AMERICAN ART DIRECTORY 1993-94

54th EDITION

The 54th edition of the AMERICAN ART DIRECTORY
was prepared by R.R. Bowker's Database Publishing Group

Senior Staff of the Database Publishing Group includes:

Senior Vice President, Database Publishing
Peter Simon

Director of Planning
Dean Hollister

Editorial Director
Edgar Adcock, Jr.

Research Director
Judy Redel

Managing Editor
Beverley McDonough

Senior Editor
Thomas B. Young

Research Manager
Tanya Hurst

Associate Editors
Mary-Anne Lutter
Teresa M. Metzger
Padi Sinegra

Research Coordinator
Ruth Ahnert

Assistant Editor
Betty Wilkerson

Assistant Research Editor
Loretta Kuhn

AMERICAN ART DIRECTORY 1993-94

54th EDITION

R.R. BOWKER
New Providence, New Jersey

Published by R.R. Bowker, A Reed Reference Publishing Company.
Copyright © 1993 by Reed Publishing (USA) Inc. All rights reserved.

International Standard Book Number: 0-8352-3202-6
International Standard Serial Number: 0065-6968
Library of Congress Catalog Number: 99-1016
Printed and Bound in the United States of America.

ISBN 0-8352-3202-6

9 780835 232029

Contents

Preface

The *American Art Directory,* first published in 1898 as the American Art Annual, continues in its tradition of excellence with the 54th edition. The directory is a standard in the field of art, and an indispensable reference to art museums, libraries, organizations, schools and corporate art holdings.

The information for the directory is collected by means of direct communication whenever possible. Forms are sent to all entrants for corroboration and updating, and information submitted by entrants is included as completely as possible within the boundaries of editorial and space restrictions. Information is provided by new entrants in response to questionnaires. In those cases where no reply is received, data is obtained from secondary sources, and an asterisk (*) is shown to the right of the institutional name. Alphabetizing in the directory is strictly letter-by-letter. Those museums, libraries, associations and organizations which bear an individual's name are alphabetized by the last name of that individual. Colleges and universities are alphabetized by the first word of their name, whether or not it is named for an individual.

Section I contains both Alphabetical and Geographic indexes. The National and Regional Organizations indexes are arranged alphabetically and contain 119 organizations which administer and coordinate the arts within the United States and Canada. Included here are libraries affiliated with these organizations. The Museums, Libraries and Associations indexes are arranged geographically, and contain listings for 1,885 main museums, 283 main libraries, 560 area associations, and 123 corporations with art holdings. There are an additional 1,301 listings for galleries, museums and libraries affiliated with main entries.

A classification key is printed to the left of each entry to designate the type:

A—Association
C—Corporate Art
L—Library
M—Museum
O—Organization

The key "M" is assigned to organizations whose primary function is gathering and preserving the visual arts.

The "O" designation is given to national and regional organizations supporting the arts through sponsorship of art activities. The "A" code is given to those supporting the arts on a more local level.

Section II lists detailed information on 1,667 art schools, and college and university departments of art, art history, and architecture in the United States and Canada.

Section III provides reference to art museums and schools abroad, state arts councils, directors and supervisors of art education, art magazines, newspapers and their art critics, art scholarships and fellowships, open exhibitions, and traveling exhibitions booking agencies.

Section IV is composed of three alphabetical indexes; institutional, personnel, and subject. The subject index includes general art subjects and specific collections, along with the name and location of the holding organization.

Every effort has been made to assure accurate reproduction of the material submitted. The publishers do not assume and hereby disclaim any liability to any party for any loss or damage caused by errors or omissions in the *American Art Directory,* whether such errors or omissions resulted from negligence, accident or any other cause. In the event of a publication error, the sole responsibility of the publisher will be the entry of corrected information in succeeding editions.

The editors express appreciation to Bruce Glaunert, Val Lowman, John Litzenberger, Mervaine Ricks, and Judith Harrison of International Computaprint Corporation for their exceptional effort in helping to produce this edition.

Please address any suggestions, comments or questions to The Editors, *American Art Directory*, R.R. Bowker, 121 Chanlon Road, New Providence, New Jersey 07974.

Beverley McDonough, *Managing Editor*

February, 1993

I ART ORGANIZATIONS

Arrangement and Abbreviations

National and Regional Organizations in the U.S.

Museums, Libraries and Associations in the U.S.

National and Regional Organizations in Canada

Museums, Libraries and Associations in Canada

ARRANGEMENT AND ABBREVIATIONS
KEY TO ART ORGANIZATIONS

ARRANGEMENT OF DATA

Name and address of institution; telephone number, including area code.

Names and titles of key personnel.

Hours open; admission fees; date established and purpose; average annual attendance; membership.

Annual figures on income and purchases.

Collections with enlarging collections indicated.

Exhibitions scheduled from 1991 onward.

Activities sponsored, including classes for adults and children, dramatic programs and docent training; lectures, concerts, gallery talks and tours; competitions, awards, scholarships and fellowships; lending programs; museum or sales shops.

Libraries also list number of book volumes, periodical subscriptions, and audiovisual and micro holdings; subject covered by name of special collections

ABBREVIATIONS AND SYMBOLS

Acad—Academic
Admin—Administration, Administrative
Adminr—Administrator
Admis—Admission
A-tapes—Audio-tapes
Adv—Advisory
AM—Morning
Ann—Annual
Approx—Approximate, Approximately
Asn—Association
Assoc—Associate
Asst—Assistant
AV—Audiovisual
Ave—Avenue
Bldg—Building
Blvd—Boulevard
Bro—Brother
C—circa
Cert—Certificate
Chap—Chapter
Chmn—Chairman
Circ—Circulation
Cl—Closed
Col—College
Coll—Collection
Comt—Committee
Coordr—Coordinator
Corresp—Corresponding
Cr—Credit
Cur—Curator
D—Day
Den—Denominational
Dept—Department
Dipl—Diploma
Dir—Director
Dist—District
Div—Division
Dorm—Dormitory
Dr—Doctor, Drive
E—East, Evening
Ed—Editor

Educ—Education
Elec Mail—Electronic Mail
Enrl—Enrollment
Ent—Entrance
Ent Req—Entrance Requirements
Est, Estab—Established
Exec—Executive
Exhib—Exhibition
Exten—Extension
Fel(s)—Fellowships
Fri—Friday
Fs—Filmstrips
Ft—Feet
FT—Full Time Instructor
GC—Graduate Course
Gen—General
Grad—Graduate
Hon—Honorary
Hr—Hour
HS—High School
Hwy—Highway
Inc—Incorporated
Incl—Including
Jr—Junior
Lect—Lecture(s)
Lectr—Lecturer
Librn—Librarian
M—Men
Maj—Major in Art
Mem—Membership
Mgr—Manager
Mon—Monday
Mss—Manuscripts
Mus—Museums
N—North
Nat—National
Nonres—Nonresident
Per subs—Period subscriptions
PM—Afternoon
Pres—President
Prin—Principal

Prof—Professor
Prog—Program
PT—Part Time Instructor
Pts—Points
Pub—Public
Publ—Publication
Pvt—Private
Qtr—Quarter
Rd—Road
Rec—Records
Reg—Registration
Req—Requirements
Res—Residence, Resident
S—South
Sat—Saturday
Schol—Scholarship
Secy—Secretary
Sem—Semester
Soc—Society
Sq—Square
Sr—Senior, Sister
St—Street
Sun—Sunday
Supt—Superintendent
Supv—Supervisor
Thurs—Thursday
Treas—Treasurer
Tues—Tuesday
Tui—Tuition
TV—Television
Undergrad—Undergraduate
Univ—University
Vol—Volunteer
Vols—Volumes
VPres—Vice President
V-tapes—Videotapes
W—West, Women
Wed—Wednesday
Wk—Week
Yr—Year(s)

*   No response to questionnnaire
†   Denotes collection currently being enlarged
A   Association
C   Corporate Art Holding
L   Library
M   Museum
O   Organization

National and Regional Organizations In The United States

O **AFRICAN AMERICAN MUSEUMS ASSOCIATION,** PO Box 548, Wilberforce, OH 45384. Tel 513-376-4611. *Pres* John Fleming; *Exec Dir* Jocelyn Robinson-Hubbuch
Open Mon - Fri 9 AM - 5 PM. Estab 1978 to represent black museums around the country. Offers consulting & networking services. Sponsors annual conferences. Mem: 496; dues institutional $100-$250
Publications: Biannual directory; Profile of Black Museums - A Survey; quarterly newsletter script for mem only

O **THE ALLIED ARTISTS OF AMERICA, INC,** National Arts Club, 15 Gramercy Park S, New York, NY 10003. Tel 212-582-6411. *Pres* Marion Roller; *VPres* Sybil Dorsi; *VPres* Gary Erbe
Open daily noon - 5 PM, Nov - Dec. Estab 1914, incorporated 1922, as a self-supporting exhibition cooperative, with juries elected each year by the membership, to promote work by American artists. Mem: 3601; dues $20 & up; annual meeting in Apr
Income: Financed by memorial funds, dues and donations
Exhibitions: Members' Regional AAA exhibitions; annual exhibition in the winter; Annual held at National Arts Club; numerous awards & medals; prizes total $16,000 each year
Publications: Catalogs; newsletter
Activities: Lect open to public, 1-3 visiting lectr per yr; gallery talks; competitions with awards

O **AMERICAN ABSTRACT ARTISTS,** 470 W End Ave, Apt 9D, New York, NY 10024. Tel 212-874-0747. *Pres* Beatrice Riese; *Treas* Katinka Mann
Estab 1936, active 1937, to promote American abstract art; develop & educate through exhibitions & publications; to provide forums for the exchange of ideas among artists. Mem: 75; dues $25; bi-monthly meetings
Income: Financed by mem
Exhibitions: (1988-1992) USA-sponsored traveling exhibit to Scandanavia, Eastern Europe, Russia & Canada.
Publications: Books and catalogs
Activities: Lect open to the public; gallery talks; individual and original objects of art lent to responsible galleries, museums and universities; originate traveling exhibitions

O **AMERICAN ACADEMY OF ARTS & LETTERS,** 633 W 155th St, New York, NY 10032. Tel 212-368-5900; FAX 212-491-4615. *Pres* Hugo Weisgall; *Executive Dir* Virginia Dajani
Open Tues - Sun 1 - 4 PM during exhibitions, by appointment other times. Estab 1898 as an honorary society of artists, writers & composers whose function it is to foster, assist & sustain an interest in literature, music & the fine arts. Formed by 1976 merger of the American Academy of Arts & Letters & the National Institute of Arts & Letters. Maintains two galleries separated by a terrace. Average Annual Attendance: 6000. Mem: 250; mem is by election; no dues; annual meeting May
Income: $1,400,000 (financed by endowment)
Purchases: $80,000-$90,000 Hassam Speicher Purchase Program
Collections: Works by members
Exhibitions: Exhibition of Candidates for Art Awards; Exhibition of Paintings Eligible for Hassam Fund Purchase; Newly Elected Members & Recipients of Honors & Awards Exhibitions, art, scores & manuscripts; Special Exhibitions
Publications: Proceedings, annual; exhibition catalogs
Activities: Awards given: Gold Medals, Richard & Hinda Rosenthal Foundation Award, Arnold W Brunner Memorial Prize in Architecture & Award of Merit of the Academy. No applications accepted
L **Library,** 633 W 155th St, 10032. Tel 212-368-6361; FAX 212-491-4615. *Librn* Nancy Johnson; *Asst Librn* Kathryn Talalay
Open Mon - Fri 9:30 AM - 5 PM by appointment only. No admis fee. Estab 1898 to collect books, papers & related articles concerning the members of the Academy-Institute; to foster, assist & sustain interest in literature, music & fine art. For reference only. Mem: 250
Income: Financed by endowment
Library Holdings: AV — Rec; Other — Clipping files, exhibition catalogs, manuscripts, memorabilia, original art works, pamphlets, photographs, sculpture
Special Subjects: Architecture, Art History, Drawings, Etchings & Engravings, Landscape Architecture, Painting - American, Portraits, Sculpture, Watercolors
Collections: †Books by and about members; manuscripts
Exhibitions: Richard Rodgers Production in Musical Theater (competition)
Activities: Competitions; scholarships & fels; individual paintings & original works of art lent; lending collection contains individual paintings, original works, paintings, photographs & sculpture

O **AMERICAN ANTIQUARIAN SOCIETY,** 185 Salisbury St, Worcester, MA 01609. Tel 508-755-5221; FAX 508-754-9069. *Pres* Ellen S Dunlap; *Cur Graphic Arts* Georgia B Barnhill
Open Mon - Fri 9 AM - 5 PM, cl Sat, Sun, holidays, third Wed in Oct, Fri after Thanksgiving. No admis fee. Incorporated 1812 to collect, preserve and encourage serious study of the materials of American history and life through 1876. Mem: 600 honorary; meetings third Wed in April & Oct
Income: Financed by endowment, gifts and grants
Purchases: $284,000
Collections: Early American portraits; Staffordshire pottery; †bookplates, †prints, †lithographs, †cartoons, †engravings; Colonial furniture; †photographs
Exhibitions: Temporary exhibitions
Publications: Proceedings, semi-annually; monographs
Activities: Undergraduate seminar in American Studies; lect; fellowships; sales shop sells books
L **Library,** 185 Salisbury St, Worcester, MA 01609-1634. Tel 508-755-5221; FAX 508-754-9069. *Assoc Librn* Nancy Burkett
Library Holdings: Micro — Prints, reels; Other — Exhibition catalogs, manuscripts, memorabilia, original art works, pamphlets, photographs, prints, reproductions
Special Subjects: Art Education, Cartoons, Decorative Arts, Etchings & Engravings, Graphic Design, Illustration, Manuscripts, Maps, Miniatures, Painting - American, Photography, Portraits, Printmaking, Prints, Woodcuts
Collections: †750,000 titles dating before 1877, including early American books on art and 20th century books and periodicals relating to the history and culture of the United States
Activities: Lect; seminar; fellowships

O **AMERICAN ARTISTS PROFESSIONAL LEAGUE, INC,** 47 Fifth Ave, New York, NY 10003. Tel 212-645-1345. *Pres* Leo Yeni; *Recording Secy* Susanne Hurt
Estab 1928 to advance the cause of fine arts in America, through the promotion of high standards of beauty, integrity and craftsmanship in painting, sculpture and the graphic arts; to emphasize the importance of order and coherent communication as prime requisites of works of art through exhibitions and publications. Mem: 1000; annual meetings
Income: Financed by membership
Exhibitions: Annually
Publications: AAPL News Bulletin, annually

O **AMERICAN ASSOCIATION OF MUSEUMS,** International Council of Museums Committee, 1225 Eye St NW, Suite 200, Washington, DC 20005. Tel 202-289-1818; FAX 202-289-6578. *Pres* Dan Moore; *Dir* Edward H Able; *Dir* Mary Louise Wood; *Deputy Executive Dir for Finance & Admin* Joseph Thompson; *Deputy Exec for Progs* Patricia Williams; *Educ* Meg McCarthy
Open 9 AM - 5 PM. No admis fee. Estab 1906, affiliated with US-ICOM in 1973, the AAM represents international museum interests within the United States & American museum interests abroad through the AAM-ICOM office which disseminates information on international conferences, publications, travel & study grants & training programs. The AAM-ICOM office also maintains an international network of museum contracts around the world. Mem: 1000; members must be museum professionals or institutions
Income: Financed by membership
Exhibitions: Annual Museum Publications Competition
Publications: AAM-ICOM page in Aviso, monthly; ICOM News, quarterly
Activities: Specialty committees; annual meeting; international meetings; professional exchanges; competition honoring excellence in museum publications design (deadline Apr 1, each yr); bookstore sells books, catalogue available

O **AMERICAN ASSOCIATION OF UNIVERSITY WOMEN,** 1111 16th St NE, Washington, DC 20036. Tel 202-785-7700; FAX 202-872-1425. *Exec Dir* Anne L Bryant
Estab 1881 to unite alumnae of different institutions for practical educational work; to further the advancement of women, lifelong learning, and responsibility to society expressed through action, advocacy, research and enlightened leadership. Mem: 175,000; holds biennial conventions
Publications: Action Alert, biweekly; Graduate Woman, bimonthly; Leader in Action, quarterly; brochures; research studies; study guides; booklets
Activities: Associations local branches develop and maintain programs in the arts. AAUW Foundation funds first professional degree in architecture, doctoral/ post doctoral candidates in the arts

O **AMERICAN CENTER FOR DESIGN GALLERY,** 233 E Ontario, Suite 500, Chicago, IL 60611. Tel 312-787-2018; FAX 312-649-9518. *Pres* Patrick Whitney; *Exec Dir* Jane Dunne
Open Mon - Fri 9 AM - 5 PM. Estab 1927 as a non-profit organization of design professionals, educators & students. Mem: 2500, dues $100, Student $50; annual meeting in June
Exhibitions: Various shows throughout the year
Publications: 100 Show Annual; annual membership directory; biannual journal; quarterly magazine; videos
Activities: Educ Foundation; design office visitation program; conferences; seminars; symposia; annual design awards program; lect open to public; tours; competitions; awards; scholarships; originate traveling exhibitions

O **AMERICAN CERAMIC SOCIETY,** 735 Ceramic Place, Westerville, OH 43081-8720. Tel 614-890-4700; FAX 614-899-6109. *Exec Dir* W Paul Holbrook
Open Mon - Fri 8:30 AM - 4 PM. No admis fee. Estab 1899 to promote the arts, science and technology of ceramics. Mem: 10,050; dues $50; annual meeting May
Income: $2,000,000 (financed by membership)
Publications: American Ceramic Society Journal, monthly; Ceramic Engineering & Science Proceedings, bi-monthly; Journal and Abstracts, bi-monthly

O **AMERICAN COLOR PRINT SOCIETY,** 4109 Locust St, Philadelphia, PA 19104. Tel 215-222-6195. *Pres* Michael Kuncevich; *VPres* Idaherma Williams; *Treas* Millicent Krouse
Estab 1939 to exhibit color prints. Mem: 150; dues $10
Activities: Sponsors annual national members exhibition of all media color prints; 6 annual prizes

O **AMERICAN COUNCIL FOR THE ARTS,** 1 E 53rd St, New York, NY 10022-4210. Tel 212-223-2787; FAX 212-223-4415. *Pres & CEO* Milton Rhodes; *Exec Dir* Linwood Oglesby; *Dir Publishing, Policy & Planning* Robert Porter; *Exec Dir* Sarah Havens
Open 9 AM - 5 PM. Mem: 2500; dues organizations $150 - $250, individual $30 - $100
Publications: ACA Update, monthly newsletter of legislative & advocacy information available to members; books on arts policy, management, education & information for artists
L Library, 1 E 53rd St, New York, NY 10022-4210. Tel 212-223-2782, Ext 224; FAX 212-223-4415; WATS 800-232-2789 (Visual Artists Information Hotline, 2 - 5 PM). *Dir* David Bosca
Research collections available on an appointment only basis for a fee; information/referral service by phone, FAX & mail. For reference only
Library Holdings: Vols 7000; Per subs 300; Vertical files
Special Subjects: Art Education, Arts Education Assessment, Arts Management, Arts Policy

O **AMERICAN CRAFT COUNCIL,** 72 Spring St, New York, NY 10012-4019. Tel 212-274-0630; FAX 212-274-0650. *Board Chmn* Carol Edelman; *Vice Chmn* Mark Levine; *Exec Dir of Council* Open ; *Editor-in-Chief American Craft Magazine* Lois Moran
Estab 1943 to stimulate interest in and appreciation of contemporary American crafts. Mem: 30,000; dues $40
Income: Financed by membership, private donations and government grants
Publications: American Craft Magazine (formerly Craft Horizons), bimonthly
Activities: Originate traveling exhibitions
L Craft Information Center, 72 Spring St, 10012-4019. Tel 212-274-0630; FAX 212-274-0650. *Librn* Mary D Hujsak
Open to ACC members Mon - Fri 1 - 5 PM
Library Holdings: Vols 5000; AV — A-tapes, slides; Other — Clipping files, exhibition catalogs 6000, pamphlets, photographs
Special Subjects: Ceramics, Crafts, Decorative Arts, Enamels, Furniture, Glass, Goldsmithing, Jewelry, Metalwork, Porcelain, Pottery, Silversmithing, Stained Glass, Tapestries, Textiles
Collections: Artists Registry & Archives: files for over 2000 craftspeople working in all media containing biographical material, slides & photographs (computerized access to the files provides indexes by artist name, geographical location, medium, process & function); Slide Study Collection: slide sets from ACC's slide & film service; newsletters & catalogs of craft organizations & educational programs on national, regional & local levels (computerized access by name, medium, location & type of organization); Archives of the American Craft Council and American Craft Museum

O **THE AMERICAN FEDERATION OF ARTS,** 41 E 65th St, New York, NY 10021. Tel 212-988-7700; FAX 212-861-2487. *Chmn* Brooke Blake; *Pres* Robert M Meltzer; *VPres* David W Steadman; *VPres* Stephanie French; *VPres* Tom L Frenderheim; *VPres* Marna Grant Monisey; *VPres* Mrs Rudolph B Schelhof; *Treas-Secy* Richard Lane; *Dir* Serena Lane; *Deputy Dir* Mark Gotlob; *Dir Exhib* Robert Workman; *Development & Membership Dir* Marita O'Hare
Estab 1909, a nonprofit visual arts museum, program & service that organizes traveling art, film & video exhibitions for art museums, art & media centers, university art galleries, schools & libraries. Mem: 1150; dues institutional members $220 - $500, individual $100 - $1,500
Income: Financed by government agencies, corporations, foundations & membership
Publications: ART: The Newsletter of the AFA, 3 per year; exhibition catalogs; Memo to Members, 6 per year for institutional members
Activities: Originate traveling exhibitions of fine arts & media arts

O **AMERICAN FINE ARTS SOCIETY,** 215 W 57th St, New York, NY 10019. Tel 212-247-4510; FAX 212-541-7024. *Pres* R A Flori; *Secy* Barbara Sherman
Open Sept - May, Mon - Fri 10 AM - 8 PM, Sat 10 AM - 4 PM. Incorporated 1889; provides facilities for art activities at the American Fine Arts Society Building. Gallery used only for Art Student League Associations, associates & members. Average Annual Attendance: 8000 - 10,000. Mem: Annual meeting Jan
Activities: Sponsors lect by prominent persons in the art world, open to public

O **THE AMERICAN FOUNDATION FOR THE ARTS,** 3814 NE Miami Ct, Miami, FL 33137. Tel 305-576-0254; FAX 305-576-0259. *Dir* May Levine
Open Mon - Fri 10 AM - 4 PM. No admis fee. Estab 1974. Mem: Dues founder $25,000, trustee $10,000, life $5000, benefactor $1000, business $250, friend $100, sustaining $50, family $25, individual $15, student annual $5
Collections: Architecture; contemporary paintings; photography

O **AMERICAN INSTITUTE FOR CONSERVATION OF HISTORIC & ARTISTIC WORKS (AIC),** 1400 16th St NW, Suite 340, Washington, DC 20036. Tel 202-232-6636; FAX 202-232-6630. *Pres* Paul Himmelstein; *VPres* Leslie M Kruth; *Exec Dir* Sarah Z Rosenberg
Open 8 AM - 5 PM. Estab 1973 for professional organization of Conservators, people who take care of our cultural and historical patrimony. Mem: 2500; dues fellows $100, professional associates $85, associates $85, student $30; meetings in early June
Income: Financed by membership
Publications: Directory, annually; journal, semi-annually; newsletter, bi-monthly
Activities: Educ Committee to keep abreast of all conservation educ facilities, programs; lect open to public; awards given

O **AMERICAN INSTITUTE OF ARCHITECTS,** 1735 New York Ave NW, Washington, DC 20006. Tel 202-626-7300; FAX 202-626-7420. *Exec VPres* James P Cramer
Open Mon - Fri 8:30 AM - 5 PM. Estab 1857 to organize and unite the architects of the United States and to promote the esthetic, scientific and practical efficiency of the profession
Income: Financed by members
Publications: AIA Memo (newsletter), monthly
Activities: Continuing education program; awards given, Gold Medal, Kemper Award, Architectural Firm Award, R S Reynolds Memorial Award and Reynolds Aluminum Prize Citation of Honor, AIA Honor Awards, Institute Honors
L AIA Library & Archives, 1735 New York Ave NW, Washington, DC 20006. Tel 202-626-7492; FAX 202-626-7420. *Sr Dir* Judy Marks
Open to the public, lending provided for members only
Income: Financed by mem
Library Holdings: Vols 30,000; Per subs 450; Micro — Fiche; AV — A-tapes, cassettes, fs, Kodachromes, lantern slides, slides, v-tapes; Other — Clipping files, manuscripts, memorabilia, original art works, photographs, sculpture
Special Subjects: Architecture, Architectural History, Landscape Architecture

O **AMERICAN INSTITUTE OF GRAPHIC ARTS,** 1059 Third Ave, New York, NY 10021. Tel 212-752-0813. *Exec Dir* Caroline Hightower
Open Mon - Fri 9:30 AM - 4:45 PM. No admis fee. Estab 1914 as a national nonprofit educational organization devoted to raising standards in all branches of the graphic arts. Art gallery maintained for A16A exhibitions resulting from design competitions; maintains library and slide archives. Mem: 5000; dues $125, junior $100, student $30
Income: Financed by membership
Exhibitions: Book Show; Communication Graphics
Publications: A1GA Graphic Design USA, hardbound annual; AIGA journal of Graphic Design, quarterly
Activities: Awards AIGA Medal for distinguished contributions to the graphic arts; originate traveling exhibitions
L Library, 1059 Third Ave, 10021. Tel 212-752-0813.
Open Mon - Fri 9:30 AM - 4:45 PM. For reference only. Art gallery maintained for AIGA exhibitions resulting from design competitions
Income: Financed by membership
Library Holdings: Vols 500; Per subs 25
Special Subjects: Advertising Design, Aesthetics, Art Education, Art History, Cartoons, Commercial Art, Graphic Arts, Graphic Design, Illustration, Industrial Design, Posters

O **AMERICAN NUMISMATIC ASSOCIATION,** Museum, 818 N Cascade, Colorado Springs, CO 80903. Tel 719-632-2646. *Pres* Edward C Rochette; *Museum Cur* Robert W Hoge
Open Tues - Sat 8:30 AM - 4 PM. No admis fee. Estab 1891 as an international organization to promote numismatics as a means of recording history. Maintains a museum and library; eight galleries display numismatic material from paper money through coins and art medals. Average Annual Attendance: 10,000. Mem: 40,000; to qualify for membership, a person must be at least eighteen years of age and interested in coin collecting; dues $21 plus one-time initiation fee of $5; annual meetings held at National Conventions in Feb and August
Income: Financed by membership, endowment, donations and miscellaneous sources
Collections: Robert T Herdegen Memorial Collection of Coins of the World; Norman H Liebman Collection of Abraham Lincoln on Paper Money; Elliott Markoff Collection of Presidential Memorabilia; general and specialized collections from all other fields of numismatics
Exhibitions: Permanent galleries exhibiting coins of the American Colonial period, the United States 1792 to date and Modern Medallic Art from contemporary medals. Temporary exhibits on selected topics, including African Emblems of Wealth
Publications: The Numismatist, monthly
Activities: Classes for adults and children; annual seminar on campus of Colorado College, Colorado Springs; lect open to public, visiting guest lectr; tours; sponsorship of National Coin Week third week in April (when members throughout the United States promote their avocations through exhibits in local areas); presentation of awards; scholarships; book traveling exhibitions; sales shop selling books, magazines, slides, medals and souvenir jewelry
L Library, 818 N Cascade Ave, Colorado Springs, CO 80903. Tel 719-632-2646. *Librn* Lynn Chen
Open Mon - Fri 8:30 AM - 4 PM, summer Mon - Sat 8:30 AM - 4 PM. No admis fee. Estab 1891 to provide research materials to the members of the Association and the general public. Open to the public for reference; lending restricted to members. Circ 4500. Mem: 28,000; dues $32 first year, $26 to renew mem; meetings twice a year
Library Holdings: Vols 35,000; Per subs 110; Auction catalogs 20,000, Micro Film; Micro — Fiche; AV — Slides, v-tapes; Other — Pamphlets
Special Subjects: Coins & Medals
Collections: Arthur Braddan Coole Library on Oriental Numismatics; books, auction catalogs & periodicals, all on numismatics
Exhibitions: Annual Summer Conference
Activities: Classes for adults & children

O **AMERICAN NUMISMATIC SOCIETY,** Broadway at 155th St, New York, NY 10032. Tel 212-234-3130; FAX 212-234-3381. *Dir & Secy* Leslie A Elam; *Chief Cur* William E Metcalf; *Librn* Francis D Campbell
Open Tues - Sat 9 AM - 4:30 PM, Sun 1 - 4 PM, cl Mon. Estab 1858 as an international organization for the advancement of numismatic knowledge.

Maintains museum & library; one exhibition hall, devoted to the World of Coins. Average Annual Attendance: 18,000. Mem: 2279; dues assoc $30; annual meeting second Sat in Oct
Income: Financed by endowment
Collections: Universal numismatics
Publications: Numismatic Literature, semi-annually; American Journal of Numismatics, annually
Activities: Lect open to public, 2 vis lectr per year; scholarships
L **Library,** Broadway at 155th St, New York, NY 10032. Tel 212-234-3130. *Librn* Francis D Campbell
For reference only
Library Holdings: Vols 100,000; Per subs 150; auction catalogs; Micro — Reels 200; AV — Fs, slides; Other — Exhibition catalogs, manuscripts, pamphlets
Special Subjects: Coins & Medals
Collections: Auction catalogs

O **AMERICAN SOCIETY OF ARTISTS, INC,** PO Box 1326, Chicago, IL 60611. Tel 312-751-2500, 708-991-4748. *Pres* Nancy J Fregin; *VPres* Helen DelValle; *Dir Promotional Servs* Arnold Jackson; *American Artisans Dir* Judy A Edborg; *Festivals Committee Dir* Kathy Chan Barnes; *Dir Lecture & Demonstration Serv* Charles J Gruner; *Special Arts Servs Dir* Patricia E Nolan; *Dir Special Events* Marge Coughin; *Midwest Representative* Paul Gallacci; *Midwest Representative* Alajos Acs; *Chicago Representative* Donald Metcoff
Estab 1972, membership organization of professional artists. Mem: 5000; qualifications for mem, must have work juried & pass jury to be accepted; dues $50, plus one initiation fee of $20; patronship, associateship & international membership also available
Income: Financed by membership
Collections: †Photographs and slides of members works
Exhibitions: Approximately 25 indoor and outdoor juried shows per year
Publications: Art Lovers' Art and Craft Fair Bulletin, quarterly; ASA Artisan, quarterly
Activities: Lect and Demonstration Service; assists members with various problems
L **Library Organization,** PO Box 1326, Palatine, 60078. Tel 312-751-2500, 708-991-4748; FAX 708-991-4748. *Librn* Donald Metcoff
Estab 1978 to provide reference material for member artists only
Income: Financed by dues and fees
Library Holdings: Per subs 8; AV — Lantern slides; Other — Photographs
Special Subjects: Art and craft supplies, exhibition and gallery information
Activities: Lecture & demonstration service

O **AMERICAN SOCIETY OF BOOKPLATE COLLECTORS & DESIGNERS,** 605 N Stoneman Ave, No F, Alhambra, CA 91801. Tel 213-283-1936. *Dir & Ed* Audrey Spencer Arellanes
Estab 1922 as an international organization to foster an interest in the art of the bookplate through the publication of a yearbook, and to encourage friendship and a greater knowledge of bookplates among members by an exchange membership list. Mem: 200 who are interested in bookplates as either a collector of artist, or just have an interest in bookplates & graphic arts; dues $50 which includes yearbook & quarterly newsletter
Income: Financed by members
Exhibitions: Bookplates, Prints in Miniature
Publications: Bookplates in the News, quarterly newsletter; Yearbook, annually
Activities: Lect given upon request; contributes bookplates to the Prints & Photographs Division of the Library of Congress & furnishes them with copies of quarterly & yearbook; originate traveling exhibitions

O **AMERICAN SOCIETY OF CONTEMPORARY ARTISTS,** c/o 3965 Sedgwick Ave, Bronx, NY 10463. Tel 718-549-2923. *Pres* Bernarl Olshan
Estab 1917. Mem: 151 elected on basis of high level of professional distinction; dues $20; annual meeting Apr
Income: Financed by members
Exhibitions: 60th & 61st Annual at National Arts Club; 62nd, 63rd & 64th Annual at Salmagundi Club; Exhibitions at Lever House Gallery and US Customhouse Museum; 65th Annual at Federal Plaza
Activities: Educ dept; demonstrations in graphics, painting & sculpture; lect open to the public; awards; originate traveling exhibitions

O **AMERICAN SOCIETY OF PORTRAIT ARTISTS (ASOPA),** 2781 Zelda Rd, Montgomery, AL 36106. Tel 205-270-1600; FAX 205-270-0150; WATS 800-235-6273. *Dir* Jennifer Frazer Williams; *Pres* Leon Loord; *VPres* Frank Tauriello; *Treas* Joy Loord McRae
Estab 1989

O **AMERICAN TAPESTRY ALLIANCE,** HC 63, PO Box 570, Chiloquin, OR 97624. Tel 503-783-2507. *Pres* Jim Brown; *VPres* Henry Ellis; *Treas* Hal Painter
Income: $40,000 (financed by mem & grants)
Exhibitions: World Tapestry Today
Publications: Exhibition catalogue & quarterly

O **AMERICAN WATERCOLOR SOCIETY,** 47 Fifth Ave, New York, NY 10003. Tel 212-206-8986. *Pres* William D Gorman; *Active Honorary Pres* Dale Meyers; *Treas* Joan Ashley Rothermel
Open during exhibitions 1 - 5 PM, cl Mon. Estab 1866 as a national organization to foster the advancement of the art of watercolor painting & to further the interests of painters in watercolor throughout the United States; occupies the galleries of the Salmagundi Club, 47 Fifth Ave, New York City for four weeks each yr for annual international exhibition. Average Annual Attendance: 4000 - 5000. Mem: 550; to qualify for mem, an artist must exhibit in two annuals within past ten yrs, then submit application to mem chairman; dues $30; annual meeting in Apr
Income: Financed by membership & donations
Publications: AwS Newsletter, demi-annually; full color exhibition catalog
Activities: Lect open to public; demonstrations during annual exhibitions; awards given at annual exhibitions; scholarships; originate traveling exhibitions

O **ARCHAEOLOGICAL INSTITUTE OF AMERICA,** 675 Commonwealth Ave, Boston, MA 02215. Tel 617-353-9361; FAX 617-353-6550. *Pres* Mark J Meister
Estab 1879 as an international organization concerned with two major areas of responsibility: facilitating archaeological research and disseminating the results to the public. Mem: 11,266 consisting of professionals & laypersons interested in archaeology; dues $50; annual meeting Dec 27-30
Income: Financed by endowment and membership
Publications: Archaeology Magazine, bimonthly; Archaeological Fieldwork Opportunities Bulletin, annual; American Journal of Archaeology, quarterly
Activities: Lect open to the public, 270 visiting lectr per year; annual award given for distinguished archaeological achievement; one or more fellowships awarded for an academic year

O **ART DEALERS ASSOCIATION OF AMERICA, INC,** 575 Madison Ave, New York, NY 10022. Tel 212-940-8590; FAX 212-940-7013. *Pres* Andre Emmerich; *VPres* Richard Gray; *VPres* Joan T Washburn; *Secy & Treas* Eric Wallach; *Admin VPres & Counsel* Gilbert Edelson; *Public Relations* Rose R Weill; *Dir of Admin* Donna Carlson
Estab 1962 as a national organization to improve the stature and status of the art-dealing profession. Mem: 133; mem by invitation
Income: Financed by membership
Exhibitions: The Art Show; annual group exhibition
Publications: Activities & Membership Roster; Update, bi-annual newsletter for members
Activities: Sponsors lect series at Metropolitan Museum of Art, 6 vis lectr per year; appraisal service for donors contributing works of art to nonprofit institutions

O **ART DIRECTORS CLUB, INC,** 250 Park Ave S, New York, NY 10003. Tel 212-674-0500; FAX 212-228-0649. *Pres* Kurt Haiman; *VPres* Seymore Chwast; *Secy* Carl Fischer; *Exec Dir* Rhoda Marshall; *Treas* Martin Solomon
Estab 1920 as an international organization to protect, promote & elevate the standards of practice of the profession of art directing. Owns gallery. Mem: 620, criteria for mem: qualified art director, at least 21 years of age, of good character & at least two years of practical experience in creating & and directing in the visual communication of graphic arts industry. Dues regular $150, nonresident $75, junior $25
Income: Financed by mem
Exhibitions: Art Directors' Annual Exhibition of Advertising, Editorial & Television Art & Design. Bimonthly shows conceived to provide a showcase for works & ideas not readily viewed otherwise. They cover new art, design, lettering & graphics by illustrators, alumni art directors, ad agencies & individuals; International Show
Publications: The Art Directors Annual; Newsletter, bimonthly
Activities: Portfolio Review Programs; seminars; lect open to public; gallery talks; annual exhibition with Gold & Silver Medals, Gold, Silver & Distinctive Merit Certificates; scholarships; originate traveling exhibitions

O **ARTISTS' FELLOWSHIP, INC,** 47 Fifth Ave, New York, NY 10003. Tel 212-255-7740. *Pres* Marc Richard Mellon; *Treas* John R McCarthy; *Correspondence Secy* Robert J Riedinger; *Historian* Kent Day Coes
Estab 1859, reorganized 1889 as Artists' Aid Society, then incorporated 1925 as Artists' Fellowship; to aid artists and their families in need because of death, illness or financial reverses. Mem: 200; annual meeting Dec
Publications: Quarterly newsletter
Activities: Awards the Gari Melchers Gold Medal for distinguished service to the arts, and Benjamin West Clinedinst Memorial Medal for outstanding achievement in the arts

O **ART LIBRARIES SOCIETY OF NORTH AMERICA,** 3900 E Timrod St, Tucson, AZ 85711. Tel 602-881-8479; FAX 602-322-6778; Elec Mail pparry@attmail.com. *Pres* Deirdre C Stam; *Exec Dir* Pamela J Parry
Open 9 AM - 5 PM, cl Sat & Sun. Estab 1972 to promote the profession of art librarianship & visual resources curatorship in North America. Mem: 1325; qualification for mem is an interest in art librarianship or related fields; dues institutional $75, individual $55; annual meeting Feb & Mar
Income: Financed by membership
Publications: Art Documentation, 4 per yr; Annual Handbook & List of Members; ARLIS/NA Update, 6 per yr; occasional papers; topical papers
Activities: Sponsors annual conference & educational programs; has 20 local chapters; Gerd Museum Award (for library school students); George Wittenborn Award (art publishing); Travel Awards (to attend annual conference); Research Fund (to assist members' research projects)

O **ART SERVICES INTERNATIONAL,** 700 N Fairfax St, Suite 220, Alexandria, VA 22314. Tel 703-548-4554. *Chief Exec Officer* Joseph Saunders; *Dir* Lynn Kahler Berg
Nonprofit, educational institution which organizes & circulates fine arts exhibitions to museums & galleries in the US & abroad

O **ARTS EXTENSION SERVICE,** c/o Div Continuing Educ, Univ of Mass, Amherst, MA 01003. Tel 413-545-2360. *Dir* Craig Dreeszen; *Educ Coordr* Dyan Wiley; *Spec Projects Coordr* Pam Korza; *Systems Coordr & Publications Mgr* Brenda Coda
Estab as a National arts service organization facilitating the continuing education of artists, arts organizations & community leaders. AES works for better access to the arts & integration of the arts in communities. AES is a nonprofit program of the Division of Continuing Education, University of Massachusetts at Amherst
Activities: Professional level arts management workshops; consulting; retreats & conferences

O **ASSOCIATION OF AMERICAN EDITORIAL CARTOONISTS,** 4101 Lake Boone Trail, Suite 201, Raleigh, NC 27607. Tel 919-787-5181; FAX 919-787-4916. *Pres* Jim Larrick; *Pres-Elect* Kevin Kallaugher; *General Mgr* Sally Nicholson; *Membership Dir* Angie Hale
Estab 1957 as an international organization of professional editorial cartoonists for newspapers and newspaper syndicates. Mem: 300; to qualify for mem, &

editorial cartoonists must be primarily employed as a cartoonist; dues $100
Income: Financed by mem
Publications: Notebook, AAEC news magazine; Best Editorial Cartoons of the Year

O **ASSOCIATION OF ART MUSEUM DIRECTORS,** 41 E 65th St, New York, NY 10021. Tel 212-249-4423. *Exec Dir* Millicent Hall Gaudieri
Estab 1916. Mem: 160; chief staff officers of major art museums
Income: Financed by membership dues
Publications: Conference Proceedings; Professional Practices in Art Museums; Annual Salary Survey

O **ASSOCIATION OF COLLEGIATE SCHOOLS OF ARCHITECTURE,** 1735 New York Ave NW, Washington, DC 20006. Tel 202-785-2324. *Exec Dir* Richard McCommons; *Asst Dir* Karen Eldridge
Open daily 9 AM - 5 PM. No admis fee. Estab 1912 as a non-profit, mem organization furthering the advancement of architectural educ. Mem: 2800 full-time architecture faculty members; mem open to schools & their faculty as well as individuals; mem rates vary; annual meeting in Mar
Income: $1-1.2 million (financed by endowment, membership, state appropriation and grants)
Publications: ACSA News, 9 times per year; Journal of Architectural Education, quarterly; Annual Meeting Proceedings; Guide to Architecture Schools in North America, biennially; Architecture Off-Campus Study Programs; Abroad-US
Activities: Educational seminars; institutes; publications; services to membership; sponsor student design competitions with awards

O **ASSOCIATION OF MEDICAL ILLUSTRATORS,** 1819 Peachtree St NE, Suite 560, Atlanta, GA 30309. Tel 404-350-7900. *Chmn* Gary Schnitz; *Pres* Craig Gosling; *Exec Dir* William Just
Estab 1945 as an international organization to encourage the advancement of medical illustration and allied fields of visual education; to promote understanding and cooperation with the medical and related professions. Mem: 804; dues active $135; annual meeting Aug
Income: Financed by membership
Exhibitions: Annual exhibition at national meeting
Publications: Journal of Biocommunications, 4 times per year; Medical Illustration, brochure; Newsletter, 6 times per year
Activities: Individual members throughout the world give lect on the profession; awards given for artistic achievements submitted to salon each year; scholarships to members of AMI accredited schools only; originate traveling exhibition

O **ATLATL,** 402 W Roosevelt, Suite C, Phoenix, AZ 85003. Tel 602-253-2731. *Exec Dir* Carla A Roberts
Open 9 AM - 5 PM. No admis fee. Estab 1981 as a national service organization for Native American Art. Altatl creates an informational network between Native American artists & art organiztions as well as between mainstream institutions & emerging organizations. Maintains a National Registry of Native American Artists which currently includes more than 1500 artists
Collections: Native American artists files
Exhibitions: The Submulou Show/Columbus Works; Artists Respond: A People in Peril
Publications: Catalogues & other publications; Native Art Update, quarterly newsletter
Activities: Workshops & training sessions; circulates audiovisual materials such as slide sets & videotapes by Native American artists; originate exhibitions of Native American art to a variety of institutions including tribal museums, community & university galleries & fine art museums

O **AUDUBON ARTISTS, INC,** 32 Union Square E, Room 612, New York, NY 10003. Tel 212-777-6795. *Pres* Stephen McNeely; *VPres* Douglas Wiltraut; *Treas* Marion Roller
Open during exhibition. Estab 1940 as a national organization for the presentation of annual exhibitions in all media, oil, acrylics, watercolors, graphics, sculpture; open to nonmembers. Exhibitions held at the National Art Club. Mem: 650; mem by invitation; dues $20; annual meeting April
Income: $15,000 (financed by membership)
Exhibitions: Annual exhibition lasting four weeks
Publications: Illustrated catalog of exhibitions, annual
Activities: Demonstrations in all media; medals & $10,000 in cash awards

C **AUTOZONE,** Autozone Corporation Collection, 3030 Poplar Ave, Memphis, TN 38111. Tel 901-325-4523; FAX 901-325-4773. *Cur* Donna Leatherman
Estab 1978 to support local artists & artists of the United States. 20th century collection of American art in a variety of media highlighting the work of artists in the South

O **COALITION OF WOMEN'S ART ORGANIZATIONS,** 123 E Beutel Rd, Port Washington, WI 53074. Tel 414-284-4458. *Pres* Dorothy Provis; *VPres-Nominations* Christine Buth-Furness; *VPres-Programs* Kyra Sullivan
Estab 1977 as a national advocacy organization dedicated to the achievement of equality for all in the arts. Mem: 22 national organizations, 30 individuals; dues $25 organizations, $10 individuals; annual meeting in Feb at College Art Association Conference
Income: Financed by mem & contributions
Publications: Coalition of Women's Art Organization News, monthly
Activities: Lect open to public

O **COLLEGE ART ASSOCIATION,** 275 Seventh Ave, New York, NY 10001. Tel 212-691-1051; FAX 212-627-2381. *Pres* Ruth Weisberg; *VPres* Larry Silver; *Exec Dir* Susan L Ball; *Asst Dir* Jeffrey Larris; *Publications Dir* Virginia Wageman
Estab 1911 as a national organization to further scholarship and excellence in the teaching and practice of art and art history. Mem: 10,000; open to all individuals & institutions interested in the purposes of the Association; dues life $1000, institution $125, individual $40-$75 (scaled to salary), student $25; annual meeting in Feb

Income: Financed by membership
Publications: The Art Bulletin, quarterly; Art Journal, quarterly; CAA Newsletter, bimonthly
Activities: Awards: Distinguished Teaching of Art History Award; Distinguished Teaching of Art Award; Charles Rufus Morey Book Award; Frank Jewett Mather Award for Distinction in Art & Architectural Criticism; Arthur Kingsley Porter Prize for Best Article by Younger Scholar in The Art Bulletin; Alfred H Barr, Jr Award for Museum Scholarship; Distinguished Artist Award for Lifetime Achievement; Award for a Distinguished Body of Work, Exhibition, Presentation or Performance

O **COLOR ASSOCIATION OF THE US,** 409 W 44th St, New York, NY 10036. Tel 212-582-6884. *Pres* Bill Bonnellgal; *Exec Dir* Marielle Bancou; *Dir Mem* Hugh Sangcola; *Assoc Dir* Margaret Walch
Open Mon - Fri 9 AM - 4 PM. Estab 1915 for the purpose of forecasting fashion colors & standards in the United States. Mem: 1500; dues $520
Income: Financed by mem
Publications: CAUS Newsletter, 8 times per year; The Color Compendium
Activities: Lect open to members, 12 vis lectrs per yr

O **CONGRESSIONAL ARTS CAUCUS,** House of Representatives, House Annex 2, H2-345, Washington, DC 20515. Tel 202-226-2456. *Acting Chmn* James Jeffords
Estab 1980 to keep members informed of the progress of arts legislation in Congress and provide them with analyses of issues affecting the arts community as a whole and within their own districts. Mem: The Caucus, which is bipartisan, is open to any member of the House of Representatives or Senate who is interested in supporting the arts

O **THE DRAWING SOCIETY,** 15 Penn Plaza, PO Box 66, New York, NY 10001. Tel 212-563-4822; FAX 212-563-4829. *Pres* Paul Cummings; *VPres* Wilder Green
Estab 1959 to encourage interest in, & understanding of, drawing of all periods & cultures. Mem: Dues $100 & up for patrons, institutional $75, associate $45
Exhibitions: Theodore Roszak: The Drawings
Publications: Drawing, bi-monthly; Books & catalogues
Activities: Originate traveling exhibitions to museums in United States

O **FEDERATION OF MODERN PAINTERS & SCULPTORS,** 234 W 21st St, New York, NY 10011. Tel 212-568-2981, 255-4858. *Pres* Haim Mendelson; *VPres* Ahmet Gursoy; *VPres* Barbara Krashes; *VPres* Theo Hios
Estab 1940 as a national organization to promote the cultural interests of free progressive artists working in the United States. Mem: 60; selected by membership committee; dues $15; meeting every two months
Income: Financed by membership
Exhibitions: Exhibition at Art Students League; A Decade for Renewal, at Lever House, New York. (1992) Krasdale Gallery, New York City
Publications: Exhibit catalog
Activities: Lectures open to public, 1 - 2 vis lectrs per yr; symposium; originate traveling exhibitions

O **GENERAL SERVICES ADMINISTRATION,** Art-in-Architecture, Public Bldg Service, 18th & F Sts NW, Washington, DC 20405. Tel 202-501-1256. *Dir* Dale M Lanzone
The Art-in-Architecture program commissions national artists to design & execute sculpture, murals, tapestries & other art works to be incorporated as part of the design of Federal Buildings. The scope of work is determined by the size & character of the building with allowances up to .5 percent of the estimated construction cost. Artists are commissioned by direct selection by the government upon recommendation by a panel of distinguished art professionals and community advisors
Income: $1,000,000

O **GUILD OF BOOK WORKERS,** 521 Fifth Ave, New York, NY 10175. Tel 212-757-6454. *Pres* Frank Mowery; *VPres* Bernadette Callery
Estab 1906 as a national organization to establish and maintain a feeling of kinship and mutual interest among workers in the several hand book crafts. Mem: 620; membership open to all interested persons; dues national $40, chapter (New York City Area Guild, New England Guild, Midwest Guild) $10 additional; annual meeting May or June
Income: Financed by membership
Exhibitions: 80th Anniversary Exhibition consisting of fine bindings, artists' books, restorations, calligraphy & decorated papers
Publications: Guild of Book Workers Journal, 2 times per year; Membership List, annually; Newsletter, 6 times per yr; Supply List, biennially; Opportunities for Study in Hand Bookbinding and Calligraphy, directory and supplement
Activities: Lectures open to members only; tours; workshops; annual seminar on Standards of Excellence in Hand Bookbinding open to public; book traveling exhibitions; originate traveling exhibitions
L **Library,** Univ of Iowa, Conservation Dept, Boston, IA 52242. Tel 914-354-7101. *Librn* Pamela Spitzmueller
Open to Guild members for lending and reference
Library Holdings: Vols 500
Special Subjects: Related to the hand book crafts; bookbinding; manuals on book & paper making crafts

O **INDUSTRIAL DESIGNERS SOCIETY OF AMERICA,** 1142 Walker Rd, Suite E, Great Falls, VA 22066. Tel 703-759-0100; FAX 703-759-7679. *Pres* Charles Pelly; *Exec Dir* Robert T Schwartz
Open daily 9 AM - 5 PM. No admis fee. Estab and incorporated 1965 as a nonprofit national organization representing the profession of industrial design. Mem: 2200; dues full, affiliate & international $213, assoc $134; annual meeting in Aug
Publications: Innovations, quarterly; IDSA Newsletter, monthly; Membership Directory; other surveys & studies
Activities: IDSA Student Chapters; IDSA Student Merit Awards; lect; competitions

O **INTERCULTURA, INC,** 3327 W Seventh St, Fort Worth, TX 76107. Tel 817-332-4691. *Interim Dir* Margaret Booher; *Dir Exhib* Marcus Sloan
Estab to organize & exhibit various art projects for museums in the US & abroad
Exhibitions: (1992) Gates of Mystery: The Art of Russia. (1993) Georgia O'Keeffe. (1994) African Zion: Sacred Art of Ethiopia

O **INTERMUSEUM CONSERVATION ASSOCIATION,** Allen Art Bldg, Oberlin, OH 44074. Tel 216-775-7331. *Pres* Emily Kass; *VPres* Anne Moore; *Secy-Treas & Dir* Francis Ashley
Estab 1952 as a non-profit conservation laboratory to aid in the maintenance of the collections of its member museums. Not open to public, maintains a technical conservation library. Mem: 29; must be non-profit cultural institution; dues $200 - $1000; meetings biannually
Activities: Lect open to public; 3 - 6 vis lectr per yr; seminars, twice a yr; scholarships for advanced training of conservators

O **INTERNATIONAL CENTER FOR ADVANCED STUDIES IN ART,** NY Univ Dept of Art & Art Education, 34 Stuyvesant St, New York, NY 10003. Tel 212-998-5700; FAX 212-505-9092. *Chmn* Leonard Lehrer
Estab 1979 to provide international studies through which the complex and multi-faceted field of visual arts can be viewed, examined, researched and developed on the highest scholarly and professional level. The most significant aspect of the Center is the firsthand contact with critics, theorists, aestheticians and other specialists and the opportunity to work with artists and other thinkers

O **INTERNATIONAL FOUNDATION FOR ART RESEARCH, INC,** 46 E 70th St, New York, NY 10021. Tel 212-879-1780; FAX 212-734-4174. *Executive Dir* Constance Lowenthal
Open Mon - Fri 9:30 AM - 5:30 PM. Estab 1968 to provide a service for impartial consideration by experts of questions concerning attribution and authenticity of major works of art; expanded in 1975 to include an Art Theft Archive for collection and cataloguing of information on art theft
Income: Financed by donations, memberships and fees
Publications: IFAR reports, 10 per year
Activities: Lectures and symposia are conducted throughout the year on subjects relating to connoisseurship, authenticity and art theft and fraud
—**Art Loss Register,** 46 E 70th St, New York, NY 10021. Tel 212-879-1780; FAX 212-734-4174. *Dir* Anna J Kisluk
The Art Loss Register at the International Foundation for Art Research is devoted to collecting & cataloguing records of art thefts & providing information on stolen objects to individuals, institutions, government agencies & others in order to prevent the circulation of stolen art & aid in its recovery. The Register contains reports from a wide range of domestic & international sources. Stolen art reports are published in its monthly IFARreports, a comprehensive report that includes stolen art listings, news coverage, authentication research, forgery news & coverage of the legal context of theft recovery
Income: Financed by fees & subscriptions
—**Authentication Service,** 46 E 70th St, New York, NY 10021. Tel 212-879-1780; FAX 212-879-1780. *Dir* Virgilia H Pancoast
Through this service, the resources of leading institutional experts, both scholarly & scientific, are made available to the public in order to answer questions relating to authenticity & proper attribution of works of art

O **INTERNATIONAL SOCIETY OF COPIER ARTISTS (ISCA),** 800 West End Ave, Suite 1313, New York, NY 10025. Tel 212-662-5533. *Dir* Louise Neaderland
Open by appt. Estab 1981
Collections: Artists Bookworks; exhibition catalogs; original art work; prints; slides
Exhibitions: ISCA Graphics; Using the copier as a creative tool
Publications: ISCA Quarterly
Activities: Educ dept, classes for adults; lect open to the public, 2 vis lectr per year; originate traveling exhibitions

O **INTER-SOCIETY COLOR COUNCIL,** Applied Color Systems, 5 Princess Rd, Lawrenceville, NJ 08648. Tel 609-924-2189. *Secy* Dr Danny C Rich
Estab 1931 as a national organization to stimulate & coordinate the study of color in science, art & industry; federation of 29 national societies & individuals interested in colors. Mem: 900; members must show an interest in color & in the aims & purposes of the Council; dues individual $25; annual meeting usually April
Income: Financed by membership
Publications: Inter-Society Color Council Newsletter, bimonthly
Activities: Lect open to public; lect at meetings; gives Macbeth Award and Godlove Award

O **KAPPA PI INTERNATIONAL HONORARY ART FRATERNITY,** 9321 Paul Adrian Dr, Crestwood, MO 63126. Tel 314-843-1273. *Pres* Arthur B Kennon; *VPres* Dr Ralph M Hudson; *Treas* Myrtle Kerr
Estab 1911 as an international honorary art fraternity for men and women in colleges, universities and art schools
Income: Financed by membership
Publications: Sketch Board Newsletter, annually in the fall; Sketch Book, annual spring magazine
Activities: Sponsors competition in photography; annual scholarships available to active members

O **ARTHUR MANLEY SOCIETY,** 12712 DuPont Circle, Tampa, FL 33626. Tel 813-855-4636. *Pres* Beverley Manley
Open Sept - May, Mon - Fri 10 AM - 8 PM, Sat 10 Am - 4 PM. Incorporated 1984; provides facilities for art activities at the American Fine Arts Society building. Gallery used only for art students. Average Annual Attendance: 9000 - 10,000. Mem: Annual meeting May
Activities: Sponsors lect by prominent people in the art world

O **MID-AMERICA ARTS ALLIANCE & EXHIBITS USA,** 912 Baltimore Ave, Suite 700, Kansas City, MO 64105. Tel 816-421-1388; FAX 816-421-3918. *Chmn* Wallace Richardson; *Pres* Edeen Martin; *Exec Dir* Mary Kennedy McCabe
A national division of Mid America Arts Alliance created to organize & tour exhibits throughout the Unites Sates & beyond
Income: $2,000,000 (financed by federal & state grants, private contributions & exhibition fees)
Exhibitions: The ABCs of Dolphins (mixed media); Aesthetic Origins: A Re-examination of American Pictorialism 1890-1930 (photography); American Indian Realism (photography); Ancestors Known and Unknown (3-D); Artists of the American West; Audubon's Aminals and Birds; Bold Strokes and Quiet Gestures; Buildings and Landscapes; Built, Thrown and Touched (ceramics); By a Clearer Light (photography); Changing American: David Plowden (photography); Chuck Close: Editions; Collective Vision: Artists and Writers Collaborate (mixed media); Connecting Lives: Documents from the AIDS Crisis (photography); John Steuart Curry's America (works on paper); Drawn to Art: William A Berry; Enlightening the Classics; Faces of Destiny (photography); Fields in Focus: Art for the Sky (photography); Fields of Dreams: Architecture and Baseball (mixed media); For God, Country and the Thrill of It (photography); Four Artists/Bon Hoa Si (mixed media); The Good Earth: Folk Art from the Chinese Countryside (mixed media); A Century of African-American Experience Greenwood: From Ruins to Renaissance (photography); Hmong Artistry: Preserving a Culture on Cloth (needlework); Benito Huerta: Attempted Not Known; Image and Identity: Recent Chicana Art (mixed media); Just Plane Screwy: Metaphysical and metaphorical Tools by Artists (mixed media); Elizabeth Layton: Drawing on Life; Warren MacKenzie (ceramics) Mojo: Keith Carter (photography); Barry Moser: Original Wood Engravings from Classical Children's Literature (wood block); Michael A Naranjo: Inner Visions (sculpture); Native American: Contemporary Realities (mixed media); Old Master Prints; On the Land: Three Centuries of American Farmlife (photography); Our Land/Ourselved (mixed media); Paradise Lost and Found: Cher Shaffer (mixed media); Photography and the Old West (photography); The Photography of Benny Joseph (photography); Please Touch (mixed media); Howardena Pindell: A Retrospective (mixed media); Ribs, Rods and Splits: Appalachian Oak Basketry (basketry); Sacred Ground/Sacred Sky (mixed media); Textile Diaries: Quilts as Cultural Markers (quilts); Through the looking Glass; Tutavoh: Learning the Hopi Way (photography); Waterways West (photography); Welty (photography); Woven Vessels (mixed media)
Publications: Exhibtion catalogs
Activities: Book traveling exhibitions; originate traveling exhibitions

O **MIDWEST ART HISTORY SOCIETY,** Univ of North Texas, PO Box 5098, Denton, TX 76203. Tel 817-565-4003. *Pres* Scott A Sullivan
Estab 1973 to further art history in the Midwest as a discipline and a profession. Average Annual Attendance: 150 at meetings. Mem: 550; membership is open to institutions, students and academic and museum art historians in the Midwest; dues institution $10, professional $5; annual meeting March 29th-31st
Income: $1200 (financed by membership)
Publications: Midwest Art History Society Newsletter, Oct & April
Activities: Lect provided

O **NATIONAL ACADEMY OF DESIGN,** 1083 Fifth Ave, New York, NY 10128. Tel 212-369-4880; FAX 212-360-6795. *Dir* Edward P Gallagher; *Cur Drawings, Prints & Paintings* Dita Amory
Open Wed - Sun noon - 5 PM, Fri evening until 8 PM, cl Mon, New Year's, Thanksgiving & Christmas. Admis $2.50. Estab 1825, honorary arts organization for American artists and architects. Mem: 425
Collections: Permanent collection consists of 5000 watercolors, drawings & graphics 2000 paintings, 250 sculptures, mostly the gifts of the artist & architectural members of the Academy from 1825 to present; American art from mid-nineteenth century to the present
Exhibitions: Annual juried exhibition of contemporary art; exhibitions of permanent collection & loan exhibitions
Publications: Annual exhibition catalogue; catalogues of exhibitions of permanent collection; catalogues of special loan exhibitions
Activities: Lectures open to public; tours by appointment; individual paintings and original objects of art lent to other museums; museum shop sells books, posters, catalogues and postcards
L **Archives,** 1083 Fifth Ave & 89th St, 10128. Tel 212-369-4880; FAX 212-360-6795. *Dir* Edward P Gallagher; *Archival Asst* Lois H Woodyatt
Open by appointment only. Admis general $3.50, sr citizens & students $2. For reference
Library Holdings: Biographical files on all members; records on The National Academy of Design; Other — Clipping files, exhibition catalogs, manuscripts, memorabilia, original art works, pamphlets, photographs, prints, sculpture
Special Subjects: National Academy of Design
Collections: Diploma works of artists elected to membership
Activities: Classes for adults & children; docent training; lect open to public; concerts; gallery talks; tours; competitions with prizes; scholarships & fels; exten dept serves art students; individual paintings & original objects of art lent to other museums; lending collection contains original art works, original prints, paintings & sculpture; book traveling exhibitions; originate traveling exhibitions

O **NATIONAL ALLIANCE FOR MEDIA ARTS & CULTURE (NAMAC),** 1212 Broadway, Suite 816, Oakland, CA 94612. Tel 510-451-2717. *National Dir* Julian Low; *Program Coordr* Mimi Zarsky; *Editor* Norman Jayo
Estab for the purpose of furthering diversity & participation in all forms of the media arts, including film, video, audio & multimedia production
Income: $200,000 (financed by grants)
Publications: Main newsletter, monthly; NAMAC Member Directory, biennial

O **NATIONAL ANTIQUE & ART DEALERS ASSOCIATION OF AMERICA,** 15 E 57th St, New York, NY 10022. Tel 212-826-9707; FAX 212-319-0471. *Pres* Mark Jacoby; *VPres* Herve Aaron; *Secy* Andrew Chait; *Treas* James McConnaughy
Estab 1954 to promote the best interests of the antique and art trade; to collect and circulate reports, statistics and other information pertaining to art; to sponsor

and organize antique and art exhibitions; to promote just, honorable and ethical trade practices
Publications: NAADA News, quarterly; NAADA Directory, every 2 years
Activities: Lect

O **NATIONAL ARCHITECTURAL ACCREDITING BOARD, INC,** 1735 New York Ave NW, Washington, DC 20006. Tel 202-783-2007; FAX 202-626-7421. *Exec Dir* John Maudlin-Jeronimo
Estab 1940 to produce and maintain a current list of accredited programs in architecture in the United States and its jurisdictions, with the general objective that a well-integrated program of architectural education be developed which will be national in scope
Publications: Criteria and Procedures, pamphlet; List of Accredited Programs in Architecture, annually

O **NATIONAL ART EDUCATION ASSOCIATION,** 1916 Association Dr, Reston, VA 22091-1590. Tel 703-860-8000. *Pres* James Clarke; *Pres-Elect* Mark R Hansen; *Exec Dir* Dr Thomas A Hatfield
Estab 1947 through the affiliation of four regional groups, Eastern, Western, Pacific and Southeastern Arts Associations. The NAEA is a national organization devoted to the advancement of the professional interests and competence of teachers of art at all educational levels. Promotes the study of the problems of teaching art; encourages research and experimentation; facilitates the professional and personal cooperation of its members; holds public discussions and programs; publishes desirable articles, reports, and surveys; integrates efforts of others with similar purposes. Mem: 29,000 art teachers, administrators, supervisors & students; fee institutional comprehensive $150, active $50; National Conference held 1991 will be in Atlanta, GA & in 1992 in Phoenix, AZ
Income: Programs financed through membership, sales of publications, and occasional grants for specific purposes
Publications: Art Education, 6 issues per year; NAEA Advisor, 4 issues per year; NAEA News, 6 issues per year; Studies in Art Education, 4 times per year; special publications

O **NATIONAL ARTISTS EQUITY ASSOCIATION INC,** Central Station, PO Box 28068, Washington, DC 20038-8068. Tel 202-628-9633; WATS 800-628-9633. *Pres* George C Koch; *VPres* Carol Sky; *Exec Dir* Catherine T Auth
Estab 1947 as a national nonprofit, aesthetically nonpartisan organization working for social, economic & legislative change for all visual artists. Mem: 4500 who are or ask to be recognized as professional contributors to the development of visual art & culture; dues chapter $60, at-large $40
Income: $100,000 (financed by membership and grants)
Publications: The National Artists Equity News, quarterly
Activities: Works for legislation & public policy favorable to visual artists; chapters occasionally organize & circulate traveling exhibitions or conduct conferences, seminars, or other educational programs

O **NATIONAL ASSEMBLY OF LOCAL ARTS AGENCIES,** 927 15th St NW, 12th Floor, Washington, DC 20005. Tel 202-371-2830; FAX 202-371-0424. *Pres & Chief Exec Officer* Robert Lynch
Open Mon - Fri 9 AM - 5:30 PM. No admis fee. Estab 1978 to provide services for and to represent the interests of local arts agencies. Mem: 800; annual meeting June
Income: $1,100,000 (financed by mem, grants & contracts)
Publications: Connections Monthly; Monographs, monthly newsletters
Activities: Annual convention, festivals conference & regional workshops

O **NATIONAL ASSEMBLY OF STATE ARTS AGENCIES,** 1010 Vermont Ave NW, Suite 920, Washington, DC 20005. Tel 202-347-6352; FAX 202-737-0526. *Chmn* Barbara Robinson; *First VChmn* Marvin Cohen; *Exec Dir* Jonathan Katz
Estab 1975 to enhance the growth and development of the arts through an informed and skilled membership; to provide forums for the review and development of national arts policy. Mem: 56; members are the fifty-six state and jurisdictional arts agencies, affiliate memberships are open to public; annual meeting Oct
Income: Financed by membership and federal grants
Publications: Annual survey of state appropriations to arts councils; newsletter, quarterly; NASAA Notes, monthly

O **NATIONAL ASSOCIATION OF ARTISTS' ORGANIZATIONS (NAAO),** 918 F St NW, Washington, DC 20004. Tel 202-347-6350. *Exec Dir* Charlotte Murphy; *Asst Dir* Penny Boyer; *Development Officer* Mary Drayton-Hill; *Admin Asst* Victoria Reis
Estab for the advancement of artist-run and artist-directed contemporary art organizations

O **NATIONAL ASSOCIATION OF SCHOOLS OF ART & DESIGN,** 11250 Roger Bacon Dr, Suite 21, Reston, VA 22090. Tel 703-437-0700. *Executive Dir* Samuel Hope
Formerly the National Conference of Schools of Design, holding its first conference in 1944. Changed name in 1948, at which time its constitution and by-laws were adopted. Changed its name again in 1960 from National Association of Schools of Design to National Association of Schools of Art. Name changed again in 1981 to National Association of Schools of Art and Design. NASAD is the national accrediting agency for higher educational institutions in the visual arts and design and is so recognized by the US Department of Education and the Council on Postsecondary Accreditation. The organization was established to develop a closer relationship among schools and departments of art and design for the purpose of educating designers and artists in the visual arts and giving evidence of permanence and stability, possessing an approved organization, administration, faculty and facilities and maintaining standards agreed upon by the Association
Income: $130,000 (financed by mem)
Publications: Directory of Member Institutions, annually; Handbook of Accreditation Standards, biennial

O **NATIONAL ASSOCIATION OF WOMEN ARTISTS, INC,** 41 Union Square W, Room 906, New York, NY 10003. Tel 212-675-1616. *Pres* Bernice Faegenburg
Estab 1889 as a national organization to provide opportunities for member women artists, to exhibit their work. Mem: 725; member work is juried prior to selection; dues $40; meetings Nov & May
Income: Financed by mem
Exhibitions: Annual members' exhibition in spring with awards; annual traveling exhibitions of oils, acrylics, works on paper, printmaking; annual New York City shows of oils, acrylics, works on paper, printmaking & sculpture
Publications: Annual Exhibition Catalog
Activities: Lect open to the public, 1 vis lectr per year; awards given to members during annual exhibition; originate traveling exhibitions

O **NATIONAL CARTOONISTS SOCIETY,** 157 W 57th St, Suite 904, New York, NY 10019. Tel 212-333-7606. *Liaison* Arnold Roth; *Pres* Mell Lazarus
Estab 1946 to advance the ideals and standards of the profession of cartooning; to assist needy, or incapacitated cartoonists; to stimulate interest in the art of cartooning by cooperating with established schools; to encourage talented students; to assist governmental and charitable institutes. Mem: 480; annual Reuben Awards Dinner in April
Collections: Milt Gross Fund; National Cartoonists Society Collection
Publications: Newsletter, monthly; The Cartoonist; annually
Activities: Educ dept to supply material and information to students; individual cartoonists to lect, chalktalks can be arranged; cartoon auctions; proceeds from traveling exhibitions and auctions support Milt Gross Fund assisting needy cartoonists, widows and children; gives Reuben Award to Outstanding Cartoonist of the Year, Silver Plaque Awards to best cartoonists in individual categories of cartooning; original cartoons lent to schools, libraries and galleries; originate traveling exhibitions

O **NATIONAL COUNCIL ON EDUCATION FOR THE CERAMIC ARTS (NCECA),** PO Box 1677, Bandon, OR 97411. Tel 503-347-4394.
Estab 1967 as a non-profit organization to promote & improve ceramic art, design, craft & educ through the exchange of information among artists, teachers & individuals in the ceramic art community
Income: Financed by annual conferences & memberships
Exhibitions: Annual Conference Exhibitions
Publications: Journal, annual; Information Annual Conference, spring; Newsletter, 4 times a year

O **NATIONAL ENDOWMENT FOR THE ARTS,** 1100 Pennsylvania Ave NW, Washington, DC 20506. Tel 202-682-5400. *Chmn* Frank Hodsoll; *Deputy Chmn for Programs* Randyy McAusland; *Deputy Chmn for Management* Laurence Daden
Open 9 AM - 5:30 PM. No admis fee. Estab 1965 to encourage & support American arts & artists. Information is to foster the excellence, diversity & vitality of the arts in the United States & to help broaden their ability & appreciation
Income: $167,731,000 (appropriation for fiscal year, programming federal funds that are given through grants to individuals and non-profit organizations. Grants to organizations must be matched at least dollar for dollar by private, state or local funds)
Publications: Annual Report; Guide to the National Endowment for the Arts
L **Library,** 1100 Pennsylvania Ave NW, 20506. Tel 202-682-5485. *Librn* M Christine Morrison
Open Mon - Fri 9 AM - 5:30 PM. Estab 1971 to provide an effective information service to staff which will support program and division activities and contribute to the accomplishment of agency goals
Income: Financed by federal appropriation
Library Holdings: Vols 8000; Per subs 150; Other — Clipping files
Special Subjects: Arts in contemporary America, arts administration, cultural policy; government and the arts

O **NATIONAL FOUNDATION FOR ADVANCEMENT IN THE ARTS,** 3915 Biscayne Blvd, Miami, FL 33137. Tel 305-573-0490; FAX 305-573-4870. *Pres* William Banchs
Estab 1981 to identify and reward young artists at critical stages in their development

O **NATIONAL INSTITUTE FOR ARCHITECTURAL EDUCATION,** 30 W 22nd St, New York, NY 10010. Tel 212-924-7000; FAX 212-366-5836. *Chmn* Robert Fox; *VChmn* Stephen Potters; *Executive Dir* Joan Bassin; *Treas* Susan Swan
Open Mon - Fri 9 AM - 5 PM, Tues 9 AM - 9 PM. Incorporated 1894 as Society of Beaux-Arts Architects, which was dissolved Dec 1941; Beaux-Arts Institute of Design estab 1916, name changed 1956 to present name. Average Annual Attendance: 2500. Mem: Approx 250; dues $25; annual meeting end of October
Exhibitions: Prize-winning drawings of competitions held during year
Publications: Yearbook, annually in October
Activities: Lect open to public, 4-5 vis lectr per year; competitions with awards; Trustee for the Lloyd Warren Fellowship (Paris Prize in Architecture) for study and travel abroad; William Van Alen Architect Memorial Award (international competition) annual scholarship for further study or research project of some architectural nature; and other trust funds for prize awards for study and travel abroad and educational activities in the United States; individual paintings & original objects of art lent; lending collection contains 200 original prints; book traveling exhibitions 3-4 per year; originate traveling exhibitions

O **NATIONAL INSTITUTE FOR THE CONSERVATION OF CULTURAL PROPERTY,** 3299 K St NW, Suite 403, Washington, DC 20007. Tel 202-625-1495; FAX 202-625-1485. *Pres* Lawrence L Reger
Estab 1974 as a national forum for conservation & preservation activities in the United States

O **NATIONAL LEAGUE OF AMERICAN PEN WOMEN,** 1300 17th St NW, Washington, DC 20036. Tel 202-785-1997. *Pres* Muriel C Freeman
Estab 1897 to support women office arts. Maintains member reference library. Mem: 6000, 212 state branches; dues $25
Income: Financed by dues and legacies
Collections: Purchase award
Exhibitions: NLAPW Biennial Arts Show
Publications: The Pen Woman, monthly magazine
Activities: Lect open to public; concerts; competitions with awards; scholarships offered

O **NATIONAL SCULPTURE SOCIETY,** 1177 Avenue of the Americas, New York, NY 10036. Tel 212-889-6960. *Pres* Stanley Bleifeld; *VPres* Domenico Facci; *Exec Dir* Gwen M Pier; *Secy* Marion Roller
Open Mon - Fri 9:30 AM - 4:30 PM. No admis fee. Estab 1893 as a national organization to spread the knowledge of good sculpture. Mem: 4000; work juried for sculptor membership; vote of Board of Directors for allied professional & patron membership; dues $20- $100; annual meeting second Tues in Jan
Income: Financed by endowment, membership & donations
Exhibitions: Annual juried exhibition open to all United States residents
Publications: Exhibition catalog, annually; membership book, triennial; National Sculpture Review, quarterly
Activities: Educ dept; lectures open to the public, 4-6 vis lectr per year; gallery talks; tours; annual exhibition; competitions; youth awards annually; exhibition prizes; Education Committee chooses recipients for NSS scholarships; scholarships offered to accredited art schools; exhibitions organized for other institutions
L **Library,** 1177 Avenue of the Americas, New York, NY 10036. Tel 212-889-6961. *Librn* Theodora Morgan
Open to the public for reference; a few volumes and periodicals, photographic and original archival materials
Library Holdings: Per subs 5000; Micro — Fiche; AV — Slides, v-tapes; Other — Clipping files, exhibition catalogs, photographs, sculpture
Special Subjects: Sculpture, American sculpture, biography, history

O **NATIONAL SOCIETY OF MURAL PAINTERS, INC,** c/o American Fine Arts Society, 215 W 57th St, New York, NY 10019. Tel 718-389-7607. *Pres* Rhoda Andors
Estab and incorporated 1895 to encourage and advance the standards of mural painting in America; to formulate a code for decorative competitions and by-laws to regulate professional practice. Mem: 200; dues $25, non-res $20
Publications: Biographies and articles pertinent to the mural painting profession; Press Sheets of photographs and articles of the executed work of the members of society
Activities: Exhibitions held in collaboration with allied professions; available for booking - a traveling show of color sketches for murals on the subject of momentous events in American History

O **NATIONAL SOCIETY OF PAINTERS IN CASEIN & ACRYLIC, INC,** 969 Catasauqua Rd, Whitehall, PA 18052. Tel 215-264-7472. *Pres* Douglas Wiltrout; *VPres* Robert Dunn; *Corresp Secy* Dorothy Barberis
Open in March during exhibition. Estab 1952 as a national organization for a showcase for artists in casein and acrylic. Galleries rented from National Arts Club. Average Annual Attendance: 800 during exhibition. Mem: 120; membership by invitation, work must pass three juries; dues $20; annual meeting April
Income: $3000 (financed by membership)
Exhibitions: Annual Exhibition
Publications: Exhibition Catalog, annually
Activities: Demonstrations; medals and $2500 in prizes given at annual exhibition; originate traveling exhibitions

O **NATIONAL WATERCOLOR SOCIETY,** 18220 S Hoffman Ave, Cerritos, CA 90701. Tel 310-925-7722. *Pres* John Selchak; *First VPs* Robert Hallet; *Treas* Linda Doll; *Dir Communications* Bonnie Price
Estab 1921 to sponsor art exhibits for the cultural & educational benefit of the public. Mem: 1560; dues $25 - $30 beginning each year in March (must be juried into mem); annual meeting Jan
Collections: Award-winning paintings from 1954 to present
Exhibitions: Spring Membership Exhibition; National Annual Exhibition. (1993) Show of permanent collection at Los Angeles Century Gallery
Publications: Society's newsletter; color annual catalog
Activities: Sponsor yearly grant to children's art program of LA Southwest Museum; originate traveling exhibitions

O **NEW ENGLAND WATERCOLOR SOCIETY,** 162 Newbury St, Boston, MA 02116. Tel 617-536-7660. *Pres* Nancy Howell
Estab 1886 to advance the fine art of aqua media. Mem: 200, assoc mem 80; annual meeting in Mar
Income: Financed by membership
Exhibitions: Annual winter membership exhibit; Biennial-North America National Show-Juried Exhibit; 2-3 exhibits per year
Activities: Demonstrations, lect & gallery works open to the public during exhibitions

O **PASTEL SOCIETY OF AMERICA,** National Arts Club Gallery, 15 Gramercy Park S, New York, NY 10003. Tel 212-533-6931. *Pres* Flora B Giffuni, MFA
Estab 1972 to promote & encourage pastel painting/artists. Mem: 600; dues full $35, assoc $25; mem open to professional artists; meetings monthly
Library Holdings: AV — A-tapes, slides, v-tapes; Other — Clipping files, exhibition catalogs, original art works
Publications: Pastelagram, bi-annual
Activities: Classes for adults; scholarships offered; exten dept serves lending collection of paintings

O **PASTEL SOCIETY OF OREGON,** PO Box 105, Roseburg, OR 97470. Tel 503-440-9171. *Pres* Laura Block
Estab 1978 to promote pastel as an art medium and to educate the public on pastel. Mem: 70; dues $20 per year; mem open to artists working in pastels; monthly working meetings
Income: $2000 (financed by membership, shows)
Library Holdings: AV — Slides, v-tapes
Special Subjects: Art Education, Video
Exhibitions: (1993) Membership Show; National Show in Bend, Oregon
Publications: Pastel Newsletter, bi-monthly
Activities: Classes for adults; hands on exhibitions for schools; scholarships offered

O **PASTEL SOCIETY OF THE WEST COAST,** Sacramento Fine Arts Center, 5330-B Gibbons Dr, Carmichael, CA 95608. Tel 916-991-2708. *Pres* Marbo Barnard; *VPres* Reif Erickson; *Memberships* Dianna Rossi
Estab 1985 to promote soft pastel medium and exhibitions, workshops. Mem: 300; dues $25; quarterly meetings in Jan, April, July & Oct 3rd Wed
Income: $20,000 (financed by membership, donations)
Library Holdings: AV — V-tapes
Exhibitions: (1993) Assoc Mem Show: Pastel in the Light; Pastel USA (International)
Publications: PSWC newsletter, quarterly; exhibit catalogs
Activities: Classes for adults; lectures open to public, 4 vis lectr per year; scholarships offered

O **PRINT CLUB CENTER FOR PRINTS & PHOTOGRAPHS,** 1614 Latimer St, Philadelphia, PA 19103. Tel 215-735-6090. *Pres* Richard P Jaffe; *VPres* Joanne Hirsh; *Dir* Kathleen Edwards; *Asst to Dir* Richard Frey; *Treas* Donald McThail
Open Tues - Sat 11 AM - 5:30 PM. No admis fee. Estab 1915 as a non-profit, educational organization dedicated to the promotion of fine prints & the support & encouragement of printmakers, photographers & collectors. Average Annual Attendance: 2000. Mem: 4000; dues contributing $50, family $30, individual $25, artists $15; annual meeting in Jan
Income: $100,000 (financed by endowment, membership and private and government grants for some activities)
Collections: The Print Club Permanent Collection (prints and photograph collection held at the Philadelphia Museum of Art); The Print Club Archives (documents, books and catalogues held at the Historical Society of Pennsylvania)
Exhibitions: Changing monthly exhibitions of prints and photographs; Annual International Competition (since 1924)
Publications: Counter Proof, bi-annual; News Print, monthly news sheet
Activities: Workshops for artists; lect series for print collectors; lect open to public, 15 visiting lectr per year; gallery talks; competitions; various prizes and purchase awards; originate traveling exhibitions

O **PRINT COUNCIL OF AMERICA,** c/o The Baltimore Museum of Art, Art Museum Dr, Baltimore, MD 21218. Tel 410-396-6345; FAX 410-396-6562. *Pres* Jay M Fisher; *VPres* Colta Ives; *Treas* Aimee Troyen
Estab 1956 as a nonprofit organization fostering the study and appreciation of fine prints, new and old. Mem: 100 museum and university professionals interested in prints; annual meeting April or May
Income: Dues & publication royalties
Publications: Occasional publications on old & modern prints; The Print Council Index to Oeuvre-Catalogues of Prints by European & American Artists

O **SALMAGUNDI CLUB,** 47 Fifth Ave, New York, NY 10003. Tel 212-255-7740. *Chmn Board* Open; *Pres* Kenith Fitch; *Correspondence Secy* John McKenna
Gallery open during exhibitions 1 - 5 PM. No admis fee. Estab 1871, incorporated 1880, to enhance the advancement of art appreciation, building purchased 1917. Clubhouse restaurant, gallery & library. Mem: 600; dues resident layman & resident artist $330, scholarship graduated to scale, Honorary & Emeritus
Income: Financed by dues, donations, bequests
Exhibitions: Seven per year by artist members with cash awards two per year by non-members (artists, photographers, sculptors) with cash awards
Publications: Centennial Roster published in 1972; Salmagundi Membership Roster, every three years; Salmagundian, three per yr
Activities: Lectures; art classes; awards; scholarships and prizes; acts as organizing and screening agency between the US Navy and US Coast Guard, and all qualified American artists; under its Naval Art Cooperation and Liaison (NACAL) Committee and Coast Guard Art Program (COGAP), artists are chosen and sent on short painting trips around the world to interpret the daily life and traditions of the US Navy & US Coast Guard; buys paintings to present to museums
L **Library,** 47 Fifth Ave, New York, NY 10003. Tel 212-255-7740. *Librn* Kenith Fitch
For reference only
Library Holdings: Vols 6000

O **SCULPTORS GUILD, INC,** 110 Greene St, New York, NY 10012. Tel 212-431-5669. *Pres* Jean Woodham; *Exec VPres* Barry Parker; *VPres Publications* Phyllis Mark; *VPres Annual Exhib* Vera Schupackitz; *VPres Admissions* M Mashiko; *VPres Spec Exhib* Renata Manasse Schwebel; *Treas* Pamela Endacott; *Secy* Carole Lewis
Open Tues & Thurs 10 AM - 5 PM & by appointment. No admis fee. Estab 1937 to promote sculpture & show members' work in an annual show & throughout the country. Mem: 114; dues $75; annual meeting in May
Income: Financed by mem dues, donations, & commissions on sales
Exhibitions: (1991) Annual Exhibition at Southern Vermont Art Center; Connecticut Commission on the Arts Showcase; The Nature of Wood; Five Sculptors from the Guild-Lobby Gallery. (1992) The Coming of Age of American Sculpture: The First Decades of the Sculptors Guilde, 1930's - 1950's, Leigh University, Iowa State University, Paine Art Center, WI, St Johns College; The Sculptors Guild at the 14th International Sculpture Conference, Philadelphia;

55th Annual Exhibition Lever House
Publications: Brochure 1985; exhibit catalogs, every other year for annual exhibitions; 50th Anniversary Catalog 1937-1938; The Guild Reporter, Vol. 1, No. 1, 1986, annually
Activities: Lectures open to public; competitions; originates traveling exhibitions

O **SOCIETY FOR FOLK ARTS PRESERVATION, INC,** 308 E 79th St, New York, NY 10021. Tel 212-734-4503. *Exec Dir* Evelyn Stern; *First VPres* Edward Lauitt; *Second VPres* Dr Erika Moser; *Secy* Robert Fertitta
Open by appointment. Estab 1977 to document on film and video, living folk art and craft traditions, worldwide. Mem: 350; dues $40
Income: Financed by donations
Collections: Folk toys & objects; Indian Textiles
Exhibitions: Warli Womens Wall Paintings from Maharashtra, India; A Sense of Beauty; Multi Image Slide Presentations - Crafts and People of Asia
Publications: Newsletter, twice a year
Activities: Educ dept; lectures open to the public, 3 vis lectr per yr; tours; originate traveling exhibitions
L Library, 308 E 79th St, New York, NY 10021. Tel 212-734-4503.
Estab 1979. Reference only
Library Holdings: Vols 500; AV — A-tapes, slides 14,000, v-tapes; Other — Clipping files, exhibition catalogs, memorabilia, original art works, pamphlets, photographs
Special Subjects: Living folk arts and crafts
Collections: Indian textiles; folk art

O **SOCIETY OF AMERICAN GRAPHIC ARTISTS,** 32 Union Square, Room 1214, New York, NY 10003. Tel 212-260-5706. *Pres* Michael DiCerbo; *VPres* Susan Carter-Carter; *VPres* Florence Putterman; *Treas* Emily Trueblood
Estab 1916 as a society of printmakers, now a society of graphic artists. Mem: 250 voted in by merit; dues $20; annual meeting May
Income: Financed by membership and associate memberships
Exhibitions: Semi-annual Open Competition National Print Exhibition; Semi-annual Closed Members Exhibit; National Traveling Exhibitions every two years
Publications: Exhibition Catalog, annually; Presentation Prints for Associate Membership
Activities: Lect open to public, 1 visiting lectr per year; sponsors competitive and members' exhibits with awards; original objects of art lent, lending collection contains original prints; originate traveling exhibitions

O **SOCIETY OF AMERICAN HISTORICAL ARTISTS,** PO Box 409, Jericho, NY 11753. Tel 516-681-8820. *Pres* John Duillo; *VPres* James Muir; *Treasurer* Ron Tunison
Estab 1980 for furthering American Historical Art, especially authenticity. Mem: 13; dues $150; meetings 3-4 per yr
Activities: Awards for excellence

O **SOCIETY OF ANIMAL ARTISTS, INC,** 151 Carroll St, PO Box 24, Bronx, NY 10464. Tel 718-885-2181. *Pres* Joseph Vance; *Treas* Eric Berg
Open during exhibitions. No admis fee. Estab 1960 to encourage international awareness of the artists who explore the beauty and habits of animals, and by so doing, help ecology and the environment. Mem: 250; artists must pass jury of admissions to become a member; dues $25, initiation fee $200; meetings twice a year, or more often if needed
Income: Financed by members
Exhibitions: Boston Museum of Science. (1991) Cleveland Museum of Science. (1992) Roger Tory Peterson Institute
Publications: Newsletter; catalogues & shows, annually
Activities: Lect for members only, 3 visiting lectr per year; gallery talks; conventions arranged with film lect and instruction; slide lect of trips with animal art by members; advisory board for those who want to study animal art and wildlife; paintings and individual objects of art lent to members, wildlife organizations, Audubon, World Wildlife Special Exhibitions; lending collection consists of catalogs, prints, color and framed reproductions, sculpture, photographs and slides; originate traveling exhibitions; prints, reproductions and original art sold at gallery shows

O **SOCIETY OF ARCHITECTURAL HISTORIANS,** 1232 Pine St, Philadelphia, PA 19107. Tel 215-735-0224, 735-0246. *Pres* Elisabeth MacDougall; *First VPres* Franklin Toker; *Second VPres* Keith Morgan; *Executive Dir* David Bahlman
Open daily 8:30 AM - 4:30 PM. Estab to provide an informal forum for those interested in architecture and its related arts, to encourage scholarly research in the field and to promote the preservation of significant architectural monuments throughout the world. Mem: 3400 who show an interest in architecture, past, present & future; dues $60; annual meeting Apr
Income: Financed by membership
Publications: Journal, quarterly; Newsletter, bimonthly; Preservation Forum, biannual
Activities: Sponsors competitions; Alice Davis Hitchcock Book Award, Founders' Award, Antoinette Forrester Downing Award & Architectural Exhibition Catalogue Award given annually; scholarships given to student members for graduate work in architecture & architectural history to attend annual domestic tour; Rosann Berry Fellowship to help advanced grad student attend annual meeting; sales shop sells architectural guides and booklets and also back issues of the Journal

O **SOCIETY OF ILLUSTRATORS,** 128 E 63rd St, New York, NY 10021. Tel 212-838-2560; FAX 212-838-2561. *Pres* Eileen Hedyschultz; *Dir* Terry Brown
Open Mon, Wed, Thurs, Fri 10 AM - 5 PM, Tues 10 AM - 8 PM. No admis fee. Estab 1901 as a national organization of professional illustrators and art directors. Gallery has group, theme, one-man and juried shows, approximately every three weeks. Mem: 1000
Publications: Illustrators Annual
Activities: Lectures open to public; holds annual national juried exhibition of best illustrations of the year; awards scholarships to college level art students; originate traveling exhibitions; sales shop sells books

O **SOCIETY OF NORTH AMERICAN GOLDSMITHS,** 5009 Londonderry Dr, Jacksonville, FL 33647. Tel 813-977-5326; FAX 813-977-8462. *Pres* Peter Jagooa; *Treas* Walt Soellner; *Bus Mgr* Robert Mitchell
Mem: 2000; dues $45; annual meetings in Aug
Income: $400,000
Exhibitions: Distinguished Members of SNAG; Jewelry USA
Publications: Metalsmith, quarterly magazine; Newsletter, bi-monthly
Activities: Lectures open to members only; competitions; scholarships

O **SPECIAL LIBRARIES ASSOCIATION,** Museum, Arts and Humanities Division, c/o Dir of Communications, 1700 18th NW, Washington, DC 20009. Tel 202-234-4700. *Pres* Katherine M Richards; *Exec Dir* David R Bender; *Bulletin Educ* Maria Barry; *Dir Communications* Mark Serepca
Estab 1929 to provide an information forum & exchange for librarians in the specialized fields of museums, arts & humanities. Mem: 582; dues $75; annual meeting early June
Publications: Museums, Arts and Humanities Division Bulletin, semi-annual

O **THE STAINED GLASS ASSOCIATION OF AMERICA,** 4050 Broadway, Suite 219, PO Box 22642, Kansas City, MO 64113. FAX 816-524-9405; WATS 800-888-7422. *Executive Secy* Kathy Murdock
Estab 1903 as an international organization to promote the development and advancement of the stained glass craft. Mem: 550; there are five categories of membership - studio member, artist designer, craft supplier member, associate member & patron member (various criteria apply to each membership); dues $300 for members with studio; associate members $100, patron members $50; semi-annual meetings Jan & June
Income: Financed by membership dues
Publications: Stained Glass magazine, quarterly
Activities: Educ dept with two and three week courses; apprenticeship program; competitions sponsored for apprentices only, every two years; cash prizes

O **UKIYO-E SOCIETY OF AMERICA, INC,** PO Box 665, New York, NY 10150. *Pres* William E Harkins; *VPres* Gabriele Grunebaum; *Secy* Martin Levitz; *Treas* Paul Steir
Estab 1972 as society of collectors of Japanese woodblock prints. Average Annual Attendance: 350. Mem: 291; dues benefactor $500, patron $100, supporting $50, contributing $40, individual $35; ten monthly meetings
Income: 10,000 (financed by mem, dues & donations)
Exhibitions: (1993) Kunisada's Japan
Publications: Impressions, annual newsletter; President's Newsletter, 10 per yr
Activities: Lect open to public, 8-10

O **UNITED STATES COMMITTEE OF THE INTERNATIONAL ASSOCIATION OF ART, INC,** Central Station, PO Box 28068, Washington, DC 20038. Tel 202-628-9633. *Pres* George Koch
Estab 1952, incorporated 1955, to promote greater appreciation of contemporary fine arts, regardless of genre; to uphold the status of the artists and to defend their rights, primarily on the national level, then on the international level, evaluating by comparison and appraisal; also to stimulate international cultural relations and exchanges of art and artists free of any aesthetic or other bias. Mem: Twelve national art organizations of painters, sculptors and graphic arts in the United States
Income: Financed by mem dues & grants
Publications: Information, three per year

O **UNITED STATES DEPARTMENT OF THE INTERIOR,** Indian Arts & Crafts Board, 1849 C St NW (Mailing add: United States Dept Interior, Room 4004, Washington, DC 20240). Tel 202-208-3773. *Gen Mgr* Robert G Hart; *Asst General Mgr* Geoffrey E Stamm
Open Mon - Fri 7:45 AM - 5 PM. No admis fee. Estab 1936 to promote contemporary arts by Indians, Eskimos & Aleuts of the United States. Board administers the Southern Plains Indian Museum, Anadarko, OK; Museum of the Plains Indian, Browning, MT; Sioux Indian Museum, Rapid City, SD. Average Annual Attendance: 150,000
Income: Financed by federal appropriation
Collections: Contemporary Native American Arts
Exhibitions: Fifteen special exhibitions among the three museums
Publications: Source Directory of Indian, Eskimo & Aleut owned & operated arts & crafts businesses
Activities: Information & advice on matters pertaining to contemporary Indian, Eskimo & Aleut arts & crafts

O **VISUAL ARTISTS & GALLERIES ASSOCIATION (VAGA),** 1133 Avenue of the Americas, 45th Fl, Suite 2626, New York, NY 10036. Tel 212-840-1805; FAX 212-840-1925. *Exec Dir* Robert Panzer
Open daily 9 AM - 5 PM, by appointment. Estab 1976 as a nonprofit venture to help artists control and police the reproduction of their works, from textile designs to photographs in textbooks; to act as a clearinghouse for licensing reproduction rights and set up a directory of artists and other owners of reproduction rights for international use. Mem: European 10,000, American 500; dues gallery & associate $300, estates $100, artist $75, renewal $50
Income: Financed by membership
Special Subjects: Copyright Law, Moral Rights, Fair Use, Droite Morale
Publications: Newsletter

O **WOMEN'S CAUCUS FOR ART,** Moore College of Art, 20th & the Parkway, Philadelphia, PA 19103. Tel 215-854-0922. *Pres* Jean Towgood; *Exec Dir* Essie Karp
Estab 1972 as a non-profit women's professional & service organization for visual arts. Average Annual Attendance: 500. Mem: 4000; annual meeting in Feb
Income: $55,000 (financed by mem)
Publications: Membership Directory, Honors Catalogue (all annual); National Update (quarterly)
Activities: Honor awards for senior women in the arts

Museums, Libraries and Associations In The United States

ALABAMA

ANNISTON

M ANNISTON MUSEUM OF NATURAL HISTORY, 800 Museum Dr, PO Box 1587, 36202-1587. Tel 205-237-6766; FAX 205-237-6776. *Dir* Christopher J Reich; *Development Officer* Lindie K Brown; *Cur National History* W Peter Conroy; *Cur Exhib* Joseph Hines; *Business Mgr* Cheryl Bragg
Open Tues - Fri 9 AM - 5 PM, Sat 10 AM - 5 PM, Sun 1 - 5 PM, cl Mon. Admis adults $3, children $2. Estab 1930, nationally accredited museum with the purpose of enhancing public knowledge, understanding & appreciation of living things & their environments. Permanent exhibit halls interpet the theme Adaptation of the Environment; changing exhibit gallery features exhibitions focusing on interrelationships between nature & art. Average Annual Attendance: 100,000. Mem: 1600; dues family $25, individual $20; annual meeting in Sept
Income: $190,000 (financed by mem, earned income, donations & city approriations)
Collections: Archaeology; Ethnology; Natural Science; Wildlife Art
Activities: Classes for adults & children; docent programs; lect open to public, 8 vis lect per year; book traveling exhibitions 5 per year; retail store sells books, original art & reproductions

BIRMINGHAM

M BIRMINGHAM MUSEUM OF ART, 2000 Eighth Ave N, 35203. Tel 205-254-2565. *Dir* Dr John Schloder; *Asst Dir* Larry Baldwin; *Cur Decorative Arts* Bryding Adams; *Cur Painting & Sculpture* Dr John Wetenhall; *Cur Education* Jeffrey York; *Cur Oriental Art* Dr Don Wood
Open Tues, Wed, Fri & Sat 10 AM - 5 PM, Thurs 10 AM - 9 PM, Sun 2 - 6 PM. No admis fee. Estab 1951 as a general art museum with collections from earliest manifestation of man's creativity to contemporary work. Its goal is to illustrate the highest level of man's artistic work in an art historical context. The 36 galleries are climate controlled; lighting system is modern and controlled to latest safety standards. Average Annual Attendance: 100,000. Mem: 6000; dues $35 - $500
Income: $3,500,000 (financed by membership, city appropriation and annual donations)
Purchases: $650,000
Collections: English ceramics and silver; American painting and sculpture; American decorative arts 19th-20th centuries; Ethnographic Collection; African, American Indian, Pre-Columbian works; Oriental Collection: Indian, Korean, Chinese & Southeast Asian works; Oriental Rug Collection; European paintings; Renaissance to 20th century art; Wedgewood Collection; photography; prints and drawings, 18th-19th centuries
Exhibitions: (1989) Idemitsu Collection; Cartier Jewels; Marie Laurencin. (1990) African Gold; Han Archaeology
Publications: Annual bulletin; bi-monthly calendar; Zorn Catalogue
Activities: Classes for adults and children; docent training; lect open to the public, 12-15 vis lectr per year; concerts; gallery talks; tours; competitions; individual paintings lent to other museums; organize and circulate traveling exhibitions; museum shop sells reproductions, prints and gifts
L Library, 2000 Eighth Ave N, 35203. Tel 205-254-2982. *Librn* Jane McRae
Open to the public by request
Income: Financed by city and private funding
Library Holdings: Vols 10,500; Per subs 63; Other — Clipping files, exhibition catalogs
Special Subjects: American Western Art, Decorative Arts, Handicrafts, Oriental Art, Traditional Arts (Pre-Columbian, African & American Indian)
Collections: Kress Collection; Wedgwood Collection; 20th century art

L BIRMINGHAM PUBLIC LIBRARY, Arts, Music & Recreation Department, 2100 Park Place, 35203. Tel 205-226-3670. *Head* Linda M Classen; *Librn* Deborah Loftis; *Librn* Angela Hall
Open Mon - Tues 9 AM - 8 PM, Thurs - Sat 9 AM - 6 PM, Sun 2 - 6 PM. Estab 1909 to serve the Jefferson County area
Library Holdings: Vols 40,000; Per subs 155; Cameras 7; Micro — Fiche; AV — A-tapes, cassettes, Kodachromes, rec; Other — Clipping files, exhibition catalogs, framed reproductions 150, memorabilia, pamphlets, photographs, sculpture
Special Subjects: Architecture, Art History, Asian Art, Decorative Arts, Folk Art, Graphic Design, History of Art & Archaeology, Islamic Art, Mixed Media, Pewter, Porcelain, Portraits, Pottery, Pre-Columbian Art, Sculpture, Applied Arts
Collections: 150 permanent collection of prints, paintings

M BIRMINGHAM SOUTHERN COLLEGE, Doris Wainwright Kennedy Art Center, PO Box A21, 35254. Tel 205-226-4925. *Dir* James Cook
Open Mon - Fri 8:30 AM - 5 PM
Exhibitions: Faculty show (all medias); juried student show; BFA show

M SLOSS FURNACES NATIONAL HISTORIC LANDMARK, PO Box 11781, 35202. Tel 205-324-1911. *Dir* James Burnham; *Asst Dir* Paige Wainwright; *Asst Cur* Margo Hays
Open Tues - Sat 10 AM - 4 PM, Sun noon - 4 PM. No admis fee. Estab as an industrial museum; former blast furnace plant; temporary exhibitions, especially in metal arts. Exhibition Center will be closed through 1993 for renovations
Exhibitions: (1992) Brent Kington & Southern Illinois Univ at Carbondale: A Metals Retrospective; Lamprecht Collection: Cast Iron in Its Own Right

M UNIVERSITY OF ALABAMA AT BIRMINGHAM, Visual Arts Gallery, 900 13th St S, 35294-1260. Tel 205-934-4941; FAX 205-975-6639; Telex 88-8826. *Pres* Charles Hays; *VPres* William A Sibley; *Cur* Antoinette Johnson
Open Mon - Thurs 1 - 6 PM, Sun 2 - 6 PM except between exhibitions, holidays & vacation. No admis fee. Estab 1973 to exhibit works of students, faculty and nationally & internationally known artists and to form and exhibit a permanent collection of art since 1750. Two galleries, each 1200 square feet and adjacent storage all on first floor of Humanities building with adjacent sculpture courtyard. All are temperature and humidity controlled and secured by alarms. Average Annual Attendance: 4100
Income: Financed by university and private donations
Purchases: $2200
Collections: †Contemporary art; †Student & faculty works since 1950; †Works on paper since 1750
Exhibitions: Paintings by Robert Sites; Photographs by Ed Willis Barnett; Terra Cotta Facades of Birmingham Architecture; Recent works by Henry Loustau; Alabama University & College Teachers of Paintings 19th Century Art & The Industrial Society; Art of the Eye; Alabama-New York: Post-Alabama Contemporary Artists; (1992) Vanishing Spain (photography); Contemporary Chinese Painting & Calligraphy; Photographs by Judy Fiskin; Christo- Prints & Lithographs. (1993) Caffery & Imes: Photo Essay of the South; Prints & Preparatory Drawings by Felix Vallotton; Recent Work by Gary Chapman
Publications: A Different Light, Stained Glass in Central Alabama; exhibition catalogs; Fin-de-siecle Faces: Portraiture in the Age of Proust; Land of 1000 Beers: Paintings, Prints & Drawings by David Sandlin; Selections I, Selections II, part of an intended series featuring the permanent collection; Terra Cotta Facades of Birmingham Architecture; Visual Arts Gallery Paper, 10 per year
Activities: Lectures open to public, 2 vis lectr per year; gallery talks; tours; competitions; awards; individual and original objects of art lent to qualified museums & galleries; book traveling exhibitions; museum shop sells gallery publications & posters

DECATUR

M JOHN C CALHOUN STATE COMMUNITY COLLEGE, Art Gallery, Hwy 31 N, PO Box 2216, 35602. Tel 205-353-3102, 800-626-3628. *Pres* Dr Richard Carpenter; *Dir* Helen C Austin, PhD; *Cur* Dr Art Bond
Open Mon - Fri 8 AM - 3 PM, special weekend openings. No admis fee. Estab 1965 to provide temporary exhibits of fine art during the school year for the benefit of the surrounding three county area and for the students and faculty of the college. Located in a fine arts building completed June 1979, the gallery has 105 linear ft of carpeted wall space with adjustable incandescent track lighting & fluorescent general lights in a controlled & well-secured environment. Average Annual Attendance: 20,000
Collections: Permanent collection consists of graphics collection as well as selected student and faculty works
Exhibitions: Student Art Exhibit; Student Photographs
Publications: Announcements; exhibition catalogs
Activities: Classes for adults; lect open to the public, 3 visiting lectr per year; gallery talks; tours; competitions with awards; scholarships and fellowships; individual paintings and original objects of art lent to museums, galleries and college art departments; lending collection contains 40 original art works and 85 original prints; book traveling exhibitions, biannually

DOTHAN

M WIREGRASS MUSEUM OF ART, 126 N College St, PO Box 1624, 36302-1624. Tel 205-794-3871. *Dir* Sam W Kates; *Educ Coordr* Gillian Crockett; *Studio Arts* Ann Hart
Open Tues - Sat 10 AM - 5 PM, Sun 1 - 5 PM, cl Mon. No Admis fee. Estab 1988 to provide exhibits & educational programs. Average Annual Attendance: 12,000. Mem: 600; dues $20 - $1000

Income: $160,000 (financed by mem, city appropriation, special events & fees)
Collections: 19th & 20th century works on paper, decorative arts, paintings & sculpture
Exhibitions: (1993) Richard Schmid. (1994) Dean Mitchell; Biennial Art Competition
Activities: Classes for adults & children; docent programs; lect open to public, 4 - 6 vis lectr per year; competitions with prizes; book traveling exhibitions, 8 - 10 per year

FAIRHOPE

A **EASTERN SHORE ART ASSOCIATION, INC,** Art Center, 401 Oak St, PO Box 443, 36533-0443. Tel 205-928-2228. *Exec Dir* David Robinson; *Admin Asst* Pat Duncan
Open Tues - Sat 10 AM - 5 PM, Sun 2 - 5 PM, cl Mon, New Years Day, Thanksgiving, Christmas. No admis fee. Estab 1952 to sponsor cultural, educational & social activities. Five galleries change exhibits monthly: Sales gallery. Average Annual Attendance: 14,000. Mem: 1000
Income: $200,000 (financed by gifts, dues, tuition fees & purchases)
Collections: Herman Bischoff, drawings, oils & watercolors; Maria Martinez, pottery; Emily Woodward Collection; contemporary American paintings from Gulf coast area
Publications: Yearbook; monthly newsletter
Activities: Classes for adults & children; lectures open to the public, 5 vis lectr per yr; concerts; gallery talks; tours; competitions with awards; outreach educational program arranges gallery tours, slide programs, and portable exhibits; book traveling exhibitions; sales shop sells original art, reproductions, prints, photographs, pottery
L **Library,** 401 Oak St, PO Box 443, 36533-0443. Tel 205-928-2228. *Librn* Elizabeth D Marsh
For lending & reference
Library Holdings: Vols 800; Other — Exhibition catalogs, pamphlets

FAYETTE

M **FAYETTE ART MUSEUM,** 530 N Temple Ave, 35555. Tel 205-932-8727. *Board Chmn & Cur* Jack Black
Open Mon, Tues, Thurs & Fri 9 AM - noon & 1 - 4 PM, also by appointment. No admis fee. Estab 1969 to offer on continuous basis exhibits of visual arts free to the public. All facilities are at Fayette Civic Center: five multi-purpose galleries plus lobby & corridors; 600 running ft of exhibition space
Income: Financed by city appropriation and Annual Art Festival
Purchases: Very limited purchases of works by local & regional artists
Collections: 2000 paintings, mostly by Lois Wilson, a former resident & by local folk artists Jimmy Lee Sudduth, Benjamin Perkins & Fred Webster
Exhibitions: Jimmie Lee Sudduth (primitive art); Rev Benjamin Perkins (folk art); Fred Webster
Activities: Lectures open to public; gallery talks; tours; individual paintings & original objects of art lent to museums & galleries; lending collection contains 1500 original prints; originate traveling exhibitions to qualified museums

GADSDEN

M **GADSDEN MUSEUM OF FINE ARTS, INC,** 2829 W Meighan Blvd, 35904-1717. Tel 205-546-7365. *Dir* Sherrie Hamil; *Pres* Robert H King; *VPres* James Ashley
Open Mon - Fri 10 AM - 4 PM, Thurs 10 AM - 8 PM, Sun 1 - 5 PM. No admis fee. Estab 1965 to promote, foster, & preserve the collection of paintings, sculpture, artifacts & antiques. 4500 sq ft. Average Annual Attendance: 10,000. Mem: 2500; dues individual $25
Income: Financed by mem, local government & grants
Collections: Snelgrove Historical Collection; Fowler Collection of Paintings, Sculpture & Porcelain
Exhibitions: Quilt exhibit; antique radios; annual juried art show
Activities: Adult & children's classes; workshops; lect open to public, 500 vis lectrs per yr; competitions with awards

HUNTSVILLE

A **HUNTSVILLE ART LEAGUE AND MUSEUM ASSOCIATION INC,** Arts Council, 700 Monroe St, 35802. Tel 205-533-6565. *Pres* Tine Purdy; *First VPres* Larry Jess; *Education Chmn* Marty Vinc; *Gallery Dir* Connie Bousson; *Treas* Becky McGehee
Open Tues - Sat 10 AM - 5 PM, Sun 1 - 5 PM. No admis fee. Estab 1957. The League is a nonprofit organization dedicated to promoting and stimulating the appreciation of the visual arts. 50 artists exhibiting, all mediums, special exhibitions. Average Annual Attendance: 3600. Mem: 200; annual dues $25; meetings held 1st Thurs each month
Income: Financed by memberships, commissions, grants
Exhibitions: Annual Fall & Spring Shows; annual juried show; continuous exhibitions throughout Huntsville; Sunday Salons
Publications: Newsletter on activities and exhibition opportunities in the Southeast, monthly; membership books
Activities: Classes for adults and children; lect open to the public, 12 vis lectr per yr; competitions; tours; individual paintings & original objects of art lent to banks, restaurants, theaters; lending collection contains original art works, original prints, paintings, photographs, sculpture; sales shop sells original art, reproductions, prints, small hand made art objects as special seasonal gifts

M **HUNTSVILLE MUSEUM OF ART,** 700 Monroe St, 35801. Tel 205-535-4350. *Dir* David M Robb Jr; *Chief Cur* Bruce Hiles; *Educ Dir* Taylor Schapiro; *Registrar* Barbara Guthrie; *Admin* Ryn Van Riper; *Development Dir* Diane Olson
Open Tues - Fri 10 AM - 5 PM, Sat 9 AM - 5 PM, Sun 1 - 5 PM, cl Mon. No

admis fee. Estab 1970. Museum is part of the Von Braun Civic Center; 23,000 sq ft total including 9000 sq ft exhibition galleries. Atmospherically controlled galleries & storage; 10 - 12 special exhibitions per year. Average Annual Attendance: 57,000. Mem: 1200; dues Champion $5000, Sustaining $2500, Participating $1000, Benefactor $500, Sponsor $200, Patron $100, Contributing $25
Income: $1,000,000 (financed by mem, city appropriation, grants & support groups)
Purchases: $25,000
Collections: †American art, 1700-present, including paintings & works on paper; local & regional art; African art; Oriental art
Exhibitions: Annual Youth Ten Staste Red-Clay Survey, juried exhibition' (1993) Space Works: The Synthesis of Art & Science; Silverpoint Etcetera; Elaine de Kooning Retrospective; American Impressionist Paintings; American Puppetry in the 1980's. (1994) Biennial Ten State Red-Clay Survey, juried exhibition;
Publications: Brochures; catalogs, occasionally; Museum Calendar, quarterly
Activities: Classes for adults & children; docent training; Partnership in Art Education program; lect open to public, 3 - 4 vis lectrs per year; concerts; gallery talks; tours; competitions with awards; scholarships offered; collection loan program; book traveling exhibitions, 8-10 per yr; originate traveling exhibitions
L Reference Library, 700 Monroe St SW, 35801. Tel 205-535-4350. *Gallery Asst* Janet Saczawa
Open Mon - Fri 8:30 AM - 5 PM. No admis fee. For reference only
Library Holdings: Vols 3000; Per subs 20; AV — Slides; Other — Clipping files, exhibition catalogs 2000, pamphlets
Special Subjects: Art Education, Art History, Asian Art, Drawings, Etchings & Engravings, Folk Art, Graphic Arts, Graphic Design, History of Art & Archaeology, Oriental Art, Painting - American, Photography, Contemporary American Art, Museum Management

M **UNIVERSITY OF ALABAMA AT HUNTSVILLE,** Gallery of Art, 35899. Tel 205-895-6114. *Gallery Adminr* Jennie Bolling
Open Mon - Fri 1 - 4:30 PM. No admis fee. Estab 1975. An intimate and small renovated chapel with a reserved section for exhibits. Average Annual Attendance: 1800
Income: Financed by administration
Exhibitions: Contemporary artwork (US and international); annual juried exhibition
Activities: Lect open to the public, 7-10 vis lectr per year; gallery talks; competitions with awards; individual paintings and original objects of art lent; book traveling exhibitions, 3 times per year; originate traveling exhibitions

MOBILE

M **ART PATRONS LEAGUE OF MOBILE,** Museum Dr, PO Box 8426, 36689. Tel 205-343-2667; Cable FAMOS. *Chmn Bd* John Gay Peake Jr; *Dir* Joseph B Schenk
Open Tues - Sun 10 AM - 5 PM. No admis fee. Estab 1964 to foster the appreciation of art and provide art education programs for the community. Average Annual Attendance: 100,000. Mem: 1000; dues business mem $1500, benefactor $500, associate $250, patron $100, supporting $50, family $25, individual $15
Income: Financed by membership, city appropriation & state grants
Purchases: $35,000
Collections: American Crafts; African Art; 19th and 20th century American and European paintings, sculpture, prints, and decorative arts; Oriental art; Miller Oriental porcelain, Indian miniatures, Chinese ceramics, Medieval art, European paintings & sculpture; 16th to 20th century and classical art; Southern furniture; Wellington Collection of Wood Engravings; †1930's - 1940's paintings & graphics
Exhibitions: Mobile Artist Assn Juried Exhibition; Watercolor Society Juried Exhibition; Gulf Coast Regional Juried Exhibit; Best of Mobile (invitational); Southeastern Juried Exhibition
Publications: Art Patrons League Calendar, quarterly
Activities: Classes for adults and children; docent training; lectures open to public, 10 vis lectr per yr; gallery talks, tours, competitions with awards; individual paintings & objects of art lent; lending collection includes art works, original prints, paintings, photographs, sculpture; museum shop sells books, original art, reproductions, prints, jewelry, toys, posters, baskets, pottery, puzzles, glass art
L Library, Langan Park, PO Box 8426, 36689. Tel 205-343-2667. *Educ Cur* Melissa Thomas
For reference only
Library Holdings: Vols 1800; Per subs 25; AV — Slides; Other — Clipping files, exhibition catalogs, framed reproductions, pamphlets, photographs, prints, reproductions
Collections: American & European paintings & decorative arts; contemporary crafts; Southern decorative arts; wood engraving

M **MUSEUM OF THE CITY OF MOBILE,** 355 Government St, 36602. Tel 205-434-7569; FAX 205-434-7686. *Dir* Open ; *Registrar* Roy V Tallon
Open Tues - Sat 10 AM - 5 PM, Sun 1- 5 PM, cl Mon & city holidays. Consists of three museums including: The Carlen House built in 1842 is a beautiful example of that style of architecture unique to this area, the Creole Cottage; the Phoenix Fire Museum occupies the home station house of the Phoenix Steam Fire Company No 6, which was organized in 1838; the Bernstein-Bush House built in 1872. Museum is located in elegantly restored Bernstein-Bush townhouse, the museum houses exhibits bearing upon the history of Mobile and the Gulf Coast area since its founding as a French colony in 1702. This building is listed on the National Register of Historic Places. Displays illustrate life in Mobile under French, British and Spanish colonial rule, the rapid growth of the city in the pre-Civil War period, the rise and fall of the fortunes of Mobile of the best defended Confederate city, and the ever international seaport and center of culture, business and scholarly institutions. Average Annual Attendance: 70,000
Income: Financed by city appropriation
Collections: CSS Hunley; Fenollosa Room collection of books, manuscripts, &

family photographs, Japanese photographs, paintings, prints, china & textiles; Roderick D MacKenzie Room; McMillan Room; Queens of Mobile Mardi Gras; Admiral Raphael Semmes collection includes probably the finest Confederate presentation sword in existence, along with a presentation cased revolver and accessories, books, paintings, documents, personal papers and ship models; Alfred Lewis Staples Mardi Gras Gallery; 80,000 items reflecting the entire span of the history of Mobile

Exhibitions: (1992) Mobile Minature Club; (1993) CSS Alabama Home at Last; Quilt Exhibit

Publications: Exhibition & collection catalogs

Activities: Classes for adults & children; docent training; lectures open to the public; tours; museum shop sells books, prints & slides

L **Reference Library,** 355 Government St, 36602. Tel 205-434-7569.
For research only
Library Holdings: Vols 25,000; Per subs 12; AV — Slides; Other — Clipping files, memorabilia, original art works, pamphlets, photographs, reproductions, sculpture

M **Carlen House,** 54 Carlen St, 36606. Tel 205-434-7569. *Dir* Open
Open Tues - Sat 10 AM - 5 PM, Sun 1 - 5 PM, cl Mon. Estab 1970 to preserve an authentic representation of Southern architecture. The Carlen House is an important representation of Mobile's unique contribution to American regional architecture. It is a fine example of the Creole Cottage as it evolved from the French Colonial form and was adapted for early American use. The house was erected in 1842; furnishings are from the collections of the Museums of the City of Mobile and are typical of a house of that period. Average Annual Attendance: 6200

Exhibitions: Sleeping Under the Stars: Exhibition of star quilts 1820- 1990, guest curator Mary Elizabeth Johnson

Activities: Lectures open to the public; group tours are conducted by guides in period costumes who emphasize aspects of everyday life in Mobile in the mid-nineteenth century. The making of material is demonstrated by the guide who cards wool, spins fibers and weaves cloth; individual paintings & original objects of art lent to other museums; sales shop sells books, slides & souvenirs

L **UNIVERSITY OF SOUTH ALABAMA,** Ethnic American Slide Library, University Blvd, 36688. Tel 205-460-6335. *Head* James E Kennedy
Open daily 8 AM - 5 PM. Estab for the acquisition of slides of works produced by Afro-American, Mexican American and native American artists and the distribution of duplicate slides of these works to educational institutions and individuals engaged in research
Library Holdings: AV — Slides
Collections: 19th and 20th century ethnic American art works in ceramics, drawing, painting, photography, printmaking, sculpture
Publications: Slide Catalog

MONTEVALLO

M **UNIVERSITY OF MONTEVALLO,** The Gallery, Station 6400, 35115. Tel 205-665-2521, Ext 285. *Acting Gallery Dir* Scott Stephens
Open Mon - Fri 9 AM - 5 PM. No admis fee. Estab Sept 1977 to supply students and public with high quality contemporary art. The gallery is 27 x 54 ft with track lighting; floors and walls carpeted; no windows. Average Annual Attendance: 2500 - 3000
Income: Financed by state appropriation and regular department budget
Publications: High quality catalogs and posters
Activities: Management classes; lect open to the public, 6 vis lectr per year; gallery talks; originate traveling exhibitions

MONTGOMERY

M **ALABAMA DEPARTMENT OF ARCHIVES AND HISTORY MUSEUM,** Museum Galleries, 624 Washington Ave, 36130. Tel 205-242-4363. *Dir* Edwin C Bridges; *Museum Cur* Robert B Bradley; *Asst Dir Public Services* Debbie Pendleton
Open Mon - Fri 8 AM - 5 PM, Sat 9 AM - 5 PM. No admis fee. Estab 1901. Reference only. Average Annual Attendance: 78,000
Income: Financed by state appropriation
Library Holdings: Vols 40,000; AV — Fs; Other — Clipping files, pamphlets, photographs
Collections: Early Alabama Indians; Children's Gallery & Grandma's Attic (for children of all ages); Military Room; the 19th Century Room; William Rufus King Room
Exhibitions: History of Alabama
Activities: Educ dept; 13 vis lectr per year; gallery talks; tours; lending to other state departments, museums & historic sites; museum shop sells books
L **Library,** 624 Washington Ave, 36130. Tel 205-242-4152; FAX 205-240-3433. *Readi Reference Librn* Frazine Taylor; *Archival Librn* Dr Norwood Kerr
Open Tues - Fri 8 AM - 5 PM, Sat 9 AM - 5 PM. Estab 1901. Department has a Manuscripts Division where original manuscript collections are maintained
Library Holdings: Vols 32,000; Micro — Fiche, reels; AV — A-tapes, cassettes, fs, lantern slides, motion pictures, rec, v-tapes; Other — Clipping files, manuscripts, pamphlets, photographs
Collections: Alabama Subjects 1700-1989; Political & Social Events; State Government Records

AMERICAN SOCIETY OF PORTRAIT ARTISTS (ASOPA)
For further information, see National and Regional Organizations

C **BLOUNT INC,** 4520 Executive Park Dr, PO Box 949, 36101. Tel 205-244-4000. *Admin Asst to Chmn* Shirley Miller Milligan
Open 8 AM - 5 PM. No admis fee. Estab 1973, original collection began in response to commemorate America's bicentennial. Collection displayed at Corporate Headquarters Building
Collections: †American art—200 years; †international sculpture; †regional artists; †works by American artists from Revolutionary period to present
Exhibitions: Greenville Co Museum of Art; Selections from the Blount

Collection; Highlights of the Blount Collection
Publications: Blount Collection Vol I, II & III, catalog; Blount Collection, quarterly newsletter
Activities: Lectures; concerts; gallery talks; tours; poster employee art competition with award; individual paintings and original objects of art lent to museums; instrumental in the formation of Art, Inc, a traveling exhibition of corporate art
L **Library,** 4520 Executive Park Dr, PO Box 949, 36101. Tel 205-272-8020. *VPres Sales* Peter Robinson
Library Holdings: Vols 75; Per subs 15; Micro — Fiche; AV — Motion pictures, rec; Other — Exhibition catalogs

M **MONTGOMERY MUSEUM OF FINE ARTS,** 1 Museum Dr, 36117. Tel 205-244-5700; FAX 205-244-5774. *Pres* John Walter Stowers; *Dir* J Brooks Joyner; *Asst Dir for Development* Grace M Hanchrow; *Asst Dir for Operations* Shirley Woods; *Registrar* Pamela Bransford; *Cur, Painting & Sculpture* Margaret Ausfeld; *Cur Exhib* Bruce Lineker; *Cur Educ* Tara Sartorius
Open Tues - Sat 10 AM - 5 PM, Thurs evening until 9 PM, Sun noon - 5 PM. No admis fee. Estab 1930 to generally promote the cultural artistic and higher education life of the city of Montgomery by all methods that may be properly pursued by a museum or art gallery. Museum opened in new 45,000 sq ft facility located on 35 acres of landscaped park, adjacent to the Alabama Shakespeare feastival. Galleries occupy lower & upper levels of two story neo-palladian structure. A new education wing, Artworks occupies 3000 sq ft & includes a hands-on, interactive gallery and studio. A recent gift of 41 American Paintings from the Blount Inc. Collection of American Art is permanently installed in spacious Blount Wing of the new museum; 240 seat auditorium. Average Annual Attendance: 50,000. Mem: 3700; dues leadership $250-$5000, associate $50-$150, individual $10-$30; annual meeting Oct
Income: Financed by membership, city and county appropriations and grants
Collections: †American & European Works on Paper; †Contemporary graphics and other works on paper by artists living in the South; decorative arts; master prints of the 15th and 19th Centuries; †paintings by American artists from early 19th Century through the present; 41 paintings from the Blount Collection of American Art
Publications: Annual Report; Calendar of Events, quarterly; exhibitions catalogs for selected shows
Activities: Classes for children; docent training; lectures open to public, 20 vis lectr per year; films; concerts; gallery talks; tours; individual paintings and original objects of art lent to galleries which meet AAM standards for security and preservation; lending collection contains 330 original prints, 250 paintings, photographs, sculpture and 3500 slides; book traveling exhibitions, 12 per year; originate traveling exhibitions, national and international; museums shop sells books, original art, reproductions, prints and gift items
L **Library,** 1 Museum Dr, PO Box 230819, 36123. Tel 205-244-5700; FAX 205-244-5774. *Librn* Alice T Carter
Open Tues - Fri 10 AM - 5 PM. Estab 1975 to assist the staff and community with reliable art research material. For reference
Income: Financed by City of Montgomery & Museum Association
Library Holdings: Vols 2200; Per subs 17; AV — Fs, motion pictures, slides; Other — Clipping files, exhibition catalogs, pamphlets, photographs, prints
Special Subjects: American Art

SELMA

M **STURDIVANT HALL,** 713 Mabry St, PO Box 1205, 36701. Tel 205-872-5626. *Pres* Captain A J Atkins; *Cur* Mrs George Tate Jr; *Cur* Mrs Carlton Steight
Open Tues - Sat 9 AM - 4 PM, Sun 2 - 4 PM. Admis adults $4, student $2, children under 6 free. Estab 1957 as a museum with emphasis on the historical South. Period furniture of the 1850's in a magnificent architectural edifice built 1852-53. Average Annual Attendance: 10,000. Mem: 480; dues $15 - $1000; annual meeting April
Income: Financed by membership, city and state appropriations
Collections: Objects of art; †period furniture; textiles
Publications: Brochure
Activities: Lect open to public; tours

THEODORE

M **BELLINGRATH GARDENS AND HOME,** 12401 Bellingrath Gardens Rd, 36582. Tel 205-973-2217; FAX 205-973-0540. *Exec Dir* J Robert Pearson
Open daily 7 AM to dusk. Admis Gardens adults $6.50, children 6 - 11 $3.25, under 6 free. Estab 1932 to perpetuate an appreciation of nature, and display man-made objects d'art. The gallery houses the world's largest public display of Boehm porcelain, and the Bellingrath Home contains priceless antiques. Average Annual Attendance: 200,000
Income: Supported by Foundation and admissions
Collections: Antiques from Europe and America; Boehm Porcelain
Activities: Classes for children; tours; lending collection contains kodachromes, motion pictures, slides; sales shop sells books, magazines, prints, reproductions and slides

TUSCALOOSA

A **ARTS COUNCIL OF TUSCALOOSA COUNTY, INC,** 600 Greensboro, 35401. Tel 205-758-8083. *Pres* Ginia McPhearson; *Exec Dir* Gail Skidmore
Open Mon - Fri 8 AM - 5 PM. No admis fee. Estab 1970 for the development, promotion and coordination of educational, cultural and artistic activities of the city and county of Tuscaloosa. Mem: 410 individual, 30 organization; dues organization $25, individual $15; annual meeting Oct, meetings quarterly
Income: Financed by endowment, membership, city, state and county appropriations
Publications: Arts calendar, monthly newsletter
Activities: Dramatic programs; concert series, Bama Fanfare (professional performances for students K - 12); sponsor of educ program called SPECTRA (Special Teaching Resources in the Arts)

M UNIVERSITY OF ALABAMA, Moody Gallery of Art, 103 Garland Hall, PO Box 870270, 35487-0270. Tel 205-348-5967. *Dir* William Dooley
Open Mon - Sat 8 AM - 5 PM, Sun 2 - 5 PM. No admis fee. Estab 1946
Collections: Small collection of paintings, prints, photography, drawings, sculpture and ceramics; primarily modern
Exhibitions: Approx 15 exhibitions per year
Activities: Originate traveling exhibitions

TUSCUMBIA

A TENNESSEE VALLEY ART ASSOCIATION AND CENTER, 511 N Water St, PO Box 474, 35674. Tel 205-383-0533. *Exec Dir* Mary Settle-Cooney; *Asst Dir* Missy Ricketts; *Dir of Visual Arts* Shirley Maize; *Exhibit Coordr* Lucie Ayers
Open Mon - Fri 1 - 5 PM, Sun 2 - 4 PM. No admis fee. Chartered 1963 to promote the arts in the Tennessee Valley. Building completed 1973. Main Gallery 60 x 40 ft; West Gallery for small exhibits, meetings and arts and crafts classes. Located one block from the birthplace of Helen Keller in Tuscumbia. During the Helen Keller Festival, TVAC sponsors the Arts and Crafts Fair. Average Annual Attendance: 10,000. Mem: Dues benefactor $100, family $50, sustaining $25, regular $15, student $10
Income: $200,000 (financed by appropriations, donations, grants & mem)
Collections: Helen Keller Crafts Collection; Reynolds Collection (paintings)
Exhibitions: Exhibition South (paintings, sculpture, prints), annual juried art show for mid-south states; Spring Photo Show, annual juried; feature work by national artists, members and students; handcraft exhibits
Activities: Classes for adults and children; dramatic programs; class instruction in a variety of arts and crafts; workshops & performances in drama; lectures open to public; concerts; gallery talks; competitions with awards; illustrated slide lecture; book traveling exhibits

TUSKEGEE INSTITUTE

M TUSKEGEE INSTITUTE NATIONAL HISTORIC SITE, George Washington Carver & The Oaks, PO Drawer 10, 36088. Tel 205-727-3200. *Park Supt* Willie C Madison; *Museum Technician* Tyrone Brandyberg
Open 9 AM - 5 PM, cl Thanksgiving, Christmas & New Years. Original museum estab 1941 and National Park in 1976 to interpret life and work of George Washington Carver and the history of Tuskegee Institute. Maintains small reference library
Income: Financed by federal funds
Collections: Artifacts interpreting life and work of George Washington Carver and history of Tuskegee Institute; life and contributions of Booker T Washington
Activities: Lectures open to public; gallery talks; guided tours; sponsor competitions with awards; individual and original objects of art lent to other parks and museums; lending limited to photos, films, slides and reproductions; book traveling exhibitions; originate traveling exhibitions; sales shop sells books, reproductions, prints and slides

ALASKA

ANCHORAGE

A ALASKA ARTISTS' GUILD, 1816 Artic Blvd, 99503. Tel 907-274-5460. *Pres* Belle Dawson; *VPres* Janaan Kitchen; *Treas* Sam McClain; *Funding* John Peirce
Estab 1954 to provide an association for the educational interaction of qualified artists and to provide an education focus for the visual arts in the community. Mem: 100; qualifications for membership include talent and training or experience in the visual arts; dues $20; meetings first Tues each month
Income: $1500 (financed by membership)
Exhibitions: All Alaska Juried Art Show; Alaska Festival of Music Art Exhibit; Exhibitions in Federal Office Building
Publications: Alaska Artists Guild Newsletter, monthly
Activities: Monthly meetings open to the public, 3 - 4 vis lectr per yr; gallery talks; competitions; $500 Betty Park Memorial Award given; annual workshop with vis instr of national repute; individual paintings and original objects of art lent to colleges and schools by members

M ANCHORAGE MUSEUM OF HISTORY AND ART, 121 W Seventh Ave, 99501. Tel 907-343-4326; FAX 907-343-6149; Elec Mail Bitnet AHDB@Alaska. *Dir* Patricia B Wolf; *Cur of Education* Sharon Abbott; *Cur of Exhibits* Dave Nicholls; *Cur of Coll* Walter Van Horn; *Archivist* M Diane Brenner
Open Winter Tue - Sat 10 AM - 6 PM, Sun 1 - 5 PM, Summer daily 9 AM - 6 PM. Admis adult $4, sr citizen $3.50, under 18 free. Estab 1968 to collect and display Alaskan art and artifacts of all periods; to present changing exhibitions of the art of the world. Average Annual Attendance: 300,000. Mem: 3000
Income: $1,900,000
Purchases: $50,000
Collections: †Alaskan art; †Alaskan Eskimo and Indian art; Alaskan history; American art; Primitive Art (non-American)
Exhibitions: (1992) The House that Jack Built (children's furniture); Earth Fire & Fibre, International Tapestries II; Northwest Tales; narrative painting
Publications: Exhibition catalogs; Newsletter, monthly; occasional papers
Activities: Educ dept; classes for adults & children; docent training; lectures open to the public; gallery talks; tours; competitions; awards; individual paintings & original works of art lent to AMA accredited museums; lending collection contains original art works, original prints, paintings, photographs, sculpture & slides; book traveling exhibitions, 10 per yr; originate traveling exhibitions; museum shop sells books, magazines, original art, prints, slides and Alaskan Native art

L Archives, 121 W Seventh Ave, 99501. Tel 907-343-6189; FAX 907-343-6149. *Museum Archivist* M Diane Brenner
Open Winter Tues - Fri 10 AM - noon, Summer Mon - Fri 9 AM - noon, evenings by appointment. No admis fee. Estab 1968 to maintain archives of Alaska materials, chiefly the Cook Inlet area. Reference only
Purchases: $4000
Library Holdings: Vols 6000; Per subs 10; original documents; Micro — Fiche, reels; AV — Kodachromes, slides, v-tapes; Other — Clipping files, exhibition catalogs, memorabilia, pamphlets, photographs
Special Subjects: American Indian Art, American Western Art, Anthropology, Eskimo Art, Historical Material, American art, Alaska history and culture, Alaska native peoples, museum techniques
Collections: Hinchey Alagco Photograph Collection of approximately 4000 pictures of the Copper River area; Alaska Railroad Collection, 19,000 historical photos; Reeve Collection, historical maps; Ward Wells Anchorage Photo Collection 1950-80, 125,000 items; FAA 1973-1975, 10,000 photos; Lu Liston Photo Collection 1920-1990, 6,000 photos; Steve McCutcheon Photo Collection, 70,000; J N Wyman (Upper Koyukon) 1989, 500 glass plates

M VISUAL ARTS CENTER OF ALASKA, PO Box 100280, 99510. Tel 907-274-9641.
Estab 1978 to provide studio space, equipment & expertise to Alaskan artists, also a public gallery for contemporary art; non-profit organization

BETHEL

M YUGTARVIK REGIONAL MUSEUM & BETHEL VISITORS CENTER, Third Ave, PO Box 388, 99559. Tel 907-543-2911. *Museum & Visitors Center Coordr* Open; *Museum Shop Mgr & Arts & Crafts Dir* Sophie Charles
Open Tues - Sat 10 AM - 5:30 PM. No admis fee. Estab 1967 to help preserve the native culture & lifestyle of the Central Yupik Eskimos of the Yukon-Kuskokwin delta. Average Annual Attendance: 10,500. Mem: 50; dues $25
Income: 165,000 (financed by city appropriation & occasional grants)
Purchases: $5000
Collections: †Traditional handmade objects of the Yupik Eskimo, both artifacts & contemporary art objects (included are full-size kayak, ivory carvings & wooden masks, wooden bowls, stone & ivory implements, grass baskets, Yupik toys, fishskin, sealgut, birdskin & fur clothing); black & white photographs
Activities: Classes for adults and children; lect open to the public; book traveling exhibitions, 3-4 times per year; museum shop sells baskets, ivory jewelry, beaded work, skin & fur garments, wooden & ivory masks, books & posters relating to Yupik Eskimos

FAIRBANKS

A FAIRBANKS ARTS ASSOCIATION, PO Box 72786, 99707. Tel 907-456-6485. *Pres* Dee Lashbrook; *VPres* Mike McGee; *VPres* George Byrdsong; *Exec Dir* Janel Thompson; *Treas* Diane Thompson
Open Mon - Fri, 9 AM - 5 PM, gallery Tues - Sat noon - 8 PM. No admis fee. Estab 1965 to provide assistance & to help coordinate & promote the programs of arts organizations; to encourage & develop educational progams designed to strengthen & improve the climate for the arts; to inform the community of performing & creative arts awareness & development in the Fairbanks area. 4000 sq ft contemporary art gallery. Average Annual Attendance: 22,000. Mem: 500; dues $25 & up; annual meeting Sept
Income: Financed by city and state appropriations, national grants, contributions
Publications: Fairbanks Arts, bi-monthly
Activities: Educ dept; classes for adults & children; performing arts programs; docent training; professional workshops; lectures open to the public, 10 vis lectr per yr; gallery talks; tours; competitions with awards; scholarships & fels offered; book traveling exhibitions, semi-annually; originate traveling exhibitions; museum shop sells books, magazines, original art, reproductions & prints

A INSTITUTE OF ALASKA NATIVE ARTS, INC, 524 Third Ave, PO Box 80583, 99708. Tel 907-456-7491. *Exec Dir* Caroline Atuk Derrick; *Prog Servs Asst* Janet Steinbright; *Admin Asst* Judy Pusti
Open daily 8 AM - 5 PM. Estab 1976 to stimulate & encourage the study & presentation of Alaska performing, literary & visual arts, & public participation therein. Small display area for exhibit of Native art works by Aleut, Eskimo & Indian artists; small reference library. Mem: 184
Collections: Athabascan Art Collection; Interwoven Expressions Works by Contemporary Alaska Native Basketmakers
Exhibitions: Alaskameut '86, exhibition of contemporary Alaska Mask
Publications: Calendar; Earth Dyes, catalog; exhibit catalogs; From Skins, Trees, Quills and Beads: The Work of Nine Athabascans, book; Journal of Alaska Native Arts, bi-monthly; posters
Activities: Workshops & residencies; conferences; seminars; lectures open to public, 5 vis lectrs per yr; scholarships & fels offered; sales shop sells books

UNIVERSITY OF ALASKA

M Museum, 907 Yukon Dr, 99775-1200. Tel 907-474-7505. *Actg Dir* Dr Paul Reichardt; *Coordr Exhibits & Exhibits Designer* Wanda W Chin; *Asst to Dir* Hazel E Daro; *Coordr Pub Servs & Educ* Terry P Dickey; *Coordr Alaska Native Heritage Film Project* Sarah M Elder; *Coordr Ethnology* Dinah W Larsen; *Coordr Fine Arts* Barry J McWayne; *Coordr Alaska Native Heritage Film Project* Leonard J Kamerling
Open May 9 AM - 5 PM, June - Aug 9 AM - 9 PM, Sept 9 AM - 5 PM, Oct - April Noon - 5 PM. Estab 1929 to collect, preserve and interpret the natural and cultural history of Alaska. Gallery contains 10,000 sq ft of exhibition space. Average Annual Attendance: 100,000. Mem: 220; dues individuals $10; annual meeting in Oct
Income: Financed by state appropriation, public and private donations, grants and contracts
Collections: †Contemporary Alaska photography; †ethnographic collection; †paintings & lithographs of Alaska subjects
Exhibitions: Temporary exhibits rotate every 2 - 3 months

Activities: Classes for adults and children; docent training; monthly children's program; lectures open to the public, three vis lectr per yr; docent tours for grades 1-12; individual paintings and original objects of art lent to other museums or in-state institutions; traveling photographic exhibitions organized and circulated; museum shop sells notecards, slides, exhibition catalogues, pamphlets, charts, posters

L **Elmer E Rasmuson Library,** 99775-1000. Tel 907-474-7224; FAX 907-474-6841. *Dir* Paul H McCarthy; *Head Information Access Servs* Robert Anderl; *Head Alaska & Polar Regions Colls* David Hales; *Acting Head Instructional Media Serv* Diane Ruess; *Collection Development Officer* Dennis Stephens; *Head of Reference & Bibliographic Instruction* Sharon West
Open Mon - Thurs 7:30 AM - 11 PM, Fri 7:30 AM - 10 PM, Sat 10 AM - 6 PM, Sun 10 AM - 10 PM, when school is not in session 8 AM - 5 PM. Estab 1922 to support research and curriculum of the university. Circ 147,000
Income: Financed by state appropriation
Library Holdings: Vols 2,260,000; film, audio tapes, goverment documents; AV — Slides, v-tapes; Other — Manuscripts, photographs
Collections: Lithographs of Fred Machetanz; paintings by Alaskan artists; C Rusty Heurlin; photographs of Early Alaskan bush pilots; print reference photograph collection on Alaska & the Polar Regions

HAINES

M **CHILKAT VALLEY HISTORICAL SOCIETY,** Sheldon Museum & Cultural Center, 25 Main St, PO Box 269, 99827. Tel 907-766-2366. *Dir Sheldon Museum* Rebecca Nelson; *Pres Chilkat Valley Historical Society* Jim Heaton; *Chairman Museum Bd of Trustees* Jan Hill; *Treas* Retha Young
Open summer daily 1 - 5 PM, winter Sun, Mon & Wed 1 - 4 PM. Admis adults $2.50, children free if with adult. Estab 1924, under operation of Chilkat Valley Historical Society since 1975, for the purpose of collecting, preserving & interpreting through exhibits, educational programs, artifacts & memorabilia the history & culture of the Chilkat Valley & Tlingit Indian People. Average Annual Attendance: 16,500. Mem: 124; dues $10; meetings second Thurs of Jan, Mar, May, July, Sept, Nov
Income: Financed by mem, user fees, Haines Borough appropriations, federal & state grants
Collections: Chilkat blankets; Tlingit Indian artifacts; ivory, silver, wood carvings; native baskets, pioneer artifacts
Publications: Haines - The First Century; A Personal Look at the Sheldon Museum & Cultural Center; Journey to the Tlingits; Newsletter
Activities: Classes for adults & children; docent training; gallery tours; book traveling exhibitions; museum store sells books, prints, slides, jewelry, wood crafts; Children's Corner

L **Library,** 25 Main St, PO Box 623, 99827
Reference use on premises only
Library Holdings: Vols 400; Per subs 8; Micro — Reels; AV — A-tapes, cassettes, motion pictures, slides; Other — Clipping files

JUNEAU

L **ALASKA STATE LIBRARY,** Historical Library Section, PO Box G, 99811-0571. Tel 907-465-2925; FAX 907-465-2665. *Head Librn* Kay Shelton; *Photographs Librn* India Spartz
Open Mon - Fri 9 AM - 5 PM. Estab 1900. Open to staff and others upon request
Library Holdings: Vols 33,000; Per subs 75; Other — Photographs 100,000
Special Subjects: Photography, Alaska
Collections: Winter & Pond; Wickersham Historical Site Collection; Skinner Collection; Grainger Post Card Collection

M **ALASKA STATE MUSEUM,** 395 Whittier St, 99801-1718. Tel 907-465-2901; FAX 907-465-2976. *Chief Cur* Bruce Kato; *Cur Coll* Steve Henrickson; *Coordr Museum Serv* Jerry Howard; *Cur Exhib* Mark Daughnette; *Registrar* Judy Hauck; *Temporary Exhibits* Paul Gardiner; *Admin Asst* Pat Montgomery
Open Tues - Sat 10 AM - 4 PM (Sept 16 - May 15), daily 9 AM - 6 PM (May 16 - Sept 15). Admis $2, students free. Estab 1898 to collect, preserve, exhibit & interpret objects of special significance or value in order to promote public appreciation of Alaska's cultural heritage, history, art & natural environment. Gallery occupies two floors; first floor houses permanent and temporary exhibits on 1400 sq ft with 14 foot ceiling; second floor houses permanent exhibits. Average Annual Attendance: 50,000 with more than 200,000 including outreach program
Income: Financed by state appropriation and grants
Collections: †Alaskan ethnographic material including Eskimo, Aleut, Athabaskan, Tlingit, Haida and Tsimshian artifacts; †Gold Rush & early Alaskan industrial & historical material; †historical & contemporary Alaskan art
Exhibitions: (Governor's Gallery 1992-93) Northwest Tales: Contemporary Narrative Printings; All Alaska Juried Art Exhibitin XXIV; Gifts from the Greatland: Alaskan Artifacts from the National Museum of Finland. (North Galleries 1992-93) Ward Wells: Alaska Photographer; Northwest Tales: Contemporary Narrative Paintings; The Alaska Oil Sketches of Lockwood De Forest; All Alaska High School Juried Art Exhibition; Gifts from the Greatland: Alaskan Artifacts ffrom the National Museum of Finland
Activities: Classes for adults & children; docent training; circulate learning kits to Alaska public schools; lect open to public, 4 - 6 vis lectr per year; gallery talks & demonstrations; individual paintings and original objects of art lent to other museums, libraries, historical societies; lending collection contains original prints, photographs; traveling exhibits of photographs and prints organized and circulated; sales shop sells books, reproductions, prints, Alaskan Native arts & crafts

KETCHIKAN

M **TONGASS HISTORICAL MUSEUM,** 629 Dock St, 99901. Tel 907-225-5600. *Dir* William Jones
Open summer Mon - Sat 8:30 AM - 5 PM, Sun 1 - 5 PM, winter Wed - Sun 1 - 5 PM. Admis adults $1. Estab 1967 to collect, preserve & exhibit area articles & collect area photographs. Maintains reference library. Average Annual Attendance: 34,000
Income: $250,000 (financed by municipal funds)
Purchases: $9950
Collections: †Ethnographic & development history, local artists contemporary artwork; †local area history artifacts; †works from local & Alaskan artists, photographs, manuscripts & newspaper archives; North West Indian Collection
Publications: Art class listings; Calendar; Newsletter
Activities: Classes for adults; docent training; lectures open to public; book traveling exhibitions, 5 vis lectr per yr

M **TOTEM HERITAGE CENTER,** 629 Dock St, 99901. Tel 907-225-5600.
Open summer daily 8 AM - 5 PM, winter Wed - Fri 1 PM - 5 PM. Admis adults $2. Estab 1976 to preserve & teach traditional Northwest Coast Indian Arts. Average Annual Attendance: 140,000
Income: $200,000
Collections: Indian arts; original totem poles; monumental sculpture
Activities: Classes for adults & children; docent training; lectures open to the public, 20 vis lectr per yr; gallery talks; tours; arts & crafts festival; scholarships; museum shop sells books, magazines, original art, reproductions, prints, slides & native art

L **Library,** 629 Dock St, 99901. Tel 907-225-5600.
For reference only
Library Holdings: Vols 250; Per subs 5; Micro — Fiche; AV — A-tapes, cassettes, Kodachromes, slides, v-tapes; Other — Clipping files, exhibition catalogs, manuscripts, original art works
Special Subjects: Northwest Coast Indian Art, Totem Poles

NOME

M **CARRIE MCLAIN MUSEUM,** 200 E Front St, PO Box 53, 99762. Tel 907-443-2566. *City Mgr* Polly Prchal; *Dir* Darlene Orr
Open Mon - Fri 1 - 8 PM, Sat 1 - 6 PM. No admis fee. Estab to show the history of Nome and its surrounding area
Income: Financed by City of Nome & supplemental grant projects & donations
Collections: Permanent collection includes examples of art from 1890 thru 1990, including basketry, carved ivory, ink, oil, skin drawings, stone carving, woodworking; extensive photography collection; gold rush & dog sledding memorabilia; Mielke Collection; Coons Collection; McLain Collection
Exhibitions: Permanent exhibitions
Activities: Demonstrations; workshops; school tours

SITKA

M **SHELDON JACKSON MUSEUM,** 104 College Dr, 99835. Tel 907-747-8981; FAX 907-747-3004. *Cur Coll* Peter Corey; *Interpretation Specialist* Rosemary Carlton; *Visitor Servs* Lisa Nicholson; *Visitor Servs* Carolyn Young
Open summer May 15 - Sept 15, 8 AM - 5 PM daily, winter Sept 16 - May 14 Tues - Sat 10 AM - 4 PM, cl Mon & Sun. Admis $2 over 18. Estab 1898, the first permanent museum in Alaska, for the purpose of collecting & preserving the cultural heritage of Alaskan Natives in the form of artifacts. The museum, a division of Alaska State Museums, occupies a concrete, octagonal structure from 1895 with permanent displays concerning Tlingit, Tsimshian, Haida, Aleut, Athabaskan & Eskimo cultures. Average Annual Attendance: 50,000
Income: $30,000 (financed by admission fee, sales, donation, State of Alaska)
Collections: Ethnographic material from Tlingit, Haida, Aleut, Athabaskan & Eskimo people; Alaskan ethnology produced through 1930
Publications: Brochures; catalogs of Ethnological Collection
Activities: Classes for adults & children; gallery interpreters & demonstrations; lect open to the public, 4 - 6 vis lectr per year; gallery talks; exten dept serves entire state through Division of Museums; original works of art lent to qualified museums; traveling exhibitions brought into the museum; museum shop sells books, original art, reproductions, Alaskan Native arts & crafts

L **Stratton Library,** 810 Lincoln St, PO Box 479, 99835. Tel 907-747-5259. *Dir Library Services* Evelyn K Bonner; *Media Servs* Walter Edgar
Estab 1944 with Collection Library for curriculum support and meeting the needs of patrons interested in the arts
Library Holdings: Vols 72,000; Per subs 412; Micro — Reels; AV — A-tapes, cassettes, fs, Kodachromes, lantern slides, motion pictures, rec, slides, v-tapes; Other — Clipping files, exhibition catalogs, framed reproductions, memorabilia, original art works, pamphlets, photographs, reproductions, sculpture
Special Subjects: Alaskan and Native American Art Books, Alaska and the Northwest Pacific Coast, Harmon original pictures
Collections: Alaska Reference Collection (containing works on Native Arts and Crafts); E W Merrill Glass Plate Photo Collection (representative of Sitka at the turn of the century)
Activities: Annual programs held in April, include dramatic presentations; lect; demonstrations

M **SITKA HISTORICAL SOCIETY,** Isabel Miller Museum, 330 Harbor Dr, 99835. Tel 907-747-6455. *Adminr* Barbara Dadd Shaffer; *Pres* John K Davis; *VPres* Nancy Ricketts; *Colls Mgr* John Hallum
Open summer daily 9 AM - 5 PM, winter Mon - Fri 10 AM - noon, 1 - 4 PM. No admis fee. Estab 1959 to preserve the history of Sitka, its people & industries. Average Annual Attendance: 80,000. Mem: 100; dues $10 - $100; annual meeting in Oct
Income: Financed by grants, memberships, donations & shop sales
Collections: 5000 photos; paintings of Alaska scenes; 5 pieces of furniture from the Russian-American era; Russian artifacts; copy of the warrant that purchased

Alaska
Exhibitions: Alaska Purchase; Diorama of Sitka in 1867 (Year of the Transfer); Forest Products Exhibit; Historic Diving Suit; Fishing Industry Exhibit
Activities: Lect open to public, 4 vis per year; shop sells books, original art, reproductions, reproductions of Tlingit totem poles, prints, video tapes & postcards

SKAGWAY

M **TRAIL OF '98 MUSEUM,** Seventh & Spring St, PO Box 415, 99840. Tel 907-983-2420. *Dir* Glenda Choate
Open 8 AM - 6 PM, May - Sept; Oct - Apr on request. Admis adults $2, students $1. Estab 1961 to preserve & display items relating to our gold rush & Skagway. Average Annual Attendance: 25,000
Income: Financed by admis
Collections: Gold Rush Era artifacts
Publications: Brochures
Activities: Sales shop sells reproductions of old newspapers & postcards

ARIZONA

BISBEE

L **BISBEE MINING & HISTORICAL MUSEUM,** Lemuel Shattuck Memorial Library, 5 Copper Queen Plaza, PO Box 14, 85603. Tel 602-432-7071. *Cur Archival Coll* Tom Vaughan
Open Mon - Fri 10 AM - 4 PM, Sat & Sun by appointment. Estab 1971 to provide research facilities on copper mining and social history of Bisbee, Arizona, Cochise County, and Northern Sonora, Mexico. For reference only
Income: $300 (financed by mem)
Purchases: $600
Library Holdings: Vols 750; Per subs 3; Micro — Reels; AV — Cassettes; Other — Clipping files, manuscripts, photographs
Special Subjects: Historical Material, Manuscripts, Maps, Photography
Activities: Classes for adults & children; docent training; lectures open to public, 5 vis lectrs per yr; originate traveling exhibitions

COTTONWOOD

A **ART QUESTERS,** 201 E Mingus Ave, 86326-3668. Tel 602-639-1661. *Owner* Richard Lambard
Estab 1987
Collections: Artist Employment/Referrals; Artist Registry; Exhibition/Performance Referrals; Information Services; Marketing/Presentation; Mixed/Multi-Disciplinary, Fundraising; Organization Services; Programs/Encourage New Art Forms

DOUGLAS

L **COCHISE COLLEGE,** Charles Di Peso Library, Art Dept, 4190 W Hwy 80, 85607. Tel 602-364-7943. *Libr Dir* Catherin Lincer
Open Mon - Fri 8 AM - 9 PM. Estab 1965
Income: Financed by state & local funds
Library Holdings: Other — Exhibition catalogs, framed reproductions, memorabilia, original art works, photographs, prints, reproductions, sculpture
Special Subjects: Oriental Art
Collections: Oriental originals (ceramics and paintings); 19th century American & European Impressionists

A **DOUGLAS ART ASSOCIATION,** Little Gallery, 11th St at Pan American Ave, PO Box 256, 85607. Tel 602-364-2633. *Pres* Ellen Klein Friskey
Open Tues - Sat 1:30 - 4 PM. No admis fee. Estab 1960 as a non-profit tax exempt organization dedicated to promoting the visual arts and general cultural awareness in the Douglas, Arizona and Agua Prieta, Sonora area. Little Gallery is operated in a city owned building with city cooperation. Average Annual Attendance: 2000. Mem: 100; dues $7.50 and $10
Income: Financed by membership and fund raising events
Collections: †Two Flags Festival International Collections for the cities of Douglas and Agua Prieta, Mexico
Publications: Newsletter, monthly
Activities: Classes for adults and children; workshops in painting and various art activities; lect open to the public; gallery talks; competitions with cash awards; sales shop sells books and donated items

DRAGOON

A **AMERIND FOUNDATION, INC,** Amerind Museum, Fulton-Hayden Memorial Art Gallery, Dragoon Rd, PO Box 400, 85609. Tel 602-586-3666; FAX 602-586-3667. *Pres* William Duncan Fulton; *VPres* Peter L Formo; *Treas* Michael W Hard; *Foundation Dir* Anne I Woosley; *Secy* Elizabeth F Husband
Open daily 10 AM - 4 PM, call for summer hours, June - Aug, Library open by appointment only. Admis adults $3, sr citizens & children (12-18) $2, under 12 free. Estab 1937 as a private, nonprofit archeological research facility & museum focusing on the native people of the Americas. Works on western themes, paintings & sculptures by 19th & 20th century Anglo & Native American artists. Average Annual Attendance: 20,000
Income: Financed by endowment income, grants, gifts
Collections: Archaeological & ethnological materials from the Americas; antique furniture; archives on film; ivory & scrimshaw; oil paintings; research & technical reports; santos; sculpture
Exhibitions: Dance in Ceremony; Southwest Art; Prehistoric Peoples of the American Southwest
Publications: Amerind Foundation Publication Series; Amerind New World Studies Series
Activities: Docent training; seminars; tours for school groups; fels offered; museum shop sells books, original art, Native American Arts & Crafts

L **Fulton-Hayden Memorial Library,** Dragoon Rd, PO Box 248, 85609. Tel 602-586-3666. *Pres* Duncan Fulton; *VPres* Peter L Formo; *Treas* Michael W Hard; *Foundation Dir* Anne I Woosley
Estab 1961. Open to scholars by appointment
Income: Financed by endowment income, grants, gifts
Library Holdings: Vols 20,000; Per subs 60; Micro — Cards, fiche, prints, reels; AV — Fs, Kodachromes, lantern slides; Other — Clipping files, exhibition catalogs, manuscripts, original art works, pamphlets, prints, sculpture
Special Subjects: Archaeology, Ethnology
Collections: Parral Archives on microfilm; collections of research and technical reports

FLAGSTAFF

M **MUSEUM OF NORTHERN ARIZONA,** Route 4, PO Box 720, 86001. Tel 602-774-5211. *Pres Board Trustees* Jim Babbitt; *Assoc Cur of Anthropology* David Wilcox
Open Mon - Sun 9 AM - 5 PM. Admis adults $3; students and children $1.50. Estab 1928 to study, preserve and interpret the art and cultural and natural history of the Colorado Plateau. Average Annual Attendance: 85,000. Mem: 4200; dues $20-$1000; annual meeting in Jan
Income: $2,500,000 (financed by endowment, membership and earned income)
Collections: †Works of Southwestern Native American artists; †non-Indian art depicting Colorado Plateau subjects; †archaeological & ethnographic artifacts & natural history specimens of the Colorado Plateau
Exhibitions: (1991) Annual Zuni, Hopi & Navajo artists exhibitions; Two changing exhibits each year: Navajo folk art/Garnet Pavatea: Hopi potter, A Separate Vision, a show of 4 innovative, contemporary Native American Art (traveling)
Publications: Bulletin, irregular; Museum Notes, bimonthly; Plateau, quarterly
Activities: Classes for adults and children; back-country expeditions; lectrs open to the public; performances; docent training lectures; gallery talks; tours; competitions with awards; scholarships offered; individual paintings and original objects of art lent to various institutions; organize and circulate traveling exhibitions; book shop sells books, magazines, videos, cassettes, prints; museum shop sells original Native American arts & crafts

M **NORTHERN ARIZONA UNIVERSITY,** Art Museum & Galleries, PO Box 6021, 86011-6021. Tel 602-523-3471; FAX 602-523-4230. *Dir* Joel S Eide
Open Mon - Fri 8 AM - 5 PM, Tues & Wed 6:30 - 8:30 PM, Sat & Sun 1 - 4 PM, special holiday hours. No admis fee. Estab 1968 for the continuing education & service to the students & the Flagstaff community in all aspects of fine arts & to national & international fine arts communities
Collections: †Contemporary ceramics; Master prints of the 20th century & American painting of the Southwest
Activities: Lect open to public, national & international workshops & conferences; concerts; tours; competitions with awards; scholarships; originate traveling exhibitions; museum shop sells books, original art works, prints & posters

GANADO

M **NATIONAL PARK SERVICE,** Hubbell Trading Post National Historic Site, PO Box 150, 86505. Tel 602-755-3475. *Supt* Charles D Wyatt; *Cur* Open
Open May - Sept 8 AM - 6 PM, Oct - Apr 8 AM - 5 PM. No admis fee. Estab 1967 to set aside Hubbell Trading Post as a historic site as the best example in Southwest of a Trader, an Indian Trading Post and people he served. Average Annual Attendance: 200,000
Income: Financed by federal appropriation
Collections: Contemporary Western artists; ethnohistoric arts & crafts; furnishings; photographs
Exhibitions: Photo contests
Activities: Educ dept; lectures open to public; tours; presentations; competitions; individual paintings & art objects are lent to certified museums; sales shop sells books, Indian arts & crafts, magazines, original art, prints & slides

KINGMAN

M **MOHAVE MUSEUM OF HISTORY AND ARTS,** 400 W Beale, 86401. Tel 602-753-3195. *Dir* Robert Yost
Open Mon - Fri 10 AM - 5 PM, Sat & Sun 1 - 5PM. Admis adults $2, children free. Estab 1960 tp preserve & present to the public the art & history of Northwest Arizona. Average Annual Attendance: 30,000. Mem: 550; dues $20-$125; annual meeting in Apr
Income: Financed by endowment, membership, city & state appropriation, sales & donations
Collections: American Indian Art; art & history of Northwest Arizona
Activities: Classes for children; docent programs; lectures open to the public; museum shop sells books, prints, original art, craft items, reproductions

MESA

M **GALERIA MESA,** Mesa Arts Center, 155 N Center, PO Box 1466, 85211-1466. Tel 602-644-2242. *Supv* Sue Hakala; *Cur* Jeffory Morris
Open Tues - Thurs noon - 8 PM, Fri & Sat noon - 5 PM. No admis fee. Estab 1981 to provide an exhibition space for new and emerging artists. Average Annual Attendance: 9000

Income: Financed by city appropriation
Collections: †Permanent collection
Activities: Classes & workshops for adults & children; lect open to public, 1 vis lectr per yr; gallery talks; tours; competitions with awards; artmobile; book traveling exhibitions annually; originate traveling exhibitions

A **XICANINDIO, INC,** PO Box 1242, 85211-1242. Tel 602-833-5875. *Pres* Jema Duarte; *VPres* Jorge Eagar; *Secy* Bryon Barabe; *Exec Dir* Dina Lopez-Woodward
Open daily 9 AM - 5 PM. Estab 1977 as a non-profit organization of Native American & Hispanic artists to promote cross cultural understanding, preserve tradition, and develop grass roots educational programs. Average Annual Attendance: 28,000. Mem: 20; annual meeting in Sept
Income: $64,000 (financed by endowment, city & state appropriation)
Publications: Papel Picado (paper cut-out techniques)
Activities: Lectures open to public, 1 vis lectr per yr

NOGALES

A **PIMERIA ALTA HISTORICAL SOCIETY,** 136 N Grand Ave, PO Box 2281, 85621. Tel 602-287-4621. *Pres* Oscar Lizardi; *Dir* Susan Clarke Spater
Open Mon - Fri 9 AM - 5 PM, Sat 10 AM - 4 PM, Sun 1 - 4 PM. Estab 1948 to preserve the unique heritage of northern Sonora Mexico and southern Arizona from 1000 AD to present; art is incorporated into interpretive exhibits. Also maintains a photo gallery. Average Annual Attendance: 15,000. Mem: 850; dues adults $7.50; meeting in Jan
Income: $55,000 (financed by memberships, fund raising events, education programs & grants)
Collections: Art and artifacts of Hohokam and Piman Indians, Spanish conquistadores and Mexican ranchers and Anglo pioneer settlement
Publications: Centennial Book of Nogales; newsletter, 10 per year; annual calendar on historic subjects
Activities: Classes for adults and children; lectures open to public, 3 vis lectr per year; tours; competitions; originate traveling exhibitions; sales shop sells books, maps and pins
L **Library,** 136 N Grand Ave, PO Box 2281, 85628-2281. Tel 602-287-4621. *Registrar* Anne B Wheeler
Collects books and archival material on Pimeria Alta, northern Sonora and southern Arizona
Income: $1000
Purchases: $500
Library Holdings: Vols 1000; Per subs 3; AV — Cassettes; Other — Clipping files, manuscripts, memorabilia, pamphlets, photographs
Collections: The Jack Kemmer Memorial Collection, books on the cattle industry of Texas, New Mexico, Arizona and California

PHOENIX

A **ARIZONA ARTIST GUILD,** 8912 N Fourth St, 85020. Tel 602-944-9713. *Pres* Betty Braig; *First VPres* Penny Peterson; *Second VPres Exhib* Larry Stewart; *Second VPres Exhib* Cathy McCormick; *Recording Secy* Diane Kent; *Corresp Secy* Maureen Fairbanks; *Treas* Cynthia Ganem
Estab 1928 to foster guild spirit, to assist in raising standards of art in the community, and to assume civic responsibility in matters relating to art. Average Annual Attendance: 550. Mem: 295 juried, 90 assoc; dues $25; membership by jury; monthly meetings
Income: Financed by endowment and membership
Exhibitions: Horizons (annually in spring, members only); fall exhibition for members only; juried exhibition
Publications: AAG news, monthly
Activities: Classes for adults; lectures sometimes open to the public, 12 or more vis lectr per year; gallery talks; competitions with awards; workshops by visiting professionals offered; paint-outs; sketch groups; demonstrations; scholarship offered
L **Library,** 8912 N Fourth St, 85020. Tel 602-944-9713, 948-8565.
Open to members for reference only
Library Holdings: Vols 200

A **ARIZONA COMMISSION ON THE ARTS,** 417 W Roosevelt, 85003. Tel 602-255-5882; FAX 602-256-0282. *Chmn* Marvin Cohen; *Executive Dir* Shelley Cohn; *Artists in Educ Dir* Sandie Campolo; *Educ Dir* Carol Jean Kennedy; *Deputy Dir* Gail Crider; *Performing Art Dir* Claire West; *Design/Organization Development Dir* Rex Gulbranson; *Visual Arts Dir* Krista Elrick; *Public Information Officer* Tonda Gorton
Open 8 AM - 5 PM. No admis fee. Estab 1966 to promote and encourage the arts in the State of Arizona. Mem: Meetings, quarterly
Income: $1,152,800 (financed by state and federal appropriation)
Exhibitions: Traveling Exhibitions 15-20 per year
Publications: Artists' Guide to Programs; monthly bulletin guide to programs
Activities: Workshops; artists-in-education program; lect open to public; scholarships; bi-cultural arts program; Art in Public Places Program; Art in Arizona Towns Program; book traveling exhibitions; originate traveling exhibitions, organization development program, design program
L **Reference Library,** 417 W Roosevelt, 85003. Tel 602-255-5882; FAX 602-256-0282. *Public Information Officer* Tonda Gorton
Library Holdings: Vols 1000; Per subs 20; AV — Slides; Other — Pamphlets
Special Subjects: Topics related to the business of the arts

A **ARIZONA WATERCOLOR ASSOCIATION,** PO Box 7574, 85011. Tel 602-584-2710. *Pres* Tom Schultz; *Treas* Jeaniene Sergio; *First VPres* Marjorie Miller; *Second VPres* Norbert Baird; *Third VPres* John Erwin; *Dir* Bette Hedblom; *Dir* Mike McDaniel; *Dir* Jim Dumble
Estab 1960 to further activity & interest in the watermedia, promote growth of individuals & group & maintain high quality of professional exhibits. Average Annual Attendance: 600. Mem: 500; qualifications for juried membership must be accepted in three different approved juried shows; all members who pay dues are considered members; dues $30

Income: Financed by dues and donations
Exhibitions: Two exhibitions yearly: Membership Show, juried in Sedona by Northern Chapter
Publications: AWA Newsletter, monthly; Directory, annual
Activities: Workshops; lectures for members only; paint outs; competitions with awards

ATLATL
For Further Information see National and Regional Organizations

C **FIRST INTERSTATE BANK OF ARIZONA,** 100 W Washington, 85003. Tel 602-229-4624. *Cur* Patsy Koldoff
Open Mon - Fri 10 AM - 3 PM. No admis fee. Collection displayed in Old West Gallery, three room gallery on second floor of Tucson Main
Collections: Western scenes
Activities: Tours; awards to various art associations around the state; objects of art lent to Tucson Museum & Phoenix Art Museum

M **HEARD MUSEUM,** 22 E Monte Vista Rd, 85004-1480. Tel 602-252-8840; FAX 602-252-9757. *Dir* Martin Sullivan; *Chief Cur* Dr Peter Welsh; *Asst Dir* Ann Marshall; *Dir of Marketing* Janice Decker; *Cur of fine Art* Margaret Archuleta; *Cur of Coll* Diana Pardue; *Registrar* Debra Slaney; *Public Information Officer* Mary Brennan; *Asst Cur* Gloria Lomahaftewa; *Exhibit Coordr* Lisa MacCollum; *Education Servs Mgr* Gina Laczko; *Librn* Mario Nick Klimiades
Open Mon - Sat 10 AM - 4:45 PM, Sun 1 - 4:45 PM. Admis adults $5, sr citizen $4, student & children $2. Estab 1929 to collect and exhibit anthropology and art; collections built around works of Indians of the Americas. Average Annual Attendance: 250,000
Collections: Fred Harvey Fine Arts Collection; C G Wallace Collection; Archeology; †Native American fine arts; †sculpture, †primitive arts from the cultures of Africa, Asia & Oceania; †American Indian
Exhibitions: Heard Museum Collection; Shaping Our Future; In the Spirit of Tradition: The Heard Museum Craft Arts Invitational; When the Rainbow Touches Down; Dan Namingha: Tewa-Hopi Reflections: May This One Grow; Recent Generations; Native American Art, 1950's - 1987; What is Native American Art?. Authority an Ornament: Art of the Sepik River; Earth, Hands, Life Southwestern Ceramic Figures; Exotic Illusions: Art Romance & the Market Place; Galbraith Collection of Native American Art; Progressions of Impressions
Publications: Amusements calendar; The Heard Museum Newsletter, quarterly; exhibition catalogs
Activities: Educ Dept; classes for adults & children; dramatic programs; docent training; lectr open to public, 10 vis lectr per year; concerts; gallery talks; tours; competitions; lect at schools; original objects of art levt to accredited museums; lending collection contains framed reproductions, original prints, 1000 paintings, photographs, sculpture & 600 slides; organize and circulate traveling exhibitions; museum shop sells books, original art, prints, reproductions and slides
L **Library & Archives,** 22 E Monte Vista Rd, 85004-1480. Tel 602-252-8840; FAX 602-252-9757. *Librn & Archivist* Mario Nick Klimiades
Open Mon - Fri 10 AM - Noon, 1 PM - 4:45 PM. Estab 1929 as a research library for museum staff, members and the public (in-house only)
Income: $11,000 (financed by membership & museum budget)
Library Holdings: Vols 24,000; Per subs 100; Micro — Fiche, prints, reels; AV — A-tapes, cassettes, lantern slides, rec, slides, v-tapes; Other — Clipping files, exhibition catalogs, manuscripts, pamphlets, photographs, prints, reproductions
Special Subjects: Anthropology, Primitive Art, Native American studies
Collections: †Native American Artists Resource Collection

A **MOVIMIENTO ARTISTICO DEL RIO SALADO, INC (MARS),** 130 N Central Ave, PO Box 20431, 85036. Tel 602-253-3541. *Chmn* Julia Emmons; *Pres* Ralph Cordova; *Art Dir* Jerry Gilmore
Open Mon - Fri 11 AM - 3 PM. No admis fee. Estab 1976 to promote Arizona, Mexican-American, Chicano artists through visual, literary & performance art. Nonprofit artist cooperative art space. Average Annual Attendance: 5000. Mem: Open to Mexican American &/or Arizona artist, submit 10 or more slides & several pieces; dues $60; monthly meetings
Income: $33,000 (financed by membership, National Endowment for the Arts, county & state appropriation)
Exhibitions: Asociacion Sonorense de Artes Plasticas; MARS '87; Alfred Arreguin & Co; Small Objects - Fundraising Exhibition; Mexican Folk Art Exhibition & Sale; Luis Bernal (photography); David Avalos (mixed media); MARS Satellite Artists Exhibition; La Phoeniquera VII
Publications: MARS Newsletter, monthly

M **PHOENIX ART MUSEUM,** 1625 N Central Ave, 85004. Tel 602-257-1880; FAX 602-253-8662. *Pres* Roy Papt; *Dir* James K Ballinger
Open Tues - Sat 10 AM - 5 PM, Wed 10 AM - 9 PM, Sun noon - 5 PM, cl Mon. Admis adults $3, students $1.50, sr citizens $2.50, members & scool tours free. Estab 1925; museum constructed 1959. Average Annual Attendance: 250,000. Mem: 7000; dues $35 and up; annual meeting April
Income: $1,900,000 (public & private funds)
Collections: Contemporary paintings, sculptures and graphics; 19th century; Baroque; Oriental arts collection; Renaissance; Thorne Miniature Rooms; Western art; Medieval art
Publications: Annual report; Calendar, monthly; exhibition catalogs
Activities: Classes for adults and children; docent training; lectures open to public, 12 vis lectr per year; concerts; gallery talks; tours; competitions; originate traveling exhibitions; museum shop sells books, magazines, reproductions, prints, slides and gifts from around the world; junior museum at same address
L **Art Research Library,** 1625 N Central Ave, 85004-1685. Tel 602-257-1880; FAX 602-253-8662. *Librn* Clayton C Kirking
Open Tues - Fri 10 AM - 4:30 PM. Estab 1959 to serve reference needs of the museum staff, docents, membership, students and public. For reference only
Income: Financed by Museum operating funds
Purchases: $22,000
Library Holdings: Vols 40,000; Per subs 97; Auction Records, Ephemera; AV —

Slides; Other — Clipping files, exhibition catalogs, memorabilia, pamphlets, reproductions
Special Subjects: American Western Art, Asian Art, Ceramics, Decorative Arts, Fashion Arts, Folk Art, Latin American Art, Painting - American, Period Rooms, Southwestern Art, Costume Design, 18th, 19th & 20th Century Western American Painting, 18th, 19th & 20th Century Chinese Painting, Ceramics, Glass
Collections: Ambrose Lansing Egyptian Collection; Arizona Artist Index; auction catalogs; museum archives; Rembrandt print catalogs; Whistler Prints

C **SECURITY PACIFIC BANK ARIZONA,** 101 N First Ave, 85002. Tel 602-262-2265. *Pres & Chief Exec Officer* James Albo
Open Mon - Thurs & Sat 9 AM - 4 PM, Fri 9 AM - 5 PM. Estab as art sponsor to provide an opportunity for Southwest art to be seen by customers and others in downtown Phoenix. Displays continually changing exhibits which benefit charitable organizations through the sale of works being shown. Collection displayed in the Galleria, and in offices statewide. Galleria exhibits, including parts of permanent collection
Collections: Approximately 400 Hopi Indian Kachinas; 350 paintings and sculpture

M **TEMPLE BETH ISRAEL,** Plotkin Juddica Museum, 3310 N Tenth Ave, 85013. Tel 602-264-4428; FAX 602-264-0039. *Dir* Plotkin Syloid; *Assoc Dir* Pamela Leoin; *Registrar* Thelma Bilsky
Open daily 10 AM - 3 PM. Admis donations accepted. Estab 1970 to promote education of Judaism. Tunisian Synagogue Gallery. Mem: 500; dues $15 - $250; annual meeting Mar 31
Income: $20,000 (financed by endowment, mem & gifts)
Collections: Contemporary art reflecting the Jewish experience; Holiday Juddica; †Jewish Life Cycle; †Tunisian Juddica
Exhibitions: 25th Anniversary Retrospective
Publications: HA-OR, three times a year
Activities: Classes for adults & children; docent programs; lect open to public, 6 vis lectr per year; films; book traveling exhibitions 3 per year; originate traveling exhibitions, 1 per year

C **VALLEY NATIONAL BANK OF ARIZONA,** Fine Arts Department, PO Box 71, 85001. Tel 602-261-2966, 253-1601. *Cur Art* Judith B Hudson; *Concourse Events Coordr* Joanne Johnson
Open to public. Estab 1933 to support emerging artists throughout the state; encourage and promote talented high school students with Scholastic Art Awards; provide the public with beautiful, integrated art in branch banks. Several thousand pieces of art collection displayed in over 200 branches, business offices, and support facilities throughout the state of Arizona
Collections: Primarily Western, Southwestern art featuring many of the now classic Western artists; earliest lithograph dates back to the 1820's and collection continues through the present
Exhibitions: Employee's Art Show; Fine Woodcarvings Show & Arizona Students Fine Art Week; Arizona Art Glass Exhibit '91
Activities: Lect; gallery talks; tours by appointment; competitions, since 1942 state sponsor for Scholastic Art Awards throughout Arizona; purchase awards throughout the state, sponsor Employees' Art Show annually, with juried and popular choice awards, underwrite local art exhibitions on the Concourse of the Home Office Building; individual objects of art lent contingent upon bank policy

PRESCOTT

M **GEORGE PHIPPEN MEMORIAL FOUNDATION,** Prescott's Phippen Museum of Western Art, 4701 N Hwy 89, PO Box 1642, 86301. Tel 602-778-1385.
Open 10 AM - 4 PM. Admis $2. Estab 1984 to promote Western art. Gallery has 4000 sq ft. Average Annual Attendance: 5500. Mem: 250; dues family $30, individual $20; annual meeting in Aug
Income: $70,000 (financed by mem & admis)
Collections: Western Art - all media
Activities: Adult classes; lect open to public, 9 vis lectr per year; sells books, prints, original art

A **PRESCOTT FINE ARTS ASSOCIATION,** Gallery, 208 N Marina St, 86301. Tel 602-445-3286. *Pres* Julie Clarke; *VPres* Kathy Sischka; *Secy* Ron Barnes
Open Wed - Sun 11 AM - 4 PM during shows. No admis fee, donations accepted. Estab 1968 to promote arts within the county and local community. Art Gallery is one large room below theater section in what was previously a Catholic Church. Average Annual Attendance: 5000. Mem: 318; dues family $50, individual $25
Income: $30,000 (financed by membership and grants from Arizona Arts and Humanities Council)
Activities: Docent training; lectrs open to public; concerts; scholarship competitions with awards; book traveling exhibitions; Sales shop sells original art, prints, woven, glass & wood items

SCOTTSDALE

A **COSANTI FOUNDATION,** 6433 Doubletree Ranch Rd, 85253. Tel 602-948-6145. *Pres* Paolo Soleri; *Asst to the Pres* Scott M Davis; *Dir of Design* Tomiaki Tamura; *Admin* Mary Hoadley
Open Mon - Sun 9 AM - 5 PM. Suggested donation $1. Estab 1956 as a non-profit educational organization by Paolo Soleri pursuing the research and development of an alternative urban environment. A permanent exhibit of original sketches, sculptures & graphics by Paolo Soleri. Average Annual Attendance: 50,000
Income: Financed by tuition, private donations and sales of art objects
Collections: Permanent collection of architectural designs and drawings by Paolo Soleri
Activities: Classes for adults & college students; academic conferences, experimental workshops; lectures open to the public; concerts; gallery talks; tours; scholarships; traveling exhibits organized and circulated; sales shop sells books, original art, prints, reproductions, slides

A **Arcosanti,** HC74 Box 4136, 86333. Tel 602-632-7135; FAX 602-632-7135; Elec Mail America Online: Arcosanti. *Pres* Paolo Soleri; *Administration* Mary Hoadley; *Asst* Scott Davis; *Planning* Tomiaki Tamura
Open Mon - Sun 9 AM - 5 PM. Suggested donation for tour $5. Estab 1970. A permanent exhibit of original sketches, sculptures & graphics by Paolo Soleri
Publications: Arcosanti Newsletter, occasional

A **FRANCHISE FINANCE CORPORATION OF AMERICA,** The Fleischer Museum, 17207 N Perimeter Dr, Suite 500, 85255-5402. Tel 602-585-3108; FAX 602-585-2225; WATS 800-528-1179. *Exec Dir* Donna H Fleischer; *Asst to Dir* Annabelle Markstein
Open 10 AM - 4 PM. No admis fee. Estab 1989 to provide a permanent home for the collection & develop a scholarly forum for education on the art period
Income: Financed by private funds
Collections: American Impressionism, California School
Exhibitions: (1990-1991) Permanent Collection: Gilcrease Comes to Scottsdale
Publications: Masterworks of California Impressionism, book; exhibition catalogs
Activities: Lect open to public; retail store sells books, prints, original art

L **Fleischer Museum Library,** 85255-5402
For reference only
Income: $18,000 (financed by private collection)
Library Holdings: Vols 264; Per subs 12; AV — Kodachromes, slides, v-tapes; Other — Clipping files, exhibition catalogs, framed reproductions, memorabilia, original art works, pamphlets, photographs, prints, reproductions, sculpture

A **SCOTTSDALE ARTISTS' LEAGUE,** PO Box 1071, 85252. Tel 602-949-9569. *Pres* Jeanne Kahn
Estab 1961 to encourage the practice of art and to support and encourage the study and application of art as an avocation, to promote ethical principals and practice, to advance the interest and appreciation of art in all its forms and to increase the usefulness of art to the public at large. Gallery in Scottsdale Memorial Hospital. Average Annual Attendance: 50 - 100 per month. Mem: 225; dues $20; monthly meetings first Tues Sept - June
Exhibitions: Yearly juried exhibition for members only; yearly juried exhibition for all Arizona artists (open shows)
Publications: Art Beat, monthly
Activities: Classes for adults; lectures open to the public, 6 vis lectr per year; gallery talks; tours; scholarships given to art students

M **SCOTTSDALE CENTER FOR THE ARTS,** 7383 Scottsdale Mall, 85251. Tel 602-994-2301; FAX 602-994-7728. *Dir* Frank Jacobson; *Dir Visual Arts* Robert Knight; *Asst Dir Visual Arts* Debra Hopkins
Open Tues - Fri 10 AM - 8 PM, Sat Noon - 8 PM, Sun Noon - 5 PM. No admis fee. Estab 1975 to provide a varied program of performance events & art exhibits. Center is a large contemporary space including two climate controlled galleries allowing viewing of large & small works in various media. Average Annual Attendance: 130,000. Mem: 2500; dues $20 and up
Income: $1,250,000 (financed by membership, city appropriation & corporate sponsorship)
Collections: Paintings, prints, sculptures
Exhibitions: (1991) Larry Rivers, Public & Private. (1992) Diamonds are Forever; Under Cover: The Book Becomes Art
Publications: Exhibition catalogs
Activities: Docent training; lectures open to public, 10 vis lectr per yr; competitions with awards; exten dept serves local schools; book traveling exhibitions; originates traveling exhibition; sales shop sells books, original art, reproductions, prints & craft items

SECOND MESA

M **HOPI CULTURAL CENTER MUSEUM,** Route 264, PO Box 7, 86043. Tel 602-734-6650. *Dir* Anna Silas
Open Mon - Fri 8 AM - 5 PM
Collections: Hopi arts & crafts; pre-historic & historic pottery; weavings; wood carvings; silver

TEMPE

ARIZONA STATE UNIVERSITY
M **University Art Museum,** Fine Arts Center, 85287-1202. Tel 602-965-2787; FAX 602-965-2787. *Dir* Marilyn A Zeitlin; *Cur* Heather Lineberry; *Registrar* Mary Jane Williams; *Installationist* Stephen Johnson; *Information Specialist* Dianne M Cripe
Open Tues - Fri 8:30 AM - 4:30 PM, Sat 10 AM - 5 PM, Sun 1 - 5 PM. No admis fee. Estab 1950 to provide esthetic and educational service for students and the citizens of the state. Permanent installations, changing galleries & various changing area; 48 shows annually. Average Annual Attendance: 55,000
Income: $250,000 (financed by state appropriations, donations and earnings)
Collections: †American crafts, especially ceramics & glass; American Crockery; †American painting & sculpture, 18th Century to present; †print collection, 15th Century to present; †Latin American Art; Folk art; African, South Seas, 20th century ceramics; 20th Century Glass; Edward Jacobson Collection of Turned-Wood bowls & Print Study Room
Exhibitions: Continuous showing of Historical & Contemporary Print Exhibitions; Showing of Historical American Ceramic Collection; Gregory Barsamian: Persistence of Vision; The Human Condition: Jacques Callot (1592 - 1635); Redefining the Lathe-Turned Object, A National Juried Exhibition; Paul Soldner: A Retrospective
Activities: Educ dept; docent training; special events; lect open to public, 12 visiting lectr per year; gallery talks; tours; competitions; individual paintings and original objects of art lent to other professional organizations; originate traveling exhibitions; museum shop sells books, original art & crafts, jewelry, cards

L **Hayden Library,** 85287-1006. Tel 602-965-6164. *Dean University Libraries* Sherri Schmidt; *Assoc Dean Coll Development* Dora Biblarz; *Art Specialist* Winberta Yao; *Architecture Librn* Berna Neal
Open Mon - Thurs 7 AM - 11:30 PM, Fri 7 AM - 7 PM, Sat 9 AM - 5 PM, Sun

noon - 11:30 PM
Income: Financed by state
Library Holdings: Vols 2,826,679; Per subs 31,694; Micro — Cards, fiche, reels; AV — Cassettes
Special Subjects: American Indian Art, American Western Art, Anthropology, Archaeology, Architecture, Art Education, Art History, Coins & Medals, History of Art & Archaeology, Interior Design

M **Memorial Union Gallery,** 85287. Tel 602-965-6649; FAX 602-965-5834. *Dir* Rosalyn Munk
Open Mon - Fri 9 AM - 5 PM. Estab to exhibit work that has strong individual qualities from the United States, also some Arizona work that has not been shown on campus. Gallery is contained in two rooms with 1400 sq ft space; fireplace; one wall is glass; 20 ft ceiling; 26 4 x 8 partitions; track lighting; one entrance and exit; located in area with maximum traffic. Average Annual Attendance: 30,000
Income: Financed by administrative appropriation
Purchases: $3000
Collections: Painting, print and sculpture, primarily Altman, Gorman, Mahaffey, Schoulder and Slater
Exhibitions: Jeff: Wood, Mixed Media; Sandra Campbell: Rock, Mixed Media Sculpture; William B Schade: Artists Books, Handmade Papers; Mary Lou Stewart: Casein, Mixed Media/Paper; Itsue Ito: Ceramic Sculpture; Martha Haley: Fibers; Robert Gischer: Oil/Mixed Media Collages; Celeste Rehm: Pen/Ink Drawings; Bruce Guttin: Wood Sculpture; George Blakely: Post Card/Photographs Installation; David E Harmon: Pastel/Paper, Oil/Canvas; Merle Perlmutter: Etchings; Melvinita Hooper: Acrylic/Paper; Pam Beyette: Woven Foil, Mixed Media
Activities: Educ dept; internships; lect open to pub, 4 visiting lectr per year; gallery talks; competitions; originate traveling exhibitions

L **Architecture and Environmental Design Library,** College of Architecture & Environmental Design, 85287. Tel 602-965-6400; FAX 602-965-1594. *Dept Head* Berna E Neal
Open Mon - Thurs 8 AM - 10 PM, Fri 8 AM - 5 PM, Sat Noon - 5 PM, Sun 5 - 10 PM. Estab 1959 to serve the architecture college and the university community with reference and research material in the subject of architecture. Circ 35,000
Income: Financed by state appropriation
Library Holdings: Vols 28,000; Per subs 150; architectural models; Micro — Fiche, prints, reels; AV — A-tapes, cassettes, motion pictures, slides, v-tapes; Other — Manuscripts, memorabilia, photographs, prints
Special Subjects: Architecture, Decorative Arts, Furniture, Jewelry, Interior Design, Landscape Architecture
Collections: †Paolo Soleri Archive; †Frank Lloyd Wright Special Research Collection

L **Architectural Image Library,** College of Architecture, 85287. Tel 602-965-5469; FAX 602-965-1594. *Coordr* Diane Upchurch
Circ 75,000
Library Holdings: AV — Slides 90,000; Other — Prints
Special Subjects: Architecture, Art History, Asian Art, Etchings & Engravings, Furniture, Graphic Design, Interior Design, Islamic Art, Landscape Architecture, Painting - American, Painting - Dutch, Painting - European, Painting - Flemish, Painting - French, Painting - German, Painting - Italian, Period Rooms, Photography, Pottery, Primitive Art, Printmaking, Sculpture, Tapestries, Textiles, Woodcuts

A **TEMPE ARTS CENTER,** 54 W First St, PO Box 549, 85280-0549. Tel 602-968-0888. *Exec Dir* Dawne Walczak; *Exhib Coordr* Patty Haberman; *Admin Asst* Kelly Gallett
Open Tues - Sun noon - 5 PM. No admis fee. Estab 1982. Contemporary craft & sculpture - outdoor sculpture garden featuring contemporary large scale sculpture on a rotating basis. Average Annual Attendance: 40,000. Mem: 200; dues $30, $50, $100, $250; annual meeting in Sept
Income: Financed by mem, city & state appropriation
Activities: Children's classes; lect open to public, 6 vis lectr per year; scholarships & fels; book traveling exhibitions 1 per year; originate traveling exhibitions 1 per year; retail store sells original art & craft only

TUBAC

A **SANTA CRUZ VALLEY ART ASSOCIATION,** Tubac Center of the Arts, PO Box 1911, 85646. Tel 602-398-2371. *Pres* Susan Aycock-Williams; *Dir* Pat Marohn
Open Tues - Sat 10 AM - 4:30 PM, Sun & holidays 1 - 4:30 PM, cl Mon. No admis fee. Estab 1963 to promote interest in regional art. Three galleries, one a Spanish Colonial Building, 139 running ft of exhibit space. Average Annual Attendance: 30,000-40,000. Mem: 800; dues $15 - $500; annual meeting in April
Collections: Works by present and former Tubac artists
Exhibitions: Invitationals; members' shows
Activities: Classes for adults and children; docent training; lectures for members only, 2 - 4 vis lectr per yr; competitions with awards; sales shop sells books, original art, pottery, jewelry, ethnic crafts (Indian, Mexican)

L **Library,** PO Box 1911, 85646. *Vol Librn* Open
Library Holdings: Vols 700; Micro — Cards; AV — Slides; Other — Exhibition catalogs
Special Subjects: Art History

TUCSON

ART LIBRARIES SOCIETY OF NORTH AMERICA
For further information, see National and Regional Organizations

M **DINNERWARE ARTIST'S COOPERATIVE,** 135 E Congress St, 85701. Tel 602-792-4503. *Exec Dir* Nora Kuhl
Open Tues - Sat noon - 5 PM. No admis fee. Estab 1979
Exhibitions: Diane Mansfield Colligan; Joseph Labate; Lance Patigian; Photography

M **TUCSON MUSEUM OF ART,** 140 N Main Ave, 85701. Tel 602-624-2333. *Dir* Robert A Yassin; *Registrar* Susan Dolan; *Dir Public Relations & Marketing* Laurie Swanson; *Business Mgr* Carol Bleck; *Controller* Ruth Sons; *School Mgr* Robert Kuegel; *Membership Secy* Dawn Briggs; *Admin Asst* Roni Thomas; *Librn* Sheila Mortonson
Open Tues - Sat 10 AM - 4 PM, Sun noon - 4 PM, cl Mon. Estab 1924 to operate a private nonprofit civic art gallery to promote art education, to hold art exhibitions and to further art appreciation for the public. Galleries display permanent collections and changing exhibitions. Average Annual Attendance: 100,000. Mem: 2500; dues Director's Circle $1000, patrons $500, sponsor $250, donor $125, friends $60, general $35; annual meeting June
Income: $950,000 (financed by grants, endowment, membership, city and state appropriations and contributions)
Collections: Contemporary Southwest; Pre-Columbian; Spanish Colonial; Western American; 20th Century art
Exhibitions: (1990-1991) Masks from Around the World; American Primitive Paintings; Larry Bell; Elmer Schooley; Women Artists of the West
Publications: Quarterly calendar; exhibition catalogs
Activities: Classes for adults and children; docent training; lectures open to public; concerts; gallery talks; tours; exten department serving Tucson school districts; traveling exhibitions organized and circulated; museum shop features contemporary crafts by southern Arizona artists

L **Library,** 140 N Main Ave, 85701. Tel 602-623-4881. *Librn* Sheila Mortonson; *Asst* Elizabeth Horner
Open Mon - Fri 10 AM - 3 PM. Estab 1974 for bibliographic and research needs of Museum staff, faculty, students and docents. Open to public for research and study
Income: Financed by gifts and fund allocations
Library Holdings: Vols 6700; Per subs 25; indexes; museum archives; Micro — Reels; AV — Cassettes, lantern slides, slides 25,000; Other — Clipping files, exhibition catalogs 500, pamphlets 3000, photographs, prints, sculpture
Special Subjects: Aesthetics, American Indian Art, American Western Art, Art Education, Art History, Ceramics, Conceptual Art, Decorative Arts, Drawings, Etchings & Engravings, Folk Art, Furniture, Glass, Gold, History of Art & Archaeology, Pre-Columbian Art, Art of Africa, Oceania, Western art, Contemporary Art, Spanish Colonial, Arizona Artists
Collections: †Biographic material documenting Arizona artists for the Archives of Arizona Art

UNIVERSITY OF ARIZONA

M **Museum of Art,** Olive & Speedway Sts, 85721. Tel 602-621-7567. *Dir & Chief Cur* Dr Peter Bermingham; *Asst Dir* Adeline Karpiscak; *Cur of Education* Joshua Goldberg; *Assoc Cur of Education* Margaret Perkins; *Cur of Coll* Dr Peter Briggs; *Admin Asst* Chris Dolezal; *Registrar* Kenneth D Little; *Asst Registrar* Richard Schaffer; *Public Relations* Brian Beck
Open Sept 1 - May 15 Mon - Fri 9 AM - 5 PM, Sun noon - 4 PM, cl Sat; May 15 - Sept 1 Mon - Fri 10 AM - 3:30 PM, Sun noon - 4 PM, cl Sat. Estab 1955 to share with the Tucson community, visitors and the university students the treasures of three remarkable permanent collections: the C Leonard Pfeiffer Collection, the Samuel H Kress Collection and the Edward J Gallagher Jr Collection. One of the museums' most important functions is to reach out to schools around Tucson through the education department. Special exhibitions are maintained on the first floor of the museum; the permanent collections are housed on the second floor. Average Annual Attendance: 45,000
Income: Financed by state appropriation
Collections: Edward J Gallagher Collection of over a hundred paintings of national and international artists; Samuel H Kress Collection of 26 Renaissance works and 26 paintings of the 15th century Spanish Retablo by Fernando Gallego; C Leonard Pfeiffer Collection of American Artists of the 30s, 40s and 50s; Jacques Lipchitz Collection of 70 plaster models
Exhibitions: (1991) Body/Culture: Chicano Figuration; Kratky Film: The Art of Czechoslovak Animation; Garo Antreasian: Recent Work; Blas-Unwanted Dead or Alive. (1992) Paintings & Drawings from the Alex Hillman Family Foundation; Brodsky/Utkin: Projects; Roland Reiss: A Seventeen Year Survey; Gustave Baumann in the West; Human Components; Raphael Collazo: Retrospective; annual faculty & MFA exhibits
Publications: Fully illustrated catalogs on all special exhibitions
Activities: Docent training; lectures open to public, 10 vis lectrs per yr; tours; gallery talks; out reach tours; book traveling exhibitions 2-3 per year; traveling exhibitions organized and circulated; sales shop sells books, cards and poster reproductions

L **Museum of Art Library,** Speedway & Olive, 85721. Tel 602-621-7567. *Librn* Barbara Kittle
Estab to assist staff and students working at museum with reference information. Not open to public; telephone requests for information answered
Library Holdings: Vols 5000; Per subs 16; AV — Cassettes, slides; Other — Clipping files, exhibition catalogs, pamphlets
Special Subjects: Art History, Museum Studies

M **Center for Creative Photography,** University of Arizona, 85721. Tel 602-621-7968; FAX 602-621-9444. *Dir* Terence Pitts; *Cur* Trudy Wilner Stack; *Registrar* Anne Sullivan; *Archivist* Amy Rule; *Librn* Tim Troy
Open Mon - Fri 9 AM - 5 PM, Sun Noon - 5 PM. Estab 1975 to house and organize the archives of numerous major photographers and to act as a research center in 20th century photography. Gallery exhibitions changing approximately every six weeks. Average Annual Attendance: 30,000
Income: Financed by state, federal, private and corporate sources
Collections: Archives of Ansel Adams, Wynn Bullock, Harry Callahan, Aaron Siskind, W Eugene Smith, Frederick Sommer, Paul Strand, Edward Weston, Richard Aredon, and others
Exhibitions: (1993) Revealing Territory: Photographs of the Southwest by Mark Klett; The Legacy of W Eugene Smith: 12 photographs in the humanistic tradition; Flor Gardun: Witness of Time; Cindy Bernard the Security Envelope Grid
Publications: The Archive, approx 3 times per year; bibliography series; exhibitions catalogs; guide series
Activities: Lectures open to public; gallery talks; tours; original objects of art lent to qualified museums; traveling exhibitions organized and circulated

L **Library,** Center for Creative Photography, 85721. Tel 602-621-1331. *Librn* Tim Troy
Open Mon - Fri 9 AM - 5 PM, Sun Noon - 5 PM. Open to the public for print viewing & research
Library Holdings: Vols 10,000; Per subs 90; Micro — Fiche, reels; AV — A-tapes, cassettes, slides, v-tapes; Other — Clipping files, exhibition catalogs, manuscripts, memorabilia, original art works, pamphlets, photographs
Special Subjects: Photography as an art form in the 20th century
Collections: Limited edition books; hand-made books; books illustrated with original photographs; artists' books
L **College of Architecture Library,** 85721. Tel 602-621-2498; FAX 602-621-8700. *Librn* Shannon L Paul; *Cataloger* Madelyn Cook; *Slide Cur* Brooks Jeffrey
Open Mon - Thurs 9 AM - 9 PM, Fri 9 AM - 5 PM, Sat noon - 5 PM, Sun noon - 9 PM. Estab 1965
Income: $34,700 (financed by state appropriation)
Library Holdings: Vols 14,000; Per subs 125; AV — Slides, v-tapes; Other — Clipping files
Special Subjects: Architecture, Drafting, Landscape Architecture, Arid Lands Architecture, Design Communications

WICKENBURG

M **MARICOPA COUNTY HISTORICAL SOCIETY,** Desert Caballeros Western Museum, 21 N Frontier St, PO Box 1446, 85358. Tel 602-684-2272. *Dir* Cheryl Taylor; *Cur* Sheila Kollasch; *Secy* Jan Heineman; *Public Relations* Antoinette Hankins; *Treas* Stephen Morris
Open Mon - Sat 10 AM - 4 PM, Sun 1 - 4 PM. Admis adults $3.50, sr citizens $3, children 6 - 16 $1, under 6 free. Estab 1960 to show the development of Wickenburg from prehistoric to present day. The museum houses western art gallery, mineral room, Indian room, period rooms and gold mining equipment. Average Annual Attendance: 30,000. Mem: 650; dues vary
Income: $50,000 - $60,000 (financed by membership, private donations, endowments)
Collections: Indian artifacts; period rooms; †Western Art; mining supply; †memorabilia George Phippen Memorial Western Bronze Collection, including Remington and Russell
Publications: A History of Wickenburg to 1875 by Helen B Hawkins; The Right Side Up Town on the Upside Down River; Museum Highlights, quarterly
Activities: Lectures open to public, 3-6 vis lectrs per yr; tours; lending collection contains original objects of art; book traveling exhibitions 2 per year; museum shop sells books, prints and postcards, gift items, manufactured & handmade
L **Library,** 21 N Frontier St, PO Box 1446, 85358. Tel 602-684-2272.
Open to members for reference only
Library Holdings: Vols 2000
Special Subjects: American Western Art, History of Wickenburg, AZ, General Arizona history

WINDOW ROCK

L **NAVAJO NATION LIBRARY,** PO Drawer K, 86515. Tel 602-871-6517. *Librn* Irving Nelson
Library Holdings: Vols 21,000
Special Subjects: History, culture & arts of Navajo Indians

M **NAVAJO TRIBAL MUSEUM,** Hwy 264, PO Box 308, 86515. Tel 602-871-6673. *Acting Dir & Cur* Clarenda Bagay
Open Mon - Fri 9 AM - 4:45 PM, cl national & tribal holidays. No admis fee. Estab 1961 to collect and preserve items depicting Navajo history and culture and natural history of region. Exhibit area approx 2500 ft. Average Annual Attendance: 16,000
Income: Financed by tribal budget & donations
Collections: †Works in all media by Navajo Indian artists, & non-Navajo artists who depict Navajo subject matter
Publications: Artist's directory & biographical file
Activities: Individual paintings and original works of art available for loan to other museums; lending collection contains 4000 nature artifacts, 300 original works of art & 30,000 photographs; sales shop sells books

YUMA

M **ARIZONA HISTORICAL SOCIETY-YUMA,** Century House Museum & Garden, 240 Madison Ave, 85364. Tel 602-782-1841. *Division Dir* Megan Reid; *Cur* Carol Brooks; *Admin Secy* Karen Roberts
Open Tues - Sat 10 AM - 5 PM. No admis fee
Income: Financed by mem, state appropriation
Collections: †Archives; †Clothing; †Furniture & Household Items; †Photos & Maps; †Trade & Business Items
Exhibitions: Lower Colorado River Region from 1540-1940; History Exhibits; Period Rooms
Publications: Newsletter

M **YUMA FINE ARTS ASSOCIATION,** Art Center, 281 Gila St, 85364. Tel 602-783-2314; FAX 602-343-9238. *Dir* Shawn Davis; *Admin Asst* Cynthia Rouillard
Open Tues - Sun 10 AM - 5 PM. Admis adult $1, children $.50, free Tues. Estab 1962 to foster the arts in the Yuma area & to provide a showing space for contemporary art & art of the Southwest. Gallery is housed in restored Southern Pacific Railway depot built in 1926. Average Annual Attendance: 30,000. Mem: 350; dues $25 - $5000
Income: Financed by endowment, membership & city appropriation, grants & fundraising events
Collections: Contemporary Art; Art of the Southwest
Exhibitions: (1990) Zarco Guerrero, Las Calacarias; Carlos Coronado Ortega, Textincos, bicultural exhibit from US & Mexico; Ceremony of Memory: Contemporary Hispanic Artists Expressions in Spirituality. (1991) A World of Kites; Annual Yuma Symposium Exhibition; Peter Jagoda; Louise Tester Pollard;

25th Southwestern Exhibition
Publications: Art Notes Southwest, quarterly
Activities: Classes for adults & children; lect open to public, 10 vis lectr per yr; concerts; gallery talks; tours; competitions; $3000 awards annually; individual paintings & original objects of art lent to other museums for specific exhibitions; book traveling exhibitions 6 - 10 times per yr; originate traveling exhibitions; museum shop sells original art & art of the Southwest

ARKANSAS

CLARKSVILLE

UNIVERSITY OF THE OZARKS
L **Dobson Memorial Library,** 415 College Ave, 72830. Tel 501-754-3839. *Library Dir* Stuart Stelzer
Estab 1891
Library Holdings: Vols 1500; Per subs 14; Micro — Fiche, reels; AV — Cassettes, rec, slides 7000, v-tapes 17
M **Stephens Gallery,** Walton Fine Arts Bldg, 72830. Tel 501-754-7119; FAX 501-754-3839, Ext 355. *Gallery Dir* Nancy Farrell
Open Mon - Fri 10 AM - 3 PM & by special arrangement. Estab 1986
Collections: Gould Ivory Collection; Pfeffer Moser Glass Collection
Exhibitions: Monthly exhibitions
Activities: Educ dept; lect open to public; concerts; gallery talks; tours

EL DORADO

A **SOUTH ARKANSAS ARTS CENTER,** 110 E Fifth St, 71730. Tel 501-862-5474. *Pres* Bill Moncries; *Exec Dir* Rueben Murray
Open Mon - Fri 10 AM - 5 PM, Sat 2 - 5 PM. No admis fee. Estab 1965 for the promotion, enrichment and improvement of the visual arts by means of exhibits, lectures and instruction, and through scholarships to be offered whenever possible. Gallery maintained. Mem: 350; dues $5; meeting second Tues every month
Income: Financed by membership, city and state appropriation
Collections: Japanese block prints (including Hokusai, Utamarro, Hiroshig); regional watercolorists; Indian Jewelry (Hopi, Zuni, Navaho)
Exhibitions: Various art shows in this and surrounding states; gallery shows, ten guest artists annually, two months dedicated to local artists, works by local artists displayed in corridor year-round;
Publications: Newsletter, quarterly
Activities: Classes for adults and children; theater and dance workshops; lectures open to public; gallery talks; competitions; scholarships
L **Library,** 110 E Fifth St, 71730. FAX 501-862-5474; *Exec Dir* Reuben Murray
Income: $250,000 (financed by mem, grants, sales & sponsorships)
Library Holdings: Vols 2000
Special Subjects: Painting - American, Painting - Japanese, Porcelain, Pottery, Southwestern Art
Exhibitions: Changing exhibits every month
Publications: SAAC newsletter

FAYETTEVILLE

UNIVERSITY OF ARKANSAS
L **Fine Arts Library,** FNAR-104, Fayetteville, AR 72701. Tel 501-575-4708. *Librn* Norma Mosby
Open Mon - Thurs 8 AM - 11 PM, Fri 8 AM - 6 PM, Sat 10 AM - 6 PM, Sun 1 - 11 PM. Estab 1951 to support the curriculum in music, art and architecture. Circ 36,000
Library Holdings: Vols 33,000; Per subs 146; Micro — Fiche, reels; AV — Slides; Other — Exhibition catalogs
Special Subjects: Architecture, Art Education, Art History, Landscape Architecture, Music

FORT SMITH

M **FORT SMITH ART CENTER,** 423 N Sixth St, 72901. Tel 501-784-2787. *Pres of Board* Dr David Harper; *Dir* Polly Crews
Open daily 9:30 AM - 4:30 PM, Sun 2 - 4 PM, cl Mon, July 4, Labor Day, Thanksgiving & Christmas Eve-New Years. No admis fee. Estab 1957 to provide art museum, art association and art education. Art Library maintained. Average Annual Attendance: 10,000. Mem: 930; dues $40
Income: $100,000 (financed by endowment, mem, contributions & sales)
Collections: †American painting, graphics and drawings; †Boehm porcelain; local & regional art
Exhibitions: Five exhibitions monthly
Publications: Bulletin, monthly
Activities: Classes for children; competitions with awards; artmobile; gallery & gift shop sells books, original art & art related gift items

HELENA

M **PHILLIPS COUNTY MUSEUM,** 623 Pecan St, 72342. Tel 501-338-3537. *Pres* Mary A Burke
Open Mon - Sat 9 AM - 5 PM, cl national holidays. No admis fee. Estab 1929 as an educational and cultural museum to impart an appreciation of local history and to display objects of art from all over the world. Average Annual Attendance: 5000. Mem: 250; dues $3-$5; annual meeting first Fri in May
Income: Financed by endowment, membership and city appropriation
Collections: China; glassware; paintings; Indian artifacts; Civil War memorabilia; Thomas Alva Edison Historical Display
Exhibitions: Blues Exhibition Chuck Berry

HOT SPRINGS

M HOT SPRINGS ART CENTER, Fine Arts Center, 514 Central Ave, 71901. Tel 501-624-0489. *Interim Exec Dir* Katherine Duncan
Open Mon - Sat 10 AM - 4 PM, Sun 1:30 - 5 PM. No admis fee. Estab 1946 as a multi-disciplinary Arts Center. The Center constitutes an amalgam of arts organizations from throughout the region, representing all forms of fine & applied art as well as performing, instructional & crafts groups. Two galleries; twenty exhibits per year of local area artists. Average Annual Attendance: 5000. Mem: 550; dues benefactor $1000, sustaining $500, sponsor $250, subscriber $100, patron $50, family $25, individual $15; annual meeting in Oct
Income: Financed by individual & corporate memberships, grants from the Arkansas Arts Council & National Endowment for the Arts
Exhibitions: Annual Open Competition; regional, state & local artist exhibition
Publications: Class schedule brochures; monthly exhibit announcements; newsletters, 4 times per year
Activities: Classes for adults and children in art, dance, theatre & music; dramatic programs; concerts; competitions with awards; scholarships offered; individual paintings & original objects of art lent to other institutions; lending collection contains books & photographs

JONESBORO

M ARKANSAS STATE UNIVERSITY-ART DEPARTMENT, JONESBORO, Fine Arts Center Gallery, Caraway Rd (Mailing add: PO Box 1920, State University, 72467). Tel 501-972-3050. *Dir* Stephen L Mayes
Open weekdays 10 AM - 4 PM. No admis fee. Estab 1967 for education objectives; recognition of contemporary artists and encouragement to students. Located in the Fine Arts Center, the well-lighted gallery measures 40 x 45 ft plus corridor display areas. Average Annual Attendance: 10,500
Income: $3956 (financed by state appropriation)
Collections: Contemporary paintings; contemporary sculpture; †historical and contemporary prints; †photographs
Publications: Exhibition catalogs
Activities: Lect open to public, 4 - 6 visiting lectr per year; gallery talks; competitions; originate traveling exhibitions
L Library, 2040 Caraway Rd (Mailing add: PO Box 1920, State University, 72467). Tel 501-972-3077. *Reference Librn* Terrie Sypoelt
Library Holdings: Vols 9100; Per subs 79; Micro — Fiche, reels; AV — Cassettes, fs, Kodachromes, motion pictures, slides
Collections: Microfilm collection for 19th century photography

LITTLE ROCK

M ARKANSAS ARTS CENTER, 501 E Ninth St, 72202. Tel 501-372-4000. *Dir & Chief Cur* Townsend D Wolfe III
Open Mon - Sat 10 AM - 5 PM, Sun & holidays noon - 5 PM. No admis fee to galleries & Decorative Arts Museum, admis charged for theatre activities. Estab 1960 to further the development, the understanding and the appreciation of the visual and performing arts. Six galleries, two for permanent collections, four for temporary exhibits & eight at the Decorative Arts Museum. Average Annual Attendance: 475,000. Mem: 4000; dues from benefactor $20,000 to basic $35; annual meeting in July
Income: Financed by endowment, membership, city and state appropriation and earned income
Purchases: Peter Paul Rubens, Hygieia Goddess of Health Feeding the Serpent; Giacomo Manzu, Bust of Woman; Alison Saar, Invisible Man; Joseph Stella, Head of a Woman in Profile; William T Wiley, Gift of Ms Givings; John Himmelfarb, Broad Daylight Meeting; Morris Graves, Chalices; Mark Tobey, Untitled, ca 1940; Hans Hofmann, Study for Fruit Bowl; Benny Andrews, Portrait of a Model & Cools
Collections: †Drawings from the Renaissance to present, with major collection of American & European drawings since 1900; 19th & 20th century paintings & prints; 20th century sculpture & photographs; Oriental & American decorative arts; contemporary crafts & toys designed by artists
Exhibitions: Annual Delta Art Exhibition; Annual Toys Designed by Artists; National Drawing Invitational; Selections from the Frederick R Weisman Collection; American Drawings: The 80s, Selections from the AAC Foundation Collection; 33rd Annual Delta Art Exhibition; National Crafts Invitational; Richard Diebenkorn: Recent Graphics; 21st Prints, Drawings & Photographs; The Quest for Self-Expression: Paintings in Moscow & Leningrad; Annual Toys Designed by Artists; Southern Quilts: A New View from the Hunter Museum of Art
Publications: Members bulletin, monthly; annual membership catalog; annual report; catalogue selections from the permanent collection; exhibit catalogues & brochures
Activities: Classes for adults and children; docent training; lect open to the public, 6 - 10 vis lectr per year; concerts; gallery talks; tours; competitions; children's theatre; exten department serving the state of Arkansas; artmobile; individual paintings and original objects of art lent to schools, civic groups and churches; lending collection contains motion pictures, original prints, paintings, 4300 phonorecords and 16,000 slides; originates traveling exhibitions; museum shop sells books, slides, gifts, jewelry and crafts
L Elizabeth Prewitt Taylor Memorial Library, MacArthur Park, 72203
Open Mon - Fri 10 AM - 5 PM. Estab 1963 to provide resources in the arts for students, educators, and interested public. For reference only
Income: $25,120
Purchases: $6800
Library Holdings: Vols 7500; Per subs 100; AV — A-tapes, cassettes, fs, Kodachromes, motion pictures, rec, slides; Other — Clipping files, exhibition catalogs, memorabilia, pamphlets
Special Subjects: Afro-American Art, American Indian Art, American Western Art, Asian Art, Decorative Arts, Eskimo Art, Folk Art, Historical Material, History of Art & Archaeology, Latin American Art
Collections: †George Fisher Cartoons; John Reid Jazz Collection

M ARKANSAS TERRITORIAL RESTORATION, 200 E Third St, 72201. Tel 501-324-9351; FAX 501-324-9345. *Dir* William B Bennett; *Educ Coordr* Starr Mitchell; *Public Relations* Hanna Bartsch Goss
Open daily 9 AM - 5 PM, Sun 1 - 5 PM, cl New Year's, Easter, Thanksgiving, Christmas Eve and Christmas Day. Admis to museum houses adults $2, sr citizens (65 and over) $1, children under 16 $.50; admis to Reception Center free. Restoration completed 1941. The Restoration is a group of homes including a recently restored log house, that represent the early and mid 19th century of Arkansas history. Average Annual Attendance: 50,000
Income: State & private funding
Collections: †Arkansas made guns & furniture; Audubon prints; furnishing of the period; porcelain hands, prints and maps from the 19th century; silver collection; watercolors
Exhibitions: (1992) African-American Arkansas History; The Ashley Family; Early Arkansas Chairs; monthly exhibitions of contemporary Arkansas Artists; May Arkansas Craft Show; Frontier Fourth of July Festivities; October Candlelight Gala; December Christmas Open House
Publications: Arkansas Made: The Decorative Mechanical and Fine Arts Produced in Arkansas 1819-1870; Territorial Times, 3 times a year
Activities: Log House activities include educational program for students and adults in candle dipping, cooking and needlework; classes for children; docent training; Reception Center has slide show, exhibits and art gallery; tours; individual paintings & original objects of art lent to other museums & cultural institutions; lending collection contains 476 books, motion pictures, 40 original prints, 10 paintings, 50 photographs, 2000 slides, loan box (artifacts); originate traveling exhibitions to area museums & schools; craft store sells books, reproductions & early Arkansas crafts
L Library, 200 E Third St, 72201. FAX 501-324-9351; *Dir* W B Worthen Jr; *Cur* Swannee Bennett; *Education Coordr* Starr Mitchell; *Public Relations* Hanna Goss
Open Mon - Sat 9 AM - 5 PM, Sun 1 - 5 PM. Admis adult $2, sr citizen $1, children $.50. Estab 1941 to preserve & promote Arkansas history. Arkansas Artist Gallery contains Arkansas artists with new display monthly, Cromwell Hall contains historical exhibits 3 times a year. Average Annual Attendance: 50,000
Income: Financed by the state & private funds
Library Holdings: Vols 500; Per subs 8; Micro — Reels; AV — A-tapes, cassettes, slides; Other — Clipping files, framed reproductions, manuscripts, original art works, pamphlets, photographs, prints, reproductions
Special Subjects: Antiques, Art, Furniture, Gardening, Historical Material, Houses, Living History
Collections: Arkansas-made decorative, mechanical & fine art
Exhibitions: Contemporary art; historical exhibits
Publications: Arkansas Made: The Decorative, Mechanical and Fine Art Produced in Arkansas 1819-1870
Activities: Educ Dept; classes for adults & children; dramatic programs; docent training; lectures open to public, 3 vis lectrs per yr; tours; individual paintings & original objects of art lent to other museums; museum shop sells books, original art, reproductions, prints

C FIRST COMMERCIAL BANK IN LITTLE ROCK, Capitol & Broadway, PO Box 1471, 72203. Tel 501-371-7000; FAX 501-371-7413. *In Charge Art Coll & Program* William Garner
Open Mon - Fri 9 AM - 4 PM. Estab 1960 to support art community. Collection displayed in two bank buildings and 20 branch offices; annual amount of contributions and grants $5000 - $15,000
Purchases: $5000
Collections: Arkansas art, chiefly paintings; some sculpture and weavings, pottery
Exhibitions: One major exhibit per year
Activities: Museum shop

M QUAPAW QUARTER ASSOCIATION, INC, Villa Marre, 1315 Scott St, 72202. Tel 501-371-0075; FAX 501-374-8142. *Exec Dir* Cheryl G Nichols; *Asst Dir* Suzanne Torrence
Open Sun 1 - 5 PM, and by appointment. Admis adults $2, sr citizens & students $1. Estab 1966. The Villa Marre is a historic house museum which, by virtue of its extraordinary collection of late 19th century decorative arts, is a center for the study of Victorian styles. Average Annual Attendance: 5000. Mem: 1000; dues $10 - $1000; annual meeting Nov
Income: $95,000 (financed by membership, corporate support, grants and fund raising events)
Collections: Artwork by Benjamin Brantley; curios appropriate to an 1881 Second Empire Victorian home, late 19th & early 20th century furniture, textiles
Publications: Quapaw Quarter Chronicle, quarterly
Activities: Classes for adults and children; docent training; lectures open to public, visiting lectr; tours; book traveling exhibitions; originate traveling exhibitions; sales shop sells books and magazines
L Preservation Resource Center, 1315 Scott St, 72202. Tel 501-371-0075.
Open Mon - Thur 9 AM - 5 PM. Estab 1976 for the assembly of materials relevant to the design and furnishing of Victorian period homes
Purchases: $500
Library Holdings: Vols 130; Per subs 12; Maps; AV — Kodachromes, lantern slides; Other — Clipping files, manuscripts, pamphlets, photographs
Collections: Architectural drawings

L UNIVERSITY OF ARKANSAS, Art Slide Library, Fine Arts Bldg, Room 251, 2801 S University, 72204. Tel 501-569-3182. *Chmn* Don Van Horn; *Slide Cur* Laura Grace
Open Mon - Fri 9 AM - 5 PM, Sun 1-4 PM. No admis fee. Estab 1978 for educational purposes. Gallery I, 2500 sq ft, is a two story space; Gallery II, 500 sq ft, is glassed on three sides; Gallery III is a hallway for student works
Income: Financed by state funds & private donations
Library Holdings: Vols 360; Per subs 15; AV — Fs, Kodachromes, slides 50,000; Other — Clipping files, exhibition catalogs, pamphlets
Special Subjects: Western & Non-Western Art & Architecture
Collections: Photographs & other works on paper
Activities: Educ dept; docent training; lectures open to public, 3 vis lectr per year; gallery talks; student competitions with awards; scholarships; originate traveling exhibitions; most exhibited art is for sale

MAGNOLIA

M SOUTHERN ARKANSAS UNIVERSITY, Art Dept Gallery & Magale Art Gallery, Jackson & S University, SAU Box 1414, 71753. Tel 501-235-4242. *Pres* Steven G Gamble; *VPres* Donald Heafner; *Chmn Art Dept* Jerry Johnson; *Asst Prof* Dianne O'Hern
Open Mon - Fri 9 AM - 10 PM. No admis fee. Estab 1970. Magale Library Art Gallery, foyer type with 120 running ft exhibition space, floor to ceiling fabric covered. Caraway Gallery preview type gallery, about 80 ft
Income: Financed by state funds
Collections: †American printmakers
Exhibitions: Mike Ellis: American Photographer; faculty exhibit; six student shows
Activities: Classes for adults & children; lectures open to public; gallery talks; tours; individual paintings & original objects of art lent to schools, non-profit organizations

MONTICELLO

M DREW COUNTY HISTORICAL SOCIETY, Museum, 404 S Main, 71655. Tel 501-367-7446. *Dir* Henri Mason; *Dir* Velma Allen
No admis fee. Estab 1969. Average Annual Attendance: 3000. Mem: dues $100, commerecial $15, individual $5; monthly meetings
Income: Financed by endowment, membership, city & county appropriation
Collections: Antique Toys & dolls; Indian Artifacts; Handwork & Clothing from early 1800's; Woodworking Tools
Exhibitions: Antique Quilts, Trunks, Paintings by Local Artists; Leather Parlor Furniture from late 1800's
Publications: Drew County Historical Journal, annually

MOUNTAIN VIEW

M OZARK FOLK CENTER, Hwy 382, PO Box 500, 72560. Tel 501-269-3280. *General Mgr* Bill Young; *Asst General Mgr* Lisa Wiede; *Music Dir* Elliott Hancock; *Crafts Dir* Kay Thomas; *Folklorist* W K McNeil
Open Mon - Fri 10 AM - 5 PM; May 1 - Oct 31 daily 8 AM - 10 PM. Admis $5.75. Estab 1973 to demonstrate various aspects of traditional culture of the Ozark Mountain region. 24 buildings for demonstration of various traditional crafts & a large auditorium for traditional music programs. Average Annual Attendance: 160,000
Income: $1,800,000 (financed by state appropriation & auxiliary committee)
Collections: †Traditional Ozark crafts; †music folios & sheet music
Activities: Sponsor workshops; lectures open to public; awards; book traveling exhibitions; sales shop sells books, magazines, slides

PINE BLUFF

A ARTS & SCIENCE CENTER FOR SOUTHEAST ARKANSAS, 220 W Martin, 71601. Tel 501-536-3375. *Dir* Helen M Brooks; *Dir Visual Art & Education* Garlan G Jenkens; *Dir Performing Arts* Galen Colbert; *Business Mgr* Sara Wright; *Children's Theatre Coordr* Don LaPlant; *Communications Mgr* Lisa Rowland
Open Mon - Fri 8 AM - 5 PM, Sat 10 AM - 4 PM. No admis fee. Opened in 1968 in Civic Center Complex; mission is to provide for the practice, teaching, performance & understanding of the Arts & Sciences. Average Annual Attendance: 55,000. Mem: 880; dues family $35
Income: $450,000
Collections: †John M Howard Memorial Collection of works by black American artists; Collection of botanical paintings by Elsie Mistie Sterling; Photographs by J C Coovert of the Southern Cotton Culture, early 1900's; †Works on paper by local, national & international artists; art deco/noveau bronze sculptures
Exhibitions: Biennial National Competition; Art Gallery Exhibitions
Activities: Classes for adults & children; dramatic programs; docent training; lect open to public; concerts; gallery talks; tours; competitions with awards; book traveling exhibitions; originate traveling exhibitions

M JEFFERSON COUNTY HISTORICAL MUSEUM, 201 E Fourth, 71601. Tel 501-541-5402. *Dir* Linda Richardson
Open daily 9 AM - 5 PM. No admis fee. Estab 1980 to collect, preserve & interpret artifacts showing the history of Jefferson County. One room in County Courthouse. Average Annual Attendance: 11,200; dues $5-$15
Income: $16,000 (financed by county Quorum Court appropriation)
Collections: Clothing dating from 1870; personal artifacts; photographs; tools & equipment; Quapau Indian artifacts
Exhibitions: Bottle Collection; Made in Pine Bluff AR; exhibit of dolls dressed in gowns worn by governors' wives; Quapace Indian Artifacts; Settlers Exhibit; Civil War Exhibit
Publications: The Jeffersonian, quarterly newsletter
Activities: Lectures, competitions

SPRINGDALE

M CITY OF SPRINGDALE, Shiloh Museum, 118 W Johnson Ave, 72764. Tel 501-750-8165. *Dir* Bob Besom; *Asst Dir* Mary Parsons; *Educ Coordr* M K Motherwell; *Exhib Designer* Katie McCoy
Open Mon - Sat 10 AM - 5 PM. No admis fee. Estab 1968 to exhibit history & culture of Northwest Arkansas. Displays in main exhibit hall of 4500 sq ft, halls, meeting room & a restored 19th century home. Average Annual Attendance: 15,000. Mem: 1000; dues $10
Income: $200,000 (financed by endowment, mem, city appropriation, private & public grants)
Collections: †Folk Arts; †Ozarks Photographers; †Charles Summey Oils; †Essie Ward Primitive Paintings
Exhibitions: Essie Ward; Charles Summey

Publications: Newsletter, quarterly
Activities: Programs & workshops for adults & children; lect open to public, 10 vis lectr per year; lending collection contains 500 items; book traveling exhibitions 2 per year; originate traveling exhibitions 1 per year; retail store sells books, magazines & original art

M COUNCIL OF OZARK ARTISTS AND CRAFTSMEN, INC, Arts Center of the Ozarks Gallery, 216 W Grove Ave, PO Box 725, 72765. Tel 501-751-5441. *Dir* Kathi Blundell; *Visual Arts Dir* Garrett Hunt; *Dir of Theatre* Harry Blundell
Open Mon - Fri 8 AM - 4 PM, gallery open Mon - Fri 9 AM - 4 PM. No admis fee. Estab 1948, merged with the Springdale Arts Center to become Arts Center of the Ozarks in 1973 to preserve the traditional handcrafts, to promote all qualified contemporary arts and crafts, to help find markets for artists and craftsmen
Income: Financed by membership & state appropriations
Exhibitions: Exhibitions change monthly
Publications: Arts Center Events, monthly; newsletter, bimonthly
Activities: Adult and children's workshops; instruction in the arts, music, dance and drama run concurrently with other activities; evening classes in painting; eight theater productions per yr, concerts & arts & crafts

STUTTGART

A GRAND PRAIRIE ARTS COUNCIL, INC, Arts Center of the Grand Prairie, 108 W 12th St, PO Box 65, 72160. Tel 501-673-1781. *Pres* Perry Yohe
Open Tues - Fri 10 AM - Noon & 2 - 4 PM, Sat & Sun 2 - 4 PM, cl Mon. No admis fee. Estab 1956 & incorporated 1964 to encourage cultural development in the Grand Prairie area, to sponsor the Grand Prairie Festival of Arts held annually in Sept at Stuttgart. Established as an arts center for junior & sr citizens. Average Annual Attendance: 2500. Mem: 250; dues $10 - $100; monthly meetings
Income: Financed by memberships & donations
Collections: Very small permanent collection started by donations
Exhibitions: Monthly exhibitions of Arkansas artists
Publications: Festival invitations; newsletter, monthly; programs
Activities: Classes for adults & children; dramatic programs; lectures open to public, 4-6 lectr per yr; gallery talks; competitions with awards; originate traveling exhibitions

CALIFORNIA

ALHAMBRA

AMERICAN SOCIETY OF BOOKPLATE COLLECTORS & DESIGNERS
For further information, see National and Regional Organizations

BAKERSFIELD

M BAKERSFIELD ART FOUNDATION, Bakersfield Museum of Art, 1930 R St, 93301. Tel 805-323-7219. *Admin Asst* Candis Gibson
Open Tues - Sat 10 AM - 4 PM, Sun Noon - 4 PM, cl Mon. Admis $1. Estab to provide the facilities & services of a municipal art museum which will nurture & develop the visual arts in Kern County. Gallery is a one story building located in Camellia Garden of Central Park. Average Annual Attendance: 50,000. Mem: 600; dues $25; Board meeting second Mon each month 5 PM
Income: Financed by corporate, state & local public, & private non-profit sources
Publications: Catalogues with each exhibit (6 yrly); Perspective, monthly
Activities: Classes for children; docent training; lect open to public; gallery talks; tours; juried competitions with prizes; scholarships & fels offered; book traveling exhibitions; originate traveling exhibitions; museum shop sells magazines & gifts

M KERN COUNTY MUSEUM, 3801 Chester Ave, 93301. Tel 805-861-2132; FAX 805-322-6415. *Dir* Carola R Enriquez; *Cur* Russ Czaplewski; *Asst Dir* David McCauley
Open Mon - Fri 8 AM - 5 PM, Sat, Sun & holidays 10 AM - 5 PM. Admis adults $3, sr citizens $2.50, children 3-12 $1.50, under 3 free. Estab 1945 to collect and interpret local history & culture, mainly through a 14 acre outdoor museum. Also has Randsburg Mining Museum. One main building, 1929 Chamber of Commerce Building, houses changing exhibitions on assorted topics; modern track lighting, temporary walls. Average Annual Attendance: 100,000. Mem: 450; dues family $25, individual $15
Income: $550,000 (financed by county appropriation and earned income)
Purchases: Pier mirror, postcards & child's lounge
Collections: †California primitive paintings; †60-structure outdoor museum covering 14 acres; †Photographic Image Collection; †Material Culture; †Paleontology; †Natural History
Exhibitions: Native American Baskets of California; Comic Book Art; Skiing in Kern; Guns of Roots: Kern County Agriculture; Routes: Motoring through Kern in the 1920s; Guns of the West; Children's Art Competitions. History of Transportation; Minerals of Kern
Publications: Brochure on the Museum; The Forgotten Photographs of Carleton E Watkins
Activities: Classes for adults & children; docent training; lectures open to public; concerts; tours; Candlelight Christmas & Heritage Days celebrations; competitions with awards; exten dept serves in eastern Kern County; individual paintings & original objects of art lent to non-profit organizations & entities with public viewing space; book traveling exhibitions, 2 per year; originate traveling exhibitions; gift shop sells books, reproductions, slides & handicrafts

L Library, 3801 Chester Ave, 93301. Tel 805-861-2132; FAX 805-322-6415.
Open Mon - Fri 8 AM - 5 PM by appointment only. Estab 1950 to support the
work of the museum. Open for reference only by appointment
Library Holdings: Vols 2200; AV — Fs, v-tapes; Other — Clipping files,
manuscripts, memorabilia, pamphlets, photographs
Special Subjects: Archaeology, Architecture, Art History, Carpets & Rugs,
Costume Design & Construction, Crafts, Decorative Arts, Furniture, Historical
Material, History of Art & Archaeology, Maps, Period Rooms, Restoration &
Conservation, Textiles, Native American Arts
Publications: Courier, quarterly newsletter
Activities: Classes for children; docent training; sales shop sells books, prints &
slides

BALBOA PARK

M MUSEUM OF PHOTOGRAPHIC ARTS, 1649 El Prado, 92101. Tel 619-239-
5262; FAX 619-238-8777. *Exec Dir* Arthur Ollman; *Asst to Dir* Cathy Boemer;
Dir of Development Richard Perry; *Development Assoc* Diane Ballard; *Exhibit
Designer* Michael Golino; *Registrar* Hetly Tye
Open daily 10 AM - 5 PM, Thurs 10 AM - 9 PM. Admis fee $2.50. Estab 1983
to collect & exhibit photographic works of art. Average Annual Attendance: 75,
000. Mem: 1600; dues $25-$10,000
Income: $930,000 (financed by city, state, & federal appropriation, endowments,
memberships, grants & corporations)
Purchases: $20,000
Collections: Photographic collection includes examples from earliest to most
recent photographs
Publications: MoPA, scholarly journal, 3 times per year
Activities: Lectures open to the public, 10-12 vis lectr per year; competitions
with awards; museum shop sells books

BELMONT

A ARTS COUNCIL OF SAN MATEO COUNTY, 1219 Ralston Ave, 94002. Tel
415-593-1816. *Pres* Barbara Hardman; *VPres* Judy Cross; *Exec Dir* Nancy
Berglass; *Treas* Robin Jaquith; *Cur* Angela Kirkner; *Office Mgr* Shawn Kaiser
Open Mon - Fri 9 AM - 5 PM, Sun 1 - 4 PM. No admis fee. Estab 1972 to
promote the cultural life of San Mateo County through programs in schools,
advocacy with business and government, to provide services for artists and arts
organizations. Galleries maintained on premises and at the Hall of Justice in
Redwood City, Calif. Each holds about 100 works of art. Average Annual
Attendance: 100,000. Mem: 1000; dues $25; annual meeting July
Income: $200,000 (financed by membership, state and county appropriation,
corporate and foundation support and programs)
Exhibitions: Bi-monthly exhibits in three galleries by local and invited artists
both regional and international
Publications: Arts Talk; cultural calendar
Activities: Classes for adults and children; volunteer and docent training; lectures
open to public; 3-5 vis lectrs per yr; concerts; gallery talks; tours; competitions
with awards; book traveling exhibitions; originate traveling; gift shop sells crafts,
fine arts, posters

BERKELEY

A BERKELEY ART CENTER, 1275 Walnut St, 94709. Tel 510-644-6893. *Exec
Dir* Michael Brown
Open Thurs - Sun 11 AM - 5 PM, cl Mon - Wed & holidays. No admis fee.
Estab 1965 to display art works of Bay Area artists. Average Annual Attendance:
12,000. Mem: 250; dues $20 - $2500; annual meeting Jan 1
Income: Financed by city appropriation and other grants
Collections: Paintings; sculptures; environments
Exhibitions: Rotating loan exhibitions & shows by Bay Area artists
Activities: Lect open to public, 8 vis lectr per year; concerts; gallery talks;
competition with prizes; original objects of art lent to non-profit & educational
institutions; originate traveling exhibitions; sales shop sells prints

L BERKELEY PUBLIC LIBRARY, Art and Music Dept, 2090 Kittredge St,
94704. Tel 510-649-3928. *Head Reference* Patricia Mullan; *Librn* Lynn Murdock
Wold; *Librn* Marti Morec; *Librn* Andrea Segall
Open Mon - Thurs 10 AM - 9 PM, Fri & Sat 10 AM - 6 PM, Sun 1 - 5 PM
Income: $60,000
Library Holdings: Vols 20,560; Per subs 116; Compact Discs 3000; AV —
Cassettes 4200, rec 15,000, slides 20,000
Activities: Lectrs on art 4 times a year

A KALA INSTITUTE, 1060 Heinz Ave, 94710. Tel 510-549-2977; FAX 510-549-
2984. *Exec Dir* Archana Horsting
Open Tues - Fri noon - 5 PM, Sat noon - 4 PM. No admis fee. Estab 1974 to
provide equipment, space, exhibition opportunities to artists. Average Annual
Attendance: 5000. Mem: 50; mem open to artists with proficiency in
printmaking; studio rental $150 - $250 per month
Income: $210,000 (financed by mem, city & state appropriation, art sales, classes
& private foundations)
Collections: Kala Institute Archive; †Works on Paper
Exhibitions: On going: Works on Paper
Activities: Classes for adults & children; lect open to public, 1 vis lectr per year;
scholarships & fels offered; book traveling exhibitions 1 per year; originate
traveling exhibitions 1 per year; retail store sells prints & original art

M JUDAH L MAGNES MUSEUM, 2911 Russell St, 94705. Tel 510-549-6950;
FAX 510-849-3650. *Dir* Seymour Fromer; *Cur* Ruth Eis; *Registrar* Marni Welch;
Public Relations Paula Friedman; *Archivist* Ruth Rafael; *Cur* Sheila Braufman;
Cur Florence Helzel; *Librn* Jane Levy; *Development & Membership* Lis Schwab
Open Sun - Thur 10 AM - 4 PM, cl Jewish and legal holidays. No admis fee.
Estab 1962 to preserve, collect & exhibit Jewish artifacts & art from around the

world; the museum also contains the Blumenthal rare books & manuscripts
library & the Western Jewish History Center archives on the Jewish community
in the Western part of the United States from 1849 to the present. Museum's
first floor has changing exhibition space and painting gallery, and the second
floor contains the permanent exhibition area; Jacques & Esther Reutlinger Hall
established 1981. Average Annual Attendance: 10,000-12,000
Income: Financed by mem, donations, & foundation grants
Purchases: Ethnic Costumes & Folk Art Pieces; Ceremonial & Fine Art
Collections: †Hannukah lamps; Synagogue art & objects; †spice boxes; †graphics;
†manuscripts; †prints; †rare books; †textiles; †genre paintings; art & ceremonial
objects from Sephardic & Indian Jewish communities
Exhibitions: A Vanished World: Roman Vishniac; Ben Zion: Tradition of
Independence; George Segal's "The Holocaust": Photographs by Ira Nowinski;
Pessach Haggadah in Memory of the Holocaust; Genre Paintings from the
Permanent Collection; The Jewish Illustrated Book; Darkness to Light: Ceramic
Sculpture by Susan Felix; Nupcias Sefardies (Sephardic Wedding); The Benno
Seegall Collection: Art Patronage in Berlin 1900-33, (prints & drawings); Forms
for Faith: 1986 Winners of the Interfaith Forum on Religion, Art and
Architecture Awards; Writes & Rituals: The Jewish Artisan; Raphael Abecassis:
Calligraphy & Illuminations (scheduled for 1987): Jewish Themes/Northern
California Artists; Treasures & Gifts: 25th Anniversary Exhibition Witnesses to
History: The Jewish Poster, 1770-1985; Personal Landscapes, Universal Visions:
A Contemporary Jewish Themes Triennial
Publications: Bibliographies; books of Western Jewish Historical themes;
exhibition catalogs; pamphlets; triannual newsletter; trade books on recent
European Jewish history
Activities: Lectures open to the public; gallery talks; tours; Rosenberg poetry
award; numismatics series; concerts; individual paintings and original objects of
art lent to museums, synagogues, exhibition halls and Jewish organizations;
traveling exhibitions organized and circulated; museum shop sells books,
magazines, original art, reproductions, prints, original jewelry, note cards, posters,
postcards

L Blumenthal Rare Book & Manuscript Library, 2911 Russell St, 94705. Tel 510-
549-6939. *Librn* Jane Levy
Estab 1966 as a center for the study and preservation of Judaica. For reference
only. Changing and permanent exhibitions of painting, sculpture, photography,
ceremonial objects
Income: Financed by mem & private gifts
Library Holdings: Vols 12,000; Per subs 15; original documents; AV — Fs,
motion pictures, slides; Other — Clipping files, exhibition catalogs, manuscripts,
memorabilia, pamphlets, reproductions
Special Subjects: Costume Design & Construction, Decorative Arts, Graphic
Arts, History of Art & Archaeology, Judaica, Painting - American, Painting -
European, Painting - Russian, Photography, Theatre Arts, Jewish art & music,
special emphasis on Yiddish theater music, History of Jewish communities
throughout the world, particularly Sephardic, rare books & manuscripts
Collections: Community collections from Cochin, Czechoslovakia, Egypt, India
and Morocco; Holocaust Material (Institute for Righteous Acts); Karaite
Community (Egypt); Passover Haggadahs (Zismer); 16th to 19th century rare
printed editions, books and manuscripts; Ukrainian programs (Belkin documents)
Exhibitions: Jewish Illustrated Books
Publications: Exhibition catalogues; Jewish Illustrated Book; The Jewish Printed
Book in India: Imprints of the Blumenthal Library
Activities: Docent training; lectures open to public, vis lectr 15 per year;
concerts; gallery talks; tours; awards; book traveling exhibitions; originate
traveling exhibitions nationwide

UNIVERSITY OF CALIFORNIA

M University Art Museum, 2626 Bancroft Way, 94720. Tel 510-642-1207; FAX
510-642-4889. *Dir* Jacquelynn Baas; *Deputy Dir* Bonnie Pitman; *Cur Film* Edith
Kramer; *Installation & Design* Nina Zurier; *Cur* Lawrence Rinder; *Cur Educ*
Sherry Goodman; *Coll & Exhib Admin* Lisa Calden; *Cur* James Steward; *Asst
Cur Video* Steve Seid; *Film Coll Mgr* Mona Nagai; *Development Dir* Janine
Sheldon
Open Wed - Sun 11 AM - 5 PM. Admis $3-$5. Estab 1965, new museum bldg
opened in 1970. Museum designed by Mario Ciampi, Richard Jorasch & Ronald
E Wagner of San Francisco; eleven exhibition galleries, a sculpture garden & a
234 seat theatre. Average Annual Attendance: Gallery 150,000, Pacific Film
Archive 150,000. Mem: 2800; dues vary
Income: $4,000,000 (financed by university sources, federal & other grants,
earned income & private donations)
Collections: Gift of 45 Hans Hoffman paintings housed in the Hans Hoffman
Gallery; pre-20th century paintings and sculpture; Chinese and Japanese
paintings; 20th century European & American painting & sculpture; over 6000
films & video tapes; 16th - 20th century works on paper; conceptual art study
center
Exhibitions: Twenty exhibitions annually; Matrix Project (a changing exhibition
of contemporary art), 600 film programs
Publications: The Calendar, bi-monthly; catalogs; handbills; exhibition brochures;
Matrix artists sheets
Activities: Lect open to the public; gallery talks; on-site performances; film
programs for classes & research screenings; film study center & library; book
traveling exhibitions, 3 per year; traveling exhibitions organized and circulated;
museum shop sells books, magazines, posters, jewelry, rental facilities available,
cafe

M Phoebe Apperson Hearst Museum of Anthropology, 103 Kroeber Hall, 94720.
Tel 510-642-3681; FAX 510-643-8557. *Dir* Burton Bennedict; *Principal
Anthropologist* Frank A Norick; *Senior Cur Anthropologist* Dave D Herod
Exhibition Hall open Tues-Fri 10 AM - 4 PM, Sat & Sun Noon - 4 PM, cl Wed
& major national holidays; access to research collections Mon - Fri 8 AM - 4:30
PM, cl Sat & Sun. Admis adults $1.50, children $.25, no admis fee Thurs. Estab
1901 as a research museum for the training and educating of undergraduate and
graduate students, a resource for scholarly research and to collect, preserve,
educate and conduct research. Average Annual Attendance: 35,000
Income: Financed principally by state appropriations
Special Subjects: Afro-American Art, American Indian Art, American Western
Art, Anthropology, Antiquities-Assyrian, Flasks & Bottles, Folk Art, Furniture,

Glass, Gold, Photography, Porcelain, Portraits, Pottery, Pre-Columbian Art
Collections: Over three million objects of anthropolgical interest, both archaeolgical & ethnological. Ethnological collections from Africa, Oceania, North America (California, Plains, Arctic & Sub-Arctic); Archaeological Collections from Egypt, Peru, California, Africa & Oceania
Publications: Annual report; exhibition guides; occasional papers of the Lowie Museum of Anthropology
Activities: Lectures open to the public; gallery talks; tours; gift shop
L **Pacific Film Archive,** 2625 Durant Ave, 94720. Tel 510-642-1412, 642-1437; FAX 510-642-4889. *Cur Film* Edith Kramer; *Library Head* Nancy Goldman; *Gen Mgr* Stephen Gong; *Assoc Film Cur* Kathy Geritz
Library Open Mon - Fri 1 - 5 PM. Estab 1971, the Archive is a cinematheque showing a constantly changing repertory of films; a research screening facility; a media information service and an archive for the storage and preservation of films
Income: Financed by earned box office income, grants, students fees and benefits
Library Holdings: Vols 5000; Per subs 75; 20,000 Stills and 5000 posters; AV — Motion pictures 6000; Other — Clipping files 60,000
Special Subjects: Film
Collections: Japanese film collection; Soviet Silents; experimental and animated films
Publications: Bi-monthly calendar
Activities: Nightly film exhibition; special daytime screening of films; lectures, fifty - seventy-five visiting filmmakers per year
L **Architectural Slide Library,** 232 Wurster Hall, 94720. Tel 510-642-3439; FAX 510-643-5607; Elec Mail slides@ced.berkeley.edu. *Librn* Maryly Snow; *Library Asst* Erica Siskind; *Photographer* Steven Brooks
Open Mon - Fri 10 AM - Noon, 1 - 4 PM. Estab 1951 for instructional support for the Department of Architecture. In 1976 Library opened circulation on a 24 hour basis for educational presentations
Income: Financed by state appropriation
Library Holdings: AV — Slides; Other — Photographs
Special Subjects: Art History, History of Architecture, Slides and Photographs, Topography, Urbanism, Design
Collections: Denise Scott Brown & William C Wheaton Collections: City Planning; Herwin Schaefer Collection: visual design
L **Environmental Design Library,** 210 Wurster Hall, 94720. Tel 510-642-4818; FAX 415-643-7891. *Head* Elizabeth Byrne; *Architectural Librn* Kathryn Wayne
Open Mon - Thurs 9 AM - 9 PM, Fri 9 AM - 5 PM, Sat 1 - 5 PM, Sun 1 - 9 PM (Sept - May). 1903. Circ 135,000
Special Subjects: Architecture, Landscape Architecture
Collections: Architecture, city & regional planning, landscape architecture

BEVERLY HILLS

L **BEVERLY HILLS PUBLIC LIBRARY,** Fine Arts Library, 444 N Rexford, 90201. Tel 310-288-2231; FAX 310-278-3387. *Supv Fine Arts Servs* Nicholas Cellini; *Fine Art Librn* Cal Davis; *Fine Art Librn* Dr Stefan Klima; *Fine Art Librn* Jeri Byrne; *Fine Art Librn* Suzy Chan; *Fine Art Librn* Sue Kaplan
Open Mon - Thurs 10 AM - 9 PM, Fri & Sat 10 AM - 6 PM, Sun noon - 5 PM. Estab 1973 to make art materials available to the general public. The library concentrates on 19th and 20th century American & British art
Income: Financed by city appropriation and Friends of Library
Library Holdings: Vols 20,000; Per subs 200; Micro — Fiche, reels; AV — Cassettes, Kodachromes, motion pictures, slides, v-tapes; Other — Clipping files, exhibition catalogs, pamphlets, photographs, prints
Special Subjects: Architecture, Film, Graphic Arts, Painting - American, Painting - European, Painting - Flemish, Painting - French, Painting - German, Painting - Russian, Painting - Scandinavian, Painting - Spanish, Photography, Prints, Sculpture, Art, Costume, Dance
Collections: †Dorthai Bock Pierre Dance Collection; Zita Zech Collection: Gifts of American Society of Interior Designers; Artists Books
Activities: Weekly film programs

BREA

M **BREA CIVIC & CULTURAL CENTER GALLERY,** Number One Civic Center Circle, 92621. Tel 714-990-7713; FAX 714-990-2258. *Cultural Arts Mgr* Emily Keller
Open Wed - Sat Noon - 5 PM, cl holidays. No admis. Estab 1980
Exhibitions: Western Sagas; American Quilt Exhibit; The Real Thing (juried realistic multimedia show); Photography Exhibit; Artists of Northern Mexico; National Watercolor Juried Show
Activities: Docent training; lectures; tours; gallery talks; concerts; workshops

BURBANK

A **BURBANK PUBLIC LIBRARY,** Warner Research Collection, 110 N Glenoaks Blvd, 91502. Tel 818-953-9743; FAX 818-953-8639. *Librn in Charge* Jerri Thomson; *Librn* Patrice Samko; *Clerk* Susan Hurlbert
Open Mon - Fri 10 AM - 5 PM by appointment only. Estab 1936 to provide visual and historical documentation for use in the pre-production phase of motion picture and television production. Also used for prototype research by artist and architects
Library Holdings: Vols 39,000; Per subs 80; License Plate Files; Other — Clipping files, exhibition catalogs, pamphlets, photographs, reproductions
Special Subjects: Advertising Design, Aesthetics, Afro-American Art, Afro-American Art, American Indian Art, American Western Art, Anthropology, Archaeology, Architecture, Costume Design & Construction, Decorative Arts, Fashion Arts, Flasks & Bottles, Folk Art, Furniture, Antiques, Glass, Graphic Arts, Graphic Design, Industrial Design, Period Rooms, Stage Design, Theater Arts
Activities: Lectures open to the public

CARMEL

M **CARMEL MISSION AND GIFT SHOP,** 3080 Rio Rd, 93923. Tel 408-624-3600. *Cur* Richard J Menn; *Shop Mgr* Katherine Ambrosio
Open Mon - Sat 9:30 AM - 4:30 PM, Sun 10:30 AM - 4:30 PM, cl Thanksgiving and Christmas. No admis fee; donations accepted. Estab 1770
Collections: California's first library, founded by Fray Junipero Serra, 1770; library of California's first college, founded by William Hartnell, 1834; Munras Memorial Collection of objects, papers, furnishings of early California; large collection of ecclesiastical art of Spanish colonial period; large collection of ecclesiastical silver and gold church vessels, 1670 - 1820; paintings, sculpture, art objects of California Mission period
Activities: Sales shop sells religious articles, souvenir books and postcards
L **Archive of Old Spanish Missions, Diocese of Monterey,** 3080 Rio Rd, 93923. Tel 408-624-1271.
Estab 1931 for research for Mission Restoration and Documents. Open to scholars by special appointment
Library Holdings: Vols 200; AV — Cassettes; Other — Clipping files, manuscripts, pamphlets, photographs
Special Subjects: Early California reference and photo library

CARMICHAEL

PASTEL SOCIETY OF THE WEST COAST
For further information, see National and Regional Organizations

CERRITOS

NATIONAL WATERCOLOR SOCIETY
For further information, see National and Regional Organizations

CHERRY VALLEY

M **RIVERSIDE COUNTY MUSEUM,** Edward-Dean Museum, 9401 Oak Glen Rd, 92223. Tel 909-845-2626. *Acting Dir* Sue Henry; *Cur* Cathy Gilbert
Open Tues - Fri 1 - 4:30 PM, Sat & Sun 10 AM - 4:30 PM. Admis adults $1, children under 12 free. Built in 1957 & given to the county of Riverside in 1964. The South Wing of the gallery displays antiques and decorative arts as permanent collections; the North Wing has monthly exhibits by contemporary artists. Average Annual Attendance: 20,000. Mem: 250; monthly meetings
Income: Financed by county funding
Collections: 17th & 18th Century European & Oriental decorative arts; Fine Arts including series of original watercolors by David Roberts
Exhibitions: (1990) Mixed Media: Turtles (Oakroom exhibit); Ivory & Jade Friends. (1991) Artists from Southern California Deserts; California Handweavers; Paintings by Jeffrey Fisher
Publications: Museum catalog
Activities: Classes for children; docent training; lectures open to public; tours; outdoor art shows; cultural festivals; concerts; gallery talks; original objects of art lent to local universities and colleges; museum and sales shop sells books, original art, reproductions, prints and slides
L **Library,** 9401 Oak Glen Rd, 92223. Tel 909-845-2626.
Open by appointment for reference only
Library Holdings: Vols 2000; Per subs 3; Micro — Cards; Other — Manuscripts, original art works, prints
Special Subjects: Art History, Asian Art, Ceramics, Costume Design & Construction, Decorative Arts, Furniture, Glass, History of Art & Archaeology, Jade, Painting - British, Painting - European, Porcelain, Watercolors, David Roberts (original lithograph set of Holy Land)

CHICO

M **CALIFORNIA STATE UNIVERSITY, CHICO,** University Art Gallery, Art Dept, 95929. Tel 916-898-5864. *Dir* Michael Bishop; *Asst Dir* Catherine Sullivan
Open Mon - Fri 10 AM - 4 PM, Sun 1 - 5 PM. No admis fee. Estab to afford broad cultural influences to the massive North California region
Income: Financed by state appropriations and private funds
Collections: University Art Collection includes Masters of Graduate Artwork Study collection of fine art print
Exhibitions: (1992) James McConnell Exhibition
Activities: Lectures open to public, 6-12 vis lectr per year; competitions with awards; individual and original objects of art lent to offices on campus
L **Meriam Library,** First & Hazel, 95929. Tel 916-898-5833. *Dir Libr Colls* William Post; *Art Librn* Carolyn Dusenbury
Open to students and the public
Library Holdings: Vols 16,600; Per subs 72; Micro — Cards, fiche, prints, reels; AV — A-tapes, cassettes, fs, motion pictures, rec, slides, v-tapes; Other — Framed reproductions, original art works, pamphlets, photographs, prints, reproductions, sculpture
Collections: Janet Turner Print Collection

M **1078 GALLERY,** 738 W Fifth St, 95928. Tel 916-343-1973. *Co-Dir* Lynette Krehe; *Co-Dir* John Ferrell
Open Tues - Sat 12:30 - 5:30 PM. No admis fee. Estab as a Nonprofit artist run arts organization showing contemporary art exhibitions & installations by artists of cultural & geographic diversity
Exhibitions: (1992) Reflections on Things at Hand (an installation by artist Brenda Louie); Isolation (mixed media sculpture by Dan Corbin); Mixed Media Painting (Bo-Joong Kin); + / - (Body) (mixed media x-ray sculpture by Jacqueline Peele). (1993) Countdown 2000 (competition)

CHULA VISTA

M SOUTHWESTERN COLLEGE, Art Gallery, 900 Otay Lakes Rd, 91910. Tel 619-421-6700. *Dean Humanities* Dr June Scopinich
Open Mon - Fri 10 AM - 2 PM; Wed - Thurs 6 - 9 PM. No admis fee. Estab 1961 to show contemporary artists' work who are of merit to the community and the school, and as an educational service. Gallery is approx 3000 sq ft. Average Annual Attendance: 10,000
Income: Financed by city and state appropriations
Collections: Permanent collection of mostly contemporary work
Exhibitions: (1991) Fall Student Exhibit; Women's Month/Black History; Bob Matheny 1961-1991, Retirement/Retrospective/Beginning; Chrisato Exhibit
Activities: Classes for adults; lect open to public, 3 vis lectr per year; gallery talks; competitions; individual paintings and original objects of art lent; lending collection contains color reproductions, photographs, and original art works; junior museum

CITY OF INDUSTRY

M WORKMAN & TEMPLE FAMILY HOMESTEAD MUSEUM, 15415 E Don Julian Rd, 91745. Tel 818-968-8492. *Dir* Karen Graham Wade; *Cur* Carol Crilly; *Dir of Education & Public Affairs* Max A van Balgooy
Open Tues - Fri 1 - 4 PM, Sat - Sun 10 AM - 4 PM, group tours by appointment, cl 4th wkend of every month & holidays. No admis fee. Estab 1981 to develop & maintain a model historic site & popular regional cultural resource. Contemporary exhibition gallery; mid-19th century Workman Family House; late 19th century watertower; 1919-23 Spanish Colonial Revival Temple Family Residence. Average Annual Attendance: 15,000. Mem: 75; dues $5
Income: Financed by city appropriation
Collections: †1840 - 1930 decorative arts, furniture, textiles, costumes, artifacts; †photographic archives; interior decorative elements (metal work, tile, wood carvings, stained glass)
Publications: The Homestead Quarterly; News 'N Notes, monthly; A Journey Through Time Teachers' Manual; A guide to El Campo Santo & the Walter Temple Memorial Mausoleum
Activities: Classes for adults & children; dramatic programs; docent training; architectural crafts fair; films; workshops; lectures open to public; museum shop sells museum-related post-cards & booklets

CLAREMONT

M GALLERIES OF THE CLAREMONT COLLEGES, 91711-6344. Tel 909-621-8283. *Dir* Marjorie L Harth; *Curatorial Asst* Elizabeth Villa; *Cur of Exhibitions* Mary McNaughton; *Galleries Mgr* Gary Keith; *Registrar* Steve Comba; *Admin Asst* Barbara Senn; *Galleries Asst* Douglas Humble
Open Wed - Sun 1 - 5 PM, cl national & college holidays. No admis fee. Estab 1974 to present balanced exhibitions useful not only to students of art history and studio arts, but also to the general public. Galleries consist of Montgomery Gallery of Pomona College & Lang Gallery of Scripps College. Average Annual Attendance: 15,000
Income: Financed jointly by Pomona & Scripps Colleges, support group, & endowment grants
Collections: Samuel H Kress Collection of Renaissance paintings; 19th century American painting; contemporary ceramics; Old Master and contemporary graphics; photographs; Oriental art; African art; Native American art
Publications: Art Publications List, annual
Activities: Lect open to the public, 2 - 3 vis lectr per year; gallery talks; tours; individual paintings & original objects of art lent to qualified museums & galleries; book traveling exhibitions biennially; originates traveling exhibitions; entrance areas sell catalogues

M SCRIPPS COLLEGE, Clark Humanities Museum, 91711. Tel 909-621-8000, Ext 3606. *Dir* Eric Haskell; *Admin Asst* Nancy Burson
Open Mon - Fri 9 AM - noon and 1 - 5 PM, cl holidays & summer. No admis fee. Estab 1970 to present multi-disciplinary exhibits in conjunction with Scripps College's humanities curriculum, and to maintain a study collection. Museum has large room with storage and study area; reception desk
Collections: Nagel Collection of Chinese, Tibetan Sculpture & Textiles; Wagner Collection of African Sculpture
Exhibitions: Hatian art; Japanese prints; masks and musical instruments
Publications: Exhibition catalogues
Activities: Lectures open to public

CUPERTINO

M DE ANZA COLLEGE, Euphrat Gallery, 21250 Stevens Creek Blvd, 95014. Tel 408-864-8836. *Dir* Jan Rindfleisch; *Asst* Patricia Alders
Open Tues - Thurs 11 AM - 4 PM, Wed 7 - 9 PM, Sat 11 AM - 2 PM. No admis fee. Estab 1971. 1700 sq ft contemporary gallery located on De Anza College Campus. Average Annual Attendance: 15,000
Income: $125,000 (financed by mem, grants, endowment, college)
Publications: Art, Religion & Spirituality; Staying Visible: The Importance of Archives; Faces in the Greater San Francisco Bay Area; Art Collectors in & Around Silicon Valley; Content Contemporary Issues; Art of the Refugee Experience; The Power of Cloth (Political Quilts 1845-1986)
Activities: Children's classes; docent programs; lectures open to public; competition with awards; sales shop sells books

CYPRESS

M CYPRESS COLLEGE, Fine Arts Gallery, 9200 Valley View St, 90630. Tel 714-826-5593. *Dir* Betty Disney; *Secy* Maureen King
Open Mon - Fri 10 AM - 2 PM during exhibitions. No admis fee. Estab 1969 to bring visually enriching experiences to the school and community. Average Annual Attendance: 5000
Income: Financed by school budget, donations, and sales
Collections: †Student works; †purchase awards; †donor gifts
Exhibitions: (1992) A Thousand Points of Light; Visual Arts Faculty Exhibit. (1993) A Digital Dialogue; Cool Caps Exhibition & Auction; annual student art exhibit
Publications: Exhibition catalogs
Activities: Lectures open to public, 2 vis lectr per year; competitions; scholarships

DAVIS

M PENCE GALLERY, 212 D St, 95616. Tel 916-758-3370. *Pres* Shirley Goldman; *Cur* Edelgard Brunelle, PhD
Open Tues - Sat Noon - 4 PM & by appointment, except holidays & between shows. No admis fee. Estab 1975 to foster & stimulate awareness of the arts & cultural heritage of California through changing exhibitions of art & objects of artistic, aesthetic & historical significance. Gallery has 90 running ft of wall space & 650 sq ft of floor space. An outdoor performing space with a small stage lies behind the Gallery. Average Annual Attendance: 6000. Mem: 300; dues business $35, family $25, individual $20; meeting 2nd Tues of each month
Income: $21,000 (financed by mem, city appropriation & fund raisings)
Exhibitions: (1992) East Is East; Home Crafts in Davisville & Early Davis; Sacred Geometry-The Measured Land. (1993) Highlights From the Collection of Dr Joseph A Baird Jr; Marek Reavis: Paintings; Ceramic Sculpture; First Year UCD Art Graduate Students Group Shop
Publications: Newsletters, 10 per year
Activities: Lect open to public & vis lectr per yr; concerts; gallery talks; tours

UNIVERSITY OF CALIFORNIA

M Memorial Union Art Gallery, Second Floor Memorial Union, 95616. Tel 916-752-2885. *Dir* Roger Hankins
Open Mon - Fri 9 AM - 5 PM, also by appointment. No admis fee. Estab 1965 to provide exhibitions of contemporary and historical concerns for the students, staff and community. Gallery consists of North Gallery and South Gallery
Collections: Northern California contemporary art
Exhibitions: (1988) Gladys Nillson; Peter Vanderberg; Leningrad Snow; Joseph Yokum Sacramento Valley Landscapes
Publications: Exhibition catalogs
Activities: Classes for adults; lectures; concerts; poetry readings; films; competitions; internships

M Richard L Nelson Gallery & Fine Arts Collection, Department of Art, 95616. Tel 916-752-8500; FAX 916-752-0795. *Dir* L Price Amerson Jr; *Coll Mgr & Registrar* Carole Rosset
Open Mon - Fri Noon - 5 PM, Sun 2 - 5 PM. No admis fee. Estab 1976 to provide exhibitions of contemporary art as well as historical importance as a service to teaching program of the department of art, the university and the public. Contains main gallery and small gallery. Average Annual Attendance: 15,000
Income: Financed by university appropriation and grants
Collections: Fine Arts Collection of the Department of Art; general collection representing various periods of historical and contemporary art, with emphasis on Northern California art; also special collection includes: The Nagel Collection of Oriental Ceramics & Sculpture
Exhibitions: Conrad Atkinson; Margaret Harrison
Publications: Exhibition catalogues
Activities: Lectures open to the public, three to five vis lectrs per year; gallery talks

L Art Dept Library, University of California, Davis, 95616. Tel 916-752-3138, 752-0152. *Vook Librn* Bonnie Holt; *Slide Librn* Vickie Aubourg
Slide Library open Mon - Fri 8 AM - noon & 1 - 5PM, Book Library open Mon - Thurs 8:30 AM - noon & 1 4:30 PM, Fri 8:30 - noon. Estab 1966 to make readily accessible reference and research material to Art Department faculty, students and the general public
Income: Financed by state appropriation and college funds
Purchases: $3500
Library Holdings: Vols 10,000; Per subs 10; DIAL (Decimal Index of Art of the Low Countries) photographs; Micro — Fiche, prints; AV — A-tapes, fs, Kodachromes, lantern slides, motion pictures, slides, v-tapes; Other — Clipping files, exhibition catalogs, photographs, reproductions
Special Subjects: Aesthetics, Afro-American Art, American Indian Art, American Western Art, Architecture, Art History, Asian Art, Conceptual Art, Film, Folk Art, Mexican Art, Oriental Art, Painting - American, Painting - British

DESERT HOT SPRINGS

M CABOT'S OLD INDIAN PUEBLO MUSEUM, Pueblo Art Gallery, 67-616 E Desert View Ave, PO Box 1267, 92240. Tel 619-329-7610; FAX 619-329-1956. *Pres* Cole H Eyraud
Open Wed - Mon 9:30 AM - 4:30 PM, cl Tues. Admis adults $2.50, sr citizens $2, juniors $1. Estab 1968 as a source of reference. 1100 sq ft art gallery representing contemporary artists through a variety of media. Artifacts of past cultures & Americana along with native American work. Average Annual Attendance: 10,000. Mem: 50; dues lifetime $1000, patron $500, donor $300, organization $100, supporting $75, family $35, individual $20, student $10
Income: Financed by donations
Purchases: Cahuilla baskets, Navajo blankets & rugs acquired
Special Subjects: Advertising Design, American Indian Art, Architecture, Carpets & Rugs, Coins & Medals, Flasks & Bottles, Furniture, Handicrafts,

Historical Material, Maps, Photography, Southwestern Art
Collections: †The Theosophical Society Collection
Exhibitions: Full Moon Shaman Ceremonies
Activities: Concerts; museum shop sells books, magazines, original art, reproductions, prints, fine mineral specimens & fossils

DOMINGUEZ HILLS

M UNIVERSITY ART GALLERY OF CALIFORNIA STATE UNIVERSITY AT DOMINGUEZ HILLS, 1000 E Victoria, 90747. Tel 213-516-3334. *Gallery Dir* Kathy Zimmerer-McKelvie
Open Mon - Thurs 10 AM - 5 PM. Estab 1973 to exhibit faculty, student, contemporary California art & multi-cultural exhibits. New 2000 sq ft gallery in 1978. Average Annual Attendance: 10,000
Income: Financed by yearly grants from CSUDH Student Assoc,; support from Friends of the Gallery, City of Carson
Exhibitions: (1992) Deanne Belinoff: Paintings & Drawings; Ron Pippin: Paradise Regained; Altered Dimensions: Photography Into Sculpture; 6 African-American Artists; Terra Fluxus: Contemporary Landscapes
Publications: Exhibition catalogues published three times per yr; yearly newsletter
Activities: Lect open to public, 10 vis lectr per year; gallery talks; tours

DOWNEY

M DOWNEY MUSEUM OF ART, 10419 Rives Ave, 90241. Tel 310-861-0419. *Dir* Scott Ward
Open Wed - Sun Noon - 5 PM. No admis fee. Estab 1957 as an aesthetic and educational facility. Located in Furman Park, it is the only art museum with a permanent collection in Southeast Los Angeles, which includes in its area 27 neighboring communities of significant ethnic range and a total population close to one million. The Museum is continuing a program for new emerging multi-ethnic artists. The facility has five gallery areas plus classroom space. Gallery I covers 15 x 39 ft, Gallery II covers approx 12 x 24 ft, Gallery III covers 15 x 20 ft, Gallery IV covers 23 x 39 ft, and Gallery V covers 24 x 24 ft. Average Annual Attendance: 12,500. Mem: 475; dues $15 - $1000; annual meeting Apr
Income: $45,000 (financed by mem, grants, donations, & fundraising)
Collections: Many pieces produced by Southern California artists over the past 20 years, including Billy Al Bengston, Corita Kent, Don Emery, Sabato Fiorello, Stephen Longstreet, Anna Mahler, Shirley Pettibone, Betye Saar, Boris Duetsch & Frederick Wight
Exhibitions: (1991) Emerging Southern California Artists; Work; Martin Mondrus - Joseph Mugniani
Publications: Exhibition catalogs
Activities: Lectures open to public, 4 vis lectr per year; gallery talks; tours; traveling exhibitions organized and circulated; museum shop selling reproductions and prints

EL CAJON

M GROSSMONT COMMUNITY COLLEGE, Hyde Gallery, 8800 Grossmont College Dr, 92020-1799. Tel 619-465-1700, Ext 277; FAX 619-461-3396. *Chmn Art Dept* Harry Lum
Open by appointment. No admis fee. Estab 1970 as a co-curricular institution which cooperates with and supports the Art Dept of Grossmont College and which provides a major cultural resource for the general public in the eastern part of the greater San Diego area. Two galleries, one 30 x 40 ft; one 30 x 20 ft. Average Annual Attendance: 20,000
Income: Financed through College
Collections: Prints; photographs; clay objects; large Tom Holland painting
Publications: Exhibition catalogs; posters
Activities: Lect open to public, 6 vis lectr per year; concerts; original objects of art lent to institutions; lending collection photographs; originate traveling exhibitions

EUREKA

A HUMBOLDT ARTS COUNCIL, Humboldt Cultural Center, 422 First St, 95501. Tel 707-442-2611. *Exec Dir* Halfrid Nelson; *Facility Dir* Alan Dismuke
Estab 1966 to encourage, promote & correlate all forms of activity in the arts & to make such activity a vital influence in the life of the community. Mem: 250; annual meeting Oct
Income: $10,000 (financed by membership)
Collections: Art Bank, consisting of the yearly award winner from the juried Redwood Art Association Spring Show; other purchase & donated works of art; photograph collection; Premier Collection of North Coast Art (traveling display); traveling import museum exhibits
Exhibitions: Annual Youth Art Exhibit
Activities: Concerts; competitions; scholarships; individual paintings & original objects of art lent; originate traveling exhibitions

FRESNO

M FRESNO ARTS CENTER & MUSEUM, 2233 N First St, 93703. Tel 209-485-4810. *Dir & Chief Cur* Robert Barrett
Open Tues - Sun 10 AM - 5 PM. Admis adults $2, students & senior citizens $1, children 16 & under, school tours & museum mem free, Sat free to public. Estab 1949 as a visual arts gallery to provide Fresno and its environs with a community oriented visual arts center. The Center exhibits works of internationally known artists, and arranges shows of local artists. Three galleries plus entry for exhibits. Average Annual Attendance: 98,000. Mem: 2500; dues $35; annual meeting in May
Income: Financed by membership and fund raising efforts

Collections: Works of prominent California artists; contemporary American artists; Mexican folk art; Mexican graphic arts; permanent collection, National & International artists; extensive Pre-Columbian folk art
Exhibitions: Contemporary exhibitions changing every 6 - 8 wks
Activities: Classes for adults and children; docent training; lect open to public, 12 vis lectr per yr; gallery talks; concerts; tours; competitions; scholarships offered; individual paintings and objects of art lent to city and county offices and other institutions; lending collection contains framed reproductions, original art works, original prints and slides; book and originate traveling exhibitions; traveling exhibitions organized and circulated; museum shop sells books, magazines, original art, reproductions, prints, cards and local crafts

M FRESNO METROPOLITAN MUSEUM, 1555 Van Ness Ave, 93721. Tel 209-441-1444. *Pres & Board of Trustees* Emory Wishon; *Dir* Ross McGuire; *Prog Dir* Richard Ambrose; *Business Adminr* Kathy Angelillo; *Development Dir* Elizabeth Olson
Open Wed 11 AM - 7 PM, Thurs - Sun 11 AM - 5 PM. Admis fee adults $2, sr citizens, students & children 3-12 $1, members & children under 3 yrs free. Estab 1984 to increase the availability of fine and educational arts to the Fresno area. Museum is housed in a refurbished 1922 newspaper plant, two stories, with other floors marked for development; equipped with elevators & facilities for the handicapped. Average Annual Attendance: 60,000. Mem: 1800; dues $15-$1000
Income: $700,000 (financed by membership, donations, service fees & grants)
Collections: Oscar & Maria Salzer Collection of still life & trompe L'oeil paintings; Oscar & Maria Collection of 16th & 17th century Dutch & Flemish paintings; Frank & Mary Alice Diener Collection of ancient snuff bottles
Exhibitions: (1991) Field of Dreams; The Realm of Giants: Sequoia - Kings Canyon National Parks; California; Day of the Dead; 9th Annual Christmas at the Met; Vanishing Views of the American West: 80 Paintings from the Anschutz Collection; 4th Annual Met in Bloom; Saroyan's Fresno; Dinosaurs II
Publications: MetReport, bi-monthly
Activities: Children's classes; docent training; lectures open to public; individual paintings & original objects of art lent; book traveling exhibitions; museum shop sells books, reproductions, prints, slides, jewelry & children's toys

FULLERTON

M CALIFORNIA STATE UNIVERSITY FULLERTON, Art Gallery, Visual Arts Center, 800 N State College Blvd, 92634. Tel 714-773-3471. *Dir* Dextra Frankel; *Asst to Dir* Marilyn Moore; *Equipment Technician* Gene Karraker
Open during exhibits, Mon - Fri Noon - 4 PM, Sun 2 - 5 PM, cl Sat. No admis fee. Estab 1963 to bring to the campus carefully developed art exhibits that instruct, inspire and challenge the student to the visual arts; to present to the student body, faculty and community exhibits of historical and aesthetic significance; to act as an educational tool, creating interaction between various departmental disciplines, and promoting public relations between campus and community. Four to five exhibits each year stemming from the Museum Studies and Exhibition Design Program. Undergraduate and graduate students have the opportunity to focus within a professionally oriented program directed toward the museum profession. Activity incorporates classes, art gallery and local museums. The Dept of Art and the Art Gallery are the holders of the permanent collection. Average Annual Attendance: 15,000-20,000
Income: Financed by state appropriation, grants and donations
Collections: Contemporary Lithographs (Gemini); works by artists in the New York Collection for Stockholm executed by Styria Studio; lithographs by Lita Albuquerque, Coy Howard, Ed Rusha and Alexis Smith; Pre-Columbian artifacts; environmental and site-specific sculpture by Lloyd Hamrol, Ray Hein, Bernard Rosenthal, Michael Todd, Jay Willis
Exhibitions: Connie Zehr: Threshold; Six Views: Contemporary Landscape Architecture; Ten Years Later: Richard Shaw, Ed Blackburn, Tony Costanzo, Robert Rasmussen (Redd Ekks), John Roloff; The Infamous Image (photography); Animals; Contemporary Humanism: Reconfirmation of the Figure; Betye Saar: Resurrection; Nature: Two Views; Models: Hand-Held Ideas
Publications: Exhibition catalogs
Activities: Lectures open to public, 8-10 visiting lectures per year; workshops; production of slide/sound interpretation programs in conjunction with specific exhibitions; gallery talks; tours; scholarships; four - six major exhibitions per year; originate traveling exhibitions

M GALLERY 57, 204 N Harbor Blvd, 92362. Tel 714-870-9194.
Open Wed - Sat noon - 5 PM, Sun noon - 3 PM. No admis fee. Estab 1984 as a venue for local emerging artists. Average Annual Attendance: 2000. Mem: 20; dues $600; monthly meetng first Thurs
Income: $15,000 (financed by mem)
Exhibitions: Intimate Spaces II
Activities: Dramatic programs; poetry readings; lectures open to public, 3-4 vis lectr per year: competition with cash awards; 12 art shows per year

A MUCKENTHALER CULTURAL CENTER, 1201 W Malvern, 92633. Tel 714-738-6595. *Dir* Judith Peterson; *Center Adminr* Denise Watson; *Exhibition Adminr* Robert Zingg; *Secy* Nancy Way
Open Tues - Sat 10 AM - 4 PM, Sun Noon - 5 PM. Suggested donation $1. Estab 1966 for the promotion and development of a public cultural center for the preservation, display and edification in the arts. Gallery is a National Historic Building, contains 2500 sq ft and is on 8 1/2 acres of land; outdoor theatre facilities. Average Annual Attendance: 60,000. Mem: 500; dues $10 and up; annual meeting in April
Income: $300,000 (financed by endowment, membership, and city appropriation)
Publications: Exhibition catalogs
Activities: Classes for adults and children; docent training; lect open tp public, 40 vis lectr per year; concerts; 3 theatre productions annually; gallery talks; tour; book traveling exhibitions; sales shop selling books, magazines and original art

GILROY

M GAVILAN COLLEGE, Art Gallery, 5055 Santa Teresa Blvd, 95020. Tel 408-847-1400. *Gallery Advisor & Humanities Division Dir* Kent Child; *Community Services Dir* Ken Cooper; *Gallery Dir* Sylvia Rios
Open Mon - Fri 8 AM - 5 PM. No admis fee. Estab 1967 to serve as a focal point in art exhibitions for community college district and as a teaching resource for the art department. Gallery is in large lobby of college library with 25 ft ceiling, redwood panelled walls and carpeted floor
Income: Financed through college
Collections: Approx 25 paintings purchased as award purchase prizes in college art competitions
Exhibitions: Monthly exhibits of student, local artist and traveling shows
Activities: Lending collection contains books, cassettes, color reproductions, film strips, Kodachromes, paintings, sculpture

GLENDALE

L BRAND LIBRARY & ART GALLERIES, 1601 W Mountain St, 91201-1209. Tel 818-956-2051; FAX 818-548-5079. *Mgr & Gallery Dir* Cindy Cleary; *Asst Mgr* Ailine Merchant; *Librn* Eve Lichtman; *Librn* Jill Conner
Open Tues & Thurs noon - 9 PM, Wed noon - 6 PM, Fri & Sat noon - 5 PM. No admis fee. Estab 1969 to exhibit Southern California artists. Large gallery, foyer gallery, glass & concrete sculpture court. Average Annual Attendance: 200,000. Mem: 375; dues $10 - $500
Income: Financed by city and state appropriations
Library Holdings: Vols 40,000; Color slides 25,000, Compact discs 8000; Micro — Fiche; AV — Cassettes 2000, rec 30,000, slides; Other — Exhibition catalogs, framed reproductions, original art works, prints, reproductions
Collections: Indexes and other guides to art and music literature; Dieterle picture collection; early photography journals; 19th & 20th century American paintings & prints
Exhibitions: 8 exhibits per year
Activities: Classes for adults & children; concerts; tours; competitions

M FOREST LAWN MUSEUM, 1712 S Glendale Ave, 91205. Tel 213-254-3131. *Dir* Frederick Llewellyn; *Mgr* Margaret Burton
Open daily 10 AM - 5 PM. No admis fee. Estab 1951 as a community museum offering education and culture through association with the architecture and the art of world masters. There are four galleries in the museum and several smaller galleries in buildings throughout the four parks. Recreation of room under the Medici Chapel in Florence, Italy, where Michelangelo's drawings were recently discovered. Average Annual Attendance: 200,000
Collections: American Western Bronzes; Ancient Biblical and Historical Coins; Crucifixion by Jan Styka (195 x 45 ft painting); Resurrection (Robert Clark), painting; reproductions of Michelangelo's greatest sculptures; stained glass window of the Last Supper by Leonardo da Vinci; originals and reproductions of famous sculptures, paintings, and documents
Exhibitions: History of Forest Lawn
Activities: Scholarships offered; lending collection contains reproductions of the crown jewels of England; originate traveling exhibitions; memento shop sells books and art works
L Library, 1712 Glendale Ave, 91205. Tel 213-254-3131.
Open 10 AM - 6 PM. For use of employees
Library Holdings: Vols 3000

C GLENDALE FEDERAL SAVINGS, 401 N Brand Blvd, 91209. Tel 818-500-2000. *Interior Designer* Joanne Kravitz
Open 9 AM - 4 PM. Collection displayed in branches

GLEN ELLEN

M JACK LONDON STATE HISTORIC PARK, House of Happy Walls, 2400 London Ranch Rd, 95442. Tel 707-938-5216.
Open daily 10 AM - 5 PM; cl Thanksgiving, Christmas, New Year's Day. Admis $20 - $40 per bus, $5 per car, sr citizens $4. Estab 1959 for the interpretation of the life of Jack London; the fieldstone home was constructed in 1919 by London's widow. The collection is housed on two floors in the House of Happy Walls, and is operated by Calif Dept of Parks & Recreation. Average Annual Attendance: 80,000
Income: Financed by state appropriation
Collections: Artifacts from South Sea Islands; original illustrations
Activities: Tours; sales shop sells some of London's books

HAYWARD

M CALIFORNIA STATE UNIVERSITY, HAYWARD, University Art Gallery, 94542. Tel 510-881-3111. *Pres* Dr Norma Rees; *Prof* Greg MacGregor; *Prof* Lew Carson
Open Mon - Wed 11 AM - 4 PM, Thurs 11 AM - 7 PM, Sun 1 - 4 PM. No admis fee. Estab 1970 to provide a changing exhibition program for the university & general public. Gallery contains 2200 sq ft. Average Annual Attendance: 11,000
Income: $13,500
Publications: Usually one catalog a yr; flyers for each show
Activities: Lectures open to public, 6 vis lectrs per year; exten dept; artmobile; book traveling exhibitions
M C E Smith Museum of Anthropology, 94542. Tel 510-881-3104; FAX 510-727-2276. *Dir* George Miller, PhD
Open Mon - Fri 9:30 - 3:30 PM. Admis free. Estab 1974 as a teaching museum. Three converted classrooms; one main entrance from center room; alarm system; smoke detectors. Average Annual Attendance: 2500. Mem: 200
Income: $22,000 (financed by state appropriation)
Exhibitions: (1992) The Ohlone Indians of the Bay Area: A Continuing Tradition
Publications: Lee Collection: Hopi Kachinas, baskets, Navajo Mat; Krone Collection: Philippine artifacts
Activities: Lect open to the public, 12 vis lectr per yr

M HAYWARD AREA FORUM OF THE ARTS, Sun Gallery, 1015 E St, 94541. *Dir* Sylvia Medeiros
Open Wed - Sat 11 AM - 5 PM, cl major holidays. No admis fee. Estab 1975. Mem: Dues sustaining $35, nonprofit organization $25, family $20, single $15, student & sr citizen $15
Income: Financed by city, county & membership funds, corporate, & foundation grants
Collections: †Contemporary art by Northern California artists
Exhibitions: San Francisco Alumni Association exhibition (photography); recent works in Monotype; contemporary Mexican painters (from Santiago Garza collection); Jack & Marilyn da Silva (metalware); art programs for the physically limited; Roger Hankins (painting, assemblage); Dicksen Schneider; Southern Alameda County Art Educators; Corita Kent; Artistas del Grupo Hermes (paintings, drawings); Recent Work in Metal; Artists With Creative Growth; The Picture: As Object, As Image (painting, assemblage, photography); Shrine & Koan (painting, sculpture); Corita & Southern Alameda County Art Educators (multi-media); HAFA members exhibition (multi-media); Art in the News (photojournalists, editorial cartoonists); Forms In Space (2-D, 3-D); Felted Fibers
Activities: Educ dept; docent training; lectures open to the public; 3 vis lectrs per year; concerts, gallery talks, tours, art festivals with awards; scholarships; individual paintings & original objects of art lent to city offices; sales shop sells original art, prints & crafts

IRVINE

M CITY OF IRVINE, Irvine Fine Arts Center, 14321 Yale Ave, 92714. Tel 714-552-1018. *Supr* Amy Aspell; *Educ Coordr* Tim Jahns; *Cur* Dori Fitzgerald; *Resources Coordr* Lisa Cone
Open Mon noon - 9 PM, Tues & Thurs 9 AM - 9 PM, Fri 9 AM - 4 PM, Sat 9 AM - 3 PM, Sun 1 - 5 PM. Estab 1980 to make the arts integral in the lives of people. Gallery contains 5000 sq ft. Average Annual Attendance: 65,000. Mem: 250; dues $25 - $100
Income: $600,000 (financed by city appropriation, grants & donations)
Exhibitions: All Media, annual competition for Orange County artists. (1992) Imperfect Order; Crossing Borders
Publications: Art Beat, quarterly
Activities: Classes for adults & children; docent programs; open studios; lect open to public, 4 vis lectr per year; competitions; originate annual traveling exhibition; retail store sells books & original art

M SEVERIN WUNDERMAN MUSEUM, 3 Mason St, 92718. Tel 714-472-1138. *Dir* Tony Clark; *Asst Dir* John Ahr; *Research Dir* William Emboden; *Research Assoc* Alison Griffith; *Installer* Phil Morrison; *Registrar* Jeanne Perry; *Project Coordr* Linda Landau; *Publicist* Mary Crost
Open Mon - Fri 10 AM - 4 PM. Admis fee adults $2, children & senior citizens $1. Estab 1985 to collect, exhibit & research the works of Jean Cocteau & other 20th century artists. Two adjoining galleries designed to exhibit drawings, pastels, paintings, tapestries, theatre properties, manuscripts & ceramics. Average Annual Attendance: 1000. Mem: 50; dues $25
Income: $500,000 (financed by endowment)
Purchases: $350,000
Collections: Actress Sarah Bernhart; †Works of Jean Cocteau; Works of Joseph Nassy: A collection of over 700 painting & drawings; †Works of contemporaries of Cocteau such as Metzinger, Dali & Leger
Exhibitions: A retrospective permanent exhibition of the works of Jean Cocteau
Publications: The Severin Wunderman Foundation: Jean Cocteau, brochure
Activities: Docent training; films; coordination of dramatic events; lecturers open to public, 2 vis lectr per year; tours; selected items are lent; originate traveling exhibitions
L Research Library, 3 Mason St, 92718. Tel 714-472-1138. *Librn* Tony Clark
Estab 1986 to collect & research the works of Jean Cocteau & other artists in the Foundation's collections. For reference only
Library Holdings: Vols 100; AV — Fs, rec, slides, v-tapes; Other — Clipping files, manuscripts, memorabilia, original art works, pamphlets, photographs, prints, reproductions, sculpture

M UNIVERSITY OF CALIFORNIA, IRVINE, Fine Art Gallery, Dept Studio Art, 92717-2775. Tel 714-856-6610, 856-8251; FAX 714-725-2450. *Dir* Catharine Lord; *Museum Scientist* Phyllis J Lutjeans
Open Oct - June, Tues - Sun noon - 5 PM. No admis fee. Estab 1965 to house changing exhibitions devoted to contemporary art
Income: Financed by city and state appropriations and by interested private collectors
Exhibitions: Nick Vaughn (1983-1987); Wayne Thiebaud: Works on Paper (1947-1987); Peter Shelton: Environmental Sculpture; Michael Hardesty, NY Artist - Site Installation; Sigmund Freud Antiquities: Fragments from a Varied Past
Publications: Exhibition catalogs; mailers
Activities: Monthly lect on each exhibit; performances; tours; field trips

KENTFIELD

M COLLEGE OF MARIN, Art Gallery, College Ave, 94904. Tel 415-485-9494. *Dir* Duane Aten
Open Mon - Fri 8 AM - 10 PM; open also during all performances for drama, music and concert-lecture series. No admis fee. Estab 1970 for the purpose of education in the college district and community. Gallery is housed in the entrance to Fine Arts Complex, measures 3600 sq ft of unlimited hanging space; has portable hanging units and locked cases. Average Annual Attendance: 100 - 300 daily
Income: Financed by state appropriation and community taxes
Collections: Art student work; miscellaneous collection
Exhibitions: Faculty and Art Student; Fine Arts and Decorative Arts
Publications: Catalogs, 1-2 per year
Activities: Gallery Design-Management course; gallery talks; tours

LAGUNA BEACH

L **ART INSTITUTE OF SOUTHERN CALIFORNIA,** Ruth Salyer Library, 2222 Laguna Canyon Rd, 92651. Tel 714-497-3309. *Pres* John W Lottes; *Chmn Visual Communications* Vito Leonard Scarola; *Chmn Fine Arts* Jonathan Burke; *Chmn Liberal Arts* Helene Garrison
Open 8 AM - 5 PM. No admis fee. Estab 1962. For lending. Circ 5000
Purchases: $9000
Library Holdings: Vols 13,140; Per subs 65; AV — Slides 22,860, v-tapes 75; Other — Clipping files, exhibition catalogs 400
Publications: Catalog, annual; newsletters, semi-annual

M **LAGUNA ART MUSEUM,** Pacific Coast Hwy at 307 Cliff Dr, 92651. Tel 714-494-8971. *Dir* Charles Desmarais; *Assoc Dir & Adminr* Bonnie Hall; *Cur Exhib* Susan Anderson; *Cur Collections* Bolton Colburn; *Public Relations* Ellen Satlof; *Finance Officer* Nancy Hightower; *Bookstore Mgr* Teresa Ferreira
Open Tues - Sun 11 AM - 5 PM. cl Mon. Admis adults $3, children free. Estab 1918 as an art association. Two large galleries, six small galleries, museum store and offices. Average Annual Attendance: 75,000. Mem: 1800; dues $35 - $1000; annual meeting in Sept
Income: Financed by endowment and membership
Collections: American Art with focus on contemporary & early 20th century California painting
Exhibitions: Permanent collection: Elmer Bischoff, Larry Bell
Activities: Classes for adults & children; dramatic programs; docent training; lectures open to public; 10 vis lectrs per year; concerts; gallery talks; tours; demonstrations; competitions with awards; museum shop sells books, magazines, original art, reproductions & prints; exten dept serves South Coast Plaza galleries; individual paintings & original objects of art lent; lending collection contains books, framed reproductions, original art works, original prints, paintings, photographs & sculpture; book traveling exhibitions; originate traveling exhibitions; museum shop sells books, magazines, original art, reproductions & prints

LA JOLLA

L **LIBRARY ASSOCIATION OF LA JOLLA,** Athenaeum Music and Arts Library, 1008 Wall St, 92037. Tel 619-454-5872. *Exec Dir & Librn* Erika Torri; *Prog Dir* Daniel Atkinson; *Membership & Public Relations Assoc* Marie Vickers Horne; *Reference Librn* Carole Shipley
Open Tues & Thurs, Sat 10 AM - 5:30 PM, Wed 10 AM - 8:30 PM. No admis fee. Estab 1899 to provide the La Jolla & San Diego communities with library resources in music & arts & an on going schedule of cultural programs, classes, concerts & exhibitions. No established gallery; changing exhibitions every 6 week. Circ 34,000. Average Annual Attendance: 45,000. Mem: 1700; dues $40 - $5000; annual meeting third Tues in July
Income: $420,000 (financed by trust fund, rents, dues, gifts, admissions & tuitions)
Purchases: $27,000
Library Holdings: Vols 9500; Per subs 78; AV — A-tapes, cassettes 4000, rec 8000, v-tapes 1000; Other — Clipping files 1800, exhibition catalogs, pamphlets, photographs
Special Subjects: Advertising Design, Aesthetics, Afro-American Art, Bookplates & Bindings, Bronzes, Architecture, Art History, Asian Art, Bookplates & Bindings, Bronzes
Exhibitions: Changing shows every 6 weeks
Publications: Bimonthly newsletter
Activities: Educ dept; classes for adults & children; lect open to public, 10 vis lectr per yr; concerts; library tours; panel discussions; vis artists workshops; outreach programs for children; bi-monthly book sales; competitions with prizes

M **MUSEUM OF CONTEMPORARY ART, SAN DIEGO** (Formerly San Diego Museum of Contemporary Art), 700 Prospect St, 92037. Tel 619-454-3541; FAX 619-454-6985. *Development Dir* Anne Farrell; *Pres Board of Trustees* Mason Phelps; *Cur* Lynda Forsha; *Dir* Hugh M Davies; *Assoc Dir* Charles Castle; *Educ Cur* Seonaid McArthur
Open Tues - Sun 10 AM - 5 PM, Wed 10 AM - 9 PM, cl Mon, New Year's, Thanksgiving & Christmas. Admis adults $4, students & sr citizens $2, children under 12 $.50, call musuem for downtown hours & admission. Estab 1941 to provide exhibitions & understanding of contemporary visual arts. Museum is a non-profit organization, tax exempt & maintains two locations, a 500 seat auditorium, 16,000 sq ft total exhibition space. Average Annual Attendance: 173,000. Mem: 2700, dues $40 - $5000; annual meeting Oct
Income: $2,000,000 (financed by private contributions, endowment, mem, National Endowment for the Arts, California Art Council, City & County of San Diego
Collections: †Contemporary Art, International, 1950 to the present
Exhibitions: Vernon Fisher; Emilio Ambasz; Ann Hamilton; Alfredo Jaar. (1991) David Hammons; Jeff Wall. (1992) Amish Kapone; Anthony Gormley; Jana Sterbak. (1993) La Fronter/The Border: Art About the US/Mexican Border Experience
Publications: Exhibition catalogs; newsletter, quarterly
Activities: Classes for adults & children; docent training; lect open to the public, 10 - 15 lectr per year; films; gallery talks; tours; concerts; individual paintings & original objects of art lent to museums & qualified art organizations; lending collection contains original art works, original prints, paintings, photographs, sculpture; book traveling exhibitions, 3 - 4 per yr; originate traveling exhibitions; museum bookstore sells books, magazines, posters, design objects

L **Helen Palmer Geisel Library,** 700 Prospect St, 92037. Tel 619-454-3541; FAX 619-234-1070. *Librn* Erika Torri
Open Mon - Fri 10 AM - 5 PM. Estab 1941. For reference use by staff and docents; by appointment only to other persons
Income: Financed by membership, gifts and grants
Library Holdings: Vols 4000; Per subs 50; artist information; Micro — Cards; AV — Slides 6000, v-tapes; Other — Clipping files 2000, exhibition catalogs, pamphlets
Special Subjects: Art History, Conceptual Art, Drawings, Latin American Art, Painting - American, Painting - British, Painting - Japanese, Photography, Sculpture, Video, Contemporary art, international in scope

M **UNIVERSITY OF CALIFORNIA-SAN DIEGO,** Mandeville Gallery, Mail Code 0327, 9500 Gilman Dr, 92093-0327. Tel 619-534-2864. *Dir* Gerry McAllister
Open Tues - Sun noon - 5 PM, cl Mon, July, Aug & Christmas break. No admis fee. Estab 1967 to provide changing exhibitions of interest to the visual arts majors, university personnel and the community at large, including an emphasis on contemporary art. Located on the west end of Mandeville Center, flexible open space approximately 40 x 70 ft. Average Annual Attendance: 15,000. Mem: 200; dues $35 & up; bi-monthly meetings
Income: Financed by state appropriations, member contributions & student registration fees
Collections: Small Impressionist Collection owned by UC Foundation, presently on loan to San Diego Fine Arts Gallery, Balboa Park
Publications: UC San Diego Catalog: At Home with Architecture; exhibit catalogs
Activities: Lectures open to public, 3-4 vis lectrs per year; gallery talks; tours; originate traveling exhibitions

LONG BEACH

M **CALIFORNIA STATE UNIVERSITY, LONG BEACH,** University Art Museum, 1250 Bellflower Blvd, 90840-1901. Tel 310-985-5761; FAX 310-985-7602. *Dir & Chief Cur* Constance W Glenn; *Assoc Dir* Ilee Kaplan; *Educ Consultant* Ann Bunn; *Registrar* Maria Mapes; *Dir Public Relations & Publications* Kirsten Schmidt
Open Tues - Thurs 11 AM - 5 PM, Fri 11 AM - 3 PM, Sat 11 AM - 4 PM, Sun 2 - 5 PM, cl Mon. Admis $1 donation suggested. Estab 1949 to be an academic and community visual arts resource. Fifth floor, University Library. Average Annual Attendance: 50,000
Income: Financed by university appropriation & private funding
Purchases: Sculpture, works of art on paper
Collections: 1965 Sculpture Symposium; contemporary prints, drawings & photographs; monumental sculpture
Exhibitions: Jim Dine Figure Drawings: 1975-1979; Kathe Kollwitz at the Zeitlin Bookshop 1937: CSULB 1979; Roy Lichtenstein: Ceramic Sculpture; Nathan Oliveira Print Retrospective; Lucas Samaras: Photo Transformations; George Segal: Pastels 1957 - 1965; Frederick Sommer at Seventy-five; The Photograph as Artifice; Renate Ponsold-Robert Motherwell: Apropos Robinson Jeffers; Francesco Clemente Recent Works; Paul Wonner: Recent Works; Jacques Hurtubise: Oeuvres Recentes-Recent Works; Bryan Hunt: A Decade of Drawings; Anders Zorn Rediscovered; Robert Longo: Sequences-Men in the Cities; A Collective Vision: Clarence White & His Students; Hirosada: Osaka Printmaker; Eric Fischl: Scenes Before the Eye; Lorna Simpson: Imagenes Liricas: New Spanish Visions; James Rosenquist: Time Dust, The Complete Graphics 1962 - 1992
Publications: Exhibition catalogs & brochures, three or four per year
Activities: Adult classes; docent training; scheduled tours; lect open to public, 6 vis lectr per year; free event Tues at noon (Museum Tues); gallery talks; book traveling exhibitions; organizes traveling exhibitions to other museums

L **University Library,** 1250 Bellflower Blvd, 90840-1901. Tel 310-985-4026; FAX 310-985-1703. *Dir* Jordan Scepanski; *Group Leader Humanities of Fine Arts* Joan E McCauley; *Art Bibliographer* Henry J DuBois
Open Mon - Thurs 7 AM - midnight, Fri 7 AM - 5 PM, Sat 9 AM - 5 PM, Sun 1 PM - midnight. Estab 1949 for delivery of information & related services to the campus & surrounding communities. For lending & reference. Circ 471,482
Income: Financed by state appropriation
Purchases: $28,600
Library Holdings: Vols 1,010,000; Art vols 37,000; art per subs 116; Micro — Cards, fiche, reels; AV — Cassettes, fs, motion pictures, rec, slides, v-tapes; Other — Exhibition catalogs, pamphlets, prints, reproductions
Special Subjects: Art Education, Art History, Asian Art, Photography, Prints, Video
Collections: Modern Photography Collection (Edward Weston, Ansel Adams), original photographic prints; Kathe Kollwitz Collection, original prints

M **LONG BEACH JEWISH COMMUNITY CENTER,** Center Gallery, 3801 E Willow St, 90815. Tel 310-426-7601. *Pres* Rita Zamost; *Exec Dir* Joe Parmet; *Asst Dir* Lynne Rosenstein; *Gallery Dir* Dr Bernard Landes
Open Sun - Fri 9 AM - 5 PM, Mon - Thurs evening 7:30 - 10 PM. Estab to provide a community service for local artists and the broader community as well as offering exhibits of particular interest to the Jewish Community. The gallery is located in the large lobby at the entrance to the building; panels and shelves are for exhibit displays
Income: Financed by membership, United Jewish Welfare Fund, United Way and Fund Raising Events
Exhibitions: Monthly exhibits throughout the year; Annual Holiday Craft and Gift Show; Annual Youth Art Show; Paintings; Photography; Portraits; Sculpture
Publications: Center News, monthly; Jewish Federation News, bimonthly
Activities: Classes for adults and children; dramatic programs; lect open to the public; concerts; competitions with awards; sales shop sells books, Israeli and Jewish Holiday art objects and gift items

M **LONG BEACH MUSEUM OF ART,** 2300 E Ocean Blvd, 90803. Tel 310-439-2119; FAX 310-439-3587. *Dir* Harold Nelson; *Development Officer* Joan Van Hooten; *Cur* Noriko Gamblin; *Media Arts Cur* Carole Ann Klonarides; *Educator* Sue Ann Robinson; *Mgr Media Arts Center* Joe Leonardi; *Business Mgr* Jim Wilson
Open Wed - Sun noon - 5 PM; cl New Year's, July 4, Thanksgiving & Christmas. Admis $2. Opened in 1951 as a Municipal Art Center under the city library department; in 1957 the Long Beach City Council changed the center to the Long Beach Museum of Art; managed by Foundation since 1985. Eight galleries & a screening room with changing exhibitions & selections from Permanent Collection. Average Annual Attendance: 50,000. Mem: 1600; dues $35
Income: Financed by annual contribution by City of Long Beach & through grants from National Endowment for the Arts, California Arts Council and private foundations & through individual & corporate contributions

Collections: †Paintings, †sculpture, †prints, †drawings, crafts & photography; 1000 items with emphasis on West Coast & California modern & contemporary art; sculpture garden; Milton Wichner Collection includes Kandinsky, Jawlensky, Feininger, Moholy-Nagy; Major collection of video art
Exhibitions: Pioneers in Paradise; Hollis Frampton: The Blue Four; Art Moderne Architecture; A Passage Repeated; Drawing & Sculpture; Life: The Second Decade; Laddie John Dill; Japan-America; Video Poetics; Art of Music Vidio; Masami Teraoka; Gary Hill Retrospective; Alexej Jawlensky Retrospective; Afro-American Quilts; Relocations & Revisions: The Japanese-American Internment Reconsidered
Publications: Announcements; exhibit catalogs; quarterly bulletin
Activities: Workshops for adults & children; docent training; screening & lecture series open to public, 12 - 20 vis lectr per year; concerts; gallery talks; tours; video art Open Channels competition; awards; book traveling exhibitions, 4 per year; originate traveling exhibitions that circulate to museums

L **Library,** 2300 E Ocean Blvd, 90803. Tel 310-439-2119.
Open Wed - Sun noon - 5 PM. Admis $2. Estab 1957 to promote understanding & appreciation of the visual & media arts; to collect & facilitate the production of significant works of art; to manage & support an institution where these works of art may be housed & displayed for the education & enjoyment of the public.
Open for staff reference with restricted lending of books, publications and slides.
Average Annual Attendance: 47,000
Library Holdings: Vols 2000; Per subs 4; AV — V-tapes; Other — Clipping files, exhibition catalogs
Special Subjects: Art History
Exhibitions: Annual Dia de los Muentos & Children's Cultural Festival
Activities: Four-part lect series, 2 - 4 vis lectr per year; poetry readings; concerts; gallery talks; tours; individual paintings & original objects of art lent to other art institutions, corporations & organizations with art programs; museum lobby sells catalogues, cards & posters

L **LONG BEACH PUBLIC LIBRARY,** 101 Pacific Ave, 90802-4482. Tel 310-437-2949; FAX 310-590-6956. *Dir Libr Servs* Cordelia Howard; *Assoc Dir Adult Servs* Eleanore Schmidt; *Fine Arts Librn* Judith Fraser
Open Mon 10 AM - 8 PM; Tues - Sat 10 AM - 5:30 PM, Sun noon - 5 PM. Estab 1897
Library Holdings: Vols 1,044,608; Micro — Fiche, reels; AV — A-tapes, cassettes, rec, v-tapes; Other — Clipping files, exhibition catalogs, framed reproductions, memorabilia, original art works, pamphlets
Collections: Miller Special Collections Room housing fine arts books with an emphasis on Asian Art and Marilyn Horne Archives

A **PUBLIC CORPORATION FOR THE ARTS,** Visual & Performing Arts Registry, 300 E Ocean Blvd, 90802. Tel 310-499-7777; FAX 310-499-7548. *Exec Dir* Sandra Gibson; *Public Arts Mgr* Jorge Pardo; *Member Serv Liaison* Susan Malmstrom; *Corporate Press Officer* David Dominquez; *Admin Asst* Richard Alexander
Open Mon - Fri 9 AM - 5 PM, cl Sat & Sun. Admis free. Estab 1977, non-profit, official arts advisory council for city of Long Beach
Income: $750,000 (financed by endowment, mem, city appropriation, private corporations & foundations)
Collections: Contemporary & archival slides; Library of Long Beach & area resident artists' work; all media-200 artists performing & visual
Publications: Newsletter, bi-monthly; quarterly events calendar; monthly media sheets
Activities: Enrichment & alternative arts programs; technical assistance; lectures open to public, 3 vis lectr per year; individual & community art grants

LOS ANGELES

A **ARMAND HAMMER MUSEUM OF ART & CULTURAL CENTER,** 10899 Wilshire Blvd, 90024. Tel 310-443-7020; FAX 310-443-7099. *Dir* Stephen Garrett; *Dir of Fine Arts* Dr Alla Hall
Collections: Five centuries of Masterpieces; European & American paintings, drawings & watercolors; Daumier Collection: paintings, drawings, sculpture, lithographs, litho stone, wood block & prints; drawings by Daumier's contemporaries; Leonardo da Vinci Codex
Exhibitions: (1992) Kazimir Malevich opening exhibition (temporary); Catherine The Great: Treasures of Imperial Russia; Splendors of the Ottoman Sultans

L **ART IN ARCHITECTURE,** Joseph Young Library, 7917 1/2 W Norton Ave, 90046. Tel 213-656-2286, 654-0990. *Dir* Dr Joseph L Young
Estab 1955 to provide background to history of art in architecture. Only availabe to students, associates and apprentices for reference only
Purchases: $2000
Library Holdings: Vols 2000; Per subs 10; AV — Kodachromes, motion pictures, slides, v-tapes; Other — Clipping files, exhibition catalogs, memorabilia, original art works, pamphlets, photographs, prints, reproductions, sculpture
Special Subjects: Architecture, Art History, Calligraphy, Drawings, Judaica, Mexican Art, Mixed Media, Mosaics, Painting - American, Painting - Dutch, Painting - European, Painting - French, Painting - Italian, Photography, Religious Art, Sculpture, Stained Glass, Mural Painting
Activities: Two vis lectrs per yr; tours; scholarships & fels offered; lending collection contains 2000 books, 200 color reproductions, 2000 Kodachromes, motion pictures, 100 original art works, 500 original prints, paintings, 500 photographs, sculpture & 2000 slides; book traveling exhibitions once a yr; originate traveling exhibitions

C **BROAD INC,** Kaufman & Broad Home Corp Collection, 11601 Wilshire Blvd, 12th Floor, 90025. Tel 310-312-5000. *Cur* Michele DeAngelus; *Asst Cur* Joanne Heyler
Estab 1981 in support and involvement of local art community
Income: Financed by corporate budget
Collections: Selection of works primarily by Southern California artists; emphasis on artists who had not had a major retrospective prior to 1975
Activities: Individual paintings & original objects of art lent

M **CALIFORNIA AFRO-AMERICAN MUSEUM,** Exposition Park 600 State Dr, 90037. Tel 213-744-7432. *Dir* Terrie S Rouse; *Deputy Dir* Angela Bonner; *Cur History* Rick Moss; *Assoc Ed Publications* Nancy McKinney
Open daily 10 AM - 5 PM, cl Mon. No admis fee. Estab to examine, collect, preserve & display art, history & culture of Blacks in The Americas with concentration on Blacks in California
Exhibitions: (1992 - 93) No Justice, No Peace; Hollywood Days, Harlem Nights; I Dream a World: Portrait of Black Women Who Changed America
Publications: Calendar of Events, every 2 months; exhibition catalogs

M **CALIFORNIA MUSEUM OF SCIENCE AND INDUSTRY,** 700 State Dr, 90037. Tel 213-744-7400. *Executive Dir* Jeffrey N Rudolph; *Deputy Dir* Bob Campbell; *Deputy Dir* Ann Muscat
Open daily 10 AM - 5 PM. Dynamically tells the story of science, industry and commerce to the public by tempting each visitor to take part in a sensory learning experience and education adventure. The museum has 9 halls housing 20 permanent exhibits and more than 60 temporary exhibits among which are Sister Cities Youth Art Exhib and Sister Cities in Focus which appear throughout the year; auditorium seating 500
Income: Financed by state appropriation and California Museum Foundation
Exhibitions: Permanent-Art Hall of Fame. Temporary-Annual Union Artist (paintings and sculpture by all unions in AFL-CIO); Bonsai, Care and Growing; children's Gametime playground exhibit; Key Art Awards (annual showing of posters, logos, word-styles promoting movies or TV shows); props from motion picture Alien
Publications: Notices of temporary exhibits, maps, pamphlets
Activities: Formal science-art education programs for school groups and the public; competitions; scholarships

M **CALIFORNIA STATE UNIVERSITY, LOS ANGELES,** Fine Arts Gallery, 5151 State University Dr, 90032. Tel 213-343-4023. *Dir* Daniel Douke
Open Mon - Thurs noon - 5 PM; Sun 1 - 4 PM. No admis fee. Estab 1954 as a forum for advanced works of art and their makers, so that education through exposure to works of art can take place. Gallery has 1400 sq ft, clean white walls, 11 ft high ceilings with an entry and catalog desk. Average Annual Attendance: 30,000
Income: Financed by endowment and state appropriation
Exhibitions: American Landscape Painting; Mark Lere; Peter Liashkoy; New Talent Exhibitions; California Painting; The Essential Modernist Framework
Publications: Exhibition catalogs, 3 per year
Activities: Educ dept; lectures open to public, 10-20 vis lectr per year; gallery talks; exten dept

M **CITY OF LOS ANGELES,** Cultural Affairs Dept, 433 S Spring St, 10th Floor, 90013. Tel 213-485-2433. *General Mgr* Adolfo V Nodal; *Performing Arts Dir* Ernest Dillihay; *Pres Cultural Affairs Commission* Elyse Grinstein; *Pres Cultural Heritage Commission* Dr Armarjit S Marwah; *Community Arts Dir* Dr Earl Shevburn
Estab 1925 to bring to the community the cultural & aesthetic aspects of Los Angeles; to encourage citizen appreciation & participation in cultural activities & developing art skills. Operates facilities, programs & classes throughout the city. Sponsors festivals, special events. Average Annual Attendance: 250,000
Income: $3,000,000 (financed by city appropriation)
Collections: Works by local area artists; Portraits of Mayors of Los Angeles; gifts to the city from other countries
Exhibitions: Various at different venues
Activities: Classes for adults and children; dramatic programs; docent training; lect open to public; concerts; gallery talks; tours; competitions; historic preservation; street murals; grants program; folk arts program; sales show sells books, original art, reproductions, and prints

M **CRAFT AND FOLK ART MUSEUM,** 6067 Wilshire Blvd, 90036. Tel 213-937-5544; FAX 213-937-5576. *Exec Dir* Patrick Ela; *Press Officer* Jean Miao; *Registrar* Carol Fulton; *Museum Educator* Phyllis Chang; *Controller* Lorraine Trippett; *Development Dir* Susan Sirkus; *Project Dir* Marcia Page; *Asst to Dir* Lisa Avalos
Open Tues - Sat 10 AM - 5 PM, Sun 11 AM - 5 PM. No admis fee. Estab 1973 as The Egg and The Eye Gallery
Collections: Contemporary American Crafts; Contemporary Design; International Folk Art, including Japanese, East Indian & Mexican works; masks of the worlds
Exhibitions: Intimate Appeal: The Figurative Art of Beatrice Wood; Ed Rossbach: 40 Years of Exploration & Innovation in Fiber Art; Biannual Festival
Publications: Calendar 5 - 6 times per year
Activities: Classes for adults & children; docent training; lect open to public, 5 vis lectr per year; gallery talks; tours; community outreach programs; book traveling exhibitions 1-2 per year; originate traveling exhibitions; museum shop sells books, magazines, original art, reproductions, prints, jewelry, folk art, ceramics, glass

L **Research Library,** 6067 Wilshire Blvd, 90036. Tel 213-934-7239, 937-5544. *Museum Librn* Joan M Benedetti; *Prog Coordr C-Sac* Nancy Downes-LeGuin
Open by appointment only. Estab 1975 to support and supplement the documentation and information activities of the Museum in regard to contemporary crafts, international folk art, design. Visual material collected equally with print. For reference only
Income: Financed by the museum & grants
Library Holdings: Vols 6000; Per subs 120; AV — Cassettes, slides; Other — Clipping files, exhibition catalogs, memorabilia, pamphlets, photographs
Special Subjects: Decorative Arts, Folk Art, Industrial Design, Masks & Masking, Vernacular domestic Architecture
Collections: Preserving Ethnic Traditions Project Archive (slides, cassette, a-tapes, and reports of LA folk artists); †Slide Registry of Contemporary Craftspeople

A **CULTURAL AFFAIRS DEPARTMENT CITY OF LOS ANGELES,** Junior Arts Center, 4814 Hollywood Blvd, 90027. Tel 213-485-4474. *Dir* Harriet S Miller; *Dir Education* Joan De Bruin; *Teacher Outreach Coordr* Laura Stickney; *Handicapped Services Coordr* Dr Mary J Martz; *Spec Events Coordr* Louise

Steinman; *International Child Art Coordr* Sandy Fine
Open Tues - Sun 12:30 - 5 PM. No admis fee. Estab 1967 to stimulate and assist in the development of art skills and creativity. The gallery offers exhibitions of interest to children and young people and those who work with the young. Average Annual Attendance: 90,000. Mem: 200; dues $25 ; annual meeting June 1
Income: Financed by city appropriation and Friends of the Junior Arts Center
Collections: International Child Art Collection; Two-dimensional works on paper; 8mm film by former students
Exhibitions: Six exhibitions a yr
Publications: Schedules of art classes, quarterly; exhibition notices
Activities: Art classes for young people in painting, dramatic programs drawing, etching, general printmaking, photography, filmmaking, photo silkscreen, ceramics, film animation; workshops for teachers; lectures, 2 - 4 vis lectr per yr; films; musical instrument making, design, video festivals for students and the general public; gallery talks; tours; scholarships
L **Library,** 4814 Hollywood Blvd, 90027
Staff use only
Library Holdings: Vols 700; AV — Slides 15,000

C **FIRST INTERSTATE BANK,** 707 Wilshire Blvd, 90017. Tel 213-614-4111, 614-4327. *VPres & Mgr* Dianne Siegel
Collections: American Art: paintings; sculpture; graphics; drawings & textiles

A **FOUNDATION FOR ART RESOURCES,** PO Box 29422, 90029. Tel 310-289-4181. *Dir* Linda Besemer; *Head Outside Art Prog* Franklin Odell
Admis exhib $1, lect $5. Estab to represent artists & art criticism theory not normally represented in main stream galleries
Income: $15,000 (financed by endowment)
Exhibitions: (1992) Far Bazzar; LA's Alternative Art Fair

C **GOLDEN STATE MUTUAL LIFE INSURANCE COMPANY,** Afro-American Art Collection, 1999 W Adams Blvd, 90018. Tel 213-731-1131. *Cur & Cunsultant* Harold Toliver
Open to public by appointment through Personnel Department. No admis fee. Estab 1965 to provide a show place for Afro-American Art; to assist in the development of ethnic pride among the youth of our community. Collection displayed throughout building
Income: Financed by the Company
Collections: Drawings, lithographs, paintings and sculpture
Publications: Afro-American Art Collection Brochure; Historical Murals Brochure
Activities: Tours by appointment

M **HEBREW UNION COLLEGE,** Skirball Museum, 32nd & Hoover Sts (Mailing add: 3077 University Ave, 90007). Tel 213-749-3424; FAX 213-749-1192. *Dir* Nancy Berman; *Adminr* Peggy Kayser; *Education Coordr* Adele Burke; *Cur* Grace Cohen Grossman; *Cur* Barbara Gilbert; *Media Resources Coordr* Susanne Kester; *Project Americana Coordr* Ellen Dryer-Kaplan
Open Tues - Fri 11 AM - 4 PM, selected Sun 10 AM - 5 PM (call for dates). No admis fee. Estab 1913 as part of library of Hebrew Union College in Cincinnati, Ohio, and moved in 1972 to the California branch of the college, and renamed the Hebrew Union College Skirball Museum; to collect, study, interpret, & exhibit materials & artifacts of Jewish culture. 5575 sq ft in gallery. Average Annual Attendance: 20,000. Mem: 1500; dues associate $1000, patron $500, sustaining $250, contemporary $150 & $125, supporting $100, contributing $50, participating $35, sr citizen & student $18
Income: Financed by mem, college appropriation; private and public grants
Collections: 2000 archaeological objects from the Near East, primarily Israeli; 6000 ceremonial objects, primarily Western Europen, but some exotic Oriental & Indian pieces as well; †2500 ethnographic objects of American Jewish Life; Chinese Torah and India Torah cases; 4000 prints & drawings from Western Europe, spanning 4 - 5 centuries
Exhibitions: Permanent exhibitions: A Walk Through The Past (Jewish histroy seen in the context of biblical archaeology & cultural anthropology); Let us give Honor to the Torah (ceremonial & related art); Reflections of Triumph: Hanukkah lamps from the collection; Celebrations (fine & folk art forms developed to celebrate Sabbath, holiday & life cycle events); Project Americana Sampler: American Judaica & objects of everyday American Jewish Life. Changing exhibitions: The Museum presents 3-6 changing exhibitions on Jewish cultural history annually
Publications: Exhibition brochures & catalogs; museum calendar, 3 per year
Activities: Docent training; lect open to public; children's workshops; lending collection contains 22,000 slides; originate traveling exhibitions

M **JAPANESE AMERICAN CULTURAL & COMMUNITY CENTER,** George J Doizaki Gallery, 244 S San Pedro St, Suite 505, 90012-3895. Tel 213-628-2725; FAX 213-617-8576. *Gallery Dir* Robert Hori
Exhibitions: (1992) Kiyoshi Awazu: Artist & Designer

A **L A ART ASSOCIATION,** 825 N LaCienega Blvd, 90069. Tel 310-652-8272. *Pres* Truda Chandlee; *Dir* Richard Campbell; *VPres* Jae Carmichael; *Secy* Inez Aldrin Kimble; *Treas* Bob Jesburg
Open Tues - Sat noon - 5 PM. Estab 1925 to discover and present young professional artists, and to exhibit the work of established California artists. Average Annual Attendance: 5000. Mem: 350; dues $50-$100 per year; biannual meetings in Apr & Oct
Income: Financed by investments; partly by membership dues
Exhibitions: All Creatures Great and Small: The Animal in Art; Burden Collection of Famous Photographers; Jubilee Show of Artists of the Forties & Fifties; Los Angeles, Yesterday and Today; Graphics, Painting & Sculpture by Southern California Artists, monthly
Publications: Announcements of exhibitions & lectures, monthly; newsletter, monthly
Activities: Exhibition receptions & gallery lectures, open to the public

A **LOS ANGELES CENTER FOR PHOTOGRAPHIC STUDIES,** 1048 W Sixth St, 90017. Tel 213-482-3566. *Pres* Josh Schweitzer; *Dir* Joe Smoke
Open Mon - Fri 10 AM - 5 PM. Estab 1974 to promote photography within the visual arts. Mem: 600; dues patron $250 - $1000, friend $100, regular $30, student & sr citizen $15
Income: $110,000 (financed by membership, city & state appropriation, federal funds, corporations & foundations)
Exhibitions: Members exhibition; group exhibitions
Publications: Frame/Work, 3 times per yr, Photo Calendar, bi-monthly
Activities: Workshops for adults; symposia; lectures open to public, 8-12 vis lectr per yr; competitions with awards; originates traveling exhibitions; sales shop sells magazines & original art

M **LOS ANGELES CONTEMPORARY EXHIBITIONS,** 1804 Industrial St, 90021. Tel 213-624-5650; FAX 213-624-6679. *Exec Dir* Gwen Darien; *Exhibit Coordr* Jinger Heffner; *Performance & Video Coordr* Tom Dennison; *Bookstore Mgr* Brad Thompson
Open Wed - Fri 11 AM - 5 PM, Sat & Sun noon - 5 PM. No admis fee, performances $10 & $12. Estab 1978, artist run interdisciplinary space. Average Annual Attendance: 25,000. Mem: 3000; dues $35 - $2500, artists $20
Activities: Lectures open to public; educational programs; originates traveling exhibitions; museum shop sells books, magazine & jewelry

M **LOS ANGELES COUNTY MUSEUM OF ART,** 5905 Wilshire Blvd, 90036. Tel 213-857-6111; FAX 213-931-7347. *Dir* Michael A Shapiro; *Deputy Dir Admin* Ronald B Bratton; *Asst Dir Operations* Arthur Owens; *Head Conservation* Pieter Meyers; *Cur Costumes & Textiles* Edward Maeder; *Asst Dir Facilities* Romalis Taylor; *Sr Cur Prints & Drawings* Victor Carlson; *Cur 20th Century Art* Stephanie Barron; *Cur Contemporary Art* Howard Fox; *Cur Far Eastern Art* George Kuwayama; *Cur European Paintings & Sculpture* Philip Conisbee; *Cur Photography* Robert A Sobieszek; *Dir Film Programs* Ronald Haver; *Dir Music Programs* Dorrance Stalvey; *Public Information Programs* Pamela Jenkinson; *Registrar* Renee Montgomery; *Librn* Eleanor Hartman; *Cur American Art* Michael Quick; *Sr Cur 20th Century Art* Maurice Tuchman; *Cur Indian & Southeast Asian Art* Pratapaditya Pal; *Cur Decorative Arts* Leslie Greone Bowman; *Asst Dir Exhib* Elizabeth Algermissen
Open Tues - Thurs 10 AM - 5 PM, Fri 10 AM - 9 PM, Sat & Sun 11 AM - 6 PM. cl Mon, Thanksgiving, Christmas & New Years Day. Admis adults $5, students & sr citizens with ID $3.50, young people 5 - 12 $1; free day second Tues of each month; museum members & children under 5 admitted free. Estab 1910 as Division of History, Science and Art; estab separately in 1961, for the purpose of acquiring, researching, publishing, exhibiting and providing for the educational use of works of art from all parts of the world in all media, dating from prehistoric times to the present. Complex of five buildings. Average Annual Attendance: 1,000,000. Mem: 80,C00; dues $45 - $5000
Income: $30,000,000 (financed by endowment, mem & county appropriation)
Collections: †American art; †ancient and Islamic art; †contemporary art; †decorative arts; †European painting and sculpture; †Far Eastern art; †Indian and South Asian art; †textiles and costumes; †modern art; †prints & †drawings; †photography
Exhibitions: (1993) When Art Became Fashion: Kosode in Edo-Period Japan; Parallel Visions: Modern Artists & Outsider Art
Publications: Members Calendar, monthly, exhibition catalogs, 6-8 yearly; exhibition education brochures, 6 yearly, permanent collection catalogs, 3 yearly
Activities: Classes for adults and children; dramatic programs; docent training; lectures open to the public, 50 vis lectr per yr; concerts; gallery talks; tours; films; individual paintings and original objects of art lent to other AAM-accredited museums for special exhibitions; lending collection contains original art works, original prints, paintings and 130,000 slides; traveling exhibitions organized and circulated; museum shop sells books, magazines, reproductions, prints, gifts, posters, postcards, calendars & jewelry
L **Library,** 5905 Wilshire Blvd, 90036. Tel 213-857-6118. *Librn* Eleanor C Hartman
Open Tues - Fri 10 AM - 4 PM. For reference only
Library Holdings: Vols 88,000; Per subs 449; Artists' Files, Auction Catalogs 27,000
L **Robert Gore Rifkind Center for German Expressionist Studies,** 5905 Wilshire Blvd, 90036. Tel 213-857-6165; FAX 213-931-7347. *Cur* Timothy Benson; *Librn* Susan Trauger; *Asst Registrar* Christine Vigiletti
Open by appointment
Library Holdings: Vols 5000; Other — Exhibition catalogs, manuscripts, memorabilia, original art works, pamphlets, photographs, prints, reproductions
Special Subjects: Decorative Arts, Drawings, Etchings & Engravings, Graphic Arts, Painting - German, Photography, Portraits, Posters, Printmaking, Prints, Sculpture, Watercolors, Woodcuts, German expressionism
Collections: German expressionist prints, †drawings, †books & periodicals
Exhibitions: (1992 - 93) Kathe Kollwitz; The Expressionist Portrait; Otto Dix: Graphic Artists; George Grosz: Social Critic
Publications: Publications relating to German Expressionist studies
Activities: Individual graphics lent to qualified institutions

M **LOS ANGELES MUNICIPAL ART GALLERY,** 4804 Hollywood Blvd, 90027. Tel 213-485-4581. *Prog Dir* Noel Korten
Open Tues - Sun 12:30 - 5 PM. Admis $1. Estab to show Los Angeles artists
Exhibitions: (1992) George Herms: The Secret Archives; LAX: The Los Angeles Exhibition

L **LOS ANGELES PUBLIC LIBRARY,** Arts & Recreation Dept, 433 S Spring St, 90013. Tel 213-612-3254. *Dept Mgr* Romaine Ahlstrom
Open Mon, Wed, Fri & Sat 10 AM - 5:30 PM, Tues & Thurs noon - 8 PM, cl Sun. No admis fee. Established 1872
Income: Financed by municipality
Library Holdings: Vols 200,000; Per subs 800; Prints including original etchings, woodcuts, lithographs & drawings; Other — Clipping files, exhibition catalogs, framed reproductions, original art works, photographs, prints
Collections: Twin Prints; Japanese prints, including a complete set of Hiroshige's Tokaido Series
Exhibitions: Museum's Artists Scrapbooks, NY Public Artist's File

M **LOYOLA MARYMOUNT UNIVERSITY,** Laband Art Gallery, Loyola Blvd at W 80th, 90045-2699. Tel 310-338-2700; FAX 310-338-4470. *Dir* Gordon Fuglie
Open Wed - Fri 10:30 AM - 4:30 PM, Sat noon - 4 PM, cl Sun & Tues. No admis fee. Estab 1971 to hold exhibitions. The new gallery which opened in 1984, is 40 ft by 50 ft with 20 ft ceilings, track lighting & closeable Skylights. Average Annual Attendance: 10,000
Exhibitions: (1991) Passover & Passion: Jewish & Christian Artists Interpretation of Their Holy Days; The biennial National exhibitions of the Los Angeles Printmaking Society. (1992) Carmen Lomas Garza: Pedacito demi Corazon
Publications: Catalogs
Activities: Lect open to public, 4 - 5 vis lectr per year; concerts; gallery talks; films; competitions with awards; sales shop sells books

M **MOUNT SAINT MARY'S COLLEGE,** Jose Drudis-Biada Art Gallery, Art Dept, 12001 Chalon Rd, 90049. Tel 310-476-2237. *Gallery Dir* Olga Seem
Open Mon - Fri noon-5 PM. No admis fee. Estab to present works of art of various disciplines for the enrichment of students and community
Income: Financed by College
Collections: Collection of works by Jose Drudis-Blada
Exhibitions: Gene Mako Collection; Sedivy & Zokosky: Recent Paintings; Works on Paper; Drucker: Constructions; Geer Installation
Publications: Exhibitions catalogs, 1 per year
Activities: Lect open to public, 2-3 vis lectr per yr; scholarships

M **MUSEUM OF AFRICAN AMERICAN ART,** 4005 Crenshaw Blvd, 3rd Floor, 90008. Tel 213-294-7071. *Founder* Dr Samella Lewis
Collections: Arts of the African & African-descendant people; Soapstone Sculpture of Shona; People of Southeast Africa; Makonde Scupiture of East Africa; Traditional Sculpture of West Africa; Sculpture, Paintings, Ceramics of the Caribbean & the South American Peoples; Contemporary North American Artists
Exhibitions: (1991) Massive Exhibition; Jamacian-California Exchange Exhibition

M **THE MUSEUM OF CONTEMPORARY ART,** 250 S Grand Ave at California Plaza, 90012. Tel 213-621-2766; FAX 213-620-8674. *Chmn* Frederick M Nicholas; *Dir* Richard Koshalek; *Assoc Dir* Sherri Geldin; *Dir Development* Erica Clark; *Dir Communications* Cynthia Hohri
Open Tues, Wed, Fri - Sun 11 AM - 6 PM, Thurs 11 AM - 8 PM, cl Mon. Admis general $4, sr citizens & students $2, children under 12 & MOCA members free. Estab 1979, emphasizing the arts since mid century, encompassing traditional & non-traditional media. Permanent building designed by Arata Isozaki opened in 1986. Average Annual Attendance: 150,000. Mem: 18,000; dues $45
Income: Financed by donations & admis fees, grants (private, corporate, NEA)
Collections: El Paso Collection; The Barry Lowen Collection; The Panza Collection; The Schreiber Collection; General Permanent Collection
Activities: Classes for children; docent training; lect open to public; gallery talks; tours; individual paintings lent to other institutions; originate traveling exhibitions; museum shop sells books, magazines, original art, posters, gifts

M **MUSEUM OF NEON ART,** 704 Traction, 90013. Tel 213-617-0274; FAX 213-620-8904. *Dir* Mary Carter
Open daily 11 AM - 11 PM. Admis $2.50. Estab 1981 to exhibit, document & preserve works of neon, electric & kinetic art. Consists of large main gallery for group or theme exhibitions & a small gallery for solo shows. Average Annual Attendance: 15,000. Mem: 300; dues $25 and up; annual meetings Dec 10
Income: Financed by memberships, donations & admission fees
Collections: †Antique electrical signs; contemporary neon art
Exhibitions: Ladies of the Night; Victoria Rivers: Neon/Fabric Construction; Electro-Kinetic Box Art. (1991) 10th Anniversary Exhibition
Publications: Transformer, quarterly
Activities: Classes for adults; lectures open to public; concerts; gallery talks; tours; original objects of art lent to motion picture sets & plays; book traveling exhibition; originates travelings exhibitions; museum shop sells books, magazines, original art, reproductions, prints, slides, electronic jewelry & posters

M **NATURAL HISTORY MUSEUM OF LOS ANGELES COUNTY,** 900 Exposition Blvd, 90007. Tel 213-744-3466; FAX 213-746-2249. *Pres Bd of Governors* Ed Harrison; *Dir* Dr Craig C Black; *Chief of Exhib* Jim Olson
Open Tues - Sun 10 AM - 5 PM, cl Mon, Thanksgiving, Christmas & New Year's Day. Admis adults $5, sr citizens & students 12 - 17 $3.50, children 5 - 12 $2, members & children under 5 free, 1st Tues of each month free. Estab 1913 to collect, exhibit and research collection in history, art and science; now focuses on American history, science and earth science. Average Annual Attendance: 1,400,000. Mem: 11,000; dues $25 - $100; annual meeting in Sept
Income: Financed by county appropriation and private donations
Collections: †American historical works and decorative arts; †California and western paintings and prints; pre-Columbian artifacts
Exhibitions: Permanent exhibits: American History Halls; Chaparral: A Story of Life from Fire; Dinosaur Fossils; Egyptian Mummy; Gem & Mineral Hall; Habitat Halls; Lando Hall of California & Southwest History; Marine Biology Hall; Megamouth; Pre-Columbian Hall; Ralph M Parsons Children's Discovery Center; Ralph M Parsons Insect Zoo; The Ralph W Schreiber Hall of Birds
Publications: Science Bulletin; Contributions in Science; Terra, bi-monthly magazine
Activities: Classes for adults and children; docent training; lectures open to the public, 6 vis lectr per yr; school tours; film program; Saturday workshops; concerts; gallery talks; tours; artmobile; individual and original objects of art lent to recognized museums, educational galleries and similar institutions; lending collection contains 30,000 color reproductions, 8653 native artifacts, 35,670 slides, 5500 small mammals, historical & scientific models; originate traveling exhibitions; museum & sales shops sell books, magazines, original art, reproductions, prints, slides & ethnic art objects

L **Research Library,** 900 Exposition Blvd, 90007. Tel 213-744-3388. *Chief Librn* Donald W McNamee
Open to staff and to the public by appointment for reference only
Library Holdings: Vols 89,472; Per subs 3000; Micro — Reels 472; AV — Slides; Other — Clipping files, exhibition catalogs, memorabilia, pamphlets, photographs, prints
Special Subjects: Anthropology, Archaeology, Photography, Posters

M **OCCIDENTAL COLLEGE,** Weingart & Coons Galleries, 1600 Campus Rd, 90041. Tel 213-259-2749. *Dir* Hendrik Stooker
Open Mon - Fri 9 AM - 4:30 PM. No admis fee. Estab 1938 to acquaint students & visitors with contemporary concerns in the visual arts. Average Annual Attendance: 50,000
Activities: Lect open to public; gallery talks

M **OTIS ART INSTITUTE OF PARSONS SCHOOL OF DESIGN GALLERY,** 2401 Wilshire Blvd, 90057. Tel 213-251-0555; FAX 213-480-0059. *Dir* Anne Ayres
Open Mon - Sat 9 AM - 5 PM. No admis fee. Estab 1954 as a forum for contemporary art. Gallery is flawless white drywall; two rooms measuring 35 x 40 ft each with 16 ft ceilings. Average Annual Attendance: 20,000. Mem: 670; dues $25 and up; meeting May and Dec
Income: Financed by endowment, membership
Collections: Contemporary art
Publications: On Kawara, 2 per yr; posters
Activities: Classes for adults; lect open to public and/or members, 2-3 visiting lectr per yr; gallery talks; individual paintings and original objects of art lent; museum shop sells books, magazines, posters, postcards

L **Library,** 2401 Wilshire Blvd, 90057. Tel 213-251-0560; FAX 213-480-0059. *Dir* Sue Maberry
Open daily 9 AM - 5 PM for student & faculty use; open to public by appointment only; cl weekends. Estab 1918 as a visual arts library
Library Holdings: Vols 35,000; Per subs 250; AV — A-tapes, cassettes, motion pictures, rec 150, slides 25,000, v-tapes 100; Other — Clipping files, exhibition catalogs, original art works, pamphlets, prints, reproductions 2500

A **PLAZA DE LA RAZA CULTURAL CENTER,** 3540 N Mission Rd, 90031-3195. Tel 213-223-2475; FAX 213-223-1804. *Exec Dir* Gema Sandoval; *School Coordr* Janet Carroll
Open 9 AM - 6 PM, Boathouse Gallery open by appointment. No admis fee. Estab 1969 to preserve, promote & present Chicano/Mexican/Latino art & culture & promote new works. Boathouse Gallery houses Plaza's permanent collection of Latino art & also hosts temporary exhibits of the work of Chicano artists. Average Annual Attendance: 10,000. Mem: 100; dues $35 - $500
Income: $800,000 (financed by endowment, mem, city & state appropriation, grants from private & public foundations)
Collections: Permanent collection of works by nationally known Latino visual artists
Exhibitions: (1992) Frank Romero at the Boathouse; Nuevo LA Chicano Visual Arts Exhibit II
Activities: Adult classes in folk arts, dance & music; children classes in music, dance, visual arts, theatre & folk arts; dramatic programs; competitions; retail store sells prints, original art, reproductions & crafts

A **SAVING & PRESERVING ARTS & CULTURAL ENVIRONMENTS,** 1804 N Van Ness, 90028. Tel 213-463-1629. *Dir* Seymour Rosen
Open by appointment only. Estab 1978 for documentation & preservation of folk art environments. Mem: Dues $15 - $250
Collections: Archival material about America's contemporary folk art environments
Activities: Lectures open to public, 6 vis lectrs per yr; gallery talks; tours; lending collection contains 20,000 photographs; originates traveling exhibitions; sales shop sells books, magazines, prints

L **Spaces Library and Archive,** 1804 N Van Ness, 90028. Tel 213-463-1629. *Consultant* Jocelyn Gibbs
Open by appointment only. Estab 1978 to provide reference for scholars, artists, preservations concerned with folk art environments. For lending & reference
Income: Financed by membership, state appropriation, government & private grants
Library Holdings: Vols 300; Per subs 3; AV — A-tapes, slides; Other — Clipping files, exhibition catalogs, manuscripts, memorabilia, photographs, sculpture
Special Subjects: Architecture, Art History, Collages, Constructions, Folk Art, Intermedia, Landscape Architecture, Folk art environments
Collections: Watts Tower Collection - photographs, documentation, archive, letters, clippings, history
Exhibitions: Divine Disorder: Folk Art Environments in California
Publications: Spaces: Notes on America's Folk Art Environments, 3 times per yr
Activities: Lectures open to public, 5 vis lectrs per yr; originate traveling exhibitions

A **SELF HELP GRAPHICS,** 3802 Brooklyn Ave, 90063. Tel 213-264-1259. *Dir* Arturo Urista
Open Tues - Fri 10 AM - 4 PM, Sat 10 AM - 2 PM. Estab 1972 to provide art opportunities for Chicano artists
Exhibitions: (1990) Bacila Hernandes: Group Show

M **SOUTHWEST MUSEUM,** 234 Museum Dr, PO Box 41558, 90041-0558. Tel 213-221-2164; FAX 213-224-8223. *Exec Dir* Dr Thomas Wilson; *Chief Cur* Kathleen Whitaker; *Registrar* Cheri Doyle; *Controller* Reginald D Huntley
Open Tues - Sun 11 AM - 5 PM, cl Mon. Admis adults $4, children $1, students & senior citizens $2. Estab 1907. Average Annual Attendance: 70,000. Mem: 5300; dues $35 & up
Income: $1,360,000 (financed by endowment & mem)
Special Subjects: American Indian Art, American Western Art, Anthropology, Archaeology, Eskimo Art, Ethnology, Mexican Art, Photography, Pre-Columbian Art, Primitive Art, Southwestern Art
Collections: Anthropology & the science of man in the New World; prehistoric,

historical, Spanish Colonial & Mexican provincial arts
Exhibitions: Permanent exhibits of Plains, Northwest Coast, California &
Southwest Indian art & culture, plus 2 changing special exhibitions
Publications: Masterkey, yearly
Activities: Classes for children & adults; docent training; lect; individual paintings
& original objects of art lent to authorized museums
L **Braun Research Library,** 234 Museum Dr, PO Box 41558, 90041-0558. Tel 213-
221-2164; FAX 213-224-8223. *Librn & Dir* Kim Walters
Open Wed - Sat 11 AM - 4:45 PM, cl Sun, Mon & Tues. Estab 1907. For
reference only
Library Holdings: Vols 50,000; Per subs 300; Micro — Cards, fiche, reels; AV —
A-tapes, cassettes, fs, Kodachromes, lantern slides, motion pictures, rec, slides, v-
tapes; Other — Clipping files, exhibition catalogs, framed reproductions,
manuscripts, memorabilia, original art works, pamphlets, photographs, prints,
reproductions
Special Subjects: Man in the New World, Indians of the Western Hemisphere,
Anthropology of the Americas, Western Americana
Collections: George Wharton James's Collection; Joseph Amasa Munk's
Collection; Charles F Lummis's Collection; Frederick Webb Hodge Collection

C **TIMES MIRROR COMPANY,** Times Mirror Square, 90053. Tel 213-237-
3819. *Supv Corporate Admin Serv* Elke G Corley
Annual amount of contributions and grants $100,000; supports museums by
providing funds for acquisitions, constructions and operating (mostly in Southern
California)
Collections: Primarily contemporary art, including works by Picasso, Steinberg,
Tamayo, Helen Frankenthaler, Richard Diebenkorn, Frank Stella, Roy
Lichtenstein & Peter Ellenshaw

UNIVERSITY OF CALIFORNIA, LOS ANGELES
M **Fowler Museum of Cultural History,** 405 Hilgard Ave, 90024-1549. Tel 310-
825-4361; FAX 310-206-7007. *Dir* Dr Christopher B Donnan; *Asst Dir & Cur
Africa, Oceania & Indonesia* Doran H Ross; *Admin Asst* Barbara Underwood;
Cur of Textiles & Folk Art Patricia B Altman; *Consulting Cur of Costumes &
Textiles* Patricia Anawalt; *Registrar* Sarah J Kennington; *Conservator* Robin
Chamberlin; *Photographer* Denis J Nervig; *Collections Mgr* Owen Moore; *Educ
Dir* Betsy Quick; *Exhib Designer* David Mayo; *Publications Dir* Daniel R Brauer;
Librn Judith Herschman
Open Wed - Sun 12 - 5 PM. Estab in 1963 to collect, preserve and make
available for research and exhibition objects and artifacts from cultures
considered to be outside the Western tradition. Changing exhibitions on view
Wed - Sun Noon - 5 PM.
Income: Financed by endowment, state appropriation and private donations
Collections: Archaeological and ethnographic collections; 150,000 objects
primarily from non-Western cultures - Africa, Asia, the Americas, Oceania, The
Near East and parts of Europe
Publications: Exhibition catalogues; filmstrips; monographs; pamphlets; papers;
posters; slide sets
Activities: Satellite Museum Program; Hall Case Program; Early Man Program;
Chumash Indian Program; Publications Program; lect open to public, 1 - 3 vis
lectr per year; seminars; symposia; book traveling exhibitions; originate traveling
exhibitions
M **Grunwald Center for the Graphic Arts,** 405 Hilgard Ave, 90024. Tel 310-825-
3783; FAX 310-206-7572. *Dir* David S Rodes; *Office Mgr* Elizabeth Gumarman;
Dir Educ & Community Develop Cindi Dale; *Assoc Dir & Cur* Cynthia
Burlingham; *Registrar* Susan Melton Lockhart
Open Tues 11 AM - 8 PM, Wed - Fri 11 AM - 5 PM, Sat & Sun 1 - 5 PM, cl
Mon and during Aug. No admis fee. Estab 1956. Gallery serves the university
and public; program is integrated with the University curricula. Average Annual
Attendance: 175,000
Collections: Grunwald Center for the Graphic Arts: 35,000 prints, drawings,
photographs & illustrated books from the 13th through 20th Centuries, including
old master prints & drawings, Frank Lloyd Wight Collection of Japanese Prints,
Tamarind Lithography Archive; Fred Grunwald Collection of Daumier, The
Rudolf L Baumfeld Collection of Landscape Drawings & Prints
Exhibitions: Three exhibitions annually
Publications: Exhibition catalogues; Jasper Johns, French Caricature, The Rudolf
L Baumfeld Collection of Landscape Drawings & Prints
Activities: Gallery talks; tours daily; book traveling exhibitions; originate
traveling exhibitions; museum shop sells books, magazines, original art,
reproductions and various gift items
M **Wight Art Gallery,** 405 Hilgard Ave, 90024-1620. Tel 310-825-1461; FAX 310-
825-1507. *Dir* Henry T Hopkins; *Admin Mgr* Patricia Capps; *Dir Educ &
Community Develop* Cindi Dale; *Cur Exhibit* Elizabeth Shepherd; *Registrar*
Susan Melton Lockhart
Open Tues 11 AM - 8 PM, Wed - Fri 11 AM - 5 PM, Sat & Sun 1 - 5 PM, cl
Mon & during Aug. No admis fee. Estab 1952. Gallery serves the university &
public; program is integrated with the University curricula. Average Annual
Attendance: 175,000
Collections: 300 paintings, including The Willitts J Hole Collection of the Italian,
Spanish, Dutch, Flemish & English schools from the 15th - 19th century;
Franklin D Murphy Sculpture Garden; 70 sculptures from the 19th - 20th
centuries, including Arp, Calder, Lachaise, Lipchitz, Moore, Noguchi, Rodin &
Smith
Exhibitions: Ten exhibitions annually. Architecture & Design: operates in close
conjunction with the Museum of Cultural History, & the Grunwald Center for
the Graphic Arts; drawings, painting, prints & sculpture
Publications: Exhibition catalogues; The Macchiaioli, California Assemblage; Silk
Route & the Diamond Path; Chicano Art
Activities: Gallery talks; tours daily; book traveling exhibitions; originate
traveling exhibitions; museum shop sells books, magazines, reproductions &
various gift items
L **Visual Resource Collection,** Department of Art History, 3239 Dickson Art
Center, 90024-1417. Tel 310-825-3725. *Dir* David Ziegler; *Asst Cur* Martha
Godfrey; *Asst Cur* Susan Rosenfeld
Library Holdings: AV — Fs, slides 260,000

L **Arts Library,** 2250 Dickson Art Center, 90024-1392. Tel 310-825-3817. *Art
Librn* Raymond Reece; *Architecture & Urban Planning Librn* Anne Hartmere;
Film & Television Librn Raymond Soto; *Arts Special Coll Librn* Brigitte
Kueppers
Founded 1952
Library Holdings: Vols 180,000; Per subs 7000; Ephemera files; Micro — Fiche,
reels; Other — Exhibition catalogs, manuscripts, photographs
Special Subjects: Artists' Books, Film Studiopapers, Iconography, Leonardo da
Vince, Photo Still Files, Press Kits, Renaissance, Scripts
Collections: †One of four copies of Princeton's Index of Christian Art; †Elmer
Belt Library of Vinciana; Judith A Hoffberg Collection of Bookworks and
Artists' Publications
L **Elmer Belt Library of Vinciana,** 405 Hilgard Ave, 90024-1392. Tel 310-825-
3817, 206-5425.
Open by appointment Mon - Fri 9 AM - 5 PM. Estab 1961
Income: Financed by state appropriation
Library Holdings: Vols 9000; original documents; Other — Clipping files,
exhibition catalogs, framed reproductions, manuscripts, original art works,
pamphlets, photographs, reproductions
Special Subjects: Architecture, Art History, Graphic Arts, Painting - French,
Painting - Italian, Painting - Italian, Sculpture, Leonardo da Vinci
Collections: Special collection of †rare books, †incunabula, and related materials
in Renaissance studies, with a focus on †Leonardo da Vinci, his manuscripts,
milieu, art and thought

UNIVERSITY OF SOUTHERN CALIFORNIA
M **Fisher Gallery,** 823 Exposition Blvd, 90089-0292. Tel 213-740-4561; FAX 213-
740-7676. *Dir* Dr Selma Holo; *Asst to Dir* Kay Allen; *Preparator* Scott
Chamberlin; *Exhib Coordr* Jennifer Jaskowiak
Open Tues - Fri noon - 5 PM, except for special exhibitions. No admis fee. Estab
1939 as the art museum of the University. Fisher Gallery consists of three rooms,
for changing exhibitions. Average Annual Attendance: 10,000
Income: Financed by endowment
Collections: Galleries house the permanent collections of paintings of 17th
century Dutch, Flemish and Italian, 18th century British, 19th century French
and American landscape and portraiture schools; Elizabeth Holmes Fisher
Collection; Armand Hammer Collection
Exhibitions: Keepers of the Flame: The Unofficial Artists of Leningrad (1993)
Israeli Contemporary Art; Los Angeles Art Festival; Edgar Ewing; collaboration
with Huntington Museum on London Types
Publications: Exhibition catalogs, three annually
Activities: Lectures open to the public; concerts; gallery talks; tours; awards;
individual paintings & original objects of art lent; lending collection contains 200
original prints, 400 paintings, 15 sculpture; originate traveling exhibitions
L **Helen Topping Architecture & Fine Arts Library,** Watt Hall 4, 90089-0182. Tel
213-740-1956. *Head Librn* Amy Navratil Ciccone; *Reference Librn* Deborah
Barlow; *Slide Cur* Howard Smith
Open Mon - Thurs 10 AM - 10 PM, Fri 10 AM - 5 PM, Sun 1 - 8 PM, cl Sat,
summer hrs Mon - Fri 10 AM - 5 PM. Estab 1925 to provide undergraduate and
graduate level students and the teaching and research faculty materials in the
areas of architecture and fine arts needed to achieve their objectives. Branch
library in the central library system is supported by the University, lending
library. Circ 65,000
Income: Financed by University funds
Purchases: $95,000
Library Holdings: Vols 61,000; Per subs 260; architectural drawings 1000;
Micro — Reels; AV — Slides 210,000, v-tapes 25; Other — Exhibition catalogs,
pamphlets
Special Subjects: Architecture, Art History, Artists' books, Fine Arts Criticism
L **Cinema-Television Library & Archives of Performing Arts,** University Library,
90089-0182. Tel 213-740-3387; FAX 213-749-1221. *Head Librn* Anne G
Schlosser
Open academic semester 8:30 AM - 10 PM. No admis fee. Estab 1960
Library Holdings: Vols 18,000; Per subs 225; Micro — Cards, reels; AV — A-
tapes, cassettes, rec, v-tapes; Other — Clipping files, manuscripts, memorabilia,
pamphlets
Special Subjects: Film, Video
Collections: Film & television: scripts, stills, posters, production records,
correspondence

A **FREDERICK R WEISMAN ART FOUNDATION,** 275 N Tarolwood, 90025.
Tel 310-277-5321; FAX 310-277-5075. *Registrar & Cur* Eddie Fumasi
Estab 1982 as a non-profit foundation focusing on exhibition, workshop & award
programs
Income: Financed by endowment
Collections: Contmporary Art: Installation Work; Mixed Media; Painting;
Sculpture; Works on Paper
Publications: Workshop publication, semi-annual
Activities: Art purchase & curatorial achievement awards distributed annually to
museum collections & professionals involved in contemporary art

C **WELLS FARGO & CO,** History Museum, 333 S Grand Ave, 90071. Tel 213-
253-7166. *Cur* Alexandra Fanning; *Asst Cur* Lacinda Luther
Open Mon - Fri 9 AM - 5 PM. Museum established to demonstrate impact of
Wells Fargo on California & American West 6500 sq ft; approx 1000 objects on
display. Average Annual Attendance: 30,000
Income: Financed by private funds
Collections: An authentic 19th century Concord stagecoach; a two-pound gold
nugget; Dorsey Gold collection of gold quartz ore; original Spanish language
documents giving Los Angeles its city status in 1835
Exhibitions: Staging; mining; express; banking; South California
Publications: Various publications concerning Wells Fargo in US history
Activities: Dramatic programs; tours & off-site presentations; lectures open to
public; museum shop sells books, reproductions of memorabilia & prints

MENDOCINO

A **MENDOCINO ART CENTER**, Gallery, 45200 Little Lake St, PO Box 765, 95460. Tel 707-937-5818. *Exec Coordr* Robert Avery; *Gallery Mgr* Marty Roderick
Open Mon - Thurs 10 AM - 4 PM, Fri - Sun 10 AM - 5 PM, winter hours daily 10 AM - 5 PM. No admis fee. Estab 1959 as a rental-sales gallery for exhibition and sales of member work; also to sponsor traveling and museum exhibits. Two major gallery rooms, 1 gallery room available for rental of one-man shows. Average Annual Attendance: 25,000. Mem: 1000; dues $35
Collections: Graphics, paintings and sculpture
Publications: Arts & Entertainment, monthly
Activities: Classes for adults and children; docent training; lectures open to the public, 4 - 10 vis lectr per yr; concerts; competitions; scholarships; individual paintings and original objects of art lent to businesses and public places; sales shop sells books, original art, reproductions, prints and crafts
L **Library,** 45200 Little Lake St, PO Box 765, 95460. Tel 707-937-5818.
Open Tues - Sat 11 AM - 2 PM. Estab 1975 to provide members with access to art books and magazines. Lending library for members of Art Center only. Circ 1350 books & 18 magazines
Income: Financed by donations & membership
Library Holdings: Vols 2500; Per subs 4; Picture File; Other — Prints, reproductions

MISSION HILLS

A **SAN FERNANDO VALLEY HISTORICAL SOCIETY**, 10940 Sepulveda Blvd, 91345. Tel 818-365-7810. *Cur* Lori Underwood
Open by appointment. No admis fee. Estab 1943. The Society manages the Andres Pico Adobe (1834) for the Los Angeles City Department of Recreation and Parks, where they house their collection. Mem: Dues; active, sustaining and organization $15, Life $100
Income: Financed by membership and donations
Collections: Historical material; Indian artifacts; paintings; costumes; decorative arts; manuscripts
Exhibitions: Permanent & temporary exhibitions
Activities: Lect; films; guided tours
L **Library,** 10940 Sepulveda Blvd, PO Box 7039, 91346. Tel 818-365-7810.
Open by appointment. Estab 1970
Income: Financed by members and gifts
Library Holdings: Vols 3650; AV — Cassettes; Other — Clipping files, manuscripts, memorabilia, original art works, pamphlets, photographs, prints
Collections: Citrus; Communities; Historical landmarks; Olive; Pioneers; San Fernando Mission; San Fernando Valley
Exhibitions: Ethnic contributions to valley history (for local school dist); 200 years valley agriculture (for SFV Fair), Valley history (local malls)
Publications: The Valley, monthly newsletter

MONTEREY

M **CASA AMESTI**, 516 Polk St, 93940. Tel 408-372-8173. *Pres* Luis Senton
Open Sat & Sun 2 - 4 PM, cl 2 wks July. Admis $1, children & members no charge. Bequeathed to the National Trust in 1953 by Mrs Frances Adler Elkins. It is an 1833 adobe structure reflecting phases of the history and culture of the part of California owned by Mexico, after the period of Spanish missions and before development of American influences from the Eastern seaboard. It is a prototype of what is now known as Monterey style architecture. The Italian-style gardens within the high adobe walls were designed by Mrs. Elkins, an interior designer, and her brother, Chicago architect David Adler. The furnishings, largely European, collected by Mrs. Elkins are displayed in a typical 1930's interior. The property is a National Trust historic house. The Old Capital Club, a private organization, leases, occupies and maintains the property for social and educational purposes
Collections: Elkins Collection of largely European furnishings
Activities: Monterey History and Art Association volunteers provide interpretive services for visitors on weekends

A **MONTEREY HISTORY AND ART ASSOCIATION**, 5 Custom House Plaza, 93940. Tel 408-372-2608. *Pres* John McCune
No admis fee. Estab 1931. The Association owns the 1845 Casa Serrano Adobe, the 1865 Doud House, the 1845 Fremont Adobe, the Mayo Hayes O'Donnell Library & the newly constructed Stanton Center - Monterey's Maritime Museum & History Center. The Association celebrates the birthday of Monterey (June 3, 1770) with the Merienda each year on the Sat nearest that date. The Association commemorates the landing at Monterey by Commodore John Drake Sloat in 1846. Mem: 1800; dues individual life membership $500, sustaining couple $75, sustaining single $50, couple $25, single $15, junior $1
Income: Financed by memberships, donations & fund raising activities
Collections: †Costumes, manuscripts and paintings, sculpture, †antique furniture, †books, †photographs
Exhibitions: Permanent & temporary exhibitions; Fourth Grade History & Art Contest
Publications: Noticias Del Puerto De Monterey, quarterly bulletin
Activities: Guided tours; competitions
M **Maritime Museum of Monterey,** 5 Custom House Plaza, 93942. Tel 408-375-2553. *Dir* Donna Penwell
Open Tues - Fri 1 - 4 PM, Sat & Sun 2 - 4 PM, Sept 1 - June 15 afternoons only, cl Mon and National holidays. Admis adults $5, children 3 - 17 $3, children 6 - 11 $2, under 6 free. Estab 1971, moved 1992 into new facility along waterfront. Maritime related artifacts & artwork; features operating light from Point Sur Lighthouse. Average Annual Attendance: 12,000. Mem: 1800; dues $30 - $50; annual meeting in Sept
Collections: Marine Artifacts, ship models, paintings, photographs, Fresnel First Order Lens from Point Sur, California (on loan from US Coast Guard)
Exhibitions: Permanent and temporary exhibitions
Activities: Lect open to public, 12 vis lectrs per year; gallery talks; tours; competitions with awards; museum shop sells books, prints, original art, reproductions & gift items

L **Library,** 155 Van Buren, PO Box 805, 93942. Tel 408-372-2608. *Librn* Martha Bently
Open Wed, Fri, Sat & Sun 1:30 - 3:30 PM. No admis fee. Estab 1971. Open for research on the premises
Library Holdings: Vols 2500; Per subs 2; Local History archive; Other — Manuscripts, memorabilia, original art works, photographs, prints
Special Subjects: Maritime history
Publications: Brochure of Museum with map

A **MONTEREY PENINSULA MUSEUM OF ART ASSOCIATION**, 559 Pacific St, 93940. Tel 408-372-7591, 372-5477; FAX 408-372-5680. *Pres* Ann T Nielsen; *VPres* William Hyland; *VPres* Jane Campbell; *Treas* Susanne Holm; *Dir* Jo Farb Hernandez; *Art Dir* Marc D'Estout; *Museum on Wheels Dir* Laura Temple; *Asst Dir Finances Admin* Buzz Hoever; *Development Dir* Donna Kneeland; *Asst Dir Museum on Wheels* Sandra S Caldewey
Open Tues - Sat 10 AM - 4 PM, Sun 1 - 4 PM, cl Mon, New Years, Christmas & Thanksgiving. No admis fee, donations requested. Estab 1959 to perpetuate knowledge of and interest in the arts; to encourage a spirit of fellowship among artists and to bring together the artist and the community at large. It recognizes the need for the collection, preservation and exhibition of art works, especially the best of those done in the area. The Frank Work Gallery (30 x 60 ft) houses temporary exhibitions; Leonard Heller Memorial Gallery, shows the William Ritschel Collection; Maurine Church Coburn Gallery, temporary exhibitions of painting, graphics & photography; five additional galleries which are used to show permanent collection as well as temporary exhibitions. Average Annual Attendance: 45,000. Mem: 2700; dues from $25 - $1000; annual meeting in July
Income: Financed by endowment, memberships and fund-raising functions
Collections: Armin Hansen Collection; †American art; †Asian & Pacific; †international folk ethnic & tribal arts; †photography & graphics; regional art, past & present; William Ritschel Collection
Exhibitions: Juried exhibitions
Publications: Newsletter, bi-monthly
Activities: Classes for adults & children; docent training; lect open to public; concerts; dramatic programs; gallery talks; tours; in service training for teachers; outreach program; scholarships; artmobile; Museum on Wheels teaches folk craft classes in schools; book traveling exhibitions 1 per year; originate traveling exhibitions; museum shop sells books, magazines, original art, reproductions, prints, & museum replicas & folk art objects

L **MONTEREY PUBLIC LIBRARY**, Art & Architecture Dept, 625 Pacific St, 93940. Tel 408-646-3932. *Dir* Paula Simpson
Open Mon - Thurs 9 AM - 9 PM; Fri 9 AM - 6 PM; Sat 9 AM - 5 PM; Sun 1 - 5 PM. Estab 1849
Income: Financed by membership and city appropriation
Purchases: $750,000
Library Holdings: Vols 10,000; Per subs 12; Micro — Reels; AV — Cassettes, motion pictures, rec, slides; Other — Clipping files, manuscripts, original art works, pamphlets, photographs, reproductions
Special Subjects: Local history
Collections: Adler; Elkins Collection on Architecture and Interior Design, especially 17th - 19th century English, Italian and French; Raiquiel; Robert Stanton

M **SAN CARLOS CATHEDRAL**, 550 Church St, 93940. Tel 408-373-2628. *Rector* Joseph Occhiuto
Open daily 8 AM - 6 PM. No admis fee. Built in 1770, now a branch of the Monterey Diocese. The art museum is housed in the 1794 Royal Presidio Chapel
Collections: Spanish religious paintings and sculpture of the 18th and 19th century
Activities: Guided tours

MONTEREY PARK

M **EAST LOS ANGELES COLLEGE**, Vincent Price Gallery, 1301 Brooklyn Ave, 91754. Tel 213-265-8841. *Dir* Thomas Silliman
Estab 1958 as a institutional art gallery serving the East Los Angeles area
Collections: Includes art from Africa, Peruvian and Mexican artifacts dating from 300 B C, North American Indian Art; important works from the Renaissance to the present day; Leonard Baskin; Daumier; Delacroix; Durer; Garvarni; Hiroshige I; Rico Lebrun; Maillol; Picasso; Piranesi; Redon; Utrillo; Howard Warshaw; Anuskiewicz; Bufano; Rouault; Tamayo

MORAGA

M **SAINT MARY'S COLLEGE OF CALIFORNIA**, Hearst Art Gallery, PO Box 5110, 94575. Tel 510-631-4379. *Dir* Ann Harlow; *Cur* Marvin Schenck
Open Wed - Sun 11 AM - 4:30 PM, cl Mon & Tues. No admis fee. Estab 1977 to exhibit a variety of the visual arts for the benefit of college students, staff and members of surrounding communities. Maintains two rooms with connecting rampway (1640 sq ft) for temporary exhibitions, William Keith Room for permanent collection. Average Annual Attendance: 10,000. Mem: 250; dues donor $50 & up, individual $20, family $30
Income: $235,000 (financed by college, donations, grants, & earned income)
Collections: Paintings by William Keith (1838-1911) & other California landscapes; icons; medieval sculpture; †thematic print collection
Publications: Exhibition catalogues, 1 - 2 per yr
Activities: Lect open to public, 5-8 vis lectrs per yr; gallery talks; tours; book traveling exhibitions, 1 - 2 per yr; loans to other museums

NEWHALL

M LOS ANGELES COUNTY MUSEUM OF NATURAL HISTORY, William S Hart Museum, William S Hart Park, 24151 San Fernando Rd, 91321. Tel 805-254-4584. *Coll Mgr* Katherine Child Debs; *Dir Admin* Carol Sandmeier
Open winter Wed - Fri 10 AM - 1 PM Sat - Sun 11 AM - 4 PM; summer mid-June to mid-Sept Wed - Sun 11 AM - 4 PM. No admis fee. Estab through the bequest of William S Hart (1946) and opened 1958 for use as a public park & museum. The retirement home of William S Hart is maintained as it was during his lifetime, His extensive collection of Western art is on display throughout the house. Average Annual Attendance: 250,000. Mem: 250; dues $15; meetings 3rd Mon of every month
Income: Financed by county appropriation & private donations
Collections: Charles Cristadoro; Sculptures (bronze ivory); Clarence Ellsworth, watercolor & oil; James M Flagg; oils, watercolors, pencil drawings; Robert L Lambdin, oils; Remington, oils, watercolor; Charles M Russell, bronzes, oils, watercolors, gouache, pen & ink; Charles Schreyvogel, oil; Joe De Yong, oils, watercolors
Activities: Classes for Adults; docent training; school outreach program; lectures open to members, 5 vis lectr per yr; tours; gallery talks; museum shop sells books, videotapes, souvenirs

NEWPORT BEACH

M NEWPORT HARBOR ART MUSEUM, 850 San Clemente Dr, 92660. Tel 714-759-1122. *Dir* Michael Botwinick; *Chief Cur* Bruce Guenther; *Dir Educ* Ellen Breitman; *Assoc Dir* Jane Piasecki; *Public Relations* Maxine Gaiber; *Dir Design & Facility* Brian Gray; *Registrar* Betsy Severance; *Dir of Development* Margie Shackelford
Open Tues - Sun 10 AM - 5 PM, cl Mon. Admis adults $4, student, sr citizen, military $2, groups of 10 $2, children 6 - 17 $1, children under 6 free, Tues free. Estab 1962 as a museum of the Art of our Time serving Orange County & Southern California. Building completed in 1977 contains four galleries of various sizes; 5000; 1600; 1200; 500 sq ft plus lobby & sculpture garden area. Average Annual Attendance: 100,000. Mem: 5500; dues business council $500, patron $150, general mem $35, student $25
Income: $1,500,000 (financed by special events, mem, government grants, private sector, sales from restaurant & bookstore)
Purchases: $100,000
Collections: Collections of contemporary American art; California artists
Exhibitions: Robert Morris: Works of the Eighties; Interpretive Link: Abstract Surrealism into Abstract Expressionism; Second Newport Biennial; New California Artists; Flemish Expressions: 20th Century Representational Painting; Chris Burden: A 20-Year Survey; John McCracken; Heroic Stance; New English Sculpture; Calarts Artists; Figurative Fifties: New York Figurative Expressionism; LA Pop in the Sixties; Gunther Forg: Paintings, Sculpture, Installation; Objectives: The New Sculpture; Erik Bulatov; Charles Ray; Tony Cragg Sculpture 1975 - 1990; Typologies; Third Newport Biennial: Mapping Histories
Publications: Bimonthly calendar; exhibition catalogs; posters
Activities: Docent training; in-service training sessions for teachers, docent tours for school & adult groups; lectures series, special guest lectures & meet-the-artist programs; gallery talks; creative art workshops, concerts & performances; film & video programs; individual paintings and original objects of art lent to qualified art museums; lending collection contains original prints; paintings and sculptures; traveling exhibitions organized and circulated; museum shop sells books, magazines, original art
L Library, 850 San Clemente Dr, 92660. Tel 714-759-1122. *Librn* Ruth Roe
Open for reference by appointment
Income: Financed by Museum
Library Holdings: Vols 5000; Per subs 11; AV — A-tapes, cassettes, slides, v-tapes; Other — Clipping files, exhibition catalogs
Special Subjects: Contemporary art

NORTH HOLLYWOOD

L WARNER BROS RESEARCH LIBRARY, 5200 Lankershim Blvd, No 100, 91601. Tel 818-506-8693; FAX 818-506-8079. *Dir* Anne G Schlosser; *Research Librn* Barbara Poland
Open Mon - Fri 9 AM - 6 PM. Estab 1929 for picture & story research
Income: Financed by endowment
Library Holdings: Vols 35,000; Per subs 85; Other — Clipping files, pamphlets, photographs
Special Subjects: Costume Design & Construction, Fashion Arts, Film, Interior Design, Military, Travel & Description, Western History
Collections: †Art & Architecture History; †Costumes; †Interior Design; †Military & Police; †Travel & Description

NORTHRIDGE

M CALIFORNIA STATE UNIVERSITY, NORTHRIDGE, Art Galleries, 18111 Nordhoff St, 91330. Tel 818-885-2156; FAX 818-885-4545. *Dir* Louise Lewis; *Exhib Coordr* Ann Burroughs
Open Mon & Sat noon - 4 PM; Tues - Fri 10 AM - 4 PM. No admis fee. Estab 1971 to serve the needs of the four art departments & to provide a source of cultural enrichment for the university & the community at large. Exhibitions in Main & South Galleries have average duration of four weeks. North Gallery for weekly MA candidate solo exhibitions. Average Annual Attendance: 35,000. Mem: Arts Council for CSUN 300; dues $25; annual meeting May
Income: $30,000 (financed by city & state appropriation, community support organizations)
Exhibitions: Nomads of the Niger; Images of the Barrio; Michael C McMillen: The Pavilion of Rain; Helen Hardin: Art as Spirit; Icons of the Divine: Lisa Lyon; Body Parts: Ilene Segalove; Women Redefining Power: International Graphics; International Chair Design; Jean Cocteau: Personalities; Artquest 87; Variations III: Emerging Artists in Southern California; Chicana Art; The

Monumental Print; Dreamtime: Art of the Australian Aborigine; California Art Pottery 1895-1920; Beverly Naidus: Activating the Audience; The Art of Fly Tying
Publications: Exhibition catalogs, 2 per yr
Activities: Docent training; 2 - 3 art performances per yr; lectures open to the public, 5-7 vis lectr per year; gallery talks; tours; competitions; sales shop sells books, magazines, original art, prints, reproductions, slides, folk art objects & gifts

OAKLAND

L CALIFORNIA COLLEGE OF ARTS AND CRAFTS LIBRARY, 5212 Broadway & College Aves, 94618. Tel 510-653-8118, Ext 176; FAX 510-655-3541. *Dir Libraries* Vanroy R Burdick; *Librn* Nina Saab; *Librn* Michael Lordi
Open Mon - Thurs 8 AM - 9 PM, Fri 8 AM - 5 PM, Sat 11 AM - 6 PM PM. Estab 1907 to support the studio & academic requirements for BFA, BArchit & MFA; Branch Library in architecture & design
Income: $266,597 (financed by tuition)
Purchases: $60,000
Library Holdings: Vols 34,000; Per subs 240; Micro — Reels; AV — Rec, slides 100,000; Other — Clipping files, exhibition catalogs
Special Subjects: Aesthetics, Architecture, Art History, Ceramics, Drawings, Film, Furniture, Glass, Graphic Design, Illustration, Industrial Design, Interior Design, Jewelry, Metalwork, Photography
Collections: Jo Sinel Collection of pioneering work in industrial design

M CREATIVE GROWTH ART CENTER, 355 24th St, 94612. Tel 510-836-2340. *Executive Dir* Irene Ward Brydon; *Studio Mgr* Ron Kilgore; *Gallery Mgr* Bonnie Haight; *Business Mgr* Timothy Sauer
Open Mon - Fri 10 AM - 4 PM. No admis fee. Estab 1974 to professionally exhibit the art of Creative Growth clients & art work by emerging & well-known artists. Average Annual Attendance: 4000
Income: $500,000
Collections: Permanent collection includes art works in all media on traditional & contemporary subjects
Exhibitions: Individual & group shows; 9 exhibitions held per year
Publications: Creative Growth Art Center newsletter, 3-4 issues per year
Activities: Docent programs; lect open to public, 6-8 vis lectr per year; competitions with awards; scholarships & fels offered; retail store sells prints, original art, reproductions

M EAST BAY ASIAN LOCAL DEVELOPMENT CORP, Asian Resource Gallery, 310 Eighth St, Suite 309, 94607. Tel 510-763-2970. *Admin Coordr* Ann G Yee
Open Mon - Fri 8 AM - 6 PM. No admis fee. Estab 1983 to promote Asian art & Asian artists
Income: $3000
Collections: Collection of photographs, paintings, mixed media; history exhibits on Asian groups from China, Japan & Korea
Exhibitions: (1989) Calvin Yau Ching; Santago Bose, wood crates. (1991) Photo Exhibition Asian Groups

L LANEY COLLEGE LIBRARY, Art Section, 900 Fallon St, 94607. Tel 510-464-3500. *Art Librn* Shirley Coaston
Open daily 8 AM - 8:45 PM. Estab 1954. Circ 78,000
Library Holdings: Vols 70,000; Per subs 300; AV — A-tapes, cassettes, fs, Kodachromes, lantern slides, motion pictures, rec, slides, v-tapes; Other — Prints, reproductions
Exhibitions: Paintings, sculpture, ceramics, fabrics, photography by students, faculty and community persons

M MILLS COLLEGE, Art Gallery, 5000 MacArthur Blvd, 94613. Tel 510-430-2164; FAX 510-430-3314. *Dir* Dr Katherine B Crum; *Asst Dir* Tim Mosman
Open Tues - Sat 11 AM - 4 PM, Sun noon - 4 PM. No admis fee. Estab 1925 to show contemporary and traditional painting, sculpture, and ceramics, exhibitions from permanent and loan collections. Gallery is Spanish colonial architecture & has 5500 sq ft main exhibition space, with skylight full length of gallery. Average Annual Attendance: 24,000
Income: Financed by college funds
Collections: †Regional collection of California paintings, drawings & prints; †extensive collection of European & American prints, drawings & ceramics; †Asian & Guatemalan textiles; †photographs
Publications: Annual bulletin; exhibition catalogs
Activities: Lect open to the public, 3 vis lectr per yr; gallery talks

NATIONAL ALLIANCE FOR MEDIA ARTS & CULTURE (NAMAC)
For further information, see National and Regional Organizations

M OAKLAND MUSEUM, Art Dept, 1000 Oak St, 94607. Tel 510-238-3005; FAX 510-238-2258. *Deputy Cur Art* Harvey L Jones; *Sr Cur Prints & Photographs* Therese Heyman; *Asst Cur* Kenneth R Trapp; *Registrar* Arthur Monroe; *Chief Cur Art* Philip Linhares; *Cur Spec Projects* Paul Tomidy
Open Wed - Sat 10 AM - 5 PM, Sun 12 - 7 PM, cl Mon, Tues, New Year's, Thanksgiving and Christmas. No admis fee. The Oakland Museum comprises three departments: Natural Sciences (formerly the Snow Museum of Natural History, founded 1922); History (formerly the Oakland Public Museum, founded 1910); and the Art Department (formerly the Oakland Art Museum, founded 1916). Internationally recognized as a brilliant contribution to urban museum design. The Oakland Museum occupies a four-square-block, three storied site on the south shore of Lake Merritt. Designed by Kevin Roche, John Dinkeloo and Associates, the Museum is a three-tiered complex of exhibition galleries, with surrounding gardens, pools, courts and lawns, constructed so that the roof of each level becomes a garden and a terrace for the one above. The Art Department has a large hall with 20 small exhibition bays for the permanent collection and a gallery for one-person or group shows as well as the Oakes Observatory and Gallery. Average Annual Attendance: 500,000

Income: Financed by city funds, private donations & Oakland Museum Association

Collections: Paintings, sculpture, prints, illustrations, photographs, artists dealing with California subjects, in a range that includes sketches and paintings by early artist-explorers; Gold Rush genre pictures; massive Victorian landscapes; examples of the California Decorative Style, Impressionist, Post-Impressionist, Abstract Expressionist, and other contemporary works

Exhibitions: Traveling exhibitions & special exhibitions

Publications: The Museum of California, bi-monthly

Activities: Docent training; lectures for members only; tours; awards; individual paintings and original objects of art lent to other museums and galleries for specific exhibitions; originate traveling exhibitions; museum shop sells books, magazines, reproductions, prints, slides & jewelry

L **Library,** 1000 Oak St, 94607-4892. Tel 510-238-3005; FAX 510-238-2258. *Chief Cur Art* Philip Linhares
Library maintained on archives of California art and artists
Income: Financed by city and state appropriation
Library Holdings: Per subs 19; Bk vols & catalogues 7000; Other — Clipping files, photographs

L **OAKLAND PUBLIC LIBRARY,** Art, Music & Recreation Section, Main Library, 125 14th St, 94612. Tel 510-273-3178. *Dir Library Servs* Martin Gomez; *Sr Librn in Charge* Gene Blinn
Open Mon - Thurs 10 AM - 8:30 PM, Fri & Sat 10 AM - 5:30 PM, cl Sun & holidays. Library cooperates with the Oakland Museum and local groups
Purchases: $30,000
Library Holdings: Vols 1,000,000; Per subs 2745; Posters; AV — A-tapes, cassettes, rec; Other — Framed reproductions, reproductions
Collections: Picture Collections
Publications: Museum catalogs

M **PRO ARTS,** 461 Ninth St, 94607. Tel 510-763-4361. *Exec Dir* Michael M Floss
Open Wed & Thurs noon - 6 PM, Fri & Sat 10 AM - 5 PM. Estab 1974 as a contemporary art exhibition space for static & non-static works, non-profit. Store-front gallery located in restored Old Oakland, 2500 sq ft, 14 ft ceiiings. Average Annual Attendance: 20,000. Mem: 1300; annual dues $25 & up
Exhibitions: (1992) Pro Arts Annual

A **SURFACE DESIGN ASSOCIATION, INC,** PO Box 20799, 94620. Tel 415-567-1992; FAX 510-567-1992. *Pres* Pat Mansfield; *VPres* Theodora Zehner; *Treas* Beverly Semmens; *Ed Surface Design Journal* Charles Talley
Estab 1976. Mem: 2000; dues regular $45, students $25, outside USA $5
Income: Financed by membership
Publications: SDA News, newsletter quarterly, Surface Design Journal, quarterly
Activities: Lect open to public; competitions with cash prize; scholarships & fels offered; originate traveling exhibitions

OJAI

A **OJAI VALLEY ART CENTER,** 113 S Montgomery, PO Box 331, 93024. Tel 805-646-0117. *Pres* Arthur Balchen; *Mgr* Teri Mettala
Open Tues- Sat noon - 4 PM. No admis fee. Estab 1936 to foster all art disciplines in community. Gallery is 40 x 50 ft, high ceilings, with a large hanging area. Average Annual Attendance: 52,000 - 60,000. Mem: 400; dues family $25, adult $10; annual meeting in Jan
Income: Financed by membership, class and special event fees
Exhibitions: Twelve monthly exhibitions; Annual Watercolor Competition
Publications: Newsletter, monthly; Ojai Review, quarterly
Activities: Classes for adults & children; dramatic programs; lectures open to public; concerts; gallery talks; competitions with awards; scholarships offered; museum shop sells books, magazines & original art

OXNARD

M **CARNEGIE ART MUSEUM,** 424 S C St, 93030. Tel 805-385-8157. *Dir* Andrew Voth; *Cur* Mary S Bellah
Open Thurs, Fri & Sat 10 AM - 5 PM, Sun 1 - 5 PM. Admis $2 donation suggested. Estab 1980 to serve as a city museum and to house permanent collection. 5000 sq ft of gallery space. Average Annual Attendance: 15,000
Income: $190,000 (financed by endowment, city appropriation, city & non-profit support)
Purchases: $8500
Collections: †California Painters: 1920 to present; Art in Public Places Program
Exhibitions: Sacha Moldovan, Russian Expressionist
Publications: Master of the Miniature: The Art of Robert Olszewski; Municipal Art Collection Catalogue; Quechuan Rug Catalogue; Theodor Lukits Catalogue
Activities: Classes for adults & children; docent programs; lect open to public, 6 vis lectrs per year; book traveling exhibitions, 4 per year; originate traveling exhibitions that circulate to other US & foreign museums

PACIFIC GROVE

A **PACIFIC GROVE ART CENTER,** 568 Lighthouse Ave, PO Box 633, 93950. Tel 408-375-2208. *Office Mgr* Connie Pearlstein; *Preparator* Michael Kainer; *Co-Dir* Barry Masteller
Open Tues - Sat noon - 5 PM; Sun 1 - 4 PM. No admis fee. Estab 1969 to promote the arts & encourage the artists of the Monterey Peninsula & California. Four galleries consist of 6000 sq ft of exhibition space, showing traditional & contemporary fine art & photography; galleries are available for classes & lectures. Average Annual Attendance: 25,000. Mem: 550; dues business & club $100, family $25, single $20, annual meeting in Nov
Income: Financed by grants, donations & income from lease of studio space
Collections: †Photography; †painting
Exhibitions: Multiple exhibits every 6 weeks throughout year
Publications: Monthly newsletter

Activities: Educ dept; classes for adults & children; dramatic programs; concerts; lect open to public, 6 - 12 vis lectr per yr; concerts; gallery talks; tours; competitions; sales shop sells books, original art, prints, photos, jewelry, t-shirts & frames

PALM SPRINGS

M **PALM SPRINGS DESERT MUSEUM, INC,** 101 Museum Dr, PO Box 2288, 92263. Tel 619-325-7186; FAX 619-327-5069. *Dir* Fritz Frauchiger; *Assoc Dir & Dir Educ* Dr Janice Lyle; *Cur Natural Science* James W Cornett; *Cur Art* Katherine Plake Hough; *Dir Performing Arts* Dr Dale Hearth
Open Sept - June Tues - Fri 10 AM - 4 PM, Sat & Sun 10 AM - 5 PM, cl Mon. Admis adults $4, students & children 6-17 $2, members & children under 6 free; Free admis the first Tues of every month Sept-June. Estab & inc 1938, includes Annenberg Theater. Average Annual Attendance: 160,000. Mem: 4000; dues life $5000, President's Circle $1000, patron $500, business & supporting $100, Active/Dual $50, individual $35
Income: Financed by private funds
Collections: Interpretation of natural sciences of the desert; 19th-20th century American painting, prints & sculpture specializing in California artists; Southwestern Native American art; William Holden Collection
Exhibitions: Approx 20 per year
Publications: Calendar of Events, bi-monthly; special exhibiton catalogs each season
Activities: Classes for adults & children; dramatic programs; docent training; lectures open to public, 20 vis lectr per yr; concerts; gallery talks; tours; individual paintings & original objects of art loaned to museums; originate traveling exhibitions; two museum shops sell books, magazines, original art, reproductions, slides, jewelry & cards (one shop annex in downtown Palm Springs)

L **Library,** 101 Museum Dr, PO Box 2288, 92263. Tel 619-325-7186; FAX 619-327-5069. *Dir* Fritz Frauchiger; *Cur* Katherine Hough; *Education* Dr Janice Lyle; *Natural Sciences* James W Cornett; *Assoc Dir & Dir Educ* Dr Janice Lyle
Open for reference only; art & natural science books available for use on premises by members
Library Holdings: Vols 6000; Per subs 82; Other — Photographs
Special Subjects: American Indian Art, American Western Art, Anthropology, Archaeology, Art Education, Art History, Bronzes, Folk Art, Graphic Arts, History of Art & Archaeology, Islamic Art, Mexican Art, Mexican Art, Mixed Media, Oriental Art, Photography, Porcelain, Portraits, Pottery, Pre-Columbian Art, Printmaking, Religious Art
Publications: Exhib Catalogues

PALO ALTO

A **PALO ALTO CULTURAL CENTER,** 1313 Newell Rd, 94303. Tel 415-329-2366; FAX 415-326-6165. *Dir* Linda Craighead; *Volunteer Coordr* Shiela Pastore; *Cur* Signe Mayfield; *Workshop Supv* Gary Clarien; *Office Mgr* Jean Dickson; *Children's Prog* Jamey Ronzone
Open Tues - Sat 10 AM - 5 PM, Tues - Thurs evening 7 - 10 PM, Sun 1 - 5 PM, cl Mon. No admis fee. Estab 1971 to stimulate aesthetic expertise & awareness in the Palo Alto & surrounding communities. Average Annual Attendance: 75,000. Mem: 400; dues $15, $25, $50, $100, $250, $500, $1000
Income: $500,000 (financed by municipal funds, private donations & earned income)
Collections: Contemporary & historical art
Publications: Palo Alto Cultural Center Newsletter/Calendar, quarterly; exhibit catalogues
Activities: Classes for adults & children; dramatic programs; docent training; lectures open to public; concerts; gallery talks; tours; competitions; museum shop sells books, original art, reproductions, prints & objects for sale related to exhibitions

M **PALO ALTO JUNIOR MUSEUM,** 1451 Middlefield Rd, 94301. Tel 415-329-2111. *Dir* John Walton; *Instructor Arts & Crafts* Debbie Hillyer
Open Tues - Sat 10 AM - 5 PM, Sun 1 - 4 PM, cl New Years, Easter, July 4, Thanksgiving & Christmas; Baylands Interpretive Center: Wed - Fri 2 - 5 PM, Sat & Sun 10 AM - 5 PM, cl Thanksgiving & Christmas. No admis fee. Estab 1932, completely renovated in 1969. Average Annual Attendance: 100,000
Income: Financed by city appropriation
Collections: Art and artifacts
Publications: Notes, monthly; Prehistoric Palo Alto (brochure)
Activities: Classes; guided tours; exten dept; sciencemobile

PASADENA

L **ART CENTER COLLEGE OF DESIGN,** James Lemont Fogg Memorial Library, 1700 Lida St, 91103-1999. Tel 818-584-5013; FAX 818-584-5027. *VPres & Dir* Elizabeth Galloway; *Catalog Librn* Alison Holt; *Slide Cur* Theresa Pendlebury; *Acquisitions Librn* George Porcari; *Circulation Supv* Jorge Pardo; *Circulations Supv* Steven Hanson; *Reference Librn* Ruth Spencer; *Photo Research Cur* Tess Norbut; *Asst Slide Cur* Diana Thater
Open Mon - Thurs 8:30 AM - 10 PM, Fri 8:30 AM - 5 PM, Sat 8:30 AM - 4 PM, cl Sun. Estab to provide reference and visual resources for the designers who study and teach at Art Center College of Design. For lending and reference. Circ 90,000
Income: Financed by institutiion & private grants
Purchases: $85,000 (books); $45,000 (periodicals); $30,000 (videos & slides)
Library Holdings: Vols 46,072; Per subs 450; AV — Cassettes, motion pictures 100, slides 90,000, v-tapes 2200; Other — Clipping files 28,000, exhibition catalogs 1850, reproductions
Special Subjects: Advertising Design, Commercial Art, Graphic Design, Illustration, Industrial Design, Photography, Environmental Design, Fine Arts, History of Design, Moving Pictures, Packaging Design

M **PACIFIC - ASIA MUSEUM,** 46 N Los Robles Ave, 91101. Tel 818-449-2742. *Dir* David Kamansky; *Asst Dir for Development* Mary Pechanec; *Asst Dir for Admin* Sherrill Livingston; *Communications Coordr* Philip Pang; *Education Coordr* Sheila Wiess; *Registrar* Debra J Bailey; *Volunteer Coordr* Liz Corey
Open Wed - Sun noon - 5 PM, cl holidays. Admis adults & non-members $2, sr citizens & students $1.50, under 12 free. Estab 1971 to promote understanding of the cultures of the Pacific and Far East through exhibitions, lectures, dance, music and concerts. Through these activities, the museum helps to increase mutual respect and appreciation of both the diversities and similarities of Eastern and Western cultures. The building was designed by Marston, Van Pelt and Mayberry, architects for Grace Nicholson. The building is listed in the national register of historic places as the Grace Nicholson Building. There is 11,000 sq ft of exhibition space. Average Annual Attendance: 50,000. Mem: dues benefactor $1000, donor $500, sponsor $250, patron $100, contributor $60, active $30
Collections: †Oriental art objects
Publications: The Past and Present Art of the Australian Aborigines; Contemporary Australian Aborigine Paintings; The Woodblock Prints of Paul Jacoulet; Chinese Jade: The Image From Within; 100 Years of Philippine Painting; Master of Tradition - The Art of Chang Ta-ch'ien
Activities: Classes for adults & children; docent training; lects open to public, 12-15 vis lectr per yr; concerts; gallery talks; tours; original objects of art lent to other museums and limited number of libraries; book traveling exhibitions, 2-3 per year; originate traveling exhibitions; museum shop sells books, oriental antiques, collectibles & contemporary gift items

M **PASADENA CITY COLLEGE,** Art Gallery, Art Dept, 1570 E Colorado Blvd, 91106. Tel 818-585-7238. *Dir* Alexander Kritselis
Open Mon - Thurs 11 AM - 4 PM; Evenings Mon, Tues & Wed 7 - 9 PM. No admis fee. Estab to show work that relates to class given at Pasadena City College. Gallery is housed in separate building; 1000 sq ft. Average Annual Attendance: 20,000. Mem: 2800 (financed by school budget)
Exhibitions: Clothing Design; painting; sculpture; Faculty Show; Advertising Design; Student Show; Print Show
Publications: Mailers for each show

M **PASADENA HISTORICAL SOCIETY,** 470 W Walnut St, 91103. Tel 818-577-1660. *Exec Dir* Judith Hunter; *Archivist* Tim Gregory; *Cur* Pam Harrison; *Educator* Sandra Gardner
Open Thurs - Sun 1 - 4 PM. Admis adults $4, students & sr citizens $3, children under 12 free. Estab 1924 for the preservation & collection of historical data relating to Pasadena. Historical house with American Impressionist Art. Average Annual Attendance: 10,000. Mem: 750; dues $35, annual meeting 4th Sun in Jan
Income: $159,000 (financed through mem, endowment & contributions)
Library Holdings: Vols 10,000; Other — Clipping files, manuscripts, memorabilia, original art works, photographs
Collections: Collection of documents & artifacts relating to Pasadena; Collection of paintings by California artists European & American furniture (antiques & reproductions); 750 photographs; rare books & manuscripts; Turn of the Century Life Style on Millionaire's Row
Exhibitions: (1992) Lingerie Exhibit; Quilt Exhibit; Watercolor Exhibit
Publications: Quarterly newsletter
Activities: Classes for adults; docent & junior docent training; lect open to public, 4 - 8 vis lectr per year; gallery talks; tours; sales shop sells books, magazines, prints & gift items

L **PASADENA PUBLIC LIBRARY,** Fine Arts Dept, 285 E Walnut St, 91101. Tel 818-405-4052. *Library Dir* Edward Szynaka; *Head Reference* Vickey Johnson
Open Mon - Thurs noon - 9 PM, Fri noon - 6 PM, Sat 9 AM - 6 PM, Sun 1-5 PM. No admis fee. Art department estab 1927
Income: Financed by endowments and gifts, for materials only
Library Holdings: Vols 27,500; Per subs 60; Compact Discs 600; Micro — Fiche, reels; AV — Cassettes 2000, rec 4800, v-tapes 1533; Other — Photographs, reproductions

M **NORTON SIMON MUSEUM,** 411 W Colorado Blvd, 91105. Tel 818-449-6840; FAX 818-796-4978. *Pres* Norton Simon; *Executive VPres* Walter Timoshuk; *Cur* Gloria Williams; *Chief Cur* Sara Campbell; *Asst Cur* Elizabeth Engels; *Registrar* Andrea Clark; *Rights & Reproductions* Liz Midas
Open Thurs - Sun noon - 6 PM. Admis Sat: adults $4, students & senior citizens $2; members & children under 12 accompanied by adults free. Estab 1974; this museum brings to the western part of the United States one of the worlds great collections of paintings, tapestries, prints & sculptures for the cultural benefit of the community at large; the museum is oriented toward the serious & meticulous presentation of masterpiece art. Average Annual Attendance: 150,000. Mem: dues $35 - $1000
Income: Financed by endowment, mem, city appropriation, tours, admissions, contributions, bookshop & grounds maintenance
Collections: Art spanning 14 centuries: including paintings, sculptures, tapestries & graphics from the early Renaissance through the 20th century; Indian & Southeast Asian sculpture
Exhibitions: Degas bronze sculptures; Goya prints; Picasso; Vangogh: Painter, Printmaker, Collector; etchings of Rembrandt; Southeast Asian and Indian Sculpture
Publications: Masterpieces from the Norton Simon Museum
Activities: Private guided tours; museum shop sells books, magazines reproductions, slides & postcards

PRESIDIO OF MONTEREY

M **DEFENSE LANGUAGE INSTITUTE FOREIGN LANGUAGE CENTER** (Formerly Unites States Army Historical Holding), Presidio of Monterey Historical Holding, Commandant, Attn: Museum, 93944-5006. Tel 408-647-5536, 647-5110; FAX 408-647-5414; Elec Mail BITNET:MCNAUGHTJ% DLI173.LEA1@KEAV-EMH.ARMY.MIL.
Open by appointment. No admis fee. Estab 1968. Depicts Presidio of Monterey from Indian, Spanish & Mexican eras to present United States Army base. One gallery of historical artifacts
Income: Financed through the US Army
Collections: Local artifacts: Rumsen Indian tools & decorations; Spanish & Mexican military items; Spanish paintings & utensils from Governor Arguello's residence; United States military items 1846 to present with emphasis on cavalry & field artillery, 1920 - 40.
Activities: Tours

QUINCY

M **PLUMAS COUNTY MUSEUM,** 500 Jackson, PO Box 10776, 95971. Tel 916-283-6320; FAX 916-283-0946. *Cur* Linda C Brennan; *Asst Cur* Scott J Lawson
Open winter Mon - Fri 8 AM - 5 PM, summer Mon - Fri 8 AM - 5 PM, Sat 10 AM - 4 PM. No admis fee. Estab 1964 to preserve the past for the enjoyment and edification of the present and future generations. Average Annual Attendance: 18,000. Mem: 300; dues life $100, general per yr $5; meetings held bi-annually
Income: Financed by members and county budget
Purchases: $300
Collections: Antique period furnishing, Indian (Maidu) artifacts, dolls, clothing, mining & logging artifacts, domestic, jewelry, guns, period furniture, Historic Home Museum adjacent; railroad collection, memorabilia
Exhibitions: Steam Forever: James E Boynton Collection
Publications: Plumas County Museum Newsletter, two times a year
Activities: Lectures open to public; bookstore

L **Museum Archives,** 500 Jackson, PO Box 10776, 95971. Tel 916-283-6320; FAX 916-283-0946. *Cur* Linda C Brennan; *Asst Cur* Scott Lawson
Open Mon - Fri 8 AM - 5 PM, Memorial Weekend - Labor Day Weekend 10 AM - 4 PM. No admis fee. Estab 1964 to preserve Plumas County's rich heritage & history. Library for reference use only. Average Annual Attendance: 22,000. Mem: 300; dues $5 & up; annual meeting June
Income: $50,000 (financed by county, memorial donations, memberships, book store sales & personal donations)
Library Holdings: Vols 2000; Per subs 1000; Negatives; Micro — Prints, reels; AV — A-tapes, cassettes, Kodachromes, motion pictures, slides; Other — Clipping files, exhibition catalogs, memorabilia, original art works, pamphlets, photographs, prints, reproductions
Special Subjects: Logging, Mining, Railroad
Collections: Crystal, china, bottles, musical instrument; Indian jewelry; Maidu Indian Basket Collection; furniture; mining; logging; agriculture; dolls; toys
Activities: Docent training; demonstrations; lectures open to public; gallery talks; tours; sales shop sells books, original art, reproductions, photographs

RANCHO PALOS VERDES

A **PALOS VERDES ART CENTER,** 5504 W Crestridge Rd, 90274. Tel 310-541-2479. *Pres* Beverly Alpay; *Exhib Dir* Anne Morris; *Public Relations Dir* June Romine
Open Mon - Fri 9 AM - 4 PM, Sat 1 - 4 PM, cl Christmas & New Years. No admis fee. Estab 19531 to provide a multifaceted program of classes, exhibits and lectures in the visual arts. Changing exhibits gallery. Average Annual Attendance: 15,000. Mem: 2000; dues $40 - $100
Income: Financed by membership & private donations
Exhibitions: Twenty-four museum exhibits per year
Publications: The Quarterly
Activities: Classes for adults & children; docent training; lect open to public, 10 vis lectrs per year; gallery talks; libr tours; competitions with awards

RED BLUFF

M **KELLY-GRIGGS HOUSE MUSEUM,** 311 Washington St (Mailing add: 311 Washington St, CA 96080). Tel 916-527-1129. *Pres* Helen McKenzie Owens
Open Thurs - Sun 2 - 5 PM, cl holidays. Donations welcome. Estab 1965, a history museum in a home built in 1880. Mem: Dues associate $10, sustaining $50, charter $100 plus $10 annually, memoriam $100, life $200, patron $500, benefactor $1000
Collections: Pendleton Art Collection spanning over a century of art; Indian artifacts; antique furniture; Victorian costumes
Exhibitions: Permanent and temporary exhibitions
Publications: Brochure; Kellygram (guides' newsletter and schedule)
Activities: Guided tours

REDDING

M **REDDING MUSEUM OF ART & HISTORY,** 56 Quartz Hill Rd, PO Box 99427, 96099-0427. Tel 916-225-4155. *Pres* Dena Moss; *Treas* Dave Howland; *Dir* Keith Foster; *Arts Cur* Rob Wilson; *Educ Coordr* Lynn Nauman; *Arts Outreach Coordr* Rosemarie Orwig
Open summer Tues - Sat 10 AM - 5 PM, Sun noon - 5 PM, winter Tues - Fri & Sun noon - 5 PM, Sat 10 AM - 5 PM, cl Mon. Estab 1963 to encourage understanding of and appreciation of human accomplishments throughout history and pre-history. Two galleries present changing monthly contemporary art exhibits. Average Annual Attendance: 100,000. Mem: 1300; dues $10 - $100; annual meeting second Wed Sept
Income: Financed by membership, city appropriation, fund raising activities
Purchases: Contemporary fine arts, Native American baskets & artifacts
Collections: Mexican & Central American Pre-Columbian pottery; †Native American baskets; †Shasta County historical artifacts and documents; †Contemporary Regional art; †photography
Exhibitions: Permanent gallery exhibition: Shasta County History. (1992) Edges & Space: Artists & Their Students in Northern California Prisons; Maria Alquilar; Annual Fine Art Competition; Survey of Kinetic Sculpture. (1993) Pluralism: Prints & Drawings of the Eighties; Acts of Conscience; American

Realism: The Urban Scene; Children's Art Competition; National Juried Art Competition - Food Art
Publications: The Covered Wagon, published by Shasta Historical Society annually; occasional papers: Winter ethnography; historical calendar
Activities: Classes for adults and children; docent training; lectures open to public, 10 vis lectr per yr; gallery talks; tours; competitions with awards; Children's Lawn Festival; Art Fair; Native American Heritage Day; Christmas Craft Show; scholarships offered; affiliated natural science museum; Community Art Rental Program; original works of art lent to other museums; originate book traveling exhibitions, 10-12 per yr; museum shop sells books, magazines & original art, consignment from local craftspeople & artists, reproductions, gifts

L **Museum Research Library,** 56 Quartz Hill Rd, PO Box 99427, 96099. Tel 916-225-4155. *Librn* Hazel McKim; *Vol* California Quint
Open Wed & Thur 10 AM - 2 PM. Open for reference only by appointment
Special Subjects: Shasta County history

REDLANDS

L **LINCOLN MEMORIAL SHRINE,** 125 W Vine St, 92373. Tel 909-798-7636, 798-7632. *Cur* Donald McCue; *Assoc Archivist* Claristie Hammond
Open Tues - Sat 1 - 5 PM, other hours by appointment; cl Sun, Mon & holidays. No admis fee. Estab 1932, operated as a section of the Smiley Public Library. Reference use only
Library Holdings: Vols 4500
Collections: Sculptures, paintings, murals
Publications: Lincoln Memorial Association Newsletter, quarterly
Activities: Docent training; temporary art exhibitions; lectures; guided tours by appointment

A **REDLANDS ART ASSOCIATION,** 215 E State St, PO Box 2273, 92373-2273. Tel 909-792-8435. *Pres* Vernon Dornbach
Open Mon - Fri 10 AM - 5 PM, Sat 10 AM - 2 PM. No admis fee. Estab 1964 to promote interest in the visual arts and to provide a gallery for artists. Average Annual Attendance: 3000. Mem: 250; dues $20; annual meeting in May
Income: Financed by dues, gifts, grants
Exhibitions: Multimedia mini juried show
Publications: Bulletin, monthly
Activities: Classes for children and adults; lectures open to public, 4 vis lectrs per yr; tours; competitions with prizes; gallery talks; scholarships; lending collection contains nature artifacts & original prints; gallery shop sells original art, reproductions, glass & ceramics

M **SAN BERNARDINO COUNTY MUSEUM,** Fine Arts Institute, 2024 Orange Tree Lane, 92374. Tel 909-798-8570. *Pres* Cindy Rinne; *VPres* Gary Holbrook; *Dir* Dr Allan Griesemer; *Cur Natural History* Gene Cardiff; *Cur Earth Sciences* Robert Reynolds; *Cur Archaeology* Ruth D Simpson; *Cur Herpetology* Robert Sanders; *Cur Entomology* Dr Charles Howell; *Registrar* Noella Benvenuti; *Artist* Vicky Hipsley; *Cur of Education* Maggie Foss
Open Tues - Sat 9 AM - 5 PM, Sun 1 - 5 PM. No admis fee. Estab 1952 for education. Maintains upper and lower dome auditoriums and foyer. Average Annual Attendance: 300,000. Mem: 2100; dues Fine Arts Institute $30, Museum Association $15 and up; annual Fine Arts Institute meeting Feb; annual Museum Association meeting May
Income: $280,000 (financed by membership)
Purchases: $1000 - $2000
Collections: Collection consists primarily of representational art pertaining to wildlife or the history of Southern California
Exhibitions: Five juried art exhibits annually for mem; three juried art exhibits for all artists
Publications: Newsletter, bi-monthly
Activities: Classes for adults and children; docent training; lect open to the public, 150 vis lectr per yr; art competitions with cash & purchase awards totaling $45,000 annually; scholarships offered; book traveling exhibition; originate traveling exhibitions; museum shop selling books, reproductions & slides, jewelry, items pertaining to natural history

M **UNIVERSITY OF REDLANDS,** Peppers Gallery, 1200 E Colton Ave, 92373. Tel 909-793-2121. *Gallery Dir* John Brownfield
Open Mon - Fri 1 - 5 PM, Sun 2 - 5 PM. No admis fee. Estab 1963 to widen students interest in art. Gallery is one large room with celestiary windows and movable panels for display. Average Annual Attendance: 1000-1500
Income: Financed by endowment
Collections: Ethnic Art; graphics; a few famous artists works
Exhibitions: Exhibitions during fall, winter, spring
Publications: Exhibition catalogs and posters
Activities: Lectures open to public, 4-5 vis lectr per year; gallery talks; tours; talent awards

RENAISSANCE

A **ARTNETWORK,** 13284 Rices Crossing Rd, PO Box 369, 95962-0369. Tel 916-692-1355; FAX 916-692-1370. *Dir* Constance Franklin-Smith
Open daily 9 AM - 5 PM. Estab 1986 to publish marketing information for fine arts
Publications: ArtSource Quarterly; Artworld Hotline; semi-monthly newsletter
Activities: Marketing seminars; lect open to public, 24 vis lectr per year; competitions; books, original art & reproductions sold through direct mail

RICHMOND

A **NATIONAL INSTITUTE OF ART & DISABILITIES (NIAD),** 551 23rd St, 94804. Tel 510-620-0290; FAX 510-620-0326. *Exec Dir* Ronald E Wray
Open Mon - Fri 9 AM - 4 PM, Sat 11 AM - 3 PM. Estab 1982 to provide freedom to create & add to the fullness of life, both for people with disabilities & for the cultural life of society. Currently there are 13 centers in California &

others in Wisconsin, Washington & Canada. Maintains a professional exhibition gallery which displays the work of NIAD artists, often alongside the work of established artists from outside the NIAD setting in order to bring the art of NIAD artists to the attention of the general public
Exhibitions: NIAD artist work
Publications: Art & Disabilities, Freedom to Create, the Creative Spirit; Freedom to Create (videotape series)
Activities: Sat children's classes; interdisciplinary visual art studio program; professional training in art & disabilities field; research, training & technical assistance; originate traveling exhibitions of NIAD artist work to regional galleries, museums, colleges, community centers & businesses; gift shop

A **RICHMOND ART CENTER,** Civic Center Plaza, Civic Center, 25th & Barrett Ave, 94804. Tel 510-620-6772; FAX 510-620-6716. *Exec Dir* Jeff Nathanson; *Admin Asst* Elizabeth Parch
Open Tues - Fri 10 AM - 4:30 PM, Sat & Sun 12 - 4:30 PM, cl Mon & holidays. No admis fee. Estab preliminary steps 1936-44; formed in 1944 to establish artists studios and community center for arts; to offer to the community an opportunity to experience and to improve knowledge and skill in the arts and crafts at the most comprehensive and highest level possible. A large gallery, small gallery and entrance gallery total 5000 sq ft, and a rental gallery covers 1628 ft; an outdoor sculpture court totals 8840 sq ft. Average Annual Attendance: 8000. Mem: 800; dues $25 up
Income: $300,000 (financed by mem, tuition, donation, grants, events, in-kind services from city & Art Center Assoc)
Collections: †Primarily contemporary art and crafts of Bay area
Exhibitions: Rotating: group theme, solo, invitational and juried annuals
Publications: Catalog for annual shows; newsletter, quarterly; show announcements for exhibitions
Activities: Classes for adults and children; lectures open to the public, 5 vis lectrs per year; gallery talks; tours; scholarships offered; outreach program serving community; rental gallery, paintings and original objects of art lent to offices, businesses and homes, members of Art Center

RIVERSIDE

M **RIVERSIDE ART MUSEUM,** 3425 Seventh St, 92501. Tel 909-684-7111. *Pres* Maureen Kane; *Dir* Mary Alice Cline
Open Mon 10 AM - 3 PM, Tues - Fri 10 AM - 5 PM, Sat 10 AM - 4 PM, cl Sun. No admis fee. Estab 1935 to display art, collect & preserve art created in the West. Three spaces - Main Gallery 72 ft x 35 ft; Upstairs Gallery 18 ft x 30 ft; Art Alliance Gallery 72 ft x 35 ft. Average Annual Attendance: 20,000. Mem: 1000; dues life mem $1000 & up, patron $200, supporting $100, family $50, individual $35, senior citizen $10; annual meeting fourth Thurs of Feb
Income: Financed by membership, grants and donations
Collections: Mixture of media dating from the late 1800s to the present; 300 pieces; art by Southern California artists (past & present) living in the west (Andrew Molles Collection)
Publications: Artifacts, monthly
Activities: Classes for adults and children; docent training; lectures open to public, 5 vis lectr per year; gallery talks; demonstrations; special events; competitions with prizes; tours; scholarships and fels offered; individual paintings & original objects of art lent; sales shop sells magazines, original art & reproductions

L **Library,** 3425 Seventh St, 92501. Tel 909-684-7111.
Open for reference upon request
Library Holdings: Vols 600; Per subs 15; Other — Exhibition catalogs, framed reproductions, pamphlets, photographs, reproductions

M **RIVERSIDE MUNICIPAL MUSEUM,** 3720 Orange St, 92501. Tel 909-782-5273. *Historic Resources Dir* William G Dougall; *Admin Cur* Alan Curl; *Museum Scientist Zoology* Ronald K Pidot; *Cur Anthropology* Christopher L Moser; *Cur History* H Vincent Moses; *Restoration Specialist* Gary Ecker; *Exhib Designer* Dasia Bytnerowicz
Collections: Archaeology; decorative arts; ethnology; historic house, 1891 Heritage House; photo & document archives

UNIVERSITY OF CALIFORNIA

M **University Art Gallery,** Watkins House, 92521. Tel 909-787-3755, 787-3786. *Dir* Katherine Warren; *Asst Dir* Deborah Dozier; *Preparator* John Dingler; *Admin Asst* Karen Speed
Open Tues - Fri noon - 5 PM, Sat & Sun noon - 4 PM. No admis fee. Estab 1963, gallery presents major temporary exhibitions. Gallery contains 2000 sq ft. Average Annual Attendance: 10,000
Exhibitions: Master Prints from the Age of Durer; program in art faculty exhibitions; Photo-Mechanical Printmaking Competition; Claire falkenstein; The Continuing Vision; From Over Function; Companeras De Mexico: Women Photograph Women; Relationship: new work by Sandra Rowe; site specific sculpture competition. (1993) African Sculpture Exhibit; Folkart & Function in Europe
Publications: Exhibition catalogs
Activities: Lectures open to public, 3-4 per yr; gallery talks; tours; competitions; book traveling exhibitions, 1-2 per yr; sales shop sells catalogs

M **California Museum of Photography,** 92521. Tel 909-787-4787; FAX 909-787-4797. *Cur* Edward W Earle; *Dir* Jonathan W Green; *Coll Mgr* Roy McJunkin; *Publicity* Helen Sanematsu; *Asst Dir, Admin* Cathleen Walling; *Community Development Officer* Concha Rivera; *Exhib Designer* Kevin Boyle; *Membership Coordr* Carol Dye; *Dir Grants & Development* Lisa Morrow
Open Wed - Sat 10 AM - 5 PM, Sun noon - 5 PM. Admis adult $2, senior citizen & youth $1, children under 12 & AAM members free. Estab 1973 to preserve, protect and exhibit photography. Museum has 5 exhibition galleries which display changing exhibitions related to historical & contemporary photography and emerging technologies. Average Annual Attendance: 16,000-20,000. Mem: 1200; dues $35
Income: $800,000 (financed by university funds, grants, private donations & mem)
Collections: Bingham camera and apparatus; Keystone-Mast stereo negatives &

prints; photographs of the 19th & 20th centuries

Exhibitions: Emperor's New Clothes: Censorship, Sexuality & the Body Politic; Smog: A Matter of Life & Breath; The Revolution will be Televised; Treasures from the permanent collection: Images & Apparatus

Activities: Lect open to public, 5 - 10 vis lectr per year; gallery talks; tours; competitions; awards; film series; Riverside Film Festival; symposia; individual photographs & original objects of art lent to qualified museums, non-profit galleries & art organizations; lending collection contains 400,000 photographs; book traveling exhibitions, 3 per year; originate traveling exhibitions; museum shop sells books, magazines, reproductions; exhibition catalogues

L **Library,** PO Box 5900, 92517-5900. Tel 909-787-3703; FAX 909-787-3285. *University Librn* James C Thompson; *Art Selector* Monica Fusich

Open Mon - Thurs 8 AM - noon, Fri 8 AM - 6 PM, Sat 10 AM - 6 PM, Sun 1 PM - 12 AM. Open to faculty, students and staff

Library Holdings: Vols 38,000; Per subs 161; Micro — Cards, fiche, reels; AV — A-tapes, cassettes, fs, motion pictures, rec, slides, v-tapes; Other — Exhibition catalogs, manuscripts, original art works

Special Subjects: Photography

ROHNERT PARK

M **SONOMA STATE UNIVERSITY,** Art Gallery, 1801 E Cotati Ave, 94928. Tel 707-664-2295; Elec Mail Michael.Schwages@Sonoma.Edu. *Dir* Michael Schwager; *Gallery Asst* Joanne Salstrom

Open Mon - Fri 11 AM - 4 PM, Sat & Sun noon - 4 PM. No admis fee. Estab 1978 to provide exhibitions of quality to the college and northern California community. 2800 sq ft of exhibition space designed to house monumental sculpture and painting

Income: Financed through University and private funds

Collections: Asnis Collection of Prints; Garfield Collection of Oriental Art

Exhibitions: (1992) Art from the Heart; Mineko Grimmer (installation); One by Two: Artists in Collaboration (mixed media); Students show

Publications: Bulletins and announcements of exhibitions; exhibition catalog

Activities: Classes for adults; lect open to public, vis lectr; gallery talks; tours; exten dept

ROSS

A **MARIN SOCIETY OF ARTISTS INC,** Sir Francis Drake Blvd, PO Box 203, 94957. Tel 415-454-9561. *Pres* Ruth McCarty; *Office Mgr* Jo Smith

Open Mon - Fri 11 AM - 4 PM; Sat & Sun 1 - 4 PM. No admis fee. Estab 1926 to foster cooperation among artists and to continually develop public interest in art. Gallery is located in a garden setting. It is approximately 3500 sq ft of well lighted exhibit space. Average Annual Attendance: 75,000. Mem: 600; Qualifications for membership: Previous exhibition in a juried show, and must reside in Bay Area if active; dues $20; meeting May & Sept

Income: Financed by membership, sale and rental of art

Activities: Lect open to the public, 2-3 vis lectr per yr; competitions with cash awards; scholarships; sales shop selling original art, original prints, handcrafted jewelry, ceramics and fiberworks

SACRAMENTO

A **CALIFORNIA CONFEDERATION OF THE ARTS,** 704 O St, 2nd Floor, 95814. Tel 916-447-7811, 213-936-4014 (LA); FAX 916-447-7891, 415-826-6850. *Exec Dir* Susan Hoffman; *Assoc Dir* Ken Larsen

Open 10 AM - 5 PM. Estab 1975 as a non-profit partnership to improve cultural opportunities. Mem: 1000; dues individual $50, organizations by budget; annual meeting May, Congress of the Arts

Income: $100,000 (financed by mem, corporate & foundation grants

Publications: Publications correspond to government & local arts activity

Activities: Referral services; lect open to public, over 10 vis lectr per year; scholarships & fels offered

CALIFORNIA STATE UNIVERSITY AT SACRAMENTO

L **Library - Humanities Reference Dept,** 2000 Jed Smith Dr, 95819. Tel 916-278-6218; FAX 916-278-7089. *Dean* Charles Martell; *Dept Head* Clifford P Wood; *Humanities Reference Librn* Marina Snow; *Humanities Reference & Slide Librn* Susan Beelick

Open Mon - Thurs 7:45 AM - 11 PM, Fri 7:45 AM - 5 PM, Sat 10 AM - 6 PM, Sun 1 - 9 PM (during school year), summer sessions vary during week. Estab 1947

Income: Financed through the University

Library Holdings: Per subs 250; Micro — Cards, fiche, reels; AV — A-tapes, cassettes, fs, slides, v-tapes; Other — Clipping files, exhibition catalogs, pamphlets, reproductions

Special Subjects: Book Arts, Decorative Arts

Publications: Women Artists: A Selected Bibliography; bibliographic handouts

M **University Union Exhibit Lounge,** University Union, CSUS, 6000 J St, 95819-6017. Tel 916-278-6595; FAX 916 278-6278. *Assoc Dir* Richard Schiffers

Open Mon - Fri 10:30 AM - 3:30 PM, Tues - Wed 5 - 8 PM, during school year; summer hours vary. No admis fee. Estab 1975 to expose students to a variety of visual arts & techniques. The Exhibit Lounge is located on the second floor of the University Union. It has 67 running feet of display space. Gallery run by students. Average Annual Attendance: 8250

Income: Student fees & commissions

Purchases: Two works purchased for permanent collection

Collections: Various prints, photographs, paintings by students; sculpture by Yoshio Taylor: Tsuki

Exhibitions: Annual student competition

Activities: Lectures open to public, 9 vis lectr per yr; gallery talks; competitions; Book traveling exhibitions once a year

M **CROCKER ART MUSEUM,** 216 O St, 95814. Tel 916-264-5423. *Dir* Barbara K Gibbs; *Cur* Janice T Driesbach; *Registrar* Paulette Hennum; *Cur Education* K D Kurutz

Open Wed - Sun 10 AM - 5 PM, Thurs 10 AM - 9 PM, cl Mon & Tues. Admis adults $3, children 7 - 17 $1.50, 6 & under free. Estab 1873; municipal art museum since 1885; original gallery building designed by Seth Babson completed in 1873; R A Herold Wing opened in 1969; Crocker Mansion Wing opened in 1989. Average Annual Attendance: 110,000. Mem: 5500; annual meeting in June

Income: $750,000 (financed by Crocker Art Museum Association and city appropriation)

Collections: †19th century California painting; American decorative arts; †contemporary California painting, sculpture and crafts; †prints and photographs; European decorative arts; †European painting 1500 - 1900; †Old Master drawings; †Oriental art

Exhibitions: (1992) A Collector's Eye: Vessels from the Hubert A Arnold Collection; Paintbrush Diplomacy: Children of the World Paint in a Single Language; The Art of Drawing: Old Masters from the Crocker Art Museum; Dalbert Castro: The Spirit of Nisenan; Harry Fonseca: The Discovery of Gold & Souls in California; Selections of Early California Painting from the Permanent Collection; Clearly Art: Pilchuck Glass Legacy; Table Manners: Scenes of the High Life from the Low Countries; Fables & Fantasies: The Art of Felix Lorieux. (1993) Tesoros De La Tierra: Ceramic Figures from Ancient; En El Ojo De Ollin: Galeria Posada RCAF (Royal Chicano Air Force) Posters; Japanese Ceramics from the Hubert Arnold Collection & Persian Miniatures; 68th Annual Crocker-Kingsley Open Art Exhibition; French Prints; Gregory Kondos: Retrospective; Olivia Parker; Chiura Obata: Travels in Yosemite; Copies After Other Artists Imitation is the Highest Form; Free Within Ourselves; Exhibition in Conjunction with Free Within Ourselves. (1994) William Allan Retrospective; To Be Assigned; Indian Miniatures from the Cleary Collection; The Age of Louis XIV: French Drawings from the Permanent Collection; Andy Warhol: Endangered Species; 69th Crocker-Kingsley Open Art Exhibition

Publications: Calendar, 6 times per year

Activities: Seminars for adults; children's programs; docent training; lect open to the public, 10 vis lectr per year; concerts; tours; annual juried competitions; individual paintings & original objects of art lent to other museums; book traveling exhibitions; originate traveling exhibitions; museum shop sells books, original art, cards & miscellaneous gifts

L **Research Library,** 216 O St, 95814. Tel 916-264-5423; FAX 916-264-7372. *Librn* Lois Courvoisier

Open Tues - Sun 10 AM - 5 PM, Thurs 10 AM - 9 PM, cl Mon. Open to staff, docent, interns and others upon application

Library Holdings: Vols 2000; Per subs 30; Dissertations; Micro — Fiche; Other — Exhibition catalogs

Activities: Educ Dept; classes for adults & children; dramatic programs; docent training; lectures open to public, some open to members only; vis lectr; concerts; artmobile; individual paintings lent

A **INSTITUTE FOR DESIGN & EXPERIMENTAL ART (IDEA),** 3414 Fourth Ave, 95817. Tel 916-452-0949. *Exec Dir* Sherry Ragan

Open Wed - Sat noon - 5 PM. Estab 1974 to produce innovative installations & performances. Average Annual Attendance: 5000

Income: $58,000 (financed by mem, city & state appropriations, foundations & National Endowment of the Arts)

Exhibitions: Installations by regional & national artists

Publications: Visions, quarterly

Activities: Classes for adults & children; dramatic programs; lect open to public, 6 vis lectr per year

M **LA RAZA-GALLERIA POSADA** (Formerly Galeria Posada), 704 O St, 95814. Tel 916-446-5133.

Open Tues - Sun noon - 6:00 PM. Estab 1981 to provide cultural art to the community

SAINT HELENA

M **SILVERADO MUSEUM,** 1490 Library Lane, PO Box 409, 94574. Tel 707-963-3757. *Dir* Norman H Strouse; *Cur* Beth Atherton

Open Tues - Sun noon - 4 PM, cl Mon. No admis fee. Estab 1969; the museum is devoted to the life and works of Robert Louis Stevenson, who spent a brief but important time in the area; the object is to acquaint people with his life and works and familiarize them with his stay. The museum has five wall cases and three large standing cases, as well as numerous bookcases. Average Annual Attendance: 5500

Income: Financed by the Vailima Foundation, set up by Mr & Mrs Norman H Strouse

Collections: All material relating to Stevenson & his immediate circle

Exhibitions: A different exhibition devoted to some phase of Stevenson's work is mounted every two months

Activities: Lectures open to public; tours; sales desk sells books and post cards

L **Reference Library,** 1490 Library Lane, PO Box 409, 94574. Tel 707-963-3757; FAX 707-963-8131. *Cur* Beth Atherton

Open Tues - Sun noon - 4 PM. 1970. For reference only

Income: Financed by Vailima Foundation

Library Holdings: Vols 3000; AV — Kodachromes 300, motion pictures

Special Subjects: Painting - American, Painting - British, Photography

Collections: †First editions, †variant editions, †fine press editions of Robert Louis Stevenson; †letters, †manuscripts, †photographs, †sculptures, †paintings and memorabilia

Exhibitions: Exhibits of two months duration 6 times a year; Christmas Exhibit

Publications: The Silverado Squatters; Prayers Written at Vailima

SALINAS

M HARTNELL COLLEGE GALLERY, 156 Homestead Ave, 93901. Tel 408-755-6700, Ext 6791. *Dir* Gary T Smith
Open Mon 10 AM - 1 PM & 7 - 9 PM, Tues - Thurs 10 AM - 1 PM, cl Fri - Sun. No admis fee. Estab 1959 to bring to students and the community the highest quality in contemporary and historical works of all media. Main gallery is 40 by 60 ft, south gallery is 15 by 30 ft, brick flooring. Average Annual Attendance: 7500
Collections: Approx 45 works on paper from the San Francisco Bay Area WPA; FSA photographs; Mrs Virginia Bacher Haichol Artifact Collection; Mrs Leslie Fenton Netsuke Collection
Exhibitions: Edward Weston; Claes Oldenburg; Edward Curtis; Oriental Porcelain from the Albert & Pat Scheopf Collection; Charles Russell & Frederick Remington; Russian Lacquer Boxes; Selections from the Hartnell Farm Security Admin Photography Collection; Christo: Wrapped Coast
Activities: Classes for adults; gallery management training; individual paintings & original objects of art lent to qualified institutions, professional galleries or museums; lending collection contains original art works; book traveling exhibitions; traveling exhibitions organized and circulated

SAN BERNARDINO

M CALIFORNIA STATE UNIVERSITY, SAN BERNARDINO, University Art Galleries, 5500 University Parkway, 92407-2397. Tel 909-880-5802. *Chmn Art Dept & Gallery Dir* Richard Johnston
Open Mon - Fri 9 AM - noon, 1 - 4 PM. No admis fee. Estab 1972 for the purpose of providing high quality exhibitions on varied subjects suitable for both campus and community. Gallery 2 opened 1978 as an exhibit area for senior shows and student work. Average Annual Attendance: 5500
Income: Financed by membership, city and state appropriations
Collections: Small collection of prints
Publications: Catalogs; Personas de los Tumbas - West Mexican tomb sculpture, 2-3 per year
Activities: Classes for adults; lect open to the public, 1-3 vis lectrs per year; gallery talks; competitions

A SAN BERNARDINO ART ASSOCIATION, INC, 780 N E St, PO Box 3574, 92404. Tel 909-885-2816. *Pres* Fern Schmidt; *First VPres* Doris Jacka; *Second VPres* Yolanda Voces; *Secy* Margaret Richards; *Corresp Secy* B Craig
Open Mon - Fri 11 AM - 3 PM. No admis fee. Estab 1934 as a non-profit organization to generate interest in art for all ages. Open to the public; maintains gallery of paintings & ceramics by local artists. Mem: 120; dues $20; meetings on 1st of each month
Publications: Newsletter
Activities: Classes for adults; artist presentations; lectures open to public, 8 vis lectr per year; gallery talks; competitions with awards; scholarships; individual paintings & original objects of art lent; sales shop sells original art, ceramics & photographs

SAN DIEGO

A BALBOA ART CONSERVATION CENTER, Balboa Park, 1649 El Prado, PO Box 3755, 92163-1755. Tel 619-236-9702; FAX 619-236-0141. *Pres* Rita Neeper; *VPres* Barbara Walbridge; *Dir & Exec Dir* Wynn Lee; *Chief Paper Conservator* Janet E Ruggles; *Chief Paintings Conservator* Elizabeth Court; *Paper Conservator* Marc Harnly; *Paper Conservator* Frances Pritchett; *Paintings Conservator* Alfredo Antognini; *Paintings Conservator* Sarah Murray; *Frames Technician* Janos Novak
Open Mon - Fri 9 AM - 4:30 PM. No admis fee. Estab 1975 for research and education in art conservation; services in exams, treatment and consultation in art conservation. Mem: 14; non-profit institutions are members, their members may contract for services; annual meeting in May
Income: $300,000 (financed by services performed)
Collections: †Illustrative photographs, †memorabilia, tools, equipment of profession; paintings for experimental & didactic purposes
Publications: BACC Newsletter, quarterly
Activities: Lectures open to public & some for members only; gallery talks; tours
L Richard D Buck Memorial Library, Balboa Park, PO Box 3755, 92163-1755. Tel 619-236-9702; FAX 619-236-0141. *Librn* Sonja Jones
Library not open to public
Income: Financed by Mellon Grant
Library Holdings: Vols 700; Per subs 35; Micro — Reels; AV — Cassettes, slides; Other — Clipping files, exhibition catalogs, memorabilia, pamphlets, photographs
Special Subjects: Art Conservation, Scientific Analysis of Materials

M CENTRO CULTURAL DE LA RAZA, 2004 Park Blvd, 92102. Tel 619-235-6135. *Board Pres* Steve E Espino; *Board VPres* Daniel Atrnandez; *Board Exec Dir* Larry Baza; *Cur* Patricio Chavez
Open Wed - Sun Noon - 5 PM. No admis fee, donations requested. Estab 1970 to create, promote, and preserve Mexican, Indian and Chicano art and culture. 2500 sq ft of gallery space with 5 sections and 8 & 15 ft walls. Average Annual Attendance: 65,000. Mem: 500; dues $10 - $1000
Income: $150,000 (financed by mem, city & state appropriation, sales & services, private grants, National Endowment for the Arts)
Purchases: $1500
Collections: Historical artifacts of Mexican and Indian culture; †contemporary artwork by Chicano artists
Exhibitions: Native American Contemporary Photography; solo exhibitions of local & regional artists; group shows; invitational group exhibitions. (1991) Order Arts Workshops; Autlan XX; Santiago Baca; Counter-Colon Ialismo; Dia-De Los Mufrtos
Publications: Exhibit catalogues, 3 per yr; literary publications, 2 per yr
Activities: Adult & children's classes; lectures open to the public, 5 - 7 vis lectrs

per yr; exten dept; lending collection includes 15 pieces of original art & prints; book traveling exhibitions, 1 - 2 per yr; originate traveling exhibits that circulate to other galleries and cultural centers; sales shop sells books, magazines, original art, reproductions, prints

A INSTALLATION GALLERY, PO Box 2552, 92112. Tel 619-260-1313; FAX 619-260-1303. *Managing Dir* Anna Gonzalez
No admis fee. Estab as a vital alternative space for San Diego, a forum for provocative ideas outside the boundaries of the museum & traditional gallery; an umbrella for community & educational outreach, for interaction with other community organizations & for art in public context, Installation is important as a dynamic intertwining of art & life & in focusing new perspectives on public issues; dedicated to promoting challenging & diverse art making without restrictions as to individuals, medium or content
Exhibitions: In Site 92; In Site 94, emphasizing artists from San Diego & Tijuana areas

M MINGEI INTERNATIONAL, INC, Mingei International Museum of World Folk Art, University Towne Centre Bldg I-5, 4405 La Jolla Village Dr, I-7 (Mailing add: PO Box 553, 92122). Tel 619-453-5300; FAX 619-453-0700. *Pres* Roger C Cornell, MD; *VPres* Alan Jaffe; *Secy* Jean Hahn; *VPres* Diane Powers; *Treas* Harold K Ticho; *Exec Dir* Martha Logenecker; *Asst Dir* James R Pahl; *Registrar* Christina Rojas; *Vol Coordr & Museum Shop Mgr* Jill Coursin; *Museum Mgr* Ann Kappes
Open Tues - Sat 11 AM - 5 PM, Fri evening to 9 PM, Sun 2 - 5 PM. Admis fee donation $2. Estab 1978 to further the understanding of arts of the people from all parts of the world. 6000 sq ft museum, architecturally designed space, white interior, hardwood floors, track lighting. Average Annual Attendance: 40,000. Mem: 1500; annual dues $20-$1000; meetings in May
Income: Financed by membership, grants and contributions
Collections: †International Folk Art (in all media including textiles, ceramics, metals, woods, stone, paper, bamboo & straw); African, American, Ethiopian, East Indian, Indonisian, Japanese, Pakistani, Himalayan & Mexican Folk Art
Exhibitions: (1993) Mingei of Japan: The Enduring Arts of the Land & People; Masterworks of West Coast American Designer/Craftsmen; Folk Toys of the World
Publications: Exhibition related publications
Activities: Docent training; illustrated lectures; films; gallery talks; tours; originate traveling exhibitions; collectors gallery sells original folk art
L Reference Library, 4405 La Jolla Village Dr I-7, 92038. Tel 619-453-5300; FAX 619-453-0700. *Librn* Nancy Andrews
Library Holdings: AV — A-tapes, cassettes, fs, Kodachromes, lantern slides, motion pictures, slides, v-tapes; Other — Clipping files, exhibition catalogs, framed reproductions, manuscripts, memorabilia, photographs

M SAN DIEGO MARITIME MUSEUM, 1306 N Harbor Dr, 92101. Tel 619-234-9153. *Pres* Morris Landon; *Exec Dir* Ken Franke; *Cur* David Brierley; *Librn* Craig Arnold
Open daily 9 AM - 8 PM. Admis family $10, adults $5, service personnel, children 13-17 & sr citizens $4, children under 12 $1.25, discount to adult groups. Estab 1948 for preservation & education of San Diego related maritime history. A maritime museum in a fleet of three ships: Star of India (1863 bark); Berkeley (1898 ferryboat); and Medea (1904 steam yacht). Average Annual Attendance: 180,000. Mem: 1600; dues life $2000, benefactor/corporate $1000, patron $500, associate $250, friend $100, active $50, family $35, individual $25; annual meeting in Nov
Collections: Antiques; maritime art; maritime artifacts; clothing; navigation instruments
Exhibitions: Temporary exhibitions
Publications: Mains'l Haul, quarterly historical journal; Books: Star of India, They Came by Sea, Transpac 1900-1979, Euterpe
Activities: Educ dept; docent training; lect for members & guests, 5 vis lectr per yr; tours; special programs; competitions for children with awards; museum store sells books, magazines, reproductions, prints, slides & related maritime items, including video tapes.

M SAN DIEGO MUSEUM OF ART, Balboa Park, PO Box 2107, 92112. Tel 619-232-7931; FAX 619-232-9367; Telex 88-3594. *Dir* Steven L Brezzo; *Dep Dir* Jane G Rice; *Head of Design & Installation* Mitchell Gaul; *Cur American Art* Martin E Peterson; *Cur European Art* Malcolm Warner; *Cur Modern Art* Mary Stofflet; *Cur Asian Art* Sung Yu; *Cur Education* Barney J Malesky; *Mem Coordr* Linda Blair; *Public Relations Coordr* Mardi Snow; *Head of Publications & Sales* David Hewitt; *Accounting Mgr* John Paterniti; *Registrar* Louis Goldich; *Planned Giving Grants Coordr* Julie Cheshire
Open Tues - Sun 10 AM - 4:30 PM; cl Mon. Admis general public $5, children 6-12 $1. Estab 1925. Gallery built in 1926 by a generous patron in a Spanish Plateresque design; the West wing was added in 1966 and the East wing in 1974. Average Annual Attendance: 417,000. Mem: 10,000; dues: Benefactor $10,000; President's Circle donor $5,000, business donor $5,000 , business partner $1,500, President's Circle $1,250, sponsoring friend $600, business associate $500, friend of museum $125, active $45, sr citizens $25, students $24
Income: $3,712,391 (financed by investment income, contributions, admissions, city and county appropriations and sales)
Purchases: $300,000
Collections: Renaissance and Baroque paintings; with strong holdings in Spanish; 19th and 20th century American and European sculpture and paintings; Asian arts - sculpture, paintings, ceramics, decorative arts; American furniture and glass, English silver; Spanish Baroque, Flemish, Dutch and English schools.
Exhibitions: (1991) Latin American Drawings Today; Four Early San Diego Painters, Braun, Fries, Mitchell, Reiffel; California Cityscapes (1993) Pacific Parallels: Artists & the Landscape in New Zealand; Sanchez Cotan; Silver, Wood, Clay, Gold: San Diego Crafts & NCECA Clay National 1993; Art Alive; The William S Paley Collection; Artists Guild Open Juried Exhibition; Helen Frankenthaler; Bruno Schulz. (1994) Giorgione: Songs of My People; Florentine Drawings; Gerald Brockhurst; Balboa's Ark; Young Art '94; Deborah Butterfield; Russian Music Covers; Passionate Visions of the American South
Publications: Biennial Reports port; catalogs of collections; exhibition catalogs;

membership calendar, monthly; gallery guide
Activities: Classes for adults and children; docent training; lectr open to the public; gallery talks; tours; competitions; traveling exhibitions organized and circulated; sales shops selling books, reproductions, prints, cards, jewelry and ceramics,

L **Art Reference Library,** Balboa Park, PO Box 2107, 92112-2107. Tel 619-232-7931. *Librn* Claire Eike; *Library Asst* Nancy Emerson
Call for hours. Estab 1926 for curatorial research. Noncirculating. Available to public on limited basis
Library Holdings: Vols 20,000; Per subs 65; AV — Slides 15,000; Other — Clipping files, exhibition catalogs, pamphlets
Special Subjects: Asian Art, Italian Renaissance, Spanish Baroque, American & Latin American Contemporary
Collections: Bibliography of artists in exhibition catalogues

L **SAN DIEGO PUBLIC LIBRARY,** Art & Music Section, 820 E St, 92101. Tel 619-236-5810. *Sr Librn* Kathleen Griffin; *Picture Specialist* Jacqueline Adams; *Librn* Christina Clifford
Open Mon - Thurs 10 AM - 9 PM, Fri & Sat 9:30 AM - 5:30 PM. No admis fee. Estab 1966 to make art available to students & the community. Two gallery spaces: smaller gallery is basically for student & classroom work; larger gallery is for invited guests. Average Annual Attendance: 8000
Income: Financed by city and state appropriation
Purchases: $32,000
Library Holdings: Vols 85,000; Per subs 200; postcards; AV — Rec 23,000; Other — Clipping files, exhibition catalogs
Collections: Former libraries of William Templeton Johnson, architect, and Donal Hord, sculptor; emphasis is on Spanish, Mediterranean, Italian and French Renaissance architecture and Oriental art, sculpture and ceramics; books on the theatre including biographies of famous actors and actresses as well as histories of the American, London and European stages, gift of Elwyn B Gould, local theatre devotee
Activities: Student show with prizes; individual paintings & original objects of art lent to faculty members on campus; book traveling exhibitions, 1 or 2 per year; sales shop sells books

M **SAN DIEGO STATE UNIVERSITY,** University Art Gallery, 5402 College Ave, 92182-0214. Tel 619-594-6511; FAX 619-594-6974. *Chmn* Fredrick Orth
Open Mon, Thurs, Sat noon - 4 PM, Tues & Wed 10 AM - 4 PM, cl Fri & Sun. No admis fee. Estab 1977 to provide exhibitions of importance to the students, faculty and public of the San Diego environment; for study and appreciation of art and enrichment of the University. Average Annual Attendance: 35,000. Mem: 270; dues $25
Income: Supported by student fees, SDSU Art Council & grants
Collections: Crafts collection; contemporary print collection; graduate student sculpture and painting
Exhibitions: Contemporary national & international artists
Publications: Exhibit catalogs
Activities: Lectures open to public, 4 vis lectr per yr; gallery talks; book traveling exhibitions, 2 per yr; originate traveling exhibitions; sales shop sells books & exhibition catalogs

L **Art Department Slide Library,** San Diego State University, 5402 College Ave, 92182-0214. Tel 619-594-6511; FAX 619-594-6974. *Slide Cur* Lilla Sweatt
Open Mon - Thurs 7:30 AM - 11 PM, Fri 7:30 AM - 5 PM, Sat 10 AM - 5 PM, Sun noon - 10 PM. Estab 1957 to aid and facilitate the faculty in teaching art and art history as well as aiding students in class reports
Library Holdings: Micro — Cards, fiche, prints, reels; AV — Cassettes, Kodachromes, slides 122,000; Other — Clipping files, exhibition catalogs, framed reproductions, manuscripts, memorabilia, pamphlets, reproductions
Exhibitions: Special Art collections, student and women's art shows

M **SUSHI-PERFORMANCE & VISUAL ART GALLERY,** 852 Eighth Ave, 92101. Tel 619-235-8466. *Dir* Lynn Schuette; *Managing Dir* Vicki Wolf; *Vis Arts Coord* Jason Tannen
Estab 1980 to present contemporary visual & performance art. Visual art gallery is 6 ft x 40 ft; performance gallery is 35 x 55 ft. Average Annual Attendance: 5000. Mem: 300; dues $15-$500
Income: $80,000 (financed by endowment, membership, city & state appropriation)
Activities: Educ dept; dramatic programs

M **TIMKEN MUSEUM OF ART,** 1500 El Prado, 92101. Tel 619-239-5548. *Pres* Robert Ames; *VPres* John Thiele; *Dir* Nancy Ames Petersen
Open Tues - Sat 10 AM - 4:30 PM, Sun 1:30 - 4:30 PM, cl Mon. No admis fee. Estab to display & preserve Europen Old Masters, 18th & 19th century American paintings & Russian icons. Six galleries. Average Annual Attendance: 90,000
Income: Financed by endowment
Collections: Dutch and Flemish, French, Spanish and American paintings; Russian icons; all paintings owned by Putnam Collection are on permanent display; Pissarro, Bords de l'Oise a Pontoise; Il Guercino - Return of the Prodigal Son; Copley, Mrs Thomas Gage
Exhibitions: (1986) Focus II: Albert Bierstadt: Cho-looke, The Yosemite Fall
Publications: Gallery Guides; exhibit catalogs; Gabriel Metsu's The Letter monograph; Eastman Johnson's The Cranberry Harvest; Island of Nantucket; Corot: View of Volterra
Activities: Lectures; tours available by request

M **UNIVERSITY OF SAN DIEGO,** Founders' Gallery, 5998 Alcala Park, 92110. Tel 619-260-4600. *Dir* Therese T Whitcomb
Open Mon - Fri noon - 5 PM. Estab 1971 to enrich the goals of the Fine Arts department and university by providing excellent in-house exhibitions of all eras, forms and media, and to share them with the community. Gallery is an architecturally outstanding facility with foyer, display area and patio, parking in central campus. Average Annual Attendance: 1500
Income: Financed by Fine Arts department & private endowment
Collections: 17th, 18th & 19th century French tapestries and furniture; South

Asian textiles and costumes of 19th and 20th centuries; Tibetan and Indian looms, Ghandi spinning wheels; 19th Century French bronze sculpture; 20th Century Paintings
Exhibitions: Seven shows each year
Publications: The Impressionist as Printmaker; Child Hassam 1859-1935; Arbol de la Vida, The Ceramic Art of Metepec
Activities: Educ dept; seminars in art history; lectures open to the public, 4 vis lectr per yr; concerts; gallery talks; tours; awards; originate traveling exhibitions

SAN FRANCISCO

A **AFRICAN AMERICAN HISTORICAL AND CULTURAL SOCIETY,** Fort Mason Ctr, Bldg C, Room 165, 94123. Tel 415-441-0640. *Pres* Ollie Bradley; *VPres* Kimberly Smith; *Exec Dir* Donetta Lane; *Admin Asst* Selina Shadle
Open Tues - Sat noon - 5 PM. Estab 1955 as an archival & presentation institution of African American thought & culture
Income: $100,000 (financed by membership & donations)
Collections: African artifacts, sculpture; Haitian art; Sargent Johnson
Publications: Ascension, biennial; Praisesinger, newsletter
Activities: Classes for adults & children; lectures open to public, 12 vis lectr per yr; gallery talks; tours; originate traveling exhibitions; sales shop sells books, magazines, original art, reproductions, prints, t-shirts, African art

L **Library,** 762 Fulton St, 94123. Tel 415-292-6172. *Librn* Amy Holloway
For reference only
Library Holdings: Vols 3000; Oral history
Collections: 1000 periodicals; African-American newspapers

A **AMERICAN INDIAN CONTEMPORARY ARTS,** 685 Market, Suite 250, 94105-4212. Tel 415-495-7600. *Exec Dir Sicangu Lakato Tribe* Janeen Antoine; *Dir Exhib & Prog Cherokee Tribe* Sara Bates
Open Tues - Sat 10 AM - 5:30 PM. No admis fee. Estab 1983 to bring to the public eye perspectives on a new generation of American Indian artists. Managed by an American Indian staff & board, it is an wsuxrional, advocacy & development organization for today's Indian artists trying to bridge the gap between traditional & contemporary art & native & non-native people
Exhibitions: (1992) Portfolio III Groups 1 & 2; Solo Exhibit - Harry Fonseca (Maidu Tribe); Indigenous People: No Boundaries; Translating Indian Memory; From the Earth VIII - A Holiday Group Exhibit. (1993) Akua, Ali'i A Me Kahuna (Gods, Chief & Holy Men) - Hawaiian Native Artist; Submuloc Wohs/ Columbus Show; Native America: Reflecting Contemporary Realities; Works on Paper: Institute of American Indian Art Student Show; Solo Exhibit - Nora Naranjo-Morse (Santa Clara Pueblo Tribe); From the Earth IX - A Holiday Group Exhibit.
Activities: On sight lect; group tours; lect at schools & universities

A **ARCHIVES OF MOCA (MUSEUM OF CONCEPTUAL ART),** 22 Hawthorne St, 94105. Tel 415-495-3193 (voice & Fax). *Dir* Tom Marioni; *Cur* Joyce Umamoto
Open by appointment. No admis fee. Estab 1970 for research, study & organization of exhibitions & events
Income: Financed by endowment
Exhibitions: Vito Acconci; Robert Barry; Bar Room Video; Chris Burden; Lowell Darling; Howard Fried; Paul Kos; Masashi Matsumoto; Restoration of Back Wall; Miniatures from San Francisco & Kyoto; Social Art, Cafe Society
Publications: Vision, annually
Activities: Classes for adults; lect, 2 vis lectr per yr; artmobile; original objects of art lent to museums & art centers; original traveling exhibitions

L **Library,** 22 Hawthorne St, 94105. Tel 415-495-3193. *Dir* Tom Marioni
For reference only
Library Holdings: Vols 1000; Original documents; Micro — Reels; AV — A-tapes, cassettes, fs, Kodachromes, motion pictures, rec, slides, v-tapes; Other — Exhibition catalogs, original art works, pamphlets, photographs, prints, sculpture
Exhibitions: Inspired by Leonardo

A **ART COM-LA MAMELLE, INC,** 70 12th St, PO Box 193123 Rincon, 94119-3123. Tel 415-431-7524, 431-7672. *Exec Dir* Carl E Loeffler; *Asst Dir* Jennifer Bender; *Distribution* Jen Tait
Open Mon - Fri 10:30 AM - 6:30 PM. Estab 1975 to support network for contemporary art
Income: Financed by endowment, membership and state appropriation
Collections: Artists' books, marginal works, video & television art, tape collection
Exhibitions: On Going - Artists Software; Artists Computer Graphics
Publications: Performance Anthology: Source book for a decade of California performance art; Correspondence Art: Source Book for the Network of International Postal Art Activity; ACEN (Art Com Electronic Network); Art Com Magazine; BBS
Activities: Distributes artists' video & television art world wide; maintains ACEN, an online artists' network for information sharing & distribution of art information; traveling exhibitions organized and circulated

L **Contemporary Art Archives,** 70 12th St, PO Box 193123 Rincon, 94119
For reference only
Special Subjects: Video, Artists' books, Alternative publishing, Performance

M **ASIAN ART MUSEUM OF SAN FRANCISCO,** Avery Brundage Collection, Golden Gate Park, 94118-4598. Tel 415-668-8921; FAX 415-668-8928; Cable SANCEMOR. *Dir* Rand Castile; *Deputy Dir* Judith Teichman; *Cur Indian Art* Terese Tse Bartholomew; *Cur Japanese Art* Yoshiko Kakudo; *Cur Educ* Richard Mellott; *Cur Chinese Art* Patricia Berger; *Cur S E Asia* Nancy Hock; *Conservator* Linda Scheifler; *Cur of Korean Art* Kumja Kim; *Librn* Fred A Cline Jr
Open Wed - Sun 10 AM - 5 PM, cl Mon, Tues & Christmas. Admis adults (18-64) $4, youth (5-17) & senior citizens $2, children under 5 free; recognized educational group free; first Wed of each month free. Founded in 1969 by the City and County of San Francisco to collect, care for, exhibit and interpret the fine arts of Asia. 40,000 sq ft of exhibition space. Average Annual Attendance:

550,000. Mem: 51,000; annual dues $45

Income: Financed by city and county appropriation and the Asian Art Museum Foundation

Collections: Nearly 12,000 objects from China, Japan, Korea, India, Southeast Asia, The Himalayas, and Middle East

Publications: Handbooks and catalogs on museum collections; exhibition catalogs

Activities: Classes for adults and children; dramtic programs; docent training; lectures open to public, 5 vis lectr per yr; concerts; gallery talks; tours; originate traveling exhibitions; museum shop sells books, magazines, original art, reproductions

L **Library,** Golden Gate Park, 94118-4598. Tel 415-668-8921; FAX 415-668-8928. *Librn* Fred A Cline Jr

Open Wed - Fri 10 AM - 4:45 PM. Estab 1967. For reference only

Income: Financed by membership, city appropriation and private gifts

Library Holdings: Vols 23,000; Per subs 160; Micro — Fiche, reels; AV — A-tapes, Kodachromes, lantern slides, motion pictures, slides; Other — Clipping files, exhibition catalogs, manuscripts, memorabilia, pamphlets, photographs

Special Subjects: Antiquities-Oriental, Antiquities-Persian, Archaeology, Architecture, Art History, Asian Art, Bronzes, Calligraphy, Carpets & Rugs, Ceramics, Decorative Arts, Dolls, Drawings, Embroidery, Enamels, Folk Art, Furniture, Glass, Gold, Goldsmithing, Handicrafts, Historical Material, History of Art & Archaeology, Islamic Art, Ivory, Jade, Jewelry, Landscape Architecture, Leather, Metalwork, Miniatures, Oriental Art, Painting - Japanese, Porcelain, Pottery, Printmaking, Prints, Religious Art, Restoration & Conservation, Sculpture, Silver, Silversmithing, Tapestries, Textiles, Watercolors, Woodcarvings, Woodcuts

Collections: Chinese painting collection; Khmer Art Collection

C **BANK OF AMERICA GALLERIES,** 555 California St, Art Program 3021, PO Box 37000, 94137. Tel 415-622-1265; FAX 415-622-2387. *Cur* Bonnie Earls-Solari

Open Plaza Gallery Mon - Fri 8 AM - 5:30 PM, Concourse Gallery Mon - Fri 8 AM - Midnight, A P Giannini Gallery Mon - Fri 8 AM - 7 PM. No admis fee. Estab 1970 to operate as a public service by Bank America Corporation for the downtown, financial district audience and art community. Average Annual Attendance: 520,000

Collections: Collection contains contemporary art in all media

Activities: Individual paintings and original objects of art lent to bonafide exhibitions and exhibiting bodies which can protect and properly install the art

M **CALIFORNIA CRAFTS MUSEUM,** Ghirardelli Square, 900 N Point, PO Box 25, 94109. Tel 415-771-1919. *Admin Dir* Margaret Wolverton

Open daily 11 AM - 6 PM. No admis fee. Estab 1978 to exhibit contemporary fine crafts. Average Annual Attendance: 20,000

Income: Financed by friends or mem, city appropriation, San Francisco Hotel Tax Fund

Activities: Lect open to the public, some to members only, 1 - 5 vis lectr per year; retail store sells books, magazines, original crafts

M **CAPP STREET PROJECT,** 250 14th St, 94103. Tel 415-626-7747. *Pres* Ann Hatch; *Prog Mgr* Mary Ceruti; *Gallery Mgr* Anastasia Shartin

Estab 1983 as a non-profit arts organization providing three month residencies in San Francisco

Exhibitions: (1991) Artists - Kate Erickson & Mel Ziegler

M **CARTOON ART MUSEUM,** 665 Third St, 94107. Tel 415-546-3922. *Dir* Valerie Cox; *Asst to Dir* Suzanne Hampton

Open Wed - Sat 11 AM - 5 PM. Admis adult $2.50, senior citizen $1.25, children $1. Estab 1984 to exhibit original cartoon art. 1000 sq ft exhibition space. Average Annual Attendance: 10,000. Mem: 500, dues individual $30

Income: $28,000

Collections: Original Cartoon Art; Books on Cartoon Art & Popular Culture

Exhibitions: 40 Years of Peanuts

Activities: Adult classes; retail store sells books, prints, magazines

A **CENTER FOR CRITICAL ARCHITECTURE,** 2AES (Art & Architecture Exhibition Space), 1700 17th St, 2nd Floor, 94103. Tel 415-863-1502; FAX 415-546-6415. *Dir* Pam Kinzie

Estab 1988 to establish awareness of design excellence & provide vehicle for exchange of critical ideas in architecture. Average Annual Attendance: 3500. Mem: 50; 1600 mailing list; dues firms $100, individuals $25

Income: Financed by endowment & mem

Exhibitions: (1993) In the Public Realm; San Francisco Embarcadero Waterfront Competition Winners

Publications: Cafe Talks

Activities: Lect open to public, 6 vis lectr per year; competitions with prizes; book traveling exhibitions 2 per year

A **CHINESE CULTURE FOUNDATION,** Chinese Culture Center Gallery, 750 Kearny St, 3rd Floor, 94108. Tel 415-986-1822; FAX 415-986-2825. *Pres* Tatwina Lee; *Exec VPres* Norman Lew; *Exec Dir* Kathleen Guan

Open Tues - Sat 10 AM - 4 PM, cl holidays. No admis fee. Estab 1965 to promote the understanding and appreciation of Chinese and Chinese-American culture in the United States. Traditional and contemporary paintings and sculpture by Chinese and Chinese-American artists, photographs and artifacts illustrating Chinese-American history, and major international and cultural exchanges from China make the center a local and national focus of Chinese artistic activities. Mem: 1500

Income: Financed by membership, city appropriation and grants

Exhibitions: Stories from China's Past; Beyond the Open Door; Landscapes of the Mind: Paintings of C C Wang; The Art of Wu Gaunzhong. (1991 - 92) Six Contemporary Chinese Women Artists

Publications: Chinese Culture Center Newsletter, quarterly; Exhibition catalogs

Activities: Classes for adults and children; dramatic programs; docent training; lect open to the public; concerts; gallery talks; tours; film programs; museum shop selling books, original art, reproductions, prints, jewelry, pottery, jade, material and papercuts

C **EMBARCADERO CENTER LTD,** 4 Embarcadero Center, Suite 2600, 94111. Tel 415-772-0500. *Public Relations Dir* Terri Lagrisola

Open to public at all hours. No admis fee. Estab 1971, modern art has been a key element in the planning and development of the Embarcadero Center complex; evidence of a desire to provide beauty on a smaller scale amid the harmony of its massive structures; to enhance the total environment, and provide a variety of dramatic views for pedestrians as they circulate through the complex. Collection displayed throughout the Center complex; Center supports San Francisco DeYoung Museum, Fine Arts Museum Downtown Center, American Conservatory Theatre, San Francisco Symphony, San Francisco Center for the Performing Arts, and others

Collections: Willi Gutmann, Two Columns with Wedge; Francoise Grossen; Michael Gibbers, Steel Sculptures; Nicholas Schoffer, Chronos XIV; Lia Cook, Space Continuum Two; Olga de Amaral, Citurs Wall; Anne Van Kleeck, Blocks, Stacks; Louise Nevelson, Sky Tree; Barbara Shawcroft, Yellow Leggs; Robert Russin, Chthonodynamis; Jean Dubuffet, La Chiffonniere; Sheila Hicks, Cristobal's Trapeze & Itaka's Cascade; John Portman Jr, The Tulip; Elbert Weinberg, Mistral; Charles O Perry, Eclipse; Adolph Gottlieb, Burst; Francoise Grossen; Olga de Amaral, Hojarasca en mil Rojos; Jagoda Buic, Souvenir en Blue; Josef Grau Garriga, Lapell D'un Poble; Candace Crockett, Revival; Armand Vaillancourt, 101 precast aggregate concrete boxes that allow visitors to walk over, under & through its waterfalls

A **EXPLORATORIUM,** 3601 Lyon St, 94123. Tel 415-563-7337; FAX 415-561-0307. *Dir* Goery Delacote; *Artist Coordr* Peter Richards; *Professional Internship Prog* Sally Duensing

Open winter Wed - Fri 1 - 5 PM, Wed 5 - 9 PM, Sat & Sun 10 AM - 5 PM, summer Wed - Sun 11 AM - 5 PM, Wed 5 - 9 PM. Admis adult $6, sr citizen $1.50, 6 - 18 $1. Estab 1969 to provide exhibits and art works centering around the theme of perception, which are designed to be manipulated and appreciated at a variety of levels by both children and adults. Average Annual Attendance: 500,000. Mem: 1500; dues $35

Income: Financed by National city & state appropriation, private foundations & corporation contributions

Publications: The Exploratorium Magazine, monthly; exhibition catalogs

Activities: Classes for artists in residence program, performing artists in residence program & teachers; lect open to the public; concerts; tours; originate traveling exhibitions; museum shop selling books, magazines, reproductions, prints, slides and science related material

M **EYE GALLERY,** 1151 Mission St, 94103. Tel 415-431-6911; FAX 415-431-1664. *Dir* Lynette Molnar; *Gallery Mgr* Michael Hofman

Open Mon - Sat noon - 5 PM. Admis, donation. Estab 1982 as a non-profit organization dedicated to presenting socially concerned photography. One large 60 ft x 20 ft gallery with sound, video & film equipment, one small 20 ft x 16 ft gallery. Average Annual Attendance: 20,000. Mem: 400; dues $25 - $500

Collections: Photographs collection

Exhibitions: 10 exhibitions through out the year, plus auction & selections

Activities: Classes for adults & children; lect, 20 vis lectr per year; gallery talks; competitions; book traveling exhibitions

A **EYES AND EARS FOUNDATION,** 870 Market St, Suite 1260, 94102. Tel 415-621-2300. *Exec Dir* Mark Rennie; *Pres* Freddie Hahne

Estab 1976 to sponsor public visual performance art projects, mostly outdoor large-scale billboard art shows & the theatre projects. Average Annual Attendance: 25,000 - 100,000 per day. Mem: 100; dues $15

Income: $57,000 (financed by endowment, membership, fundraising, individual & corporate contributions)

Exhibitions: Artists Television Access; Lynn Hershman & Lisa English's Endangered Species; Sando Counts, Sideshow; weekly exhibitions. (1991) Comedia Bowl

M **FINE ARTS MUSEUMS OF SAN FRANCISCO,** M H de Young Memorial Museum and California Palace of the Legion of Honor, Golden Gate Park, 94118. Tel 415-750-3600. *Dir* Harry S Parker III; *Secy* Delores Malone; *Dir Educ* Louis Gordon; *Deputy Dir Admin* Stephen E Dykes; *Assoc Dir & Chief Cur* Steven Nash; *Cur American Decorative Arts* Donald L Stover; *Cur Prints & Drawings* Robert F Johnson; *Cur African, Oceania & the Americas* Kathleen Berrin; *Mgr Exhib* Bill White; *Cur Interpretation* Renee Dreyfus; *Dir Development* James Forbes; *Cur Textiles* Melissa Levitan; *Registrar* Ted Greenberg; *Conservator Paper* Robert Futernick; *Cur American Painting* Marc Simpson; *Publications Mgr* Ann Karlstrom; *Cur Rugs* Cathryn Cootner; *General Mgr Museum Stores* Couric Payne; *Editor Triptych* Pamela Forbes

Open Wed - Sun 10 AM - 5 PM. Admis adults $5, sr & youth 12 - 17 $3, under 12 free. Estab 1895 to provide museums of historic art from ancient Egypt to the 20th century. Two separate buildings are maintained, one in the Golden Gate Park (de Young Museum) with 65 galleries, and the other in Lincoln Park (California Palace of the Legion of Honor) with 22 galleries. Average Annual Attendance: 800,000. Mem: 50,000; dues patron $1000, sponsor $500, donor $250, supporting $100, sustaining $60, participating $45, individual $25, senior dual $20, senior single $15

Income: $7,500,000 (financed by endowment, membership, city appropriations, & grants)

Purchases: Portrait of a Lady by Frans Pourbus the Younger (1569/70-1622), Roscoe & Margaret Oakes Fund

Collections: African Art; American Art; Ancient Art; Art from Central & South America & Mesoamerica; Textiles graphic arts of all schools and eras; primitive arts of Africa, Oceania and the Americas; Rodin sculpture collection

Exhibitions: The Search for Alexander; The Vatican Collections: The Papacy and Art; The New Painting: Impressionism 1874-1886

Publications: Triptych, bi-monthly magazine; exhibition and collection catalogues

Activities: Docent tours; symposia; teacher's workshops; lectures; concerts; films; museum shop sells books, magazines, reproductions, prints, slides & jewelry

L **Library,** Golden Gate Park, 94118. Tel 415-750-7603. *Librn* Gerald Smith

Estab 1955 to serve museum staff in research on collections, conservation, acquisition, interpretations. Graphic arts are housed in the Achenbach Foundation Library in the California Palace of the Legion of Honor

Income: Financed by membership and city appropriation
Library Holdings: Vols 45,000; Per subs 125; Micro — Fiche 613, reels; AV — Slides 30,000; Other — Exhibition catalogs
Special Subjects: American Indian Art, African, American, French and Oceanic art
Collections: Achenbach Foundation for Graphic Arts (prints and drawings)

A **The Museum Society,** c/o de Young Museum, Golden Gate Park, 94118. Tel 415-750-3636; FAX 415-750-7686. *Membership Mgr* Paula March
Estab 1971 as a membership organization for Fine Arts Museums of San Francisco and the Asian Art Museum of San Francisco. Mem: 45,000; dues $50
Income: $2,770,000 (financed by membership and bookshop revenues)
Publications: Triptych, bimonthly magazine
Activities: Museum shop sells books, reproductions, prints and slides

A **THE FRIENDS OF PHOTOGRAPHY,** Ansel Adams Center for Photography, 250 Fourth St, 94103. Tel 415-495-7000. *Pres* C David Robinson; *VPres* David Vena; *Exec Dir* Andy Grundberg; *Treas* Geoffrey Yang; *Secy* Rena Bransten
Open Tues - Sun 11 AM - 5 PM. Admis adults $4, students $3, sr citizens & youth 12 - 17 $2, members & children free. Estab 1967 to promote creative photography through exhibitions, workshops, publications & critical inquiry. Maintains an art gallery with continuous exhibitions. Average Annual Attendance: 36,400. Mem: 5500; dues $35
Income: $1,000,000 (financed by endowment, membership, city and state appropriations, federal grants and patrons)
Collections: Photographs by Ansel Adams
Publications: Untitled, book series published by the Friends of Photography, 2 times per year; newsletter, 6 issues per year; monographic publications
Activities: Classes for adults; educational outreach to children; lect open to the public, 6 vis lectr per year; competitions with awards; scholarships; book traveling exhibitions; originate traveling exhibitions; sales shop sells books

M **GALERIA DE LA RAZA,** Studio 24, 2851 & 2857 24th St, 94110. Tel 415-826-8009. *Dir* Maria Pinedo
Open Tues - Sat 1 - 6 PM, Galeria; Mon - Sat noon - 6 PM, Studio 24. Estab 1969 as a community gallery and museum to exhibit works by Chicano-Latino artists, contemporary as well as cultural folk art. Average Annual Attendance: 35,000. Mem: 135; annual dues $25
Income: Financed by NEA, California Arts Council, private foundations and earned income from sales in studio
Exhibitions: Changing monthly
Publications: Exhibition catalogs, small publications, yearly calendar, children's coloring book and postcards; bi-monthly newsletter
Activities: Classes for adults and children; folk art demonstrations; lectures open to public, 4 vis lectr per yr; concerts; gallery talks; awards; galeria tours; originate one traveling exhibition per year; museum shop sells books, magazines, original art, reproductions, prints, folk art
L **Chicano-Latino Arts Resource Library,** 2857 24th St, 94110. Tel 415-826-8009.
Open Mon - Fri noon - 6 PM. Estab 1978 as a reference and archive of Chicano and Latino arts
Income: $1000
Purchases: $500
Library Holdings: Vols 300; Per subs 5; AV — Slides; Other — Clipping files, exhibition catalogs, memorabilia, original art works, pamphlets, photographs, prints, reproductions
Special Subjects: El Dia de Los Muertas artifacts and resources
Collections: Chicano and Latino murals; Chicano Latino Youth; car clubs Mexican Folk Art; Mexican and Latin American Contemporary Art

A **INTERSECTION FOR THE ARTS,** 446 Valencia, 94103. Tel 415-626-2787. *Dir* Francis Phillips
Open Tues - Sat noon - 4:30 PM. Estab 1965 to represent visual & performing arts. Average Annual Attendance: 10,000
Exhibitions: (1990) A Installation: From Here to There by Kate Connel & John Santof

A **JAPANTOWN ART & MEDIA WORKSHOP,** 1840 Sutter St, Suite 207, 94115. Tel 415-922-8700. *Exec Dir* Dennis Taniguchi; *Creative Dir* Alex Mizuno
Open daily 10 AM - 5 PM. No admis fee. Estab 1977 as an Asian-American art center. Mem: 120; dues $20
Income: $100,000 (financed by endowment, mem, foundations, city & state appropriations)
Collections: Silkscreen posters & other art works
Exhibitions: Layer Exhibition; Asia-American Film & Video Exhibit
Publications: Enemy Alien; Yoisho
Activities: Classes for adults & children; concerts; competitions with awards; lending collection contains posters

L **MECHANICS' INSTITUTE LIBRARY,** 57 Post St, 94104. Tel 415-421-1750. *Dir* K T Pabst; *Reference Librn* Craig Jackson
Open for members only Mon - Thurs 9 AM - 9 PM, Fri & Sat 9 AM - 6 PM, Sun 1 - 5 PM. Estab 1854 to serve the needs of 7000 members with a general collection emphasizing the humanities. Circ 285,000
Income: Financed by city appropriation, building rents, endowment
Library Holdings: Vols 180,000; Per subs 685; Newspapers; Micro — Fiche; AV — Cassettes, v-tapes; Other — Clipping files
Special Subjects: American Western Art, Architecture, Art History, Crafts, Decorative Arts, Embroidery, Etchings & Engravings, Fashion Arts, Furniture, Handicrafts, Painting - American, Painting - Australian, Painting - British, Painting - French, Painting - German, Japanese Painting, Photography, Watercolors

M **MEXICAN MUSEUM,** Fort Mason Center, Bldg D, Laguna & Marina Blvd, 94123. Tel 415-441-0445. *Exec Dir* Marie Acosta-Colon; *Deputy Dir* Gloria Jaramillo; *Interim Cur* Jonathan Yorba; *Cur Cultural Prog* Rene Yanez; *Financial Mgr* Chris Kovach; *Acting Dir Development* Amy Schoenborn
Open Wed - Sun noon - 5 PM. Admis adults $3, students & sr citizens $2, suggested donation $40 per group up to 35. Estab 1975 to foster the exhibition,

conservation & dissemination of Mexican & Mexican American & Chicano culture for all people. Average Annual Attendance: 60,000. Mem: 720, dues $25
Income: Financed by state grants, corporate & individual support, earned income through gift shop, memberships, educational tours & workshops
Collections: Chicano, Colonial, Folk, Mexcian, Mexican-American & pre-Hispanic Fine Arts
Exhibitions: (1992) The Chicano Codices; Encountering Art of the Americas; The Fifth Element: Recent Acquisitions of Contemporary Art. (1993) Carlos Almaraz: A Retrospective; Visiones Del Pueblo: The Folk Art of Latin America; Gronk: A Multi-media exhibition; El Dia De Los Muertos; Ceremony of Memory II: New Expressions in Spirituality Among Contemporary Chicano & Latino Artists
Publications: Exhibit catalogs
Activities: Summer internship program; docent program; lect open to public; gallery talks; tours; exten dept serves San Francisco Bay area; lending collection contains slides and educational kits; book traveling exhibitions; museum shop sells folk art objects, books, original art, reproductions, prints, posters, clothing & woven goods

M **MUSEO ITALO AMERICANO,** Fort Mason Center, Bldg C, 94123. Tel 415-673-2200; FAX 415-673-2292. *Pres* Eugene Bertorelli; *VPres* Stephanie Wilhelm; *VPres* Paola Bagnatori; *Secy* Claudio Tarchi; *Cur* Robert Whyte; *Chmn* Modesto Lanzone; *Adminr* Jovanne D Reilly
Open Wed - Sun noon - 5 PM. Admis $2, sr & students $1. Estab 1978 to research, preserve and display works of Italian and Italian-American artists and to foster educational programs for the appreciation of Italian and Italian-American art, history and culture. The Museo is located on San Francisco's waterfront at Fort Mason Center. Average Annual Attendance: 12,000-20,000. Mem: annual dues $35 & up
Income: Financed by membership, city appropriation, foundations & corporate contributions
Collections: Over 100 donated works by Italian & Italian American artists
Exhibitions: The Work of David Bottini (sculpture); Frank Spadarella (photography); Palcoscenico e Spazio Scenico (stage design; Emerging Artists Show
Publications: Calendar of Events, quarterly
Activities: Classes for adults and children; Italian language classes; lectures open to public; concerts; gallery talks; tours; museum shop sells books, original art, reproductions, prints, jewelry & wide range of objects created by Italians & Italian Americans
L Fort Mason Ctr, Bldg C, 94123-1380. Tel 415-673-2200; FAX 415-673-2292. *Pres* Eugene Bertorelli
Estab 1978 to serve as a resource center of Italian & Italian-American materials
Library Holdings: Vols 300; Per subs 3

M **NEW LANGTON ARTS,** 1246 Folsom St, 94103. Tel 415-626-5416; FAX 415-255-1453. *Exec Dir* Nancy Gonchar; *Prog Dir* Shauna O'Donnell; *Mgr* Arnold Kemp; *Development Dir* Heather Tissue
Estab 1975 to support artists in experimental art, non-profit organization
Exhibitions: David Wilson: Museum of Jurassic Technology. (1991) George Stone; Irwin; Beliz Brothers; Chris Daubert; Trimpin; Bruce Tomb & John Randolph. (1992) Millie Wilson: Living in Someone Else's Paradise; The Abortion Project; Daniel Martinez: I Pissed on the Man who Called Me a Dog

M **RANDALL MUSEUM JUNIOR MUSEUM** (Formerly Josephine D/Randall Junior Museum), 199 Museum Way, 94114. Tel 415-554-9600. *Dir* Amy Dawson; *Cur Natural Sciences* John Dillon; *Cur Arts* Chris Boetcher; *Art Instr* Dennis Treanor; *Art Instr* Julie Dodd Tetzlaff
Open Tues - Sat 10 AM - 5 PM, cl holidays. No admis fee. Estab 1937 as part of the San Francisco Recreation & Park Dept. Average Annual Attendance: 50,000. Mem: 300; dues $15 - $250; annual meeting June
Collections: Animals; Children's Art; Indian Artifacts; Insects, Minerals
Activities: Classes for adults & children; dramatic programs; docent training; lect open to public; concerts; tours; competitions with awards; scholarships

L **SAN FRANCISCO ACADEMY OF COMIC ART,** Library, 2850 Ulloa St, 94116. Tel 415-681-1737. *Dir* Bill Blackbeard
Open daily by appointment 10 AM - 10 PM. Estab 1967 to locate, preserve and house all elements of American popular narrative culture in danger of destruction through oversight or misunderstanding. Gallery maintained
Income: Financed by grants, donations, fees from personnel writing and lect, research charges
Library Holdings: Vols 28,000; Per subs 42; AV — Cassettes, motion pictures, rec, slides, v-tapes; Other — Clipping files, exhibition catalogs, framed reproductions, manuscripts, memorabilia, original art works, pamphlets, photographs, prints, reproductions
Collections: †Adventure fiction; †the American comic strip; †the American newspaper; †the American popular fiction magazine; †children's books since 1850; †detective fiction; †motion pictures; †the popular illustrated periodical; radical and underground publications; †science fiction; †Victorian illustrated book; western fiction
Exhibitions: Permanent collection: Original art in the comic strip and popular fiction; comic strip exhibit; national science fiction
Activities: Lect, 10 visiting lectr per year; gallery talks; tours; originate traveling exhibitions

M **SAN FRANCISCO ART INSTITUTE,** Galleries, 800 Chestnut St, 94133. Tel 415-771-7020. *Gallery Dir* Jeanie Weiffenbach
Open Mon - Fri 9 AM - 5 PM. No admis fee. Estab 1871, incorporated 1889 to foster the appreciation & creation of the fine arts & maintain a school & museum for that purpose. Walter McBean Gallery, two-level, used for exhibitions of contemporary artists of international repute; Diego Rivera Gallery, one room with Rivera miral, used for exhibitions of work by SFAI students; SFAI Photo Gallery, for photo students. Average Annual Attendance: 60,000. Mem: 1300; dues $15 - $100 & up; annual meeting June
Exhibitions: Walter McBean (six exhibitions per yr)
Publications: Exhibition catalogs
Activities: Lectures open to public, some for members only; 20 vis per yr; gallery talks; tours; competitions; scholarships & fels offered; exten dept; Traveling exhibitions organized & circulated; sales shop sells art supplies

L **Anne Bremer Memorial Library,** 800 Chestnut St, 94133. Tel 415-771-7020, ext 59. *Media Dir* C Stephanian; *Librn* Jeff Gunderson; *Catalog Librn* Carolyn Franklin; *Library Asst* Claudia Marlowe; *Catalog Asst* Deborah White; *Media Asst* Trish Carney
Open Mon - Thurs 9 AM - 8 PM, Fri 9 AM - 5 PM during school sessions. Estab 1871 to develop a collection & services which will anticipate, reflect & support the objectives & direction of the San Francisco Art Institute & the contemporary arts community. Circ 12,795
Library Holdings: Vols 26,000; Per subs 200; AV — Cassettes 600, fs, Kodachromes, motion pictures, slides 60,000; Other — Clipping files, exhibition catalogs, manuscripts, memorabilia, pamphlets, photographs
Collections: Archives documenting the history of the Art Institute; artists' books; audio-tapes of artists working in sound (experimental music, etc)
Exhibitions: 1960's Rock Posters; Artists' Book Contest; Living First Ladies Mural
Activities: Poetry-Book Readings; current events roundtable

A **SAN FRANCISCO ARTSPACE & ARTSPACE ANNEX,** 1286 Folsom St, 94103. Tel 415-626-9100; FAX 415-431-6612. *Dir* Anne MacDonald; *Prog Dir* Maureen Keefe
Open Tues - Sat. Estab 1985 for contemporary exhibitions & installations; video editing & sound systems. 2 galleries, 3000 sq ft
Income: Financed by endowment, mem, city & state appropriation
Exhibitions: Jessica Diamond
Publications: Shift Magazine, quarterly
Activities: Children's classes; lect open to public, 5 vis lectr per year; grants offered; retail store sells books, magazines

A **SAN FRANCISCO CAMERAWORK INC,** 70 - 12th St, 94103. Tel 415-621-1001. *Dir* Marnie Gillett; *Assoc Dir* Rupert Jenkins
Open Tues - Sat noon - 5 PM. Estab 1973 to encourage and display contemporary photography & related visual arts through exhibitions, lectures, publications & communication services. Two large galleries in a loft space as well as bookstore display area. Average Annual Attendance: 35,000. Mem: 850; dues $35 per yr
Income: Financed by government agencies & private contributions, membership
Exhibitions: (1991) Nuclear Matters
Publications: San Francisco Camerawork Quarterly
Activities: Educ dept; lect open to public, 25 vis lectr per yr; workshops; gallery talks; book traveling exhibition annually; originate traveling exhibitions; museum shop sells books and magazines, postcards, artists' books

A **SAN FRANCISCO CITY & COUNTY ARTS COMMISSION,** 25 Venice, Room 240, 94102. Tel 415-558-3463. *Pres* Ann Healey; *Dir Cultural Affairs* Joan Winship; *Dir Neighborhood Art Prog* Sonia Gray; *Coordr Street Artist Prog* Howard Lazar; *Art Coordr* Jill Manton; *Cur Capricorn Asunder Gallery* Ann Meisner; *Art Coordr* Tonia Macneil
Open daily 8 AM - 5 PM. No admis fee. Estab 1932. Average Annual Attendance: 100,000. Mem: Consists of 9 professional and 3 lay-members appointed by the Mayor with advice of art societies, and 5 ex-officio members; monthly meetings. Passes on all buildings and works of art placed on property of City or County; supervises and controls all appropriations made by the Board of Supervisors of music and the advancement of art and music; may volunteer advice to private owners who submit plans for suggestions; maintains a State/Local Partnership Program and a Neighborhood Arts Program; administers ordinance providing two percent of cost of public construction for art; also, a municipal collection for art for embellishing public offices; maintains art gallery and Annual Symphony Pops Concerts and Annual Arts Festival; licenses street artists; responsible for cataloging and maintaining all public works of art
Activities: Classes for adults and children; dramatic programs; docent training; lectures open to the public; concerts; gallery talks; tours; competitions with awards; individual paintings & original objects of art lent

M **SAN FRANCISCO CRAFT AND FOLK ART MUSEUM,** Fort Mason Center, Landmark Bldg A, 94123-1382. Tel 415-775-0990. *Dir* J Weldon Smith, PhD; *Cur* Carole Austin; *Adminr* Mary Ann McNicholas
Estab 1982 to provide a permanent showplace for contemporary craft, folk art and traditional ethnic art. 1500 sq ft, two stories. Average Annual Attendance: 90,000. Mem: 756
Income: $250,000 (financed by endowment, membership fees, city and state appropriations and private foundations)
Publications: A Report, scholarly quarterly; 1989-90 The Arts & Crafts Studio of Dirk Van Erp; The Quiet Eye: Pottery of Shoji Hamada and Bernard Leach
Activities: Lectures open to the public, 6 lectr per year; special events; sales shop sells books, original art, crafts

M **SAN FRANCISCO MARITIME NATIONAL HISTORICAL PARK** (Formerly National Maritime Museum - San Francisco), National Maritime Museum, Bldg E, Lower Fort Mason, 94123. Tel 415-556-1659; FAX 415-556-1624. *Supt* William G Thomas; *Chief Cur* Karl Kortum
Open winter daily 10 AM - 5 PM, summer daily 10 AM - 6 PM. Admis adults $3, sr citizens & children free. Estab 1951; museum built in 1939; a terazzo and stainless steel structure with a nautical theme
Income: Financed by federal funding, private support from National Maritime Museum Association, National Maritime Museum Library & donations
Purchases: A S Palmer Film Collection
Special Subjects: Maritime history with emphasis on San Francisco & Pacific Coast
Collections: †Ship models; paintings; square-rigged sailing ship; paddlewheel ferry; paddlewheel tug; 3-mast schooner; steam schooner; scow schooner; steam tug, small craft
Exhibitions: Tugboats; San Francisco Bay Ferryboats
Publications: Sealetter; booklets, irregular
Activities: Slide lectures; environmental living program; sales shop sells books, magazines, reproductions and misc materials

L **J Porter Shaw Library,** Lower Fort Mason, Bldg E, 94123. Tel 415-556-9870; FAX 415-556-1624. *Principal Librn* David Hull; *Reference* Irene Stachura; *Technical Services* Herbert Beckwith
Open to the public for research on premises
Library Holdings: Vols 18,000; Per subs 150; Archives, Vessel Plans, Oral History; Micro — Fiche, reels; AV — A-tapes, cassettes, motion pictures; Other — Clipping files, manuscripts, memorabilia, pamphlets, photographs 250,000

M **SAN FRANCISCO MUSEUM OF MODERN ART,** 401 Van Ness, 94102. Tel 415-252-4000; FAX 415-863-0603. *Dir* John R Lane; *Deputy Dir* Inge Lise Eckmann; *Chief Cur* Richard Siegesmund; *Controller* Ikuko Satoda; *Dir, Public Relations* Chelsea Brown; *Dir Development* Virginia C Rubin
Open Tues - Wed & Fri 10 AM - 5 PM, Thurs 10 AM - 9 PM, Sat & Sun 11 AM - 5 PM. Admis adults $4, sr citizens & students $2, Thurs $2 after 5 PM, members & children under 13 free. Estab 1935 to collect and exhibit art of the 20th century. Museum occupies two floors; four major galleries 35 x 180 ft; six corridor galleries; six smaller galleries. Average Annual Attendance: 300,000. Mem: 13,000; dues $15 - $1000
Income: Financed by endowment, membership, city hotel tax, earnings & grants
Collections: Clyfford Still; †painting, †photography, †sculpture †architecture & design, †media & video works
Exhibitions: (1992) Robert Rauschenberg: The Early 1950s; Typologies: Nine Contemporary Photographers; Jackson Pollock: Psychoanalytic Drawings; Wright Morris: Origin of a Species; 1992 SECA Art Award; Luciano Fabro: A Retrospective; Linda Connor; Richard Diebenkorn; Jeff Koons; California Graphic Designers. (1993) On Kawara: Date Paintings in 89 Cities; Shin Takamatsu; Clyfford Still; Richard Prince; Thresholds & Enclosures; Carrie Mae Weems; General Idea's Fin de Siecle; John Heartfield Photomontages; Cady Noland: New Work; Max Beckmann Prints from the Collection of The Museum of Modern Art
Publications: Calendar, monthly
Activities: Classes for adults and children; docent training; lect open to public, 6-8 visiting lectrs per year; concerts; gallery talks; tours; traveling exhibitions organized and circulated; museum shop selling books, magazines, reproductions and slides

L **Louise Sloss Ackerman Fine Arts Library,** 401 Van Ness Ave, 94102-4582. Tel 415-252-4120; FAX 415-431-6590. *Librn* Eugenie Candau
Open to the public for reference, Tues & Wed 1 - 5 PM, by appointment
Library Holdings: Vols 18,000; Per subs 400; artists files; museum archives; Other — Exhibition catalogs
Special Subjects: Afro-American Art, American Indian Art, Fashion Arts, Film, Folk Art, Mexican Art, Oriental Art, Painting - American, Pre-Columbian Art, Southwestern Art, Modern and contemporary art including photography, architecture and design
Collections: Margery Mann Collection of books in the history of photography

L **SAN FRANCISCO PUBLIC LIBRARY,** Art and Music Dept, Civic Center, 94102. Tel 415-557-4525; FAX 415-864-8351. *Dir* Kenneth E Dowlin; *Art & Music* Faun McInnis
Open Mon, Wed, Thurs, Sat 10 AM - 6 PM, Tues Noon - 9 PM, Fri Noon - 6 PM, Sun 1 - 5 PM. Estab 1878
Income: Financed by city and state appropriations
Library Holdings: Vols 45,000; Per subs 250; Micro — Cards, fiche, reels; AV — Motion pictures, rec, v-tapes; Other — Clipping files, exhibition catalogs, framed reproductions, photographs, prints

L **SAN FRANCISCO STATE UNIVERSITY,** J Paul Leonard Library, 1630 Holloway, 94132. Tel 415-338-1455; Elec Mail dtong@SFSUVAX1SFSuEDU. *Dir* Open ; *Art Librn* Darlene Tong
Open Mon - Thurs 9 AM - 9 PM, Fri 9 AM - 4 PM, Sat & Sun noon - 5 PM. Estab 1890
Library Holdings: Vols 700,000; Per subs 4500; Bound Periodial Vol 110,000; Micro — Cards, fiche, prints, reels; AV — A-tapes, cassettes, fs, motion pictures, rec, v-tapes; Other — Exhibition catalogs, framed reproductions, manuscripts, memorabilia, original art works
Special Subjects: Advertising Design, Aesthetics, Afro-American Art, American Indian Art, American Western Art, Antiquities-Etruscan, Antiquities-Greek, Antiquities-Roman, Archaeology, Architecture
Collections: John Magnani Collection of Arts & Crafts; Frank deBellis Collection on Italian Culture; Juliet Bredon Collection of Chinese Textiles; H Wilder Bentley Brush Painting Collection; Simeon Pelenc Collection of Paintings & Drawings
Activities: Book traveling exhibitions; originate traveling exhibitions; sales shop sells books & reproductions

M **SOUTHERN EXPOSURE GALLERY,** 401 Alabama St, 94110. Tel 415-863-2141. *Dir* Jon Winet
Estab to give exposure of contemporary California art by emerging and established artists

M **TATTOO ART MUSEUM,** 837 Columbus Ave, 94133. Tel 415-775-4991. *Dir* Lyle Tuttle; *Consultant* Judith Tuttle
Open daily Noon - 6 PM. Admis donations. Estab 1974. Average Annual Attendance: 5000. Mem: 50; monthly meetings
Collections: Lyle Tuttle Collection, tattoo art, Memorabilia & Equipment, especially tattoo machines & primitive tools; George Burchett Collection
Publications: Magazine of the Tattoo Art Museum; Tattoo Historian, bi -annual; Annual Tattoo Calendar
Activities: Lect open to public, 12 vis lectr per yr; awards; Tattoo Hall of Fame; individual paintings and objects of art lent; bookstore sells books, original art work, reproductions, prints & slides

SAN JOSE

M ROSICRUCIAN EGYPTIAN MUSEUM AND ART GALLERY, 1342 Naglee Ave, 95191-0001. Tel 408-947-3636; FAX 408-947-3677. *Acting Adminr* Cynthia Stretch; *Exhib Cur* Susan Wageman
Open daily 9 AM - 5 PM. Admis adults $6, sr citizens $4, children 7 - 15 $3.50, under 7 free. Estab 1929, in present location 1966, to publicly show a collection of the works of the ancient Egyptians, reflecting their lives and culture. Collections include Bronzes of Egyptian Gods & Goddesses; Funerary Models; full size walk-in tomb replica; human & animal mummies; Tel-El-Armana room with amulets, cosmetics & writing implements; jewelry, pottery & King Zoser's tomb complex; Mesopotanian collection - cuneiform tablets & seals from Babylon, Sumer & Assyna; a contemporary art gallery. Average Annual Attendance: 100,000
Income: Financed by Rosicrucian Order, AMORC
Purchases: Regular acquisitions of Egyptian antiquities
Collections: Collections include Bronzes of Egyptian Gods & Goddesses; Funerary Models; full size walk-in tomb replica; human & animal mummies; Tel-El-Armana room; amulets, cosmetics, writing implements, jewelry, pottery, scale model of King Zoser's tomb complex; Mesopotanian collection - cuneiform tablets & seals from Babylon, Sumer & Assyna; a contemporary art gallery
Exhibitions: Monthly contemporary exhibitions in Art Gallery; mainly one-man
Publications: About Mummies; The Hieroglphic Coloring Book
Activities: Tours for children; lectures; gift shop sells books, magazines, reproductions, prints, slides, jewelry & posters

M SAN JOSE INSTITUTE OF CONTEMPORARY ART, 2 N Second St, Suite 100, 95113. Tel 408-998-4310, 283-8155. *Dir* Kathryn Funk
Open Tues, Wed, Fri & Sat 11 AM - 5 PM, Thurs 11 AM - 8 PM & by appointment. No admis fee. Estab 1980, SJICA is a non-profit visual arts organization highlighting emerging & established artists from the Greater Bay Area. One large store front space plus mezzanine. Average Annual Attendance: 20,000. Mem: 700; dues $25 & up
Income: Financed by membership & cultural grants
Exhibitions: Monthly exhibitions
Activities: Lect open to public; gallery talks & tours by appointment

M SAN JOSE MUSEUM OF ART, 110 S Market St, 95113. Tel 408-294-2787; FAX 408-294-2977. *Dir* Josi I Callan; *Cur* Peter Gordon; *Deputy Dir* Deborah Norberg; *Art School Dir* Diane Levinson; *Book & Gift Shop Mgr* Christina Miller
Open Wed, Fri - Sun 10 AM - 5 PM, Thurs 10 AM - 8 PM. Admis $4, sr citizens & students $2, Thurs free. Estab 1968; provides San Jose and Bay Area residents with contemporary art from the region, nation and abroad through exhibitions and public education; maintains an art school providing classes taught by practicing artists. The museum is housed in facilities which wed an 1892 Romanesque revival building originally designed as a post office, and a contemporary addition. Average Annual Attendance: 85,000. Mem: dues $15 - $250, patrons $500 - $2500; annual meeting June
Income: Financed by City of San Jose, private sector contributions, state & federal government
Collections: Permanent Collection features work by †nationally recognized artists, †artists of the CA region, †American prints, †sculptures, & †paintings by American masters
Exhibitions: (1991-92) Compassion & Protest: Recent Social & Political Art from the Eli Broad Family Foundation Collection; Rodin Bronzes in the Round; Lynda Benglis; Dual Natures; David Best: Faith & Fantasy; Arneson, DeForest, Hudson & Wiley: Selections from the Anderson Collection; Drawing Redux; Gronk: Fascinating Slippers/Pantunflas
Publications: Exhibition catalogs; newsletter, quarterly
Activities: Classes for adults and children; docent training; lect open to the public, 10 - 15 vis lectr per year; tours; gallery talks; individual paintings & original objects of art lent to institutions, museums & galleries; lending collection contains original art works, prints, paintings, photographs, sculpture; book traveling exhibitions, 4 per yr; traveling exhibitions organized and circulated; museum shop sells books, original art, reproductions

L Library, 110 S Market St, 95113. Tel 408-294-2787. *Librn* Jean Wheeler
Open to the museum staff and volunteers for reference only
Income: Financed by donations
Library Holdings: Vols 1950; AV — Slides 1200, v-tapes; Other — Clipping files, exhibition catalogs 3000, pamphlets, photographs
Special Subjects: Children's Art Books
Publications: SJMA Frameworks, 6 times a year

SAN JOSE STATE UNIVERSITY

M Art Gallery, Art Dept, 95192-0089. Tel 408-924-4328. *Dir* Andy Ostheimer
Open Tues - Fri 11 AM - 4 PM during term. No admis fee. Estab 1960 as part of the university Art Dept. Gallery is 34 x 28 ft with 12 ft ceiling. Average Annual Attendance: 9000
Income: Financed by city and state appropriations
Publications: Exhibition catalogs; brochures
Activities: Lectures open to the public, 6 vis lectr per yr; concerts; gallery talks; tours; catalogs sometimes sold

M Union Gallery, S Ninth St, Student Union, 95192. Tel 408-924-6330. *Dir* Ted Gehrke; *Registrar* Alice Liang; *Cur Permanent Coll* David Gruss; *Asst Dir* Bob Yanes
Open Mon - Fri 9:30 AM - 4 PM, Wed & Thurs 6 - 8 PM. No admis fee. Estab 1968 to supplement the available art at San Jose State and to broaden the student's appreciation of art. The gallery consists of two main spaces: main gallery, with an additional back gallery for smaller exhibitions. Average Annual Attendance: 30,000
Income: Financed by state appropriation and through the University
Publications: Exhibition catalogs
Activities: Lect open to public, 9 vis lectr per year; gallery talks; paintings and original art objects lent to other galleries or museums; lending collection contains cassettes

L Robert D Clark Library, Washington Square, 95192-0028. Tel 408-924-2738. *Art Reference Librn* Edith Crowe; *Slide Cur* Elizabeth Antrim
Purchases: $48,597
Library Holdings: Vols 34,155; Per subs 103; Micro — Cards, fiche, prints, reels; AV — A-tapes, cassettes, fs, lantern slides, motion pictures, rec, slides, v-tapes; Other — Exhibition catalogs, framed reproductions, original art works, photographs, prints, reproductions

SAN LUIS OBISPO

L CALIFORNIA POLYTECHNIC STATE UNIVERSITY, College of Architecture & Environmental Design-Art Collection, Instructional Resource Center, 93407. Tel 805-756-2165; FAX 805-756-5986. *Dir of IRC* Martha J Steward
Open Mon - Fri 9 AM - 5 PM, cl Sat & Sun. Admis free. Estab 1969; 180,000 slides for lending & reference. Circ 20,000 (slides)
Income: $11,500 (financed by state appropriation)
Library Holdings: Vols 4000; Per subs 30
Special Subjects: Architecture, Interior Design, Landscape Architecture
Collections: Architecture & Landscape Architecture slide collection

L CUESTA COLLEGE, Cuesta College Art Gallery, PO Box 8106, 93403-8106. Tel 805-546-3202; FAX 805-546-3904. *Dir* Marta Peluso
Open Mon - Thurs 7:30 AM - 9 PM, Fri 7:30 AM - 4 PM, Sun 11 AM - 6 PM, vacation hrs vary. Estab 1966 to support the educational program of the college. Contemporary fine art gallery featuring rotating exhibitions of national, regional & local artists. Average Annual Attendance: 10,000
Library Holdings: Vols 3130; Per subs 18; Micro — Fiche, reels; AV — A-tapes, cassettes, fs, motion pictures, rec, slides, v-tapes; Other — Pamphlets
Collections: 20 works of art primarily of California artists; 2 Japanese artists
Activities: Educ dept; Lectr open to public, 6 vis lectrs a year; gallery talks; tours; originate traveling exhibitions

SAN LUIS REY

M MISSION SAN LUIS REY MUSEUM, 4050 Mission Ave, 92068. Tel 619-757-3651; FAX 619-757-4613. *Local Minister* Evan Howard; *Cur* Mary Whelan; *Adminr* Ed Gabarra
Open Mon - Sat 10 AM - 4 PM, Sun noon - 4 PM. Admis adults $3, children $1. Estab 1798 to protect, conserve & display artifacts which reflect the history of the Mission. Average Annual Attendance: 75,000
Income: Financed by property of Franciscan Friars Inc of California
Collections: Artifacts, furniture, paintings, statuary, religious vestments & vessels & other historical objects from early mission days in California
Activities: Individual paintings & original objects of art lent to qualified museums; sales shop sells books, slides & religious items

SAN MARCOS

M PALOMAR COMMUNITY COLLEGE, Boehm Gallery, 1140 W Mission Rd, 92069. Tel 619-744-1150. *Gallery Dir* Louise Kirtland-Boehm
Open Mon - Thurs 8 AM - 8 PM, Fri 8 AM - 4 PM, Sat 10 AM - 2 PM. No admis fee. Estab 1964 to provide the community with fine art regardless of style, period or approach. The gallery is 35 x 35 ft, no windows, 18 in brick exterior, acoustic ceiling and asphalt tile floor. Average Annual Attendance: 50,000
Income: $8000 (exhibition budget). Financed by city and state appropriations
Collections: †Contemporary art by nationally acclaimed artists; 16th - 20th century art; California artists
Exhibitions: Annual Student Art Show; Three Photographers: Edward, Cole and Kim Weston; Roland Reiss, The Morality Plays: An Installation Work; Eleanor Antin, A Look-Back 1969-1975; Robert Freeman; Native American; Etchings and Richard White; Table; Kazuo Kadonaga; Sculpture; D J Hall; Recent Paintings and Drawings Richard Allen Morris: Painting Retrospective; Christine Oatman: Fantasy Landscapes; Sam Richardson: Ten Year Retrospective of Sculpture and Drawing; Italo Sconga: Recent Sculpture; Masami Teraoka: Recent Paintings and Prints; Wayne Thiebaud: Recent Paintings and Drawings; William Wiley: Recent Sculpture and Drawings
Activities: Lect open to public, 12 vis lectr per year; competitions; individual paintings and original objects of art lent to reputable museums and galleries; lending collection contains original paintings, prints and sculpture

SAN MARINO

M CALIFORNIA HISTORICAL SOCIETY, El Molino Viejo, 1120 Old Mill Rd, 2090 Jackson St, 91108-1840. Tel 818-449-5450. *Dir* Margaret Eley; *Pres* David Hudnut; *Dir Southern California* Margaret Eley
Open Tues - Sun 1 - 4 PM, cl holidays. Historic adobe grist mill with changing exhibit room. Mem: dues centennial $1000, benefactor $500, associate $250, patron $150, contributing $75, sustaining $40, active $25, student $15
Income: Financed by mem dues & contributions
Collections: Fine arts include California lithography & other graphics; oils; watercolors; drawings; furniture & artifacts to 1915; research materials both original & published on California & Western artists
Exhibitions: National traveling photographic exhibitions; The American Farm; changing thematic exhibits relating to California history in the galleries of the Whittier House from the society's collection. Permanent exhibition in San Francisco from the Society's collections
Publications: California History, quarterly magazine
Activities: Classes for adults; docent training; programs; lectures, tours & films throughout the state; lectures open to the public; concerts; gallery talks; tours; awards given for participation in the field of California history; traveling exhibitions organized & circulated; bookshop

L **Schubert Hall Library,** 2099 Pacific Ave, 94109-2235. Tel 415-567-1848.
Estab 1922 to collect books, manuscripts, photographs, ephemera, maps and
posters pertaining to California and Western history. For in-house reference and
research only
Library Holdings: Vols 45,500; Per subs 150; original documents; 3-dimensional
artifacts; Micro — Fiche, reels; AV — A-tapes, cassettes, Kodachromes, lantern
slides, motion pictures, slides; Other — Clipping files, framed reproductions,
manuscripts, memorabilia, original art works, pamphlets, photographs 500,000,
prints, reproductions
Special Subjects: Early California imprints; county and municipal histories; early
voyages of exploration, Genealogy; Gold Rush; Printing; Publishing
Collections: C Templeton Crocker Collections; Florence Keen Collection of
Western Literature; San Francisco Chronicle Collection; Kemble Collection of
Western Printing and Publishing
Exhibitions: The American Farm; Executive Order 9006

M **HENRY E HUNTINGTON LIBRARY, ART COLLECTIONS &
BOTANICAL GARDENS,** 1151 Oxford Rd, 91108. Tel 818-405-2100; FAX
818-405-0225. *Pres* Robert Allen Skotheim; *Cur Art Div* Edward J Nygren;
Communications Dir Catherine Babcock; *Dir Library* William A Moffett; *Dir
Botanical Gardens* James Folsom; *Cur British & Continental Art* Shelley M
Bennett; *Cur American Art* Amy Meyers
Grounds open Tues - Sun 1 - 4:30 PM, Main Library open Mon - Sat 8:30 AM -
5 PM. No admis, call (818) 405-2100 for information regarding free Sun
reservations. Estab 1919 by the late Henry E Huntington as a free research
library, art gallery, museum and botanical garden; exhibitions open to the public
in 1928 for educational and cultural purposes. Virginia Steele Scott Gallery for
American art opened in 1984. Average Annual Attendance: 500,000. Mem:
3500, supporters of the institution who give $35 - $999 annually are known as
the Friends of the Huntington Library, Fellows give $1500 or more per year
Income: Financed by endowment and gifts
Collections: British and European art of the 18th and early 19th centuries with a
strong supporting collection of French furniture, decorative objects and sculpture
of the same periods; American Art (1700-1940)
Exhibitions: Rotating exhibitions from the permanent collection, some loan
exhibitions from public and private collections
Publications: The Calendar, biomonthly; Huntington Library Quarterly; various
monographs & exhibition catalogs
Activities: Classes for children; docent training; Lectures open to public;
concerts; gallery talks; tours; dramatic programs; scholarly symposia; fels offered;
sales shop sells books, postcards, prints, reproductions and slides
L **Art Reference Library,** 1151 Oxford Rd, 91108. Tel 818-405-2228; FAX 818-
405-0225. *Art Reference Librn* Linda Kay Zoeckler
Open Mon - Fri 8:30 AM - Noon, 1 - 5 PM. No admis fee. Estab 1940 for
research. Open to qualified scholars for reference. Average Annual Attendance:
1500
Income: Financed by endowments and gifts
Library Holdings: Vols 30,000; Per subs 300; Photographic archive 100,000;
Micro — Fiche, reels; AV — Cassettes, lantern slides, slides, v-tapes; Other —
Clipping files, exhibition catalogs, manuscripts, memorabilia, pamphlets,
photographs
Special Subjects: British art of the 18th and early 19th centuries; American Art
1730-1940
Collections: British drawings and watercolors; probably the largest collection of
books, photographs and other materials for the study of British art that exists
outside London

L **UNIV OF SOUTHERN CALIFORNIA,** Greene & Greene Library of the Arts
& Crafts Movement, The Scott Gallery of the Huntington Library, 1151 Oxford
Rd, 91108. Tel 818-405-2232. *Dir* Edward Bosley III; *Library Chmn* Doris N
Gertmenian
Open Tues & Thurs 1 - 4PM by appointment. Estab 1968 as a concentrated
collection of archival material on the work of architects Charles & Henry
Greene, their contemporaries, and the Arts and Crafts movement. For research
only
Library Holdings: Vols 800; Per subs 4; blueprints, client files, drawings; AV —
Rec, slides 800; Other — Clipping files, exhibition catalogs, manuscripts 10,
memorabilia, pamphlets, photographs
Special Subjects: Architecture, Decorative Arts, Historical Material
Collections: †Art, architecture, and decorative arts of architects Charles Sumner
Greene and Henry Mather Greene
Activities: Docent training; lect open to members only

SAN MIGUEL

M **MISSION SAN MIGUEL MUSEUM,** Mission St, PO Box 69, 93451. Tel 805-
467-3256. *Dir* Father Clifford Herle; *Pastor* Peter Krieg
Open daily 10 AM - 5 PM, cl New Year's, Easter, Thanksgiving and Christmas.
Admis by donation. Estab 1797 as The Old Mission church, the original still in
use as the parish church, and the entire Mission has been restored. The Mission
contains paintings dating back to the 18th century, also original, untouched
frescoes. Average Annual Attendance: 50,000
Income: Financed by Franciscan Friars
Activities: Concerts; tours; sales shop sells books, reproductions, prints, slides,
gifts & religious articles

SAN RAFAEL

M **CITY OF SAN RAFAEL,** Falkirk Cultural Center, PO Box 151560, 94915. Tel
415-485-3328. *Dir* Carol Adney; *Cur* Carrie Lederer; *Arts Coordr* Lisa Launer
Gallery Open Tues - Fri 10 AM - 5 PM, Thurs 10 AM - 9 PM, Sat 10 AM - 1
PM. Estab 1974 to provide classes, lectures, concerts. Contemporary art gallery.
Average Annual Attendance: 45,000. Mem: Dues Business/Corporate $1000,
patron $500, donor $250, sponsor $100, family $50, regular $30, sr citizen &
student $15
Income: Financed by City of San Rafael appropriation, rentals, classes & grants

Publications: Exhibition catalogues
Activities: Classes for adults and children; docent training; lectures open to
public, 6 vis lect per yr; concerts; tours; juried annual competition; cash awards;
bookstore sells books, prints, & poetry readings

M **PUBLIC ART WORKS,** PO Box 150435, 94915-0435. Tel 415-457-9744. *Exec
Dir* Judy Moran
Estab 1979 to sponsor art in public places
Exhibitions: (1992) Aspirations by Horace Washington, a temporary public
sculpture in Marin City, CA, Dial 1-800-585-FEAR by Jeanne C Finley & John
Muse, a multi-site, multi-media installation for Mill Valley, CA

SANTA ANA

M **BOWER'S MUSEUM,** 2002 N Main St, 92706. Tel 714-972-1900; FAX 714-
835-5937. *Registrar* Teresa M Ridgeway; *Exec Dir* Dr Peter Keller; *Chief Cur*
Armand J Labbe; *Cur Native American Art* Paul Opodocer; *Chief Cur of Educ*
Janet Baker; *Cur of Exhibit* Paul Johnson
Open Tues - Sat 10 AM - 5 PM, Sun 1 - 5 PM, cl Mon. No admis fee. Estab
1934 to provide an active cultural arts museum for the community. Housed in an
authentic California mission-style structure amid expansive fountain-studded
grounds, originally devoted to the display of antique furniture, Indian relics &
historical items of early California families, is currently undergoing a major
expansion of its physical plant. The new 51,000 sq ft addition includes major
galleries, new collection storage rooms, administrative offices, library, restaurant
peoples of the Americas & the Pacific rim. Average Annual Attendance: 225,000.
Mem: 1800; dues from student $15 - life $1000
Income: Financed by city appropriation
Collections: Pre-Columbian, North American Indian, Asian, Pacific & African;
California history; late 19th century Oriental costumes; 19th & early 20th
century North & South American costumes; Northwest American Indian; 19th &
20th century American Indian baskets; 19th century American textiles,
decorative arts & patterned glass; Oceania; Orange County history
Publications: Brochures; Calendar, monthly; exhibition catalogs
Activities: Classes for adults and children; docent guild; lect open to public; films;
gallery talks; tours; study clubs; paintings and original art objects lent to other
museums; organize and circulate traveling exhibitions; sales shop sells books,
magazines, original art, reproductions, prints, jewelry, imported clothing, gift
items

M **ORANGE COUNTY CENTER FOR CONTEMPORARY ART,** 3621 W Mac
Arthur Blvd, Suite 111, 92704. Tel 714-549-4989. *Dir* Jefferey Frisch; *Advisor to
Board* Gene Isaacson; *Treas* Jacquie Rieder-Hudd
Open Wed - Sun 11 AM - 4 PM. No admis fee. Estab 1980 as a non-profit
exhibit space, alternative to commercial galleries and to provide support and
exposure to contemporary work in visual arts; gallery houses artists slide registry.
Average Annual Attendance: 3000. Mem: 200; general membership requires only
annual dues, affiliate is a juried process; annual dues affiliate $480, general $25
Income: Financed by membership & donations
Exhibitions: The gallery shows run 4 wks & 3 artists are shown concurrently
Publications: Art Week, monthly; Art Scene, monthly
Activities: Lectures open to public; concerts; gallery talks; sponsors juried exhibit
annually; awards donated by local businesses

SANTA BARBARA

L **BROOKS INSTITUTE PHOTOGRAPHY LIBRARY,** 1321 Alameda Padre
Serra, 93103. Tel 805-966-3888. *Librn* James B Maher; *Librn* Isabelle Higgins
Lend to students only, reference to non-students
Library Holdings: Vols 6342; Per subs 133; AV — V-tapes 158
Special Subjects: Photography

A **SANTA BARBARA CONTEMPORARY ARTS FORUM,** 653 Paseo Nuevo,
93101. Tel 805-966-5373; FAX 805-962-1421. *Pres Board of Dir* John Bishop;
Dir Nancy Doll; *VPres* Susan Rose; *VPres* Tim Schiffer; *Treas* Priscilla Diamond;
Secy Jill Kitnick
Open Tues - Sat 10 AM - 5 PM. Estab 1976; committed to the presentation of
contemporary art. Klausner Gallery 2345 sq ft & Norton Gallery 378 sq ft. Mem:
800; dues $25; annual meeting in July
Income: $265,000 (financed by federal, state, county & city grants, corporate &
private contributions, fund raising events)
Publications: Addictions; Carl Cheng: John Doe Co; exhibit catalogues; Focus/
Santa Barbara; Jene Highstein: Gallery/Landscape; Teraoka Erotica
Activities: Educ dept; school & organization presentations; Lectures open to the
public, 6 - 8 vis lectrs per year; concerts; gallery talks; competitions; originate
traveling exhibitions to other non-profit galleries

M **SANTA BARBARA MUSEUM OF ART,** 1130 State St, 93101-2746. Tel 805-
963-4364, 963-2240 (hearing impaired). *Dir* Paul N Perrot; *Asst Dir Admin*
Michael Kwan; *Asst Dir Curatorial Affairs* Robert Henning Jr; *Development Dir*
Barbara Luton; *Cur Educ* Deborah Borrowdule-Cox; *Registrar* Cherie Summers;
Cur 20th Century Art Diana duPont; *Cur Asian Art* Susan Shin-Tsu Tai; *Cur
Photography* Karen Sinsheimer; *Public Relations* Virginia Cochran
Open Tues - Sat 11 AM - 5 PM, Thurs 11 AM - 9 PM, Sun noon - 5 PM. Admis
adults $3, sr citizens $2.50, students 6 - 16 $1.50, members & children under 6
free, Thurs & first Sun of month free. Estab 1941 as an art museum. Average
Annual Attendance: 125,000. Mem: 3600; dues director's circle $1250 & up,
patron $600, master member $300, gallery guild $150, assoc $60, general $40,
student $20
Income: 2,600,000 (financed by earnings including endowment, mem, grants
<government & foundations> & contributions)
Collections: Preston Morton Collection of American Art; Asian Art; Classical
Art; International Modern Art; 19th Century French Art; prints & drawings;
photography; 20th Century Art
Exhibitions: (1992 - 93) Prized Possessions: Selections from the Permanent
Collection; Venice: The City of All Seasons; Santa Barbara's Own: The

Architecture of Lutah Maria Riggs; Cambios: The Spirit of Transformation in Spanish Colonial Art; Mexican Colonial Paintings: From the Old World to the New; Photographs of China by Lois Conner; In Dialogue: The Art of Elsa Rady & Robert Mapplethorpe; Brushstrokes: Styles & Techniques of Chinese Painting; Auguste Rodin: Selections from the Fine Arts Museums of San Francisco; In Rodin's Studio: Photographs; Seeing Straight: The F/64 Revolution in Photography; Egypt Through the Lens; Werner Bischof; The Splendid Centuries: 18th & 19th Century French Paintings From the Fine Arts Museums of San Francisco; 19th Century French Prints from the Permanent Collection; The Santa Barbara Connection: Contemporary Photography

Publications: Bulletin, bi-monthly newsletter; exhibit & collection catalogs; Update, semi-annual periodical

Activities: Classes for adults & children; docent training; lectures; gallery talks; tours; performances; community outreach programs; travel programs; films; competitions; paintings and original art objects lent to museums and University galleries; originate traveling exhibitions; museum shop sells books, jewelry & various items

L **Library,** 1130 State St, 93101. Tel 805-963-4364, Ext 351. *Librn* Ron Crozier
Open to public on an appointment basis. For reference only
Library Holdings: Vols 2500; Per subs 37; Other — Exhibition catalogs, pamphlets

L **SANTA BARBARA PUBLIC LIBRARY,** Faulkner Memorial Art Wing, 40 E Anapamu St, PO Box 1019, 93102. Tel 805-962-7653; FAX 805-962-8972. *Dir* Carol Keator; *Reference Librn* Margot Collin
Open Mon - Thurs 10 AM - 9 PM, Fri & Sat 10 AM - 5:30 PM, Sun 1 - 5 PM. Estab 1930 and administered by the library trustees as a municipal art reading room and gallery
Library Holdings: Vols 200,000; Per subs 500; Micro — Fiche, prints, reels; AV — Cassettes, rec; Other — Clipping files, framed reproductions, pamphlets, reproductions
Exhibitions: Local contemporary paintings and sculpture
Activities: Lectures, programs and meetings; lending collection contains reproduction paintings

UNIVERSITY OF CALIFORNIA, SANTA BARBARA

M **University Art Museum,** Arts Bldg, 1626-B, 93106. Tel 805-893-2951, 893-3013; FAX 805-893-7206. *Dir* Marla Berns; *Cur* Elizabeth Brown; *Designer of Exhib* Paul Prince; *Cur of Education* Corinne Gilletz Horowitz; *Registrar* Sandra Rushing; *Public Relations Coordr* Sharon Major; *Preparator* Rollin Fortier; *Cur of Architectural Drawings* Dr David Gebhard; *Adjunct Cur Ethnic Art* Dr Herbert M Cole; *Adjunct Cur Photography* Dr Ulrich Keller; *Adjunct Cur Drawings* Dr Alfred Moir
Open Tues - Sat 10 AM - 4 PM, Sun & holidays 1 - 5 PM, cl Mon, New Year's, Thanksgiving, Christmas, Easter and between exhibits. No admis fee. Estab 1959 & direct at both the needs of the university & the community; with a wide range of contemporary & historical exhibitions. Located on the UCSB campus the Arts Building complex; three galleries for changing exhibits; two which exhibit part of the permanent collection. Average Annual Attendance: 30,000
Income: Financed by university funds
Collections: Collection of Architectural Drawings by Southern California Architects, including Irving Gill, R M Schindler, George Washington Smith and Kem Weber; Morgenroth Collection of Renaissance Medals and Plaquettes; Sedgwick Collection of 16th - 18th Century Italian, Flemish and Dutch Artists; Ala Story Print Collection; Grace H Dreyfus Collection of Ancient Peruvian & Middle Eastern Art; Fernand Lungren Bequest
Exhibitions: (1993) Deep Cover: The Deadly Art of Illusion; Pierson, Thomas (sculpture); Intimate Works, Rickey; Master of Fine Arts Exhibitions; Annual Undergraduate Exhibition
Publications: Exhibition catalogs, 3 - 6 per year
Activities: Classes for adults & children,; Lectures upon request; regulary schedule of docent training; gallery talks; lending collection contains 6000 original art works, 1000 original prints, 300 paintings, sculpture, 300,000 architectural drawings; book traveling exhibitions; originate traveling exhibitions; sales shop sells exhibition catalogs, books, prints, slides, reproductions, t-shirts, gifts

L **Arts Library,** 93106. Tel 805-893-3613; Elec Mail BM.A3Z@RLG.BITNET. *Head Arts Library* Lynette Korenic
Open Mon - Thurs 9 AM - 10 PM, Fri & Sat 9 AM - 6 PM, Sun 2 - 10 PM. Estab 1966 to support academic programs. Circ 60,000
Income: Financed by state appropriation
Library Holdings: Vols 84,000; Per subs 540; Auction Catalogs 42,000; Micro — Fiche 75,000, reels 1300; AV — V-tapes 165; Other — Exhibition catalogs 77,000, pamphlets 11, photographs 5000
Special Subjects: Aesthetics, American Western Art, Antiquities-Byzantine, Antiquities-Greek, Antiquities-Roman, Architecture, Art History, Asian Art, Bronzes, Drawings, Etchings & Engravings, Furniture, History of Art & Archaeology, Latin American Art, Mexican Art, Oriental Art, Painting - American, Painting - European, Painting - Flemish, Painting - French, Painting - Italian, Photography, Pre-Columbian Art, Primitive Art, Prints, art theory & criticism, Greek, Roman & Etruscan art, Islamic art & architecture, Medieval art & architecture, primitive & exotic art, Renaissance & Baroque art
Publications: Catalogs of the Art Exhibition, Catalogs of the Arts Library, University of California, Santa Barbara; Cambridge, England, Chadwyck-Healey, 1978
Activities: Tours

SANTA CLARA

M **SANTA CLARA UNIVERSITY,** de Saisset Museum, 500 El Camino Real, 95053. Tel 408-554-4528. *Academic Pres* Rev Paul Locatelli, SJ; *Academic VPres* Rev Stephen A Privett, SJ; *Dir* Rebecca M Schapp; *Preparator* Fred Shepard; *Coll Mgr & Public Relations Officer* Ann Koster; *Secy* Marianne Oswald
Open Tues - Sun 11 AM - 4 PM, cl Mon and all holidays. No admis fee. Estab 1955 as a major cultural resource in Northern California. In recent years the museum has dramatically broadened its scope, exhibiting some of the world's leading avant-garde artists while not losing sight of the traditional. The gallery

has 20,000 sq ft of floor space in a concrete structure adjacent to the Mission Santa Clara, two stories of galleries with a mezzanine for small exhibitions, plus offices & workrooms. Average Annual Attendance: 25,000. Mem: Dues friend $500, benefactor $250, sponsor $100, family $50, individual $35, faculty & staff $25, student & senior citizen $15
Income: Financed by endowment, membership, University operating budget & grants
Purchases: All media
Collections: Kolb Collection of 17th and 18th century graphics; Arnold Mountfort Collection; D'Berger Collection of French furniture and ivories; African collection; New Deal art repository; photography, paintings, antiques, sculpture, prints, china, silver and ivory collections; 17th and 18th century tapestries; Henrietta Shore Collection (paintings and prints); Focus Gallery Collection: Helen Johnston Bequest (photographs)
Exhibitions: Quarterly exhibitions of contemporary & modern art
Publications: Newsletter, quarterly; exhibition catalogs
Activities: Lect open to public; gallery talks; tours; paintings lent to campus offices; originate traveling exhibitions

M **TRITON MUSEUM OF ART,** 1505 Warburton Ave, 95050. Tel 408-247-3754; FAX 408-247-3796. *Dir* Bill Atkins; *Asst to Dir* Preston Metcalf; *Pres* Louis Castro; *Cur* George Rivera
Open Mon, Wed - Fri 10 AM - 5 PM, Sat & Sun noon - 5 PM, Tues 10 AM - 9 PM. No admis fee. Estab 1965 to offer a rich and varied cultural experience to members of the community through the display of 19th & 20th century American art, particularly artists of California, and through related special events and programs. The museum consists of a new state of the art facility designed by San Francisco architect Barcelon Jang. The building opened in Oct, 1987 & sits on a 7 acre park site with four Oriental/Spanish style pavilions & sculpture garden. Average Annual Attendance: 120,000. Mem: 600; dues $15 - $1000
Income: $550,000 (financed by endowment, mem & city appropriation)
Collections: Paintings by Frank Duveneck; The Austen D Warburton Native American Art & Artifacts Collection; American painting, prints and sculpture; oil paintings by Theodore Wores; international folk art
Exhibitions: (1993) Transitional Realities; Arinori Ichihara Large Works on Paper; Roy Ragle Retrospect; 11th Biennial Drawing & Print Competition
Publications: Exhibition catalogs; newsletter, bimonthly
Activities: Classes for children; docent training; lect open to public; gallery talks; tours; museum shop sells books, postcards & reproductions, handmade jewelry & gift items

L **Library,** 1505 Warburton Ave, 95050. Tel 408-247-3754; FAX 408-247-3796. *Pubic Relations* Jill Bryant
Open by appointment only. Estab 1967 to enhance the resource of the art museum. Open to members for reference
Library Holdings: Vols 500; Per subs 10
Special Subjects: Folk Art, Twentieth Century American Art
Collections: †Special collection of artists books
Exhibitions: Working with Glass: A Survey of Bay Area Artists; Art of New Guinea; The Art of Instruments: 1450-1800; Scientific Inventions and Curiosities by Clayton Bailey; Miniatures
Publications: Newsletter, bi-monthly; exhibition catalogs
Activities: Workshops for adults & children; docent training; lect open to public; tours; annual rotating print & drawing or watercolor competitions with awards; originate traveling exhibitions to local & regional institutions; museum shop sells books & original art

SANTA CLARITA

L **CALIFORNIA INSTITUTE OF THE ARTS LIBRARY,** 24700 McBean Parkway, 91355. Tel 805-253-7885; FAX 805-254-4561. *Dean* Frederick Gardner; *Music Librn & Cataloger* Joan Anderson; *Head, Computer Serv* Frederick Gardner; *Film & Reference Librn* Margie Hanft; *Dance & Theater Librn* Lucy Harrison; *Art & Slide Librn* Evelyn Horigan
Open Mon - Thurs 9 AM - Midnight, Fri 9 AM - 9 PM, Sat noon - 5 PM, Sun 1 PM - Midnight. Estab 1961, first classes 1970, designed to be a community of practicing artists working in schools of art, design, film, music, theatre and dance
Income: Financed by endowment
Library Holdings: Vols 63,204; Per subs 643; Performance music: 12,190 scores; Micro — Cards 3900, fiche 991, reels 7375; AV — A-tapes, cassettes, fs 731, motion pictures 873, rec 12,937, slides 93,805, v-tapes 1572; Other — Exhibition catalogs 10,247, pamphlets
Special Subjects: Film, Theatre Arts, Video, Art & Design, Critical Studies, Dance, Music
Exhibitions: Student work, approximately 20 per year
Publications: California Institute of the Art Library Handbook

SANTA CRUZ

M **THE ART MUSEUM OF SANTA CRUZ COUNTY,** 705 Front St, 95060. Tel 408-429-1964. *Dir* Charles Hilger
Admis $1 general public, free to members, children, teachers with school groups. Estab 1981 to encourage and support the study of fine arts and to foster and support educational and artistic interests in the county. 2200 sq ft galleries. Average Annual Attendance: 10,000. Mem: 1200; dues $15 - $5000
Income: $100,000
Publications: Catalogues; quarterly newsletter
Activities: Docent training; lectures open to public, 12 vis lectr per yr; gallery talks; tours; competitions; originate traveling exhibitions; Art Box, a mobile museum which travels to county elementary schools

A **CHILDREN'S ART FOUNDATION,** 915 Cedar St, PO Box 83, 95063. Tel 408-426-5557; FAX 408-426-1161. *Pres* William Rubel; *VPres* Gerry Mandel; *Admin Asst* Laura Shafer
Open Mon - Fri 1 - 5:30 PM & by appointment. No admis fee. Estab 1973 to improve the quality of American art education. Gallery has 800 sq ft with rotating displays of art by children from around the world. Average Annual

Attendance: 3500. Mem: 15,000; dues $23; quarterly meetings
Income: $130,000
Purchases: $5000
Collections: American children's drawings; drawings, paintings & prints from 40 countries
Exhibitions: Exhibit of 55 works from international children's art collection at Portland Art Museum; Exhibit of 50 paintings by Nelly Toll, made when she was a 10-year-old in hiding from the Nazis in Poland in 1943-44, at the University of California, Santa Cruz
Publications: Stone Soup, magazine 5 times per yr
Activities: Classes for children; individual paintings & original objects of art lent; originates traveling exhibitions; sales shop sells magazines & reproductions

A **SANTA CRUZ ART LEAGUE, INC,** 526 Broadway, 95060. Tel 408-426-5787. *Pres* Bill Bagnall; *Exec Dir* Susan Kirkpatrick Bischof
Open Tues - Sun 11 AM - 4 PM, cl Mon. No admis fee, $1 donation. Estab 1919. Incorporated 1949, to further interest in art. Monthly gallery displays of paintings by members. Average Annual Attendance: 11,000. Mem: 225; membership qualifications, Executive Board of Art League judge three original artworks; dues life $200, active artists $25, assoc artists $15, mem $10, annual meeting 2nd Wed each month
Income: Financed by donations
Collections: Permanent display of life size wax figures of Last Supper from DaVinci painting
Exhibitions: 56th Annual Statewide Juried Show
Publications: Bulletin, monthly
Activities: Classes for adults; classes in painting; demonstration by professional artist at monthly meetings; 12 vis lectr per yr; gallery talks; competitions with awards; scholarships offered to senior high schools in Santa Cruz County

M **UNIVERSITY OF CALIFORNIA - SANTA CRUZ,** Eloisa Pickard Smith Gallery, Cowell College, 95064. Tel 408-459-2953. *Dir* Linda Pope
Open Tues - Sun 11 AM - 5 PM
Exhibitions: Futzie Nutzle; Tobin Keller; Barbara Guenther
Publications: Exhibition catalog, annually

SANTA MONICA

L **GETTY CENTER FOR THE HISTORY OF ART & THE HUMANITIES TRUST MUSEUM,** 17985 Pacific Coast Highway (Mailing add: 401 Wilshire Blvd, Suite 700, Santa Monica, 90401-1455). Tel 310-458-9811; FAX 310-458-6661; Telex 82-0268; TWX 910-343-6873. *Assoc Dir* Thomas W Reese; *Cur of European Sculpture & Works of Art* Peter Fusco; *Cur Paintings & Drawings* George Goldner; *Cur Antiquities* Marion True; *Cur Photographs* Weston Naef; *Cur Decorative Arts* Gillian Wilson; *Cur Manuscripts* Thom Kren; *Head Public Information* Lori Starr
Open by appointment only. No admis fee, parking reservations required, call 213-458-2003. Estab 1983 for the purpose of advancing research in art history & related disciplines. The museum building is a re-creation of an ancient Roman villa and consists of 47 galleries. Average Annual Attendance: 400,000
Income: Financed by Foundation
Library Holdings: Vols 650,000; Per subs 1500; Micro — Fiche, reels; Other — Exhibition catalogs, pamphlets
Special Subjects: Architectural treatises, antiquities reference works, early 20th century archival & library materials
Collections: Art historical archives; photo archives
Publications: Calendar, monthly; Museum Journal, annually
Activities: Docent training; slide show for children; classroom materials; Res scholar program by invitation only, 20 vis scholars per yr; original objects of art lent to other museums for special exhibitions; museum shop sells books, reproductions, slides & museum publications

L **The J Paul Getty Museum,** 17985 Pacific Coast Highway (Mailing add: PO Box 2112, Santa Monica, 90407-2112). Tel 310-459-7611; FAX 310-454-6633. *Dir* John Walsh Jr; *Cur of European Sculpture & Works of Art* Pet Fusco; *Cur Paintings & Drawings* George Goldner; *Cur Antiquities* Marion True; *Cur Photographs* Weston Naef; *Cur Decorative Arts* Gillian Wilson; *Cur Manuscripts* Thomas Kren; *Head Public Information* Lori Starr
Open Tues - Sun 10 AM - 5 PM, cl New Year's Day, Independence Day, Thanksgiving & Christmas. No admis fee, parking reservations required, call 310-458- 2003. Founded 1953. Research in fields pertaining to collections & conservation. The museum building is a re-creation of an ancient Roman villa with interior & exterior gardens. Average Annual Attendance: 400,000
Income: $Financed by endowment
Library Holdings: Vols 450,000; Per subs 1500; Micro — Fiche, reels; Other — Exhibition catalogs, pamphlets
Special Subjects: Architectural treatises, antiquities reference works, early 20th century archival & library materials
Collections: †Greek & Roman antiquities; †French decorative arts; †Western European paintings, drawings, sculpture; illuminated manuscripts; deocrative arts; 19th & 20th century photographs
Publications: Calendar, quarterly; Museum Journal, annually
Activities: Educ dept; classes for adults & children; lect; concerts; gallery talks; scholarships & fels offered; museum shop sells books

M **SANTA MONICA COLLEGE ART GALLERY,** 1900 Pico Blvd, 90405. Tel 310-452-9230, Ext 9550. *Gallery Chmn* Mauricio Baraetucci
Open Mon - Fri 10 AM - 3 PM, Thurs 7 - 9 PM, cl academic holidays. No admis fee. Estab 1973 to provide a study gallery for direct contact with contemporary and historic works of art. Average Annual Attendance: 25,000
Income: Financed by membership, city and state appropriations
Collections: Southern California prints and drawings
Exhibitions: 8 per year
Activities: Lect open to public; gallery talks; tours; original art objects lent

SANTA ROSA

SANTA ROSA JUNIOR COLLEGE
M **Art Gallery,** 1501 Mendocino Ave, 95401. Tel 707-527-4298; FAX 707-527-4298. *Dir* Donna Larsen
Open Tues - Fri & Sun noon - 4 PM. No admis fee. Estab 1973. 1700 sq ft exhibit space with movable walls. Average Annual Attendance: 10,000
Exhibitions: Four exhibits during the school year generally of contemporary artists of national and local prominence and of emerging new artists
Activities: Lectures open to the public, 1-2 vis lectrs per year; gallery talks

SARATOGA

A **MONTALVO CENTER FOR THE ARTS,** 15400 Montalvo Rd, PO Box 158, 95071. Tel 408-741-3421; FAX 408-741-5592. *Exec Dir* Elizbeth Challener
Open Tues - Sun 1 - 4 PM, cl Mon and holidays. Admis $1, 18 and under free. Estab 1930; administered by Montalvo Association, Villa Montalvo is part of a cultural center for the development of art, literature, music and architecture by artists and promising students. There are facilities for five artists-in-residence. The home of the late US Senator and Mayor of San Francisco, James Duval Phelan, was bequeathed as a cultural center, and is conducted as a non-profit enterprise by the Board of Trustees of the Montalvo Association. Average Annual Attendance: 7000. Mem: 1250; dues $25 and up; annual meeting in Nov
Income: $350,000 (financed by donation, grants & investments)
Exhibitions: 20 solo exhibitions per year of emerging artists in all media; occasional special or group exhibitions
Publications: Calendar, monthly
Activities: Lectures open to public, 8 vis lect per year; concerts; gallery talks; tours; competitions with awards; plays; winter workshops; scholarships; museum shop sells books, original art, reproductions, prints & gift items

SAUSALITO

A **HEADLANDS CENTER FOR THE ARTS,** 944 Fort Barry, 94965. Tel 415-331-2787. *Exec Dir* Jennifer Dowley; *Program Dir* Ann Chamberlain; *Development Dir* Linda Martin; *Facilities Mgr* Bruce Kremer; *Communications Dir* Elaine Sit
Open daily noon - 5 PM. No admis fee. Estab 1982 to support artists in their research of the Marin Headlands, a National Park. Average Annual Attendance: 18,000. Mem: 300
Income: $380,000 (financed by endowment, city appropriation, donations from foundations & corporations)
Publications: Bi-monthly calendar, annual journal

STANFORD

M **STANFORD UNIVERSITY,** Art Gallery, Serra St, 94305. Tel 415-724-0462; FAX 415-725-0464. *Dir* Thomas K Seligman; *Assoc Dir & Cur Coll* Dr Carol Osborne; *Cur of Prints & Drawings* Betsy G Fryberger; *Cur of Oriental Art* Patrick Maveety; *Cur of Photography* Joe Leivick; *Registrar & Asst Cur* Susan Roberts-Manganelli; *Registrar & Asst Cur* Susan Roberts-Manganelli; *Cur of Modern & Contemporary* Dr Hilarie Faberman; *Cur of African & Oceanic Art* Ruth Franklin
Open Tues - Fri 10 AM - 5 PM, Sat & Sun 1 - 5 PM. No admis fee. Estab 1891 as a teaching museum and laboratory for University's Department of Art. Average Annual Attendance: 85,000. Mem: 1600; dues $10 - $200; annual meeting in May
Income: Financed by endowment, mem & university funds
Collections: †Native American art; †African art; †Ancient art; †B G Cantor Gallery of Rodin Sculpture; †Oriental art; Stanford Family Collection; †European art 16th-20th century; †American art of 19th & 20th centuries †Photography; †Pre-Columbian art; †Contemporary Art; †Western Art of the 20th Century
Exhibitions: Recent Acquisitions, 1984 - 1990; paintings, sculpture, drawings, prints, photographs & decorative arts; Summer Fields -- Montotypes by Kritina Brancy; Mark Tobey: Works on Paper; Barbara Morgan -- paintings & photographs. (1991) The Sigmund Freun Antiquities -- Fragments from a Buried Past; Joel Leivick -- Carrara & Other Recent Photographs of Italy; Homage to Grant Wood -- American Gothic as Cultural Icon; Master of Fine Arts. (1992) The Anderson Print Collection, prints, multiples & monotypes
Publications: The Stanford Museum, biennial journal; exhibition catalogs; handbook of the collection
Activities: Classes for adults & children; docent training; lect open to the public, 15 vis lectr per year; gallery talks; tours; book traveling exhibitions; originate traveling exhibitions
L **Art Library,** 102 Cummings Art Bldg, 94305-2018. Tel 415-723-3408; Elec Mail CN.ART@STANFORD.BITNER, CN.ART@FORSYTHE.STANFORD.EDU. *Librn* Alex Ross; *Asst Librn* Open
Open Mon - Thurs 9 AM - 10 PM, Fri & Sat 9 AM - 5 PM, Sun 1 - 10 PM. Limited service to non-Stanford students
Library Holdings: Vols 130,000; Per subs 500; Micro — Fiche; Other — Exhibition catalogs
Special Subjects: Aesthetics, Afro-American Art, American Indian Art, American Western Art, Antiquities-Assyrian, Antiquities-Byzantine, Antiquities-Egyptian, Antiquities-Etruscan, Antiquities-Greek, Antiquities-Oriental, Antiquities-Persian, Antiquities-Roman, Archaeology, Architecture, Art History

STOCKTON

M **SAN JOAQUIN PIONEER AND HISTORICAL SOCIETY,** The Haggin Museum, 1201 N Pershing Ave, 95203-1699. Tel 209-462-4116, 462-1566. *Dir & Cur of History* Tod Ruhstaller; *Admin Asst* Setsuko Ryuto; *Cur Exhib & Design* Mike Ferrell; *Registrar* Faith Bilyeu; *Librn & Archivist* Open
Open Tues - Sun 1:30 - 5 PM. No admis fee. Estab 1928 to protect, preserve and interpret for present and future generations historical and fine arts collections

that pertain to the museum's disciplines. The museum covers 34,000 sq ft of exhibit space housing art and history collections. Average Annual Attendance: 69,000. Mem: 1500; dues $25 and up; annual meeting third Tues in Jan
Income: $500,000 (financed by endowment, mem, city & county appropriation & foundation grant)
Collections: 19th Century French, American and European paintings; Oriental & European decorative arts; graphics; Japanese woodblock prints; American Illustrators
Exhibitions: Six - eight temporary exhibits per year; Stockton National Print & Drawing juried exhibition; Stockton Art League Exhibition; Robert T McKee Student Art Exhibition
Publications: Museum Calendar, quarterly
Activities: Summer art classes for children; docent training; lectures open to the public; concerts; gallery talks; tours; competitions; awards; individual paintings and original objects of art lent; book traveling exhibitions, 2 - 3 per year; sales shop sells books, postcards, posters, notecards

L **Petzinger Memorial Library,** Victory Park, 1201 N Pershing Ave, 95203-1699. Tel 209-462-4116, 462-1566. *Acting Librn* Tod Ruhstaller
Open Tues - Sat by appointment only. Estab 1941 to supply material to those interested in the research of California and San Joaquin County history as well as the history of Stockton. For reference only
Income: $15,000 (financed by endowment for Historical Libraries)
Purchases: $400
Library Holdings: Vols 7000; original documents; AV — Cassettes, Kodachromes, lantern slides, motion pictures, slides; Other — Clipping files, exhibition catalogs, manuscripts, memorabilia, pamphlets, photographs, prints
Special Subjects: California, Central San Joaquin Valley & Stockton History
Collections: Earl Rowland Art Reference Library

M **UNIVERSITY OF THE PACIFIC,** McCaffrey Center, 3601 Pacific Ave, 95211. Tel 209-946-2814. *Dir* Carla Malone
Open Mon - Fri 9 AM - 8 AM, Sat & Sun 3 - 9 PM. No admis fee. Estab 1975 to expose the University community to various art forms. Gallery is 1200 sq ft witn 80 ft wall space, well equiped ceiling spots and flat panels. Average Annual Attendance: 10,000
Income: Financed by student fees and sales
Exhibitions: Rotating schedule of contemporary California artists
Activities: Lectures open to the public, 3-4 vis lectr per year; gallery talks; juried contests; awards; tours

THOUSAND OAKS

M **CONEJO VALLEY ART MUSEUM,** 193A N Moorpark Rd, 91360. Tel 805-373-0054. *Pres* Maria Dessornes; *VPres* Gayle Simpson; *Exhibit Dir* Ginger Worthley
Open Wed - Sun noon - 5 PM. No admis fee, donation suggested. Estab 1975 to exhibit works of nationally and internationally known artists. Average Annual Attendance: 8000. Mem: 200; dues family $25, single $15
Income: Financed by membership, donations & grants
Collections: Large Serigraph by Ron Davis
Activities: Lectrs open to the public, 6 vis lectrs per year; concerts; gallery talks; competitions with awards; scholarships offered; museum shop sells books, original art, reproductions, prints, jewelry & folkart

TORRANCE

M **EL CAMINO COLLEGE ART GALLERY,** 16007 Crenshaw Blvd, 90506. Tel 310-532-3670, Ext 4568. *Dir* Susanna Meiers
Open Mon - Fri 9 AM - 3 PM, Mon & Thurs 5:30 - 8:30 PM. No admis fee. Estab 1970 to exhibit professional, historical and student art. Gallery has 2300 sq ft of exhibit space located on the ground floor of the Art Building on campus. Average Annual Attendance: 5000
Collections: Small print collection; small sculpture collection
Exhibitions: Juried student exhibit; organizational & guild competitions
Publications: Exhibit catalogs
Activities: Classes for adults; docent training; lectures open to public, 25 vis lectr per yr; concerts; gallery talks; tours; competitions with awards; scholarships offered through the Library; exten dept serves the South Bay Community; collections or parts of collections are exchanged; lending collection contains books & sculpture; sales shop sells original art & posters

TURLOCK

CALIFORNIA STATE UNIVERSITY STANISLAUS
M **University Art Gallery,** 801 Monte Vista, 95380. Tel 209-667-3431. *Dir* Dr Hope B Werness; *Cur & Registrar* Jamie Gwyn Hoover
Open Tues - Fri noon - 3:30 PM. No admis fee. Estab 1967, for the purpose of community and cultural instruction. Gallery is small, covering 250 ft running. Average Annual Attendance: 10,000
Income: Financed by state appropriation
Purchases: $500
Collections: †Permanent collection of graphics & small contemporary works; Chinese pottery & artifacts; contemporary paintings, graphics; ancient Egyptian & Greek artifacts; Japanese artifacts; Italian Renaissance Jewelry; Pre-Conquest artifacts; William Wendt paintings (California landscapes)
Exhibitions: (1992) Warrington Colescott Retrospective; Stephanie Weber: Recent Paintings & Drawings. (1993) Charles Moore: Civil Rights Photographs; Faculty exhibition; Hograth Exhibition; Celebrate
Central Valley Women Artists; California Printmaking Exhibiton: An Historical Perspective
Publications: Exhibition catalogs
Activities: Classes for adults; lect open to the public, 11 visiting lectrs per year; concerts; gallery talks; tours; exten dept serving summer school; individual paintings & original objects of art lent to qualified museums & galleries & campus community; lending collection contains film strips, 35mm lantern slides, motion pictures, original art works, original prints; book traveling exhibitions 1 - 2 per year; originate traveling exhibitions to University Art Galleries

L **Vasche Library,** 801 Monte Vista, 95380. Tel 209-667-3232. *Dean Library Serv* John Amrhein
Open Mon - Thurs 9 AM - 9 PM, Fri 9 AM - 5 PM, Sat 9 AM - 5 PM, Sun 1 - 5 PM. Estab 1960, a regional state university
Purchases: $8300
Library Holdings: Vols 10,500; Per subs 45; Micro — Fiche, prints, reels; AV — A-tapes, cassettes, v-tapes
Special Subjects: Emphasis on 19th and 20th century art

UKIAH

M **CITY OF UKIAH,** Grace Hudson Museum & The Sun House, 431 S Main St, 95482. Tel 707-462-3370. *Dir* Suzanne Abel-Vidor, MA
Open Tues - Sat 10 AM - 4:30 PM, Sun Noon - 4:30 PM. No admis fee. Estab 1975. Average Annual Attendance: 11,500. Mem: 450; dues $5 - $500; annual meeting in June
Income: $130,000 (financed by endowment, membership, city appropriation & grants)
Collections: Hudson & Carpenter Family Collection; Grace Hudson Art Collection; Collection of Pomo Indian arts & material cult; Photographic & manuscript archives
Exhibitions: Grace Hudson (art). (1989) Mendocino Co (textiles); L P Latimer (paintings). (1990) False Needs & True: Resources of Scarcity, Waste of Plenty; What Style Is It? (SITES exhibition). (1991) Shadowcatchers: Pioneer California Women Photographers
Activities: Classes for adults & children in docent programs; lect open to the public, 2 -3 vis lectr per yr; book traveling exhibitions once per yr; originating traveling exhibitions, once per yr; museum shop sells books, magazines, slides, original art, reproductions & jewelry

VAN NUYS

M **LOS ANGELES VALLEY COLLEGE,** Art Gallery, 5800 Fulton Ave, 91401. Tel 818-781-1200, Ext 400. *Dir* Jim Marin
Open Mon - Thurs noon - 3 PM & 7 - 9 PM. No admis fee, donation requested. Estab 1960 to show changing exhibitions of ethnic, historical, & contemporary art. Single gallery
Income: $25,000 (financed by state appropriation & fundraising)
Exhibitions: (1991) Paintings by June Harwood; student exhibition
Activities: Lectures open to public, 2 vis lectr per yr

VENICE

A **BEYOND BAROQUE FOUNDATION,** Beyond Baroque Literary/Arts Center, 681 Venice Blvd, 90291. Tel 310-822-3006. *Dir* D B Finnegan; *Prog Dir* Erica Bornstein
Open Tues - Fri 10 AM - 5 PM, Sat noon - 4 PM. Admis $8 non-members, $4 members & students. Estab 1968 to promote & support literary arts projects, writers & artists in Southern Calif & nationally. Mem: 1200; dues $30 annually for 2 people
Income: $200,000 (financed by grants from National Endowment for the Arts, California Art Council, City of Los Angeles, other government & private grants as well as donations from the public)
Publications: Annual magazine
Activities: All types of writing workshops; art lect open to public; weekly reading & performance series; art gallery; film program

A **SOCIAL & PUBLIC ART RESOURCE CENTER,** (SPARC), 685 Venice Blvd, 90291. Tel 310-822-9560. *Artistic Dir* Judith F Baca; *Asst to Artistic Dir* Regan McNeill; *Gallery Coordr* Marietta Bernstorff
Open Mon - Fri 9:30 AM - 5:30 PM, Sat 10 AM - 4 PM. Admis donations requested. Estab 1976 as a non-profit multi-cultural art center that produces, exhibits, distributes & preserves public artworks. Average Annual Attendance: 10,000. Mem: 200; dues $25 & up; mem open to public
Exhibitions: Hispanic show
Publications: California Chicano Muralists; Signs from the Heart
Activities: Classes for adults & children; lect open to public, 6 - 10 vis lectr per year; gallery talks; mural tours; competitions; book traveling exhibitions; museum & sales shop sells books, reproductions, prints, slides, ethnic trinkets, cards, jewelry t-shirts & postcards

VENTURA

M **VENTURA COUNTY HISTORICAL SOCIETY MUSEUM,** 100 E Main St, 93001. Tel 805-653-0323. *Pres* Charles A Covarrubias; *VPres* W B Mariott Jr; *VPres* Gregory H Smith; *Exec Dir* Edward Robings; *Cur* Meg Phetts; *Res Librn* Charles Johnson
Open Tues - Sun 10 AM - 5 PM, cl Mon. No admis fee. Estab 1913 to collect, study, & interpret the history of Ventura County. Hoffman Gallery houses changing exhibits every 6-8 weeks. Average Annual Attendance: 150,000. Mem: 1800; dues $25 - $500; annual meeting in May
Income: $300,000 (financed by endowment, mem, county appropriation)
Collections: Farm implements & machines; fine arts; historical artifacts; historical figures; prehistoric artifacts
Exhibitions: California on Canvas: The Gardena Collection; George Stuart Historical Figures; Annual Assembly of the Arts; permanent collection
Publications: Heritage & History, monthly; Ventura County Historical Quarterly
Activities: Docent training & networking; school outreach; lectures open to public, 6 vis lectr per yr; competitions with awards; museum shop sells books, original art, jewelry, and clothing

WALNUT CREEK

M WALNUT CREEK REGIONAL CENTER FOR THE ARTS, Bedford Gallery, 1601 Civic Dr, 94596. Tel 510-295-1400; FAX 510-943-7222. *Prog Dir* Marti Klinkner; *Co-Cur* Warren Drehrer
Open Tues - Sun noon - 5 PM, Fri 7:30 - 9 PM, cl national holidays. No admis fee. Estab 1963, to offer varied and educational changing exhibitions to the community and surrounding area. Gallery contains 396 running ft, 2300 sq ft, including mezzanine gallery. Average Annual Attendance: 24,000. Mem: 500; dues $15
Income: Funded by city, public & private grants
Purchases: $2000
Collections: General city collection consisting of paintings, prints, photographs and crafts
Publications: City Scene (newsletter); three catalogs per year
Activities: Classes for adults and children; dramatic programs; docent training; lectures open to public, 6 - 10 vis lectr per year; concerts; gallery talks; tours; competitions; sales shop sells books, original art, slides and catalogs

WHITTIER

M RIO HONDO COLLEGE ART GALLERY, 3600 Workman Mill Rd, 90608. Tel 310-908-3428. *Gallery Dir* Chris Akuna-Hanson; *Division Dean* Lance Carlton
Open Mon - Fri 11 AM - 4 PM & 6:30 - 9 PM. No admis fee. Estab 1967 to bring to the college students a wide variety of art experiences that will enhance and develop their sensitivity and appreciation of art. Small gallery about 1000 sq ft located within the art facility. Average Annual Attendance: 8000
Income: Financed through college
Collections: Contemporary paintings and graphics by Southern California artists
Exhibitions: Landscapes by Paul Donaldson, Carl Aldana, James Urstrom; Sculptures by Joyce Kohl; Self Portraits by Selected California Artists; student shows and area high school honor show
Activities: Classes for adults; lectures open to public

WILLITS

M MENDOCINO COUNTY MUSEUM, 400 E Commercial St, 95490. Tel 707-459-2736. *Dir* Daniel Taylor; *Cur* Mary Beth Shaw
Open Wed - Sat 10 AM - 4:30 PM. No admis fee. Estab 1972 to collect, interpret & exhibit material culture of Mendocino County. Average Annual Attendance: 16,500
Income: $100,000 (financed by county funds)
Collections: General collections relating to Mendocino County History including Pomo Indian & contemporary objects
Exhibitions: A Promise Kept
Activities: Lending collection contains paintings & art objects; originate traveling exhibitions 1 - 3 per yr to Western region museums; museum store sells books, crafts & original art

YOSEMITE NATIONAL PARK

M YOSEMITE MUSEUM, National Park Service, PO Box 577, 95389. Tel 209-372-0281, 372-0297. *Chief Cur* David M Forgang; *Cur Ethnography* Craig D Bates; *Registrar* Martha J Lee; *Coll Mgr* Barbara Beroza
Open daily 9 AM - 5 PM summer, Fri - Tues 9 AM - 5 PM winter. No admis fee. Estab 1926 to interpret the natural sciences and human history of the Yosemite area. Mem: 1700; dues $10 and up
Income: Financed by federal appropriation
Collections: Indian cultural artifacts; †original paintings & photos of Yosemite; photographs (special collection on early Yosemite); pioneer artifacts; Yosemite related emphemera
Activities: Classes for adults and children; lectures open to public; paintings and original art objects lent on special exhibits only; lending collection contains prints, photographs; shop sells books, magazines, reproductions, prints, slides; junior museum
L Research Library, PO Box 577, 95389. Tel 209-372-0280.
For reference only
Library Holdings: Vols 10,000; Per subs 100; Micro — Fiche, reels; AV — Lantern slides, slides; Other — Clipping files, exhibition catalogs, manuscripts, memorabilia, pamphlets, photographs, reproductions
Special Subjects: Yosemite history

COLORADO

ASPEN

M THE ASPEN ART MUSEUM, 590 N Mill St, 81611. Tel 303-925-8050; FAX 303-925-8054. *Dir* Suzanne Farver
Open Tues, Wed, Fri, Sat & Sun noon - 6 PM, Thurs noon - 8 PM, cl New Years, July 4, Thanksgiving & Christmas. Admis $2. Estab 1979. Maintains small reference library
Activities: Classes for adults and children; docent training; lectures; tours; films; gallery talks; concerts; originates traveling exhibitions

BLACKHAWK

M BLACKHAWK MOUNTAIN SCHOOL OF ART GALLERY, 251 Main St, 80422. Tel 303-582-5235. *Dir* Michael S Parfenoff; *Regional Dir* Michael J Reardon
Open 10 AM - 5 PM June, July and Aug. No admis fee. Estab 1972 to exhibit works of art by students, faculty & friends of the school. The Gallery is part of the educational experience for the students. They organize exhibits, staff the gallery and carry out all necessary functions of the gallery. There is 300 sq ft of exhibition space

BOULDER

A BOULDER ART CENTER, 1750 13th St, 80302. Tel 303-443-2122. *Pres* Susan Soklin; *Interim Dir* Don Hobbs; *Office Mgr* Alice Grubb
Open Tues - Sat 11 AM - 5 PM, Sun 1 - 5 PM. Admis exhibitions free, lectures $1-$5. Estab 1976 to promote contemporary visual arts & appreciation of quality in the community. Two galleries totaling 5000 sq ft; lecture space; exhibitions focus on contemporary, experimental, Colorado & regional art. Average Annual Attendance: 20,000. Mem: 700; dues from $12-$1000; annual meeting in Oct
Income: 180,000 (financed by endowment, membership, city appropriation & grants)
Collections: Tom Hicks, Another Boulder, large outdoor sculpture; Doug Wilson, untitled, large outdoor sculpture
Publications: The 13th Street Journal, 8 times annum
Activities: Classes for adults and children; docent training; lect open to public, 3-5 vis lectr per yr; concerts; gallery talks; tours; competitions with awards; sales shop sells magazines

A BOULDER HISTORICAL SOCIETY INC, Museum of History, 1206 Euclid Ave, 80302. Tel 303-449-3464. *Dir* Tom Meier; *Cur Educ* Wendy Gordon; *Cur Costumes* Phyllis Plehaty
Open Tues - Sat noon - 4 PM. Admis adults $1. Estab 1944 to promote history of Boulder Valley. Average Annual Attendance: 5000. Mem: 400; dues $15 - $100; annual meeting in Nov
Income: $90,000 (financed by endowment & mem)
Purchases: Quilts, photographs, costumes, agricultural tools, glass
Collections: Costumes; Local Historical Material; Manuscripts & Photographs
Exhibitions: Period Kitchen & Sitting Room; 19th Century Businesses; Bicycles; Millenary Shop; Agriculture; Mining; Education
Publications: Quarterly newsletter
Activities: Adult classes; lect open to public, 400 vis lectr per year; lending collection contains 5000 paintings; book traveling exhibitions 1 per year; originate traveling exhibitions 2 per year; retail store sells books, local history artifacts & costumes

L BOULDER PUBLIC LIBRARY AND GALLERY, Dept of Fine Arts Gallery, 1000 Canyon Blvd, PO Drawer H, 80306. Tel 303-441-3100; FAX 303-442-1808. *Library Dir* Marcelee Gralapp; *Asst Library Dir* Randy Smith; *Exhib Coordr* Clark Richert; *City of Boulder Arts Commission* Donna Gartenmann
Open Mon - Fri 9 AM - 9 PM, Sat 9 AM - 6 PM, Sun noon - 6 PM. Estab to enhance the personal development of Boulder citizens by meeting their informational needs. Bridge Gallery, three shows change monthly. Average Annual Attendance: 300,000
Income: Financed by city appropriations, grants and gifts
Library Holdings: Micro — Cards, fiche, prints; AV — A-tapes, cassettes, fs, slides, v-tapes; Other — Clipping files, exhibition catalogs, framed reproductions, manuscripts, original art works, pamphlets, photographs, prints, reproductions, sculpture
Special Subjects: Colorado Artists Register
Activities: Classes for adults and children; lectures open to public; concerts; tours; competitions; awards

M LEANIN' TREE MUSEUM OF WESTERN ART, PO Box 9500, 80301. Tel 303-530-1442; FAX 303-530-7283. *Art Adminr* Jackie Lloyd
Open Mon - Fri 8 AM - 4:30 PM, Sat 10 AM - 4:30 PM. No admis fee. Estab 1974
Purchases: March of the Brave Dogs, original painting by Stan Davies, Racing to the Wagon by John Hampton
Collections: Contemporary western cowboy and Indian art; western bronze sculptures; paintings by major contemporary western artists
Activities: Self guided tours; museum shop sells prints, greeting cards, coffee mugs, t-shirts with Western art

M UNIVERSITY OF COLORADO, Art Galleries, Sibell-Wolle Fine Arts Bldg, Campus Box 318, 80309-0318. Tel 303-492-8300; FAX 303-492-4886. *Dir* Michael Crane
Open Mon - Fri 8 AM - 5 PM; Tues till 8 PM; Sat noon - 4 PM. No admis fee. Estab 1939 to maintain & exhibit art collections & to show temporary exhibits. The galleries have 450 linear ft of wall space & a total of 5000 sq ft
Income: Financed through University, gifts & grants
Collections: †19th & 20th century paintings & †prints; †photographs, †prints, drawings, watercolors, sculptures & ceramics
Exhibitions: (1991) Andres Serrano; Robert Colescott; Faces of Aids by Lynn Sloan-Theodore; The Presence of Absence; Pepon Osorio; A Different War: Vietnam in Art; Deborah Small; David Avalos; Hachivi Edgar Heap of Birds. (1992) Visiting Artist Program: 20th Anniversary Show; Between Worlds: Contemporary Mexican Photography; American Renegades: Kenneth Patchen, d a levy, D R Wagner; The Nearest Edge of the World; Art & Cuba Now; Betye Saar; Columbus Workshop; Chicano/Latino Art: Images in the Age of Aids; Mr Imagination. (1993) Hybrid State; May Stevens; Garrison Roots; Dale Chisman; Days of the Dead; Rimma & Valerie Gerlovin; Chuck Forsman
Publications: Brochures; exhibition catalogs
Activities: Lect open to public, 15 vis artists per year; paintings and original art objects lent to museums; lending collection contains original art works and prints, paintings, photographs, sculpture, original drawings

L **Art and Architecture Library,** PO Box 184, 80309. Tel 303-492-7955; FAX 303-492-1881. *Head Art & Architecture Library* Liesel Nolan; *Library Technician* Mary Larson; *Library Asst* Anna Frajzyngier
Open Mon - Fri 8 AM - Midnight, Sat 10 AM - 5 PM, Sun Noon - Midnight; summer hours Mon - Thurs 7:30 AM - 10 PM, Fri 7:30 AM - 5 PM, Sat 10 AM - 5 PM, Sun Noon - 10 PM. Estab 1966 to support the university curriculum in the areas of fine arts, art history, environmental design, architecture, planning, landscape and interior design. For lending only
Income: Financed by state appropriation
Library Holdings: Vols 80,000; Per subs 500; MFA thesis statements; museum & gallery publications; Micro — Fiche 5950, reels; Other — Exhibition catalogs
Special Subjects: Afro-American Art, American Indian Art, American Western Art, Eskimo Art, Folk Art, History of Art & Archaeology, Latin American Art, Mexican Art, Oriental Art, Painting - American, Religious Art, Southwestern Art, Artists books

BRECKENRIDGE

M **COLORADO MOUNTAIN COLLEGE,** Fine Arts Gallery, 103 S Harris St, 80424. Tel 303-453-6757; FAX 303-453-2209. *Dir* Tim Hoopingarner
Exhibitions: Harry Callahan, color photographs; The Cranbrook Show, Polaroid still lifes; Betty Hahn, images from the series It's a Mystery; Robert Fichter, recent works; William Larson & Henry Wessel, Jr, recent works; Meridel Rubenstein: Low Riders portfolio

BRIGHTON

M **ADAMS COUNTY HISTORICAL SOCIETY,** Museum & Cultural Center, 9601 Henderson Rd, 80601. Tel 303-659-7013. *Adminr* Patricia Erger
Open Tues - Sat 10 AM - 4:30 PM, cl Mon & Sun. Admis donations requested. Historical Society estab 1974, museum estab 1987. Average Annual Attendance: 5000. Mem: 150; dues $5 - $1000; annual meeting in Jan
Income: $50,000 (financed by mem, bazaars, gift shop & donations)
Purchases: Three small bronze pieces
Collections: Blacksmith Shop/Earth Science; Barber Shop Equipment; 1940's Doll House; Uniforms; Spanish & American/WW I & WW II
Exhibitions: Photographs; Carvings; Quilts; Iceland Art; Indian
Publications: Hi Story News, quarterly newsletter
Activities: Docent programs; children's Christmas programs; bi-monthly lect open to public; originate traveling exhibitions 10 per year; retail store sells books
L **Library,** 9601 Henderson Rd, 80601
For reference. Different artists & groups exhibited throughout the year
Income: $50,000 (financed by mem, dues, craft shows, gifts & grants)
Library Holdings: Vols 300; AV — Lantern slides; Other — Clipping files, framed reproductions, memorabilia, original art works, pamphlets, photographs, sculpture

CENTRAL CITY

A **GILPIN COUNTY ARTS ASSOCIATION,** Eureka St, PO Box 161, 80427. Tel 303-582-5952, 582-5574. *Pres* Harrison Shaffer; *Corresponding Secy* Kay Russell; *Gallery Mgr* Marti Niman
Open daily 11 AM - 5:30 PM. No admis fee. Estab 1948 to offer a juried exhibition of Colorado artists & to support the local school arts program. Six wings on two floors; outdoor sculpture garden; memorial fountain in Newbury Wing sculpted by Angelo di Benedetto; gallery is open June - Sept 15; oldest juried art exhibition in Colorado; non-profit organization. Average Annual Attendance: 25,000. Mem: 200; annual dues $1000; annual meeting, 3rd Sun in Aug
Income: Financed by membership, sales and entry fee
Purchases: Over $60,000 annually
Publications: Annual exhibit catalog
Activities: Juried competitions with awards; sponsor elementary & secondary school art program; all art work is original & for sale

COLORADO SPRINGS

AMERICAN NUMISMATIC ASSOCIATION
For further information, see National and Regional Organizations

M **COLORADO SPRINGS FINE ARTS CENTER,** 30 W Dale St, 80903. Tel 719-634-5581; FAX 719-634-0570. *Dir* David Wagner; *Dir of Exhib* Cathy Wright; *Dir Public Relations* Julie Morrill; *Dir Sales Shop* Ellie Jeffers; *Dir Museum Servs* R E Zendejas; *Assoc Exec Dir* Robert Howsam; *Dir of Performing Arts* Kenneth M Wohlford; *Librn* Rod Dew; *Bemis Art School Dir* Judith Ann Polus
Open Tues - Fri 9 AM - 5 PM, Sat 10 AM - 5 PM, Sun 1 - 5 PM, cl Mon. Admis adults $2.50, sr citizens $1.50, students between 13 & 21 $1.50; 6 - 12 $1; 5 & under free. Estab 1936 as a forum, advocate and programmer of visual and performing arts activities & art school for the community. Eleven galleries range in size from quite small to large. Exhibits range from international to national to regional.. Average Annual Attendance: 122,000. Mem: 2500; dues $20 - $1000; annual meeting Oct
Income: $1,600,000 (financed by endowment, membership, business & industry contributions, revenue producing enterprises, city, state & federal appropriations)
Library Holdings: Vols 27,000; Per subs 50; Other — Clipping files, exhibition catalogs, memorabilia, pamphlets
Collections: †Taylor Museum Collection of Southwestern Spanish Colonial and Native American art; †American paintings, sculptures, graphics and drawings with emphasis on art west of the Mississippi; ethnographic collections; fine arts collections; 19th and 20th century art
Exhibitions: Sacred Land: Indian & Hispanic Cultures of the Southwest
Publications: Artsfocus, bi-monthly calendar; educational programs and tours; exhibition catalogs; gallery sheets; scholarly publications; catalogue of the collections

Activities: Art classes for pre-school arts program; gifted and talented classes (grades 3-6) in visual arts and drama; docent lecture/presentations to children and adults; creative dramatics; docent training; lectures open to public; concerts; films; gallery talks; competitions; art lent to AAM accredited museums; shop sells books, art and gifts
L **Library,** 30 W Dale St, 80903. Tel 719-634-5581; FAX 719-634-0570. *Librn* Roderick Dew
Open Tues - Fri 9 AM - 5 PM, Sat 10 AM - 12 noon and 1 - 5 PM, cl Mon & Sun. Estab 1936 as a fine arts reference library in support of the museum's collection and activities. Open for public reference, lending is restricted to members of the center and local university students and faculty
Income: Financed by endowment & membership
Library Holdings: Vols 27,000; Per subs 50; Other — Clipping files, exhibition catalogs, memorabilia, pamphlets
Special Subjects: Aesthetics, American Indian Art, American Western Art, Anthropology, Art Education, Art History, Ceramics, Collages, Crafts, Decorative Arts, Embroidery, Eskimo Art, Etchings & Engravings, Ethnology, Folk Art, Art and anthropology of the Southwest; Guatemalan textiles; Mexican Folk Art; Santos of the Southwestern US
Collections: Taylor Museum Collection on the art & anthropology of the Southwest
Activities: Tours

M **UNITED STATES FIGURE SKATING ASSOCIATION,** World Figure Skating Hall of Fame and Museum, 20 First St, 80906. Tel 719-635-5200; FAX 719-635-9548. *Pres* Claire Ferguson; *VPres* Carolyn Kruse; *Dir* Dale Mitch; *Secy* Robert Watson
Open winter Mon - Fri 10 AM - 4 PM, summer Mon - Sat 10 AM - 4 PM. No admis fee. Estab 1979 to preserve the art and history of figure skating. Maintains 18,000 sq ft exhibition area. Average Annual Attendance: 25,000
Income: Financed by Association's general fund & mem
Collections: Skating in Art, the Gillis Grafstrom Collection; costumes of the champions; Pierre Brunet Collection, Gladys McFerron Collection, Rloss Photo Collection, Dorothy Stevens Collection
Exhibitions: Olympic Figure Skating 1908 - 1992; Scott Hamilton: Portraiture of a Champion; Sonja Henie Remembered
Publications: Skating Magazine
Activities: Gallery talks; tours; competitions with awards; video tape showings; originate traveling exhibitions to skating organizations, clubs and members; gift shop sells books, reproductions, jewelry, decals, cards, decorations
L **Library,** 20 First St, 80906. Tel 719-635-5200; FAX 719-635-9548.
Open Tues - Sat 10 AM - 4 PM
Library Holdings: Micro — Reels; AV — A-tapes, cassettes, fs, lantern slides; motion pictures, rec, slides, v-tapes; Other — Clipping files, exhibition catalogs, framed reproductions, memorabilia, original art works, pamphlets, photographs, prints
Special Subjects: Skating, the best reference collection in the world
Collections: First books published in English, French & German on skating

M **UNIVERSITY OF COLORADO AT COLORADO SPRINGS,** Gallery of Contemporary Art, Austin Bluffs Pkwy, PO Box 7150, 80933-7150. Tel 719-593-3567. *Dir & Cur* Gerry Riggs; *Admin Asst* Crace Gerstner
Open Mon - Fri 10 AM - 4 PM, Sat 1 - 4 PM. Admis fee adults $1, sr citizen & students $.50, children under 12 free. Estab 1981 to organize & host exhibitions primarily of contemporary art by artists of international, national, & regional significance. 411 linear ft & 6000 sq ft of exhibitioin space; adjoining classroom, auditorium & workshop/storage room. Average Annual Attendance: 25,000
Income: $130,000 (financed by state appropriation & private donations)
Exhibitions: (1991) The International Pinhole Photography Exhibit; Colorado Collects; Chicago Art Today. (1992) Crossing Over/Changing Places; Fabric Gardens
Publications: Gallery of Contemporary Art News, spring, summer & fall; Sin Frontiers, Crossing Borders; Crossovers: Contemporary Fibers; Colorado Collects: Art of the 20th Century
Activities: Classes for adults & children; docent training; museum training program; lect open to public, 7 vis lectr per year; concerts; book traveling exhibitions, 4 per year; museum shop sells catalogues, postcards & posters

CRIPPLE CREEK

M **CRIPPLE CREEK DISTRICT MUSEUM,** 500 E Bennett Ave, PO Box 1210, 80813. Tel 719-689-2634. *Dir* Erik Swanson
Open Fall & Summer daily 10 AM - 5:30 PM, Spring & Winter weekends only. Admis adults $2.25, children 7 - 12 $.50, children under 7 free. Estab 1953 as a showplace for local artists. Average Annual Attendance: 35,000
Income: Financed by donations
Collections: Archival Collection; small collection of locally produced paintings
Exhibitions: Victorian Gambling; Gold Ore
Activities: Museum shop sells books

DENVER

AURARIA HIGHER EDUCATION CENTER
M **Auraria Library Gallery,** Campus Box S, PO Box 173361, 80217-3361. Tel 303-556-8337; FAX 303-556-3447. *Dir* Carol Keller
Open Mon - Fri 11 AM - 5 PM. Estab 1982. Library Gallery is located in the Auraria Library and exhibits small one-person and group exhibitions. Average Annual Attendance: 30,000
Income: Financed by colleges and Auraria Higher Education Center
Activities: Book traveling exhibitions
M **Emmanuel Gallery,** Campus Box S, PO Box 173361, 80217-3361. Tel 303-556-8337; FAX 303-556-3447. *Dir* Carol Keller
Open Mon - Fri 11 AM - 5 PM. Estab 1976. Gallery is in the oldest standing church structure in Denver which has been renovated for exhibit space. This historically designated building is used by the Community College of Denver,

Metropolitan State College, the University of Colorado at Denver and the Denver community. Average Annual Attendance: 30,000
Income: Financed by above colleges and Auraria Higher Education Center
Activities: Book traveling exhibitions

A **CHICANO HUMANITIES & ARTS COUNCIL,** 4136 Tejon St, PO Box 2512, 80201. Tel 303-477-7733; FAX 303-433-3660. *Exec Dir* Rick F Menzonares; *Prog Dir* Isabel Armijo-Beeson; *Admin Asst* Alberto Torres
Open Mon - Sat 1 - 5 PM. Estab 1979 to promote & preserve Chicano/Latino art, culture & humanities. Average Annual Attendance: 25,000. Mem: 300; dues $20; annual meeting in Jan
Income: $170,000 (financed by mem, city & state appropriation, giftshop sales & contributions)
Collections: From Mexico to Xicano: Codex Prophecies & Revelations; The Art We Love to Hate (Black Velvet)
Exhibitions: Dia los Muertos, CHAC y Amigos (Art Auction); Chile Harvest Festival (Spanish Colonial Folk Art)
Publications: The CHAC Reporter, monthly
Activities: Youth program; lect open to public, 3 vis lectr per year; lending collection contains 19 paintings; retail store sells books, prints, magazines, original art, reproductions, cards, folk art & jewelry

M **COLORADO HISTORICAL SOCIETY,** Museum, 1300 Broadway, 80203. Tel 303-866-3682; FAX 303-866-5739. *VPres* Andrew E Masich; *State Archaeologist* Susan Collins; *Cur Decorative & Fine Arts* Georgiana Contiguglia; *Cur Photography* Eric Paddock; *Dir Publications* David Wetzel; *Dir Educ* Carol Schreider; *Cur Material Culture* Anne Wainstein Bond; *Cur Books & Manuscripts* Stan Oliner; *Coll Mgr* Jeanne Brako; *Dir Coll Servs* Katherine Kane; *Dir Design & Production* Kevin Scott
Open Mon - Sat 10 AM - 4:30 PM, Sun noon - 4:30 PM, cl Christmas. Admis adults $3, children 6 - 16 yrs & sr citizens $1.50, children under 6 free. Estab 1879 to collect, preserve & interpret the history of Colorado. Main level exhibit space of 35,000 sq ft; special exhibit galleries. Average Annual Attendance: 200,000. Mem: 7800; dues $35; annual meeting varies
Income: $1,600,000 (financed by endowment, mem, state & federal appropriations)
Exhibitions: 20th Century Colorado; Artist of America
Publications: Colorado Heritage, quarterly; Colorado History News, monthly; Essays & Monographs
Activities: Classes for children; docent training; lect open to the public; gallery talks; museum shop sells books & magazines
L **Stephen H Hart Library,** 1300 Broadway, 80203. Tel 303-866-2305.
Open to public for reference
Library Holdings: Vols 40,000; maps; Micro — Reels 26,000; AV — A-tapes, rec; Other — Manuscripts 9,000,000, photographs 500,000
Special Subjects: American Western Art, Archaeology, Architecture, Maps, Painting - American, Photography, Southwestern Art
Collections: William Henry Jackson Glass Plate Negatives of Views West of the Mississippi

M **DENVER ART MUSEUM,** 100 W 14th Ave Parkway, 80204. Tel 303-640-2793; FAX 303-640-5627. *Dir* Lewis Sharp; *Public Relations Dir* Daphne Holmes
Open Sun Noon - 5 PM, Tues - Sat 10 AM - 5 PM. Admis adults $3, senior citizens & students $1.50, children under 6 & members free. Estab 1893, new building opened 1971, to provide a number of permanent and rotating art collections for public viewing, as well a variety of art education programs and services. The Museum, a seven story building contains 210,000 sq ft of space, 117,000 of which is exhibit space. Average Annual Attendance: 400,000. Mem: 19,000; dues family $35, individual $25; annual meeting in Apr
Income: Financed by membership, city and state appropriations and private funding
Collections: †American art; †Contemporary art; †European art; †Native American art; †Native arts; †New World art; †Oriental art; †Quilts; Photography
Publications: Calendar, monthly; catalogues for exhibitions
Activities: Classes for adults and children; dramatic programs; docent training; lectures open to the public, 10 vis lectr per year; individual paintings and original objects of art lent to museums; book traveling exhibitions, 5 - 6 per year; originate traveling exhibitions to national & international museums & galleries; museum shop sells books, jewelry, prints, reproductions, slides, Native American Art, magazines, gift items & stationery
L **Frederic H Douglas Library,** 100 W 14th Ave Parkway, 80204. Tel 303-640-1613; FAX 303-640-5627. *Librn* Margaret Goodrich; *Cur Native Arts Department* Richard Conn
Open Tues & Thurs 10 AM - 5 PM, by appointment for research. Estab 1935 to facilitate research in anthropology and native arts. Reference only
Purchases: $1000
Library Holdings: Vols 7000; Per subs 300; Basketry, pottery; Micro — Fiche; Other — Clipping files, exhibition catalogs, manuscripts, memorabilia, original art works, pamphlets, photographs, sculpture
Special Subjects: Africa, American Indians, Native American linguistics, Oceania
Collections: †Native American; †African & Oceanic linguistics

L **DENVER PUBLIC LIBRARY,** Humanities Dept, 1357 Broadway, 80203. Tel 303-640-8830. *Librn* Rick J Ashton; *Head Dept* James Kroll
Open Mon - Wed 10 AM - 9 PM, Thurs - Sat 10 AM - 5:30 PM, Sun 1 - 5 PM. No admis fee. Estab 1889
Income: Financed by city and county taxes
Library Holdings: Vols 80,000; Per subs 100; original documents; Micro — Fiche, reels; AV — A-tapes, cassettes, fs, rec 1500; Other — Clipping files, exhibition catalogs, manuscripts, memorabilia, original art works, pamphlets 177,726, photographs 14,752, prints 1384, reproductions, sculpture
Special Subjects: American Western Art
Collections: †Western art
Exhibitions: Frequent exhibitions from the book and picture collections
Activities: Lectures open to public; concerts; tours

M **MUSEUM OF WESTERN ART,** 1727 Tremont Place, 80202. Tel 303-296-1880. *Pres* William C Foxley
Open Tues - Sat 10 AM - 4:30 PM. Admis adults $3, children & sr citizens $1.50. Estab 1983 to collect & interpret the art of the American West. Located in the National Register Navarre Building, the museum features 8000 sq ft of temperature and humidity controlled exhibit space, plus store, work, and reserve collection space. Average Annual Attendance: 20,000. Mem: 500; dues commercial $100, family $35, single $25
Income: Financed by admissions, sales, rental income, sponsorships
Collections: Collection of masterworks spanning the period from the Civil War to World War II, including works by many of the West's major artists suag as Bierstadt, Moran, Remington, Russell, Blumenschein and O'Keeffe
Publications: Frontier Spirit; Catch the Frontier Spirit, newsletter
Activities: Educ dept; docent programs; book traveling exhibitions twice a yr; museum shop sells books, magazines, original art, reproductions, prints, slides, Native American jewelry

C **SLA ARCH-COUTURE INC,** Art Collection, 2088 S Pennsylvania St, 80210. Tel 303-777-8255; FAX 303-778-8259. *Pres & Chief Exec Officer* Leslie Atkinson; *Exec Asst* Karen Boyles; *Asst* Cecil Burns
Open by appointment only. Estab 1980 for education & enjoyment. Sculpture, paintings, artifacts, African art, New Guine, bone, skull & skelton collections, BC & AD coins, art library, Native American, extensive photo & slide collection of Tarahumara Indians of Old Mexico. Average Annual Attendance: 500
Purchases: Rinoserous Skin Sheld, African & Bird Wing Collection
Collections: †SLA Corporation Collection: African & New Guine; Animal; Artifacts; Figurative; Landscape; Portraits; drawing, etching, litho, oil & watercolor; clay, sculpture/bronze, stone & wood
Exhibitions: Deceased Artists 1890 - 1930; Evolving Young Artists
Activities: Classes for adults & children; lect open to public, 4 - 8 vis lectr per year; tours by appointment; art appraisals; art brokering & locating; art collection consulting; environmental enrichment design

M **THE TURNER MUSEUM,** 773 Downing St, 80218. Tel 303-832-0924. *Founder & Treas* Douglas Graham; *Dir & VPres* Linda Graham; *Dir & Secy* K L Vaggalis
Open Mon - Fri 2 - 5 PM, Sun 10 AM - 2 PM. Admis $7.50 including tour. Estab 1973 to carry out the last will of J M W Turner & to publicly display his works & also his principal admirer's (Thomas Moran) works. The Atlantic Richfield Gallery; The Mediterranean Gallery; The Kurt Pantzer Gallery. Average Annual Attendance: 5000. Mem: 800; dues family $25, corporate $100; annual meeting first Sun in Dec
Income: 10,000 (financed by endowment, membership & fund raising)
Purchases: J M W Turner; Thomas Moran
Collections: Thomas Moran Collection; J M W Turner Collection
Exhibitions: Turner's Cosmic Optimism; England & Wales
Publications: Turner & Moran, yearly; Turner on Paper
Activities: Classes for adults & children; seminars, courses in art appreciation; lect open to public, 6 vis lectr per year; concerts; gallery talks; tours; individual paintings and original objects of art lent to other museums and similar organizations; lending collection contains books, color reproductions, original art works, original prints, slides and posters; originate traveling exhibitions; museum shop sells books, magazines, original art, reproductions, prints & posters

EVERGREEN

M **JEFFERSON COUNTY OPEN SPACE,** Hiwan Homestead Museum, 4208 S Timbervale Dr, 80439. Tel 303-674-6262. *Adminr* Jennifer Karber; *Educ Coordr* Sue Ashbaugh
Open Tues - Sun noon - 5 PM, cl Mon. No admis fee. Estab 1975 to collect, preserve & exhibit Jefferson County history. History House is furnished to 1900; 17 room log mansion with original furnishings & displays on local history. Average Annual Attendance: 18,000. Mem: 175; dues couple $15, individual $10; monthly meetings
Income: $20,000 (financed by mem & memorial donations)
Collections: †Decorative & Fine Arts; Farm Machinery; Manuscripts; †Native American Arts & Crafts; Photographs; Textiles
Exhibitions: (1992-94) Home on the Range
Publications: The Record, quarterly
Activities: Children's classes, docent programs; historic lect series open to public, 4 vis lectr per year

FORT COLLINS

M **COLORADO STATE UNIVERSITY,** Curfman Gallery. Lory Student Center, 80523. Tel 303-491-6626. *Dir* Miriam B Harris
Open Mon - Fri 8:30 AM - 4:30 PM & 7 - 9:30 PM, Sun 1 - 4 PM. No admis fee. Estab 1965 to exhibit multi-cultural works from all over the world plus student works. 20 x 26 ft with fabric covered movable interior walls; some wood paneling on outer walls; handicapped accessible. Average Annual Attendance: 50,000
Income: $10,000 (financed by student government money, state appropriated funds through college administration)
Exhibitions: (1992) The Nature of Miriam Schapiro; Random Access Memories by Barbara Nessim; Sacred Ground/Sacred Sky
Activities: Lectures open to public

C **FIRST INTERSTATE BANK OF FORT COLLINS,** 205 W Oak, 80521. Tel 303-482-4801; FAX 303-484-2311. *Dir of Marketing* Duane Rowe
Open 9 AM - 5:30 PM. No admis fee. Estab 1977 to invest in art for enjoyment of bank customers. Collection displayed in lobby and mezzanine of main bank; supports Council on Arts and Humanities, Colorado State University, Symphony, Theater
Collections: Prints by Boulanger, Calder, Sam Francis, Japser Johns, Pali, Rauschenberg, Vasarely, Dave Yust and local artists
Activities: Originate traveling exhibitions; sponsors Colorado State University Traveling Print Collection

M ONE WEST ART CENTER, 201 S College Ave, 80524. Tel 303-482-2787.
Open Tues - Sat 10 AM - 5 PM. No admis fee. Estab 1989. 2 galleries, 5000 sq
ft housed in former 1911 post office on historic register. Average Annual
Attendance: 10,000. Mem: 500; dues $20; annual meeting in Dec
Income: $75,000 (financed by mem, fund raisers & tenant rent
Activities: Childrens classes; retail store sells original art

FORT MORGAN

M FORT MORGAN HERITAGE FOUNDATION, 414 Main St, PO Box 184,
80701. Tel 303-867-6331. *Pres Heritage Foundation* Sue Spencer; *VPres* Gerald
Danford; *Dir* Marne Jurgemeyer; *Admin Asst* Michelle David
Open Mon - Fri 10 AM - 5 PM, Tues - Thurs evenings 6 - 8 PM, Sat 1:30 - 4:30
PM. No admis fee. Estab 1975 to interpret the history & culture of the area.
Museum exhibits on a temporary basis fine art exhibits, both local artists &
traveling exhibits. Average Annual Attendance: 10,000. Mem: 275; dues $10-
$500; annual meeting 4th Thurs in Jan
Income: $110,000 (financed by endowment, membership, city appropriation &
local, state & federal grants)
Collections: Hogsette Collection; primarily cultural & historical material
Activities: Classes for adults & children; docent programs

GOLDEN

A FOOTHILLS ART CENTER, INC, 809 15th St, 80401. Tel 303-279-3922.
Exec Dir Carol V Dickinson
Open Mon - Sat 9 AM - 4 PM, Sun 1 - 4 PM, cl holidays. No admis fee. Estab
1968 to provide a cultural center which embrases all the arts, to educate and
stimulate the community in the appreciation and understanding of the arts, to
provide equal opportunities for all people to participate in the further study and
enjoyment of the arts, and to provide artists and artisans with the opportunity to
present their work. Housed in the former First Presbyterian Church of Golden,
the original structure was built in 1872, the manse (a part of the whole layout)
was built in 1892; there are five galleries, offices, a kitchen and classrooms.
Average Annual Attendance: 15,000. Mem: 950; dues $20; annual meeting in
December
Income: $165,000 (financed by membership, city appropriation, donations,
commissions and rental of rooms)
Exhibitions: North American Sculpture Exhibitions; Rocky Mountain National
Watermedia Exhibition; numberous open juried competitions
Publications: Bimonthly newsletter; one chapbook per year-winner of poetry;
Catalogs of major national shows
Activities: Classes for adults and children; lectures open to the public, 2 - 3 vis
lectr per year; concerts; tours; competitions with awards; individual paintings and
original objects of art lent to businesses
L Art Library, 809 15th St, 80401. Tel 303-279-3922.
Open to members only
Library Holdings: Vols 800; Per subs 3

GRAND JUNCTION

L MUSEUM OF WESTERN COLORADO, 248 S Fourth St, PO Box 20,000-
5020, 81502-5020. Tel 303-242-0971; FAX 303-244-1639. *Archivist* Judy
Prosser; *Dir* Kenneth Perry
Open Mon - Fri 10 AM - 4:45 PM, cl Sun, Christmas wk & major holidays. No
admis fee. Estab 1965 to collect preserve, interpret social & natural history of
Western Colorado. For reference only. Mem: Dues benefactor $1000, patron
$500, sponsor $150, contributer & business $50, family $20, retired adult $12
Income: Financed by mem & Mesa County
Library Holdings: Vols 2500; Per subs 15; Micro — Prints, reels; AV —
Cassettes, lantern slides, motion pictures, slides; Other — Manuscripts,
memorabilia, original art works, pamphlets, photographs
Special Subjects: Natural History; Social History of Western Colorado
Collections: Frank Dean Collection; †Al Look Collection; †Warren Kiefer
Railroad Collection; Wilson Rockwell Collection; artwork, books, manuscripts &
photographs on the history & natural history of Western Colorado; †Mesa
County Oral History Collection
Exhibitions: Denny Sanders Exhibit; Country School Legacy; Otavolo Indian
Exhibit; Keith Phillips/Sheri Dunn Art Show; Lydia & Bob Maurer Art Show;
World War I Exhibition & Lecture Series; Pearl Harbor Exhibition & Lecture
Series; Classic Film Festival; Al Look Lecture Series
Publications: Dino Tracks, monthly newsletter; Legacy, journal; A Bibliography
of the Dinosauria; Cross Orchards Coloring Book; Dinosaur Valley Coloring
Book; Familiar Insects of Mesa County, Colorado; Footprints in the Trail;; Mesa
County, Colorado: a 100 Year History; Mesa County Cooking with History;
More Footprints in the Trail; Paleontology & Geology of the Dinosaur Triangle
Activities: Classes for children; docent training; lectures open to the public, 10
vis lectr per year; concerts; tours; Cross Ranch Apple Jubilee; Cross Ranch
Artisan's Festival; slides/tape & video tape presentations

A WESTERN COLORADO CENTER FOR THE ARTS, INC, 1803 N Seventh,
81501. Tel 303-243-7337. *Dir* David M Davis
Open Tues - Sat 10 AM - 5 PM. No admis fee. Art Center - Museum
incorporated in 1952 to provide an appropriate setting for appreciation of and
active participation in the arts. Two exhibition galleries of 2000 sq ft each; small
stage; four studio classrooms. Average Annual Attendance: 20,000-24,000. Mem:
800; dues family $15, individual $7.50; annual meeting in Feb
Income: Financed by endowment, membership, tuition, gifts & grants
Collections: Ceramics, needlework, paintings; Navajo weavings
Exhibitions: Changing exhibits only in gallery
Publications: Newsletter for members, monthly
Activities: Classes for adults and children; dramatic programs; Childrens Theatre
Company and Class Program; Community Theatre; docent training; lectures open
to the public, 4-5 vis lectr per yr; concerts; gallery talks; tours; competitions;
book traveling exhibitions, 8-10 per yr; originate traveling exhibitions; sales shop
sells books, magazines, original art, reproductions, Southwest Indian &
contemporary craft items & notecards

L Library, 1803 N Seventh, 81501
Open to members and public for reference
Library Holdings: Vols 1000; Other — Exhibition catalogs

GREELEY

M UNIVERSITY OF NORTHERN COLORADO, John Mariani Art Gallery,
Department of Visual Arts, Eighth Ave & 18th St, 80639. Tel 303-351-2184;
FAX 303-351-2299. *Dir* Tom Stephens
Open Mon - Fri 9 AM - 4 PM. No admis fee. Estab 1973, to provide art
exhibitions for the benefit of the University and the surrounding community
Income: Financed by endowment and city and state appropriations
Publications: Schedule of Exhibitions, quarterly
Activities: Classes for adults; lectures open to public; gallery talks; tours;
competitions with awards

GUNNISON

M WESTERN STATE COLLEGE OF COLORADO, Quigley Hall Art Gallery,
81231. Tel 303-943-2045. *Chmn* Charles Tutor; *Art Area Coordr* Lee Johnson;
Gallery Dir Harry Heil
Open Mon - Fri 1 - 5 PM. No admis fee. Estab 1967 for the purpose of
exhibiting student, staff and traveling art. Nearly 300 running ft composition
walls, security lock-up iron grill gate is contained in the gallery. Average Annual
Attendance: 7500
Income: Financed by state appropriation
Collections: Original paintings and prints
Exhibitions: (1992) Dennis Dalton; Marlene Birr; Larry Runner; Terri Lennon;
Senior exhibitions
Activities: Competitions; originates traveling exhibitions

LA JUNTA

M KOSHARE INDIAN MUSEUM, INC, 115 W 18th, PO BOX 580, 81050. Tel
719-384-4411. *Exec Dir* Michael J Menard
Open summer 9 AM - 5 PM, winter 12:30 - 4:30 PM. No admis fee. Estab 1949
for the exhibition of Indian artifacts and paintings. 15,000 sq ft display space. For
reference to members only or by special arrangement. Average Annual
Attendance: 100,000. Mem: 250; annual meeting 2nd Tues in Dec
Income: Financed by donations & shows
Special Subjects: American Indian Art, American Western Art, Anthropology,
Archaeology, Eskimo Art, History of Art & Archaeology, Pottery, Primitive Art,
Southwestern Art
Collections: †Indian arts and crafts, of and by Indians; Taos Ten; †prominent
southwestern artists
Activities: Classes for children; tours; Paintings and original art works lent to
qualified museums; book traveling exhibitions; museum shop sells books, original
art, reproductions, souvenirs, Indian jewelry & pottery
L Library, 115 W 18th, 81050. Tel 719-384-4411. *Librn* Sharon E Johnson
Open for reference only to members
Library Holdings: Vols 1700; Other — Clipping files
Special Subjects: American Indian Art, American Western Art, Anthropology,
Archaeology, Eskimo Art, History of Art & Archaeology, Pottery, Primitive Art,
Southwestern Art

LEADVILLE

A LAKE COUNTY CIVIC CENTER ASSOCIATION, INC, Heritage Museum
and Gallery, 100-102 W Ninth St, PO Box 962, 80461. Tel 719-486-1878, 486-
1421. *Pres Board of Dir* Annie Cavalli; *Dir* Ann Peniston
Open Memorial Day - Sept 30 daily 10 AM - 4:30 PM, July 15 - Aug 31 daily
10 AM - 8 PM. Admis adults $1.50, sr citizens $1, children 6 - 16 $.75, under 6
free, members free. Estab 1971 to promote the preservation, restoration and
study of the rich history of the Lake County area, and to provide display area for
local and non-local art work, and also to provide an educational assistance both
to public schools and interested individuals. The Museum and Gallery own no art
work, but display a variety of art on a changing basis. Average Annual
Attendance: 10,000. Mem: 250; dues donor $100, contributing $50, patron $25,
associate $12.50; annual meeting Feb
Income: 10,000 - $15,000 (financed by membership & admission fees)
Purchases: $500 - $1000
Collections: Diorama of Leadville history; mining & Victorian era artifacts;
Victorian furniture
Exhibitions: Changing displays of paintings, photography and craft work
Publications: Mountain Diggings, annual; The Tallyboard, newsletter, quarterly
Activities: Lectures open to public; competitions; shop sells books, slides, papers,
postcards, rock samples

M TABOR OPERA HOUSE MUSEUM, 306-310 Harrison Ave (Mailing add: 815
Harrison Ave, 80461). Tel 719-486-1147. *Cur* Evelyn E Furman
Open June - Oct Sun - Fri 9 AM - 5:30 PM, Nov - May by appointment only.
Admis adults $3, children under 12 $1.50. Estab 1955 as a historic theatre
museum
Collections: Costumes; paintings
Exhibitions: Original scenery live shows
Activities: Lectures; tours; films; concerts; arts festivals; sales shop sells books,
cards, pictures & souvenirs

LITTLETON

M ARAPAHOE COMMUNITY COLLEGE, Colorado Gallery of the Arts, 2500 W College Dr, PO Box 9002, 80160. Tel 303-797-5650; FAX 303-797-5935. *Dir* Wayne Henry
Open Mon - Thurs 9 AM - 2 PM & 6 - 9 PM, Fri 9 AM - 2 PM, Sat 1 - 4 PM. Admis adults $1, sr citizens & students $.50, Arapahoe students, staff, gallery members & children under 12 free. Gallery contributes significantly to the cultural growth of the Denver-metro area. Average Annual Attendance: 13,000. Mem: 550; dues patron $100, associate $35-$99, family $20, individual $15, student & sr citizens $10
Income: $80,000 (Financed by membership, state & federal grants, corporate & private donations)
Collections: Small Costume Collection (for educational purposes & outreach program)
Exhibitions: (1991) Architectural Dozen; Hot Rocks Return; ACC Art Students; Colorado Arts Education Association Exhibit
Publications: Artline, quarterly newsletter; Clay: Beyond Function, catalog
Activities: Classes for children; docent training; workshops; lectures open to public, 10 vis lectr per yr; tours; concerts; book traveling exhibitions

LOVELAND

M LOVELAND MUSEUM AND GALLERY, 503 Lincoln, 80537. Tel 303-962-2410; FAX 303-962-2900. *Dir* Susan Ison; *Cur Exhibits* Judy Eakin; *Cur Education* Tom Katsimpalis; *Secy* Karla Wilson; *Cur Coll* Monica Gould
Open Tues, Wed & Fri 10 AM - 5 PM, Thurs 9 AM - 9 PM, Sat 10 AM - 4 PM, Sun noon - 4 PM. No admis fee. Estab 1956 to preserve and interpret history of Loveland area. Average Annual Attendance: 28,000. Mem: 120; dues individual $15
Income: Financed by city appropriation
Collections: Archaeology; art; dioramas; historical material; period rooms
Exhibitions: Victorian period rooms; pioneer cabin; Bureau of Reclamation relief map of Big Thompson Project; art gallery
Activities: Classes for adults and children; lectures open to public; tours; inter-museum loan programs; museum shop sells books, magazines, original art, reproductions & prints

PUEBLO

M ROSEMOUNT VICTORIAN HOUSE MUSEUM, 419 W 14th St, PO Box 5259, 81002. Tel 719-545-5290; FAX 719-545-5290. *Exec Dir* Lisa A Higbee; *Dir of Public Relations* Margaret Ekiss; *Registrar* Martha Valle; *Pres* Sonia Clark
Open June - Aug, Tues - Sat 10 AM - 4 PM, Sun 2 - 4 PM, Sept - May Tues - Sat 1 - 4 PM, Sun 2 -4 PM. Admis adults $2, sr citizens & children 6-16 $1, under 6 free. Estab 1970 as an historic house museum devoted to portraying lifestyle of a wealthy Victorian family. 37 room Victorian mansion contains 75 percent of original furnishings including many decorative objects & art from late 19th century. Average Annual Attendance: 18,000. Mem: 800; dues $15-$500; annual meeting in May
Income: $250,000 (financed by endowment, mem, rental, gift shop, auxiliary organization, fundraisers, admissions, donations & grants)
Purchases: $250,000
Collections: Permanent collections are displayed in a 37 room Victorian mansion and are one of the finest intact collection of the American Aesthetic Movement; Collections include furnishings, decorative objects, paintings, sculpture, drawings, photographs, all pertaining to the life of the Thatcher Family
Activities: Children's classes; docent training; lectures open to public, 2-3 vis lectr per yr; museum shop sells books, prints, postcards, stationery, games, toys

A SANGRE DE CRISTO ARTS & CONFERENCE CENTER, 210 N Santa Fe, 81003. Tel 719-543-0130; FAX 719-543-0134. *Dir* Maggie Divelbiss; *Asst Dir* David Supancic; *Visual Art Cur* Jennifer Cook; *Rentals Coordr* Lori Sheehan; *Marketing Coordr* Stacy Everhart; *Dir Educ* Donna Stinchcomb
Open Mon - Sat 11 AM - 4 PM. No admis fee. Estab 1972 to promote the educational & cultural activities related to the fine arts in Southern Colorado including 4 gallery spaces & a hands on children's museum, a conference area with over 7000 sq ft of rentable space for conventions, receptions, meetings, including a 500 seat theater. The Helen T White Gallery provides four gallery spaces with changing exhibitions by local, regional & international artists, including the Francis King Collection of Western Art on permanent display. PAWS Children's Museum displays over 2 dozen hands-on exhibits. Average Annual Attendance: 40,000. Mem: 1200, dues $15 - $1500
Income: $993,000 (financed by mem, city & County appropriation, grants, grants, private underwriting, donations & in-kind services)
Collections: Francis King Collection of Western Art, on permanent display
Publications: Town & Center Mosaic, nine times a yr; Catalogue of Francis King Collection, annual report exhibition catalogues; brochures for workshop & dance classes, quarterly; performing arts series, children's series, children's museum
Activities: Year-round workshop program, wide selection of disciplines for children & adults; special facilities for ceramics, painting & photography; school of dance; artists-in-residence; lect & seminars coinciding with exhibits; Theatre Arts - Town & Crown Performing Arts Series; Children's Playhouse Series; outdoor summer concerts, Repertory Theatre Company presenting 2 performances a yr, resident modern dance conpany; scholarships offered; individual paintings & objects of art lent to museums, galleries & art centers; lending collection contains 320 original art works, 50 original prints, 150 paintings, photographs, nature artifacts & sculptures; book traveling exhibitions, 1-3 per yr; Three Peaks shop sells hand-crafted & imported gifts & southwestern artifacts, posters, books, jewelry

M UNIVERSITY OF SOUTHERN COLORADO, College of Liberal & Fine Arts, 2200 Bonforte, 81001-4901. Tel 719-549-2835. *Art Dept Chmn* Carl Jensen; *Gallery Dir* Robert Hench
Open daily 10 AM - 4 PM. No admis fee. Estab 1972 to provide educational exhibitions for students attending the University. Gallery has a 40 x 50 ft area with 16 ft ceiling; vinyl covered wooden walls; carpeted and adjustable track lighting. Average Annual Attendance: 6000
Income: Financed through University and student government
Collections: Basketry of the Plains Indian, clothing of the Plains Indian; Orman Collection of Indian Art of the Southwest including Indian blankets of the Rio Grande and Navajo people; pottery of the Pueblo Indians (both recent and ancient)
Exhibitions: Art Director's Club of Denver Exhibition; Colorado Drawings; Colorado Art Educator's Association Exhibition. (1991) 70th National Watercolor Exhibition
Publications: Catalogs
Activities: Lectures open to the public; individual paintings and original objects of art lent; book traveling exhibitions 2-6 per year; traveling exhibitions organized and circulated

TRINIDAD

M ARTHUR ROY MITCHELL MEMORIAL INC, Museum of Western Art, 150 E Main St, 81082-0095. Tel 719-846-4224. *Pres* Bernard Parsons; *VPres* Clara Dunning; *Dir* Peggy Weurding; *Treas* Eugene Aiello
Open daily 10 AM - 4 PM, cl Sun Apr - Sept. No admis fee. Estab 1981 to preserve & display art of the American West. 20,000 sq ft of exhibit space. Average Annual Attendance: 8000. Mem: 950
Income: $45,000 (financed by endowment, mem, donations, gifts, grants & gift shop)
Activities: Classes in docent programs; lect open to the public, 1 vis lectr per year; competitions; exten dept lending collection contains over 300 paintings; book traveling exhibitions; museum shop sells books, original art, Indian jewerly & Indian rugs

CONNECTICUT

AVON

A FARMINGTON VALLEY ARTS CENTER, 25-27 Art Center Lane, Avon Park N, 06001. Tel 203-678-1867, 674-1877. *Exec Dir* Betty Friedman; *Admin Coordr* Jean Swanson; *Shop Mgr* Sally Bloomberg
Open Mon - Sat 10 AM - 4 PM. No admis fee. Estab 1971 to provide a facility with appropriate environment and programs, to serve as a focal point for public awareness of and participation in the visual arts by furthering quality arts education and exposure to dedicated artists and their works. Maintains 20 studios. Average Annual Attendance: 20,000. Mem: 1200; dues family $25, individual $20, Board of Directors annual meeting in April
Income: 300,000 (financed by shop, mem, grants, tuitions, donations from corporations & individuals, special event earning)
Exhibitions: American artists/craftspeople featured in Fisher Gallery & Shop
Activities: Classes for adults and children; lectures open to the public; tours; competitions; visits to artist's studios; annual holiday sale of fine crafts

BLOOMFIELD

A HANDWEAVERS GUILD OF AMERICA, 120 Mountain Ave, B-101, 06002. Tel 203-242-3577; FAX 203-242-3982. *Development Dir* Janet H Hutson; *Advertising Dir* Sandra Bowles; *Editor* Judy Robbins
Estab 1969 to promote fiberarts. Mem: 10,000; annual dues $25; annual meeting summer
Income: Financed by city appropriation, contributions, advertising & conferences
Publications: Shuttle, Spindle & Dyepot, quarterly publication for members
Activities: Scholarships & fels offered

BRIDGEPORT

M THE BARNUM MUSEUM, 820 Main St, 06604. Tel 203-331-1104; FAX 203-331-1405. *Exec Dir* Linda Altshuler; *Cur* Robert Pelton
Open Tues - Sat 10 AM - 4:40 PM, Sun noon - 4:30 PM. Admis adults $5, sr citizens $4 & children $3. Estab 1893 to exhibit the life & times of P T Barnum. Average Annual Attendance: 50,000. Mem: 500; dues family $45, individual $25
Income: Financed by city appropriation, admission, annual fund & fundraising events
Exhibitions: (1992) Pop Goes the Book: Pop-up & Moveable Books, cards & advertisements. (1993) Barnum, The Beatles & Batman: A Century of Promotion in American Life; Kids' Bridge
Publications: The Barnum Hearld newsletter, 2 times per year
Activities: Gallery talks; tours; films; workshops; lectures open to the public; book traveling exhibitions, 1 per yr; originate traveling exhibitions; sales shop sells books, souvenirs

M HOUSATONIC COMMUNITY COLLEGE, Housatonic Museum of Art, 510 Barnum Ave, 06608. Tel 203-579-6727; FAX 203-579-6993. *Head Cur* Jeanne DuBois
Open Mon - Thurs 8 AM - 10 PM, Fri 8 AM - 4 PM. No admis fee. Estab 1968 for educational purposes. Collection is located on five floors throughout college facilities with changing exhibition galleries on the second and fourth floors. Average Annual Attendance: 12,000
Income: Financed by student government, other groups and donations
Collections: Extensive 19th and 20th Century drawings, paintings and sculpture: Avery, Baskin,Calder, Cassat, Chagall, Daumier, DeChirico, Derain, Dubuffet, Gottlieb, Lichtenstein, Lindner, Marisol, Matisse, Miro-Moore, Pavia, Picasso, Rauchenberg, Rivers, Shahn, Vasarely, Warhol, Wesselmann and others.

Extensive ethnographic collections, including Africa, South Seas and others; smaller holdings from various historical periods
Exhibitions: Several exhibitions per year
Publications: Exhibition catalogs
Activities: Classes for adults; college art courses; !ectures open to public, 2-4 vis lectr per year; concerts; gallery talks; tours; individual paintings and original objects of art lent to institutions; limited lending collection contains 2000 paintings, 25,000 slides; originate traveling exhibitions
L **Library,** 510 Barnum Ave, 06608. Tel 203-579-6465; FAX 203-579-6993. *Dir* Bruce Harvey
Extensive art section open to students and community
Library Holdings: Vols 1500; Micro — Fiche

M **MUSEUM OF ART, SCIENCE AND INDUSTRY,** Discovery Museum, 4450 Park Ave, 06604. Tel 203-372-3521. *Exec Dir* Mary Ann C Freeman; *Cur Art* Lee Scharf; *Dir Admin* Kathleen B Derringer
Open Tues - Sat 10 AM - 5 PM, Sun noon - 5 PM, cl major holidays. Admis adults $5.50, children, sr citizens & students $3.50, members free. Estab 1958 to provide exhibitions and educational programs in the arts and sciences for a regional audience. Average Annual Attendance: 90,000. Mem: 1500, dues $20 - $1000; annual meeting June
Collections: Paintings, prints & works on paper
Exhibitions: Temporary & permanent exhibitions; hands-on physical science exhibits; New Hands-on Art Gallery
Publications: American Artists Abroad, catalog; Milton Avery, catalog
Activities: Classes for adults & children; docent training; lectures open to public, 6 vis lect per yr; gallery talks; competitions with awards; planetarium shows; individual paintings & original objects of art lent to other museums & galleries; book traveling exhibitions, 1 per yr; curate own exhibitions; museum shop sells books, reproductions, cards, calendars, gifts, & toys for children & adults

M **UNIVERSITY OF BRIDGEPORT,** Carlson Gallery, Bernhard Center, 06601. Tel 203-576-4402. *Art Dept Chmn* Ketti Kupper
Open Mon - Fri 11 AM - 5 PM, Sat & Sun 1 - 5 PM. No admis fee
Collections: Contemporary art; prints
Activities: Lectures; gallery talks; concerts; originates traveling exhibitions

BROOKFIELD

M **BROOKFIELD CRAFT CENTER, INC,** Gallery, Route 25, PO Box 122, 06804. Tel 203-775-4526. *Exec Dir* John I Russell; *VPres* Fred Marden; *Secy* Barrie Karasch
Open daily 10 AM - 5 PM. No admis fee. Estab 1954 to provide a wide spectrum of craft education and exhibition to the local and national audiences. Average Annual Attendance: 5500. Mem: 1200; dues $20-$1000
Income: $203,500 (financed by endowment, membership & tuition)
Exhibitions: Contemporary craft exhibitions changing every six weeks
Publications: Catalogs
Activities: Classes for adults and children; lectures open to public, vis lectr 180 per yr; concerts; gallery talks; tours; scholarships; book traveling exhibitions to other craft organizations; sales shop sells original art and handmade craft items
L **Video Library,** Route 25, PO Box 122, 06804. Tel 203-775-4526. *Registrar* Dee Wagner
Open Mon - Sat 10 AM - 4 PM, Sun 2 - 5 PM. Estab 1954 to aid students & members of the Center with resource craft information. Reference only
Purchases: $250
Library Holdings: Vols 1200; Per subs 25; Other — Exhibition catalogs

BROOKLYN

M **NEW ENGLAND CENTER FOR CONTEMPORARY ART,** Route 169, PO Box 302, 06234. Tel 203-774-8899; FAX 203-774-4840. *Dir* Henry Riseman; *Cur* Eva Pape; *Traveling Exhib Dir* Martha Henry
Open Apr - Dec Mon - Sat 10 AM - 5 PM, Sun noon - 5 PM, cl Christmas. No admis fee. Estab 1975. Mem: Dues corporate $100, supporting $50, family $15, individual $10, senior citizen $6
Collections: Contemporary paintings and sculpture; print collection by Russian artists; woodblock print collection from the People's Republic of China
Activities: Classes for adults and children; lectures; tours; films; gallery talks; originates traveling exhibitions; sales shop sells paintings, prints and books

COS COB

M **HISTORICAL SOCIETY OF THE TOWN OF GREENWICH, INC,** Bush-Holley House, 39 Strickland Rd, 06807. Tel 203-869-6899; FAX 203-869-6727. *Chmn* Claire F Vanderbilt; *Dir* Susan Tritsehler; *Pres* Suzanne Schutz
Open Tues - Sat noon - 4 PM; business hrs 9 AM - 5 PM. Admis adults $2, senior citizens & students $1, children under 12 $.50. Average Annual Attendance: 3000. Mem: 1500; dues $15 & up; annual meeting in Sept
Income: Financed by contributions, mem, special events, fees
Collections: Outbuildings housing toys and collection of John Rogers groups; 18th and 19th century decorative arts; paintings of American impressionists; antiques
Exhibitions: On Home Ground, Elmer Livingston; At Holly House; The Dear Old House at it's Best; The Holly House at the Turn of the Twentieth Century
Publications: Pamphlets
Activities: Classes for adults and children; docent training; children's summer program; lect open to the public, 5 vis lectr per year; concerts; tours

DANBURY

M **DANBURY SCOTT-FANTON MUSEUM AND HISTORICAL SOCIETY, INC,** 43 Main St, 06810. Tel 203-743-5200. *Dir* Lucy E Boland
Mus open Wed - Sun 2 - 5 PM, cl Mon, Tues & holidays; office open Tues - Fri 10 AM - 5 PM. No admis fee. Estab June 24, 1941 as historic house. Merged with Museum and Arts Center by Legislative Act 1947. Operates the 1785 John and Mary Rider House as a museum of early Americana, and the 1790 Dodd Hat Shop with exhibits relating to hatting. Huntington Hall houses frequently changing exhibits. Ives Homestead, located at Rogers Park in Danbury is to be restored and opened to the public as a memorial to American composer Charles Edward Ives. At present there is a Charles Ives Parlor in the Rider House, recreating the period with Ives furnishings and memorabilia. Average Annual Attendance: 5000. Mem: 500; dues student $2 up to life $1000; annual meeting in Nov
Income: Financed by endowment and membership
Publications: Newsletter, monthly; reprints
Activities: Classes for adults and children; dramatic programs; lectures open to public; concerts; open house; special exhibits; gallery talks; tours; slide shows
L **Library,** 43 Main St, 06810. Tel 203-743-5200. *Dir & Cur* Lucy E Boland
Historic information & photographs for reference only
Library Holdings: Other — Clipping files, manuscripts, memorabilia, photographs
Collections: Charles Ives Photograph Collection

A **WOOSTER COMMUNITY ART CENTER,** 73 Miry Brook Rd, 06810. Tel 203-744-4825. *Exec Dir* Nancy M Rogers; *Admin Asst* Ida Swenson
Open Mon - Thurs 9 AM - 10 PM, Fri 9 AM - 5 PM. Estab 1965 as a Community Art Center. Reception center gallery 500 sq ft. Average Annual Attendance: 1500. Mem: 100
Exhibitions: Nancy Tholen; P Warfield; A Werner; Faculty Exhibits
Publications: Arts News (newsletter), 3 times a yr
Activities: Lectures open to public; gallery talks; awards; originate traveling exhibitions; sales shop sells art supplies
L **Library,** 73 Miry Brook Rd, 06810. Tel 203-744-4825.
Library Holdings: AV — Slides 2200

EAST WINDSOR

M **EAST WINDSOR HISTORICAL SOCIETY, INC,** Scantic Academy Museum, 115 Scantic Rd, 06088. Tel 203-623-3149, 623-7736. *Pres* Bruce Colgate; *Secy* Flicka Thrall; *Treas* Margaret Hoffman
Open by appointment only. Estab 1965 to display household & farm implement used in East Windsor 1800-1930. Average Annual Attendance: 250. Mem: 100; dues $5; annual meeting fourth Wed in May
Income: $2000 (financed by membership and donations)
Collections: Paintings by local artists
Publications: East Windsor, Through the Years: a local history
Activities: Museum shop sells books

ESSEX

A **ESSEX ART ASSOCIATION, INC,** N Main St, PO Box 193, 06426. Tel 203-767-8996. *Pres* Boyce Price; *Treas* Jesse Mayer; *Secy* Margaret Wilson
Open daily 1 - 5 PM June - Labor Day. No admis fee. Estab 1946 as a non-profit organization for the encouragement of the arts and to provide and maintain suitable headquarters for the showing of art. Maintains a small, well-equipped one-floor gallery. Average Annual Attendance: 2500. Mem: 360; dues artists $25, assoc $20; annual meeting in Fall
Income: Financed by membership & donations
Exhibitions: Three annual exhibits each year plus one or two special exhibits

FAIRFIELD

A **FAIRFIELD HISTORICAL SOCIETY,** 636 Old Post Rd, 06430. Tel 203-259-1598. *Cur* Christopher B Nevins
Open Mon - Fri 9 AM - 5 PM, Sun 1 - 5 PM. Suggested donation adults $1, children $.50. Estab 1902 to collect, preserve and interpret artifacts and information relating to the history of Fairfield. Average Annual Attendance: 3000. Mem: 750; dues $20 - $500; meeting date varies
Income: $100,000 (financed by endowment, membership, admissions, donations and town contributions)
Collections: Ceramics, furniture, greeting cards, jewelry, paintings, photographs, prints, silver; local history; textiles & costumes
Publications: Newsletter, quarterly
Activities: Classes for adults & children; dramatic programs; docent training; docent lectures open to public for a fee; gallery talks; tours
L **Library,** 636 Old Post Rd, 06430. Tel 203-259-1598. *Librn* Linda M Mulford
Open Mon - Fri 9 AM - 5 PM, Sun 1 - 5 PM. Estab 1902. Open to the public for reference only. Mem: 1000; dues $25; annual meeting in Oct
Library Holdings: Vols 7000; diaries, documents, maps; Micro — Fiche; AV — Lantern slides, slides; Other — Clipping files, manuscripts, original art works, pamphlets, photographs, prints
Special Subjects: Genealogy & local history
Activities: Classes for adults & children; docent training; lect; gallery talks; tours; individual paintings & original objects of art lent; museum shop sells books, original art, prints

M **FAIRFIELD UNIVERSITY,** Thomas J Walsh Art Gallery, Quick Center for the Arts, N Benson Rd, 06430. Tel 203-254-4242; 203-254-4113. *Dir Walsh Art Gallery* Dr Philip Eliasoph
Open Tues - Sat 11 AM - 5 PM, Sun noon - 4 PM. No admis fee. Estab 1990. Multi-purpose space with state of the art security & environmental controls requirement; 2200 sq ft
Income: Financed by endowment & university funds

Exhibitions: Thematic & social context art exhibitions; Renaissance Baroque, 19th & 20th centuries. (1992) Fairfield Collects; Loans from Friends of Fairfield University; Art as Activist: Revoluntary Posters from Central & Eastern Europe. (1993) Our Land/Ourselves: American Indian Contemporary Art; The Golden Age of Jazz: Photographic Portraits by William Gottlieb; Alumni Art Exhibition: A Reunion of Fairfield's Artists; The National Sculpture Society's Centennial Exhibition; National Drawing Association: Juried Exhibition; Richard McDaniel: Winter Approaches. (1994) Africa's Legacy in Mexico: Photo Documents by Tony Gleaton; Fresh Paint: Fine Arts Department Student Exhibition
Publications: Educational materials; exhibition catalogues
Activities: Adult classes; lect open to public; book traveling exhibitions 3 per year; originate traveling exhibitions 2 per year

FARMINGTON

A **THE ART GUILD,** Church St, 06032. Tel 203-677-6205. *Pres* William Godfrey; *Exec Dir* Donna Gorman
Open Tues - Fri 11 AM - 4 PM, when exhibits are ongoing. No admis fee. Estab 1976 to provide instruction in art and crafts and provide facilities for local artists. 18' x 18' with moveable walls. Displaying painting, sculpture, crafts, photography. Mem: 300; dues $25
Income: $40,000 (financed by membership, state, local and corporate grants, sales and fees)
Exhibitions: Faculty show; Xmas Crafts Show; individual & group shows; Members Show; Distinguished Artists Exhibition
Activities: Classes for adults and children; lectures open to public, 1 vis lectr per year; competitions; awards

M **FARMINGTON VILLAGE GREEN AND LIBRARY ASSOCIATION,** Stanley-Whitman House, 37 High St, 06032. Tel 203-677-9222. *Chmn* Lisa Johnson; *Dir* Jean Martin
Open May - Oct Wed - Sun noon - 4 PM; Mar, Apr & Nov - Dec noon - 4 PM. Admis adults $3, children & sr citizens $2. Estab 1935. The museum is governed by a branch of the Farmington Village Green & Library Association & is housed in the circa 1720 Stanley-Whitman House. Mem: Dues life $500, supporting $150, contributing $75, sustaining $50, family $25, individual $15
Collections: American costumes and textiles; decorative arts; furniture; musical instruments; 18th century garden
Exhibitions: Permanent and changing exhibitions
Publications: A Guide to Historic Farmington, Connecticut; A Short History of Farmington, Connecticut
Activities: Lectures open to public; guided tours; shop sells books & pamphlets, folk art & colonial reproductions

C **HEUBLEIN, INC,** 16 Munson Rd, PO Box 388, 06034-0388. Tel 203-231-5000; FAX 203-674-8916. *Corporate VPres* Peter M Seremet; *Admin Services* K Gaillard
Open to public by appointment. Estab 1973 for the benefit of employees and to complement the building interior design
Purchases: $15,000
Collections: Contemporary American art, large oils & sculptures, acrylics, watercolors, drawings, prints, photographs & tapestries
Activities: Selected pieces are loaned to qualifying organizations who must provide for all necessary packing requirements, insurance & transportation

M **HILL-STEAD MUSEUM,** 35 Mountain Rd, 06032. Tel 203-677-4787; FAX 203-677-9064. *Pres* Mary T Sargent; *Trustee* Charles F Ferguson; *Trustee* John C Pope; *Trustee* Karen Langmann; *Trustee* Susan A Galvin; *Dir* Sarah A Lytle
Hours change seasonally, call for current schedule. Admis adults $6, sr citizens & students over 12 $5, under 12 $3. Estab 1946. Colonial Rivival style house designed by Theodate Pope in colaboration with McKim, Mead and White, and built around 1900 for industrialist Alfred Atmore Pope. Set on 150 acres including a sunken garden designed by Beatrix Farrand, the house contains Mr Pope's early collection of French Impressionist paintings and decorative arts. Average Annual Attendance: 15,000
Income: Financed by endowment, contributions, individual, corporate & foundations, admissions & sales
Collections: Paintings by Cassatt, Degas, Manet, Monet & Whistler; prints by Durer, Piranesi, Whistler & other 19th century artists; American, English & other European furniture Oriental & European porcelain; Japanese prints
Publications: Catalog of Hill-Stead Paintings; Theodate Pope Riddle, Her Life & Work; Hill-Stead Museum House Guide
Activities: Guide training; concerts; museum talks; tours; shop sells books, postcards, posters & gifts

GOSHEN

M **GOSHEN HISTORICAL SOCIETY,** Old Middle St, 06756-2001. Tel 203-491-2665. *Pres* Margaret K Wood; *Cur* Hazel Wadhams
Open year round Tues 10 AM - noon, July & Aug Sat 2 - 4 PM. Estab 1955 to interpret the past & present of our area. Average Annual Attendance: 400. Mem: 300; meetings in May & Sept
Income: Financed by endowment
Collections: Collection of Indian art, farm tools, household items used through town's history & photographs
Exhibitions: Exhibits focused on 250 years of town's history
Activities: Classes for children; 2 vis lectr per year; scholarships

GREENWICH

M **THE BRUCE MUSEUM,** Museum Dr, 06830. Tel 203-869-0376; FAX 203-869-0963. *Dir* John B Clark; *Cur Art* Nancy Hall-Duncan
Open Tues - Sat 10 AM - 5 PM, Sun 2 - 5 PM. Donations. Estab 1909 by Robert M Bruce as regional education center that collects & exhibits objects of artistic, historic & scientific importance to the development of our American

culture. Small reference library for staff use only. Average Annual Attendance: 80,000. Mem: 1500; dues $15 - $5000; annual meetings in May
Income: $530,000 (financed by the town of Greenwich $280,000 & by the Bruce Museum Associates, Inc $250,000)
Collections: †19th & 20th century American paintings & costumes; North American Indian ethnology; Orientalia; American natural sciences
Publications: Exhibition Catalogs, 6 per yr; calender of events, 12 per yr
Activities: Classes for adults and children; dramatic programs; docent training; lectures open to public, 12-15 vis lectr per yr; concerts; gallery talks; tours; exten dept serves 15 mile radius; originate traveling exhibitions; museum shop sells books, original art, reproductions & ethnic artifacts

M **CONNECTICUT INSTITUTE OF ART GALLERIES,** 581 W Putnam Ave, 06830. Tel 203-869-4430; FAX 203-869-0521. *Pres & Dir* August Propersi; *VPres* Joann Propersi; *Adminr* Michael Propersi; *Asst* Linda Propersi
Open Mon - Fri 9 AM - 5 PM. No admis fee. Estab 1954. Gallery to exhibit professional works of art
Activities: Classes for adults; lectures for members only; scholarships

A **THE GREENWICH ART SOCIETY INC,** 299 Greenwich Ave, 06830. Tel 203-629-1533. *Co-Pres* John Howard; *Co-Pres* Paul Egen; *Dir of Classes* Fran Brooks; *Treasurer* Richard Bishop
Estab 1912 as a nonprofit organization to further art education and to awaken and stimulate broader interest in arts and crafts in the town of Greenwich. Art Center studio is used for classes, exhibitions and meetings. Mem: 400; dues family $35, regular $25, student 19-24 yrs $10
Income: Financed by membership, fees & contributions
Exhibitions: Albert Hulbutt Gallery (annual); Bank & Corporate Show (annual)
Publications: The History of the Greenwich Art Society, booklet; bulletin of program for the year and class schedule
Activities: Day and evening classes for adults, special classes for children; critiques and demonstrations; lectures open to public; scholarships

L **GREENWICH LIBRARY,** 101 W Putnam Ave, 06830-5387. Tel 203-622-7900; FAX 203-622-7959. *Dir* Elizabeth Mainiero; *Art & Music Librn* David Waring; *Media Librn* Wayne Campbell
Open Mon - Fri 9 AM - 9 PM, Sat 9 AM - 5 PM, Sun 1 - 5 PM Oct - May. Estab 1878 to provide free & convenient access to the broadest possible range of information & ideas. Hurlbutt Gallery features exhibits of paintings, prints, sculpture, photos, antiques, and objects d'art, sponsored by Friends of the Greenwich Library. Circ 1,063,950
Income: $3,378,992 (financed by city appropriation)
Purchases: Art & Music $19,925, video $39,913, records & audio cassettes $46,285
Library Holdings: Vols 288,217; Per subs 599; Art related books 16,990, Per sub 56, CDs 4886; AV — Cassettes 6550, rec 8770, v-tapes 7698; Other — Framed reproductions 438
Collections: †Book arts collection (fine press books)
Exhibitions: (1991-92) Greenwich Art Society; Annual Juried Show; Landscapes; Tony Walton; After Columbus; Suzanne Benton; Pamela Perrari; Fresh Paint: 8th Annual Emerging Artists Show
Publications: Monthly book lists
Activities: Lectures open to public, 3-5 vis lectr per yr; individual paintings lent to Greenwich residents; lending collection contains approx 438 items

GUIFORD

A **CONNECTICUT WOMEN ARTISTS, INC,** 17 Wingate Rd, 06437. Tel 203-645-1370. *Pres* Penny Weinstein; *VPres* Joan Thompson; *Secy* Ann Langdon
Estab 1929 to provide a forum for serious Connecticut women artists. Mem: 220; mem must have three juried acceptances in CWA exhibitions; dues $15; annual meeting in June
Income: Financed by members
Exhibitions: (1991) 62nd Annual Exhibition: John Slade Ely House, New Haven CT
Activities: Competitions with CWA awards; scholarships

HAMDEN

L **PAIER COLLEGE OF ART, INC,** Library, Six Prospect Court, 06517. Tel 203-777-7319, 287-3023 (library). *Pres* Edward T Paier; *VPres* Jonathan E Paier; *Library Dir* Gail J Nochin
Open daily 8 AM - 8 PM. Admis free. Estab 1946, library estab 1978
Library Holdings: Vols 13,000; Per subs 85; AV — A-tapes, slides, v-tapes; Other — Clipping files, exhibition catalogs, pamphlets, prints, reproductions
Special Subjects: Advertising Design, Architecture, Art History, Calligraphy, Commercial Art, Conceptual Art, Decorative Arts, Drawings, Folk Art, Graphic Arts, Graphic Design, History of Art & Archaeology, Illustration, Interior Design, Lettering

HARTFORD

A **CONNECTICUT HISTORICAL SOCIETY,** 1 Elizabeth St, 06105. Tel 203-236-5621; FAX 203-236-2664. *Dir* Christopher P Bickford; *Asst Dir* Paul B Parvis; *Cur* Elizabeth P Fox; *Dir of Education* Christine Ermenc; *Cur Prints & Photographs* Kate Steinway; *Registrar* Richard C Malley; *Editor* Everett C Wilkie Jr; *Public Information Officer* Diana McCain
Open Tues - Sun 12 - 5 PM; cl Sat (June 1 - Sept 1). Admis fee $2, children 3 -12 $1, members free. Estab 1825 to collect and preserve materials of Connecticut interest and to encourage interest in Connecticut history. Exhibition space totals 6500 sq ft, half of which is devoted to permanent exhibitions, the other half to changing exhibits. Average Annual Attendance: 20,300. Mem: 2300; annual dues $20; annual meeting Oct
Income: Financed by endowment and membership
Collections: Historical Collections (decorative arts)

Exhibitions: Connecticut History Day
Publications: Connecticut Historical Society Bulletin, quarterly; Annual Report; Notes and News, five times a year
Activities: Classes for adults & children, dramatic programs, docent training; Lectures open to public, 12 vis lectr per yr; gallery talks; tours; competitions with awards; exten dept serves Connecticut State; individual paintings and original objects of art lent; lending collection contains books, lent to qualified institutions; book traveling exhibitions annually; originate traveling exhibitions; museum shop sells books, reproductions, prints

L **Library,** 1 Elizabeth St, 06105. *Head Librn* Everett C Wilkie Jr
Open Tues- Sat 9 AM - 5 PM, cl Sun, Sat & holidays (June 1 - Sept 1). Reference only
Library Holdings: Vols 100,000; Per subs 62; AV — Lantern slides, rec, v-tapes; Other — Clipping files, exhibition catalogs, framed reproductions, original art works, pamphlets, photographs, prints, reproductions
Special Subjects: Connecticut structures & artists
Collections: Frederick K & Margaret R Barbour Furniture Collection; George Dudley Seymour Collection of Furniture; Morgan B Brainard Tavern Signs
Publications: Bulletin, quarterly; Notes & News, five times per year
Activities: Docent training; lectures open to public, 10 vis lectr per year; gallery talks; tours

L **CONNECTICUT STATE LIBRARY,** Museum of Connecticut History, 231 Capitol Ave, 06106. Tel 203-566-3056; FAX 203-566-2133. *Museum Adminr* Dean Nelson; *Cur* David J Corrigan; *Cur* Deborah Barone
Open Mon - Fri 9 AM - 4:45 PM, Sat 9 AM - 1 PM, cl holidays. Estab 1910 to collect, preserve and display artifacts and memorabilia reflecting the history and heritage of Connecticut. For reference only
Library Holdings: Vols 500,000; original documents; Micro — Fiche, reels; AV — Cassettes, motion pictures, v-tapes; Other — Clipping files, manuscripts, memorabilia, original art works, pamphlets, photographs, prints
Special Subjects: Coins & Medals, Conneticut, firearms
Collections: Collection of Firearms; Portraits of Connecticut's Governors
Exhibitions: Changing exhibits

L **HARTFORD PUBLIC LIBRARY,** Art Dept, 500 Main St, 06103. Tel 203-293-6071. *Dept Head* Vernon Martin
Open hours vary. Estab 1774 as a free public library
Income: Financed by endowment, membership, and city appropriation
Library Holdings: 300,000 pictures; AV — Motion pictures, rec, v-tapes

M **OLD STATE HOUSE,** 800 Main St, 06103. Tel 203-522-6766; FAX 203-522-2812. *Chmn* David Whelehan; *Pres* David Coffin; *Exec Dir* Wilson H Faude
Open Tues - Sat 10 AM - 5 PM, Sun noon - 5 PM. No admis fee. Estab 1975 to preserve oldest state house in the nation and present variety of exhibitions on historic and contemporary subjects. Former executive wing is used for exhibitions of contemporary artists and craftsmen, paintings, decorative arts on a rotating basis. Average Annual Attendance: 200,000. Mem: 1500; dues individual $10, family $15, life $1000; annual meeting in the fall
Income: Financed by endowment, membership and appeals
Collections: †Connecticut portraits; documents; Restored Senate Chamber
Activities: Education department; lectures open to the public, 25 vis lectr per yr; concerts; gallery talks; tours; individual paintings and original objects of art lent to museums for special exhibitions; museum shop sells books, magazines, original art, reproductions, prints, slides, Connecticut arts and crafts

M **REAL ART WAYS (RAW),** 56 Arbor St, 06106. Tel 203-232-1006; FAX 203-233-6691. *Dir* Will K Wilkins; *Gallery Cur* Anne Pasternak
Estab 1974 to present artists of many disciplines working at the forefront of creative activity in their respective fields

A **STOWE-DAY FOUNDATION,** Harriet Beecher Stowe House, 77 Forest St, 06105. Tel 203-522-9258. *Dir* Jo Blatti; *Cur* Renee Tribert Williams; *Education Coordr* Earl French
Open Tues - Sat 9:30 AM - 4 PM, Sun noon - 4 PM, Mon 9:30 AM - 4 PM, June 1- Columbus Day & Dec. Estab 1941 to maintain and open to the public the restored Harriet Beecher Stowe House. The Foundation operates the Stowe-Day Library, oversees a publishing program of reprints of H B Stowe's works and new books and provides workshops and lectures. Average Annual Attendance: 22,000. Mem: 300; dues sustaining $150, supporting $50, family $30, individual $20; fall & spring meetings
Collections: 19th Century Decorative Arts, Domestic Furnishing, Fine Arts; Wallpaper & Floor Treatment Sample Collections
Publications: The Harriet Beecher Stowe House & Library Newsletter, 6 times per year; catalog available upon request
Activities: Classes for adults; teacher workshops; lect open to public, 1-2 visiting lectr per year; paintings & original decorative, domestic or fine art objects lent to institutions; shop sells books, prints, slides, Victorian gift items

L **Library,** 77 Forest St, 06105. Tel 203-728-5507. *Dir* Jo Blatti; *Head Librn* Diana Royce; *Asst Librn* Suzanne Zack; *Photo Archivist* Beverly Zell
Open Mon - Fri 9 AM - 4:30 PM, cl national holidays. Estab 1965 to concentrate on the architecture, decorative arts, history and literature of the United States in the 19th century emphasizing a Hartford neighborhood known as Nook Farm. Reference only
Library Holdings: Vols 15,000; Per subs 18; original documents; Micro — Fiche, reels; AV — Lantern slides, slides; Other — Clipping files, exhibition catalogs, manuscripts, memorabilia, pamphlets, photographs
Special Subjects: Architecture, Decorative Arts, Furniture, Historical Material, Pewter, Hartford 19th Century Literature Community, Nook Farm & Residents; Mark Twain; Harriet Beecher Stowe; Chas Dudley Warner, William Gillette
Collections: Architecture & Decorative Arts of 19th Century: books, plans, drawings, trade catalogs †Hartford 19th Century Literary Community, Nook Farm & Residents; Mark Twain; Harriet Beecher Stowe; Chas Dudley Warner; William Gillette
Activities: Library tours

M **TRINITY COLLEGE,** Austin Arts Center, 300 Summit St, 06106. Tel 203-297-2498; FAX 203-297-5380. *Dir* Jeffry Walker; *Chmn Dept Fine Arts* Michael Mahoney; *Dir Studio Arts Prog* Robert Kirschbaum
Open daily 1 - 5 PM (when college is in session). No admis fee. Estab 1965. A building housing the teaching & performing aspects of music, theater dance & studio arts at a liberal arts college. Widener Gallery provides exhibition space mainly for student & faculty works, plus outside exhibitions
Income: Financed by college appropriation
Collections: Edwin M Blake Memorial and Archive; College Collection; Samuel H Kress Study Collection; George F McMurray Loan Collection
Activities: Lectures open to public, 6 vis lectr per year; lending collection contains 500 original art works and 100,000 slides

M **MARK TWAIN MEMORIAL,** 351 Farmington Ave, 06105. Tel 203-247-0998 (admin office), 525-9317, 525-9318 (visitor center); FAX 203-278-8748. *Executive Dir* John Boyer; *Cur* Marianne Curling
Open Tues - Sat 9:30 AM - 5 PM, Sun noon - 5 PM, June 1 - Columbus Day & Dec 9:30 AM - 5 PM. Admis adults $6.50, children $2.75, under 6 free, group rates available. Estab 1929 to restore & maintain Mark Twain's Hartford home, to collect research materials needed for the project & to keep before the public the life & work of Mark Twain. Maintains Historic House Museum with period interiors, museum room of memorabilia. National Historic Landmark status, US Dept of Interior. Average Annual Attendance: 55,000. Mem: 1200; dues $25 & up; annual meeting
Collections: Lockwood deForest Collection; Mark Twain memorabilia (photographs, manuscripts); period & original furnishings; Tiffany Collection; Candace Wheeler Collection
Exhibitions: National Symposia
Publications: Exhibition catalogues
Activities: Classes for adults & children; docent training; lectures open to public; group tours; open house; Victorian Christmas; gallery talks; college internships offered; individual paintings & original objects of art lent to approved museums & organizations; lending collection contains books, color reproductions, film strips, lantern slides, prints, paintings, photographs, sculpture & slides; museum shop sells books, slides & items related to Victorian lifestyle; junior museum

L **Research Library,** 351 Farmington Ave, 06105. Tel 203-247-0998 (admin office); FAX 203-278-8148. *Exec Dir* John Boyer; *Cur* Marianne Curling
For reference only
Library Holdings: Vols 6000; Per subs 15; Micro — Fiche, reels; AV — A-tapes, fs, lantern slides, motion pictures, rec, slides, v-tapes; Other — Clipping files, manuscripts, memorabilia, original art works, pamphlets, photographs, reproductions, sculpture

M **WADSWORTH ATHENEUM,** 600 Main St, 06103-2990. Tel 203-278-2670; FAX 203-278-2670, Ext 440. *Dir* Patrick McCughey; *Cur European Paintings, Sculpture, Drawings & Prints* Jean Cadogan; *Acting Cur Art Educ* Anne Stellwagen; *Head Conservator* Stephen Kornhauser; *Cur of Contemporary Art* Andrea Miller-Keller; *Cur Costume & Textiles* Carol Krute; *Cur Decorative Arts* William Hosley; *Registrar* Martha Small
Open Tues - Fri 11 AM - 7 PM, Sat & Sun 11 AM - 5 PM, cl Mon. Estab 1842 by Daniel Wadsworth as Atheneum Gallery of Fine Arts. There are more than 60 galleries in 5 interconnected buildings, plus lecture room, classrooms and 299-seat theater. 1968 renovation of facilities includes James Lippincott Goodwin Building, along with sculpture court, restaurant, additional classrooms, and offices. Average Annual Attendance: 152,000. Mem: 6000; dues $25 & up; annual meeting Nov
Income: Financed by private funds
Library Holdings: Vols 27,000; Micro — Fiche, reels; AV — A-tapes, rec, slides, v-tapes; Other — Clipping files, exhibition catalogs, manuscripts, memorabilia, pamphlets, photographs
Special Subjects: Decorative Arts, Museology; Visual Arts
Collections: Archival materials (Wadsworth Atheneum); titles from the Watkinson Library of Reference, 19th century; Hetty Gray Baker Bookplate Collection
Exhibitions: (1991) Francesco Clemente; 3 Worlds; Masters of Baroque; Sacred & Secular: Late Medieval & Early Renaissance Art. (1992 - 93) The Spirit of Lenius; Art at the Wadsworth Atheneum
Publications: Newsletter, monthly to members; collections and exhibitions catalogs
Activities: Lectures and gallery talks by staff; docent talks; seasonal concerts; gallery tours; outside lect; members' exhibition previews and various special events; Atheneum Shop selling books, reproductions, photographs, cards and gifts

L **Auerbach Art Library,** 600 Main St, 06103. Tel 203-278-2670, Ext 342; FAX 203-527-0803. *Librn* John W Teahan; *Asst Librn* Anne Lyons
Open Tues, Thurs, Sat 11 AM - 5 PM, cl Sun, Mon, Wed, Fri. Estab 1934 as a reference service to the museum staff, members and public; to provide materials supporting work with museum collection. For reference only
Library Holdings: Vols 27,000; Per subs 150; Micro — Fiche, reels; AV — Lantern slides, rec; Other — Clipping files, exhibition catalogs, pamphlets
Special Subjects: Decorative Arts, Art sales and collections, museology
Collections: Sol Lewitt (contemporary art); Elizabeth Miles (English silver); Watkinson Collection (pre-1917 art reference)

KENT

M **CONNECTICUT HISTORICAL COMMISSION,** Sloane-Stanley Museum, Rt 7 (Mailing add: Connecticut Historical Commission, 59 S Prospect St, Hartford, 06106). Tel 203-566-3005. *Dir* John W Shannahan; *Museum Dir* David O White
Open May - Oct Wed - Sun 10 AM - 4:30 PM. Admis adults $3, sr citizens $1.50, children $1.50. Estab 1969 to collect, preserve, exhibit historic American tools, implements and paintings of American scenes. Average Annual Attendance: 4000
Income: Financed by state appropriation
Collections: Paintings by Eric Sloane; American tools and implements
Activities: Museum shop sells books & prints

A **KENT ART ASSOCIATION, INC,** Gallery, 21 S Main St, PO Box 202, 06757. Tel 203-927-3989. *Pres* Barbara Goodspeed; *VPres* Gloria Malcolm-Arnold; *Second VPres* Charles Dransfield; *Recording Secy* Maggie Smith; *Corresp Secy* Dorothy Stewart; *Treas* Lee Bardenheuer
Open during exhibitions only Tues - Sun 1 - p PM, cl Mon. Estab 1923, incorporated 1935. Maintains gallery for changing exhibitions. Average Annual Attendance: 2000. Mem: 400; dues assoc $15, sustaining $25, patron $40, life $200; annual meeting Oct
Income: Financed by mem, donations
Exhibitions: Spring Show; Member's Show; President's Show; Fall Show
Publications: Exhibition catalogues, 4 per year
Activities: Lect; demonstrations

LITCHFIELD

A **LITCHFIELD HISTORICAL SOCIETY,** On-the-Green, PO Box 385, 06759. Tel 203-567-4501; FAX 203-567-3565. *Dir* Catherine Keene Fields; *Cur* Jennifer de Simos; *Educ Coordr* Lisa Kightlinger
Open Tues - Sat 11 AM - 5 PM, Sun 1 - 5 PM; Mid Apr - Mid Nov. Admis $2, children under 16 free. Estab 1856, incorporated 1897 for the preservation and interpretation of local historical collections. A gallery of portraits by Ralph Earl is maintained. Average Annual Attendance: 8000 - 10,000. Mem: 500; dues benefactor $250, donor $100, contributing $50, family $25, individual $15; annual meeting second Fri in Sept
Income: $220,000 (financed by endowment, mem & fundraising)
Collections: American and Connecticut fine & decorative arts, pewter, costumes, textiles, paintings, silver, pottery, and graphics
Exhibitions: Changing exhibitions on area art & history
Activities: Educ dept; classes for adults & children; docent training; lect open to public, 6 vis lectr per year; concerts; gallery talks; tours; individual and original objects of art lent to accredited museums with board approval; originate traveling exhibitions for circulation to other museums in Connecticut; sales shop sells books, reproductions & prints
L **Ingraham Memorial Research Library,** Seven South St, PO Box 385, 06759. Tel 203-567-4501. *Dir* Catherine Keene Fields; *Librn* Nancy Beveridge
Open Tues - Sat 10 AM - 12 noon, 1 - 4 PM. Estab 1856 as a center of local history and genealogy study
Income: $10,000 (financed by endowment and membership)
Library Holdings: Vols 10,000; Per subs 10; 50,000 original documents; Micro — Reels; Other — Clipping files, exhibition catalogs, manuscripts, memorabilia, pamphlets, photographs, prints
Special Subjects: Litchfield & Connecticut history 1700-1975
Collections: †40,000 manuscripts in local history

MERIDEN

A **ARTS AND CRAFTS ASSOCIATION OF MERIDEN INC,** Gallery 53, 53 Colony St, PO Box 348, 06450. Tel 203-235-5347. *Pres* Fred Peterson
Open Tues - Fri noon - 4 PM, weekends on special exhibits. No admis fee. Estab 1907 to encourage appreciation of the arts in the community. One floor gallery to hold exhibits and art work studios above with meeting room. Average Annual Attendance: 1000. Mem: 400; dues $12 and up; annual meeting June
Income: Financed by membership and fund raising
Collections: †Permanent collection of paintings & sculptures includes works by Eric Sloan, Emile Gruppe, Stow Wengenroth as well as works by Meriden artists
Exhibitions: Annual Members Show; Photography Show; Student Show; One man & group shows; theme shows & alternating exhibits of works from permanent collection
Activities: Classes for adults and children; dramatic programs; lectures open to the public, 8 vis lectr per yr; workshops; gallery talks; tours; competitions with awards; scholarships; individual paintings and original objects of art lent to banks & public buildings; originate traveling exhibitions; sales shop sells original art & crafts
L **Library,** PO Box 348, 06450. Tel 203-235-5347.
Library Holdings: Vols 250
Collections: Indiana Thomas Book Collection

MIDDLETOWN

M **WESLEYAN UNIVERSITY,** Davison Art Center, 301 High St, 06459-0487. Tel 203-347-9411, Ext 2401; FAX 203-343-3904. *Cur* Ellen G D'Oench; *Registrar* Janine Mileaf
Open Tues - Fri noon - 4 PM, Sat & Sun 2 - 5 PM, cl Mon & academic vacations. No admis fee. Part of the collection was presented to Wesleyan University by George W and Harriet B Davison. Since 1952 the collection with its reference library has been housed in the historic Alsop House, now the Davison Art Center
Collections: The print collection, extending from the 15th century to present day includes Master E S, Nielli, Mantegna, Pollaiuolo, Durer, Cranach, Rembrandt, Canaletto, Piranesi, Goya, Millet, Meryon, Jim Dine, & others; Japanese & contemporary American prints; 1840s to present, photographs
Exhibitions: Regularly changing prints, drawings and photograph exhibitions and other works on paper
Publications: Exhibition catalogues
Activities: Lectures open to the public, 5-10 per yr; gallery talks; tours; original objects of art lent; lending collection contains 20,000 original prints, drawings & photographs; traveling exhibitions organized & circulated
—**Art Library,** 06459-0487. Tel 203-347-9411, Ext 2697. *Art Librn* Susanne Javorski
Open Mon - Thurs 9 AM - 11 PM, Fri 9 AM - 5 PM, Sat noon - 5 PM, Sun 1 - 11 PM. Estab 1950 as research/reference library primarily supporting university courses in art history
Library Holdings: Vols 24,000; Per subs 125
Collections: †Print Reference Collection (books pertaining to the history of the graphic arts)

A **Friends of the Davison Art Center,** 301 High St, 06459-0487. Tel 203-347-9411, Ext 2401; FAX 203-343-3904.
Estab 1961 for the support and augmentation of the activities and acquisition fund of the Davison Art Center by its members
Income: Financed by membership dues & contributions
Purchases: Photographs, Prints
M **Ezra and Cecile Zilkha Gallery,** Center for the Arts, 06459-0442. Tel 203-347-9411. *Cur Exhibitions* Klaus Ottmann
Open Tues - Fri noon - 4 PM, Sat & Sun 2 - 5 PM, cl Mon & academic vacations. No admis fee. Estab 1974. Exhibitions of contemporary art. Average Annual Attendance: 10,000
Exhibitions: Changing exhibitions of contemporary art
Publications: Exhibition catalogs & brochures
Activities: Educ Dept; lectures, 4 per yr; gallery talks; tours; sales shop sells catalogs

MYSTIC

A **MYSTIC ART ASSOCIATION, INC,** 9 Water St, PO Box 259, 06355. Tel 203-536-7601. *Exec Dir* Marjorie Ciminera; *Pres* William Topkin; *Treas* Anthony P Halsey; *VPres* Paul Lowell White
Open daily 11 AM - 5 PM. No admis fee. Estab 1920 to maintain an art museum to promote cultural education, local philanthropic and charitable interests. The association owns a colonial building on the bank of Mystic River with spacious grounds; there is one small gallery and one large gallery with L-shaped corridor. Average Annual Attendance: 6000 - 8000. Mem: 700, artist mem must have high standards of proficiency and be elected by 2/3 vote; dues active $20, assoc $15; meetings held Sept
Income: Financed by membership
Collections: Original artwork by notable artists
Exhibitions: Juried Members' Show (all media); Annual Regional (all media)
Activities: Educ committee; classes for children; lect open to public, 3 or 4 vis lectr per year; concerts; gallery talks; competitions with cash awards; individual paintings lent

NEW BRITAIN

M **CENTRAL CONNECTICUT STATE UNIVERSITY,** Art Dept Museum, 1615 Stanley St, 06050. Tel 203-827-7322; FAX 203-827-7046. *Dir* A Walter Kendra
Estab to collect, display and interpret works of art and ethnic materials relating to the art education program. Center will be constructed within two years and collection will be on display in center, whole collection will not be on permanent display
Exhibitions: (1991) Polish Folk Art & Contemporary Polish Prints; Youth Art Month Exhibitions; Connecticut State University Faculty Exhibition, including Eastern, Western, Southern & Central Universities; Erick Sloane Exhibition

M **NEW BRITAIN INSTITUTE,** New Britain Museum of American Art, 56 Lexington St, 06052. Tel 203-229-0257. *Dir* Daniel DuBois; *Business Mgr* Mel Ellis; *Cur* Janice LaMotta; *Cur of Education* Deborah Frizzell
Open Tues - Sun 1 - 5 PM, cl holidays. No admis fee. Estab 1903 to exhibit, collect and preserve American art. 19 galleries. Average Annual Attendance: 24,000. Mem: 1400; dues patron $100, contributing $50, family $25, individual $15
Income: Financed by endowment
Collections: Traces American Art from Colonial Period (1740) to Contemporary (paintings, graphics, & sculpture)
Publications: Newsletter, quarterly
Activities: Educ dept; docent training; lect open to public, 6 vis lectr per year; concerts; gallery talks; tours; competitions with prizes; original objects of art lent to other museums; originate traveling exhibitions; museum shop selling books, reproductions, prints, slides and postcards and gifts

NEW CANAAN

M **NEW CANAAN HISTORICAL SOCIETY,** 13 Oenoke Ridge, 06840. Tel 203-966-1776. *Exec Dir* Janet Lindstrom; *Librn* Marilyn O'Rourke
Open Wed, Thurs, Sun 2 - 4 PM, Town House open Tues - Sat 9:30 AM - 12:30 PM & 2 - 4:30 PM. Admis $2. Estab 1889 to bring together & arrange historical events & genealogies, collect relics, form a museum & library. Society consists of 7 museums & library. Rogers' studio contains sculpture groups by John Rogers. Exhibit room houses changing displays of costumes, photos & paintings. Average Annual Attendance: 2000-5000. Mem: 900; dues family $35, individual $25; meetings 2nd Mon in Mar, June, Sept, Dec
Income: Financed by memberships & contributions
Collections: Costume collection, including fans, purses & shoes; document collections; pewter; period furniture; photo collection; Rogers' sculpture groups; quilts
Exhibitions: Costume and History; permanent exhibition of Rogers' sculptures
Activities: Seminars; children's classes; docent training; lectures open to public, 4 vis lectrs per yr; awards

A **SILVERMINE GUILD ARTS CENTER,** Silvermine Galleries, 1037 Silvermine Rd, 06840. Tel 203-966-5617. *Pres Bd Trustees* Richard Rothchild; *Gallery Mgr* Dona Everson; *Guild Dir* Carol Sims; *Artistic Exec Dir* Brian Gormley; *School Dir* Michael J Costello
Open Tues - Sat 11 AM - 5 PM, Sun 12:30 - 5 PM, cl Mon. No admis fee. Estab 1922 as an independent art center to foster, promote and encourage activities in the arts and art education and to provide a place for member artists and invited artists to show and sell their work, and to offer the community a wide variety of artistic, cultural and educational activities. Four exhibition galleries and Farrell Gallery which contains paintings and sculpture for purchase. Average Annual Attendance: 20,000. Mem: 800; dues sustaining $125, individual $25
Income: Financed by membership, sale of art, contributions and tuitions
Collections: †Permanent print collection containing purchase prizes from International Print Exhibition

Exhibitions: Biennial International Print Exhibition; Art of Northwest USA - Exhibition of Painting and Sculpture (juried); 14 one-person exhibitions (juried); 2 group shows (juried); 2 invitational exhibitions (juried)
Publications: Exhibition catalogs; member newsletter, quarterly
Activities: Classes for adults and children; docent training; workshops; lectures open to the public, 10 vis lectr per yr; concerts; gallery talks; tours; competitions with awards; scholarships; individual paintings and original objects of art lent to corporations and banks; lending collection contains books & original prints; originate traveling exhibitions; museum shop sells books, original art, reproductions & prints
L **Library,** 1037 Silvermine Rd, 06840. Tel 203-966-5617.
Library Holdings: Vols 2000; Per subs 6; AV — Slides

NEW HAVEN

M **KNIGHTS OF COLUMBUS SUPREME COUNCIL,** Headquarters Museum, 1 Columbus Plaza, 06507. Tel 203-772-2130; FAX 203-773-3000. *Cur & Registrar* Mary Lou Cummings
Open Mon - Fri 8:30 AM - 4 PM. No admis fee. Estab 1982 as a corporate history museum revealing the history & activities of the Knights of Columbus. Average Annual Attendance: 3000
Collections: Fine & decorative arts
Exhibitions: Christopher Columbus; Founder Father Michael J McGivney; gifts & items from Knights of Columbus state & local councils; Knights of Columbus War Activities; Tributes (interactions with the Catholic Church & the Vatican)
Publications: Museum tour brochure
Activities: Lectures open to the public; corporate archives research history of Knights of Columbus; individual paintings & original objects of art lent under special arrangements & careful consideration

M **MUNSON GALLERY,** 33 Whitney Ave, 06511. Tel 203-865-2121. *Pres* Dolores Pelton
Open Tues - Fri 10 AM - 5:30 PM, Sat 11 AM - 5 PM. No admis fee. Estab 1860 to encourage interest in the arts by regular exhibitions of painting, sculpture, graphics, framing and restoration. Located in restored foundry building in New Haven Audubon Street Arts complex
Collections: Contemporary art in all mediums
Exhibitions: One person exhibits; regional work; international artists

A **NEW HAVEN COLONY HISTORICAL SOCIETY,** 114 Whitney Ave, 06510. Tel 203-562-4183. *Pres* F Farny Eilers; *Dir* Robert Egleston; *Cur* Lisa Broberg-Quintana
Open Tues - Fri 10 AM - 5 PM, Sat, Sun 2 - 5 PM, cl Mon & major holidays. Admis adults $2, sr citizens $1.50, children 6 - 16 $1, members & Tues free. Estab 1862 for the preservation, exhibition and research of local history. Average Annual Attendance: 11,300. Mem: 1100; annual meeting Nov
Income: $250,000 (financed by private contributions)
Special Subjects: Genealogy
Collections: Morris House (c 1685 - 1780); decorative arts; ceramics; 18th & 19th Century Collection of portraits of the New Haven area personages; maritime collection of shops paintings; paintings by local artists Corne, Durrie, Jocelyn, Moulthrop
Exhibitions: Permanent exhibition includes paintings by local artists such as Jocelyn, Moulthrop & George H Durrie; landscape portraits; maritime historicl paintings; New Haven Illustrated: From Colony, Town to City; Maritime New Haven; Table Wares 1640 - 1840; Ingersoll Collection of Furniture & Decorative Arts; Two changing exhibitions per year minimumm
Publications: Newsletter; Quarterly Journal
Activities: Classes for adults & children; hands-on programs; docent training; lect open to public, 4 vis lectr per year; slideshows; concerts; gallery talks & tours; individual paintings & objects of art lent to other approved museums; museum shop sells reproductions, prints, antiques & collectibles
L **Whitney Library,** 114 Whitney Ave, 06510-1025. Tel 203-562-4183. *Librn* James Campbell; *Archivist* Carol McHugh-Griger
Open Tues - Fri 1 - 5 PM. Admis $2 for nonmembers for library use. Estab 1862 to collect, preserve, make available, and publish historical and genealogical material relating to the early settlement and subsequent history of New Haven, its vicinity and incidentally, other parts of the USA. The Society has four departments: museum, library-archives, photograph and educational, with the museum staff taking care of the galleries, the library is primary for reference
Income: Financed by endowment, membership, and grants
Library Holdings: Vols 30,000; Per subs 55; original documents; 30,000 glass plate negatives; Micro — Fiche, reels; AV — A-tapes, cassettes, fs, motion pictures, rec, v-tapes; Other — Clipping files, exhibition catalogs, manuscripts, memorabilia, pamphlets, photographs, prints
Special Subjects: Architecture, Art History, Decorative Arts, Historical Material, Landscape Architecture, Marine Painting, Painting - American, Period Rooms, Portraits, Pottery, Genealogy
Collections: Afro-American Coll; Architectural Drawings; John W Barber Coll; Dana: New Haven Old and New; Durrie Papers; Ingersoll Papers; National & Local Historic Figures, A-Z; Ezra Stiles Papers; Noah Webster Collection
Publications: Journal, irregular; News and Notes, irregular; monographs; exhibition catalogs
Activities: Arrangement with local colleges for internship programs and work-study programs; students from Southern Connecticut State University Library School do on-site field work and give seminars for graduate students in library science; classes for children; docent training; lectures open to public & members, 7 vis lectr per year; tours; individual paintings and objects of art lent to other institutions; museum shop sells books, reproductions, prints & antiques

A **NEW HAVEN PAINT AND CLAY CLUB, INC,** The John Slade Ely House, 51 Trumbull St, 06510. Tel 203-624-8055. *Pres* Nan Tussing; *Secy* Christy Gallagher
Open Tues - Fri 12:30 - 4 PM; Sat & Sun 2 - 5 PM; cl Mon. Estab 1900, incorporated 1928. Mem: 270; open to artists working in any media whose work has been accepted two times in the Annual Juried Show; dues life $200, sustaining $20, active $25, assoc $10; annual meeting May

Income: $4000 (financed by dues)
Purchases: $3000
Collections: †Permanent Collection
Exhibitions: Annual April Exhibition (New England & New York artists); Annual Fall Exhibition (active members only); Permanent Collection
Publications: Catalog of spring show; newsletter
Activities: Lecture at annual meeting; scholarships; individual paintings & original objects of art lent

M **SOUTHERN CONNECTICUT STATE UNIVERSITY,** Art Gallery, PO Box 3144, 06515. Tel 203-397-4262. *Dir* Tony Bonadies
Estab 1976 to build a collection of works of art for educational purposes, gallery developing now. Mem: 750; dues $5 and up
Income: $10,000 (financed by membership, state appropriation, and fund raising)
Collections: African & Pre-Columbian art
Activities: Travelogues; lectures open to public, 6 vis lectrs per year; gallery talks; national and international tours; original objects of art lent to administrative offices

YALE UNIVERSITY

M **Art Gallery,** 1111 Chapel St, Yale Station, PO Box 2006, 06520. Tel 203-432-0600. *Dir* Mary G Neill; *Cur Prints, Drawings & Photographs* Richard S Field; *Assoc Cur Ancient Art* Susan Matheson; *Cur American Painting* Helen Cooper; *Cur American Decorative Arts* Patricia Kane; *Registrar* Rosalie Reed; *Membership, Sales & Publications* Caroline Rollins; *Supt* Robert Soule; *Cur Education* Janet S Dickson
Open Tues - Sat 10 AM - 5 PM, Sun 2 - 5 PM, cl Mon. No admis fee. Estab 1832 to exhibit works of art from ancient times to present. Building designed by Louis Kahn and completed in 1953. Average Annual Attendance: 120,000. Mem: 1500; dues $25 and up
Income: Financed by endowment, membership and annual fund-raising
Collections: †American and European painting and sculpture; †Chinese painting and ceramics; †Japanese painting & ceramics; Dura-Europos Archaeological Collection; †Garvan Collection of American Decorative Arts; History paintings and miniatures by John Trumbull; Jarves Collection of Italian Renaissance Painting; Societe Anonyme Collection of twentieth century art; Stoddard Collection of Greek Vases; 20th Century Art; †25,000 prints, drawings & photographs
Exhibitions: (1993) Discovered Lands; Prince Drawings, Photographs & Watercolors, 3 yrs of acquisitions; Cosmic Dancer - Shiva Nataraja; At the Dragon Court; Chinese Embroidered Mandarin Squares; A Private View; Sally Mann - Immediate Family. (1994) Jade Studio; Masterpieces of Ming & Quing Painting
Publications: Exhibition catalogues; Yale University Art Gallery Bulletin, 2 times a yr
Activities: Sunday programs; gallery tours three times per week; Art a la Carte (lunchtime mini-lect); sales desk sells books, catalogues, reproductions, jewelry and postcards

M **Yale Center for British Art,** 1080 Chapel St, Yale Station, PO Box 2120, 06520. Tel 203-432-2800; FAX 203-432-9695. *Dir* Duncan Robinson; *Asst Dir* Constance Clement; *Cur Paintings* Malcolm Cormack; *Cur Prints Drawings & Rare Books* Patrick Noon; *Registrar* Timothy Goodhue
Open Tues - Sat 10 AM - 5 PM, Sun noon - 5 PM, cl Mon. no admis fee. Estab 1977 to foster appreciation and knowledge of British art, to encourage interdisciplinary use of the collections. Reference library & photograph archive for reference;. Average Annual Attendance: 100,000. Mem: 1800
Income: Financed by endowment, annual gifts, membership & museum shop
Collections: Paintings; drawings; prints; rare books & sculpture
Exhibitions: (1991 - 92) Maggi Hambling: An Eye through a Decade; Richard Parkes Bonington: On the Pleasure of Painting; Peter Nadin: Recent Work; Roads to Rails: Revolution in British Transport. (1992 - 93) Victorian Landscape Watercolors; Martin Naylor: Selected Works 1972 - 1992; Gold on Cloth: Bookbinding in 19th century England; Works by Augustus & Gwen John; Contemporary British Letterpress; Sir Thomas Lawrence, Portraits of an Age, 1790 - 1830; C R Cockerell; Horatio Ross; Turner Prints; A Nation of Shopkeepers
Publications: Calendar of Events-Preview of Exhibitions, bi-annually; exhibition catalogues, five per year
Activities: Docent & information volunteer training; symposia; lectures; concerts; gallery talks; tours; films open to the public; scholarships & fels offered; individual paintings and objects of art lent to other museums; originate traveling exhibitions; museum shop sells books, reproductions, postcards & exhibitions catalogs
—**Art Reference Library,** 1080 Chapel St, Yale Station, PO Box 2120, 06520. Tel 203-432-2818; FAX 203-432-9695. *Librn* Dr Anne-Marie Logan
Open Tues - Fri 10 AM - 4:30 PM. No admis fee. Estab 1977 to support collection of British Art. Reference library
Library Holdings: Vols 14,000; Per subs 56; Micro — Cards, fiche 75,000, reels 860; AV — V-tapes; Other — Exhibition catalogs, pamphlets, photographs 150,000
Special Subjects: Art History, Drawings, Etchings & Engravings, Maps, Marine Painting, Painting - British, Portraits, Restoration & Conservation, British Art since 16th century
Collections: British Art from age of Holbein to present
Activities: Classes for adults & children; docent training; lect open to public; concerts; gallery talks; tours; scholarships; originate traveling exhibitions; museum shop sells books, reproductions, slides
L **Art and Architecture Library,** 180 York St, Yale Station, PO Box 1605A, 06520. Tel 203-432-2640. *Acting Librn* Sue Curckford-Peters; *Asst Librn* Christine deVallet; *Slide & Photograph* Helen Chillman
Estab 1868. Serves Schools of Art & Architecture, History of Art Dept & the Yale University Art Gallery
Library Holdings: Vols 100,000; Photographs & color prints 173,000; Micro — Fiche; AV — Slides 293,000; Other — Exhibition catalogs
Collections: †Faber Birren Collection of Books on Color
Publications: Faber Birren Collection of Books on Color: A Bibliography

NEW LONDON

M LYMAN ALLYN ART MUSEUM, 625 Williams St, 06320. Tel 203-443-2545.
Dir Elizabeth P Knowles; *Secy* Mrs David Miller; *Registrar* Nicole Pelto; *Educ Coordr* Kathrine Walker; *Conservator* Lance Mayer; *Conservator* Gay Myers; *Pub Relations Officer* Karen Asher; *Dir Development* Elizabeth McGinley
Open Tues - Sun 1 - 5 PM; cl Mon. No admis fee. Estab 1930 for the education and enrichment of the community and others. The current building consists of nine permanent galleries and four galleries for changing exhibitions. Average Annual Attendance: 500,000. Mem: 1500; dues range from individual $15 to life $10,000
Income: $220,000 (financed by endowment, membership, and gifts)
Purchases: $10,000
Collections: Egyptian, Greek & Roman antiquities; Medieval & Renaissance art; Oriental material primitive art; American & European paintings; furniture; silver; decorative arts; Baratz Collection of dolls, doll houses & toys
Exhibitions: Museology: Photographs of Richard Ross; Ladies Fashion Emporium & Victorian Toy Shop; Afro-American; 4 corporate collections; The Devotion Family of 18th Century Connecticut: In Life & in Art; Lines, Letters, Image: An International Calligraphy Exhibition; Connecticut Women Artists; The Artist Sees New London
Publications: Handbook of the Museum's Outstanding Holdings; New London County Furniture from 1640-1840; New London Silver
Activities: Classes for adults and children; docent training; school tours and programs; lectures open to public; museum shop sells small antiques, books & reproductions
L Library, 625 Williams St, 06320
Open Tues - Sat 11 AM - 5 PM. Estab 1932 to provide an art reference library as an adjunct to the material in the Lyman Allyn Art Museum. Reference only
Library Holdings: Vols 10,000; Per subs 32; Micro — Fiche; AV — Slides; Other — Clipping files, exhibition catalogs, pamphlets, photographs, reproductions
Special Subjects: Decorative Arts, Artists & Related Areas; Art Objects
Collections: Decorative arts, furniture, drawings
Activities: Docent training; lectures open to public, 2 vis lectr per year; gallery talks; tours

A NEW LONDON COUNTY HISTORICAL SOCIETY, 11 Blinman St, 06320. Tel 203-443-1209. *Dir* William E Hare II
Open Wed - Fri 1 - 4 PM, Sat 10 AM - 4 PM by appointment. Admis $2. Estab 1871 for preservation of New London County history. 300; dues $20; annual meeting in Sept. Average Annual Attendance: 2000
Income: $6000 (financed by endowment, mem, admissions)
Purchases: Manuscripts
Collections: Six Portraits by Ralph Earle; furniture & decorative arts owned by Shaw & Perkins families; furniture made in New London County; miscellaneous portraits, miniatures
Exhibitions: Temporary Exhibitions
Publications: NLCHS Bulletin, quarterly; books
Activities: Lect open to public, 6 vis lectr per yr; retail store sells books

M US COAST GUARD MUSEUM, US Coast Guard Academy, 15 Mohegan Ave, 06320-4195. Tel 203-444-8511. *Dir* Valarie J Kinkade
Open Mon - Fri 9 AM - 4:30 PM, Sat 10 AM - 5 PM, Sun noon - 5 PM. No Admis fee. Estab 1967 to preserve historical heritage of US Coast Guard, US Life Saving Service and US Lighthouse Service. Average Annual Attendance: 20,000
Income: Financed by federal appropriations and private donations
Purchases: $12,000
Collections: Ship & aircraft models; paintings; photographs & manuscripts representing the Coast Guard; military artifacts from WWI, WWII & Vietnam;
Exhibitions: Life Savings at Sea; permanent collection. (1991) Origins of Coast Guard. (1992) Only Medal of Honor ever awarded to a Coast Guardsman
Activities: Museum studies internships, graduate level; individual paintings & original objects of art lent to federal museums & qualified organizations for educational purposes only; lending collection contains 200 framed reproductions, 300 paintings, sculpture; book traveling exhibitions, biennial; originate traveling exhibitions to other Coast Guard facilities; Sales shop sells Coast Guard souvenirs

NORFOLK

M NORFOLK HISTORICAL SOCIETY INC, Museum, 13 Village Green, PO Box 288, 06058-0288. Tel 203-542-5761, 542-5231. *Pres & Dir* Cay Fields; *Archivist* Ann Havemeyer; *Cur Photography* Michaela A Murphy; *Cur Rare Books* Laura Byers; *Exhib Designer* Kathleen Bordelon
No admis fee. Estab 1960
Collections: †Marie Kendall Photography Collection (1884 - 1935), era during which she worked in Norfolk; Collection of works by Alfred S G Taylor, noted architect - his blueprints, drawings, photographs plus documents for 40 of his buildings in Norfork listed as a Thematic Group in the National Register of Historic Places; Small collection of Connecticut clocks; Fine 1879 dollhouse with elegant original furnishings; photographs & memorabilia of the Norfolk Downs, one of the very first New England golf courses (1897)
Exhibitions: Norfolk General Stores, Post Offices & Early Norfolk Merchants
Publications: Exhibition catalogs; books, pamphlets & maps, irregularly

NORWALK

M LOCKWOOD-MATHEWS MANSION MUSEUM, 295 West Ave, 06850. Tel 203-838-9799. *Dir* David J Byrnes; *Asst Dir* Kathleen Maher
Open Tues - Fri 11 AM - 3 PM, Sun 1 - 4 PM. Admis, suggested donation $5, students & sr citizens $3. Estab 1968 to completely restore this 19th century 50-room mansion as a historic house museum. Now a registered National Historic Landmark. Average Annual Attendance: 25,000. Mem: 1200; annual meeting

May
Income: $37,000 (financed by membership, city and state appropriation, federal grant)
Collections: †Furniture original to the mansion; 19th century decorative arts, painting & textiles
Exhibitions: (1991) Hudson River School Painting; Celebrate Norwalk; Tiffany Exhibit; AIA Exhibit; Christmas Tree Exhibit
Publications: Newsletter, quarterly
Activities: Educ dept; classes for adults & children; docent training; lect open to public, 6 vis lectr per year; gallery talks; tours; book traveling exhibitions, 1 - 2 per year; museum shop sells books & magazines

NORWICH

M NORWICH FREE ACADEMY, Slater Memorial Museum & Converse Art Gallery, 108 Crescent St, 06360. Tel 203-887-2505, Ext 218. *Dir* Joseph P Gualtieri; *Asst to Dir* Frances E Kornacki; *Docent* Mary-Anne Hall; *Registrar* Carolyn J Baker
Open Sept - June Mon - Fri 9 AM - 4 PM; Sat & Sun 1 - 4 PM; July - Aug Tues - Sun 1 - 4 PM; cl holidays throughout the year. No admis fee. Estab 1888. The collection is housed in two buildings. Average Annual Attendance: 35,000. Mem: 600; lifetime individual $150, patron $50, contributing $25, family $15, individual $10, sr citizen $7.50; annual meeting usually Apr
Income: Financed by endowment
Collections: Vanderpoel Collection of Asian Art; African Art; American Art & Furniture from the 17th - 20th Centuries; Native American Artifacts; Egyptian Art Objects & Textiles; Greek, †Roman & Renaissance Plaster Cast Collection (major collection)
Exhibitions: Special exhibitions changed every 4 - 6 wks; Work of the Norwich Art School children & students displayed
Publications: Greek Myths for Young People; Catalogue of the Plaster Cast Collection
Activities: Lect open to public; competitions; individual paintings and original objects of art lent to museums and historical societies; shop sells postcards

OLD LYME

A LYME ART ASSOCIATION, INC, Lyme St, PO Box 222, 06371. Tel 203-434-7802. *Pres* William Babcock; *VPres* Thomas Torrenti; *Recording Secy* Sultana Hanniford; *Treas* H Gil-Roberts
Open Tues - Sat noon - 5 PM, Sun & holidays 1 - 5 PM. No admis fee, donations accepted. Estab 1914 to promote art & advance education. Four large sky-lighted galleries are maintained. Present building built in 1922 by early Lyme artists. Average Annual Attendance: 2000. Mem: 38; dues invitational juried members $35, associate membership, $10; meetings in May & Sept
Income: Financed by membership and associate members dues, donations & sales commissions
Collections: Collection is under custodianship of Florence Griswold Museum
Exhibitions: Six annual exhibitions: 3 open, 3 member only
Activities: Lectures for members only, 2 vis lectrs per year; concerts; tours; competitions with awards; sales shop sells original art

M LYME HISTORICAL SOCIETY, Florence Griswold Museum, 96 Lyme St, 06371. Tel 203-434-5542. *Pres* Wilson G Bradford; *Dir* Jeffrey W Andersen; *Cur & Librn* Debra A Fillos
Open June - Oct, Tues - Sat 10 AM - 5 PM, Sun 1 - 5 PM; Nov - May, Wed - Sun 1 - 5 PM. Admis $3. Estab 1936 for the purpose of collecting, preserving & exhibiting the art & history of the Lyme region. Average Annual Attendance: 11,000. Mem: 1530; dues family $30, individual $25; annual meeting in June
Income: $450,000 (financed by endowment, mem, grants & town appropriation)
Collections: Old Lyme Art Colony paintings; Clara Champlain Griswold Toy Collection; Evelyn McCurdy Salisbury Ceramic Collection; decorative arts & furnishings; local historical collections
Exhibitions: The Ancient Town of Lyme; The Art Colony at Old Lyme; 19th Century Period Rooms; Walker Evans Photographs; Clark Voorhees 1971 - 1933; Old Lyme: The American Barbizon; Dressed for Any Occasion: Patterns of Fashion in the 19th Century; Thomas W Nason, 1889-1971, A Personal Vision of New England; The Notable Women of Lyme; The Whites of Waterford: An American Landscape Tradition; Childe Hassam in Connecticut; En Plein Air: The Art Colonies of East Hampton & Old Lyme; The Harmony of Nature: Frank Vincent DuMond
Publications: The Connecticut Impressionists at Old Lyme; The Lieutenant River; The Lymes Heritae Cookbook; The Lyme Ledger, quarterly; Report of the Lyme Historical Society, annually; Miss Florence & The Artists of Old Lyme; A New Look at History
Activities: Classes for adults & children; docent training; lectures open to public; tours; museum shop selling books
L Archives, 96 Lyme St, 06371. Tel 203-434-5542. *Cur* Debra A Fillos
Open Mon - Fri 10 AM - 5 PM. Estab 1953 as a research facility for museum programs and for the public. Open to the public for reference by appointment
Purchases: $1500
Library Holdings: Vols 1200; Per subs 15; AV — Cassettes, Kodachromes, motion pictures, slides; Other — Clipping files, exhibition catalogs, manuscripts, memorabilia, pamphlets, photographs, prints, reproductions
Special Subjects: The Art Colony at Old Lyme, American landscape paintings, local history

RIDGEFIELD

M ALDRICH MUSEUM OF CONTEMPORARY ART, 258 Main St, 06877. Tel 203-438-4519; FAX 203-438-0198. *Dir* Barry A Rosenberg; *Cur Educ* Harry Philbrick
Open Tues - Sun 1 - 5 PM; group visits by appointment. admis adults $3, students $2. Estab 1964 for the presentation of contemporary painting and sculpture and allied arts; to stimulate public awareness of contemporary art

through exhibitions and education programs. Nine galleries on three floors of a totally renovated colonial building provide well-lit exhibition space; outdoor sculpture garden. Mem: 600; dues $35 - $10,000
Income: $130,000 (financed by membership, federal and state grants, corporate and private foundations)
Collections: Aldrich Collection; †extended loan collection; †museum collection of emerging artists; print collection
Exhibitions: (1993) Simply Made in America
Publications: Exhibition catalogs; Newsletter, quarterly
Activities: Classes for adults & children; docent training; lect open to public, 10 vis lectr per year; concerts; gallery talks; tours; film; competitions with prizes; scholarships & fels offered; Artreach Program sends docents with slide lect into Fairfield County, CT & Westchester County, NY, art classes; originate traveling exhibitions; sales shop sells books, reproductions, jewelry & gift items

STAMFORD

L FERGUSON LIBRARY, One Public Library Plaza, 06904. Tel 203-964-1000.
Pres Ernest A DiMattia Jr; *Dir of Admin Servs* Arleen Arnold; *Dir of Personnel* Kevin McCarthy; *Dir of Public Relations* Nancy Goss; *Dir of Public Servs* Katherine Golomb; *Dir of Branch Servs* Cenetta Lee; *Business Office Supvr* Marie Giuliano; *Arts & Media Supvr* Phyllis Massar; *Dir of Computer Serv* Hye Ok Park
Open Mon - Thurs 10 AM - 9 PM, Fri 10 AM - 6 PM, Sat 10 AM - 5 PM, mid Sept - mid May Sun 1 - 5 PM. Estab 1880 as a public library dedicated to serving the information needs of the community
Income: Financed by city appropriation
Purchases: $15,000 (art & music books), $50,000 (films & videocassettes), $20,000 (records, tapes & CD's)
Library Holdings: Vols 15,500; Circulating sculpture and frame art; AV — Cassettes, motion pictures, rec, slides, v-tapes; Other — Framed reproductions
Collections: Photography of Old Stamford
Exhibitions: Painting, sculpture, photography & posters under sponsorship of Friends of Ferguson Library
Publications: Focus on Ferguson quarterly newsletter, Art Currents for the Whitney Museum, Musical Notes for the Stamford Symphony and the Connecticut Grand Opera

M STAMFORD MUSEUM AND NATURE CENTER, 39 Scofieldtown Rd, 06903. Tel 203-322-1646. *Pres* Monroe Silverman; *Dir* Gerald E Rasmussen; *Asst Dir* Philip Novak; *Dir of Art* Dorothy Mayhall
Open Mon - Sat 9 AM - 5 PM, Sun & holidays 1 - 5 PM, cl Thanksgiving, Christmas & New Year's Day. Admis adults $2.50, Stamford residents $1.25, Children accompanied by adult $.75, mem free. Estab 1936, Art Department 1955. Museum has an art wing for changing exhibitions of 19th & 20th century art. Average Annual Attendance: 250,000. Mem: 3000; dues $30 & up; annual meeting June
Income: Financed by mem, private & corporate donations & city appropriation
Collections: †American crafts, †American Indian, †painting, †photography, †prints, †sculpture, †sculpture garden
Exhibitions: Annual Connecticut Artists; Four Winners Exhibition; Ellen Lanyon: Strange Games; Private Expressions: Personal Experiences; Color: Pure & Simple; American Art at the Turn of the Century; American Printmaking; The Natural Image; New American Paperworks; Connecticut Craftsmen; Bernstein; Button; Johnson, Margolies; Krushenick; Fiberforms
Publications: American Art: American Women; Animals; brochures; exhibit catalogs; Folk Art: Then & Now; monthly newsletter
Activities: Educ dept, classes for adults & children in art, dance, nature & science; docent training; lectures open to public, 12 vis lectr per year; concerts; gallery talks; tours; competitions with awards; individual paintings & original objects of art lent to other museums; originate traveling exhibitions; museum shop sells books, magazines, slides, & 19th century collectibles & gifts

C XEROX CORPORATION, Art Collection, 800 Long Ridge Rd, 06904. Tel 203-968-3000; FAX 203-968-3330. *Mgr Cultural & Community Affairs* Bob Gudger
Collection on display at Xerox Headquarters
Collections: The art collection represents a broad spectrum of American fine art as well as art forms from other countries. The works range from abstraction to realism and consist of sculpture by David Lee Brown located in the lobby, fiberwork by Gerhardt Knodel located in the dining facility, collages, etchings, lithographs, graphics, mezzotints, mono-prints, montages, pastels, photography, pochoir, silkscreens, watercolors and xerography

STORRS

UNIVERSITY OF CONNECTICUT
M William Benton Museum of Art - Connecticut's State Art Museum, 245 Glenbrook Rd, 06269-2140. Tel 203-486-4520; FAX 203-486-0234. *Dir* Paul F Rovetti; *Cur Furniture & Decorative Arts* Charles F Scott; *Cur of Education* Hildegard Cummings; *Cur of Collections* Thomas P Bruhn; *Registrar* George Mazeika; *Museum Shop Mgr* Ann Ryan
Open during exhibitions Mon - Sat 10 AM - 4:30 PM, Sun 1 - 5 PM. No admis fee. Estab 1966, a museum of art, operating as an autonomous department within the University, serving the students, faculty & general public; contributing to the field at large through research, exhibitions & publications & by maintaining a permanent collection of over 3500 objects. The main gallery measures 36 x 116 ft with a balcony (with exhibit walls) running on three walls and two pendant galleries 20 x 31 ft. Average Annual Attendance: 25,000. Mem: 1100; dues double $25
Income: $700,000 (financed by membership, state appropriation, grants, gifts & donations)
Collections: †American painting and graphics early 20th Century; †German and French graphics late 19th and 20th Century; †selected 17th and 18th Century European paintings, sculptures and graphics; Western European and American c 1600 to present; paintings, graphics
Publications: Exhibition catalogs,annually

Activities: Lectures open to the public, 5-8 vis lectr per year; concerts; gallery talks, tours; individual paintings and original objects of art lent to accredited institutions for exhibition purposes; lending collection contains original prints, paintings and sculpture; book traveling exhibitions; originate traveling exhibitions; sales shop sells books, original art, prints, reproductions and museum related art objects and jewelry

M Jorgensen Gallery, U-104 2132 Hillside Rd, 06269-3104. Tel 203-486-4228.
Operations Dir Gary Yakstis
Open Mon - Fri 9 AM - 4 PM, cl Sat & Sun. No admis fee. Estab 1967 to present work by leading contemporary North American artists. Serves the public as well as the university community. The gallery is 2872 square feet. Average Annual Attendance: 25,000
Activities: Gallery talks

L Art & Design Library, PO Box U-5AD, 06269-1005. Tel 203-486-2787; FAX 203-486-3593. *Head* Thomas J Jacoby; *Asst Head* Tim Ann Parker
Open Mon - Thurs 9 AM - 10 PM, Fri 9 AM - 5 PM, Sat noon - 6 PM, Sun noon - 10 PM. Estab 1979 to support the Departments of Art, Landscape Architecture, Garden History & William Benton Museum of Art. Circ 16,000
Income: Financed by state appropriation & private funds
Library Holdings: Vols 60,000; Per subs 200; Posters; Micro — Cards, fiche; Other — Exhibition catalogs, pamphlets
Special Subjects: Afro-American Art, Antiquities-Assyrian, Antiquities-Byzantine, Antiquities-Egyptian, Antiquities-Etruscan, Antiquities-Greek, Antiquities-Oriental, Antiquities-Roman, Architecture, Art History, Asian Art, Commercial Art, Costume Design & Construction, Decorative Arts, Drawings, American Art, Artistic Photography, Western European Art

STRATFORD

A STRATFORD HISTORICAL SOCIETY, 967 Academy Hill, PO Box 382, 06497. Tel 203-378-0630. *Cur* Hiram Tindall
Open mid-Apr through Oct Wed - Sun. Admis $2. Estab 1926 to promote the history of Stratford. Permanent & changing exhibits of local history. Average Annual Attendance: 2000. Mem: 500
Collections: 18th century house with period furnishings; collection of baskets, ceramics, cooking items, paintings, quilts, military items & weapons
Exhibitions: China Trade Exhibit; Indian Exhibit
Publications: Newsletter

L Geneological Library, 967 Academy Hill, PO Box 382, 06497
Office open Tues & Thurs
Income: $50,000 (financed by mem & city appropriation)
Library Holdings: Vols 500; AV — Rec, slides; Other — Clipping files, manuscripts, memorabilia, original art works, pamphlets, photographs, prints

WASHINGTON DEPOT

A WASHINGTON ART ASSOCIATION, 4 Bryon Plaza, PO Box 173, 06794-0173. Tel 203-868-2878. *Pres* Elizabeth Rives; *VPres* Francis Patnaude; *VPres* Brooke Gloger
Open Mon - Sat 10 AM - 5 PM, Sun 2 - 5 PM, cl Wed. Estab 1952 to make available to the community a variety of art experiences through exhibitions and activities. Three connected galleries downstairs for individual & group shows; small members sales gallery upstairs. Average Annual Attendance: 10,000. Mem: 850; dues family $30, individual $20; annual meeting third Sun in Aug
Income: $32,000 (financed by endowment, membership and fund-raising events)
Exhibitions: (1992) Young Talent; Members Show - 40th Anniversary; Black & White Show: Garden Photographs; Three Painters; Andrew Forge; Ruth Miller; Architects Who Do Other Things; 40th Anniversary Celebration Exhibition; Tommy Simpson; Missy Stevens; Emily McClennen; Chris Spiesel; Shaw Stuart; Folk Visionaries; Christmas Show & Sale
Publications: Events Bulletin, quarterly
Activities: Classes for adults and children; lect open to public, 8 vis lectr per year; gallery talks; sales shop sells original art & crafts by members

L Library, 4 Bryon Plaza, PO Box 173, 06794. Tel 203-868-2878. *Librn* Jean McAdams
Open to members and teachers for reference
Library Holdings: Vols 400; Per subs 2; Other — Clipping files, exhibition catalogs
Special Subjects: Aesthetics, Crafts, Decorative Arts, Graphic Arts, Illustration, Landscapes, Painting - American, Photography, Porcelain, Portraits, Printmaking

WATERBURY

L SILAS BRONSON LIBRARY, Art, Theatre & Music Services, 267 Grand St, 06702. Tel 203-574-8222; FAX 203-574-8055. *Dir* Leo Flanagan; *Fine Arts* Eugenia Benson
Open Mon & Wed 9 Am - 9 PM, Tues, Thurs & Sat 9 AM - 5:30 PM, Fri 9 AM - 5:30 PM. Estab 1869 to provide a free public library for the community. A spotlighted gallery wall and locked glass exhibition case used for art exhibits
Income: Financed by endowment and city appropriation
Exhibitions: Local artists in various media
Publications: Books & Happenings, monthly newsletter
Activities: Lect open to the public; concerts; individual framed art prints lent

M MATTATUCK HISTORICAL SOCIETY MUSEUM, 144 W Main St, 06702. Tel 203-753-0381. *Pres* Julia Q Keggi; *VPres* Paul A Gimbel; *VPres* Orton P Camp Jr; *Dir* Ann Smith; *Asst Dir* Laurie Ryer; *Education Dir* Dorothy Cantor; *Secy* Ann Lilley
Open Tues - Sat 10 AM - 5 PM, Sun noon - 5 PM, cl Mon, cl Sun in July & Aug. No admis fee. Estab 1877 to collect and preserve the arts, history of the state of Connecticut, especially of Waterbury and adjacent towns. An art gallery is maintained. Average Annual Attendance: 100,000. Mem: 1175; dues $40 - $5000; annual meeting in Nov
Income: Financed by endowment, mem & grants
Collections: †Connecticut artists collection; †decorative arts collection; †local

history and industrial artifacts; †period rooms
Publications: Annual Report
Activities: Educ dept; classes for adults and children; dramatic programs; docent training; lectures; gallery talks; group tours by appointment; competitions; individual paintings & original objects of art lent to other museums; lending collection contains paintings, photographs & slides; museum shop sells books, original art, reproductions, prints, decorative arts

L **Library,** 144 W Main St, 06702. Tel 203-753-0381.
Open for reference by appointment only
Library Holdings: Vols 3000; Per subs 10; CT artist files; Other — Exhibition catalogs, manuscripts, memorabilia, pamphlets, photographs
Special Subjects: Architecture, Art Education, Art History, Ceramics, Coins & Medals, Collages, Decorative Arts, Drawings, Etchings & Engravings, Furniture, Local industrial history

WEST HARTFORD

M **NOAH WEBSTER FOUNDATION & HISTORICAL SOCIETY OF WEST HARTFORD, INC,** Noah Webster's House, 227 S Main St, 06107. Tel 203-521-5362. *Dir* Sally Williams; *Educ Dir* Colette Breault; *Admin Asst* Patricia Barker
Estab 1965 to preserve & promote 18th century daily life, Noah Webster & West Hartford history. Average Annual Attendance: 11,000. Mem: 500; annual meeting in Jan
Exhibitions: Changing art exhibitions - painting, photography, sculpture; Annual Spelling Bee
Publications: The Spectator, bi-monthly member newsletter
Activities: Classes for adults & children; docent programs; lect open to public; competitions with awards; retail store sells books, prints

M **UNIVERSITY OF HARTFORD,** Joseloff Gallery, Harry Jack Gray Center, 200 Bloomfield Ave, 06117. Tel 203-243-4098. *Dir* Zina Davis
Open Tues - Fri 11 AM - 4 PM, Sat & Sun noon - 4 PM. No admis fee. Comprehensive exhibition program focusing on established and emerging artists
Exhibitions: Milton Avery; The Poetice Vision; Mia Weserlund Roosen (sculptures, maquettes, drawings). George McNeil, Large Scale Recent Paintings & Prints; Arakawa; The Process in Question; The Photographs of Aaron Siskind. (1991) Sandy Skoglund/John Coplans, Investigation in Perception. (1992) Betye Saar, The Ritual Journey; Josef Albers
Activities: Classes for adults

L **Anne Bunce Cheney Library,** University of Hartford, 200 Bloomfield Ave, 06117. Tel 203-243-4397. *Library Coordr* Anna Bigazzi; *Library Asst* Anna Bigazzi
Open Mon - Fri 8:30 AM - 9 PM, cl Sat & Sun. Estab 1964. Circ 9689
Income: Financed through university library
Library Holdings: Vols 14,000; Per subs 90; Other — Exhibition catalogs, pamphlets, reproductions

WESTON

A **THE COLEY HOMESTEAD & BARN MUSEUM,** 104 Weston Rd, PO Box 1092, 06883. Tel 203-222-1804.
Estab 1961 for preservation of local history and for education. Average Annual Attendance: 300. Mem: 250; dues $15; annual meeting in Mar
Income: Financed by mem, endowment
Collections: Furniture, farm tools and implements, artisan's tools
Publications: The Chronicle, quarterly
Activities: Children's classes in schools; lectures open to public

WESTPORT

L **WESTPORT PUBLIC LIBRARY,** Arnold Bernhard Plaza, 06880. Tel 203-227-8411. *Dir* Sally H Poundstone; *Head of AV Services* Thelma Gordon
Open Labor Day - Memorial Day Mon, Tues & Thurs 9 AM - 9 PM, Wed & Fri 9 AM - 6 PM, Sat 9 AM - 5 PM, Sun 1 - 5 PM. Estab 1907. Circ 500,107
Income: $2,204,440 (financed by endowment, city & state appropriations, fines, rentals & gifts)
Purchases: $272,307
Library Holdings: Vols 182,451; Per subs 381; Micro — Fiche; AV — Cassettes, fs, rec, v-tapes; Other — Clipping files, memorabilia, pamphlets, photographs
Collections: Picture collection (for pictorial research by artists, illustrators, & designers)
Publications: News from Your Library, bi-monthly
Activities: Lectures open to public

WETHERSFIELD

A **WETHERSFIELD HISTORICAL SOCIETY INC,** Old Academy Library, 150 Main St, 06109. *Dir* Nora Howard
Open Tues - Thurs 1 - 4 PM, Sat 1 - PM & by appointment. Estab 1932. Average Annual Attendance: 8000. Mem: dues family $25; annual meeting in mid May
Income: $150,000 (financed by endowment, mem, programs, donations, rentals)
Collections: Wethersfield History & Genealogy
Exhibitions: Woodworkers Guild; Embroiderer's Guild; Wethersfield History
Publications: Quarterly newsletter
Activities: Classes for adults & children; docent programs; lect open to public, 4 vis lectr per yr; book traveling exhibitions 4 per yr; retail store sells books, prints, & more

A **WETHERSFIELD HISTORICAL SOCIETY INC,** 150 Main St, 06109. Tel 203-529-7656. *Dir* Nora Howard
Open Tues - Sat 1 - 4 PM. Estab 1932 to preserve local history. Two changing exhibit rooms. Average Annual Attendance: 18,000. Mem: 800; dues family $30, individual $20; annual meeting in mid - May

Income: $190,000 (financed by endowment, mem, programs & fundraising)
Collections: Local history
Publications: Newsletter, quarterly
Activities: Children's programs; docent programs; lect open to public, 4 vis lectr per year; book traveling exhibitions 8 per year; retail store sells books & prints

DELAWARE

DOVER

M **HISTORICAL AND CULTURAL AFFAIRS,** Delaware State Museums, 102 S State St, PO Box 1401, 19903. Tel 302-739-5316; FAX 302-739-6267. *Div Dir* Daniel Griffith; *Cur Coll* Ann Horsey; *Cur Exhib* Dominique Coulet du Gard; *Cur Education* Madeline Thomas; *Adminr* James A Stewart; *Cur Registration* Claudia F Melson; *Cur Historic Bldgs* Steven Curtis
John Dickinson Plantation: Tues - Sat 10 AM - 3:30 PM, Apr - Dec 1:30 - 4:30 PM; Johnson Victrola Museum, Meeting House Galleries I & II: Tues - Sat 10 Am - 3:30 PM; Old State House, Zwaanendael, New Castle Courthouse: Tues - Sat 8:30 AM - 4:30 PM, Sun 1:30 - 4:30 PM. No admis fee. Historic house museums were opened in the 1950s, Zwaanendael Museum 1931, to reflect the pre-historic and historic development of Delaware by exhibiting artifacts and interpreting the same through various facilities-those of early times. Average Annual Attendance: 93,000
Income: $1,500,000 (state appropriations)
Collections: Allee House furniture & decorative arts; Meeting House Galleries I & II: Prehistoric & Historic Archaeology; Main Street Delaware; John Dickinson Plantation: Decorative arts, furniture & Dicksinson family artifacts; New Castle Court House: Portraits of famous Delawareans, archaeological artifacts, furniture & maps; Old State House: legislative judicial & governmental furniture & decorative arts; Zwaanendael Museum: HMS Debraak Artifacts, Mary Gregory Glass, Dolls etc; Commemorative gifts to the State of Delaware from Holland, china, glass, & silver; Johnson Victoria Museum: Talking machines, Victrolas, early recordings & Johnson memorabilia associated with the Victor Talking Machine Company (RCA)
Publications: Delaware State Museum Bulletins; Delaware History Notebook; miscellaneous booklets and brochures
Activities: Classes for children; docent training; special educational programs for school groups and adults which reflect the architecture, government, education and aspects of social history relevant to Delaware; individual paintings are lent to governmental facilities; inservice programs relating to Delaware history are offered to Delaware teachers; traveling trunk program circulated to elementary schools; museum shop sells books, magazines, prints & Delaware souvenirs

MIDDLETOWN

A **COUNCIL OF DELAWARE ARTISTS,** 1322 Bayview Rd, 19709. Tel 302-378-7274; FAX 302-378-1600. *Pres* Nancy C Willis
Estab 1955 to educate the membership and the public about significant aspects of the creative arts including discussions, lectures and exhibitions pertaining to the visual arts and to provide continuous exposure of member's work through exhibitions; to establish an atmosphere of fellowship and cooperation among professional artist members. Mem: 100; dues $20; meetings once per month
Income: Financed by membership dues
Publications: Newsletter, 9 per year
Activities: Lect open to public; 9 vis lectr per year; individual paintings lent to schools, public offices, retirement homes, banks and museums; originate traveling exhibitions

NEWARK

UNIVERSITY OF DELAWARE
M **University Gallery,** 19716. Tel 302-831-1251. *Dir* Belena S Chapp
Open daily noon - 5 PM, shorter hours during vacation. Estab 1976 to enlarge the student's acquaintance with art in its various aspects. Average Annual Attendance: 10,000
Exhibitions: The African American Art: The Paul Jones Collection; Russian & Greek Icons from the Burgess' Jastak Collection
Activities: Book traveling exhibitions
M **University Gallery,** 114 Old College, 19716-2509. Tel 302-831-8242; FAX 302-831-4330. *Dir/Cur* Belena S Chapp; *Asst Cur* Jan Lopéz
Open Mon - Fri 11 AM - 5 PM, Sat & Sun 1 - 5 PM, cl university holidays. No admis fee. Estab 1978 to promote excellence in arts & humanities at the University of Delaware through exhibitions, acquisitions, preservation, interpretation of art collection & through providing support system to Museum studies curriculum. Average Annual Attendance: 10,000
Collections: 19th & 20th century American works on paper; Pre-Columbian textiles & ceramics; African Artifacts; early 20th century photographs
Exhibitions: (1991) Brandywine Valley to the Bay: Art from private collections. (1993) African American Art: The Paul R Jones Collection
Publications: Exhibit catalog
Activities: Lectures open to public, 5 vis lectr per year; gallery talks; competitions with awards; individual and original objects of art lent to other museums and universities; book traveling exhibitions, 1 per yr; originate traveling exhibitions which circulate nationally to museums & universities
L **Morris Library,** S College Ave, 19717-5267. Tel 302-831-2965, 831-2231; FAX 302-831-1046. *Dir Libraries* Susan Brynteson; *Reference Librn (Art & Art History)* Susan A Davi; *Head Reference Dept* Shirley Branden
Income: Financed through the University
Purchases: $100,000
Library Holdings: Vols 2,000,000; Per subs 350; Maps; Micro — Cards, fiche, prints, reels; AV — A-tapes, cassettes, fs, motion pictures, rec, slides, v-tapes; Other — Exhibition catalogs, manuscripts, pamphlets, photographs, prints
Collections: American art and architecture; early 20th century European art; material on ornamental horticulture

REHOBOTH BEACH

A **REHOBOTH ART LEAGUE, INC,** 12 Dodds Lane, Henlopen Acres, 19971.
Tel 302-227-8408. *Pres of Board* Susan M Townsend; *Dir* Charles Palmer; *Asst
Dir* Carolyn Wright
Open Mid May - Mid Oct, Mon - Sat 10 AM - 4 PM, Sun noon - 4 PM. No
admis fee. Estab 1938 to provide art education and creative arts in Rehoboth
Beach community and Sussex County, Delaware. Two galleries, the Corkran and
the Tubbs built for exhibitions; plus Homestead, circa 1743, gallery & studio.
Average Annual Attendance: 30,000. Mem: 1200; dues $20 and up
Income: Financed by membership, donation and fund raising and sales of
paintings
Collections: Small permanent collection from gifts, includes many Ethel P B
Leach, Orville Peats & Howard Pyle
Exhibitions: Annual Members Fine Arts Crafts Exhibition; Annual Member Fine
Arts Exhibition; Outdoor Fine Art; Inland Bays
Publications: Brochure of yearly events
Activities: Classes for adults and children; lect open to public, 3 vis lectr per yr;
concerts; gallery talks; competitions with awards; scholarships offered; sales shop
selling original art and prints

WILMINGTON

M **DELAWARE ART MUSEUM,** 2301 Kentmere Parkway, 19806. Tel 302-571-
9590. *Dir* Stephen T Bruni; *Assoc Dir & Chief Cur* Rowland P Elzea; *Dir Educ*
Lial Jones; *Registrar* Mary Holahan
Open Wed - Sat 10 AM - 5 PM, Tues 10 AM - 9 PM, Sun noon - 5 PM, cl
Mon. Admis adults $4, sr citizens & students $2.50, children 8 & under free.
Incorporated 1912 as the Wilmington Society of Fine Arts; present building
expanded 1987; a privately funded, non-profit cultural & educational institution
dedicated to the increase of knowledge & pleasure through the display &
interpretation of works of art & through classes designed to encourage an
understanding of & a participation in the fine arts. Nine galleries are used for
exhibitions; six usually hold permanent or semi-permanent exhibitions which
change at six week intervals. Average Annual Attendance: 100,000. Mem: 3200;
dues family $50, individual $30; annual meeting in March
Income: $1,800,000 (financed by endowment, mem & grants)
Purchases: $20,000
Collections: †Bancroft Collection of English Pre-Raphelite Paintings; †Copeland
Collection of Work by Local Artists; Phelps Collection of Andrew Wyeth Works;
†American paintings & sculpture, including many Howard Pyle works &
complete etchings & lithographs of John Sloan; †American illustrations
Exhibitions: (1993) 19th Century British Watercolors; Focus on Found; Art in
Bloom; Biennial '93
Publications: DAM Magazine, quarterly
Activities: Classes for adults & children; docent training; workshops; lectures
open to the public & occasionally to members only, 6 vis lectr per year; concerts;
gallery talks; tours; competitions; exten dept serving schools & community groups
offering two-week programs in visual education; originate traveling exhibitions;
museum & sales shops sell books, candles, jewelry, note cards, paper, original art,
prints, reproductions, slides & crafts
L **Helen Farr Sloan Library,** 2301 Kentmere Parkway, 19806. Tel 302-571-9590;
FAX 302-571-0220. *Head Librn* Iris Snyder
Open Tues, Wed, Thurs 1 - 4 PM, Fri by appointment. Estab 1923. Open to
public for reference only
Library Holdings: Vols 40,000; Per subs 70; AV — V-tapes 30; Other —
Clipping files, exhibition catalogs, manuscripts, memorabilia, original art works,
pamphlets, photographs, prints
Special Subjects: Art History, Illustration, Painting - American, American Art
19th - 20th Century, American Illustration, Pre-Raphaelite Art
Collections: John Sloan Archives and Library; †Howard Pyle Archives and
Library; †Samuel Bancroft Pre Raphaelite Library; †Everett Shinn Archives;
Frank Schoonover Archives

HISTORICAL SOCIETY OF DELAWARE

M **Old Town Hall Museum,** 512 Market Sts, 19801. Tel 302-655-7161; FAX 302-
655-7844. *Exec Dir* Dr Barbara E Benson; *Dir Museum Division* Anne S
Woodward; *Registrar* Thomas Veckman
Open Tues - Fri Noon - 4 PM, Sat 10 AM - 4 PM. No admis fee. Estab 1864 to
preserve, collect & diplay material related to Delaware History. Old Town Hall
Museum is the main museum gallery for the Historical Society of Delaware.
Mem: 1200; dues $35; annual meeting in April
Collections: Regional decorative arts; children's toys; costumes
Exhibitions: (1993) Treasures of the Collections of Historical Society of
Delaware. (1994) Delaware & WWII
Publications: Delaware Collections by Deborah D Waters; Delaware History,
twice a year
Activities: Lectures open to public, 3 - 7 vis lectr per yr; concerts; gallery talks;
tours; originate traveling exhibitions in conjunction with other history museums;
museum shop sells books, reproductions, prints
M **George Read II House,** 42 The Strand, 19720. Tel 302-322-8411. *Site Dir*
Timothy J Mullin
Open Tues - Sat 10 AM - 4 PM, Sun Noon - 4 PM, cl New Year's,
Thanksgiving and Christmas. Admis adults $3, children $1.50. Average Annual
Attendance: 20,000. Mem: 1000; dues $10 and up
Collections: Federal Period decorative arts and architecture
Activities: Walking tours; sales shop sells books & crafts
L **Library,** 505 Market St, 19801. Tel 302-655-7161. *Exec Dir* Dr Barbara E
Benson
Open Mon 1 - 9 PM, Tues - Fri 9 AM - 5 PM
Library Holdings: Vols 75,000; Per subs 73; Micro — Fiche, reels; AV —
Cassettes, fs, Kodachromes, lantern slides, motion pictures, rec, slides; Other —
Clipping files, exhibition catalogs, manuscripts, memorabilia, pamphlets,
photographs, prints
Special Subjects: American and Delaware history
Publications: Delaware History, twice a year; Newsletter, once a year

M **NEMOURS MANSION & GARDENS,** Rockland Rd, PO Box 109, 19899. Tel
302-651-6912. *Tour Supv* B J Whiting
Open May - Nov tours Tues - Sat 9 & 11 AM, 1 & 3 PM, Sun 11 AM, 1 & 3
PM. Admis fee. Estab 1977. 300 acre estate of Alfred du Pont; 102 room
modified Louis XVI chateau built 1909 - 10; formal French-style gardens and
natural woods
Collections: Collection of European furniture, tapestries, & paintings dating back
to the 15th century

C **WILMINGTON TRUST COMPANY,** Rodney Square N, 19890. Tel 302-651-
8381. *VPres* Lewis B Hyman; *Art Consultant* Jean Athan
Open to public by appointment only. No admis fee. Estab 1942 to support
regional artists. Collection displayed statewide in branch offices
Collections: Primarily Delaware scenes by Delaware artists

WINTERTHUR

M **WINTERTHUR MUSEUM AND GARDENS,** Route 52, 19735. Tel 302-888-
4600, 888-4907; FAX 302-888-4880; WATS 800-448-3883. *Chmn* Walter J Laird
Jr; *Dir* Dwight P Lanmon; *Deputy Dir Coll* Brock Jobe; *Deputy Dir Finance &
Admin* Richard F Crozier; *Head of gardens* Thomas Buchter; *Registrar* Karol A
Schmiegel; *Dir Public Relations* Janice Roosevelt; *Deputy Dir External Affairs*
Carol S Harding
Museum open Tues - Sat 9:30 - 5 PM, Sun noon - 5 PM, cl Mon, New Years,
July 4, Thanksgiving, Dec 24 & 25. Admis adults $6, sr citizens & youth 12 - 16
$4.50, children 5 - 11 $1.50. Corporation estab in 1930, museum opened in 1951.
Museum collection housed in two buildings, the Period Rooms (guided tours) &
the Galleries (self guided) featuring decorative arts made or used in America
from 1640 - 1840; vast naturalist garden. Average Annual Attendance: 165,000.
Mem: 16,000
Income: Financed by endowment, membership, grants for special projects,
admission, commercial activities
Collections: Over 89,000 American decorative arts made or used from 1640 -
1860; ceramics, furniture, glassware, interior architecture, metals, needlework,
paintings, prints & textiles
Exhibitions: Point to Point Steeplechase Race
Publications: Publications and articles by staff, including Winterthur Portfolio,
quarterly; Annual Report
Activities: School programs for K - 12; classes for adults & children; Winterthur
Program in Early American Culture; Winterthur Program in the Conservation of
Artistic & Historic objects, & PhD programs in the History of American
Civilization, a graduate program co-sponsored with the University of Delaware;
lect open to the public & to members; Yuletide tours; competitions; fellowships;
individual paintings and original objects of art lent to museums and historical
societies; museum shop sells books, postcards, plants and slides; Winterthur
reproduction gallery sells over 200 reproductions of museum objects
L **Library,** Route 52, 19735. Tel 302-888-4627; FAX 302-888-4870. *Dir & Librn*
Waldron Phoenix Belknap Jr; *Research Librn of American Painting* Dr Katharine
Martinez; *Assoc Conservator for Libr Colls* Maria Fredericks; *Librn in Charge
Visual Resources Coll* Bert Denker; *Librn in Charge Joseph Downs Coll of
Manuscripts & Printed Ephemera* Richard McKinstry; *Librn in Charge Printed
Books & Periodical Coll* Nelville Thompson
Open Mon - Fri 8:30 AM - 5 PM. Estab in 1951 to support advanced study in
American artistic, cultural, social and intellectual history up to the early
twentieth century. For reference only
Library Holdings: Vols 75,000; Per subs 300; Auction Catalogs; Architectural
Drawings; Micro — Cards, fiche 9200, prints, reels 3450; AV — A-tapes, fs,
Kodachromes, lantern slides, motion pictures, slides 170,000; Other — Clipping
files, exhibition catalogs, manuscripts 73,000, memorabilia, original art works,
pamphlets, photographs 150,000, prints, reproductions
Special Subjects: Architecture, Decorative Arts, Painting - American, Museology
Collections: †Waldron Phoenix Belknap, Jr Research Library of American
Painting; †Edward Deming Andrews Memorial Shaker Collection; †Decorative
Arts Photographic Collection; Henry A duPont and Henry F duPont Papers;
†Thelma S Mendsen Card Collection; †Maxine Waldron Collection of Children's
Books and Paper Toys
Publications: Catalogs of collections of printed books: General (9 volumes);
Trade Catalogs; Andrews Shaker Collection; America Cornucopia (thematic
guide to library collections)
M **Historic Houses of Odessa,** Main St, PO Box 507, Odessa, 19730. Tel 302-378-
4069. *Site Adminr* Steven M Pulinka; *Exhib & Prog Coordr* Deborah Buckson
Open Tues - Sat 10 AM - 4 PM, Sun 1 - 4 PM, cl Mon & holidays. Admis adults
(combined) $6, (house) $3, students & senior citizens (combined) $5, (house) $2.
25. Estab 1958 for interpretation of regional lifestyle, architecture & material
culture. Historic Houses of Odessa is a cluster of 18th & 19th century domestic
structures composing a historic village within the community of Odessa. Gallery
is humidity-controlled & contains seven gallery spaces. Average Annual
Attendance: 20,000
Income: Financed by endowment
Special Subjects: Architecture, Delaware furniture, Belter furniture
Collections: Corbit-Sharp House containing Chippendale, Federal & Queen Anne
furniture; Wilson-Warner House; 19th century Brick Hotel Gallery; Federal
Decorative Arts †Brick Hotel contains largest collection of early Victorian Belter
Furniture in Nation
Exhibitions: (1992) Alice In Wonderland at Wilson Warner House
Activities: Tours

DISTRICT OF COLUMBIA

WASHINGTON

M AMERICAN ARCHITECTURAL FOUNDATION, The Octagon, 1799 New York Ave NW, 20006-5292. Tel 202-638-3105; FAX 202-626-7420. *Dir* Nancy Davis
Open Tues - Fri 10 AM - 4 PM; Sat & Sun Noon - 4 PM. Admis by donation; groups over 10 charges $3 per person except student and senior citizens groups $1 per person. Opened as house museum in 1970; formerly a federal townhouse designed by the first architect of the United States Capitol, Dr William Thornton for Col John Taylor III to serve as a winter home; used by President & Mrs Madison as temporary White House during war of 1812. Furnished with late 18th and early 19th century decorative arts; changing exhibition program in second floor galleries. Average Annual Attendance: 25,000
Collections: Permanent collection of furniture, paintings, ceramics, kitchen utensils
Publications: Competition 1792-Designing a Nation's Capitol, 1976 book; exhibition catalogs; Octagon being an Account of a Famous Residence: Its Great Years, Decline & Restortaion , 1976 book; William Thornton: A Renaissance Man in the Federal City, book; The Architect & the British Country House, book; Architectural Records Management, 1985 booklet; the Architecture of Richard Morris Hunt, 1986 book; Building the Octagon, 1989 book; Ambitious Appetites: Dining, Behavior & Patterns of Consumption in Federal Washington, 1990 book; In the Most Fashionable Style: Making a Home in the Federal City, 1991 book; Creating the Federal City, 1774-1800: Potomac Fever, 1988 book; The Frame in American, 1700-1900: A survey of Fabrication, Techniques & Styles, 1983 catalog; Robert Mills, Architect, 1989 book; Sir Christopher Wren: The Design of St Paul's Cathedral, 1987 book; & exhibit catalogs
Activities: Educ dept; docent training; tours; lect open to public, 6 vis lectrs per year; museum shop sells books & reproductions
L The Octagon Museum, The Octagon, 1799 New York Ave, NW, 20006-5292. Tel 202-638-3105; FAX 202-626-7420. *Dir* Nancy Davis
Open to the public for reference but primarily used by staff
Library Holdings: Vols 200; Per subs 10
Special Subjects: Architecture, Decorative Arts, History of the Octagon and the Tayloe Family

AMERICAN ASSOCIATION OF MUSEUMS
For further information, see National and Regional Organizations

AMERICAN ASSOCIATION OF UNIVERSITY WOMEN
For further information, see National and Regional Organizations

AMERICAN INSTITUTE FOR CONSERVATION OF HISTORIC & ARTISTIC WORKS (AIC)
For further information, see National and Regional Organizations

AMERICAN INSTITUTE OF ARCHITECTS
For further information, see National and Regional Organizations

M AMERICAN UNIVERSITY, Watkins Collectiony, 4400 Massachusetts Ave NW, 20016. Tel 202-885-1670. *Dir* Ron Haynie; *Cur* Steve Dykstra
Open Mon - Fri 10 AM - noon & 1 - 4 PM. No admis fee. Estab 1943 to exhibit art of interest to public and university art community; schedule includes occasional education or theme shows and student exhibits. Maintains large room with moveable panels and one small exhibit room with attendant's desk. Average Annual Attendance: 2000 plus art students
Collections: Watkins Collection of 19th and 20th century American and European paintings; drawings & prints
Activities: Lectures open to the public, 3 - 5 vis lectr per year; individual paintings and original objects of art lent to museums and university galleries; traveling exhibitions organized and circulated on occasion

M ANACOSTIA MUSEUM, 1901 Fort Pl SE, 20020. Tel 202-287-3369; FAX 202-287-3183. *Dir* Steven Newsome; *Deputy Dir* Sharon Reinckens; *Acting Dir Educ & Research* Zora Martin-Felton; *Education Specialist* Robert Hall; *Historian* Portia P James
Open Mon - Fri 10 AM - 6 PM, Sat, Sun and holidays 1 - 6 PM, cl Christmas. No admis fee. Estab 1967, as a non-profit federally chartered corporation to record and research African, Black American and Anacostia history and urban problems
Income: Federally funded bureau of Smithsonian Institute
Collections: Afro-American and African art; Afro-American history
Exhibitions: (1991) Gathered Visions: selected works by African-American women artists; To Achieve these Rights. (1993) Alvin Alley; Quilt Exhibition; Bob Marley
Publications: Educational booklets; exhibit programs; museum brochures accompany each major exhibit
Activities: Programs for children and adults; lect; tours; gallery talks; art festivals; competitions; extension department serves groups unable to visit the museum; traveling exhibitions organized and circulated
L Research Library, 1901 Fort Pl SE, 20020. Tel 202-287-3380; FAX 202-287-3183. *Librn* Timothy Carr
Open to the public for research on the premises
Library Holdings: Vols 1500

M ARCHIVES OF AMERICAN ART, AA-PG Bldg Smithsonian Institute, Rm 331, Balcony, 20560. Tel 202-357-2781. *Dir* Richard J Wattenmaker
Open Mon - Fri 9 AM - 5 PM. No admis fee. The Archives of American Art, founded in 1954, has assembled the world's largest collection of material documenting the history of the visual arts in this country. Eight million items of original source material are available on microfilm to scholars, students, writers and researchers. Affiliated with the Smithsonian Institution since 1970, the Archives preserves its original documents in Washington with microfilm copies in its regional branches. Mem: 2000; dues $65 & up

Income: Financed by federal appropriation, private contributions, gifts & foundation grants
Collections: †Manuscript collection pertinent to the study of art in America
Publications: Finding aids & guides, video: From Reliable Sources - The Archives of American Art
—New York Regional Center, 1285 Avenue of the Americas, Lobby Level, New York, NY 10019. Tel 212-399-5015. *Dir* Stephen Polcari; *Supervisory & Archivist* Cathy Stover
Open daily 9 AM - 5 PM. Estab 1956 to collect papers of artists, critics, dealers & collectors. 3000 sq ft. Average Annual Attendance: 5000. Mem: 1200; dues $65; annual meeting varies
Collections: Letters, diaries, artwork, writings, photographs & oral histories of the American art world
Exhibitions: American Art of the 19th & 20th centuries
Activities: Lect open to members only, 200 vis lectr per yr; gallery talks
—Midwest Regional Center, 5200 Woodward Ave, Detroit, MI 48202. Tel 313-226-7544; FAX 313-226-7620. *Librn* Adrienne Aluzzo
Open Mon - Fri 9:30 AM - 5 PM. Estab 1954 to document the history of art in America
Income: Financed trust funds
Activities: Lectures open to the public, 3-4 vis lectrs per yr
—New England Regional Center, 87 Mount Vernon St, Boston, MA 02108. Tel 617-565-8444; FAX 617-565-8466. *Dir* Robert Brown
—Huntington Library Memorial Museum, 1151 Oxford Rd, San Francisco, CA 91108. Tel 818-405-7847; FAX 818-405-7207. *Regional Dir* Paul J Karlstrom
Open by appointment only Mon - Fri 9 AM - noon & 1 - 5 PM. Estab 1954 as a manuscript repository of American artists. Reference only
Library Holdings: Micro — Reels; AV — Fs
Special Subjects: Art History, American Art History
Collections: Manuscripts, correspondence, journals, diaries of American painters, sculpters, craftsmen, designers & architects
Publications: The Archives of American Art Journal, quarterly

M ART MUSEUM OF THE AMERICAS (Formerly Museum of Modern Art of Latin America), 1889 F St NW (Mailing add: 17th & Constitution Ave NW, 20006). Tel 202-458-6016. *Dir* Dr Belgica Rodriguez; *Cur Reference Center* Maria Leyva
Open Tues - Sat 10 AM - 5 PM, cl holidays. No admis fee. Estab 1976 by organization of American States to bring about an awareness and appreciation of contemporary Latin American art. The museum maintains an art gallery with the focus on contemporary Latin American art. Average Annual Attendance: 100, 000
Collections: Contemporary Latin American and Caribbean art including paintings, prints, drawings & sculpture
Exhibitions: Images of Silence; Photography from Latin America & the Caribbean in the 80's; The Figure in Latin American & Caribbean Art
Activities: Lect open to public, 10 vis lectr per year; gallery talks; tours; paintings and original art objects lent to museums & educational institutions; originate traveling exhibitions; sales shop sells films on Latin American art and artists
L Archive of Contemporary Latin American Art, 1889 F St, 20006. Tel 202-458-6016.
Open to scholars for research only
Library Holdings: books; Micro — Fiche, reels; AV — A-tapes, slides, v-tapes; Other — Clipping files, exhibition catalogs, pamphlets, photographs, reproductions
Special Subjects: Aesthetics, Art History, Film, Latin American Art, Mexican Art, Painting - Spanish

A ART PAC, 729 Eighth St, Suite 300, 20003. Tel 202-546-1804; FAX 202-543-2405. *Treas* Robert J Bedard
Estab 1981 to lobby for art's legislation & assist federal candidates supporting the arts. Mem: Dues $40
Income: Financed by membership
Publications: Newsletter/ART PAC News, quarterly
Activities: Legislator of Year Award

M ARTS CLUB OF WASHINGTON, James Monroe House, 2017 I St NW, 20006. Tel 202-331-7282. *Pres* Evelyn Woolson; *Mgr* Alma Gensler
Open Tues & Thurs 10 AM - 5 PM, Wed & Fri 2 - 5 PM, Sat 10 AM - 2 PM, Sun 1 - 5 PM, cl Mon. No admis fee. Founded 1916. The James Monroe House (1803-1805) was built by Timothy Caldwell of Philadelphia. It is registered with the National Register of Historic Places, the Historical Survey 1937 and 1968, and the National Trust for Historic Preservation. James Monroe, fifth President of the United States, resided in the house while he was Secretary of War and State. During the first six months of his Presidency (1817-1825) the house served as the Executive Mansion, since the White House had been burned in the War of 1812 and had not yet been restored. Garden, rooms & stairhalls serve as galleries. Average Annual Attendance: 10,000. Mem: 250; annual meeting April
Income: Financed by mem, catering functions & fundraising
Purchases: obtained through gifts & bequests
Collections: Washington, DC art
Publications: Monthly news bulletin to members
Activities: Lectures open to public & for members, 40 vis lectrs per yr; concerts, gallery talks; tours; awards; scholarships

ASSOCIATION OF COLLEGIATE SCHOOLS OF ARCHITECTURE
For further information, see National and Regional Organizations

M B'NAI B'RITH INTERNATIONAL, B'nai B'rith Klutznick National Jewish Museum, 1640 Rhode Island Ave NW, 20036. Tel 202-857-6583. *Museum Resources Assoc* Lisa Rosenblatt; *Dir* Ori Z Soltes; *Assoc Dir* Amy Kostant; *Shop Mgr* Dolores Porter
Open Sun - Fri 10 AM - 5 PM, cl Sat & legal & Jewish holidays. No admis fee; suggested donation adults $2, children, students & sr citizens $1. Estab 1957 to exhibit & preserve Jewish art & culture. Two changing exhibition galleries; five permanent collection galleries, including Life & Holiday cycles; sculpture garden; Jewish American Sports Hall of Fame. Average Annual Attendance: 35,000.

Mem: 600; dues $25 - $5000
Income: General operations financed by parent organization; programs & exhibitions financed by Museum members, private & corporate donations
Collections: Permanent collection of Jewish ceremonial & folk art; ancient coins; archives of B'nai B'rith; contemporary paintings; lithographs
Exhibitions: (1991) Intimitions of Immortality. (1992) Ceramics of Otto Natzler; Paintings of Malcah Zeldis; Old Voices, New Faces; (Soviet) Jewish Artists from the 1920s; Agri-culture; Jewish Immigrants, Farmers, Artists in New Jersey; Where Did They Go? Where Are They Now?
Publications: Exhibitions brochures; Members Newsletter, semi-annual; Permanent Collection Catalogue
Activities: Holiday family education program; children's program; docent training; workshops; lect open to public; films; gallery talks; exhibit tours; individual paintings & original objects of art lent to museums; originate traveling exhibitions; museum shop sells books, original art, reproductions, posters, Judaica & giftware

L **CATHOLIC UNIVERSITY OF AMERICA,** Humanities Division, Mullen Library, 620 Michigan Ave NE, 20064. Tel 202-319-5075. *Head Humanities Division* B Gutekunst
Open fall & spring terms Mon - Thurs 9 AM - 10 PM, Fri & Sat 9 AM - 5 PM, Sun 1 - 10 PM. Estab 1958 to offer academic resources and services that are integral to the work of the institution
Library Holdings: Vols 12,000
Special Subjects: Early Christian & Medieval Art

CONGRESSIONAL ARTS CAUCUS
For further information, see National and Regional Organizations

M **CORCORAN GALLERY OF ART,** 17th St and New York Ave NW, 20006. Tel 202-638-3211. *Pres* David Levy; *Assoc Dir* Jack Cowart; *Cur* Terrie Sultan; *Registrar* Cynthia Rom
Open Tues - Sun 10 AM - 5 PM. No admis fee. Founded 1869 primarily for the encouragement of American art. The nucleus of the collection of American Paintings was formed by its founder, William Wilson Corcoran, early in the second half of the 19th century. In 1925 a large wing designed by Charles A Platt was added to house the European collection bequested by Senator William Andrews Clark of Montana. The Walker Collection, formed by Edward C and Mary Walker, added important French Impressionists to the collection upon its donation in 1937. Average Annual Attendance: 400,000. Mem: 4500; dues contributing $500 and up, sponsor $250, Friends of the Corcoran $125, family $50, single $35, student and senior citizen $15
Collections: The American collection of paintings, watercolors, drawings, sculpture and photgrphy from the 18th through 20th centuries; European collection includes paintings and drawings by Dutch, Flemish, English and French artists; 18th century French salon, furniture, laces, rugs, majolica; Gothic and Beauvais tapestries; Greek antiquities; 13th century stained glass window and bronzes by Antoine Louise Barye; tryptich by Andrea Vanni; Walker Collection of French Impressionists
Exhibitions: Changing exhibitions of Contemporary Art; Fine Art Photography; works by regional artists; works drawn from the permanent collection
Publications: Calendar of Events (for members); Corcoran Shop Catalogue
Activities: Classes for adults and children; docent training; lectures open to public; concerts; gallery talks; tours; originates traveling exhibitions; shop sells books, magazines, reproductions, prints & slides
L **Library,** 500 17th St NW, 20006. Tel 202-628-9484, Ext 750; FAX 202-737-2664. *Librn* Ann Maginnis
Available for inter-library loan and for public use by appointment only
Purchases: 51,200
Library Holdings: Vols 14,300; Per subs 130; Micro — Fiche; AV — Slides; Other — Exhibition catalogs
Special Subjects: Art History

M **DAR MUSEUM,** National Society Daughters of the American Revolution, 1776 D St NW, 20006. Tel 202-879-3237. *Museum Dir & Chief Cur* Diane Dunkley; *Dir of Museum Serv* Catherine Tuggle
Open Mon - Fri 8:30 AM - 4 PM, Sun 1 - 5 PM. No admis fee. Estab 1890 for collection & exhibition of decorative arts used in America from 1700 - 1840; for the study of objects, & the preservation of Revolutionary artifacts & documentation of American life. There are 33 period rooms which reflect the decorative arts of particular states, also a museum which houses large collections grouped by ceramics, textiles, silver, glass, furniture & paintings. Average Annual Attendance: 12,000. Mem: 215,000; dues $15 - $17; annual meeting in April
Income: Under $200,000 (financed by membership)
Purchases: Under $20,000
Collections: †Ceramics, †furniture, †glass, †paintings, †prints, †silver, textiles
Exhibitions: Special exhibitions arranged and changed periodically, usually every 2 - 3 months
Activities: Classes for children; docent training; lectures; gallery talks; tours; paintings and original art works lent to museums; sales shop sells books, slides, stationery, dolls and handcrafted gift items
L **Library,** 1776 D St NW, 20006
Open to public by advance notice; for reference only
Purchases: $1000
Library Holdings: Vols 2500; Per subs 4
Special Subjects: American Decorative Arts

M **FEDERAL RESERVE BOARD,** Art Gallery, 20th St & Constitutioin Ave NW, 20551. Tel 202-452-3686; FAX 202-452-3102. *Dir* Mary Anne Goley
Open daily 11:30 AM - 2 PM. Estab 1975 to promote art in the work place. Two story atrium space with travertine, marble walls. Works are hung on four landings & one very long hall. Average Annual Attendance: 800. Mem: 1500
Income: Financed by the Federal Reserve Board
Collections: American & European paintings; 19th century - present sculpture; Works on paper
Exhibitions: Swiss Folk Art
Publications: Exhibition catalogs
Activities: Docent programs; book traveling exhibitions 4 per year; originate traveling exhibitions 4 per year

L **FOLGER SHAKESPEARE LIBRARY,** 201 E Capitol St SE, 20003. Tel 202-544-4600; FAX 202-544-4623. *Dir* Werner Gundersheimer; *Assoc Dir* Philip A Knachel
Open (exhibition gallery) Mon - Sat 10 AM - 4 PM, Sun also from April 15 - Labor Day. Estab 1932 as an international center for the study of all aspects of the European Renaissance and civilization in the 16th and 17th centuries. Maintains an art gallery and a permanent display of Shakespearean items and changing topical exhibits of books, manuscripts, paintings and sculpture. Contemporary art is exhibited in the lower gallery
Income: Financed by endowment
Library Holdings: Vols 230,000; Per subs 180; rare books 100,000; Micro — Reels; AV — A-tapes, fs, motion pictures, rec, slides; Other — Exhibition catalogs, manuscripts, memorabilia, original art works, pamphlets, photographs, prints, reproductions, sculpture
Collections: Shakespeare, playbills and promptbooks; Continental and English Renaissance, 1450-1700
Publications: Newsletter, three times per yr; Shakespeare Quarterly
Activities: Seminars for advanced graduate students; lectures open to public; concerts; gallery talks; scholarships offered; originate traveling exhibitions

M **FONDO DEL SOL,** Visual Art & Media Center, 2112 R St NW, 20008. Tel 202-483-2777. *Executive Dir* Mark Zuver; *Asst Dir Spec Projects* Irma Talabi Francis
Estab 1973 to promote Latin American culture, non-profit organization
Collections: Permanent collection, Religious artifacts of artistry, ceramics, sculpture, paintings - Columbian, South American

M **FREER GALLERY OF ART,** 1050 Independence Ave SW, 20560. Tel 202-357-4880; FAX 202-357-4911. *Dir* Milo Beach; *Asst Dir* Tom Lentz; *Cur Chinese Art* Shen Fu; *Cur Near Eastern Art* Marianna Simpson; *Assoc Cur Japanese Art* Ann Yonemura; *Head Conservator & Technical Laboratory* W T Chase; *Conservation Scientist* John Winter; *Admin Officer* Sarah Newmeyer
Estab 1906 under Smithsonian Institution to exhibit its outstanding masterpieces of American and Oriental art; to carry out research and publication in the history of civilizations represented by objects in the collections
Income: Financed by endowment and Federal appropriation
Purchases: Oriental art
Collections: †Art of the Near and Far East: paintings, sculpture, objects in stone, wood, jade, glass, porcelain, bronze, gold, silver, lacquer, metalwork; manuscripts (early Christian); Collection of works by James McNeill Whistler and some of his contemporaries Linda Merrill: American Art
Exhibitions: Asian art; Whistler exhibition
Activities: Lectures, six vis lectr per year; tours; museum shop sells books, reproductions, slides, needlepoint, desk accessories, postcards, greeting cards and note cards

M **FREER GALLERY OF ART & THE ARTHUR M SACKLER GALLERY GALLERY** (Formerly Arthur M Sackler Gallery), 1050 Independence Ave SW, 20560. Tel 202-357-4880. *Dir* Milo C Beach
Open daily 10 AM - 5:30 PM, cl Christmas Day. No admis fee. Estab 1987 for exhibition, research & education on the arts of Asia. Average Annual Attendance: 500,000
Income: Financed by endowment & federal appropriation
Collections: Chinese, Japanese, Islamic, Ancient Near Eastern & South & Southeast Asia
Exhibitions: (1993) Joined Colors: Decorative & Meaning in Chinese Porcelain; The Golden Age of Sculpture from Sri Lanka
Publications: Asian Art, quarterly; Arthur M Sackler Gallery Calendar, bi-monthly
Activities: Programs for adults & children; dramatic programs; docent training; lectures open to public, 5-6 vis lectr per yr; concerts; gallery talks; tours; films; individual paintings & original objects of art lent to other art institutions; originate traveling exhibitions; museum shop sells books, magazines, reproductions, prints, slides, jewelry, cards & gifts
L **Library,** 1050 Independence Ave SW, 20560. Tel 202-357-4880. *Head Librn* Lily C J Keckses; *Librn* Kathryn D Phillips; *Librn* Reiko Yoshimura; *Archivist* Colleen Hennessey
Open to public for reference
Library Holdings: Vols 52,000; Per subs 350; Sales catalogs Micro — Fiche, reels; AV — A-tapes, cassettes, lantern slides, slides; Other — Clipping files, exhibition catalogs, reproductions
Special Subjects: Antiquities-Oriental, Antiquities-Persian, Architecture, Asian Art, Bronzes, Calligraphy, Ceramics, Coins & Medals, Decorative Arts, Embroidery, Folk Art, Glass, Gold, Islamic Art, Volumes related to cultural & historical background of the collection

GENERAL SERVICES ADMINISTRATION
For further information, see National and Regional Organizations

M **GEORGETOWN UNIVERSITY,** Art and History Museum, PO Box 2269, Hoya Station, 20057. Tel 202-687-4406; FAX 202-687-4452. *Cur* Clifford T Chieffo; *Assoc Cur* Patricia H Chieffo
Open during University hours according to yearly schedule, cl holidays. No admis fee. University estab 1789. The museum is on the Georgetown University campus in Healy Hall (1879)
Income: Financed by University budget
Collections: American portraits; Works by Van Dycke and Gilbert Stuart; graphics, historical objects, paintings, religious art, paintings
Publications: Collection catalog, exhibit catalogs
Activities: Educational programs for undergraduate students; gallery talks; guided tours; art festivals, temporary exhibitions
L **Lauinger Library-Special Collections Division,** 37th & O Sts NW, PO Box 37445, 20013-7445. Tel 202-687-7444; FAX 202-687-7501. *Special Collections Librn* George M Barringer
Open Mon - Fri 9 AM - 5:30 PM. Estab 1796 to support Georgetown's academic programs
Library Holdings: Other — Original art works, photographs, prints

Special Subjects: Bookplates & Bindings, Cartoons, Drawings, Illustration, Woodcuts
Collections: †Editorial Cartoon Collection - Originals (American) c 1910 to present; Elder Collection - Artist Self - Portraits, prints, drawings, watercolors, paintings , c 1925-1975; †Jesuit Collection - American fine prints, c 1900-1950 Eric F Menke Collection - prints, drawings, watercolors, paintings; Murphy Collection - American Fine Prints, c 1900 - 1950; †Eric Smith Collection - original editorial cartoon; Lynd Ward Collection- prints, drawings, watercolors, paintings, c 1925 - 1980; Printmakers' Collections: John DePol, Norman Kent, Clare Leighton, Barry Moser
Publications: Annual print exhibition handlists; Graphic Arts in the Special Collections Division, Georgetown University Library; Special Collections at Georgetown

M **GEORGE WASHINGTON UNIVERSITY,** The Dimock Gallery, Lower Lisner Auditorium, 730 21st St NW, 20052. Tel 202-994-1525. *Dir* Lenore D Miller; *Asst Cur* Penny Dwyer
Open Tues - Fri 10 AM - 5 PM, Sat noon - 5 PM, cl Sun, Mon & national holidays. No admis fee. Estab 1967 to enhance graduate & undergraduate programs in fine art & research in art history; documentation of permanent collections; feature historical & contemporary exhibitions related to university art dept programs. Average Annual Attendance: 10,000
Collections: U S Grant Collection of Photographs; W Lloyd Wright Collection of Washingtoniana; Joseph Pennell Collection of Prints; graphic arts from the 18th, 19th and 20th centuries, with special emphasis on American art; historical material; paintings; prints; sculpture; works pertaining to George Washington
Exhibitions: 8 - 10 temporary exhibitions staged per yr, including faculty, alumni, student, permanent collection shows & Washington DC area invitational exhibitions
Publications: Exhibition catalogs
Activities: Lectures open to public, concerts and gallery talks; individual paintings & original objects of art lent; book traveling exhibitions

M **HARVARD UNIVERSITY,** Dumbarton Oaks Research Library and Collections, 1703 32nd St NW, 20007. Tel 202-342-3200; Cable: HARDOAKS. *Dir* Angeliki Laiou
Open daily (Gardens) Apr - Oct 2 - 6 PM, Nov - Mar 2 - 5 PM, (Collections) Tues - Sun 2 - 5 PM, cl holidays. Conveyed in 1940 to Harvard University by Mr and Mrs Robert Woods Bliss as a research center in the Byzantine and Medieval humanities and subsequently enlarged to include pre-Columbian studies & studies in landscape architecture. Average Annual Attendance: 100,000
Collections: †Byzantine devoted to early Christian & Byzantine mosaics, textiles, bronzes, sculpture, ivories, metalwork, jewelry, glyptics & other decorative arts of the period; pre-Columbian devoted to sculpture, textiles, pottery, gold ornaments & other objects from Mexico, Central & South America, dating from 800 BC to early 16th century; European & American paintings, sculpture & decorative arts
Publications: Handbooks and catalogs of the Byzantine and pre-Columbian collection; scholarly publications in Byzantine, pre-Columbian and landscape architecture studies
Activities: Lectures; conferences

L **Library,** 1703 32nd St NW, 20007. Tel 202-342-3200, Ext 241. *Librn* Irene Vaslef; *Serials Librn* Patricia Hardesty
Important resources for Byzantine research
Library Holdings: Vols 123,500; Per subs 870; Micro — Fiche, reels; Other — Exhibition catalogs
Special Subjects: Landscape Architecture, Pre-Columbian Art, Byzantine Studies
Collections: Dumbarton Oaks Census of Early Christian and Byzantine Objects in American Collection; Photographic copy of the Princeton Index of Christian Art; collection of photographs

L **Studies in Landscape Architecture & Garden Library,** 1703 32nd St NW, 20007. Tel 202-342-3280. *Librn* Linda Lott-Gerlach; *Assoc Librn* Anne Thacher; *Dir Studies* Dr Joachim Wolschke-Bulmahn
For reference
Library Holdings: Vols 14,059; Per subs 42; Drawings of Garden, Seed catalogs; Micro — Fiche, reels; AV — Slides; Other — Exhibition catalogs, manuscripts, memorabilia, original art works, pamphlets, photographs, prints
Special Subjects: Architecture, Landscape Architecture, History of Landscape Architecture, History of Horticulture, History of Botanical Illustration
Collections: †Rare books (3337)
Exhibitions: The French Garden; The Poetic Dimension in Contemporary Garden Design: Ian Hamilton Findlay & Bernard Lassus; The Regional American Gardener's Library; New World Symphony: The Introduction of Exotic Plants into European Culture; From Art to Comic: A Glimpse into Five Centuries of Discussion about Garden Design
Publications: Dumbarton Oaks Reprints & Facsimiles in Landscape Architecture; History of Landscape Architecture (Colloquium Series); other titles in garden history
Activities: Departmental lect; roundtables; symposium

M **HIRSHHORN MUSEUM AND SCULPTURE GARDEN,** Seventh & Independence Ave SW, 20560. Tel 202-357-3091; FAX 202-786-2682. *Dir* James Demetrion; *Deputy Dir* Stephen Weil; *Adminr* Beverly Pierce; *Chief Cur* Neal Benezra; *Chief Education Dept* Edward P Lawson; *Registrar* Douglas Robinson; *Chief Exhib* Edward Scheiser; *Chief Conservator* Lawrence Hoffman; *Chief Photography* Lee Stalsworth; *Public Affairs Officer* Sidney Lawrence
Open Mon - Sun 10 AM - 5:30 PM, cl Christmas Day. No Admis Fee. Estab 1966 under the aegis of the Smithsonian Institution; building designed by Gordon Bunshaft of the architectural firm of Skidmore, Owings & Merrill. Opened in 1974. Average Annual Attendance: 908,000
Income: Financed by federal funds
Collections: †12,900 paintings, sculptures, drawings & prints, the majority donated to the nation by Joseph H Hirshhorn, emphasizing the development of modern art from the latter half of the 19th century to the present; †American art beginning with a strong group of Thomas Eakins and going on to Sargent, Chase, Hartley, Gorky, De Kooning, Rothko, Noland, Rivers and Frank Stella; †European paintings of the last 3 decades represented by Agam, Bacon, Balthus, Leger, Miro and Vasarely; †extensive sculpture collection includes works by Arp, Caro, Daumier, Brancusi, Degas, Giacometti, Manzu, Moore, Nadelman, Rodin and David Smith
Exhibitions: Permanent collection and special loan exhibitions
Publications: Exhibition catalogs; collection catalogs; seasonal events calendar, 3 times per yr
Activities: Docent training; education outreach; lect open to public, 8 - 10 vis lectrs per yr; concerts; gallery talks; tours; films; individual and original objects of art lent to museums; book traveling exhibitions one-four times per yr; sales shop sells books, magazines, reproductions, slides, jewelry and various gift items

L **Library,** Seventh & Independence Ave SW, 20560. Tel 202-357-3222. *Librn* Anna Brooke
Estab 1974. For reference only by appointment
Income: Financed by federal funds
Library Holdings: Vols 40,000; Per subs 50; Auction Cats; Micro — Fiche, reels; AV — A-tapes, cassettes, slides, v-tapes; Other — Clipping files, exhibition catalogs, memorabilia, photographs
Special Subjects: American painting 1850 to the present, international modern sculpture
Collections: Armory Show Memorabilia; Eakins Memorabilia; 5 Samuel Murray Scrapbooks

M **HISTORICAL SOCIETY OF WASHINGTON DC,** Christian Heurich Mansion, 1307 New Hampshire Ave NW, 20036. Tel 202-785-2068; FAX 202-331-1979. *Pres* Kathryn S Smith; *Exec Dir* John V Alviti; *Cur* Candace Shireman; *Cur* Cheryl Miller
Open Wed - Sat noon - 3 PM. Admis adults $3, sr citizens $1.50, members, students, children under 18 free. Estab 1894. Historic house museum; 1894 Richardsonian Romanesque, with ornate interiors & furnishings original to house; painted ceilings, wallstenciling & carved mantels, woodwork, furniture. Average Annual Attendance: 8000. Mem: 1800; annual dues $40-$2000
Income: $385,000 (financed by endowment, mem, grants & earned income)
Exhibitions: Small exhibitions, largely using photographs, manuscripts, maps, memorabilia from Washington history library collections
Publications: Washington History, semi-annual magazine
Activities: Tours; children's classes on request; workshops on preserving local history; teacher training in DC history; outreach program to schools; lect open to public, 12 - 15 vis lectrs per year; museum shop sells books, cards, reproduction maps & prints

L **Research Collections,** 1307 N Hampshire Ave, 20036
Open Wed, Fri, Sat 10 AM - 4 PM. Estab 1894 for collection of materials related to Washington, DC history. For reference only
Library Holdings: Vols 14,000; Micro — Cards, fiche; AV — A-tapes, lantern slides, motion pictures, slides; Other — Clipping files, manuscripts, memorabilia, original art works, pamphlets, photographs, prints, reproductions
Special Subjects: Architecture of Washington, DC
Activities: Individual paintings & original objects of art lent; sales shop sells books, magazines & prints

M **HOWARD UNIVERSITY,** Gallery of Art, College of Fine Arts, 2455 Sixth St NW, 20059. Tel 202-806-7047.
Open Mon - Fri 9 AM - 5 PM, cl Sat & Sun. No admis fee. Estab 1928 to stimulate the study and appreciation of the fine arts in the University and community. Three air-conditioned art galleries are in Childers Hall, James V Herring Heritage Gallery, James A Porter Gallery, and the Student Gallery along with Gumbel Print Room. Average Annual Attendance: 24,000
Collections: †Agnes Delano Collection of contemporary American watercolors and prints; Irving R Gumbel Collection of prints; Kress Study Collection of Renaissance paintings and sculpture; Alain Locke Collection of African art; †University collection of painting, sculpture and graphic arts by Afro-Americans
Exhibitions: Changing monthly exhibits
Publications: Catalogue of the African and Afro-American collections; exhibition catalogues; informational brochures; Native American Arts (serial)
Activities: Bimonthly gallery lect and community programs

L **Architecture & Planning Library,** 2366 Sixth St NW, 20059. Tel 202-806-7773. *Librn* Gertis Fenuku
Library Holdings: Vols 27,000; Per subs 400; Doc 600; Micro — Reels 1,300; AV — Fs, lantern slides, slides 29,000; Other — Photographs
Special Subjects: Architectural History, Construction & Design, City Planning, Environmental Design
Collections: Dominick Collection of pre-1900 books & periodicals on architecture; K Keith Collection of books & photographs on indigenous African architecture

M **INTERNATIONAL SCULPTURE CENTER,** 1050 17th St NW, Suite 250, 20036. Tel 202-785-1144; FAX 202-965-7318. *Exec Dir* David Furchgott; *Deputy Dir* Nina Ozlu
Estab 1960, dedicated to expand the base of understanding & support of contemporary sculpture through its programs & services. The ISC serves the needs & interests of sculptors, educators, arts supporters & the general public

A **THE JOHN F KENNEDY CENTER FOR THE PERFORMING ARTS,** 20566. Tel 202-416-8000; FAX 202-416-8421. *Chmn of the Board of Trustees* James D Wolfensohn
Open Mon - Sun 10 AM - 12 Midnight. No admis fee for building, ticket prices vary. The Center opened in Sept 1971. Facilities include the 2200-seat Opera House, 2750-seat Concert Hall, 1130-seat Eisenhower Theater, 500-seat Terrace Theater, 224-seat film theater & 350-seat Theater Lab operated by the American Film Institute.
Estab in 1958 by Act of Congress as the National Cultural Center. A bureau of the Smithsonian Institution, but administered by a separate independent Board of Trustees; the Center is the sole official memorial in Washington to President Kennedy. Although the Center does not have an official collection, gifts in the form of art objects from foreign countries are on display throughout the Center. Average Annual Attendance: 1,500,000 ticketed, 2,500,000-3,000,000 visitors. Mem: Friends of the Kennedy Center 40,000; dues from $30-$2000
Income: $30,000,000 (financed by ticket revenue and private contributions)
Exhibitions: Changing exhibits on the performing arts are displayed in the

Center's Performing Arts Library, a cooperative effort between Kennedy Center and the Library of Congress. Exhibits frequently include portraits, prints, engravings, sketches, etc, of relevance to the performing arts
Publications: John F Kennedy Center for the Performing Arts; Kennedy Center News, bi-monthly
Activities: Classes for adults and children; dramatic programs; performing arts series for young audiences; lectures open to public, 50 vis lectr per yr; concerts; tours; originate traveling exhibitions to Library of Congress; sales shop sells books, original art, reproductions, slides, souvenirs, needle point and posters

L **Performing Arts Library,** Roof Terrace Level, 20566. Tel 202-416-8780. *Chief of Music* Dr James W Pruett
Open Tues - Fri 11 AM - 8:30 PM, Sat 10 AM - 6 PM, cl Mon & Sun. Estab 1979 to provide a national information and reference facility for all areas of the performing arts, including film and broadcasting. For reference only. Access to all Library of Congress collections
Library Holdings: Vols 7000; Per subs 400; Micro — Fiche, reels; AV — A-tapes, cassettes, rec, slides, v-tapes; Other — Clipping files, exhibition catalogs, framed reproductions, manuscripts, memorabilia, pamphlets, reproductions
Special Subjects: Kennedy Center History, performing arts information

A **LAWYERS COMMITTEE FOR THE ARTS,** Volunteer Lawyers for the Arts, 918 16th St, NW, Suite 400, 20006. Tel 202-429-0229. *Exec Dir* Joshua Kaufman
Open Mon - Fri 9 AM - 5 PM. Estab 1977 to provide pro bono legal referral services. A small library provides access to art law books & forms
Publications: Art of investing in Art
Activities: Lectures to public or groups on request

L **LIBRARY OF CONGRESS,** Prints and Photographs Division, Madison Bldg, Room 339, 101 Independence Ave SE, 20540. Tel 202-707-6394 (reference), 707-5836 (offices); FAX 202-707-6647. *Librn* James H Billington; *Chief* Stephen E Ostrow; *Head Reference Section* Mary M Ison; *Cur Architecture* C Ford Peatross; *Fine Prints* Carol Pulin; *Photographs* Beverly W Brannan; *Photographs* Verna Curtis; *Popular & Applied Graphic Arts* Bernard F Reilly; *Posters* Elena G Millie
Exhib Halls Open Mon - Fri 8:30 AM - 9:30 PM, Sat 8:30 AM - 6 PM, Sun 1 - 5 PM, Reading Room of the Division open Mon - Fri 8:30 AM - 5 PM, cl legal holidays. Estab 1897. For reference only
Income: Financed by congressional appropriation, gifts and endowments
Purchases: Fine prints, master photographs, posters, architectural drawings & historical prints & drawings
Library Holdings: Architectural Items 2,000,000; Posters 80,000; Popular & Applied Graphic Art Items 108,500; Master Photographs 3800; Fine Prints 110,000; Negatives & Transparencies 6,750,000; Other — Photographs 12,000,000
Special Subjects: Americana, universal coverage of visual subjects
Collections: Archive of Hispanic Culture; Japanese Prints; †Pennell Collection of Whistleriana; †Civil War drawings, prints, photographs and negatives; †early American lithographs; †pictorial archives of early American architecture; †Historic American Buildings Survey; Historic American Engineering Record; Cabinet of American Illustration; †original fine prints of all schools & periods; Yanker Collection of Propaganda posters; †originally designed posters for all periods, dating 1840s - present; Seagram County Court House Collection; †Swann Collection of Cartoons & Caricatures; †American Political Cartoons; †outstanding among the collection of photographs & photographic negatives are the Brady-Handy Collection, Farm Security Administration Collection, Alexander Graham Bell Collection, Arnold Genthe, J C H Grabill, F B Johnston, Tony Frissell, Detroit Photographic Co W H Jackson Collection, George Grantham Bain Collection, H E French Washington Photographs, Matson Near Eastern Collection; †Presidential, †geographical, †biographical & †master photograph groupings & captured German photographs of the WW II period
Exhibitions: Permanent collection
Publications: A Century of Photographs, 1846-1946; American Prints in the Library of Congress; American Revolution in Drawings & Prints; COPAR Newsletter (1975-1985) (Cooperative Preservation of Architectural Records), quarterly; Graphic Sampler; Historic America: Buildings, Structures & Sites; Historic American Buildings Survey; Middle East in Pictures; Viewpoints; Special Collections in the Library of Congress; Fine Prints in the Library of Congress; The Poster Collection in the Library of Congress; Popular & Applied Graphic Art in the Library of Congress
Activities: Academic Internship program for advanced undergraduates & graduates who wish to work with & study the collections of the division

M **MARINE CORPS MUSEUM,** Art Collection, Marine Corps Historical Center, Bldg 58 Washington Navy Yard, 20374. Tel 202-433-3840; FAX 202-433-7265. *Dir* E H Simmons; *Deputy Dir* F B Nihart; *Cur Art* J T Dyer
Open Mon - Sat 10 AM - 4 PM, Sun & Holidays noon - 5 PM. No admis fee. Estab 1960. Large 20 ft x 100 ft gallery available for temporary exhibits; maintains 30,000 volume library directly relating to military and Naval history. Average Annual Attendance: 25,000
Income: Financed by US government
Collections: Marine Corps art (original art work by, of and about Marines with the major emphasis of the collection on the Vietnam War & peace time operations); military music; personal papers
Publications: Exhibit publications
Activities: Tours; museum shop sells prints, books, models, miniatures and jewelry

M **MERIDIAN HOUSE INTERNATIONAL,** 1624-30 Crescent Pl NW, 20009. Tel 202-667-6800, FAX 202-667-1475. *Pres, Ambassador* Walter L Cutler; *VPres for Development* Patricia Johnson; *VPres for Mgt* William Muldoon
Open 1 - 4 PM. Estab 1960
Income: Financed by endowment & contributions
Exhibitions: (1990) Artists in National Parks; Color & Form: Contemporary Art from Yugoslavia; New Art from Singapore
Activities: Lect open to public, 2 - 3 per yr

M **NATIONAL ACADEMY OF SCIENCES,** Arts in the Academy, 2101 Constitution Ave, NW, 20418. Tel 202-334-2436; FAX 202-334-1597. *Dir* Fredrica W Wechsler
Open Mon - Fri 9 AM - 5 PM. No admis fee
Exhibitions: (1991) Burko, Cantrell, Ginsberg, Kirschbaum, Lardiere, O'Connell, Okoshi, Rosenthal. (1992) Chemistry Imagined, Torrence/Hoffman; Behnke, Kimes; Information Art Diagramming Microchips; The Astronomical Image
Activities: Concerts; individual paintings & original objects of art lent to other galleries

M **NATIONAL AIR AND SPACE MUSEUM,** Sixth & Independence Ave SW, 20560. Tel 202-357-2700. *Dir* Dr Martin Harwit
Open daily 10 AM - 5:30 PM, cl Dec 25. No admis fee. Estab 1946 to memorialize the national development of aviation and space flight. One gallery comprised of 5000 sq ft devoted to the theme, Flight and the Arts. Average Annual Attendance: 8,000,000
Income: Financed through the Smithsonian Institution
Collections: Paintings, prints and drawings include: Alexander Calder, Lamar Dodd, Richard Estes, Audrey Flack, Francisco Goya, Lowell Nesbitt, Robert Rauschenberg, James Wyeth; major sculptures by Richard Lippold, Alejandro Otero, Charles Perry; Stuart Speiser Collection of Photo Realist Art
Exhibitions: Exhibitions change annually
Publications: Various publications relating to aviation and space science
Activities: Education dept; handicapped services; regional resource program; lectures open to public, 15 - 20 vis lectr per year; concerts; gallery talks; tours; scholarships; individual paintings and original objects of art lent to non-profit educational institutions; book traveling exhibitions; originate traveling exhibitions; museum shop sells books, magazines, reproductions, prints, slides, posters, stamp covers, kites, models and jewelry

L **Library MRC 314,** Seventh & Independence Ave SW, 20560. Tel 202-357-3133. *Branch Librn* David M Spencer
Open 10 AM - 5:15 PM. Estab 1972 to support research in aerospace field; Library is part of the Smithsonian Institution Libraries system. For reference. Average Annual Attendance: 4000
Income: Financed by federal funds
Library Holdings: Vols 40,000; Per subs 300; Micro — Fiche 200,000, reels 2000
Special Subjects: Ballooning (prints), Earth & Aerospace, Astronomy and Planetary Science
Collections: Aerospace Event Files; Aviation and Space Art; Illustrated Sheet Music; Archives of Personalities
Publications: NASM Library Guide; NASM Library Periodical Index
Activities: Educ dept; classes for children; docent training; lectures open to public; tours; awards; scholarships

NATIONAL ARCHITECTURAL ACCREDITING BOARD, INC
For further information, see National and Regional Organizations

NATIONAL ARTISTS EQUITY ASSOCIATION INC
For further information, see National and Regional Organizations

NATIONAL ASSEMBLY OF LOCAL ARTS AGENCIES
For further information, see National and Regional Organizations

NATIONAL ASSEMBLY OF STATE ARTS AGENCIES
For further information, see National and Regional Organizations

NATIONAL ASSOCIATION OF ARTISTS' ORGANIZATIONS (NAAO)
For further information, see National and Regional Organizations

M **NATIONAL CENTER ON ARTS & AGING-NATIONAL COUNCIL ON THE AGING,** NCOA Gallery Patina, 409 Third St SW, 20024. Tel 202-479-1200; FAX 202-479-0735. *Pres* Daniel Thursz; *VPres* Nancy Peavy; *Dir Art Center* Sylvia Riggs Liroff; *Gallery Coordr* Marie Martin
Open Mon - Fri 9 AM - 5 PM. No admis fee. Estab 1981 as a showcase for the works of older professional & emerging artists & display exhibits about aging. Located in entrance to NCOA, Gallery Patina has 720 sq ft of exhibit space plus adjoining conference facilities for lectures & performances. Average Annual Attendance: 4000
Income: Financed by NCOA general revenue plus corporate, institutional & co-sponsors
Exhibitions: Through the Looking Glass: Works by Elizabeth Layton; Photographs by Lucian Aigner; Creative Progressions: Art & Craftwork by Kentucky Senior Artists; Elders of the Tribe: Contemporary Artists Over 70
Activities: Lectures open to public

NATIONAL ENDOWMENT FOR THE ARTS
For further information, see National and Regional Organizations

M **NATIONAL GALLERY OF ART,** Constitution Ave at Fourth St NW, 20565. Tel 202-737-4215; TWX 202-842-6176. *Chmn Bd of Trustees* Dr Franklin D Murphy; *Pres* John R Stevenson; *Dir* Earl A Powell III; *Deputy Dir* Roger Mandle; *Dean, Center for Advanced Study in Visual Arts* Henry A Millon; *Chief Librn* Neal Turtell; *Special Events Officer* Genevra Higginson; *Cur Photo Archives* Ruth Philbrick; *Cur American Art* Nicholai Cikovsky; *Cur Northern Baroque Painting* Arthur Wheelock; *Cur Renaissance Painting* David Brown; *Cur Southern Baroque Painting* Diane DeGrazia; *Sr Cur Print, Drawing & Sculpture* Andrew Robison; *Cur Sculpture* C Douglas Lewis; *Cur Educ* Linda Downs; *Chief of Design & Installation* Gaillard Ravenel; *Chief Photographic Services* Richard Amt; *Head Educ Resources Progs* Ruth Perlin; *Horticulture* Donald Hand; *Editor* Frances Smyth; *Chief Conservation* Ross Merrill; *Gallery Archivist* Maygene Daniels; *Admnr* Anne B Evans; *Secy & Gen Counsel* Philip C Jessup; *Treas* Daniel Herrick; *Registrar* Sally Freitag; *Coordr of Photography* Ira Bartfield; *Asst to Dir of Music* George Manos; *Public Information Officer* Ruth Kaplan; *Corporate Relations Officer* Elizabeth Perry; *Development Officer* Laura Smith-Fisher; *Visitor Services* Sandra Creighton; *Publication Sales Mgr* Keith Webb
Open Mon - Sat 10 AM - 5 PM; Sun 11 AM - 6 PM; cl Christmas & New Years

Day. No admis fee. Administered by a board of trustees which consists of Chmn Dr Franklin D Murphy, US Chief Justice, US Secy of State, Treasury, Smithsonian Institution, John R Stevenson, Robert Smith Alexander M Laughin & Ruth Carter Stevenson. Estab 1941; East Building opened 1978. West Building was a gift from Andrew W Mellon; the East Building was a gift of Paul Mellon, Ailsa Mellon Bruce & Andrew Mellon Foundation. Average Annual Attendance: 6,500,000
Income: Financed by private endowment and federal appropriation
Collections: The Andrew W Mellon Collection of 126 paintings and 26 pieces of sculpture includes Raphael's Alba Madonna, Niccolini-Cowper's Madonna, and St George and the Dragon; van Eyck Annunciation; Botticelli's Adoration of the Magi; nine Rembrandts. Twenty-one of these paintings came from the Hermitage. Also in the original gift were the Vaughan Portrait of George Washington by Gilbert Stuart and The Washington Family by Edward Savage. The Samuel H Kress Collection, given to the nation over a period of years, includes the great tondo The Adoration of the Magi by Fra Angelico and Fra Filippo Lippi, the Laocoon by El Greco, and fine examples by Giorgione, Titian, Grunewald, Durer, Memling, Bosch, Francois Clouet, Poussin, Watteau, Chardin, Boucher, Fragonard, David and Ingres. Also included are a number of masterpieces of Italian and French sculpture. In the Widener Collection are paintings by Rembrandt, van Dyck, and Vermeer, as well as major works of Italian, Spanish, English and French painting and Italian and French sculpture and decorative arts. The Chester Dale Collection includes masterpieces by Braque, Cezanne, Degas, Gauguin, Manet, Matisse, Modigliani, Monet, Picasso, Pissarro, Renoir, Toulouse-Lautrec, van Gogh, and such American painters as George Bellows, Childe Hassam, and Gilbert Stuart. Several major works of art by Cezanne, Gauguin, Picasso and the American painter Walt Kuhn were given to the Gallery in 1972 by the W Averell Harriman Foundation in memory of Marie N Harriman. Paintings to round out the collection have been bought with funds provided by the late Ailsa Mellon Bruce. Most important among them are: portrait of Ginevra de' Benci (the only generally acknowledged painting by Leonardo da Vinci outside Europe), Georges de la Tour's Repentant Magdalen, Picasso's Nude Woman-1910, Rubens' Daniel in the Lions' Den, Claude Lorrain's Judgment of Paris, St George and the Dragon attributed to Rogier van der Weyden, and a number of American paintings, including Thomas Cole's second set of the Voyage of Life. The National Gallery's rapidly expanding graphic arts holdings, in great part given by Lessing J Rosenwald, numbers about 50,000 items and dates from the 12th century to the present. The Index of American Design contains over 17,000 watercolor renderings and 500 photographs of American crafts and folk arts. The National Gallery's Collection continues to be built by private donation, rather than through government funds, which serve solely to operate and maintain the Gallery
Exhibitions: Temporary exhibitions from collections both in the United States and abroad
Publications: A W Mellon Lectures in the Fine Arts; Studies in the History of Art; exhibition catalogs; annual report; monthly calendar of events
Activities: Sunday lect by distinquished quest speakers & members of the staff are given throughout the year; the A W Mellon Lect in the Fine Arts are delivered as a series each spring by an outstanding scholar; concerts are held in the West Garden Court, West Building each Sunday evening between October & June at 7 PM without charge; general tours & lect are given in the Gallery by members of the Education Department throughout the week; special tours are arranged for groups; films on art are presented on a varying schedule; color slide programs, films & video cassettes on gallery exhibitions & collections, free of charge, free catalog; sponsors Metropolitan Opera auditions; programs to 4900 communities; provides art loans to galleries around the world; lending collection contains books, cassettes, color reproductions, film strips, framed reproductions, Kodachromes, sculpture & slides; museum shop sells books, magazines, reproductions, prints, slides & video-cassettes

L **Library,** Constitution Ave at Fourth St NW, 20565. Tel 202-737-4215. *Exec Librn* Neal Turtell; *Reader Services Librn* Lamia Doumato; *Catalogue Librn* Roger Lawson
Open Mon Noon - 4:30 PM, Tues - Fri 10 AM - 4:30 PM. Estab 1941 to support the national curatorial, educational and research activities and serve as a research center for graduate & undergraduate students, visiting scholars and researchers in the visual arts. Supports the research programs of the Center for Advanced Study in the Visual Arts. For reference only
Income: Financed by federal appropriations and trust funds
Library Holdings: Vols 160,000; Per subs 950; Vertical Files 125,000; Micro — Fiche, reels; AV — A-tapes; Other — Exhibition catalogs, manuscripts, pamphlets, photographs
Special Subjects: Western European & American art & architecture, illuminated manuscripts; surrealism, Leonardo da Vinci, auction catalogues
Collections: Art exhibition, art auction and private art collection catalogs; artist monographs; Leonardo da Vinci, catalogues raisonne
Exhibitions: Changing exhibitions; art & history of books, printing & graphic arts
Publications: Guide to the Library, annual
Activities: Library tours on request

L **Photographic Archives,** Constitution Ave at Fourth St NW, 20565. Tel 202-842-6027; FAX 202-789-2681. *Cur* Ruth Philbrick
Open daily 10 AM - 4:30 PM. Reference only
Library Holdings: Micro — Cards, fiche 4,680,000, prints, reels; Other — Photographs 1,350,000
Special Subjects: Black-white photographs & microforms of American & Western European art

L **Slide Library,** Fourth & Constitution Ave NW, 20565. Tel 202-842-6100; FAX 202-408-8530. *Chief Slide Librn* Gregory P J Most
Library Holdings: AV — Slides 155,000
Special Subjects: Graphic Arts, Western European & American painting & sculpture

L **Index of American Design,** Sixth & Constitution Ave NW, 20565. Tel 202-842-6605; FAX 202-842-6859. *Asst Cur* Carlotta Owens; *Asst Cur* Charles Ritchie
Open daily 10 AM - noon & 2 - 4 PM. No admis fee. Acquired by National Gallery in 1943 to serve as a visual archive of American decorative arts, late 17th through 19th centuries. Study room with National Gallery print galleries available for exhibitions; offices; storeroom
Library Holdings: Water colors 17,000; Micro — Fiche; Other — Photographs
Special Subjects: Architecture, Ceramics, Costume Design & Construction, Decorative Arts, Folk Art, Furniture, Glass, Jewelry, Religious Art, Silver, Textiles, Woodcarvings
Activities: Original objects of art lent to institutions complying with National Gallery lending rules; lending collection contains 11 slide programs available through National Gallery dept of exten programs

NATIONAL INSTITUTE FOR THE CONSERVATION OF CULTURAL PROPERTY
For further information, see National and Regional Organizations

NATIONAL LEAGUE OF AMERICAN PEN WOMEN
For further information, see National and Regional Organizations

M **NATIONAL MUSEUM OF AFRICAN ART,** 950 Independence Ave SW, 20560. Tel 202-357-4600; FAX 202-357-4879. *Dir* Sylvia H Williams; *Assoc Dir* Roy Sieber; *Chief Cur* Philip Ravenhill; *Senior Scholar & Founding Dir Emeritus* Warren M Robbins; *Cur* Lydia Puccinelli; *Cur* Roslyn Walker; *Cur Education* Edward Lifschitz; *Public Affairs Dir* Janice Kaplan; *Exhibition Production Chief* Basil Arendse
Open Mon - Sun 10 AM - 5:30 PM, cl Christmas Day. No admis fee. Estab 1964 to foster public understanding & appreciation of the diverse cultures & artistic achievements in Africa; museum joined the Smithsonian Institution in 1979. Closed until Sept 1987 when the Museum was re-opened to the public as part of the Smithsonian's new museum complex, the Quadrangle. Average Annual Attendance: 500,000
Income: $2,500,000 (financed by federal funding, membership and contributions)
Collections: African art works in wood, metal, ceramic, ivory & fiber (6000 objects); Eliot Elisofon Photographic Archives of 200,000 slides & 78,000 black & white photographs & 140,000 ft of motion picture film & videotape
Publications: Exhibition Catalogs; multimedia slide kit; pamphlets; booklets
Activities: Classes for adults & children; docent training; lect open to public; concerts; gallery talks; films; tours; residency fellowship program; museum sales shop sells books, magazines, reproductions, prints, slides, quality crafts, original art, jewelry and other imports from Africa

L **The Warren M Robbins Library,** 950 Independence Ave SW, 20560. Tel 202-357-4875; FAX 202-357-4879. *Librn* Janet L Stanley
Open Mon - Fri 9 AM - 5 PM. Estab 1971 to provide major resource center for African art and culture; Library is part of the Smithsonian Institution Libraries system. For reference only
Income: Financed through Smithsonian budget
Library Holdings: Vols 25,000; Per subs 200; Other — Clipping files, exhibition catalogs, pamphlets
Special Subjects: Afro-American Art, African Art: African artistic retentions in the New World
Publications: Libr Acquisitions List, monthly

M **NATIONAL MUSEUM OF AMERICAN ART,** Eighth & G Sts NW, 20560. Tel 202-357-2700; FAX 202-786-2607. *Dir* Elizabeth Broun; *Deputy Dir* Charles Robertson; *Chief Cur* Virginia Mecklenburg; *Cur Painting & Sculpture* Richard Murray; *Cur Painting & Sculpture* William H Truettner; *Cur Painting & Sculpture* Harry Rand; *Cur Photography* Merry Foresta; *Cur Graphic Arts* Joann G Moser; *Cur Research* Lois M Fink; *Chief External Affairs* W Robert Johnston; *Registrar* Melissa Kroning; *Chief of Design & Production* Val Lewton; *Sr Conservator* Stefano Scafetta; *Actg Chief Research & Scholars Center* Rachel Allen; *Ed-in-Chief* Steve Dietz; *Intern Origrams Officer* Patricia H Chieffo; *Admin Officer* Maureen Damaska
Open daily 10 AM - 5:30 PM; cl Christmas. Estab 1829, and later absorbed by the Smithsonian Institution, it was designated the National Gallery of Art in 1906. The museum's name was changed to the National Collection of Fine Arts in 1937 and, in 1980, to the National Museum of American Art. The museum now focuses upon the acquisition, study and presentation of American art from its beginning to the present. Barney Studio House, administered by the museum, is a unique showplace built by artist Alice Pike Barney as her home, studio and salon; it is open for guided tours by reservation only and for special programs. Average Annual Attendance: 500,000
Income: $5,000,000 annually (financed by federal appropriation, gifts, grants & trust income)
Collections: The collection of paintings, sculpture, photographs, folk art, prints, drawings & crafts number over 34,000, and include outstanding masterworks aswell as important holdings by lesser-known artists. The works represent a wide range of American work, particularly late 19th and early 20th century. Major collections include those of Harriet Lane Johnston (1906), William T Evans (1907), John Gellatly (1929), the S C Johnson & Son Collection (1967), Container Corporation of America Collection (1984) , Sara Roby Foundation Collection (1984), Herbert Waide Hemphill Jr Collection (1986), and Patricia and Phillip Frost Collection . There is a sizeable collection of portrait miniatures. All works not on display are available for examination by scholars. Research resources include: Inventory of American Paintings Executed Before 1914, a computerized index; Smithsonian Art Index; Pre-1877 Art Exhibition Catalogue Index; Peter A Juley & Son Collection of 127,000 historic photographic negatives; Inventory of American Sculpture
Exhibitions: A representative selection of works from the collection are on permanent display in the galleries, providing a comprehensive view of the varied aspects of American art. Most temporary exhibitions, some ten a year, are originated by the staff, many as part of the program to investigate less well-known aspects of American art. They include both studies of individual artists and thematic studies.
Publications: Major exhibitions are accompanied by authoritative publications; smaller exhibitions usually are accompanied by checklists
Activities: The Office of Education Programs carries on an active program with the schools and the general public, offering imaginative participatory tours for children, as well as lectures and symposia for adults. A research program in American art is maintained for visiting scholars and training is carried on through internship in general museum practice and conservation; the museum also circulates exhibitions throughout the United States on a regular basis

L Library of the National Museum of American Art and the National Portrait Gallery, Eighth & G Sts NW, 20560. Tel 202-357-1886; FAX 202-786-2565. *Chief Librn* Cecilia Chin; *Asst Librn* Patricia Lynagh; *Cataloger* L Kimball Clark
Open Mon - Fri 10 AM - 5 PM. Estab 1964 to serve the reference and research needs of the staff and affiliated researchers of the National Collection of Fine Arts, the National Portrait Gallery, the Archives of American Art, and other Smithsonian bureaus. Open to graduate students and other qualified adult researchers. Circ 7940
Income: $160,000 (financed by federal appropriation)
Purchases: $30,000
Library Holdings: Vols 65,000; Per subs 800; Original documents; Micro — Fiche, reels; Other — Clipping files, exhibition catalogs, manuscripts, pamphlets, reproductions
Special Subjects: American art, especially printing, drawing, sculpture and graphic arts, contemporary art, American history and biography
Collections: Ferdinand Perret Art Reference Library: collection of scrapbooks of clippings and pamphlets; special section on California art and artists consisting of approx 325 ring binders on art and artists of Southern California; vertical file of 400 file drawers of material on art and artists, with increasing emphasis on American art and artists
Activities: Library tours by appointment only

M Renwick Gallery, 17th St & Pennsylvania Ave NW, 20560. Tel 202-357-2531; FAX 202-786-2810. *Cur-in-charge* Michael Monroe
Open daily 10 AM - 5:30 PM; cl Christmas. Designed in 1859 by architect James Renwick, Jr, as the Corcoran Gallery of Art, the building was renamed for the architect in 1965 when it was transferred by the Federal government to the Smithsonian Institution for restoration. Restored to its French Second Empire elegance after 67 years as the United States Court of Claims, the building has two public rooms with period furnishings, the Grand Salon and the Octagon Room, as well as eight areas for its permanent collection and temporary exhibitions of American crafts
Collections: American crafts
Exhibitions: (1988-89) New American Furniture; Glassworks; Structure & Surface: Beads in Contemporary American Art; Masterworks of Louis Comfort Tiffany
Publications: Major exhibitions are accompanied by publications, smaller exhibitions by checklists
Activities: Docent training; film programs; lectures emphasizing the creative work of American craftsmen; tours; concerts

M NATIONAL MUSEUM OF AMERICAN HISTORY, 14th St & Constitution Ave, 20560. Tel 202-357-2700; FAX 202-357-4256. *Dir* Roger G Kennedy; *Deputy Dir* Spencer Crew
Open daily 10 AM - 5:30 PM, Apr 1 - Labor Day 10 AM - 9 PM, cl Christmas Day. No admis fee. Estab 1964. The Museum, a bureau of the Smithsonian Institution, is devoted to the collection, care, study & exhibition of objects that reflect the experience of the American people. Average Annual Attendance: 6 million
Collections: Agriculture, armed forces, automobiles, †ceramics, †glass, locomotives, musical instruments, †numismatics, †philately, political history, †textiles
Exhibitions: American Encounters, American Pressed Pattern Glass; First Ladies: Political Role & Public Image; Yeoman F; The Tool Chest; From Parlor to Politics: Women & Reform in America; We the People: Winning the Vote; A More Perfect Union: Japanese Americans & the United States Constitution; Field to Factory: Afro-American Migration 1915 - 1940; What are Archives: Who Uses Archives; After the Revolution: Everyday Life in America; Information Age: People, Information & Technology; The Ceremonial Court; A Material World; Engines of Change: The American Industrial Revolution 1790 - 1860; Infantry Machine Guns in the United States Service 1861 - present. (1992-93) Kiowa Culture in Transition 1925 - 1955: The Photographs of Horace Poolaw; Navajo: Portrait of a Nation; Put the City Up: Chicago Architecture; Trees of Christmas 1992. (1993) Hidden Americans; The American Revival in Pipe Organ Building; G I: The American Soldier Experience in World War ii; Manufactured Weather; Edison After Forty; Seeing is Believing: Photos of the Civil Rights Movement; The Past as Memory & Model; Beyond Catergory: The Musical Genius of Duke Ellington; Land of Promise / Land of Paradox
Publications: Exhibition brochures & catalogs; related research publications
Activities: Classes for adults & children; docent training; internship & fellowship programs; lectures open to public; concerts; museum shop sells books, magazines, reproductions, prints and slides

A Society For Commercial Archeology, Room 5010, 20560 FAX 202-882-5424; Estab 1976 to promote public awareness, exchange information & encourage selective conservation of the commercial landscape. Mem: 800; dues $15; annual meetings
Income: Financed by mem & dues
Publications: News Journal, three times a year

L Branch Library, 14th St & Constitution Ave, 20560. Tel 202-357-2036, 357-2414; FAX 202-357-4256. *Librn* Rhoda Ratner
Open Mon - Fri 8:45 AM - 5:15 PM. Library is part of the Smithsonian Institution Libraries system. Open to staff and visiting scholars
Income: Financed through SIL budgets
Library Holdings: Vols 165,000; Per subs 450; Micro — Fiche, reels
Special Subjects: Carpets & Rugs, Decorative Arts, Furniture, Graphic Design, Historical Material, Metalwork, Photography, Pottery, Silver, Textiles, American History, World's Fairs Reference

M NATIONAL MUSEUM OF WOMEN IN THE ARTS, 1250 New York Ave NW, 20005. Tel 202-783-5000; FAX 202-393-3235. *Admin Dir* Rebecca Phillips-Abbott
Open Mon - Sat 10 AM - 5 PM, Sun noon - 5 PM, cl Thanksgiving, Christmas & New Year's Day, group tours by appointment. Admis suggested donation adults $3, srs, students & children $2. Estab 1981 to promote knowledge & appreciation of women artists through exhibits, publication, special events & library services
Income: Private non-profit
Exhibitions: Selections from the permanent collection; (1992) A Personal Statement: Arkansas Women Artists; Stitches in Air: Belgian Lace &

Contemporary Interpretations; Women Photographers in Camera Work; Calligraphic Artists' Books; Kathe Kollwitz: A Self-Portrait; Forefront: Pat Oleszko; The Book as Art V; Breaking the Rules: Audrey Flack, a Retrospective, 1950 - 1990. (1993) Carrie Mae Weems; Out of Land: Utah Women Artists; Association of Women Artists in Berlin
Publications: Exhibit catalogs

L Library & Research Center, 1250 New York Ave NW, 20005. Tel 202-783-5000; FAX 202-393-3235. *Head Librn* Krystyn A Wasserman; *Library Asst* Wendy Bellion
Open Mon - Fri 10 AM - 5 PM, by appointment only. Admis suggested donation adults $3, srs & students $2. Estab 1982, to highlight the artistic achievement of women past, present & future. Gallery has over 1500 works by more than 500 artists from Renaissance to the present, in a variety of media. Average Annual Attendance: 95,000. Mem: 60,000; dues $20 & up
Library Holdings: Vols 6500; Per subs 50; AV — A-tapes 32, cassettes, slides, v-tapes; Other — Clipping files, exhibition catalogs, manuscripts, memorabilia, original art works, pamphlets, photographs, prints, reproductions, sculpture
Special Subjects: For reference only
Collections: Irene Rice Pereira Library; Collection of Artists' Books; Collection of Bookplates; Archives of the International Festival of Women Artists in Copenhagen, Denmark, 1980
Activities: Lects; concerts; gallery talks; tours; original objects of art & individual paintings lent to museums; book traveling exhibitions 2 - 3 per year; originate traveling exhibition to museums; museum shop sells books, magazines, reproductions, prints, slides

M NATIONAL PORTRAIT GALLERY, F St at Eighth NW, 20560. Tel 202-357-2700. *Dir* Alan Fern; *Deputy Dir* Carolyn Carrl; *Assoc Dir for Admin* Barbara A Hart; *Cur Paintings & Sculpture* Robert G Stewart; *Chief Design & Production* Nello Marconi; *Cur Exhib* Beverly Cox; *Cur Education* Harry Jackson; *Cur Photographs* Mary Panzer; *Cur Prints* Wendy W Reaves; *Registrar* Suzanne Jenkins; *Keeper Catalog of American Portraits* Linda Thrift; *Ed Charles Wilson Peale Papers* Lillian B Miller; *Conservator* Cindylou Ochershausen; *Chief Photographer* Roland White; *Public Affairs Officer* Brennan Rash; *Publications Officer* Frances Stevenson
Open daily 10 AM - 5:30 PM; cl Dec 25. No admis fee. The National Portrait Gallery was estab by Act of Congress in 1962 as a museum of the Smithsonian Institution for the exhibition and study of portraiture depicting men and women who have made significant contributions to the history, development, and culture of the people of the United States. One of the oldest government structures in Washington, the former US Patent Office Building constructed between 1836 & 1867, on the very site which Pierre L'Enfant, in his original plan for the city, had designated for a pantheon to honor the nation's immortals. The first floor is devoted to major loan exhibitions & photographs, prints & drawings from the permanent collection. Special galleries housing a collection of portrait engravings by CBJF de Saint-Memin, silhouettes by Auguste Edouart, portrait sculptures by Jo Davidson & selections from the Time Cover Collection. Second floor features the permanent collection of portraits of eminent Americans & the Hall of Presidents, containing portraits & associative items of our Chief Executives. The two-story Victorian Renaissance Revival Great Hall on the third floor is used for special events & exhibitions. The third floor mezzanine houses a permanent collection civil war gallery with portaits, engravings & photographs. Average Annual Attendance: 414,000
Income: $3,000 (financed by federal appropriation & private contributions)
Collections: The collections, which are constantly being expanded, include portraits of significant Americans, preferably executed from life, in all traditional media: oils, watercolors, charcoal, pen and ink, daguerreotypes, photographs; portraits of American Presidents from George Washington to Ronald Reagan. 900 original works of art from the Time Magazine Cover collection; more than 5000 glass plate negatives by Mathew Brady & studio in the Meserve Collection
Exhibitions: (1992) Poster Portraits; Arnold Newman's Americans; Recent Acquisitions; Noble Heritage; Five Centuries of Portraits from the Hosokawa Family; The Spirit of Party: Hamilton & Jefferson at Odds; In Pursuit of Fame: Rembrandt Peale 1778 - 1860. (1993) Recent Acquisitions; The Telling Image: Photographs from the Archives of American Art; The Family 1976: Richard Avedons Portraits for Rolling Stone; Revisiting the White City: American Art at the 1893 World's Fair; To the President: Presidential Portraits by the People; Contemporary Self-Portraits from the James Goode Collection; James Vanderzee: Portraits
Publications: Large-scale, richly illustrated publications accompany major shows and provide comprehensive analysis of exhibition themes; descriptive brochures about the gallery; documentary, audio, and visual materials designed to be used as teaching guides; illustrated checklist; American portraiture; biographies
Activities: Outreach programs for elementary and secondary schools, senior citizens groups, hospitals, and nursing homes; docent training; teacher workshops; scheduled walk-in tours for special groups, adults, families & schools; programs for handicapped & other special audiences; Cultures In Motion (special musical & dramatic events); museum shop sells books, magazines, reproductions, prints, and slides

L Library, Eighth & G Sts NW, 20560. Tel 202-357-1886; FAX 202-786-2565, 633-9351. *Chief Librn* Cecelia H Chin; *Asst Librn* Pat Lynagh; *Cataloger* Kinball Clark
Shared with the National Museum of American Art; see library entry under National Museum of American Art
Library Holdings: Vols 80,000; Per subs 900; Micro — Fiche, reels; Other — Clipping files, exhibition catalogs, manuscripts, reproductions

M NATIONAL TRUST FOR HISTORIC PRESERVATION, 1785 Massachusetts Ave NW, 20036. Tel 202-673-4000; FAX 202-673-4038. *Pres* Richard Moe
Open to the public, hours and fees vary with the property, cl Christmas, New Years. Founded 1949, the National Trust for Historic Preservation is the only national, non-profit, private organization chartered by Congress to encourage public participation in the preservation of sites, buildings and objects significant in American history and culture. Its services, counsel and education on preservation, and historic property interpretation and administration, are carried out at national and regional headquarters in consultation with advisors in each state and U.S. Territory. Mem: 175,000; dues sustaining $100, active $15, student

$10
Income: Financed by membership dues, contributions and matching grants from the U.S. Department of the Interior, National Park Service, under provision of the National Historic Preservation Act of 1966
Collections: Fine and decorative arts furnishing nine historic house museums: Chesterwood, Stockbridge, MA; Cliveden, Philadelphia, PA; Decatur House and Woodrow Wilson House, Washington, DC; Drayton Hall, Charleston, SC; Lyndhurst, Tarrytown, NY; Oatlands, Leesburg, VA; The Shadows-on-the-Teche, New Iberia, LA; Woodlawn/Pope-Leighey Plantation House, Mt Vernon, VA. (For additional information, see separate listings)
Publications: Historic Preservation, bi-monthly; Preservation News, monthly newspaper

M **Decatur House,** 748 Jackson Pl NW, 20006. Tel 202-842-0920; FAX 202-842-0030. *Dir* Vicki Sopher; *Asst Dir* Sarah Saville Shaffer
Open Tues - Fri 10 AM - 3 PM, Sat & Sun noon - 4 PM, cl Mon. Admis adults $3, students & sr citizens $1.50, National Trust Members free. Estab 1958, bequeathed to National Trust for Historic Preservation by Mrs Truxton Beale to foster appreciation & interest in the history & culture of the city of Washington, DC. The House is a Federal period townhouse designed by Benjamin Henry Latrobe & completed in 1819. Average Annual Attendance: 19,000. Mem: National Trust members
Income: Financed by endowment & membership
Collections: Furniture & memorabilia of the Federal period; Victorian house furnishings
Exhibitions: Special exhibits
Activities: Lectures open to the public, 2-3 vis lectr per yr; concerts; individual paintings & original objects of art lent; sales shop sells books, magazines, reproductions, prints & Christmas decorations

M **NAVAL HISTORICAL CENTER,** The Navy Museum, Washington Navy Yard, Ninth & M Sts SE, 20374-0571. Tel 202-433-4882; FAX 202-433-8200. *Dir* Dr Oscar P Fitzgerald; *Assoc Dir* Claudia L Pennington; *Cur* Dr Edward Furgol; *Public Prog* Susan Silverstein
Open Sept - May Mon - Fri 9 AM - 4 PM, June - Aug daily 9 AM - 5 PM. Parking and admis free. Estab 1961 to present history & preserve heritage of US Navy. 48,000 sq ft exhibit area. Average Annual Attendance: 300,000
Income: Financed by federal appropriations
Collections: History of US Navy from 1775 to Space Age; Naval Art; Paintings; Prints; Watercolors; Naval Artifacts; Fighting Top of Constitution; WW II Corsair (744 plane)
Exhibitions: Changing art exhibitions; Polar Exploration; 75 Years of Naval Aviation; Submarine Museum Annex; WW II
Activities: Docent training; tours; internships; individual paintings & original objects of art lent to public institutions; museum shop sells books, reproductions, prints, postcards, jewelry, t-shirts, models & nautical accessories

M **THE PHILLIPS COLLECTION,** 1600 21st St NW, 20009. Tel 202-387-2151, 387-0961; FAX 202-387-2436. *Dir* Charles S Moffett; *Asst to Dir* Barbara Grupe; *Chief Cur* Eliza Rathbone; *Assoc Cur* Elizabeth Hutton Turner; *Asst Cur* Elizabeth Chew; *Consulting Cur* Willem de Looper; *Dir of Music* Charles Crowder; *Registrar* Joseph Holbach; *Librn* Karen Schneider; *Dir of Public Affairs* Laura Lester; *Dir of Development* Penelope de Bordenave Saffer; *Dir of Corporate & Foundation Relations* Cathy Card Sterling; *Adminr* Jose Tain-Alfonso; *Dir of Personnel* Elizabeth Hubbard; *Visual Resources Coordr* Ignacio Moreno; *Education Dir* Donna McKee; *Facilities & Security Mgr* Tom Gilleylen
Open Mon - Sat 10 AM - 5 PM, Sun noon - 7 PM, cl Christmas, Thanksgiving, July 4 & New Years. Weekday admis is suggested contribution, weekend admis adults $5, sr citizens & students $2.50. Opened to the public 1921 to show and interpret the best of contemporary painting in the context of outstanding works of the past; to underscore this intent through the presentation of concerts and lectures. The original building, a Georgian Revival residence designed in 1897 by Hornblower & Marshall, was added to in 1907 & renovated in 1983-84. A modern annex connected by a double bridge to the old gallery was opened to the public in 1960 and renovated in 1987-89. Average Annual Attendance: 150,000. Mem: 3000; individual dues range from $45 - $5000 & up, corporate memberships at 2500, $5000 & $10,000
Income: $4,000,000 (financed by endowment, mem, contributions, grants, sales, rental fees & exhibition fees)
Collections: 19th & 20th century American & European painting with special emphasis on units of particular artists such as Bonnard, Braque, Cezanne, Daumier, de Stael, Dufy, Rouault, & Americans such as Avery, Dove, Gatch, Knaths, Marin, O'Keeffe, Prendergast, Rothko & Tack. The best known painting is Renoir's Luncheon of the Boating Party
Exhibitions: (1993) Two Lives: Georgia O'Keeffe & Alfred Stieglitz - A Conversation in Paintings & Photographs; Augustus Vincent Tack. (1994) Jacob Lawrence's The Migration of the Negro - 1941; A Dialogue with Nature: Nine Contemporary Sculptors, Parts I, II & III Indian Art Today: Four Artists from the Chester & Davida Herwitz Family Collection; Ralston Crawford; Duncan Phillips: 100th Anniversary Celebration; Elmer Bischoff: 1947-1985; Gauguin & His Circle in Brittany: The Prints of the Pont Aven School
Publications: The Phillips Collection: A Summary Catalogue; News & Events, bi-monthly; childrens guides; exhibition catalogs & brochures; membership brochures & communications
Activities: Classes for adults & children; lectures open to public & to mem only, 10-15 vis lectr per year; weekly concerts; gallery talks; tours; individual paintings & original objects of art lent to national & international museums; book traveling exhibitions, 3 per year; originate traveling exhibitions to national and international museums; museum sales shop sells books, magazines, reproductions, prints, slides, jewelry & original crafts

L **Library,** 1600 21st St NW, 20009. Tel 202-387-2151; FAX 202-387-2436. *Librn* Karen Schneider
Available to serious students, researchers & museum professionals, by appointment; reference only
Library Holdings: Vols 5000; Per subs 30; Vertical Files; Micro — Reels 60; Other — Exhibition catalogs, pamphlets
Special Subjects: Aesthetics, Art History, Drawings, Graphic Arts, Painting - American, Painting - British, Painting - European, Painting - French, Photography, Sculpture, Monographs on Phillips Collection artists, 19th & 20th century European & American art, books by Duncan Phillips

M **MARJORIE MERRIWEATHER POST FOUNDATION OF DC,** Hillwood Museum, 4155 Linnean Ave NW, 20008. Tel 202-686-8500, 686-5807. *Pres* Ellen MacNeile Charles; *Cur* Anne Odom; *Dir* Fred J Fisher
Open Tues - Sat 9 - 10:30 AM & noon - 1:30 & 3 PM for tours. Admis adults $10, students $5, children under 12 not admitted. Estab 1976 to enable the general public to see extensive collection of Russian and French decorative art. Mansion in the Georgian style, home of the late Marjorie Merriweather Post, situated on 25 acres of landscaped grounds. Average Annual Attendance: 22,000
Income: Financed by endowment & admis
Collections: Russian decorative arts; French decorative arts, furnishings & memorabilia
Publications: Notes on Hillwood, Russian Art at Hillwood
Activities: Lectures open to public, 2-3 vis lectr per year; special tours; tours; museum shop sells books, original art, reproductions, prints & slides

PUBLIC LIBRARY OF THE DISTRICT OF COLUMBIA

L **Art Division,** Martin Luther King Memorial Library, 901 G St NW, 20001. Tel 202-727-1291; FAX 202-727-1129. *Dir Library* Dr Hardy R Franklin; *Chief Art Div* Bonnie C Kryszak
Open winter Mon - Thurs 9 AM - 9 PM, Fri & Sat 9 AM - 5:30 PM; summer Mon & Thurs 9 AM - 9 PM, Tues, Wed, Fri, Sat 9 AM - 5:30 PM. No admis fee
Income: Financed by city government appropriation
Library Holdings: Vols 1,870,005; Per subs 95; Micro — Reels; Other — Clipping files, exhibition catalogs, pamphlets
Collections: †Reference and circulating books and periodicals on architecture, painting, sculpture, photography, graphic and applied arts; †extensive pamphlet file including all art subjects, with special emphasis on individual American artists and on more than 800 artists active in the area; †circulating picture collection numbering over 65,000 mounted reproductions
Exhibitions: Special exhibitions held occasionally

L **Audiovisual Division,** Martin Luther King Memorial Library, 901 G St NW, Room 226, 20001. Tel 202-727-1265. *Chief* Eric White
Open Mon - Thurs 9 AM - 9 PM, Fri 9 AM - 5:30 PM
Purchases: 16 mm, VHS
Library Holdings: Books-on-tape; AV — Cassettes, motion pictures, rec, v-tapes

M **SMITHSONIAN INSTITUTION,** 1000 Jefferson Dr, 20560. Tel 202-357-2700. *Secy* Robert Adams; *Under Secy* Constance Berry Newman; *Asst Secy for Arts & Humanities* Tom Freudenheim; *Asst Secy for the Sciences* Dr Robert Hoffmann; *Asst Secy for Educ & Public Progs* James Early; *Asst Secy for External Affairs* Tom Lovejoy; *Asst Secy for Institutional Initiatives* Alice Burnette
Open daily 10 AM - 5:30 PM, cl December 25. Estab 1846, when James Smithson bequeathed his fortune to the United States, under the name of the Smithsonian Institution, an establishment in Washington for the increase & diffusion of knowledge. To carry out the terms of Smithson's will, the Institution performs fundamental research; preserves for study & reference about 137 million items of scientific cultural & historical interest; maintains exhibits representative of the arts, American history, aeronautics & space exploration; technology; natural history; & engages in programs of education & national & international cooperative research & training. See separate listings for complete information on the bureaus listed below. Average Annual Attendance: 30,000,000
Activities: Classes for adults & children; dramatic programs; docent training; lectures open to the public; concerts; gallery talks; tours; awards; scholarships & fels; museum shop sells books, magazines, original art, reproductions, prints, slides, & gifts
—**Archives of American Art,** AA-PG Bldg Smithsonian Institute, 20560
—**Cooper-Hewitt Museum,** 2 E 91st St, New York, NY 10128
—**Hirshhorn Museum and Sculpture Garden,** Seventh & Independence Aves, SW, 20560
—**John F Kennedy Center for the Performing Arts,** 20566
Administered under a separate Board of Trustees
—**National Air and Space Museum,** Seventh & Independence Ave, SW, 20560
—**National Museum of American Art,** Eighth & G Sts, NW, 20560
Includes the Renwick Gallery
—**National Gallery of Art,** Constitution Ave at Fourth St, NW, 20565
Open Mon - Sat 10 AM -5 PM, Sun 11 AM- 6 PM, cl Dec 25 & Jan 1. No admis fee. Estab 1937, the National Gallery of Art & its collection belong to the people of the United States. Administered under a separate Board of Trustees
Special Subjects: Italian Renaissance & Baroque Impressionism
Exhibitions: European & American paintings, sculpture, decorative arts & works on paper on permanent display. Exhibitions from different countries & cultures throughout the world are presented on a regular basis
Activities: Classes for adults & children; dramatic programs; docent training; lect open to public; concerts; gallery talks; tours; individual paintings & original objects of art lent to other museums; museum shop sells books, magazines, reproductions & slides
—**National Museum of American History,** 14th St & Constitution Ave, 20560
—**National Portrait Gallery,** F St at Eighth, NW, 20560. Tel 202-357-2700.
—**Arthur M Sackler Gallery,** 1050 Independence Ave SW, 20560
—**Freer Gallery of Art,** Jefferson Dr at 12th St SW, 20560
—**National Museum of African Art,** 950 Independence Ave, SW, 20560
—**National Museum of the American Indian,** 3753 Broadway at 155th ST, New York, NY 10032. Tel 212-283-2420; FAX 212-491-9302. *Dir* Richard West Jr; *Asst Dir* Duane H King; *Librn* Mary Davis
Open Tues - Sat 10 AM - 5 PM, Sun 1 - 5 PM. Admis adults $3, children & seniors $2, free to museum members & children under 7. Estab 1916 for the preservation, study & exhibitions of Native American artifacts of North, Central & South America. The museum will move in 1994 to the Alexander Hamilton Custom House. Average Annual Attendance: 46,000. Mem: 40,000; dues charter members $20, other $35 - $100
Special Subjects: Native Americans Culture
Collections: The collection includes materials not only of cultural, historic, aesthetic & scientific significance, but also objects of profound spiritual & religious significance. It is the largest collection in the world
Exhibitions: (1992-93) Pathways of Tradition at the Alexander Hamilton Custom House lower Manhatten. (1994) Inaugural Exhibition at the Custom House with

name changing to the George Custer Hege Center of the National Museum of the American Art
Activities: Educ dept has demonstrations of music & craft by Native Americans; dramatic programs; tours; outreach program; original objects of art lent to other museums in country; originate traveling exhibitions to museums around the country; museum shop sells books, reproductions, prints & slides
—**Anacostia Museum,** 1901 Fort Pl, SE, 20020

M **SOCIETY OF THE CINCINNATI,** Anderson House Museum, 2118 Massachusetts Ave NW, 20008. Tel 202-785-2040; FAX 202-785-0729. *Dir* Katheleen Betts
Open Tues - Sat 1 - 4 PM, special hours on request by groups for guided tours, cl National holidays. No admis fee. The Society of the Cincinnati was founded in May 1783; the museum was opened to the public in 1938. Anderson House serves as the national headquarters museum of The Society of the Cincinnati. The House is a national museum for the custody & preservation of historical documents, relics & archives, especially those pertaining to the American Revolution.. Because of its superb building (1905, Little & Browne, Boston architects), original furnishings & collections of European & Oriental art, Anderson House is also a Historic House Museum. On the first floor of the house are portraits of founding members of the Society by Gilbert Stuart, George Catlin, Ezra Ames, Ralph Earl & other early American painters. Average Annual Attendance: 10,000. Mem: 3300
Income: Privately funded
Collections: Figurines of the French regiments that fought at Yorktown, Virginia in 1781 and others; †historical material; Japanese screens, bronzes, ceramics, jade; Asian works of art; 17th & 18th Century Flemish tapestries, sculpture & period furniture; paintings
Exhibitions: Rotating exhibitions; the permanent collection
Publications: Annual Report of the Museum Director; A Few Questions & Answers Regarding the Society of the Cincinnati, brochures
Activities: Lectures open to the public; concerts; tours; scholarships offered; individual paintings and original objects of art lent
L **Anderson House Library,** 2118 Massachusetts Ave NW, 20008. *Dir* Sandra L Powers
Open Mon - Fri 10 Am - 4 PM, by appointment. Serves as the national headquarters library of the Society of the Cincinnati
Library Holdings: Vols 30,000; Per subs 100; Micro — Fiche, reels 300; Other — Clipping files, manuscripts, memorabilia, pamphlets, photographs, prints
Special Subjects: American Revolution; Art of War, 18th century
Publications: Annual Report of the Library Director

SPECIAL LIBRARIES ASSOCIATION
For further information, see National and Regional Organizations

M **STUDIO GALLERY,** 2108 R St NW, 20008. Tel 202-232-8734. *Dir* June Linowitz; *Co-Chmn* Pamela Wedd Brown; *Co-Chmn* Martha Tabor
Open Wed - Sat 11 AM - 5 PM, Sun 1 - 5 PM. No admis fee. Estab 1964 as a showcase for local artists. Average Annual Attendance: 10,000-20,000. Mem: 30; dues $920; monthly meetings
Income: Non-profit
Exhibitions: 4-week exhibitions of gallery artists & special out-reach exhibitions
Activities: Lect open to public; gallery talks; individual paintings & original works of art lent to Embassies

M **SUPREME COURT OF THE UNITED STATES,** 1 First St, NE, US Supreme Court Bldg, 20543. Tel 202-479-3298; FAX 202-479-2971. *Cur* Gail Galloway; *Coll & Exhibits Coordr* Catherine Fitts; *Visitor Prog Coordr* Priscilla Goodwin; *Photograph Coll Coordr* Lois Long
Open Mon - Fri 9 AM - 4:30 PM, cl federal holidays. No admis fee. Curator's office estab 1973. Two exhibit spaces on ground floor; portrait collection displayed on ground floor & in restricted areas of the building. Average Annual Attendance: 798,233
Collections: Portraits of all former Justices throughout history; marble busts of the Chief Justices and certain Associate Justices; historic images such as photos, etchings and drawings of the Justices and the architecture of the building; memorabilia, archival & manuscript materials on the Supreme Court history; 18th & 19th century American & English furniture & decorative arts
Exhibitions: Permanent and temporary exhibits
Publications: Exhibit brochures
Activities: Lectures in the courtroom every hour on the half hour; continuously running film describing the functions of the Supreme Court; tours; individual paintings & original objects of art lent to museums & historical organizations; sales shop operated by Supreme Court Historical Society sells gift items

M **TEXTILE MUSEUM,** 2320 S St NW, 20008. Tel 202-667-0441; FAX 202-483-0994. *Pres* Edwin M Zimmerman; *Dir* Ursula E McCracken; *Admin Asst* Josephine Tucci; *Cur New World* Ann P Rowe; *Cur Eastern Hemisphere* Carol Bier
Open Mon - Sat 10 AM - 5 PM, Sun 1 - 5 PM. Admis by contribution, $5 suggested. Estab 1925 for the acquisition, study & exhibition of rugs & textiles. The gallery contains eight rooms for exhibition, storage areas, museum shop, conservation laboratory, library & offices. Average Annual Attendance: 40,000. Mem: 3000; dues Washington, DC area $40, out-of-town $35
Income: Financed by endowment, mem & grants
Collections: †Oriental rugs from antiquity to the present, as well as rugs & textiles from the Old & New Worlds with the general exception of Western Europe & the United States. The collection contains 12,000 textiles & 1500 rugs; Coptic, Islamic textiles; Central & South American ethnographic textiles
Exhibitions: (1991) Visions of Infinity: Design & Pattern in Oriental Carpets; Trailing the Tiger -- To Golden Cloths of Sumatra's Minangkabau; New Quilts: Interpretations & Innovations; Adean Four-Cornered Hats: Ancient Volumes; Mamluk Carpets; Fabric of the Inca Empire Aegean Crossroads: Greek Island Embroideries; The Scent of Flowers: Kashmir Shawls; Turkmen: Tribal Carpets & Traditions; Master Dyers to the World; Flat-Woven Textiles: The Arthur D Jenkins Collection; (1992 - 93) Bukhara: Traditional Weavings from Pre-Soviet Central Asia; A Kurdish Reed Screen; Textiles & the Tai Experience in Southeast Asia; Patterns of Prestige: The Development & Influence of the Saltillo Sarape; Mexican Samplers: Patterns of Continuity & Change; Inspirations: Exploring the Art of Faith Ringgold; Beyond the Tanabata Bridge: A Textile Journey in Japan
Publications: Irene Emery Round Table on Museum Textiles, irregular; Museum journal, annual; museum newsletter, quarterly; exhibition catalogs
Activities: Docent training; internships in conservation & museum studies; lectures open to public; gallery talks; tours; original objects of art lent to other museums for special exhibitions; originate traveling exhibitions; museum shop & sales shop selling books, original art, patterns, yarn & floss, ethnic folk jewelry, woven & knitted articles
L **Arthur D Jenkins Library,** 2320 S St NW, 20008. Tel 202-667-0441; FAX 202-483-0994. *Librn* Mary Samms; *Library Asst* Deborah Koslowsky
Open Wed - Sat 10 AM - 2 PM. Estab 1925 as a reference library dealing with ancient and ethnographic textiles and rugs of the world
Income: Financed by endowment, membership and gifts
Library Holdings: Vols 14,000; Per subs 164; AV — Cassettes, slides, v-tapes; Other — Clipping files, exhibition catalogs, manuscripts, pamphlets, photographs
Special Subjects: American Indian Art, Decorative Arts, Folk Art, Historical Material, History of Art & Archaeology, Islamic Art, Latin American Art, Mexican Art, Oriental Art, Pre-Columbian Art
Collections: †Oriental rugs; †Peruvian, †Indonesian, †American Indian and †Indian Textiles

L **TRINITY COLLEGE LIBRARY,** 125 Michigan Ave NE, 20017. Tel 202-939-5171; FAX 202-939-5134. *Dir* Karen Leider; *Public Serv* Mary Ann Babendreier; *Periodicals* Doris Gruber
Open during school semesters, Mon - Thurs 9 AM - 11 PM, Fri 9 AM - 8 PM, Sat 10 AM - 5 PM, Sun noon - 11 PM. Estab 1897 as an undergraduate college library, serving the college community
Income: $253,548 (financed by college budget)
Library Holdings: Vols 5200; Per subs 16; Micro — Reels; AV — Cassettes, slides
Special Subjects: Art collection in both books and slides is general in content, including works on painting, sculpture and architecture principally

M **UNITED STATES CAPITOL,** Architect of the Capitol, 20515. Tel 202-225-1222. *Architect of the Capitol* George M White; *Chief Cur* Dr Barbara A Wolanin
Open daily 9 AM - 4:30 PM. No admis fee. Cornerstone layed 1793. Capitol is working building with museum value. Restored historic chambers; paintings & sculptures scattered through rooms & halls of Congress; reference library. Average Annual Attendance: 10,000,000
Income: Financed by United States Congressional appropriation and appropriate donations
Collections: Works by Andrei, Brumidi, Crawford, Cox, Franzoni, French, Greenough, Leutze, Peale, Powers, Rogers, Trumbull, Vanderlyn, Weir; approx 800 paintings & sculptures, manuscripts
Exhibitions: Art and Architecture of the United States Capitol, changes periodically. Hall of the House of Representatives; Arts Caucus Annual Exhibition; changing exhibitions sponsored by Members of Congress
Publications: Art in the Capitol, periodically; catalog of collections; occasional pamphlets; press releases
Activities: US Capitol Guide Service tours; fellowships; individual paintings and original art objects lent to major museums and exhibitions in Washington, DC
L **Art Reference Library,** Office of the Curator, HT - 3, US Capitol, 20515. Tel 202-225-1222. *Cur* Barbara A Wolanin; *Archivist* Sarah H Turner; *Registrar* Pamela Violante; *Architect* George M White
Open 9 AM - 4:30 PM. Estab for research on United States Capitol, its art and artists
Library Holdings: Vols 5000; Per subs 10; Correspondence; Micro — Reels; AV — Slides 5000, v-tapes; Other — Clipping files, exhibition catalogs, manuscripts, memorabilia, original art works, pamphlets, photographs, prints
Special Subjects: Architecture, Architecture of the US Capitol, Capitol Collection, History of Washington, DC
Collections: 100,000 architectural drawings; 60,000 photographs; archives pertaining to Capitol art and architecture 1793 to present
Exhibitions: Permanent educational exhibits

A **UNITED STATES COMMISSION OF FINE ARTS,** Pension Bldg, Suite 312, 441 F St NW, 20001. Tel 202-504-2200; FAX 202-504-2195. *Chmn* J Carter Brown; *Secy* Charles H Atherton
Open daily 8:30 AM - 5 PM. Estab by Act of Congress in 1910 to advise the President, members of congress, and various governmental agencies on matters pertaining to the appearance of Washington, DC. The Commission of Fine Arts is composed of seven members who are appointed by the President for four-year terms. Report issued periodically, principally concerned with architectural review. Plans for all new projects in the District of Columbia under the direction of the Federal and District of Columbia Governments which affect the appearance of the city, and all questions involving matters of design with which the Federal Government may be concerned must be submitted to the Commission for comment and advice before contracts are made. Also gives advice on suitability of designs of private buildings in certain parts of the city adjacent to the various departments and agencies of the District and Federal Governments, the Mall, Rock Creek Park, and Georgetown
Income: Financed by annual appropriations enacted by Congress
Publications: 15 publications on area architecture, 1964-1978; Commission of Fine Arts, 1910-1985

UNITED STATES COMMITTEE OF THE INTERNATIONAL ASSOCIATION OF ART, INC
For further information, see National and Regional Organizations

M **US DEPARTMENT OF STATE,** Diplomatic Reception Rooms, 2201 C St NW, 20520-7310. Tel 202-647-1990; FAX 202-647-3428. *Cur* Harry H Sahnabel; *Assoc Cur* Gail F Serfaty; *Asst Cur* Mary K Itsell; *Secy* Tamara Payton; *Chmn Fine Arts Committee* Clement E Conger; *Fine Arts Support Specialist* Patricia

Heflin
Open for three public tours by reservations only Mon - Fri 9:30 AM, 10:30 AM
& 2:45 PM. No admis fee. Estab unofficially 1961, officially 1971 to entertain
foreign dignitaries. These rooms allow foreign & American visitors to view
furniture & art of the American & Federal periods. A total of 42 rooms (only
twelve are open to public) are furnished in 18th & early 19th Century American
furniture & silver, Chinese export porcelain, antique Orienty rugs, American
portraits & paintings. Average Annual Attendance: 110,000
Income: Financed by private donations, foundation and corporate grants and
loans of furnishings and paintings
Purchases: American Fine & decorative arts
Collections: †American furniture (1740-1825; †American portraits & paintings;
†Chinese export porcelain; †American silver
Publications: Treasures of the US Dept of State; PBS documentary film:
America's Heritage
Activities: Tours given Mon - Fri; fine & decorative art objects lent to special
museum exhibitions

UNITED STATES DEPARTMENT OF THE INTERIOR, Indian Arts &
Crafts Board
For further information, see National and Regional Organizations

M **UNITED STATES DEPARTMENT OF THE INTERIOR MUSEUM,** C St
between 18th & 19th Sts NW, Dept of the Interior, 20240. Tel 202-208-4743.
Museum Cur Debra Berke; *Museum Technician* Anne Howell
Open Mon - Fri 8 AM - 4 PM. No admis fee. Estab 1938 to visualize and
explain to the public through works of art and other media the history, aims and
activities of the Department. Museum occupies one wing on the first floor of the
Interior Department Building. Average Annual Attendance: 10,000
Income: Federally funded
Collections: Leland Curtis (paintings) ; Colburn Collection of Indian basketry;
†general collection of Indian, Eskimo, South Sea Islands and Virgin Islands arts
and crafts, documents, maps, charts, etc; Gibson Collection of Indian materials;
Indian arts and crafts; murals; dioramas of interior history scenes; oil paintings of
early American survey teams by William Henry Jackson; oil paintings of western
conservation scenes by Wilfrid Swancourt Bronson; sculpture groups; watercolor
& black & white illustrations; wildlife paintings by Walter Weber
Exhibitions: (1991) Overview of Interior history & activities; architectural history
of the headquarters building; interpretation of a turn of the century totem pole

M **UNITED STATES NAVY,** Art Gallery, Bldg 67, Washington Navy Yard, Ninth
& M St SE, 20374. Tel 202-433-3815; FAX 202-433-9553. *Acting Cur* John D
Barnett
Open Monday - Friday 8 AM - 4 PM. Estab 1941. Average Annual Attendance:
3000
Income: Financed by Naval Historical Center
Collections: Graphic arts, paintings, sketches
Exhibitions: Quarterly exhibits of art work from WWII through 1979 from the
permanent collection; Navy art WWII permanent collection
Publications: United States Navy Combat Art
Activities: Lending collection contains original objects of art

A **UNITED STATES SENATE COMMISSION ON ART,** United States Capitol
Bldg, Room S-411, 20510-7102. Tel 202-224-2955. *Chmn* George Mitchell;
VChmn Bob Dole; *Cur* James R Ketchum; *Registrar* John B Odell; *Registrarial
Asst* Melinda K Smith; *Curatorial Asst* Richard L Doerner; *Museum Specialist*
Scott M Strong; *Assoc Cur* Melinda Y Frye
Rooms in Capitol under jurisdiction of Commission are open daily 9 AM - 4:30
PM. No admis fee. Commission estab 1968 to acquire, supervise, hold, place and
protect all works of art, historical objects, and exhibits within the Senate wing of
the United States Capitol and Senate Office Buildings. Average Annual
Attendance: 1,000,000
Income: Financed by United States Senate appropriation
Collections: Paintings, sculpture, historic furnishings and memorabilia located
within the Senate wing of the Capitol and Senate Office Buildings; Preservation
Projects: Old Senate and Old Supreme Court Chamber restored to their
appearances 1850
Exhibitions: The Senate Seal; The Supreme Court of the United States, the
Capitol Years 1801-1935; Life Under the Dome: Prints from the U S Senate
collection 1861-1897
Publications: The Senate Chamber 1810-1859; The Supreme Court Chamber
1810-1860; A Necessary Fence: The Senate's First Century; An Assembly of
Chosen Men: Popular Views of the Senate's Chambers 1847-1886
L **Reference Library,** United States Capitol Bldg Room S-411, 20510-7102. Tel
202-224-2976. *Librn* Roger Haley
A reference collection on fine and decorative arts; supplemented by the United
States Senate Library
Income: $1000 (financed by United States Senate appropriation to the
Commission)
Library Holdings: Vols 250,000; Per subs 30; Micro — Cards; AV — Slides;
Other — Clipping files, exhibition catalogs, manuscripts, memorabilia, pamphlets,
photographs
Special Subjects: Architecture, Decorative Arts, United States Senate

M **THE WASHINGTON CENTER FOR PHOTOGRAPHY,** 1731 21st St NW,
20009. Tel 202-234-5517. *Chmn* Ingrid Hansen; *Treas* Suzanne Quinlan; *Secy*
Liz McGrath; *Publicity* Jerry Smith
Open Wed - Sun noon - 5 PM, cl Mon & Tues. Admis free. Estab 1986 as an
educational resource center. Office space, 1000 sq ft of exhibition wall space.
Average Annual Attendance: 9000. Mem: 300; dues $25 - $200; annual meeting
in Aug
Income: Financed by mem, & grants
Exhibitions: (1992) Lawyers, Guns & Money
Publications: Contact, semi-annual; Update, bi-monthly
Activities: Educ dept; classes for adults; workshops; lect open to public, 1 - 2 vis
lectr per year; gallery talks; competitions; exhibitions; portfolio review; book
traveling exhibitions semi-annually

A **WASHINGTON PROJECT FOR THE ARTS,** 400 Seventh St NW, 20004. Tel
202-347-4813; FAX 202-347-8383. *Exec Dir* Donald Russell
Open 11 AM - 6 PM, cl Mon. No admis fee. Estab 1975, provides space for
contemporary artists spanning the visual, media, literary, performing & book arts.
Mem: Annual dues $35
Income: Financed by members & the public
Exhibitions: (1992) Face to Face: John Aheam & Rigoberto Torres
Publications: Exhibition catalogs; WPA Newsletter, quarterly
Activities: Educ dept; Lect open to public, Open City outreach program

M **WHITE HOUSE,** 1600 Pennsylvania Ave NW, 20500. Tel 202-456-1414; FAX
202-456-2883. *Cur* Rex W Scouten; *Assoc Cur* Betty C Monkman
Open Tues - Sat 10 AM - Noon, cl Sun, Mon, most holidays. No admis fee
Income: Financed by Federal government appropriation
Collections: †18th & 19th century period furniture; 18th, 19th & 20th century
†paintings & †prints; †glassware; †manuscripts; †porcelain; †sculpture
Exhibitions: Temporary & permanent exhibits on White House & its collections
Publications: Art in the White House: A Nation's Pride; The First Ladies; The
Living White House; The President's House: A History; The Presidents of the
United States; The White House: a Historic Guide; White House History,
magazine; White House Glassware: Two Centuries of Presidential Entertaining

M **WOODROW WILSON HOUSE,** 2340 S St, NW, 20008. Tel 202-387-4062;
FAX 202-483-1466. *Dir* Michael T Sheehan; *Asst Dir* Frank J Aurellan; *Prog
Asst* Karen Walsh
Open Tues - Sun 10 AM - 4 PM, cl Mon. Admis adults $4, students & sr citizens
$2.50, National Trust members free. Estab 1963, owned by the National Trust
for Historic Preservation, it works to foster interest & appreciation of the 28th
President, Woodrow Wilson. Wilson House is a 1915 Georgian-Revival
townhouse designed by Waddy B Wood, with formal garden. From 1921 it
served as the home of President & Mrs Wilson. Average Annual Attendance: 16,
000. Mem: 275; dues $35 & up
Income: Financed by endowment, mem, admissions & sales
Collections: Early 20th century art, furnishings, clothing; presidential
memorabilia; decorative arts
Publications: Woodrow Wilson News, quarterly
Activities: Provide lect; individual paintings & objects of art lent to qualified
museums; museum shop sells books & reproductions

FLORIDA

BELLEAIR

A **FLORIDA GULF COAST ART CENTER, INC,** 222 Ponce de Leon Blvd,
34616. Tel 813-584-8634; FAX 813-586-0782. *Trustee Adminr* Amelia B
Coward; *Cur* Barbara Anderson Hill; *Educ Coordr* Donna Sinicrope; *Dir
Community Relations* Nancy Kelly
Open Mon - Fri 10 AM - 4 PM, Sat & Sun noon - 4 PM, cl holidays. No admis
fee, donations accepted. Estab 1936 as a regional center for the visual arts.
Gallery has 2,200 sq ft of space, white walls, track lighting and a security system.
Average Annual Attendance: 10,000. Mem: 1000; dues life mem $5000,
president's circle $1000, director's circle $500, patron $250, sustaining $125,
recriprocal $50, family $35, individual $25; annual meeting in Sept
Income: Financed by tuition, membership dues, donations & grants
Exhibitions: Average 12 exhibitions a year including regional artists, traveling
exhibits and those organized by Art Center
Publications: Bulletin, bi-monthly newsletter; catalogue; exhibition brochures
Activities: Classes for adults and children; workshops; lectures; gallery talks
L **Art Reference Library,** 222 Ponce de Leon Blvd, 34616. Tel 813-584-8634; FAX
813-586-0782. *Educ Coordr* Donna Sinicrope
Open Tues - Sat 10 AM - 4 PM, Sun 2 - 5 PM, cl Aug. Estab 1949 to provide
reference material and current periodicals to Art Center members and students.
Average Annual Attendance: 8000. Mem: 1300; dues $20 and up; annual
meeting in March or April
Library Holdings: Vols 1200; Per subs 3; AV — Fs, slides; Other — Exhibition
catalogs
Activities: Classes for adults and children; docent training; lectures open to
public, 8 vis lectr per year; concerts; gallery talks; tours; competitions with
awards; book traveling exhibitions 2 per yr

BOCA RATON

A **BOCA RATON MUSEUM OF ART,** 801 W Palmetto Park Rd, 33486. Tel
407-392-2500; FAX 407-391-6410. *Pres* Fern Lingner; *VPres* Harold Perper;
VPres Henry Deppe; *Exec Dir* Roger Selby
Open Mon - Fri 10 AM - 4 PM, Sat & Sun Noon - 4 PM, cl holidays. No admis
fee, suggested donation $2. Estab 1951 to foster and develop the cultural arts.
Large Main Gallery, museum shop contained in one building. Second building
houses art school and storage. 4500 sq ft expansion houses a permanent
collection. Average Annual Attendance: 40,000. Mem: 2500; annual dues single
$40, family $60; annual meeting April
Income: Financed by membership, fund raising, art school and grants
Exhibitions: Changes every 4-6 wks; State-wide competition and show
Publications: Exhibition catalogues; newsletter, 11 per year
Activities: Classes for adults and children; docent training; lect for members and
guests; tours; juried exhibition; national outdoor art festival with awards given for
Best in Show and Merit; museum shop sells books, original art, reproductions,
prints
L **Library,** 801 W Palmetto Park Rd, 33486. Tel 407-392-2500. *Librn* Emanuel
Schechter
Open Mon - Fri 10 AM - 4 PM, Sat & Sun Noon - 4 PM. Estab 1970
Library Holdings: Vols 4000

M FLORIDA ATLANTIC UNIVERSITY, Ritter Art Gallery, 500 NW 20th St, 33431. Tel 407-367-2661. *Dir* Robert Watson
Open Tues - Fri 10 AM - 4 PM. No admis fee. Estab 1970 to provide exhibit space for faculty and students and to provide an opportunity to bring to the area exhibits which would expand the cultural experience of the viewers. Gallery is located at the center of the University campus. Average Annual Attendance: 15,000
Income: Financed by city, state & county appropriations and student activities fees
Collections: Slide collection; student work
Exhibitions: Annual juried student show; faculty & former students; work from area junior colleges; traveling exhibitions; Dre Devens: Dutch Constructivist; Arnulf Rainer: the Self -Portraits; Jan Schoonhoven: A Retrospective
Publications: We Call This Art, newsletter; exhibit catalogues
Activities: Classes for adults; dramatic programs; lect open to public & some for members only; concerts; gallery talks; tours; competitions with awards; originate traveling exhibitions; traveling exhibitions organized and circulated

M INTERNATIONAL MUSEUM OF CARTOON ART (Formerly Museum of Cartoon Art), 200 Plaza Real, PO Box 1643, 33429. Tel 407-391-2200. *Chmn* Mort Walker; *Pres* Joseph D'Angelo; *Dir* Charles Green; *Dir* Brian Walker; *Mgr* Ashley Hunt
Open Tues - Fri 10 AM - 4 PM, Sun 1 - 5 PM, cl major holidays. Admis adults $1.50, sr citizens and children under 12 $.75. Estab 1974 as world's first museum dedicated solely to the unique art form of cartooning. Consists of two floors with a total of 10 large display rooms with historical & contemporary permanent exhibs. Special exhibs 4 per yr. Average Annual Attendance: 15,000. Mem: 400; dues $30-$35
Income: Financed by contributions & earned income
Collections: Animated Film Collection, videotape; Cartoon Hall of Fame; Comics collection from 1896 to the present; early and contemporary original cartoon art
Exhibitions: Original artwork from all of the various genres of illustration; annual children's cartoon contest for age under 17; Peanuts Retrospective; Uncle Sam; Defenders of the Earth; Disney '86/'87
Publications: Tad Dorgan, Story of America in Cartoons; Dick Tracy: The Art of Chester Gould
Activities: Lectures open to public, 12 vis lectr per year; competitions with cash, prize, print & certificate awards; individual paintings & original objects of art lent to other museums, galleries, schools & universities & arts organizations; originate traveling exhibitions; museum sales shop sells books, magazines, original art, reproductions, prints & various cartoon oriented souvenirs, toys, T-shirts
L Library, Comly Ave, 10573
Income: $160,000 (financed by contributions)
Library Holdings: Vols 1500; Per subs 5; AV — Motion pictures, slides, v-tapes; Other — Clipping files, memorabilia, photographs, prints, reproductions
Collections: Archives collection
Activities: Celebrity Guest Cartoonist program

BRADENTON

A ART LEAGUE OF MANATEE COUNTY, Art Center, 209 Ninth St W, 34205. Tel 813-746-2862. *Office Mgr* Laura Avery; *Office Asst* Sandra French
Open Sept - May, Mon - Fri 9 AM - 4:30 PM, Sat 1 - 4 PM, Sun 2 - 4 PM, cl June, July, Aug and holidays. No admis fee. Estab 1937 to offer opportunities in further education in the visual arts by providing space for exhibitions, classes, demonstrations, critiques & the exchange of ideas & information by visiting artists. Average Annual Attendance: 25,000. Mem: 600; dues $5 and up; annual meeting in April
Exhibitions: Work by members, one person shows and circulating exhibitions changing at three week intervals from Oct to May
Activities: Art school instruction in painting, drawing, clay techniques and variety of handcrafts; creative development for children; special art programs; gallery talks
L Library, Art Center, 209 Ninth St W, 33505. Tel 813-746-2862. *Mgr* Laura Avery; *Office Asst* Sandra French
Open Mon - Fri 9 AM - 4:30 PM, Sat 10 AM - 4 PM, Sun 1 - 4 PM
Income: Financed by donations
Library Holdings: Vols 850; Other — Clipping files

CLEARWATER

L NAPOLEONIC SOCIETY OF AMERICA, Library, 1115 Ponce de Leon Blvd, 34616. Tel 813-586-1779. *Pres* Robert M Snibbe
Open 9 AM - 5 PM. No admis fee. Estab 1983
Income: $130,999 (financed by mem)
Library Holdings: Vols 450; Per subs 4; AV — V-tapes; Other — Memorabilia, photographs
Special Subjects: Historical Material, Miniatures, Painting - French
Publications: Members bulletin, quarterly

CORAL GABLES

M UNIVERSITY OF MIAMI, Lowe Art Museum, 1301 Stanford Dr, 33146. Tel 305-284-3536. *Dir* Brian Dursum; *Cur of Exhib* Denise Gersan; *Registrar* Jose Guitian
Open Tues - Sat 10 AM - 5 PM, Sun noon - 5PM, cl Mon. Admis general $4, sr citizens $3, students $2, members, Univ of Miami students & children under 6 free, group rates available. Estab 1952 to bring outstanding exhibitions and collections to the community and to the University; gallery maintained. Average Annual Attendance: 95,000
Collections: †African Art; Washington Allston Trust Collection; †Virgil Barker Collection of 19th & 20th Century American Art; Alfred I Barton Collection of Southwestern American Indian Art; Esso Collection of Latin American Art; Samuel H Kress Collection of Renaissance & Baroque Art; Samuel K Lothrop Collection of Guatemalan Textiles; Asian Art; †Pre-Columbian; American &

European Paintings; Cintas Foundation Collection of Spanish Old Master Paintings
Exhibitions: Varied, changing exhibitions throughout the year. (1992 - 93) The University of Miami Studio Art Faculty Exhibition; From Peale to Pearlstein: American Portraiture from the Permanent Collection; Donald Sultan: A Print Retrospective; Architectural Drawings: Arabian Fantasies for Opa-Locka; Bold Strokes & Quiet Gestures: 20th Century Drawings & Watercolors from the Santa Barbara Museum of Art; Art that Works: The Decorative Arts of the Eighties, Crafted in America; Chihuly Works in Glass; University of Miami Undergraduate/Master of Fine Arts Student Exhibition; Consuelo Kanaga: An American Photographer
Publications: Exhibition catalogs; newsletter, bimonthly
Activities: Classes for children; docent training; lect open to public, 6 vis lectr per year; concerts; gallery talks; tours; individual paintings & original objects of art lent to other museums; originate traveling exhibitions; museum shop sells books, magazines, ceramics, jewelry, children's art toys; decorative gifts

L Lowe Art Museum Reference Library, 1301 Stanford Dr, 33124-6310. Tel 305-284-3535, 284-3536. *Cur* Denise Gersan
For reference only
Library Holdings: Vols 5000; Per subs 1500; Micro — Cards; AV — Kodachromes, slides; Other — Clipping files, exhibition catalogs, photographs
Special Subjects: Art History
Publications: Newsletter, quarterly
Activities: Classes for children; docent training; lectures open to public, 6 vis lectr per year; concerts; gallery talks; tours

DAYTONA BEACH

M DAYTONA BEACH COMMUNITY COLLEGE, Southeast Museum of Photography, PO Box 2811, 32120-2811. Tel 904-254-4475; FAX 904-254-4487. *Dir* Alison Nordstrom
Open Mon 10 AM - 7 PM, Tues - Fri 10 AM - 4 PM. Estab 1960
Collections: Photographic Collection of Karsch, Chartier - Breson, Friedlander, Perlmutter

M HALIFAX HISTORICAL SOCIETY, INC, Halifax Historical Museum, 252 S Beach St, 32114. Tel 904-255-6976. *Pres* Dr William Doremus; *Pres Emeritus* Robert B Wood; *1st VPres* William Wood; *2nd VPres* Lorraine Freeman; *3rd VPres* Dr Palmera Kabana; *Acting Dir* Elizabeth B Baker
Open Tues - Sat 10 AM - 4 PM. Admis adult $2, children 12 & under $.50, members & children free on Sat. Estab 1949 to preserve & interpret history of the Halifax area. Ames Gallery contains modern art. Average Annual Attendance: 18,000. Mem: 423; dues $18 & up; annual meeting 1st Thurs in Jan
Income: Financed by dues, donations, grants, gift shop, fund raising
Collections: Digget Collection of wooden models of boats, cars & trains; †18th century Spanish & English artifacts; Indian arrowheads, canoe, pottery; racing memorabilia; Victorian clothing & furniture
Publications: Monthly newsletter; Six Columns & Fort New Smyrna; various pamphlets
Activities: Lectures open to public, 7 vis lectrs per yr; recognition plaques; book traveling exhibitions, 4 per yr; museum shop sells books, magazines, reproductions, plates

M MUSEUM OF ARTS AND SCIENCES, Cuban Museum, 1040 Museum Blvd, 32114. Tel 904-255-0285; FAX 904-255-0285. *Dir* Gary Russell Libby
Open Tues - Fri 9 AM - 4 PM, Sat & Sun noon - 5 PM, cl Mon & national holidays. Admis $3, museum members free. Estab 1955 to offer both educational and cultural services to the public. Large hexagonal main exhibition galleries, hall gallery & lobby gallery are maintained; Museum includes Planetarium, A Frischer Sculpture Garden, Gallery of American Art, Root Hall & Gallery. Average Annual Attendance: 100,000. Mem: 5000; dues $30; annual meeting Nov
Income: $800,000 (financed by endowment, mem, city & county appropriations & donations)
Purchases: American contemporary art 1720 - 1900
Collections: American Art 1620 - 1900; Aboriginal art including Florida Indian; American Illustration: Norman Rockwell; Cuban Collection; decorative arts including silver & furniture; Florida Contemporary Collection; African Art; Pre-Columbian Art
Exhibitions: (1992-93) Spirit Societies: African Objects; Fine & Decorative Arts from the Age of Napoleon; From the Age of Optimism: The Arts in America; Conquistador: Spain in 16th Century La Florida; The Multiple is Unique: A Primer on Printmaking; The New World in the Eyes of Explorers; Gizmos & Gadgets; Thomas A Edison: The Evolution of Sound Reproduction 1877 - 1914; Bold Marks: New Expressionist Paintings; The Beginnings of a National Style: American Art before 1830; Stopping Time: The Photographs of Harold Edgerton; Faces on Fossils; Contemporary Prints from Topaz Editions; Chinese Decorative Arts from the Permanent Collection; Tuscawilla: A Natural History; A Treasury of Indian Miniature Paintings
Publications: Catalogs, monthly; magazine, quarterly
Activities: Classes for adults and children; docent training; lectures open to public, 10 vis lectrs per year; gallery talks; concerts; tours; competitions with awards; scholarships; exten dept serves Volusia County; individual paintings and original objects of art lent to other museums municipalities & public spaces; lending collection contains books, nature artifacts, original art works, original prints, paintings & photographs; traveling exhibitions organized and circulated; museum shop sells books, magazines, original art, reproductions, prints & slides
L Library, 1040 Museum Blvd, 32114. *Librn* Marge Sigerson
Open to members and school children; reference library
Income: Financed by Museum
Purchases: Periodicals & reference materials
Library Holdings: Vols 10,000; Per subs 10; AV — Slides, v-tapes; Other — Clipping files, exhibition catalogs, manuscripts, photographs, prints
Special Subjects: Cuban Art
Collections: Cuban: Jose Marti Library

DELAND

M **DELAND MUSEUM OF ART,** 600 N Woodland Blvd, 32720-3447. Tel 904-734-4371. *Exec Dir* Harry Messersmith; *Asst to Dir* Jan Stein
Open Tues - Sat 10 AM - 4 PM, Sun 1 - 4 PM. Admis adults $2, children $1. Estab 1951 to provide art education. Lower gallery: 12 ft carpeted walls, 3100 sq ft; upper gallery: 12 ft carpeted walls, 2100 sq ft. Average Annual Attendance: 15,000. Mem: 800; dues family $50, individual $30, sr citizens $25
Income: $152,000 (financed by mem, city & state appropriation & Volusia County)
Purchases: $1000
Collections: Contemporary Florida Artists 1900 - Present; North American Indian Baskets
Exhibitions: (1992) Jerimiah Miller Momentary Solitude; Southeastern Watercolor, juried competition
Activities: Classes for adults & children; docent programs; lect open to public, 8 vis lectr per year; competitions with awards; book traveling exhibitions 1 per year; originate traveling exhibitions 5 per year; retail store sells books, original art & reproductions

M **STETSON UNIVERSITY,** Duncan Gallery of Art, 32720. Tel 904-822-7266. *Dir* Gary Bolding
Open Mon - Fri 9 AM - 4 PM, Sat & Sun 1 - 4 PM. No admis fee. Estab 1964 as an educational gallery to augment studio teaching program. There is a large main gallery, 44 x 55 ft, with a lobby area 22 x 44 ft. Average Annual Attendance: 5000
Income: University art budget
Purchases: $1000
Collections: 20th Century American Prints, Ceramics, Drawings, Oils, Watercolors
Exhibitions: Various regional & national artists exhibitions; themed group exhibitions
Publications: Catalogs; monthly exhibition announcements
Activities: Lect open to public, 8 vis lectr per year, gallery talks; student competitions with prizes

DELRAY BEACH

M **PALM BEACH COUNTY PARKS & RECREATION DEPARTMENT,** Morikami Museum & Japanese Gardens, 4000 Morikami Park Rd, 33446. Tel 407-495-0233; FAX 407-499-2557. *Dir* Larry Rosensweig; *Cur* Thomas Gregersen; *Educ Dir* Reiko Nishioka; *Museum Store Mgr* Helene Buntman; *Admin Assoc* Nancy Azzole; *Garden Cur* Norman Nelson; *Cur Exhib* Shoko Brown; *Dir of Development* Anne Merrill
Open Tues - Sun 10 AM - 5 PM. No admis fee; donations accepted. Estab 1977 to preserve & interpret Japanese culture & Japanese-American culture. Five small galleries in Japanese style building. Average Annual Attendance: 65,000. Mem: 850; dues $35; annual meeting June
Income: $650,000 (financed by mem & county appropriation)
Purchases: $9000
Collections: †Japanese folk arts (ceramics, dolls, tools, baskets, home furnishings); †Japanese art (paintings, prints, textiles); †Japanese-American historical & art objects
Exhibitions: (1993) Japanese Art; Personal Selections from the Collection of Mary & Jackson Burke; Second Biennial Contemporary Japanese Print Exhibition
Publications: Newsletter, quarterly; Calendar bi-monthly; Exhibition catalogs 1-2 per yr
Activities: Classes for adults & children; dramatic programs; docent training; concerts; gallery talks; tours; book traveling exhibitions biannually; originate traveling exhibitions; museum shop sells books, reproductions, Japanese clothing, folk toys, original art, prints & cards
L **Donald B Gordon Memorial Library,** Morikami Museum, 4000 Morikami Rd, 33446. Tel 407-495-0233; FAX 407-499-2557. *Librn* Gert Berman
Open by appointment. Estab 1977 to provide printed & recorded materials on Japan. For reference only
Income: Financed by donations
Purchases: $1000
Library Holdings: Vols 600; Per subs 10; AV — Cassettes, fs, Kodachromes, rec, slides, v-tapes; Other — Clipping files, exhibition catalogs, memorabilia, pamphlets
Special Subjects: Japan, Japanese-Americans
Collections: Memorabilia of George S Morikami

FORT LAUDERDALE

L **ART INSTITUTE OF FORT LAUDERDALE,** Technical Library, 1799 SE 17th St, 33316. Tel 305-463-3000, Ext 541. *Library-LRC Dir* Merrill Murray; *Asst Librn* Joyce Kaiser-Brinklow
Open daily 7:45 AM - 5:15 PM. Estab 1973 as a technical library for the applied and fine arts
Purchases: $8000
Library Holdings: Vols 1200; Per subs 157; AV — A-tapes, cassettes 50, fs, Kodachromes, motion pictures, v-tapes 600; Other — Clipping files 2000
Activities: Educ dept; lect open to public; competitions; scholarships & fels offered; sales shop sells books, prints & supplies

M **MUSEUM OF ART, FORT LAUDERDALE,** 1 E Las Olas Blvd, 33301-1807. Tel 305-525-5500; FAX 305-524-6011. *Exec Dir* Dr Kenworth W Moffett; *Cur Coll* Jorge Santis; *Cur Exhib* Lawrence Pamer
Open Tues 11 AM - 9 PM, Wed - Sat 10 AM - 5 PM, Sun noon - 5 PM, cl Mon & national holidays. Admis non-members $3.25, sr citizens $2.75, student with identification card $1.25, no charge for members & children under 12. Estab 1958 to bring art to the community and provide cultural facilities and programs. Library, exhibit space & auditorium are maintained. Average Annual Attendance:

33,000. Mem: 5000; dues corporate $5000 & $2500, benefactor $1000, patron $500, contributing $250, sustaining $125, family - dual $50, individual $35
Collections: American & European paintings, sculpture & graphics from late 19th century - present; pre-Columbian & historic American Indian ceramics, basketry & stone artifacts; West African tribal sculpture; Golda & Meyer B Marks Cobra Art Collection
Exhibitions: (1991) Wolf-Kahn Paintings; 20th Century Flower Paintings; Duane Hanson Sculptures. (1993) Vorot to Cezanne
Publications: Annual Report; Bulletin, quarterly; Calendar of Events, monthly; Exhibition Catalogs
Activities: Classes for adults and children; docent training; slide lecture program in schools by request; lect; gallery talks; tours; films; competitions; individual paintings & original objects of art lent to other museums; sales shop
L **Library,** 1 E Las Olas Blvd, 33301-1807. Tel 305-525-5500; FAX 305-524-6011. *Librn* Katherine Darr
Founded 1958. Staff and members only
Library Holdings: Vols 5500; Per subs 15; AV — Slides

M **MUSEUM OF DISCOVERY & SCIENCE,** 401 SW Second St, 33312. Tel 305-467-6637; FAX 305-467-0046. *Exec Dir* Kim L Maher; *Trustee Pres* Steven Josias
Open Mon - Fri 10 AM - 5 PM, Sat 10 AM - 8:30 PM, Sun noon - 5 PM, cl Christmas Day, open on all other holidays; Blockbuster IMAX Theater open Mon - Sun with daily showings. Admis adults $6, sr citizens $5, children 3 - 12 $5, special group rates available. Estab 1977 to increase science literacy. Average Annual Attendance: 500,000. Mem: 1114; dues $25 - $250
Income: $3,000,000
Exhibitions: Florida EcoScapes; Technology; Solar; Sound Tracks; Space Base; Body Works; KidScience; No Place Like Home
Publications: Modulations, quarterly
Activities: Classes for adults & children; camps; sleepovers; outreach programs; films daily; lect open to public, some to members only, 7 vis lectr per year; book traveling exhibitions 5 per year; originate traveling exhibitions one per year; retail store sells books, prints, magazines & reproductions

FORT MYERS

M **EDISON COMMUNITY COLLEGE,** Gallery of Fine Art, 8099 College Parkway, PO Box 06210, 33906. Tel 813-489-9314. *Cur* Jay Williams; *Registrar* Dorothy Causey
Open Tues - Fri 10 AM - 4 PM, Sat 11 AM - 3 PM, Sun 1 - 5 PM. No admis fee. Estab 1979 to provide exhibitions of national & regional importance & related educational programs. Main gallery 2000 sq ft, high security; adjunct auditorium gallery. Average Annual Attendance: 15,000. Mem: 200; annual dues $30
Income: Financed by endowment and state appropriation
Exhibitions: (1992) Earth, Sea & Sky: Paintings of Charles H Woodbury; O'Appalachia (folk art of the southern mountains); Spiral Journey: Photographs by Linda Conner. (1993) Paintings by Larry Francis Lebby; The Tactile Vessel; Robert Rauschenberg, Recent Paintings
Activities: Tours for adults & children; docent training; lect open to public, 2 - 4 vis lectr per year; gallery talks; book traveling exhibitions 2 - 4 per year; originate traveling exhibitions to other museums in Florida; sales shop sells posters & catalogs

GAINESVILLE

M **CITY OF GAINESVILLE,** Thomas Center Galleries - Cultural Affairs, 302 NE Sixth Ave, 32602-0490. Tel 904-334-2197; FAX 904-334-2314. *Mgr* Cani Gesualdi; *Gallery Coordr* Mallory O'Connor
Open Mon - Fri 8 AM - 5 PM, Sat & Sun 1 - 4 PM. Estab 1979 to increase local arts awareness. Average Annual Attendance: 9000
Income: $8000 (financed by city appropriation, grants & donations)
Exhibitions: Exhibits with historical focus; Minority Artists; Special constituencies
Publications: Exhibition brochures, catalogues
Activities: Classes for adults & children; seminars; gallery hops; demonstrations & workshops; book traveling exhibitions semi-annually; originate traveling exhibitions

UNIVERSITY OF FLORIDA
M **University Gallery,** 32611. Tel 904-392-0201. *Acting Dir* Karen W Val Des; *Registrar* Janice Everidge
Open Mon - Fri 9 AM - 5 PM, Sun 1 - 5 PM, cl Sat & holidays. No admis fee. Estab 1965 as an arts exhibition gallery, open 11 months of the year, showing monthly exhibitions with contemporary and historical content. Gallery located in independent building with small lecture hall, limited access and completely secure with temperature and humidity control, carpet covered walls and adjustable track lighting; display area is in excess of 3000 sq ft. Average Annual Attendance: 40,000. Mem: 300; dues professional $100 and up, family $20, individual $10; annual meeting May
Income: $70,000 (financed by state appropriation and community memberships)
Purchases: $2000
Collections: †European and American prints, paintings and photographs; †Oriental (India) miniatures and sculptures; †pre-Columbian and Latin American art (also folk art)
Exhibitions: Changing monthly exhibitions; Annual University of Florida Art Faculty (January)
Publications: Exhibition catalogs; periodic bulletins
Activities: Docent training; lectures open to public; exten dept serving area schools; lending collection contains cassettes, original art works, photographs and slides; traveling exhibitions organized and circulated
L **Architecture and Fine Arts Library,** 32611. Tel 904-392-0222. *Architecture Fine Arts Bibliographer & Head Librn* Edward H Teague
Open Mon - Thurs 8 AM - 10 PM, Fri 8 AM - 5 PM, Sat 1 - 5 PM, Sun 2 - 10 PM. Library estab 1853 as a state art & architecture information center

Library Holdings: Vols 65,000; Per subs 550; Micro — Fiche, reels; AV — V-tapes; Other — Exhibition catalogs, manuscripts, pamphlets, photographs, reproductions
Special Subjects: Architecture, Art History, Constructions
Collections: Rare book collection

HOLLYWOOD

M **ART AND CULTURE CENTER OF HOLLYWOOD,** 1650 Harrison St, 33020. Tel 305-921-3274, 921-3275. *Chmn* Johnnie Glantz; *Dir* Wendy M Blazier; *Educ Cur* Marina D Whitman
Open Tues - Sat 10 AM - 4 PM, Thurs 7 - 9 PM, Sun 1 - 4 PM. Admis Wed - Sat $2, Sun $3, Tues free. Estab 1975 for the study, education & enjoyment of visual & performing arts. Great Gallery, major exhibit space, is 6300 sq ft with 400 running ft; concerts are also held there. Two Hall galleries. Average Annual Attendance: 30,000. Mem: 1250; annual dues $25-$500
Income: $200,000 (financed by membership, city appropriation, private & public contributions, grants)
Collections: 19th & 20th century American & contemporary Florida artists; African & 18th - 19th century European silver
Exhibitions: (1991) Ed Smith: Sculpture & Drawings; Moments in Time: Recent Paintings by Ramon Carullo; Dreams & Nightmares: The Artists' Organization; Exploring 19th Century America: The Great Tradition of Landscape Painting; An Atristic Discovery: 16th Congressional District High School Art Competition; China Through the Eyes of Her Artists; Five Views: South Florida Cultural Consortium 1990 Award Winners. (1992) As Scene by Both Sides. The American War in Vietnam as Seen by 40 American & Vietnamese Artists; Chaim Gross: Watercolors, Drawings & Sculpture
Publications: Calendar of Events, bi-monthly; exhibit catalogs
Activities: Educ dept; lectures open to public, 8 vis lectrs per yr; competitions with awards; individual paintings & original objects of art lent to museums; lending collection contains 50 motion pictures & 100 original art works; originate travelling exhibitions; museum shop

L **Art Reference Library,** 1650 Harrison St, 33020. *Librn* Lois Harvey
Open by appointment or request. Estab 1983 as an art research facility for staff, docents & members. For reference only. Average Annual Attendance: 43,000
Income: $1000
Purchases: $1000
Library Holdings: Vols 1200; Per subs 3; Micro — Cards; AV — Motion pictures; Other — Exhibition catalogs, pamphlets
Collections: African Collection of English Silver; International, national & regional artists
Activities: Classes for adults & children; docent training; lect open to pub, 6 vis lectr per year; concerts; gallery talks; tours; original paintings & original objects of art lent to other museums & children's museums; originate traveling exhibitions to national, state & regional institutions

M **HOLLYWOOD ART MUSEUM,** 4000 Hollywood Blvd, 33021. Tel 305-927-6455. *VPres* Dave Racalbuto; *Dir* Herbert Tulk; *Treas* Lilyan Beckerman; *Secy* Gert Tulk
Open Sept - June Mon - Fri 1 - 4 PM. No admis fee. Estab 1962 to encourage artists, instruct students & establish museum arts, science & technology. On site have limited art showcases in prominent locations. Mem: Dues $5-$20
Income: Financed by fund raising events - i.e. Golf Classics etc
Collections: Bakuba Collection
Exhibitions: Permanent and temporary exhibits
Publications: H.A.M., annual magazine
Activities: Educ dept, classes for children, docent training, teach in school; lecture open to public, gallery talks, tours, competition awards, scholarships to children; artmobile; originate traveling expeditions to schools in Broward County

JACKSONVILLE

M **CUMMER GALLERY OF ART,** DeEtte Holden Cummer Museum Foundation, 829 Riverside Ave, 32204. Tel 904-356-6857; FAX 904-353-4101. *Asst to Dir* Jean C Hall; *Asst to Dir* L Vance Shrum; *Asst to Dir* Mary Campbell Gristina; *Dir Admin* Stuart B Evans
Open Tues - Fri 10 AM - 4 PM, Sat noon - 5 PM, Sun 2 - 5 PM, cl Mon and national holidays. No admis fee. Estab 1961 as a general art museum, collecting and exhibiting fine arts of all periods and cultures. Eleven galleries of paintings & decorative arts surround garden court sited on two acres of formal gardens. Average Annual Attendance: 60,000. Mem: 2000; dues $15-$5000
Income: $1,000,000
Purchases: $600,000
Collections: †European and American painting, sculpture, graphic arts, tapestries and decorative arts; Netsuke, Inro and porcelains; Oriental Collection of jade, ivory; Early Meissen porcelain
Exhibitions: (1992) Joseph Jeffers Dodge Paintings & Drawings; An Artist Collects: Joseph Jeffers Dodge Collection; Cornelia Morse Carithers Memorial Print Exhibition; John Steuart Curry's America. (1993) Image Impact: Gefter, Hope, Johnson, Tomczak; Festival of Trees; The Life of Christ Print Exhibiton; William Keith; Florida Landscapes & Spaces; Indian Miniatures; Collectors' Choice Exhibition
Publications: Collection handbooks; exhibition catalogs; yearbooks
Activities: Lectures, 4 vis lectr per yr; concerts; gallery talks; tours; individual paintings lent to major retrospective exhibitions & reciprocating fine arts museums; museum shop sells books, prints & small objects of art associated with museum collections
L **Library,** 829 Riverside Ave, 32204. Tel 904-356-6857.
Open for reference
Income: $3500
Purchases: $3500
Library Holdings: Vols 3100; Per subs 17; AV — Slides 10,000; Other — Exhibition catalogs 1200
Special Subjects: German porcelain, Meissen

M **FLORIDA COMMUNITY COLLEGE AT JACKSONVILLE,** South Gallery, 11901 Beach Blvd, 32246-7625. Tel 904-646-2023; FAX 904-646-2209. *Dir* Mary Joan Hinson; *Docent* Mary Worthy-Dumbleton
Open Mon 10 AM - 9 PM, Tues - Thurs 10 AM - 5 PM, Fri 10 AM - 1 PM, cl weekends. No admis fee. Estab 1985
Collections: FCCJ Permanent Collection
Exhibitions: (1992) Gerald Dante Flores (abstract & sculptural works); FCCJ Art Faculty; Holiday Arts Festival; Bette Bates & Robert Tynes (graphite art & painting); B J Adams & Georgina Holt (fiber art & ceramics). (1993) Spring '93, A Student Annual; Celebration of Printmaking

M **JACKSONVILLE ART MUSEUM,** 4160 Boulevard Center Dr, 32207. Tel 904-398-8336. *Dir* Bruce H Dempsey; *Assoc Dir* John S Bunker; *Art Librn* Barbara Salvage
Open Tues, Wed & Fri 10 AM - 4 PM, Thurs 10 AM - 10 PM, Sat & Sun 1 - 5 PM, cl Mon, holidays. No admis fee. Estab 1947 as an art center for the greater Jacksonville area. Average Annual Attendance: 100,000. Mem: 3200; dues $25; annual meeting spring
Income: Financed by membership
Collections: Pre-Columbian art; 20th century paintings, prints and sculpture
Exhibitions: Photons; Phonons - Kinetic Art; The Nature of Sculpture; Wyeth Family Exhibition
Publications: Calendar, monthly; exhibition catalogues
Activities: Classes for adults and children; docent training; art enrichment program; dramatic programs; lectures open to the public, 10 vis lectr per yr; concerts; gallery talks; tours; competitions; scholarships; book traveling exhibitions; originate traveling exhibitions; museum shop sells books, magazines, original art, reproductions, prints, jewelry & children's toys
L **Library,** 4160 Boulevard Center Dr, 32207. Tel 904-398-8336; FAX 904-348-3167. *Art Librn* Barbara Salvage
Open to teachers in Duval County schools
Library Holdings: Vols 200

L **JACKSONVILLE PUBLIC LIBRARY,** Fine Arts & Recreation Dept, 122 N Ocean St, 32202. Tel 904-630-2665. *Dir* Judith L Williams; *Dept Head* Tricia Coutant
Open Mon - Thurs 10 AM - 9 PM, Fri & Sat 10 AM - 6 PM. No admis fee. Estab 1905 to serve the public by giving them free access to books, films, phonograph recordings, pamphlets, periodicals, maps, plus informational services and free programming
Income: Financed by city appropriation
Library Holdings: Vols 47,000; AV — Motion pictures 2125, rec 15,000, slides 5100, v-tapes 2500; Other — Photographs 3000
Publications: Annual Report
Activities: Weekly film programs; bi-weekly concerts

M **JACKSONVILLE UNIVERSITY,** Alexander Brest Museum & Gallery, 2800 University Blvd, 32211. Tel 904-744-3950; FAX 904-744-010. *Dir* M Lauderdale
Open Mon - Fri 9 AM - 4:30 PM, Sat noon - 5 PM. No admis fee. Estab 1972 to exhibit decorative arts collection. Three galleries exhibiting decorative arts. One gallery contains contemporary art by local artists. Average Annual Attendance: 18,000
Income: Financed by endowment & private funds
Collections: Porcelain; Ivory; †Pre-Columbian; †Steuben; Tiffany
Exhibitions: Gypsies (paintings); Eleanor Allen
Activities: Docent programs

M **MUSEUM SCIENCE & HISTORY,** 1025 Museum Circle, 32207. Tel 904-396-7062, Ext 214. *Executive Dir* Margo Dundon; *Prog Developer* Dee Dee Honaman
Open Mon - Fri 9 AM - 5 PM; Sat 11 AM - 5 PM; Sun 1 - 5 PM; cl Mon, Sept and major holidays. Admis adults $2, children 4-18 $1. Estab 1941. Lobby and three floors contain exhibit areas, classrooms, and studios. Average Annual Attendance: 225,000. Mem: 825; dues vary
Income: Financed by membership, city appropriation, and grants
Collections: Historical; Live Animal Collection; Physical Science Demonstrations
Exhibitions: Alexander Brest Planetarium (16th largest in US); health; science; wildlife
Publications: Teacher's Guide, annually; brochures, bimonthly; annual report
Activities: Classes for adults and children; dramatic programs; docent training; lect open to public; tours; Art in the Park; traveling exhibitions organized and circulated; museum shop and sales shop selling books, prints, museum-oriented items and toys for children

SOCIETY OF NORTH AMERICAN GOLDSMITHS
For further information, see National and Regional Organizations

KEY WEST

M **KEY WEST ART AND HISTORICAL SOCIETY,** East Martello Museum and Gallery, 3501 Roosevelt Blvd, 33040. Tel 305-296-3913. *Pres* Bob Feldman; *VPres* Thomas Pope; *VPres* Helen Harrison; *Recording Secy* Janet Hayes; *Corresp Secy* Max McQuillin; *Exec Dir* Susan Olsen
Open Mon - Sun 9:30 AM - 5 PM; cl Christmas. Admis $3 adults, children 7 - 15 $1, active military free. Estab 1962 to preserve history of the Florida Keys. Two air-conditioned contiguous galleries with arched ceilings. Average Annual Attendance: 25,000. Mem: 1200; annual dues $25, individual $15, student $2; annual meeting in Apr
Income: Financed by membership, donations, admissions & gift shop sales
Collections: Carvings & paintings of Mario Sanchez; folk art of Stanley Papio
Exhibitions: Monthly exhibits by Key West artists during winter; Art & History Fair
Publications: Martello; two newsletters
Activities: Lectures open to public, 6 vis lectrs per yr; competitions with prizes; individual paintings & original objects of art lent to qualifying museums; book traveling exhibitions; originate traveling exhibitions; museum shop sells books, magazines, original art, reproductions, prints

A **OLD ISLAND RESTORATION FOUNDATION INC,** Wrecker's Museum, 322 Duval St (Mailing add: 1501 Olivia St, 33040). Tel 305-294-9502. *Dir* Nancy O Jameson
Open 10 AM - 4 PM. Admis $2. Estab 1975 to present the maritime history of Key West's wrecking industry in the 19th century. Furnished period house with paintings throughout. Average Annual Attendance: 20,000. Mem: 200; dues $15 - $20; annual meeting in Apr
Income: $36,000 (financed through admis fees & fundraising)
Purchases: $6000 for sailships in sunset, 19th century American School
Collections: Oil on canvas by Edward Moran; All Sailing Ships & Scenes; Watercolors by Marshall Joyce; Watercolors by unkonwn artists

LAKELAND

M **ARTS ON THE PARK,** 115 N Kentucky Ave, 33801. Tel 813-680-2787. *Pres* Lo Alexander; *VPres* Penelope Pinson; *Exec Dir* Dudley Uphoff; *Treas* Steve Hamic
Open Tues - Fri 10 AM - 5 PM. No admis fee. Estab 1979 to encourage Florida artists through shows, competitions, classes.. 1600 sq ft ground floor, plus 2nd floor library, office, studio, in restored contributing structure in Lakeland's Munn Park Historic District. Average Annual Attendance: 30,000. Mem: 1200; dues sponsor $100 - $999, individual $35, sr citizens $25
Income: $80,000 (financed by membership, city, business & industry)
Exhibitions: (1992) Our Town; Mixed Media; Fall Festival; Artwear; Members Juried Show; Ikebana; IMC Family Show; A Gift of Art; Snowfest. (1993) Florida Artists Group; Senior Artists Showcase; Arts Explosion; Doors; Wordart Competition; Porcelain Artists of Lakeland; IMC Mayshow; Members Annual; Summer Sale
Publications: Art Paper, quarterly newsletter; Onionhead, quarterly literary magazine
Activities: Classes for adults & children, docent training; lect open to the public, 2 vis lectr per year; concerts; gallery talks; tours; competitions with awards; scholarships & fels offered; exten dept serves county; originate traveling exhibitions

M **FLORIDA SOUTHERN COLLEGE,** Melvin Art Gallery, 111 Lake Hollingsworth Dr, 33801-5698. Tel 813-680-4224, 680-4225. *Dir* Downing Barnitz
Open Mon - Fri 1:30 - 4:30 PM. No admis fee. Estab 1971 as a teaching gallery. Large 3000 sq ft main gallery; small one room adjacent gallery. Average Annual Attendance: 3000 - 5000
Collections: Brass Rubbings Collection in Roux Library; Laymon Glass Collection in Annie Pfeiffer Chapel; permanent collection in various offices and buildings
Exhibitions: (1990) James Michaels; The Ten: Women In Art, Bette Buck, Louise Cherwak, Nancy Baur Dillen, Carol Garutti, Liz Hanson, Mona Jordan, Rebecca D Lee, Susan Martin, Ellen Pavlakos, Nancy Strange Seib; Four Pastelists: Greg Biolchini, Rick Olson, Richard Segalman, Gene Sparkman (1991) F S C Art Faculty: Downing Barnitz, Gale Doak, Beth Ford, William Melvin, John Obrecht; Lakeland Art Guild - Juried Show #20; Florida Artist Group; F S C Annual Student Exhibit
Activities: Lectures open to public, 3 vis lectr per yr; gallery talks; concerts; awards

M **POLK MUSEUM OF ART,** 800 E Palmetto, 33801. Tel 813-688-7743. *Executive Dir* Ken Rollins; *Cur Educ* Jane Parkerson; *Pres* Dorothy Jenkins; *Controller* Debbie Tibbs
Open Mon - Sat 10 AM - 4 PM, Sun noon - 4 PM. No admis fee. For reference. Average Annual Attendance: 125,000. Mem: 1600; dues patron $1000, benefactor $500, advocate $250, sponsor $100, general $35, 10% discount on general mem for senior citizens
Income: Financed by mem, cities of Lakeland & Winter Haven, Polk County School Board, grants, county government, endowment
Library Holdings: Vols 1200; Per subs 27; Other — Exhibition catalogs
Collections: Ellis Verink Photographs; 15th - 19th Century European ceramics; Pre-Columbian Collection; assorted decorative arts; contemporary paintings featuring Florida artists; oriental arts
Exhibitions: Changing exhibitions, approximately every eight weeks
Activities: Classes for adults & children; workshops; Meet-the-Artist series; circulating exhibits; docent training; lectures open to public; tours; art films; docent-guided tours
L **Penfield Library,** 800 E Palmetto, 33801. Tel 813-688-7743. *Co-Chmn* Corinne Sherwood; *Co-Chmn* Mary Kay Smith; *Librn* Martha Bier
Open Tues - Fri 10 AM - 5 PM, Sat 10 AM - 4 PM, Sun 1 - 4 PM. Estab 1970 as a reference library for Polk County residents
Library Holdings: Vols 1200; Per subs 27; Other — Exhibition catalogs, photographs, prints
Special Subjects: American Indian Art, American Western Art, Art Education, Art History, Folk Art, History of Art & Archaeology, Latin American Art, Mexican Art, Oriental Art, Pre-Columbian Art, Southwestern Art

LAKE WORTH

M **PALM BEACH COMMUNITY COLLEGE FOUNDATION,** Museum of Art, 601 Lake Ave, 33460. Tel 407-582-00006. *Dir* Kip Eagen
Open 10 AM - 5 PM. Admis $2 Donation. Estab 1989 for exhibition of contemporary art. Mus is a renovated 1939 Art Deco Movie Theature with 5 separate galleries on 2 floors. Average Annual Attendance: 4000. Mem: 500; average dues $100
Income: Financed by endowment, mem
Collections: Contemporary Ceramics; Contemporary Glass; Kinetic Sculpture
Exhibitions: Changing exhibits & permanent collection
Publications: Catalogs; posters
Activities: Children's classes; docent programs; lectures open to public, some to members only, 3 vis lectrs per yr; lending collection contains art objects; book traveling exhibitions 1-2 per yr

MAITLAND

M **MAITLAND ART CENTER,** 231 W Packwood Ave, 32751-5596. Tel 407-539-2181. *Exec Dir* James G Shepp; *Educ Coordr* Ann E Spalding; *Prog Coordr* Julie Mimms; *Staff Coordr* Carol B Shurtleff; *Traveling Exhib Cur* Dorothy T Van Arsdale
Open Mon - Fri 10 AM - 4:30 PM, Sat & Sun noon - 4:30 PM, cl major holidays. No admis fee. Estab 1938 to promote exploration and education in the visual arts and contemporary crafts; listed in National Register of Historic Places. Four galleries totaling 202 running ft. Average Annual Attendance: 45,000. Mem: 625; dues $15-$1000; annual meeting in April
Income: Financed by membership, city and state appropriations, donations, special events, endowment
Collections: Architectural work including 6-acre compound and memorial chapel designed by Smith; graphics; paintings & sculptures of Andre Smith; etchings & drawings
Exhibitions: Coins & Medals: Twenty Centuries of French Art; Collector's Collect IV: Grady Kimsey: To the Future; 1789 The French Revolution & Architectural Drawings of Andre Smith; Maury Hurt: Recent Works; Carol Bechtel: Recent Works; Isabelle Rouault; The Dragon Throne, Chinese Imperial Art Out from Africa; Selections from the Permanent Collection; Japanese Netsuke; Roger Dumas, A Retrospective; Heirloom Swedish Textiles; George Spivey, A Retrospective. (1991) 1990 Members Juried Exhibition; Woody Walters, Florida The Land; Barbara Tiffany-Eginton and Jeanne Welch; Sports Feelings; Winifred Johnson Clive, A Retrospective Vessels; The Architect As Artist; 1991 Members Juries Exhibition; Jon Barron Farmer. (1992) Columbus Through the Eyes of Florida Artists; Art Three by Three, 1992; 1992 Juried Competition; Andre Smith: Part II of Greenberg Collection & Recent Acquisitions; The People, Art of Native Americans; The Artist's Table (MACA); Selections from the Collection of the Univ of South Florida; Jan Chenoweth; J Andre Smith, The Greenberg Collection
Publications: Exhibit catalogs; quarterly class schedules; quarterly newsletter
Activities: Classes for adults and children; art training classes; docent training; lect open to public; gallery talks; tours; competitions with awards; individual paintings & original objects of art lent; book traveling exhibitions, annually; originate traveling exhibitions; museum shop sells original art, reproductions, cards, jewelry & children's items
L **Library,** 231 W Packwood Ave, 32751-5596. Tel 407-539-2181; FAX 407-539-6282. *Dir* James G Shepp; *Cur Traveling Exhib* Dorothy T Van Arsdale; *Admin Asst* Julia M Mimms; *Educ Coordr* Carol B Shurtleff; *Community Relations Coordr* Catherine T Simmons
Open Mon - Fri 10 AM - 4:30 PM, Sat & Sun noon - 4:30 PM, cl major holidays. No admis fee. Estab 1970 to promote knowledge & education in American Art. Open for reference. Average Annual Attendance: 55,000
Income: Financed by City of Maitland, mem, tuition, special events, grants, contributions, gallery donations
Library Holdings: Vols 900; Per subs 10; Other — Exhibition catalogs
Special Subjects: American Indian Art, American Western Art, Art Education, Art History, Decorative Arts, History of Art & Archaeology, Mixed Media, Painting - American, Sculpture, Theatre Arts
Collections: †Works by Andre Smith (1880 - 1959); exhibiting artists

MELBOURNE

M **BREVARD ART CENTER AND MUSEUM, INC,** 1463 Highland Ave, PO Box 360835, 32936-0835. Tel 407-242-0737; FAX 407-242-0798. *Pres* Caryl Wright; *Executive Dir* Randall Hayes; *Asst Dir Business Management* Ruth Ann Pippin
Open Tues - Fri 10 AM - 5 PM, Sat 10 AM - 4 PM, Sun noon - 4 PM, cl Mon. Estab 1978 to exhibit art for the education, information, and enjoyment of the public. Exhibition facility with three changing and two permanent collection galleries with approx 6000 sq ft of exhibition space. Average Annual Attendance: 40,000. Mem: 1700; dues individual $20, family $35, patron $100 and up; annual meeting third Tues in May
Income: $400,000 (financed by membership, city & county appropriation, corporate gifts & grants)
Purchases: $1500
Collections: †Contemporary regional & national artists; drawings, paintings, prints of Ernst Oppler; small objects collection of Ethnic Art: Eskimo, African Egyptian, Pre-Columbian
Exhibitions: Ernst Oppler & the Russian Ballet; Annual Members Juried Exhibition
Publications: Bi-monthly newsletter; calendar for members; handouts & catalogues for changing exhibitions
Activities: Classes for adults and children; docent training; artist-in-residence program; lectures open to the public; concerts; gallery talks; tours; competitions with awards; book traveling exhibitions, 6-8 per yr; museum shop sells original art, reproductions, prints, small objects & cards

MIAMI

THE AMERICAN FOUNDATION FOR THE ARTS
For further information, see National and Regional Organizations

M **BAKEHOUSE ART COMPLEX, INC,** 561 NW 32nd St, 33127. Tel 305-576-2828. *Dir* Helene M Pancoast; *Adminr* Donna Wilt Sperow
Open Tues - Fri 10 AM - 4 PM. No admis fee. Estab 1985. Cultural complex with artist studios, galleries & classrooms; main gallery: 3200 sq ft, 16' ceilings, track lighting; Swenson Gallery: 800 sq ft, carpeted floor. Average Annual Attendance: 8000. Mem: 200; dues donor $500, supporter $100, family $50, friend $35
Income: $135,000 (financed through mem, studio rents, grants & contributions)
Exhibitions: Art from Andrew: Holiday Exhibition: 1993 - 6th Anniversary; Women's Caucus for Art; Three Person Award Exhibition; 4th Annual Membership Exhibition
Activities: Classes for adults & children; lect open to public, 6 - 8 vis lectr per year; competitions; scholarships & fels; retail store sells original art

M **CENTER FOR THE FINE ARTS,** 101 W Flagler St, 33130. Tel 305-375-3000, 375-1700; FAX 305-375-1725. *Dir* Mark Ormond; *Asst Dir* Brenda Williamson; *Registrar* Arlene Dellis; *Development* Emeilo Alonso-Mendoza; *Mem & Volunteer Coordr* Roanne Katcher
Open Tues - Sat 10 AM - 5 PM, Thurs 10 AM - 9 PM, Sun noon - 5 PM, cl Mon. Admis adults $3, children $2, groups $2.50 (20 or more). Estab 1984 to originate & receive major traveling art exhibitions. 16,000 sq ft of gallery space on two levels; 3300 sq ft sculpture court; 1800 sq ft auditorium. Average Annual Attendance: 15,000. Mem: 6800; dues $35
Exhibitions: Elisa Armany Sculputre; Rodin Bronzes from B Geraco Canter Collections; Hans Hoffman; Edward Manchmaster Prints from the Epstein Collection; Fact & Fiction:State of Florida Photography; Joel Shapiro; Goya's Los Caprichos; Jasper Johns; Landscape in 20th Century American Art, selections from the Metropolitan Museum of Art
Publications: CFA News, quarterly; exhibit brochures, quarterly
Activities: Docent programs; films; concerts; dance performances; lect open to public, 12 vis lectr per yr; book traveling exhibitions, 10 per yr; originate traveling exhibitions; museum shop sells books, reproductions, prints, jewelry, art-greeting cards, posters

M **FLORIDA INTERNATIONAL UNIVERSITY,** The Art Museum at FIU, University Park, PC 112, 33199. Tel 305-348-2890; FAX 305-348-2762. *Dir* Dahlia Morgan; *Coordr Univ Colls* Regina C Bailey
Open Mon 10 AM - 9 PM, Tues - Fri 10 AM - 5 PM, Sat noon - 4 PM. No admis fee. Estab 1977. 4000 sq ft of flexible exhibition space in the main administration building. Average Annual Attendance: 50,000. Mem: 50; dues $250 & up
Income: Financed by state appropriation & supported by FIU Student Government Assn
Collections: The Metropolitan Collection
Exhibitions: (1990) New Acquisition: The Metropolitan Collection; Of Time & the City: American Modernism from the Sheldon Memorial Art Gallery; American Art Today: The City
Publications: Exhibition catalogs
Activities: Dade County Public Schools Museum Education Program; lectopen to the public, 4 vis lectrs per yr; gallery talks; tours; competitions; awards; book traveling exhibitions; originate traveling exhibitions that circulate to Florida Atlantic University

M **METRO-DADE CENTER,** Center for the Fine Arts, 101 W Flagler St, 33130. Tel 305-375-1700, 375-3000 (business office). *Dir* Mark Ormond; *Cur Exhib* Louis Grachos
Open Tues - Sat 10 AM - 5 PM, Thurs evening until 9 PM, Sun noon - 5 PM. Admis $5, Tues is contribution day. Estab 1984 as a county facility to host major traveling exhibitions of art. 34,000 sq ft including 16,000 sq ft of gallery space on two levels, 3300 sq ft sculpture court, 1800 sq ft auditorium & 637 sq ft book store
Exhibitions: Twelve new exhibitions each year. (1992) Treasures of Faberge; Three Centuries of French Paintings; Miami Architecture in the Tropics; Interrogating Identity; Out of the Ordinary; Max Beckmann (1993) Masterworks of American Impressionism

M **MIAMI-DADE COMMUNITY COLLEGE,** Kendal Campus, Art Gallery, 11011 SW 104th St, 33176-3393. Tel 305-237-2322, 237-2281; FAX 305-237-2658. *Dir & Cur* Robert J Sindelir; *Asst to Dir* Lilia M Fontana
Open Mon, Thurs & Fri 8 AM - 4 PM, Tues - Wed 12 - 7:30 PM. No admis fee. Estab 1970 as a teaching laboratory and public service
Income: Financed by state appropriation
Purchases: $250,000
Collections: Contemporary American paintings, photographs, prints, sculpture includes: Beal, Boice, Bolotowsky, Christo, Ferrer, Fine, Gibson, Henry, Hepworth, Hockney, Judd, Komar, Lichtenstein, Marisol, Melamid, Michals, Motherwell, Nesbitt, Oldenburg, Parker & Pearlstein
Exhibitions: Tom Doyle; Max Cole; Ed McGowin; Lynn Gelfman; Vito Acconci; Marilyn Pappas; Tom Balbo; Phillip Tsiaras; Jene Highstein; Jim Jacobs; Robert Peterson
Publications: 6 catalogs per yr
Activities: Lectures open to public, 4 - 6 vis lectrs per year; gallery talks; individual paintings and original objects of art lent; lending collection contains original art works, original prints, paintings, photographs, sculpture; traveling exhibitions organized and circulated

M **MIAMI-DADE COMMUNITY COLLEGE, WOLFSON CAMPUS,** Frances Wolfson Art Gallery, 300 NE Second Ave, Fifth Floor, 33132. Tel 305-237-3278; FAX 305-237-3645. *Gallery Dir* Kate Rawlinson; *Dir Cultural Affairs* Olga Garay; *Academic & Community Liaison* Joanne Butcher
No admis fee. Gallery estab 1976 to exhibit contemporary art for students & community. Atrium/lobby space; 2000 sq ft & 157 linear ft; two smaller secured galleries. Average Annual Attendance: 3000
Income: $230,000, as part of Wolfson Campus Galleries (financed by endowment, annual grants & state appropriation)
Collections: †Wolfson Campus Collection - all media & subjects
Exhibitions: Second Time Around: Photo Exhibit; Transforms: Mixed-Media Student Exhibit; Glen Gentele: The Genetic Trail, sculptures
Activities: Educational packets; workshops; symposia; lect open to public, 12 vis lectr per year

M **InterAmerican Art Gallery,** 627 SW 27th Ave, No 3104 (Mailing add: c/o Centre Gallery, 300 NE Second Ave, 33132). Tel 305-237-3278; FAX 305-237-3645. *Gallery Dir* Kate Rawlinson; *Dir Cultural Affairs* Olga Garay; *Academic & Community Liaison* Joanne Butcher
No admis fee. Gallery estab 1986 to exhibit contemporary art for students & community. Large main gallery, small side gallery, secured space; 1214 sq ft & 136 linear ft. Average Annual Attendance: 2000
Income: $230,000, as part of Wolfson Campus Galleries (financed by endowment, annual grants & state appropriation)
Exhibitions: Barbara Strassen: Primordial Present, paintings & installation
Activities: Educational packets; workshops; symposia

M **Centre Gallery,** 300 NE Second Ave, No 1365, 33132. Tel 305-237-3278; FAX 305-237-3645. *Gallery Dir* Kate Rawlinson; *Dir Cultural Affairs* Olga Garay; *Academic & Community Liaison* Joanne Butcher
No admis fee. Gallery estab 1990 to exhibit contemporary art for students & community. Secured space with alarm system, no windows; 2500 sq ft & 200 linear ft. Average Annual Attendance: 4000
Income: $230,000, as part of Wolfson Campus Galleries (financed by endowment, annual grants & state appropriation)
Collections: †Wolfson Campus Collection - all media & subjects
Exhibitions: Sevilla: New Crossings; Gloria Luria Gallery Years; Afrika: Sergei Bugaev; Alvin Lucier: Sound Installation
Publications: Exhibition catalogs
Activities: Educational packets; workshops; symposia; lect open to public, 12 vis lectr per year; book traveling exhibitions 2 per year; originate traveling exhibitions 1 per year

L **MIAMI-DADE PUBLIC LIBRARY,** 101 W Flagler St, 33130. Tel 305-375-2665. *Dir* Ronald S Kozlowski; *Asst Dir* Mary Somerville; *Asst Dir* Raymond Santiago; *Asst Dir & Media Relations* William Urbizu; *Technical Serv Adminr* Susan Mead-Donaldson; *Supv Branches* Harriet Schwanke; *Supv Branches* Sharon Bart; *Art Servs Librn* Barbara Young; *Artmobile Librn* Thomas Jenks; *Youth Serv Adminr* Sylvia Mavrogenes
Open Mon - Wed & Fri - Sat 9 AM - 6 PM, Thurs 9 AM - 9 PM, Sun (Oct - May) 1 - 5 PM. No admis fee. Estab 1947 to provide the informational, educational and recreational needs of the community. Gallery maintained, Artmobile maintained
Income: Financed by special millage
Library Holdings: Per subs 140; Micro — Fiche, reels; AV — Cassettes 2000, motion pictures 5500, rec 4000, v-tapes 6000; Other — Clipping files, exhibition catalogs, framed reproductions 800, original art works 1200, pamphlets, photographs, prints, reproductions
Special Subjects: Afro-American Art, Latin American Art
Collections: African American original graphics; Latin American original graphics; Oriental collection of original graphics
Exhibitions: (1991) Vassily Gladkow: Landscape Drawings from Soviet Union; Miami Thriving in Change (1940 - 1990): 50 Years of Collection. (1992) Still Life a Visual Feast. (1993) The International Art of Printing: Ediciones Poligrafa, 1964 - 1993
Publications: Exhibition catalogs
Activities: Lectures open to public; concerts; gallery talks; tours; exten dept; artmobile; reproductions lent; book traveling exhibitions, 1-2 per year; originate traveling exhibitions, permanent collection of works on paper

NATIONAL FOUNDATION FOR ADVANCEMENT IN THE ARTS
For further information, see National and Regional Organizations

M **VIZCAYA MUSEUM AND GARDENS,** 3251 S Miami Ave, 33129. Tel 305-579-4626; FAX 305-285-2004. *Chief Cur* Doris B Littlefield; *Cur* Michele A McDonald; *Chief Conservator* Emilio Cianfoni
Open daily 9:30 AM - 5 PM, cl Christmas. Admis house and gardens $5, group, senior citizens, children $3.50. Estab 1952 to increase the general public's appreciation of the European decorative arts, architecture and landscape design through lectures and tours conducted by trained volunteer guides. Vizcaya is a house museum with a major collection of European decorative arts and elaborate formal gardens. The Villa, formerly the home of James Deering, was completed in 1916 and contains approximately 70 rooms. Upper Gallery, changing special exhibitions. Average Annual Attendance: 225,000. Mem: 1500; dues $35 and up; annual meeting third Wed in April
Income: $1,039,725 (financed by admission fees)
Collections: Italian and French Furniture of the 16th - 18th and Early 19th Centuries; Notable Specialized Collections of Carpets, Tapestries, Roman Antiques and Bronze Mortars
Exhibitions: Four - six changing annually
Publications: Vizcayan Newsletter, quarterly
Activities: Classes for children; docent training; lectures open to the public; concerts; tours; individual paintings and original objects of art lent to accredited museums; museum shop sells books, magazines, original art, reproductions, prints and slides

L **Library,** 3251 S Miami Ave, 33129. Tel 305-579-2708, Ext 242. *Vol Librn* Don Gayer
Open to museums volunteers and students of the decorative arts for reference only
Income: Financed by donations
Library Holdings: Vols 4000; Per subs 8; archival material; AV — Cassettes, Kodachromes, slides; Other — Exhibition catalogs, memorabilia, photographs
Special Subjects: Decorative Arts, Furniture, Interior Design
Collections: Slide collection for reference and teaching

MIAMI BEACH

M **BASS MUSEUM OF ART,** 2121 Park Ave, 33139. Tel 305-673-7530; FAX 305-673-7062. *Dir* Diane W Camber
Open Tues - Sat 10 AM - 5 PM, Sun 1 - 5 PM. Admis adults $5, students $4, donations on Tues. Estab 1964 for the collection & exhibition of works of art. Collection features European art, architectural drawings & contemporary art. The museum is a two-story 1930 art deco structure. Average Annual Attendance: 100,000
Income: $1,150,000 (financed by city, mem & grants from state, county & federal government)
Collections: Permanent collection of European textiles, Old Master paintings, Baroque sculpture, Oriental art, ecclesiastical artifacts, 19th & 20th century graphics, paintings & architectural drawings & arts
Exhibitions: (1991 - 92) Designing for the Theatre: Selections from the RLB Tobin Collection; The Drawings of Federico Garcia Lorca; The Palaces of St Petersburg; Santos de Palo: The Household Saints of Puerto Rico; Saints & Madonnas from the Bass Collection; Between Worlds: Contemporary Mexican Photography. (1992) Encuentro by Regina Silveira; Five Centuries of European

Portraits; Twentieth Century American Portrait Photography; Eye for I: Video Self-Portraits; Photos de Notre Jumelage; The Normandie: Floating Art Deco Palace; From Media to Metaphor: Art About AIDS; Russian Painting 1900 - 1940 from the State Russian Museum; Photostroika: New Photography from the Soviet Union & Baltic Republics
Publications: Quarterly magazine; exhibition catalogues; permanent collection catalogue
Activities: Lectures open to public; concerts; films; individual and original objects of art lent to other museums; originate traveling exhibitions; sales shop selling cards, jewelry & objects of fine design

L **MIAMI DADE PUBLIC LIBRARY,** Miami Beach Branch, 2100 Collins Ave, 33139. Tel 305-535-4219. *Chief Librn* Susan Stringfield
Open Mon & Wed 10 AM - 8 PM, Tues & Thurs - Sat 10 AM - 5:30 PM. Estab 1927 to serve the citizens of Miami Beach. Circ 350,000
Income: $850,000 (financed by city appropriation)
Purchases: $125,000
Library Holdings: Vols 70,000; Per subs 250; Micro — Reels; AV — A-tapes, motion pictures, rec, v-tapes; Other — Clipping files, pamphlets

A **WOLFSONIAN FOUNDATION,** 1001 Washington Ave, 33139. Tel 305-531-1001; FAX 305-531-2133. *Dir* Peggy A Loar; *Assoc Dir* James J Kamm; *Head Librn* James Findlay; *Head Register* Christine Giles
Estab 1986
Income: Financed by private foundation
Collections: †Architecture & Design Arts; †Decorative & Propaganda Arts (pertaining to period 1885-1945); †Fine Arts; †Rare & Reference Library

NAPLES

M **NAPLES ART GALLERY,** 275 Broad Ave S, 33940. Tel 813-262-4551. *Pres* William B Spink; *VPres & Treas* Warren C Nelson
Open Mon - Sat 9.30 AM - 5 PM. No admis fee. Estab 1965 to present works of prominent American artists for display in home or office. Contains foyer with fountain & four additional gallery rooms & sculpture garden; 4600 sq ft of gallery space. Average Annual Attendance: 10,000-15,000
Income: $1,000,000 (financed by sales)
Exhibitions: One or two-person shows
Publications: Exhibit brochures

NORTH MIAMI

M **NORTH MIAMI CENTER OF CONTEMPORARY ART,** 12340 NE Eighth Ave, 33161. Tel 305-893-6211. *Dir* Lou Anne Colodny
Open Mon - Fri 10 AM - 4 PM, Sat 1 - 4 PM. No admis fee. Estab 1981 to feature Florida artists. Average Annual Attendance: 10,000. Mem: 500; dues $20-$150
Income: Financed by mem, city appropriation, private donations, corporations foundations
Exhibitions: (1992) Florida Fellowships; Book, Box, Word; Primitives: A State of Mind; High Heeled Art; Rethinking Sculpture; changing exhibits of multi media & large scale installations
Publications: Catalogs; newsletter, semi-annually
Activities: Docent programs; film videos; lect open to public; originate traveling exhibitions & performances

NORTH MIAMI BEACH

M **SAINT BERNARD FOUNDATION AND MONASTERY,** 16711 W Dixie Hwy, 33160. Tel 305-945-1462. *Exec Dir* Barbara Bambrick
Open Mon - Sat 10 AM - 5 PM, Sun noon - 5 PM. Admis adults $4, sr citizens $2.50, children 7-12 $1, under 6 free. A reconstruction of a monastery built in Segovia, Spain, in 1141, with original stones brought to the United States by William Randolph Hearst
Income: Financed by members & donations of visitors
Collections: Historic and Religious Material; paintings; sculpture
Activities: Tours; arts festivals; sales shop sells books, slides & religious objects

OCALA

M **CENTRAL FLORIDA COMMUNITY COLLEGE ART COLLECTION,** 3001 SW College Rd, PO Box 1388, 32678. Tel 904-237-2111; FAX 904-237-0510. *Pres* William Campion
Open Mon - Fri 8 AM - 4:30 PM. No admis fee. Estab 1962 as a service to the community. Gallery is the lobby to the auditorium. Average Annual Attendance: 5000
Income: Financed by state appropriations
Collections: Contemporary Artists of Varies Media; CFCC Foundation Permanent Collection
Exhibitions: Student Art Exhibitions
Activities: Classes for adults; scholarships

M **FLORIDA STATE UNIVERSITY FOUNDATION - CENTRAL FLORIDA COMMUNITY COLLEGE FOUNDATION,** The Appleton Museum of Art, 4333 E Silver Springs Blvd, 34470-5000. Tel 904-236-5050; FAX 904-236-5056. *Dir* Sandra Talarico; *Registrar* Brenda McNeal; *Facilities Dir* Russell Days; *Cur Museum Educ* Edgar H H Mathews IV
Open Tues - Sat 10 AM - 4:30 PM, Sun 1 - 5 PM. Admis adults $3, studens with ID $2, children under 18 free. Estab 1987 to provide cultural & educational programs. Fine arts collection including European, Pre-Columbian, African, Asian & decorative arts. Average Annual Attendance: 60,000. Mem: 2500; dues $10 - $500
Income: $1,000,000 (financed by endowment, mem & city appropriation)
Purchases: $2700

Collections: †Arthur I Appleton Collection; †Appleton Museum of Art Collection
Exhibitions: Divine Light: The Art of the Russian Icon; Art Deco Sculpture; European & American Glass from the 18th and early 19th centuries; Tiffany Lamps
Publications: Museum catalog; Newletter, quarterly
Activities: Educ dept; classes for adults & children; docent training; lect open to public, 10 vis lectr per year; concerts; gallery talks; tours; individual paintings & original objects of art lent to other institutions; lending collection contains books, photographs & slides; book traveling exhibitions, 8 - 10 per year; originate traveling exhibitions to state institutions; museum shop sells books, original art, reproductions, posters & jewelry

ORLANDO

A **ORLANDO MUSEUM OF ART,** 2416 N Mills Ave, 32803. Tel 407-896-4231. *Dir* Marena Grant Morrisey
Open Tues - Sat 9 AM - 5 PM, Sun noon - 5 PM, cl Mon. Admis donation required, suggested adult $4, children 4 - 11 $2, members & children under 4 free. Estab 1924 to encourage the awareness of and participation in the visual arts. Accredited by the American Association of Museums. Seven galleries including exhibitions of 19th & 20th Century American Art, Pre-Columbian and African Art. Average Annual Attendance: 100,000. Mem: 2250; dues $30 & up; annual meeting in Sept
Income: Financed by membership, United Arts of Central Florida, Inc., State of Florida
Collections: †19th & 20th Century American painting, sculpture, prints & photography; †Pre-Columbian from Central & South America; African Art
Publications: Members Magazine, 2 times per year; mem newsletter, 6 times per year; exhibition catalogues
Activities: Classes for children; docent training; lect open to public, 4 - 6 vis lectr per year; concerts; gallery talks; tours; competitions; exten dept serving central Florida; individual prints lent to museums; book traveling exhibitions; originate traveling exhibitions; museum shop sells books, magazines, reproductions & art exhibit & art related merchandise

L **Art Library,** 2416 N Mills Ave, 32803. Tel 407-896-4231. *Executive Dir* Marena Grant Morrisey
Library Holdings: Vols 3200; Per subs 10; Other — Clipping files, exhibition catalogs, pamphlets
Special Subjects: Aesthetics, Afro-American Art, American Western Art, Art Education, Art History, Ceramics, Decorative Arts, Furniture, Glass, History of Art & Archaeology, Landscape Architecture, Mexican Art, Painting - American, Prints, Sculpture

A **PINE CASTLE FOLK ART CENTER,** 6015 Randolph St, 32809. Tel 407-855-7461. *Pres* Doris Hunt; *Dir* Diane Sarchet
Open 9 AM - 5 PM. No Admis fee, tours $3. Estab 1965 as a non-profit community cultural center which provides programs in visual arts, folk crafts, local history, music and drama, and sponsors special projects for handicapped and senior citizens. One room 15 x 15 ft in main building; 85 yr old cracker farm house. Average Annual Attendance: 25,000. Mem: Annual meeting in March
Income: Financed by membership, private foundation, state grants & United Arts Fund
Collections: Oral histories of area Old-timers, along with photographs, memorabilia and antiques
Exhibitions: Members' Exhibition
Publications: Pioneer Days Annual Historical Magazine; quarterly newsletter
Activities: Classes for adults and children; dramatic programs; lect open to the public, 2 vis lectr per yr; Folk Art Events; concerts

M **VALENCIA COMMUNITY COLLEGE,** Art Gallery-East Campus, 701 N Econlockhatchee Trail, PO Box 32802, 32802. Tel 407-299-5000, Ext 2298. *Chmn* Qurenzia Throm; *Pres* Paul Gianini
Open Mon - Fri 12:30 - 4:30 PM. No admis fee. Estab 1982
Income: Financed by state appropriation, grants & private donations
Purchases: $750
Collections: †Permanent collection: Mixed Media; Small Works: Mixed Media
Exhibitions: Forceful Gesture by Mimi Smith; Small Works competition
Activities: Individual paintings & original objects of art lent; lending collection contains 250 items; originate traveling exhibitions 2 per year

ORMOND BEACH

M **ORMOND MEMORIAL ART MUSEUM AND GARDENS,** 78 E Granada Blvd, 32176. Tel 904-677-1857. *Cur* Leslie Scheiblberg
Open Tues - Fri 11 AM - 4 PM, Sat & Sun noon - 4 PM, cl Mon & month of Aug. No admis fee. Estab 1946 to house the symbolic oil paintings of Malcolm Fraser. Four connecting rooms; rear gallery opens with French doors onto wooden patio deck with a gazebo; lattice work windows. Average Annual Attendance: 6000-8000. Mem: 350; dues $15, $20, $25, $50, $100 & $500; monthly meetings & annual meeting in Jan
Income: $32,000 (financed by endowment, membership & city appropriation)
Collections: Malcolm Fraser Symbolic Paintings - permanent collection; Catherine Combs lusterware
Exhibitions: Paintings, photography, crafts, sculpture & multi-media exhibits
Activities: Classes for adults & children; lect open to the public; workshops & children's events; private tours available; gallery tours

M **TOMOKA STATE PARK MUSEUM,** Fred Dana Marsh Museum, 2099 N Beach St, 32174. Tel 904-676-4045; FAX 904-676-4060. *Coordr* William C Egan
Open Sun - Sat 9:30 AM - 4:30 PM. No admis. Estab 1967
Income: Financed by state appropriation
Collections: Fred Dana Marsh Art Collection; Tomoka Basin Geology; Tomoka Basin Indian Artifacts
Exhibitions: Florida geology; Florida history; Indian artifacts; wildlife
Publications: Richard Oswald: Tomoka State Park's Hero of the Revolution, brochure; The Legend of Tomokie, brochure
Activities: Tours

PALM BEACH

M HENRY MORRISON FLAGLER MUSEUM, Whitehall Mansion, Cocoanut Row, P0 Box 969, 33480. Tel 407-655-2833; FAX 407-655-2826. *Dir* Charles B Simmons
Open Tues - Sat 10 AM - 5 PM, Sun noon - 5 PM, cl Mon. Admis adults $3.50, children 6 - 12 $1.25, under 6 free. Estab 1960 for preservation and interpretation of the Whitehall mansion, the 1901 residence built for Standard Oil partner and pioneer developer of Florida's east coast, Henry Morrison Flagler. Fifty-five room historic house with restored rooms and special collections, special events & exhibitions. Average Annual Attendance: 130,000. Mem: 1700; dues $35 - $1000; annual meeting Fri preceding first Sat in Feb
Income: Financed by endowment, membership and admissions
Collections: †Original family furnishings, †china, †costumes; †furniture; †glassware; †paintings and †silver
Exhibitions: Various temporary exhibits
Publications: The Henry Morrison Flagler Museum booklet; Members' Newsletter, bimonthly
Activities: Guide training; lectures open to public; gallery talks; concerts; tours competitions; museum sells books & postcards contains gift shop

M EDNA HIBEL ART FOUNDATION, Hibel Museum of Art, 150 Royal Poinciana Plaza, PO Box 10607, 33480. Tel 407-833-6870; FAX 407-848-9640. *Dir* Mary Johnson; *Asst Dir* Janet E Tanis; *Pres* Theodore Plotkin; *Exec Trustee* Andy Plotkin, PhD
Open Tues - Sat 10 AM - 5 PM, Sun 1 - 5 PM, cl Mon. No admis fee. Estab 1977 to extend the appreciation of the art of Edna Hibel specifically & visual art in general. 14 galleries and spaces devoted to paintings, litographs, sculpture and porcelain art by artist Edna Hibel, also features antique furniture, snuff botles, paper weights and art book collections. Average Annual Attendance: 20,000. Mem: 10,000; dues $20; meeting Feb & Mar
Income: $80,000 (financed by city appropriation & museum store sales)
Purchases: $80,000
Special Subjects: Art History, Painting - American, Painting - European
Collections: Craig Collection of Edna Hibel's Work; English & Italian 18th century furniture; ancient Chinese snuffbottles; 18th & 19th century paperweights; Japanese dolls; 19th & 20th century library art books; Paintings; Porcelain Art, Lithographs; Serigraphs, Sculpture
Exhibitions: Moscow, Leningrad. (1992) Grenchen, Switzerland
Publications: Edna Hibel Society Newsletter, 3 per year; exhibition catalogs; exhibition posters
Activities: Classes for children; docent training; Lectures open to public, 4 vis lectr per yr; concerts; gallery talks; tours; book traveling exhibitions; originate traveling exhibitions; museum shop sells books and reproductions
L Library, 150 Royal Poinciana Plaza, 33480. Tel 407-833-6870; FAX 407-848-9640. *Dir* Mary Johnson; *Exec Trustee* Andy Plotkin, PhD; *Asst Dir & Dir Educ* Janet Tanis
Open Tues - Sat 10 AM - 5 PM, Sun 1 - 5 PM. No admis fee. For reference only. Average Annual Attendance: 25,000
Purchases: $300
Library Holdings: Vols 400; AV — A-tapes, cassettes, fs, motion pictures, slides, v-tapes; Other — Clipping files, exhibition catalogs, framed reproductions, memorabilia, original art works, pamphlets, photographs, prints, reproductions, sculpture
Special Subjects: Antique art books on European & Oriental art; Stone lithography
Exhibitions: Annual Festival of Animals. (1992) Peace through Wisdom: The Year of Europe, Grenchen Art Museum, Switzerland
Activities: Classes for adults & children; docent training; lect open to public, 2 vis lectr per year; lect to school classes & cultural activities for elementary school children; museum shop sells books, reproductions, collectable art plates, gift boxes, jewelry, posters

A THE SOCIETY OF THE FOUR ARTS, 4 Arts Plaza, 33480. Tel 407-655-7226; FAX 407-655-7233. *Pres* F Eugene Dixon Jr; *VPres* Mrs James A dePeyster; *VPres* Wiley R Reynolds; *VPres* Mrs Robert A Magowan; *VPres* Hollis M Baker; *Dir* Robert W Safrin; *Deputy Dir* Nancy Mato; *Treas* Henry P McIntosh IV; *Secy* William S Gubelmann
Open Dec to mid-April Mon - Sat 10 AM - 5 PM, Sun 2 - 5 PM. Admis to exhibition galleries free; $3 donation suggested. Estab 1936 to encourage an appreciation of the arts by presentation of exhibitions, lectures, concerts, films and programs for young people and the maintenance of a fine library and gardens. Five galleries for exhibitions, separate general library, gardens and auditorium. Average Annual Attendance: 72,000 (galleries and library). Mem: 1500; duea life $10,000, sustaining $450; annual meeting third Fri in March
Income: Financed by endowment, membership, city appropriation toward maintenance of library and contributions
Exhibitions: 52nd Annual National Exhibition of Contemporary American Paintings; Portraits & Prospects, British & Irish watercolors & drawings from the collection of the Ulster Museum Belfast; Andre Ostier: Masques et Bergam as ques; For the Table: Masterworks in silver from the Chrysler Museum Lace thru the Centuries; Of Time & the City: American Modernism from the Sheldon Memorial Art Gallery
Publications: Calendar; schedule of events, annual
Activities: Programs for young people; lectures open to the public when space permits, otherwise limited to members, 13 vis lectr per year; concerts; films; competitions open to artists resident in United States; juror selects about 70 paintings for inclusion in annual exhibition
L Library, 4 Arts Plaza, 33480. Tel 407-655-2766; FAX 407-655-7233. *Librn* Joanne Rendou
Open Mon - Fri 10 AM - 5 PM, cl Sat May to Nov. Estab 1936. Circ 38,000
Income: Financed by endowment, membership and city appropriation
Library Holdings: Vols 35,000; Per subs 75
Collections: Addison Mizner Collection which consists of over 300 reference books and scrapbooks in Mizner's personal library
Publications: Booklist, semi annual
Activities: Library tours

PANAMA CITY

M VISUAL ARTS CENTER OF NORTHWEST FLORIDA, 19 E Fourth St, 32401. Tel 904-769-4451. *Exec Dir* Mary Bradshaw Jeanes; *Asst Dir* Cheryl Amato
Open Tues - Sat 9 AM - 4 PM, Thurs 9 AM - 8 PM, Sun 1 - 4 PM. No admis fee. The Center occupies the old city hall, jail & fire station on the corner of Fourth St & Harrison Ave in downtown Panama City. Main gallery hosts contemporary artists, juried competitions & museum coordinated collections. The lower galleries feature emerging artists & community sponsored competitions & collections. Average Annual Attendance: 9000. Mem: 390; individual $25, student $10
Income: $95,000 (financed by mem, grants & corporate sponsors)
Collections: †Permanent collection contains works of artists from Northwest Florida
Exhibitions: Exhibits change approx every 6 weeks
Publications: Images, newsletter, every 6 weeks
Activities: Classes for adults & children; docent programs; lect open to public, 3 vis lectr per year; book traveling exhibitions 2 per year
L Visual Arts Center Library, 19 E Fourth St, 32401
For reference & limited lending
Library Holdings: Vols 200; AV — V-tapes

PEMBROKE PINES

M BROWARD COMMUNITY COLLEGE - SOUTH CAMPUS, Art Gallery, 7200 Hollywood Blvd, 33024. Tel 305-963-8895, 963-8969; FAX 305-963-8802. *Gallery Dir* Kyra Belan
Open Mon - Fri 10 AM - 3 PM. No admis fee. Estab 1991 to offer contemporary art exhibitions & cultural enrichment activities to college students & to the surrounding community. Gallery is 31 ft x 31 ft with a glass wall & high ceilings
Income: Financed by grants
Exhibitions: Studio Art Club Annual Juried Exhibition. (1992) Carol Cornelison: Mixed Media; Jean-Claude Rigaud: Sculpture & Paintings; Amalia Padilla-Gregg: Paintings; Elena Presser: Works on Paper
Activities: Lect open to public, 6 vis lectr per year; competitions

PENSACOLA

A HISTORIC PENSACOLA PRESERVATION BOARD, Historic Pensacola Village, 120 Church St, Suite A, 32501. Tel 904-444-8905; FAX 904-444-8641. *Dir* John P Daniels; *Museum Adminr* Tom Muir
Open Mon - Fri 8 AM - 4:30 PM, Sat 10 AM - 4:30 PM, cl New Years, Thanksgiving, Christmas. No admis fee. Estab 1967 for collection, preservation, and interpretation of artifacts dealing with the history and culture of Pensacola and West Florida. Multi-building complex includes 2 museums & 3 historic houses; main gallery includes history of development of West Florida as well as area for temporary exhibits. Average Annual Attendance: 45,000
Income: $500,000 (financed by city, county, and state appropriations, sales and rentals)
Collections: Costumes; decorative arts; Early 19th & 20th century local artists; Archives; Marine lumbering & farming tools & equipment
Activities: Educ dept; docent training; sales shop selling books, reproductions and local crafts
L Library, 120 Church St, Suite A, 32501. Tel 904-444-8905; FAX 904-444-8641. *Museum Adminr* Tom Muir
Open to the public for reference
Library Holdings: Vols 800; Per subs 15; AV — Slides; Other — Photographs
Special Subjects: Architecture, Decorative Arts, Historical Material, Regional history

M PENSACOLA JUNIOR COLLEGE, Visual Arts Gallery, 1000 College Blvd, 32504. Tel 904-484-1000; FAX 904-484-1826. *Dir* Allan Peterson; *Secy* Betty Larson
Open Mon - Thurs 8 AM - 9 PM, Fri 8 AM - 3:30 PM, cl weekends. No admis fee. Average Annual Attendance: 20,000
Income: Financed by state appropriation
Collections: †Contemporary ceramics, †glass, †drawings, †paintings, †prints, †photographs, †sculpture
Exhibitions: The Glassmaker: Historic and Contemporary; Pensacola National Crafts Exhibition; Pensacola National Printmaking Exhibition; Pensacola National Watermedia Exhibition; New Orleans Sculpture Invitational; Realism: A Close Look; Kim Irwin & Lisa Williamson-Fabric Collage; Texas Sculpture Invitational; Pensacola National Portrait Exhibition; Robert Fichter photography; Pensacola National Calligraphy Exhibition; Pensacola National Landscape Exhibition
Publications: Catalog, brochure or poster for each exhibition
Activities: Lect open to the public, 3 - 6 vis lectr per yr; workshops; gallery talks; competitions with awards given; scholarships offered for second year students; individual paintings and original objects of art lent to other museums and lending collection contains original art works; traveling exhibitions organized and circulated

M PENSACOLA MUSEUM OF ART, 407 S Jefferson St, 32501. Tel 904-432-6247. *Dir* Dr Carol Malt; *Admin Asst* Sandra Gentry
Open Tues - Fri 10 AM - 5 PM, Sat 10 AM - 4 PM, cl Sun & Mon. No admis fee. Estab 1954 to further and disseminate art history and some studio instruction with regard to the general public and to increase knowledge and appreciation thereof. Museum is a historical building, old city jail built in 1908, and has 13,000 sq ft of exhibition area. Average Annual Attendance: 32,000. Mem: 1000; dues $20 & up; annual meeting in Oct
Income: Financed by membership
Collections: Contemporary art
Exhibitions: Changing loan exhibitions
Publications: Monthly newsletter
Activities: Studio classes for children; docent training; art history lect open to public; film series; book traveling exhibitions; originate traveling exhibitions

L **Harry Thornton Library,** 407 S Jefferson St, 32501. Tel 904-432-6247. *Dir* Dr Carol Malt
Open Tues - Sat 10 AM - 5 PM, Sat 10 AM - 4 PM. Estab 1968 to provide reference material for public and members
Income: Financed by membership, city appropriation and grants by state and federal government
Purchases: $250
Library Holdings: Vols 300; Per subs 10; Other — Exhibition catalogs
Collections: Complete set of E Benezit's Dictionaire des Peintres, Sculpteurs, Dessinateurs et Graveurs; Encyclopedia of World Art and other art references books
Publications: Exhibitions catalogs; newsletter, 10 per year
Activities: Lect open to public, 5 visiting lectr per year; films; concerts; tours; competitions; purchase and category awards; fels

M **UNIVERSITY OF WEST FLORIDA,** Art Gallery, 11000 University Parkway, 32514. Tel 904-474-2696. *Dir* Duncan E Stewart; *Asst Dir* E George Norris
Open Tues - Thurs 10 AM - 5 PM; Fri - Sat 10 AM - 1 PM; cl Sun. No admis fee. Estab 1970 to hold exhibitions which will relate to our role as a senior level university. Galleries include a foyer gallery 10 x 40 ft & a main gallery of 1500 sq ft. It is fully air-conditioned & has carpeted walls with full facilities for construction & display. Average Annual Attendance: 4500
Income: Financed by state appropriation
Collections: Photographs and prints by a number of traditional and contemporary artists
Activities: Lectures open to public, 3 vis lectr per year; gallery talks; tours; competitions with awards; films; scholarships offered; individual paintings & original objects of art lent to univ offices; book traveling exhibitions
L **Library,** 11000 University Parkway, 32514-5750. Tel 904-474-2213; FAX 904-474-3338. *Dir Special Collections* Dean DeBolt
Estab 1967
Income: Financed by state appropriations & Friends of the Library
Library Holdings: Vols 8345; Per subs 176; AV — Fs; Other — Memorabilia
Special Subjects: George Washington Sully, Watercolor sketches, Mardi Gras Float Designs

M **T T WENTWORTH JR MUSEUM,** Florida State Museum, 330 S Jefferson, 32501. Tel 904-444-8586, 444-8905; FAX 904-444-8641. *Cur* Tom Muir; *Deputy Dir & Secy* T W Wentworth
Open Sat - Sun 2 - 6 PM. No admis fee. Estab 1957 to conserve historical items & make them available to the public; art sections to encourage art & exhibit local art work. Mem: Annual meeting Aug
Income: Financed by mem & founder's contributions
Collections: Works of local & some nationally famous artists; Indian artifacts; coins; porcelain
Exhibitions: Special yearly art exhibit of some distinguished local artist

PUNTA GORDA

A **FLORIDA ARTIST GROUP INC,** 25363 Aysen Dr, 33983. Tel 813-743-2542. *Pres* Anne L Atz; *Sr VPres* Margaret E Kelly; *VPres* Marcelle Bear; *Recording Secy* Dorothy C Stewart; *Treas* Susan Stevens
Estab 1949 for the stimulation of finer standards of the creative effort within the state of Florida. Mem: 200, qualification for mem by invitation based on artistic merit; dues $20; annual meeting April or May
Income: $4700 (financed by membership and donations)
Exhibitions: Annual juried exhibition
Publications: Newsletter, 3 per year
Activities: Lectures and workshops open to members and public; competitions, one annual competition open to members only; five memorial awards, five corporate awards; originate traveling exhibitions

SAFETY HARBOR

M **SAFETY HARBOR MUSEUM OF REGIONAL HISTORY,** 329 S Bayshore Dr, 34695. Tel 813-726-1668. *Pres* Larry Horn; *VPres* Dean Hollihan; *Treasurer* Mary Pruss; *Historical Preservation Dir* Ruth Pedigo
Open daily 10 AM - 4 PM. Admis adult $1, children $.50. Estab 1977 to promote, encourage, maintain and operate a museum for the preservation of knowledge and appreciation of Florida's history; to display and interpret historical materials and allied fields. Indian art in the form of murals, pottery & artifacts. Average Annual Attendance: 8000. Mem: 60; dues $15 - $500; quarterly meetings
Income: $2000 (financed by membership and donations)
Collections: †Fossils; †dioramas, Heritage Gallery furniture; †Indian artifacts; †natural history exhibits; possessions of Count Philippe: Antiques; Spanish artifacts
Activities: Docent training; lectures open to public, 7 vis lectr per yr; gallery talks; tours; originate traveling exhibitions

SAINT AUGUSTINE

A **HISTORIC SAINT AUGUSTINE PRESERVATION BOARD,** PO Box 1987, 32085. Tel 904-825-5033; FAX 904-825-5096. *Cur* Tracy Spikes; *Exec Dir* Earle W Newton; *Info Officer* Cookie O'Brien
Open daily 9 AM - 5:15 PM, cl Christmas. Admis to six buildings adults $2.50, students $1.25, children under 6 free. Estab 1959 to depict daily life in the 1740's (Spanish) through its living history museum
Collections: Spanish artifacts; fine and decorative arts; restored and reconstructed colonial buildings from the 18th and 19th centuries
Exhibitions: Permanent and temporary exhibitions
Publications: Brochures and booklets

M **LIGHTNER MUSEUM,** 75 King St, Museum-City Hall Complex, PO Box 334, 32085. Tel 904-824-2874. *Exec Dir* Robert W Harper III; *Cur* James McBeth; *Registrar* Irene L Lawrie; *Chief Visitors Services* Helen Ballard
Open 9 AM - 5 PM, cl Christmas. Admis adults $4, students $1, children under 12 free when accompanied by adult. Estab 1948. Average Annual Attendance: 160,000
Income: Financed by admissions
Collections: 19th century material culture & decorative arts
Activities: Classes for adults and children; dramatic programs; docent training; lectures open to public, 4 vis lectr per year; concerts; gallery talks; tours; Individual paintings & original objects of art lent to museums; book traveling exhibitions; originate traveling exhibitions to other museums; museum shop sells books, magazines, reproductions, prints, slides, dolls, jewelry, procelain, games & cards
L **Library,** PO Box 334, 32085-0334. Tel 904-824-2874. *Librn* Open
Library for reference only
Income: Financed by the Museum
Library Holdings: Vols 4600; Per subs 10; Other — Clipping files, exhibition catalogs, memorabilia, original art works, pamphlets, photographs, prints, reproductions, sculpture
Special Subjects: 19th Century Decorative Arts

A **SAINT AUGUSTINE ART ASSOCIATION GALLERY,** 22 Marine St, 32084. Tel 904-824-2310. *Pres* Les Thomas; *VPres* Ken McMillan; *Dir* Kay Burtin
Open Tues - Sat 11 AM - 3 PM, Sun 2 - 5 PM. No admis fee. Estab 1924, inc 1934 as a non-profit organization to further art appreciation in the community by exhibits and instructions, also to provide a gallery where local artists may show their work & public & tourists may see them free.. Gallery is 50 ft x 90 ft with carpeted walls for exhibits. Average Annual Attendance: 8000. Mem: 425; dues $20 and up; annual meeting in Mar
Income: Financed by memberships & development grant
Collections: Donations of art works by St Augustine artists or members representing St Augustine
Exhibitions: Oct to June changing monthly
Activities: Classes for adults & children; docent training; shows with various themes changing every 3 wks; lectures open to public, 3-5 vis lectr per year; gallery talks; tours; competitions with prizes

SAINT AUGUSTINE HISTORICAL SOCIETY
M **Oldest House and Museums,** 14 Saint Frances St, 32084. Tel 904-824-2872. *Dir* Page Edwards; *Vol Coordr* Eddie Joyce Geyer
Open Mon - Fri 9 AM - 5 PM; cl Christmas Day. Admis adults $3.50, students $1.75. Estab 1883 to preserve the Spanish heritage of the United States through exhibits in historic museum with collection of furnishings appropriate to the periods in Saint Augustine history (1565 to date). The Oldest House was acquired in 1918; it is owned and operated by the Saint Augustine Historical Society; it has been designated a National Historic Landmark by the Department of the Interior and is listed in the national register of historic sites and places. Average Annual Attendance: 90,000. Mem: 600; dues $20; annual meeting Jan
Income: Financed by admissions
Collections: Archaeological material recovered from this area, both aboriginal and colonial; period furnishings: Spanish America (1565-1763 & 1783-1821); British (1763-1783); American (1821-present)
Exhibitions: Saint Johns Railway
Publications: El Escribano, annual; East Florida Gazette, quarterly
Activities: Classes for adults and children; docent training; lectures open to the public, 9 vis lectr per yr; original objects of art lent; museum shop sells books, reproductions, prints & slides
L **Library,** 271 Charlotte St, 32084. Tel 904-824-2872. *Library Dir* Jean Trapido Rosenthal; *Ed & Dir Research* Jacqueline Fretwell; *Librn* Sheherzad Navidi
Open Mon - Fri 9 AM - noon and 1 - 5 PM, cl holidays. Research library
Income: Financed by endowment and admissions from Oldest House
Library Holdings: Vols 10,000; Per subs 40; original documents; Micro — Reels; AV — A-tapes, cassettes, Kodachromes, motion pictures, rec, slides; Other — Clipping files, manuscripts, memorabilia, original art works, pamphlets, photographs, prints, reproductions, sculpture
Special Subjects: Anthropology, Archaeology, Architecture, Ceramics, Coins & Medals, Costume Design & Construction, Furniture, Glass, Historical Material, History of Art & Archaeology, Manuscripts, Maps, Painting - American, Painting - Spanish, Period Rooms, Pottery, Religious Art, Restoration & Conservation, Florida history (to 1821) with emphasis on early periods of Saint Augustine history to the present
Collections: Paintings of early artists and of early Saint Augustine; 200 linear feet of maps, photographs, documents and photostats of Spanish Archival Materials as touching directly on Saint Augustine's History during the early Spanish, British and American periods (1565 to present)
Publications: East Florida Gazette, quarterly; El Escribano, annually
Activities: Lect open to public, 9 vis lectr per year

SAINT PETERSBURG

M **MUSEUM OF FINE ARTS, SAINT PETERSBURG, FLORIDA, INC,** 255 Beach Dr NE, 33701. Tel 813-896-2667; FAX 813-894-4638. *Dir* Michael Milkovich; *Asst Dir & Cur Decorative Arts* Cynthia Duval; *Sr Cur of Coll & Exhib* Dr Diana Lesko; *Admin Asst* Bobbye Hoover; *Membership & Coordr* Donna Fletcher; *Coordr Exhib* Carol K Allen; *Registrar* Margarita Laughlin; *Finance Officer* Thomas S Metts; *Museum Shop* Kathy Stover
Open Tues - Sat 10 AM - 5 PM; Sun 1 - 5 PM; cl Mon. Admis by voluntary donation. Estab 1961 to increase and diffuse knowledge and appreciation of art; to collect and preserve objects of artistic interest; to provide facilities for research and to offer popular instruction and opportunities for esthetic enjoyment of art. Twenty galleries of works including American & European painting, drawing, print, sculpture & photographs; Oriental sculpture; decorative arts; pre-Columbian art. Average Annual Attendance: 110,000. Mem: 3200; dues $20 and higher; annual meeting May
Income: $700,000 (financed by endowment, membership, fund raising, city & state grants)

Purchases: $150,000
Collections: †Decorative arts; †drawings; †paintings; †photographs; †prints; †sculpture
Exhibitions: (1992) Rodin Bronzes from the Iris & B Gerald Cantor Foundation; ABC's if Art: An Exhibition of Techniques & Material; 18th, 19th & early 20th century fans: The Elsa James Zelley Collection; African Art from Florida Museums; Walter O Evans Collection of African Art; Access to Art: All Creatures Great & Small; Please Touch: Art from MFA Collection; The Intriguing World of Glass: from two prominent Florida collections; large contemporary prints from MFA collection
Publications: Mosaic, bi-monthly newsletter; Pharos, bi-annual scholarly magazine
Activities: Classes for adults and children; docent training; lect open to public, 3 vis lectr per yr; films; concerts; tours; individual paintings & original objects of art lent to other museums; lending collection contains color reproductions, films on art; originate traveling exhibitions; museum shop sells books, reproductions, prints, museum replicas, jewelry, pottery and crafts by local artisans
L **Art Reference Library,** 255 Beach Dr N, 33701. Tel 813-896-2667; FAX 813-894-4638. *Library Vol* Muriel S Kirk
Open Tues - Fri 10 AM - 5 PM, cl Mon. Estab 1962 as reference library
Income: Financed by grants & contributions
Purchases: $4200
Library Holdings: Vols 9500; Per subs 30; AV — A-tapes, slides 20,000, v-tapes; Other — Exhibition catalogs, reproductions
Special Subjects: American Indian Art, Architecture, Art History, Bronzes, Carpets & Rugs, Ceramics, Folk Art, Glass, Gold, Graphic Design, History of Art & Archaeology, Islamic Art, Painting - European, Painting - Flemish, Painting - French, Painting - German, Stained Glass, Tapestries
Collections: †Photography
Publications: Mosaic, bi-monthly membership bulletin; Pharos, biennial
Activities: Classes for adults and children; lectures open to the public, 6 vis lectr per year; concerts; gallery talks; exten dept serves public schools

M **SALVADOR DALI MUSEUM,** 1000 Third St S, 33701. Tel 813-823-3767, 822-6270; FAX 813-894-6068. *Pres* A Reynolds Morse; *Acting Dir* T Marshall Rousseau; *Vol Coordr* Gwenda Barnitz; *Bookstore Mgr* Kathy White
Open Tues - Sat 10 AM - 5 PM, Sun Noon - 5 PM, cl Mon. Admis $3. Estab 1971 to share the private Dali Collection of Mr and Mrs A Reynolds Morse with the public; formerly in Cleveland, Ohio, the museum re-opened March 7, 1982 in St Petersburg, Fla. Average Annual Attendance: 75,000
Income: Financed by private collector, State University System and donations
Collections: †93 oils and 5 large masterworks by Dali make up a retrospective of his work from 1914 to the present; numerous drawings and watercolors
Exhibitions: Important Dali Statements & Surrealist Documents; Women - Dali's View; Erotic Art by Dali; Homage to Gala; The Secret Life Drawings; Flor Dali; Dali & Halsman Photography; Dali's Surrealist Fruits and Flowers (graphic show); Hiram College Graphic Exhibit; Important Dali Statements & Surrealist Documents; Women - Dali's View; Erotic Art by Dali; Dali and Halsman Photography; Dali Alchemy; Dali Les-Chants-De Maldoror; Alice in Wonderland
Publications: Dali Adventure; Dali - A Panorama of His Art; Dali Draftmanship; Guide to Works by Dali in Public Museums; Introductionto Dali; Dali-Picasso; Poetic Homage to Gala-Dali; Dali Primer; Dali's World of Symbols: Workbook for Children; Dali Newsletter; exhibition catalogues
Activities: Adult classes; docent training; lectures open to public 2, vis lectr per year; film series; gallery talks; tours; museum shop sells books, reproductions, prints, slides, postcards
L **Library,** 1000 Third St S, 33701. Tel 813-823-3767; FAX 813-894-6068. *Librn* Leslie Tabor
Restricted use at present; contains 5000 references to Dali in books, periodicals and newspapers
Income: Financed privately by Salvador Dali Foundation
Purchases: $15,000-$20,000
Library Holdings: Vols 32; Per subs 20; Illustrated editions by Dali; AV — A-tapes, cassettes, Kodachromes 3000, motion pictures 10, slides, v-tapes 50; Other — Clipping files, exhibition catalogs, framed reproductions 1028, manuscripts, memorabilia, original art works 165, pamphlets, photographs, prints 750
Collections: Films and Tapes on or by Dali

SARASOTA

M **FOSTER HARMON GALLERIES OF AMERICAN ART,** 1415 Main St, 34236. Tel 813-955-1002. *Dir* Foster Harmon; *Asst Dir* Donn Roll
Open Mon - Sat 10 AM - 5 PM. No admis fee. Estab 1964 in Naples, 1980 in Sarasota to exhibit major 20th century American artists. Three exhibition galleries; vault storage room; shipping room. Average Annual Attendance: 40,000
Exhibitions: 22 exhibitions per yr; Annual Major Florida Artists Show
Activities: Lectures; competitions; scholarships offered; individual paintings lent to museums; book traveling exhibitions; originate traveling exhibitions; sales shop sells original art & prints
L **Library,** 1415 Main St, 34236. Tel 813-955-1002. *Dir* Foster Harmon; *Asst Dir* Donn Roll
Open Mon - Sat 10 AM - 5 PM. Estab 1980 for gallery & public reference
Library Holdings: Vols 1000; AV — Kodachromes, v-tapes; Other — Clipping files, exhibition catalogs, original art works, pamphlets, photographs, prints, sculpture
Exhibitions: Twenty-five exhibitions scheduled per year

L **RINGLING SCHOOL OF ART & DESIGN LIBRARY,** 2700 N Tamiami Trail, 34234. Tel 813-359-7584; FAX 813-359-7517. *Library Dir* Open ; *AV Librn* Allen Novak; *Library Technician* Patti Roberts
Open Mon - Thurs 8 AM - 10 PM, Fri 8 AM - 4:30 PM, Sat noon - 4 PM, Sun 4 - 10 PM. Estab 1932 to serve the curriculum needs of an undergraduate, visual arts college. Art gallery is maintained. Circ 30,000
Income: $40,000 (Financed by library association, parent institution & capital expense)
Purchases: $40,000

Library Holdings: Vols 14,545; Per subs 315; AV — Cassettes 250, fs 24, slides 30,000; Other — Exhibition catalogs
Special Subjects: Art History, Graphic Design, Illustration, Interior Design, Photography, Computer Design, Fine Arts

A **SARASOTA VISUAL ART CENTER,** 707 N Tamiami Trail, 34236. Tel 813-365-2032. *Pres* Samuel Shapiro; *Gallery Dir* Max P Muller
Open Oct - May, Mon - Fri 10 AM - 4 PM; Sat & Sun 1 - 4 PM. No admis fee. Estab 1926, inc 1940, to promote the educational & cultural advantages of Sarasota in the field of contemporary art. Three large exhibiting galleries. Average Annual Attendance: 12,000. Mem: 981; dues $25; annual meeting in Apr
Income: Financed by membership & donations
Exhibitions: (1992) From Abstract to Realism; Annual SVAC Ethnic Exhibit: Hispanic-American Art; Ikenobo-Ikebana Workshops; Georgia O'Keeffe, Painter Extraordinaire, a dramatic presentation by Jenny Aldrich; The Peter Max Exhibit; Remembering Valfred Thelin. (1993) Members Show, Performing Arts Through the Eye of the Beholder; Ikenobo-Ikebana Demonstrations & Workshops; Ikenobo- Ikebana Annual Exhibit; Second Annual Artists' Costume Ball; Annual Arts & Crafts Festival; SVAC Artist of the Year Exhibit; Artists of Florida '93; Women's Caucus for Statewide Juried Exhibition; Student Exhibit
Publications: Bulletin, monthly; yearbook
Activities: Classes for adults; workshops; lectures open to the public, 5 - 6 vis lectr per yr; demonstrations; competitions with cash awards; gallery talks; museum shop sells books, original art, prints, crafts
L **Library,** Civic Center, 707 N Tamiami Trail, 34230. *Head Librn* Heather Newman
Open for art reference
Library Holdings: Vols 325

M **STATE ART MUSEUM OF FLORIDA,** John & Mable Ringling Museum of Art, 5401 Bay Shore Rd, PO Box 1838, 34243. Tel 813-355-5101. *Dir* David Ebitz; *Registrar* Edward Amatore; *Conservator* Michelle Scalera; *Dir Public Affairs* Patricia R Buck; *Dept Dir Finance & Admin* Barbara Bruening; *Dir Adult Educ* Elisa Hansen; *Dir Student Educ* Susan Hazelroth; *Librn* Lynell Morr
Open daily 10 AM - 5:30 PM. Admis adults $8.50, children under 12 free. Estab 1928. Bequeathed to the State of Florida by John Ringling & operated by the state; built in Italian villa style around sculpture garden on 38 landscaped acres; original 19th century theater from Asolo, near Venice, in adjacent building; Ringling Residence & Circus Galleries on grounds. Average Annual Attendance: 250,000 paid combination, 700,000 free attendance and special events. Mem: 3000; dues benefactor $10,000, patron $5000, fellow $1000, friend $250, centennial $100, family $50, individual $30
Collections: Archaeology of Cyprus; Baroque pictures, especially those of Peter Paul Rubens; European painting, sculpture, drawings & prints from the 16th, 17th & 18th centuries; medals & 18th century decorative arts; developing collection of 19th & 20th century painting, sculpture, drawings & prints
Exhibitions: Selections from the Permanent Collection: Old Masters. (1992) William Wegman: Painting, Drawings, Photographs, Videotapes; Jackie Ferrara Sculpture: A Retrospective; Recent Acquisitions 1990 - 1992. (1993) Statewide Juried Exhibition; Strike a Pose (1992) William Wegman: Painting, Drawings, Photographs, Videotapes; Jackie Ferrara Sculpture: A Retrospective
Publications: Calendar, bi-monthly; Collection Catalogues; Exhibition Catalogues; Newsletter, quarterly
Activities: Education dept; docent training; state services; lect open to public & some for members only; concerts; gallery talks; extension dept serves the state; 1000 individual paintings and 1000 original objects of art lent to affiliates and other qualified museums nationally and internationally on board approval; originate traveling exhibitions to affiliates; sales shop sells books, reproductions, prints and slides
L **Art Research Library,** 5401 Bay Shore Rd, 34243. Tel 813-355-5101; FAX 813-351-7959. *Librn* Lynell A Morr; *Archivist* Deborah Walk
Open Wed & Fri 10 AM - 5 PM. Reference only
Library Holdings: Vols 25,000; Per subs 100; Art Auction Catalogues, Rare Books; Other — Clipping files, exhibition catalogs, reproductions
Special Subjects: Art History, Painting - Dutch, Painting - Flemish, Painting - Italian, Emblem books, iconography, Renaissance & Baroque art

STUART

M **HISTORICAL SOCIETY OF MARTIN COUNTY,** Elliott Museum, 825 NE Ocean Blvd, 34996-1696. Tel 407-225-1961. *Dir* Elizabeth Press
Open daily 1 - 4 PM, including holidays. Admis adults $2.50, children between 6 & 13 $.50. Estab 1961. Average Annual Attendance: 30,000. Mem: 1000; dues $20-$1000
Collections: Contemporary American artists (realistic): Walter Brightwell, Nina D Buxton, Cecilia Cardman, E I Couse, James Ernst, Jo Gabeler, Diana Kan, Hui Chi Mau, Rose W Traines
Activities: Concerts; local school tours, morning; bookstore sells jewelry & children items

TALLAHASSEE

M **FLORIDA STATE UNIVERSITY,** Fine Arts Gallery & Museum, 250 Fine Arts Bldg, Copeland & Tennessee Sts, 32306-2037. Tel 904-644-6836. *Dir* Allys Palladino-Craig; *Registrar of Coll* Jan Robison; *Cur* John Woodworth; *Registrar of Exhib* Viki D Wylder
Open Mon - Fri 10 AM - 4 PM, Sat & Sun 1 - 4 PM, 7 - 8 PM preceding Mainstage performances; cl school holidays. No admis fee. Estab 1950. Three upper galleries; two lower galleries, one for permanent collection; sculpture courtyard. Average Annual Attendance: 55,000. Mem: 300, friends of the Gallery; 150, Artists' League
Income: Financed by state appropriations, grants & private sector
Collections: Asian prints; Carter Collection of pre-Columbian Art; contemporary American graphics, photography & paintings; European painting
Exhibitions: Permanent Collections; changing schedule of major art historical

works & contemporary American & European art
Publications: Exhibition catalogues
Activities: Lectures open to public, 4-6 vis lectrs per yr; concerts; gallery talks; tours; competition with awards; exten dept; individual paintings & original objects of art lent by appropriate request; book traveling exhibitions, 1-2 per yr; originate traveling exhibitions

M **LEMOYNE ART FOUNDATION, INC,** 125 N Gadsden St, 32301. Tel 904-222-8800. *Pres* Thomas A Deans; *Dir* Richard L Puckett
Open Tues - Sat 10 AM - 5 PM; Sun 2 - 5 PM; cl Mon. No admis fee. Estab 1964 as a non-profit organization to serve as gallery for contemporary, quality art; class center; sponsor the visual arts in Tallahassee; an educational institution in the broadest sense. Located in Meginnes-Munroe House, built c 1840; four main galleries and gallery shop. Average Annual Attendance: 7000. Mem: 800; dues $25 - $1000
Income: Financed by membership, sales, classes and fund raisers
Collections: Contemporary Florida Artists; William Watson Collection of Ceramics; Karl Zerbe Serigraphs
Publications: Newsletter, bi-monthly
Activities: Classes for adults and children; lect open to public, 4 vis lectr per year; gallery talks; tours; competitions; individual paintings and original objects of art lent to businesses and members; lending collection contains original art works, original prints; paintings and sculpture; sales shop sells original fine art, craft items and prints

M **TALLAHASSEE MUSEUM OF HISTORY & NATURAL SCIENCE,** 3945 Museum Dr, 32310. Tel 904-575-8684. *Dir* Russell S Daws; *Assoc Dir* Gwendolyn Waldorf; *Education Dir* Claude Stephens; *Cur of Coll & Exhib* Linda Deaton; *Animal Cur* Mike Jones
Open Mon - Sat 9 AM - 5 PM; Sun 12:30 - 5 PM. Admis adults $5, children 4 - 15 $3, members free. Estab 1957 to educate children and adults about natural history, native wildlife, North Florida history, art and culture. Facilities include 1880's farm, historic buildings, exhibit and class buildings, 40 acres of nature trails, and animal habitats. Average Annual Attendance: 125,000. Mem: 6000; dues $25 - $1000; annual meeting third Thurs in Oct
Income: $1,000,000 (financed by mem, fundraisers, admis & government appropriation)
Collections: Pre-Columbia Florida Indian Pottery; Historic Buildings; Furnishings
Exhibitions: Changing exhibit on art, clothing, crafts, history, and science; permanent or semi-permanent (3 years) exhibits on local history and natural history
Publications: Guidebook Series; Newsletter, monthly; School Handbook
Activities: Classes for adults and children; lectures open to public, 8 - 12 vis lectr per year; concerts; tours; original objects from other countries lent to local school groups & to civic organizations; lending collection contains 150 boxed exhibits on art, culture, history & science; sales shop sells books, science & history objects & folk crafts
L **Library,** 3945 Museum Dr, 32310. Tel 904-575-8684; FAX 904-574-8243.
Open to members
Library Holdings: Vols 500; Per subs 7
Collections: Ivan Gundrum Pre-Columbian Florida Indian Artifacts (reproductions) representing the Weeden Island culture 500 - 1500 AD

TAMPA

C **CASPERS, INC,** Art Collection, 4908 W Nassau St, 33607. Tel 813-287-2231.
Pres Joseph Casper; *VPres* Chuck Peterson; *Marketing Mgr* Molly Lawrence
Open Mon - Fri 8 AM - 5 PM. Estab 1981 to enhance the employees' environment
Collections: Collection features works by artists with some relationship to Florida

A **CITY OF TAMPA,** Art in Public Places, 1420 N Tampa St, 33803. Tel 813-227-7736; FAX 813-227-7744. *Prog Coordr* Marianne Eggler-Gerozissis; *Adminr Parks, Recreation & Cultural Serv* Joe Abrahams
Estab 1985 to visually enhance & enrich the public environment for both residents & visitors of Tampa. Mem: Public Art Committee & members meet monthly
Income: $40,000 (financed by city appropriation)
Publications: Public Art Brochure
Activities: Lect & tours on public art open to teachers & the public

C **FIRST NATIONAL BANK OF FLORIDA,** First Florida Tower, PO Box 31265, 33631-3265. Tel 813-224-1111. *Chmn of Board* A Bronson Thayer
Open 8:30 AM - 5 PM. Estab 1973. Collection displayed on all floors of bank
Collections: Acrylic on canvas, aluminum sculpture, ceramic raku, collages (paper, Plexiglas and serigraph), lithographs, oils, silk screen, silk screen on mirrored Plexiglas and plastic, sculpture, serigraphs and wool tapestries
Activities: Tours; individual objects of art lent to Tampa Museum

M **FLORIDA CENTER FOR CONTEMPORARY ART-ARTIST ALLIANCE INC,** 1513 E Eighth Ave, 33605. Tel 813-248-1171. *Exec Dir* Barbara A Rigall
Estab as a nonprofit alternative gallery providing venue for new work of Florida artists
Exhibitions: (1991) AIDS Artreach. (1992) Women, Art & Power. (1993) Intermedia Installation; 3-D Works

ARTHUR MANLEY SOCIETY
For further information, see National and Regional Organizations

M **TAMPA MUSEUM OF ART,** 601 Doyle Carlton Dr, 33602. Tel 813-223-8130; FAX 813-223-8732. *Dir* Andrew Maass; *Cur Contemporary* Doug Dreisthoon; *Cur Antiquity* Pamela Russell; *Preparator* Bob Hellier
Open Tues - Sat 10 AM - 5 PM, Wed 10 AM - 9 PM, Sun 1 - 5 PM. No admis fee. Estab 1970 to present varied art exhibitions & activities. Six galleries with changing exhibitions. Average Annual Attendance: 120,000. Mem: 2500; dues $45; monthly meetings

Income: $1,250,000 (financed by local govt grants, mem & contributions)
Purchases: $1,080,000
Collections: †Contemporary American Art; †Greek & Roman Antiquities; Decorative arts: Pre-Columbia artifacts; C Paul Jennewein Collection; Otto Neuman
Exhibitions: (1993) Goddess Polis; Art of the Himalayans
Publications: Catalogs; Newsletter, bi-monthly; school calander
Activities: Classes for adults & children; dramatic programs; docent training; films; workshops; lectures open to public; 10 vis lectr per yr; concerts; gallery talks; tours; competitions; awards; individual paintings & original objects of art lent to fellow museums, lending collection contains cassettes, color reproductions, Kodachromes, phonorecords, photographs, slides & videos; book traveling exhibitions; originate traveling exhibitions to other museums; museum shop sells books, reproductions, prints, jewelery, toys, T-shirts, cards & stationary
L **Library,** 601 Doyle Carlton Dr, 33602. Tel 813-223-8130; FAX 813-223-8732. *Registrar Asst* Anette Gordan
For reference only
Library Holdings: Vols 1200; Per subs 32; Micro — Fiche; AV — A-tapes, cassettes, slides, v-tapes; Other — Exhibition catalogs 700, pamphlets
Special Subjects: Antiquities-Egyptian, Antiquities-Etruscan, Antiquities-Greek, Antiquities-Roman, Art Education, Art History, Coins & Medals, Decorative Arts, Painting - American, Painting - European, Photography, Pre-Columbian Art, Primitive Art, Prints, Sculpture, Southwestern Art, Watercolors

M **UNIVERSITY OF SOUTH FLORIDA,** Contemporary Art Museum, College of Fine Arts, 4202 E Fowler Ave, 33620-7360. Tel 813-974-2849. *Dir & Chief Cur* Margaret A Miller; *Assoc Dir* Alexa A Favata; *Cur* Michelle S Juristo
Open Mon - Fri 10 AM - 5 PM; Sat & Sun 1 - 4 PM. No admis fee. Estab 1961 to provide visual art exhibitions of American & European contemporary art. Museum located on W Holly Dr on Tampa Campus. Average Annual Attendance: 55,000. Mem: Dues corporate $1000-$100,000, private $5-$1000
Income: Financed by state appropriation, grants, membership fees & corporate art program
Collections: African art, Pre-Columbian artifacts; art bank collection of loan traveling exhibitions (approx 60 small package exhibitions); contemporary photography; †contemporary works on paper; †painting, sculpture, ceramics
Publications: Exhibition catalogs
Activities: Educ dept; docent training; lectures open to public, 4 vis lectrs per year; gallery talks; tours; awards; through Art Bank program original prints, paintings & records are lent to institutions, universities & arts organizations; book traveling exhibitions, 2 per year; traveling exhibitions organized and circulated to universities, galleries & colleges
L **Library,** 4202 E Fowler Ave, 33620. Tel 813-974-2729. *Dir* Sam Fustukian; *Art Reference Librn* Irene Frank
Open to students and public
Library Holdings: Vols 865,276; Per subs 5041; Micro — Cards, fiche, reels; AV — A-tapes, cassettes, fs, motion pictures, v-tapes; Other — Clipping files, framed reproductions, manuscripts, pamphlets, photographs, prints, reproductions
Special Subjects: Historical Material, contemporary
Collections: Rare art books

UNIVERSITY OF TAMPA
M **Henry B Plant Museum,** 401 W Kennedy Blvd, 33606. Tel 813-254-1891. *Dir* Cynthia Gandee; *Admin Asst* Heather Brabham; *Cur & Registrar* Susan Carter; *Museum Relations* Darby Miller; *Cur Educ* Harriett Lenfestey; *Museum Store Mgr* Sue Blankinship
Open Tues - Sat 10 AM - 4 PM, Sun noon - 4 PM, cl holidays. Admis suggested donation $3. Estab 1933 in the former Tampa Bay Hotel built in 1891, to explain the importance of the Tampa Bay Hotel & Henry Plant to the area. This building which contains Victorian furnishings & artifacts, original to the Tampa Bay Hotel, is now on the register as a National Historical Landmark built by the railroad industrialist H B Plant. Average Annual Attendance: 25,000. Mem: 500
Income: Financed by city appropriation, University of Tampa, mem & donations
Collections: †Late Victorian furniture and objects d'art of same period; Venetian mirrors; Wedgwood, Oriental porcelains
Exhibitions: Exhibits relating to 19th century life; Plant system railroads & steamships
Publications: Henry B Plant Museum, Today & Moments In Time, a pictorial history of the Tampa Bay Hotel; Tampa Bay Hotel: Florida's First Magic Kingdom (video); member newsletter, quarterly
Activities: Docent training; lect open to public, & lect for members only, 4 vis lectrs per yr; tours; museum store sells books, original art reproductions, Victorian style gifts, Chinese & Japanese artifacts, antique estate jewelry, estate silver, linens
M **Lee Scarfone Gallery,** 410 W Kennedy Blvd, 33606. Tel 813-253-3333, Ext 217. *Pres* Bruce Samson; *Dir* Dorothy Cowden
Open Mon - Fri 9 AM - 5 PM, Sat 1 - 4 PM, cl Sat in June & July. No admis fee. Estab 1977 to exhibit works of art as an extension of the classroom and to utilize the space for public functions which would benefit from the artistic environment created by showing current trends of all art forms of artistic merit. Average Annual Attendance: 12,000. Mem: 75; donation dues $25-$400
Income: Financed by donations & fundraisers
Collections: Contemporary artists
Exhibitions: All Florida Art Competition; Faculty & Student Exhibitions; Pedro Perez; O V Shaffer; William Haney; Otto Neuman; William Pachner; William Walmsley; Kenneth Kerslake; Michael Minardi; Cheryl Goldsleger, Judy Chicago; Edward Hopper; Florida Artist Group
Publications: Exhibiton brochures, 10 times a yr
Activities: Classes for adults; lectures open to public; gallery talks; awards; scholarships; lend artwork to other art or educational institutions; lending collection contains 100 pieces of original art; originate traveling exhibitions

TEQUESTA

M LIGHTHOUSE GALLERY, 373 Tequesta Dr, Gallery Sq N, 33469. Tel 407-746-3101, 746-4654. *Pres* Bruce Spencer
Open Tues - Sat 10 AM - 4 PM; cl Mon. No admis fee. Estab 1964 to create public interest in all forms of the fine arts. Average Annual Attendance: 50,000. Mem: 850; dues $40; annual meeting in April
Exhibitions: Temporary and Traveling Exhibitions; PSA International Photo Salon
Publications: Calendar of Events, monthly
Activities: Classes for adults & children; dramatic programs; lectures open to the public, 15 vis lectrs per yr; concerts; gallery talks; tours; competitions; cash awards; museum shop sells books, original art, reproductions, prints
L Library, 373 Tequesta Dr, Gallery Sq N, 33458
Small library of art books and art magazines
Library Holdings: Vols 600; Per subs 10; Other — Clipping files, exhibition catalogs, pamphlets, prints, reproductions

VALPARAISO

M HISTORICAL SOCIETY OF OKALOOSA & WALTON COUNTIES, INC, Historical Society Museum, 115 Westview Ave, PO Box 488, 32580. Tel 904-678-2615. *Dir* Mrs Christian S LaRoche
Open Tues - Sat 11 AM - 4 PM. No admis fee. Estab 1971 to collect, preserve, & display items related to the history & development of the area. Average Annual Attendance: 6000. Mem: 100; dues $10
Income: $16,000 (financed by mem, city & county appropriation, fundraising, donations)
Collections: Paleo & archaic stone artifacts; pioneer household utensils, agricultural implements, artisans' tools, tools used in the turpentine & lumber industries; photos & files of research materials
Activities: Adult & children's classes; docent programs; lectures open to the public; gallery talks; tours; shop sells books, oroginal art, baskets, pillows, jewelry, quilts

WEST PALM BEACH

A HISTORICAL SOCIETY OF PALM BEACH COUNTY, 3650 Summit Blvd, 33406. Tel 407-471-1492. *Dir* Nan Dennison, PhD
Open Tues - Thurs 10 AM - 4 PM, Fri 10 AM - Noon. No admis fee. Estab 1937 to preserve & disseminate history of Palm Beach County. Average Annual Attendance: 1000. Mem: 600; dues $20; annual meeting 2nd Tues of month from Nov - Apr
Income: $50,000 (financed by mem)
Library Holdings: Vols 5000; 160 Bound periodical vols, postcards; Micro — Reels 1000; AV — A-tapes, slides 5000; Other — Clipping files, pamphlets, photographs 10,000
Collections: Addison Mizner architectural drawings; History of Palm Beach County; other local architect drawings
Publications: Newsletter, monthly Oct - May
Activities: Lectures open to public, 6 vis lectrs per yr; sales shop sells books, slides, photos

M NORTON GALLERY AND SCHOOL OF ART, 1451 S Olive Ave, 33401. Tel 407-832-5194; FAX 407-659-4689. *Dir* Christina Orr-Cahall; *Pres* R B Snyder; *Dir Development* Elizabeth Beasley; *Cur* David Setford; *Mem Secy* Theresa Hickman; *Public Relations Dir* Susan Gottlieb; *Supt* Franklyn Slocumb; *Registrar* Pamela Parry; *Cur Educ* Lynn Anderson
Open Tues - Sat 10 AM - 5 PM; Sun 1 - 5 PM. Admis voluntary donation. The Norton Gallery of Art was founded in 1940, dedicated in 1941 for the education and enjoyment of the public; additions were made in 1946, 49, 52 and 66. Acquisitions and gifts are continually being made to the museum. Building and major collections were given by Ralph Hubbard Norton and Elizabeth Calhoun Norton. The Gallery, designed by the Palm Beach architects, Wyeth, King and Johnson, opened to the public in 1941, with an original collection of one hundred paintings. Mr Norton continued to acquire works of art for the museum until his death in 1953, when the remainder of his private collection was given to the museum. Sculptures are exhibited throughout the Gallery & in the patio garden. Average Annual Attendance: 120,000. Mem: 4000; dues family $60 & $40; annual meeting Nov
Income: Financed by endowment, membership, city appropriation, Palm Beach County Tourist Development Council, donations & fund raising events
Collections: French Collection contains late 19th & early 20th century paintings including Impressionist & Post-Impressionist masterpieces; American holdings include works of art from 1900 to the present; Chinese collections contain archaic bronzes, archaic jades, Buddhist sculpture, jade carvings & ceramics
Publications: Monthly calendar; exhibition catalogs
Activities: Public school tours; dramatic programs; docent training; lectures open to public, 8 vis lectrs per year; films; concerts; gallery talks; tours; competitions with awards; individual paintings and original objects of art lent to museums around the world; originate traveling exhibitions; museum shop sells books, magazines, reproductions, prints & slides
L Library, 1451 S Olive Ave, 33401. Tel 407-832-5194; FAX 407-659-4689. *Dir* Dr Christina Orr-Cahall; *Cur* David F Setford Sr
Open Tues - Sat 10 AM - 5 PM, Sun 1 - 5 PM. Admis voluntary donation. Estab 1941. Average Annual Attendance: 120,000
Purchases: $3000
Library Holdings: Vols 3800; Per subs 30; Micro — Fiche, reels; AV — A-tapes, fs, Kodachromes, slides; Other — Clipping files, exhibition catalogs, memorabilia, pamphlets, photographs
Collections: †Individual Artist Reviews, †Catalogues, etc
Publications: Bi-monthly calendar of events
Activities: Classes for adults & children; dramatic programs; docent training; lect open to public, 10 vis lectr per year; concerts; gallery talks; tours; original & individual paintings lent; museum shop sells books, reproductions, prints, slides, table art

WHITE SPRINGS

M FLORIDA DEPARTMENT OF NATURAL RESOURCES, Stephen Foster State Folk Culture Center, PO Drawer G, 32096. Tel 904-397-2733. *Park Mgr* Darrell R Krause
Open 8 AM - Sunset daily. Admis Florida res vehicle operator $1, each passenger $.50, children under 6 free; out-of-state vehicle operator $2, each passenger $1. Estab 1950 as a memorial to Stephen Collins Foster; operated by the State Department of Natural Resources. Museum contains eight dioramas of Foster's best known songs. The North wing holds a collection of minstrel materials; the South wing 19th century furniture & musical instruments; the 200 foot tall Foster Tower, a collection of pianos. Average Annual Attendance: 90,000

A FLORIDA FOLKLIFE PROGRAMS, PO Box 265, 32096. Tel 904-397-2192; FAX 904-397-2915. *Dir* Ormond H Loomis; *Folklife Adminr* David Reddy; *Folk Arts Coordr* Robert L Stone
Open Mon - Fri 8 AM - 5 PM. No admis fee. Estab 1979. The Bureau is under Secretary of Jim Smith and carries on a year-round calendar of folk activities in an effort to encourage statewide public interest and participation in the folk arts and folklore
Special Subjects: Ethnology, Folk Art
Activities: Classes for adults and children; Lectures open to public; concerts; gallery talks and tours; Florida Folk Heritage Award; apprenticeships offered; originate traveling exhibitions
L Library, PO Box 265, 32096. Tel 904-397-2192; FAX 904-397-2915.
Open to public for reference Mon - Fri 8 AM - 5 PM
Library Holdings: Vols 500; Per subs 12; Micro — Cards; AV — A-tapes, cassettes, fs, Kodachromes, rec, slides, v-tapes; Other — Clipping files, exhibition catalogs, manuscripts, original art works, pamphlets, photographs
Special Subjects: Ethnology, Folk Art, Florida folklife

WINTER PARK

A ARCHITECTS DESIGN GROUP INC, 333 N Knowles Ave (Mailing add: PO Box 1210, 32790). Tel 407-647-1706; FAX 407-645-5525. *Pres* I S K Reeves V
Open by appointment. Estab 1971
Collections: †Antique American Indian Art

M CHARLES MORSE MUSEUM OF AMERICAN ART, 133 E Welbourne Ave (Mailing add: 151 E Welbourne Ave, 32789). Tel 407-644-3686; FAX 407-647-1284. *Chmn of the Board & Dir* Hugh F McKean; *Pres of Association* Ann MacArthur
Open Tues - Sat 9:30 AM - 4 PM, Sun 1 - 4 PM, cl Mon, Christmas Day, New Years Day, Fourth of July, Thanksgiving, Labor Day & Memorial Day. Admis adults $2.50, students & children $1, members free. Estab to display work of Louis Comfort Tiffany and his contemporaries from an extensive collection on a rotating basis. A small, intimate jewel box of a gallery consists of nine rooms and display areas. Mem: 732; dues from $5-$10,000
Income: $141,000 (financed by endowment and membership)
Collections: Art Nouveau Furnitures by Galle, Guimard, Majorelle, & others; Louis Comfort Tiffany collection of lamps, paintings, personal correspondence & effects, personal windows & photographs; Tiffany & other America art pottery numbering several hundred items; Tiffany studios photographers; items of blown glass; complete inventory of metalware desk sets; paintings by Tiffany's contemporaries; personal windows of others; photographs
Exhibitions: Art That Swings: European Art Nouveau; With Love From the Past: A Celebration of the Winter Park Centennial; Art That Sparkles: American Cut Glass; America the Beautiful: Landscape Paintings from the McKean Collection; Mysteries from Laurelton Hall; The Art of Printing; personal windows & lamps, vases, metal wares & paintings of Louis Comfort Tiffany; decorative art objects, paintings, contemporaries
Publications: INSIDER, monthly newletter to members
Activities: Classes for adults; docent training; lect; concerts; gallery talks; tours; competitions with awards; exten dept serves schools, nursing homes and public parks; original objects of art lent to nursing homes, bank lobbies and art center; museum shop sells books, prints, slides, postcards, posters & notepaper

M ROLLINS COLLEGE, George D and Harriet W Cornell Fine Arts Museum, 32789. Tel 407-646-2526; FAX 407-646-2524. *Dir* Dr Arthur R Blumenthal; *Registrar* Mary Ann Bowie; *Exhibit Designer* Richard D Colvin; *Admin Asst* Roz Sontag
Open Tues - Fri 10 AM - 5 PM; Sat & Sun 1 - 5 PM; cl Mon. No admis fee. Formerly the Morse Gallery of Art, estab 1942. New Fine Arts Center completed in 1976, dedicated & opened on Jan 29, 1978. Rollins College is a liberal arts college & the Cornell Fine Arts Museum is part of the college. Cornell Fine Arts Museum was accredited by the American Association of Museums in 1981. The museum houses the college's permanent collection of 4000 works & provides a focus for the arts in central Florida. Museum consists of the McKean, the Yust & Knapp Galleries. Average Annual Attendance: 20,000. Mem: Dues benefactor $500, sponsor $100, donor $50, family $35, assoc $30, active $20
Income: $125,000 (financed by endowment & grants)
Collections: American paintings and portraits; European paintings from the 15th to 20th centuries; print; bronzes; decorative arts; Smith Watch Key Collection of 1200 keys
Exhibitions: Whistler & Friends; Italian Renaissance & Baroque Paintings from Florida Museums
Activities: Five vis lectr per yr; concerts; gallery talks; tours; originates traveling exhibitions

GEORGIA

ALBANY

M ALBANY MUSEUM OF ART, 311 Meadowlark Dr, 31707. Tel 912-439-8400, 435-0977; FAX 912-434-4289. *Exec Dir* Paula Bacon; *Cur* E Michael Whittington
Open Tues - Sat 10 AM - 5 PM, Sun 2 - 5 PM, cl Mon, also by special appointment. Admis contribution adults $3, sr citizens $2, students $1, Tues, members & children under 12 free. Estab 1964; new museum facility opened 1983. Average Annual Attendance: 35,000. Mem: 1200; dues patron family $250, patron individual $130, young patron family $125, young patron individual $65, sustaining $100, associate $75, contributing $50, family $35, individual $25; monthly trustee & committee meetings
Income: $500,000 (financed by state, federal & foundation grants, mem & special events)
Purchases: Recent purchases include photographs by Henri Cartier Besson
Collections: African Collection; 20th Century American Art; Art of the Southern Region; Ancient Art - Greek, Roman & Egyptian; Community Collection
Exhibitions: Children's Art Fair
Publications: Bimonthly newsletter; exhibition catalogs
Activities: Classes for adults & children; workshops; docent training; lect open to public, 6 vis lectr per year; gallery; films; talks; tours; Children's Art Fair; individual paintings & original objects of art lent to other museums; originate traveling exhibitions to other museums; museum shop

AMERICUS

M GEORGIA SOUTHWESTERN COLLEGE, Art Gallery, 31709. Tel 912-928-1279; FAX 912-928-1630. *Chmn Fine Arts* Duke Jackson; *Art Coordr* Jack R Lewis
Open Mon - Fri 8 AM - 5 PM. No admis fee. Estab 1971
Collections: Contemporary prints; Indian art of the southwest

ATHENS

M US NAVY SUPPLY CORPS SCHOOL, Museum, Prince Ave & Oglethorpe St, 30606-5000. Tel 706-345-7349. *Cur* Dan Roth
Open Mon - Fri 8:30 AM - 5 PM. No admis fee. Estab 1974 to promote history & activities of US Navy Supply Corps. Museum housed in National Register Carnegie Library building (c1910). Average Annual Attendance: 2000
Income: Financed by federal appropriation
Collections: Nautical painting, ship models, gallery gear, navigational equipment, uniforms, personal memorabilia

UNIVERSITY OF GEORGIA

M Georgia Museum of Art, Jackson St, 30602-1719. Tel 706-542-3255. *Actg Museum Adminr* William Eiland; *Actg Preparator* Jim Stipe Maas; *Cur Education* Susan Longhenry; *Registrar* Lynne Bowenkamp; *Dir Public Affairs & Publications* Bonnie Uter
Open Mon - Wed, Fri, Sat 9 AM - 5 PM, Thurs 9 AM - 9 PM, Sun noon - 6 PM. No admis fee. Estab 1945; open to the public 1948 as a fine arts museum. Five exhibition galleries. Average Annual Attendance: 40,000. Mem: 565; dues $15 - $1000; annual meeting Feb
Income: Financed through university, mem & grants
Purchases: American & European prints & paintings
Collections: †American Paintings (19th & 20th century); †Drawings; †European & American Graphics, 15th century to the present; †Japanese Graphics, 15th century to the present
Exhibitions: (1992) Prints & Drawings of Italy: The 16th Century; Charles Meryon & Jean-Francois Millet: Etchings of Urban & Rural 19th Century France. (1993) Gerald L Brockhurst; The 14th Annual School of Art Symposium
Publications: Newsletter, four times annually; gallery notes, biannually; exhibtion catalogs; annual report bulletin
Activities: Classes for adults & children; docent training; sr citizen program; volunteer docents program; lectures open to the public, 3 - 5 vis lectr per year; tours; gallery talks; competitions with awards; individual paintings and original objects of art lent to other museums and galleries; traveling exhibitions organized and circulated; Museum shop sells books, magazines, original art, notecards, reproduction jewelry
L University of Georgia Libraries, Fine Arts Collection, Jackson St, 30602. Tel 706-542-7462. *Art Librn* Marilyn Halkovic
Open Mon - Thurs 7:30 AM - Midnight, Fri 7:30 AM - 9 PM, Sat 9 AM - 6 PM, Sun 1 PM - Midnight; between quarters Mon - Fri 8 AM - 6 PM, Sat 9 AM - 6 PM, cl Sun
Income: Financed by state appropriation
Library Holdings: Vols 58,500; Per subs 265; Micro — Cards, fiche, prints, reels; AV — A-tapes, cassettes, motion pictures, rec, slides, v-tapes; Other — Exhibition catalogs, manuscripts, photographs
Special Subjects: History of Art & Architecture, History of Photography
Collections: †Rare books & manuscripts collection; †illustration archives on microfiche; stereographs from William C Darrah Collection; †private press collection; †handmade paper collections
L Dept of Art, Visual Arts Bldg, Jackson St, 30602. Tel 706-542-1511. *Librn* David Koffman; *Dept Head* Evan Firestone
Open 8 AM - 5 PM and by special arrangement. Estab 1955 to house slides and AV equipment for use by faculty and students for classroom lecturing. Reference & instructional library
Library Holdings: AV — Cassettes, slides 150,000, v-tapes
Special Subjects: 19th Century Albumen Prints

ATLANTA

ASSOCIATION OF MEDICAL ILLUSTRATORS
For further information, see National and Regional Organization

L ATLANTA COLLEGE OF ART LIBRARY, 1280 Peachtree St NE, 30309. Tel 404-898-1166. *Dir* Barbara Hutsell; *Visual Coll Cur* Kevin Fitzgerald; *Asst Librn* Jessica Seiler
Open Mon & Fri 9 AM - 5 PM, Tues, Wed, Thurs 9 AM - 8 PM. Estab 1950 to provide art information and research facility to the Atlanta College of Art community and the southeast art community. Library has a small exhibition space for art. Circ 12,000
Purchases: $22,800
Library Holdings: Vols 26,000; Per subs 320; Artists' book collection; Micro — Fiche; AV — Cassettes, rec, slides, v-tapes; Other — Exhibition catalogs
Special Subjects: Graphic Design, Interior Design, 20th century American art, with emphasis on art since 1950
Collections: †Artists' Books; †rare books
Exhibitions: Exhibitions of art by students & faculty
Activities: Films; visiting artists program

A ATLANTA HISTORICAL SOCIETY INC, Atlanta History Center, 3101 Andrews Dr NW, 30305. Tel 404-814-4000; FAX 404-814-4186. *Exec Dir* Rick Beard; *Asst Dir* Katherine G Farnham; *Dir Prog* Darlene Roth; *Dir Library & Archives* Anne Salter; *Dir Gardens* Allen Sistrunk
Open Mon - Sat 9 AM - 5:30 PM, Sun noon - 5:30 PM. Admis $6, discount for sr citizens, youth, children & groups. Estab 1926, dedicated to presenting the stories of Atlanta's past, present & future through exhibits, programs, collections & research. 32 acres of gardens & woodlands; two National Historic Register houses: Swan House, a 1928 classically styled mansion with original furnishings, & the 1840s Tullie Smith Farm with outbuildings & livestock; an 1890s Victorian playhouse; woodland trails labeled for self-guided tours; McElreath Hall, housing an extensive library/archives, exhibit galleries, a visitors' center, a museum shop, a members room & a 400 seat auditorium. Average Annual Attendance: 115,000. Mem: 5000, dues $30 - $1000; annual meeting mid-Oct
Income: $3,400,000 (financed through endowment, mem, county appropriation)
Purchases: $22,500
Collections: Burrison Folklife Collection; Thomas S Dickey Civil War Ordinance Collection; DuBose Civil War Collection
Exhibitions: Atlanta & the War, 1861 - 1865; Atlanta Resurgens; On the Set of Gone With the Wind: Photographs by Fred A Parrish; America & the New Republic: The Classical Ideal
Publications: Atlanta History, quarterly; A Journal of Georgia & the South
Activities: Classes for adults & children; dramatic programs; docent programs; lect open to public, 20 vis lectr per year; symposia; workshops; special events; book traveling exhibitions; originate traveling exhibitions; retail store sells books, prints, magazines, slides, original art, reproductions, folk crafts, educational toys

M ATLANTA MUSEUM, 537-39 Peachtree St NE, 30308. Tel 404-872-8233. *Dir* J H Elliott Jr; *Cur* Mary Gene Elliot
Open Mon - Fri 10 AM - 5 PM, cl Sat, Sun & holidays. Admis adults $2, children $1, special group rates. Estab 1938
Collections: Bronzes; Confederate Money; Decorative Arts; Early Chinese Art; Furniture; Indian Artifacts; Paintings; Porcelains; Sculpture; Glass
Activities: Lect; tours; sales shop sells antiques, china, furniture, gifts, glass, paintings, porcelain, rugs and silver

L ATLANTA PUBLIC LIBRARY, Art-Humanities Dept, 1 Margaret Mitchell Square NW, 30303. Tel 404-730-1700; FAX 404-730-1990. *Dir* Ronald A Dubberly; *Mgr* Julie M Compton
Open weekdays 9 AM - 9 PM; Sat 9 AM - 6 PM. Estab 1950 to provide materials in the fine arts. Some exhibit space maintained
Income: Financed by city and state appropriation
Library Holdings: AV — Cassettes, motion pictures 1100, rec; Other — Prints
Activities: Classes for adults; lect open to the public

M CENTER FOR PUPPETRY ARTS, 1404 Spring St NW, 30309. Tel 404-873-3089; FAX 404-873-9907. *Exec Dir* Vincent Anthony; *Admin Dir* Lisa Rhodes; *Producer* Rita Carter; *Museum Dir* Clarice DeProspero; *Educ Dir* Claire Ritzler
Estab 1978. Puppetry - International Exhibits. Mem: dues $25 - $1000 & up
Income: $1,300,000 (financed by endowment, mem, city & state appropriations)
Collections: Global collection of puppets
Exhibitions: Puppetry of Canada; Echoes of Society
Publications: Articles, brochures, catalogs & reports
Activities: Classes for adults & children; dramatic programs; lect open to public, 3 vis lectr per year; scholarships; artmobile; lending collection contains art objects; book traveling exhibitions 3 per year; originate traveling exhibitions 2 per year; retail store sells books & prints
Library, 1404 Spring St NW, 30309
For reference only. Library estab 1978
Library Holdings: Vols 400; Per subs 100; AV — A-tapes, cassettes, rec, slides, v-tapes; Other — Clipping files, exhibition catalogs, framed reproductions, memorabilia, original art works, pamphlets, photographs, reproductions

M EMORY UNIVERSITY, Museum of Art & Archaeology, Carlos Hall, 571 S Kilgo, 30322. Tel 404-727-4282; FAX 404-727-4292. *Dir* Dr Maxwell L Anderson; *Asst Dir* Catherine T Howett; *Exhib Design Supv* W Clayton Bass; *Coordr Education Progs* Elizabeth S Hornor; *Secy* Catherine Howett
Open Tues - Sat 10 AM - 4:30 PM, Sun noon - 5 PM. No admis fee. Admis suggested donation $2. Museum redesigned in 1985 by Michael Graves, Post-Modernist architect; 15,400 sq ft; permanent exhibition galleries & special exhibition galleries. Average Annual Attendance: 43,055. Mem: 400; dues $25 & up
Income: $1,072,000
Collections: †Old World art & archaeology, including works·from Egypt, Mesopotamia, ancient Palestine; Pre-Columbian, American Indian & Far Eastern holdings; †art collection from Renaissance to present, classical Greek, Roman &

Egyptian
Exhibitions: (1988-1989) Roman Portraits in Context: Imperial & Private Likenesses from the Museo Nazionale Romano; Monuments & Mummies: The Shelton Expedition to Egypt; The Fragrant Past: Perfumes of Cleopatra & Julius Ceasar. (1989-1990) Syracuse the Fairest Greek City: Ancient Art from the Museo Archeologico Regionale Paolo Orsi; Radiance in Stone: Sculptures in Colored Marble from the Museo Nazionale Romano. (1990-1991) Beyond the Pyramids: Egyptian Regional Art from the Museo Egizio, Turin
Publications: Exhibition catalogues
Activities: Dramatic programs; docent programs; demonstratons; storytelling; gallery talks; lectures open to public, 30 vis lectrs per yr; objects from permanent collection loaned to other institutions; book traveling exhibitions, 2-4 per yr; originate traveling exhibitions; museum shop sells postcards, note cards, exhibition catalogues, posters & gift items

A **GEORGIA COUNCIL FOR THE ARTS,** 530 Means St NW, 30318. Tel 404-651-7920. *Exec Dir* Betsey Weltner
Open Mon - Fri 8 AM - 5 PM. Estab 1968 as a state agency providing funding to non-profit, tax-exempt organizations & individual Georgia artists for arts programming. Mem: 24 members appointed by governor; meetings four times per yr
Income: $3,900,000 (financed by state appropriation plus federal funding)
Publications: Guide to Programs, annual (one for organizations & one for artists)

L **GEORGIA INSTITUTE OF TECHNOLOGY,** College of Architecture Library, 225 North Ave NW, 30332. Tel 404-894-4877. *Librn* Kathryn S Brackney
Income: Financed by state appropriation
Library Holdings: Vols 23,7000; Per subs 150; Architectural drawings; AV — Slides; Other — Pamphlets

L **GEORGIA STATE UNIVERSITY,** School of Art & Design, Visual Resource Library & Reading Room, University Plaza, 30303. Tel 404-651-2257. *Cur* Joan W Tysinger; *Photographer Asst* Ann England
Open Mon - Fri 8:30 AM - 5 PM. No admis fee. Estab 1970 to make visual and literary resource materials available for study, teaching and research. Average Annual Attendance: 20,000
Library Holdings: Vols 2500; Per subs 18; AV — A-tapes, slides 145,000, v-tapes 45; Other — Exhibition catalogs, original art works, pamphlets, reproductions
Exhibitions: (1992) The Third Culture: Illlustrations of Leo & Diane Dillon; Ice Fishing Houses of the Great North; Lilienthal (ceramics); Lily (photography); Davis (mixed media); See (Sculpture); Fall Senior Exhibition. (1993) Four Chicano Artists; Faculty Exhibition; Gurty (photography); Jachomowicz (photography); Ginsberg (printmaking); Winter Senior Exhibition; Rogers: Recent Works; Annual Student Art Exhibition; Tucker, Lawrence, Pindell
Activities: Lectures open to public, 5-10 vis lectr per yr; films; artist's slide presentations; discussions
M **Art Gallery,** University Plaza, 30303. Tel 404-651-2257; FAX 404-651-1032. *Dir* Tina Dunkley
Open Mon - Sat 8 AM - 8 PM, Sun 10 AM - 8 PM. No admis fee
Exhibitions: (1991) Figurative Clays; Helen Cohen. (1992) Sue Coe
Publications: Catalogues
Activities: Gallery talks; lending collection contains original art works

A **GEORGIA VOLUNTEER LAWYERS FOR THE ARTS, INC,** 141 Pryor St SW, Suite 2030, 30303. Tel 404-525-6046; FAX 404-730-5798. *Exec Dir* Gail Centini; *Dep Dir* Patricia Prusak PhD
Open Mon - Fri 10 AM - 5 PM. Estab 1975 as legal reference for the arts
Income: Financed by city & state funds & private foundations
Collections: Copyrights; fundraising; art law related to literature
Publications: An Artists Handbook on Copyright; Handbook on the Georgia Print Law
Activities: Educ dept; lectures open to public, 5 vis lectr per yr

M **HIGH MUSEUM OF ART,** 1280 Peachtree St NE, 30309. Tel 404-892-3600; FAX 404-898-9578. *Dir* Ned Rifkin; *Chmn Board of Dir* Richard A Denny Jr; *Cur American Art* Judy Larson; *Cur Decorative Art* Donald Pierce; *Cur European Art* Ronni Baer; *Cur 20th Century Art* Susan Krane; *Assoc Cur 20th Century Art* Carrie Przybilla; *Cur Photography* Ellen Dugan; *Cur Media Art* Linda Dubler; *Registrar* Frances Francis; *Mgr Exhib* Marjorie Harvey
Open Mon - Thurs & Sat 10 AM - 5 PM, Fri 10 AM - 9 PM, Sun noon - 5 PM, cl Mon. Admis adults $5, sr citizens & students $3, children ages 6 - 17 $1, children under 6 & members free, Thurs 1 - 5 PM free. Estab 1926 to make the best in the visual arts available to the Atlanta public in exhibitions & supporting programs. Four floors (46,000 sq ft) exhibition space; top floor for traveling exhibitions; semi-flexible space (moveable walls); ramp & elevator for accessibility. Average Annual Attendance: 500,000. Mem: 23,000; dues $25 & up
Income: $7,500,000 (financed by endowment, mem, Members Guild of the High Museum of Art, city & state appropriations, museum shop sales, grants & foundations, ticket sales & operating income)
Collections: American painting & sculpture; European painting & sculpture; 20th Century painting, photography & sculpture; African Art; works on paper; 19th Century decorative art featuring Herter Brothers, William Whitehead & John Henry Belter; contemporary crafts; 20th Century furniture; regional historical decorative arts & English ceramics; 19th Century American landscape paintings; contemporary art since 1970 †Western art early Renaissance - present; decorative arts; graphics; sculpture; African & sub-Saharan; †19th - 20th century photography
Exhibitions: (1993) Abstract Expressionism: Selections from the Metropolitan Museum of Art; Ralph Eugene Meatyrad: An American Visionary; African Reflections: Art from Northeastern Zaire; Art at the Edge: Alison Saar; Annie Leibovitz: Photographs 1970 - 1990; In Praise of Painting: The Art of Gerrit Dou; Small Pictures from the Mangooian Collection. (1994) The Royal Art of Benin; Old Master Drawings from the Steiner Collection; Equal Rights & Justice; Willem de Kooning from the Hirshhorn Collection; The Schlossberg Collection of Drawing & Sculpture; The Herter Brothers: European Furniture Makers in the American Gilded Age. (1995) Venetian Paintings from the Museum of Fine Arts in Budapest; Sean Scully

Publications: Calendar of Events, monthly; exhibition catalogues
Activities: Workshops for adults, children & families; docent training; lect open to public; family days; tours; performing arts programs; sr citizen programs; gallery talks; speakers bureau; traveling exhibitions organized and circulated; two museum shops sell books, reproductions, slides, prints, stationery, children's books & toys, crafts, jewelry & gift items; junior museum
L **Library,** 1280 Peachtree St NE, 30309. Tel 404-892-3600, Ext 360; FAX 404-898-9252. *Librn* Jack Miller
Library Holdings: Vols 8500; Per subs 50; AV — Slides; Other — Clipping files, exhibition catalogs
Special Subjects: Aesthetics, Afro-American Art, American Western Art, Antiquities-Oriental, Architecture, Art Education, Art History, Ceramics, Conceptual Art, Constructions, Crafts, Decorative Arts, Drawings, Etchings & Engravings, Film, Folk Art, Furniture, Glass, Graphic Arts, Graphic Design

M **NEXUS CONTEMPORARY ART CENTER,** 535 Means St, 30318. Tel 404-688-1970; FAX 404-577-5856. *Exec Dir* Louise Shaw; *Dir Nexus Gallery* Ann Holcomb; *Dir Nexus Press* Michael Goodman
Open Tues - Sat 11 AM - 5 PM. No admis fee. Estab 1973 to promote & present contemporary art in all media. Average Annual Attendance: 45,000. Mem: 1600; dues $15-$40; annual meeting in June
Activities: Educ dept; classes for adults & children; lectures open to public, 4 vis lectr per year; gallery talks; sales shop sells Nexus Press publications

M **PHOTOGRAPHIC INVESTMENTS GALLERY,** 468 Amour Dr, 30324. Tel 404-876-7260. *Pres* Edwin C Symmes Jr
Open daily 10 AM - 4 PM. No admis fee. Estab 1979 to display & produce traveling exhibits of classical photography. Two gallery spaces. Average Annual Attendance: 10,000
Collections: 19th century photographic images in all media; 20th century black & white & color photos by masters
Exhibitions: 19th Century Albumen Prints of Westminster Cathedral; Netsuke: An Insight into Japan; Color Photography by E C Symmes; 19th & 20th Century Images of China
Activities: Lectures open to public; original objects of art lent; lending collection contains 1500 19th century Albumen prints; originate traveling exhibitions; original art sold

C **RITZ-CARLTON HOTEL COMPANY,** Art Collection, 3414 Peachtree Rd NE, Suite 300, 30326. Tel 404-237-5500; FAX 404-261-2289. *Chmn* William B Johnson; *Cur* Lynne M Kortenhaus; *Fine Arts Advisor* Lynne M Kortenhaus
Open 24 hrs. No admis fee. Estab 1983 to reflect & communicate the history & tradition of Ritz-Carlton Hotels
Purchases: $7,500,000
Special Subjects: Painting - American, Painting - British, Prints, Sculpture
Collections: †18th & 19th century European & American paintings, prints, sculpture †18th & 19th century English & Continental antiques & decorations
Publications: The Ritz-Carlton Art Collections, catalogs
Activities: Lectures open to public on request; sales shop sells books & reproductions

AUGUSTA

M **AUGUSTA RICHMOND COUNTY MUSEUM,** 540 Telfair St, 30901. Tel 706-722-8454. *Dir* Richard Wescott
Open Tues - Sat 10 AM - 5 PM, Sun 2 - 5 PM, cl holidays. No admis fee. Estab 1937; owns 1850 historic Brahe House at 426 Telfair St. Mem: Dues $5-$250
Collections: Archaeology; Decorative Arts; Graphics; Historical Material; Paintings; Sculpture
Activities: Training program for professional museum personnel; workshops; films; lect; guided tours; volunteer council; book traveling exhibitions

M **GERTRUDE HERBERT MEMORIAL INSTITUTE OF ART,** 506 Telfair St, 30901. Tel 706-722-5495; FAX 706-722-3670. *Dir* Dee Templeton
Open Tues - Fri 10 AM - 5 PM, Sun 1 - 4 PM, groups by special appt, Sun 2 - 5 PM, cl Mon, Thanksgiving, Christmas & New Years. No admis fee. Estab 1937 for the advancement & encouragement of art & education in art. Main gallery located on first floor of historic home. Average Annual Attendance: 5000. Mem: 250
Income: $20,000
Collections: European Renaissance; modern paintings, sculpture, graphics
Exhibitions: Circulating exhibitions; monthly exhibitions; one-person and group exhibitions; the Southeastern Annual Juried Exhibition
Activities: Classes for adults & children; docent training; lectures open to public, 4 vis lectr per yr; concerts; gallery talks; tours; competitions with awards; scholarships; book traveling exhibitions

C **MORRIS COMMUNICATIONS CORPORATION,** 725 Broad St, PO Box 936, 30913. Tel 706-724-0851; FAX 706-722-7125. *Chmn & CEO* W S Morris III
Collections: Alaskan Art; Western Bronzes; Wildlife (birds)
M **Morris Museum of Art,** 1 Tenth St, 30901-1134. Tel 706-724-7501; FAX 706-724-7612. *Dir* Louise Keith Claussen; *Cur* Estill Curtis Pennington; *Chmn Board* W S Morris III; *Store Mgr* Melinda Murphy
Open Tues - Sat 10 AM - 5:30 PM, Sun 1 - 5 PM. Admis adults $2, sr citizens 65 & over $1, students $1. Estab 1992 to emphasize painting in the South. Mem: dues $15 - $5000; quarterly meetings
Income: Financed by endowment, mem & foundation funds
Collections: Birds of North America; Bird Paintings; Robin Hill; †Southern American Art
Exhibitions: A Southern Collection: Masterworks from a Permanent Collection of Painting in the South
Activities: Docent programs; lect open to public, 6 vis lectr per year; book traveling exhibitions 3 - 4 per year; originate traveling exhibitions 1 per year; retail store sells books

COLUMBUS

M COLUMBUS COLLEGE, The Gallery, Dept of Art, 3600 Algonquin Dr, 31907-2079. Tel 706-568-2047. *Dept Head* Jarrell Hethcox
Open Mon - Fri 9 AM - 5 PM. No admis fee. Average Annual Attendance: 6000
Income: $8000 (financed by student activities)
Purchases: Permanent collection
Exhibitions: Annual art students show; faculty show; regional guest artist & nationally prominent artist
Activities: Classes for adults & college students; lectures open to the public, 1 - 5 vis lectr per yr; tours; competitions with awards; scholarships offered

M COLUMBUS MUSEUM, 1251 Wynnton Rd, 31906. Tel 706-649-0713; FAX 706-649-1070. *Dir* Anne Timpano; *Chief Cur* Karol Anne Peard Lawson; *Dir of Educ* Anne King; *Cur of Archaeology* Frank T Schnell; *Dir of Development* Betsy Covington; *Communications Dir* Dannell Pitts; *Museum Resource Specialist* Marjorie Drury; *Registration Asst* Sue Cagle; *Asst to the Dir* Patricia Butts; *Art Handler* Chris Land; *Preparator* Steve Ellis; *Membership Coordr* Lucia Swift; *Educ Assoc* Pam Pruett; *Exhibit Designer* Tim Flick; *Business Mgr* Doug Star; *Spec Events* Becky Williams
Open Tues - Sat 10 AM - 5 PM, Sun 1 - 5 PM, cl Mon, Thanksgiving & Christmas. No admis fee. Estab 1953 to build a permanent collection; encourage work by Georgia & Southern artists; establish loan shows & traveling exhibitions in all fields of American art & history. Average Annual Attendance: 80,000. Mem: 2100; dues $25 & up; annual meeting Sept
Collections: †American Art; early Federal to modern, includes painting, sculpture & graphic arts; Doll Collection; †Georgia Craftsmen; †Regional history section with extensive Collection of Historical & Archaeological Material relating to local history; †Prints; Southern Folk Art; Gun Collection; †Sculpture permanent collection includes Landscapes, Paintings & Portraits by Early & Contemporary American Painters, with strong Collection of American Impressionism paintings
Exhibitions: Milton Avery; Masks; Masques, Masx; Southeastern Baskets; East Meets West: Chen Chi Watercolors, 1940 - 1987; A Select View, American Paintings from the Columbus Museum; The Art of A Henry Nordhausen; Light After Dark: Photography by Karekin Goekjian; Training the Hand & Eye (1991) African - American Artists, 1880 - 1987: Selections from the Evans - Tibbs Collection; Home Again: The Return of Six Artists Native to the Chattahoochee Valley; Travel with Gerry: The Art of Gerry Bosch. (1992) An Other World; Contrast, Confluence & the Columbian Encounter; The Perry Morgan Collection of Tucker Porcelain; African - American Folk & Decorative Art from the permanent collection
Publications: Annual report; gallery guides; newsletter, quarterly
Activities: Workshops for adults and children; docent training; lect open to public, 10 - 12 vis lectr per year; tours; gallery talks; book traveling exhibitions, 6-10 per yr; originate traveling exhibitions; museum shop sells books, reproductions, prints & gift items

DALTON

A CREATIVE ARTS GUILD, 520 W Waugh St, PO Box 1485, 30722-1485. Tel 706-278-0168; FAX 706-278-6996. *Pres* J Mike Brown; *Dir* Bernice Spigel
Open Mon - Fri 9 AM - 5 PM; Sat 11 AM - 2 PM. No admis fee. Estab 1963 to recognize, stimulate & popularize creative excellence in the arts for the benefit of the entire community. Average Annual Attendance: 121,000. Mem: 1000; dues family $20, annual meeting in June
Income: $500,000 (financed by mem, commissions, grants, tuitions & fund raising events)
Collections: Permanent collection of regional art
Exhibitions: Changing monthly shows of Crafts; Graphics; Photography; Original Art; Sculpture; Fiber
Publications: Bulletins to members, monthly
Activities: Classes for adults and children; dramatic programs; visual and performing arts programs for schools; concerts; gallery talks; competitions with awards; arts and crafts festivals; individual paintings & original objects of art lent to area schools & organizations

DECATUR

M AGNES SCOTT COLLEGE, Dalton Gallery, E College Ave, 30030. Tel 404-371-6366. *Chmn Art Dept* Terry McGehee
Open Mon - Fri 9 AM - 9 PM; Sat 9 AM - 5 PM; Sun 2 - 5 PM. No admis fee. Estab 1965 to enhance art program. Gallery consists of 4 rooms, 300 running ft of wall space, light beige walls and rug; Dana Fine Arts Bldg designed by John Portman
Income: Financed by endowment
Collections: Clifford M Clarke; Harry L Dalton; Steffen Thomas; Ferdinand Warren
Activities: Lect open to public

FORT BENNING

M NATIONAL INFANTRY MUSEUM, Bldg 396, Baltzell Ave, 31905-5273. Tel 706-545-2958. *Dir* Dick Dewayne Grube; *Cur* Frank Hanner
Open Tues - Fri 10 AM - 4:30 PM; Sat - Sun 12:30 - 4:30 PM. No admis fee. Estab 1959 to honor the infantryman and his two centuries of proud history. Gallery contains 30,000 sq ft; Hall of Flags, Gallery of Military Art, Benning Room, West Gallery: 1750 - 1865, Center Galleries 1870 - 1970, Medal of Honor Hall and Airborne Diorama. Average Annual Attendance: 100,000. Mem: 9000; dues $10
Income: $200,000 (financed by federal funds)
Collections: †Military related art; Presidential Documents & Memorabilia; Regimental Quartermasters Sales Store
Exhibitions: (1993) War in the Gulf; Military Heritage of the Chattahoochee Valley, 1492-1992 (current through 1995); Observing the Fiftieth Anniversary of World War II
Activities: Lect open to public

L Library, Bldg 396, Baltzell Ave, 31905-5273. *Librn* Donna Lowe
Open Tues - Fri 10 AM - 4:30 PM, Sat & Sun 12:30 - 4:30 PM. Estab 1959 to preserve the collection of field manuals and other military information. For reference only
Library Holdings: Vols 8000; AV — Fs, motion pictures, slides; Other — Clipping files, manuscripts, memorabilia, original art works, pamphlets, photographs, prints, sculpture
Special Subjects: The Infantryman

FORT VALLEY

L FORT VALLEY STATE COLLEGE, H A Hunt Memorial Library, 1005 State College Dr, 31030-3298. Tel 912-825-6342; FAX 912-825-6916. *Library Dir* Carole Taylor
Open 8 AM - 5 PM. No admis fee. Estab 1939
Special Subjects: Afro-American Art, Art Education, Art History, Graphic Arts, Graphic Design
Collections: Afro - American Art; Graphic Arts
Exhibitions: History of College

JEKYLL ISLAND

M JEKYLL ISLAND MUSEUM, 375 Riverview Dr, 31527. Tel 912-635-4036 (Tours), 635-2119 (Office). *Exec Dir Jekyll Island* George Chambliss; *Cur of Educ* Leslie Hicks
Open Memorial Day - Labor Day Mon - Sun 9 AM - 6 PM, Labor Day - Memorial Day Mon - Sun 9:30 AM - 5 PM. Admis $6, students $4 (6-18 years). Estab 1954. Average Annual Attendance: 51,000
Income: Financed by fees & admissions
Collections: 1890 Furniture; Tiffany Stained Glass Windows; portraits
Activities: Programs for adults & children; lectures open to public; tours; book traveling exhibitions, 4 per year; museum shop sells books, reproductions, slides & turn-of-the century related items

LAGRANGE

M CHATTAHOOCHEE VALLEY ART MUSEUM, 112 Hines St, 30240. Tel 706-882-3267. *Exec Dir* Keith Rasmussen; *Cur Educ* Gregory Morton; *Asst Cur* Anise Morrison; *Finance Officer* Renee Warrick; *Admin Officer* Owen Holleran
Open Tues - Fri 9 AM - 5 PM, Sat 11 AM - 5 PM, Sun 1 - 5 PM, cl Mon. Estab 1963 to provide visual art experience & education to people of West Georgia. 100 year old former Troup County Jail refurbished for use as galleries having about 350 running ft of wall space & 7000 sq ft of floor space on two floors. Average Annual Attendance: 22,000. Mem: 380; dues $10 - $5000; annual meeting in Jan
Income: $150,000 (financed by foundation grant, civic organizations & fundraisers)
Purchases: $10,000, Purchase Awards, LaGrange National XVII Competition
Collections: Contemporary American art of all types & media
Exhibitions: Outsider art from private collections
Publications: Quarterly newsletter
Activities: Classes for adults & children; lect open to public; competitions with awards; lending collection contains 400 paintings & art objects; book traveling exhibitions 2 per year; retail store sells books, prints, original art & reproductions

M LA GRANGE COLLEGE, Lamar Dodd Art Center Museum, 601 Broad St, 30240. Tel 706-882-2911; FAX 706-884-6567. *Dir* John D Lawrence
Estab 1988
Collections: 20th Century Photography; American Indian Collection; Retrospective Collection
Exhibitions: Two shows every six weeks

MACON

M MUSEUM OF ARTS AND SCIENCES, INC, 4182 Forsyth Rd, 31210. Tel 912-477-3232; FAX 912-477-3251. *Exec Dir* Nancy B Anderson; *Dir of Educ* Mary Ann Ellis; *Dir of Fine Arts* Suzanne Harper
Open Mon - Thurs 9 AM - 5 PM, Fri 9 AM - 9 PM, Sat 9 AM - 5 PM, Sun 1 - 5 PM. Admis adults $2, children $1, members no charge, Mon 9 AM - 5 PM, Fri 5 - 9 PM no admis fee. Estab 1956 as a general art & science museum with a planetarium. South Gallery 50 ft x 60 ft; North Gallery 25 ft x 35 ft; Hall Gallery 8 ft x 32 ft; Newberry Hall 1759 sq ft. Average Annual Attendance: 70,000. Mem: 1700; dues $15 - $250
Collections: American art with emphasis on the Southeast drawings, paintings, prints & sculpture; gems & minerals; doll collection; quilt collection; ethnographic
Publications: Museum Muse, bi-monthly newsletter; catalogues
Activities: Classes for adults and children; docent training; summer children's camps; guided tours; lectures open to public, 2 - 6 vis lectr per yr; concerts; gallery talks; movies; special events; individual paintings & original objects of art lent to other museums; book traveling exhibitions, 5 - 10 per year; originate traveling exhibitions to circulate to schools or appropriate institutions in Georgia & Southeast; museum shop sells books, magazines, original art, reproductions, prints, small educational toys, t-shirts, gem & minerals, gift items, rocks, shells, science kits

MADISON

M MORGAN COUNTY FOUNDATION, INC, Madison-Morgan Cultural Center, 434 S Main St, 30650. Tel 706-342-4743. *Chmn Board* Lyn Hunt; *Exec Dir* Open; *Admin Dir* Peggy Kempton; *Dir Marketing* Margaret Ligon; *Dir Visual Arts* Jackson Cheatham; *Secy Admin Asst* Barbara D Engle
Open Tues - Sat 10 AM - 4:30 PM, Sun 2 - 5 PM. Admis fee adults $2, students $1, members free. Estab 1976 to enhance the educational & cultural life of

Georgia and the Southeast. Four galleries for changing exhibits, housed in former classrooms (approx 25 ft x 35 ft of historic 1895 school facility; heart pine floors, no daylight, tungsten track lighting only, with heat, air conditioning & electronic security. Average Annual Attendance: 30,000. Mem: 1500; dues $15-$1000; annual meeting 2nd Mon in July
Income: $460,000 (financed by endowment, mem, state grants, admissions fees for services & sponsorship contributions)
Exhibitions: Usually two simultaneous exhibits, each 8-12 wks, of work by regional artists &/or collections of museums & private collections from the region or across the nation; Annual Juried Regional Art Exhibit
Publications: Exhibit brochures & catalogs, 4-5 per yr; Madison Georgia - An Architectural Guide
Activities: Performing arts programs; docent training; gallery tours; demonstrations; lectures open to public, 5-10 vis lectrs per yr; competitions with awards; book traveling exhibitions, 5-10 per yr; originate traveling exhibitions; museum shop sells books, posters, note cards, postcards

MOUNT BERRY

M BERRY COLLEGE, Moon Gallery, Art Dept Berry College, 30149. Tel 706-232-9109; FAX 706-236-2248. *Pres* Dr Gloria Shatto; *VPres* Dr Doyle Mathis; *Secy* Joyce Morris
Open weekdays 9 AM - 4 PM. No admis fee. Estab 1971. Medium size gallery, carpeted floors and walls, tracking spots. Average Annual Attendance: 3500
Exhibitions: (1993) Barbara Moss: Works on Paper; David Vanderpoel & Martin Kahnle; Photographs by Richard Tichich
Activities: Classes for adults and children; lectures open to the public, 8 - 10 vis lectr per yr; gallery talks; competitions with awards; scholarships offered; individual paintings and original objects of art lent; lending collection contains books, cassettes, color reproductions, 20 original prints, paintings, records, photographs and 5000 slides; book traveling exhibitions; originate traveling exhibitions
L Memorial Library, 30149. Tel 706-236-2221; FAX 706-236-2248. *Dir* Ondina Gonzalez; *Prof of Art* Dr T J Mew III
Open daily 9 AM - 4 PM. Estab 1972 for educational purposes
Library Holdings: Vols 350; Per subs 25; AV — A-tapes, cassettes, fs, motion pictures, rec, slides, v-tapes; Other — Clipping files, exhibition catalogs, manuscripts, memorabilia, original art works, pamphlets, photographs, prints
Special Subjects: Ceramics, Contemporary women artists

SAVANNAH

M KIAH MUSEUM, 505 W 36th St, 31401. Tel 912-236-8544. *Dir & Founder* Virginia J Kiah
Open Tues - Thurs 11 AM - 5 PM. No admis fee. Estab 1959 to expose this type of culture to the masses; to teach the relationship of art to everyday life
Collections: Civil War Period Collection; Harmon Foundation Collection of African Wood Carvings; Howard J Morrison Jr Osteological Collection; Marie Dressler Collection; Fine Arts Exhibit of all art work of students and adult artists from 18 countries; Folk Art; 18th & 20th Century Furniture; Hobby Collection; Indian Artifacts
Exhibitions: Ten paintings from the House of Representatives
Activities: Docent training; gallery talks; tours; paintings & original objects of art lent to schools

M SHIPS OF THE SEA MUSEUM, 503 E River St, 31401. Tel 912-232-1511. *Exec Dir* David T Guernsey Jr
Open Mon - Sun 10 AM - 5 PM. Admis adults $2, senior citizens $1, children between 7 & 12 $.75. Estab 1966 to bring a greater awareness to the general public of the great part in history that ships have played. Four floors of ship models & items which pertain to the sea with an outstanding exhibit of ships-in-bottles & scrimshaw. Average Annual Attendance: 50,000
Income: Financed privately
Collections: Figureheads; Porcelains; Scrimshaw; Ships Models, etc
Activities: Classes for children; museum shop sells books, magazines & slides
L Library, 503 E River St, 31401. *Librn* Barbara Anchors
Reference only
Library Holdings: Vols 500; Per subs 10; Micro — Cards; Other — Clipping files, framed reproductions, memorabilia, original art works, pamphlets, photographs, prints
Special Subjects: Maritime
Activities: Children summer classes in nautical lore

M TELFAIR ACADEMY OF ARTS AND SCIENCES INC, 121 Barnard St, PO Box 10081, 31401. Tel 912-232-1177. *Dir* Gregory Allgire Smith; *Admin* Sandra S Hadaway; *Cur Registrar* Pamela King; *Preparator* Miutin Pavovic; *Cur Educ* Harry H DeLorme
Open Tues - Sat 10 AM - 5 PM; Sun 2 - 5 PM; cl Mon. Admis adults $2.50, students $1, children under 12 $.50; free on Sun. Estab 1883; it is the oldest art museum in the southeast. The collections are housed in an 1818 Regency Mansion (with an 1883 Art Museum Wing) designed by English architect William Jay; Telfair has been designated a National Historic Landmark. Average Annual Attendance: 110,00. Mem: 1375; dues family $35, individual $25, junior citizen and senior citizen $10; annual meeting Apr
Income: Financed by endowment, membership, city and state appropriation, banks and corporate foundations and federal government
Collections: American Impressionism; Ash Can Realism; Collections of 18th and 19th Century American Portraiture; Decorative Arts and Period Rooms; works of art on paper; costumes; 19th and 20th century French and German paintings
Exhibitions: Special and traveling exhibitions
Publications: The Octagon Room; We Ain't What We Used to Be; Christopher P H Murphy (1869-1939): A Retrospective
Activities: Classes for children; docent training; adult & children's programs; special tours; lect open to the public, 4-10 vis lectr per yr; concerts; gallery talks; family Sunday programs; exten dept serving public schools and retired citizens centers; museum shop sells books, posters, postcards

L Library, 121 Barnard St, PO Box 10081, 31401. Tel 912-232-1177.
For reference only, for scholars and the public
Library Holdings: Vols 1200; AV — Slides; Other — Clipping files, exhibition catalogs, manuscripts, pamphlets, photographs, reproductions
Special Subjects: American Art

VALDOSTA

M VALDOSTA STATE COLLEGE, Art Gallery, N Patterson St, 31601. Tel 912-333-5835. *Gallery Dir* Stephen Andersen; *Head Art Dept* Dr Lanny Milbrandt
Open Mon - Thurs 10 AM - 4 PM, Fri 10 AM - 3 PM. No admis fee. Estab 1970 for educational purposes serving students, faculty, community & region. Gallery is an open rectangular room with approximately 122 running ft of exhibition space. Average Annual Attendance: 20,000
Income: Financed by state appropriations
Exhibitions: 8-9 exhibitions per year; national juried Valdosta works on paper exhibition
Activities: Classes for adults; dramatic programs; docent training; lectures open to public, 3-5 vis lectrs per year; concerts; gallery talks; tours; competitions; scholarships; originate traveling exhibitions

WAYCROSS

M OKEFENOKEE HERITAGE CENTER, INC, 1460 N Augusta Ave (Mailing add: Route 5, PO Box 406A, 31501). Tel 912-285-4260, 285-0733; FAX 912-283-2858. *Dir* John H Karew
Open Tues - Sat 10 AM - 5 PM, Sun 2 - 4 PM, cl holidays. Admis adults $2, youth 5-18 $1, under 4 & members free. Estab 1975 to house displays on arts & history. Two gallery areas. Average Annual Attendance: 18,000. Mem: 350; annual meeting 3rd week in Oct
Income: $85,000 (financed by endowment, membership, grants, contributions, admis, special activities, gift shop)
Collections: Prints, crafts, paintings and photographs
Publications: Newsletter, monthly; exhibition catalogues
Activities: Classes for adults and children; dramatic programs; docent training; films; demonstrations; workshops; slide show; lectures open to public, 12 vis lectrs per year; concerts; gallery talks; tours; competitions; purchase awards; book traveling exhibitions, 6-12 per yr; museum shop sells books, original art, reproductions, prints, gifts and souvenirs

HAWAII

HAWAII NATIONAL PARK

M VOLCANO ART CENTER, PO Box 104, 96718-0104. Tel 808-967-7511 (gallery), 967-8222 (office). *Exec Dir* Susan McGovern; *Gallery Dir* Natalie Pfeifer
Open daily 9 AM - 5 PM. No admis fee. Estab 1974 to promote Hawaiian arts & crafts. Mem: dues $25
Collections: Hawaiian fine arts & crafts: art-to-wear, books, ceramics, glass, jewelry, native woods, photographs, posters, sculpture
Publications: Volcano Gazette, bi-monthly
Activities: Classes for adults & children; dramatic programs; docent programs; Elderhostel, camps, marathon run; lect open to public; retail store sells books, prints, original art, reproductions, crafts, clothes, jewelry

HILO

M STATE OF HAWAII, DEPT OF LAND & NATURAL RESOURCES, Wailoa Visitor Center, Piopio St, PO Box 936, 96721. Tel 808-933-4360. *Dir* Kathleen Lassiter; *Asst Dir* Betty L King
Open Mon, Tues, Thurs & Fri 8 AM - 4:30 PM, Wed noon - 8:30 PM, Sat 9 AM - 3 PM, cl Sun & State holidays. Estab 1968 as a place of interest in Hilo for local residents as well as visitors to the island
Exhibitions: Main Gallery (1993) Impressions from the West; Splendors of Art; Twelve Moons in the Forest; Merrie Monarch Quilt Show; Spring Arts Festival; One Hundred Years Ago; Big Island Bonsai; Hono, Hono, Hono; Big Island Wood Show; Art by the Foot; Poetry in Light; A Holiday Spectacular. Downstairs Gallery (1993) Images of Kona; Edwin Kayton & Diane Moore; Ceramics, Memories on Tour; Hand Made Fabrics; David Deardorf; Spring Things; Big Island Amateur Radio Club; Mixed Media Delights; To Set the Mood; Robbie LaLonde; Damascus Aquarian; The Volcano Art Center; Santa's Workshop

HONOLULU

A ASSOCIATION OF HAWAII ARTISTS, PO Box 10202, 96816. Tel 808-955-6100. *Pres* Jack Adams
Estab 1934 to promote congeniality and stimulate growth by presenting programs; to contribute to the cultural life of the State of Hawaii. Average Annual Attendance: 1000. Mem: 350; dues $12, monthly meeting every third Tues
Income: Financed by membership
Publications: Paint Rag, monthly
Activities: Lect open to public, 12 visiting lectr per year; demonstrations; competitions; cash awards, plaques and rossettes; scholarships

M **BERNICE PAUAHI BISHOP MUSEUM,** 1525 Bernice St, PO Box 19000-A, 96817-0916. Tel 808-847-3511; FAX 808-841-8968. *Dir* W Donald Duckworth
Open Mon - Sun 9 AM - 5 PM, cl Christmas. Estab 1889 to preserve & study the culture & natural history of Hawaii
Exhibitions: The Space Expo '92
L **Library,** 1525 Bernice St, 96817-0916. Tel 808-848-4147; FAX 808-841-8968. *Reference Librn* Patty Belcher
Open Tues - Fri 10 AM - 3 PM, Sat 9 AM - noon. Estab 1889
Library Holdings: Vols 40,000
Special Subjects: Anthropology, Archaeology, Ethnology, Folk Art, Historical Material, History of Art & Archaeology, Hawaii & the Pacific Cultural & Natural History
L **Archives,** 1525 Bernice St, 96817-0916. Tel 808-848-4182.
Open Tues - Fri 10 AM - 3 PM, Sat 9 AM - noon. Estab 1991
Library Holdings: Other — Manuscripts 3500, photographs 1,000,000
Collections: Cylinders, discs & reel to reel tapes; Maps; Moving Images; Oils on Canvas; Works of Art on Paper

M **THE CONTEMPORARY MUSEUM,** 2411 Makiki Heights Dr, 96822. Tel 808-526-1322; FAX 808-536-5973. *Dir* Merrill Rueppel; *Assoc Dir* James Jensen
Open Tues - Sat 10 AM - 4 PM, Sun noon - 4 PM, cl Mon. Admis adults $3, children under 14 & members free. Estab 1961 as Contemporary Arts Center to provide a showcase for contemporary artists of Hawaii.. Reorganized & opened in 1988 in present facility situated in 3 1/2 acres of gardens; five galleries comprise 5,000 sq ft of exhibitions space. Also includes exhibition annex, Honolulu Advertiser Gallery, in downtown Honolulu.. Average Annual Attendance: 30,000. Mem: 2500; dues $35 & up
Income: $1,500,000 (financed by endowment, mem, grants, contributions, admissions)
Collections: Permanent collection of over 1100 works from 1945 to present in all media by local, national & international artists
Exhibitions: Approximately 25 termporary exhibitions annually of artists of local, national, international reputation. Masami Teraoka: Waves & Plagues; Sataru Abe (paintings & sculpture); Suzanne Wolfe (ceramics)
Publications: Masami Teraoka: Waves & Plagues, (90 page catalogue)
Activities: Educ dept; docent training; lect open to public; gallery talks; tours; Museum shop sells books, original art, reproductions, prints & jewelry

M **HONOLULU ACADEMY OF ARTS,** 900 S Beretania St, 96814. Tel 808-532-8700; FAX 808-532-8787; Cable HONART. *Dir* George R Ellis; *Assoc Dir* David de la Torre; *Cur Western Art* Jeniffer Saville; *Cur Textile Coll* Reiko Brandon; *Cur Asian Art* Stephen Little; *Cur Educ* Karen Thompson; *Cur Public Prog* James H Furstenberg; *Cur Art Center* Carol Khewhok; *Keeper, Lending Center* Kiersten Cox; *Slide Coll* Gwen Harada; *Registrar* Sanna Deutsch; *Fund Development* Susan Lampe; *Public Relations Officer* Mickey Wittig-Harby; *Asst Cur Western Art* Sarah Bremser
Open Tues - Sat 10 AM - 4:30 PM, Sun 1 - 5 PM, cl Mon & major holidays. Admis suggested donation. Estab 1927 as the only art museum of a broad general nature in the Pacific; to provide Hawaii's people of many races with works of art representing their composite cultural heritage from both East and West. Main building is a Registered National Historic Place. Average Annual Attendance: 250,000. Mem: 5000; dues $10 and up
Income: $3,456,000
Collections: European and American Decorative Arts, Painting, Prints, Sculpture; Ancient Mediterranean and Medieval Christian Art; Kress Collection of Italian Renaissance Painting; Chinese Bronze, Ceramics, Furniture, Lacquerware, Painting, Sculpture; Islamic Ceramics; Japanese Ceramics, Folk Arts, Painting, Prints, Screens, Sculpture; Korean Ceramics; Traditional Arts of Africa, Oceania and the Americas; Western and Oriental Textiles
Exhibitions: Approx 50 temporary exhibitions annually
Publications: Art Books and Pamphlets; Catalog of the Collection; Catalogs of Special Exhibitions; Honolulu Academy of Arts Journal
Activities: Classes for children; lectr; films & videos illustrating contemporary & historic range of the medium; guided tours; gallery talks; arts festivals; workshops; music programs; research in Asian & Western Art; lending collection contains paintings, prints, textiles, reproductions, photographs. slides and ethnographic objects (about 21,000); sales shop sells books and gifts
L **Robert Allerton Library,** 900 S Beretania St, 96814. Tel 808-532-8755; FAX 808-532-8787. *Librn* Anne T Seaman
Open Tues - Sat 10 AM - noon & 1 - 4 PM, cl Sun & Mon. Estab 1927. Reference library for staff and members
Library Holdings: Vols 40,000; Per subs 250; Micro — Fiche, reels; AV — Slides; Other — Clipping files, exhibition catalogs, pamphlets, photographs
Special Subjects: Art History, Oriental Art, National Palace Museum Photographic Archives

M **JUDICIARY HISTORY CENTER,** 417 S King St, 96813. Tel 808-548-3163; FAX 808-536-5054. *Dir* Lani Lapilio; *Educ Spec* Victoria Kneubuhl; *Cur* Ruth Tamura
Open Tues - Thurs 10 AM - 3 PM. No admis fee. Estab to interpret the history of Hawaii's courts & legal system. Average Annual Attendance: 25,000. Mem: 150; dues $2, $15, $25, $100, $1000
Income: $28,000 (financed by state appropriation)
Collections: Art (paintings, prints); Artifacts; Documents (judicial & legal); furniture
Exhibitions: The Monarchy Courts; Martial Law in Hawaii 1941 - 1944; Restored Court Room 1913
Activities: Educ dept; dramatic programs; docent programs; tours; originate 2 travelling exhibits per year

C **PERSIS CORPORATION** (Formerly Honolulu Advertiser), Art Collection, 605 Kapiolani Blvd, 96802. Tel 808-525-8015; FAX 808-521-7691. *Cur* Sharon Carter-Smith, MA
Open 8:30 AM - 5:30 PM. Art Collection estab 1961 for contemporary art. Gallery located on 1st floor near entrance; changing exhibits every 6 weeks: local artists, nationally known artists, group shows & annual showcase of recent corporate acquisitions
Purchases: Jennifer Bartlett painting, Richard Estes print, Paul Wonner painting
Activities: Docent training; lect open to public; many purchases & prizes awarded to local exhibits, special projects funded

M **QUEEN'S MEDICAL CENTER AUXILIARY,** Queen Emma Gallery, 1301 Punchbowl St, PO Box 861, 96813. Tel 808-547-4397; FAX 808-547-4646. *Dir* Masa Morioka Taira; *Assoc Dir* David Landry; *Secy* Ellyn Fukuda; *Treas* Dori Thurman
Open daily 8 AM - 4 PM. No admis fee. Estab 1977 as a showcase for local & regional artists. 13 ft x 24 ft alternative space in largest, oldest hospital in Hawaii. Average Annual Attendance: 15,000
Income: Financed by sales & donations
Collections: Queen Emma's Medallion (wall mural); Hawaiian Moon Calendar (pastels); linocut prints by Dietrick Varez; glass spheres; batik hangings
Exhibitions: Human Form Traveling Exhibit; monthly exhibits
Activities: Individual paintings & original objects of art lent to medical personnel or prospective buyers

M **TENNENT ART FOUNDATION GALLERY,** 203 Prospect St, 96813. Tel 808-531-1987. *Dir* Elaine Tennent
Open Tues - Sat 10 AM - noon; Sun 2 - 4 PM or by appointment. No admis fee. Estab 1954; dedicated to aesthetic portrayal of Hawaiian people and to house works of Madge Tennent. Gallery is set in a terraced garden with a variety of plants & trees. Average Annual Attendance: 300. Mem: Dues individual $15, family $25; annual meeting in Feb
Income: Financed by trust
Collections: Madge Tennent's Personal Art Books Collection
Publications: Prospectus, quarterly newsletter
Activities: Special exhibitions and social events sponsored by Friends of Tennent Art Gallery; lect; tours; concerts; museum shop sells note cards, art coloring books
L **Library,** 203 Prospect St, 96813
Open for reference
Library Holdings: Vols 350

M **UNIVERSITY OF HAWAII AT MANOA,** Art Gallery, 2535 The Mall, 96822. Tel 808-956-6888; FAX 808-942-9008. *Chmn Dept Art* Robert Jay; *Dir* Tom Klobe; *Assoc Dir* Sharon Tasaka
Open Mon - Fri 10 AM - 4 PM; Sun noon - 4 PM; cl Sat. No admis fee. Estab 1976 to present a program of local, national and international exhibitions. Gallery is seen as a major teaching tool for all area of specialization. It is located in the center of the art building and is designed as a versatile space with a flexible installation system that allows all types of art to be displayed. Average Annual Attendance: 50,000
Collections: Japanese & Polish posters
Exhibitions: Facing the Gods: Ritual Masks of the Himalayas; Prints & Process; Symbol & Surrogate: The Picture Within; The Presence of Absence; Jean Charlot: A Retrospective; The Image & the Word; The Fourth International Shoebox Sculpture Exhibition. (1992) Treasures of Hawaiian History
Publications: Exhibition catalogs
Activities: Lect open to public; gallery talks; book traveling exhibitions; originate traveling exhibitions

KANEOHE

M **THE GALLERY AT HAWAII LOA COLLEGE,** Marinda Lee Gallery, 45-045 Kamehameha Hwy, 96744-5297. Tel 808-233-3100; FAX 808-233-3190. *Gallery Dir* Mollie Foti; *Gallery Dir* Gail Hazelhurst; *Gallery Dir* Hoppy Smith
Open Mon - Thurs 8 AM - 10 PM, Fri 8 AM - 6 PM, cl weekends & holidays. No admis fee. Estab 1983 as a cultural & academic resource for students & community. Average Annual Attendance: 2500
Income: Financed by college funds & private donations

LAHAINA

A **LAHAINA ARTS SOCIETY,** Art Organization, 649 Wharf St, 96761. Tel 808-661-0111. *Pres* Eileen Jones; *VPres* Dan Skinner; *Secy* Liz Singer; *Bookkeeper* Theo Morrison; *Gallery Dir* Mona Harris
Open daily 10 AM - 4 PM. No admis fee. Estab 1968 as a nonprofit organization interested in perpetuating culture, art & beuty by providing stimulating art instruction, lectures & art exhibits. Gallery located in old Lahaina Courthouse; Main Gallery is on ground floor; Old Jail Gallery is in the basement. Average Annual Attendance: 36,000. Mem: 350; dues $30; annual meeting Oct
Income: $12,000 (financed by membership and annual fundraising event, Beaux Arts Ball)
Exhibitions: Exhibits change each month; group, special or theme exhibits in Main Gallery; one or two-person member shows are in Old Jail Gallery
Publications: Newsletter, monthly; exhibition catalogs
Activities: Classes for children; lectures for members only; gallery talks; competitions with scholarships; workshops; scholarships; gallery sales shop sells original art, prints, cards, ceramics, handcrafted jewelry & sculptures

LAIE

A **POLYNESIAN CULTURAL CENTER,** 55-370 Kamehameha Hwy, 96762. Tel 808-293-3001; FAX 808-293-3022. *Chmn Bd* Dallin H Oaks; *Pres & Gen Mgr* Lester Moore; *Dir* Bryan Bowles
Open Mon - Sat 11 AM - 9 PM, cl Sun, Thanksgiving, New Years & Christmas. Admis adults $14, children $7. Estab 1963 by the Church of Jesus Christ of Latter Day Saints as an authentic Polynesian village. Center is a 42 acre living museum with two amphitheaters, it represents villages of Hawaii, Samoa, Tonga, Fiji, Tahiti, New Zealand & the Marquesas. Average Annual Attendance: 1,000,000
Income: Financed by admissions
Collections: Decorative arts, ethnic material, graphics, paintings and sculpture
Publications: Polynesia in a Day, magazine
Activities: Classes for adults & children; workshop training in Polynesian arts & crafts; lectures open to public; scholarships; sales shop sells Polynesian handicrafts, books, reproductions, prints, slides, tapa cloth, Hawaiian quilting & pandanus-leaf items

LIHUE

M KAUAI MUSEUM, PO Box 248, 96766. Tel 808-245-6931. *Pres* David Goodale; *Dir* Carol Lovell; *Cur* Margaret Lovett; *Mgr Museum Shop* Helen Riznik
Open Mon - Fri 9:30 AM - 4:30 PM, Sat 9 AM - 1 PM, cl Sun. Admis adults $3, children thru age 17 free when accompanied by an adult. Estab 1961 to provide the history through the permanent exhibit, the Story of Kauai and through art exhibits; ethnic cultural exhibits in the Wilcox Building to give the community an opportunity to learn more of ethnic backgrounds. Average Annual Attendance: 22,000. Mem: 800; dues $10 - $100; annual meeting in Nov
Collections: Hawaiian artifacts; Oriental works
Exhibitions: Upstairs: Quilts; Downstairs: Hawaiian History
Publications: Hawaiian Quilting on Kauai; Early Kauai Hospitality; Amelia; Moki Goes Fishing; Kauai: The Separate Kingdom
Activities: Classes for adults & children; lectures open to public, 8 per yr; concerts; tours; competitions with awards; individual objects of art lent to local institutions; book traveling exhibitions, 3 per yr; museum shop sells books, original art, reproductions, prints

L KAUAI REGIONAL LIBRARY, 4344 Hardy St, 96766. Tel 808-245-3617; FAX 808-246-2001.
Open Mon - Wed 8 AM - 8 PM, Thurs - Fri 8 AM - 4:30 PM, Sat 8 AM - noon. Estab 1922 to serve the public of Kauai through a network of a regional library, three community libraries, community-school library, reading room in community center and a bookmobile service. These libraries provide exhibition space for a variety of art works and individual art shows as well as participate in joint art exhibits with the local schools, community college and museum. Gallery provides display and exhibit area for one-man and group art shows. Library will be closed until Fall 1991. Circ 431,678
Income: $794,942 (financed by state appropriation)
Library Holdings: Vols 173,656; Per subs 801; AV — A-tapes, cassettes, fs, rec, slides, v-tapes; Other — Clipping files, pamphlets
Collections: Curator for art in State Buildings Collection for the Island of Kauai funded through the statewide program by the State Foundation on Culture and the Arts. This collection is a revolving collection available for all state buildings and public schools
Exhibitions: Series of small one-man exhibits; average thirteen per year
Activities: Dramatic programs; film programs; lectr open to public, 4 - 8 vis lectr per year; library tours; craft exhibits; contests

WAILUKU

A MAUI HISTORICAL SOCIETY, Bailey House, 2375A Main St, 96793. Tel 808-244-3326; FAX 808-242-4878. *Pres* Barbara Long; *Adminr* Tamara L Horcajo; *Dir* Kealii Reichel
Open daily 10 AM - 4:30 PM. Donation requested adults $2, students $.50. Estab 1957 to preserve the history of Hawaii, particularly Maui County; housed in former residence of Edward Bailey (1814-1903). Average Annual Attendance: 21,000. Mem: 800; dues $10 - $100, annual meeting Jan
Income: $100,000 (financed by membership, gift shop purchases & admission fees)
Collections: Landscape Paintings (1860-1900); Paintings of Hawaiian Scenes by Edward Bailey; Prehistoric Hawaiian Artifacts
Exhibitions: Exhibits depicting missionary life, throughout the year
Publications: LaHaina Historical Guide; La Perouse on Maui; Hale Hoikeike - A House and Its People; Index to the Maui News 1900-1932
Activities: Classes for children; docent training; lect open to public, 4-6 vis lectrs per year; tours; originate traveling exhibitions to schools & other museums; museum shop sells books, reproductions, prints, slides & arts & crafts

IDAHO

BOISE

M BOISE ART MUSEUM, 670 S Julia Davis Dr, 83702. Tel 208-345-8330. *Dir* Dennis O'Leary; *Adminr* Barbara Streng; *Cur of Educ* Michael Riley; *Cur of Exhibitions* Sandy Harthorn; *Community Development Coordr* Nancy McDaniel
Open Tues - Fri 10 AM - 5 PM, Sat & Sun noon - 5 PM, cl Mon & holidays. Admis general $3, sr citizens & college students $2, grades 1 - 12 $1, children under 6 free, first Thurs of month free. Estab 1931, incorporated 1961, gallery opened 1936. Average Annual Attendance: 147,000. Mem: 1600; dues family $35, individual $25; annual meetings in May
Income: Financed by mem, Beaux Arts Societe, grants, private & corporate donations, art festival
Collections: African Sculpture (masks); American, †European & Oriental Collections of Painting, The Minor Arts, Sculpture; collection of works by Northwest Artists; Arranged Image Photography; Contemporary Prints; Glenn C Janss; American Realism
Exhibitions: Biennial exhibition for Idaho artists; 20 exhibitions annually of all media, regional to international; Contemporary & Historical rotating shows; Frederick J Waugh; Strange Vistas, Imagined Histories; Ansel Adams: Transforming the Western Image; John Stuart Curry: Lone Star Art; A Sumptuous Past; Spirits; Creative Clays
Publications: Annual report; bulletin, 4 per year; catalogs & posters of exhibitios, occasionally
Activities: Classes in art & art appreciation; lect open to public; docent tours; concerts; films; outdoor arts festival; Beaux Arts Societe (fund raising auxiliary); exten dept serves 50 mile radius; artmobile; book traveling exhibitions; originate traveling exhibitions statewide & Northwest region; museum shop sells books, original art, reproductions, cards & jewelry

M IDAHO HISTORICAL MUSEUM, 610 N Julia Davis Dr, 83702. Tel 208-334-2120. *Museum Adminr* Kenneth J Swanson; *Registrar* Jody Ochoa; *Cur* Joe Toluse
Open Mon - Sat 9 AM - 5 PM, Sun & holidays 1 - 5 PM. No admis fee
Exhibitions: Story of Idaho

CALDWELL

M ALBERTSON COLLEGE OF IDAHO, Rosenthal Art Gallery, 83605. Tel 208-459-5426; FAX 208-454-2077. *Dir* Lynn Webster; *Asst Dir* Stephen Fisher
Open Tues, Thurs & Sun 1 - 4 PM, cl academic holidays. No admis fee. Estab 1980
Collections: Luther Douglas, Sand Paintings; Paintings; Prints Collection
Exhibitions: Temporary and traveling exhibitions on an inter-museum loan basis
Publications: Exhibit Brochures
Activities: Lect; gallery talks; guided tours; films

MOSCOW

M APPALOOSA MUSEUM, INC, Moscow-Pullman Hwy, PO Box 8403, 83843. Tel 208-882-5578; FAX 208-882-8150. *Pres* King Rockhill; *Cur* Claudia McGehee; *Cur* Marianne Emmendorfer
Open Mon - Fri 8 AM - 5 PM, June - Sept Sat 9 AM - 3 PM. No admis fee. Estab 1974 to collect, preserve, study & exhibit those objects that illustrate the story of the Appaloosa Horse. Average Annual Attendance: 5000. Mem: 22,000; annual meeting on May 1
Income: $6000 (financed by grants from Appaloosa Horse Club)
Purchases: $1600
Collections: Bronzes by Shirley Botoham, Less Williver, Don Christian & William Menshew; reproductions of Chinese, European & Persian Art relating to Appaloosas; reproductions of Charles Russellart; original Western by George Phippen, Reynolds
Activities: Lectures open to the public; tours; museum shop sells books & Appaloosa Horse reproductions

POCATELLO

M IDAHO STATE UNIVERSITY, John B Davis Gallery of Fine Art, 83209. Tel 208-236-2361; FAX 208-236-4000. *Acting Dir* Tony Martin
Open Mon - Fri 10 AM - 5 PM. No admis fee. Estab 1956 to exhibit art. Gallery contains 130 running ft of space with 8 ft ceilings. Average Annual Attendance: 2600
Income: $2600 (financed by city appropriation)
Purchases: $350
Collections: †Permanent collection
Exhibitions: Big Sky Biennial Exhibit; Regional Group Graduate Exhibit; exhibitions & national exhibitions; MFA Thesis Exhibits, bi-weekly one-man shows; student exhibits
Activities: Lectures open to public, 5-10 vis lectr per year; gallery talks; tours; competitions with awards; scholarships; exten dept servs surrounding communities; individual paintings lent to school offices & community

TWIN FALLS

M COLLEGE OF SOUTHERN IDAHO, Herrett Museum & Art Gallery, 315 Falls Ave, PO Box 1238, 83303. Tel 208-733-9554, Ext 355; FAX 208-734-2362. *Dir* James Woods; *Cur Colls* Phyllis Oppenheim; *Gallery Dir* Mike Green; *Display Artist* Bill West; *Display Technician* Nick Peterson; *Office Mgr* Wilma Titmus
Open Tues 9:30 AM - 8 PM, Wed - Fri 9:30 AM - 4:30 PM, Sat 1 - 4:30 PM, cl holidays. No admis fee. Estab 1965. Average Annual Attendance: 10,000
Collections: Pre-Columbian, Pre-Historian & Ethnographic Indian Artifacts
Activities: Classes for adults & children; lectures open to public; gallery talks; tours for school groups

WEISER

M INTERMOUNTAIN CULTURAL CENTER & MUSEUM, 2295 Paddock Ave, PO Box 307, 83672. Tel 208-549-0205. *Mgr* Carol Odoms
Open summer Thurs - Mon noon - 4:30 PM, winter Fri - Mon noon - 4:30 PM. Admis $2. Estab 1962 to preserve the history of Washington County, Idaho. Housed in a 1923 three story, solid concrete building of the Intermountain Institute. Average Annual Attendance: 2200. Mem: 200; dues family $25, couple $15, individual $10
Income: $20,000 (financed by membership, county appropriation, gifts & fundraising)
Collections: Washington County memorabilia & artifacts
Publications: Museum newsletter; quarterly bulletin
Activities: Tours; sales shop sells books, magazines & gift items

ILLINOIS

AURORA

M AURORA UNIVERSITY, Schingoethe Center for Native American Cultures, Dunham Hall, 1400 Marseillaise, 347 S Gladstone, 60506-4892. Tel 708-844-5402; FAX 708-844-5463. *Cur* Marcia Lautanen-Raleigh; *Asst Cur* Denyse M Cunningham; *Educ Mgr* Rachel Kay Schimelfenig; *Cur Asst* Elizabeth Crane

Open Mon, Tues, Thurs & Fri 10 AM - 4:30 PM, Sun 1 - 4 PM. No admis fee. Estab 1990 to advance cultural literacy about Native peoples. Two permanent exhibit galleries with rotating displays from the museum collection; one temporary exhibit gallery with museum collection displays & borrowed materials. Total of 3500 sq ft. Average Annual Attendance: 10,000. Mem: 50; dues individual $30, donor $50 - $500; annual meeting second weekend in Dec
Income: $78,000 (financed by mem & endowment)
Collections: †Ethnographic material from North, Central & South America; †Native American Fine Art; Prehistoric/Pre-Columbian material
Exhibitions: Storyteller Pottery; Biennial Native American Fine Arts Show. (1992) Effects of Columbus. (1993) American Indians of 1893
Publications: Spreading Wings; quarterly newsletter to membership
Activities: Workshops for adults; summer classes for children; outreach materials for educators; docent programs; lect open to public, 3 - 4 vis lectr per year; competitions with awards

BISHOP HILL

M ILLINOIS HISTORIC PRESERVATION AGENCY, Bishop Hill State Historis Site, PO Box D, 61419. Tel 309-927-3345. *Site Mgr* Martha J Downey; *Asst Site Mgr* Cheryl Dowell
Open daily 9 AM - 5 PM, cl Thanksgiving, Christmas, New Years, Veteran's Day, Martin Luther King's Birthday, & President's Day. No admis fee. Estab 1946 to interpret history of Bishop Hill Colony. Average Annual Attendance: 75,000
Income: Financed by state appropriation
Collections: Artifacts pertaining to Bishop Hill Colony 1846-1861; primitive paintings by Olof Krans
Activities: Lect open to public

BLOOMINGTON

M ILLINOIS WESLEYAN UNIVERSITY, Merwin & Wakeley Galleries, Alice Millar Center for Fine Arts, 61702. Tel 309-556-3077, 556-3150; FAX 309-556-3411. *Dir* Ann E Taulbee
Open Mon - Fri noon - 3 PM, Tues evening 7 - 9 PM, Sat & Sun 1 - 4 PM. Estab 1945
Income: Financed by endowment, and membership
Collections: 250 drawings, paintings & prints including works by Baskin, Max Beckmann, Helen Frankenthaler, Philip Guston, John Ihle, Oliviera, Larry Rivers & Whistler
Exhibitions: Gary Justis; Dann Nardi
Publications: Exhibition Posters; Gallery Schedule, monthly;
Activities: Dramatic programs; concerts; lectures open to public, 5 vis lectr per year; tours; competitions; original objects of art lent, on campus only; book traveling exhibitions; traveling exhibitions organized and circulated
L Slide Library, 201 E University St, 61702-2899. Tel 309-556-3077. *Fine Arts Librn* Robert C Delvin
Library Holdings: AV — Slides 35,000

A MCLEAN COUNTY ART ASSOCIATION, Arts Center, 601 N East St, 61701. Tel 309-829-0011. *Pres* Nancy S Merwin
Open Tues 10 AM - 7 PM, Wed - Fri 10 AM - 5 PM, Sat noon - 4 PM. No admis. Estab 1922 to enhance the arts in McLean County. Provides display galleries, sales & rental gallery featuring local professional artists. Brandt Gallery is 2500 sq ft hosting local shows & traveling exhibits.. Mem: 600; annual meeting first Fri in May
Income: Financed by mem, art & book sales
Exhibitions: Annual Amateur Competition & Exhibition; Annual Holiday Show & Sale; 10 - 12 other exhibits, local & traveling
Publications: Quarterly newsletter
Activities: Classes for adults & children; lectures open to public; gallery talks; tours; competitions with awards; gift shop sells fine crafts & original art, conservation framing shop

M MCLEAN COUNTY HISTORICAL SOCIETY, 200 N Main, 61701. Tel 309-827-0428; FAX 309-827-0100. *Exec Dir* Greg Koos; *Librn & Archivist* William Todtz; *Cur* Susan Hartzad; *Museum Educ* Patty Wagner
Open Mon - Sat 10 AM - 5 PM. Admis adults $2, children $1, members free. Estab 1892 to promote history of McLean County. Average Annual Attendance: 5000. Mem: 1000
Income: Financed by endowment & mem
Collections: Civil War; Illinois History; local history; Maternal Culture
Exhibitions: Encounter on the Prairie
Activities: Classes for adults & children; lect open to public; retail store sells books, prints & locally trademarked items

CARBONDALE

M SOUTHERN ILLINOIS UNIVERSITY, University Museum, 62901. Tel 618-453-5388. *Dir* Dr John J Whitlock; *Museology* Dr Robert Lorinskas; *Prog Educational-Community Servs Coordr* Robert De Hoet; *Cur Colls* Lorilee Huffman; *Exhibits Designer* Alan Harasimowicz; *Adj Cur Archaeology* Dr Robert L Rands; *Adj Cur Anthropology* Dr Joel Maring; *Adj Cur Geology* Dr George Fraunfelter; *Adjunct Cur Botany* Dr Donald Ugent; *Adjunct Cur Zoology* Dr Brooks Burr
Open Mon - Fri 9 AM - 3 PM; Sun 1:30 - 4:30 PM. No admis fee. Estab 1874 to reflect the history and cultures of southern Illinois and promote the understanding of the area; to provide area schools and the University with support through educational outreach programs; to promote the fine arts in an unrestricted manner through exhibitions and provide support to the School of Art MFA program through exhibition of MFA graduate students. One art gallery of 1700 sq ft, shared gallery spaces totalling 1500 sq ft, sculpture garden & 2 semi-permanent exhibit halls with 3500 sq ft featuring exhibitis on southern Illinois. Average Annual Attendance: 50,000

Income: Financed by state appropriated budget, federal, state & private grants, donations & University museum associates
Purchases: Michael Dunbar; Richard Hunt; Ke Francis
Collections: Decorative Arts; European & American paintings, drawings & prints from 13th - 20th century with emphasis on 19th & 20th century; photography, sculpture, blacksmithing & art & crafts; Oceanic Collection; Southern Illinois history; 20th century sculpture, metals, ceramics; Asiatic holdings; archaeology; costumes; textiles; geology; zoology
Exhibitions: A variety of changing exhibitions in all media; ethnographic arts; history & the sciences
Publications: Annual report; annual museum newsletter; exhibition catalogs
Activities: Museum studies program; docent training; tours; lect; films; inter-museum loan; public outreach programs; active volunteer program; originates traveling exhibitions; museum gift shop
L Humanities Library, 62901. Tel 618-536-3391. *Acting Humanities Librn* Loretta Koch
Primarily lending
Library Holdings: Vols 32,500; Per subs 150; Micro — Cards, fiche, reels; AV — Cassettes 475, rec; Other — Exhibition catalogs, framed reproductions

CHAMPAIGN

M PARKLAND COLLEGE, Art Gallery, 2400 W Bradley Ave, 61821-1899. Tel 217-351-2485. *Gallery Dir* Denise Seif; *Admin Asst* Paulette Deckard
Open Mon - Fri 10 AM - 3 PM. No admis fee. Estab 1981 to exhibit contemporary fine art. Average Annual Attendance: 10,000
Income: Non-profit, supported by Parkland College & in part by Illinois Arts Council, a state agency
Exhibitions: State of the Art - a Biennial National Watercolor Invitational; Midwest Ceramics Invitational - Biennial, 2-person shows
Publications: Bi-annual exhibitional catalogs & brochures
Activities: Lectures open to students, 2-3 vis lectr per year; originate traveling exhibitions

UNIVERSITY OF ILLINOIS

M Krannert Art Museum, 500 E Peabody Dr, 61820. Tel 217-333-1860. *Acting Dir* Ted Zernich; *Assoc Dir* Jim Peele; *Cur* Maarten Van de Guchte; *Cur* Eunice Maguire; *Registrar* Kathleen Jones
Open Tues - Sat 10 AM - 5 PM, Wed evenings until 8 PM, Sun 2 - 5 PM. No admis fee. Estab 1961 to house and administer the art collections of University of Illinois, to support teaching and research program, and to serve as an area art museum. Gallery is 48,000 sq ft, with 30,000 devoted to exhibition space. Average Annual Attendance: 100,000. Mem: 800; dues $25 and up
Income: Financed by membership, state appropriation, grants
Collections: †American paintings, †sculpture, †prints & drawings; †Ancient Near Eastern Classical & Medieval Art; European Paintings; European & American Decorative Arts; Pre-Columbian Art; †Asian Art; African Art
Publications: Catalogs, 3 or 4 annually
Activities: Classes for children; docent training; symposia; lectures open to the public, 15 vis lectrs per year; concerts; gallery talks; tours; original objects of art lent to museums and university galleries; book traveling exhibitions; originate traveling exhibitions; museum shop
M World Heritage Museum, 484 Lincoln Hall, 702 S Wright St, Urbana, IL 61801. Tel 217-333-2360. *Dir* Dr Barbara E Bohen; *Cur Numismatics* Dr James Dengate; *Asst Dir* Carol Knauss; *Project Coordr* Diana Johnson
Open Mon - Fri 9 AM - 5 PM, Sun 2 - 5 PM when classes in session. No admis fee. Estab 1911. Galleries devoted to different historic and ethnographic cultures. Average Annual Attendance: 30,000. Mem: 800
Income: $120,000
Purchases: John Needles Chester Vase - Apulian Krater ca 320 BC
Collections: Original works and reproductions of Greek, Roman, Egyptian, Mesopotamian, African, Oriental and European art, including sculpture, pottery, glass, implements, coins, seals, clay tablets, inscriptions and manuscripts
Exhibitions: Of Kings, Crusaders & Craftsmen; Beyond the Himalayas. (1991) Bound for Eternity. (1992) An American Encounter
Publications: Heritage, bi-annual newsletter; exhibition brochures
Activities: Lectures open to the public, 1 - 2 vis lectr per yr; concerts; gallery talks; tours; bus trips; workshops; competitions with awards; original objects of art lent for special shows in established museums; book traveling exhibitions; museum shop sells books & reproductions
M Museum of Natural History, 1301 W Green, Urbana, 61801. Tel 217-333-2517. *Dir* Daniel Blake; *Museum Cur* Joanna Kluessandorf; *Museum Cur* Charles Stout; *Assoc Dir* Douglas Brewer; *Cur Malacology* Lowell Getz
Open Mon - Sat 9 AM - 5 PM, Sun 2 - 5 PM. No admis fee. Estab 1868 for research and education in anthropology, botany, geology and zoology. Hall of the Past: Native North Americans, especially Midwest. Average Annual Attendance: 40,000. Mem: 100
Income: Financed by State University support
Collections: Anthropology, Herpetology, Malacology, Mammalogy & Paleontology collections, 400,000 specimens
Activities: Classes for children; docent training; lectures open to public, 2-3 vis lectr per yr; tours; original objects of art lent to other museums; museum shop sells books, native artwork
L Ricker Library of Architecture and Art, 208 Architecture Bldg, 608 E Lorado Taft Dr, 61820. Tel 217-333-0224. *Librn* Dr Jane Block
Open Mon - Thurs 8 AM - 10 PM, Fri 8 AM - 5 PM, Sat 10 AM - 5 PM, Sun 1 - 10 PM. Estab 1878 to serve the study and research needs of the students and faculty of the university and the community. Ricker Library lends material through UIUC Interlibrary Loan. Circ 50,000
Income: $60,200 (financed by state appropriation, blanket order, gifts and UIUC Library Friends)
Purchases: $65,000
Library Holdings: Vols 45,000; Per subs 350; Micro — Fiche, reels; Other — Clipping files, exhibition catalogs, pamphlets, photographs, reproductions, sculpture
Special Subjects: Architecture, Art Education, Art History, Asian Art, Ceramics, Collages, Conceptual Art, Crafts, Decorative Arts, Drawings, Graphic Design,

Handicrafts, History of Art & Archaeology, Illustration, Interior Design, Landscape Architecture, Manuscripts, Mixed Media, Painting - American, Photography, Portraits, Pottery, Restoration & Conservation, Sculpture, Stained Glass, Watercolors, Woodcarvings, History of Art & Architecture; Philosophy of Art, Practice and History of Painting, Vernacular Architecture
Collections: Architectural Folio; Prairie School Architects; Ricker Papers; Frank Lloyd Wright
Publications: Acquisitions list, 4 per year; annual periodicals list

CHARLESTON

M **EASTERN ILLINOIS UNIVERSITY,** Tarble Arts Center, S Ninth St at Cleveland Ave, 61920. Tel 217-581-5832, 581-2787. *Dir* Michael Watts; *Cur of Educ* Donna Meeks; *Registrar* David Pooley
Open Tues - Fri 10 AM - 5 PM, Sat 10 AM - 4 PM, Sun 1 - 4 PM, cl Mon & major holidays. No admis fee. Estab 1982 to encourage the understanding of & participation in the arts. Main Gallery consists of fifteen 20 ft x 20 ft modular units with natural & incandescent lighting; Brainard Gallery, 20 ft x 50 ft; Reading Room, 20 ft x 20 ft; Sales/Rental Gallery, 20 ft x 20 ft. Average Annual Attendance: 18,000. Mem: 300; dues $10 - $1000
Income: Financed by state appropriation, membership contributions, sales & rental commissions, grant & foundation funds
Collections: †Contemporary Printmaking by Midwest artists; †American Scene Prints; Paul Turner Sargent paintings; †Contemporary American Art; †Indigenous Contemporary Illinois Folk Arts
Exhibitions: Solo Exhibitions: Rudy Pozzatti: Recent Works; William L Hawkins: Transformations; Nathan Lerner: 50 Years of Photographic Inquiry; Lasting Impressions: Drawings by Thomas Hart Benton; Group Shows: Echo Press: A Decade of Printmaking; Old Master Prints from Collegiate Collections; Spirited Visions: Portraits of Chicago Artists; A Celebration of Contemporary Illinois Folk Arts; African American Prints from the Ruth Waddy Collection; Wall Ceramics: Cary Esser, Karen Gunderman & Jim Stephenson; Portraits & Prospects: British & Irish Drawings & Watercolors; Annual Exhibitions: Art Faculty Exhibition, All-Student Show (juried, undergraduate), Graduate Art Exhibition (group thesis), Watercolor: Illinois (biennial juried compeition), International Children's Exhibition; Folk Arts from the Collection
Publications: Exhibition catalogs
Activities: Classes & workshops for children & adults; dramatic programs; docent training; lectures open to public; concerts; gallery talks; tours; competitions with awards; films & videos; individual paintings & original objects of art lent to qualified professional galleries, arts centers & museums; book traveling exhibitions, 2 - 4 per yr; originate traveling exhibitions; sales shop sells books, original art & craft pieces; Sales/Rental Gallery rents & sells original works

CHICAGO

AMERICAN CENTER FOR DESIGN GALLERY
For further information, see National and Regional Organizations

AMERICAN SOCIETY OF ARTISTS, INC
For further information, see National and Regional Organizations

M **ARC GALLERY,** 1040 W Huron St, 60622. Tel 312-733-2787. *Chmn* Katherine Rosing
Exhibitions: The Sound & Light Show; Self-Portrait Show; How I Didn't Spend My Summer Vacation

M **ARTEMISIA GALLERY,** 700 N Carpenter, 60622. Tel 312-226-7323. *Pres Emeritus* Fern Shaffer
Open Tues - Sat 11 AM - 5 PM. No admis fee. Estab 1973 to promote public awareness of women artists. Five areas to show five different artists or group shows including a photography gallery. Average Annual Attendance: 12,000. Mem: 18; dues $600; annual meeting in Aug; mem is judged by quality of art work
Income: Financed by grants, donations, gallery members & benefits
Exhibitions: Regular exhibitions by members; annual exhibit of established contemporary women artists; new artists & educational exhibits
Activities: Classes for adults; dramatic programs; lect open to public, 6 - 7 lectr per yr; gallery talks; book traveling exhibitions 1 - 2 per yr; originate traveling exhibitions; shop sells original art, books & magazines

A **THE ART INSTITUTE OF CHICAGO,** Michigan Ave at Adams St, 60603. Tel 312-443-3600; FAX 312-443-0849. *Chmn Board of Trustees* Marshall Field; *Pres & Dir* James N Wood; *Acting Pres of School* Peter Brown; *Exec VPres Admin Affairs* Robert E Mars; *Exec VPres Development & Public Affairs* Larry Ter Molen; *Secy* Phyllis L Robb; *Deputy Dir* Teri J Edelstein; *Cur American Arts* Judith Barter; *Cur European Painting* Douglas Druick; *Cur European Painting Before 1750* Martha Wolff; *Acting Dir Conservation* Frank Zuccari; *Exec Dir Museum Educ* Ronne Hartfield; *Exec Dir Photographic Serv* Alan B Newman; *Cur Photography* David Travis; *Cur Africa, Oceania & the Americas* Richard F Townsend; *Cur Prints & Drawings* Douglas Druick; *Cur Prints & Drawings* Suzanne McCullagh; *Cur Architecture* John Zukowsky; *Dir of Government Affairs & Foundation Relations* Mary Jane Keitel; *Cur Textiles* Christa C Mayer Thurman; *Cur European Decorative Arts, Sculpture & Classical Art* Ian Wardropper; *Cur 20th Century Painting & Sculpture* Charles Stuckey; *Exec Dir of Museum Registration* Mary Solt; *Exec Dir Public Affairs* Eileen E Harakal; *Exec Dir Publications* Susan F Rossen
Open Mon, Wed, Thurs & Fri 10:30 AM - 4:30 PM, Tues 10:30 AM - 8 PM, Sat 10 AM - 5 PM, Sun & holidays noon - 5 PM, cl Christmas. Admis adults $6 suggested, sr citizens and children $3 suggested, Tues no admis fee. Estab and incorporated 1879 to found, build, maintain and operate museums of fine arts, schools and libraries of art, to form, preserve and exhibit collections of objects of art of all kinds, and to carry on appropriate activities conducive to the artistic development of the community. Average Annual Attendance: 1,400,000. Mem: 90,000; dues family $50, individual $40, national associates & students $30
Income: $100,000,000 (financed by endowments, gifts & grants)
Collections: Paintings, sculpture, oriental art, prints and drawings, photographs, decorative arts, primitive art and textiles; The painting collection reviews Western art, with an especially fine sequence of French Impressionists and Post Impressionists; the print collection illustrates the history of printmaking from the 15th - 20th centuries with important examples of all periods. It is particularly rich in French works of the 19th century including Meryon, Redon, Millet, Gauguin and Toulouse- Lautrec; textiles are displayed in the Agnes Allerton Textile Galleries which includes a study room and new conservation facilities; the collection of primitive art consists of African, Oceanic and ancient American objects; The Architecture Collection includes all the 19th & 20th century drawings and architectural fragments in the Institute's permanent collection including the more than 40,000 architectural drawings that are in the Burnham Library of Architecture; The Columbus Drive Facilities include the reconstructed Trading Room from the Chicago Stock Exchange; Arthur Rubloff Paperweight collection is on view; the America Windows, monumental stained glass windows designed by Marc Chagall, are on view in the gallery overlooking McKinlock Court.
Exhibitions: Continual special exhibitions; exhibitions of permanent collections. (1992 - 93) The Ancient Americas: Art from Sacred Landscapes; Building in a New Spain: Contemporary Spanish Architecture; Soviet Propaganda Plates from the Tuber Collection; Magritte; Chicago Architecture & Design, 1923 - 1993: Reconfiguration of an American Metropolis; Gates of Mystery: The Art of Holy Russia from the Russian Museum, St Petersburg; Max Ernst: Dada & the Dawn of Surrealism; Chicago's Dream, A World's Treasure: The Art Institute of Chicago 1893 - 1993; Thonet Furniture from the Collection of Mr & Mrs Manfred Steinfeld & German & Austrian Textiles from the Permanent Collection 1900 - 1930s
Publications: News & Events every two months; Museum Studies; catalogs; Annual Report
Activities: Classes & workshops for adults & children; teacher training; docent training; lect open to public; concerts; gallery walks & talks; guided lect tours; competitions; individual paintings and original objects of art lent to museums around the world; originate traveling exhibitions to selected museums; museum shop sells books, magazines, original art, reproductions, prints, slides, decorative accessories, crafts, jewelry, greeting cards and postcards

L **Ryerson and Burnham Libraries,** Michigan Ave at Adams St, 60603. Tel 312-443-3666; FAX 312-443-0849; Elec Mail bm.aic@rlg. *Dir of Libraries* Jack Perry Brown; *Assoc Librn & Head Reference Dept* Susan Glover Godlewski; *Head Technical Services* Louis Hammack; *Head Slide Librn* Leigh Gates; *Serials Librn* Ann Jones; *Inter-Library Loan Librn* Maureen Lasko; *Architecture Librn* Mary Woolever; *Archivist* John Smith
Open Wed - Fri 12:30 - 4:30 PM, Tues 12:30 AM - 7:45 PM, Sat 10 AM - 4:30 PM, cl Sat from June - Labor Day & legal holidays. Open to museum members, staff of museum, students and faculty of the School of Art Institute and visiting scholars and curators, for reference only
Income: $1,410,000
Purchases: $410,000
Library Holdings: Vols 250,000; Per subs 1500; Micro — Fiche, reels; AV — Slides 380,000; Other — Clipping files, exhibition catalogs, manuscripts, memorabilia, pamphlets, photographs
Special Subjects: Afro-American Art, Art History, Asian Art, Decorative Arts, Folk Art, History of Art & Archaeology, Marine Painting, Painting - American, Pre-Columbian Art, Primitive Art
Collections: Burnham Archive: Chicago Architects, letters, reports; including special Louis Sullivan, Frank Lloyd Wright, and D H Burnham collections; Percier and Fontaine Collection; Chicago Art and Artists Scrapbook: newspaper clippings from Chicago papers from 1880 to present; Mary Reynolds Collection: Surrealism; Bruce Goff Archive; Collins Archive of Catalan Art & Architecture
Publications: Architectural Records In Chicago, research guide; Burnham Index to Architectural Literature (1990)

A **Woman's Board,** 60603. Tel 312-443-3629. *Pres* Mrs Vernon M Wagner
Estab 1952 to supplement the Board of Trustees in advancing the growth of the Institute and extending its activities and usefulness as a cultural and educational institution. Mem: 98; annual meeting May
Income: Financed by contributions

A **Auxiliary Board,** 60603. Tel 312-443-3674. *Pres* Jennifer D Ames
Estab 1973 to promote interest in programs and activities of the Art Institute amoung younger men and women. Mem: 60; dues $100; annual meeting June

A **Antiquarian Society,** 60603. Tel 312-443-3641. *Pres* Mrs Morris S Weeden; *Secy* Suzanne Pattou
Open Tues & Wed 9 AM - 5 PM. Estab 1877. Makes gift of decorative arts to the Institute. Mem: 557; by invitation; annual meeting Nov
Income: Financed by donations, benefits, annual dues
Exhibitions: European Decorative Arts & Sculpture Exhibition
Publications: Antiquarian Society Catalogue, every 10 years
Activities: Lectures and seminars for members; tours; trips

A **Print and Drawing Dept,** 60603. Tel 312-443-3660. *Pres* Edward Blair
Estab and incorporated 1922 to study prints and drawings and their purchase for the institute. Mem: 190; dues $35-50
Income: Financed by membership contributions
Activities: Lectures; gallery talks

A **Society for Contemporary Arts,** 60603. Tel 312-443-3630; FAX 312-443-0849. *Pres* Terry Moritz
Estab and incorporated 1940 to assist the Institute in acquisition of contemporary works. Mem: 180; annual dues $300 - $500; annual meeting May
Income: Membership contributions
Activities: Lectures, seminars & biennial exhibition at the Institute

A **Department of Asian Art,** 60603. Tel 312-443-3834. *Cur Asian Art* Yutaka Mino; *Assoc Cur Chinese Art* Elinor Pearlstein; *Assoc Cur Japanese Art* James T Ulak
Estab 1925 to promote interest in the Institute's collection of Asian art. Mem: 50; dues $50
Purchases: Tang Dynasty Lu-shan Ware, 9th Century Chinese Cermaics
Collections: Chinese furniture; bronze; jade; ceramics; Buddhist arts & paintings Collections; Clarence Buckingham Japanese Woodblock Print Collection; Japanese Buddhist art; ceramic & painting Collection; Korean Ceramics Collection

Exhibitions: Ice and Green Clouds: Traditions of Chinese Celadon; Todai-ji: The Great Eastern Temple; The Light of Asia Suleyman
Publications: Exhibition catalogues
Activities: Lectures open to public; symposia on exhibitions
A **Textile Society,** 60603. Tel 312-443-3696. *Pres* Diana Senior
Open daily 10 AM - 4 PM by appointment only. Estab 1978 to promote appreciation of textiles through lectures, raising of funds, special publications and exhibitions for the Department of Textiles
M **Kraft General Food Education Center Museum,** Michigan Ave at Adams St, 60603. Tel 312-443-3680. *Assoc Dir of Museum Educ* Jean Sousa
Open Mon, Wed - Fri 10:30 AM - 4:30 PM, Tues 10:30 AM - 8 PM, Sat 10 AM - 5 PM, Sun & holidays noon - 5 PM. Admis free with Art Institute of Chicago discretionary admis, no admis fee Tuesday. Estab 1964. The facility will be renovated beginning in Feb of 1991 & will reopen in the fall of 1992. The new center will include a main exhibition gallery, family room, classrooms, a Teacher Resource Center, a seminar room, an auditorium, conference room & staff offices. Average Annual Attendance: 150,000
Income: Financed by grants, gifts & endowment; renovation financed by Kraft General Foods & the Woman's Board; exhibitions supported by grants from Chicago Community Trust & NEA
Exhibitions: Art Inside Out: Exploring Art & Culture Through Time
Publications: Family Self Guides to permanent collections & special exhibitions; Forms in Space I; gallery games; Heritage Hike I, II, III, IV; yearly publications: Volunteer Directory; Information for Students & Teachers; quarterly brochures on family programs, teachers' services, school & general programs
Activities: Docent training; teacher & family workshops; lect open to the public; gallery walks & games; tours; performances; artist demonstrations
L **Teacher Resource Center,** Michigan Ave at Adams St, 60603. Tel 312-443-3680.
Open Tues 3 - 7 PM, Sat 10 AM - 4 PM. Open for reference only. Average Annual Attendance: 20,000
Income: Financed by endowment
Library Holdings: Vols 1500
Activities: Center for junior museum activities such as gallery games and architectural walks

A **ARTS CLUB OF CHICAGO,** 109 E Ontario St, 60611. Tel 312-787-3997; FAX 312-787-8664. *Dir* Robbin Lockett; *Pres* Stanley M Freehling; *First VPres* John Cartland; *Secy* Marshall Holeb
Open 10 AM - 5:30 PM. No admis fee. Estab 1916 to maintain club rooms for members and provide public galleries for changing exhibitions. Gallery has 200 running ft of wall space. Average Annual Attendance: 15,000. Mem: 1150; annual meeting in Nov
Income: Financed by membership dues
Purchases: Occasional purchases gifts & bequests
Exhibitions: (1991) Islamic Prayer Rugs from Oberlin College Collection; Artist members Exhibition (sculpture & painting); Hans Belmer: Forty Year Retrospective (photographs)
Publications: Exhibition Catalogs
Activities: Dramatic programs; lectures; concerts; traveling exhibitions organized and circulated
L **Reference Library,** 109 E Ontario St, 60611
Library Holdings: Vols 3000; Per subs 6; Other — Exhibition catalogs
Special Subjects: 20th Century paintings, sculpture, drawings, prints & photography

M **BALZEKAS MUSEUM OF LITHUANIAN CULTURE,** 6500 S Pulaski Rd, 60629. Tel 312-582-6500; FAX 312-582-5133. *Pres* Stanley Balzekas Jr; *VPres* Joseph Katauskas; *Exec Dir* Val Ramonis
Open seven days a week 10 AM - 4 PM. Admis adults $3 sr citizens $2, children $1. Estab 1966 as a repository for collecting and preserving Lithuanian cultural treasures. Mem: 2000; annual dues $25
Income: $10,00 (financed by membership and donations)
Collections: †Amber; Philately; †Coins; †Textiles; †Wooden folkart; †Maps; †Paintings; †Graphics
Exhibitions: Various exhibits of paintings, graphics & sculpture (1993) Amber
Publications: Lithuanian Museum Review, bi-monthly
Activities: Classes for adults and children; workshops; lectures open to the public, 5 vis lectrs per year; concerts; gallery talks; tours; individual paintings & original objects of art lent to other institutions; originate traveling exhibitions; museum shop sells books, reproductions, prints, amber, gift items, textiles, dolls & coins; junior museum
L **Research Library,** 6500 S Pulaski Rd, 60629. Tel 312-582-6500; FAX 312-582-5133. *Head Librn* Dr David Fainhauz; *Librn* Jessie Daraska
Open daily 10 AM - 4 PM. Estab 1966 to preserve Lithuanian-American literature & culture. Open to public for reference only
Library Holdings: Vols 20,000; Per subs 20; Micro — Cards, prints; AV — A-tapes, cassettes, rec, slides; Other — Clipping files, exhibition catalogs, manuscripts, memorabilia, pamphlets, prints, reproductions
Collections: †Reproductions of Lithuanian artists †Information on Lithuanian artists and their works
Exhibitions: Rare Book & Map Exhibits

M **BEACON STREET GALLERY,** Uptown, Hull House, 4520 N Beacon St, 60640. Tel 312-528-4526. *Dir & Cur* Patricia Murphy; *Exhib Coordr* Martha Ehrlich
Open Wed - Sat 11 AM - 4 PM. No admis fee. Estab to exhibit folk & ethnic art & avant-garde work
Exhibitions: (1992) Discovering America (contemporary Native American painting); Subversive Acts (Hmong Pandau in transition). (1993) Contemporary Asian American Painting
M **Gallery at the School,** 1225 W School, 60657. Tel 312-528-4526. *Exhib Coordr* Martha Ehrlich
Open Wed - Sat 11 AM - 4 PM. No admis fee. Estab to exhib folk & ethnic art & avant-garde work
Exhibitions: (1992) Aborigine Prints & Batiks from Australs; Long Road Home (Guatemalan prints & photos). (1993) From Traditional to Contemporary Chinese Painting; Contempoary Euritrian Painting & Sculpture Show

M **ROY BOYD GALLERY,** 739 N Wells St, 60610-3520. Tel 312-642-1606; FAX 312-642-2143. *Co-Dir* Ann Boyd; *Co-Dir* Roy Boyd; *Assoc Dir* Leslie Wolfe
Open Tues - Sat 10 AM - 5:30 PM. No admis fee. Estab 1972 to exhibit art
Collections: Contemporary American paintings; Russian & Baltic photography; sculpture & works on paper

M **CHICAGO ARCHITECTURE FOUNDATION,** 224 S Michigan Ave, 60604. Tel 312-922-3432. *Mgr* Sally Hess; *Exec Dir* John Engman
Open Mon - Fri 9 AM - 6 PM, Sat 9 AM - 5 PM, Sun noon - 4:30 PM. Comprehensive program of tours, lectures exhibitions & special events to enhance public awareness & appreciation of Chicago architecture. Average Annual Attendance: 160,000. Mem: 5000; dues $35
Income: Financed by mem, shop & tour center, foundation, government & private grants
Activities: Classes for adults; dramatic programs; docent training; lect open to public, 35 vis lectr per year; concerts; tours; sales shop sells books, magazines, architecturally inspired gift items, stationery & posters
M **Glessner House,** 1800 S Prairie Ave, 60616. Tel 312-922-3432. *Cur* Carol Callahan
Open Wed & Fri noon - 3 PM, Sat & Sun noon - 4 PM. Admis adults $5, students & sr citizens $3. Estab 1967 to save and restore Glessner House, the last remaining building in Chicago designed by reknown late 19th century architect Henry Hobson Richardson. Glessner House was completed in 1887 on Prairie Avenue, Chicago's most elegant residential neighborhood. The museum is furnished with original period furnishings in the English Arts and Crafts and Aesthetic Movement styles. Average Annual Attendance: 10,000. Mem: 4400; dues $35
Income: Financed by membership, tours, programs & grants
Collections: †House Furnishings
Publications: Chicago Architecture Foundation Members' Newsletter, bimonthly
Activities: Classes for adults & children; docent training; dramatic programs; lect open to public, 60 vis lectr per yr; forum discussions, symposia; original objects of art lent to galleries which are mounting exhibitions on architecture; lending collection contains architectural ornaments; sales shop sells books, magazines, reproductions, prints, posters, stationery & small gift items
M **Henry B Clarke House Museum,** 1800 S Prairie Ave, 60616. Tel 312-922-3432. *Cur* Janice Griffin
Admis $5 ($8 for joint tour with Glessner House). Estab 1982. The oldest building in Chicago; includes period rooms. Average Annual Attendance: 8000
Collections: History & †Decorative Arts of the 1830's, 40's, 50's
Activities: Classes for adults & children; dramatic programs; docent training; Lectures open to the public, 45 vis lectr per yr; tours; individual paintings & original objects of art lent; museum shop sells books, magazines, reproductions, slides

A **CHICAGO ARTISTS' COALITION,** 5 W Grand Ave, 60610. Tel 312-670-2060; FAX 312-670-2521. *Exec Dir* Arlene Rakoncay
Open Mon - Fri 9 AM - 5 PM. Estab 1975 to provide services, benefits, information & support to visual artists. Resource center includes reference books, pamphlets & catalogs. Mem: 2800; mem open to professional fine & graphic artists; dues $30; monthly board meetings; annual meeting in Sept
Income: $130,000 (financed by membership, city & state appropriation, donations, earned income projects, corporations & foundations)
Publications: Artists' Gallery Guide; Artists' Resource Book; Artists' Bookkeeping Book; Chicago Artists News, 11 times per yr
Activities: Lectures open to public, 25 vis lectrs per yr

M **CHICAGO CHILDREN'S MUSEUM** (Formerly Express-Ways Children's Museum), 465 E Illinois St, 2nd Floor, 60611. Tel 312-527-1000; FAX 312-527-9082. *Executive Dir* Dianne L Sautter; *Assoc Executive Dir* Judy Chiss
Open Tues - Fri 12:30 - 4:30 PM, Sat & Sun 10 AM - 4:30 PM, cl Mon. Admis adults $3, children $2, Thurs 5 - 8 PM free. Estab 1982 to inspire discovery & self-expression in children through interactive exhibits & programs. Average Annual Attendance: 3500 families. Mem: dues $35
Income: $1,200,000 (financed by mem, foundation, corporate, government, individual support, earned income)
Exhibitions: Amazing Chicago; City Hospital; Touchy Business; The Art & Science of Bubbles; Lies About Animals; Magic & Masquerades
Activities: Classes for adults & children; docent programs; retail store sells books, prints, educational toys & games

A **CHICAGO HISTORICAL SOCIETY,** Clark St at North Ave, 60614. Tel 312-642-4600; FAX 312-266-2077. *Chmn* Richard H Needham; *VChmn* Edgar D Jannotta; *VChmn* W Paul Kruss; *Treas* Philip W Hummer; *Pres* Ellsworth H Brown; *Cur Decorative Arts* Robert Goler; *Cur Costumes* Barbara Schreier; *Ed* Russell Lewis; *Dir Educ & Public Prog* Amina Dickerson; *Cur Architecture* Wim de Wit; *Cur Manuscripts Collections* A J Motley; *Librn* Janice McNeill
Open Mon - Sat 9:30 AM - 4:30 PM; Sun & holidays noon - 5 PM. Admis adults $3, children (6 - 17) $2, sr citizens $1; no admis fee Mon. Estab 1856 to maintain a museum and library of American history with special emphasis on the Chicago region. Average Annual Attendance: 175,000. Mem: 8500; dues $30; annual meeting in Oct
Income: $6,200,000 (financed by endowment, mem, city & state appropriations & public donations)
Collections: Architectural Archive; Chicago Decorative Arts; Costumes; Graphics; Manuscripts; Printed Collection
Exhibitions: We the People: Creating a New Nation; a House Divided: America in the Age of Lincoln; Chicago History Galleries; City Goes to War: Chicago During WW II; World's Columbian Exposition; The Art of Archibald J Motley, Jr
Publications: Books, Calendar of Events & newsletter, quarterly; catalogs; Chicago History, quarterly
Activities: Classes for adults and children; lect open to public, 8-10 vis lectr per year; gallery talks; tours; sales shop selling books, magazines, prints, reproductions, slides

L **CHICAGO PUBLIC LIBRARY,** Harold Washington Library Center, Art Information Center, Visual & Performing Arts Div, 400 S State St, 60605. Tel 312-747-4800; FAX 312-747-4832. *Acting Commissioner* Robert R Remer; *Head Visual & Performing Arts Div* Rosalinda I Hack; *Head Special Projects* Gerald Zimmerman; *Head Art Information Center* Yvonne S Brown; *Picture Coll Librn* Margaret K Gross; *Coll Development* Karen Kuntz; *Serials* Laura Morgan
Open Mon - Thurs 9 AM - 7 PM, Fri 9 AM - 5 PM, Sat 9 AM - 5 PM. Estab 1872 as a free public library and reading room. The original building was built in 1897. New location of central library. The Harold Washington Library Center was opened to the public in 1991. Audio-visual materials are restricted for use by Chicago area residents
Income: $258,230 (financed by city & state appropriations)
Library Holdings: Vols 101,399; Per subs 539; Micro — Fiche 6192, reels 7684; AV — V-tapes 307; Other — Clipping files, exhibition catalogs, pamphlets, photographs
Special Subjects: Afro-American Art, American Indian Art, American Western Art, Decorative Arts, Folk Art, Historical Material, Islamic Art, Judaica, Oriental Art, Painting - American, Chicago Architecture; Dance
Collections: Exhibition catalogues beginning in 1973, primarily English language catalogues; folk dance collection of 50 loose leaf volumes; picture collection of over one million items of secondary source material covering all subject areas; dance videocassettes documenting history, styles & local choreography; Chicago Artists Archives
Activities: Dramatic programs; lect open to public; concerts; interlibrary loan

A **CHICAGO SOCIETY OF ARTISTS, INC,** 2548 N McVicker, 60639. Tel 312-889-5348. *Pres* Barry Skurkis; *VPres* Annette Okner; *VPres* John Duffy; *Treas* Janine Collier-Charlton; *Recording Secy* Rita Doyle Leavitt; *Corresponding Secy* Dolores Minkoff
Estab 1887 to unite artists in fellowship, to maintain high professional standards, and to advance art with exhibitions. Average Annual Attendance: 5000. Mem: 106; mem qualifications include professional standing as a visual artist & passing a jurying of at least 6 art works by board of directors; dues $25; meetings 4th Sun in Apr & 1st week in Dec
Income: $7000 (financed by mem & sales of calendars)
Exhibitions: Held at various commercial, non-profit & civic galleries
Publications: The Chicago Society of Artists Lino-Cut Calendar, annual; Role and Impact: the Chicago Society of Artists
Activities: Lecture services by members; lectures open to public, 4 vis lectrs per yr; competitions with awards; exten dept serves Chicago & suburbs; sells books & calendars

COLUMBIA COLLEGE
L **Library,** 600 S Michigan Ave, 60605. Tel 312-663-1600; FAX 312-663-1707. *Dir* Mary Schellhorn; *Head Technical Serv* Patricia Smith; *Fine Arts Librn* Wendy Hall
Open Mon - Thurs 8 AM - 10 PM, Fri 8 AM - 6 PM, Sat 9 AM - 5 PM. Estab 1893 to provide library & media services & materials in support of the curriculum & to serve the college community as a whole. For lending & reference
Library Holdings: Vols 107,000; Per subs 300; Micro — Fiche, reels; AV — Cassettes, slides, v-tapes; Other — Clipping files, exhibition catalogs, pamphlets
Special Subjects: Advertising Design, Art Education, Commercial Art, Film, Graphic Arts, Theatre Arts, Video
Collections: †George Lurie Fine Arts Collection; Film & Television Script Collection
Publications: Film/Videotape List; Index to Filmscripts; Periodicals List
M **The Museum of Contemporary Photography,** 600 S Michigan Ave, 60605-1996. Tel 312-663-5554; FAX 312-663-1707. *Dir* Denise Miller Clark; *Asst Dir* Ellen Ushioka; *Curatorial Asst Preparator* Jennifer Hill; *Museum Coordr & Chmn Dept Art & Photography* John Mulvany
Open Sept - May, Mon - Fri 10 AM - 5 PM, Sat noon - 5 PM; June & July, Mon - Fri 10 AM - 4 PM, Sat noon - 4 PM, cl Aug. Estab 1976 to exhibit, collect & promote contemporary photography. 4000 sq ft on two levels; newly designed 1500 sq ft main exhibition gallery permits a spacious installation of 200 photographs; upper level gallery can accommodate an additional 200-300 prints. Mem: 450; dues $10 - $1,000
Collections: Contemporary American photography, including in-depth holdings of works by Harold Allen, Harry Callahan, Barbara Crane, Louise Dahl-Wolfe, Dorothea Lange, Danny Lyon, Barbara Morgan, David Plowden, Anne Noggle & Jerry Uelsmann
Exhibitions: (1992) Open Spain/Espana Abierta: Contemporary Documentary Photography in Spain. (1993) Within this Garden: Photographs by Ruth Thorne-Thomsen
Publications: Exhibit catalogs
Activities: Lectures open to public, 6 vis lectrs per yr; lending collection of photographs; book traveling exhibitions, 1-2 per yr; originate traveling exhibitions; museum shop sells books, catalogs & posters

A **CONTEMPORARY ART WORKSHOP,** 542 W Grant Place, 60614. Tel 312-472-4004. *Co-Dir* John Kearney; *Co-Dir* Lynn Kearney
Open daily 12:30 - 5 PM, Sat 2 - 5 PM. No admis fee. Estab 1949 as an art center & a Workshop-Alternative Space for artists; it is the oldest artist-run art workshop in the country. Studios for 20 artists & two galleries for exhibition of developing & emerging artists from Chicago & other parts of the country are maintained. Average Annual Attendance: 7000
Income: Financed by contributions, foundations, Illinois Arts Council, Chicago Council on Fine Arts, National Endowment for the Arts, & earnings by the workshop fees
Exhibitions: John Kearney; Mat Williams; Didier Nolet; Nick Blosser; Peter Roos; Doug Jeck; Joe Seigenthaler; Delia Seigenthaler John Slavik; Perry Pollock; Willie Kohler; Tom Gengler; Dawn Guernsey; Anna Kunz Paula Martinez; Catherine Arnold; Denise Falk; Mark Ottens
Activities: Classes for adults; lectures open to public, 5 vis lect per yr; gallery talks; tours; gallery sells artwork

C **CONTINENTAL BANK CORPORATION,** Art Collection, 231 S LaSalle St, 60697. Tel 312-828-2345. *Art Consultant* Emily Nixon
Collections: †Vintage photographs; †contemporary master prints; †folk art; †American Indian art & artifacts; †Pre-Columbian art & artifacts; †African art; †ancient art; †art of the American West

M **DUSABLE MUSEUM OF AFRICAN AMERICAN HISTORY,** 740 E 56th Pl, 60637. Tel 312-947-0600; FAX 312-947-0677. *Founder* Margaret T Burrough; *Chief Cur* Ramon Price; *Registrar* Theresa Christopher
Open Mon - Fri 9 AM - 5 PM, Sat & Sun noon - 5 PM. Admis adults $2, children & students $1, groups by appointment. Estab 1961 as history and art museum on African American history. Mem: dues corp $1000, family $35, general $25, student & sr citizen $15
Collections: Historical archives; paintings; photographs; prints; sculpture
Publications: Books of poems, children's stories, African and African-American history; Heritage Calendar, annually
Activities: Lect; guided tours; book traveling exhibitions; sales shop selling curios, sculpture, prints, books and artifacts

C **EXCHANGE NATIONAL BANK OF CHICAGO,** 120 S LaSalle St, 60603. Tel 312-781-8076; FAX 312-750-6467. *Cur* Herbert Kahn
Open Mon - Fri 8 AM - 4 PM. No admis fee. Estab 1968 as a community service by making a meaningful cultural contribution to the community. Collection displayed in public areas of the bank
Collections: Approximately 2000 photographs by important photographers since the founding of photography up to the present
Activities: Tours

M **FIELD MUSEUM OF NATURAL HISTORY,** Roosevelt Rd at Lake Shore Dr, 60605. Tel 312-922-9410; FAX 312-427-7269. *Pres* Willard L Boyd
Open daily 9 AM - 5 PM, cl Thanksgiving, Christmas, New Years. Admis family (maximum) $10, adults $3, students $2, sr citizens $2, no charge on Thurs. Estab 1893 to preserve and disseminate knowledge of natural history. 22 anthropological exhibition halls, including a Hall of Primitive Art are maintained. Average Annual Attendance: 1,400,000. Mem: 23,172; dues $30 & $35
Income: $20,000,000 (financed by endowment, mem, city & state appropriations & federal & earned funds)
Collections: Anthropological, botanical, geological & zoological collections totaling over 19,000,000 artifacts & specimens, including 100,000 art objects from North & South America, Oceania, Africa, asia & prehistoric Europe
Exhibitions: Permanent exhibitions: Ancient Egypt Exhibition; Prehistoric Peoples Exhibition; Dinosaur Hall; The American Indian; Pacific Exhibition
Publications: In the Field, monthly; Fieldiana (serial)
Activities: Classes for adults and children; lectures open to the public, 25 vis lectrs per year; concerts; gallery talks; tours; exten dept serving Chicago area; original objects of art lent to qualified museum or other scholarly institutions; traveling exhibitions organized & circulated; museum shop selling books, magazines, prints, slides
L **Library,** Roosevelt Rd at Lake Shore Dr, 60605. Tel 312-922-9410, Ext 282; FAX 312-427-7269. *Librn* W Peyton Fawcett
Open Mon - Fri 8:30 AM - 4:30 PM
Library Holdings: Vols 235,000; Per subs 4000
Special Subjects: American Indian Art, Anthropology, Antiquities-Egyptian, Archaeology, Asian Art
Collections: Rare Book Room housing 6000 vols

C **THE FIRST NATIONAL BANK OF CHICAGO,** Art Collection, 1 First National Plaza, Suite 0523, 60670. Tel 312-732-5935. *Dir Art Prog* John Hallmark Neff; *Cur* Daniel T Mills; *Asst* John W Dodge
Open to public by appointment only. No admis fee. Estab 1968 to assemble works of art to serve as a permanent extension of daily life. Collection displayed throughout bank building and overseas offices
Collections: Art from Africa, America, Asia, Australia, the Caribbean Basin, Europe, Latin America, Near East and the South Seas ranging from 6th Century BC to the present
Exhibitions: (1991) The Age of the Marvelous, Hood Museum, Dartmouth; Marvin D Cone - 100 Birthday Anniversary, Cedar Rapids Museum of Art; Leaves from the Bodhi Tree: The Art of Pala India & its International Legacy, Dayton Art Institute; Lenore Tawney: A Retrospective, American Craft Museum; Tom Shannon, Moderna Museet, Stockholm
Activities: Individual objects of art lent only to major exhibitions in museums; originate traveling exhibitions

L **HARRINGTON INSTITUTE OF INTERIOR DESIGN,** Design Library, 410 S Michigan Ave, 60605. Tel 312-939-4975; FAX 312-939-8005. *Library Dir* Adeline Schuster; *Asst Librn Cataloging* Elaine Lowenthal; *Circulation Specialist* Elaine Lowenthal; *Library Technical Asst* Jeff Dawson
Open Mon, Wed & Fri 8 AM - 5 PM, Tues & Thurs 8 AM - 9 PM, summer daily 9 AM - 5 PM. Estab 1960
Purchases: 30,000 (books, periodicals & AV materials)
Library Holdings: Vols 15,000; Per subs 95; AV — Slides 10,000, v-tapes 100; Other — Clipping files, exhibition catalogs, pamphlets 200
Special Subjects: Architecture, Furniture, Interior Design, Pure Design, 20th Century Design
Collections: Furniture Manufacture Catalogs
Publications: current Awareness; subject bibliographies; recent acquistions

M **HYDE PARK ART CENTER,** 1701 E 53rd St, 60615. Tel 312-324-5520. *Exec Dir* Eileen M Murray
Open Tues - Sat 11 AM - 5 PM. No admis fee. Estab 1939 to stimulate an interest in art. Average Annual Attendance: 14,000. Mem: 800; dues family $35
Income: $195,000 (financed by endowment, mem, city & state appropriation, foundations, corporations & private contributions)
Exhibitions: Annual Holiday Show & Sale
Publications: Quarterly newsletter, exhibition catalogues
Activities: Classes for adults & children; lect open to the public; scholarships; gallery sells artwork

C **ILLINOIS BELL,** 225 W Randolph St, 60606. Tel 312-727-1480. *Corp Art Dir* Dina Sigmund
Lobby gallery open 8 AM - 5 PM. Estab 1967 to support the arts; to make the company a responsive member of the community; to provide uplifting atmosphere for employees. Collection displayed throughout building and in offices; Lobby exhibits art (not from company collection)
Collections: 725 works, mostly prints by contemporary Illinois artists
Activities: Gallery talks; tours for groups; originate traveling exhibitions from Lobby exhibits to various galleries and other public locations in Illinois

M **ILLINOIS STATE MUSEUM,** State of Illinois Art Gallery, 100 W Randolph, Suite 2-100, 60601. Tel 312-814-5322; FAX 312-814-3891. *Admin Asst & Registration* Jane Stevens; *Preparations* Luke Dohner; *Educ & Public Relations* Judith Lloyd
Open Mon - Fri 10 AM - 6 PM. No admis fee. Estab 1985 for the purpose of promoting an awareness of the variety of art found and produced in Illinois. 3 large galleries & 2 smaller galleries provide a flexible space for a diverse exhibition program. Exhibits are produced by the Illinois State Museum & the State of Illinois Art Gallery. Average Annual Attendance: 47,000
Exhibitions: (1991) Moholy-Nagy: A New Vision for Chicago; Gertrude Abercrombie (paintings); Ed Shay: My Back Yard; Spirited Vision: Portrait of Chicago Artists, Patty Carroll; Edith Altman (paintings & books). (1992) John Warner Norton; Computer Art: Pushing the Boundaries
Publications: Exhibit catalogs
Activities: Book traveling exhibitions, 6 per year; originate traveling exhibitions; museum shop sells books and original art

M **Illinois Artisans Shop,** 100 W Randolph St, 60601. Tel 312-814-5321; FAX 312-814-3891. *Dir ILL Artisans Prog* Ellen Gantner; *Mgr ILL Artisans Shop* Kasha Yankovich
Open Mon - Fri 9 AM - 5 PM. No admis fee. Estab 1985. A not-for-profit program to showcase the craft work of Illinois artisans accepted in a consignment shop & to educate the public about the scope of craft art. Mem: 1100 artists in prog; qualification for men: juried art work
Income: Financed by state appropriation & retail sales of art work
Activities: Demonstrations; lect open to public

M **Southern Illinois Arts & Crafts Marketplace,** PO Box 69, 62897. Tel 618-629-2220; FAX 618-629-2559. *Dir ILL Artisans Prog* Ellen Gantner; *Dir SIACM* Leo Packard; *Mgr IL Artisans Shop* Mary Lou Galloway
Open daily 9 AM - 5 PM. No admis fee. Estab 1990. A not-for-profit program to showcase the craft work of Illinois artisans accepted in a consignment shop & to educate the public about the scope of craft art. Mem: 1100 artists in prog; qualification for mem: juried art work
Income: Financed by state appropriation & retail sales of art work
Activities: Demonstrations; lect open to public

M **Lincoln Home National Historic Site,** 406 S Eighth St, 61701. Tel 217-524-1520. *Dir IL Artisans Prog* Ellen Gantner; *Mgr IL Artisans Shop* Gloria Redemer
Open Mon - Sat 9 AM - 5 PM, Sun noon - 5 PM. No admis fee. Estab 1990. A not-for-profit program to showcase the craft work of Illinois artisans accepted in a consignment shop & to educate the public about the scope of craft art. Mem: 1100 artists in program
Income: Financed by state appropriation & retail sales of art work
Activities: Demonstrations; lect open to public

M **LOYOLA UNIVERSITY OF CHICAGO,** Martin D'Arcy Gallery of Art, 6525 N Sheridan Rd, 60626. Tel 312-508-2679; FAX 312-508-2993. *Dir* David Robertson; *Cur* Rita McCarthy
Open Mon - Fri noon - 4 PM, Tues & Thurs 6 - 9 PM, Sun 1 - 4 PM. No admis fee. Estab 1969 to display the permanent university collection of Medieval, Renaissance & Baroque decorative arts & paintings. One gallery set up as a large living room with comfortable seating, classical music, view of Lake Michigan & art objects in view
Income: Financed by gifts
Collections: †Bronze, †enamel, †gold, †ivory, paintings, †sculpture, †silver, †textiles, †wax
Activities: Gallery talks; tours on request; paintings & original objects of art lent to qualified museums; lending collection contains original art works, paintings & sculpture

L **Library,** 6525 N Sheridan Rd, 60626-5385. Tel 312-508-2658; FAX 312-508-2993. *Dir* David Robertson; *Cur* Rita McCarthy
Open to university students & scholars
Library Holdings: Vols 14,100; Per subs 45
Publications: The Art of Jewelry, 1450 - 1650; Enamels, the XII to the XVI century; The First Ten Years, Notable Acquisitions of Medieval Renaissance & Baroque Art

M **MEXICAN FINE ARTS CENTER MUSEUM,** 1852 W 19th St, 60608. Tel 312-738-1503; FAX 312-738-9740. *Pres* Helen Valdez; *Executive Dir* Carlos Tortolero; *Visual Arts Coord* Rene Arceo
Open Tues - Sun 10 AM - 5 PM. No admis fee. Estab 1982. Average Annual Attendance: 70,000. Mem: 1100; dues $20
Income: $535,000 (financed by mem, city, state & federal appropriation, corporation & foundations)
Collections: Mexican prints, photography & folk art collection; Latino art collection
Exhibitions: Jose Guadalupe Posada
Activities: Classes for children in docent programs; lect open to the public, 4 vis lectr per year; museum shop sells books, original art, folk art & prints

M **MUSEUM OF CONTEMPORARY ART,** 237 E Ontario St, 60611. Tel 312-280-2660; FAX 312-280-2687. *Chief Cur* Richard Francis; *Dir* Kevin Consey; *Assoc Dir* Mary I Ittelson; *Educ Dir* Roger Dell; *Adminr* Helen Dunbeck; *Assoc Cur* Lynne Warren; *Dir Development* Carolyn Stolper; *Registrar* Lela Hersh; *Store Mgr* Janet Smith; *Controller* Nancy Cook; *Dir Public Marketing* Maureen King
Open Tues - Sat 10 AM - 5 PM, Sun noon - 5 PM, cl Mon, Thanksgiving, Christmas & New Year's Day. Suggested admis adults $6, students, sr citizens &

children under 16 $3, members & children under 10 free, Tues free. Estab 1967 as a forum for contemporary arts in Chicago. Average Annual Attendance: 110,000. Mem: 5700
Income: $1,000,000 (financed by endowment, membership, public and private sources)
Collections: Permanent collection of 20th century and contemporary, constantly growing through gifts and purchases
Exhibitions: (1991) CUBA - USA: The First Generation; Options 40: Cheri Samba; Options 41: Julia Wachtel; Jean-Pierre Raynaud; Remy Zaugg; Options 42: Daniel Senise; Sigmar Polke; Memory & Metaphor: The Art of Romare Bearden; Rosemarie Trockel. (1992) Donald Lipski: The Bells; Alfredo Jaar: Geography Equals War; Artists' Books from the Permanent Collection; Modeling the Future: The New Museum & Key Works from the Permanent Collection; Conceptualism - PostConceptualism: The 1960s to the 1990s; Art at the Armory: Occupied Territory. (1993) Emmet Gown: Photographs; Alexander Calder from the Collection of the Ruth & Leonard J Horwich Family; Lorna Simpson: For the Sake of the Viewer; Options 45: Libby Wadsworth; Conceptual Photography from the Gerald S Elliott Collection; Hand-Painted Pop: American Art in Transition, 1955 - 62
Publications: Bimonthly calendar, exhibition catalogs
Activities: Docent training; teacher workshops; lectures; performance, tours, films; book traveling exhibitions; originate traveling exhibitions; museum store selling books, designer jewelry and other gifts, magazines, original art & reproductions

L **Library,** 237 E Ontario St, 60611. Tel 312-280-2692; FAX 312-280-2687. *Librn* Sonja Staum; *Librn* Sonja Staum
Library collection
Library Holdings: Vols 15,000; Per subs 110; Artist Files 125 drawers; AV — Cassettes 400, slides 45,000, v-tapes 300

A **MUSEUM OF HOLOGRAPHY - CHICAGO,** 1134 W Washington Blvd, 60607. Tel 312-226-1007; FAX 312-829-9636. *Dir* Loren Billings; *VPres* Patrick McCallig; *Secy* Robert Billings; *Dir Display & Design* Constance Kasprzak; *Dir Educ* Dr Ted Niemiec; *Dir Research* John Hoffmann; *Dir System Development* Terry Kay; *Dir Electronics & Kinetics* John General
Open Wed - Sun 12:30 - 5 PM, group tours Mon, Tues by appointment. Admis $2.50. Estab 1976 to perform all functions of a museum. 15,000 sq ft of exhibition space, oak panel walls, special display wings, sales gallery; school facilities comprise 4600 sq ft of fully equipped laboratories and darkrooms with additional lecture facilities. Average Annual Attendance: 25,000
Income: $780,000 (financed by sales, research grants, teaching, consulting, museum store, school, tours & rentals)
Collections: Holograms from throughout the world
Exhibitions: Holography. (1993) Artistic States of Light, Energy & Matter
Publications: Holography; class text books
Activities: Classes for adults; lectures open to public, 6 vis lectr per yr; book traveling exhibitions; museum shop sells books, originals & holograms

L **David Wender Library,** 1134 W Washington Blvd, 60607. FAX 312-829-9636; *Exec Dir* Loren Billings
Open Wed - Sun 12:30 - 5 PM
Library Holdings: Vols 350; Per subs 10; AV — Kodachromes, motion pictures, slides, v-tapes; Other — Exhibition catalogs, framed reproductions

M **MUSEUM OF SCIENCE AND INDUSTRY,** 57th St & Lake Shore Dr, 60637. Tel 312-684-1414; FAX 312-684-7141. *Pres & Dir* Dr James S Kahn; *VPres for Admin* Dr David E Hennage; *VPres Prog* Dr Peter Anderson; *Dir Education* Theodore H Ansbacher; *Dir Operations* Thomas Dabertin; *Dir Exhibits* Paul Hoffer
Open summer Mon - Sun 9:30 AM - 5:30 PM, winter Mon - Fri 9:30 AM - 4 PM, Sat, Sun & holidays 9:30 AM - 5:30 PM. No admis fee. Estab 1926 to further public understanding of science, technology, industry, medicine & related fields. Visitor-participation exhibits depicting scientific principles, technological applications & social implications in fields of artscience. Average Annual Attendance: 4,000,000. Mem: 8090; dues life $1000, contributing $100, family $30, individual $20
Income: $16,200,000 (financed by endowment, membership, city & state appropriation, contributions & grants from companies, foundations & individuals)
Collections: Artscience Gallery, artworks based on scientific & technological principles; This is Photography, scientific, industrial & popular uses of photography; Chicago, industrial & scientific development; Newspaper in America, world events in photos; Colleen Moore's Fairy Castle
Exhibitions: Learning & Learning disabilities
Publications: Progress, bimonthly; calendar of events, bimonthly
Activities: Classes for adults & children; dramatic programs; field trips; summer camps; teacher workshops; lectures open to public, 4 vis lect per yr; competitions; outreach activities; lending collection contains communications, transportation & textile equipment; book traveling exhibitions; originate traveling exhibitions; museum shop sells books, magazines, prints, slides, postcards & souvenirs

M **NAB GALLERY,** 1433 Wolfram, 60657. Tel 312-525-5418. *Assoc Dir* Robert Horn; *Assoc Dir* Craig Anderson
Open Sat & Sun. No admis fee. Estab 1974 as an artist-run space to show original artworks. Average Annual Attendance: 5000. Mem: 5; open to artists with portfolio; dues $500; monthly meetings
Income: $15,000 (finaced by mem)
Exhibitions: Bob Horn; Larry Kolden; Craig Anderson; Local Artist Juried Exhibit
Activities: Classes for adults; dramatic progams; competitions

M **NAME,** 700 N Carpenter St, 60622. Tel 312-226-0671. *Executive Dir* Irene Tsatsos
Open Tues - Sat noon - 6 PM. Estab 1973, as a non-profit alternative art gallery. Gallery has 4500 sq ft of space. Average Annual Attendance: 12,500
Income: Financed by city, state & federal grants, private donations & corporate/foundation grants
Exhibitions: Edith Altman (review); Esther Parada (review); Engaged Objects; Colliding Fronts: Art & Science; Collage at N.A.M.E.; Convincing Lies;

Photography as Unfaithful Witness
Publications: Exhibition catalogues
Activities: Lectures open to the public, 4 vis lectr per year; gallery talks; book traveling exhibitions; originate traveling exhibitions

L **NAME Documents,** 700 N Carpenter, 60622-5901. Tel 312-226-0671. *Dir* Irene Tsatsos
Open Tues - Sat noon - 6 PM. Estab 1973
Library Holdings: AV — Slides; Other — Clipping files, exhibition catalogs, memorabilia, prints

L **NEWBERRY LIBRARY,** 60 W Walton St, 60610-3394. Tel 312-943-9090. *Pres & Librn* Charles T Cullen; *Academic VPres* Richard Brown; *Librn* Mary Wyly; *VPres Finance* Melody Savage
Open Tues - Thurs 10 AM - 6 PM, Fri & Sat 9 AM - 5PM. Estab 1887 for research in the history & humanities of Western Civilization. For reference only. Two small galleries are maintained for exhibitions. Mem: 1950; annual dues $35; annual meeting in Oct
Income: $4,500,000 (financed by endowment, mem, gifts, federal, corporate & foundation funds)
Purchases: $400,000
Library Holdings: Vols 1,400,000; Per subs 1500; Micro — Cards, fiche, reels; AV — A-tapes, motion pictures, rec, v-tapes; Other — Clipping files, exhibition catalogs, manuscripts 5,000,000, memorabilia, original art works, pamphlets, photographs
Special Subjects: American Indian Art, American Western Art, Art History, Ethnology, Graphic Arts, History of Art & Archaeology, Manuscripts, Maps, Southwestern Art
Collections: †Edward Ayer Collection, manuscripts & maps related to European expansion to the Americas & the Pacific; †Everett D Graff Collection of Western Americana books & manuscripts; †John M Wing Foundation Collection on history of printing & aesthetics of book design; †Rudy L Ruggles Collection on American constitutional & legal history
Publications: A Newberry Newsletter, quarterly; Center for Renaissance Studies Newsletter, 3 times per yr; Mapline, quarterly newsletter; Meeting Ground, bi-annual newsletter; Origins, quarterly newsletter
Activities: Classes for adults; dramatic programs; docent training; lectrs open to public, some open to members only, 35 vis lectr per yr; concerts; gallery talks; tours; scholarships & fels offered; individual paintings & original objects of art lent to museums & libraries on restricted basis; book traveling exhibitions 1-2 per yr; sales shop sells books, reproductions, slides

M **NORTHEASTERN ILLINOIS UNIVERSITY,** Gallery, Art Dept, 5500 N St Louis Ave, 60625. Tel 312-583-4050, Ext 3324. *Coordr & Prof* Mary Stoppert
Open Mon - Fri 1 - 5 PM. No admis fee. Estab Feb 1973 for the purpose of providing a link between the University and the local community on a cultural and aesthetic level, to bring the best local and Midwest artists to this community. Gallery is located in the commuter center on the University campus. Average Annual Attendance: 5000
Income: Financed by Department of Art funds and personnel
Publications: Flyers on each show
Activities: Competitions

M **NORTHERN ILLINOIS UNIVERSITY,** Art Gallery in Chicago, 212 W Superior St, Suite 306, 60610. Tel 312-642-6010. *Dir* Peggy Doherty
Open Tues - Sat 11 AM - 5 PM. No admis fee. Estab 1985. 1700 sq ft, 200 linear ft, movable walls, 10.5 ft ceilings. Average Annual Attendance: 3000
Income: Financed by state appropriation
Publications: Occasional catalogues
Activities: Adult classes; lectrs open to public, 5 vis lectrs a year; panel discussions & seminars; concerts; gallery talks; book traveling exhibitions; originate traveling exhibitions

M **NORTH PARK COLLEGE,** Carlson Tower Gallery, 3225 W Foster, 60625. Tel 312-583-2700; FAX 312-583-0858. *Gallery Dir* Gayle V Bradley-Johnson
Open Mon - Fri 9 AM - 4 PM, occasional weekend evenings. No admis fee. Educational development of aesthetic appreciation
Collections: Original contemporary Christian, Illinois & Scandinavian art
Activities: Classes for adults; lectures open to public, 1-2 vis lectrs per year; concerts; exten dept serves Chicago; book traveling exhitions, 1-2 per year

M **PALETTE & CHISEL ACADEMY OF FINE ARTS,** 1012 N Dearborn St, 60610. Tel 312-642-4400. *Pres* Joe Vangsness; *Exec Dir* Karen Lambeth
Gallery open Fri 2 - 6 PM, Sat 12 - 4 PM, workshops are open to the public on a regular basis. No admis fee. Estab & incorporated 1985 to provide a meeting/work place for the visual arts. Building contains galleries, classrooms, studios & library. Mem: 203; dues $200; patron & nonresident membership available
Collections: Permanent Collection: works by James Montgomery Ward; J Jeffery Grant; A W Mauach; Richard Schmid & others
Exhibitions: Five Members Award shows; guest artists & organizations frequently exhibited; local & regional juried shows
Publications: The "COW BELL", quarterly
Activities: Educ events, classes for artists; lectures open to public; tours; competitions; awards; scholarships & fels offered

M **PEACE MUSEUM,** 350 W Ontario, 60610. Tel 312-440-1860. *Dir* Peter Ratajczak
Open Tues, Wed, Fri - Sun noon - 5 PM, Thurs noon - 8 PM, cl Mon. Admis adults $2, senior citizens, students & children $.50, members free. Estab 1981 to provide peace education through the arts; presents issue-oriented exhibits. Gallery has changing exhibits; museum presents four exhibits per yr. Administrative Office: 78 E Washington, Chicago, IL 60602. Average Annual Attendance: 2500; dues $25 - $500
Income: Financed by foundation grants, donations & memberships
Collections: Artists and peace; collection of segments from the Ribbon; music, musicians and peace
Exhibitions: Play Play: An Exhibit on Toys & Games for Parents, Teachers, Children; The Ribbon: A Celebration of Life, segments from the handcrafted

peace ribbon that was wrapped around the Pentagon; Visions: Works by Contemporary Sculptors; Dr Martin Luther King, Jr: Peacemaker. Forced out:Photographs of Refugees; Highlights of Permanent Collection; John Hartfield: photographs of Nazi Period
Publications: Notes from the Peace Museum - quarterly membership newsletter
Activities: Lect open to public, 10 - 15 vis lectr per yr; competitions; individual paintings & original objects of art lent to other galleries, art directors of publications & universities; lending collection contains 100 original art works, 100 original prints, 150 photographs, 2000 slides & peace posters; book traveling exhibitions; traveling exhibitions to library exhibit spaces, galleries, schools & community centers; museum shop sells books, reproductions, posters, buttons, jewelry & cards

C **PLAYBOY ENTERPRISES, INC,** 680 N Lake Shore Dr, 60611. Tel 312-751-8000; FAX 312-751-2818. *VPres & Art Dir* Tom Staebler; *Business Mgr & Cur* Barbara Hoffman
Open to public by appointment only in groups. No admis fee. Estab 1953 to gather and maintain works commissioned for reproduction by Playboy Magazine
Collections: Selected works from 4000 illustrations and fine art pieces, works include paintings and sculpture representing 20th Century artists such as Robert Ginzel, Roger Hane, Larry Rivers, James Rosenquist, Seymour Rosofsky, Roy Schnackenberg, George Segal, Andy Warhol, Robert Weaver, Tom Wesselman, Karl Wirsum, and others
Publications: Catalogs pertaining to Beyond Illustration - The Art of Playboy; The Art of Playboy - from the First 25 Years
Activities: Lectures; tours; annual illustration awards; individual paintings & original objects of art lent to museums & schools; originate traveling exhibitions to galleries, universities, museums and cultural centers

L **Library,** 680 N Lake Shore Dr, 60611. Tel 312-751-8000; FAX 312-751-2818.
Library Holdings: Other — Clipping files, exhibition catalogs, original art works, photographs

M **POLISH MUSEUM OF AMERICA,** 984 N Milwaukee Ave, 60622. Tel 312-384-3352; FAX 312-384-3799. *Pres* Tom Podl; *Cur* Krzysztof Kamyszew
Open daily noon - 4 PM. No admis fee. Estab 1937, to promote & preserve Polish & Polish-American culture. A specialized Museum and Gallery containing works of Polish artists, and Polish-American artists is maintained. Average Annual Attendance: 30,000. Mem: dues $25
Income: Financed by donations & fundraising
Collections: Originals dating to beginning of 20th century, a few older pieces; Pulaski at Savannah (Batowski); works of Polish artists, Polish-American artists and works on Polish subject; Nikifor, Jan Styka, Wojciech Kossak; paintings from the collection of the Polish Pavilion from 1939 World's Fair in NY
Exhibitions: Modern Polish Art; folk art; militaria
Publications: Polish Museum Quarterly; catalogs
Activities: Lectures & film presentations open to public, 15 vis lectrs pr yr; concerts; gallery talks; tours; paintings & original objects of art lent to other museums or cultural institutions; book traveling exhibitions, 2 per yr; originate traveling exhibitions circulated to schools, universities & cultural institutions; sales shop sells books, magazines, reproductions, folk art from Poland

L **Research Library,** 984 N Milwaukee Ave, 60622. Tel 312-384-3352; FAX 312-384-3799. *Librn* Maria Karpowicz; *Cur* Krzysztof Kamyszew
For reference only; interlibrary circulation
Library Holdings: Vols 63,000; Per subs 125; Micro — Fiche, reels; AV — A-tapes, cassettes, fs, motion pictures, rec, slides 2000, v-tapes; Other — Clipping files, exhibition catalogs, framed reproductions, manuscripts, memorabilia, original art works, pamphlets, photographs 3000, prints, reproductions 1000, sculpture
Special Subjects: Maps, Coins & Medals, Posters, Poland & works by Polish-American authors, philatelic, kosciuszko
Collections: Haiman; Paderewski; Polish Art
Activities: Lect

M **RANDOLPH STREET GALLERY,** 756 N Milwaukee Ave, 60622. Tel 312-666-7737; FAX 312-666-8585. *Exec Dir* Peter Taub; *Asst Dir* Guy Nickson; *Communications Coordr* Marie Shurkus
Open Tues - Sat 12 noon - 6 PM. Estab 1979 dedicated to the development & understanding of new & innovative art. 1600 sq ft, 14 ft ceiling ht, white walls, sprung wood floors; exhibition space in one room, performance space in adjoining room of same dimensions with lighting grid, basic theatrical lighting & sound system, video playback equipment. Average Annual Attendance: 10,000
Income: $190,000 (financed by endowment, membership, city & state appropriation & private foundation grants)
Exhibitions: In Evidence: by Nayland Blane, Jesica Holt & Andres Serrano
Publications: Performance Art Journal, bi-monthly
Activities: Educ dept, panel discussions with artists; gallery talks

A **THE RENAISSANCE SOCIETY,** Bergman Gallery, 5811 S Ellis, 60637. Tel 312-702-8670; FAX 312-702-9669. *Dir* Susanne Ghez
Open Tues - Fri 10 AM - 4 PM, Sat & Sun noon - 4 PM, cl summer. No admis fee. Founded 1915 to advance the understanding & appreciation of the arts in all forms. Mem: 500; annual dues $40; annual meeting June
Exhibitions: Six changing exhibitions per yr
Publications: Exhibit catalogs
Activities: Classes for adults; lectures open to public; gallery talks; film programs; performances

L **SAINT XAVIER UNIVERSITY,** Byrne Memorial Library, Art Dept, 3700 W 103rd St, 60655. Tel 312-779-3300, Ext 365; FAX 312-779-5231. *Dir* JoAnn Ellingson
Open daily 8 AM - 10 PM. Estab 1847
Library Holdings: Vols 129,000; Per subs 649; Micro — Cards; AV — Kodachromes, motion pictures, rec, slides 10,000, v-tapes; Other — Original art works
Collections: Permanent art collection

L SCHOOL OF ART INSTITUTE OF CHICAGO, Video Data Bank, 37 S Wabash, Colulmbus Dr at Jackson Blvd, 60603. Tel 312-899-5172; FAX 312-263-0141. *Dir* Kate Horsfield; *Assoc Dir* Mindy Faber
Open 9 AM - 6 PM. No admis fee. Estab 1892
Income: $350,000 (financed by grants & earned income)
Library Holdings: AV — V-tapes 3000
Special Subjects: Art History, Film, Mixed Media, Painting - American, Painting - British, Painting - German, Photography, Sculpture, Video, On Art & Artists - over 200 interviews with contemporary artists on video, performance
Collections: Video Tapes: Early Video History, Independent Video/Alternative Media, On Art & Artists
Publications: Annual catalog of holdings

L SCHOOL OF THE ART INSTITUTE OF CHICAGO, John M Flaxman Library, 37 S Wabash, 60603. Tel 312-899-5097; FAX 312-443-0849. *Dir* Nadene Byrne; *Head Readers Services* Roland Hansen; *Asst Dir & Head Technical Services* Fred Hillbruner
Open Mon - Thurs 8:30 AM - 9 PM, Fri 8:30 AM - 5 PM, Sat 9 AM - 5 PM, Sun 10 AM - 6 PM. Estab 1967 to provide a strong working collection for School's programs in the visual and related arts. Circ 39,300
Income: $260,100 (financed through the operational budgets of the School of Art Institute of Chicago)
Purchases: $57,800
Library Holdings: Vols 32,000; Per subs 320; AV — Cassettes, motion pictures, rec, v-tapes; Other — Exhibition catalogs, pamphlets, prints
Special Subjects: Art, Humanities
Collections: †Erens Film Scripts; Whitney Halstead Art History; †Film Study Collection; †Artists Interview Series; †Artist's Book Collection; Mary McCarty Art History
Publications: Book SAIC, quarterly newsletter; Artist produced periodicals, 1986; International Artists Book Show Catalog; Library Handbook for patrons, annually; Ferret collection guides

M SPERTUS MUSEUM, 618 S Michigan Ave, 60605. Tel 312-922-9012, Ext 248. *Dir* Morris A Fred; *Exhibits Cur* Mark Akgulian; *Registrar & Cur of Permanent Collection* Olga Weiss; *Educational Cur* Kathi Lieb; *Membership Coordr* Barbra Lovell; *Tour Coordr* Susan Shore; *Artifact Center Cur* Susan Bass Marcus
Open Sun - Thurs, 10 AM - 5 PM, Fri 10 AM - 3 PM, Artifact Center open Sun - Thurs 1 - 4:30 PM. Admis adults $3.50 children, students and senior citizens, $2, Fri free. Estab 1967 for interpreting and preserving the 3500-year-old heritage embodied in Jewish history. Museum houses a distinguished collection of Judaica from many parts of the world, containing exquisitely designed ceremonial objects of gold, silver, bronze and ivory. Average Annual Attendance: 25,000
Income: Financed by contributions and subsidy from Spertus College
Collections: A pertinent collection of sculpture, paintings and graphic art; ethnographic materials spanning centuries of Jewish experience; a permanent holocaust memorial; Judaica, paintings, ceremonial silver, textiles, archaeology
Exhibitions: Three changing exhibitions per year in permanent gallery; Ann C Field Gallery; features works by contemporary Jewish artists
Publications: Special publications with exhibits; Annual Calendar of Events
Activities: Educ dept; docent training; lectures; gallery talks and tours; lending collection contains 1500 slides & archaeological replicas; traveling exhibitions organized and circulated; museum store selling books, original art reproductions, slides and jewelry from Israel; The Artifact Center is a hands on exhibit on art & archaeology in ancient Israel
L Asher Library, 618 S Michigan Ave, 60605. Tel 312-922-9012, 922-9020; FAX 312-922-6406. *Admin Librn* Kathleen Bloch; *Reference Librn* Dan Sharon; *Dir* Michael Terry; *Cataloger* Ahuva Rosenberg
Reference library open to public. Includes Badona Spertus Art Library
Library Holdings: Vols 1400
Special Subjects: Judaica

M SWEDISH AMERICAN MUSEUM ASSOCIATION OF CHICAGO, 5211 N Clark St, 60640. Tel 312-728-8111. *Pres* Wayne Moky; *Exec Dir* Kerstin B Lane; *First VPres* Joan Papadopoulos; *Treas* Bertha Carlson; *Treas* June Carlson; *Secy* Marcia Youngberg
Open Tues - Fri 11 AM - 4 PM, Sat 11 AM - 3 PM. No admis fee, donations appreciated. Estab 1976 to display Swedish arts, crafts, artists, scientists, and artifacts connected with United States, especially Chicago. Material displayed in a store front in Andersonville, once a predominantly Swedish area in Chicago. Average Annual Attendance: 25,000. Mem: 12,000; dues $5-$500; metings Apr, June & Oct
Income: $200,000 (financed by mem & donations)
Collections: Artifacts used or made by Swedes, photographs, oils of or by Swedes in United States
Publications: Bulletins, bi-monthly
Activities: Educ dept for Swedish language and culture study; classes for adults; dramatic programs; docent training; lectures open to public, 2 vis lectr per year; concerts

M TERRA MUSEUM OF AMERICAN ART, 664 N Michigan Ave, 60611. Tel 312-664-3939; FAX 312-664-2052. *Pres* Daniel J Terra; *Dir* Robert Donnelley; *Controller* Stuart Popowcer; *Dir Retail Operations* Chris Kennedy; *Staff Asst* Holly Wagoner; *Dir Educ* Roberta Gray Katz; *Mgr School & Teacher Prog* Virginia Spindler; *Registrar* Jayne Johnson; *Cur* D Scott Atkinson; *Librn* Catherine Wilson; *Membership Coordr* Stephanie Sokolec
Open Tues noon - 8 PM, Wed - Sat 10 AM - 5 PM, Sun noon - 5 PM, cl Mon. Admis adults $4, sr citizens, college students with ID & children 12-18 $2.50, members & children under 12 free. Estab 1980 to educate the public through the exhibition of the Terra Collection and visiting exhibitions of American paintings. Average Annual Attendance: 174,872. Mem: 2000; dues $25-$2000
Income: Financed by endowment and memberships
Collections: †Terra Collection of 18th, 19th and 20th century American oil, watercolor and pastel paintings
Exhibitions: (1993) The Drawings of Stuart Davis: The Amazing Continuity; Theme & Improvisation: Kandinsky & the American Abstraction at the Addison

Gallery of American Art
Publications: Exhibition catalogues
Activities: Docent training; gallery talks; guided tours; individual and original objects of art lent to other museums; sales shop sells books, prints, slides and posters
L Library, 664 N Michigan Ave, 60611. Tel 312-664-3939; FAX 312-664-2052. *Librn* Catherine Wilson
Reference library
Income: Privately financed
Library Holdings: Vols 4500; Per subs 9; Auction Catalogs; Other — Exhibition catalogs, manuscripts, pamphlets
Special Subjects: American Western Art

M UKRAINIAN NATIONAL MUSEUM AND LIBRARY, 2453 W Chicago Ave, 60622. Tel 312-276-6565. *Dir & Pres* Dr George Hrycelak; *Cur* Oksana Teodorowych
Open Sun 11 AM - 4 PM. Estab 1954, to collect and preserve Ukrainian cultural heritage
Income: Financed through membership and donations
Library Holdings: Vols 18,000; Per subs 100; Micro — Cards; AV — Kodachromes, slides; Other — Clipping files, framed reproductions, manuscripts, memorabilia, original art works, pamphlets, photographs, sculpture
Special Subjects: Large collection of Ukrainian Folk Arts: easter egg painting, embroidery, woodcarving
Activities: Classes for adults and children; tours; Book traveling exhibitions; traveling exhibitions organized and circulated

UNIVERSITY OF CHICAGO
M Lorado Taft Midway Studios, 6016 Ingleside Ave, 60637. Tel 312-753-4821. *Dir* Thomas Mapp
Open Mon - Fri 9 AM - 5 PM, cl Sun. Studios of Lorado Taft and Associates, a Registered National Historic Landmark; now University of Chicago, Committee on Art & Design
Activities: Special performances
M David and Alfred Smart Museum of Art, 5550 S Greenwood Ave, 60637. Tel 312-702-0200; FAX 312-702-3121. *Dir* Richard Born; *Registrar* Bruce Linn; *Preparator* Rudy Bernal; *Public Information Officer* Rachel Lerner-Rosenberg; *Operations Mgr* Priscilla Stratton; *Educ Coordr* Cathleen Gibbons; *Asst Cur* Tiffany D'Alessandro; *Educ Asst* Vipule Patel; *Public Information Asst* Jessica Clark
Open Tues, Wed, Fri 10 AM - 4 PM, Sat - Sun noon - 6 PM. No admis fee. Estab 1974 to assist the teaching and research programs of the University of Chicago by maintaining a permanent collection and presenting exhibitions & symposia of scholarly and general interest. Gallery designed by E L Barnes; exhibit space covers 9500 sq ft & also contains print & drawing study room, Elden Sculpture Garden. Average Annual Attendance: 35,000. Mem: 400; dues individual $35
Income: Financed by membership, university and special funds, corporations and foundations, goverment grants
Collections: †American, †Ancient, †Baroque, †decorative arts, †drawings, †Medieval, †Modern European, †Oriental & Renaissance paintings , †photographs, †prints, †sculpture
Exhibitions: Four major exhibitions yearly
Activities: Docent training; lectures open to public, 5-10 vis lectrs per year; symposia; gallery talks; tours; concerts; individual paintings & original objects of art lent to professional art museums; book traveling exhibitions, 1-3 per year; originate traveling exhibitions; sales shop sells books, post cards, posters, papers and photographs
M Oriental Institute Museum, 1155 E 58th St, 60637. Tel 312-702-9520; FAX 312-702-9853. *Dir* William M Sumner; *Cur* Karen L Wilson; *Registrar* Raymond Tindel; *Archivist* John Larson; *Asst Cur* Emily Teeter
Open Tues, Thurs - Sat 10 AM - 4 PM, Wed 10 AM - 8:30 PM, Sun noon - 4 PM, cl Mon. No admis fee. Estab 1894 as a museum of antiquities excavated from Egypt, Mesopotamia, Assyria, Syria, Palestine, Persia, Anatolia and Nubia, dating from 7000 years ago until the 18th Century AD. Average Annual Attendance: 58,000 - 62,000. Mem: 2650; dues $30 and up
Income: Financed by endowment, membership, federal and state grant
Collections: Ancient Near Eastern antiquities from pre-historic times to the beginning of the present era plus some Islamic artifacts; Egypt: colossal statue of King Tut, mummies; Iraq: Assyrian winged human-headed bull (40 tons); Mesopotamina temple & house interior, reconstructions, sculpture, jewelry; Iran: Persian bull; column & capital from Persepolis; Palestine: Megiddo ivories & horned altar
Exhibitions: (1992 - 93) Sifting the Sands of Time: The Oriental Institute & the Ancient Near East; Vanished Kingdoms of the Nile: The Rediscovery of Ancient Nubia
Publications: Annual report; News & Notes, bimonthly; museum guidebook; brochures
Activities: Classes for adults & children; lectures open to the public, 8 - 10 vis lectr per yr; gallery talks; tours; original objects of art lent to museums and institutions; museum shop sells books, magazines, reproductions, prints, slides, original art, crafts, and near Eastern jewelry
—**Oriental Institute Research Archives,** 1155 E 58th St, 60637-1569. Tel 312-702-9537; FAX 312-702-9853. *Librn* Charles E Jones; *Asst Archivist* Terry Wilfong
Open to staff, students and members for reference
Library Holdings: Vols 25,000; Per subs 500; Micro — Cards, fiche, reels; AV — A-tapes, cassettes, Kodachromes, lantern slides, motion pictures, slides; Other — Clipping files, exhibition catalogs, manuscripts, memorabilia, pamphlets, photographs
Special Subjects: Anthropology, Antiquities-Assyrian, Antiquities-Byzantine, Antiquities-Egyptian, Antiquities-Greek, Antiquities-Persian, Archaeology, Asian Art, Historical Material, History of Art & Archaeology, Islamic Art, Textiles, The ancient Near East
L Art Slide Collection, 5540 S Greenwood, 60637. Tel 312-702-0261. *Cur* Olivera Mihailovic
Open Mon - Fri 8:30 AM - 4 PM; cl Sat & Sun. Estab 1938. For reference only
Library Holdings: AV — Slides 296,000

L Max Epstein Archive, 420 C Joseph Regenstein Library, 60637. Tel 312-702-7080. *Cur* Benjamin Withers
Open Mon - Fri 9 AM - 5 PM; cl Sat & Sun. Estab 1938. For reference only
Income: Financed by gifts and donations
Library Holdings: Vols 55,500; Mounted photographs of art 500,000; catalogued and mounted photographs added annually 8000; auction sales catalogs, Union Catalog of Art Books in Chicago
Collections: Photographs of architecture, sculpture, painting, drawing & decorative arts illustrating Far Eastern, South Asian & Western art history; illustrated Bartsch Catalogue; DIAL Index; Marburger Index; Papal Medals Collection; Courtauld Institute Illustrated Archive; Courtauld Photo Survey

M UNIVERSITY OF ILLINOIS AT CHICAGO, Gallery 400, 400 S Peoria, 60607. Tel 312-996-6114; FAX 312-996-5378. *Dir* Karen Indeck
Open during exhibitions. No admis fee. Estab 1983 to highlight current trends in art & architecture. Loft space approx 130 ft x 30 ft serving primarily as exhibition hall, as well as for lectures, films & video screenings
Income: $120,000 (financed by state & federal grants, college of AAUP)
Exhibitions: (1989) Dwight Heald Perkins: Social Consciousness & the Prairie School; Colors: Color Laser Copier Art; Irwin Kremen: per se Collages & other Works; Studio Arts Faculty
Publications: Exhibit Catalogs, 2 per yr
Activities: Lectures open to public, 10 vis lectrs per yr; book traveling exhibitions, 1-2 per yr

M UPTOWN CENTER HULL HOUSE ASSN, Beacon Street Gallery & Performance Company, 1225 W School St, 60657. Tel 312-528-4526; FAX 312-528-7153. *Cur* Susan F Field
Open Mon - Fri 10 AM - 5 PM. No admis fee. Estab 1983 as a contemporary arts & folk art gallery. Average Annual Attendance: 40,000
Income: Financed by endowment, city & state appropriation
Exhibitions: Mexican Mask Show; Avant Guard Productions
Activities: Classes for adults & children; dramatic programs

DANVILLE

M VERMILION COUNTY MUSEUM SOCIETY, 116 N Gilbert St, 61832. Tel 217-442-2922. *Prog Dir* Susan Richter; *Asst Dir* June Larson
Open Tues - Sat 10 AM - 5 PM, Sun 1 - 5 PM, cl Mon, Thanksgiving and Christmas. Admis 15 years over $1, 6 - 14 $.50, under 6 years no admis fee, school and scout groups no admis fee. Estab 1964; in 1855 doctor's residence and carriage house. Average Annual Attendance: 5500. Mem: 1001; dues life $150, patron $50, contributing $25, organization $10, family $12, individual $10, student & sr citizen $8
Collections: Costumes; decorative arts; graphics; historical material; paintings; sculpture
Exhibitions: (1992) 135th Mann's Chapel Commemorative Service; Candlelight Christmas Walk. (1993) Lincoln Birthday Open House; Rock & Mineral Show Open House; Focus on History, Photography Contest; 11th Annual Midwest Heritage Quilt Show
Publications: Heritage, quarterly magazine
Activities: Lectures open to public; museum shop sells books, magazines & prints
L Library, 116 N Gilbert St, 61832. Tel 217-442-2922. *Prog Dir* Susan E Richter
Open to the public for reference
Income: Financed by endowment fund
Library Holdings: Vols 400; AV — Slides, v-tapes; Other — Clipping files, photographs
Collections: Medical equipment, furniture, photographs, arrowheads
Publications: The Heritage of Vermilion County, quarterly; bimonthly newsletter

DECATUR

M MILLIKIN UNIVERSITY, Perkinson Gallery, Kirkland Fine Arts Center, 1184 W Main St, 62522. Tel 217-424-6227; FAX 217-424-3993. *Dir* Marvin L Klaven
Open Mon - Fri noon - 5 PM. No admis fee. Estab 1970. Gallery has 3200 sq ft & 224 running ft of wall space
Income: Financed by university appropriation
Collections: Drawings; painting; prints; sculpture; watercolors
Publications: Monthly show announcements
Activities: Lectures; guided tours; gallery talks

DE KALB

M NORTHERN ILLINOIS UNIVERSITY, NIU Art Museum, Altgeld Hall, 2nd Floor, 60115. Tel 815-753-1936. *Dir* Lynda Clark
Open Mon - Fri 10 AM - 6 PM. No admis charge. Estab 1970. Main Gallery is 6000 sq ft, Gallery 200 is 3000 sq ft. Average Annual Attendance: 50,000
Income: Financed by state appropriation & grants from public agencies & private foundations
Collections: †Contemporary & †Modern paintings, †prints, †sculptures, & †photographs, †Burmese Art; Native American Art
Publications: Kathryn Bloom: Innovation in Arts Education; exhibit catalogs
Activities: Classes for adults & children; dramatic programs; docent training; lectures open to public, 10 vis lectr per yr; gallery talks; tours; competitions sponsored vary; original objects of art lent to accredited museums; book traveling exhibitions; sales shop sells original limited edition prints
L Library, 60115. Tel 815-753-1634. *Arts Librn* Charles Larry
Estab 1977 to provide reference service and develop the collection
Library Holdings: Vols 32,035; Per subs 217; rare books 250, art book titles 937, art book volumes; Micro — Cards, fiche, reels; AV — Motion pictures, slides, v-tapes; Other — Exhibition catalogs

EDWARDSVILLE

L SOUTHERN ILLINOIS UNIVERSITY, Lovejoy Library, Fine Arts Dept, PO Box 1063, 62026. Tel 618-692-2711; FAX 618-692-2381. *Friends of Lovejoy Library* Donna Bardon; *Fine Arts Librn* Therese M Zoski
Open Mon - Thurs 8 AM - 11 PM, Fri 8 AM - 5 PM, Sat 9 AM - 6 PM, Sun noon - 10 PM. Estab 1957, as a source for general University undergraduate and graduate instruction, and faculty research
Library Holdings: Vols 500,000; Per subs 6000
Exhibitions: Louis Sullivan Collection of Terra Cotta
Activities: Photography contest; scholarships

ELMHURST

M LIZZADRO MUSEUM OF LAPIDARY ART, 220 Cottage Hill Ave, 60126. Tel 708-833-1616. *Dir* John S Lizzadro; *Prog Dir* Dorothy Anderson
Open Tues - Sat 10 AM - 5 PM, Sun 1 - 5 PM, cl Mon. Admis adults $2.50, sr citizens $1.50, students $1, under 13 free, no charge on Fri. Estab 1962 to promote interest in the lapidary arts & the study & collecting of minerals & fossils. Main exhibit area contains hardstone carvings, gemstone materials, minerals; lower level contains education exhibits. Average Annual Attendance: 30,000. Mem: 350; dues $30 per yr
Income: Financed by endowment
Collections: Hardstone Carving Collection
Exhibitions: Educational exhibits
Publications: Biannual
Activities: Lect open to the public, 12 vis lectr per year; educational films; tours; demonstrations; sales shop sells books, jewelry, magazines, hardstone & gemstone souvenirs

ELSAH

M PRINCIPIA COLLEGE, School of Nations Museum, 62028. Tel 618-374-2131, Ext 312; FAX 618-374-5122. *Cur* Bonnie Gibbs
Open Tues & Fri by appointment only
Collections: American Indian collection including baskets, bead work, blankets, leather, pottery, quill work and silver; Asian art collection includes arts and crafts, ceramics, textiles from China, Japan and Southeast Asia; European collections include glass, metals, snuff boxes, textiles and wood; costumes and dolls from around the world
Exhibitions: Changing exhibits on campus locations; permanent exhibits in School of Nations lower floor
Activities: Special programs offered throughout the year; objects available for individual study

EVANSTON

A AMERICAN JEWISH ART CLUB, 9545 N Drake, Apt 8E, 60203. Tel 312-676-3187. *Pres* Louise Dunn Yochim; *VPres* Michael Karzen; *Treas* Ruth Zwick; *Publicity Dir* Debra Jacobson
Estab to achieve pride in heritage, to expand exhibition outlets & to educate. Average Annual Attendance: 5000. Mem: 70; mem based on professional standing & jurying by general membership; dues $25; ten meetings per yr
Income: Financed by membership dues & contributions
Exhibitions: Juried exhibitions
Publications: Monthly newsletter
Activities: Educ dept; lectures open to public, 10 vis lectrs per yr; competitions with awards; traveling exhibitions; sales shop sells original art

A EVANSTON ART CENTER, 2603 Sheridan Rd, 60201. Tel 708-475-5300; FAX 708-475-5330. *Dir School* Jessica Breslauer
Open Tues - Sat 10 AM - 4 PM, Thurs evening 7 - 10 PM, Sun 2 - 5 PM. No admis fee. Estab 1929 as a community visual arts center with exhibits, instruction, and programs. Focuses primarily on the contemporary visual arts with emphasis on emerging & under-recognized Midwest artists. Average Annual Attendance: 35,000. Mem: 1500; dues $30, annual meeting in April
Income: Supported by state & city arts councils & memberships
Exhibitions: Primarily artists of the Midwest, all media
Publications: Concentrics, quarterly; exhibition catalogs
Activities: Classes for adults and children; lect, 6 vis lectr per year

M EVANSTON HISTORICAL SOCIETY, Charles Gates Dawes House, 225 Greenwood St, 60201. Tel 708-475-3410. *Acting Dir* Mary McWilliams
Open Mon, Tues, Thurs, Fri & Sat 1 - 5 PM. Admis $3, $1. Estab 1960. Average Annual Attendance: 2500. Mem: 1500; dues $15-$25; annual meeting in June
Income: $200,000,000 (financed by mem & city appropriation)
Collections: Original furnishings of Vice President Nobel Laureate Dawes; Gwen Simpson costume collection; historical artifacts; WW I guns & weapons; doll collection
Exhibitions: Changing costume exhibitions
Publications: Evanston Historical Society newsletter, 6 times per year

NORTHWESTERN UNIVERSITY

M Mary & Leigh Block Gallery, 1967 Sheridan Rd, 60208. Tel 708-491-4000; FAX 708-491-2261. *Dir* David Mickenberg; *Cur* Jennifer Holmes; *Public Relations & Development* Lynne Remington; *Educ & Tours* Corinne Granof
Open Tues & Wed Noon - 5 PM, Thurs - Sun Noon - 8 PM. No admis fee. Estab 1980, to serve the university, Chicago and North Shore communities. Average Annual Attendance: 30,000. Mem: 500; dues $25-$1000
Exhibitions: (1991) The Modernist Tradition in American Watercolors. (1992) Modernism in Chicago, Professional of the XVI Century, German Prints During the Weimar years. (1993) Special Collection: The Photographic Order From Pop to Now; Constantin Brancusi: The Photographs; The Graven Image: The Rise of Professional Print Makers Antwerp & Naarlem; Fluxus: A Conceptual Country
Publications: Exhibition catalogs
Activities: Lectures open to public; concerts; gallery talks; tours; book traveling exhibitions; originate traveling exhibitions circulated through other university galleries and museums; sales shop sells catalogs and posters

L Art Library, 1935 Sheridan Rd, 60208-2300. Tel 708-491-7484, 491-3635. *Head Special Art Library* R Russell Maylone; *Bibliographer* Rochelle S Elstein
Open Mon - Thurs 8:30 AM - 10 PM, Fri & Sat 8:30 AM - 5 PM, Sun 1 - 10 PM. Estab 1970 as a separate collection. Serves curriculum & research needs of the Art & Art History Departments
Income: Financed through the university & endowment funds
Library Holdings: Vols 64,000; Other — Exhibition catalogs
Special Subjects: History of Art & Archaeology, 20th Century Art Movements

FREEPORT

M FREEPORT ART MUSEUM & CULTURAL CENTER, 121 N Harlem, 61032. Tel 815-235-9755. *Dir* Becky Connors; *Business Mgr* Sherry Roskam
Open Wed - Sun, 12 PM - 5 PM and by appointment. Admis adults $1, srs & students $.50. Estab 1975 to house W T Rawleigh Art Collection and to promote the arts in the region. Five permanent galleries & three galleries featuring temporary exhibitions. Average Annual Attendance: 13,000. Mem: 300; dues $20; annual meeting May
Income: $90,000 (financed by endowment, mem, city & state appropriations, & other grants)
Collections: American Indian pottery, basketry & beadwork; art from Madagascar; European 19th century oil paintings; †oil paintings; †prints; †sculpture; †textiles; †antiquities from Egypt, Greece, Rome & MesoAmerica; †Oriental art
Exhibitions: (1992) Newell Gallery: Carole Komarek; Masks in Motion; Inuit Art; Ferguson Gallery: Peter New McRowland; Masks in Motion; Inuit Art. (1993) Newell Gallery: Michael Johnson; Art From the Freeport Public Schools; Mary Phelan; Textiles; Young Regional Artists Invitational; Robert Sunday; Ferguson Gallery: Michael Johnson; Art From the Freeport Public Schools; John Bakker; Textiles; Young Regional Artists Invitational; Frances Cox. (1994) Newell Gallery: Roland Poska; Art From the Freeport Public Schools; Invent America ; Lill St Pottery/Table settings; Ferguson Gallery: Roland Poska; Art From the Freeport Public Schools; Invent America ; Lill St Pottery/Table Settings
Activities: Classes for adults and children; docent training; lectures open to public; gallery talks; tours; competitions; exten dept serving Ogle, Carroll, Jo Daviess Counties; individual paintings and original objects of art lent to bona fide galleries with full insurance; lending collection contains paintings & sculpture; book traveling exhibitions; organize and circulate traveling exhibitions
L Library, 121 N Harlem, 61032. Tel 815-235-9755. *Dir* Becky Connors
Open to members and public for research and reference
Library Holdings: Vols 500; Per subs 10
Special Subjects: Afro-American Art, American Indian Art, Antiquities-Egyptian, Antiquities-Greek, Antiquities-Oriental, Antiquities-Roman, Flasks & Bottles, Historical Material, Laces, Painting - American, Painting - British, Southwestern Art, Textiles
Publications: Annual report; quarterly newsletter

GALESBURG

A GALESBURG CIVIC ART CENTER, 114 E Main, 61401. Tel 309-342-7415. *Pres* John Burgland; *VPres* Shardlow Hansen; *Dir* Paulette Thenhaus
Open Tues - Fri 10:30 AM - 4:30 PM, Sat 10:30 AM - 3 PM, cl Sun & Mon. No admis fee. Estab 1923 as a non-profit organization for the furtherance of art. The main gallery has about 100 running feet of wall space for the hanging of exhibits. The sales-rental gallery is on a commission basis and is open to professional artists as a place to sell their work under a consignment agreement. Average Annual Attendance: 20,000. Mem: 400; dues begin at $15; annual meeting 2nd Wed in June
Income: Financed by membership and grants
Collections: Regional artists in a variety of media (change monthly)
Exhibitions: (1992) By Hand: Holiday Art Market; GALEX - national juried competition, all media. (1993) Exotic Fibers
Publications: The Artifacts, newsletter
Activities: Classes for adults and children; gallery talks; tours; competitions with awards; lending collection contains original art works, paintings, photographs & sculpture; museum shop sells original art, prints

GREENVILLE

M GREENVILLE COLLEGE, Richard W Bock Sculpture Collection, 62246. Tel 618-664-1840, Ext 321. *Dir & Cur* Guy M Chase
Open Mon - Wed 3:30 - 5:30 PM, Sat 10:30 AM - 12:30 PM & by appointment, cl summer & holidays. No admis fee. Estab 1975 to display an extensive collection of the life work of the American sculptor in a restored home of the mid-19th century period. Five large rooms and two hallways have approximately 320 running ft of exhibition space. Average Annual Attendance: 5000
Income: Financed by endowment, college appropriation, gifts and donations
Collections: Furniture and furnishings of the 1850-1875 era; Japanese prints; late 19th and early 20th century drawing, painting and sculpture; late 19th and early 20th century posters; Frank Lloyd Wright artifacts, designs and drawings
Publications: General museum brochures
Activities: Lect open to the public, 1-2 vis lectr per year; gallery talks; individual paintings and original objects of art lent to museums only; lending collection contains original art works, paintings, photographs, sculpture and drawings; traveling exhibitions organized and circulated; museum shop sells books, magazines
L The Richard W Bock Sculpture Collection & Art Library, 62246. Tel 618-664-1840, Ext 321. *Librn* Guy M Chase
For reference only
Library Holdings: Vols 1000; AV — Rec; Other — Exhibition catalogs
Special Subjects: Richard W Bock, The Prairie School of Architecture, Frank Lloyd Wright

HIGHLAND PARK

C STROUD WALLER INC, 246 Beech St (Mailing add: 180 Scott Ave, Winnetka, 60093). Tel 708-835-4676, 835-8424. *Partner* Jane Stroud; *Partner* Marlene Waller
Estab 1974
Collections: AT&T Midwest Corp Center; United Stationers Inc; W W Grainger Inc; Illinois Tool Works Inc; McDermott, Will & Emery Law Offices; Chapman & Culter Law Offices; Katten, Muchin & Zavis Law Offices

JACKSONVILLE

M ART ASSOCIATION OF JACKSONVILLE, David Strawn Art Gallery, 331 W College (Mailing add: PO Box 1213, 62651). Tel 217-243-9390. *Dir* Kelly M Gross; *Pres* Susi Newman
Open Sept - May, Tues - Sat 4 - 6 PM, Sun 1 - 3 PM. No admis fee. Estab 1873, endowed 1915, to serve the community by offering monthly shows of visual arts and weekly classes in a variety of media. The two main rooms house the monthly exhibitions and a third large room houses a collection of Pre-Columbian pottery. The Gallery is in a large building, previously a private home. Average Annual Attendance: 1800. Mem: 550; dues $10 & up; annual meeting July
Income: Financed by endowment & mem
Collections: Pre-Columbian Pottery; pottery discovered in the Mississippi Valley
Activities: Classes for adults and children; lect workshops open to public

JOLIET

M JOLIET JUNIOR COLLEGE, Laura A Sprague Art Gallery, J Bldg, 1216 Houbolt Ave, 2nd Floor, 60436. Tel 815-729-9020, Ext 2423, 2223. *Gallery Dir* Joe B Milosevich
Open Mon 9 AM - 2 PM, Tues, Wed & Thurs 6 PM - 8 PM. Estab 1978, to present exhibitions related to academic programs, the college and the community. Gallery, approx 20 x 25 ft, has burlap covered panels mounted on the walls, and also has track lighting
Income: Financed by college appropriations
Collections: Permanent collection of student work, annual
Exhibitions: (1991) Fabrycki. (1992) Maakestad, Gniech, Hahn, Helbine, Crawford; Joliet Junior College Art Faculty Exhibition; Joliet Junior College Area High School Art Exhibition. (1993) Dragovan; Illinois Community College Juried Art Exhibition; Joliet Junior College Art Students' Juried Exhibition (1988) Leslie Scruggs; Marion Kryczka. (1989) Gamil Arida
Activities: Lect open to public, 2 - 3 vis lect per yr; gallery talks; tours; sponsor student competitions with awards

LAKE FOREST

L LAKE FOREST LIBRARY, Fine Arts Dept, 360 E Deerpath, 60045. Tel 708-234-0636; FAX 708-234-1453. *Admin Librn* Kaye Grabbe; *Adult Servs Coordr* Cynthia Infantino; *Graphic Artist* Patricia Kreischer
Open Mon - Thurs 9 AM - 9 PM, Fri 9 AM - 6 PM, Sat 9 AM - 5 PM, Sun 1 - 5 PM (Sept - May). Estab 1898 to make accessible to the residents of the city, books and other resources and services for education, information and recreation. Gallery carries sculpture reproductions. Circ 341,497
Income: $1,732,500 (financed by city & state appropriations)
Purchases: $171,000 (materials); $1,520,000 (total expenditure)
Library Holdings: Pamphlets, sculpture reproductions
Special Subjects: Local architects
Collections: Folk art; painting
Publications: The Open Book, four times per year

LOMBARD

L HELEN M PLUM MEMORIAL LIBRARY, 110 W Maple St, 60148. Tel 708-627-0316; FAX 708-627-0336. *Dir* Robert A Harris; *Readers' Services* Donna Slyfield
Open Mon - Fri 9 AM - 9 PM, Sat 9 AM - 5 PM, cl Sun. Estab as a public library. Art gallery maintained for monthly displays by Addison Art League. Circ 438,331
Income: $1,427,162 (financed by local government)
Purchases: $722,485
Library Holdings: Vols 178,384; Per subs 380; Micro — Fiche, prints, reels; AV — A-tapes, cassettes, fs, motion pictures, rec, slides, v-tapes; Other — Framed reproductions, pamphlets, prints, reproductions, sculpture
Special Subjects: Art History, Crafts, Decorative Arts, Folk Art, Handicrafts, Painting - American
Activities: Lectures open to public; original objects of art lent to public

LONG GROVE

C KEMPER NATIONAL INSURANCE COMPANIES, Kemper Dr, F-3, 60049. Tel 312-540-2502. *Art Cur* Joan E Robertson
Open to public in groups of 5 - 25, by three weeks prior appointment. Estab 1973 to provide a better working environment for employees and to support Chicago and Midwest artists. Collection displayed in halls and offices of headquarters
Collections: †Approximately 78 percent Chicago & Midwest artists, contemporary, with many young emerging artists
Exhibitions: One-person shows in private exhibition area
Publications: Art collection brochure (1978)
Activities: Lect; gallery talks; purchase awards at Chicago area shows and art fairs; individual objects of art lent to artists for retrospectives and shows, and to institutions

MACOMB

M WESTERN ILLINOIS UNIVERSITY, Art Gallery-Museum, 61455. Tel 309-298-1587; FAX 309-298-2400. *Pres* Ralph Wagoner; *Cur Exhib* John R Graham
Open Mon, Wed - Fri 9 AM - 4 PM & Tues 6 - 8 PM. No admis fee. Estab 1945 to present art as an aesthetic and teaching aid. Building has three galleries with 500 running ft. Average Annual Attendance: 20,000
Income: Financed through state appropriation
Activities: Classes for adults; lectures open to the public, 8 vis lectr per year; gallery talks; tours; competitions with awards; individual paintings lent; lending collection contains 100 paintings; traveling exhibitions organized and circulated

MOLINE

C DEERE & COMPANY, John Deere Rd, 61265. Tel 309-765-8000; FAX 309-765-4735. *Coll Conservator* Laurence Jonson AACR
Guided tours Mon - Fri 10:30 AM - 1:30 PM. Estab 1964 to complement the offices designed by Eero Saarinen & Kevin Roche; to provide opportunities for employees & visitors to view & enjoy a wide variety of art pieces from many parts of the world. Collection displayed at Deere & Company Administrative Center
Collections: Artifacts, paintings, prints, sculpture & tapestries from over 25 countries
Activities: Concerts; tours

MOUNT VERNON

M MITCHELL MUSEUM, Richview Rd, PO Box 923, 62864. Tel 618-242-1236; FAX 618-242-9530. *Dir* Michael Stephenson
Open Tues - Sat 10 AM - 5 PM, Sun 1 - 5 PM, cl Mon & national holidays. No admis fee. Estab 1973 to present exhibitions of paintings, sculpture, graphic arts, architecture and design representing contemporary art trends; to provide continued learning and expanded education. Marble faced structure houses two galleries for exhibition, 3000 sq ft & 1300 sq ft; flexible designs. Average Annual Attendance: 60,000. Mem: 800; dues $25; annual meeting in Nov
Income: Financed by endowment and membership
Collections: Paintings by late 19th and early 20th century American artists; some drawings and small sculptures; silver, small stone, wood and ivory carvings; vases; jade; cut glass; small bronzes; †outdoor sculpture; †graphics
Exhibitions: Changing exhibits; Southern Illinois Artists Open Competition
Publications: Form Beyond Function: Recent Sculpture by North American Metalsmiths; quarterly newsletter; Recent Graphics from American Print Shops; Sculpture at Cedarhurst, catalogue
Activities: Classes for adults & children; dramatic programs; docent training; workshops; demonstrations; field trips; lectures open to public, 8-10 vis lectr per year; concerts; gallery talks; tours; competitions with awards; scholarships; individual paintings & original objects of art lent to qualified institutions & museums; book traveling exhibitions, 3-5 per year; originate traveling exhibitions to qualified museums & college galleries with adequate staff & facilities; sales shop selling books, reproductions, slides, postcards & small items for children
L Library, Richview Rd, PO Box 923, 62864. *Librn* Beth Brennan
Open to public for reference only
Library Holdings: Vols 1000; Per subs 15; AV — A-tapes, cassettes, Kodachromes, slides; Other — Exhibition catalogs, pamphlets
Special Subjects: Painting - American

NAPERVILLE

L NORTH CENTRAL COLLEGE, Oesterle Library, 320 E School, 60566. Tel 708-420-3425; FAX 708-357-8393. *Dir* Carolyn A Sheehy; *Techician* Belinda Cheek; *Public Services Librn* Kelly Collins; *Public Services Librn* Jacklyn Egolof; *System Librn* Sharon Takacs
Open Mon - Thurs 8 AM - 11 PM, Fri 8 AM - 6:30 PM, Sat 9 AM - 5:30 PM, Sun noon - 11 PM. Estab 1861 to provide academic support. For lending & reference. Art Gallery houses 4-5 exhibitions per yr
Library Holdings: Vols 120,000; Per subs 751; Micro — Fiche, reels; AV — A-tapes, cassettes, fs, lantern slides, motion pictures, rec, v-tapes; Other — Clipping files, manuscripts, memorabilia, original art works, pamphlets, photographs
Collections: Sang Collection of Fine Bindings
Exhibitions: Barry Skurkis; Hopi Art
Activities: Book traveling exhibitions, 4 per yr

NILES

M THE BRADFORD MUSEUM OF COLLECTOR'S PLATES, 9333 Milwaukee Ave, 60714. Tel 708-966-2770; FAX 708-966-2121. *Mgr Public Relations* Ginny Sexton; *Tour Coordr* Marianne Mercado
Open Mon - Fri 9 AM - 4 PM, Sat & Sun 10 AM - 5 PM. Admis adult $2, sr citizens $1, children under 12 accompanied by adult free, free on Sun. Estab 1978 to house and display limited-edition collector's plates for purposes of study, education and enjoyment. Average Annual Attendance: 10,000
Income: Financed by The Bradford Exchange
Collections: Traded Limited-Edition Collector's Plates, including Bing & Grondahl, Haviland, Lalique, Lenox, Rosenthal, Royal Copenhagen, Royal Doulton, & many more; more than 1300 plates produced by more than 62 makers from 16 different countries, each plate series is updated yearly
Publications: The Bradford Book of Collector's Plates, annually
Activities: Docent training; lect open to public; tours; original objects of art lent for temporary exhibition purposes; lending collection contains motion pictures and limited-edition collector's plates; book traveling exhibitions; originate traveling exhibitions

NORMAL

ILLINOIS STATE UNIVERSITY
L Museum Library, 61761. Tel 309-438-8800. *Registrar* Sharon Hardey
Museum library open to scholars, students and staff
Library Holdings: Vols 201; Per subs 22
Special Subjects: Decorative Arts, American Indian Art, Pre-Columbian Art, African Art and History
M University Galleries, 110 Center For Visual Arts, Beaufort St, 61761. Tel 309-438-5487; FAX 309-438-8318. *Dir* Barry Blinderman; *Cur* Debra Risberg
No admis fee. Estab 1973 to provide changing exhibits of contemporary art for the students & community at large. The main gallery I contains rotating exhibitions; gallery II & III display student & faculty work, graduate exhibitions, studio area shows & works from the permanent collection. Average Annual Attendance: 29,000
Income: $100,000 (financed by university)
Collections: †Contemporary art emphasis †prints & drawings & 1500 object colletion of African Art, primarily West African
Exhibitions: (1991) Jeanne Dunning: Bodies of Work. (1992) Dennis Oppenheim: Drawings & Selected Sculpture; Paintings by Mark Forth & David Hodges
Publications: exhibition catalogs
Activities: Lectrs open to the public, 7 vis lectr per year; gallery talks; tours; individual paintings and original objects of art lent for other exhibitions; lending collection contains original art works, original prints, paintings, photographs and sculpture; book traveling exhibitions, one per year; originate traveling exhibitions

NORTHBROOK

C IMCERA GROUP INC (Formerly International Minerals & Chemicals Corp), 2315 Sanders Rd, 60062. Tel 708-564-8600; FAX 708-205-2166. *Art Coordr* Mary Ann King
Collections: Contemporary paintings & sculpture, primarily artistic expressionism

OAKBROOK

C MCDONALD'S CORPORATION, Art Collection, 1 McDonald's Plaza, 60521. Tel 708-575-3000; FAX 708-575-5361. *Cur* Susan Pertl
Open to group tours by appointment. Estab 1971
Collections: Collection of contemporary paintings & sculpture & of works by established & emerging artists
Activities: Lectures; The Spirit of McDonald's Competition; individual paintings & original objects of art lent, lending collection consists of more than 1000 pieces

PARIS

M BICENTENNIAL ART CENTER & MUSEUM, 132 S Central Ave, 61944. Tel 217-466-8130. *Exec Coordr* Thelma M Sturgeon
Open Tues - Fri noon - 4 PM, Sat 2 - 4 PM, Sun 1 - 3 PM. No admis fee. Estab 1975 to encourage & bring art to area. Four galleries, 1037 sq ft. Average Annual Attendance: 3000. Mem: 300; annual meeting Oct
Income: $30,000 (financed by membership, contributions, fundraising)
Collections: Paintings & sculpture primarily 20th century period, including extensive collection of Alice Baber work
Exhibitions: Changing exhibits each month
Publications: Monthly newsletter
Activities: Classes for adults & children; lect open to public, 6 vis lectr per yr; traveling exhibitions, 2 per yr

PEORIA

M BRADLEY UNIVERSITY, Hartman Center Gallery, Heuser Art Center, 61625. Tel 309-677-2967; FAX 309-677-2330. *Dir Div of Art* Robert Reedy; *Assoc Prof Art & Cur Installations* Jim Hansen; *Gallery Dir* George Ann Danehower
Open Mon - Fri 9:30 - noon, 1 - 4 PM. Exhibition space 639 sq ft. Average Annual Attendance: 2000
Income: Financed by University
Exhibitions: (1992) Personal narratives: Faculty Exhibit. (1993) Bradley National Print & Drawing Exhibition; The Clay Cup
Activities: Classes for adults; lect open to the public; gallery talks; tours; competitions with awards; master print program; individual paintings lent on campus

M LAKEVIEW MUSEUM OF ARTS AND SCIENCES, 1125 W Lake Ave, 61614. Tel 309-686-7000; FAX 309-686-0280. *Dir* Michael H Sanden; *Assoc Dir* Judy Geary-Furniss; *Cur Coll & Exhib* John Heintzman; *Cur of Exhib* Cori Tibbitts; *Cur of Education* Barbara Greenberg; *Science Planetarium Dir* Sheldon Schafer
Open Tues - Sat 10 AM - 5 PM, Sun 1 - 5 PM, Wed 7 - 9 PM, cl Mon. Estab 1960, new building opened 1965, to provide enjoyment and education by reflecting the historical, cultural and industrial life of the Central Illinois area. Average Annual Attendance: 250,000. Mem: 3600; dues family $25, individual $15, student $10; annual meeting in June
Income: $500,000
Collections: Archaeological; †decorative arts; extensive entomological & paleontological collections; paintings & graphics; fine arts; anthropology, natural sciences
Exhibitions: Monthly exhibitions dealing with the arts and sciences
Publications: Bi-monthly bulletin; Lake Views, bi-monthly; exhibition catalogues
Activities: Classes for adults and children; dramatic programs; docent trainings; lectures open to public, 8-10 vis lectrs per year; concerts; gallery talks; tours; competitions with awards; individual and original objects of art lent to sister institutions; sales shop sells books, magazines, original art, reproductions, prints and craft items

A PEORIA ART GUILD, 1831 N Knoxville, 61603. Tel 309-685-7522. *Dir* Sue Widdows
Open Tues - Sat 10 AM - 5 PM, cl Mon. No admis fee. Estab 1878 to encourage development of the arts. Average Annual Attendance: 10,000. Mem: 952; dues $25
Income: Financed by membership, Illinois Arts Council, sales & rental & private donations
Collections: †Framed & unframed 2-D design, ceramics, sculpture, jewelry, weaving & wood designs; winning works from the Bradley National Print & Drawing Exhibition
Exhibitions: One-person shows; group theme shows, 11 shows annually
Activities: Classes for adults and children; workshops; lect open to public, 5 - 6 vis lect per year; gallery talks; tours; awards; individual paintings rented to business & members of the community; lending collection contains original art work, prints, paintings, photographs & sculptures; sales shop sells books, magazines, original art, reproductions & prints

M PEORIA HISTORICAL SOCIETY, 942 NE Glen Oak, 61603. Tel 309-674-1921. *Pres* David Puterbaugh; *Dir* Keith L Barr
Judge John C Flanagan House open for tours Mon - Fri 10 AM - 4 PM; Pettengill-Morron House open Tues - Sat 10 AM - 4 PM. Admis adults $3, children 15 & under $1. Estab 1934 to acquire, preserve and display artifacts and records relating to the history of Peoria and the Central Illinois Valley; to encourage and support historical research and investigation and to promote and sustain public interest in history of Peoria and the Central Illinois Valley. Two historic house museums: Flanagan House is post-colonial, Pettengill-Morron house is Victorian. Average Annual Attendance: 5000. Mem: 700; annual dues $25, annual meeting third Mon in May
Income: Financed by mem, endowments; private gifts & grants
Collections: Household items & artifacts from 1840; Library housed in special collections center of Bradley University; Peoria Pottery
Exhibitions: Rennick Award (art works relating to historic sites)
Publications: Monthly Newsletter to members
Activities: Classes for children; lect open to public, 6 vis lectr per yr; monthly meetings Sept - May relating to history of the area; competitions with prizes; Boutique at Pettengill-Morron House; museum shop sells books, cards, reproductions

QUINCY

A QUINCY ART CENTER, 1515 Jersey St, 62301. Tel 217-223-5900. *Pres* Ridgely Pierson
Open Tues - Fri 1 - 4 PM, Sat & Sun 2 - 5 PM, cl Mon, holidays, July & Aug. Estab 1923, incorporated 1951 to foster public awareness and understanding of the visual arts. Average Annual Attendance: 6000. Mem: 400; dues life membership $250, sustaining $100, annual patron $30, family $15, individual $10, student $5; annual meeting in July
Income: Financed by grants, donations, membership fees, antique shows and Beaux Art Ball
Collections: Crafts, graphics, †painting and sculpture by contemporary American and European artists
Exhibitions: Annual Quincy Art Show; annual students art show; Art Club's Artist Guild Show
Publications: Calendar, brochures and/or catalogs for temporary exhibitions; Quarterly Bulletin
Activities: Classes for adults and children; lectures open to public, 6 visiting lecturers per year; films; gallery talks; tours; competitions with awards; scholarships; inter-museum loan; traveling exhibitions organized and circulated
L Library, 1515 Jersey St, 62301. *Pres* Ridgely Pierson
Library Holdings: Vols 350

A QUINCY SOCIETY OF FINE ARTS, 428 Maine, 62301-3930. Tel 217-222-3432; FAX 217-222-3556. *Dir* Rob Dwyer
Open Mon - Fri 8 AM - 5 PM. Estab 1947 as a community arts council to coordinate & stimulate the visual & performing arts in Quincy & Adams County. Mem: 30 art organizations
Income: Financed by endowment, membership & contribution, Illinois Arts Council, National Endowment for the Arts
Publications: Cultural Calendars, monthly; pamphlets & catalogs
Activities: Workshops for adults and students in visual and performing arts

M QUINCY UNIVERSITY, The Gray Gallery, 1800 College Ave, 62301-2699. Tel 217-228-5371. *Gallery Dir* Robert Lee Mejer
Open Mon - Thur 8 AM - 10 PM, Fri 8 AM - 8 PM, Sat 11 AM - 5 PM, Sun 1 - 10 PM. No admis fee. Estab 1968 for cultural enrichment & exposure to contemporary art forms in the community. Exhibitions are held in the Brenner library foyer & The Gray Gallery. Average Annual Attendance: 6000
Income: Financed through the College & Student Activities Association
Collections: †19th century Oriental and European prints; †permanent collection of student and faculty works; †20th century American prints and drawings
Exhibitions: (1991) Kevin McGrath, mixed media constructions; Sonia Gechtoff, works on paper; James Kelly, collage. (1992) Anita Jung, works on paper; Quincy University Art Department Faculty Anniversary (Teaching): Tom Brown (40 yrs/retrospective), Robert Lee Mejer (25 yrs), Richard Mammer (20 yrs); Daniel Burke, works on paper. (1993) Lee Bomhoff, pastel drawings; Ralph Murrell Larmann, handmade paper/acrylic reliefs
Publications: Brochures, 1-2 times annually; gallery calendars, annually
Activities: Lectures open to public, 1 vis lectr per year; gallery talks; tours; student show with awards; individual paintings & original objects of art lent; book traveling exhibitions 1 - 2 per year
L Brenner Library, 1800 College Ave, 62301. Tel 217-222-8020; FAX 217-228-5354. *Dir* Victor Kingery
Reference only for public; lending for faculty & students
Income: $1600 (financed by college revenues)
Purchases: $1600 annually for books
Library Holdings: Vols 7200; Per subs 20; AV — Cassettes, fs, lantern slides, motion pictures, rec, slides, v-tapes; Other — Exhibition catalogs, prints

ROCKFORD

A ROCKFORD ART MUSEUM, 711 N Main St, 61103. Tel 815-968-2787. *Dir* Barbara Sellett; *Cur* Peter Baldaia; *Financial Officer* Curtis Kleckler; *Educ Dir* Laura Johnson
Open Tues - Sat 11 AM - 5 PM, Sun 1 PM - 5 PM, cl Mon & holidays. Admis suggested donation adults $2, students & children $1. Estab 1913 to promote and cultivate an active interest in all fields of fine and applied art, past and present, in the surrounding area. 20,000 sq ft exhibition space. Average Annual Attendance: 100,000. Mem: 1000
Income: Financed by mem, state appropriation & private donations
Collections: Permanent collection 19th & 20th century American oil paintings, graphics, sculpture, photography, ceramics, glassware, textiles, watercolors and mixed media
Exhibitions: Annual Rockford & Vicinity Show; Annual Young Artist's Exhibition; numerous one-person and group shows
Publications: Exhibition brochures & catalogs; newsletter, monthly
Activities: Classes for adults & children; docent training; artist-in-residence; museum school program; lectures open to public, 5 vis lectr per year; gallery talks; tours; competitions with cash awards; book traveling exhibitions; museum shop sells books, original art, reproductions, prints, jewelry, ceramics & crafts
L Library, 711 N Main St, 61103. Tel 815-968-2787; FAX 815-965-0642. *Educ Dir* Laura Johnson
Open to the public and members by appointment. For reference only
Library Holdings: Vols 500; Per subs 15
Special Subjects: The visual arts

ROCK ISLAND

M AUGUSTANA COLLEGE, Art Gallery, NW Corner Seventh Ave & 38th St, 61201. Tel 309-794-7469; FAX 309-794-7678. *Gallery Dir* Sherry C Maurer
Open Tues - Sat noon - 4 PM. No admis fee. Estab 1973 for the display of visual arts exhibits commensurate with a liberal arts college curriculum. Main gallery serves as an entrance to large auditorium; lower gallery is smaller than main gallery; two galleries total 217 ft wall space. Average Annual Attendance: 55,000
Income: $53,785
Purchases: $3000
Collections: Contemporary, Eastern & Western prints; Swedish American Art; modern Oriental
Publications: Exhibit catalogs
Activities: Classes for children; lectures open to public; 3 - 4 vis lectrs per year; concerts; gallery talks; tours; competitions, awards ranging from $1900-$2500; scholarships; art works lent to campus offices for display; book traveling exhibitions, 3 per yr; originate traveling exhibitions

SKOKIE

L SKOKIE PUBLIC LIBRARY, 5215 Oakton, 60077. Tel 708-673-7774; FAX 708-673-7797. *Dir* Carolyn Anthony; *Assoc Dir for Public Services* Barbara Kozlowski; *Asst Dir for Technical Services* Camille Cleland
Open Mon - Fri 9 AM - 9 PM, Sat 9 AM - 5 PM, Sun 1 - 5 PM. Estab 1941 as a general public library serving the residents of Skokie; reciprocal borrowing privileges offered to members of public libraries in North Suburban Library System. Art gallery is maintained
Income: $2,800,000 (financed by independent tax levy)
Purchases: 450,000
Library Holdings: Vols 360,954; Per subs 789; Micro — Fiche, reels; AV — A-tapes, cassettes, slides, v-tapes; Other — Clipping files, framed reproductions, original art works, pamphlets, reproductions, sculpture
Special Subjects: Architecture, Art History, Crafts, Dolls, Embroidery, Handicrafts, Painting - American, Painting - European, Sculpture, Watercolors
Activities: Lectures open to public; framed art prints & posters lent; book traveling exhibitions

SPRINGFIELD

M ILLINOIS STATE MUSEUM, Illinois Art Gallery & Lockport Gallery, Spring & Edwards St, 62706. Tel 217-782-7440. *Dir* R Bruce J McMillan; *Dir of Art* Kent J Smith; *Cur Decorative Arts* Janice Wass; *Cur Asst Decorative Art* Irene Boyer; *Registrar for Art* Carole Peterson; *Ed Art* Amy Jackson; *Exhibits Designer Art* Philip Kennedy
Open Mon - Sat 8:30 AM - 5 PM; Sun noon - 5 PM. No admis fee. Estab 1877 as museum of natural history, art added in 1928. Collection, exhibition & publication of art produced by or of interest to Illinois & its citizens. Six major changing exhibitions annually. Changing exhibition space: Springfield Art Gallery 3000 sq ft; Arts of Sciences Gallery (six changing exhibitions), 1364 sq ft; permanent collection galleries present fine, decorative & ethnographic arts, 6400 sq ft permanent exhibit of Illinois Decorative Arts, At Home in The Heartland 3000 sq ft. Average Annual Attendance: 300,000. Mem: 650; dues $25 - $500
Income: $266,000. Art Section only (Springfield program financed by state appropriation); Chicago & Lockport programs privately funded
Purchases: $5000
Collections: Decorative art including †ceramics, †metal work, †textiles, †glass, †furniture; fine art including †paintings, †sculpture, †prints, †drawings, †photography, †contemporary crafts, †folk art
Exhibitions: 18 exhibitions annually featuring contemporary & historical paintings, sculpture, photography, graphics, decorative arts & history, with emphasis on Illinois material
Publications: Living Museum (also in Braille), quarterly; exhibit & collection catalogs; Biennial report
Activities: Programs for adults & children; dramatic programs; lect & symposia open to public; concerts; gallery talks; tours; competitions with awards; film series; individual paintings lent to other museums, historical sites & galleries; book traveling exhibitions, 3 per year; traveling exhibitions organized & circulated, 3 per year; museum shop selling books & original art; Illinois Artisans Shop sells consigned work by Illinois Artisans, facilities in Chicago, Springfield & near Rend Lake

L **Library,** Spring & Edwards St, 62706. Tel 217-782-6623. *Librn* Orvetta
Robinson; *Library Asst* Ronald Sauberli
Open Mon - Sat 8:30 AM - 5 PM, Sun noon - 5 PM. Estab to provide
informational materials and services to meet the requirements of the museum
staff in fields pertinent to the purpose and work of the museum. Circ 100 per
month
Income: Financed by state appropriation
Purchases: $2600
Library Holdings: Vols 1500; Per subs 27; AV — Slides, v-tapes; Other —
Clipping files, exhibition catalogs, manuscripts, memorabilia, pamphlets
Special Subjects: Anthropology, art and natural sciences
Collections: Anthropology and Ornithology

A **SPRINGFIELD ART ASSOCIATION OF EDWARDS PLACE,** 700 N
Fourth, 62702. Tel 217-523-2631, 523-3507. *Exec Dir* Rod Buffington
Open Daily 9 AM - 4 PM, Sat, Sun 1 - 3 PM. No admis fee. Estab 1913 to
foster appreciation of art, to instruct people in art and to expose people to quality
art. Mem: 1000; dues $25 - $2000; monthly meeting
Income: $138,000 (financed by membership and grants, interests, tuition, and
benefits)
Collections: †Contemporary American Indian; African sculpture; early American
paintings; furniture; Mexican; Oriental and Japanese artifacts and textiles;
†paintings; †pottery; †prints; †textiles
Exhibitions: Twelve to fifteen exhibitions are scheduled annually with 2 or 3
juried exhibitions; work is borrowed from museum and artist nationwide
Publications: Newsletters, membership brochures, membership roster, 12 - 15 per
year
Activities: Classes for adults and children; docent training; art outreach program
in school in community; lectures open to the public; gallery talks; tours;
scholarships; book traveling exhibitions; sales shop sells original art, prints
L **Michael Victor II Art Library,** 700 N Fourth, 62702. Tel 217-523-0092. *Librn*
Joan Ekiss
Open 9 AM - 4 PM daily, Mon - Thurs 6:30 - 9:30 PM, Sat 9 AM - noon, cl
Sun. Estab 1965 to provide total community with access to art and art related
books
Income: $900
Purchases: $700
Library Holdings: Vols 5000; Per subs 10; Micro — Cards; AV — Slides;
Other — Clipping files, exhibition catalogs, pamphlets, reproductions
Special Subjects: Aesthetics, Afro-American Art, American Indian Art,
American Western Art, Architecture, Art Education, Art History, Asian Art,
Calligraphy, Carpets & Rugs, Cartoons, Ceramics, Collages, Commercial Art,
Conceptual Art
Activities: Film program; lecture series

WATSEKA

M **IROQUOIS COUNTY HISTORICAL SOCIETY MUSEUM,** Old Courthouse
Museum, 103 W Cherry, 60970. Tel 815-432-2215. *Pres* Hubert Lytle; *VPres*
Mary Hartke
Open Mon - Fri 10:30 AM - 4:30 PM, Sat & Sun 1 - 4:30 PM. Estab 1967 to
further the interest in history, art & genealogy. Two rooms for county artists.
Average Annual Attendance: 10,000. Mem: 800; dues $5 - $100
Income: Financed by donations by visitors, artists & art committee sells crafts
Collections: Paintings, prints, posters & pictures
Publications: Genealogical Stalker, quarterly; newsletter, monthly; historic
reprints
Activities: Lectures open to public; concerts; tours; competitions with awards;
museum shop sells books, original art, maps & Indian items

WHEATON

A **DUPAGE ART LEAGUE SCHOOL & GALLERY,** 219 W Front St, 60187. Tel
708-653-7090. *Pres* Susan Moesch; *Treas* Betty Bell; *VPres Educ* Mary Dorell;
VPres Exhibits Virginia Gould; *VPres Organization* Rose Holan; *VPres Activities*
Carol Kincaid; *VPres Building & Grounds* Earl Steinke; *Secy* Barbara Rothman
Open daily 9 AM - 5 PM, Sat 9 AM - 2 PM. No admis fee. Estab 1957, is
primarily an educational organization founded to encourage artists and promote
high artistic standards through instruction, informative programs and exhibits.
Three galleries are maintained where members exhibit & sell their work. Mem:
450; dues $30; annual meeting May
Income: Financed through membership, gifts and donations
Exhibitions: Monthly exhibits; 9 juried shows per yr; holiday gift gallery; Fine
Art Gallery with monthly exhibits of local artists (Gallery I), one-man or one-
woman shows (Gallery II), Fine Crafts (Gallery III)
Publications: Newsletter, monthly
Activities: Classes for adults and children; programs; demonstrations; lect open to
the public, 8 vis lectr per year; gallery talks; competitions; awards; scholarships;
individual paintings & original objects of art lent to local libraries & businesses;
sales shop selling original art & fine crafts (jewerly, ceramics, woodworks fiber &
glass)

WINNETKA

A **NORTH SHORE ART LEAGUE,** Winnetka Community House, 620 Lincoln,
60093. Tel 312-446-2870. *Pres* Pam Elesh; *First VPres* Nancy Koltun; *Second
VPres* Giedre Zumbakis
Open Mon - Sat 9 AM - 6 PM. Estab 1924, inc 1954, to promote interest in
creative art through education, exhibition opportunities, scholarship and art
programs. Average Annual Attendance: 100,000. Mem: 650; dues $30, annual
meeting May
Exhibitions: Midwest Craft Festival - New Horizons in Art; Old Orchard Art
Festival - Members Show; Midwest Print Show
Publications: Art League News, quarterly
Activities: Classes for adults and children; sponser juried competitions with
awards; scholarships offered for children

INDIANA

ANDERSON

A **ANDERSON FINE ARTS CENTER,** 226 W Historical Eighth St, 46016. Tel
317-649-1248. *Exec Dir* Deborah McBratney-Stapleton; *Pres Board Trustees*
Charles Dillman; *Cur* Christine Green; *Educ Coordr* Mark Vanek; *Gallery Asst*
Tim Swain
Open Sept - July Tues - Sat 10 AM - 5 PM, Sun 2 - 5 PM, cl Mon & national
holidays. No admis fee. Estab 1967 to serve the community by promoting &
encouraging interest in the fine arts through exhibitions, programs & education
activities & the development of a permanent collection. Three galleries contain
1705 sq ft; also a small sales & rental gallery & a studio/theatre. Average Annual
Attendance: 30,000. Mem: 700; dues sponsor $1000 or more, sustaining $500-
$999, benefactor $250-$499, patron $100-$249, contributor $50-$99, friend $25-
$49; annual meeting in May
Income: Financed by memberships, endowments, grants, individual & corporate
contributions
Special Subjects: Contemporary American Art
Collections: Midwestern & 20th century American prints, paintings & drawings
Exhibitions: Annual Winter Show Exhibits; annual Christmas Tree Exhibit;
annual Indiana Artists - Local Exhibit; annual photo exhibits; one-man shows
Publications: Calendar of Events, quarterly; catalogue of the permanent
collection; exhibition catalogs
Activities: Classes for adults & children; dramatic programs; docent training;
educational outreach; lectures open to public, 4-6 vis lectr per yr; concerts;
gallery talks; tours; competitions with awards; Art Lady Project in the Public
Schools; individual paintings & original objects of art lent to businesses,
educational facilities & other museums; lending collection contains 300 original
art works, 150 original prints, 300 paintings, 10 sculpture & 1000 slides; book
traveling exhibitions; museum shop sells books, original art, reproductions, prints,
slides, pottery, handcrafted items, glass, fine cards & note papers
L **Library,** 226 W Historical Eighth St, 46016. Tel 317-649-1248.
Open Tues - Sat 10 AM - 5 PM, Sun 2 - 5 PM. Estab 1967 for reference needs
& enjoyment by members of Arts Center & the community
Purchases: $500
Library Holdings: Vols 400; Per subs 14; AV — Cassettes, Kodachromes, motion
pictures, slides; Other — Clipping files, exhibition catalogs, pamphlets
Collections: Contemporary American art

BLOOMINGTON

M **BELLEVUE GALLERY,** 104 1/2 Kirkwood Ave, 47401. Tel 812-333-6206.
Estab 1989 to show emerging artists. Two rooms on second floor of Allen
Building in downtown Bloomington. Average Annual Attendance: 4000. Mem:
12; dues $180; monthly meetings first Fues of month
Income: $5000 (financed by mem & contributions)

INDIANA UNIVERSITY
M **Art Museum,** E Seventh St, 47405. Tel 812-855-5445; FAX 812-855-5445; Cable
ARTMUSEUM INDVERS. *Dir* Adelheid Gealt; *Deputy Dir* Gwen Bruce; *Assoc
Dir Editorial Servs* Linda Baden; *Cur Ancient Art* Adriana Calinescu; *Registrar*
Deb Garland; *Cur Educ* EdMaxedon; *Cur African & Oceanic Pre Columbian Art*
Diane Pelrine; *Cur 19th & 20th Century Art* Kathleen Foster
Open Wed, Thurs, Sat 9 AM - 5 PM, Fri 10 AM - 8 PM, Sun noon - 5 PM, cl
Mon & Tues. No admis fee. Estab 1941 to serve as a teaching & cultural
resource for the University community & the public at large. Average Annual
Attendance: 100,000
Collections: †African, †ancient to modern, Far Eastern, Oceanic, the Americas,
†prints, drawings & photographs
Exhibitions: (1991) Henry Radford Hope School of Fine Arts Faculty Show;
Highlights from the Hope Collection in the Indiana University Art Museum;
AFRI-COBRA: A Retrospective; Richard Andriessen; MGA Thesis Shows;
Silver: New Forms & Expressions II (1992) A Golden Year: Gifts in Honor of
the Indiana University Art Museum's Fifieth Anniversary; An American Picture
Gallery: Recent Gifts from Morton C Bradley, Jr; Color/Form: The Geometric
Sculpture of Morton C Bradley, Jr; The Artist as Explorer: Albrecht Durer;
Treasures from Polynesia; From Myth to Reality: Bovines in Art; MFA Thesis
Shows
Publications: Guide to the collection, exhibition catalogs, occasional papers,
newsletter
Activities: Classes for adults & children; docent training; Lect open to public;
gallery talks; tours; concert series; competition with awards; Book traveling
exhibitions; originate traveling exhibitions; museum shop sells books, magazines,
reproductions, prints, slides
M **William Hammond Mathers Museum,** 601 E Eighth St, 47405. Tel 812-885-
6873; FAX 812-855-0205. *Dir* Geoffrey W Conrad; *Designer* Elaine Gaul; *Coll
Mgr* Tristine Perkins; *Exhibits Mgr* David Bruker; *Conservator* Judith Sylvester;
Asst Dir Judith Kirk; *Cur Coll* Thomas Kavanagh; *Business Mgr* Sandra Warren
Open Tues - Fri 9 AM - 4:30 PM, Sat & Sun 1 - 4:30 PM. No admis fee. Estab
1964 as Indiana University Museum, institute renamed in 1983. Museum of
World Cultures housing over 30,000 artifacts
Collections: Anthropology, folklore & history with collections of American
primitives, Latin American primitives & folk art
Exhibitions: Eskimo: Life from the Tundra & Sea: A Missionary Collects: John
White Among the Tetela
Publications: Papers & monograph series
Activities: Docent program; museum training classes; lectures; tours; film series;
school loan collection

L **INDIANA UNIVERSITY,** Fine Arts Library, Art Museum Bldg, 47405. Tel
812-855-3314; FAX 812-855-3443; Elec Mail Bitnet.IRVINE&atsIUBACS. *Head
Librn* Betty Jo Irvine; *Asst Librn* Rosann Auchstetter; *Slide Librn* Eileen Fry
For lending
Income: Financed by state & student fees

Library Holdings: Vols 80,000; Per subs 390; Micro — Fiche 16,000; AV — Slides 325,000; Other — Clipping files 50,000, exhibition catalogs, reproductions 50,000

Special Subjects: Advertising Design, Aesthetics, Afro-American Art, American Indian Art, American Western Art, Antiquities-Byzantine, Antiquities-Greek, Antiquities-Oriental, Antiquities-Roman, Architecture, Art History, Asian Art, Ceramics, Conceptual Art, Decorative Arts, Drawings, Eskimo Art, Etchings & Engravings, Folk Art, Goldsmithing, Graphic Arts, Graphic Design, History of Art & Archaeology, Islamic Art, Jewelry, Manuscripts, Mixed Media, Oriental Art, Painting - American, Painting - British, Painting - Dutch, Painting - European, Painting - Flemish

ELKHART

M MIDWEST MUSEUM OF AMERICAN ART, 429 S Main St, PO Box 1812, 46515. Tel 219-293-6660. *Pres* Dr Richard D Burns; *VPres* Michael Nickol; *Dir* Jane Burns; *Cur Exhibitions & Education* Brian D Byrn
Open Tues - Fri 11 AM - 5 PM, Thurs 7 PM - 9 PM, Sat - Sun 1 - 4 PM. Admis adults $1.50, student & senior citizens $.75. Estab 1979 to provide high quality exhibitions, educational programs, & permanent collection of 19th & 20th century American art for the public. Seven galleries on two floors (approx 9000 sq ft of exhibit space). Average Annual Attendance: 15-20,000. Mem: 900; dues $10 - $250
Income: $100,000 (financed through membership, grants, foundations, contributions)
Collections: Paintings: Arthur Bowen Davies; Joan Mitchell; Robert Natkin; Maurice Pendergast; †Grant Wood; Red Grooms; Carl Olaf Seltzer; Norman Rockwell; LeRoy Neiman; Roger Brown; Art Green; George Luks; Glen Cooper Henshaw; Pennerton West; Robert Reid; Sculpture: Louise Nevelson; Mark DiSuvero; Felix Eboigbe; Frederick MacMonnies; Photographs: Ansel Adams; Imogen Cunningham; Walker Evans; W Eugene Smith; Edward Steichen; Alfred Stieglitz; Clarence White; Minor White; Bernice Abbott; Edward Curtis; Arnold Genthe
Exhibitions: Changing Walls: Tactile Environment; Midwest Photo '80
Publications: Midwest Museum Bulletin, bimonthly
Activities: Classes for adults and children; dramatic programs; docent training; lect open to the public, 6 visiting lectrs per year; concerts; gallery talks; tours; competitions with awards; individual paintings and original objects of art lent; book traveling exhibitions, 10-12 per year; traveling exhibitions organized and circulated

EVANSVILLE

M EVANSVILLE MUSEUM OF ARTS AND SCIENCE, 411 SE Riverside Dr, 47713. Tel 812-425-2406, 421-7506 (TTY); FAX 812-421-7507. *Pres Board Dir* Patrick Shoulders; *Dir* John W Streetman; *Dir Emeritus* Siegfried Weng; *Cur Educ* Sam Longmire; *Cur of Coll* Mary Schnepper; *Registrar* Susan P Colaricci; *Asst Cur* Thomas R Lonnberg; *Science Planetarium Dir* Mitch Luman
Open Tues - Sat 10 AM - 5 PM, Sun noon - 5 PM, cl Mon. No admis fee. Estab 1926 to maintain and perpetuate a living museum to influence and inspire the taste and cultural growth of the community, to provide facilities for the collection, preservation and exhibition of objects and data and programs related to the arts, history, science and technology. First Level: 19th century village of homes, shops, offices & town hall, America at War Gallery, two science & technology galleries, classrooms; Second Level: furnished Gothic Room with linefold paneling; Sculpture Gallery: galleries for Dutch & Flemish art, 18th century English art, 19th & 20th century American & European art, Anthropology Gallery; two galleries for monthly exhibits; Third Level: Planetarium. Average Annual Attendance: 100,000. Mem: Dues benefactor $1000, sponsor $250, donor $250, patron $100, contributing $50, family $25, individual $15; annual meeting third Tues in May
Income: $174,000 (financed by mem, city & state appropriations)
Collections: †American & European paintings & drawings; †20th century American crafts; †history archives; Oriental art; sculpture from BC to contemporary; †Victorian decorative arts; anthropological collections
Exhibitions: (1992) 10th Annual Realism Today; 45th Annual Mid-States Art Show; Evansville Artists Guild Annual Show
Publications: Bulletin, monthly; catalogs of exhibitions
Activities: Classes for adults and children; dramatic programs; docent training; lect open to public; concerts; gallery talks; tours; competitions; exten dept serving area schools; individual paintings and original objects of art lent to institutions; traveling exhibitions organized and circulated; museum shop selling books, original art, reproductions, prints, jewelry, and pottery
L Henry R Walker Jr Memorial Art Library, 411 SE Riverside Dr, 47713. Tel 812-425-2406. *Cur* Mary Schnepper
Open Tues - Sat 10 AM - 5 PM, Sun Noon - 5 PM. For reference only
Library Holdings: Vols 4000; Per subs 25; AV — Slides; Other — Clipping files, exhibition catalogs, manuscripts, memorabilia, original art works, pamphlets, photographs, prints, reproductions, sculpture

UNIVERSITY OF EVANSVILLE
M Krannert Gallery, 1800 Lincoln Ave, 47722. Tel 812-479-2043. *Chmn Art Dept* Les Miley
Open Mon - Sat 9 AM - 5 PM. No admis fee. Estab 1969-70 to bring to the University and public communities exhibitions which reflect the contemporary arts, ranging from crafts through painting and sculpture. Public access exhibition space 80 x 40 ft and located in Fine Arts Building
Income: Financed by Department of Art funds
Exhibitions: Drawing Exhibition; Indiana Ceramics; New Aquisitions; Student Scholarship Exhibition; Undergraduate BFA Exhibition; Faculty Exhibition; Painting Invitational; Sculpture Invitational; Evansville Artists Guild Show; Photography Exhibition (1988-89) Ceramic Sculpture & Drawing; Annual Student Show
Activities: Lectures open to the public, 2 vis lectrs per yr; gallery talks; competitions; awards; individual paintings and original objects of art lent to university community

L University Library, 1800 Lincoln Ave, 47722. Tel 812-479-2482; FAX 812-479-2009. *Acquistions Librn* Marvin Guilfoyle
Open 8 AM - 11 PM
Library Holdings: Vols 4000; Per subs 27; Micro — Fiche, prints; AV — A-tapes, rec, slides; Other — Original art works, pamphlets, prints

L WILLARD LIBRARY, Dept of Fine Arts, 21 First Ave, 47710. Tel 812-425-4309. *Head Librn* William Goodrich; *Adult Serv* David Locker; *Spec Coll* Joan Elliott-Parker; *Childrens Librn* Anne Lambert
Open Tues - Fri 9 AM - 5:30 PM, Sat 9 AM - 5 PM, Sun 1 - 5 PM. Estab 1885
Income: $3000 (financed by endowment and city appropriation)
Library Holdings: Vols 600; Per subs 16; AV — Rec; Other — Original art works, photographs

FORT WAYNE

L ALLEN COUNTY PUBLIC LIBRARY, Fine Arts Dept, 900 Webster St, 46802. Tel 219-424-7241; FAX 219-422-9688. *Dir* Jeffrey R Krull; *Assoc Dir* Steven Fortreide; *Head Fine Arts Dept* Bob Brubaker
Open Mon - Thurs 9 AM - 9 PM, Fri 9 AM - 6 PM, Sat 9 AM - 6 PM, Sun 1 - 6 PM. Estab 1968 to provide a reference collection of the highest quality and completeness for the community and its colleges, and a place where local artists and musicians could exhibit their works and perform; and to provide a circulating collection of art prints, slides and musical scores sufficient to meet the demand. The gallery is reserved for painting, sculpture, graphics, ceramics and other art crafts; photography exhibits are held in the lobby area
Income: $100,000 (financed by local property taxes)
Library Holdings: Vols 60,000; Per subs 170; Mounted pictures; AV — Cassettes 3000, motion pictures 2600, rec 20,000, slides 22,000, v-tapes 1000; Other — Exhibition catalogs, framed reproductions 200, prints, reproductions
Activities: Concerts

A ARTS UNITED OF GREATER FORT WAYNE, The Canal House, 114 E Superior St, 46802. Tel 219-424-0646; FAX 219-424-2783. *Pres* Robert E Bush Jr; *Chmn* Robert L Delaney; *Asst Dir* Kathi Nadolny; *Comptroller* Camille Douglas-Edwards; *Mgr Arts Center* Janet McCaulay; *Dir Marketing* Gregory Manifold; *Dir Development* Kimberly Bastin
Estab 1955 to raise funds for cultural organizations in Fort Wayne & to foster a positive atmosphere for arts growth
Income: Financed by public allocations & private donations
Collections: Bicentennial Collection
Publications: Discovery, quarterly newspaper; fine arts calendar
Activities: Own and manage the Performing Arts Center, umbrella organization for 36 arts organizations

M FORT WAYNE MUSEUM OF ART, INC, 311 E Main St, 46802. Tel 219-422-6467; FAX 219-422-1374. *Dir* Emily Kass
Open Tues - Fri & Sat (June-Aug) 10 AM - 5 PM, Sat (Sept-May) 10 AM - 8 PM, Sun Noon 5 PM, cl Mon. No admis fee. Estab 1921 to heighten visual perception of fine arts and perception of other disciplines. Average Annual Attendance: 85,000. Mem: 1591; dues $25 for an individual & up; annual meeting July
Income: Financed by endowment, memberships, Arts United & grants
Collections: Paintings, prints, sculpture and minor art; Dorsky and Tannenbaum Collection of contemporary Graphics; Fairbanks Collection of Paintings and Prints; Hamilton Collection of Paintings and Sculpture; Thieme Collection of Paintings; Weatherhead Collection of Contemporary Paintings & Prints; William Moser Collection of African Art; Contemporary pieces by living American artists; African, Pre-Colombian, Greek & Roman artifacts
Exhibitions: (1989) Mary Beth Edelson: Shape Shifter-Seven Mediums; Jose Guadalupe Posada Prints; Mexico Nueve; Mexican Works on Paper; Question of Drawing; Sculptors on Paper; Artful Objects: Recent American Crafts; Amish Quilts from the Museum of American Folk Art; Bill Jensen Works on Paper (1990) Heirs to Impressionism: Berthe and Andre Noufflard; Italy: One Hundred Years of Photography; The Art of Paul Manship; American Modernism; Alice and Look Who Else Through the Lookingglass; Reginald Marsh: Coney Island (1991) (planned) Ceramics of the Weimar Republic; Experimental Traditions: 25 Years of American Architecture; Larry Rivers: Public and Private; African American Artists: 1880-1987; The American Scene: Art of the 30's
Publications: Books; calendar, bi-monthly; catalogs; fact sheets; posters
Activities: Classes for adults and children; docent training; lectures open to public; 15 vis lectr per year; gallery talks; tours; five to six traveling exhibitions per year; originate traveling exhibitions; museum and sales shop sells books, magazines, original art, reproductions and prints

C LINCOLN NATIONAL LIFE INSURANCE CO, Lincoln Museum, 1300 S Clinton St, 46801. Tel 219-455-3864; FAX 219-455-6922. *Asst* Ruth Cook
Open Mon - Thurs 9 AM - 5 PM, Fri 8 AM - 12:30 PM, May - Sept Mon - Fri 8 AM - 4:30 PM, Sat 10 AM - 4:30 PM. No admis fee. Estab 1928 for collection of Lincolniana; as research library and museum. Average Annual Attendance: 14,000
Special Subjects: Bronzes, Calligraphy, Cartoons, Coins & Medals, Etchings & Engravings, Historical Material, Portraits, Posters, Sculpture
Collections: †Lincolniana; †Civil War; †19th Century Art (1809-1865)
Publications: Lincoln Lore, monthly; R Gerald McMurry Lecture, annually
Activities: Lect open to public; 1 vis lectr per yr; individual paintings & original objects of art lent to qualified institutions; originate traveling exhibitions

M SAINT FRANCIS COLLEGE, John Weatherhead Gallery, 1901 Spring St, 46808. Tel 219-434-3100.
Open Mon - Fri 10 AM - 5 PM. No admis fee. Estab 1965, to provide art programs to students and community. Gallery, approx 25 x 15 ft each, is maintained in two rooms, located on the third floor, Bonaventure Hall. Average Annual Attendance: 1000
Activities: Lectures open to public, 1-2 visiting lecturers per year; tours; competitions with awards; traveling exhibitions organized and circulated

HAMMOND

M **PURDUE UNIVERSITY CALUMET,** Bicentennial Library Gallery, 46323-2094. Tel 219-989-2249. *Admin & Chmn Art Committee* John Carlisle
Open Mon - Thurs 8 AM - 9:30 PM, Fri 8 AM - 5 PM, Sat 10 AM - 4 PM, Sun 1 - 5 PM. No admis fee. Estab 1976 to present varied art media to the university community & general public. Average Annual Attendance: 25,000
Income: $2000
Collections: 19th century Chinese Scroll collection; 1930 art deco bronze sculptured doors from City Hall
Exhibitions: Area Professional Artists & Students Shows; group shows; traveling shows (Smithsonian Institution, French Cultural Services, Austrian Institute)
Activities: Book traveling exhibitions

HUNTINGTON

M **HUNTINGTON COLLEGE,** Robert E Wilson Art Gallery, Center for the Arts, 2303 College Ave, 46750-1299. Tel 219-356-6000; FAX 219-356-9448. *Dir* Dwight Ericsson
Open Mon - Fri 8 AM - 5 PM. No admis fee. Estab 1990 to provide community with art shows & support college art program. Gallery is 25 x 44 ft. Average Annual Attendance: 1500
Income: $5000 (financed by gifts)
Collections: Wilson Collection (paintings)
Activities: Art in the schools; docent programs; book traveling exhibitions 4 per year

INDIANAPOLIS

M **CHILDREN'S MUSEUM,** Rauh Memorial Library, 300 N Meridian, PO Box 3000, 46206. Tel 317-924-5431; FAX 317-921-4019. *Pres* Peter Sterling; *VPres* Paul Richard; *VPres* Margaret Maxwell; *VPres* John Grogan
Open 10 AM - 5 PM. Admis $4, $3. Estab 1926 to enrich the lives of children. History, physical science, natural science, world cultures, pastimes, center of exploration, trains, dolls, playscape, planetarium, theater. Average Annual Attendance: 1,100,000. Mem: 6800; dues family $50; annual meeting Apr
Income: $10,000,000 (funded by endowment, mem, fundraising)
Collections: Caplan Collection
Exhibitions: (1990) Field to Factory; Pagagnini Violin Exhibit; Dinomania; Super Heros
Publications: Quarterly newsletter
Activities: Children's classes; dramatic programs; docent programs; lect open to public, 6 vis lectr per year; competitions in theatre, visual arts, vocal music, literature, dance & instrumental music; lending collection contains 730 educational kits; book traveling exhibitions, 3 per year; retail store sells books

M **EITELJORG MUSEUM OF AMERICAN INDIAN & WESTERN ART,** 500 W Washington, 46204. Tel 317-636-9378; FAX 317-264-1724. *Chmn* Harrison Eiteljorg; *Exec Dir* Michael Duty
Open Tues - Sat 10 AM - 5 PM, Sun noon - 5 PM. Dedicated to the preservation & interpretation of the history of the American frontier experience, particularly as it relates to the culture & art of North American Indians & to the exploration, settling & development of the continent
Collections: Collections of Taos Artists; 19th & 20th Century Art Work
Exhibitions: (1990) New Art of the West by Group Artists

M **HISTORIC LANDMARKS FOUNDATION OF INDIANA,** Morris-Butler House, 1204 N Park Ave, 46202. Tel 317-636-5409; FAX 317-636-2630. *Adminr* Tiffany C Sallee
Open Tues - Sat 1 - 4 PM, Sun 1 - 4 PM (tours on the hour), cl Mon. Admis adult $2, students & children $1. Home built 1865 and restored by Historic Landmarks Foundation of Indiana. Estab in 1969 to document age of picturesque eexlecticism in architecture & interior decoration. Interpretation, exhibition & preservation of Victorian lifestyle, customs and objects (1850-1890). 16 rooms completely furnished. Facilities for receptions and meetings. All paintings by Indiana artists previously owned by Mid-Victorian homeowners (1850-1890). Average Annual Attendance: 10,000. Mem: Annual dues $15-$100
Income: Financed by private funds & admis fees
Collections: †Rococo, †Renaissance & Gothic Revival furniture; †paintings by early Indiana artists; †Victorian ceramics, silver & glass; †Victorian textiles
Publications: Victorian Wedding Primer; Victorian Christmas Sampler
Activities: Educ Dept; classes for children & adults; docent training; lect open to public, 10 vis lectr per year; individual paintings & original objects of art lent to professional museums; lending collection contains original art work & paintings

L **Information Center Library,** 340 W Michigan St, 46202. Tel 317-639-4534; FAX 317-639-6734. *Pres* J Reid Williamson Jr; *VPres* James D Conley; *Dir Community Servs* Marsh Davis
For Reference only
Library Holdings: Vols 3000; Per subs 100; AV — A-tapes, Kodachromes, motion pictures, slides, v-tapes; Other — Clipping files

A **HOOSIER SALON PATRONS ASSOCIATION,** Hoosier Salon Art Gallery, 6434 N College Ave, 46220. Tel 317-253-5340. *Pres* Henry B Blackwell; *First VPres* Jamia Jacobsen; *Treas* Thomas Fairchild
Main gallery open Mon - Fri 9:30 AM - 4 PM. No admis fee. Estab 1925 to promote work of Indiana artists. Average Annual Attendance: Annual exhibit 4000; daily attendance 10-50. Mem: Artists 650, patrons 700; dues patrons $35 & up, artists $20; annual meeting in June
Income: Financed by memberships and art sales
Collections: Paintings, prints, sculpture
Exhibitions: Annual Hoosier Salon in spring & then on tour
Publications: Annual Salon Exhibition Catalog; History of the Hoosier Salon; Hoosier Salon Newsletter, three times a year
Activities: Gallery talks & tours at annual exhibit; Juried competition with awards; original prints & paintings lent to qualified organizations; gallery sells original art & prints

A **INDIANAPOLIS ART LEAGUE,** Churchman-Fehsenfeld Gallery, 820 E 67th St, 46220. Tel 317-255-2464; FAX 317-284-0486. *Exec Dir* Joyce Sommers; *Education Dir* David Thomas; *Exhib Cur* Julia Muney Moore
Open Mon - Thur 9 AM - 10 PM, Fri 9 AM - 5 PM, Sat 9 AM - 3 PM, Sun noon - 3 PM. No admis fee, donations accepted. Estab 1934 to promote Indiana & Midwestern artists through classes & exhibitions. Average Annual Attendance: 119,000. Mem: 2000
Income: Financed by endowment, membership, city & state appropriation
Exhibitions: (1992) Studio Furniture Indiana; Transformations: Feminist Art by Louisville Artists; Amanda Block: A Retrospective; Essential Systems: Cross, Gray, Hayward; Indiana Directions '92. (1993) Six Indiana Fiber Artists; Two in Clay: Harris Deller/Dorothy Feibleman; Baltic/Midwestern Enamels; Indiana Woodcraft; Regional '93
Publications: Paper Canvas, 3 times a year
Activities: Over 90 art classes offered for all ages & skill levels in all ages & skill levels in all medias. Outdoor riverfront stage has music, theatre and dance; summer fine arts camps; workshops; lectures open to the public; competitions with awards; scholarship & fels offered; book traveling exhibitions; library; slide and resume bank for regional artists; corporate consulting

L **Library,** 820 E 67th St, 46220. Tel 317-255-2464. *Resource Coordr* Julia Muney Moore
Open Mon - Fri 9 AM - 10 PM. Estab 1976. For reference only
Library Holdings: Vols 1200; Per subs 10; AV — A-tapes, slides, v-tapes; Other — Clipping files, exhibition catalogs, pamphlets, photographs

L **INDIANAPOLIS MARION COUNTY PUBLIC LIBRARY,** Arts Division, 40 E St Clair St, 46204. Tel 317-269-1764. *Division Head* Dan Gann
Open Mon - Fri 9 AM - 9 PM, Sat 9 AM - 5 PM, Sun 1 - 5 PM. Estab 1873
Income: Financed by state appropriation and county property tax
Library Holdings: Vols 25,000; Per subs 200; Micro — Reels; AV — Cassettes, fs 1250, motion pictures, rec 25,000; Other — Clipping files, exhibition catalogs, framed reproductions, pamphlets, photographs, prints
Collections: Julia Connor Thompson Collection on Finer Arts in Homemaking
Activities: Lect open to public; concerts; tours

M **INDIANAPOLIS MUSEUM OF ART,** 1200 W 38th St, 46208. Tel 317-923-1331; FAX 317-926-8931. *Chmn Board of Trustees* Anna S White; *Pres Board of Trustees* Richard D Wood; *Dir* Bret Waller; *Chief Cur* Ellen Lee; *Cur Oriental Art* Dr James Robinson; *Asst Cur Textiles & Costumes* Niloo Imami-Paydar; *Cur Contemporary Art* Holliday T Day; *Cur Decorative Arts* Barry Shifman; *Cur Prints & Drawings* Martin F Krause; *Cur African, S Pacific, Pre-Columbian* Ted Celenko; *Dir Educ* Daryl Fischer; *Chief Conservator* Martin J Radecki; *Registrar* Vanessa Burkhart; *Dir Educational Resources* Carolyn J Metz; *Dir Marketing, Communications, Mem & Development* Mary T Bergrson; *Dir Institutional Advancement* Mack P McKinzie; *Dir Human Resources* Kathleen Mason; *Business Mgr* Matthew Cornacchione
Open Tues - Sun 11 AM - 5 PM; cl Mon, Thanksgiving, Christmas & New Year's Day. No admis fee to permanent collection; Charge for special exhibitions. Estab 1883 to maintain a museum, the grounds, pavilions, and other facilities for the display of art, a library for the collection of books, manuscripts, periodicals, photographs and other similar data or facilities relating to art of all kinds; to promote interest in art of all kinds by lectures, exhibitions, publications, programs and general sponsorship of art and artists in the City of Indianapolis and State of Indiana; to cooperate with national state and city government and civic, educational and artistic groups foundations. Maintains 4 pavilions, the Krannert, Hulman, Clowes & Lilly Pavilions, as part of a 152 acre complex. Average Annual Attendance: 500,000. Mem: 12,000; dues reciprocal $110, sustaining $60, family-double $30, individual $20
Collections: Classical to contemporary watercolors, including †J M W Turner Collection; †American period rooms, †costumes and textiles; †decorative arts, including watch collection; †18th century English portraiture; †18th - 19th century European porcelain and furniture; †ethnographic art of North and South America, Africa and Oceania; Indiana paintings; †Oriental bronzes, ceramics, jade and paintings; †19th - 20th century American and European paintings; †Holliday Collection of Neo-Impressionist paintings; †17th century European paintings; †Renaissance to contemporary drawings and prints; Western American art
Publications: Brochures; handbook of permanent collections; Bi-monthly magazine (Previews) for members; catalogues for IMA-organized exhibitions
Activities: Classes for adults and children; docent training; lect open to public, 15 - 20 vis lectrs per yr; concerts; gallery talks; tours; scholarships offered; exten dept; individual paintings & original objects of art lent; originate traveling exhibitions; museum shop and sales shop selling books, magazines, original art, reproductions, prints, slides & jewelry; Alliance Art Rental Gallery rents paintings to members and sells to members and public

M **Clowes Fund Collection,** Clowes Pavilion, 1200 W 38th St, 46208. Tel 317-923-1331; FAX 317-926-8931. *Cur* A Ian Fraser
Open Tues - Sun 11 AM - 5 PM, cl Mon. No admis fee. Estab 1958 to display paintings of the Old Masters from the collection of the late Dr G H A Clowes. Average Annual Attendance: 62,000
Income: Financed by endowment
Collections: Italian Renaissance: Duccio, Fra Angelico, Bellini, Luini, Tintoretto, and others; Spanish-El Greco, Goya and others; Northern Renaissance-17th and 18th century Dutch, Hals, Rembrandt and others; French-Clouet, Corneille de Lyon; English-Reynolds, Constable and others; Flemish-Breughel, Bosch and others
Exhibitions: (1991) Richard Pousette-Dart; Seurat at Gravelines: The Last Landscapes. (1992) William S Paley Collection. (1993) Tales of Japan: Three Centuries of Japanese Painting; Per Kirkeby Paintings & Drawings; Max Ernst; The Sculpture

L **Stout Reference Library,** 1200 W 38th St, 46208. Tel 317-923-1331, Ext 276; FAX 317-926-8931. *Dir Educational Resources* Carolyn J Metz; *Reference Librn* Ursual Kolmstetter; *Librn Asst* Anne Marie Quets
Open Tues - Fri 10 AM - 5 PM, Sat & Sun 1 PM - 4 PM. Estab 1908 to serve needs of Museum staff and Indianapolis community. For reference only
Income: Financed by endowment, mem, city appropriation & federal grants
Library Holdings: Vols 27,000; Per subs 150; Micro — Fiche, reels; Other —

Clipping files, exhibition catalogs, pamphlets
Special Subjects: Architecture, Decorative Arts, Ethnology, Oriental Art, Painting - American, Sculpture, Textiles
Collections: Indiana Artists
Publications: Exhibition catalogs as needed; Indianapolis Museum of Art Bulletin, irregularly; newsletter, bimonthly; 100 Masterpieces

L **Slide Collection,** 1200 W 38th St, 46208. Tel 317-923-1331, Ext 126; FAX 317-926-8931. *Slide Coordr* Joni Back
Open Tues - Sat 1 - 5 PM. Estab 1972 to provide visuals on the history of art and to document and record the museum programs and activities. Circ 50,000
Income: Financed by endowment and museum budget
Purchases: $5000
Library Holdings: AV — Slides 120,000
Special Subjects: Art History
Collections: Exhibits and installation documentation of programs

M **Indianapolis Museum of Art at Columbus,** Fifth and Franklin Sts, 47201. Tel 812-372-4622. *Coordr* Kitty Uhrich
Open Mon - Sat 10 AM - 2 PM; Apr - Oct Sun noon - 4. No admis fee. Estab 1974. Gallery contains 1200 sq ft on upper floor of Columbus Visitors Center. Average Annual Attendance: 5500. Mem: 250; dues family $30, individual $20; annual meeting in May
Income: Financed by auction & Indianapolis Museum of Art
Exhibitions: Exhibitions from the permanent collection quarterly; exhibitions of IMA permanent collection & of local interest
Activities: School programs; resource kits; lectures open to public, 6 - 8 vis lectrs per yr; concerts; gallery talks; tours; purchase awards

M **INDIANA STATE MUSEUM,** 202 N Alabama St, 46204. Tel 317-232-1637; FAX 317-232-7090. *Exec Dir* Richard A Gontz; *Dir Public Programs* Lynda Blackwelder; *Dir Budget & Finance* William Bruggen; *Cur in Charge* Ronald Richards; *Cur Fine Arts* Claudia Kheel; *Cur Costumes* Debra Siewart; *Cur Flat Textiles* Kathleen McClary; *Cur History* Dale Ogden; *Cur Popular Culture* William Wepler; *Registrar* Jeffrey Tenuth; *Coll Mgr* Linda Badger; *Textile Conservator* Delores Keesee; *Cur Biology* William McKnight; *Dir Design & Graphics* Wade Carmichael; *Dir Public Relations* Cindy Busch; *Media Relation Specialist* Melanie Maxwell; *Dept of Education* Nancy Wolfe
Open daily 9 AM - 4:45 PM, Sun noon - 4:45 PM. No admis fee. Estab 1869 for collections; current museum building opened 1967 to collect, preserve and interpret the natural and cultural history of the state. Numerous galleries. Average Annual Attendance: 260,000. Mem: 1300; dues $5 and up; annual meeting Apr
Income: Financed by state appropriation
Exhibitions: Three Indiana art shows annually; Pottinger Amish Quilt Collection; Indiana Sports Hall of Fame
Publications: On-the-Move, quarterly; brochures for individual historic sites
Activities: Docent training; in-school programs; lect open to public, 4 vis lectr per year; sales shop selling books, reproductions and prints

INDIANA UNIVERSITY - PURDUE UNIVERSITY AT INDIANAPOLIS

M **Indianapolis Center for Contemporary Art-Herron Gallery,** 1701 N Pennsylvania St, 46202. Tel 317-920-2420; FAX 317-920-2401. *Dir & Cur Art Gallery* Lese Hilgeman; *Gallery Asst* James E May
Open Mon - Thurs 10 AM - 7 PM, Fri 10 AM - 5 PM, Sat 10 AM - 2 PM. No admis fee. School estab 1860. Gallery estab 1978 and is located in the Museum Building & exhibits contemporary art on an international scale. 3000 sq ft, 14 ft ceilings, marble floors, climate control. Average Annual Attendance: 40,000. Mem: 250; dues $25 - $500
Income: Financed by state appropriation, grants & private support
Exhibitions: (1993) Invasions of Privacy; Patrick Dougherty: Enclosures A Site Specific Installation
Activities: Educ dept; docent training; tours; lectures open to public; 15 vis lectrs per year; gallery talks; tours; competitions; awards; exten dept serving Indianapolis and surrounding communities; facilitators of civic art projects; book traveling exhibitions, 2 per year; originate traveling exhibitions; museum shop sells t-shirts, posters, catalogs
—**Herron School of Art Library,** 1701 N Pennsylvania St, 46202-2402. Tel 317-920-2433; FAX 317-920-2430. *Head Librn* Ophelia Roop; *Assoc Librn* Jennifer Hehman
Open Mon - Thurs 8 AM - 7 PM, Fri 8 AM - 5 PM, Sat 8:30 AM - 12:30 PM. Estab 1970 as a visual resource center for the support of the curriculum of the Herron School of Art. Circ 110,000
Income: $35,000 (financed by state appropriation)
Purchases: $17,000
Library Holdings: Vols 21,000; Per subs 100; Laser disc; AV — A-tapes, lantern slides, slides, v-tapes; Other — Clipping files, exhibition catalogs, pamphlets, photographs, prints, reproductions
Special Subjects: Advertising Design, Afro-American Art, American Indian Art, American Western Art, Antiquities-Greek, Architecture, Art Education, Art History, Ceramics, Collages, Commercial Art, Conceptual Art, Crafts, Display, Drawings, Visual communication, painting, Woodworking

C **LAUGHNER BROTHERS, INC,** 4004 US Hwy 31S, 46227. Tel 317-783-2907; FAX 317-783-3126. *Pres* Richard Tierney
Open Mon - Sun 11 AM-8:30 PM. Estab 1960 to promote Indiana artists. Collection displayed in dining establishments, Mr Laughner uses original paintings from several artists as his main decor in all 10 locations in Indiana
Purchases: $2000

M **MARIAN COLLEGE,** Allison Mansion, 3200 Cold Spring Rd, 46222. Tel 317-929-0299, 929-0123; FAX 317-929-0263. *Dir of Conferences & Events* Vicky Welch
Conference Center open by appointment. Donations accepted. Estab 1970, in the National Register of Historical Places. The interior of the mansion is a work of art with its magnificent treatment of walls of hand carved marble and wood: oak, white mahogany and walnut. The grand stairway in the main hall leads to the balcony overlooking the hall, all hand-carved walnut. A private collection of 17th century paintings complement its beauty
Income: Financed by donations
Activities: Concerts; tours; corporate meeting site

M **THE NATIONAL ART MUSEUM OF SPORT,** Bank One Center & Tower, Suite 200, 111 Monument Circle, 46204. Tel 317-687-1715; FAX 317-687-1718. *Pres* Germain G Glidden; *VPres* Angelica Heller; *Secy* James Q Bensen
Open Mon - Fri 9 AM - 5 PM. No admis fee. Estab 1964 to expose the direct connection between art and sport. Average Annual Attendance: 1000. Mem: 3003; dues up to $1000; annual meeting in Jan
Income: $50,000 (financed by membership and corporate donations)
Collections: Paintings, sculpture and prints of leading past and present US sports champions
Publications: Newsletter, 2-3 per year
Activities: Lect open to public, 2 vis lectrs per year; individual and original objects of art lent to leading museums and corporate offices; originate traveling exhibitions

M **NATIONAL ART MUSEUM OF SPORT,** Bank One Tower, Suite 200, 111 Monument Circle, 46204. Tel 317-687-1715; FAX 317-687-1718. *Exec Dir* Reilly Rhodes; *Asst to Dir* Melissa Copper; *Registrar* Rebecca Ryan; *Comptroller* Eric Scott; *Membership Coordr* Diane Huser; *Media Relations Asst* Amy Beam; *Cur Educ* Virginia Hamm; *Marketing & Prog Coordr* Laura Orgera; *Registrar Asst* Gay Lewis; *Exhib Asst* Larry Giacoletti; *Secy* Kristi McCaffrey
Open Mon - Fri 9 AM - 5 PM, Sat 10 AM - 4 PM. Admis free, donations accepted. Estab 1959 as a fine art museum covering sports. Mem: 167
Collections: Works by George Bellows, Fletcher Martin, Winslow Homer, Alfred Boucher, Willard Mullin, John Groth
Exhibitions: (1992) Inuit Games: Traditional Sport & Play of the Eskimo; Tiffany Sporting Themes: The Belmont Humidor; The Sport of Kings & Thoroughbred Racetracks; Selections from the Permanent Collection (works collected from 1960); Artists at Ringside; Winslow Homer Sporting Scenes; Indiana Pacers in Art. (1993) Spirit of America: One Nation Under Sport
Publications: News from the Museum, quarterly newsletter; catalogs
Activities: Docent training; teach workshops; lect open to public; gallery talke; tours; individual paintings & original objects of art lent to archivally sound institutions with adequate security & qualified staff; book traveling exhibitions 5 - 6 per year; originate traveling exhibitions; museum shop sells books, reproductions, prints, clothing, games, cards & stationery, jewelry

M **UNIVERSITY OF INDIANAPOLIS,** Leah Ransburg Art Gallery, 1400 E Hanna Ave, 46227. Tel 317-788-3253. *Dir* Earl G Snellenberger
Open Mon - Fri 9 AM - 4 PM. No admis fee. Estab 1964 to serve the campus and community. Average Annual Attendance: 40,000
Income: Financed by institution support
Purchases: $15,000
Collections: †Art Department Collection; †Krannert Memorial Collection
Publications: Announcements; annual catalog and bulletin
Activities: Classes for adults; lectures open to public; concerts; gallery talks; competitions with prizes; scholarships

LAFAYETTE

M **GREATER LAFAYETTE MUSEUM OF ART** (Formerly Lafayette Art Association), 101 S Ninth St, 47901. Tel 317-742-1128. *Pres* Tom Greives; *Dir* Sharon A Theobald; *Cur* Ellen E Fischer; *Development* Julie L Weiland; *Asst to Dir* Debbie Black
Open Tues - Sun 1 PM - 5 PM, cl Mon & Aug. No admis fee. Estab 1909 to encourage and stimulate art and to present exhibitions of works of local, regional and national artists and groups as well as representative works of American and foreign artists. Average Annual Attendance: 10,000. Mem: 1000; dues family $30, individual $20, student & sr citizen $15; annual meeting Oct
Income: Financed by art association foundation, endowment, membership, school of art & special events
Collections: Permanent collection of over 526 works of art obtained through purchase or donation since 1909 Laura Anne Fry American Art Pottery & Art Glass; Alice Baber Collection of Contemporary American Art; American art collection specializing in Hoosier artist's work
Publications: In Perspective, quarterly newsletter; exhibition catalogs; annual report
Activities: Classes for adults & children; docent training; lect open to the public, 8 - 10 vis lectr per year; gallery talks; tours; competitions with awards; Akeley Memorial lecture series; scholarships; individual paintings & original objects of art lent to Museum members on a monthly basis & to corporations; originate book traveling exhibitons, 1 - 2 per year; sales shop selling books, original art, prints, reproductions

L **Library,** 101 S Ninth St, 47901. Tel 317-742-1128; FAX 317-742-1120. *Pres* Tom Greives
Open to members
Library Holdings: Vols 1000; Per subs 15; AV — V-tapes; Other — Clipping files, exhibition catalogs, framed reproductions, prints

M **TIPPECANOE COUNTY HISTORICAL MUSEUM,** 909 South St, 47901. Tel 317-742-8411. *Exec Dir* Patrick Daily; *Develop Dir* Kathleen Atwell; *Cur of Educ* Paula Woods; *Asst Cur Educ* Cindy Bedell; *Exhibition Dir* William Dichtl
Open daily 1 - 5 PM, cl Mon. No admis fee. Estab 1925 to collect, preserve, research and interpret the history of Tippecanoe County and the immediate surrounding area. Housed in a Victorian house (1851-52), there are exhibits of various phases of county history in nine rooms. Average Annual Attendance: 20, 000. Mem: 1000; dues $10 - $500; annual meeting Jan
Income: Financed by endowment, membership, county and state appropriation, sales and programs
Collections: Broad range, incorporating any object relative to county history
Exhibitions: Changing exhibits; fixed exhibits include Pioneer Development, Woodland Indians, The Building Years 1840-1900, miniature rooms, paintings & porcelains. (1993) Communications; Mourning A Loved One, Mourning Practices of 19th Century; a photo exhibit on the Columbian Exposition; photo exhibition on banks
Publications: Tippecanoe Tales, occasional series on various phases of Tippecanoe County history; Weatenotes, 11 times a year; Books on various historical topics, every 2 yrs
Activities: Classes for adults and children; docent training; lect open to the public; tours; individual paintings and original objects of art lent to other museums; sales shop selling books, reproductions, original crafts on consignment

L **Alameda McCollough Library,** 909 South St, 47901. Tel 317-742-8411. *Librn* Nancy Weirich; *Archivist* Sarah Cooke
Open to serious researchers for reference only
Library Holdings: Vols 6000; Per subs 21; maps; Micro — Reels 575; AV — A-tapes; Other — Clipping files, manuscripts, pamphlets, photographs

MADISON

M **JEFFERSON COUNTY HISTORICAL SOCIETY MUSEUM,** 615 W First St, 47250. Tel 812-265-2335. *Pres* John Wurtz
Open Fri, Sat & Sun 1 - 4 PM. Estab 1900 to preserve and display art and artifacts worthy of note and pertinent to local area history and culture. Museum is on the grounds of the Madison Jefferson County Public Library and was the carriage house for the owners of the original mansion which later became the library. Average Annual Attendance: 1500. Mem: 45, dues $2 single, $5 family, $10 patron, monthly meetings on the fourth Thurs 8 PM
Collections: William McKendree Snyder Collection, paintings, portraits
Activities: Lectures open to public, 6 vis lectr per yr; paintings & art objects are lent to organization sponsored events

MUNCIE

BALL STATE UNIVERSITY
M **Museum of Art,** 47306. Tel 317-285-5242; FAX 317-285-3790. *Dir* Alain Joyaux; *Asst to Dir* Lisa Carmichael; *Cur Educ & Asst Dir* Nancy Huth; *Preparator* Terrence McIntee
Open Mon - Fri 9 AM - 4:30 PM, Sat & Sun 1:30 - 4:30 PM, cl legal holidays. Estab 1936 as a university & community art museum. Four galleries, sculpture court & mezzanine. Average Annual Attendance: 27,000
Income: Financed by University, community & fedral govt
Collections: Ball-Kraft Collection of Roman and Syrian glass; Italian Renaissance art and furniture; 18th, 19th & 20th century European & American paintings, prints, and drawings
Exhibitions: (1993) Biennial Art Faculty Exhibit; Annual Art Student Exhibit; Annual Drawing & Small Sculpture Show; Contemporaries Servies; Gods, Saints, Heros & Villians; Art that Works: Decorative Arts of the 80s crafted in America; WPA Exhibition
Publications: Exhibition catalogs; biennial report
Activities: Docent training; Lect open to public, 2 - 5 vis lectr per year; gallery talks; competitions; tours; Scholarships; individual paintings and original objects of art lent to other art galleries and museums; book traveling exhibitions, 6-7 per yr; originate traveling exhibitions

L **Architecture Library,** College of Architecture & Planning, McKinley at Neely, 47306-0160. Tel 317-285-5857, 285-5858. *Librn* Wayne Meyer
Open Mon - Thurs 8 AM - 10 PM, Fri 8 AM - 5 PM, Sat 9 AM - 5 PM, Sun 1 - 10 PM; interims Mon - Fri 8 AM - 5 PM, cl Sat & Sun. Estab 1965 to provide materials necessary to support the academic programs of the College of Architecture & Planning. Average Annual Attendance: 22,000
Income: Financed through University
Library Holdings: Vols 26,000; Per subs 95; Manufacturers' catalogs; architectural drawings; maps and student theses; Micro — Fiche 7050, reels 340; AV — Slides 70,000; Other — Clipping files, exhibition catalogs 600, pamphlets
Special Subjects: Landscape architecture

NASHVILLE

A **BROWN COUNTY ART GALLERY ASSOCIATION INC,** 1 Artist Dr, PO Box 443, 47448. Tel 812-988-4609. *Pres* Carol Bland; *First VPres* Sue McAllister; *Second VPres* Martha Callaway; *Dir* Charles P Keefe
Open year round 10 AM - 5 PM. No admis fee. Estab 1926 to unite artists and laymen in fellowship; to create a greater incentive for development of art and its presentation to the public; to estab an art gallery for exhibition of work of members of the Association. Average Annual Attendance: 35,000. Mem: 53 artists; 400 supporting members; dues life $500, individual $10; annual meeting Oct
Income: Financed by memberships, foundation and trust
Collections: 75 oil paintings & pastels by the late Glen Cooper Henshaw; permanent collection of art by early Indiana artists
Exhibitions: Three exhibits each year by the artist members
Publications: Annual catalog
Activities: Competitions with awards

M **T C STEELE STATE HISTORIC SITE,** RR 1, PO Box 256, 47448. Tel 812-988-2785. *Cur* Andrea Smith
Open Wed - Sat 9 AM - 5 PM, Sun & Tues 1 - 5 PM. No admis fee. Estab 1945 to protect, collect & interpret the art & lifestyle of T C & Selma Steele. 1200 sq ft, with 80 T C Steele paintings on display at any one time. Average Annual Attendance: 16,000-17,000
Income: Financed by state appropriation
Collections: 347 paintings, historic furnishing, decorative arts photos, books. No purchases, all part of willed estate
Activities: Lect open to public; concerts; gallery talks; tours; four annual special events; individual paintings & original objects of art lent to other museums & universities; lending collection contains original art works & paintings; framed reproductions; originate traveling exhibitions to other museums & historic sites; museum shop sells books & prints

NEW ALBANY

M **FLOYD COUNTY MUSEUM,** 201 E Spring St, 47150. Tel 812-944-7336. *Pres* John Geltmaker; *Art Dir* Jonas Howard; *Coordr* Sally Newkirk
Open Tues - Sat 10 AM - 4 PM. No admis fee. Estab 1971, to exhibit professional artists work on a monthly basis & to promote the arts & history of our community. Two galleries are maintained, approx dimensions: 18 x 25 ft and

15 x 25 ft. Average Annual Attendance: 7000. Mem: 300; dues $10-$500, annual meeting Dec
Income: Financed by county appropriation, memberships & fund raising
Collections: Permanent collection of †historical items
Exhibitions: Floyd County in World War I; 1920s to Depression Years; A History Sampler; Annual July Juried Art Exhibit; Hand Carved, Animated Folk Art Diorama on permanent display
Publications: Bulletins
Activities: Classes for adults and children; lect open to the public; concerts; tours; competitions; awards; book traveling exhibitions annually

NEW HARMONY

M **THE NEW HARMONY GALLERY OF CONTEMPORARY ART,** 506 Main St, 47631. Tel 812-682-3156. *Dir* Connie Weinzapfel; *Asst Dir* Curtis R Uebelhor
Open Tues - Sat 9 AM - 5 PM, Sun 1 - 5 PM, cl Mon. No admis fee. Estab 1975 for exhibition of contemporary midwest art and artists. Average Annual Attendance: 25,000
Income: Financed by contributions and grants
Exhibitions: Monthly changing exhibitions
Activities: Lect open to the public, 4 vis lectr per yr; gallery talks; tours; awards; book traveling exhibitions; originate traveling exhibitions; sales shop sells magazines & original art

NOTRE DAME

M **SAINT MARY'S COLLEGE,** Moreau Gallery, 46556. Tel 219-284-4655; FAX 219-284-4716. *Gallery Dir* Bill Tourtillotte
Open Tues - Fri 10 AM - noon & 1 - 4 PM, Sun 1 - 3 PM, Sat 10 AM - noon. Estab 1956 for education and community-related exhibits. Gallery presently occupies two spaces; all exhibits rotate. Average Annual Attendance: 6000
Collections: Cotter Collection; Dunbarton Collection of prints; Norman LaLiberte; various media
Publications: Catalogs, occasionally
Activities: Classes for adults; dramatic programs; lect open to public; tours; concerts; gallery talks; competitions with awards; scholarships offered; individual paintings and original objects of art lent; originate traveling exhibitions

UNIVERSITY OF NOTRE DAME
M **Snite Museum of Art,** 46556. Tel 219-239-5466; FAX 219-239-8501. *Dir* Dean A Porter; *Cur* Stephen B Spiro; *Cur* Douglas Bradley; *Educ Coordr* Gina Zachman; *Coordr Community Prog* Diana Matthias; *Registrar* Robert Smogor; *Head Preparator* Greg Denby; *Executive Secy* Anne Mills; *Auditorium Mgr & Book Store Mgr* Iris Mensing; *Exhibition Designer* John Phegley; *Secy* Sue Fitzpatrick
Open Tues - Sat 10 AM - 4 PM, Thurs 4 - 8 PM, Sun 1 - 4 PM (when classes are in session). No admis fee. Estab 1842; Wightman Memorial Art Gallery estab 1917; O'Shaughnessy Art Gallery estab 1952; Snite Museum estab 1980 to educate through the visual arts; during a four year period it is the objective to expose students to all areas of art including geographic, period & media, open 1980. Galleries consist of 35,000 sq ft. Average Annual Attendance: 95,000. Mem: 650; dues from $15 - $5000; annual meeting in May
Income: $600,000 (financed by endowment, university appropriation & gifts)
Purchases: $600,000
Collections: †African art; American Indian & pre-Columbian art; Baroque paintings, northern and Italian; 18th and 19th century American, English, 17th, 18th & 19th Century French paintings & Master drawings; Kress Study Collection; 19th century French oils; Reilly Collection of Old Master Drawings through 19th century; Sanderson Collection of Rembrandt Collections
Exhibitions: Renaissance Drawings from the Ambrosiana; Rembrandt Etchings; George Rickey in South Bend; A Curator's Choice: Art of Africa & the Americas; Selected Works from the Snite Museum of Art; Victor Higgins, Realism to Impressionism to Modernism
Publications: Exhibition catalogs, 3-5 times per yr; Calendar of Events, semi-annually
Activities: Docent training; lectures open to public, 4-6 vis lectr per year; concerts; gallery talks; tours; individual paintings and original objects of art lent to qualified institutions; book traveling exhibitions, 2-3 per year; originate traveling exhibitions; museum shop sells books, posters, post cards, sweat shirts, tote bags & T-shirts

L **Snite Museum Library,** 46556. Tel 219-239-5466; FAX 219-239-8501.
Open Tues - Sat 10 AM - 4 PM, Sun 1 - 4 PM. No admis fee. Estab 1980. Open to students and faculty for reference only
Library Holdings: Other — Exhibition catalogs

L **Architecture Library,** 46556. Tel 219-631-6654. *Librn* Sheila Curl; *Library Assoc* Linda Messersmith
Open Mon - Thurs 8 AM - 10 PM, Fri 8 AM - 5 PM, Sat 9 AM - 5 PM, Sun 1 - 10 PM, vacations Mon - Fri 8 AM - 5 PM. Estab 1890 as a branch of the university library. Circ 10,000
Income: $70,000 (financed by university)
Purchases: 25,000
Library Holdings: Vols 15,000; Per subs 100; Micro — Fiche, reels; AV — Fs; Other — Clipping files, pamphlets, reproductions
Special Subjects: Architecture, History of Art & Archaeology, Landscape Architecture, Restoration & Conservation, art, engineering, planning environment
Collections: Rare folio books on architecture
Exhibitions: Models of Student Work; Student Thesis Projects; visiting exhibits
Publications: Architecture Library New Books List, monthly
Activities: Lectures open to public, 8 vis lectr per year; tours; awards; scholarships; exten dept serves Rome

RICHMOND

A ART ASSOCIATION OF RICHMOND, Richmond Art Museum, 350 Whitewater Blvd, 47374. Tel 317-966-0256. *Dir* Ruth B Mills-Varnell
Open Sept - Dec & Feb - July, Mon - Fri 9 AM - 4 PM, Sun 1 - 4 PM, cl Sat and school holidays. No admis fee. Estab 1898 to promote creative ability, art appreciation and art in public schools. Maintains an art gallery with four exhibit rooms: 2 rooms for permanent collection and 2 rooms for current exhibits. Average Annual Attendance: 10,000. Mem: 600; dues from students $2 - $1000
Income: Financed by membership
Collections: Regional and state art; American, European, Oriental art
Exhibitions: Annual Area Professional Artists Exhibition; Crafts Exhibition; Amateur Area Artists Exhibition; Annual Photographic Exhibition; High School Art Exhibition; Hands-On Exhibition for grade school children
Publications: Art in Richmond - 1898 - 1978; newsletter, quarterly
Activities: Docent training; lect open to public, 6 vis lectr per year; gallery talks; tours; competitions with merit and purchase awards; scholarships; individual paintings and original objects of art lent to businesses and schools; lending collection contains books, original art works, original prints and photographs; originate traveling exhib
L Library, 350 Whitewater Blvd, 47374. Tel 317-966-0256. *Dir* Ruth B Mills-Varnell
Open to members
Library Holdings: Vols 200; Per subs 3
Special Subjects: Art museums, art techniques

M EARLHAM COLLEGE, Leeds Gallery, National Rd W, 47374-4095. Tel 317-983-1200; FAX 317-983-1304. *Pres College* Richard Woods; *Art Dept* Richard Rodgers; *Dir Permanent Coll* Laura Nies
Open daily 8 AM - noon. No admis fee. Estab 1847 as a liberal arts college; Leeds Gallery estab 1970
Collections: Regional artist: George Baker, Bundy (John Ellwood), Marcus Mote; prints by internationally known artists of 19th & 20th centuries; regional artists; rotating collections from all areas
Activities: Dramatic programs; lect open to public, 5-6 vis lectr per yr; concerts; individual paintings and original objects of art lent; traveling exhibitions organized and circulated; sales shop selling books

ROCHESTER

M FULTON COUNTY HISTORICAL SOCIETY INC, Fulton County Museum & Round Barn Museum, 37 E 375 N, 46975-9412. Tel 219-223-4436. *Pres* Shirley Willard; *Treas* Wilma Thomas; *Admin Asst* Melinda Clinger
Open 9 AM - 5 PM. No admis fee. Estab 1988 to preserve Fulton County & Northern Indiana history. 20 x 24 ft; new exhibit quarterly. Average Annual Attendance: 20,000. Mem: 700; dues $15; annual meeting 3rd Mon in Nov
Income: $72,000 (financed by mem, sales & festivals, grants & donations)
Collections: Antiques; Elmo Lincoln, first Tarzan; old farm equipment; old household furniture; Woodland Indians
Exhibitions: Boy's toys & banks; Round Barn Festival; Trail of Courage; Redbud Trail Rendezvous
Publications: Fulton County Images, annual
Activities: Classes for adults & children; dramatic programs; docent programs; Indian dances; living history festivals, 10,000 vis lectr per year; lect open to public; competitions with prizes; retail store sells books, prints, magazines, original art & reproductions
L Fulton County Museum Reference Room, 37 E 375 N, 46975-9412
For reference
Income: $72,000
Purchases: $1000
Library Holdings: Vols 7500; Per subs 80; Wood Carvings; AV — Cassettes, Kodachromes, motion pictures, slides, v-tapes; Other — Clipping files, manuscripts, memorabilia, original art works, pamphlets, photographs, prints

SOUTH BEND

A SOUTH BEND REGIONAL MUSEUM OF ART, 120 S Saint Joseph St, 46601. Tel 219-284-9102. *Exec Dir* Susan R Visser; *Cur* Leisa Rundquist
Warner Gallery open Tues - Sun noon - 5 PM; WAL Gallery open Tues - Fri 12:30 - 4 PM, Sat & Sun noon - 5 PM. No admis fee. Estab in 1947 for museum exhibitions, lectures, film series, workshops, and studio classes. The Art Center is located in a three-story building designed by Philip Johnson. There are two galleries: the Warner Gallery features travelling shows or larger exhibits organized by the Art Center, and The WAL Upper Level Gallery features one or two-person shows by local or regional artists. Average Annual Attendance: 40,000. Mem: 1,000; dues sustaining $100, family $35, active $20, student & senior citizens $10
Income: Financed by membership, corporate support, city and state appropriations
Collections: European and American paintings, drawings, prints and objects; †20th century American art with emphasis on regional and local works
Publications: Bi-monthly newsletter, exhibition catalogues, and checklists
Activities: Studio classes for adults and children; docent training and tours; outreach educational program conducted by Women's Art League; workshops; lectures open to public, 3 lectr per yr; gallery talks; artist studio tours; competitions with prizes; film series; scholarships; paintings and original works of art lent to accredited museums; lending collection contains prints, paintings, phono records and sculpture; museum shop sells gift items and original works of art
L Library, 120 S Saint Joseph St, 46601. Tel 219-284-9102.
Estab 1947 to provide art resource material to members of the Art Center
Library Holdings: Vols 963; Per subs 49; AV — Motion pictures, rec; Other — Exhibition catalogs

TERRE HAUTE

M INDIANA STATE UNIVERSITY, Turman Art Gallery, Fine Arts Bldg, 47809. Tel 812-237-3697. *Chmn Art Dept* Wayne Enstice; *Dir* Craig McDaniel
Open Tues - Fri noon - 4:30 PM, Sun 1 - 5 PM, cl last two weeks in Aug. No admis fee
Collections: Paintings & sculpture
Exhibitions: Changing exhibitions of national & regional contemporary art during school terms; periodic student & faculty exhibitions
Activities: Lect

M SHELDON SWOPE ART MUSEUM, 25 S Seventh St, 47807-3692. Tel 812-238-1676; FAX 812-232-6115. *Dir* Edward R Quick; *Registrar* Carolyn Anderson; *Cur* Thomas Delaney; *Office Mgr* Paul Arroyo; *Preparator* Elizabeth Petrulis
Open year round Tues - Fri 10 AM - 5 PM, Sat - Sun noon - 5 PM. No admis fee. Estab 1942 to present free of charge works of fine art for the education and enjoyment of the public. Average Annual Attendance: 15,000. Mem: 750; dues individual $20; annual meeting third Wed in Sept
Income: $130,000 (financed by membership, city appropriation and trust fund)
Collections: American art of 19th and 20th centuries; European art from 14th century to present; ancient, Far Eastern and ethnographic art; decorative arts; glass
Publications: Membership newsletter, bimonthly; catalogs to special exhibitions
Activities: Docent training; lectures open to the public, 10 vis lectr per yr; concerts; gallery talks; tours; competitions with awards; individual paintings & original objects of art lent to other museums; originate traveling exhibitions; museum shop sells books, original art, reproductions, note cards, gift items & prints
L Research Library, 25 S Seventh St, 47807-3692. Tel 812-238-1676; FAX 812-232-6115. *Dir* Edward Quick
Open Tues - Sun Noon - 4:50 PM. Open to the public
Library Holdings: Vols 3000; Per subs 25; AV — Slides; Other — Clipping files, exhibition catalogs, memorabilia, pamphlets, photographs
Collections: American Modern; American Regionalist; European

UPLAND

M TAYLOR UNIVERSITY, Chronicle-Tribune Art Gallery, Art Dept, 46989. Tel 317-998-2751, Ext 5306; FAX 317-998-4910. *Dir* Craig Moore
Open Mon - Sat 11 AM - 4 PM and Mon, Wed and Fri 7 - 9 PM, cl Sun. No admis fee. Estab 1972 as an educational gallery
Activities: Classes for children; competitions

VALPARAISO

M VALPARAISO UNIVERSITY, Museum of Art, 46383. Tel 219-464-5365; FAX 219-464-5381. *Dir & Cur* Richard H W Brauer
Open Mon - Fri 8 AM - 10 PM, Sat 9 AM - 5 PM, Sun 1 - 10 PM. No admis fee. Estab 1953 to present significant art to the student and citizen community for their education in the values of art. Gallery areas located in Moellering Library, Christ College Building and the Union
Income: $14,000 (financed by endowment)
Purchases: $10,000
Collections: †Sloan Collection: 19th and 20th Century American Landscape Paintings, Prints, and Drawings; Valparaiso University Collection: Art on Biblical Themes
Exhibitions: Rotating Exhibits
Activities: Lectures open to the public; gallery talks; individual paintings and original objects of art lent to museums and art centers

WEST LAFAYETTE

M PURDUE UNIVERSITY GALLERIES, Creative Arts Bldg 1, 47907-1352. Tel 317-494-3061; FAX 317-496-1198. *Gallery Dir* Mona Berg; *Asst Dir* Michael Atwell
Open Mon - Fri 10 AM - 5 PM & 7 - 9 PM, Sun 1 - 5 PM. No admis fee. Estab 1972 to provide aesthetic & educational programs for art students, the university & greater Lafayette community. Galleries are located in four different buildings to provide approximately 5000 sq ft of space for temporary exhibitions. Average Annual Attendance: 60,000
Income: Financed through the university
Purchases: $1500
Collections: Contemporary paintings, †prints, sculpture; †ceramics; Pre-Columbian textiles; American Indian baskets
Exhibitions: 40 per yr including work by faculty, students, regionally & nationally prominent artists
Publications: Exhibit catalogs
Activities: Lectures open to public; concerts; gallery talks; competitions with awards; individual paintings & original objects of art lent to university administrative offices; book traveling exhibitions, 1-2 per year; traveling exhib organized and circulated

IOWA

AMES

M IOWA STATE UNIVERSITY, Brunnier Gallery Museum, Scheman Bldg, 50011. Tel 515-294-3342; FAX 515-294-3349. *Dir* Lynette Pohlman; *Registrar & Assoc Cur* Mary Atherly; *Educ Coordr* Deborah Lombard; *Grants Writer* Peggy Fay; *Publicity* Ray Bentor; *Shop Mgr* Jan Rathke
Open Tues, Wed, & Fri 11 AM - 4 PM, Thurs 11 AM - 9 PM, Sat & Sun 1 - 4 PM, cl Mon. No admis fee. Estab 1975, to provide a high level of quality, varied and comprehensive exhibits of national and international scope; and to develop and expand a permanent decorative arts collection of the western world. Gallery is maintained and comprised of 10,000 sq ft of exhibit space, with flexible space arrangement. Average Annual Attendance: Approx 30,000-50,000
Income: $300,000 (financed through state appropriations & grants)
Collections: Permanent collection of ceramics, dolls, furniture, glass, ivory, wood, sculpture, fine arts
Activities: Classes for children; docent training; lect open to public, 10 - 15 vis lectr per year; book traveling exhibitions, 3-4 per year; traveling exhibitions organized and circulated; museum shop sells books, slides, catalogs, jewelry, dolls, glass, original works

A OCTAGON CENTER FOR THE ARTS, 427 Douglas, 50010. Tel 515-232-5331. *Pres* Barbara Atha, *VPres* Warren Sargent, *Treas* Beverly Wandling, *Dir* Helene J Kaplan; *Dir Educ* Suann Rosenberger
Open Mon - Fri 9 AM - 5 PM, Sat 10 - 5 PM, Sun 2 - 5 PM. Admis suggested donation or contribution adults $1, children under 12 $1, family $3. Estab 1966 to provide year-round classes for all ages; exhibitions of the work of outstanding artists from throughout the world and also special programs in the visual and performing arts. Average Annual Attendance: 32,000. Mem: 600, open to anyone who is interested in supporting or participating in the arts; dues $15 - $500, annual meeting in Apr
Income: $300,000 (financed by membership, city and state appropriations, class fees and fund raising)
Exhibitions: (1993) Aspects of the Environment: Recycled Creations; Annual Scholastic Art Awards; 1993 Year of the Craft: Octagon Clay & Fiber Exhibition; Ames High School Seniors Art Show; The Octagon Community of Artists Exhibition; The Shell Game: The Button as Craft. (1994) Annual Scholastic Art Awards; Salute to Seniors: A Exhibition of Artists Over 60; Ames High School Senior Art Show; Rub Brass With the Past: A Hands-on Historical Art Experience; Masks. (1995) Annual Scholatic Art Awards; 1995 Octagon Craft Exhibition: Clay, Paper, Metal, Wood & Glass; Ames High School Seniors Art Show
Publications: Exhibition catalogs; newsletter, b-monthly
Activities: Classes for adults and children; dramatic programs; special classes for elderly & handicapped; lectures open to public, 2-3 lectr per year; gallery talks; tours; competitions with awards; scholarships & fels offered; lending collection of 500 lantern slides; book traveling exhibitions; originate traveling exhibitions; museum shop sells books, original art, prints & original crafts

ANAMOSA

A PAINT 'N PALETTE CLUB, Grant Wood & Memorial Park Gallery, RR 3, 52205. Tel 319-462-2680. *Pres* Mildred Brown; *VPres* Thelma Darrow; *Exec Dir* Dr Gerald F Brown; *Executive Dir* Wilbur Evarts; *Secy* Ann Potter
Open June 1 - Oct 15; Sun 1 - 4 PM; other times by appointment. No admis fee (donations accepted). Estab 1955 to maintain Antioch School, the school attended by Grant Wood, a famous Iowa artist; to provide a studio and gallery for local artists and for public enjoyment. A log cabin art gallery on the grounds of the Grant Wood Memorial Park contains the work of some local and visiting artists. Average Annual Attendance: 2000 - 3000. Mem: 37, members must have art experience; dues $15
Income: $700 - $800 (financed by endowment and donations)
Collections: Prints of Grant Wood, Iowa's most famous artist; original amateur art
Exhibitions: Special exhibits throughout the season
Activities: Occasional classes for adults and children; films; lect open to public, 6-7 vis lectr per yr; tours; competitions; sales shop selling magazines, original art, prints, reproductions, memorial plates and coins, postcards

BURLINGTON

A ART GUILD OF BURLINGTON, Arts for Living Center, Seventh & Washington St, PO Box 5, 52601. Tel 319-754-8069. *Dir* Lois Rigdon; *Pres* Tim Gerard; *Pres Elect* Renee Faud; *VPres* John Siekert; *Treas* Julie Taylor; *Secy* Geri Lloyd
Open Tues - Fri noon - 5 PM, weekends 2 - 5 PM, cl Mon & all major holidays, with the exception of Thanksgiving. No admis fee. Estab 1966, the Art Guild purchased the Center (a church building built 1868) in 1974, which has now been placed on the National Register of Historic Places. Average Annual Attendance: 8000. Mem: 425; dues benefactor $1000, down to student $5, meeting first Thurs of the month
Income: Financed by membership and donations
Exhibitions: Exhibitions of regional professional artists
Publications: Newsletter, monthly
Activities: Classes for adults and children; films; special workshops; lectures open to the public, 6 vis lectr per yr; concerts; gallery talks; tours; book traveling exhibitions, 2 - 3 per yr; traveling exhibitions organized and circulated; sales shop sells books, original art, reproductions, prints

CEDAR FALLS

M CITY OF CEDAR FALLS, IOWA, James & Meryl Hearst Center for the Arts, 304 W Seerley Blvd, 50613. Tel 319-273-8641; FAX 319-273-8641. *Dir* Mary Huber
Open Tues - Fri 11 AM - 4 PM, Tues & Thurs evening 6 - 9 PM, Sat & Sun 1 - 4PM. No admis fee. Estab 1988

Income: $140,000 (financed by city appropriation, individual contributions, program fees & grants)
Exhibitions: Annual competition exhibition; 28 exhibitions per year
Activities: Classes for adults & children; dramatic programs; docent training; lect open to public, 3 - 5 vis lectr per year

M UNIVERSITY OF NORTHERN IOWA, Gallery of Art, 27th St at Hudson Rd, 50614. Tel 319-273-2077; FAX 319-273-2731. *Dir* Julie D Nelson
Open Mon - Thurs 9 AM - 4:30 PM, Sat & Sun 1 - 4 PM, Mon evenings 7 - 9 PM. No admis fee. Estab 1978 to bring to the University and the community at large the finest quality of art from all over the world. The 4700 sq ft gallery is divided into 5 separate exhibition rooms; high security museum space with climate control and a highly flexible light system; the Gallery adjoins a public reception space and a new 144 seat auditorium; the facility also has two permanent collections' storage areas, a work shop, a general storage room and a fully accessible loading dock. Average Annual Attendance: 11,000
Income: Financed by state appropriation
Purchases: 20th century art work
Collections: †20th century American & European Art
Exhibitions: (1991) Magic Silver Show; Odessyeus Suite by Romare Beardon; Yoshishige Furukawa: New Paintings & Drawings; Drawing Beyond Nature: Recent Abstract Drawings by Michelle Amato, Fontaine Dunn, Clarence Morgan & James Perry; Sally Hutchison: Small Paintings; North American Tattoos & Tattoo Artists (photographs); Annual Juried Student Exhibition; Summer Solos: Byrd, Stancliffe, Zlotsky, Yuen; MA Thesis Exhibition; UNI Art Faculty Exhibition; Portraits; Bird Kingdom (prints & drawings); Dream Pictures; Woodcuts; The Excavation of the Apashi; Recent Sculptures. (1992) Uncle Charlie & His Family; Up to Now: Paintings by Steve Sornman 1974-1991; Linda Slobodin, Aftermath (photography, video & audio materials); Field Effects: Recent Work by Eleven Fairfield Artists; Sandy Hale, Child Mothers (photograph); Etching & Handmade Paper Exhibition; JoAnne Walters (photography); John Page Exhibition; Diana Horowitz, April Funke, Langden Quinn, Amy Weiskopf Exhibition; Karl Baden (photography). (1993) Diane Neumaier (photography); Selections from the UNI Permanent Collection; Catherine Angel (photography); Annual High School Art Scholarship Competition Day; In-House Art Scholarship Reviews
Publications: Exhibition catalogs
Activities: Docent training; lect open to public, 20 vis lectr per year; concerts; gallery talks; tours; competition; individual paintings & original objects of art lent; book traveling exhibitions 2 - 8 per yr; originate traveling exhibitions; sales shop sells catalogs, postcards, posters

L Art & Music Section Rod Library, 50614. Tel 319-273-6252; FAX 319-273-2913. *Dir* Herbert D Safford; *Asst Dir* Robert Rose; *Librn* Dr Alberto H Hernandez
Open Mon - Thurs 7:30 AM - midnight, Fri 7:30 AM - 6 PM, Sat 10 AM - 6 PM, Sun 1:30 PM - midnight. Main Library estab 1964, addition 1975, to serve art and music patrons. For lending and reference. Circ 18,872
Income: Financed by state
Purchases: $35,266
Library Holdings: Vols 46,089; Per subs 169; Micro — Fiche, prints; AV — A-tapes, cassettes 600, rec, slides 7000; Other — Clipping files, exhibition catalogs, original art works, pamphlets, prints, reproductions 200

CEDAR RAPIDS

M CEDAR RAPIDS MUSEUM OF ART, 410 Third St SE, 52401. Tel 319-366-7503; FAX 319-366-4111. *Dir* Joseph S Czestochowski
Open Tues - Sat 10 AM - 4 PM, Thurs 10 AM - 7 PM, Sun noon - 3 PM. Estab art association 1905, art center 1966. First and second floors maintain changing exhibits and the third floor maintains the Permanent Collection. Mem: 1000; dues family $35, individual $25, students and sr citizens $15
Income: Financed by endowment, membership, city and state appropriations
Collections: Largest concentrated collection of Grant Wood, Marvin Cone and Mauricio Lasansky art in existencne; print collection
Exhibitions: Rotating exhibitions
Publications: Newsletter, bi-monthly
Activities: Classes for adults and children; docent training; lectures open to public, 2 - 3 vis lectr per yr; gallery talks; tours; individual paintings and original objects of art lent on request; book traveling exhibitions, 5 - 6 per yr; originate traveling exhibitions; museum shop sells books, original art, reproductions, prints & craft items including pottery, weaving, jewelry

L Herbert S Stamats Library, 410 Third Ave SE, 52401. Tel 319-366-7503; FAX 319-366-4111.
Open Tues - Sat 10 AM - 4 PM, Thurs 10 AM - 7 PM, Sun noon - 3 PM. For reference
Library Holdings: Vols 1200; Per subs 5; AV — Cassettes, fs
Special Subjects: Archival materials on American Regionalism, Grant Wood, James Swann, Chicago Society of Etchers, Prairie Printmakers, Mauricio Lasansky, Bertha Jaques, Malvina Hoffman, Marvin Cone

M COE COLLEGE, Gordon Fennell Gallery & Marvin Cone Gallery, 1221 First Ave NE, 52402. Tel 319-399-8559. *Chmn Art Dept* John Beckelman; *Gallery Dir* Shirley Donaldson
Open daily 3 - 5 PM. No admis fee. Estab 1942 to exhibit traveling exhibitions and local exhibits. Two galleries, both 60 x 18 ft with 125 running ft of exhibit space & 200 works on permanent exhibition. Average Annual Attendance: 5000
Income: $6120 (financed through college)
Collections: Coe Collection of art works; Marvin Cone Alumni Collection; Marvin Cone Collection; Conger Metcalf Collection of paintings; Hinkhouse Collection of contemporary art
Exhibitions: Circulating exhibits; one-person & group shows of regional nature
Publications: Exhibition brochures, 8 - 10 per year
Activities: Lectures open to public, 5 - 6 vis lectr per year; gallery talks; tours; competitions; individual paintings & original objects of art lent to colleges & local galleries; lending collection contains original art work, original prints, paintings, sculpture & slides; traveling exhib organized and circulated

M Stewart Memorial Library & Gallery, 1220 First Ave NE, 52402-5092. Tel 319-399-8559.
Collections: 200 permanent collection works

M MOUNT MERCY COLLEGE, McAuley Gallery, 1330 Elmhurst Dr NE, 52402. Tel 319-363-8213; FAX 319-363-5270. *Dir* David Van Allen
Open Mon - Thurs 7 AM - 9 PM. No admis fee. Estab 1970 to show work by a variety of fine artists. The shows are used by the art department as teaching aids. They provide cultural exposure to the entire community. One room 22 x 30 ft; 2 wall are glass overlooking a small courtyard. Average Annual Attendance: 1000
Income: Financed through the college
Purchases: $300
Collections: †Small collection of prints & paintings
Exhibitions: Annual High School Art Exhibit; Senior Thesis Exhibit
Publications: Reviews in Fiber Arts; American Craft & Ceramics Monthly
Activities: Classes for adults; dramatic programs; lectures open to the public; gallery talks; competitions with awards; scholarships
L **Library,** Art Dept, 1330 Elmhurst Dr NE, 52402-4797. Tel 319-363-8213, Ext 244; FAX 319-363-5270. *Librn* Marilyn Murphy
Library Holdings: Vols 1000; Per subs 30; Micro — Cards, fiche, prints, reels; AV — A-tapes, cassettes, fs, Kodachromes, lantern slides, motion pictures, rec, slides, v-tapes; Other — Exhibition catalogs, framed reproductions, original art works, pamphlets, photographs, prints, reproductions, sculpture

CLINTON

A CLINTON ART ASSOCIATION GALLERY, 708 25th Ave N, PO Box 132, 52733. Tel 319-243-3300, 242-8055. *Dir* Hortense Blake
Open Sat & Sun 1 - 5 PM, cl Christmas and New Years. No admis fee. Estab 1968 to bring visual art to the community. Small gallery is housed in an abandoned building of an army hospital complex and is loaned to the association by the Clinton Park and Recreation Board. A separate Pottery School has been maintained since 1975. Average Annual Attendance: 15,000. Mem: 400; dues single membership $10; annual meeting first Tues in May
Income: Financed by membership and through grants from the Iowa Arts Council
Collections: Painting (watercolor, oil, acrylic, pastel); beaded loin cloth; photographs; lithograph; engraving; sculptures; etching; prints; pottery; fabric; pencil; wood; slate; Ektaflex Color Printmaking System; glass; ink; lucite; rugs; woodcarving
Publications: Newsletter every two months
Activities: Classes for adults and children in watercolor, oil, rosemaling, macrame, photography and pottery making; docent training; lectures open to public; gallery talks; tours; individual paintings lent by members to businesses; lending collection contains books, lantern slides and slides; sales shop selling original art and prints; sales shop

DAVENPORT

M DAVENPORT MUSEUM OF ART, 1737 W 12th St, 52804. Tel 319-326-7804; FAX 319-326-7876. *Dir* Wm Steven Bradley; *Asst Dir* Mark Towner; *Admin Secy* Rebecca Hipple; *Cur of Coll* Brady Roberts; *Museum Educator* Ann Marie Hayes; *Research Librn* Sheryl Haut; *Supt* Robert Rose; *Curatorial Registrar* Patrick Sweeney
Open Tues - Sat 10:30 AM - 4:30 PM, Sun 1 - 4:30 PM, cl Mon & holidays. No admis fee. Estab 1925 as a museum of art and custodian of public collection and an education center for the visual arts. Consists of three levels including a spacious main gallery, exhibition area and two additional floors with galleries; six multipurpose art studios, printmaking & ceramic gallery, studio workshop; and an outdoor studio-plaza on the lower level. Average Annual Attendance: 100,000. Mem: 1009; dues family $40, individual $25, sr citizens $20, student $15; annual meeting June
Income: $900,000 (financed by private & city appropriation)
Collections: 19th & 20th Century American; Regionalism including Grant Wood, Thomas Hart Benton, John Steuart Curry; European; Mexican- Colonial; Haitian; Oriental
Exhibitions: Beverly Pepper: The Moline Makers; Byron Burford; Mississippi Corridor; Grandma Moses; Selections: The Union League of Chicago Collection; Thomas Eakins (photographs); Joseph Sheppard; Mauricio Lasansky; Sol LeWitt; Stephen Antonakos - Neons; Frederic Carder: Portrait of a Glassmaker; Paul Brach Retrospective; David Hockney (photographs); Rudie (holograms); McMichael Canadian Collection; Kassebaum Medieval and Renaissance Ceramics Collected Masterworks: The International Collections of the Davenport Museum of Art; Mexico Nueve; A Differnt War: Vietnam In Art; Judaica: Paintings by Nathan Hilu & Ceramics by Robert Lipnick; Faith Ringgold: 25 Year Survey
Publications: Bi-monthly newsletter; biennial report; Focus 1: Michael Boyd - Paintings from the 1980's; Focus 2: Photo Image League - Individual Vision/ Collective Support; Focus 3: A Sense of Wonder - The Art of Haiti; Focus 4: Artists Who Teach: Building our Future; Haitian Art: The Legend & Legacy of the Naive Tradition; Three Decades of Midwestern Photography, 1960 - 1990
Activities: Educ Dept; classes for adults and children; docent training; lect open to the public; concerts; gallery talks; tours; competitions with prizes; scholarships and fels offered; traveling exhibitions organized and circulated; originate traveling exhibitions; Museum shop selling books, original art; Arterarium environmental installation
L **Art Reference Library,** 1737 W 12th St, 52804. Tel 319-326-7804; FAX 319-326-7876. *Librn* Sheryl Haut
Open for reference
Library Holdings: Vols 6000; Per subs 20; AV — V-tapes
Special Subjects: General visual arts

M PUTNAM MUSEUM OF HISTORY & NATURAL SCIENCE, 1717 W 12th St, 52804. Tel 319-324-1933. *Dir* Michael J Smith; *Asst Dir Curatorial Servs* Janice Hall; *Asst Dir Educ* Karen Larson; *Cur of Historical Coll* Scott Roller
Open Tues - Fri 9 AM - 5 PM, Sat 10 AM - 5 PM, Sun noon - 5 PM, cl Mon & national holidays. Admis adults $3, senior citizens $2, ages 7-17 $1, Putnam members & children 6 & under free. Estab 1867 as Academy of Science. Average Annual Attendance: 60,000. Mem: 4360; dues contributing $75, family $35, individual $25, sr citizen $22

Income: $300,000 (financed by endowments & earned income)
Collections: Natural history; American Indian, pre-Columbian; anthropology; arts of Asia, Near & Middle East, Africa, Oceanic; botany; ethnology; paleontology; decorative arts; local history
Exhibitions: Permanent and changing exhibition programs
Activities: Formally organized education programs for children and adults; films; lect; gallery talks; guided tours
L **Library,** 1717 W 12th St, 52804. Tel 319-324-1933; FAX 319-324-6638.
Available for use by special request
Library Holdings: Vols 50,000

DECORAH

M VESTERHEIM NORWEGIAN-AMERICAN MUSEUM, 502 W Water St, 52101. Tel 319-382-9682. *Dir* Darrell D Henning; *Cur & Conservator Objects* Dana Jackson; *Textiles Cur & Conservator* Laurann Figg; *Asst Cur & Site Mgr* Steve Johnson
Open May - Oct 9 AM - 5 PM daily, Nov - Apr 10 AM - 4 PM, cl Thanksgiving, Christmas, Easter & New Years. Admis adults $4, children (7 - 18) $2, (summer), adults $3, children $1.50 (winter). Estab 1877 for the collection, preservation and exhibition of all artifacts on the life of the people in the United States of Norwegian birth and descent, in their home environment in Norway and in their settlements in America. Numerous historic buildings, including two from Norway, make up the complex of Vesterheim. Average Annual Attendance: 30,000. Mem: 7000; dues $10; annual meeting Oct
Income: $400,000 (financed by endowment, mem, donations, admissions, sales)
Collections: Extensive collections combine those of Luther College and the Museum Corporation through house furnishings, costumes, tools and implements, church furniture, toys and the like, the Museum tells the story of the Norwegian immigrant
Exhibitions: Annual competitive exhibitions in Norwegian rosemaling, weaving & woodcarving; American rug hooking
Publications: Newsletter, quarterly; Norrona Sketchbook; Norwegian Tracks, quarterly; Time Honored Norwegian Recipes; Rosemaling Letter, quarterly; Vesterheim: Samplings from the Collection; Rosemaler's Recipes Cookbook; Woodworker's Newsletter, quarterly
Activities: Classes for adults; genealogy center; workshops in & tours to Norway; competitions; museum shop books, original art, prints, and slides, related gift items, woodenware, artist supplies for rosemaling
L **Reference Library,** 502 W Water St, 52101. Tel 319-382-9681. *Librn* Carol Hasrold
Reference library open to the public
Library Holdings: Vols 10,000
Special Subjects: Norwegian history, culture, crafts, genealogy

DES MOINES

M EDMUNDSON ART FOUNDATION, INC, Des Moines Art Center, 4700 Grand Ave, 50312-2099. Tel 515-277-4405; FAX 515-279-3834. *Dir* I Michael Danoff; *Pres Board Trustees* Jane A Gordon
Open Tues - Sat 11 AM - 5 PM, Sun noon - 5 PM, cl Mon. Admis $2, student & sr citizen $1, Thurs free; members, children 12 & under & scheduled docent tours free. Estab 1948 for the purpose of displaying, conserving and interpreting art. Large sculpture galleries in I M Pei-designed addition; the main gallery covers 36 x 117 ft area. New Meier wing, opened 1985, increased space for exhibitions 50 percent. Average Annual Attendance: 140,000. Mem: 3000, dues $25 and up
Income: $935,000 (financed by endowment, membership, state appropriation)
Collections: African art; graphics; American & European sculpture & painting of the past 200 years
Exhibitions: (1993) Anish Kapoor (sculptures); Rescuers of the Holocaust: Portraits by Gay Block; Jean-Michel Basqulat (drawings & paintings); Iowa Artists; American Indian Parfleche: A Tradition of Abstract Painting
Publications: Bulletin, bimonthly; annual report; catalogs of exhibitions
Activities: Classes for adults and children; docent training; lectures open to members only, 6 visiting lectr per year; concerts; gallery talks; tours; competitions; traveling exhibitions organized and circulated; museum shop sells books, original art, prints, and postcards
L **Library,** 4700 Grand Ave, 50312-2099. Tel 515-277-4405; FAX 515-279-3834. *Librn* Margaret Buckley
Open Tues - Fri 11 AM - 5 PM. Estab 1948 for research for permanent collection, staff for acquisitions, exhibition preparation, class preparation & lectures. Open to the public for reference only by appointment
Income: $28,000
Purchases: $2000
Library Holdings: Vols 11,657; Per subs 31; Other — Exhibition catalogs
Special Subjects: 20th Century Art

M IOWA STATE EDUCATION ASSOCIATION, Salisbury House, 4025 Tonawanda Dr, 50312. Tel 515-279-9711; FAX 515-279-2659. *Exec Dir* Fred Comer; *Assoc Exec Dir* C William Pritchard
Open daily 8 AM - 4:30 PM. Admis adults $2, 12 years & under $1. Estab 1954 as a cultural center. Gallery is maintained as a replica of King's House in Salisbury, England and contains Tudor age furniture, classic paintings, and sculpture from East and West, tapestries, Oriental rugs. Average Annual Attendance: 17,000
Income: Financed through membership and endowment
Collections: Collection of paintings by Raeburn, Romney, Sir T Lawrence, Van Dyck; permanent collection of tapestries by Brussels Brabant, Flemish, French Verdure; permanent collection of sculpture by Archapinko, Bordelle, Martini; permanent collection of Chinese, India & Oriental (Persian) rugs
Exhibitions: Permanent collection
Activities: Lect; tours; individual paintings and original objects of art lent; lending collection contains motion pictures, original art works, paintings; museum shop sells reproductions, brochures, postcards, stationery

L   PUBLIC LIBRARY OF DES MOINES, Fine Arts Dept, 100 Locust St, 50308. Tel 515-283-4267; FAX 515-283-4503. *Head Librn* Pam Deitrick; *Art Librn* Carla Tibboel
Open Mon - Thur 9 AM - 9 PM, Fri 9 AM - 6 PM, Sat 9 AM -5 PM, cl Sun. Estab 1866, dept estab 1970 to serve art & music patrons. Circ 10,000
Income: $3000 (financed by membership)
Library Holdings: Vols 6000; Per subs 9; AV — V-tapes

DUBUQUE

M   DUBUQUE ART ASSOCIATION, Dubuque Museum of Art, 36 E Eighth St, 52001. Tel 319-557-1851. *Pres* Wayne Norman Jr; *Dir* Martha L Lovejoy
Open Tues - Fri 10 AM - 5 PM, Sat & Sun 1 - 5 PM, cl Mon. No admis fee. Estab 1911, inc 1956 to preserve, collect, exhibit, interpret & teach the fine arts to those in the Dubuque area & surrounding communities. Occupies Old County Jail (now National Historic Landmark), built in 1857, converted in 1976. Average Annual Attendance: 20,000. Mem: 500; dues $15 - $1000; annual meeting in May
Income: Financed by dues and donations
Collections: †Permanent collection consists of regional & historic art, drawings, paintings, prints, sculptures & watercolor
Exhibitions: Crafts show; ceramics, drawing, paintings, sculptures
Activities: Classes for adults & children; lect open to public, 12-14 vis lectr per yr; concerts; gallery talks; tours; competitions with awards; book traveling exhibitions; museum shop sells original art, prints

FAIRFIELD

L   FAIRFIELD PUBLIC LIBRARY, Fairfield Art Association, 114 S Court, 52556. Tel 515-472-6551. *Librn* James Rubis; *Chmn Museum Committee* Paul Selz; *Pres Art Assoc* Nancy Horras
Open Mon - Fri 9:30 AM - 8:30 PM, Sat 9:30 - 4:30 PM, Winter Sun 1:30 - 4:30 PM, cl national holidays. No admis fee
Income: Library and museum financed by endowment and city appropriation; Art Association financed by endowment and membership
Library Holdings: Vols 70,000; Per subs 180
Collections: †Graphics; Indian art; †paintings
Activities: Classes for adults and children; lect open to the public; competitions

A   INSTITUTE FOR CREATIVE ARTS, c/o MIU-Faculty Mail, PO Box 1019, 52557. Tel 515-472-6966. *Dir* C Gregory Thatcher; *Cur* Terrence Kennedy
Open daily 10 AM - 4:30 PM. No admis fee. Estab 1985 to foster development of the arts in the region. One gallery 20 ft X 40 ft for exhibition of contemporary & historic art; 20 artist studios; event room for lectures & performances; classrooms for teaching visual arts courses. Average Annual Attendance: 2000
Income: Financed by endowment
Collections: Contemporary art in all media
Exhibitions: Sales and Rental Exhibition; Annual Juried Show; Selected Masterworks; David Hanson: Coal Strip, Montana (photography)
Publications: Exhibit catalogues
Activities: Classes for adults & children; dramatic programs; lectures open to public, 15 vis lectrs per yr; competitions with awards

FORT DODGE

M   BLANDEN MEMORIAL ART MUSEUM, 920 Third Ave S, 50501. Tel 515-573-2316; FAX 515-573-2317. *Dir* Philip A LaDouceur; *Educ* Meg Adams
Open Tues, Wed & Fri 10 AM - 5 PM, Thurs 10 AM - 8:30 PM, Sat & Sun 1 - 5 PM. No admis fee. Estab 1930 as a permanent municipal, non-profit institution, educational & aesthetic in purpose; the museum interprets, exhibits & cares for a permanent collection & traveling exhibitions. Houses works of art in permanent collection. Average Annual Attendance: 14,000. Mem: 325; dues $10 - $500
Income: $250,000 (financed by city & state appropriation, membership, Blanden Art Gallery Charitable Foundation & private support)
Collections: †Arts of China & Japan; †Decorative Arts; †15th - 20th Century Works on Paper; Pre-Columbian & African Art; †Regional Art; †Twentieth century American & European masters, paintings & sculpture
Exhibitions: George Bottini: Painter of Montmartre; Aerial Imagery: Nazca & American Landscapes; Patterns & Sources of Navajo Weaving; Robert McKibbin: The Landscape; Thomas Patrick Gormally: Selection of sculpture, painting & drawing; Jose Luis Cuevas: Intolerance; The Photography of James Vander Zee; Genre Scenes: Works on paper from the Hirshhorn Museum & Sculpture Garden; War & Children: Lewis Hine's Photography in Europe; Artists & Models: Portraits from the Hirshhorn Museum & Sculpture Garden; Studio C Series Photographs by Dan Powell, Paper Innovations; Edna Hogan: A One Person Show Harold Edgerton (photography) Chen Chi in America; Iowa Collects Asian Art. (1992) Visions of Color; Six Women Artists; Modern Prints from the Permanent Collection
Publications: Quarterly bulletin; Charitable Foundation brochure; exhibition catalogues; annual report; membership information; handbook of the permanent collection
Activities: Classes for adults & children; docent training; art appreciation program in the community schools; lectures open to public, 5-10 vis lectrs per yr; gallery talks; tours; competitions; scholarships offered; exten outreach art appreciation program; loans to art museums meeting necessary professional requirements including climate conditions, security & other physical needs specifications of the art collection; lending collection contains color reproductions & film strips; book traveling exhibitions, 6-10 per yr; originate traveling exhibitions; museum shop sells books, original art by Iowa artists
L   Museum Library, 920 Third Ave S, 50501. Tel 515-573-2316; FAX 515-573-2317. *Dir* Philip A LaDouceur
Open Tues, Wed & Fri 10 AM - 5 PM, Thurs 10 AM - 8:30 PM, Sat & Sun 1 - 5 PM. Estab 1972 as reference library for museum
Income: $90,000 (financed by membership, city appropriation and charitable foundation)
Library Holdings: Vols 4100; Per subs 12; Micro — Cards; AV — Fs, slides, v-tapes; Other — Clipping files, exhibition catalogs, framed reproductions 148, pamphlets, reproductions, sculpture 9

GRINNELL

M   GRINNELL COLLEGE, Print & Drawing Study Room/Gallery, 50112. Tel 515-269-3371. *Dir* Kay Wilson
Open Sun - Fri 1 - 5 PM. No admis fee. Estab 1983. Average Annual Attendance: 4000
Income: $75,000 (financed by endowment)
Purchases: 30,000
Exhibitions: (1991) Keith Jacobshagen: Works on Paper; Paul Cadmus. (1992) Keith Jacobshagen (photographs); Aleksandr Kalugin: New Work
Publications: Exhibition catalogs
Activities: Lectures open to the public, 4 vis lectr per year; book traveling exhibitions 8 times per year; originate traveling exhibitions 4 times per year; museum shop sells original art

INDIANOLA

M   SIMPSON COLLEGE, Farnham Gallery, 701 N C, 50125. Tel 515-961-1561; FAX 515-961-1498. *Head Art Dept* Janet Heinicke
Open Mon - Fri 8 AM - 4:30 PM. No admis fee. Estab 1982 to educate and inform the public. 2 small gallery rooms each 14 ft 4 in x 29 ft. Average Annual Attendance: 1200
Collections: Small permanent collection being started
Exhibitions: (1991) Senior shows - Joan Vitale, Jean Salem; Farnham East - Photographs of China, Miriam Jenkins; Farnham West - 6 x 6 drawings & prints by students of 6 Iowa colleges, Mt Mercy, Luther, Iowa Wesleyan Central, Simpson & Grandview; Bruce Bobick (watercolor paintings & quilts), Carrollton, GA; Campus workshop (painting) Faculty show - recent work by Mary Schaeffer (sculpture); Janet Heinicke (painting & drawing); Senior shows - Kris Coltrain, Waverly; Cori Brown, Farragut; Craig Brown, Eldora; Edith Kuitert, Pella; Thad White, Indianola; Sue Curtis, Indianola; Dollie Stout, Randolph; Indianola Area Artists Show; critique with guest artist
Activities: Classes for adults; lectrs open to public, 4 vis lectr per year; gallery talks; scholarships offered; individual paintings lent; originate traveling exhibitions

IOWA CITY

A   IOWA CITY - JOHNSON COUNTY ARTS COUNCIL, Arts Center, 129 E Washington, 52240. Tel 319-337-7447. *Pres* Naomi Schedl; *Vol Coordr* Marjorie Donovan; *Treas* Sharon Stubbs
Open Mon - Sat 10 AM - 3 PM. No admis fee. Estab 1975. Large gallery space for group or theme shows; solo room for single artist shows; installation space. Average Annual Attendance: 5000. Mem: 250 - 300; dues family $30, individual $20; meeting 1st Tues of month
Income: $20,000 (financed by membership, sales & grants)
Exhibitions: Eleven exhibitions per yr are mounted. In April a national exhibition of works using paper &/or fiber as a medium is organized & installed. Monthly exhibitions include works of local artists & from local collections. Each group show is accompanied by a solo show and an installation in separate gallery spaces
Publications: Paper Fiber Show Catalog, annually; membership pamphlet; monthly newsletter
Activities: Workshops; competitions with awards; T V forums; fiscal agent for individual artists; co-sponsor of arts festival

UNIVERSITY OF IOWA

M   Museum of Art, 150 N Riverside Dr, 52242. Tel 319-335-1727; FAX 319-335-3677. *Dir* Stephen S Prokopoff; *Cur Educ* Emily J G Vermillion; *Cur Graphic Arts* Jo-Ann Conklin; *Technical Dir* David Dennis; *Registrar* Jeff Martin
Open Tues - Sat 10 AM - 5 PM, Sun noon - 5 PM, cl Thanksgiving, Christmas & New Year's Day. No admis fee. Estab 1969 to collect, exhibit and preserve for the future, works of art from different cultures; to make these objects as accessible as possible to people of all ages in the state of Iowa; to assist the public, through educational programs and publications, in interpreting these works of art and expanding their appreciation of art in general. 48,000 sq ft in 16 galleries, including a central sculpture court. Average Annual Attendance: 50,000. Mem: 1000; dues student $10, sr citizen $25, individual $35, household $50, sponsor $125, patron $250, benefactor $500, directors circle $1000
Income: Financed by membership, state appropriation and private donations
Collections: African and Pre-Columbian art; Chinese and Tibetan bronzes; Oriental jade; 19th and 20th century European and American paintings and sculpture; prints, drawings, photography, silver
Exhibitions: The Elliott Collection of 20th Century European paintings, silver and jade; a major collection of African sculpture and a selection of prints by Mauricio Lasansky are on permanent exhibition. Approximately 14 changing exhibitions each year, both permanent collection and traveling exhibitions
Publications: Calendar (brochure), twice/year; exhibition catalogs; newsletter
Activities: Docent training; lect open to the public, 8 vis lectr per year; concerts; gallery talks; tours; works of art lent to other museums; originate traveling exhibitions; sales shop sells posters, postcards and catalogs
L   Art Library, 150 N Riverside Dr, 52242. Tel 319-335-3089. *Interim Librn* Rijn Templeton
Open Mon - Fri 8 AM - 5 PM, Mon - Thurs 7 - 10 PM, Sat & Sun 1 - 4 PM. Estab 1937 to support the University programs, community and state needs. Circ 40,000
Income: Financed by state appropriation
Purchases: $76,000
Library Holdings: Vols 70,000; Per subs 230; Micro — Fiche, reels; Other — Clipping files, exhibition catalogs, memorabilia, pamphlets

KEOKUK

A KEOKUK ART CENTER, Keosippi Mall, PO Box 862, 52632. Tel 319-524-8354. *Pres* Joan Schleier; *Dir* Tom Seabold; *VPres* Jim Dennis; *Treas* Helen Gammon
Open Tues - Sat 9 AM - noon. No admis fee. Estab 1954 to promote art in tri-state area. Gallery maintained in Keokuk Public Library, 210 N Fifth St. Average Annual Attendance: 2000. Mem: Dues sustaining $50, patron $25, family $12, individual $6, student $2; annual meeting first Mon in May
Collections: Paintings, sculpture
Publications: Newsletter, quarterly
Activities: Classes for adults and children; docent training; lect open to the public; gallery talks; tours; competitions with cash awards; scholarships; book traveling exhibitions; originate traveling exhibitions

LEMARS

M TEIKYO WESTMAR UNIVERSITY, Westmar Art Gallery, 51031. Tel 712-546-7081, Ext 231. *Gallery Dir* Anne Lubbin
Open daily 8 AM - 5:30 PM, Sat 2 - 5 PM; inactive during summer. No admis fee. Estab 1973. The purpose of the gallery is to provide a forum for cultivating the sensitivity of our student body and the community to a variety of visual arts through a regular schedule of art exhibits. Gallery covers 2000 sq ft floor space, 170 linear feet of display space, with track lighting. Average Annual Attendance: 7500
Income: Financed by endowment, college appropriation and private gifts
Collections: Haitian Art Collection
Publications: Westmar College Fine Arts Schedule of Events
Activities: Educ dept; lectures open to the public; concerts; gallery talks
L Mock Library Art Dept, 51031. Tel 712-546-7081. *Dir* Ann Lubbin
Open to students
Library Holdings: Vols 1675; Per subs 9; AV — Slides

MARSHALLTOWN

A CENTRAL IOWA ART ASSOCIATION, INC, Fisher Community Center, 709 S Center, 50158. Tel 515-753-9013. *Dir* Susan Malloy
Open Mon - Fri 8 AM - 11 PM, Sat 8 AM - 5 PM, Sun 2 - 5 PM. Estab 1942, incorporated 1959. The large auditorium has changing monthly exhibitions of varied art; glass cases in corridor & studio display contemporary ceramics of high quality. Average Annual Attendance: 3000. Mem: 330; dues $15; annual meeting June 30
Income: Financed by mem, contributions & United Way
Collections: Fisher Collection—Utrillo, Cassatt, Sisley, Vuillard, Monet, Degas, Signac, Le Gourge, Vlaminck and Monticelli; sculpture—Christian Petersen, Rominelli, Bourdelle; ceramic study collection—Gilhooly, Arneson, Nagle, Kottler, Babu, Geraedts, Boxem, Leach, Voulkos; traditional Japanese wares
Exhibitions: Monthly art & craft exhibits in Fisher Community Center Auditorium
Publications: Newsletter, monthly; brochures
Activities: Classes for adults and children in ceramics, sculpture, jewelry, painting; lectures open to the public, 3 vis lectr per yr; gallery talks; tours; awards; individual paintings & original objects of art lent; book traveling exhibitions; originate traveling exhibitions; sales shop sells original art, reproductions, prints, pottery, wood, fiber & metal
L Art Reference Library, Fisher Community Center, 50158. Tel 515-753-9013. *Dir* Susan Malloy
For reference only
Library Holdings: Vols 300; AV — Cassettes, slides; Other — Original art works, photographs, sculpture

MASON CITY

M CHARLES H MACNIDER MUSEUM, 303 Second St SE, 50401-3988. Tel 515-421-3666. *Dir* Richard E Leet; *Coordr Educ* Mary Mello-nee; *Registrar & Cur Asst* Robin Wagner
Open Tues & Thurs 10 AM - 9 PM, Wed, Fri & Sat 10 AM - 5 PM, Sun 1 - 5 PM, cl Mon & holidays. No admis fee. Estab 1964, opened 1966 to provide experience in the arts through development of a permanent collection, through scheduling of temporary exhibitions, through the offering of classes & art instruction, through special programs in film, music & other areas of the performing arts. The museum was estab in an English-Tudor style of brick & tile, enhanced by modern, design coordinated additions. It is located in a scenic setting, 2 1/2 blocks from the main thoroughfare of Mason City. Gallery lighting and neutral backgrounds provide a good environment for exhibitions. Average Annual Attendance: Over 35,000. Mem: 890; dues from contributions $15-$500or more
Income: $320,000 (financed by mem, city appropriation & grants)
Collections: Permanent collection being developed with an emphasis on American art, with some representation of Iowa art; contains paintings, prints, pottery; artists represented include Baziotes, Benton, Burchfield, Burford, Calder, Cropsey, Davies, De Staebler, Dove, Flannagan, Francis, Gottlieb, Graves, Guston, Healy, Hurd, Lasansky, Levine, Martin, Maurer, Metcalf, Sloan & Oliveira; Bil Baird: World of Puppets
Exhibitions: Impressionist Paintings from the Phillips Collection; Annual Area Competitive Show; Annual Iowa Crafts Competition; Art of the Puppet by Bil Baird; Bentons Bentons; Sam Francis: Works on Paper; Magic Carpets—Rugs of the Orient; Remington's Early Years; Rembrandt's Etchings, Neon Art by Lili Lakich
Publications: Newsletter, bi-monthly; occasional exhibit fliers or catalogs
Activities: Classes for adults and children; docent training; seminars and workshops; lect open to public, 2-4 vis lectr per yr; concerts; gallery talks; tours; competitions; individual paintings and original objects of art lent to other museums and art centers; museum shop selling original art

L Library, 303 Second St SE, 50401. Tel 515-421-3666.
Reference library within the structure of the museum. For reference only
Library Holdings: Vols 1000; Per subs 24; AV — Slides, v-tapes
Special Subjects: Architecture, Art Education, Art History, Ceramics, Decorative Arts, Drawings, Folk Art, Graphic Design, Painting - American, Photography, Pottery, Sculpture, Watercolors, American art

L MASON CITY PUBLIC LIBRARY, 225 Second St SE, 50401. Tel 515-423-7552. *Dir* Andrew Alexander; *Reference* Bev Elder; *Childrens Room* Margaret Hanawalt; *Young Adult* Fern Robinson; *Art Librn* Elizabeth Camarigg
Open Mon - Thurs 9 AM - 9 PM; Fri & Sat 2 - 5 PM; Sun 1 - 5 PM. No admis fee. Estab 1869 to service public in providing reading material and information. Permanent collection of regional artists on display in auditorium; monthly exhibits of local & regional artists located in main lobby of library. Circ 197,635
Income: $327,909 (financed by city, county appropriation and Federal Revenue Sharings)
Purchases: $85,000
Library Holdings: Vols 103,000; Per subs 356; original documents; Micro — Fiche, reels; AV — Cassettes, fs 350, motion pictures, rec; Other — Clipping files, framed reproductions, memorabilia, original art works, pamphlets, prints
Collections: Permanent collection of regional artists; signed letters of authors
Exhibitions: Rotating exhibitions
Activities: Ext dept serves general public; gallery holdings consist of seven art works & ten original paintings which are lent to the public

MOUNT VERNON

M CORNELL COLLEGE, Armstrong Gallery, 52314. Tel 319-895-8811. *Dir Gallery* Anthony Plaut; *Chmn Dept of Art* Doug Hanson
Open Mon - Fri 9 AM - 4 PM. Estab to display artists work
Income: Financed by Cornell College
Collections: Thomas Nast drawings & prints; Sonnenschein Collection of European Drawings of the 15th - 17th Century
Exhibitions: Four exhibits per yr plus 10-20 student thesis shows
Activities: Lect open to public, 1 vis lectr per yr

MUSCATINE

M MUSCATINE ART CENTER, 1314 Mulberry Ave, 52761. Tel 319-263-8282. *Pres* William Snydacker; *Dir* Barbara C Longtin
Open Tues - Fri 11 AM - 5 PM, Sat & Sun 1 - 5 PM, Thurs eve 7 - 9 PM, cl Mon and legal holidays. No admis fee. Estab 1965. Mem: 600; dues sponsor $500 - $999, supporting $200 - $499, contributing $100 - $199, sustaining $50 - $99, family $30, individual $20, senior citizens $12.50 or senior citizen couple $20
Income: Financed by city appropriation and Muscatine Art Center Support Foundation
Collections: Muscatine History; Button Collection; Paperweight Collection; decorative arts, graphics, paintings; Great River Collection, prints and paintings depicting the Mississippi River and its environs
Publications: Newsletter, quarterly
Activities: Classes for children and adults; lectures open to the public, 6 vis lectr per yr; concerts; gallery talks; tours; competitions with awards; individual paintings & original objects of art lent; book traveling exhibitions
L Library, 1314 Mulberry Ave, 52761. Tel 319-263-8282.
For reference only
Library Holdings: Vols 2500; Per subs 10; Other — Memorabilia, pamphlets

ORANGE CITY

M NORTHWESTERN COLLEGE, Te Paske Gallery of Rowenhorst, Student Center, 51041. Tel 712-737-4821, ext 156. *Exhib Coordr* John Kaericher
Open Mon - Sat 8 AM - 10 PM. No admis fee. Estab 1968 to promote the visual arts in northwest Iowa and to function as a learning resource for the college and community. Average Annual Attendance: 1500 - 2000
Income: Financed by school budget
Collections: Approx 75 original works of art: etchings, woodcuts, serigraphs, lithographs, mezzotints, paintings, sculpture and ceramics by modern and old masters of Western World and Japan
Exhibitions: Contemporary American Artists Series; student and faculty shows
Activities: Classes for adults; lect open to the public, 2 - 3 vis lectr per yr; gallery talks; competitions; individual prints and original objects of art lent to schools and libraries

SIOUX CITY

A SIOUX CITY ART CENTER, 513 Nebraska St, 51101. Tel 712-279-6272; FAX 712-279-6309. *Board Trustees* Christie Metz; *Board Dirs Pres* Sandy Ellis; *Dir* Jim Zimmer
Open Tues - Sat 10 AM - 5 PM, Sun 1 - 5 PM, Mon 5 - 8 PM, cl holidays. No admis fee. Estab 1938 to provide art experiences to the general public. Four exhibition galleries consisting of nationally known artists from the midwest regional area; includes a graphics gallery and changing exhibitions. Average Annual Attendance: 40,000. Mem: 750; dues $15 - $5000; monthly meetings
Income: Financed by membership, city and state appropriation
Collections: Permanent collection of over 700 works; consists of †paintings and †prints of nationally known regional artists, contemporary photography and sculpture and crafts; Grant Wood Mural
Exhibitions: Youth Art Month Exhibition; Annual Juried Exhibition
Publications: Annual Report; Artifact, monthly magazine; exhibition catalogs
Activities: Classes for adults and children; docent training; workshops; outreach programs to schools; lectures open to public, 5 - 6 vis lectr per year; gallery talks, tours; film series; concerts; competitions; scholarships; original objects of art & individual paintings lent to qualified institutions with approved facilities and security; book traveling exhibitions, 3 - 4 per yr; traveling exhibitions organized and circulated to regional art museums; museum & sales shops sell books, original art, posters and prints; junior museum

L   **Library,** 513 Nebraska St, Sioux City, 51101. Tel 712-279-6272; FAX 712-279-6309. *Dir* Jim Zimmer
Reference library - non-circulating
Library Holdings: Vols 1500; Per subs 20; AV — Cassettes, slides; Other — Exhibition catalogs

STORM LAKE

M   **WITTER GALLERY,** 609 Cayuga St, 50588. Tel 712-732-3400. *Pres* Therese Daniel; *Dir* Andriette Wickstrom; *Educ Coordr* Judy Ferguson
Open Mon - Fri 1:30 - 4 PM, Sat 10 AM - 12 PM. No admis fee. Estab 1972 to encourage the appreciation of fine arts and to support fine arts education, exhibits, lectures and workshops. Gallery occupies a wing of the Storm Lake Public Library building. It has about 1800 sq ft of floor space and 120 linear ft of hanging wall space. Average Annual Attendance: 10,000. Mem: 300; dues patron $1000, benefactor $500, sponsor $250, supporting $100, sustaining $50, family $25, single $15
Income: $20,000 (financed by endowment, membership, city appropriation, fund raising projects)
Collections: Paintings & collected artifacts of Miss Ella Witter; prints by Dorothy D Skewis
Exhibitions: Iowa Women in Art: Pioneers of the Past- touring exhibition of work by Ella Witter and Dorothy Skewis
Publications: Witter Gallery News & Events
Activities: Classes for adults; art appreciation program in area schools; lect open to public, 10 vis lectr per yr, gallery talks; concerts; tours; biennial juried competition with cash awards; originate traveling exhibits; museum shop sells notecards and tote bags

WATERLOO

A   **WATERLOO ART ASSOCIATION,** 501 Sycamore St (Mailing add: PO Box 1496, 50704). Tel 319-232-1984. *Pres* James L Smith; *Secy* Helen Kennedy
Open Tues - Sat 10 AM - 4 PM. No admis fee. Estab 1944 to encourage area artists and provide for the exhibition of their work. Gallery is maintained in a rented building providing gallery rooms, workshop, art supply sales room and storage. Average Annual Attendance: 2000. Mem: 150; dues $20; annual meeting last Tues Jan
Income: Financed by membership
Collections: Small collection of work by former members
Exhibitions: Amateur Iowa Artists Regional Show; Black Hawk County Art Show; Monthly exhibits by area professionals
Publications: Bulletin published six times a yr
Activities: Classes for adults; workshops; lectures open to public, 8-10 vis lectr per yr; gallery talks; tours; competitions with awards; sales shop sells original art, prints, pottery & sculpture & gift shop items

M   **WATERLOO MUSEUM OF ART,** 225 Commercial St, 50701. Tel 319-291-4491. *Dir* Clarence Alling
Open Mon - Fri 10 AM - 5 PM, Sun 2 - 5 PM, cl Sat. No admis fee. Estab 1957 to provide an art forum for the Waterloo area. Average Annual Attendance: 35,000, plus junior museum attendance of 16,000. Mem: 500; dues individual $15 & up; annual meeting second Thurs of July
Income: Financed by city funds and memberships
Collections: Small new collection of contemporary American paintings, prints and †sculpture; †Haitian paintings and sculpture
Exhibitions: Schedule changing exhibitions of regional painting, sculpture, prints & fine crafts
Activities: Classes for adults and children; docent training; lectures open to public; concerts; gallery talks; tours; scholarships & fels offered; originate traveling exhibitions; sales shop sells original art; junior museum located at 225 Commercial St

WEST BRANCH

L   **HERBERT HOOVER PRESIDENTIAL LIBRARY & MUSEUM,** Parkside Dr, 52358. Tel 319-643-5301; FAX 319-643-5825. *Library Dir* Richard Norton Smith; *Asst Dir* Timothy Walch
Open daily 9 AM - 5 PM, cl Thanksgiving, Christmas, New Year's Day. Admis $1, children 15 & under free. Estab 1962 as a research center to service the papers of Herbert Hoover and other related manuscript collections; a museum to exhibit the life & times of Herbert Hoover from his 90 years of public service and accomplishments
Income: Financed by federal appropriation
Library Holdings: Vols 25,000; Per subs 67; original documents, still photographs; Micro — Reels; AV — A-tapes, motion pictures, rec, slides; Other — Clipping files, manuscripts, memorabilia, pamphlets
Collections: 64 Chinese porcelains; oil paintings; 190 Original Editorial Cartoons; 340 posters; 26 World War I Food Administration; 464 World War I Painted and Embroidered Flour Sacks
Exhibitions: Permanent exhibits on Herbert and Lou Henry Hoover; subjects related to Hoover and the times; temporary exhibits cover subjects related to the memorabilia collection, the decades & activities of Hoover's life, & state & national interest
Activities: Lectures open to public; 2-3 vis lectrs per year; sales shop sells books, prints, slides and medals

KANSAS

ABILENE

L   **DWIGHT D EISENHOWER PRESIDENTIAL LIBRARY,** 200 SE Fourth St, 67410. Tel 913-263-4751. *Dir* Daniel Holt; *Museum Cur* Dennis Medina
Open daily 9 AM - 4:45 PM, cl Thanksgiving, Christmas & New Years. Admis $1.50, sr citizens $1, under 16 free. Estab 1961 as library, in 1954 as museum. Average Annual Attendance: 126,000
Income: Financed by Federal Government appropriation
Library Holdings: Vols 22,850; Micro — Prints, reels; AV — A-tapes, cassettes, fs, motion pictures, rec, slides, v-tapes; Other — Clipping files, manuscripts, memorabilia, original art works, photographs, prints, sculpture
Collections: Research Library and Museum contains papers of Dwight D Eisenhower and his associates, together with items of historical interest connected with the Eisenhower Family. Mementos and gifts of General Dwight D Eisenhower both before, during, and after his term as President of the United States
Activities: Educ dept; docent training; lect open to the public, 5 vis lectr per year; libr tours; individual paintings & original objects of art lent; lending collection contains original art work & prints, paintings & sculpture; originate traveling exhibitions; museum shop sells books, prints, reproductions & slides

ALMA

M   **WABAUNSEE COUNTY HISTORICAL MUSEUM,** 227 Missouri, PO Box 387, 66401. Tel 913-765-2200. *Dir & Cur* Joanne Stroup
No admis fee. Estab 1968 for the purpose of preserving art in Wabaunsee County. Paintings are hung throughout the museum in available space. Average Annual Attendance: 2000. Mem: 300; dues $5; annual meeting last Sat in May
Income: $30,000 (financed by mem & endowment)
Collections: Blacksmith shop; postal display; clothing; farm tools & equipment; 1923 reel firetruck; mainstreet USA-historical town; old time telephone shop; indian arrowhead display; General Louis Walt display
Publications: Historical Society Newsletter, quarterly

ASHLAND

M   **CLARK COUNTY HISTORICAL SOCIETY,** Pioneer - Krier Museum, 430 W Fourth St, PO Box 862, 67831-0862. Tel 316-635-2227. *Cur* Floretta Carter
Open daily 1 - 5 PM. Admis donations requested. Estab 1967 to collect & preserve Southwest Kansas history. Displays set up as mortuary, bank, general store, barber shop, doctor's office, saddle shop, blacksmith shop; rooms in homes, such as bedroom, parlor, kitchen, music room, kraft room; aerobatic plane; farm machinery; buggies. Average Annual Attendance: 1400. Mem: 300; lifetime $10; annual meeting in Nov
Income: $20,277 (financed by mem, county taxes & donations)
Collections: Archeological Collection; Barbed Wire Collection; Early Settlers Collection; Elephant Collection; Gun Collection
Exhibitions: 1992 Kansas Day Demonstrations
Publications: Notes on Eary Clark County, Kansas, book; Kings & Queens of the Range, book
Activities: Demonstrations & group tours; retail store sells books

ATCHISON

M   **MUCHNIC FOUNDATION AND ATCHISON ART ASSOCIATION,** Muchnic Gallery, 704 N Fourth St, PO Box 12, Route 2, 66002. Tel 913-367-1317. *Cur* Mrs Pennell Snowden
Open weekends. Estab 1970 to bring art to the people of Atchison. 19th century home furnished with original family belongings downstairs; upstairs there are 5 rooms devoted to the art gallery. Average Annual Attendance: 2000. Mem: 20; annual meeting second Tues of each month
Income: Financed by Muchnic Foundation, Atchison Art Asn art shows
Purchases: $7000
Collections: †Paintings by regional artists: Don Andorfer; Thomas Hart Benton; John Stuart Curry; Raymond Eastwood; John Falter; Jim Hamil; Wilbur Niewald; Jack O'Hara; Roger Shimomura; Robert Sudlow; Grant Wood; Jamie Wyeth; Walter Yost
Activities: Classes for adults; docent training; gallery talks; tours; book traveling exhibitions, annually; originate traveling exhibitions; sales shop sells original art

BALDWIN CITY

M   **BAKER UNIVERSITY,** Old Castle Museum, 515 Fifth, PO Box 65, 66006. Tel 913-594-6809; FAX 913-594-2522. *Dir* Brenda Day
Open Tues - Sun 2 - 5 PM, cl Mon. Admis by donation. Estab 1953 to display items related to life in early Kansas. Average Annual Attendance: 1500
Income: Financed by endowment, University & donations
Collections: Country store; Indian artifacts & pottery; 19th century print shop; quilts; silver & pewter dishes & table service; tools; old quilts; old cameras
Exhibitions: John Brown material; Indian Pottery; Indian artifacts; old guns
Activities: Lectures open to public

CHANUTE

M   **MARTIN & OSA JOHNSON SAFARI MUSEUM, INC,** 16 S Grant, 66720. Tel 316-431-2730. *Dir* Conrad G Froehlich; *Cur* Barbara E Henshall
Open Mon - Sat 10 AM - 5 PM, Sun 1 - 5 PM. Admis adults $2.50, students $1, children under 12 free with adult. Estab 1961 to be the repository of the Johnson Archives. Average Annual Attendance: 4500. Mem: 275; dues $15; annual

meeting in Oct
Income: $80,000 (financed by membership, city appropriation, donations & gifts shop)
Exhibitions: The story of Martin and Osa Johnson; African Tribal Culture
Publications: Wait-A-Bit, quarterly newsletter; Books: Exploring with Martin and Osa Johnson; Empty Masks
Activities: Educ dept; tours; museum boxes for school use; individual paintings & original objects of art lent to qualified institutions; museum shop sells books, imported carvings, brass, fabric & ethnic toys
—**Imperato Collection of West African Artifacts,** 66720. Tel 316-431-2730. *Dir* Conrad G Froehlich
Estab 1974
Collections: West African sculpture including masks, ancestor figures & ritual objects, household items, musical instruments
Exhibitions: African culture exhibit of East & West African items; narrow strip loom; ceremonial masks
Publications: Collection catalogs
—**Johnson Collection of Photographs, Movies & Memorabilia,** 66720. Tel 316-431-2730. *Dir* Conrad G Froehlich
Collections: Photographs & movie footage of the South Seas, Borneo & East Africa between 1917-1936; Manuscript material, archival collection, & artifacts collected by the Johnsons
Exhibitions: Life of the Johnsons
—**Selsor Gallery of Art,** 66720. Tel 316-431-2730. *Dir* Conrad G Froehlich
Estab 1981
Collections: Original paintings; scratch boards & sketches; bronze, ivory & amber sculpture; lithographs
—**Scott Explorers Library,** 66720. Tel 316-431-2730. *Dir* Conrad G Froehlich
Estab 1980 for research and reference
Library Holdings: Vols 14,000
Special Subjects: Natural History, Exploration

EL DORADO

M **WARREN HALL COUTTS III MEMORIAL MUSEUM OF ART,** 110 N Main St, 67042. Tel 316-321-1215. *Chmn Board* Rhoda Hodges
Open Mon - Fri 1 - 5 PM & by special arrangements. No admis fee. Estab 1970 as a Fine Arts museum. Average Annual Attendance: 4000
Income: Financed by endowment & gifts
Collections: †Fredrick Remington sculpture collection completed in 1992 (recasts)
Activities: Classes for adults & children; lect open to public, 1 - 2 lectr per yr; concerts; gallery talks; tours; competitions with awards; scholarships offered; individual paintings & original objects of art lent on a limited basis

ELLSWORTH

M **ROGERS HOUSE MUSEUM GALLERY,** 102 E Main S, 67439. *Dir* Ruth E Rogers
Open Mon - Sat Noon - 5 PM, cl Sun & holidays. Adults $.50, children 6-12 $.25. Estab 1968 in a historic cowboy hotel
Collections: Original paintings, prints; miscellaneous art
Publications: Art Observations (book); Country Neighbor; The Great West; Quill of the Kansan (books)
Activities: Sales shop sells original paintings and prints

EMPORIA

M **EMPORIA STATE UNIVERSITY,** Norman R Eppink Art Gallery, 1200 Commercial, 66801. Tel 316-343-1200. *Dir* Donald Perry
Open Mon - Fri 9 AM - 4 PM, cl university holidays. No admis fee. Estab 1939 to bring a variety of exhibitions to the campus. Main Gallery is 25x50 ft & has a 50 ft wall for hanging items; adjacent gallery is 16x50 ft; display gallery contains 18 40 inch x 28 inch panels. Average Annual Attendance: 10,000
Income: Financed by state, grant & endowment funds
Purchases: Annual purchase of contemporary drawings from the Annual National Invitational Drawing Exhibition, and works on paper from the Annual Summer Art Festival
Collections: Artifacts; †contemporary drawings and paintings; †sculpture
Publications: Exhibition catalogs
Activities: Lectures open to public, 6 vis lectr per yr; concerts; gallery talks; tours; scholarships; individual paintings & original objects of art lent to university offices; book 4-6 traveling exhibitions per yr; originate traveling exhibitions to schools

HAYS

M **FORT HAYS STATE UNIVERSITY,** Moss-Thorns Gallery of Arts, 600 Park St, 67601. Tel 913-628-4247; FAX 913-628-4087. *Chmn* Gary Coulter
Open Mon - Fri 8:30 AM - 4 PM, weekends on special occasions. No admis fee. Estab 1953 to provide constant changing exhibitions for the benefit of students, faculty and other interested people in an education situation. Rarick Hall has 2200 sq ft with moveable panels that can be used to divide the gallery into four smaller galleries. Mem: 88
Income: Financed by state appropriation
Purchases: $2000
Collections: Vyvyan Blackford Collection; †contemporary prints; †national exhibition of small paintings, prints and drawings; regionalist collection (1930s); Oriental scroll collection
Exhibitions: (1992) Annual Faculty Exhibition; MFA Graduate Thesis Exhibition; Daniel Johnson: Printmaking. (1993) Senior Graduation Exhibition; Kansas 18th National Small Painting, Drawing & Print Exhibition; Annual Student Honors Exhibition; Chaiwat Thumsujarit: Sabbatical Leave Exhibition; Kathleen Kuchar: Leave of Absence Exhibition; Dave Chalfant (drawing); Donna

Roberts (painting)
Publications: Exhibitions brochures; Art Calendar, annually
Activities: Lectures open to public, 4 vis lectr per yr; gallery talks; tours; competitions with prizes; concerts; Exten dept serving western Kansas; individual paintings and original objects of art lent to individuals, organizations and institutions; lending collection of original art works and prints, paintings, sculpture and slides; traveling exhibitions organized and circulated

L **Forsyth Library,** 600 Park St, 67601. Tel 913-628-4431; FAX 913-628-4096. *Interim Dir* Dr Louis Caplan; *Reference Librn* Phyllis Schmidt
Reference Library
Library Holdings: Vols 6000; Per subs 1181; AV — Fs; Other — Exhibition catalogs

HUTCHINSON

A **HUTCHINSON ART ASSOCIATION GALLERY,** 1520 N Main, 67501. Tel 316-663-1081, 662-8652. *Dir* Del Knauer; *Pres* Jinx Wright; *VPres* Jane Dronberger; *Treas* Larry Bolton; *Secy* Shirley Johnson
Open Tues - Fri 11 AM - 5 PM, Sat & Sun 2 - 4 PM. Estab 1949 to bring exhibitions to the city of Hutchinson and maintain a permanent collection in the public schools. Two galleries. Average Annual Attendance: 3000; dues $10 & up or $15 for two; monthly meetings
Income: Financed by memberships, profits on spring fair, corporations
Collections: Permanent collection of watercolors, prints, ceramics, glass, wood, oils & metals
Exhibitions: Two all-member shows per yr; one traveling show per month
Activities: Annual Art Fair with prizes; lectures open to the public, 3 vis lectr per yr; gallery talks; tours; monthly public receptions to meet artists currently exhibiting; scholarships; book traveling exhibitions; shop sells original art, prints, cards, ceramics, handblown glass, jewelry, sculpture, carved wood & stoneware

INDEPENDENCE

M **LADIES LIBRARY AND ART ASSOCIATION,** Independence Museum, PO Box 294, 67301. Tel 316-331-3515.
Open Sept - May, Thurs, Fri, Sat 1 - 4 PM, June - Aug 9:30 AM - 1 PM. Donations. Estab 1882 to provide library facilities & to secure an art collection for the community. The museum has a large 19 ft gallery which contains original paintings; Indian art & artifacts; Mexican Room, late 1800 & early 1900 costume Room, country store, War & Peace Room, Oriental room, period bedroom, early 1900 kitchen, childrens room, William Inge Memorabilia Room & historical oil room. Presently establishing a blacksmith shop. Average Annual Attendance: 3000. Mem: 125; dues $15 - $50; meeting monthly Oct - May
Income: Financed by membership, bequests, gifts, art exhibits and various projects
Collections: †William Inge Memorabilia Collection; †Oriental Collection
Exhibitions: Annual Art Exhibit; Photography Shows; various artists & craftsmen exhibits; Quilt Fair; Doll Fair; Gun Show; Afghan Fair; Needlework Show
Activities: Classes for adults & children; lectures open to public, 9 vis lect per yr; concerts; gallery talks; tours; competitions with awards; individual paintings lent to State House, library, & bank; lending collection contains original prints & paintings

LAWRENCE

M **UNIVERSITY OF KANSAS,** Spencer Museum of Art, 66045. Tel 913-864-4710; FAX 913-864-3112. *Dir* Andrea Norris; *Asst Dir* Douglas Tilghman; *Cur Prints* Stephen Goddard; *Cur Photography* John Poltz; *Research Cur* Marilyn Stokstad, PhD; *Registrar* Janet Dreiling; *Exhib Designer* Mark Roeyer; *Managing Ed & Public Relations* Sally Hayden; *Membership* Linda Bailey; *Programs* Carissa McKenzie; *Docents* Betsy Weaver; *Bookshop* Kathleen McVay; *Cur European & American Art* Nancy Corwin; *Cur Education* Pat Villenue; *Graphic Designer* Susan Hyde
Open Tues - Sat 8:30 AM - 5 PM, Sun noon - 5 PM, cl Mon. No admis fee. Dedicated in Spooner Hall 1928, Spencer dedicated 1978. The Museum has traditionally served as a laboratory for the visual arts, supporting curricular study in the arts. Primary emphasis is placed on acquisitions and publications, with a regular schedule of changing exhibitions. Museum has a two level Central Court, seven galleries devoted to the permanent collections, and three galleries for temporary exhibitions; altogether affording 29,000 sq ft. Mem: dues $35
Income: Financed by membership, state appropriation and state and federal grants, contributions
Collections: †American Paintings; †ancient art; †graphics; †Medieval art; †17th and 18th century art, especially German; †19th century European and American art; †Oriental art; †20th century European and American art
Exhibitions: (1991) Landscape Prints and Drawings from the Bequest of Rudolph L Baumfeld; Art with a Mission: Objects of the Arts and Crafts Movement from Local Collections; Quilt National '89; Italian Master Drawings from the Horvitz Collection; Southern Light, Southern Land: Painting in New Zealand, 1840-1990; Spencer Museum Celebrates Ten Years of Art; The Art of Teaching: Sixteenth-Century Allegorical Prints and Drawings; Innovators of American Illustration; Japanese women Artists, 1600-1900; A Kansas Collection; Prairie Print Makers; New Work New York; The World in Miniature: Engravings by the German Little Masters,1500-1550; Mind Landscapes: The Paintings of C C Wang; Megalith: Photographs by Paul Caponigro.
Publications: The Register of the Spencer Museum of Art, annually; monthly calendar; Murphy Lectures, annually; exhibit catalogs, 1 - 2 per year
Activities: Classes for children, docent training; lect open to the public, 24 vis lectr per yr; concerts; gallery talks; tours; traveling exhibitions organized and circulated; museum shop sells books, magazines, posters & postcards

L **Murphy Library of Art and Architecture,** University of Kansas, 66045. Tel 913-864-3020. *Librn* Susan V Craig
Open Mon - Thurs 8 AM - 10 PM, Fri 8 AM - 8 PM, Sat 9 AM - 5 PM, Sun noon - 10 PM. Estab 1970 to support academic programs and for research. Open to faculty, students and public
Library Holdings: Vols 90,000; Per subs 700; Micro — Fiche, reels; Other — Clipping files, exhibition catalogs, pamphlets
Special Subjects: Oriental Art, Photography

L **Architectural Resource Center,** School of Architecture &Urban Design, 66045.
Tel 913-864-3244; FAX 913-864-5393. *Dir* Ursula Stammler
Open Mon - Fri 9 AM - noon & 1 PM - 5 PM, Sun - Thurs 7:30 PM - 9:30 PM.
Slide Library, estab 1968, is primarily a teaching tool for faculty, but also
accessible to students; Donald E & Mary Bole Hatch Architectural Reading
Room, estab 1981, is adjacent to studios in School of Architecture & supports the
immediate reference needs of students. For reference only
  Income: Financed by endowment & state appropriation
  Library Holdings: Vols 2000; Per subs 30; AV — Slides 68,000

LINDSBORG

BETHANY COLLEGE
L **Library,** 235 E Swensson, 67456. Tel 913-227-3311, Ext 166. *Librn* Dixie M
Lanning; *Asst Librn* John Stratton; *Inter-Library Loan Librn* Denise Cummings
Open Wed - Sun 1 - 5 PM. Estab 1957 for use by art students. For reference
only
  Library Holdings: Vols 110,000; Per subs 600; Booktitles 65,000; Other —
Clipping files, exhibition catalogs, pamphlets, photographs
M **Mingenback Art Center,** 401 N First St, 67456. Tel 913-227-3311, Ext 146.
Chmn Dept Carolyn Kahler; *Prof* Ray Kahmeyer; *Asst Prof* Mary Kay; *Asst Prof*
Kent Breeding; *Asst Prof* Dr Bruce Kahler
Materials are not for public display, for educational reference only
  Collections: Oil paintings, watercolors, prints, etchings, lithographs, wood
engravings, ceramics and sculpture
  Exhibitions: Messiah Festival of Music & Art Exhibition; St Louis Student
Exhibition

M **BIRGER SANDZEN MEMORIAL GALLERY,** 401 N First St, PO Box 348,
67456. Tel 913-227-2220. *Dir* Larry L Griffis
Open Wed - Sun 1 - 5 PM, cl Mon, Tues & major holidays. Admis adults $1,
grade & high school students $.25. Estab 1957 to permanently exhibit the
paintings & prints by the late Birger Sandzen, teacher at Bethany College for 52
years. Ten exhibition areas. Average Annual Attendance: 7000 - 9000. Mem:
350; dues $5 - $1000; annual meeting May for Board of Directors
  Income: Financed by admission fees, sales & membership
  Collections: H V Poor, Lester Raymer, Birger Sandzen, John Bashor, Elmer
Tomasch, Dale Reed & Carl Milles
  Exhibitions: Spring & Fall: Guest artist & special exhibits; Winter & Summer:
Work from permanent collections
  Publications: The Graphic Work of Birger Sandzen
  Activities: Classes for children; docent training; lectures open to public 2 - 4 vis
lectrs per year; concerts; gallery talks; tours; sales desk sells books, reproductions,
stationary

LOGAN

M **DANE G HANSEN MEMORIAL MUSEUM,** PO Box 187, 67646. Tel 913-
689-4846; FAX 913-689-4833. *Dir* Renee McElroy
Open Mon - Fri 9 AM - noon & 1 - 4 PM, Sat 9 AM - noon & 1 - 5 PM, Sun &
holidays 1 - 5 PM, cl Thanksgiving, Christmas & New Year's. No admis fee.
Estab 1973. Traveling exhibitions. Average Annual Attendance: 9000. Mem:
Dues sustaining $50, patron $15, benefactor $5
  Collections: Coins; guns; paintings; prints; sculptures
  Exhibitions: (1992) Sea Stars & Moths by John Cody; Paintings by John Thorns;
Wrench Collection by Sonny Ruff; Capturing The Spirit: Portraits of
Contemporary Mexican Artists. (1993) Victorian Gardens: A Horticultural
Extravaganza; Floyd Riggs Memorial Comic Book Collection; High School Art
'93; Perpetual Campaign: How Presidents Try to Persuade The People; Paintings
by Betty Baird Hmong Artistry: Preserving A Culture on Cloth; Ribs, Rods,
Splits: Appalachian Oak Basketry; Textile Diaries: Quilts as Cultural Markers;
Keepers Of The Kiln: Seven Contemporary Ceramic Artists
  Activities: Classes for adults & children; lectures open to public, 3 vis lectr per
yr; concerts; tours

MANHATTAN

L **KANSAS STATE UNIVERSITY,** Paul Weigel Library of Architecture &
Design, 323 Seaton Hall, College of Architecture & Design, 66506. Tel 913-532-
5968. *Librn* Patricia Weisenburger; *Library Asst* Sonja Melton
Open Mon - Thurs 8 AM - 10 PM, Fri 8 AM - 5 PM, Sat 11 AM - 5 PM, Sun 2
- 10 PM. Estab 1917. Circ 29,861
  Income: $40,000 (financed by state appropriations & gifts)
  Library Holdings: Vols 36,150; Per subs 225; Micro — Fiche, reels; Other —
Clipping files
  Special Subjects: Architecture, Drafting, Graphic Design, Historical Material,
Landscape Architecture, Restoration & Conservation, Architectural history,
Community & regional planning, Historic preservation, Interior architecture,
Landscape architecture
  Publications: Subject catalog

M **RILEY COUNTY HISTORICAL MUSEUM,** 2309 Claflin Rd, 66502. Tel 913-
537-2210. *Dir* D Cheryl Collins; *Archivist* Jeanne C Mithen
Open Tues - Fri 8:30 AM - 5 PM; Sat & Sun 2 - 5 PM. No admis fee. Estab
1916 to exhibit history and current & historical arts & crafts. Average Annual
Attendance: 25,000. Mem: 900; dues $10; meetings in Jan, Apr, July, Oct
  Income: Financed by Riley County budget
  Exhibitions: Household Work Week (1991 - 1992) Riley County: The Land &
The People; (1992) The Riley County Home Front in WWII
  Publications: Tracing Traditions, a coloring book for children
  Activities: Classes for children, dramatic programs, docent programs; lectures
open to public; book traveling exhibitions, 2 per yr; originate traveling exhibitions
to schools & club meetings; sales shop sells books, Kansas crafts, wheatweaving,
wood cuts, pottery & wood carvings

L **Seaton Library,** 66502. *Archivist* Jeanne C Mithen
Reference, non-circulating collection
  Library Holdings: AV — A-tapes, fs, slides, v-tapes; Other — Clipping files,
memorabilia, pamphlets, photographs
  Special Subjects: Architecture, Historical Material, Manuscripts, Maps,
Manhattan/Riley County Architecture - homes & buildings
  Collections: Photo Collection

MCPHERSON

M **MCPHERSON COLLEGE GALLERY,** Friendship Hall, 1600 E Euclid, 67460.
Tel 316-241-0731; FAX 316-241-0731. *Dir* Susan W Dodson
Open Mon - Fri 8 AM - 10 PM. No admis fee. Estab 1960 to present works of
art to the college students and to the community. A long gallery which is the
entrance to an auditorium, has four showcases and 11 panels 4 x 16 ft. Average
Annual Attendance: 2500
  Income: Financed through college
  Collections: Oils, original prints, watercolors
  Activities: Classes for adults; scholarships; book traveling exhibitions

M **MCPHERSON MUSEUM,** 1130 E Euclid, 67460. Tel 316-241-1716. *Museum
Dir* Shirley Ade; *Display Arrangement* Nadine Logback; *Office* Patty Johnson
Open Tues - Sun 1 - 5 PM, cl Mon & holidays. Admis adult $1. Estab 1890.
Average Annual Attendance: 7000
  Income: Financed by city appropriation
  Collections: Fossils of mammoths, mastodons, saber tooth tigers & many other
fossils; oriental & African collection; Pioneer artifacts & Indian artifacts
  Exhibitions: Fall Festival; Victorian Christmas; Quilt Show
  Publications: McPherson Museum Memoranda

NORTH NEWTON

L **BETHEL COLLEGE,** Mennonite Library & Archives, PO Drawer A, 67117-
9989. Tel 316-283-2500, Ext 213; FAX 316-284-5286. *Archivist* John D Thiesen
Open Mon - Fri 10 AM - 5 PM. No admis fee. Estab 1936 to preserve resources
related to Mennonite history for the use of researchers
  Income: $70,000 (financed by college & church conference support)
  Library Holdings: Micro — Fiche, reels; AV — A-tapes, cassettes, fs,
Kodachromes, lantern slides, motion pictures, rec, slides, v-tapes; Other —
Clipping files, exhibition catalogs, framed reproductions, manuscripts,
memorabilia, original art works, pamphlets, photographs, prints, reproductions
  Collections: 500 paintings and etchings by Mennonite artists
  Exhibitions: Photographs of Hopi and Cheyenne Indians; The Dutch Setting:
Mennonite Personalities & Their Environment; Children of Yesterday; Weddings
of Yesterday
  Publications: Gleanings from the Threshing Floor, bi-annual newsletter;
Mennonite Life, quarterly journal

NORTON

C **FIRST STATE BANK,** 105 W Main, 67654. Tel 913-877-3341; FAX 913-877-
5808. *Pres* L O Concannon; *VPres* Ann R Hazlett
Open Mon - Fri 9 AM - 3 PM. Estab 1965 as a gallery of those who ran for
President of the United States and lost
  Collections: Also Ran Gallery

SALINA

M **SALINA ART CENTER,** 242 S Santa Fe, 67401. Tel 913-827-1431. *Dir* Saralyn
Reece Hardy
Open daily noon - 5 PM, cl Mon. No admis fee. Estab 1979 as an international
& national private non- profit, non-collecting contemporary art & education
center. Average Annual Attendance: 30,000. Mem: 500; dues $30
  Income: $300,000 (financed by mem & private donations)
  Exhibitions: Contemporary Art; changing exhibitions; Annual Juried Show
  Publications: Brochures; newsletters
  Activities: Classes for adults & children; docent programs; lect open to public, 6 -
8 vis lectr per year; competitions; traveling exten dept serves rural Kansas; book
traveling exhibitions 4 per year; originate traveling exhibitions 5 per year

TOPEKA

M **KANSAS STATE HISTORICAL SOCIETY,** Kansas Museum of History, 6425
SW Sixth, 66615-1099. Tel 913-272-8681; FAX 913-296-1005. *Exec Dir* Ramon
Powers; *Museum Dir* Robert Keckeisen; *Cur Fine Art* Anne Marvin; *Cur of
Decorative Art* Blair Tarr
Open Mon - Sat 9 AM - 4:30 PM, Sun 12:30 - 4:30 PM. No admis fee. Estab
1875 to collect, preserve and interpret the historical documents and objects of
Kansas history. Average Annual Attendance: 140,000. Mem: 3400; dues life
$1000, special $50 - $1000, family $35, individual $25, student $15; meetings in
spring & fall
  Income: $784,000 (financed by endowment & state)
  Collections: Regional collection for period from middle 19th century to present,
especially portraiture, native art, political cartoons and folk art
  Exhibitions: Rotating Exhibits
  Publications: Kansas History: Journal of the Great Plains, quarterly; exhibit
catalogs
  Activities: Classes for adults & children; dramatic programs; docent training;
craft demonstration program; lectures open to public; provided by staff to public organizations on request; tours; slide tape programs;
exten dept serves entire state of Kansas; traveling trunks on Kansas topics; book
traveling exhibitions, 1-2 per year; sales shop sells books, prints, cards, slides,
postcards, folk art, crafts, souvenirs and jewelry; junior museum

M TOPEKA PUBLIC LIBRARY, Gallery of Fine Arts, 1515 W Tenth St, 66604.
Tel 913-233-2040, Ext 27; FAX 913-233-2055. *Dir* David L Leamon; *Asst Dir*
Tom J Muth; *Fine Arts Dept Head* Mark Rustman; *Gallery Dir* Larry D Peters;
Adult Serv Dept Jim Rhodes; *Childrens Dept Head* Eleanor Strecker
Open Mon -Fri 9 AM - 9 PM, Sat 9 AM - 6 PM, Sun 2 - 6 PM (Labor Day -
Memorial Day). No admis fee. Estab 1870 to serve the city and the Northeast
Kansas Library System residents with public information, both educational and
recreational; to be one of the areas cultural centers through services from the
unique Fine Arts Dept and Gallery of Fine Arts within the library. Gallery is 40
ft x 30 ft, with track lighting, carpet covered walls & security system; gallery
furniture. Circ 1,240,000. Average Annual Attendance: 2400
Income: $2,500,000 (financed by endowment & city appropriations)
Purchases: $72,713
Library Holdings: Vols 267,782; Per subs 497; Documents, Postcards; Micro —
Fiche, reels; AV — Cassettes, fs, rec, slides, v-tapes; Other — Clipping files,
exhibition catalogs, framed reproductions, manuscripts, memorabilia, original art
works, pamphlets, photographs, reproductions, sculpture
Special Subjects: Topeka Room of Topeka artists and authors
Collections: Hirschberg Collection of West African Arts; Johnson Collection of
Art; Rare Book Room; Wilder Collection of Art Glass & Pottery; †Regional
painting & crafts, prints; Glass paperweight collection
Exhibitions: Timock, Babu, Ferguson, Leedy, Pinnel, Edward Navone; Pitchers
at an Exhibition; Tex; Wounded Face-Sculpture; Charles Stoch painting; Don
Perry & Steven Hill; Topeka Crafts Competition; Macy Dorf-Steueware; Dalton
Howard; Joan Foth; Randall Exon; The Painting of Dwight D Eisenhower;
Elizabeth Layton drawings; Robert Sudlow: a Retrospective
Publications: Creative Expression in Rural West Africa; Rookwood Pottery: One
Hundred Year Anniversary
Activities: Dramatic programs; concerts; gallery talks; competitions with awards;
exten dept serves outlying areas within city limits; lending collection for Fine
Arts Dept only contains 30,000 books, 340 cassettes, 35,000 color reproductions,
1500 framed reproductions, over 500 videos, 8826 phonorecords & 16,000 slides;
book traveling exhibitions annually

M WASHBURN UNIVERSITY, Mulvane Art Museum, 17th & Jewell, 66621. Tel
913-231-1010, Ext 1324; FAX 913-231-1089. *Dir* Donald Bartlett Doe; *Registrar*
Carol Emert; *Admin Asst* Elizabeth V Wunder; *Educ Specialist* Rachel Melton
Open 9 AM - 4 PM, Sun 2 - 5 PM, cl Sat & holidays. Estab 1924.
Building gift of Margaret Mulvane: provides three galleries with 319 running ft of
hanging space with carpeted walls and temperature and humidity controlled.
Average Annual Attendance: 30,000. Mem: 1000; dues $15 and up
Income: $250,000
Purchases: $10,000
Collections: 19th & 20th Century American and European paintings and prints
Exhibitions: Continuous program of exhibitions of mountain plains contemporary
art; students exhibition; annual Kansas artists competition
Publications: Exhibition brochures
Activities: Classes for adults and children, docent training; lectures open to
public, 12 vis lectr per yr; concerts; gallery talks; competitions with awards;
tours; films open to the community without charge; scholarships; individuals
painting and original objects of art lent to art institutions; book traveling
exhibitions, 5-6 times per yr; museum shop sells original art, books, prints,
reproductions, slides, gift items

WICHITA

FRIENDS UNIVERSITY
M Whittier Fine Arts Gallery, 2100 University, 67213. Tel 316-261-5877; FAX
316-263-1092. *Dir* Ted Crone
Open daily 7:45 AM - 10 PM. No admis fee. Estab 1963 to bring art-craft
exhibits to campus as an educational learning experience and to supply the local
community with first class exhibits. 1224 sq ft of exhibit space. Average Annual
Attendance: 15,000-20,000
Exhibitions: (1990) Dennis Southwick; Terry Russel; Wichita Oil Painting
Society; Faculty Exhibition
Publications: Exhibition catalogs
Activities: Lectures open to public, 4 vis lectr per year; gallery talks; tours; exten
dept
L Edmund Stanley Library Gallery, 2100 University Ave, 67213. Tel 316-261-
5880; FAX 316-263-1092. *Dir* Jonathan Sparks; *Asst to Dir* Kathy Gaynor
Estab 1979. 500 sq ft of exhibition space, ideal for crafts and locked cases
Library Holdings: Vols 85,000; Per subs 640

A KANSAS WATERCOLOR SOCIETY, Wichita Art Museum, PO Box 12010,
67277-2010. Tel 316-722-6007. *Pres* Kay McCrea; *Exec Dir* Ruth E Sanderson
Open during shows Tues - Sat 10 AM - 4:50 PM, Sun 1 - 4:50 PM. No admis.
Estab 1968 to promote watercolor in Kansas. Three levels, space is triangulated,
sales-rental gallery & childrens area. Average Annual Attendance: 9000. Mem:
257; dues $15; annual meeting in Mar
Income: Financed by membership, entry fees & patrons
Publications: Newsletter, quarterly
Activities: Demonstrations & workshops; lect open to public, 2 vis lectr per year;
gallery talks; tours; competions with awards; traveling exhibitions organized and
circulated; sales shop

M MID-AMERICA ALL-INDIAN CENTER, 650 N Seneca, 67203. Tel 316-262-
5221. *Exec Dir* Jerry L Aday; *Gift Shop Mgr & Tours* Jerry P Martin
Open Mon - Sat 10 AM - 5 PM, Sun 1 - 5 PM, cl Mon Oct 1 - May 1. Admis
adults $1.89, children 6 - 12 $.94, under 6 free. Estab 1976 to preserve the
Indian heritage, culture & traditions. Average Annual Attendance: 36,000. Mem:
300 - 400; dues benefactor $500 & up, patron $250 - $499, friend $100 - $249,
contributor $50 - $99, family $35 - $49, individual $25 - $34
Income: Financed by admissions, donations, memberships & gift shop sales
Collections: Native American arts and artifacts; Mildred Many Memorial
Collection; Lincoln Ellsworth Collection; Plains beadwork; Northwest Coast &
Eskimo crafts; Southwest pottery, paintings, sculpture, carvings & basketry
Exhibitions: Four changing exhibits per year, prehistory or speciality exhibits; 3

dimensional traditional art; 2 & 3 dimensional contemporary art
Publications: Gallery Notes, quarterly newsletter
Activities: Classes for adults; lectures open to the public; gallery talks; tours;
museum shop sells books, original art, reproductions, prints, Indian items,
beadwork & beading supplies
L Library, 650 N Seneca, 67203. Tel 316-262-5221. *Dir* Jerry P Martin; *Registrar*
Sue Cowdery
Reference only
Library Holdings: Vols 400; Indian art & history; AV — Fs, motion pictures,
slides; Other — Pamphlets

M WICHITA ART MUSEUM, 619 Stackman Dr, 67203. Tel 316-268-4921; FAX
316-268-4980. *Dir* Inez Wolins; *Chief Cur* Novelene Ross; *Asst Dir* Douglas
King; *Registrar* Barbara Odevseff
Open Tues - Sat 10 AM - 5 PM, Sun Noon - 5 PM, cl Mon and holidays. No
admis fee. Estab 1935 to house and exhibit art works belonging to permanent
collection; to present exhibits of loaned art works, to ensure care and maintain
the safety of works through security, environmental controls and appropriate
curatorial functions and to interpret collections and exhibitions through formal
and educational presentations. Facility designed by Edward Larrabee Barnes
opened Oct 1977. Average Annual Attendance: 85,000 - 100,000. Mem: Dues
$25 up
Income: $1,200,000
Collections: Roland P Murdock, American Art; M C Naftzger Collection of
Charles M Russell (paintings, drawings and sculpture); Kurdian Collection of Pre-
Columbian Mexican Art; Virginia and George Ablah Collection of British
Watercolors; L S & Ida L Naftzger Collection of Prints & Drawings; Gwen
Houston Naftzger Collection of Boehm and Doughty Porcelain Birds; Florence
Naftzger Evans Collection of Porcelain and Faience; Hands-on Collection for the
Blind
Exhibitions: (1991) The Artists Series: Monotypes of Joyce Treiman; Ritual
Dances & Ceremonials: Prints by Potawatomi Artist Woody Crumbo;
Masterpieces of the American West: Selections from the Anschutz Collection;
Ancient Echoes/Silent Messengers, Sculpture by Steve Kestrel; Folk: The Art of
Benny & George Andrews; Clara Sipprell: a Pictorial Photographer. (1992)
Visionary Artists Bill Traylor & Minnie Evans; New Mexico Patterns: Paintings
by Dick Mason; Gift Prints of the Prairie Print Makers; Lloyd Foltz: A
Retrospective; That's All Folks
Original Art from Warner Bros Animation Studio; Jose Guadalupe Posada; Luis
Jimenez; European & American Masterpieces from the William I Koch
Collection
Publications: Bi-monthly newsletter; Catalog of Roland P Murdock Collection;
Charles M Russell Collection; exhibition brochures and catalogues
Activities: Classes for adults & children; dramatic prog; docent training;
competitions with awards; sales shop sells books, magazines, orginal art,
reproductions, prints, slides, jewelry & art related objects
L Library, 619 Stackman Dr, 67203. Tel 316-268-4921; FAX 316-268-4980. *Librn*
Lois F Crane
Open Tues - Fri 10 AM - 5 PM. Estab 1963 as research library for museum staff.
Reference only
Income: $5220 budgeted (1992)
Library Holdings: Vols 5057; Per subs 29; auction catalogs, museum handbooks;
Other — Exhibition catalogs, pamphlets
Special Subjects: American Indian Art, American Western Art, Art History,
Decorative Arts, Drawings, Etchings & Engravings, Folk Art, Landscapes,
Painting - American, Pre-Columbian Art, Prints, Sculpture, Watercolors, History
of American Art
Collections: Elizabeth S Navas Collection; Gene Morse Collection Charles M
Russell Collection of Western Art, paintings, graphics, sculpture
Activities: Classes for children; docent training; lect open to public; museum shop
sells books, magazines, original art, reproductions, slides

A WICHITA CENTER FOR THE ARTS, 9112 E Central, 67206. Tel 316-634-
2787; FAX 316-634-0593. *Chmn Board* Barry L Downing; *Pres* Dr William
Otton; *Treas* Carol Sbarra
Open Mon - Fri 10 AM - 5 PM, Sat & Sun 1 - 5 PM, cl August, national
holidays. Admis $2. Estab 1920, inc April 1932, as an educational & cultural
institution. Gallery contains 1000 running ft of exhibit space; up to 6 exhibits
each four-week period. Average Annual Attendance: 25,000. Mem: 750; dues
$25 and up; annual meeting 2nd Tues in May
Income: Financed by private contributions
Collections: Prints and drawings, paintings, sculpture, †American decorative arts
& contemporary crafts
Exhibitions: Exhibitions change each month; one man shows, special programs;
Annual National Craft Exhibit; Annual Small Oil Painting Exhibit
Publications: Monthly newsletter, Sept - May
Activities: Classes for adults & children; dramatic programs; docent training;
lectures open to public, up to 6 vis lectr per year; gallery talks; competitions with
awards; scholarships; individual paintings & original objects of art lent to other
art museums; book traveling exhibitions; originate traveling exhibitions; sales
shop sells books & original art
L Maude Schollenberger Memorial Library, 9112 E Central, 67206. Tel 316-634-
2787; FAX 316-634-0593. *Pres* Dr William Otton
Open Tues - Fri 10 AM - 5 PM, Sat & Sun 1 - 5 PM, cl Mon. Estab 1965. For
reference
Income: Financed by private contributions
Library Holdings: Vols 3000; Per subs 4; Other — Clipping files, exhibition
catalogs, manuscripts, memorabilia, original art works, photographs, sculpture

L WICHITA PUBLIC LIBRARY, 223 S Main, 67202. Tel 316-262-0611. *Head
Librn* Richard J Rademacher; *Asst Librn* Gary D Hime; *Adult Serv Division
Coordr* Myrna Hudson; *Public Support Serv* Diana Williams; *Youth Serv
Division Coordr* Judy Nichols
Open Mon - Thurs 8:30 AM - 9 PM, Fri & Sat 8:30 AM - 5:30 PM. Estab 1876
and grown to be informational center and large free public library to improve the
community with educational, cultural and recreational benefits through books,
recordings, films, art works and other materials. Circ 1,100,000

Income: $4,000,000 (from local taxes)
Library Holdings: Micro — Reels; AV — Motion pictures, rec; Other — Framed reproductions
Special Subjects: Advertising Design, Afro-American Art, American Indian Art, American Western Art, Anthropology, Architecture, Bookplates & Bindings, Coins & Medals, Crafts, Decorative Arts, Film, Folk Art, Furniture, Glass, Graphic Arts
Collections: Kansas Book Collection; John F Kennedy Collection; Harry Mueller Philately Book Collection; Driscoll Piracy Collection
Exhibitions: Preview of Oscar Shorts
Activities: Lect; tours

M **WICHITA STATE UNIVERSITY,** Edwin A Ulrich Museum of Art, PO Box 46, 67208. Tel 316-689-3664; FAX 316-689-3898. *Dir* Donald E Knaub; *Registrar* Maria T Ciski; *Asst Cur* Amy L Young; *Asst Cur* Stephen Murillo
Open Wed & Fri 10 AM - 4 PM, Wed & Thurs 6 - 9 PM, Sun & holidays 1 - 4 PM. No admis fee. Estab 1974 to provide exhibitions of contemporary & 20th century art for the benefit of the university & community. The museum was established to provide members of the university community with an educational & research facility for art, to exhibit traveling shows by nationally & internationally recognized artists & to organize touring exhibitions from the permanent collection. A 6000 sq ft main gallery has movable walls that can be changed to accommodate different exhibitions
Income: Financed by endowment & state funds
Collections: †The Outdoor Sculpture Collection of 53 pieces featuring a 28 x 52 ft mosaic mural designed by Joan Miro; The Permanent Collection, with emphasis on contemporary & 20th century American & European artwork; Ulrich Collection of Frederick J Waugh (painting); collection of prints by Honore Daumier, Arthur B Davies, Albrecht Altdorfer, Harry Sternberg, Anthony van Dyck; collections of sculpture by Ernest Trova & Charles Grafly; photographs by Gordon Parks; prints & drawings by William Gropper; paintings by Josef Presser
Exhibitions: (1988) Ernst Neizvestny: Sculptures & Paintings; Contemporary German Prints; Figure as Subject: From the Whitney Museum of American Art; Kathe Kollwitz, Drawings & Prints. (1989) Three Generations of Photograph's from Edward Cole & Kim Weston; Honore Daumier (lithographs); Frank Lloyd Wright (furniture); Carl Milles: Sculptures & Drawings. (1990) The works of John Steuart Curry; The Humanist Icon; Neonics
Publications: Philip Reisman, The Sculptures of Duane Hanson
Activities: Lectures open to public; concerts; gallery talks; tours by arrangement; traveling exhibits organized and circulated; sales shop sells books

WINFIELD

L **SOUTHWESTERN COLLEGE,** Memorial Library - Art Dept, 100 College, 67156. Tel 316-221-8225; FAX 316-221-3725. *Dir* Gregory J Zuck
Open school year Mon - Thurs 8 AM - 10 PM, Fri 8 AM - 4 PM, Sat noon - 4 PM, Sun 3 - 10 PM, summer Mon - Fri 8 AM - 4 PM. Estab 1885 as a four-year liberal arts college. Circ 30,000
Income: Financed by college budget
Library Holdings: Vols 93,000; Per subs 300; Micro — Fiche, reels
Collections: Arthur Covey Collection of paintings, mural sketches, etchings, lithographs, drawings and watercolors; Cunningham Asian Arts Collection of books, catalogues & exhibition catalogs
Exhibitions: Exhibits of the College's Art Department
Activities: Tours

KENTUCKY

ASHLAND

C **ASHLAND OIL, INC,** PO Box 391, 41114. Tel 606-329-3333; FAX 606-329-3559. *Corporate Art Admin* Sharon Walker
Collection may be viewed through special arrangements. Estab 1972, primary function may be decorative art, but also to establish a creative atmosphere; to enhance community cultural life. Collection displayed in public areas of corporate office buildings
Collections: Mainly contemporary printmaking, emphasis on Americans; paintings, sculpture, wall hangings
Activities: Tours; competitions, sponsorship consists of purchase awards for local art group and museum competitions; provides purchase and merit awards for certain museum and university competitions; individual objects of art lent; originate traveling exhibitions to museums, colleges, universities and art centers in general marketing areas

BEREA

M **BEREA COLLEGE,** Doris Ulmann Galleries, Art Dept, CPO 2342, 40404. Tel 606-986-9341, Ext 5530. *Dir* Robert Boyce
Open Mon - Fri 8 AM - 5 PM, Sun 1 - 5 PM. No admis fee. Estab 1936 for educational purposes. Three gallery areas; exhibitions change monthly; loan and rental shows, regional artists, work from Berea College collections
Income: Financed by college budget
Collections: Kress Study Collection of Renaissance art; Doris Ulmann photographs; prints, textiles, paintings, sculpture, ceramics; Asian Art
Activities: Education Dept; lectures open to the public, 2 - 6 vis lectr per yr; gallery talks; tours; scholarships offered; individual paintings and original objects of art lent to other colleges, museums, and galleries; lending collection contains 500 framed reproductions

L **Art Dept Library,** CPO 2342, 40404. Tel 606-986-9341, Ext 5530. *Dept Chair* Walter Hyleck
Open Mon - Fri 8 AM - 5 PM. Estab 1936. Reference library only
Income: Financed by college budget
Purchases: $1200 annually
Library Holdings: Vols 3500; Per subs 30; AV — Cassettes, fs, Kodachromes, lantern slides, rec, slides, v-tapes; Other — Clipping files, exhibition catalogs, framed reproductions, manuscripts, memorabilia, original art works, pamphlets, photographs, prints, reproductions, sculpture

A **KENTUCKY GUILD OF ARTISTS AND CRAFTSMEN INC,** 128 Main St, 40403. Tel 606-986-3192. *Dir* Anna Reiss
Open Mon - Sat 10 AM - 5 PM. No admis fee. Estab 1961 for the pursuit of excellence in the arts and crafts and to encourage the public appreciation thereof. Maintains an art gallery. Average Annual Attendance: 20,000. Mem: 500; must be a Kentucky resident and be juried for exhibiting status; dues individual $15; annual meeting Nov
Income: $62,000 (financed by grants, contributions, admissions and membership fees)
Exhibitions: Two annual fairs include a members exhibit
Publications: The Guild Record, 6 times per yr
Activities: Classes for adults and children; docent training; workshops; lect open to public, 4 - 5 vis lectr per yr; demonstrations; competitions with awards; individual and original objects of art lent to corporate offices and museums; traveling exhibitions organized and circulated

BOWLING GREEN

WESTERN KENTUCKY UNIVERSITY

M **Kentucky Museum,** 42101. Tel 502-745-2592; FAX 502-745-5943. *Dir* Larry Scott; *Cur of Exhib* Donna Parker; *Cur of Coll & Registrar* Sandra Staebell; *Cur Educ* Dianne Watkins
Open Tues - Sat 9:30 AM - 4 PM, Sun 1 - 4 PM. Admis family $5, adult $2, children $1, members free. As well as offering exhibits and programs of wide interest, the museum also serves as a research and educational resource for scholars, specialists, and academic units of the University. The museum's subject area is the history and art of Kentucky, with supportive areas in American art and decorative arts, and European art. Average Annual Attendance: 36,000
Income: Financed by state appropriation and University
Activities: Workshops for adults and children; docent training; lectures open to the public, 2 vis lectr per yr; gallery talks; tours; individual paintings & original objects of art lent to public institutions & museums; originate traveling exhibitions; museum shop sells books, magazines, reproductions, contemporary arts & crafts, toys, textiles
L **Kentucky Library,** 42101. Tel 502-745-5083.
Open to the public for reference
Library Holdings: Vols 34,000; Per subs 1800; Maps, broadsides, postcards; Micro — Reels; AV — A-tapes, cassettes, Kodachromes, lantern slides, rec, slides; Other — Clipping files, framed reproductions, manuscripts, memorabilia, original art works, pamphlets, photographs
Collections: Ellis Collection of steamboat pictures; Gerard Collection of Bowling Green Photographs; McGregor Collection of rare books; Neal Collection of Utopian materials
M **University Gallery,** Ivan Wilson Center for Fine Arts, Rm 443, 42101. Tel 502-745-3944. *Dir* Leo Fernandez
Open Mon - Fri 8:30 AM - 4:30 PM. No admis fee. Estab 1973 for art exhibitions relating to university instruction and regional cultural needs. Average Annual Attendance: 12,000
Income: Financed by state appropriation
Exhibitions: (1992) Recent Work by Barry Fleming; Computer Generated Installation & Monotypes by Hui-Chu Ying; Recent Sculptures by Dennis Whitcopf; WKU Art Faculty Exhibition. (1993) Duck Blinds - Recent Work by Ivan Schieferdecker; 32nd Annual WKU Juried Art Student Exhibition; National Craft Invitational; WKU Art Senior Exhibition

CRESTVIEW

M **THOMAS MORE COLLEGE,** TM Gallery, 333 Thomas More Parkway, 41017. Tel 606-344-3420; FAX 606-344-3345. *Dir* Moria Hobbs; *Asst Dir* Joan Enzweiler
Open Mon - Thurs 8 AM - 9:45 PM, Fri 8 AM - 4:30 PM, Sat noon - 4 PM, Sun 1 - 5 PM. No admis fee. Estab for cultural & educational enrichment for the institution & area. Average Annual Attendance: 2000
Exhibitions: Full academic season of exhibitions
Activities: Lectures open to public, 1-2 vis lectr per yr; book traveling exhibitions

DANVILLE

M **EPHRAIM MCDOWELL-CAMBUS-KENNETH FOUNDATION,** McDowell House & Apothecary Shop, 125 S Second St, 40422. Tel 606-236-2804. *Cur* George Grider; *Dir* Carol Johnson Senn; *Asst Dir* Alberta Moynahan
Open Mon - Sat 10 AM - noon & 1 - 4 PM, Sun 2 - 4 PM, cl Mon Nov 1 - Mar 1. Admis adults $3, sr citizens $2, students $1, children $1, group rates available. Estab 1935 to preserve the home of the Father of Abdominal Surgery in Danville, 1795 - 1830. Average Annual Attendance: 5000. Mem: 600; dues $20-$1000
Income: $36,000 (financed by endowment, members, private contribution from groups & individuals)
Collections: All furnishings pre-1830; apothecary collection: late 18th & early 19th Century, 320 pieces; portraits & folk art, 1795-1830
Publications: Annual newsletter
Activities: Docent training; lect open to public, 50 vis lectr per year; tours; sales shop sells books, prints, slides, pewter mugs

FORT KNOX

M **CAVALRY - ARMOR FOUNDATION,** Patton Museum of Cavalry & Armor, 4554 Fayette Ave, PO Box 208, 40121-0208. Tel 502-624-3812; FAX 502-624-6968. *Dir* John M Purdy; *Cur* Charles R Lemons
Open year round weekdays 9 AM - 4:30 PM, holidays & weekends May 1 - Sept 30 10 AM - 6 PM, Oct 1 - Apr 30 10 AM - 4:30 PM, cl Dec 24 & 25 & Dec 31 - Jan 1. No admis fee. Estab 1975 to preserve historical materials relating to Cavalry & Armor & to make these properties available for public exhibit & research. The Museum is administered by the US Army Armor Center, Fort Knox & is one of the largest in the US Army Museum System. Galleries feature a variety of armored equipment & vehicles, weapons, art & other memorabilia which chronologically present the development of the Armor branch from the beginning of mechanization to the present
Activities: Retail store sells books & prints

FRANKFORT

M **KENTUCKY HISTORICAL SOCIETY,** Old State Capitol & Annex, Broadway at St Clair, PO Box H, 40602. Tel 502-564-3016; FAX 502-564-4701. *Dir* Dr James Klotter
Open Mon - Sat 9 AM - 4 PM, Sun 1 - 5 PM. No admis fee. Estab 1836 as a general history and art museum emphasizing the history, culture and decorative arts of the Commonwealth of Kentucky and its people. The Old Capitol Galleries located in the Old State House consist of two rooms totaling 2740 sq ft which are used by the Museum to display its fine arts exhibitions, painting, silver, furniture and sculpture, one temporary exhibits gallery in Old Capitol Annex. Average Annual Attendance: 50,000. Mem: 6000; dues for life $300 individual $25
Income: 560,000 (financed by state appropriation)
Collections: Kentucky and American furniture coverlets, furniture, paintings, quilts, silver, textiles
Publications: The Register, The Bulletin, quarterly
Activities: Lect open to public, 4 vis lectrs per year; tours; individual paintings and original objects of art lent to qualified museums; lending collection consists of original art works, original prints; paintings; sculpture and historical artifacts; book traveling exhibitions; traveling exhibitions organized and circulated; museum shop sells books and reproductions
L **Library,** Old Capitol Annex, 3rd Floor, PO Box H, 40602. Tel 502-564-3016; FAX 502-564-4701. *Dir* Dr James Klotter
Library Holdings: Vols 50,000

M **KENTUCKY NEW STATE CAPITOL,** Office of Historic Properties, Capitol Ave, Berry Hill Mansion, 40601. Tel 502-564-3000; Capitol Tour Desk 502-564-3449. *Cur & Exec Dir* Jolene Greenwell
Open Mon - Fri 8 AM - 4:30 PM, Sat 9 AM - 4 PM, Sun 1 - 5 PM. No admis fee
Income: Funded by city appropriation
Collections: First Lady, Miniature Dolls; Oil Paintings of Chief Justices; Statues of Famous Kentuckians including Abraham Lincoln & Jefferson Davis
Publications: Brochures; exhibition catalogs

M **KENTUCKY STATE UNIVERSITY,** Jackson Hall Gallery, Art Dept, Room 205, E Main St, 40601. Tel 502-227-5995. *Gallery Coordr* Jo Leadingham
Open Mon - Fri 8 AM - 4:30 PM. No admis fee. Gallery. Average Annual Attendance: 2000
Income: Financed through small grants and University appropriations
Collections: A small collection of students & faculty work
Exhibitions: Rotating exhibits every 4 wks
Activities: Lect open to the public, 4 visiting lectrs per year; competitions; scholarships; book traveling exhibitions, 2-3 per year

M **LIBERTY HALL HISTORIC SITE,** Liberty Hall Museum, 218 Wilkinson St, 40601. Tel 502-227-2560. *Dir* Carter Lively; *Cur* Mary Elizabeth Smith
Open Tues - Sat 10 AM - 5 PM, Sun 2 - 5 PM, cl Mon & holidays. Admis adults $2, children and students $.50. Estab 1937 as an historic museum. A Georgian house built in 1796, named Historic Landmark in 1972
Collections: 18th century furniture; china; silver; portraits
Activities: Guided tours
L **Library,** 218 Wilkinson St, 40601. Tel 502-227-2560. *Dir* Carter Lively
Open Tues 11 AM - 3PM. Non-circulating library
Library Holdings: Vols 2000
Collections: Books belonging to John Brown, Kentucky's first US senator & builder of Liberty Hall
M **Orlando Brown House,** 202 Wilkinson St, 40601. Tel 502-875-4952. *Dir* Carter Lively
Open Tues - Sat 10 AM - 4 PM, Sun 2 - 4 PM, cl Mon and holidays. Admis adults $1.50, children $.50. Estab 1956. Built in 1835 by architect Gilbert Shryock
Collections: Paul Sawyier paintings; original furnishings
Activities: Guided tours

GEORGETOWN

M **GEORGETOWN COLLEGE GALLERY,** Mullberry St, PO Box 201, 40324. Tel 502-863-8106; FAX 502-868-8888. *Chmn* James McCormick
Open Mon, Wed & Fri noon - 4:30 PM. No admis fee. Estab 1959 as educational gallery with various mediums & styles. Gallery has 100 running ft wall space, portable screens. Average Annual Attendance: 1200
Collections: †Contemporary graphics; †contemporary painting & sculpture; crafts; artifacts
Exhibitions: (1991) Kevin Booher, Electronic generated images; Techniques: Contemporary prints lent by Associated American Artists, N Y (Frankenthaler, Boker, Kahn, Etc). (1992)W Leet Computer Art; Gayle Williamson, Fabric Icons; Student Competition, Senior Exhibition
Activities: Classes for children; lect open to public; 1-2 vis lectr per year;; scholarships & fels offered; exten dept; individual paintings & original objects of art lent to museums

HARRODSBURG

M **OLD FORT HARROD STATE PARK MANSION MUSEUM,** S College St, PO Box 156, 40330. Tel 606-734-3314. *Supt* Susan T Barrington
Open daily 9 AM - 5:30 PM. Admis $2. Estab 1925. Average Annual Attendance: 60,000
Collections: Antique China; Confederate Room; Daniel Boone & George Rogers Clark Room; furniture; gun collection; Indian artifacts; Lincoln Room; musical instruments; silver
Exhibitions: Permanent collection

M **SHAKER VILLAGE OF PLEASANT HILL,** 3500 Lexington Rd, 40330. Tel 606-734-5411. *Pres & Chief Exec Officer* James C Thomas; *Dir of Coll* Laurie Curry
Open daily 9:30 AM - 5 PM from mid-Mar through Nov, hours vary in winter. Admis adults $5.50, children 12-high school $2.50, children 6-11 $1. Estab 1961 to restore, preserve & interpret the architecture, artifacts & culture of Shakers. 2800 acres, 30 historic buildings (1805-1855) Primary Exhibition Building: 40 room center; family dwelling (1824-34) stone three story dwelling full of artifacts & furniture of Shakers. Average Annual Attendance: 140,000. Mem: 2300; dues individual $15, family $25; annual meeting in Spring
Income: Financed by mem, endowment, inn & lodging, sales, village-generated income
Collections: Shaker culture including furniture, textiles, manuscripts, cultural artifacts, architecture & period rooms & shops
Activities: Classes for children; Shaker music programs; lect open to public & members by appointment; tours; museum shop sells books, magazines, reproductions, prints, slides & handmade crafts

HIGHLAND HEIGHTS

M **NORTHERN KENTUCKY UNIVERSITY GALLERY,** Room 338, Nunn Dr, 41099-1002. Tel 606-572-5421. *Dir* David Knight
Open Mon - Fri 8 AM - 10 PM, Sat & Sun 10 AM - 5 PM. No admis fee. Estab 1968, new location 1976, to provide an arts center for the University and community area. Two galleries are maintained, the smaller 15 X 30. Average Annual Attendance: 2500
Income: Financed by university and state funds
Collections: Permanent collection of Red Grooms Monumental Sculpture in Metal; Donald Judd Monumental Sculpture; earth works, other outdoor sculpture, prints, painting, photographs, folk art
Exhibitions: Student exhibitions; state, regional & national visiting artists
Publications: Bulletins, 4-5 per year
Activities: Lectures open to public, 3-5 vis lectr per yr; gallery talks; individual paintings & original objects of art lent to university members to be used in their offices only; lending collection contains 379 prints, paintings, photographs & ceramics

LEXINGTON

M **HEADLEY-WHITNEY MUSEUM,** 4435 Old Frankfort Pike, 40510. Tel 606-255-6653. *Pres* Kathryn Gentry; *VPres* Charles Mitchell; *Interim Dir* James E Seidelman
Open Mon - Fri 10 AM - 5 PM, Sat & Sun noon - 5 PM, Apr - Oct cl Mon, Nov - Mar cl Mon & Tues. Admis adults $3, sr $2.75, AAA $2.75, students $1.25, children 6 & under free. Estab 1968 in central Kentucky for the collection, preservation & interpretation of fine examples of visual arts with an emphasis on the decorative arts. Five principal galleries are maintained. Average Annual Attendance: 20,000. Mem: 500; dues $10, $25, $35, $45, $100
Income: Financed by admissions, membership, benefits, sales, grants & contributions
Collections: Antique boxes, gemstones, jeweled bibelots, minerals; Oriental porcelains; seashells; Objects of nature
Exhibitions: Monthly exhibitions
Publications: Headley Treasure of Bibelots & Boxes (catalog of Bibelot Collection); newsletters, quarterly
Activities: Educ dept; docent training; symposia; lect open to the public; concerts; tours; individual paintings and original objects of art lent; lending collection contains slides, selected works from permanent collections by special arrangement; book traveling exhibitions; museum shop sells books, original art, reproductions, slides, jewelry, shell items & porcelains
L **Library,** 4435 Old Frankfort Pike, 40504. *Dir* James E Seidelman
Open Wed - Sun 10 AM - 5 PM. Estab 1968. For reference, research and visitors' use
Library Holdings: Vols 1500; Other — Exhibition catalogs, memorabilia, original art works, pamphlets, photographs, reproductions, sculpture
Special Subjects: Goldsmithing, Oriental Art, Gemstones, minerals, seashells

A **LEXINGTON ART LEAGUE, INC,** Loudoun House, 209 Castlewood Dr, 40505. Tel 606-254-7024. *Exec Dir* Hal C Harned
Open Tues - Fri noon - 4 PM, Sat & Sun 1 - 4 PM. No admis fee. Estab 1957, to encourage an active interest in the visual arts among its members & community as a whole. Three visual art galleries. Average Annual Attendance: 5000. Mem: 420; dues $25; annual meeting in Apr
Income: Financed by mem, art fairs, donations, grants
Exhibitions: Changing monthly exhibitions; member, group, one person exhibitions
Publications: Annual Membership Book; newsletter, bi-monthly
Activities: Classes for adults & children; lectures, 4 vis lectrs per year; gallery talks; tours; competitions; originate traveling exhibitions

M **LIVING ARTS & SCIENCE CENTER, INC,** 362 N Martin Luther King Jr Dr, 40508. Tel 606-252-5222. *Dir* Marty Henton
Open Mon - Fri 9 AM - 4 PM, Sat 10 AM - 1 PM. No admis fee. Estab 1968 to provide enrichment opportunities in the arts and sciences. Galllery features 8-10

exhibits per year with regional art. Average Annual Attendance: 25,000. Mem: 400; dues $15-500; annual meetings
Income: Financed by grants & fundraising events
Exhibitions: Ten temporary art exhibits per year
Publications: Exhibition catalogs
Activities: Classes for adults and children; lectures open to public; tours; design and children's art competition with cash awards; class scholarships offered; book traveling exhibitions once per year; museum shop

M **TRANSYLVANIA UNIVERSITY,** Morlan Gallery, Mitchell Fine Arts Center, 300 N Broadway, 40508. Tel 606-233-8210. *Dir* Nancy Wolsk
Open Mon - Fri 11:30 AM - 5 PM. No admis fee. Gallery is housed in The Mitchell Fine Arts Building. Average Annual Attendance: 3000
Income: Financed by endowment
Collections: 19th century portraits; 19th century natural history works
Exhibitions: Temporary exhibitions, primarily contemporary works, various media
Activities: Lectures open to public; gallery talks; competitions; originate traveling exhibitions

UNIVERSITY OF KENTUCKY
M **Art Museum,** Center for the Arts, 40506-0241. Tel 606-257-5716; FAX 606-258-1994. *Dir* Harriet Fowler; *Registrar* Barbara Lovejoy; *Preparator* Michael Brechner; *Designer* Rebecca Simmermacher; *Cur* William Henning
Estab 1975 to collect, preserve, exhibit and interpret world art for the benefit of the University community and the region. New building completed and opened November 1979; 20,000 sq ft of galleries and work space. Average Annual Attendance: 30,000. Mem: 485; dues $25 & up
Income: $225,000 (financed by state appropriation and gifts)
Collections: African; American Indian; European and American paintings, sculpture and graphics, 15th - 20th century; Oriental; Pre-Columbian
Publications: Museum Newsletter; exhibitions catalogs; posters
Activities: Classes for children; docent training; lectures open to the public, 5 vis lectrs per year; concerts; gallery talks; book traveling exhibitions, 5 per year; originate traveling exhibitions; museum shop sells books
L **Edward Warder Rannells Art Library,** M I King Library N, 40506. Tel 606-257-3938; FAX 606-257-4908; Elec Mail megshaw@ukcc.uky.edu. *Librn* Meg Shaw
Open to students, faculty & general public
Library Holdings: Vols 40,198; Per subs 212; Micro — Fiche 812, reels 169; Other — Clipping files, pamphlets
Special Subjects: Art Education, Art History, Photography, Theatre Arts
L **Photographic Archives,** 40506-0039. Tel 606-257-8611, 257-8634; FAX 606-257-1563. *Dir Special Collections & Archives* William J Marshall; *Photographic Archivist* Thomas House
Library Holdings: Vols 100,000; Per subs 130,000; Exhibition catalogs, manuscript materials; AV — A-tapes, motion pictures; Other — Exhibition catalogs
Collections: Over 300,000 photographs documenting the history of photography as well as Kentucky, Appalachia and surrounding areas

L **UNIVERSITY OF KENTUCKY,** Hunter M Adams Architecture Library, 200 Pence Hall, 40506-0041. Tel 606-257-1533; FAX 606-257-4305. *Librn* Faith Harders; *Library Technician* Joe Staggs
Open Mon - Thurs 8 AM - 10 PM, Fri 8 AM - 6 PM, Sat 2 - 5 PM, Sun 3 - 10 PM, Summer Mon - Fri 8 AM - 4:30 PM
Library Holdings: Vols 28,000; Per subs 229; Architectural drawing; Micro — Cards 1828, fiche 1903, reels 606; AV — A-tapes, cassettes, slides; Other — Clipping files, exhibition catalogs, sculpture
Special Subjects: Architecture, Furniture, Interior Design, Landscape Architecture, Construction, Historic preservation, LeCorbusier, Urbanism
Publications: News of the Hunter M Adams Architecture Library, quarterly

LOUISVILLE

A **THE FILSON CLUB,** 1310 S Third St, 40208. Tel 502-635-5083; FAX 502-635-5086. *Dir* R R Von Stockum; *Museum Cur* Candice Perry
Open Mon - Fri 9 AM - 5 PM, cl national holidays. Admis $2 non-member fee. Estab 1884 to collect, preserve and publish historical material, especially pertaining to Kentucky. Average Annual Attendance: 15,000. Mem: 3000; dues life $500; annual $30
Income: Financed by membership dues & private funds
Collections: †Books and manuscripts; large collection of portraits of Kentuckians; artifacts, textiles, silver, photographs, maps, prints
Publications: Filson Club History Quarterly; Series 1 and Series 2 Publications (39 volumes)
Activities: Lectures open to public, 6 vis lectrs per yr
L **Reference and Research Library,** 1310 S Third St, 40208. Tel 502-635-5083. *Librn* Dorothy Rush
Open Mon - Fri 9 AM - 5 PM, Sat 9 AM - noon. Estab 1884 to collect, preserve and publish Kentucky historical material and associated material
Income: Financed by endowments, memberships and gifts
Library Holdings: Vols 55,000; Micro — Reels; Other — Clipping files, manuscripts, memorabilia, original art works, pamphlets, photographs, prints, sculpture
Exhibitions: Portraits of Kentuckians
Publications: Filson Club History Quarterly; Series & Series 2 publication (40 vols)
Activities: Lect open to public 6 - 10 per year; tours; individual paintings & original objects of art lent to other organizations for special exhibits; museum shop sells books, reproductions & prints

M **KENTUCKY ART & CRAFT GALLERY,** 609 W Main St, 40202. Tel 502-589-0102; FAX 502-589-0154. *Exec Dir* Rita Steinberg; *Cur* Open; *Gallery Sales Mgr* Kay O Wicks; *Dir Marketing* Sue Rosen
Open Mon - Sat 10 AM - 4 PM. Estab 1981 to advance and perpetuate Kentucky's art and craft heritage. Works by over 400 Kentucky Crafts people

displayed and sold in restored 19th century building. Average Annual Attendance: 60,000. Mem: 600; dues $500, $250, $100 & $25
Income: Financed by membership dues, state appropriation, corporations, foundations and fund-raising events
Exhibitions: Rotating Exhibits
Publications: Made in Kentucky, newsletter three times yearly
Activities: Adult classes; dramatic programs; workshops for artists & crafts people; lect open to the public, 2 vis lectr per year; scholarships & fels offered; book traveling exhibitions, 6 per year; originate traveling exhibitions annually; sales shop sells original art and crafts

M **KENTUCKY DERBY MUSEUM,** 704 Central Ave (Mailing add: PO Box 3513, 40201). Tel 502-637-1111; FAX 502-636-5855. *Exec Dir* Randy Roy; *Deputy Dir External Affairs* Jenan Dorman; *Exhibit Specialist* David McElrath; *Cur* Lynn Renau; *Public Relations & Promotions* Susanne Wright
Open daily 9 AM - 5 PM. Admis fee adults $3.50, sr citizens $2.50, children (5 - 12) $1.50, children under 5 free. Estab 1985 for the Thoroughbred Racing Industry. Average Annual Attendance: 200,000. Mem: 1000; dues $25 - $100
Income: $1,000,000 (financed by Earned revenues)
Collections: 19th & 20th century Equine Art; Archives from Industry; Kentucky Derby Memorabilia
Exhibitions: Permanent exhibits about Derby & Thoroughbred Racing Industry; African-Americans in Thoroughbred Racing
Publications: Inside Track newsletter, quarterly
Activities: Classes for adults & children; docent training; lectures open to public, 2-4 vis lectr per year; student art competitions; originate traveling exhibitions statewide; museum shop sells books, magazines, slides & equine related gifts

C **LIBERTY NATIONAL BANK,** Liberty Gallery, 416 W Jefferson, 40202. Tel 502-566-2081; FAX 502-566-1800. *Dir* Jacque Parsley; *Gallery Coordr* Teresa Gemme
Open Mon - Thurs 9 AM - 4 PM, Fri 9 AM - 5 PM. No admis fee. Estab 1976. Non-profit gallery, local & regional exhibits, national exhibit in fall
Income: Financed by Liberty National Bank
Exhibitions: (1991) United Way Photography Exhibit; Totally Transparent
Publications: Catalogues, 1 - 2 per yr
Activities: Craft instruction; lectures open to public; school tours; invitational exhibits with purchase awards; traveling exhibitions

A **LOUISVILLE VISUAL ART ASSOCIATION,** The Water Tower, 3005 Upper River Rd, 40207. Tel 502-896-2146; FAX 502-896-2148. *Pres* Ronald J Murphy; *Exec Dir* John P Begley; *Gen Mgr* Lisa Work
Open Mon - Fri 9 AM - 5 PM, Sun noon - 4 PM, cl Sat. No admis fee. Estab 1909 to provide programs for local & regional artists, adults & children; slide registry. Gallery area: Price Gallery 125-150 running ft, Brown Hall 125-150 running ft, 3500 sq ft total. Average Annual Attendance: 200,000. Mem: 5000; dues $20 - $500; monthly meeting of Board of Dir
Income: $750,000 (financed by endowment, mem, state appropriation, Greater Louisville Fund for the Arts, grants, rental of space & annual fundraising ev
Exhibitions: Group Invitational; regional artist emphasis; regional competitions
Publications: Visual Art Review, 6 times per yr; exhibit catalogs
Activities: Classes & workshops for adults & children; docent; lectures open to the public, 50 vis lectrs per yr; concerts; gallery talks; tours; competitions with awards; scholarships; exten dept serves Jefferson, Bullitt, Oldham & Shelby Counties in Kentucky & Clark, Floyd & Harrison Counties in Indiana; individual paintings & original objects of art lent to prospective buyers; book traveling exhibitions; originate traveling exhibitions; sales shop sells magazines, original art, crafts and prints

M **SOUTHERN BAPTIST THEOLOGICAL SEMINARY,** Joseph A Callaway Archaeological Museum, 2825 Lexington Rd, 40280. Tel 502-897-4141. *Cur* Dr Joel F Drinkard Jr
Open Mon - Fri 8 AM - 5 PM, other hours by special arrangement. No admis fee. Estab 1961
Collections: Biblical archeology; glass; numismatics; religious materials from Caesarea, Machaerus; Ostiaca; mummy; pottery; sculpture; textiles
Activities: Guided tours; films

M **J B SPEED ART MUSEUM,** 2035 S Third St, PO Box 2600, 40201-2600. Tel 502-636-2893. *Chmn Board of Governors* John W Barr III; *Pres Board Governor* John S Speed; *Dir* Peter Morrin; *Registrar* Charles Pittenger; *Communications Officer* Mark Stewart; *Business Mgr* David Knopf; *Cur* Ruth Cloudman
Open Tues - Sat 10 AM - 4 PM, Sun 1 - 5 PM. Donation. Estab 1925 for the collection and exhibition of works of art of all periods and cultures, supported by a full special exhibition program and educational activities. Galleries are arranged to present painting, sculpture and decorative arts of all periods and cultures; special facilities for prints and drawings. Average Annual Attendance: 120,000. Mem: 4500; dues family $40
Income: Financed by endowment
Collections: Comprehensive permanent collection
Exhibitions: In Pursuit of Perfection: The Art of J A D Ingres; Breaking the Rules: Audrey Flack, A Retrospective 1950 - 1990
Publications: Newsletter, quarterly; Bulletin, occasional
Activities: Classes for children; docent training; lect open to public, 10 - 12 vis lectr per yr; concerts; gallery talks; tours; competitions; individual paintings and original objects of art lent to members; lending collection contains 200 paintings; museum shop sells books, original art, reproductions
L **Art Reference Library,** 2035 S Third St, PO Box 2600, 40201-2600. Tel 502-636-2899. *Librn* Mary Jane Benedict
Open Tues - Fri 1 - 4 PM
Income: Financed by general budget
Purchases: $10,000
Library Holdings: Vols 14,732; Per subs 73; Vertical Files 48; AV — Slides; Other — Clipping files, exhibition catalogs, manuscripts, pamphlets, photographs
Special Subjects: Aesthetics, American Indian Art, Antiquities-Roman, Architecture, Art Education, Art History, Calligraphy, Ceramics, Costume Design & Construction, Decorative Arts, Drawings, Etchings & Engravings,

Furniture, Historical Material, History of Art & Archaeology, Landscapes, Oriental Art, Painting - American, Painting - British, Painting - Dutch
Collections: J B Speed's Lincoln Books; Frederick Weygold's Indian Collection
Publications: Acquisitions list, bibliographies, in-house periodical index, index to J B Speed Art Museum bulletins, index to dealers catalogs

UNIVERSITY OF LOUISVILLE
M **Allen R Hite Art Institute Gallery**, Belknap Campus, 40292. Tel 502-588-6794. *Chmn* John Whitesell; *Secy* Linda Sheehan; *Prog Asst* Matt Landus; *Admin Secy* Andra Jean Owen
Open Mon - Fri 8:30 AM - 4 PM, cl Sat & Sun. No admis fee. Estab 1935 for education and enrichment. There are three galleries: the main gallery, a small gallery & a student gallery
Income: Financed by endowment, and state appropriation
Collections: †Teaching collection; paintings; drawings; prints
Exhibitions: (1993) Arazio & Barbara Fumagalli; Annual Metroversity Juried Exhibition; American Society of Interior Designers; Debra Clem; Allen R Hite Arts Institute Student Show; MA Thesis Exhibiton, BFA Exhibition
Publications: Exhibition catalogs
Activities: Lect open to public, 3 vis lectr per yr; gallery talks; tours; Winthrop Allen Memorial Prize for creative art; scholarships; original objects of art lent to other departments on campus & to other exhibitions; lending collection includes 1000 prints, 36 drawings, 36 paintings; book traveling exhibitions
L **Margaret M Bridwell Art Library**, Belknap Campus, 40292. Tel 502-588-6741; Elec Mail GRGILB01&@ULKYVM(Bitnet). *Head Art Library* Gail R Gilbert; *Asst to Art Librn* Kathleen Moore
Open Mon - Thurs 8 AM - 9 PM, Fri 8 AM - 5 PM, Sat 10 AM - 2 PM, Sun 2 - 6 PM. Estab 1956 to support the programs of the art department. For reference only
Income: Financed by endowment and state appropriation
Purchases: $36,300
Library Holdings: Vols 56,000; Per subs 265; Micro — Fiche, reels; AV — Rec; Other — Clipping files, exhibition catalogs, manuscripts, memorabilia, pamphlets
Special Subjects: Architecture, Art History, Photography, American Art
Collections: †Original Christmas cards; †posters
L **Photographic Archives**, 40292. Tel 502-588-6752; FAX 502-588-8753; Elec Mail BITNEY:JCAND01&@ULKYVM. *Cur* James C Anderson; *Assoc Cur* Cynthia Stevenson
Open Mon - Fri 10 AM - 4 PM. No admis fee. Estab 1967 to collect, preserve, organize photographs and related materials; primary emphasis on documentary photography
Income: Financed through the University
Library Holdings: Vols 500; Micro — Reels; Other — Clipping files, exhibition catalogs, photographs 750,000
Collections: Antique Media & Equipment; Lou Block Collection; Will Bowers Collection; Bradley Studio--Georgetown; Theodore M Brown--Robery J Doherty Collection; Caldwell Tank Co Collection; Caulfield & Shook, Inc; Lin Caulfield Collection; Cooper Collection; Flexner Slide Collection; Erotic Photography; Fine Print Collection; Arthur Y Ford Albums; Forensic Photographic Collection; Vida Hunt Francis Collection; K & IT Railroad Collections; Mary D Hill Collections; Goiswold Collections; Joseph Krementz Collection; Kentucky Mountain Schools Collection; The Macauley Theater Collection; Manvell Collection of Film Stills; Boyd Martin Collection; Kate Matthews Collection; J C Rieger Collections; Roy Emerson Stryker Collections
Publications: Exhibition catalogues; collections brochures
Activities: Lectures open to public, vis lectr per yr varies; gallery talks; educational groups; individual paintings lent to museums & galleries; book traveling exhibitions; originates traveling exhibitions; sales shop sells reproductions, prints, slides & postcards
L **Slide Collection**, 40292. Tel 502-588-5917. *Cur Slides* Ann S Coates; *Asst to Cur* Karen Knowles; *Asst to Cur* Eddie Sue McDowell
Open Mon - Fri 8:30 AM - 4:30 PM. Estab 1930's to provide comprehensive collection of slides for use in the University instructional program; 300,000 catalogued slides primarily illustrating history of Western art. Circ 50,000
Library Holdings: AV — Kodachromes, slides 350,000; Other — Clipping files
Special Subjects: Architecture, Painting - American, Photography, Porcelain, Pottery, Decorative Arts
Collections: American Studies; Calligraphy; Manuscript of Medieval Life

MAYSVILLE

M **MASON COUNTY MUSEUM**, 215 Sutton St, 41056. Tel 606-564-5865. *Dir* Jean W Calvert; *Pres* Bill Hendrickson; *Librn* M M Kendall
Open Tues 10 AM - 4 PM. Admis adults $1, children $.50, students in groups $.25. Estab 1879 to maintain historical records and artifacts for area. Average Annual Attendance: 500. Mem: 200; dues $10-$25
Income: $30,000 (financed by endowment and members)
Collections: Paintings & maps related to area; genealogical library
Activities: Gallery talks; tours; individual paintings and original objects of art lent; book traveling exhibitions; bookstore sells books, prints and postcards

MOREHEAD

MOREHEAD STATE UNIVERSITY
M **Claypool-Young Art Gallery**, Art Dept, 40351. Tel 606-783-2193. *Dir* Thomas Sternal
Open Mon - Fri 8 AM - 4 PM, by appointment. Estab 1922 to provide undergraduate & graduate programs in studio and art education. An exhibition gallery is maintained for traveling exhibitions, faculty & student work. The Claypool-Young Art Gallery is tri-level with 2344 sq ft of exhibition space. Average Annual Attendance: 8000
Income: Financed by appropriation
Collections: Establishing a permanent collection which to date consists principally of prints by major contemporary figures; several works added each year through purchase or bequest. Additions to lending collection include: The Maria Rilke Suite of lithographs by Ben Shahn consisting of 23 pieces; the Laus

Pictorum Suite by Leonard Baskin, consisting of 14 pieces; and three lithographs by Thomas Hart Benton: Jesse James, Frankie and Johnny, and Huck Finn Permanent display of several hundred Eastern Kentucky Folk Art pieces
Exhibitions: A large number of solo exhibitions along with invitational shows & group exhibits
Activities: Educ dept; lect open to the public, 5 vis lectr per year; concert; gallery talks; tours; competitions; individual paintings lent to schools; lending collection contains 200 items, prints, photographs; traveling exhibition organized and circulated; museum shop sells folk art
L **Camden-Carroll Library**, University Blvd, 40351. Tel 606-783-2143; FAX 606-784-3788. *Dir* Larry X Besant
Library Holdings: Vols 1500; Per subs 50; Micro — Cards, fiche, reels; AV — A-tapes, cassettes, fs, motion pictures, rec, slides, v-tapes; Other — Framed reproductions, original art works, pamphlets, photographs, prints, reproductions, sculpture

MURRAY

M **MURRAY STATE UNIVERSITY**, Eagle Gallery, Price Doyle Fine Arts Center, 1 Murray St, 42071-3303. Tel 502-762-3052; FAX 502-762-6335. *Chmn* Dick Dougherty; *Gallery Dir* Albert Sperath
Open Mon - Fri 8 AM - 9 PM, Sat 10 AM - 4 PM, Sun 1 - 4 PM. No admis fee. Estab 1971. Gallery houses the permanent art collection of the University; the Main Gallery is located on the fourth floor & its dimensions are 100 x 40 ft; the upper level is divided into three small galleries that may be used as one or three. Average Annual Attendance: 10,000
Income: Financed by state appropriation and grants
Collections: Asian Collection (given by Asian Cultural Exchange Foundation); Collection of Clara M Eagle Gallery; Harry L Jackson Print Collection; WPA prints, drawings
Exhibitions: Biennial Magic Silver Show (even years); Annual Student Exhibition; Biennial Faculty Exhibitions (odd years)
Publications: Brochures and posters for individual shows
Activities: Vis artists; workshops; demonstrations; lect open to public, 8 vis lectr per year; gallery talks; tours; competitions with merit & purchase awards; exten dept serving Jackson Purchase Area of Kentucky; individual paintings & original objects of art lent; lending collection consists of original prints, paintings, photographs & sculpture; books traveling exhibitions; traveling exhibitions organized and circulated

OWENSBORO

M **BRESCIA COLLEGE**, Anna Eaton Stout Memorial Art Gallery, 717 Frederica, 42301. Tel 502-685-3131. *Chmn Dept Art* Sr Mary Diane Taylor; *Gallery Dir* Herb Weaver
Open Mon - Fri 8 AM - 4:30 PM, Sat 8 AM - noon. No admis fee. Estab 1950. Gallery space is 20 x 30 ft, walls are covered with neutral carpeting. Average Annual Attendance: 4000
Exhibitions: (1990-91) Lawson, Scott, Green; Robbye Clark-Senior Exhibition; Always a River Water Colors of the Ohio; Kathe Baggarly; Aleata Howard: Senior Exhibitions; Tammy Hoffman & Lisa Clary: Senior Exhibitions; Rollie Rhodes & Lisa Howard: Senior Exhibitions; High School Regional Juried Art Competition; Area Women Artists Invitational; Laura Bennett & Molly Hoffman: Senior Exhibitions; Randy Halbec: Senior Exhibition; Brescia Student Juried Art Exhibition; Brescia Art Faculty
Activities: Lectures open to public, 2-3 vis lectr per yr; competitions with awards; scholarships; book traveling exhibitions; originate traveling exhibitions

M **OWENSBORO MUSEUM OF FINE ART**, 901 Frederica St, 42301. Tel 502-685-3181. *Dir* Mary Bryan Hood; *Asst Dir* Jane Wilson; *Dir Operations* Joe Bland; *Educ Dir* Laura Bennett; *Business Mgr* Edith McGuire
Open Mon - Fri 10 AM - 4 PM, Sat & Sun 1 - 4 PM. No admis fee. Estab 1976. Average Annual Attendance: 60,000. Mem: 1000; annual dues $5-$10,000
Income: Financed by endowment, membership, city and county appropriations, grants
Collections: 14th - 18th century drawings, graphics, decorative arts; 19th - 20th century American, French and English paintings and sculpture
Exhibitions: The Regionalists: Three Dimensional Forms (1992) Mid-American Biennial
Publications: Exhibition catalogues; newsletters
Activities: Classes for adults and children; docent training; dramatic programs; seminars & critiques led by major American artists; lectures open to the public, 6 vis lectrs per year; concerts; gallery talks; tours; purchase awards; pre-tour visits to the classroom; film series; individual & original objects of art lent to museums; book traveling exhibitions, 1 -2 per yr; museum shop sells books, original art, giftware
L **Art Library**, 901 Frederica St, 42301. Tel 502-685-3181. *Dir* Mary Bryan Hood
Books for reference; software for lending
Library Holdings: Vols 2000; Art Education Software; Other — Clipping files, exhibition catalogs, manuscripts, pamphlets, photographs, reproductions

PADUCAH

A **YEISER ART CENTER INC**, Paducah Art Guild Inc Gallery, 200 Broadway, 42001. Tel 502-442-2453. *Exec Dir* Dan Carver
Open Tues - Sat 10 AM - 4 PM, Sun 1 - 5 PM, cl Mon & major holidays. No admis fee. Estab 1957 as a non profit cultural and educational institution to provide the community and the membership with visual art exhibitions, classes and related activities of the highest quality. Average Annual Attendance: 16,000. Mem: 600; monthly programs & membership meetings
Income: $80,000 (financed by mem fees, donations, commissions & grants)
Collections: Primarily regional/contemporary with some 19th century works on paper & Japanese prints; teaching collection; Collection includes R Haley Lever; Matisse; Goya
Exhibitions: Changing exhibitions of historical and contemporary art of regional,

national, and international nature; 2-D Competition; Crafts Competition
Publications: Monthly Newsletter
Activities: Lectures open to public; gallery talks; tours; competitions with awards; scholarships offered; individual and original objects of art lent to qualified institutions; lending collection contains original art works, prints and paintings; originate traveling exhibitions; sales shop sells original art & regional crafts

WHITESBURG

C **APPALSHOP INC,** Appalshop Films Media Center, 306 Madison St, 41858. Tel 606-633-0108; FAX 606-633-1009; 800-545-7467 (orders only).
Open 9 AM - 5 PM. Estab 1969 as the Community Film Workshop of Appalachia, part of a national program to train poor & minority young people in the skills of film & television production, now a incorporated non-profit media arts center. In 1982 a renovated 13,000 sq ft warehouse, became the Appalshop Center with offices, video & radio editing suites, a 150 seat theater, an art gallery & educational facilities. Recently a community radio station was added
Activities: Films, plays, music & educational programs to schools, college, museums, libraries, churches, festivals, conferences & community in the region, throughout the US & in Europe, Asia & Africa

WILMORE

M **ASBURY COLLEGE,** Student Center Gallery, 1 Macklem Dr, 40390. Tel 606-858-3511; FAX 606-858-3921. *Head Art Dept* Dr Rudy Medlock
Open 1 - 9 PM. No admis fee. Estab 1976 for the purpose of exhibiting the works of national, local, and student artists. Carpeted walls, and tract lighting in a 20 by 20 ft space. Average Annual Attendance: 2000
Publications: Newsletter
Activities: Classes for children; dramatic programs; lect open to public, 6 vis lectr per yr; gallery talks; competitions

LOUISIANA

ALEXANDRIA

M **ALEXANDRIA MUSEUM OF ART,** 933 Main St, PO Box 1028, 71309-1028. Tel 318-443-3458. *Dir* Mark Tullos; *Cur* Elizabeth Cubbeck-Meche; *Cur Educ* Dorenda J Gifford
Open Tues - Fri 9 AM - 5 PM, Sat 10 AM - 4 PM. Admis fee. Estab 1977 to explore American art of 20th century with emphasis on contemporary art of the south. National Register Building in Downtown Historic District; 2900 sq ft gallery remodeled in 1984; 933 window works - installation gallery visible through 8 x 8 street front window; accredited by AAM. Average Annual Attendance: 35,000. Mem: 600; dues $15 - $500 individual; $250 - $5000 business
Income: $250,000 (financed by membership, grants & donations)
Purchases: $5000 - $30,000
Collections: †Contemporary Louisiana Art; N Louisiana Folk Crafts; †Contemporary Southern Art; Prints & Drawings; †Artist's Books
Publications: Catalogs: Doing it Right & Passing it on; North Louisiana Folk Crafts; Lynda Benglis & Keith Sonnier; Robert Gordy & Robert Warrens; Lin Emery & Emery Clark; quarterly newsletter; September Competition catalog, annual; Richard Johnson/John Scott (March, 1991)
Activities: Classes for adults & children; docent training; workshops; lect open to public, 6 vis lectr per yr; gallery talks; tours; annual Sept competition, international, all media with awards; exten dept serves 7 parishes in Central Louisiana; individual paintings & original objects of art lent; lending collection contains color reproductions, 1500 kodachromes, original art works & video cassettes; book traveling exhibitions; traveling exhibitions organized and circulated; museum shop sells books, original art; junior museum located at 927 Main St

BATON ROUGE

M **EAST BATON ROUGE PARKS & RECREATION COMMISSION,** Baton Rouge Gallery Inc, 1442 City Park Ave, 70808-1037. Tel 504-383-1470. *Dir* Anne Boudreau
Estab 1966 to educate & promote contemporary art. Non-profit, cooperative, contemporary gallery made up of general members from community & artist members. Average Annual Attendance: 10,000. Mem: 40 artist, 200 community; dues artist $80, community $30; annual meeting in Nov
Income: $50,000 (financed by mem & East Baton Rouge Parks & Recreation Commission)
Activities: Dramatic programs; docent programs; multidisciplinary arts (performance oriented); lect open to public

M **LOUISIANA ARTS AND SCIENCE CENTER,** 100 S River Rd, PO Box 3373, 70821. Tel 504-344-5272. *Exec Dir* Carol S Gikas; *Cur* Maia Jalenak
Open Tues - Sat 10 AM - 4:30 PM, Sun 1 - 4:30 PM, cl Mon. Admis Planetarium only adults $1.50, children $.50. Estab 1960. General museum - art, history and science. Center administers the Riverside Museum in the renovated Old Illinois Central Railroad Station with an auditorium, restaurant & sculpture garden. Museum contains changing & permanent exhibits of art, Louisiana history & science. Center administers the Zeiss Planetarium & Old Governor's Mansion, a restored historic house. Average Annual Attendance: 300,000. Mem: Dues $15 - $1000
Income: Financed by membership, city appropriation and donations
Collections: 18th & 20th century European & American paintings; contemporary photographs; Clementine Hunter paintings; Ivan Mestrovic; sculpture; Egyptian

artifacts; Eskimo graphics & soapstone carvings; North American Indian crafts; Tibetan religious art; memorabilia of former Louisiana governors;
Exhibitions: Country Store & Acadian House; Egyptian Mummies & Artifacts; Miniature Train; Discovery Depot, a participatory gallery that introduces children to art (1991) Prints by Richard Diebenkorn; Of Time & the City: American Modernism 1910-1930, from the Sheldon Memorial Art Gallery: American Watercolor; From the Old World to the New: Mexican Paintings
Publications: Happenings, Heavenly Facts, quarterly
Activities: Classes for adults & children; docent training; lectures open to public; concerts; gallery talks; tours; book traveling exhibitions; museum shop

L **Library,** 100 S River Rd, PO Box 3373, 70821. Tel 504-344-5272. *Exec Dir* Carol S Gikas
Small reference library open to staff only

LOUISIANA STATE UNIVERSITY

M **Museum of Arts,** 114 Memorial Tower, 70803. Tel 504-388-4003. *Pres* Linda Bowsher; *Secy* Mark Worthen; *Dir & Cur* H Parrott Bacot; *Admin Asst* Mibs Bartkiewicz
Open Mon - Fri 8 AM - 4:30 PM, Sat 9 AM - Noon & 1 - 4 PM, Sun 1 - 4 PM. No admis fee. Estab 1959 to serve as a constant reminder of the major cultural heritage the United States received from the British People. Two temporary galleries house loan exhibitions and local art work. Average Annual Attendance: 55,000. Mem: 400; dues $10 - $500
Income: Financed by endowment, membership & state funds
Special Subjects: Hogarth and Caroline Durieux Graphics Collection, New Orleans Silver
Collections: Hogarth & Caroline Durieux graphic works; early Baton Rouge subjects; early New Orleans-made silver; English and American drawings, decorative arts, paintings, watercolors Newcomb Crafts: 19th century lighting devices
Publications: Catalogues; newsletter
Activities: Lect, 2 vis lectr per year; gallery talks; tours; competitions; originate traveling exhibitions

L **Library,** 114 Memorial Tower, 70803. Tel 504-388-4003.
Open Mon - Fri 8 AM - 4 PM, Sat 10 AM - noon & 1 - 4 PM, Sun 1 - 4 PM, cl university holidays. No admis fee, guided tours $2 per person. Reference library. Average Annual Attendance: 7500. Mem: 480; dues $20, $25 $100; annual meeting in spring
Library Holdings: Vols 600; Per subs 3; Other — Clipping files, exhibition catalogs, original art works, photographs, prints, sculpture
Special Subjects: Anglo-American decorative arts, drawings, paintings
Collections: English - American decorative arts, drawings, paintings
Exhibitions: English period rooms 17th & 19th century; American period rooms 18th & 19th century; Collection of Newcomb Crafts; New Orleans made Silver; Hogarth Prints; Work by Caroline Durieux; 18th century lighting devices
Publications: exhibit catalogs
Activities: Lect for members only, 1 - 2 per year; tours; individual paintings & objects of art lent to other museums

M **Union Art Gallery,** PO Box 25123, 70894-5123. Tel 504-388-5162. *Art Dir* Judith R Stahl
Open Mon - Fri 9 AM - 9 PM, Sat & Sun 11 AM - 5 PM. Estab 1964, designed for exhibitions for university and community interests. Gallery is centrally located on the main floor of the LSU Union with 1725 sq ft. Average Annual Attendance: 55,000. Mem: 4000; dues $35
Income: Financed by student activity fee, fundraising & grants
Exhibitions: Louisiana Contemporary Craft Exhibition; Compact Competition
Publications: Brochures for local exhibitions, quarterly
Activities: Classes for adults & children; lectures open to public, 2 vis lectr per yr; concerts; gallery talks; competitions; awards

M **School of Art Gallery,** 111 Foster Hall, 70803. Tel 504-388-5402. *Dir* Robert Lyon
Open Mon - Fri 10 AM - 4 PM, Sun 1 - 5 PM. No admis fee. Estab 1934 for special exhibitions planned by faculty committee. Circulates exhibitions of student's arts consisting of 30 - 40 works by students. Average Annual Attendance: 10,000
Collections: Department collection of contemporary graphic works, prints and drawings
Activities: Classes for adults; lectures open to the public, 5 vis lectr per yr; gallery talks; scholarships & fels offered

L **Design Resource Center,** 104 New Design Bldg, 70803. Tel 504-388-2665; Elec Mail BITNET:NOTSTM@LSU.VM. *Librn* Sandra Mooney
Estab 1959. Lending library
Library Holdings: Vols 9,043; Per subs 100; VF 16 drawers; AV — Slides 29,107
Special Subjects: Advertising Design, Architecture, Commercial Art, Decorative Arts, Drafting, Drawings, Furniture, Graphic Arts, Graphic Design, History of Art & Archaeology, Industrial Design, Interior Design, Landscape Architecture, Photography, Restoration & Conservation, Sculpture

L **SOUTHERN UNIVERSITY,** Art and Architecture Library, Southern University Post Office Branch, 70813. Tel 504-771-3290. *Librn* Dorothy Davis; *Librn* Lucille Bowie
Open Mon - Fri 8 AM - 10:45 PM. Estab 1971 to encourage support of fine arts and architecture. Circ 12,000
Income: Financed by state appropriation
Library Holdings: Vols 6500; Per subs 92; Micro — Fiche, reels; AV — Cassettes, motion pictures, slides; Other — Pamphlets

COVINGTON

A **ST TAMMANY ART ASSOCIATION,** 129 N New Hampshire St, PO Box 704, 70434. Tel 504-892-8650. *Pres* Madeline Gill; *VPres & Exec Dir* Don Marshall; *Coordr* Marie-Louise Adams
Open Tues - Sat 10 AM - 4 PM, Sun 1 - 4 PM. No admis fee. Estab 1958 to act as a center for art in the community. Average Annual Attendance: 5000. Mem: 850; dues family $30, individual $20; annuarl meeting in May
Income: $45,000 (financed by endowment & mem)
Exhibitions: Crafts Conference; monthly exhibits; Literary Festival; Photographic

Club
Publications: Newsletter, 3 times per yr
Activities: Classes for adults & children, Artists in the Schools Program; docent training; lect open to public, 10 vis lectr per year; gallery talks; tours; competition with cash awards

CROWLEY

A **CROWLEY ART ASSOCIATION,** The Gallery, 220 N Parkerson, PO Box 2003, 70527-2003. Tel 318-783-3747. *Coordr* Jean Oubre
Open daily 10 AM - 4 PM. No admis fee. Estab 1980 to promote art in all forms. Average Annual Attendance: 50. Mem: 200; dues $10; monthly meetings
Income: Financed by mem
Exhibitions: Rice Festival Poster Contest; Juried Art Show
Publications: Monthly newsletter
Activities: Classes for adults & children; lect open to public, 3 vis lectr per year; competitions; retail store sells original art

JENNINGS

M **ZIGLER MUSEUM,** 411 Clara St, 70546. Tel 318-824-0114. *Pres Board Trustees* Richard Boisture
Open Tues - Sat 9 AM - 5 PM, Sun 1 - 5 PM, cl Mon. No admis fee. Estab 1963 to place the art of western civilization and the area in a historical context. West Wing has permanent collection of American and European paintings and sculptures. East Wing contains a gallery of wildlife art. Central galleries are reserved for a new art exhibit each month. Average Annual Attendance: 20,000
Purchases: 23 paintings by William Tolliver; 1 painting by Vlaminck; 1 painting by Whitney Hubbard; 1 painting by van Dyck; 1 painting by Herring
Collections: Bierstadt; Chierici; Constable; Crane; Gay; Heldner; George Inness Jr; Pearce; Pissarro; Reynolds; Sloan; Frank Smith; Vergne; Whistler; Gustave Wolff; Robert Wood; Sculpture: J Chester Armstrong; Wildlife Art; Louisiana Art
Exhibitions: Rotating exhibits
Publications: Brochure
Activities: Classes for adults; docent training; lectures open to public; tours; individual paintings & original objects of art lent; originates traveling exhibitions that travel to other museums; sales shop sells books, magazines, reproductions; prints

LAFAYETTE

M **LAFAYETTE MUSEUM ASSOCIATION,** Lafayette Museum, 1122 Lafayette St, 70501. Tel 318-234-2208. *Pres* Kathryn Breaux
Open Tues - Sat 9 AM - 5 PM. Admis $3, student $2. Estab 1954 as a historical house. Average Annual Attendance: 2000-3000
Income: $35,000 (financed by endowment, city appropriation)
Purchases: Refurbishing 2 rooms in mus
Collections: Historical †Costumes & Dress, †Documents, †Furnishings, †Objects
Activities: Children's tours

M **LAFAYETTE NATURAL HISTORY MUSEUM, PLANETARIUM AND NATURE STATION,** 637 Girard Park Dr, 70503. Tel 318-261-8350. *Dir* James Whelan; *Cur Exhibits* Cliff Deal; *Cur Natural Science* Bill Fontenot; *Cur Planetarium* David Hostetter; *Registrar* Kathy Ball; *Secy* Karen Miller
Open Mon, Wed, Fri 9 AM - 5 PM, Tues, Thurs 9 AM - 9 PM, Sat, Sun 1 - 5 PM. No admis fee except to out of parish school groups-$1 per student. Estab 1969 to provide a focus on the physical world in order to benefit the citizens of the community. 30 by 130 ft space with architectural glass window walls, interior walls constructed as needed. Average Annual Attendance: 60,000. Mem: 750; annual meeting in Oct
Income: $350,000 (financed by membership, city appropriation)
Purchases: $4000
Collections: Acadian artifacts; Audubon prints; Historical Louisiana maps; Louisiana Indian artifacts; Louisiana landscape art; Louisiana related Harper's Weekly prints; Louisiana shells; Louisiana moths & butterflies
Exhibitions: Rain or Shine: Louisiana Weather; Travailler C'est Trop Dur: The Tools of Cajun Music; Audubon's World: A Window Into Nature; Louisiana Snakes Alive; Louisiana Crawfish: Perspectives on a New World Traveler Outlook Universe; Waterways of Louisiana; Wildflowers of Louisiana; Rain or Shine: Louisiana Weather
Activities: Classes for adults and children; docent training; lectures open to public, 2 vis lectr per yr; lending collection contains 20 nature artifacts, original art works, 400 photos, 1000 slides, 200 Louisiana Indian & Acadian artifacts; book traveling exhibitions; originate traveling exhibitions in Louisiana; shop sells books, regional crafts, posters and souvenirs

UNIVERSITY OF SOUTHWESTERN LOUISIANA

M **University Art Museum,** PO Drawer 42571, 70504. Tel 318-231-5326; FAX 318-231-5907. *Dir* Herman Mhire; *Dir Foundation* Nancy Richard; *Asst to Dir* Della Viator
Open Mon - Fri 9 AM - 4 PM, Sun 2 - 5 PM, cl Sat. Admis fee. Estab 1968 as an art museum, for education of the population of the region. Average Annual Attendance: 15,000. Mem: Dues $1000 - $10
Income: Financed by membership, university, university foundation, state & federal grants
Collections: Paintings by 19th & 20th century Louisiana artists; 19th & 20th century Japanese prints; Henry Botkin: Paintings, Drawings, Collages; Contemporary Louisiana Photography
Exhibitions: (1991) Chuck Close: Editions. (1992) Clarence John Laughlin: Visionary Photographer; Nikken Sekkei 1900 - 1990: Its Ninety Years; The Modernization of Japan; Louisiana Contemporaries: Selections from the ARCO Collection Art in the American South 1733 - 1989: Selections from the Ogden Collection
Publications: Books; exhibition catalogues
Activities: Lectures open to the public; concerts; gallery talks; tours; traveling exhibitions organized and circulated

LAKE CHARLES

M **IMPERIAL CALCASIEU MUSEUM,** 205 W Sallier, 70601. Tel 318-439-3797. *Dir* Jane G Barham
Open Mon - Fri 10 AM - 5 PM, Sat & Sun 1 - 5 PM. Estab March 1963 by the Junior League of Lake Charles and housed in City Hall. After several moves in location, the museum is now housed in a building of Louisiana Colonial architecture which incorporates in its structure old bricks, beams, balustrades, and columns taken from demolished old homes. In December 1966 administration was assumed by The Fine Arts Center and Museum of Old Imperial Calcasieu Museum, Inc, with a name change in 1971. Site of the building was chosen for its historic value, having been owned by the Charles Sallier family, the first white settler on the lake, and the town named for him. The museum depicts the early history of the area. Average Annual Attendance: 12,500. Mem: 150; dues $25 - $1000
Income: Financed by membership
Collections: Artifacts of the Victorian Period, especially Late Victorian
Exhibitions: American Indian Artifacts in Calcasieu Collections; Antique Quilts and Coverlets; Calcasieu People and Places in 19th Century Photographs; Christmas Around The World; special exhibitions every six weeks, with smaller exhibits by other organizations at times
Activities: Tours; Book 6 to 8 traveling exhibitions pr yr; museum shop sells books and museum stationery

M **Gibson Barham Gallery,** 204 W Sallier St, 70601. Tel 318-439-3797. *Coordr* Mary June Malus
Open Tues - Fri 10 AM - 5 PM, Sat & Sun 1 - 5 PM, cl Mon. Admis $1. 2500 sq ft in gallery with approx 200 running ft for temporary exhibits (6 - 8 per yr). Average Annual Attendance: 10,000
Activities: Lectures open to the public; gallery talks; Museum shop sells books & slides

L **Gibson Library,** 205 W Sallier, 70601. *Coordr* Mary June Malus
Open Mon - Fri 10 AM - 5 PM, Sat & Sun 1 - 5 PM. Estab 1971, to display early school books & bibles. Reference Library
Income: Financed by memberships, memorials & gifts
Library Holdings: Vols 100; Per subs 100; AV — A-tapes, cassettes, slides, v-tapes; Other — Memorabilia, original art works, pamphlets, photographs, sculpture
Collections: Audubon animal paintings; Audubon bird paintings; Calcasieu photographs; Boyd Cruise
Exhibitions: History of Imperial Calcasieu Parish, with settings & objects

MINDEN

L **WEBSTER PARISH LIBRARY,** 521 East & West Sts, 71055. Tel 318-371-3080. *Librn* Barbara Slack; *Asst Librn* Beverly Hammett
Open Mon, Wed, Thurs 9 AM - 8 PM, Tues, Fri, Sat 9 AM - 5 PM. Estab 1929 to serve as headquarters & main branch for county. Circ 145,508
Income: $221,353 (financed by parish tax)
Library Holdings: Vols 83,062; Per subs 107; Micro — Fiche, reels; AV — Cassettes, fs, motion pictures, rec, slides; Other — Clipping files, framed reproductions, original art works, pamphlets, photographs
Activities: Exten dept serves the elderly; individual paintings lent to registered borrowers; lending collection contains 54 art prints & 50 b & w photographs depicting parish history

MONROE

M **NORTHEAST LOUISIANA UNIVERSITY,** Bry Gallery, 700 University Ave, Stubbs 141, 71209. Tel 318-342-1000. *Head* Ron J Alexander, MFA
Open 8 AM - 4 PM. No admis fee. Estab 1931. Gallery is 24 sq ft x 26 sq ft with 14 ft ceilings. Average Annual Attendance: 8000
Collections: Kit Gilbert; Pave Brou of New Orleans
Activities: Classes for adults & children; docent training; 6 vis lectr per year; gallery talks; exten dept

M **TWIN CITY ART FOUNDATION,** Masur Museum of Art, 1400 S Grand St, 71202. Tel 318-329-2237. *Dir* William C Pratt
Open Tues - Thurs 9 AM - 5 PM, Fri - Sun 2 - 5 PM. No admis fee. Estab 1963 to encourage art in all media and to enrich the cultural climate of this area. Gallery has 500 running ft hanging space. Average Annual Attendance: 5000. Mem: 380; dues $250, $100, $35
Income: $58,000 (financed by membership & appropriations)
Purchases: $3000
Collections: †Contemporary art all media, approximately 100 works
Publications: Brochures of shows, monthly
Activities: Classes for adults and children; lectures open to public, 4 vis lectr per yr; tours; competitions; book traveling exhibitions

NEW IBERIA

M **SHADOWS-ON-THE-TECHE,** 317 E Main St, PO Box 9703, 70562-9703. Tel 318-369-6446; FAX 318-369-5213. *Dir* Shereen H Minvielle
Open daily 9 AM - 4:30 PM, cl Christmas, New Years Day and Thanksgiving Day. Admis adults $4, children 6-11 $2, group rates available. The Shadows is a property of the National Trust for Historic Preservation. Preserved as a historic house museum; operated as a community preservation center, it is a National Historic Landmark. On the Bayou Teche, it faces the main street of modern New Iberia, but is surrounded by three acres of landscaped gardens shaded by live oaks. Built in 1831, the Shadows represents a Louisiana adaptation of classical revival architecture. The life & culture of a 19th century southern Louisiana sugar plantation are reflected in the possessions of four generations of the Weeks family on display in the house. It fell into ruin after the Civil War, but was restored during the 1920's by Weeks Hall, great-grandson of the builder Mr Hall bequeathed the Shadows to the National Trust in 1958. Property serves as a focal point for advancement of historic preservation, it develops new relationships

among cultural community preservation groups and National Trust members in its area. Responds to community preservation needs by acting as a link between community and appropriate regional or headquarters offices of National Trust. Average Annual Attendance: 30,000. Mem: 300
Income: Financed by memberships in Friends of the Shadows, admission fees & special events
Collections: Paintings by Louisiana's itinerant artist Adrien Persac (1857-72) paintings by Weeks Hall; furnishings typical of those owned by a planter's family between 1830 and 1865
Activities: Docent training; interpretive programs which are related to the Shadows historic preservation program; Members Day during National Historic Preservation Week; concerts; tours; museum shop sells books, original art and prints

NEW ORLEANS

A **CONTEMPORARY ARTS CENTER,** 900 Camp St, 70130. Tel 504-523-1216; FAX 504-528-3828. *Exec Dir* Annette Carlozzi
Open Wed - Sun 11 AM - 5 PM. Admis $3, members free. Estab 1976 to support experimentation & innovative products of work in visual arts & performing arts. Interdisciplinary arts center. Average Annual Attendance: 55, 000. Mem: 3200; annual dues $25 & up; annual meeting in May
Exhibitions: (1992) Impostorphobia; It'll Come True: Eleven Artists First & Last; Discovering Columbus: Louisiana Artists' Open Forum; Arts Against Aids; Architectonic: Reflections on a Sense of Place; Borrello; Avenues of Departure; Twelve Houston Artists. (1993) Soul Shadows: Urban Warrior Myths; Under a Spell; Out of the Ordinary; Arts Connection; Los Angeles Contemporary Artists; The Transparent Object
Activities: Educ dept; classes for adults & children; provides concerts; gallery talks; tours; competitions with awards

M **LONGUE VUE HOUSE AND GARDENS,** 7 Bamboo Rd, 70124. Tel 504-488-5488; FAX 504-486-7015. *Dir* Florence Coyle Treadway; *Asst Dir* Mary E D'Aquin Fergusson; *Cur* Lydia H Schmalz; *Museum Shop Mgr* Kathryn B Youngberg; *Vol Dir* Angelle Thompson
Open Tues - Fri 10 AM - 4:30 PM, Sat 10 AM - 4:30 PM, Sun 1 - 5 PM, cl Mon except for group tours. Admis adults $5, students & children $3. Estab 1980 to preserve and interpret Longue Vue House & Gardens and collect decorative and fine arts. Period 1930-40 house. Average Annual Attendance: 45, 000. Mem: 1000; dues family $25, individual $12, student & senior citizen $7; biannual meetings in Spring & Fall
Income: $450,000 (financed by endowment)
Collections: 18th - 19th century English & American furniture; textile collection of 18th - 20th century English, French, & American fabrics, needlework, Karabagh & Aubusson rugs, 19th - 20th century French wallpapers; 18 th - 20th century British ceramics; Chinese exports; contemporary & modern art, including Vasarely, Gabo, Picasso, Michel, Agam, Hepworth, & Laurens
Publications: The Decorative Arts at Longue Vue; The Queen's Table
Activities: Docent programs; lectures open to public, 8 - 10 vis lectrs per yr; museum shop sells books, reproductions, prints, slides, decorative arts

M **LOUISIANA DEPARTMENT OF CULTURE, RECREATION AND TOURISM,** Louisiana State Museum, 751 Chartres St, PO Box 2448, 70176. Tel 504-568-6968; FAX 504-568-6969. *Chmn* Dr E Ralph Lupin; *Dir Spec Projects* Vaughn L Glasgow; *Dir Coll* Larry Tanner; *Dir of Programs* Tamra Carboni; *Registrar* Deena Bedigian
Open Tues - Sun 10 AM - 5 PM. Admis adult $3, student $1.50, educational groups free by appointment. Estab 1906, to collect, preserve and present original materials illustrating Louisiana's heritage. Gallery is maintained, and has eight historic buildings containing paintings, prints, maps and photographs. Average Annual Attendance: 320,000. Mem: 3000; dues $20 - $35; annual meeting May
Income: $2,000,000 (financed by state appropriation)
Purchases: $40,000
Collections: Carnival costumes (200 items); Colonial documents (500,000 folios); †decorative art (8000 items); †flat textiles (1000 items); historic costumes (6000 items); jazz and Louisiana music (40,000 objects); Louisiana silver (300); maps and cartography (3000); Newcomb pottery and allied arts (750); †paintings (1500 canvases); †photography (70,000 images); †post Colonial manuscripts (500,000); †prints (3000 works); †rare Louisiana books (40,000); sculpture (125 works)
Publications: Louisiana's Black Heritage; Louisiana Portrait Gallery, Vol I; A Social History of the American Alligator; exhibit catalogs
Activities: Classes for adults & children; docent training; dramatic programs; lect open to the public, 6 - 10 vis lectrs per year; tours; individual paintings & original objects of art lent to museums; book traveling exhibitions, 2 - 3 per year; originate traveling exhibitions; museum shop sells books, original art, reproductions, prints, maps and crafts

L **Louisiana Historical Center Library,** 400 Esplande Ave (Mailing add: PO Box 2448, 70176). Tel 504-568-8214; FAX 504-568-6969. *Dir* James F Sefcik; *Archivist & Cur Maps & Manuscripts* Kathryn Page
Archives open by appointment only Wed - Fri 10 AM - 4 PM. Estab 1930, to collect materials related to Louisiana heritage
Library Holdings: Vols 40,000; Per subs 5; Non-circulating Louisiana historical material; Other — Clipping files
Special Subjects: Colonial judicial documents

A **LOUISIANA HISTORICAL ASSOCIATION,** Confederate Museum, 929 Camp St, 70130. Tel 504-523-4522. *Chmn Memorial Hall Committee* Bill Meneray; *Cur* Pat Eymard
Open Mon - Sat 10 AM - 4 PM. Admis adults $2, students & sr citizens $1, children $.50. Estab 1891 to collect and display articles, memorabilia and records from Louisiana history and particularly the era surrounding the Civil War. Gallery is maintained in a one story brick building; one main hall paneled in cypress, one side hall containing paintings of Civil War figures and display cases containing artifacts. Average Annual Attendance: 15,000. Mem: 2000; dues $15; annual meeting Mar
Income: Financed by membership and admissions
Publications: Louisiana Historical Association Newsletter; Louisiana History, quarterly
Activities: Lect open to the public; competitions; sales shop sells books, reproductions and novelties

M **NEW ORLEANS ACADEMY OF FINE ARTS,** Academy Gallery, 5256 Magazine St, 70115. Tel 504-899-8111. *Pres* Dorothy J Coleman; *Dir* Auseklis Ozols; *Gallery Dir & Admin Asst* Patsy Collins Baker
Open Mon - Fri 9 AM - 4 PM, Sat 10 AM - 4 PM. No admis fee. Estab 1978 to provide instruction in the classical approaches to art teaching adjunct to school. Average Annual Attendance: 300
Activities: Classes for adults; lectures open to members only, 3 vis lectrs per yr; academic awards in painting, drawing, sculpture

M **NEW ORLEANS MUSEUM OF ART,** 1 Collins Diboll Circle, PO Box 19123, 70124. Tel 504-488-2631; FAX 504-484-6662. *Pres of Board* Louis M Freeman; *Dir* E John Bullard; *Asst Dir for Art* William A Fagaly; *Asst Dir for Admin* Jacqueline Sullivan; *Asst Dir for Develop* Sharon Litwin; *Asst Dir Educ* Lee Morais; *Chief Cur Exhib* Daniel Piersol; *Cur Decorative Arts* John W Keefe; *Cur Photography* Nancy Barrett; *Editor Arts Quarterly* Wanda O'Shello; *Asst Cur Educ* Ann Moore; *Public Relations Officer* Virginia Weaver; *Registrar* Paul Tarver; *Asst Registrar & Cur Traveling Exhib* Patricia Pecoravo; *Asst to Dir* Alice Rae Yelen; *Librn* Carl Penny; *Chief Preparator* Thomas E Herrington
Open Tues - Sun 10 AM - 5 PM, cl Mon & legal holidays. Admis adults (18 - 64) $6, children (3 - 17) $3. Estab 1910; building given to city by Issac Delgado, maintained by municipal funds & private donations to provide a stimulus to a broader cultural life for the entire community. Stern Auditorum, Ella West Freeman wing for changing exhibitions; Wisner Education wing for learning experiences; Delgado Building for permanent display. Museum opens April 1993 after complete renovations & expansion; gallery spaced doubled & new Courtyard Cafe restaurant & expanded shop. Average Annual Attendance: 150,000. Mem: 10,000; dues $35 - $1000, annual meeting Nov
Income: Financed by membership, city appropriation, federal, state & foundation grants, corporate contributions & individual donations
Collections: Old Master paintings of various schools; Kress Collection of Italian Renaissance & Baroque Painting; Chapman H Hyams Collection of Barbizon & Salon Paintings; Pre-Columbian & Spanish colonial painting & sculpture; works by Edgar Degas; 20th century English & Continental art, including Surrealism & School of Paris; Japanese Edo period painting; African Art; photography; graphics; Melvin P Billups Glass Collection; 19th & 20th century United States & Louisiana painting & sculpture; Latter- Schlesinger Collection of English & Continental Portrait Miniatures; Victor Kiam Collection of African, Oceanic American Indian, & 20th century European & American Painting & Sculpture; The Matilda Geddings Gray Foundation Collection of Works by Peter Carl Faberge; Rosemunde E & Emile Kuntz Federal & Louisiana Period Rooms; 16th - 20th century French art; Bert Piso Collection of 17th century Dutch painting Imperial Treasures by Peter Carl Faberge from the Matilda Geddings Gray Foundation Collection; 18th, 19th & 20th Century French Paintings; Morgan-Whitney Collection of Chinese Jades; Rosemonde E & Emile Kuntz Rooms of Late 18th - Early 19th Century American Furniture
Exhibitions: (1993) Bon Temps Rouler: Mardi Gras Photographs by Sydney Byrd; Between Home & Heaven: Contemporary American Landscape Photography; New Art for a New Building; Treasures of the Church: 200 Years of Faith & Service; Sculpture 1860 - 1960 from New Orleans Collections; Fritz Bultman Retrospective; Passioniate Visions of the American South: Self-Taught Artists from 1940 to the Present. (1994) Songs of My People
Publications: Arts Quarterly; catalogs of New Orleans Museum of Art organized exhibitions; History of New Orleans Museum of Art
Activities: Classes for children; docent training; teacher workshops; lectr open to public, 20 vis lectr per year; concerts; gallery talks; tours including multi-language; VanGo Museum on Wheels; competitions; individual paintings and original objects of art lent to museums; book traveling exhibitions 5 per year; originate traveling exhibitions; museum shop sells books, original art, reproductions, prints, cards, toys and jewelry

L **Felix J Dreyfous Library,** 1 Collins Diboll Circle, PO Box 19123, 70124. FAX 504-484-6662; *Librn* Carl O Penny
Open Mon - Fri 9 AM - 5 PM. Estab 1971 to provide information for reference to the curators, museum members and art researchers. Open to staff and members; general public by appointment
Income: Financed by membership, donations and gifts
Library Holdings: Vols 20,000; Per subs 50; Micro — Fiche, reels; AV — A-tapes, cassettes, slides, v-tapes; Other — Clipping files, exhibition catalogs, memorabilia, pamphlets
Special Subjects: Photography, African art, Pre-Columbian art
Collections: WPA Project - New Orleans Artists

TULANE UNIVERSITY

M **University Art Collection,** Tulane University Library, 7001 Freret St, 70118. Tel 504-865-5389. *Chmn* Richard Powell
Open Mon - Fri 8:30 AM - 5 PM, cl school holidays and Mardi Gras. No admis fee. Estab 1889
Collections: Architectural Drawings; Photograph Collection; 19th and 20th century European and American Paintings and Prints; 19th and 20th century Japanese Block Prints
Activities: Lectures

M **Dept Art Newcomb Col Art Galleries,** 1229 Broadway, 70118. Tel 504-865-5327; FAX 504-862-8710. *Chmn* Richard Tuttle; *Dir* Sally Stanola; *Adminr* Linda Turpie
Open Tues - Fri 9 AM - 4:30 PM, Sat & Sun (during exhibitions) 1 - 5 PM. Average Annual Attendance: 5000 - 7000
Exhibitions: (1993) Stone Sculpture by Jack Kehoe & Horace Farlowe; Undergraduate Student Exhibition; MFA Thesis Exhibit
Activities: Lectures open to the public, 10 - 12 vis lectr per yr; gallery talks; tours; awards; scholarships; book traveling exhibitions, 2 - 3 per yr; originate traveling exhibitions

L **Architecture Library,** Howard-Tilton Memorial Library, Rm 202 Richardson Memorial Hall, 70118. Tel 504-865-5391; FAX 504-865-6773. *Head* Frances E Hecker
Open fall & spring Mon - Thurs 8 AM - 9:50 PM, Fri 8 AM - 4:50 PM, Sat 10 AM - 4:50 PM, Sun 2 - 9:50 PM; summer Mon - Fri 8:30 AM - noon & 1 - 4:50 PM, cl Sat & Sun
Library Holdings: Vols 11,400; Per subs 218; Other — Clipping files, prints
Special Subjects: Architecture

M **Gallier House Museum,** 1118-1132 Royal St, 70116. Tel 504-523-6722. *Dir* Ann M Masson; *Cur* Daisy D Tarver; *Business Mgr* Barbara Lopez; *Educ Coordr* Michele Bray; *Gift Shop Mgr* Cynthia Steward
Open Mon - Sat 10 - 4:30 PM, Sun noon - 4:30 PM. Admis family $9, adult $4, children $2.25. Estab 1971 to preserve & exhibit the house of James Gallier Jr & 19th century decorative arts. Average Annual Attendance: 20,000. Mem: 150; dues $10-$250
Library Holdings: Vols 1000; Per subs 10; AV — Slides, v-tapes; Other — Clipping files, manuscripts, original art works, pamphlets, photographs, prints, sculpture
Special Subjects: Architecture, Art History, Decorative Arts, Furniture, Period Rooms, Porcelain, Silver, Textiles
Collections: 19th century architecture, art, decorative arts, New Orleans lifestyles
Exhibitions: Architectural Details
Publications: Quarterly newsletter
Activities: Classes for adults & children; docent training; lectures open to the public; 2 vis lectrs per year; Retail store sells books, prints, slides, Victorian gifts

M **UNIVERSITY OF NEW ORLEANS,** Fine Arts Gallery, 2000 Lake Shore Dr, 70148. Tel 504-286-6493. *Gallery Dir* Annette Fournet; *Secy* Vernoica Thompson
Open Mon - Fri 8 AM - 4:30 PM. No admis fee. Estab 1974 to expose the students and community to historic and contemporary visual arts. Gallery consists of 1800 sq ft, 165 lineal ft of wall space, 20 ft ceilings, natural and artificial lighting. Average Annual Attendance: 15,000
Income: Financed by state appropriation
Activities: Credit & non-credit classes for adults in conjunction with University of New Orleans; lectures open to public, 20 vis lectr per yr

L **Earl K Long Library,** Lakefront, 70148. Tel 504-286-6354; FAX 504-286-7277. *Chair Reference Servs* Robert T Heriard
Open Mon - Thurs 8 AM - 12 AM; Fri 8 AM - 4:30 PM, Sat 9 AM - 5 PM, Sun 1 PM - 9 PM. Estab 1958 for scholarly & professional research. For lending & reference. Circ 110,140
Income: $2,401,104 (financed by state appropriation)
Purchases: $797,407
Library Holdings: Vols 394,729; Per subs 4500; Art Vols 12,974; art per subs 250; Micro — Cards, fiche, reels

M **KEMPER & LEILA WILLIAMS FOUNDATION,** 533 Royal St, 70130. Tel 504-523-4662. *Pres of Board* Mary Louise Christovich; *Dir Emerita* Dode Platou; *Dir* Jon Kukla; *Chief Cur* John Lawrence; *Cur of Manuscripts* Alfred Lemmon; *Syst Dir* Charles Patch; *Coll Mgr* Priscilla Lawrence; *Registrar* Maureen Donnelly; *Education Cur* Elsa Schneider; *Dir Publications & Academic Affairs* Patricia Brady; *Head Librn* Florence Jumonville
Open Tues - Sat 10 AM - 4:45 PM. No admis fee to Gallery, admis to Williams Residence and ten gallery tour by guide $2. Building constructed in 1792 by Jean Francois Merieult; renovated by Koch & Wilson to accommodate the ten galleries which house a collection of paintings, prints, documents, books & artifacts relating to the history of Louisiana from the time of its settlement, gathered over a number of years by the late L Kemper Williams & his wife. The foundation was established with private funds to keep original collection intact & to allow for expansion. Research Center for State and Local History/Museum. Average Annual Attendance: 35,000
Income: Financed by endowment
Collections: Charles L Franck, photographs (1900-1955); Dan Leyrer, photographs (1930-1970); Clarence Laughlin, photographs (1935-1965); James Gallier Jr & Sr, architectural drawings (1830-1870); Morries Henry Hobbs, prints (1940); B Lafon, drawings of fortifications (1841); B Simon, lithographs of 19th-century businesses; Alfred R & William Waud, drawings of Civil War & post-war; †maps, †paintings, †photographs, †prints, †three-dimensional objects
Exhibitions: Alfred R Waud, Special Artist on Assignment (Profiles of American Cities 1850-1880); Crescent City Silver (19th-Century New Orleans Silver & Silversmiths); The Changing Face of Canal Street; The Roast of the Town (coffee); It's the Law; Charles H Reinike (watercolors); Joseph Rusling Meeker: Images of the Mississippi Delta, painting; Off the Track: Southern Plantation Photographs; Piney Woods People; In Dixieland I'll Take My Stand: Confederate Music of Civil War; Orleans Gallery: The Founders, painting & sculpture; Bound to Please, books; Music in the Street: Photographs by Ralston Crawford; I Remember New Orleans: The Movies; Sugar Bowl 50th Anniversary; Rex, Mardi Gras Memorabilia; Louisiana Alphabet; Comus, Mardi Gras Memorabilia; Kemper & Leila Williams: Collectors/Founders; Stuart Lynn; Louisiana Constitution; Fine Print: Printing in New Orleans 1764 - 1864; A Creole Legacy: Decorative Arts from the Clarisse Claiborne Grima House
Publications: Guide to Research at the Historic New Orleans Collection; exhibition brochures & catalogs; historic publications; monograph series; quarterly newsletter
Activities: Docent training; lectures open to public; tours; competitions with awards; gallery talks; individual paintings & original objects of art lent to museums, institutions, foundations, libraries & research centers; sales shop sells books, original art, reproductions and prints; research collections

L **Historic New Orleans Collection,** 533 Royal St, 70130. Tel 504-523-4662. *Head Librn* Florence M Jumonville; *Reference Librn* Pamela D Arceneaux; *Reference Librn* Jessica Travis
Open Tues - Sat 10 AM - 4:30 PM. Open to researchers
Income: Financed by private endowment
Library Holdings: Vols 15,000; Per subs 30; Maps 500; AV — Motion pictures 100; Other — Pamphlets 7000
Special Subjects: Material pertaining to Louisiana; New Orleans architecture; sheet music; New Orleans imprints; New Orleans City Directories

Collections: Manuscripts Division: unique textual sources on New Orleans and Louisiana History and Culture (family papers and other collections, †newspapers); Curatorial Division: †visual materials, biographical information on regional artists
Publications: Guide to The Vieux Carre Survey, a guide to a collection of material on New Orleans architecture; Bibliography of New Orleans Imprints, 1764-1864

PORT ALLEN

M **WEST BATON ROUGE HISTORICAL ASSOCIATION,** Museum, 845 N Jefferson Ave, 70767. Tel 504-336-2422. *Dir* Karen Babb
Open Tues - Sat 10 AM - 4:30 PM, Sun 2 - 5 PM. No admis fee. Estab 1968, Museum opened 1970, to foster interest in history, particularly that of West Baton Rouge Parish; to encourage research, collection and preservation of material illustrating past and present activities of the parish; to operate one or more museums; to receive gifts and donations; to accept exhibits and historical materials on loan. One room housing a collection of American Empire (circa 1840) bedroom furniture; a large room housing a scale model of a sugar mill (one inch to one foot, dated 1904) & parish memorabilia, two old printing presses; a room 31 x 40 ft for art exhibits; restored plantation quarters cabin (circa 1850). Average Annual Attendance: 3000. Mem: 235; dues $10; annual meeting Jan
Income: $70,000 (financed by mem, gifts & millage levied on parish)
Collections: †Art collection of parish artists; c1830 French Creole Cottage; †Contemporary Louisiana (drawings, paintings, prints & sculpture); †Needlework; †Newcomb Pottery; Old Duck Decoys
Exhibitions: Gallery with 6 shows yearly
Publications: Ecoutez, twice a year
Activities: Gallery talks; tours; competitions; annual Ethel Claiborne Dameron Memorial Series, varied programs

SAINT MARTINVILLE

M **LONGFELLOW-EVANGELINE STATE COMMEMORATIVE AREA,** Hwy 31, 1200 N Main, 70582. Tel 318-394-4284, 394-3754. *Mgr* Reinaldo Barnes; *Site & Museum Cur* Donna Chisolm
Open daily 9 AM - 5 PM. Admis adults $2, children free. Estab 1931 to display & describe 18th & 19th century French lifeways & folk items. Artworks are displayed in an 18th & 19th century plantation home, in the interpretive center of the site & in the 18th century cabin. Average Annual Attendance: 50,000
Income: Financed by state appropriations
Collections: Early 19th century portraits; 18th, 19th & 20th century textile arts; religious art of the 19th century; wood carvings; local craft & folk art
Activities: Docent training; lect open to public, tours; sales shop sells books, postcards & audio-tapes

SHREVEPORT

M **CENTENARY COLLEGE OF LOUISIANA,** Meadows Museum of Art, 2911 Centenary Blvd, PO Box 41188, 71134-1188. Tel 318-869-5169; FAX 318-869-5026. *Dir* Judy Godfrey
Open Tues - Fri 1 - 5 PM, Sat & Sun 1 - 4 PM, cl weekends June - Aug. No admis fee. Estab 1975 to house the Indo-China Collection of Drawings & Paintings by Jean Despujols. Eight galleries; main gallery on first floor 25 x 80 ft; other galleries 25 x 30 ft; linen walls, track lights and no windows. Average Annual Attendance: 18,000
Income: $80,000 (financed by endowment)
Collections: 360 works in Indo-China Collection, dealing with Angkor Region, The Cordillera, Gulf of Siam, Laos, The Nam-Te, The Thai, Upper Tonkin, Vietnam
Exhibitions: Degas Pastel Society; Dutch & Flemish; Italian Renaissance Paintings; Souchon, painting; Twentieth Century Art
Publications: Partial Catalog of Permanent Collection with 21 color plates
Activities: Docent training; lectures open to public, 4 vis lectr per yr; gallery talks; tours; individual paintings & original objects of art lent to qualified museums; lending collection includes one motion picture

M **CLYDE CONNELLY CENTER FOR CONTEMPORARY ARTS** (Formerly Stoner Arts Center), c/o Janis T Woods, 826 Ontario, 71106-1119. Tel 318-226-7412. *Chmn* Bill McElroy
Open Tues - Sat Noon - 5 PM. No admis fee. Estab 1972. Two exhibit areas totaling 700 sq ft. Average Annual Attendance: 5000. Mem: 500; dues $15-$35; monthly board meetings
Income: $100,000 (financed by membership)
Exhibitions: Rotating exhibits of adult contemporary art & childrens art work
Activities: Classes for adults & children; lectures open to public

M **LOUISIANA STATE EXHIBIT MUSEUM,** PO Box 38356, 71133. Tel 318-632-2020; FAX 318-632-2056. *Dir* Dr George Ward Shannon Jr
Open Tues - Sat 9 AM - 4:30 PM, cl Christmas. No admis fee. Estab 1939 to display permanent and temporary exhibitions demonstrating the state's history, resources and natural beauty. Art Gallery is maintained. Average Annual Attendance: 200,000
Income: Financed by state appropriation
Collections: Archaeology; dioramas; historical relics; Indian artifacts; murals
Publications: History of Art; brochures
Activities: Public Archaeology program; films; concerts

M **R W NORTON ART GALLERY,** 4747 Creswell Ave, 71106-1899. Tel 318-865-4201; FAX 318-869-0435. *Pres of the Board* Mrs Richard W Norton Jr; *VPres of the Board* A W Coon; *Secy of the Board* Jerry M Bloomer
Open Tues - Fri 10 AM - 5 PM, Sat & Sun 1 - 5 PM, cl Mon & holidays. No admis fee. Estab 1946, opened 1966. Founded to present aspects of the development of American and European art and culture through exhibition and interpretation of fine works of art and literature, both from the Gallery's own

collections and from those of other institutions and individuals. Average Annual Attendance: 25,000
Income: Financed by endowment
Collections: American miniatures and colonial silver; contemporary American & European painting and †sculpture; painting and sculpture relating to Early American history; †Paintings by 19th century American artists of the Hudson River School; Portraits of famous confederate leaders; 16th Century Flemish tapestries; Wedgwood pottery; paintings and sculpture by western American artists Frederic Remington & Charles M Russell
Exhibitions: Arts for the Parks; Majesty in Motion: The Paintings of Frederick Waugh; American Impressionism; Wildlife: The Artist's View; Images of Louisiana: Paintings by Elton Louviere; The Schmidgall Animal Sculpture Collection; Guy Coheleach Wildlife Paintings; American Historical Paintings by J L G Ferris
Publications: Announcements of special exhibitions; catalogs (47 through 1992); catalogs of the Frederic Remington & Charles M Russell Collections & of the Wedgwood Collection
Activities: Educ dept; lect open to public; gallery talks; tours; museum shop sells magazines, exhibition catalogs, catalogs of permanent collection
L **Library,** 4747 Creswell Ave, 71106-1899. Tel 318-865-4201; FAX 318-869-0435. *Librn* Jerry M Bloomer; *Asst Librn* Eva W Moses
Open Tues - Sat 1 - 5 PM. Estab 1946 to acquire and make available for public use on the premises, important books, exhibition catalogs, etc relating to the visual arts, literature, American history and genealogy, as well as other standard reference and bibliographic works for reference only
Income: Financed by endowment
Library Holdings: Vols 7000; Per subs 100; Original documents; Auction catalogs; Micro — Reels; AV — Slides; Other — Clipping files, exhibition catalogs, manuscripts, memorabilia, pamphlets, photographs
Special Subjects: American Western Art, Architecture, Art History, Bronzes, Carpets & Rugs, Ceramics, Coins & Medals, Crafts, Decorative Arts, Dolls, Drawings, Etchings & Engravings, Folk Art, Painting - European, Painting - Flemish, Furniture, Painting - French, Glass, Painting - German, Goldsmithing, Graphic Arts, History of Art & Archaeology, Illustration, Pewter, Photography, Porcelain, Portraits, Pottery, Printmaking, Prints, Landscapes, Manuscripts, Sculpture, Silver, Marine Painting, Silversmithing, Metalwork, Southwestern Art, Miniatures, Stained Glass, Tapestries, Watercolors, Painting - American, Painting - British, Bibliography, fine arts, history, literature, ornithological works by J J Audubon (elephant folio edition of Birds of America) and John Gould (complete set), rare books and atlases
Collections: James M Owens Memorial Collection of Early Americana (725 volumes on Colonial history, particularly on Virginia)

L **SOUTHERN UNIVERSITY LIBRARY,** 3050 Martin Luther King Jr Dr, 71107. Tel 318-674-3400. *Dir* Orella R Brazile
Estab 1967 to supplement the curriculum and provide bibliographic as well as reference service to both the academic community and the public
Library Holdings: Vols 45,762; Per subs 365; Micro — Fiche 22,990, reels; AV — Cassettes 1121, fs 414, motion pictures 59, rec 293, slides 22,871, v-tapes 16; Other — Clipping files, framed reproductions, original art works, pamphlets 750, prints, reproductions 12, sculpture
Collections: Black Collection, pictures, clippings & motion pictures; Louisiana Collection
Exhibitions: Show Local Artists Exhibitions
Activities: Book traveling exhibition annually; originate traveling exhibitions to YWCA

MAINE

AUGUSTA

M **UNIVERSITY OF MAINE AT AUGUSTA,** Jewett Gallery, University Heights, 04330. Tel 207-621-3000. *Dir* Keran Gilg
Open Mon - Thurs 9 AM - 7 PM, Fri 9 AM - 5 PM. No admis fee. Estab 1970 to provide changing exhibitions of the visual arts for the university students and faculty and for the larger Augusta-Kennebec Valley community; the principal exhibition area is a two level combination lounge and gallery. Average Annual Attendance: 9000
Income: Financed by university budget
Collections: Drawings, paintings, outdoor sculpture
Exhibitions: Six major art exhibits
Activities: Lect open to public, 2 - 3 vis lectr per year; gallery talks; tours

BATH

M **MAINE MARITIME MUSEUM,** 243 Washington St, 04530. Tel 207-443-1316. *Exec Dir* Jean M Weber; *Cur* Robert Webb
Open daily 9:30 AM - 5 PM, cl Thanksgiving, Christmas, New Years Day. Admis adults $6, children under 16 $2.50, under 6 free, group rates available. Estab 1964 for the preservation of Maine's maritime heritage. Average Annual Attendance: 45,000. Mem: 1700; dues $25 & up; annual meeting Aug
Income: Financed by membership, gifts, grants & admissions
Collections: †Marine art; †ship models; †shipbuilding tools; †shipping papers; †navigational instruments; †traditional watercraft
Exhibitions: Maritime History of Maine; Lobstering & the Maine Coast; Family Fleets; Historical Percy & Small Shipyard; other rotating exhibits
Publications: Long Reach Log, quarterly
Activities: Classes for adults and children; docent training; Apprenticeshop Boatbuilding School; lectures open to public, 20 vis lectr per yr; group tours; concerts; gallery talks; individual paintings and original objects of art lent to non-profit institutionswith proper security and climate control; museum shop sells books,reproductions, prints and related novelties

L **Archives Library,** 243 Washington St, 04530. Tel 207-443-1316. *Library Dir* Nathan Lipfert
Open Mon - Fri & by appointment. Small reference library
Income: Financed by membership, admis, gifts and grants
Library Holdings: Vols 6500; Per subs 50; manuscripts; AV — A-tapes, Kodachromes, motion pictures, slides, v-tapes; Other — Clipping files, memorabilia, original art works, pamphlets, photographs
Special Subjects: Historical Material, Manuscripts, Maps, Marine Painting, Painting - American, Painting - Australian, Scrimshaw, Maine maritime history & art, especially shipbuilding
Collections: Sewall Ship Papers, shipbuilding firms business papers
Exhibitions: Maritime History of Maine, Lobstering & the Maine Coast

BLUE HILL

M **PARSON FISHER HOUSE,** Jonathan Fisher Memorial, Inc, 04614. Tel 207-374-2459. *Pres* Margaret Beardsley
Open July - Sept Mon - Sat 2 - 5 PM. Admis $1. Estab 1965 to preserve the home & memorabilia of Jonathan Fisher. The house was designed & built by him in 1814. Average Annual Attendance: 300. Mem: 260; dues endowment $1000, contributing $100, sustaining $25, annual $5; annual meeting Aug
Income: Financed by admis fees, dues, gifts & endowment funds
Purchases: Original Fisher paintings or books
Collections: Furniture, Manuscripts, †Paintings & †Articles made by Fisher
Activities: Lect open to public, 1 - 2 vis lectr per yr; individual paintings & original objects of art lent to state museum or comparable organizations for exhibit; sales shop sells reproductions, & slides

BOOTHBAY HARBOR

A **BOOTHBAY REGION ART FOUNDATION, INC,** Brick House Gallery, Brick House (Mailing add: PO Box 124, 04538). Tel 207-633-2703. *Pres* Lois Goldstone; *VPres* James Wilmot; *Treas* William Burley
Open Mon - Sat 11 AM - 5 PM; Sun noon - 5 PM (June 24 through Sept 16). Estab 1956, originated to help develop an art curriculum in the local schools, presently functions to bring art of the region's artists to enrich the culture of the community. Located in historic Brick House, built in 1807, two exhibition rooms on the first floor and two on the second, one of which features prints, drawings and small watercolors. Average Annual Attendance: 3000. Mem: 465; dues $1 - $25; annual meeting first Tues in Oct
Income: Financed by mem, contributions & commissions
Exhibitions: Three juried shows of graphics, paintings and sculpture by artists of the Boothbay Region and Monhegan Island
Activities: Scholarships

BRUNSWICK

M **BOWDOIN COLLEGE,** Peary-MacMillan Arctic Museum, 04011. Tel 207-725-3416, 725-3062; FAX 207-725-3132. *Dir* Susan A Kaplan; *Cur* Gerald F Bigelow; *Technician* Cathy Brann
Open Tues - Sat 10 AM - 5 PM, Sun 2 - 5 PM, cl Mon & holidays. No admis fee. Estab 1967. Museum consists of 3 galleries containing ivory, fur & soapstone Inuit artifacts, Arctic exploration equipment, natural history specimens, prints & paintings. Average Annual Attendance: 18,000
Library Holdings: Other — Clipping files, manuscripts, memorabilia, original art works, photographs, prints
Special Subjects: Ivory, Manuscripts, Photography, Primitive Art, Sculpture
Collections: †Inuit artifacts & drawings; †exploration equipment; †Arctic photos & films; †Arctic related manuscripts & books
Exhibitions: One permanent exhibition on Arctic exploration & Inuit culture; temporary exhibits annually
Activities: Docent training; lect open to the public, 3 - 7 per year; tours; individual paintings & original art or ethnographic objects lent to other museums; originate traveling exhibitions in Maine & to Arctic communities; sales shop sells books, cards, original art

M **Museum of Art,** Walker Art Bldg, 04011. Tel 207-725-3275. *Dir* Katharine J Watson
Open Tues - Sat 10 AM - 5 PM, Sun 2 - 5 PM, cl Mon & holidays. No admis fee. Estab 1891-1894. Ten galleries containing paintings, medals, sculpture, decorative arts, works on paper, antiquities & Winslow Homer memorabilia. Average Annual Attendance: 28,000
Collections: Assyrian reliefs; Greek & Roman antiquities; European & American paintings, prints, drawings, sculpture, photographs & decorative arts; Kress Study Collection; Molinari Collection of Medals & Plaquettes; Winslow Homer memorabilia; Far Eastern ceramics; Pre-Columbian sculpture
Exhibitions: 14 - 20 temporary exhibitions per year; three major exhibitions per year
Activities: Evening slide lect, gallery talks; film series; story hours; docent training; lect open to the public, 6 - 10 vis lectrs per year; guided tours by appointment only; individual paintings & original objects of art lent to accredited museums; museum shop sells books, reproductions, slides, jewelry

DAMARISCOTTA

M **ROUND TOP CENTER FOR THE ARTS INC,** Arts Gallery, PO Box 1316, 04543. Tel 207-563-1507. *Pres* Nancy Freeman
Open Mon - Sat 9 AM - 5 PM. Estab 1988 for presentation & participation in quality arts with emphasis on education. Average Annual Attendance: 5000. Mem: 1200; dues $15 - $1000; annual meeting in Mar
Income: $150,000 (financed by mem)
Collections: All facets & eras of visual arts history; classical music collection; theatre script collection
Publications: Catalogues, gallery booklets & newsletters
Activities: Classes for adults & children; dramatic programs; lect open to public, 5 - 10 vis lectr per year; retail store sells prints

L **Round Top Library,** PO Box 1316, 04543
Estab 1989 for arts research & reference. For reference only
Income: $150,000 (financed by endowment)
Library Holdings: Vols 2500; AV — Rec; Other — Exhibition catalogs, original art works, pamphlets, sculpture
Special Subjects: Afro-American Art, American Indian Art, American Western Art, Architecture, Art History, Historical Material, Mexican Art, Mixed Media, Oriental Art, Primitive Art

DEER ISLE

M **HAYSTACK MOUNTAIN SCHOOL OF CRAFTS,** Gallery, PO Box 518, 04627-0518. Tel 207-348-2306. *Chmn Board* William Daley; *Pres* Richard Howe; *Dir* Stuart J Kestenbaum; *Treas* Ingrid Menken
Open 10 AM- 4 PM daily. No admis fee. Estab 1980, provide exhibition space for artists & instructors. Gallery maintained for continuous summer exhibition of important American and other national craftsmen, one room 24' X 40'. Average Annual Attendance: 325
Income: $150,000 (financed by tuition income plus annual donations)
Collections: †American Ceramics; †Jewelry
Publications: Annual brochure
Activities: 13 week summer session in ceramics, graphics, glass, jewelry, weaving, blacksmithing, papermaking & fabrics; lectures open to the public, 130 vis lectr per yr; gallery talks; concerts; scholarships; individual paintings and original objects of art lent to schools and banks
L **Library,** 04627-0087. Tel 207-348-2306. *Dir* Stuart J Kestenbaum
For reference only
Library Holdings: Vols 500; Per subs 10; AV — Kodachromes

ELLSWORTH

M **COLONEL BLACK MANSION,** 81 W Main St, 04605. Tel 207-667-8671. *Pres* John Lynch; *Secy* Barbara Ann Foster; *Caretaker/Hostess* Bernadette Keenan-McCormick; *Committee Chmn* Jane Lord
Open June 1 - Oct 15, Mon - Sat 10 AM - 4:30 PM; cl Sun & July 4th. Admis adults $5, Students under 12 $2. Estab 1929. Historical mansion operated by the Hancock County Trustees of Public Reservations. Average Annual Attendance: 3000. Mem: 225; annual meeting second Wed in Aug
Income: Financed by private trust fund, donations & admissions
Collections: Authentic period china, decorative objects, glass, furniture in original setting; carriages & sleighs
Publications: Colonel John Black of Ellsworth (1781 - 1856); David Cobb an American Patriot; Legacy of the Penobscot Million
Activities: Docent training; guided tours; Guided tours; museum shop sells books, magazines, post cards & dried arrangements

HALLOWELL

A **KENNEBEC VALLEY ART ASSOCIATION,** Harlow Gallery, 160 Water St, PO Box 213, 04347. Tel 207-622-3813. *Gallery Dir* Adele Nichols; *Treas* Madge Ames
Open Tues - Sat 1 - 4 PM, cl Mon & Sun. No admis fee. Estab 1963 to foster an interest in and appreciation of fine art. Single gallery on ground level having central entrance and two old storefront windows which provide window display space, peg board covering walls, with two large display screens providing extra display area. Average Annual Attendance: 700. Mem: Approx 100; dues $15; annual meeting first Mon in Jan
Income: Financed by membership and donations
Publications: Newsletter, monthly
Activities: Classes for adults; lectures open to the public, 10 - 12 vis lectrs per year; gallery talks; scholarshps & fels offered; museum shop sells original art

KENNEBUNK

M **BRICK STORE MUSEUM,** 117 Main St, PO Box 177, 04043. Tel 207-985-4802. *Dir* Susan C S Edwards
Open Tues - Sat 10 AM - 4:30 PM. Admis $2. The Museum is composed of a block of 29th century restored commercial buildings, including William Lord's Brick Store. Average Annual Attendance: 10,000. Mem: 1200; dues $15 - $50; annual meeting June
Income: Financed by endowment, mem, small grants, programs, admissions
Collections: Taylor-Barry Period House (circa 1803, sea captain's house); 19th century Americana; costumes; household furnishings; marine artifacts; paintings; tools; manuscripts
Exhibitions: Crafts, fine arts, local history, decorative arts
Publications: Exhibition catalogs
Activities: Lect series; architectural walking tours; field trips; teas & receptions at Taylor-Barry House; sales shop sells books, crafts & gifts
L **Library,** 117 Main St, PO Box 177, 04043. Tel 207-985-4802. *Manuscripts Cur* Joyce Butler
Open Tues - Sat 10 AM - 4:30 PM. Estab 1936 to preserve & present history & art of southern Maine. Non-circulating reference library only
Library Holdings: Vols 3000; Per subs 8; Other — Manuscripts
Special Subjects: Architecture, Fine Arts, Local & State History, New England 19th Century Decorative Arts
Collections: 40,000 items: photographs, documents, fine art & decorative arts
Exhibitions: Through the Artist's Eye: A Maine Woman in the World, Home from the Seas: Kennebunkport's Fabled Sea Captain
Publications: Chapters in Local History, semi annual

KENNEBUNKPORT

M **ROGER DEERING STUDIO - GALLERY,** Ocean Ave & Elm St, PO Box 123, 04046. Tel 207-967-2273. *Dir* Winifred Deering
Open to the public during the summer season and by appointment only the remaining months
Collections: Deering Painting Collection

KINGFIELD

M **STANLEY MUSEUM, INC,** School St, PO Box 280, 04947. Tel 207-265-2729. *Dir* Susan S Davis, MA; *Secy* Rose B Oswald, BA
Admis $2. Estab 1982. Average Annual Attendance: 2000. Mem: 525; dues $10 - $1000; annual meetings in July
Income: $50,000 (financed by endowment, membership, donations & grants)
Purchases: $35,000 (steam car)
Collections: Collection of †steam cars, †photography & †violins
Exhibitions: Steam cars, violins & photography
Publications: Newsletter; quarterly
Activities: Classes for adults & children in dramatic & docent programs; lect open to the public, 2 vis lectr per yr; museum shop sells books, magazines & prints

LEWISTON

M **BATES COLLEGE,** Museum of Art, Olin Art Center, 04240. Tel 207-786-6158; FAX 207-786-6123. *Dir* Genetta McLean; *Asst Cur* Bill Low
Open Tues - Sat 10 AM - 4 PM, Sun 1 - 5 PM; cl Mon & major holidays. No admis fee. Estab in the Olin Arts Center, Oct 1986 to acquaint the student body and the community with works recognized artists
Collections: Marsden Hartley Drawings (99) Paintings (2); 19th & 20th Century American and European Paintings and Prints; 17th & 18th Century Dutch, English, French and Italian Paintings One Zorach Sculpture; The Little Family Antique Collection; 19th & 20th Century American and European Paintings and Prints; 17th & 18th Century Dutch, English, French and Italian Landscapes and Portraits
Exhibitions: Changing monthly exhibitions
Activities: Lectures open to public; concerts; gallery talks; individual paintings & original objects of art lent to museums, college & university galleries

OGUNQUIT

A **BARN GALLERY ASSOCIATES, INC,** Bourne's Lane, PO Box 2029, 03907. Tel 207-646-5370, 363-6131 (winter). *Pres* Adrian Asherman; *VPres* Patricia Pope; *Dir* Donna McNeil; *Treas* Timothy Ellis; *Asst Dir* Scottie Frier
Open Mon - Sat 10 AM - 5 PM; Sun 2 - 5 PM (mid-June through mid-Sept), evenings Tues & Thurs 7 - 9 PM, Thurs 10 AM - 9 PM. No admis fee for exhibits, nominal fee for programs. Estab 1959 as a charitable, educational institution. Maintains two main galleries, the Collector's Gallery of unframed works and J Scott Smart outdoor sculpture court. Average Annual Attendance: 15,000. Mem: Dues $500 - $15; annual meetings in Aug
Income: Financed by memberships, endowment fund, program admissions
Exhibitions: Exhibitions during the summer
Publications: A Century of Color: 1886-1986
Activities: Classes for adults and children; workshops; films and demonstrations; art auction; lect open to public; concerts; gallery talks

M **OGUNQUIT MUSEUM OF AMERICAN ART** (Formerly Museum of Art of Ogunquit), 183 Shore Rd, PO Box 815, 03907. Tel 207-646-4909. *Dir* John Dirks; *Cur* Michael Culver; *Assoc Dir* A B Brook
Open July 1 - Sept 15 Mon - Sat 10:30 AM - 5 PM, Sun 2 - 5 PM. No admis fee. Estab 1952 to collect, preserve & exhibit 20th century American art. Museum consists of 4 interior galleries; central gallery provides an expansive view of the Atlantic Ocean & the rockbound coast; outdoor sculpture garden. Average Annual Attendance: 10,000. Mem: 330; dues Benefactor $5000, Patron $1000, Donor $500, Business $250, Associate $100, Couple $50, Individual $25
Income: Financed by endowment, membership, donations
Purchases: Recent additions to Collection: works by Charles Woodbury, Isabel Bishop, Gertrude Fiske, Dozier Bell, Jack Levine
Collections: Paintings, drawings & sculpture by 20th Century contemporary Americans, including Marsh, Burchfield, Hartley, Lachaise, Tobey, Kuhn, Strater, Graves, Levine & Marin
Exhibitions: (1991) John Laurent Retrospectivetrospectives. (1992) Walt Kuhn & Jack Levine Retrospectives
Publications: Exhibition catalog, annually; Museum Bulletin
Activities: Individual paintings and original objects of art lent (restricted list only, available for short periods to museums and galleries); museum shop sells posters, postcards, museum catalogs, art books
L **Reference Library,** PO Box 815, 03907. Tel 207-646-4909.
Library Holdings: Vols 250; Other — Clipping files, exhibition catalogs, manuscripts, memorabilia, original art works, pamphlets, photographs, reproductions

ORONO

M **UNIVERSITY OF MAINE,** Museum of Art, 109 Carnegie Hall, 04469. Tel 207-581-3255. *Dir* Charles A Shepard III; *Admin Asst* Faye Boyle; *Exhibits Preparator* Stephen Ringle
Open Mon - Fri 9 AM - 4:30 PM, Sat 1 - 4 PM, wkend hrs by appointment. Estab 1946 to add to the cultural life of the university student; to be a service to Maine artists; to promote good & important art, both historic and modern. Average Annual Attendance: 15,000. Mem: 180; dues $25 - $100
Income: Financed by mem & state appropriation
Collections: The University Collection has grown to a stature which makes it a

nucleus in the state for historic & contemporary art, in all media. It includes more than 5200 original works of art
Exhibitions: John Buck: New Prints; Acadian Hard Times: The St John Valley During the Depression; Edmund Schildknecht: Small Towns; James Linehan: Retrospective
Publications: Biennial catalogs & exhibition notes
Activities: Lectures open to public; individual paintings lent to campus offices; traveling exhibitions, 89 per year; originate traveling exhibitions

PEMAQUID POINT

A **PEMAQUID GROUP OF ARTISTS,** Lighthouse Park (Mailing add: c/o Mrs Edward Wise, New Harbor, 04554). Tel 207-677-2560, 677-2752. *Pres* Edward B Wise; *Secy* Mrs Edward Wise; *Gallery Hostess* Sheila Jackovich; *Treas* Maude Olson
Open Mon - Sat 10:30 AM - 5 PM, Sun 1 - 5 PM. Admis by donation. Estab 1929 to exhibit and sell paintings, sculpture, carvings by members, and to give scholarships. Maintains an art gallery, open July through Columbus Day. Average Annual Attendance: 8000. Mem: 31, must be residents of the Bristol Peninsula; annual meeting Oct 13
Income: Financed by dues, patrons, commissions on paintings and sculpture
Exhibitions: Summer members exhibition
Activities: Scholarships; gallery sells original art

POLAND SPRING

M **UNITED SOCIETY OF SHAKERS,** Shaker Museum, Sabbathday Lake, 04274. Tel 207-926-4597. *Dir* Leonard L Brooks; *Archivist* Ann Gilbert; *Cur* Br Arnold Hadd
Open Mon - Sat 10 AM - 4:30 PM. Admis for tours: adults $3, children (6-12) $1.50, under 6 free with adult. Estab 1931, incorporated 1971, to preserve for educational and cultural purposes Shaker artifacts, publications, manuscripts and works of art; to provide facilities for educational and cultural activities in connection with the preservation of the Shaker tradition; to provide a place of study and research for students of history and religion
Collections: †Drawings & paintings by Shaker artists; †Shaker textiles; †community industries; †furniture; †manuscripts; †metal & wooden ware
Exhibitions: Shaker Oval Box Making; Winter Life
Publications: The Shaker Quarterly
Activities: Classes for adults; workshops in summer for herb dyeing, oval box making, cultivating, weaving, spinning, photography, baskets; lect open to public; concerts; tours; individual paintings & original objects of art lent to institutions mounting exhibits; museum shop sells books, reproductions, prints, slides, herbs produced in the community, yarn from flock, woven items
L **The Shaker Library,** Sabbathday Lake, 04274. Tel 207-926-4597. *Dir* Leonard Brooks; *Archivist* Anne Gilbert; *Cur* Br Arnold Hadd
Open Mon - Fri 8:30 AM - 4:30 PM. For reference only
Library Holdings: Vols 10,000; Per subs 70; ephemera; Micro — Prints 317, reels 353; AV — A-tapes, cassettes, fs, motion pictures, rec, slides, v-tapes; Other — Clipping files, exhibition catalogs, manuscripts, photographs, prints
Special Subjects: Architecture, Crafts, Folk Art, Furniture, Historical Material, History of Art & Archaeology, Manuscripts, Maps, Mixed Media, Photography, Posters, Textiles, Video, Woodcuts, American Communal Societies, Early American Technology, Herbology
Collections: The Koreshan Unity; The Religious Society of Friends
Publications: The Shaker Quarterly

PORTLAND

A **MAINE HISTORICAL SOCIETY,** 485 Congress St, 04101. Tel 207-774-1822. *Dir* Elizabeth J Miller
Open June - Sept Mon - Fri 10 AM - 5 PM, cl State & Federal holidays. No admis fee. Estab 1822 to collect, preserve & teach the history of Maine; the society owns & operates a historical research library & the Wadsworth - Longfellow House of 1785. Mem: 2100; dues $20; annual meeting 3rd Sat of June
Publications: Maine Historical Society, quarterly; tri-annual monograph
M **Wadsworth-Longfellow House,** 485 Congress St, 04101. Tel 207-774-1822, 772-1807. *Head Museum Servs* Nan Cumming
Open June - mid-Oct Tues - Sat 10 AM - 4 PM. Admis adults $3, children $1. Average Annual Attendance: 9500.
Income: Financed by donations, admis, dues & endowment income
Collections: Maine furniture; glass; historic artifacts; paintings; photographs; pottery; prints; textiles; Maine artists; Maine portraits, seascapes
Publications: Quarterly, special publications
Activities: Educ dept; docent training; individual paintings & original objects of art lent to museums; museum shop sells books, reproductions, prints & slides
L **Library,** 485 Congress St, 04101. Tel 207-774-1822. *Dir Library Servs* Nicholas Noyes; *Research & Reference Asst* Stephen T Seames; *Cur Museum Coll & Longfellow House* Nan Cumming
Open Tues, Wed & Fri 9 AM - 5 PM, Thurs 9 AM - 7 PM, 2nd Sat of each month 9 AM - 5 PM. Admis $3. Average Annual Attendance: 4000. Mem: 2000
Library Holdings: Vols 65,000; Other — Manuscripts
Activities: Classes for adults & children; workshops; lectures open to the public, 6 vis lectr per year; tours; lending collection contains original objects of art

M **PORTLAND MUSEUM OF ART,** 7 Congress Square, 04101. Tel 207-775-6148. *Dir* Barbara Shissler Nosanow; *Cur Coll* Jessica Nicoll; *Registrar* Michelle Butterfield; *Educ Dir* Wes LaFountain; *Public Relations Dir* Lisa Austin; *Development Dir* Marilyn Pyhrberg; *Financial Officer* Elena Murdoch
Open Tues - Sat 10 AM - 5 PM, Thurs until 9 PM, Sun noon - 5 PM. Admis adults $3.50 sr citizens & students $2.50, children 6 -16 yrs $1, children under 6 free, Thurs 5 - 9 free. Estab 1882 as a non-profit educational institution based on the visual arts and critical excellence. The Museum includes the McLellan-Sweat House, built in 1800, a Registered National Historic Landmark; the LDM Sweat Memorial Galleries, built in 1911; & the Charles Shipman Payson Building, built

in 1983, designed by Henry N Cobb. This building is named for Mr Charles Shipman Payson, whose gift of 17 Winslow Homer paintings spurred expansion. Average Annual Attendance: 100,000. Mem: 3400; dues $20 - $5000
Income: $1,291,855 (financed by endowment, membership, private & corporate donations, grants from national, state & municipal organizations)
Purchases: $62,000
Collections: †19th & 20th century American & European paintings; neo-classic American sculpture; †contemporary prints; †State of Maine Collection of artists associated with Maine including Winslow Homer, Andrew Wyeth & Marsden Hartley; †American decorative arts of the Federal period; †American glass
Exhibitions: Rockwell Kent; John Hultberg; On the Line: The New Color Photojournalism; Skowhegan: A Ten-Year Retrospective 1975-1985
Publications: Bulletin, monthly; exhibition catalogs; general information brochure
Activities: Classes for adults & children; docent training; lectures open to public; tours; gallery talks; concerts; films; competitions; members' openings of exhibitions; individual paintings and original objects of art lent to museums; museum shop sells books, reproductions, prints, posters, cards, jewelry, gifts & items by Maine craftsmen

L **PORTLAND PUBLIC LIBRARY,** Art Dept, 5 Monument Square, 04101. Tel 207-871-1700. *Dir* Sheldon Kaye; *Art Specialist* Steven Goldberg
Open Mon, Wed & Fri 9 AM - 6 PM, Tues & Thurs Noon - 9 PM, Sat 9 AM - 5 PM. Estab 1867 as the public library for city of Portland. Circ 51,700
Income: Financed by endowment, city & state appropriation
Purchases: $32,000
Library Holdings: Vols 17,400; Per subs 96; Micro — Fiche, reels; AV — Cassettes, motion pictures, rec, v-tapes; Other — Clipping files, exhibition catalogs, original art works, pamphlets, sculpture
Collections: †Costume Book Collection; †Maine Sheet Music; Press Books - †Anthoensen Press, Mosher Press
Exhibitions: Monthly exhibits concentrating on Portland & Maine artists
Activities: Lect open to the public; gallery talks

L **PORTLAND SCHOOL OF ART,** Library, 619 Congress St, 04101. Tel 207-775-5153. *Librn* Edna Keyes; *Technical Services Librn* Mark Knierim
Open Mon - Thurs 8 AM - 9:30 PM, Fri 8 AM - 5 PM, Sat & Sun 11 AM - 4 PM. Estab 1973, to support the curriculum and serve the needs of students and faculty. Circ 12,000
Income: $20,000
Purchases: $15,000
Library Holdings: Vols 18,000; Per subs 110; AV — A-tapes 56, cassettes, lantern slides, slides 40,000, v-tapes; Other — Clipping files, exhibition catalogs, pamphlets
Special Subjects: Advertising Design, Art History, Crafts, Decorative Arts, Etchings & Engravings, Furniture, Graphic Arts, Graphic Design, Printmaking, Prints, Sculpture, Textiles, Woodcuts, Antiquities, Costumes, Crafts, Decorative Arts, Dolls, Drafting, Drawings, Enamels, Etchings & Engravings, Ethnology
M **Baxter Gallery,** 04101. Tel 207-775-5152. *Dir* Susan Waller
Open Tues, Wed, Fri - Sun 11 AM - 4 PM, Thurs 11 AM - 9 PM. No admis fee. Gallery estab 1983 to present temporary exhibitions of contemporary art & design. 1800 sq ft gallery located on third floor of Romanesque revival building. Average Annual Attendance: 10,000
Income: $38,700
Exhibitions: (1991-92) Imperiled Shores; As Seen By Both Sides: American & Vietnamese Artists Look at the War
Publications: Exhibition catalogues, 2 yearly
Activities: Tours of exhibitions; lectures open to public; originate traveling exhibitions

M **VICTORIA SOCIETY OF MAINE,** Victoria Mansion - Morse Libby House, 109 Danforth St, 04101-4504. Tel 207-772-4841. *Pres* Beth Holmes; *Dir* Bruce T Sherwood
Open Tues - Sat 10 AM - 4 PM, Sun 1 - 4 PM June - Aug, Tues - Sat 10 AM - 1 PM, Sun 1 - 4 PM Sept, other months by appointment. Admis adults $2, children under 12 $.50. Estab 1943 to display Italian Villa, Victorian Period, built by Henry Austin of New Haven, Connecticut in 1858-1860. Average Annual Attendance: 9000. Mem: 550; dues $15; annual meeting Apr
Income: Financed by membership, tours & special activities, grants & donations
Special Subjects: Architecture, Decorative Arts, Furniture, Glass, Historical Material, Interior Design, Landscape Architecture, Landscapes, Painting - American, Period Rooms, Restoration & Conservation
Collections: Original Interior-Exterior and Original Furnishings, Gifts and Loans of the Victorian Period
Exhibitions: 19th century architecture & life
Activities: Classes for children; dramatic programs; docent training; lect open to public; 2 vis lectr per yr; concerts; tours; museum shop sells books & slides

ROCKLAND

M **WILLIAM A FARNSWORTH LIBRARY AND ART MUSEUM,** 19 Elm St, PO Box 466, 04841. Tel 207-596-6457. *Dir* Christopher B Crosman; *Development Dir* Mary Alice Bird; *Registrar* Edith Murphy; *Education Coordr* Debra Vendetti
Open Tues - Sat 10 AM - 5 PM, Sun 1 - 5 PM, Mon (June - Sept) 10 AM - 5 PM. Admis $3. Estab 1948 to house, preserve & exhibit American art. Six galleries house permanent & changing exhibitions. Average Annual Attendance: 60,000. Mem: 2200; dues $25 & up
Income: Financed by endowment & public support
Collections: American Art; American Decorative Arts; European Fine Arts
Publications: Annual report, quarterly newsletter, exhibit catalogs
Activities: Classes for adults & children; lect open to public; concerts; gallery talks; competitions; individual paintings & original objects of art lent to other museums & galleries; originate traveling exhibitions; museum shop sells books, original art, reproductions & prints

L **Library,** 19 Elm St, 04841. Tel 207-596-6457. *Librn* Barbara C Watson
Estab 1948. Art reference only. Archives on American artists, including papers of
Louise Nevelson, Andrew Wyeth, N C Wyeth, George Bellows, Robert Indiana
& Waldo Peirce
Library Holdings: Vols 4000; Per subs 10; Other — Clipping files, exhibition
catalogs
Special Subjects: Art History, Etchings & Engravings, Folk Art, History of Art
& Archaeology, Marine Painting, Painting - American, Period Rooms,
Printmaking, Watercolors
Collections: American, Oriental & European art & decorative arts

ROCKPORT

A **MAINE COAST ARTISTS,** Art Gallery, Russell Ave, PO Box 147, 04856. Tel
207-236-2875. *Dir* Paula M Paulette
Open Tues - Wed & Fri - Sun 10 AM - 5 PM, Thurs 10 AM - 9 PM (May 23 -
Sept 27). No admis fee. Estab 1952 to show the works of contemporary Maine
artists. Gallery building was an old livery stable & fire station overlooking
Rockport Harbor. Average Annual Attendance: 14,000. Mem: 800; dues $30 -
$500; annual meeting Nov
Income: Financed by mem, contributions, grants, handling fees, annual art
auction
Exhibitions: Seasonal: varied exhibitions of contemporary Maine art
Publications: Quarterly newsletter; exhibition catalogues; brochures
Activities: Educ dept; classes for adults & children; docent training; lect open to
the public, 5 vis lectr per year; concerts; gallery talks; tours; originate traveling
exhibitions to museums, galleries & universities who meet facility requirements;
sales shop sells books, magazines, original art, prints, fine crafts & t-shirts

A **MAINE PHOTOGRAPHIC WORKSHOPS,** 2 Central St, 04856. Tel 207-236-
8581. *Founder & Dir* David H Lyman
Open Mon - Sun 9 AM - 5 PM & 7 - 9 PM June - Aug. Admis lectures $2.50.
Estab 1973 as photographic center. Contains four separate spaces for the display
of vintage & contemporary photographers. Average Annual Attendance: 10,000.
Mem: 1400; dues $20; annual meetings Nov
Income: $2,000,000 (financed by membership, tuitions, sales & accommodations
Collections: Eastern Illustrating Archive containing 100,000 vintage glass plates;
The Kosti Ruohomaa Collection, prints of Life photographers; Master Work
Collection; Paul Caponigro Archive, prints
Exhibitions: Forty photographic exhibitions
Publications: The Work Print, bi-monthly newsletter; Catalogues - Programs,
semi-annual
Activities: Classes for adults & children; dramatic programs; lectures open to
public, 50 vis lectr per yr; competitions with awards; scholarships offered; lending
collection contains photographs; book traveling exhibitions; originate traveling
exhibitions; sales shop sells books, magazines, original art, reproductions, prints,
photographic equipment & supplies

L **Workshop Library,** Union Hall, 2 Central St, 04856. *Librn* Deanna Bonner-
Ganter
Open Mon - Wed 9 AM - 5 PM & 7 - 9 PM, Thur - Sun 9 AM - 5 PM. Estab
1975 to support student studies
Purchases: $2500
Library Holdings: Vols 600; Per subs 45; Micro — Cards, prints; AV — A-tapes,
cassettes, fs, Kodachromes, lantern slides, motion pictures, rec, slides, v-tapes;
Other — Clipping files, exhibition catalogs, framed reproductions, memorabilia,
original art works, pamphlets, photographs, reproductions
Special Subjects: Photographic technical & esthetic subjects, photographic
history

SACO

M **YORK INSTITUTE MUSEUM,** 371 Main St, 04072. Tel 207-282-3031, 283-
3861. *Exec Dir* Emerson W Baker
Open Tues, Wed & Fri 1 - 4 PM, Thurs 1 - 8 PM May - Oct, also Sat 1 - 4 PM
July & Aug, Tues & Wed 1 - 4 PM, Thurs 1 - 8 PM Nov - Apr. Admis adult $2,
sr citizens & student $1, groups $.50. Estab 1867 as a museum of regional history
& culture. Permanent collections feature Maine furniture, decorative arts &
paintings, 1780-1820. Special exhibitions on regional art, social history, industrial
history. Average Annual Attendance: 4500. Mem: 300; dues, perpetual $1000,
life $500, contributing $50, family $25, sr citizen family $20, single $15; annual
meeting 3rd Wed in Sept
Income: Financed by endowment, private & corporate contributions, federal,
state & municipal support
Collections: Federal period Maine decorative arts; glass; historical material;
paintings; pewter; sculpture; silver
Activities: Classes for adults & children; dramatic programs; docent training; lect
open to public, 8 vis lectr per year; concerts; gallery talks; tours; exten dept;
individual paintings and original objects of art lent to other museums; museum
shop sells books

SEARSPORT

M **PENOBSCOT MARINE MUSEUM,** Church St, 04974. Tel 207-548-2529;
FAX 207-548-2520. *Dir* Renny A Stackpole. *Museum Teacher* Janice Kasper;
Dir of Development Judith Demott; *Publicist* Ann Moffitt; *Librn* Paige Lilly; *Cur*
Samuel W Shogren
Open Memorial Day weekend - Oct 15, Mon - Sat 9:30 AM - 5 PM, Sun 1 - 5
PM. Admis adults $4, senior citizens $3.50, youth 7-15 $1.50, 6 & under free.
Estab 1936 as a memorial to the maritime record of present and former residents
of the State of Maine in shipbuilding, shipping and all maritime affairs. The
Museum consists of seven historic buildings, including the Old Town Hall
(1845), Nickels-Colcord Duncan House (1880); Fowler True Ross House (1825);
Capt Merithew House; Dutch House; two new buildings: Stephen Phillips'
Memorial Library (1983) & Douglas & Margaret Carver Memorial Art Gallery/
Auditorium (1986) & a classroom building. Average Annual Attendance: 15,000.

Mem: 950; dues $25 & up; annual meeting June
Income: Financed by mem, grant, gifts & admissions
Collections: Marine Artifacts; China Trade Exports; 450 paintings; Ship Models;
water craft; decorative arts; ceramics; glass; textiles & extensive archives
Exhibitions: Permanent exhibit: The Challenge of the Downeasters; Marine
Painting of Thomas and James Buttersworth
Publications: Searsport Sea Captains, 1989; annual report; newsletter, when
appropriate
Activities: Educ dept; classes for adults & children; docent training; lect open to
public, 12 vis lectr per year; concerts; scholarships; individual paintings & original
objects of art lent to other institutions in accordance with museum policies;
originate traveling exhibitions; sales shop sells Marine books, magazines, original
art & reproductions & prints

L **Stephen Phillips Memorial Library,** Church St, 04974. Tel 207-548-6634. *Librn*
Paige Lilly
Open for reference to researchers
Library Holdings: Vols 6000; Per subs 30; nautical charts; Micro — Fiche, reels;
AV — A-tapes, cassettes, fs, lantern slides, slides, v-tapes; Other — Clipping
files, exhibition catalogs, manuscripts, memorabilia, original art works, pamphlets,
photographs, prints
Special Subjects: Architecture, Art History, Asian Art, Ceramics, Decorative
Arts, Drafting, Etchings & Engravings, Flasks & Bottles, Folk Art, Furniture

SOUTHWEST HARBOR

M **WENDELL GILLEY MUSEUM,** Main St & Herrick Rd, PO Box 254, 04679.
Tel 207-244-7555. *Pres* Steven C Rockefeller; *Exec Dir* Nina Z Gormley; *VPres*
Robert L Hinckley
Open June & Oct Tues - Sun 10 AM - 4 PM, July - Aug Tues - Sun 10 AM - 5
PM, May, Nov & Dec Fri - Sun 10 AM - 4 PM. Admis fee adults $3. Estab
1981 to house collection of bird carvings & other wildlife related art. Gallery
occupies 3000 sq ft on one floor of a solar heated building; handicapped access.
Average Annual Attendance: 15,000 - 17,000. Mem: 2000; dues $15-$500;
annual meeting Oct or Nov
Income: $125,000 (financed by membership, admissions, sales, fundraising
events)
Collections: Decorative wood carvings of birds & working decoys by Wendell
Gilley; Birds of America, 1972 ed J J Audubon; Birds of Mt Desert Island by
Carroll S Tyson (prints); Photos by Eliot Porter
Exhibitions: Bird Carvings by Wendell Gilley (rotating); The Canoe in American
Art & Life; Audubon prints (rotating); Fly-fishing Art Summer. (1990) Inspiring
Artists
Publications: The Eider, bi-annual newsletter
Activities: Classes for adults & children; films; lectures open to public, 20 vis
lectrs per yr; book traveling exhibitions once or twice a yr; originate traveling
exhibitions for libraries & schools; museum shop sells books, original art,
reproductions, carving tools, gift items

WATERVILLE

M **COLBY COLLEGE,** Musuem of Art, 04901-4799. Tel 207-872-3228; FAX 207-
872-3555. *Dir* Hugh J Gourley III; *Asst Dir* Lynn Marsden-Atlass; *Secy* Alice
Fitzgerald
Open Mon - Sat 10 AM - noon, 1 - 4:30 PM, Sun 2 - 4:30 PM, cl major
holidays. No admis fee. Estab 1959 to serve as an adjunct to the Colby College
Art Program & to be a museum center for Central Maine. Mem: Friends of Art
at Colby, 625; dues $15 & up
Income: Financed by college funds, mem & donations
Collections: Bernat Oriental ceramics & bronzes; American Heritage collection;
The Helen Warren & Willard Howe Cummings Collection of American Art;
American Art of the 18th, 19th & 20th centuries; Jette Collection of American
painting in the Impressionist Period; John Marin Collection of 25 works by
Marin; Adelaide Pearson Collection; Pre-Columbian Mexico; Etruscan art
Publications: Exhibition catalogs; periodic newsletter
Activities: Docent training; lectures open to public; gallery talks; tours; individual
paintings lent to other museums; originate traveling exhibitions; museum shop
sells gift items, jewelry & sundries

L **Bixler Art & Music Library,** 04901. Tel 207-872-3232. *Librn* Anthony P Hess
For reference & academic lending to college community
Library Holdings: Vols 14,000; Per subs 65; Music; Micro — Reels; AV — A-
tapes, cassettes, Kodachromes, lantern slides, rec, slides 50,000, v-tapes; Other —
Clipping files, exhibition catalogs, prints
Special Subjects: Afro-American Art, American Indian Art, American Western
Art, Asian Art, Folk Art, History of Art & Archaeology, Islamic Art, Judaica,
Latin American Art, Mexican Art, Oriental Art

M **THOMAS COLLEGE ART GALLERY,** W River Rd, 04901. Tel 207-873-0771.
Dir Sally Keene
Open Mon - Fri 8 AM - 5 PM. No admis fee. Estab 1968 for presentation of
instructional shows for student & community audiences. Average Annual
Attendance: 1500
Exhibitions: Monthly exhibitions by local artists

L **Library,** W River Rd, 04901. Tel 207-873-0771. *Dir Public Relations* Sally
Keene
For reference only
Library Holdings: Vols 21,500; Per subs 400; AV — Slides

M **WATERVILLE HISTORICAL SOCIETY,** Redington Museum, 64 Silver St,
04901. Tel 207-872-9439. *Pres Historical Society* Willard B Arnold III; *Resident
Cur* Richard Danz; *Resident Cur* Lidia Danz; *Librn* William B Miller
Open Memorial Day - Labor Day Tues - Sat 10 AM - 4 PM. Admis adults $2,
children 12 - 17 $2, under 12 free. Estab 1903. Average Annual Attendance:
1500. Mem: 450; dues sponsor $100, family $15, single $12.50; annual meeting
first Thurs in June
Income: Financed by membership and city appropriation & limited endowment
Collections: 19th century drug store, 18th & 19th century furniture, portraits of
early local residents, early silver and china, Victorian clothing
Activities: Lect open to public, 3 vis lectr per year; tours

WISCASSET

A   LINCOLN COUNTY HISTORICAL ASSOCIATION, Pownalborough Court
House, PO Box 61, 04578. Tel 207-882-6817. *Dir* Martha Stetson
Inc 1954, to preserve buildings of historic interest. Presents 200 years of Maine's
crafts and skills including the work of craftsmen who spend part of the year in
Maine. Gallery presents the works of contemporary professional artists, working
in Maine, by means of two juried summer exhibitions. Two museums and one art
gallery maintained. Average Annual Attendance: 3000. Mem: 650; dues $20 and
up; annual meeting July
  Income: Financed by dues, fundraisers, admis
  Collections: Furniture; hand tools; household articles; prison equipment; textiles
  Exhibitions: Changing exhibits on 200 years of Maine crafts and skills; Lincoln
  County Museum, permanent exhibit on the history of punishment
  Publications: Newsletter and occasional monographs
  Activities: School programs; tours; slide shows; lect
L   Library, 04578. Tel 207-882-6817. *Dir* Martha Stetson
  Open by appointment for reference and research
M   Lincoln County Museum & Pre-Revolutionary Court House, Federal St, PO Box
  61, 04578. Tel 207-882-6817. *Dir* Martha Stetson
  Open July - Aug, Tues - Sun 11 AM - 4:30 PM; Sun noon - 4 PM; Court House
  open July - Aug, Wed - Sat 10 AM - 4 PM. Admis adults $2, children 12 &
  under $1; Court House admis adults $3, children $1. Average Annual
  Attendance: 2000. Mem: 600; dues $20 & up, annual meeting in July
  Income: Mem, donations, restricted funds & bequests
  Activities: Lectures open to the public; tours
M   Maine Art Gallery, Old Academy, Warren St, PO Box 315, 04578. Tel 207-882-
  7511. *Chmn & Dir* Martha Oatway; *Treas* Linda Stetson; *Secy* Edith Barnett
  Open summer daily 10 AM - 4 PM, Sun 1 - 4 PM, winter Fri & Sat 10 AM - 4
  PM, Sun 1 - 4 PM. No admis fee, donations appreciated. Estab 1958 as a
  cooperative, non-profit gallery created by the Artist Members of Lincoln County
  Cultural & Historical Association to exhibit the work of artists living or working
  in Maine. Gallery occupies a red brick federal two-story building built in 1807 as
  a free Academy. The building is now on National Historical Register. Average
  Annual Attendance: 6000. Mem: 185; annual dues $20; annual meeting Sept
  Income: Financed by patrons
  Exhibitions: Summer Exhibition: A juried show in parts of 8 weeks featuring
  approx 100 painters & sculptors living or working in Maine. Winter series of one-
  person invited exhibitions
  Activities: Lect open to public; gallery talks; school art classes visits

YORK

A   OLD YORK HISTORICAL SOCIETY, PO Box 312, 03909. Tel 207-363-4974.
Dir Richard Borges; *Membership & Vol Coordr* Cheryl St Germain
Open mid-June - Sept Tues - Sat 10 AM - 5 PM. Admis adults $6, children 6-16
$2.50, children under 6 free; rates are available for individual buildings. Estab
1941 to operate buildings of historical interest & to inspire an awareness &
appreciaton of York's past in order to protect the town's environment for the
present & for future. Administers Old Gaol, oldest jail in US; 18th Century
Jefferds Tavern; Elizabeth Perkins House; John Hancock Wharehouse; Emerson-
Wilcox House; Schoolhouse. Average Annual Attendance: 10,000. Mem: 600;
dues $25 & up; annual meeting in August
  Collections: American & European furniture; decorative arts from southern
  Maine; ceramic & glass collection; tools & maritime artifacts
  Activities: Classes for adults & children; docent training; lectures open to public,
  3 per yr; concerts; tours; fellowship; originate traveling exhibitions that circulate
  to other museums; sales shop sells books, reproductions, prints, Maine crafts &
  books & other gift items
M   Elizabeth Perkins House, 03909. Tel 207-363-4974.
  Open mid-June - Sept daily 1 - 5 PM. Admis adults $2. A Colonial house as
  lived in by a Victorian family, built in 1730; contains 18th and 19th century
  furniture, china, and prints. Average Annual Attendance: 2300
M   Old School House, 03909. Tel 207-363-4974.
  Open mid-June - Sept. Original school built in 1755; figures of the schoolmaster
  and children are in period costumes. Average Annual Attendance: 6000
M   Jefferds Tavern, Lindsey Rd, 03909. Tel 207-363-4974. *Exec Dir* Richard Borges
  Open Memorial Day - Mid-October Mon - Sat 10:30 AM - 5 PM. Admis adults
  $1, children under 12 free. An ancient hostelry built before the Revolution by
  Captain Samuel Jefferds
M   John Hancock Warehouse, Lindsey Rd, 03909. Tel 207-363-4974. *Exec Dir*
  Richard Borges
  Open Mon - Sat 10:30 AM - 5 PM, Sun 1:30 - 5 PM. Admis adults $.50,
  children under 12 free. Owned by a signer of the Declaration of Independence at
  the time of his death; listed in the National Register of Historic Places. Average
  Annual Attendance: 1000
  Income: Financed by endowment
  Exhibitions: Old tools; Antique Ship Models; Life & Industry on the York River
  Activities: Lectures open to public, 12 visiting lecturers per year; originate
  traveling exhibitions
M   Gaol Museum, Lindsey Rd, 03909. Tel 207-363-4974. *Exec Dir* Richard Borges;
  Cur John Labranche; *Educator* Sarah Giffen
  Open June - Oct Mon - Fri 10:30 AM - 4:30 PM, Sun 1:30 - 4:30 PM. Admis
  $3. Estab 1900 as a local history museum to maintain, care for and develop
  historical collections of a regional nature and to promote historic research and
  historically educational programs. Museum consists of the oldest jail in the
  United States and an 18th century tavern arranged as period rooms. Two
  exhibition rooms house traveling shows & temporary exhibitions of an historical
  nature. Average Annual Attendance: 10,000. Mem: 600; dues family $15, single
  $10; annual mccting Aug
  Income: $70,000 (financed by endowment)
  Collections: Regional collection of American furniture & decorative arts; rare
  books; manuscripts
  Publications: Old Gaol Museum (history), E H Pendleton; York Maine Then &
  Now; Enchanted Ground, George Garrett; Old Gaol Newsletter, quarterly
  Activities: Classes for adults & children; dramatic programs; docent training;
  lectures open to public, 6 vis lect per yr; sales shops sells books

L   George Marshall Store Library, Lindsey Rd, 30909. Tel 207-363-4974. *Librn*
Virginia Speller
Open daily 10 AM - 4 PM. Reference only
  Library Holdings: Vols 5000; Original documents; Micro — Prints, reels; AV —
  Kodachromes, slides, v-tapes; Other — Clipping files, exhibition catalogs,
  manuscripts, memorabilia, pamphlets, photographs
  Special Subjects: Decorative Arts, Genealogy, Local history

MARYLAND

ANNAPOLIS

M   HAMMOND-HARWOOD HOUSE ASSOCIATION, INC, 19 Maryland Ave,
21401. Tel 410-269-1714. *Exec Dir* Stephen E Patrick
Open Nov - March Tues - Sat 10 AM - 4 PM, Sun 1 - 4 PM, Apr - Oct Tues -
Sat 10 AM - 5 PM, Sun 2 - 5 PM. Admis adults $4, students between 6 & 18 $3.
Estab 1938 to preserve the Hammond-Harwood House (1774), a National
Historic Landmark; to educate the public in the arts and architecture of
Maryland in the 18th century. Average Annual Attendance: 15,000. Mem: 400;
dues varied; meeting May and Nov
  Income: Financed by endowment, membership, attendance and sales
  Collections: Paintings by C W Peale; Chinese export porcelain; English and
  American furnishings, especially from Maryland; prints; English & American
  silver; colonial architectural interiors designed by William Buckland
  Publications: Maryland's Way (Hammond-Harwood House cookbook);
  Hammond-Harwood House Guidebook
  Activities: Interpretive programs; docent training; lect open to public; individual
  paintings and original objects of art lent to bonafide museums within reasonable
  transporting distance; sales shop sells books, slides, postcards, notepaper & gifts

M   MARYLAND HALL FOR THE CREATIVE ARTS, Cardinal Gallery, 801
Chase St, 21401. Tel 410-263-5544; FAX 410-263-5114. *Exec Dir* Michael R
Bailey; *Dir Exhib* Mike Purvis
Open Mon - Fri 9 AM - 8 PM, Sat 10 AM - 2 PM, cl Sun. Admis free. Estab
1986 to expose regional talent within a national context. Two room post modern
space with 100 ft of wall space & 1100 sq ft of floor area. Contemporary grid-
track lighting. Limited, portable, double sided walls for larger exhibits. Average
Annual Attendance: 6000
  Income: Operating on a budget through Board of Trustees, Foundation Trustees,
  local & state & special grant funding
  Exhibitions: Inside The Mid Atlantic
  Publications: Exhibition catalog

M   SAINT JOHN'S COLLEGE, Elizabeth Myers Mitchell Art Gallery, 60 College
Ave, 21404. Tel 410-263-2371, Ext 443, 450, (Direct line) 626-2556; FAX 410-
263-4828. *Dir* Heidi Schaller; *Asst Dir* Donna Schueler
Open Sept - May Tues - Sun Noon - 5 PM, Fri 7 - 8 PM. No admis fee. Estab
1989 for museum quality exhibits for the area. One gallery of 1300 sq ft,
rectangle with corner windows, one gallery of 525 sq ft, rectangular, no windows.
Average Annual Attendance: 3500. Mem: 77; dues $5 - $1000
  Exhibitions: (1990) Twentieth Century Sculpture; Art of Our Time: Works on
  Paper from the Olga Hirshhorn Collection. (1991) Drawings of Koni Voshi
  Activities: Educ dept offers studio courses in painting, lifedrawing and sculpture
  for adults and children; lectr open to public, 7 vis lectr per year; gallery talks;
  tours

M   UNITED STATES NAVAL ACADEMY MUSEUM, 118 Maryland Ave,
21402. Tel 410-267-2108. *Dir* Dr Kenneth Hagan; *Senior Cur* James W
Cheevers; *Cur of Ship Models* Robert F Sumrall; *Cur of Robinson Coll* Sigrid
Trumpy; *Sr Exhibit Specialist* Ronald Corder
Open Mon - Sat 9 AM - 5 PM, Sun 11 AM - 5 PM. No admis fee. Estab 1845
as Naval School Lyceum for the purpose of collecting, preserving and exhibiting
objects related to American naval history. Museum contains two large galleries
totaling 9000 sq ft, with other exhibits in other areas of the campus. Average
Annual Attendance: Approx 600,000
  Income: Financed by Federal Government appropriations and private donations
  Purchases: $36,170
  Collections: †Ceramicwares; Drawings, †Paintings, †Prints, †Sculpture of Naval
  Portraits and Events; †Medals; †Naval Uniforms; †Ship Models; †Silver;
  †Weapons.
  Exhibitions: Selections from the Permanent Art Collection; John Sloan, A
  Printmaker; Dutch Seapower in the 17th Century; The Bradshaw Collections of
  Marine Paintings; Target Angle Zero; Selections from the Permanent Art
  Collection; Edward Seager (1809-86)
  Publications: Collection catalogs and special exhibition brochures, periodically
  Activities: Lect; tours upon request; individual paintings and original objects of
  art lent to other museums and related institutions for special, temporary
  exhibitions; originate traveling exhibitions
L   Library, 118 Maryland Ave, 21402. Tel 410-267-2108. *Dir* Dr Kenneth J Hagan
  Open to students, scholars and public with notice, reference only
  Library Holdings: Vols 200; Per subs 15; Other — Exhibition catalogs
  Special Subjects: Naval History, Marine Art

BALTIMORE

M   BALTIMORE CITY COMMUNITY COLLEGE (Formerly New Community
College of Baltimore), Art Gallery, Fine & Applied Arts Dept, 2901 Liberty
Heights Ave, 21215. Tel 410-396-7980. *Gallery Dir* Allyn O Harris
Open Mon - Fri 10 AM - 4 PM. No admis fee. Estab 1965 to bring to the
Baltimore and college communities exhibitions of note by regional artists, and to
serve as a showplace for the artistic productions of the college art students and
faculty. Consists of one large gallery area, approx 120 running ft, well-lighted

through the use of both natural light (sky domes) and cove lighting which provides an even wash to the walls
Income: Financed through the college
Collections: Graphics from the 16th century to the present; paintings by notable American artists and regional ones
Exhibitions: Group shows and three-man shows representing a broad cross section of work by regional artists; art faculty show; three-man show featuring graphic designs and paintings; exhibition of portraits by 15 artists; annual student show
Publications: Gallery anouncements
Activities: Lect open to public; gallery talks

M **BALTIMORE CITY LIFE MUSEUMS,** 800 E Lombard St, 21202-4523. Tel 410-396-3524; FAX 410-396-1806. *Pres* Kevin Byrnes; *Dir* Nancy Brennan; *Asst Dir* John W Durel
Hours vary by site. No admis fee. Estab 1931 to collect, interpret & exhibit objects related to Baltimore history. Five sites: Carroll Mansion, Peale Museum, H L Mencken House, 1840 House, Baltimore Center for Urban Archaeology. Average Annual Attendance: 50,000. Mem: 300; dues $20; annual meeting in Sept
Income: Financed by city government & other sources
Collections: †Archaeological artifacts; †Baltimore historic photographs; †Baltimore paintings; †H L Mencken's personal effects; †Peale family paintings; †prints of Baltimore
Exhibitions: (1991) Mermaid, Mummies & Mastodons: The Evolution of American Museums
Publications: City Past-Time, quarterly newsletter
Activities: Dramatic programs; docent training; lectures open to public, 5-10 vis lectrs per yr; gallery talks; tours; individual paintings & original objects of art lent to other museums; museum shop sells books & postcards

L **Library,** 800 E Lombard St, 21202. Tel 410-396-1164. *Supv* Mary Markey
Open to staff & public for reference, by appointment only
Library Holdings: Vols 1400; Per subs 20; Maps, Printed Ephemera; Micro — Reels; AV — Lantern slides, motion pictures, rec, slides, v-tapes; Other — Clipping files, exhibition catalogs, framed reproductions, manuscripts, memorabilia, original art works, pamphlets, photographs, prints, reproductions
Special Subjects: Architecture, Baltimore History, Maritime

M **BALTIMORE MUSEUM OF ART,** Art Museum Dr, 21218. Tel 410-396-7101; FAX 410-396-6562. *Dir* Arnold L Lehman; *Dir Education* Schroeder Cherry; *Deputy Dir Admin* Zoe Pindak; *Dir Public Information* Marge Lee; *Deputy Dir & Cur Modern Paintings & Sculpture* Brenda Richardson; *Deputy Dir Museum Development* Elspeth Udvarhelyi; *Cur Decorative Arts* Wendy Cooper; *Consultant Cur Decorative Arts* William Voss Elder III; *Assoc Cur Prints Drawings & Photographs* Jan Howard; *Asst Cur Decorative of Arts* M B Munford; *Cur Painting & Sculpture Before 1900* Sona Johnston; *Consultant Cur Textiles* Open; *Assoc Cur Textiles* Anita Jones; *Cur Art of Africa, Americas, Oceania* Frederick Lamp; *Assoc Cur Art Of Africa, Americas, Oceania* Katharine Ferstrom
Open Wed, Thurs & Fri 10 AM - 4 PM, Sat & Sun 11 AM - 6 PM, cl Mon, Tues & holidays. Admis $5 for non-members over 19. Estab 1914 to house & preserve art works, to present art exhibitions, art-related activities & offer educational programs & events. The original building was designed by John Russell Pope in 1929; new wing opened 1982 with cafe, auditorium & traveling exhibition galleries; sculpture gardens opened in 1980 and 1988. Average Annual Attendance: 300,000. Mem: 17,000; dues $15 - $50
Income: $8,000,000 (financed by city & state appropriation; corporate, individual & foundation gifts; mem, earned revenue & endowment income; county support)
Collections: Blanche Adler Collection of Graphic Art; Antioch Mosaics; Ellen H Bayard Collection of 18th & 19th Century American Paintings, European Ceramics, Chinese Export Porcelain, American & English Silver; General Lawrason Riggs Collection of Old Master Prints & Chinese Ceramics; Thomas E Benesch Memorial Collection of Drawings by 20th Century American & European artists; Harry A Bernstein Memorial Collection of Contemporary American Paintings; Cone Collection of 19th & 20th Century French Paintings, Sculpture; Drawings & Prints, Near Eastern & European Textiles Laces, Jewelry, Furniture & other Decorative Arts; Elise Agnus Daingerfield Collection of 18th Century English, French & American Paintings with emphasis on Portraiture; Hanson Rawlings Duval Jr Memorial Collection of 19th Century Baltimore Architectural Elements, American Furniture, Paintings, European & Chinese Ceramics; Abram Eisenberg Collection of Paintings, primarily 19th Century French; Jacob Epstein Collection of Old Master Paintings; Edward Joseph Gallagher III Memorial Collection of American Paintings between 1921 & 1955; T Harrison Garrett Collection of Graphic Art 15th - 19th Century; Nelson & Juanita Greif Gutman Memorial Collection of 20th Century Paintings, Sculpture & Drawings; Charles & Elsa Hutzler Memorial Collection of Contemporary Sculpture; Mary Frick Jacobs Collection of 15th - 18th Century European Paintings, Tapestries, Furniture & Objects d'Art; Julius Levy Memorial Fund Collection of Oriental Art; George A Lucas Collection of 19th Century Drawings, Prints, Paintings & Bronzes; Saidie A May Collection of 20th Century Paintings, Sculpture & Graphics, Ancient, Medieval & Renaissance Sculpture & Textiles; McLanahan Memorial Collection of 1720 Bedchamber & its Furnishings; Samuel & Tobie Miller Memorial Collection of Contemporary Painting & Sculpture; J G D'Arcy Paul Collection of 18th Century American Furniture; Peabody Institute Collection of 19th & 20th Century American Paintings; White Collection of Ceramics, Furniture, Needlework, Glass & Decorative Art Books; White Collection of Early Maryland Silver; William Woodward Collection of 18th & 19th Century Paintings of English Sporting Life; Wurtzburger Collection of Art of Africa, the Americas & Oceania; Janet & Alan Wurtzburger Collection of 20th Century Sculpture; Robert H and Ryda Levi Collection of Contemporary Sculpture
Exhibitions: Painting, sculpture, textiles, furniture & other decorative arts, prints, drawings and photography
Publications: Exhibition catalogs; monthly calendar; members newsletter; posters and postcards
Activities: Classes for children; docent training; lectures open to the public; concerts; gallery talks; tours; competitions; dance performances; film series; museum shop selling books, original art, reproductions, prints, slides and art-related gifts

L **E Kirkbride Miller Art Research Library,** Art Museum Dr, 21218. Tel 410-396-6317. *Librn* Cindy Tripoulas
Open by appointment only
Library Holdings: Vols 40,800; Per subs 225; Auction Catalogs; Micro — Fiche, reels; Other — Clipping files, exhibition catalogs, pamphlets
Special Subjects: Photography, American decorative arts, 19th and 20th century French art, arts of Africa, the Americas & Oceania

M **THE CONTEMPORARY,** Museum for Contemporary Arts, 601 N Howard St, 21201. Tel 410-333-8600. *Dir* George Ciscle; *Asst Dir* Lisa Corrin; *Museum Asst* Jed Dodds
Estab 1989 to explore connections between the art of our time & our world. Average Annual Attendance: 25,000. Mem: 400; dues $35; annual meeting in June
Income: Financed by endowment, mem, grants & private donations
Exhibitions: Mining the Museum: an installation by Fred Wilson; Catfish Dreamin'; A Sculpture on a Truck by Alison Saar
Publications: Mining the Museum; Outcry; Artists Answer AIDs
Activities: Classes for adults & children; dramatic programs; docent programs; lect open to public, 5 vis lectr per year; book traveling exhibitions 1 per year; originate traveling exhibitions 1 per year

JOHNS HOPKINS UNIVERSITY

M **Archaeological Collection,** 3400 N Charles St, 21218. Tel 410-516-7561. *Cur* Dr Lori-Ann Touchett; *Cur Near Eastern & Egyptian Art* Dr Betsy Bryan
Estab 1876. Small exhibit space in Gilman Hall
Collections: Egyptian through Roman material 3500 BC to 500 AD

M **Evergreen House,** 4545 N Charles St, 21210. Tel 410-516-0341. *Dir* Lili Ott
Open Mon - Fri 10 AM - 4 PM, Sun 1 - 4 PM. Admis fee $5. Estab 1952 for promotion of cultural and educational functions and research. Formerly the residence of Ambassador John W Garrett which he bequeathed to the University. Average Annual Attendance: 10,000. Mem: Annual dues $25
Collections: Bakst Theater Decorations; European Ceramics; Japanese Inro, Netsuke & Lacquer: Chinese Ceramics; Oriental Rugs; Rare Book Collection; Tiffany Glass; Twentieth Century European Paintings
Exhibitions: Changing exhibitions
Activities: Lect open to public & various groups; concerts; gallery talks; tours; individual paintings and original objects of art lent to other museums, national and international; museum shop sells books, jewelry, original art, reproductions, prints

L **George Peabody Library,** 17 E Mount Vernon Place, 21202. Tel 410-659-8197. *Head Librn* Robert Bartram; *Admin Asst* J Jenkins
Open Mon - Sat 9 AM - 5 PM
Library Holdings: Vols 283,000
Special Subjects: Architecture, Decorative Arts

M **Homewood House Museum,** 3400 N Charles St, 21218. Tel 410-516-5589; FAX 410-516-7859. *Dir* Mary Butler Davies
Open 11 AM - 5 PM. Admis $5. Estab 1987; a historic house museum. Restored Federal Period country seat of Charles Carroll, Jr, with period furnishings. Average Annual Attendance: 10,000. Mem: Annual dues $25
Special Subjects: Domestic Life & Social History of Early 19th Century
Collections: English & American decorative arts of the late 18th & early 19th Century
Activities: Classes for adults; historically relevant activities for children & young people; concerts; tours; internships offered; museum shop sells books, original art, object reproductions, prints, slides, exclusive Homewood items & jewelry

M **MARYLAND ART PLACE,** 218 W Saratoga St, 21201. Tel 410-962-8565. *Exec Dir* Jack Rasmussen; *Development Dir* Coleen West; *Program Dir* Charlotte Cohen
Open Tues - Sat 11 AM - 5 PM. No admis fee. Estab 1981, to provide opportunities for artists to exhibit work, nurture & promote new ideas & forms. 3 floors of exhibition space, including the 14 Karat Caberet used for performance art, music, films and dance. Average Annual Attendance: 30,000. Mem: 900; annual dues $25 - $1000
Income: $299,000 (financed by mem, federal, state & corporate appropriation)
Exhibitions: Back To The Future: Maryland Artists 1950s-1980s; (1991) Empire-Monument Express; Maryland-On-View; Street of Gold; The Gathering
Publications: Catalogs, annual; exhibition brochures, 4-6 per year; newsletters, 2 per year
Activities: Critics' residencies including writing workship & annual public forum; lect open to public, 4 vis lectr per yr; concerts; gallery talks; tours; originate traveling exhibitions, 1 - 2 per yr

M **MARYLAND HISTORICAL SOCIETY,** Museum of Maryland History, 201 W Monument St, 21201. Tel 410-685-3750, Ext 70; FAX 410-385-2105. *Dir* Charles T Lyle; *Chief Cur* Jennifer F Goldsborough
Open Tues - Fri 10 AM - 4:30 PM, Sat 9 AM - 4:30 PM. Admis adults $3.50, sr & students $2.50, children $1.50. Estab 1844 to collect, display & interpret the history of the State of Maryland. Average Annual Attendance: 70,000. Mem: 6500; dues family $45; annual meeting in June
Income: Financed by endowment, mem, city & state appropriations
Collections: †Architectural drawings; †crystal and glassware; †ethnic artifacts, all of Maryland origin or provenance; †metalwork; †paintings, both portrait and landscape; †porcelain and †pottery; †silver; †textiles and †costumes; †furniture
Exhibitions: Continually changing exhibitions reflecting the history and culture of the state
Publications: Maryland Historical Society Magazine, quarterly; News and Notes, bimonthly
Activities: Educ dept; classes for adults; docent training; lect open to the public; concerts; gallery talks; tours; competitions with awards; exten dept; individual paintings & original objects of art lent to other organizations; originate traveling exhibitions; museum shop sells books, magazines, original art, reproductions, prints, slides, crafts, decorative arts items, jewelry

L **Library,** 201 W Monument St, 21201. Tel 410-685-3750; FAX 410-385-2105.
Dir Charles Lyle; *Chief Cur* Jennifer Goldsborough
Open Tues - Fri 10 AM - 5 PM, Sat 9 AM - 5PM. Estab 1844. Library for
reference only. Average Annual Attendance: 80,000. Mem: 6000
Library Holdings: Vols 60,000; Per subs 125; Micro — Fiche, reels; AV — A-
tapes, cassettes, fs, Kodachromes, lantern slides, motion pictures, rec, slides, v-
tapes; Other — Clipping files, exhibition catalogs, manuscripts, memorabilia,
pamphlets, photographs, prints, reproductions

M **MARYLAND INSTITUTE,** College of Art Exhibitions, 1300 Mount Royal Ave,
21217. Tel 410-225-2519; FAX 410-669-9206. *Pres* Fred Lazarus IV; *Dir* David
Brown
Open Mon, Tues, Wed & Sat 10 AM - 5 PM, Thurs & Fri 10 AM - 9 PM, Sun
noon - 5 PM. No admis fee. Estab 1826, including the Decker & Meyerhoff
Galleries & the Graduate Thesis Gallery. Average Annual Attendance: 10,000
Income: Financed by endowment and student tuition
Collections: Maryland Institute-George A Lucas Collection donated in 1909
comprising over 400 paintings and drawings by Corot, Daumier, Delacrox,
Greuze, Manet, Millet, Pissarro, Whistler; bronzes by Antoine Barye, and a
collection of 17,000 graphics
Exhibitions: Changing exhibitions of contemporary work in Meyerhoff & Fox
Galleries
Publications: Handouts of the works in the Lucas Collection; several small
catalogs; two major publications per year
Activities: Dramatic programs; lect open to the public; concerts; gallery talks;
tours; original objects of art lent; traveling exhibitions organized and circulated
L **Library,** 1400 Cathedral St, 21201. Tel 410-225-2311. *Librn* John Stoneham
Library Holdings: Vols 47,000; Per subs 200

M **MEREDITH GALLERY,** 805 N Charles St, 21201. Tel 410-837-3575; FAX
410-837-3577. *Dir* Judith Lippman; *Assoc Dir* Terry Heffner
No admis fee. Estab 1977 to exhibit a variety of contemporary art by living
American artists, including art furniture, ceramics, glass, handmade paper,
paintings & prints. The building is divided into two floors with regular monthly
exhibits & ongoing representation of gallery artists. Average Annual Attendance:
3500-4000
Exhibitions: Ed Baynard; Gene Davis; Dorothy Gillespie; Paul Jenkins; Margie
Hughto; Alex Katz; David Lund; Robert Motherwell; Bennett Bean; John
Dunnigan; Elizabeth Osborne; Michael Graves; Judy Kensley McKie; Alphonse
Mattia; Rosanne Somerson; Stanley Tigerman; Robert Stern
Activities: Classes for adults and children; educational lect on current exhibitions;
lect open to public; gallery talks; tours

MORGAN STATE UNIVERSITY
M **James E Lewis Museum of Art,** Cold Spring Lane & Hillen Rd, 21239. Tel 410-
319-3030, 319-3306; FAX 410-319-3835. *Dir & Cur* Gabriel S Tenabe
Open Mon - Fri 9 AM - 5 PM, Sat, Sun, holidays by appointment only, cl
Easter, Thanksgiving, Christmas. No admis fee. Estab 1950. Average Annual
Attendance: 5000
Income: $5500
Collections: 19th & 20th century American and European sculpture; graphics;
paintings; decorative arts; archaeology; African and New Guinea Sculptures
Exhibitions: (1993) Elizabeth Catlet (prints & sculpture); Wearable Art Exhibit;
Bahamian Artist Exhibit
Publications: Catalogs, monthly
Activities: Lectures open to public, vis lectrs; lending collection contains 500
kodachromes; traveling exhibitions organized & circulated
L **Library,** Cold Spring Lane & Hillen Rd, 21239. Tel 410-319-3488. *Dir* Karen
Robertson
Library Holdings: Vols 8800; Other — Photographs

A **MUNICIPAL ART SOCIETY OF BALTIMORE CITY,** 135 E Baltimore St,
21202. Tel 410-727-1700 (Compton). *Mgr* William Rienhoff
Estab 1899; the society contributes primarily public sculpture and worthy public
art projects in Baltimore City
Income: Financed by endowment
Activities: Support public art in Baltimore City

M **NATIONAL SOCIETY OF COLONIAL DAMES OF AMERICA IN THE
STATE OF MARYLAND,** Mount Clare Mansion, Carroll Park, 21230. Tel 410-
837-3262. *Admin* Margaret Sobel
Open Tues - Fri 10 AM - 4:30 PM, Sat & Sun Noon - 4:30 PM. Admis adults
$3, students & sr citizens $2, children under 12 $.50. Estab 1917 to preserve the
home of Charles Carroll, Barrister & teach about the colonial period of Maryland
history. Maintained by the National Society of Colonial Dames. Rooms of the
house are furnished with 18th & early 19th century decorative arts, much of
which belonged to the Carroll family who built the house in 1756. Average
Annual Attendance: 7000-8000
Income: Financed by admission, gift shop sales and contributions from public and
private sectors
Collections: American paintings; 18th and early 19th century English and
American furniture; English silver; Irish crystal; Oriental export porcelain;
archaeological artifacts found on property; other English and American
decorative arts
Publications: Brochure on Mount Clare; Mount Clare: Being an Account of the
Seat Built by Charles Carroll, Barrister Upon His Lands at Patapsco; booklet on
the house
Activities: Historical slide shows for schools and organizations; tours; original
objects of art lent to historical societies; museum shop sells books, reproductions,
slides, gift items & historical replicas
L **Library,** Carroll Park, 21230. Tel 410-837-3262.
Open to members and the public for reference only
Library Holdings: Vols 1000; AV — Slides; Other — Framed reproductions,
original art works, pamphlets, photographs
Special Subjects: Decorative Arts, 18th Century Culture
Collections: 18th century furniture; decorative arts; part of the library of Charles
Carroll, Barrister-at-law, builder of the house, 1756

L **ENOCH PRATT FREE LIBRARY OF BALTIMORE CITY,** Fine Arts Dept,
400 Cathedral St, 21201. Tel 410-396-5430. *Dir* Anna Curry; *Chief Public
Relations Division* Averil Kadis; *Dept Head* Ellen Luchinsky
Open Mon, Tues & Wed 10 AM - 8 PM, Sat 10 AM - 5 PM, Sun 1 - 5 PM Oct
- May, cl Fri. Estab 1882 to provide materials, primarily circulating on the visual
arts and music. Exhibition space in display windows, interior display cases,
corridors and special departments
Income: Financed by city and state appropriation
Purchases: $11,000
Library Holdings: Framed prints, unframed pictures; AV — Fs, motion pictures,
rec, slides; Other — Framed reproductions, reproductions
Publications: Booklets, periodically
Activities: Lect & film showings

PRINT COUNCIL OF AMERICA
For further information, see National and Regional Organizations

A **SCHOOL 33 ART CENTER,** 1427 Light St, 21230. Tel 410-396-4641; FAX
410-625-2634. *Dir* Claudia Amory
Open Tues - Sat 11 AM - 4 PM. Estab 1979 to promote the development &
growth of contemporary visual art. Provide services & special events for artists &
the public
Exhibitions: (1992) Situations; The King of Print Comes to Town; Forged
Futures; Elements; New Work by Kuhne & Nadeau; Los Desaparecidos; Form
As Metaphor; Conversations; Time Out. (1993) Growth & Atrophy: The
Empathetic Landscape; New Photographs, Work by Rookchin, Ueda, Taylor;
Cryptics; New Work by Clark, Hirsche & Pettus; Work by Ueda, Smith

A **STAR-SPANGLED BANNER FLAG HOUSE ASSOCIATION,** Flag House &
1812 Museum, 844 E Pratt St, 21202. Tel 410-837-1793. *Pres* J Prentiss Browne;
VPres Clifford Bruck; *VPres* Gordon M F Stick Jr; *Treas* Harry F Reid
Open Mon - Sat 10 AM - 4 PM, cl Sun. Admis adults $1.50, students 13 - 18 $1,
children 6 - 12 $.50, under 6 free. Estab 1928 for the care and maintenance of
1793 home of Mary Pickersgill, maker of 15 star, 15 stripe flag used at Fort
McHenry during Battle of Baltimore, War of 1812, which inspired Francis Scott
Key to pen his famous poem, now our national anthem; also to conduct an
educational program for public and private schools. Museum houses artifacts,
portraits and library. 1793 house furnished and decorated in Federal period to
look as it did when Mary Pickersgill was in residence. Average Annual
Attendance: 15,000. Mem: 500; dues $15; annual meeting May
Income: Financed by memberships, admissions, special events fundraisers & sales
from museum shop
Collections: Flag collection; original antiques of Federal period
Publications: The Star (newsletter), quarterly
Activities: Educ dept; lectures open to public; concerts; gallery talks; tours;
museum sales shop sells books, reproductions, prints, slides, Baltimore souvenirs,
flags from all nations, maps, country crafts & small antiques
L **Library,** 844 E Pratt St, 21202. Tel 410-837-1793, 837-1812. *Adminr* Mary
Helen Nippard
Open to public for reference
Library Holdings: Vols 500; Per subs 4; Government Documents; AV — A-
tapes, slides; Other — Clipping files, exhibition catalogs, framed reproductions,
manuscripts, memorabilia, original art works, pamphlets, photographs, prints,
reproductions
Special Subjects: Mary Pickersgill, flagmaker, War of 1812 (Battle of Baltimore)

M **UNITED METHODIST HISTORICAL SOCIETY,** Lovely Lane Museum,
2200 Saint Paul St, 21218. Tel 410-889-4458. *Pres* Helen Wicklein; *Executive
Secy* Edwin Schell
Open Mon & Fri 10 AM - 4 PM, Sun after church; groups by appointment. No
admis fee. Estab 1855; a religious collection specializing in Methodism. The main
museum room contains permanent exhibits; three other galleries are devoted
largely to rotating exhibits. Average Annual Attendance: 4000. Mem: 765; dues
$5 - $150; annual meeting May
Income: $43,000 (financed by mem & religious denomination)
Collections: †Church edifices, †furniture, †medallions and emblems,
†photographs, †quilts, †statuary, †artifacts
Publications: Third Century Methodism, quarterly; annual report
Activities: Docent training; lectures open to public, 1 vis lectr per year; gallery
talks; tours; competitions with awards; sales shop sells books, prints, and cards
L **Library,** Lovely Lane Museum, 2200 Saint Paul St, 21218. Tel 410-889-4458.
Librn Edwin Schell; *Asst Librn* Betty Ammons
Open Mon & Fri 10 AM - 4 PM & by appointment. Estab 1855 specializing in
United Methodist history & heritage. Open to general public for reference.
Average Annual Attendance: 4000. Mem: 700
Income: $43,000
Purchases: $600
Library Holdings: Vols 5000; Per subs 23; Archives; Micro — Reels; AV — A-
tapes, cassettes, fs, Kodachromes, lantern slides, motion pictures, rec, slides;
Other — Clipping files, manuscripts, memorabilia, original art works, pamphlets,
photographs, prints, sculpture
Special Subjects: Archaeology, Architecture, Bookplates & Bindings, Etchings &
Engravings, Film, Prints, Religious Art, Historical Material, Manuscripts, Maps,
Painting - American, Portraits, Posters, Textiles, United Methodist History, Local
Church History, Baltimore Conference Archives
Collections: Fountain of Youth: The Epwerth League Mar 31 - Dec 31, 1990
Publications: Third Century Methodism, 3 times per yr

M **WALTERS ART GALLERY,** 600 N Charles St, 21201. Tel 410-547-9000; FAX
410-783-7969. *Pres Board of Trustees* Jay M Wilson; *Dir* Robert P Bergman;
Assoc Dir William R Johnston; *Asst Dir Admin* Roy G Corbett; *Asst Dir
Curatorial Affairs & Cur of Medieval Art* Gary Vikan; *Cur of Ancient Art* Ellen
Reeder; *Research Cur of Manuscripts and Rare Books* Lilian M C Randall; *Dir
of Development* Kate Sellers; *Dir of Education* Diane Brandt Stillman; *Ed of
Publications* Valerie Arnade; *Dir of Conservation & Technical Research* Terry
Drayman Weisser; *Registrar* Leopoldine Prosperetti; *Sales Mgr* William O'Brien
Open Tues - Sun 11 AM - 5 PM, cl Mon, New Year's Day, Fourth of July,

Thanksgiving, Christmas Eve, Christmas. Admis adults $4, sr citizens $3, members, students & children free, free admis on Sat 11 AM - noon. Estab 1931 by the will of Henry Walters & opened in 1934 as an art museum. Hackerman House Museum of Asian Art opened in 1990. A Renaissance revival museum of 1905 with a contemporary wing of five floors opened in 1974, covering 126,000 sq ft of exhibition space with auditorium, library and conservation laboratory. Average Annual Attendance: 222,000. Mem: 5000; dues $15 - $5000

Income: $2,850,000 (financed by endowment, membership, city and state appropriation and grants)

Collections: The Collection covers the entire history of art from Egyptian times to the beginning of the 20th century. It includes important groups of Roman sculpture, Etruscan, Byzantine & medieval art; Oriental art; Sevres porcelains; Near Eastern Art & Euorpean paintings

Exhibitions: Sharing Traditions: Five Black Artists in Nineteenth-Century America, from the Collection of the National Museum of American Art; Harlem Portraits: Photographs by Carl Van Vechten; Silver Treasure from Early Byzantium; Renaissance to Rococo: Italian Paintings from the Walters Collection; Master Drawings from Titian to Picasso: The Curtis O Baer Collection; Dutch Masterworks from The Bredius Museum: A Connoisseur's Collection; Northern European Masterworks from the Walters Collection; Frederick Carder: Portrait of a Glassmaker; Objects of Adornment: Five Thousand Years of Jewelry from The Walters Art Gallery; Stories from China's Past, Han Dynasty Pictorial Tomb Tiles from Sichuan, People's Republic of China; Time Sanctified; Holy Image, Holy Space; From Alexander to Cleopatra

Publications: Bulletin, bi-monthly; journal, annually; exhibition catalogues

Activities: Classes for adults & children; dramatic programs; docent training; seminars; lectures open to the public; concerts; gallery talks; tours; films; exten dept serves Baltimore City & nearby counties; book traveling exhibitions, 3 - 4 per yr; originate traveling exhibitions; museum shop sells books, reproductions, slides, Christmas cards, notepaper

L **Library,** 600 N Charles St, 21201. Tel 410-547-9000, Ext 274; FAX 410-783-7969. *Librn* Muriel L Toppan; *Asst to Librn* Elizabeth Fishman

Open Tues - Fri 11 AM - 5 PM. Estab 1934 chiefly to serve the curatorial staff; also provides art reference services for students and the general public. For reference only

Income: $68,000

Purchases: $36,300

Library Holdings: Vols 80,000; Per subs 500; Other — Exhibition catalogs

Special Subjects: American Western Art, Antiquities-Assyrian, Archaeology, Architecture, Ceramics, Decorative Arts, Drawings, History of Art & Archaeology, Painting - American, Religious Art, History of art from prehistoric times to the end of the 19th century, with emphasis on manuscript illumination and decorative arts

CHESTERTOWN

A **HISTORICAL SOCIETY OF KENT COUNTY,** 101 Church Alley, PO Box 665, 21620. Tel 410-778-3499. *Pres* Open

Open May - Oct Sat & Sun 1 - 4 PM. Admis adults $1, children & students $.50. Estab 1936 to foster an appreciation of our colonial heritage, to encourage restoration, to enlighten and to entertain. Headquarters are in an early 18th century town house, beautifully restored and furnished. Mem: 525; dues family $10, single $7; annual meeting Apr

Income: Financed by membership and a Candlelight Tour

Collections: Furniture, pictures; Indian artifacts; fans

Exhibitions: Annual Decorative Arts Forum

Activities: Lect for members & community, 4 vis lectr per year; tours; open house with traditional costuming

COLLEGE PARK

M **UNIVERSITY OF MARYLAND, COLLEGE PARK,** Art Gallery, Art-Sociology Bldg, 20742. Tel 301-405-2763. *Dir* Terry Gips; *Asst to Dir* Debra Firmani

Open Mon - Fri noon - 4 PM, Wed evening until 9 PM, Sat & Sun 1 - 5 PM, cl summer & holidays. No admis fee. Estab 1966 to present historic & contemporary exhibitions. Gallery has 4000 sq ft of space, normally divided into one large & one smaller gallery. Average Annual Attendance: 10,000

Income: Financed by university & dept funds, grants, catalog sales

Collections: 20th century paintings, prints & drawings, including WPA mural studies, paintings by Warhol, Prendergast & Gottlieb; prints by Hundertwasser, Appel, Kitaj, Rivers & Chryssa; 20th century Japanese prints by Hiratsuka, Kosaka, Matsubara, Iwami, Ay-O & others; West African sculpture

Exhibitions: Louis Faurer: Photographs from Philadelphia & New York, 1937-1973; David Driskell: A Survey; Ralston Crawford Photographs: Art & Process; Traditional Forms & Modern Africa: West African Art at the University of Maryland; 350 Years of Art & Architecture in Maryland (1991) Dreams, Lies & Exaggerations: Photomontage in American

Publications: Exhibition catalogs, 1 - 2 per year

Activities: Lect, symposiums & films open to public; 3 vis lectr per year; gallery talks; tours; individual paintings & original objects of art lent; lending collection contains original art work & print, paintings, photographs & sculpture; originate traveling exhibitions; exhibition catalogs sold in gallery

L **Art Library,** Art-Sociology Bldg, 20742. Tel 301-405-2061. *Head Art Library* Courtney Shaw; *Asst Librn* Lynne Woodruff; *Libr Asst* Marilyn Valentine; *Libr Technical Asst II* Susan Mazur

Open Mon - Thurs 8:30 AM - 10 PM, Fri 8:30 AM - 5 PM, Sat 10 AM - 5 PM, Sun 1 - 10 PM. Estab 1979 in new building to serve the needs of the art & art history departments and campus in various art subjects

Income: Financed by university library system

Library Holdings: Vols 75,000; Per subs 234; Micro — Fiche, reels; Other — Exhibition catalogs, reproductions 30,000

Special Subjects: Advertising Design, Afro-American Art, American Indian Art, American Western Art, Art Education, Art History, Bronzes, Calligraphy, Carpets & Rugs, Ceramics, Folk Art, Furniture, Graphic Arts, Graphic Design, History of Art & Archaeology, Illustration, Interior Design, Islamic Art, Ivory,

Jade, Laces, Painting - American, Painting - European, Painting - Flemish, Painting - French, Photography, Portraits, Posters, Pottery, Prints

Collections: Art & Architecture in France; Index photographic de l'art de France; Index Iconologicus; Decimal Index to art of Low Countries; †Marburg index; Index of American Design; Deloynes Collections; Southeast Asia Collection

Publications: Bibliography; Checklist of Useful Tools for the Study of Art

Activities: Tours

L **Architecture Library,** 20742. Tel 301-405-6317 (architecture), 405-6320 (Libr Colls). *Acting Head* Cindy Larimer; *Cur NTL* Sally Sims Stokes

Open Mon - Thurs 8:30 AM - 10 PM, Fri 8:30 AM - 5 PM, Sat 1 - 5 PM, Sun 5 - 10 PM. Estab 1967 for lending & reference; NTHP collection is for reference only. Circ 23,000

Library Holdings: Vols 41,000; Per subs 450; Bd per 6200; Micro — Fiche 200, reels 600

Special Subjects: Architecture, Landscape Architecture

Collections: †World exhibitions: books & pamphlets on buildings, art work & machinery; †National Trust for Historic Preservation Library Collection of UMCP

Publications: NTHP Library Acquisitions List, monthly; Architecture Library (brochure), annual; Access to Architectural Literature: Periodical Indexes, annual

L **Historic Preservation Library,** 20742. Tel 301-405-6319. *Librn* Sally Sims Stokes

Open Mon - Fri 9 AM - 5 PM. For reference only

Income: Financed by the University of Maryland

Library Holdings: Vols 11,000; Per subs 300; Micro — Fiche; AV — A-tapes, cassettes, motion pictures, v-tapes; Other — Clipping files, pamphlets

Special Subjects: Architecture, Historical Material, Period Rooms, Restoration & Conservation, all aspects of preservation of historic buildings

COLUMBIA

M **MARYLAND MUSEUM OF AFRICAN ART,** 5430 Vantage Point Rd, Historic Oakland at Town Center, PO Box 1105, 21044. Tel 410-730-7105; FAX 410-730-1823. *Exec Dir* Doris Hillian Ligon; *Dir* Claude M Ligon

Open Tues - Fri 10 AM - 4 PM, Sun noon - 4 PM. No admis fee. Estab 1980 working towards better understanding of African art. Mem: Dues contributing $100, family $25, individual $15, student $10

Collections: African art consisting of sculpture, textiles, masks and musical instruments

Publications: Museum Memos, quarterly

Activities: Workshops for children & families; docent training; lectures open to public, 7 vis lectr per year; gallery talks; tours; awards given

CUMBERLAND

M **ALLEGANY COUNTY HISTORICAL SOCIETY,** History House, 218 Washington St, 21502. Tel 301-777-8678. *Dir* Martha Hahn; *Pres* James S Bryner; *VPres* Roseanne Shuttleworth

Open Tues - Sat 11 AM - 4 PM, May - Oct, Sun 1:30 - 4 PM. Admis $2. Estab 1937. 18 room Victorian house, each room furnished with furniture, antiques, pictures. Average Annual Attendance: 4000. Mem: 600; dues $10 individual, $15 couple; meetings Jan, May, Sept, Nov

Income: $16,000 (financed by mem)

Publications: Quarterly newsletter

Activities: Originates traveling exhibitions to area schools; sales shop sells books and prints

EASTON

M **ACADEMY OF THE ARTS,** 106 South St, 21601. Tel 410-822-0455; FAX 410-822-5997. *Dir & Cur* Christopher Brownawell

Open Mon, Tues, Fri & Sat 10 AM - 4 PM, Wed & Thurs 10 AM - 9 PM, Sun 1 - 4 PM, cl bank holidays. No admis fee. Estab 1958 to promote the knowledge, appreciation & practice of all the arts; a private non-profit art center. Two large rooms in a historic building (old schoolhouse) in Easton's historic district. The Academy is housed in two 18th century structures-the original schoolhouse in Easton and an adjacent residence that has been renovated and linked with new construction. Begun in 1989, the renovation project expands the Academy's 6500 square feet to 26,000 square feet and includes four galleries, five studios, a 500 volume resource center and an Artist's slide registry. Average Annual Attendance: 20,000. Mem: 1500; dues benefactor $5000, patron $1000, sustaining $500, contributing $250, friend $100, dual family $50, individual $30

Income: Financed by memberships, contributions, government, corporate & foundation grants, admissions, tuitions, endowment & investments

Collections: Permanent art collection includes 19th and 20th century prints and paintings, including artists Felix Burot, James McNeill Whistler and Anders Lorn-the majority, however, have been produced by contemporary eastern shore artists

Exhibitions: The Academy mounts 24 exhibits per year featuring local, regional and nationally known artists

Publications: Academy of the Arts Newsletter, bimonthly; Eastern Shore Calendar of the Arts & Humanities, quarterly

Activities: Classes in drawing, painting, sculpture, fine crafts plus weekend workshops and open studio sessions; dance and music classes for all ages; childrens' summer arts program in all disciplined and arts media; dramatic programs; annual juried show & annual members shows with prizes awarded for both; exten dept serving Mid-Shore Talbot, Caroline, Queen Annes, Dorchester and Kent

FORT MEADE

M **FORT GEORGE G MEADE MUSEUM,** 4674 Griffin Ave, Attn: AFKA-ZI-PTS-MU, 20755-5094. Tel 410-677-7054; FTS 923-6966. *Cur* Robert S Johnson; *Museum Technician* Cynthia L Hayden
Open Wed - Sat 11 AM - 4 PM, Sun 1 - 4 PM, cl Mon, Tues and holidays. No admis. Estab 1963 to collect, preserve, study and display military artifacts relating to the United States Army, Fort Meade and the surrounding region. Average Annual Attendance: 40,000
Income: Financed by federal and military funds
Collections: Military art; World War I, World War II and Civil War Periods
Exhibitions: History of First US Army; History of Fort George G Meade
Activities: Lect open to the public, 4 vis lectr per yr; gallery talks; tours; living history programs

FROSTBURG

M **FROSTBURG STATE UNIVERSITY,** The Stephanie Ann Roper Gallery, 21532. Tel 301-689-4000. *Head* Dustin P Davis; *Coordr* Nancy Rosnow
Open Sat - Tues 1 - 4 PM, Wed 7 - 9 PM. No admis fee. Estab 1972 for educational purposes. Average Annual Attendance: 3000
Income: Financed by state appropriation
Collections: Folk art; prints
Exhibitions: Duane Hanson; Mid-Atlantic Region Print Exhibition; Tenth Street Days
Activities: Educ dept; lectures open to the public, 5 vis lectr per yr; gallery talks; competitions with awards; individual and original objects of art lent for exhibition; book traveling exhibitions, 4 per yr; junior museum
L **Lewis J Ort Library,** 21532. Tel 301-689-4395. *Dir* Dr David M Gillespie; *Exhib Librn* Mary Jo Price
Library Holdings: Vols 500,000; Per subs 1300; Micro — Fiche; AV — A-tapes, cassettes, fs, Kodachromes, motion pictures, slides, v-tapes; Other — Exhibition catalogs, prints, reproductions

HAGERSTOWN

M **WASHINGTON COUNTY MUSEUM OF FINE ARTS,** City Park, PO Box 423, 21741. Tel 301-739-5727. *Dir* Jean Woods; *Admin Asst* Christine Shives
Open Tues - Sat 10 AM - 5 PM, Sun 1 - 6 PM, cl Mon. No admis fee. Estab 1930 to exhibit, interpret & conserve art. The museum consists of the William H Singer Memorial Gallery, Sculpture Court, Concert Gallery, South Gallery and North Gallery. Average Annual Attendance: 40,000. Mem: 800; dues $25
Income: Financed by government, mem & donations
Collections: American pressed glass; antique laces; †contemporary painting, drawing, prints & sculpture; †European & †American sculpture, †prints & drawings; Oriental jades & art; †ethnographic art; decorative art; textiles; folk art; 19th & 20th century American art
Exhibitions: Annual Exhibition of Cumberland Valley Artists; Annual Photographic Salon; Fiber and Metal; Old Master Drawings; Paintings by Alice Neel; Paintings by American Indians; Paintings by the Peale Family; American Drawings II; English Landscapes by Philip Jackson; Victorian Art Glass; Crafts Invitational; Data-Paintings by Charles Field and Richard Lutzke; David Hatfield; Discovery in Stone; American Indian Baskets; Sculpture Fibers; Germanic Heritage; Cullen Yates: American Impressionist; Dorothy Gillespie; William H Singer, Jr (1868-1943)
Publications: The Fiftieth Year; American Pressed Glass; Old Master Drawings; annual reports; bulletin, monthly; catalogs of major exhibitions; catalog of the permanent collection; bi-monthly bulletin
Activities: Classes for adults and children; dramatic programs; docent training; lectures open to public, 10 vis lectr per yr; concerts; gallery talks; tours; competitions with awards; original objects of art lent to accredited museums; originate traveling exhibitions; sales shop sells books & original art
L **Library,** City Park, PO Box 423, 21741. Tel 301-739-5727.
Open Tues - Sat 10 AM - 5 PM, Sun 1 - 6 PM. Open to the public for reference only
Library Holdings: Vols 4000; Per subs 7; Micro — Cards; AV — Cassettes, fs, motion pictures, rec, slides, v-tapes; Other — Clipping files, exhibition catalogs, pamphlets

LAUREL

M **MARYLAND-NATIONAL CAPITAL PARK & PLANNING COMMISSION,** Montpelier Cultural Arts Center, 12826 Laurel-Bowie Rd, 20708. Tel 301-953-1993, 410-792-0664; FAX 301-206-9682. *Dir* Richard Zandler; *Asst Dir* Nancy Sausser; *Office Mgr* Janet Henderson
Open daily 10 AM - 5 PM. No admis fee. Estab 1979 to serve artists regionally and to offer high quality fine arts experiences to public. Main Gallery houses major invitational exhibitions by artists of regional & national reputation; Library Gallery houses local artists' exhibitions; Resident Artists' Gallery provided to artists who rent studio space; Small library of donated volumes. Average Annual Attendance: 35,000
Income: $300,000 (financed by county appropriation, grants, classes & studio rentals)
Exhibitions: (1990) Sculptural Furniture; Spirit Soundings; Photography Retropsective of Aubrey Bodine
Publications: Exhibit catalogs; promotional invitations, monthly
Activities: Classes for adults & children; lect open to public, 5 vis lectr per yr; competitions with awards; book traveling exhibitions, annually; originate traveling exhibitions

RIVERDALE

A **PYRAMID ATLANTIC,** 6001 66th Ave, Suite 103, 20737. Tel 301-459-7154. *Exec Dir* Cynthia Wayne; *Artistic Dir* Helen C Frederick; *Resident Printer* Susan Goldman
Open Mon - Sat 10 AM - 4 PM. Estab 1981 to support artists, foster the art of hand papermaking, printmaking & book arts
Income: Financed by grants from federal, state & local funding agencies, foundations & corporate support, mem
Collections: Archives of Prints, paper works & books
Exhibitions: What Path Now: Contemporary Artist Book, By Josh Heller. (1992) Crossing Over/Changing Places, by Jane Former

ROCKVILLE

M **JEWISH COMMUNITY CENTER OF GREATER WASHINGTON,** Jane L & Robert H Weiner Judaic Museum, 6125 Montrose Rd, 20852. Tel 301-881-0100. *Pres* Dr Richard Reff; *Exec Dir* Lester Kaplan; *Dir* Karen Falk
Open Mon - Thur noon - 4 PM & 7:30 - 9:30 PM, Sun 2 PM - 5 PM. No admis fee. Estab 1925 to preserve, exhibit and promulgate Jewish culture. Center houses museum and Goldman Fine Arts Gallery. Average Annual Attendance: 25,000
Income: Financed by endowment, corporate, private and public gifts and grants and sales
Exhibitions: Beth Ames Swartz: Israel Revisited; The Jews in the Age of Rembrandt; First Generation: Jewish Immigrant Artists in America; Charlotte: Life or Theater; 7-8 temporary exhibitions yearly including Israel Artists & American & emerging artists
Publications: Exhibition catalogues; brochures
Activities: Classes for adults & children; docent training; lectures open to public; concerts; gallery talks; tours; book traveling exhibitions; originate traveling exhibitions; museum shop sells books, original art, reproductions & prints

SAINT MARY CITY

M **ST MARY'S COLLEGE OF MARYLAND,** The Dwight Frederick Boyden Gallery, SMC, 20686. Tel 301-862-0246; FAX 301-862-0958. *Dir* Jonathan Ingersoll; *Gallery Asst* DiAnne Mita; *Registrar* Jan Kiphart
Open Mon - Thurs 10:30 AM - 5 PM, Fri 10:30 AM - 4:30 PM. No admis fee. 1600 sq ft exhibition space for temporary exhibits of art; five bldgs with art hung in public areas
Income: Financed by St Mary's College
Purchases: Collection is from donation
Collections: Study; developmental; Long Term Loan; SMC; Permanent
Exhibitions: Mac Wells, Clayton Pond, Ric Wagner
Activities: Gallery talks; individual paintings & original objects of art lent to local, non-profit organizations; lending collection contains original art works & prints, paintings & sculptures

SAINT MICHAELS

M **CHESAPEAKE BAY MARITIME MUSEUM,** Navy Point, PO Box 636, 21663. Tel 410-745-2916; FAX 410-745-6088. *Dir* John R Valliant; *Cur* Pete Lesher
Open Oct - May, Thurs - Sun 10 AM - 4 PM; cl Mon; Jan-March weekends only; May - Oct daily 10 AM - 5 PM. Admis adults $6, children $3. Estab 1965 as a waterside museum dedicated to preserving the maritime history of the Chesapeake Bay. Consists of twenty buildings on approximately 18 acres of waterfront property including Hooper's Strait Lighthouse, 1879. Average Annual Attendance: 85,000. Mem: 4500; dues $25 - $60
Income: Financed by membership, admissions & endowment
Collections: Paintings; ship models; vessels including skipjack, bugeye, log canoes, and many small crafts; waterfowling exhibits; working boat shop
Publications: Weather Gauge (newsletter), semi-annually
Activities: Classes for adults & children; docent training; lectures open to public, 10 vis lectr per year; concerts; gallery talks; tours; museum shop sells books, original art, reproductions, prints, slides
L **Library,** Navy Point, PO Box 636, 21663. Tel 410-745-2916; FAX 410-745-6088. *Cur* Pete Lesher
Estab 1965 for preservation of Chesapeake Bay maritime history & culture. One room with 2 - 3 exhibits per year. Average Annual Attendance: 15,000
Income: Financed by endowment
Library Holdings: Vols 3500; Per subs 5; Micro — Cards; Other — Clipping files, pamphlets
Special Subjects: Local art, maritime history

SALISBURY

SALISBURY STATE UNIVERSITY
M **University Gallery,** College & Camden Aves, Art Department, 21801. Tel 410-543-6271. *Art Dept Chmn* James L Burgess; *Interim Gallery Dir* Heather Timmons
Open Sept - Dec & Feb - May Mon & Wed 10 AM - 8 PM, Tues & Thurs 10 AM - 5 PM, Sat & Sun 1 - 5 PM, cl Fri. No admis fee. Estab 1967, to provide a wide range of art exhibitions to the University and community, with emphasis on educational value of exhibitions. Gallery open to public, and is located on the second floor of Blackwell Library. Average Annual Attendance: 4000
Income: Financed mainly by Salisbury State University with additional support from the Maryland State Arts Council, The Salisbury/Wicomico Arts Council and other agencies
Exhibitions: Annual faculty and student shows; wide range of traveling exhibitions from various national and regional arts organizations and galleries; occasional regional and local exhibitions
Publications: Announcements
Activities: Workshops for children, students and general public; film series; lectures open to the public, 1-2 vis lectr per yr; museum shop

L **Blackwell Library,** 1101 Camden Ave, 21801. Tel 410-543-6130. *Library Dir* James R Thrash
Open Mon - Thurs 8 AM - midnight, Fri 8 AM - 10 PM, Sat 10 AM - 8 PM, Sun noon - midnight. Estab 1925, to support the curriculum of Salisbury State University. Library has total space of 66,000 sq ft. Circ 2500
Library Holdings: Vols 220,580; Per subs 1632; Micro — Cards, fiche, reels; AV — A-tapes, cassettes, fs, motion pictures, rec, slides, v-tapes; Other — Clipping files, pamphlets

M **WARD FOUNDATION,** Ward Museum of Wildfowl Art, 909 S Schumaker, 21801. Tel 410-749-6104, 742-4988; FAX 410-742-3107. *Exec Dir* Van Baker; *Chmn* Marshall Moore; *Membership* Jean Henning; *Archives* Barbara Gehrm; *Gift Shop Mgr* Doug Johnson; *Events Coordr* Jane Rollins; *Cur Educ* Ann Anderson; *Pub Information Coordr* Joe Forsthoffer; *Business Mgr* Tim Lanids
Open Tues - Sat 10 AM - 5 PM, Sun 1 - 5 PM, cl Mon. Admis $2, mem & children under 12 free. Estab 1968 as a non-profit organization dedicated to preservation & conservation of wildfowl carving. Main gallery & balcony contain 2000 carvings , prints & paintings of wildfowl-related items, including World Championship carvings. Average Annual Attendance: 8000. Mem: 7000; dues family $40, individual $25
Income: $1,000,000 (financed by members, city & state appropriations, grants, donations, gift shop sales)
Exhibitions: Annual Fall Exhibition of paintings & sculptures; Antique decoy auction; The Ward Exhibition of Wildfowl Art
Publications: Wildfowl Art Journal, quarterly; Ward Foundation News, quarterly
Activities: Classes for adults & children; docent training; lectrs open to public; tours; competition with awards; carving workshops held in Apr, June & Feb; individual paintings & original objects of art lent; lending collection contains color reproductions, framed reproductions, original art works, original prints, paintings, photographs, sculpture; museum shop sells books, magazines, original art, reproductions, prints, slides, decoys and video shows

SILVER SPRING

L **MARYLAND COLLEGE OF ART & DESIGN LIBRARY,** 10500 Georgia Ave, 20902. Tel 301-649-4454. *Head Librn* Teresa Cummings Stevens
Open Mon - Fri 8:30 AM - 4:30 PM. Estab 1977 to facilitate & encourage learning by the students & to provide aid for the faculty. College maintains Gudelsky Gallery. Circ 7200
Purchases: $4000
Library Holdings: Vols 12,000; Per subs 25; AV — Cassettes 10, motion pictures, slides 16,000; Other — Clipping files
Special Subjects: Art History, Calligraphy, Commercial Art, Graphic Design, Illustration, Painting - American, Painting - British, Painting - Canadian, Painting - Dutch, Painting - European, Painting - Flemish, Painting - French, Painting - German, Painting - Italian, Painting - Japanese, Painting - New Zealander, Painting - Polish, Painting - Russian, Painting - Scandinavian, Painting - Spanish, Posters, Woodcuts, French, German, Italian, Photography, Spanish

SOLOMONS

M **CALVERT MARINE MUSEUM,** PO Box 97, 20688. Tel 410-326-2042; FAX 410-326-6691. *Dir* C Douglass Alves Jr; *Registrar* Robert J Hurry; *Exhib Designer* S Curtis Bowman; *Master Woodcarver* LeRoy Langley; *Cur of Education* Craig DeTample; *Cur Maritime History* Richard J Dodds; *Cur of Estuarine Biology* Kenneth Kaumeyer; *Cur of Paleontology* Michael D Gottfried
Open Mon - Sun 10 AM - 5 PM. Admis $2 & $3. Estab 1970, to provide the public with a marine oriented museum on maritime history, estuarine natural history, marine paleontology and natural & cultural history of the Patuxent River region. 5,500 sq ft gallery is maintained on maritime history of the region, 3-4 shows per yr. Average Annual Attendance: 50,000. Mem: 2000; dues family $25, individual $15
Income: $900,000 (financed by county appropriation & Calvert Marine Society)
Purchases: $1000
Collections: J S Bohannon Folk Art Steamboat Collection; local Chesapeake Bay Ship Portraits; Tufnell Watercolor Collection; Louis Feuchter Collection A Aubrey Bodine Collection; C Leslie Oursler Collection; August H O Rolle Collection
Publications: Newsletter Bugeye Times, quarterly; Flotilla: Battle for the Patuxent; War on the Patuxent, 1814: A Catalog of Artifacts; miscellaneous special publications on history; A History of Drum Point Lighthouse; Fossils of Calvert Cliffs; Watercraft Collection, brochure; The Drum Point Lighthouse, brochure; Early Chesapeake Single-Log Canoes: A Brief History & Introduction to Building Techniques; Cradle of Invasion: A History of the US Amphibious Training Base, Solomons, Maryland, 1942 - 45; The Othello Affair; The Pursuit of French Pirates on the Patuxent River, Maryland, August 1807; Working the Water: The Commercial Fisheries of Maryland's Patuxent River; The Last Generation: A History of a Chesapeake Shipbuilding Family
Activities: Classes for adults and children; docent training; lectures open to the public, 8 lectrs per year; concerts; gallery talks; tours; individual paintings & original objects of art lent to other appropriately qualified non-profit organizations; lending collection contains 3000 black & white photographs, lantern slides, art works, original prints, 2800 slides; originate traveling exhibitions, circulated to other professional museums; sales shop sells books, magazines, original art, prints, reproductions, slides, hand crafts

L **Library,** PO Box 97, 20688. Tel 410-326-2042. *Librn* Paul Berry
Open Mon - Fri 10 AM - 4:30 PM, cl weekends. Estab 1970. Library open for research and reference
Income: $1000 (financed by Calvert County government, membership, giftshop, donations, grants)
Purchases: $800
Library Holdings: Vols 3000; Per subs 25; Micro — Cards, fiche; AV — A-tapes, fs, Kodachromes, motion pictures, rec, slides, v-tapes; Other — Clipping files, exhibition catalogs, manuscripts, memorabilia, original art works, pamphlets, photographs, prints, reproductions
Special Subjects: Southern Maryland, Patuxent River, Chesapeake Bay

TOWSON

M **GOUCHER COLLEGE,** Rosenberg Gallery, Department of Art, 1021 Dulaney Valley Rd, 21204. Tel 410-337-6333, 337-6073. *Exhib Dir & Coll Coordr* Helen Glazer
Open Mon - Fri 9 AM - 5 PM during the academic calendar and on evenings and weekends of public events. No admis fee. Estab 1964 to display temporary and continuously changing exhibitions of contemporary and historically important visual arts. Gallery space located in the lobby of the Kraushaar Auditorium; 150 running feet of wall space. Average Annual Attendance: 60,000
Income: Financed privately
Collections: Ceramics; coins; drawings; paintings; prints; sculpture; †photography
Exhibitions: (1991) Books & Bookends - Sculptural Approaches; Neal Gallico, Paintings & James Sherwood, Color Photographs; Tim Thompson, Architectural Installation; Outcry: Artists Answer AIDS. (1991-92) Shaping Space; Photographs by Ed Worteck; Seeking - Through the Medium of Paper, Works by E H Sorrells-Adewale; Woman as Protagonist. (1992-93) Approaching the Quincentenary: Latino Art 1982-92; Shrines: Shelly Hull & Jenni Lukac; Photographs by Gary Cawood; An American in Japan
Publications: Exhibit brochures, 4 per year
Activities: Lect open to public; gallery talks; individual paintings and original objects of art lent to museums and university galleries; book traveling exhibitions 1 per year

TOWSON STATE UNIVERSITY

M **The Holtzman Art Gallery,** Osler Dr, 21204. Tel 410-321-2808. *Dir* Christopher Bartlett
Open Tues - Sat 11 AM - 4 PM. Estab 1973 to provide a wide variety of art exhibitions, primarily contemporary work, for students, faculty and community. The main gallery is situated in the new fine arts building directly off the foyer. It is 30 x 60 ft with 15 ft ceiling and 15 x 30 ft storage area. Average Annual Attendance: 10,000
Income: $18,000 (financed by state appropriation, cultural services fees and private gifts)
Purchases: $1000
Collections: African art; †Asian arts, through Roberts Art Collection; †contemporary painting and sculpture
Exhibitions: Annual Student Exhibition; Annual Faculty Exhibition; Annual Summer Exhibition Color and Image, American Enamels; Mary Ann Krutsick, visiting artist
Publications: Calendar, each semester; exhibition posters and catalogs
Activities: Lectures open to public, 5 - 10 vis lectr per year; gallery talks; tours; artmobile; book 2 - 3 traveling exhibitions per year; sales shop selling exhibition catalogs and posters

M **Asian Arts Center,** Fine Arts Bldg, Osler Dr & Cross Campus Dr, 21204. Tel 410-830-2807. *Cur* Suewhei T Shieh
Open during academic year Mon - Fri 10 AM - 4 PM, Sat 2 - 4 PM, summer Mon - Fri 11 AM - 3 PM. No admis fee. Estab 1972 to provide an area to display the Asian art collections of the University and for the benefit of both the university community and the public. The gallery is located on the second floor of the Fine Arts Building; also includes a small reference library. Average Annual Attendance: 3500
Income: Financed by state funding
Collections: Asian Ceramics; ivory; metalwork; furniture; paintings; prints; textiles; sculptures
Exhibitions: Permanent collection; special loan exhibitions
Activities: Lectures open to public; 2 vis lectr per year; gallery talks; tours; workshops; concerts; performances; individual and original objects of art lent to educational and cultural institutions

WESTMINSTER

M **WESTERN MARYLAND COLLEGE,** Gallery One, Department of Art, 21157. Tel 410-848-7000, Ext 596. *Gallery Dir* Wasyl Palijczuk
Open Mon - Fri 10 AM - 4 PM. No admis fee. Estab to expose students to original works by professional artists
Income: Financed by college funds
Exhibitions: Six visiting artists shows; student shows; faculty & alumni show

MASSACHUSETTS

AMESBURY

M **THE BARTLETT MUSEUM,** 270 Main St, PO Box 692, 01913. Tel 508-388-4528. *Pres* Lars Johannessen; *Cur* Hazele Kray
Open Memorial Day to Labor Day Wed - Sun 1 - 4 PM. Estab 1968. Two-room Victorian-style Ferry School built in 1870. Name later changed to The Bartlett School in honor of Josiah Bartlett, signer of America's Declaration of Independence, near whose home the school was sited. Mem: dues patron $100 & up, contributing $25, family $15, individual $5, student $1
Collections: Natural science artifacts
Exhibitions: (1993) Costume Exhibit; Hat-Making Exhibit
Activities: Workshops

AMHERST

M **AMHERST COLLEGE,** Mead Art Museum, 01002. Tel 413-542-2335; FAX 413-542-2117. *Dir* Martha Sandweiss; *Cur European Art* Ross Fox
Open Mon - Fri 10 AM - 4:30 PM, Sat & Sun 1 - 5 PM (summer) Tues - Sun 1 - PM, cl Mon. No admis fee. Estab 1949. Average Annual Attendance: 13,500. Mem: 500; annual meetings in the spring

Collections: Ancient art; †American art; †English art; Western European & †Oriental collections
Exhibitions: Images of Alexsei Remisov; Delacroix & the Romantic Image; Progressive Geometric Abstraction in America; Willard Boepple Sculpture; changing exhibitions for college curriculum.
Publications: American Art at Amherst: A Summary Catalogue of the Collection at the Mead Art Gallery; American Watercolors & Drawings from Amherst College; Mead Museum Monographs; catalogues for major exhibitions
Activities: Educ dept; lectures open to public; 3 vis lect per yr; gallery talks; tours; individual paintings & original objects of art lent for exhibition only to other museums
L **Frost Library,** 01002. Tel 413-542-2373. *Fine Arts Librn* Elizabeth M Kelly
Circulating to Amherst College students and five college faculty
Library Holdings: Vols 40,000; Per subs 82; Micro — Fiche; AV — Slides; Other — Exhibition catalogs

ARTS EXTENSION SERVICE
For further information, see National & Regional Organizations

L **JONES LIBRARY, INC,** 43 Amity St, 01002. Tel 413-256-4090. *Dir* Bonnie Isman; *Asst Dir* Sondra M Radosh; *Reference Librn* Pauline M Peterson; *Adult Service Librn* Beth Girshman; *Cur* Dan Lombardo
Open Mon, Wed, Fri and Sat 9 AM - 5 PM, Tues & Thurs 9 AM - 9:30 PM, Sun 1 PM - 5 PM; Special Collections has limited hours. Estab 1919 as a public library. Gallery. Circ 210,000. Average Annual Attendance: 100,000
Income: Financed by endowment and city appropriation
Library Holdings: Micro — Reels; AV — A-tapes, cassettes, rec, slides; Other — Clipping files, framed reproductions, manuscripts, memorabilia, original art works, pamphlets, photographs, sculpture
Collections: †Emily Dickinson; Harlan Fiske Stone; Ray Stannard Baker; †Robert Frost; †Sidney Waugh Writings; †local history & geneology
Activities: Lect open to public; concerts; tours

UNIVERSITY OF MASSACHUSETTS, AMHERST
M **University Gallery,** Fine Arts Center, Room 35 D, 01003. Tel 413-545-3670; FAX 413-545-0132. *Dir* Betsy Siersma; *Cur* Regina Coppola; *Registrar* Jennifer Lind; *Gallery Mgr* Craig Allaben
Open Tues - Fri 11 AM - 4:30 PM, Sat & Sun 2 - 5 PM during school year. No admis fee. Estab 1975. Main gallery 37 x 40 ft; East, West and Lower Galleries 20 x 40 ft each. Average Annual Attendance: 15,000. Mem: 150; dues $25 and up
Collections: †20th century American works on paper including drawings, prints and photographs
Exhibitions: Vito Acconci; Michael Brewster; Daniel Buren; Donna Dennis; Naum Gabo Monoprints; Jenny Holzer; Mel Kendreck; The Prints of Barnett Newman; Judy Pfaff; Martin Puryear; Jim Roche; Fred Sandback; Italo Scanga; Judith Shea; Peter Shelton; Alan Shields; Mauro Staccioli; Fransesc Torres; Allan Wexler; Recent Museum Architecture in New England; The Shadow of the Bomb; Beyond Light; Infra-Red Photography
Publications: Exhibition catalogs
Activities: Lect open to the public; gallery talks; tours; film program; individual art works from the permanent collection loaned to other institutions; originate traveling exhibitions
L **Dorothy W Perkins Slide Library,** Bartlett Hall, 01003. Tel 413-545-3314. *Cur of Slides & Art History* Louise Bloomberg; *Slide Librn* Nathalie Sulzner
Open Mon - Fri 12:15 PM - 3:30 PM. Circ 60,000 (slides)
Library Holdings: Magnetic Disks 50; Study Plates 7000, interactive video disks; AV — Slides 260,000
Exhibitions: (1986) Exhibit of over 200 early architectural photographs

ANDOVER

M **PHILLIPS ACADEMY,** Addison Gallery of American Art, Chapel Ave, 01810. Tel 508-749-4015. *Dir* Jock Reynolds; *Cur Photography* James L Sheldon; *Asst Dir* Susan Faxon; *Cur Paintings, Sculpture, Prints & Drawings* Susan Faxon; *Registrar* Denise Johnson; *Registrar* Alison Karamer; *Curatorial Asst Preparator* Leslie Maloney; *Membership Public Relations* Duncan Will
Open Tues - Sat 10 AM - 5 PM, Sun 1 - 5 PM. No admis fee. Estab 1931 in memory of Mrs Keturah Addison Cobb, to enrich permanently the lives of the students by helping to cultivate and foster in them a love for the beautiful. The gift also included a number of important paintings, prints and sculpture as a nucleus for the beginning of a permanent collection of American art. Maintains small reference library for museum use only. Average Annual Attendance: 35,000
Income: Financed by endowment
Collections: 18th, 19th and 20th century drawings, paintings, prints, sculpture; photographs; film; videotapes
Exhibitions: (1990) Winslow Homer at the Addison; Stephen Davis - Jacob & His Twelve Sons
Activities: Lect open to public, 8-10 vis lectrs per year; concerts

ASHLAND

M **ASHLAND HISTORICAL SOCIETY,** 2 Myrtle St, PO Box 145, 01721. Tel 508-881-8183.
Estab 1909
Publications: Monthly newsletter for members

ATTLEBORO

M **ATTLEBORO MUSEUM, CENTER FOR THE ARTS,** Capron Park, 199 County St, 02703. Tel 508-222-2644. *Pres* David Laferriere; *VPres* Steven Fallon; *Treas* Scott Smith; *Dir* John Chandler
Open Tues - Fri 12:30 - 5:30 PM, Sat 9 AM - 5 PM, Sun 12:30 - 5 PM, cl Mon. No admis fee. Estab 1927 to exhibit the works of contemporary New England artists, as well as the art works of the museum's own collection. These are public

openings plus several competitive exhibits with awards and an outdoor art festival. Three galleries with changing monthly exhibits of paintings, drawings, sculpture, ceramics, jewelry, glass, metals & prints. Mem: 230; dues life mem $1000, benefactor $500, patron $250, sponsor $200, supporting & corporate $1000, assoc $40, family $35, artist mem $25 student & senior citizen $15
Income: Financed by mem, gifts, local & state grants
Collections: Paintings and prints
Exhibitions: Holiday Show; Annual Area Artist Exhibit; Individual & Group Exhibits of Various Media & Subject; Competitive Painting Show; Summer Members Show; Competitive Photography Show; Selections from the Permanent Collection
Publications: Newsletter
Activities: Classes for adults and children; lect open to public; concerts; gallery talks; competitions, painting and photography; original objects of art lent

BEVERLY

M **BEVERLY HISTORICAL SOCIETY,** Cabot, Hale and Balch House Museums, 117 Cabot St, 01915. Tel 508-922-1186. *Pres* John W Murray; *Cur* Katherine Pinkham; *Treas* Richard Carr
Cabot Museum open yearly Wed - Fri 10 AM - 4 PM & alternate Sat; Balch House open May 20 - Oct 15; Hale House open June - Sept. Admis adults $2 (all three museums for $5), children under 16 $.50 (all three museums for $1). The Balch House built in 1636 by John Balch contains period furniture. The Hale House was built in 1694 by the first minister, John Hale. Cabot House built in 1781-82 by prominent merchant and private owner, John Cabot. Average Annual Attendance: 2000. Mem: 450; dues families $15, single $10; annual meeting Oct
Collections: 120 paintings containing portraits, folk & Revolutionary War scenes; 1000 pieces furniture, toys, doll houses, military & maritime items & pewter, books, manuscripts & photographs
Exhibitions: Beverly Mariners and the China Trade; Two Hundred Years at the House of Cabot; Collection of 19th Century Accessories
Publications: Quarterly newsletter
Activities: Docent training; lectures open to public and some for members only; gallery talks by arrangement; tours; individual paintings and original objects of art lent to other museums and libraries; sales shop sells books and postcards
L **Library,** 117 Cabot St, 01915. Tel 508-922-1186.
Library Holdings: Vols 4000; Per subs 2; AV — A-tapes, motion pictures, slides; Other — Clipping files, manuscripts, memorabilia, pamphlets, photographs, prints, sculpture
Special Subjects: New England Maritime and Transportation History; Beverly History

BOSTON

ARCHAEOLOGICAL INSTITUTE OF AMERICA
For further information, see National and Regional Organizations

M **THE ART INSTITUTE OF BOSTON,** Gallery East, 700 Beacon St, 02215. Tel 617-262-1223; FAX 617-437-1226. *Pres* Stan Trecker; *Dir Gallery* Bonnie Robinson; *Dir Gallery* Martin Mugar
Open Mon - Fri 9 AM - 4:30 PM, Sat noon - 4 PM. No admis fee. Estab 1969 to present major contemporary & historical exhibitions of the work of established & emerging artists, & to show work by students & faculty of the Institute. 3000 sq ft of gallery. Average Annual Attendance: 4000
Exhibitions: Four Venezualan Photographers; Checkoly Poster Show. (1991) Contemporary Landscape Show, Gina Wesch & Herni Pardee; Louis Finkelstein; Zen Art
Activities: Classes for adults & children; professional programs in fine & applied arts & photography; lectures open to the public, five visiting lecturers per year; lecture series coordinated with exhibitions; gallery talks; competitions, local and regional; exten dept serves Greater Boston area; individual paintings & original objects of art lent to other galleries; curate & mount exhibitions for major public spaces
L **Library,** 700 Beacon St, 02215. Tel 617-262-1223. *Librn* Valda Bolis
Open Mon - Thurs 7:30 AM - 9:30 PM, Fri 7:30 AM - 6 PM, Sat 8 AM - 2 PM. Estab 1969 to support school curriculum
Purchases: $15,000
Library Holdings: Vols 7000; Per subs 50; Vertical File 260; AV — Kodachromes, slides 30,000, v-tapes 150; Other — Clipping files 10,000, exhibition catalogs
Special Subjects: Advertising Design, Art Education, Art History, Ceramics, Commercial Art, Conceptual Art, Drawings, Film, Graphic Arts, Graphic Design, Illustration, Photography, Posters, Pottery, Printmaking, Prints, Watercolors

C **BANK OF BOSTON,** Gallery, 100 Federal St, 02110. Tel 617-434-2200. *Dir & Cur* Lillian Lambrechts; *Technical Dir* James Field
Collections: Contemporary paintings; non-contemporary paintings & textiles, sculpture
Publications: Exhibition catalogues, 6-10 times per yr

A **BOSTON ARCHITECTURAL CENTER,** 320 Newbury St, 02115. Tel 617-536-3170; FAX 617-536-5829. *Dir* Diane Sparrow; *Pres* George Terrien; *Dean* Arcangelo Cascieri
Open Mon - Thurs 9 AM - 11 PM, Fri - Sun 9 AM - 5 PM. No admis fee. Estab 1889 for education of architects & designers. Small exhibition space on first floor. Average Annual Attendance: 2000. Mem: 300; dues $25; annual meeting June
Activities: Classes for adults; lect open to public, 16 vis lectrs per year; competitions; exten dept serving professional architects; traveling exhibitions organized and circulated
L **Memorial Library,** 320 Newbury St, 02115. Tel 617-536-9018; FAX 617-536-5829. *Chief Librn* Susan Lewis; *Asst Librn* Sarah Dickinson
Open by appointment only
Income: $2000
Library Holdings: Vols 2000

Special Subjects: 19th century European & American Architecture
Collections: 18th, 19th & early 20th century architectural books from the collections of practicing architects
Exhibitions: (1989) For the Record

A BOSTON ART COMMISSION OF THE CITY OF BOSTON, 1 City Hall Square, 02201. Tel 617-635-3245. *Chmn* Robert Cormier; *Exec Secy* Mary O Shannon; *Commissioner* Bruce R Rossley; *Commissioner* William B Osgood; *Commissioner* Donald L Stull; *Commissioner* Bruce Beal
Estab 1890 to accept & maintain the art collection owned by the City of Boston. Mem: 5; one representative from each organization: Boston Society of Architects, Director of Office of Arts & Humanities, Boston Public Library, Copley Society, & Boston Museum of Fine Arts; meetings once per month
Income: Financed by city appropriation
Purchases: Commissions through private trust fund
Collections: City of Boston art collection, including fountains, paintings, sculpture, statuary
Publications: Catalog and guide to the art work owned by the City of Boston, in preparation; Passport to Public Art
Activities: Competitions

L BOSTON ATHENAEUM, 10 1/2 Beacon St, 02108. Tel 617-227-0270; FAX 617-227-5266. *Dir & Librn* Rodney Armstrong; *Cur of Collections* Michael Wentworth; *Art Gallery Dir* Donald C Kelley; *Print Dept Cur* Sally Pierce; *Honorary Cur of Prints* Charles E Mason Jr
Open Mon - Fri 9 AM - 5:30 PM, Sat 9 AM - 4 PM; cl Sun also Sat June 1 - Oct 1. Estab 1807 to exhibit fine arts and crafts of New England and national artists. Large exhibition gallery in conjunction with library. Average Annual Attendance: 20,000.
Income: $1,400,000 (financed by endowment and membership)
Purchases: $75,000
Library Holdings: Vols 100,000; Per subs 100; Original documents; Micro — Reels; Other — Clipping files, exhibition catalogs, manuscripts, memorabilia, original art works, pamphlets, photographs, prints, reproductions, sculpture
Collections: †19th century Boston prints and photographs; †American and European painting and sculpture; †World War I posters
Exhibitions: Change monthly
Publications: Exhibition catalogs
Activities: Lectures open to public, 15 vis lectrs per yr; concerts; tours; individual paintings & original art lent to qualified museums and institutions; book traveling exhibitions; originate traveling exhibitions; museum shop

M THE BOSTONIAN SOCIETY, Old State House Museum, 206 Washington St, 02109. Tel 617-720-3290. *Exec Dir* Joan C Hull; *Dir Coll* Carolyn Hughes
Open daily 9:30 AM - 5 PM. Admis adults $2, older adults & students $1.50, children ages 6 -18 $.75. Estab 1881 to collect & preserve the history of Boston. Average Annual Attendance: 90,000. Mem: 1250; dues benefactor $500, supporter $100, family $50, individuals $30, students $20, sr citizens $20; annual meeting
Income: Financed by endowment, membership, admissions, grants, state & federal appropriations
Collections: Paintings and artifacts relating to Boston history; Maritime art; Revolutionary War artifacts; prints
Exhibitions: Ongoing exhibitions
Publications: Proceedings of The Bostonian Society; The Bostonian Society Newsletter
Activities: Workshops; lect open to public; gallery talks; walking tours; individual paintings & original objects of art lent to other museums; museum shop sells books, reproductions, prints, pewter & children's products

L Library, 15 State St, 3rd fl (Mailing add: Old State House, 206 Washington St, 02109). Tel 617-720-3285; FAX 617-720-3289. *Librn* Philip S Bergen
Open Mon - Fri 9:30 AM - 4:30 PM. Estab 1881 to collect and preserve material related to the history of Boston
Purchases: $1500
Library Holdings: Vols 8000; Per subs 10; Postcards, Ephemera, Scrapbooks, Documents; AV — Slides 1000; Other — Clipping files, manuscripts, memorabilia, original art works, pamphlets, photographs 8500, prints 2000, reproductions
Special Subjects: History of Boston
Exhibitions: (1992-94) The Last Tenement: Community & Urban Renewal in Boston's West End
Publications: Bostonian Society Newsletter, quarterly

A BOSTON PRINTMAKERS, c/o Emmanuel College, 400 The Fenway, 02115. Tel 617-735-9898. *Pres* Marjorie Javan
Estab 1947 to aid printmakers in exhibiting their work; to bring quality work to the public. Average Annual Attendance: 15,000. Mem: 200; dues $25; annual meeting June
Income: Financed by membership, entry fees, and commission on sales
Purchases: $4700
Exhibitions: ?Prints, artist books, etchings, lithograph, mixed media, monotypes, serigraph & woodcut
Publications: Exhibition catalogs
Activities: Lectures open to the public; gallery talks; competitions with awards and prizes; individual paintings and original objects of art lent to local museums, galleries, libraries and schools; book 5 traveling exhibitions per year; traveling exhibitions organized and circulated

BOSTON PUBLIC LIBRARY
L Central Library, Copley Square, 02117. Tel 617-536-5400. *Dir* Arthur Curley
Building contains mural decorations by Edwin A Abbey, John Elliott, Pierre Puvis de Chavannes, & John Singer Sargent; bronze doors by Daniel Chester French; sculptures by Frederick MacMonnies, Bela Pratt, Louis Saint Gaudens; paintings by Copley and Duplessis; & bust of John Deferrari by Joseph A Cole tti
Income: Financed by city and state appropriation
Library Holdings: Vols 6,000,000; Per subs 16,704
Publications: Exhibition catalogues
Activities: Lect open to the public; concerts; tours

L Fine Arts Dept, Copley Square, 02117. Tel 617-536-5400, Ext 275. *Cur of Fine Arts* Janice Chadbourne
Open Mon - Thurs 9 AM - 9 PM, Fri & Sat 9 AM - 5 PM. Non-circulating
Library Holdings: Vols 156,000; Per subs 320; Auction Catalogs; Micro — Cards, fiche 12,000, reels 81; Other — Clipping files, exhibition catalogs, manuscripts, memorabilia, pamphlets, photographs, reproductions
Collections: Vertical files on local artists, architects & organizations; Connick Stained Glass Archives; W G Preston Architectural Drawings; Peabody & Stearns Architectural Drawings; Society of Arts & Crafts Archives
Publications: Fine Arts Department (a description)

M Albert H Wiggin Gallery & Print Department, Copley Square, 02117. Tel 617-536-5400, Ext 280. *Keeper of Prints* Sinclair H Hitchings; *Asst Keeper of Prints* Karen Smith Shafts
Open Gallery Mon - Thurs 9 AM - 9 PM, Fri & Sat 9 AM - 5 PM, cl Sun; Print Study Room Mon - Fri 9 AM- 5 PM, cl Sat & Sun
Library Holdings: Architectural drawings 100,023, prints, drawings, paintings 75, 539, negatives 40,810 & postcards 135,280; AV — Lantern slides 6,623; Other — Clipping files, exhibition catalogs, photographs 650,379
Collections: Collection of 18th, 19th & 20th century French, English & American prints & drawings, including the Albert H Wiggin Collection; 20th century American prints by Boston artists; 19th century photographs of the American West & of India & the Middle East; Boston Pictorial Archive; architectural archives; paintings; postcards; Boston Herald Traveler Photo Morgue
Exhibitions: Eight or nine per year drawn from the print department's permanent collections
Activities: Lectures open to the public, 1-2 vis lectr per year; Internships offered

L Rare Book & Manuscripts Dept, Copley Square, 02117. Tel 617-536-5400, Ext 425. *In Charge Keeper* Dr Laura Monti; *Cur of Rare Books* Roberta Zonghi; *Cur of Manuscripts* Giusseppe Bissaccia; *Librn* Eugene Zepp
Open 9 AM - 5 PM Weekdays. Estab 1934. Average Annual Attendance: 1400
Income: Financed by trust funds
Purchases: Books, manuscripts & maps
Library Holdings: Vols 260,000; Per subs 4; Micro — Prints, reels; AV — Lantern slides; Other — Clipping files, exhibition catalogs, manuscripts, memorabilia, pamphlets, photographs
Special Subjects: Landscapes, Antiquities-Greek, Antiquities-Roman, Bookplates & Bindings, Calligraphy, Costume Design & Construction, Etchings & Engravings, Graphic Design, Illustration, Mosaics, Photography, Posters, Prints, Restoration & Conservation, Stage Design, Woodcuts, Landscape; Navigation & Travel, Sciences, Spanish & Portugese, West Indies; anti-slavery; gardening; women's history; religion
Collections: †Americana; †anti-slavery, †history, †colonization & discovery; †Spanish & Portugese: literature, history & economics; †theater: playbills, plays, programs; juvenilia; †Women: authors, marriage, manners & customs; †science: astronomy, physics & mathematics; †English: literature, history & laws; †classical literature; †history of printing; †botany; †landscape & gardening; †religion
Exhibitions: Irwin D Hoffman: a retrospective exhibition; A Medieval Christmas & Little Bit More; the National Teachers Book Award; George Washington; Barcelona & its Publishing; the New England Church in the 17th Century; Continuation of the Exhibit "Collectors' Choice"; the Artist & Child; From Bondage to Freedom; Calderon de la Barca & his contemporaries; Jefferson - a tribute; Engravings of 16th & 17th centuries: A Technique of Book Illustration; Images of Christmas; the World Beyond; Boston Latin School; Three Hundred & Fiftieth Anniversary 1635-1985; Numismatics; Barcelona Imprints; Medieval Manuscripts; Wilfred Beaulieu & Le Travailleur; France in America; A Man of our Times; Saint Francis of Assisi; Boston Reveres the Brownings; Simon Bolivar: a Bicentennial Tribute; The Highlights of the Ticknor Collection; the Written Word of the Christian Faith; the Multiple Facets of Dwiggins; We the People: American Constitution; Nathaniel Bowditch: His Work; The Stinehour Press; Christopher Columbus: The Genoese; Robert & Elizabeth Browning; Lafayette: American & French Hero; W B Yeats; Italian Treasures; North American Indians. (1991) The Civil War: People & Places; John Adams Library; Portuguese Discoverers; Splendid Editions of the Works of Shakespeare. (1992) New England's Many Faces of Slavery; Geo Cruikshank's World Revisited
Activities: Seminars; lectures open to the public, 3 vis lectrs per yr; concerts; tours; sales shop sells postcards & pamphlets

M BOSTON UNIVERSITY, Art Gallery, 855 Commonwealth Ave, 02215. Tel 617-353-3329. *Dir* Kim Sichel; *Asst Dir* Mary Drach
Open Mon - Fri 10 AM - 4 PM, Sat & Sun 1 - 5 PM. No admis fee. Estab 1960. One exhibition space, 250 running ft, 2500 sq ft
Collections: Contemporary & New England Art
Activities: Lectures open to public; gallery talks; book traveling exhibitions, 2 per year; originate traveling exhibitions

A BOSTON VISUAL ARTISTS UNION, 33 Harrison Ave, 7th Fl, 02111. Tel 617-695-1266. *Business Dir* Carol Spack; *Admin Asst* James Roszel
Open Mon, Wed & Thur noon - 5 PM, Sat 10 AM - noon. No admis fee. Estab 1970 to bring the artist out of the studio & into the market. A small reference library, slide registry & print bins of members' works are maintained. Mem: 400; dues $40; monthly meetings
Income: (Financed by endowment, mem, city & state appropriation
Publications: BVAU News, bi-monthly
Activities: Professional workshops; lectures open to public, 20 vis lectrs per year; books sold

M BROMFIELD GALLERY, 107 South St, 02111. Tel 617-451-3605. *Dir* Christina Lanzl
Open Tues - Sat 10 AM - 5:30 PM. No admis fee. Estab 1972 to exhibit art. 3 galleries, about 2000 sq ft. Average Annual Attendance: 3000. Mem: 20; dues $750; monthly meetings
Income: Financed by mem
Activities: Lect open to public, 5 vis lectr per year; gallery talks

M **CRANE COLLECTION GALLERY,** 218 Newbury St, 02116. Tel 617-262-4080. *Pres* Bonnie L Crane; *Asst to Pres* Gael Crasco
Open Tues - Sat 10 AM - 5 PM. Estab 1983 to exhibit 19th and early 20th century American paintings. Five rooms in 19th century building with period furnishings. Average Annual Attendance: 2500
Collections: 19th century & early 20th century American paintings, including Hudson River School, Boston School & regional artists
Exhibitions: Boston School: Then & Now; Summer Scenes II; Bruce Crane; Tonalism; Inspiration of Cape Ann; City Scenes

C **FEDERAL RESERVE BANK OF BOSTON,** PO Box 2076, 02106-2076. Tel 617-973-3454, 973-3368; FAX 617-973-3621. *Cultural Affairs Coordr* Anne Belson; *Cultural Affairs Asst* Gail Carson
Open Mon - Fri 9 AM - 5 PM by appointment only. Estab 1978 for educational & cultural enrichment. Collection displayed on 3rd, 4th, 31st and 32nd floors and elsewhere throughout building. A permanent gallery, 28 x 183 ft with an adjoining 420 seat auditorium, located on the ground floor; open Mon - Fri 10 AM - 4 PM; is reserved for temporary exhibitions
Collections: †Focus of the collection is on United States art since the mid-1950's
Publications: Art at the Federal Reserve Bank of Boston; Lithographs: The Federal Reserve Bank of Boston Collection
Activities: Lect; gallery talks; tours; book temporary exhibitions by New England groups

M **ISABELLA STEWART GARDNER MUSEUM,** 280 Fenway (Mailing add: 2 Palace Rd, 02115). Tel 617-566-1401; FAX 617-566-7653. *Dir* Anne Hawley; *Cur* Hilliard T Goldfarb; *Development* Susan Courtemanche; *Business* Susan Davy
Open Tues - Sun 11 AM - 5 PM, cl Mon & national holidays. Admis $6, sr citizen & student $3. Estab 1903, the museum houses Isabella Stewart Gardner's various collections. Museum building is styled after a 16th century Venetian villa; all galleries open onto a central, glass-roofed courtyard, filled with flowers that are changed with the seasons of the year. Average Annual Attendance: 155,000. Mem: 2000; dues $25 & up
Income: Financed by endowment, fundraising, mem donations & door charge
Collections: Gothic and Italian Renaissance, Roman and classical sculpture; Dutch and Flemish 17th century; Japanese screens; Oriental and Islamic ceramics, glass, sculpture; 19th century American and French paintings; major paintings of John Singer Sargent and James McNeill Whistler
Publications: Guide to the Collection; Oriental & Islamic Art in the Isabella Stewart Gardner Museum; European & American paintings in The Isabella Stewart Gardner Museum; Drawings-Isabella Stewart Gardner Museum; Mrs Jack; A Checklist of the Correspondence of Isabella Stewart Gardner at the Gardner Museum; Sculpture in the Isabella Stewart Gardner Museum; Textiles - Isabella Stewart Gardner Museum; children's books - Isabella Stewart Gardner Museum; Fenway Court
Activities: Classes for children; lectures open to public 10 vis lectrs per year; concerts; gallery talks; tours; symposia; sales shop selling books, reproductions, prints, slides, postcards & annual reports, jewelry, gifts

L **Rare Book Collection & Archives,** 2 Palace Rd, 02115. Tel 617-566-1401; FAX 617-566-7653. *Librn & Archivist* Susan Sinclair
Open by appointment Mon, Wed, Fri. Estab 1903. Open to scholars who need to work with museum archives; building designed in style of 15th century Venetian palace. Mem: 2000; annual dues $25 & up
Library Holdings: Vols 800; Per subs 19; Other — Clipping files, exhibition catalogs, manuscripts, memorabilia, photographs
Special Subjects: Art History
Collections: Objects spanning 30 centuries; 1000 rare books spanning 6 centuries including papers of museum founder; rich in Italian Renaissance painting
Activities: Educ program; lect open to public, 6 - 8 vis lectrs per year; symposia; concerts; gallery talks; tours; Sales shop sells books, reproductions, prints, slides, postcards

M **GIBSON SOCIETY, INC,** Gibson House Museum, 137 Beacon St, 02116-1504. Tel 617-267-6338. *Adminr* Edward Gordon
Open May - Oct, Wed - Sun, Nov - Apr, Sat & Sun 2 - 5 PM, cl holidays. Admis $3. Estab 1957 as a Victorian House museum; memorial to Gibson family. Victorian time capsule, early Back Bay Town House, 8 rooms with Victorian & Edwardian era furnishings. Average Annual Attendance: 1500
Income: Trust fund, admissions
Collections: Decorative arts; paintings; sculpture; Victorian period furniture; objects associated with Gibson & related families
Activities: Guided tours; original objects of art lent to museums & galleries; sales shop sells postcards

A **GUILD OF BOSTON ARTISTS,** 162 Newbury St, 02116. Tel 617-536-7660. *Pres* Robert J Cormier; *Treas* Roger W Curtis; *Gallery Mgr* Barbara A Smith
Open Tues - Sat 10 AM - 5 PM; cl Sun, Mon & July & Aug. No admis fee. Estab and incorporated 1914, cooperative organization. Guild owns building; one gallery with continuous exhibitions in which each member is entitled to show one work; second gallery devoted to one-man shows, each member by turn at regular intervals. Mem: Active 65-80, associates under 100; annual meeting April
Income: Financed by membership dues
Exhibitions: Three yearly general exhibitions; two educational exhibits

M **INSTITUTE OF CONTEMPORARY ART,** 955 Boylston St, 02115-3194. Tel 617-266-5151; FAX 617-266-4021. *Dir* Milena Kalinovska; *Asst to Dir* Christa Balderacchi; *Dir Membership* Valessia Samaras; *Dir Development* Teil Silverstein; *Dir & Video Producer* Branka Bogdanov; *Cur* Matthew Teitelbaum; *Exhib Mgr & Registrar* Matthew Siegal; *Asst Registrar* Lia Gangitano; *Mgr Public Information* Lisa Rivo; *Development Assoc* Barbara Vejvoda; *Special Events Coordr* Kate Shamon; *Controller & Chief Financial Officer* Richard Lappin; *Financial Asst* Yat-May Wong; *Gallery & Bookstore Mgr* Anne Taupier; *Production Asst* John Miazga; *Production Asst* Tim Obetz
Open Wed 5 - 9 PM, Thurs noon - 9 PM, Fri, Sat & Sun noon - 5 PM. Admis $5, students with ID $3, sr citizens & children $2, members free. Estab 1936 to organize, document, & exhibit works of contemporary masters of new &

innovative talents, showing a range of artistic media, including paintings, sculpture, photography, film & video performance. Average Annual Attendance: 55,000. Mem: 2500; dues $30 & up; annual meeting in Sept
Income: Financed by membership, gifts and grants, earned income
Publications: Exhibition catalogs
Activities: Programs for adults & children; lectures open to public, 20 vis lectr per yr; film series; video; concerts; gallery talks; tours; competitions; book traveling exhibitions annually; originate traveling exhibitions, circulating to other national & international contemporary art museums; museum shop sells books, magazines, t-shirts, catalogues, cards, posters

MASSACHUSETTS COLLEGE OF ART
L **Morton R Godine Library,** 621 Huntington Ave, 02115. Tel 617-232-1555. *Dir* George Morgan; *Librn* Margot Isabelle; *Librn* Mary Curtin-Stevenson; *Slide Cur* Staci Stull; *Archivist* Paul Dobbs; *Librn* John Keating; *Librn* Mary Van Winkle
For lending
Library Holdings: Vols 95,000; Per subs 491; Micro — Cards, fiche 8000; AV — A-tapes, cassettes, fs, motion pictures, rec, slides, v-tapes; Other — Exhibition catalogs, memorabilia, original art works, pamphlets, photographs, prints, sculpture
Special Subjects: Art Education, Art History

A **MASSACHUSETTS HISTORICAL SOCIETY,** 1154 Boylston St, 02215. Tel 617-536-1608. *Dir* Louis L Tucker
Open Mon - Fri 9 AM - 4:45 PM, cl Sat, Sun & holidays. No admis fee. Estab 1791
Income: Financed by endowment
Collections: Archives; historical material; paintings; sculpture
Exhibitions: Temporary exhibitions
Publications: Annual brochure; irregular leaflets; various books
Activities: Lectures; special exhibits for members and their guests
L **Library,** 1154 Boylston St, 02215. Tel 617-536-1608. *Librn* Peter Drummey; *Photography* Chris Steele
Open Mon - Fri 9 AM - 4:45 PM. Average Annual Attendance: 3000
Library Holdings: Vols 250,000; Other — Manuscripts 3500, prints
Special Subjects: Coins & Medals, Manuscripts, Maps, Miniatures, Painting - American, Photography, Portraits, Prints
Publications: Portraits in the Massachusetts Historical Society, Boston 1988 (one edition)
Activities: Lectures

A **MOBIUS INC,** 354 Congress St, 02210. Tel 617-542-7416. *Co-Dir* Marilyn Arsem; *Co-Dir* Nancy Adams
Estab 1977 to support artists producing experimental work in all media. Average Annual Attendance: 4000
Exhibitions: Weekly exhibition for Boston & Regional Artists in experimental work in all media; Sculpture for Moments; installations & performances throughout the year

M **MUSEUM OF AFRO-AMERICAN HISTORY,** Abiel Smith School, 46 Joy St, 02114. Tel 617-742-1854. *Executive Dir* Monica Fairbairn
A non-profit education institution founded to study the social history of New England's Afro American communities & to promote an awareness of that history by means of educational programs, publications, exhibits & special events. The African Meeting House is the chief artifact of the Museum of Afro American History
Activities: Lect open to public, 4 vis lectr per year; concerts; gallery talks; tours; individual paintings & original objects of art lent; book traveling exhibitions; museum shop sells books

M **MUSEUM OF FINE ARTS,** 465 Huntington Ave, 02115. Tel 617-267-9300; FAX 617-247-2312. *Dir* Alan Shestack; *Deputy Dir* Morton Golden; *Dir Development* Patricia Jacoby; *Asst Dir Exhibit* Desiree Caldwell; *Comptroller* Thomas Fitzgerald; *Registrar* Linda Thomas; *Cur American Decorative Arts* Jonathan Fairbanks; *Cur European Decorative Arts & Sculpture* Anne Poulet; *Cur Asiatic Art* Wu Tung; *Cur European Paintings* Peter Sutton; *Cur Prints & Drawings* Clifford Ackley; *Asst Dir Special Projects & Prog* Brent Benjamin; *Cur Classical Art* Cornelius C Vermeule; *Asst Dir Operations* David Moffatt; *Cur American Painting* Theodore E Stebbins Jr; *Cur Egyptian & Ancient Near Eastern Art* Rita Freed; *Dir Research* Arthur Beale; *Dir Education* William Burback; *Cur Contemporary Art* Trevor Fairbrother
Open Tues 10 AM - 5 PM, Wed 10 AM - 10 PM, Thurs - Sun 10 AM - 5 PM, cl Mon. Admis adults $7, sr citizens $6, members free. Estab and inc 1870; present building opened 1909. Average Annual Attendance: 800,000. Mem: 55,000; dues assoc $100, family $50, individual $40
Collections: Outstanding Chinese, Japanese and Indian art; exceptional †Egyptian, †Greek and †Roman art; †master paintings of Europe and America; †superb print collection from 15th century to present; †sculpture, †decorative and minor arts including period rooms, porcelains, †silver, †tapestries, †textiles, †costumes, †musical instruments
Exhibitions: Specially organized exhibitions are continually on view; exhibitions of the permanent collections. (1993) Age of Rubens; Building a Collection - Dept of Contemporary Art Part I; John Singleton Copley's Watson and the Shark
Publications: Journal, yearly; calendar of events, bi-monthly; exhibition catalogs; collection catalogs
Activities: Classes for adults & children; lectures open to public; concerts; gallery talks; tours; films; museum shop sells books, magazines, original art, reproductions, prints & slides
L **William Morris Hunt Memorial Library,** 465 Huntington Ave, 02115. Tel 617-267-9300; FAX 617-267-0280. *Chief Librn* Nancy S Allen
Admis adults $7, sr citizens & students $6, youths 6 - 17 $3.50. Estab 1870 to house, preserve, interpret & publish its collections. For reference only. Average Annual Attendance: 1,000,000. Mem: 59,000
Income: $290,000 (financed by endowment & mem)
Purchases: $105,000
Library Holdings: Per subs 650; Other — Clipping files, exhibition catalogs, pamphlets 117,000

Special Subjects: Carpets & Rugs, Ceramics, Decorative Arts, Drawings, Etchings & Engravings, Furniture, Painting - American, Prints, Sculpture, Textiles, Mosaics, Painting - American, Painting - European, Restoration & Conservation, Sculpture, Antiquities
Activities: Classes for adults and children; docent training; dramatic programs; lectures open to public; concerts; gallery talks; tours; book traveling exhibitions

L **Dept of Photographic Services,** Slide & Photographic Library, 465 Huntington Ave, 02115. Tel 617-267-9300; FAX 617-247-2312. *Dir* Janice Sorkow
Library Holdings: AV — Slides 120,000
Special Subjects: Architecture, Decorative Arts, Painting - American, Photography, Prints, Sculpture

M **MUSEUM OF THE NATIONAL CENTER OF AFRO-AMERICAN ARTISTS,** 300 Walnut Ave, 02119. Tel 617-442-8014. *Dir & Cur* Edmund B Gaither; *Asst Dir* Harriet F Kennedy; *Artistic Dir* Elma Lewis
Open June - Aug daily 1 - 6 PM, Sept - May daily 1 - 5 PM. Admis adult $1.25, children $.50. Estab 1969 to promote visual art heritage of Black people in the Americas and Africa. Suite of three special exhibition galleries; suite of three African Art Galleries; suite of three permanent collection galleries; one local artist gallery. Average Annual Attendance: 10,000. Mem: 250; annual dues $25
Income: $250,000 (financed by private gifts, contracts, etc)
Collections: Art from Western Africa; Early 20th century Afro-American Prints & Drawings; visual fine arts of the Black world
Exhibitions: African Artists in America; Stone Churches of Ethiopia; Preying Shoes, Praying Shoes-A Video Installation, James Mintford; African Outlook; Recent Fashion Design, C S Okkeke; Afro-American Artist in Paris 1919-1937
Publications: Newsletter, quarterly
Activities: Dramatic programs; lectures open to the public; concerts; gallery talks; tours; competitions with awards (Edward Mitchell Barrister Award); book traveling exhibitions; traveling exhibitions organized and circulated; sales shop sells books, magazines, prints and small sculpture

M **NATIONAL ARCHIVES AND RECORDS SERVICE,** John F Kennedy Library and Museum, Columbia Point, 02125. Tel 617-929-4500. *Dir* Charles Daly; *Cur* Dave Powers
Open daily 9 AM - 5 PM. Admis adult $5, children 5 - 15 $1. Estab 1964 to preserve collections of Kennedy papers and other material pertaining to his career; to educate public about J F Kennedy's career and political system; to make materials available to researchers. Library is a nine-story building overlooking Boston Harbor, has two theaters and an exhibition floor. Average Annual Attendance: 500,000
Income: Financed by federal government and national archives trust fund
Library Holdings: Micro — Cards, fiche, prints; AV — A-tapes, cassettes, fs, lantern slides, motion pictures, slides, v-tapes; Other — Memorabilia, original art works, pamphlets, photographs, prints, reproductions
Collections: 32,000,000 documents and personal papers of John F Kennedy, Robert Kennedy and many others associated with life and career of John F Kennedy; 6,000,000 ft of film relating to political career, 150,000 photographs, 1200 oral histories, 11,000 paintings and museum objects (personal); manuscripts of Ernest Hemingway, 10,000 photographs of him with family & friends; 800 glass plates collection of Josilh Johnson Hanes
Activities: Tours; museum shop sells books, reproductions, prints and slides

L **NEW ENGLAND SCHOOL OF ART & DESIGN,** Library, 28 Newbury St, 02116. Tel 617-536-0383. *Librn* Brian Tynemouth, MLS
For lending
Purchases: $5000
Library Holdings: Vols 5500; Per subs 55; AV — Slides, v-tapes; Other — Clipping files, pamphlets
Special Subjects: Advertising Design, Architecture, Art History, Calligraphy, Commercial Art, Furniture, Graphic Design, Illustration, Interior Design, Landscape Architecture, Lettering, Photography, Posters

NEW ENGLAND WATERCOLOR SOCIETY
For further information, see National and Regional Organizations

M **NICHOLS HOUSE MUSEUM, INC,** 55 Mount Vernon St, 02108. Tel 617-227-6993. *Cur* William H Pear
Open 1 - 5 PM. Admis $3. Estab 1961. Average Annual Attendance: 3000. Mem: 315; dues $25; annual meeting in May
Income: $50,000 (financed by endowment, membership, rentals)
Collections: Decorative Arts Collection

L **PAYETTE ASSOCIATES ARCHITECTS PLANNERS,** Library, 285 Summer St, 02210. Tel 617-342-8201, Ext 234; FAX 617-342-8202. *Librn* Ann Collins; *Archivist* Bob Drake
Library Holdings: Vols 1500; Per subs 120; AV — Slides; Other — Clipping files
Special Subjects: Architecture
Collections: Interiors Sample Library; †Manufacturer's Catalogs; †Medical & Laboratory Planning

M **PHOTOGRAPHIC RESOURCE CENTER,** 602 Commonwealth Ave, 02215-2400. Tel 617-353-0700; FAX 617-353-1662. *Dir* Brenda Sullivan; *Cur* John Jacob; *Dir Publications* Dan Younger
Open Tues - Sun noon - 5 PM, Thurs noon - 8 PM. Admis general $3, sr & students $2, free Thurs 5 PM - 8 PM. Estab 1977 for the photographic arts. Mem: 2600; dues $25
Library Holdings: Vols 3500; Other — Exhibition catalogs
Activities: Educ dept; photography workshops with guest artists; lectures open to public, 5 vis lectr per year; gallery talks; tours; competitions; book traveling exhibitions 2 - 3 per year; originate traveling exhibitions

A **SOCIETY FOR THE PRESERVATION OF NEW ENGLAND ANTIQUITIES,** Harrison Gray Otis House, 141 Cambridge St, 02114. Tel 617-227-3956; FAX 617-227-9204. *Dir* Jane Nylander
Open Tues - Fri 12 - 5 PM, Sat 10 AM - 5 PM. Admis adults $3, children under 12 $1.50. Estab and inc 1910, the Otis House serves as both headquarters and

museum for the Society. Society owns over 30 historic houses throughout New England, 23 of which are open to the public. Average Annual Attendance: 3000. Mem: 3200; dues $15 and up; annual meeting May or June
Special Subjects: Historic preservation, interpretation of historic properties
Collections: American and European decorative arts and antiques with New England history; photographs; houses
Publications: Old Time New England, occasional bulletin; SPNEA News, quarterly; house guide, annual
Activities: Classes for adults; lectures open to public, 5-10 vis lectr per yr; originate traveling exhibitions; museum shop sells books

L **Archives,** Harrison Gray Otis House, 141 Cambridge St, 02114. Tel 617-227-3956; FAX 617-227-9204. *Cur Archives* Lorna Condon
Admis $4 - $5. Estab 1910 to preserve & interpret New England domestic architecture & daily life 1820 - 1900. For reference. Mem: 3000; dues $35; annual meeting in June
Library Holdings: Other — Clipping files, manuscripts, memorabilia, original art works, pamphlets, photographs, prints
Collections: Study collections of New England Architecture in the form of decorative arts, interior decoration, landscape; †400,000 photographs, †pattern books; other collections include textiles, wallpaper
Exhibitions: Portsmouth Furniture: Masterworks from the New Hampshire Seacoast
Activities: Classes for adults & children; lect open to public; concerts; tours; museum shop sells books, reproductions & slides

A **THE SOCIETY OF ARTS AND CRAFTS,** 175 Newbury St, 02116. Tel 617-266-1810. *Pres* Ellen Grossman; *Exec Dir* Barbara Baker; *Gallery Mgr* Randi Lathrop
Open Mon, Tues Thurs & Fri 10 AM - 6 PM, Wed 10 AM - 7 PM, Sat 10 AM - 5 PM, Sun noon - 5 PM. No admis fee. Estab 1897 to promote high standards of excellence in the arts & crafts & to educate the public in the appreciation of fine craftsmanship. Two galleries on the second level house special exhibitions. Average Annual Attendance: 8000. Mem: 800; dues party or joint $50, single $30; annual meeting in May or June
Income: $110,000 (financed by membership, gallery sales, grants)
Collections: Contemporary one-of-a-kind furniture
Exhibitions: Special exhibitions on a single craft medium presented year round; Furniture Interiors I, II & III
Activities: Lect open to public, 4 - 5 vis lectr per yr; gallery talks; awards; sales shop sells fine handmade crafts in ceramics, wood, glass, metal, fiber & leather

C **STATE STREET BANK & TRUST CO,** 225 Franklin St, 02101. Tel 617-654-3938. *Art Cur* Rhonda Berchuck
Collections: American & European Paintings from the 17th to 19th Centuries; engravings; lithographs; ship models & figureheads; maritime artifacts; decorative arts

M **USS CONSTITUTION MUSEUM FOUNDATION INC,** Boston National Historical Park, Museum, Charlestown Navy Yard, Bldg 22, PO Box 1812, 02129. Tel 617-426-1812; FAX 617-242-0496. *Exec Dir* Ellen Kraft; *Dir Finance & Administration* Bob Hassey; *Cur* Anne Gimes Rand; *Dir Educ* Dan Schwartz; *Dir Development* Margot Emery
Open 9 AM - 5 PM, varies by season. Admis $3 & under. Estab 1972 to collect, preserve & display items relating to USS Constitution. Average Annual Attendance: 100,000. Mem: 1100; dues $25 - $1,000; annual meeting in the fall
Income: $1,400,000 (financed by endowment, mem, admis, gift shop, federal, state & private grants)
Collections: †Documents relating to Constitution; †Personal possessions of crew members; †Shipbuilding & navigational tools; †Souvenirs depicting old ironsides; †USS Constitution images (paintings, prints & photos)
Exhibitions: A Century of Service; Life at Sea; A Look Below the Waterline: Preserving Old Ironsides; Annual Juried Ship Model Show
Publications: Chronicle, quarterly newsletter
Activities: Classes for adults & children; family programs; docent programs; lect open to public, 4-6 vis lectr per year; tours; competitions; book traveling exhibitions; originate traveling exhibitions; retail store sells books, prints, magazines, slides, reproductions, clothing & souvenirs

A **VOLUNTEER LAWYERS FOR THE ARTS OF MASSACHUSETTS INC,** PO Box 8784, 02114. Tel 617-523-1764; FAX 617-523-1764.
Estab 1989 to provide arts related legal assistance to artists & arts organizations
Activities: Lect open to public

BROCKTON

L **BROCKTON PUBLIC LIBRARY SYSTEM,** Joseph A Driscoll Art Gallery, 304 Main St, 02401-5390. Tel 508-580-7890. *Dir* Ernest J Webby Jr
Open Mon - Thurs 9 AM - 9 PM, Fri & Sat 9 AM - 5 PM, cl Sun. No admis fee. Special room for monthly art exhibitions. Average Annual Attendance: 20,000
Library Holdings: Vols 294,000
Collections: W C Bryant Collection of 19th and 20th century American paintings, chiefly New England artists; gifts of 20th century paintings which includes four paintings by Hendricks Hallett and an oil painting by Mme Elisabeth Weber-Fulop; loan collection of 20th century painters from the Woman's Club of Brockton; mounted photographs of Renaissance art and watercolors by F Mortimer Lamb
Exhibitions: Monthly exhibitions by local and nationally known artists

A **FULLER MUSEUM OF ART,** 455 Oak St, 02401. Tel 508-588-6000. *Dir* Caroline Graboys; *Dir Visual Display* Otto Erbar; *Dir Development* Beth Galer; *Dir Educ* Linda Keating; *Dir Exhib* Donna Barnes
Open Wed - Sun noon - 5 PM. Admis adults $2, children $1. Estab 1969 to provide a variety of art exhibitions & education programs of regional & national interest. The center houses six galleries; one gallery is reserved for important works of art on loan from the Museum of Fine Arts, Boston. Average Annual Attendance: 35,000. Mem: 1500; dues $20

Income: $784,000 (financed by endowment, mem, gifts & government grants)
Collections: Contemporary American art; Early American & Sandwich glass; 19th century American paintings; contemporary regional crafts
Publications: Newsletter & calendar of events, 3 per year
Activities: Classes for adults & children; docent training; special programs for children; lect open to the public, 4 vis lectr per year; gallery talks; tours; competitions; concerts; scholarships; 0ndividual paintings & original objects of art lent to accredited museums of the American Association of Museums; lending collection contains paintings & slides; originate traveling exhibitions; museum shop sells original art, reproductions, prints & contemporary crafts
L **Library,** 455 Oak St, 02401. Tel 508-588-6000.
Open to members, staff & students
Library Holdings: Vols 5000

CAMBRIDGE

A **CAMBRIDGE ART ASSOCIATION,** 25 R Lowell St, 02138. Tel 617-876-0246. *Dir* Kathryn Zuckerman
Open Tues - Sat 11 AM - 5 PM, cl in July and Aug. No admis fee. Estab 1944 to exhibit, rent and sell members' work and to encourage an interest in fine arts and crafts in the community. Mem: 400; dues artists $50, friends $30, students $10; annual meeting Jan
Exhibitions: Invited shows in Rental Gallery and Craft Gallery; foreign exhibition each year; members' juried exhibitions in Main Gallery every month
Publications: Bulletin, monthly
Activities: Classes for adults; dramatic programs; open workshops; lect and demonstrations; competitions with prizes; sales shop sells books, original art, prints, cards, jewelry and crafts

HARVARD UNIVERSITY
M **Harvard University Art Museums,** 32 Quincy St, 02138. Tel 617-495-9400; FAX 617-495-9936. *Dir* James Cuno; *Deputy Dir* Frances A Beane; *Mgr Corporate & Foundation Relations* Susan L Kany; *Registrar* Jane Montgomery; *Cur Chinese Art* Robert Mowry; *Archivist* Phoebe Peebles; *Membership* Rebecca Wright; *Visitor Servs* Margaret Howland; *Dir Center for Conservation & Technical Studies* Henry Lie; *Public Relations* Cynthia Friedmann; *Dir of Fellows & Special Programs* Mary Rose Maybank
Open Tues - Sun 10 AM - 5 PM, cl Mon & holidays. Admis (applies to all 3 museums) adults $4, students & sr citizens $2.50, children under 18 free admis, no admis fee Sat mornings. 225,000 vol fine arts library (Fogg Art Museum) & Rubel Asiatic Research Collection (Sackler) available for use by request only; extensive visual collection; reading room; classrooms. Average Annual Attendance: 245,000. Mem: 2200; dues patron $1000, donor $500, contributor $100, couple $50, individual $35, student $25, admis only $20
Income: Financed by endowment, mem & federal grants
Publications: Director's report, quarterly newsletter; exhibit catalogs; gallery guides
Activities: Lectures; gallery talks; tours; seminars; concerts
—**Busch-Reisinger Museum,** 32 Quincy St, 02138. Tel 617-495-2317; FAX 617-495-9936. *Cur* Peter Nisbet; *Curatorial Assoc* Emile Norris
Estab 1901 and opened in 1920, it has one of the most important and extensive collections of Central & European art outside of Europe, ranging from the Romanesque to the present day. This collection serves the teaching program of the Department of Fine Arts, outside scholars and the general public
Collections: Late Medieval, Renaissance & Baroque sculpture; 16th century paintings & 18th century porcelain; 20th century German works; sculpture, paintings, drawings & prints; largest collection of Bauhaus material outside Germany
Exhibitions: Paul Klee Drawing Exhibition; George Grosz
Publications: Newsletter
Activities: Tours by appointment; lecture open to the public; gallery talks; originate traveling exhibitions
—**William Hayes Fogg Art Museum,** 32 Quincy St, 02138. Tel 617-495-9400; FAX 617-495-9936. *Dir* James Cuno; *Deputy Dir* Frances A Beane; *Cur Drawings* William W Robinson; *Cur Prints* Marjorie B Cohn; *Archivist* Phoebe Peebles; *Dir Conservation* M Cohn Beale; *Cur Painting* Ivan Gasnell
Open Tues - Sun 10 AM - 5 PM, cl Mon & holidays. Admis adults $4, students $2.50, Sat mornings free. University estab 1891; museum estab 1927; serves both as a public museum and as a laboratory for Harvard's Dept of Fine Arts, which trains art historians and museum professionals. The Center for Conservation and Technical Studies operates a training program for conservators and technical specialists. Average Annual Attendance: 200,000. Mem: 2200; dues $35 & up
Income: Financed by endowment, membership and federal grants
Collections: European & American paintings, sculpture, decorative arts, photograhs, prints & drawings; English & American silver; Wedgwood; Maurice Wertheim collection of impressionist & past- impressionist art
Publications: Annual report; newsletter, 4 - 5 per year
Activities: Docent training; lectures open to the public, up to 50 vis lectrs per yr; concerts; gallery talks; tours; individual paintings and original objects of art lent to exhibitions; book traveling exhibitions, 1 - 2 per yr; originate traveling exhibitions; museum shop sells books, reproductions and prints
—**Arthur M Sackler Museum,** 485 Broadway, 02138. Tel 617-495-9400; FAX 617-495-9936. *Dir* James Cuno; *Deputy Dir* Frances A Beane; *Cur Chinese Art* Robert Mowry; *Cur Islamic & Later Indian Art* Stuart Cary Welch; *Honorary Cur Rugs* Walter Denny
Estab 1985 to serve both as a public museum & as a laboratory for Harvard's Dept of Fine Arts, which trains art historians & museum professionals
Collections: Ancient coins; Greek red & black figure vases; Greek & Roman bronze & marble sculpture; Greek, Roman & Near Eastern metalwork & jewelry; Egyptian antiquities; Asian bronzes, ceramics, jades, painting, prints & sculpture; Islamic & Indian paintings, illuminated manuscripts, ceramics, metalwork & textiles
Activities: Museum shop sells books, prints & reproductions

L **Fine Arts Library,** 02138. Tel 617-495-3373; FAX 617-496-4889. *Librn* Jeffrey L Horrell; *Assoc Librn Book Coll* Patricia J Rogers; *Cur of Visual Coll* Helene Roberts; *Chief Cataloguer* Susan Myerson
Open to Harvard Community Mon - Thur 9 AM - 10 PM, Fri 9 AM - 5 PM, Sat 10 AM - 5 PM. Estab 1895 to support the teaching department of fine arts & the research needs of the curatorial departments of the Fogg Art Museum & an international community of scholars in art history. Circ 116,000
Income: $1,956,510 (financed by endowment)
Purchases: $352,172
Library Holdings: Vols 247,929; Per subs 1426; Ephemera; Micro — Fiche, reels; AV — Slides 587,300; Other — Exhibition catalogs, pamphlets 57,435, photographs 941,776
Special Subjects: All areas of art history with emphasis on Italian primitives, architectural history, art and architecture of Western & Eastern Europe, conservation and restoration of works of art, Dutch 17th Century, history of photography, master drawings, Romanesque sculpture, Far Eastern art, Islamic art & architecture
Collections: DIAL Index; Marburger Index; The Index of Jewish Art; The Knoedler Libray Library on Microfiche; Manuscript Archives of American artists and art scholars; Oriental and Islamic Art; Rubel Asiatic Research Collection: Library collection on the arts of the Far East; 40,000 catalogued auction sales catalogs
Publications: Catalog of Auction Sales Catalogs; Fine Arts Library Catalog (1971); Dictionary Catalog; The Catalogs of the Rubel Asiatic Research Collection (microfiche editions, 1984); Guide to the Card Catalogs of Harvard University, 1895 - 1981 (1984); Iconographic Index to Old Testament (1987); Iconographic Index to New Testament (1992); Vol I: Narrative Paintings of the Italian School (1992)
L **Frances Loeb Library,** Graduate School of Design, Gund Hall, 02138. Tel 617-495-2574. *Librn* Hinda F Sklar
Estab 1900 to serve faculty and students of graduate school of design. Circ 55,000
Income: $996,000 (financed by endowment & tuition)
Purchases: $233,000
Library Holdings: Vols 248,000; Per subs 1500; Drawings; Micro — Fiche, reels; AV — A-tapes, cassettes, fs, Kodachromes, lantern slides, motion pictures, rec, slides, v-tapes; Other — Clipping files, exhibition catalogs, manuscripts, pamphlets, photographs
Special Subjects: Architecture, City and Regional Planning; Landscape Architecture, Urban Design
Collections: Cluny; Le Corbusier; Charles Eliot; John C Olmsted; H H Richardson; Charles Mulford Robinson; Hugh Stubbins; Josep Lluis Sert
Publications: Frances Loeb Library Users' Guide, annual
Activities: Tours
M **Semitic Museum,** 6 Divinity Ave, 02138. Tel 617-495-4631, 495-3123; FAX 617-496-8904. *Dir & Prof* Lawrence Stager; *Exec Dir* Dr Carney E S Gavin; *Cur Exhibits* Nitza Rosovsky
Open Mon - Fri 11 AM - 5 PM. No admis fee, $2 donation. Estab 1889 to promote sound knowledge of Semitic languages and history; an archaeological research museum. Average Annual Attendance: 3000-15,000. Mem: 250; dues $20 and up
Income: Financed by endowment, mem, federal research grants and contracts
Collections: †Historic photographs, Collection; Excavated material from Nazi & various other Palestinian & near Eastern sites; Islamic metal weapons, garments (Ottoman Empire); Pheonician glass, (1870's Mid East photographs, Mid East costumes)
Exhibitions: (1990-91) The Tumen Collection of Judaica; The Holy Land Then & Now
Publications: Harvard Semitic Series; exhibit catalogs
Activities: Docent training; lecture-film series; lectures open to public, 5-8 vis lectr per yr; gallery talks; tours; exten dept serves Harvard Unversity; original objects of art lent to universities and museums; book traveling exhibitions; originate traveling exhibitions; sales shop sells books, reproductions & prints

M **LONGFELLOW NATIONAL HISTORIC SITE,** 105 Brattle St, 02138. Tel 617-876-4491. *Cur* Jim Shay; *Supervisory Park Ranger* Brian Doherty
Open daily 10 AM - 4:30 PM. Admis $2 (under 16, over 62 free). Estab 1972 to acquaint the public with the life, work, and time of the American poet Henry W Longfellow. Average Annual Attendance: 18,000
Income: Financed by US Department of the Interior
Collections: Paintings, sculpture, prints, furniture and furnishings once belonging to Henry W Longfellow and his daughter Alice; 19th century photographic collection including views of China and Japan
Activities: Lectures open to public; concerts; tours; individual paintings and original objects of art lent to qualified institutions; sales shop sells books

MASSACHUSETTS INSTITUTE OF TECHNOLOGY
M **List Visual Arts Center,** Wiesner Bldg E 15 - 109, 20 Ames St, 02139. Tel 617-253-4400. *Dir* Katy Kline; *Cur* Helaine Posner; *Registrar* Jill Aszling; *Admin Officer* Toby Levi; *Gallery Mgr* Jon Roll
Open Mon - Fri noon - 6 PM, Sat & Sun 1 - 5 PM. No admis fee. Estab 1963 to organize exhibitions of contemporary art in all media. Average Annual Attendance: 20,000
Income: Financed by MIT, public and private endowments, art councils, corporations and individuals
Collections: Major public sculpture, paintings, drawings, prints, photographs and site-specific commissions all publicly sited through the campus. All collections are being enlarged through donations & purchases
Exhibitions: Twelve exhibitions per year of contemporary art in all mediums
Publications: Exhibition catalogs
Activities: Educ Dept; tours; films; lectures open to public, 20 vis lectr per yr; lending collection of original art; Student Loan Print Collection of over 350 pieces; book traveling exhibitions, one per yr; originate traveling exhibitions to major museums; museum shop sells books

M MIT Museum, Bldg N52, 265 Massachusetts Ave, 02139. Tel 617-253-4444; FAX 617-253-8994. *Dir* Warren A Seamans; *Facilities Mgr* Barbara Linden; *Asst Dir Exhibits* Joan Loria; *Asst Dir Coll* Michael Yeates; *Asst Cur Exhibits* Donald Stidsen; *Asst Dir Education & Community Relations* Marcia Conroy; *Asst Dir Marketing* Kathleen Thruston; *Asst Dir Admin* Phoebe Hackett
Open Tues - Fri 9 AM - 5 PM, Sat & Sun 1 - 5 PM. Admis for people outside MIT community $2. Estab 1971 as a museum facility documenting the development of the Institute and of 19th and 20th century science and technology and the interrelationships of art, science, and technology. 14-18 galleries of varying sizes. Average Annual Attendance: 200,000
Income: Financed by University & outside funding
Collections: Architectural drawings; biographical information; furniture; objets d'art; scientific instruments and apparatus; paintings; portraits; photographs
Exhibitions: (1993) The Hudson Studio; the Sporting Woman
Publications: The MIT Museum Newsletter, quarterly; exhibition catalogs; gallery exhibition notes
Activities: Classes for adults and children; lectures open to the public; 4 - 6 vis lectr per yr; gallery talks; tours; book traveling exhibitions, 2 - 4 per yr; originate traveling exhibitions; museum shop sells books, prints, MIT - & exhibit-related items
—Hart Nautical Galleries and Collections, 265 Massachusetts Ave, 02139. Tel 617-253-5942. *Cur* Kurt Hasselbalch
Gallery open daily 9 AM - 8 PM; reference Mon - Fri 9 AM - 5 PM by appointment only. Estab 1922 to preserve history of naval architecture, shipbuilding, yachts. Galleries include permanent exhibit of ship models & changing exhibits
Income: Financed by University
Collections: Forbes Collection of whaling prints; rigged models & half models of merchant and warships, engine models, marine paintings & drawings
Exhibitions: (1993) Exhibition on 100 Year Anniversary of MIT Department of Ocean Engineering
Activities: Lectures open to the public, 5 vis lectr per yr; individual paintings & original objects of art lent to qualified museums; lending collection contains prints, slides & models; museum shop sells books
L Rotch Library of Architecture & Planning, 77 Massachusetts Ave, Room 7-238, 02139. *Librn* Margaret DePopolo; *Assoc Librn & Col Mgr* Merrill W Smith; *Librn Aga Khan Program for Islamic Architecture* Omar Khalidi
Open Mon - Thurs 8:30 AM - 10 PM, Fri 8:30 AM - 7 PM, Sat 10 AM - 6 PM, Sun 2 - 10 PM, special hours when school is not in session. Estab 1868 to serve the students and faculty of the School of Architecture and Planning and other members of the MIT community
Library Holdings: Vols 175,000; Per subs 650; Micro — Fiche, reels; AV — A-tapes, cassettes, Kodachromes, lantern slides, motion pictures, slides, v-tapes; Other — Exhibition catalogs, pamphlets, photographs
Special Subjects: Architectural Designs History & Theory, Art History, Urban & Environmental Designs, Contemporary Islamic Architecture
Publications: Selected Rotch Library Acquisitions; Selected Publications of the Faculty, School of Architecture and Planning, annually; The Aga Khan Program

CHATHAM

M CHATHAM HISTORICAL SOCIETY, Old Atwood House, 347 Old Harbor Rd, PO Box 381, 02633. Tel 508-945-2493. *Pres* Daniel Buckley; *Cur* Jeannette Fontaine
Open Mon, Wed & Fri June - Sept 9 hrs per wk. Admis fee $3. Estab 1926 to preserve local Chatham history. Murals Barn houses Alice Stallknecht murals of Chatham people, The New Gallery houses Frederick Wight paintings of local sea captains. Average Annual Attendance: 1500. Mem: Dues $10; meetings in Aug & Feb
Income: Financed by mem
Collections: †Harold Brett (paintings); Harold Dunbar (paintings); Frederick Wight (paintings); Sandwich Glass; 17th & 18th century furnishings

CHESTNUT HILL

M BOSTON COLLEGE, Museum of Art, Devlin Hall 108, 02167. Tel 617-552-8587; FAX 617-552-8577. *Dir* Nancy Netzer; *Cur* Alston Conley; *Adminr* Helen Swartz
Estab 1863. Average Annual Attendance: 30,000 - 50,000. Mem: 250
Income: Financed through University funds
Activities: Lect open to public, some open to only members; book traveling exhibitions 3 per year; originate traveling exhibitions 3 per year

COHASSET

M COHASSET HISTORICAL SOCIETY, Caleb Lothrop House, Elm St (Mailing add: 14 Summer St, 02025). Tel 617-383-6930. *Pres* Bartram J Pratt; *VPres T* Gerard Keating; *Sr Cur* David Wadsworth
Headquarters open by appointment only; Maritime Museum & Wilson House open daily 1:30 - 4:30 PM, cl Mon June - Sept. Admis by donations. Estab 1974 as the headquarters house of the Cohasset Historical Society. Paintings of local significance are displayed in various rooms; Cohasset Historical Society's library & archives located here. Mem: 400; dues life member $250, sustaining $30, family $20, single $10; annual meetings in Nov & Mar
Collections: Old furniture, local art work
Publications: Historical Highlights, newsletter 4 times per yr
Activities: Educ dept
M Cohasset Maritime Museum, Elm St (Mailing add: 14 Summer St, 02025). Tel 617-383-6930.
Estab 1957 to display the seafaring history of Cohasset. Average Annual Attendance: 700
Collections: Artifacts, artworks, documents & models depicting Cohasset's history as a seafaring & fishing community during the 18th & 19th centuries; general collection of local historical artifacts

M Captain John Wilson Historical House, Elm St (Mailing add: 14 Summer St, 02025). Tel 617-383-6930.
Estab 1936. Paintings of local subjects & topics, some by local artists, are displayed upon walls of the several rooms. Average Annual Attendance: 700
Collections: Old household furnishings, toys, kitchenware & artwork from the old homes of Cohasset

CONCORD

A CONCORD ART ASSOCIATION, 37 Lexington Rd, 01742. Tel 508-369-2578. *VPres* Loring W Coleman; *Cur* Patsy B McVity; *Treas* Abbie Page; *Secy* Alice Moulton
Open Tues - Sat 11 AM - 4:30 PM, Sun 2 - 4:30 PM. Admis adult $1, members, children under 14, student groups & sr citizens free. Estab 1916 for the encouragement of art & artists. Average Annual Attendance: 10,000. Mem: 600; dues life member $500, business & patron $30, associate $20, artist $15, student $2
Income: Financed by membership
Collections: Bronze sculptures; colonial glass
Exhibitions: Changing exhibition per year
Publications: Exhibition notices
Activities: Lect open to public, 4 - 6 vis lectr per year; tours; sales gallery sells original art, prints and reproductions

M CONCORD MUSEUM, 200 Lexington Rd, PO Box 146, 01742. Tel 508-369-9609; FAX 508-369-9660. *Pres* Richard Clayton; *Dir* Dennis Fiori; *Cur* David Wood; *Business Mgr* Cathy Tilney; *Coordr of Educ* Jayne Gordon
Open Apr - Dec Mon - Sat 10 AM - 5 PM, Sun 1 - 5 PM, Jan - Mar Mon - Sat 11 AM - 4 PM, Sun 1 - 4 PM. Admis adults $5, sr citizens $4, children $2, members & family free. Estab 1886 to collect and preserve objects of antiquarian interest to Concord and towns originally a part of Concord; to interpret life in Colonial America, range of American arts, role of Concord in the American Revolution, and contributions of Concord authors-Thoreau, Emerson, Alcotts and Hawthorne-to American literature. Fifteen Period rooms & galleries showing. Average Annual Attendance: 36,000. Mem: 950; dues $30 & up; annual meeting Mar or May
Income: $500,000 (financed by membership, admission, grants, endowment & giving)
Publications: Newsletter, quarterly; Concord: Climate for Freedom by Ruth Wheeler; Forms to Sett On: A Social History of Concord Seating Furniture; Musketaquid to Concord: The Native & European Experience; Native American Source Book: A Teacher's Guide to New England Natives
Activities: Classes for adults and children; docent training; lectures open to the public; 8 vis lectrs per yr; concerts; gallery talks; tours; museum shop sells books, reproductions, prints, slides, gift items and crafts made by local craftspeople which compliment the museum collection
L Library, 200 Lexington Rd, 01742. Tel 508-369-9763; FAX 508-369-9660. *Cur* David Wood
Open to members only for research
Purchases: American Decorative Arts
Library Holdings: Vols 800; Per subs 14
Special Subjects: Decorative Arts, Concord Collection, Costumes, Early American Decorative Arts

A LOUISA MAY ALCOTT MEMORIAL ASSOCIATION, Orchard House, 399 Lexington Rd, PO Box 343, 01742. Tel 508-369-4118. *Dir* Stephanie Upton; *Asst Dir* Maria Baranchuk
Open weekends & by appointment. Estab 1911, preservation of house & family effects for educational purposes. Historic House Museum. Average Annual Attendance: 30,000. Mem: 500; dues individual $25, family $35; friends & corporations by invitation; annual meeting in spring
Income: Financed by mem, admissions, gift shop sales & donations
Collections: Books & photographs of Alcott's; Household furnishings; House where Little Women was written; May Alcott's paintings & sketches
Publications: Portfolio, journal
Activities: Classes for adults & children; dramatic programs; docent programs; lect open to public, 10 vis lectr per year; retail store sells books & prints

CUMMINGTON

M TOWN OF CUMMINGTON HISTORICAL COMMISSION, Kingman Tavern Historical Museum, Main St, RR1, PO Box 5, 01026. Tel 413-634-5335. *Chmn* Merrie Bergmann; *Archivist* Daphne Morris; *VChmn* B D Goldsmith
Open 2 - 5 PM, Sat July & Aug by appointment. Admis donation suggested. Estab 1968 to have and display artifacts of Cummington and locality. 17 room house with artifacts of Cummington and area including 17 miniature rooms, 2 fl barn, tools, equipment, carriage shed, cider mill. Average Annual Attendance: 300. Mem: 7, appointed by selectmen
Income: $5000 (financed by endowment and donations)
Publications: Only One Cummington, history of Cummington
Activities: Demonstrators; sales shop sells books and souvenirs

DEERFIELD

M HISTORIC DEERFIELD, INC, The Street, PO Box 321, 01342. Tel 413-774-5581; FAX 413-773-7415. *Pres* Henry N Flynt Jr; *VPres* John D Ong; *Executive Dir & Secy* Donald R Friary; *VPres* Mary Maple Dunn; *Dir Academic Programs* Kenneth Hafertepe; *Business Mgr* Carol Wenzel; *Cur* Philip Zea
Open Mon - Sat 9:30 - 4:30 PM, Sun 11 AM - 4:30 PM. Admis adult $7.50, children $4. Estab 1952 to collect, study and interpret artifacts related to the history of Deerfield, the culture of the Connecticut Valley and the arts in early American life. Maintains 13 historic house museums. Average Annual Attendance: 60,000. Mem: Dues $25; annual meeting 2nd or 3rd Sun in Sept
Income: $1,923,527 (financed by endowment, mem, rental, royalty & museum store income)

Purchases: $163,694
Collections: †American and English silver; †American and European textiles and costume; †American needlework; †American pewter; †Chinese export porcelain; †early American household objects; †early American paintings and prints; †early New England furniture; †English ceramics
Exhibitions: (1993) Ebenezer Hinsdale Williams House (1838)
Publications: Historical Deerfield Quarterly; Annual Report
Activities: Educ dept; lect open to public, 17 vis lectr per year; gallery talks; tours; scholarships and fellowships; museum shop sells books, reproductions, slides and local crafts

L **Henry N Flynt Library,** Memorial St, PO Box 53, 01342. Tel 413-774-5581, Ext 125; FAX 413-773-7415. *Librn* David R Proper; *Asst Librn* Sharman Prouty; *Library Aide* Shirley Majewski
Open Mon - Fri 8:30 AM - 5 PM. Estab 1970 to support research on local history and the museum collections; also for staff training
Income: Grants & Historic Deerfield budget
Purchases: 1000 vols per year
Library Holdings: Vols 14,500; Per subs 45; Micro — Reels 325; Other — Exhibition catalogs, manuscripts, pamphlets
Special Subjects: American Indian Art, Decorative Arts, Folk Art, Furniture, Historical Material, Painting - American, Painting - British, Portraits, Restoration & Conservation, Textiles, Manuscripts, Metalwork, Painting - American, Photography, Porcelain
Collections: †Decorative Arts; works dealing with the Connecticut River Valley
Publications: Research at Deerfield, An Introduction to the Memorial Libraries
Activities: Museum sales shop sells books, reproductions, slides, craft items, souvenirs, ceramics, glass and candles

A **POCUMTUCK VALLEY MEMORIAL ASSOCIATION,** Memorial Hall, Memorial St, PO Box 428, 01342. Tel 413-774-7476. *Pres* Amelia Miller; *VPres* William Hubbard; *Secy* Donald Frizzle; *Dir* Timothy C Neumann; *Cur* Suzanne Flint
Open May 1 - Oct 31 Mon - Fri 10 AM - 4:30 PM, Sat - Sun 12:30 PM - 4:30 PM. Admis adults $2, students $1.50, children (6-12) $.75, tour $1. Estab 1870 to collect the art and other cultural artifacts of the Connecticut River Valley and Western Massachusetts. Maintains 15 galleries. Average Annual Attendance: 17,000. Mem: 800; dues $10; annual meeting last Tues in Feb
Income: $400,000 (financed by endowment, membership, sales & fundraising)
Collections: Folk art; furniture; Indian artifacts; paintings; pewter; textiles; tools; toys; dolls
Publications: PVMA Newsletter, quarterly
Activities: Classes for children; lect open to the public; concerts; tours; artmobile; individual paintings and original objects of art lent to other museums; lending collection contains original art works, original prints, paintings and artifacts; museum shop selling books, original art, reproductions and slides

DUXBURY

M **ART COMPLEX MUSEUM,** 189 Alden St, PO Box 2814, 02331. Tel 617-934-6634. *Museum Dir* Charles A Weyerhaeuser; *Cur* Wendy Tarlow Kaplan; *Publicity Coordr* Bonnie Jernigan; *Education Coordr* Diane Muliero; *Curatorial Asst* Joanne Olson; *Secy* Patricia O'Donnell
Open Wed - Sun 1 - 4 PM. No admis fee. Estab 1971 as a center for the arts. Average Annual Attendance: 10,000
Income: Financed by endowment
Collections: American paintings, prints & sculpture; European paintings and prints; Asian art; Native American art; Shaker furniture
Exhibitions: (1991) Carrie May Weems. (1992) Tim Harding; Beyond the Borders: Seven Quilters; Richard Bertman; Work & Whimsey; Bridge of Fire; Human/Nature; Critic's Choice
Publications: —Complexities (newsletters); exhib catalogues
Activities: Education dept, workshops for children and adults; docent training; lect open to public; concerts; gallery talks; tours of visiting groups; individual art works lent to other institutions

L **Library,** 189 Alden St, PO Box 2814, 02331. Tel 617-934-6634. *Librn* Nancy W Grinnell
Open to the public for reference
Income: Financed by endowment
Library Holdings: Vols 4000; Per subs 12; AV — Slides; Other — Clipping files, exhibition catalogs, pamphlets
Special Subjects: Asian Art, Prints, American art
Exhibitions: (1990) Asian books & manuscripts
Activities: Docent reading group

ESSEX

M **ESSEX HISTORICAL SOCIETY,** Essex Shipbuilding Museum, PO Box 277, Main St, 01929. Tel 508-768-7541. *Admin* Diana H Stockton; *Cur* James Witham; *Pres* John D Cushing; *Historian* Dana A Story; *Treas* Charlotte Bengston
Open May - Oct Thurs - Sat 11 AM - 4 PM, Sun 1 - 4 PM. Admis $2, sr citizens $1.50, children under 12, members & Essex res free. Estab 1976 to preserve & interpret Essex history with special emphasis on its shipbuilding industry. Average Annual Attendance: 3000. Mem: 350; dues $10; annual meeting second Tues in May
Income: $30,000 (financed by endowment, mem, business, individual contributions & grants)
Purchases: $11,500 (climate control & Macintosh printer)
Collections: Collection of shipbuilding tools, documents, paintings, plans & photographs, models-both scale & builders
Exhibitions: Five rigged ship models & 15 builder's models on loan from the Smithsonian Institution's Watercraft Collection; Frame-Up (on going); Caulkerr Art (on going)
Publications: A list of vessels, boats & other craft built in the town of Essex 1860-1980, a complete inventory of the Ancient Burying Ground of Essex 1680 - 1868; Essex Electrics, 1981; Dubbing, Hooping & Lofting

Activities: Classes for adults & children; lect open to the public, 2 - 3 vis lectr per year; gallery talks; tours; competition with prizes; exten dept lends paintings, art objects, tools & models; museum shop sells books, prints, original art, reproductions, & audio-video cassettes, t-shirts, models, plans, magazines & notecards

FALL RIVER

M **FALL RIVER HISTORICAL SOCIETY,** 451 Rock St, 02720. Tel 508-679-1071. *Registrar* Debra Collins; *Cur* Michael Martins; *Pres* J Thomas Cottrell; *VPres* Harriet Remington Chase
Open Tues - Fri 9 AM - 4:30 PM, Sat & Sun 2 PM - 4 PM. Admis adult $3, children under 12 $1.50. Estab 1921 to preserve the social & economic history of Fall River. Average Annual Attendance: 6000. Mem: 659; dues $20
Income: Financed by endowment, mem
Collections: †Fall River School Still Life Paintings & Portraits; Antonio Jacobsen marine paintings; †Period costumes, furs, fans; †Victorian furnishings & decorative arts
Exhibitions: Victorian Decorative Stenceling: A Lost Art Revived; More Than Just Mourning: Fashionable Black in the Collection of the Fall River Historical Society
Activities: Small private tours for local schools; lectures open to public, 4 vis lectrs per yr; individual paintings lent; shop sells books, prints, postcards, paperweights

FITCHBURG

M **FITCHBURG ART MUSEUM,** 185 Elm St, 01420. Tel 508-345-4207. *Pres* Georgia Barnhill; *VPres* Malte Lukas; *Dir* Peter Timms; *Asst to the Dir* Aliki Katsaros; *Secy* Nelde Drumm; *Treas* Jay Rome; *Dir Educ* Jean McCrosky; *Dir of Docents* Ursula Pitman; *Cur* Linda Poras; *Asst Dir* Joan Hathaway
Open Tues - Sat 10 AM - 4 PM, Sun 1 - 4 PM. Admis fee $3. Estab 1925. Three building complex incl two museums, with eight large galleries & two entrance halls & one administration bldg. Average Annual Attendance: 15,000. Mem: 1300; dues $25 - 1000; annual meeting Dec
Income: Financed by endowment and membership
Collections: †Drawings, †paintings and †prints; †A Walk Through The Ancient World (household & sacred articles from ancient cultures)
Publications: Exhibitions catalogs; event notices
Activities: Classes for adults & children; docent training; lect open to public, 5 vis lectr per year; gallery talks; tours; competitions with award; scholarships; individual paintings & original objects of art lent to colleges & museums; sales shop sells original art & reproductions

M **FITCHBURG HISTORICAL SOCIETY,** 50 Grove St, PO Box 953, 01420-0953. Tel 508-345-1157. *Exec Dir* E F West
Open Mon 10 AM - 4 PM, 6 - 9 PM, Tues - Thurs 10 AM - 4 PM, Sept - June Sun 2 - 4 PM. Members free, non-members $2. Estab 1892 to preserve & transmit local history. 3 floors of Fitchburg items. Mem: 450; annual dues individual $15, family $25, $50 & $100; annual meeting third Mon in May
Income: Financed by endowment & mem
Collections: Books, printed items, artifacts of all kinds made in or living in Fitchburg
Exhibitions: Fitchburg artifacts (some permanently displayed, others changing)
Publications: Monthly newsletter
Activities: Lect open to public, 6 vis lectr per year; gallery talks; tours; competitions

FRAMINGHAM

M **DANFORTH MUSEUM OF ART,** 123 Union Ave, 01701. Tel 508-620-0050. *Dir* Robert J Evans; *Development & Public Relations Dir* Marillyn Gray; *Educ Coordr* Ann I Person; *Museum Asst* Sarah M Lawler; *Financial Dir* Leslie Archer; *Museum Shop Mgr* Marilyn Ross
Open Wed - Sun noon - 5 PM. Admis adults $3, students & sr citizens $2, children free. Estab 1974 to provide fine arts and art-related activities to people of all ages in the South Middlesex area. There are six galleries, including a children's gallery with hands-on activities. Average Annual Attendance: 30,000. Mem: 1000; dues vary from $15 - $45, annual meeting in Oct
Income: Financed by membership, Framingham State College and Town of Framingham, federal & state grants; foundations & corporate support
Collections: †Old master & contemporary prints, drawings & photography; †19th & 20th century American paintings; African & Oceanic art
Exhibitions: Varied program of changing exhibitions, traveling shows, selections from the permanent collection, in a variety of periods, styles & media
Publications: Newsletter; exhibition brochures & catalogues, museum school brochure
Activities: Classes for adults and children; docent training; programs for area schools; lect open to public, 5-10 vis lectr per yr; concerts; gallery talks; tours; trips; book traveling exhibitions; originate traveling exhibitions to other museums; museum shop sells publications, original art, prints, art glass, crafts, jewelry & ceramics; junior gallery

L **Library,** 123 Union Ave, 01701. Tel 508-620-0050.
Open Wed - Fri Noon - 4:30 PM, Sat & Sun 1 - 4:30 PM. Estab 1975 as an educational resource of art books and catalogues. For reference only; research as requested
Library Holdings: Vols 4000; Per subs 10; Other — Clipping files, exhibition catalogs, pamphlets
Special Subjects: Rare and valuable books; Whistler books & catalogues
Collections: Bibliographies for the museum exhibitions; museum school book collection

GARDNER

M **MOUNT WACHUSETT COMMUNITY COLLEGE**, Art Galleries, 444 Green St, 01440. Tel 508-632-6600, Ext 180. *Chmn Dept Art* Jean C Tandy; *Dir Fine Arts Gallery* Gene Cauthen
Open Mon - Thurs 8 AM - 9 PM, Fri 8 AM - 5 PM. No admis fee. Estab 1971 to supply resources for a two-year art curriculum; develop an art collection. Well-lighted gallery with skylights & track lighting, white panelled walls; two open, spacious levels with Welsh tile floors. Average Annual Attendance: 8000-10,000
Income: Financed by city and state appropriations
Purchases: Pottery by Makato Yabe, print by Bob Boy, 17 student paintings, 10 student prints, 5 student ceramic works, 8 student sculpture, 2 bronze works
Collections: †Approx 100 works; framed color art posters and reproductions; prints; ceramic pieces; student collection
Exhibitions: Annual student competition of painting, sculpture, drawing, ceramics, printmaking; local, national & international artists and former students' works
Publications: Annual brochure
Activities: Lectures open to the public, 8-10 vis lectr per yr; gallery talks; tours; competitions; awards; exten dept serves Mount Wachussett
L **Library**, 444 Green St, 01440. Tel 508-632-6600, Ext 126. *Dir* Linda R Oldach; *Asst Librn* Christina Coolidge
Open Mon - Thurs 8 AM - 9:30 PM, Fri 8 AM - 5 PM, Sun 2 - 6 PM (when school is in session). Estab 1964. Circ 12,998
Income: Financed by state appropriation
Library Holdings: Vols 70,000; Per subs 320; Micro — Fiche, reels; AV — Cassettes, fs, rec, slides; Other — Memorabilia, pamphlets
Exhibitions: Periodic exhibitions

GLENDALE

M **NATIONAL TRUST FOR HISTORIC PRESERVATION**, Chesterwood Museum, 4 Williamsville Rd (Mailing add: PO Box 827, Glendale Rd, Stockbridge, 01262-0826). Tel 413-298-3579; FAX 413-298-3973. *Dir* Paul W Ivory; *Asst Dir* Susan Frisch Lehrer; *Admin Asst* Rolaine D Ball
Open daily 10 AM - 5 PM, May 1 through Oct 31. Admis adults $5.50, children 13 - 18 $3, 6 - 12 $1, group rates available by advanced arrangement, free to National Trust Members & Friends of Chesterwood. Estab 1955 to preserve & present the summer home & studio of Daniel Chester French. Chesterwood, a museum property of the National Trust for Historic Preservation, was the summer estate of Daniel Chester French (1850 - 1931), sculptor of the Lincoln Memorial, Minute Man & Leading figure of the American Renaissance. The 150 acre property includes: French Studio (1898) & Residence (1900 - 1901), both designed by Henry Bacon, architect of the Lincoln Memorial; Barn Gallery, a c1825 barn adapted for use as exhibition space, a museum gift shop in a c1925 garage & country place garden with woodland walk laid out by French. Average Annual Attendance: 33,000. Mem: 155,000; individual dues $25
Collections: Plaster models, marble & bronze casts of French's work & paintings Period furnishings; memorabilia
Exhibitions: Annual Outdoor Contemporary Sculpture Exhibition; Annual Antique Car Show; Christmas at Chesterwood; special exhibits dealing with aspects of historic preservation in the Berkshire region & French's life, career, social & artistic milieu, & summer estate
Activities: College summer intern programs; volunteer & guide training program; sculptor in residence program; lect open to the public, 5 vis lectrs per yr; gallery talks; tours; museum shop sells books, magazines, reproductions, prints, slides & gift items
L **Museum Library & Archives**, 4 Williamsville Rd (Mailing add: PO Box 827, Glendale Rd, Stockbridge, 01262-0827). Tel 413-298-3579. *Asst Museum Dir* Susan Frisch Lehrer; *Archivist* Wanda Magdeleine Styka
Open by appointment only. Estab 1969. Library consists of books on sculpture, historic preservation, decorative arts, history of art, reference, gardening, architecture & landscape architecture, personal books collected by sculptor Daniel Chester French, Mary Adams French (wife), & Margaret French Cresson (daughter) as well as archival material; serves art, social, landscape & architectural historians & historic preservationists
Library Holdings: Vols 5000; Per subs 5; Micro — Reels; AV — A-tapes, cassettes, lantern slides, motion pictures, slides, v-tapes; Other — Clipping files, exhibition catalogs, manuscripts, memorabilia, original art works, pamphlets, photographs, prints, sculpture
Special Subjects: Architecture, Art History, Coins & Medals, Decorative Arts, Furniture, Historical Material, Landscape Architecture, Painting - American, Period Rooms, Restoration & Conservation, Chesterwood, late 19th & early 20th century classical sculpture, Lincoln Memorial, American Renaissance, Country Place Era
Collections: Oral histories: Daniel Chester French and Chesterwood; Berkshire region historic preservation clipping file; maps; blueprints and plans of work; period photographs of Daniel Chester French and his family, summer estate and sculptures; papers, photographs albums & scrapbooks of D C French & Margaret French Cresson, sculptor, writer & preservationist; period photographs of sculptures by contemporary & non-contemporary sculptors
Publications: The Chesterwood Pedestal, newsletter twice a yr; educational brochures; annual exhibit catalogues
Activities: Intern archivist program

GLOUCESTER

A **CAPE ANN HISTORICAL ASSOCIATION**, Gallery, 27 Pleasant St, 01930. Tel 508-283-0455. *Cur* Britt Crews; *Admin* Judith McCulloch
Open Tues - Sat 10 AM - 5 PM, cl Sun, Mon & holidays. Admis adults $2, senior citizens & students $1, children under 12 free. Incorporated in 1876 for the preservation of ancient houses. One built in 1650, one in 1750 & one in 1799. Average Annual Attendance: 5000. Mem: 1300; dues $10 & up; annual meeting May
Income: Endowment, contribution & mem
Collections: Antique furniture, glass, jewelry & mementos of the Revolutionary

period; fishing gear, equipment & schooner models; paintings & drawings of Fitz Hugh Lane; porcelain; ship models; silver
Publications: Quarterly newsletter; exhibition catalogs, annual
Activities: Educ dept; classes for children; docent training; lectures open to public, 4 vis lectrs per yr; concerts; gallery talks; tours; museum shop sells books & reproductions

M **Museum**, 27 Pleasant St, 01930. Tel 508-283-0455. *Admin* Judith McCulloch
Open Tues - Sat 10 AM - 5 PM. Admis adults $3.50, sr citizens $3, students $2 & members free. Estab 1873 to foster appreciation of the quality & diversity of life on Cape Ann past & present. Two galleries of fine arts, decorative arts & American furniture; Fisheries/maritime gallery; 1804 furnished house. Average Annual Attendance: 10,000. Mem: 1650; dues $15 & up
Special Subjects: Cape Ann art history; Gloucester & New England fishing industry
Collections: Fitz Hugh Lane Collection, paintings
Activities: Lect open to public, 2-3 lectr per yr; individual paintings & original objects of art lent to museums, galleries & local businesses; museum shop sells books, reproductions, prints, slides, jewelry, postcards & note papers
L **Library**, 27 Pleasant St, 01930. *Cur* Britt Crews
Estab 1876. Reference only
Library Holdings: Vols 2000; AV — Motion pictures, rec; Other — Clipping files, exhibition catalogs, manuscripts, memorabilia, original art works, pamphlets, photographs, prints, reproductions, sculpture

M **HAMMOND CASTLE MUSEUM**, 80 Hesperus Ave, 01930. Tel 508-283-2080, 283-2081. *Executive Dir & Cur* John W Pettibone
Open daily 9 AM - 5 PM. Admis adults $5, seniors & students $4, children between 6 & 12 $3. Estab 1931 by a famous inventor, John Hays Hammond Jr. Incorporated in 1938 for the public exhibition of authentic works of art, architecture and specimens of antiquarian value and to encourage and promote better education in the fine arts, with particular reference to purity of design and style. Built in style of a medieval castle with Great Hall, courtyard and period rooms, Dr Hammond combined elements of Roman, Medieval and Renaissance periods in his attempt to recreate an atmosphere of European beauty. Average Annual Attendance: 60,000. Mem: 300; dues vary
Income: Financed by tours, concerts, membership and grants, special events
Collections: Rare collection of European artifacts; Roman, Medieval and Renaissance Periods
Publications: Museum guidebook; exhibition catalogs; Hammond Biography
Activities: Classes for children; docent training; educational & teacher workshops; lectures open to public; concerts; tours; extension dept serves neighboring schools; individual paintings and original objects of art lent to sister institutions for special exhibitions; sales shop sells books, reproductions, crafts, jewelry, art cards, postcards & audio tapes

A **NORTH SHORE ARTS ASSOCIATION, INC**, Art Gallery, 197 E Main St (Rear), 01930. Tel 508-283-1857. *Pres* Harold Kloongian; *VPres* Theresa Wonson; *Treas* Roger Curtis
Open 10 AM - 5:30 PM, Sun 2:30 - 5:30 PM, July, Aug & Sept. No admis fee. Estab in 1922 to promote American art by exhibitions. Gallery owned by Association. Average Annual Attendance: 4000. Mem: 350; dues artist $25, patron $10, associate $5; annual meeting Aug
Income: Financed by dues, contributions & rentals
Publications: Calendar of Events
Activities: Art classes in painting & drawing from life; lect open to public, 4 vis lectr per yr; gallery talks; competitions with awards

GRAFTON

M **WILLARD HOUSE AND CLOCK MUSEUM, INC**, 11 Willard St, 01519. Tel 508-839-3335. *Pres* Dr Roger W Robinson; *VPres* George McEvoy; *Dir* Mrs Roger W Robinson; *Secy* Bernice Norton
Open Tues - Sat 10 AM - 4 PM, Sun 1 - 5 PM. Admis adults $2, children $.75. Estab 1968 for education in fields of decorative arts and antiques. Maintains nine rooms open in house museum. Average Annual Attendance: 3000. Mem: 200; dues $15; annual meeting Oct
Income: Financed by endowment, mem, admissions, gifts & sales
Purchases: Six Willard Clocks
Collections: Early Country Antique Furniture, 17th & 18th Century; 68 Willard Clocks by Benjamin, Simon, Ephraim & Aaron Willard; 16 paintings of various members of the Willard Clockmaking Family
Exhibitions: Doll Show; Fashion Show of 18th & 19th Century Gowns
Activities: Lect, 4 visiting lectr per year; museum shop sells books & antiques

GREAT BARRINGTON

M **SIMON'S ROCK COLLEGE OF BARD**, 84 Alford Rd, 01230. Tel 413-528-0771. *Chmn Art Dept* Arthur Hillman
Open Mon - Thurs 8 AM - midnight, Fri 8 AM - 9 PM, Sat noon - 9 PM, Sun noon - midnight. No admis fee. Estab 1964 as a liberal arts college
Exhibitions: A continuing exhibition program of professional and student works in drawing, painting, graphics, sculpture and crafts; Graphic Design Workshop of Simon's Rock (poster); Barbara Baranowska (photographs); Jim Cave (prints); Peter Homestead (sculpture); Tom Shepard (sculpture and drawings); Evan Stoller (sculpture); Niki Berg, photograph; Dennis Connors, sculpture; Cynthia Picchi, painting; Lyalya, painting & sculpture; Nick Farina, photography; Richard Webb, painting; William Jackson, sculpture; Jane Palmer, ceramics; Arthur Hillman, prints; The African-Afro-American Connection, photos; Brigitte Keller, painting; Harriet Eisner, painting; Linda Kaye-Moses, jewelry; Taff Fitterer, painting
Activities: Gallery talks; tours
L **Library**, 84 Alford Rd, 01230. Tel 413-528-0771, Ext 370. *Librn* Joan Goodkind
Library Holdings: Vols 60,000; Per subs 300; Micro — Fiche, reels; AV — Cassettes, rec

HADLEY

M PORTER-PHELPS-HUNTINGTON FOUNDATION, INC FOUNDATION, INC, Historic House Museum, 130 River Dr, 01035. Tel 413-584-4699. *Pres* James Boylan; *Dir* Susan J Lisk; *VPres* Gregory Farmer
Open May 15 to Oct 15 Sat - Wed 1 - 4:30 PM. Admis fee $4, children under 12 $1. Estab 1955. Historic house built in 1752; twelve rooms house the accumulated belongings of ten generations of one family; carriage house; corn barn; historic gardens; sunken garden. Average Annual Attendance: 4000. Mem: 500; dues $5 - $100; annual meeting in May
Income: $47,000 (financed by endowment & membership)
Collections: Porter-Phelps-Huntington family collection of 17th, 18th & 19th century furniture, paintins, papers, decorative arts; clothing collection; archives at Amherst
Publications: Annual report; Forty Acres, newsletter, quarterly
Activities: Provides concerts; tours; individual paintings & objects of art lent to other museums; museum shop sells books & prints

HARVARD

M FRUITLANDS MUSEUM, INC, 102 Prospect Hill Rd, Prospect Hill, 01451. Tel 508-456-3924. *Dir* Robert D Farwell; *Asst to Dir* Joanne Myers; *Cur* Maggie Stier
Open Tues - Sun 10 AM - 5 PM (mid-May - mid-Oct), cl Mon. Admis adults $5, students $2.50, ages 7-16 $1. Estab 1914, incorporated 1930 by Clara Endicott Sears. Fruitlands was the scene of Bronson Alcott's Utopian experiment in community living. The Fruitlands Farmhouse contains furniture, household articles, pictures, handicrafts, books & valuable manuscript collection of Alcott, Lane & Transcendental group. The Shaker House, built in 1794 by the members of the former Harvard Shaker Village, was originally used as an office. Moved to its present location, it now forms the setting for the products of Shaker Handicrafts & Community Industries. American Indian museum contains ethnological exhibits. Picture gallery contains portraits by itinerant artists of the first half of the 19th Century & landscapes by Hudson River School. Average Annual Attendance: 12,000. Mem: 650; schedule of mem fees; annual meeting in June
Income: Financed by Sears Trust, mem fees, gifts & grants
Purchases: Books, paintings & ethnographic materials
Publications: Under the Mulberry Tree, quarterly
Activities: Docent training; lect open to public, 2-4 vis lectr per yr; concerts; individual & original objects of art lent to other museums in the area; lending collection includes original art works, prints, paintings; book traveling exhibitions; museum shop sells books, magazines, reproductions & prints

L Library, 102 Prospect Hill Rd, 01451. Tel 508-456-3924. *Cur* Margaret Stier
Open year round by appointment. Estab 1914 for staff resource & scholarly research
Library Holdings: Vols 10,000; Per subs 10; Micro — Reels; AV — Fs, motion pictures, rec, slides, v-tapes; Other — Manuscripts, memorabilia, original art works, photographs
Special Subjects: Art History, Transcendental Movement, Shakers, American Indian North of Mexico

HAVERHILL

L HAVERHILL PUBLIC LIBRARY, Art Dept, 99 Main St, 01830. Tel 508-373-1586. *Dir* Howard W Curtis
Open Mon & Tues 1 - 5 PM & 6 - 8 PM, Wed & Thurs 1 - 5 PM, Sat 10 AM - noon & 1 - 5 PM, cl Fri. Estab 1873
Income: Financed by private endowment
Library Holdings: Vols 8500; Per subs 16; AV — A-tapes, cassettes, fs, Kodachromes, lantern slides, motion pictures, v-tapes; Other — Clipping files, manuscripts, original art works, photographs, prints, sculpture
Special Subjects: Manuscripts, Photography, Prints
Collections: Illuminated manuscripts; mid-19th century photographs, work by Beato and Robertson, Bourne, Frith, Gardner, Naya, O'Sullivan, and others; small group of paintings including Joseph A Ames, †Henry Bacon, †Sidney M Chase, †William S Haseltine, Thomas Hill, Harrison Plummer, Winfield Scott Thomas, Robert Wade
Exhibitions: Matthew Brady, photographer, from the National Portrait Gallery
Publications: Architectural Heritage of Haverhill
Activities: Slide presentations; lectures open to public; concerts; periodic films

HOLYOKE

M CITY OF HOLYOKE MUSEUM-WISTARIAHURST, 238 Cabot St, 01040. Tel 413-534-2216. *Chmn Holyoke Historical Commission* Jill Hodnicki
Open Wed - Sun 1 - 5 PM, cl national & state holidays. Admis adult $2, sr citizen $1.50, members & children under 12 free. Historic house museum estab to show history of Holyoke 1850- 1930. Sponsored by the City of Holyoke under the jurisdiction of the Holyoke Historical Commission. Average Annual Attendance: 18,000. Mem: annual meeting May
Income: $60,000 (financed by city appropriation)
Collections: Late 19th & early 20th century furniture, paintings, prints, decorative arts & architectural details; period rooms; natural history & native Armenian ethno-graphic material
Activities: Workshops, courses & special programs for adults & children; contemporary art exhibits and historic exhibits; gallery talks; lectures; concerts; special events and holiday programs; group and school tours; sales shop selling booklets and items relating to exhibitions

LEXINGTON

M MUSEUM OF OUR NATIONAL HERITAGE, 33 Marrett Rd, PO Box 519, 02173. Tel 617-861-6559. *Dir* Clement M Silvestro; *Dir Educ* Robert MacKay; *Cur of Exhibits* Cara Sutherland; *Gen Servs* June Cobb; *Librn* Nola Skousen; *Cur Colls* John Hamilton; *Designer* Serena Furman
Open Mon - Sat 10 AM - 5 PM, Sun noon - 5 PM. No admis fee. Estab 1972 as an American history museum, including art and decorative art. Five modern galleries for changing exhibits, flexible lighting & climate control. Two galleries of 3000 sq ft, two 1500 sq ft, atrium area used for print & photo exhibits. Average Annual Attendance: 60,000. Mem: 200; dues friend for life $250, family $20, individual $15
Income: $1,500,000 (financed by endowment & appeal to Masons)
Purchases: $45,000
Collections: General American & American Paints; American decorative art; objects decorated with Masonic, patriotic & fraternal symbolism
Publications: Exhibition catalogs
Activities: Docent training; lect open to public; concerts; gallery talks; tours for school groups; paintings and art objects lent; originate traveling exhibitions; museum shop sells books and a variety of gift items related to exhibit program

LINCOLN

M DECORDOVA MUSEUM & SCULPTURE PARK, 51 Sandy Pond Rd, 01773-2600. Tel 617-259-8355; FAX 617-259-8249. *Dir* Paul Master-Karnik; *Assoc Dir Development* Denise Trapani; *Cur* Rachel Lafo; *Membership Dir* Susan Diachisin; *Corp Program Dir* Sandra Mongeon; *Public Relations Dir* Michael Sockol; *Assoc Dir Education* Eleanor Lazarus
Open Tues - Fri 10 AM - 5 PM, Sat & Sun noon - 5 PM. Admis adults $4, 6 - 21 & sr citizens $3, students & members free. Esab 1948 to exhibit, to interpret, to collect & to preserve modern & contemporary American art.. 8000 sq ft is broken into five galleries. Average Annual Attendance: 95,000. Mem: 2000; dues $35 - $1000
Income: $1,700,000 (financed by endowment, individual/corporate mem, foundation & government grants)
Purchases: $10,000
Collections: American art; 20th century American painting, graphics, sculpture & photography; emphasis on artists associated with New England
Exhibitions: (1991) Contemporary Sculpture: Howard Ben Tre; Photographs by Aaron Siskind; Video Artists Address AIDS; Playing Around: Toys by Artists; Embracing the Personal: Drawings by Roger Kizik; The Boston Printmakers 43rd North American Print Exhibition; Commemoration & Collaboration: The Art of Roy & Mara Superior; 9 Artists/9 Visions; Op & Pop: Prints from the Permanent Collection; Land Sea & Sky: Maps in Contemporary Art; Crossings: A Collaboration between Civia Rosenberg & May Stevens; DeCordova Museum School Juried Exhibition. (1992) Art that Works: The Decorative Arts of the Eighties; Animals in Art: Selections from the Permanent Collection; The Politics of Cloth: Selection from the Fabric Workshop; Philip Sirois: New Paintings; Post Modern Baroque: Contemporary Paintings & Photographs; Lee Friedlander: Nudes; 11 Artists/11 Visions; New Videos: Selections from the 17th Annual NE Film & Video Festival; Good-Bye to Apple Pie: Contemporary Artists View the Family in Crisis; Reframing the Family; The Above-Below: An Installlation by Bart Uchida
Publications: Exhibition catalogs; newsletter
Activities: Classes for adults & children; lectures, guided tours; films; concerts; arts festivals; outreach programs; paintings and original objects of art lent to corporate membership; traveling exhibitions organized and circulated

L DeCordova Museum Library, 51 Sandy Pond Rd, 01773-2600. Tel 617-259-8355; FAX 617-259-8249. *Librn* Barbara Stecher
Open Mon - Fri 9 AM - 5 PM, for students & members of the museum only
Library Holdings: Vols 2500; Per subs 15; AV — Slides, v-tapes; Other — Exhibition catalogs, pamphlets
Special Subjects: Fine Arts & Studio Arts, 20th Century Contemporary Art

LOWELL

A LOWELL ART ASSOCIATION, Whistler House Museum of Art, 243 Worthen St, 01852. Tel 508-452-7641. *Pres* Mary Lou Doherty; *VPres* George Duncan; *Exec Dir* Carol Durand
Open Wed - Fri 11 AM - 4 PM & Sun 1 - 4 PM, cl Mon. Admis $2. Estab 1878 to preserve the birthplace of James McNeil Whistler; to promote the arts in all its phases; and to maintain a center for the cultural benefit of all the citizens of the community. Average Annual Attendance: 5000. Mem: 500; dues adults $25, sr citizens & students $15
Income: Financed by endowment, mem, admissions, grants & earned income
Collections: Mid 19th through early 20th century American Art: Hibbard, Benson, Noyes, Spear, Paxton, Phelps; Whistler etchings & lithographs
Exhibitions: Galleries of works from permanent collection & periodic exhibits by contemporary artists
Publications: Brochures; S P Howes: Portrait Painter, catalog
Activities: Educ dept, classes for adults & children; docent training; lect open to public, 3 vis lectr per year; concerts; gallery talks; tours; programs of historical interest; book traveling exhibitions, 1 or 2 per year; originate traveling exhibitions to small museums & schools; museum shop sells books, original art, reproductions, prints, postcards, jewelry, Victoriana

MALDEN

L MALDEN PUBLIC LIBRARY, Art Dept & Gallery, 36 Salem St, 02148. Tel 617-324-0218; FAX 617-324-4467. *Librn* Dina G Malgeri
Open Mon - Thurs 9 AM - 9 PM, Fri & Sat 9 AM - 6 PM, cl Sun & holidays, cl Sat during summer months. Estab 1879, incorporated 1885 as a public library and art gallery. Maintains an art department with three galleries. Circ 239,493
Income: $421,530 (financed by endowment, city and state appropriations)
Purchases: $91,000

Library Holdings: Other — Exhibition catalogs, framed reproductions, manuscripts, memorabilia, original art works, pamphlets, photographs, prints, reproductions, sculpture
Publications: Thirty Paintings in the Malden Collection (art catalog); annual report; art reproduction note cards
Activities: Lect open to public, 6-12 vis lectr per year; concerts; gallery talks; tours

MARBLEHEAD

A **MARBLEHEAD ARTS ASSOCIATION, INC,** King Hooper Mansion, 8 Hooper St, 01945. Tel 617-631-2608. *Pres* En Marquis Brown; *Executive Secy* Eleanor Livengood; *Executive Secy* Lillian Remington
Open Tues - Sun 1 - 4 PM, cl Mon. Admis $1 for tours, no admis to art galleries. Estab 1922. Owns & occupies the historic King Hooper Mansion, located in historic Marblehead. Contains fine paneling, ballroom, gallery, and garden by Shurclif. Maintains an art gallery. Mem: 400; membership upon application (open); dues family $20, individuals $16; annual meeting June
Income: Financed by mem & mansion rentals
Exhibitions: (1992) Artist Member Show; monthly exhibits shown
Activities: Classes for adults; lectures open to the public; concerts; gallery talks; tours; competitions with cash & ribbon awards

A **MARBLEHEAD HISTORICAL SOCIETY,** 161 Washington St, PO Box 1048, 01945. Tel 617-631-1069. *Executive Secy* Mrs John P Hunt
Open Mon - Sat 10 AM - 4 PM (May 15 - Oct 15), cl Sun. Admis $2.25. Estab 1898, incorporated 1902 for the preservation of Lee Mansion & historical material & records of Marblehead. Average Annual Attendance: 3000
Income: Financed by endowment, mem & admissions
Collections: China & glass; collection of portraits, documents, furniture & pictures of ships
Activities: Lect open to the public; tours; sales shop selling books, prints & reproductions
L **Library,** 161 Washington, PO Box 1048, 01945. Tel 617-631-1069. *Historian* Janice Rideout
Open to qualified visitors for reference only

MARION

A **MARION ART CENTER,** 80 Pleasant, PO Box 602, 02738. Tel 508-748-1266. *Pres* Trudy Kingery; *Dir* Wendy Bidstrup
Open Tues - Fri 1 - 5 PM, Sat 10 AM - 2 PM. Estab 1957 to provide theater, concerts & visual arts exhibitions for the community & to provide studio & music classes for adults & children. Two galleries, 125 ft of wall space, 500 sq ft floor space; indirect lighting; entrance off Main St. Average Annual Attendance: 2000. Mem: 650, dues corporate $350, patron $100, sponsor $50, basic $25; annual meeting in Jan
Income: Financed by mem dues, donations and profit from ticket and gallery sales
Collections: Cecil Clark Davis (1877-1955), portrait paintings
Exhibitions: Monthly one person and group shows
Publications: Annual membership folder; monthly invitations to opening; Newsletter, monthly
Activities: Classes for adults and children; dramatic programs; lect open to the public, 6 vis lectr per yr; concerts; gallery talks; competitions; scholarships; student art competition held annually; awards for student art & best portfolio; sales shop sells fine crafts, small paintings, prints, cards, original art and reproductions

MEDFORD

M **TUFTS UNIVERSITY,** Art Gallery, Aidekman Arts Center, 02155. Tel 617-627-3518. *Dir* Elizabeth Wylie
Open fall & spring semesters, Tues - Sun 11 AM - 5 PM, Thurs 11 AM - 9 PM. No admis fee. Estab 1955 to display works of art by University students and faculty and special exhibitions of traditional and experimental works in all visual art media. Average Annual Attendance: 5000
Income: Financed through the Fine Arts Department, private, corporate & foundation sources, state & federal agencies
Purchases: Roger Kizik, Animal; Danny Lyon, photographs; Paul Stopforth, oils & drawings
Collections: Primarily 19th & 20th Century American paintings, prints & drawings; contemporary paintings, photographs & works on paper
Exhibitions: Fourteen shows annually, including theses exhibits of candidates for the MFA degree offered by Tufts in affiliation with the School of the Boston Museum of Fine Arts; Added Dimensions; Danny Lyon: Pictures from Films/Films from Pictures; Collaborations/Rugg Road; Private Lives: Personal Narrative Painting; Chuck Close: Handmade Paper Editions; Olga Antonova, Susan Schwall & Pauna Blacklow: Three Women, Three Visions; Mitchell Gordon Exterior/Interior: Alice Neel; The Life & Art of Esphyr Slobodkina
Publications: Exhibition brochures
Activities: Lect open to the public, 1 - 2 vis lectrs per year; gallery talks; tours; competitions; individual and original objects of art lent to locations on campus and occasionally outside sources; book traveling exhibitions

MILTON

M **CAPTAIN ROBERT BENNET FORBES HOUSE,** 215 Adams St, 02186. Tel 617-696-1815. *Dir* Dana D Ricciardi, PhD; *Admin Asst* Alessandra Smith; *Exec Secy* Nadine Leary
Open Wed & Sun 1 - 4 PM, Thurs by appointment. Admis $3, srs & students $1.50, children under 12 free. Estab 1964 as a Historic House museum; for preservation, research, education: 19th century through Forbes family focus. Average Annual Attendance: 1000. Mem: 400; dues life member $500, sponsor

$250, donor $100, friend $50, family $30, individual $20
Income: $70,000 (financed by endowment, membership & fundraising)
Library Holdings: Vols 2500; Per subs $0; Micro — Prints; Other — Exhibition catalogs, manuscripts, memorabilia, original art works, pamphlets, photographs, prints
Collections: Abraham Lincoln Civil War Collections & Archives; Forbes Family Collection of China trade & American furnishings
Exhibitions: Annual Abraham Lincoln essay contest for grades 5 - 12
Publications: Forbes House Jottings, four times per year
Activities: Classes for adults & children; docent training; lect open to public, 3 vis lectr per year; competitions & awards; lending collection contains decorative arts, Lincoln memorabilia, original art works, original prints & sculpture; museum shop sells books, cards, gifts & prints

NANTUCKET

A **ARTISTS ASSOCIATION OF NANTUCKET,** PO Box 1104, 02554. Tel 508-228-0722. *Pres* William Welch
Open Mon - Sat 10 AM - 5 PM, 7 - 10 PM, Sun 1 - 5 PM, 7 - 10 PM. No admis fee. Estab 1944 to provide a place for Nantucket artists of all levels & styles to show their work, & encourage new artists. Maintains one gallery: The Little Gallery, two floors in historic building. Average Annual Attendance: 50,000 - 70,000. Mem: 500; dues patron $500, artist $50; annual meeting Aug
Income: $75,000 - $100,000 (financed by mem, fundraising & commissions, large patron gifts)
Collections: 160 pieces, most by Nantucket artists
Exhibitions: Annual Craft Show; juried shows; changing one-person & group member shows during summer; occasional off-season shows
Publications: Monthly newsletter; annual brochure
Activities: Classes for adults & children; workshops; lect open to public, 5-6 vis lectr per yr; gallery talks; competitions with awards; scholarships; individual paintings & original objects of art lent to local hospital & public offices; sales shop sells original art, prints & lithographs

M **NANTUCKET HISTORICAL ASSOCIATION,** Historic Nantucket, S Washington, PO Box 1016, 02554. Tel 508-228-1894; FAX 508-228-5618. *Exec Dir* Maurice E Gibbs
Open June - Oct 10 AM - 5 PM. Admis: a visitor pass to all buildings, adults $5, children 5 - 14 $2.50; individual building admis $1 - $3. Estab 1894 to preserve Nantucket & maintain history. Historic Nantucket is a collection of 13 buildings throughout the town, open to the public & owned by the Nantucket Historical Association. Together they portray the way people lived & worked as Nantucket grew from a small farming community to the center of America's whaling industry. Mem: 3000; dues families $40, individuals $25; annual meeting July
Income: $450,000 (financed by endowment, membership and admissions)
Collections: Portraits, Oil Paintings, Watercolors, Needlework Pictures and all other manner of artifacts related to Nantucket & Maritime History; all objects exhibited in our historic houses & museums which cover the period 1686 - 1930
Publications: Art on Nantucket; Historic Nantucket, quarterly, magazine for members
Activities: Classes for children; lect open to public; 12 vis lectr per year; tours; individual paintings lent to other museums; museum shop sells books, reproductions, prints, slides, period furniture, silver, bone & ivory scrimshaw, candles & children's toys

NEW BEDFORD

L **NEW BEDFORD FREE PUBLIC LIBRARY,** Art Dept, 613 Pleasant St, 02740. Tel 508-991-6275. *Dir* Rosemary Medeiros; *Dept Head Reference* Paula Wallace; *Dept Head Genealogy & Whaling Coll* Paul Cyr; *Dept Head Technical Service* Vicki A Lukas
Open Mon 9 AM - 9 PM, Tues & Thurs - Sat 9 AM - 5 PM, Wed 1 - 9 PM, cl Sun & holidays. Circ 399,947
Income: $1,038,291 (financed: $108,515 by endowment; $829,726 by city, $100,050 by state appropriation)
Purchases: $121,165
Library Holdings: Micro — Reels; AV — Cassettes, fs, motion pictures, rec, slides, v-tapes; Other — Framed reproductions, photographs
Special Subjects: American Western Art, Etchings & Engravings, Landscapes, Marine Painting, Painting - American, Watercolors, Woodcarvings, Whaling, New Bedford Artists
Collections: Paintings by Clifford Ashley, Albert Bierstadt, F D Millet, William Wall
Activities: Scholarships; individual and original objects of art lent to city offices

M **OLD DARTMOUTH HISTORICAL SOCIETY,** New Bedford Whaling Museum, 18 Johnny Cake Hill, 02740. Tel 508-997-0046; FAX 508-997-0018. *Dir* Anthony M Zane; *Sr Cur* Richard C Kugler; *Registrar* Judith N Lund
Open Mon - Sat 9 AM - 5 PM, Sun 1 - 5 PM. Admis adults $3.50, sr citizens $3, children 6 - 14 $2.50, children under 6 free. Estab 1903 to collect, preserve & interpret objects including printed material, pictures & artifacts related to the history of the New Bedford area & American whaling. Average Annual Attendance: 60,000. Mem: 2300; dues $15-$850; annual meeting May
Income: $713,000 (financed by endowment, mem, special events & admissions)
Collections: Russell-Purrington Panorama of a Whaling Voyage; domestic crafts; furniture & domestic arts; New Bedford artists; paintings & prints; scrimshaw; ship models; Whaleship Lagoda: 1/2 scale model that vistors may board; whaling arts & crafts
Exhibitions: Highlights From the Glass Museum's Collection; The Scope of History: How a Museum Collects; The Fishing Industry
Publications: Bulletin from Johnny Cake Hill, quarterly; exhibition catalogs; calendar, quarterly
Activities: Classes for adults & children; docent training; lect open to public, 6 vis lectr per yr; gallery talks; tours; individual paintings & original objects of art lent to other museums; traveling exhibitions organized & circulated; museum shop sells books, magazines, reproductions, prints & gift items

L **Whaling Museum Library,** 18 Johnny Cake Hill, 02740. Tel 508-997-0046. *Librn* Virginia M Adams
For reference only
Library Holdings: Vols 15,000; Per subs 12; Micro — Reels; Other — Clipping files, exhibition catalogs, manuscripts, memorabilia, pamphlets
Special Subjects: Charles F Batchelder Whaling Collection, Charles A Goodwin Collection, History of Whaling Industry, Andrew Snow Logbook Collection

NEWBURYPORT

M **HISTORICAL SOCIETY OF OLD NEWBURY,** Cushing House Museum, 98 High St, 01950. Tel 508-462-2681. *Cur* Suzanne Simon
Open Tues - Sat 10 AM - 4 PM, cl Sun & Mon. Admis adults $2. Estab 1877 to preserve heritage of Old Newbury, Newbury, Newburyport & West Newbury. Average Annual Attendance: 2000. Mem: 800; dues individual life $350, annual benefactor &100, annual sustaining $35, family $20, individual $15
Income: $50,000 (financed by dues, tours, endowments, fund-raisers)
Collections: China; dolls; furniture; glass; miniatures; needlework; paintings; paperweights; sampler collection; silver; military & other historical material
Publications: Old-Town & The Waterside, 200 years of Tradition & Change in Newbury, Newburyport & West Newbury - 1635 1835
Activities: Lect open to public, 10 vis lectr per yr; tours for children; Garden Tour; annual auction; individual paintings & original objects of art lent; museum shop sells books

M **NEWBURYPORT MARITIME SOCIETY,** Custom House Maritime Museum, 25 Water St, 01950. Tel 508-462-8681. *Dir & Cur* Janet Howell
Open Mon - Sat 10 AM - 4 PM, Sun 1 - 5 PM. Admis adults $1.50, children to 15 $.75, under 5 free. Estab 1975 to exhibit the maritime heritage of the Merrimack Valley. Housed in an 1835 custom house designed by Robert Mills. The structure is on the National Register of Historic Places. Average Annual Attendance: 8000. Mem: 600; dues $2 - $1000, annual meeting in Dec
Income: $75,000 (financed by membership, admission, fundraisers, public, private & government grants)
Collections: Collection of portraits, ship models and decorative art objects 1680-1820; original collection of ethnographic items owned by Newburyport Marine Society Members, half hull models of Merrimack River Valley Ships; portraits of sea captains; navigational instrument and models
Exhibitions: Lithographs of George C Wales; Run of the Mill - Photos of New England Milling Industry
Publications: Newsletter, bimonthly
Activities: Classes for adults and children; lectures open to the public, 10 vis lectrs per year; gallery talks; tours; individual paintings and original objects of art lent to other museums and historical agencies; book traveling exhibitions; museum shop selling nautical items

NORTHAMPTON

L **FORBES LIBRARY,** 20 West St, 01060. Tel 413-584-8550, 586-0489. *Dir* Blaise Bisaillon; *Art & Music Librn* Faith Kaufmann
Open Mon - Tues 9 AM - 6 PM, Wed 9 AM - 9 PM, Fri & Sat 9 AM - 5 PM, cl Thurs & holidays. Estab 1894 to serve the residential and academic community as a general public library and a research facility. Gallery and exhibit cases for regional artists, photographers and craftspeople. Circ 292,950
Income: $750,000 (financed by endowment, city & state appropriation, federal funds)
Purchases: $53,500
Library Holdings: Vols 18,000; Per subs 47; CD 1500, original documents; Micro — Reels; AV — Cassettes 1700; Other — Clipping files, exhibition catalogs, original art works, photographs, prints, reproductions
Special Subjects: Art, music
Collections: Bien Edition of Audubon Bird Prints; Library of Charles E Forbes; Japanese Books; Walter E Corbin Collection of Photographic Prints and Slides; The Coolidge Collection; Connecticut Valley History; Genealogical Records; Official White House Portraits of President Calvin Coolidge and Grace Anna Coolidge; World War I and II Poster Collection; Local History Photograph Collection & Print Collection
Exhibitions: Monthly exhibits of works by regional artists, photographers and craftspeople
Activities: Lect program; concerts; tours; exten dept to elderly and house bound

M **HISTORIC NORTHAMPTON MUSEUM,** 46 Bridge St, 01060. Tel 413-584-6011. *Exec Dir* Pamela Toma; *Cur Colls* Lynne Bassett; *Admin Asst* Terrie Korpita
Open Mon - Fri 9 AM - 5 PM. Estab 1905 to collect, preserve & exhibit objects of human history in Northhampton & the Connecticut Valley. The museum maintains 3 historic houses from about 1728, 1798 & 1813; a barn from about 1825 with newly added education center; a non-circulating reference library. Average Annual Attendance: 9500. Mem: 500; dues business $100 - $500, individual $20 - $100; annual meeting in Nov
Income: $95,000 (financed by endowment, mem, gifts)
Collections: Collections focus on material culture of Northampton & the upper Connecticut River Valley, costumes, textiles, ca. 1900 Howes Brothers photographs; archaeological artifacts from on-site excavation, decorative arts oil paintings of local personalities and scenes; Collection of costumes, textiles, furniture & decorative art
Publications: Newsletter, quarterly; booklets on local subjects; brochures & flyers
Activities: Classes for adults & children; docent programs; workshops; internships; lectures open to the public; gallery talks; scholarships offered; museum shop sells books, merchandise related to museum's collections, reproductions of collection items, maps, period toys & games

M **SMITH COLLEGE,** Museum of Art, Elm Street at Bedford Terrace, 01063. Tel 413-585-2760; FAX 413-585-2782. *Dir & Chief Cur* Suzannah J Fabing; *Assoc Cur Prints* Ann H Sievers; *Assoc Cur Paintings* Linda Muehlig; *Prog Coordr & Archivist* Michael Goodison

Open Tues - Sat noon - 4 PM, Thurs until 8 PM, cl Mon & academic holidays, call for summer hours. No admis fee. Collection founded 1879; Hillyer Art Gallery built 1882; Smith College Museum of Art established 1920; Tryon Art Gallery built 1926; present Smith College Museum of Art in Tryon Hall opened 1973. Average Annual Attendance: 36,000. Mem: 800; dues student $10 & up
Collections: Examples from most periods and cultures with special emphasis on European and American paintings, sculpture, drawings, prints, photographs and decorative arts of the 17th-20th centuries
Exhibitions: Temporary exhibitions and installations 12-24 annually
Publications: Catalogues
Activities: Gallery tours; lectures; gallery talks; concerts; individual works of art lent to other institutions; sales desk selling publications, post and note cards, posters

L **Hillyer Art Library,** Elm Street at Bedford Terrace, 01063. *Librn* Amanda W Bowen
Open Mon - Thurs 7:45 AM - 11 PM, Fri 7:45 AM - 10 PM, Sat 10 AM - 10 PM, Sun noon - 10 PM. Estab 1900 to support courses offered by art department of Smith College. For reference use only
Income: Financed by endowment
Library Holdings: Vols 61,261; Per subs 200; Micro — Fiche, reels; AV — Cassettes; Other — Exhibition catalogs

NORTH ANDOVER

M **MUSEUM OF AMERICAN TEXTILE HISTORY,** 800 Massachusetts Ave, 01845. Tel 508-686-0191. *Pres* Edward B Stevens; *Dir* Paul Rivard; *Cur* Laurence F Gross; *Textile Conservator* Kathleen Francis
Open Tues - Fri 10 AM - 5 PM, Sat & Sun 1 - 5 PM. Admis adults $2, minors and sr citizens $1. Estab 1960 to preserve artifacts, documents and pictorial descriptions of the American textile industry and related development abroad. Two permanent exhibit galleries: Homespun to Factory Made; Woolen Textiles in America, 1776-1876. Average Annual Attendance: 17,000
Income: Financed by endowment
Collections: Hand looms, industrial machinery, spinning wheels, †textile collection
Exhibitions: Celebration & Remembrace: Commemorative Textiles in America, 1990-1990
Publications: Exhibition catalogs
Activities: Classes for adults; docent training; tours; competitions; lending collection contains slides; originate traveling exhibits; sales desk selling books, prints and postcards

L **Library,** 800 Massachusetts Ave, 01845. Tel 508-686-0191. *Librn* Clare Sheridan
Open by appointment. For reference only
Income: Financed by endowment
Library Holdings: Vols 25,000; Per subs 56; ephemera, original documents, trade literature; Micro — Reels; AV — Motion pictures; Other — Exhibition catalogs, manuscripts, memorabilia, original art works, pamphlets, photographs, prints, reproductions, sculpture
Special Subjects: History of textile industry, textile design and manufacturing, textile mill architecture
Publications: Checklist of prints and manuscripts

NORTON

WHEATON COLLEGE
M **Watson Gallery,** E Main St, 02766. Tel 508-285-7722, Ext 428; FAX 508-285-2908. *Dir* Ann Murray
Open daily 12:30 - 4:30 PM. No admis fee. Estab 1960, gallery program since 1930 to provide a wide range of contemporary one person & group shows as well as exhibitions from the permanent collection of paintings, graphics & objects. Gallery is of fireproof steel-frame, glass and brick construction; there are no windows. Average Annual Attendance: 5000
Income: Financed by college budget
Purchases: Marble portrait bust of Roman boy; Etruscan antefix head; Head of Galienus, Roman c 260 AD; Head of Abba, Egyptian c 700 BC, Cycladic Figurine
Collections: 19th & 20th century prints & drawings; decorative arts; Wedgewood, 18th & 19th century glass; ancient bronzes, sculptures & ceramics
Exhibitions: Changing exhibitions including student, faculty & outside exhibitions
Publications: Exhibition catalogs; Prints of the 19th Century: A Selection from the Wheaton College Collection; Collage; Eleanor Norcross; Amy Cross; Edith Loring Getchell; Hugh Townley; Patterns: Period Costumes; Francesco Spicuzza; Waterworks; Dime Store Deco; Spirituality in Contemporary Art by Women
Activities: Lectures open to the public, five - eight vis lect per year; concerts; gallery talks; tours; individual paintings and original objects of art lent to colleges & other museums & galleries; traveling exhibitions organized and circulated; original prints and reproductions for annual rental

L **Madeleine Clark Wallace Library,** 02766. Tel 508-285-7722, Ext 503. *Fine Arts Librn Liaison* Faith Dickhaut Kindness
Open Mon - Fri 8:30 AM - 10 PM, Sat 9 AM - 10 PM, Sun 10:30 AM - 10 PM. Estab 1962 in Watson Hall; consolidated in 1980 as special collection in Main library to support curricular and other needs of the Wheaton community
Library Holdings: Vols 300,000; Per subs 1450; Micro forms; AV — Cassettes, slides; Other — Clipping files, exhibition catalogs, pamphlets

PAXTON

M **ANNA MARIA COLLEGE,** Saint Luke's Gallery, Moll Art Center, Sunset Lane, 01612. Tel 508-849-3441. *Chmn Art Dept* R A Parente Jr
Open 10 AM - 3 PM. No admis fee. Estab 1968 as an outlet for the art student and professional artist, and to raise the artistic awareness of the general community. Main Gallery is 35 x 15 ft with about 300 sq ft of wall space. Average Annual Attendance: 600
Collections: Small assortment of furniture, paintings, sculpture
Exhibitions: Annual senior art exhibit; local artists; faculty & students shows
Publications: Exhibit programs
Activities: Educ Dept; lect open to public; individual paintings & original objects of art lent to campus offices

PITTSFIELD

L BERKSHIRE ATHENAEUM LIBRARY, Music and Arts Department, 1 Wendell Ave, 01201. Tel 413-499-9487. *Dir* Ron Latham; *Head Dept Music & Arts Serv* Mary Ann Knight
Open Mon - Thurs 10 AM - 9 PM, Fri & Sat 10 AM - 5 PM. Estab 1872, music and arts dept 1937
Income: Financed by city & state appropriations
Library Holdings: Vols 8500; Compact Discs 500; AV — Cassettes 1200, rec 12,000; Other — Prints 2000
Collections: Mary Rice Morgan Ballet Collection: a reference room of programs, prints, original art, rare & current books on dance; 1350 piece sheet music reference collection
Exhibitions: Changing monthly exhibits of fine arts, crafts, antiques & collectables

M BERKSHIRE MUSEUM, 39 South St, 01201. Tel 413-443-7171. *Dir* Barry Dressel; *Dir of Development* Tracy Wilson; *Dir Art Educ* Marion Grant; *Aquirium Dir* Thomas G Smith; *Librn* Mary Mace; *Registrar* Tim Decker
Estab 1903 as a museum of art, natural science & history. Average Annual Attendance: 85,000. Mem: 2400; dues sustaining $30 & up, family $25, single $20; annual meeting Feb
Income: Financed by endowment, mem, fundraising & gifts
Collections: Paintings of the Hudson River School (Inness, Moran, Blakelock, Martin, Wyant, Moran, Church, Bierstadt & others); American Abstract: Art of the '30s; early American portraits; Egyptian, Babylonia & Near East arts; grave reliefs from Palmyra; Paul M Hahn Collection of 18th century English & American silver; Old Masters (Pons, de Hooch, Van Dyck & others); contemporary painting & sculpture; two Norman Rockwell paintings
Exhibitions: A E Gallatin & His Circle; Nancy Graves; George H Seeley; Patricia Johanson: Drawings & Models for Environmental Projects; A J Russell; Pat Adams: Paintings, 1968-1988; Museum presents changing exhibits relating to art, natural science & history, some drawing on the Museum's own collections; educational programs for children & adults presented throughout the year
Publications: Schedule of events, quarterly
Activities: Classes for adults & children; lect open to the public; 40 vis lectr; concerts gallery talks; individual paintings & original objects of art lent to corporate & individual members; museum shop sells gifts

M CITY OF PITTSFIELD, Berkshire Artisans, 28 Renne Ave, 01201-4720. Tel 413-499-9348. *Commissioner of Cultural Affairs & Artistic Dir* Daniel M O'Connell, MFA
Open Mon - Fri 11 AM - 5 PM. No admis fee. Estab 1976. 3 story of 100 yr old brownstone, municipal gallery. Average Annual Attendance: 5100. Mem: 1200; annual dues $5000; annual meeting Sept
Income: $100,000 (financed by endowment, mem, city, state & federal appropriations)
Exhibitions: Doe, Warner Freidman, Dave Novak, Jay Tobin, Daniel Galvez, John Dilg, Sally Fine, Linda Bernstein, David Merritt
Publications: The Berkshire Review
Activities: Classes for adults & children; dramatic programs; docent training; lectures open to public, 12 vis lectr per year; scholarships & fels offered; competitions; artmobile; lending collection contains paintings, art objects; traveling exhibition, 12 per yr; originate traveling exhibitions, 12 per yr; museum shop sells books, prints, magazines, slides, original art, public murals

M HANCOCK SHAKER VILLAGE, INC, US Route 20, PO Box 898, 01202. Tel 413-443-0188. *Dir* Lawrence J Yerdon; *Cur Coll* June Sprigg; *Cur Educ Serv* Todd Burdick
Open June 1 - Nov 1 9:30 AM - 5 PM daily. Admis adults $6, senior citizens & students $5.50, children between 6 & 12 $2. Estab 1960 for the preservation and restoration of Hancock Shaker Village and the interpretation of Shaker art, architecture and culture. Period rooms throughout the village. Exhibition Gallery contains Shaker inspirational drawings and graphic materials. Average Annual Attendance: 50,000. Mem: 1300; dues individual $20
Income: Financed by membership, donations
Special Subjects: Conceptual Art, Display, Folk Art, Furniture, Handicrafts, Historical Material, Manuscripts, Maps, Period Rooms, Religious Art, Reproductions, Textiles
Collections: Shaker architecture, furniture and industrial material; Shaker inspirational drawings
Publications: Newsletter, quarterly; specialized publications
Activities: Classes for adults and children; docent training; workshops; seminars; lect open to public; gallery talks; tours; individual paintings & original objects of art lent to qualified museums with proper security & environmental conditions; museum shop selling books, magazines, reproductions, prints, slides

L Library, US Route 20, PO Box 898, 01201. Tel 413-443-0188. *Librn* Robert F W Meader; *Assoc Librn* Magda Gaber-Hotchkiss
Reference library open to students and scholars by appointment
Library Holdings: Vols 3800; graphic, maps; Micro — Fiche, reels; AV — Rec; Other — Clipping files, exhibition catalogs, framed reproductions, manuscripts, photographs, prints
Special Subjects: Shaker crafts & culture, agricultural & mechanical books
Collections: Buildings; †furniture; inspirational drawings; †farm & crafts artifacts

PLYMOUTH

M PILGRIM SOCIETY, Pilgrim Hall Museum, 75 Court St, 02360. Tel 508-746-1620. *Pres* Peter J Gomez; *Dir* Ernest Buchner; *Cur Exhib* Karen Goldstein; *Cur Manuscripts & Books* Peggy Timlin
Open daily 9:30 AM - 4:30 PM. Admis adults $4, sr citizen $3.50. children $1.50. Estab 1820 to depict the history of the Pilgrim Colonists in Plymouth Colony. Average Annual Attendance: 27,000. Mem: 809; dues $20; annual meetings in Dec
Income: Financed by endowment, membership & admissions
Special Subjects: Historical Material, Manuscripts, Maps, Painting - American

Collections: Arms & armor, decorative arts, furniture & paintings relating to the Plymouth Colony settlement (1620-1692) and the later history of Plymouth
Exhibitions: Permanent collections; 200 Years of Needles & Thread
Publications: The Pilgrim Journal, bi-annually
Activities: Lectures open to public, 8 vis lectrs per yr; Museum shop sells books, magazines, reproductions, prints, slides, ceramics, souvenir wares

L Library, 75 Court St, 02360. Tel 508-746-1620. *Cur Manuscripts & Books* Peggy M Timlin
Open Apr - Nov daily 9:30 AM - 4:30 PM, Dec - Mar noon - 4:30 PM. Admis adults $5, children $2.50. Estab 1820 to collect material relative to the history of Plymouth. For reference only
Library Holdings: Vols 20,000; Per subs 5; Micro — Reels; AV — A-tapes, cassettes, Kodachromes, lantern slides, motion pictures, rec, slides; Other — Clipping files, exhibition catalogs, manuscripts, memorabilia, original art works, pamphlets, photographs, prints, reproductions, sculpture

A PLYMOUTH ANTIQUARIAN SOCIETY, PO Box 1137, 02362. Tel 508-746-0012. *Dir & Cur* Barbara J Milligan; *Cur* Dorthea Anderson; *Registrar* Dorothy B Reed
Open May, June & Sept Fri - Sun 10 AM - 5 PM, July & Aug daily 10 AM - 5 PM. Admis adults $2.50, children $.50. Estab 1919 to maintain and preserve the three museums: Harlow Old Fort House (1677), Spooner House (1747), and Antiquarian House (1809). Average Annual Attendance: 2000. Mem: 500; dues $10-$100; annual meeting Nov
Income: Financed by membership & donations
Collections: Antique dolls, artwork, china, furniture, costumes, & toys
Activities: Classes for adults & children; lect open to the public; sales shop at Harlow House sells selected items

PROVINCETOWN

A PROVINCETOWN ART ASSOCIATION AND MUSEUM, 460 Commercial Street, 02657. Tel 508-487-1750. *Dir* Robyn S Watson
Open daily noon - 4 PM & 7 - 10 PM. Admis adult $2, sr citizens & children $1. Estab in 1914 to promote and cultivate the practice and appreciation of all branches of the fine arts, to hold temporary exhibitions, forums, and concerts for its members and the public. Four galleries are maintained. Average Annual Attendance: 60,000. Mem: 1000; mem open; dues range from $35 - $50
Income: Financed by membership, private contributions, state agencies, IMS, NEA & others
Collections: Permanent collection consists of artists work who have lived or worked on the Lowe Cape
Exhibitions: Permanent collection, members' exhibitions
Publications: Exhibitions catalogues and newsletters
Activities: Classes for adults & children; lect open to public, 6 vis lectr per year; concerts; gallery talks; individual paintings and original objects of art lent to other museums; book traveling exhibiton; originate traveling exhibition; museum shop sells books, magazines, original art, prints, reproductions, slides

L Library, 460 Commercial Street, 02657
Open to members & researchers by appointment
Library Holdings: Vols 500; Other — Clipping files, exhibition catalogs, pamphlets, photographs
Special Subjects: Provincetown artists
Collections: Memorabilia of WHW Bicknell; Provincetown Artists

QUINCY

M ADAMS NATIONAL HISTORIC SITE, 135 Adams St, PO Box 531, 02269. Tel 617-773-1177; FAX 617-471-9683. *Cur* Judith McAlister; *Supt* Marianne Peak
Open daily April 19 - Nov 10 9 AM - 5 PM. Admis adults $2, children under 16 admitted free if accompanied by an adult. Estab 1946. The site consists of a house, part of which dates to 1731; a library containing approx 14,000 books, a carriage house, a woodshed & grounds which were once owned & enjoyed by four generations of the Adams family. Average Annual Attendance: 31,000
Income: Financed by Federal Government
Collections: Original furnishings belonging to the four generations of Adamses who lived in the house between 1788 and 1937
Activities: Lectures (one week each spring); tours

ROCKPORT

A ROCKPORT ART ASSOCIATION, Old Tavern, 12 Main St, 01966. Tel 508-546-6604. *Pres* John Caggiano; *Exec Dir* Ann Fisk
Open summer daily 9:30 AM - 5 PM, Sun 1 - 5 PM, winter daily 10 AM - 4 PM, Sun 1 - 5 PM. No admis fee. Estab 1921 as a non-profit educational organization established for the advancement of art. Four galleries are maintained in the Old Tavern Building; two large summer galleries are adjacent to the main structure. Average Annual Attendance: 75,000. Mem: 1300; mem open to Cape Ann resident artists (minimum of one month), must pass mem jury; contributing mem open to public; photography mem subject of resident/jury restrictions
Income: Financed by endowment, mem, gifts, art programs & sales
Collections: Permanent collection of †works by Cape Ann artists of the past, especially those by former members
Exhibitions: Special organized exhibitions are continually on view; fifty exhibitions scheduled per year
Publications: Quarry Cookbook; Rockport Artists Book 1990; Reprints (recent); Rockport Artists Book 1940; Rockport Sketch Book
Activities: Classes & workshops for adults & children; lect open to the public; painting lectr/demonstrations; Tavern Door shop sells books, cards and notes by artist members

A SANDY BAY HISTORICAL SOCIETY, Sewall Scripture House-Old Castle, 40 King St & Castle Lane, PO Box 63, 01966. Tel 508-546-9533. *Cur* Cynthia A Peckam
Open summer 2 - 5 PM. No admis fee. Estab 1925. Average Annual Attendance: 300. Mem: 500; dues $7; annual meeting first Fri in Sept
Income: $8000 (financed by endowment, mem)
Collections: Extensive Granite Tools & Quarry Materials; 55 local paintings in oil, prints, watercolor; old quilts, samplers, textiles
Exhibitions: A Town That Was; Some Rockporters Who Were (for the Sesqui-centennial of the town)
Publications: Membership bulletins, 3-4 annually; brochures

SALEM

M PEABODY & ESSEX MUSEUM, East Indian Square, 01970. Tel 508-744-3390, 745-1876. *Dir* Peter Fetchko; *Dir Admin & Finance* Ira Schlosser
Open Mon - Sat 10 AM - 5 PM, Sun noon - 5 PM, cl Thanksgiving, Christmas Day, & New Years Day. Admis adults $2, children $1.25, senior citizens $1.50. Estab 1848 to display the Institute's collections of artifacts & historic houses representing the richness of Salem's & Essex County's material culture from the early 17th into the 20th centuries. The Museum is housed in Plummer Hall built in 1857 & is an excellent example of Victorian Italian Revival architecture. The Essex site (across the Street) was founded in 1821 to preserve & interpret the history of Essex County, Massachusetts from the 17th century to the present. It includes 15 buildings, all on the National Historic Register, including three with National Landmark status. On the first floor is the John A McCarthy Gallery devoted to changing displays and loan exhibitions. The second floor has a portrait gallery, and the main gallery containing three early period rooms; a special collections and print room used for small exhibitions. Average Annual Attendance: 100,000. Mem: 4800; dues $30 - $60; annual meeting Apr
Income: $687,542 (financed by endowment, membership, gifts and admissions)
Collections: Architectural fragments, buttons, ceramics, clocks, dolls, furniture, glassware, pewter, sculpture, silver and toys all associated with the civil history of Essex County and adjacent areas since the early 17th century
Exhibitions: Images from the Peabody Tanneries; Paintings by Joseph Peinchinsky; Step Forward Step Back: 3 Centuries of American Footwear Fashions Essex County Landscape Artist; Fashions and Draperies for Windows and Beds; Library Exhibit - Conservation: Some Problems and Solutions; Life and Times in Shoe City: The Shoe Workers of Lynn; Nathaniel Hawthorne Exhibition;
Publications: Historical Collections, quarterly; newsletter, quarterly; occasional books
Activities: Classes for adults and children; docent training; courses regarding Museum's collections; lect open to public & for members only, 6 vis lectr per year; gallery talks; tours; concerts; films; scholarships; paintings and original objects of art lent to museums and institutions; sales shop sells folk art, books, magazines, reproductions, prints and slides

L James Duncan Phillips Library, 132 Essex St, 01970. Tel 508-744-3390; FAX 508-744-0036. *Dir* William T La Moy
Open Mon - Fri 10 AM - 5 PM. For reference only
Library Holdings: Vols 400,000; Other — Manuscripts, memorabilia, pamphlets
Special Subjects: Architecture, Asian Art, Bookplates & Bindings, Carpets & Rugs, Cartoons, Ceramics, Crafts, Decorative Arts, Dolls, Drawings, Embroidery, Etchings & Engravings, Ethnology, Flasks & Bottles, Folk Art, Furniture, Glass, Gold
Collections: The history of Essex County, Massachusetts, in its regional national & global contexts; Western language material on Imperial China
Publications: Essex Institute Historical Collecions; quarterly journal

M Gardner-Pingree House, 128 Essex St, 01970. Tel 508-744-3390.
Open Tues - Sat 10 AM - 4 PM, Sun 1 - 4:30 PM (June 1 - Oct 5). Admis adults $1.50, sr citizens $1, children $.75. Built in 1804-1805 and illustrates the Federal Style of Salem master-builder and carver, Samuel McIntire; furnished in that period

M Crowninshield-Bentley House, 126 Essex St, 01970. Tel 508-744-3390.
Open Tues - Sat 10 AM - 4 PM, Sun 1 - 4:30 PM (June 1 - Oct 31). Admis adults $1.50, sr citizens $1, children $75. Built in 1727, added to and remodeled after 1800. It illustrates the styles of interior architecture and furnishings of much of the 18th century in Salem

M John Ward House, 132 Essex St, 01970. Tel 508-744-3390.
Open Tues - Sat 10 AM - 4 PM, Sun 1 - 4:30 PM (June 1 - Oct 31). Admis adults $1.50, sr citizens $1, children $.75. Built 1684, restored 1910-1912 under direction of George Francis Dow, architectural historian. Furnished in the manner of the time. The rear lean-to contains a later apothecary's shop, a weaving room with operable loom and a small cent shop

M Andrew-Safford House, 13 Washington Square, 01970. Tel 508-744-3390.
Open Thurs 2 - 4:30 PM. Admis $1.50. Built in 1818-1819, and purchased by the Institute in 1947 for the purpose of presenting a vivid image of early 19th century urban life. It is the residence of the Institute's director

M Peirce-Nichols House, 80 Federal St, 01970. Tel 508-745-9321.
Open Tues - Sat 2 - 4:30 PM, open to public by appointment only. Admis adult $1.50, sr citizen $1, children $.75. Built in 1782 by Samuel McIntire. Maintains some original furnishings and a counting house

M Cotting-Smith-Assembly House, 138 Federal St, 01970. Tel 508-744-2231. *Dir* Whitney Lamy
Open for functions & by special appointment. Admis adult $1.50, sr citizen $1, children $.75. Built in 1782 as a hall for social assemblies; remodeled in 1796 by Samuel McIntire as a home residence. The interior features a Victorian sitting room and an unusual Chinese parlor

M Lyle-Tapley Shoe Shop & Vaughn Doll House, 132 Essex St, 01970. Tel 508-744-3390.
Open June 1 - Oct 31 Tues - Sat 9 AM - 4:30 PM, Sun 1 - 5 PM. Accommodates special collections

M Derby-Beebe Summer House, 132 Essex St, 01970. Tel 508-744-3390.
The Summer House (c. 1800) is the focal point of the Institute Gardens

SANDWICH

M THORNTON W BURGESS SOCIETY, INC, Museum, 4 Water St, PO Box 972, 02563. Tel 508-888-4668. *Exec Dir* Jeanne Johnson; *VPres* David O'Conner
Open Mon - Sat 10 AM - 4 PM, Sun 1 - 4 PM. Admis by donation. Estab 1976 to inspire reverence for wildlife & concern for the natural environment. 1756 house. Average Annual Attendance: 80,000. Mem: 2900; dues family $20, individual $12; annual meeting in Feb
Income: Financed by mem, gift shop & mailorder sales
Collections: Collection of Thornton Burgess's writings; the original Harrison Cady illustrations from the writings of the children's author & naturalist
Publications: Newsletter, 3 times per yr; program schedule, 4 times per yr
Activities: Classes for adults & children; docent programs; lectures open to public

M HERITAGE PLANTATION OF SANDWICH, Grove and Pine Sts, PO Box 566, 02563. Tel 508-888-3300. *Dir* Gene A Schott; *Asst Dir* Nancy Tyrer; *Cur Military History* James Cervantes; *Cur Botanical Science* Jean Gillis; *Registrar* Allota Whitney; *Cur Art Museum* Brian Culity; *Cur Antique Auto Museum* James A Harwick
Open daily 10 AM - 5 PM, May - Oct. Admis adults $5, children $2. Estab 1969 as a museum of Americana. Heritage Plantation is a Massachusettes charitable corporation. Maintains three galleries which house collections. Average Annual Attendance: 100,000. Mem: 3000; dues $25-$1000
Income: Financed by endowment, membership, admissions
Collections: †American Indian artifacts; folk art; primitive paintings; †Scrimshaw Antique Automobiles; †Folk Art; †Fine Arts; Tools; Weapons; Military Miniatures; Native American Art
Exhibitions: Western Art; Landscape Paintings; Pennsylvania German Art; Young American Chinese Experimental Art Antique & Classic Automobiles; Hand painted Military Miniatures & Antique Firearms; Restored 1912 Charles I D Looff Carousel; Currier & Ives prints. (1993) Drums A beating, Trumpets Sounding: Artistically Carved Powder Horns in the Provincial Manner; The Songless Aviary: The World of A E Crowell & Son; The Eye of the Angel;
Publications: Quarterly newsletter; exhibit catalogues
Activities: Classes for adults and children; docent training; lect for members only, 7 - 10 vis lectrs per year; concerts; gallery talks; tours; exten dept serving Cape Cod area; artmobile; individual paintings and original objects of art lent; lending collection includes 300 film strips, 50 original prints, 100 paintings & nature artifacts; museum shop sells books, original art, reproductions, prints, slides

M THE SANDWICH HISTORICAL SOCIETY, INC, Sandwich Glass Museum, 129 Main St, PO Box 103, 02563. Tel 508-888-0251. *Dir* Dorothy G Hogan, BA; *Cur Glass* Kirk J Nelson, MA; *Cur Hist* Lynne M Horton, BA
Open April - Oct daily 9:30 AM - 4:30 PM, Nov, Dec, Feb & March, Wed - Sun 9:30 AM - 4 PM, cl Mon & Tues, Jan. Admis adults $3, children 6-12 $.50. Estab 1907 to collect, preserve local history. Thirteen galleries contain the products of the glass companies that operated in Sandwich from 1825-1907. Also displayed are artefacts and memorabilia relating to the history of Sandwich. Average Annual Attendance: 63,000. Mem: 605; annual dues family $18 individual $10; meeting dates: 3rd Tues in Feb, Apr, June, Aug & Oct
Income: $382,000 (financed by endowment, membership, admissions and retails sales
Special Subjects: Glass
Collections: Glass-Sandwich, American, European; Artifacts relating to the history of Sandwich
Exhibitions: (1993) Pressed Glass Cup Plates of Albert C Marble 1825-1850
Publications: The Cullet, 3 times per yr; Acorn annually
Activities: Classes for adults and children; docent training; lecures open to public, 11 vis lectr per yr; scholarships & fels offered; lending collections contains 5000 items; museum shop sells books, slides, original art, reproductions

L Library, 129 Main St, PO Box 103, 02563. Tel 508-888-0251. *Dir* Dorothy G Hogan, BA
For reference only
Purchases: $900
Library Holdings: Vols 3000; Per subs 21; Micro — Reels; AV — A-tapes, lantern slides, motion pictures, slides, v-tapes; Other — Clipping files, exhibition catalogs, manuscripts, memorabilia, photographs, prints
Special Subjects: Decorative Arts, Glass

SHARON

M KENDALL WHALING MUSEUM, 27 Everett St, PO Box 297, 02067. Tel 617-784-5642. *Dir* Stuart M Frank; *Registrar* Ellen Z Hazen
Open Tues - Sat 10 AM - 5 PM, Mon holidays; cl New Years, Memorial Day, Independence Day, Thanksgiving and Christmas. Admis family $5, adults $2, student $1.50, children under 14 $1. Estab 1956 to collect, preserve & interpret art works & artifacts relating to the history & fine arts of whaling & the natural history of the whale. Ten galleries hold the maritime collections. Average Annual Attendance: 20,000. Mem: 750; dues $20
Income: Financed by foundations, grants, admissions, gifts and publications
Collections: †Dutch & Flemish marine painting of 17th -18th century; †American, British, European & Japanese prints & paintings, 16th-20th century; †Scrimshaw; †ship models; †tools; †small craft; †decorative arts & carvings; †Eskimo (Inuit) art; †maritime art
Exhibitions: Recent acquisitions (annual): Dutch Old Master paintings; Japanese Whaling Art, 1680 - 1980; Northwest Coast Indian Art; Afro-American Contributions to the Whaling Industry
Publications: Kendall Whaling Museum Newsletter, quarterly; original publications; exhibition catalogs; monograph series
Activities: Classes for adults & children; musical programs; lectures open to public, 30 vis lectr per year; concerts; gallery talks; tours; awards; scholarships offered; exten dept serves New England & anywhere else by arrangement; individual paintings & original objects of art lent to qualified museums; museum shop sells books, magazines, original art, reproductions, prints, slides, records, jewelry, crockery, stationery, gifts, curriculum kits, & educational material

L **Library,** 27 Everett St, PO Box 297, 02067. Tel 617-784-5642. *Librn* Sara Riley
For reference only
Library Holdings: Vols 9000; Per subs 15; Micro — Cards, fiche, prints, reels; AV — A-tapes, cassettes, fs, Kodachromes, lantern slides, motion pictures, rec, slides, v-tapes; Other — Clipping files, exhibition catalogs, framed reproductions, manuscripts, memorabilia, original art works, pamphlets, photographs, prints, reproductions, sculpture
Special Subjects: Whaling history & literature; maritime art 17th - 20th century; natural history: 15th century to present; marine mammal preservation, seal hunting, cetology, fine arts
Publications: Monographic series, 3 per year; quarterly newsletter

SOUTH HADLEY

M **MOUNT HOLYOKE COLLEGE,** Art Museum, 01075-1499. Tel 413-538-2245; FAX 413-538-2050. *Dir* Kristin A Mortimer; *Cur* Wendy Watson; *Bus Mgr* Amy Wehle; *Registrar & Preparator* Sean Tarpey
Open Tues - Fri 11 AM - 5 PM, Sat - Sun 1 - 5 PM. No admis fee. Estab 1876, museum now occupies a building dedicated in 1970. In addition to its permanent collections, museum also organizes special exhibitions of international scope. Art museum with five galleries houses the permanent collection and special exhibitions. Mem: Dues $25 - $500
Income: Financed by endowment, membership and college funds
Collections: †Asian art, †European & American paintings, †sculpture, †prints & drawings; †Egyptian, Greek, Roman, Pre-Columbian
Publications: Newsletter, annually; exhibition catalogues
Activities: Symposia; docent training; lectures open to public, 5 -6 vis lectr per yr; concerts; films; tours; individual paintings lent to exhibitions sponsored by museums; Museum shop sells exhibition catalogues, cards

L **Art Library,** 01075. Tel 413-538-2225. *Dir* Anne Edmonds
Open to college community only
Library Holdings: Vols 15,550; Per subs 64; AV — Slides

SOUTH SUDBURY

M **LONGFELLOW'S WAYSIDE INN MUSEUM,** Wayside Inn Rd off Route 20, 01776. Tel 508-443-1776. *Innkeeper* Robert H Purrington; *Chmn Trustees* Richard Davidson
Open daily 9 AM - 6 PM cl Christmas Day. Admis $.50; no charge for dining room and overnight guests. Estab 1702 as the oldest operating Inn in America. The ancient hostelry continues to provide hospitality to wayfarers from all over the world. 18th century period rooms including Old Barroom, Longfellow Parlor, Longfellow Bed Chamber, Old Kitchen, Drivers and Drovers Chamber. Historic buildings on the estate include Redstone School of Mary's Little Lamb fame, grist mill, and Martha Mary Chapel. Average Annual Attendance: 170,000
Collections: Early American furniture and decorative arts; Howe family memorabilia; paintings; photographs of the Inn; prints
Activities: Classes for adults; docent training; colonial crafts demonstrations and workshops; lect open to public, 5 vis lectr per year; gallery talks; tours; sales shop selling books, original art, reproductions, prints and slides

SPRINGFIELD

M **MUSEUM OF FINE ARTS,** 49 Chestnut St, 01103. Tel 413-732-6092; FAX 413-734-3688. *Dir* Hollister Sturges; *Cur Education* Kay Nichols; *Registrar* Karen Papineau; *Cur Coll* Heather Haskell; *Spec Events Coordr* Laurie Dellecese
Open Wed, Fri - Sun noon - 4 PM, cl Mon, Tues, Thurs & holidays. No admis fee. Estab 1933 as a unit of the Springfield Library and Museums Association through the bequests of Mr & Mrs James Philip Gray, to collect, preserve & display original artwork. Building contains 18 galleries, theater, offices. Average Annual Attendance: 76,000. Mem: 4500; dues $50
Collections: †American paintings, sculpture, and graphics, primitve to contemporary; Chinese, Prehistoric to 19th Century; †European paintings and sculpture, early Renaissance to contemporary; †Japanese woodblock prints
Exhibitions: Special exhibitions, historic to contemporary are continually on view in addition to permanent collection; changing exhibitions
Publications: Handbook to the American and European Collection,Museum of Fine Arts, Springfield; exhibition catalogs
Activities: Classes for adults & children; dramatic programs; docent training; lectures open to public, 65 vis lectr per yr; concerts, gallery talks & tours; scholarships; individual paintings & original objects of art lent to museums & galleries; lending collection contains original art works, original prints, paintings, sculpture, color transparencies & black & white photographs; book traveling exhibitions 1 - 3 per yr; originate traveling exhibitions; museum shop sells books, children's items, gift items, jewelry, posters, reproductions, prints & slides

L **Reference Library,** 49 Chestnut St, 01103. Tel 413-732-6092; FAX 413-734-3688. *Asst to Registrar* Stephen Fisher
Library Holdings: Vols 5000; AV — Slides; Other — Photographs

M **GEORGE WALTER VINCENT SMITH ART MUSEUM,** 222 State St, 01103. Tel 413-733-4214. *Chmn Trustee Committee* Roger Tutnam; *Dir* Hollister Sturges; *Registrar* Karen Papineau; *Cur Education* Kay Nichols; *Asst Cur Educ* Mary Franks; *Conservator* Emil G Schnorr; *Cur* Kay Nichols
Open Tues - Sun noon - 5 PM. No admis fee. Estab 1889 to preserve, protect, present, interpret, study and publish the collections of fine and decorative arts; administered by the Springfield Library & Museums Association. Maintains eleven galleries housing permanent collection and one gallery reserved for changing exhibitions. Average Annual Attendance: 35,000. Mem: 2000; dues $15 and up; annual meeting June
Income: Financed by endowment, mem, city & state appropriations
Collections: 19th century American & European Paintings; Japanese Bronzes-Arms & Armor; Near Eastern Carpets; Oriental Arts (calligraphy, ceramics, lacquer, painting, sculpture, textiles); Oriental Cloisonne; plaster casts of ancient & Renaissance sculptural masterworks
Publications: Annual report; quadrangle calendar; special exhibition catalogs
Activities: Classes for adults and children; docent training; lectures open to public, 30 vis lect per yr; concerts; gallery talks; tours; scholarships; original objects of art lent to members; lending collection contains framed reproductions; book traveling exhibitions, one per yr; originate traveling exhibitions

A **SPRINGFIELD ART LEAGUE,** George Walter Vincent Smith Art Museum, 222 State St, 01103. Tel 413-733-4214. *Pres* Mary Massidda
Estab 1918 to stimulate art expression and appreciation in Springfield. Mem: Dues $15; annual meeting May
Income: Financed solely by membership
Exhibitions: Non-juried show in Oct open to all members. (1991) Annual juried exhibition open to all artists; Invitational Exhibit; Council Member Exhibit
Activities: Lectr open to public; demonstrations; tours; workshops

A **SPRINGFIELD CITY LIBRARY & MUSEUMS ASSOCIATION,** Art & Music Dept, 220 State St, 01103. Tel 413-739-3871. *Pres* Thomas Costello; *Head Art & Music Dept* Karen A Dorval; *Co-Dir* Ann Keefe; *Co-Dir* Marcia Lewis; *Co-Dir* Emily Bader; *Co-Dir* Lee Fogerty
Open Mon & Wed noon - 9 PM, Tues & Thurs 9 AM - 5 PM, Fri & Sat noon - 5 PM, cl holidays & weekends in summer. No admis fee. Estab 1857, Department opened 1905. In addition to the City Library system, the Springfield Library and Museums Association owns and administers, as separate units, the George Walter Vincent Smith Museum, the Museum of Fine Arts, the Science Museum and the Connecticut Valley Historical Museum
Income: $140,000 (financed by city appropriations & private endowments)
Library Holdings: Vols 20,000; Per subs 96; CDs 6500; AV — Cassettes 2000, rec 18,000; Other — Clipping files, exhibition catalogs, pamphlets, reproductions
Exhibitions: Monthly exhibitions from the library's collections and of work by local artists

M **SPRINGFIELD COLLEGE,** Hasting Gallery, 263 Alden St, 01109. Tel 413-748-3000. *Coordr* Ronald Maggio
Open Mon - Thurs 8 AM - 12 AM, Fri 8 AM - 8 PM, Sat 9 AM - 8 PM, Sun Noon - 12 AM. Estab 1975 to bring a wide range of quality exhibits in all areas of the visual arts to the Springfield College campus and surrounding community
Income: Financed by Cultural Affairs Committee
Library Holdings: Vols 112,000; Per subs 10; Micro — Prints; AV — Cassettes, fs, motion pictures, v-tapes; Other — Original art works, prints
Activities: Dramatic programs; lect open to public,; original prints, color reproductions, photographs lent to faculty & administration on campus

M **SPRINGFIELD LIBRARY & MUSEUMS ASSOCIATION,** Connecticut Valley Historical Museum, 194 State St, 01103. Tel 413-732-3080; FAX 413-734-3688. *Dir* Joseph Carvalho; *Cur Coll* Gail N Colglazier; *Cur Education* Alice Smith; *Head of Library & Archive Coll* Guy A McLain Jr
Open Thurs - Sun noon - 4 PM. No admis fee. Estab 1876 to interpret history of Connecticut River Valley. Average Annual Attendance: 25,000. Mem: 3900; dues $30; annual meeting in Sept
Library Holdings: Vols 23,000; Other — Manuscripts, photographs 25,000
Collections: Decorative arts of Connecticut Valley, including furniture, paintings & prints, pewter, glass, silver; early games
Exhibitions: Many exhibits pertaining to history & decorative arts of Connecticut River Valley
Publications: Founders & Colonizers (1636-1702); Springfield 1636-1986); Springfield Fights the Civil War; Springfield Furniture 1700-1850; The Paintings & the Journal of Joseph Whiting Stock; The Pynchons of Springfield; William Pynchon, Merchant & Colonizer
Activities: Classes for adults and children; docent training; lectures open to the public, 25 vis lectr per yr; school programs; tours; craft demonstrations; book traveling exhibitions 1 - 2 per yr; sales shop sells books

M **ZONE ART CENTER,** 395 Dwight St, 2nd Floor, 01103. Tel 413-732-1995. *Dir* Brendan Stecchine
Open Fri, Sat & Sun 2 - 5 PM, or by appointment. Estab 1980 to encourage & present contemporary innovative arts in all media
Exhibitions: The Holy Ghost's, Richard Yade in collaboration with William G Bauer; Changing exhibitions: poetry readings, jazz concerts

STOCKBRIDGE

M **NORMAN ROCKWELL MUSEUM AT STOCKBRIDGE,** Main St, PO Box 308, 01262. Tel 413-298-3822. *Pres* Lila W Berle; *Dir* Laurie Norton Moffatt; *VPres* David Klausmeyer; *Asst Dir for Prog & Education* Maud V Ayson; *Development Dir* Philip S Deely; *Cur* Maureen Hart Hennessey; *Asst Dir for Finance & Admin* Henry H Williams Jr
Open May - Oct daily 10 AM - 5 PM, Nov - Apr Mon - Fri 11 AM - 4 PM, Sat & Sun 10 AM - 5 PM, cl Thanksgiving, Christmas, New Years Day. Admis adult $8, youth 6 - 18 $1, children 5 & under free, Stockbridge res & museum members free. Estab 1967 to preserve and present the art & life of Norman Rockwell. Museum includes Rockwell's own collection, his studio & extensive archives. Average Annual Attendance: 146,000. Mem: 1500; dues $25-$5000; annual meeting in Oct
Income: Financed by endowment, mem, sales & admissions
Collections: Largest permanent collection of original Rockwell art (500 original paintings & drawings); artifacts and furnishings of Norman Rockwell's studio; archives including business records, letters, memorabilia, negatives, photographs
Exhibitions: Exhibits from the permanent collections
Publications: Norman Rockwell: A Definitive Catalogue; The Portfolio, three times a year
Activities: Docent training; lectrs open to public; gallery talks; tours; scholarships offered; museum shop sells books, reproductions, prints, Rockwell memorabilia & collectibles

L **Library,** PO Box 308, 01262. Tel 413-298-4100. *Cur* Maureen Hart Hennessey; *Curatorial Asst* Linda Szekely
Open by appointment
Library Holdings: Vols 100; Per subs 10; AV — A-tapes, cassettes, lantern slides, motion pictures, rec, slides, v-tapes; Other — Clipping files, manuscripts, memorabilia, photographs, prints, reproductions
Special Subjects: Norman Rockwell

M **THE TRUSTEES OF RESERVATIONS,** The Mission House, PO Box 792, 01262. Tel 413-298-3239. *Adminr* Mark Baer
Open Memorial Day through Columbus Day Tues - Sat 10 AM - 5 PM, Sun 11 AM - 4 PM. Admis. Built 1739, the home of John Sergeant, first missionary to the Stockbridge Indians, it is now an Early American Museum containing an outstanding collection of Colonial furnishings. Museum opened in 1930. Average Annual Attendance: 3000

TAUNTON

M **OLD COLONY HISTORICAL SOCIETY,** Museum, 66 Church Green, 02780. Tel 508-822-1622. *Pres* Marcus A Rhodes Jr; *Dir* Lisa A Compton; *Cur* Jane M Emack-Cambra
Open Tues - Sat 10 AM - 4 PM. Admis adults $2, sr citizens & children 12 - 18 $1. Estab 1853 to preserve & perpetuate the history of the Old Colony in Massachusetts. Four exhibition halls. Average Annual Attendance: 7000. Mem: 700; dues $10 - $250; annual meeting third Thurs in Apr
Income: $120,000 (financed by endowment, mem, service fees, grants)
Collections: Fire fighting equipment; furniture, household utensils, Indian artifacts, military items; portraits, silver, stoves
Publications: Booklets; pamphlets
Activities: Classes for adults & children; docent training; workshops; lectures open to public, 8-10 vis lectrs per yr; fels; museum shop sells books & souvenirs
L **Library,** 66 Church Green, 02780. Tel 508-822-1622. *Dir* Lisa A Compton; *Asst Librn* Greta Smith; *Cur* Jane Emack-Cambra
Open Tues - Sat 10 AM - 4 PM. Admis genealogy $5, other research $2. Estab 1853. For reference only
Library Holdings: Per subs 10; Micro — Reels; AV — A-tapes, slides; Other — Exhibition catalogs, manuscripts, memorabilia, pamphlets, photographs, prints
Special Subjects: Architecture, Art History, Ceramics, Coins & Medals, Decorative Arts, Dolls, Flasks & Bottles, Folk Art, Furniture, Glass, Historical Material, Manuscripts, Maps, Metalwork, Painting - American, Pewter, Photography, Porcelain, Portraits, Silver, Silversmithing, Textiles, Genealogy

TYRINGHAM

M **TYRINGHAM ART GALLERIES,** Tyringham Rd, 01264. Tel 413-243-0654, 243-3260. *Co-Dir* Ann Marie Davis; *Co-Dir* Donald Davis Jr
Admis $1, children under 12 free. Estab 1953 to exhibit and sell paintings, prints and sculptures by recognized artists, including world masters. The building was designed as a sculpture studio by the late Sir Henry Kitson. Average Annual Attendance: 30,000
Income: Financed privately
Collections: Santarella Sculpture Gardens
Exhibitions: Frequent one-person shows by established artists
Publications: Occasional auction catalogs
Activities: Gallery talks; tours

WALTHAM

A **AMERICAN JEWISH HISTORICAL SOCIETY,** 2 Thornton Rd, 02154. Tel 617-891-8110; FAX 617-899-9208. *Pres* Ronald C Curhan; *Exec Dir* Michael Feldberg
Open Summer Mon - Fri 8:30 AM - 5 PM, Winter Mon - Thurs 8:30 AM - 5 PM, Fri 8:30 AM - 2 PM. No admis fee. Estab 1892 to collect, preserve, catalog and disseminate information relating to the American Jewish experience. Two galleries with exhibitions mounted, 15 x 50 ft. Average Annual Attendance: 3000. Mem: 3300; dues $50; annual meeting May
Income: $500,000 (financed by endowment, membership, Jewish Federation allocations, grants and donations)
Collections: Manuscripts; Portraits; Yiddish Motion Pictures; Yiddish Theater Posters
Exhibitions: Gustatory Delights in the New World; German Jews in America; Emma Lazarus, Joseph Pulitzer & The Statue of Liberty; Yiddish Theatre in America; American Jewish Colonial Portraits; Sebhardim in America
Publications: American Jewish History, quarterly; Heritage; Local Jewish Historical Society News; books; newsletters
Activities: Lect open to public, 10 vis lectr per year; gallery talks; tours; competitions with awards; individual paintings & original objects of art lent to museums & historical societies; lending collection contains motion pictures, paintings, books, original art works, original prints & photographs; originate traveling exhibitions
L **Lee M Friedman Memorial Library,** 2 Thornton Rd, 02154. Tel 617-891-8110; FAX 617-899-9208. *Librn* Open
Open Mon - Fri 8:30 AM - 5 PM, winter hours on Fri 8:30 AM - 2 PM, Sun 2 - 5 PM. Estab 1892 to collect, preserve & catalog material relating to American Jewish history. Open to qualified researchers for reference
Income: $514,000 (financed by endowment, mem, contributions, grants, allocations from Jewish welfare funds)
Purchases: $10,000
Library Holdings: Vols 90,000; Per subs 100; archives; AV — Cassettes, motion pictures, rec, slides; Other — Exhibition catalogs, manuscripts, memorabilia, original art works, pamphlets, photographs, prints, reproductions, sculpture
Special Subjects: Colonial American Jewry, philanthropic institutions, synagogues
Collections: Stephen S Wise Manuscripts Collection; Archives of Major Jewish Organizations
Exhibitions: Colonial American Jewry; 19th Century Jewish Families; On Common Ground: The Boston Jewish Experience, 1649-1980; Statue of Liberty; German American Jewry; Moses Michael Hays & Post- Revolutionary Boston
Publications: American Jewish History, quarterly; Heritage, bi-annually
Activities: Lectures open to public, 2-3 vis lectr per year; gallery talks; tours; sponsor competitions; awards; originate traveling exhibitions to libraries, museum societies, synagogues

M **BRANDEIS UNIVERSITY,** Rose Art Museum, PO Box 9110, 02254. Tel 617-736-3434. *Dir* Carl I Belz; *Cur* Susan Stoops; *Registrar* Lisa Leary; *Preparator* Roger Kizik; *Coordr Patrons & Friends* Corinne Zimmermann
Open Tues - Wed & Fri - Sun 1 - 5 PM, Thurs 1 - 9 PM, cl Mon & holidays. No admis fee. Estab 1961 for the organization of regionally and nationally recognized exhibits of contemporary painting and sculpture. All galleries are used for changing exhibitions; there are no permanent exhibitions; two levels & wing gallery. Average Annual Attendance: 20,000
Collections: The permanent collections consist of: African art; American Indian art; contemporary art (post World War II); Japanese prints; modern art (1800 to World War II), including the Riverside Museum Collections and the Teresa Jackson Weill Collection; Pre-Columbian art; pre-modern art (before 1800); Mr and Mrs Edward Rose Collection of early ceramics; Helen S Slosberg Collection of Oceanic art; Tibetian art
Exhibitions: Stephen Antonakos; William Beckman & Gregory Gillespie; Eva Hesse; Katherine Porter; Friedel Dzubas; Dorothea Rockburne; Lester Johnson; Jake Berthot; Jene Highstein
Publications: Exhibition catalogs
Activities: Docent training; lectures open to public; gallery talks; tours; individual paintings and original objects of art lent to students and individuals within the university; lending collection contains original art works, original prints, paintings; book traveling exhibitions, one per year
L **Leonard L Farber Library,** Norman & Rosita Creative Arts Center, 415 South St, 02254. Tel 617-736-4681; FAX 617-736-4675; Elec Mail SHORT@BINAH. CC.BRANDEIS.EDU. *Creative Arts Librn* Bradley H Short
Open Mon - Fri 8:30 AM - 1 AM, Sat 9 AM - 10 PM, Sun noon - 1 AM. Estab 1948 to provide materials & services for the teaching, research, & public interest in the arts of the Brandeis community. For lending & reference
Library Holdings: Vols 35,000; Per subs 130; Micro — Cards, fiche, prints, reels; AV — Cassettes, rec; Other — Exhibition catalogs, photographs
Special Subjects: Art History
Collections: †Dr Bern Dibner Collection of Leonardo Da Vinci - Books; Benjamin A & Julia M Trustman Collection of Honore Daumier Prints (4000); extensive collection of books on Daumier
Exhibitions: Rotating exhibition of Daumier Prints

WELLESLEY

WELLESLEY COLLEGE

M **Museum,** Jewett Arts Center, 106 Central St, 02181. Tel 617-235-0320, Ext 2051; FAX 617-283-2064. *Dir* Susan Taylor; *Asst Dir* Lucy Flint-Gohlke; *Asst Dir for Public Relations & Development* Nancy Gunn; *Cur* Juidth Hoos Fox
Open Mon - Sat 10 AM - 5 PM; Sun 2 - 5 PM; cl New Years Day, Thanksgiving, Dec 24, 25 and 31, mid-June, July and Aug. No admis fee. Estab 1889, dedicated to acquiring a collection of high quality art objects for the primary purpose of teaching art history from original works. Main gallery houses major exhibitions; Corridor Gallery, works on paper; Sculpture Court, permanent installation, sculpture, reliefs, works on wood panel. Average Annual Attendance: 18,000. Mem: 650; dues donor $100, contributor $50, regular $25
Income: Financed by membership, through college and gifts
Collections: Paintings; sculpture; graphic & decorative arts; Asian, African, ancient, medieval, Renaissance, Baroque, 19th & 20th century European & American art; photography
Exhibitions: On the Boards: 19th Century Boston Architectural Drawings; A Timely Encounter: 19th Century Photographs from Japan; 1976-1986: Ten Years of Collecting Contemporary American Art, Selections from the Edward R Downe Jr Collection; Francesca Woodman: Photographic
Publications: Exhibition catalogs; Wellesley College Friends of Art Newsletter, annually
Activities: Docent training; lectures open to public and members only; gallery talks; tours; original objects of art lent to students; lending collection contains original prints; book traveling exhibitons; originate traveling exhibitions; sales desk sells catalogs, postcards and notecards
L **Art Library,** 02181. Tel 617-283-3258; FAX 617-283-3647; Elec Mail Internet: RMCELROY@LUCY.WELLESLY.EDU. *Librn* Richard McElroy
Circ 18,000
Income: Financed by College appropriation
Purchases: $48,000
Library Holdings: Vols 48,500; Per subs 158; Micro — Fiche 1700; AV — Kodachromes, lantern slides; Other — Exhibition catalogs, pamphlets, photographs
Special Subjects: Antiquities-Greek, Antiquities-Roman, Archaeology, Architecture, Art History, Asian Art, History of Art & Archaeology, Oriental Art, Painting - American, Painting - European, Painting - Italian, American art and architecture, Western European art and architecture, Far Eastern art, Ancient art and architecture

WELLFLEET

M **WELLFLEET HISTORICAL SOCIETY MUSEUM & RIDER HOUSE,** Main St, PO Box 58, 02667. Tel 508-349-9157. *Cur* Joan Hopkins Coughlin; *Co-Cur* Durand Echeverria
Open June - 2nd week of Sept, Tues - Sat 2 - 5 PM. Admis $2. Estab 1953. Average Annual Attendance: 200. Mem: 350; dues $3; 5 general meetings per yr
Income: $4000 (financed by mem)
Purchases: $1000
Collections: Shipwreck & marine items; shellfish & finfish exhibit; whaling tools; ship models; china & glass; pewter; Indian artifacts; farm equipment; herb & flower gardens; photography; Victorian parlor
Publications: Beacon, annual
Activities: Educ dept, classes for children; lectrs open to public, 5 vis lectr per year

WENHAM

A **WENHAM MUSEUM,** 132 Main St, 01984. Tel 508-468-2377. *Dir* Eleanor E Thompson; *Pres* Elizabeth Stone; *Office Admin* Felicia Connolly; *Doll Cur* Diane Buck; *Cur* Ann Folley
Open Mon - Fri 11 AM - 4 PM, Sat 1 - 4 PM, Sun 2 - 5 PM, groups by appointment. Admis adults $1.50, children (6-14) $.50. Estab 1921 as Historical Society, incorporated 1953, to acquire, preserve, interpret, and exhibit collections of literary and historical interest; to provide an educational and cultural service and facilities. Maintains three permanent galleries and one gallery for changing exhibits. Average Annual Attendance: 10,000. Mem: 650; dues family $10, individual $5; annual meeting April
Income: Financed by endowment, membership, earned income
Collections: Dolls; doll houses; figurines; costumes and accessories 1800 - 1960; embroideries; fans; needlework; quilts; toys
Exhibitions: Ice Cutting Tool Exhibit; 19th Century Shoe Shops; Still Lifes; Quilts Old & New; Samplers; Tin & Woodenware; Weavers; Wedding Dresses
Publications: Annual report; newsletter
Activities: Classes for children; lectures open to the public; gallery talks; tours; museum shop sells books, miniatures, original needlework, dolls and small toys
L **Timothy Pickering Library,** 132 Main St, 01984. *Librn* Marilyn Corning
Open to members and the public for reference
Library Holdings: Vols 2200; Other — Manuscripts, memorabilia, pamphlets, photographs

WESTFIELD

M **WESTFIELD ATHENAEUM,** Jasper Rand Art Museum, 6 Elm St, 01085. Tel 413-568-7833. *Pres* Barbara Bush; *Treas* Leslie A Chapin; *Dir* Patricia T Cramer
Open Mon - Thurs 8:30 AM - 8 PM, Fri & Sat 8:30 AM - 5 PM, cl Sat in summer. No admis fee. Estab 1927 to provide exhibitions of art works by area artists and other prominent artists. Gallery measures 25 x 30 x 17 feet, with a domed ceiling and free-standing glass cases and wall cases. Average Annual Attendance: 13,500. Mem: Annual meeting fourth Mon in Oct
Income: Financed by endowment, city appropriation
Exhibitions: Changing exhibits on a monthly basis

WESTON

M **REGIS COLLEGE,** L J Walters Jr Gallery, 235 Wellesley St, 02193. Tel 617-893-1820, Ext 2330-2607. *Dir* Sr Louisella Walters
Open Mon - Fri 9 AM - 4:30 PM. No admis fee. Estab 1964 for education, visiting exhibits and student use. Gallery is one room, 20 x 30 ft. Average Annual Attendance: 1500
Income: Financed by donations
Exhibitions: Local painters and sculptors; student exhibits

WILLIAMSTOWN

M **STERLING AND FRANCINE CLARK ART INSTITUTE,** 225 South St, PO Box 8, 01267. Tel 413-458-9545. *Dir* David S Brooke; *Assoc Dir* John H Brooks; *Cur Prints & Drawings* Rafael A Fernandez; *Cur of Paintings* Steven Kern; *Cur of Decorative Arts* Beth Carver Wees; *Registrar* Martha Asher; *Asst Comptroller* Valerie Schueckler; *Asst Comptroller* Karin Watkins; *Supt* Alan Chamberland; *Dir of Public Relations* Mary Jo Carpenter
Open Tues - Sun 10 AM - 5 PM, cl Mon, New Year's Day, Thanksgiving & Christmas. No admis fee. Estab 1955 as a museum of fine arts with galleries, art research library and public events in auditorium. Average Annual Attendance: 100,000
Collections: Antique silver; Dutch, Flemish, French, Italian Old Master paintings from the 14th-18th centuries; French 19th century paintings, especially the Impressionists; 19th century sculpture; Old Master prints and drawings; porcelains; selected 19th century American artists (Homer and Sargent)
Exhibitions: The Permanent Collection and Traveling Exhibitions
Publications: Calendar of Events, quarterly
Activities: Educ dept; docent training; lectures open to public; concerts; gallery talks; tours for school children; book traveling exhibitions, 4-6 per year; originate traveling exhibitions; museum shop sells books, reproductions, prints, slides, jewelry, glass, games, puzzles
L **Clark Art Institute Library,** 225 South St, PO Box 8, 01267. Tel 413-458-9545. *Librn* Sarah S Gibson; *Photograph & Slide Librn* J Dustin Wees
Open Mon - Fri 9 AM - 5 PM, cl holidays. Estab 1962. For reference only
Purchases: $113,000
Library Holdings: Vols 100,000; Per subs 685; Auction sales catalogues 28,000; Micro — Fiche, reels; Other — Exhibition catalogs, photographs, reproductions
Special Subjects: Art History, Decorative Arts, Etchings & Engravings, Painting - American, Painting - British, Porcelain, Prints, Sculpture, Silver, Watercolors, European and American Art
Collections: †Mary Ann Beinecke Decorative Art Collection; †Duveen Library & Archive; †Juynboli Collection

M **WILLIAMS COLLEGE,** Museum of Art, Main St, 01267-2566. Tel 413-597-2429; FAX 413-458-9017. *Dir* Linda Shearer; *Assoc Dir* W Rod Faulds; *PR-Development Dir* Zelda Stern; *Prendergast Cur* Nancy Mowll Mathews; *Assoc Cur Exhib* Deborah Menaker Rothschild; *Educ Coordr* Barbara Robertson; *Public Relations Coordr* Susan Dillman; *Assoc Cur Coll* Vivian Patterson; *Registrar* Diane Hart; *Asst to Dir* Judith M Raab; *Preparator* Timothy Sedlock
Open Tues - Sat 10 AM - 5 PM, Sun 1 - 5 PM. No admis fee. Estab 1926 for the presentation of the permanent collection and temporary loan exhibitions for the benefit of the Williams College community and the general public. Original 1846 Greek Revival building designed by Thomas Tefft; 1983 & 1986 additions and renovations designed by Charles Moore & Robert Harper of Centerbrook Architects & Planners. Building also houses Art Department of Williams College. Average Annual Attendance: 50,000
Collections: 18th - 20th century American art; modern & contemporary art; Asian & African art; ancient & medieval art; 20th century American photography
Exhibitions: (1992) The Prendergasts & the History of Art; Suzy Frelinghuysen & George L K Morris, American Abstract Artists: Aspects of their Work & Collection; Sites of Recollection: Four Altars & A Rap Opera; Georgia O'Keeffe: National Issues, 1918 - 1924; Assuming the Guise: African Masks Considered & Reconsidered (1989-90) Mary Cassatt: The Color Prints; Maurice Prendergast.
Publications: Exhibition catalogs, 3 - 4 per year; brochures
Activities: Classes for children; docent training; lect open to public; gallery talks; tours; individual paintings and original objects of art are lent to other museums; originate traveling exhibitions; museum shop sells books, jewelry, magazines, posters & postcards
L **Sawyer Library,** 01267-2566. Tel 413-597-2501; FAX 413-597-4106. *Librn* Phyllis L Cutler
Income: $22,367
Library Holdings: Vols 697,023; Per subs 3024; AV — Slides 22,800
L **Chapin Library,** Stetson Hall, PO Box 426, 01267-0426. Tel 413-597-2462. *Asst Librn* Wayne G Hammond
Open Mon - Fri 10 AM - noon & 1 - 5 PM. Library estab 1923. For reference only
Library Holdings: AV — A-tapes, cassettes, motion pictures, rec, slides, v-tapes; Other — Clipping files, exhibition catalogs, manuscripts, memorabilia, pamphlets, photographs
Special Subjects: Advertising Design, Architecture, Bookplates & Bindings, Calligraphy, Decorative Arts, Film, Graphic Arts, Illustration, Lettering, Manuscripts, Maps, Photography, Printmaking, Theatre Arts, Woodcuts

WORCESTER

AMERICAN ANTIQUARIAN SOCIETY
For further information, see National and Regional Organizations

M **CLARK UNIVERSITY,** The University Gallery at Goddard Library, 950 Main St, 01610. Tel 508-793-7113. *Dir* Sarah Buie
Open Tues - Sun noon - 5 PM, cl University holidays & vacations. No admis fee. Estab 1976 to provide the Clark community & greater Worcester community the opportunity to view quality exhibitions of art, primarily, but not exclusively, contemporary. Gallery 24 ft x 32 ft, 9 ft ceiling height, with moveable panels. Average Annual Attendance: 5000
Income: Financed through the University
Exhibitions: 6-8 exhibitions per year of, primarily lesser known young artists and well-known artists
Publications: Announcements of exhibitions
Activities: Lectures open to public; gallery talks; Senior Art Purchase Award

L **COLLEGE OF THE HOLY CROSS,** Dinand Library, 1 College St, 01610-2349. Tel 508-793-3372; FAX 508-793-2372. *Dept Chmn Visual Arts* John Reboli; *Music & Visual Arts Librn* Lisa Redpath; *College Librn* Dr James Hogan
Estab 1843 to support the academic study & research needs of a liberal visual arts department
Library Holdings: Vols 10,000; Per subs 30; AV — Slides 50,000; Other — Exhibition catalogs, original art works, sculpture
Special Subjects: Antiquities-Byzantine, Antiquities-Greek, Architecture, Art Education, Art History, Commercial Art, Decorative Arts, Fashion Arts, Film, Graphic Arts, Industrial Design, Painting - American, Theatre Arts
Publications: Art reference bibliographies, semi-annual

M **HIGGINS ARMORY MUSEUM,** 100 Barber Ave, 01606-2434. Tel 508-853-6015; FAX 508-852-7697. *Pres* Dale R Harger; *Dir* Joseph Karl Schwarzer II
Open Tues - Sat 10 AM - 4 PM, Sun noon - 4 PM, cl Mon & national holidays. Admis adults $4.25, children 6 - 16 $3.25, sr citizens $3.50. Estab 1929 to collect & maintain arms, armor & related artifacts. Museum has a Gothic Hall with high vaulted ceilings. Average Annual Attendance: 40 - 50,000. Mem: 300; dues $15 - $1000; annual meeting Apr
Income: Financed by admissions, membership, grants, gift shop and endowment
Collections: Arms & armor from antiquity through the 1800s art from related periods: paintings; tapestries; stained glass; woodcarvings
Publications: Knightly News, quarterly
Activities: Classes for children; dramatic programs; lectures open to public, 2 vis lectr per yr; concerts; gallery talks; tours; original objects of art lent to other museums, lending collection contains 60 paintings, 15 sculptures, several thousand objects of armor; museum shop sells books, magazines, reproductions & souvenirs
L **Library,** 100 Barber Ave, 01606-2444. Tel 508-853-6015; FAX 508-852-7697. *Cur & Librn* Walter J Karcheski Jr
Library closed at present due to renovations; no opening date set
Library Holdings: Vols 3000; Per subs 5; Other — Clipping files, exhibition catalogs, manuscripts, memorabilia, photographs
Special Subjects: Archaeology, Art History, Bronzes, History of Art & Archaeology, Islamic Art, Metalwork, Mixed Media, Painting - European, Portraits, Stained Glass, Woodcuts, Arms & armor, medieval & Renaissance history & warfare to c1870
Publications: Higgins Catalogue of Armor (out-of-print); Higgins Catalogue of Books; Knightly News quarterly

M **WORCESTER ART MUSEUM,** 55 Salisbury St, 01609-3196. Tel 508-799-4406. *Dir* James A Welu; *Deputy Dir* Anthony G King; *Dir Development & Membership* Susan Courtemanche; *Assoc Dir Development* Clare O'Connell; *Asst Dir Development* Sarah Cecil; *Dir Public Affairs* Gina Lionette; *Dir Public Information* Barbara Feldstein; *Dir Publications* Ann McCrea; *Dir Education* Honee A Hess; *Dir Curatorial Affairs* Susan E Strickler; *Cur Asian Art* Elizabeth de Sabato Swinton; *Cur Contemporary Art* Donna Harkavy; *Cur Photography* Stephen B Jarecke; *Cur Prints & Drawings* David L Acton; *Registrar* Joan-Elisabeth Reid; *Chief Preparator & Exhibition Designer* John R Reynolds; *Chief Conservator* Jennifer Spohn; *Dir Building Servs* James Sanders; *Coordr Spec Events* Brenda Welch

Open Wed & Fri 11 AM - 4 PM, Thurs 11 AM - 8 PM, Sat 10 AM - 5 PM, Sun 1 - 5 PM, cl Mon & major holidays. Admis adult $4, sr citizens & full-time students with current ID $2.50 members & children under 18 free, Sat 10 AM - noon free to all. Estab Museum 1896, School 1898. The Museum and School were founded for the promotion of art and art education in Worcester; for the preservation and exhibition of works and objects of art and for instruction in the industrial, liberal and fine arts. There are 42 galleries housed in a neoclassical building. The Higgins Education Wing, built in 1970, houses studios and classrooms and contains exhibition space for shows sponsored by the Education Department. Average Annual Attendance: 130,000. Mem: 4500; dues $15 - $1000 & over; annual meeting in Nov
Income: $4,000,000 (financed by endowment, mem, private corporate contributions & government grants)
Collections: John Chandler Bancroft Collection of Japanese Prints; †American Paintings of 17th - 20th Centuries; †British Paintings of 18th and 19th Centuries; †Dutch 17th and 19th Century Paintings; †Egyptian, Classical, Oriental and Medieval Sculpture; †French Paintings of 16th - 19th Centuries; †Flemish 16th - 17th Century Paintings; †Italian Paintings of the 13th - 18th Centuries; Mosaics from Antioch; †Pre-Columbian Collection; 12th Century French Chapter House
Exhibitions: (1992) Insights: Lawrence Gipe: Century of Progress; Clarence John Laughlin: Visionary Photographer; American Portrait Miniatures: Selections from the Worcester Art Museum Collection; Keith Haring, Andy Warhol & Walt Disney; Clinton Hill: Paperworks & Constructions. (1993) Ottocento: Romanticism & Revolution in 19th Century Italian Painting; Master Printmakers: Piranesi's Dream of Ancient Rome; Master Printmakers: Erik Levine; The Carribean & Latin American World 500 Years Later: Photographs by Ann Parker; Master Printmakers: Goya, Moralist Amid Chaos; Master Printmakers: The Poetic Vision of Odilon Redon; Judith Leyster: A Dutch Master of the Golden Age; Insights: A Distant View
Publications: American Portrait Miniatures: The Worcester Art Museum Collection; In Battle's Light: Woodblock Prints of Japan's Early Modern Wars; Calendar of Events, quarterly; The Second Wave: American Abstractions of the 1930s & 1940s; A Spectrum of Innovation: American Color Prints, 1890 - 1960
Activities: Classes for adults & children; docent training; lect open to public, 10-15 vis lectr per year; symposia; concerts; gallery talks; tours; film series; videos; scholarships offered; museum shop sells books, reproductions, prints, jewelry & exhibition-related merchandise
L **Library,** 55 Salisbury St, 01609-3196. Tel 508-799-4406, Ext 206. *Librn* Kathy L Berg; *Slide Librn* Debby Aframe; *Asst* Donna Winant; *Cataloger* Pauline McCormick
Open Tues & Thurs 11 AM - 4 PM, & by appointment during academic year. Estab 1909 to provide resource material for the Museum Departments. Participate in Worcester Area Cooperating Libraries. Maintains non-circulating collection only
Income: $85,200 (financed by endowment, grants and gifts)
Purchases: $25,000
Library Holdings: Vols 34,000; Per subs 106; Auction & sale catalogues; Micro — Fiche; AV — Kodachromes, lantern slides, slides; Other — Exhibition catalogs, pamphlets
Special Subjects: European & American paintings, prints & drawings; Japanese prints; auction & sale catalogues; museum exhibition catalogues
Exhibitions: Periodic book displays related to museum exhibitions and special library collections
Activities: Tours

M **WORCESTER CENTER FOR CRAFTS,** 25 Sagamore Rd, 01605. Tel 508-753-8183. *Executive Dir* Cyrus D Lipsitt
Open Mon - Thurs 9 AM - 8 PM, Sat 9 AM - 5 PM. No admis fee. Estab 1856 for educational exhibits of historic & contemporary crafts. Professionally lighted & installed 40 x 60 gallery with six major shows per yr in main gallery. Atrium Gallery hosts 4-6 smaller exhibitions per year. Average Annual Attendance: 8000. Mem: 800; dues $35 & up
Income: Financed by mem, grants & contributions
Collections: Collection contains 200 books, 2000 Kodachromes, 300 photographs
Exhibitions: Five exhibits annually, juried, invitational or traveling; It's About Time: American Woodcarvers; Michael James: Quiltmaker; Fabric Constructions: The Art Quilt; Precious Objects
Publications: Exhibition catalogs; On-Center, newsletter
Activities: Classes for adults and children; weekend professional workshops; 2 yr full-time program in professional crafts; lectures open to the public, 12 vis lecturers per yr; gallery talks; tours; scholarships offered; book traveling exhibitions 2 per year; traveling exhibitions organized and circulated; supply shop and gift shop sell books, original craft objects

MICHIGAN

ADRIAN

M **SIENA HEIGHTS COLLEGE,** Klemm Gallery, Studio Angelico, 1247 E Siena Heights Dr, 49221. Tel 517-263-0731; FAX 517-265-3380. *Dir* Christine Reising
Open Mon - Fir 9 AM - 4 PM, Tues evening 6 - 9 PM, cl Easter. No admis fee. Estab 1919 to offer cultural programs to Lenawee County & others. Average Annual Attendance: 6000
Collections: Drawings; graphics; paintings; sculptures; textiles
Exhibitions: Invitational Artists Shows; temporary exhibitions
Activities: Classes for adults & children; lect open to public, 6 vis lectr per yr; gallery talks; tours; competitions with awards; scholarships & fels
L **Art Library,** 1247 E Siena Heights Dr, 49221. Tel 517-263-0731; FAX 517-265-3380. *Dir Instructional Servs* Mark Dombrowski; *Public Servs Librn* Jean S Baker
Library Holdings: Vols 10,000; Per subs 35; Micro — Cards, fiche, reels; AV — A-tapes, cassettes, fs, lantern slides, rec, slides, v-tapes; Other — Clipping files, exhibition catalogs, manuscripts, memorabilia, original art works, pamphlets, photographs, reproductions, sculpture

ALBION

M **ALBION COLLEGE,** Bobbitt Visual Arts Center, 49224. Tel 517-629-0246. *Gallery Dir* Frank Machek
Open Mon - Thurs 9 AM - 4:45 PM & 6:30 - 10 PM, Fri 9 AM - 4:45 PM, Sat 10 AM - 1 PM, Sun 2 - 5 PM. No admis fee. Estab 1835 to offer art education at college level and general art exhibition program for campus community and public. Maintains one large gallery and three smaller galleries
Income: Privately funded
Purchases: $2000 - $4000
Collections: African Art; ceramics; glass; †prints
Exhibitions: From The Print Collection; Pieces from the Permanent Collection; various one-man and group shows
Activities: Lect open to public, 2 - 4 vis lectr per year; gallery talks; original objects of art lent to faculty and students

ALPENA

M **JESSE BESSER MUSEUM,** 491 Johnson St, 49707. Tel 517-356-2202. *Pres* John Milroy; *Dir* Dennis R Bodem; *First VPres* Shirley Houston; *Treas* Lillian Banas
Open Mon - Fri 10 AM - 5 PM, Thurs 10 AM - 9 PM, Sat & Sun noon - 5 PM. Admis adults $2, children $1. Estab association 1962, building open to public 1966, an accredited museum of history, science & art serving northern Michigan. Museum has a research library, a planetarium, a Foucault Pendulum, Indian artifact collection, Avenue of shops, lumbering exhibits & preserved furnished historical buildings on grounds. Also on grounds, sculptured fountain by artist Glen Michaels. Three galleries are utilized for shows, traveling exhibits, & changing exhibitions of the Museum's collection of modern art & art prints, decorative arts & furniture. There are 260 running ft of wall space on lower level, 1250 sq ft & 1645 sq ft on upper level galleries. Average Annual Attendance: 29,000
Income: Financed by Besser Foundation, federal & state grants, private gifts & donations, Museums Founders Society, Operation Support Grant from Michigan Council for the Arts, & other sources
Collections: †Art prints; †Clewell pottery; †contemporary native american art; †maps of the Great Lakes; †modern art; †photography
Exhibitions: Changing exhibitions of all major collecting areas & touring exhibits; Northeast Michigan Juried Art
Activities: Classes for adults & children; art workshops; seminars; docent training; lect open to public, 5 vis lectr per year; gallery talks; tours; competitions with awards; book traveling exhibitions 8 per year; originate traveling exhibitions; museum shop sells books, magazines, original art, handicrafts
L **Philip M Park Library,** 491 Johnson St, 49707. Tel 517-356-2202. *Dir* Dennis R Bodem; *Librn* Sandy Mitchell
Open to public for reference only
Library Holdings: Vols 2750; Per subs 42; Micro — Fiche, reels; Other — Clipping files, exhibition catalogs, manuscripts, pamphlets
Special Subjects: American Indian Art, Architecture, Art History, Ceramics, Decorative Arts, Dolls, Flasks & Bottles, Folk Art, Glass, Painting - American, Pottery, Printmaking, Prints, Restoration & Conservation, Antiques, Museum Management

ANN ARBOR

A **ANN ARBOR ART ASSOCIATION,** 117 W Liberty, 48104. Tel 313-994-8004. *Pres* Jeff Colton; *VPres* Jack Reinelt; *Executive Dir* Marsha Chamberlin; *Dir of Operations* Susan Monaghan; *Gallery Dir* Martine Perreault; *Educ Dir* Mary Hafeli; *Development Dir* Julie Burgess
Open Mon noon - 5 PM, Tues - Sat 10 AM - 5 PM. Estab 1909 to provide for the well-being of the visual arts through programs that encourage participation in & support for the visual arts, as well as foster artistic development. Maintains 750 square feet of exhibit gallery space with monthly shows; sales - rental gallery next to exhibit area; classes in studio art & art appreciation; special events. Average Annual Attendance: 52,000. Mem: 1000; dues $35; annual meeting June
Income: Financed by mem, Michigan Council for the Arts grant, rental of studios & retail sales
Exhibitions: Monthly Shows; The Annual, membership competition; The Print, annual printmaking competition; Youth Art, for annual high school students competition
Publications: Class catalog, quarterly; gallery announcements, monthly; lecture listings, quarterly; newsletter, quarterly
Activities: Classes for adults and children; lect open to the public, 4-6 visiting lectr per year; gallery talks; tours; awards; scholarships; exten dept lends individual paintings & original objects of art to organizations & community facilities; sales shop selling original art

A **ARTRAIN, INC,** N E W Center, 1100 N Main St, 48107. Tel 313-747-8300. *Chmn* Ronald Weiser; *Pres* David Griffith; *Dir Community Relations* Wendy Paskus
No admis fee. Estab 1971 to tour major art exhibits throughout the nation and provide catalyst for community arts development. Consists of converted railroad cars with large walls and cases. Average Annual Attendance: 122,000
Income: Financed by endowment, state appropriation, individual foundation and corporation campaigns
Exhibitions: (1989-91) Treasures of Childhood: 150 Years of American Toys.
Publications: Exhibition catalogs; newsletter
Activities: Classes for children; docent training; lectures open to public; competitions; book traveling exhibitions; museum shop sells exhibit related items

A **MICHIGAN GUILD OF ARTISTS & ARTISANS,** Michigan Guild Gallery, 118 N Fourth Ave, 48104. Tel 313-662-3382. *Exec Dir* Mary Strope; *Membership Servs Coordr* Joe Jaworek; *Art Fair Dir* Shary Brown
Open Mon - Fri 9 AM - 5 PM. No admis fee. Estab as an art service organization offering exhibition opportunities, referrals, group health insurance;

specializing in contemporary work of all media by member artists. Average Annual Attendance: 1000. Mem: 2500; dues $45 - $55; annual meeting in Jan
Income: Financed by membership fees & art fair fees
Exhibitions: (1993) Schedule dedicated to the Year of American Crafts
Publications: Membership newsletter, bi-monthly
Activities: Business classes for artists; art fairs

UNIVERSITY OF MICHIGAN

M **Museum of Art,** 525 S State St, 48109-1354. Tel 313-764-0395; FAX 313-764-3731. *Dir* William Hennessey; *Cur of Asian Art* Marshall Wu; *Assoc Admin* Janet E Torno; *Registrar* Carole A McNamara
Open (Sept - May) Tues - Fri 10 AM - 5 PM, Sat & Sun 1 - 5 PM; (June - Aug) Tues - Sat 11 AM - 5 PM, Sun 1 - 5 PM. No admis fee. Estab 1946, as a university art museum and museum for the Ann Arbor community. Average Annual Attendance: 60,000. Mem: 1100; dues individual $35
Income: Financed by state appropriation
Collections: Arts of the Western World from the 6th Century AD to the Present; Asian, Near Eastern, African & Oceanic, including ceramics, contemporary art, decorative art, graphic arts, manuscripts, painting, sculpture
Exhibitions: (1991) Greece vs Rome: The Search for the Classical Spirit; Photographs by Walker Evans; The Art of Science; Wide World of Whistler; Art Words from the Brush; Rembrandt Etchings from notre Dame; I See America Dancing: Photographs by Barbara Morgan; Klimt & Schiele; Bladwin Lee; Jasper Johns: Prints from the Kaufman Collection. (1992-93) Paintings by Tan Tee Chie; Picasso & Gris: Paintings from the Carey Walker Foundation; Paul Klee; The Pear: French Graphic Art in the Golden Age of Caricature; Comedy & the Artist's Eye; Realist Prints: Then & Now (1970 - 1990); Faith Ringgold: Story Quilts; Not Losing Her Memory: Stories in Photography, Words & Collages; Syliva Plimack Mangold: Works on Paper 1968 - 1991; Joseph Hampl; Beyond the Plane: Relief Paintings by Judith Rothschild; Emil Weddige; Tiffany Interiors from the H O Havemeyer House; Old Master Drawings from the Collection of Joseph F McCrindle; Janice Gordon: Recent Constructions; Photographs by Carlo Naya; Four Treasures of the Chinese Scholar's Studio; African Art from the Museum Collection: A Celebration; Michael Kenna Photographs
Publications: Bulletin of the Museum of Art & Archaeology, irregular
Activities: Educ dept; docent training; 10 vis lectr per yr; gallery talks; tours; museum shop selling publications, posters, postcards & gifts

M **Kelsey Museum of Archaeology,** 434 State St, 48109-1390. Tel 313-763-3559; FAX 313-764-2697. *Dir* Elaine K Gazda; *Cur* Sharon Herbert; *Assoc Cur* Margaret C Root; *Asst Cur* Thelma Thomas; *Coodr of Coll* Robin Meador-Woodruff; *Asst Dir & Asst Cur Educ* Lauren E Talalay
Open Sept - April Mon - Fri 9 AM - 4 PM, Sat & Sun 1 - 4 PM; May - Aug Tues - Fri 11 AM - 4 PM, Sat & Sun 1 - 4 PM, cl Mon. No admis fee. Estab 1928. Four small galleries are maintained. Average Annual Attendance: 25,500
Collections: †Objects of the Graeco-Roman period from excavations conducted by the University of Michigan in Egypt & Iraq; Greece, Etruria, Rome & provinces: sculpture, inscriptions, pottery, bronzes, terracottas; Egyptian antiquities dynastic through Roman; Roman & Islamic glass, bone & ivory objects, textiles, coins; 19th century photographs
Exhibitions: (1991) The Sigmund Freud Antiquities Fragments from a Buried Past; Writing in the Ancient World. (1993) Riches to Rags: Gujarati Textiles
Publications: Bulletin of the Museums of Art and Archaeology
Activities: Lect open to the public, 10-12 visiting lectr per year; gallery talks; tours; book traveling exhibitions; originate traveling exhibitions to museums with similar collections; sales shop selling books and exhibition catalogs

M **Slusser Gallery,** School of Art, 2000 Bonisteel Blvd, 48109. Tel 313-936-2082. *Interim Dean* John H Stephenson; *Secy Exhib* H Dornoff
Open Tues - Sat 11 AM - 5 PM. No admis fee. Estab 1974, primarily used as an educational facility with high volume of student and faculty participation. Gallery is located on the main floor of the Art & Architecture Building & is comprised of 3,600 sq ft of exhibition space & is a well lighted area. Average Annual Attendance: 11,000
Income: Financed by School of Art general fund & gifts of the Friends of the Jean Paul Slusser Gallery
Collections: Artifacts of the School's history; works by faculty & alumni of the University of Michigan School of Art
Exhibitions: Faculty & student exhibitions; traveling exhibitions
Publications: Occasional catalogues
Activities: Lect open to the public, 10-15 visiting lectr per year; gallery talks

L **Asian Art Archives,** 48109-1357. Tel 313-764-5555, 936-3050; FAX 313-747-4121. *Sr Assoc Cur* Wendy Holden
Open Mon - Fri 9 AM - 5 PM. Estab 1962 for study & research. Contains 80, 0000 black & white photographs of Asian art objects or monuments. Library also houses the Asian Art Photographic Distribution, a non-profit business selling visual resource materials dealing with Chinese & Japanese art
Income: $4000 - $5000 (financed by endowment, federal funds)
Purchases: $4000 - $5000
Library Holdings: Vols 50; Black/white negatives 26,000; Micro — Reels; AV — Slides; Other — Clipping files, exhibition catalogs, photographs 80,000, reproductions 3000
Special Subjects: Archaeology, Architecture, Art History, Asian Art, Bronzes, Ceramics, Decorative Arts, Graphic Arts, History of Art & Archaeology, Islamic Art, Landscapes, Oriental Art, Painting - Japanese
Collections: National Palace Museum, Taiwan, photographic archive; †Chinese art, painting, decorative arts; Southeast Asian Art Archive, sculpture, architecture; Islamic Art Archive; †Asian Art Archive, Chinese & Japanese arts, painting
Publications: Newsletter, East Asian Art & Archaeology (three issues per year)

L **Fine Arts Library,** 260 Tappan Hall, 48109. Tel 313-764-5405. *Head Fine Arts Library* Deirdre Spencer; *Library Technical Asst* Barbara Peacock
Open Mon - Thurs 8 AM - 11 PM, Fri 8 AM - 5 PM, Sat 10 AM - 6 PM, Sun 1 - 10 PM, summer hours vary. Estab 1949, to support the academic programs of the History of the Art Dept, including research of faculty and graduate students. Circ 17,200
Income: Financed by state appropriation
Library Holdings: Vols 65,000; Per subs 232; Marburger index of photographic documentation of art in Germany; Micro — Fiche, reels; Other — Exhibition catalogs, pamphlets
Special Subjects: Afro-American Art, Antiquities-Byzantine, Antiquities-Etruscan, Antiquities-Greek, Antiquities-Roman, Art History, History of Art & Archaeology, Islamic Art, Oriental Art, Painting - American, Painting - British, Painting - Dutch, Painting - European, Painting - Flemish

L **Slide and Photograph Collection,** History of Art Department, 20A Tappan Hall, 48109. Tel 313-763-6114; FAX 313-747-4121. *Cur* Joy Blouin; *Sr Cur* Rebecca Hoort; *Photographer* Patrick Young; *Sr Assoc Cur & Asian Art Archives* Wendy Holden
Open Mon - Fri 8:30 AM - 1 PM, 2 - 5 PM. Estab 1911, as a library for teaching and research collection of slides and photos of art objects; limited commercial distribution; non-profit slide distribution projects; (Asian Art Photographic Distribution; Univ of Mich Slide Distribution). Circ 3,600 weekly
Income: Financed by state appropriation
Library Holdings: AV — Lantern slides, slides 290,000; Other — Photographs 200,000, reproductions
Special Subjects: History of Art & Archaeology
Collections: Berenson's I Tatti Archive; Courtauld Institute Illustration Archive; Palace Museum Archive (Chinese painting); Romanesque Archive (sculpture and some architecture concentrating on Burgundy, Southwestern France, †Spain and southern Italy); †SE Asian and Indian Archives; †Islamic Archives
Activities: Materials lent only to University of Michigan faculty and students

L **Art & Architecture Library & Computer Lab,** 2106 Bonisteel Blvd, 48109-2069. Tel 313-764-1303. *Librn* P A Kusnerz; *Asst Librn* D H Shields
Estab to support the teaching and research activities of the School of Art and the College of Architecture & Urban Planning
Library Holdings: Vols 65,000; Per subs 550; Micro — Cards, fiche 1000, prints, reels 150; AV — A-tapes, cassettes, fs, Kodachromes, lantern slides 1000, slides 60,000, v-tapes; Other — Clipping files, exhibition catalogs, manuscripts 1000, original art works, pamphlets, photographs, sculpture 10
Special Subjects: Architecture of all places & periods, Contemporary art & design, History of Photography, Studio art collections in graphic design
Collections: Jens Jensen Archive of Landscape Architecture & Drawings
Activities: Computer workstations with various software

BATTLE CREEK

M **ART CENTER OF BATTLE CREEK,** 265 E Emmett St, 49017. Tel 616-962-9511. *Dir* Ann Worth Concannon; *Educ Dir* Susan Eckhardt
Open Tues - Fri 10 AM - 5 PM, Sat & Sun 1 - 4 PM, cl Aug & legal holidays. No admis fee. Estab 1948 to offer classes for children and adults, and to present monthly exhibitions of professional work. Four galleries of varying sizes with central vaulted ceiling gallery, track lighting and security. Average Annual Attendance: 30,000. Mem: 765; annual dues $10-$500; annual meeting Sept
Income: Financed by mem, endowment fund, grants, MCA, MCH, UAC, special projects, tuition, sales of artwork
Collections: Michigan Art Collection featuring 20th century Michigan artists
Exhibitions: Group & Solo Shows: Paintings; Photography; Prints; Sculpture; Crafts; American Art 40's & 50's; Artist's competitions
Publications: Newsletter, bi-monthly
Activities: Classes for adults and children; docent training, workshops & programs; lect open to public; gallery talks; tours; competitions with prizes; scholarships offered; traveling shows from Michigan Art Collection lent to professional art agencies; book traveling exhibitions, 3-5 per yr; originate traveling exhibitions to museums & art centers; museum shop sells original art by Michigan artists

L **Michigan Art & Artist Archives,** 1265 E Emmett St, 49017. Tel 616-962-9511. *Dir* Ann Concannon; *Office Mgr* Barbara Adams
Library Holdings: Vols 450; Per subs 5; AV — Slides; Other — Clipping files, exhibition catalogs, original art works, photographs, sculpture
Special Subjects: Afro-American Art, American Indian Art, Antiquities-Egyptian, Art History, Middle American Art

BAY CITY

M **BAY COUNTY HISTORICAL SOCIETY,** Historical Museum of Bay County, 321 Washington Ave, 48708. Tel 517-893-5733. *Pres* Leon Katzinger; *Exec Dir* Gay McInerney
Open Mon - Fri 10 AM - 5 PM, Sun 1 - 5 PM. No admis fee. Estab 1919 to preserve, collect, & interpret the historical materials of Bay County. Average Annual Attendance: 4000. Mem: 300; dues corporate $500, patron $100, small business $50, sustaining $25; annual meeting in May
Income: Financed by mem, state grant, county funds
Collections: Hand crafts, photographs, portraits, quilts; mid-1800s - post WW II historical material; native American materials & paintings
Exhibitions: Sportsman's Holiday; hunting, fishing & outdoor activities are featured
Publications: Anishinabe - People of Saginaw; Ghost Towns & Place Names; Vanished Industries; Women of Bay County
Activities: Hands-on classes for children; docent training; home tours; traveling displays & educational kits; lectures open to public, 2-3 vis lectrs per yr; museum shop sells books, reproductions, hand crafts

BIRMINGHAM

A **BIRMINGHAM-BLOOMFIELD ART ASSOCIATION,** 1516 S Cranbrook Rd, 48009. Tel 313-644-0866; FAX 313-644-7904. *Pres* Susie Citrin; *VPres* Evie Wheat; *Dir* Kenneth R Gross; *Asst Dir* Kathy Dowling; *Office Mgr* Ann Garrison; *Business Mgr* Frances St Lawrence
Open Mon - Thurs 9 AM - 10 PM, Fri 9 AM - 7 PM, Sat 9 AM - 5 PM, cl Sun. No admis fee. Estab 1956 to provide a community-wide, integrated studio-gallery art center. Average Annual Attendance: 10,000. Mem: 1300; dues $25 and up; annual meeting May
Income: $400,000 (financed by membership, tuitions, special events funding, operational support from Michigan Council for the Arts & donations)

Collections: Very small collection of craft objects & prints by local artists; also have originals by local artists
Exhibitions: Michigan Fine Arts Competitions; faculty, students & area art organizations
Publications: Newsletter, eleven a year
Activities: Classes for adults and children; docent training; Picture Lady Program; Career Program; Teen Volunteer Service; lectures open to public, 6 - 10 vis lectrs per year; gallery talks; tours; competitions, cash awards, ribbons & certificates; local scholarships; exten dept serving public schools; individual paintings lent to public on a rental basis; lending collection contains books, original art works & prints, paintings, photographs & sculpture; sales & rental gallery; sales shop sells original art & craft items

BLOOMFIELD HILLS

M CRANBROOK ACADEMY OF ART MUSEUM, 1221 N Woodward, PO Box 801, 48303-0801. Tel 313-645-3312; FAX 313-646-0046. *Dir Museum* Roy Slade; *Cur Coll* Greg Wittkopp; *Asst Cur* David D J Rau
Open Tues - Sun 1 - 5 PM, cl Mon and major holidays. Admis adults $3, students & senior citizens $2, group rates available. Estab 1942 as part of Cranbrook Academy of Art. Average Annual Attendance: 40,000. Mem: 1500; dues general $35
Collections: Artists associated with Cranbrook Academy of Art: ceramics by Maija Grotell; architectural drawings & decorative arts by Eliel Saarinen; porcelains by Adelaide Robineau; sculpture by Carl Milles; contemporary paintings; 19th century prints; study collection of textiles; prints and ceramics
Exhibitions: Annual Student Exhibition; Contemporary architecture, craft-media, design, paintings and sculpture
Activities: Lectures open to public & for members only; gallery talks; tours; individual paintings & original objects of art lent to other museums; book traveling exhibitions; originate traveling exhibitions & circulate to other museums national & international; museum shop sells books & slides
L Library, 500 Lone Pine Rd, PO Box 801, 48303-0801. Tel 313-645-3355; FAX 313-646-0046. *Head Librn* Judy Dyki
Open Mon - Fri 9 AM - 5 PM & 7 PM - 10 PM, Sat & Sun 1 - 5 PM. Estab 1928 to support research needs of Art Academy and Museum. Library is for Academy students, faculty and staff; open to public for reference only
Income: Financed by academy
Library Holdings: Vols 25,000; Per subs 150; masters theses; AV — A-tapes, cassettes 600, slides 32,500, v-tapes; Other — Clipping files, exhibition catalogs
Special Subjects: Ceramics, Graphic Arts, Sculpture, Architecture, Design, Fiber Arts, History of Art, Metal Working, Photography, Printmaking

DEARBORN

C FORD MOTOR COMPANY, American Rd, 48121. Tel 313-845-8741.
Educational Affairs Lee Collins
Collection not available for public viewing
Collections: 20th century American art, primarily watercolors

DETROIT

L CENTER FOR CREATIVE STUDIES, College of Art & Design Library, 201 E Kirby, 48202. Tel 313-872-3118, Ext 263. *Librn* Jean Peyrat; *Slide Librn* Evelyn Malles
Open Mon - Thurs 8:30 AM - 9 PM, Fri 8:30 AM - 4:30 PM, Sat 11 AM - 3 PM. Estab 1966 to serve students & faculty of an undergraduate art school. Primarily a how-to, illustrative collection. Gallery has 3 rooms located at 15 E Kirby
Income: Financed by private school
Library Holdings: Vols 22,000; Per subs 72; AV — Slides 58,000; Other — Exhibition catalogs
Special Subjects: Advertising Design, Crafts, Graphic Design, Industrial Design, Photography

M DETROIT ARTISTS MARKET, 300 River Place, Suite 1650, 48207. Tel 313-393-1770; FAX 313-393-1772. *Board Chmn* Carol Roberts; *VChmn* Tom Cliff; *VChmn* Robert Cassey; *VChmn* Nancy Cunningham; *VChmn* Charles Glass; *VChmn* Evie Wheat; *Art Dir* Gerry Craig; *Mgr* Nancy Follett
Open Mon - Sat 11 AM - 5 PM. No admis fee. Estab 1932 to educate public & bring work by local artists within 90 mile radius to the attention of the public. Average Annual Attendance: 10,000. Mem: 1200; dues $15 - $1000
Income: $250,000 (financed by endowment, membership, state appropriation, mini-grants, MCA, contributions, percent of art work sales)
Exhibitions: Small Group Exhibition; All Media Juried Exhibition; The Garden Sale. (1992) Retro-Perspective: Cass Corridor Continuum; Serendipitous Season: Holiday Gifts. (1993) All Media Juried Exhibition; In & Just Out; Michigan Potters Association Juried Show; New Work; Reform Function: Furniture & Costume; Willing Disbelief
Publications: Catalogs, 1-2 per yr; quarterly newsletter; Journal of exhibitions available for each exhibition including an essay & biographical information of participating artists
Activities: Educ dept; lect open to public; tours; competitions with awards; scholarships; sales shop sells magazines, original art

M DETROIT FOCUS, 743 Beaubien, 48226. Tel 313-882-1624. *Dir* Gere Baskin
Open Wed - Sat noon - 6 PM. No admis fee. Estab 1978 as an exhibition space for Michigan visual artists. Average Annual Attendance: 10,000. Mem: 400; dues from $25; meetings annually
Income: $70,000 (financed by mem, city & state appropriation, fundraising)
Exhibitions: Juried exhibitions
Publications: Detroit Focus Quarterly; exhibition catalogues
Activities: Lectures open to public, 9 vis lectrs per yr; competitions; awards; originate traveling exhibitions

M DETROIT INSTITUTE OF ARTS, 5200 Woodward Ave, 48202. Tel 313-833-7900, 833-2323. *Dir* Samuel Sachs II; *Deputy Dir* Maurice Parrish; *Cur American Art* Nancy Rivard-Shaw; *Cur Ancient Art* William H Peck; *Cur African, Oceanic & New World Cultures Art* Michael Kan; *Cur European Paintings* J Patrice Marandel; *Cur Education* Patience Young; *Graphic Arts* Ellen Sharp; *Cur Twentieth Century* J van der Mark; *Cur of Asian Art* Laurie Barnes; *Photographer* Dirk Bakker; *Head Conservator* Barbara Heller; *Cur European Sculpture & Decorative Arts* Alan Darr; *Registrar* Suzanne Quigley
Open Wed - Sun 11 AM - 4 PM, cl Mon, Tues & holidays. Estab and incorporated 1885 as Detroit Museum of Art; chartered as municipal department 1919 and name changed; original organization continued as Founders Society Detroit Institute of Arts; present building opened 1927; Ford Wing addition completed 1966; Cavanagh Wing addition opened 1971. Midwest area office of Archives of American Art
Collections: Elizabeth Parke Firestone Collection of 18th Century French Silver; William Randolph Hearst Collection of Arms and Armor and Flemish Tapestries; Grace Whitney Hoff Collection of Fine Bindings; German Expressionist Art; African, Oceanic & New World Cultures; Graphic Art, Photography; Modern Art; 20th century Art; American Art: Painting, Sculpture, Furniture, and Decorative Arts; European Painting, sculpture and Decorative Art; Asian Art; Ancient Art
Exhibitions: (1991) Revelaciones: The Art of Manuel Alvarez Bravo; Fair Scenes & Glorious Wonders: Thomas Cole's Travels in Italy, Switzerland, France & England; Richard Pousette-Dar: Inner Realms & Outer Space; Florence Henri: Artist-Photographer of the Avant Garde; Contemporary Studio Glass: The David Jacob Chodorkoff Collection; Detroit Public School Exhibition; Henry Ossawa Tanner; Emmet Gowin: Photographs; Collaboration in Print: Stewart & Stewart Prints, 1980-1990
Publications: Exhibition catalogues; bulletin; annual report; collection catalogues
Activities: Classes for adults and children; docent training; lectures open to the public; gallery talks; tours; live Youtheatre for youngsters, concerts, Detroit filmtheatre; individual paintings & original objects of art lent; book traveling exhibitions; originate traveling exhibitions; museum shop sells books, magazines, prints & slides
L Research Library, 5200 Woodward Ave, 48202. Tel 313-833-7926. *Librn* Constance Wall
Open Wed - Fri 9 AM - 5 PM by appointment only. Estab 1905 to provide material for research, interpretation and documentation of museum collection. For reference only
Income: Financed by city
Library Holdings: Vols 500,000; Per subs 168; Micro — Cards, reels; AV — Lantern slides, slides; Other — Clipping files, exhibition catalogs, pamphlets, photographs
Special Subjects: Archaeology, Architecture, Art History, applied arts
Collections: Albert Kahn Architecture Library; Paul McPharlin Collection of Puppetry; Grace Whitney-Hoff Collection of Fine Bindings
A Founders Society, 5200 Woodward Ave, 48202. Tel 313-833-7900; Cable DETINARTS. *Pres* Richard Manoogian; *Exec VPres* Joseph P Bianco; *VPres* Margaret K Gillis; *VPres* Henry B Frank; *Treas* Gilbert B Silverman; *Secy* Marianne S Schwartz
Estab and incorporated 1885; public membership philanthropic society contributing to the growth of the Detroit Institute of Arts; underwrites Educ Dept activities, publications, special exhibitions and purchases of works of art. Mem: 26,000; dues corporate patron $10,000, corporate sponsor $5000, corporate contributor $1000, corporate $250, patron $150, family $40, individual $25
Activities: Museum shop rents original work by Michigan artists and reproductions

L DETROIT PUBLIC LIBRARY, Art & Literature Dept, 5201 Woodward Ave, 48202-4093. Tel 313-833-1470; FAX 313-833-1474. *Library Dir* Jean T Curtis; *Chief Art & Literature Dept* Shirley Solvick; *First Asst Art & Literature Dept* Jean Comport
Open Tues, Thurs, Fri & Sat 9:30 AM - 5:30 PM, Wed 1 - 9 PM. Estab 1865. Serves residents of Michigan with circulating and reference materials
Income: Financed by city and state appropriation
Purchases: $32,000
Library Holdings: Vols 71,000; Per subs 200; Micro — Fiche, reels; Other — Clipping files, exhibition catalogs, pamphlets, photographs, reproductions
Activities: Tours

M DETROIT REPERTORY THEATRE GALLERY, 13103 Woodrow Wilson, 48238. Tel 313-868-1347. *Gallery Dir* Gilda Snowden
Estab 1957 to show Detroit Art
Income: Financed by endowment & state appropriation
Exhibitions: One person shows for emerging Detroit Area Artists; Felecia Hunt, Charzette Torrence, Michael Ragins, Shirley Woodson
Publications: Exhibition catalogs
Activities: Adult classes; dramatic programs

M PEWABIC SOCIETY INC, 10125 E Jefferson, 48214. Tel 313-822-0954. *Artistic Dir* Ronald Streitz Jr
Estab to continue its tradition of leadership in the areas of ceramic & education
Collections: The work of the founder (Mary Chase Stratton)
Exhibitions: (1989) Contemporary exhibitions by Heino, Mary & Edward Schiers

M WAYNE STATE UNIVERSITY, Community Arts Gallery, 450 Reuther Mall, 48202. Tel 313-577-2985. *Dir* John Slick
Open Mon - Fri 9 AM - 5 PM. No admis fee. Estab 1956 as a facility for university and community oriented exhibitions and programs. Has a slide library
Collections: Small collection of American and European graphics, painting, sculpture
Exhibitions: (1989) Urbanology, Artists View Urban Experience
Activities: Lect for adults, students and the community; concerts; scholarships

M YOUR HERITAGE HOUSE, 110 E Ferry Ave, 48202. Tel 313-871-1667. *Dir* Josephine H Love; *Asst Dir* Arianne King
Open daily 10 AM - 4 PM. Estab 1980. Average Annual Attendance: 15,000 - 20,000. Mem: 100; dues $50; annual meeting Sept
Income: Financed by endowment, membership, city and state appropriation, individuals, groups and business donations
Collections: †Art for Youth; Black Heritage; graphics; Puppetry; Paintings; objects and works of interest to children; dolls
Publications: Catalogues: imprints; I Remember a Southern Christmas, book
Activities: Classes for adults and children; lect open to the public, 3-6 visiting lectr per year; concerts; gallery talks; tours; scholarships; artmobile; sales shop selling books, cards and catalogues of exhibits
L Library, 110 E Ferry Ave, 48202. Tel 313-871-1667. *Librn* Open
Open daily 10 AM - 4 PM. Estab 1969 to provide fine arts material for children. For reference only
Library Holdings: Rare books & music scores; Micro — Cards; Other — Clipping files, exhibition catalogs, manuscripts, memorabilia, pamphlets, photographs, prints
Special Subjects: Fine Arts for Youth
Collections: Black Heritage; Music for children by notable French composers; Puppetry of the World

EAST LANSING

M MICHIGAN STATE UNIVERSITY, Kresge Art Museum, 48824. Tel 517-355-7631. *Dir* Dr Susan Bandes; *Dir Emeritus* Joseph Ishikawa; *Educ Coordr* Dr Carol Fisher; *Registrar* Lynne Campbell; *Cur* Dr Phylis Floyd
Open Mon - Wed & Fri 9:30 AM - 4:30 PM, Thurs noon - 8 PM, Sat & Sun 1 - 4 PM, summer hours: Mon - Fri 11 AM - 4 PM, Sat & Sun 1 - 4 PM, cl Aug - mid-Sept. No admis fee. Estab 1959. Average Annual Attendance: 35,000. Mem: 500; dues $15 - $1000
Income: Financed by Michigan State University & Friends of Kresge Art Museum
Purchases: Paolo di Giovanni Fei triptych, 1985; John Marin watercolor, 1986; Gaston Lachaise, 1987; Jasper Johns
Collections: †Work from neolithic period to present; †European paintings & sculpture; †American paintings & sculpture; †prints from 1500 to present; †complete prints of Peter Takal; Small †Asian, African, †pre-Columbian collections
Exhibitions: Shows making up a yearly calendar of about 12 exhibitions supplementing the permanent collection; special exhibits; staff and student shows
Publications: Kresge Art Museum Bulletin, annually; Exhibition calender and publications
Activities: Docent training; workshops; lectures open to public; symposia; gallery talks; tours; off-campus breakfast lectures; individual paintings and original objects of art lent to qualified institutions or galleries; originate traveling exhibitions
L Art Library, 48824-1048. Tel 517-353-4593. *Head Art Library* Patricia T Thompson
Open Mon - Fri 8 AM - 10:45 PM, Sat 10 AM - 10:45 PM, Sun noon - 10:45 PM. Estab 1973 to support the research and teaching needs in the visual arts of Michigan State University
Income: Financed by state appropriation
Library Holdings: Vols 60,000; Per subs 175; Other — Clipping files, exhibition catalogs
Special Subjects: Architecture, Art History, Decorative Arts, Furniture, Graphic Arts, History of Art & Archaeology, Interior Design, Painting - American, Painting - British, Painting - Dutch, Painting - European, Painting - Flemish, Painting - German, Painting - Italian, African Art; illuminated manuscript facsimiles in special collections

ESCANABA

M WILLIAM BONIFAS FINE ART CENTER GALLERY, Alice Powers Art Gallery, Seventh St & First Ave S, 49829. Tel 906-786-3833. *Gallery Dir* Norbert Laporte; *Adminr* Vicki Soderberg
Open Tues - Fri noon - 4 PM, Thurs 7 - 9 PM. No admis fee. Estab 1974 to advance the arts in the area. 40 x 80, small gallery inside Center. Mem: Dues club $50, patron $30 and up, family $25, individual $15, student and senior citizen $10
Collections: Local artists work
Publications: Passage North, monthly newsletter
Activities: Classes for adults & children; dramatic programs; lectures open to public, 3 vis lectr per year; tours; individual paintings & original objects of art lent to arts organizations & businesses in return for promotional assistance

FLINT

M FLINT INSTITUTE OF ARTS, 1120 E Kearsley St, 48503. Tel 313-234-1695; FAX 313-234-1692. *Dir* John A Mahey; *Asst to Dir* Deborah S Gossel; *Cur* Christopher R Young; *Cur of Education* Jean Forell; *Public Relations & Membership Coordr* Suzanne G Walters; *Business Mgr* Barbara F Gerholz; *Museum Shop Mgr* Peggy Shedd; *Development Officer* Sarah E Warner
Open Tues - Sat 10 AM - 5 PM, Sun 1 - 5 PM, Fri (May - Oct) 7 - 9 PM. No admis fee. Estab 1928 as a community art museum serving the citizens of the area. Average Annual Attendance: 70,000. Mem: 2200; dues $15 & up; annual meeting third Tues in June
Collections: African Sculpture; French Paperweights; Modern Art; 19th Century Germanic Glass; Oriental Gallery; 17th - 20th Century European & American Art; Renaissance & Baroque Gallery
Exhibitions: (1992) The Art of Drawing: Old Masters from the Crocker Art Museum, Sacramento, California; The Art of Giving: Recent Gifts to the Permanent Collection; Highlights from the Nelson A Rockefeller Collection of Mexican Folk Art. (1993) Recent Works by Rafael Caduuro; William Keith: California's Poet Painter; Gardens of Paradise, Oriental prayer rugs from the

Huntington Museum of Art; Access to Art - All Creatures Great & Small, tactile exhibition for the visually impaired; The Purloined Image, explores works from contemporary artists who have incorporated images borrowed from artists of the past; That's All Folks
Bugs Bunny & Friends of Warner Brothers Cartoons; Morris Graves - Reconciling Inner & Outer Realities; Before Discovery - Art of the Americas Before Columbus. (1994) The Polemic Image: Social Commentary of the 1930s & 40s; Eighteenth Century Dutch Watercolors from the Rijksmuseum Amsterdam; All that Glitters: Gems, Jewelry & Goldsmith Masterpieces from the Hungarian National Museum; Wayne Thiebaud Prints; Walter O Evans Collection of African-American Art
Publications: Exhibition catalogs; monthly calendar for members
Activities: Classes for adults and children; docent training; lect open to public, 12 vis lectr per year; concerts; gallery talks; tours; Flint Art Fair; individual paintings & original objects of art lent to other museums; museum shop sells books, gift items, stationery, cards and jewelry; original art, reproductions
L 48503. Tel 313-234-1695; FAX 313-234-1692. *Registrar* Beth Fedorko
Open to members and staff for reference
Library Holdings: Vols 3000; Per subs 4; Other — Exhibition catalogs

L FLINT PUBLIC LIBRARY, Fine Arts Dept, 1026 E Kearsley, 48502. Tel 313-232-7111. *Dir* Gloria Coles; *Head Art, Music & Drama Dept* Debra Rubey
Open Mon - Thurs 9 AM - 9 PM, Fri & Sat 9 AM - 6 PM. Art, Music and Drama Department established in 1958 as a division of Flint Board of Education. Primarily lending library
Library Holdings: Vols 43,000; Per subs 172; AV — A-tapes, cassettes, motion pictures, rec; Other — Clipping files, exhibition catalogs, framed reproductions, memorabilia, photographs, reproductions

GRAND RAPIDS

M CALVIN COLLEGE, Center Art Gallery, 49546. Tel 616-957-6326; FAX 616-957-8551. *Dir of Exhib* Virginia Bullock
Open Sept - May Mon - Thurs 9 AM - 9 PM, Fri 9 AM - 5 PM, Sat noon - 4 PM, Summer 9 AM - 4:30 PM, cl Sun. No admis fee. Estab 1974 to provide the art students, and the college community and the public at large with challenging visual monthly exhibitions. Gallery is well lighted, air-conditioned 40 x 70 ft with 10 ft ceiling along the sides and 8 ft ceiling in the center. Average Annual Attendance: 12,000
Income: Financed through private budget
Collections: Dutch 17th & 19th century paintings and prints; Japanese prints; †contemporary paintings, prints, drawings, sculpture, weaving and ceramics
Exhibitions: Invitational exhibits by various artists, exhibits of public and private collections and faculty and student exhibits
Publications: Various exhibition brochures
Activities: Classes for adults; lectures open to public; concerts; gallery talks; competitions

M GRAND RAPIDS ART MUSEUM, 155 Division N, 49503. Tel 616-459-4677; FAX 616-459-8491. *Dir* Judith Sobol; *Education Dir* Linda Thompson; *Development Dir* Van Edgerton
Open Tues & Sun noon - 4 PM, Wed, Fri & Sat 10 AM - 4 PM, Thurs 10 AM - 9 PM, cl Mon & legal holidays. Admis adults $2, students, sr citizens & children $.50. Museum allocated a 1910 Beaux Arts former post office and courthouse, renovated and opened in Sept 1981. Average Annual Attendance: 100,000. Mem: 2750; dues corporate benefactor $2500, corporate patron $1000, corporate donor $600, corporate $300, benefactor $2500, grand patron $500 - $1000, collections patron $300, donor $150, patron $74, family $45, individual $35, full-time student $15; annual meeting in Sept
Income: $919,000 (financed by endowment, membership, state appropriation and federal grants)
Purchases: $30,000
Collections: Staffordshire Pottery; American 19th & 20th century paintings; decorative arts; drawings; French 19th century paintings; German expressionist paintings; master prints of all eras; Renaissance paintings; sculpture
Publications: Catalogs of major exhibitions; bi-monthly newsletter
Activities: Classes for children; dramatic programs; docent training; lectures open to public, 15 vis lectr per year; gallery talks; tours; competitions; concerts; scholarships; individual paintings and original objects of art lent to museums; lending collection contains books, color reproductions, framed reproductions, original art works, original prints, paintings, photographs, sculpture and slides; book traveling exhibitions; originate traveling exhibitions; museum & sales shops sell books, reproductions, jewelry, arts and crafts objects; Passage-ways Children's Gallery
L McBride Art Reference Library, 155 Division N, 49503. Tel 616-459-4677. *Library Chmn* Luci King
Open Tues & Sun noon - 4 PM, Wed, Fri & Sat 10 AM - 4 PM, Thurs 10 AM - 9 PM. Estab 1969. Reference library
Income: Financed by membership, gifts, museum general budget allowance
Purchases: $2000
Library Holdings: Vols 6680; Per subs 7; AV — A-tapes, cassettes, slides; Other — Clipping files, exhibition catalogs 10,000, pamphlets, reproductions
Special Subjects: Art Education, Art History
Activities: Docent Training

L GRAND RAPIDS PUBLIC LIBRARY, Music & Art Dept, 60 Library Plaza NE, 49503. Tel 616-456-3608. *Dir Library* Robert Raz
Open Mon, Tues & Wed 9 AM - 9 PM, Thurs, Fri & Sat 9 AM - 5:30 PM. No admis fee. Estab 1871 to provide information and library materials for people in Grand Rapids and Lakeland Library Federation area. Circ 1,031,274
Income: $4,064,791 (financed by city & state appropriations)
Purchases: $200,000
Library Holdings: Vols 20,000; Per subs 44; Micro — Fiche, reels; AV — Cassettes, motion pictures, rec; Other — Clipping files, exhibition catalogs, original art works, pamphlets
Special Subjects: Furniture
Collections: The Furniture Design Collection
Activities: Tours

L **KENDALL COLLEGE OF ART & DESIGN,** Frank & Lyn Van Steenberg Library, 111 Division Ave N, 49503-3194. Tel 616-451-2787; FAX 616-451-9867. *Pres* Charles L Deihl; *VPres for Academic Affairs* Carl Hayano; *Chmn Art History & Liberal Arts* Robert Sheardy; *Chmn Foundation & Fine Arts* Margaret Vega; *Chmn Design Studies* Ed Wong-Lida; *Dean of Student Affairs* Sue Hamady
Open Mon - Thurs 8 AM - 8:30 PM, Fri 8 AM - 4:30 PM. Estab 1928 to serve Kendall students and faculty; also available to artists and designers as a reference library
Income: Financed by tuition
Library Holdings: Vols 14,500; Per subs 95; Micro — Prints, reels; AV — Rec, slides, v-tapes; Other — Clipping files, exhibition catalogs, reproductions
Special Subjects: Advertising Design, Art History, Commercial Art, Decorative Arts, Furniture, Graphic Design, Illustration, Industrial Design, Interior Design, Photography, Video
Collections: Furniture Collection

M **PUBLIC MUSEUM OF GRAND RAPIDS,** 54 Jefferson SE, 49503. Tel 616-456-3977. *Dir* Timothy J Chester; *Asst Dir* Kay A Zuris; *Admin Asst* Jana M Wallace; *Planning Coordr* Mary Esther Lee; *Colls Mgr* Marilyn Merdzinski
Open Mon - Fri 10 AM - 5 PM, Sat & Sun 1 - 5 PM. Admis adults $2, senior citizens & students $.50. Estab 1854 for the interpretation of environment & culture of West Michigan & Grand Rapids. Average Annual Attendance: 400,000. Mem: 1500; dues $10-$500; annual meeting in May
Income: $2,000,000 (financed by endowment, mem, city & state appropriations, grants, contributions & foundations)
Collections: Costumes & household textiles; Decorative arts; Ethonogical; Furniture of the 19th & 20th century; Industrial & agricultural artifacts
Exhibitions: Field to Factory
Publications: Museum, quarterly; Discoveries, monthly
Activities: Classes for adults & children; docent training; lectures open to public, 4 vis lectr per year; sales shop sells books, magazines, slides, toys, clothing & stationary

M **URBAN INSTITUTE FOR CONTEMPORARY ARTS,** Race Street Gallery, 1064 Race St NE, 49503. Tel 616-454-7000. *Exec Dir* Paula Wilkerson
Open Tues, Thurs, Fri noon - 5 PM, Wed noon - 8 PM, Sat 1 - 5 PM. No admis fee. Estab 1976, dedicated to the development of a vital cultural community. Average Annual Attendance: 15,000
Income: Financed by grants, donations, mem, ticket sales, studio rental & fundraising events
Exhibitions: Invitational Artist - Generated Dolls; Artist Frank Fantauczi; Jazz Guitarist Spencer Barefied, Artist in Res (1992) Outcry - Artists Answer AIDS; Voices from the Front; World AIDS Day; The Normal Heart
Activities: Film program & literature readings; lect open to public, 3 vis lectr per year; book traveling exhibitions; sales shop sells t-shirts

GROSSE POINTE SHORES

M **EDSEL & ELEANOR FORD HOUSE,** 1100 Lake Shore Rd, 48236. Tel 313-884-4222; FAX 313-884-5977. *Pres* Open ; *Head Cur & Registrar* Maureen Devine; *Dir Tours* Donna Oliver
Open Wed - Sun 1 - 5 PM, Apr - Dec Wed - Sun noon - 5 PM. Admis adult $4, sr citizen $3, children $2. Estab 1978 to help educate public on local history, fine & decorative arts. Average Annual Attendance: 38,000
Income: Financed by endowment
Collections: Collection paintings, prints, archival photographs, French & English antique furniture, silver, glass, ceramics, historic textiles
Exhibitions: Lawrence Scripps Wilkinson Toy Collection, annual holiday exhibit. (1993) Creative Clays: Art Pottery; Gardens of Paradise: Oriental Prayer Rugs. (1994) Imperial Russian Porcelain
Activities: Classes for adults & children, seasonal children's programs; docent training.; lect open to public, 4 - 6 vis lectr per year; tours; individual paintings & original objects of art lent to other museums; book traveling exhibitions 2 - 3 per year; museum shop sells books, reproductions, souvenirs & postcards

HARTLAND

A **HARTLAND ART COUNCIL,** PO Box 290126, 48353. Tel 313-632-6324. *Pres* Bob Salo
Estab 1973 to promote arts in Hartland community. Gallery space in local library and adjacent school building. Mem: 35; dues $10 - $100; annual meeting in May
Income: $3000-$4000 (financed by mem & summer art camp)
Collections: Paintings, photographs, sculptures, fibers, works of Michigan artists exhibited in local public buildings
Exhibitions: Local artists exhibit annually
Publications: Recollections, exhibit catalog
Activities: Classes for adults & children; lectures open to public; competitions with awards; scholarships; exten dept serving Michigan art councils and schools, lending collection contains kodachromes & photographs; originate traveling exhibitions

HOLLAND

M **HOPE COLLEGE,** De Pree Art Center & Gallery, 275 Columbia Ave, 49423. Tel 616-394-7500. *Dir* John Montgomery Wilson
Open Mon - Sat 10 AM - 9 PM, Sun 1 - 9 PM. No admis fee. Estab as a place for the college & community to enjoy art. Average Annual Attendance: 5000
Exhibitions: Pre-modern Art of Vienna; Prints of Japan; New Deal: Government Art of the 30's & 40's; Movers & Shakers: sculpture that affects change in time; Power over the Clay; Days of Saints & Souls: A Celebration of the Day of the Dead
Publications: Exhibition catalogs
Activities: Lect open to the public; tours; gallery talks; individual paintings and original objects of art lent to faculty; lending collection contains original art works; original prints, paintings and sculpture

INTERLOCHEN

L **INTERLOCHEN** (Formerly Center for the Arts), PO Box 199, 49643. Tel 616-276-7200, Ext 7420; FAX 616-276-6321. *Head Librn* Evelyn R Weliver
Open daily 8 AM - 5 PM & 6:30 - 9:30 PM. Estab 1963. Special music library with over 50,000 titles. Circ 9000
Library Holdings: Vols 17,000; Per subs 140; Micro — Reels; AV — Cassettes, fs, rec
Publications: Interlochen Review, annual
Activities: Dramatic programs; lect open to the public; concerts; tours; competitions; awards; scholarships or fellowships; originate traveling exhibitions

JACKSON

M **ELLA SHARP MUSEUM,** 3225 Fourth St, 49203. Tel 517-787-2320. *Dir* Robert Kret; *Dir of Public Relations* Kathy Spring; *Cur of Art Educ* Mark Packer; *Registrar, Librn & Archivist* Gregg Larson; *Cur Historical Educ* Alice Cernighia; *Membership Secy* Barbara Stanton; *Office Mgr* Cynthia Parker; *Outreach Coordr* Lynnea Lottis; *Marketing* Jan Bellamy
Open Tues - Fri 10 AM - 5 PM, Sat & Sun noon - 5 PM, cl Mon and major holidays. Admis adults $2.50, children $1, sr citizens $2, family $5. Estab 1965 to serve the people of Jackson and to provide a place for cultural education in the community and a temporary gallery where a variety of exhibits are held. Included are a large and small gallery; small library is maintained. Average Annual Attendance: 200,000. Mem: 2,000; dues $2000, $1000, $500, $250, $125, $65, $50, $30, $20, $10; annual meeting June
Income: Financed by endowment and membership along with grants
Collections: China; coverlets and quilts; furniture from Victorian period; †oil paintings; porcelain; †prints
Publications: Annual Report; bulletins and catalogs; newsletter, monthly; research material as requested
Activities: Classes for adults and children; dramatic programs; lect open to public, 7 vis lectr per yr; concerts; gallery talks; tours; competitions; art objects lent to schools; lending collection contains photographs; gift shop

KALAMAZOO

M **KALAMAZOO INSTITUTE OF ARTS,** 314 S Park St, 49007. Tel 616-349-7775; FAX 616-349-9313. *Executive Dir* James A Bridenstine
Open Tues - Sat 10 AM - 5 PM, Sun 1 - 5 PM, cl Aug, Sun during June, July & holidays. No admis fee. Incorporated 1924 to further interest in the arts, especially in the visual arts; new building opened in 1961. There is one large gallery, four small exhibition galleries, with exhibitions changed monthly. One or more galleries always devoted to pieces from the permanent collection. Average Annual Attendance: 150,000. Mem: 1800; dues $25 & up; annual meeting Sept
Income: $800,000 (financed by endowment & mem)
Collections: †Art on Paper - drawings, graphics, photographs & watercolors; †sculpture; †20th century American art
Exhibitions: Bronson Park Art Fair; Kalamazoo Area Show;
Publications: Exhibition catalogs, issued irregularly; newsletters, monthly
Activities: Classes for adults & children; docent training; lectures open to the public; concerts; tours; scholarships; individual paintings & original objects of art lent to other institutions; lending collection contains books & slides; originate traveling exhibitions; museum shop sells craft items, jewelry & cards

L **Library,** 314 S Park St, 49007. Tel 616-349-7775; FAX 616-349-9313. *Head Librn* Rebecca D Steel
Open Tues - Sat 10 AM - 5 PM. Estab 1961, reference for Kalamazoo Institute of Arts curatorial staff and school faculty. For public reference only, open to members for circulation
Library Holdings: Vols 10,000; Per subs 65; AV — Slides; Other — Clipping files 1000, exhibition catalogs, pamphlets
Special Subjects: Art History, Ceramics, Etchings & Engravings, Folk Art, Jewelry, Lettering, Painting - American, Painting - British, Painting - European, Photography, Pottery, Printmaking, Watercolors, Woodcuts, American Art, especially art of the 20th century printmaking, history, technique & Weaving
Activities: Lect; tours

M **WESTERN MICHIGAN UNIVERSITY-ART DEPT,** Gallery II, Department of Art, 49008. Tel 616-387-2455; FAX 616-387-2828. *Chmn* Phil Vander Weg; *Exhib Dir* Jacquelyn Ruttinger
Open Mon - Fri 10 AM - 5 PM. No admis fee. Estab 1965 to provide visual enrichment to the university and Kalamazoo community. Gallery II is a space located in the ground floor of Sangren Hall; outdoor sculpture exhibit space. Average Annual Attendance: 15,000
Income: $8500 (financed by state appropriation)
Collections: Contemporary print collection; 19th & 20th century American & European Art
Exhibitions: Jean Van Harlingen (Environmental installation, handmade paper, multi-media infatable sculpture); Doug Moran (drawings); Jan Ballard (photography); Calvin Niemeyer (paintings); Richard Hunt (prints) (1991-92) Ardine Nelson (photographs); Mary Hatch (painting); Bert Browwer (paintings); Don King (paintings); Al LaVergne & Curtis Ray Patterson (sculpture); Carol Hannum & Eve Reid (paintings & handmade paper) Richard Loving (paintings); Lester Johnson (sculpture); Video on Art; Art on Video (Video); Frederik Marsh (photography)
Publications: Sculpture Tour 92 - 93
Activities: Educ dept; lect open to public; gallery talks; tours; scholarships; collection contains 1900 original art works, 350 original prints

LAKESIDE

M LAKESIDE STUDIO, 15251 S Lakeshore Rd, 49116. Tel 616-469-1377; FAX 616-469-1101. *Exec Dir* Laurie Wilson
Estab 1968, international. Represents international artists, American, Soviet, Chinese, Dutch work done by Artists-in-Residence
Activities: Award placement in Artist-in-Residence Program through selection process; museum shop sells original art

LANSING

M LANSING ART GALLERY, 425 S Grand Ave, 48933. Tel 517-374-6400. *Dir* Karen Stock; *Pres* Sharon Ellis
Open Mon - Fri 10 AM - 4 PM, Sun 1 - 4 PM. No admis fee. Estab 1965 as a private non-profit gallery to promote the visual arts in their many forms to citizens of the greater Lansing area. Maintains large exhibit area, gallery shop and rental gallery. Average Annual Attendance: 18,000. Mem: 500; dues $20 - $2500; annual meeting June
Income: $180,000 (financed by mem, sales, grants, contributions & fees)
Exhibitions: Monthly invitational shows & competitions
Publications: Gallery News, monthly
Activities: Docent training; lectures open to the public, 10 vis lectr per yr; gallery talks; tours; competitions with awards; individual paintings & original objects of art available for lease or purchase, including original art works, original prints, paintings, photographs & sculpture; book traveling exhibitions, 1-2 per year; sales shop selling books, jewelry, pottery, original art and prints

LELAND

M LEELANAU HISTORICAL MUSEUM, 203 E Cedar St, PO Box 246, 49654. Tel 616-256-7475. *Cur & Admin* Laura Quackenbush
Open June 15 - Labor Day Tues - Sat 10 AM - 4 PM, Labor Day - June 14 Fri, Sat & Sun 1 - 4 PM. Admis adult $1, student $.50. Estab 1959 for the preservation & exhibition of local history. One gallery for temporary exhibits of traditional & folk arts, 40 ft x 20 ft. Average Annual Attendance: 5,000. Mem: 450; dues $15; annual meeting last Mon in Aug
Income: $52,000 (financed by endowment, mem, fundraising & activities)
Collections: Small collection of local paintings, both folk and fine art, small collection of Leelanau County Indian baskets, birch bark crafts
Exhibitions: (1992) Ladies of the Great Lakes: models, renderings & relics of working boats
Publications: Lee Muse newsletter, 2 per yr
Activities: Educ dept; Sales shop sells books, reproductions, local crafts & original needlework kits

MARQUETTE

M NORTHERN MICHIGAN UNIVERSITY, Lee Hall Gallery, 49855. Tel 906-227-1481. *Gallery Dir* Wayne Francis
Open Mon - Fri 9 AM - 5 PM, Sun 1 - 4 PM. No admis fee. Estab 1975 to bring exhibits of the visual arts to the University, community and the upper peninsula of Michigan. Gallery covers approx 2000 sq ft of space, with security system & smoke detectors. Average Annual Attendance: 6,000-10,000
Income: $6500 (financed by University funds)
Collections: Contemporary printing & sculpture; student collection; Japanese & American illustration; Japanese prints and artifacts; †permanent collection
Exhibitions: Average of one to two major exhibits each month
Publications: Exhibit Announcement, monthly
Activities: Educ dept; Lect open to the public, 5 visiting lectrs per year; gallery talks; competitions; individual paintings and original objects of art lent; traveling exhibitions organized and circulated

MIDLAND

L GRACE A DOW MEMORIAL LIBRARY, Fine Arts Dept, 1710 W Saint Andrews, 48640. Tel 517-835-7151; FAX 517-835-9791. *Dir* Rosemarie Byers; *Fine Arts Reference Librn* Margaret Allen
Open Mon - Fri 10 AM - 9 PM, Sat 10 AM - 5 PM; during school year, Sun 1 - 5 PM. Estab 1955 as a public library. Maintains art gallery
Income: Financed by city appropriation and gifts
Purchases: $27,000
Library Holdings: Vols 12,000; Per subs 80; Compact discs; AV — A-tapes, cassettes, motion pictures, rec, v-tapes; Other — Clipping files, framed reproductions, original art works, pamphlets, prints, reproductions
Collections: Alden B Dow Fine Arts Collection
Exhibitions: Exhibits form local artists, art groups & schools
Activities: Films

A MIDLAND ART COUNCIL, 1801 W St Andrews, 48640. Tel 517-631-3250. *Dir* Hilary Bassett; *Prog Coordr* Daria Potts; *Office Mgr* Bonnie Datte; *Studio School Coordr & Public Relations Coordr* B B Winslow
Open Mon - Sun 1 - 5 PM. No admis fee. Estab 1956 to generate interest in and foster understanding and enjoyment of the visual arts. Exhibition space consists of three galleries, one 40 x 80 ft and two smaller 20 x 40 ft space; spot tracking lighting. Average Annual Attendance: 20,000. Mem: 650; dues sr citizen $7.50, family $30; annual meeting in May; monthly board meetings
Income: $200,000 (financed by endowment, mem, grants, fees for services, fundraising events)
Exhibitions: Annual Mid Michigan Competition; All Media Juried Exhibition (open to all Michigan artists age 18 & over)
Publications: Calendar of events; Artscape, monthly newsletter for members; yearly report
Activities: Classes for adults & children; docent training; workshops; Picture Parent; Midland Art Reach; lect open to public, 4 vis lectr per yr; gallery talks;

self-guiding tours; tours; juried art fairs; competitions with awards; scholarships; book 5 - 10 traveling exhibitions per yr; originate traveling exhibitions; museum shop sells books, magazines, original art, jewelry, children's art toys, reproductions, original crafts

M MIDLAND COUNTY HISTORICAL SOCIETY, 1801 W St Andrews, 48640. Tel 517-835-7401. *Dir* Gary Skory, BS; *Asst Dir* Shelley Wegner, BS
Open 9 AM - 6 PM. Estab 1952. Average Annual Attendance: 100. Mem: 350; dues $10, $15, $25, $50 & $100
Income: $105,000 (financed by endowment & membership)
Collections: Collection of local history photographs; Collection of local books
Exhibitions: Oriental Dolls: Blair-Murrah
Publications: Salt of the Earth, Yates; Midland Log
Activities: Classes for children; docent programs; lectures open to the public, 3 vis lectr per year; museum shop sells books, original art & reproductions

MONROE

A MONROE CITY COMMUNITY COLLEGE (Formerly Monroe City-County Fine Arts Council), Fine Arts Council, 1555 S Raisinville Rd, 48161. Tel 313-242-7300, Ext 345. *Pres* Elaine Rugila
Estab 1967 to promote the arts. Average Annual Attendance: 120. Mem: 50; dues $5
Income: $3000 (financed by endowment, membership & county appropriation)
Activities: Classes for children; gallery talks; competitions with awards; scholarships

MOUNT CLEMENS

A THE ART CENTER, 125 Macomb Place, 48043. Tel 313-469-8666. *Exec Dir* Jo-Anne Wilkie
Open Tues - Sat 11 AM - 5 PM, Sun 1 - 4 PM, cl Mon. No admis fee. Estab 1969 to foster art appreciation and participation for people of Macomb County. The only public facility of its kind in the northeast Detroit metro area; The Center has two rooms, 17 x 27 ft, connected by lobby area in the former Carnegie Library Bldg, a Historical State Registered building. Average Annual Attendance: 10,000. Mem: 500; dues individual $15; annual meeting June
Income: Financed by membership, city and state appropriation, commissions from sales, class fees, special fund raising events & the Michigan Council for the Arts
Exhibitions: Several all state open competitive exhibitions, including painting and sculpture, crafts; two county wide student shows, one is regional scholastic art awards shows
Publications: Newsletter, quarterly
Activities: Classes for adults and children; docent training; tours; competitions; gallery & gift shops sell original art

MOUNT PLEASANT

M CENTRAL MICHIGAN UNIVERSITY, Art Gallery, Whitman 132, 48859. Tel 517-774-3341. *Dir* Marcia Polenberg
Open Mon - Fri 10 AM - 4 PM, Tues 7 - 9 PM, Sat 10 AM - 4 PM. No admis fee. Estab to serve Mount Pleasant and university community; offer contemporary and traditional forms of art. Gallery is located in lower level of Woldt Emmons Food Commons; 125 ft of wall space & 900 sq ft of unobstructed floor space. Average Annual Attendance: 5000
Income: Financed by art department
Collections: Small collection of contemporary prints
Exhibitions: Six temporary exhibitions per year; BFA/MFA student exhibitions
Activities: Lect open to public, 10 vis lectrs per yr; gallery talks; tours; lending collection contains 30 original prints; book traveling exhibitions, 1 or 2 per year

MUSKEGON

M MUSKEGON MUSEUM OF ART, 296 W Webster Ave, 49440. Tel 616-722-2600; FAX 616-728-6335. *Dir* Al Kochka; *Asst Dir & Cur Coll & Exhib* Henry Matthews; *Cur Graphic Arts* Robert Youngman; *Coordr Development & Public Relations* Melissa Freye; *Coordr Museum Guides* Gail Phinney; *Registrar* Babs Vaughn; *Gift Shop Mgr* Mickey Kroesing
Open Tues - Fri 10 AM - 5 PM, Sat, Sun noon - 5 PM. Estab 1912, Hackley Gallery designed by S S Beman, Chicago architect. Average Annual Attendance: 40,000. Mem: 1100; dues benefactor $1000, patron $250, sponsor $100, contributing $50, family $25, individual $15, students & sr citizens $5
Income: $500,000 (financed by endowment, underwriting, mem & fundraising)
Collections: American paintings; glass by Louis Comfort Tiffany, Harvey Littleton, Lipofsky, & others; The Home Signal by Winslow Homer; Impressionist paintings; modern & Old Masters prints; Study in Rose & Brown by James Whistler; Tornado Over Kansas by John Steuart Curry; New York Restaurant by Edward Hopper
Exhibitions: 64th Annual West Michigan Juried competition; Michigan Masterpieces
Publications: Catalogs of American & European paintings from the Permanent Collection
Activities: Classes for adults and children; docent training; workshops; lectures open to public; gallery talks; tours; competitions with awards; individual and original objects of art lent to qualified museums; book traveling exhibitions; originate traveling exhibitions; museum shop sells books and reproductions
L Library, 296 W Webster, 49440. Tel 616-722-2600; FAX 616-728-6335. *Librn* Pat Dake
Membership estab 1977. Open to public

OLIVET

M OLIVET COLLEGE, Armstrong Museum of Art and Archaeology, 49076. Tel 616-749-7000. *Interim Pres* Gretchen Kreuter; *Dir* Donald Rowe
Open Mon - Fri 9 AM - 5 PM, while college is in session. Estab 1960 to collect artifacts and display for educational purposes. Average Annual Attendance: 1200
Collections: American Indian, Mesopotamian, Philippine and Thailand Artifacts; Modern American Prints; Primitive Art; Sculpture
Exhibitions: Invitational shows; one-man shows; student shows; traveling shows
Activities: Book traveling exhibitions
L Library, 49076. Tel 616-749-7608. *Head* Todd F Trevorrow
Library Holdings: Vols 75,000; Micro — Prints

ORCHARD LAKE

M ST MARY'S GALERIA (Formerly Orchard Lake School Galeria), 3535 Indian Trail, 48324. Tel 313-682-1885. *Dir* Marian Owczarski
Open Mon - Fri 1 - 5 PM, first Sun of the month 1 - 4 PM and anytime upon request. No admis fee. Estab to house major Polish and Polish-American art. Average Annual Attendance: 8000
Collections: Contemporary Polish Painting by Andrzej Luczynski; John Paul II: The First Year (Pictorial exhibit); Sculpture by Marian Owczarski; History of Polish Printing: Rare Books and Documents; Polish Folk Art; Polish Tapestry; Paintings of A Wierusz Kowalski; Watercolors by J Falat; Watercolors by Wojciech Gierson; Louvre by Night, a sketch by Aleksander Gierymski; Oil paintings by Jacek Malczewski; lithographs by Irena Snarski and Barbara Rosiak
Activities: Lectures open to the public; concerts; tours

PETOSKEY

M CROOKED TREE ARTS COUNCIL, Virginia M McCune Community Arts Center, 461 E Mitchell St, 49770. Tel 616-347-4337. *Dir* Sean Ley; *Pres* Mary Fink; *VPres* Pat Bass; *Sales Coordr* Anne Thurston
Open Mon - Sat 10 AM - 5 PM. No admis fee. Estab 1981 as a non-profit arts council and arts center. 40 ft x 25 ft exhibition gallery featuring monthly shows, modern lighting and security systems; 85 x 45 ft gallery featuring work of Michigan artists on consignment. Average Annual Attendance: 20,000. Mem: 1400; dues $15 individual, $25 annual; annual meeting in Sept
Income: $250,000 (financed by endowment, city & state appropriation, ticket sales, tuition income, fundraisers)
Exhibitions: Monthly exhibits shown
Publications: Art news, bimonthly
Activities: Adult and children's classes, dramatic programs, docent programs, music and dance classes; 3 competitions per yr (crafts, fine arts, photography), cash prizes; book 7 traveling exhibitions per yr; sales shop sells original art, reproductions, prints, art postcards

PONTIAC

A CREATIVE ARTS CENTER, 47 Williams St, 48341. Tel 313-333-7849. *Interim Dir* Angela Petroff
Open Tues, Wed, Thurs & Sat 10 AM - 4 PM, cl holidays. No admis fee. Estab 1964 to present the best in exhibitions, educational activities, & community art outreach. Main gallery is a 2 storey central space with carpeted walls; Clerestory Gallery is the 2nd floor balcony overlooking the main gallery. Average Annual Attendance: 80,000. Mem: 200; dues organizational $50, general $35, artists & citizens $20, annual meeting March
Income: Financed by endowment, mem, city & state appropriation, trust funds, United Way, Michigan Council for the Arts
Exhibitions: Temporary exhibits of historic, contemporary & culturally diverse works
Activities: Classes for adults & children; dramatic programs, music, dance, visual arts programs; lect open to the public, 30 vis lectr per year; gallery talks; concerts; tours; competitions with awards; book traveling exhibitions semi-annually; originate traveling exhibitions; sales shop sells books & original art work

PORT HURON

M MUSEUM OF ARTS AND HISTORY, 1115 Sixth St, 48060. Tel 313-982-0891. *Dir* Stephen R Williams
Open Wed - Sun 1 - 4:30 PM. No admis fee. Estab 1968 to preserve area historical and marine artifacts; exhibit living regional artists; exhibit significant shows of national and international interest. Two galleries are maintained for loaned exhibitions & the permanent collection; also a decorative arts gallery & a sales gallery. Average Annual Attendance: 120,000. Mem: 1400; dues family $17.50
Income: $200,000 (financed by endowment, membership, city appropriation, state & federal grants & earned income through program fees)
Collections: Thomas Edison; Civil War; Marine Artifacts; 19th Century American Decorative Arts, Painting and Prints
Publications: Newsletter, monthly; exhibit catalogs
Activities: Classes for adults and children; docent training; lect open to public, 6 vis lectr per year; gallery talks; tours; competitions with awards; film series; festivals; music & theatre programs; book traveling exhibitions, 8 per year; museum shop sells books, magazines, original art

M ST CLAIR COUNTY COMMUNITY COLLEGE, Jack R Hennesey Art Galleries, 323 Erie St, PO Box 5015, 48061-5015. Tel 313-984-3881. *Coordr of Galleries* John Henry
Open Mon - Fri 8 AM - 4 PM. No admis fee. Estab 1975 to serve the community as an exhibition site and to serve the faculty and students of the college as a teaching tool. Maintains three galleries connected by common hall with approximately 2,000 sq ft. Average Annual Attendance: 3000
Collections: Paintings, print, and sculpture (wood and metal)
Activities: Educ dept; lect open to the public; concerts; competitions with awards; scholarships

ROCHESTER

M OAKLAND UNIVERSITY, Meadow Brook Art Gallery, 48309-4401. Tel 313-370-3005. *Dir Office Cultural Affairs Oakland Univ* Stewart Hyke; *Dir* Kiichi Usui; *Pres Meadow Brook Gallery Assocs* James B Fitzpatrick
Open Tues - Fri 1 - 5 PM, Sat & Sun 2 - 6:30 PM, evening 7:30 - 8:30 PM in conjunction with Meadow Brook Theater Performances. No admis fee. Estab 1962 to provide a series of changing exhibitions and to develop an art collection to serve the university community and the greater community of southern Michigan. Average Annual Attendance: 50,000. Mem: 300; dues $20 - $500
Income: Financed by university budget, mem, fees & contributions
Collections: Art of Africa, Oceania and Pre-Columbian America; contemporary art and Sculpture Park; Oriental art
Exhibitions: Installation of six outdoor sculpture in the Meadow Brook Sculpture Park
Publications: Exhibition catalogs
Activities: Educ dept; lect open to public, 2 visiting lectr per year; slide presentations in conjunction with exhibitions; paintings and original art objects lent within university; originate traveling exhibitions

SAGINAW

M SAGINAW ART MUSEUM, 1126 N Michigan Ave, 48602. Tel 517-754-2491. *Dir* Ann M Knoll
Open Tues - Sat 10 AM - 5 PM, Sun 1 - 5 PM. No admis fee. Estab 1947 as an art exhibition center & education department. Housed in 1899, former residence of Clark L Ring family, designed by Charles Adams Platt. Average Annual Attendance: 19,300. Mem: 547; dues $10 - $1000; annual meetings on 2nd Thurs of September
Income: $164,500 (financed by endowment, membership and grants)
Collections: 14th century through present European & American paintings; contemporary graphics; Visionarea (children's hands-on)
Publications: Annual report; monthly
Activities: Classes for adults and children; docent training; lectures open to the public; gallery talks; tours; competitions; awards; exten dept serves grade schools; individual paintings & objects of art lent to other museums; book traveling exhibitions, 10 per yr; originate traveling exhibitions which circulate to other museums
L Couse Memorial Library, 1126 N Michigan Ave, 48602. Tel 517-754-2491.
Open to public for reference only by appointment
Library Holdings: Vols 3000; Per subs 15; AV — Kodachromes, slides; Other — Clipping files, exhibition catalogs, original art works, pamphlets, photographs, prints, sculpture

TRAVERSE CITY

M NORTHWESTERN MICHIGAN COLLEGE, Dennos Museum Center, 1701 E Front St, 49684. Tel 616-922-1055; FAX 616-922-1597. *Museum Dir* Eugene A Jenneman
Open Mon - Sat 10 AM - 5 PM, Sun 1 - 5 PM. Estab 1991. 40,000 sq ft complex features three changing exhibit galleries & a sculpture court; a hands on Discovery Gallery; & a Gallery of Inuit Art, the museum's major permanent collection. The 367 seat Milliken Auditorium offers theater & musical performances throught-out the year
Income: $400,00 (financed by earned income/endowment)
Library Holdings: Other — Prints
Collections: Canadian Inuit sculpture & prints

TROY

C K MART CORP, 3100 W Big Beaver Rd, 48084. Tel 313-643-1077. *Pub Relations* Michelle DeLand; *VPres Government & Pub Relations* Robert Stevenson; *Public Communication Coordr* Jan Potter
Collections: Contemporary art of all media; sculpture; ancient, pre 19th century & 19th century art

YPSILANTI

M EASTERN MICHIGAN UNIVERSITY, Ford Gallery, 48197. Tel 313-487-1268; FAX 313-487-3600. *Dept Head* John Van Haren; *Gallery Dir* Gretchen Otto
Open Mon - Fri 8 AM - 5 PM. No admis fee. Estab 1925, in present building since 1982, for educational purposes. Art Dept gallery is maintained displaying staff and student exhibitions from a wide variety of sources; also one large, well-lighted gallery with lobby and a satellite student-operated gallery are maintained
Income: Financed by state appropriation
Purchases: $500
Exhibitions: Seven changing exhibitions annually. (1993) Bowling Green Faculty Show; Annual Student Show; Honors Student Thesis Show; Graduate Thesis Exhibits
Publications: Campus Life, bi-annual bulletin
Activities: Classes for adults; lect open to public, 6 visiting lectr per year; gallery talks; concerts; competitions; Community Art House
L Art Dept Slide Collection, Ford Hall, Room 214, 48197. Tel 313-487-1213. *Librn* Carole Judy
Open 8 AM - 5 PM. Estab 1978 as reference source for faculty and graduate students
Library Holdings: Vols 350; AV — Slides 85,000
Special Subjects: Afro-American Art, American Indian Art, American Western Art, Furniture, History of Art & Archaeology, Mexican Art, Oriental Art, Painting - American, Pre-Columbian Art, Restoration & Conservation

MINNESOTA

BLOOMINGTON

M BLOOMINGTON ART CENTER, 10206 Penn Ave S, 55431. Tel 612-887-9667. *Dir* Susan Anderson
Open Mon - Fri 8:30 AM - 9:30 PM. No admis fee. Estab 1976 to serve emerging local artists. Average Annual Attendance: 12,000. Mem: 700; dues individual $15, family $35; annual meeting in Jan
Income: $179,000 (financed by mem & city appropriation)
Activities: Classes for adults & children in dramatic programs; lecturess open to public, 3 vis lectr per year; competitions & prizes

BRAINERD

M CROW WING COUNTY HISTORICAL SOCIETY, 320 W Laurel St, PO Box 722, 56401. Tel 218-829-3268. *Exec Dir* Open
Open June - Aug, Mon - Fri 9 AM - 5 PM, Sept - May, Mon - Fri 1 - 5 PM. Admis $1 adults. Estab 1927 to preserve & interpret county history. Average Annual Attendance: 6000. Mem: 750; dues $10 - $500; annual meeting 2nd Tues in Apr
Income: $90,000 (financed by mem, county, state grants, private donations)
Exhibitions: 19th Century Uses of Rails; Sarah Thorp Heald & Freeman Thorp Paintings: Home & Community: Rotating Artifacts Reflecting County Life; Native American Tools & Beadwork; When Lumber Was King
Publications: The Crow Wing County Historian, quarterly newsletter
Activities: Docent training; lect open to public; tours; competitions with awards; museum shop sells books, reproductions, prints

BROOKLYN PARK

M NORTH HENNEPIN COMMUNITY COLLEGE, Art Gallery, 7411 85th Ave N, 55445. Tel 612-424-0907, 424-0811. *Dir* Susan McDonald
Open Mon - Fri 8 AM - 7:30 PM. No admis fee. Estab 1966 to make art available to students & community. Two gallery spaces: smaller gallery is for one person exhibitions & installation; larger gallery is for group exhibitions. Average Annual Attendance: 8000
Income: Financed by state appropriation & foundation grants
Collections: Student works and local artists in Minnesota
Exhibitions: Mid-West Artist on regular basis
Activities: Lect open to the public; concerts; gallery talks; tours; student show with prizes; individual paintings & original objects of art lent to faculty members on campus; book traveling exhibitions, 1 - 2 per year; sales shop sells books

DULUTH

M SAINT LOUIS COUNTY HISTORICAL SOCIETY, 506 W Michigan St, 55802. Tel 218-722-8011. *Dir* JoAnne Coombe
Open Mon - Sat 10 AM - 5 PM, Sun noon - 5 PM. Admis adults $4, sr citizen $3, jrs $2, family $11, 5 & under free. Estab in 1922. Housed in the St Louis County Heritage & Arts Center along with A M Chisholm Museum, Duluth Ballet, Duluth-Superior Symphony, Duluth Playhouse, Duluth Art Institute, Matinee Musicale & Lake Superior Museum of Transportation. Society exhibit areas consist of three galleries interspersed in viewing areas. Average Annual Attendance: 100,000. Mem: 900; annual dues $9 & up; annual meeting
Income: $236,000 (financed by public support, dues, earned profit, & volunteer service)
Collections: E Johnson Collection; drawings; paintings; Ojibwe & Sioux beadwork, quillwork, basketry; Logging Exhibit; Herman Melheim hand-carved furniture
Exhibitions: Changing exhibits on topics related to the history of northeastern Minnesota & Lake Superior region
Publications: Newsletter, quarterly; books and pamphlets on topics related to the history of northeastern Minn
Activities: Workshops; lectures; tours to places of historical interest within the region

M UNIVERSITY OF MINNESOTA, DULUTH, Tweed Museum of Art, 10 University Dr, 55812. Tel 218-726-8222; FAX 218-726-8503. *Dir* Martin DeWitt; *Technician* Larry Gruenwald
Open Mon, Wed - Fri 9 AM - 4:30 PM, Sat & Sun 1 - 5 PM, Tues 9 AM - 8 PM. No admis fee. Estab 1950 to serve both the University and community as a center for exhibition of works of art and related activities. Nine galleries within the museum. Average Annual Attendance: 80,000. Mem: 680; dues $10 - $250
Income: Financed by membership, state appropriation and foundation
Purchases: $10,000 - $50,000
Collections: Jonathan Sax Collections of 20th Century American Prints; George P Tweed Memorial Art Collections of 500 paintings with emphasis on Barbizon School and 19th Century American; †20th century American paintings & sculptures; Old Master European paintings
Exhibitions: (1991) Porcelain: Six Minnesota Women; Jim Tittle: New Photographs; Book Arts, Betty Bright, Judy Nunnelly Minneapolis College of Art & Design; Nicholas Africano: Innocence & Experience; Annual Art Student Exhibition; Arrowhead Artists Exhibition Series; Steve Sorman Paintings; American & European Paintings, Selections from the Permanent Collection. (1992) Morgan Park: Continuity & Change in Company Town; Glenn C Nelson: A Tribute Exhibition. (1993) Contemporary Photographers Series; Sara Singer: New Work; Minnesota Ceramics Today: Other Traditions; Joan Simmons: Paintings & Works on Paper; Annual Art Student Juried Exhibition; American Art from the Frederick R Weismann Collection; Craig Blacklock: Lake Superior Images
Publications: Catalogues, irregular
Activities: Docent training; lect open to public, 6-8 vis lectr per yr; concerts;

gallery talks; tours; individual paintings and original objects of art lent to qualifying museums and institutions; lending collection contains original art works, original prints and paintings; traveling exhibitions organized and circulated; museum shop sells books, reproductions, craft objects & cards

EAGAN

C WEST PUBLISHING COMPANY, Art & the Law, 610 Opperman Dr, 55123. Tel 612-687-7893. *VPres* Gerard L Cafesjian; *Cur* Otto S Theuer
Average Annual Attendance: 100,000 at 5 sites nationwide
Purchases: $40,000
Collections: †West Collection of Contemporary American Art
Exhibitions: Annual Art & the Law National Invitiational; Travel Shows-Editions from the West Collection
Publications: The West Collection (coffee table art book); annual exhibition catalogues
Activities: Docent programs; awards; individual paintings lent to museums only; originate traveling exhibitions that circulate to art museums & similar public institutions; direct sales of books & reproductions

ELYSIAN

M LESUEUR COUNTY HISTORICAL, Museum, Chapter One, PO Box 240, 56028-0240. Tel 507-267-4620, 362-8350. *VPres* Michael LaFrance; *Dir & Museologist* Dorothy I Hruska
Open May - Sept Sat & Sun 1:30 - 5:30 PM; June - Aug Wed - Sun 1:30 - 5:30 PM. No admis fee. Estab 1966 to show the works of Adolf Dehn, Roger Preuss, David Maass; Lloyd Herfindohl and Albert Christ-Janer to preserve early heritage and artifacts of the pioneers of LeSueur County. Museum is depository of Dehn, Preuss, Maass and Lloyd Herfindahl; examples of originals, prints and publications of the artists are on display. Average Annual Attendance: 5000. Mem: 700; dues life $25, annual $1; annual meeting quarterly
Income: $12,000 (financed by mem, county appropriation, county government & grants)
Purchases: $51,000
Collections: †Adolf Dehn; David Maass; Roger Preuss; Lloyd Herfindahl; Albert Christ-Janer
Exhibitions: (1993) Exhibitions of works by Adolf Dehn, David Maass, Roger Preuss, Lloyd Herfindohl, Albert Christ-Janer
Publications: Newsletters, quarterly
Activities: Slide carousel to show the sites and early history of the County and works of the Artists; lect open to public; gallery talks; tours; lending collection contains 300 books, cassettes, color reproductions, 400 lantern slides, original prints, paintings, motion pictures and 300 photographs; museum shop sells books, original art and prints

L Collections Library, PO Box 240, 56028-0240. Tel 507-362-8350, 267-4620. *Dir* Dorothy I Hruska
Open by appointment only. Estab 1970 to collect locally and state-wide for purposes of genealogy; history of the artists
Library Holdings: Vols 350; Per subs 3; Micro — Reels 120; AV — A-tapes, cassettes, lantern slides, slides; Other — Clipping files, framed reproductions, original art works, prints, reproductions
Special Subjects: Prints of four Artists
Collections: Original Adolf Dehn Watercolors and Lithographs; Duck Stamp Prints of Roger Preuss and David Maass; Lloyd Herfindahl; All Media
Exhibitions: Lloyd Herfindahl
Publications: Newsletters, 4 per yr

FOUNTAIN

A FILLMORE COUNTY HISTORICAL SOCIETY, Rt 1, PO Box 81D, 55935. Tel 507-268-4449. *Executive Dir* Jerry D Henke; *Asst Dir* Alma Syvertson
Open 9 AM - 4 PM. No admis fee, donations accepted. Estab 1934 to preserve & illustrate the written & photographic history. Average Annual Attendance: 5000. Mem: 350; dues $5 - $100; annual meeting 2nd Sat in Oct
Income: $50,000 (financed by mem, county appropriations, donations)
Purchases: An Original Bernard Pietenpol Airplane
Collections: Bue Photography; Antique Agricultural Equipment; Hand Made Wooden Tools; Vintage Clothing & Tractors
Publications: Rural Roots, quarterly
Activities: Gift shop sells books

GLENWOOD

M POPE COUNTY HISTORICAL SOCIETY MUSEUM, S Hwy 104 (Mailing add: 809 S Lakeshore Dr, 56334). Tel 612-634-3293. *Pres* Don Rosholt; *VPres* George Harvey; *Office Supv* Merlin Berglin
Open Mon - Fri 9 AM - 4:30 PM, Sat & Sun 1 - 5 PM. Admis adults $3, children under 12 $.50. Estab 1932 to display & preserve artifacts & geneology files. Average Annual Attendance: 3000. Mem: 325; dues $5; annual meeting 2nd Sat in Feb
Income: $36,000 (financed by county appropriation, admissions & gifts)
Publications: Semi-annual newsletter
Activities: Educ dept; guided tours for students

INTERNATIONAL FALLS

M KOOCHICHING COUNTY HISTORICAL SOCIETY MUSEUM, 214 Sixth Ave, PO Box 1147, 56649. Tel 218-283-4316. *Pres* Einar Sundin; *VPres* Steven Earley; *Exec Dir* Sandra Boen
Open Mon - Sat 10 AM - 4 PM. Admis adults $.50, children $.25. Estab 1967 to collect, preserve and interpret the history of Koochiching County and of the state of Minnesota

Income: Financed by county, membership & admission funds
Collections: 50 paintings relating to the history of the county, including many by local artists, and six of which were commissioned for the museum
Exhibitions: Permanent collection
Publications: Gesundheit, monthly newsletter; descriptive brochure about paintings
Activities: Classes for adults and children; dramatic programs; lectures open to public, 1-2 vis lectr per year; tours; originate traveling exhibitions; sales shop sells books, Indian craft items, note and post cards

LESUEUR

M **LESUEUR MUSEUM,** 709 N Second St, 56058. Tel 612-357-4488. *Pres* Helen Meyer; *Cur* Mary Gartner; *Treas* Ann Burns
Open Memorial Day - Labor Day 1 - 5 PM. No admis fee. Estab 1976
Exhibitions: Green Giant & Canning; Agriculture; Veterinary Medicine; War in the Valley

MANKATO

M **MANKATO STATE UNIVERSITY,** Conkling Gallery Art Dept, MSU Box 42, PO Box 8400, 56002-8400. Tel 507-389-6412. *Dir* Louise McLaughlin
Open Mon - Wed 9 AM - 9 PM, Thurs & Fri 9 AM - 5 PM, Sun 1 - 4 PM. No admis fee. Estab 1979 to provide cultural enrichment in the visual arts to the campus and community through a program of exhibitions from local, regional, and national sources, and student exhibitions. Gallery has 150 running feet of carpeted display area, track lighting and climate controlled
Income: Financed by university
Collections: American bookplates; contemporary prints, drawings, paintings, photographs, sculpture and crafts; student works in all media

MINNEAPOLIS

M **AMERICAN SWEDISH INSTITUTE,** 2600 Park Ave, 55407. Tel 612-871-4907; FAX 612-871-8682. *Dir* Open
Open Tues, Thurs, Fri & Sat noon - 4 PM, Wed noon - 8 PM, Sun 1 - 5 PM, cl Mon & national holidays. Admis adults $3, students under 18 & sr citizens $1, children under 6 free. Estab & incorporated 1929 to preserve, collect, procure & exhibit objects related to the Swedish-American in the Midwest from 1845. Building donated by Swan J Turnblad and contains, in a home setting, a fine collection of Swedish artifacts, plus many items of general cultural interest pertaining to Scandinavia. The Grand Hall, paneled in African mahogany, is considered to be the finest example in US. Throughout the gallery there are eleven porcelain tile fireplaces; nine Swedish and two German design. Average Annual Attendance: 50,000. Mem: 7000; dues, life $2000, patron $150, supporting $100, sustaining $75, family (husband, wife & all children under age 18, living at home) $40, regular (single) $30, non-resident single, or husband & wife outside of fifty mile radius of Twin Cities $25, students attending school, below the age of 18 $15
Collections: Paintings, sculpture, tapestries, ceramics, china, glass, pioneer items & textiles, immigration related objects
Publications: ASI Posten (newsletter), monthly; ASI catalog
Activities: Classes for children & adults; dramatic programs; docent training; lect open to public; concerts; gallery talks; tours; awards; scholarships & fels offered; individual paintings lent to other museums; book traveling exhibitions, 1 - 2 per yr; museum shop sells books, magazines, original art

M **BELL MUSEUM OF NATURAL HISTORY,** University of Minnesota, 10 Church St, 55455. Tel 612-388-0755. *Dir* Byron Webster
Estab 1872 to educate the public in the appreciation of the out-of-doors & man's relationship to nature through historic & contemporary visual arts. Average Annual Attendance: 60,000
Collections: Art library; memorabilia; original art; prints; records; watercolors & oils

C **FEDERAL RESERVE BANK OF MINNEAPOLIS,** 250 Marquette Ave, 55480. Tel 612-340-6928. *Cur* Christine T Power
Open to public by appointment with Art Dir or Asst. No admis fee. Estab 1973 to enhance the working environment of bank; to support the creative efforts of 9th district artists. Collection displayed throughout the bank in offices, lounges, public areas and work areas
Collections: Regional collection consists of works by artists living & working in the 9th Federal Reserve District
Activities: Tours; individual objects of art loaned for special exhibitions upon request

C **FIRST BANK MINNEAPOLIS,** Art Collection, 120 S Sixth St, 55402. Tel 612-973-1111. *Art Coll Mgr* Jane Swingle
Collections: Contemporary art

C **GENERAL MILLS, INC,** Art Collection, 1 General Mills Blvd, 55440. Tel 612-540-7269. *Art Cur* Donald B McNeil
Open to public by appointment only. No admis fee. Estab 1959 to enhance employee work areas and alternative community art resource. Collection displayed in office building
Collections: 20th Century multi-media works, original prints, paintings & sculptures (1200 pieces)
Activities: Lect; gallery talks; tours; individual objects of art lent at request of museums, galleries, and artists for specific exhibitions; originate traveling exhibitions to colleges, art centers and museums

C **HONEYWELL INC,** Art Collection, Honeywell Plaza, 55408. Tel 612-951-3394. *Cur* Caren Olsen; *Asst Cur* Patricia Ryan
Open Mon - Fri 9 AM - 4 PM. Collection displayed in main lobby, second and fifth floors
Collections: Variety of paintings, abstracts and statues

M **INTERMEDIA ARTS MINNESOTA,** 425 Ontario St SE, 55414. Tel 612-627-4444; FAX 612-627-4430. *Exec Dir* Tom Borrup; *Development Dir* Susan Jacob; *Distribution Dir* Margret Weinstein; *Marketing & Public Relations Dir* Kathleen Maloney
Open 10 AM - 6 PM. No admis fee. Estab 1973. 2000 sq ft space used for installations, screenings and performances. Average Annual Attendance: 6000. Mem: $250; annual dues $25
Income: Financed by endowment, membership
Collections: Video as Art Form; History of Video; Computer Graphics; Artificial Intelligence & Art
Exhibitions: (1990) Endangered; Art by Men of Color Jerome Media Art Commissions
Publications: Video handbook, Fundraising for Media, Meeting Your Maker, Making Your Message
Activities: Scholarships & fels offered

M **LUTHERAN BROTHERHOOD GALLERY,** 625 Fourth Ave S, 55415. Tel 612-340-7000. *Art Consultant* Richard L Hulstrom
Open Mon - Fri 10 AM - 4 PM. No Admis fee. Estab 1982 as a cultural & educational gallery. Art is exhibited in a modest sized gallery & in the corporate library
Collections: Bing & Grondahl Plate Collection; Martin Luther Commemorative Medals 16th - 20th centuries
Exhibitions: 8-10 Exhibitions per year
Activities: Originate traveling exhibitions

M **MHIRIPIRI GALLERY,** 100 N Sixth St, No 110, 55403. Tel 612-332-7406. *Co-Owner* Rex Mhiripiri; *Co-Owner* Julie Mhiripiri
Open 10 AM - 8 PM. Estab 1986

L **MINNEAPOLIS COLLEGE OF ART & DESIGN,** Library & Media Center, 2501 Stevens Ave S, 55404. Tel 612-874-3791 (Library), 874-3672 (Media Center). *Dir* Mary Manning; *Slide Librn* Allan Kohl; *Media Center Dir* Brad Smith
Open Mon - Thurs 8:30 AM - 10 PM, Fri 8:30 AM - 5 PM, Sat & Sun noon - 4:30 PM, summer 11:30 AM - 4:30 PM, slide library & media center have different hours. Estab to provide library and media services and materials in support of the curriculum of the College; includes a library, slide library and media center. Circ 37,000, circ limited to students, staff & alumni
Income: Financed by student tuition, grants and gifts
Library Holdings: Vols 58,000; Per subs 227; Micro — Fiche; AV — Cassettes, rec, slides, v-tapes; Other — Clipping files, exhibition catalogs, pamphlets
Special Subjects: Drawings, Film, Graphic Design, Illustration, Photography, Printmaking, Sculpture, Video, Contemporary painting, Product design
Publications: Monthly accessions list; guide to MCAD Library (irregular); annual serials lists; bibliographic guides to collection

M **MINNEAPOLIS SOCIETY OF FINE ARTS,** Minneapolis Institute of Arts, 2400 Third Ave S, 55404. Tel 612-870-3000; FAX 612-870-3004. *Dir* Evan Maurer; *Assoc Dir* Timothy Fiske; *Chmn Education* Kathryn C Johnson; *Cur Prints & Drawings* Richard Campbell; *Cur Photography* Carroll T Hartwell; *Cur Oriental Arts* Robert Jacobsen; *Registrar* Catherine Ricciardelli; *Chief Cur & Cur Decorative Arts* Michael Conforti; *Cur Paintings* George Keyes; *Cur Textiles* Lotus Stack; *Cur Ethnographic Arts* Louise Lincoln; *Asst Cur* Daniel Oleary; *Cur African Oceanic New World Cultures* Louise Lincoln
Open Tues - Sat 10 AM - 5 PM, Thurs 10 AM - 9 PM, Sun noon - 5 PM, cl Mon. Admis to museum's permanent collection free; exhibitions adults $2, student $1, free to members, sr citizens, those under 12 & AFDC Cardholders. Estab 1883 to foster the knowledge, understanding and practice of the arts. The first gallery was opened in 1889, and the original building was constructed in 1911-15. The south wing was added in 1926, and the entire structure features the classical elements of the day. The museum was expanded to twice the original size in 1972-74, and has incorporated modern themes designed by Kenzo, Tange and URTEC of Tokyo. Average Annual Attendance: 400,000. Mem: 18,000; dues household $40, individual $30; annual meeting in Oct
Income: Financed by endowment, membership, county and state appropriations, and admissions
Collections: Collection representing all schools and periods of art: American and European paintings, decorative arts, period rooms, photography, prints and drawings, sculpture; Ancient, African, Oceanic, Oriental and native North and South American arts and textiles
Exhibitions: (1993) Images of a Queen's Power: Royal Tapestries of France; The Westward Migration of Chinese Blue & White Porcelain; American Masters: Selections from the Collection of Richard Lewis Hillstrom; Two Lives: Georgia O'Keefe & Alfred Stieglitz - A Conversation in Paintings & Photographs; Alfred Stieglitz's Camera Notes; Minnesota 1990. (1994) Visions of Antiquity: Neoclassic Figure Drawings
Publications: Bulletin, biannually; exhibitions catalogs; member's magazine, monthly
Activities: Classes for adults and children; docent training; workshops; lect open to public, 15 visiting lectr per year; concerts; gallery talks; tours; paintings and original art objects lent to other professional arts organizations; originate traveling exhibitions; museum shop sells books, reproductions, prints, slides and jewelry

L   *Art Reference Library,* 2400 Third Ave S, 55404. Tel 612-870-3046; FAX 870-3004. *Librn* Harold Peterson; *Asst Librn* Michael Boe
Open Tues, Wed & Fri 10 AM - 5 PM, Thurs 10 AM - 8 PM, Sat noon - 4 PM. Estab 1915 to provide a reference collection based around the museum's collection of works of art. Maintains an art gallery, Leslie Memorial Room and has exhibitions of books and prints
Library Holdings: Vols 40,000; Per subs 100
Special Subjects: History of books, printings, decorative arts, prints and photography
Collections: Leslie Collection: History of Books and Printing; Minnick Collection: Botanical, Floral and Fashion Books
Exhibitions: (1992) Five Hundred Years of Sporting Books, Manuscripts, Prints & Drawings; C R Ashbee & The Essex House Press. (1993) Jean Cocteau
Publications: History & Guide to the Library; A Long Chain of Words by John Parker; I Tatti by Jane Satheowski

A Friends of the Institute, 2400 Third Ave S, 55404. Tel 612-870-3046. *Pres* Joan Hutton
Estab 1922 to broaden the influence of the Institute in the community and to provide volunteer support within the museum. Mem: 1900; annual meeting May
Activities: Coordinates docent program, museum shop, sales and rental gallery, speaker's bureau, information desk, special lect, exhibitions and fund-raising projects

C NORWEST BANK OF MINNEAPOLIS, Art Collection, Sixth & Marquette Ave, 55479-1025. Tel 612-667-5136. *Cur Coll* David Ryan
Exhibitions: Primarily prints, as well as sculpture, paintings & photography

C THE PILLSBURY COMPANY, Art Collection, Pillsbury Center, 200 S Sixth St, 55402. Tel 612-330-4718. *Chief Exec Officer* I A Martin; *Mgr Bldg Servs* Jean Hardginski
Estab to create exciting and attractive environment and support the arts. Collection displayed on internal walls of corporate headquarters building
Collections: Contemporary and Western American art, primarily oil paintings, prints and watercolors

UNIVERSITY OF MINNESOTA

M University Art Museum, 110 Northrop Memorial Auditorium, 84 Church St SE, 55455. Tel 612-624-9876. *Dir* Lyndel King; *Development Officer* Kathleen Fluegel; *Assoc Admin* Gwen Sutter; *Cur* Patricia McDonnell; *Asst Dir for Touring* Colleen Sheehy; *Registrar* Karen Duncan; *Public Information & Special Events* Robert Bitzan; *Preparator* William Lampe; *Preparator* John Sonderegger; *Preparator* Tim White
Open Mon - Fri 11 AM - 5 PM, Sun 2 - 5 PM, cl Sat & holidays. Estab 1934; the program of the University Art Museum is one geared to meet broad objectives of an all-University museum, as well as the specific teaching and research needs of various University of Minnesota departments. Average Annual Attendance: 50,000
Income: Financed by state appropriation, grants and gifts
Purchases: Earth Projects, 1969, by Robert Morris; Warm on Cool, 1958, Cameron Booth; The Plainsman, 1945, John Steuart Curry
Collections: Paintings, drawings and prints by American artists working in the first half of the 20th century, and contains notable works by Avery, Dove, Feininger, Hartley, MacDonald-Wright, Marin, Maurer and O'Keefe; Nordfeldt collection on extended loan from Mrs B J O Nordfeldt; print collection includes works by artists of all schools and periods; sculpture collection of major works by contemporary artists including: Baizerman, Bertoia, Richier, David Smith and others; Third Ave El at 14th St, 1931: Edward Laning; Study of New York 1939 Worlds Fair Mural, 1938: Ilya Bolotowsky; decorative arts
Exhibitions: The University Art Museum stresses a program of major loan exhibitions, held concurrently with smaller exhibitions organized for specific teaching purposes or from the permanent collection
Activities: Programs; lending program to University, staff & students of Minnesota faculty of framed two-dimensional material; originate traveling exhibitions

M Coffman Union Third Floor Gallery, 300 Washington Ave SE, 55455. Tel 612-625-9918, 625-9617. *Coordr* Mishawn J Cook
Open Mon - Thurs 7 AM - 9 PM, Fri - Sat 7 AM - 1 AM, cl Sun. No admis fee. Estab 1976 to make art accessible to university community & general public. Average Annual Attendance: 30,000
Income: Financed by student fees
Activities: Educ dept; lectures; gallery talks

L Art Book Collection, 5 Wilson Library, 55455. Tel 612-624-7343; Elec Mail H. SCH@UMINN1.BITNET. *Librn* Herbert G Scherer
Open Mon - Fri 7 AM - 1 AM, Sat & Sun 9 AM - 1 PM. Estab 1950 to serve undergraduate and graduate teaching programs in Art History & Humanities to PhD level, and in Studio Art to MA level; to provide art related books to other departments and to the entire academic community as best we can
Library Holdings: Vols 70,000; Per subs 339; Micro — Fiche 7000; AV — Cassettes 52; Other — Exhibition catalogs, pamphlets
Special Subjects: Art History, Scandinavian art history
Activities: Tours; single lectures

L Architecture Library, 89 Church St SE, 55455. Tel 612-624-6383. *Library Head* Joon Mornes
Open Mon - Fri 8 AM - 4:30 PM. Circ 20,641
Income: Financed by University
Library Holdings: Vols 35,522; Per subs 229; Micro — Reels 244; AV — V-tapes 571; Other — Manuscripts, pamphlets
Special Subjects: Architecture, Decorative Arts, Graphic Arts, Interior Design, Landscape Architecture, Energy Conservation, Environmental Psychology

L Children's Literature Research Collections, 109 Walter Library, 117 Pleasant St SE, University of Minnesota Libraries, 55455. Tel 612-624-4576; FAX 612-625-5525, 626-8518. *Cur* Karen Nelson Hoyle
Open Mon - Fri 8:30 AM - 4:30 PM. Estab 1949 to collect books, manuscripts & illustrations for use by researchers & for exhibits
Income: Financed by endowment, University of Minnesota libraries
Library Holdings: Vols 140,000; Per subs 140; toys; AV — Cassettes, rec, v-tapes; Other — Clipping files, manuscripts, original art works, pamphlets
Special Subjects: Illustration, Manuscripts, Painting - American
Publications: Kerlan Newsletter, 4 times per yr
Activities: Lectures; book traveling exhibitions, 6 per yr; originate traveling exhibitions

M WALKER ART CENTER, Vineland Place, 55403. Tel 612-375-7600. *Pres* Gary Capen; *Chmn Board* Lawrence Perlman; *Dir* Kathy Halbreich; *Admin Dir* David Galligan; *Cur* Gary Garrels; *Cur* Elizabeth Armstrong; *Registrar* Gwen Bitz; *Assoc Registrar* Pamela Young; *Dir Development* Kathi DeShaw; *Dir Education* Margy Ligon; *Dir Performing Arts* John Killacky; *Dir Film & Video* Bruce Jenkins; *Public Information* Margaret Patridge; *Graphic Designer* Laurie Makela; *Dir Membership* Rebecca Olson
Open Tues - Sat 10 AM - 8 PM; Sun 11 AM - 5 PM, cl Mon. Admis $3. Estab 1879 by T B Walker, reorganized 1939 as Walker Art Center, Inc; building erected 1927; new museum building opened 1971. The Center consists of nine galleries, three sculpture terraces, the Center Bookshop, 0 acre Sculpture Garden, Conservatory & the Gallery 8 Restaurant. Average Annual Attendance: 450,000. Mem: 5000; dues household $35, individual $25, special $20; annual meeting September
Income: $1,983,625 (financed by endowment, membership, state appropriation, grants and book shop)
Collections: †Prints & drawings; photography; †sculpture; †20th century paintings
Exhibitions: (1993) In the Spirit of Fluxus; Jeff Koons. (1994) Helio Oiticica; Bruce Nauman
Publications: Brochures; calendar of events, 11 issues a year; Design, Quarterly; exhibition catalogs
Activities: Classes for adults and children; docent training; internships; lectures open to public, 25 vis lectrs per yr; concerts; gallery talks; school & adult tours; films; exten dept serving Minnesota and surrounding states; individual paintings and original objects of art lent to museums; traveling exhibitions organized and circulated; museum shop selling books, magazines, posters, jewelry and gift items

L Staff Reference Library, Vineland Place, 55403. Tel 612-375-7680. *Librn* Rosemary Furtak
Open to museum personnel & scholars by appointment. For reference only
Library Holdings: Vols 25,000; Per subs 140; AV — A-tapes 1700, v-tapes; Other — Clipping files, exhibition catalogs
Special Subjects: Architecture, Film, Photography, Sculpture, Design, Graphics, catalogs dating back to 1940

MOORHEAD

M PLAINS ART MUSEUM, 521 Main Ave, PO Box 2338, 56560. Tel 218-236-7383. *Pres Board Dir* Cindy Phillips; *VPres Board Dir* Jan Larson; *Dir* Elizabeth Hannaher; *Business Mgr* Paul Carlson; *Cur Educ* Marla Green; *Mem & Development* Cher Hersrud; *Registrar* Michelle Smith; *Communications Mgr* Laurie Baker
Open Tues - Sat 10 AM - 5 PM, Sun noon - 5 PM, cl holidays. No admis fee. Estab 1960 to foster and promote a knowledge and love of art in the community and to provide a repository for the artistic heritage of this area; to operate and maintain an art gallery and museum, to promote the extension and improvement of education in the arts; to provide facilities for the exhibition and conservation of the art in this area, past and present. Former Moorhead Federal Building (1913), Oscar Wenderoth, architect, houses the museum. This stately classical revival style building has a vari-colored marble lobby, ionic columns and tall arched windows; a major restoration-reconstruction project completed in 1987. Average Annual Attendance: 21,000. Mem: 500; dues $10 - $1000; annual meeting Apr
Income: Financed by membership, NEH, NEA & foundation grants & charitable gaming, special events, state & business grants
Collections: Contemporary American, American Indian & West African; The Rolling Plains Art Gallery (traveling gallery)
Exhibitions: (1993) Collection Revealed (a special exhibition from the permanent collection); Santos de Palo: Household Saints of Puerto Rico; Woven Vessels
Publications: Plains Art Museum, quarterly; exhibition checklist & catalogs with each exhibition
Activities: Classes for adults; docent training; lect open to public; concerts; gallery talks; tours; family art workshops; book traveling exhibitions, 7-10 per yr; originate traveling exhibitions circulated to galleries and museums in a 6 state area: ND, SD, MN, WI, IA, MT; museum shop sells books, magazines, original art, posters and prints, reproductions, t-shirts, jewelry, postcards and local craft items

OWATONNA

A OWATONNA ARTS CENTER, Community Arts Center, 435 Dunnell Dr, PO Box 134, 55060. Tel 507-451-0533. *Board Dirs* Sally Lane; *VPres* Allison Waggoner; *Secy* Cheryl Spear; *Dir & Cur* Silvan A Durben; *Asst to Dir* Judy Srsen; *Development Dir* Pat Abbe; *Treas* Tom Crosbie
Open Tues - Sun 1 - 5 PM, Sun 2 - 5 PM. No admis fee except for specials. Estab 1974 to preserve local professional artists' work & promote the arts in the community. The West Gallery (32 x 26 x 12 ft) and the North Gallery (29 x 20 x 12 ft) provide an interesting walk through space and a versatile space in which to display two and three dimensional work; the two galleries can be combined by use of moveable panels; and the Sculpture Garden which was completed in 1979 of multi-level construction. Average Annual Attendance: 7000. Mem: 400; dues basic $25 & up, sustaining $200 & up; annual meeting third Sun in Oct
Income: $80,000 (financed by mem & fund raising activities plus sustaining fund from industries & business)
Special Subjects: Architecture, Art Education, Art History, Ceramics, Commercial Art, Decorative Arts, Furniture, Graphic Arts, Graphic Design, Jewelry, Painting - American, Photography, Sculpture, Watercolors
Collections: Marianne Young World Costume Collection of garments and jewelry from 27 countries; painting, prints, sculpture by local professional artists; 3 Bronzes by John Rood, Paul Grandland & Charles Gagnon
Exhibitions: Annual Outdoor Arts Festival; Annual Steele County Show; Annual Christmas Theme Display
Publications: Monthly newsletter to members & other Arts Organizations
Activities: Classes for adults and children; festivals; concerts monthly; tours; original objects of art & Costume Collection lent to other arts organizations

L Library, 435 Dunnell Dr, 55060
Open to members only; for reference
Library Holdings: Vols 255

PARK RAPIDS

M NORTH COUNTRY MUSEUM OF ARTS, Third and Court Streets, PO Box 328, 56470. Tel 218-732-5237. *Cur* Johanna M Verbrugghen; *Treas* Blanche Szuszitzky
Open May - Oct Tues - Sun 11 AM - 5 PM. Admis $1. Estab 1977 to provide a cultural and educational center to house a permanent study collection of old school European paintings and to house traveling exhibitions for the benefit of persons of all ages through contact and work with art in its many forms.
Maintains Great Gallery, Members Gallery, four Revolving Galleries and studio. Average Annual Attendance: 6000. Mem: 120; dues family $20, individual $15; annual meeting Oct
Income: $25,000 (financed by membership, individual & corporate grants & gifts)
Collections: †Nigerian arts, crafts & artifacts; †45 Old School European paintings; †18 Contemporary Prints; 19 Drawings of Native American Children
Exhibitions: Annual Juried High School Fine Arts Exhibition
Activities: Classes for adults and children; docent training; lect open to the public, 2-3 lectr per year; concerts; gallery talks; tours; competitions; book traveling exhibitions, 5-6 per year; originate traveling exhibits; museum shop selling original art

ROCHESTER

A ROCHESTER ART CENTER, 320 E Center St, 55904. Tel 507-282-8629. *Dir* Betty Jean Shigaki
Open Tues - Sat 10 AM - 5 PM, Sun noon - 5 PM, cl Mon. No admis fee. Estab 1946 as a center for contemporary visual arts and crafts, Rochester Art Center sponsors an on-going program of exhibitions, educational classes, lectures, workshops and community services in the arts. Two separate galleries offer a combined exhibition space of 8000 sq ft. Average Annual Attendance: 25,000. Mem: 1000; dues $20-$50; annual meeting in Nov
Income: Financed by endowment, contributions, city and state appropriations, fund raising and tuition
Collections: Local and regional artists' work, including prints, sculpture & watercolors
Exhibitions: Varied exhibits in Contemporary Fine Arts and Crafts
Publications: Newsletter, quarterly
Activities: Classes for adults and children; lectures open to public; gallery talks; tours; scholarships & fels offered; original objects of art lent to corporations & other arts organizations; originate traveling exhibitions

SAINT CLOUD

SAINT CLOUD STATE UNIVERSITY

M Atwood Center Gallery Lounge, Atwood Center, 56301. Tel 612-255-2205; FAX 612-654-5190. *Prog Dir* Margaret Vos; *Asst Dir* Toshiko Schwerdtfeger
Open Mon - Fri 7 AM - 11 PM, Sat 8 AM - 11 PM, Sun noon - 11 PM. No admis fee. Estab 1967 as a university student union facility. Gallery area is part of program, designed for maximum exposure, where students may relax or study while enjoying exhibits; space is flexible; also area for music listening and small theatre; additional exhibits displayed in prominent area
Income: Financed by student enrollment fee assessment
Collections: Collections of artists work from the central Minnesota area
Exhibitions: Monthly exhibits in various media
Activities: Artists' residencies, lectures & workshops that coincide with exhibits
M Kiehle Gallery, 720 S Fourth Ave, 56301. Tel 612-255-4283. *Dir* Michael W Stowell
Open Mon - Fri 8 AM - 4 PM. No admis fee. Estab 1974 to expose college community to ideas and attitudes in the field of visual arts. The gallery has 1600 sq ft of enclosed multi use gallery floor space and 2500 sq ft outside sculpture court. Average Annual Attendance: 15,000
Income: Financed by student fund appropriation
Activities: Lectures open to the public, 5 vis lectr per yr; gallery talks; competitions; individual paintings and original objects of art lent to other departments on campus; lending collection contains original prints, paintings, photographs and sculpture; traveling exhibitions organized and circulated

SAINT JOSEPH

M COLLEGE OF SAINT BENEDICT, Art Gallery, Benedict Arts Center, 56374-2099. Tel 612-363-5777. *Dir Fine Arts* Karen L Mrja; *Chmn of Art Dept* Bela Petheo; *Exhib Coordr* Russ Nordman
Open daily 9 AM - 4:30 PM. No admis fee. Estab 1963
Income: Financed by college
Collections: Contemporary collection of crafts, drawings, paintings, prints and sculpture; East Asian Collection of ceramics, crafts, drawings, fibers and prints; Miscellaneous African, New Guinea, Indian and European
Activities: Lect open to the public, 8 vis lectr per year; gallery talks; tours; scholarships; individual paintings and original objects of art lent to faculty and staff members of the college

SAINT PAUL

M ARCHIVES OF THE ARCHDIOCESE OF ST PAUL & MINNEAPOLIS, 226 Summit Ave, 55102. Tel 612-291-4429; FAX 612-290-1629. *Archivist* Steven T Granger
Open Mon - Fri 9 AM - 5 PM. No admis fee. Estab 1987 to collect & preserve materials of archival value relating to the Catholic church of the Archdiocese of Saint Paul & Minneapolis. Average Annual Attendance: 300
Income: Financed by Diocesan funds
Collections: Artifacts; documents; letters; painting; papers & photographs
Activities: Lect, 2 vis lectr per year

C BURLINGTON NORTHERN, 30 Crocus Pl, 55102. Tel 612-222-2403. *Cur Coll* Dr Ann T Walton
Estab 1910
Collections: American art of the first half of the 20th century; landscape of North Western US; Blackfeet Indian portraits
Activities: Lectures; Collection travels to museums throughout the US 4 times a year

M COLLEGE OF THE ASSOCIATED ARTS, 344 Summit Ave, 55102. Tel 612-224-3416. *Pres* Robert E Hankey
Open Mon - Fri 9 AM - 4 PM. No admis fee. Estab 1948; galleries were established in adjunct to art education. Average Annual Attendance: 400-500
Income: Financed by endowment
Exhibitions: Ten shows per year of the work of local artists, faculty, students, traveling shows, and work from our own collection. The emphasis is on Modern Art
L Library, 344 Summit Ave, 55102. Tel 612-224-3416. *Librn* Mary Beth Frasczak
Estab 1948 to have reference material for our own students. Not open to public. Maintains an art gallery
Library Holdings: Vols 2000; Per subs 24; AV — Slides; Other — Original art works, pamphlets, photographs, reproductions

M FILM IN THE CITIES GALLERY, 2388 University Ave, 55114. Tel 612-646-6104. *Dir* James Dozier
Open Mon - Fri 9 AM - 5 PM, Sat noon - 4 PM. No admis fee. Estab 1970 as a non-profit photography gallery
Collections: Small permanent film study & photography collections
Activities: Classes for adults & children; lectures open to public, 7-15 lectr per year; scholarships & fels offered; sales shop sells books & magazines

M HAMLINE UNIVERSITY LEARNING CENTER GALLERY, 55104. Tel 612-641-2387, 641-2296. *Cur Permanent Colls & Exhib Dir* James D Conaway
Open Mon - Fri 8:30 AM - 10 PM. No admis fee. Estab 1943 to display outstanding works of art in all media for instruction of and appreciation by the public and students. Average Annual Attendance: 12,000
Income: Financed by the University
Collections: Contemporary paintings, prints, drawings and sculpture
Exhibitions: (1987-88) Connie Lowe drawings; Diane Williams paintings; Marilyn Cool paintings; Ruth Brophy paintings. (1988-89) Mary Walker sculpture; Ann Labovitz paintings
Publications: Exhibition catalog
Activities: Classes for adults; lectures open to the public, 6 vis lectr per year; gallery talks; individual paintings and original objects of art lent to faculty and staff; originate traveling exhibitions to galleries, historical societies and colleges
L Library, 1536 Hewitt Ave, 55104. Tel 612-641-2373, 641-2375. *Chmn* Michael Price; *Dir & Cur* John Noell Pray
Rental Library of original modern works and reproductions; extensive color slide library of paintings, architecture, sculpture, minor arts and graphics

M MACALESTER COLLEGE, Galleries, 1600 Grand Ave, 55105. Tel 612-696-6416; FAX 612-696-6689. *Cur* Cherie Doyle Riesenberg
Open Mon - Fri 10 AM - 9 PM, cl June - Aug, national holidays & school vacations. No admis fee. Estab 1964 as a college facility to bring contemporary art exhibitions to the students, faculty and community. Average Annual Attendance: 10,000 - 18,000
Collections: African Art; Oriental Art; contemporary & historical prints, paintings, sculpture & crafts
Exhibitions: Temporary, traveling & student exhibitions with special emphasis on international & multi-cultural
Activities: Lectures open to the public; concerts; gallery talks; tours; competitions with awards; individual paintings and original objects of art lent; lending collection contains original prints, paintings & sculpture; book traveling exhibitions; traveling exhibitions organized and circulated; sales shop selling art books and supplies
L DeWitt Wallace Library, 1600 Grand Ave, 55105. Tel 612-696-6345. *Library Dir* Joel Clemmer
Circ 66,531
Library Holdings: Vols 273,668; Per subs 1311; Micro — Cards, fiche, reels; AV — Cassettes; Other — Framed reproductions, pamphlets
Special Subjects: Art History
Activities: Individual paintings & original objects of art lent to students, faculty & staff of the college

A MINNESOTA HISTORICAL SOCIETY, 345 Kellogg Blvd W, 55102-1906. Tel 612-296-2747, 296-6126. *Pres* Charles Arnason; *Dir* Nina M Archabal; *Deputy Dir* Ian R Stewart; *Asst to Dir for Libraries & Museum Coll* Lila J Goff
Open Mon - Sat 8:30 AM - 5 PM, Sun 11 AM - 4 PM. Estab 1849 to collect, preserve and make available to the public the history of Minnesota. Average Annual Attendance: 100,000. Mem: 5000; dues $20; annual meeting in October
Income: Financed by endowment, membership and state appropriation
Collections: Archives; †art works; †books; †maps; †manuscripts; †museum artifacts relating to the history of Minnesota; newspapers; †photographs
Exhibitions: Images of Minnesota; Alexis Jean Fourvier; Lines of Expression
Publications: Minnesota History, quarterly; Minnesota History News, 6 issues per year; books & exhibit catalogs
Activities: Classes for adults & children; lect open to the public; tours; gallery talks; book traveling exhibitions; originate traveling exhibitions; sales shop sells books, magazines, prints, reproductions, original art & slides
L Library, 345 Kellogg Blvd W, 55102-1906. Tel 612-296-2143. *Cur Art* Thomas O'Sullivan; *Head Reference Serv* Denise Carlson
No admis fee. For reference
Library Holdings: Vols 500,000; Micro — Fiche, reels; AV — A-tapes, cassettes, fs, Kodachromes, motion pictures, rec, slides, v-tapes; Other — Clipping files, exhibition catalogs, manuscripts, memorabilia, pamphlets, prints, sculpture
Special Subjects: Minnesota Art
Collections: 19th & 20th century art relating to Minnesota
Activities: Individual paintings & original objects of art lent to qualified museums & galleries

M MINNESOTA MUSEUM OF AMERICAN ART, Landmark Center, Fifth at Market, 55102-1486. Tel 612-292-4355. *Dir* M J Czarniecki III; *Acting Asst Dir Development & Membership* Ricka Kohnstamm; *Deputy Dir* Paul Orman; *Assoc Cur* Paul Spencer; *Media Relations Supv* Tim Jennen; *Personnel Supv* Ramona Weselmann; *Acting Plant & Security Supvr* Dave Koepke; *Chief Cur* Katherine Van Tassell; *Coll Outreach Programs Supv* Holly Wolhart; *Assoc Cur* Leanne Klein
Open Tues - Fri 10:30 AM - 4:30 PM, Thurs 10:30 AM - 7:30 PM, Sat & Sun 1 - 4:30 PM. Admis by donation. Estab 1927 as the St Paul Gallery & School of Art. The museum occupies two locations in downtown St Paul. In its Landmark Center Galleries, MMA hosts traveling exhibitions of regional & national importance. Work from the museum's collections are shown in the Jemne Building, which is listed on the National Register of Historic Places; it is a handsome blend of Art Deco & International styles of architecture of the 1930's. Average Annual Attendance: 120,000. Mem: 1200; dues household $35, individual $25; annual meeting Sept
Income: $1,042,000 (financed by endowment, individual contributions, mem, allocation from United Arts Fund & foundation & government grants)
Collections: American Art; contemporary art of the Upper Midwest; E S Curtis collection; Paul Manship collection and several non-western cultures: Korean, Japanese, Chinese, Oceanic, African, Native American
Exhibitions: (1992) Shared Visions: Native American Painters & Sculptores in the 20th Century; Minnesota Voices. (1993) Spirits: The Collection of Geoffrey Holder & Carmen de Lavallade; The American Hand: Twentieth Century Crafts; As Seen by Both Sides: American & Vietnamese Artists Look at the War; Charles Burchfield; Breaking Boundaries: American Puppetry in the 1980's. (1994) Seeing Straight: The F64 Revolution in Photography
Publications: Exhibition catalogs; gallery guides (periodic); Newsletter, bi-monthly; annual report
Activities: Classes for adults and children; docent training; lectures open to public, free to members, 20-25/years; art works are lent to museums; education collection lent to non-museum entities (schools, libraries, goverment, businesses, and professional offices) for a specified fee; circulating exhibitions, program (9 exhibitions titles); originate traveling exhibitions; museum shop sells books, slides & gifts
L Library, St Peter at Kellogg Blvd, 55102-1486. Tel 612-292-4350. *Assoc Cur Coll Management* Leanne Klein
For reference only
Library Holdings: Vols 2500; Per subs 10
Special Subjects: Asian Art, American Art of the 20th century
Collections: Art of Korea; Paul Manship Files
M Jemne Building, St Peter at Kellogg Blvd, 55102-1486. Tel 612-292-4355.
Open Tues, Wed, Fri, Sat 10 AM - 5 PM, Thurs 10 AM - 8 PM, Sun 1 - 5 PM. No admis fee
Income: Financed by Minnesota Museum of Art
Exhibitions: (1992-93) Garden of Delights: Nature in Asian Art; The Still Life in American Art: Minnesota Museum of Art & Area Collections: Animals: Selections from the Collection of Minnesota Museum of Art
Publications: Bimonthly calendar of events

C NORTH CENTRAL LIFE INSURANCE COMPANY, Art Collection, 445 Minnesota St, PO Box 64139, 55164. Tel 612-227-8000, Ext 290. *Corp Council* Frank McCarthy
Not open to public
Collections: Works by Charles Beck, Alexis Fournier, John Gordon, Michael Heindorf, Catherine Ingebretsen, Valerie Jaudon, Bruce McClain, William Murray, Malcolm Myers, Roger Laux Nelson, John Page, Bela Petheo, Marjorie Pohlman, Birney Quick, Joan Seifert, Cynthia Starkweather Nelson, Terry Striech, Richard Sussman

L SAINT PAUL PUBLIC LIBRARY, Art & Music Dept, 90 W Fourth St, 55102. Tel 612-292-6186. *Dir Library* Gerald W Steenberg; *Supv Art & Music Dept* Sue A Ellingwood
Open Mon & Thurs 9 AM - 9 PM, Tues, Wed, Fri & Sat 9 AM - 5:30 PM, cl Sat during Summer. Estab 1882. Circ 92,642
Income: Financed by city appropriation
Purchases: $18,800
Library Holdings: Vols 16,000; Per subs 95; Compact discs; AV — Cassettes, rec, slides 2000; Other — Clipping files, exhibition catalogs, framed reproductions 450, sculpture 110
Collections: Field collection of old time sheet music

C 3M, Art Collection, 3M Center, Bldg 225-1S-01, 55144-1000. Tel 612-737-3335; FAX 612-737-4555. *Cur, Art Coll* Charles Helsell
Estab 1902, dept estab 1974. Concourse Gallery provides changing exhibitions drawn from the collection
Collections: Collection of paintings, drawings, sculpture, watercolors, original prints, photographs & textiles
Activities: Individual paintings & original objects of art are lent to scholary exhibitions

M UNIVERSITY OF MINNESOTA, Paul Whitney Larson Gallery, 2017 Buford, 55108. Tel 612-625-7200, 625-0214. *Gallery Cur* Linda Billings; *Prog Dir* Marlene Vernon
Open Mon - Fri 10 AM - 4 PM, Wed 10 AM - 8 PM, Sun 1 - 5 PM, cl Sat. No admis fee. Estab 1979 to bring art of great variety into the daily lives of students & university community. Intimate gallery featuring traditional & contemporary visual arts
Income: Financed by student fee
Publications: Annual Report and Activity Summary
Activities: Mini-courses; lectures open to public, arts & crafts sales; films & videos
M Goldstein Gallery, Dept of Design, Housing & Apparel, 241 McNeal Hall, 55108. Tel 612-624-7434; FAX 612-624-2750. *Dir* Dr Suzanne Baizerman; *Costume Cur* Dr Marilyn DeLong; *Cur Decorative Arts* Dr Timothy T Blade; *Textile Cur* Karen LaBat
Open Mon - Fri 10 AM - 4 PM, Thurs until 8 PM, Sat & Sun 1:30 - 4:30 PM.

Estab 1976 as an exhibit facility serving as an educational tool in teaching & research. Mem: 315; mem $15-$5000; annual meeting in June
Income: $128,000 (financed by private gifts, mem & grants)
Collections: Historic costumes; 20th century designer garments; historic & contemporary decorative arts; furniture; glass; metal ceramics; historic flat textiles
Exhibitions: The Essential Gourd, Putting on the Ritz: Fact and Fantasy in 30's Fashion, Basketweave. Here Comes the Bride, Then & Now. Alexander Girard Designs: Fabric & Furniture; Applied Design & Commercial Art: Student Exhibit; Danish Immigrant Homes: Glimpses from Southwestern Minnesota; Finnish Women's Handicrafts: Past & Present; Kashmire to Pailsey: Cultural Interactions (1991) Mention the Unmentionables: 100 years of Underwear. (1992) Shopping Bag Design: People, Process, Product
Publications: Exhibition catalogs
Activities: Lectures open to public, 10 vis lectrs per yr; tours; original objects of art lent to other institutions

A WOMEN'S ART REGISTRY OF MINNESOTA GALLERY, 2402 University Ave W, 55114. Tel 612-649-0059. *Admin Dir* Vicki MacNabb
Estab 1975. Maintains gallery. Mem: 2800; dues $25 - $250
Income: Financed by membership, grants for projects & operating expenses
Collections: Members work on display in one area
Exhibitions: Local & national exhibitions; Annual Juried Members Exhibit
Activities: Educ dept; lect open to the public; competitions with awards; scholarships and fels offered; individual paintings lent and original objects of art lent to non-profit groups for fee; originate traveling exhibitions

WORTHINGTON

A NOBLES COUNTY ART CENTER GALLERY, 318 Ninth St, PO Box 313, 56187. Tel 507-372-8245. *Co - Dir* Jean Bunge; *Co - Dir* Martin Bunge
Open Mon - Fri 2 - 4:30 PM, cl holidays. No admis fee. Estab 1960 to nourish the arts and encourage artists of the Nobles County Area. Located on the ground floor of the county administration building, 84 ft x 30 ft with ell 22 ft x 15 ft. Average Annual Attendance: 2500 - 3000. Mem: 125; dues $5 - $100; annual meeting in Jan
Income: Financed by membership dues, donations, memorial gifts & county appropriation
Collections: Midwestern art
Exhibitions: Art in the Courtyard; monthly exhibitions; two juried fine art shows per year; annual student exhibition the work of area artists
Publications: Monthly newsletter
Activities: Classes for adults; gallery talks; tours; competitions with awards; scholarships offered

MISSISSIPPI

BILOXI

A BILOXI ART ASSOCIATION INC & GALLERY, 137 Lameuse St, PO Box 667, 39530. Tel 601-432-5682. *Pres* Ellen M O'Brian; *VPres* Sue Henry; *Treas* Lilly Holliman
Open Thurs - Sat 11:30 AM - 4:30 PM. No admis fee. Estab 1965 to promote art & educate general public. Gallery maintained on volunteer basis by 23 members of Biloxi Art Assn & Gallery. Average Annual Attendance: 5000. Mem: 48; mem open to artists at all levels; dues $10, students $2.50; meetings third Tues of each month
Income: $750 (financed by mem)
Collections: Works by local artists
Publications: Biloxi Art Assn & Gallery Newsletter, monthly
Activities: Workshops; lect open to public; competitions with awards; individual paintings & original objects of art lent; lending collection contains original art works, original prints, paintings & sculpture; revolving art exhibit in 10 locations on Mississippi Gulf Coast; sale shop sells & exhibits original art & prints

CLARKSDALE

M CARNEGIE PUBLIC LIBRARY, Delta Blues Museum, 114 Delta Ave, PO Box 280, 38614. Tel 601-624-4461; FAX 601-627-7263. *Dir* Sid F Graves Jr; *Acting Cur* John Ruskey
Open Mon - Fri 9 AM - noon & 1 - 5 PM, Sat 10 AM - 2 PM. No admis fee. Estab 1979 to preserve & promote understanding of MS Delta blues music & heritage. Average Annual Attendance: 12,000
Collections: Books & tapes; †Interpretative exhibits; †memorabilia; †photography & art (sculpture, paintings); †recordings; †stage & music; †videos
Exhibitions: All Shook Up: MS Roots of American Music; Vintage American Guitar Collection
Publications: Delta Blues Museum Brochure
Activities: Blues performances; lect open to public, 10 vis lectr per year; retail store sells books, prints, magazines, original art, reproductions, souvenirs, gifts, audiotapes

CLEVELAND

M DELTA STATE UNIVERSITY, Fielding L Wright Art Center, PO Box D-2, 38733. Tel 601-846-4720. *Chmn Dept* Collier B Parker; *Exhib Chmn* Terry K Simmons; *Chmn Art Education* Carolyn Stone, PhD
Open Mon - Fri 8 AM - 5 PM, Sun 3 - 5 PM on opening shows, cl school holidays. No admis fee. Estab 1968 as an educational gallery for the benefit of the students, but serves the entire area for changing art shows; it is the only

facility of this nature in the Mississippi Delta Region. Three gallery areas.
Average Annual Attendance: 2500-3000
Income: Financed by state appropriation
Collections: Delta State University permanent collection; Ruth Atkinson Holmes Collection; Marie Hull Collection; Smith-Patterson Memorial Collection; Whittington Memorial Collection; James Townes Medal Collection; Joe and Lucy Howorth Collection; John Miller Photography Collection; Photography Study Collection;
Exhibitions: (1992) C-Farings, an Exhibit of Sculpture, John C Cassibry; Bill Lauderdale, Paintings. (1993) Paper: USA/Finland; Affinities; Jones Fort; Lytle Cory; Sang Robertson
Publications: Announcements of exhibitions, monthly during fall, winter and spring; exhibit catalogs
Activities: Classes for adults & children; lect open to public, 10 vis lectr per yr; gallery talks; tours; competitions; exten department serving the Mississippi Delta Region; individual paintings and original objects of art lent to offices of campus; lending collection contains color reproductions, film strips, motion pictures, original art works, 30,000 slides; traveling exhibitions organized and circulated

L Library, 38733. Tel 601-846-4440. *Coordr Library Servs* Jo Wilson
Reference only
Library Holdings: Vols 25,000; Per subs 52; Micro — Cards, fiche, prints, reels; AV — A-tapes, cassettes, fs, Kodachromes, motion pictures, rec, slides, v-tapes; Other — Clipping files, exhibition catalogs, framed reproductions, original art works, photographs, prints

COLUMBUS

M COLUMBUS AND LOWNDES COUNTY HISTORICAL SOCIETY,
Florence McLeod Hazard Museum, 316 Seventh St N, 39701. Tel 601-327-8888.
Cur Carolyn Neault
Open Tues & Thurs 1 - 4 PM or by appointment. No admis fee. Estab 1960 for a memorabilia 1832-1907 pertaining to Lowndes County preserved & exhibited.
Average Annual Attendance: 2000. Mem: 210; dues $3; annual meeting third Thurs in Nov
Income: $600 (financed by membership, bequests, donations, memorials, sale of souvenirs)
Collections: 100 years of artifacts, books, †china, †crystal, clothes, flags, †furniture, †jewelry, pictures, portraits, swords, wedding gowns
Activities: Docent training; tours for school children; awards; museum shop sells books and souvenirs

M MISSISSIPPI UNIVERSITY FOR WOMEN, Fine Arts Gallery, Fine Arts Bldg, 39701. Tel 601-329-7341. *Dir of Gallery, Cur of Museum & Permanent Coll* Larry Feeney
Open Mon - Fri 8 AM - 5 PM. No admis fee. Estab 1948. Average Annual Attendance: 1200
Income: Financed by state appropriation & private funds
Collections: †American Art; †paintings, sculpture, photographs, drawings, ceramics, prints; †Permanent collection of Mississippi artists
Exhibitions: Frequent special and circulating exhibitions; Selections from permanent collection, periodically
Activities: Visiting artists program; workshops; lectures open to public, 4 vis lectrs per year; gallery talks; tours; scholarships; individual paintings & original objects of art lent to offices & public student areas on the campus; lending collection contains 400 original prints, 300 paintings, 100 records; book traveling exhibitions; originate traveling exhibitions

GREENWOOD

M COTTONLANDIA MUSEUM, Hwy 49-82 Bypass W, 38930. Tel 601-453-0925; FAX 601-453-6680. *Exec Dir* Peggy H McCormick; *Secy* Jane M Montgomery
Open Mon - Fri 8 AM - 5 PM, Sat - Sun 2 - 5 PM. Admis adults $2.50, children $.50. Estab 1969 as a museum for tourism & learning facility for schools. Two well lighted rooms plus available space in museum for temporary & competition, permanent hangings in some corridors. Average Annual Attendance: 15,000.
Mem: 500; dues vary; annual meeting early Dec
Income: Financed by mem, county appropriation, donations
Collections: †Permanent collection of works of past Cottonlandia Collection; competition winners; other accessions by Mississippi Artists
Publications: Cottonlandia newsletter, bimonthly
Activities: Classes for adults; lect open to the public, 2 vis lectr per year; talks; tours; competitions with awards; individual paintings lent; lending collection contains nature artifacts; museum shop sells books, original art, reproductions, prints

HATTIESBURG

M TURNER HOUSE MUSEUM, 500 Bay, 39401. Tel 601-582-1771. *Dir & Cur* David Sheley
Open by appointment. No admis fee. Estab 1970
Collections: 18th century furniture; silver; crystal chandelier; Persian rugs; old masters; tapestries
Activities: Tours

L UNIVERSITY OF SOUTHERN MISSISSIPPI, McCain Library & Archives, Hardy St & US Route 49, Southern Station, PO Box 5148, 39406-5148. Tel 601-266-4345. *Dir* Kay L Wall MLS; *Cur* Dolores A Jones MLS; *Archivist* Terry S Latour, MA; *Librn* Henry L Simmons, MS; *Reference Librn & Cataloger* Angela R Jones
Open Mon, Wed & Thurs 8 AM - 6 PM, Tues 8 AM - 8 PM, Fri 8 AM - 5 PM, Sat 10 AM - 2 PM. No admis fee. University estab 1912, libr estab 1976. For reference only
Collections: De Grummond Children's Literature Research Collection (historical children's literature & illustrations); Mississippiana Collection (all documentary media); Editorial Cartoon Collection
Publications: Juvenile Miscellany, 3 times per yr

JACKSON

M CRAFTSMEN'S GUILD OF MISSISSIPPI, INC, Agriculture & Forestry Museum, 1150 Lakeland Dr, 39216. Tel 601-981-0019. *Exec Dir* Marjorie Bates; *Adminr* Lauren Dixson
Estab 1973 to preserve, promote, educate, market & encourage excellence in regional crafts. Two galleries: Mississippi Crafts Center, PO Box 69, Ridgeland 39158, sales demonstrations, festival of regional crafts; Capital Street Crafts Gallery, sidewalk museum changing monthly exhibits of regional crafts. Mem: 200; annual dues $30; annual meeting Feb
Income: $200,000 (financed by membership, state arts commission grant, corporate & private contributions, earned income)
Activities: Classes for adults & children; lect open to public, 2 vis lectr per yr; lending collection; museum shop sells books, original art, postcards

L MISSISSIPPI DEPARTMENT OF ARCHIVES AND HISTORY, State Historical Museum, 100 S State St, PO Box 571, 39205-0571. Tel 601-359-6850, 359-6920. *Pres Board Trustees* William F Winter; *Dir* Elbert R Hilliard; *Dir State Historical Museum* Donna Dye; *Dir Archives & Library* H T Holmes; *Dir Historic Preservation* Kenneth M P'Pool; *Dir Public Information* Christine Wilson; *Dir Special Projects* Dr Patricia Galloway; *Dir Historic Properties* James F Barnett Jr; *Dir Records Management* William J Hanna
Open Mon - Fri 8 AM - 5 PM, Sat 9:30 AM - 4:30 PM, Sun 12:30 - 4:30 PM.
Estab 1902 for the care and custody of official archives; to collect material relating to the history of the State from the earliest times and to impart a knowledge of the history and resources of the State. Maintains the State Historical Museum. Maintains a portrait gallery of distinguished Mississippians and holds monthly exhibitions, concerts & lectures. Average Annual Attendance: 65,000
Income: Financed by state appropriation
Library Holdings: Vols 40,000; Per subs 250; original documents; Micro — Fiche, reels; AV — A-tapes, cassettes, fs, motion pictures, rec, slides, v-tapes; Other — Clipping files, exhibition catalogs, manuscripts, pamphlets, photographs, prints
Special Subjects: Archaeology, Civil War, genealogy, Mississippiana
Collections: Maps; photographs; newspapers; museum artifacts; all pertaining to Mississippi
Exhibitions: (1991) Beyond the Porches; Biloxi's Ethnic Heritage; Delta Blues Today; Eudora; Gold of El Dorado; The Natchez Passion for Greek Revival Architecture; Eudora Welty (photographs); Steamboating in Style; Walthall County; Welty I; Welty II
Publications: Journal of Mississippi History, quarterly; Mississippi History Newsletter, monthly
Activities: Folk crafts programs; lectures; concerts; gallery talks; tours; exten dept serves other museums & libraries; individual paintings & original objects of art lent; book traveling exhibitions, 3-4 per year; originate and circulate traveling exhibitions; sales shop sells books, original art, reproductions, prints, slides and folk crafts

M MISSISSIPPI DEPARTMENT OF ARCHIVES & HISTORY, Mississippi State Historical Museum, 100 S State St, PO Box 571, 39201. Tel 601-354-6222. *Pres* William Winter; *Dir* Donna Dye; *Cur Exhib* Cavett Taff; *Cur Colls* Mary Lorenz; *Progs Coordr* Ann Morrison
Open Mon - Fri 8 AM - 5 PM, Sat 9:30 AM - 4:30 PM, Sun 12:30 - 4:30 PM.
No admis fee. Estab 1961 for education in Mississippi history & culture through interpretation of the collection. Oil portraits hung throughout the 3-story Greek Revival former capitol; four rooms set aside for temporary exhibits. Average Annual Attendance: 80,000
Income: $850,000 (financed by state appropriations)
Collections: 98 oil portraits; artifacts of Mississippi history & culture from earliest times to the present
Activities: Talks for children and adult groups; docent training; concerts; gallery talks; tours; dramatic programs; statewide social studies teachers workshop; lect open to the public, 4-5 vis lectr per yr; book traveling exhibitions, 3-4 per year; originate traveling exhibitions; circulate to institutions throughout the state; museum shop sells books, magazines, original art, prints, reproductions, slides & Mississippi Craftsmen's Guild items; films; school films loan service

M MISSISSIPPI MUSEUM OF ART, 201 E Pascagoula St, 39201. Tel 601-960-1515; FAX 601-960-1505; WATS 800-423-4971. *Exec Dir* Linda S Sullivan; *Asst Cur & Registrar* Laura Leggett; *Dir Finance* Michele Harris
Open Mon - Sat 10 AM - 5 PM, Sun noon - 5 PM. Admis fee. Chartered in 1911. Museum opened April 22, 1978; East Exhibition Galleries, 6400 sq ft; West Exhibition Galleries, 2600 sq ft; Graphics Study Center, 800 sq ft; houses exhibition area, study and storage rooms; Impressions Gallery, 400 sq ft Open Gallery, 2000 sq ft, includes special power,lighting and water requirements for technological media; Upper and Lower Atrium Galleries, 4500 sq ft; & outdoor Sculpture Garden; Non-Profit Corporation. Average Annual Attendance: 110,000. Mem: 3400; dues individual $15, artist $20, family $25, patron $100, donor $250, benefactor $500, Rembrandt Society $1000
Income: $130,000 (financed by endowment, membership, contributions, public sector grants & appropriations, earned income)
Purchases: A Bierstadt, Edward Potthast, Eugene Auffrey, Birney Imes III (45 color photographs) Thomas Salley Croprey, A B Davies
Collections: 19th & 20th Century American; Smaller non-western art collection, oceanic, Eskimo, Native American, Asian, African; Southern Photographers; Western art history sample collection
Exhibitions: (1993) Overstreet: Two Generations of Architecture in the South; Annual Spring Symposium & Antique Show; Scholastic Art Awards; William Dunlap - Reconstructed Recollections; Mississippi Craft Exhibit; Official Images: New Deal Photographs; Songs of My People; Mississippi National Watercolors Grand Exhibition. (1994) Discoveries - African Art from the Smiley Collection; Master Silver by Paul Storr & his Contemporaries; Privileged Eye - Photographs by Carl Vechten
Publications: Newsletter, bi-monthly; selected exhibition catalogs
Activities: Classes for adults and children; docent training; lect open to public, some for members only, 6 vis lectr per yr, 10 vis artists per yr; tours;

competitions; music series; scholarships offered; Art Cart; travel lect program; original objects of art lent to accredited museums; branches in Biloxi & Tupelo; book traveling exhibitions 4-6 per yr; originate traveling exhibitions; museum shop sells books, magazines, reproductions, prints, slides, paper goods, designer items, Mississippi crafts
L **Media Center Library,** 201 E Pascagoula St, 39201. Tel 601-960-1515.
For reference only, open to the general public
Library Holdings: Vols 10,000; Per subs 12; AV — Kodachromes, motion pictures, slides, v-tapes; Other — Clipping files, exhibition catalogs, pamphlets
Collections: Walter Anderson Collection on Slides; Marie Hull Collection of Art Reference Books; Metropolitan Miniature Album; Museums permanent collection

LAUREL

M **LAUREN ROGERS MUSEUM OF ART,** Fifth Ave & Seventh St, PO Box 1108, 39440. Tel 601-649-6374; FAX 601-649-6379. *Dir* Mary Anne Pennington; *Registrar* Amorita Gordon; *Public Information Officer* Kim Thomson; *Asst Dir* Marna Ward; *Head Librn* Tammy D Atkinson
Open Tues - Sat 10 AM - 5 PM, Sun 1 - 4 PM, cl Mon. No admis fee. Estab 1923 as a reference and research library and museum of art for public use and employment. Six smaller galleries open off large American Gallery; these include European Gallery, Catherine Marshall Gardiner Basket collection, Gibbons Silver Gallery plus 2 temporary exhibit galleries. Average Annual Attendance: 20,000. Mem: Dues $20 - $1000
Income: Financed by endowment (Eastman Memorial Foundation), mem, donations, fundraising, events government appropriations, grants
Collections: European Artists of the 19th Century 18th Century English Georgian Silver; 18th & 19th Century Japanaese Ukiyo-e Woodblock Prints; 19th & 20th Century American Paintings North American Indian Basketry
Exhibitions: Annual schedule of exhibitions by regional and nationally recognized artists; collections exhibits
Publications: Gibbons Silver Catalog; Jean Leon Gerome Ferris, 1863-1930: American Painter Historian; Handbook of The Collections; Mississippi Portraiture
Activities: Workshop for adults and children; musical concerts; docent education; lectures open to public, gallery talks; tours; bi-annual symposium on southern art cultures; individual art objects lent to AAM Accredited museums or galleries; museum shop sells books, magazines, reproductions, slides, gifts, postcards, posters, jewelry, works by local craftsmen
L **Library,** 39440. Tel 601-649-6374. *Head Librn* Tammy Atkinson; *Asst Librn* Donna Smith
For reference only
Income: Financed by endowment (Eastman Memorial Foundation), mem, donations
Library Holdings: Vols 11,000; Per subs 150; Micro — Fiche, reels 200; AV — A-tapes, slides 500; Other — Clipping files, exhibition catalogs, manuscripts, memorabilia, pamphlets, photographs, reproductions
Special Subjects: American Indian Art, Art History, Bookplates & Bindings, Folk Art, Painting - American, Painting - European, Portraits, Silver, Art, Mississipiana, Laurel history
Collections: Museum archives

MERIDIAN

M **MERIDIAN MUSEUM OF ART,** Seventh St at Twenty-fifth Ave, PO Box 5773, 39302. Tel 601-693-1501. *Dir* Terence Heder
Open Tues - Sun 1 - 5 PM, cl Mon. No admis fee. Estab 1970 to provide exhibition space for local, state & nationally known artists. Museum has four galleries. Housed in a national landmark building, the museum offers over twenty exhibitions annually in four galleries. Average Annual Attendance: 6500. Mem: 300; dues $15 - $1000; annual membership meeting first week of Jan
Income: Financed by membership and appropriation
Collections: 20th century Southern fine arts & photography; 18th century European portraits; contemporary & traditional crafts & decorative arts
Exhibitions: (1991) Meridian Museum of Art Annual Members' Show; Meridian Museum of Art 18th Annual Bi-State Competition; Jeffrey Lewis- Painting; Portraits & Landscape Paintings of Jason Bouldin of Clarksdale, Mississippi; Photographs of the Sugarditch by Jane Rule Burdine; Southern Paintings from the Everette James Collection; Photography of George Ohr: The Mad Potter of Biloxi; Beverly Erdreich (paintings); Contemporary Crafts from FAMOS; Photography at the MMA; Gardens of Paradise (oriental carpets); Formed & Fired: American Art Pottery; Works on Paper from the MMA permanent collection; Emerging Modernism: 20th century American Art Movements; Steuben Glass from a Meridian collection; Black Women: Achievement Against the Odds; Journey in Search of Lost Images (contemporary western paintings); New Forms in Old Clay; Meridan Camera Club annual exhibition in the Weidmann Gallery; Meridian Museum of Art: Entries for 19th Annual Bi-State; Mississippi State Faculty Show; Photographs of Ken Stocker; Japanese Porcelain from the High Museum, Atlanta. (1993) Alex Loeb Collection Mississippi Art Colony
Activities: Classes for adults & children; youth art classes held each summer; symposia lectures open to public; gallery talks; tours; competitions with awards; original objects of art lent to museums, traveling shows & offices in the city; book traveling exhibitions, 2 per yr; originate traveling exhibitions for circulation to museums & galleries; museum shop sells original art, reproductions & crafts

A **MISSISSIPPI ART COLONY,** 2741 38th St, 39305. Tel 601-482-2827. *Dir* Mrs Jamie Tate; *Pres* George Ann McCulla; *VPres* Amelia Crumbley; *Secy & Treas* Jean R Loeb
Estab 1945 to hold workshops at least twice yearly, for painting & drawing instruction and occasionally other areas; to organize juried show, with prizes awarded, that travels state of Mississippi between workshops. Average Annual Attendance: 40 at each of the two four-day workshops. Mem: 55; dues $15; annual fall workshop last week of Sept
Income: Financed by membership
Exhibitions: Two travel exhibitions each year
Publications: Bulletin, newsletter
Activities: Competitions sponsored; awards; scholarships; traveling exhibitions organized & circulated to libraries & museums in Mississippi

OXFORD

M **UNIVERSITY OF MISSISSIPPI,** University Museums, University Ave & Fifth St (Mailing add: University of Mississippi, University, 38677). Tel 601-232-7073. *Dir* Bonnie J Krause; *Museum Educator* Amy DeWys-VanHecke; *Prog Coordr* Susan Hannah
Open Tues - Sat 10 AM - 4 PM, Sun 1 - 4 PM, cl Mon. No admis fee. Estab 1977 to collect, conserve and exhibit objects related to history of the University of Mississippi and to the cultural and scientific heritage of the people of the state and region. Main gallery contains 3000 sq ft with 12 ft ceilings for permanent collections and 800 sq ft with 18 ft ceilings for temporary exhibits; meeting room has 1100 sq ft for temporary wall hung exhibits; each of the four galleries of the Mary Buie Museum contains 400 sq ft for permanent collection
Income: $163,000 (financed by state appropriation)
Collections: Theora Hamblett Collection (paintings, glass, drawings); Lewisohn Collection of Caribbean Art; Fulton-Meyer Collection of African Art; Millington-Barnard Collection of 18th and 19th Century Scientific Instruments; David Robinson Collection of Greek and Roman antiquities; antique dolls; Victorian memorabilia; American decorative arts; Southern folk art
Exhibitions: (1991-92) National Works on Paper Competition/Exhibition; Olynthus 348 BC: The Destruction & Resurrection of a Greek City
Activities: Classes for children; docent training; gallery talks and tours; school outreach program
L **University Museums Library,** 38677. Tel 601-232-7073. *Dir* Bonnie J Krause
Open to members, students, researchers for reference
Library Holdings: Vols 600; Per subs 8
Special Subjects: Antiquities-Greek, Antiquities-Roman, Art History, Graphic Arts, Victorian Decorative Arts, American Art, American folk art
M **University Gallery,** Fine Arts Center, 38677. Tel 601-232-7193; FAX 601-232-7010. *Dir* Margaret Gorove
Open daily 8:30 AM - 4:30 PM. No admis fee. Estab 1954 as a teaching gallery. Average Annual Attendance: 1000
Income: Financed by state appropriation & tuition
Collections: Faculty & student work; some work bought from traveling exhibitions
Exhibitions: Faculty, students, junior colleges & alumni
Publications: Gallery Schedule, annual
Activities: Lectures open to public, 1-2 vis lectrs per yr; gallery talks; individual paintings & original objects of art lent to departments within the University Complex; lending collection contains original art works, original prints, paintings & sculpture

RAYMOND

M **HINDS JUNIOR COLLEGE DISTRICT,** Marie Hull Gallery, 39154. Tel 601-857-3275. *Dir* Gayle McCarty; *Chmn* Russell Schneider
Open Mon - Thurs 8 AM - 3 PM, Fri 8 AM - noon. No admis fee. Estab 1971 as a community service and cultural agent for the visual arts. Main gallery measures 60 x 60 ft; an adjacent gallery 8 x 45 ft; reception area 15 x 25 ft. Average Annual Attendance: 2500
Income: $2900 (financed by Art Department budget)
Collections: †Permanent collection of state artist, with 150 pieces in prints, sculptures and paintings
Exhibitions: Sponsors 7 exhibits during college session
Activities: Lect open to the public; gallery talks; tours; competitions; individual paintings and original objects of art lent to faculty and staff offices on three campuses; lending collection contains original art works

RIDGELAND

M **MISSISSIPPI CRAFTS CENTER,** Natchez Trace Parkway, PO Box 69, 39158. Tel 601-856-7546. *Dir* Martha Garrott
Open Mon - Sun 9 AM - 5 PM. No admis fee. Estab 1975. Average Annual Attendance: 30,000. Mem: 200; dues $50; annual meeting in Dec
Income: Financed by sales & grants
Activities: Classes for adults & children; store sells books, original art & crafts

TOUGALOO

TOUGALOO COLLEGE
M **Art Collection,** 39174. Tel 601-977-7743; FAX 601-977-7714. *Pres* Dr Adib Shakir; *Dir* Ron Schnell; *VPres Academic Affairs* Dr Betty Parker-Smith; *Photographer* Ann Schnell
No admis fee. Estab 1963 to service the community and the metropolitan Jackson area. Located in Student Union Building and Library. Average Annual Attendance: 1000
Income: Financed by endowment and department budget
Collections: †Afro-American; African; International Print Collection with emphasis on European art; New York School (abstract, expressionism, minimal art, surrealism)
Exhibitions: African Collection; Afro-American Collection; Faculty & Student Show; Local artists; FDrancisco Mora: Painting; Social & Political Protest in Art
Publications: Mississippi Museum of Art, African Tribal Art; Calder-Hayter-Miro; G M Designs of the 1960's; Hans Hofmann, Light Prints; brochure; catalog; newspaper of special events
Activities: Dramatic programs; lect open to public, 2-3 vis lectr per year; concerts; gallery talks; tours by appointment; scholarships; exten dept; individual paintings and original objects of art lent to libraries, universities and museums; lending collection contains 8000 lantern slides, 700 original art works, 350 original prints, 140 paintings, 150 sculpture, industrial designs and typography; originate traveling exhibitions
L **Coleman Library,** 39174. Tel 601-977-7704; FAX 601-977-7714. *Dir Library Servs* Charlene Cole
Open Mon - Thurs 8 AM - midnight, Fri 8 AM - 5 PM, Sat 1 - 4 PM, Sun 3 - 9 PM. No admis fee. Estab 1963. Open to students and faculty

Income: Financed by rental fees
Library Holdings: Vols 135,000; Per subs 432; Micro — Cards, fiche, reels; AV — A-tapes, cassettes, fs, Kodachromes, motion pictures, rec, slides; Other — Clipping files, exhibition catalogs, framed reproductions, manuscripts, memorabilia, original art works, pamphlets, photographs, prints, reproductions, sculpture
Special Subjects: Advertising Design, Aesthetics, Afro-American Art, American Indian Art, American Western Art, Anthropology, Antiquities-Egyptian, Antiquities-Greek, Antiquities-Oriental, Antiquities-Persian, Antiquities-Roman, Archaeology, Folk Art, Glass, Graphic Arts, Graphic Design, Historical Material, History of Art & Archaeology, Interior Design, Latin American Art, Lettering, Manuscripts, Maps, Prints, Religious Art, Reproductions, Restoration & Conservation, Sculpture, Stained Glass, Video, Watercolors
Collections: Tracy Sugerman (wash drawings, civil rights studies 1964); African masks & sculpture
Exhibitions: Four major exhibits per year
Publications: Tougaloo College Art Collections
Activities: Lectures open to public, 2 vis lectr per yr; symposium; gallery talks; tour

TUPELO

C **BANK OF MISSISSIPPI,** Art Collection, 1 Mississippi Plaza, PO Box 789, 38802. Tel 601-680-2000. *Pres* Aubrey B Patterson Jr
Open 9 AM - 4:30 PM. Estab to encourage local artists and provide cultural enrichment for customers and friends
Purchases: $500
Collections: Oils, prints, watercolors
Activities: Grants available

L **LEE COUNTY LIBRARY,** 219 Madison, 38801. Tel 601-841-9029. *Chmn Board of Trustees* J D McGill, Jr; *Acting Dir* Louann Hurst; *Technical Services Librn* Barbara Anglin
Open Mon - Thurs 9:30 AM - 8:30 PM, Fri 11 AM - 2 PM, Sat 9 AM - 5 PM, cl Sun. Estab 1941 to provide books and other sources of information to serve the intellectual, recreational and cultural needs of its users. Maintains art gallery; The Mezzanine Gallery and Helen Foster Auditorium are used as exhibit space for works by University Art students, local professional artists and traveling exhibitions
Income: $469,000 (financed by city, state and county appropriations)
Library Holdings: AV — Cassettes, rec; Other — Framed reproductions
Collections: The Tupelo Gum Tree Festival purchase prizes, these include †paintings and pottery
Publications: Bi-monthly newsletter
Activities: Book traveling exhibitions

MISSOURI

ARROW ROCK

M **ARROW ROCK STATE HISTORIC SITE,** 65320. Tel 816-837-3330. *Admin* Mike Dickey
Tours available daily June - Aug, Apr, May, Sept & Oct Sat & Sun only, & by appointment. Admis $3. Estab 1923 to preserve, exhibit and interpret the cultural resources of Missouri, especially those associated with George Caleb Bingham and his era in central Missouri. The 1837 home of G C Bingham serves as a museum house and the 1834 Tavern has exhibition space for the Bingham Collection. Average Annual Attendance: 80,000
Income: Financed by state appropriation
Collections: Bingham Collection; Central Missouri Collection (textiles, furnishing and glass of the 19th century)
Exhibitions: Annual Art Fair; Annual Summer Workshop Exhibit; Annual Craft Festival
Activities: Classes for children; tours

CAPE GIRARDEAU

L **SOUTHEAST MISSOURI STATE UNIVERSITY,** Kent Library, 1 University Plaza, 63701. Tel 314-651-2235. *Dir* James Zink
Open Mon - Thur 8 AM - 10:30 PM, Fri 8 AM - 6 PM, Sat 9 AM - 5 PM, Sun 1:30 - 10:30 PM. Exhibition areas on second and third levels; Atrium Gallery on fourth level. The Jake K Wells Mural, 800 sq ft covers the west wall of the library foyer, depicting the nature and the development of the southeast region of the state
Collections: Charles Harrison Collection (rare books including some of the finest examples of the book arts); books and manuscripts from the 13th to the 20th century
Exhibitions: Missouri Arts Council touring exhibits; exhibits by local artists
Activities: Tours

COLUMBIA

L **DANIEL BOONE REGIONAL LIBRARY,** 100 W Broadway, 65203. Tel 314-443-3161. *Dir* Tom Strange
Open Mon - Thurs 9 AM - 9 PM, Fri 9 AM - 6 PM, Sat 9 AM - 5 PM, Sun 1 - 5 PM. Estab 1959
Library Holdings: AV — Cassettes
Exhibitions: Exhibits by local artists through the year

A **STATE HISTORICAL SOCIETY OF MISSOURI,** 1020 Lowry, 65201. Tel 314-882-7083; FAX 314-884-4950. *Exec Dir* Dr James W Goodrich; *Cur* Sidney Larson
Open Mon - Fri 8:30 AM - 4 PM. No admis fee. Estab 1898 to collect, preserve, make accessible & publish materials pertaining to the history of Missouri & Western America. Major art gallery 54 ft x 36 ft; corridor galleries. Average Annual Attendance: 30,000. Mem: 8000; dues $10; annual meeting in fall
Income: Financed by state appropriation
Collections: Works by Thomas H Benton, George C Bingham, Karl Bodmer, Fred Geary, Carl Gentry, William Knox, Roscoe Misselhorn, Frank B Nuderscher, Charles Schwartz, Fred Shane, Frederick Sylvester; contemporary artists collection containing work of over fifty outstanding Missouri related artists; original cartoon collection of works by Tom Engelhardt, Daniel Fitzpatrick, Don Hesse, Bill Mauldin, S J Ray and others
Publications: Missouri Historical Review, quarterly; R Douglas Hurt and Mary K Dains, eds; Thomas Hart Benton, Artist: Writer and Intellectual (1989)
Activities: Individual paintings lent, loans based on submitted requests

L **Library,** 1020 Lowry St, 65201. Tel 314-882-7083. *Dir & Librn* James W Goodrich
Open to public for reference use only
Income: Financed by state appropriation
Library Holdings: Vols 435,000; Per subs 900
Special Subjects: Painting - American, Cartoons, Missouri & the Midwest
Collections: George Caleb Bingham Paintings Collection; The Thomas Hart Benton Collection; Karl Bodmer Ninety colored engravings Eugene Field Collection; Mahan Memorial Mark Twain Collection; Bishop William Fletcher McMurray Collection; Francis A Sampson Collection of rare books

M **STEPHENS COLLEGE,** Lewis James & Nellie Stratton Davis Art Gallery, 65215. Tel 314-876-7173. *Dir* Irene Alexander; *Actg Dir* Sarah Riley-Land
Open Mon - Fri 10 AM - 4 PM, Sat noon - 4 PM, cl school holidays, Summer. No admis fee. Estab 1964 to provide exhibitions of art for the general interest of the local community and for the education of the student body in general. Average Annual Attendance: 500
Income: Operating budget $2000 (financed by endowment)
Collections: †Modern paintings; †modern graphics; primitive sculpture
Exhibitions: Elizabeth Layton's Drawing on Life; Margaret Peterson Paintings
Activities: Lect open to the public, 6 vis lectr per yr; gallery talks; exhibitions; competitions; awards

UNIVERSITY OF MISSOURI

M **Museum of Art and Archaeology,** One Pickard Hall, 65211. Tel 314-882-3591; FAX 314-884-4039. *Dir* Morteza Sajadian; *Asst Dir* Jacque F Dunn; *Assoc Cur European & American Art* Christine Crafts Neal; *Cur Ancient Art* Jane C Biers; *Registrar* Jeffrey Wilcox; *Asst Conservator* Aimee Leonhard; *Cur Educ* Luann Andrews
Open Tues - Fri 9 AM - 5 PM, Sat & Sun noon - 5 PM, cl Mon & holidays. No admis fee. Estab 1957 to exhibit a study collection for students in Art History and Archaeology; a comprehensive collection for the enjoyment of the general area of Missouri. Housed in renovated 1890's building, 8 galleries for permanent collection & special exhibitions. Average Annual Attendance: 35,000. Mem: 800
Income: $250,000 (financed by membership, and state appropriation)
Collections: †Ancient Art—Egypt, Western Asia, Greek and Roman; European & American painting and sculpture; †Early Christian—Byzantine and Coptic; †Modern paintings and sculpture; †Prints and drawings; African, Pre-Columbian; Oriental—Chinese and Japanese; South Asian—Indian, Thai, Tibetan, Nepalese
Exhibitions: (1993) From the Pasture to Polis: Art in the Age of Homer. Changing exhibitions from permanent collections
Publications: Muse, annually; exhibition catalogues; The News, 3 per yr
Activities: Classes for adults & children; docent training; workshops on conservation; lect open to public, 5 - 10 vis lectr per yr; concerts; tours; gallery talks; original objects of art lent to institutions; book traveling exhibitions, 2 - 3 per year; originate traveling exhibitions; museum shop sells books, prints, reproductions

L **Art, Archaeology & Music Collection,** Ellis Library, Ninth & Lowry St, 65201. Tel 314-882-7634.
Estab 1841 to house material for the faculty and students of the University
Income: Financed by state appropriation
Library Holdings: Vols 65,000; Per subs 300; Micro — Fiche, reels; AV — Rec; Other — Exhibition catalogs
Special Subjects: European prehistory, Near Eastern & Mediterranean art & archeology, Renaissance art history

CRESTWOOD

KAPPA PI INTERNATIONAL HONORARY ART FRATERNITY
For further information, see National and Regional Organizations

FENTON

L **MARITZ, INC,** Library, 1400 S Highway Dr, 63099. Tel 314-827-1501; FAX 314-827-5505. *Mgr* Mary Anne Walton; *Librn* Jeffrey L Sherk
Library estab 1968. For reference & lending. Circ 12,000
Library Holdings: Vols 6000; Per subs 350; Micro — Fiche 1600; Other — Clipping files
Special Subjects: Advertising Design, American Indian Art, American Western Art, Architecture, Calligraphy, Cartoons, Commercial Art, Folk Art, Graphic Arts, Illustration, Photography, Posters
Collections: Graphic Arts

FULTON

M WESTMINSTER COLLEGE, Winston Churchill Memorial & Library in the United States, 501 Westminster Ave, 65251. Tel 314-642-3361, 642-6648. *Dir* Judith Novak Pugh; *Asst to the Dir* Randy P Hendrix; *Archivist* Warren Hollrah
Open Mon - Sat 10 AM - 4:30 PM, Sun 12:30 - 4:30 PM. Admis adults $2, seniors $1.50, children 12 & under free; group rates. Estab 1969 to commemorate life & times of Winston Churchill & attest to ideals of Anglo-American relations. Special exhibits gallery changes quarterly; ecclesiastical gallery contains historic robes & communion vessels; connecting gallery houses historic map collection. Average Annual Attendance: 22,000. Mem: 900
Income: Financed by endowment, mem, admissions, friends fundraising, gift shop sales
Collections: Churchill & family memorabilia, including documents, manuscripts & photographs; Churchill oil paintings; rare maps
Exhibitions: Churchill paintings; Iron Curtain speech memorabilia
Publications: MEMO, quarterly newsletter
Activities: Churchill classes for WC students; docent training; lect open to public; concerts; tours; scholarships & fels offered; individual paintings & original objects of art lent to other museums & libraries; book traveling exhibitions, 2-4 per yr; originate traveling exhibitions; museum shop sells books, original art, reproductions, prints, slides, Churchill busts & memorabilia, English china, posters, collectible English toy soldiers

M WILLIAM WOODS COLLEGE, Art Gallery, 65251. Tel 314-642-2251, Ext 367. *Dir* Paul Clervi
Open Mon - Fri 9 AM - 4:30 PM. No admis fee. Estab 1967 to be used as a teaching aid for the Art Center. Maintains 3200 sq ft sky-lighted gallery with a mezzanine
Income: Financed by endowment
Activities: Lect open to the public, 2 per year; gallery talks; scholarships

HOLLISTER

L WORLD ARCHAEOLOGICAL SOCIETY, Information Center & Library, Lake Rd 65-48, HCR-1-PO Box 445, 65672. Tel 417-334-2377. *Dir* Ron Miller; *Asst Dir* Mrs Steve Miller
Not open to public. Estab 1971 to research worldwide mail & telephone queries. Lending & reference by special arrangement
Income: Financed by endowment
Library Holdings: Vols 6000; Per subs 32; AV — Slides; Other — Clipping files, original art works, photographs, prints
Special Subjects: American Indian Art, American Western Art, Anthropology, Antiquities-Egyptian, Antiquities-Greek, Antiquities-Oriental, Antiquities-Roman, Archaeology, Architecture, Art History, Asian Art, History of Art & Archaeology, Oriental Art, Pre-Columbian Art, Primitive Art, Religious Art
Collections: Steve Miller Library of Archaeology
Publications: WAS Newsletter, occasional; special publications, occasional
Activities: Educ dept; special tapes on request; consulting; competitions; awards; exten dept answers questions globally

INDEPENDENCE

M CHURCH OF JESUS CHRIST OF LATTER DAY SAINTS, Mormon Visitors' Center, 937 W Walnut, 64050. Tel 816-836-3466. *Dir* Allen Rozsa
Open daily 9 AM - 9 PM. No admis fee. Estab 1971 as a center of Latter Day Saints beliefs & history for residents of Missouri, Ohio, & Illinois. Average Annual Attendance: 50,000
Collections: Large 30 ft mural of Christ; painting; computer reproductions; 2 and a half ton statue
Exhibitions: Paintings; audio-visual shows; historical maps exhibits
Publications: Brochures
Activities: Lectures open to the public; tours; sales shop sells books & reproductions

M JACKSON COUNTY HISTORICAL SOCIETY, 1859 Jail, Marshal s Home & Museum, 217 N Main St, 64050. Tel 816-252-1892. *Dir* Gay Clemenson; *Operating Committee Chmn* Nancy Williams
Open Mon - Sat 10 AM - 5 PM, Sun 1 - 4 PM, cl Jan & Mon Feb - Mar. Admis adults $2.50, sr citizens $1.75, group rates available. Estab 1958 for interpretation of Jackson County history. 1859 Federal town house of county marshal, attached limestone jail which served as federal headquarters during the Civil War. Restored historical interior c 1860's. Restored cell of Frank James c 1882. Average Annual Attendance: 12,000. Mem: 1000; dues $15 - $500
Income: Financed by membership, tours, fundraising events
Collections: Jackson County history, 1800-present; home furnishings of mid-19th century in restored areas
Exhibitions: Permanent exhibits on Jackson County history; changing exhibits
Publications: Jackson County Historical Society Journal, bi-annual
Activities: Educ dept; classes for children; docent training; Lectures open to public; tours; museum shop sells books
L Research Library and Archives, Independence Square Courthouse, Room 103, 64050. Tel 816-252-7454. *Site Dir* Kathleen Halcro; *Archivist* Jennifer Parker
Open Mon & Wed 9:30 AM - 2:30 PM, Tues & Fri noon - 5 PM, Sat noon - 3 PM. Estab 1966
Income: Financed by memberships, fees, donations, sales
Library Holdings: Vols 2000; Per subs 15; Micro — Reels; AV — A-tapes, fs, Kodachromes, lantern slides, motion pictures, slides, v-tapes; Other — Clipping files, photographs
Special Subjects: Collection limited to the history of Jackson County & surrounding region
Collections: Photograph collection for reference; extensive manuscript collection

M John Wornall House Museum, 146 W 61 Terrace, 64113. Tel 816-444-1858. *Dir* Abby Mink; *Asst to Dir* Sally Gibbs; *Asst to Dir* Amy Nuetzmann
Open Tues - Sat 10 AM - 4 PM, Sun 1 - 4 PM. Admis adults $2.50, sr citizens $2, children under 12 $1, group rates available. Estab 1972 restored to interpret the daily lives of frontier farm families in the 1830s-1860s in early Kansas City. House was used as field hospital during the Civil War. Built in 1858; opened to public in 1972. Average Annual Attendance: 10,000. Mem: 400; dues $15 - $100
Income: Financed by memberships, tours & fund raisings
Collections: Home furnishings of prosperous farm families
Exhibitions: Special exhibitions on subjects dealing with interpretation of home & Civil War period
Activities: Classes for adults & children; docent training; concerts; tours; museum shop sells books, herbs, holiday & gift items

L NATIONAL ARCHIVES & RECORDS ADMINISTRATION, Harry S Truman Library, 24 Hwy & Delaware, 64050. Tel 816-833-1400. *Dir* Benedict K Zobrist; *Asst Dir* George H Curtis
Open 9 AM - 5 PM, cl Thanksgiving, Christmas & New Years. Admis $2. Estab 1957 to preserve and make available for study and exhibition the papers, objects and other materials relating to President Harry S Truman and to the history of the Truman administration. Gravesite of President & Mrs Truman in the courtyard. Administered by the National Archives and Records Administration of the Federal Government. Average Annual Attendance: 200,000
Income: Financed by federal appropriation and federal trust fund
Library Holdings: Vols 40,000; Per subs 23; Documents; Micro — Reels; AV — A-tapes, motion pictures, rec, slides; Other — Clipping files, framed reproductions, manuscripts, memorabilia, original art works, pamphlets, photographs, prints, sculpture
Collections: Papers of Harry S Truman, his associates, and of officials in the Truman administration; Portraits of President Truman; paintings, prints, sculptures & artifacts presented to President Truman during the Presidential & Post-Presidential periods; original political cartoons; mural by Thomas Hart Benton
Exhibitions: Permanent and temporary exhibits relating to the life and times of Harry S Truman; the history of the Truman administration; the history and nature of office of the Presidency
Publications: Historical materials in the Truman Library
Activities: Educ dept; tours for school groups; sales shop sells books, reproductions, slides and postcards

JEFFERSON CITY

M DEPARTMENT OF NATURAL RESOURCES OF MISSOURI, Missouri State Museum, State Capitol, Room B-2, 65101. Tel 314-751-2854. *Dir* John Hensley; *Cur Exhib* Bill Fannin; *Cur Coll* L T Shelton; *Cur Field Exhib* Beth Prevost
Open daily 8 AM - 5 PM, cl holidays. No admis fee. Estab 1920. Average Annual Attendance: 250,000
Income: Financed by state appropriation, affiliated with Missouri Department of Natural Resources
Collections: Art murals by T H Benton, Berninghaus, Frank Brangwyn, N C Wyeth; historical material and natural specimens representing Missouri's natural and cultural resources; Indian artifacts; History hall & reference center
Exhibitions: Permanent and temporary exhibits
Publications: Pamphlets
Activities: Guided tours of Capitol; audio-visual presentations; book traveling exhibitions, 4-5 per year
M Elizabeth Rozier Gallery, State Capitol, Room B-2, 65101. Tel 314-751-4210. *Dir* John Hensley
Open 10 AM - 4 PM. No admis fee. Estab 1981 to provide art, crafts & educational exhibits. Located in mid-nineteenth century building with a large & small gallery. Average Annual Attendance: 6000
Activities: Lectures open to public, 15 vis lectr per yr; concerts; gallery talks; tours; competitions with awards; book traveling exhibitions

JOPLIN

L WINFRED L & ELIZABETH C POST FOUNDATION, Post Memorial Art Reference Library, 300 Main St, 64801. Tel 417-782-5419; FAX 417-624-5217. *Dir* Leslie T Simpson
Open Mon & Thurs 10 AM - 9 PM, Tues, Wed & Fri 10 AM - 5 PM, Sat 10 AM - 4 PM. No admis fee. Estab 1981 to provide information on the fine and decorative arts to members of the community. Located in a wing of the Joplin Public Library. Average Annual Attendance: 6500
Income: Financed by private endowment
Library Holdings: Vols 2600; Per subs 25; Other — Clipping files, exhibition catalogs, original art works, pamphlets, photographs, reproductions, sculpture
Special Subjects: Architecture, Art History, Decorative Arts, Furniture, Historical Material, Photography
Collections: 16th-17th Century Antiques & Artworks; †Joplin, Mo historic architecture collection; †fine arts books collections; †mounted reproductions
Exhibitions: Monthly exhibits of works by area artists
Activities: Educ dept; film & slide programs

A SPIVA ART CENTER, INC, 3950 Newman Rd, Missouri Southern State College Campus, 64801. Tel 417-623-0183. *Dir* V A Christensen
Open Tues - Sat 10 AM - 4 PM, Sun 2 - 5 PM, cl Mon & national holidays. Estab June 1959, inc 1969, as a non-profit, cultural center with the purpose of increasing knowledge and appreciation of the visual arts in Joplin and surrounding area; to offer educational classes, workshops, and to exhibit works of educational and artistic value. Average Annual Attendance: 15,000. Mem: 650; dues $5 - $1000; annual meeting in Dec
Exhibitions: (1993) Floored Art: Exhibitions of Rugs & Related Arts; Iro Sohn, Helwig Putter & Eddy Hoyt; Photo Spiva; 45th Annual Membership Show. (1994) Missouri Arts Bi-Annual; Adolf Dehn: Midwest Landscapes; 44th Spiva Annual; MSSC Seniors; Our Land/Ourselves: Native Americans; Women in

Print
Publications: Calendar; newsletter
Activities: Classes in various phases of the visual arts for adults and children; lectures open to public; gallery tours; competitions with prizes

KANSAS CITY

M **AVILA COLLEGE**, Thornhill Art Gallery, 11901 Wornall Rd, 64145. Tel 816-942-8400. *Aceadmic Dean* Sr Marie Joan Harris; *Chmn Humanities* Daniel Larson; *Pres* Larry Kramer; *Dir* George Chrisman
Open Mon - Fri 10 AM - 4 PM. No admis fee. Estab 1978 to present the visual arts in a contemporary sense to the student community as well as the Greater Kansas City community. Gallery space 60 x 35 ft is maintained with carpeted floor and walls, an Artist-in-Residence studio, and track lighting. Average Annual Attendance: 2000
Income: Financed through school budget
Activities: Classes for adults; dramatic programs; lectures open to public; gallery talks

C **COMMERCE BANCSHARES, INC,** Art Collection, 1000 Walnut St, PO Box 13686, 64199. Tel 816-234-2968; FAX 816-234-2356. *Chief Exec Officer & Pres* David W Kemper; *Dir Art Coll* Laura Kemper Fields; *Cur Art Coll* Karen Duethman
Open Mon - Sat 8 AM - 5 PM. Estab 1964. 125 ft barrel vaulted gallery with 13 ft ceiling to exhibit museum quality paintings
Exhibitions: Contemporary American Realist Art, paintings & drawings
Activities: Individual paintings lent on restricted basis

HALLMARK CARDS, INC
C **Fine Art Programs,** 25th & McGee, 64108. Tel 816-274-4726; FAX 816-545-6591. *Dir Fine Art Prog* Keith F Davis
Estab 1949
Collections: Hallmark Photographic Collection; Hallmark Art Collection; drawings; paintings; photographs; prints
Exhibitions: (1991-93) Clarence John Laughlin: Visionary Photographer; The Passionate Observer: Photographs by Carl Van Vechten
Publications: Exhibition catalogues; New Acquisitions brochures, annually
Activities: Lect; purchase awards for art shows; individual objects of art lent to reputable institutions for temporary exhibitions; originate traveling exhibitions
L **Creative Library,** No 146, PO Box 419820, 64141-6820. Tel 816-274-5525; FAX 816-274-7245. *Mgr Library Services* Jon M Henderson; *Reference Librn* Mary Knebel
Open to Hallmark personnel only. Estab to provide pictorial research
Income: Financed by corp funds
Library Holdings: Vols 22,000; Per subs 140
Special Subjects: Illustration, Design, Fine Arts, Children's Books
Collections: Old & rare collection

M **KANSAS CITY ART INSTITUTE,** Kemper Museum of Contemporary Art & Design, 4415 Warwick Blvd, 64111. Tel 816-561-4852; FAX 816-561-6404. *Chmn Board of Governors* Donald Pratt; *Dir Exhib* Sherry Cromwell-Lacy
Average Annual Attendance: 34,000
Exhibitions: Changing contemporary art exhibitions
Activities: Classes for adults; lectures open to public, 12 vis lectrs per yr; tours; awards; scholarships; exten dept serves community
L 4415 Warwick Blvd, 64111. Tel 816-561-4852; FAX 816-561-6404. *Library Dir* Allen Morrill
Open Mon - Thurs 8:30 AM - 9 PM, Fri 8:30 AM - 5 PM, Sat noon - 5 PM, Sun 1 - 5 PM. Estab 1924 to serve students and faculty of Art Institute
Income: $75,622 (financed by Art Institute budget)
Library Holdings: Vols 37,000; Per subs 120; Picture file; Other — Exhibition catalogs
Special Subjects: Photography, Fine arts

M **KANSAS CITY ARTISTS COALITION,** 201 Wyandotte, 64105. Tel 816-421-5222. *Executive Dir* Janet F Simpson; *Forum Ed* Betsy O'Hara
Open Wed - Sat 11 AM - 4 PM. No admis fee. Estab 1972 to promote contemporary art & artists from Kansas City & the Midwest; non-profit organization. Average Annual Attendance: 6000. Mem: 420; dues $40
Exhibitions: (1990-91) Image & Word; Constructs; David Shapiro; Eastern European Artists (Geringer, Luebs & Satz); Regional Profiles: Fiber; River Market Regional Exhibition
Publications: Forum, 5 times a year; newsletter
Activities: Lectures open to public, 1-2 vis lectrs a year; competitions with awards

L **KANSAS CITY PUBLIC LIBRARY,** 311 E 12th St, 64106. Tel 816-221-2685. *Central Reference Coordr* Lillie Brack
Open Mon - Thurs 9 AM - 9 PM, Fri & Sat 9 AM - 5 PM, Sun 1 - 5 PM. Established 1873
Library Holdings: Vols 1,459,336; Per subs 1575; Micro — Fiche, reels; AV — Motion pictures, rec, slides; Other — Clipping files, exhibition catalogs, framed reproductions, memorabilia, pamphlets, prints, reproductions

M **LIBERTY MEMORIAL MUSEUM & ARCHIVES,** 100 W 26th St, 64108. Tel 816-221-1918. *Dir* Doran L Cart; *Archivist* Cynthia J Rogers
Open Wed - Sun 9:30 AM - 4:30 PM. Admin adults $2. Estab 1919 to exhibit World War I memorabilia. Two rectangular spaces 45 x 90 ft; permanent & temporary exhibits
Income: Financed by city appropriation & admis fees
Collections: †WWI: books, documents, militaria, original sketches & paintings, photos, posters, sheet music
Exhibitions: Trench Warfare; Aviation; Artillery; Medical Care; Uniforms; Women at War
Publications: Signals, quarterly newsletter
Activities: Children's programs; docent programs; retail store sells books & prints

MID-AMERICA ARTS ALLIANCE & EXHIBITS USA
For further information, see National and Regional Organizations

M **NELSON-ATKINS MUSEUM OF ART,** 4525 Oak St, 64111-1873. Tel 816-561-4000; FAX 816-561-7145. *Dir & Cur Oriental Art* Marc F Wilson; *Dir Development* Michael Churchman; *Registrar* Ann E Erbarcher; *Samuel Sosland Cur American Art* Dr Henry Adams; *Cur Decorative Arts & Assoc Cur European Decorative Arts* Christina H Nelson; *Cur of Exhib & Designs* Andrew Meredith; *Cur Prints, Drawings & Photography* George L McKenna; *Cur European Painting & Sculpture* Dr Roger B Ward; *Sanders Sosland Cur 20th Century Art* Deborah R Emont Scott; *Assoc Cur Southeast Asian & Indian Art* Dr Dorothy H Fickle; *Assoc Cur Africa, Oceania & the Americas* Dr David A Binkley; *Assoc Cur Ancient Art* Dr Robert Cohon; *Consult Cur Medieval Art* Dr Marilyn Stokstad; *Res Cur Far Eastern Art* Chu-tsing Li; *Conservator* Forrest Bailey; *Assoc Conservator of Paper* Open; *Asst Conservator* Scott Heffley; *Asst Cur European Art* Eliot Rowlands; *Asst Cur 20th Century Art* Deni McHenri; *Research Asst Oriental Art* Joseph Chang; *Asst Cur American Art* Margaret C Conrads
Open Tues - Sat 10 AM - 5 PM, Sun 1 - 5 PM, cl Mon, New Year's Day, July 4, Thanksgiving, Christmas. Admis adults $3, students & children 6 to 18 $1, children 5 & under free, Sat no admis fee. Estab 1933 to enrich, enliven and present the arts of the ancient and modern world to the Midwest and the remainder of the US; develop activities relating to art education, the interpretation of the collections and their general enjoyment. Average Annual Attendance: 425,440. Mem: 13,000; dues $40 - $2500
Income: Financed by endowment, membership and gifts
Collections: †Burnap Collection of English pottery, Oriental ceramics, paintings, sculpture, bronze, Egyptian tomb sculpture, American painting, period rooms & furniture; Coloisters; †contemporary works of art; †Impressionist painting; the finest Oriental furniture collection outside of the Orient; sculpture garden; †Oriental Art
Exhibitions: Christo's Wrapped Walkways Documentation; Richard Estes Urban Landscape; Monet's Water Lilies Triptych; various loan shows & displays of permanent collection; Inside Looking In; Rookwood Pottery
Publications: Calendar, 10 times per year
Activities: Classes for children; docent training; workshops; symposia; lectures open to the public & for members only, 20 vis lectrs per yr; concerts; gallery talks; tours; individual paintings and original objects of art lent to qualified organizations & exhibitions; museum sales shop sells books, magazines, original art, reproductions, prints, slides, posters, postcards; sales and rental gallery sells or rents original art
L **Kenneth and Helen Spencer Art Reference Library,** 4525 Oak St, 64111-1873. Tel 816-751-1216; FAX 816-561-7154. *Head Librn* Susan Malkoff Moon; *Cataloger* Jane Cheng; *Cataloger* Jane Zander; *Slide Librn* Jan B McKenna
Open Tues - Thurs, Sat & Sun 10 AM - 4 PM, Fri 10 AM - 9 PM. For reference only
Library Holdings: Vols 65,000; Per titles 1200, auction catalogues, international auction; Micro — Fiche; AV — Cassettes, motion pictures, slides 60,000, v-tapes; Other — Clipping files, exhibition catalogs, manuscripts, pamphlets, photographs
Special Subjects: Afro-American Art, Asian Art, Decorative Arts, Folk Art, Graphic Arts, Oriental Art, Painting - American, Period Rooms, Pre-Columbian Art, Southwestern Art, Auction Catalogues
Collections: Bender Library is comprised of books on prints and drawings; Oriental study collection of materials on Oriental art with enphasis on Chinese art
Publications: Calendar, 10 times per year
A **Friends of Art,** 4525 Oak St, 64111-1873. Tel 816-561-4000, Ext 246; FAX 816-561-7145. *Dir* Marc Wilson; *VPres* Open; *Secy* Open; *Asst Dir of Development & Membership* Judith M Cooke
Open Tues - Sat 10 AM - 5 PM, Sun 1 - 5 PM. Admis adults $2, children free. Estab 1934 as a non-profit organization supporting the Nelson Gallery and now serves as membership department. Mem: 7000; dues $35-$250
Income: Financed by membership and contributions
Publications: Membership communication
Activities: Classes for adults and children; docent training; lectures open to public; gallery talks; tours; sales shop sells books, magazines, reproductions and slides; junior museum
M **Creative Arts Center,** 4525 Oak St, 64111-1873. Tel 816-751-1236; FAX 816-561-7154. *Dir* Ann Brubaker
Open Tues - Sat 10 AM - 5 PM, Sun 1 - 5 PM. Estab 1960 to create a greater awareness of the world around us through art
Activities: Creative art classes for children sculpture, drawing, painting, Oriental, brushwork & design classes; workshops; docent training; tours

THE STAINED GLASS ASSOCIATION OF AMERICA
For further information, see National and Regional Organizations

C **UNITED MISSOURI BANCSHARES, INC,** PO Box 419226, 64141-6226. Tel 816-860-7000. *Chmn* R Crosby Kemper
Estab 1973 to provide good art for viewing by customers. Collection is displayed in lobbies and customer access areas in various United Missouri Banks
Collections: Americana Collection, including American portraits (George Caleb Bingham, Benjamin Blythe, Gilbert Stuart, Charles Wilson Peale), regional collection (William Commerford, Peter Hurd, J H Sharp, Gordon Snidow), modern art (Fran Bull, Olive Rush, Wayne Thiebaud, Ellsworth Kelly)
Activities: Objects of art lent to galleries for special exhibits

M **UNIVERSITY OF MISSOURI-KANSAS CITY,** Gallery of Art, 5100 Rockhill Rd, 64110. Tel 816-235-1502. *Dir* Craig Subler
Open Mon - Fri noon - 5 PM, Sun noon - 5 PM, Summer Mon - Fri noon - 5 PM. No admis fee. Estab 1977 to bring a broad range of art to both students and the community. Average Annual Attendance: 5000
Income: Financed by endowment, city & state appropriation, contribution
Publications: Exhibition catalogues
Activities: Adult classes; lectures open to the public, 5 vis lectrs per yr; originate traveling exhibitions that circulate to museums & galleries in Missouri & Pennsylvania

MARYVILLE

M NORTHWEST MISSOURI STATE UNIVERSITY, DeLuce Art Gallery, Dept of Art, 64468. Tel 816-562-1326; FAX 816-562-1900. *Chmn Dept Art* Lee Hageman; *Olive DeLuce Art Gallery Coll Cur* Philip Laber; *Percival DeLuce Art Gallery Coll Cur* Robert Sunkel
Open Mon - Fri 1 - 4 PM. No admis fee. Estab 1965 to provide exhibitions of contemporary works in all media as part of the learning experiences in the visual arts. Gallery is maintained with 150 running feet exhibition space with high security, humidity controlled air conditioning and flexible lighting. Average Annual Attendance: 6000
Income: Financed by city appropriation
Collections: Percival DeLuce Memorial Collection consisting of American paintings, drawings, prints and decorative arts; some European furniture and prints
Activities: Classes for adults; lect open to public, 6 vis lectr per yr; gallery talks; tours; scholarships; individual and original objects of art lent within the institution; lending collection contains original art works, original prints, paintings and drawings; book 3 traveling exhibitions per year

MEXICO

M AUDRAIN COUNTY HISTORICAL SOCIETY, Graceland Museum & American Saddlehorse Museum, 501 S Muldrow Ave, PO Box 3, 65265. Tel 314-581-3910. *Exec Dir* Leta Hodge
Open Tues - Sun 1 - 4 PM, cl Monday, Jan & holidays. Admis $1. 1959. Average Annual Attendance: 2500. Mem: 766; dues $5 and up
Income: $25,000 (financed by endowment & membership
Collections: Currier & Ives; Photographs; Lusterware; Dolls; Tom Bass Artifacts
Publications: Graceland Gazzette, 4 times yearly

L MEXICO-AUDRAIN COUNTY LIBRARY, 305 W Jackson, 65265. Tel 314-581-4939. *Dir* Kurt H Lamb; *Children's Librn* Margaret Jones; *Acquisitions Librn* Violet Lierheimer; *Reference Librn* Christal Brunner
Open winter hours, Mon - Thurs 9 AM - 9 PM, Fri & Sat 9 AM - 5:30 PM. No admis fee. Estab 1912 to provide library services to the residents of Audrain County, Missouri. Exhibit room with different exhibits each month; childrens department has a continuously changing exhibit
Income: Financed by donations
Library Holdings: Vols 112,529; Per subs 127; art print reproductions; newspapers; AV — Fs, Kodachromes, motion pictures, rec
Collections: Audrain County history; paintings by Audrain County artists
Exhibitions: Local Federated Womens Club sponsored a different exhibit each month during the fall, winter and spring, these included local artists, both adult and young people, and recognized artists of the area; The Missouri Council of the Arts also provide traveling exhibits that we display
Activities: Classes for children; story hour 1 hr 4 days a week; individual paintings and original objects of art lent

SAINT CHARLES

M LINDENWOOD COLLEGE, Harry D Hendren Gallery, Department of Art, 63301. Tel 314-949-4862. *Chmn* W Dean Eckert
Open Mon - Fri 9 AM - 5 PM, Sat & Sun noon - 4 PM. No admis fee. Estab 1969 as a college exhibition gallery. Gallery is approximately 3600 sq ft with skylight and one wall of side light. Average Annual Attendance: 4000
Income: Financed by endowment
Collections: Contemporary American and European prints in various media including works by Paul Jenkins, William Hayter, Will Barnet, Mauricio Lazansky
Exhibitions: Photographs by Tim Smith
Activities: Lectures open to the public, 5-6 vis lectr per year; gallery talks; tours; original objects of art lent; lending collection contains photographs; traveling exhibitions organized and circulated through the Missouri State Council on the Arts

SAINTE GENEVIEVE

M ST GENEVIEVE MUSEUM, Merchant & DuBourgh St, 63670. Tel 314-883-3461. *Pres* Carrol Fallert; *Treas* Delores Koetting
Open winter noon - 4 PM, summer 9 - 11 AM, noon - 4 PM. Admis adults $1, students $.35. Estab 1935. Average Annual Attendance: 7000 - 8000. Mem: Dues family $5, individual $3
Income: Financed by mem, admis, sales

SAINT JOSEPH

M THE ALBRECHT-KEMPER MUSEUM OF ART, 2818 Frederick Blvd, 64506. Tel 816-233-7003; FAX 816-233-3413. *Dir* Marianne Berardi; *Registrar* Ann Tootle; *Communications Dir* Stanley Harris
Open Tues - Fri 10 AM - 4 PM, Sat & Sun 1 - 4 PM, cl Mon. No admis fee. Estab 1914 to increase public knowledge & appreciation of the arts. Mem: 650; dues $25 & up, students $5; annual meeting in Apr
Income: Financed by mem & fundraising events
Collections: Collections of American Art consisting of paintings by George Bellows, Thomas Hart Benton, Albert Bierstadt, Alfred Bricher, William Merritt Chase, Francis Edmonds, George Hall, Robert Henri, Edward Hopper, George Inness, Eastman Johnson, Fitz Hugh Lane, Ernest Lawson, William Paxton, Rembrandt Peale, John Sloan, Gilbert Stuart, Andrew Wyeth; drawings by Leonard Baskin, Robert Birmelin, Isabel Bishop, Paul Cadmus, Kenneth Callahan, William Gropper, Gabor Peterdi, Robert Vickrey, & John Wilde. Prints by John Taylor Arms, George Catlin, Thomas Nason, Bruce McCombs, Evan Lindquist; sculpture by L E Gus Shafe, Ernest Trova & Larry Young
Exhibitions: (1993) Under the Influence: The Students of Thomas Hart Benton;

Paintings by Paul Pletha; Catlin's Indians: The Kemper Portfolio
Publications: Annual report including catalog of year's acquisitions, exhibition catalogs & brochures; Artmail, monthly newsletter
Activities: Classes for adults & children; docent training; lect open to public, 8 vis lectr per year; performances & programs in fine arts theater; concerts; gallery talks, tours, competitions; individual paintings & original objects of art lent to other museums; book traveling exhibitions 1 - 2 per year; originate traveling exhibitions to other museums; museum shop sells books, magazines & miscellaneous items

M MISSOURI WESTERN STATE COLLEGE, Fine Arts Gallery, 4525 Downs Dr, 64507. Tel 816-271-4282. *Pres* Dr Janet Murphy; *VPres* Dr James Roever; *Chmn Department of Art* William Eickhorst, EdD
Open 8 AM - 4:30 PM. No admis fee. Estab 1971 to bring an awareness of contemporary directions in art to students and to the community. Foyer gallery is in front of building, next to theater; 120 ft long, 30 ft wide, with 25 ft high ceiling; rug paneling on walls; modern decor, gallery 206 is on 2nd floor; 25 ft square, 10 ft ceiling; rug paneling on walls, carpeted. Average Annual Attendance: 10,000
Income: Financed by state appropriation
Exhibitions: Invitational of juried art exhibitions
Activities: Classes for adults; lect open to public; gallery talks; tours; competitions; scholarships; exten dept; individual paintings and original objects of art lent to staff offices within college; lending collection contains original art works, original prints, paintings and sculpture; book traveling exhibitions

M SAINT JOSEPH MUSEUM, 11th and Charles, 64501. Tel 816-232-8471; FAX 816-232-8482. *Dir* Richard A Nolf; *Registrar & Cur Collection* Bonnie K Watkins; *Cur Ethnology* Marilyn S Taylor; *Cur Hist & Librn* Jacqueline Lewin
Open Mon - Sat 9 AM - 5 PM, Sun & holidays 1 - 5 PM. Admis adults $1, children between 7 & 15 $.50, under 7 free. Estab 1926 to increase and diffuse knowledge and appreciation of history, art and the sciences and to aid the educational work that is being done by the schools of Saint Joseph and other educational organizations. Mini-gallery, usually for small, low security traveling exhibits. Average Annual Attendance: 100,000. Mem: 209; dues $15 and up; annual meeting Jan
Income: $100,000 (financed by membership, and city appropriation)
Collections: †Harry L George Collection of Native American Art
Publications: The Happenings (newsletter), bimonthly
Activities: Classes for children; craft program; lect open to public; museum shop selling books, reproductions, prints, slides, gift items

L Library, 11th & Charles, 64501. Tel 816-232-8471; FAX 816-232-8482. *Dir* Richard A Wolf
Open Apr - Sept Mon - Sat 9 AM - 5 PM, Sun 1 - 5 PM. Estab 1926 to hold museum collections. Mini gallery for traveling exhibits
Purchases: $1200
Library Holdings: Vols 5000; Per subs 40; Other — Clipping files, framed reproductions, manuscripts, memorabilia, original art works, photographs, prints, sculpture
Special Subjects: Area History; Native American; Natural History
Publications: The Happenings, bi-monthly newsletter
Activities: Classes for children; docent training; tours; originate traveling exhibitions to schools

SAINT LOUIS

A ARTS & EDUCATION COUNCIL OF GREATER SAINT LOUIS, 3526 Washington Ave, 63103. Tel 314-535-3600. *Chmn* Ted C Wetterau; *Pres* Patricia Rich; *Dir Public Information* Renee Bazin
Estab 1963 to coordinate, promote and assist in the development of cultural and educational activities in the Greater St. Louis area; to offer planning, coordinating, promotional and fundraising service to eligible organizations and groups, thereby creating a valuable community-wide association. Mem: 138
Income: Financed by funds from private sector
Publications: Calendar of cultural events, quarterly; Arts Directory, annually; Newsletter, quarterly; annual report

M ATRIUM GALLERY, Old Post Office Bldg, 815 Olive, 63101. Tel 314-621-1066. *Dir* Carolyn Miles
Open Mon - Fri 9 AM - 5 PM, Sat noon - 5 PM, also by appointment. Estab 1986. Commercial gallery featuring contemporary artists who are active regionally & nationally featuring one-person shows
Activities: Buffet luncheon/lecture art series; 15 vis lectrs per year

C THE BOATMEN'S NATIONAL BANK OF ST LOUIS, Art Collection, 1 Boatmen's Plaza, 800 Market St, 63101. Tel 314-466-6000. *Pres & Chmn* Andrew B Craig; *Sr VPres Advertising & Public Relations* Alfred S Dominick Jr
Open Mon - Fri 8 AM - 4 PM. Bank estab 1938; corporate art collection estab for purposes of investment & the pleasure of art. Art emphasizes Western theme & bank's affiliation with opening of the West
Collections: The Political Series by George Caleb Bingham; †Transportation Series by Oscar E Berninghause; Exhibition into the Rockies Mountains - watercolors by Alfred Jacob Miller; Tarahumara Series by George Carlson

M CHATILLON-DEMENIL HOUSE FOUNDATION, DeMenil Mansion, 3352 DeMenil Place, 63118. Tel 314-771-5828. *Dir* Donna Marin; *Educ Dir* Rachelle Reeg
Open Tues - Sat 10 AM - 4 PM. Admis $3. Estab 1965 to educate & inform the community on 19th century life & culture. Average Annual Attendance: 8000. Mem: 650; dues $35 - $1000; annual meeting in May
Income: Financed by mem, grants & donations
Collections: Decorative art from c1770 through 19th century; period rooms with furnishings; paintings
Activities: Children's programs; dramatic programs; docent progams; internships; lect open to public, 6 vis lectr per year; retail store sells books

M **CONCORDIA HISTORICAL INSTITUTE,** 801 DeMun Ave, 63105. Tel 314-721-5934. *Dir* Dr August R Suelflow
Open Mon - Fri 8 AM - 5 PM, cl international holidays. No admis fee. Estab 1847, to collect & preserve resources on the history of Lutheranism in America. Affiliated with The Lutheran Church, Missouri Synod. Average Annual Attendance: 12,000. Mem: 1600; dues Life $500, over 65 $300, organization $75, patron $50, sustaining $30, active & subscription $20
Collections: Church archives and vast historical materials; crafts; handcrafts; Reformation and Lutheran coins and medals; Works by Lutheran artists and paintings and artifacts for Lutheran worship; Native artwork from Foreign Mission Fields, especially China, India, Africa & New Guinea
Exhibitions: Temporary exhibitions
Publications: Concordia Historical Institute Quarterly; Historical Footnotes, a quarterly newsletter; Regional Archivist, a newsletter and 'how to' serial for archives; bulletins
Activities: Lect open to public; competitions with awards; Distinquished Service Award & awards of commendation for contributions to Lutheran History & archives; sales shop sells books, slides & craft items

M **CRAFT ALLIANCE GALLERY & EDUCATION CENTER,** 6640 Delmar Blvd, 63130. Tel 314-725-1151, 725-1177; FAX 314-725-1180. *Exec Dir* James Reed; *Chief Cur* Barbara Jedda; *Dir Educational Center* Barbara-Decker Franklin; *Dir Development* Ned Mitchell; *Shop Mgr* Susan Nanna
Open Tues - Fri noon - 5 PM, Sat 10 AM - 5 PM. No admis fee. Estab 1964 for exhibition and sales of craft objects. Average Annual Attendance: 12,000. Mem: 650
Income: Financed by mem, Missouri Arts Council, St Louis Arts & Education Council, National Endowment for the Arts, Regional Arts Commission
Exhibitions: Monthly exhibits by national artists. (1991) Animals of Power. (1992) Woven Vessels (basketry) (1993) Tales & Traditions: Storytelling in 20th Century American Craft
Publications: Animals of Power, (1991); Exhibition catalogs; Old & New Faces, Vols 1 & 2 (1987 & 88); Works Off The Lathe
Activities: Classes for adults & children; lectures open to public, 3 vis lectrs per yr; Scholarships; book one traveling exhibition per yr; originate traveling exhibitions; sales shop sells books, magazines and original art

A **FORUM FOR CONTEMPORARY ARTS,** 3540 Washington Ave, 63103. Tel 314-535-4660. *Pres* Emily Rauh Pulitzer; *Exec Dir* Elizabeth Wright Millard
Open Tues - Fri noon - 5 PM. No admis fee, donations accepted. Estab 1980 to promote & advocate the visual & performing arts. Multi-disciplinary visual & performing arts center. Average Annual Attendance: 150,000. Mem: 350; dues $30 & up
Income: $400,000 (financed by membership, corporations & foundation funds)
Exhibitions: Pop & After: Sculpture by Johns, Lichtenstein, Oldenburg & Segal; Selections From the Fabric Workshop; On Site: Three St Louis Sculptures, works by Serra, Miss, Sonfist; Contemporary Aboriginal Art; Art of Music Video
Activities: Educational outreach; workshops; lect open to public; 12 - 15 vis lectr per yr; concerts; gallery talks; tours; book traveling exhibitions; originates traveling exhibitions

M **LAUMEIER SCULPTURE PARK,** 12580 Rott Rd, 63127. Tel 314-821-1209. *Dir* Dr Beej Nierrengarten-Smith; *Cur* Debbie Reinhardt; *Cur* Michele Krevenas
Park open daily 8 AM - half hour past sunset; Gallery open Wed - Sat 10 AM - 5 PM, Sun noon - 5 PM. Estab 1976 to exhibit contemporary sculpture by internationally acclaimed artists. Average Annual Attendance: 350,000. Mem: 500; dues corporate $500, patron $200, contributing $100, regular $35 & students $10
Income: Financed by membership, corporate gifts & grants
Collections: Outdoor contemporary sculpture collection by Jackie Ferrara, Charles Ginnever, Richard Hunt, William King, Alexander Liberman, Mary Miss, Robert Morris, Jene Highstein Vito Acconci, Beverly Pepper, Tony Rosenthal, David Von Schlegell, Richard Serra, Michael Steiner, Mark Di Suvero, Ernest Trova, Dennis Oppenheim, Donald Judd, Arman, Hera, George Tickey, Ursula von Rydingsvard, Dan Graham, Richard Fleischner
Activities: Classes for adults & children; docent training; lect open to the public, 3 vis lectr per yr; concerts; gallery talks; tours; original objects of art lent to established institutions; lending collection contains 40 sculptures; book traveling exhibitions; originate traveling exhibitions; museum shop sells books, original art, slides

C **MARK TWAIN BANCSHARES,** 8820 Ladue Rd, 63124. Tel 314-727-1000. *Chief Exec Officer* John Dubinsky
Collections: Sculpture; American paintings; graphics; photography

M **MARYVILLE UNIVERSITY SAINT LOUIS,** Morton J May Foundation Gallery, 13550 Conway Rd, 63141. Tel 314-576-9300. *Gallery Dir* Nancy N Rice
Open Mon - Thurs 9 AM - 10 PM, Fri & Sat 8 AM - 5 PM, Sun 2 - 10 PM. No admis fee. Estab to show work of artists, many of whom have no gallery affiliation. Average Annual Attendance: 3000
Income: $2901
Activities: Lect open to public, 4 vis lectr per year; gallery talks; individual paintings & original objects of art lent to organizations, art guilds & schools

M **MISSOURI HISTORICAL SOCIETY,** Jefferson Memorial Bldg, PO Box 11940, 63112-0040. Tel 314-746-4599. *Pres* Robert Archibald; *Exec VPres* Karen M Goering; *VPres* Marsha Bray; *Dir Educ* James Powers; *Cur Photographs* Duane Sneddeker
Open Tues - Sun 9:30 AM - 5 PM. No admis fee. Estab 1866 to collect and preserve objects and information relating to the history of St Louis, Missouri and the Louisiana Purchase Territory. Estab 1866 to preserve the history of St Louis & the American West. Average Annual Attendance: 200,000. Mem: # 5500; dues from $35; annual meeting Sept
Income: Financed by private endowment, mem, special events, city & county taxes
Collections: †19th & 20th century art of St Louis and the American West;

†paintings; †photographs; †prints
Exhibitions: Lindbergh Memorabilia; Decorative Arts; St. Louis 1904 Worlds Fair ; Growing up in St. Louis
Publications: Focus, quarterly; Gateway Heritage, quarterly journal
Activities: Classes for adults & children; dramatic programs; docent training; outreach program festivals; lectures open to public, 3-5 vis lectr per year; gallery talks; tours; individual paintings & original objects of art lent to qualified museums & galleries that meet AAM standards; book traveling exhibitions; originate traveling exhibitions; sales shop sells books, prints, slides, souvenirs, china

L **Library & Collections Center,** 225 S Shinker St, PO Box 11940, 63112-0040. Tel 314-746-4599. *Dir Library & Archives* Peter Michel; *Dir Museum Colls* Magdalyn Sebastian
Open Mon - Sat 10 AM - 5 PM
Library Holdings: Vols 70,000; Per subs 317; Micro — Reels; AV — Cassettes; Other — Clipping files, manuscripts, pamphlets, photographs 500,00, prints 2000, sculpture 150
Special Subjects: Midwestern and Western Artists: Bodmer, Catlin and Russell

A **SAINT LOUIS ARTISTS' GUILD,** 227 E Lockwood, 63119. Tel 314-961-1246. *Pres* Gretchen Brighamy; *Treas* Rob Sadlerner
Open daily noon - 4 PM, Sun 1 - 5 PM, cl Tues. No admis fee. Estab for the purpose of promoting excellence in the arts. Average Annual Attendance: 5000. Mem: 600, dues $45
Income: Financed by membership
Exhibitions: Eleven exhibits per yr
Publications: Monthly newsletter
Activities: Educ dept; competitions with awards

M **THE SAINT LOUIS ART MUSEUM,** 1 Fine Arts Dr, 63110. Tel 314-721-0067; FAX 314-721-6172. *Dir* James D Burke
Open Tues 1:30 - 8:30 PM, Wed - Sun 10 AM - 5 PM, cl Mon. No admis fee except for special exhibitions. Estab 1907, erected as Palace of Art for 1904 World's Fair; designed by Cass Gilbert in Beaux Arts architecture style. The main sculpture hall is fashioned after Roman Baths of Caracalla. Average Annual Attendance: 650,000. Mem: 16,000; dues $2500, $1000, $500, $100, $50, $45, $25
Income: Property tax provides 65% of operating income & balance from grants & private donations
Collections: A comprehensive museum of global interest with collections ranging from prehistoric times to the present. A new department of prints, drawings and photographs display works from the Museum's 6000 holdings; outstanding art collection of works from Oceania, Africa, Pre-Columbian and American Indian objects; paintings emphasize Northern European works from the Renaissance to Rembrandt as well as colonial to contemporary American, French Impressionist and Post Impressionist and German Expressionist works; 20th century European sculpture, American and European decorative art; Chinese bronzes and porcelains
Publications: The St Louis Art Museum Bulletin, semi-annual; annual report; bi-monthly magazine/calendar
Activities: Classes for adults and children; lectures open to public; films; special programs and performances; gallery talks; tours; exten dept serves state of Missouri; individual paintings and original objects of art lent to other museums; traveling exhibitions organized and circulated

L **Richardson Memorial Library,** Forest Park, 63110-1380. Tel 314-721-0067; FAX 314-721-6172. *Librn* Stephanie C Sigala; *Assoc Librn* Marianne L Cavanaugh; *Archivist* Norma Sindelar; *Archives Technician* Polly Coxe; *Admin Asst* Pamela Paterson; *Slide Cur* Cheryl Vogler; *Technical Services Asst* Bette Gorden
Open Tues - Fri 10 AM - 5 PM. Estab 1915 to provide reference and bibliographical service to the museum staff and the adult public; to bibliographically support the collections owned by the museum
Income: Financed by endowment and city appropriation
Library Holdings: Vols 54,000; Per subs 300; Art auction catalogs since 1824; Micro — Fiche, reels; AV — Lantern slides, slides 36,000; Other — Clipping files, exhibition catalogs, pamphlets
Collections: Museum Archives, includes records of Louisiana Purchase Expo (1904) and papers of Morton W May

L **SAINT LOUIS PUBLIC LIBRARY,** Fine Arts Dept, 1301 Olive St, 63103. Tel 314-241-2288; FAX 314-241-3840. *Mgr Fine Arts Dept* Suzy Enns Frechette
Open Mon 10 AM - 9 PM, Tues - Fri 10 AM - 6 PM, Sat 9 AM - 5 PM. Estab Art Department in 1912
Library Holdings: Vols 100,000; Micro — Fiche, reels; AV — Cassettes, motion pictures, rec, slides 17,500; Other — Clipping files 135, exhibition catalogs, pamphlets, reproductions
Collections: Steedman Architectural Library; Local Artists Files

M **UNIVERSITY OF MISSOURI, SAINT LOUIS,** Gallery 210, Art Department, 8001 Natural Bridge Rd, 63121. Tel 314-553-5975. *Dir* Thomas H Kochheiser
Open Mon & Tues 9 AM - 8 PM, Wed - Fri 9 AM - 5 PM. Estab 1972 to exhibit contemporary art of national importance & to provide visual enrichment to campus & community. Average Annual Attendance: 5000
Income: Financed by state appropriation
Publications: Exhibition catalogs: Color Photography; Light Abstractions
Activities: Educ dept on art history; lect open to public; originate traveling exhibitions

WASHINGTON UNIVERSITY
M **Gallery of Art,** Steinberg Hall, Campus Box 1214, 63130. Tel 314-935-5490. *Act Dir* Joseph H Ketner; *Cur* Chris Scoates; *Registrar* Marie Nordimann; *Facilities Tech* David Lobbig; *Admin* Jane Franklin
Open Mon - Fri 10 AM - 5 PM, Sat & Sun 1 - 5 PM, cl Mon from mid-May - Labor Day. No admis fee. Estab 1881, present building opened 1960, for the students of Washington University & the community at large. A modern building containing two floors of gallery space for exhibit of the permanent collection & special exhibitions. Also houses a library of art, archaeology, architecture &

design
Income: Financed by university & private support
Collections: Emphasis on †modern artists, including Miro, Ernst, Picasso, Leger, Moore; many †Old Masters, 19th & 20th century European & American paintings, sculpture, drawings & prints
Publications: Exhibition catalogs
Activities: Lect open to public, 24 vis lectr per year by artists, art historians & architects; symposia; music concerts; films; scholarships; book traveling exhibitions; originate traveling exhibitions; sales shop sells exhibition catalogs & postcards

L **Art & Architecture Library,** 1 Brookings Dr, PO Box 1060, 63130. Tel 314-935-5268; FAX 314-935-4045; Elec Mail AADB@WULIBS.BITNET. *Art & Architecture Librn* Dana Beth; *Circulation & Reserve Supv* Betty Daniel
Open Mon - Thurs 8:30 AM - 10 PM, Fri 8:30 AM - 5 PM, Sat 11 AM - 5 PM, Sun 1 - 9 PM, cl nights & weekends during vacations & intersessions. Supports the academic programs of the School of Fine Arts, the School of Architecture & the Department of Art History & Archaeology
Income: Financed through the university
Library Holdings: Vols 75,000; Per subs 330; Micro — Cards, fiche 1354, prints, reels 245; Other — Exhibition catalogs, pamphlets, reproductions

M **WEBSTER UNIVERSITY,** Loretto-Hilton Center Gallery, 130 Edgar Rd, 63119. Tel 314-968-7171. *Admnr* Tom Lang
Open Mon - Fri 9 AM - 6 PM, Sat & Sun 1 - 5 PM, cl Christmas. No admis fee. Estab 1966
Exhibitions: Cecille Hunt Gallery, May Gallery
Publications: Monthly news releases; exhibition catalogs; books
Activities: Lectures open to the public; concerts; gallery talks; tours; competitions; awards; individual paintings & original objects of art lent

L **Library,** 475 E Lockwood Ave, 63119. Tel 314-968-6951; FAX 314-968-7113. For reference & lending
Library Holdings: Vols 221,897; Per subs 932; Micro — Cards, fiche, prints, reels; AV — A-tapes, cassettes, fs, motion pictures, rec, slides, v-tapes; Other — Exhibition catalogs, manuscripts, pamphlets, photographs, prints, reproductions
Special Subjects: 20th century paintings, prints, sculpture and photography

SPRINGFIELD

A **SOUTHWEST MISSOURI MUSEUM ASSOCIATES INC,** 1111 E Brookside Dr, 65807. Tel 417-866-2716. *Pres* Sharon Deal
Estab 1928 to inform and interest citizens in appreciation of art, and to maintain an art museum as an essential public institution. Mem: 1300; dues sustaining life $1000, life $500, supporting $50, family $40, at large $30, art group: resident $20, extension groups $10
Income: $14,000 (financed by membership)
Publications: Bi-monthly newsletter, in cooperation with the Museum
Activities: Gift shop sells books, original art, prints, reproductions, stationary & gift items; maintain a sales gallery

M **SPRINGFIELD ART MUSEUM,** 1111 E Brookside Dr, 65807. Tel 417-866-2716. *Dir* Jerry A Berger; *Cur of Coll* Greg G Thielen; *Cur Education* Faith Yorty; *Librn* Wanda Rudolph; *Secy* Warren Meadows
Open Tues - Sat 9 AM - 5 PM Wed 6:30 - 9 PM, Sun 1 - 5 PM, cl Mon. No admis fee. Estab 1928 to encourage appreciation and foster education of the visual arts. Museum has three temporary exhibition galleries totaling approximately 7500 sq ft; new wing opened in 1975 contains 400-seat auditorium and sales gallery. Average Annual Attendance: 50,000. Mem: 1300; dues $10 - $1000; annual meeting second Wed in May
Income: $500,000 (financed by mem, city & state appropriations)
Purchases: $40,000
Collections: †American drawing and photography; †American painting and sculpture of all periods; †American print of all periods with emphasis on the 20th Century; †European prints, drawings and paintings from the 17th - 20th Centuries
Activities: Classes for adults and children; lect open to public; concerts; gallery talks; tours; competitions with awards; originate traveling exhibition; sales shop selling books, original art, prints

L **Library,** 1111 E Brookside Dr, 65807. Tel 417-866-2716. *Librn* Wanda Rudolph
Open Tues, Thurs - Sat 9 AM - 5 PM, Wed 9 AM - 5 PM & 6:30 - 9 PM, Sun 1 - 5 PM. Estab 1928 to assist those persons interested in securing information regarding art & artists, craftsmen from ancient times to the present. Circ 1800. Average Annual Attendance: 50,000
Income: Financed by city
Purchases: $4000
Library Holdings: Vols 4300; Per subs 40; Art Access Kits, slide kits & exhibition cards; AV — Cassettes, slides, v-tapes; Other — Clipping files, exhibition catalogs, pamphlets
Collections: American & European paintings, prints & sculpture primarily 19th & 20th Century
Exhibitions: WUSA - Watercolor USA, open to residents & MOAK, Missouri, Oklahoma, Arkansas, Kansas arts & crafts show

ST LOUIS

M **TROVA FOUNDATION,** Philip Samuels Fine Art, 8112 Maryland Ave, 63105. Tel 314-727-2444; FAX 314-727-6084. *Pres* Philip Samuels; *Dir* Clifford Samuels
Open Mon - Fri 10:30 AM - 5:30 PM by appointment. Estab 1988.
Contemporary painting, collage, drawing & sculpture

STOUTSVILLE

M **MARK TWAIN BIRTHPLACE MUSEUM,** Route, PO Box 54, 65283. Tel 314-565-3449. *Site Admin* John Cunning; *Guide* Madeline Loutenschlager
Open Mon - Sat 10 AM - 4 PM, Sun noon - 5 PM. Admis adults $1.25, children between 6 & 12 $ .75. Estab 1960 to preserve the birth cabin of Samuel L Clemens, interpret his life and inform visitors of local history. Foyer and two large exhibit areas. Average Annual Attendance: 24,000
Income: Financed by state appropriation
Collections: Samuel Clemens memorabilia; manuscripts; period furnishings and paintings
Exhibitions: Permanent exhibits depicting the life of Samuel Clemens
Activities: Lectures; tours; craft demonstrations

WARRENSBURG

M **CENTRAL MISSOURI STATE UNIVERSITY,** Art Center Gallery, 64093. Tel 816-543-4498; FAX 816-543-8006. *Gallery Dir* Billi Rothove
Open Sept - Apr, Mon - Fri 8 AM - 5 PM, June & July, Mon - Fri 8 AM - 4 PM. No admis fee. Estab 1984 for the purpose of education through exhibition. Small outer gallery & large main gallery located in the university Art Center. Average Annual Attendance: 3500
Income: Financed by state appropriation and university funding
Collections: †University permanent collection
Exhibitions: Greater Midwest International Annual Visual Art Competition
Activities: Classes for adults; 4 vis lectrs per year; gallery talks; tours; competitions with awards; scholarships & fels offered; individual paintings & original objects of art sold & rented to corporations & college community; traveling exhibitions organized and circulated

MONTANA

ANACONDA

A **COPPER VILLAGE MUSEUM & ARTS CENTER,** 401 E Commercial, 59711. Tel 406-563-2422. *Dir* Linda Talbott; *Pres & Board Dir* Susan Fischer
Open Tues - Fri 10 AM - 5 PM, Sat & Sun 11 AM - 4 PM, cl Mon & holidays. No admis fee. Estab 1971 as Community Arts Center, gallery and regional historical museum. Average Annual Attendance: 15,000. Mem: 150; dues $5-$100
Income: Financed by endowment, membership, city appropriation, fundraising events & individual donations
Collections: Permanent collection holds paintings & prints
Exhibitions: Monthly exhibits of local, national & international art work
Publications: Quarterly newsletters, brochures
Activities: Classes for adults and children; dramatic programs; docent training; lectures open to public; 4 vis lectrs per yr; concerts; gallery talks; tours; awards; scholarships & fels; book traveling exhibitions, 4-8 per yr; originate traveling exhibitions which circulate to Montana Galleries; sales shop sells books, original art, prints, pottery, glass & jewelry

L **Library,** Courthouse, 401 E Commercial, 59711. Tel 406-563-2422. *Dir* Linda Talbott
Library open to the public for reference
Library Holdings: Vols 45; Per subs 11; AV — Motion pictures, slides; Other — Clipping files, memorabilia, pamphlets, reproductions, sculpture
Special Subjects: Western History and Art
Publications: Newletters, quarterly; brochures
Activities: Book traveling exhibitions

BILLINGS

M **PETER YEGEN JR YELLOWSTONE COUNTY MUSEUM,** Logan Field, PO Box 959, 59103. Tel 406-256-6811.
Open 10:30 AM - 5 PM. No admis fee. Estab 1953. Average Annual Attendance: 13,000. Mem: 150; dues $15-$1000; annual meeting in July
Income: $17,000 (financed by county)
Collections: Indian artifacts; settlement of Montana historical items; books; photos
Exhibitions: Dinosaur bones; Indian artifacts military items
Activities: Docent programs

A **YELLOWSTONE ART CENTER,** 401 N 27th St, 59101. Tel 406-256-6804; FAX 406-256-6817. *Pres of Board* Douglas Richardson; *Dir* Donna M Forbes; *Asst Dir* Gordon McDonnell; *Cur* Sheila Miles
Open Tues - Sat 11 AM - 5 PM, Sun noon - 5 PM, Thurs 7 - 9 PM. No admis fee. Estab 1964 to offer a broad program of art exhibitions, both historical and contemporary, of the highest quality, to provide related educational programs. Two large galleries and four smaller ones in a large brick structure. Average Annual Attendance: 25,000. Mem: 850; dues $20 and up; annual meeting third Wed June
Income: $700,000 (financed by membership, contributions & county appropriations, grants, museum shop)
Purchases: Current work by Montana artists
Collections: †Contemporary Print Collection; Poindexter Collection of Abstract Expressionists; †Contemporary Montana Artists
Exhibitions: Jim Roche, Sign Times; Universal Limited Art Editions; Winter Country; Historic & Contemporary Western Winter Paintings, Vernon Fisher; Fred Longan Collection; Historic & Contemporary Photographs, Bruce Charlesworth; Neltje (paintings); 23rd Annual Auction (paintings)
Publications: Bi-monthly exhibition announcements; newsletter, bi-monthly; exhibition catalogues, 4-6 per yr

Activities: Docent training; lectures open to public, 6 vis lectrs per yr; gallery talks; tours; chamber concerts; individual paintings and original art objects lent to museums and art centers; originate traveling exhibitions; museum shop selling books, original art, reproductions, prints, jewelry, pottery and posters

BOZEMAN

MONTANA STATE UNIVERSITY
M **Museum of the Rockies,** 59717. Tel 406-994-2251; FAX 406-994-2682. *Dir* Arthur H Wolf; *Asst Dir* Judy Weaver; *Cur Art & Photography* Steve Jackson
Open 9 AM - 9 PM Memorial Day - Labor Day; winter, Tues - Sat 9 AM - 5 PM, Sun 1 - 5 PM, cl Mon. Admis family $10, adult $3, children 5-18 & MSU students $2, children under 5 free. Estab in 1958 to interpret the physical and cultural heritages of the Northern Rockies region. Rotation gallery features changing exhibitions. Average Annual Attendance: 160,000. Mem: 4200; dues directors circle $500, sustaining $250, contribution $100, family $45, non-resident family $30, individual $20, MSU student $10
Income: Financed by MSU, fundraising, grants & revenue
Collections: Art Works by R E DeCamp; Edgar Paxton; C M Russell; O C Seltzer; William Standing; geology; paleontology; astronomy, archaeological artifacts; history and western art; regional native Americans
Publications: Quarterly newsletter; papers
Activities: Classes for adults & children; docent training; dramatic programs; lectures open to public & members, planetarium shows, classes, field trips, field schools, gallery talks; tours; traveling portable planetarium, book traveling exhibitions; originate traveling exhibitions; museum shop sells books, magazines, original art, reproductions, prints, slides, crafts, toys, hats, t-shirts, stationery
M **Haynes Fine Arts Gallery,** School of Art, Haynes Hall Rm 213, 59717. Tel 406-994-2562; FAX 406-994-2893. *Gallery Dir* John Anacker
Open Mon - Fri 8 AM - 5 PM. No admis fee. Estab 1894 to present exhibitions of national interest. A new building with a small gallery space adjacent to offices and studio classrooms. Average Annual Attendance: 10,000
Income: Financed by university appropriation
Collections: Japanese Patterns, Native American Ceramics, WPA Prints
Activities: Lectures open to the public, 5 visiting lecturers per year; gallery talks; competitions
L **Creative Arts Library,** 207 Cheever Hall, Creative Arts Complex, 59717. Tel 406-994-4091. *Librn* Kathy Kaya
Open Mon - Thurs 7:45 AM - 10 PM, Fri 7:45 AM - 5 PM, Sat & Sun 1 - 5 PM. Estab 1974 to support the Schools of Architecture and Art
Income: Financed by state appropriation
Library Holdings: Vols 17,000; Per subs 100; Matted reproductions; AV — Slides 79,000

BROWNING

M **MUSEUM OF THE PLAINS INDIAN & CRAFTS CENTER,** US Hwy 89 & 2, 59417. Tel 406-338-2230. *Cur* Loretta F Pepion
Open June - Sept, daily 9 AM - 5 PM, Oct - May Mon - Fri 10 AM - 4:30 PM, cl New Year's Day, Thanksgiving Day and Christmas. No admis fee. Estab 1941 to promote the development of contemporary Native American arts & crafts, administered and operated by the Indian Arts and Crafts Board, US Dept of the Interior. Average Annual Attendance: 80,000
Income: Financed by federal appropriation
Collections: Contemporary Native American arts & crafts; historic works by Plains Indian craftsmen & artists
Exhibitions: Historic arts created by the tribal peoples of the Northern Plains; Traditional costumes of Northern Plains men, women & children; Art forms related to the social & ceremonial aspects of the regional tribal cultures; Winds of Change: Five Screen Multi-Media Presentation of the Evolution of Indian Cultures on the Northern Plains; One-Person exhibitons of Native American artists & craftsmen; Architectural decorations, including carved wood panels by sculptor John Clarke & a series of murals by Victor Pepion
Publications: Continuing series of brochures for one-person shows, exhibition catalogues
Activities: Gallery talks; tours; demonstrations of Native American arts & crafts; traveling exhibitions organized and circulated; sales shop sells books, original art

BUTTE

M **BUTTE SILVER BOW ARTS CHATEAU,** 321 W Broadway, 59701. Tel 406-723-7600. *Dir* Sharon Knauth
Open Sept - May Tues - Sun 1 - 4 PM, June - Aug Tues - Sat 10 AM - 5 PM, Sun 1 - 4 PM, cl major holidays. Admis donation. Estab 1977 to further all forms of art. 1898 French Chateau converted to galleries. Mem: 350; dues Business: benefactor $1000, patron $750, sustaining $500, contributing $100, active $10; Individual: benefactor $1000, patron $500, sustaining $100, contributing $50, family $25, active $10; annual meeting Jan
Collections: Contemporary regional art
Publications: Newsletter
Activities: Classes for adults, dramatic programs; lectures open to public, 10 vis lectr per year; gallery talks; tours; book traveling exhibitions, 4 per year; sales shop sells original art, reproductions & prints

CHESTER

M **LIBERTY VILLAGE ARTS CENTER AND GALLERY,** Main St, PO Box 269, 59522. Tel 406-759-5652. *Dir* Jennie Hollister-Didier
Open Tues - Fri Sun 1 - 5 PM, cl New Years, Easter, Thanksgiving & Christmas. No admis fee. Estab 1976 to provide community with traveling exhibitions & education center. Average Annual Attendance: 1500-2000. Mem: 50; dues patron $100 & up, Friend of the Arts $50 - $99, family $25, individual $20; annual meeting Oct
Collections: Works by local artists, paintings & quilts

Activities: Classes for adults & children; workshops; film series; lectures open to public, 5 vis lectr per yr; gallery talks; competitions with awards; book traveling exhibitions; originate traveling exhibitions; museum shop sells books, original art & prints

DILLON

M **WESTERN MONTANA COLLEGE,** Art Gallery/Museum, 710 S Atlantic, 59725-3598. Tel 406-683-7126. *Interim Dir* Laura Kat Hawkins; *Cur* Jim Corr
Open Mon - Fri noon - 3 PM, Tues 7 PM - 9 PM. No admis fee. Estab 1970 to display art works of various kinds, used as an educational facility. Located in the south end of Old Main Hall Seidensticker Wildlife Collection. Average Annual Attendance: 7000
Income: Financed through college funds
Collections: †Emerick Art Book Collection; Seidensticker Wildlife
Activities: Education dept; scholarships; artmobile
L **Lucy Carson Memorial Library,** 710 S Atlantic, 59725-3598. Tel 406-683-7541; FAX 406-683-7493. *Head Librn* Mike Schultz
Library open to the public
Library Holdings: Vols 4500; Per subs 12; AV — V-tapes 140

GREAT FALLS

M **CASCADE COUNTY HISTORICAL SOCIETY,** Cascade County Historical Museum & Archives, 1400 First Ave N, 59401. Tel 406-452-3462. *Dir & Cur* Cindy Kittredge; *Cur Colls* Barbara Brewer; *Archives* Julianne Ruby; *Bookkeeper* Kim Hulten; *Gift Shop Mgr* Claudette Bourcier
Open summer, Mon - Fri 10 AM - 5 PM, Sat & Sun noon - 5PM, winter, Tues - Fri 10 AM - 5 PM, Sat & Sun noon - 5 PM, cl holidays. No admis fee. Estab 1976 to preserve & interpret the history of the Cascade County area & the diverse area heritage. The historical museum is housed in a school building built in 1895, which is functioning as an art center and historical museum. Auxiliary site open in the summer at State Fairgrounds. Open Thurs - Sun noon - 5 PM (Memorial Day to Labor Day). Average Annual Attendance: 9000. Mem: 400; dues corporate $250; patron $200; sustainer $50; sponsor $100; family $20; individual $15; senior citizen $10; annual meeting third Thurs in Feb
Income: $102,000 (financed by mem dues, donations, memorials, sales shop, grants)
Collections: Art, documents, manuscripts, photographs, objects reflecting the history of the local area; clothing, furniture & memorabilia from Great Falls & Cascade County
Exhibitions: Exhibits from the permanent collections, changed quarterly
Activities: Educ dept, classes for adults & childrens; Lect open to public; tours; 10 lect per year; individual paintings & original objects of art lent to other museums; Book traveling expedition once a yr; originate traveling expedition to schools & smaller areas town businesses; museum shop sells books, original arts, reproductions & prints

M **PARIS GIBSON SQUARE,** Museum of Art, 1400 First Ave N, 59401. Tel 406-727-8255. *Dir* Elizabeth Kennedy; *Cur* Barbara Racker
Open Tues - Fri 10 AM - 5 PM, Sat & Sun 12 - 5 PM, cl Mon. No admis fee. Estab 1976 to exhibit contemporary & historical art. Maintains 3 galleries which consist of 1100 ft of running wall space. Average Annual Attendance: 57,000. Mem: 550-650; mem open to public; dues $20; annual meetings in June
Income: $300,000 (financed by mem, grants, contributions & county mill)
Collections: †Contemporary regional artists; Montana folk-art naive sculptures (polychromed wood), Lee Steen
Exhibitions: (1989) Western States Art Foundation. (1991) Robert Cardbas, James Craig, Tom Ferris; Tactice Vessel Paul Slaton; All City Student Art Show; Portraits
Publications: Artist postcards, bi-monthly exhibition announcements, Exhibition Quarterly
Activities: Classes for adults & children; docent training; lect open to public, 10-15 vis lectr per yr; gallery talks; tours; book traveling exhibitions, 1-3 per year; originate traveling exhibitions; Museum shop sells Montana original art, reproductions, prints, ceramics, museum cards & gift items

M **C M RUSSELL MUSEUM,** 400 13th St N, 59401. Tel 406-727-8787; FAX 406-727-2402. *Dir* Lorne E Render; *Cur* Elizabeth Dear; *Registrar* Janet W Postler
Open during winter Tues - Sat 10 AM - 5 PM, Sun 1 - 5 PM, cl Mon; summer (May 1 - Oct 30) Mon - Sat 9 AM - 6 PM, Sun 1 - 5 PM. Admis adults $4, students $2, sr citizens $3, children under 5 free. Estab 1953 to preserve art of Charles M Russell, western painter. Museum includes Russell's home & original studio; has seven galleries of Western art/photographs & Indian artifacts. Average Annual Attendance: 65,000. Mem: 1750; dues $20 - $1000; annual meeting in May
Income: Financed by operating budget
Collections: Works by Charles M Russell & other Western works including Seltzer, Couse, Wieghorst, Heikka, Reiss, Farny. Historical & contemporary
Exhibitions: Traveling exhibitions of western art permanent exhibitions. (1993) Robert M Scriver; Taos Artists; Contemporary Indian Art
Publications: Magazine, semi-annually; newsletter, quarterly
Activities: Classes for children; docent training; lectures open to public; gallery talks; tours; Annual C M Russell Auction; individual paintings & original objects of art lent to other appropriate institutions; museum store sells books, magazines, reproductions, prints, jewelry, pottery
L **Frederic G Renner Memorial Library,** 400 13th St N, 59401. Tel 406-727-8787; FAX 406-727-2402. *Librn* Janet W Postler
Open same hrs as museum. Estab 1965 to provide research material on Western art & artists, primarily C M Russell & The History of Montana & The West. For reference only
Income: $2500 (financed by private contributions)
Library Holdings: Vols 2500; Per subs 6; AV — Motion pictures, slides, v-tapes; Other — Clipping files, exhibition catalogs, manuscripts, memorabilia, pamphlets, photographs, reproductions

Special Subjects: American Western Art, Art History, Painting - American, Southwestern Art
Collections: Joseph Henry Sharp Collection of Indian Photographs; Yost Archival Collection; Flood Archival Collection
Publications: C M Russell Museum Newsletter, quarterly; Russell's West, semi-annual magazine

HAMILTON

M **RAVALLI COUNTY MUSEUM,** 205 Bedford, Old Court House, 59840. Tel 406-363-3338. *Dir* Helen Ann Bibler; *Treas* Open
Open summer Mon - Thurs 10 AM - 4 PM, Sun 2:30 - 5 PM, winter Mon - Thurs 1 - 4 PM. No admis fee. Estab 1979 to preserve the history of the Bitterroot Valley. Museum contains Flathead Indian exhibit, Rocky Mt Spotted Fever display, pioneer rooms, schoolroom, tack & trophy room extensive archives. Average Annual Attendance: 9000. Mem: 160; dues regular $5, sr citizen $2, family $10; meetings third Mon of each month
Income: Financed by county appropriation & gifts from Bitterroot Valley Historical Society
Purchases: $5000
Collections: Home furnishings reflecting early life of the Bitterroot Valley; Indian Railroad
Exhibitions: Daly Days; Porcelain Artists Exhibit; Quilt Shows; local collections exhibited; traveling art shows
Publications: An Old Bitter Rooters Thoughts in Poetry, Joe Hughes; Bitterroot Trails, Bitterroot Historical Society; McIntosh Apple Cookbook; Historic Survey of Hamilton Buildings 1890 - 1940; The Vicbor Story, Jeffrey H Langton; The Yellow Pine; May Vallance
Activities: Lectures open to public; concerts, gallery talks; book traveling exhibitions; sales shop sells locally made china art, cards, books, original arts & prints

HELENA

A **MONTANA HISTORICAL SOCIETY,** 225 N Roberts, 59620. Tel 406-444-2694; FAX 406-444-2695. *Dir* Brian Cockhill; *Business Mgr* Sharon McCabe
Open Mon - Fri 8 AM - 5 PM, Sat 9 AM - 5 PM, Sun (Memorial Day - Labor Day) 9 AM - 5 PM. No admis fee. Estab 1865 to collect, preserve and present articles relevant to history and heritage of Montana and the Northwest. Mackay Gallery of C M Russell Art; temporary exhibits gallery. Average Annual Attendance: 93,000. Mem: 4000; dues $40
Income: $27,000 (financed by State of Montana General Fund, private gifts and grants; federal grants, earned revenue)
Collections: †Haynes Collection of Art and Artifacts; MacKay Collection of C M Russell Art; Poindexter Collection of Contemporary Art; Montana artists; late 19th & 20th century Western art; ethnographic & decorative arts
Exhibitions: Bronzes of the American West; Mackay Gallery of C M Russell Art
Publications: Montana, Magazine of Western History, quarterly; Montana Post (newsletter), quarterly
Activities: Educational programs for adults & children; docent training; lect open to public, 10 vis lectr per year; concerts; gallery talks; tours; scholarships & fels; individual paintings & original objects of art lent to museums, galleries, historical societies, bonafide organizations & corporations; lending collection includes 300 color transparencies, 200 original art works, 500,000 photographs, 40 sculptures, 1000 slides; book traveling exhibitions; traveling exhibitions organized and circulated; sales shop selling books, magazines, prints, reproductions, slides
L **Library,** 225 N Roberts, 59620. Tel 406-444-2694. *Dir* Brian Cockhill; *Cur Coll* Kirby Lambert; *Photograph Cur* Delores Morrow
For reference and research only
Income: Financed by State of Montana
Library Holdings: Vols 4000; Per subs 100; Other — Clipping files, exhibition catalogs, manuscripts, pamphlets, photographs
Special Subjects: American Indian Art, American Western Art, Anthropology, Archaeology, Ethnology, Historical Material, Painting - American, Montana history
Collections: Historical artifacts; Late 19th & 20th century art; photo collection; manuscripts
Publications: Montana: The Magazine of Western History, quarterly

KALISPELL

A **HOCKADAY CENTER FOR THE ARTS,** Second Ave E & Third St, PO Box 83, 59901. Tel 406-755-5268. *Dir* Magee Nelson
Open Tues - Sat 10 AM - 5 PM. No admis fee. Estab 1968 to foster and encourage a growing interest in and understanding of all the arts; to provide the opportunity to take a place in the main current of the arts today, as well as to observe and learn from the arts of the past. Center is housed in the former Carnegie Library near downtown Kalispell; has five spacious exhibition galleries & a sales gallery. Mem: 1000; dues benefactor $50; patron $35; family $30; individual $15; student & sr citizen $8
Income: $110,000 (financed by memberships, contributions, grants, exhibition sponsors, corporate donations and city-county funds)
Collections: Main collection includes eight portrait studies by Hugh Hockaday, artist of regional significance & the center's late namesake, as well as the works of Theodore Waddell, David Shaner, Russell Chatham & others
Exhibitions: Eight to twelve traveling & regional exhibitions per yr
Publications: Exhibition catalogs; newsletter, monthly
Activities: Classes for adults & children; drama programs; docent training; gallery talks open to public; annual film tour; summer and winter art festival; sponsors competitions with awards; book traveling exhibitions, 3-7 per year; originate traveling exhibitions; sales shop sells local artists' paintings

LEWISTOWN

A **LEWISTOWN ART CENTER,** 801 W Broadway, 59457. Tel 406-538-8278. *Dir* Ellen Gerharz
Open Tues - Sat 11:30 AM - 5:30 PM, cl Mon. Estab 1971 for advancement & education in the arts. The gallery exhibitions change monthly showing a variety of local, state & national art work. A sales gallery features Montana artists & local artists. Average Annual Attendance: 5000. Mem: 500; dues $1 - $15; annual meeting in July
Income: $52,000 (financed entirely by mem, donations, sponsorships by local businesses, & art grants)
Exhibitions: In-state shows; Juried Art Auction; regional shows
Publications: Newsletter, bimonthly
Activities: Arts classes & workshops for adults & children; dramatic programs; lect open to the public, 3 - 4 vis lectr per year; gallery talks; tours; scholarships; individual paintings & original objects of art lent to schools, churches & businesses; sales shop sells books, original art, reproductions, prints, sculpture, pottery, wall hangings, jewelry, fiber arts & wood crafts

MILES CITY

A **CUSTER COUNTY ART CENTER,** Water Plant Rd, PO Box 1284, 59301. Tel 406-232-0635, 232-0637. *Exec Dir* Susan McDaniel; *Asst Dir* Ronda Worlie
Open Tues - Sun 1 - 5 PM, cl holidays. No admis fee. Estab 1977 to open an arts program of exhibits and educational activities to residents of Southeastern Montana. Maintains The Water Works Gallery, located in the former holding tanks of the old Miles City Water Works. Average Annual Attendance: 10,000. Mem: 500; dues benefactor $500, patron $300, sponsor $100, sustaining $75, contributing $50, family $30, individual $20, student & sr citizens $10
Income: $110,000 (financed by mem, fundraising events & grants)
Collections: Edward S Curtis Photographic Collection; Contemporary Montana Artists
Exhibitions: Custer County Art Center annual juried art exhibit; annual Art Auction Exhibit; plus eight additional temporary exhibits per year; Western Art Roundup & Quick Draw during Bucking Horse Sale Weekend
Publications: Newsletter, quarterly; exhibit catalogs, biannually
Activities: Classes for adults & children; lect open to the public, 4 vis lectr per yr; gallery talks; tours; competitions; films; exten dept serves schools; book traveling exhibitions; originate traveling exhibitions; museum store sells pottery, jewelry, books, prints, original art & gifts from regional crafts people

MISSOULA

M **FORT MISSOULA HISTORICAL MUSEUM,** Bldg 322, Fort Missoula, 59801. Tel 406-728-3476. *Dir* Robert Brown; *Cur* L Jane Richards
Open Tues - Sun noon - 5 PM. No admis fee. Estab July 4, 1976 to collect and exhibit artifacts related to the history of western Montana. Changing gallery, 900 sq ft used for temporary exhibits; Meeting room gallery, 200 sq ft; Permanent gallery, 1200 sq ft. Average Annual Attendance: 14,000. Mem: 225; annual dues $10; meetings third Thursday in May
Income: $70,000 (financed by membership, county appropriation and fund raising events)
Collections: Photograph collection
Exhibitions: Timber: Fort Missoula 1877-1947; Missoula: a Community Evolved
Activities: Classes for adults and children; lectures open to public; gallery talks; tours; book traveling exhibitions; sales shop sells books, magazines, original art

M **MISSOULA MUSEUM OF THE ARTS,** 335 N Pattee, 59802. Tel 406-728-0447. *Dir* Laura J Millin; *Cur* Deborah Mitchell; *Adminr* Billie Bloom
Open Mon - Sat noon - 5 PM. No admis fee. Estab 1975. Housed in renovated Carnegie Library (1903) featuring soft-panel covered walls; moveable track lighting; approx 3500 sq ft of exhibits space on two floors; fire and security alarm systems; meeting rooms. Average Annual Attendance: 20,000. Mem: 600
Income: $135,000 (financed by membership, grants, fund raising events & annual permissive mill levy by Missoula County)
Purchases: Contemporary Art of Western Montana
Collections: †Contemporary Art of Western Montana
Publications: Exhibit catalogs; membership newsletter; mailers & posters advertising shows
Activities: Classes for adults & children; docent training; lect open to public, 6 - 8 vis lectrs per year; gallery talks; tours; competitions; prize & purchase awards; films; book traveling exhibitions 8-10 per year; museum shop sells artists made jewelry, toys & video

UNIVERSITY OF MONTANA
M **Gallery of Visual Arts,** School of Fine Arts, 59812. Tel 406-243-2019, 243-4970. *Dir* Dennis D Kern; *Admin Officer* Bryan D Spellman
Open Tues - Sat 11 AM - 3 PM. No admis fee. Estab 1981 to present faculty, student & outside exhibitions of contemporary emphasis for community interest. Gallery has 220 linear ft, 2800 sq ft; adjustable lighting. Average Annual Attendance: 15,000
Exhibitions: (1992) Art Department Faculty Exhibit. (1993) Jeff Key & Bruce Guttin (sculpture); Bachelor of Fine Art Exhibit; MFA Thesis Exhibits
Activities: Educ dept; internships for gallery management; lectures open to public, 1 - 3 vis lectrs per year; gallery talks; tours; competitions; campus art awards; Thomas Wickes Award
M **Paxson Gallery,** School of Fine Arts, Performing Arts/Radio-TV Bldg, 59812. Tel 406-243-2019. *Dean* James D Kriley; *Cur* Dennis D Kern; *Admin Officer* Bryan D Spellman
Open Mon - Fri 9 AM - noon & 1 - 4 PM. No admis fee. Estab 1985 to exhibit permanent art collection & selected traveling exhibitions. Gallery has 190 linear ft, 670 sq ft; adjustable space & lighting. Average Annual Attendance: 50,000 - 60,000
Collections: Autio Ceramics Collection; Dana Collection; Duncan Collection; McGill Collection; contemporary †ceramic sculpture & †paintings; historical

furniture; Western genre paintings
Exhibitions: (1992) Walter Hooks, Last Works. (1993) Centennial Exhibit; Ron Klien (sculpture); MFA Thesis Exhibit
Activities: Educ dept; internships for collection & gallery management; lectures open to public; original objects of art lent to Montana Art Gallery Directors' Association members; loans of historical objects to Montana museums; lending collection contains 25 original prints, 250 paintings & 105 photographs; book traveling exhibitions, 1 - 5 per year; originate traveling exhibitions to any museum or gallery meeting staff & security requirements

PRYOR

M CHIEF PLENTY COUPS MUSEUM, PO Box 100, 59066. Tel 406-252-1289. *Regional Mgr* Ray Bernsten; *Dir* Rich Pittsley; *Int* Lawrence Flat Lip
Open May 1 - Sept 30 daily 10 AM - 5 PM. Admis $3 per vehicle (park entrance fee includes museum). Estab 1972. Average Annual Attendance: 5000
Income: Financed by state appropriation; affiliated with Montana Fish, Wildlife and Parks
Collections: Ethnographic materials of the Crow Indians; paintings; drawings; prehistoric artifacts
Exhibitions: Crow clothing and adornment
Activities: Tours; sales shop sells books, prints, stationary notes, Crow crafts & beadwork

SIDNEY

M MONDAK HERITAGE CENTER, 120 Third Ave SE, PO Box 50, 59270. Tel 406-482-3500. *Exec Dir* Bert Sawyer; *Exec Dir* Marie Sawyer; *Admin Asst* Becky Dige
Open Tues - Sun 1 - 5 PM. No admis fee. Estab 1972 to preserve history of area and further interest in fine arts. Average Annual Attendance: 13,000. Mem: 300; dues $5 & up; annual meeting Mar
Income: Financed by county appropriations, membership dues, grants & donations
Collections: J K Ralston originals; Mortensen woodcut prints
Exhibitions: (1992) Quilt Display; 13th Annual Juried Quilt Show; Youth Art Show; Edna Loughney; Ed Frank; Quiet Shadows: Women in the Pacific War; Rising Star Studio Show; Ken Jorgenson; Freeman Butts; Japanese Folk Toys; 3rd Annual MonDak Photography Show; Sheepranching in Paradise; 15th Annual Custer County Juried Art Show; Decline of the Empire; Docent Sponsored Teddy Bear Show; MonDak Juried Art Show; Ethnic Christman Celebration: Russia; Artists in Retrospect; Sidney Artists
Publications: MonDak Historical & Arts Society Newsletter, 6 times yearly
Activities: Educ dept; docent training; classes for adults & children; dramatic programs; lect open to public; 2 vis lectr per year; gallery talks; tours; competitions with awards; individual paintings & original objects of art lent to other museums & galleries; lending collection contains books; sales shop sells books, magazines, original art, reproductions, prints, pottery & calendars
L Willo Ralston Library for Historical Research, 120 Third Ave SE, PO Box 50, 59270. Tel 406-482-3500. *Exec Dir* Bert Sawyer; *Exec Dir* Marie Sawyer
Open to the public for historical reference
Income: Financed by County Mill levy
Library Holdings: Vols 1500; Micro — Reels; Other — Clipping files, exhibition catalogs, manuscripts, memorabilia, pamphlets, photographs
Activities: Tours

NEBRASKA

AURORA

M PLAINSMAN MUSEUM, 210 16th, 68818. Tel 402-694-6531. *Dir* Gwen Allen; *Asst Dir* John Green
Open April 1 - Oct 31 Mon - Sat 9 AM - 5 PM, Sun 1 - 5 PM, Nov 1 - Mar 31 Mon - Sun 1 - 5 PM. Admis adults $3.50, sr citizens $2.50, children $1. Estab 1976 to tell the story of Plainsman using mosaics, murals, & period homes, boardwalk with many shops, other settings to add to use of artifacts. Museum rotunda is exhibit area for eight 20 ft x 8 ft murals & mosaic tile floor, octagonal in shape measuring 58 ft across & depicting the birds & the animals of the prairie with plainsman centered. Agricultural Museum dedicated 1986. Houses homestead dating 1881-house, barn, workshop, windmill. Large collection of horsedrawn equipment & vintage machinery. Replicas of Hamilton County Court House and Nebraska State Capitol. Average Annual Attendance: 15,000. Mem: 350; dues family $15, singles $8; annual meeting third Thurs in Jan
Income: $60,000 (financed by membership, county allowance and individual donations)
Collections: Murals by Sidney E King; †Pioneer Scene Mosaic Floor; 2 large murals by Ernest Ochsner; 1 large pen & ink mural (20 ft x 8 ft) by Larry Guyton
Activities: Docent training; lect open to public; concerts, tours; museum shop sells books, reproductions, Hamilton County Bicentennial plates, post cards & note cards

CHADRON

M CHADRON STATE COLLEGE, Arts Gallery, Tenth and Main Sts, 69337. Tel 308-432-4451, Ext 6317. *Coordr* Dr Noel Gray
Open Mon - Fri 8 AM - 5 PM. No admis fee. Estab 1967 to offer opportunities for students, faculty and local artists to present their works; to bring in shows to upgrade the cultural opportunities of students and the general public. Main gallery has space for traveling and larger shows; little gallery suffices for small

shows. Average Annual Attendance: 5000
Income: Financed by college budget and state appropriation
Exhibitions: Arts and Crafts Fair; Bosworth, Rickenbach Exhibits; Da Vinci Model Show by IBM; Edges: Hard and Soft; Faculty Art Show; Former Students Works; Hands in Clay; Greg Lafler: Ceramics and Crafts; Photographs of the Farm Security Administration; Roten Galleries: Graphics Show; National Cone Box Traveling Show; Iowa Arts & Crafts; Mathew Brady, photographs State of the Print; Student Art Show; Of Dustbowl Descent
Activities: Lectures open to public; gallery talks; competitions with awards

CHAPPELL

L CHAPPELL MEMORIAL LIBRARY AND ART GALLERY, 289 Babcock, PO Box 248, 69129. Tel 308-874-2626. *Head Librn* Dixie Riley; *Asst Librn* Doris McFee
Open Tues - Thurs 2 - 5 PM, Tues & Thurs evening 7 - 9 PM. No admis fee. Estab 1935 by gift of Mrs Charles H Chappell
Income: Financed by city of Chappell
Library Holdings: Vols 10,398; Per subs 31
Collections: Permanent personal collection of art works from many countries, a gift from Mrs Charles H Chappell; Aaran Pyle Collection
Activities: Gallery talks; library tours

GERING

M OREGON TRAIL MUSEUM ASSOCIATION, Scotts Bluff National Monument, Hwy 92 W, PO Box 27, 69341. Tel 308-436-4340; FAX 308-436-7611. *Supt* JoAnn Kyral; *Chief Ranger* Palma Wilson; *Business Mgr* Jolene Kaufman; *Museum Technician* Audrey Barnhart
Open June - Sept 8 AM - 8 PM, Oct - May 8 AM - 5 PM, cl Christmas & New Year's Day. No admis fee. Estab 1919 to preserve & display Oregon Trail landmark, artifacts, art & natural resources. 3 exhibit rooms. Average Annual Attendance: 170,000. Mem: 75; dues $3
Income: Financed by sales of Oregon Trail Museum Association
Collections: Watercolors, drawings, & photographs by William H Jackson; surface finds from the Oregon Trail vicinity; paleontological specimens from within Monument boundaries
Exhibitions: 6 exhibits depicting geological, prehistoric, archaeological, ethnological history of the area; 15 exhibits depicting history of western migration from 1840-1870s; photos, drawings & paintings by W H Jackson; 2 dioramas depicting interaction between white man & buffalo
Publications: The Overland Migration; brochures & handbooks
Activities: Slide presentation of history of Oregon Trail & Scotts Bluff; Living History presentation of life on the trail; lectures open to public; museum shop sells books, prints, slides, postcards

HASTINGS

M HASTINGS MUSEUM, 1330 N Burlington Ave, 68901. Tel 402-461-2399; FAX 402-461-2379. *Dir* Ed Bisaillon; *Pres Board Trustees* Jack Osbrone; *Cur Exhib* Burton R Nelson; *Museum Coordr* Geraldine S Shuman; *Cur Astronomy* Mark A Hartman; *Exhib Specialist* Jerome Dierfeldt; *Educ Coordr* Joan Janzen
Open Mon - Sat 9 AM - 5 PM, Sun 1 - 5 PM. Admis adults $2, children (7-15) $1, tots free. Estab 1926 for a program of service and exhibits to augment and stimulate the total educative program of schools and the general public. Animal displays in natural habitat settings. Average Annual Attendance: 35,000. Mem: 1750; dues life $100, family $7.50, individual $4
Income: Financed by city appropriation
Collections: Glassware; Irma Kruse Collection; Richards Coin Collection; George W Cole Smith and Wesson Gun Collection; American Indian Artifacts
Exhibitions: People on the Plains; Natural Habitats
Publications: Yester News, monthly except July, August & Sept
Activities: Sales shop selling books and selected gift items

HOLDREGE

M PHELPS COUNTY HISTORICAL SOCIETY, Phelps County Museum, PO Box 164, 68949-0164. Tel 308-995-5015. *Pres* Don Lindgren; *VPres* Eileen Schrock; *Treas* Bernice Lindgren
Open Mon - Sat 10 AM - 5 PM, Sun 1 - 5 PM, cl Jan 1, July 4, Thanksgiving, Armistice Day & Christmas. No admis fee. Estab 1966 for preservation of County history and artifacts. Average Annual Attendance: 9500. Mem: 450; dues life $100, annual $5; annual meeting May
Income: Financed by membership, county mill levy, state contributions & estate gifts
Collections: Agriculture equipment, china, furniture, historical items, photos
Publications: History of Phelps County, 1873-1980; Centennial History of Holdrege, 1883; Holdrege Centennial Coloring Book
Activities: Lectures open to the public, 4 vis lectr per yr; tours; book traveling exhibitions; sales shop sells books, labels, souvenir plates, original art
L Library, 68949
Open Mon - Sat 10 AM - 5 PM, Sun 1 - 5 PM. Admis donations only. Estab 1966 for historic preservation & education. Collections available for in museum research only. Average Annual Attendance: 10,000. Mem: 350; dues $5; annual meeting in May
Library Holdings: Vols 1000; AV — A-tapes, cassettes, Kodachromes, lantern slides, motion pictures, v-tapes; Other — Clipping files, manuscripts, pamphlets, photographs, prints
Activities: Classes for adults & children; lect open to public, 4 vis lectr per year; tours; sales shop sells books, reproductions, prints, toys, ceramics

LEXINGTON

M DAWSON COUNTY HISTORICAL SOCIETY, Museum, PO Box 369, 68850-0369. Tel 308-324-5340. *Dir* Bob Wallace; *Asst Dir* Genice Gordening; *Cur* Open
Open Mon - Sun 9 AM - 5 PM. Admis $1. Estab 1958 to preserve Dawson County's heritage. Art gallery features exhibits by local artists; exhibits change monthly. Average Annual Attendance: 6000. Mem: 450; dues life $100, family $7.50, individual $5
Income: Financed by endowment, mem, grants, county appropriation
Library Holdings: Per subs 4
Collections: Agricultural Equipment; Furniture; Glassware; Household Implements; Textiles; Tools
Exhibitions: 1919 McCoto Aeroplane
Publications: Dawson County Banner newsletter, quarterly
Activities: Docent programs; lectures open to public, 3 vis lectr per yr; book traveling exhibitions 4 per yr; retail store sells books, original art, fossils

LINCOLN

M HAYMARKET ART GALLERY, 119 S Ninth St, 68508. Tel 402-475-1061. *Dir* Louise Holt; *Pres* Dorothy Thompson; *VPres* Elaine Williams
Open Tues - Sat 10 AM - 5 PM, cl Sun & Mon. No admis fee. Estab 1968 as a non-profit organization to exhibit, promote & sell works by regional artists. Located in 100 yr old building near downtown Lincoln; main floor & basement include over 3000 sq ft exhibit area, office, storage & kitchen; second floor contains rented artist studios & classrooms. Mem: 172; dues fr o $15; annual meeting 2nd Fri in June
Income: Financed by mem, commissions on sales
Exhibitions: Monthly exhibits of gallery artists' work; Christman at Haymarket
Publications: Exhibit announcements 9 - 10 per yr
Activities: Classes for adults & children; competitions with awards; scholarships offered to Lincoln high school students pursuing art in college

A LINCOLN ARTS COUNCIL, PO Box 83051, 68501. Tel 402-434-2787. *Pres* Al Hamersky; *Exec Dir* Steve Tremble
Open 8 AM - 5 PM. Estab 1966 to promote & encourage the community at large & all its arts organizations to grow, develop, use all the resources available, avoid overlapping of energy, money, talent; clearing house for arts activities scheduling. Mem: 400; 60 groups; dues prorated; meetings monthly Sept - May
Income: Financed by endowment, membership, city and state appropriation, community arts fund
Publications: Arts calendar; newsletter
Activities: Educ dept; classes for adults & children; lect open to the public; 5 vis lectr per year; concerts; gallery talks; tours; arts festival; awards; outreach to handicapped

M NEBRASKA STATE CAPITOL, 1445 K St, 68509-4924. Tel 402-471-3191; FAX 402-471-0421. *Mgr Capitol Restoration & Promotion* Robert C Ripley; *Preservation* Thomas L Kaspar
Open Mon - Fri 8 AM - 5 PM, Sat 10 AM - 5 PM, Sun & holidays 1 - 5 PM. Stone carvings of BAS reliefs; mosaic tile vaulting & floor panels; painted & mosaic murals; vernacular architectural ornamentation. Average Annual Attendance: 100,000
Income: Financed by state appropriation & private donations
Purchases: Eight murals commissioned to complete Capitol Thematic Program
Collections: Lee Lawrie, building sculptor; Hildreth Meiere, mosaicist; muralists - Augustos V Tack, Kenneth Evett, James Penny, Elizabeth Dolan, Jean Reynal, Reinhold Marxhausen, F John Miller, Charles Clement
Publications: A Harmony of the Arts - The Nebraska State Capitol
Activities: Univ of Nebraska lect & service organization lect; retail store sells books & prints

M NEBRASKA WESLEYAN UNIVERSITY, Elder Gallery, 50th & Huntington, 68504. Tel 402-466-2371, 465-2230. *Dir* Betty Wallace
Open Tues - Fri 10 AM - 4 PM, Sat & Sun 1 - 4 PM. No admis fee. Estab 1966 as a cultural addition to college and community. Average Annual Attendance: 10,000
Collections: Campus collection; †permanent collection of prints, paintings and sculpture
Exhibitions: Annual Fred Wells 10-state juried exhibition; Nebraska Art Educators; faculty show; students shows; other changing monthly shows
Activities: Classes for adults

UNIVERSITY OF NEBRASKA, LINCOLN
M Sheldon Memorial Art Gallery, 12th & R St, 68588-0300. Tel 402-472-2461. *Dir* George W Neubert; *Education Coordr* Karen Janovy; *Cur* Mary Riepma Ross *Film Theater* Dan Ladely; *Cur* Daphne Anderson Deeds; *Adminr* P J Jacobs
Open Tues - Sat 10 AM - 5 PM, Thurs, Fri & Sat 7 - 9 PM, Sun 2 - 9 PM. No admis fee. Estab 1888 to exhibit the permanent collections owned by the University and to present temporary exhibitions on an annual basis. These activities are accompanied by appropriate interpretive programs. The Sheldon Gallery, a gift of Mary Frances & Bromley Sheldon, was opened in 1963 & is the work of Philip Johnson. Facilities in addition to 15,000 sq ft of exhibition galleries, include an auditorium, a print study, members room a a 5 acre outdoor sculpture garden. Average Annual Attendance: 110,000
Income: Financed by endowment, state appropriation and Nebraska Art Association
Purchases: $200,000
Collections: Frank M Hall Collection of contemporary paintings, sculpture, prints, drawings, photographs and ceramics; Nebraska Art Association Collection of American paintings and drawings; University Collections
Exhibitions: (1993) Ansel Adams; Chicanismo: Photos by Louis Bernal; Louis Sullivan; Craig Roper & Cameron Show; Brancusi Photographs; Augustus Vincent Tack
Publications: Exhibition catalogs

Activities: Docent training; lectures open to public, 4 vis lectrs per yr; gallery talks; tours; campus loan program; individual paintings and original objects of art lent to campus offices & other museums; circulate traveling exhibitions; art shop sells reproductions of works of original art within the permanent collection, prints, jewelry, ceramics and unique gifts

L Architecture Library, 308 Architecture Hall, 68588-0108. Tel 402-472-1208. *Assoc Prof* Kay Logan-Peters
Open Mon - Thurs 8 AM - 10 PM, Fri 8 AM - 5 PM, Sat 1 - 5 PM, Sun 2 - 10 PM, summer hours Mon - Fri 8 AM - 5 PM. Circ 21,000
Purchases: $25,000
Library Holdings: Vols 43,000; Per subs 203; Micro — Fiche, reels; AV — A-tapes, cassettes, fs, rec, slides 30,000; Other — Clipping files, exhibition catalogs, photographs
Special Subjects: Architecture, Architecture; Community and Regional Planning
Collections: American Architectural Books (microfilm); Architecture: Urban Documents (microfiche); Fowler Collection of Early Architectural Books (microfilm); National Register of Historic Places (microfiche); Historic American Building Survey Measure and Drawings

M The Gallery of the Department of Art & Art History, 102 Richards Hall, Tenth & T Sts, 207 NC Woods Hall, 68588-0114. Tel 402-472-5541, 472-2631 (Main Art Office). *Chmn & Dir* Joseph M Ruffo
Open Mon - Thurs 9 AM - 5 PM. No admis fee. Estab 1985 to exhibit contemporary art by national artists; student & faculty exhibitions. 2300 sq ft with 238 running feet of exhibition space in two spacious rooms; track lights. Average Annual Attendance: 8000
Collections: Collection of UNL Student Work from BFA & MFA degree program
Exhibitions: Contemporary Czechoslovak Posters
Publications: Exhibition catalogues

MCCOOK

M HIGH PLAINS MUSEUM, 421 Norris Ave, 69001. Tel 308-345-3661. *Chmn Bd* Russell Dowling
Open Tues - Sun noon - 5 PM, cl Mon & holidays. No admis fee, donations accepted. Estab 1963 to preserve the items pertaining to the local history and to interpret them for the public. Museum is located in new building. New additions include complete pioneer kitchen; railroad section (inside & out); complete Old Time Pharmacy. Morning tours by appointment. Average Annual Attendance: 8000. Mem: 210; mem qualification is art display by local art club; dues $5 - $200; annual meeting in Mar
Income: Financed by membership
Collections: Paintings made on the barracks walls of prisoner of war camp near McCook; paintings donated by local artists
Exhibitions: Quilt Show
Activities: Lect open to the public, 8 vis lectrs per yr; tours; competitions; original objects of art lent; lending collection contains books, framed reproductions & motion pictures; museum shop sells books, magazines & original art; repair shop

MINDEN

M HAROLD WARP PIONEER VILLAGE FOUNDATION, PO Box 68, 68959-0068. Tel 308-832-1181; FAX 308-832-2750; WATS 800-445-4447. *Pres* Harold Warp; *Gen Mgr* Marvin Mangers
Open daily. Admis adults $5, children $2.50, children under 6 free; special rates to groups. Estab 1953 to preserve man's progress from 1830 to present day. Foundation includes a 90 unit motel, 350 seat restaurant & 135 site camp ground. Average Annual Attendance: 100,000
Collections: Folk art; graphics; historical materials; paintings; sculpture
Publications: History of Man's Progress (1830-present); Sister Clara's Letters (Over Our Hill-Past Our Place)
Activities: Classes for adults; elder hostel; lectures for members only; tours; museum shop sells books, reproductions, prints & slides

NEBRASKA CITY

M GAME AND PARKS COMMISSION, Arbor Lodge State Historical Park, PO Box 15, 68410. Tel 402-873-7222. *Dir* Rex Amack; *Supt* Randall Fox; *Asst Supt* Mark Kemper
Open Apr - May, Mon - Sun 11 AM - 5 PM, May - Sept, Mon - Sun 9 AM - 5 PM, Sept - Oct, Mon - Sun 11 AM - 5 PM. Admis adults $3, children 6-15 $1, children under 5 no charge. Estab 1923. Art collection of members of the J S Morton family and outdoor scenes spread through a 52 room mansion. Average Annual Attendance: 40,000
Income: Financed by state appropriation
Activities: Lect open to public; tours; awards, Arbor Day Tree plantings on April 22; sales shop sells books, Arbor Day tree pins & postcards

OMAHA

M ARTISTS' COOPERATIVE GALLERY, 405 S 11th St, 68102. Tel 402-342-9617. *Pres* Margie Schimenti; *VPres* David McCallum; *Board Dir* Jerry Jacoby; *Board Dir* Sally Dreyer; *Board Dir* Ulla Gallahen; *Board Dir* Pamela King; *Board Dir* Ruth Harris Urban
Open Tue - Thurs 11 AM - 5 PM, Fri & Sat 11 AM - 10 PM, Sun noon - 5 PM. No admis fee. Estab 1975 to be gathering place for those interested in visual art; to display quality local, contemporary art; to offer programs, panels & discussions on related issues to the public. Gallery contains 4000 sq ft consisting of large open area with 1 small, self-contained gallery. Average Annual Attendance: 21,000. Mem: 29; dues $300; monthly meetings
Income: $10,000
Exhibitions: Each month a different show features 2 - 4 members of the gallery with a major show. December features an all member show; exchange exhibits & special exhibits are featured by arrangement
Activities: Lectures open to public, 3-4 vis lectr per yr; book traveling exhibitions; originates traveling exhibitions

M **BEMIS FOUNDATION,** New Gallery, 614 S 11th St, 68102. Tel 402-341-7130; FAX 402-341-9791. *Dir* Ree Schonlau; *Program Dir* Joan Batson; *Development Asst* Christina Narwicz
Open daily 11 AM - 5 PM. No admis fee. 3500 sq ft, 12 - 13 ft ceilings, dark wood floors, off-white walls. Average Annual Attendance: 8000 - 10,000
Collections: Bemis collection of international contemporary art
Exhibitions: (1992) David Simpson; Wojciech Pakowski & Yun-Dong Nam; Patrick Siler; Norbert Kleinlein; Seven Artists (Who Happen to be Women); Brook Levan/Life in General; Bemis Retrospective; Terra Incognita: New Landscape Painting (1990) Mixed Media Work
Activities: Lect open to public, 25 - 30 vis lectr per year; concerts; awards

M **CREIGHTON UNIVERSITY,** Fine Arts Gallery, 2500 California St, 68178. Tel 402-280-2509; FAX 402-280-2320. *Dir* John Thein; *Chmn Fine & Performing Arts Dept* Jerome K Horning
Open Mon - Sat 10 AM - 4 PM, Sun noon - 4 PM. Mus estab 1973. Gallery handles 8 exhibits per academic year; space provided for student thesis exhibits; 150 running ft. Average Annual Attendance: 2000
Income: $4200 (financed by school's general funding)
Collections: Ceramics; drawings; graphics; paintings; photography; pottery and sculpture; printmaking
Exhibitions: (1990-91) Bonnie Manriquez & Nancy Samotis (painting); John Thein (painted glass); Senior Thesis Exhibits; Creighton University Faculty Exhibit; Chris Weaver (sculpture); Student Juried Exhibit
Activities: Lect open to the public

M **JOSLYN ART MUSEUM,** 2200 Dodge St, 68102. Tel 402-342-3300; FAX 402-342-2376. *Dir* Graham W J Beal; *Deputy Dir* Audrey Kauders; *Chief Cur, Cur Material Culture* Marsha V Gallagher; *Cur Western American Art* David Hunt; *Dir Marketing & Public Relations* Linda Rejcevich; *Assoc Cur 20th Century Art* Janet Farber; *Coll & Exhib Mgr* Theodore James; *Museum Shop Mgr* Liala Ralph; *Cur Educ* Carol Wyrick; *Art Librn* Kathryn Corcoran
Open Tues - Sat 10 AM - 5 PM, Thurs 10 AM - 9 PM, Sun 1 - 5 PM, cl Mon & holidays. Admis adults $3, children under 12 & sr citizens $1.50, Sat AM free, members free. Estab in 1931 as a cultural center for the community. Joslyn houses works from antiquity to the present, with a special emphasis on 19th & 20th century European & American art. In addition to the art galleries, there is the 1200 seat Witherspoon Concert Hall, the 200 seat Lecture Hall, Members Room & the Storz Fountain Court. Museum was a gift of Mrs Sarah H Joslyn in memory of her husband, George A Joslyn. Museum is a marble building covering a two-block area; contains ten large galleries with small exhibit areas surrounding the large central Storz Fountain Court and 1200-seat Witherspoon Concert Hall on the main floor. The concert hall is used for programs by major community music and cultural organizations. The ground floor includes exhibit areas, library, classroom, lecture hall, museum shop and office. Average Annual Attendance: 130,000. Mem: 7000; dues $15 - $35
Collections: †Ancient through modern art, including European & American paintings, sculpture, graphics; †Art of the Western Frontier; †Native American art
Exhibitions: Temporary exhibitions include traveling shows of national significance; Joslyn-organized shows; one-person & group shows in all media; Midlands Invitational
Publications: Members calendar, bi-monthly; exhibition catalogs; art books
Activities: Creative and art appreciation classes for adults and children (pre-school through high school); special workshops; film programs; special tour program of permanent collections and special exhibitions maintained for public school children; lect and exhibition gallery talks; tours of the collections and special exhibitions; museum shop sells books, magazines, reproductions, prints, slides, cards, collectibles & posters

L **Art Reference Library,** 2200 Dodge St, 68102. Tel 402-342-3300; FAX 402-342-2376. *Art Librn* Kathryn L Corcoran
Open Tues - Sat 10 AM - 5 PM, Sun 1 - 5 PM. Estab 1931, reference only
Library Holdings: Vols 22,000; Per subs 250; 150 vertical files; AV — Slides 20,000; Other — Reproductions
Special Subjects: 19th & 20th century European & American art

L **NEBRASKA ARTS COUNCIL LIBRARY,** 1313 Farnam On-the-Mall, 68102-1873. Tel 402-595-2122; FAX 402-595-2217. *Chmn* Robert Duncan; *Exec Dir* Jennifer S Clark
Open Mon - Fri 8 AM - 5 PM. Estab circa 1970 to provide information on arts administration topics to constituents
Library Holdings: Vols 700; AV — Motion pictures, slides, v-tapes; Other — Pamphlets
Publications: Guidelines, annually; Nebraska touring program brochures, annually; newsletters, quarterly
Activities: Grants to non-profit community organizations and schools for projects related to the arts; workshops; lect open to public, 2 - 3 visiting lectr per year; grant awards to non-profit organizations in Nebraska for arts projects

M **OMAHA CHILDRENS MUSEUM, INC,** 500 S 20th St, 68102. Tel 402-342-6164. *Dir* Elizabeth Brownrigg; *Finance Mgr* Jim O'Conner; *Public Relations Dir* Betsye Paragas
Open Tues - Sat 10 AM - 5 PM, Sun 1 - 5 PM, cl Mon. Admis $3. Estab 1978 to provide high-quality participation & educational experiences in the arts, humanities & science. Average Annual Attendance: 100,000. Mem: 1500 families; dues $30
Income: Financed by mem, admissions, grants, donations from individuals, foundations & corporations
Exhibitions: Hands-on exhibits which promote learning in the arts, science & humanities; traveling exhibits; workshops by local professional educators & artists
Publications: Bi-monthly calendar; museum newsletter, quarterly
Activities: Classes for adults & children; docent training; originate traveling exhibitions; museum shop sells books, educational games & toys

M **UNION PACIFIC RAILROAD,** Historical Museum, 1416 Dodge St, 68179. Tel 402-271-3530; FAX 402-271-5572. *Museum Dir* Donald Snoddy
Open Mon - Fri 9 AM - 3 PM, Sat 9 AM - noon, cl major holidays

M **UNIVERSITY OF NEBRASKA AT OMAHA,** Art Gallery, Fine Arts Bldg, Room 137, 68182-0012. Tel 402-554-2796. *Dir* Nancy Kelly
Open Mon - Fri 9:30 AM - 4:30 PM. Estab 1967 to heighten cultural and aesthetic awareness of the metropolitan and midlands area. Average Annual Attendance: 14,000
Income: Financed by state appropriation
Purchases: $5000
Collections: University Visiting Printmaker's Collection
Exhibitions: Wayne Kimball, lithographs; Dennis Guastella, paintings; Juergen Strunck, relief prints; Drawings: Terry Allen, Power Boothe, Harold Boyd, Ann Karlsen, Fran Noel & Jim Roche
Publications: Exhibition catalogs
Activities: Lect open to public, 2 vis lectr per year; gallery talks; tours; competitions; scholarships

SEWARD

M **CONCORDIA COLLEGE,** Marx Hausen Art Gallery, 800 N Columbia Ave, 68434. Tel 402-643-3651. *Dir* Lynn Soloway
Open weekdays 8 AM - 5 PM, Sun 2 - 5 PM. No admis fee. Estab 1959 to provide the college and community with a wide variety of original art; both monthly exhibitions and permanent collection serve primarily an educational need; spacious gallery has additional showcases
Collections: Ceramics; †Contemporary Original Prints
Exhibitions: Wood: A Common Material; Nebraska Places & Spaces; 1 & 2 artists exhibitions; shows drawn from Permanent Collection and Annual Student Exhibitions; The Art of Cartoons; Animal Show; The Computer and its Influence on Art and Design: Part II; Contemporary Artists Christian Themes; The Human Image (from the permanent collection)
Activities: Gallery talks; original objects of art lent; lending collection of framed reproductions, original prints and paintings; book traveling exhibitions, 6 per year

WAYNE

M **WAYNE STATE COLLEGE,** Nordstrand Visual Arts Gallery, Fine Arts Center, 68787. Tel 402-375-2200, Ext 360; FAX 402-375-7204. *Division Chmn of Fine Arts* Dr Jay O'Leary
Open Mon - Fri 9 AM - 5 PM. No admis fee. Estab January 1977 to provide art students with a space to display work; to enhance student's education by viewing incoming regional professional work; to enrich cultural atmosphere of college and community. Small gallery, carpeted floors and walls, ceiling spotlights on tracts. Average Annual Attendance: 800
Income: Financed by city and state appropriation, as well as Wayne State Foundation
Collections: †Wayne State Foundation Print Collection
Activities: Lect open to public, 1 - 2 vis lectr per year; competitions

WILBER

M **WILBER CZECH MUSEUM,** 321 S Harris, PO Box 253, 68465. Tel 402-821-2485. *Pres* Irma Ourecky
Open daily 1 - 4 PM & by appointment, cl holidays. No admis fee. Estab 1962 to preserve Czech culture & artifacts. Average Annual Attendance: 4000. Mem: annual meeting in Dec
Income: Financed by donations & shop sales
Collections: Model rooms of homes & businesses of pioneer days
Exhibitions: (1991) 30th Annual Czech Festival. (1993) 32nd Annual Czech Festival
Activities: Tours for adult & school groups; sales shop sells books, quilted items, Czech crystal & crafts

NEVADA

ELKO

M **NORTHEASTERN NEVADA HISTORICAL SOCIETY MUSEUM,** 1515 Idaho St, 89801. Tel 702-738-3418; FAX 702-753-9863. *Museum Dir* Howard Hickson
Open Mon - Sat 9 AM - 5 PM, Sun 1 - 5 PM. No admis fee; admis charge for theatre program. Estab 1968; general museum concentrating on Northeastern Nevada; also area cultural center. Gallery is 4000 sq ft, 12 exhibits per year local, state, regional and national artists. Average Annual Attendance: 52,000. Mem: 2500; dues $10 - $1000; annual meeting date varies; membership dues
Income: $18,000 (financed by grants, contributions, dues sales shop and memorials)
Collections: History; Pre-Hsitory; Natural History; Art
Exhibitions: Annual statewide touring photography exhibitions; sound slide show - Nevada subjects; Michael Johnson American Artwork
Publications: Historical, quarterly; Northeastern Nevada Historical Society Quarterly
Activities: Classes for children; docent training; lectures open to public, 10 vis lectr per year; concerts; gallery talks; tours; photography competitions with awards; Nevada photography exhibit tours to 13 Nevada communities; exten dept serving Nevada; lending collection of 35 film strips, 4000 slides (complete programs); 5000 photographs; 1700 books & 12 cassettes; originate traveling exhibitions; museum shop sales books, magazines, prints, and local craft items

L **Library,** 1515 Idaho St, 89801. Tel 702-738-3418. *Dir* Howard Hickson; *Asst Dir* Shawn Hall
Open Mon - Sat 9 AM - 5 PM, Sun 1 - 5 PM. Rotating art exhibits, two local artists display at all times

Income: $5000 (finance by contributions, dues, sales shop, memorials
Library Holdings: Vols 4000; Per subs 10; AV — A-tapes, cassettes, fs, slides, v-tapes; Other — Clipping files, exhibition catalogs, framed reproductions, manuscripts, memorabilia, original art works, pamphlets, photographs 23,000, prints, reproductions
Special Subjects: American Indian Art, American Western Art, Film, Flasks & Bottles, Folk Art, Historical Material, History of Art & Archaeology, Period Rooms, Southwestern Art, Theatre Arts, Video, Concentration on Northeastern Nevada History
Collections: Newspaper and negative files
Publications: Quarterly historical publication

LAS VEGAS

M **LAS VEGAS ART MUSEUM,** 3333 W Washington, 89107. Tel 702-647-4300; FAX 702-647-0319. *Pres* Marilyn Green; *Dir* Helen E Gaines
Open Tues - Sat 10 AM - 3 PM, Sun noon - 3 PM, cl Mon. No admis fee. Estab 1950 to offer fine arts to the community of Las Vegas; to offer artist a place to show, work and study; to offer good education in fine arts to adults and children of the community. Three galleries that change monthly. Average Annual Attendance: 9000. Mem: 500; dues benefactor $1000, patron $500, sponsor $200, family $30, individual $21, sr citizens (55 & over) $10; meetings third Thurs each month
Income: Financed by mem, donation & commissions on sales gift shop
Collections: Contemporary artists
Exhibitions: State & County Art Show; local & international exhibits; National Finals Art Show
Publications: Bulletin, monthly; The Art Beat newsletter, monthly
Activities: Classes for adults presented by leading artists & craftsmen; museum sponsors classes for youths; self-help workshops; docent training; competitions; sales shop sells original art; junior museum

L **LAS VEGAS-CLARK COUNTY LIBRARY DISTRICT,** 4020 S Maryland Parkway, 89119. Tel 702-733-7810. *Dir* Charles W Hunsberger; *Asst Dir* Nancy Hudson; *Extension Serv* Ann Langevin; *Branch Adminr* Beryl Andrus; *Branch Adminr* Doug Henderson; *Branch Adminr* Sally Feldman; *Branch Adminr* Darrell Batson; *Branch Adminr* Jane Lorance; *Branch Adminr* Vlasta Honsa; *Branch Adminr* Jack Gardner; *Branch Adminr* Joel McKee; *Young People's Library* Gale Zachariah; *Reference* David Welles; *Technical Serv* Alice Dopp; *Business Serv* Irene Voit; *Library Development* Stan Colton; *Periodicals* Laura Lawrence; *Programming* Margaret Trasatti
Open Mon - Thurs 9 AM - 9 PM, Fri & Sat 9 AM - 5 PM, Sun 1 - 5 PM. Estab 1965 to provide informaton in all its varieties of form to people of all ages; nine branch libraries, including three art galleries. Galleries provide regularly rotating art exhibitions of regional & national repute as well as ten solo shows a year, & a regional mixed media competition every spring. Circ 1,770,951
Income: $5,500,000 (financed by state and county appropriation)
Purchases: $700,000
Library Holdings: Per subs 586; Micro — Fiche, reels; AV — A-tapes, cassettes, fs, motion pictures, rec; Other — Clipping files, framed reproductions, original art works, pamphlets, photographs, prints, reproductions, sculpture
Collections: Model ship collection; †Nevada materials
Exhibitions: Art-a-Fair; Nevada Watercolor Society; All Aboard: Railroads, Memorabilia; Neon: Smithsonian Exhibition; Expressions in Fiber; Graham & Breedlove; Sand & Water; Dottie Burton; Woodworks: Christian Brisepierre & Jack Daseler; KNPR Craftworks; It's a Small, Small World: Dollhouses, Kimberly House
Publications: Exhibition brochures, monthly; library program, bimonthly
Activities: Lectures open to the public; concerts; tours; competitions with awards; exten dept & regional service dept serving the area; individual paintings & original objects of art lent; book traveling exhibitions; originate traveling exhibitions; used book store sells books, magazines, original art & handcrafts

M **Flamingo Gallery,** 4020 S Maryland Parkway, 89119. Tel 702-733-7810; FAX 702-732-7271. *Dir* Denise Shapiro
Open Mon - Thurs 9 AM - 9 PM, Fri 9 AM - 5 PM, Sat 9 AM - 5 PM, Sun 1 - 5 PM. Estab 1970. Gallery is located in Clark County Library, main gallery has 80 running feet of exhibit space, upstairs gallery is used for photographic displays. Average Annual Attendance: 36,000 - 40,000. Mem: 500; dues $15, annual meeting in summer
Income: Financed by tax support, federal and state grants
Exhibitions: Art-A-Fair (judged and juried); Spirit Impressions; The Potter & the Weaver; Nevada Watercolor Society Annual exhibit
Publications: Bi-monthly library calendar of events
Activities: Classes for adults and children; dramatic programs; string quartet; feature films; lectures open to public, 10 vis lectr per year; concerts; Art-A-Fair competition; monetary awards

M **UNIVERSITY OF NEVADA, LAS VEGAS,** Art Gallery, 4505 Maryland Parkway, 89154. Tel 702-739-3893. *Dir* Jerry Schefcik
Open Sept - June Tues - Sat noon - 4 PM. Gallery measures 26 x 22 ft. Average Annual Attendance: 5000. Mem: 50; dues $10
Income: Financed by membership and appropriation
Collections: †Ceramics; Oriental Art; †Paintings; Prints; †Sculpture
Exhibitions: (1993) Julia Couzens (charcoal drawings); Robert Venturi Show (Learning from Las Vegas); Photographs; Paintings; Prints
Activities: Classes for adults and children; dramatic programs; lect open to the public, 2 vis lectr per year; concerts; gallery talks; tours; competitions; scholarships; lending collection contains 15,000 Kodachromes and 70,000 slides; originate traveling exhibitions

RENO

M **NEVADA MUSEUM OF ART,** 160 W Liberty St, 89501. Tel 702-329-3333; FAX 702-329-1541. *Pres* Frank Gallagher; *Educ Coordr* Kathy Dewey; *Development Officer* Jenny Rudy; *Admin Asst* Jennifer Smalley; *Exec Dir* Richard R Esparza; *Cur* Howard DaLee Spencer; *Cur Educ* Wendy Thomas Felling; *Registrar* Susie Aker; *ARTLINKS Coordr* Leslie Dandois
Open Tues - Sat 10 AM - 4 PM, Sun 12 - 4 PM. Admis adult $3, sr citizen $1.50, children $.50, free admis Fri. Estab 1931 to collect, conserve & exhibit 19th & 20th century American art, with an emphasis on the art of this region, including contemporary & Native American art, for the enrichment & heritage of the citizens of Nevada & the surrounding Great Basin. The facility is a 60,000 sq ft state of the art building which holds three exhibitions simultaneously. Average Annual Attendance: 45,000. Mem: 1000; dues corporation $250, family $35; annual meeting Apr
Income: Financed by endowment, mem, federal & private foundation grants, individual grants & earned income
Collections: †E L Wiegnad Art Collection (emphasis on the American work ethic); †Permanent Collection (includes 19th & 20th century American Art with an emphasis on the Great Basin region)
Exhibitions: (1992) Mexican Masters of the Post-Muralist Period; Arneson, De Forest, Hudson & Wiley: Selections from the Anderson Collection; Jeff Nicholson: Nevada Realist; Original Animation Cells George I Sturman Collection; Italian American Folklife in the West; Richard Hunt: Contemporary Master of Sculpture. (1993) Ingrid Evans: Paper Sculpture; Richard Guy Walton Retrospective; Roger Shimomura: Paintings; California Impressionist Paintings
Publications: Annual Bulletin; brochures; catalogues; calendar newsletter, quarterly; postcards for events, twice a month
Activities: Classes for adults & children; dramatic programs; hands on exhibits; lect open to the public, 20 vis lectr per year; gallery talks; tours; concerts; scholarships; outreach services to schools, senior citizens & other community groups in Greater Reno-Carson-Tahoe area; exchange program with other museums; originate traveling exhibitions; museum shop sells books, original art & reproductions

L **Art Library,** 160 W Liberty St, 89501. Tel 702-329-3333; FAX 702-329-1541. *Exec Dir* Richard Esparza; *Cur Educ & Library Coordr* Wendy Thomas Felling
Open Tues - Sat 10 AM - 4 PM, Sun noon - 4 PM. Admis adults $3, students & sr $1.50, children 6 - 12 yrs $.50, members free. Estab 1931
Library Holdings: Vols 1350; Per subs 6; Other — Clipping files, exhibition catalogs, manuscripts, memorabilia, pamphlets, photographs, reproductions
Special Subjects: Advertising Design, Aesthetics, Afro-American Art, American Indian Art, American Western Art, Anthropology, Antiquities-Byzantine, Antiquities-Egyptian, Antiquities-Etruscan, Antiquities-Greek, Antiquities-Oriental, Antiquities-Roman, Archaeology, Architecture, Art Education

A **SIERRA ARTS FOUNDATION,** 200 Flint St, 89501. Tel 702-329-1324; FAX 702-329-1328. *Pres* David Line; *First VPres* Joan Dyer; *Second VPres* Kathie Bartlett; *Exec Dir* Patricia Smith; *Secy* Duffy Bride
Open Mon - Fri 8:30 AM - 5 PM. Estab 1971 as a non-profit, private community arts agency, shows works of emerging, regional artists. Mem: 800
Income: Financed by endowment, corporate & individual mem, city, state & federal appropriations & gifts
Publications: Art Works; How Do I Feel? What Do I Need?; Marketing Survey Report; A Celebration, Encore, monthly newsletter; Master Calendar; Services Booklet; Art Resources Guide
Activities: Educ dept; Arts-In-Education; concerts; festivals; competitions; exten dept; Endowment Income Grants Program for local arts organizations and individual artists

M **UNIVERSITY OF NEVADA,** Sheppard Fine Art Gallery, Church Fine Arts Bldg, 89557. Tel 702-784-4636. *Gallery Cur* Walter McNamara; *Art Dept Chmn* James McCormick
Open Mon - Fri 9 AM - 4 PM, cl Sat, Sun & holidays. Estab 1960. Gallery has 1800 sq ft finished exhibition space. Average Annual Attendance: 15,000-24,000
Activities: Lectures open to public, 3-6 vis lectr per yr; gallery talks; tours; competitions with awards; scholarships; individual paintings & original objects of art lent; museum shop

NEW HAMPSHIRE

CENTER SANDWICH

M **SANDWICH HISTORICAL SOCIETY,** Maple St, 03227. Tel 603-284-6269. *Dir* Virginia Heard, MSLS; *Cur* Suzita Myers
Open June - Sept Mon - Sat 1 - 5 PM, July & Aug Mon - Sat 11 AM - 5 PM, cl Sun. Admis free. Estab 1917
Collections: Painting by Albert Gallatin Hoit (oil & water); Paintings by E Wood Perry (oil)
Exhibitions: Mothers & Daughters of Sandwich: Photographs by Susan L Nicolay
Publications: Annual Excursion Bulletin 1920, annually; Newsletter, 4 per year

CONCORD

A **LEAGUE OF NEW HAMPSHIRE CRAFTSMEN,** League Gallery, 205 N Main St, 03301. Tel 603-224-1471; FAX 603-225-8451. *Dir* Mary G White; *Gallery Coordr* Jill Snyder Wallace
Open Mon - Fri 9 AM - 5 PM. Estab 1932 to encourage the economic development & education of the crafts; gallery displaying exhibits of members' works. Average Annual Attendance: 5000. Mem: 3000; dues $20-individual; annual meeting in Oct
Exhibitions: Annual Craftsmen's Fair; Living with Crafts; Annual Juried Exhibit
Publications: Newsletter, quarterly
Activities: Classes for adults;; Exhibits; Competitions with awards; scholarships offered; lending collection of books

L **Library,** 205 N Main St, 03301. Tel 603-224-1471; FAX 603-225-8452. *Dir* Mary White
Open to members
Income: Financed by league operating funds
Library Holdings: Vols 1100; Per subs 30; AV — Cassettes, slides; Other — Clipping files, exhibition catalogs 10, manuscripts, original art works, pamphlets, photographs
Special Subjects: Crafts, Marketing Crafts

A **NEW HAMPSHIRE HISTORICAL SOCIETY,** 30 Park St, 03301. Tel 603-225-3381. *Pres* David G Stahl; *Dir* John Frisbee; *Cur* D B Garvin; *Librn* William Copeley
Open Mon - Fri 9 AM - 4:30 PM, Sat & Sun noon - 4:30 PM. Admis $2 donation suggested. Estab 1823 to collect, preserve and make available books, manuscripts and artifacts pertaining to the history of New Hampshire; art gallery maintained. Exhibition gallery maintained. Average Annual Attendance: 20,000. Mem: 3000; dues family $50, active $30; annual meeting first Sat in Apr
Income: $700,000 (financed by endowment, mem, grants & sales)
Purchases: $20,000
Special Subjects: Archaeology, Architecture, Bookplates & Bindings, Costume Design & Construction, Crafts, Decorative Arts, Dolls, Furniture, Glass, Historical Material, Landscapes, Manuscripts, Maps, Painting - American, Pewter, Photography, Portraits, Posters, Pottery, Prints, Restoration & Conservation, Silver, Textiles, Watercolors
Collections: †Artifacts made or used in New Hampshire including collections of †glass, †furniture, †metals, †paintings, †silver and †textiles; †Fine and Decorative Arts; †Historical Memorabilia
Exhibitions: Highways & Hotels: On the Road in New Hampshire. (1992-93) At What Cost: Land use in NH
Publications: Historical New Hampshire, quarterly; annual report; exhibition catalogues; bi-monthly newsletter
Activities: Classes for adults & children; docent training; lect open to public, 4 vis per year; programs & tours for children; gallery talks; bus tours; museum shop sells books, reproductions, prints
L **Library,** 30 Park St, 03301. Tel 603-225-3381. *Pres* David G Stahl
Admis $3 per day. Reference library only
Library Holdings: Vols 50,000; Per subs 150; newspapers; Micro — Reels; AV — A-tapes, cassettes, fs, lantern slides, motion pictures, rec, slides, v-tapes; Other — Exhibition catalogs, framed reproductions, manuscripts, memorabilia, original art works, pamphlets, photographs, prints
Special Subjects: New Hampshire History

M **SAINT PAUL'S SCHOOL,** Art Center in Hargate, 03301. Tel 603-225-3341, Ext 258; FAX 603-225-2156. *Dir Art Center* Karen Burgess Smith; *Gallery Asst* Carol Shelton
Open Tues - Sat 10 AM - 4:30 PM, during school year. Estab 1967 to house the Art Department of St Paul's School, to provide a cultural center for the school community as well as the central area of New Hampshire. Secure gallery consisting of subdivided room approximately 60 x 40 ft. Average Annual Attendance: 10,000
Income: Financed by endowment
Collections: Painting, sculpture, drawings, graphics, chiefly gifts to the school; collection represents varied periods and nationalities
Exhibitions: (1993) Winnie Owens-Hart, Ceramic Works; Helena Chapellin-Wilson, Gum bichromate images
Activities: Lectures & classes for students & school community only; Gallery receptions & lectures open to the public; tours; original objects of art lent to qualifying institutions
L **Ohrstrom Library,** 325 Pleasant St, 03301. Tel 603-225-3341, Ext 212; FAX 603-225-2156. *Librn* R Cassels-Brown
Estab 1967 for art reference only. Circ 600
Income: $1000
Purchases: Approx $1000
Library Holdings: Vols 50,000; Per subs 150; AV — Slides; Other — Exhibition catalogs, reproductions

CORNISH

M **SAINT-GAUDENS NATIONAL HISTORIC SITE,** New Hampshire Route 12A (Mailing add: RR 3, PO Box 73, 03745). Tel 603-675-2175; FAX 603-675-2701; FTS 834-1620. *Supt & Cur* John H Dryfhout
Open daily 8:30 AM - 4:30 PM (end of May - Oct 31). Admis (16 and over) $.50. Estab 1926, transferred to Federal Government (National Park Service) in 1965 to commemorate the home, studios & works of Augustus Saint-Gaudens (1848-1907), one of America's foremost sculptors. The site has historically (1907) furnished rooms, studios & gardens displaying approximately half of the work of Augustus Saint-Gaudens. Average Annual Attendance: 40,000
Income: Financed by federal appropriation (National Park Service)
Purchases: Works by Augustus Saint Gaudens; original furnishings of the Cornish Property
Collections: Historic furnishings & sculpture; plaster, bronze & marble works by Augustus; Saint Gaudens
Exhibitions: Paintings by Deborah Berningham
Publications: Brochures
Activities: Individual paintings & original objects of art lent to museums & societies; sales shop sells books, slides & souvenir items
L **Library,** Saint Gaudens Rd, RR 2 PO Box 73, 03745. Tel 603-675-2175; FAX 603-675-2701.
Open for reference
Library Holdings: Vols 500
Special Subjects: 19th and early 20th Century American art

DURHAM

M **UNIVERSITY OF NEW HAMPSHIRE,** The Art Gallery, Paul Creative Arts Center, 03824-3538. Tel 603-862-3712, 3713 (outreach). *Dir* Vicki C Wright; *Asst Dir* M Lora Lytjen; *Educ Coordr* Helen K Reid
Open Mon - Wed 10 AM - 4 PM, Thurs 10 AM - 8 PM, Sat & Sun 1 - 5 PM, cl Fri & Univ holidays; The Art Gallery features exhibitions from September through mid June each year. No admis fee. Estab 1960 renovated 1973, teaching collection for university faculty & students outreach & public service functions for the non-university community. Upper mezzanine & lower level galleries with a total of 3800 ft of exhibition space; 900 ft storage room to house permanent collection & temporary loans; additional storage & office space. Average Annual Attendance: 15,000. Mem: 200
Collections: 19th century American landscapes, 19th century Japanese prints, and 20th century works on paper
Exhibitions: Temporary exhibitions
Publications: Exhibition catalogs; miscellaneous booklets
Activities: Educational program for area schools; workshops; docent training; lect open to public, 8-10 vis lectrs per yr; concerts; gallery talks; tours; fels offered; individual paintings & original objects of art lent to other qualified museums for exhibitions; lending collection contains slides and video tapes; book traveling exhibitions, 1-3 per yr; originate traveling exhibitions; sales shop sells books, magazines & note cards
L **Dept of the Arts Slide Library,** Paul Creative Arts Center, 03824. Tel 603-862-3818. *Slide Librn* Barbara Scroggins
Estab as a teaching collection for the university. Slides do not circulate off-campus
Library Holdings: AV — Slides 132,000
Special Subjects: Western art

EXETER

M **PHILLIPS EXETER ACADEMY,** Frederic R Mayer Art Center & Lamont Gallery, Front St & Tan Lane, 03833. Tel 603-772-4311, Ext 324. *Principal* Kendra O'Donnell; *Dir* Margaret Hanni
Open Mon - Sat 9 AM - 5 PM, Wed 9 AM - 1 PM & Sun 2 - 5 PM. No admis fee. Estab 1953 to provide an Art Center and studios for art instruction dedicated to the memory of Thomas William Lamont II, lost in action in 1945. Four bays with moveable walls to alter number and size of bays, sky lit with sol-r-veil screen
Exhibitions: (1990) Montford & Hendricks: Art After 45; Carol Aronson - Paintings; Photographs: Athletes 1860-1986. (1991) Art Department Faculty Show; Jon Brooks - Sculpture; British Watercolors from the Harrow School Collection; Student Show
Activities: Classes for Academy students; dramatic programs; lect open to public, 4 vis lectr per year

HANOVER

M **DARTMOUTH COLLEGE,** Hood Museum of Art, 03755. Tel 603-646-2808. *Dir* Timothy Rub; *Sr Cur & Cur for Ethnographic Art* Tamara Northern; *Cur for American Art* Barbara MacAdam; *Cur for European Art* Richard Rand; *Cur for Exhib* Evelyn Marcus; *Registrar* Kellen Haak; *Preparator* James Watkinson; *Financial Mgr* Nancy McLain; *Assoc Registrar* Kathleen O'Malley; *Asst Registrar* Cynthia Gilliland; *Cur Arts Educ Servs* Leslie Wellman; *Cur Academic Progs* Katherine Hart
Open Tues - Fri & Sun 11 AM - 5 PM, Sat 11 AM - 8 PM. No admis fee. Estab 1772 to serve the Dartmouth community & Upper Valley region. New building, designed by Charles Moore & Chad Floyd of Centerbrook, completed in 1985, houses ten galleries. Average Annual Attendance: 70,000. Mem: 2100; dues $30 - $1000; annual meeting in July
Income: Financed through Dartmouth College, endowment income, contributions and grants
Collections: The Hood Museum has about 15,000 art objects and about 35,000 anthropology objects; especially strong in areas such as 19th and 20th century American art, 17th century paintings and European and American prints; also has a survey of Native American, African, Oriental and Pre-Columbian artifacts
Exhibitions: Approximately fifteen temporary exhibitions per year on a wide range of subjects. Exhibitions include those organize by the museum, travelling exhibitions and exhibitions drawn from permanent collections
Publications: Museum catalogues, annually
Activities: Classes for adults & children; docent training; lectures open to public, 8 - 10 vis lectr per yr; gallery talks; tours; awards; individual paintings & original objects of art lent to other museums and campus departments; book traveling exhibitions, 1 - 2 per year; museum shop sells books, cards & posters
L **Sherman Art Library,** 6033 Carpenter Hall, 03755-3570. Tel 603-646-2305; FAX 603-646-1218. *Librn* Barbara E Reed
Open Mon - Thurs 8 AM - 12 PM, Fri 8 AM - 6 PM, Sat 9 AM - 6 PM, Sun 1 - 12 PM, during school terms (reduced hours in summer & during intersessions). Estab 1928
Library Holdings: Vols 82,000; Per subs 500; Micro — Cards 328, fiche 100,000, prints 1529, reels 111; Other — Exhibition catalogs, pamphlets
Special Subjects: Architecture, Photography

HOPKINTON

M **NEW HAMPSHIRE ANTIQUARIAN SOCIETY,** 300 Main St, 03229. Tel 603-746-3825. *Exec Dir* Kathleen Belko
Open Mon & Fri 1 - 5 PM. No admis fee. Estab 1875 to preserve local & state historical & genealogical records & collections, and to provide the community with cultural & historical programs of local significance. Gallery houses primative portraits of local citizens by itinerant artists. Average Annual Attendance: 1000. Mem: 400; dues $5
Income: $7000
Collections: Early American furniture, clothing, china, portraits; local historical material
Exhibitions: 18th - 20th century local handicrafts
Activities: Children's classes; docent training; lectures open to public

KEENE

M HISTORICAL SOCIETY OF CHESHIRE COUNTY, Colony House Museum, 104 West St, PO Box 803, 03431. Tel 603-352-1895. *Dir* Alan Rumrill, MLS; *Tour Guide* Joan Nichols; *Admin Asst* Roxanne Roy
Open Tues - Sat 11 AM - 4 PM. Admis fee $2. Estab 1973 to exhibit Cheshire County History. Average Annual Attendance: 1000. Mem: 450; dues $10; annual meeting in April
Income: $7000 (financed by endowment & membership)
Purchases: $1500
Collections: †New Hampshire Glass Collection; Hampshire Pottery Collection; †Newburyport Silver Collection
Publications: Newsletter
Activities: Lectures open to the public, 5 vis lectr per yr; museum shop sells books
L Archive Center of the Society, 246 Main St, PO Box 803, 03431. Tel 603-352-1895. *Dir* Alan Rumrill, MLS
Open Mon - Fri 9 AM - 4 PM. Estab 1927 as a reference library
Income: $3000 (financed by endowment & membership)
Purchases: $1000
Library Holdings: Vols 5000; Per subs 3; Micro — Prints; AV — Slides; Other — Clipping files, exhibition catalogs, manuscripts, original art works, pamphlets, photographs, reproductions
Special Subjects: Flasks & Bottles, Glass, Historical Material, Pottery, Silver
Publications: Newsletter, 5 times annually

M KEENE STATE COLLEGE, Thorne-Sagendorph Art Gallery, Appian Way, 03431. Tel 603-352-1909, Ext 382. *Dir* Maureen Ahearn
Open Sept - May Mon - Fri noon - 4 PM, Wed evenings 6 - 8 PM, June - Aug Mon - Thurs 9 AM - 3 PM. No admis fee. Estab 1965 to provide a year-round calendar of continuing exhibitions; to sponsor related programs of artistic and educational interest; and to maintain small permanent collection displayed on campus. Two adjacent galleries occupy space in a wing of Mason Library on campus. Average Annual Attendance: 9000. Mem: 400; dues $10
Income: Financed by endowment, state appropriation and annual College budget
Collections: Paintings and Prints of Historical Interest included: Pierre Alechinsky; Milton Avery; Chuck Close; Robert Mapplethorpe; Paul Pollero; Gregorio Prestopino; George Rickey; Sidney Twardowicz Artists of National Prominence; Paintings by Regional Artists
Exhibitions: (1990) New Art/New Hampshire IV
Publications: Small catalogs or brochures to accompany exhibitions
Activities: Lectures open to public; concerts; gallery talks; competitions; individual paintings lent to departments on campus, other museums and galleries; lending collection consists of original prints, paintings and sculpture; book traveling exhibitions; originate traveling exhibitions; sales shop sells catalogues

MANCHESTER

M THE CURRIER GALLERY OF ART, 192 Orange St, 03104. Tel 603-669-6144. *Pres* Kimon S Zachos; *VPres* John H Morison; *Treas* Davis P Thurber; *Clerk* Mrs Norman F Milne; *Dir* Marilyn F Hoffman; *Coordr Public Relations* Catherine A Wright; *Mgr Museum Progs* Virginia H Eshoo; *Supv Currier Art Center* Robert Eshoo; *Dir Educ* Barbara A Pitsch; *Cur* Michael Komanecky; *Dir Development* Stephanie B Neal
Open Tues, Wed, Fri, Sat 10 AM - 4 PM, Thurs 10 AM - 10 PM, Sun 2 - 5 PM, cl Mon & national holidays. No admis fee. Estab & incorporated 1915 by will of Mrs Hannah M & Governor Moody Currier, which included endowment, building opened in 1929. Building contains six galleries, library & auditorium, two pavilions. Currier Art Center is housed in adjacent building acquired in 1938 & offers after school & Sat classes for children. Average Annual Attendance: 40,000. Mem: 1200; dues $15 & up; annual meeting in Mar
Income: Financed by endowment
Collections: American Furniture, glass & textiles 18th - 20th century; †American Paintings & Sculpture 18th century to present; European Paintings, prints & sculpture, 13th - 20th century; †European Masters 13th - 20th century; †Fine American Decorative Art 17th - 19th century including furniture, glass textiles & silver; Frank Lloyd Wright designed Zimmerman House, opened seasonally for tours
Publications: Bulletin, semi-annually; calendar, quarterly; exhibition catalogs, occasionally; Annual Report
Activities: Classes for children; docent training; lectures open to public; concerts; gallery talks; tours; awards; exten dept serves New Hampshire schools; individual paintings & original objectds of art lent
L Library, 192 Orange St, 03104. Tel 603-669-6144. *Librn* Maria K Graubart
Open to gallery staff, docents and research students by appointment for reference only
Library Holdings: Vols 10,000; Per subs 40; Other — Exhibition catalogs

L MANCHESTER CITY LIBRARY, 405 Pine St, 03104. Tel 603-624-6550. *Fine Arts Librn* Beverly M White
Open Mon, Tues & Thurs 9 AM - 9 PM, Wed & Fri 9 AM - 5:30 PM, Sat 9 AM - 5 PM
Income: Financed by city appropriations
Purchases: $6000
Library Holdings: Vols 22,694; mounted pictures; Micro — Reels; AV — A-tapes, cassettes 6010, fs 100, motion pictures 175, rec 5477, v-tapes 1312; Other — Framed reproductions 99
Exhibitions: Patron's art works, crafts, collectibles
Activities: Monthly summer film program to public

A MANCHESTER HISTORIC ASSOCIATION, 129 Amherst St, 03101. Tel 603-622-7531. *Pres* Fred Matuszawski; *Dir* John Mayer
Open Tues - Fri 9 AM - 4 PM, Sat 10 AM - 4 PM, cl Sun & Mon, national & state holidays, & Tues following Mon holidays. Estab 1896 to collect, preserve and make known Manchester's historical heritage. Average Annual Attendance: 10,000. Mem: 400; dues sponsor $500, benefactor $250, patron $100, supporting

$50, contributing $25, individual $15, annual meeting in April
Income: $100,000
Collections: †Furniture, †glass, †pewter, †maps, †prints, †paintings, †ceramics, †costumes, †textiles, †artifacts of all types; †Indian artifact collection of over 10,000 pieces found at Manchester sites; historical material
Exhibitions: Permanent and changing exhibitions reflecting all aspects of Manchester history
Publications: Annual report; bulletin, quarterly; catalogs, occasionally
Activities: Spring and fall program series; docent training; lectures open to public, 4 vis lectr per year; concerts; gallery talks; tours; competitions; individual and original objects of art lent to educational, business organizations and other museums; book traveling exhibitions; sales shop sells books, original art, reproductions and prints
L Library, 129 Amherst St, 03104. Tel 603-622-7531. *Librn* Elizabeth Lessard; *Asst Librn* Arlene Crossett
Income: $47,000 (financed by endowment)
Library Holdings: Vols 500; Per subs 14; maps; early textiles mill records; swatch sample books; 19th century music; Amoskeag Mfg Co Archives, publications of local history; AV — Cassettes; Other — Clipping files, manuscripts, memorabilia, pamphlets, photographs, prints, reproductions
Exhibitions: Quarterly exhibits reflecting history of city of Manchester
Publications: Manchester Historic Association, quarterly bulletin; annual report

M MANCHESTER INSTITUTE OF ARTS AND SCIENCES GALLERY, 148 Concord St, 03104. Tel 603-623-0313. *Dir* Angelo Randazzo; *Program & Educ Coordr* Kim Keegan; *Admin Asst* Nancy Banian; *Public Relations & Membership Coordr* Linda Seabury
Open Mon - Thurs 9 AM - 9 PM, Fri & Sat 9 AM - 5 PM, cl Sun. No admis fee. Estab 1898, as a private non-profit educational institution in order to promote, encourage and stimulate education in the arts and sciences. Gallery has limited space which is devoted to a variety of exhibitions including historical as well as contemporary themes. Mem: 670; dues family $35, individual $25; annual meeting in June
Income: Financed by endowment, membership, tuition and grants
Publications: Exhibition catalogs; schedule of courses, exhibitions and programs, 2 or 3 times per year
Activities: Classes for adults; films; lect; concerts; sales shop selling handcrafted items & fine arts prints

A NEW HAMPSHIRE ART ASSOCIATION, INC, PO Box 3096, 03303. Tel 603-796-6414. *Admin* Angus Locke
Estab 1940, incorporated 1962, as a non-profit organization, to promote the public's understanding and appreciation of the arts; to provide artists with a forum for their work and ideas. It offers a year-round exhibition and sales gallery at its headquarters in Manchester; an August exhibition at Sunapee State Park. Mem: 400; dues $25; annual meeting June
Income: Financed by grants, dues, patrons, rental art & sales
Exhibitions: Annuals at Currier Gallery of Art; Summer Annual combined with New Hampshire League of Arts and Crafts at Mount Sunapee State Park; Summer Annual Juried Exhibition at Prescott Park; Year-Round exhibits at N.E. Center; Durham NH; various one-person & group shows
Activities: Educ program for schools; patron program; lect demonstrations by member artists; awards; originate traveling exhibitions

M SAINT ANSELM COLLEGE, Chapel Art Center, PO Box 1718, 03102. Tel 603-641-7470; FAX 603-641-7116. *Dir* Dr Donald Rosenthal; *Coordr Exhib* Adrian LaVallee; *Secy* Denise Beaule
Open Mon - Fri 10 AM - 4 PM. No admis fee. Large gallery, formerly college chapel with painted, barrel-vaulted ceiling, stained glass windows. Average Annual Attendance: 5000
Income: Financed through College
Collections: New Hampshire artists & craftsmen; Prints
Exhibitions: (1992) Guatemala: Holy Week, Photographs by Peter Randall & Gary Samson. (1993) Recent Landscape Painting; Contemporary Religious Art
Publications: Exhibition catalogues
Activities: Lect open to public; gallery talks; concerts

PLYMOUTH

L PLYMOUTH STATE COLLEGE, Herbert H Lamson Library, 03264. Tel 603-535-2258. *Dir Library Services* Philip Wei; *Coordr Public Servs* Gary McCool; *Slide & Ill Librn* William Kietzman
Open Mon - Thurs 7 AM - 11:30 PM, Fri 7 AM - 9 PM, Sat 10 AM - 9 PM, Sun noon - 11:30 PM. Estab 1871 to serve the academic and personal needs of the college's students and faculty. Maintains exhibition space, an 18 ft exhibition wall. Circ 106,000
Income: $705,000 (one-fourth financed by state appropriation)
Purchases: $250,000
Library Holdings: audio discs 6300; Micro — Fiche 275,000, reels 7600; AV — Cassettes 1770, fs 3200, rec 32,700, slides 32,700; Other — Pamphlets
Exhibitions: Lucien Aigner; Patricia Benson; James Fortune; Margaret Houseworth; Winthrop Pratt; Leslie Snow; Viola Sutton; John McDonnell; Warren Mason
Publications: Brochures; handbook
Activities: Lect open to public; library tours; bibliographic instruction

PORTSMOUTH

A NATIONAL SOCIETY OF THE COLONIAL DAMES OF AMERICA, Moffatt-Ladd House, 154 Market St (Mailing add: 123 Mill Rd, 03862). Tel 603-436-8221.
Open Mon - Sat 10 AM - 4 PM, Sun 2 - 5 PM. Admis adults $4, children $1; garden $1; free to school groups. Society estab 1892, museum estab 1913. Moffatt-Ladd House was built in 1763. Average Annual Attendance: 2000. Mem: 215
Income: $54,000 (financed by endowment, mem, rents & donations)

Collections: Original china & porcelain, furniture, documents, letters & papers, portraits, wallpaper & documented wallpaper
Exhibitions: Costumes
Publications: George Mason & Gunston Hall (video); George Mason & The Bill of Rights (video); The Great Seal (audiotape)
Activities: School tours; lect open to members only, 4 vis lectr per year; competitions with awards; scholarships; sales table sells books & prints

M **PORTSMOUTH ATHENAEUM,** 9 Market Square, PO Box 848, 03801. Tel 603-431-2538. *Pres* Ronan Donoho; *Treas* Kevin LoaFond; *Librn* Jeannette Mitchell; *Keeper* Jane M Porter
Historic Reading Room open yearly Thurs 1 - 4 PM or by appointment. No admis fee. Estab 1817 to house museum of historical objects of local, statewide and national interest and is listed on National Register of Historical Sites. Average Annual Attendance: 2800. Mem: 200; dues $50; annual meeting 2nd Wed in Jan
Income: Financed by endowment and membership
Collections: American paintings; Colonial portraits; ship models & half-models; New England history; maritime history
Exhibitions: American Portraiture in the Grand Manner, 1720-1920
Activities: Lectures; gallery talks; tours; lending collection contains individual paintings & original objects of art and has lent to the Los Angeles County Museum of Art & National Portrait Gallery

L **Library,** 9 Market Square, PO Box 848, 03801. Tel 603-431-2538. *Librn* F Jeannette Mitchell
Open Tues & Thurs 1 - 4 PM or by appointment. Estab 1817. For reference only
Library Holdings: Vols 31,000; Per subs 45; AV — Cassettes, lantern slides; Other — Clipping files, manuscripts, memorabilia, original art works, pamphlets, photographs, prints
Special Subjects: 18th Century American Shipping; United States Marine History

M **PORTSMOUTH HISTORICAL SOCIETY,** John Paul Jones House, Middle and State St, PO Box 728, 03802-0728. Tel 603-436-8420. *Pres* Carl W Brage; *Dir* Priscilla Walker
Open Mon - Sat 10 AM - 4 PM, Sun noon - 4 PM. Admis adults $4, children $2, children under 6 free. Estab 1920 to identify and retain local history. The House was built in 1758 by Gregory Purcell, a merchant sea-captain. Purchased and restored in 1920 by the Portsmouth Historical Society. Average Annual Attendance: 7000. Mem: 250; dues $15; annual meeting May
Income: Financed by membership, investment and admission fees
Collections: Guns, books, china, costumes, documents, furniture, glass, portraits and silver pertaining to the early history of Portsmouth
Activities: Lectures, 1-2 vis lectr per year; daily tours; museum shop sells books, prints, slides, cards & jewelry

M **WARNER HOUSE ASSOCIATION,** MacPheadris-Warner House, 150 Daniel St, PO Box 895, 03802-0895. Tel 603-436-5909. *Chmn* Clinton Springer
Open June - Oct, Tues - Sat 10 AM - 4:30 PM, Sun 1 - 4:30 PM, cl Mon. Admis $4. Estab 1931
Income: $30,000 (financed by endowment, membership & admissions)
Collections: Stair Murals Collection
Exhibitions: Period Furniture & Decorative Accessories Joseph Blackburn: Portraits (1761)
Activities: Lect open to public, 5 vis lectr per year; tours; sales shop sells books reproductions, prints & slides

SHARON

M **SHARON ARTS CENTER,** Route 123, 03458. Tel 603-924-7256. *Dir* Marilyn Ash; *Gallery Mgr* Randall Hoel; *Registrar* Luann Hightower; *Shop Mgr* Carol Underwood
Open Mon - Sat 10 AM - 5 PM, Sun 1 - 5 PM. No admis fee. Estab 1947 to promote the education, sales, & enjoyment of the arts. Center consists of a gallery, store, & classroom facility. Average Annual Attendance: 15,000. Mem: 700; dues family $40, individual $25; annual meeting in Sept
Income: Financed by endowment, mem & state appropriation
Collections: Nora S Unwin Collection of Wood Engravings, Drawings, Watercolors
Exhibitions: Seven exhibits per yr featuring fine artists & craftsmen throughout the region; New Images in the Folk Tradition; Regional Juried Exhibition of Paintings & Drawings
Activities: Classes for adults & children; lectures open to public; competitions with awards; sales shop sells crafts

NEW JERSEY

ATLANTIC CITY

L **PRINCETON ANTIQUES BOOKSERVICE,** Art Marketing Reference Library, 2915-17 Atlantic Ave, 08401. Tel 609-344-1943; FAX 609-344-1944. *Pres* Robert E Ruffolo Jr; *Cur* Martha Ireland; *Adminr* Robert Eugene
Open by appointment 10 AM - 4 PM. Estab 1974 for pricing documentation of books and antiques. Open by appointment only; maintains art gallery. Average Annual Attendance: 1000
Income: $25,000 - $30,000
Purchases: $20,000
Library Holdings: Vols 12,500; Per subs 20; exhibition catalogs, original art works and prints; AV — Slides
Special Subjects: The function in US of art and the book market, Price information history from 1900
Collections: 19th century art; Post-card Photo Library Information Bank, 1900 - 1950, consisting 250,000 post-cards
Activities: Sales shop sells books & original art

BAYONNE

L **BAYONNE FREE PUBLIC LIBRARY,** Art Dept, 697 Avenue C, 07002. Tel 201-858-6981. *Library Dir* Sneh Bains
Open Mon, Tues, Thurs 9 AM - 12 noon, 1 - 5 PM, 6 - 9 PM, Wed, Fri, Sat 9 AM - 12 noon, 1 - 5 PM. Estab 1894. Art Gallery has 194 running feet exhibition space
Income: Financed by city appropriation and state aid
Library Holdings: Vols 222,000; Per subs 517; AV — Fs, rec 8101, slides 736; Other — Clipping files
Activities: Concerts; adult and children film programs weekly

BLOOMFIELD

M **HISTORICAL SOCIETY OF BLOOMFIELD,** 90 Broad St, 07003. Tel 201-429-9292; FAX 201-429-0170. *Pres* Jean Kuras; *Dir* Dorothy Johnson
Open Wed 2 - 4:30 PM by appointment. No admis fee. Estab circa 1968 to collect, preserve & exhibit items which may help to establish or illustrate the history of the area. Museum located in the gallery of the Bloomfield Public Library. Average Annual Attendance: 1436. Mem: 232; dues life $50, commercial organization $25, non-profit organization $10, couple $8, individual $5, student under 18 $1; meeting second Wed of alternate months Sept - May
Income: Financed by mem, Ways & Means Committee
Collections: Miscellaneous items of books, †clothing & accessories, †deeds & other documents, †dioramas, †early maps & newspapers, furniture, †household articles, letters, †memorabilia, †paintings, postcards, posters, tools, toys
Exhibitions: Permanent exhibitions
Activities: Lectures open to public, 3 - 5 vis lectrs per year; tours; sales shop sells books, prints, postcards, mugs, notepaper, medallions, & fruit cake (seasonal)

BURLINGTON

A **BURLINGTON COUNTY HISTORICAL SOCIETY,** 457 High St, 08016. Tel 609-386-4773. *Pres* Theodore B Codding; *VPres* James Greene; *Dir* M M Pernot
Open Mon - Thurs 1 - 4 PM, Sun 2 - 4 PM. Admis $2. Estab 1915 to preserve & interpret Burlington County history. Average Annual Attendance: 5000. Mem: 800; dues $15 & up; annual meeting fourth Thurs in May
Income: Financed by endowment & donations
Special Subjects: Historical Material, Burlington County & South Jersey history, Genealogy
Collections: Decorative arts; Quilts; Sampler
Publications: Newsletter, quarterly
Activities: Tours for children; docent training; lectures open to public, 3 vis lectrs per year; tours; museum shop sells books, magazines & reproductions

CALDWELL

M **CALDWELL COLLEGE,** Art Gallery, 07006. Tel 201-228-4424. *Dir* Sr M Gerardine
Open Mon - Fri 8:30 AM - 5 PM, weekends by appointment. No admis fee. Estab 1970 to provide students and area community with exposure to professional contemporary talent, to afford opportunities for qualified artists to have one-person shows
Income: Financed by college budget
Exhibitions: George Mueller (painting); Mary Ansgar of Norway Painting; Bob Lahm (painting); Alan Brown (painting); Alumni Show
Activities: Education department in connection with the college art department; lect open to public, 3 vis lectr per yr; scholarships offered; lending collection contains 12,000 kodachromes, motion pictures

CAMDEN

C **CAMPBELL MUSEUM,** Campbell Place, 08101. Tel 609-342-6440. *Pres* Ralph Collier; *Museum Asst* Bess Brock
Open Mon - Fri 9 AM - 4:30 PM. No admis fee. Estab 1966, a non-profit educational institution chartered by State of New Jersey, to collect soup tureens of silver, porcelain and pewter from the royal European houses of 18th &19th centuries. Collection displayed at Campbell Museum. Museum has red velvet walls and Plexiglas cases. Average Annual Attendance: 35,000
Income: Financed by Campbell Soup Company
Purchases: Soup tureens & eating vessels from European houses of 18th & 19th centuries
Collections: 18th Century soup tureens by leading porcelain makers and silversmiths
Exhibitions: Juried tureen exhibitions
Publications: Catalogue
Activities: Lectures; gallery talks; tours; film; competitions with awards; original objects of art lent; book traveling exhibitions; originate traveling exhibitions to museums only

M **RUTGERS UNIVERSITY,** Stedman Art Gallery, Fine Arts Center, 08102. Tel 609-225-6245, 225-6350. *Dir* Virginia Oberlin Steel; *Asst Dir for Progs & Admin* Nancy Maguire; *Asst Dir Educ* Noreen Scott Garrity
Open Mon - Sat 10 AM - 4 PM. No admis fee. Estab 1975 to serve educational needs of the campus and to serve community of southern New Jersey. Average Annual Attendance: 12,000
Income: Financed by endowment, state appropriation and gifts from private sources
Collections: Modern & contemporary art; †works on paper
Exhibitions: Changing exhibitions of visual arts & interdisciplinary exhibitions
Publications: Catalog for a major exhibition, yearly
Activities: Visiting lecturers, symposia, concerts & gallery talks open to public; competition with purchase prizes

CLINTON

M CLINTON HISTORICAL MUSEUM VILLAGE, 56 Main St, PO Box 5005, 08809. Tel 908-735-4101; FAX 908-735-0914. *Dir* David Breslauer; *Cur* Kathryn Jordan; *Registrar* Jean Daly
Open Apr 1 - Oct 31, Tues - Sun 10 AM - 4 PM. Admis adults $3, seniors $2, children under 12 $1.50, pre-schoolers free. Estab 1960 for the preservation and display of artifacts from the 18th and 19th century for educational and cultural purposes. Four-floor grist mill, blacksmith shop, general store, schoolhouse, log cabin and herb garden. Average Annual Attendance: 26,000. Mem: 630; dues $15 - $2500; annual meeting March
Income: $100,000 (financed by mem & donations)
Collections: Artifacts pertaining to 18th, 19th & early 20th centuries
Exhibitions: Craft Show; Antique Show; Harvest Jubilee; toy exhibit. (1991) Motorcycles
Publications: The Old Mill Wheel, newsletter, four times a year
Activities: Classes for children; docent training; lectures; concerts; tours; sales shop selling books and gift items
L Library, 56 Main St, PO Box 5005, 08809. Tel 908-735-4101; FAX 908-735-0914. *Registrar* Jean Daly
For historical reference
Library Holdings: Vols 600

A HUNTERDON ART CENTER, 7 Lower Center St, 08809. Tel 908-735-8415; FAX 908-735-8416. *Exec Dir* Sue Knapp-Steen; *Pres* Ellen Rosenthal; *VPres* Helen Axel; *Dir Educ* Ruth S Claus
Open Thurs & Fri 12:30 - 4:30 PM, Sat & Sun 1 - 5 PM. Admis adult $3, sr $1.50, children $1. Estab 1952 as a non-profit organization to provide arts enrichment through fine & performing arts. The first and second floors provide gallery space. The old stone mill has been remodeled retaining the original atmosphere with open broad wooden beams, white walls and plank flooring. Average Annual Attendance: 22,000. Mem: 750; dues patron $150, endowment $100, sustaining $75, family $35, single $25, student & sr citizens $10
Income: Financed by membership, city, state and county appropriations, federal funding, donations
Purchases: $100
Collections: †Print collection
Exhibitions: National Print Exhibit
Publications: Biannual newsletter.
Activities: Classes for adults & children; lect open to public, 4 vis lectr per year; tours; scholarships offered; individual paintings and original objects of art lent to Newark Museum and corp membership; originate traveling exhibitions to Newark Museum and corp membership; sales shop sells books, original art, reproductions, prints & handmade items

CRANBURY

C M GRUMBACHER INC, 30 Englehard Dr, 08512-9545. Tel 609-655-8282. *In Charge Art Awards Prog* Sandy DuBuske; *Public Relations* Dawn Lerch; *Dir Human Resources* Jim Preston
Exhibitions: Emerging Artists Exhibition
Publications: Palette Talk magazine, quarterly
Activities: Lectures; factory tours; cash awards; medallions; certificates to various art societies

DOVER

A ASSOCIATED ARTISTS OF NEW JERSEY, 452 Rockaway Rd, 07801. Tel 201-625-4810. *Pres* Ann Steele-Marsh; *VPres* Open ; *Treas* Hella Bailin
Estab 1941 to hold one or two exhibitions a year, with informal meetings in summer. Mem: Members selected by invitation of the board; dues $30; annual meeting Apr-May
Income: Financed by membership

A BLACKWELL STREET CENTER FOR THE ARTS, 32-34 W Blackwell St, 07801. Tel 201-328-9628. *Dir* Annette Adrian Hanna
Estab 1983. Average Annual Attendance: 2100. Mem: 25 artist, 12 public; qualifications for mem: artist members juried by Credentials Commission; dues $35 - $450; monthly meeting third Thurs of month
Income: $20,000 (financed by mem, grants & donations)
Exhibitions: Ten or more exhibitions scheduled per year
Activities: Lect open to public, 2 vis lectr per year

EAST HANOVER

C NABISCO BRANDS, INC, DeForest Ave, 07936. WATS 800-526-0896. *Archivist* David Stivers
Art collection viewed only while on tour
Collections: A History of the Golden Age of Illustration; Illustrations for Cream of Wheat Cereal Advertising in Magazines, on Posters & Signs, from 1900-1955, includes oil on canvas, oil on board, watercolors, sketches & photo montages
Exhibitions: Cream of Wheat Art Collection Traveling Exhibit

ELIZABETH

L FREE PUBLIC LIBRARY OF ELIZABETH, Fine Arts Dept, 11 S Broad St, 07202. Tel 201-354-6060. *Dir* Joseph Keenan; *Asst Dir & Head Art Dept* Roman Sawycky
Open Mon - Fri 9 AM - 9 PM, Sat 9 AM - 5 PM, cl Sun. No admis fee. Estab 1913, the art department functions within the Linx library system; it offers free service to patrons of Elizabeth & Union County. Special exhibit area displays paintings and miscellaneous objects d'art
Income: Financed by city and state appropriations
Library Holdings: Vols 15,000; Photographs & Illustrations 200,000; Other —

Reproductions 800
Collections: Japanese prints by various artists
Exhibitions: Works by artists and photographers; other special exhibitions from time to time
Activities: Dramatic programs; lect open to the public, 15 visiting lectrs per year; concerts; material available to patrons of Union County; lending collection contains film strips, projection equipment & motion pictures; printed catalogues of film strips & films available to the public - 4500 VHS videotapes (circulating)

ENGLEWOOD

L ENGLEWOOD LIBRARY, Fine Arts Dept, 31 Engle St, 07631. Tel 201-568-2215; FAX 201-568-8199. *Dir Library* Maryann Heaphy; *Head Programming Dept* Mary Beall
Open Mon - Thurs 9 AM - 9 PM, Fri & Sat 9 AM - 5 PM, Sun 1 - 5 PM (Oct-May). Estab 1901 to establish a free public library for citizens
Income: $510,000 (financed by endowment, city and state appropriation)
Library Holdings: Micro — Reels; AV — Cassettes, fs, motion pictures, rec, slides; Other — Clipping files, framed reproductions, original art works, pamphlets
Exhibitions: Members of Salurre to Women In The Arts; Quilts; Rare Books & Manuscripts; World of Renaissance
Activities: Lect open to public; concerts

HOPEWELL

M HOPEWELL MUSEUM, 28 E Broad St, 08525. Tel 609-466-0103. *Pres* David Mackey; *Cur* Beverly Weidl
Open Mon, Wed & Sat 2 - 5 PM, cl national holidays. No admis fee, donations suggested. Estab 1922 as a museum of local history from early 1700 - 1900, to show what the community was like for almost 300 years. Average Annual Attendance: 2000
Income: Financed by endowment, membership and donations
Collections: Antique china, glass, silver & pewter; colonial furniture; colonial parlor; early needlework; Indian handicrafts; photograph collection; Victorian parlor
Publications: Hopewell Valley Heritage; Pioneers of Old Hopewell; maps

JERSEY CITY

M JERSEY CITY MUSEUM, 472 Jersey Ave, 07302. Tel 201-547-4514. *Chmn* Audrey Winkler; *Dir* Nina S Jacobs; *Cur* Gary Sangster
Estab 1901 for the purpose of preserving & interpreting its permanent collection of art & historical objects. Maintains three gallery spaces for contemporary & historical exhibitions. Average Annual Attendance: 25,000. Mem: 500; dues $25 - $100, student & sr citizens $10
Income: Financed by state, county, city, federal appropriations as well as foundation, corporate & private support
Collections: Paintings, drawings & watercolors by 19th century artist August Will; 19th & 20th century paintings & prints; Jersey City & New Jersey related artifacts, documents, decorative & historical objects
Exhibitions: Changing exhibitions
Publications: Exhibition catalogs, posters, reproductions of art work on cards
Activities: Educ dept, classes for adults & children; workshops; lect open to public; gallery talks; tours; slide & panel talks; historical tours; video & performance arts

M JERSEY CITY STATE COLLEGE, Courtney Art Gallery, Dept of Art, 2039 Kennedy Blvd, 07305. Tel 201-200-3214. *Dir* Harold Lemmerman
Open Mon - Fri 10 AM - 5 PM. No admis fee. Estab 1969 to bring examples of professional work to the campus in each of the areas in which students are involved: Painting, sculpture, film, photography, textiles, weaving, ceramics, graphic design. Gallery is operated by students, and with the Jersey City Museum form a student internship training program. Average Annual Attendance: 5000
Income: Financed by city, state appropriation, and Art Department
Collections: Small collection of prints and paintings
Exhibitions: (1992) Ben Jones Exhibit; Sister John Steans (watercolor)
Activities: Lect open to public, 5 visiting lectrs per year; gallery talks; exten dept serving community organizations; individual paintings and original objects of art lent; lending collection contains color reproductions, film strips, Kodachromes, motion pictures, photographs; traveling exhibitions organized and circulated
M Art Space, 2039 Kennedy Blvd, 07305. Tel 201-200-3214. *Dir* Dr Harold Lemmerman
Gallery maintained for student & professional exhibitions
Exhibitions: (1992) Alexander Viscio; Master of Arts; Laura McDonald; AIDS Awareness

M SAINT PETER'S COLLEGE, Art Gallery, 2641 Kennedy Blvd, 07306. Tel 201-333-4400. *Dir* Oscar Magnan
Open Mon, Tues, Fri & Sat 11 AM - 4 PM, Wed & Thurs 11 AM - 9 PM. No admis fee. Estab 1971 to present the different art trends. Gallery is maintained with good space, lighting and alarm systems
Income: Financed by the college
Activities: Classes for adults; docent training; lectures open to public, 20 vis lectrs per year; concerts; gallery talks; tours; exten dept serving students

LAKEWOOD

M GEORGIAN COURT COLLEGE GALLERY, M Christina Geis Gallery, Lakewood Ave, 08701. Tel 908-364-2200, Ext 48. *Dir* Sr Mary Christina Geis
Open Mon - Fri 9 AM - noon & 1 - 4 PM. No admis fee. Estab 1964 to offer art students the opportunity to view the works of professional artists and also to exhibit student work. Gallery is one large room with 100 running feet of wall

area for flat work; the center area for sculpture. Average Annual Attendance: 1000
Income: Financed through the college
Exhibitions: Monthly exhibitions

LAWRENCEVILLE

INTER-SOCIETY COLOR COUNCIL
For further information, see National and Regional Organizations

M **RIDER COLLEGE,** Art Gallery, 2083 Lawrenceville Rd, PO Box 6400, 08648-3099. Tel 609-896-5192, 896-5168. *Assoc Prof of Art & Dir* Harry I Naar
Open Mon - Thurs 1 - 10 PM, Fri - Sun 1 - 5 PM. No admis fee. Estab 1970 to afford members of the community & college the opportunity to expand their knowledge and exposure to art. Gallery has 1513 sq ft of space divided into two rooms of different height. Average Annual Attendance: 5000
Income: $8000 (college funded)
Collections: †African Art; Contemporary Art; paintings, drawings, sculpture
Exhibitions: (1990) Tony Rosati (works on paper); Louis Draper, Aubrey J Kauffman (photographs); Johnathan Shalrn (sculprure-drawings); Princeton Artists Alliance (group show-paintings, prints); Robert Godfrey (paintings, drawings); Johnson Atelier (sculpture & drawings); AIDS Quilts. (1991) Diane Horn (paintings); Robert Birmelin (paintings- drawings); Ruth Fine (paintings on paper)
Activities: Docent training; internships; lect open to public, 4 - 6 vis lectr per yr; gallery talks; individual paintings lent to museums, group shows, one person shows; book traveling exhibitions

LAYTON

L **PETERS VALLEY CRAFT CENTER,** 19 Kuhn Rd, 07851. Tel 201-948-5200; FAX 201-948-0011. *Exec Dir* Jeanie Eberhardt; *Asst Dir* Sandra Ward
Open 10 AM - 5 PM. Estab 1970 as a non profit craft education center to promote & encourage traditional & contemporary crafts through exhibitions, demonstrations, workshops & educational programs. Located at Valley Brook Farm Administrative Offices. Mem: 500; dues $25; annual meeting in Oct
Income: Financed in part by a grant from NJ State Council on the Arts/Dept of State & the Geralding R Dodge Foundation
Activities: Educ dept; classes for adults & children;; lect open to public, 80 vis lectr per year; tours; workshops; competitions; sales shop sells original crafts

LINCROFT

M **MONMOUTH MUSEUM AND CULTURAL CENTER,** PO Box 359, 07738. Tel 908-747-2266; FAX 908-747-8592. *Prog Adminr* Catherine Jahos; *Pres* Dorothy V Morehouse; *First VPres* Barbara Goldfarb; *Second VPres* Jane McCosker; *Chmn of Board* Raymond Herter
Open Tues - Sat 10 AM - 4:30 PM, Sun 1 - 5 PM. Admis adults $2, children and senior citizens $1, free to Museum members & Brookdale Community College students. Estab 1963 to advance interest in art, science and nature. Museum houses two large galleries & the Becker Children's Wing. Exhibitions are changed four times a year; also an educational area and a conference area. Average Annual Attendance: 50,000. Mem: 1600; dues family $30, individual $20; annual meeting Jan
Income: $450,000 (financed by membership, donations, county funds & benefits)
Exhibitions: Annual Monmouth County Arts Council Juried Exhibition; From this Day Forward (Wedding Gowns 1810-1030); Keep the Home Fires Burning; WW II Homefront; Tom Toms to Tranquilizers (History of Medicine); New Jersey Watercolor; The Horse (Man's Noble Companion); Exploring Palentology, Dig We Must: The Fantistic Fossil Find
Publications: Calendar of events; catalogues of exhibitions; newsletter
Activities: Classes for adults and children; docent training; lect open to public; originate traveling trunks for use in schools; museum shop sells books and gift items

LONG BRANCH

M **LONG BRANCH HISTORICAL MUSEUM,** 1260 Ocean Ave, 07740. Tel 201-229-0600, 222-9879. *Pres* Edgar N Dinkelspiel
Open by appointment only. No admis fee. Estab 1953 as post Civil War historical museum. Average Annual Attendance: 10,000. Mem: Dues $1
Collections: Period furniture

MADISON

M **DREW UNIVERSITY,** Elizabeth P Korn Gallery, 07940. Tel 201-408-3553. *Dean* Paolo Cucchi; *Chmn Art Dept* Livio Saganic
Open Tues - Sun 12:30 - 4 PM & by appointment. No admis fee. Estab 1968 to provide exhibitions each school year to augment program of courses & to serve the community
Income: Financed by University instructional budget, general budget & donations
Collections: Ancient Near-East archaeological collection; colonial America; †contemporary abstraction; native American artifacts; 19th century academic; Oriental art
Exhibitions: (1992) Weaving & Womens Prowess; Tai Textiles from Mainland SE Asia Mavis Pusey; Steven Siegel; Shamanic Voices; Fiber Arts; Jill Levine & Karen Harris; George Grosz prints; 55 Mercer; Spanish Civil War;
Activities: Lectures open to public, 3-4 vis lectr per yr
L **Art Dept Library,** Rt 24, 07940. Tel 201-408-3588. *Dir* Dr Caroline M Coughlin; *Reference Librn* Jody Caldwell
Library maintained for art history courses
Purchases: $5777 annually (for purchases to support art history courses at the college level)
Library Holdings: Vols 350,000; Per subs 2033; Micro — Fiche; AV — A-tapes, fs, rec, slides, v-tapes; Other — Exhibition catalogs, manuscripts, original art works, pamphlets, photographs

L **FAIRLEIGH DICKINSON UNIVERSITY,** Florham Madison Campus Library - Art Dept, 285 Madison Ave, 07940. Tel 201-593-8500; FAX 201-593-8525. *Libr Dir* James Fraser
Open Mon - Fri 8:30 AM - 10:30 PM. Estab 1958. Circ 40,000
Library Holdings: Vols 200,000; Per subs 960; Archives of NY Cultural Art Center 30,000; AV — Rec 5000, slides 50,000; Other — Exhibition catalogs 6000, original art works 6000, photographs 50,000
Collections: †Czech Graphic Design, 1919-1939; †Cartoon & Graphic Satire; †Outdoor Advertising; †book arts
Exhibitions: (1990) Anna Mackova, woodcut. (1990-91) Lithuanian Posters of the 1980s; Hiroshi Hamaya: Photos of Urumchi
Publications: Exhibition catalogues

M **UNITED METHODIST CHURCH COMMISSION ON ARCHIVES AND HISTORY,** PO Box 127, 07940. Tel 201-822-2787; FAX 201-408-3909. *Secy* Dr Charles Yrigoyen Jr
Open Mon - Fri 9 AM - 5 PM. No admis fee. Estab 1885 as a religious history museum. The Archives & History Center is located on Drew University Campus, & it contais a museum, a library & a spacious 180,000 cubic ft archival vault
Collections: Letters; Photographs
Exhibitions: Chinese Missionaries
Publications: Historian's Digest, bimonthly; Methodist History, quarterly
Activities: Guided tours; sales shop sells books, plates, cards, slides and prints
L **Library,** PO Box 127, 07940. Tel 201-408-3590. *Dir* Kenneth Rowe
Library Holdings: Vols 50,000; Per subs 25
Collections: Methodist materials; pamphlets & manuscripts of John Wesley & his associates; materials pertaining to women & ethnic minorities

MAHWAH

M **THE ART GALLERIES OF RAMAPO COLLEGE,** 505 Ramapo Valley Rd, 07430. Tel 201-529-7587.
Open Mon - Thurs 11 AM - 4 PM, Sun 3 - 6 PM. No admis fee. Estab 1979 as outreach for community, faculty, staff & students to support undergraduate curriculum. Three galleries: thematic changing exhibitions gallery; permanent collection gallery; alternate space gallery. Average Annual Attendance: 5000. Mem: 300 (friends); dues $15
Income: Financed by state appropriation & grants
Collections: †Rodman Collection of Popular Art, including works by Henry Rousseau, Pippin & Edmondson; †Study Collection of Prints; fine art printmaking from 15th century to present
Exhibitions: New Horizons in Printmaking; Sculpture Inside & Out; Leonardo da Vinci's inventions made into working models; Inside Tracts: Jeff Gates (Photographer); American Immigration History (Photo Exhibit); SOHO Summer Sampler (mixed)
Publications: Exhibit catalogs
Activities: Classes for adults & children; dramatic programs; docent training; lectures open to public, 10 vis lectrs per yr; competitions; scholarships & fels offered; individual paintings lent to institutions, colleges & museums; book traveling exhibitions; originate traveling exhibitions

MERCERVILLE

L **JOHNSON ATELIER TECHNICAL INSTITUTE OF SCULPTURE,** Johnson Atelier Library, 60 Ward Ave Extension, 08619. Tel 609-890-7777. *Librn* Eden R Bentley
Not open to public. Estab 1977 to provide an information center for apprentices, instructors and staff on sculpture, art appreciation and art history. Library provides space for lectures, movies, slides, classes on art history & critique sessions
Income: $3000 (privately financed)
Purchases: $3000
Library Holdings: Vols 3000; Per subs 28; AV — Cassettes, slides; Other — Clipping files, exhibition catalogs
Special Subjects: Art History, Sculpture, Art Appreciation, Health & Legal Issues Concerning Art
Collections: Exhibition catalogues on sculptors and group shows; slides of about 90 sculptor's work

MILLVILLE

M **WHEATON CULTURAL ALLIANCE INC,** Wheaton Village, 1501 Glasstown Rd, 08332. Tel 609-825-6800; FAX 609-825-2410. *Pres* Barry Taylor
Estab 1970, a cultural center dedicated to American folklore, craft & heritage

MONTCLAIR

M **MONTCLAIR ART MUSEUM,** 3 S Mountain Ave, 07042-1747. Tel 201-746-5555; FAX 201-746-9118. *Pres* James Mills; *Dir* Ellen Harris; *Dir Communications* Anne-Marie Nolin; *Curatorial Registrar* Martin Beck; *Comptroller* Sonyia Woloshyn; *Dir Development* Elyse Reissman; *Cur Educ* Janet Cook; *Cur Coll* Alehandro Anreus
Open Tues, Wed, Fri & Sat 11 AM - 5 PM, Thurs & Sun 1 - 5 PM. Admis suggested contribution $4. Estab 1914. Five galleries of changing exhibitions; one gallery of permanent exhibitions; student gallery. Average Annual Attendance: 70,000. Mem: 2700; individual $30
Income: Financed by endowment and membership
Collections: American costumes; The Rand Collection of American Indian Art Whitney Silver Collection; †American paintings, 18th - 20th century; bookplate collection; †prints & drawings
Exhibitions: (1992) The American Landscape: From Cole to Blakelock Dottie Atty: The Anxious Object; Three Hispanic-American Masters; Robert Kushner: Seasons; Brave Against the Enemy: Plains Indian Art from the Montclair Art Museum; Arctic Imagery: Contemporary Inuit Drawing from a Private New

Jersey Collection. (1993) Hans Weingaertner: A Retrospective; The Crayon; June Brides; Currier & Ives: Selections from the George Raimes Beach Collection; Henri & The Ash Can School
Publications: Bulletin, bi-monthly; exhibition catalogues
Activities: Classes for adults and children; docent training; workshops coordinated programs with school groups; dramatic programs; lectures open to the public; concerts; gallery talks every Sunday; tours; museum shop sells books, notecards, reproductions, slides, Native American jewelry & crafts, jewelry & games/toys for children

L **LeBrun Library,** 3 S Mountain Ave, 07042. Tel 201-746-5555; FAX 201-746-9118. *Librn* Edith A Rights
Open Tues, Wed, Fri, Sat 10 AM - 5 PM, Thurs & Sun 2 - 5 PM, cl Mon & major holidays. Admis suggested donation general $4, senior citizen & students over 18 with ID $2, members & children under 18 free. Estab 1924 to support research and exhibitions of the museum. For reference only
Library Holdings: Vols 13,000; Per subs 50; Bookplates; Micro — Fiche; AV — A-tapes, slides; Other — Clipping files, exhibition catalogs
Special Subjects: American Art, American Indian, Japanese Culture
Collections: †Bookplates; †posters
Exhibitions: Selected bookplates of Arthur Nelson Macdonald; The Book Plate Work of David McNeely Stauffer
Publications: The Bookplates of Arthur Nelson MacDonald

MORRISTOWN

L **COLLEGE OF SAINT ELIZABETH,** Mahoney Library, 2 Convent Rd, 07960-6989. Tel 201-292-6476. *Dir of Library* Open
Open Mon - Thurs 8:30 AM - 10 PM, Fri 8:30 AM - 6 PM. Estab 1899 for academic purposes
Income: Financed by private funds
Library Holdings: Vols 7200; Per subs 40; Micro — Fiche, reels; AV — Cassettes, fs, rec; Other — Exhibition catalogs, original art works, photographs, prints, reproductions, sculpture
Special Subjects: The Madonna
Exhibitions: Sculpture, paintings, prints by the Art Dept faculty
Activities: Original objects of art lent

M **MORRIS MUSEUM,** 6 Normandy Heights Rd, 07960. Tel 201-538-0454; FAX 201-538-0154. *Exec Dir* John D Peterson; *Public Relations Dir* Jill Kimbaris
Open Mon - Sat 10 AM - 5 PM, Sun 1 - 5 PM; cl major holidays. Admis adults $4, students, sr citizens & children $2; groups of 20 or more $2 per person. Estab 1913 to educate diverse public on topics in art, anthropology & history, as well as the sciences. Average Annual Attendance: 310,000. Mem: 3000; dues benefactor $250, corporate $150, patron $100, associate $75, sponsor $50, non-profit organizations $40, family $40, couple $40, individual $25, students & sr ctizens $20
Collections: American historic & foreign; decorative arts; dolls; North American Indians; Art; Rock & Mineral
Exhibitions: History Gallery features early American kitchen & general store; North American Indian & Woodland Indian Galleries; Rock & Mineral Gallery; Live Animal Gallery; Dinosaur Gallery; Children's Room; Mammal Gallery; Model Train Gallery
Activities: Classes for adults & children; dramatic programs; docent training; lect open to the public; concerts; gallery talks for schools; individual paintings & original objects of art lent to other museums & art organizations; originate traveling exhibitions; museum shop sells books, original art, reproductions, prints, slides, jewelry, games & crafts from around the world

L **Library,** 6 Normandy Heights Rd, 07960. Tel 201-538-0454; FAX 201-538-0154. *Librn* Betty Addison
Library Holdings: Vols 2500; Per subs 10; AV — Slides
Special Subjects: Anthropology, Archaeology, Art Education, Ceramics, Costume Design & Construction, Decorative Arts, Dolls, Painting - American, Painting - British, Painting - Dutch, Painting - European, Painting - Flemish, Painting - French, Painting - German, Painting - Italian, Painting - Japanese, Painting - Scandinavian, Painting - Spanish, Pottery, Pre-Columbian Art, Textiles

M **SCHUYLER-HAMILTON HOUSE,** 5 Olyphant Place, 07960. Tel 201-267-4039. *Regent* Martha Ann King
Open Tues & Sun 2 - 5 PM, other times by appointment. Admis adults $1, children under 12 free. Estab 1923 for preservation of historical landmark. House is furnished with 18th Century antiques; five large portraits of General & Mrs Philip Schuyler, their daughter, Betsey Schuyler Hamilton, Alexander Hamilton and Dr Jabez Campfield; old lithographs, silhouette of George Washington, needle and petit point. Average Annual Attendance: 1500. Mem: 90; dues $30; annual meeting 1st Thurs in May, Chapter meets Oct - May
Income: Financed by membership, Friends of Schuyler-Hamilton, foundations & matching gifts
Collections: China - Canton, blue willow, Staffordshire; doll china; pewter; brass candlesticks; rugs; tunebooks
Activities: Docent training; lect for members; tours; competitions with awards; scholarships; sales shop sells stationery, cards & reproductions

NEWARK

A **ALJIRA CENTER FOR CONTEMPORARY ART,** 2 Washington Place, 4th floor, PO Box 7506, 07107. Tel 201-643-6877. *Exec Dir* Victor Davson; *Art Dir* Carl Hazelwood
Open Wed - Sun noon - 6 PM. Estab 1983 as a multi-cultural visual art organization
Exhibitions: (1991) Living Space - Interior Exterior; Decorative Impulse

M **NEWARK MUSEUM ASSOCIATION,** The Newark Museum, 49 Washington St, PO Box 540, 07101. Tel 201-596-6550; FAX 201-642-0459. *Pres & Chmn Bd of Trustees* Kevin Shanley; *Dir* Samuel C Miller; *Deputy Dir* Mary Sue Sweeney Price; *Business Adminr* Dominic A Lisanti; *Curatorial Adminr & Registrar* Audrey Koenig; *Cur Classical Collection* Dr Susan H Auth; *Cur Coin Collection* Dr William L Bischoff; *Cur Decorative Arts* Ulysses G Dietz; *Cur Oriental Coll* Valrae Reynolds; *Cur Ethnological Coll* Anne M Spencer; *Dir Education* Susan Newberry; *Lending Dept Supv* Helene Konkus; *Cur Earth Sciences* Dr Alice Blount; *Arts Workshop Supv* Stephen McKenzie; *Dir of Mem & Museum Servs* Barbara Lowell; *Gift Shop Supv* Lorelei Rowars; *Dir of Exhibitions* David Palmer; *Prog Coordr* Jane W Rappaport; *Public Relations Officer* Donna Brion; *Dir Science Dept & Cur Biology* Dr Carol Bossert; *Dir Development* Peggy Dougherty; *Cur Painting & Sculpture* Joseph Jacobs
Open Wed - Sun noon - 5 PM, cl Christmas, New Year's Day, July 4 & Thanksgiving. No admis fee. Estab 1909 to exhibit articles of art, science, & technology, & for the study of the arts and sciences. The building was a gift of Louis Bamberger, opened 1926; held in trust by the Museum Association for the City of Newark, which gave the site. The adjoining buildings were acquired by the Museum in 1937 & 1982. Major renovation designed by Michael Graves reopened in 1989, with 60,000 sq ft of gallery space, as well as new education facilities & a 300 seat auditorium & won the 1992 American Institute of Architects Honor Award for Design Excellence. Average Annual Attendance: 350,000. Mem: 7900; dues $35 and up; annual meeting Jan
Income: $5,800,000 (financed by city & state appropriations, county funds)
Collections: †American painting and sculpture of all periods with primitives well represented; †African, †American Indian, †Chinese, †Indian, †Islamic, †Japanese, †South Pacific, †Tibetan; †Mediterranean Antiquities, including Eugene Schaefer Collection of ancient glass; †decorative arts; †Pre-Columbian material; crosses & crucifixes; †numismatics
Exhibitions: American Folk Art; American paintings and sculptures; Tibet: A Lost World; Japanese Art; Chinese Ceramics; Ritual & Ceremony in African Life; Victorian Furniture; The Ballantine House; Art of Coptic Egypt; Southwest Indian Pottery; Japan The Enduring Heritage; 2000 Years of Chinese Ceramics; Murals Without Walls; Arshile Gorky's Aviation Murals Rediscovered; American Art Pottery; American Bronze Sculpture; American Silver; Navajo Textiles; American Impressionists; Edmondson/Butler Folk Art; Twentieth Century Afro-American Artists; Money & Medals of Newark; Against the Odds; Dragon Threads; In the Wake of Columbus: American Treasure, Demographic Upheaval, Global Economy
Publications: Newsletter, bimonthly; catalogs and bulletins on major exhibitions
Activities: Extensive educational programs including classes for adults & children; docent training; lect open to the public, 15 - 20 vis lectr per year; films; concerts; gallery talks; tours; competitions; exten dept serving community neighborhoods; individual paintings & original objects of art lent to other museums; lending collection contains cultural, scientific & historic objects & models; museum shop sells catalogues, reproductions, prints, original craft items from around the world

L **Newark Museum Library,** 49 Washington St, PO Box 540, 07101. Tel 201-596-6622; FAX 201-642-0459. *Librn* Margaret DiSalvi
Open Wed - Fri 9 AM - 5 PM. Estab 1926 to serve the Museum staff and to provide information on the collections
Library Holdings: Vols 27,000; Per subs 200; AV — Kodachromes, lantern slides, slides; Other — Clipping files, exhibition catalogs, pamphlets, photographs
Special Subjects: American Indian Art, Decorative Arts, Oriental Art, Primitive Art, Native American Art

M **Junior Museum,** 53 Washington St, PO Box 540, 07101. Tel 201-596-6605; FAX 201-642-0459. *Junior Museum Supv* Jane Caffrey Reid; *Asst Supv* Kevin Heller; *Art Asst* Alejandro H Ramirez; *Art Asst* Enola R Romano
Open Oct - Dec & Feb - May Tues - Fri 9 AM - 5 PM, Sat 9 AM - 1 PM. No admis fee. Estab 1926 to provide art and science programs designed to stimulate the individual child in self discovery and exploration of the world, and to teach effective use of the Museum as a whole, which may lead to valuable lifetime interests. Average Annual Attendance: 17,000. Mem: 3500 active; $.10 lifetime membership; annual meeting May
Income: Financed through The Newark Museum
Exhibitions: Changing exhibitions of childrens' artwork; annual spring & summer exhibitions in Junior Gallery; Stepping into Ancient Egypt: The House of the Artist Pashed
Activities: Weekday Pre-School, Saturday morning & summer workshops for ages 3-16, parents' workshops, community outreach & school enrichment programs, special events workshops & holiday festivals & hospital outreach, Junior Gallery offering a self guided gallery game

L **NEWARK PUBLIC LIBRARY,** Art & Music Div, 5 Washington St, PO Box 630, 07101. Tel 201-733-7840; FAX 201-733-5648. *Supv Art & Music Div* Frances Beiman
Open Sept - June Tues - Thurs 9 AM - 8:30 PM, Mon & Fri 9 AM - 5:30 PM, Sat 9 AM - 5:30 PM. Estab 1888, provides materials on all aspects of the visual arts to the New Jersey Library Network of New Jersey. Maintains an art gallery: a total of 200 running ft. Circ 70,000
Income: Financed by city & state appropriations
Library Holdings: Vols 75,000; Per subs 240; original documents; Micro — Fiche, reels; AV — Slides 18,000; Other — Clipping files, exhibition catalogs, manuscripts, original art works, photographs, prints
Special Subjects: Bookplates & Bindings, Artist's Books, Fine Prints, Illustrated Books, Japanese Books & Prints, Shopping Bags, Shopping Bags
Collections: †Autographs; †Bookplates; †Fine Print Collection (18,000); †Picture Collection (1,000,000 illustrations); †Posters (4000)
Exhibitions: Posters from the Olympic Games: 1964-1984; Prints by Clarence Carter: A 60 year retrospective; Movable Books: A Paradise of Pop Ups, A Feast of Fold Outs, & a Mix of Mechanicals Melded with a Marvelous Melange on the Same Theme; A Celebration of Great Books from the Limited Editions Club, 1988; Prints by Joseph Pennell: 1857-1926; Charles Breed: Early Photographs, 1900-1923, 1989; Contemporary American Printmaking 1989; Poster & Prints from Puerto Rico, 1950-1990
Publications: Calendar of events, bimonthly
Activities: Gallery talks; tours

M **NEW JERSEY HISTORICAL SOCIETY MUSEUM,** 230 Broadway, 07104. Tel 201-483-3939; FAX 201-483-1988. *Chmn Board* Katharine Auchincloss; *Cur & Registrar* Open
Open Wed - Sat 10 AM - 4 PM. Admis adults $2.50, students & senior citizens

$2, groups $1.50 per person. Estab 1845 to collect, preserve, exhibit and make available for study the materials pertaining to the history of New Jersey and its people. The museum has five period rooms and lobby display cases on the main floor; three galleries on second floor totaling 3900 sq ft devoted to permanent or changing exhibitions. Average Annual Attendance: 45,000. Mem: 3163; dues adults $25 and up; annual meeting third Wed in April
Income: Financed by endowment, membership, gifts, grants and benefits
Collections: Ceramics; glassware; furniture; important technical drawings from 1790-1815; Indian relics; New Jersey portraits, landscapes, prints and photographs; sculpture; silhouettes and miniatures; silver; toys; World War I posters; New Jersey History Artifacts
Exhibitions: Painted in Crayon: Pastel Portraits from the Collection; Steam: Power to Move the World; Things Once Common, a collection of household implements and every day tools from the late 18th - 19th centuries interpreting the social history of New Jersey's past; Period Rooms, four Victorian & one Colonial; Rembrandt Peale and Gilbert Stuart from permanent collection
Publications: Exhibition catalogs; New Jersey History, quarterly; New Jersey Messenger, monthly newsletter; Instructional Bulletin; Crossroads, Jersey Journeys
Activities: Classes for children; docent training; school history clubs; lectr open to the public; tours; competitions; individual paintings and original objects of art lent to established institutions; traveling exhibitions organized and circulated; sales shop selling books, reproductions, prints and items for children

M **New Jersey State Museum at Morven,** 55 Stockton St, Princeton, 08540. Tel 609-683-4495; FAX 609-599-4098. *Cur Cultural History* Suzanne Crilley; *Development Dir* Robin Austin; *Admin* Ken Mailloux
Open Wed 10 AM - 2 PM, Sat 10 AM - 1 PM. Admis adults $2, children $1. Built by Richard Stockton, a signer of the Declaration of Independence, and later the residence of New Jersey Governors; tours and exhibitions highlight landscape archaeology and architectural preservation currently in progress. Average Annual Attendance: 5000
Income: Program of the New Jersey State Museum; financed by gifts, grants & benefits
Collections: Artifacts Archaeology
Exhibitions: Period rooms of Federal and Jacksonian Eras; Statesmen Gallery
Activities: Tours; Sandbox Archaeology Program for New Jersey school children; museum shop

L **NEW JERSEY INSTITUTE OF TECHNOLOGY,** Architectural Information Center, 323 Martin Luther King Blvd, 07102. Tel 201-596-3083; FAX 201-596-8296. *Supvr* Rachel Roth
Open Mon - Fri 8:30 AM - 4:30 PM. Estab 1975 to serve the needs of the school of architecture. For lending & reference
Purchases: $12,000
Library Holdings: AV — A-tapes, cassettes, fs, slides; Other — Clipping files, pamphlets
Special Subjects: Architecture, Art History, Constructions, History of Art & Archaeology, Interior Design, Landscape Architecture, Maps, Period Rooms, Photography, Restoration & Conservation

C **PRUDENTIAL INSURANCE COLLECTION,** 213 Washington St, 07101. Tel 201-877-6000. *Dir Art Program* Helene Zucker Seeman; *Adminr* Naomi Baigell
Estab 1969 to enhance the surroundings and living up to social responsibility in supporting art as a genuinely important part of life
Collections: Approximately 12,000 holdings of paintings, sculptures & unique works on paper; 2558 signed graphics; 1182 posters; 241 billboards; 200 photographs

NEW BRUNSWICK

M **DOUGLASS COLLEGE-RUTGERS THE STATE UNIVERSITY,** Mary H Dana Women Artists Series, Mable Smith Douglas Library, Chapel Dr, 08903. Tel 908-932-9346. *Cur* Francoise S Puniello
Open Mon - Thurs 8 AM - 1 AM, Fri 8 AM - 11 PM, Sat 10 AM - 8 PM, Sun 11 AM - 1 AM. No admis fee. Estab 1971 to exhibit the work of living women artists. Located in lobby of Mabel Smith Douglass Library on women's campus of Rutgers University
Income: Financed from gifts from endowment, student groups & departmental funds
Exhibitions: Four exhibits each academic yr, all are one or two-women exhibits
Publications: Annual exhibition catalogue
Activities: Lect open to public; visiting lect; artists selected by jury

C **JOHNSON & JOHNSON,** Art Program, One Johnson & Johnson Plaza, 08933. Tel 201-524-3698. *Art Cur* Michael J Bzdak; *Asst Cur* Phillip Earenfight
Collections: Works on paper from the 1960s, 70s & 80s; photographs; works by New Jersey artists
Exhibitions: Paul Robeson: Artist & Activist; Images of an Icon: Photographs of the Statue of Liberty Stated as Fact; Photographic Documents of New Jersey

RUTGERS, THE STATE UNIVERSITY OF NEW JERSEY
M **Jane Voorhees Zimmerli Art Museum,** George & Hamilton Sts, 08903. Tel 908-932-7203; FAX 908-922-8201. *Dir* Phillip Dennis Cate; *Asst Dir, Curatorial Affairs* Jeffrey Wechsler; *Assoc Dir* Carma C Fauntleroy; *Cur Educ* Dr Laura Fattal; *Cur Prints & Drawings* Trudy Hansen; *Registrar* Barbara Trelstad
Open Mon, Tues, Thurs & Fri 10 AM - 4:30 PM, Sat & Sun noon - 5 PM, cl Wed, Dec 25 - Jan 1, Sat in July. No admis fee. Estab 1966 to house Fine Arts Collection & present exhibitions through the school year. Average Annual Attendance: 30,000. Mem: 900; dues $35, $10 student
Income: Financed by state appropriation & public & private sources
Purchases: $150,000
Collections: †Original artwork & manuscripts for children's books; 15th & 17th century Italian; 17th century Dutch; 18th, 19th & 20th century American; 18th & 19th century English paintings; †19th & 20th century French & American prints; †Rutgers University Collection of Children's Literature; †Rutgers Archives for Printmaking Studios; Japonisme: Western Art Influenced by

Japanese Art; †Russian Art
Exhibitions: (1993) Focus Four: Aspects Four Collection at Rutgers; Expression Abstracted: Heads by Pepi Rosenborg & Seliger & Sirugo; Masters of Fine Arts Exhibition; Opulence in an Age of Industry: Collections from the Sigmund Freedman Collection; Mikado's Empire: Early photography of Japan 1868 - 1912
Publications: Friends Newsletter; exhibition catalogs; Interntional Center for Japonisme Newsletter
Activities: Classes for adults & children; docent training; lect open to public; concerts; gallery talks; tours; individual paintings & original objects of art lent to museums; traveling exhibitions organized & circulated; museum shop sells books

L **Art Library,** Voorhees Hall, 08903. Tel 908-932-7739; FAX 908-932-6743. *Art Librn* Halina Rusak; *Asst Librn* Marguerite Barrett
Open Mon - Thurs 9 AM - 12 PM, Fri & Sat 9 AM - 5 PM, Sun 1 - 12 PM. Estab 1966 for academic research. For reference only
Library Holdings: Vols 59,000; Per subs 240; Micro — Fiche; Other — Clipping files, exhibition catalogs, pamphlets
Special Subjects: Architectural History; Western Art
Collections: Mary Barlett Cowdrey Collection of America Art; Louis E Stern Collection of Contemporary Art; Howard Hibbard Collection; Western Art-Architectural History
Activities: Bibliographic instruction; tours; lect

NEW PROVIDENCE

M **CAMBRIA HISTORICAL SOCIETY,** 121 Chanlon Rd, 07974. Tel 908-665-2846. *Dir* Tamika Borden; *Cur* Donald Bruce
Open Mon - Thurs & Sat 10 AM - 4 PM. Admis adult $3. Estab 1950 as a historic house museum. Average Annual Attendance: 25,00. Mem: 1750; dues $40; annual meeting in August
Income: $140,000 (financed by membership)
Collections: China; dolls; furniture; glass; paintings

NORTH BRANCH

A **PRINTMAKING COUNCIL OF NEW JERSEY,** 440 River Rd, 08876. Tel 908-725-2110. *Development Dir* Sarah M Muccifori
Open Tues - Fri 10 AM - 4 PM, Sat 1 - 4 PM, cl Sun. No admis fee. Estab 1973 to promote fine art/original printmaking. Average Annual Attendance: 30,000. Mem: 315; dues $35 & up; annual meeting in Oct
Income: Financed by endowment, NJ State Council on the Arts, Somerset County Parks Commission, Geraldine R Dodge Foundation, corporations
Activities: Adult classes; lect open to public, some to members only; competitions with awards contains art objects; lending collection contains art objects, lent to corporate members & libraries; book traveling exhibitions 9 per yr; originate traveling exhibitions 9 per yr

NORTH BRUNSWICK

A **MIDDLESEX COUNTY CULTURAL & HERITAGE COMMISSION,** Artists League of Central New Jersey, 841 Georges Rd, 08902. Tel 908-745-4489. *VPres* Cynthia Walling; *Treas* Edmund Spiro; *Exhibit Chmn* Wend Enger Gibson
Estab 1979 to provide exhibition opportunities and information services for members, and educational and cultural opportunities for the general public. Slide file of members' art work is maintained. Mem: 177; dues family or friend $25, mem $15, students & sr citizens $10; monthly board meetings
Income: Financed by mem, state grants, fundraising
Exhibitions: New Brunswick Tommorrow; Annual Statewide Show
Publications: ALCNJ Newsletter, monthly
Activities: Demonstrations open to public; competitions with awards

OCEAN CITY

A **OCEAN CITY ART CENTER,** 1735 Simpson Ave, 08226. Tel 609-399-7628. *Exec Dir* Eunice Bell; *Board Pres* Scott Griswold Jr
Open Mon - Sat 9 AM - 4 PM, evenings Mon - Fri 7 - 10 PM. Estab 1967 to promote the arts. Two galleries are maintained; upper gallery houses the permanent collection; lower gallery is for monthly changing exhibitions throughout the year. Average Annual Attendance: 10,000. Mem: 1000; dues individual $8, family $15; annual meeting in mid-March
Income: $70,000 (financed by membership, city appropriation, New Jersey State Council on the Arts Grant 1981)
Exhibitions: Annual: Membership Show, Juried Show, Boardwalk Art Show Winners Exhibition, Christmas Crafts Fair, Juried Photography Show
Publications: Newsletters, quarterly
Activities: Classes for adults and children; lect open to the public, 12 vis lectr per year; concerts; competitions with awards; scholarships offered; museum shop sells books, original art and crafts

L **Art Library,** 1735 Simpson Ave, PO Box 97, 08226. Tel 609-399-7628. *Exec Dir* Eunice Bell
Open 9 AM - 4 PM daily, & Mon - Sat, 7 - 10 PM evenings
Income: $70,000
Library Holdings: Vols 400; Per subs 2; AV — Slides; Other — Exhibition catalogs
Special Subjects: Art History, Photography

OCEANVILLE

M **NOYES MUSEUM,** Lily Lake Rd, 08231. Tel 609-652-8848; FAX 609-652-6166. *Dir* Robert J Koenig; *Asst Dir* Bonnie Bird Pover; *Curatorial Asst & Registrar* Stacy Smith
Open Wed - Sun 11 AM - 4 PM. Admis adults $3, sr citizens $1.50, full-time students & children $.50, Fri free. Estab 1983 to foster awareness & appreciation of contemporary American art & crafts & folk art from the mid- Atlantic region.

Four wing galleries & central gallery space devoted to rotating exhibitions of contemporary American art, folk art, wildlife art & local/regional history. Average Annual Attendance: 12,000-15,000. Mem: 750; dues corporate sponsor $500 - $1500, benefactor $250, sponsor $125, patron $75, family $35, individual $20, students $10

Income: $335,000 (financed by endowment, membership, state appropriation)

Purchases: Purple Martin Palace by Leslie Christofferson

Collections: Contemporary American Fine Art & Crafts; 19th & 20th century folk art from the mid-Atlantic region

Exhibitions: (1991) The Last Portfolio of Henry Moore; American abstract paintings by Charles Evans II. (1992) New Jersey Arts Annual: Fine Arts; Points of the Compass: Contemporary Works by Four Artists

Activities: Free tours, educational handouts for classes K - 12; Meet the Artist Days; family festivals; educ outreach programs; lect & special programs open to the public, 5 per year; gallery talks; tours; individual paintings & original objects of work lent to other professional museums or exhibition spaces; book traveling exhibitions 2 - 6 per year; originate traveling exhibitions to other professional museums or exhibition spaces; gift shop sells posters, tote bags, notecards, handmade crafts, jewelry baskets, glassware, ornaments

L **Library,** Lily Lake Rd, 08231. Tel 609-652-8848. *Asst to Dir* Bonnie Bird Pover Estab 1983

Special Subjects: American art, American Bird Decoys

Collections: †Contemporary American Art rotating exhibitions of Contemporary American Art; crafts; folk art; Meet the Artist Days

Exhibitions: Crafts & folkart

Publications: Exhibition catalogs

Activities: Tours available for school and community groups; concerts; gallery talks; lectures open to public; 4 vis lectr per yr

PARAMUS

M **BERGEN MUSEUM OF ART & SCIENCE,** 327 Ridgewood Ave, 07652. Tel 201-265-1248, 265-1255. *Dir* David Messer

Open Tues - Sat 10 AM - 5 PM; Sun 1 - 5 PM, cl Mon & some holidays. Admis adults $2.50, sr citizens & students $1, group rates. Estab May 1956 to maintain a museum which will provide a creative & recreative museum to stimulate youth & adult interest in art & science. Average Annual Attendance: 15,000. Mem: 800

Income: Financed by mem, contributions, county appropriations, grants & corporation

Collections: Mainly works of New Jersey artists; painting, sculpture, prints

Publications: Newsletter, quarterly

Activities: Classes for adults & children; docent training; lectures open to public, 8 - 10 vis lectrs per year; concerts; gallery talks; tours; competitions with awards; exten dept serves county; museum shop sells books, jewelry, dolls, toys, rocks, minerals

PATERSON

M **PASSAIC COUNTY HISTORICAL SOCIETY,** Lambert Castle, Three Valley Rd, 07503-2932. Tel 201-881-2761; FAX 201-881-2762. *Dir* Kate Gordon; *Cur* Andrew Shick

Open Wed - Sun 1 - 4 PM. Admis adults $1.50, sr $1, children under 15 free. Estab 1926. Located in Lambert Castle built in 1892. Average Annual Attendance: 25,000. Mem: Dues sustaining $50; family $35; regular $20; sr $15; student $5

Collections: Koempel Spoon Collection; textiles; local historical material; paintings; photographs; decorative arts; folk art

Exhibitions: Passaic Falls; Gaetano Federici; Victorian Costumes; quilts & coverlets; World War I posters; Passaic County Folk Art, Life and Times in Silk City

Publications: Castle Lite, bi-monthly newsletter; pamphlets; exhibition catalogues

Activities: Docent training; lectures open to the public, 4 vis lectr per yr; gallery talks; tours; museum shop sells publications, postcards, souvenirs, gifts

L **Library,** Lambert Castle, Three Valley Rd, 07503-2932. Tel 201-881-2761; FAX 201-881-2762.

Open Mon - Fri 9 AM - 4 PM by appointment only

Library Holdings: Vols 10,000

Special Subjects: Local History, Silk Industry, Local Genealogy

PLAINFIELD

L **PLAINFIELD PUBLIC LIBRARY,** Eighth St at Park Ave, 07060-2514. Tel 908-757-1111; FAX 908-754-0063. *Dir* Karen Thorburn

Open Mon - Thur 9 AM - 9 PM; Fri - Sat 9 AM - 5 PM. Estab 1881. Maintains an art gallery with original artworks on permanent display, group shows as scheduled. Circ 135,000

Income: Financed by endowment, city and state appropriation, and Federal funds

Library Holdings: Vols 190,000; Per subs 400; Micro — Fiche, reels; AV — Cassettes, fs, Kodachromes, motion pictures, rec slides, v-tapes; Other — Exhibition catalogs, original art works, photographs

Special Subjects: Arts of the United States (slides), Lincoln Fine Arts Collection (books & periodicals)

PRINCETON

C **BRISTOL-MYERS SQUIBB CO,** PO Box 4000, 08543-4000. Tel 609-252-4076, 252-4000. *Dir Cultural Relations* Pamela Sherin

Estab as a community service, in appreciation of beauty. Maintains a Fine Arts Gallery which mounts 6-10 exhibitions per yr

Activities: Competitions; financial assistance to museums and art association's juried shows throughout New Jersey; for medical charities, have initiated large photograph exhibitions; awards; originate traveling exhibitions

PRINCETON UNIVERSITY

M **The Art Museum,** 08544-1018. Tel 609-258-3788; FAX 609-258-5949. *Dir* Allen Rosenbaum; *Assoc Cur* Michael Padgett; *Assoc Cur* Betsy Rosasco; *Assoc Cur* Barbara Ross; *Registrar* Maureen McCormick; *Managing Ed* Jill Guthrie

No admis fee. Estab 1890 to make original works of art available to students in the Department of Art & Archeology and also for the enjoyment of the University, community and general public. About 65,600 sq ft of gallery space for permanent, semi-permanent and changing installations. Average Annual Attendance: 70,000. Mem: 1250; dues $25 and up

Income: Financed by endowment and the University and by government, corporate and private sources

Collections: †Ancient Mediterranean; †British & American; †Chinese ritual bronze vessels; †Far Eastern, especially Chinese and Japanese paintings; †mediaeval & later European; †Pre-Columbian; Northwest Coast Indian; African

Exhibitions: 20th Century Master Works on Paper & Sculpture from the Nowinski Collection; Sleep of Reason, Reality & Fantasy in the print series of Goya; American Drawings from the Feld Family Collection; Class of 1953 Collections Goddess & Polis; Panathenaic Festival in Ancient Athens; Franz Photos; What Photographs Look Like; Contemporary Photographs. (All exhibitions tentative)

Publications: Catalogs, occasionally; Record of the Art Museum, semi-annually; newsletter, three times per yr

Activities: Docent training; lect; gallery talks; tours

L **Index of Christian Art,** 107 McCormick Hall, 08544-1018. Tel 609-258-3773. *Dir* Brendan Cassidy

Open Mon - Fri 9 AM - 5 PM, cl holidays. Estab 1917 as a division of the Department of Art and Archaeology. It is a research and reference collection of cards and photographs designed to facilitate the study of Christian iconography in works of art before 1400. Duplicate copies exist in Washington, DC in the Dumbarton Oaks Research Center and in Los Angeles in the Library of the University of California. European copies are in Rome in the Vatican Library and in Utrecht in the University

L **Marquand Library,** McCormick Hall, 08544. Tel 609-258-3783; FAX 609-258-0103. *Librn* Janice J Powell; *Asst Librn* Denise Gavio

Not open to public. Estab 1908 to serve study & research needs of the students & faculty of Princeton University in the History of Art, Architecture, Photography, Classical & Archaeology. For reference only

Income: Financed by endowments

Library Holdings: Vols 185,000; Per subs 900; 837 Film Titles; Micro — Fiche 12,728

RED BANK

A **NEW JERSEY WATER-COLOR SOCIETY,** 40 Whittman Dr, 07701. Tel 908-747-0122. *Pres* Fran McIlvan; *First VPres* Pat Brannigan; *Second VPres* Debbie Tintle; *Treas* Pat Shamy

Estab 1938 to bring to the public the best in New Jersey watercolorists - teachers. Mem: 125; dues $20; open to exhibitors in the Annual Open Exhibition whose work conforms to standards of the Society & are legal residents of the State of NJ

Exhibitions: Annual Members Show in spring; Annual Open Statewide Juried Exhibition in fall - alternating between Nabisco Brands USA Gallery, East Hanover, NJ and the Monmouth Museum, Lincroft, NJ

Publications: Illustrated Catalogue; Newsletter, 2 per yr

Activities: Classes for adults & children; workshops; lectures open to public, 2—4 vis lectrs per yr; competitions with awards; annual dinner; reception for Open & Members Shows

RINGWOOD

M **RINGWOOD MANOR HOUSE MUSEUM,** Sloatsburg Rd, PO Box 1304, 07456. Tel 201-962-7031; FAX 201-962-7658. *Cur* Elbertus Prol

Open May - Oct Tues - Fri 10 AM - 4 PM; Sat, Sun & holidays 10 AM - 5 PM. No admis fee. Estab 1935

Income: Financed by state appropriation & funds raised by private organization sponsored special events

Collections: Decorative arts; furniture; graphics; historical material; paintings; New Jersey iron making history

Activities: Guided tours; special events; sales shop sells books, magazines, reproductions & prints

RIVER EDGE

M **BERGEN COUNTY HISTORICAL SOCIETY,** Steuben House Museum, 1201 Main St, PO Box 55, 07661. Tel 201-343-9492, 487-1739 (museum). *Adminr* Open

Open Wed - Sat 10 AM - noon, Sun 2 - 5 PM. No admis fee. Estab 1902 to collect & preserve historical items of Bergen County. Average Annual Attendance: 10,000. Mem: 535; dues $12; annual meeting in June

Income: Financed by membership, grants & corporate support

Collections: Collection of artifacts of the Bergen Dutch 1680-1914

Publications: In Bergen's Attic, quarterly newletter

Activities: Classes for children; docent programs; lectures open to public, 8 vis lectr per yr; museum shop sells books

RIVER VALE

L **RIVER VALE PUBLIC LIBRARY,** Art Dept, 412 River Vale Rd, 07675. Tel 201-391-2323; FAX 201-391-6599. *Dir* Eleanor Horchler

Open Mon - Thurs 10 AM - 9 PM, Fri 10 AM - 5 PM, Sat 10 AM - 4 PM, cl Sat July and Aug

Income: $163,000 (financed by city appropriation)

Library Holdings: Per subs 120; Sculpture reproductions; AV — Cassettes, rec; Other — Framed reproductions

Special Subjects: Art History, Theatre Arts
Collections: Fine arts: music and art, history, artists, techniques; Theatre history: Broadway; movies; Beginning photography collection
Exhibitions: Local artists exhibits
Activities: Individual paintings lent to valid library card holders

SOUTH ORANGE

M **SETON HALL UNIVERSITY,** 400 S Orange Ave, 07079. Tel 201-761-9543, 761-9000; FAX 201-761-9432. *Dir* Petrateu Doesschate Chu
Open Mon - Fri 10 AM - 5 PM, Sat & Sun 2 - 4 PM. No admis fee. Estab 1963. Troast Memorial Gallery, estab 1974, houses permanent collection of contemporary American art; Wang Fang-Yu Collection of Oriental art was estab in 1977. Average Annual Attendance: 35,000
Collections: †Archaeology Collections
Exhibitions: Arts of American Indians Beadwork; Indians of New Jersey 10,000 BC-AD 1758.
Activities: Lectures open to the public; gallery talks
L **Library,** 405 S Orange Ave, 07079. Tel 201-761-9431; FAX 201-761-9432. *Acting Dean* Robert Jones; *Assoc Dean* Paul Chao
Open Mon - Thurs 8 AM - 12 PM, Fri 8 AM - 5 PM, Sat 9 AM - 5 PM, Sun 1 - 11 PM
Library Holdings: Vols 2000; AV — Slides 12,000

SPRINGFIELD

L **SPRINGFIELD FREE PUBLIC LIBRARY,** Donald B Palmer Museum, 66 Mountain Ave, 07081-1786. Tel 201-376-4930; FAX 201-376-1334. *Head Circulation Dept* Rose Searles; *Head Technical Servs* Joan L Meyer; *Ref Dept* Henriann Robins; *Head Childrens Dept* Nancy Shacklette; *Bookkeeper* Erna Kitzing
Open Mon, Wed, Thurs 10 AM - 9 PM, Tues, Fri, & Sat 10 AM - 5 PM. No admis fee. Estab 1975 as a museum addition to a public library established to preserve local history. The library, including a meeting room, serves as a cultural center
Collections: †Permanent collection of circulating framed art reproductions
Activities: Films; lectures; puppet shows; individual reproductions lent to library patrons; lending collection contains books, framed reproductions, records, photographs, slides & periodicals

SUMMIT

A **NEW JERSEY CENTER FOR VISUAL ARTS,** 68 Elm St, 07901. Tel 908-273-9121; FAX 908-273-1457. *Pres* Deborah Cave; *Exec Dir* George S Bolge; *Dir Educ* William G Ruby; *Dir Development & Public Relations* Doris Ackerman
Open daily noon - 4 PM, Sat & Sun 2 - 4 PM. No admis fee. Estab 1933, incorporated 1956. Two gallery spaces, containing 5000 ft of exhibition space, specializing in visual art. Average Annual Attendance: 50,000. Mem: 2400; dues Friends Membership $45, general membership $35; annual meeting May
Exhibitions: Changing exhibitions of contemporary visual art; Members' Show; Juried Show; Outdoor Show
Publications: Class & exhibition catalogs; monthly newsletter
Activities: Art classes for adults, children & community groups; workshops & open studios; docent training; lectures open to public & for members, 10 vis lectrs per yr; concerts; gallery talks; tours; competitions with awards; scholarships; individual paintings & original objects of art lent; organize traveling exhibitions of borrowed work; sales shop sells original art

TRENTON

A **ARTWORKS,** The Visual Art School of Princeton and Trenton, 19 Everett Alley, 08611. Tel 609-394-9436. *Chmn Bd of Trustees* Laurence G Capo; *VChmn* Winn Thompson III; *Treas* Alisas Harris; *Exec Dir* Lawrence Snider
Open Tues - Fri 11 AM - 4 PM, call for Sat hours. Estab 1964 to establish & maintain educational & cultural programs devoted to visual arts. Skylit gallery, 2000 sq ft, in downtown Trenton. Average Annual Attendance: 7500. Mem: 850; dues $35 - $50; annual meeting in May
Income: Financed by friends, class fees, workshops & demonstration fees, trip fees, entry fees, grants, corporate & private contributions
Exhibitions: Exhibitions are held at the Trenton Gallery & at various locations throughout the community
Publications: The Artworks Reader, quarterly
Activities: Classes for adults and children; lectures open to the public, 3-10 vis lectr per yr; tours; competitions with awards; scholarships offered
L **Library,** 45 Stockton St, 08540. Tel 609-921-9173, 394-9436; FAX 609-394-9551. *Exec Dir* Laurence Snider
Reference library
Library Holdings: Vols 200; AV — Slides

L **FREE PUBLIC LIBRARY,** Art and Music Dept, 120 Academy St, PO Box 2448, 08607-2448. Tel 609-392-7188, Ext 24; FAX 609-396-7655. *Dir* Robert E Coumbe; *Head Art & Music Dept* Shirley Michael
Open Mon, Wed, Thurs 9 AM - 9 PM, Tues, Fri & Sat 9 AM - 5 PM, cl Sun & holidays. Estab 1900
Income: Financed by city appropriation
Library Holdings: Vols 8000; Per subs 35; 5500 Mounted pictures; Micro — Reels; AV — Motion pictures 300, rec; Other — Clipping files, exhibition catalogs, memorabilia, pamphlets, photographs, prints, reproductions
Exhibitions: Paintings; photographs; crafts; antiques collections

M **MERCER COUNTY COMMUNITY COLLEGE,** The Gallery, 1200 Old Trenton Rd, 08690. Tel 609-586-4800, Ext 589. *Gallery Dir* Henry Hose
Open Mon - Sat 11 AM - 3 PM, Thurs 5 - 8 PM. No admis fee. Estab 1971 as an educational resource for students. Gallery of 2000 sq ft primarily for exhibiting work by New Jersey artists. Average Annual Attendance: 3600
Income: Financed by public funding & sales commissions
Purchases: Annual purchases from exhibits
Collections: Cybis Collection; Painting by Wolf Kahn; Sculptures by Salvadore Dali & Isaac Whitkin; Paintings by Reginald Neal; Darby Bannard; B J Nordfeldt; NJ artist collection; Art Work by Frank Ivera
Exhibitions: Faculty, student & children's art exhibits as well as exhibits from the permanent collection & exhibitions by NJ artists Deadre McErail; Faculty Works by Joan Needham
Activities: Classes for adults and children; dramatic programs; lectures open to public, 12 vis lectrs per yr; concerts; gallery talks by appointment; tours; competitions with purchase awards; scholarships offered; individual paintings & original objects of art lent to other galleries & museums; lending collection contains original prints
L **Library,** 1200 Old Trenton Rd, 08690. Tel 609-586-4800. *Library Dir* Pam Price
Estab 1891 to provide library services for the college; portion of the main floor is devoted to permanent display cabinets. In addition display panels are used for faculty exhibits, community exhibits and traveling exhibits
Library Holdings: Vols 64,518; Per subs 718; AV — A-tapes 1460, fs, rec 3107, slides 17, v-tapes 2878; Other — Pamphlets 644, photographs, prints
Publications: Library handbook, annually; Videocassette catalog, annually

M **NEW JERSEY STATE MUSEUM,** 205 W State St, CN-530, 08625. Tel 609-292-6300. *Dir* Leah P Sloshberg; *Cur Fine Arts* Zoltan Buki; *Cur Cultural History* Sue Crilley; *Cur Exhibits* John Mohr; *Cur Education* Karen Cummins; *Cur Archaeology-Ethnology* Lorraine Williams; *Cur Science* David Parris
Open Tues - Sat 9 AM - 4:45 PM, Sun noon - 5 PM, cl Mon & most state holidays. No admis fee. Estab 1891 by legislation to collect, exhibit and interpret fine arts, cultural history, archaeology-ethnology and science with a New Jersey focus; changing exhibit gallery, Hall of Natural Science, fine & decorative arts galleries; ethnology gallery. Average Annual Attendance: 350,000. Mem: 1000; dues $25 and up; annual meeting June
Income: $2,000,000 (financed by state appropriation)
Purchases: $60,000, plus $30,000 - $60,000 from Friends
Collections: American fine & decorative arts of the 18th, 19th & 20th century; †American painting from 1910 - 1950 with special emphasis on the Steiglitz Circle Regionalist, Abstract Artists; New Jersey fine & decorative arts; Christopher Columbus Collection of Arts
Exhibitions: Changing exhibitions focus on New Jersey artists & cultural history; Long-term exhibition galleries on the fine & decorative arts, ethnology & the natural sciences; Weaving Around the World
Publications: Bulletins; catalogs, and irregular serials; Investigators; reports; NEWS, bi-monthly; annual report
Activities: Classes for adults & children; dramatic programs; docent training; lectures open to the public, 10 vis lectr per yr; concerts; gallery talks; tours; individual paintings & original objects of art lent to other institutions; lending collection contains 3000 motion picture titles, 2613 reels, nature artifacts, original art works, original prints, paintings, photographs, sculpture, slides; book traveling exhibitions; traveling exhibitions organized and circulated; museum shop sells books, international folk crafts or items related to collection

M **OLD BARRACKS MUSEUM,** Barrack St, 08608. Tel 609-396-1776; FAX 609-777-4000. *Dir* Cynthia Koch; *Assoc Dir* Sara Cureton; *Cur* Diane Gutenkauf; *Cur Education* Sharon Misik; *Development Dir* Sara Hill; *Military Historian* Lawrence Schmidt; *Chief Historical Interpreter* Jeffrey Macechak
Open Tues - Sat 11 AM - 5 PM, Sun 1 - 5 PM, Mon by appointment. Admis adults $2, children 12 & under $.50, educational groups free. Built 1758, estab 1902 as museum of history and decorative arts. Located in English barracks that housed Hessian Soldiers Dec 1776. Average Annual Attendance: 28,000. Mem: 460; dues $10 - $200; annual meeting May
Income: Financed by membership, state appropriation & donations
Collections: †American decorative arts 1750 - 1820; Archaeological materials; †early American tools and household equipment; †military artifacts; 19th century New Jersey Portraits; patriotic paintings and prints
Exhibitions: The Trenton Barrack 1758 - 1918; Washington & The Battle of Trenton; 18th century Period Rooms and Soldiers Quarters; changing exhibitions; Of War, Law, and the Third Amendment; Hail the Conquering Hero Comes: Washington's Triumphal Entry into Trenton; The Restoration of the Old Barracks
Publications: The Barracks Bugle, quarterly newsletter; The Old Barracks at Trenton, book
Activities: Classes for children; dramatic programs; docent training; lectures open to the public, 3 vis lectr per yr; tours; exten dept serves elementary schools; individual paintings & original objects of art lent to museums; lending collection contains slides & reproduction military objects/costumes; book traveling exhibitions; museum shop sells books, reproductions, prints, slides, historical toys, ceramics

M **TRENTON STATE COLLEGE,** College Art Gallery, Holman Hall CN 4700, Hillwood Lakes, 08650-4700. Tel 609-771-2198, 771-2652. *Pres* Dr Harold Eickoff; *Chmn* Dr Howard Goldstein; *Gallery Coordr* Judith P Masterson
Open Mon - Fri noon - 3 PM, Thurs 7 - 9 PM, Sun 1 - 3 PM. No admis fee. Estab to present students and community with the opportunity to study a wide range of artistic expressions and to exhibit their work. Average Annual Attendance: 2000
Income: Financed by art dept budget and grants including NJ State Council on the Arts, Mercer County Cultural and Heritage Commission
Purchases: Works from National Print Exhibition, National Drawing Exhibition & Mercer County Photography Exhibition
Collections: Purchases from National Print and Drawing Show
Exhibitions: Craft Show; Faculty Show; Mercer County Competitive Art; Mercer County Competitive Photography; National Drawing Exhibition; National Print Exhibition; Selections from the State Museum; Sculpture Shows; Student Show;

Contemporary Issues; African Arts
Publications: Catalog for National Print Exhibition; catalog for National Drawing Exhibition; catalog for Contemporary Issues; catalog for African Arts
Activities: Classes for adults and children; lectures open to the public, 5 vis lectrs per year; gallery talks; tours; competitions with awards; individual paintings and original objects of art lent to other offices and departments on campus; lending collection contains original art works; original prints; paintings; traveling exhibitions organized and circulated to other state colleges and art schools

UNION

M KEAN COLLEGE OF NEW JERSEY, College Gallery, Morris Ave, 07083. Tel 908-527-2307, 527-2347. *Pres* Elisa Gomez; *Gallery Dir* Eugenie Eugenietsai
Open Mon - Thurs 10 AM - 2 PM, 5 - 7 PM, by appointment at other times. No admis fee. Estab 1971 as a forum to present all art forms to students and the community through original exhibitions, catalogues, fine art, by guest curators, art history and museum training students. One gallery 22 x 34 ft plus an alcove 8 x 18 ft on first floor of arts and humanities building. Average Annual Attendance: 3000
Income: Financed by state appropriation and private grants
Collections: American painting, prints sculpture by Audobon, L Baskin, Robert Cooke, Max Ernst, Lamar Dodd, W Homer, P Jenkins, J Stella, Tony Smith, Walter Darby Bannard, Werner Drewes, B J O Norfeldt, James Rosenquist, Robert Rauschenberg, Odilon Redon; photographs, rare books, and 1935-50 design and furniture; Ben Yamimoto Art Work
Exhibitions: Robin Krueger Gallery 1935 - 1974: Reconstructed; Local Limners; Another side of Thoman Nast; Giulio Bonasone; John Button; Fine Arts Faculty 83; Local Limners; Mount, Homer & their contemporaries; Piranesi: Real & Imaginary; Problems in Connoisseurship; Tony Smith, 81 More & the Sculptural Process; Art Directors Club of New Jersey Awards Exhibition; Hans Weingaertner 1896-1970, paintings; works by candidates for graduate degree; exhibition of works by undergraduate fine arts majors; Native American Image; Let's Look at Pictures; A Survey of Latin American Drawings & Prints; Cooperative Gallery; Style & Theme in Japanese art from 13th-20th centuries; I Hang Up My Hat After Dark
Publications: Catalogues for exhibitions
Activities: Dramatic programs; lectures open to the public; individual paintings lent to colleges, institutions, corporations, and departments on the campus
L Nancy Thompson Library, Morris Ave, 07083. Tel 908-527-2017. *Librn* Barbara Simpson
Open Mon - Thurs 8 AM - 11:30 PM, Fri 8 AM - 10 PM, Sat 8 AM - 5 PM, Sun 1 - 8 PM. Estab 1855 to support instruction
Purchases: $6000
Library Holdings: Vols 243,000; Per subs 1350; AV — A-tapes 150, fs, slides; Other — Exhibition catalogs, pamphlets

UPPER MONTCLAIR

M MONTCLAIR STATE COLLEGE, Art Gallery, 07043. Tel 201-893-5113. *Dir* Lorenzo Pace; *Pres* Irvin Reid; *VPres* Richard Lynde; *Dean* Geoffrey Newman; *Chmn Fine Arts Dept* Anne Betty Weinshenker
Open Mon - Fri 10 AM - 4 PM. No admis fee. Estab 1973. Three galleries with 1200 sq ft, 600 sq ft & 600 sq ft. Average Annual Attendance: 5000
Collections: Cosla Collection of Renaissance Art, Lida Hilton Print Collection, Wingert Collection of African & Oceanic Art
Exhibitions: (1991) Four Native Americans; Japanese Fibers. (1992) Don Miller: Painting the African Pageant
Activities: Classes for adults; lectures open to public; concerts; gallery talks; scholarships offered
L Slide Library, Fine Arts Department, 07043. Tel 201-893-4151. *Slide Librn Cur* Lynda Hong
Open Mon - Thurs 8:30 AM - 8 PM, Fri 8:30 AM - 1:30 PM. Estab 1968 to provide audio visual material and information about the art world for faculty, visiting artists and community. Circ 40,000
Library Holdings: Vols 13,600; Per subs 118; AV 300; AV — Cassettes, fs, Kodachromes, lantern slides, slides; Other — Clipping files, exhibition catalogs, framed reproductions, pamphlets, photographs, reproductions
Special Subjects: Prehistoric to contemporary art

WAYNE

M WILLIAM PATERSON COLLEGE OF NEW JERSEY, Ben Shahn Galleries, 300 Pompton Rd, 07470. Tel 201-595-2654; FAX 201-595-3273. *Dir* Nancy Einreinhofer
Open Mon - Thurs 10 AM - 5 PM. No admis fee. Estab 1969 to educate & instruct students & visitors through exhibits & programs. 5000 sq ft space divided into three gallery rooms specializing in the exhibition of contemporary art. Average Annual Attendance: 10,000
Collections: Permanent collection of WPC 19th century landscapes; paintings & sculptures from 1950's to present
Exhibitions: Three gallery rooms of rotating exhibits of contemporary art that change twice during each semester
Publications: Exhibition catalogs
Activities: Art at Lunch program; docent programs; lect open to public, 15 vis lectr per year

WESTFIELD

A FEDERATED ART ASSOCIATIONS OF NEW JERSEY, INC, PO Box 2195, 07091. Tel 201-232-7623, 763-3335. *Pres* Helen Poulos; *Dir* Jane Whipple Green; *VPres for South Jersey* Ethel Fishberg; *VPres for North Jersey* Eugenia Gore
Estab 1969 to provide communications and exchange of ideas among visual art groups. Mem: 9000 (50 member groups); dues per club $25, individuals $15;

composed of four districts which meet separately, annually
Income: $6000 (financed by dues, advertising, donations)
Publications: Directory of Visual Art Organizations in New Jersey, periodically; FAA NJ Views, quarterly; Judge & Jury Selector; Living Library of New Jersey Visual Artists; Videos of Artists in Their Own Studios
Activities: Annual Art Forum; lectures open to the public, 8 vis lectr per yr

WOODBRIDGE

M WOODBRIDGE TOWNSHIP CULTURAL ARTS COMMISSION, Barron Arts Center, 582 Rahway Ave, 07095. Tel 908-634-0413. *Chmn* Dr Dolores Gioffre; *Dir* Stephen J Kager; *Prog Coordr* Nancy Casteras
No admis fee. Estab 1977 to provide exhibits of nationally recognized artists, craftsmen & photographers, & of outstanding NJ talent. Gallery is housed in an 1877 Richardsonian Romanesque Revival building on the National Register of Historic Places. Average Annual Attendance: 8000
Income: $71,000 (financed by endowment & city appropriation)
Activities: Lect open to public, 5 vis lectr per yr; awards; concerts; poetry readings

NEW MEXICO

ABIQUIU

M GHOST RANCH LIVING MUSEUM, Carson National Forest, Canjilon District, General Delivery, 87510. Tel 505-685-4312. *Dir* Albert Martinez; *Environmental Educ* Diego Martinez
Open April - Sept 8 AM - 5:30 PM, Oct - Mar 8 AM - 4:30 PM, cl Mon. No admis fee. Estab 1959 as an outdoor interpretive project for the conservation of natural resources. Average Annual Attendance: 105,000
Income: $140,000 (financed by government appropriations & corporate contributions)
Collections: Paintings and prints related to natural resources conservation; art objects
Publications: Ghost Ranch Museum & More, bulletin; Museum at Ghost Ranch, bulletin; We Called it Ghost Ranch, book
Activities: Classes for children; lectures open to the public; tours; museum shop sells books & prints; gift shop

ALBUQUERQUE

M ALBUQUERQUE MUSEUM OF ART, HISTORY & SCIENCE, 2000 Mountain Rd NW, PO Box 1293, 87103. Tel 505-243-7255; FAX 505-764-6546. *Dir* James C Moore; *Asst Dir* Irene Kersting; *Cur of Art* Ellen J Landis; *Cur of History* Byron Johnson; *Cur of Exhibits* Robert Woltman; *Cur of Collections* Tom Lark; *Cur of Education* Chris Steiner
Open Tues - Sun 9 AM - 5 PM. No admis fee. Estab 1967 as a city museum with the purpose of diffusing knowledge & appreciation of history, art & science, establishing & maintaining a museum & related reference library, of collecting & preserving objects of historic, artistic & scientific interest, of protecting historic sites, works of art & works of nature from needless destruction, of providing facilities for research & publication & of offering popular instruction & opportunities for aesthetic enjoyment. Average Annual Attendance: 123,000. Mem: 1075; dues Friend $100, Corporate $100, Patron $75, Family $40, Individual $25, Sr Citizen Family $25, Sr Citizen $15
Income: Financed by city appropriation and Albuquerque Museum Foundation
Collections: Decorative arts; costumes; †fine arts and crafts; objects and artifacts relevant to our cultural history from 20,000 BC to present; photography
Publications: Las Noticias, monthly
Activities: Classes for adults & children; docent training; lect; gallery talks; tour; competition with awards; original objects of art lent to other museums; book traveling exhibitions, 3 per yr; originate traveling exhibitions; sales shop selling books, original magazines, reproductions, prints, Indian jewelry, local crafts & pottery

M ALBUQUERQUE UNITED ARTISTS, PO Box 1808, 87103. Tel 505-243-0531. *Pres* Barbara Grothus; *Office Mgr* Pascale Vial
Estab 1978 to represent/show work of member artists, statewide shows. Various locations, shows held at galleries around Albuquerque as donated spaces. Average Annual Attendance: 400. Mem: open to contemporary artists; dues $25; monthly meeting 2nd Tues
Exhibitions: Visions of Excellence; exhibits at various locations
Publications: Bimonthly bulletin

M AMERICAN CLASSICAL COLLEGE, Classical Art Gallery, 11501 Menaul St NE, PO Box 4526, 87112. Tel 505-296-2320. *Pres* Dr C M Flumiani
Open daily 10 AM - 12 noon & 3 - 5 PM. No admis fee. Estab 1969 to foster the classical approach to the arts and art education. 2500 sq ft building. Mem: 15; dues $200
Income: Financed by endowment
Collections: Italian masters classical paintings
Publications: Art & Life, quarterly
Activities: Classes for adults; lectures; book shop
L Trecento Art Library, 607 McKnight St NW, PO Box 4526, 87102. Tel 505-296-2320. *Pres* Dr C M Flumiani
Open 10 AM - 4 PM. Estab 1971. For reference only
Income: Financed by College
Library Holdings: Vols 4500; Per subs 15; Other — Framed reproductions, original art works, reproductions
Special Subjects: Painting - American, Painting - Dutch, Painting - French, Painting - German, Painting - Italian, Flagellanti Art

A **INDIAN ARTS & CRAFTS ASSOCIATION,** 122 La Veta Dr NE, Suite B, 87108. Tel 505-265-9149. *Exec Dir* Helen Skredergard
Estab 1974 to promote, preserve, protect & enhance the understanding of authentic handmade American Indian arts & crafts. Mem: 580; semi-annual meeting in Jan & Aug
Income: Financed by membership dues, markets
Exhibitions: Annual Indian IACA Artists of the Year
Publications: Annual directory; brochures on various Indian arts & crafts; newsletter, 10-11 times per year
Activities: Marketing seminars for Indian artists & crafts persons; lect are open to public, 4-5 vis lectr; competitions

M **INDIAN PUEBLO CULTURAL CENTER,** 2401 12th St NW, 87102. Tel 505-843-7270. *Dir* Rafael Gutierrez; *Exec Asst* Joyce Merrill; *Museum Coordr* Pat Reck; *Retail Marketing Mgr* Judy Fairbanks
Open 9 AM to 5:30 PM. Admis adults $2.50, sr citizen $1.50, student $1. Estab 1976 to advance understanding and insure perpetuation of Pueblo culture. Pueblo Gallery houses monthly Native American artist exhibits. Average Annual Attendance: 80,000. Mem: 800 - 1000; dues family $25, individual $15, students & sr citizens $7.50; annual meeting 3rd Tues in Feb
Income: Financed by admissions, restaurant revenue, & office space rental
Collections: †Jewelry, †paintings, †photos, †pottery, †rugs, †sculptures, †textiles
Exhibitions: Monthly exhibits of Native American art; Pueblo Children's Art Contest
Publications: Pueblo Horizons, 4 times per yr
Activities: Classes for adults & children; docent training; lectures open to public, 6-12 lectrs per yr; competitions with awards; museum shop sells books, original art, reproductions, prints, slides, Native American arts & crafts (pots, rugs, kachinas)

C **LOVELACE MEDICAL FOUNDATION,** Art Collection, 5400 Gibson Blvd, SE, 87108. Tel 505-262-7000; FAX 505-262-7729. *Chief Exec Officer* Derick Pasternack
No admis fee. Estab 1940. Foundation utilizes patient waiting lobbies throughout medical clinic and hospital complex to display collection
Collections: Indian (American Southwest) Textiles; Santa Fe School paintings; Taos School paintings
Activities: Tours; individual paintings lent to requesting museums

A **NEW MEXICO ART LEAGUE,** Gallery, 3407 Juan Tabo NE, 87111. Tel 505-293-5034. *Pres* John Beyer; *VPres* Dick Wimberly; *Treas* Joan Bedeaux
Open Tue - Sat 10 AM - 4 PM, Sun 1 - 4 PM, cl Mon. No admis fee. Estab 1929 to promote artists of New Mexico; art gallery. Members' works exhibited in space 3000 sq ft. Average Annual Attendance: 2500. Mem: 366; dues $30; annual meeting in Aug
Income: Financed by membership and sales
Collections: Best of show of National Small Painting Show
Exhibitions: 15th annual Small Painting Show (national competition)
Publications: Catalog of National Small Painting Show; newsletter, monthly
Activities: Workshops for adults; lectures open to the public; 9-10 vis lectr per year; gallery talks; competitions with awards; paintings & original objects of art lent locally; sales shop sells original art

A **SOCIETY OF LAYERISTS IN MULTI MEDIA,** 1408 Georgia NE, 87124. Tel 505-268-1100. *Founder* Mary Carroll Nelson
Estab 1981
Income: $2500 (financed by mem)
Collections: Mixed Media

UNIVERSITY OF NEW MEXICO
M **University Art Museum,** Fine Arts Center, 87131. Tel 505-277-4001. *Dir* Peter Walch; *Registrar* Kitty Longstreth-Brown; *Cur Exhibits* Lee Savary; *Assoc Dir* Linda Bahm; *Cur Educ* Jeannette Entwistle
Open Tues - Fri 9 AM - 4 PM, & Tues evening 5 - 9 PM, Sun 1 - 4 PM. No admis fee. Estab 1963. Maintains four galleries; a print and photograph room which is open to the public at certain hours. Average Annual Attendance: 49,000. Mem: 200; dues $10 - $500; annual meeting May
Income: Financed by university appropriations, grants and donations
Collections: Field Collection of Spanish Colonial Silver; Tamarind Archive of lithographs; 19th & 20th century American painting & sculpture, drawings; prints by American & European masters; 19th & 20th century lithographs & photography.
Exhibitions: (1993) The Mediated Image; Ralph E Meatyard Kinetic Esthetic; Miguel Gandort Pictorialism; 20th century art
Publications: Bulletin; exhibition catalogs
Activities: Lectures open to the public; inter-museum loans; traveling exhibitions organized and circulated; museum shop sells books, catalogs, magazines, cards
M **Jonson Gallery,** 1909 Las Lomas Rd NE, 87131-1416. Tel 505-277-4967; FAX 505-277-7215. *Cur* Joseph Traugott; *Assoc Cur* Tiska Blankenship
Open Tues - Fri 9 AM - 4 PM; Tues 5 - 9 PM; cl Sat - Sun and holidays. No admis fee. Estab 1950 for the assemblage and preservation of a comprehensive collection of the works of Raymond Jonson; a depository for works of art by other artists and their preservation, with emphasis on the Transcendental Painting Group (1938-42); the exhibition of contemporary works of art. The structure includes a main gallery, four storage rooms, work room & office, a reception room and living quarters for the curator. Average Annual Attendance: 10,000
Income: Financed through University & Jonson Trust
Collections: Jonson reserved retrospective collection; †other artists works & works by Jonson students
Exhibitions: (1991) 2000 years of Contemporary New Mexico Ceramic; Raymond Johnson Centennial Exhibitions. (1993) Media/Contra/Media, Paula Hocks Retrospect; Living with the Enemy; Annual Summer Raymond Johnson Exhibition
Publications: Exhibition announcements; The Art of Raymond Jonson; The Transcendental Painting Group, New Mexico 1938-1941
Activities: Lectures open to public, 5 vis lectrs per yr; gallery talks; tours;

Scholarships; individual paintings & original works of art lent to museums & campus president's office; lending collection contains 1000 books, 800 color reproductions, 2000 original art works, 40 original prints, 2000 paintings, 25 sculpture & 800 slides; originate traveling exhibitions; books sold by order
L **Jonson Library,** 1909 Las Lomas Rd NE, 87131-1416. Tel 505-277-4967, 277-1844; FAX 505-277-7215. *Assoc Cur* Tiska Blankenship
For reference only, exceptions made for special projects
Library Holdings: Vols 500; Per subs 3; AV — Slides; Other — Clipping files, exhibition catalogs, manuscripts, memorabilia, pamphlets, photographs, reproductions
Special Subjects: Transcendentalism
Collections: The Jonson Archives containing books and magazines relating to Raymond Jonson, his letters, his diaries, catalogs, clippings, photographs and slides of works
L **Fine Arts Library,** Fine Arts Center, 87131-1501. Tel 505-277-2357; FAX 505-277-6019. *Dir* James Wright; *Assoc Cur* Nancy Pistorius
Open Mon - Thurs 8 AM - 10 PM; Fri 8 AM - 6 PM, Sat 10 AM - 6 PM; Sun noon - 10 PM. Estab 1963 to provide library assistance, literature, microforms and sound recording materials to support the programs of the university in the areas of art, architecture, music and photography
Library Holdings: Vols 109,200; Per subs 197; Micro — Cards, fiche, reels; AV — A-tapes, cassettes, fs, rec, v-tapes; Other — Exhibition catalogs, pamphlets
Special Subjects: American Indian Art, American Western Art, Architecture, Art Education, Art History, Ceramics, Conceptual Art, Decorative Arts, Drafting, Drawings, Furniture, Goldsmithing, Graphic Arts, Islamic Art, Jewelry, History of Photography, Modern American & European, Native American, Spanish Colonial, Southwest Music, Opera

ARTESIA

M **ARTESIA HISTORICAL MUSEUM & ART CENTER,** 505 W Richardson Ave, 88210. Tel 505-748-2390. *Dir* Nancy Dunn; *Curatorial Asst* Millie McQuade; *Registrar* Merle Rich
Open Tues - Sat 10 AM - noon & 1 - 5 PM. No admis fee. Estab 1970 to preserve & make available local history. Gallery showcases local & regional artists, exhibits drawn from permanent art collection
Income: Financed by city appropriation
Collections: Art; early Area Histroy; Farm; Kitchen; Ranch; Native American Artifacts; Oil & Mineral; WWI & WWII
Exhibitions: Russell Floore Memorial Southwest Art Show
Activities: School & civic club programs; book traveling exhibitions 2 - 3 per year

CHURCH ROCK

M **RED ROCK STATE PARK,** Museum, PO Box 328, 87311. Tel 505-863-1337. *Dir* Joan Barnette; *Asst Cur* Marquis Dann
Open Mon - Fri 8 AM - 4:30 PM, Memorial Day - Labor Day daily 8 AM - 9:30 PM. Admis adults $1, children $.50. Estab 1959 to acquaint visitors with the arts & crafts of the Navajo, Zuni & Hopi Indians & other tribes of the Four Corners area. A small museum manned by Red Rock State Park; displaying Indian arts and crafts and exhibitions on natural history. Average Annual Attendance: 20,000. Mem: Dues $8
Income: Financed by city of Gallup, private contributions and admission fees
Collections: Kachina carving doll collection; arts & crafts of Navajo, Zuni & Hopi & other Pueblos; specimens of geological, herbarium, archeological & cultural materials
Exhibitions: Permanent exhibits: Navajo Hogan; Pueblo Culture; Elizabeth Andron Houser Collection of Native American Arts; Gallup Intertribal Indian Ceremonial Posters, temporary exhibits vary
Publications: Exhibitions catalog; quarterly newsletter
Activities: Lect open to public; gallery talks; tours; concerts; rodeos; individual paintings & original objects of art lent to other museums; book traveling exhibitions, 1 - 4 per year; originate traveling exhibitions; circulate to museums & arts & educational organizations; sales shop sells books, reproductions, magazines, prints, slides, sandpaintings, pottery, jewelry & other Native American crafts
L **Library,** PO Box 328, 87311. Tel 505-722-6196.
Open Mon - Fri 8 AM - 4:30 PM, Memorial Day - Labor Day daily 8 AM - 9 PM. Admis suggested donation adults $1, children $.50
Library Holdings: Vols 350; Per subs 5; Micro — Cards; Other — Clipping files, exhibition catalogs, manuscripts, pamphlets, photographs, prints
Special Subjects: Anthropology, Southwest Indians, science, sociology, geology

CIMARRON

M **PHILMONT SCOUT RANCH,** Philmont Museum, Philmont Scout Ranch, 87714. Tel 505-376-2281. *Dir* Stephen Zimmer
Open Mon - Fri 8 AM - 5 PM. No admis fee. Estab 1967 to exhibit art & history of Southwest United States. Average Annual Attendance: 30,000
Income: Financed by endowment & sales desk revenue
Collections: Art by Ernest Thompson Seton; American Indian Art; History of Boy Scouts of America; History of New Mexico
Exhibitions: Ernest Thompson Seton's Collection of Plains Indian Art
Activities: Docent programs; lectures open to public; lending collection contains over 6000 items; retail store sells books, magazines, prints
L **Seaton Memorial Library,** Philmont Scout Ranch, 87714. *Dir* Stephen Zimmer
Estab as a lending & reference facility
Income: Financed by endowment
Library Holdings: Vols 6500; Per subs 17; Other — Clipping files, exhibition catalogs, framed reproductions, manuscripts, memorabilia, original art works, pamphlets, photographs, prints

DEMING

M LUNA COUNTY HISTORICAL SOCIETY, INC, Deming Luna Mimbres Museum, 301 S Silver St, 88030. Tel 505-546-2382. *Coordr* Katy Hofacket; *Dir* Ted Southerland; *Asst Dir* Ruth Brown; *Treas* John Plantz; *Archives* Dolly Shannon; *Dolls & Toys* Louise Southerland
Open Mon - Sat 9 AM - 4 PM, Sun 1:30 - 4 PM, cl Thanksgiving & Christmas Day, open by appointment during evenings for special interest groups. Admis free with donations. Estab 1955, moved into Old Armory 1978, to preserve Luna County history, historical items & records for reference. Art gallery is in a passageway 50 ft x 10 ft, no windows; open to local artists for displays. Average Annual Attendance: 20,000. Mem: 200; dues $3; annual meeting in Jan
Income: Financed by donations & endowment earnings
Collections: Chuck wagon, vintage clothing, dolls, frontier life objects & other items on the local history; Mimbres Indian artifacts; mine equipment; minerals; paintings & saddles; camera display; phone equipment; quilt room; old lace display; National Guard display; Bataan-Corregidor display & momument; facsimile of front of Harvey House; bell collection; bottle collection, china, ceramics & silver displays; antiques; Military Room; Art Gallery
Publications: History of Luna County & Supplement One
Activities: Dramatic programs; docent training; tours; service awards; museum shop sells Indian jewelry, postcards & pottery

LAS CRUCES

M NEW MEXICO STATE UNIVERSITY, University Art Gallery, PO Box 30001, 88003. Tel 505-646-2545. *Gallery Dir* Karen R Mobley; *Asst Cur* Rosemary McLaughlin
Open Mon - Fri 10 AM - 4 PM, Thurs 7 - 9 PM, Sun 1 - 4 PM. No admis fee. Gallery estab in 1974 as an educational resource for the University & southern New Mexico. 4000 sq ft with incandescent lighting, temperature/humidity control, electronic security. Average Annual Attendance: 17,000. Mem: Dues beginning at $5
Purchases: Peggy Cyphers, Sabina Ott, Diane Marsh
Collections: Photographs; prints & drawings & works on paper; collection of Retablos; paintings on canvas
Exhibitions: Landscape, Politics & Culture; The Figure in Indian Art; Federico Armyo
Publications: Exhibit catalogs, two per year
Activities: Educ dept - docent training; lectures open to public, 10-12 vis lectr per yr; gallery talks; competitions with awards; individual paintings & original objects of art lent to museums & galleries; lending collection contains original prints, paintings, phonorecords, photographs, sculptures & retablos; book traveling exhibitions; originate traveling exhibitions

LAS VEGAS

M NEW MEXICO HIGHLANDS UNIVERSITY, Arrott Art Gallery, Donnelly Library, National Ave, 87701. Tel 505-425-7511, 454-3338. *Art Dir* Bob Read
Open Mon - Fri 8 AM - 5 PM. No admis fee. Estab 1956 to acquaint University and townspeople with art of the past and present. Gallery dimensions approx 20 x 40 ft. Average Annual Attendance: 4000 - 5000
Income: Financed by state appropriation
Collections: †Permanent collection
Exhibitions: Twelve individual & group shows; one statewide show
Publications: University general catalog, annually
Activities: Classes for adults & children; lectures open to public, 1 vis lectr per yr; concerts; gallery talks; tours; competitions; scholarships & fels offered; book traveling exhibitions, 1-2 per year

LOS ALAMOS

M FULLER LODGE ART CENTER, 2132 Central Ave, PO Box 790, 87544. Tel 505-662-9331; FAX 505-662-6455. *Dir* Patricia Chavez
Open Mon - Sat 10 AM - 4 PM, Sun 1 - 4 PM. No admis fee. Estab 1977 to provide an art center to the regional area; to foster the interests of the artists and art interested public of the Community. Center is approx 210 running ft; located in the Fuller Lodge; national Historical Site; gallery area has been renovated. Average Annual Attendance: 12,000. Mem: 350; dues memorial $1500, life $1000, corporate $300, patron $100, sponsor $50, contributing $30, member $20
Income: Financed by membership, county appropriation, grants, gallery shop sales, annual art sale
Collections: †Northern New Mexico Art (all media)
Exhibitions: (1993) The Beauty of Los Alamos; Of Life's Beauty; Protege; Que Pasa: Art in New Mexico; Works by The Rocky Mountain Region of the Embroiders' Guild of America Inc; Biennial Painting, Drawing, Print, Photography & Sculpture 6 State Juried Exhibition; A Look Back in Time: The Fuller Lodge Reunion Show; Summer Fair; From the Spirit; The Glass Menagerie; Through the Looking Glass: A Photography Juried Exhibition; Early Christmas Fair; Affordable Arts; Kalcidoscope
Publications: Bulletin, quarterly
Activities: Classes for children; docent training; seminars for artists; competitions with awards; gallery talks; individual paintings & original objects of art lent; book traveling exhibitions; originate traveling exhibitions; museum shop sells books, original art, cards, art related toys & calendars

MESILLA

M GADSDEN MUSEUM, W Barker Rd, PO Box 147, 88046. Tel 505-526-6293. *Owner* Mary Veitch Alexander
Open Mon - Sun 9 - 11 AM & 1 - 6 PM, cl Easter, Thanksgiving, Christmas. Admis adults $1.07, children $.54. Estab 1931 to preserve the history of Mesilla Valley. Average Annual Attendance: 3000
Income: $2000 (financed by donations)

Collections: Civil War collection; clothing; gun collection; Indian artifacts, including pottery; paintings; Santo collection
Activities: Educ dept; tours for school children; original objects of art lent; museum shop sells books

PORTALES

M EASTERN NEW MEXICO UNIVERSITY, Dept of Art, Dept of Art 105, 88130. Tel 505-562-2510. *Dir* Greg Erf
Open 7 AM - 9 PM. No admis fee. Estab 1935 for exhibiting student artwork; gallery is room coverted for student works
Income: Financed by University funds
Collections: Student works in Art Department Collection
Exhibitions: Seen & Unseen
Activities: Individual paintings and original objects of art lent to the University

L Golden Library, Station 32, 88130. Tel 505-562-2624. *Art Exhib Dir* Larry Schwartwood
Public exhibitions & artist presentations
Income: $3000 (financed by University & grants)
Purchases: Some student art is purchased
Library Holdings: Vols 10,000; Per subs 35; Micro — Cards, fiche, prints, reels; AV — A-tapes, cassettes, fs, Kodachromes, motion pictures, rec, slides, v-tapes; Other — Exhibition catalogs, framed reproductions, original art works, pamphlets, photographs, prints, sculpture
Exhibitions: (1990) Margaret Quintuna; Faculty Show. (1991) Emerging New Mexico Photographs

ROSWELL

M ROSWELL MUSEUM AND ART CENTER, 100 W 11th St, 88201. Tel 505-624-6744. *Pres Board Trustees* Brad Pretti; *VPres* Helen Elliot; *Treas* Juanita Stiff; *Dir* William D Ebie; *Asst Dir* Laurie J Rufe; *Cur Coll* Wesley A Rusnell; *Registrar* Teresa Ebie
Open Mon - Sat 9 AM - 5 PM, Sun & holidays 1 - 5 PM, cl Christmas & New Year's Day. No admis fee. Estab 1937 to promote and cultivate the fine arts. The basis of the fine arts collection being paintings and sculptures with emphasis on the artistic heritage of the Southwest. 16 galleries are maintained for art works; plus Robert H Goddard rocket display; 24,000 sq ft of exhibition space. Average Annual Attendance: 50,000. Mem: 1340; dues $15 and up
Income: $500,000 (financed by mem, city & county appropriation)
Collections: †Regional & Native American fine arts & crafts & Western historical artifacts; †international graphics collection; †20th century Southwestern paintings & sculpture, drawings; †Hispanic Art
Exhibitions: Permanent collection plus 10-14 temporary exhibitions annually
Publications: Bulletin, quarterly; Exhibition Catalogs
Activities: Classes for adults & children; docent training; school outreach program; artist-in-residence grants; lectures open to public, 6-12 vis lectr per year; concerts; gallery talks; tours; individual paintings & original art objects lent to museums; book traveling exhibitions; museum shop sells books, magazines, reproductions, cards, Indian jewelry & Native American art

L Library, 11th and Main Sts, 88201. Tel 505-624-6744.
Reference only
Library Holdings: Vols 7500; Per subs 35; Micro — Cards; AV — A-tapes, cassettes, motion pictures, slides, v-tapes; Other — Exhibition catalogs, prints
Special Subjects: Southwestern Art

SANTA FE

A THE CENTER FOR CONTEMPORARY ARTS OF SANTA FE, 291 E Barcelona Rd, 87501. Tel 505-982-1338; FAX 505-982-9854. *Dir* Robert B Gaylor; *Co-Dir* Linda Klosky
Gallery open 10 AM - 4 PM, open evenings for performances or cinema screenings. admis gallery free, media arts $3.50 - $5, other $6 - $15. Estab 1979, as a multidisciplinary contemporary arts organization. Hosts performance art: dance, poetry, musical, mixed media. Exhibition space for changing shows; theatre; dance space; new performance space & Teen Project space. Average Annual Attendance: 65,000 (all events)
Exhibitions: Visual arts exhibitions
Activities: Teen Project-performing, visual, mixed media, music, radio & video workshops & projects for teens; lect open to public, 12 vis lectr per year; concerts; junior museum

M GUADALUPE HISTORIC FOUNDATION, Santuario de Guadalupe, 100 Guadalupe, 87501. Tel 505-988-2027. *Pres* Mikki Anaya; *VPres* Felice Gonzales; *VPres* Dino De Kleden; *Treas* Waldo Anton; *Dir* Emilio I Ortiz
Open Mon - Sat 9 AM - 4 PM, Sun noon - 4 PM, cl weekends Nov - Apr. Admis - donation. Estab 1790, became an international museum 1975 to preserve and extend the community's awareness through education and in culture areas. Gallery space is used for exhibits of local artists, with emphasis on Hispanic art. Average Annual Attendance: 37,000. Mem: 400; dues $15 & up: annual meeting Apr
Income: $41,000 (financed by membership, grants, corporate & private donations)
Collections: Archdiocese Santa Fe Collection, 16th century books, 18th -19th century religious artifacts; Mexican Baroque paintings; Our Lady of Guadalupe mural by Jose de Alzibar; Renaissance Venetian painting
Publications: Flyers; noticias; quarterly newsletter
Activities: Dramatic programs; docent training; performing arts; visual arts; poetry readings; lectures open to public, 1-2 vis lectr per year; concerts; tours

M INSTITUTE OF AMERICAN INDIAN ARTS MUSEUM, 108 Cathedral Place, 87501. Tel 505-988-6281; FAX 505-988-6273; WATS 800-476-1281. *Dir* Paul Gonzales
Open summer Mon - Sat 10 AM - 5 PM, winter daily 9 AM - 5 PM, weekends by appointment only. No admis fee. Estab 1962 to train Native American

students to own, operate and manage their own museums; to collect, preserve and exhibit materials relating to the Native American; act as a resource area for Indian Museums nationwide. Small museum of 5 principal galleries; approx 10, 000 ft of exhibit area. Average Annual Attendance: 15,000
Income: $250,000 (financed by Congressional appropriation)
Purchases: $5000
Collections: National collection of contemporary Indian arts & crafts in America; Vital & comprehensive collection in fields of paintings, graphics, textiles, ceramics, sculpture, jewelry, photographs, printed textiles, costumes, ethnological materials such as drums & paraphernalia for general living
Exhibitions: Annual Faculty & Alumni; Annual High School Indian Art Show; Annual Graduating Students; Beyond Prison Gates
Publications: Exhibition catalogs; museum workbooks
Activities: Assisting any Indian reservation in setting up their own visitor centers or museums in America; material available to Indian reservations, museum, cultural centers and universities, with fees, transportation and insurance provided; classes for adults; lect open to public, 2-3 visiting lectr per year; concerts; gallery talks; competitions; awards; scholarships; individual paintings and original objects of art lent; book traveling exhibitions 6-8 per year; originate traveling exhibitions; sales shop sells student arts and crafts, books, magazines, original art, and prints

L **Alaska Native Culture and Arts Development,** PO Box 20007, Santa Fe, 87504. Tel 505-988-6423; FAX 505-988-8446. *Librn* Mary Young; *Library Asst* Grace Nuvayestewa
Open Mon - Fri 8 AM - 5 PM & 6 - 9 PM, Sat 11 AM - 3 PM, Sun 1 - 5 PM. Estab 1962 to support college curriculum. Circ 30,000
Income: $31,000; private fundraising and goverment
Purchases: $2500
Library Holdings: Vols 14,000; Per subs 150; Indian Reference Books 1142; Micro — Prints, reels; AV — A-tapes, Kodachromes 40,000, motion pictures, v-tapes 957; Other — Clipping files, exhibition catalogs 50, original art works, photographs, prints, sculpture
Special Subjects: American Indian Art, Eskimo Art, Native American subjects

M **MUSEUM OF NEW MEXICO,** 113 Lincoln Ave, PO Box 2087, 87504-2087. Tel 505-827-6451; FAX 505-827-6427. *Dir* Thomas Livesay; *Deputy Dir* Marsha Jackson
Open daily 10 AM - 5 PM, cl Christmas, New Year's Day. Admis adults $3.50 single visit, $6 multiple visits, 2-day pass, children under 17 free. Estab 1909. Museum is a state institution and operates in four major fields of interest: Fine Arts, International Folk Art, History and Anthropology. Four separate buildings, each with galleries: Southwestern art, Indian arts and crafts. Average Annual Attendance: 850,000. Mem: 800; dues $35 - $1000, annual meeting in Nov
Income: Financed by state appropriation, federal grants & private funds
Collections: Over 500,000 objects, artifacts and works of art in the fields of art, archaeology, folk art and history
Publications: Annual report; books; El Palacio, quarterly; exhibition catalogs; guides; magazines; monographs; pamphlets
Activities: Educ kits with hands-on materials are sent to schools throughout the state; docent program serving 15,000 school children; films; lectures open to public, 12 vis lectr per year; gallery talks; tours; extension dept serves United States & Mexico; original objects of art lent to other cultural institutions; lending collection 7000 original art works; book traveling exhibitions 2-3 per yr; originate traveling exhibitions; museum-sales shop sells books, magazines, reproductions, prints, slides, posters and Indian arts & crafts

L **Palace of Governors Library,** PO Box 2087, 87504-2087. Tel 505-827-6451; FAX 505-827-6497. *Librn* Orlando Romero
Museum houses four separate research libraries on folk art, fine arts, history and anthropology
Library Holdings: Vols 15,000; 40 journals
Special Subjects: Spanish colonial history, Southwestern art and archaeology, worldwide folk art

M **Museum of Fine Arts,** 107 W Palace, PO Box 2087, 87503. Tel 505-827-4452; FAX 505-827-4473. *Dir* David Turner; *Cur Painting* Sandra D'Emilio; *Cur Photography* Steve Yates; *Asst Cur Contemporary Art* Sandy Ballatore; *Asst Cur Coll* Joan Tafoya; *Librn* Phyllis Cohen; *Preparator* Charles Sloan
Open daily 10 AM - 5 PM, cl Mon in Winter. Admis adults $2, children $1, 2-day & annual passes available. Estab 1917 to serve as an exhibitions hall, chiefly for New Mexican and Southwestern art. Building is of classic Southwestern design (adobe); attached auditorium used for performing arts presentations. Average Annual Attendance: 290,000
Income: Financed by state appropriation
Collections: Drawings, paintings, photographs, prints and sculpture with emphasis on New Mexican and regional art, including Native American artists
Publications: Exhibition catalogs; gallery brochures
Activities: Docent training; lect open to public, 10 visiting lectr per year; concerts; gallery talks; tours; competitions; individual paintings and original objects of art lent to art museums; lending collection contains original prints, paintings, photographs and sculpture; originate traveling exhibitions; museum shop sells books, magazines, reproductions and slides

L **Museum of Fine Arts Library,** 105 W Palace, PO Box 2087, 87504-2087. Tel 505-827-4453; FAX 505-827-4473. *Librn* Phyllis Cohen
Open Mon - Fri 9 AM - 4 PM, cl Mon in winter. Estab 1917 to provide fine arts research materials to museum staff, artists, writers and community
Purchases: $4000
Library Holdings: Vols 5000; Per subs 45; Micro — Fiche; AV — Slides; Other — Clipping files, exhibition catalogs, manuscripts, memorabilia, pamphlets
Special Subjects: American art and artists with emphasis on Southwestern art and artists
Collections: Biography files of artists

M **Museum of International Folk Art,** 706 Camino Lejo, 87504-2087. Tel 505-827-6350; FAX 505-827-6349. *Dir* Charlene Cerny; *Asst Dir* Joyce Ice; *Cur American & Latin American Coll* Barbara Mauldin; *Cur European & American Coll* Judith Chiba Smith; *Cur Spanish Colonial Coll* Robin Farwell Gavin; *Cur Textiles* Nora Fisher; *Conservator* Claire Munzenrider; *Cur of New Mexico Hispanic Crafts & Textiles* Helen Lucero; *Prog Mgr* Carol Steiro; *Librn* Judith Sellars
Open daily 10 AM - 5 PM, cl Mon Jan & Feb. Admis adults $3.50, children free.

Estab 1953 to collect, exhibit and preserve worldwide folk art. Average Annual Attendance: 200,000
Income: Financed by endowment, grants and state appropriation
Collections: †Arts of Traditional Peoples, with emphasis on Spanish Colonial and Hispanic-related cultures; †costumes & textiles
Exhibitions: (1991) Hojalateria: Tinwork in New Mexico. (1993) Familia y Fe; Turkisk Traditional Art Today; Folk Art of Brazil's Northeast; Across Generations; Mud, Mirror & Thread: Folk Art of India. (1994) Swedish Folk Art
Publications: American Folk Masters, 1992; The Spirit of Folk Art, 1989
Activities: Docent training; public programs; tours; original objects of art lent to responsible museums nationwide; originate traveling exhibitions; museum shop sells books & original art

L **Library,** 706 Camino Lejo, PO Box 2087, 87504-2087. Tel 505-827-6350. *Librn* Judith Sellars
Open Mon - Fri 10 AM - noon & 1 - 5 PM, cl Mon Nov - Apr. Estab 1953 to support museum's research needs. Reference library
Income: Financed private and state support
Purchases: $4000
Library Holdings: Vols 11,000; Per subs 180; AV — A-tapes, cassettes, rec, slides; Other — Clipping files, exhibition catalogs, manuscripts, pamphlets, photographs
Special Subjects: Textiles, Folk costume design & construction, Folk art of various countries, religious folk art of New Mexico
Collections: Folk literature and music of the Spanish Colonist in New Mexico circa 1800-1971

M **Palace of Governors,** PO Box 2087, 87504-2087. Tel 505-827-6483. *Assoc Dir* Thomas Chavez
Built in 1610
Exhibitions: Society Defined; Another Mexico

M **Laboratory of Anthropology,** Old Santa Fe Trail, 87501. Tel 505-827-6344; FAX 505-827-6497. *Librn* Laura Holt
Open Mon - Sat 8 AM - noon and 1 - 5 PM. Estab 1936 as a research laboratory in archaeology and ethnology
Collections: Materials from various Indian cultures of the Southwest: jewelry, pottery and textiles
Exhibitions: From this Earth: Pottery of the Southwest; Changing exhibitions

M **MUSEUM OF NEW MEXICO,** Office of Cultural Affairs of New Mexico, The Governor's Gallery, State Capitol, PO Box 2087, 87504. Tel 505-827-3064, 827-4464. *Cur* Stuart Ashman; *Asst Dir Research Progs* Victoria Andrews
Open Mon - Fri 8 AM - 5 PM. No admis fee. Estab 1977 to promote New Mexico artists. Gallery located in Governor's reception area in the State Capitol. Average Annual Attendance: 20,000
Income: Financed by state appropriation & the Museum of New Mexico
Exhibitions: Exhibits of New Mexico Art (all media); New Mexican Governor's Awards Show
Activities: Docent training; Lect open to public, 4-6 vis lectr per year; concerts; gallery talks; tours; A Governor's Award for Excellence in the Arts; exten dept serves entire state; artmobile; book traveling exhibitions, 1 per yr; originate traveling exhibitions to other public galleries

M **PUEBLO OF SAN ILDEFONSO,** Maria Martinez Museum, Route 5, PO Box 315-A, 87501. Tel 505-455-2031 (business office), 455-3549 (visitors' center). *Tourism Mgr* Harold Torres
Open Mon - Fri 8 AM - 4 PM. Museum admis is included with $3 entrance fee to the Pueblo. Estab to display pottery: history, artists & methods of pottery making
Collections: Arts & Crafts; Clothing; Painting; Pottery

M **SCHOOL OF AMERICAN RESEARCH,** PO Box 2188, 87504. Tel 505-982-3584; FAX 505-989-9809. *Dir* Douglas W Schwartz; *Mgr Coll* Michael J Hering
Estab 1907. Dedicated to advance studies in anthropology, support advanced seminars for post-doctoral scholars, archaeological research, anthropological publication, and a public education program. Open to members and special scholars by appointment. Southwest Indian Arts Building houses collections for research. Mem: 1100; dues family $50, individual $40
Income: Financed by endowment, membership, special grants and individuals
Purchases: J J Mora prints
Collections: Basketry, paintings, Southwest Indian pottery, silver jewelry, textiles, Kachinas
Publications: Explorations, once a year; Publications of Advanced Seminar Series
Activities: Lectures for members only, 5 vis lectr per yr; scholarships

L **Library,** PO Box 2188, 87504. Tel 505-982-3583. *Librn* Jane Gillentine
Open to scholars of the School of American Research; staff and members by appointment
Library Holdings: Vols 6000; Per subs 27; Government publications
Special Subjects: Anthropology

M **WHEELWRIGHT MUSEUM OF THE AMERICAN INDIAN,** PO Box 5153, 87502. Tel 505-982-4636; FAX 505-989-7386. *Dir* Jonathan Batkin; *Cur* Lynette Miller
Open Mon - Sat 10 AM - 5 PM, Sun 1 - 5 PM, cl Mon Dec - Feb. No admis fee. Estab 1937 to preserve Navajo ceremonialism & promote the culture of the American Indian. Main gallery has changing exhibitions dealing with contemporary Indian themes; lower gallery is a recreation of a turn-of-the-century trading post & functions as a museum shop. Average Annual Attendance: 60,000. Mem: 1400; dues $25 & up; annual meeting
Income: Financed by endowment & mem
Collections: Baskets; jewelry; masks; photographs; ritual material; rugs; sandpainting reproductions of various Navajo ceremonies; tapes
Exhibitions: (1991) Tsonakwa & Yolaika: Legends in Stone, Bone & Wood; David Dawangyumptewa; Rolland D Lee. (1992) Da'iili Hozho' Hooghan: A Home for Beautiful Thoughts; A Bridge Across Cultures: Pueblo Painters in Santa Fe 1910 - 1930; A Man Made of Words & Images: N Scott Momaday
Publications: Bulletins & books on Navajo culture; exhibition catalogs
Activities: Lectures open to public, 5 vis lectrs per year; tours; individual paintings & original objects of art lent to museums; lending collection contains

books, color reproductions, framed reproductions, Kodachromes, nature artifacts, original art works, original prints, paintings & phonorecords; museum shop selling books, magazines, original art, reproductions, prints, slides & authentic American Indian arts & crafts

L Mary Cabot Wheelwright Research Library, 704 Camino Lejo, PO Box 5153, 87502. Tel 505-982-4636; FAX 505-989-7386. *Cur* Lynette Miller
Open to researchers for reference
Library Holdings: Vols 4000; Per subs 3000; Per Issues 3000
Special Subjects: American Indian Art, Anthropology, Carpets & Rugs, Ethnology, Religious Art, Textiles

TAOS

M BENT MUSEUM & GALLERY, 117 Bent St, PO Box 153, 87571. Tel 505-758-2376. *Owner* Otto T Noeding; *Owner* Faye S Noeding
Open daily 10 AM - 4 PM. Admis adults $1, children 8 - 15 $.50, under 8 free. Estab 1959. Home of the first territorial governor of New Mexico - Site of his death in 1847
Collections: American Indian Art; old Americana; old Taos art
Activities: Sales shop sells books, prints, Indian jewelry, pottery & dolls

A KIT CARSON HISTORIC MUSEUM, PO Drawer CCC, 87571. Tel 505-758-0505. *Executive Dir* Neil Poese
Estab 1949 to maintain and operate the home of Kit Carson and to perpetuate his name and deeds. The Kit Carson Home is now classified as a Registered National Historic Landmark. In 1962 the home of Ernest L Blumenschein was given to the Foundation by Miss Helen C Blumenschein; it is now classified as a Registered National Landmark. In 1967 Mrs Rebecca S James gave the Foundation the Ferdinand Maxwell House and Property. In 1972, acquired the Hacienda de Don Antonio Severino Martinez, prominent Taos merchant and official during the Spanish Colonial Period; designated a Registered National Historic Landmark. Acquired in 1972, site of the Simeon Turley Trading Post, Grist Mill and Distillery, built in 1830 and destroyed in Taos Rebellion of 1847; entered in National Register of Historic Places. Acquired in 1977 La Morada de Don Fernando de Taos, Chapel and meeting place of Los Penitentes, an early religious organization; entered in National Register of Historic Places. Average Annual Attendance: 53,000. Mem: 230; dues patron $1000, sponsor $750, benefactor $500, supporting $250, subscribing $100, sustaining $50, share $25, participating $15; annual meeting Mar
Income: $400,000 (financed by admissions, museum shops, rentals, donations & grants)
Purchases: $70,000
Collections: †Historical and Archaeological Collection; Western Americana
Publications: Director's Annual Report, monthly; Las Noticias Alegres de Casa Kit Carson, quarterly newsletter; publications on the historic sites; technical reports
Activities: Tours; lect
L Foundation Library, PO Drawer CCC, 87571. Tel 505-758-0505. *Dir* Neil Poese
For reference only
Purchases: $500-$1000
Library Holdings: Vols 5300; maps; AV — Cassettes, Kodachromes, lantern slides, motion pictures, rec, slides; Other — Clipping files, exhibition catalogs, framed reproductions, manuscripts, memorabilia, original art works, pamphlets, photographs, prints, reproductions, sculpture
Special Subjects: Archaeology, Kit Carson
M Ernest Blumenschein Home, PO Drawer CCC, 87571. Tel 505-758-0330.
Open daily 9 AM - 5 PM. Admis family rate $7, adults $3, sr citizens $2.50, youths $2, children under 6 years free with parents, group tour rates available & combination tickets available to Martinez Hacienda & Kit Carson Museum. Home of world renowned artist and co-founder of famous Taos Society of Artists. Restored original mud plaster adobe dating to 1789 with traditional furnishings of New Mexico & European furnishings. Average Annual Attendance: 20,000
Collections: Original antique furniture; pieces of art by the Blumenschein family and members of Taos Society of Artists and other Taos artists - 1890-1930
Exhibitions: Temporary exhibits of arts and crafts of the Taos area and of New Mexico
Activities: Education dept; docent training; tours; annual children art show; original objects of art lent to qualified art museums; book traveling exhibiton; museum shop sells books, reproductions, prints and slides
M Home & Museum, PO Drawer CCC, 87571. Tel 505-758-4741.
Open daily 9 AM - 5 PM. Admis family rate $7, adults $3, sr citizens $2.50, youths $2, children under 6 years free with parents, group tours available. Home of the famous Western Scout and Fur Trapper. Built in 1825, bought by Kit in 1843 as a wedding gift for his beautiful bride, Josefa Jaramillo, member of prominent Taos family. They lived in the home for 25 years, their lifetime together as both died in 1868
Income: Financed by donations, admissions
Collections: Period furniture and furnishings
Exhibitions: Life of Kit Carson and Personal Items; clothing; guns; saddles; tools; Spanish articles; archaeological artifacts, mountain man exhibits
M Martinez Hacienda, PO Drawer CCC, 87571. Tel 505-758-1000.
Open Mon - Sun 9 AM - 5 PM. Admis family rate $7, sr citizens $2.50, adults $3, youth $2, children under 6 free with parents, group tours rates & combination tickets available to Kit Carson Museum & Blumenschein Home. Built and occupied by Don Antonio, Martinez 1800-1827. Last remaining hacienda open to public in New Mexico. Martinez, an important trader with Mexico, also served as Alcalde of Northern New Mexico. Spanish Colonial fortress hacienda having 21 rooms & two large patios. Living museum program daily
Income: Financed by admissions, donations
Collections: †Furniture, †furnishings, †tools, and †other articles of Spanish Colonial period and personal family articles

M MILLICENT ROGERS MUSEUM, PO Box A, 87571. Tel 505-758-2462; FAX 505-758-5751. *Dir* Patrick T Houlihan; *Asst Cur Exhib* Vincente Martinez; *Chief Cur* Guadalupe Tafoya; *Cur Native Americans* Soge Track; *Asst Dir Admin* Dennis Cruz

Open Mon - Sun 9 AM - 5 PM, cl holidays. Admis adults $3 ($2 groups of 10 or more), under 16 $1, family groups $6. Estab 1956 for the acquisition, preservation, research, display and interpretation of art and material cultures of Native American and Hispanic cultures of the southwest focusing on northern New Mexico. The museum's permanent home is a traditional adobe building, once the private residence of Claude J K Anderson. Average Annual Attendance: 20,000. Mem: 600; semi-annual Board of Directors meeting in spring and fall
Income: Financed by endowment, membership, donations, admissions, grants and revenue from museum store
Collections: American Indian Art of Western United States, emphasis on Southwestern groups; paintings by contemporary Native American artists; religious arts and non-religious artifacts of Hispanic cultures; Nucleus of collection formed by Millicent Rogers
Exhibitions: (1993) Tutavoh; Learning the Hopi Way; Hozhoogo Nitsehakees; Thoughts of Beauty; Abiquin Country; Photographs by Mark Kane. (1994) Hispanic Women of New Mexico
Publications: Las Palabras, quarterly newsletter for members of the museum
Activities: Classes for adults and children; lectures open to the public, 2 - 3 visiting lecturers per year; gallery talks; tours; competitions; field trips; seminars; film series; individual paintings and original works of art lent to similar institutions and special interest groups; book 1 - 3 traveling exhibitions per year; museum shop sells books, magazines, original art, reproductions, prints, art and craft work by contemporary Southwest Indian and Hispanic artisans
L Library, 1504 Museum Rd, 87571. Tel 505-758-2462; FAX 505-758-5751. *Librn* Ann Lamont McVicar
Open daily 9 AM - 5 PM. Estab 1953, emphasis on Native American, Chicano/Hispanic northern New Mexican Anglo artists. Average Annual Attendance: 45,000. Mem: 350
Library Holdings: Vols 2500; Per subs 25; Other — Clipping files, exhibition catalogs, manuscripts, pamphlets
Special Subjects: American Indian Art, Archaeology, Art Education, Art History, Decorative Arts, Eskimo Art, Folk Art, Historical Material, Latin American Art, Mexican Art, Primitive Art, Southwestern Art, Art & Architecture, Material Culture & Art, Museology, Southwestern Hispanic History
Collections: Limited edition, special edition & out of print books on Southwestern Americana; Maria Martinez pottery; over 600 Native American & Hispanic textiles; Native American costumes

A TAOS ART ASSOCIATION INC, Stables Art Center, 133 Paseo de Pueblo Norte, 87571. Tel 505-758-2052; FAX 505-758-2036. *Pres* Larry Martinez; *Exec Dir* Judith Fritz; *Dir Stables Gallery* Leah Sobol; *Museum Shop Mgr* Barbara Lafon
Open Mon - Sat 10 AM - 5 PM, Sun noon - 5 PM. No admis fee. Estab Oct 1981 as a nonprofit community art center to promote the arts in Taos for the benefit of the entire community. Average Annual Attendance: 30,000. Mem: 1000; annual meeting Apr
Income: Financed by memberships, contributions, grants and sales of art works
Exhibitions: Annual Awards Show for Taos County; 14 exhibitions per yr, including Artist of Taos; Taos Impressionism; Spirit in Art; SW Furniture; Taos Non Representational Technology
Publications: Monthly calendar of events to membership and with map to hotels
Activities: Classes for adults and children; children's program in painting and theater; dramatic programs; lect open to the public; concerts; competitions; traveling exhibitions organized and circulated; sales shop sells books, magazines, original art, reproductions, prints, slides & posters

M UNIVERSITY OF NEW MEXICO, The Harwood Foundation, PO Box 4080, 87571. Tel 505-758-9826. *Dir* Robert M Ellis; *Cur* David Witt
Open Mon - Fri noon - 5 PM, Sat 10 AM - 4 PM. No admis fee. Estab 1923, Buildings and contents given to the University by Elizabeth Case Harwood, 1936, to be maintained as an art, educational and cultural center; maintained by the University with all activities open to the public. Building was added to the National Register of Historic Places in 1976; two main galleries plus smaller display areas
Income: Financed by University of New Mexico, private contributions & grants, government grants, endowment income
Collections: †Permanent collection of works by Taos artists
Exhibitions: Four changing exhibits each year; New Mexico Impressions; Three Generations of Hispanic Photographers
Publications: Exhibit catalogs; newsletter, 4 per yr
Activities: Tours; individual paintings and original objects of art lent to museums; lending collection contains original prints, paintings, photographs and sculpture
L Library, PO Box 766, 87571. Tel 505-758-3063; FAX 505-758-7864. *Librn* Tracy McCallum
Open Mon, Thurs 10 AM - 8 PM; Tues, Wed, Fri 10 AM - 5 PM; Sat 10 AM - 4 PM. Estab 1936 as a public library. Circ 59,000
Library Holdings: Vols 45,000; Per subs 70; AV — Slides; Other — Clipping files, exhibition catalogs, framed reproductions, manuscripts, original art works, pamphlets, photographs, prints, reproductions, sculpture
Special Subjects: Southwestern Art
Activities: Lect; concerts; films; plays

NEW YORK

ALBANY

M ALBANY INSTITUTE OF HISTORY AND ART, 125 Washington Ave, 12210. Tel 518-463-4478; FAX 518-462-1522. *Chmn* Robert Krackeler; *Dir* Christine M Miles; *Acting Librn* Mary Schifferli
Open Tues, Wed & Fri 10 AM - 5 PM, Thurs 10 AM - 8 PM, Sat & Sun noon - 5 PM, cl Mon & most NY state holidays. No admis fee. Estab 1791, inc 1793 as the Society for the Promotion of Agriculture, Arts, and Manufactures; 1829 as Albany Institute; 1900 as Albany Institute and Historical and Art Society. Present name adopted 1926. Provides curatorial services to Empire State Plaza

contemporary art collection. Maintains luncheon gallery, museum shop & sales-rental gallery. Average Annual Attendance: 90,000. Mem: 3500; dues $35 and up; annual meeting May
Income: Financed by endowment, membership, sales, city, county, state and federal appropriations, special gifts
Collections: †Art & historical material, chiefly related to regional artists & craftsmen or people who lived in the area; †contemporary paintings & sculpture; †17th - 19th century painting & sculpture by artists of the Hudson River area; paintings; ceramics, especially Staffordshire with local historic scenes & export ware; †New York (especially Albany) furniture, glass; pewter silver & other regional decorative arts; textiles; costumes; 18th - 19th century pottery
Exhibitions: Hudson River School paintings from the Institute's collections; Remembrance of Patria: Dutch Arts and Culture in Colonial America; All Aboard: Railroad Images; Cast with Style: 19th Century Cast-iron Stoves; Visions & Vistas; City Neighbor: An Albany Community Album; Art that Works: The Decorative Arts of the 80s; Shoulder-to-Shoulder: Wrapped in Splendor; The Eyes Have It: Spectacular Spectacles; PotteryWorks: Albany Area Pottery
Publications: Catalogues; several books about the history of New York State; Remembrance of Patria: Dutch Arts and Culture in Colonial America; members' newsletter and calendar
Activities: Classes for adults and children; dramatic programs; lectures open to the public, 5 - 12 vis lectr per yr; gallery talks; tours; competitions with awards; exten dept serving area schools; originate traveling exhibitions; sales-rental gallery sells books, original art & prints

L **McKinney Library,** 125 Washington Ave, 12210. Tel 518-463-4478. *Acting Librn* Mary Schifferli
Open Tues - Fri 9 AM - 3 PM. Estab 1793 to collect historical material concerning Albany and the Upper Hudson region, as well as books on fine and decorative art related to the Institute's holdings. For reference only
Library Holdings: Vols 12,500; Per subs 65; Other — Clipping files, exhibition catalogs 50, manuscripts, memorabilia, pamphlets, photographs
Special Subjects: Ceramics, Decorative Arts, Historical Material, Jewelry, Manuscripts, Painting - American, Photography, Sculpture, Silver, Textiles, Albany social and political history, American painting and sculpture, Dutch in the Upper Hudson Valley, 17th to 19th century manuscripts

M **COLLEGE OF SAINT ROSE,** Picotte Art Gallery, 324 State Street, 12210. Tel 518-485-3900. *Dir* Jeanne Flanagan
Open Mon - Fri 11:30 AM - 4:30 PM, Sun 1 - 4 PM, cl Sat. No admis fee. Estab 1969 to act as a forum for contemporary art in the downtown Albany area. Average Annual Attendance: 5000 - 10,000
Income: Financed by college funds
Collections: Paintings, prints, sculpture
Activities: Lectures open to public; concerts; gallery talks; competitions

M **HISTORIC CHERRY HILL,** 523-1/2 S Pearl St, 12202. Tel 518-434-4791. *Dir* Liselle La France; *Cur* Kristine Robinson; *Educ Dir* Rebecca Watrous
Open Tues - Sat 10 AM - 3 PM, Sun 1 - 3 PM. Admis adults $3.50, sr citizens $3, students $2, children $1. Estab 1964 to preserve and research about the house and contents of Cherry Hill, built for Philip Van Rensselaer in 1787, and lived in by him and four generations of his descendents until 1963. Georgian mansion having 14 rooms of original furniture, ceramics, paintings and other decorative arts spanning all five generations & garden. Average Annual Attendance: 5000. Mem: 250; dues $15 & up
Income: Financed by endowment fund, admis, mem, program grants, sales shop revenue
Collections: Catherine Van Rensselaer Bonney Collection of Oriental decorative arts; New York State furniture; silver; ceramics; textiles and paintings dating from the early 18th thru 20th centuries
Publications: New Gleanings, quarterly newsletter
Activities: Educ dept; classroom materials; lectures open to public; tours; paintings and art objects are lent to other museums and exhibitions; museum shop sells books, postcards & reproductions

A **NEW YORK OFFICE OF PARKS, RECREATION & HISTORIC PRESERVATION,** Natural Heritage Trust, Empire State Plaza, Agency Building One, 12238. Tel 716-493-2611. *Dir* Mark Lyons; *Chief of Grants, State of NY* Kevin Burns; *Regional Prog Specialist* Leo Downey
Estab to administer individual gifts & funds; funding appropriated by state legislatures for various purposes

L **NEW YORK STATE LIBRARY,** Manuscripts and Special Collections, 11th floor, Cultural Education Center, Empire State Plaza, 12230. Tel 518-474-6282; FAX 518-474-5786; Elec Mail James Cosaro, FLIN e-mail:bm.n2a. *State Librn-Assoc Commissioner for Libraries* Joseph Shubert; *Dir* Jerome Yavarkovsky; *Assoc Librn* James Corsaro
Open Mon - Fri 9 AM - 5 PM
Income: Financed by State
Special Subjects: Art History, Historical Material, Manuscripts, Photography, New York State History
Collections: Over 50,000 items: black & white original photographs, glass negatives, daguerreotypes, engravings, lithographs, bookplates, postcards, original sketches & drawings, cartoons, sterograms & extra illustrated books depicting view of New York State & Portraits of its citizens past & present
Exhibitions: Exhibit program involves printed and manuscript materials

M **NEW YORK STATE MUSEUM,** Cultural Education Center, Empire State Plaza, 12230. Tel 518-474-5877. *Dir & Asst Commissioner* Louis D Levine
Open 10 AM - 5 PM. No admis fee. Estab 1836 to research, collect, exhibit and educate about the natural & human history of New York State for the people of New York; to function as a cultural center in the Capital District of the Empire State. Museum has 1 1/2 acres of exhibit space; three permanent exhibit halls devoted to people & nature (history & science) themes of Adirondack Wilderness, Metropolitan New York, Upstate New York; three temporary exhibit galleries of art, historical & technological artifacts. Average Annual Attendance: 900,000
Income: $5,700,000 (financed by state appropriation, government and foundation grants and private donations)
Collections: Ethnological artifacts of Iroquois-Algonkian (New York area) Indians; circus posters, costumes, decorative arts, paintings, photographs, postcards, prints, toys, weapons
Exhibitions: The Adirondeck Wilderness; New York Metropolis; UP State Hall
Activities: Classes for adults and children; lect open to public; concerts; individual paintings and original objects of art lent to museums; lending collection contains nature artifacts, original art works, original prints, paintings, photographs and slides; book traveling exhibitions, 6 per year; originate traveling exhibitions; museum shop sells books, magazines, original art, reproductions, prints, slides, toys, baskets, pottery by local artists, jewelry, stationery and posters

A **PRINT CLUB OF ALBANY,** Museum, 140 N Pearl St (Mailing add: Ft Orange Station, PO Box 6578, 12206-6578). Tel 518-432-9514. *Pres* Charles Semowich; *Librn & Archivist* William Clarkin; *VPres* Paul Lengyel; *Print Selection Committee Chmn* Thomas Andress; *Facilities Chmn* James Otis
Estab 1933 for those interested in all aspects of prints & printmaking. Average Annual Attendance: 2000. Mem: dues $60; mem open to artists who have national recognition, non-artists need interest in prints
Income: Financed by mem, city & state appropriation, sales, commissions & Albany Fine Art Fair
Purchases: Prints & printmakers' archives
Collections: Drawings; Plates; Prints from all periods & countries concentrating on 20th century America
Exhibitions: (1991) Dorothy Lathrop Respective. (1992) 17th National Open Competitive Print Exhibition
Publications: Exibition catalogues; newsletter, 5 per year
Activities: Trips; workshops; lect open to public, 6 - 7 vis lectr per year;; originate traveling exhibitions to other museums & art centers; sales shop sells prints & original art

M **SCHUYLER MANSION STATE HISTORIC SITE,** 32 Catherine St, 12202. Tel 518-434-0834. *Site Mgr* Susan Haswell; *Historic Site Asst* Mary Ellen Grimaldi
Open Wed - Sat 10 AM - 5 PM, Sun 1 - 5 PM, cl Mon & Tues, mid-Apr - Oct, call for winter hrs. No admis fee. Estab 1917 for the preservation and interpretation of the 18th century home of Philip Schuyler, one of the finest examples of Georgian architecture in the country. The house boasts a substantial collection of Schuyler family pieces & fine examples of Chinese export porcelain, delftware & English glassware. Average Annual Attendance: 15,000
Income: Financed by state appropriation
Collections: American furnishings of the Colonial and Federal Periods, predominantly of New York and New England origins
Publications: Schuyler Mansion: A Historic Structure Report; Schuyler Genealogy: A Compendium of Sources Pertaining to the Schuyler Families in America Prior to 1800; vol 2 prior to 1900
Activities: Educ dept; lect; tours

M **STATE UNIVERSITY OF NEW YORK AT ALBANY,** University Art Gallery, 1400 Washington Ave, 12222. Tel 518-442-4035; FAX 518-442-5075. *Interim Dir* Marijo Dougherty; *Preparator* Zheng Hu; *Admin Asst* Joanne Lue
Open Tues - Fri 10 AM - 5 PM, Sat & Sun 1 - 4 PM, cl Mon. No admis fee. Estab 1968 to augment the teaching program of the Fine Arts Department, to present exhibitions of community interest, and to be of service to the University System, particularly Albany. Gallery has 6400 sq ft on first floor, 3200 sq ft on second floor. Medium security gallery, students as security personnel. The University Art Gallery is custodian for the Fine Arts Study Collection, a collection of contemporary prints which is available on premises for study purposes. Average Annual Attendance: 25,000
Income: Financed by state appropriation
Collections: Paintings, prints, drawings & sculpture of 20th century contemporary art; photographs
Exhibitions: (1993) Particular Voices: Portraits of Gay & Lesbian Writers; Jasper Johns: Prints & Multiples; Printmaking by O'Connor, Cartnell, Bernstein; The Atmosphere: Art & Science; Thesis Exhibtions. (1994) Nelson A Rockfeller: Public Arts & Public Policy; 150 Years of American Art from Collections of Alumni, Faculty & Friends; Faculty Exhibitions; Thesis Exhibition
Publications: Exhibition catalogs
Activities: Lectures open to public, some for members only; gallery talks; tours; competitions with awards; individual paintings lent to offices on the university campus only; lending collection contains 300 art works, 150 original prints and 75 sculptures; book traveling exhibitions; originate traveling exhibition

L **Art Dept Slide Library,** Fine Arts Bldg, Room 121, 12222. Tel 518-442-4018. *Art Historian* Roberta Bernstein; *Art Historian* Sarah Cohen
Open daily 9 AM - 4 PM. Estab 1967 to provide instruction and reference for the university and community
Library Holdings: Per subs 5; AV — Fs, Kodachromes, lantern slides, slides 80,000; Other — Exhibition catalogs, pamphlets, photographs
Collections: Slides, mainly of Western art and architecture

ALFRED

L **NEW YORK STATE COLLEGE OF CERAMICS AT ALFRED UNIVERSITY,** Scholes Library of Ceramics, Harder Hall, State St, 14802. Tel 607-871-2494; FAX 607-871-2349; Elec Mail BITNET:FCONNOLLY@CERAMICS. *Dir* Bruce E Connolly; *Cataloging & Serials Librn* Martha A Mueller; *Technical Ref & ILL Librn* Paul T Culley; *Reference Librn & Archivist* Elizabeth Gulacsy; *Art Librn* Carla C Freeman
Open academic year Mon - Thurs 8 AM - 11 PM, Fri 8 AM - 8 PM, Sat 10 AM - 6 PM, Sun 10 - 11 AM, other periods Mon - Fri 8 AM - 4:30 PM. Estab 1947 to service art education to the Master's level in fine art and the PhD level in engineering and science related to ceramics. The College has a 2500 sq ft Art Gallery which is managed by the Art and Design Division
Income: $620,000 (financed by endowment & state appropriation)
Purchases: $55,000
Library Holdings: Vols 22,000; Per subs 150; College archives & NCECA

archives; Micro — Fiche, reels; AV — A-tapes, cassettes, fs, lantern slides, motion pictures, slides 130, v-tapes 150; Other — Clipping files, exhibition catalogs, original art works, pamphlets

Special Subjects: Ceramics, Glass, Graphic Arts, Painting - American, Photography, Pottery, Printmaking, Sculpture, Video, Fine Art, Wood Design

Collections: Silverman Collection (glass)

Activities: Tours

ALMOND

M **ALMOND HISTORICAL SOCIETY, INC,** Hagadorn House The 1800-37 Museum, 11 N Main St, PO Box 209, 14804. Tel 607-276-6465, 276-6380. *Pres* Charlotte K Baker; *VPres* Judy Coleman; *Treas* Frederick Bayless
Open Fri 2 - 4 PM & by appointment. Admis by donations. Estab 1965 to preserve local history, genealogy & artifacts. The Little Gallery 4 ft x 12 ft, burlap covered walls, 4 display cases, 8-track lighting system. Average Annual Attendance: 2000. Mem: 385; mem open to those interested in local history; dues $2.50, family $6, business or professional $10, life member $100; $100; annual meeting in Nov
Income: $25,908 (financed by endowment, mem, city appropriations)
Collections: 1513 genealogies of local families; town & village records; slide collection of local houses; 1500 costumes & hats; 50 quilts; toys; school books; maps; cemetary lists; photographs, scrapbooks
Exhibitions: Local architecture: drawings & photographs; history of the local post office
Publications: The Cooking Fireplace in the Hagadorn House; My Father's Old Fashioned Drug Store; When My Grandfather Ran a General Store; Forgotten Cemeteries of Almond; School Days; Recollections of Horace Stillman
Activities: Childrens' classes; lectures open to public, 4 vis lectrs per year

AMENIA

A **AGES OF MAN FELLOWSHIP,** Sheffield Rd, 12501. Tel 914-373-9380. *Pres* Dr Nathan Cabot Hale; *VPres* Niels Berg
Open 10 AM - 5 PM. Estab 1968 for the building and design of a sculpture chapel based on the thematic concepts of the Cycle of Life. Mem: 20; dues $100; meetings May and Nov
Income: Financed by membership and contributions
Collections: Sculpture and architectural models of the chapel
Publications: Project report, yearly
Activities: Art history; apprenticeship and journeyman instruction in Cycle of Life design; lect open to the public, 20 vis lectr per yr; gallery talks; original objects of art lent to museums, art associations, educational institutions; originate traveling exhibitions

AMHERST

M **DAEMEN COLLEGE,** Fanette Goldman & Carolyn Greenfield Gallery, Duns Scotus Hall, 4380 Main St, 14226. Tel 716-839-3600, Ext 241. *Dir* Dennis Barraclough
Open Mon - Fri 9 AM - 4 PM. No admis fee. Estab to add dimension to the art program and afford liberal arts students opportunity to view art made by established artists as well as art students. Gallery area is part of main building (Duns Scotus Hall), recently renovated exterior & entrance. Average Annual Attendance: 1500
Income: Financed by College Art Department
Activities: Lect open to public, 4 - 5 vis lectr per year
L **Marian Library,** 4380 Main St, 14226-3592. Tel 716-839-3600; FAX 716-839-8475. *Head Librn* Glenn V Woike; *Ref Librn* Mary Joan Gleason; *Ref Librn* Randolph Chojecki; *Technical Servs Librn* Lee Vitale
Library Holdings: Vols 130,000; Per subs 850; Micro — Cards; AV — Slides; Other — Pamphlets
Special Subjects: Art Education, Art History, Calligraphy, Graphic Arts, Graphic Design, Painting - American, Textiles

AMSTERDAM

M **MOHAWK VALLEY HERITAGE ASSOCIATION, INC,** Walter Elwood Museum, 300 Guy Park Ave, 12010-2228. Tel 518-843-5151. *Pres* Lionel H Fallows; *Dir* Mary M Gage; *Supt Greater Amsterdam School Dist* H Arthur P Cotugno
Open Sept - June Mon - Fri 8:30 AM - 4 PM & weekend by appointment; July 1 - Labor Day Mon - Thurs 8:30 AM - 3:30 PM, Fri 8:30 AM - 1 PM. Estab 1940 to preserve local heritage & natural history. Gallery displays changing exhibits, local & professional collections & museum's works of art. Mem: 675; dues $5 - $500; annual meeting 3rd Tues in June
Income: $25,000 (financed by mem & fundraisers)
Collections: Oil paintings by turn of the century local artists; photographs of early Amsterdam & vicinity; steel engravings by turn of the century artists
Exhibitions: Paintings by the Monday Art Group (local area artists)
Activities: Adult classes; museum shop sells books, maps

ANNANDALE-ON-HUDSON

M **BARD COLLEGE,** William Cooper Procter Art Center, 12504. Tel 914-758-6822. *Dir* Tom Wolf
Open daily 10 AM - 5 PM. Estab 1964 as an educational center. Art center has a gallery, slide library and uses the college library for its teaching
Collections: Assorted contemporary paintings and sculptures; photograph collection of prints
Exhibitions: Two student exhibitions per year; faculty and traveling exhibitions
Publications: Catalogs
Activities: Children's art classes; lect open to the public; gallery talks; scholarships

ARDSLEY

C **CIBA-GEIGY CORPORATION,** Art Collection, 444 Saw Mill River Rd, 10502. Tel 914-479-2605. *Dir, Corporate Art Servs* Markus J Low
Open to public by appointment. Estab 1959 to add color and warmth to interior of its new headquarters, and to support of promising artists. Collection displayed at various company facilities
Collections: †New York School of Painting, abstract expressionist, geometric and figurative art; Swiss Art
Exhibitions: Ciba Geigy Collects: Aspects of Abstraction, Figural Art of the New York School: Selections from the Ciba - Geigy Collection
Publications: Catalogues of collection and exhibition
Activities: Individual objects of art lent upon request to museums and educational institutions for limited periods; originate traveling exhibitions upon request to museums and educational institutions

ASTORIA

M **AMERICAN MUSEUM OF THE MOVING IMAGE,** 35th Ave & 36th St, 11106. Tel 718-784-4520; FAX 718-784-4681. *Dir* Rochelle Slovin, MA; *Head of Colls* Richard Koszarski, PhD; *Head of Film & Video* David Schwartz
Open Tues - Fri noon - 4 PM, Sat & Sun noon - 6 PM. Admis adults $5, children $2.50. Estab 1981, devoted to art, history, technique & technology of moving image media. Temporary gallery on first floor, 1800 sq ft, 2nd floor installations "Behind the Screen", 3rd floor 5500 sq ft of exhibitions, performances. Average Annual Attendance: 100,000. Mem: 1500; annual dues $35 - $1000
Collections: The museum has a collection of over 70,000 artifacts relating to the material art form of movies & television, magazines, dolls, costumes, clothing
Exhibitions: The Living Room Candidate; Changing Faces: History of Hollywood Hair & Make-up; From Harlem to Hollywood: The American Race Movies 1912 - 1948; 1989 Peabody Award Winners: Red Scare; Betty Boop
Publications: Behind the Screen; Who Does What in Motion Pictures & Television
Activities: Classes for children; ESL programs; docent training; adult tours; lect open to public, 50 vis lectr per year; gallery talks; tours; museum shop sells books, magazines, & reproductions

AUBURN

M **CAYUGA MUSEUM OF HISTORY AND ART,** 203 Genesee St, 13021. Tel 315-253-8051. *Dir* Peter Jones; *Cur* Peter Gabak
Open Mon - Fri 1 - 5 PM, Sat 9 AM - 5 PM, Sun 2 - 5 PM, cl New Year's, Labor Day, Thanksgiving, Christmas. No admis fee. Estab 1936 for research and Indian history. Average Annual Attendance: 40,000. Mem: 700; dues $10 - $30; annual meeting in Jan
Income: Financed by endowment, membership, county and city appropriation
Collections: American Pottery; Beardsley Filipino; Herter textiles; †sound on film; †permanent painting by Americans
Exhibitions: Bicentennial, 12 Ethnic Group Shows; Auburn 200 Year Anniversary Show
Activities: Classes for adults and children; docent training; lect open to public, 6 visiting lectr per year; gallery talks, tours; competitions; lending collection contains motion pictures, paintings, slides; museum shop sells original art, reproductions and small gifts
L **Library,** 203 Genesee St, 13021. Tel 315-253-8051. *Acting Librn* Peter Gabak
Open to researchers for reference
Library Holdings: Vols 16,000; Per subs 10
Special Subjects: Indians, local history
Collections: Clarke Collection

M **SCHWEINFURTH ART CENTER,** 205 Genesee St, 13021. Tel 315-255-1553. *Dir* Lisa Pennella; *Educ Coordr* Susan Marteney; *Admin Asst* Dawn Maskerman
Open Tues - Fri 12 noon - 5 PM, Sat 10 AM - 5 PM, Sun 1 - 5 PM. Admis adult $1. Estab 1975 to exhibit & sponsor multi arts activities for a rural audience. 700 sq ft contemporary gallery & 5 galleries 250 sq ft. Average Annual Attendance: 15,000. Mem: 400; dues $15 - $1000
Income: $143,000 (financed by endowment, membership, city & state appropriation, federal & private)
Exhibitions: Annual adult exhibitions; local artist solo exhibitions
Publications: Monthly calendar
Activities: Classes for adults & children; lect open to the public, 2 vis lectr per yr; book traveling exhibitions, twice per yr; museum shop sells books

AURIESVILLE

M **KATERI GALLERIES,** The National Shrine of the North American Martyrs, 12016. Tel 518-853-3033. *Dir* John J Paret; *Asst Dir* John M Doolan
Open 9 AM - 5 PM. No admis fee. Estab 1885 as a religious and historic shrine. Average Annual Attendance: 100,000
Publications: The Pilgrim, quarterly

BALDWIN

M **BALDWIN HISTORICAL SOCIETY MUSEUM,** 1980 Grand Ave, 11510. Tel 516-223-6900. *Pres* Vincent B Schuman; *Cur* Glenn F Sitterly
Open to the public Mon, Wed, Fri 9 AM - 11:30 AM, Sun 1 - 4 PM by appointment. No admis fee. Estab 1971, museum estab 1976 to preserve Baldwin history memorablia including historical photographs. Average Annual Attendance: 500. Mem: 225; dues family $10, individual $5; monthly meetings except Jan, Feb, July & Aug
Income: $5000 (financed by mem, fundraising)
Collections: Collection of local history photographs, postal cards, advertising objects, decorative art objects, manuscripts

Exhibitions: Selection of Baldwin's memorabilia
Publications: Newsletter
Activities: Educ dept; classes for adults & children in local history programs; lect open to the public, 4 vis lectr per year; gallery talks; annual American History award given to a senior in History; museum shop sells books, reproductions, prints & post cards

BALLSTON SPA

A **SARATOGA COUNTY HISTORICAL SOCIETY,** Brookside Museum, Six Charlton St, 12020. Tel 518-885-4000. *Exec Dir* David Mitchell; *Colls Mgr* William Garrison; *Education Dir* Claudia McLaughlin
Open Tues - Fri 10 AM - 4 PM, Sat & Sun noon - 4 PM, cl Mon. Admis adults $2, children $1. Estab 1965 to inform pubic on the history of Saratoga County. 4 small galleries. Average Annual Attendance: 10,000. Mem: 500; dues individual $15
Income: $100,000 (financed by endowment, mem, city appropriation & grants)
Collections: History of Saratoga County, books, manuscripts, objects, photographs
Exhibitions: Dairying in Saratoga County
Publications: Gristmill, 4 per year
Activities: Classes for adults & children; lectures open to public, 4 vis lectr per yr; Sales shop sells books & gifts

BAYSIDE

M **QUEEBSBOROUGH COMMUNITY COLLEGE,** Art Gallery, 22-05 56th Ave, 11364-1497. Tel 718-631-6396; FAX 718-423-9620, 279-1792. *Dir* Faustino Quintanilla; *Gallery Asst* Oscar Sossa
Open 9 AM - 5 PM. No admis fee. Esatb 1981 to provide the college & Queens Community with up to date documentation outline on the visual arts. Average Annual Attendance: 12,000. Mem: 300; dues associate $25; student $10
Income: $214,793 (financed by endowment & mem)
Purchases: Ruth Rothschild & Hampton Blake
Collections: Contemporary Art; works on paper; Richard Art Schwager; Roger Indiana; Paul Jenkins; R Dichtenstein; Larry Rives; Frank Stella; Judy Ritka; Alfonso Ossorio; Jules Allen; Jimmy Ernst; Josef Albers; Sirena
Exhibitions: Siri Berg-Suzane Winkler: Works on Paper; Permanent Collection: Larry Rives
Publications: Signal; Politics & Gender; Romanticism & Classicism; Power of Popular Imagery; Art & Politics
Activities: Lectures open to public, 6 vis lectr per year; gallery tours; scholarships offered; exten dept provides lending collection of 150 paintings; originate traveling exhibitions annually

L **QUEENSBOROUGH COMMUNITY COLLEGE LIBRARY,** 56th Ave & Springfield Blvd, 11364. Tel 718-631-6226. *Chief Librn* Kyu Hugh Kim; *Music & Art Librn* Donald Bryk
Open Mon - Thurs 8:30 AM - 9 PM, Fri 8:30 AM - 5 PM, Sat 10 AM - 5 PM. Estab 1961 to serve the students and faculty of the college
Income: $1,200,000
Purchases: $75,000
Library Holdings: Book and periodical collection which includes material on painting, sculpture and architecture; reproductions of famous paintings on walls throughout the library and reproductions of artifacts and sculpture
Collections: Extremely valuable vertical file collection; print collection

BINGHAMTON

M **ROBERSON MUSEUM & SCIENCE CENTER,** 30 Front St, 13905. Tel 607-772-0660; FAX 607-771-8905. *Dir* Robert W Aber; *Dir Exhib & Prog* Carolyn S Brown PhD; *Dir Science* Jay Sarton; *Chief Designer* Peter Klosky; *Registar* Eve Daniels; *Coll Documentation Systems Mgr* Gary Noce; *Cur History* Timothy Weidner; *Cur Art* Carol Wood; *Cur Folklife* Catherine Schwoeffermann
Open Tues - Thurs & Sat 10 AM - 5 PM, Fri 10 AM - 9 PM, Sun noon - 5 PM, cl Mon. Admis $2 - $3. Estab 1954 as a regional museum of art, history, folklore & science educ center. The Roberson Mansion, built in 1905-06 contains eight galleries; the Martin Building, built in 1968, designed by Richard Neutra, contains five galleries; the A Ward Ford Wing, completed in 1983 contains the Irma M Ahearn Gallery. Average Annual Attendance: 100,000. Mem: 1500, dues $30 - $35
Income: $1,500,000 (financed by endowment, mem, city, county & state appropriations, federal funds & foundations)
Collections: Loomis Wildlife Collection: Northeastern Birds & Mammals; Regional fine & decorative arts, crafts, furniture; archeological & ethnological collections; natural history specimens; historical archives & photographic collections; Hands-on science displays & interactive art
Exhibitions: (1993) Threaded Memories: A Family Quilt Collection; Barbara Insalaco; Exceptional Artworks; Climbing Jacob's Ladder; Bell Watch Collection; Childhood From Field to Factory
Publications: Exhibition catalogs; quarterly newsletter
Activities: Classes for adults & children; school programs; public programs & workshops; lect open to the public; 5 vis lectr per year; concerts; gallery talks; tours; scholarships; programs sent to schools in eleven counties; individual paintings & original objects of art lent; lending collection contains slide tape programs with hands-on-activities for groups; book traveling exhibitions 2 - 3 per year; originate traveling exhibitions to other museums; museum & sales shops sell books, original art, reproductions, prints, slides & a wide range of contemporary crafts

BLUE MOUNTAIN LAKE

M **ADIRONDACK HISTORICAL ASSOCIATION,** Adirondack Museum, 12812. Tel 518-352-7311; FAX 518-352-7603; WATS 800-352-7603. *Pres* Robert R Worth; *Dir* Jacqueline Day; *Cur* Caroline Welsh; *Cur* Hallie Bond; *Education Dir* Daisy Kelly; *Registrar* Tracy Meehan
Open Memorial Day Oct 15 daily 9:30 AM - 5:30 PM. Estab 1957 to relate history and art to the Adirondack region. Museum contains two large galleries for paintings. Average Annual Attendance: 100,000. Mem: 1300; annual meeting August
Collections: †Paintings, †Prints, †Photographs, †Wood Sculpture
Exhibitions: Adirondack Centennial Exhibit; one special exhibition each year (has included the work of Frderic Remington, Allen Blagden, Matthias Oppersdorf)
Publications: Newsletters, books
Activities: Classes for adults and children; lectures open to public, 8-10 vis lectrs per year; concerts; tours; individual paintings and original objects of art lent to museums and galleries; sales shop sells books, magazines, reproductions, prints, slides and postcards

L **Library,** 12812. Tel 518-352-7311; FAX 518-352-7603. *Librn* Jerold L Pepper
Open Mon - Fri 9:30 AM - 5 PM by appointment. Estab to provide research materials for museum staff (exhibit documentation) and researchers interested in the Adirondack, and to preserve written materials relating to the Adirondack. For research only
Library Holdings: Vols 10,000; Per subs 13; maps; Micro — Fiche, reels; AV — A-tapes 25, cassettes, Kodachromes, motion pictures, rec, slides; Other — Clipping files, exhibition catalogs, manuscripts, memorabilia, original art works, pamphlets, photographs
Special Subjects: All Adirondackiana

A **ADIRONDACK LAKES CENTER FOR THE ARTS,** 12812. Tel 518-352-7715. *Dir* Deborah Evans; *Prog Coordr* Paige Macdonald
Open Mon - Fri 9 AM - 4 PM, summer Sat & Sun 10 AM - 5 PM. Admis concerts films $3 - $5, concerts $10 - $12. Estab 1967; this Community Art Center offers both concerts and artist - craftsmen the opportunity for creative exchange. 7000 sq ft facility with 4 studios and black-box theatre. Average Annual Attendance: 30,000. Mem: 600; annual meeting in July
Income: $180,000 (financed by private contributions, county, state & federal assistance, foundations, local businesses, government, mem & fundraising events)
Exhibitions: Exhibits change every month
Publications: Newsletter - Program, quarterly
Activities: Classes for adults and children; lectures open to public, 8 vis lectr per yr; concerts; competitions; gallery talks; tours; scholarships; exten dept serves Adirondack Park; sales shop sells original art, prints, crafts made locally and records by musicians appearing at the art center

BOLTON LANDING

A **MARCELLA SEMBRICH MEMORIAL ASSOCIATION INC,** Opera Museum, Lake Shore Dr, PO Box 417, 12814-0417. Tel 518-644-9839. *Admin Dir* Anita Richards; *Assoc Pres* David Lloyd; *Cur* Richard Wargo
Open June 15 - Sept 15 10 AM - 12:30 PM & 2 - 5:30 PM. Estab 1937 to exhibit memorabilia of Marcella Sembrich & the Golden Age of Opera. Exhibits in Sembrich's former teaching studio on the shore of Lake George. Average Annual Attendance: 1800. Mem: 316; dues $35 & $50; annual meeting in Jan
Income: $30,000 (financed by mem & gifts)
Collections: Memorabilia of the life & career of Marcella Sembrich, opera star of international acclaim (1858 - 1935); paintings, sculpture, furnishings, photographs, costumes, art works, gifts & trophies from colleagues & admirers
Publications: Newsletter, annual; Recollection of Marcella Sembrich, Biography
Activities: Lect open to public, 4 vis lectr per year; retail store sells books, postcards & cassettes

BROCKPORT

M **STATE UNIVERSITY OF NEW YORK, COLLEGE AT BROCKPORT,** Tower Fine Arts Gallery, Dept of Art, 14420. Tel 716-395-2209. *Dir* Anna Calluori Holcombe
Open Tues - Sat noon - 5 PM, Tues & Wed evenings 7 - 9 PM. Estab to present quality exhibitions for purpose of education. 160 running ft, 1900 sq ft. Average Annual Attendance: 7000
Income: Financed by state appropriation & student government
Collections: e e cummings paintings & drawings
Exhibitions: The Faculty Selects: Alumni Invitational III; Thomas R Markusen: A Decade of Metal, 1980 - 1990; Martha Jackson-Jarvis: Hands of Yemaya. (1991) The National Council on Education for the Ceramic Arts; East Asian Festival; Annual Student Exhibition; Bachelor of Fine Arts Graduates. (1992) Margaret Bourke White; Haudenosaunee Artists: Common Heritage; mono prints by painters
Activities: Lectures open to public, 6 vis lectrs per yr; book traveling exhibitions, 1-2 per yr; originate traveling exhibitions

BRONX

AMERICAN SOCIETY OF CONTEMPORARY ARTISTS
For further information, see National and Regional Organizations

M **BRONX COUNCIL ON THE ARTS,** Longwood Arts Gallery, 965 Longwood Ave (Mailing add: 1738 Hone Ave, 10461-1486). Tel 718-931-9500; FAX 718-409-6445. *Council Dir* William Aguado; *Admin Dir* Betti-Sue Hertz
Open Mon - Fri noon - 5 PM, Sat noon - 4 PM, also by appointment. No admis fee. Estab 1985 for exhibits of interest to artists & the Bronx communities. The Gallery, housed in a former Bronx Public School building at 925 Longwood Ave, presents solo & group exhibitions centering on contemporary themes of interest to artists & the Bronx communities

Income: Financed by city, state & federal grants, foundation & corporate support
Exhibitions: (1992 - 93) Vietnamese Artists; Post-Colonialism; Feminism & the Body; Puerto Rican Taino Imagery in Contemporary Art; Real Life Comics; Like Butter; Maze-phantasm; Mini-Murals; Sovereign State; Here & Now, Now & Then
Publications: Catalogues, 2 per year
Activities: Lect open to public, 3 vis lectr per year; fel; book traveling exhibitions 2 per year; originate traveling exhibitions 5 per year

M **BRONX MUSEUM OF THE ARTS,** 1040 Grand Concourse, 10456. Tel 718-681-6000; FAX 718-681-6181. *Chmn of Board* Carlos Cuevas; *Pres* Elizabeth Cooke; *Dir* Grace Stanislaus; *Deputy Dir* Jeffrey Ramirez
Open Wed - Fri 10 AM - 5 PM, Sat & Sun 1 - 6 PM, cl Mon & Tues. Admin adults $3, students $2, sr citizens $1, children under 12 & members free. Estab 1971 with a primary purpose of making arts & educational programming more accessible & relevant to the Borough's 1.2 million ethnically diverse residents; to stimulate community participation through the visual arts within a central museum space & a network of four Satellite Galleries in public spaces in the Bronx; exhibiting diverse collections & schools of art with special concern accorded Bronx artists; to provide educational programs in the arts while serving as a catalyst for its continued creative development. Mem: 987; corporate sponsor $1000, patron $500, associate $250, sustaining $100, family $50, individual $35, student & sr citizen $25
Income: Financed by membership, city, state & federal appropriations, foundations & corporations
Collections: Collection of 20th century works on paper by artists from the geographical areas of Latin America, Africa & Southeast Asia as well as works by American descendents of these areas; File on Bronx artists
Publications: Exhibition catalogs; educational workbooks; walking tours of the Bronx
Activities: Classes for adults, children & seniors; lect open to public; concerts; gallery talks; tours; films; annual arts & crafts festival; traveling exhibitions; museum shop sells books, posters, catalogs, original art, prints, jewelry, childrens & museum gift items

M **BRONX RIVER ART CENTER,** Gallery, 1087 E Tremont Ave, 10460. Tel 718-589-5819. *Exec Dir* Lynn Seeney; *Gallery Coordr* Amir Bey
Open Tues - Thurs 3 - 6 PM. No admis fee. Estab 1980 as a professional, multi-cultural art center. 2000 sq ft, handicapped accessible, ground floor gallery. Two main gallery rooms, natural light. Average Annual Attendance: 5000
Exhibitions: Exhibitions of contemporary artists focusing on innovative multi-cultural, multi-media work
Activities: Classes for adults & children; lect open to public, 16 vis lectr per year; originate traveling exhibitions 1 per year

M **EN FOCO, INC,** 32 E Kingsbridge Rd, 10468. Tel 718-584-7718. *Exec Dir* Charles B Biasiny-Rivera; *Assoc Dir* Betty Wilde
Estab to support publications of Nueva Luz, a bilingual journal of photography, and the establishment of a slide library
Collections: Photographs of Minority Cultures
Exhibitions: Annual Seminar in Puerto Rico & Touring Gallery

M **LEHMAN COLLEGE ART GALLERY,** 250 Bedford Park Blvd W, 10468. Tel 718-960-8731; FAX 212-960-8935. *Dir* Susan Hoeltzel; *Asst to Dir* Skowmon Hastanan
Open Tues - Sat 10 AM - 4 PM. No admis fee. Estab 1985 to exhibit work of 20th century artists. Two galleries housed in Fine Arts building on Lehman College campus, City University NY, designed by Marcel Breuer. Average Annual Attendance: 10,000. Mem: 100; dues $30-$1000
Income: Financed by endowment, mem, city & state appropriation
Publications: Exhibition catalogs; gallery notes
Activities: Children's classes; docent programs; lectures open to public, 6 vis lectrs per yr; book traveling exhibitions; originate traveling exhibitions

SOCIETY OF ANIMAL ARTISTS, INC
For further information, see National and Regional Organizations

M **VAN CORTLANDT MANSION & MUSEUM,** W 246th & Broadway, 10471. Tel 718-543-3344; FAX 718-543-3315. *Dir* Jane Herrick
Open AM - 4:30 PM, Sun 2 - 4:30 PM, cl Mon. Admis adult $.50, children under 12 free, Fri & Sat free to all. Estab 1898. Average Annual Attendance: 30,000
Collections: Furniture & objects of the 18th century
Activities: Classes for children; slide programs for visitors

M **WAVE HILL,** 675 W 252 St, 10471. Tel 212-549-3200; FAX 212-884-8952. *Exec Dir* Kate Pearson French; *Public Relations Dir* Marilyn Oser
Open daily 10 AM - 4:30 PM. No admis weekdays, weekends adults $2, sr citizens & students $1, children under 14 free. Estab 1960 as a public garden & cultural center. Wave Hill House Gallery; Glyndor Gallery; Outdoor Sculpture Garden. Average Annual Attendance: 80,000. Mem: 2000; dues $30
Income: Financed by mem, city & state appropriation, private funding
Collections: †Toscanini Collection: Recordings, Tapes, Photos, Memorabilia
Publications: Calendar, 4 per yr; exhibit catalogues, annually
Activities: Adult & children's classes; dramatic programs; natural history/environmental workshops; lect open to public, 3 vis lectr per yr; concerts; originate traveling exhibitions; shop sells books, magazines, reproductions

BRONXVILLE

L **BRONXVILLE PUBLIC LIBRARY,** 201 Pondfield Rd, 10708. Tel 914-337-7680. *Dir* Jane Cumming Selvar
Open winter Mon, Wed & Fri 9:30 AM - 5:30 PM, Tues 9:30 AM - 9 PM, Thurs 1 - 9 PM, Sat 9:30 AM - 5 PM, Sun 1 - 5 PM, summer Mon, Wed, Thurs & Fri 9:30 AM - 5:30 PM, Sat 9:30 AM - 1 PM. No admis fee
Income: Financed by city and state appropriations

Special Subjects: Painting - American, Prints
Collections: American painters: Bruce Crane, Childe Hassam, Winslow Homer, William Henry Howe, Frederick Waugh; Japanese Art Prints; 25 Original Currier and Ives Prints
Exhibitions: Current artists, changed monthly; original paintings and prints

L **SARAH LAWRENCE COLLEGE LIBRARY,** Esther Raushenbush Library, Glen Washington Rd, 10708. Tel 914-337-0700. *Librn* Charlin Chang Fagan; *Exhibits Librn* Carol Shaner; *Slide Librn* Renee Kent
Open 9 AM - 5 PM. Estab to provide library facilities for students and members of the community with an emphasis on art history. Slide collection closed to the public; non-circulating reference materials available to the public
Library Holdings: Vols 200,000; Per subs 917; AV — Slides 65,000
Exhibitions: Changing exhibits
Activities: Lectures in connection with exhibits; tours on request

BROOKLYN

A **BROOKLYN ARTS COUNCIL,** BACA Downtown, 195 Cadman Plaza W, 11201. Tel 718-625-0080. *Dir* Warren Rosenzweig; *Gallery Coordr* Paul Remirez; *Technical Dir* Kyle Chepulis; *Theater Coordr* Scott Smith; *Exec Dir* Charlene Victor
Gallery open Tues - Sat 1 - 6 PM, theater Fri & Sat 8 - 11 PM. No admis fee to gallery, theater $5 - $8. Estab 1979 to promote experimentation, excellence, and exchange in the visual & performing arts. Two professionally equipped galleries exhibit recent work by contemporary artists working in all media; painting, sculpture, video, installation, mixed media, and performance are presented through solo, group, and thematic guest-curated shows. Average Annual Attendance: 15,0000
Income: $200,000 (financed by endowment, city & state appropriation, theater admissions, gallery sales, corporate & foundation support)
Exhibitions: Solo exhibitions by Brooklyn-based, non-affiliated artists; Artist & Guest-curated group & thematic exhibitions
Publications: BACA Downtown Calendar, bimonthly
Activities: Workshops for adults & children; lect open to public, seminars; gallery talks; competitions with awards

A **BROOKLYN HISTORICAL SOCIETY,** 128 Pierrepont St, 11201. Tel 718-624-0890. *Pres* Carl Ferenbach; *Exec Dir* David M Kahn
Open Tues - Sat 10 AM - 5 PM. Estab in 1863 to collect, preserve and interpret documentary and other materials relating to the history of Brooklyn and the adjoining geographical areas. Gallery used for exhibits on Brooklyn history. Average Annual Attendance: 15,000. Mem: 1750; dues $15 - $1000; annual meeting May
Income: $650,000 (financed by grants, endowment, membership)
Collections: Paintings, drawings, watercolors, prints, sculpture, decorative arts, archeological artifacts relating to Brooklyn's history and key citizens
Exhibitions: Old Dutch Homesteads of Brooklyn; Black Women of Brooklyn; Indian Life in 17th century Brooklyn; Henry Ward Beecher; Brooklyn Baseball & the Dodgers; Rediscovering Greenwood Cemetery; Aids Brooklyn
Publications: Bimonthly newsletter
Activities: Educ dept; docent training; lect open to the public, 15 vis lectr per year; gallery talks; individual paintings and original objects of art lent to other institutions; lending collection contains 3000 original prints, 275 paintings, 20 sculptures
L **Library,** 128 Pierrepont St, 11201. Tel 718-624-0890. *Dir & Librn* Irene Tichenol
Open Tues - Sat 10 AM - 4:45 PM. General admis $2. Estab 1863 for the purpose of collecting, preserving and interperting the history of Brooklyn. Open to general public. Mem: dues $25
Library Holdings: Vols 170,000; Other — Clipping files, manuscripts, original art works, pamphlets, photographs 90,000
Special Subjects: Brooklyn History; Genealogy
Activities: Classes for adult and children; Lectures open to public

M **BROOKLYN MUSEUM,** 200 Eastern Parkway, 11238. Tel 718-638-5000; FAX 718-638-3731; Telex 12-5378; Cable BRKLYN-MUSUNYK. *Chmn Board of Trustees* Robert S Rubin; *Dir* Robert T Buck; *Deputy Dir* Roy R Eddey; *Chief Cur and Cur American Paintings & Sculpture* Linda S Ferber; *Vice Dir Development* Karen H Putnam; *Asst Dir Public Information* Sally Williams; *Cur Egyptian & Classical Art* Richard Fazzini; *Cur European Paintings & Sculpture* Sarah Faunce; *Cur American Paintings & Sculpture* Linda Ferber; *Cur Contemporary Art* Charlotta Kotik; *Cur Asian Art* Amy Poster; *Cur Decorative Arts* Kevin Stayton; *Cur African, Oceanic & New World Cultures* William Siegman; *Cur Prints & Drawings* Linda Kramer; *Chief Conservator* Ken Moser; *Chmn African, Oceanic & New World Art* Diana Fane; *Registrar* Liz Reynolds; *Librn* Deirdre Lawrence; *VDir Marketing* Rena Zurofsky
Open daily 10 AM - 5 PM, cl Tues. Voluntary admis fee. Estab 1823 as an art museum with educational facilities. Five floors of galleries maintained, seventh largest museum of art in the United States. Average Annual Attendance: 350,000. Mem: 9000; dues donor $600, patron $300, contributor $125, family $65, individual $45, senior citizens & students $30
Income: $14,374,000 (financed by endowment, membership, city & state appropriation, gifts)
Collections: Art from the Americas and South Pacific; American period rooms; European and American paintings, sculpture; prints and drawings; costumes and textiles, decorative arts; Major collections of Egyptian and Classical; Oriental, Middle Eastern and African art; Sculpture Garden of ornaments from demolished New York buildings
Exhibitions: (1993) West Wing Opening: Contemporary Art Installation; Milton & Edith Lowenthal Bequest of 31 American Paintings & Sculptures; Leon Polk Smith: Promised Gift; Consuelo Kanaga: An American Photographer; A Grand Lobby Installation by Donald Lipski; West Wing Opening: Egyptian Reinstallation; Arata Isozaki: Architecture 1960 - 1990; Indian Miniatures
Publications: Annual Report; newsletter, monthly; catalogs of major exhibitions; handbooks
Activities: Classes for adults and children; docent training; lect open to the

public, 150 vis lectr per year; gallery talks; tours; individual paintings and original objects of art lent to other museums; originate traveling exhibitions; museum shops sell books, original objects, reproductions, prints, slides for adults & children

L **Libraries/Archives,** 200 Eastern Parkway, 11238. Tel 718-638-5000, Ext 307; FAX 718-638-3731; Elec Mail RLINE-MAIL BM.GML. *Librn* Deirdre E Lawrence
Open by appointment, call in advance. Estab 1823 to serve the staff of the museum and public for reference by appointment only
Income: Financed by city, state and private appropriation
Purchases: $50,000
Library Holdings: Vols 180,000; Per subs 400; Micro — Fiche; AV — A-tapes, slides 50,000, v-tapes; Other — Clipping files, exhibition catalogs, pamphlets
Special Subjects: Afro-American Art, American Indian Art, American Western Art, Anthropology, Antiquities-Assyrian, Antiquities-Egyptian, Antiquities-Greek, Antiquities-Roman, Archaeology, Art History, Asian Art, Decorative Arts, Drawings, Embroidery, Fashion Arts, American Painting & Sculpture, African, Oceanic & New World Cultures, 19th & 20th century prints, costumes & textiles
Collections: Fashion plates; original fashion sketches 1900-1950, 19th century documentary photographs
Publications: Newsletter, bi-monthly
Activities: Classes for children; docent training; programs relating to current exhibitions; lectures open to public, 30 vis lectr per year; gallery talks; tours; originate traveling exhibitions to other museums

L **Wilbour Library of Egyptology,** 200 Eastern Parkway, 11238. Tel 718-638-5000, Ext 215; FAX 718-638-3731. *Librn* Diane Guzman
Open Mon, Wed & Fri 10 AM - 5 PM, cl Tues. Estab 1916 for the purpose of the study of Ancient Egypt. For reference by appointment only
Income: Financed by endowment and city appropriation
Purchases: $16,000
Library Holdings: Vols 35,000; Per subs 150; original documents; Micro — Fiche; Other — Exhibition catalogs, pamphlets
Collections: Seyffarth papers
Publications: Wilbour Monographs; general introductory bibliographies on Egyptian art available to visitors

L **BROOKLYN PUBLIC LIBRARY,** Art and Music Division, Grand Army Plaza, 11238. Tel 718-780-7784. *Division Chief* Sue Sharma; *Chief AV Div* G Verdini
Open Mon - Thurs 9 AM - 8 PM; Fri & Sat 10 AM - 6 PM; Sun 1 - 5 PM. No admis fee. Estab 1892
Income: Financed by city and state appropriation
Library Holdings: Vols 168,500; Per subs 420; mounted picture; Micro — Cards, prints, reels; AV — A-tapes, cassettes, fs, motion pictures, rec, slides, v-tapes; Other — Exhibition catalogs, pamphlets
Collections: Checkers Collection; Chess Collection; Costume Collection
Publications: Brooklyn Public Library Bulletin, bimonthly
Activities: Classes for children; programs; films

M **THE FUND FOR THE BOROUGH OF BROOKLYN,** The Rotunda Gallery, Brooklyn War Memorial, Cadman Plaza W (Mailing add: 16 Court St, Suite 1400 W, 11241). Tel 718-855-7882 (Office), 875-4031 (Gallery); FAX 718-802-9095. *Dir* Janet Riker; *Dir of Educ* Meridith McNeal
Open Tues - Fri noon - 5 PM, Sat 11 AM - 4 PM. No admis fee. Estab 1981 to exhibit the works of professional Brooklyn affiliated artists. Average Annual Attendance: 14,000
Income: Financed by federal, state & municipal sources, private foundations, corporations & individuals
Exhibitions: Seasonal group exhibits of paintings, sculpture, works on paper, photography as well as site specific indoor & outdoor installations & video programs
Activities: Classes for adults & children; lectures open to the public; gallery talks; computerized slide registry

M **KINGSBOROUGH COMMUNITY COLLEGE, CITY UNIVERSITY OF NEW YORK,** Art Gallery, 2001 Oriental Blvd, 11235. Tel 718-368-5000. *Dir* Lilly Wei; *Gallery Asst* Peter Malone
Open Mon - Fri 9 AM - 4 PM. No admis fee. Estab 1975 to show a variety of contemporary artistic styles. 44 ft x 44 ft gallery with moveable walls & 30 ft x 25 ft outdoor sculpture courtyard. Average Annual Attendance: 10,000
Income: Financed by Kingsborough Community College Assn
Exhibitions: Annual Student Exhibition
Activities: Lectures open to public, 4 - 8 vis lectr per yr; competitions with awards

L **NEW YORK CITY TECHNICAL COLLEGE,** Namm Hall Library and Learning Resource Center, 300 Jay St, 11201. Tel 718-260-5469; FAX 718-260-5467. *Dir Librn* Darrow Wood; *Admin Services Librn* Prof Paul T Snerman; *Chief Cataloguer* Prof Joseph Viscarra; *Reference Coordr* Prof Eustace O Burnett
Open Mon - Fri 9 AM - 9 PM, Sat & Sun 10 AM - 2 PM. Estab 1947
Library Holdings: Other — Reproductions
Special Subjects: Advertising Design, Graphic Arts
Publications: Library Alert & Library Notes, occasional publications
Activities: Tours; Library Instruction; BRS Data Base Searching

A **NEW YORK EXPERIMENTAL GLASS WORKSHOP,** 647 Fulton St, 11217. Tel 718-625-3685. *Dir* Tina Yalle; *Asst to Dir* Patricia Pullman
Open Mon - Fri 10 AM - 6 PM, Sat & Sun noon - 6 PM. No admis fee. Estab 1978 to provide facility for artists who work in glass
Publications: Glass Magazine, quarterly
Activities: Educ dept; classes for adults; lectures open to public, 7 vis lectr per year; gallery talks; tours; competitions; scholarships and fels offered

L **PRATT INSTITUTE LIBRARY,** Art & Architecture Dept, 200 Willoughby Ave, 11205. Tel 718-636-3545. *Dean* F William Chickering; *Asst Dean* Dr Sydney Starr Keaveney; *Art & Architecture Librn* Jean Hines
Open Mon - Thurs 9 AM - 11 PM, Fri 9 AM - 5 PM, Sat & Sun noon - 5 PM

for students, faculty & staff, others by appointment or with METRO or ALB card. Estab 1887 for students, faculty, staff & alumni of Pratt Institute. The school has several galleries, the library has exhibitions in display cases
Income: $50,000
Library Holdings: Vols 60,000; Per subs 150; Micro — Fiche, reels; AV — Slides; Other — Clipping files, exhibition catalogs, prints, reproductions
Special Subjects: Architecture, Photography, Contemporary Art, Design

M **Rubelle & Norman Schafler Gallery,** 200 Willoughby Ave, 11205. Tel 718-636-3517; FAX 718-636-3455. *Dir Exhib* Eleanor Moretta; *Registrar* Nicholas Battis; *Exhibit Designer* Katherine Davis
Open Mon - Fri 9 AM - 5 PM, summer 9 AM - 4 PM. No admis fee. Estab 1960. Average Annual Attendance: 14,000
Collections: Permanent collection of fiber art, paintings, pottery, prints, photographsm sculpture
Exhibitions: Revered Earth & Cross Cut/Piedra Lumbre; Nature of Science; What is Socially Responsible Design
Activities: Guest lectures; lectures open to the public, 2 vis lectrs per year; traveling exhibitions, 1 per year; originate traveling exhibitions

BROOKVILLE

M **C W POST CAMPUS OF LONG ISLAND UNIVERSITY,** Hillwood Art Museum, 11548. Tel 516-299-2788, 299-2789. *Dir* Dr Judy Collischan; *Deputy Dir* Margaret Kerswill
Open Mon - Fri 10 AM - 5 PM, Sun 1 - 5 PM, during academic year. No admis fee. Estab 1973. Museum has great appeal to the surrounding North Shore community as well as the student body. The museum is located in a multimillion dollar student complex; it occupies a space of approx 46 x 92 ft. Average Annual Attendance: 25,000
Income: Financed by university budget, grants and donations
Collections: Contemporary graphics, including works by Rauschenberg, Max Ernst, Pearlstein, Mark di Suvero and Salvador Dali
Exhibitions: Monumental Drawings, including R Serra, R Nonas, M Westerlund-Roosen, J Highstein; Painting from the Mind's Eye, including B Jensen, T Nozkowski, N Brett, D Nelson, L Fishman; The Raw Edge: Ceramics of the 80's, including M Lucero, T Rosenberg, P Gourfain, A Gardner, V Frey; Floored, including L Benglis, C Andre, T Girouard, K Park, H Hammond; The Expressionist Vision, including A Rattner, J Solmon, M Hartley, K Schrag, Ben-Zion, U Romano, K Zerbe; Futurism and Photography; The Artist in the Theatre, including R Grooms, R Lichtenstein, J Shea, E Murray, V James, R Kushner, A Katz Reflections: New Conceptions of Nature, including P Norvell, J Bartlett, L Nesbitt, A Sonfist, M Stuart, T Winters, J Robbins; Michelle Stuart, Donald Lipski & Seymour Lipton, sculpture
Publications: Exhibition catalogs
Activities: Lectures open to public, 6 - 10 vis lectrs per year; concerts; museum talks; tours; individual paintings & original objects of art lent; lending collection contains books, cassettes, 3000 prints; originate traveling exhibitions

BUFFALO

L **BUFFALO AND ERIE COUNTY PUBLIC LIBRARY,** Lafayette Square, 14203. Tel 716-858-8900; FAX 716-858-6211. *Dir* Donald H Cloudsley; *Deputy Dir Public Services* Diane J Chrisman; *Deputy Dir Support Services* Wallace D Mohn
Open Mon, Tues, Wed, Fri, Sat 8:30 AM - 6 PM, Thurs 8:30 AM - 9 PM. Estab 1954 through a merger of the Buffalo Public, Grosvenor, and Erie County Public Libraries
Income: $19,287,833 (financed by county appropriation & state aid)
Library Holdings: Vols 2,500,000; Per subs 3600; AV — Motion pictures; Other — Exhibition catalogs, manuscripts 4178, original art works, photographs, prints
Collections: Drawings by Fritz Eichenberg; etchings by William J Schwanekamp; Niagara Falls prints; original woodcuts of J J Lankes; posters (mostly WW I); Rare Book Room with emphasis on fine printing
Publications: Library Bulletin, monthly; Western NY Index, monthly, annual cumulation
Activities: Dramatic programs; consumer programs; gallery talks; tours; concerts; book talks; architectural programs

M **THE BUFFALO FINE ARTS ACADEMY,** Albright-Knox Art Gallery, 1285 Elmwood Ave, 14222. Tel 716-882-8700; FAX 716-882-1958. *Pres* Seymour H Knox; *VPres* Mrs John T Elfvin; *VPres* Northrup R Knox; *VPres* William J Magavern II; *Treas* Richard W Cutting; *Dir* Douglas G Schultz; *Chief Cur* Michael G Auping; *Cur* Cheryl A Brutan; *Cur Education* Jennifer Bayles; *Registrar* Laura Catalano
Open Tues - Sat 11 AM - 5 PM, Sun noon - 5 PM, cl Thanksgiving, Christmas and New Year's Day. Admis adults $4, students & sr citizens $3, children 12 & under free. Estab 1862 as The Buffalo Fine Arts Academy. Gallery dedicated in 1905, with a new wing added in 1962. Average Annual Attendance: 210,000. Mem: 6400; dues individual $35; annual meeting in Oct
Income: $3,100,000 (financed by contributions, mem, endowment, county appropriations, individual & corporate grants, earned income & special projects)
Collections: †Painting & drawings; †prints & sculpture ranging from 3000 BC to the present with special emphasis on †American & European contemporary art; †sculpture & constructions
Exhibitions: (1991) Jenny Holzer: The Venice Installation. (1992) Susan Rothenberg: Paintings & Drawings. (1993) Clyfford Still: The Buffalo & San Francisco Collections
Publications: Annual report; calendar (monthly); exhibition catalogs
Activities: Classes for adults and children; docent training; family workshops & programs; programs for the handicapped; lectures open to public; concerts; gallery talks; tours; lending collections contain paintings, photographs & sculptures; originate traveling exhibitions; gallery shop sells books, magazines, original art, reproductions, prints, slides

L **G Robert Strauss Jr Memorial Library,** 1285 Elmwood Ave, 14222. Tel 716-882-8700, Ext 225; FAX 716-882-8773. *Librn* Kari E Horowicz; *Asst Librn* Janice Lurie
Open Thurs & Fri 2 - 5 PM, Sat 1 - 3 PM & by appointment. Estab 1933 to support the staff research and to document the Gallery collection, also to serve the fine art and art history people doing research in the western New York area. Exhibits are prepared in a small vestibule, rare items in the library collection & print collection are displayed
Library Holdings: Vols 30,000; Per subs 100; original documents; Micro — Fiche; AV — A-tapes, cassettes, v-tapes; Other — Clipping files, exhibition catalogs, manuscripts, memorabilia, original art works, pamphlets, photographs, prints, reproductions
Special Subjects: History of Art & Archaeology, Painting - American, Photography, Pre-Columbian Art, Printmaking, Prints, Sculpture, American Art; Contemporary Art; Artists' Books; Illustrated Books
Collections: †Artists books; †illustrated books; †Graphic Ephemera
Exhibitions: Books and Prints of Maillol; Photography in Books; Rare Art Periodicals; Woodcuts from the Library Collection; Artists' Books; Illustrated Books; Derriere Le Mirroir; From the Gallery Archives; General Ide; Books with a Diffrence Circle Press Publications

L **BUFFALO MUSEUM OF SCIENCE,** Research Library, Humboldt Parkway, 14211. Tel 716-896-5200, Ext 239. *Research Librn* Lisa A Seivert
Open Mon - Fri 10 AM - 5 PM (by appointment only). Estab 1861 to further the study of natural history among the people of Buffalo. Reference only to members. Museum has exhibition space for permanent and temporary exhibitions. Circ 650
Income: Financed by endowment, membership, county & state appropriation, grants, gifts
Purchases: $12,000
Library Holdings: Vols 12,000; Per subs 600; Micro — Fiche, reels; AV — A-tapes; Other — Clipping files, exhibition catalogs, manuscripts, pamphlets, photographs
Special Subjects: Afro-American Art, American Indian Art, Anthropology, Archaeology, Ethnology, Jade, Oriental Art, Pre-Columbian Art
Collections: African, Asian, American, European, Oceanic & Oriental Art; E W Hamlin Oriental Library of Art & Archaeology; Milestones of Science: First Editions Announcing Scientific Discoveries or Advances
Publications: Bulletin of the Buffalo Society of Natural Sciences, irregular; Collections, bi-monthly
Activities: Classes for adults and children; docent training; travel talks; lectures open to public, 5 vis lectr per year; tours; sponsor Camera Club Photo Contests; book traveling exhibitions, 2-3 per yr

M **BURCHFIELD ART CENTER,** 1300 Elmwood Ave, 14222. Tel 716-878-6011; FAX 716-878-6003. *Dir* Anthony Bannon; *Charles Cary Rumsey Cur* Nancy Weekly; *Archivist & Registrar* Michelle Weekly; *Dir of Development* Catherine Carfagna; *Admin Asst* Lisa Brown; *Business Operations Mgr* Micheline Lepine; *Educ Cur* Gerald Mead
Open Tues - Sat 10 AM - 5 PM, Sun 1 - 5 PM. No admis fee. Estab 1966 to develop a regional arts center for the exhibition, study and encouragement of artistic expression in the Western New York area. This includes a permanent collection of works by Charles Burchfield and other historic and contemporary artists who have lived or worked in the area. Museum has eight exhibition galleries. Average Annual Attendance: 40,000. Mem: 1600; dues sustaining $50, family $30, regular $20, student, artist & sr citizen $10
Income: Financed by grants, endowment, membership, SUNY and other sources
Collections: †Charles Burchfield; †works by contemporary and historical artists of the western New York area
Exhibitions: Charles Burchfield, permanent collection; Tyrone Georgiou: Archaeology Today Tomorrow; The State of Upstate: New York Women Artists; Kleinhans Music Hall: The Saarinens in Buffalo, 1940; Natural Selection: Sculpture by Christy Rupp; Rosalind-Kimball Moulton: Photography & Light Drawings; Tom Toles: Pulitzer Prize Winning Cartoons; Robert Lax & Concrete Poetry. (1991-92) Science as Spectacle: Gary Nickard; Buffalo Society of Artists 100th Anniversary Exhibition; Treasures from the Turtle: Art from the Iroquois; Frederick Law Olmsted - Designs for Buffalo's Parks & Parkways (1868 - 98)
Publications: Exhibition catalogues
Activities: Docent training; lect open to the public; concerts; tours; poetry readings; competitions; dept serves area schools and community organizations; original objects of art lent to teachers; lending collection contains books, cassettes, color reproduction, film strips, framed reproductions, slides, magazine articles, periodicals; originate traveling exhibitions; shop sells books, catalogues, craft art, reproductions and wallpapers designed by Charles Burchfield

L **Archives,** 1300 Elmwood Ave, 14222. Tel 716-878-4143; FAX 716-878-6003. *Researcher* Robert Slammon
Open Mon - Fri 10 AM - 5 PM. Estab 1967. For public reference only
Library Holdings: Vols 2500; Monographs, Periodicals, Study Collection; AV — A-tapes, cassettes, motion pictures, slides, v-tapes; Other — Clipping files, exhibition catalogs, manuscripts, memorabilia, photographs
Special Subjects: Architecture, Art Education, Art History, Historical Material, Manuscripts, Painting - American, Photography, Printmaking, Watercolors, Western New York State Regional Arts
Collections: Archives relating to Charles E Burchfield, George William Eggers, Charles Cary Rumsey, Frank K M Rehn Gallery, J J Lankes, Martha Visser't Hooft, Buffalo Society of Artists, Patteran Society; Artpark; Artist Gallery
Exhibitions: Archival materials relating to the life and career of Charles Burchfield

M **CENTER FOR EXPLORATORY & PERCEPTUAL ART,** CEPA Gallery, 700 Main St, 4th Floor, 14202. Tel 716-856-2717. *Pres* Lynette Hamister; *Exec Dir* Gail Nicholson
Open Tues - Fri 10 AM 5 PM, Sat noon - 4 PM. No admis fee. Estab 1974 as a non-profit art center for the advancement of contemporary ideas & issues expressed through photographically related work. five gallery rooms, 225 running ft of wall space, tracklight, hardwood floors. Average Annual Attendance: 50,000. Mem: 200; dues $20 - $1000
Income: $100,000 (financed by mem, city & state appropriation, NY State Council on the arts, National Endowment for the Arts)
Publications: CEPA Quarterly; Artist Project Publications, 2 artist books per year
Activities: Adult classes; lectures open to public, vis lectrs; competitions with awards; book one traveling exhibition per year; shop sells books, original art

L **CEPA Library,** 700 Main St, 4th Floor, 14202. Tel 716-856-2717.
Reference library only
Library Holdings: AV — Lantern slides, rec, slides, v-tapes; Other — Clipping files, exhibition catalogs, pamphlets
Special Subjects: Photography

M **HALLWALLS CONTEMPORARY ARTS CENTER,** 700 Main St, 14202. Tel 716-854-5828; FAX 716-855-3959. *Dir* Edmund Cardoni
Open Tues - Fri noon - 6 PM, Sat 1 - 5 PM. Admis fee varies; Hallwall members free. Estab 1974 to provide exhibition space for artists whose careers are just beginning to emerge into the mainstream of art activity; besides exhibition, programming includes film, literature, music, performance art & video. The gallery is comprised of 1 large & 3 smaller viewing galleries. Average Annual Attendance: 25,000. Mem: 200; dues $20-$300
Income: Financed by the National Endowment for the Arts, city, county & state appropriations, the Institute of Museum Services, New York State Council of Art, contributions from private corporations & founations
Activities: Lectures open to the public; gallery talks; originate traveling exhibitions

CANAJOHARIE

M **CANAJOHARIE ART GALLERY,** 2 Erie Blvd, 13317. Tel 518-673-2314. *Pres of Board* Mrs John Fenno; *Dir* Eric Trahan; *Cur* Edward Lipowicz; *Historical Cur* Elena Borowski
Open Mon - Wed and Fri 9:30 AM - 4:45 PM, Thurs 9:30 AM - 8:30 PM, Sat 9:30 AM - 1:30 PM, cl Sun. No admis fee. Estab 1927 as a memorial to Senator James Arkell. Two galleries exhibit works from permanent collection including major collection of paintings by Winslow Homer. Average Annual Attendance: 3000 - 5000. Mem: Annual meeting in Jan
Income: Financed by endowment and village grants
Collections: †Paintings by American artists, colonial period - present
Exhibitions: Permanent collection
Publications: Catalog of Permanent Art Collection varies
Activities: Gallery talks; tours; individual paintings & original objects of art lent to community residents & businesses or institutions

L **Library,** 2 Erie Blvd, 13317. Tel 518-673-2314. *Dir Library* Eric Trahan; *Pres of Board* Mrs John Fenno; *Historical Cur* Elena Borowski
Library Holdings: Vols 38,000; Per subs 145
Activities: Lectures open to public, 5 vis lectr per year; concerts; gallery talks; tours; lending collection contains 29,022 books, cassettes, framed reproductions & 788 phono records; sales shop sells prints & catalog at Permanent Art Collection

CANTON

M **ST LAWRENCE UNIVERSITY,** Richard F Brush Art Gallery, Romoda Dr, 13617. Tel 315-379-5174. *Dir* Catherine Tedford; *Acting Colls Mgr* laura Desmond
Open Mon - Fri noon - 6 PM, by appointment. No admis fee. Estab 1968 as an adjunct of the Department of Fine Arts. The Gallery's programs are intended to complement the University's curriculum as well as benefit the general public of Northern New York state & Southern Canada
Income: Financed by university funds
Collections: †20th Century American & European prints, drawings & photographs; 16 - 20th Century European & American paintings, sculpture & prints; Oriental & African Art
Publications: Annual report; exhibition brochures
Activities: Lect open to public, 6 vis lectr per year; art objects lent to museums

CARMEL

A **NEW YORK TAPESTRY ARTISTS,** PO Box 1290, 10113-0940. Tel 212-924-2478, 914-225-8276; FAX 914-225-0382. *Artist* Betty Vera; *Artist* Bojana H Leznicki; *Artist* Mary-Ann Sievert; *Artist* Rita R Gekht
Estab 1987 as an artists' collaboration to work on group projects, exhibits & promote/educate the public about contemporary fine art tapestry & related work in other mediums. Mem: 5; members must be selected & accepted as professional fiber artist by current members
Income: Financed by endowment
Activities: Adult classes; lect open to public; originate traveling exhibitions 1-3 per year

CAZENOVIA

M **CAZENOVIA COLLEGE,** Chapman Art Center Gallery, 13035. Tel 315-665-9446, Ext 162; FAX 315-655-2190. *Dir Art Prog* John Aistars
Open Mon - Fri 1 - 4 PM & 7 - 9 PM, Sat 10 AM - 7 PM, Sun 1 - 5 PM. No admis fee. Estab 1977 as a college gallery for students and community. Gallery is 1084 sq feet with track lighting and movable display panels. Average Annual Attendance: 1000
Income: Financed through College
Collections: A small permanent collection of work donated to college
Exhibitions: Annual shows of faculty, students & invitational work; Cazenovia Watercolor Soc

CHAUTAUQUA

M **CHAUTAUQUA ART ASSOCIATION GALLERIES,** PO Box 999, 14722. Tel 716-357-2771. *Pres* Atta Korol; *VPres* Joan Reed; *Dir* Donald R Haug
Open Mon - Sun 11 AM - 5 PM July - Aug. No admis fee. Estab 1952 to promote quality art, culture & appreciation of the arts. Main gallery with 3 smaller galleries. Average Annual Attendance: 20,000. Mem: 250; dues $12; monthly meetings
Income: Financed by membership, grants, donations & fundraising activities
Exhibitions: Twenty-four exhibitions per yr including crafts, prints, paintings, glass, metals & sculpture; Annual Chautauqua National Exhibition of Americna Art (entering 36th yr)
Publications: Chautauqua National, catalog, yearly; Calendar of Events, yearly; Chautauqua National Prosetus, yearly; Annual Report; promotional materials; exhibition brochures; membership brochures
Activities: Classes for adults & children; art appreciation; docent training; lect open to public, 17 vis lectr per yr; concerts; gallery talks; docent tours; competitions; annual juried National Exhibition of American Art; awards; individual paintings & original objects of art lent to area libraries, exhibition sites, area galleries & theatres; book traveling exhibitions annually; originate traveling exhibitions; sales shop sells books, original art, reproductions, prints, original jewelry, small gifts & handicraft from around the world

CLINTON

M **HAMILTON COLLEGE,** Fred L Emerson Gallery, 13323. Tel 315-859-4396; FAX 315-859-4969. *Dir* David Butler
Open Tues - Sun 11 AM - 5 PM, Sat & Sun 1 - 5 PM. No admis fee. Estab 1982. Housed in 1914 building. Average Annual Attendance: 20,000
Income: Financed by Hamilton College appropriations
Purchases: Martin Lewis, Rainy Day on Murray Hill, etching; George Bellows Between Rounds 1916, lithograph; Jefferson David Chalfant Working Sketch for the Chess Players, pencil; Roman, c 2nd Century AD; Two Sarcophagi Fragments, marble
Collections: Greek vases, Roman glass; †16th - 20th century prints, †19th - 20th century paintings; Native American artifacts
Exhibitions: (1991) Leon Golub Portraits. (1992) Philip Hooker & His Contemporaries, 1796 - 1836
Publications: Exhibition catalogues
Activities: Lectures open to the public, 2-3 vis lectrs per yr; concerts; gallery talks; tours; individual paintings & original objects of art lent; originate traveling exhibitions

A **KIRKLAND ART CENTER,** E Park Row, PO Box 213, 13323. Tel 315-853-8871. *Dir* Dare Thompson
Open Tues - Fri 9:30 AM - 5 PM, Sun 2 - 5 PM, cl Mon; Tues - Fri 9:30 - 3 PM, Sun 2 - 5 PM July & Aug. No admis fee. Estab 1960 to promote the arts in the town of Kirkland & surrounding area. The center has a large main gallery, dance studio & studio space for classes. Average Annual Attendance: 15,000 - 17,000. Mem: 1350; dues adults $15; annual meeting June
Income: Financed by endowment, mem, state, county & town appropriation, fund raising events, thrift, gallery shop, United Way & United Arts Funds
Exhibitions: Works by contemporary artists
Publications: Newsletter, monthly
Activities: Classes for adults & children; performances for children; bluegrass & folk music series; film series; lectures open to public; competitions; art shop sells original art

COLD SPRING

M **PUTNAM COUNTY HISTORICAL SOCIETY,** Foundry School Museum, 63 Chestnut St, 10516. Tel 914-265-4010. *Cur* Charlotte Eaton
Open Tues - Wed 10 AM - 4 PM, Thurs 1 - 4 PM, Sun 2 - 5 PM, cl Mon, Fri & Sat. No admis fee. Estab 1906 to present local history artifacts. Average Annual Attendance: 1000. Mem: 500; dues family $25, individual $15, srs & students $10; juniors 10 - 13 $1; annual meeting in June
Income: $30,000 (financed by endowment, mem, fundraising events)
Collections: 19th Century Country Kitchen, West Point Foundry; Country Store; Furnishings & Hudson River Paintings
Exhibitions: (1992) Paintings of Michael Kelly; Hotels & Inns of Philipstown; Columbus & Cold Spring's Italian Heritage; Christmas Comes to the Foundry School Museum; 4 exhibits a year.
Activities: School programs; lect open to public, 2 vis lectr per year; competitions with awards; individual paintings & original objects of art lent

COOPERSTOWN

A **COOPERSTOWN ART ASSOCIATION,** 22 Main St, 13326. Tel 607-547-9777. *Dir* Abigail Amols
Open Mon - Sat 11 AM - 4 PM, Sun 1 - 4 PM. Estab 1928 to provide a cultural program for the central part of New York State. An art gallery is maintained. Average Annual Attendance: 14,000. Mem: 1283; dues $15 & up
Income: Financed by membership
Collections: †Crafts; †paintings; †sculpture
Exhibitions: Annula National Juried Exhibitions; 51st Annual National Art Exhibition (juried show)
Publications: Newsletter, annual
Activities: Classes for adults; lect open to public, 1 - 3 vis lectr per year; concerts; awards; scholarships; individual paintings and original objects of art lent; lending collection contains paintings, sculpture, crafts

A **LEATHERSTOCKING BRUSH & PALETTE CLUB INC,** PO Box 446, 13326. Tel 607-547-8044. *Publicity* Dorothy V Smith
Estab 1965 to encourage original arts and crafts work and foster general art appreciation and education. Mem: 75; dues $5, meetings quarterly

Income: Financed by membership and outdoor show revenues
Exhibitions: Annual Labor Day Weekend Outdoor Arts & Crafts Show; Annual Fine Arts Exhibition; Leatherstocking Gallery Arts & Crafts Shop
Publications: Information Bulletin, quarterly
Activities: Classes for adults; All activities offered to public; member tours to art museums & exhibits; scholarships; originate traveling exhibitions

M **NATIONAL BASEBALL HALL OF FAME AND MUSEUM, INC,** Art Collection, Main St, PO Box 590, 13326. Tel 607-547-9988; FAX 607-547-5980. *Dir* Howard C Talbot Jr; *Assoc Dir* William J Guilfoile; *Registrar* Peter P Clark; *Historian* Thomas R Heitz; *Cur Exhibits* William T Spencer
Open May - Oct daily 9 AM - 9 PM, Nov - April daily 9 AM - 5 PM. Admis adults $4, children ages 7-15 $1.50. Estab 1936 to collect, preserve and display memorabilia pertaining to the national game of baseball. Average Annual Attendance: 200,000
Income: $1,500,000 (financed by admis & gift shop sales, Hall of Fame Game & contributions)
Collections: Baseball & sport-related art & memorabilia
Publications: National Baseball Hall of Fame & Museum Yearbook, annually; Newsletter, quarterly
Activities: Orginate traveling exhibitions to museums, banks, baseball clubs, shopping malls; bookstore sells books, t-shirts, caps, glassware, postcards, mugs and jackets

NEW YORK STATE HISTORICAL ASSOCIATION

M **Fenimore House,** Route 80, Lake Rd, PO Box 800, 13326. Tel 607-547-2533; FAX 607-547-5384. *Pres* Dr William Tramposch; *Assoc Dir* Milo V Stewart; *Cur Coll* A Bruce MacLeish
Open May - Oct daily 9 AM - 6 PM, Nov & Dec, Tues - Sun 10 AM - 4 PM, cl all Jan - Apr. Admis adults $5, children $2, members free. Estab 1899 as a historical society whose purpose is to promote the study of New York State through a statewide educational program, the operation of two museums, and graduate programs offering master's degree in conjunction with the State University College at Oneonta. Fenimore House is an art museum with an extensive collection of folk, academic & decorative art. Average Annual Attendance: 45,000. Mem: 5800; dues $25; annual meeting July
Collections: American folk art; Browere life masks of famous Americans; James Fenimore Cooper (memorabilia); genre paintings of New York State; landscapes; portraits
Exhibitions: (1993) Worlds of Art - Worlds Apart
Publications: Director's Report, annual; New York History, quarterly journal; Heritage, quarterly membership magazine
Activities: Classes for adults and children; docent training; seminars on American culture; junior program; conferences; lect open to the public; gallery talks; tours; individual paintings and original objects of art lent to selected museums

M **Farmers' Museum, Inc,** Route 80, Lake Rd, PO Box 800, 13326. Tel 607-547-2593; FAX 607-547-5384. *Pres* Dr William Tramposch
Open May - Oct daily 9 AM - 6 PM; Nov, Dec & Apr Tues - Sun 10 AM - 4 PM: cl Jan - Mar (open by appointment only). Admis adults $6, children between 7-15 $2.50, under 7 & members free. Estab 1943 as an outdoor museum of rural life in upstate New York, 1785 - 1860. Main exhibit building with exhibits & craft demonstrations; recreated village with 13 buildings brought in from nearby area. Average Annual Attendance: 100,000
Income: Financed by endowment, self-sustaining
Collections: 19th century tools & implements; horse-drawn vehicles & farm equipment; 19th century rural home & interior furnishings
Exhibitions: The Sheltered Nest: Mechanizing the Victorian Household; Beginnings: New York State Agriculture; Textile Loft; Tradesman's Tool Chest (22 New York Crafts)
Activities: Classes for adults & children; docent training; lectures open to public, 2-3 vis lectr per yr; concerts; tours; special events; book traveling exhibitions; museum shop sells reproductions & gifts

L **Library,** Route 80, Lake Rd, 13326. Tel 607-547-2509. *Librn* Amy Barnum
Open to public for reference only
Library Holdings: Vols 70,000; Per subs 160; Micro — Reels; AV — Cassettes, rec; Other — Manuscripts
Special Subjects: Decorative Arts, Folk Art, New York State History

CORNING

M **CORNING MUSEUM OF GLASS,** One Museum Way, 14830-2253. Tel 607-937-5371; FAX 607-937-3352. *Dir* David Whitehouse; *Research Scientist* Robert H Brill; *Cur 20th Century Glass* Susanne Frantz; *cur American Glass* Jane Spillman; *Registrar* Priscilla B Price; *Managing Editor* Richard W Price
Open all year daily 9 AM - 5 PM. Admis family $13, adult $5, sr citizen $4, children 6 - 17 $3, children under 6 free. Estab 1951 to collect & exhibit the finest glass from 1500 BC to the present. New building opened May 1980. Average Annual Attendance: 450,000. Mem: 800; annual dues $125 & up
Income: $3,000,000 (financed by gifts, interest & sales)
Collections: †Over 25,000 objects representing all periods of glass history from 1500 BC to the present
Exhibitions: Drinking vessels from our Collection
Publications: Journal of Glass Studies annually; New Glass Review, annually; annual catalog for special exhibitions
Activities: Classes for children; docent training; annual seminar on glass; lectures open to the public, 20 vis lectr per year; film series; gallery talks; tours; competitions; awards; scholarships & fels; original art objects lent to the other museums; lending collection contains 50,000 books, 350 lantern slides; originate traveling exhibitions; sales shop sells books, postcards, prints & slides

L **Rakow Library,** One Museum Way, 14830-2253. Tel 607-937-5371; FAX 607-937-3352. *Librn* Norma P H Jenkins; *Assoc Librn* Virginia L Wright
Open Mon - Fri 9 AM - 5 PM. Estab 1951 for the purpose of providing comprehensive coverage of the art, history, archaeology and early manufacture of glass. The library is primarily for research reference use.
Library Holdings: Vols 27,400; Per subs 765; Original documents; 670 rare books; Micro — Fiche 12,500, reels 685; AV — A-tapes, cassettes, motion pictures, slides 160,000, v-tapes 560; Other — Clipping files, exhibition catalogs,

original art works, pamphlets, photographs, prints 550
Special Subjects: Antiquities-Assyrian, Antiquities-Byzantine, Antiquities-Egyptian, Antiquities-Etruscan, Antiquities-Greek, Antiquities-Oriental, Antiquities-Persian, Antiquities-Roman, Archaeology, Crafts, Decorative Arts, Flasks & Bottles, Glass, Glass history, manufacturing, painting and staining, glassware, ornamental glass
Collections: Archival and historical materials relating to glass and its manufactures; 3900 manufacturers' trade catalogs on microfiche

M **THE ROCKWELL MUSEUM,** 111 Cedar St, 14830. Tel 607-937-5386; FAX 607-974-4536. *Dir* Dr Kent Ahrens; *Registrar* Susan Kowalczyk; *Cur* Robyn G Peterson; *Asst Dir Admin* Mercedes C Skidmore; *Public Relations & Marketing Mgr* Lilita Bergs; *Supv Public Programs* P Jensen Monroe; *Museum Shop Mgr* Juanita Malavet
Open Sept - June Mon - Sat 9 AM - 5 PM, Sun noon - 5 PM, July & Aug Mon - Fri 9 AM - 7 PM, Sat 9 AM - 5 PM, Sun noon - 5 PM. Admis family $10, adults $4, sr citizens $3.60, students 6 - 17 $2. Estab 1976 to house & exhibit the collection of the Robert F Rockwell Foundation and to collect & exhibit American Western art, Carder glass, antique toys. The 3rd floor Western art gallery has bronzes, paintings, antique firearms & artifacts & Reifschlager Gallery displays Carder Steuben glass. Average Annual Attendance: 50,000. Mem: 700; dues $25 - $1000; meetings in June & Dec
Income: $400,000 (financed by a grant from the Corning Glass Works)
Purchases: $50,000
Collections: †Carder Steuben glass (1903 - 1933); bronzes; etchings; †19th & 20th century American Western paintings & illustrations; Plains Indian beadwork & artifacts; prints; †Pueblo Indian pottery; Navajo rugs; †19th century popular Western fiction
Exhibitions: (1992) California Grandeur & Genre; Transforming the Western Image in Twentieth Century American Art. (1993) Finding New Worlds: American Frontier Photography; Red Grooms' Ruckus Rodeo; Brilliance in Glass: The Lost Wax Castings of Frederick Carder
Publications: Exhibition catalog; Newsletter, bi-monthly
Activities: Classes for adults & children; docent training; film series; lect open to public; annual symposia on American Western art; gallery talks; tours; paintings, original objects of art lent to established museums; lending collection contains reproductions, original art works, original prints, Victorian toys, Carder Steuben Glass; originate traveling exhibitions; shop sells books, magazines, reproductions, prints, Indian jewelry, postcards, crafts from the Southwest, T-shirts, Pueblo pottery, Hopi Kachinas, toys, glass
L **Library,** 111 Cedar St, 14830. Tel 607-937-5386; FAX 607-974-4536. *Dir* Kent Ahrens
For reference only
Income: Financed by membership, bequests, grants, corporate donations from Corning Glass Works
Library Holdings: Vols 3000; Per subs 40; Micro — Cards; AV — Cassettes, fs, slides, v-tapes; Other — Clipping files, exhibition catalogs, manuscripts, original art works, pamphlets, photographs

CORNWALL ON HUDSON

M **MUSEUM OF THE HUDSON HIGHLANDS,** The Boulevard, PO Box 181, 12520. Tel 914-534-7781. *Pres* James W Rathbun; *Dir* Charles Keene; *Admin Dir* Susan Brander; *Cur Art* Audrey Hall; *Wildlife Biologist* M Sillings
Open Mon - Thurs 11 AM - 5 PM, Sat noon - 5 PM, Sun 1:30 - 5 PM, cl Fri. Admis $1 suggested donation. Estab 1962; primarily a children's natural history & art museum. A large octagonal gallery & a small gallery. Average Annual Attendance: 33,000. Mem: 450; artists qualify by approval of slides; dues $15-$25
Income: $140,000 (financed by membership, city appropriation & grants)
Activities: Classes for adults & children; lectures open to public, 2 vis lectrs per yr; competitions with awards; lending collection contains nature & history kits; book traveling exhibitions, annually; museum shop sells books, magazines, original art, reproductions, prints, toys, pottery, jewelry, batik scarfs

CORTLAND

M **CORTLAND COUNTY HISTORICAL SOCIETY,** Suggett House Museum, 25 Homer Ave, 13045. Tel 607-756-6071. *Pres* James Sarvay; *Treas* Robert Ferris; *Dir* Mary Ann Kane
Open Tues - Sat 1 - 4 PM, mornings by appointment. Estab 1925 to collect, store and interpret the history of Cortland County through programs, exhibits and records in our 1790 Suggett House. Average Annual Attendance: 30,000. Mem: 602; dues $15; meetings second Sat of Jan, Apr, June & Oct
Income: $50,000 (financed by endowment, memberships, county appropriations, grants, sales and fund raisers)
Purchases: Antique furniture & paintings from Cortland County
Collections: †Antique furniture, †children's toys, †china, †folk art, †glass, †military memorabilia, †paintings, †textiles & clothing
Publications: Roots & Branches, 4 times per yr; books on local history; bulletin, 4 times per yr; newsletter, 6 times per yr
Activities: Classes for adults & children; docent training; lectures open to public, 12 vis lectr per yr; gallery talks; tours; exten dept serves Cortland & surrounding counties; individual paintings & original objects of art lent to other museums & college galleries; book traveling exhibitions; originates traveling exhibitions; museum shop sells books, reproductions & prints
L **Kellogg Memorial Research Library,** 13045. Tel 607-756-6071. *Librn* Shirley Heppell; *Coll Mgr* Anetta Wright
Open Tues - Sat 1 - 5 PM, mornings by appointment. Estab 1976 to collect, preserve and interpret information about the history of Cortland County
Purchases: $500
Library Holdings: Vols 3000; Per subs 25; Micro — Reels; AV — Slides; Other — Clipping files, exhibition catalogs, manuscripts, memorabilia, original art works, pamphlets, photographs, prints

L **CORTLAND FREE LIBRARY,** 32 Church St, 13045. Tel 607-753-1042. *Dir* Warren S Eddy
Open Mon - Thurs 10 AM - 8:30 PM, Fri & Sat 10 AM - 5:30 PM, cl Sun. No admis fee. Estab 1938
Purchases: $1700
Library Holdings: Vols 1600
Exhibitions: Occasiional monthly exhibitions held

M **THE 1890 HOUSE-MUSEUM & CENTER FOR VICTORIAN ARTS,** 37 Tompkins St, 13045-2555. Tel 607-756-7551. *Dir* John H Nozynski; *Admin Asst* Grace Nicholas
Open daily 9 AM - 5 PM, tours 9 AM - 5 PM. Estab 1978
Collections: †Decorative arts; †Oriental Furnishings; †Paintings; †1890 - 1900 Documentary Photographs; †Victorian Furniture; †Victorian Silver
Exhibitions: Late Victorian Cast Iron Lawn Ornaments; Victorian Lighting; Documentary Photographs of Restoration
Publications: Whispers Near the Inglenook, quarterly
L **Kellogg Library & Reading Room,** 37 Tompkins St, 13045-2555
For lending & reference
Library Holdings: Vols 1800; Per subs 12

L **STATE UNIVERSITY OF NEW YORK COLLEGE AT CORTLAND,** Art Slide Library, 13045. Tel 607-753-4318; FAX 607-753-5999. *Cur* Jo Schaffer
Open Mon - Fri 8:30 AM - 5 PM, and by appointment. Estab 1967 to provide visual resources to faculty, students and community
Income: Financed by state appropriation
Library Holdings: Vols 1000; Per subs 10; Micro — Fiche; AV — Fs, Kodachromes, lantern slides 5000, slides 125,000, v-tapes 100; Other — Exhibition catalogs, photographs 10,000
Special Subjects: Pop Art

COXSACKIE

M **GREENE COUNTY HISTORICAL SOCIETY,** Bronck Museum, Route 9W, 12051. Tel 518-731-6490, 731-6822. *Pres* Robert Stackman; *Librn* Raymond Beecher; *Cur* Shelby Kriele
Open June - Sept 10 AM - 4 PM. Admis $3. Estab 1929
Publications: Greene County Historical Journal, quarterly

DOUGLASTON

A **NATIONAL ART LEAGUE INC,** 44-21 Douglaston Parkway, 11360. Tel 718-229-9495. *Pres* Mary Ann Heinzen; *VPres* Al Camurati
Estab 1932, inc 1950, as Art League of Long Island, Inc. Mem: 230
Income: Financed by membership dues & contributions
Exhibitions: Six annual major shows, one national; gallery exhibitions
Publications: Brochures; bulletins; catalogs; newsletter, monthly
Activities: Art classes for adults and children; demonstrations; lectures open to public, 10 vis lectr per yr; gallery talks; competitions with awards

EAST HAMPTON

L **EAST HAMPTON LIBRARY,** Pennypacker Long Island Collection, 159 Main St, 11937. Tel 516-324-0222. *Librn* Dorothy King
Open Mon - Wed & Fri - Sat 1 - 4:30 PM, cl Thurs & Sun. Estab 1897
Library Holdings: Maps; Other — Clipping files, exhibition catalogs, manuscripts, original art works, pamphlets, prints
Collections: Pennypacker Long Island Collection contains material relating to the history & people of Long Island; Thomas Moran Biographical Art Collection contains original pen & ink & pencil sketches by Thomas Moran, lithographs, etchings & engravings by Moran & other members of the family, biographical material, exhibit catalogues, books & pamphlets

M **GUILD HALL OF EAST HAMPTON, INC,** Guild Hall Museum, 158 Main St, 11937. Tel 516-324-0806; FAX 516-324-2722. *Chmn* Jo Raymond; *1st VChmn* James Marcus; *2nd VChmn* Karen Karp; *Treas* Roy L Furman; *Secy* Susanne B Bullock; *Exec Dir* Joy L Gordon; *Cur* Christina Mossaides Strassfield; *Assoc Cur & Registrar* Tracey R Bashkoff
Open Winter - Spring Wed - Sat 11 AM - 5 PM, Sun noon - 5 PM, Summer open daily 11 AM - 5 PM, Fall same as Spring. No admis fee for members, non-members $2. Estab 1931 as a cultural center for the visual and performing arts with a State Board of Regents Educational Charter. Emphasis in art collection and exhibiton is chiefly on the many artists who live or have lived in the area. Museum has four galleries, art library & a sculpture garden. Average Annual Attendance: 80,000. Mem: 4000; dues $25 - $2500; annual meeting May
Income: $1,400,000 (financed by mem, federal, state, county & town appropriations, corporate, foundation, individual contributions, benefits, fund drives & museum shop)
Collections: Focuses on American artists associated with the region of Eastern Long Island, including James Brooks, Jimmy Ernst, Adolf Gottlieb, Childe Hassam, William de Kooning, Roy Lichtenstein, Thomas Moran, Jackson Pollock, Larry Rivers, as well as contemporary artists such as Eric Fischl, Donald Sultan & Lynda Benglis, paintings, works on paper, prints, photographs, sculpture
Exhibitions: (1991) The Montauk: Native Americans of Eastern Long Island; East Hampton: The 19th Century Artists' Paradise; 53rd Annual Guild Hall Artist Members' Exhibition; Aspect of Collage; Eric Fischl: A Cinematic View; Chuck Close: Up Close; A View from the Sixties: Selections from the Leo Castelli & Michael & Ileana Sonnabend Collection; Robert Dash: Darkness; Philip Pavia: Abstract Marble Sculpture; Hans Namuth: Permanent Faces; Contemporary Craft. (1992) 54th Annual Members' Exhibition; Esteban Vincente: A Forty Year Survey; Miriam Schapiro: The Politics of the Decorative; Percival Goodman: Visionary Drawings; Volume: 6 Contemporary Sculptors; Roy Lichtenstein: Three Decades of Sculpture; Donald Sultan: Paintings 1978-1992; Relative Truths: East End Photography
Publications: Newsletter, exhibition catalogues, annual report, monthly calendar

Activities: Classes for adults; docent training; cooperative projects with area schools; lect open to public, 12 vis lectr per year; concerts, gallery talks; tours, competitions; original art objects lent to museums, libraries, schools, public building; lending collection contains cassettes, original art works and prints, paintings, photographs, sculpture, slides; book traveling exhibitions; originate traveling exhibitions; museum shop sells mainly posters created for Guild Hall by artists of region; also gift items and local crafts

EAST ISLIP

M **ISLIP ART MUSEUM,** 50 Irish Lane, 11730. Tel 516-224-5402. *Exec Dir* Mary Lou Cohalan; *Dir of Coll & Exhib* Catherine Valenza; *Cur* Karen Shaw
Open Wed - Sat 10 AM - 4 PM, Sun 2 - 4:30 PM. No admis fee, suggested donation $1. Estab 1979 for group showings of contemporary art from local & city based artists. 3000 sq ft of exhibition space divided among 4 rooms & a hallway on the Brookwood Hall estate. The main building housing the Museum also houses the town offices & the Islip Arts Council. Average Annual Attendance: 9500. Mem: 250; dues $25-$5,000
Income: $150,000 (financed by mem, city & state appropriation, & National Endowment for the Arts)
Exhibitions: Myths & Rituals for the 21st Century; The Vivid Pastel. (1989) Quilts, A Voice in Silence. (1990) Comtemporary Folk Carving from Mexico
Publications: Exibition brochures; Newsletter: Islip Art Muse, bi-monthly
Activities: Classes for adults & children; internships; lectures open to public, 3 - 5 vis lectrs per year; book traveling exhibitions, 2 per yr; originate traveling exhibitions for local libraries & banks; museum shop sells books, handmade gifts, jewelry, original art, postcards, posters, reproductions

EAST OTTO

A **ASHFORD HOLLOW FOUNDATION FOR VISUAL & PERFORMING ARTS,** Griffis Sculpture Park, 6902 Mill Valley Rd, 14729. Tel 716-886-3616. *Dir* Mark Griffis; *Assoc Dir* Simon Griffis; *Chief Exec Officer* Larry Griffis
Open May - Oct 9 AM - dusk. No admis fee, donations welcomed. Funds for the 400 acre sculpture park donated by Ruth Griffis in memory of her husband, L W Griffis Sr. The original park accomodates the work of Larry Griffis Jr. The expanded areas now include works of numerous other sculptors. Materials include welded steel, wood, aluminum & bronze, most of which has been cast at the Essex St Foundry. Sculpture park festival stage is an open-air platform for regional artist's performance of dance, music, poetry & drama
Income: Financed by donations, postcard sales & public funds
Exhibitions: Twelve distinctly different groups of work by Larry Griffis Jr are displayed
Publications: Brochure; postcards
Activities: Retail store sells prints, original art, reproductions, metal sculptures; jr museum, Big Orbit, 30 Essex St, Buffalo, NY

ELMIRA

M **ARNOT ART MUSEUM,** 235 Lake St, 14901. Tel 607-734-3697; FAX 607-734-5687. *Dir* John D O'Hern; *Cur Collection* Rachael Sadinsky
Open Tues - Sat 10 AM - 5 PM, Sun 2 - 5 PM, cl Mon & national holidays. Admis $2. Estab 1911 to serve the people of the community with a regular schedule of changing exhibits of the permanent collection, traveling shows & regional artists, as well as providing other free cultural activities not ordinarily available in the area. Permanent installations: 17th to 19th-century European art in period room of original donor, Matthias H Arnot; 19th-20th century American paintings. Average Annual Attendance: 50,000. Mem: 850; dues $25 and up
Collections: †American & European sculpture; Flemish, Dutch, †French, English, German, Italian, Spanish & †American paintings & works on paper Matthias H Arnot Collection—permanent installation in restored 1880s picture gallery
Exhibitions: Annual Regional Art Exhibition with prizes; Annual Arts & Crafts Exhibition with prizes
Publications: Books; catalogs
Activities: Classes for adults & children, two wk summer adult painting school, docent training, & outreach programs for community groups through educ center; lectures and gallery talks open to public; tours; competitions; individual paintings lent; book traveling exhibitions, 5-8 per yr; originate traveling exhibitions to US museums; museum shop sells books, catalogues, original art & craft work, reproductions, slides, prints

M **ELMIRA COLLEGE,** George Waters Gallery, Park Place, 14901. Tel 607-734-3911, Ext 354. *Dir* Leslie Kramer
Open Tues - Sat 1 - 4 PM, cl Mon & Sun. No admis fee. The Gallery is located in the Elmira Campus Center. Average Annual Attendance: 1000
Income: Financed by school budget

FLUSHING

A **BOWNE HOUSE HISTORICAL SOCIETY,** 37-01 Bowne St, 11354. Tel 718-359-0528. *Pres* Virginia Bowen; *VPres* Dougald MacLean; *Dir* Donna Russo; *Corresp Secy* Madeline Schau; *Recording Secy* Catherine Campbell; *Treas* Kenneth Kupferberg
Open Tues, Sat & Sun 2:30 - 4:30 PM. Admis adults $3, sr citizens $2, children $1. Estab 1945 for historic preservation, education, collection of 17th, 18th & 19th century furnishing & decorative & fine art. Examples of colonial life are excellent. Average Annual Attendance: 5000. Mem: 620; dues $250, $100, $50, $25, $10; annual meeting third Tues in May
Income: Financed by mem & private & public contributions
Collections: Furnishings from the 17th, 18th and early 19th Centuries Furniture, pewter, fabrics, china, portraits, prints and documents
Exhibitions: (1992) Photo Documentation of ongoing Restoration
Publications: Booklets regarding John Bowne and the House; quarterly newsletter
Activities: Educ dept; classes for adults & children; docent training; lect open to the public; museum shop sells books, reproductions, prints, slides, products of herb garden, plates and tiles

A **HUDSON VALLEY ART ASSOCIATION,** 148-45 60th Ave, 11355. Tel 718-353-6887. *Pres* Al Camurati; *Treas* Perry Alley; *Secy* Mary Hargrove
Estab 1928, inc 1933 to perpetuate the artistic traditions of American artists such as made famous the Hudson River School of painting through exhibitions of painting and sculpture with public support. Mem: 300; membership by invitation; dues $25, special exhibits extra; annual meeting May
Exhibitions: Annual juried exhibition each May, open to all artists of the US who work in realistic tradition, to compete for money awards and gold medals of honor; other exhibits from time to time
Activities: Free demonstrations, exhibitions, lectures

M **QUEENS COLLEGE, CITY UNIVERSITY OF NEW YORK,** Godwin-Ternbach Museum, Kissena Blvd, 11367. Tel 718-997-4747. *Dir & Cur* Marilyn L Simor; *Asst Cur* Eleanor Glick
No admis fee. Estab 1957 for a study collection for Queens College students & in 1981 independently chartered. Collection located in one large exhibition gallery on Queens College Campus. Average Annual Attendance: 10,000. Mem: 60, dues $25
Income: Financed by state appropriation, Friends of the Museum, federal state and local grants
Library Holdings: Per subs 200; AV — Slides 15,000; Other — Exhibition catalogs 20,000, photographs 20,000, reproductions 50,000
Collections: Ancient & antique glass; Egyptian, Greek, Luristan antiquities, Old Master & WPA prints; Renaissance & later bronzes; 16th - 20th century paintings
Exhibitions: 20th Century Prints; Joseph Ternback: Collector, Connoisseur; Italian Art; 15th - 18th Century Art of the East; Recent Acquisitions 1981 - 1985; Herb Aach Memorial Exhibition; Summerscape; Ancient & Islamic Art: Selections from the Godwin-Ternbach Museum; Gerald Hahn Amemorial Exhibition; Helen Benz Schiavo: A Memorial Exhibition; Alliance of Queens Artists
Publications: Brochures, exhibition catalogs; newsletter
Activities: Classes for adults; high school creative arts program; lect open to public, 3-4 vis lectr per yr; gallery talks; individual paintings & original objects of art lent to qualified art organization & museums

M **Queens College Art Center,** 65-39 Kissena Blvd, 11367. Tel 718-997-3770; FAX 718-793-8049; Elec Mail ADLQC@CUNYVM.BITNET. *Dir* Suzanna Simor; *Cur* Alexandra deLuise
Open Mon - Thurs 9 AM - 8 PM, Fri 9 AM - 5 PM. No admis fee. Estab 1937. Average Annual Attendance: 20,000
Exhibitions: (1992-1993) Diane Atkatz (paintings; Augustin Victor Casasola (photographs); Pier Paolo Pasoline; Greenbriar Workshop: Recent Works; Mexican Revolution; Luisella Carretta: Natural Writings; Carel Blazer: Dutch Photojournalist; Photographs of the Spanish War; Elias Friedensohn: Airports & Escapes (paintings & drawings); Anna Bisso (drawings, paintings, mixed media); Hans Namuth: Los Todos Santeros (photographs); Lois Polansky: Bookworks
Publications: exhibition catalogues
Activities: Gallery talks; lect open to the public, 2 - 3 vis lectr per yr

L **Art Library,** 65-30 Kissena Blvd, 11367. *Head* Suzanna Simor; *Art Librn* Alexandra deLuise
Open 52 hrs wk when classes are in session. Estab 1937 to support instruction. Circ 30,000
Library Holdings: Vols 50,000; Per subs 200; Micro — Fiche 1000, reels; AV — Slides 15,000; Other — Clipping files, exhibition catalogs 20,000, pamphlets, photographs, reproductions 50,000
Activities: Lending collection contains 30,000 books, 30,000 color reproductions & 12,000 slides

M **THE QUEENS MUSEUM OF ART,** New York City Bldg, Flushing Meadows-Corona Park, 11368-3398. Tel 718-592-2405; FAX 718-592-5778. *Exec Dir* Sharon Vatsky; *Asst Dir* Beth Henriques; *Dir Exhib* Louis P Grachos; *Cur* Marc H Miller; *Cur* Barbara Matilsky; *Asst Cur* Phyllis Bilick; *Dir Admin* Barbara Sperber; *Pres* Donald R Miller; *VPres* John Ottulich; *Secy* Rose Ciampa
Open Tues - Fri 10 AM - 5 PM, Sat & Sun noon - 5:30 PM, cl Mon. Admis by contribution, adult $2, students & sr citizens $1, children under 5 & members free. Estab 1972 to provide a vital cultural center for the more than 2.5 million residents of Queens County; it provides changing, high-quality, fine art exhibitions & a wide-range of educational & public programs. Museum has approx 25,000 sq ft gallery space, The Panorama of New York City (9,335 sq ft architectural scale model of New York City), theatre, workshops, offices. Average Annual Attendance: 100,000. Mem: 1000; dues $10 - $1000
Income: Financed by membership, city & state appropriations, corporation, foundation, National Endowment for Arts & individual grants
Collections: The Panorama of New York City (world's largest architectural scale model); Small collection of paintings, photographs & prints; Collection of materials from 1939 - 1940 & 1964 - 1965 New York World's Fairs
Publications: Catalogs; newsletter, quarterly; World's Fair newsletter, bi-annually; Bunorama brochure
Activities: Guided tours for adults & children; docent training; projects involving elementary school children; films; drop-in arts & crafts workshops on Sun during school year & certain weekdays in summer; lect open to public with vis lectr; concerts; gallery talks; tours; competitions; City Safari Program about The Panarama, satellite gallery at Bulova Corporate Center in Jackson Heights, NY; book traveling exhibitions, 4 per yr; museum shop sells books, reproductions, prints, exhibition catalogs and children's items

FREDONIA

M **STATE UNIVERSITY OF NEW YORK COLLEGE AT FREDONIA,** M C Rockefeller Arts Center Gallery, 14063. Tel 716-673-3217; FAX 716-673-3397. *Center Dir* Jefferson Westwood
Open Wed & Thurs 11 AM - 3 PM, Fri & Sun 3 PM - 8 PM. No admis fee. Estab 1963 and relocated in 1969 to new quarters designed by I M Pei and Partners. The gallery serves as a focal point of the campus, uniting the college with the community. Average Annual Attendance: 5000
Income: Financed by state appropriation and student groups
Collections: Primarily 20 century American art and architectural archival

material, with an emphasis on prints and sculpture
Exhibitions: Graduating Seniors I; Graduating Seniors II; Graduating Seniors III
Publications: Exhibition catalogs
Activities: Individual paintings and original objects of art lent to offices and public lobbies on campus; traveling exhibitions organized and circulated

GARDEN CITY

L **ADELPHI UNIVERSITY,** Fine & Performing Arts Library, 11530. Tel 516-877-3000; FAX 516-877-8592. *Fine Arts Librn* Erica Doctorow; *Performing Arts Librn* Gary Cantrell
Open Mon - Thurs 8:30 AM - 11 PM, Fri & Sat 10 AM - 6 PM, Sun 1 - 11 PM. The Fine & Performing Arts Library builds print and nonprint collections and provides reference service in fine and applied arts, music, dance, theater, photography, university archives and special collections
Income: Financed by state appropriations and through the University
Library Holdings: Vols 35,000; Per subs 125; original documents; Micro — Fiche, reels; AV — Cassettes, fs, motion pictures, rec 9000, slides 1500, v-tapes 50; Other — Exhibition catalogs, manuscripts, memorabilia, original art works, pamphlets, photographs, prints, reproductions
Collections: Americana; William Blake; Cuala Press; Expatriate Writers; Cobbett; Morley; Hauptmann; Whitman; University Archives; Spanish Civil War Robert McMillian Papers; Christopher Morley
Exhibitions: 85 Golden Florins
Activities: Lectures

M **Swirbul Library Gallery,** 11530. Tel 516-877-3000; FAX 516-877-3592. *Dir* Erica Doctorow
Open Mon - Thurs 8 AM - 11 PM, Sat 10 AM - 6 PM, Sun 1 - 11 PM. No admis fee. Estab 1963 to enrich cultural life, provide a showcase for faculty research and art works and interdisciplinary exhibitions. Average Annual Attendance: 30,000. Mem: 150
Collections: †William Blake
Exhibitions: Walt Whitman Exhibition
Publications: Exhibit catalogs
Activities: Lectures open to the public, 4 vis lectr per yr; gallery talks; individual and original objects of art lent to university offices only

M **NASSAU COMMUNITY COLLEGE,** Firehouse Art Gallery, 11530. Tel 516-222-7165. *Dir* Robert Lawn; *Cur* Janet Marzo; *Cur* Elizabeth Karoly; *Cur* Ray Horton
Open Mon - Thurs 11:30 AM - 4:30 PM, Tues - Thurs 7 AM - 10 PM, Sept - May. Estab 1964 to exhibit fine art and varied media. Two exhibition spaces, carpeted fabric walls, and track lighting
Income: Financed by state, college & county appropriation
Collections: Painting; sculpture; prints
Exhibitions: Invitational exhibits, national or regional competition; faculty & student exhibits per year
Activities: Lectures open to the public; competitions with awards

GARDINER

M **HUGUENOT HISTORICAL SOCIETY OF NEW PALTZ,** Locust Lawn, Route 32 (Mailing add: Route 32, New Paltz, 12525). Tel 914-255-1660. *Pres* Kenneth E Hasbrouck Sr
Open Memorial Day - Sept 30 Wed - Sun 10 AM - 4 PM. Admis house alone $2, full tour (outbuildings) $3. Estab to exhibit furniture & art of the area & early 19th century and in particular, the furnishings belonging to the Col Josiah Hasbrouck family. The house was built in 1814. Architect by James Cromwell. There are also farm outbuildings with pertinent displays. House acquired in 1958. Historic house. Mem: 5500; annual dues $10; annual meeting in June
Income: Financed by mem, endowment
Collections: American primitive paintings; early 19th century furnishings & paintings including Ammi Phillips portraits of Hasbrouck family
Exhibitions: Revolving in-house displays
Publications: Hasbrouck Family in America, vol I & II; Crispell Family in America; genealogies & histories
Activities: Educ dept; docent training for house tours; tours; Sales shop sells books and items relating to local history, geneology

GARRISON

L **ALICE CURTIS DESMOND & HAMILTON FISH LIBRARY,** Hudson River Reference Collection, Routes 9D & 403, PO Box 265, 10524. Tel 914-424-3020; FAX 914-424-4061. *Libr Dir* Geraldine Baldwin; *Adminr* Pamela Read
Open by appointment only. No admis fee. Estab 1983
Special Subjects: Art Education, Art History, Dioramas, Display, Landscape Architecture, Landscapes, Painting - American, Photography, Restoration & Conservation
Collections: Slide Archive: Hudson River views in 19th century painting
Exhibitions: Shows annually: Contemporary artists as well as Hudson River School Works

GENESEO

M **LIVINGSTON COUNTY HISTORICAL SOCIETY,** Cobblestone Museum, 30 Center St, 14454. Tel 716-243-9147. *Pres* Stanley Johnson
Open May - Oct Sun & Thurs 2 - 5 PM. No admis fee. Estab 1877 to procure, protect & preserve Livingston County history. Average Annual Attendance: 1500. Mem: 230; dues $5 per year; meetings first Sun in Nov & May
Income: $2500 (financed by mem)
Collections: China & Silver; Indian Artifacts; primitive tools; Shaker items; toy collection; war items
Activities: Lect open to public, 6 vis lectr per year

M **STATE UNIVERSITY OF NEW YORK AT GENESEO,** Bertha V B Lederer Gallery, 14454. Tel 716-245-5814; FAX 716-245-5005. *Dir & Chmn Exhib Committee* Jan Jackson
Open 2 - 5 PM for exhibitions. No admis fee. Estab 1967; the gallery serves the college and community. Average Annual Attendance: 6000
Income: Financed by state appropriation
Collections: Ceramics, furniture, graphics, paintings, sculpture
Publications: Exhibition catalogs
Activities: Lectures open to public; lending collection contains 400 - 600 books

GLENS FALLS

M **HYDE COLLECTION TRUST,** 161 Warren St, 12801. Tel 518-792-1761; FAX 518-792-9197. *Dir* Cecilia Esposito
Open Tues - Sun noon - 5 PM. Admis adults $2, children, students, senior citizens $1. Estab 1952 to promote & cultivate the study & improvement of the fine arts. Average Annual Attendance: 15,000. Mem: 900; dues $15-$5000
Income: Financed by endowment, membership, contributions, municipal support and grants
Collections: Drawings by da Vinci, Degas, Tiepolo, Matisse, Lorraine and others; Paintings by El Greco, Rembrandt, Rubens, Botticelli, Tintoretto, Renoir, Picasso, Homer and others; furniture, sculpture, tapestries
Exhibitions: Six temporary exhibitions throughout the year; Electric Garden; John Singer Sketch Book; Joseph C Parker Sculpture
Publications: American Quilts: European and American Samplers; Annual Report; The Art of Henry Ossawa Tanner; Rembrandt's Christ; The Sculpture of John Rogers; David Smith of Bolton Landing; Rockwell Kent (1882-1971); Elihu Vedder; Hyde Collection Catalogue; History of Glens Falls; Family Pride; The Italian Renaissance House & its Furnishings; Splendid Innovations: The World of French Design 1650-1785
Activities: Classes for adults; docent training; lectures open to the public, 5-10 vis lectr per year; concerts; gallery talks; tours; competitions with purchase awards; scholarships; original objects of art lent to accredited museums; book traveling exhibitions; originate traveling exhibitions; museum sales shop sells books, reproductions, prints & slides

L **Library,** 161 Warren St, 12801. Tel 518-792-1761; FAX 518-792-9197. *Dir* Cecilia Esposito
Income: Financed by the Hyde Collection Trust
Purchases: Books & periodicals
Library Holdings: Vols 1000; Per subs 8; Hyde Family Archives containing 3000 original documents; Other — Clipping files, exhibition catalogs, memorabilia, photographs

GOSHEN

M **TROTTING HORSE MUSEUM,** 240 Main St, 10924. Tel 914-294-6330. *Dir* Philip A Pines; *Adminr & Asst Treas* Gail Cunard; *Registrar* Walter Latzko
Open Mon - Sat 10 AM - 5 PM, Sun & holidays noon - 5 PM. Admis adults $1.50, children $.50. Estab 1951 to preserve the artifacts of harness racing. There are two galleries; one usually has the museum's permanent collection; the smaller one is used for visiting art shows. Average Annual Attendance: 10,000. Mem: 800; dues $100, $50, $35; annual meeting in July
Income: Financed by endowment and membership
Collections: Large collection of lithographs by Currier and Ives pertaining to harness racing, plus other leading printers of the 19th century; bronzes, dioramas, statuary, wood carvings
Exhibitions: Visiting art shows
Publications: Newsletter, quarterly
Activities: Classes for children; lect open to public; concerts; gallery talks; tours; museum shop sells books, reproductions, prints, jewelry, harness racing memorabilia & other horse-related items

HAMILTON

M **COLGATE UNIVERSITY,** Picker Art Gallery, Charles A Dana Arts Center, 13346. Tel 315-824-7634; FAX 315-824-7787. *Dir* Dewey F Mosby, PhD; *Registrar & Asst Cur* Jenni Schlossman; *Secy* Jeanie Newlun; *Gallery Asst* Elvia Bona
Open daily 10 AM - 5 PM. No admis fee. Estab 1966, as an educative adjunct to study in the fine arts and liberal arts curriculum. Building designed by architect Paul Rudolph. Average Annual Attendance: 15,000. Mem: 147; dues lifetime $5000, patron $1000, sustaining $500, supporting $100, sponsoring $50, contributing $25, student $10
Income: Financed by the University and Friends of the Visual Arts at Colgate
Collections: Herman Collection of Modern Chinese Woodcuts; †Gary M Hoffer '74 Memorial Photography Collection; Luis de Hoyos Collection of pre-Columbian Art; paintings; photographs; posters; prints; †sculpture
Publications: Annual report; bulletins; exhibition catalogs
Activities: Lectures open to the public & some for members only; individual paintings & original objects of art lent; book traveling exhibitions; originate traveling exhibitions

HEMPSTEAD

M **FINE ARTS MUSEUM OF LONG ISLAND,** 295 Fulton Ave, 11550. Tel 516-481-5700; FAX 516-481-8007. *Sir* Eleanor Flomenhaft; *Asst* Geraldine Morley; *Registrar* Paul Andersen
Open 10 AM - 4:30 PM. Admis $2. Estab 1979. A contemporary hall for rotating exhibits; a computer imaging center with hand-on equipment; a pre-columbian & primitive art hall; a window environment for solo shows; 20,000 sq ft exhibition space. Average Annual Attendance: 25,000. Mem: 1400; dues $35
Income: $379,000 (financed by endowment, mem, state appropriation)
Exhibitions: Selections from FAMLI's Permanent Collection: Pre-Columbia Artifacts, Photography, Paintings, Sculpture, Computer art; Annual Juried Art

Exhibition
Activities: Classes for adults & children; docent programs; lectures open to public, 5 vis lectr per year; competitions with awards; originate traveling exhibitions 2 per year—yr; retail store sells books, prints, original art

M HOFSTRA UNIVERSITY, Hofstra Museum, Emily Lowe Gallery, Hempstead Turnpike, 11550. Tel 516-560-5672, 560- 5673. *Acting Dir* David C Christman; *Cur Coll* Elearnor Rait; *Exhibit Designer & Preparation* Karen Albert; *Registrar* Mary Wakeford
Open Wed - Fri 10 AM - 5 PM, Tues 10 AM - 9 PM, Sat & Sun 1 - 5 PM. No admis fee. Estab 1963; a university museum that serves the needs of its student body and the surrounding Nassau County community. Museum includes 5 exhibition facilities. Average Annual Attendance: 10,000 - 15000. Mem: 500; dues $20 - $100
Income: Financed by endowment, membership, foundation and University
Collections: †American paintings & prints; African, Pre-Columbian, New Guinea, Japanese & Indian art; 17th & 18th century European painting; contemporary prints, painting & photographs
Exhibitions: Mother & Child: the Art of Henry Moore; Shapes of the Mind: African Art from L I Collections; People at Work: 17th Century Dutch Art; Seymour Lipton; 1979 - 1989: American, Italian, Mexican Art for the Collection of Francesco Pellizzi; The Coming of Age of America: The First Decades of the Sculptors Guild; The Transparent Thread: Asian Philosophy in Recent American Cart. (1991) Street Scenes: 1930's - '50's; Leonard Bramer's Drawing of the 17th Century Dutch Life (1986) T.V. Sculpture; R.B. Kitaj (Art and Literature); Indian Miniatures; Maelstrom; Preserving Our Heritage: A Celebration of the Restoration of Hofstra's Collection of Currier and Ives Prints; The Mountain Retreat: Modern Chinese Landscape Paintings
Publications: Exhibition catalogs
Activities: Lect open to public, 10 - 15 vis lectr per year; gallery talks; tours for school groups & community organizations; originate traveling exhibitions

HEWLETT

L HEWLETT-WOODMERE PUBLIC LIBRARY, 1125 Broadway, 11557. Tel 516-374-1967; FAX 516-569-1229. *Art Librn* Nancy Delin
Open Mon - Thurs 9 AM - 9 PM, Fri 9 AM - 6 PM, Sat 9 AM - 5 PM, Sun 1 - 5 PM (except summer). Estab 1947 as a Co-Center for art and music. Gallery maintained
Income: Financed by state appropriation and school district
Library Holdings: Vols 124,980; Per subs 473; Micro — Reels; AV — Fs, Kodachromes, motion pictures, rec, slides; Other — Exhibition catalogs, pamphlets, photographs, reproductions
Special Subjects: Architecture, Crafts, Film, Photography, antiques
Exhibitions: Hold local exhibits
Publications: Index to Art Reproductions in Books (Scarecrow Press)
Activities: Classes for adults and children; lect open to the public; concerts; gallery talks; tours

HOWES CAVE

M IROQUOIS INDIAN MUSEUM, Caverns Rd, PO Box 7, 12092. Tel 518-296-8949; FAX 518-296-8955. *Dir* Christina Johannsen; *Dir Children's Museum* Colette Lemmon; *Cur* Stephanie Shultes; *Museum Educator* Perry Ground; *Nature Park Mgr* Mike Butler
Open 10 AM - 5 PM. Admis adult $5, sr citizen $4, children 7 - 17 $2.50. Estab 1980 to teach about Iroquois culture today & in the past. Exhibits follow a time line from the earliest times to present day. Archaeology exhibits trace the development of native culture from the time of Paleo-Indians (8000 BC) through the 1700s, when the Iroquois & colonists lived side-by-side in the Schoharie Valley. Mem: 900; dues donor $45, family $25, individual $20, sr $10
Income: $300,000 (financed by mem, admis, sales shop, fundraising & grants)
Collections: †Historic beadwork & cornhusk work; †extensive collection of contemporary art (painting & sculpture) & crafts (baskets, woodwork items & beadwork); †Paleo Indian to 18th century artifacts mainly from known sites in Schoharie County, NY
Exhibitions: (1992) Visual Voices of the Iroquois (painting & sculpture from 1821 - 1992). (1993) Indian Stereotypes as External Avatars
Publications: Exhibition catalogs; Museum Notes, quarterly
Activities: Classes for adults & children; school programs; lect open to public; scholarships; exten dept includes lending collection; retail store sells books, prints, magazines, slides & original art; Iroquois Indian Children's Museum

HUDSON

M OLANA STATE HISTORIC SITE, RD 2, Off Route 9-G, 12534. Tel 518-828-0135. *Cur* Karen Zubowski; *Historic Site Mgr* James Ryan; *Interpretive Programs Asst* Robin Eckerle; *Site Asst* Heidi Hill
Open May 1 to Labor Day, Wed - Sat 10 AM - 4 PM, Sun noon - 4 PM, by tour only, Wed after Labor Day to Oct 31 Wed - Sun noon - 4 PM. Opened as a museum June 1967 to promote interest in and disseminate information of the life, works and times of Frederic Edwin Church, landscape painter of the Hudson River School. The building is a Persian-style residence overlooking the Hudson River. Average Annual Attendance: House 24,000; Grounds 200,000. Mem: 615; dues $25 - $5000; annual meeting May or June
Income: Financed by state appropriation
Collections: Extensive 19th Century Furniture Collection; Oil Sketches & Drawings by Church; †Paintings by Church †and other artists; Textile Collection; Decorative Arts
Publications: The Crayon, quarterly (journal produced by Friends of Olana)
Activities: Slide programs; lectures; concerts; original objects of art lent to other institutions who qualify

L Archives, Rd 2, Off Route 9-G, 12534. Tel 518-828-0135. *Historic Site Mgr* James Ryan
Open to the public with approval of Site Manager; for reference only
Library Holdings: Other — Exhibition catalogs 10, memorabilia 200, original art works, photographs, prints
Collections: Family papers, photographs, books, correspondence diaries, receipts
Publications: Crayon, quarterly

HUNTINGTON

M HECKSCHER MUSEUM, 2 Prime Ave, 11743-7702. Tel 516-351-3250; FAX 516-423-2145. *Chairman Board Trustees* John W B Hadley; *Dir* Dr John E Coraor; *Cur* Anna C Noll; *Coordr Educ* Melissa Erb; *Registrar* William Titus; *Development Officer* Anne Howell
Open Tues - Fri 10 AM - 5 PM, Sat & Sun 1 - 5 PM, cl Mon & holidays. No admis fee, suggested donation $2. Estab 1920, inc 1957, for the maintenance, preservation and operation of the museum building together with the preservation, exhibition and display of all objects and works of art therein. Four galleries, each 20 x 40 ft with 15 ft ceilings, track incandescent and diffused ultraviolet-free fluorescent lighting. Two galleries are used for changing exhibition and two for permanent collections. Average Annual Attendance: 40,000. Mem: 680; dues $35 and up; annual meeting in June
Income: $740,000 (financed by endowment, membership, town appropriations and grants)
Collections: Major works by the Moran family, George Grosz, Lucas Cranach the Elder, R A Blakelock, Arthur Dove, Helen Torr, Thomas Eakins, James M & William Hart, Asher B Durand; sculpture, drawings & prints by 16th - 20th century artists, primary American with some European
Exhibitions: Land of Whitman; Watercolors and Drawings by Stanton MacDonald Wright; The Photo Secession: The Golden Years of Pictorial Photography in America; From the Pens of the Masters: Eighteenth Century Venetian Drawings From the Robert Lehman Collection of the Metropolitan Museum of Art; A Feast for the Eyes: Contemporary Representations of Food; Tonalism, An American Experience; The Paintings of Edward Steichen; Sights for Small Eyes; Long Island Painters & Portraits; Huntington Township Art League sponsors annual Long Island Artists Exhibition; regional artists are featured in contemporary exhibitions
Publications: Bi-monthly newsletter; Catalog of the collection; exhibition catalogs
Activities: Classes for adults and children; dramatic programs; docent training; lect open to the public, 10-12 vis lectrs per yr; concerts; gallery talks; tours; Heckscher Award, monetary prize connected with annual Long Island Artists juried show; scholarships offered for children's summer art programs; individual paintings & original objects of art lent to other museums for exhibitions or short term exchanges; lending collection contains original art works, paintings, sculpture & original prints; book traveling exhibitions 2-3 per year; originate traveling exhibitions to other museums; sales shop sells books, reproductions & slides; children's shop sells toys, books, games

L Library, 2 Prime Ave, 11743-7702. *Vol Librn* Shirley Brevda
Open Tues - Fri 10 AM - 4 PM. Estab to provide range of research materials and unique resources. Open to researchers & public by appointment. For reference only
Library Holdings: Vols 2000; Per subs 10; Micro — Cards; AV — A-tapes, slides; Other — Clipping files, exhibition catalogs, memorabilia, pamphlets, reproductions
Special Subjects: Museum & dealer exhibit catalogs, 19th Century - present American & European art

HYDE PARK

M NATIONAL ARCHIVES & RECORDS ADMINISTRATION, Franklin D Roosevelt Museum, 511 Albany Post Rd, 12538. Tel 914-229-8114; FAX 914-229-0872. *Dir* Verne W Newton
Open daily 9 AM - 5 PM, cl Thanksgiving, Christmas & New Year's Day. Admis adults $3.50 for combination ticket to the Roosevelt Home & Museum, children, senior citizens & school groups free. Estab 1939; contains displays on President and Mrs Roosevelt's lives, careers and special interests, including personal items, gifts and items collected by President Roosevelt. Average Annual Attendance: 175,000
Income: $1,002,000 (financed by congressional appropriation, trust fund)
Purchases: $154,000
Collections: Papers of President & Mrs Roosevelt & of various members of his administration; prints, paintings & documents on the Hudson Valley; paintings, prints, ship models, documents & relics of the history of the United States Navy as well as other marine items; early juvenile books
Exhibitions: Winston Churchill Paintings; Hard Life after FDR
Publications: The Museum of The Franklin D Roosevelt Library; Historical Materials in the Franklin D Roosevelt Library; The Era of Franklin D Roosevelt
Activities: Individual paintings & original objects of art lent to museums; lending collection contains 45,000 books, nature artifacts, 9443 paintings, phonorecords, sculptures & drawings; reproductions available for a fee;; sales shop sells books, prints, reproductions, slides, souvenir items & toys

L Library, 511 Albany Post Rd, 12538. Tel 914-229-8114; FAX 914-229-0872. *Librn* Sheryl Griffith; *Chief Archivist* Frances M Seeber
Open Mon - Fri 9 AM - 4:30 PM. Estab 1939 to preserve, interpret & make available for research archives & memorabilia relating to Franklin & Eleanor Roosevelt, their families & associates. Open to scholars on appointment only
Income: $325,000 (financed by US government & trust fund)
Purchases: $4000
Library Holdings: Newspapers, maps, broadsides; Micro — Fiche, reels; AV — A-tapes, cassettes, fs, motion pictures, rec, slides, v-tapes; Other — Clipping files 500, exhibition catalogs, manuscripts, memorabilia 300, original art works, pamphlets, photographs 200, prints, sculpture
Special Subjects: Franklin-Eleanor Roosevelt; American History & Politics, 1913-45; NY Colonial History; Hudson Valley History; US Naval History
Collections: Naval history; Hudson River Valley history; early juvenile books; illustrated ornithology; Eleanor and Franklin Roosevelt; US History: 20th

Century
Publications: The Era of Franklin D Roosevelt: A Selected Bibliography of Periodicals, Essays & Dissertation Literature, 1945-1971; Franklin D Roosevelt and Foreign Affairs

M **ROOSEVELT-VANDERBILT NATIONAL HISTORIC SITES,** 519 Albany Post Rd, 12538. Tel 914-229-9115. *Superintendent* Duane Pearson
Open daily 9 AM - 5 PM Apr - Oct, cl Tues & Wed Nov - Mar, cl Thanksgiving, Christmas & New Year's Day, Eleanor Roosevelt NHS open daily Nov, Dec, Mar & Apr, by appt only Thurs - Sun, Jan - Mar, Groups of 10 or more require reservations. Admis $1.50, under 16, over 62 and school groups free admis. Vanderbilt Mansion NHS estab 1940; home of Franklin D Roosevelt NHS 1944; Eleanor Roosevelt NHS, 1977. Average Annual Attendance: 330,000
Income: Financed by Federal Government
Collections: Vanderbilt & Home of FDR collections consist of original furnishings; Eleanor Roosevelt site collections are combination of originals, reproductions & like items
Publications: Vanderbilt Mansion, book; Art in the Home of Franklin D Roosevelt, brochure
Activities: Tours; sales shop sells books, postcards and slides

M **EDWIN A ULRICH MUSEUM,** Wave Crest on-the-Hudson, Albany Post Rd, 12538. Tel 914-229-7107. *Dir* Edwin A Ulrich
Open May 1 - Sept 30 Fri - Mon 11 AM - 4 PM, & by appointment. Admis $1. Estab 1956 to exhibit three generations of the Waugh family of painters, 1813 - 1973, and to promote American art. Average Annual Attendance: 500
Income: Financed by owner and director
Collections: Collections by Samuel Bell Waugh, 1813-1884; Fred J Waugh 1860-1940; Coulton Waugh, 1896-1973
Exhibitions: Fine art and works by the Waugh family
Publications: Complete Biography of Frederick J Waugh; Frederick Waugh's Paintings of the Sea; Landscape Painting with a Knife; Seascape Painting, Step by Step
Activities: Lect open to the public; gallery talks; tours; individual paintings lent to other recognized museums; lending collection contains 300 Kodachromes; sales shop selling books, reproductions, slides and prints
L **Library,** Wave Crest on-the-Hudson, Albany Post Rd, 12538. Tel 914-229-7107. *Dir* Edwin A Ulrich
Open May 1 - Sept 30 Fri - Mon 11 AM - 4 PM, & by appointment. Estab 1956. For reference only
Library Holdings: Vols 125; Per subs 2; Micro — Prints; AV — Kodachromes, slides; Other — Clipping files, exhibition catalogs, framed reproductions, memorabilia, original art works, pamphlets, photographs, prints, reproductions
Collections: Works of three generations of the Waugh family

ISLAND PARK

A **LONG BEACH ART LEAGUE,** PO Box 123, 11558. Tel 516-431-5082. *Pres* Susan Kornblum; *VPres* Mary Mendoza
Founded in 1952 by a group of interested residents determined to form an organization to promote art activity and appreciation with emphasis on quality
Exhibitions: (1993) North by South
Publications: Exhibitions brochures
Activities: Workshops; demonstrations; lect; discussions

ITHACA

M **CORNELL UNIVERSITY,** Herbert F Johnson Museum of Art, 14853-4001. Tel 607-255-6464; FAX 607-255-9940. *Co-Dir* Richard J Schwartz; *Co-Dir* Franklin W Robinson; *Cur Prints & Photographs* Nancy E Green; *Assoc Cur Painting & Sculpture* Nancy Allyn Jarzombek; *Adjunct Cur Film & Video* Richard Herskowitz; *Asst Dir Colls & Progs & Cur Asian Art* Martie Young; *Registrar* Nancy Harm; *Chief Adminr* Cheryl L H Muka; *Community Educator* Penny Dietrich; *Community Relations Coordr* Jill Hartz; *Asst Dir Public Affairs* Dorothy Reddington; *Asst Dir Business Operations* Rob Paratley; *Ames Coordr for Univrsity Educ* Cathy Klimaszewski
Open Tues - Sun 10 AM - 5 PM, cl Mon. No admis fee. Estab 1973, replacing the Andrew Dickson White Museum of Art, originally founded in 1953 as Cornell University's Art Museum to serve students, the Tompkins County community & the Finger Lakes region. The collection & galleries are housed in an I M Pei designed building on Cornell University campus overlooking downtown Ithaca & Cayuga Lake. Average Annual Attendance: 85,000. Mem: 1000; dues $20 - $2500
Income: Financed by endowment, mem, grants & university funds
Purchases: $100,000
Collections: †Asian art; †arts of ethnographic societies; †European & American paintings, †drawings, †sculpture, †graphic arts, †photographs, †video
Exhibitions: Earth Art, Hans Hinterreiter, Wingtrace: The Sign of its Track; Joyce Cutler Shaw; Frank Lloyd Wright & the Johnson Wax Buildings: Creating a Corporate Cathedral; Bryan Hunt: Falls & Figures; Joan Mitchell; The Landscapes & Still Lifes of David Johnson (1827 - 1908); Paintings & Drawings by American artists R Knight & A Knight; Arthur Wesley Dow; NYS Artists Series IX: Message to the Future; Made to Remember: American Commemorative Quilts; Electric Spaces; Nature's Changing Legacy; Photographs of Robert Alan Ketchum; Cornell Collects; Agnes Denes: A Retrospective
Publications: Seasonal newsletter; exhibition catalogs
Activities: Workshops for adults and children; lect open to public, 5 - 10 vis lectr per year; gallery talks; tours; individual paintings and original objects of art lent to other institutions for special exhibitions; originate traveling exhibitions; museum shop sells exhibition catalogs, postcards & notecards
L **Museum Library,** 14853. Tel 607-255-6464; FAX 607-255-9940. *Dir* Franklin W Robinson
Open Tues - Sun 10 AM - 5 PM, print room open to public by appointment only. Estab 1956. Open to scholars & students by special appointments. Average Annual Attendance: 16,000
Library Holdings: Vols 5000; Per subs 15; Monographs; Other — Exhibition catalogs

L **Fine Arts Library,** Sibley Dome, 14853. Tel 607-255-3710. *Librn* Judith Holliday; *Asst Librn* Patricia Sullivan
Open Sat 10 AM - 5 PM, Sun 1 - 11 PM, Mon - Thurs 9 AM - 11 PM, Fri 9 AM - 6 PM, hours change for University vacation and summer session. Estab 1871 to serve Cornell students. Circ 90,280
Income: Financed through University funds
Purchases: $174,000
Library Holdings: Vols 145,000; Per subs 1800; Micro — Fiche 5928, reels 424; Other — Exhibition catalogs

M **DEWITT HISTORICAL SOCIETY OF TOMPKINS COUNTY,** 116 N Cayuga St, 14850. Tel 607-273-8284. *Dir* Margaret Hobbie
Open Tues - Sat 11 AM - 5 PM. No admis fee. Estab 1935 to collect, preserve & interpret the history of Tompkins County, New York. Average Annual Attendance: 10,000. Mem: 750; dues $15-$500; annual meeting in last quarter
Income: $200,000 (financed by endowment, membership, county appropriation, state & federal grants, earned income, foundations)
Collections: Decorative arts; local historical objects; painting & sketches by local artists; portraits; photographers - Charles Jones, Henry Head, Robert Head, Sheldon Smith, Verne Morton
Publications: DeWitt Historical Society Newsletter, quarterly; DeWitt Historical Society Calender & Newsnotes
Activities: Classes for adults & children; lectures open to public, 12 vis lectrs per yr; competitions with awards; book traveling exhibitions, 1-2 per yr; originate traveling exhibitions; museum shop sells books, reproductions of photographs; gift items

M **HINCKLEY FOUNDATION MUSEUM,** 410 E Seneca St, 14850. Tel 607-273-7053. *Dir* Macleah Carlisle
Open Sat 10 AM - 4 PM & by appointment. Admis donations accepted. Estab 1970 to collect & preserve 18th, 19th & early 20th century domestic, decorative & folk arts artifacts. One main gallery with three small galleries. Average Annual Attendance: 500. Mem: 150; dues family $15, individual $10; annual meeting in Mar
Income: $19,000 (financed by endowment, mem, grants & rent)
Purchases: 19th century washing machine, c1870 log cabin quilt; three bonnets
Collections: Clothing; lighting devices; petwer; quilts; toys; trivets
Exhibitions: (1991) Early American Folk Magic; Early Religious Movements of New York State. (1992) Gardens; 18th & 19th Century Cooking. (1993) Toys
Activities: Children's classes; lect open to public, 1 - 2 vis lectr per year; lending collection contains approx 20 art objects; book traveling exhibition one per year; retail store sells books

JAMAICA

M **JAMAICA ARTS CENTER,** 161-04 Jamaica Ave, 11432. Tel 718-658-7400; FAX 718-658-7922. *Board Pres* Jacquline Arrington; *Exec Dir* Veronique LeMelle; *Dir Public Prog* Howard Asch; *Performing Arts Dir* Claudia Bostick; *Visual Arts Dir* Robert Craddock
Open Mon, Tues, Fri & Sat 9 AM - 5 PM, Wed & Thurs 9 AM - 9 PM. Estab 1974 to provide educational opportunity in the visual and performing arts, exhibitions and performances. Three museum quality spaces, total 3500 sq ft. Average Annual Attendance: 65,000
Income: $939,000 (financed by city dept of cultural affairs, New York State Council on the Arts, foundations, corporations & workshop tuitions)
Exhibitions: (1990) Streets of Gold; Colin Chase
Publications: Exhibition catalogs & posters
Activities: Classes for adults, teens & children; dramatic programs; concerts; gallery talks; tours; competitions; scholarships; exten dept serves New York City; photographs and blow ups of original photograghs lent; book traveling exhibitions annually

L **QUEENS BOROUGH PUBLIC LIBRARY,** Fine Arts & Recreation Division, 89-11 Merrick Blvd, 11432. Tel 718-990-0755; FAX 718-658-8312. *Dir* Constance B Cooke; *Division Mgr* Claire Kach; *Asst Mgr* Sharon Kugler
Open Mon - Fri 10 AM - 9 PM, Sat 10 AM - 5:30 PM, Sun, Sept - May, noon - 5 PM. Estab 1933 to serve the general public in Queens, New York
Income: Financed by city & state appropriations
Library Holdings: Vols 129,800; Per subs 398; CDs 3500; Micro — Fiche, reels 4100; AV — A-tapes, cassettes 10,500, rec 9000; Other — Clipping files, exhibition catalogs, original art works, pamphlets, photographs, prints, reproductions 500,000
Collections: The WPA Print Collection
Activities: Concerts

M **SAINT JOHN'S UNIVERSITY,** Chung-Cheng Art Gallery, Sun Yat Sen Hall, Grand Central and Utopia Parkways, 11439. Tel 718-990-6161, Ext 6583. *Cur* Abraham P Ho
Open Mon - Fri 10 AM - 8 PM, Sat & Sun 10 AM - 4 PM. No admis fee. Estab Oct 1977 to make available Oriental art objects to the public, and to expose the metropolitan area to the Oriental culture through various exhibits and activities. Gallery displays contemporary as well as ancient objects, mainly Oriental with a few western subjects. Average Annual Attendance: 50,000
Income: Financed by the University, endowments and private contributions
Collections: Harry C Goebel Collection containing 595 pieces of rare and beautiful art objects dating from the 7th - 19th century - jades; ivory carvings; netsuke; procelains; lacquerware and paintings from Japan and China; permanent collection containing 700 pieces of Chinese porcelain, paintings, textiles, calligraphy & paper cuttings dating from 7th - 20th century
Exhibitions: Two Great Textiles of Modern Chinese Paintings; The Chinese Ancient Coin Exhibit
Publications: Exhibition catalogues
Activities: Lectures open to the public, 3 vis lectr per yr; concerts; gallery talks; tours; competitions with awards; individual paintings & original objects of art lent; lending collection contains 200 original art works; original prints; 200 paintings; traveling exhibitions organized and circulated

L **Asian Collection,** Grand Central and Utopia Parkways, 11439. Tel 718-990-6161, Ext 6722. *Librn* Kenji Niki
Open to the public for reference only
Library Holdings: Vols 50,500; Per subs 90; Micro — Cards, fiche, prints, reels; Other — Exhibition catalogs, manuscripts
Collections: Collected Works of Chinese and Japanese Calligraphy; Japan Foundation Collection includes 200 volumes on various Japanese art subjects; Series of Chinese Arts

JAMESTOWN

M **JAMESTOWN COMMUNITY COLLEGE,** The Forum Gallery, 525 Falconer St, 14701. Tel 716-665-9107; FAX 716-665-9110; Elec Mail INTERNET: DTALLEY@TMN.COM. *Dir* Dan R Talley; *Asst to Dir* Michelle Henry
Open Tues - Sat 11 AM - 5 PM, Wed evening until 8 PM. No admis fee. Estab 1979 to show significant regional, national & international contemporary art. Facility includes 1000 sq ft exhibition area. New facility planned for 1995 with approx 3000 sq ft exhibition area
Income: $93,000 (financed through city appropriation, Faculty Student Association & private foundation funds)
Exhibitions: (1992) Cletus Johnson; Theaters & Collages; Beyond Boundaries: Contemporary Art by Scandinavian Artists
Publications: Exhibition catalogs, 4 per year
Activities: Lect open to public, 200 vis lectr per year

L **JAMES PRENDERGAST LIBRARY ASSOCIATION,** 509 Cherry St, 14701. Tel 716-484-7135; FAX 716-483-6880. *Dir* Murray L Bob; *Head Reference Librn* Kim Morris
Open Mon - Fri 9 AM - 9 PM, Sat 9 AM - 5:30 PM, Sun 1 - 4 PM, shorter hours in summer. Estab 1891 as part of library. Maintains art gallery
Income: Financed by state & local funds
Library Holdings: Vols 248,373; Per subs 504; Micro — Prints; AV — Motion pictures, rec, slides; Other — Reproductions, sculpture
Special Subjects: Prints
Collections: Prendergast paintings, 19th & 20th century paintings; Roger Tory Peterson, limited edition print collection; Alexander Calder mats
Exhibitions: Traveling Exhibitions; local one-person and group shows
Publications: Mirror Up To Nature, collection catalog
Activities: Lectures open to the public; concerts; competitions; lending collection contains books, cassettes, film strips, framed reproductions, Kodachromes, phonorecords & slides; books traveling exhibitions

JERICHO

SOCIETY OF AMERICAN HISTORICAL ARTISTS
For further information, see National and Regional Organizations

KATONAH

M **CARAMOOR CENTER FOR MUSIC & THE ARTS, INC,** Caramoor House Museum, Girdle Ridge Rd, PO Box R, 10536. Tel 914-232-5035. *Chmn Bd of Trustees* Peter Gottsegen; *Exec Dir* Howard Herring; *Admnr* Hilton Bailey
Open winter Mon - Fri by appointment; summer Wed & Fri by appointment, Thurs & Sat 11 AM - 4 PM, Sun 1 - 4 PM. Admis adults $4. Estab 1970 to preserve the house & its collections, the legacy of Walter T Rosen, & to provide interpretive & education programs. Period rooms from European palaces are showcase for art collection from Europe & the Orient, spanning 6 centuries
Income: $42,000
Collections: Period rooms - European & fine & decorative arts from Europe & the Orient (1800 - 1950)
Publications: Guidebook to collection
Activities: Classes for children; docent training; concerts; lectures open to public, 6 - 8 vis lectr per yr; museum shop sells books, prints, slides

M **KATONAH MUSEUM OF ART,** Route 22 at Jay St, 10536. Tel 914-232-9555. *Pres* Betty Himmel; *VPres* Leslie Jacobson; *Dir* George G King; *Treas* William Eggleston
Open Tues - Fri 2 - 5 PM, Sat 10 AM - 5 PM, Sun 1 - 5 PM, cl Mon. No admis fee. Estab 1953 to present exhibitions created with loaned works of art, programs for schools, films, lectures, demonstrations and workshops. The Katonah Museum consists of 3000 sq ft of exhibition space with a sculpture garden. Average Annual Attendance: 50,000. Mem: 1200; dues $35 and up
Income: $700,000 (financed by mem, contributions & grants)
Exhibitions: Fairfield Porter; Navajo Weavings; Navajo Ways; Bloomsbury Artists at Charleston; An American Luminist; Charles Henry Gifford; Edouard Vuillard, Master of Intimism; Odilon Redon; George Rickey
Publications: Forgotten Instruments, 1980; exhibition catalogs; Shelter: Models of Native Ingenuity, 82; Many Trails: Indians of the Lower Hudson Valley, 1983
Activities: Docent training; teacher workshops; programs for schools; lect & films open to the public, 2 - 10 vis lectr per year; gallery talks; tours; original paintings, prints & photos lent; member school lending collection contains AV programs & slides; originate traveling exhibitions

M **NEW YORK STATE OFFICE OF PARKS RECREATION & HISTORIC PRESERVATION,** John Jay Homestead State Historic Site, New York State Route 22, PO Box AH, 10536. Tel 914-232-5651. *Historic Site Mgr II* Linda M Connelly; *Interpretive Programs Asst* Julia M Warger
Open Wed - Sat 10 AM - 4 PM, Sun noon - 4 PM, May - Sept; after Labor Day call for fall and winter hours. No admis fee. Estab 1968 to inform public on John Jay and his contributions to national, state & local history. Ten restored period rooms reflecting occupancy of the Jay family at its height; art distributed throughout. Average Annual Attendance: 25,000. Mem: 400; annual dues $15 and up; annual meetings in April
Income: Financed by state appropriation
Collections: American art and American decorative arts; John Jay memorabilia and archives; Westchester mansion with estate & out-buildings
Exhibitions: Federal Period Decorations
Publications: John Jay and the Constitution, a Teacher's Guide; John Jay 1745-1829; The Jays of Bedford; The Jay Genealogy
Activities: Classes for adults and children; dramatic programs; docent training; lectures open to public; concerts; gallery talks; group tours by advance reservation; school outreach; craft demonstrations; special exhibits

KENMORE

A **BUFFALO SOCIETY OF ARTISTS,** 33 Delaware Rd, 14217. Tel 716-875-7571. *Pres* Rita Argen Averbach; *First VPres* Carol Townsend; *Second VPres* Larry Bell; *Treas* Noreer Spurling; *Recording Secy* Daniel Haskin; *Corresp Secy* Anita Johnson
Estab 1891 for practicing and exhibiting artists. Mem: 160; dues $20; annual meeting May/June
Income: Financed by membership dues
Exhibitions: Annual Juried Exhibition
Publications: Annual Exhibition Catalogue
Activities: Lectures open to the public; competitions with awards

KENOZA LAKE

M **MAX HUTCHINSON'S SCULPTURE FIELDS,** Fulton Hill Rd, PO Box 94, 12750. Tel 914-482-3669 (voice & fax). *Pres* Max Hutchinson
Open by appointment. No admis fee. Estab 1986 to exhibit large scale & outdoor sculpture. permanent & changing exhibits of sculpture mostly oriented to outdoor locations
Exhibitions: Twenty-five sculptures by Ju Ming; Eight sculptures by Charles Ginnever; individual works by Mel Chin, Linda Howard, Peter Barton, Ronald Bladen, Donna Byers, Jackie Ferrara, Ann Gillen, Ruth Hardinger, Marcia Kaplan, Marion Kaselle, Bridget Kennedy, Bernard Kirschenbaum, Henner Kuckuck, Wendy Lehman, John Pohanka, Christy Rupp, Frank Sansome, Heidi Schlatter, Robert Stackhouse, William Tucker, Brian Wall, Mac Whitney, Robert Wick, Roger Williams
Activities: Original art sold

KINDERHOOK

M **COLUMBIA COUNTY HISTORICAL SOCIETY,** Columbia County Museum, PO Box 311, Five Albany Ave, 12106. Tel 518-758-9265. *Pres* James Elliott Lindsley; *Exec Dir* Sharon S Palmer; *Museum Asst* Jeanette Johnson; *Cur* Helen McLallen
Open Mar - Oct, Mon - Fri 10 AM - 4 PM, Sat 11 AM - 5 PM, Sun 1 - 5 PM. No admis fee. Estab 1916 as House of History & Van Alen House to interpret local and regional, colonial and federal period history, including art of 18th and 19th century and decorative arts. In large hall, wall space 40 ft x 38 ft used for 3 exhibitions of paintings per yr. Average Annual Attendance: 12,000. Mem: 700; dues $15-$500; annual meeting third Sat in Oct
Income: $125,000 (financed by membership, endowment, activities, projects, events, private donations, admissions, government & corporate grants)
Collections: Historical objects pertaining to history of county; †New York regional decorative arts; furniture & costumes; paintings of 18th and 19th centuries
Exhibitions: Local history & cultural exhibit; Black history Columbia County 1750-1900. (1993) Sons & Daughters of Italia
Publications: A Visible Heritage: The History of Columbia County through Art & Architecture; exhibit catalogs; quarterly newsletter; brochures
Activities: Classes for children; docent training; lectures open to the public, 4 vis lectr per yr; concerts; originate traveling exhibitions; museum shop sells books, gifts, prints

L **Library,** PO Box 311, Five Albany Ave, 12106. Tel 518-758-9265. *Pres* James Elliott Lindsley
Open Mon - Fri 10 AM - 4 PM, June - Aug Sat 11 AM - 5 PM, Sun 1 - 5 PM. Estab 1926 to maintain research files on the county and regional art history. For reference only
Library Holdings: Vols 3300; Per subs 3; AV — Cassettes, Kodachromes, slides; Other — Clipping files, exhibition catalogs, manuscripts, memorabilia, original art works, pamphlets, photographs, prints
Special Subjects: Architecture, Decorative Arts, Folk Art, County History
Collections: †County & Regional history; †Hudson Valley architecture; Dutch culture; †Local & Regional paintings & decorative arts; Federalists

KINGSTON

M **PALISADES INTERSTATE PARK COMMISSION,** Senate House State Historic Site, 296 Fair St, 12401. Tel 914-338-2786. *Historic Site Mgr* Rich Goring
Open Apr - Dec Wed - Sat 10 AM - 5 PM, Sun 1 - 5 PM, Jan - Mar Sat 10 AM - 5 PM, Sun 1 - 5 PM. No admis fee. Estab 1887 as an educational community resource which tells the story of the growth of state government as well as the stories of the lives & works of local 19th century artists. Average Annual Attendance: 20,000
Collections: 18th and 19th century decorative arts; 18th and 19th century paintings and other works of art, particularly those by James Bard, Jervis McEntee, Ammi Phillips, Joseph Tubby and John Vanderlyn
Publications: Exhibition catalogs
Activities: Classes for adults & children; docent training; lectures open to the public, 2 vis lectr per yr; individual paintings & original objects of art lent to well-established institutions, lending collection contains 200 color reproductions, 200 original art works, 300 original prints, 200 paintings & 10 sculptures; book traveling exhibitions

L **Reference Library,** 296 Fair St, 12401. Tel 914-338-2786. *Historic Site Mgr* Rich Goring
Open Wed - Sat 10 AM - 5 PM, Sun 1 - 5 PM, cl Jan - Mar. Estab 1887. Open by appointment to scholars, students & researchers for reference only
Library Holdings: Vols 10,000; Per subs 10; Other — Exhibition catalogs, manuscripts, memorabilia, pamphlets
Special Subjects: Ulster County history; government; genealogies; local artists
Collections: Collection of letters relating to the artist John Vanderlyn
Publications: Exhibit catalogs

LAKE GEORGE

M **LAKE GEORGE ARTS PROJECT,** Courthouse Gallery, Canada St, 12845. Tel 518-668-2616; FAX 518-668-3788. *Dir* John Strong; *Asst Dir* Barbara Hancock
Open Tues - Fri noon - 5 PM. Estab 1977, gallery estab 1985 to provide income & exposure for regional artists. 30 ft by 30 ft. Average Annual Attendance: 400. Mem: 350; dues $15-$100; annual meeting in Dec
Income: $90,000 (financed by mem & by city & state appropriation

LEROY

A **LEROY HISTORICAL SOCIETY,** 23 E Main St, 14482. Tel 716-768-7433. *Dir* Lynne Belluscio
Estab 1940
Income: $42,000 (financed by endowment, mem, city & state appropriations)
Collections: Decorative Arts; 19th Century Art; Textiles; Tools; Western NY Redware
Exhibitions: (1991) Piecing It All Together: Quilts
Publications: Quarterly newsletter

LONG BEACH

L **LONG BEACH PUBLIC LIBRARY,** 111 W Park Ave, 11561. Tel 516-432-7201; FAX 516-889-4641. *Dir* George Trepp
Open Oct - May Mon, Wed, Thurs 9 AM - 9 PM, Tues & Fri 9 AM - 6 PM, Sat 9 AM - 5 PM, Sun 1 - 5 PM. Estab 1928 to serve the community with information and services, including recreational, cultural and informational materials. The Long Beach Art Association in cooperation with the library presents monthly exhibits of all types of media
Library Holdings: Micro — Fiche, reels; AV — Cassettes, fs, rec, v-tapes; Other — Memorabilia, pamphlets, photographs
Collections: Local history; 300 photographs of Long Beach
Exhibitions: Local talent; membership shows; juried exhibitions
Publications: Monthly newsletter
Activities: Dramatic programs; lect open to public, 18-20 vis lectr per yr; concerts; gallery talks; films; tours

LONG ISLAND CITY

C **CITIBANK, NA,** One Court Sq, 8th Floor, 11120. Tel 718-248-1864; FAX 718-248-1834. *Cur* Suzy Lemakis
Estab to enhance the environment. Collection displayed in offices of the corporate headquarters
Collections: Art reflects the working environment of the various departments, including international, American and New York themes
Activities: Individual objects of art lent for museum exhibitions

INSTITUTE FOR CONTEMPORARY ART
M **The Clocktower Gallery,** 46-01 21st St, New York, 11101. Tel 212-233-1440. *Clocktower Coordr* Miranda Banks
Open Thurs - Sun noon - 6 PM. Admis donation $1. Estab to present a broad range of artistic activities in various media. Located in the top two floors of a turn-of-the-century municipal building owned by the city. Average Annual Attendance: 15,000
Income: Financed by city & state appropriations, corporate & private patrons, National Endowment for the Arts
Collections: Sculpture; painting; photography
Publications: Exhibit catalogues
Activities: Classes for adults & children, dance, film, video, photography, architectural presentations; lectures open to public, concerts, tours, competition for studio program with awards of studio residency; original works of art lent to not-for-profit institutions with appropriate facilities; book traveling exhibitions; originate traveling exhibitions; sales shop sells books, catalogues, posters
M **Project Studio One (P S 1),** 46-01 21st St, 11101. Tel 718-784-2084; FAX 718-482-9454. *Exec Dir Institute* Alanna Heiss; *Managing Dir* Anthony Vasconcellos; *Building Dir* Hank Stahler; *Educ Coordr* George York; *Publications Dir* Carole Kismaric
Open Wed - Sun noon - 6 PM. Admis donation $2. Estab 1972 as artists studio & exhibition contemporary & experimental art. Located in a vast renovated 19th century Romanesque school-house, the gallery contains 25,000 sq ft of space. Average Annual Attendance: 35,000. Mem: Dues leadership council $5000, patrons council $1000
Income: Financed by city & state appropriations, corporate & private donations, National Endowment for the Arts
Collections: Painting; sculpture; photography; fashion; video; film; architecture
Exhibitions: The Knot: Arte Povera; About Place: Contemporary American Landscape; Images of the Unknown; John McCracken; Dennis Oppenheim; David Hammons
Publications: Exhibit catalogues; Studio Artists' Yearbook, annually
Activities: Classes for adults & children, dance, film, video, photography, architectural presentations; lectures open to public; concerts; tours; competition for studio program with awards of studio residency; original works of art lent to not-for-profit institutions with appropriate facilities; book traveling exhibitions; originate traveling exhibitions; sales shop sells books, catalogues, posters, postcards

M **ISAMU NOGUCHI FOUNDATION,** Garden Museum, 32-37 Vernon Blvd, 11106. Tel 718-721-1932. *Dir* Bruce Altshuler; *Dir of Education* Lawre Stone
Open Apr 1 - Nov 30 Wed & Sat 11 AM - 6 PM. Suggested contribution $4. Estab 1985 to preserve, protect & exhibit important sculptural, environmental & design work of Isamu Noguchi. Twelve galleries and a garden exhibiting over 250 sculptures, models, drawings and photos. 24,000 sq ft factory converted by the artist. Average Annual Attendance: 12,000
Income: $400,000 (financed by Noguchi Foundation, New York City Department of Cultural Affairs & private donations)
Collections: Sculptures in stone, wood, metal, paper, clay; models and drawings; photos of Noguchi's gardens and plazas; stage sets
Exhibitions: Permanent exhibition
Activities: Educ Dept; tours for adults & children; docent training; lectures open to public; concerts; gallery talks; tours; museum shop sells books, magazines, slides & Akari lamps

MOUNTAINVILLE

M **STORM KING ART CENTER,** Old Pleasant Hill Rd, 10953. Tel 914-534-3115; FAX 914-534-4457. *Dir* David R Collens
Open daily 11 AM - 5:30 PM, Apr 1 - Nov 30. Admis adults $5, sr citizens & students $3, children under 5 free. Estab 1960. Average Annual Attendance: 50,000. Mem: dues $35 individual, $50 family, $100 contributor, $250 donor, $500 sponsor, $1000 patron
Collections: 400 acre sculpture park with over 100 large scale 20th century American & European sculptures, including works by Aycock, Armajani, Bourgeois, Calder, Caro, di Suvero, Grosvenor, Hepworth, LeWitt, Liberman, Moore, Nevelson, Noguchi, Rickey, Serra, Smith, Snelson, Streeter, Witkin
Exhibitions: Changing annual exhibition of contemporary sculpture in museum building & sculpture park. (1991) Enclosures & Encounters: Recent Aspects of Architectural Sculpture. (1992) Ursula von Rydingsvard: Sculpture. (1993) Work by Siah Armajani
Publications: A landscape for Modern Sculpture: Storm King Art Center; exhibition catalogs; poster
Activities: Educ dept; lect open to public, lectr series, courses in sculpture history & modern art; concerts; gallery talks, guided tours of sculpture park, outdoor concerts; museum shop sells books, slides, postcards, posters, t-shirts, totes & maps

MOUNT VERNON

L **MOUNT VERNON PUBLIC LIBRARY,** Fine Art Dept, 28 S First Ave, 10550. Tel 914-668-1840. *Dir* E L Mittelgluek
Open Mon - Thurs 9 AM - 9 PM, Fri 9 AM - 6 PM, Sat 9 AM - 5 PM, Sun 1 - 5 PM, cl Sat & Sun during July and Aug. No admis fee. Estab 1854. Library contains Doric Hall with murals by Edward Gay, NA; Exhibition Room with frescoes by Louise Brann Soverns; and Norman Wells Print Alcove, estab 1941
Income: $2,200,000 (financed by city & other funds)
Library Holdings: Vols 415,000; Art books 17,000; AV — A-tapes 1293, cassettes 1293, rec 11,500; Other — Photographs 11,500
Special Subjects: Architecture, Ceramics, Costume Design & Construction, Decorative Arts, Painting - American, Photography, Prints
Exhibitions: Costume dolls; fans; metalwork; one-man shows of painting, sculpture & photographs porcelains; silver; woodcarving; jewelry; other exhibits changing monthly cover a wide range of subjects from miniatures to origami
Activities: Lectures open to public, 6 vis lectr per yr; concerts; gallery talks; tours; individual paintings & original objects of art lent to library members

MUMFORD

M **GENESEE COUNTRY MUSEUM,** John L Wehle Gallery of Sporting Art, 1410 Flint Hill Rd (Mailing add: PO Box 310, Rochester, 14603). Tel 716-538-6822; FAX 716-538-2887. *Dir* Stuart B Bolger; *Adminr* Scott Adamson
Open Tues - Fri 10 AM - 4 PM Sat, Sun & holidays 10 AM - 5 PM, cl Mon, May, June, Sept & Oct. Admis adults $9, sr citizens $8, youth $6, children & students $4.50. Estab 1976. Gallery has over 600 paintings & sculptures dealing with wildlife, sporting art & western art. Average Annual Attendance: 120,000. Mem: 2000; dues Hosmer Inn Society $500, Crier $325, Selectman $150, Family $75, Friend & one $75, Friends $50
Income: Financed by self-generated income
Collections: Decorative arts, restored 19th Century buildings, paintings & sculpture
Publications: Booklets; Four Centuries of Sporting Art; Genesee Country Museum; monthly newsletter
Activities: Classes for adults & children; docent training; lect open to public; concerts; gallery talks; tours; museum shop sells books, magazines, original art, reproductions, prints & slides

NEW CITY

M **HISTORICAL SOCIETY OF ROCKLAND COUNTY,** 20 Zukor Rd, 10956. Tel 914-634-9629. *Exec Dir* Debra Walker; *Dir Progs* Stephen Hadley; *Cur Coll* Alison Geiger; *Publications* Marianne Leese
Open 9:30 AM - 4 PM. Admis $2 donation. Estab 1965 to preserve & interpret history of Rockland County. Average Annual Attendance: 15,000. Mem: 2000; dues $20
Income: $25,000 (financed by endowment, membership, state appropriation)
Activities: Classes for adults & children; docent programs; lect open to public, 6 visiting lectr per yr; History Awards Program for high school seniors; lending collection contains 10,000 items; book traveling exhibition annually; retail store sells books

NEW PALTZ

M THE COLLEGE AT NEW PALTZ STATE UNIVERSITY OF NEW YORK
(Formerly State University of New York at New Paltz), College Art Gallery, 75
S Manheim, 12561. Tel 914-257-3844; FAX 914-257-3854. *Dir* Neil C Trager;
Asst Dir Christine De Lape
Open Mon - Fri 10 AM - 4 PM, Tues 7 AM - 9 PM, Sat & Sun 1 - 4 PM. No
admis fee. With an exhibition schedule of 10 exhibitions per year, the College
Art Gallery provides support for the various art curricula & serves as a major
cultural resource for the College & surrounding community. There are two
adjoining galleries, South Gallery 59 x 56 ft, North Gallery 42 x 23 ft. Average
Annual Attendance: 15,000 - 20,000
Collections: Artifacts, Folk Art, Oriental Prints; Painting, principally 20th
century America; †Photographs; Posters; Pre-Columbian Art; Prints, Primative
African & New Guinea; Sculpture
Exhibitions: Coroplast's Art: Greek Terracottas of the Hellenistic World;
Uncommon Ground, 23 Latin American Artists; The Search for Freedom:
African American Art 1945 - 1975
Activities: Lect open to public; concerts; gallery talks; competitions; individual
paintings and original objects of art lent to museums and galleries; lending
collection contains artifacts; original prints; paintings, photographs, sculpture, folk
art, textiles, drawings, posters
L Sojourner Truth Library, 12561. Tel 914-257-3701; FAX 914-257-3854. *Dir*
William E Connors; *Coordr of Reader Serv* James R Goodrich; *Coordr of
Technical Serv* Jean S Sauer; *Coordr of Computer Serv* Chui-chun Lee; *Head of
Reference* Gerlinde Barley; *Head of Circulation* Nancy Nielson
For lending & reference. Circ 259,000
Income: Financed by state appropriation
Purchases: $411,900
Library Holdings: Vols 375,000; Per subs 1950; Micro — Cards, fiche, prints,
reels; AV — Rec; Other — Exhibition catalogs, pamphlets

NEW ROCHELLE

M COLLEGE OF NEW ROCHELLE, Castle Gallery, Castle Place, 10805. Tel
914-654-5423; FAX 914-654-5290. *Exec Dir* Susan Shoulet; *Asst Dir* Karen
Convertino; *Assoc Dir* Anne Robertson
Open Mon - Fri 10 AM - 5 PM, weekends noon - 4 PM. No admis fee. Estab
1979 as a professional art gallery to serve the college, city of New Rochelle &
lower Westchester & provide exhibition & interpretation of fine arts, material
culture. Located in Leland Castle, a gothic revival building, listed in National
Register of Historic Places; gallery is modern facility, with flexible space
Publications: Newsletter
Activities: Docent training; lectures; open to public, 6 vis lectrs per year;
originate traveling exhibitions
L NEW ROCHELLE PUBLIC LIBRARY, Art Section, One Library Plaza,
10801. Tel 914-632-7878. *Dir* Patricia Anderson; *Head of Reference* Marjorie
Sha
Open Oct - May Mon 10 AM - 6 PM, Tues 10 AM - 9 PM, Wed noon - 6 PM,
Thurs noon - 9 PM, Fri & Sat 10 AM - 5 PM, Sun 1 - 5 PM. Estab 1894
Library Holdings: Vols 8000; Per subs 4; Micro — Fiche, reels; AV — Cassettes,
rec, slides, v-tapes; Other — Clipping files, exhibition catalogs, original art works,
pamphlets, photographs
Exhibitions: All shows, displays and exhibits are reviewed and scheduled by
professional advisory panel
Activities: Lectures and demonstrations; lending collection contains framed prints
and art slides
A New Rochelle Art Association, One Library Place, 10801. Tel 914-632-7878.
Pres Bill Tamraz
Estab 1912 to encourage art in the area. Mem: 200; dues $20; monthly meeting
Income: Financed by membership
Exhibitions: Four exhibitions per year
Activities: Classes for adults; Lectures open to public, 4 vis lectr per year;
competitions with awards

NEW YORK

M LOUIS ABRONS ART CENTER, 466 Grand, 10002. Tel 212-598-0400; FAX
212-505-8329. *Dir* Susan Fleminger
Open Mon - Fri 9 AM - 6 PM, Sat 10 AM - 6 PM, Sun noon - 6 PM. Estab
1974 as a mulitple arts community based center for the performing & visual arts
programs

A ACTUAL ART FOUNDATION, 7 Worth St, 10013. Tel 212-226-3109. *Pres*
Valerie Shakespeare; *Treasurer* Margaret Thatcher
Estab 1983 to promote Actual Art
Income: $75,000 (financed by endowment & public fund raising)

A AESTHETIC REALISM FOUNDATION, Eli Siegel Collection, 141 Greene St,
10012. Tel 212-777-4490; FAX 212-777-4426. *Librn* Richita Anderson; *Librn*
Leila Rosen; *Librn* Meryl Simon
Open by appointment. Estab 1973. The Collection houses the books &
manuscripts of Eli Siegel (1902-1978), American poet, critic & founder of the
philosophy Aesthetic Realism
Library Holdings: Vols 30,000; AV — A-tapes; Other — Manuscripts
Special Subjects: Aesthetics, Anthropology, Art History, Manuscripts, Painting -
American, Painting - European, Photography, Art Criticism
M Terrain Gallery, 141 Greene St, 10012. Tel 212-777-4490; FAX 212-777-4426.
Coordr Jane Hall; *Coordr* Nancy Huntting; *Coordr* Marcia Rackow; *Coordr*
Carrie Wilson
Open Sat 1 - 3:15 PM & other times by appointment. Estab 1955 with a bases in
this principle stated by Eric Siegel, founder of the philosophy Aesthetic Realm:
All beauty is a making one of opposites & the making one opposites is what we
are going after in ourselves

Collections: Permanent collection of paintings, prints, drawings & photographs
with commentary
Activities: Gallery talks open to the public every Sat at 2:30 PM & by
appointment for groups during the week
L Library, 141 Greene St, 10012-3201. Tel 212-777-4490; FAX 212-777-4426.
Librn Richita Anderson
Open by appointment. Estab 1973 by Eric Siegel on the principle: The world, art,
& self explain each other - each is the aesthetic oneness of opposites
Special Subjects: Aesthetics, Anthropology, Architecture, Art Education, Art
History, History of Art & Archaeology, Painting - American, Painting - British,
Painting - European, Painting - Japanese, Photography, Theatre Arts
Collections: Published poems & essays by Eli Siegel; published & unpublished
lectures by Eli Siegel
Publications: The Right of Aesthetic Realism to be Known, weekly periodical

M A I R GALLERY, 63 Crosby St, 10012. Tel 212-966-0799. *Coordr* Nancy Waits
Open Tues - Sat 11 AM - 6 PM. No admis fee. Estab 1972 as cooperative
women's gallery representing 20 American women artists; also provides programs
and services to women artists community. Average Annual Attendance: 20,000.
Mem: 20; 10 national affiliates
Income: Financed by membership, city and state appropriation
Exhibitions: One-woman exhibitions; invitational which can be international,
regional and performance or theme shows
Publications: Invitational exhibition catalogues, bi-annually
Activities: Lect open to public

THE ALLIED ARTISTS OF AMERICA, INC
For further information, see National and Regional Organizations

M ALTERNATIVE MUSEUM, 594 Broadway, 10012. Tel 212-966-4444; FAX
212-226-2158. *Dir* Geno Rodriguez; *Assoc Cur* Francis X Resch
Exhibitions: Philadelphia Artists (all art forms); Nexus: the Art of Syncritism

AMERICAN ABSTRACT ARTISTS
For further information, see National and Regional Organizations

AMERICAN ACADEMY OF ARTS & LETTERS
For further information, see National and Regional Organizations

AMERICAN ARTISTS PROFESSIONAL LEAGUE, INC
For further information, see National and Regional Organizations

AMERICAN COUNCIL FOR THE ARTS
For further information, see National and Regional Organizations

M AMERICAN CRAFT COUNCIL, American Craft Museum, 40 W 53rd St,
10019. Tel 212-956-3535; FAX 212-459-0926. *Dir* Janet Kardon; *Registrar* Doris
Stowens
Open Wed - Sun 10 AM - 5 PM, Tues 10 AM - 8 PM. Estab 1956 by the
American Craft Council (see National Organizations). Gallery displays
contemporary art in craft media. Average Annual Attendance: 47,000. Mem: 35,
000; dues benefactors $1000, patrons $500, friends $250, sponsors $100, family/
dual $50, subscribing $39.50
Income: Financed by memberships, government grants, private & corporate
donation
Collections: Works of American craftsmen since 1900 in ceramics, paper, fiber,
wood, metal, glass, plastics, enamels
Publications: American Craft, bi-monthly magazine; exhibition catalogs;
bibliographies, directories and manuals on crafts
Activities: Docent training; lectures open to public, 30 vis lectrs per yr; gallery
talks; tours; competitions; awards; Meet the Artist program; Book traveling
exhibitions, annually; sales shop sells books, magazines, slides

AMERICAN CRAFT COUNCIL
For further information see National and Regional Organizations

THE AMERICAN FEDERATION OF ARTS
For further information, see National and Regional Organizations

AMERICAN FINE ARTS SOCIETY
For further information, see National and Regional Organizations

AMERICAN INSTITUTE OF GRAPHIC ARTS
For further information, see National and Regional Organizations

M AMERICAN MUSEUM OF NATURAL HISTORY, Central Park West at 79th
St, 10024-5192. Tel 212-769-5000. *Pres* George Langdon; *Dir* William J
Maynihan
Open Mon, Tues, Thurs & Sun 10 AM - 5:45 PM, Wed, Fri & Sat 10 AM - 9
PM, cl Thanksgiving and Christmas. Admis by contribution (suggested, adults $3.
50, children $1.50). Estab 1869 as a museum for the study and exhibition of all
aspects of natural history. Exhibition spaces include Roosevelt Memorial Hall,
Gallery 3, Naturemax Gallery, Akeley Gallery, Gallery 1. Average Annual
Attendance: 2,500,000. Mem: 500,000
Income: Financed by special presentations, contributions
Exhibitions: Permanent exhibitions include: Hall of Asian Peoples; Hall of Ocean
Life & Biology of Fishes; Arthur Ross Hall of Meteorites; Guggenheim Hall of
Minerals; Margaret Mead Hall of Pacific Peoples. (1993) Bear Imagination &
Reality: The Hall (1994) Shark
Fact & Fantasy
Publications: Natural History, magazine; Curator; Bulletin of the American
Museum of Natural History; Anthropological Papers of the American Museum of
Natural History; American Museum of Natural History Novitates; annual report
Activities: Classes for adults and children; dance & music programs; lectures
open to the public; tours; scholarships

L **Library,** Central Park W at 79th St, 10024. Tel 212-769-5400; FAX 212-769-5009. *Dir Library Servs* Nina J Root
Library Holdings: Vols 410,000; AV — A-tapes, fs, Kodachromes, lantern slides, motion pictures, rec, slides, v-tapes; Other — Clipping files, exhibition catalogs, manuscripts, memorabilia, original art works, pamphlets, photographs, prints, reproductions, sculpture
Special Subjects: Afro-American Art, American Indian Art, Anthropology, Archaeology, Architecture, Bronzes, Carpets & Rugs, Ceramics, Coins & Medals, Costume Design & Construction, Dioramas, Display, Drawings, Embroidery, Eskimo Art, Etchings & Engravings, Ethnology, Gold, Goldsmithing, Historical Material, Mexican Art, Painting - American, Portraits, Pottery, Primitive Art

AMERICAN NUMISMATIC SOCIETY
For further information, see National and Regional Organizations

A **AMERICAN-SCANDINAVIAN FOUNDATION,** 725 Park Ave, 10021. Tel 212-879-9779; FAX 212-249-3444. *Pres* Lena Biorck Kaplan; *Dir* Lynn Carter; *Prog Dir* Patricia Splendore
Foundation estab 1910 since 1980 exhibitions of contemporary art from Denmark, Finland, Iceland, Norway & Sweden have been presented. Mem: 3500; annual dues $40
Exhibitions: Contemporary Scandinavian painting, sculpture, design and crafts; artwork is selected for exhibition by a committee of professional art advisors
Publications: Calendar of Nordic Events, 2 times a year; The Scandinavian Review, 3 times a year; SCAN, newsletter 4 times a year
Activities: Lect open to public; awards; scholarships

AMERICAN WATERCOLOR SOCIETY
For further information, see National and Regional Organizations

M **AMERICAS SOCIETY,** 680 Park Ave, 10021. Tel 212-249-8950; FAX 212-517-6247; Telex 42-9169. *Dir Visual Arts Program* Fatima Bercht
Open Tues - Sun noon - 6 PM, cl Mon (during exhibitions). Admis suggested $2 contribution. Estab 1967 to enlarge knowledge & appreciation in the United States of the art & cultural heritage of other countries in the Western Hemisphere. One large gallery with 3-4 loan exhibitions a year of Latin American & Canadian art. Average Annual Attendance: 10,000. Mem: 900; dues $35
Income: $120,500
Collections: Collection of Mexican art & furniture as well as contemporary Latin American
Exhibitions: (1990) Aspects of Contemporary Mexican Painting. (1991) Contemporary Art from Chile; Masks of the Americas
Publications: Exhibition catalogs
Activities: Classes for adults & children in conjunction with exhibitions; lect open to the public, 50-100 vis lectr per yr; gallery talks; concerts; tours; paintings lent to museums & major exhibitions; originate traveling exhibitions; sales shop sells books

A **ARCHITECTURAL LEAGUE OF NEW YORK,** 457 Madison Ave, 10022. Tel 212-753-1722; FAX 212-371-6048. *Pres* Paul S Byard; *Executive Dir* Rosalie Genevro
Admis seminars $5, mem free. Estab 1881 to promote art and architecture; serves as a forum for new and experimental ideas in the arts. Mem: 1000; dues over 35 years $85, under 35 years $50, students $25; annual meeting in June
Exhibitions: Annual Juried Exhibition of Young Architects Competition
Publications: Exhibition catalogs; posters
Activities: Lect; slide lect; competitions; awards

A **ART COMMISSION OF THE CITY OF NEW YORK,** City Hall, 3rd floor, 10007. Tel 212-788-3071; FAX 212-788-3086. *Pres* Edward A Ames
Open by appointment only. No admis fee. Estab 1898 to review designs for city buildings landscape architecture & works of art proposed for city owned property. Portraits are installed in Governors Room and other areas in City Hall. Mem: 11
Income: Financed by city appropriation
Collections: 100 portraits of historic figures, state, city and national
Publications: The Art Commission and Municipal Art Society Guide to Outdoor Sculpture by Margot Gayle and Michele Cohen; New York Re-Viewed, Exhibition Catalogue of 19th and 20th Century Photographs from the Collection of the Art Commission; Imaginary Cities, European Views from the Collection of the Art Commission
A **Associates of the Art Commission, Inc,** City Hall, 3rd floor, 10007. Tel 212-566-5528; FAX 212-788-3086. *Acting Dir* Vivian Millicent Warfield; *Commissioner* Eliott C Nolen; *Commissioner* Robert Ryman; *Commissioner* John T Sargent; *Commissioner* Anita Soto; *Commissioner* John Willen Bicher
Estab 1913 to advise and counsel Art Commission as requested. Mem: 35; dues $35; annual meeting in Jan
Income: Financed by membership

ART DEALERS ASSOCIATION OF AMERICA, INC
For further information, see National and Regional Organizations

ART DIRECTORS CLUB, INC
For further information, see National and Regional Organizations

A **ART INFORMATION CENTER, INC,** 280 Broadway, Room 412, 10007. Tel 212-227-0282. *Pres* Anne Chamberlain; *Dir* Dan Concholar; *Treas* George Tanier; *Board Dir Member* Jacob Lawrence; *Board Dir Member* Sylvan Cole; *Board Dir Member* Inger Tanier
Open 10 AM - 5 PM. Organized 1959, inc 1963, as a tax-deductible clearing house of contemporary fine arts. Maintains international files of living artists with their gallery affiliations and where they have shown since 1960 (c 65,000 artists); files of galleries, their rosters of artists and catalogs of current and recent shows (c 550 in New York, 300 in other US cities, 50 in foreign cities); files of slides of work by unaffiliated artists (c 750 artists and 8-12 slides each) for use by dealers looking for new talent. The Center helps to channel the many artists in New York, and those coming to New York, seeking New York outlets for their work. It aids new galleries to start and furnishes information on many aspects of contemporary art to museums, art schools, collectors and the public. All documentation kept up-to-date
Income: $20,000 (financed by donations & small grants)

A **ART IN GENERAL,** 79 Walker St, 10013-3523. Tel 212-219-0473. *Exec Dir* Holly Block; *Gallery Coordr* Ruth Libermann; *Writer* Kerri Sakamoto
Open Thurs - Sat noon - 6 PM. No admis fee. Estab 1981 as a nonprofit organization. Non-profit arts organization which relies on private & public support to meet its expenses. Average Annual Attendance: 10,000
Income: Financed by endowment, state & private funds
Exhibitions: (1992) Salon Show
Activities: Group tours

A **ARTIST-CRAFTSMEN OF NEW YORK,** 165 E 83rd St, 10028. Tel 212-686-0135. *Pres* Monona Rossol; *VPres* Kathe Berl
Estab 1958 as successor to New York Society of Craftsmen and New York Society of Ceramic Arts. Exhibitions and demonstrations are arranged for the purpose of broadening public interest in and knowledge of crafts; developing standards of taste in design and workmanship. Affiliated with American Craftsmen's Council. Mem: 300; qualification for mem: by submission of work by artist-craftsman member to membership jury with emphasis laid upon professional standards of craftsmanship and the quality of work; non-craftsman may become associate or contributing member on election by the Board of Governors; annual meeting in March, with six membership meetings per year
Exhibitions: Annual exhibition in New York City; periodic exhibitions at National Design Center and other New York City locations
Publications: Newsletter

ARTISTS' FELLOWSHIP, INC
For further information, see National and Regional Organizations

A **ARTISTS SPACE,** 223 W Broadway, 10013. Tel 212-226-3970; FAX 212-966-1434. *Pres* Hermine Ford; *VPres* Meryl Meltzer; *Dir* Carlos Gutierrez-Solana; *Treas* Phillip E Aarons; *Secy* Beverly Wolff; *Development Dir* Lori Blount Radford; *Progm Coordr* Gary Nicard; *Slide File Coordr* Christopher Nahas; *Development Assoc* Alan Kleinman; *Exec Assoc* Amy Wanggaard; *Registrar & Preparator* Ken Buhler; *Finance Dir* Peter Siegel
Open Tues - Sat 11 AM - 6 PM. Estab 1973 as a non-profit contemporary art exhibition space & artists services organization that provides artists with professional & financial support while presenting the most exciting new art developments to the public
Activities: Administers two grant programs
M **Artists Space Gallery,** 223 W Broadway, 10013. Tel 212-226-3970. *Dir* Carlos Gutierrez-Solana; *Developmental Assoc* Alan Kleinman
Open Tues - Sat 11 AM - 6 PM. No admis fee for exhibitions, films & events $4. Estab 1973 to assist emerging & unaffiliated artists. Five exhibition rooms & hall gallery. Average Annual Attendance: 20,000
Income: Financed by National Endowment for the Arts, New York State Council, corporate & foundation funds & private contributions
Activities: Gallery talks by appointment; financial aid to artists for public presentation; book traveling exhibitions; originate traveling exhibitions; junior museum
L **Unaffiliated Artists File,** 223 W Broadway the Visual Arts, 10013. Tel 212-226-3970. *Slide File Coordr* Hendrika ter Elst
Open Tues - Sat 11 AM - 4 PM. Slide file of over 2500 New York state artists. Available to dealers, critics, curators & artists for reference only

A **ART STUDENTS LEAGUE OF NEW YORK,** 215 W 57th St, 10019. Tel 212-247-4510. *Exec Dir & Dir Libr* Rosina A Florio
Gallery open 10 AM - 8 PM. No admis to members. Estab 1875 to maintain art school and membership activities. Maintains an art gallery open to public for league exhibits. Average Annual Attendance: 8000-9000. Mem: 6000; dues $10; annual meeting Dec
Income: Financed by tuitions and investments
Exhibitions: Exhibitions by members, students and instructors
Publications: Art Students League News, monthly
Activities: Lectures open to public, 12 vis lectr per yr; individual paintings & original objects of art lent to museums
L **Library,** 215 W 57th St, 10019. Tel 212-247-4510. *Dir* Rosina A Florio
Reference library for students and members
Library Holdings: AV — A-tapes, cassettes, fs, slides, v-tapes; Other — Clipping files, exhibition catalogs, manuscripts, original art works, pamphlets, photographs, prints, reproductions, sculpture

A **ASIAN AMERICAN ARTS CENTRE,** 26 Bowery, 10013. Tel 212-233-2154; FAX 212-766-1287. *Dir* Robert Lee
Open Mon - Fri 10 AM - 6 PM. No admis fee. Estab 1974 to promote Asian American artists & preserve Asian heritage. Gallery has multi-purpose exhibition space. Average Annual Attendance: 12,000. Mem: 500; dues $25
Income: Public & private grants, sponsorships, donations
Collections: Permanent collection of works commemorating Tiananmen Square; China June 4; collection of works by contemporary Asian American artists; folk arts collection (predominantly Chinese)
Publications: Arts Spiral, bi-annual
Activities: Educ dept; lectures open to public; 15 vis lectrs per year; gallery talks; tours; competitions with awards; originate traveling exhibitions; sales shop sells books, magazines & original art

M **THE ASIA SOCIETY GALLERIES,** 725 Park Ave, 10021. Tel 212-288-6400; Telex 22-4953 ASIA URCable ASIAHOUSE NEW YORK. *Chmn Society Board of Trustees* John C Whitehead; *Pres* Nicholas Platt; *Dir Galleries* Vishakha Desai; *Cur Galleries* Denise P Leidy
Open Tues - Sat 11 AM - 6 PM, Sun noon - 5 PM. Admis fee $2. Estab in 1956 as a non-profit organization to further greater understanding & mutual appreciation between the US & peoples of Asia. The Asia House Gallery was

inaugurated in 1960 to acquaint Americans with the historic art of Asia. In 1981 the Asia Society came into possession of its permanent collection, the Mr & Mrs John D Rockefeller 3d Collection of Asian Art, which is shown in conjunction with three to four temporary exhibitions each year. Average Annual Attendance: 60,000. Mem: 6000; dues $50 and up; annual meeting in May
Income: $750,000 (financed by endowment, mem, & grants from foundation, individual, federal & state government)
Collections: †Mr & Mrs John D Rockefeller 3d Collection of Asian Art; loans obtained from the US and foreign collections for special exhibitions
Activities: Lectures by guest specialists in connection with each exhibition & recorded lectures by the gallery education staff available to visitors; forty vis lectr per year; concerts, gallery talks, tours; loan exhibitions originated; book traveling exhibitions twice per year; sales shop sells books, magazines, prints, slides

A **ASSOCIATION OF ARTIST-RUN GALLERIES,** 164 Mercer St, 10012. Tel 212-924-6520. *Exec Dir* Geoff Homan
Open Tues & Thurs 11 AM - 4 PM. No admis fee. Estab 1974 as a non-profit membership association composed of artist-run galleries & spaces. Sponsors an information resource center for member galleries, artists & general public. Thirty five artist-run galleries. Mem: Dues patron $100, sponsor $50, contributor $25, individual $10
Income: Financed by endowment, membership, city and state appropriation
Exhibitions: US Customhouse-World Trade Center; Museum of the City of New York
Publications: AAR Guide; Fly Tracks, reviews; Time & Space Concepts in Art; The 10th St Days; How to Begin & Maintain an Artist Run Space; Newsletter
Activities: Educ program in conjunction with various schools off-campus programs; lectures open to public; concerts; gallery talks; tours

ASSOCIATION OF ART MUSEUM DIRECTORS
For further information, see National and Regional Organizations

A **ASSOCIATION OF HISPANIC ARTS,** 173 E 116 St, 10029. Tel 212-860-5445; FAX 212-427-2787. *Exec Dir* Jane Arce Bello; *Dir Technical Assistance* Daniela Montana
Eatab in 1975, the Association of Hispanic Arts, Inc. is a not-for-profit art service organization dedicated to the advancement of Latino arts. We highlight and promote the achievements of Latino artists and provide technical assistance to arts organizations. AHA is an innovative forum for cultural exchange, with programs designed to foster the appreciation, development and stability of the Latino cultural community
Income: Financed by grants & contracts from public & private sector
Publications: Hispanic Arts News, 10 times per yr; weekly listing of arts activities (in English & Spanish)

M **ATLANTIC GALLERY,** 164 Mercer St, 10012. Tel 212-219-3183. *Mgr* Carol Hamann
Open Tues - Sat 11 AM - 5 PM. No admis fee. Estab 1974 as an artist-run gallery presenting the work of members and guests artists in solo exhibitions and group shows. Gallery is 25 x 75 ft second-floor space. Average Annual Attendance: 1200. Mem: 32; dues $90 a month; monthly meetings
Income: Financed by membership and artists of the gallery
Exhibitions: Roslyn Fassett; Invitational. (1991) Horowitz, McD'Miller, Jacobson, O'Toole, Brody, Ed Herman. (1992) Brody, Hamann, Hawkins, Herman
Publications: Periodic flyers
Activities: Lect open to public; life-drawing sessions; concerts; poetry readings; sales shop sells original art

AUDUBON ARTISTS, INC
For further information, see National and Regional Organizations

M **AUSTRIAN CULTURAL INSTITUTE,** Gallery, 11 E 52nd St (Mailing add: 11 E 52nd St, 10022). Tel 212-759-5165; FAX 212-319-9636; Telex 17-7142; Cable AUSTRO-CULT. *Dir* Dr Wolfgang Waldner
Open Mon - Fri 9 AM - 5 PM. Estab 1962 for presentaiton of Austrian Art & culture in America. 10 exhibitions per year, focus on contemporary Austrian art mainly
Exhibitions: Walter Weer, Rudolf Haas, Oskar Hofinger, Haut und Hulle - Photo exhibition, Schmuck Jewelry, The Window - Friedrich Eckhardt
Publications: Austria Kutur, bi-monthly; monthly events calendar

A **LEO BAECK INSTITUTE,** 129 E 73rd St, 10021. Tel 212-744-6400; FAX 212-988-1305. *Exec Dir* Robert A Jacobs; *Pres* Ismar Schorsch; *Art Cur* Jacqueline Rea
Open daily 9 AM - 5 PM; Fri 9 AM - 3 PM Nov - March. No admis fee. Estab 1955 for history of German-Speaking Jewry. Center includes library & archives. Average Annual Attendance: 1000. Mem: 1500; dues $50-$1000
Collections: Drawings, paintings, prints, sculpture, ritual objects, textiles from 15th - 20th centuries; 19th - 20th Century German-Jewish Artists, including Max Liebermann, Lesser Ury, Ludwig Meidner, Hugo Steiner-Prag
Exhibitions: Portraits of German Jews
Publications: Year Book; LBI News, semi-annually
Activities: Educ dept; lectures open to the public, 7 - 10 vis lectr per yr; individual paintings & original objects of art lent to qualified museums
L **Library,** 129 E 73rd St, 10021. Tel 212-744-6400. *Archivist* Diane Spielmann
Open winter Mon - Fri 9 AM - 5 PM, Fri 9 AM - 4 PM; July - Aug 9 AM - 4 PM. Estab 1955 to collect & preserve materials by & about history of German-speaking Jews. For reference only
Income: Financed by endowment & membership
Library Holdings: Vols 50,000; Per subs 150; Micro — Fiche; Other — Original art works 6300, photographs 30,000, prints 5000, sculpture 30
Special Subjects: Drawings, Folk Art, Historical Material, History of Art & Archaeology, Judaica, Painting - German, Portraits, Prints, Stage Design, Watercolors
Collections: †Archival collections relating to German-Jewish life

M **BARTOW-PELL MANSION MUSEUM AND GARDEN,** Shore Rd, Pelham Bay Park, 10464. Tel 718-885-1461; FAX 718-885-1461. *Pres* Lynn Zurcher
Open Wed, Sat & Sun 12 - 4 PM, cl 3 wks in summer. Admis adults $2, children under 12 free. Estab 1914
Collections: Greek revival restoration; period furnishings; paintings; sunken gardens

M **BARUCH COLLEGE OF THE CITY UNIVERSITY OF NEW YORK,** Gallery, 135 E 22nd St (Mailing add: 17 Lexington Ave, PO Box 821, New York, NY 10010). Tel 212-387-1006. *Dir* Sandra Kraskin, PhD
Open Mon - Fri noon - 5 PM, Thurs noon - 7 PM. No admis fee. Estab 1983. 2400 sq ft. Average Annual Attendance: 10,000
Income: $60,000 (financed by endowments, state appropriation)
Publications: Exhibition catalogues
Activities: Lect open to the public, 3 vis lectr per yr; scholarships; book traveling exhibitions once per yr; originate traveling exhibitions once per yr

M **BLUE MOUNTAIN GALLERY,** 121 Wooster St, 10012. Tel 212-226-9402. *Dir* Donna Maria de Creeft
Open Tues - Sun noon - 6 PM. No admis fee. Estab 1980 to exhibit contemporary works of gallery members. 15 ft x 33 ft, white walls, grey floor, & black ceiling. Mem: 25, members must be artists willing to exhibit & sell own work & must be chosen by existing members; memb enrollment fee $450, mem monthly intern $70, out of town $120 monthly; meetings held eery 4-6 weeks

M **CARIBBEAN CULTURAL CENTER,** 408 W 58th St, 10019. Tel 212-307-7420; FAX 212-315-1086. *Exec Dir* Marta Moreno Vega; *Deputy Dir* Laura Moreno; *Dir Special Projects* C Daniel Dawson
Open Tues - Fri 11 AM - 6 PM. Admis $2. Estab 1976. Mem: dues $25
Income: Financed by endowment, mem, city & state appropriations, foundation support
Publications: Caribe Magazine, irregular; occasional papers
Activities: Adult classes; lect open to public, 5-10 vis lectr per year; scholarships offered; retail store sells books, prints, magazines, slides, original art, reproductions, artifacts from the Caribbean, Latin America & Africa

M **CATHEDRAL OF SAINT JOHN THE DIVINE,** 1047 Amsterdam Ave, 10025. Tel 212-316-7493. *Dir* Peggy Harrington
Open Mon - Fri 11 AM - 4 PM, Sat & Sun 1 PM - 4 PM. No admis fee. Estab 1974. The museum building was erected in the 1820's and forms part of the complex of the Cathedral of Saint John the Divine. Average Annual Attendance: 500,000
Income: Financed by federal government appropriations and Cathedral assistance
Collections: Old Master Paintings; decorative arts; sculptures; silver; tapestries; vestments
Exhibitions: Monthly Photography Exhibitions; annual exhibitions planned to spotlight specific areas of the Cathedral's permanent art collection
Activities: Lect open to public, 10 vis lectr per year; concerts; gallery talks; tours

M **CENTER FOR BOOK ARTS, INC,** 626 Broadway, 10012. Tel 212-460-9768. *Dir* Brian Hannon
Open Mon - Fri 10 AM - 6 PM. Estab 1974 as a reference library
Collections: Archive of Book Arts Collection
Publications: Book art review: exhibition catalogues

L **CENTER FOR SAFETY IN THE ARTS,** Art Hazards Information Center, 5 Beekman St, Room 1030, 10038. Tel 212-227-6220. *Exec Dir* Michael McCann
Open by appointment. Estab to make more available research in art hazards. For reference only
Library Holdings: Vols 500
Special Subjects: Visual & performing arts, health & safety
Activities: Adult classes; lectures

C **THE CHASE MANHATTAN BANK, NA,** Art Collection, One Chase Manhatten Plaza, 9th Floor, 10081. Tel 212-552-4794; FAX 212-552-0695. *Exec Dir & VPres* Manuel Gonzalez; *Mgr* Margaret della Cioppa; *Registrar* Katherine Gass; *Asst Cur* Stacy Gershon
Estab 1959 to support young and emerging artists and enhance bank offices world-wide. Collection displayed in branches, offices in New York City, state and world-wide
Collections: Largely contemporary American, 11,500 works in all media
Exhibitions: Selection from the Chase Manhattan Bank Art Collection
Publications: Acquisitions report, annual; Art at Work: The Chase Manhattan Bank
Activities: Lectures for employees; individual objects of art lent to museum and gallery exhibitions; originate traveling exhibitions

M **CHILDREN'S MUSEUM OF MANHATTAN,** 212 W 83rd St, 10024. Tel 212-721-1234. *Assoc Dir* Robert Blandford; *Educ Dir* Valerie Winkler; *Public Program Dir* Gail Tipton
Open Tues - Fri 2 - 5 PM, Sat, Sun & holidays 10 AM - 5 PM. Admis $4. Estab 1973 as a children's museum & art center featuring participatory art, science, & nature exhibits. Average Annual Attendance: 150,000. Mem: 1700; dues $40 - $5000
Income: $2,300,000 (financed by city, state, federal, corporate & foundation support, admis, mem, donations, program fees & tuition, sales shop)
Exhibitions: The Performing Arts & Early Childhood Ed; Time Warner Center for Media; Scholastic Gallery. (1991) Braingames; Magical Patterns
Publications: Monthly calendars; program brochures
Activities: Educ dept with parent/child workshops, toddler programs, summer day camp, outreach, performing artists, volunteer/intern training, teacher training program; scholarships offered; museum sales shop sells books, games, toys

M **CHINA INSTITUTE IN AMERICA,** China House Gallery, 125 E 65th St, 10021. Tel 212-744-8181; FAX 212-628-4159. *Dir* J May Lee
Open Mon - Sat 10 AM - 5 PM. Contribution. Estab 1966 to promote a knowledge of Chinese culture. Two-room gallery. Average Annual Attendance:

12,000. Mem: 1500; dues resident $50, non-resident $35, academic $30, student, $20
Income: $30,000 (financed by membership, government grants and sponsors)
Exhibitions: Art of the Han; Embroidery of Imperial China; Origins of Chinese Ceramics; Treasures from The Metropolitan Museum of Art; Treasures from The Newark Museum; Chinese Porcelain in European Mounts; Tz'u-chou Ware; Masterpieces of Sung & Yuan Dynasty Calligraphy; Communion of Scholars: Chinese Art at Yale; Chinese Bamboo Carving; Chinese Ceramics of the Transitional Period: 1620-1683; Chinese Traditional Architecture; Chinese Printed Books
Publications: Exhibition catalogs
Activities: Classes for adults & children; lectures open to public; concerts; gallery talks; tours; originate traveling exhibitions; sales shop sells books

L **CITY COLLEGE OF THE CITY UNIVERSITY OF NEW YORK,** Morris Raphael Cohen Library, Convent Ave & 138th St, 10031. Tel 212-650-7292. *Acting Chief Librn* Ruth Henderson; *Chief Reference Div* Sally Lyon
Open Mon - Thurs 9 AM - 8 PM, Fri 9 AM - 5 PM, Sat Noon - 6 PM. Estab 1847 to support the education at the City College
Library Holdings: Vols 22,000; Per subs 40; Micro — Fiche; Other — Clipping files, exhibition catalogs, memorabilia, pamphlets
Collections: History of Costume
L **Architecture Library,** 408 Shepard Hall, Convent Ave & 138th St, 10031. Tel 212-650-8768. *Librn* Judy Connorton
Reference use for public; circulation for patrons with CUNY ID's
Library Holdings: Vols 20,000; Per subs 60; Micro — Fiche, reels; AV — A-tapes; Other — Clipping files
Special Subjects: Architecture, Landscape Architecture, Urban Planning

COLLEGE ART ASSOCIATION
For further information, see National and Regional Organization

COLOR ASSOCIATION OF THE US
For further information, see National and Regional Organizations

L **COLUMBIA UNIVERSITY,** Avery Architectural and Fine Arts Library, 117th St W of Amsterdam Ave, 10027. Tel 212-854-3501; FAX 212-854-8904. *Librn* Angela Giral
Open Mon - Thurs 9 AM - 11 PM, Fri 9 AM - 9 PM, Sat noon - 6 PM, Sun 2 - 10 PM. Estab 1890 for reference only. Primarily for reference
Library Holdings: Vols 250,000; Per subs 1000; original documents; Micro — Fiche, reels; Other — Manuscripts, memorabilia, photographs, prints
Special Subjects: Architecture, Art History, City Planning
Collections: Over 200,000 original architectural drawings, mainly American
Publications: Catalog of Avery Memorial Architectural Library; Avery Index to Architectural Periodicals, annually, also available as a data base
L **Dept of Art History & Archeology,** Photograph Collection, 820-825 Schermerhorn Hall, 10027. Tel 212-854-3044; FAX 212-854-7329. *Cur Visual Resources Coll* Linda Strauss
Library Holdings: Gallery announcements 15,000; Other — Photographs 250,000
Collections: Berenson I-Tatti Archive; Dial Iconographic Index; Haseloff Archive; Bartsch Collection; Gaigleres Collection; Arthur Kingsley Porter Collection; Ware Collection; Courtauld Index; Marburger Index; Windsor Castle; Chatsworth Collection; Millard Meiss Collection
M **Art Gallery, Gallery,** Schermerhorn Hall, 8th Floor, 10025. Tel 212-854-7288; FAX 212-854-7329. *Dir* Sarah Elliston Weiner
Open Wed - Sat 1 - 5 PM. Estab 1986 to complement the educational goals of Columbia University & to embody the research interests of Faculty & graduate students in art history. 5 rooms, 2300 sq ft, 310 running ft 4 exhibitions annually during the academic year
Income: $35,000 (financed by endowment & university
Collections: Temoorary exhibitions only
Exhibitions: Money Matters: A critical Look at Bank Architecture

M **CONGREGATION EMANU-EL,** 1 E 65th St, 10021-6596. Tel 212-744-1400; FAX 212-570-0826. *Dir* Reva G Kirschberg; *Cur* Cissy Grossman, MA
Open daily 10 AM - 4 PM. No admis fee. Estab 1928 as a Judaica museum & to show history of congregation. Building is a landmark & is open for touring
Income: Financed by subvention from congregation
Collections: Congregational Memorabilia; Graphics; Judaica; Paintings
Exhibitions: Seasonal exhibits; Congregational History; Photographic exhibit of stained glass; A Temple Treasury, The Judaica Collection of Congregation Emanu-El of the City of New York

M **COOPER-HEWITT, NATIONAL MUSEUM OF DESIGN,** 2 E 91st St, 10128. Tel 212-860-6868; FAX 212-860-6909. *Dir* Dianne Pilgrim; *Cur Decorative Arts* David McFadden; *Cur Drawings & Prints* Marilyn Symmes; *Cur Textiles* Milton Sonday; *Exhib Coordr* Dorothy Twining Globus; *Librn* Stephen Van Dyk
Open Tues 10 AM - 9 PM, Wed - Sat 10 AM - 5 PM, Sun noon - 5 PM, cl Mon & federal holidays. Admis Adults $3, seniors & students $1.50, free admis to members & after 5 PM on Tues. Founded 1895 as the Cooper Union Museum, to serve the needs of scholars, craftsmen, students, designers and everyone who deals with man's living world. Museum is based on large and varied collections of decorative arts, architecture and a library strong in those fields. Exhibitions are based on the Museum's vast collections or loan shows illustrative of each phase of design, and make available the best examples of man's creative genius from the past and present. Its emphasis on education is expanded by special courses and seminars related to design in all forms and of all periods. The Main galleries occupy the first and second floors; exhibitions relate to the collections and some aspects of design; the Design Gallery has changing exhibitions from the permanent collection of architecture and design. Average Annual Attendance: 200,000. Mem: 7000; dues $45-$1000
Income: Financed by private contributions, membership and partly Smithsonian Institution
Collections: Drawings and paintings including works by Frederic Church,

Winslow Homer, Thomas Moran and other 19th century American artists; ceramics, furniture and woodwork, glass, original drawings and designs for architecture and the decorative arts; 15th - 20th century prints; textiles, lace, wallpaper; 300,000 works representing a span of 300 years
Exhibitions: Intimate World of Alexander Calder; Color, Light, Surface: Contemporary Fabrics; Flora Danica & The Heritage of Danish Porcelain; The Doghouse (1992-93) The Power of Maps; Revolution, Life & Labor: Sonet Porcelains 1918 - 1985; From Background to Foreground: Looking at an 18th Century Wallpaper; Czech Cubism
Publications: The Smithsonian Illustrated Library of Antiques; books on decorative arts; collection handbooks; exhibition catalogues; quarterly newsletter
Activities: Classes for adults and children; dramatic programs; docent training; Master's Degree program in European Decorative Arts through Parsons & New School; lect open to public; tours; seminars; concerts; gallery talks; paintings and original objects of art lent to museums and cultural institutions; lending collection contains over 300,000 original prints; book traveling exhibitions; originate traveling exhibitions; museum and sales shop sells books, reproductions, slides, posters
L **Cooper-Hewitt Museum Branch Library,** 2 E 91st St, 10128. Tel 212-860-6887; FAX 212-860-6909. *Librn* Stephen Van Dyk
Open Mon - Fri 9 AM - 5:30 PM
Income: Financed through SIL budgets
Library Holdings: Vols 50,000; Per subs 200; pictures and photographs 1,500, 900, original documents; Other — Exhibition catalogs, manuscripts, memorabilia, photographs, prints, reproductions
Special Subjects: Advertising Design, Decorative Arts, Graphic Design, Industrial Design, Interior Design, Color, Materials of Design
Collections: Donald Deskey Archive; Henry Dreyfuss Archive; Nancy McCelland Archive; Ladislav Sutnar Archive

L **COOPER UNION FOR THE ADVANCEMENT OF SCIENCE & ART,** Library, 41 Cooper Square, 10003. Tel 212-353-4186; FAX 212-353-4345. *Head Librn* Elizabeth Vajda; *Art & Architecture* Ulla Volk; *Slide & Picture* Tom Micchelli; *Engineering & Science* Carol Salomon
Estab 1859 to support the curriculum of the three professional schools: Art, Architecture, Engineering
Library Holdings: Vols 86,500; Per subs 370; Micro — Fiche 3500, reels 3800; AV — Lantern slides, slides 50,000; Other — Clipping files 90,000
Special Subjects: Architecture, Calligraphy, Collages, Commercial Art, Drawings, Etchings & Engravings, Film, Graphic Arts, Graphic Design, Islamic Art, Landscape Architecture, Manuscripts, Maps, Painting - American, Painting - British, Painting - Dutch, Painting - Flemish, Painting - French, Painting - German, Painting - Italian, Painting - Japanese, Painting - Russian, Painting - Spanish, Photography, Posters, Pre-Columbian Art, Prints, Sculpture, Photography
Activities: Non-degree classes for adults; lectures open to the public, 20 - 30 vis lectr per yr; scholarships

A **CREATIVE TIME,** 131 W 24th St, 10011. Tel 212-206-6674; FAX 212-255-8467. *Exec Dir* Cee Brown; *Dir Development* Joyce Lawler
Open Mon - Fri 10 AM - 5 PM, exhibition hrs vary depending on site. Admis performances $8, exhibitions usually free. Estab 1973 to present visual, architecture & performing art programs in public spaces throughout New York City. Spaces include a variety of temporarily unused public locations. Average Annual Attendance: 50,000. Mem: 200; members give tax-deductible contributions
Income: $500,000 (financed by National Endowment for the Arts, NY State Council of the Arts, NYC Dept of Cultural Affairs, private corporations & foundations)
Exhibitions: Art in the Anchorage
Publications: Creative Time; biannual program/project catalogs
Activities: Multi-media, dance & performance art events

M **CULTURAL COUNCIL FOUNDATION,** Fourteen Sculptors Gallery, 164 Mercer St, 10012. Tel 212-966-5790. *Chmn Board of Dir* Siena Porta
Open Tues - Sun 11 AM - 6 PM. No admis fee. Estab 1973 to exhibit emerging & established sculptors. Invitational, curated & traveling exhibitions held annually of artists throughout the US. Average Annual Attendance: 35,000. Mem: 22; mem qualifications: reviewed & interviewed by current gallery artists; dues $700; annual meeting in June
Income: Financed by membership
Publications: Catalogs
Activities: Gallery talks; tours; competitions; originate traveling exhibitions

A **DIA CENTER FOR THE ARTS,** 548 W 22nd St, 10012. Tel 212-431-9232; FAX 212-226-6326. *Exec Dir* Charles B Wright
Estab 1974 for planning, realization and presentation of important works of contemporary art. Committment to artist's participation in display of works in long term, carefully maintained installations. Galleries in US & abroad
Collections: Works by 13 contemporary American & European artists, retrospective in nature; works by Walter De Maria
Exhibitions: (1992) Joseph Beuy: Arena; Robert Gober; Dan Graham
Publications: The Foundation has published collections of poetry & translations of poetry
Activities: Exhibit catalogues; Series of discussions on contemporary cultural issues

A **THE DRAWING CENTER,** 35 Wooster St, 10013. Tel 212-219-2166. *Dir* Ann Philbin; *Dir Operations* Peter Gilmore; *Dir Development* Caroline Harris; *Registrar* Meryl Cohen
Open Tues - Sat 11 AM - 6 PM, Wed 11 AM - 8 PM. Estab 1977 to express the quality and diversity of drawing through exhibition and education. Average Annual Attendance: 125,000. Mem: 300; dues $35 -and up
Exhibitions: Group shows of emerging artists: Selections; The Northern Landscape: Flemish, Dutch, & British Drawings From The Courtauld Collections
Publications: Exhibition catalogs
Activities: Classes for adults and children; lectures open to the public

THE DRAWING SOCIETY
For further information, see National and Regional Organizations

A **ELECTRONIC ARTS INTERMIX, INC,** 536 Broadway, 10012. Tel 212-966-4605; FAX 212-941-6118. *Dir* Lori Zippay; *Editing Post Production Facility* Ivar Smedstad
Open daily 9:30 AM - 5:30 PM. Estab as a non-profit corporation to assist artists seeking to explore the potentials of the electronic media, particularly television, as a means of personal expression
Income: Financed by videotape and editing fees and in part by federal and state funds and contributions
Collections: Several hundred video cassettes
Publications: Electronic Arts Intermix Videocassette Catalog, annual

M **EL MUSEO DEL BARRIO,** 1230 Fifth Ave, 10029. Tel 212-831-7272; FAX 212-831-7927. *Exec Dir* Petra Barreras del Rio; *Chief Cur* Susana Torruella Leval
Open Wed - Sun 11 AM 5 PM, cl Mon & Tues. Admis adults $2, senior citizens & students with ID $1, children under 12 free when accompanied by adult. Estab 1969 to conserve and display works by Puerto Rican artists and other Hispanic artists. Located on Museum Mile. Gallery space divided into 4 wings: Northwest Wing houses Santos de Palo, East Gallery will house Pre-Columbian installation, F-Stop Gallery devoted to photography and Childrens Wing opened fall of 1982. Average Annual Attendance: 19,450. Mem: 250; patron, organization & business $1000, associate $500, sustaining $250, support $100, contributing $50, family $35, individual $25, special $15
Collections: 16mm Films on History, Culture and Art; †300 Paintings and †5000 Works on Paper, by Puerto Rican and other Latin American Artists; Pre-Columbian Caribbean Artifacts; Santos (Folk Religious Carvings)
Activities: Classes for adults and children; dramatic programs; children's workshops; lectures open to public, 25 visiting lecturers per year; concerts; gallery talks; tours; awards; scholarships; individual and original ojbects of art lent to other museums and galleries; originate traveling exhibitions; Junior Museum

M **AMOS ENO GALLERY,** 594 Broadway No 404, 10012. Tel 212-226-5342. *Dir* Daniel B Ferris
Open Tues - Sun 11 AM - 6 PM. No admis fee. Estab 1974
Collections: Contemporary Art

C **EQUITABLE LIFE ASSURANCE SOCIETY,** 787 Seventh Ave, 10019. Tel 212-554-1234. *Cur* Pari Spave; *Asst Cur* Babette Allina
Annual amount of contributions and grants $75,000; supports employee gifts to all arts organizations; direct grants to 8 national arts service organizations
Collections: Commissioned Art Works by: Roy Lichetenstein, Scott Burton, Sol Lewitt, Sandro Chia & The America Today Murals by Thomas Hart Benton
Activities: Support technical assistance programs

M **EXIT ART,** 548 Broadway, 2nd Floor, 10012. Tel 212-966-7745; FAX 212-925-2928. *Dir* Jeannette Ingberman; *Asst Dir* Stuart Anthony; *Admin* Gisella Bacacan; *Co-Founder-Official Poet* Papo Colo
Estab 1982, dedicated to multi-cultural, multi-media enlightenment through presentations & publications, film festivals, exhibitions

M **FASHION INSTITUTE OF TECHNOLOGY GALLERIES,** Seventh Ave at 27th St, 10001-5992. Tel 212-760-7675, 760-7700; FAX 212-760-7978. *Dir* Richard Martin
Open Tues - Fri noon - 8 PM, Sat 10 AM - 5 PM, cl Sun, Mon & holidays. No admis fee. Estab May 1975 to bring to the student body and the community at large a variety of exhibitions in the applied arts. Gallery contains 11,500 sq ft of space divided into four galleries. The gallery on the main floor is used for small exhibits while the three galleries located in the lower level are used for major exhibitions. Average Annual Attendance: 70,000
Income: Financed by endowment and grants
Purchases: Costumes & textile collections, Edward C Blum Design Laboratory
Collections: Largest working costume and textile collection in the world
Publications: Exhibit catalogs
Activities: Classes for adults; docent training; lect open to the public, gallery talks; tours; exten dept serving the museum personnel; individual paintings and original objects of art lent to major museums and art institutions; traveling exhibitions organized and circulated
L **Library,** Seventh Ave at 27th St, 10001-5992. Tel 212-760-7590; FAX 212-760-7268. *Dir* Rochelle Sager; *Ref Head* Beryl Rentof; *Ref & Special Collections* Marjorie Miller; *Ref & Vertical Files* Lorraine Weberg; *Ref & Ill* Stephen Rosenberger; *Acq Head* Judy Wood; *Cat Head* Janette Rozene
Open Mon - Thurs 9 AM - 9 PM, Fri 9 AM - 6:30 PM, Sat & Sun noon - 5 PM. Estab 1948 to meet the academic needs of the students and faculty and to serve as a resource for the fashion industry. Open for reference only
Library Holdings: Vols 98,332; Per subs 527; Artist Books; Micro — Cards, fiche 1313, prints, reels; AV — A-tapes 96, cassettes 794, fs 357, motion pictures 295, rec 335, slides 86,596; Other — Clipping files 7829, exhibition catalogs, memorabilia, original art works 500,000, pamphlets, photographs, prints, reproductions
Special Subjects: Artists Books
Collections: Oral History Project on the Fashion Industry; several sketchbook collections

FEDERATION OF MODERN PAINTERS & SCULPTORS
For further information, see National and Regional Organizations

M **55 MERCER,** 55 Mercer St, 10013. Tel 212-226-8513. *Pres* Robert Sussman
Open Tues - Sat 10 AM - 6 PM. No admis fee. Estab 1970 to give unaffiliated artists a space to show their work. Average Annual Attendance: 8000. Mem: 16; dues $1200; meeting every 2 months
Income: Financed by mem dues
Exhibitions: One Person & Group shows including Anne Barnard, Eric Deiratsch, Hank DeRicco, Charles Farless, Bill Giersbach, Gloria Greenberg,

Betti-Sue Hertz, Eliot Label, Mike Metz, Nancy Olivier, Joyce Robins, Robert Segall, Carol Steen, Robert Sussman, Joy Walker, Diane Whitcomb, Tyler Smith, Carl Plansky, Leslie Wayne, Fran Schalom, Ethlin Honig, Joan Gardner, Bill Hochhausen, Pierre Louaver
Activities: Apprenticeship program; competitions; individual paintings and original objects of art lent to college shows

M **FIRST STREET GALLERY,** 560 Broadway, 10012. Tel 212-226-9127. *Acting Dir* Rallou Hamshaw
Estab 1969 to promote figurative art & artists throughout the US. Artist-run cooperative exhibiting contemporary Realist work. Mem: 25; dues $100; open to Realist artists only; monthly meetings

C **FORBES INC,** 62 Fifth Ave, 10011. Tel 212-620-2389; FAX 212-620-2426. *Cur* Margaret Kelly
Collections: Faberge Imperial Eggs Collection; Peter Paul Rubens canvas; van Gogh drawing; Renoir oil; Victorian paintings Presidential papers; Antique Toys; Contemporary American Art

A **FOTOGRAFICA,** 484 W 43rd St, Suite 22T, 10036. Tel 212-244-5182. *Exec Dir* Perla de Leon; *Asst Dir* Evelyn Collazo, AA
Estab 1982 to promote Latin American photography. Average Annual Attendance: 500. Mem: dues individual $25, group $50, associate $250, patron $500, corporate $1500
Collections: El Dia de Los Muertos

L **FRANKLIN FURNACE ARCHIVE, INC,** 112 Franklin St, 10013. Tel 212-925-4671. *Executive Dir* Martha Wilson; *Dir Coll Management* Michael Katchen; *Prog Dir* Isabel Samaras; *Dir of Development* Jacqueline Shiffman; *Adminr* Harley Spiller
Open Tues - Fri noon - 6 PM, Sat 1 - 6 PM. No admis fee. Estab 1976 as a non-profit corporation dedicated to the cataloging, exhibition & preservation of book-like work by artists, performance art & temporary installations. Mem: dues $45, artists $30
Library Holdings: Vols 9000; AV — A-tapes, slides; Other — Clipping files, exhibition catalogs, memorabilia, original art works, pamphlets, photographs
Special Subjects: Artists' use of language, book works & artists' periodicals, artists' books, mail art, performance art documentation
Publications: FLUE, irregular periodical
Activities: Intern training program; performance program; lectures open to public; gallery talks; tours; original objects of art lent to qualified institutions; book traveling exhibitions; originate traveling exhibitions; museum shop sells magazines

M **FRAUNCES TAVERN MUSEUM,** 54 Pearl St, 10004-2429. Tel 212-425-1778; FAX 212-509-3467. *Dir & Cur* Lauren Kaminsky; *Development Assoc* Lisa Reninger; *Education Coordr* Debbie Longman; *Public Relations Officer* Susan George; *Museum Asst* Maureen Sarro
Open Mon - Fri 10 AM - 4:45 PM. Admis adults $2.50, students, children & senior citizens $1. Estab 1907 for focus on early American history, culture, historic preservation & New York City history. Museum is housed in the site of eighteenth-century Fraunces Tavern and four adjacent nineteenth-century buildings. The museum houses two fully furnished period rooms: the Long Room, site of George Washington's farewell to his officers at the end of the Revolutionary War, and the Clinton Room. a nineteenth-century dining room. Mem: 500; dues $20-$1000
Collections: 17th, 18th, 19th & 20th century prints, paintings, artifacts & decorative arts relating to early American history, culture & historic preservation; New York City history; George Washington & other historic figures in American history
Exhibitions: The Healing Arts in Early America; Tavern Revels; Capital City; NY After the Revolution; Watercolors of Harry Ogden; Education in the Young Republic; The Changing Image of George Washington; To Establish Justice: The 200th Anniversary of the US District Court in New York; Wall Street: Changing Fortunes; Come All You Gallant Heroes; To Please Every Taste
Publications: Exhibit catalogs
Activities: Educ dept; docent training; lectures open to public; tours; demonstrations; films; off-site programs; individual paintings lent to qualified museums & historical organizations, lending collection contains 750 original works of art, 150 original prints, & 1300 decorative art & artifacts; book traveling exhibitions; museum shop sells books, reproductions, prints & slides

L **FRENCH INSTITUTE-ALLIANCE FRANCAISE,** Library, 22 E 60th St, 10022-1077. Tel 212-355-6100; FAX 212-935-4119. *Library Dir* Fred J Gitner; *Asst Librn* Odelia Levanovsky; *Catalog Librn* Eva Goldschmidt
Open Mon - Thurs 10 AM - 8 PM, Fri 10 AM - 6 PM, Sat 10 AM - 1:30 PM (Oct - May). Admis first visit free, $5 daily use fee for non-members. Estab 1911 to encourage the study of the French language and culture. Library lends to members, reference only for non-members; maintains art gallery
Income: Financed by endowment & membership, tax deductible contributions & foundation grants
Library Holdings: Vols 45,000; Per subs 110; AV — Cassettes 900, rec 1350; Other — Exhibition catalogs
Special Subjects: Film, French Art
Collections: †Architecture, †costume, †decorative arts, †paintings
Exhibitions: Rogi Andre: Portraits; Sam Levin: French Stars, portraits; Andre Ostier, portraits
Publications: Acquisitions list, quarterly
Activities: Classes given; lect open to public, 25 vis lectr per yr; concerts; weekly film showings; closed circuit TV screenings

L **FRICK ART REFERENCE LIBRARY,** 10 E 71st St, 10021. Tel 212-288-8700. *Librn* Helen Sanger; *Librn* Andrew W Mellon; *Cataloguer* Patricia D Siska; *Reference Librn, Reading Room* Irene Avens; *Reference Letters* Lydia Dufour; *Assoc Librn* Marie C Keith
Open Sept - July, Mon - Fri 10 AM - 4 PM; Sept - May, Sat 10 AM - noon, cl Sun, holidays & month of Aug. Estab 1920 as a reference library to serve adults

and graduate students interested in the history of European and American painting, drawing, sculpture, illuminated manuscripts. For reference only
Library Holdings: Vols 181,544; 65,581; Micro — Fiche 61; Other — Exhibition catalogs 78,014, photographs 421,183
Publications: Frick Art Reference Library Original Index to Art Periodicals; Frick Art Reference Library Sales Catalogue Index (microform); The Story of the Firck Art Reference Libary: The Early Years, by Katharine McCook Knox

M **FRICK COLLECTION,** One E 70th St, 10021. Tel 212-288-0700; FAX 212-628-4417. *Pres* Henry Clay Frick II; *Dir* Charles Ryskamp; *Cur* Edgar Munhall; *Research Cur* Bernice Davidson; *Deputy Dir Admin* Robert B Goldsmith; *Mgr Sales & Info* Deborah Charlton; *Mgr Bldgs & Secy* Robert J Brady; *Registrar* William G Stout
Open Tues - Sat 10 AM - 6 PM, Sun 1 - 6 PM; cl Jan 1, July 4, Thanksgiving, Dec 24 & 25. Admis adults $3, students & sr citizens $1.50, children under 10 not admitted. Estab 1920; opened to public 1935 as a gallery of art. The Frick Collection is housed in the former residence of Henry Clay Frick (1849-1919), built in 1913-14 and alterations and additions were made 1931-1935 and a further extension and garden were completed in 1977. The rooms are in the style of English and French interiors of the 18th century. Average Annual Attendance: 225,000. Mem: 600 Fellows; dues $500 minimum contribution
Income: $7,780,000 (financed by endowment, membership, admissions)
Collections: 15th-18th century sculpture, of which Renaissance bronzes are most numerous; 14th-19th century paintings, with fine examples of Western European masters and suites of Boucher and Fragonard decorations; Renaissance and French 18th century furniture; 17th-18th century Chinese and French porcelains; 16th century Limoges enamels; 16th-19th century drawings and prints
Exhibitions: In Pursuit of quaility (paintings from the Kimbell Art Museum, Fort Worth). (1991) From Pontormo to Seurat; Nicholas Lancret, 1690 - 1743. (1992) An Album of 19th Century Interiors, Pollaiuolo & Hercules
Publications: French Clocks in North American Collections; The Frick Collection, an Illustrated Catalog; Guide to the Galleries; Handbook of Paintings; Ingres & the Comtesse d'Haussonville; Watercolors by Francois-Marius Granet; exhibition catalogs
Activities: Lect open to public; concerts; museum shop selling books, prints, slides, postcards, greeting cards

C **FRIED, FRANK, HARRIS, SHRIVER & JACOBSON,** Art Collection, One New York Plaza, 10004. Tel 212-820-8000; Telex 747-1526. *Chmn* Arthur Fleischer Jr; *Cur* Brooke Alexander; *Cur* Paula Cooper
Open by appointment. Estab 1979 intended as a survey
Purchases: Over 400 pieces in all offices (NY, DC & LA)
Collections: †Fried, Frank, Harris, Shriver & Jacobson Art Collection; Contemporary Art
Exhibitions: Permanent exhibition
Activities: Tours

M **GALLERY OF PREHISTORIC PAINTINGS,** 30 E 81st St, 10028. Tel 212-861-5152. *Dir* Douglas Mazonowicz
Open by appointment. No admis fee. Estab 1975 to make available to the public the art works of prehistoric peoples, particularly the cave paintings of France, Spain and the Sahara Desert. Large display area. Average Annual Attendance: 10,000
Income: Financed by private funds
Collections: Early American Indian Rock Art; Rock Art of Eastern Spain; Rock Art of the Sahara; serigraph reproduction editions of Cave Art of France and Spain
Publications: Newsletter, quarterly
Activities: Classes for adults and children; Cave Art-in-Schools Program; lect open to the public; gallery talks; tours; lending collection contains books, cassettes, framed reproductions, 1000 Kodachromes, motion pictures, original prints, 1000 photographs, 2000 slides; traveling exhibitions organized and circulated; sales shop selling books, magazines

L **Library,** 30 E 81st St, 10028. Tel 212-861-5152. *Dir* Douglas Mazonowicz
Open Mon - Fri 9 AM - 5 PM, Sat 9 AM - noon. Estab 1975 to make information available to the general public concerning the art works of prehistoric peoples. For reference only
Library Holdings: Vols 250; Per subs 9; AV — Cassettes, Kodachromes, motion pictures, slides; Other — Clipping files, exhibition catalogs, framed reproductions, manuscripts, pamphlets, photographs, prints, reproductions, sculpture

C **THE GILMAN PAPER COMPANY,** 111 W 50th St, 10020. Tel 212-246-3300; FAX 212-582-7610. *Cur* Pierre Apraxime
Collections: Al Reinhardt; Robert Mangold; Ellsworth Kelly; Dan Flavin; Robert Morris; conceptual art; Robert Smithsons Script for the Spiral Jetty; Claes Oldenburg drawing Potatoe; architectural drawings; photography; Cameron; Duchamp; Steiglitz; Sheeler; Moholy-Nagy
Activities: Tours

A **GRAPHIC ARTISTS GUILD,** 11 W 20th St, 10011. Tel 212-463-7730; FAX 212-463-8777. *Exec Dir* Paul Basista
Estab 1967 to improve the economic & social condition of graphic artists; to provide legal & credit services to members; to increase public appreciation of graphic art (including illustration, cartooning & design) as an art form. Mem: 275
Income: Financed by mem & publication sales
Publications: GAG Directory of Illustration, annual; GAG Handbook, Pricing & Ethical Guidelines, biennial; monthly newsletter; cartooning books
Activities: Walter Hortens Memorial Awards for Distinguished Service & Outstanding Client

L **GROLIER CLUB LIBRARY,** 47 E 60th St, 10022. Tel 212-838-6690; FAX 212-838-2445. *Pres* Kenneth A Lohf; *Librn* Martin Antonetti
Open Mon - Sat 10 AM - 5 PM, cl Sun, Sat in the Summer. No admis fee. Estab 1884, devoted to the arts of the book. Mem: 700; annual meetings fourth Thurs of Jan
Purchases: $15,000
Library Holdings: Vols 65,000; Per subs 35; Other — Prints

Special Subjects: Bibliography
Collections: †Bookseller and auction catalogs from 17th century
Exhibitions: Italian & French 16th Century Bookbindings; With Weapons & Wits (WW II); Contemporary American Bookbindings; Modern German Fine Printing
Publications: Rudolph Ruzicka: Speaking Reminiscently (1986); Exhibition Catalog (1989)
Activities: Lect for members only

A **JOHN SIMON GUGGENHEIM MEMORIAL FOUNDATION,** 90 Park Ave, 10016. Tel 212-687-4470. *Pres* Joel Conarroe; *VPres & Secy* G Thomas Tanselle; *Dir Planning & Latin America Prog* Peter Kardon; *Assoc Secy* Sue Schwager; *Treas* Coleen Higgins-Jacob; *Development Officer* Nancy McCabe
Estab & incorporated 1925; offers fellowships to further the development of scholars & artists by assisting them to engage in research in any field of knowledge & creation in any of the arts, under the freest possible conditions & irrespective of race, color or creed. For additional information see section devoted to Scholarships and Fellowships

M **SOLOMON R GUGGENHEIM MUSEUM,** 1071 Fifth Ave, 10128. Tel 212-360-3500. *Dir* Thomas Krens; *Deputy Dir* Diane Waldman; *Admin* Gail Harrity; *Cur* Vivian Endicott Barnett; *Cur Emer* Louise Averill Svendsen; *Comptroller* Stephen Dewhurst; *Asst Cur* Susan B Hirschfeld; *Asst Cur* Lisa Dennison; *Archivist* Ward Jackson; *Conservator* Paul Schwartzbaum; *Photographer* David Heald; *Public Affairs Coordr* Glory Jones; *Asst to Dir* Ann Kraft; *Librn* Sonja Bay; *Asst Librn* Tara Massarsky
Open Wed - Sun 11 AM - 5 PM, Tues 11 AM - 8 PM, cl Mon & holidays. Admis general $3.50, students with valid ID cards and visitors over 62 $2, group rates for students when accompanied by a teacher, children under seven free, Tues eve free. Estab 1937 as a nonprofit organization which is maintained by the Solomon R Guggenheim Foundation; founded for the promotion and encouragement of art and education in art; to foster an appreciation of art by acquainting museum visitors with significant paintings and sculpture of our time. The gallery was designed by architect Frank Lloyd Wright. Average Annual Attendance: 530,000. Mem: 2000; dues $35 - $1000
Income: Financed by endowment, membership and state and federal appropriations
Purchases: Anthony Caro, Richard Long, Robert Rauschenberg, Cy Twombly
Collections: Reflects the creative accomplishments in modern art from the time of the Impressionists to the constantly changing experimental art of today. The collection of nearly four thousand works, augmented by the Justin K Thannhauser Collection of 75 Impressionists and Post-Impressionist masterpieces, including the largest group of paintings by Vasily Kandinsky; one of the largest and most comprehensive collection of paintings by Paul Klee; largest number of sculptures by Constantin Brancusi in any New York museum; paintings by Chagall, Delaunay, Lager, Marc, Picasso, Bacon, Bonnard, Braque, Cezanne, Malevitch, Modigliani, Moore, Reusseau and Seurat, with concentration of works by Dubuffet, Miro and Mondrian among the Europeans; Americans such as Davis, deKooning, Diebenkorn, Gottlieb, Guston, Johns, Lichenstein, Agnes Martin, Motherwell, Nevelson, Noguchi, Pollack, younger artists include Andre, Flavin, Judd, Christensen, Hamilton, Hesse, Mangold, Nauman, Stella and Serra; paintings, drawings and sculpture collections are being enlarged
Exhibitions: (1989) German Painting
Publications: Exhibition catalogs
Activities: Lect open to the public; concerts; gallery talks; acoustiguide tours; individual paintings & original objects of art lent to other museums & galleries; lending collection contains original art works, original prints, painting, sculpture, 10,000 slides; originates traveling exhibitions; museum shop sells books and jewelry

L **Library,** 1071 Fifth Ave, 10028. Tel 212-360-3538, 360-3541. *Librn* Sonja Bay; *Asst Librn* Tara Massarsky
Open by telephone appointment only, Mon - Fri 11 AM - 5 PM. Estab 1952 to document the Museum's collection of 20th century art. For reference only
Library Holdings: Vols 25,000; Per subs 50; Micro — Reels; AV — A-tapes, slides; Other — Clipping files, exhibition catalogs
Collections: Rebay Library

GUILD OF BOOK WORKERS
For further information, see National and Regional Organizations

A **HARVESTWORKS, INC,** 596 Broadway, Suite 602, 10012. Tel 212-431-1130; FAX 212-431-1134. *Dir* Brian Karl; *Dir* Carol Parkinson; *Studio Mgr* Alex Noyes; *Prog Coordr* John McGeehan
Open Mon - Fri 10 AM - 6 PM. Estab 1977 to provide support & facilities for audio art & experimental music. Average Annual Attendance: 2000. Mem: 250; dues $35
Income: $150,000 (financed by endowment, mem, city & state appropriations, recording studio)
Purchases: Pro-tools by Digi Design, Digital Audio Editing
Publications: Tell Us, the Audio Series, 3 - 4 per year
Activities: Adult classes; artist in residence program; lect open to public, 12 vis lectr per year; competitions; scholarships offered; emergency audio services remote recording; retail store sells audio art & music cassettes & CD's

M **HISPANIC SOCIETY OF AMERICA,** Museum, Broadway, Between 155th and 156th Sts, 10032. Tel 212-926-2234. *Pres* George S Moore; *Dir* Theodore S Beardsley Jr; *Cur Mus Paintings & Metalwork* Priscilla E Muller; *Cur Archaeology* Vivian A Hibbs; *Cur Emeritus Sculpture* Beatrice G Proske
Open Tues - Sat 10 AM - 4 PM, Sun 1 - 4 PM. No admis fee. Estab 1904 by Archer Milton Huntingon as a free public museum and library devoted to the culture of Hispanic peoples. Average Annual Attendance: 15,000. Mem: 100 plus 300 corresponding members; membership by election
Income: Financed by endowment
Purchases: Hispanic objects in various media
Collections: †Archaeology; †costumes; customs; †decorative arts of the Iberian peoples; †paintings; †photographic reference files; †sculpture; †prints
Exhibitions: Permanent gallery exhibits are representative of the arts and cultures of Iberian Peninsula from prehistory to the present. Sorolla, an 80th Anniversary

Exhibition
Publications: Works by members of the staff and society on Spanish art, history, literature, bibliography, with special emphasis on the collections of the society
Activities: Sales shop selling books, reproductins & prints

L **Library,** 613 W 155th St, 10032. Tel 212-926-2234. *Cur* Gerald J MacDonald; *Cur Manuscripts & Rare Bks* Sandra Sider
Open Tues - Fri 1 - 4:15 PM, Sat 10 AM - 4:15 PM, cl Aug, Christmas holidays & other holidays. Estab 1904 as a free reference library to present the culture of Hispanic peoples. Reference only
Income: Financed by endowment
Library Holdings: Vols 250,000; Micro — Fiche, prints, reels; AV — Cassettes, fs, lantern slides, motion pictures, rec, slides, v-tapes; Other — Clipping files, exhibition catalogs, manuscripts, memorabilia, original art works, pamphlets, photographs, prints, reproductions, sculpture
Special Subjects: Art, history, literature, general culture of Spain & Portugal

M **HUDSON GUILD NEIGHBORHOOD HOUSE,** Art Gallery, 441 W 26th St, 10001. Tel 212-760-9800. *Gallery Dir* Haim Mendelson
Estab 1948 for exhibition of contemporary art. A modern facility within the Hudson Guild Building. The Art Gallery is also open for all performances of the Hudson Guild Theatre
Income: Financed by the Joe & Emily Lowe Foundation
Exhibitions: (1992) Hispanic Artists in New York. (1993) A Small World Art Festival; A Celebration of Black Creativity; a Celebration of Women's Creativity; Forty Fifth Anniversary Exhibition

M **ILLUSTRATION HOUSE INC,** Gallery, 96 Spring St, 7th floor, 10012. Tel 212-966-9444; FAX 212-966-9425. *Pres* Walt Reed; *VPres* Roger Reed; *Asst Dir* Fred Taraba; *Gallery Mgr* Jim Pratzon; *Painting Restorer* Jill Pratzon
Open 10:30 AM - 5:30 PM. Estab 1974 devoted to exhibition & selling original paintings & drawings of America's great illustrators (1880-1990)
Collections: Illustration Art Reference
Exhibitions: Art Pertaining to illustration (1880-1980) Semi-annual auction of original illustration art of full range of media & genre. (1992) The New Rochelle Nexus; Harvey Dunn: The Heart of Illustration; Vladislaw Benda: Theatre Masks & Exotic Drawings
Publications: The Illustration Collection, subscription
Activities: Sales shop sells books & original art

A **INDEPENDENT CURATORS INCORPORATED,** 799 Broadway, Suite 205, 10003. Tel 212-254-8200; FAX 212-477-4781. *Exec Dir* Susan Sollins; *Assoc Dir* Judith Olch Richards; *Registrar* Jack Coyle
Estab 1975 as a non-profit traveling exhibition service specializing in contemporary art
Income: $230,000
Exhibitions: Selections from the Sol Lewitt Collection; Drawings: After Photography; Large Scale Drawings; After Matisse; Video Transformations; The Analytical Theatre: New Art from Britain; Life & Image; The American Experience: Contemporary Immigrant Artists; Tradition & Conflict: Images of a Turbulent Decade; No Laughing Matter; Contemporary Illustrated Books: Word & Image, 1967 - 1988; Imagenes Liricas; New Spanish Visions; Eye for I: Video Self-Portraits; Dark Decor; Team Spirit; A Different War: Vietnam in Art; Eternal Metaphors: New Art from Italy
Publications: Exhibition catalogs
Activities: Originate traveling exhibitions

M **INTAR LATIN AMERICAN GALLERY,** 420 W 42nd St, 10036. Tel 212-695-6135; FAX 212-268-0102. *Dir* Inverna Lockpez
Open Mon - Fri noon - 6 PM. No admis fee. Estab 1978. Assists and exhibits artists of diverse racial backgrounds. Devoted to artists who inhabit a dimension of their own in which the tension between singularity and universality has been acknowledged successfully. Only Hispanic gallery in area. Average Annual Attendance: 7000
Income: Financed by endowment
Publications: Exhibition catalogues
Activities: Lect open to public; gallery talks; Originates traveling exhibitions

M **THE INTERCHURCH CENTER,** The Interchurch Center Galleries, 475 Riverside Dr, 10115. Tel 212-870-2933; FAX 212-870-2440. *Cur* Dorothy Cochran
Open daily 9 AM - 4:30 PM. No admis fee. Estab 1969
Exhibitions: Rotating exhibits, 10 per year
Publications: 475, monthly

L **The Interchurch Center Library,** 475 Riverside Dr, 10115
For lending & reference. Circ 2000
Income: $6,000,000
Purchases: $6000
Library Holdings: Vols 14,000; Per subs 95
Special Subjects: Religious Art

C **INTERNATIONAL BUSINESS MACHINES CORP,** IBM Gallery of Science & Art, 590 Madison Ave, 10022. Tel 212-745-6100, 745-5214; FAX 212-745-5172. *Dir Cultural Prog* R P Berglund
Open Tues - Sat 11 AM - 6 PM. No admis fee. Estab 1939 to present high quality museum, organized art & science exhibitions; recent facility opened 1983. 11,000 sq ft of exhibition space, 200 seat auditorium. Average Annual Attendance: 500,000
Activities: Docent program; Gallery talks; tours; book traveling exhibitions, 10 - 12 per yr

INTERNATIONAL CENTER FOR ADVANCED STUDIES IN ART
For further information, see National and Regional Organizations

A **INTERNATIONAL CENTER OF MEDIEVAL ART, INC,** The Cloisters, Fort Tryon Park, 10040. Tel 212-928-1146. *Pres* Walter Cahn; *Pres* Marilyn Stokstad; *Treas* Paula Gerson
Estab 1956 as The International Center of Romanesque Art, Inc. The

International Center of Medieval Art was founded to promote greater knowledge of the arts of the Middle Ages, & to contribute to & make available the results of new research. Mem: 1000; dues benefactor $1000, sustaining $500, contributing $100, institutions $50, active foreign countries $35, active US $30, student $15; annual meeting Feb, in conjunction with College Art Association of America
Publications: Gesta (illustrated journal), two issues per year; ICMA Newsletter, 3 issues per year; Romanesque Sculpture in American Collections, New England Museums; Gothic Sculpture in American Collections
Activities: Sponsor sessions at the annual conferences of The Medieval Institute of Western Michigan University, Kalamazoo; keeps its members informed as to events of interest to medievalists; public lect, exhibitions and symposia

M **INTERNATIONAL CENTER OF PHOTOGRAPHY,** 1130 Fifth Ave, 10128. Tel 212-860-1777; FAX 212-360-6490. *Dir* Cornell Capa; *Deputy Dir for Prog* Willis Hartshorn; *Dir Educ* Philip Block; *Deputy Dir for Development* Ann Doherty; *Deputy Dir for Adminr* Steve Rooney; *Public Information Dir* Phyllis Levine; *Cur of Coll* Miles Barth
Open Tues 11 AM - 8 PM, Wed - Sun 11 AM - 6 PM, cl Mon. Admis adults $4, students & sr citizens $2.50, no admis fee Tues 5 - 8 PM. Estab 1974 to encourage and assist photographers of all ages and nationalities who are vitally concerned with their world and times, to find and help new talents, to uncover and preserve forgotten archives and to present such work to the public. Maintains five exhibition galleries showing a changing exhibition program of photographic expression and experimentation by over 350 photographers. Average Annual Attendance: 100,000. Mem: 7000; dues $40 and up
Income: Financed by public and private grants
Collections: The core of the collection is 20th century documentary photography, with a companion collection of examples of master photographs of the 20th century including Siskind, Abbott, Callahan, Feininger, Hine and Cartier-Bresson. Major holdings include works from the documentary tradition as well as fashion and other aesthetic genres
Exhibitions: (1993) Mexico Through Foreign Eyes
Publications: Annual report; monographs; exhibition catalogs
Activities: Classes for adults and children; docent training; workshops; lect open to public, 75 vis lectr per yr; gallery talks; tours; scholarships; original objects of art lent to other museums and educational institutions; book traveling exhibitions; originate traveling exhibitions; museum shop selling books, magazines, prints and postcards

L **Library,** 1130 Fifth Ave, 10128. Tel 212-860-1787.
Reference only
Library Holdings: Vols 4000; Per subs 25; AV — A-tapes, cassettes, fs, Kodachromes, slides, v-tapes; Other — Clipping files, exhibition catalogs, pamphlets
Collections: Archives contains films, video tapes & audio recordings of programs related to photographs in the collections as well as programs about the subject & history of photography

M **Midtown,** 1133 Avenue of the Americas, 10036. Tel 212-768-4682; FAX 212-368-4688. *Dir* Cornell Capa
Open Tues 11 AM - 8 PM, Wed - Sun 11 AM - 6 PM, cl Mon. Admis $4, students & sr citizens $2.50. Estab 1989. Maintains eight exhibition galleries
Activities: Educ dept; classes for adults & children; docent training; lect open to public; gallery talks; tours; scholarships & fels; originate traveling exhibitions; museum shop sells books, magazines, prints & slides

INTERNATIONAL FOUNDATION FOR ART RESEARCH, INC
For further information, see National and Regional Organizations

M **INTERNATIONAL MUSEUM OF AFRICAN ART,** 593 Broadway, 10012. Tel 212-966-1313; FAX 212-966-1432. *Exec Dir* Dr Susan Vogel; *Chmn* Adrian Mnuchin; *Asst Cur* Polly Nooter; *Deputy Dir* Thomas H Wilson; *Comptroller* Albert Hutchinson; *Admin Asst* Carol Braide; *Educ Coordr* Carol Thompson
Open Tues 10 AM - 8 PM, Wed - Fri 10 AM - 5 PM, Sat 11 AM - 5 PM, Sun noon - 5 PM. Voluntary contribution adults $2.50, students, sr citizens, & children $1.50. Estab 1983 to exhibit the best in traditional African art. 5 galleries housed in 2 adjacent recently-restored turn-of- century townhouses. Average Annual Attendance: 12,500. Mem: 800; dues vary
Income: $1,100,000 (financed by mem, foundation grant entrance fees, exhibition fee & tours)
Purchases: $425,000
Exhibitions: African Aesthetics: The Carl Monzin Collection; The Essential Gourd: African Art from the Obvious to the Ingenious; African Masterpieces from Munich: The Staatliches Museum fur Volkerkunde. (1991) Closeup: Lessons in the Art of Seeing African Sculpture
Publications: African Masterpieces from the Musee de L'Homme; Sets, Series & Ensembles in African Art; Exhibition Catalogues
Activities: Docent training; lectures Sundays open to public; 5-10 vis lectr per year; tours; gallery talks; book traveling exhibitions, 1-2 per yr; originate traveling exhibitions to circulate to other museums; museum shop sells catalogues, books

INTERNATIONAL SOCIETY OF COPIER ARTISTS (ISCA)
For further information, see National and Regional Organizations

JAPAN SOCIETY, INC
M **Japan Society Gallery,** 333 E 47th St, 10017. Tel 212-832-1155, 755-6752. *Pres Japan Society* William H Gleysteen Jr; *Dir* Dr Gunhild Avitabile
Open Tues - Sun 11 AM - 5 PM, cl Mon. No admis fee; suggested contribution. Estab 1907, bi-cultural membership organizations to deepen understanding and friendship between Japan and the United States. Reference library. Average Annual Attendance: 50,000 - 100,000. Mem: 3500 individual; dues $750, $500, $250, $125, $60, $45, $20; annual meeting Oct
Income: Financed by mem, grants & donations
Collections: Japan Society permanent collection: ceramics, paintings, prints, sculpture & woodblocks
Exhibitions: (1992) Japanese Folk Art: A Triumph of Simplicity; The Dragon King of the Sea: Japanese Decorative Art of the Meiji Period from the John R Young Collection
Publications: Japan Society Newsletter, monthly; exhibition catalogs
Activities: Classes for adults; lectures; concerts; movies; tours; exhibitions; workshops

L Library, 333 E 47th St, 10017. Tel 212-832-1155; FAX 212-715-1279. *Dir* Reiko Sassa; *Asst Librn* Yozo Horiuchi
Open Tues - Thurs 10 AM - 5 PM. Estab 1971
Income: Financed by membership
Library Holdings: Vols 10,000; Per subs 113; Other — Clipping files, pamphlets
Publications: What Shall I Read on Japan

M THE JEWISH MUSEUM, 1109 Fifth Ave, 10128. Tel 212-423-3200; FAX 212-423-3232. *Dir* Joan H Rosenbaum; *Adminr* Samantha Gilbert; *Chief Cur* Susan T Goodman; *Asst Dir Adminr* Claudette Donlon; *Dir Public Relations* Anne J Scher; *Dir Educ* Judith Siegel; *Asst Dir Programs* Ward Mintz; *Dir Museum Shop* Robin Cramer; *Dir Public Affairs* Philip Meranus; *Cur of Collections* Norman Kleeblatt; *Cur of Judaica* Dr Vivian B Mann
Open Sun, Mon, Wed & Thur 11 AM - 5:45 PM, Tues 11 AM - 8 PM, Fri 11 AM - 3 PM. Admis adults $6, students with ID cards & senior citizens $4, members & children under 12 free. Estab 1904 to preserve and present the Jewish cultural tradition. Three exhibition floors devoted to the display of ceremonial objects and fine art in the permanent collection, special exhibitions from the permanent collections and photographs and contemporary art on loan. Average Annual Attendance: 189,000. Mem: 9300; dues $20 - $300 and up
Income: Financed by membership, grants, individual contributions and organizations
Collections: †Contemporary art; graphics; †Jewish ceremonial objects; †paintings; †textiles; comprehensive collection of Jewish ceremonial art; Harry G Friedman Collection of Ceremonial Objects; Samuel Friedenberg Collection of Plaques & Medals; Rose & Benjamen Mintz Collection of Eastern European Art; Harry J Stein-Samuel Freidenberg Collection of Coins from the Holy Land
Exhibitions: Gardens & Ghettos: The Art of Jewish Life in Italy; Getting Comfortable in New York: The American Jewish Home, 1880 - 1950. (1991) Jacques Lipschitz: A Life in Sculpture (1992) Bridges & Boundaries: African Americans & American Jews
Publications: Newsletter, quarterly; exhibition catalogs; program brochures; posters and graphics; annual report
Activities: Classes and programs for children; docent training; lect open to public; concerts; film screenings; traveling exhibitions organized and circulated museum trips to Europe, once or twice per year; museum shop selling books, magazines, original art, reproductions, prints, slides, needlecrafts, posters, catalogs and postcards
L Library, 1109 Fifth Ave, 10128. Tel 212-423-3200; FAX 212-423-3232. *Cur of Judaica* Dr Vivian B Mann
Reference library open to staff only
Income: Financed by Jewish Museum budget & private sources
Purchases: $3000
Library Holdings: Vols 1250; AV — A-tapes, cassettes, slides, v-tapes; Other — Clipping files, exhibition catalogs, pamphlets, photographs
Special Subjects: Judaica
Collections: Esther M Rosen Slide Library (contains slides of objects in the museum's collection)

A KENKELEBA HOUSE, INC, Kenkeleba Gallery, 214 E Second St, 10009. Tel 212-674-3939. *Dir* Corrine Jennings; *Art Dir* Joe Overstreet
Open Wed - Sat 11 AM - 6 PM. No admis fee. Committed to the goals of presenting, preserving & encouraging the development of art excluded from the cultural mainstream. Supports experimental & interdisciplinary approaches. Features exhibitions of contemporary & modern painting, sculpture, experimental media, performance, poetry readings & literary forums
Collections: 20th Century African American Artists
Exhibitions: (1992) Eleanor Magid & Tom Kendall; Frank Stewart & Adal (photography)

M KENNEDY GALLERIES, Art Gallery, 40 W 57th St, 10019. Tel 212-541-9600; FAX 212-333-7451. *Chmn* Lawrence Fleischman
Open to public with restrictions
Library Holdings: Vols 6500; Per subs 25; VF 10
Special Subjects: American Painting & Sculpture
Exhibitions: (1991) Clarice Smith; Joe O'Sicky; John Marin Show
Publications: American Art Journal

M THE KITCHEN CENTER, 512 W 19th St, 10011. Tel 212-255-5793; FAX 212-645-4258. *Exec Dir* Lauren Amazeen; *Prog Dir* Scott Macaulay; *Publicity Dir* Eric Latzki
Estab 1971 as a center for video art and a showcase for experimental & avant-garde music
Exhibitions: Exhibitions held in the gallery, often incorporating video, audio & experimental performing arts, including dance & performance art

L M KNOEDLER & CO, INC, Library, 19 E 70th St, 10021. Tel 212-794-0567; FAX 212-772-6932. *Librn* Melissa DeMedeiros
Open Mon - Fri 10 AM - 5 PM to researchers by appointment only. Research by appointment on a fee basis, for scholars, museum curators & students use
Income: Financed by usage fees
Library Holdings: Vols 50,000; Per subs 20; auction catalogs; Micro — Fiche; Other — Clipping files, exhibition catalogs, pamphlets, photographs
Special Subjects: Painting - American, Painting - European, Modern & Contemporary Art

M LAMAMA LA GALLERIA, 6 E First St, 10003. Tel 212-505-2476. *Dir & Cur* Lawry Smith
Open Tues - Sun 1 - 6 PM. Admis by donation. Estab 1983 for exhibition of emerging artists. 2500 sq ft, bi-level. Average Annual Attendance: 10,000. Mem: 3000; dues $20; biennial meetings in Oct & May
Activities: Classes for adults & children; lectures open to public, 6 vis lectr per year; concerts; gallery talks

M LINCOLN CENTER FOR THE PERFORMING ARTS, Cork Gallery, 132 W 65th St, 10023. Tel 212-875-5151; FAX 212-769-1551. *Pres* Nathan Leventhal; *Community Relations* Jenneth Webster
Open Mon - Sun 10 AM - 10 PM. No admis fee. Estab in 1971 to provide a show case for young & unknown artists. One 60 ft x 10 ft wall covered in white linen, two smaller walls, 11 ft & 8 ft 6 inches, respectively, plus two 15 ft bay windows. Average Annual Attendance: 15,000
Exhibitions: (1992) Medarts International Exhibition; Phil Sherrod & Street Painters Society; National Academy of Design; Art Students League; West Side Arts Coalition; Queens Center for Independent Living; Ana Pellicer's Hulama Project; Hell's Kitchen Aids Project, Creative Artists' Network

M MANHATTAN PSYCHIATRIC CENTER'S SCULPTURE GARDEN, Ward's Island, 10035. Tel 212-369-0500, Ext 3022. *Project Coordr* Helen Thomas
Open Mon - Sun 10 AM - sundown. No admis fee. Estab 1977 to enhance hospital environment & offer exhibition area to new as well as established sculptors. 122 acres of hospital grounds are used to site outdoor sculpture, mostly on temporary basis. Project is organized in affiliation with the art organization, Artists Representing Environmental Art (AREA) through Apr 1987. After that date artists may contact Manhattan Psychiatric Center directly to arrange for possible display of work
Collections: The Emerging Sun, Vivienne Thaul Wechter; Silent Columns, Penny Kaplan; Rock Garden Sanctuary, Gigi & Paul Franklin; Map of Time, Time of Map, Toshio Sasaki; The Gazebo, Helene Brandt; Revolve, Jiro Naito
Exhibitions: Sculpture on Shoreline Sites; Ward's Island Inland Show Continued; Roman Garden Sites Continued; Steel Toys, Elizabeth Egbert; Untitled, Stephen Keltner; Clovis, Glen Zwygardt; A Pleasant Square, Raphaela Pivetta

C MANUFACTURERS HANOVER, 270 Park Ave, 11th Floor, 10017. Tel 212-270-5141. *Cur* Claudia Mengel
Collections: 19th century American paintings and prints; 20th century and contemporary paintings; sculpture; graphics; antique furniture; decorative arts; textiles

M THE MARBELLA GALLERY INC, 28 E 72, 10021. Tel 212-288-7809.
Estab 1971 to buy & sell American art of the 19th century & early 20th century
Activities: Lect open to public; book traveling exhibitions 2 per year

M MARYMOUNT MANHATTAN COLLEGE GALLERY, 221 E 71 St, 10021. Tel 212-517-0400. *Dir* Karen Harris
Open 12:30 - 8 PM. No admis fee. Estab 1982 as a showcase for unaffiliated artists. Gallery is 30 x 40 ft. Average Annual Attendance: 2500
Exhibitions: Dorothy Gillespie; Liz Whitney Quisgar
Activities: Lectures by artist

M THE METROPOLITAN MUSEUM OF ART, Main Bldg, 1000 Fifth Ave, 10028. Tel 212-535-7710 (General Information), 879-5500 (Museum Offices); FAX 212-570-3970. *Chmn Board Trustees* Arthur Ochs Sulzberger; *Pres* William H Luers; *Dir* Philippe de Montebello; *Assoc Dir* Penelope K Bardel; *Deputy Dir Educ* Kent Lydecker; *Dir Communiations* Harold Holzer; *Exec VPres & Counsel* Ashton Hawkins; *VPres Operations* Richard Morsches; *VPres Finance & Treas* Diana T Murray; *VPres Development & Membership* Emily Rafferty; *VPres Merchandising Activities* John Curran; *Admin Human Resources* Carol S Cantrell; *Chmn American Art Dept* John K Howat; *Cur American Decorative Art* Morrison H Hecksher; *Chmn Ancient Near Eastern Art* Prudence O Harper; *Cur Arms & Armor* Stuart Pyhrr; *Chief Librn* William B Walker; *Assoc Cur Drawings* Helen Mules; *Cur Egyptian Art* Dorothea Arnold; *Lila Acheson Wallace Research Cur Egyptology* Christine Lilyquist; *Chmn European Paintings* Everett Fahy; *Cur-in-Charge Prints & Illustrated Books* Colta Ives; *Chmn European Sculture & Decorative Arts* Olga Raggio; *Sr Cur Asian Art* James C Y Watt; *Cur Asian Art* Martin Lerner; *Cur-in-Charge Greek & Roman Art* Carlos A Picon; *Cur Greek & Roman Art* Joan R Mertens; *Cur Robert Lehman Collection* Laurence Kanter; *Cur Musical Instruments* Laurence Libin; *Cur American Paintings & Sculpture* H Barbara Weinberg; *Cur Arts of Africa, Oceania & the Americas* Julie Jones; *Cur Costume Institute* Richard Martin; *Special Consultant for Asian Affairs* Wen Fong; *Cur Islamic Art* Daniel Walker; *Chmn Medieval Art & the Cloisters* William D Wixoma; *Chmn Twentieth Century Art* William S Lieberman; *Conservator Objects* James H Frantz; *Conservator Paintings* Hubert von Sonnenberg; *Conservator-in-Charge Paper* Helen K Otis; *Conservator Textiles* Nobuko Kajitani; *Cur Photographs* Maria Hambourg; *Program Mgr Concerts & Lectures* Hilde Limondjian
Open Tues - Thurs & Sun 9:30 AM - 5:15 PM, Fri & Sat 9:30 AM - 8:45 PM, cl Mon. Admis suggested for adults $6, students & sr citizens $3. Estab 1870 to encourage and debelop the study of the fine arts, and the application of arts to life; of advancing the general knowledge of kindred subjects, and to that end of furnishing popular instruction and recreation. Average Annual Attendance: 4,700,000. Mem: 97,245; dues $4000, sponsor $2000, donor $900, contributing $600, sustaining $300, dual $125, individual $70, student $30, national associate $35
Income: $78,146,461 (financed by endowment, mem, city & state appropriations & other)
Collections: †Acquisitions-Departments: Africcna, Oceanic; American decorative arts, paintings & sculpture; †Ancient Near Eastern art; †arms & armor; †Asian art; †Costume Institute; †drawings; †Egyptian art; †European paintings, sculpture & decorative arts; †Greek & Roman art; †Islamic art; Lehman Collection, †medieval art & The Cloisters; †musical instruments; †prints; †photographs; †Twentieth Century Art Exhibitions
Publications: Bulletin, quarterly; Calendar, bi-monthly; The Journal, annually; exhibition catalogs, scholarly books
Activities: Classes for adults and children; docent training; films; programs for the disabled touch collection; lectures open to public; concerts; gallery talks; tours; outreach; scholarships; extin serves community programs for greater New York City area; color reproductions, individual paintings & original objects of art lent to other institutions; book traveling exhibitions; originate traveling exhibitions to US museums; museum shop sells books, magazines, original art, reproductions, prints, slides, children's activities, records, post cards & posters

L **Thomas J Watson Library,** Fifth Ave at 82nd St, 10028. Tel 212-879-5500, Ext 3221. *Chief Librn* William B Walker; *Acquisitions Librn & Bibliographer* Doralynn Pines; *Systems Reference Librn* Patricia J Barnett; *Serials Librn* Trevor Hadley; *Reader Servs Librn* Linda Seckelson; *Conservation Librn* Mindell Dubansky
Open Tues - Fri 10 AM - 4:45 PM, cl holidays and Aug. Estab 1880 for the use of the curatorial, educational and other staff; privileges are extended to qualified researchers and graduate students with appropriate identification. Reference library
Income: Financed by endowment
Library Holdings: Vols 300,000; Per subs 2250; original documents, auction catalogs; Micro — Fiche, reels; AV — Fs; Other — Clipping files, exhibition catalogs, manuscripts, memorabilia, pamphlets
Special Subjects: Aesthetics, Afro-American Art, American Western Art, Antiquities-Assyrian, Antiquities-Byzantine, Antiquities-Egyptian, Antiquities-Etruscan, Antiquities-Greek, Antiquities-Oriental, Antiquities-Persian, Painting, Prints and Drawings of all Countries and Periods
Collections: Art Auction Catalogs

L **Dept of Prints & Illustrated Books,** 1000 Fifth Ave, 10028-0198. Tel 212-570-3920; FAX 212-570-3879. *Cur in Charge* Colta Ives; *Cur* Mary L Myers
Open Tues - Fri 10 AM - 12:30 PM & 2 - 5 PM by appointment. Estab 1917 to collect & preserve prints, illustrated books & drawings for ornament & architecture. Has 3 exhibition galleries
Library Holdings: Other — Original art works, prints
Special Subjects: Architecture, Art History, Decorative Arts, Drawings, Etchings & Engravings, Illustration, Landscape Architecture, Portraits, Printmaking, Prints, Woodcuts, Bookplates, Lithographs, Illustrated Books

L **Photograph and Slide Library,** Fifth Ave at 82nd St, 10028. Tel 212-879-5500, Ext 3261. *Chief Librn* Priscilla Farah; *Librn* Susan Melick; *Assoc Museum Librn* Mary Doherty; *Asst Museum Librn* Beatrice Epstein; *Asst Museum Librn* Carolyn Lucarelli
Open Tues - Fri 10 AM - 4:45 PM, cl holidays and Aug. Estab 1907 to provide a circulation (rental) library of slides covering the history of art; to provide color transparencies and photographs of the collections of the Metropolitan Museum of Art for publication purposes. Circ 100,000
Library Holdings: Color transparencies; AV — Lantern slides, slides 400,000; Other — Photographs
Special Subjects: Art History, Collections of the Metropolitan Museum of Art, particularly complete coverage of Western and European decorative arts
Collections: William Keighley Slide Collection covering Asia Minor, Austria, France, Germany, Italy and Spain; architecture and other arts of various periods

L **Robert Goldwater Library,** 1000 Fifth Ave, 10028-0198. Tel 212-570-3707. *Librn* Peter Blank; *Asst Museum Librn* Ross Day
Open Tues - Fri 10 AM - 4:30 PM. Estab 1957 as the library of the Museum of Primitive Art; holding of the Metropolitan Museum as of 1976; open Feb 1982
Income: Financed by endowment
Library Holdings: Vols 30,000; Per subs 175; Micro — Fiche, reels
Special Subjects: Anthropology, Archaeology, Ethnology, African, American Indian, Eskimo, Oceanic, Pre-Columbian and Primitive art
Publications: Primitive Art Bibliographies (1963 - 1971); Catalog of the Robert Goldwater Library (1982, 4 vols)

L **Robert Lehman Collection Library,** Fifth Ave at 82nd St, 10028. Tel 212-879-5500, Ext 3662. *Librn* Nicole Leibow-Giegerich
Estab 1975 to provide museum staff & researchers with a resource from which to obtain information about the Lehman Collection. Open by appointment only
Income: Financed by endowment
Library Holdings: Vols 15,000; Per subs 54; Original documents; Other — Clipping files, exhibition catalogs, manuscripts, memorabilia, pamphlets, photographs, reproductions
Special Subjects: Western European arts from the 13th - 20th Centuries with special emphasis on the art of Siena, Old Master drawings and Renaissance decorative arts
Collections: Archives containing books, correspondence, manuscripts and reproductions; photograph collection

L **Irene Lewisohn Costume Reference Library,** 1000 Fifth Ave, 10028. Tel 212-879-5500, Ext 3908; FAX 212-570-3970. *Head Librn* Robert C Kaufmann; *Ref Librn & Cataloger* Dorothy K Hesselman
Open Tues - Thurs by appointment. Estab 1946 to study costume history, fashion and theatre design and any subject related to the subject of dress. For reference only
Income: Financed by bequest
Library Holdings: Vols 10,000; Per subs 52; fashion plates, original fashion sketches; Other — Clipping files, memorabilia, photographs, prints
Special Subjects: Costume Design & Construction, Fashion Arts, Jewelry
Collections: Mainbocher Fashion Sketches

L **Uris Library,** Fifth Ave at 82nd St, 10028. Tel 212-879-5500, Ext 3788. *Asst Museum Librn* Mary Grace Whalen
Open Tues - Thurs, Sun 10 AM - 4:30 PM, Fri & Sat 10 AM - 8:30 PM. The Uris Library & Resource Center is part of the educ department
Library Holdings: Vols 4000; AV — Cassettes 500, fs 1250
Special Subjects: Art Education, Art History, Antiquities, Portraits, Primitive art, Sculpture, Tapestries

M **The Cloisters,** Fort Tryon Park, 10040. Tel 212-923-3700; FAX 212-795-3640; Cable CLOMUSE. *Chmn* William D Wixom; *Cur* Jane Hayward; *Assoc Cur* Timothy Husband; *Head Admin* George Lonsdors
Open Tues - Sat 10 AM - 4:45 PM, Sun & holidays Oct - April 1 - 4:45 PM, May - Sept noon - 4:45 PM. Estab 1938 to display in an appropriate setting works of art and architecture of the Middle Ages. Medieval French cloisters incorporated into the building, as well as the chapter house, a chapel, and Romanesque apse; also Medieval herb garden. Average Annual Attendance: 240, 000
Library Holdings: Vols 360,000; Per subs 1800
Collections: Frescoes, ivories, precious metalwork, paintings, polychromed statues, stained glass, tapestries, and other French and Spanish architectural elements
Exhibitions: The Wild Man: Medieval Myth and Symbolism; The Royal Abbey of Saint-Denis in the Time of Abbot Suger (1122-1151)
Publications: A Walk Through The Cloisters; exhibition catalogs
Activities: Classes for adults and children; dramatic programs; lect open to public; concerts; original objects of art lent to other museums; museum shop sells books, reproductions and slides

L **The Cloisters Library,** Fort Tryon Park, 10040. Tel 212-923-3700, Ext 154; FAX 212-795-3640. *Asst Museum Librn* Lauren Jackson Beck
Open Tues - Fri 9:30 AM - 4:30 PM. Estab 1938 to be used as a small highly specialized reference library for the curatorial staff at The Cloisters; scholars and accredited graduate students are welcome and qualified researchers by appointment only. For reference only
Income: Financed by endowment
Library Holdings: Vols 10,000; Per subs 53; original documents; Micro — Fiche 9000; AV — Slides 20,000; Other — Exhibition catalogs, photographs 22,000
Collections: George Grey Barnard Papers; Demotte Photograph Archive; Archives of The Cloisters

L **MIDMARCH ASSOCIATES,** Women Artists News Archive, 300 Riverside Dr, Apt 8A, 10025. Tel 212-666-6990. *Ed* Rena Hansen; *Exec Dir* Cynthia Navaretta
Open by appointment. Estab 1975 to maintain archival material on women artists world wide
Income: Financed by public funding & contributions
Library Holdings: Other — Clipping files, exhibition catalogs, manuscripts, memorabilia, original art works, pamphlets, photographs, sculpture
Special Subjects: Architecture, Art History, Ceramics, Conceptual Art, Constructions, Crafts, Decorative Arts, Drawings, Film, Latin American Art, Mixed Media, Pre-Columbian Art, Sculpture, Theatre Arts, Watercolors
Publications: Essays on Women Photographers 1840 - 1930; guide to Women's Art Organizations & Directory for the Arts, bi-annually; Regional Series on Women Artists (New England, Texas, California, Pacific Northwest), annually; Voices of Women; Women Artists of the World; Women Artists News, bimonthly; Talk That Changed Art, 1975 - 1990; Beyond Walls & Wars: Art, Politics & Multiculturalism
Activities: Education department; lectures provided

L **PIERPONT MORGAN LIBRARY,** 29 E 36th St, 10016. Tel 212-685-0008; FAX 212-685-4740. *Pres* S Parker Gilbert; *Dir* Dr Charles E Pierce Jr; *Asst Dir* William M Jackson; *Cur Printed Books & Bindings* H George Fletcher; *Cur Medieval & Renaissance Manuscripts* Dr John H Plummer; *Cur Medieval & Renaissance Manuscripts* William M Voelkle; *Emeritus Cur Drawings & Prints* Felice Stampfle; *Cur Drawings & Prints* Cara D Denison; *Cur Autograph Manuscripts* Robert Parks; *Cur Music Manuscripts* J Rigbie Turner; *Cur Gilbert & Sullivan Coll* Frederic W Wilson; *Assoc Cur Printed Books* Anna Lou Ashby; *Head Reader Serv* Inge Dupont; *Registrar* David W Wright; *Public Affairs* Elizabeth Wilson; *Honorary Cur Seals & Tablets* Dr Edith Porada
Open Tues - Sat 10:30 AM - 5 PM, Sun 1 - 5 PM, cl Mon & Sun during July & Aug; reading room open to scholars Mon - Fri 9:30 AM - 4:45 PM. No admis fee; suggested donation $5. Estab 1924 for research & exhibition purposes. The Gallery has changing exhibition with Old Master drawings, Medieval and Renaissance illuminated manuscripts, rare printed books, and literary, historical, and music manuscripts. Average Annual Attendance: 200,000. Mem: 1100; dues $35, $50
Income: $4,000,000 (financed by endowment and membership)
Purchases: $1,000,000
Library Holdings: Vols 50,000; Per subs 170; original documents; AV — Slides; Other — Manuscripts, original art works
Collections: Ancient written records including seals, cuneiform tablets and papyri; art objects; †autograph manuscripts; †book bindings; †early children's books; †Medieval & Renaissance illuminated manuscripts; †later printed books; †letters and documents; mezzotints; modern calligraphy; †music manuscripts; †original drawing from 14th-19th centuries; †printed books before 1500; Rembrandt prints
Exhibitions: Small Mischief; Master Drawings from the Albertina; Drawings from the E V Thaw collection; the Apocalypse: 950 - 1800; Italian drawings from the collection of Duke Roberto Ferretti; Merchants to Emperors: British Artists in India; Mahler & Liszt
Publications: Report to the Fellows, triennial; books; catalogs; facsimiles
Activities: Lect open to the public, 8 vis lectr per year; tours; sales shop sells books, reproductions, prints, slides, cards, calendars, address books and posters

M **MORRIS-JUMEL MANSION, INC,** 1765 Jumel Terrace, 10032. Tel 212-923-8008. *Pres* Carolyn Denerstein; *Dir* Penelope Savalas
Open Tues - Sun 10 AM - 4 PM. Admis adults $3. Estab 1904 as a Historic House Museum. Morris-Jumel Mansion consists of ten period rooms which are restored to represent the colonial, revolutionary & nineteenth century history of the mansion, highlighting its interesting owners & inhabitants (the Morris family, George Washington, M Jumel & Aaron Burr). Average Annual Attendance: 30, 000. Mem: 26; contributors 700; dues $25 - $5000
Income: Financed by mem, contributions, federal, state, city & private sources
Collections: Architecture; †decorative art; †furniture of the 18th & 19th centuries
Publications: Morris-Jumel News, quarterly; exhibitions catalogs
Activities: Educ dept; docent training; lectures open to the public; concerts; tours; traveling exhibitions organized and circulated; sales shop sells books, postcards, souveniers

A **MUNICIPAL ART SOCIETY OF NEW YORK,** 457 Madison Ave, 10022. Tel 212-935-3960; FAX 212-753-1816. *Pres* Kent Barwick; *Chmn* Steve Swid
Estab 1892, incorporated 1898. The Society is the one organization in New York where the layman, professional and business firm can work together to encourage high standards for public art, architecture, planning, landscaping and preservation in the five boroughs. Mem: 4500; dues $25 and up; annual meeting June
Collections: Photographs
Exhibitions: Reviewing the City's Edge; Rare Photographs by Stanford White
Publications: The Livable City, quarterly

L **Information Exchange,** 457 Madison Ave, 10022. Tel 212-935-3960; FAX 212-753-1816. *Acting Dir* Ann Anielewski
Open Mon - Fri 10 AM - 1 PM. Estab 1979. For reference only
Library Holdings: Vols 1000; Per subs 100; Other — Clipping files, exhibition catalogs, pamphlets
Special Subjects: Architecture, Historic Preservation, Landscape Architecture, Public Art, Urban Planning in New York City
Publications: Information sheets, irregular

M **MUSEUM OF AMERICAN FOLK ART,** 2 Lincoln Square, 61 W 62nd St, 10023. Tel 212-977-7298, Gallery 595-9533. *Dir* Gerard C Wertkin
Open Tues - Sun 11:30 AM - 7:30 PM, cl Mon. No admis fee, suggested donation $2. Estab 1961 for the collection & exhibition of American folk art in all media, including painting, sculpture, textiles & painted & decorated furniture. Single floor, cruciform shape gallery approx 3000 sq ft. Average Annual Attendance: 100,000. Mem: 5000; dues $35 & up
Income: Financed by membership, state appropriation, personal donations
Collections: American folk paintings & watercolors; folk sculpture including shop & carousel figures, shiphead figures, decoys, weathervanes, whirligigs, wood carvings & chalkware; painted & decorated furniture; tradesmen's signs; textiles including quilts, coverlets, stenciled fabrics, hooked rugs & samplers
Publications: The Clarion, quarterly magazine
Activities: Educ dept; classes for adults; docent training; lect open to public; gallery talks; tours; scholarships & fels; outreach programs; book traveling exhibitions; originate traveling exhibitions to qualifying art & educational institutions; museum shop sells books, reproductions & prints

L **Library,** 2 Lincoln Square, 10023. Tel 212-977-7298, 977-7170. *Librn* Jill Keefe
Not open to public; reference library
Library Holdings: Vols 5000; Per subs 32; AV — Fs, motion pictures, slides, v-tapes; Other — Clipping files, exhibition catalogs, manuscripts, memorabilia, pamphlets, photographs, prints, reproductions

M **MUSEUM OF MODERN ART,** 11 W 53rd St, 10019-5498. Tel 212-708-9400, (Exhibit & Film Info) 708-9480; FAX 212-708-9889; Telex 6-2370; Cable MODERNART. *Chmn of Board* David Rockefeller; *Pres Emeritus* Mrs John D Rockefeller III; *Pres* Agnes Gund; *Chmn Emeritus* William S Paley; *VChmn Emeritus* Mrs Henry Ives Cobb; *VChmn* Mrs Frank Y Larkin; *VChmn* Donald B Marron; *VChmn* Gifford Phillips; *VPres* Ronald S Lauder; *VPres* Richard E Solomon; *VPres & Treas* John Parkinson III; *Dir Museum* Richard E Oldenburg; *Deputy Dir, Development & Public Affairs* Sue B Dorn; *Deputy Dir, Planning & Prog Support* James Snyder; *Deputy Dir Curatorial Affairs* Riva Castleman; *Dir Dept Film* Mary Lea Bandy; *Coordr Exhib* Richard Palmer; *Dir International Prog* Waldo Rasmussen; *Dir Public Information* Jeanne Collins; *Actig Dir Educ* Carol Morgan; *Dir Publications* Osa Brown; *Dir Development* Dan Vecchitto; *Dir Visitor Servs* Jo Pike; *Dir Dept Painting & Sculpture* Kirk Varnedoe; *Dir Dept Drawings* John Elderfield; *Dir Dept Architecture & Design* Terence Riley; *Dir Dept Photography* Peter Galassi
Open Mon, Tues, Fri, Sat & Sun 11 AM - 6 PM; Thurs 11 AM - 9 PM; cl Wed and Christmas. Admis adults $7.50, students & sr citizens $4.50, children under 16 accompanied by adult free, Thurs 5 - 9 PM pay what you wish. Estab 1929, the Museum offers an unrivaled survey of modern art from 1880 to the present. Designed in 1939 by Phillip Goodwin & Edward Durell Stone, the building is one of the first examples of the International Style in the US. Subsequent expansions took place in the 1950s & 1960s under the architect Philip Johnson, who also designed the Abby Aldrich Rockefeller Sculpture Garden. A major renovation, completed in 1984, doubled the Museum's gallery space & enhanced visitor facilities. Average Annual Attendance: 1,300,000. Mem: 52,000; dues student $25, others $45 & up
Income: Financed by admissions, membership, sales of publications and other services and contributions
Collections: †Painting & sculptures over 2963; †drawings 5090; †prints 15,822; †illustrated books 20,423; †photographs 15,000; †architectural drawings; †architectural models; †design objects; †posters & graphics 5777; films 10,000; †film stills over 3,000,000
Exhibitions: (1991) The Gardens of Roberto Burle Marx: The Unnatural AA of the Garden (landscape architecture); Liubov Popova (paintings, works on paper, textile); British Photography from the Thatcher Years; Art of the Forties; Projects: Michael Craig-Martin (contemporary British art); Seven Master Printmakers: Innovations in the 1980s; Hines V: Tadao Ando (Japanese architecture); Ad Reinhardt (paintings, collages, & drawings); Pleasures & Terros of Domestic Comfort (photography). (1992) Projects: Art Spiegleman; Master Prints from the Collection; For Twenty-Five Years: Gemini GEL; Lighting from the Sixties & Seventies; Richard Serra: Afangar Icelandic Series; Gay Block: Rescuers of the Holocaust; Frank Gehry: New Furniture Prototypes; The William S Paley Collection; Allegories of Modernism: Contemporary Drawing; Gertrude Kasebier; Kaj Franck: Designer; Antoni Tapies in Print; Projects: Felix Gonzalez-Torres; Louis I Kahn: In the Realm of Architecture; Henri Matisse: A Retrospective; The Artist & the Book in Italy; The Indy Race Car. (1993) Thinking is Form: Drawings of Joseph Beuys; Latin American Artists of the Twentieth Century
Publications: Annual report; books on exhibitions & artists; Members Quarterly; Members Calendar; monographs; catalogs; exhibitions catalogs
Activities: Symposia; film showings, international in scope, illustrating the historic and esthetic development of the motion picture; lectr; concerts; art advisory service; originates traveling exhibitions; circulating film programs and video programs; bookstore selling publications, postcards, note and seasonal cards, posters, slides, calendars, design objects & furniture

L **Library,** 11 W 53rd St, 10019-5498. Tel 212-708-9433, 708-9430; FAX 212-708-9889; Telex 6-2370. *Dir* Clive Phillpot; *Asst Dir* Janis Ekdahl; *Assoc Librn Cataloguing* Daniel Starr; *Assoc Librn Reference* Eumie Imm
Open Mon - Fri 11 AM - 5 PM. Estab 1929 as a research library. For museum staff, art researchers & the public
Library Holdings: Vols 100,000; Per subs 250; 25,000 Artists files; Micro — Reels; AV — Cassettes, v-tapes; Other — Clipping files, exhibition catalogs, manuscripts, pamphlets
Special Subjects: Architecture, Drawings, Film, Graphic Arts, Mixed Media, Photography, Sculpture, Design, Painting, Intermedia
Collections: †Archives of artists' groups; †artists' books; †avant-garde art; †Dada & Surrealism; †archive of museum publications; †Latin American art; personal papers of artists, writers, dealers; political art documentation/archives
Exhibitions: Fluxus: Selections from the Gilbert & Lila Silverman Collection, 1988-89 (catalog)
Publications: Annual Bibliography of Modern Art; catalog of the Library of the Museum of Modern Art

M **MUSEUM OF THE CITY OF NEW YORK,** 1220 Fifth Ave, 10029. Tel 212-534-1672; FAX 212-534-5974. *Dir* Robert R Macdonald; *Deputy Dir for Admin & Finance* Ed Henry; *Assoc Dir Public Prog* Dr Andrew Svedlow; *Deputy Dir Membership & Development* Dr Sally Yerkovich
Open Tues - Sat 10 AM - 5 PM, Sun & holidays 1 - 5 PM, cl Mon. No admis fee. Estab 1923 to preserve the cultural accomplishments of New York City and to meet the needs and interests of the community of today. Average Annual Attendance: 200,000. Mem: 2500; dues $20 and up
Income: $3,000,000 (financed by private & non-profit institutions, individual contributions, city, state & federal funds)
Collections: †Costume collection; †decorative arts collection; †paintings, sculpture, prints and †photographs collection; theatre and †music collection; †toy collection
Exhibitions: (1991) The Gibson Girl; Within Bohemia's Borders: Greenwich Village 1830 - 1930, Paintings of Theresa Bernstern; Artistic New York of Louis Comfort; Tiffany. (1993) Jews in Colonial New York - The Levy Franks Family Portraits; Growing Old in Spanish Harlem; Broadway - 125 Years of Musical Theatre; Songs of My People - An African-American Self- Portrait
Publications: Annual Report; Newsletter, Fall, Spring, Winter, & Summer; Quarterly, Programs Brochure for Members
Activities: Classes for adults and children; dramatic programs; demonstrations; docent training; lectures open to public; gallery talks; concerts; city walking tours; individual paintings and original objects of art lent to affiliated institutions; museum shop selling books, reproductions, cards

L **Library,** 1220 Fifth Ave, 10029. Tel 212-534-1672; FAX 212-534-5974. *Rights & Reproductions* Marguerite Lavin
Library Holdings: Vols 8000; Per subs 10; Other — Clipping files, manuscripts, memorabilia, original art works, photographs, prints, reproductions
Special Subjects: History of New York City

NATIONAL ACADEMY OF DESIGN
For further information, see National and Regional Organizations

NATIONAL ANTIQUE & ART DEALERS ASSOCIATION OF AMERICA
For further information, see National and Regional Organizations

NATIONAL ASSOCIATION OF WOMEN ARTISTS, INC
For further information, see National and Regional Organizations

NATIONAL CARTOONISTS SOCIETY
For further information, see National and Regional Organizations

A **NATIONAL COUNCIL ON ART IN JEWISH LIFE,** 15 E 84th St, 10028. Tel 212-879-4500. *Pres* Julius Schatz; *VPres* Michael Ehrenthal; *Treasurer* Sam Levine
Open to public. Estab 1965 to advance Jewish art & aid Jewish artists. Average Annual Attendance: 500. Mem: 200; dues $15-$100
Income: Financed by memberships & grants
Collections: Bibliographic & resource files
Publications: First Jewish Art Annual; Art in Judaism; art pamphlets
Activities: Classes for adults; lectures open to public; sales shop sells books, original art, prints & slides

L **Library,** 15 E 84th St, 10028. Tel 212-879-4500. *Pres* Julius Schatz
Open Mon - Fri by appointment. Estab 1965
Library Holdings: Micro — Cards; Other — Clipping files, exhibition catalogs, manuscripts, memorabilia, pamphlets, reproductions

NATIONAL INSTITUTE FOR ARCHITECTURAL EDUCATION
For further information, see National and Regional Organizations

M **NATIONAL MUSEUM OF THE AMERICAN INDIAN,** Broadway at 155th St, 10032. Tel 212-283-2420; FAX 212-491-9302. *Dir* Dr Dwane King; *Assoc Cur* Mary Jane Lenz; *Asst Cur* Cecile R Ganteaume; *Development Pub Affairs Officer* Elizabeth Beim; *Cur Exhibits* Peter S Brill; *Registrar* Lee A Callander; *Designer* Don Werner; *Librn* Mary B Davis
Open Tues - Sat 10 AM - 5 PM, Sun 1 - 5 PM, cl Mon & major holidays. Admis adults $3, sr citizens & students $2. Estab in 1916 by George G Heye & devoted to the collection, preservation, study & exhibition of all things connected with the anthropology of the aboriginal peoples of North, Central & South America. 15,000 sq ft of exhibits arranged geographically and in terms of archaeology & ethnology of major regions; visitors guide in braille & interpreter-on-request program is available. Average Annual Attendance: 45,000. Mem: 1500; dues benefactor $5000, patron $1000, supporting $500, associate $250, contributing $100, sustaining $50, family $35, regular $20, sr citizen & student $10
Income: Financed by trust, endowments & revenues, gifts, grants, contributions, memberships & funds appropriated by Congress
Collections: Pre-Columbian art and historical materials; world's largest collection of art and the culture of the Indians of North, Central and South America
Publications: Books, occasionally; catalogs; monographs
Activities: Guided tours for children; lectures open to public; outreach program to classrooms & audience beyond museum's immediate location; originate traveling exhibitions; museum shop sells Indian crafts, jewelry, masks, pottery, beadwork, basketry, weavings, carvings, paintings & prints, books slides, postcards & notepaper

M **THE NATIONAL PARK SERVICE, UNITED STATES DEPARTMENT OF THE INTERIOR,** The Statue of Liberty National Monument, Liberty Island, 10004. Tel 212-363-7620, 363-5804; FAX 212-363-8347. *Chief Cur* Diana Pardue; *Cur Coll* Felice Ciccione; *Cur of Exhibits* Mary Davidson; *Libr*

Technician Barry Moreno; *Registrar* Geraldine Santoro
Open 9:30 AM - 5 PM. No admis fee, donations accepted. Estab 1972. Exhibit areas in base of Statue of Liberty & in Ellis Island Immigration Museum
Collections: Statue of Liberty Collection; Ellis Island Collection; Furniture Art Work, oral histories, prints, manuscripts, films & videos, archives, books, periodicals, historic structures
Exhibitions: AMI exhibition on the immigration history of the USA; Statue of Liberty exhibit
Activities: Educ dept; docent training; classes for children; dramatic programs; lect open to public; gallery talks; tours; individual paintings & original objects of art lent to other museums; book traveling exhibitions; sales shop sells books, magazines, original art, prints & slides

NATIONAL SCULPTURE SOCIETY
For further information, see National and Regional Organizations

NATIONAL SOCIETY OF MURAL PAINTERS, INC
For further information, see National and Regional Organizations

M **THE NEW MUSEUM OF CONTEMPORARY ART,** 583 Broadway, 10012. Tel 212-219-1222; FAX 212-431-5328. *Dir* Marcia Tucker
Open Wed - Fri & Sun noon - 6 PM, Sat noon - 8 PM, cl Mon & Tues. Estab 1977 to present to the public new, provocative art that does not yet have wide public exposure or critical acceptance. Average Annual Attendance: 80,000. Mem: 800; dues $35 & up
Income: Financed by endowment, membership, state appropriation, corporations, foundations and Federal grants
Collections: Semi-permanent collections of paintings, prints, photos, sculptures
Publications: Newsletter; exhibition catalogs
Activities: Classes for adults & children; docent training; lect open to public; 3 - 4 vis lectr per yr; gallery talks; tours; exten dept serves high schools in metropolitan area; book traveling exhibitions, 1 - 2 times per yr; originate traveling exhibitions
L **The Soho Center Library,** 583 Broadway, 10012. Tel 212-219-1222; FAX 212-431-5328. *Dir* Marcia Tucker
Open 12 noon - 6 PM. Admis $3.50. Estab 1985. Reference library
Income: Financed by membership & city appropriation
Library Holdings: Vols 200; Per subs 150
Special Subjects: Architecture, Art History, Conceptual Art, Film, Painting - American, Painting - Australian, Painting - British, Painting - Canadian, Painting - Dutch, Painting - European, Painting - French, Painting - German, Painting - Italian, Painting - Japanese, Painting - New Zealander, Painting - Russian, Painting - Scandinavian, Painting - Spanish, Photography, Prints, Sculpture

A **NEW YORK ARTISTS EQUITY ASSOCIATION, INC,** 498 Broome St, 10013. Tel 212-941-0130. *Pres* Regina Stewart; *VPres* Violet Baxter; *VPres* Arthur Coppedge; *VPres* Marianne B Schnell; *VPres* Doris Wyman; *Treas* Jo Ann Leiser; *Secy* Dorothy Roatz Myers
Open 10 AM - 6 PM. Estab 1947 as a politically non-partisan group to advance the cultural, legislative, economic and professional interest of painters, sculptors, printmakers, and others in the field of visual arts. Various committees concerned with aims. Administrators of the Artists Welfare Fund, Inc. Mem: Over 3000; dues $30, meetings monthly
Income: Financed by dues
Publications: The Artists Proof newsletter, quarterly
Activities: Lectures open to public; 6 - 8 vis lectr per yer; symposiums & seminars Oct - May Art Thursday; trips to cultural institutions; advocacy; information services; artists benefits

A **NEW YORK HISTORICAL SOCIETY,** 170 Central Park W, 10024-5194. Tel 212-873-3400; FAX 212-874-8706. *Chmn* Norman Pearlstine; *Admin Exhib & Registration* Albina DeMeio; *Sr Cur* Annette Blaugrund
Open Tues - Sun 10 AM - 5 PM, cl Mon & national holidays. Admis adults $3, senior citizens $2, children under 12 $1. Estab 1804 to collect and preserve material relating to the history of New York City and State. Maintains art gallery. Average Annual Attendance: 50,000. Mem: 2870; dues benefactor $25,000, patron $10,000, associate $5000, pintard friend $1000, pintard fellow $250, New-Yorker $100, participating $50, individual $35, sr citizen, non-resident & student $25
Income: $8,000,000 (financed by endowment, grants, contributions, federal, state & local government, mem, admissions)
Collections: The Birds of America: Audubon's 433 original watercolors; architectural drawings, decorative arts, drawings, paintings, photographs, prints & sculpture. American paintings from the Colonial period to 20th century, including genre scenes, portraits & landscapes by major artists of this period
Activities: Docent training; films; concerts; symposia; annual Why History? program; tours & workshops for children & adults; teachers workshops; gallery tours for the public; individual paintings & original objects of art lent to museums; lending collection contains 2700 paintings, 5000 drawings, 675 sculptures, 800 miniatures; book traveling exhibitions, 3 per yr; museum shop sells books, magazines, prints, reproductions, cards
L **Library,** 170 Central Park W, 10024. Tel 212-873-3400. *Dir* Jean Ashton
Open Labor Day - Memorial Day, Tues - Sat 10 AM - 5 PM, Memorial Day to Labor Day, Mon - Fri 10 AM - 5 PM, cl Sun. For reference only
Library Holdings: Vols 650,000; Per subs 300; AV Maps 30,000, VF 10,000 (including menus); Micro Film 50,000; Micro — Cards 10,000, fiche, reels; AV — Fs 7500; Other — Clipping files, exhibition catalogs, manuscripts, memorabilia, original art works, pamphlets, photographs, prints, sculpture
Special Subjects: American Art to 1900; American History; New York City & State; Naval History, New York Genealogy
Collections: American Almanacs; American Genealogy; American Indian (accounts of & captivities); Early American Imprints; Early Travels in America; Early American Trials; Circus in America (Leonidas Westervelt); Civil War Regimental Histories & Muster Rolls; Jenny Lind (Leonidas Westervelt) Maps; Military History (Military Order of the Loyal Legion of the United States, Commandery of the State of New York) Military History & Science (Seventh Regiment Military Library); Naval & Marine History (Naval History Society);

18th & 19th Century New York City & New York State Newspapers; Slavery & the Civil War; Spanish American War (Harper); Among the Manuscript Collections; Horatio Gates, Alexander McDougall, Rufus King, American Fur Company, Livingston Family, American Art Union, American Academy of Fine Arts

L **THE NEW YORK PUBLIC LIBRARY,** Astor, Lenox & Tilden Foundations, Fifth Ave & 42nd St, 10018. Tel 212-930-0830. *Pres* Timothy S Healy
Estab 1895. Entire library contains over 30,000,000 items
L **Print Room,** Fifth Ave & 42nd St, Room 308, 10018. Tel 212-930-0817, 930-0837. *Cur of Prints* Roberta Waddell; *Cur of Photographs* Julia Van Haaften
Open by application to Special Collection Office, Mon, Tues, Wed, Fri & Sat 1 - 6 PM, cl Sun, Thurs & holidays. Estab 1899
Library Holdings: Vols 25,000; Stereographs 72,000; Other — Photographs 15,000, prints 175,000
Special Subjects: Graphic artists and catalogs of their works, original fine prints of the past six centuries with special emphasis on 19th century French and American, contemporary American and European, prints, techniques and illustrated books, photographers & history of photography, original 19th century topographical photographs & photo-illustrated books, American & European
Collections: Samuel Putnam Avery Collection (primarily 19th century prints); Radin Collection of Western European bookplates: British and American caricatures; Beverly Chew bequest of Milton and Pope portraits; Eno Collection of New York City Views; McAlpin Collection of George Washington Portraits; Smith Collection of Japanese Prints; Phelps Stokes Collection of American Views; Lewis Wickes Hine Collection; Robert Dennis Collection of Stereoscopic Views; Pageant of America Collection; Romana Javitz Collection
L **Spencer Collection,** Fifth Ave & 42nd St, Room 308, 10018. Tel 212-930-0817. *Asst Dir for Art, Prints & Photographs & Cur Spencer Coll* Robert Rainwater
Open by application to Special Collection Office, Mon - Sat 1 - 6 PM, cl Sun & holidays
Library Holdings: Vols 9000
Special Subjects: Rare illustrated and illuminated manuscripts and books in all languages of all countries and of all periods, constituting the development of book illustration and fine bindings
L **Art, Prints and Photographs Division,** Fifth Ave & 42nd St, Room 313, 10018. Tel 212-930-0834. *Asst Dir* Robert Rainwater; *Cur Art & Arch Coll* Paula A Baxter
Open Mon, Tues, Wed, Fri & Sat 10 AM - 6 PM, cl Sun & Thurs. Estab 1911 for reference
Library Holdings: Vols 230,000; Other — Clipping files, exhibition catalogs, pamphlets
Special Subjects: Architecture, Art History, Ceramics, Costume Design & Construction, Decorative Arts, Drawings, Furniture, Glass, Goldsmithing, Interior Design, Ivory, Jade, Jewelry, Latin American Art, Metalwork, Mexican Art, Oriental Art, Painting - American, Pewter, Porcelain
Collections: †Private and public collection catalogs; individual artists and architects
L **Schomburg Center for Research in Black Culture,** 515 Lenox Ave, 10037. Tel 212-491-2200. *Chief* Howard Dodson
Open for research & exhibitions Mon - Wed noon - 8 PM, Fri & Sat 10 AM - 6 PM. A reference library devoted to Black people throughout the world; small gallery in lobby for rotating exhibition program
Library Holdings: Vols 125,000; broadsides, maps, playbills, programs; Micro — Reels; AV — Fs, rec; Other — Clipping files, photographs, prints
Special Subjects: Black people throughout the world with major emphasis on Afro-American, Africa and Caribbean, nucleus of collected rarities of Arthur A Schomburg, a Puerto Rican of African descent
Collections: Largest collection in the country of books on Black Culture and Art; a research collection containing African Art, American Art by Black artists, Afro-Caribbean art and artifacts
Activities: Lectures open to public; gallery talks; tours; scholarships offered; originate traveling exhibitions; sales shop sells reproductions, exhibition catalogs & cards
L **Mid-Manhattan Library, Art Collection,** 455 Fifth Ave, 10016. Tel 212-340-0871. *Supervising Librn* Ann C S Benton
Open Mon & Wed 9 AM - 9 PM, Tues & Thurs 11 AM - 7 PM, Fri & Sat 10 AM - 6 PM
Library Holdings: Vols 36,000; Per subs 200; Vertical files of clippings on artists & New York City art institutions; Micro — Fiche, reels; AV — V-tapes; Other — Clipping files
—**Mid-Manhattan Library, Picture Collection,** 455 Fifth Ave, 10016. Tel 212-340-0878. *Supervising Librn* Mildred Wright
For current schedule call 212-340-0878, 0849. Estab 1915
Library Holdings: Vols 20,000; Per subs 100
Collections: Approximately 5,000,000 classified pictures; Encyclopedic in scope; Approximately half of collection available for loan with a valid NYPL card, remainder available for studying & copying, not for classroom or exhibition use
M **Shelby Cullom Davis Museum,** Lincoln Center, 111 Amsterdam Ave, 10023. Tel 212-870-1630. *Exec Dir* Robert Marx; *Museum Head* Donald Vlack; *Dance Cur* Madeleine Nichols; *Theatre Cur* Robert Taylor; *Music Cur* Jean Bowen; *Recordings Cur* Donald McCormick; *Chief Librn Circulations Coll Mgr* Susan Sommer; *Public Relations Dir* Carlee Drummer; *Publications Dir* Karen Van Westering; *Cur Exhibits* Barbara Stratyner
Hours open change each summer & fall; for information call 212-870-1630, 340-0849. No admis fee. Estab 1965 to present exhibitions of high quality pertaining directly with the performing arts. Main Gallery is 140 x 40 x 20 ft & has large glass space designed by Saarinsen; Astor Gallery measures 25 x 57 x 12 ft; Amsterdam Gallery is 30 x 48 x 10 ft
Income: Financed by endowment and city appropriation
Collections: Prints; letters; documents; photographs; posters, films; video tapes; memorabilia; dance music; recordings
Exhibitions: (1993) Jazz

L NEW YORK SCHOOL OF INTERIOR DESIGN LIBRARY, 155 E 56th St, 10022. Tel 212-753-5365; FAX 212-753-2034. *Librn* Malcolm E Scheer
Open Mon - Thurs 9 AM - 7 PM, Fri 9 AM - 2 PM. Estab 1924 to supplement the courses given by the school and to aid students and faculty in their research and projects
Income: $4484 (financed by New York State grant)
Purchases: $6345
Library Holdings: Vols 4800; Per subs 68; AV — Slides; Other — Exhibition catalogs
Special Subjects: Interior Design, Architecture

A NEW YORK SOCIETY OF ARCHITECTS, 275 Seventh Ave, 15th floor, 10001. Tel 212-675-6646; FAX 212-675-5922. *Pres* John Anastasi; *Second VPres* Shirley Klein; *Treas* Sal Bracco; *Exec Dir* Diane Elmendorf
Open 9:30 AM - 4:30 PM. Incorporated 1906. Mem: 750; dues $125
Income: $100,000 (financed by dues and sales)
Publications: Bulletin, bi-monthly; New York City Building Code Manual; New York City Fire Prevention Code
Activities: Educational programs; educational seminars; lect open to public, 6-10 per yr; Matthew W. DelGaudio Award for Excellence in Design to architectural students, Honorary Membership Certificate to other than architect, Distinguished Service Award to members, Sidney L Strauss Memorial Award to architect or layman, Fred L Uebmann Book Award; scholarships

M NEW YORK STUDIO SCHOOL OF DRAWING, PAINTING & SCULPTURE, Gallery, 8 W Eighth St, 10011. Tel 212-777-0996. *Chmn* Charles Cowles; *Dean* Graham Nickson
Open daily 10 AM - 4 PM or 5 PM. No admis fee. Estab 1964, a non-profit organization. Gallery is located on ground floor of the Studio School, site of the original Whitney Museum of Art; 2 large rooms on courtyard. Average Annual Attendance: 1000
Income: Financed by private funding
Exhibitions: Founding Faculty Show, including works by Meyer Schapiro, Esteban Vicente, Mercedes Matter, Nicholas Carone, Peter Agostini; occasional drawing exhibitions. Works from the Drawing Marathon
Activities: Educ dept; drawing instruction; lectures open to public, 30 vis lectrs per yr; scholarship & fels offered
L Library, 8 W Eighth St, 10011. Tel 212-673-6466.
Estab 1964 for pedagogical purposes. Not open to public
Library Holdings: Vols 5000; Per subs 4; AV — A-tapes, cassettes, slides, v-tapes; Other — Clipping files, reproductions
Activities: Lectures open to public, weekly

NEW YORK UNIVERSITY
M Grey Art Gallery and Study Center, 33 Washington Place, 10003. Tel 212-998-6780; FAX 212-995-4024. *Dir* Thomas W Sokolowski; *Asst to Dir & Librn* Mary Beth Shine; *Registrar* Michele Wong; *Gallery Mgr* Wendell Walker; *Gallery Monitor* Debra Whitney
Open Tues & Thurs 10 AM - 6:30 PM; Wed 10 AM - 8:30 PM; Fri 10 AM - 5 PM; Sat 1 - 5 PM; summer Mon - Fri 10 AM - 5 PM. No admis fee; suggested contribution. Estab 1975 as university art museum to serve public as well as university community. The New York University Art Collection of approx 3500 works is now under the Grey Art Gallery. Gallery space of approx 4000 sq ft used for changing exhibitions. Average Annual Attendance: 50,000. Mem: 250
Collections: American and European 20th Century Paintings, Watercolors, and Prints; Ben and Abby Grey Foundation Collection of Comtemporary Asian and Middle Eastern Art; New York University Art Collection
Exhibitions: Modern Redux: Critical Alternatives for Architecture in the Next Decade; A E Gallatin & His Circle/Abstract Appropriations
Publications: Exhibition catalogs
Activities: Lectures open to public, 2-3 vis lectr per yr; Individual paintings and original objects of art lent to other cultural institutions and sister organizations for exhibitions; originate traveling exhibitions; sales shop selling exhibition catalogs
M 80 Washington Square East Galleries, 80 Washington Sq E, 10003. Tel 212-998-5747; FAX 212-998-5752. *Faculty Dir* Dr Marilynn Karp; *Dir* Ruth D Newman
Open Tues 11 AM - 7 PM, Wed & Thurs 11 AM - 6 PM, Fri & Sat 11 AM - 5 PM. No admis fee. Estab 1975 for exhibitions of works by graduate student artists. Eight gallery rooms containing one man shows. Average Annual Attendance: 10,000
Exhibitions: 70 one man shows annually; Annual Small Works Competition
Publications: Press releases
Activities: Annual International Art Competition, Small Works
L Stephen Chan Library of Fine Arts, One E 78th St, 10021. Tel 212-772-5825.
Dir Sharon Chickanzeff; *Supvr* Robert Stacey; *Reference Librn* Max Marmor
Estab to provide scholarly materials for graduate studies in art history and archaeology. Reference library
Library Holdings: Vols 129,000; Per subs 725; Micro — Fiche, reels
Special Subjects: Antiquities-Byzantine, Antiquities-Etruscan, Antiquities-Greek, Antiquities-Oriental, Antiquities-Persian, Archaeology, Islamic Art, Oriental Art, Restoration & Conservation
L Institute of Fine Arts Visual Resources Collection, One E 78th St, 10021. Tel 212-772-5821; FAX 212-772-5807. *Cur* Jenni Rodda; *Asst Cur* Dorothy Simon
Library open to qualified researchers
Collections: Offner, Florentine painting; Coor, Sienese painting; Berenson, Italian painting; DIAL Collection; I Tatti Archive; Gernsheim Corpus, 60,000 drawings

M NIAGARA UNIVERSITY, Castellani Art Museum, Niagara University, 14109. Tel 716-286-8200. *Registrar* Kathleen Fraas; *Dir* Sandra H Olsen, PhD; *Gallery Mgr* Kim Yarwood; *Museum Shop* Anne LaBarbera; *Museum Shop* Carla Castellani
Open Wed - Sat 11 AM - 5 PM, Sun 1 - 5 PM. No admis fee. Estab 1978. The gallery is a 10,000 sq ft museum that displays the permanent collection of over 3000 works of art encompassing 19th century to present with a concentration contemporary art. Mem: 300
Income: $120,000
Collections: Modern paintings, sculpture & works on paper (19th -20th

centuries); Pre-Columbian Pottery
Exhibitions: Glass art: Arnold Mesches; John Moore; Michael Kessler; Arcadia Revisted: Niagara River & Falls from Lake Erie to Lake Ontario, Photographs by John Pfahl
Publications: Exhibition catalogs, 4 per yr
Activities: Classes for adults & children; Public Art Project on Underground Railroad; docent training; learning disabled prog; sr citizen outreach prog; lect open to the public, 1-6 vis lectrs per yr; concerts; gallery talks; tours; competitions; awards; scholarships & fels offered; individual paintings & original objects of art lent to qualified museums; originate traveling exhibitions

M NIPPON CLUB GALLERY, 145 W 57th St, 10019. Tel 212-581-2223. *Dir* Thom Donovan
Open Mon - Sat 11 AM - 7 PM, cl Sun & holidays. No admis fee. Estab 1981 for the purpose of international cultural exchange of arts & crafts from Japan & US. Located in the main lobby of a 6 storey club house; gallery space is 900 sq ft with high ceiling & multiple lighting system. Mem: 2700; dues $400
Income: Financed by mem
Publications: The Nippon Club Dayori, monthly; The Nippon Club Directory, annual; The Nippon Club News, annual
Activities: Classes for adults; lectures for mem only, 5 vis lectrs per yr

A THE ONE CLUB FOR ART & COPY, 32 E 21st St, 10010. Tel 212-979-1900. *Dir* Mary Warlick; *Asst to Dir* Kristin Overson
Open Mon - Fri 10 AM - 6 PM. Estab 1975 to support the craft of advertising, informal interchange among creative people, develop advertising excellence through advertising students who are tomorrow's professionals. Exhibits feature different advertising agencies. Mem: 700; dues individual $75, student $45; annual meeting in Jan
Income: $200,000 (financed by membership & awards show)
Publications: The One Show Annual, Advertising's Best Print, Radio & TV, annually
Activities: Educ dept; lect open to public & some for members only; gallery talks; competitions with awards; scholarships; individual ads lent to various ad clubs & sometimes to various schools; shop sells books & TV reels

A ORGANIZATION OF INDEPENDENT ARTISTS, 19 Hudson St, No 402, 10013. Tel 212-219-9213; FAX 212-219-9216. *Pres* Susan Fetterolf; *VPres* Debra Feiman; *Exec Dir* Joseph Stasko; *Admin Asst* Nicole Herz
Open Tues & Thurs 1 - 7 PM, Wed & Fri 1 - 5 PM. Estab 1976 to facilitate artist-curated group exhibitions in public spaces throughout NY. Exhibit in public spaces. Average Annual Attendance: 20,000. Mem: 1000; patrons $500, sponsors $100, friends $30, artists $30
Income: $60,000 (financed by mem, state appropriation, federal funds, corporate & foundation funds)
Exhibitions: South Beach Psychiatric Center Sculpture Garden; Latitudes of Time; The Ways of Wood; New Geometric Abstractions
Publications: Quarterly newsletter
Activities: Tours; Warren Tanner Memorial Art Fund Award; scholarships; slide registry

C PAINE WEBBER INC, 1285 Avenue of the Americas, 10019. Tel 212-713-2869; FAX 212-713-1087. *Pres* Donald B Marron; *Cur* Jennifer Wells
Collection displayed throughout offices
Collections: Contemporary American & European drawings, sculptures, paintings & prints
Activities: Tours; individual paintings & objects of art lent

L PARSONS SCHOOL OF DESIGN, Adam & Sophie Gimbel Design Library, 2 W 13th St, 10011. Tel 212-229-8914; FAX 212-929-2456. *Library Dir* Hikemt Dogu; *Reference Librn* Claire Petrie
Open Mon - Thurs 10 AM - 9 PM, Fri & Sat 10 AM - 6 PM. Estab as a school in 1896, the Gimbel Library moved to its present location in 1974; collections & services support the curriculum of the school as well as general design research. Lending to Parsons students & library consortium members; limited reference to general public
Library Holdings: Vols 37,000; Per subs 160; Pictures 30,000; AV — Slides 60,000; Other — Exhibition catalogs, memorabilia, original art works, prints
Special Subjects: Architecture, Art History, Crafts, Fashion Arts, Furniture, Graphic Design, Industrial Design, Interior Design, Photography, Textiles, Design Concepts, Typography
Collections: Claire McCardell Fashion Sketchbooks

PASTEL SOCIETY OF AMERICA
For further information, see National and Regional Organizations

A PEN AND BRUSH, INC, 16 E Tenth St, 10003. Tel 212-475-3669. *Pres* Sarah E Wright; *First VPres* Marion Roller; *Treas* Barbara Adrian
Open 1 - 4 PM Tues - Sun except holidays during exhibitions; cl during July & August. Estab 1893, incorporated 1912. The Clubhouse was purchased in 1923, and contains rooms, dining room & 3 exhibition galleries. Mem: Approx 325; dues $80 professional women writers, artists, sculptors, craftsmen; musicians; annual meeting Feb
Collections: Paintings; graphics; pastels; sculpture; crafts
Exhibitions: Ten annual exhibitions of members' work; occasional one-man shows
Activities: Classes for adults in watercolors; lectures open to public; 2-3 vis lectr per yr; concerts; gallery talks; concerts; competitions & awards
L Library, 16 E Tenth St, 10003. Tel 212-475-3669. *Pres* Sarah E Wright
For members only
Library Holdings: Vols 1000; Per subs 5
Publications: Bulletin, monthly

C PHILIP MORRIS COMPANY INC, 120 Park Ave, 10017. Tel 212-880-3575; FAX 212-878-2167. *VPres Corporate Contributions & Cultural Affairs* Stephanie Fre nch
Estab 1960's to enhance the creative and aesthetic environments of offices.

Collection displayed in offices and corridors; annual amount of contributions and grants $1,000,000; supports museums, exhibitions, theater, groups, symphony orchestras, art associations, libraries, historical societies, opera companies, commissions

Collections: Prints by artists around the world, tobacco memorabilia, works by emerging artists

Activities: Supports arts organizations located in Philip Morris plant communities; individual objects of art lent to museums exhibitions only

L **PLAYERS,** Hampden-Booth Theatre Library, 16 Gramercy Park, 10003. Tel 212-228-7610. *Cur & Librn* Raymond Wemmlinger
Open Mon - Fri 10 AM - 5 PM & by appointment. Estab 1957 to provide scholarly & professional research on American & English theater with emphasis on 19th century
Purchases: $10,000
Library Holdings: Vols 10,000; Micro — Reels; AV — A-tapes, cassettes, rec; Other — Clipping files, exhibition catalogs, framed reproductions, manuscripts, memorabilia, original art works, pamphlets, photographs, prints, reproductions, sculpture
Special Subjects: Coins & Medals, Costume Design & Construction, Etchings & Engravings, Painting - American, Painting - British, Photography, Portraits, Prints, Sculpture, Stage Design, Reproductions, Theatre Arts
Collections: Documents, letters, photos, paintings, memorabilia, promptbooks of †Walter Hampden, †Edwin Booth, Max Gordon, Union Square Theater; English playbills (18th & 19th century)

M **PORT AUTHORITY OF NEW YORK & NEW JERSEY,** Art Collection, 1 World Trade Center, 82 W, 10048. Tel 212-435-3325; FAX 212-435-3382. *Admnr* Saul Wenegrat; *Cur* Christine Moss Lassiter; *Registrar* Kimberly Beard
Open 24 hrs. Estab 1969 as a public arts program. John F Kennedy International Airport, International Arrivals Bldg; World Trade Center; Port Authority Bus Terminal. Average Annual Attendance: 10,000,000
Purchases: $250,000
Exhibitions: Memories of Surrealism, Salvador Dali; Wind Circus of Susumu Shingu (World Trade Center); Barrier Murals by Franco the Great Gaskin; The Wonder Woman Wall by Graupe Pillard (Port Authority Bus Terminal); American - for the People of Bathgate by Tim Rollins & KOS (Bathgate Industrial Park); Smug by Tony Smith (Saint John's Rotary, Holland Tunnel)
Publications: Art for the Public, collection catalog
Activities: Competitions sponsored, awards given; lending collection of original objects of art & paintings; 6 traveling exhibitions booked per yr; originate traveling exhibitions

L **PRATT MANHATTAN,** 295 Lafayette St, 10012. Tel 212-925-8481; FAX 212-941-6397. *Chmn* Elliott Gordon
Library Holdings: Per subs 32; VF 8
Special Subjects: Decorative Arts, Interior Design, Costume Design & Construction, Textiles, Photography

M **PRINCE STREET GALLERY,** 121 Wooster St, 10012. Tel 212-226-9402. *Dir* Iona Fromboluti
Open Tues - Sun noon - 6 PM. Estab 1970 to provide a showing place for members, mainly figurative art; cooperative artist run gallery. Gallery has about 30 members who have shown in New York as well as throughout the country & internationally. Average Annual Attendance: 6000. Mem: 30; membership enrollment fees $450, membership $70 per month for 10 months; monthly meetings
Income: Financed by membership
Exhibitions: Gallery Artists: David Paulson, Ginger Levant, Kevine Donahue; Guest Artists: Janice Becker, Claire Rosenfeld, Nancy Prusinowski, Susan Grabel, Gina Werfel, Sharyn Finnegan, Chris Semergieff, Pearl Rosen
Publications: Annual catalog

C **PRINTED MATTER, INC,** 77 Wooster St, 10012. Tel 212-925-0325. *Dir* John Goodwin
Open Tues - Sat 10 AM - 6 PM, cl major holidays
Exhibitions: Conceptual artists books from the 70's & early 80's

A **PRINTMAKING WORKSHOP,** 55 W 17th St, 10011. Tel 212-989-6125, 242-9884; FAX 212-206-8398. *Dir* Robert Blackburn
Open Mon - Fri 8 AM - midnight, Sat & Sun 10 AM - 7 PM. Estab 1949 as a workshop space for artists to print etchings & lighographs, relief printing, photographics, including night classes & edition printing; outreach program. Mem: 800; dues vary
Income: Financed by earned income, membership, city, federal & state appropriation, donations from individuals, some foundation & corporate support
Collections: Impressions-Expressions, Black American Graphics; Artists Who Make Prints, Independent Artists; Prints & Monotypes From Bob Blackbur
Activities: Classes for professional artists; outreach workshops for young people; lectures; art resource referral; scholarship; traveling exhibitions organized and circulated

A **PUBLIC ART FUND, INC,** One E 53rd St, 10022. Tel 212-980-4575; FAX 212-980-3610. *Pres* Susan K Freedman; *Exec Dir* James M Clark; *Project Dir* Fernando Hoffroy; *Dir Development* Judy R Marklay
Open Mon - Fri 10 AM - 6 PM. Estab 1977 to incorporate contemporary art at sites throughout New York City; one of the first organizations solely dedicated to securing a place for art work within the landscape & is recognized world-wide for its pioneering support of temporary public art installation
Income: $220,000 (financed by National Endowment for the Arts, New York State Council of the Art, endowments, private & corporate contributions)
Exhibitions: William Fullbrooks: Bill of Rights; Andrew Menard Multimedia Installation: With or Without Reason; Joe Shapiro: Untitled; Ben Bursztyn: Telepathic Mailbox & Migrant Letters; Martin Wong: Traffic Signs for the Hearing Impaired
Publications: Catalogues; manuals on public art; newsletter; postcards
Activities: Competitions to commission new works of art; site assistance; temporary exhibition program

L **Library,** 1 E 53rd St, 10022. Tel 212-980-4575; FAX 212-980-3610. *Project Dir* Fernando Hoffory
Estab as a reference library on public art
Library Holdings: Documentation of public art projects; AV — Slides 4000
Collections: Murals; outdoor sculpture; sponsors temporary installations throughout New York City

C **R J R NABISCO, INC,** 1301 Avenue of the Americas, 34th Floor, 10019. Tel 212-258-5600. *Facilities Dept* Doug Hall
Collection shown in Corporate Headquarters Plaza & Reynolds Buildings
Collections: Works of living 20th century artists, including paintings, prints, photography, sculpture, crafts & mixed media; glass cases display Art Deco smoking memorabilia; 30 ft mural tracing the history of tobacco by Dennis Abbe

M **NICHOLAS ROERICH MUSEUM,** 319 W 107th St, 10025. Tel 212-864-7752; FAX 212-864-7704. *Pres* Edgar Lansbury; *Exec Dir* Daniel Entin
Open daily 2 - 5 PM; cl Mon & holidays. No admis fee. Estab 1958 to show a permanent collection of paintings by Nicholas Roerich, internationally known artist, to promote his ideals as a great thinker, writer, humanitarian, scientist, and explorer, and to promote his Pact and Banner of Peace. There is a gallery in which works of contemporary artists are shown. Average Annual Attendance: 8000. Mem: Dues sustaining $50, contributing $25, assoc $10
Income: Financed by membership and donations
Collections: Permanent collection of paintings by Nicholas Roerich
Exhibitions: Monthly exhibitions by young artists; Zavalniuk Exhibit of Paintings from Moscow
Publications: Altai-Himalaya, A Travel Diary; Flowers of Morya, The Theme of Spiritual Pilgrimage in the Poetry of Nicholas Roerich; The Invincible; Nicholas Roerich, An Annotated Bibliography; Nicholas Roerich, A Short Biography; Nicholas Roerich 1874-1974 Centenary Monograph; Roerich Pact & Banner of Peace; Shambhala
Activities: Lect open to public; concerts; tours; museum shop selling books, reproductions and postcards

C **RUDER FINN & ROTMAN INC,** 301 E 57th St, 10022. Tel 212-593-6400; FAX 212-715-1507. *Pres* Philippa Polskin
Estab to link corporations which support the arts with museum exhibitions and performing arts events, to develop major corporate sponsored exhibitions and special projects created for public spaces. Assistance given for marketing and publicity assignments for cultural institutions and the selection, installation and documentation of corporate art collections. We are in the business of linking corporations with museums and other arts organizations in support of exhibitions; also council both small business and large corporations on how they can contribute to their communities through the visual arts. Ruder & Finn Fine Arts is a division of the public relations firm of Ruder & Finn Inc
Activities: Originate traveling exhibitions to museums nationwide

SALMAGUNDI CLUB
For further information, see National and Regional Organizations

M **SCALAMANDRE MUSEUM OF TEXTILES,** 950 Third Ave, 10022. Tel 718-361-8500; FAX 212-688-7531. *Mgr* Leslie Stein
Open Mon - Fri 9 AM - 5 PM. Estab 1947 to encourage interest in textile design for decoration
Collections: Contemporary textiles showing modern motifs in textured weaves of today; reproductions of old textiles; 2000 old documentary pieces of textile
Exhibitions: 15 small student exhibits for art schools, colleges (must be requested by faculty member); permanent display of textiles used in Historic Restorations
Activities: Lect given on history of textile design, including the classification of textiles, both period and modern; traveling exhibits in the various periods of decorative art for circulation throughout the United States to museums only

L **SCHOOL OF VISUAL ARTS LIBRARY,** 380 Second Ave (Mailing add: 209 E 23rd St, 10010). Tel 212-679-7350, Ext 412; FAX 212-725-3587. *Chief Librn* Robert Lobe; *Cataloger* Rosyln D Mylorie; *Reference* Nina Nazionale; *Slide Cur* Matthew Haberstroh
Open Mon - Thurs 9 AM - 7:30 PM, Fri 9 AM - 5 PM, Sat 11 AM - 4 PM. Estab 1962 to serve needs of School of Visual Arts students and faculty. Exclusively for student & faculty use, lending to students. Circ 32,500
Income: Financed by tuition
Purchases: $50,000
Library Holdings: Vols 57,000; Per subs 250; AV — A-tapes, cassettes, rec, slides, v-tapes; Other — Clipping files, exhibition catalogs, framed reproductions, original art works, pamphlets, photographs, reproductions, sculpture
Special Subjects: Art History, Film, Photography, Sculpture, Graphic Arts, Graphic Design, Illustration, Painting - American, Photography, media arts, painting
Publications: Library Handbook; monthly accessions lists

SCULPTORS GUILD, INC
For further information, see National and Regional Organizations

M **SCULPTURE CENTER INC,** 167 E 69th St, 10021. Tel 212-737-9870. *Pres* Kathy Southern; *VPres* Edwin Nochberg; *VPres* Jan Abrams; *Treas* Arthur Abelman; *Gallery Dir* Marion Giffiths; *School Dir* Michael Cochran; *Asst Dir* Jay Gibson; *Asst Dir* Elizabeth Eder
Open Tues - Sat 11 AM - 5 PM. No admis fee. Estab 1928 as Clay Club of New York to further the interest of student and professional sculptors. Incorporated in 1944 as the Sculpture Center, a nonprofit organization for the promotion of the art of sculpture and to provide work facilities. Moved into the new building in 1950, when the present name was adopted. Slide file maintained for unaffiliated sculptors for use by consultants, curators, collectors & architects. A gallery is maintained, and has represented in it professional sculptors. School and studio space can be provided for beginning, intermediate and advanced students. Average Annual Attendance: 35,000
Exhibitions: Solo & group exhibitions of emerging & mid-career sculptors; selection from the Sculptor Center Slide File; Three man show: Ellen Kruger,

Anne Chu, Henry MacNeil; Video Installations; Spring Major Installation by Donna Dennis; ongoing series of installations on AIDS as well as monthly readings by poets & writers
Publications: Announcements (for the gallery and school); brochures; exhibition catalogs
Activities: Classes for adults and children; lectures open to public; concerts; gallery talks; tours; scholarships; original objects of art lent to private galleries and corporate lobbies; sales shop sells tools and supplies for sculptors
L **Library,** 167 E 69th St, 10021. Tel 212-737-9870. *School Dir* Michael Cochran
Library Holdings: Vols 200; Per subs 3; Other — Exhibition catalogs, memorabilia, original art works, pamphlets, photographs, sculpture

C **JOSEPH E SEAGRAM & SONS, INC,** Gallery, 375 Park Ave, 10152. Tel 212-572-7379. *Cur* Carla Caccamise Ash; *Asst Cur* Barry M Winiker
Open to public. Estab 1958 for the enjoyment of Seagram employees. Collection displayed in offices and reception areas; permanent gallery on 4th floor, used for temporary art exhibitions, both for loan and in-house
Collections: 19th and 20th century American photographs of urban life; antique glass, European and American; 20th century drawings, graphics, paintings, posters and tapestries
Exhibitions: Temporary installations of notable sculpture on Plaza; several loan exhibitions
Publications: Exhibit catalog
Activities: Lect; tours of public areas Tues 3 PM; individual objects of art lent for selected musuem exhibitions; originate traveling exhibitions

M **ABIGAIL ADAMS SMITH MUSEUM,** 421 E 61st St, 10021. Tel 212-838-6878. *Dir* Suzanne Stirn-Ainslie
Open Mon - Fri 10 AM - 4 PM, Sun 1 - 5 PM. Admis adults $2, senior citizens $1. Estab 1939, historic house museum representing early 19th century New York City. Nine period rooms in original 1826 interiors; 1799 Landmark building. Mem: dues $25 - $500, annual meeting in Apr
Collections: †Decorative arts-furniture, †ceramics, †metals, †porcelain, †silver, †textiles; †documents & †manuscripts
Exhibitions: Period rooms in original 1820s interiors; American Decorative Arts
Publications: Biannual newsletter
Activities: Classes for adults & children; docent programs; musical performances; craft demonstrations; lect open to public, 5 - 10 vis lectr per year; scholarships & fels offered; retail store sells books, slides, historical reproduction items

SOCIETY FOR FOLK ARTS PRESERVATION, INC
For further information, see National and Regional Organizations

SOCIETY OF AMERICAN GRAPHIC ARTISTS
For further information, see National and Regional Organizations

SOCIETY OF ILLUSTRATORS
For further information, see National and Regional Organizations

M **SOCIETY OF ILLUSTRATORS,** Museum of American Illustration, 128 E 63rd St, 10021. Tel 212-838-2560. *Dir* Terrence Brown; *Asst Dir* Phillis Harvey
Open Mon, Wed, Thurs & Fri 10 AM - 5 PM, Tues 10 AM - 8 PM, cl Aug & legal holidays. No admis fee. 1901. Average Annual Attendance: 30,000
Collections: Original illustrations from 1838 to present, all media
Exhibitions: Seventeen exhibitions a year
Activities: Lect open to public, 18 vis lectr; sponsor competitions for professional illustrators; awards; individual paintings & original objects of art lent to museums & universities; lending collection contains 1200 art works; original traveling exhibitions; museum shop sells books, prints, t-shirts & gift items

A **SOCIETY OF SCRIBES, LTD,** PO Box 933, 10150. Tel 212-861-4880. *Pres* Margaret Neiman Harber; *VPres* Joanna Mezzatesta; *Treas* Judith B Kastin
Estab 1974. Mem: 1000; dues $35 USA, $30 Canada & Mexico, $32 overseas; annual meeting in Feb, annual Holiday Fair in Dec
Exhibitions: (1992) Open Exhibit of Members Work; Master Eagle Gallery; Annual Young Calligraphers Contest & Exhibition, Donnell Library, New York City
Publications: Newsletter, 4 per yr; Journal, annual
Activities: Workshops; lectures open to public

M **SOHO 20 GALLERY,** 469 Broome St, 10013. Tel 212-226-4167. *Dir* Eugenia C Foxworth
Open Tues - Sat noon - 6 PM. Estab 1973 as a women's co-operative gallery. 2600 sq ft for exhibition. Main gallery 400 sq ft invitational space located in the Gunther Building. Average Annual Attendance: 50 per day. Mem: 27; annual dues $2400, meetings first Tues each month
Income: Financed by funding programs, sponsored exhibitions
Exhibitions: (1993) Soho 20 Strikes Gold; Judith Steinberg; Jessica Lenard; Yong Soon Min
Activities: Lect open to the public; 52 vis lectr per yr; gallery talks; tours; individual paintings and original objects of art lent to corporations, universities & other galleries; originate traveling exhibitions to other museums

M **SOUTH STREET SEAPORT MUSEUM,** 207 Front St, 10038. Tel 212-669-9400; FAX 212-732-5168. *Pres* Peter Neill; *Dir Educ* Janet Rassweiler; *Historian & Librn* Norman Brouwer
Open daily 11 AM - 5 PM. Admis adults $3.50, children $1.50, members no charge. Estab 1967 to preserve the maritime history and traditions of the Port of New York. Several gallery spaces: The Seaport Gallery for art exhibits; the printing press gallery at Bowne & Co Staioners; the museum children's center. Average Annual Attendance: 300,000. Mem: 9000; dues family $25, individual $15; annual meeting May
Income: Financed by membership and corporate grants
Collections: Restored historic buildings; fleet of historic ships; permanent collection of marine art & artifacts; collections of ship models; archive of ship plans, photos & negatives
Exhibitions: Recent Archeology in Lower Manhattan; My Hammer Hand; New

York Trades Transformed; Mens Lives; Titanic
; Waterfront Photography
Publications: Seaport Magazine, quarterly
Activities: Classes for children; walking tours of area; lect open to public, 10 - 15 visiting lectr per year; concerts; individual paintings and original objects of art lent to institutions; museum shop sells books, magazines, reproductions & prints
L **Library,** 207 Front St, 10038. Tel 212-669-9400; FAX 212-732-5168. *Historian & Librn* Norman Brouwer
For reference
Library Holdings: Vols 9500; Per subs 30; negatives; AV — Motion pictures, slides; Other — Clipping files, exhibition catalogs, manuscripts, memorabilia, original art works, pamphlets, photographs, prints, reproductions

C **STERLING PORTFOLIO INC,** 444 E 58th St, 10022. Tel 212-755-2733. *Cur* Lois Wagner
Open by appointment only. Estab 1978
Collections: American Impressionism & Realism from 1880-1930; figurative, landscape & still-life paintings

M **STOREFRONT FOR ART & ARCHITECTURE,** 97 Kenmare St, 10012. Tel 212-431-5795. *Dir* Shirin Neshat; *Founder* Kyong Park; *Spec Dir Ecotec* Amerigo Murras
Open Tues - Sat noon - 6 PM. No admis charge. Estab to show interdisciplinary & experimental works of art & architecture, often never previously shown in New York. Organizes large events or competitions of an experimental nature
Exhibitions: (1992) Ecotec Forum, held in Corsica, France; Future Systems; Gunther Domeney (Austrian architect); Mark West (Canadian artist)
Publications: Exhibition catalogs; monthly bulletin; quarterly reports

M **THE STUDIO MUSEUM IN HARLEM,** 144 W 125th St, 10027. Tel 212-864-4500; FAX 212-666-5753. *Exec Dir* Kinshasha Holman Conwill; *Deputy Dir Progs* Patricia Cruz; *Cur* Dr Sharon Patton; *Museum Shop Mgr* Michelle Lee
Open Wed - Fri 10 AM - 5 PM, Sat & Sun 1 - 6 PM. Admis adults $1.50, children, students & sr citizens $.50, members free. Estab 1967 to exhibit the works of contemporary Black American artists, mount historical and informative exhibitions, and provide culturally educational programs and activities for the general public. 10,000 sq ft of exhibition and education space. Average Annual Attendance: 40,000. Mem: 11,000; dues $15 - $1000
Income: Financed by membership, city and state appropriation, corporate and foundation funding, federal funding, rental income, gift shop sales & individual contributions
Collections: James Van Der Zee Collection of Photography; over 1000 works of art by African-American artists including sculpture, painting and works on paper; Caribbean art
Exhibitions: (1991) Romare Bearden: A Retrospective
Publications: Catalogues of major black artists; exhibition catalogues
Activities: Classes for adults & children; docent training; workshops; panel discussions; demonstrations; cooperative school program; internship program; lectures open to public, 10 vis lectr per yr; concerts; gallery talks; tours; scholarships; book traveling exhibitions; originate traveling exhibitions; museum shop sells books, magazines, original art, reproductions, prints, jewelry, baskets, crafts, pottery & catalogues

M **SWISS INSTITUTE,** 35 W 67, 10023. Tel 212-496-1759. *Admin* Ariane Braillard; *Dir* Carin Kuoni
Open Mon, Tues, Thurs, Fri, Sat & Sun 2 - 7 PM, cl Wed. No admis fee. Estab 1986 to showcase swiss artists & culture. 1500 sq ft. Average Annual Attendance: 1500. Mem: 300; dues $50; annual meeting in May
Income: Financed by endowments, mem & sponsersp & sponsors
Publications: Catalogs
Activities: Lect open to public, 5 vis lectr per year; concerts; book traveling exhibitions; originate traveling exhibitions; sales shop sells books, prints & original art

A **LOUIS COMFORT TIFFANY FOUNDATION,** Canal Station, PO Box 480, 10013. Tel 212-431-3685. *Pres* Angela K Westwater; *VPres* Paul Smith; *Secy* Gerard Jones
Estab 1918 to encourage talented artists - painters, sculptors & crafts artists - by awarding a limited number of grants biennially. Mem: Annual meeting May
Income: Financed by endowment
Activities: Bi-annual grants selected from nominations of professionals around the US; This is a closed competition; no direct applications accepted

UKIYO-E SOCIETY OF AMERICA, INC
For further information, see National and Regional Organizations

A **UKRAINIAN INSTITUTE OF AMERICA, INC,** 2 E 79th St, 10021. Tel 212-288-8660. *Pres* Walter Baranetski; *Admin Dir* Wolodymyr Lysniak; *Cur* Daria Hoydysh
Open Tues - Sat 11 AM - 6 PM, Sun by appointment. Admis by contribution. Estab 1948 to develop, sponsor and promote educational activities which will acquaint the general public with history, culture and art of Ukrainian people. Average Annual Attendance: 8500. Mem: 280; dues life $100, associate $25; annual meeting Nov 6
Income: $60,000 (financed by endowment, membership and contributions)
Purchases: $2500
Collections: Church & religious relics; folk art, ceramic & woodwork; patents of Ukrainian-American engineers; Gritchenko Foundation Collection; sculptures by Archipenko, Kruk, Mol & others; Ukrainian paintings
Exhibitions: Arka Petryshyn, International Art Exhibit
Publications: UIA Newsletter, monthly; Fifteenth Anniversary of UIA; Thirtieth Anniversary of UIA
Activities: Classes for adults; dramatic programs; seminars; symposiums; workshop seminars; literary evenings; lectures open to public; conceerts; gallery talks; tours

M **THE UKRAINIAN MUSEUM,** 203 Second Ave, 10003. Tel 212-228-0110; FAX 212-228-1947. *Dir* Maria Shust; *Admin Dir* Daria Bajko; *Educational Dir* Lubow Wolynetz; *Public Relations* Lydia Hajduczok; *Archivist* Chrystyna Pevny
Open Wed - Sun 1 - 5 PM. Admis adults $1, sr citizens, students & children $. 50. Estab 1976 to collect, preserve, maintain & exhibit its permanent collection of Ukrainian folk art, fine art & its photographic & document collection of Ukrainian immigration; special exhibitions organized on various aspects of the Ukrainian culture. Average Annual Attendance: 13,000. Mem: 1700; dues family $50, adults $25, sr citizens & students $10
Income: $214,000 (financed by membership, donations and grants)
Collections: Major crafts in Ukrainian folk art: woven & embroidered textiles (including costumes & kilims), woodwork, ceramics, metalwork, Ukrainian Easter eggs; fine arts; photographic/documentary archival collection on Ukrainian immigration in the USA, also including photographs depicting Ukrainian cultural heritage, among them photographs of individuals in their native dress, architectural landmarks as well as photographic records of historic events
Exhibitions: (1993) Two Folk Art Exhibitions: Burshchiv & Sokal Region; Primative Artists Exhibition - John Peernock
Publications: Annual report; bulletins; bilingual exhibition catalogs or brochures
Activities: Classes for adults & children; lectrs open to the public, 2 - 3 vis lectrs per year; gallery talks; tours; individual paintings & original objects of art lent; lending collection contains 1000 original prints, 100 paintings, 500 phonorecords & 1000 sculptures; originate traveling exhibitions; museum shop sells books, magazines, original art & reproductions

L **Library,** 203 Second Ave, 10003. Tel 212-228-0110; FAX 212-228-1947. *Dir* Maria Shust
Library for internal use only
Library Holdings: Vols 2000; AV — Slides 600; Other — Exhibition catalogs, photographs
Special Subjects: Ukrainian Fine and Folk Art
Publications: Extensive catalogues with major exhibitions; Annual reports

L **UNION OF AMERICAN HEBREW CONGREGATIONS,** Synagogue Art and Architectural Library, 838 Fifth Ave, 10021. Tel 212-249-0100. *Dir* Joseph C Bernstein
Open Mon - Fri 9:30 AM - 5 PM; cl Sat & Sun and Jewish holidays. Estab 1957. Books for use on premises only
Income: Financed by budgetary allocation plus rental fees for slides
Library Holdings: Vols 200; AV — Slides 3000
Special Subjects: Synagogue architecture, ceremonial objects and Judaic art
Publications: An American Synagogue for Today and Tomorrow (book); Contemporary Synagogue Art (book)
Activities: Slide rental service

M **UNION SQUARE GALLERY,** 47 Irving Place, 10003. Tel 212-777-8393. *Dir* Todd Weinstein
Open by appointment. Estab 1980 to celebrate work
Activities: Retail store sells books, prints & original art

L **UNIVERSITY CLUB LIBRARY,** One W 54th St, 10019. Tel 212-572-3418; FAX 212-586-9095. *Dir* Andrew Berner; *Asst Dir* Jane Reed
Open to members & qualified scholars (inquire by letter or telephone first) Mon - Fri 10 AM - 7 PM. Estab 1865 for the promotion of the arts & culture in post-university graduates. Art is displayed in all areas of the building. Average Annual Attendance: 7000. Mem: 4250
Income: Financed by endowments & mem
Library Holdings: Vols 90,000
Collections: Art; architecture, fine printing, book illustration, works by George Cruikshank
Publications: The Illuminator, occasional

M **VIRIDIAN GALLERY,** 24 W 57th St, 10019. Tel 212-245-2882. *Dir* Karl Staubo
Estab 1968 to exhibit work by emerging artists. Average Annual Attendance: 10,000
Exhibitions: Juried exhibitions, biannual
Publications: Gallery Artists; Gallery Catalogue
Activities: Exten dept lends paintings, sculpture & photographs; book traveling exhibitions once per yr; originate traveling exhibitions, twice per yr

VISUAL ARTISTS & GALLERIES (VAGA)
For further information, see National and Regional Organizations

M **WARD-NASSE GALLERY,** 178 Prince St, 10012. Tel 212-925-6951. *Dir* Robert Curcio; *Chmn of the Board* Harry Nasse
Open Tues - Sat 11 AM - 6 PM, Sun 1 - 4 PM. No admis fee. Estab 1969 to provide an artist-run gallery; also serves as resource center for artists and public; to provide internships for students. Cooperative gallery with four-person and larger salon shows. Average Annual Attendance: 7000. Mem: 150; dues $700 for 2 years: 4 person show, slide and salon, $200 for sustaining membership
Income: Financed by membership
Exhibitions: Seventeen exhibitions per year ranging from 3 person shows, up to large salon shows with 100 artists
Publications: Brochure; gallery catalog, every two years
Activities: Work study programs; lectures open to public; concerts; poetry readings; multi-arts events; extension dept

M **WHITE COLUMNS,** 142-54 Christopher St, 10014. Tel 212-924-4212. *Exec Dir* Bill Arning; *Asst Dir* Catherine Howe; *Gallery Mgr* Elaine TinNyo
Estab 1970 to showcase the works of emerging artists
Exhibitions: (1990) Taro Suzuki-Suzanne Jolson New Paintings. (1991) Lyric: Uses of Beauty in the 90's, Bill Arning; Photo Projects; Benefit Show: On to Thirty; Installations by Fred Thomaselli, Charles Long; Guest Curated Show

M **WHITNEY MUSEUM OF AMERICAN ART,** 945 Madison Ave, 10021. Tel 212-570-3600. *Dir* David A Ross; *Deputy Dir Internal Affairs* Jennifer Russell; *Deputy Dir External Affairs* Amory Houghton; *Asst Dir Development & Membership* James Kraft; *Cur* Barbara Haskell; *Cur Film & Video* John G Hanhardt; *Cur* Richard Marshall; *Cur* Lisa Phillips; *Cur* Elisabeth Sussmann; *Adjunct Cur Drawings* Klaus Kertess; *Advisor Hopper Collection* Deborah Lyons; *Cur Educ* Constance Wolf; *Head Branch Museums* Pamela G Perkins; *Public Relations Officer* Steven Schlough; *Chief Financial Officer* Michael Wolfe; *Adminr Colls & Exhib* Nancy McGary; *Head Publications* Doris Palca; *Librn* May Castleberry; *Head Independent Study Prog* Ronald Clark; *Personnel Dir* Mary McGoldrich; *Sales Adminr* Kaarin Lemstrom-Sheedy
Open Wed, Fri - Sun 11 AM - 6 PM, Thurs 1 - 8 PM, cl Mon, Tues & national holidays. Admis $6, sr seniors 62 & over $4, students with ID $4, children under 12 free. Estab 1930, incorporated 1931 by Gertrude Vanderbilt Whitney for the advancement of contemporary American art; Museum opened 1931 on Eigth Street and moved to 54th Street in 1954; new building opened in 1966. Average Annual Attendance: 500,000. Mem: 5000; dues $50 and up
Income: Financed by endowment, admissions, grants, membership
Purchases: Numerous annual acquisitions
Collections: †Drawings, †paintings, †prints, †sculpture of mainly 20th century American artists
Exhibitions: Figurative Works from the Permanent Collection; Trans-Voices; Alfonso Ossorio Drawings, 1940-48: The Anatomy of a Surrealist Sensibility; Jean-Michel Basquiat; Robert Gardner: The Impulse to Preserve; Agnes Martin; Jonas Mekas; The Geometric Tradition in 20th Century American Art; Thersea Hak Kyung Cha; 1993 Biennial Exhibition; In the Spirit of Fluxus; Hand-Painted Pop: American Art in Transition, 1955-62
Publications: Annual report; brochures, cards, posters; calendars; exhibition catalogues; gallery brochures
Activities: Classes for adults; docent training; symposia & panel discussions; teachers' workshops; lectures open to the public; gallery talks; tours; Artreach provides introductory art education to elementary and high school students; individual paintings and original objects of art lent; originate traveling exhibitions for museums here and abroad; sales shop sells books, magazines, reproductions, slides, cards & posters

L **Library,** 945 Madison Ave, 10021. Tel 212-570-3648. *Librn* May Castleberry
Open Tues - Fri 10 AM - noon & 2 - 5 PM by appointment for advanced research. No admis fee. Estab 1931 for encouragement and advancement of American art and art scholarship
Purchases: $15,000
Library Holdings: Vols 30,000; Per subs 100; Micro — Cards, fiche, reels; AV — A-tapes, cassettes, rec, slides; Other — Clipping files, exhibition catalogs, manuscripts, memorabilia, pamphlets, photographs, reproductions
Special Subjects: Focuses on 20th century American drawing, graphics, painting and sculpture

M **Downtown at Federal Reserve Plaza,** 33 Maiden Lane at Nassau St, 10038. Tel 212-943-5655; FAX 212-425-8384. *Dir* Karl E Willers; *ISP Coordr* Miwon Kwon; *Gallery Asst* Gioia Whittemore
Open Mon - Fri 11 AM - 6 PM. No admis fee
Income: Financed by Park Tower Realty Corp & IBM
Exhibitions: Changing exhibitions every 2 1/2 months
Publications: Exhibit catalogs

M **Whitney Museum at Philip Morris,** 120 Park Ave at 42nd St, 10017. Tel 212-878-2550. *Branch Dir* Thelma Golden
Sculpture court open Mon - Sat 7:30 AM - 9:30 PM, Sun & holidays 11 AM - 7 PM, gallery open Mon - Fri 11 AM - 6 PM, Thurs 11 AM - 7:30 PM. No admis fee. Estab 1982 to extend American art to wider audience. Sculpture court with major works & adjacent gallery for changing exhibitions. Average Annual Attendance: 45,000
Income: Financed by Philip Morris Companies Inc
Exhibitions: Y David Chung: Turtle Boat Head; Glenn Ligon: Good Mirrors Art Not Cheap; Suzanne McClelland
Publications: Free brochures for each exhibition
Activities: Gallery talks Mon, Wed & Fri at 1 PM; films; performances

M **Whitney at Equitable Center,** 787 Seventh Ave, 10019. Tel 212-554-1113. *Branch Dir* Kathleen Monaghan
Open Mon - Fri 11 AM - 6 PM, Thurs 11 AM - 7:30 PM, Sat noon - 5 PM. No admis fee. Estab 1986. Two galleries for permanent collection & changing exhibitions
Income: Financed by Equitable Life Assurance Society of the US
Exhibitions: 20th Century American Art: Highlights of the Permanent Collection; Figure as Subject: The Last Decade; Hugh Ferriss: Metropolis; Master American Photographs: 1910-1980; The Interpretive Link: Abstract Surrealism into Abstract Expressionism
Publications: Free brochures for each exhibition
Activities: Free gallery talks

M **Whitney Museum of American Art at Champion,** 10021. *Mgr* Cynthia Roznoy; *Gallery Coordr* Jennifer Landes; *Educ Coordr* Holly Williams
Open Tues - Sat 11 AM - 5 PM. No admis fee. Estab 1981
Income: Financed by Champion International Corporation
Activities: Lect; gallery talks; films; performances

A **CATHARINE LORILLARD WOLFE ART CLUB, INC,** 802 Broadway, 10003. Tel 212-254-2000. *Pres* Karin Strong
Estab 1896, incorporated in as a non-profit club to further fine, representational American Art. A club of professional women painters, graphic artists & sculptors. Mem: 290; dues $30, associate membership $15; monthly meetings
Income: Financed by mem
Exhibitions: Members Exhibition (spring); Open Annual Exhibition (fall)
Activities: Metropolitan Museum Benefit, annually; lect; demonstration programs

A **WOMEN IN THE ARTS FOUNDATION, INC,** 1175 York Ave, No 2G, 10021. Tel 212-751-1915. *Executive Coordr* Roberta Crown; *Recording Coordr* Sari Menna; *Newsletter Editor* Jackie Skiles; *Financial Coordr* Alice Philipps
Estab 1971 for the purpose of overcoming discrimination against women artists both in government and the private sector. Sponsors discussions, workshops, panels and exhibits the work of women artists, both established & unknown.

Average Annual Attendance: 1000. Mem: 200; dues $40
Income: $12,000 (financed by endowment & mem)
Exhibitions: Arsenal Gallery: Patterns of Nature; Broadway Gallery, Passaic Community College: Perspectives '86; Cork Gallery: Color Reflections
Publications: Women in the Arts, bulletin-newsletter, quarterly
Activities: Public educ as to the problems & discrimination faced by women artists; lect open to the public; individual paintings & original objects of art lent to museum & university art galleries for special exhibitions; original art works for exhibitions are obtained from member artists; traveling exhibitions organized & circulated

M WOMEN'S INTERART CENTER, INC, Interart Gallery, 549 W 52 St, 10019. Tel 212-246-1050. *Dir of Programming* Ronnie Geist; *VPres* Bill Perlman; *Artistic Dir* Margot Lewitin
Open Mon - Fri 1 - 6 PM. No admis fee. Estab 1970 to present to the public the work of significant, emerging women artists. Average Annual Attendance: 9000. Mem: Dues $35
Income: Financed by state appropriation, National Endowment for the Arts, private foundations, corporations & individuals
Exhibitions: (1993) Community as Planner
Publications: Women's Interart Center Newsletter, quarterly
Activities: Classes for adults; lect open to public, 2 visiting lectr per year; originate traveling exhibitions

M YESHIVA UNIVERSITY MUSEUM, 2520 Amsterdam Ave at W 185th St, 10033. Tel 212-960-5390, 960-5268; FAX 212-960-5406. *Dir* Sylvia A Herskowitz; *Educ Dir* Jeannette Ornstein; *Office Mgr* Eleanor Chiger; *Asst Cur* Bonni-Dara Michaels; *Asst Cur* Gabriel Goldstein; *Adminr* Randy R Glickberg; *Special Events Coordr* June B Aranoff; *Registrar* Ellin Burke
Open Tues - Thurs 10:30 AM - 5 PM, Sun noon - 6 PM. Admis adults $3, students & senior citizens $1.50. Estab 1973 to collect, preserve & interpret Jewish art & objects of material culture in the light of Jewish history. 8000 sq ft of upper & lower galleries. Average Annual Attendance: 25,000. Mem: 400; dues $18-$1000
Collections: Architectual models, ceremonial objects, documents, ethnographic material, fine & decorative art, manuscripts, photographs, sculpture, textiles
Exhibitions: Ashkenaz: The German Jewish Heritage; Jewish Themes in Electronic Art; Mordecai Manuel Noah: The First American Jew; The Sephardic Journey: 1492-1992; The Serendipitous Years: 15 Years of Unplanned Gifts
Publications: Catalogs
Activities: Workshops for adults & children; docent programs; lect; tours; live prformances; museum shop sells books, original art, reproductions, prints & slides

NIAGARA FALLS

M NATIVE AMERICAN CENTER FOR THE LIVING ARTS, 25 Rainbow Blvd, 14303. Tel 716-284-2427. *Executive Dir* Elwood Green
Open Mon - Fri 9 AM - 5 PM, Sat & Sun noon - 5 PM; summer daily 9 AM - 6 PM, cl New Years, Thanksgiving, Christmas. Admis adult $3.50, sr citizens $3, children between 5 & 13 & students with ID $2, children under 5 free. Estab 1970 to preserve & promote American Indian art & culture. Average Annual Attendance: 100,000. Mem: 500; dues family $35, individual $25
Income: $1,500,000 (Financed by earned income & state arts councils programs funding)
Collections: Native American Archaeological, Ethnographic & Contemporary Art from Mexico, US & Canada; Native American Archive & Iconography
Publications: Turtle, quarterly tabloid; art catalogues
Activities: Classes for adults & children; dramatic programs; docent training; lectures open to public, 10 vis lectr per yr; concerts; gallery talks; tours; AV presentations; competitions with awards; individual paintings & original objects of art lent to museums & galleries; originate traveling exhibition; sales shop sells books, magazines, original art, reproductions, prints, slides, crafts & records

NORTHPORT

L NORTHPORT-EAST NORTHPORT PUBLIC LIBRARY, Art Dept, 151 Laurel Ave, 11768. Tel 516-261-6930. *Dir* Stephanie Heineman; *Asst Dir* Eileen Minogue
Open Sept - June Mon - Fri 9 AM - 9 PM, Sat 9 AM - 5 PM, Sun 1 - 5 PM. Estab 1914. Circ 451,778
Income: $1,956,852 (financed by local tax levy)
Purchases: $200,000
Library Holdings: Vols 17,000; Per subs 68; Micro — Fiche; AV — A-tapes, cassettes, fs, rec, slides, v-tapes; Other — Clipping files, exhibition catalogs, framed reproductions, manuscripts, pamphlets, prints, reproductions, sculpture
Activities: Lectures open to public, 5 vis lectrs per yr; concerts; competitions; original paintings and art objects lent

NORTH SALEM

M HAMMOND MUSEUM & JAPANESE STROLL GARDEN, Cross-Cultural Center, Deveau Rd, 10560. Tel 914-669-5033. *Chmn of Board of Trustees* Gail Pantezzi
Open May - Dec, Wed - Sun 10 AM - 4 PM. Admis to Museum adults $2, children $1; to the Gardens adults $4, children $2. A Museum of the Humanities, it presents changing exhibitions of international scope and varied historic periods and topics, supplemented by programs of related special events. The Japanese Stroll Gardens comprising 15 individual gardens on 3 1/2 acres, include a lake, a reflecting pool, a dry landscape, a waterfall, and a Zen Garden. A Museum of the Humanities, it presents changing exhibitions of international scope and varied historic periods and topics, supplemented by programs of related special events. The Oriental Stroll Gardens comprising 15 individual gardens on 3 1/2 acres, include a lake, a reflecting pool, a dry landscape, a waterfall, and a Zen Garden. Average Annual Attendance: 35,000. Mem: 1800; Qualifications for mem: Open to all who are in sympathy with its aims and

purposes
Income: Financed by memberships, matching funds, private foundations & corporations
Activities: Dramatic programs; lect open to the public; concerts; documentary films; museum shop; Terrace Restaurant, luncheon by reservation

NYACK

A OIL PASTEL ASSOCIATION, PO Box 587, 10960. Tel 914-353-2483. *Pres* John T Elliott; *Executive Dir* Sheila Elliott
Estab 1983 exhibition forum for new & traditional types of pastel paintings. Average Annual Attendance: 2000. Mem: 350; dues $25 per year
Income: $4000 (financed by donations & mem)
Exhibitions: Oil pastels; soft pastels; water soluble pastels
Publications: Art & Artists, USA
Activities: Classes for adults; workshops; scholarships offered

OGDENSBURG

M FREDERIC REMINGTON ART MUSEUM, 303 Washington St, 13669. Tel 315-393-2425; FAX 315-393-4464. *Dir* Lowell McAllister
Open May 1 - Oct 31 Mon - Sat 10 AM - 5 PM, Sun 1 - 5 PM, Nov 1 - Apr 30 Tues - Sat 10 AM - 5 PM, cl legal holidays. Admis general $3, senior citizens & students between 13 & 16 $2, children under 12 free. Estab 1923 to house and exhibit works of art of Frederic Remington (1861-1909), a native of northern New York. The museum is in the converted Parish Mansion, built 1809-10, and the recently constructed Addie Priest Newell Wing. Remington's last studio has been reconstructed with most of the original furnishings. Average Annual Attendance: 15,000
Income: Financed by endowment and city appropriation
Collections: Remington paintings, bronzes, watercolors, drawings, photographs, letters & personal art collection; studies in plaster by Edwin Willard Deming; sculpture by Sally James Farnham; Haskell Collection of 19th century American and European paintings; Parish Collection of Belter furniture; Sharp Collection of period glass, china, silver and cameos
Exhibitions: The Children's Exhibit; The Frederic Remington Exhibit
Activities: Educ dept; lectures open to the public; tours; sales shop sells books, prints, slides, post cards, plates, spoons and rings
L Library, 303 Washington St, 13669. Tel 315-393-2425; FAX 315-393-4464. *Exec Dir* Lowell McAllister
Remington's own personal library for viewing purposes only
Library Holdings: Vols 200; Per subs 5

OLD CHATHAM

M SHAKER MUSEUM, Shaker Museum Rd, 12136. Tel 518-794-9100. *Dir* Viki Sand; *Asst Dir Coll & Research* Jerry Grant; *Finance Mgr* Pam Cook
Open May - Oct daily 10 AM - 5 PM. Admis adults $6, reduced rates for senior citizens, children & groups. Estab 1950 to promote interest in and understanding of the Shaker cultural heritage. The exhibits are housed in a complex of eight buildings. Average Annual Attendance: 20,000. Mem: 325; dues $35 - $1000
Income: $430,000; financed by earned revenue, endowment, contributions, private & public grants
Purchases: $3000
Collections: 35,000 artifacts representing 200 years of Shaker history and culture
Exhibitions: Orientation to Shaker History; Shakers in the 20th Century; Shaker Cabinetmakers and Their Tools; study storage related to individual collections
Publications: Members update; The Shaker Adventure; Shaker Seed Industry; pamphlets; booklets; gallery guide; catalogs; postcards, reprints, and broadsides
Activities: Seminars; School & adult tours; lectures; symposia; festivals; family events; museum shop sells Shaker reproduction furniture, craft items & publications
L Emma B King Library, Shaker Museum Rd, 12136. Tel 518-794-9100, Ext 111. *Dir* Viki Sand
Open by appointment. Admis research use fee
Library Holdings: Vols 2000; Per subs 22; Micro — Reels 189; AV — A-tapes, cassettes, fs, Kodachromes, motion pictures, rec, slides, v-tapes; Other — Manuscripts, memorabilia, original art works 100, pamphlets, photographs 3500
Collections: Manuscripts and records; Photographic and map archive

OLD WESTBURY

M NEW YORK INSTITUTE OF TECHNOLOGY, Gallery, 11568. Tel 516-686-7542. *Chmn* John Murray
Open Mon - Fri 9 AM - 5 PM. Estab 1964. Gallery maintained for the many exhibits held during the year. Average Annual Attendance: 5000
Exhibitions: Annual faculty and student shows; some traveling exhibitions
Publications: Graphic Guild Newsletter, quarterly
Activities: Classes in custom silk-screen printmaking; gallery talks; awards; scholarships; Exten Dept serves all areas
L Art & Architectural Library, Education Hall, 11568. Tel 516-686-7579. *Librn* Clare Cohn-Brown
Open Mon - Thurs 8:30 AM - 9 PM, Fri 8:30 AM - 5 PM, Sat noon - 4 PM. No admis fee. Estab 1976
Library Holdings: Vols 13,000; Per subs 252; Micro — Reels 1255; AV — Cassettes, motion pictures 23, slides 30,000, v-tapes 80; Other — Clipping files, exhibition catalogs, pamphlets
Special Subjects: Afro-American Art, American Western Art, Antiquities-Egyptian, Art History, Asian Art, Calligraphy, Cartoons, Decorative Arts, Folk Art, Mexican Art, Southwestern Art
Exhibitions: Architecture dept student projects
Activities: Tours

M STATE UNIVERSITY OF NEW YORK COLLEGE AT OLD WESTBURY,
Amelie A Wallace Gallery, Rt 107 (Broadway), PO Box 210, 11568. Tel 516-876-3148. *Dir* Eugenie Tsai
Open Mon, Tues & Sat noon - 4 PM, Wed - Thurs noon - 6 PM. No admis fee. Estab 1976 to serve as a teaching aid and for community enlightenment. 334 sq ft on three levels. Average Annual Attendance: 3000
Income: $9750 (financed by endowment)
Publications: Exhibit catalogues
Activities: Lect open to public, 4 vis lectr per yr; originate traveling exhibitions

ONEIDA

M MADISON COUNTY HISTORICAL SOCIETY, Cottage Lawn, 435 Main St, PO Box 415, 13421. Tel 315-363-4136. *Pres* James Cleary; *VPres* Harold Chamberlain
Open Tues - Sat 1 - 5 PM & by appointment. No admis fee. Estab 1898 to collect, preserve and interpret artifacts indigenous to the history of Madison County. 1849 AJ Davis Gothic dwelling with period rooms, library and Craft Archive. Average Annual Attendance: 4000. Mem: 700; dues $15; annual meeting second Tues of Nov
Income: $87,000 (financed by endowment, mem, county, city & state appropriation, Annual Craft Fair)
Collections: Locally produced and or used furnishings, paintings, silver, textiles and ceramics
Exhibitions: (1993) Gerrit Smith & the Anti-Slavery Movement
Publications: Quarterly Newsletter; Madison County Heritage, published annually; Country Roads Revisited
Activities: Educational outreach programs for nursing homes and schools; lectures open to public, 6 vis lectrs per year; slides; tapes & movies documenting traditional craftsmen at work; individual paintings and original objects of art lent to qualified museums and galleries for special exhibits; sales shop sells books, magazines, prints and slides
L Library, 435 Main St, 13421. Tel 315-363-4136. *Librn* Mary King
Open Tues - Sat 1 - 5 PM. Estab 1975 as a reference library of primary and secondary sources on Madison County History
Library Holdings: Vols 2500; Per subs 5; AV — Cassettes, lantern slides, motion pictures, rec, slides, v-tapes; Other — Clipping files, exhibition catalogs, manuscripts, memorabilia, pamphlets, photographs, prints
Special Subjects: Madison County and New York State History, Civil War, Oneida Indians
Collections: Gerrit Smith family papers

ONEONTA

M HARTWICK COLLEGE, Foreman Gallery, Anderson Center for the Arts, 13820. Tel 607-431-4827. *Cur* John Wineland
Open Mon - Thurs 1 - 5 PM & 7 - 9 PM, or by appointment; cl last half of Dec. No admis fee. Estab 1928, college collections and exhibitions for benefit of faculty, students and community
Collections: Painting, prints, drawings, sculpture, ceramics, and tapestry from 16th through 20th centuries: Renaissance and Baroque paintings and drawings; 19th century American Landscapes; 260 American political cartoons by John H Cassell
Exhibitions: Changing exhibitions to meet curriculm needs; Annual Student Exhibition; There Are No Heros; Paul Owens, Portfolio for the Homeless; Artists' Relief
Publications: Exhibition catalogues
Activities: Classes in museum studies; lectures open to the public; book traveling exhibitions, 5 - 10 per yr; originate traveling exhibitions
M Yager Museum, Hartwick College, 13820. Tel 607-431-4488. *Dir* Jane des Grange
Open Mon - Sat 10 AM - 4 PM, Sun 1 - 4 PM. No admis fee. Estab 1928
Collections: Collection of North American, Mexican & South American Indian art & artifacts
Exhibitions: Changing exhibitions; 19th Century Family Life of the Native Americans; Bruce North; Affair of the Heart
Activities: Classes in museum studies; lectures; tours; films

M STATE UNIVERSITY OF NEW YORK COLLEGE AT ONEONTA, Art Gallery & Sculpture Court, Fine Arts Center, 13820. Tel 607-431-3717. *Chmn Art Dept* Ernest D Mahlke
Open Mon - Fri 11 AM - 4 PM, Tues & Thurs 7 - 9 PM, Sat 1 - 4 PM. No admis fee. Art Gallery and Sculpture Court are major features of the Art Wing, separate fine arts and student galleries. Average Annual Attendance: 3384
Income: Financed by city and state appropriation

ORIENT

M OYSTERPONDS HISTORICAL SOCIETY, Museum, Village La, PO Box 844, 11957. Tel 516-323-2480. *Dir* Mickie McCormic; *Pres* Richard Frank; *VPres* Fredrica Wachsberger; *VPres* Reginald Tuthill; *VPres* Frederick Letson; *Treas* Nancy Douglass; *Secy* Christine Letson
Open July & Aug Wed, Thurs, Sat & Sun 2 - 5 PM, June & Sept weekends only. Admis adults $3, children $.50, mem free. Estab 1944 to discover, procure, & preserve material related to the civil & military history of Long Island, particularly the East Marion & Orient Hamlets. Mem: 500; dues family $30, individual $15; annual meeting in July
Income: $90,000 (financed by endowment, mem, state appropriation, fund raising)
Collections: Early Indian artifacts, including arrowheads, baskets & clay vessels; 18th century furniture & decorative arts; late 19th century Victorian furniture; marine & portrait paintings; photographs; textile collection, including quilts, scarves, fans; tools & equipment related to the agricultural & sea-related occupations of this area
Exhibitions: The Sea Around Us; Toys & Dolls; Clothing of an Orient Midget

Family; Indian Artifacts. (1991) Civil War Memorabilia; Traveling Companions: Trunks & Valeses
Publications: Historical Orient Village, book; Historical Review, book; monthly newsletter
Activities: Classes for adults & children; docent training; lectures open to public; museum shop sells books, magazines, original art, reproductions & prints

OSSINING

M MUSEUM OF OSSINING HISTORICAL SOCIETY, 196 Croton Ave, 10562. Tel 914-941-0001. *Pres* Gerard Dorian; *Dir* Roberta Y Arminio
Open Mon, Weds and Sun 2 - 4 PM & by appointment. No admis fee. Estab 1931 to educate the public in the history and traditions of the vicinity. East Gallery contains changing exhibitions and a portion of the permanent collection; West Gallery contains permanent collection. Average Annual Attendance: 2500.
Mem: 497; dues patron $100, civic, commercial & contributing $25, family $15, individual $10, sr citizens & student $5
Income: Financed by membership and town appropriation
Library Holdings: AV — V-tapes 32
Special Subjects: Antiquities-Etruscan, Antiquities-Roman, Architecture, Art History, Conceptual Art, Flasks & Bottles, Folk Art, Graphic Design, Handicrafts, History of Art & Archaeology, Painting - Italian, Sculpture, Italian Art & Architecture
Collections: Costumes; textiles & quilts; slides & films of old Ossining; old photographs & daguerreotypes; Victorian dollhouse complete in minute detail, contains antique dolls, toys, miniatures, old school books & photographs; oil portraits; fine arts
Publications: Monthly brochure
Activities: Education dept; class visits; special assignment guidance; lectures open to public, 4 vis lectr per yr; gallery talks; tours; competitions & awards; individual paintings & original objects of art lent to schools, banks & industry; sales shop sells books, magazines
L Library, 196 Croton Ave, 10562. Tel 914-941-0001. *Librn* John Drittler
Library Holdings: Vols 1000; Micro — Reels; AV — A-tapes, cassettes, lantern slides, slides, v-tapes 32; Other — Clipping files, exhibition catalogs, framed reproductions, memorabilia, original art works, photographs, prints, reproductions

OSWEGO

M STATE UNIVERSITY OF NEW YORK AT OSWEGO, Tyler Art Gallery, Tyler Hall, 13126. Tel 315-341-2113. *Dir* Coy L Ludwig; *Asst Dir* Mindy Ostrow
Open Mon - Fri 9:30 AM - 4:30 PM, Sept - May; summer hours as posted. No admis fee. Estab 1969 to provide cultural stimulation and enrichment of art to the college community and to the residents of Oswego County. Two gallery spaces in Tyler Hall, the North Gallery is approximately 2400 sq ft and the South Gallery is approximately 1300 sq ft. Average Annual Attendance: 20,000
Income: Financed by University funds
Collections: Arnold Collection of Fine Prints; Contemporary American Prints and Paintings
Exhibitions: Two galleries show a combined total of 14 exhibitions per school year
Publications: Brochures; occasional catalogs for exhibitions; posters
Activities: Lect open to public, 8-10 vis lect per year; concerts, gallery talks; lending collection contains individual and original objects of art; originates traveling exhibitions
L Penfield Library, 13126-3514. Tel 315-341-4232; FAX 315-341-3194. *Dir* Michael McLane
Library Holdings: Vols 410,000; Per subs 1756; AV — A-tapes, cassettes, motion pictures, slides, v-tapes; Other — Framed reproductions, original art works, pamphlets

OYSTER BAY

L PLANTING FIELDS FOUNDATION, Coe Hall at Planting Fields Arboretum, Planting Fields Rd, 11771. Tel 516-922-0479. *Cur* Lorraine Gilligan; *Archivist* Eugenia Clarke
Open Apr - Sept Mon - Fri 1 - 3:30 PM. Admis adults $2, sr citizens & children 6 - 12 $1. Archives estab 1979 for Coe family papers, architectural drawings, photos, Planting Fields Foundation documents. For reference only. Coe Hall, a Tudor revival mansion being restored to its 1920's appearance, contains 17th-20th century paintings
Income: Financed by endowment
Library Holdings: AV — A-tapes, cassettes, fs, lantern slides, motion pictures, slides, v-tapes; Other — Clipping files, manuscripts, memorabilia, original art works, pamphlets, photographs, prints
Special Subjects: American Western Art, Architecture, Decorative Arts, Historical Material, Landscape Architecture, Painting - British, Painting - Dutch, Painting - European, Painting - Italian, Period Rooms, Photography, Porcelain, Portraits, Restoration & Conservation, Stained Glass
Activities: Educ dept; classes for children; docent training; lectures open to public, 5 vis lectr per yr; concerts; guided tours of historic house

PELHAM

M PELHAM ART CENTER, 155 Fifth Ave, 10803. Tel 914-738-2525; FAX 914-738-2686. *Exec Dir* Alison Paul; *Prog Coordr* Kathi Dinan
No admis fee. Estab 1975 as a community art center. Average Annual Attendance: 20,000. Mem: 500; dues $25 - $100; annual meeting in June
Income: $280,000 (financed by mem, tuition, earned income & gift shop sales)
Activities: Classes for adults & children; studio classes; docent programs; lect open to public, 2 - 3 vis lectr per year; scholarships & fels offered; retail store sells books & prints

PLATTSBURGH

M CLINTON COUNTY HISTORICAL ASSOCIATION, Clinton County
Historical Museum, 48 Court St, PO Box 332, 12901-0332. Tel 518-561-0340.
Dir & Cur Helen W Allan
Open 1 - 4 PM daily except Wed & Thurs. Admis adults $2, children $1. Estab
in 1973 to preserve and publicize the history of Clinton County, New York.
Average Annual Attendance: 4000-5000. Mem: 420; dues $500, $100, $50, $25,
$15, Business/Institution $25
Income: $70,000 (financed by membership, NYSCA & federal grants and county
appropriation)
Collections: Glass & ceramics, paintings & prints, furniture & textiles collection;
Military and Naval history; Redford Glass (19th Century handblown)
Exhibitions: (1988) Original People: Natives American in the Champlain Valley.
(1989) Fur & Feather. (1991) The History of Fire & Fire Control in Clinton
County
Publications: Antiquarian, annual magazine; North Country Notes, monthly
newsletter
Activities: Lect open to the public, 10 vis lectr per year; writing (historical-North
Country Topics) competition & prize; museum shop sells books, collectables,
prints and reproductions

M STATE UNIVERSITY OF NEW YORK, SUNY Plattsburgh Art Museum,
12901. Tel 518-564-2813 Kent, 564-2288 Myers. *Dir* Edward R Brohel
Open Tues - Wed & Fri 10 AM - 5 PM, Thurs 10 AM - 9 PM, Sun 2 - 5 PM, cl
university holidays. No admis fee. Estab 1978
Collections: Rockwell Kent Collection, paintings, prints, drawings, sketches,
proofs & designs, books; china; ephemera
Exhibitions: Sixteen exhibitions each year; antique and contemporary, all media
Publications: Exhibition catalogs; monthly exhibition announcements; semi-
annual calendar of events
Activities: Programs for undergrad students, elementary and secondary schools
and community groups in area; docent programs; lectures open to the public, 10
vis lectr per yr; tours; competitions with awards; individual paintings lent

PLEASANTVILLE

M PACE UNIVERSITY GALLERY, Bedford Rd, 10570. Tel 914-773-3694; FAX
914-773-3785. *Gallery Dir* Beth A Treadway
Open Sun - Fri 1 - 5 PM, cl Sat. No admis fee. Estab 1978 to exhibit the works
of nationally known professional artists and groups, and to serve as a focal point
for artistic activities within the university and surrounding communities. The
gallery is located on the ground floor of the Arts Building and has a commanding
view of the center of campus; it is both spacious and modern
Income: Financed by the university
Activities: Lectures open to public, 8-10 visiting lecturers per year; gallery talks;
tours

C THE READER'S DIGEST ASSOCIATION INC, World Headquarters, 10570.
Tel 914-241-5797. *Cur* Frances Chaves; *Asst Cur* Marianne Brunson Frisch
Art collection located throughout corporate headquarters; public viewing by
appointment only
Collections: †Over 5000 works of art, French Impressionists & Post -
Impressionists as well as 19th century & contemporary American artists &
International artists; graphics; decorative arts; sculpture; painting; mixed media;
works on paper

PORT CHESTER

L PORT CHESTER PUBLIC LIBRARY, Fine Arts Dept, One Haseco Ave,
10573. Tel 914-939-6710. *Dir* Robin Lettieri
Open Mon 9 AM - 9 PM, Tues & Wed 9 AM - 8 PM, Thurs - Sat 9 AM - 5
PM. Estab 1876 to circulate books, records, magazines, to the general public to
provide reference services. Maintains an art gallery. A small gallery with about
ten shows per year, mostly local artists. Circ 103,598. Average Annual
Attendance: 2000
Income: $494,600 (financed by endowment, villages and state appropriations)
Purchases: $50,500
Library Holdings: Vols 73,861; Per subs 185; Micro — Reels; AV — Fs, rec,
slides; Other — Framed reproductions, pamphlets, prints
Exhibitions: Water colors, oils, acrylics, photographs
Activities: Educ dept; lectures, films; open to the public; films; career seminars
and workshops; individual paintings lent

PORT WASHINGTON

M LONG ISLAND GRAPHIC EYE GALLERY, 301 Main St, 11050. Tel 516-
883-9668. *Pres* Myrna Turtletaub; *Secy* Angela Milner; *Treas* Esta Rubin
Open Wed - Sun noon - 5 PM. No admis fee. Chartered 1974 as a non-profit
educational gallery to educate the public in the understanding & appreciation of
prints, and to promote art techniques. Average Annual Attendance: 3500. Mem:
25; dues $500; open to professional artists & art instructors; monthly meetings
Income: Financed by memberships & individual project grants
Collections: †Slide collection
Exhibitions: Angela Milner; Christmas Show: Windows
Activities: Education dept; lect & demonstrations in print media open to public,
3 - 4 vis lectr per yr; competitions with awards; sales shop sells original art &
prints

L PORT WASHINGTON PUBLIC LIBRARY, One Library Dr, 11050-2794. Tel
516-883-4400; FAX 516-944-6855. *Dir* Edward De Sciora; *Dir of Media Serv*
Lillian R Katz; *Cur of Spec Coll* Janet West
Open Mon - Fri 9 AM - 9 PM, Sat 9 AM - 5 PM, Sun 1 - 5 PM. No admis fee.
Estab 1892. Circ 303,500
Income: Financed by state appropriation & school district

Library Holdings: Vols 123,000; Per subs 750; Micro — Cards, reels; AV — A-
tapes, cassettes, fs, rec, v-tapes; Other — Clipping files, manuscripts, pamphlets,
photographs, prints
Collections: Robert Hamilton Ball Theatre Collection of over 2000 books,
journals, pictorial & ephemeral items on theatre history & research; Ernie Simon
Collection of photographs & newspaper articles on the history of Port
Washington; Mason Photograph Archive of photographic negatives spanning over
75 years of Port Washington social history; P W Play Troupe Archive of
memorabilia covering the 60 year history of the oldest theatre group on Long
Island; Collection of drawings by children's illustrator Peter Spier
Exhibitions: (1990) Art Gallery monthly exhibits: sculpture, drawings, painting,
fabric, industrial design & photography; Photography Gallery monthly or
bimonthly exhibits; Photography Club of Long Island annual exhibition; Hajime
Okubo (box constructions); Paul Wood (oil painting & watercolors); Lita
Kelmenson (drawings & wood sculpture); Photographers: Dency Ann Kane,
Marion Fuller, Christine Osinski
Publications: Monthly guide catalog

POTSDAM

M POTSDAM COLLEGE OF THE STATE UNIVERSITY OF NEW YORK,
Roland Gibson Gallery, Pierrepont Ave, 13676. Tel 315-267-2254, 267-2250,
267-2481. *Dir* Mark Sloan; *Cur* Diana Cooper
Open daily noon - 5 PM. No admis fee. Estab 1967 to serve college and
community as a teaching gallery. Gallery has 4800 square feet of exhibition space
on three levels with security & environmental controls. Average Annual
Attendance: 18,000. Mem: 200; dues $10 - $100; annual meeting Oct
Collections: †Contemporary Japanese, Italian & American art (painting, sculpture
& prints); †contemporary drawing collection
Publications: Exhibition catalogs
Activities: Docent training; lect open to public, 10-12 vis lectr per yr; concerts;
gallery talks; tours; competitions; original objects of art lent to public institutions,
art museums and art organizations; book traveling exhibitions, 1-3 times per yr;
traveling exhibitions organized and circulated

M VILLAGE OF POTSDAM PUBLIC MUSEUM (Formerly Potsdam Public
Museum), Civic Center, 13676. Tel 315-265-6910. *Pres of Board* Beverly
Washburn; *Dir* Betsy Travis
Open Tues - Sat 2 - 5 PM, cl Sun & Mon. No admis fee. Estab 1940 as an
educational institution acting as a cultural and historical center for the Village of
Potsdam and surrounding area. Educational services taken to area schools.
Museum occupies a sandstone building, formerly a Universalist Church built in
1876. Maintains small reference library. Average Annual Attendance: 12,000
Income: Financed by village, town, state & federal appropriation
Collections: Burnap Collection of English Pottery; costumes of the 19th and 20th
centuries; Mandarin Chinese hangings, china and costumes; photograph
collection and artifacts and material on local history; pressed glass and art glass
of the 19th and early 20th century
Exhibitions: Changing exhibitions
Publications: Newsletter, 3 - 4 times per year
Activities: Classes for adults & children; programs for schools; lectures open to
public, 8 vis lectr per year; concerts; tours

POUGHKEEPSIE

M DUTCHESS COUNTY ARTS COUNCIL, 39 Market St, 12601. Tel 914-454-
3222. *Executive Dir* Sherre Wesley; *Office Mgr* Lauren R Zoppa; *Development
Assoc* Mary Koniz Arnold
Open Mon - Fri 9 AM - 5 PM. No admis fee. Estab 1965 in mid-Hudson region
as premiere location for arts cultural activities. Mem: 325; dues $25-$250; annual
meeting in Jan
Income: $650,000 (financed by mem, county & state appropriation & Dutchess
Arts Fund)
Publications: Artscene, quarterly newsletter; Arts in Education Quarterly
Activities: Coordinate arts-in-education programs in schools; lect open to public;
technical assistance workshops; poetry; scholarships & fels offered

M MID-HUDSON ARTS AND SCIENCE CENTER, 228 Main St, 12601. Tel
914-471-1155. *Pres* Robert Sanderson; *Exec Dir* Janet Jappen
Open Tues - Sat 11 AM - 4 PM, 1st Sun noon - 4 PM. Admis adults $2, children
$1. Estab 1977 as a museum for all people. Main gallery approx 35 x 60 ft,
community gallery approx 15 x 20 ft, theatre gallery approx 35 x 35. Average
Annual Attendance: 5000. Mem: 350; dues $35 family, $25 individual, $10
student
Income: Financed by mem, gallery sales, gift shop & foundation grants
Activities: Classes for adults and children; dramatic programs; lectures open to
the public; concerts; gallery talks; tours; competitions with awards; individual
paintings and original objects of art lent to local businesses, schools, government
buildings; traveling exhibition organized and circulated to schools, government
buildings; museum shop sells books, magazines, original art, reproductions, prints
and import gift items

M VASSAR COLLEGE, Vassar Art Gallery, Raymond Ave, 12601. Tel 914-437-
5235. *Dir* James Mundy; *Cur* Rebecca E Lawton; *Registrar* Joann Potter;
Preparator John P Miller
Open Wed - Sat 10 AM - 5 PM, Sun noon - 5 PM, cl Mon - Tues & holidays.
No admis fee. Estab 1864; collects Eastern and Western art of all periods. The
museum has 6000 sq ft of exhibition space in 1915 Gothic style building.
Average Annual Attendance: 12,000. Mem: 1100; dues $35 & up; bi-annual
meeting fall & spring
Income: Financed by Vassar College, endowment and membership
Purchases: $60,000
Collections: Charles M Pratt gift of Italian Renaissance paintings; †Matthew
Vassar collection of 19th century American paintings of Hudson River School
and 19th century English watercolors; †Felix M Warburg Collection of medieval
sculpture and graphics including Duerer & Rembrandt; Charles Pratt Collection

of Chinese Jades; †20th century art of all media including photography; †European paintings, sculpture and drawings ranging from the Renaissance to the 20th century, including Bacchiacca, Cezanne, Salvator Rosa, Claesz, Tiepolo, Robert, Corot, Cezanne, Delacroix, Gifford, Van Gogh, Tanner, Munch, Klee, Bourdelle, Laurent, Davidson, Gabo, Calder, Moore; †20th Century American and European paintings including Henri, Hartley, O'Keeffe, Bacon, Nicholson, Rothko, de Kooning, Hartigan, Weber; graphics ranging from Barocci to Rembrandt to Goya to Picasso, Matisse, Braque, Kelly, Grooms and Graves; photography from Anna Atkins, Cameson, Gilpin, Steichen, Abbott, Lange, Lynes and Linda Connor; †The Classical Collection includes Greek vases, Egyptian, Etruscan, and Mycenaean objects, Roman glass, portrait busts, jewelry; other archaeological finds
Exhibitions: Recent Latin American Drawings; Works on Paper from Winston-Malbin Coll; Vanessa Bell; Nancy Graves
Publications: Gallery, biannually
Activities: Lectures open to public, 10 - 12 vis lectr per yr; gallery talks; tours; concerts; internships offered; individual paintings and original objects of art lent to other museums; book and originate traveling exhibitions

L **Art Library,** Raymond Ave, 12601. Tel 914-437-5790. *Librn* Tom Hill
Open Mon - Thurs 8:30 AM - midnight, Fri 8:30 AM - 10 PM, Sat 9 AM - 10 PM, Sun 10 AM - noon, cl Summer. Estab 1937. Circulation to students and faculty only
Library Holdings: Vols 38,500; Per subs 250; Micro — Fiche, reels; Other — Exhibition catalogs

PURCHASE

M **MANHATTANVILLE COLLEGE,** Brownson Art Gallery, Brownson Bldg, 10577. Tel 914-694-2200, Ext 331; FAX 914-694-2386. *Chmn* Randolph Williams; *Dean of Faculty* James B Bryan
Open 9 AM - 4:30 PM. No admis fee. Average Annual Attendance: 300 per wk
Income: Financed by endowment and tuition
Collections: Sculpture
Exhibitions: Leslie Lowinger, Graveyards & Other Places; Anthony & Ann Woiner, Exploring Spaces
Publications: Magazine, bimonthly; catalogs
Activities: Lectures open to public, 5 vis lectr per yr; concerts; gallery talks; scholarships; original objects of art lent; originate traveling exhibitions; sales shop sells books, magazines, reproductions & prints

L **Library,** 125 Purchase St, 10577-0560. Tel 914-694-2200, Ext 274; FAX 914-694-2386. *Librn* Edward O'Hara
Library Holdings: Vols 250,000; Per subs 1100

C **PEPSICO INC,** Anderson Hill Rd, 10577. Tel 914-253-2900. *Executive Committee Chmn* Donald M Kendall; *Dir Art Prog* Katherine F Niles
Open Mon - Sun 9 AM - 5 PM. No admis fee. Estab 1970 to present sculpture of museum quality. Average Annual Attendance: 10,000
Collections: Forty-two large outdoor sculptures, works by Alexander Calder, Henry Moore, Louise Nevelson, David Smith, Arnaldo Pomodoro, Jacques Lipchitz, Henry Laurens, Auguste Rodin, Miro, Giacometti, Max Ernst, Jean DuBuffet, Tony Smith, George Segal, Claes Oldenburg, George Rickey, Richard Erdman & Barbara Hepworth

M **STATE UNIVERSITY OF NEW YORK AT PURCHASE,** Neuberger Museum, 735 Anderson Hill Rd, 10577. Tel 914-251-6100; FAX 914-253-5552. *Dir* Lucinda H Gedeon; *Museum Mgr* Douglas Caulk; *Registrar* Joan Hendricks; *Cur Asst* Olga D'Angelo; *Coordr of Public Information* Patricia Greenhill; *Head of Musuem Education* Eleanor Brackbill; *Development Assoc* Jewel Hoogstoel; *Cur Contemporary Art* Cornelia Butler
Open Tues - Fri 10 AM - 4 PM, Sat & Sun 11 AM - 5 PM, cl Mon and major holidays. Suggested contribution $2. Estab 1968, opened May 1974 to serve university and residents of New York State and Connecticut. 78,000 sq ft facility designed by Johnson Burgee, with nine total galleries, five outside sculpture courts. Average Annual Attendance: 58,000. Mem: Dues sustaining $1000, patron $500, donor $250, contributing $100, family-dual $50, individual $35
Income: Financed by State University of New York, endowment fund, government grants, private foundations, donors and membership
Collections: The Neuberger Museum's permanent collection includes 3600 objects featuring 20th century European & American paintings, sculpture, drawings, prints, photographs & audio works; African and ancient art; large scale sculpture
Exhibitions: Changing contemporary art exhibitions
Publications: Exhibition catalogues; brochures; quarterly calendars
Activities: Docent training; internships for Purchase College students; tours for children, adults and citizens with special needs; lectures open to public, 10-12 vis lectr per year; concerts; gallery talks; tours; internships; original objects of art lent to other museums; book traveling exhibitions, 2-3 per year; originate traveling exhibitions to other museums; sales shop sells books, magazines, prints, small gift items and cards

L **Library,** 735 Anderson Hill Rd, 10577-1400. Tel 914-251-6435; FAX 914-251-6437. *Dir* Lawrence E Randall; *Reference-Visual Arts Specialist* Carol Abatelli
Library Holdings: Vols 20,000; Per subs 73; Micro — Cards, fiche, reels; AV — A-tapes, cassettes, motion pictures, rec, slides, v-tapes; Other — Reproductions
Special Subjects: 20th Century American Art

RIVERHEAD

A **EAST END ARTS & HUMANITIES COUNCIL,** 133 E Main St, 11901. Tel 516-727-0900. *Exec Dir* Judith Kaufman Weiner
Open Mon - Fri 10 AM - 5 PM, Sat 12 - 5 PM. No admis fee. Estab 1972. Average Annual Attendance: 11,000. Mem: 900; dues $10 - $25
Income: Financed by public and private sector
Publications: East End Arts News, monthly; East End Calendar of Cultural Events
Activities: Classes for children; lectures open to public, competitions with awards, gallery talks, tours; sales shop sells books, original art & crafts, hand crafted items

ROCHESTER

A **DEAF ARTISTS OF AMERICA INC,** 87 N Clinton Ave, Suite 408, 14604. Tel 716-325-2400. *Executive Dir* Tom Willard; *Prog Dir* Tracey Willard
Open Wed - Sat 1 - 4 PM, Thurs 7 AM - 9 PM, cl Sun - Tues. No admis fee. Estab 1985 to support & recognize America's deaf artists. 600 sq ft, one-room gallery on 4th floor. Average Annual Attendance: 500. Mem: 350; dues $25; biennial meeting in odd numbered years
Income: $35,000 (financed by mem, state appropriation, earned income)
Purchases: Assorted artwork
Collections: Permanent collection of artwork by deaf artists - all media included
Exhibitions: 4-6 changing art exhibits per year
Publications: Directory of American Deaf Artists, annual; Uncharted: Exploring the World of Deaf Artists, quarterly magazine
Activities: Adult classes; workshops & conferences; lect open to public, 1-2 vis lectr per yr; retail store sells books, prints, crafts

M **INTERNATIONAL MUSEUM OF PHOTOGRAPHY AT GEORGE EASTMAN HOUSE,** 900 East Ave, 14607. Tel 716-271-3361; FAX 716-271-3970. *Chmn* Bruce B Bates; *Dir* James L Enyeart; *Cur Film Coll* Jan-Christopher Horak; *Controller* Paul J Piazza; *Dir Technology Coll* Philip Condax; *Mgr Information Technologies* Andrew Eskind; *Dir Development* Eleanor Herman; *Sr Cur* Marianne Fulton; *Sr Cur* William F Stapp; *Operations & Finance* Daniel Y McCormick
Open Tues - Sun. Admis adults $2, students & senior citizens $1.50, children under 12 $.75. Estab 1949 for photography exhibitions, research and education. Restored landmark & gardens. Average Annual Attendance: 110,000. Mem: 3000; dues family $45, individual $35, students & senior citizens $25
Income: Financed by corp & individual gifts, foundation & government grants, earned income
Collections: Equipment (photographic); film; 19th and 20th century photography
Exhibitions: Blacks in America: A Photographic Record; Cameron: Her Work & Career; This Edifice is Colossal: 19th Century Photography; Images of Excellence: Stieglitz, 25 Years of Space Photography; (1988) The Snapshot at 100, Charles Zoller & John Collins
Publications: Image, quarterly; books & catalogs
Activities: Classes for children; docent training; teacher workshops; school exhibition program; lectures open to the public; gallery talks; tours; scholarships; exten dept; lending collection contains photographs & original objects of art; book traveling exhibitions; traveling exhibitions organized and circulated; museum shop sells books, magazines & reproductions; junior museum

L **Library,** 900 East Ave, 14607. Tel 716-271-3361. *Archivist* David A Wooters; *Librn* Rachel Stuhlman
Open Tues by appointment only
Library Holdings: Vols 40,000; Per subs 375; Micro — Fiche, reels 75; AV — A-tapes, rec, slides; Other — Clipping files, exhibition catalogs, manuscripts, pamphlets, reproductions
Special Subjects: History and Aesthetics of Photography; Motion Pictures
Collections: Largest collection in the US of photographs, camera technology & Library dealing with the history & aesthetics of photography: 600,000 photographs including major collections of Edward Steichen, Alvin Langdon Coburn, Southworth & Howes, Louis Walton Sipley, Lewis Hine, Edward Muybridge & Nickolas Muray
Publications: Image, quarterly
Activities: Educ dept; docent training; Discovery Room for children

M **LANDMARK SOCIETY OF WESTERN NEW YORK, INC,** 133 S Fitzhugh St, 14608-2204. Tel 716-546-7029; FAX 716-546-4788. *Dir* Henry McCartney
Campbell-Whittlesey House & Stone-Tolan House open Fri - Sun noon - 4 PM. Admis adults $2, children under 14 $.25. Estab 1937. Campbell-Wittlesey House, 123 S Fitzhugh St; Stone-Tolan House, 2370 East Ave. Mem: dues life $1000, cornerstone $250, pillar $100, patron $50, family $30, active $25
Collections: Art, furnishings & decorative arts of the 1830s; furnishings & decorative arts of early 19th century
Publications: Bi-monthly newsletter; booklets; brochures; guides; postcards
Activities: Docent program; workshops; lectures; tours

L **Wenrich Memorial Library,** 133 S Fitzhugh St, 14608-2204. Tel 716-546-7029; FAX 716-546-4788. *Asst Dir* Ann B Parks; *Res Coordr* Cynthia Howk
Open Tues - Fri 10 AM - 2 PM & by appointment. Estab 1970 to preserve landmarks in Western New York; information center containing drawings, photographs, slides, books & periodicals, as well as archives of local architecture & information on preservation & restoration techniques
Income: Financed by membership & special grants
Purchases: $900
Library Holdings: Vols 4000; Per subs 25; AV — Kodachromes, slides; Other — Clipping files, exhibition catalogs, manuscripts, pamphlets, photographs
Special Subjects: Architecture, Historical Material, Landscape Architecture, Restoration & Conservation, Architectural History, Historic Preservation, Local Architecture
Collections: Claude Bragdon Collection of Architectural Drawings; Historic American Buildings: Survey Drawings of Local Architecture; John Wenrich & Walter Cassebeer Collection of Prints & Watercolors
Exhibitions: Adaptive Use: New Uses for Old Buildings; The Architecture of Ward Wellington Ward; Rochester Prints, from the drawings of Walter Cassebeer
Publications: Newsletter, bi-monthly
Activities: Classes for adults & children; docent training; lectures open to public, tours; originate traveling exhibitions to area schools, colleges, banks, community centers

M **PYRAMID ARTS CENTER,** 274 N Goodman St, Village Gate Square, 14607. Tel 716-461-2222. *Asst Dir* Fred Wagner; *Asst Dir* Pamela S Hawkins; *Public Relations Dir* Krysia Mnick; *Gallery Mgr* Peter-Michael Kinney
Open Wed - Sun 11 AM - 5 PM. Admis $1 donation. Estab 1977 to hold exhibitions & performances, non-profit organization. 17,000 sq ft exhibition & performance space with 2 theatres & marley floor. Average Annual Attendance: 15,000 - 20,000. Mem: 400; dues $15 - $50
Exhibitions: Deaf Artists of America; Invitational & Juried shows
Activities: Educ dept; workshops with guest artists; lect open to public, 10 vis lectr per year; concerts; gallery talks; competitions; book traveling exhibitions, 1 per year; originate travel exhibitions

A **ROCHESTER HISTORICAL SOCIETY,** 485 East Ave, 14607. Tel 716-271-2705. *Pres* Elizabeth G Holahan; *First VPres* David Hislop; *Cur* Nancy Schneiderman; *Cur* Meghan Lodge; *Treas* Clinton Steadman
Open Mon - Fri 10 AM - 4 PM. Admis adults $1.25, students & sr citizens $1, children under 12 $.50. Estab 1860, refounded 1888, to obtain & preserve relics & documents & publish material relating to Rochester's history. Headquaters at Woodside, Greek Revival Mansion built in 1839. Early Rochesterians portraits displayed throughout the house. Average Annual Attendance: 3000. Mem: 700; annual meeting in Spring
Income: Financed by membership
Collections: Rochester costumes, furnishings & portraits
Exhibitions: 19th century mansion with gardens
Publications: Genesee Valley Occasional Papers; The Rochester Historical Society Publication Fund Series, 25 volumes; Woodside's First Family, catalog
Activities: Lect open to public, 6 vis lectr per yr; concerts; tours; individual paintings & original objects of art lent to museums & other institutions with adequate security

L **ROCHESTER INSTITUTE OF TECHNOLOGY,** Technical & Education Center of the Graphic Arts, One Lomb Memorial Dr, 14623-0887. Tel 716-475-2411; FAX 716-475-7052. *Librn* Helga Birth
The library houses an extensive international collection of graphic arts periodicals, technical reports and conference proceedings. These are used to compile a monthly publication which offers subject-categorized, fully indexed informative abstracts of the literature. It represents an expanded effort into current awareness and retrospective retrieval capability. The library is open to Rochester Institute of Technology graduate printing students, industry professionals, RIT staff & faculty for research. It is a closed stock, non-lending library
Publications: Graphic Arts Literature Abstracts, monthly; T&E Center News, monthly
Activities: Seminars for the graphic arts industry

M **STRONG MUSEUM,** 1 Manhattan Square, 14618. Tel 716-263-2700; FAX 716-263-2493. *Public Relations* Susan Trien
Open Mon - Sat 10 AM - 5 PM, cl Thanksgiving, Christmas & New Year's Day. Admis adults $4, sr citizens $3, students with ID $2, children (3 - 16) $1.50, children 2 & under free, museum members free, groups of 20 or more $3 per person. Children's learning center; cafe; shop; accessible to people with disabilities
Collections: 500,000 objects including dolls, furniture, glassware, miniatures & toys
Exhibitions: At Home on the Home Front; Selling the Goods: origins of American Advertising 1840 - 1940; Neither Rich nor Poor: Searching for the American Middle Class. (1992) Robots, Rockets & Realities: Frankenstein to the Final Frontier; Altered States: Alcohol & Other Drugs in America; Holiday Display; Natural Visions (paintings). (1993) Bridges & Boundaries: African Americans & American Jews; As We See It (photographs); There's Always Room for Jell-O; Fitting In: Four Generations of College Life; Montage 93: International Festival of the Image; Great Transformations 1820 - 1920; Margaret Woodbury Strong, Collector; One History Place; Changing Patterns: Household Furnishings 1820 - 1939
Activities: Family programs; Wed music & lect series; pre-school performance series

UNIVERSITY OF ROCHESTER
M **Memorial Art Gallery,** 500 University Ave, 14607-1415. Tel 716-473-7720; TDD 716-473-6152. *Pres Bd of Mgrs* Emille Allen; *Dir* Grant Holcomb; *Dir Development* Peggy Hubbard; *Asst Dir Admin* Kim Hallatt; *Asst Dir Educ* Susan Dodge Peters; *Public Relations Mgr* Deborah Rothman; *Membership Mgr* Judie Van Bramer
Open Tues 12:30 - 9 PM, Wed - Fri 10 AM - 4 PM, Sat 10 AM - 5 PM, Sun noon - 5 PM, cl Mon. Admis adults $4, sr citizens & students $2.50, children 6 - 18 $1, 5 & under free; no admis fee Tues 5 - 9 PM to members & University of Rochester students. Estab 1913 as a university art museum and public art museum for the Rochester area. The original building is in an Italian Renaissance style. Average Annual Attendance: 160,000. Mem: 7200; dues $40 & up
Income: Financed by endowment, mem, grants, earned income & University support
Collections: Covers all major periods and cultural areas from Assyria and predynastic Egypt to the present, paintings, sculpture, prints, drawings, decorative arts; special strengths are medieval & 17th century Dutch painting, 19th & eearly 20th century French painting, American art & American folk art
Exhibitions: (1992) Ceramic Figures From Ancient America; After Columbus: The First Hundred Years of Mapping America; Light, Air, & Color: American Impressionist Paintings from the Collection of the Pennsylvania Academy of the Fine Arts; Traditional Masterpieces from Zaire: Royal Kuba Art. (1993) Rochester-Finger Lakes Exhibition; Iteration: The New Digital Imaging; Sites of Recollection: Four Altars & a Rap Opera
Publications: Gallery Notes, 6 times yr; Porticus, journal of the Memorial Art Gallery; exhibition catalogs
Activities: Studio art classes for adults and children; docent training; lect open to the public; gallery talks; tours; exten dept serving Rochester area and surrounding nine counties; lending collection contains books, cassettes, color reproductions, framed reproductions, kodachromes, motion pictures, original art works, original paintings, photographs, sculpture and slides; traveling exhibitions organized and circulated; gallery store sells original art, fine crafts, prints, books & paper products
L **Charlotte W Allen Memorial Art Gallery Library,** 500 University Ave, 14607. Tel 716-473-7720, Ext 322. *Librn* Lucy Bjorklund Harper
Open Tues 1 - 9 PM, Wed - Fri & Sun 1 - 4 PM, cl Sat. Estab as a research library
Income: Financed by endowment, mem & city appropriation
Library Holdings: Vols 25,000; Per subs 60; Auction catalogues; Other — Clipping files, exhibition catalogs, pamphlets
Special Subjects: American Western Art, Architecture, Art History, Decorative Arts, Drawings, Etchings & Engravings, Folk Art, Graphic Arts, History of Art & Archaeology, Laces, Landscapes, Painting - American, Painting - British, Painting - European, Pre-Columbian Art

L **Art Library,** River Campus, 14627. Tel 716-275-4476; FAX 716-473-1906. *Librn* Stephanie J Frontz; *Slide Cur* Kim Kopatz
Open Mon - Thurs 9 AM - 10 PM, Fri 9 AM - 6 PM, Sat noon - 5 PM, Sun 1 - 10 PM. Estab to support academic programs of Department of Art and Art History and other academic departments within the University. Small gallery is maintained by Art & Art History Department & Library
Library Holdings: Vols 40,000; Per subs 200; Micro — Fiche; AV — Kodachromes, lantern slides, motion pictures, slides; Other — Exhibition catalogs

M **VISUAL STUDIES WORKSHOP,** 31 Prince St, 14607. Tel 716-442-8676. *Dir* Nathan Lyons; *Chmn Board of Trustees* William Edwards; *Coordr Exhib* James Wyman; *Coordr Book Distribution* Dina Baumel; *Coordr Summer Institute* Barbara Day
Open Mon - Fri 9 AM - 5 PM. No admis fee. Estab 1969 to establish a center for the transmission and study of the visual image. Visual Studies Workshops produce & or present approximately 20 exhibitions pr year encompassing contemporary & historical issues; subjects vary from photography, film, video, artists book works & related media. Average Annual Attendance: 300,000. Mem: 2300; dues $30
Income: $460,000 (financed by mem, state appropriation, federal & corporate resources & earned income)
Purchases: $5000
Special Subjects: Photography, Prints, Artist's Books
Collections: 19th & 20th century photographs, mechanical prints & artists books
Exhibitions: (1991 - 94) Chile from Within: Black & White Photographs from 1973-1988; Joseph Jachna; Mario Fiacomelli; Joan Lyons; Eric Renner; Murray Riss; Museum Musings by Diane Neumaier
Publications: Afterimage, monthly
Activities: Classes for adults; workshop program in museum studies; Summer Institute program with intensive short term workshops for artists & museum professionals; lectures open to the public, 15 vis lectr per year; gallery talks; tours (by appointment); original objects of art lent to institutions with proper exhibition facilities; lending collection contains 27,000 photographs of original artwork; traveling exhibitions organized & circulated to museums, colleges & universities; museum shop sells books, magazines, original art & prints
L **Research Center,** 31 Prince St, 14607. Tel 716-442-8676. *Coordr Research Center* John Rudy
Open Mon - Fri 9 AM - 6 PM. Estab 1971 to maintain a permanent collection for the study of the function and effect of the visual image. For reference only
Income: $80,000 (financed by grants)
Purchases: $5000
Library Holdings: Vols 15,000; posters; AV — A-tapes, cassettes, fs, Kodachromes, lantern slides, motion pictures, slides, v-tapes; Other — Clipping files, exhibition catalogs, manuscripts, original art works, photographs, prints, reproductions
Special Subjects: Photography
Collections: Illustrated book collection; photographic print collection
Publications: Various publications
Activities: Internship programs; workshops; graduate museum studies program; visual studies; lectures open to public; gallery talks; tours

ROME

A **ROME ART AND COMMUNITY CENTER,** 308 W Bloomfield St, 13440. Tel 315-336-1040. *Dir* Leo Crandall
Open Mon - Sat 9 AM - 5 PM, Mon - Thurs evenings 6:30 - 9 PM. No admis fee. Estab 1968 for art exhibits and classes. Three galleries. Average Annual Attendance: 30,000. Mem: 1000; dues family with 2 children $10, individual $5
Income: Financed by city appropriation, New York State Council on the Arts, Oneida County, United Arts Fund-Mohawk Valley, mem, donations & private foundations
Exhibitions: Various art and craft exhibitions every six weeks
Publications: Newsletter, bimonthly; community calendar, quarterly; class brochures, quarterly
Activities: Classes for adults and children; lectures open to the public, 20 vis lectrs per yr; tours; readings; concerts; weekly films; scholarships to gifted children

M **ROME HISTORICAL SOCIETY MUSEUM,** 200 Church, 13440. Tel 315-336-5870. *Pres* Mary Grow; *Dir* Jon Austin; *First VPres* Bill Jackson
Open Mon - Fri 9 AM - 4 PM & by appointment, additional weekend hrs July & Aug; cl holidays. No admis fee. Estab 1936 as a historical museum and society. Average Annual Attendance: 11,500. Mem: 500; dues $1.50 - $150; annual meeting in Aug
Income: Financed by membership, city appropriation, private foundations, federal & state grants
Collections: E Buyck; P F Hugunine; Forest Moses; Ann Marriot; Will Moses; Revolutionary War period paintings
Exhibitions: Variety of exhibitions examining local history using objects and 2-D materials
Publications: Annals and Recollections, quarterly; bi-monthly newsletter
Activities: School programs; docent training; lect open to the public, 8 vis lectr per year; tours; gallery talks; museum shop sells books, prints & slides
L **William E Scripture Memorial Library,** 200 Church St, 13440. Tel 315-336-5870. *Cur Colls* Barbara Schaeffer; *Cur Educ* James Crawford; *Archivist* Tim Lewis
Open Mon - Fri 9 AM - noon & 1 - 4 PM, weekends by appointment. Estab 1936 for historical research of Rome and the Mohawk Valley
Library Holdings: Vols 2500; Per subs 5; Other — Clipping files, manuscripts, pamphlets, photographs, prints, reproductions
Special Subjects: Maps, Local history
Collections: Area paintings from the Revolutionary War period to the present; Frederick Hodges Journals; The Hathaway Papers; Local Malitia Records 1830-1840; La Bita: Local newspaper printed in Rome New York 1918-1950

ROSENDALE

A WOMEN'S STUDIO WORKSHOP, INC, 262 Binnewater Lane, PO Box 489, 12472. Tel 914-658-9133. *Exec Dir* Ann Kalmbach; *Prog Dir* Lisa Kellogg; *Artistic Dir* Tana Kellner
Open Tues - Fri 10 AM - 5 PM, Sat noon - 4 PM. Estab 1974. Mem: 814, dues $25
Income: $200,000 (financed by sales, tuition & grants)
Publications: Artists' books, 5-7 per yr
Activities: Adult classes; lect open to public, 45 vis lectr per year; tours; scholarships; book traveling exhibitions, annually; originate traveling exhibitions; sales shop sells workshop products, books & handmade paper

ROSLYN

L BRYANT LIBRARY, Paper Mill Rd, 11576. Tel 516-621-2240; FAX 516-621-7211. *Dir* Elizabeth McCloat
Estab 1878 as a public library. Gallery houses monthly exhibits, mostly paintings. Circ 236,000
Income: $1,400,000
Purchases: $325,000
Library Holdings: Vols 148,725; Per subs 500; Micro — Fiche, reels; AV — Cassettes 895, fs, rec 4141, v-tapes; Other — Clipping files, manuscripts 10,933, pamphlets 12,364, photographs 7126
Special Subjects: Architecture, Historical Material
Collections: William Cullen Bryant; Christopher Morley; local history of Roslyn, Long Island, New York
Exhibitions: At Liberty with Liberty (multi-media); Hudson Talbott (drawings, greeting card & poster designs); New Faces; Going Places; Beyond the Status Quo
Publications: Bryant Library Calendar of Events, monthly; Bryant Library Newsletter, bi-monthly; The Bryant Library: 100 Years, 1878-1978, exhibit catalogue; W C Bryant in Roslyn, book; exhibit catalog
Activities: Lect open to public, 30-40 vis lectrs per yr; book traveling exhibitions

M NASSAU COUNTY MUSEUM OF FINE ART, Northern Blvd, PO Box D, 11576. Tel 516-484-9337; FAX 516-484-0710. *Dir Admin & Chief Cur* Constance Schwartz; *Operations Mgr* Robert Bertlesman; *Admin Asst* Christine Standridge; *Comptroller* Ann Gelles; *Registrar* Fernanda Bennett; *Coordr Young People's Program* Jean Henning
Open Tues - Fri 10 AM - 4:30 PM, Sat & Sun 1 - 5 PM, cl Mon. No admis fee. Estab 1975 for exhibits of historical and contemporary nature for Nassau County Residents. Art museum housed in c 1900, three story Neo-Georgian brick mansion, former estate of Childs Frick. Average Annual Attendance: 250,000. Mem: 2500; dues $20 - $1000
Income: Financed by membership and county appropriation
Collections: 20th century American prints; drawings; outdoor sculpture; architectural blueprints & drawings relating to the Museum building & property
Publications: Catalogs for exhibitions
Activities: Classes for adults and children; dramatic programs; docent training; lectures open to the public; gallery talks; tours; original paintings and original objects of art lent to other qualified institutions; book traveling exhibitions; traveling exhibitions organized and circulated to the Gallery Association of New York State; sales shop sells art books, catalogs, crafts & other museum related items for sale

SAINT BONAVENTURE

M SAINT BONAVENTURE UNIVERSITY, Art Collection, 14778. Tel 716-375-2000. *Dir & Cur* Bro John Capozzi
Open Mon - Thurs 8 AM - midnight, Fri 8 AM - 5 PM, Sat 8 AM - 8 PM, Sun 10 AM - midnight. No admis fee. Estab 1856 to provide artistic surroundings for students. Average Annual Attendance: 4000
Income: Financed by university budget
Collections: Paintings; porcelains and American Indian pottery; ivories, jade miniatures; cloisonne
Exhibitions: Rotating exhibitions
Publications: Art Catalog of Collection
Activities: Museum shop sells reproductions

SANBORN

M NIAGARA COUNTY COMMUNITY COLLEGE ART GALLERY, 3111 Saunders Settlement Rd, 14132. Tel 716-731-3271, Ext 390. *Gallery Dir* Alice Dudko
Open Mon - Thurs 10 AM - 4:30 PM, Fri 10 AM - 2 PM. No admis fee. Estab 1973 for varied exhibits that will be of interest to students and the community. Gallery has 270 sq ft of area & approx 250 running ft. Average Annual Attendance: 9000
Income: $4500
Collections: Prints (contemporary)
Exhibitions: (1992) Celebrating Craft: 11 Craftman from Western New York; The Full Circle: 6 Contemporary Native American Artists; Mini Exhibit; Student Art Exhibit; Three Alumni. (1993) African Treasures; Faculty Exhibit; Spring Student Exhibit; Student Art Exhibit; Student Illustration Exhibit/Suny Buffalo; Three Photographers Rural Vistas-Rediscovery of the American Landscape; paintings by Coniglie, Headrick, Hucke, Ram & Spurling; Yuppidreams in Darthvader Frames by Kim Yarwood (paintings); NCCC Student Exhibition; Architecture in Contemporary Prints; Dixon, Godsisz, Runca-NCC Alumni Exhibition (paintings, mixed media); Mary Roehm (architectural ceramics)
Publications: Catalogs
Activities: Classes for adults; dramatic programs; lectures open to the public, 6 vis lectr per year; 3 concerts per year; tours

SARATOGA SPRINGS

M NATIONAL MUSEUM OF RACING AND HALL OF FAME, Union Ave, 12866. Tel 518-584-0400; FAX 518-584-4574. *Dir* Peter Hammell
Open Mon - Sat 10 AM - 4:30 PM, Sun Noon - 4:30 PM. No admis fee, children under 12 must be accompanied by parents. Estab 1950 as a museum for the collection, preservation and exhibition of all kinds of articles associated with the origin, history and development of horse racing. There are 10 galleries of sporting art. The handsome Georgian-Colonial design brick structure houses one of the world's greatest collections of equine art along with trophies, sculptures and memorabilia of the sport from its earliest days. Average Annual Attendance: 25,000. Mem: Annual meeting Aug
Income: Financed through annual appeal and individual contributions
Collections: Oil paintings of thoroughbred horses, trophies, racing silks, bronzes, prints, racing memorabilia
Exhibitions: (1992) More than a Likeness: Saratoga Portraits
Publications: Catalog; Hall of Fame booklets
Activities: Classes for adults & children; docent training; lect; exten dept serving Northeast; original objects of art lent on special occasions; museum shop selling books, reproductions, prints, jewelry, figurines and other items
L Reference Library, Union Ave, 12866. Tel 518-584-0400; FAX 518-584-4574. Open to researchers, students and authors by appointment
Library Holdings: Per subs 6; AV — Fs; Other — Clipping files, exhibition catalogs, memorabilia, original art works, pamphlets, photographs
Special Subjects: Thoroughbred racing, horses

M SKIDMORE COLLEGE, Schick Art Gallery, N Broadway, 12866. Tel 518-584-5000, Ext 2370. *Dir* David Miller; *Slide & Photograph Asst* Jackie Pardon
Open Sept - May Mon - Fri 9 AM - 5 PM, Sat & Sun 1 - 3:30 PM; summer: hours variable according to summer class schedules. No admis fee. Estab 1927 for educational enrichment of the college and community. Exhibitions are intended to bring awareness of both contemporary and historical trends in art. Average Annual Attendance: 12,000
Income: Financed through College
Library Holdings: Vols 392,014; Per subs 1653
Collections: American and European Prints; Saratoga Springs Historical Collection
Exhibitions: (1991) Out of Abstract Expressionism, Roy DeForest, Sonia Gechtoff & Philip Wofford. (1992) Joan Semmel Paintings; Annual Art Faculty Exhibit; Patterns & Layers; Michael Moschen. (1993) Annual Student Exhibit; Two-Person Faculty; Grace Hartigan & the Poets; Senior Thesis Exhibit
Publications: Exhibition catalogs, occasionally
Activities: Lect open to public, 5-6 visiting lectr per year; gallery talks; traveling exhibitions organized and circulated
L Lucy Scribner Library, Art Reading Area, North Broadway, 12866. Tel 518-584-5000, Ext 640. *Fine & Performing Arts Librn* Jane Graves; *Fine Arts & Photograph Asst* Heather Ferguson
Open Mon - Sat 8 AM - 11 PM, Sun noon - 11 PM. Estab 1925
Library Holdings: Vols 392,014; Per subs 1653; Micro — Cards; AV — Fs, Kodachromes, lantern slides, motion pictures, rec, slides 53,000; Other — Exhibition catalogs, memorabilia, original art works, photographs, prints 600, reproductions, sculpture
Collections: Anita Pohndorff Yates Collection of Saratoga History

SCHENECTADY

A SCHENECTADY COUNTY HISTORICAL SOCIETY, 32 Washington Ave, 12305. Tel 518-374-0263. *Pres* John Van Schaick; *Coordr Exhib* Jo Mordecai
Open Mon - Fri 1 - 5 PM, cl national holidays. Admis adults $1, children $.50. Estab 1905, for the preservation of local historical materials. Located within area of original Schenectady stockade by the Dutch in 1661; contains 50 paintings of the 19th century dealing with prominent Schenectady residents. Average Annual Attendance: 7500. Mem: 850; dues patron, $25, regular $10; annual meeting 2nd Tues of Apr
Collections: Decorative arts; historical material; Indian artifacts; paintings; photographs; documents, genealogy
Exhibitions: Temporary exhibitions from other museums
Publications: Newsletter, monthly
Activities: Lectures open to public, 20 vis lectrs per yr; tours; exten dept serves elementary schools; sales shop sells books & slides
L Library, 32 Washington Ave, 12305. *Archivist Librn* Elsie Maddaus; *Learning Librn Intern* Scott Haefner
Open Mon - Fri
Library Holdings: Vols 3000; Per subs 10; Micro — Reels; AV — Cassettes, motion pictures, slides; Other — Clipping files, manuscripts 16,000, memorabilia, pamphlets, photographs

M SCHENECTADY MUSEUM, PLANETARIUM & VISITORS CENTER, Nott Terrace Heights, 12308. Tel 518-382-7890. *Dir* Roger E Calkins; *Cur Exhibits* John Davis; *Cur Educ* Maria Brown; *Public Information* Carol J Hudson
Open Tues - Fri 10 AM - 4:30 PM, Sat & Sun noon - 5 PM. Museum only admis adults $3, children $1.50; museum & planetarium adults $5, children $2.50. Founded 1934, chartered by the New York State Regents in 1937 to increase and diffuse knowledge in appreciation of art, history, industry, and science by providing collections, exhibits, lectures and other programs. Sales and rental gallery is maintained. Average Annual Attendance: 80,000. Mem: 2200; dues annual individual $30, student & senior citizens $15, family membership $45; annual meeting Oct
Collections: African Art; decorative arts; 19th and 20th century art; 19th and 20th century costumes and textiles; North American Indian Art
Exhibitions: Electron City; Out of the Ordinary; Sense & Perception; Heart Treasure Chest; Continuous Costume Exhibits
Publications: Annual Report; Calendar, monthly; Museum Notes, monthly; exhibition catalogues
Activities: Art and craft classes; Festival of Nations; Crafts Fair; Rock Festival; Haunted House; Museum Ball; docent training; lectures open to the public; concerts; gallery talks; tours; loan materials and exhibits for area schools, colleges and libraries; book traveling exhibitions, 3 - 4 per yr; museum shop sells books, original art, reproductions, prints & crafts

L **Library,** 12308. Tel 518-382-7890. *Librn* Open
For reference and technical information only
Library Holdings: Vols 5000

SENECA FALLS

M **SENECA FALLS HISTORICAL SOCIETY MUSEUM,** 55 Cayuga St, 13148.
Tel 315-568-8412. *Pres* Ann Cramer; *VPres* Janette Pfeiff; *Exec Dir* Sylvia
Farrer-Bornarth; *Education Coordr* Frances Barbieri; *Librn & Registrar* Sheldon
King; *Photo Archivist* George Covert
Open Mon - Fri 9 AM - 5 PM. Admis adult $2, children & students $1. Estab
1896 as an educational institution dedicated to the preservation & interpretation
of Seneca County. Victorian 23 room house with decorative arts collection.
Average Annual Attendance: 9000. Mem: 400; dues family $25, singel $15;
annual meeting in Feb
Income: $85,000 (financed by endowment, membership, city, state & federal
appropriation, United Way)
Collections: Local painters; central New York State folk art & crafts; Currier &
Ives prints; nineteenth century decorative arts
Publications: Reprints of archival material
Activities: Classes for adults and children; docent training; school group
programs; lect open to public, 8 vis lectr per year, concerts; gallery talks, tours;
original objects of art lent to other institutions; sales shop sells books and
reproductions

SETAUKET

M **GALLERY NORTH,** 90 N Country Rd, 11733. Tel 516-751-2676. *Pres* Vinnie
Fish; *VPres* James Lecky; *Dir* Louise Kalin; *Treas* Levan Merrihew
Open Tues - Sat 10 AM - 5 PM, Sun 1 - 5 PM. No admis fee. Estab 1965 to
exhibit the work of contemporary Long Island artists & crafts people. Gallery is
housed in Victorian building with 3 main exhibition rooms. Average Annual
Attendance: 10,000. Mem: 150; dues $10 - $100; quarterly meetings
Income: $57,000 (financed by membership & sales)
Exhibitions: Eight changing exhibitions per yr; annual outdoor art show open to
artists & crafts people
Activities: Lectures open to public; competitions with awards; sales shop sells
crafts from local artists & imported crafts

SKANEATELES

M **JOHN D BARROW ART GALLERY,** 49 E Genesee St, 13152. Tel 315-685-
5135. *Chmn of Trustees* Frances Milford
Open Thurs & Sat 2 - 4 PM, Summer Mon - Sat 2-4 PM. No admis fee. Estab in
1900 to exhibit paintings of John D Barrow. Three rooms with unusual feature of
tiered paintings built in a wainscoting. Mem: 160
Income: Financed by donations
Activities: Lectures open to public

A **SKANEATELES LIBRARY ASSOCIATION,** 49 E Genesee St, 13152. Tel
315-685-5135. *Pres* Robert Soderberg
Open Mon, Wed, Fri, Sat 10 AM - 5 PM, Tues & Thurs 10 AM - 8:30 PM, and
by request. Estab 1900 to display paintings of John D Barrow. 2 rooms, one with
single and one with triple wainscoting of paintings. Average Annual Attendance:
1150. Mem: Annual meeting 4th Thurs in Jan
Income: Financed by annual fund raising drive and endowments
Collections: Paintings by American artists; etchings by American and foreign
artists; 300 paintings by John D Barrow, in separate wing; 19th century
landscapes & portraits
Exhibitions: Occasional special exhibitions
Activities: Annual guided tours for 4th graders; docent training; occasional open
lectures; gallery talks; tours; paintings lent for one year on the condition that
borrower pays for restoration; shop sells prints, postcards, calendars

SOUTHAMPTON

M **THE PARRISH ART MUSEUM,** 25 Jobs Lane, 11968. Tel 516-283-2118;
FAX 516-283-7006. *Dir* Trudy Kramer; *Assoc Dir* Anke Jackson; *Cur* Donna
DeSalvo; *Educ Dir* Kent dur Russell
Open Mon, Thurs, Fri & Sat 10 AM - 5 PM, Sun 1 - 5 PM; cl Tues & Wed Sept
16 - June 14 & Wed June 15 - Sept 15. No admis fee. Estab 1898 to exhibit, care
for and research permanent collections and loaned works of art with emphasis on
American 19th and 20th century paintings. Three main galleries are maintained;
total dimensions 4288 sq ft, 355 running feet. Average Annual Attendance: 70,
000. Mem: 2000; dues $25 - $1000 & up; annual meeting Dec
Income: Financed by contributions & grants
Collections: †American paintings, 19th and 20th century; Dunnigan Collection of
19th century etchings; Japanese woodblock prints and stencils; Samuel Parrish
Collection of Italian Renaissance panel paintings; William Merritt Chase
Collection and Archives; Fairfield Porter Bequest
Exhibitions: (1990) School Art Festival; Louis H Sullivan: Unison with Nature;
Masterpieces of American Painting from the Brooklyn Museum: A Celebration of
American Ideals; Half-Truths; Drawing Highlights: Eric Fischl, Roy Lichtenstein,
Esteban Vicente & Selections from the Collection; 32nd Juried Exhibition: Works
on Paper; Frames
Activities: Classes for adults and children; docent training; films; lectures open to
the public 3 vis lectr per yr; concerts; gallery talks; tours; competitions; exten
dept serving area schools; individual paintings lent to museums; traveling
exhibitions organized and circulated; museum shop sells books, magazines,
reproductions, prints, craft items
L **Aline B Saarinen Library,** 25 Jobs Lane, 11968. Tel 516-283-2118; FAX 516-
283-7006. *Librn* Eva Balamuth
Reference library
Library Holdings: Vols 4200; Per subs 6; Other — Clipping files, exhibition

catalogs, memorabilia
Special Subjects: Architecture, Art History, Drawings, Oriental Art, Painting -
American
Collections: William Merritt Chase Archives; original documents, photographs,
memorabilia, research materials pertaining to the life and work of Chase (1849-
1916)

STAATSBURG

M **NEW YORK STATE OFFICE OF PARKS, RECREATION & HISTORICAL
PRESERVATION,** Mills Mansion State Historical Site, Old Post Rd, PO Box
308, 12580. Tel 914-889-4100; FAX 914-889-8321. *Historic Site Mgr* Melodye
Moore
Open May 26 - Oct 31, Wed - Sun 10 AM - 4:30 PM. No admis fee. Estab 1938
to interpret lifestyle of the very affluent segment of American society during the
period 1890-1929. Average Annual Attendance: 10,000
Collections: Original furnishings, paintings, prints, decorative art objects and
tapestries from Mr and Mrs Mills
Activities: Docent training; workshops; lectures open to the public; concerts;
gallery tours; loans of paintings or original art objects have to be approved by
New York State Office of Parks and Recreation, Division of Historic
Preservation

STATEN ISLAND

M **JACQUES MARCHAIS CENTER OF TIBETAN ART,** Tibetan Museum, 338
Lighthouse Ave, New York, 10306. Tel 718-987-3478, 987-3500; FAX 718-351-
0402. *Dir* Barbara Lipton; *Asst Dir* Dorothy Reilly
Open Wed - Sun 1 - 5 PM. Admis adults $3, sr citizens $2.50, children under 12
$1. Estab 1946 for maintenance of library & museum in Buddhist philosophy, art
& religion, with particular emphasis on Tibetan Buddhism & art. Buildings
planned for and collection amassed by Mrs Harry Klauber, (known professionally
as Jacques Marchais) who ran an Oriental art gallery from 1938 until her death
in 1948. Average Annual Attendance: 10,000. Mem: 300; dues $20 & up
Income: Financed by contributions, admissions, mem, city, state & federal
appropriations, gift shop sales, foundation & corporate grants
Purchases: Tibetan art & ethnographic materials; books on related subjects
Collections: †Jacques Marchais permanent collection of Tibetan and Buddhist
Art
Activities: Educ programs are offered for school groups, adult groups, sr citizens
& blind & visually impaired audiences, appointment required; dramatic programs,
dance; poetry readings; lectures open to public, 20 vis lectr per year; concerts;
gallery talks; tours; exten servs New York City; individual paintings & original
objects of art lent to museums for special exhibits; museum shop sells books,
Tibetan carpets, wooden masks, jewelry, music tapes, posters, textiles, gift ware &
unique items from various Asian countries

M **THE JOHN A NOBLE COLLECTION,** 1000 Richmond Terrace, 10301. Tel
718-447-6490. *Dir* Erin Urban
Open weekdays 1 - 5 PM. No admis fee. Estab 1986 to present art & maritime
history. Permanent installation of John A Noble's Houseboat Studio; art; gallery
for changing exhibitions of prints & maritime history. Average Annual
Attendance: 5000. Mem: 500; dues $25; annual meeting in Apr
Income: $100,000 (financed by mem, state & city appropriation)
Collections: Archives; †Art; Maritime Artifacts
Publications: Hold Fast
, quarterly newsletter
Activities: Classes for adults & children; lect open to public; lending collection
contains 80 paintings & art objects

M **ORDER SONS OF ITALY IN AMERICA,** Garibaldi & Meucci Meuseum, 420
Tompkins Ave, 10305. Tel 718-442-1608. *Dir* Carol Quinby
Open Tues - Fri 9 AM - 5 PM, Sat & Sun 1 - 5 PM. No admis fee. Estab 1956
to collect, preserve & interpret material pertaining to Italian culture. Average
Annual Attendance: 3300. Mem: 125; dues $25
Income: $100,000 (financed by endowment, mem, city & state appropriation,
Order Sons of Italy in America)
Collections: Bronzes; Coins; Decorative Arts; Medals; Paintings; Paper; Prints;
Stamps
Exhibitions: Garibaldi, Champion of Freedom; Through the Golden Door, Lewis
Hine (Photos); Antonio Meucci, The First Inventor of the Telephone
Activities: Classes for adults & children; lectures open to public, 4 vis lectr per yr

M **SNUG HARBOR CULTURAL CENTER,** Newhouse Center for Contemporary
Art, 1000 Richmond Terrace, 10301. Tel 718-448-2500; FAX 718-442-8534. *Dir
Visual Arts* Olivia Georgia
Open Wed - Sun noon - 5 PM. Admis donation. Estab 1977 to provide a forum
for regionally & nationally significant visual art. Average Annual Attendance: 50,
000
Income: Financed by mem, city & state appropriation, corporate funds
Collections: Changing exhibits
Publications: Exhibition catalogs
Activities: Children's programs; docent programs; lectures open to public, 3 vis
lectr per year; retail store sells books, prints, original art, reproductions

M **STATEN ISLAND INSTITUTE OF ARTS AND SCIENCES,** 75 Stuyvesant
Pl, 10301. Tel 718-727-1135; FAX 718-273-5683. *Chmn Board* Robert
O'Connor; *Pres & Chief Exec Officer* Hedy Hartman; *Archivist* John-Paul
Richiuso
Open Mon - Sat 9 AM - 5 PM, Sun 1 - 5 PM. No admis fee, donations accepted.
Estab 1881, inc 1906. Average Annual Attendance: 105,000. Mem: 750; dues
$15 & up
Collections: †American paintings of the 19th and 20th centuries; Oriental,
Greek, Roman and primitive art objects; †prints and small sculptures
Exhibitions: Decorative arts; design exhibitions in various media; major loan
shows of paintings and prints; special exhibitions of graphic arts and of

photography;
Publications: Annual Reports; catalog
Activities: Fall & spring terms for adults & children classes; docent training; lect on art & science open to public; complete program of lectr, art & natural history for school children with annual registration of 45,000; 40 vis lectr per year; gallery talks; tours; competitions with awards; museum shop sells books, original art & reproductions

L **Archives Library,** 75 Stuyvesant PL, 10301. Tel 718-727-1135; FAX 718-273-5683. *Cur Archives & Library* Vincent Sweeney
Library Holdings: Vols 30,000; Per subs 10
Collections: George W Curtis Collection of books, manuscripts, and memorabilia; reference collection of 30,000 publications in science and art history; a choice collection of Staten Island newspapers from 1834-1934 on microfilm; letters, documents, journals, files of clippings and old photographs relating to the history of Staten Island and the metropolitan region
Publications: Proceeding of Staten Island Institute of Arts and Sciences

STONE RIDGE

M **ULSTER COUNTY COMMUNITY COLLEGE,** Muroff-Kotler Visual Arts Gallery, 12484. Tel 914-687-5000. *Coordr* Prof Allan L Cohan
Open Mon - Fri 10 AM - 3 PM, fall and spring semesters, cl summer. No admis fee. Estab 1963 as a center for creative activity. Gallery is maintained as an adjunct to the college's cultural and academic program; John Vanderlyn Hall has 40 x 28 ft enclosed space and is located on the campus. Average Annual Attendance: 3000
Income: Financed by college funds
Purchases: $750
Collections: Contemporary drawings, †paintings, photographs, prints, sculpture, historical works
Publications: Flyers announcing each exhibit, every four to six weeks
Activities: Lect open to the public, 2-3 visiting lectrs per year; concerts

STONY BROOK

M **THE MUSEUMS AT STONY BROOK,** 1208 Route 25A, 11790. Tel 516-751-0066; FAX 516-751-0353. *Pres* Deborah J Johnson; *Dir Institutional Development* Joseph Dunworth
Open Wed - Sat 10 AM - 5 PM, Sun noon - 5 PM, cl Mon & Tues, Thanksgiving, Dec 24, 25, Jan 1. Admis adults $6, students & sr citizens $4, children 6 - 12 $3, under 6 & members free. Chartered 1942 as a nonprofit educational institution whose purpose is to collect and preserve objects of historic and artistic interest. The Museums' 22 buildings, 13.5 acre complex include a History Museum, Art Museum, Carriage Museum, various period buildings, a museum store, & the Hawkins-Mount House (currently not open to the public). Average Annual Attendance: 50,000. Mem: 1000; dues $25-$5000
Collections: Paintings & drawings by †William Sidney Mount & other American Artists including †Shepard Alonzo Mount, †Henry S Mount, †William M Davis, †Edward Lange, †Charles H Miller; costumes; toys & dolls; decoys; textiles; carriages & carriage accoutrements; miniature rooms; American historical artifacts
Exhibitions: Changing exhibitions in Art Museum and History Museum
Publications: Annual Report; Quarterly Newsletter; exhibition catalogs; brochures
Activities: Classes for adults & children; docent training; lectures open to public, 3-5 vis lectr per year; concerts; gallery talks; tours; competitions; individual paintings & original objects of art lent to other museums; originate traveling exhibitions to history & art museums; museum shop sells books, reproductions, prints, gifts and paper goods related to collections

L **Kate Strong Historical Library,** 1208 Route 25A, 11790. Tel 516-751-0066.
Reference library open to researchers by appointment
Library Holdings: Vols 2194; Per subs 62; trade catalogs; Micro — Reels; AV — Motion pictures, slides, v-tapes; Other — Exhibition catalogs, manuscripts, pamphlets, photographs
Special Subjects: American Art History
Collections: William Cooper, shipbuilder, 19th century, Sag Harbor; Israel Green Hawkins, Edward P Buffet, Hal B Fullerton; Archives: Papers of William Sidney Mount and family; Daniel Williamson and John Williamson, Stony Brook

M **STATE UNIVERSITY OF NEW YORK AT STONY BROOK,** Art Gallery, 11794-5425. Tel 516-632-7240. *Dir* Rhonda Cooper
Open Tues - Sat noon - 4 PM. No admis fee. Estab 1967 to serve both the campus and the community by exhibiting professional artists. One gallery 41 x 73 with 22 ft ceiling; second space 22 x 73 ft with 12 ft ceilings. Average Annual Attendance: 1500 students and members of the community per show
Income: Financed by state appropriation
Exhibitions: Fiber Explorations; Herman Cherry 1984 - 1989; Robert Kushner: Silent Operas Kit-Yin Snyder: Enrico IV; Poetic License; Prints by Printmakers. City Views; Adolph Gottlieb: Epic Art; Reuben Kadish; Julius Tobias
Publications: Catalogues, five times a year
Activities: Lectures open to the public, bi-monthly, 4 - 6 vis lectrs per year; traveling exhibitions

SYRACUSE

M **EVERSON MUSEUM OF ART,** 401 Harrison St, 13202. Tel 315-474-6064.
Pres Stephen Johnson; *VPres* Bruce A Kenan; *VPres* David W Burns; *Dir* Ronald A Kuchta; *Assoc Dir* Sandra Trop; *Cur* Thomas Piche Jr; *Development Officer* Kristine Waelder; *Public Information Officer* Linda M Herbert
Open Tues - Fri noon - 5 PM, Sat 10 AM - 5 PM, Sun noon - 5 PM, cl Mon. No admis fee. Estab 1896 to present free exhibitions by lending artists, chiefly American to serve as an educational element for the cultural and general community. Houses a new facility: The Syracuse China Center of the Study of American Ceramics provides 4022 sq ft of open storage for the museum's collection of 1000 pieces of American ceramics, ranging from Native American

pots, circa AD 1000, to contemporary ceramic sculpture & vessel forms, also to include study collections of world ceramics, numbering 1500 objects. Average Annual Attendance: 150,000. Mem: 2427: dues general $35, senior citizens $25
Income: Financed by mem, county & state appropriation, New York State Council of the Arts, National Endowment for the Arts, Institute for Museum Services, private corporate grants, individual grants
Collections: African Collection; †contemporary American ceramics; †contemporary American painting & sculpture; 17th, 18th & 19th century English porcelain; †traditional American painting & portraiture; video-tape collection; Cloud Wampler Collection of Oriental Art
Exhibitions: (1993) 29th Ceramic National Exhibition; Adrienne Salinger Photographs; The Adirondacks: An American Treasure (photographs by Nathan Farb)
Publications: Art books; bulletin, monthly; Educational materials; exhibition catalogs
Activities: Educ dept; docent training; lect open to the public, 10 visiting lectr per year; concerts; gallery talks; tours; competitions; exten dept serves public schools of Syracuse;; book traveling exhibitions, 5 per yr; originate traveling exhibitions; museum and sales shop selling books, magazines, original art, reproductions, prints, slides, ceramics, local and national arts and crafts

M **LEMOYNE COLLEGE,** Wilson Art Gallery, Le Moyne Heights, 13214. Tel 315-445-4331. *Chmn & Librn* Dr Tanya Popovic; *Asst Prof Philosophy* Dr Donald Arentz; *Periodical Librn* Lynnette Stevens
Open Mon - Thurs 9 AM - 11 PM, Fri 9 AM - 9 PM, Sat & Sun 9 AM - 5 PM. No admis fee. Estab 1966. Average Annual Attendance: 1500
Income: Financed through the Faculty Art Gallery Committee
Collections: Paintings, etchings, prints and watercolors
Activities: Individual painting and original objects of art lent

A **LIGHT WORK,** 316 Waverly Ave, 13244-3010. Tel 315-443-1300. *Dir* Jeff Hoone; *Asst Dir* Gina Murtagh
Estab 1973, artist-run photography center, laboratory facilities, exhibitions, publications & residency programs for artist
Exhibitions: Temporary exhibitions held throughout the year

SYRACUSE UNIVERSITY

M **Joe and Emily Lowe Art Gallery,** Sims Hall, 13244. Tel 315-443-4098. *Dir* Edward A Aiken; *Registrar & Preparator* Bradley Hudson
Open Tues - Sun noon - 5 PM. No admis fee. Estab 1952 to present art exhibitions to inform university and communities of central upstate New York areas of international heritage of art, new advances in contemporary art with emphasis on the discovery of regional values, outstanding local art including faculty and student work. Museum Training Program complements our exhibition program. 7134 sq ft of space normally divided into separate galleries by movable walls. Average Annual Attendance: 20,000
Income: Financed through University with additional outside grants
Exhibitions: (1992 - 93) Cartoons, Characters & Comics; A Tale of Two Cities; Studio Arts Department; MSA Exhibition 1 & 2; A Summer Exhibition; Selections from the permanent collections
Publications: Exhibition catalogs each show
Activities: Private tours on request; traveling exhibitions organized and circulated

M **Art Collection,** Sims Hall, 13244. Tel 315-443-4097. *Dir* Alfred T Collette; *Asst Dir* Domenic J Iacono; *Cur* David Prince; *Preparator* David Gabel
The Art Collection is housed in a temperature & humidity-controlled area of Sims Hall, adjacent to the Art Gallery. Used primarily for storage & care of the 35,000 object collection, this facility also includes a teaching display area to accommodate classes & individuals involved in research
Income: financed by university funds and endowments
Purchases: WPA Federal Art Projects Prints, Contemporary American Prints
Collections: West African tribal art; Korean, Japanese & American ceramics; Indian folk art; Pre-Columbian & contemporary Peruvian ceramics; Scandinavian designs in metal, wood, clay & textiles; 20th century American works with an emphasis on the Depression & War years (prints & paintings); 19th century European Salon paintings; history of printmaking (emphasis on American artists); decorative arts; Mary Petty-Alan Dunn Center for Social Cartooning

L **Library,** Fine Arts Dept, 458 Bird Library, 13244-2010. Tel 315-443-2440. *Fine Arts Librn* Randall Bond; *Architecture Librn & Dept Head* Barbara A Opar
Open Mon - Thurs 8 AM - 10 PM, Fri 8 AM - 6 PM, Sat 10 AM - 6 PM, Sun 10 AM - 10 PM. Estab 1870 for reference and research in the history of art
Library Holdings: Vols 55,000; Per subs 335; Picture file 27,000, compact discs 1500; Micro — Cards, fiche, prints, reels; AV — A-tapes, cassettes 1500, fs, motion pictures, rec 20,000, slides 300,000, v-tapes; Other — Exhibition catalogs 15,000, manuscripts, photographs
Collections: Manuscript Collections of many American artists

TARRYTOWN

M **HISTORIC HUDSON VALLEY,** 150 White Plains Rd, 10591. Tel 914-631-8609; FAX 914-631-0089. *Dir Admin & Finance* Wadell Stillman; *Cur* Joseph T Butler; *Public Affairs* Sally Johnston
Open 10 AM - 5 PM, cl Thanksgiving Day, Christmas, New Year's Day & Tues Dec - Mar. Admis to Sunnyside, Philipsburg Manor and Van Cortlandt Manor adults $4 each property, sr citizens and juniors 6-14 $2.50 each property; three visit tickets valid one year, adults $10, sr citizens and juniors $6.50; groups of 20 or more must make reservations in advance. Chartered 1951 as a nonprofit educational foundation. Owns and operates historic properties which are Sunnyside in Tarrytown, the home of author Washington Irving; Philipsburg Manor in North Tarrytown, a Dutch-American gristmill-farm site of the early 1700s; Van Cortlandt Manor in Croton-on-Hudson, a manorial estate of the Revolutionary War period. Average Annual Attendance: 150,000
Collections: Memorabilia of Washington Irving, Van Cortlandt and Philipse families; 17th, 18th and 19th century decorative arts; Philipsburg Manor, Upper Mills, Four Centuries of History, A Decade of Restoration
Exhibitions: Union Church of Pocantico Hills; stained glass windows by Marc Chagall; Henri Matisse; 19th & 20th century toys; Candellight Tours
Publications: American Industrialization, Economic Expansion, and the Law;

America's Wooden Age; Aspects of Early New York Society and Politics; Bracebride Hall; Business Enterprise in Early New York; Diedrich Knickerbocker's A History of New York; An Emerging Independent American Economy: 1815-1875; The Family Collections at Van Cortlandt Manor; The Howe Map; The Hudson River 1850-1918, A Photographic Portrait; Life Along the Hudson; Life of George Washington; The Loyalist Americans; Material Culture of the Wooden Age; The Mill at Philipsburg Manor, Upper Mills, and a Brief History of Milling; Old Christmas; Party and Political Opposition in Revolutionary America; Philipsburg Manor: A Guidebook; A Portfolio of Sleepy Hollow Prints; Rip Van Winkle & the Legend of Sleepy Hollow; Six Publications related to Washington Irving; An American Treasure: The Hudson River Valley
Activities: Classes for adults and children; docent training; demonstrations of 17th and 18th century arts and crafts; lectures open to the public; guided tours; gallery talks; sales shop sells books, reproductions & slides
L **Library,** 150 White Plains Rd, 10591. Tel 914-631-8609. *Librn* Kate Johnson; *Asst Librn* Claudia Dovman
Specialized reference library with particular emphasis on 17th, 18th and 19th century living in the Hudson River Valley
Library Holdings: Per subs 123; Micro — Reels; Other — Exhibition catalogs, manuscripts
Special Subjects: Washington Irving

M **LYNDHURST,** 635 S Broadway, 10591. Tel 914-631-0046. *Dir* Susanne Brendel-PanDich
Open May - Oct, Tues - Sun 10 AM - 5 PM, Nov - Apr, weekends only 10 AM - 5 PM. Admis adults $6, sr citizens $5, students $3, group rates by arrangement; free to National Trust Members. A property of the National Trust for Historic Preservation as a National Historic Landmark. Lyndhurst is a Gothic revival castle designed in 1838 for General William Paulding by Alexander Jackson Davis, one of America's most influential 19th century architects. Comissioned by second owner, George Merritt, to enlarge the house. Davis, in 1865, continued the Gothic revial style in the additions. It was purchased in 1880 by Jay Gould & willed to his daughter, Helen. Later acquired by another daughter, Anna, Duchess of Talleyrand-Perigord, Lyndhurst was left to National Trust in 1964. The property is located on spacious grounds along the Hudson River. Visitors are invited to explore the magnificent park. Other highlights include a carriagehouse, stocked with period vehicles, stables, and the remains of private greenhouses. Windows attributed to L C Tiffany. The preservation of Lyndhurst is a composite of the contributions of the three families who lived in it. Property serves as a focal point for advancement of historic preservation. Through it are developed new relationships amoung cultural, community preservation groups and National Trust members in its area. Responds to community preservation needs by acting as a link between community and appropriate regional or headquarter offices of National Trust. Provides interpretive programs which are related to Lyndhurst's particular case study in historic preservation. The National Trust Restoration Workshop, located in a portion of the stable complex carries out restoration craft services for National Trust properties. Average Annual Attendance: 80,000
Income: Financed by admission fees, memberships, private contributions, special events and federal appropriations
Collections: Collection of Gothic furniture designed by architect A J Davis in the 1830s and 1870s; 19th century furnishings and paintings; Tiffany glass
Exhibitions: Seasonal exhibitions
Activities: Summer outdoor concerts; antique and auto shows; Christmas programs; guided tours; individual paintings and original objects of art lent as requested for special exhibitions by museums and historical societies; museum shop sells books, reproductions, slides and gift items

TICONDEROGA

M **FORT TICONDEROGA ASSOCIATION,** PO Box 390, 12883. Tel 518-585-2821; FAX 518-585-2210. *Pres* John B Pell; *Exec Dir* Nicholas Westbrook; *Cur* Bruce M Moseley
Open daily May 10 - mid-Oct 9 AM - 5 PM, July & Aug 9 AM - 6 PM. Admis adults $7, children $5. Estab 1909 to preserve and present the Colonial and Revolutionary history of Fort Ticonderoga. The Museum is in the restored barracks of the Colonial fort. Average Annual Attendance: 100,000. Mem: 450; dues $20 & up
Income: Financed by admission fees, museum shop sales & donations.
Collections: Artifacts; manuscripts; paintings
Exhibitions: Held in mid-May - mid-Oct
Publications: Bulletin of the Fort Ticonderoga Museum, semi-annual
Activities: Classes for adults & children, docent training; lect open to public, 5 vis lectr per year; concerts; tours; scholarships & fels offered; individual paintings and original objects of art lent to qualified museums; sales shop sells books, reproductions, slides
L **Thompson-Pell Research Center,** PO Box 390, 12883. Tel 518-585-2821; FAX 518-585-2210. *Exec Dir* Nicholas Westbrook; *Cur* Bruce M Moseley
Open by appointment for reference only
Income: Financed by grants, contributions & earned income
Purchases: $30,000 per year
Library Holdings: Vols 10,000; Per subs 30; AV — A-tapes, cassettes, fs, Kodachromes, lantern slides, motion pictures, rec, slides, v-tapes; Other — Clipping files, exhibition catalogs, manuscripts, pamphlets, photographs, prints
Special Subjects: Archaeology, Bookplates & Bindings, Etchings & Engravings, Historical Material, Manuscripts, Maps, Painting - American, Painting - British, Restoration & Conservation, Military History
Publications: The Bulletin of the Fort Ticonderoga Museum, annual; The Haversack, semi-annual newsletter

TROY

A **RENSSELAER COUNTY HISTORICAL SOCIETY,** Hart-Cluett Mansion, 1827, 59 Second St, 12180. Tel 518-272-7232. *Pres* Ellen S Hogarty; *Dir* Anne W Ackerson; *Cur* Stacy F Pomeroy Draper; *Educ Dir* Marcy Shaffer
Open Tues - Sat 10 AM - 4 PM. Admis donation for adults $2. Estab 1927 to promote historical research and to collect and exhibit materials of all kinds

related to the history of the Rensselaer County area including books, papers, fine and decorative arts. The Hart-Cluett Mansion is a historic house museum with 11 period rooms. Average Annual Attendance: 13,000. Mem: 600; dues $25; annual meeting second Mon in Sept
Income: $200,000 (financed by endowment & mem)
Collections: Ceramics; costumes; Elijah Galusha 19th century furniture; paintings by local artists including C G Beauregard, Joseph Hidley and Abel Buel Moore; portraits; quilts and coverlets; silver
Exhibitions: Canes; Currier and Ives; Troy-Bilt Rototiller
Publications: Annual report; quarterly newsletter
Activities: Classes for children, docent training; lect open to public; gallery talks; tours; book traveling exhibitions; traveling exhibitions organized and circulated; sales shop sells books, prints, original art & reproductions
L **Library,** 59 Second St, 12180. Tel 518-272-7232. *Cur* Stacy Pomeroy Draper
Primarily for reference
Income: Financed by endowment, membership, grants, events
Library Holdings: Vols 2000; Per subs 4; AV — Lantern slides, motion pictures, slides; Other — Clipping files, framed reproductions, manuscripts, memorabilia, photographs
Special Subjects: Local history

M **RENSSELAER NEWMAN FOUNDATION CHAPEL AND CULTURAL CENTER,** The Gallery, 2125 Burdett Ave, 12180. Tel 518-274-7793. *Pres* Michael Duffy; *Dir* William McQuiston; *Treas* Thomas Phelan; *Secy* Mairin Quinn
Open 9 AM - 11 PM. Estab 1968 to provide religion and culture for members of the Rensselaer Polytechnic Institute and Troy area, a broadly ecumenical service. Gallery maintained. Average Annual Attendance: 100,000
Income: $150,000 (financed by contributions)
Collections: Contemporary paintings, sculpture and needlework; liturgical vestments and artifacts; medieval sculpture
Exhibitions: Laliberte banners; Picasso traveling exhibition New York State Council on the Arts; Smithsonian Institution Traveling Exhibition; local one man shows
Publications: Sun and Balance, three times a year
Activities: Dramatic programs; classes for adults and children; lect open to public, 10 vis lectr per yr; concerts; Poetry Series; Peace Fair; Festival of Religion and the Arts

M **RUSSELL SAGE COLLEGE,** Gallery, Schacht Fine Arts Center, 12180. Tel 518-270-2248. *Gallery Dir* Harold Lohner
Open Mon - Fri 9 AM - 5 PM, Sun 2 - 5 PM. No admis fee. Estab 1970 for exhibition of contemporary art for college and public. Gallery is one room, with 150 running ft. Average Annual Attendance: 3000
Income: Financed by the college
Collections: Drawings (contemporary); paintings (contemporary); sculpture of New Guinea and Africa
Exhibitions: Faculty and student shows; paintings, drawings, sculpture from New York City galleries and area artists; photography; traveling exhibitions
Activities: Gallery talks; original objects of art lent on campus; lending collection contains original prints, paintings, sculpture; traveling exhibitions organized and circulated

UTICA

M **MUNSON-WILLIAMS-PROCTOR INSTITUTE,** Museum of Art, 310 Genesee St, 13502-4799. Tel 315-797-0000; FAX 315-797-5608. *Dir* Paul D Schweizer; *Museum Educator* Elaine DePalma-Sadzkoski
Open Tues - Sat 10 AM - 5 PM, Sun 1 - 5 PM, cl Mon. No admis fee. Estab 1919 through an endowment granted a provisional charter by the Board of Regents of the University of the State of New York, changed to an absolute charter in 1941, and amended in 1948 to empower the Institute to provide instruction at the college level in the field of fine arts. The Institute became active in 1935 with the purpose of establishing & maintaining a gallery & collection of art to give instruction & to have an auxiliary library. It consists of a School of Art estab 1941; a Museum of Art opened in 1960; Fountain Elms, a house-museum was restored in 1960; a Meetinghouse opened in 1963 & a Performing Arts Division. Average Annual Attendance: 200,000. Mem: 3400; dues family $30, individual $20, senior citizen $15, student $10
Income: Financed by endowment, tuition and private contributions, voluntary donations at entrances
Purchases: 19th & 20th century American, European paintings, sculpture, graphic & decorative arts
Collections: †Arts of Central New York; †19th & 20th century European paintings and sculpture; Greek, Persian and Pre-Columbian art; †18th, 19th and 20th century American paintings, sculpture, and decorative arts; †drawings and prints
Exhibitions: Next to Nature; Evolution of the American Chair; Rodney Ripps; Monotype of Maurice Prendergast; The Rivendell Collection; Side by Side by Cole: The Two Versions of Thomas Cole's Voyage of Life Series of Paintings; Filmmakers of Central New York; The Blue & the Gray: Stoneware of Oneida Country; The Painter's Music; The Musician's Art; Masters of Contemporary Polish Art; The Highway as Habitat; Spendors of the New World; Splendors of the Pre-Columbian Era; Rivers of Gold
Publications: Bulletin, monthly; exhibition catalogues
Activities: Educ dept; docent training; lectures open to public; films; recitals; concerts; drama; art and gift shop sells books, original art, reproductions, prints, slides
L **Art Reference Library,** 310 Genessee St, 13502. Tel 315-797-0000, Ext 23. *Librn* Cynthia M Barth; *Music Librn* Michael Schuyler
Open Tues - Sat 10 AM - 5 PM. Estab 1940 to support School of Art, Museum of Art staff, Institute Membership and general public; circulation only to members of the Institute. Circ 5000
Purchases: $5000
Library Holdings: Vols 22,000; Per subs 60; Micro — Fiche; AV — Rec 5400, slides 23,000; Other — Clipping files, pamphlets
Special Subjects: Art History, Decorative Arts, Painting - American, Painting -

European, Photography, Pre-Columbian Art
Collections: Fountain Elms Collection; autographs, rare books and manuscripts, book plates;
Publications: Bibliographies related to museum exhibitions; bibliographic instructional materials

M **SCULPTURE SPACE, INC,** 12 Gates St, 13502. Tel 315-724-8381. *Exec Dir* Sylvia de Swaan; *Studio Mgr* Jonathan Kirk
Open by appointment only. No admis fee. Estab 1975 to provide professional artists with studio space. Average Annual Attendance: 300
Income: $75,000
Publications: Sculpture Space News, semi-annual
Activities: Awards (funded residences); scholarships & fels offered

VALLEY COTTAGE

L **VALLEY COTTAGE LIBRARY,** Gallery, Route 303, 10989. Tel 914-268-7700. *Library Dir* Ellen Simpson; *Exhib Dir* Claudette Doran
Open Mon - Thurs 10 AM - 9 PM, Fri & Sat 10 AM - 5 PM. Estab 1959. 27 x 7, artificial & natural light
Publications: Focus, quarterly

VESTAL

M **STATE UNIVERSITY OF NEW YORK AT BINGHAMTON,** University Art Gallery, 13901. Tel 607-777-2634; FAX 607-777-4000. *Dir* Lyn Gamwell; *Cur* Lucie Nelson; *Technical Coordr* Matthew Zupnick; *Secy* Norma Moses
Open Tues - Fri 9 AM - 4:30 PM, Thurs evening 6 - 8 PM, Sat & Sun 1 - 4:30 PM, cl university holidays. Estab 1967
Income: $20,000 (financed by state appropriations)
Collections: †Teaching collection from Egyptian to contemporary art
Exhibitions: (1993) Century of Silence. (1994) Madness in America
Publications: Exhibit catalogs
Activities: Lectures open to the public; gallery talks; seminars; internships

WATERTOWN

M **ROSWELL P FLOWER MEMORIAL LIBRARY,** 229 Washington St, 13601. Tel 315-788-2352. *Dir* Kenneth Hodosy
Open Sept - June Mon - Thurs 9:30 AM - 9 PM; Fri 9:30 AM - 5 PM, Sat 9 AM - 5 PM; July & Aug Mon 9:30 AM - 8:30 PM, Tues - Fri 9:30 AM - 5 PM, cl Sat. Estab 1904. The library contains murals, paintings and sculptures scattered throughout the building. Circ 184,325
Income: $471,000 (financed by the City of Watertown)
Special Subjects: Murals and paintings of local history and local interest
Collections: Military history (US); New York State material and genealogy
Exhibitions: Local Artists Guild; North Country Artist Guild
Activities: Lectures open to public; concerts; library tours; film programs

M **JEFFERSON COUNTY HISTORICAL SOCIETY,** 228 Washington St, 13601. Tel 315-782-3491. *Dir* Dr Persijs Kolberg; *Cur Educ* Melissa Widrick
Estab 1886. Average Annual Attendance: 11,500. Mem: 560; annual meeting May
Income: $142,000 (financed by endowment, membership, county appropriation, grants, private foundations and gifts)
Collections: Tyler Coverlet Collection; Costume Collection; Kinne Water Turbine Collection; 19th century Furniture; Prehistoric Indian Arts, Jefferson County
Exhibitions: The Homefront: WW II Exhibit
Publications: Bulletin, 1-2 times per yr; Musuem Musings; 4 times per yr; Abraham Tuthill (catalogue)
Activities: Classes for adults and children; in-school local history programs; lectures open to public, 5-6 plus 3 local vis lectr per yr; lending collection includes: artifacts, 155 items; traveling exhibitions, 1-2 per yr; originate traveling exhibitions; museum shop sells books, prints, antiques, collectables; Made in NYS: Handwoven Coverlets, 1820 to 1860 (Coverlets, damask tablecloths and ingrain carpet)
L **Library,** 228 Washington St, 13601. Tel 315-782-3491. *Dir* Dr Persijs Kolberg
Library Holdings: Vols 2211; Other — Clipping files, exhibition catalogs, framed reproductions, manuscripts, memorabilia, original art works, pamphlets, prints
Special Subjects: Architecture, Decorative Arts, Furniture, Glass, Historical Material
Publications: Museum Musings Newsletter, quarterly; Bulletin, annualy

WESTFIELD

L **PATTERSON LIBRARY & ART GALLERY,** 40 S Portage St, 14787. Tel 716-326-2154. *Dir* Deborah Williams; *Arts Specialist* Korene Korol
Open Mon - Wed 9 AM - 8 PM, Thurs - Sat 9 AM - 5 PM. Estab 1896 (Octagon Gallery estab 1971) to provide opportunity for education and recreation through the use of literature, music, films, paintings and other art forms; Rotunda Gallery estab 1986. Octagon Gallery is 1115 sq ft with 11 ft ceilings & 100 ft running space. Circ 72,000. Average Annual Attendance: 14,000
Income: Financed by endowment and private sources
Library Holdings: Vols 34,000; Per subs 164; AV — A-tapes, cassettes 125, fs, motion pictures, rec, slides; Other — Framed reproductions, memorabilia, original art works, pamphlets, photographs 10,000, sculpture
Special Subjects: Glass plate negatives of local history, WW I posters, seashells, mounted birds
Exhibitions: Annual Westfield Revisited Exhibition
Activities: Classes for children; docent training; lect open to public, 2 vis lectr per yr; concerts; gallery talks; tours; individual paintings & original objects of art lent to public; traveling exhibitions organized and circulated

WEST NYACK

M **ROCKLAND CENTER FOR THE ARTS,** 27 S Greenbush Rd, 10994. Tel 914-358-0877. *Exec Dir* Julianne Ramos , MFA
Open Mon-Fri 9 AM - 10 PM, Sat - Sun 9 AM - 4 PM. No admis fee. Estab 1947 to present excellence in the arts, education & services. 40 ft by 70 ft gallery space. Average Annual Attendance: 50,000. Mem: 3000; dues family $35, singles $20; annual meeting in Oct
Income: 400,000 (finance by membership, state appropriations, corporations, foundations & earned income)
Collections: Contemporary painting & drawing collection
Exhibitions: (1990) Expressions; American Housing
Publications: Artline Newsletter; art school catalogues; exhibition catalogue
Activities: Classes for adults & children in visual, literary & performing arts; lect open to the public; performances in classical, jazz, folk music

WEST POINT

M **UNITED STATES MILITARY ACADEMY,** West Point Museum, 10996. Tel 914-938-2203; Autovon 8-688-2203-3201. *Dir Museum* Michael E Moss; *Cur Weapons* Robert W Fisch; *Cur History* Michael J McAfee; *Cur Art* David Meschutt; *Museum Specialist* Walter J Nock; *Registrar* Pat A Dursi; *Cur Design* Richard Clark
Open daily 10:30 AM - 4:15 PM. No admis fee. Estab 1854, supplementing the academic, cultural & military instruction of cadets; also disseminates the history of the US Army, the US Military Academy & the West Point area. Collections open to the public. Average Annual Attendance: 300,000
Purchases: $5000
Collections: Rindisbacher watercolors; Sully Portrait Collection; †cadet drawings from 1820 - 1940; †military paintings and prints; †military artifacts including weapons, flags, uniforms, medals, etc; paintings and prints of West Point; Jonas Lie Collection of Panama Canal Oils; Liedesdorf Collection of European Armor; European and American posters; extensive holdings from World War I and World War II, military and homefront subjects
Exhibitions: The Toy Soldier: A Historical Review; Whistler and Others: Cadet Drawings from the 19th Century to World War I; Jonas Lie and the Building of the Panama Canal; The Land of Counterpane: Toy Soldiers; The US Cavalry in the West; Exhibition of Don Spaulding's art and private collection; American and French Zouaves
Publications: Posters for Victory; The West Point Museum: A Guide to the Collections; West Point Museum Bulletin, irregularly
Activities: Gallery talks; tours; Individual paintings & original objects of art lent to accredited museums; book traveling exhibitions 2 per year to accredited museums; museum shop sells books, reproductions, prints & military souvenirs

WOODSTOCK

A **CATSKILL CENTER FOR PHOTOGRAPHY, INC,** 59 Tinker St, 12498. Tel 914-679-9957. *Exec Dir* Colleen Kenyon
Estab 1977, a non-profit organization, an art & education center, an artists space
Collections: Permanent collection contains 5000 photographic prints & art work which incorporates photography
Exhibitions: (1989) Two part exhibition: Revamp Review, Television for Real; Woodstock Remembered; 150 Years of Architectural Photography in America

A **WOODSTOCK ARTISTS ASSOCIATION,** 28 Tinker St, 12948. Tel 914-679-2940. *Head Archives* Allice Lewis
Open Apr - Oct, Thurs - Mon noon - 5 PM, Nov - Mar Fri - Sun noon - 5 PM, cl Feb. Estab 1922 to exhibit the work of artists of the region. Upstairs Gallery - Group member show; Downstairs Gallery - Solo exhibits; exhibiting members must live within 25 miles of Woodstock. Mem: 800; dues individual $30; meetings in June & Nov
Income: $40,000 (financed by endowment, membership, city appropriation)
Collections: The Permanent Collection of Woodstock Artists includes oils, prints & sculpture
Publications: Woodstock Art Heritage: The Permanent Collection of the Woodstock Artists Association (1987)
Activities: Classes for children; dramatic programs; film; Lect open to public; concerts; gallery talks; awards; competitions with awards; individual paintings & original objects of art lent; lending collection includes 650 original art works, 120 original prints, 472 paintings, 40 photographs & 18 sculptures; book traveling exhibitions; sales shop sells books & prints
L **WAA Archives,** 28 Tinker St, 12498. Tel 914-679-2940.
For reference only
Library Holdings: Other — Clipping files, memorabilia, original art works, photographs, prints, sculpture
Special Subjects: Woodstock Artists, past-present

YONKERS

M **HUDSON RIVER MUSEUM,** Trevor Park-on-Hudson, 511 Warburton Ave, 10701. Tel 914-963-4550; FAX 914-963-8558. *Dir* Philip Berre; *Cur* Laura Vookles Hardin; *Dir Education* Kathryn Adamchick; *Tech* John Matherly
Open Wed, Fri & Sat 1 - 5 PM, Thurs 10 AM - 9 PM, Sun noon - 5 PM. Admis by voluntary contribution. Estab 1924 as a general museum of art, history and science
Income: $700,000 (financed by membership, city and county appropriation, state arts council, federal grants, donations)
Collections: 19th & 20th century American art, decorative arts, furniture, toys, dolls, costumes, accoutrement, silver, china, paintings, sculpture, photography
Exhibitions: In Plural America; The Old Croton Aqueduct
Publications: Bimonthly calendar of events; special exhibitions catalogs; annual report
Activities: Docent training; lectures and special events open to public; concerts; gallery talks; tours; art lent to other museums for exhibition purposes; lending

collection contains original art works, paintings, photographs, sculpture; book traveling exhibitions; traveling exhibitions organized and circulated to museums, college galleries - regional & national; museum shop sells books, inexpensive items for children

M **PHILIPSE MANOR HALL STATE HISTORIC SITE,** 29 Warburton Ave, PO Box 496, 10702. Tel 914-965-4027. *Project Dir* Alix Sandra Schnee
Open by appointment only. No admis fee. Estab 1908 to preserve Georgian manor house owned by the Frederick Philipse family; to interpret Philipse Manor Halls architecture, its significance as the home of an American Loyalist and its importance as an example of 17th and 18th century Anglo-Dutch patterns in landholding and development. The State Historic Site is part of the New York State Office of Parks and Recreation; the Hall houses contemporary style exhibits of history, art and architecture hung against a backdrop of fine 18th and 19th century architectural carvings
Income: Financed by state appropriation
Collections: Cochran Portrait of Famous Americans; Cochran Collection of Windor Chairs
Activities: Lectures open to public; concerts; tours; demonstrations; films

L **YONKERS PUBLIC LIBRARY,** Fine Arts Dept, 1500 Central Park Ave, 10710. Tel 914-337-1500, Ext 311. *Librn III & Head Dept* Joanne Roche
Open Mon - Fri 9AM - 9 PM, Sat 9 AM - 5 PM, Sun noon - 5 PM, cl Sat & Sun during summer. Estab 1962 to serve the general public with a special interest in the arts, especially the fine arts, performing arts, and the decorative and applied arts. Circ printed material approx 22,000; recorded material approx 66,000
Income: $65,000 (financed by city appropriation & gifts)
Purchases: $65,000
Library Holdings: Vols 14,000; Per subs 82; Scores 3000; Micro — Fiche, reels; AV — A-tapes 3100, cassettes 1000, rec 15,000, slides 2000, v-tapes 200; Other — Clipping files, pamphlets 7000

L **Will Library,** 1500 Central Park Ave, 10710. Tel 914-337-1500. *Librn* Leslie Dickinson
Library Holdings: Vols 126,000; Per subs 75
Exhibitions: Exhibits work by local artists and craftsmen

NORTH CAROLINA

ASHEVILLE

M **ASHEVILLE ART MUSEUM,** 2 S Park Square, PO Box 1717, 28802. Tel 704-253-3227; FAX 704-251-5652. *Exec Dir* Edwin Ritts Jr; *Assoc Dir Educ* Diane Dufilho; *Dir Development* Harryette Cox; *Cur* Frank Thomson
Open Tues - Sat 10 AM - 6 PM, Fri 10 AM - 8 PM, Sun 1 - 5 PM, cl Mon. Admis adults $4, children 6 - 15 $2.50, under 6 free, Sat free, members free. Estab 1948 to provide art experiences to the Western North Carolina area through exhibitions. Six galleries maintained,. Average Annual Attendance: 50,000. Mem: 750; dues family $35, single $25, annual meeting July
Income: Financed by membership, United Arts Fund Drive & auxiliary
Purchases: James Chapin, Romane Bearden, George Luks
Collections: 20th Century American Art
Publications: Quarterly membership; newsletter, catalogues
Activities: Classes for adults & children docent training; lectures open to public; gallery talks; tours; competitions; original objects of art lent to other museums

A **SOUTHERN HIGHLAND HANDICRAFT GUILD,** Folk Art Center, Riceville Rd Blue Ridge Parkway, PO Box 9545, 28815. Tel 704-298-7928. *Dir* Robert Gabriel; *Educ Dir* Andrew Glasgow
Open Mon - Sun 9 AM - 5 PM, cl Thanksgiving, Christmas and New Year's. No admis fee. Estab 1930 to encourage wider appreciation of mountain crafts; raise and maintain standards of design and craftsmanship, and encourage individual expression. Mem: 700; open to eligible craftsmen from Southern Appalachian Mountain Region upon approval of applicant's work by Standards Committee and Board of Trustees; dues group $40, single $20; annual meeting in Apr
Income: Financed by membership and merchandising
Publications: Highland Highlights; monthly newsletter
Activities: Education dept; workshops for adults and children; lectures open to public and some for members only; gallery talks; tours; competitions; retail shops open

BREVARD

M **BREVARD COLLEGE,** Sims Art Center, 28712. Tel 704-883-8292, Ext 245. *Dir* Tim Murray
Open Mon - Thurs 8 AM - 10 PM, Fri 8 AM - 5 PM. No admis fee. Estab 1969 as Art Department with gallery. Center has three areas, 160 ft running space, and 1500 sq ft floor space
Income: Financed by departmental appropriation
Collections: Contemporary art; 1940-1970 paintings and watercolors; print and pottery collection
Exhibitions: Student and visiting artist exhibitions
Activities: Classes for adults; dramatic programs; college classes and continuing education; 4 vis lectr per yr; 4 gallery talks; competitions with cash awards; scholarships; lending collection contains books, cassettes, color reproductions, film strips, photographs, slides

L **James A Jones Library,** 28712. Tel 704-883-8292, Ext 2268, 2298; FAX 704-884-5424. *Librn* Michael McCabe
Open Mon - Fri 8:30 AM - 4:30 PM. Estab 1934. For reference & circulation
Income: Financed by parent institution
Library Holdings: Vols 3325; Per subs 16; AV — Cassettes, fs, slides, v-tapes 55; Other — Clipping files, pamphlets, prints
Publications: New book list, monthly
Activities: Film series, weekly during academic year

CHAPEL HILL

UNIVERSITY OF NORTH CAROLINA AT CHAPEL HILL

M **Ackland Art Museum,** Campus Box 3400, 27599-3400. Tel 919-966-5736; FAX 919-966-1400; TDD 919-962-0837. *Dir* Charles Millard; *Cur* Sarah Schroth
Open Tues - Sat 10 AM - 5 PM, Sun 1 - 5 PM, cl Mon and University holidays. No admis fee. Estab 1958 as an art museum which serves the members of the university community as well as the public. The Museum houses a permanent collection and presents a program of changing exhibitions. Average Annual Attendance: 30,000. Mem: 830; dues $25, $45, $100 & $500
Income: Financed by endowment, membership and state appropriation
Publications: Newsletter, fall and spring; The Ackland Art Museum (handbook)
Activities: Dramatic programs; docent training; lect open to public, 3 vis lectr per year; gallery talks; tours; exhibition catalogs available for sale

L **Joseph Curtis Sloane Art Library,** Hanes Art Center, Campus Box 3405, 27599-3405. Tel 919-962-2397. *Art Librn* Philip Rees; *Libr Asst* Rachel Frew
Open Mon - Thurs 8 AM - 10 PM, Fri 8 AM - 5 PM, Sat 10 AM - 5 PM, Sun 2 - 10 PM
Income: Financed by state appropriation
Library Holdings: Vols 76,000; Micro — Fiche 14,500, reels 320; Other — Exhibition catalogs, pamphlets
Special Subjects: Architecture, Art History, Painting - American, Painting - British, Painting - Dutch, Painting - Flemish, Painting - French, Painting - Italian

CHARLOTTE

C **BRANCH BANKING & TRUST COMPANY,** Art Collection, 200 S Tryon ST, 28202. Tel 704-342-7000.
Open Mon - Thurs 9 AM - 5 PM, Fri 9 AM - 6 PM. Estab 1978. Works chosen from local & North Carolina artists only; lower level of bank devoted to student art

C **KNIGHT PUBLISHING COMPANY,** 600 S Tryon St, PO Box 32188, 28232. Tel 704-358-5000. *Community Events Mgr* Carlton Montgomery
Open 8 AM - 8 PM. No admis fee. Collection estab 1971 to enhance the interior decoration of the building; monthly changing exhibits in lobby gallery. Lobby gallery is 30 x 100 for showing regional arts, crafts & photography. Average Annual Attendance: 500-1000
Purchases: $2500
Collections: Collection contains wide variety of regional contemporary art, paintings, drawings, weavings and pottery
Activities: Purchase awards in regional art competitions

M **THE LIGHT FACTORY, INC,** 311 Arlington Ave, (ADP) PO Box 32815, 28203. Tel 704-333-9755. *Exec Dir* Linda Ford; *Prog Coordr* Rhonda Harris
Estab 1975 as a photographic arts center serving the public interest by advancing an awareness, understanding & appreciation of photography as a means of personal expression & development through programs, publications, exhibitions, workshops & lectures
Exhibitions: Through the Looking Glass; Gloria De Filippes Brush & Sharon Anglin Kuhne; Platinum & Palladium by Bill Wylie; Carl Bergaman & Stuart Klipper; Pinky Bass & Clara Couch Eastern European Photography

M **MINT MUSEUM OF ART,** 2730 Randolph Rd, 28207. Tel 704-337-2000; FAX 704-337-2101. *Dir* Bruce Evans; *Deputy Dir* Steve Marsh; *Dir Curatorial Serv* Charles Mo
Open Tues 10 AM - 10 PM, Wed - Sat 10 AM - 5 PM, Sun 1 - 6 PM, cl Mon & holidays. Admis $2, children 12 & under & members free. Estab 1936 as an art museum in what was the first branch of the US mint erected in 1837. Museum houses three changing galleries: a permanent gallery, Delhom Decorative Arts Gallery. Average Annual Attendance: 150,000. Mem: 1850; dues Mint Master $1000, benefactor $500, sponser $250, patron $120, family $45, individual $30, sr citizen or student 20% discount
Income: Financed by endowment, membership and city appropriation
Collections: Decorative arts, paintings, sculpture with emphasis on Baroque, Renaissance, 18th century English, 19th and 20th century European and American paintings, and pre-Columbian art
Publications: Mint Museum Newsletter and calendar of events, six times a year
Activities: Classes for adults; docent training; lect open to the public, 25 visiting lectrs per year; concerts; gallery talks; tours; competitions; original objects of art lent to other museums; museum shop selling books, original art, prints, gifts, museum replicas, jewelry, cards

L **Library,** 2730 Randolph Rd, 28207. Tel 704-337-2000; FAX 704-337-2101. *Librn* Sara Wolf
Open to the public for reference only
Library Holdings: Vols 10,000

L **PUBLIC LIBRARY OF CHARLOTTE AND MECKLENBURG COUNTY,** 310 N Tryon St, 28202-2176. Tel 704-336-2801. *Dir* Robert Cannon; *Assoc Dir* Judith Sutton; *Art Librn* Carolyn Hunter
Open Mon - Fri 9 AM - 9 PM, Sat 9 AM - 6 PM, Sun 2 - 6 PM, cl Sun June - Aug. Estab 1903 to provide free public library service to citizens of Mecklenburg County. Gallery contains 90 linear feet of wall space
Income: $10.9 million (financed by state and county appropriations)
Purchases: $713,068
Library Holdings: Vols 792,393; maps 6865; AV — Cassettes, fs, motion pictures 2772, rec 27,869, slides 9261; Other — Prints 424, sculpture
Exhibitions: Local artists exhibit for one month

M **SCIENCE MUSEUMS OF CHARLOTTE, INC,** Discovery Place, 301 N Tryon St, 28202. Tel 704-372-6261; FAX 704-337-2670. *Chief Exec Officer* Freda Nicholson; *Dir Educ & Prog* Beverly Sanford; *Marketing Public Relations Specialist* Lynn Grayson
Open Sept - May Mon - Fri 9 AM - 5 PM, June - Aug 9 AM - 6 PM, Sat 9 AM - 6 PM, Sun 1 - 6 PM. Admis adult $4, students & sr citizens $3, children 3-5 w/ parent $2 & under 2 yrs free, no charge for members. Estab 1981 as a science

museum with hands on concept of learning by doing. A small staff reference library is maintained. Average Annual Attendance: 400,000. Mem: 5000; dues - family $40, sr citizen $25, student $20

Income: $1,350,000 (financed by city & county appropriations, fees & sales shop)

Collections: Arthropods; gems & minerals; Lepidoptera; †Pre-Columbian: Mayan, North American, Peruvian; †primitive art: African, Alaskan Eskimo, Oceania, South America; reptillia

Publications: Science Magazine, quarterly; activities bulletin, quarterly

Activities: Classes for adults and children; docent training; volunteer training program for demonstrators & guides; major programming for school lectures; tours; acceptable for internship from UNCC and Queens College; book traveling exhibitions, 4 per yr; originate traveling exhibitions that circulate to science museum collaborations; museum shop sells books, prints, shells, jewelry, school supplies & souvenirs; junior museum is primarily geared to pre-school and early elementary age children

A **SPIRIT SQUARE CENTER FOR THE ARTS,** 345 N College St, 28202. Tel 704-372-9664; FAX 704-377-9808. *Pres* Joe Golden, PhD; *VPres of Arts & Educ* Joe Jefcoat MFA; *Cur Exhib* Ken Bloom
Open Tues - Sat noon - 6 PM. Estab 1983. Seven art galleries. Average Annual Attendance: 20,000

Income: $3,000,000 (financed by mem, city & state appropriation & local arts drive)

Activities: Classes for adults & children; dramatic programs; docent training; lect open to the public, 18 vis lect per year; concerts; gallery talks; tours; scholarships; artmobile; museum shop sells books & original art

DALLAS

M **GASTON COUNTY MUSEUM OF ART & HISTORY,** 131 W Main St, PO Box 429, 28034-0429. Tel 704-922-7681; FAX 704-922-7683. *Pres* David Q Bumgardner; *VPres* Pam Warlick; *Dir* Alan D Waufle; *Cur of Education* Cecilia Benoy; *Cur of Coll & Exhib* James W Hollomon Jr
Open Tues - Fri 10 AM - 5 PM, Sat 1 - 5 PM, Sun 2 - 5 PM. No admis fee. Estab Nov 1975, opened July 1976 to promote the fine arts and local history in Gaston County, through classes, workshops and exhibitions; to preserve Historic Dallas Square; promote the history of the textile industry. The museum is located in an 1852 Hoffman Hotel; the Hands-On Gallery includes sculpture & weaving which may be touched; the two small galleries are on local history, with the major gallery for changing & traveling exhibits. Average Annual Attendance: 53,000. Mem: 715; dues $20 - $1000; annual meeting Nov, with quarterly meetings the first Thurs in Feb, May August & Nov

Income: $320,000 (financed by mem & county appropriation)

Purchases: $1000 per yr for regional art

Collections: †Antique furniture; †contemporary sculpture; †documents; †19th - 20th century American art; objects of local history; †paintings by North Carolina artists living & dead photographs; †textile history

Exhibitions: Toys Were Us

Publications: The Register, quarterly newsletter

Activities: Classes for adults and children; docent training; dramatic programs; outreach classes to schools; lectures open to the public, 6 vis lectr per year; gallery talks; tours; competitions with cash & purchase awards; exten dept serves Gaston County; individual paintings & original objects of art lent to qualified institutions; book traveling exhibitions, 3 per year; sales shop sells books, magazines, original art, reproductions, prints, stationery, postcards, gifts & jewelry

L **Library,** 131 W Main St, PO Box 429, 28034. Tel 704-922-7681. *Dir* Alan D Waufle
Open to public for reference only
Library Holdings: Vols 650; Per subs 13; AV — A-tapes, fs, slides; Other — Clipping files, exhibition catalogs, framed reproductions, memorabilia, pamphlets, photographs, prints

DAVIDSON

M **DAVIDSON COLLEGE ART GALLERY,** PO Box 10, 28036. Tel 704-892-2000. *Dir* Herb Jackson
Open Mon - Fri 10 AM - 5 PM. No admis fee. Estab 1952 to provide exhibitions of educational importance. Gallery covers 4000 sq ft. Average Annual Attendance: 6000
Income: Financed by college budget
Collections: Primary emphasis in graphics
Activities: Lectures open to public, 6 vis lectr per year; gallery talks
L **Library,** PO Box 10, 28036. Tel 704-892-2000, Ext 358. *Librn* Dr Leland Park
Open to students and visitors
Library Holdings: Vols 200; Per subs 2

DURHAM

M **DUKE UNIVERSITY MUSEUM OF ART,** 6845 College Station, PO Box 90732, 27708-0732. Tel 919-684-5135. *Dir* Michael P Mezzatesta; *Admin Asst* Lilian Antonovics; *Cur Pre-Colombian Art* Dorie Reents-Budet; *Asst Cur* Louise Brasher; *Registrar* Jessie Petcoff
Open Mon - Fri 9 AM - 5 PM, Sat 11 AM - 2 PM, Sun 2 - 5 PM. No admis fee. Estab 1969 as a study museum with the collections being used and studied by various university departments, as well as the public school system and surrounding communities. The museum is located on the East Campus in a renovated two-story Georgian building; gallery space includes part of the first floor and entire second floor with the space divided into eight major gallery areas. Average Annual Attendance: 8000 - 10,000
Income: Financed by University
Collections: African; classical; graphics; Medieval decorative art and sculpture; Oriental jade and porcelain; paintings; †Pre-Columbian; textiles (Peruvian, Navajo)
Exhibitions: Old Master Drawing; Medieval Elimination; Portrait of a Sacred

Myan Cave
Publications: Exhibition catalogs, 1 - 2 per year
Activities: Lect open to public, 2 - 4 lectr per year; gallery talks; tours; individual paintings and original objects of art lent to other museums which are equipped with proper security and insurance

L **East Campus Library,** 6857 College Station, 27708. Tel 919-684-6227, 684-3244; FAX 919-681-8678. *Librn & Art Bibliographer* Lee Sorensen
Open 8 AM - 2 AM. Estab 1930 to support the study of art at Duke University
Income: Financed by budget & endowment
Purchases: $53,800, excluding approval plan expenditure
Library Holdings: Vols 85,000; Per subs 416; Micro — Cards, fiche, reels; Other — Clipping files, exhibition catalogs, pamphlets 3250
Special Subjects: Afro-American Art, American Western Art, Architecture, Art History, Graphic Arts, History of Art & Archaeology, Judaica, Painting - American, Painting - British, Painting - Dutch, Painting - European, Painting - Flemish, Painting - French, Painting - German, Painting - Italian
Collections: Emphasis on European and American Art

M **DUKE UNIVERSITY UNION,** Duke University, 27706. Tel 919-684-2911. *Union Dir* Jon J Phelps; *Assoc Dir* Peter Coyle; *Asst Dir Programs* Beth Budd; *Specialist Ceramic Educ* Sharon Adams
Louise Jones Brown Gallery open Sun - Sat 7 AM - 1 AM; West Gallery & Hanks Gallery open Mon - Fri 8 AM - 5 PM; East Gallery open Sun - Sat 8 AM - midnight. No admis fee. Estab to bring to the university community exhibits of every type of graphic arts; to bring artists to campus for workshops. East Campus Gallery, room with waist high bookshelves in east campus library; West Gallery, exhibit walls & freestanding display cases in West Campus Library used for student work; Hanks Gallery & Louise Jones Brown Gallery, two galleries in Bryan Center (performing arts complex). Mem: 15; monthly meetings
Income: Financed by endowment, commission on exhibit works sold & student fees
Exhibitions: Professional & local artists, approx 3 monthly (1 in each gallery); plus Duke student artists in 1 gallery monthly
Activities: Classes for adults; lectures open to public, 1 vis lect per year; competitions; gallery talks

M **DURHAM ART GUILD INC,** 120 Morris St, 27701. Tel 919-560-2713. *Gallery Coordr* Susan Lopez Hickman
Open Mon - Sat 9 AM - 9 PM, Sun 1 - 9 PM. No admis fee. Estab 1948 to exhibit work of regional artists. 3600 sq ft gallery located in Arts Council Bldg. Average Annual Attendance: 10,000. Mem: 400; dues $20; annual meeting in June
Income: $50,000 (financed by mem, city & state appropriations)
Exhibitions: Exhibitions of work by regional artists, 8 - 10 per year; annual juried art shows
Publications: Juried Show Catalogue, annual; quarterly newsletter
Activities: Lect open to public, 3 vis lectr per year; competitions with awards; originate traveling exhibitions 2 per year

M **NORTH CAROLINA CENTRAL UNIVERSITY,** Art Museum, PO Box 19555, 27707. Tel 919-560-6211; FAX 919-560-5012. *Dir* Norman E Pendergraft
Open Tues - Fri 9 AM - 5 PM, Sun 2 - 5 PM. No admis fee. Estab 1971 in a former black teaching institution with a collection of contemporary art, many Afro-American artists, reflecting diversity in style, technique, medium and subject. Three galleries are maintained; one houses the permanent collection and two are for changing shows. Average Annual Attendance: 4000
Income: Financed by state appropriation
Collections: African & Oceanic; †Contemporary American with a focus on minority artists
Exhibitions: (1989) Gullah Life Reflections - Paintings of Jonathan Green. Black Women Artists - NC Connections. (1991) Where Myth Stirs: Paintings by Jim Moon
Publications: Artis, Bearden & Burke: A Bibliography & Illustrations List; exhibition catalogs
Activities: Lect open to public; gallery talks; tours

FAYETTEVILLE

M **FAYETTEVILLE MUSEUM OF ART, INC,** 839 Stamper Rd, PO Box 35134, 28303. Tel 919-485-5121. *Dir* Tom Grubb; *Educ Dir* Olga McCoy; *Admin Asst* Diana Campbell
Open Tues - Fri 10 AM - 5 PM, Sat & Sun 1 - 5 PM. No admis fee. Estab 1971 to promote in the area an active interest in the fine and applied arts; to establish and maintain a permanent collection. Front & main galleries are 996 sq ft, 143 ft wall space (231 ft wall space with temporary walls). Average Annual Attendance: 20,000. Mem: 600; dues $5000, $1000, $250, $100, $45, $25, $20; annual meeting in the spring
Income: $200,000 (financed by fundraisers, membership, grants & city)
Collections: American art of all media, with concentration on Southeastern artists; African Art
Exhibitions: (1991) James Beaman (paintings); 19th Annual Competition for North Carolina Artists; Michael Northuis (paintings); Capital Art League
Publications: Annual competition catalogue; quarterly calendar
Activities: Classes for adults and children; docent training; lect open to public, 12-15 visiting lectr per year; concerts; gallery talks; competitions with cash awards; book traveling exhibitions 3 - 4 per year

GREENSBORO

M **GREEN HILL CENTER FOR NORTH CAROLINA ART,** 200 N Davie St, 27401. Tel 919-333-7460. *Exec Dir & Cur* Jennifer W Moore; *Educ Dir* Lynn Lazich; *Gallery Mgr* Mary Pearson
Open Tues - Fri 10 AM - 5 PM, Sat 11 AM - 5 PM, cl Sun & Mon. No admis fee. Estab and incorporated 1974 as a non-profit institution offering exhibitions and educational programming featuring the visual arts of North Carolina. Average Annual Attendance: 35,000. Mem: 600; dues $20 - $2500

Income: Financed by mem, United Arts Council of Greensboro, Institute of Museum Services, North Carolina Arts Council
Exhibitions: (1991) Taking a Stand: Art & Social Vision; Phil Link: Recent Works; Revising the View: NC Women Artists; Art & Music (Working title); Welcome to Fantastic Art: A Herman Finney Retrospective; The Winter Show
Publications: Newsletter; catalogues
Activities: Classes for adults & children; docent training; artists-in-the-schools program; lectures open to public, 5-6 vis lectr per yr; concerts; gallery talks; tours; competitions with awards; originate traveling exhibitions; sales shop sells books, magazines & original art

A **GREENSBORO ARTISTS' LEAGUE,** 200 N Davie St, 27401. Tel 919-333-7485. *Exec Dir* William Calhoun
Open Tues - Fri 10 AM - 5 PM, Sat noon - 5 PM. No admis fee. Estab 1956 to encourage members to show & sell their works. Twenty-five exhibitions per year in the gallery; mostly one- person exhibitions & invitational group shows. Average Annual Attendance: 30,000. Mem: 400; dues patron $100, supportive $50, family $40, single $30, sr citizen $20; annual meeting last Tues in Jan
Exhibitions: African American Arts Festival Celebration; All Members Exhibitions; National Traveling Competition
Publications: Bi-monthly newsletter
Activities: Classes & workshops for adults; lectures open to public; annual international competition with monetary prizes & merit awards

M **GREENSBORO COLLEGE,** Irene Cullis Gallery, 815 W Market St, 27401. Tel 919-272-7102. *Assoc Prof* Robert Kowski
Open Mon - Fri 10 AM - 4 PM, Sun 2 - 5 PM. Estab to exhibit visual art by visiting professional artists, Greensboro College art students and others. Average Annual Attendance: 1500

M **UNIVERSITY OF NORTH CAROLINA AT GREENSBORO,** Weatherspoon Art Gallery, Spring Garden & Tate St, 27412. Tel 919-334-5770. *Dir* Ruth K Beesch; *Asst to Dir* Ann Dortch; *Cur of Exhib* Trevor Richardson; *Registrar* Barbara Brady
Open Tues, Thurs & Fri 10 AM - 5 PM, Wed 10 AM - 8 PM, Sat & Sun 1 - 5 PM, cl Mon, University holiday periods and between academic sessions. No admis fee. Estab 1942. The gallery houses modern art; new facility, 46,000 sq ft. Average Annual Attendance: 18,000. Mem: 750; dues $20 & up; annual meeting May
Purchases: $110,000
Collections: †Contemporary American paintings, drawings, prints & sculpture; Japanese scrolls, Japanese prints; Cone Collection: Matisse, Picasso, prints & Matisse bronzes
Exhibitions: (1990) Artists in the Abstract; Falk Visiting Artist Exhibition: Peter Agostini; American Modernism; Henri Matisse: Lithographs and Bronzes from the Cone Collection; The Postwar Spirit; Changing Perceptions: The Evolution of 20th Century American Art; A Snazzy, Jazzy Black Tie Affair (preview party for Weatherspoon Gallery Association members); Weatherspoon Art Gallery Lecture Series; Falk Visiting Artist Lecture Series; Falk Visiting Artist Exhibition: Jeff Joyce; Action and Artifact; Art on Paper; Carl Billingsley: Sculpture Installation; Masked Figures by David Finn. (1991) MFA Thesis Exhibition; The Quest for Self Expression: Painting in Moscow & Leningrad, 1965-1990; Falk Visiting Artist Exhibition; William Willis: Paintings; Falk Visiting Artist Exhibition: Juried Senior Exhibition; Spring Acquisitions; American Prints in Black & White, 1900-1950: Selections from The Reba and David Williams Collection; Edvard Munch: The Early Years; MFA Thesis Exhibition
Publications: Art on Paper Catalogue, annually; Weatherspoon Gallery Association Bulletin, biennially
Activities: Classes for adults; docent training; trips to national exhibitions; lectures open to the public, 20 vis lectrs per year; gallery talks; tours; individual paintings and original objects of art lent to other museums, and local corporate and individual benefactors contributing $1000 or more per year; lending collection consists of original art works, original prints, paintings, photographs, sculpture and videotapes; originate traveling exhibitions; postcard reproductions sold at reception desk

GREENVILLE

M **EAST CAROLINA UNIVERSITY,** Wellington B Gray Gallery, Jenkins Fine Arts Center, 27858-4353. Tel 919-757-6336; FAX 919-757-6441. *Gallery Dir* Charles Muir Lovell
Open Mon - Sat 10 AM - 5 PM, Thurs evenings until 8 PM year round, cl University holidays. No admis fee. Estab 1977, the Gallery presents 15 exhibitions annually of contemporary art in various media. Understanding of exhibitions is strengthened by educational programs including lectures, workshops, symposia & guided tours. The gallery is a large, modern 6000 sq ft facility with track lighting and modular moveable walls. Average Annual Attendance: 23,000
Income: Financed by state appropriation, Art Enthusiasts of Eastern Carolina, state & federal grants, corporate & foundation donations
Special Subjects: 20th Century Art; Historical Art from Different Cultures and Civilizations
Collections: Larry Rivers: The Boston Massacre - Color Lithographs
Exhibitions: (1992) Recherche, African American artist group from Philadelphia, Pennsylvania; William Fick: Linocuts; Joyce Ogden: Personal View, Site Specific Installation; Jack Troy: Salt Fired Ceramics; Sigmund Abeles Retrospective, organized by New England College Gallery; Leland Wallin - Straight from the Eye: Toys Observed. (1993) Open Spain: Espana Abierta, 147 documentary photographs of Spain (1980 - 1990), organized by the Museum of Contemporary Photography, Chicago; Carol Shinn: Machine Stitching; Phyllis Rosenblatt: Drawings; The Dream Realm of Minnie Evans, 53 paintings by the acclaimed African American folk artist from Wilmington, North Carolina, sponsored in part by a grant from the National Endowment for the Arts, organized by the Wellington B Gray Gallery; Norman Keller Retrospective; Marsha Burn Photographs; Anders Knuttson: Light Paintings. (1994) Gregory Amenoff: Works on Paper, organized by the DeCordova Museum & Sculpture Park, Lincoln, Massachusetts; Angela Bourodimos & Jane Hammond: A Question of Gender;

Joseph Beuys: Drawings, Objects & Prints, organized by the Goethe Institute, Atlanta; Annual Undergraduate Competition; National Juried Competition, The Figure in Drawing & Painting
Publications: The Dream World of Minnie Evans; Jacob Lawrence: An American Master; exhibition catalogs
Activities: Lect open to public, 18 vis lectr per year; workshops & symposia; gallery talks; tours; originate traveling exhibitions

L **Art Library,** Leo Jenkins Fine Arts Center, 27858. Tel 919-757-6785. *Librn* Paul Evans
Open daily 8 AM - 5 PM. Estab 1977 for Art School study of current and selected periodicals and selected reference books and slides. For lending and reference
Library Holdings: Vols 3500; Per subs 62; Micro — Cards, prints 30; AV — A-tapes, cassettes, fs, motion pictures, slides 80,000, v-tapes; Other — Exhibition catalogs, manuscripts, prints

A **GREENVILLE MUSEUM OF ART, INC,** 802 S Evans St, 27834. Tel 919-758-1946. *Exec Dir* Barbour Strickland; *Asst to Dir* Beth Collier; *Preparator* Christopher Daniels
Open Tues - Fri 10 AM - 5 PM, Sat & Sun 1 - 4 PM, cl Mon. No admis fee. Estab 1939, incorporated in 1956, to foster public interest in art & to form a permanent collection. Six galleries 2000 sq ft including a children's gallery. Average Annual Attendance: 24,000. Mem: 600; dues $35 and higher; annual meeting each Spring
Income: $100,000 (plus Foundation income for acquisition of art; financed by contributions, memberships, appropriations & grants)
Collections: †20th Century Contemporary paintings; drawings; graphics; †regional and national sculpture
Exhibitions: Exhibitions featuring work of regional artists; National traveling exhibits; Collection exhibits
Publications: Annual Report; A Visit to GMA, brochure; monthly exhibit announcements; quarterly members' newsletter
Activities: Classes for adults & children; demonstrations; dramatic programs; docent training; workshops; lectures open to public, 8 vis lectrs pr yr; gallery talks; tours; artmobile; individual paintings & original objects of art lent to museums & educational institutions; lending collection contains prints, paintings, sculpture & drawings; book traveling exhibitions, 3-5 per yr; museum shop sells books, original art, crafts & jewelry

L **Reference Library,** 802 S Evans St, 27834. Tel 919-758-1946. *Exec Dir* Barbour Strickland
Library Holdings: Vols 300; Per subs 150

HICKORY

M **HICKORY MUSEUM OF ART, INC,** 243 Third Ave NE, PO Box 2572, 28603. Tel 704-327-8576. *Exec Dir* Mildred M Coe; *Communications Officer* Angela Chapman; *Technical Advisor* Ladell Herman; *Cur Education* John Post; *Registrar* Ellen Schwarzbek
Open Tues - Fri 10 AM - 5 PM, Sat & Sun 1 - 4 PM, cl Mon. No admis fee. Estab 1944 to collect and foster American art and serve the western Piedmont area as an exhibiting and training art center. Located in a renovated 1926 high school building; 10,000 sq ft gallery space for exhibition of permanent collection & traveling shows. Average Annual Attendance: 35,000. Mem: 1400; dues $30 - $5000; annual meeting 1st Tues in May
Income: Financed by mem, donations, local United Arts Fund grants
Collections: Small European collection; very fine collection of 19th and 20th century American paintings; Oriental works, Pre-Columbian
Exhibitions: (1993) North Carolina Invitational; Jacob Lawrence, An American Master
Publications: Quarterly newsletter; calendar; exhibition catalogs
Activities: Classes for adults and children; dramatic programs; docent training; periodic art classes; films; lectures open to the public, 4 vis lectr per year; concerts; gallery talks; tours; competitions with awards; exten dept serves Catawba County & surrounding area; individual paintings & original objects of art lent to other museums & galleries; book traveling exhibitions, twice a yr; originate traveling exhibitions which circulate to qualifying museums & galleries; museum shop sells books, reproductions & gift items

L **Library,** PO Box 2572, 28603. Tel 704-327-8576.
Library Holdings: Vols 2000; Per subs 8; AV — Cassettes 50, motion pictures, slides 500; Other — Clipping files, exhibition catalogs, manuscripts, memorabilia, pamphlets, photographs, reproductions

HIGH POINT

A **HIGH POINT HISTORICAL SOCIETY INC,** Museum, 1805 E Lexington Ave, 27262. Tel 919-885-6859. *Cur Exhib & Colls* Vince Cannino; *Cur Educ & Progs* Sherri Simon
Open Tues - Sat 10 AM - 4:30, Sun 1 - 4:30 PM. No admis fee. Estab 1970 to preserve the history of High Point. Military History Gallery: Revolutionary War up to Desert Storm; NC Pottery Gallery: Transportation/Communication/Manufacturing Exhibits. Average Annual Attendance: 17,000. Mem: 275; dues $25 - $150; annual meeting 4th Tues in May
Activities: Adult classes; docent programs; lect open to public, 14 vis lectr per year; book traveling exhibitions 2 - 4 per year; originate traveling exhibitions 2 per year; retail store sells books & prints

KINSTON

A **COMMUNITY COUNCIL FOR THE ARTS,** 400 N Queen st, PO Box 3554, 28501. Tel 919-527-2517. *Pres* Sue Ellen Maddux; *VPres* William C Coley III; *Dir* Carol Tokarski; *Asst Dir & Art Coordr* Mark Brown; *Bookkeeper* Odelle Taylor
Open Tues - Fri 9 AM - 5 PM, Sat 10 AM - 5 PM. No admis fee. Estab 1965 to promote the arts in the Kinston-Lenoir County area. Maintains a library of art magazines available for research by approval, five exhibition galleries & one sales

gallery. Mem: dues renaissance $1000, sustainer $500 - $999, patron $250 - $499, donor $150 - $249, sponsor $75 - $149, family $40 - $74, individual $25 - $39
Income: Financed by county appropriations
Publications: Kaleidoscope, monthly newsletter
Activities: Arts festivals; classes for adults and children; tours; gallery talks; competitions with awards; lending collection contains original art works, 52 original prints, 102 paintings, sculpture; book traveling exhibitions; sales shop sells original art; Art Center Children's Gallery

LEXINGTON

M **DAVIDSON COUNTY ART GUILD GALLERY, INC,** 224 S Main St, 27292. Tel 704-249-2742. *Pres* Rochelle T Grubb; *VPres* Bonnie Gobble; *Exec Dir* Melinda Smith
Open Mon - Fri 10 AM - 4:30 PM, Sun 2 - 4:30 PM. No admis fee. Estab 1968 to expose & to educate the public in different art forms. Four galleries - two main floor, 2 mezzanine floor in a Greek revival-style building built in 1911; 1986 building was renovated into an arts center. Average Annual Attendance: 20,000. Mem: 400; dues $500 Benefactor, $250 Patron, $100 Donor, $50 Family, $25 individual, artists, student & sr citizen $15; annual meeting second week in Oct
Income: $70,000 (financed by endowment, mem, city appropriation, sales)
Exhibitions: Katherine Skipper; Photography Invitational; Annual Members Open; Spotlight
Publications: Davidson County Art Guild Newsletter, quarterly; annual yearbook
Activities: Adult & children's classes; docent programs; workshops; demonstrations; museum trips; classes for sr citizens, mentally handicapped; lect open to public, 4 - 6 lectr per year; concerts; gallery talks; tours; competitions with awards; book traveling exhibitions, annually

LOUISBURG

M **LOUISBURG COLLEGE,** Art Gallery, 501 N Main St, 27549. Tel 919-496-2521. *Dir & Cur* William Hinton
Open Jan - Apr, Aug - Dec Mon - Fri 10 AM - 5 PM, cl holidays. No admis fee. Estab 1957
Collections: American Impressionist Art; Primitive Art
Activities: Arts festivals; lectures; gallery talks; tours

MONROE

M **UNION COUNTY PUBLIC LIBRARY GALLERY,** 316 E Windsor St, 28112. Tel 704-283-8184. *Dir* Daniel S MacNeill
Open Mon, Wed & Fri 9 AM - 6 PM, Tues & Thurs 9 AM - 8 PM, Sat 9 AM - 5 PM, Sun 2 - 5:30 PM. Gallery accommodates 25 large paintings & monthly exhibits of local work or traveling exhibitions
Collections: North Carolina collection
Exhibitions: Various local artists exhibitions

MORGANTON

M **BURKE ARTS COUNCIL,** Jailhouse Galleries, 115 E Meeting St, 28655. Tel 704-433-7282. *Exec Dir* Gail Ross; *Pres* Vesna Draxler
Open Mon - Fri 9 AM - 5 PM, 1st Sun of the month 1 - 4 PM. No admis fee, gifts accepted. Estab 1977 to provide high quality art shows in all media. Galleries in two old jails, third in the new civic auditorium. Average Annual Attendance: 2500. Mem: 500; dues from $5; annual meeting in May
Income: $55,000 (financed by mem, city & state appropriations, foundations & grants)
Publications: Arts in Burke County, every 3 - 4 yrs; Catalogue of the Southern Appalachian Regional Show, annual
Activities: Adult classes in conjunction with the Community College; children's classes; docent programs; lectures open to the public, 5 - 10 vis lectrs per yr; Southern Appalachian Painting & Drawing Competition, Waldensian International Postcard Art Competition; cash awards; book traveling exhibitions, 1 per yr; sales shop sells magazines, original art, prints, local & regional crafts

NEW BERN

M **TRYON PALACE HISTORIC SITES & GARDENS,** 610 Pollock St, 28560. Tel 919-638-1560; FAX 919-638-9031. *Dir* Kay P Williams; *Communications Specialist* Maria L Muniz; *Cur Interpretation* Hilarie M Hicks; *Cur Coll* John B Green III; *Horticulturist* J A Dove; *Asst Horticulturist* Susan K Ferguson; *Historian* John R Barden; *Conservator* Philippe Lafargue
Open Mon - Sat 9:30 AM - 4 PM, Sun 1:30 - 4 PM. Admis adults $12, children $6. Estab 1959. Maintained are the historic house museums & galleries (Tryon Palace, Dixon-Stevenson House, John Wright Stanly House & New Bern Academy) with 18th & 19th century English & American furniture, paintings, prints, silver, ceramic objects & textiles. Average Annual Attendance: 75,000
Income: Financed by state & private bequests
Collections: Paintings by Nathaniel Dance; Thomas Gainsborough; School of Sir Godfrey Kneller; Claude Lorrain; David Martin; Richard Paton; William Peters; Charles Phillips; Alan Ramsay; Jan Siberechts; E Van Stuven; Richard Wilson; Graphics
Exhibitions: Temporary exhibitions on history & decorative arts, 3 per yr
Publications: Books & leaflets; Tryon Palace Newsletter, 3 per yr
Activities: Crafts demonstrations for adults & children; audio-visual orientation program; annual symposium on 18th & 19th century decorative arts; interpretive drama program; docent training; lectures open to public, 10 vis lectr per yr; concerts; tours; 0cholarships offered; museum shop sells books, magazines, reproductions, prints, slides & ceramics

L **Library,** 610 Pollock St, PO Box 1007, 28560. Tel 919-638-1560; FAX 919-638-9031. *Librn* John Barden
For reference; open for use with permission
Income: Financed by state
Library Holdings: Vols 5000; Per subs 50; AV — Slides, v-tapes; Other — Clipping files, pamphlets, photographs
Special Subjects: Royal Governor William Tryon's Inventory, bks, 18th Century Collection of Books, Decorative Arts
Collections: †18th & early 19th century decorative arts

NORTH WILKESBORO

M **WILKES ART GALLERY,** 800 Elizabeth St, 28659. Tel 919-667-2841. *Mgr* Edie Hutchens; *Dir* Paula Morris
Open Mon - Fri 10 AM - 5 PM, Sat noon - 4 PM, evenings for special events, cl New Year's Day, Easter, Easter Monday, Thanksgiving, Labor Day, Memorial Day & Christmas. No admis fee. Estab 1962 to take art to as many areas as possible. Gallery is housed in a 1928 renovated structure; there are two galleries, one with 650 sq ft & one with 400 sq ft. Average Annual Attendance: 10,400. Mem: 400; dues patron & corp $250 & up, donor $150, sponsor $75, family $20; annual meeting in May
Income: Financed by membership, local governments, state arts council & corporations
Collections: Contemporary paintings, graphics, sculpture, primarily of NC artists
Exhibitions: Artist League Juried Competition; Blue Ridge Overview (amateur photography); temporary exhibitions Apple's, Art & Apple Pie Competition; Northwest Artist League Competition
Publications: Title of Exhibition, monthly brochures & catalogues; Wilkes Art Gallery Newsletter, monthly
Activities: Classes for adults & children; docent training; arts festivals; films; art & craft classes; lect open to public, 3 vis lectrs per yr; gallery talks; tours, competitions with awards; concerts; individual paintings & original objects of art lent to patron, donor & benefactor organizations, schools, hospitals, nursing homes & county offices; sales shop sells, books, crafts, original art, pottery, prints & reproductions

RALEIGH

A **ARTSPACE INC,** 201 E Davie St, PO Box 27331, 27611. Tel 919-821-2787. *Executive Dir* Rock Kershaw; *Assoc Dir* Ann Tharrington; *Facility Mgr* Angie Morris
Open Tues - Fri 9 AM - 6 PM, Sat 10 AM - 5 PM, Sun 1 -5 PM. No admis fee. Estab 1986. Mem: Annual meeting in Apr
Income: $400,000 (financed by mem, city & state appropriation, rental income)
Exhibitions: Fantasy Art; Henley SE Spectrum; The Art is in the Mail; Holiday Showcase; New Works; Get A Start in the Arts; Triangle Clay Show
Activities: Classes for adults & children; dramatic programs; docent programs; artists business workshops; lectures open to public, 6 vis lectr per year; competitions with cash awards; scholarships & fels offered; book traveling exhibitions 2 per yr; originate traveling exhibiton, annually

ASSOCIATION OF AMERICAN EDITORIAL CARTOONISTS
For further information, see National and Regional Organizations

M **CITY GALLERY OF CONTEMPORARY ART,** 220 S Blount St, PO Box 66, 27601-0066. Tel 919-839-2077. *Dir* Denise Dickens
Open Tues - Sat 10 AM - 5 PM, Sun 1 - 5 PM. No admis fee. Estab 1983. 8000 sq ft building with 5000 sq ft of exhibition space. Average Annual Attendance: 20,000. Mem: 500
Income: $300 (financed by membership, city & state appropriation, contributions & foundations)
Publications: Exhibition catalogues
Activities: Lect open to the public, 6 vis lectr per yr; book traveling exhibitions 5 times per yr; originate traveling exhibitions 2 - 3 times per yr

A **CITY OF RALEIGH ARTS COMMISSION,** Municipal Building Art Exhibitions, 222 W Hargett St, PO Box 590, 27612. Tel 919-831-6234. *Chmn* Harold Jeffreys; *Exec Dir* Elaine Lorber; *Coordr* Beverly Ayscue
Open Mon - Fri 8:30 AM - 5:15 PM. Estab 1984 to showcase Raleigh-based artists/art collections in the local area. First & second floor lobbies of the Raleigh Municipal Building
Income: $4675 (financed by city & state appropriation)

M **NORTH CAROLINA MUSEUM OF ART,** 2110 Blue Ridge Rd, 27607. Tel 919-833-1935; FAX 919-733-8034. *Dir* Richard S Schneiderman; *Assoc Dir Admin* Hal McKinney; *Chief Cur* Tony Janson; *Dir Education* Joseph F Covington; *Chief Designer* Dan Gottlieb; *Chief Conservator* David Goist; *Registrar* Peggy Jo Kirby; *Librn* Anna Dvorak; *Asst to Dir Development* Anne C Jones
Open Tues - Thurs, Sat 9 AM - 5 PM, Fri 9 AM - 9 PM, Sun 11 AM - 6 PM, cl Mon & holidays. No admis fee. Estab 1947, open to public 1956, to acquire, preserve, and exhibit works of art for the education and enjoyment of the people of the state, and to conduct programs of education, research, and publications designed to encourage interest in and an appreciation of art. Average Annual Attendance: 265,000. Mem: 7900; dues $25 & up
Income: Financed by state appropriation
Collections: Ancient art; Mary Duke Biddle Education Gallery; European and American painting, sculpture & decorative arts; Samuel H Kress Collection; Pre-Columbian, African, Oceanic & New World art
Exhibitions: North Carolina Artists Exhibitions; wide range of temporary exhibitions
Publications: Bulletin, annual; Preview, trimestral; exhibition & permanent collection catalogs
Activities: Classes for adults & children; docent training; lectures open to public; concerts; gallery talks; tours; exten dept serving North Carolina;; originate traveling exhibitions to North Carolina museums & galleries; museum shop sells books, magazines, reproductions, prints and slides

L **Reference Library,** 2110 Blue Ridge Rd, 27607. Tel 919-833-1935; FAX 919-733-8034. *Librn* Dr Anna Dvorak
Open Tues - Fri 9 AM - 5 PM. Open to public for reference
Income: Financed by State and NCMA Foundation
Purchases: $24,125
Library Holdings: Vols 27,430; Per subs 86; AV — Slides 25,000; Other — Clipping files, exhibition catalogs, pamphlets
Special Subjects: Decorative Arts, Fine Arts

A **NORTH CAROLINA MUSEUMS COUNCIL,** PO Box 2603, 27602. Tel 919-733-7450; FAX 919-733-1048. *Pres* Robert G Wolk; *VPres* Dwaine Coley; *Treas* Martha Battle; *Secy* JoAnne Powell
Estab 1964 to stimulate interest, support and understanding of museums. Mem: 250; dues individual $15; meetings spring and fall (annual meeting)
Income: Financed by membership
Publications: NCMC Newsletter, quarterly
Activities: Awards given

L **NORTH CAROLINA STATE UNIVERSITY,** Harrye Lyons Design Library, 209 Brooks Hall, 27695-7701. Tel 919-515-2207; FAX 919-515-7330. *Librn* Caroline Carlton; *Librn Asst* Lynn Crisp; *Librn Asst* Dot Hunt; *Librn Asst* Sherry Johnson
Open Mon - Thurs 8 AM - 9 PM, Fri 8 AM - 5 PM, Sat 9 AM - 1 PM, Sun 2 - 9 PM. Estab 1942 to serve the reading, study, reference and research needs of the faculty, students and staff of the School of Design and the University campus, as well as off-campus borrowers. Primarily for lending. Circ 56,058
Income: Financed by state appropriation, private funds and membership
Purchases: $48,000
Library Holdings: Vols 35,955; Per subs 782; trade literature, vertical files; AV — A-tapes, slides, v-tapes; Other — Pamphlets
Special Subjects: Architecture, Art History, Furniture, Graphic Design, History of Art & Archaeology, Landscape Architecture, Urban and Product Design, Visual and Basic Design
Collections: File on measured Drawings of North Carolina Historic Sites; 458 maps & plans; 300 bibliographies compiled by the Design Library staff
Publications: Index to the School of Design, student publication book Vols 1 - 25

M **Visual Arts Programs,** Cates Ave, PO Box 7306, 27695-7306. Tel 919-515-3503; FAX 919-515-7473. *Dir* Charlotte V Brown; *Cur* Open
Open 7 AM - 11 PM, except student holidays. No admis fee. Estab 1979 to provide changing exhibitions in the decorative & fine arts. Two small shared spaces, 200 running ft. Average Annual Attendance: 15,000. Mem: 150; dues $25-$1500; annual meeting last Wed in Oct
Income: $200,000 (financed by state appropriation & student fees)
Purchases: $10,000
Collections: †American regional & national graphics; †American, Indian, Oriental & pre-Columbian textiles; †ceramics (fine, ironstone, porcelain, traditional); †product design; †furniture
Exhibitions: Siggraph 85; Vernacular Pottery of North Carolina; Items of Everyday Use from Japan; Seeing an Idea; A Blessing from the Source: The Annie Hooper Bequest; Finery
Publications: Exhibit catalogs
Activities: Docent & self-guided tours; lectures open to public, 3-6 vis lectrs per yr; competitions

A **PORTRAITS SOUTH,** 4008 Barrett Dr, Suite 106, 27609. Tel 919-782-1610. *Pres* Jac F ReVille
Estab 1980, agent for professional portrait artists. Mem: 100 represented artists
Publications: Newsletters for artists, twice a year
Activities: Book traveling exhibitions 100 per year; originate traveling exhibitions 100 per year

REIDSVILLE

M **NORTH CAROLINA STATE UNIVERSITY,** Chinqua-Penn Plantation House, Garden & Greenhouses, Route 3, PO Box 682, 27320. Tel 919-349-4576. *Dir* Linn Keller; *House Mgr* Vivian Forrester; *Supt of Grounds* Keith E Davis; *Admin Sec* Betty Citty
Open Wed - Sat 10 AM - 4 PM, Sun 1:30 - 4:30 PM; cl to the public. Admis adults $6, senior citizens $5, children $2.50. Estab 1966 as part of University's total educational program to make the house with its collection and the gardens available to the public. Average Annual Attendance: 30,000
Income: Financed by state appropriation and admis fee
Collections: Antique European Furniture; Oriental Art Objects; Botanical (growing)
Activities: Sales shop sells unique items from around the world & chinqua - Penn materials

RESEARCH TRIANGLE PARK

C **BURROUGHS WELLCOME COMPANY,** Art Collection, 3030 Cornwallis Rd, 27709. Tel 919-248-3000, Ext 4449. *Dir Public Affairs* Thack Brown
Open 9 AM - 4 PM, groups only by prior arrangement. No admis fee. Estab 1979 to develop a meaningful collection of American Contemporary Art for enjoyment and enrichment for employees and communities. Collection displayed in Corporate Headquarters Building
Collections: Paintings and sculpture from permanent collection and on-loan from The Whitney Museum in New York City
Activities: Tours

ROCKY MOUNT

A **ROCKY MOUNT ARTS CENTER,** 1173 Nashville Rd, PO Box 4031, 27803-4031. Tel 919-972-1163, 972-1164. *Dir* Angela Jolly
Open Mon - Fri 8:30 AM - 5 PM, Sun 2 - 4 PM, cl Sat except for classes. No admis fee. Estab 1957 to promote the development of the creative arts in the community through education, participation and appreciation of music, dance, painting, drama, etc; to provide facilities and guidance for developing talents and enriching lives through artistic expression and appreciation. Maintains the Hines Art Gallery. Average Annual Attendance: 25,000. Mem: 600; dues $10 & up; annual meeting in Oct
Income: Financed by City Recreation Department with supplemental support by membership
Exhibitions: Outdoor Art Exhibition in the Spring; Permanent collection & traveling shows change each month
Activities: Conducts art classes; year-round theatre program; classes for adults and children; lect open to public, 2-4 vis lectr per year; concerts; gallery talks; tours; competitions; book traveling exhibitions 5-6 per year

SALISBURY

M **HORIZONS UNLIMITED SUPPLEMENTARY EDUCATIONAL CENTER,** Art Gallery, 1637 Parkview Circle, 28144. Tel 704-639-3004. *Dir* Cynthia B Zeger
Open Mon - Fri 8 AM - 4 PM. No admis fee. Estab 1968 to exhibit art work of public schools, supplemented by exhibits of local artists from time to time during the school year; primary purpose is to supplement art education activities in the public schools. The Center is comprised of two areas, one approximately 24 x 65 ft, the other 15 x 70 ft with an adjoining classroom for instruction and demonstrations. Average Annual Attendance: 4500
Income: Financed by membership, state and county appropriation, and from local foundations
Activities: Classes for adults and children; lectures open to public, 5 visiting lecturers per year; gallery talks; tours; individual and original objects of art lent

M **WATERWORKS VISUAL ARTS CENTER,** One Water St, 28144. Tel 704-636-1882. *Exec Dir* Ronald L Crusan; *Asst Dir* Barbara Setzer
Open Tues - Sat 10 AM - 4 PM, Sun 1 - 4 PM. No admis fee. Estab 1977 for exhibition & instruction of visual arts. Four galleries with changing exhibitions. Average Annual Attendance: 20,000. Mem: 700; dues $20
Income: $144,000 (financed by mem, city, county, appropriation, United Arts Fund, exhibition & educational corporate sponsors)
Exhibitions: (1992) Eurique Vega; Maud Gatewood; Wolf Kahn; Linda Brown; Paul Rousso; Willie Ann Wright
Publications: Charlotte Gallery Arts, catalogue; Salisbury Rennaisance, Understanding Abstract Art
Activities: Classes for adults & children; classes for special populations; classes for children in public housing; in-school programs; lect open to public, 5 vis lectr per year; gallery talks, tours; book traveling exhibitions; originate traveling exhibitions

STATESVILLE

M **ARTS AND SCIENCE CENTER,** 1335 Museum Rd, 28677. Tel 704-873-4734. *Exec Dir* Rita Rhodes; *Asst Dir* Diana Bromley
Open Tues - Sat 11 AM - 5 PM, Sun 2 - 5 PM. No admis fee. Estab 1956 to aid the community in the promotion of art history & science. Bowles, Grier & Henkel Galleries features monthly changing exhibits; Artifacts Room features permanent displays. Average Annual Attendance: 14,000. Mem: 650; dues $15 & up; monthly meetings
Income: Financed by mem, CAFD (Cooperative Arts Fund Drive), grants & sponsorships
Collections: Collections entail †Ancient Arts, †Decorative Arts, †Fine Arts, †Natural History
Exhibitions: Annual Iredell Photography Club; Mitchell Community Art Students & Faculty; Statesville Artists' Guild & Mooresville Artists Guild Sale & Show
Activities: Art classes; classes for children; community booths; lect; gallery talks; tours; sponsors competitions with awards; individual and original objects of art lent to museums and responsible organizations; book traveling exhibitions, 2 - 3 per year, traveling educational trunks, annual NC Heritage Festival, annual Native American Evening with exhibits reflecting heritage

TARBORO

M **EDGECOMBE COUNTY CULTURAL ARTS COUNCIL, INC,** Blount-Bridgers House, Hobson Pittman Memorial Gallery, 130 Bridgers St, 27886. Tel 919-823-4159. *Dir* Meade B Horne; *Educ* Mellissa Matson; *Asst to Dir* Susan M Spain
Open Mon - Fri 10 AM - 4 PM, Sat - Sun 2 - 4 PM. No admis fee. Estab 1982, to present local culture as it relates to state & nation. Located in a restored 1810 plantation house, 5 rooms in period interpretation, 3 used as gallery space for 20th century art permanent & traveling exhibits
Income: $100,000 (financed by city & state appropriation, corporate & private donations)
Collections: Pittman Collection of oil, w/c & drawings; American Collection of oils, watercolor & drawings; Decorative arts 19th century Southern
Exhibitions: Hobson Pittman retrospect; period rooms, 1810-1870
Activities: Classes for adults & children, docent programs; lect open to the public, 5 vis lectr per year; concerts; gallery talks; tours; exten dept lends out paintings; book traveling exhibitions, 6 times per year; originate traveling exhibitions, once per year; museum shop sells original art

WADESBORO

M ANSON COUNTY HISTORICAL SOCIETY, INC, 209 E Wade St, PO Box 732, 28170. Tel 704-694-6694. *Pres* Linn D Garibaldi; *VPres* Robbie Liles
Open Apr - Sept, 1st Sun of each month 3 - 5 PM & by appointment. No admis fee. Estab 1960 as a museum of 18th & 19th century furniture. Average Annual Attendance: 1000. Mem: 240; dues family $15, single $10; annual meeting Nov
Income: $12,000 (financed by mem)
Collections: Collection of 18th & 19th century furniture
Publications: History of Anson County, 1750 - 1976

WILMINGTON

M BATTLESHIP NORTH CAROLINA (Formerly USS North Carolina Battleship Memorial), Battleship Dr Eagle Island, PO Box 417, 28402. Tel 919-251-5797; FAX 919-251-5807. *Dir* David R Scheu; *Asst Dir* Roger Miller; *Prom Dir* LuAnn Olason; *Cur* Kim Robinson Sincox; *Sales Dir* Kim Whitfield
Open daily 8 AM to approx sunset. Admis adult $6, children between 6 & 11 $3, under 6 free. Estab 1961 as historic ship museum to memorialize the World War Two dead of the state of North Carolina. Average Annual Attendance: 250,000
Income: Financed by admissions, sales in gift shop & snack bar
Collections: Artifacts associated with or appropriate to the ships bearing the name North Carolina: BB-55 (1936 - 1947); CA-12 (1905 - 1930) & Ship-of-the-line (1818 - 1867); also artifacts associated with the memorial itself.
Publications: Battleship North Carolina; Ship's Data 1
Activities: Lectures open to public; sales shop sells books, reproduction prints, slides, souveniers & post cards

M SAINT JOHN'S MUSEUM OF ART, 114 Orange St, 28401. Tel 919-763-0281. *Dir* C Reynolds Brown; *Asst Dir* Pamela A Jobin; *Cur of Education* Tiffany Lee; *Cur of Registry & Coll* Anne Brennan
Open Tues - Sat 10 AM - 5 PM, Sun noon - 4 PM. No admis fee. Estab 1962 to promote the visual arts in southeastern North Carolina, and to provide exhibitions for the enjoyment of creative ability and artistic achievement. Average Annual Attendance: 30,000. Mem: 950; dues $25 - $1000; annual meeting in May
Income: Financed by membership, city, county and state appropriation, and grants
Collections: †Jugtown Pottery, †Mary Cassatt's color prints The Ten
Exhibitions: Bi-monthly exhibitions including artwork from regional artists, loans from North Carolina Museum of Art and other museums in Southeastern United States
Publications: Quarterly bulletin; exhibition announcements
Activities: Classes for adults and children; docent training; lect open to public, 12 vis lectr per year; concerts; gallery talks; tours; book traveling exhibitions; originate traveling exhibitions; sales shop sells books, original art
L Library, 114 Orange St, 28401. Tel 919-763-0281. *Asst Dir* Pamela A Jobin
Estab 1962. For reference only
Library Holdings: Vols 200; AV — Cassettes, motion pictures, v-tapes; Other — Clipping files, exhibition catalogs, photographs

WILSON

M BARTON COLLEGE, Case Art Gallery & Rackley Room Gallery, 27893. Tel 919-237-3161, Ext 264. *Gallery Dir* Lora Stutts
Open Mon - Fri 10 AM - 4:30 PM, Sat 1 - 3 PM. No admis fee. Estab 1967 to provide art exposure for our students and community. Gallery is 50 x 50 ft. Average Annual Attendance: 3000
Income: Financed by college budget
Collections: Ceramics; recent drawings; painting; prints; sculpture; African masks
Activities: Gallery talks; competitions; scholarships offered; book traveling exhibitions, 2 per yr
L Library, Whitehead & Gold Sts, 27893. Tel 919-399-6500; FAX 919-237-4957. *Dir* Shirley Gregory
For reference only
Library Holdings: Vols 2500; Per subs 94; AV — Fs, Kodachromes, rec, slides, v-tapes 50; Other — Exhibition catalogs, original art works, pamphlets, sculpture
Special Subjects: Art History

WINSTON-SALEM

A ARTS COUNCIL, INC, 305 W Fourth St, PO Box 10935, 27108. Tel 919-722-2585. *Pres & Exec Dir* David C Hudson; *Exhib Cur* Amy Fundenburke; *Dir Communications* Judy Sutherin
Open Mon - Fri 9 AM - 5 PM. Estab 1949 as a housing, coordinating, promoting and fund-raising organization for 11 funded & 39 associate member groups, including Associated Artists, Sawtooth Center for Visual Design, the Winston-Salem Symphony Association, the Little Theatre, Southeastern Center for Contemporary Art and Children's Theatre Board; member groups are independently incorporated. Housing facilities include Hanes Community Center: theatre & rehearsal rooms, Sawtooth Building: art and craft studios and exhibition galleries. Mem: Annual meeting May
Income: Financed by fund drives, public and private grants and endowments

A ASSOCIATED ARTISTS OF WINSTON-SALEM, 226 N Marshall St, 27101. Tel 919-722-0340. *Exec Dir* Rosemary H Martin; *Asst Dir* Andrea Bronzo
Open Mon - Sat 9 AM - 9 PM. No admis fee. Estab 1956 to promote & conduct activities that support the awareness, education, enjoyment & appreciation of visual fine art. The Association rents the walls of the Gallery from the Arts Council. Average Annual Attendance: 75,000. Mem: 400; dues $15 - 40; monthly meetings
Income: $100,000 (financed by membership & Arts Council funds)
Exhibitions: One Southeastern regional show; two national shows; various member exhibitions
Publications: Newsletter, bi-monthly

Activities: Membership programs; workshops; lect; demonstrations; lect open to public, 7 vis lectr per yr; gallery talks; tours; competitions with awards; scholarships & fels offered; exten dept serves city; originate traveling exhibitions; gallery sells original art

M OLD SALEM INC, Museum of Early Southern Decorative Arts, 924 S Main St, PO Box 10310, 27108. Tel 919-721-7360. *Dir Emeritus* Frank L Horton; *Dir of Research* Brad Rauschenberg; *Adminr* Madelyn Moeller; *Educ Coordr* Sally Gant; *Assoc Educ* Ruth Brooks; *Pub Dir* Forsyth Alexander; *Research Assoc* Martha Rowe; *Photographer Technician* Wes Stewart
Open Mon - Sat 10:30 AM - 5 PM, Sun 1:30 - 4:30 PM. Admis adult $5, children $3. Estab 1965 to bring to light the arts and antiquities produced in Maryland, Virginia, Kentucky, Tennessee, North and South Carolina, and Georgia through the first two decades of the 19th century. Three galleries are furnished with Southern decorative arts or imported objects used in the South, and fifteen period settings from Southern houses dating from 1690 to 1821. Average Annual Attendance: 25,000. Mem: 1250; dues $25 & up; annual meeting Spring
Income: $225,000 (financed by endowment, membership, state appropriation, and other funds)
Purchases: $50,000
Collections: †Southern decorative arts in general, and specifically furniture, paintings, silver, ceramics, metalwares, and woodwork of southern origin
Exhibitions: Ongoing Research in Southern Decorative Arts
Publications: Journal of Early Southern Decorative Arts, semiannually; catalog of the collection 1991, Museum of Early Southern Decorative Arts; The Luminary, newsletter, semiannually
Activities: Classes for adults and children; graduate Summer Institute; lectures open to public, 15 vis lectr per year; gallery talks; scholarships; exten dept serves eight Southern States; individual paintings & original objects of art lent to museums & cultural institutions & with special permission from staff are available for special exhibits; lending collection contains 2000 original art works, 100 paintings, 18,000 photographs & 30,000 slides; originate traveling exhibitions; sales shop selling books, slides
L Library, PO Box 10310, 27108. Tel 919-721-7367. *Dir of Research* Bradford L Rauschenberg; *Research Assoc* Martha Rowe
Open Mon - Sat 10:30 AM - 5 PM, Sun 1:30 - 4:30 PM. Estab 1965 to display and research early southern decorative arts through 1820
Library Holdings: Vols 5500; Per subs 1000; Computer data base index of early Southern Artists & Artisans; Micro — Fiche, prints, reels; AV — Slides; Other — Photographs
Special Subjects: Aesthetics, Afro-American Art, American Indian Art, Archaeology, Architecture, Art History, Carpets & Rugs, Ceramics, Costume Design & Construction, Crafts, Research of regional artists
Publications: Journal of Early Southern Decorative Arts, bi-annually; Luminary, bi-annually

M REYNOLDA HOUSE MUSEUM OF AMERICAN ART, Reynolda Rd, PO Box 11765, 27116. Tel 919-725-5325; FAX 919-721-0991. *Exec Dir* Nicholas B Bragg; *Cur of Educ* Marjorie Northup; *Development Dir* Elizabeth Morgan
Open Tues - Sat 9:30 - 4:30 PM, Sun 1:30 - 4:30 PM, cl Mon. Admis adults $5, sr citizens $4, students $3. Estab 1964 to offer a learning experience through a correlation of art, music and literature using the house and the Collection of American Art as resources. Gallery located in the 40 rooms of the former R J Reynolds mansion. Average Annual Attendance: 45,000. Mem: 600; annual meeting of Board of Directors in May and Nov
Income: Financed by endowment, Friends' contributions, local and state government grants for specific programs, as well as foundation grants
Collections: Doughty Bird Collection; costume collection; †permanent Collection of paintings, prints and sculpture on permanent loan
Exhibitions: William Sidney Mount
Publications: Annual Report; Calendar of Events, 3 per year
Activities: Classes for adults and children; dramatic programs; docent training; lect open to public, 20 vis lectr per year; concerts; gallery talks; tours; individual paintings and original objects of art lent to specific museums with reciprocity agreement; lending collection contains original prints, paintings; museum shop sells slides of paintings
L Library, Reynolda Rd, PO Box 11765, 27116. FAX 919-725-5325; *Librn* Ruth Mullen
Open to public
Library Holdings: Vols 2000; Per subs 30

M SOUTHEASTERN CENTER FOR CONTEMPORARY ART, 750 Marguerite Dr, 27106. Tel 919-725-1904; FAX 919-722-6059. *Pres* Diane Eshelman; *Dir* Susan Lubowsky; *Asst Dir* Vicki Kopf; *Educ Coordr* Terri Dowell-Dennis; *Asst Cur* Jeff Fleming; *Business Mgr* Susan Boon
Open Tues - Sat 10 AM - 5 PM, Sun 2 - 5 PM, cl Mon. Admis adults $3, students & senior citizens $2. Estab 1956 to indentify & exhibit the country's major contemporary artists of exceptional talent; to present educational programs for children & adults; to bring the viewing public in direct contact with artists & their art. Maintained are nine indoor and outdoor exhibition areas. Average Annual Attendance: 90,000. Mem: 2000; dues varying categories; annual meeting May
Income: Financed by endowment, membership, local and state arts councils, grants and sales commissions
Exhibitions: (1992) Terry Allen: Youth in Asia; Adrian Piper; Accounts Southeast: Joyce J Scott; Assemblage
Publications: Catalogs, 3-4 per yr; newsletter, quarterly
Activities: Classes for adults and children; docent training; workshops; lectures open to public; concerts; gallery talks; tours; competitions with awards; scholarships; original objects of art lent to non-profit tax exempt organizations; originate traveling exhibitions; center shop sells books, magazines, original art, gifts, paper products, crafts

C WACHOVIA BANK OF NORTH CAROLINA, 300 N Main St, PO Box 3099, 27150-3099. Tel 919-770-6143. *Asst VPres* Linda G Cooper
Estab to support the arts and enhance the environment for customers and employees. Collection displayed throughout the 204 offices
Collections: Traditional and contemporary work, primarily by North Carolina and Southeastern United States artists

WAKE FOREST UNIVERSITY

L **A Lewis Aycock Art Slide Library & Print Collection,** PO Box 7232, Reynolda Sta, 27109-7232. Tel 919-759-5078; FAX 919-759-4691. *Cur Slides & Prints* Martine Sherrill
Open Mon - Fri 9 AM - 5 PM. Estab 1968. Circ 15,000 (slides)
Library Holdings: Per subs 19; Laserdisks; AV — Kodachromes, lantern slides, motion pictures, rec 128,088, slides 136,000, v-tapes; Other — Clipping files, exhibition catalogs, original art works, pamphlets, photographs, prints
Special Subjects: Afro-American Art, American Indian Art, Folk Art, History of Art & Archaeology, Islamic Art, Mexican Art, Oriental Art, Period Rooms, Pre-Columbian Art, Religious Art
Collections: Art Department Slide Collection; University Print Collection

M **Fine Arts Gallery,** Scales Fine Arts Center, PO Box 7232, Reynolda Sta, 27109-7232. Tel 919-759-5585; FAX 919-759-5795. *Dir* Victor Faccinto
Open Mon - Fri 10 AM - 5 PM, Sat & Sun 1 - 5 PM. No admis fee. Estab 1976 for international contemporary & historical exhibitions. 3500 sq ft of exhibition space in two separate galleries. Average Annual Attendance: 9000
Income: Financed by university
Exhibitions: Light & Sound
Activities: Lectures open to the public, 6 vis lectr per year

M **Museum of Anthropology,** Wingate Dr, PO Box 7267, 27109-7201. Tel 919-759-5282; FAX 919-759-9831. *Dir* Mary Jane Berman; *Ed Cur* Beverlye Hancock; *Museum Educ* Candi Lavender; *Vol Coordr* Katie Shugart
Open Tues - Fri 10 AM - 4:30 PM, Sat & Sun 2 - 4:30 PM. Estab 1963. Mem: 265; dues $5 - $50
Income: $19,586 (financed by mem & University)
Purchases: $1,693.75
Exhibitions: Cartoons; Tatavoh: Learning the Hopi Way
Activities: Courses for adults & children; dramatic programs; docent training; lectures open to the public, 5 vis lectrs per year; traveling exhibitions, 1 per year; store sells books, prints & slides

NORTH DAKOTA

BELCOURT

M **TURTLE MOUNTAIN CHIPPEWA HISTORICAL SOCIETY,** Turtle Mountain Heritage Center, PO Box 257, 58316. Tel 701-477-6140. *Dir* Gaylene Martin; *Sales* Rita Martin; *Sales* Stella Davis
Open 8 AM - 4:30 PM, summer weekends 1 - 5 PM. No admis fee. Estab 1985 to promote & preserve culture. Small, well arranged, attractive gallery consisting of historical photos, memorabilia, artifacts, art works, beadwork, all pertaining to the Turtle Mountain Chippewa. Average Annual Attendance: 4000. Mem: 132; family $15, individual $10; annual meeting in Aug
Income: $98,496 (financed by mem, sales, bazaars & promotions)
Collections: †Ancient tools & implements; †basketry; †beaded artifacts; †contemporary Indian crafts; †costumes; †memorabilia; †paintings; †pottery; †sculpture; †stones
Exhibitions: Paintings; Jingle Dress - Male Costume
Publications: Newsletter, twice a year
Activities: Classes for adults & children; lect open to public; book traveling exhibitions 2 per year; originate traveling exhibitions 1 per year; retail store sells books, prints & original art

L **Heritage Center Archives,** PO Box 257, 58316
Estab 1986. For reference
Income: Financed by city appropriation
Library Holdings: Vols 200; AV — A-tapes, fs, rec, slides; Other — Clipping files, original art works, pamphlets, photographs, reproductions, sculpture

DICKINSON

M **DICKINSON STATE UNIVERSITY,** Mind's Eye Gallery, 58601-4896. Tel 701-227-2312. *Dir* Katrina Callahan-Dolcater; *Assoc Dir* Benni Privatsky
Open Mon - Thurs 8 AM - 10 PM, Fri 8 AM - 4 PM, Sat 1 - 4 PM, Sun 6 - 10 PM. No admis fee. Estab 1972 as a visual arts gallery presenting monthly exhibits representing the work of local, national and international artists. Gallery is a secure, large room approx 50 x 20 ft, with a 20 ft ceiling and approx 120 running ft of sheetrock display space. Average Annual Attendance: 5000
Income: Financed by North Dakota Council on the Arts grants,students activities fees and memberships
Purchases: $1000
Collections: Zoe Beiler paintings; contemporary graphics
Exhibitions: Bela Petheo; A Long Way to See: Photographs of North Dakota by Wayne Gudmundson; S U Art Faculty: Biennial Exhibit; Chambered Vessels Metalsmithing by Ellen Auyong; Early Dakota Quilting; North Dakota Centennial Juried Exhibition; Dakotas 100: International Competition of Works on Paper
Publications: Exhibit announcements
Activities: Lectures open to public, 2 - 4 vis lectr per year; gallery talks; originate traveling exhibitions

L **Stoxen Library,** 58601. Tel 701-227-2135; FAX 701-227-2006. *Librn Dir* Bernnett Reinke; *Acquisition Dir* Jim Martz; *Public Servs Dir* Eileen Kopran; *Cataloging Dir* Lillian Sormson
Open Mon - Thurs 8 AM - 10 PM, Fri 8 AM - 4 PM, Sat 1 - 4 PM, Sun 6 - 10 PM. Open to college students & general public
Library Holdings: Vols 3325; Per subs 20

FARGO

M **NORTH DAKOTA STATE UNIVERSITY,** Memorial Union Art Gallery, 58105. Tel 701-237-8239, 237-7900. *Dir* Barbara Hatfield
Open Sept - May Mon - Fri 10 AM - 5 PM, Sat & Sun 1 - 5 PM. Estab 1975 to educate through exposure to wide variety of artwork. 37 ft x 28 ft track lighting, gray carpet, attendent & security system
Income: $17,000 (financed by student activity fee allocation)
Collections: Permanent collection of contemporary work by American artists
Exhibitions: Contemporary works by American artists
Activities: Lectures open to public, 3 vis lectrs per year; gallery talks; book traveling exhibitions, 5-7 per year to museums & galleries in North Dakota & Minnesota

FORT RANSOM

M **SVACA - SHEYENNE VALLEY ARTS AND CRAFTS ASSOCIATION,** Bjarne Ness Gallery, 58033. Tel 701-973-2821. *Chmn* Edward Hiller; *Prog Coordr* Lucy Carlblom
Open Sat, Sun and holidays 1 - 6 PM, June 1 - Sept 30. No admis fee, donations accepted. Estab 1966 to promote & encourage the arts in a rural setting. The Gallery is the former studio of the late Bjarne Ness. Average Annual Attendance: 2400. Mem: 180; dues couple $8; annual meeting Oct
Income: Financed by membership, grants & Annual Festival
Collections: Paintings of Bjarne Ness; paintings and wood carvings by area artists in SVACA's Bear Creek Hall
Exhibitions: Annual Arts and Crafts Festival; one or two members' shows
Activities: Classes for adults & children

L **Library,** RR 1, PO Box 59, 58033. Tel 701-973-2821.
Open to members for reference
Library Holdings: Vols 100; Per subs 3
Special Subjects: Arts and crafts

FORT TOTTEN

A **FORT TOTTEN STATE HISTORIC SITE,** Pioneer Daughters Museum, PO Box 224, 58335-0224. Tel 701-766-4441. *Site Supv I* Vance Nelson; *Site Supv III* J C Mattson
Open summer site 8 AM - 5 PM, museum 1 - 5 PM. No admis fee. Estab 1960 to preserve & interpret fort buildings & drawings
Income: Financed by state appropriation, donations
Collections: Buildings of historic site, outdoor museum; Pioneer Artifacts;
Activities: Classes for adults & children; guided group tours; lectures open to public; book traveling exhibition annually; museum shop sells books, Native American Crafts (beadwork), postcards, souvenirs

GRAND FORKS

M **NORTH DAKOTA MUSEUM OF ART,** PO Box 7305, Univ Station, 58202. Tel 701-777-4195; FAX 701-777-4425. *Dir & Head Cur* Laurel J Reuter; *Exhib Coordr* Marilyn Fundingsland; *Asst to Dir* Nina Lewis; *Dir Audience Development* Madelyn Camrud; *Coordr Special Projects* Tracy Wilborn; *Office Mgr* Elaine McKenzie
Open Mon - Fri 9 AM - 5 PM, Thurs until 9 PM, Sat & Sun 1 - 5 PM. No admis fee. Estab 1971 as a contemporary art museum. In 1986 the museum moved into a renovated 1907 campus building. Average Annual Attendance: 50,000. Mem: 500; dues individual $25; annual meeting in June
Income: Financed by university, state & private endowments, gifts, mem & earned income
Collections: Native American; American Art
Publications: Exhibition catalog
Activities: Dramatic programs; docent training; workshops; lect open to the public, 25 vis lectr per year; gallery talks; tours; book traveling exhibitions; originate traveling exhibitions for circulation to US museums & abroad; museum shop sells books, magazines, folk & ethnic art

M **UNIVERSITY OF NORTH DAKOTA,** Hughes Fine Arts Center, Dept of Visual Arts, Room 127, 58202-8134. Tel 701-777-2257.
Open 7 AM - noon. Estab 1979 to augment teaching & offer another location to display art. 96 running ft of wall space. Average Annual Attendance: 1200
Collections: Collection chosen from Annual Print & Drawing Juried Exhibit
Exhibitions: Bill Leaf, Large Drawings; Annual Print & Drawing Juried Exhibit
Activities: Lect open to public, 6 - 10 lectr per year; lending collection contains over 200 items; book traveling exhibitions 1 per year; retail store sells original art

MAYVILLE

M **MAYVILLE STATE UNIVERSITY GALLERY,** 58257. Tel 701-786-2301, Ext 811. *Dir* Lila Hauge
Open Mon - Fri 9 AM - 5 PM
Exhibitions: Contemporary American & North Dakota artists; student exhibitions

MINOT

M **MINOT ART ASSOCIATION,** Minot Art Gallery, State Fair Grounds, PO Box 325, 58701. Tel 701-838-4445. *Dir* Judith Allen
Open Jan - Dec, Wed - Sun 1 - 5 PM. Estab 1970 to promote means and opportunities for the education of the public with respect to the study and culture of the fine arts. Average Annual Attendance: 2500. Mem: 300; dues $15 - $1000, board meeting 2nd Wed of month
Income: Financed by endowment, mem, contributions & sales
Purchases: $500

Collections: Original art works; paintings; pottery; printmaking; sculpture; all done by local & national artists
Exhibitions: Art competitions; artfests; one-person exhibits; traveling art exhibits; exhibitions change monthly
Publications: Calendar of Exhibits; monthly newsletter
Activities: Classes for adults and children; gallery talks; tour; competitions; scholarships; book traveling exhibitions, 2 - 3 per yr; traveling exhibitions organized and circulated

M MINOT STATE UNIVERSITY, University Galleries, 500 University Ave W, 58707. Tel 701-857-3836. *Dir* Linda Olson; *Chmn of Art Dept* Open
Open Mon - Fri 7 AM - 7 PM. No admis fee. Estab 1975 as a supplementary teaching aid, resource for Minot State University, Northwest & Central North Dakota. Gallery one room 600 sq ft, with movable pylons. Average Annual Attendance: 1000
Income: $8000 (financed by student fees)
Purchases: $2500
Collections: †Over 300 2-D works on paper in all media on paper (printmaking, drawing, painting).
Exhibitions: (1993) 22nd National Works on Paper Exhibition
Publications: Calendar of exhibits, annual; posters
Activities: Lect open to public, 2-3 vis lectr per yr; competitions with awards; lending collection of 300 individual paintings, prints, drawings; book exhibitions, 18 - 20 per yr

VALLEY CITY

M VALLEY CITY ARTS & GALLERY ASSOCIATION, Second Crossing Gallery Staus Mall, 200 Central Ave N, 58072. Tel 701-845-2690. *Dir* Cynthia Hagel; *Asst Dir* Kleda Kuehne
Open Mon - Fri 10 AM - 4 PM, Sat 1 - 4 PM. No admis fee. Estab 1973 to provide local, state, national and international shows for people in this area. Small but professional gallery consists of a 1250 sq ft room with track lighting and movable standards; maintain a Mezzanine gallery for exhibits of local and area artists. Average Annual Attendance: 5000. Mem: 150; dues $15 and up
Income: $20,000 (financed by endowment, mem & grants)
Exhibitions: 11 or 12 exhibitions a year of material from American Federation of Arts, North Dakota Art Gallery Association, Western Association of Art Museums, local, national & state shows
Publications: Calendar, annually
Activities: Classes for adults and children; Video-Brown Bag; Gallery talks; competitions with awards biennial juried national; scholarships; original objects of art lent to campus offices; book traveling exhibitions; Sales shop sells original art, original gift cards and prints

OHIO

AKRON

M AKRON ART MUSEUM, 70 E Market St, 44308. Tel 216-376-9185. *Dir* Mitchell Kahan; *Cur Art* Barbara Tannenbaum; *Dir Educ* Marcianne Herr; *Registrar* Jane Falk; *Admnr* Anne Palmer; *Dir Development* Arlene Rossen
Open Tues - Fri 11 AM - 5 PM, Sat 10 AM - 5 PM, Sun noon - 5 PM. No admis fee. Estab 1922 as a musem to exhibit & collect art. In Sept 1981, opened new Akron Art Museum in restored and reconstructed 1899 Neo-Renaissance style old post office; total of eleven galleries; three house the permanent collection and eight have changing exhibitions. Average Annual Attendance: 55,000. Mem: 2000; dues general $45; annual meeting in Sept
Income: $1,063,000 (financed by mem, endowment, corporate, foundation & government grants)
Collections: Photography; 20th century American and European painting and sculpture; Mark Di Suvero; Philip Pearlstein; Sol Lewitt; Richard Estes; Lois Lane; Philip Guston; Cindy Sherman
Exhibitions: (1992) Ralph Eugene Meatyard: An American Visionary
Publications: Calendar, bi-monthly; exhibition catalogs; annual report
Activities: Education dept; docent training; lect open to public, 6 - 8 lectr per year; gallery talks; concerts; tours; artist demonstration-workshop series; originates traveling exhibitions; sales desk sells books & catalogues
L Martha Stecher Reed Art Library, 70 E Market St, 44308. Tel 216-376-9185; FAX 216-376-1180. *Educ Dir* Marcianne Herr
Open for reference, not open to public
Income: $3500
Library Holdings: Vols 10,000; Per subs 75; Contemporary Art; AV — A-tapes, cassettes, Kodachromes, slides, v-tapes 50; Other — Clipping files, exhibition catalogs, pamphlets
Special Subjects: Photography, Contemporary art
Collections: Edwin Shaw Volumes, to accompany collection of American Impressionist art

L AKRON-SUMMIT COUNTY PUBLIC LIBRARY, Fine Arts Division, 55 S Main St, 44326. Tel 216-762-6623; FAX 216-762-6623. *Librn & Dir* Steven Hawk; *Head of Fine Arts Div* Karla Steward
Open Mon - Thurs 9 AM - 9 PM, Fri 9 AM - 6 PM, Sat 9 AM - 5 PM. Estab 1904 to serve the educational & recreational needs of the general public of Summit & contiguous counties
Income: $50,000 (fine arts div)
Library Holdings: Vols 25,000; Per subs 175; AV — A-tapes, cassettes, motion pictures, rec, v-tapes; Other — Clipping files, exhibition catalogs, original art works, pamphlets, sculpture
Special Subjects: Architecture, Art History, Ceramics, Costume Design & Construction, Decorative Arts, Crafts, Drawings, Embroidery, Folk Art, Graphic Arts, Glass, Illustration, Jewelry, Photography
Activities: Book traveling exhibitions, 4-6 per yr

M STAN HYWET HALL & GARDENS, INC, 714 N Portage Path, 44303. Tel 216-836-5533; FAX 216-836-2680. *Exec Dir* John Franklin Miller; *Supt of Grounds* Carl Ruprecht; *Dir Public Relations* Kelly A Kleinschmidt
Open Tues - Sat 10 AM - 4 PM, Sun 1 - 4 PM, cl Mon & major national holidays. Admis adults $6, children 6 - 12 $3, children under 6 free. Incorporated 1957, Stan Hywet Hall is a house museum, serving as a civic and cultural center. All restoration and preservation work is carefully researched to retain the original concept of the property, which represents a way of life that is gone forever. The mansion, the focal point of the estate, is a 65-room Tudor Revival manor house, furnished with priceless antiques and works of art dating from the 14th century. The property is the former home of Frank A Seiberling, (Akron rubber industrialist and co-founder of Goodyear Tire and Rubber) and was completed in 1915. There are 70 acres of formal gardens, meadows, woods and lagoons. Average Annual Attendance: 175,000. Mem: 3100; dues $25 and up; annual meeting in May
Income: $1,000,000 (financed by endowment, membership, admissions, gifts grants, rentals and special events
Collections: Antique furniture; china; crystal; paintings; porcelain; rugs; sculpture; silver; tapestries
Exhibitions: Holiday Festival
Publications: Stan Hywet Hall and Gardens Annual Report, yearly; Stan Hywet Hall Newsletter, monthly
Activities: Childrens programs; dramatic programs; docent training; lectures open to public, year round special events; concerts; exten dept serves libraries; original objects of art lent to historical societies & museums; lending collection includes 5000 books & 250 slides; sales shop sells books, original art, slides and wide variety of gift items

M SUMMIT COUNTY HISTORICAL SOCIETY, 550 Copley Rd, 44320-2398. Tel 216-535-1120; FAX 216-762-6623. *Dir* Stephen H Paschen; *Pres* Phillip Bradley; *VPres* John V Miller; *VPres* Kathleen Schmats
Open Tues - Sun 1 - 5 PM. Admis adults $3, children under 16 & senior citizens $2. Estab 1926 for the collection, preservation and display of items of an historical nature from Summit County. Average Annual Attendance: 3500. Mem: 900; dues $20 - $500; annual meeting late Jan
Income: $150,000 (financed by endowment, membership, county appropriation)
Collections: 19th & 20th century costumes and accessories; 1810 - 1900 era furniture; 19th century chinaware, glassware, silverware, and pottery; 19th century portraits; 19th & 20th century tools, household items and toys
Publications: Old Portage Trail Review, monthly
Activities: Educ dept; docent training; awards; sales shop sells books, magazines, crafts, souvenirs, toys, notepaper

UNIVERSITY OF AKRON

M University Galleries, 44325. Tel 216-972-5950; FAX 216-972-5960. *Dir* Andrew Borowic; *Asst Dir* Susan McKiernan; *Gallery Dir* Rod Bengstrom
Open Mon, Tues & Fri 10 AM - 5 PM, Wed & Thurs 10 AM - 9 PM. Estab 1974 to exhibit the work of important contemporary artists working in all regions of the United States, as well as to provide a showcase for the work of artists working within the university community. Two galleries: Emily H Davis Art Gallery, 2000 sq ft of floor space; 200 running ft of wall space; Guzzetta Hall Atrium Gallery, 120 running ft of wall space. Average Annual Attendance: 12,000-15,000
Income: Financed by university funds & grants
Collections: Southeast Asian Ceramics & Artifacts; Contemporary Photography
Exhibitions: Arakawa; Michiko Itatani; Eric Fischl; Georges Rouault; Takaaki Matsamoto; Vito Acconci; film installations
Publications: Catalogs and artists books in conjunction with exhibitions
Activities: Lectures open to the public; gallery talks; competitions; awards for Student Show; Scholarships and fels offered; book traveling exhibitions; originate traveling exhibitions, circulation to other university galleries & small museums with contemporary program

ASHLAND

M ASHLAND COLLEGE ARTS AND HUMANITIES GALLERY, College Ave, 44805. Tel 419-289-4142. *Chmn* Albert Goad
Open Tues - Sun 1 - 4 PM, Tues evenings 7 - 10 PM. No admis fee. Estab 1969. Gallery maintained for continuous exhibitions
Exhibitions: Mostly contemporary works, some historical, occidental and Oriental
Activities: Classes for children; dramatic programs; lect open to public; 2 - 3 gallery talks; tours and regular tours to leading art museums; concerts; scholarships; original objects of art lent to Akron Art Institute and Cleveland Museum of Art

ASHTABULA

A ASHTABULA ARTS CENTER, 2928 W 13th St, 44004. Tel 216-964-3396. *Exec Dir* Beth Lieber; *Admin Asst & visual Arts & Exhibit Coordr* Meeghan Humphery; *Business Mgr* Elaine Barr; *Theatre Coordr* John Hubbard; *Public Relations Coordr* Michelle McGinnis; *Technical Coordr* Charles Fike; *Pres* Serene Farmer
Open Mon - Sat 9 AM - 5 PM. No admis fee. Estab 1953 as a non-profit, tax exempt art organization, to provide high quality instruction. One major gallery area with smaller anex-fixed panels on all walls. Average Annual Attendance: 5000. Mem: 1000, dues family $35, individual $20; annual meeting in Oct
Income: Financed by mem, NEA, OAC, WSL, JTPA
Collections: Local and regional contemporary work, small international contemporary print collection, regional wood sculpture (major portion of collection represents local and regional talent)
Publications: Ashtabula Arts Center News, bimonthly; monthly exhibit information
Activities: Classes for adults and children; dramatic program; lect open to public, 5 - 10 vis lectr per yr; concerts; gallery talks; tours; competitions; cash awards; scholarships & fels offered; exten dept serves Ashtabula County hospitals and

public buildings; individual paintings and original objects of art lent to schools and public buildings; lending collection contains books, cassettes, color reproductions, framed reproductions, original art works, original prints, paintings, phonorecords, photographs, sculpture and slides; book traveling exhibitions; originate traveling exhibitions

ATHENS

M **OHIO UNIVERSITY,** Trisolini Gallery, 48 E Union St, 45701-2979. Tel 614-593-1304. *Dir* John Gerber; *Gallery Coordr* Jennifer Kelly
Open Mon - Sat noon - 4 PM. No admis fee. Estab 1974 to provide cultural exposure to the university community and to the residents of the surrounding region. Gallery has four rooms with carpeted walls and floors. Average Annual Attendance: 5000. Mem: 300; dues $10; monthly meeting
Income: Financed by state appropriation
Purchases: $10,000 (plus grant funds)
Collections: †Contemporary prints, some paintings, photographs and sculpture Southwest Native American Collection
Exhibitions: Southwest Native American Collection of Edwin L & Ruth E Kennedy; Henry Lin Retrospective; Alumni Invitational
Publications: Scholarly exhibition catalogues, two or three times a yr; Permanent Collection of Twentieth Century Prints; Clarence H White: the Reverence for Beauty
Activities: Lect open to public, 5-7 visiting lecturers per year; gallery talks; tours; sponsors competitions with awards; traveling exhibitions organized and circulated; museum shop sells books, original art, prints, crafts, pottery, handmade jewelry, quilts
M **Seigfred Gallery,** School of Art, Seigfred Hall 528, 45701. Tel 614-593-4286. *Dir* Joe Bova
Open Tues - Fri 10 AM - 4 PM. No admis fee. Gallery is used for faculty exhibitions, student exhibitions and visiting artist shows
L **Fine Arts Library,** Alden Library, Park Place, 45701-2878. Tel 614-593-2663. *Art Librn* Anne Braxton
Open Mon - Thurs 8 AM - midnight, Fri 8 AM - 10 PM, Sat 10 AM - 10 PM, Sun noon - midnight
Income: Financed by state appropriation
Library Holdings: Vols 48,000; Micro — Fiche; Other — Clipping files, exhibition catalogs, manuscripts, photographs, prints, reproductions
Collections: Research collection in history of photography; small collection of original photographs for study purposes

BAY VILLAGE

A **BAYCRAFTERS, INC,** Huntington Metropark, 28795 Lake Rd, 44140. Tel 216-871-6543. *Dir* Sally Irwin Price
Open Mon - Fri 9 AM - 5 PM, weekends during shows. Estab 1948 for advancement & enjoyment of arts & crafts in the area. Average Annual Attendance: 30,000. Mem: 1800, dues $15 & $20
Exhibitions: Christmas Show; Emerald Necklace Juried Art Show; Juried Art Show; Octoberfair; Renaissance Fayre; student competition; individual gallery shows; floral juried art show; corporate juried art show
Publications: Bulletins & competition notices
Activities: Classes for adults and children; lectures open to public, 9-12 vis lectr per yr; gallery talks; tours; sponsors two juried art shows for adults and one for children; monetary prizes awarded; scholarships; originate traveling exhibitions to local libraries; shop sells original art, reproductions, prints, pottery & other crafts work from local & out-of-town artists

BEREA

M **BALDWIN-WALLACE COLLEGE,** Fawick Art Gallery, 275 Eastland Rd, 44017. Tel 216-826-2152. *Dir* Dean Drahos
Open Mon - Fri 2 - 5 PM, cl weekends & holidays. No admis fee. The Art Gallery is considered to be a part of the art program of the department of art; its purpose is that of a teaching museum for the students of the college and the general public. Average Annual Attendance: 2500
Income: Financed through budgetary support of the college
Collections: Approx †200 paintings and sculptures by Midwest artists of the 20th century; approx †1900 drawings and prints from 16th - 20th century, with a concentration in 19th & 20th century examples
Exhibitions: Traveling and student exhibitions
Publications: Exhibition catalogs are published for important exhibitions, 1 - 2 per year
Activities: Lect open to public; gallery talks; tours; competitions; individual paintings lent to schools; book traveling exhibitions

BOWLING GREEN

M **BOWLING GREEN STATE UNIVERSITY,** School of Art, Fine Arts Bldg, 43403-0211. Tel 419-372-2787. *Exhib Prog Adminr* Jacqueline S Nathan
Open Mon - Fri 9 AM - 4:30 PM, Sun 2 - 5 PM, cl holidays. Estab 1964 to provide enrichment to School of Art program by furnishing research materials, exhibitions and related events; to provide for the growth of public sensitivity to the visual arts. Gallery is a multi-level facility located in the Fine Arts building with approximately 2850 running feet of exhibition space. Average Annual Attendance: 7500
Income: Financed by the University, state grants & donations
Collections: Contemporary prints
Activities: Lects open to the public, 6-8 vis lectrs a year; competitions; book traveling exhibitions; originate traveling exhibitions

BROOKLYN

M **BROOKLYN HISTORICAL SOCIETY,** 4442 Ridge Rd, 44144. Tel 216-749-2804. *Pres* Barbara Stepic; *VPres* Barbara Schieve; *VPres* Edward Koschmann; *Treas* Helen Nedelka
Open Tues 10 AM - 2 PM, Sun 2 - 5 PM, & tours by appointment. No admis fee. Estab 1970 to preserve history of area. Average Annual Attendance: 1000. Mem: 150; dues $3; meetings last Wed of month, except July, Aug, Nov
Income: $10,000 (financed by fundraisers)
Collections: †China; †dolls; †pre-1900 & 1920's furniture; †glass; †kitchenware; †old tools; †quilts & linens
Exhibitions: World War I & Brooklyn Airport
Activities: Educ dept; lect open to public; sales shop sells handicrafts, rag rugs, quilted items, dried herb products

CANTON

M **CANTON ART INSTITUTE,** 1001 Market Ave N, 44702. Tel 216-453-7666; FAX 216-452-4477. *Pres* Thomas M Hague; *VPres* Nan Johnston; *Treas* William Pincoe; *Gallery Dir* Manuel J Albacete; *Business Mgr* Mrs Kenneth D Adams
Open Tues - Thurs 10 AM - 5 PM, 7 - 9 PM, Fri & Sat 10 AM - 5 PM, Sun 2 - 5 PM. No admis fee. Estab 1935, incorporated 1941. Nine modern gallery areas of varios sizes. Average Annual Attendance: 50,000. Mem: 1200; dues $15 and higher; annual meeting Fall
Collections: American, Italian and Spanish paintings; art objects; costumes; decorative arts; 18th & 19th century English & American portraiture; graphics; sculpture; 20th century regional art; Italian sculpture
Exhibitions: Approx 40 to 50 traveling or collected exhibitions of commercial and industrial arts; painting; sculpture annually; French Music Hall Posters from 1890 to 1940's (1991) National Ceramics Invitational. (1992) All Ohio 1992; Mac Sigan Reality Sculpture; Beyond the Surface by CAI
Activities: Formally organized education programs for adults and children; docent training; guided tours; lectures open to public, 10 vis lectr per year; films; gallery talks; arts festivals; competitions with awards; scholarships; individual and original objects of art lent; book traveling exhibitions; originate traveling exhibitions; museum shop sells books, original art, prints
L **Art Library,** 1001 Market Ave N, 44702. Tel 216-453-7666; FAX 216-452-4477. *Exec Dir* Manuel J Albacete
Library Holdings: Vols 2500; Per subs 25; AV — A-tapes, slides, v-tapes; Other — Clipping files, exhibition catalogs, pamphlets, prints

CINCINNATI

A **CINCINNATI ART CLUB,** 1021 Parkside Place, 45202. Tel 513-241-4591. *Pres* Thomas Eckley; *VPres & Treas* Ben Baker
Open daily except Wed Sept - May, call for hours. No admis fee. Estab 1890, incorporated 1923 for purpose of advancing love & knowledge of fine art. Gallery contains a small collection of paintings by American artists; modern building 100 ft x 50 ft. Average Annual Attendance: 3500. Mem: 300; open to all who show interest & appreciation of art; active members must be judged by proficency of works; dues active $85, associate $75
Income: Financed by dues, rental of gallery, sales commissions, bequests
Collections: Small collection of works by former members
Exhibitions: Exhibition of members' work changed monthly. Annual Club Shows Sept, Jan, Spring (March-April) & Christmas Art Bazaar; juried annual show
Publications: Dragonfly (monthly member newsletter)
Activities: Lectures for members only, 6 - 8 vis lectr demonstrations per yr; competitions with awards; scholarships offered to Cincinnati Art Academy

A **CINCINNATI ARTISTS' GROUP EFFORT,** 344 W Fourth St, 45202. Tel 513-381-2437. *Adminr Coordr* Krista Campbell
Open Thurs - Sat, noon - 4 PM. No admis fee. Estab 1978 as an artist-run alternative space exhibiting visual, media, & performance art. Store-front gallery on two floors in the gallery district of Cincinnati; permanent video screening facility. Average Annual Attendance: 15,000 gallery, 500,000 public art viewers. Mem: 250; dues $20 - $500; annual meeting in June
Income: $70,000 (financed by foundations, Ohio Arts Council, City of Cincinnati Arts Allocation, mem, & National Endowment for the Arts)
Publications: Artists' Pulp; catalogs, 2 Mid-Career
Activities: Lect open to public, 3-5 vis lectr per year; concerts; gallery talks; sales shop sells books, magazine & original art

M **CINCINNATI INSTITUTE OF FINE ARTS,** Taft Museum, 316 Pike St, 45202-4293. Tel 513-241-0343; FAX 513-241-7762. *Dir Taft Museum* Dr Ruth K Meyer; *Asst Dir & Cur Colls* David T Johnson; *Cur of Education* Abby S Schwartz; *Chmn Cincinnati Inst of Fine Arts* Lee Ault Carter; *Chmn Museum Committee* Robert E Stautberg; *Admin Asst* Carolyn Rison; *Business Mgr* Angela Larimer; *Publications* Cate O'Hara
Open Mon - Sat 10 AM - 5 PM, Sun & holidays noon - 5 PM, cl New Year's Day, Thanksgiving & Christmas. No admis fee; suggested donation adults $2, sr, mems & children $1. Estab 1927, a gift of Mr and Mrs Charles P Taft's art collection to the Cincinnati Institute of Fine Arts including the house and an endowment fund for maintenance. Active control was taken in 1931; museum opened in 1932. The historic house, built in 1820, is one of the finest examples of Federal architecture in this country, and was designated a National Landmark. Its interior is decorated in the style of the period. An architectural formal (green) garden was opened in 1949. Average Annual Attendance: 50,000. Mem: 1200; dues $25 - $5000
Income: $1,250,000 (financed by endowment & annual fine arts fund drive)
Collections: Furnishings include antique toiles and satins and a notable collection of Duncan Phyfe furniture; paintings include works by Rembrandt, Hals, Turner, Goya, Corot, Gainsborough, Raeburn; Whistler and other Old Masters; 200 notable Chinese Porcelains Kangxi, Yongzheng & Qianlong; 120 French Renaissance enamels; Renaissance jewelry & 16th - 18th century watches from Europe

Exhibitions: Four to five exhibitions scheduled per year
Activities: Classes for adults & children, docent training; lect open to public, 6-10 vis lect per yr; chamber music; concerts; gallery talks; tours; scholarships; individual paintins lent to special museum exhibitions; lending collection contains 600 color reproductions, 600 Kodachromes, 500 original art works, 160 paintings, 600 phtographs, sculptures & 1500 slides; museum shop sells books, magazines, reproductions, prints, slides, needlework & titles

A **CINCINNATI INSTITUTE OF FINE ARTS,** 2649 Erie Ave, 45208. Tel 513-871-2787. *Chmn Bd & Pres* Lee A Carter; *VPres* Daniel W LeBlonde; *Exec Dir* Ervin Oberschmidt
Estab and inc 1927 to provide for the continuance and growth of education and culture in the various fields of fine arts in the metropolitan community of Cincinnati. Mem: Annual meeting Oct
Income: Financed through endowments by Cincinnati Symphony Orchestra, Cincinnati Art Museum, Cincinnati Opera, Taft Museum, May Festival, Cincinnati Ballet, Contemporary Arts Center, Playhouse in the Park, Special Projects Pool & Annual Community Wide fine Arts Fund Drive
Publications: Quarterly Calendar

M **CINCINNATI MUSEUM ASSOCIATION,** Cincinnati Art Museum, Eden Park, 45202-1596. Tel 513-721-5204; FAX 513-721-0129. *Dir* Millard F Rogers; *Asst Dir for Operations* George E Snyder; *Cur Decorative Arts* Anita Ellis; *Cur Costumes, Textiles* Otto Thieme; *Cur Prints & Drawings* Kristin L Spangenberg; *Cur Classical, Near Eastern Art* Glenn E Markoe; *Cur Painting* John Wilson; *Cur Contemporary Art* Jean E Feinberg; *Assoc Cur Far Eastern Art* Ellen Avril; *Assoc Cur Photography & Design* Dennis Kiel; *Asst Dir for Coll* Elisabeth Batchelor; *Asst Dir Developemtn* James Edgy; *Ed* Ann Cotter; *Registrar* Mary Ellen Goeke; *Asst Dir Marketing* Gretchen Mehring
Open Tues - Sat 10 AM - 5 PM, Sun 11 AM - 5 PM, cl Mon & holidays. Admis adults $5, college students $4, sr citizens $4, children free, free to members, special rates for tour groups. Estab 1881 to collect, exhibit, conserve & interpret works of art from all periods & civilizations (range of 5000 years of major cultures of the world) paintings (European and American); world costumes, textiles; arts of Africa and the Americas; world prints, drawings and photographs; world sculpture, world decorative arts and period rooms. Exhibition galleries cover an area of approx 4 acres, occupying three floors, assembly areas & social center on ground level; altogether some 80 galleries given over to permanent collections, with additional galleries set aside for temporary exhibitions. Average Annual Attendance: 215,000. Mem: 8700; dues $30 & up
Income: $6,300,000 (financed by endowment, admis & Cincinnati Fine Arts Fund, museum shop earnings, federal, state, city & private grants)
Collections: Artists; art in Cincinnati; Egyption, Greek, Roman, Near and Far Eastern arts; musical instruments; paintings (European & American); world costumes, textiles; arts of Africa & the Americas; world prints, drawings & photographs; world sculpture; world decorative arts & period rooms
Exhibitions: (1993) Six Centuries of Master Prints: Treasures from the Herbert Greer French Collection; Photographic Treasures from the Cincinnati Art Museum; Rookwood Pottery: The Glorious Gamble; With Grace & Favour: Fashion from the Victorian & Edwardian Eras
Publications: Annual Report; bi-monthly magazine; catalogues for exhibitions and collections
Activities: Seminars; lectures open to public; gallery talks; tours; museum shop
L **Mary R Schiff Library,** Eden Park, 45202-1596. Tel 513-721-5204, Ext 223; FAX 513-721-0129. *Head Librn* Mona L Chapin
Open Tues - Fri 10 AM - 5 PM, Sat 10 AM - 5 PM, Sun noon - 5 PM. Admis $5. Estab to satisfy research needs of museum staff, academy faculty and students. For reference
Income: Financed by endowment
Library Holdings: Vols 55,279; Per subs 135; Micro — Fiche; Other — Clipping files, exhibition catalogs, manuscripts, pamphlets, photographs, reproductions
Collections: †Files on Cincinnati Artists, †Art in Cincinnati, †the Cincinnati Art Museum, & the Art Academy of Cincinnati; encyclopedia collection covering 5000 years of art & art history

M **COLLEGE OF MOUNT SAINT JOSEPH,** Studio San Giuseppe, Art Department, 5701 Delhi Pike, 45233-1670. Tel 513-244-4314; FAX 513-244-4222. *Dir* Gerald Bellas
Open Mon - Fri 8:30 AM - 5 PM, Sun 1:30 - 4:30 PM. No admis fee. Estab 1962 to exhibit a variety of art forms by professional artists, faculty & students. Average Annual Attendance: 5000
Exhibitions: (1993) Fiber/Fabric Now; '93 Senior Thesis
Activities: Lectures open to public; concerts; gallery talks; tours
L **Archbishop Alter Library,** 5701 Delhi Pike, 45233-1670. Tel 513-244-4350; FAX 513-244-4222. *Dir* Ann Chase
Estab 1920 to serve students of art department. Circ 1200
Library Holdings: Vols 78,917; Per subs 664; AV — A-tapes, fs, slides; Other — Exhibition catalogs, prints

M **CONTEMPORARY ARTS CENTER,** 115 E Fifth St, 45202. Tel 513-721-0390; FAX 513-721-7418. *Chmn* Roger Ach; *Pres* Richard Rosenthal; *VPres* Thomas L Williams; *Treas* Kenneth Butler; *Businexx Mgr* Nancy Glier; *Membership & Gallery Coordr* Jennifer Adams; *Preparator* Dennis Herrington; *Cur* Jan Riley; *Public Relations* Bronwen Howell
Open Mon - Sat 10 AM - 6 PM. Admis adults $2, students & sr citizens $1, mem free. Estab 1939. The Center is a museum for the presentation of current developments in the visual and related arts. It does not maintain a permanent collection but offers changing exhibitions of international, national and regional focus. Average Annual Attendance: 110,000. Mem: 3200; dues from $15 - $150
Income: $1,340,000 (financed by endowment, fine arts fund drive, city, state arts council & federal groups, corporate sponsorship)
Special Subjects: Advertising Design, Afro-American Art, American Indian Art, American Western Art, Antiquities-Assyrian, Antiquities-Byzantine, Antiquities-Egyptian, Antiquities-Etruscan
Exhibitions: Mike & Doug Stara; Organic Architecture; Mechanika
Publications: Catalogues of exhibitions, 4 - 7 times per year
Activities: Classes for adults and children; docent training; perfomance programs; lectures open to public, 8-12 vis lectr per year; concerts; gallery talks; programs for adults and children; tours; lending collection contains slides and videotapes; book traveling exhibitions, 2-5 per yr; traveling exhibitions organized and circulated; museum shop sells books, cards, reproductions & prints
L **Library,** 115 E Fifth St, 45202. Tel 513-721-0390; FAX 513-721-7418.
For in-house only
Library Holdings: Per subs 10; Other — Exhibition catalogs

M **HEBREW UNION COLLEGE - JEWISH INSTITUTE OF RELIGION,** Skirball Museum-Cincinnati Branch, 3101 Clifton Ave, 45220. Tel 513-221-1875; FAX 513-221-1842. *Dir* Marilyn F Reichert; *Cur* Judith S Lucas
Open Mon - Thurs 11 AM - 4 PM, Sun 2 - 5 PM. No admis fee. Estab 1913 to interpret Judaism to the general public through Jewish art & artifacts; also the archaeologic work of the college in Israel. 2450 sq ft of exhibition space; traveling exhibition gallery. Average Annual Attendance: 4000
Income: Financed by endowment, donations & grants
Collections: Jewish ceremonial art; archaeologic artifacts; paintings, drawings & sculpture by Jewish artists; photography; textiles
Exhibitions: (1991) An Eternal People: The Jewish Experience
Publications: A Walk Through The Past
Activities: Docent training; lectures open to public; tours; individual and original objects of art lent; sales shop sells books & Judaica subject matter

M **HILLEL FOUNDATION,** Hillel Jewish Student Center Gallery, 2615 Clifton Ave, 45220-2885. Tel 513-221-6728; FAX 513-221-7134. *Exec Dir* Rabbi Abie Ingber
Open Mon - Thurs 9 AM - 5 PM, Fri 9 AM - 3 PM. Estab 1982 to promote Jewish artists & educate students. Jewish artists in various media (exhibit & sale) & collection of antique Judaica from around the world. Listed in AAA guide
Collections: Antique Judaica

L **PUBLIC LIBRARY OF CINCINNATI & HAMILTON COUNTY,** Art & Music Department, 800 Vine St, Library Square, 45202-2071. Tel 513-369-6955; FAX 513-369-6063. *Head Art & Music Dept* Charles Ishee; *First Asst* Anna Horton; *Dir & Treas* Robert Stonestreet
Open Mon - Fri 9 AM - 9 PM, Sat 9 AM - 6 PM, Sun 1 PM - 5 PM. Estab 1872 to provide the community with both scholarly and recreational materials in area of fine arts. Display cases in the department to exhibit collections
Income: $72,500 (financed by taxes, state, county appropriations)
Library Holdings: Vols 149,387; Per subs 713; Vertical file; Micro — Cards, fiche 22,091, prints, reels; AV — Cassettes, fs, lantern slides, motion pictures, rec, slides, v-tapes; Other — Clipping files 790,139, exhibition catalogs, manuscripts 6950, memorabilia, original art works, pamphlets, photographs, prints, reproductions
Special Subjects: Advertising Design, Aesthetics, Afro-American Art, American Indian Art, American Western Art, Antiquities-Assyrian, Archaeology, Art History, Calligraphy, Drawings, Folk Art, History of Art & Archaeology, Landscape Architecture, Mexican Art, Mixed Media, Painting - American, Photography, Pre-Columbian Art, Religious Art, Southwestern Art, American Art, Cincinnati & regional art, Picasso
Collections: Langstroth Collection - Chromolithographs of the 19th Century: also scrapbooks on the history of Chromolithography; Eda Kuhn Loeb Collection - The Artist & the Book 1875 to present; 61 Titles with Original signed Lithographs by Artists from Manet to Dali; Valerio Collection - Italian Art
Exhibitions: (1992) Valentines; Theodore Langstroth & Lithography; Movies, Movies, Movies; Pre-Columbian Art
Activities: Tours; sales shop sells books, reproductions, prints, tote bags, toys & stationery items

UNIVERSITY OF CINCINNATI
M **Tangeman Fine Arts Gallery,** 403 Tangeman, Mail Location 136, 45221. Tel 513-556-3462. *Dir* Susan Heekin; *Dir* Pam Seyring Boyle
Open Mon - Fri 9 AM - 5 PM, Sat 1 - 3 PM. No admis fee. Estab 1967 to preserve and maintain the University's art collection; Gallery reorganized and separated from University Collection in 1978. Gallery is maintained and presents quality contemporary and historical exhibitions of works by artists of local, regional and national reputation. Average Annual Attendance: 39,000
Income: Financed through university, grants & co-sponsorships
Collections: Julius Fleischman Collection
Publications: Fragments, catalogue
Activities: Lectures open to the public; concerts; performances; film & dance; gallery talks; tours; book traveling exhibitions, 1 - 3 per yr; originate small traveling exhibitions
L **Design, Architecture, Art & Planning Library,** 800 Alms Bldg, 45221-0016. Tel 513-556-1320; FAX 513-556-3288. *DAAP Librn* Jane Carlin
Open Mon - Thurs 8 AM - 10 PM, Fri 8 AM - 5 PM, Sat 9 AM - 5 PM, Sun 1 - 8 PM (Academic Year); summer hours vary. Estab 1925 to support the programs of the College of Design, Architecture, Art and Planning. Circ 42,000. Average Annual Attendance: 78,000
Purchases: $50,000
Library Holdings: Vols 55,000; Per subs 300; Artists' Book Collection; Micro — Fiche, reels 1000; AV — V-tapes; Other — Exhibition catalogs
Special Subjects: Art Education, Art History, Architecture, Graphic Design, Industrial Design, Interior Design, Collection of artists' publications
L **DAAP Slide Library,** Art History Dept, 45221. Tel 513-556-0279. *Cur* Adrienne Varady
Library contains 210,000 slides

M **XAVIER UNIVERSITY,** Xavier Art Gallery, 3800 Victory Pkwy, 45207. Tel 513-745-3811. *Dir* Bernard L Schmidt
Open Mon - Fri 1 - 5 PM, 1 - 4 PM (fall and winter), cl Sat. No admis fee. Estab 1987 as academic facility for students, faculty & community. Spacious galleries with white walls & hardwood floors; main gallery 21 x 50 ft, adjacent gallery 20 x 20 ft
Income: Privately financed
Exhibitions: Professional artists; qualified students of Xavier University
Activities: Classes for adults; Lect open to public, 5 per yr; gallery talks; tours; book traveling exhibitions

CLEVELAND

C AMERITRUST COMPANY NATIONAL ASSOCIATION, Art Collection, 900 Euclid Ave, 44101. Tel 216-737-5552. *Coordr* Rob Verderber
Collection estab 1971 to enhance the executive offices of the bank; supports and promotes the performing and visual arts. Collection displayed in executive offices
Collections: Primarily 19th Century American oils with few contemporary pieces
Activities: Tours; individual objects of art lent to traveling exhibit touring United States and Europe

C B P AMERICA, 200 Public Square, 44114. Tel 216-586-4592. *Art Admin Consultant* Jane B Tesso
Estab to enhance quality of life in communities where the company has employees or operations. Supports performing theatres, museums, orchestras and art education
Collections: Contemporary American Art
Activities: Operating support, facilities and production sponsorship

M CLEVELAND CENTER FOR CONTEMPORARY ART, 8501 Carnegie Ave, 44106. Tel 216-421-8671; FAX 216-421-0737. *Dir* Marjorie Talalay; *Chief Cur* David Rubin; *Chief Preparator & Registrar* Dan Witczak; *Dir of Sales* Lendy Bannett; *Dir Development* Susan Murray; *Dir Educ* Pam Esch; *Staff Asst* Douglas Zulio; *Dir Development* Kathy Charlton
Open Tues - Wed 11 AM - 6 PM, Thurs - Fri 11 AM - 8:30 PM, Sat & Sun noon - 5 PM, cl Mon. No admis fee. Estab 1968 to present the best and most innovative works by national figures in the contemporary visual arts as well as works by talented area artists. Five galleries which change exhibits every 6-8 wks. Located in a renovated building which is part of the Cleveland Playhouse complex. Mem: 600; dues center circle $500; sustaining $129; contributing $50; family $35; single $25; student or artist $15
Income: $175,000 (financed by membership, state appropriation, federal and state agencies and local foundations)
Exhibitions: (1992-93) Peter Eisenman & Frank Gehry: The Venice Biennale Exhibition; Robert Stackhouse: White Star; Symbols & Meanings: Five Native American Artists; Peter Campus: Digital Photographs; Inaugural Exhibition; Carrie Mae Weems: Family Pictures & Stories; Elaine Reichek: Native Intelligence; Luis Cruz Azaceta: The Aids Epidemic Series; Alison Saar: Allegorical Sculpture; The Gift of Art; Kevin Everson; Ellen Brooks: Nature as Artifice; Malcolm Cochran: The Difference Between Religion & a Relationship with Christ; Penny Rakoff; Nigel Rolfe: Frozen Moments; Suzanne Giroux: Giverny, Le Temps Mauve; About Nature; Ricchard Long; Neil Winokur. (1993-94) Director's Choice; Ana Mendieta; Martin Puryear; Artists of Gateway; Gary Bower; Outside the Frame: Performance & the Object; Old Glory: The American Flag in Contemporary Art
Publications: Exhibition catalogues
Activities: Classes for children, docent training; family workshops; adult night classes; lectures open to the public; gallery talks; tours; scholarships; individual and original objects of art lent to corporate members; originate traveling exhibitions; sales shop sells original art works, books, magazines & prints
L Library, 8501 Carnegie Ave, 44106. Tel 216-421-8671; FAX 216-421-0737. *Dir* Marjorie Talalay
Mem: 600; dues $25
Library Holdings: Vols 2000; Per subs 10; AV — Slides; Other — Clipping files, exhibition catalogs, photographs

M CLEVELAND INSTITUTE OF ART, Reinberger Galleries, University Circle, 11141 East Blvd, 44106. Tel 216-421-7407. *Gallery Dir* Bruce Checefsky; *Pres* Robert A Mayer
Open Mon - Fri 9 AM - 4:30 PM, Tues & Wed 7 - 9 PM, Sat 9 AM - noon, Sun 2 - 5 PM. No admis fee. Estab 1882 as a five-year, fully accredited professional college of art. Gallery is integrated with extensive exhibitions
Exhibitions: (1993) Bob Blackburn Printmaking Workshop; Annual Independent Student Exhibition; Pepin Ozario Show
Publications: Link (alumni magazine), quarterly; posters to accompany each exhibit; bi-annual school catalog
Activities: Classes for adults and children; lect open to public
L Jessica Gund Memorial Library, 11141 East Blvd, 44106. Tel 216-421-7440; FAX 216-421-7439. *Library Dir* Cristine Rom; *Circulation Supvr* Lori Nofziger; *Technical Servs Librn* Hyosoo Lee; *Slide Librn* Michelle Rossman
Open Mon - Thurs 8 AM - 9:30 PM, Fri 8 AM - 5 PM, Sat 10 AM - 5 PM, Sun hours vary. Estab 1882 to select, house and distribute library material in all media that will support the Institute's studio and academic areas of instruction
Income: Financed by tuition, gift, endowments
Library Holdings: Vols 42,000; Per subs 225; Artists' Books 570; Micro — Fiche, prints; AV — A-tapes, cassettes, slides, v-tapes; Other — Clipping files, exhibition catalogs, manuscripts, memorabilia, original art works, pamphlets, photographs, prints, reproductions
Special Subjects: Industrial Design, Art, Artists' Books, Artists' Books; Industrial Design
Activities: Library tours
A Art Association, University Circle, 11141 East Blvd, 44106. Tel 216-421-7000; FAX 216-421-7438. *Pres* Robert Mayer
Estab & inc 1916, re-incorporated 1950 as a non-profit organization, to unite artists & art lovers of Cleveland into a working body whose purpose it shall be to advance, in the broadest possible way, the art interest of the city. Mem: 140; dues $50, active membership fees $10, assoc membership $1; annual meeting in Nov
Income: $30,000 (financed through endowment, sales & dues)
Purchases: $9300
Collections: Collection of art by Cleveland artists which includes ceramics, drawings, glass, paintings, prints & small sculpture
Exhibitions: Lending collection exhibited annually
Activities: Competitions; awards; scholarships; works of art lent to members for one-year period

M CLEVELAND MUSEUM OF ART, 11150 East Blvd, 44106. Tel 216-421-7340; FAX 216-421-0411; Cable MUSART CLEVELAND. *Pres* Michael Sherwin; *Dir* Dr Evan H Turner; *Asst Dir Admin* William S Talbot; *Asst Dir Operations & Finance* John P McGann; *Cur Contemporary Art* Tom E Hinson; *Chief Cur Later Western Art* Henry Hawley; *Cur Paintings* Alan Chong; *Cur Early Western Art* Renate Eikelmann; *Cur Textiles* Anne E Wardwell; *Cur Japanese Art* Michael R Cunningham; *Cur SE Asian Art* Stanislaw Czuma; *Asst in East Indian Art & Museum Designer* William E Ward; *Cur Ancient Art* Arielle P Kozloff; *Cur Education* James A Birch; *Chief Cur Musical Arts* Karel Paukert; *Chief Ed Museum Publications* Laurence Channing; *Mgr Public Information* Adele Z Silver; *Registrar* Delbert R Gutridge
Open Tues, Thurs, Fri 10 AM - 6 PM, Wed 10 AM - 10 PM, Sat 9 AM - 5 PM, Sun 1 - 6 PM, cl Mon & four holidays. No admis fee. Estab and incorporated 1913; building opened 1916. Gallery addition in 1958; Education Wing in 1971; New Library & Gallery addition in 1984. Average Annual Attendance: 500,000. Mem: 10,000; dues $25 & up; annual meeting in Dec
Income: $8,527,687 (financed by trust & endowment income, mem, gifts & grants)
Purchases: $6,757,978
Collections: Ancient Near Eastern, Egyptian, Greek, & Roman art; drawings & prints; European & American paintings, sculpture, and decorative arts of all periods, with notable collections of medieval art, 18th-century French decorative arts, & 17th-century European painting & 19th-century European & American painting; Islamic art; North American Indian, African, & Oceanic art; Oriental art, including important collections of Chinese & Japanese painting & ceramics, and Indian sculpture; photographs; Pre-Columbian American art; textiles, especially from Eygpt & medieval Persia
Exhibitions: Contemporary American Photographs; Victorian Landscape Watercolors
Publications: Bulletin, 10 times per yr; News & Calendar, monthly; collection catalogs; exhibition catalogs
Activities: Classes for adults & children, studio workshops; teacher resource center; lectures open to public, 14 vis lectr per yr; concerts; gallery talks; tours; exten dept serves local schools & public buildings; individual paintings & original objects of art lent to schools, libraries & cultural art centers; book traveling exhibitions; originate traveling exhibitions; museum shop sells books, reproductions & slides
L Ingalls Library, 11150 East Blvd, 44106. Tel 216-421-7340; FAX 216-421-0411; Elec Mail BM.CMA@RLG.BITNET. *Librn* Ann B Abid
Estab 1916. Open to Museum members, visiting graduate students, faculty, curators; general public on Wed only
Library Holdings: Vols 175,000; Per subs 3101; Auction catalogues; Micro — Fiche, reels; AV — Lantern slides, slides; Other — Clipping files, exhibition catalogs, pamphlets, photographs, prints
A Print Club of Cleveland, 11150 East Blvd, 44106. Tel 216-421-7340; FAX 216-421-0411. *VPres* Diane Stupay; *VPres* Virginia Foley; *Treas* Robert Milne; *Secy* Anne Landefeld
Estab 1919 to stimulate interest in prints and drawings through education, collecting and commissioning of new works and enhancement of the museum's collection by gifts and purchases. Mem: 250; dues $100 and up; annual meeting Jan
Income: Financed by membership
Publications: The Print Club of Cleveland 1919-1969. Available at Museum Sales Desk, $10 plus postage
Activities: Lect open to the public

L CLEVELAND PUBLIC LIBRARY, Fine Arts & Special Collections Dept, 325 Superior Ave, 44114. Tel 216-623-2848, 623-2848; FAX 216-623-7050. *Dir* Marilyn Gell Mason; *Head Fine Arts & Special Colls Dept* Alice N Loranth; *Head Main Library* Joan Clark
Open Mon - Sat 9 AM - 6 PM, Sept - June Sun 1 - 5 PM. Estab 1869. Circ 5, 624,099
Income: $34,577,461
Library Holdings: Vols 179,008; Per subs 628; original documents; Special Collection vol 151,864 & per sub 410; CD's 2442; Micro — Fiche 11,508, prints, reels 1947; AV — Cassettes 7454, rec 17,916, slides 457, v-tapes; Other — Clipping files, exhibition catalogs, manuscripts, pamphlets, photographs, prints
Special Subjects: Architecture, Art History, Decorative Arts, Oriental Art, Primitive Art, All art media
Collections: Cleveland Artist Original Graphics; Architectural plans, blueprints & drawings of five Cleveland buildings by Hubbel & Benes architectural firm
Publications: Descriptive pamphlets of holdings
Activities: Lect & collections open to public; tours available for groups; competitions; Sales shop sells books, reproductions, prints & gift items

L CLEVELAND STATE UNIVERSITY, Library & Art Services, Rhodes Tower 322, 44115. Tel 216-687-2492. *Supvr Art Serv* Pamela Eyerdam
Estab 1965 to house collection of visual arts
Purchases: $16,000
Library Holdings: Vols 15,000; Per subs 96; Color Reproductions; Micro — Cards, fiche, prints, reels; AV — A-tapes, cassettes, fs, motion pictures, rec, slides 65,000, v-tapes; Other — Clipping files, exhibition catalogs, original art works, pamphlets, photographs, prints, reproductions
Collections: 19th & 20th century European & American art; medieval art; Indian & West African art
M Art Gallery, 2307 Chester Ave, 44115. Tel 216-687-2103; FAX 216-687-9366. *Dir* Robert Thurner; *Preparator* Scott Simmerly
Open Mon - Fri 9 AM - 5 PM, Sat 1 PM - 4 PM. Admis free. Estab 1965 to present important art to University & Northeast Ohio community. 4500 sq ft floor space carpeted, 260 running ft wall space, 14 ft high track lighting, air conditioned, humidity controlled, motion detectors & closed circuit 24 hr surveillance by university police. Average Annual Attendance: 54,000
Income: $70,000 (financed by student fees & grants)
Collections: African; African American
Exhibitions: Ninth annual People's Art Show
Publications: Exhibition Catalog
Activities: Educ dept; docent training; workshops; symposia; lect open to public, 24 vis lectr per yr; competitions with awards; book traveling exhibitions; originate traveling exhibitions

C **NATIONAL CITY BANK,** Atrium Gallery, 1900 E Ninth St, PO Box 5756, 44101. Tel 216-575-2000; FAX 216-575-2353. *Personnel Officer* Ellen M Kynkor
Open Mon - Fri 8 AM - 5 PM, cl Sat & Sun. Admis free. Estab 1980 to support regional artists in the community. Open area of atrium joining buildings. Average Annual Attendance: 500,000
Collections: National City Art Collection (Contemporary art created by regional artists from Cleveland & Northeast Ohio area)
Exhibitions: Eleven exhibits annually, (changed monthly); Holiday Tree in Dec
Activities: Book traveling exhibitions; originate traveling exhibitions

M **NEW ORGANIZATION FOR THE VISUAL ARTS,** (NOVA), 4614 Prospect Ave, No 410, Prospect Park Bldg, 44103. Tel 216-431-7500. *Exec Dir* Janus Small
Estab 1972 as a non-profit artists' service organization

L **NORTHEAST OHIO AREAWIDE COORDINATING AGENCY (NOACA),** Information Resource Center, Atrium Office Plaza, 668 Euclid Ave, 44114-3000. Tel 216-241-2414, Ext 240; FAX 216-621-3024. *Information Specialist* Kenneth Goldberg
Open Mon - Fri 8 AM - 5 PM. Library established 1963, staff use only
Library Holdings: Vols 9000; Per subs 75; Micro — Fiche, reels; AV — A-tapes, cassettes, fs, slides, v-tapes; Other — Clipping files, exhibition catalogs, manuscripts, memorabilia, original art works, pamphlets, photographs, prints, reproductions
Special Subjects: Architecture, Art Education, Art History, Costume Design & Construction, Ethnology, Folk Art, Graphic Arts, Historical Material, Mixed Media, Reproductions, Theatre Arts
Collections: Architectural History; Preservation & Restoration; Urban Planning & Urban Design
Publications: NOACA News; various reports related to planning, transportation & environment issues

M **SAINT MARY'S ROMANIAN ORTHODOX CHURCH,** Romanian Ethnic Museum, 3256 Warren Rd, 44111. Tel 216-941-5550. *Pres* George Ittu; *VPres & Dir* Jane Martin
Open Mon - Fri 8:30 AM - 4:30 PM, and on request. No admis fee. Estab 1960. Average Annual Attendance: 5000
Income: Financed by parish appropriation
Collections: Anisoara Stan Collection; O K Cosla Collection; Gunther Collection; Romanian art, artifacts, costumes, ceramics, painters, rugs, silver and woodwork; icons on glass & wood; books
Activities: Lect open to public; tours; individual paintings and original objects of art lent to other ethnic museums and faiths for exhibits; lending collection contains 100 original art works, 250 original prints, 50 paintings, sculpture, 2000 costumes, rugs and artifacts

M **SPACES,** 2220 Superior Viaduct, 44113. Tel 216-621-2314. *Dir* Susan R Channing; *Assoc Dir* Julie Fehrenbach; *Mgr & Video Art Coordr* Gail Rickards
Open Tues - Sat 11 AM - 5 PM. No admis fee. Estab 1978 to show innovative work by living artists. Single room, 6000 sq ft & 12 ft ceiling. Exhibitions, usually 3 artists per show, change monthly. Average Annual Attendance: 10,000. Mem: 300
Income: $1,000,000 (financed by endowment, membership, state appropriation, foundations)
Exhibitions: Monthly rotating exhibits
Publications: Exhibition catalogs, 3 per year
Activities: Dramatic programs & other performance art; video art series; lectures open to the public, 15 vis lectr per year; competitions; book traveling exhibitions, one per year; originate traveling exhibitions, one per year

M **THE TEMPLE,** The Temple Museum of Religious Art, University Circle at Silver Park, 44106. Tel 216-791-7755. *Sr Rabbi* Benjamin Alon Kamin; *Museum Dir* Claudia Z Fechter
Open daily 9 AM - 3 PM by appointment. No admis fee. Estab 1950 for the display & teaching of Judaica. Two galleries, each housed in a national landmark temple. Average Annual Attendance: 5000. Mem: 15,000; annual meeting
Collections: Archaeology; ceremonial art; decorative arts; paintings; prints; sculpture
Activities: Lectures open to the public; competitions; awards; tours; museum shop
L **Library,** 44106. Tel 216-791-7755, 831-3233; FAX 216-719-7043. *Cur* Mrs Richard M Fechter
Permanent collection of silver, manuscripts and fabrics of Judaica over the last 100 yrs. Pottery from antiquity. Two buildings
Library Holdings: Vols 45,000; Per subs 100; AV — A-tapes, cassettes, fs, rec, slides, v-tapes; Other — Clipping files, exhibition catalogs, manuscripts, photographs
Special Subjects: Anthropology, Antiquities-Egyptian, Antiquities-Roman, Architecture, Art History, Calligraphy, Ceramics, Coins & Medals, Costume Design & Construction, Decorative Arts, Crafts, Drawings, Embroidery, Ethnology, Folk Art, Glass, Graphic Arts, Handicrafts, Historical Material, Judaica, Manuscripts, Coins & Medals, Painting - Israeli, Photography, Pottery, Religious Art, Restoration & Conservation, Sculpture, Textiles
Exhibitions: In the Beginning - Jewish Birth Customs; The Loom & the Cloth: an exhibition of the fabrics of Jewish life; Abba Hillel Silver: a remembrance
Publications: The Loom and the Cloth: an exhibition of the fabrics of Jewish life

M **WESTERN RESERVE HISTORICAL SOCIETY,** 10825 East Blvd, 44106. Tel 216-721-5722. *Exec Dir* Theodore A Sande; *Dir Museum* Steven Miller; *Business Mgr* Sally Adams; *Librn* Kermit J Pike
Museums open Tues - Sat 10 AM - 5 PM, Sun noon - 5 PM. Admis adults $4, sr citizens & students $2, group rates available. Estab 1867 to discover, collect & perserve whatever relates to the history, biography, genealogy & antiquities of Ohio & the West. Average Annual Attendance: 85,000
Collections: Airplanes; automobiles; costumes; decorative, fine & domestic arts
Exhibitions: People at the Crossroads-Settling the Western Reserve, 1796- 1870;

Chisholm Halle Custom Wing; Crawford Auto-Aviation collection
Publications: Books on Regional History; Western Reserve Historical Society News, bi-monthly
Activities: Docent training; classes for adults and children; lect open to public, 25 vis lectrs per year; tours; gallery talks; awards; individual paintings & objects of art lent to qualified institutions; sales shop sells books, magazines, reproductions & prints
L **Library,** 10825 East Blvd, 44106. Tel 216-721-5722; FAX 216-721-0645. *Librn Dir* Kermit J Pike
For reference only
Library Holdings: Vols 250,000; Per subs 100; Micro — Cards 200, fiche 2000, reels 25,000; AV — A-tapes, lantern slides, rec, slides; Other — Exhibition catalogs, manuscripts 5,000,000, pamphlets, photographs, prints
Special Subjects: Architecture, Decorative Arts, Folk Art, Maps, Photography, Prints

COLUMBUS

A **ACME ART CO,** 737 N High St, 43215. Tel 614-299-4003. *Dir* Lori McCargish; *Exec Dir* Leslie Constable; *Exec Dir* Charles Wince
Open Wed - Sat 1 - 5 PM, or by appointment. Admis free. Estab 1986 to provide programming that emphasizes emerging experimental & obscure art forms. Non profit gallery. Presents 12 major shows per year, in addition we also provide artist lectures fundraisers that involve & benefit both local artists and the gallery itself and performance and video programs. Average Annual Attendance: 150, 000. Mem: 100
Income: $31,000 (financed by endowment, membership, Hio Arts, Columbus Arts & private funding
Exhibitions: Alan Crockett; John Sanborn; Bathroom Artists
Activities: Dramatic programs; lectures open to public, 2-5 vis lectr per year

M **CAPITAL UNIVERSITY,** Schumacher Gallery, 2199 E Main St, 43209. Tel 614-236-6319. *Dir* Dr Cassandra Lee Tellier; *Asst Dir* Jan Popp
Open Mon - Fri 1 - 5 PM, Sat & Sun 2 - 5 PM. No admis fee. Estab 1964 to provide the best available visual arts to the students; to serve the entire community with monthly traveling shows, community programming and permanent collections. Gallery is 16,000 sq ft, that includes six display galleries of permanent holdings, gallery area for temporary monthly exhibits, galleries, fabrication room, community reception room, lecture area seating 60 and lecture space seating 250. Average Annual Attendance: 9000
Income: Financed by foundation grants & individual gifts
Collections: †Ethnic Arts (including American Indian, Inuit, Oceanic); †American paintings, sculpture & graphics of 20th century; Period works from 16th - 19th century; †Major Ohio Artists; †Graphics; †Asian Art
Exhibitions: Seven individual & group visiting shows per year; individual exhibits include contemporary artists & loans from individuals & other museums
Activities: Lect open to public; gallery talks; competitions; individual paintings and original art objects lent by special request only; gallery shop open to the public
L **Art Library,** 2199 E Main St, 43209. Tel 614-236-6615; FAX 614-236-6490. *Dir* Dr Albert Maag
Open to students, faculty, staff, and for reference only to the public
Library Holdings: Vols 5000; Per subs 15

L **COLUMBUS COLLEGE OF ART & DESIGN,** Packard Library, 107 N Ninth St, 43215-1758. Tel 614-224-9101. *Librn* Chilin Yu
Open Mon & Fri 8 AM - 5 PM, Tue - Thurs 8 AM - 8 PM. Estab 1879. Open to public for reference only
Income: $279,000 (financed by tuition fees & grants)
Purchases: $71,000
Library Holdings: Vols 32,000; Per subs 214; AV — Cassettes, Kodachromes, lantern slides, rec, slides, v-tapes; Other — Clipping files, exhibition catalogs, original art works, pamphlets, photographs, reproductions, sculpture
Special Subjects: Advertising Design, American Indian Art, Architecture, Art History, Asian Art, Commercial Art, Decorative Arts, Drawings, Etchings & Engravings, Fashion Arts, Film, Folk Art, Goldsmithing, Graphic Arts, Graphic Design, History of Art & Archaeology, Illustration, Interior Design, Landscape Architecture, Mixed Media, Painting - American, Painting - European, Photography, Portraits, Pre-Columbian Art, Prints, Religious Art, Silversmithing, Theatre Arts, Video, Woodcarvings
Exhibitions: Students' work
Publications: Botticelli, annually
Activities: Classes for adults and children; lectures open to the public, 25 vis lectr per year; tours; competitions with awards; scholarships

M **COLUMBUS CULTURAL ARTS CENTER,** 139 W Main St, 43215. Tel 614-645-7047. *Dir* Jennifer Johnson
Open Mon - Fri 8 AM - 5 PM, Mon - Thurs 7 - 10 PM, Sat & Sun 1 - 5 PM. No admis fee. Estab 1978, visual arts facilities & gallery. Maintains small reference library. Average Annual Attendance: 50,000. Mem: 50; dues $25; annual meeting May 15
Income: Financed by city appropriation
Activities: Classes for adults & children; lect open to public, 58 vis lectr per year; concerts; gallery talks; tours; festivals; book traveling exhibitions, 2 per year

M **COLUMBUS MUSEUM OF ART,** 480 E Broad St, 43215. Tel 614-221-6801; FAX 614-221-0226. *Pres* Don M Casto III; *Dir* Merribell Parsons; *Cur European Art* E Jane Connell; *Development Dir* James F Weidman; *Asst Registrar* Rod Bouc; *Dir of Education* Sharon Kokot; *Dir of Finance* Elizabeth Roush; *Dir Public Relations & Marketing* Mary K Ellison; *Dir Coll* Roger Clisby
Open Tues - Fri & Sun 11 AM - 5 PM, Sat 10 AM - 5 PM, Wed until 9 PM, cl Mon & holidays. No Admis fee, charge for special exhibitions, adults $3.50, children (6-17), senior citizens & students with valid school ID $1. Estab 1878. Present main building constructed in 1931 in an Italianate palatial style; addition built in 1974; Sculpture Park and Garden added in 1979. Average Annual Attendance: 160,000. Mem: 6000; dues $45 annually

Income: Financed by annual contributions, endowment, membership and public support

Collections: 16th - 20th century European paintings, drawings & prints; 19th & 20th century American paintings, works on paper; 19th & 20th century European & American sculpture Chinese & Japanese ceramics; pre-Columbian sculpture

Exhibitions: (1992) Reckoning with Winslow Homer: His Late Paintings & Their Influence; Poetics of the Real: American Landscape Photography; Setting the Stage: Contemporary Artists Design for the Performing Arts; Columbus Art League's 81st Annual Exhibition. (1993 - 94) Weaving: A Legacy, Don & Jean Stuck Coverlet Collection

Publications: Exhibition & permanent collection catalogs; interpretive materials; montly members calendar of events; three-month guide to programs & events; gallery handouts

Activities: Workshops for adults , youth, parents & children; docent training; lect open to public, 24 vis lectr per year; concerts; gallery talks; tours; Friday film series; members trips; sales & rental gallery; book traveling exhibitions, 8 - 10 per year; originate traveling exhibitions; museum shop sells books, ceramics, jewelry, greeting cards, original art, reproductions, Ohio & contemporary crafts

L   Resource Center, 480 E Broad St, 43215. Tel 614-221-6801; FAX 614-221-0226.
Educator for Schools, Prog & Resources Carole Genshaft
Estab 1974 as a reference center for staff, mem, teachers & docents
Library Holdings: Vols 5000; Per subs 25; AV — Motion pictures, slides 15,000; Other — Clipping files, exhibition catalogs, pamphlets
Special Subjects: Antiquities-Oriental, Art Education, Art History, Eskimo Art, Folk Art, Oriental Art, Painting - American, Painting - Dutch, Painting - European, Painting - Flemish, Painting - French, Portraits, Pre-Columbian Art, American Coverlets

A   DIALOGUE INC, 9 Buttles Ave, Suite 318, PO Box 2572, 43216. Tel 614-621-3704. *Exec Ed* Ann Marie Slaughter; *Assoc Ed* Lorrie Dirkse
Estab 1975 to promote the sharing of arts resources
Income: $200,000 (financed by endowment, mem, state appropriation)
Publications: Dialogue, bimonthly journal

A   OHIO HISTORICAL SOCIETY, I 71 & 17th Ave, 43211. Tel 614-297-2300.
Dir Gary C Ness; *Chief Educ Division* Dr Amos Loveday; *Head Archaeology* Martha Otto; *Actg Head History* Don Hutslar; *Head Natural History* Carl Albrecht; *Head Historic Preservation* Ray Luce
Open Mon - Sun 9 AM - 5 PM. No admis fee. Estab 1885, Ohio Historical Society was chartered on this date, to promote a knowledge of history, natural history and archaeology, especially of Ohio; to collect and maintain artifacts, books and archives relating to Ohio's history. Main gallery covers over one acre of floor space and includes exhibits on history, natural history, archaeology; also houses a natural history demonstration laboratory and audio- visual theatre. Average Annual Attendance: 500,000. Mem: 12,000; dues individual $32; annual meeting September
Income: Financed by endowment, membership, state appropriation and contributions
Collections: Archaeology; †artifacts; ceramics; †clothing; †furniture; †glassware; †paintings
Publications: Museum Echoes, newsletter, monthly; Ohio History, scholarly journal, quarterly; Timeline, popular journal, bi-monthly
Activities: Classes for adults & children; docent training; lectures open to public; photographic competitions with awards; individual paintings and original art objects lent; lending collection to museum and art galleries; books traveling exhibitions, originate traveling exhibitions; sales shop sells books, magazines, reproductions, prints, slides and other souvenir items, post cards, jewelry

L   Archives-Library Division, 1982 Velma Ave, 43211. Tel 614-297-2510. *Division Chief & State Archivist* George Parkinson; *Head Collections* William G Myers; *Head Conservation* Vernon Will; *Asst State Archivist* John Stewart
Open Tues - Sat 9 AM - 5 PM. Estab 1885, to collect, preserve and interpret evidences of the past. For reference only. Average Annual Attendance: 12,200
Income: $1,100,000 (financed by state appropriation and private revenue)
Purchases: $56,000
Library Holdings: Vols 148,600; Per subs 300; maps 5000; Micro — Reels 45,000; AV — A-tapes, cassettes 2500, fs, Kodachromes, lantern slides, motion pictures, rec, slides, v-tapes; Other — Exhibition catalogs, manuscripts 1000, memorabilia, pamphlets, photographs 50,000, prints, reproductions
Collections: †Broadsides; †Ohio government documents; †Ohio newspapers; †Temperance collection †maps; papers of early Ohio political leaders; †posters; †rare books; †trade catalogs; †photographs; †manuscripts
Publications: Ohio History (bi-annual); Timeline (bi-monthly)
Activities: Educ Dept, classes for adults, classes for children, docent training

OHIO STATE UNIVERSITY

M   Wexner Center for the Arts, N High St at 15th Ave, 43210-1393. Tel 614-292-0330; FAX 614-292-3369. *Acting Dir* William Cook; *Chief Cur & Dir Exhib* Sarah Rogers-Lafferty; *Registrar* Maureen Sagan Alvim; *Exhib Designer* Jim Scott; *Exhib Designer* Ben Knepper; *Dir Development* Deborah Addison
Open Tues, Wed & Fri 10 AM - 6 PM, Thurs & Sat 10 AM -8 PM, Sun noon - 5 PM, cl Mon. No admis fee. Estab 1989 to provide quality contemporary exhibitions for students & faculty, to promote interaction with the regional art community & to maintain & extend collection of contemporary art. Administers the permanent collection and exhibitions in 4 professionally equipped galleries and is the center for long-range planning in visual arts
Income: $2,500,000 (financed by state & federal grant, funds raised through the University development fund, & state appropriation)
Collections: †Contemporary collection; graphic arts; manuscript collection; Wiant collection of Chinese art
Exhibitions: Solo Exhibits: Elizabeth Murray: Recent Works; Terry Allen's a Simple Story. Group Exhibits: Art in Europe & America The 1950s & 1960s; Art in Europe & America The 1960s & 1970s; New Works for New Spaces: Into the Nineties; Will/Power
Publications: Exhibition catalogs
Activities: Schools in gallery; lectures open to public, 12 vis lectr per year; concerts; gallery talks; tours; invitational juried exhibitions; rent traveling exhibitions, 1-5 per year; originate traveling exhibitions

L   Fine Arts Library, 035L Wexner Center for the Arts, 27 W 17th Ave Mall, 43210. Tel 614-292-6184. *Head Librn* Susan E Wyngaard; *Asst* Diana Druback
Open Mon - Thurs 8 AM - 10 PM, Fri 8 AM - 5 PM, Sat noon - 6 PM, Sun 2 - 10 PM, while classes are in session; vacation, 10 AM - 5 PM daily. Estab during 1930's to support teaching & research in art, art education, design, history of art & photography. Average Annual Attendance: 150,000
Income: $80,000
Purchases: $80,000
Library Holdings: Vols 95,000; Per subs 300; Micro — Cards, fiche, reels; AV — Slides; Other — Exhibition catalogs, original art works
Special Subjects: Asian Art, Medieval & Renaissance, 19th Century French art, photography

L   Slide & Photograph Library, 204 Hayes Hall, 108 N Oval Mall, 43210. Tel 614-292-0520. *Cur* John J Taormina
Open Mon - Fri 8 AM - 5 PM. Estab 1925 to provide visual resources for instruction and research in history of art. Teaching - Reference Collection, restricted circulation
Income: Financed by state funds through State University System
Library Holdings: Vols 150; Per subs 2; AV — A-tapes 30, slides 260,000; Other — Exhibition catalogs, framed reproductions, original art works, photographs 230,000, prints, reproductions
Collections: †Asian art & architecture; history of Western art & architecture; African art & architecture

L   Cartoon, Graphic & Photographic Arts Research Library, 023L Wexner Center, 27 W 17th Ave Mall, OH 43210-1393. Tel 614-292-0538; FAX 614-292-7859. *Cur* Lucy Shelton Caswell
Open Mon - Fri 8 AM - 5 PM. Estab 1977
Income: Financed by state Appropriation
Library Holdings: Micro — Reels; AV — Cassettes, motion pictures, rec, slides; Other — Clipping files, exhibition catalogs, manuscripts, memorabilia, original art works, photographs
Special Subjects: Cartoons, Illustration, Manuscripts, Photography, Posters
Collections: †Milton Caniff Collection; Walt Kelly Collection; Jon Whitcomb Collection; Floyd & Marion Rinhart Collection; Woody Gelman Collection; Will Eisner Collection; John Fischetti Collection; Karl Hubenthal Collection; Charles Kuhn Collection; Mike Peters Collection; Jim Borgman Collection; Noel Sickles Collection

L   Human Ecology Library, 1787 Neil Ave, 43210-1295. Tel 614-292-4220. *Librn* Leta Hendricks
Open Mon - Thurs 8 AM - 8 PM, Fri 8 AM - 5 PM, Sat 10 AM - 2 PM, Sun 1 - 3 PM
Library Holdings: Vols 23,000; Per subs 200; Micro — Fiche; AV — A-tapes, cassettes, fs, motion pictures, slides, v-tapes; Other — Exhibition catalogs, pamphlets
Special Subjects: Carpets & Rugs, Crafts, Decorative Arts, Embroidery, Fashion Arts, Folk Art, Furniture, Jewelry, Textiles
Collections: †Costumes; †Crafts; †Textiles & Clothing

L   PUBLIC LIBRARY OF COLUMBUS AND FRANKLIN COUNTY,
Columbus Metropolitan Library, 96 S Grant Ave (Mailing add: 28 S Hamilton Rd, OH 43213). Tel 614-645-2690. *Dir* Larry Black; *Division Head* Susan Malloy; *Exhib Coordr* Susan Olcott; *Library Dir* Meribah Mansfield
Open Mon - Thurs 9 AM - 9 PM, Fri & Sat 9 AM - 6PM, cl Sun. Estab 1873 to serve informational, educational and cultural needs of Columbus and Franklin County. Gallery is 130 running ft
Income: $141,000 (financed by state and county appropriation)
Library Holdings: Vols 62,000; Classified picture file; Micro — Reels; AV — Cassettes, motion pictures, rec, v-tapes; Other — Exhibition catalogs, pamphlets
Special Subjects: Architecture, Decorative Arts, Film, Photography, Theatre Arts, Antiques, Music, Television
Exhibitions: Milton Caniff: Art for Everybody; The Wonderful T: The Art of James Thurber; innovative and informative exhibits with emphasis on local professional artists and traveling exhibits; Creative Best of Columbus Society of Communicating Arts; Ohio Folk Traditions: A New Generation
Publications: Novel Events, newsletter, bimonthly
Activities: Classes for adults and children; film series; lect open to public; concerts; tours; exten dept serves Franklin County; book traveling exhibitions 3 - 4 per year; originate traveling exhibitions

COSHOCTON

M   JOHNSON-HUMRICKHOUSE MUSEUM, 300 Whitewoman St, Roscoe Village, 43812. Tel 614-622-8710. *Dir* Midge Derby
Open daily noon - 5 PM May through Oct, 1 - 4:30 PM Nov through April, cl Mon, Thanksgiving, Christmas and New Year's Day. No admis fee. Estab 1931, as a gift of two pioneer residents. Museum is located in historical Roscoe Village in a newly constructed building (1979) managed by the Library Board
Collections: American Indian baskets and bead work; Aztec, Toltec and Mayan pottery heads; Chinese and Japanese amber, brass, bronze, cloisonne, copper, embroideries, ivory, jade, lacquers, pewter ware, porcelains, prints, wood carvings; European glass, laces, pewter, porcelains, prints; Eskimo artifacts; material from Coshocton County Mound Builders; Miller-Preston bequest of furnishings and implements used by Coshocton County pioneer families
Exhibitions: Permanent collection exhibitions changed periodically; traveling exhibitions. (1993) Space Exhibit
Activities: Educ Dept; gallery talks, lect

L   Library, 300 Whitewoman St, Roscoe Village, 43812. Tel 614-622-8710.
Technical books for research supplied by City Library on permanent loan

CUYAHOGA FALLS

M   RICHARD GALLERY AND ALMOND TEA GALLERY, Divisions of Studios of Jack Richard, 2250 Front St, 44221. Tel 216-929-1575. *Dir* Jack Richard; *Agent* Jane Williams
Open Tues - Fri 11:30 AM - 5 PM, Sat 11 AM - 1:30 PM, Tues Eve 7 - 10 PM, cl Sun & Mon, other hours by appointment. No admis fee. Estab Richard Gallery

1960, for exhibition of local, regional and national works of art. Average Annual Attendance: 12,000
Income: Financed privately
Collections: Ball; Brackman; Cornwell; Grell; Gleitsmann; Loomis; Terry Richard; †Oriental
Exhibitions: 50 Women Plus; student exhibits; Japanese Prints; members exhibits; 30 one-person exhibits; Pastel Exhibit Great American Nude; Flowers, Flowers, Flowers; Age Old Masters; Progress and Change in Paintings; Brackman Masterpieces
Activities: Classes for adults and children; lectures open to public; 5 visiting lectrs per year; 20 gallery talks; 20-25 tours; competitions with awards; scholarships; individual paintings and original objects of art lent; lending collection contains 300 paintings and prints, and 300 cassettes; book traveling exhibitions; originate traveling exhibitions; sales shop sells books, magazines, original art, reproductions prints and slides; frame shop
L **Library,** 2250 Front St, 44221. Tel 216-929-1575.
For reference and limited lending only
Library Holdings: Vols 1000; AV — Kodachromes, motion pictures, rec, slides, v-tapes; Other — Clipping files, framed reproductions, original art works, photographs, prints, reproductions

DAYTON

M **DAYTON ART INSTITUTE,** Forest & Riverview Ave, PO Box 941, 45401-0941. Tel 513-223-5277; FAX 513-223-3140. *Dir* Alex Nyerges; *Cur of European & Graphic Arts & Registrar* Dominique Vasseur; *Cur Asian Art* Clarence Kelley; *Dir Development* Lois Mann; *Public Relations* Pat Koepnick
Open Tues - Sun noon - 5 PM. Admis adults $2, sr citizens & students $1, children under 18 free. Estab 1919 for the public benefit. Some of the galleries include: Ancient Gallery, Contemporary Gallery, European 16th-18th Century Gallery, Experiencenter Gallery, Print Corridor, Special Exhibitions Gallery and an Asian Wing and an American wing. Average Annual Attendance: 170,000. Mem: 3800; dues $3-$1000; annual meeting Sept
Income: $1,300,000 (financed by federal, state & local funds, mem dues, endowment & corporate grants)
Collections: †American Collection; European Art From Medieval Period to Present; Oriental Collection;
Exhibitions: (1992 - 93) Kandinsky Exhibit
Publications: Annual report; bulletin; Calendar of Events, bi-monthly; gallery guides & catalogs, periodically
Activities: Docent training; classes for adults and children; lect open to public, 3-6 per year; gallery talks; tours; concerts; annual Oktoberfest; annual style show; Guild Volunteer Organization; scholarships; book 6 traveling exhibitions per year; museum store selling books, original art, toys and jewelry
L **Library,** Forest & Riverview Aves, PO Box 941, 45401-0941. Tel 513-223-5277; FAX 513-223-3140. *Librn* Jane Dunwoodie; *Asst Librn* Julie Martin; *Ref Librn* Alice Saidel
Open Mon - Fri 9 AM - 5 PM, cl month of Aug. Estab 1922. Open to the public for art reference only
Income: Financed by Dayton Art Institute budget
Library Holdings: Vols 26,500; Per subs 111; Auction catalogs; Micro — Fiche; AV — Slides; Other — Clipping files, exhibition catalogs, pamphlets
Special Subjects: Architecture
Collections: Louis J P Lott and Walter G Schaeffer, architectural libraries

M **PATTERSON HOMESTEAD,** 1815 Brown St, 45409. Tel 513-222-9724. *Dir* Mollie Lee Williams; *Staff Site Interpreter* Anne Lykins
Open Apr - Dec Tues - Fri 10 AM - 4 PM, Sun 1 - 4 PM, cl legal holidays. No admis fee. Estab 1953. Patterson Homestead is an 1816 Federal style farmhouse
Collections: Antique & period furniture, ranging from the hand-hewn to highly decorative Victorian Eastlake pieces, including Chippendale, Hepplewhite, Sheraton & American Empire styles; Oil Portraits of members of the Patterson family; Manuscript Collection
Exhibitions: Temporary exhibitions
Activities: Programs for children & grad students affiliated with Wright State Univ; docent program; lectures; tours

WRIGHT STATE UNIVERSITY
M **Dayton Art Institute,** 45435. Tel 513-873-2978; FAX 513-873-4082. *Curatorial Consultant* Teresa Schalnat
Open Mon - Fri 10 AM - 4 PM, Sat & Sun noon - 4 PM, cl holidays. No admis fee. Estab 1974, devoted to exhibitions & research in contemporary art. Four galleries; multi-level contemporary building with 5000 sq ft & 500 running ft of wall space. Available also are areas outside on the campus & selected sites in Dayton. Average Annual Attendance: 25,000. Mem: 200; dues $25 & up
Income: Financed through the university & grants
Collections: Collection of Contemporary Art
Exhibitions: regional artists & traveling exhibitions; Sites of Recollection: Four Atlers & A Rap Opera
Publications: Artist's books & exhibition catalogs, 2 per year
Activities: Classes for adults; lect open to public, 7-8 vis lectrs per year; gallery talks; tours; individual paintings & art objects lent to faculty and administrative areas; lending collection contains original art works, original prints, paintings, photographs & sculpture; originate traveling exhibitions; sales desk sells catalogs, periodicals
L **Dept of Art and Art History Resource Center & Slide Library,** 45435. Tel 513-873-3567. *Slide Cur* Pat Robinow
Open Mon, Wed, Fri 9 AM - 5 PM, Tues & Thurs 10 AM - 2 PM. Estab 1970 to serve Wright State University and art professionals in the greater Dayton area. For lending and reference. Circ Approx 300 slides per week
Library Holdings: Vols 200; Per subs 10; Art school catalogs; AV — A-tapes, cassettes, slides, v-tapes; Other — Exhibition catalogs
Special Subjects: Architecture, Art History, Drawings, Etchings & Engravings, History of Art & Archaeology, Painting - American, Painting - British, Painting - Dutch, Painting - European, Painting - Flemish, Painting - French, Painting - German, Painting - Italian, Painting - Polish, Painting - Russian

DELAWARE

L **BEEGHLY LIBRARY,** 43 University Ave, 43015. Tel 614-368-3246. *Dir* Kathleen List; *Technical Servs* Lois Ward
Library Holdings: Vols 437,000; Per subs 1163; Micro — Reels; AV — Cassettes, v-tapes; Other — Memorabilia

DOVER

M **WARTHER MUSEUM INC,** 331 Karl Ave, 44622. Tel 216-343-7513. *Pres* David Warther; *General Mgr* Mark Warther
Open daily 9 AM - 5 PM. Admis $5.50. Estab 1936 to display carvings. Average Annual Attendance: 100,000
Income: $250,000 (financed by admis)
Collections: Carvings of America; Railroad History; Carvings of ivory, ebony & walnut depicting the evolution of the steam engine
Exhibitions: Carvings of America; Railroads by Ernest Warther
Activities: Retail store sells books magazines & prints

FINDLAY

M **FINDLAY COLLEGE,** Egner Fine Arts Center, 1000 N Main St, 45840. Tel 419-422-8313. *Dir* Douglas Salveson
Open Mon - Fri 9 AM - 4:30 PM. Estab in 1962 as an auxiliary to the college art department. Gallery is maintained
Income: Financed by endowment
Collections: †Contemporary prints; student works
Exhibitions: Contemporary Art & Crafts
Activities: Classes for adults and children; dramatic programs; lectures open to public, 2-3 vis lectrs per yr; concerts; competitions with awards; scholarships; individual paintings & original objects of art lent, primarily to College offices; book traveling exhibitions, biennially

GALLIPOLIS

A **FRENCH ART COLONY,** 530 First Ave, PO Box 472, 45631. Tel 614-446-3834. *Dir* Lee Miller; *Cur* Janice M Thaler; *Secy* Doug Combs; *Treasurer* Peggy Evans
Open Tues & Thurs 10 AM - 3 PM, Sat & Sun 1 - 5 PM. No admis fee. Estab 1964 to promote the arts throughout the region. Mem: 325; dues $15 and up
Income: Financed by membership and donations
Exhibitions: Photography, bi-annual; visual arts - annual
Publications: Newsletter, monthly
Activities: Classes for adults and children; dramatic programs; community programs; creative writing; visual art programs and classes; lect open to public; concerts; tours; competitions; 10 - 12 purchase awards; book traveling exhibitions
L **Library,** 530 First Ave, PO Box 472, 45631. Tel 614-446-3834. *Vol Librn* Vilma Pikkoja
Open Tues & Thurs 10 AM - 3 PM, Sat & Sun 1 - 5 PM. Estab 1972 as small reference library dealing primarily with visual arts
Library Holdings: Vols 2000; Per subs 5; AV — Cassettes, lantern slides, slides; Other — Clipping files, exhibition catalogs, memorabilia, pamphlets, photographs, prints, reproductions
Special Subjects: Fine Arts

GAMBIER

M **KENYON COLLEGE,** Art Gallery, Olin Library, Kenyon College, 43022. Tel 614-427-5000. *Coordr* Judy Beckman
Open daily 8:30 AM - 8:30 PM, through school year only. No admis fee. Estab 1973 as teaching arm of the Art Department of Kenyon College
Income: Financed by college
Collections: Art collection and items of some historical importance
Activities: Lectures open to public; gallery talks; tours; Honors Day cash awards

GRANVILLE

M **DENISON UNIVERSITY,** Art Gallery, Burke Hall of Music & Art, 43023. Tel 614-587-6255, 587-6596. *Dir* Michael Jung; *Registrar & Cur* Letha Schetzsle
Open Mon - Sat 10:30 AM - 4 PM, Mon - Fri evenings 7 - 9 PM, Sun 1 - 4 PM. No admis fee. Estab 1946 for educational and exhibition purposes. Four galleries for exhibitions; one seminar room; storage for permanent collections173. Average Annual Attendance: 25,000
Income: Financed through University
Collections: American and European paintings, †prints, †drawings and sculpture; Burmese textiles, lacquerware and Buddhist sculpture; Chinese bronzes, robes and porcelains; Cuna Indian Molas, Uchus and ceremonial objects; American Indian pottery, baskets and rugs; African sculpture and basketry
Exhibitions: Visiting artists exhibitions; student and senior shows; faculty show; in house show
Activities: Lectures open to public, 4 - 6 vis lectrs per yr; gallery talks; tours; exten dept; individual paintings & original objects of art lent to secured areas on campus only; book traveling exhibitions, 2 - 4 per yr
L **Art Dept Slide Library,** Cleveland Hall Annex, 43023. *In Charge* Gerard J Gauthier
Open to students and faculty for reference only
Library Holdings: AV — Slides 75,000

JEFFERSON

M DEZIGN HOUSE, PO Box 284, 44047. Tel 216-294-2778. *Dir* Ramon J Elias; *Assoc* Margery M Elias
Open only to clients. Estab 1962 for the encouragement of original art. Private gallery
Income: Financed privately
Collections: Original American and European
L Library, PO Box 284, Jefferson, 44047. Tel 216-294-2778. *Dir* Ramon J Elias
Estab 1953. Open for private research only
Library Holdings: Vols 7000; Per subs 40; AV — Kodachromes 2000, rec; Other — Clipping files, exhibition catalogs, manuscripts, memorabilia, original art works, pamphlets, photographs, prints, sculpture
Special Subjects: North Eastern Ohio Art of the 60's

KENT

KENT STATE UNIVERSITY

M School of Art Gallery, 44242. Tel 216-672-7853. *Dir* Dr Fred T Smith
Open Mon - Fri 10 AM - 4 PM, Sun 2 - 4 PM, cl school holidays. No admis fee. Estab 1950 as part of the instructional program at Kent State. One main gallery 2200 sq ft; two student galleries; Eells Gallery; Blossom Music Center. Average Annual Attendance: 22,000. Mem: 76; annual dues $10; annual meeting in June
Income: Financed by University, grants & fundraising
Collections: Michener Collection, contemporary prints & paintings; permanent collection sculpture, paintings, prints, crafts & photography
Exhibitions: Annual Invitational; faculty & student one-man & group exhibitions; traveling exhibitions from museums; William Schock: The Drawings; National Crafts Invitational; America at War: WW II Posters & Prints; Vito Acconci: Prints 1970-85; An Installation by Patrick Ireland; African Dress & Textile Arts; A New Generation of Ohio Artists; European Glass Art. (1993) Scholastic Arts: High School & Junior High School; Student Annual Show; Contemporary Platinum Prints & Photographs
Publications: Brochures; catalogs, 2-3 times per yr
Activities: Classes for students in museum preparation; lectures open to public, 10-15 vis lect per yr; gallery talks; tours; competitions; individual paintings and original objects of art lent to offices on campus; book traveling exhibitions, 3 per yr

LAKEWOOD

A BECK CENTER FOR THE CULTURAL ARTS, 17801 Detroit Ave, 44107. Tel 216-521-2540. *Pres Bd Trustees* Rosemary E Corcoran; *Managing Dir* Andrea Krist
Open Mon, Wed, Thurs, Fri, Sat & Sun 2 - 5 PM, performance evenings 7 - 9 PM, cl Tues. No admis fee. Estab 1976 to present a wide variety of the fine and graphic arts including exhibits from the Cleveland Museum of Art. A North and South Gallery separated by an indoor garden under a skylight roof; total sq footage: approx 3400 sq ft; part of a cultural center which includes a legitimate theatre. Average Annual Attendance: 50,000
Income: Financed by operating cost of the center
Collections: Contemporary pieces including acrylics, collages, etchings, oils, sculpture and watercolors
Exhibitions: (1992) Contemporary Russian Art; Proscenium, Annual Juried Show. (1993) Kwo, Miller, Thurmer (paintings & sculpture); Touching Stories, from Cleveland Museum of Art; Hungarian Art; Krabill (paintings)
Publications: Bulletins; Programs, every five weeks
Activities: Classes for adults and children; dramatic programs; lect open to public; concerts; gallery talks; tours; competitions; cash awards; book traveling exhibitions, 5 per year; sales shop sells original art and prints

MANSFIELD

A MANSFIELD FINE ARTS GUILD, Mansfield Art Center, 700 Marion Ave, 44903. Tel 419-756-1700. *Dir* H Daniel Butts III
Open Tues - Sat 11 AM - 5 PM, Sun 12 - 5 PM, cl Mon & national holidays. No admis fee. Estab 1945, incorporated 1956 to maintain an art center in which exhibitions, lectures, gallery talks, special programs, symposia and series of classes for adults and children are provided for the North Central Ohio area; maintained by membership, commission on sales and classes. Gallery dimensions 5000 sq ft with flexible lighting, movable walls, props, etc to facilitate monthly exhibition changes. Average Annual Attendance: 25,000. Mem: 1050; dues $15 - $1000; annual meeting in Apr
Exhibitions: Changing exhibitions of member artists' work; traveling shows & locally organized one-man, group and theme exhibitions changing monthly throughout the year
Publications: Catalogs; class schedules; monthly newsletter
Activities: Classes for adults and children; lectures open to public, 6 vis lectr per year; gallery talks mainly for school groups; competitions; scholarships
L Library, 700 Marion Ave, 44903. Tel 419-756-1700. *Art Dir* H Daniel Butts III
The library is basically a collection of monographs and studies of styles and periods for teacher and student reference
Library Holdings: Vols 500

MARIETTA

M MARIETTA COLLEGE, Grover M Hermann Fine Arts Center, 45750. Tel 614-374-4696. *Chmn* Valdis Garoza
Open Mon - Fri 8 AM - 10:30 PM, Sat & Sun 1 - 10:30 PM. No admis fee. Estab 1965. Gallery maintained. Average Annual Attendance: 20,000
Collections: Permanent collection of contemporary American paintings, sculpture and crafts; significant collection of African and pre-Columbian art
Activities: Lect open to public; competitions; book shop

M THE OHIO HISTORICAL SOCIETY, INC, Campus Martius Museum and Ohio River Museum, 601 Second St, 45750. Tel 614-373-3750. *Mgr* John B Briley; *Asst Mgr* Kim McGrew
Campus Martins Museum open in Mar, Apr, Oct & Nov, Wed - Sat 9:30 AM - 5 PM, Sun noon - 5 PM, May thru Sept Mon - Sat 9:30 AM - 5 PM, Sun & holidays noon - 5 PM, cl Dec, Jan, Feb. Admis fee age 13 & up $3, ages 6 - 12 $1, members & children under 6 free. Estab 1929 as part of the Ohio Historical Society to collect, exhibit & interpret historical items, including art & manuscripts, pertaining to the history of Marietta, the Northwest Territory (Ohio portion) & in 1941 the Ohio Rier. Campus Martius Museum has 2500 sq ft of exhibition space on three floors plus a two-story home, a portion of the original fort of 1790-95 enclosed within the building. The Ohio River Museum has approximately 1500 sq ft of exhibition space in three separate buildings connected by walkway. Average Annual Attendance: 40,000
Income: Financed by state appropriation, mem, grants, fund raising, admissions & sales
Collections: Tell City Pilothouse, a replica of the 18th century flatboat; Steamer W P Snyder Jr; decorative arts from 19th century Ohio; early Ohio Paintings, prints, and photographs; items from early Putnam, Blennerhassett and other families; Ohio Company and Marietta materials; Ohio River landscapes
Activities: Classes for adults and children; museum tours; sales shop sells books, reproductions, prints, slides, crafts, and souvenir items

MASSILLON

M MASSILLON MUSEUM, 212 Lincoln Way E, 44646. *Dir* John Klassen; *Registrar* Margaret Vogt
Open Tues - Sat 9:30 AM - 5 PM, Sun 2 - 5 PM. No admis fee. Estab 1933 as a museum of art and history. The museum places emphasis on the Ohio area by representing the fine arts and crafts and the Massillon area with an historical collection. Average Annual Attendance: 24,000. Mem: 1254; dues $10 & higher
Income: Financed by local property tax
Collections: †Ceramics, china, costumes, drawings, furniture, †glass, †jewelry, †paintings, prints
Exhibitions: Monthly exhibitions
Publications: Pamphlet of activities & exhibitions, quarterly
Activities: Classes for adults and children; docent training; lectures open to public; 3 vis lectr per yr; gallery talks; tours; exten dept serves public schools; individual paintings & original objects of art lent to area museums; museum shop sells local arts & crafts

MAYFIELD VILLAGE

L MAYFIELD REGIONAL LIBRARY, 6080 Wilson Mills Rd, 44143. Tel 216-473-0350. *Art Librn* Dian Disantis
Open Mon - Thurs 9 AM - 9 PM, Fri & Sat 9 AM - 5:30 PM, Sun 1 - 5 PM (during school months). Estab 1972
Exhibitions: Original art works by local artists

MIDDLETOWN

A MIDDLETOWN FINE ARTS CENTER, AIM Bldg, 130 N Verity Parkway, 45042. Tel 513-424-2416. *Pres* Joann Grimes; *Adminr* Peggy Davish
Open Tues - Thurs 9 AM - 9 PM, Mon 9 AM - 4 PM, Sat 9 AM - noon. Estab 1957 to provide facilities program and instruction, for the development of interests and skills in the visual arts, for students of all ages from Middletown and its surrounding communities. Average Annual Attendance: 5000
Income: Endowment through funds donated to Arts in Middletown (funding agency)
Exhibitions: 10 - 12 exhibitions per year including Annual Area Art Show; Annual Student Show; plus one and two-man invitational shows of regional artists
Publications: Brochures publicizing exhibitions, schedule of classes, bi-monthly
Activities: Classes for adults and children Sat mornings; competitions; awards; scholarships; original art work available for sale
L Library, 130 N Verity Parkway, 45042. Tel 513-424-2416. *Librn* Beth Townsley
Open Tues - Thurs 9 AM - 9 PM, Mon 9 AM - 4 PM, Sat 9 AM - noon, cl Sun. Estab 1963, to provide information and enjoyment for students and instructors. Library open for lending or reference. Circ 30
Income: Financed through annual budget & donations
Purchases: $150
Library Holdings: Vols 750; Per subs 4; AV — Slides
Collections: All books pertain only to art subjects: Art history; ceramics; crafts; illustrations; references; techniques; theory

NEWARK

M LICKING COUNTY ART ASSOCIATION GALLERY, 391 Hudson Ave, 43055. Tel 614-349-8031. *Pres* Jeri Clark; *Exec Dir* Claire Wright
Open Oct - July Tues - Sun 1 - 4 PM; school tours by appointment. No admis fee. Estab 1959 to offer nine monthly art exhibits of Ohio and mid-west artists. Three large rooms for monthly shows, also a youth gallery, members gallery and a permanent collection. Second building located at 19 North St adjoining, for art classes and houses a large kiln for ceramics. Average Annual Attendance: 6000. Mem: 600; dues $15 - $500; annual meeting third Tues in May
Income: Financed by membership, annual art auction and Action for Arts Campaign
Collections: Paintings
Publications: Art Print, monthly newsletter
Activities: Classes for adults and children; docent training; monthly programs; lect open to public, 9 visiting lectr per year; gallery talks; tours; demonstrations; competitions; cash awards; fellowships; book traveling exhibitions; gallery shop sells, books, original art, prints, craft items, ceramics, jewelry, wood mirrors and stitchery

NORTH CANTON

L NORTH CANTON PUBLIC LIBRARY, Little Art Gallery, 185 N Main St, 44720. Tel 216-499-4712. *Library Dir* Eileen Flowers; *Chmn Art Committee* Virginia West; *Cur* Judee DuBourdieu
Open Mon - Thurs 10 AM - 9 PM, Fri 10 AM - 6 PM, Sat 9 AM - 5 PM. No admis fee. Estab 1936 to encourage and promote appreciation and education of fine art, graphic arts, commercial art and other related subjects; also recognizes and encourages local artists by promoting exhibitions of their work. Circ 446. Average Annual Attendance: 5000. Mem: 175; annual dues $10, meetings Sept, Nov & Apr
Income: Financed by city and state appropriation
Purchases: $500
Library Holdings: Vols 54,014; Per subs 180
Collections: †Original works by contemporary artists; †religious reproductions; †reproductions for juvenile; †reproductions for circulation
Exhibitions: Monthly exhibits; Stark County Competitive Artists Show
Activities: Classes for adults & children; lect open to the public, 1 vis lectr per yr; gallery talks; tours; competitions with awards; scholarships offered; individual paintings lent, lending collection contains color reproductions

OBERLIN

A FIRELANDS ASSOCIATION FOR THE VISUAL ARTS, 80 S Main St, 44074-1683. Tel 216-774-7158. *Gallery Dir* Susan Jones; *Educ Dir* Jane MacDonald-McInerney; *Office Mgr* Holly Whiteside Thompson
Gallery open Tues - Sat noon - 4 PM, Sun 2 - 4 PM. No admis fee. Estab 1979 as a non-profit community art organization. Average Annual Attendance: 4000. Mem: 325; dues basic $6 - $25, contributors up to $500, annual meeting in Nov
Income: $25,000 (financed by endowment, mem, fees, tuitions & commissions)
Exhibitions: (1992); The Artist as Quiltmaker, biennial; Double Take; Prime Images; FAVA Members' Holiday Show '92; Art 6 (1993) Six-State Photography '93; Breaking with Tradition; 3 from Oberlin
Activities: Classes for adults, teens & children; family workshops; lect open to public, 6 vis lectr per year; competitions with awards; scholarships for low income children; retail store sells books & gifts

INTERMUSEUM CONSERVATION ASSOCIATION
For further information, see National and Regional Organizations

M OBERLIN COLLEGE, Allen Memorial Art Museum, Main & Lorain Sts, 44074. Tel 216-775-8665; FAX 216-775-8799. *Dir* Anne F Moore; *Acting Registrar* Kimberly Fixx; *Acting Cur Educ Prog* Corinne Fryhle; *Cur Special Events* Leslie Miller; *Museum Technician & Preparator* Scott Carpenter
Open Tues - Sat 10 AM - 5 PM, Sun 1 - 5 PM, cl Mon. No admis fee. Estab 1917 to serve teaching needs of Oberlin College & provide cultural enrichment for Northern Ohio region. Original building was designed by Cass Gilbert, a new addition opened in 1977 and was designed by Venturi, Rauch & Scott Brown. Average Annual Attendance: 35,000. Mem: 450; dues sustaining fellow $1000, sponsor $500 supporting memo $100, contributing mem $50, family $35, individual $25, student & sr citizen $10
Income: Financed by endowment, membership, and Oberlin College general fund
Collections: The collection which ranges over the entire history of Art is particularly strong in the area of Dutch & Flemish paintings of the 17th century, European Art of the late 19th & early 20th centuries, contemporary American art, old masters & Japanese prints
Exhibitions: Frequent traveling exhibitions and special in-house exhibitions
Publications: Allen Memorial Art Museum Bulletin twice yearly; catalogues of permanent collections; exhibition catalogues
Activities: Classes for adults & children; docent training; lectures open to public, 10 vis lectr per yr; gallery talks; concerts; tours; travel programs; Original objects of art lent to other institutions for special exhibition; lending collection contains 250 original art works for lending to students on a semester basis; book traveling exhibitions, 2-4 per yr; traveling exhibitions organized and circulated; Museum shop sells books, prints, slides & museum publications

L Clarence Ward Art Library, Allen Art Bldg, Main & Lorain Sts, 44074. Tel 216-775-8635; Elec Mail PWEIDMAN@OBERLIN. *Art Librn* Dr Jeffrey Weidman
Open Mon - Thurs 8:30 AM - 5:30 PM & 7 - 11 PM, Fri 8:30 AM - 5:30 PM, Sat 1 - 6 PM, Sun 1 - 5 PM & 7 - 11 PM. Estab 1917 to serve the library needs of the Art Department, the Allen Memorial Art Museum and the Oberlin College community in the visual arts
Income: Financed by appropriations from Oberlin College Libraries
Library Holdings: Vols 65,000; Per subs 250; Auction sales catalogs 10,000; Micro — Fiche, reels; Other — Clipping files, pamphlets
Special Subjects: Advertising Design, Aesthetics, Afro-American Art, American Indian Art, American Western Art, Anthropology, Antiquities-Assyrian, Antiquities-Byzantine, Antiquities-Egyptian, Antiquities-Etruscan, Artists' books; rare books and periodicals
Collections: Jefferson and Artz Collections of Early Architectural Books; †artists' books
Publications: Bibliographies and library guides, irregular
Activities: Classes for adults & children; tours

OXFORD

M MIAMI UNIVERSITY ART MUSEUM, Patterson Ave, 45056. Tel 513-529-2232. *Dir* Bonnie G Kelm; *Cur of Coll* Edna Southard; *Cur of Educ* Bonnie C Mason; *Registrar* Beverly Bach; *Preparator* Nopchai Ungkavatanapong; *Admin Secy* Alice Kettler
Open Tues - Sun 11 AM - 5 PM, cl Mon & university holidays. Estab 1972, Art Museum facility opened Fall 1978, to care for and exhibit University art collections, to arrange for a variety of traveling exhibitions and for the educational and cultural enrichment of the University and the region. Museum is maintained with exhibition space of 9000 sq ft, consisting of 5 galleries in contemporary building; it also operates The McGuffey Museum, home of

William Holmes McGuffey, a national historic landmark; it is accredited by the American Association of Museums. Average Annual Attendance: 50,000. Mem: 1000; dues $25 and up
Income: Financed by gift and state appropriation
Collections: Charles M Messer Leica Camera Collection; Ancient Art; Decorative Arts; International Folk Art, largely Middle European, Middle Eastern, Mexican, Central & South America; European & American paintings, prints & sculpture; African art; Chinese Art; Gandharan art; Native American Art; Oceanic Art; photography; textiles
Exhibitions: Twelve per year
Publications: Brochures; catalogs, approx 6-8 per year; quarterly newsletter
Activities: Programs for adults & children; docent training; lectures open to the public, 5-6 vis lectr per yr; concerts; gallery talks; tours; individual paintings & original objects of art lent to qualified museums in US; book traveling exhibitions, 2-3 per yr; originate traveling exhibitions

L Wertz Art & Architecture Library, 130 Alumni Hall, 45056. Tel 513-529-6638. *Librn* Joann Olson
Open Mon - Thurs 9 AM - 10 PM, Fri 9 AM - 5 PM, Sat 1 - 5 PM, Sun 1 - 10 PM during academic yaer. Estab to support the programs of the Schools of Art & Architecture & related disciplines
Library Holdings: Vols 50,000; Per subs 256; Micro — Cards, fiche, reels
Special Subjects: Architecture, Art Education, Art History, Decorative Arts, Graphic Arts, Landscape Architecture, Photography

PAINESVILLE

M ARCHAEOLOGICAL SOCIETY OF OHIO, Indian Museum of Lake County, Ohio, 391 W Washington, 44077. Tel 216-352-1911. *Dir* Gwen G King; *Asst Dir* Christine Walick; *Asst Dir* Ann Dewald
Open Mon - Fri 9 AM - 4 PM, Sat & Sun 1 - 4 PM, cl major holiday weekends. Admis donations accepted. 7000. Mem: 300; dues $18 - $1000
Income: Financed by mem
Collections: Early Indians of Ohio; North American Native American Cultures; Reeve Village Site, Lake County, Ohio
Exhibitions: Quill Boxes of the Ottawa, Ojibwe & Mic Mac; Eastern Woodland Indians; Native American Awareness 1992, student competition
Activities: Children's workshops; teacher workshops; lect open to public; competitions with awards; retail stores sells books

L Indian Museum Library, 391 W Washington, 44077. *Dir* Gwen King
For reference
Income: Financed by mem
Library Holdings: Vols 700; Per subs 4
Special Subjects: American Indian Art, Archaeology, Eskimo Art

PORTSMOUTH

M SOUTHERN OHIO MUSEUM CORPORATION, Southern Ohio Museum & Cultural Center, 825 Gallia St, PO Box 990, 45662. Tel 614-354-5629. *Pres* Tom Reynolds; *Co-Dir* Kay Bouyack; *Co-Dir* Sara Johnson; *Cur of Educ* Dennis Stewart
Open Tues & Fri 10 AM - 5 PM, Sat & Sun 1 - 5 PM. Admis adults $1, children $.75. Estab 1977 to provide exhibitions & performances. Museum facility is a renovated & refurbished neo-classical building, 21,000 sq ft, constructed in 1918 as a bank. Facility has two temporary exhibit galleries & a theatre. Average Annual Attendance: 30,000. Mem: 1000; dues family $25
Income: $200,000 (financed by endowment, mem, & city appropriation)
Collections: Clarence Carter Paintings; watercolors & prints
Exhibitions: Contemporary and traditional arts, history, science or humanities
Publications: Annual report; exhibition catalogs
Activities: Classes for adults & children; dramatic programs; docent training; lect open to public, 5 vis lectr per yr; exten dept serves county; book traveling exhibitions; originates traveling exhibitions; museum shop sells books, gift items, jewelry & prints

SALEM

A G G DRAYTON CLUB, 864 Heritage Lane, 44460. Tel 216-332-0959. *Pres* Patricia Bauman; *VPres* Thomas Bauman; *Treasurer* Jerry Wine
Estab 1979 to research Grace Drayton's art work. Mem: 80; dues $6 per yr
Income: $500 (financed by membership)
Collections: †Grace G Drayton Collection
Publications: International G G Drayton Association Newsletter, quarterly
Activities: Lectures open to public

SPRINGFIELD

M CLARK COUNTY HISTORICAL SOCIETY, PO Box 2157, 45501. Tel 513-324-0657. *Pres* James Kenney; *Exec Dir & Cur Museum* Floyd Barmann
Open Mon - Fri 10 AM - 4 PM; Sat 9 AM - 1 PM. Estab 1897 for collection and preservation of Clark County history and historical artifacts. Average Annual Attendance: 4000-5000. Mem: 600; dues patron $50, family $15, individual $10, senior citizen $7.50; annual meeting Nov
Income: $55,000 (financed by appropriation)
Collections: European Landscapes; Oil Paintings, mostly mid-late 19th century, of prominent Springfielders; artifacts
Publications: Newsletter, monthly; annual monograph
Activities: Monthly meetings and lect open to public; tours; restoration project: The David Crabill Homestead (1826), located at Lake Lagonda in Buck Creek State Park; individual paintings & original objects of art lent to museums; lending collection contains 150 original artworks, 50 original prints, 75 paintings & 2000 photographs; sales shop sells books
L Library, 818 N Fountain, 45504. Tel 513-324-0657. *Dir* Floyd Barmann
Open Mon - Fri 10 AM - 4 PM, Sat 9 AM - 1 PM. For reference only
Library Holdings: Vols 4000; Micro — Reels; Other — Clipping files, manuscripts, memorabilia, original art works
Collections: Photograph Collection

M SPRINGFIELD MUSEUM OF ART, 107 Cliff Park Rd, 45501. Tel 513-325-4673; FAX 513-325-4674. *Pres* Glenn W Collier; *First VPres* Peter Gus Geil; *Second VPres* Lori Bartell; *Treas* Robert E Zinser; *Dir* Mark J Chepp
Open Tues - Fri 9 AM - 5 PM; Sat 9 AM - 3 PM; Sun 2 - 4 PM; cl Mon. No admis fee. Estab 1951 for educational and cultural purposes, particularly the encouragement of the appreciation, study of, participation in and enjoyment of the fine arts. Average Annual Attendance: 30,000. Mem: 1000; dues benefactor $100, sustaining $50, family $35, individual $25; meetings third Tues in June
Income: $250,000 (financed by endowment, mem & tuition fees)
Collections: 19th & 20th Century Artists (mostly American, some French)
Exhibitions: (1993) The Decorative & Ceremonial Arts of West Africa; An Unexpected Orthodoxy: The Paintings of Lorenzo Scott; American Paintings from the Permanent Collection; Annual Springfield Museum of Art Student Exhibition; Alice Trumbull Mason: Home Grown Abstraction; The Biennial SMA Faculty Exhibition; Annual Members' Juried Exhibition; God's Garden: Spiritualism in 19th Century American Landscape Painting; American Paintings from the Permanent Collection; The Western Ohio Watercolor Society Juried Exhibition; The Watercolor Paintings of Frances Hynes; New Additions to the Springfield Collection: 3; Miracles of Mexican Folk Art: Retablos & Ex-Votos
Publications: Newsletter, bi-monthly
Activities: Classes for adults and children; docent training; lectures open to public, 6 vis lectr per year; tours; gallery talks; competitions with prizes; scholarships offered; individual paintings and original objects of art lent; book traveling exhibitions; originate traveling exhibitions; sales shop selling original art and prints
L Library, 107 Cliff Park Rd, 45501. Tel 513-325-4673; FAX 513-325-4671. *Librn* Mary M Miller
Open Tues - Fri 9 AM - 5 PM, Sat 9 AM - 3 PM, Sun 2 - 4 PM. Estab 1973 for art study. For reference only. Average Annual Attendance: 35,000
Income: Financed by endowment & mem
Library Holdings: Vols 2500; Per subs 20; AV — Slides 400; Other — Clipping files, exhibition catalogs, framed reproductions, pamphlets
Special Subjects: Art Education, Art History, Photography
Collections: Axel Bahnsen Photograph Collection
Activities: Lectures open to public; scholarships

SYLVANIA

L LOURDES COLLEGE, Duns Scotus Library, 6832 Convent Blvd, 43560. Tel 419-885-3211. *Librn* Sr Mary Thomas More
Estab 1949. Art pieces exhibited on walls of three academic bldgs; classroom & library
Library Holdings: Vols 60,000; Per subs 400; Micro — Fiche 8594; AV — A-tapes, cassettes, fs, rec, slides, v-tapes; Other — Manuscripts, memorabilia, original art works, pamphlets, prints, reproductions, sculpture
Special Subjects: Afro-American Art, American Indian Art, American Western Art, Art Education, Asian Art, Commercial Art, Etchings & Engravings, Handicrafts, History of Art & Archaeology, Illustration, Jewelry, Landscapes, Leather, Lettering, Manuscripts
Collections: †350 art pieces in library cataloged
Activities: Lect open to public; tours; scholarships & fels offered

TOLEDO

M BLAIR MUSEUM OF LITHOPHANES AND CARVED WAXES, 2032 Robinwood Ave, PO Box 4557, 43620. Tel 419-243-4115. *Cur* Laurel G Blair
Open by appointment for groups of 10-20. Admis $5, senior citizens $3. Estab 1965 for the purpose of displaying lithophanes and carved waxes; the only museum of its kind in the world. There are five galleries showing 1000 lithophanes & 200 carved waxes. Average Annual Attendance: 2000. Mem: 175; dues $16; meetings bi-annually
Income: Financed by mem, donations, sales of merchandise
Collections: Lithophane Collection, with 2300 examples is the world's largest (only 1000 can be shown at once); †Wax Collection, with over 500 examples from Egyptian period to present
Publications: Bulletin, bi-monthly
Activities: Lectures open to the public; book traveling exhibitions
L Library, 2032 Robinwood Ave, 43620. Tel 419-243-4115.
For reference only
Library Holdings: Vols 100; Per subs 35; AV — V-tapes

C OWENS-CORNING FIBERGLASS CORPORATION, Art Collection, Fiberglas Tower, Jefferson & Saint Clair Sts, 43659. Tel 419-248-6179. *Cur* Penny McMorris
Open to public by appointment only. Estab 1968 to create a pleasant and stimulating work environment for employees; to provide a focal point for contemporary art; supporting the arts both through purchase of works and display of the collection. Collection displayed in company offices in Toledo and other cities
Collections: Approximately 1000 works of art by contemporary American artists

A SPECTRUM GALLERY & ART CENTER OF TOLEDO, Toledo Botanical Garden, 5403 Elmer Dr, 43635-2948. Tel 419-531-7769. *Coordr* Pat Johnson
Open Tues - Sun 1 - 5 PM; cl Mon. No admis fee. Estab 1975 to encourage & support public appreciation of fine art & to organize & promote related activities; promote mutual understanding & cooperation among artists, artist groups & the public; promote beautification of Toledo through use of art work. Clubhouse (3 galleries, sales room office & working studio) part of Artist Village in Toledo Botanical Garden; large adjacent Art Education Center. Average Annual Attendance: 15,000-20,000. Mem: 350; dues adult $25 - $75; sr citizens & students $15; annual meeting April
Income: $15,000 - $20,000 (financed by mem & fund-raising events, sales of art, donations & art classes)
Exhibitions: Juried Membership Show; Crosby Festival of the Arts; Toledo Festival; spot exhibitions
Publications: Spectrum (newsletter), bi-monthly
Activities: Classes for adults and children; lectures open to the public, 4-5 vis lectr per year; competitions; traveling exhibitions organized and circulated; sales shop selling original art

A TOLEDO ARTISTS' CLUB, Toledo Botanical Garden, PO Box 7430, 43615. Tel 419-531-4079. *Pres* Judy Reese; *VPres* Virginia Kret
Open Mon - Fri 12 - 4 PM, Sat 9 AM - 1 PM. Estab 1943. New Clubhouse-Gallery opened at Crosby Gardens, Toledo in August 1979. Mem: 400-500; dues $15 (variable)
Income: Financed by membership and exhibitions
Exhibitions: Approximately 80 pieces of artwork exhibited each month in new Gallery; includes paintings, pottery, sculpture, stained glass
Publications: Newsletter, monthly
Activities: Classes for adults and children; workshops; demonstrations; lect open to the public; competitions; jointly present Crosby Gardens Arts Festival in June with Crosby Gardens, Toledo Forestry Division & the Arts Commission of Greater Toledo; sales shop selling original art

A TOLEDO FEDERATION OF ART SOCIETIES, INC, 2445 Monroe St, 43620. Tel 419-255-8000; FAX 419-244-2217. *Dir* David Steadman; *First VPres* Helen Zeller; *Second VPres* Nathalie Davis; *Treas* Scott Heacock; *Corresp Secy* Joyce Rice; *Museum Contact* Steve Frushour
Open 10 AM - 4 PM. No admis fee. Juried exhibition each spring of local artist. State of the art display gallery, 6000 sq ft, track lighting, environmentally controlled. Average Annual Attendance: 5000. Mem: 15 area clubs; dues $10; meetings first Sat after first Fri (Oct - May)
Income: Financed by mem, community contributions & exhibition entry charges
Collections: †Permanent collection
Exhibitions: Annual Exhibition
Publications: Annual Exhibit Catalogue
Activities: Competitions with cash awards; individual paintings & original objects of art lent to area civic & public institutions; lending collection contains original art works

M TOLEDO MUSEUM OF ART, Toledo Museum of Art, 2445 Monroe St at Scottwood Ave, PO Box 1013, 43697. Tel 419-255-8000; Cable TOLMUSART. *Pres* Duane Stranahan; *Dir* David W Steadman; *Deputy Dir* Roger M Berkowitz; *Registrar* Patricia Whitesides; *Asst to Dir* John S Stanley; *Chmn Museum Educ* Stef Stahl; *Chmn University Education* Elizabeth Cole; *Cur of Contemporary Art* Robert F Phillips; *Cur of Ancient Art* Kurt T Luckner; *Cur Graphic Arts* Christine Swenson; *Mgr Performing Arts* Joyce Smar; *Public Information* Barbara Van Vleet; *Mgr Personnel* Robert Oates; *Cur of 19th & 20th Century Glass* Davira Taragin; *Cur European Painting & Sculpture Before 1900* Lawrence Nichols
Open Tues - Sat 10 AM - 4 PM, Sun 1 - 5 PM, cl Mon & legal holidays; Collector's Corner open Tues - Sat 10 AM - 4 PM, Sun 1 - 4:30 PM. No admis fee. Estab and incorporated 1901; building erected 1912, additions 1926 and 1933. Museum contains Canaday Gallery, Print Galleries, Glass Gallery, School Gallery, Collector's Corner for sales & rental, a bookstore & an art supply store. Average Annual Attendance: 265,000. Mem: 8000; dues $20 & up
Collections: Ancient to modern glass; European paintings, sculpture & decorative arts; American paintings, sculpture & decorative arts; books & manuscripts; Egyptian, Greek, Roman, Near & Far East art, African art
Exhibitions: (1992) A Mediterranean Holiday: 18th Century Italian Prints from the Collection; Other Languages, Other Signs, The Books of Antonio Frasconi. (1993) Noah's Raven: A Video Installation by Mary Lucier; Max Beckmann Prints from the Collection of the Museum of Modern Art; Toledo Area Artists 75th Annual Exhibition; Athena Society 90th Anniversary Exhibition; The Saxe Contemporary Studio Crafts Collection; The Toledo Museum of Art Education Exhibitions; Celebrating Children's Art; Mugs, Mugs, Mugs: More Than A Cup; New Glass 1993
Publications: American Paintings; Ancient Glass; Art in Glass; Corpus Vasorum Antiquorum I & II; European Paintings; Guide to the Collections
Activities: Classes for adults & children; lect; concerts; tours; book traveling exhibitions; originate traveling exhibitions
L Library, PO Box 1013, 43697. Tel 419-255-8000, Ext 37. *Librn* Anne O Morris; *Assoc Librn* Judith Friebert; *Cataloger* Sharon Scott
Open Tues - Fri 10 AM - 4 PM, Mon 5 - 8:30 PM, Tues - Thurs 4 - 8:30 PM during university sessions, Sun 1 - 4:30 PM. Estab 1901 to provide resources for the museum's staff. Primarily for reference but does lend to certain groups of users
Library Holdings: Vols 58,500; Per subs 300; Micro — Fiche, reels 75; Other — Clipping files, exhibition catalogs 17,000
Special Subjects: Art History, Decorative Arts, Glass, Graphic Arts, Painting - American, Painting - European, Photography

VAN WERT

M WASSENBERG ART CENTER, 643 S Washington St, 45891. Tel 419-238-6837. *Dir* Michele L Smith; *Office Mgr* Kay R Sluterbeck
Open daily 1 - 5 PM, cl Mon. No admis fee. Estab 1961 to encourage the arts in the Van Wert area. Two large gallery areas, basement classroom; maximum exhibit 150 pieces. Average Annual Attendance: 1500. Mem: 350; dues individual $15, various other; annual meeting in Jan, date varies
Income: $20,000 (financed by endowment, mem, fundraisers)
Library Holdings: Vols 250; Per subs 6; AV — A-tapes, cassettes, fs, slides, v-tapes; Other — Original art works, prints, reproductions, sculpture
Collections: Wassenberg Collection; Prints & Original Art; All subjects/all media
Exhibitions: Annual June Art Exhibit; Annual Oct Photography Exhibit
Publications: Gallery Review, bi-monthly
Activities: Classes for adults & children; docent programs; lect open to public, some only to members; competitions; scholarships & fels offered; book traveling exhibitions 6-8 per year

VERMILION

M GREAT LAKES HISTORICAL SOCIETY, 480 Main St, 44089. Tel 216-967-3467; FAX 216-967-1519. *Pres* Timothy J Runyan; *VPres* Alexander B Cook; *Business Mgr* Martha Long
Open daily 10 AM - 5 PM. Admis adults $4, children $2. Estab 1944 to promote interest in discovering and preserving material about the Great Lakes and surrounding areas. Maintains an art gallery as part of the Maritime History Museum. Average Annual Attendance: 35,000. Mem: 3000; dues from $22 - $1000; meetings May & Oct
Income: $130,000 (financed by endowment, membership and sales from museum store)
Collections: †Collection of Ship Models, †Marine Relics, †Paintings and †Photographs dealing with history of the Great Lakes
Exhibitions: Annual Model Boat Show Exhibition
Publications: Chadburn (newsletter), quarterly; Inland Seas, quarterly journal
Activities: Educ dept; lect open to public, 2 vis lectr per year; tours; competitions; awards; book traveling exhibitions, 2 per year; sales shop selling books, magazines, original art, reproductions, prints, slides and gifts

WELLINGTON

M SOUTHERN LORAIN COUNTY HISTORICAL SOCIETY, Spirit of '76 Museum, 201 N Main, PO Box 76, 44090. Tel 216-647-4367. *Pres* Charles Oney; *VPres* Ralph Wright; *Cur* Albert Grimm
Open April - Nov Sat & Sun 2:30 - 5 PM, groups of ten or more any time by reservation. No admis fee. Estab 1970 to memorialize Archibald M Willard who created the Spirit of '76, nation's most inspirational painting. Average Annual Attendance: 2000. Mem: 259; dues couple $10, individual $5; annual meeting Apr
Income: $10,000 (financed by membership, gifts and gift shop)
Purchases: $10,000
Collections: Archibald M Willard Paintings; artifacts of local interest; memorabilia of Myron T Herrick
Publications: Newsletters
Activities: Sales shop sells books, reproductions, prints and miscellaneous items

WESTERVILLE

AMERICAN CERAMIC SOCIETY
For further information, see National and Regional Organizations

WEST LIBERTY

M PIATT CASTLES, 10051 Rd 47, 43357. Tel 513-465-2821. *Dir* Margaret Piatt; *Prog Mgr* James Nash
Castle Piatt Mac-A-Cheek open Apr - Oct daily 11 AM - 5 PM, Mar Sat & Sun 11 AM - 5 PM; Castle Mac-O-Chee May - Sept daily 11 AM - 5 PM, Apr & Oct Sat & Sun 11 AM - 5 PM. Admis adults $5, children 6 - 12 $3. Paintings & sculptures displayed throughout both homes - room like settings. Average Annual Attendance: 40,000
Collections: Early American & French period family furnishings; Rare Art; Indian artifacts; European & Asian antiques; weapons
Publications: Brochures
Activities: Tours

WILBERFORCE

AFRICAN AMERICAN ASSOCIATION
For further information, see National and Regional Organizations

WILLOUGHBY

A FINE ARTS ASSOCIATION, School of Fine Arts, 38660 Mentor Ave, 44094. Tel 216-951-7500. *Pres* Robert H Wigton; *Executive Dir* Charles Frank
Open Mon - Fri 9 AM - 8 PM, Sat 9 AM - 5 PM. No admis fee. Estab 1957 to bring arts education to all people regardless of their ability to pay, race or social standing. Main Floor Gallery houses theme, one-man & group monthly exhibitions; 2nd Floor Gallery houses monthly school exhibits. Average Annual Attendance: 70,000. Mem: 500; dues $25 and up; annual meeting Sept
Income: Financed by class fees and donations
Exhibitions: Monthly exhibitions, theme, one man & group; Annual juried exhibit for area artists
Activities: Classes for adults and children; dramatic programs; lectures open to the public, 10 vis lectrs per year; gallery talks; tours; concerts; competitions with awards; scholarships

WOOSTER

M WAYNE CENTER FOR THE ARTS, 237 S Walnut St, 44691. Tel 216-264-8596. *Exec Dir* Roberto Looney; *Asst to Dir* Isabel Matson
Open Sun - Fri 2 - 5 PM. No admis fee. Estab 1944 to provide an opportunity for students, faculty and the local community to view original works of art. The gallery is housed in a former library; Main floor has large open areas and upper balcony more intimate exhibition space. Average Annual Attendance: 5000
Income: $20,000 (financed through college)
Collections: Chinese bronzes & porcelains; paintings; prints; tapestries; African artifacts; contemporary American ceramics
Exhibitions: Traveling & monthly exhibitions
Publications: Exhibition catalogues, 2 per yr
Activities: Lect open to public, 10 - 15 vis lectr per year; gallery talks; books traveling exhibitions

M WAYNE COUNTY HISTORICAL SOCIETY, 546 E Bowman St, 44691. Tel 216-264-8856. *Pres* Larry Drabenstott; *VPres* Ray Leisy; *Treas* Rachel Fetzer; *Treas* Mary Knight
Open daily 2 - 4:30 PM. Admis adults $1, students $.50, under 14 free. Estab 1954 to discover, preserve, & pass on the history of Wayne County. Main building built in 1815 is furnished partially as a home; one room school house, log cabin, building with model carpenter shop, model blacksmith shop. Average Annual Attendance: 2000. Mem: 650; dues $10 - $200; annual meeting in Apr, quarterly meetings Jan, Apr, July, Oct
Income: Financed by mem, county commissioners
Collections: Memorabilia of Wayne County inhabitants, furnishings, artisans' tools
Publications: Baker's 1856 Map of Wayne Co, 1820 Tax Lists: Census, 1826 tax lists with details Wayne Co, Caldwell's Atlas of Wayne Co 1873 & 1897, Wayne Co Will Abstracts, Estates & Guardianships 1813 - 1852 Vol 1852 - 1900 Vol II, Wayne Co Abstracts of Naturalization 1812 - 1903, 75 years of Wayne Co marriages, History of Wayne Co, Wayne Co Burial Records, Early Land Records Wayne Co; quarterly newsletter
Activities: Adult & children's classes; docent programs

XENIA

A GREENE COUNTY HISTORICAL SOCIETY, 74 W Church St, 45385-2902. Tel 513-372-4606. *Exec Secy* Joan Baxter
Open 9 AM - noon & 1 - 3:30 PM. Admis $2. Estab 1929 to preserve the history of Greene County, OH. Average Annual Attendance: 2000. Mem: 400; dues individual $7.50, sr $5; annual meeting in June
Income: Financed by mem & county appropriation
Collections: Clothing; Medical; Military; †Railroad (historic model)
Exhibitions: Log House & furnishings; Victorian House & furnishings; Railroad; Conestoga Wagon
Activities: Lect open to public, 12 vis lectr per year; retail store sells books, note paper, materials relating to county

YELLOW SPRINGS

M ANTIOCH COLLEGE, Noyes & Read Galleries, 45387. Tel 513-767-7331, Ext 467. *Project Dir* Demi Reber
Open Mon - Fri 1 - 4 PM. No admis fee. Estab 1972. Noyes Gallery to offer works to students and the community that both challenge and broaden their definitions of Art; Read Gallery is primarily a student gallery

YOUNGSTOWN

M BUTLER INSTITUTE OF AMERICAN ART, Art Museum, 524 Wick Ave, 44502. Tel 216-743-1107; FAX 216-743-9567. *Dir* Dr Louis A Zona; *Assoc Dir* Clyde Singer; *Dir Educ* Carole O'Brien; *Dir of Research & Archives* Peggy Kaulback
Open Tues, Thur - Sat 11 AM - 4 PM; Wed 11 AM - 8 PM; Sun noon - 4 PM. No admis. Estab 1919, and is the first museum building to be devoted entirely to American Art. Eighteen galleries containing 11,000 works of American artists. Average Annual Attendance: 212,000. Mem: 4000; dues $5 - $3000; annual meetings in May
Income: Financed by endowment, grants and gifts
Collections: Comprehensive collection of American art covering three centuries; American Impressionism; the American West & Marine & Sports Art collections; Principle artists: Winslow Homer, Albert Bierstadt, Martin Johnson Heade, Georgia O'Keeffe, Charles Sheeler, Helen Frankenthaler, John S Sargent, JM Whistler, Mary Cassatt, Thomas Cole, Edward Hopper, Romare Bearden & Andy Warhol †American Glass Bells†Miniatures of all the Presidents of the United States (watercolor)
Exhibitions: Jasper Johns: Drawings & Prints from the collection of Leo Castelli; Charles Burchfield; Larry Rivers: Public & Private; Fireworks; American Artists Celebrate the Eighth Art; Sounding the Depths; annual midyear show (national painting survey); Area Artists Annual; Youngstown State University Annual; one-person exhibitions
Publications: Exhibition catalogues; bi-monthly newsletter; biannual report
Activities: Classes for children & adults; docent training; lectures open to the public, 15 vis lectr per year; concerts; gallery talks; tours; competitions with awards; individual paintings and original objects of art lent to qualified museums, institutions, world wide; book traveling exhibitions, 10 per yr; traveling exhibitions organized and circulated; museum shop sells books, original art, reproductions, prints, slides, crafts, jewelry, original pottery & art related materials

L Hopper Resource Library, 524 Wick Ave, 44502. Tel 216-743-1107, 743-1711. *Dir Research & Archives* Peggy Kaulback
Open Tues & Thurs 11 AM - 4 PM, Wed, Fri & Sat 11 AM - 8 PM, Sun noon - 4 PM. No admis fee. For reference only. Average Annual Attendance: 122,000. Mem: 3090
Income: Financed by endowment, grants and gifts
Library Holdings: Vols 1500; Per subs 10; AV — Kodachromes, slides; Other — Clipping files, exhibition catalogs, framed reproductions, memorabilia, pamphlets, photographs
Special Subjects: American Art

ZANESVILLE

A ZANESVILLE ART CENTER, 620 Military Rd, 43701. Tel 614-452-0741. *Dir* Dr Charles Dietz; *Secy & Registrar* Mrs Joseph Howell; *Pres Board Trustees* Walker Huffman; *Pres Board Dir* Susan Hendley; *Cur Oriental Art* Mrs Willis Bailey; *Cur Glass* William Brown
Open Tues - Sun 1 - 5 PM; cl Mon & holidays. No admis fee. Estab 1936 to provide a public center for the arts and crafts, permanent collections and temporary exhibitions, classes in art and crafts, library of art volumes and a

meeting place for art and civic groups. There are fifteen galleries for Old & Modern Masters' paintings, sculpture, prints, ceramics, glass, photography, children's art & gift art; handicapped facilities. Average Annual Attendance: 25, 000. Mem: 350; dues $10 & up
Income: Financed by endowment & mem
Collections: †American, European and †Oriental Paintings, Sculptures, Ceramics, Prints, Drawings, and Crafts; †Children's Art; †Midwestern and †Zanesville Ceramics and Glass
Exhibitions: (1989) Annual AAUW Children's Art Shows; selections from Zanesville Art Center permanent collections; Sue Wall paintings, Flowers in Art; Southeastern Ohio Watercolor Society shows; Sarah Becker oriental art collection selections ; Primative Paintings of Paul Patton; Commercial Art Selections; 48th Annual May Art and Craft exhibition; Murray Tinkleman Graphics; Pottery Lover's Festival exhibition; Recent Mexican Art & Craft Accessions & selections of Mexican Masks & Ceramics from Z.A.C. collections; Ohio Watercolor Society shows; one person exhibitions
Publications: Bulletin, tri-monthly
Activities: Classes for adults & children; docent training; lectures open to public, 5 vis lectr per year; concerts; gallery talks; tours; competitions with awards; individual paintings lent to public institutions; lending collection contains 6000 pieces of original art works, 500 original prints, 2000 paintings, 200 photographs & 50 sculpture; sales shop sells books & original art
L **Library,** 620 Military Rd, 43701. Tel 614-452-0741. *Registrar & Librn* Mrs Joseph Howell
Open Tues - Sun 1 - 5 PM, cl Mon and major holidays. Estab 1936 to provide fine arts and crafts information & exhibitions
Income: Financed by endowment, membership, trust funds and investments
Library Holdings: Vols 7000; Per subs 10; AV — Fs 20, Kodachromes 10,000, lantern slides, slides 10,000; Other — Clipping files, exhibition catalogs, framed reproductions 10, original art works, pamphlets, photographs, prints, reproductions, sculpture
Special Subjects: Midwestern Glass and Ceramics
Publications: Bulletins; gallery brochures

OKLAHOMA

ANADARKO

M **NATIONAL HALL OF FAME FOR FAMOUS AMERICAN INDIANS,** PO Box 548, 73005. Tel 405-247-5555. *Dir & Exec VPres* Joe McBride; *Treas* George F Moran; *Secy* Carolyn N McBride
Open Mon - Sat 9 AM - 5PM, Sun 1 - 5 PM. No admis fee. Estab 1952 to honor famous American Indians who have contributed to the culture of America, including statesmen, innovators, sportsmen, warriors; to teach the youth of our country that there is a reward for greatness. An outdoor Museum in a landscaped area containing bronze sculptured portraits of honorees. Average Annual Attendance: 20,000. Mem: 250; dues life $100, Individual or Family $25; annual meeting Aug
Income: Finance by mem, city & state appropriation & donation
Purchases: $2500 - $20,000
Collections: †Bronze sculptured portraits & bronze statues of two animals important to Indian culture
Publications: Brochure
Activities: Dedication ceremonies for honorees in August; Sales shop sells books & postcards

M **SOUTHERN PLAINS INDIAN MUSEUM,** US Hwy 62, PO Box 749, 73005. Tel 405-247-6221. *Cur* Rosemary Ellison
Open June - Sept Mon - Sat 9 AM - 5 PM; Sun 1 - 5 PM; Oct - May Tues - Sat 9 AM - 5 PM, Sun 1 - 5 PM; cl New Year's Day, Thanksgiving & Christmas. No admis fee. Estab 1947-48 to promote the development of contemporary native American arts and crafts of the United States. Administered and operated by the Indian Arts and Crafts Board, US Department of the Interior. Average Annual Attendance: 80,000
Income: Financed by federal appropriation
Purchases: Primarily dependent upon gifts
Collections: Contemporary native American arts and crafts of the United States; Historic Works by Southern Plains Indian Craftsmen
Exhibitions: Contemporary Southern Plains Indian Metalwork; continuing series of one-person exhibitions; changing exhibitions by contemporary native American artists and craftsmen; Historic Southern Plains Indian Arts
Publications: One-person exhibition brochure series, monthly during Fall & Winter
Activities: Gallery talks; traveling exhibitions organized and circulated

ARDMORE

A **CHARLES B GODDARD CENTER FOR THE VISUAL AND PERFORMING ARTS,** First & D St SW, PO Box 1624, 73402. Tel 405-226-0909. *Chmn* Regina Turrentine; *Treas* John Snodgrass; *Dir* Mort Hamilton
Open Mon - Fri 9 AM -4 PM, Sat & Sun 1 - 4 PM. No admis fee. Estab March 1970 to bring fine art programs in the related fields of music, art and films to local community at minimum cost; gallery to bring traveling exhibitions to Ardmore. Four exhibit galleries. Average Annual Attendance: 35,000. Mem: 400; dues $10-$1000; monthly advisory board meetings, & monthly primary board meeting
Income: $200,000
Collections: †Western & Contemporary Art, paintings, sculpture, prints; †Small collection of Western Art & bronzes; †American Graphic Art; †photography
Exhibitions: Ardmore Art Exhibition
Publications: Outlook, bi-monthly
Activities: Classes for adults & children in dancing, art; docent training; dramatic programs; lect open to the public, 5 vis lectr per yr; concerts; gallery talks; competitions with awards; tours; individual paintings & original objects of art lent to qualified institutions-museums

BARTLESVILLE

M **FRANK PHILLIPS FOUNDATION INC,** Woolaroc Museum, State Hwy 123, Route 3, 74003. Tel 918-336-0307; FAX 918-336-0084. *Dir* Robert R Lansdown; *Cur Art* Linda Stonelaws; *Cur Coll* Ken Meek
Open Tues - Sun 10 AM - 5 PM, cl Mon, Thanksgiving & Christmas. Admis 16 & older $2, children under 16 free. Estab 1929 to house art and artifacts of the Southwest. Museum dedicated by Frank Phillips. Gallery has two levels, 8 rooms upstairs and 4 rooms downstairs. Average Annual Attendance: 200,000
Income: Financed by endowment & revenues generated by admission fees & sales
Collections: American Indian artifacts; prehistoric artifacts; paintings, drawings, graphics, minerals, oriental material, sculpture, weapons
Exhibitions: (1993) Blanket Exhibit
Publications: Woolaroc Story; Woolaroc, museum guidebook
Activities: Gallery talks; tours; lending collection contains transparencies to be used to illustrate educational publications; book traveling exhibitions; museum & sales shops sell books, magazines, original art, reproductions, prints, slides, Indian-made jewelry and pottery, postcards
L **Library,** State Hwy 123, Route 3, 74003. Tel 918-336-0307; FAX 918-336-0084. *Dir* Robert R Lansdown
Circ Reference library open to employees only
Library Holdings: Vols 1000; AV — Kodachromes, slides; Other — Clipping files, exhibition catalogs, pamphlets, photographs

CLAREMORE

M **WILL ROGERS MEMORIAL AND MUSEUM,** W Will Rogers Blvd, PO Box 157, 74018. Tel 918-341-0719; FAX 918-341-8246. *Dir* Joseph Carter; *Cur* Gregory Malak
Open daily 8 AM - 5 PM. No Admis Fee donations accepted. Estab 1938 to perpetuate the name, works, and spirit of Will Rogers. There are three main galleries, diorama room, foyer and gardens. The large Jo Davidson statue of Will Rogers dominates the foyer; the north gallery includes photographs and paintings of Will Rogers and his ancestors (including a family tree, explaining his Indian heritage), and many other personal items; east gallery has saddle collection and other Western items; Jo Mora dioramas; additional gallery, research library and theatre. Average Annual Attendance: 350,000
Income: $300,000 (financed by state appropriation)
Collections: Borein Etchings; Bust by Electra Wagoner Biggs; Collections of Paintings by Various Artists commissioned by a calendar company with originals donated to Memorial; Count Tamburini Oil of Will Rogers; Jo Mora Dioramas (13); Large Equestrian Statue by Electra Wagoner Biggs; Mural by Ray Piercey; Original of Will Rogers by Leyendecker; Paintings of Will and his Parents by Local Artists; original of Will Rogers by Charles Banks Wilson
Publications: Brochures and materials for students
Activities: Lect; films; assist with publishing project of Will Rogers works at Oklahoma State University; lending collection contains motion pictures, 50 photographs, 144 slides, 20 minute documentary of Will Rogers available to non-profit organizations; originate traveling exhibitions; museum shop selling books, magazines, reproductions of orginial photographs in sepiatone, slides, VHS tapes, Will Rogers & Oklahoma items
L **Media Center Library,** 1720 W Will Rogers Blvd, PO Box 157, 74018-0157. Tel 918-341-0719; FAX 918-341-8246; WATS 800-324-9455. *Dir* Joseph Carter; *Librn* Patricia Lowe; *Cur* Greg Malak
Reference library for research by appointment only
Library Holdings: Vols 2500; Per subs 15; original writings; AV — A-tapes, cassettes, fs, Kodachromes, motion pictures, rec, slides, v-tapes; Other — Clipping files, framed reproductions, manuscripts, memorabilia, original art works, pamphlets, photographs, prints, reproductions, sculpture
Collections: Will Rogers Collection

ENID

M **PHILLIPS UNIVERSITY,** Grace Phillips Johnson Art Gallery, University Station, PO Box 2000, 73702. Tel 405-237-4433. *Cur Dir* Prof Mary Phillips
Open Tues - Fri 10 AM - 5 PM; Sat, Sun & holidays by appointment only, cl national holidays. No admis fee. Estab 1966
Collections: Decorative arts; historical material of the University; paintings, prints, sculpture
Exhibitions: Exhibitions from the collection; traveling exhibitions
Publications: Exhibition catalogs, bi-annual
Activities: Lect open to the public, 2 vis lectr per year; concerts; gallery talks; book traveling exhibitions

GOODWELL

M **NO MAN'S LAND HISTORICAL SOCIETY MUSEUM,** Sewell St, PO Box 278, 73939. Tel 405-349-2670. *Pres* Henry C Hitch, Jr; *VPres* Gerald Dixon; *Museum Dir* Dr Harold S Kachel; *Cur & Secy* Joan Overton Kachel
Open Tues - Fri 9 AM - 5 PM, Sun 1 - 5 PM; cl Mon, Sat & holidays. No admis fee. Estab 1934 to procure appropriate museum material with special regard to portraying the history of No Man's Land (Oklahoma Panhandle) and the immediate adjacent regions. The gallery is 14 ft x 40 ft (560 sq ft). Average Annual Attendance: 4000. Mem: 59; dues life $100, organization $10, individual $10
Income: Financed by state appropriation and donations
Collections: Duckett Alabaster Carvings; Oils by Pearl Robison Burrows Burns
Exhibitions: Nine exhibits each year by local artists; six exhibits by local craftsmen each year
Activities: Lect open to public, 2 vis lectr per year; gallery talks; tours

LANGSTON

M **LANGSTON UNIVERSITY,** Melvin B Tolson Black Heritage Center, PO Box 907, 73050. Tel 405-466-2231. *Dir Library* Alberta Mayberry; *Cur* Ronald L Keyes
Open Mon - Fri 8 AM - 5 PM. No admis fee. Estab 1959 to exhibit pertinent works of art, both contemporary and traditional; to serve as a teaching tool for students. Average Annual Attendance: 6000
Income: Financed by state appropriation
Collections: African American Art & Artifacts; Paintings & Photographs
Activities: Classes for adults; lect, 2 vis lectr per year; gallery talks; tours

LAWTON

M **INSTITUTE OF THE GREAT PLAINS,** Museum of the Great Plains, 601 Ferris, PO Box 68, 73502. Tel 405-581-3460. *Dir* Steve Wilson; *Achaeologist* Joe Anderson; *Cur Anthropology* Joe Hayes; *Photo Lab Technician* Brian Smith; *Cur Spec Coll* Debby Baroff
Open Mon - Fri 8 AM - 5 PM, Sat 10 AM - 5:30 PM, Sun 1:30 - 5:30 PM. Estab 1961 to collect, preserve, interpret and exhibit items of the cultural history of man in the Great Plains of North America. Galleries of the Museum of the Great Plains express a regional concept of interpreting the relationship of man to a semi-arid plains environment. Average Annual Attendance: 90,000. Mem: 700; dues $15
Income: Financed by endowment, city and state appropriations
Collections: Archaeological, ethnological, historical and natural science collections relating to man's inhabitance of the Great Plains; photographs relating to Plains Indians, agriculture, settlement, ranching
Exhibitions: History, archaeology & ethnological exhibits
Publications: Great Plains Journal, annual; Contributions to the Museum of the Great Plains 1-9, irregular; Museum Newsletter, irregular
Activities: Classes for children; dramatic programs; docent training; lect open to public, 6 vis lectr per year; gallery talks; museum shop selling books, magazines, original art, reproductions, prints
L **Research Library,** PO Box 68, 73502. Tel 405-581-3460. *Cur Spec Coll* Deborah Baroff
Open Mon - Fri 8 AM - 5 PM. Estab 1961 to provide research materials for the 10-state Great Plains region. Lending to staff only
Income: Financed by endowment, city and state appropriations
Library Holdings: Vols 22,000; Per subs 100; Documents 300,000; Micro — Reels; Other — Photographs 22,000
Special Subjects: Archaeology, Anthropology
Collections: Archives; photographic collections
Publications: Great Plains Journal, annual; Museum of the Great Plains Newsletter, irregularly

MUSKOGEE

M **ATALOA LODGE MUSEUM** (Formerly Bacone College Museum), 2299 Old Bacone Rd, 74403-1797. Tel 918-683-4581, Ext 283; FAX 918-683-4588. *Dir* Thomas R McKinney
Open Mon - Fri 10 AM - 4:30 PM. No admis fee. Estab to enhance Indian culture by having a collection of artifacts from various Indian tribes. Three large rooms. Average Annual Attendance: 2000
Income: Financed through Bacone College
Collections: Indian crafts and artifacts: silverwork, weapons, blankets, dolls, beadwork, pottery, weaving and basketry; Indian Art
Activities: Tours; Sales shop sells books, magazines, original art, reporductions, prints, ceramics, beadwork, silver smithing work, baskets & handcrafted items

M **FIVE CIVILIZED TRIBES MUSEUM,** Agency Hill, Honor Heights Dr, 74401. Tel 918-683-1701. *Pres* W S Warner Jr; *Dir* Dianne S Haralson
Open Mon - Sat 10 AM - 5 PM, Sun 1 - 5 PM. Admis adults $2, senior citizens $1.75, students $1, children under 6 free. Estab 1966 to exhibit artifacts, relics, history, and traditional Indian art of the Cherokee, Chickasaw, Choctaw, Creek, and Seminole Indian Tribes. Average Annual Attendance: 50,000. Mem: 1000; dues vary; annual meeting in Dec
Income: $48,000 (financed by mem & admissions)
Collections: †Traditional Indian art by known artists of Five Tribes heritage, including original paintings & sculpture; large collection of Jerome Tiger originals
Exhibitions: Four Annual Judged Exhibitions & Sale of Beadwork, Pottery, Basketry & Silver; Competitive Art Show; Students Competitive Show; Craft Competition & Masters' Exhibition
Publications: Newsletter, 4 times a year
Activities: Gallery talks; tours; competitions with awards; museum shop selling books, original art, reproductions, prints, beadwork, pottery, basketry and other handmade items
L **Library,** Agency Hill, Honor Heights Dr, 74401. Tel 918-683-1701. *Dir* Dianne Haralson
Open Mon - Sat 10 AM - 5 PM, Sun 1 - 5 PM by appointment only. Estab 1966 to preserve history, culture, traditions, legends, etc of Five Civilized Tribes (Cherokee, Creek, Choctaw, Chickasaw, and Seminole tribes). Maintains an art gallery
Income: Financed by museum
Library Holdings: Vols 3500; Per subs 5; original documents; AV — Cassettes, lantern slides; Other — Clipping files, exhibition catalogs, framed reproductions, manuscripts, memorabilia, original art works, pamphlets, photographs, prints, reproductions, sculpture
Publications: Newsletter, every three months

NORMAN

M **FIREHOUSE ART CENTER,** 444 S Flood, 73069. Tel 405-329-4523. *Exec Dir* Nancy McClellan
Open Mon - Fri 9 AM - 5 PM, Sat 10 AM - 4 PM. Estab 1971. 7-8 exhibits per year of contemporary work by local, state, regional & national artists. Average Annual Attendance: 5000. Mem: 350; dues family $25; annual meeting in Aug
Income: $60,000 (financed by mem, city & state appropriation, grants, donations, fundraising)
Exhibitions: (1991) Biennial photo competition; Anniversary Show
Activities: Classes for adults & children; lect open to public, 2 vis lectr per year; competitions; scholarships & fels offered; retail store sells original art

UNIVERSITY OF OKLAHOMA

M **Fred Jones Jr Museum of Art,** 410 W Boyd St, 73019. Tel 405-325-3272; FAX 405-325-7696. *Dir* Thomas R Toperzer; *Asst Dir* Edwin J Deighton; *Museum Educator* Susan G Baley; *Preparator* T Ashley McGrew; *Registrar* Gail Anderson; *Public Information Officer* Jill Johnson
Open Tues - Fri 10 AM - 4:30 PM, Thurs 10 AM - 9 PM, Sat & Sun 1 - 4:30 PM, cl Mon. Estab 1936 to provide cultural enrichment for the people of Oklahoma; to collect, preserve, exhibit and provide research in art of all significant periods. Approx 15,000 sq ft for permanent and temporary exhibitions on two indoor levels;. Average Annual Attendance: 50,000. Mem: 360; dues $15 - $100; meetings Sept & Jan
Income: Financed by university allocation, foundation endowment & Board of Visitors
Purchases: Focus upon contemporary art
Collections: African sculpture; †American all media; Asian; †crafts; European all media; oceanic art; †photography
Exhibitions: Wayne Thiebuad: Works on Paper 1947-1987; Bruce Goff: Toward Absolute Architecture; The New Expeditionary Photographers; The best of Times: Intimate American Paintings From the Turn of the Century; Carolyn Brady: Watercolors; New Work: Joseph Glasco; University of Oklahoma Art Faculty & Graduate Student Centennial Exhibition; 76th Annual Art Students' Exhibition; R E Gillet: March of the Forgotten; Anton Henning: New Work; Joe Andoe: New Work; Edward Knippers: Violence & Grace; Alumni Collects; Oscar B Jacobson: Oklahoma Painter; Lines of Vision: Drawings by Contemporary Women; 77th Annual Art Student's Exhibition Francesco Clemente: Departure of the Argonaut; In Context: Georgia O'Keeffe; US Biennial III: A National Photo Exhibition; Dr Seuss: From Then to Now; Robert Colescott: A Retrospective; New Work: Rodney Carswell; Ellsworth Kelly: A Print Retro; New Work: Tom Berg; Frank Stella: The Circuits Prints
Publications: Calender of activities; posters; announcements; exhibition catalogues
Activities: Docent training; lect open to public; concerts; gallery talks; tours; competitions; individual paintings and original objects of art lent to other museums and galleries; lending collection contains original art works and prints, paintings; museum shop selling books, magazines, original art, slides
L **Architecture Library,** Gould Hall, 73019. Tel 405-325-5521. *Library Technician* Ilse Davis
Library Holdings: Vols 16,200; Per subs 48
Special Subjects: Architecture, Interior Design, Landscape Architecture, Urban & Environmental Design
L **Fine Arts Library,** Catlett Music Center, Room 007, 73019. Tel 405-325-4243; FAX 405-325-7618. *Fine Arts Librn* Jan E Seifert
Open Mon - Thurs 8 AM - 10 PM, Fri 8 AM - 5 PM, Sat 10 AM - 5 PM, Sun 1 - 10 PM. Estab to provide instructional support to the academic community of the university and general service to the people of the state. Circ 6900
Income: Financed by state appropriation
Library Holdings: Vols 27,000; Per subs 50; Micro — Fiche, reels; AV — V-tapes

OKLAHOMA CITY

M **INDIVIDUAL ARTISTS OF OKLAHOMA,** 2850 NW 63rd, PO Box 60824, 73146. Tel 405-843-3441. *Dir* Michael Freed
Open Tues - Sat noon - 5 PM. No admis fee. Estab 1979 to promote Oklahoma artists of all disciplines. Average Annual Attendance: 3500. Mem: 400; dues $20; annual meeting in spring
Income: Financed by membership, state arts council & fundraising
Exhibitions: Monthly exhibits of Oklahoma artists plus a traveling exhibit
Publications: IAO Newsletter, quarterly
Activities: Lect open to public, 6 vis lectr per year; competitions; traveling exhibitions, 1 per yr; originate traveling exhibition, 1 per yr

M **NATIONAL COWBOY HALL OF FAME AND WESTERN HERITAGE CENTER,** 1700 NE 63rd St, 73111. Tel 405-478-2250; FAX 405-478-4714. *Exec Dir* B Byron Price; *Asst Dir* Bobby Weaver; *Art Dir* Ed Muno; *Coll Cur* Don Reeves
Open daily 8:30 AM - 6 PM summer; 9 AM - 5 PM winter, cl New Year's Day, Thanksgiving & Christmas Day. Admis adults $5, senior citizens $4, children 6 - 12 $2 , group rates available. Estab 1957, opened 1965 to preserve the American Western Heritage through art & artifacts. Museum includes western history and art. Average Annual Attendance: 200,000. Mem: 2000; dues $35
Income: Financed by membership
Collections: Albert K Mitchell Russell-Remington Collection; †Contemporary Western Art; Fechin Collection; Schreyvogel Collection; Taos Collection; John Wayne Collection, kachinas, guns, knives & art; western art; James Earle & Laura G Fraser Studio Collection; Great Western Performers Portrait Collection; Rodeo Portrait Collection
Exhibitions: Annual National Academy of Western Art & Western Heritage Awards. (1993) Fort Marion Experience: Beyond the Prison Gates; National Academy of Western Art Exhibit
Publications: Persimmon Hill Magazine, quarterly
Activities: Lectures open to public, 5 vis lectrs per yr; concerts; gallery talks; tours; competitions with prizes; Western Heritage Awards in Apr; Rodeo Hall of Fame Inductions in Dec; originate traveling exhibitions, circulated to requesting agencies, universities, museums, galleries; gift shop sells books, magazines, reproductions & prints

M **Museum,** 1700 NE 63rd St, 73111. Tel 405-478-2250. *Executive Dir* B Byron Price
Open 8:30 AM - 6 PM, May - Sept, 9 AM - 5 PM Sept - May. Admis: adults $4, sr citizens $3, children 6-12 $1.50. Estab 1965 to interpret the heritage of the American west. Four permanent and two temporary galleries. Average Annual Attendance: 200,000. Mem: 3800; annual dues $35
Income: Financed by private donation
Library Holdings: Vols 10,000; Per subs 75; Other — Exhibition catalogs, manuscripts, pamphlets, photographs, reproductions
Collections: Historical Western Art; Contemporary Western Art
Publications: Persimmon Hill, quarterly magazine
Activities: Lectures open to the public, 4 vis lectr per yr; gallery talks; tours; sponsor competitions; award; Individual paintings and original objects of art lent to qualifying institutions; lending collections contain 100 original art works, 100 original paints & 100 original sculptures; Museum shop sells books, magazines, reproductions, prints and slides

M **OKLAHOMA CENTER FOR SCIENCE AND ART,** Kirkpatrick Center, 2100 NE 52nd, 73111. Tel 405-424-5545 (Omniplex); 427-5461 (Kirkpatrick Center); 427-5461 (Air Space Museum). *Exec Dir* Billy Bowden; *Cur* Linda Raulston; *Coordr Indian Gallery* Terri Cummings; *Coordr Sanamu African Gallery* Bruce Fisher; *Coordr Photography Hall Fame* Michael Harris; *Dir Omniplex* Marilyn Rippee; *Dir Air Space Museum* Don Finch
Open Mon - Sat 9 AM - 5 PM, Sun noon - 5 PM. Admis adults $5, children & sr citizens $3, one price for entire center. Estab 1958 to focus on the interrelationships between science, arts and the humanities and to supplement educational facilities offered in the public schools in the areas of arts and sciences. The Kirkpatrick Center houses Omniplex, a hands-on science museum; museum shop; George Sutton bird paintings; Oklahoma Aviation and Space Hall of Fame and Museum; Center of American Indian Gallery; Sanamu African Gallery; Oriental Art Gallery; International Photography Hall of Fame; Oklahoma Zoological Society Offices; Kirkpatrick Planetarium; miniature Victorian house; antique clocks; US Navy Gallery; retired sr volunteer program; Oklahoma City Zoo offices. Average Annual Attendance: 350,000
Income: Financed by membership, private donations, Allied Arts Foundation, admission fees, and class tuition
Collections: European and Oriental Ivory Sculpture; Japanese Woodblock Prints; Oceanic art; Pre-Columbian and American Indian art; Sutton paintings; Traditional and Contemporary African art; 1,000 photographs in Photography Hall of Fame
Exhibitions: Changing exhibitions every six to ten weeks
Publications: Insights, quarterly; Omniplex Newsletter, monthly
Activities: Classes for adults and children; docent training; lect open to public; tours; book traveling exhibitions; museum shop sells books, prints, science related material, cards & jewelry

M **OKLAHOMA CITY ART MUSEUM,** 3113 Pershing Blvd, 73107. Tel 405-946-4477; FAX 405-946-7671. *Dir* Jean Cassels Hagman; *Asst Cur* Alyson B Stanfield; *Cur Educ* Doris McGranahan; *Dir Public Relations & Marketing* Shauna Lawyer; *Asst to Dir* Susie Bauer; *Membership & Museum Store* Jackie Meeks; *Preparator* Jim Meeks; *Registrar* Jayne Hazleton; *Adminr* Karen Eckstein; *Development Asst* Adrien Werts
Open Tues, Wed, Fri & Sat 10 AM - 5 PM, Thurs 10 AM - 8PM, cl Mon & major holidays. Admis adults $3.50, students & sr citizens $2.50, children under 12 & members free. Estab 1989 with the merger of the Oklahoma Art Center & the Oklahoma Museum of Art. Permanent collection exhibited in upper galleries. Average Annual Attendance: 35,000. Mem: 1300; dues $25 - $5000; annual meeting in June
Income: Financed by membership, private contributions, grants & earned income
Collections: †19th - 20th century European & American paintings including works by Bellows, Tiffany, Chase, Cropsey, Benton, Moran, Hassam; †19th - 20th century French paintings & sculpture including works by Courbet, Michel, Boudin, Jacques, Lacroix de Marseilles; Harpignies; †20th century American paintings & graphics, including: Henri Marin, Kelly, Indiana, Francis, Davis, Warhol; American Sculpture by Bertoia, Bonlecon, Calder
Exhibitions: Ongoing: selections from the permanent collection of European & American painting; The Rowdy London of William Hogarth; The Rodin Bronzes: Sculpture from The B Gerald Cantor Collections; Metaphors & Realities in Contemporary Hungarian Art; French Paintings of Three Centuries from the New Orleans Museum of Art; 18th century British Engravings after Claude Lorrain; Matisse's Secret: Kuba Textiles from Zaire; Edward Steichen: The Early Years, 1900 - 1927. (1993) Familiar Faces: Portraits from the Permanent Collection; Selected American Paintings from the Daywood Collection, Huntington Museum of Art
Publications: Calendar, bi-monthly, exhibition catalogs, posters
Activities: Studio classes for children; fine arts & crafts fairs; dramatic programs; docent training; lect open to public, 10 vis lectrs per yr; concerts; gallery talks; tours; films; individual paintings & original objects of art lent to other museums; book traveling exhibitions 4 - 6 per year; originate traveling exhibitions; museum shop sells books, magazines, reproductions, prints, original art, jewelry

L **Library,** 3113 Pershing Blvd, 73107. Tel 405-946-4477. *Dir* Jean Hagman; *Dir Public Relations* Shauna Lawyer; *Cur* Alyson B Stanfield; *Cur Educ* Doris McGravahan; *Business Mgr* Karen Eckstein
Open Mon - Sat 10 AM - 5 PM, Thurs until 8 PM, Sun 1 - 5 PM. General admis $3.50, sr citizens & students $2.50, children 12 & under free. Estab 1989 to bring a quality fine arts museum & related educational progamming to Oklahoma. Library for reference only. Average Annual Attendance: 20,000. Mem: 1500
Income: Non-profit organization financed through private contribution
Library Holdings: Vols 2000; Per subs 15; Other — Clipping files, exhibition catalogs
Special Subjects: Medieval Art, 19th Century French & American Paintings & Sculpture

M **OKLAHOMA CITY UNIVERSITY,** Hulsey Gallery-Norick Art Center, 2501 N Blackwelder, 73106. Tel 405-521-5226; FAX 405-521-5264. *Dir* Brunel Faris; *Admin Asst* Maria Amos
Open Mon - Fri 10 AM - 4 PM, Sat & Sun 1 - 5 PM. Admis free. Estab 1904 to educ in the arts. Gallery is 2200 sq ft with fabric covered walls & moveable display forms. Average Annual Attendance: 2000. Mem: 140
Income: Financed by endowment, membership & the University
Collections: †Oklahoma City University Art Collection; Art donated by individuals & organizations from Oklahoma
Exhibitions: Oklahoma City University Student Exhibit; Oklahoma High School Print & Drawing Exhibit; Annual exhibits change monthly
Publications: NAC Notes, quarterly; DepARTures, bi-annually
Activities: Classes for adults & children; dramatic programs; docent training; lectures open to the public, 2-3 vis lectr per yr; scholarships offered; individual/paintings & original works of art lent to various departments of the Oklahoma City University campus; sales shop sells books, magazines

L **Linda Garrett Reference Library,** 2501 N Blackwelder, 73106. Tel 405-521-5226.
For lending & reference
Income: Financed by endowment, donation & University
Library Holdings: Vols 207; AV — V-tapes; Other — Exhibition catalogs, original art works, photographs, prints, reproductions, sculpture

M **OKLAHOMA HISTORICAL SOCIETY,** State Museum of History, Wiley Post Historical Bldg, 2100 N Lincoln Blvd, 73105. Tel 405-521-2491; FAX 405-525-3272. *Pres Board Trustees* Martin A Hagerstrand; *Exec Dir* J Blake Wade; *Publications* Mary Blochowiak; *Museums Division* Kathy Dickson; *Historical Sites* John R Hill; *Library Resources* Ed Shoemaker; *Preservation Dir* Melvena Heisch; *State Museum Dir* Bill Pitts; *Indian Archives & Manuscripts* William Welge
Open Mon - Sat 8 AM - 5 PM, cl State holidays. No admis fee. Estab 1893 to provide an historical overview of the State of Oklahoma, from prehistory to the present, through interpretive exhibits, three dimensional artifacts, original art & photographs. Average Annual Attendance: 150,000. Mem: 3500; dues $15; annual meeting Apr
Income: Financed by state appropriations and membership; Society depends on donations for additions to its collections
Collections: Anthropology; archaeology; historical artifacts; documents; American Indian art; Oklahoma art; Western art
Exhibitions: Permanent exhibits depicting pre-history, Oklahoma Indian Tribes' history, the Five Civilized Tribes' occupancy of Indian Territory, the land openings of the late 19th and early 20th centuries, statehood, and progress since statehood; special exhibits 2-3 times per yr
Publications: Mistletoe Leaves, monthly newsletter; The Chronicles of Oklahoma, Society quarterly; various brochures and reprints
Activities: Special presentations and films for children & adults; interpretive programs; self-guided tours; individual paintings & original objects of art lent to qualified museums; lending collection contains paintings, 19th century beadwork & Indian artifacts; originate traveling exhibitions; sales shop sells books, magazines

L **Library Resources Division,** 2100 N Lincoln Blvd, 73105. Tel 405-521-2491; FAX 405-525-3272. *Dir Library Resources Div* Edward C Shoemaker
Open Tues - Sat 9 AM - 5 PM, Mon 9 AM - 8 PM. Estab 1893 to collect & preserve historical materials & publications on Oklahoma history. For reference only
Library Holdings: Vols 61,305; Per subs 80; Micro — Fiche, reels 12,493; Other — Clipping files, manuscripts, pamphlets, photographs
Special Subjects: American Indian Art, American Western Art, Ethnology, Historical Material, Maps, American Indian, Genealogy, Oklahoma & Indian Territories, The West
Publications: Chronicles of Oklahoma, quarterly; Mistletoe Leaves, monthly newsletter

OKMULGEE

M **CREEK COUNCIL HOUSE MUSEUM,** Town Square, 74447. Tel 918-756-2324. *Dir* Tommy A Steinsiek
Open Tues - Sat 9 AM - 5 PM. No admis fee. Estab 1867, first Council House built, present Council House erected in1878 to collect and preserve artifacts from Creek history. Five rooms downstairs containing artifacts; four rooms upstairs showing art work, early time of Okmulgee; rooms of House of Warriors and House of Kings. Average Annual Attendance: 8000-10,000
Income: Financed by membership and city appropriation
Collections: †Creek Artifacts
Exhibitions: Annual Oklahoma Indian Art Market (juried competitions)
Activities: Seminars on Creek Culture and history; Annual Wild Onion Feast (traditional tribal foods); lectures open to public, 5-10 per yr; gallery talks; artmobile; book traveling exhibitions; museum shop sells books, original art, reproductions, prints and Native American art and craft items

L **Library,** Town Square, 74447. Tel 918-756-2324. *Project Dir* Annette B Fromm
Open Tues - Fri 9 AM - 5 PM. Estab to collect Creek and related books and documents for research and historical purposes. For reference only
Library Holdings: Vols 250; Per subs 10; Micro — Reels; AV — A-tapes, motion pictures; Other — Clipping files, exhibition catalogs, framed reproductions, manuscripts, memorabilia, original art works, pamphlets, photographs, prints, sculpture

PONCA CITY

A **PONCA CITY ART ASSOCIATION,** 819 E Central, PO BPox 1394, 74601. Tel 405-765-9746. *Office Mgr* Donna Secrest
Open Wed - Sun 1 - 5 PM. No admis fee. Estab 1947 to encourage creative arts, to furnish place and sponsor art classes, art exhibits and workshops. Mem: 600; dues $10 family; annual meeting third Tues in April
Income: $10,000 (financed by membership and flea market)
Collections: Permanent fine arts collection; additions by purchases and donations
Exhibitions: Eight per year
Publications: Association Bulletin, 6 per yr
Activities: Classes for adults and children; lectures open to public; tours; competitions for members only with awards; scholarships offered; individual paintings lent to city-owned buildings; sales shop sells original art, reproductions and prints

M PONCA CITY CULTURAL CENTER & MUSEUM, 1000 E Grand Ave, 74601. Tel 405-767-0427. *Dir* La Wanda French
Open Mon, Wed - Sat 10 AM - 5 PM, Sun and holidays 1 - 5 PM; cl Tues, Thanksgiving, Christmas Eve and Christmas Day, New Year's Eve and New Year's Day. Admis adults $1. The Cultural Center & Museum, a National Historic House since 1976, houses the Indian Museum, the Bryant Baker Studio, the 101 Ranch Room, and the DAR Memorial Museum. The Indian Museum, established in 1936, places an emphasis on materials from the five neighboring tribes (Ponca, Kaw, Otoe, Osage, and Tonkawa) whose artistic use of beading, fingerweaving and ribbon-work are displayed throughout the Museum. The Bryant Baker Studio is a replica of the New York Studio of Bryant Baker, sculptor of the Pioneer Woman Statue, a local landmark, and the studio contains original bronze and plaster sculpture. The 101 Ranch Room exhibits memorabilia from the world renowned Miller Brothers' 101 Ranch, located south of Ponca City in the early 1900s. The Museum is the former home of Ernest Whitworth Marland, oilman and philanthropist, and the tenth governor of Oklahoma. Average Annual Attendance: 25,000
Income: Financed by the City of Ponca City and donations
Collections: Bryant Baker original sculpture; 101 Ranch memorabilia; Indian ethnography and archeology of Indian tribes throughout the United States
Exhibitions: Smithsonian Indian Images; Indian costumes, jewelry, pottery, baskets, musical instruments & tools. (1993) Native American Games
Publications: Brochure
Activities: Tours; sales shop selling books, arrowheads, Indian arts and crafts
L Library, 1000 E Grand Ave, 74601. Tel 405-767-0427. *Dir* La Wanda French; *Asst* Roberta Gartrell
Open Mon, Wed, Thurs, Fri, Sat 10 AM - 5 PM, Sun 1 - 5 PM, cl Tues. Primarily research library
Income: Financed by Ponca City
Library Holdings: Vols 230; Per subs 13
Special Subjects: Anthropology, Archaeology, Indian art

L PONCA CITY LIBRARY, Art Dept, 515 E Grand, 74601. Tel 405-767-0345. *Dir* Steve Skidmore; *Head Public Servs* Holly LaBossiere; *Head Technical Servs* Judi Anderson
Open Mon - Thurs 9 AM - 9 PM, Fri & Sat 9 AM - 5 PM, cl Sun. Estab 1904 to serve the citizens of Ponca City. Gallery maintained. Circ 150,000
Library Holdings: AV — Cassettes; Other — Framed reproductions, original art works, pamphlets, photographs, sculpture
Collections: Oriental Art Collection; Sandzen Collection; paintings

SHAWNEE

M SAINT GREGORY'S ABBEY AND COLLEGE, Mabee-Gerrer Museum of Art, 1900 W MacArthur Dr, 74801. Tel 405-878-5300; FAX 405-878-5198. *Dir* Bro Benedict, ASB; *Conservator* Bro Justin Jones, OSB; *Registrar* Melissa Strickland; *Coll Mgr* Bro Julian Cutler
Open daily 1 - 4 PM, cl Mon. No admis fee. Estab 1904 to contribute to the cultural growth and appreciation of the general public of Oklahoma as well as of the student body of Saint Gregory's College. A new 16,000 sq foot gallery was completed in 1979. In 1990 1500 sq ft was added which includes a new gallery, a multi- purpose room & theater. Collections are being enlarged by purchases and by gifts. Average Annual Attendance: 40,000
Income: Financed by endowment, Abbey, membership and foundation funds
Collections: Artifacts from ancient civilization; African, Eqyptian, Roman, Grecian, Babylonian, Pre-Columbian North, South and Central American Indian, and South Pacific; †etchings, †engravings, †serigraphs and †lithographs; †oil paintings by American and European artists; †Native American; Icons: Greek, Russian & Balkan; Retablos from Mexico & New Mexico
Activities: Classes for adults and children; docent training; lectures open to public, 4 vis lectr per yr; gallery talks; tours; individual paintings & original objects of art lent to other museums

STILLWATER

M OKLAHOMA STATE UNIVERSITY, Gardiner Art Gallery, Dept of Art, Bartlett Center of the Studio Arts, Morrill & Knoblock Sts, 74078-0120. Tel 405-744-9086; FAX 405-744-7074. *Dir* B J Smith
Open Mon - Fri 8 AM - 5 PM, Sun 1 - 5 PM. No admis fee. Estab 1970 as a visual and educational extension of the department's classes and as a cultural service to the community and area. One gallery located on the ground floor in new annex behind the renovated building. 250 running feet of wall space, 12 ft ceiling. Average Annual Attendance: 5000
Income: Financed by college
Collections: 200 prints, mostly post World War II
Exhibitions: Exhibitions changed every 3 - 4 weeks year round; faculty, student, invitational and traveling shows
Publications: Exhibition schedules, exhibition brochures
Activities: Book traveling exhibitions
L Architecture Library, 74078-0185. Tel 405-744-6047. *Architecture Librn* Teresa Anne Fehlig
Open fall & spring semesters Mon - Thurs 8 AM - 5 PM & 7 - 10 PM, Fri 8 AM - 5 PM, Sun 1 - 5 PM, summer hrs vary. Estab 1976 to meet the combined needs of the faculty & students of the School of Architecture
Purchases: $14,000
Library Holdings: Vols 11,267; Per subs 50; AV — Slides
Special Subjects: Underground Housing

TAHLEQUAH

A CHEROKEE NATIONAL HISTORICAL SOCIETY, INC, PO Box 515, 74465. Tel 918-456-6195. *Pres* Gary Chapman; *Admin* Myrna Moss; *Office Mgr* Debbie Duvall
Open Mon - Sat 10 AM - 5 PM, Sun 1 - 5 PM. Admis adult $2.50, children $1. 25. Estab 1963 to commemorate and portray the history, traditions and lore of a

great Indian tribe, and to assist in improving local economic conditions. Maintains an art gallery, primarily Indian art. Average Annual Attendance: 130,000. Mem: 1500; dues $25 and up
Income: Financed by membership, admissions and grants
Collections: Indian artists interpretations of Trails of Tears
Exhibitions: Trail of Tears Art Show, annually; Retrospective by famous Cherokee artist, annually; frequent one-artist shows
Publications: The Columns, quarterly
Activities: Lectures open to public; competitions with cash awards; museum shop sells books, reproductions, prints & slides
L Library, PO Box 515, 74465. *Librn* Tom Mooney
Open Mon - Sat 8 AM - 5 PM, Sun 1 - 5 PM. Estab 1976 to preserve remnants of Cherokee history and to educate the general public about that cultural heritage; a repository of Indian art and documents. Maintains an art gallery with work by artists of several different tribes; heavy emphasis given to the Cherokee experience
Income: Financed by membership, admissions and grants
Library Holdings: Vols 3000; Per subs 10; manuscripts; archival materials in excess of 500 cu ft; Micro — Reels 127; AV — A-tapes, cassettes, fs, Kodachromes, slides; Other — Clipping files, framed reproductions, manuscripts, memorabilia, original art works, pamphlets, photographs, prints, sculpture
Special Subjects: Cherokee history
Exhibitions: Annual Trail of Tears Art Show (Indian artists' interpretation of the Trail of Tears theme); Cherokee Artists Exhibition; rotating exhibitions; special exhibitions, periodically (primarily Indian artists)
Publications: Quaterly columns

TULSA

C BANK OF OKLAHOMA NA, Art Collection, PO Box 2300, 74192. Tel 918-588-6370. *Chmn Executive Committee* Leonard J Eaton
Open 8 AM - 5 PM. No admis fee. Estab 1968 to enhance work environment. Collection displayed on 7 floors of the Bank of Oklahoma Tower
Purchases: $15,000
Collections: Approximately 425 pieces of Modern Art
Activities: Lect; tours; scholarships offered to University of Tulsa

M GERSHON & REBECCA FENSTER MUSEUM OF JEWISH ART, 1223 E 17th Place, 74110. Tel 918-582-3732. *Exec Dir* Diana Aaronson
Open Tues - Fri 10 AM - 4 PM, Sun 1 - 4 PM. No admis fee. Estab 1966 to collect, preserve & interpret cultural, historical & aesthetic materials attesting to Jewish cultural history. Average Annual Attendance: 3000. Mem: 200; dues $35, annual meeting in Dec
Income: $45,000 (financed by endowment & mem)
Collections: Anti-semitica; archeology of old world; ethnographic materials; fine art by Jewish artists & on Jewish themes; ritual & ceremonial Judaica
Exhibitions: Permanent collections; quarterly exhibits
Publications: Fenster Museum News, quarterly
Activities: Classes for adults & children, docent training; lectures open to public; gallery talks; tours; individual paintings & original objects of art lent to other museums & religious institutions

M THOMAS GILCREASE INSTITUTE OF AMERICAN HISTORY & ART, 1400 Gilcrease Museum Rd, 74127. Tel 918-582-3122. *Dir* Fred A Myers; *Dir Public Relations* Paula Eliot
Open Mon - Sat 9 AM - 5 PM, Sun & holidays 1 - 5 PM, cl Christmas. No admis fee. Estab by the late Thomas Gilcrease as a private institution; acquired by the City of Tulsa 1954 (governed by a Board of Directors & City Park Board); building addition completed 1963 & 1987. Average Annual Attendance: 100,000. Mem: 1600; dues $15 and up
Income: Financed by city funds
Collections: American art from Colonial period to 20th century with emphasis on art of historical significance, sculpture, painting, graphics. Much of the work shown is of documentary nature, with emphasis on the Native American material & the opening of the Trans-Mississippi West. Art Collections include 10,000 paintings by 400 American artists; artifact collections include 250,000 objects including both prehistoric & historic materials from most of the Native American cultures in Middle & North America
Exhibitions: Special exhibitions periodically; rotating exhibits during fall, winter, spring seasons; Gilcrease Student Art Festival; Gilcrease Rendezvous
Publications: The Gilcrease Magazine, bi-annual
Activities: Film program; lect on art & history; gallery tours; lect to school groups outside the museum; museum shop
L Library, 1400 Gilcrease Museum Rd, 74127. Tel 918-582-3122; FAX 918-592-2248. *Cur Archival Colls* Sarah Erwin
Open daily, cl weekends & holidays. Library open for research by appointment, contains 90,000 books & documents, many rare books & manuscripts of the American discovery period, as well as materials concerning the Five Civilized Tribes
Income: Financed by city appropriation
Library Holdings: Vols 40,000; Per subs 10; Other — Exhibition catalogs, manuscripts, memorabilia, pamphlets, photographs
Special Subjects: Discovery & development of America; American Indian History

M PHILBROOK MUSEUM OF ART, 2727 S Rockford Rd, PO Box 52510, 74152-0510. Tel 918-749-7941; FAX 918-743-4230. *Dir* Marcia Manhart; *Dir Exhib & Coll* Christine Kallenberger; *Dir Annual Giving* Doris Frampton; *Hardman Cur* Richard Townsend; *Deputy Dir* David Singleton; *Dir Communications* Lynne Butterworth; *Museum Shop Mgr* M J Barbre; *Preparator* Charles Taylor; *Dir of Education* Jeannette Lawson; *Dir of Development* Chica Sanderson; *Facility Coordr* Charisse Cooper; *Museum School Dir* Norman Nilsen
Open Tues - Sat 10 AM - 5 PM, Thurs 10 AM - 8 PM, Sun 1 - 5 PM. Admis adults $3, college students and sr citizens $1.50, high school students and younger free. Estab 1939 as a general art museum in an Italian Renaissance Revival Villa, the former home of philanthropist & oil baron Waite Phillips. Twenty-three acres of formal and natural gardens. Also contains a special

exhibition gallery. Average Annual Attendance: 120,000. Mem: 4500; dues $25 and up; annual meeting April

Income: Financed by endowment, membership, earned income, corporate & private gifts & public grants

Collections: Laura A Clubb Collection of American & European Paintings; Clark Field Collection of American Indian Baskets and Pottery; Gillert Collection of Southeast Asian Ceramics; Gussman Collection of African Sculpture; Samuel H Kress Collection of Italian Renaissance Paintings and Sculpture; Roberta C Lawson Collection of Indian Costumes and Artifacts;Tabor Collection of Oriental Art; American Indian paintings and sculpture; European, early American and contemporary American oils, watercolors and prints; period furniture

Exhibitions: (1992) On the Road: Selections from the Permanent Collection of the San Diego Museum of Contemporary Art; Masterworks of American Impressionism from the Pfeil Collection; Goya's Disasters of War & The Proverbs; Objects & Drawings from the Sanford M & Diane Besser Collection. (1993) Paul Manship: Changing Taste in America; Baroque Gold & Jewelry from the Hungarian National Museum; From Elizabeth I to Elizabeth II: 400 Years of Drawing from the National Portrait Gallery, London; Glass from Ancient Craft to Contemporary Art: 1962 - 1992 & Beyond

Publications: Bi-monthly bulletin; exhibition catalogs

Activities: Classes for adults and children; dramatic programs; docent training; lects open to public, 27 vis lectr per year; concerts; gallery talks; tours; scholarships; individual and original objects of art lent to museums, corporations and city government; book traveling exhibitions, 3-5 per year; originate traveling exhibitions; museum shop sells books, magazines, original art, reproductions, prints, slides and gift items

L **Chapman Library,** 2727 S Rockford Rd, PO Box 52510, 74152. Tel 918-748-5306; FAX 918-743-4230. *Librn* Thomas E Young

Open Tues - Fri by appointment. Reference-resource center for the curatorial staff, teaching faculty, volunteers and membership

Library Holdings: Vols 10,000; Per subs 125; AV — Slides; Other — Clipping files, exhibition catalogs, pamphlets, reproductions

Special Subjects: American Indian Art, American Western Art, Decorative Arts, Folk Art, History of Art & Archaeology, Landscape Architecture, Oriental Art, Painting - American, Pre-Columbian Art, Southwestern Art, Painting - Italian, Photography, Pottery, Primitive Art, Prints, Sculpture

Collections: Roberta Campbell Lawson Library of source materials on American Indians

M **UNIVERSITY OF TULSA,** Alexandre Hogue Gallery, Art Dept, 600 S College Ave, 74104. Tel 918-631-2202; FAX 918-631-2033. *Dir* Thomas A Manhart

Open Mon - Fri 8:30 - 4:30 PM. No admis fee. Estab 1966 to display the works of regionally & nationally known artists. 176 running ft. Average Annual Attendance: 1000

Exhibitions: Annual Student Art Competition; National Scholastic Art Awards Scholarships & Competition

Activities: Lectures open to public, 6 vis lectrs per yr; competition with awards; scholarships offered; individual paintings & original objects of art lent

WOODWARD

M **PLAINS INDIANS & PIONEERS HISTORICAL FOUNDATION,** Museum & Art Center, 2009 Williams Ave, PO Box 1167, 73802. Tel 405-256-6136. *Dir & Cur* Frankie Herzer; *Admin Asst* Bwetty Semmel

Open Tues - Sat 10 AM - 5 PM, Sun 1 - 4 PM, cl Mon. No admis fee. Estab 1957 to preserve local history and to support visual arts. Average Annual Attendance: 15,000. Mem: 450; dues $15 - $500; annual meeting Nov

Income: Financed by membership and trust fund

Collections: Early day artifacts as well as Indian material

Exhibitions: Juried contests for high school students & photographers; Fine Arts, Creative Crafts (guest artist featured each month in the gallery)

Publications: Below Devil's Gap (historical book); brochures; quarterly newsletter; Oklahoma's Northwest Territory Map; Woodward County Pioneer Families, 1907-57 (2 volumes)

Activities: Classes for adults and children; docent training; lectures open to public, 3 vis lectr per year; tours; competitions with prizes; book traveling exhibitions, 3 per year; museum shop sells books, magazines, original art and prints & Northwest Okla artisans crafts

OREGON

ASHLAND

SOUTHERN OREGON STATE COLLEGE

M **Stevenson Union Gallery,** 1250 Siskiyou Blvd, 97520. Tel 503-552-6465; FAX 503-552-6440. *Dir* Phil Campbell; *Mgr* Doug Graneto

Open Mon - Thurs 8 AM - 7 PM, Fri 8 AM - 6 PM. No admis fee. Estab 1972 to offer college and community high quality arts. Located on the third floor of Stevenson Union, the gallery is about 1200 sq ft. Average Annual Attendance: 20,000

Income: Financed by student fees

Collections: Small permanent collection of prints, paintings by local artists and a sculpture by Bruce West

Exhibitions: Ceramics, paintings, photography, prints, sculpture, faculty & student work. Clinton Brown; Carol Setterland; Robert Wilson; Annual Student Art Show

Activities: Lectures open to public, 3 vis lectrs per yr; competitions

M **Central Art Gallery,** 97520. Tel 503-552-6386; FAX 503-552-6429. *Gallery Dir* Rick Martinez; *Chmn Dept Art* Margaret L Sjogren

Open Mon - Fri 8:30 AM - 5 PM

Income: Financed by Department of Art

Exhibitions: (1993) Exhibition of BFA Students; Sharon Boyer; Georgia Glennon; Jill Frank; Diana Muhs; Anthony Kerwin; Angelica Carpenter; Printmaking Class; Teresa Montgomery; Lizbeth Gieseler

ASTORIA

M **COLUMBIA RIVER MARITIME MUSEUM,** 1792 Marine Dr, 97103. Tel 503-325-2323; FAX 503-325-2331. *Exec Dir* Jerry Ostermiller

Open daily 9:30 AM - 5 PM, cl on Thanksgiving & Christmas. Admis adults $5, sr citizens $4, children $2, children under 6 free. Estab 1962 as a maritime museum, to collect, preserve & interpret maritime history of Pacific NW. Maintains seven galleries of nautical history including works of art. Average Annual Attendance: 97,000. Mem: 2000; dues $15; annual meeting in Oct

Income: $500,000 (financed by admissions, sales, memberships & individual & corporate donations)

Collections: †Maritime Paintings, †Prints & Photography; †Ship Models & †nautical artifacts; Lightship Columbia

Exhibitions: Rotating & temporary exhibit space in Great Hall; visiting vessels as available

Publications: The Quarterdeck, quarterly

Activities: Classes for adults; volunteer opportunities; docent training; lectures open to the public, 6 vis lectr per year; tours; competitions; outreach program to schools; individual paintings & original objects of art lent to accredited museums; Museum shop sells books, limited edition prints, posters, reproductions, contemporary scrimshaw & jewelry

L **Library,** 1792 Marine Dr, 97103. Tel 503-325-2323. *Cur* Anne Witty

Library for use on the premises; majority of contents are not relevant to art

Income: Financed by admissions, trusts, membership dues and donations

Library Holdings: Vols 6000; Per subs 196; AV — Cassettes, motion pictures; Other — Clipping files, exhibition catalogs, manuscripts, original art works, pamphlets, photographs, prints, reproductions

Special Subjects: Drafting, Historical Material, Maps, Marine Painting, Scrimshaw, Maritime & Pacific Northwest history, ship models

Publications: The Quarterdeck Review, quarterly

BANDON

NATIONAL COUNCIL ON EDUCATION FOR THE CERAMIC ARTS (NCECA)

For further information, see National and Regional Organizations

BEND

M **HIGH DESERT MUSEUM,** 59800 S Hwy 97, 97702-8933. Tel 503-382-4754; FAX 503-382-5256. *Pres* Donald M Kerr; *Dir of Operations* Jerry Moore; *Communications Dir* Jack Cooper; *Cur of Exhibits* Susan Harless

Open 9 AM - 5 PM. Admis adults $4.50, sr citizens $4, children between 6-12 $2.50. Estab 1974. Brooks Gallery, Spirit of the Southwest Gallery & Nancy R Chandler Memorial Gallery. Mem: 4185; dues $25 & up; annual meeting in Sept

Income: Financed by membership, donations & grants

Collections: Historical artifacts; Western art; wildlife sculpture, oils, watercolor, photography; Sherry Sandler, sculpture; Georgia Gerber, sculpture; Joe Halco, sculpture; Rod Frederick, prints; Philip Hyde, photography

Exhibitions: (1990-91) Birds in Art; art & artifacts of high desert history; high desert landscape photography

Activities: Classes for adults & children; docent programs; lectures open to the public, 8-10 vis lectr per yr; competitions with awards, The Earle A Chiles Award; book traveling exhibitions, 3 per yr; museum shop sells books, magazines, original art, reproductions, prints, kewelry, science toys, cards, apparel, folk arts & crafts

CHILOQUIN

AMERICAN TAPESTRY ALLIANCE

For further information, see National and Regional Organizations

COOS BAY

M **COOS ART MUSEUM,** 235 Anderson Ave, 97420-1610. Tel 503-267-3901. *Pres Board* Wineva Johnson; *1st VPres Board* Marianna Mattecheck; *Executive Dir* Larry Watson

Open Tues - Fri 11 AM - 5 PM, Sat & Sun 1 - 4 PM. Admis donations requested. Estab 1966 (relocated to an historic former Post Office Building in downtown district) to bring contemporary art to Southwestern Oregon through collections, exhibitions & educational programming. Five galleries with portable furniture walls. Average Annual Attendance: 15,000. Mem: 800; dues family $30, single $20; annual meeting first quarter of year

Income: $100,000 (financed by mem, fund raisers, memorials, contributions, endowments & grants)

Collections: †Contemporary American Printmakers; †paintings, †photographs, †sculpture

Exhibitions: Contemporary art, historic art, folk art & industrial art exhibitions which change approx every 2 months; Northwest Prints & Paintins Biennial; Public Hanging annually. (1992) Oregon Spotlight '92: Rick Bartow & Frank Boyden; Wild & Scenic Rivers of Oregon: Photographs by Larry N Olson; The Art of Haniwa: An Interpretive Vision; A Gathering of Angels. (1993) A Public Hanging; Museum Collection; Oregon: Crossroads on the Rim

Publications: Annual Museum Brochure; exhibit announcements, every 6 wks

Activities: Classes & workshops for adults & children; Artists-in-Education Program for public schools; dramatic programs; docent training; lect open to public, 6 vis lectr per yr; concerts; gallery talks; tours; scholarships; rental/sales gallery & museum gift shop sells books, original art prints, reproductions, prints, slides, Oregon handcrafted gift items & educational items

COQUILLE

A **COQUILLE VALLEY ART ASSOCIATION,** Myrtle Pt Hwy, 97423. Tel 503-396-3294. *Pres* Anna Crosby; *VPres* Katherine Castello; *Treas* Savannah Bentcourt
Open Tues - Sun 1 - 4 PM, cl Mon & holidays. No admis fee. Estab 1950 to teach art and art appreciation. Gallery maintained on main floor of Art Association owned old refurbished schoolhouse. Mem: 220; dues $15, sr citizens $12; annual meetings first Wed in April
Income: Financed by membership, annual bazaar & Coos County Fair
Exhibitions: Exhibits by local members, as well as by others throughout the state
Publications: Monthly newsletter
Activities: Classes for adults and children; lectures open to public, 4-5 vis lectr per yr; gallery talks; tours; awards; scholarships; individual paintings lent to banks, lobbies, automobile showrooms & music stores; traveling exhibitions organized and circulated; sales shop sells original art, miniatures & handicraft
L **Library,** Myrtle Pt Hwy, 97423. Tel 503-396-3294.

CORVALLIS

OREGON STATE UNIVERSITY
M **Horner Museum,** Gill Coliseum, 26th St, 97331. Tel 503-737-2951. *Dir* Lucy Skjelstad
Open Tues - Fri 10 AM - 5 PM, Sat noon - 4 PM, Sun 2 - 5 PM, cl Mon, winters; Mon - Fri 10 AM - 5 PM, Sun 2 - 5 PM, cl Sat, summers. No admis fee. Estab 1925 to collect, preserve and exhibit the history and natural history of Oregon. Average Annual Attendance: 40,000. Mem: 195; dues individual $10
Income: Financed by state appropriations and donations
Collections: †Ethnographic, Worldwide; Geological and Biological Specimens; †Historic Objects, Pioneer Period to Present; †Oral History
Publications: Horner Museum Tour Guide Series, a set of thematic history guidebooks; exhibition catalogs
Activities: Lectures open to public; tours; individual paintings & original objects of art lent to museums & non-profit agencies; museum shop sells books, reproductions, posters, T-shirts & ethnic craft items
M **Fairbanks Gallery,** Fairbanks Hall, 97331-3702. Tel 503-737-4745; FAX 503-737-2420. *Gallery Dir* Douglas Russell
Open 8 AM - 5 PM. No admis fee. Estab 1933 to display work of contemporary American artists. Gallery space 1100 sq ft
Income: Financed by state appropriation and grants
Collections: Goya to Rauschenberg; Japanese Print Collection; Wendel Black Print Collection
M **Memorial Union Art Gallery,** 97331. Tel 503-737-2416; 737-1566. *Secy & Dir* William Edwards; *Asst Dir* Donald Johnson
Open daily 8 AM - 10 PM. Estab 1928. Average Annual Attendance: 50,000. Mem: 15,000; annual meeting May
Income: $70,000
Collections: William Henry Price Memorial Collection of Oil Paintings
Publications: Calendar and exhibition pamphlets
Activities: Educ program; lect; exten dept serving the State; individual paintings lent to schools; material available to responsible galleries for fees; traveling exhibitions organized and circulated
M **Giustina Gallery,** LaSells Stewart Center, 26th & Western Blvds, 97331. Tel 503-737-2402; FAX 530-737-2420. *Gallery Dir* Douglas Russell
Open Mon - Fri 8 AM - 5 PM, additional hrs during special events at LaSells Stewart Center. No admis fee. Estab 1981 to display work of contemporary artists. Gallery is 4800 sq ft
Income: Financed by grants & state appropiation
Exhibitions: Exhibitions changing monthly

THE DALLES

A **THE DALLES ART ASSOCIATION,** Oregon Trail Art Gallery, The Dalles Art Center, 220 E Fourth & Washington, 97058. Tel 503-296-4759. *Dir* Judi B Timmons
Open Tues - Sat 11 AM - 5 PM. No admis fee. Estab 1959 for presentation of community arts activities. Gallery maintained. Average Annual Attendance: 4500. Mem: 180, dues corporate $250, patron $100, business $50, family $30, individual $20, sr $15; meeting held quarterly 1st month
Income: Financed by dues, fund-raising events, grants, sponsorships
Exhibitions: Member and guest exhibits; state services exhibits
Publications: Monthly bulletin
Activities: Classes for adults & children; docent training; summer children's program; lect open to public; competitions; gallery sells original art, jewelry, pottery, basketry

EUGENE

M **CITY OF EUGENE, HULT CENTER,** Jacobs Gallery, One Eugene Center, 97401. Tel 503-687-5087; FAX 503-687-5426. *Visual Arts Coordr* Suzanne Pepin; *Public Art Coordr* Kirsten Jones
Open Mon - Fri 9 AM - 5 PM, Sat 11 AM - 3 PM. No admis fee. Estab 1982 for art appreciation & education. Gallery in lower level of Hult Center for the Performing Arts. Functions as a meeting & reception area, as well as a gallery
Income: $31,400 (financed by city appropriation, gallery sales commissions & cost reimbursements from artists)
Exhibitions: Exhibits selected by committee of local artists, Hult Center representative & Cultural Affairs Commission representative; Christopher Burkett; Art in Education

M **MAUDE I KERNS ART CENTER,** Henry Korn Gallery, 1910 E 15th Ave, 97403. Tel 503-345-1571. *Admin Dir* M Clare Feighan; *Pres* JoLayne McDow
Open Tues - Fri 10 AM - 5 PM, Sat 1 - 5 PM, Sun 1 - 5 PM. Admis Suggested $2 donation. Estab 1951, the Center is a nonprofit educational organization dedicated to promoting quality in the arts and crafts through classes, exhibitions,

workshops, community projects, and special events. The Center houses the Henry Korn Gallery, the Main Gallery featuring monthly shows of contemporary artists; the Mezzanine Gallery, suited to photographs, prints, drawings & smaller works of art, Printmakers Co-op & Ceramics Co-op. Average Annual Attendance: 9000. Mem: 600; dues family $35, individual $20; annual meeting second Mon in Apr
Income: $100,000 (financed by membership, class tuition, art sales, contributions, grants)
Collections: †Sculpture & painting of Oregon Artists
Exhibitions: Every 6 weeks exhibits featuring individual & group shows by Pacific Northwest artists
Publications: State of the Crafts, Maude Kerns; membership newsletter
Activities: Classes for adults and children; dramatic programs; volunteer program; lect open to the public & for members only on request; concerts; gallery talks; tours; competitions

M **LANE COMMUNITY COLLEGE,** Art Dept Gallery, 4000 E 30th Ave, 97405. Tel 503-747-4501. *Dir* Harold Hoy
Open 8 AM - 5 PM. Estab 1970
Income: Financed through county funds
Exhibitions: Paintings by David Selleck
Activities: Lectures

UNIVERSITY OF OREGON
M **Museum of Art,** 1430 Johnson Lane, 97403. Tel 503-346-3027. *Dir* Stephen C McGough; *Cur Exhib* Tommy Griffin; *Asst Cur Asian Art* Diana Tenckhoff; *Admin Asst* Ethel Weltman; *Registrar* Lawrence Fong
Open Wed - Sun noon - 5 PM, cl Mon, Tues & university holidays. No admis fee. Estab 1930 to promote among university students and faculty and the general public an active and continuing interest in the visual arts of both Western and Oriental cultures. Average Annual Attendance: 55,000. Mem: 600; dues $10-$500; annual meeting May
Income: $201,000 (financed by state appropriation and private donations)
Collections: African; Contemporary Northwest Collection; Greater Pacific Basin Collection; Asian Art representing the cultures of China, Japan, Cambodia, Korea, Mongolia, Tibet, Russia, and American and British works executed in the traditional Oriental manner; 19-20th century European and American
Exhibitions: (1992) Masters of Fine Arts Exhibition; American Prints from the Collection; Christopher Burkett Photography; Oregon Biennial 1991; La Verne Krause: Painter & Printmaker (1924 - 1987). (1993) Sculpture by Auguste Rodin; Thomas Hart Benton on the Oregon Trail; Taking Pictures Home: Oliver Gaglianti's Life Work in Photographs; Masters of Fine Arts Exhibition
Publications: exhibition catalog
Activities: Docent training; lect open to public, 4 or more vis lectr per year; sales shop sells books, slides, cards, gifts
M **Aperture Photo Gallery - EMU Art Gallery,** ERB Memorial Union, 97403. Tel 503-346-4373; FAX 503-346-4400. *Dir* Dusty Miller; *Asst Dir* Frank Geltner; *Craft Center Coordr* Thomas Urban; *Cur* Jan McLaughlin; *Cur* Eric Geddes
Open Mon - Sat 7:30 AM - 11:30 PM, Sun Noon - 11:30 PM. No admis fee. Estab 1981 to provide space for work of university community
Income: Financed by student fees
Collections: †Pacific Northwest Art
Exhibitions: Periodic art exhibitions on portable display boards in various rooms; display in the art gallery of selections from the permanent collection
Activities: Classes for adults; craft workshops; lectures
L **Architecture and Allied Arts Library,** 200 Lawrence Hall, 97403. Tel 503-346-3637. *Head Librn* Sheila M Klos; *Reference Librn* James H Carmin; *Slide Cur* Christine L Sundt
Open Mon - Thurs 8 AM - 11 PM, Fri 8 AM - 9 PM, Sat 10 AM - 9 PM, Sun 10 AM - 11 PM. Estab 1915 to provide resources for the courses, degree programs & research of the departments in the School of Architecture & Allied Arts. Primarily for lending
Income: Financed by state appropriation
Library Holdings: Vols 50,000; Per subs 400; Micro — Fiche; AV — Slides 225,000; Other — Exhibition catalogs, photographs 30,000

FOREST GROVE

M **PACIFIC UNIVERSITY,** Old College Hall, Pacific University Museum, 97116. Tel 503-357-6151. *Contact* Rick Read
Open Tues & Thurs 9:30 AM - Noon & 12:30 - 4:30 PM, Wed 9:30 AM - Noon, Sat - 11 AM - 3 PM & by appointment, cl school vacations. No admis fee. Estab 1949
Collections: Indian Artifacts; Oriental Art Objects; Pacific Univ & Forest Grove Artifacts
Publications: Annual of the Curator; Friends of Old College Hall Newsletter, bi-annual
Activities: Tours

JACKSONVILLE

M **SOUTHERN OREGON HISTORICAL SOCIETY,** Jacksonville Museum of Southern Oregon History, 206 N Fifth St, PO Box 480, 97530. Tel 503-773-6536; FAX 503-776-7994. *Exec Dir* Samuel J Wegner; *Historic Resource Dir* Bradford Linder; *Development Dir* Janice Farmer; *Finance Dir* Maureen Smith; *Cur Coll* Janette Merriman; *Staff Development Specialist* Dawna Curler; *Communications Serv* Natalie Brown; *Membership Coordr* Susan Cox-Smith; *Coordr Children's Prog* Amelia Chamberlain; *Research Specialist* Paul Richardson; *Exhib Designer* Rich Chavka; *Prog Dir* Joy B Dunn; *Oral Historian* Marjorie Edens
Open Mon - Sat 10 AM - 5 PM, Memorial Day - Labor Day open Mon - Sun 10 AM - 5 PM. Modest admis fee. Estab 1946 to preserve & interpret the history of southern Oregon. Included are the Peter Britt Gallery (19th Century photography artifacts); Children's Museum (next door in old county jail, a hands-on museum, incls the Pinto Gallery of Bozo the Clown). The historic sites include the Cornelius C Beekman House (1876), Beekman Bank (1863), Catholic

Rectory (circa 1861), US Hotel (1880). Average Annual Attendance: 150,000.
Mem: 1800; dues vary from active $30 to jr historian $5
Income: Financed by membership, public & private grants, & county historical fund
Exhibitions: Making Tracks: The Impact of the Railroad on the Rogue Valley; Hanna Pottery; Jacksonville: Boomtown to Hometown. (1993) Oregon Trail Sesquicentennial; Peter Britt
Publications: Table Rock Sentinel, bimonthly; ArtiFACTS, monthly newsletter
Activities: Handcraft workshops for children; docent training; film program; lect open to the public; museum shop sells books, magazines, reproductions, prints
L **Library,** 106 N Central Ave, Medford, 97501-5926. Tel 503-773-6536; FAX 503-776-7994. *Library Mgr* Carol Harbison; *Cur Coll* Janette Merriman
Open Tues - Sat 1 - 5 PM. Open to public for reference only
Income: Financed by membership, sales and county tax
Library Holdings: Vols 4000; Per subs 75; Ephemera, art on paper; Other — Manuscripts, photographs
Special Subjects: Historic preservation, museum techniques, Southern Oregon History

KLAMATH FALLS

M **FAVELL MUSEUM OF WESTERN ART & INDIAN ARTIFACTS,** 125 W Main, PO Box 165, 97601. Tel 503-882-9996. *Pres* Gene H Favell; *VPres & Treas* Winifred L Favell; *Admin* Bev Jackson; *Cur* Don Allen
Open Mon - Sat 9:30 AM - 5:30 PM, cl Sun. Admis adults $4, sr citizens 65 & over $3, youth 6 - 16 years $2. Estab 1972 to preserve Western heritage as represented by Indian artifacts and contemporary western art. Gallery features contemporary western artists combined with art and artifacts displays. Average Annual Attendance: 15,000 - 20,000. Mem: dues $75; annual meeting May
Income: $200,000 - $250,000 (financed by owners)
Purchases: Paintings by: Grace Hudson, McCarthy, Arlene Hooker Fay & James Bama; 800 works of art by 300 artists
Collections: †Contemporary western art; †western Indian artifacts: pottery, stonework, baskets, bead and quiltwork; †miniature firearms
Publications: A treasury of our Western Heritage (book on cross section of museum collection)
Activities: Lectures open to public; gallery talks; museum shop selling books, original art, reproductions, prints, slides

M **KLAMATH COUNTY MUSEUM,** 1451 Main St, 97601. Tel 503-883-4208. *Dir* Patsy McMillan
Open Tues - Sat 9 AM - 5 PM; cl Sun & Mon. Admis free. Estab 1953 to tell the story of the Klamath Country and to preserve and exhibit related material. Average Annual Attendance: 30,000
Income: Financed by county appropriation
Collections: Indian and pioneer artifacts; four original Rembrandt etchings; Healey painting; photograph document files
Publications: Museum Research Papers
Activities: Lectures open to public; guided tours for 4th grade students; book traveling exhibitions; traveling exhibitions and circulated; museum shop sells books & original art
L **Research Library,** 1451 Main St, 97601. Tel 503-882-6953. *Dir* Patsy McMillan
Open to the public for reference Tues - Sat 9 AM - 4:30 PM by appointment. Estab 1955 to collect, preserve, document & interpret the local history
Income: Financed by County General Fund
Library Holdings: Vols 10,000; Micro — Reels; AV — Motion pictures, slides; Other — Clipping files, manuscripts, original art works, pamphlets, photographs 5000
Collections: Modoc Indian War Books, Documents and Manuscripts
Activities: Guided tours for 4th grade students; school kits lent to area schools; sales shop sells books, prints, paintings, ceramic & other miscellaneous items
M **Baldwin Hotel Museum Annex,** 31 Main St, 97601. Tel 503-883-4207. *Dir* Patsy McMillan
Open Tues - Sat 10 AM - 4 PM, June - September. Admis adults $3, students & sr citizens $2, family $6, under 3 free. A state and national historic landmark purchased by Klamath County in January 1978. Restoration of building began in February 1978 and it was dedicated as a museum by Oregon's Governor Robert Straub June 3, 1978. Opened to the public August 19, 1978. May be viewed by tour only
Exhibitions: (1993) Wedding Gowns
Activities: Guided tours for 5th grade students; museum shop sells books & original art

A **KLAMATH FALLS ART ASSOCIATION,** Klamath Art Gallery, 120 Riverside Dr, PO Box 955, 97601. Tel 503-883-1833. *Pres* Mary Hyde Martin; *Chmn Exhib* Melissa Drew
Open Mon - Sat 1 - 4 PM, Sun 2 - 5 PM, and special occasions. No admis fee. Estab 1948 to provide art training for local residents. Gallery estab 1960 to provide display and teaching space for the Association's activities. Average Annual Attendance: 5000. Mem: 200; dues $7 and higher; annual meeting Sept
Income: Financed by membership, gallery sales, tuition
Collections: Ceramics; paintings; weaving (owned by members)
Exhibitions: Twelve annually; one membership show, one juried show, and the remainder varies
Activities: Classes in painting, drawing, ceramics, weaving; children's summer art classes; workshops; lect, visiting lectrs; annual arts festival, mid-Sept

MEDFORD

A **ROGUE VALLEY ART ASSOCIATION,** Rogue Gallery, 40 S Bartlett, PO Box 763, 97501. Tel 503-772-8118. *Pres* Lois Cousineau; *Dir* Nancy Jo Mullen; *Admin Asst* Kenton Gould
Open Tues - Fri 10 AM - 5 PM, Sat 10 AM - 4 PM, cl Sun & Mon. Estab 1960 to provide a full range of programs, exhibits & classes to the region. Gallery 6000 sq ft, 2200 sq ft, sales & rental space, 2000 sq ft & 200 running ft of sliding panels. Average Annual Attendance: 15,000. Mem: 650; dues $20 - $500; annual

meeting Jan
Income: Financed by mem dues, grants, fund raising events
Collections: Contemporary Northwest prints
Exhibitions: (1992) Faye Cummings (drawings), Darryla Green-McGrath (video, prints); Festival of Trees; Irkutsk Print Co-op, Oregon Printmakers' Studio, Eugene (lithographs, etchings, prints); What is not Forbidden, Soviet Outsider Artists (paintings, prints); local artists. (1993) Angelina M A Hekking, Shad Gierlich (photography); Jean LaMarr; Monique Passicot; Victoria Rivers; Art to Art; Artists Who Teach & Mentor; Matriarchs, Pioneering Women in Oregon Architecture; State of Jefferson, bi-annual invitational; Valley Vistas, Landscapes of Time, Place & Duration, Jack Teeters, Bob Inlow.
Publications: Newsletter, 6 per yr
Activities: Educ dept; classes for adults & children; lect open to public, 2 vis lectr per year; gallery talks; tours; scholarships & fels offered; individual paintgns lent through a rental program to members; lending collection contains art works, paintings, photographs & sculpture; book traveling exhibitions, 2 - 3 per year; sales shop sells original art, crafts, books, prints, sculpture, pottery, jewelry, greeting cards

MONMOUTH

M **WESTERN OREGON STATE COLLEGE,** Campbell Hall Gallery, 345 Monmouth Ave, 97361. Tel 503-838-8340. *Head Art Dept* Don Hoskisson
Open Mon - Fri 8 AM - 5 PM during scheduled exhibits. No admis fee. Estab to bring contemporary art work to the community and the college for study and visual understanding. Library maintained. Average Annual Attendance: 3000-4000
Income: $3000 (financed by state appropriation and student fees)
Collections: †Permanent collection
Exhibitions: Contemporary Northwest Visual Art; rotating faculty and student exhibits
Activities: Lectures open to the public, 3 - 5 vis lectr per year; gallery talks; tours; competitions with awards; lending collection contains 10,000 slides; originate traveling exhibitions

NORTH BEND

M **COOS COUNTY HISTORICAL SOCIETY MUSEUM,** 1220 Sherman, 97459. Tel 503-756-6320. *Dir* Ann Koppy
Open Tues - Sat 10 AM - 4 PM. Admis $1. Estab 1891 to collect, preserve & interpret history of Coos County. Average Annual Attendance: 7255. Mem: 400; dues $10 - $250; annual meeting in June
Income: $31,100 (financed by endowment, mem, admissions, sales & donations)
Collections: Native American Artifacts; Tools/Implements of Pioneer Lifeways; Photographs; Maritime Objects
Exhibitions: Pioneer Kitchen; Formal Parlor (c1900); rotating Exhibits; Maritime
Publications: Coos Historical Journal, annua; bi-monthly newsletter
Activities: Lectures open to public, vis lectr;; lending collection contains 100 items; retail store sells books

PORTLAND

L **BASSIST COLLEGE LIBRARY,** 2000 SW Fifth Ave, 97201. Tel 503-228-6528. *Pres* Donald H Bassist; *VPres & Secy* Norma Bassist; *Librn* Nancy Thurston; *Librn* Joseph Schiwek Jr; *Librn* Norma Bassist
Open 8 AM - 5 PM. No admis fee. Estab 1964 to provide practical instruction in retail merchandising, interior design, display, fashion design, advertising and promotion, fashion history and textiles. Average Annual Attendance: 200
Library Holdings: Vols 14,000; Per subs 120; AV — Slides; Other — Clipping files
Special Subjects: Art History, Costume Design & Construction, Fashion Arts, Furniture, Industrial Design, Interior Design, Textiles
Collections: Collection of Fashion and Costume History Books; Collection in Furniture and Interior Decoration Fields
Activities: Scholarships offered

M **BLUE SKY,** Oregon Center for the Photographic Arts, 1231 NW Hoyt St, 97209. Tel 503-225-0210. *Dir* Chris Rauschenberg
Exhibitions: Monthly rotating exhibits

M **CONTEMPORARY CRAFTS ASSOCIATION AND GALLERY,** 3934 SW Corbett Ave, 97201. Tel 503-223-2654. *Exec Dir* Marlene Gabel
Open Tues - Fri 11 AM - 5 PM, Sat noon - 5 PM, Sun 1 - 5 PM, cl Mon. No admis fee. Estab 1937 to promote, exhibit and sell contemporary crafts. Gallery is maintained also as a consignment outlet, and holds exhibits monthly. Average Annual Attendance: 30,000. Mem: 1000; dues $30
Income: $114,000 (financed by membership)
Collections: †Contemporary crafts in clay, fiber, glass, metal & wood
Publications: Contemporary Crafts News, quarterly
Activities: Artists-in-Education Prog; docent training; lectures open to the public, some for members only; 10-12 vis lectrs per yr; gallery talks; tours; competitions; artist-in-residence; originate traveling exhibitions; sales shop sells books, fine crafts, original art
L **Library,** 3934 SW Corbett Ave, 97201. Tel 503-223-2654. *Acting Librn* Beulah Parisi
Open to members
Library Holdings: Vols 430; Per subs 260

A **METROPOLITAN ARTS COMMISSION,** Metropolitan Center for Public Arts, 1120 SW Fifth, Room 1023, 97204. Tel 503-823-5111; FAX 503-796-3388. *Chmn* Michael Powell; *Dir* Bill Bulick
Open Mon - Fri 8 AM - 5 PM. No admis fee. Estab 1973, to promote and encourage programs to further the development and public awareness of and interest in the visual and performing arts
Income: Financed by city and county appropriation

Purchases: Visual Chronicle of Portland, one percent for Public Art projects
Collections: Works by local artists
Publications: Newsletter, bi-monthly
Activities: Competitions with awards; individual paintings & original objects of art lent

L **MULTNOMAH COUNTY LIBRARY,** Henry Failing Art and Music Dept, 801 SW Tenth, 97205. Tel 503-248-5281. *Dir* Ginnie Cooper; *Head Art & Music Dept* Ella Seely
Open Mon - Thurs 10 AM - 8 PM, Fri & Sat 10 AM - 5:30 PM. Estab 1864 as a public library service to Multnomah County
Library Holdings: Vols 23,000; AV — Rec, slides; Other — Clipping files

A **OREGON HISTORICAL SOCIETY,** 1200 SW Park Ave, 97205. Tel 503-222-1741; FAX 503-221-2035. *Exec Dir* Chet Orloff; *Educ Dir* Barbara Abrans; *Chief Cur* Dale Archibald; *Cur of Coll* J D Cleaver
Open Mon - Sat 10 AM - 5 PM. No admis fee. Estab 1873, incorporated 1898, to collect, preserve, exhibit and publish materials pertaining to the Oregon country. Approx 20,000 sq ft of exhibit space; Society maintains historic 1856 James F. Bybee House, Howell Territorial Park, Sauvie Island. Average Annual Attendance: 150,000. Mem: 8500; dues individual & family $25 - $49, senior $20, student $15; annual meeting Nov
Income: $3,363,000 biennially (financed by state appropriation, membership, grants, gifts & donations)
Collections: †Artifacts, †Manuscripts, †paintings, †photographs, collection by Oregon Country & Oregon State artists
Publications: Oregon Historical Quarterly; books; maps; pamphlets; newsletter
Activities: Seminars for adults; classes for children; docent training; educational programs; lectures open to the public; tours, gallery talks; competitions; individual paintings & original objects of art lent; originate traveling exhibitions; sales shop sells books, original art, reproductions & prints

L **Library,** 1200 SW Park Ave, 97205. FAX 503-221-2035; *Chief Librn* Louis Flannery; *Quarterly Ed* Rick Harmon
Open Mon - Sat 10 AM - 5 PM. For reference only
Library Holdings: Vols 100,000; Per subs 620; original documents; Micro — Cards, fiche, prints, reels; AV — A-tapes, cassettes, fs, lantern slides, motion pictures, rec, slides, v-tapes; Other — Clipping files, exhibition catalogs, framed reproductions, manuscripts, memorabilia, original art works, pamphlets, photographs, prints, reproductions, sculpture
Special Subjects: History of the Pacific Northwest & the Oregon Country; political & economic growth of Pacific Northwest; Northwest Exploration & voyages
Collections: 3500 separate manuscript collections containing 17,500,000 pieces; 1,500,000 historic photographs; 15,000 maps

M **OREGON SCHOOL OF ARTS AND CRAFTS,** Hoffman Gallery, 8245 SW Barnes Rd, 97225. Tel 503-297-5544; FAX 503-297-9651. *Pres* Paul Magnusson; *Chief Academic Officer* Jane Kyle
Open Mon - Thurs 9 AM - 9:30 PM, Fri 9 AM - 5 PM, Sat 10 AM - 5 PM, Sun 10 AM - 4 PM. No admis fee, except for special events and classes. Estab 1906 to teach seven disciplines in the arts and crafts. Hoffman Exhibition Gallery features national & international craftspeople. Average Annual Attendance: 1500. Mem: 600; dues $35 - $1000; annual meeting in June
Income: Financed by tuitions, endowment, membership, state appropriation and National Endowments of the Arts, Washington, DC
Special Subjects: Art History, Asian Art, Bookplates & Bindings, Calligraphy, Carpets & Rugs, Ceramics, Collages, Costume Design & Construction, Crafts, Decorative Arts, Embroidery, Enamels, Etchings & Engravings, Folk Art, Furniture, Glass
Collections: Permanent collection of historic, traditional craftwork
Exhibitions: (1993) Chronicles: Nuclear Materials into Art; Folk Art of Mexico; Native American Crafts; Cross Currents: Books from the Pacific Rim; Student Show; Thesis Show; Past Artists in Residence Show; Summer Craft Show; 1993 Artists in Residence Show; An Installation by Christine Bourdette; Holiday Gift Show
Publications: Course schedules, quarterly; gallery announcements, 12 per year; newsletter to members, 4 per year; 2 year catalog
Activities: Classes & workshops for adults; lectures open to public; gallery talks; tours; scholarships; sales shop sells books, magazines and original art

L **Library,** 8245 SW Barnes Rd, 97225. Tel 503-297-5544; FAX 503-297-9651. *Librn* Christine Peterson
Open Mon - Thurs 9 AM - 8 PM, Fri - Sat 10 AM - 1 PM. Estab 1979 to serve as a craft reference library for students and faculty and others interested in crafts
Library Holdings: Vols 3000; Per subs 72; Micro — Fiche; AV — A-tapes, slides; Other — Clipping files, exhibition catalogs, pamphlets, photographs
Special Subjects: Architecture, Ceramics, Drawings, Glass, Metalwork, Photography, Printmaking, Textiles, Book Arts, Craft History, Ethnic/Pattern, Metals, Nature, Wood
Activities: Interlibrary loan services available

M **PORTLAND ART MUSEUM** (Formerly Oregon Art Institute), 1219 SW Park Ave, 97205. Tel 503-226-2811; FAX 503-226-4842. *Pres & Chief Exec Officer* Dan L Monroe; *Development* Craig Vincent-Jones; *Cur Asian Art* Donald Jenkins; *Cur Photography* Terry Toedtemeier; *Cur Contemporary Art* John Weber; *Cur American & European Art* Prudence Roberts; *Cur Educ* Amy Osaki; *Registrar* Marc Pence; *Conservator* Sonja Sopher
Open Tues - Sat 11 AM - 5 PM, Sun 1 - 5 PM. Admis adults $4.50, students $2.50, children 6 - 12 $1.50, members & children under 6 free. Estab 1892 to make a collection of works of art & to erect & maintain a suitable building in which the same may be studied & exhibited; to develop & encourage the study of art. Average Annual Attendance: 175,000. Mem: 6500; dues $35 & up; annual meeting Sept
Income: Financed by admissions, endowment, grants, contributions & mem
Collections: †American painting, 19th & 20th centuries; Elizabeth Cole Butler Collection; Gebauer Collection of Cameroon Art; †Vivian & Gordon Gilkey Graphics Art Collection; Hirsch Collection of Oriental Rugs; Samuel H Kress Collection of Renaissance Painting & Sculpture; Mary Andrews Ladd Collection of Japanese Prints; Lawther Collection of Ethiopian Crosses; Lewis Collection of Classical Antiquities; †Alice B Nunn Collection of English Silver; †Oriental sculptures, paintings, bronzes, ceramics & other decorative arts; Persian & Hindu miniatures; Pre-Columbian Art; Rasmussen Collection of Northwest Coast Indian & Eskimo Arts; Evan H Roberts Memorial 19th & 20th Century Sculpture Collection; Margery H Smith Collection of Asian Art; †20th century photographs
Publications: Annual report; Art of Cameroon; Calendar, monthly; exhibition catalogs; Art in the Life of the Northwest Coast Indian; collection catalogs
Activities: Docent training; lect open to the public, 20 vis lectr per yr; gallery talks; tours; individual paintings & original objects of art lent; book traveling exhibitions, 8 - 12 per yr; originate traveling exhibitions; museum shop sells books, gifts & cards

L **Rex Arragon Library,** 1219 SW Park Ave, 97205. Tel 503-226-2811, Ext 215; FAX 503-226-4842. *Library Dir* Dan Lucas
Estab 1892 to provide reference for museum staff, Pacific Northwest College of art students & public
Library Holdings: Vols 22,000; Per subs 80; Artist files; AV — Slides; Other — Clipping files, exhibition catalogs
Special Subjects: Afro-American Art, American Indian Art, American Western Art, Art History, Asian Art, Folk Art, Islamic Art, Mexican Art, Oriental Art, Painting - American, Pre-Columbian Art, Southwestern Art, Northwest Coast Indian art & culture

A **Northwest Film Center,** 1219 SW Park Ave, 97205. Tel 503-221-1156; FAX 503-226-4842. *Dir* Bill Foster
Admis $5. Estab 1972 as a regional media arts center. Maintains film archive, circ film library, film & video exhibition program & classes. Average Annual Attendance: 40,000
Exhibitions: Annual Northwest Film & Video Festival; Young Peoples Film Festival; Portland International Film Festival
Activities: Film screening program; courses in film and video; video/filmmaker-in-schools program; lectures open to public, 24 vis lectrs per yr; competitions with awards; exten dept

M **PORTLAND CHILDREN'S MUSEUM,** 3037 SW Second Ave, 97201. Tel 503-823-2227; FAX 503-823-3667. *Dir* Robert G Bridgeford
Open daily 9 AM - 5 PM, cl National Holidays. Admis adults $3.50, children over 1 $3. Extab 1949; sponsored jointly by Friends of the Children's Museum & the Portland Bureau of Parks & Recreation. Average Annual Attendance: 130,000. Mem: 2500; dues $40 family
Income: Financed by city appropriation 50% & Friends of the Children's Museum 50%
Collections: Children's art; natural history, toys, dollhouses, miniatures; multicultural artifacts relating to children's culture
Exhibitions: Baby Room; Customs House & Clay Shop; Kid City Grocery Store, H2 Oh; 10 Best & 10 Worst Toys; Grocery Store; rotating exhibitions quarterly
Publications: Museum Program Guide, quarterly
Activities: Classes for children; docent training; lectures; tours; book traveling exhibitions; museum shop sells toys

M **PORTLAND COMMUNITY COLLEGE,** North View Gallery, 12000 SW 49th Ave, 97219. Tel 503-244-6111; FAX 503-452-4947. *Dir* Hugh Webb
Open Mon - Fri 8 AM - 5 PM. No admis fee. Estab 1970. Gallery's primary focus on comtemporary Northwest artists, throuhg solo shows, group invitations, installations & new genres
Exhibitions: Contemporary art of the Northwest

PORTLAND STATE UNIVERSITY

M **Littman Gallery,** 725 SW Harrison, 97201. Tel 503-725-4452; FAX 503-725-4882.
Open Mon - Fri noon - 4 PM. No admis fee. Estab 1980 to exhibit art in variety of media, style & geographic distribution. Gallery space has 1500 sq ft
Exhibitions: (1993) Jeff Whipple (paintings); Don Gray (paintings); Oregon & Washington Womens Show; David Fish (sculpture); Karen Waaler (paintings); Faye Cummings; Chris Gander; Zack Kircher (sculptures)
Activities: Lectures open to public; gallery talks

M **White Gallery,** 1825 SW Broadway, 97201. Tel 503-725-3020; FAX 503-725-4882.
Open Mon - Fri 8 AM - 10 PM, Sat 9 AM - 7 PM. No admis fee. Estab 1970 as a student operated gallery exhibiting works by professional artists representing primarily photography
Collections: Permanent collection contains work by local professional artists with a few nationally recognized artists
Exhibitions: (1993) Cindy Hatfield; Dale Strouse; Lori McDonald; Thomas Nolan; George Osterag; Paullette Reef-Davis
Activities: Lectures open to public; gallery talks; individual paintings & original objects of art lent to other schools or museums; lending collection contains original prints, paintings & sculpture

M **REED COLLEGE,** Douglas F Cooley Memorial Art Gallery, 3203 SE Woodstock Blvd, 97202-8199. Tel 503-771-1112, Ext 251. *Cur* Susan Fillin-Yeh
Open Tues - Sun noon - 5 PM, Drawings Room open by appointment for study of works on paper. No admis fee. Estab 1989 to enhance the teaching of art, art history & the humanities. The program brings to the college & the community exhibitions of art from a variety of periods & traditions as well as significant contemporary art not previously available in the Northwest
Collections: †Pre-20th century prints; 20th century prints, drawings, paintings, photographs and sculptures
Activities: Public openings; lectures; gallery talks

L **UNIVERSITY OF PORTLAND,** Wilson W Clark Memorial Library, 5000 N Willamette Blvd, PO Box 83017, 97283-0017. Tel 503-283-7111; Elec Mail BROWNE@UOFPORT.BITNET. *Dir* Joseph P Browne; *Reference Librn* Pam Horan; *Technical Services Librn* Susan Hinken; *Spec Serv Librn* Michael Storwick
Open Sun 11 AM - 12 AM, Mon - Thurs 8 AM - noon, Fri 8 AM - 9 PM, Sat 9 AM - 4 PM. Estab 1901 to support the University curriculum. Maintains an art gallery with a rotating exhibit. Circ 50,000
Income: Financed through the University
Collections: Rotating collections
Publications: Art Objects, holdings list

A **WEST HILLS UNITARIAN FELLOWSHIP,** 8470 SW Oleson Rd, 97223. Tel 503-246-3351, 244-1379. *Pres* Jan Tuttle; *VPres* Beverly Conaway; *Office Admin* Doll Gardner; *Fine Arts Chmn* Helen Johnson
Open Mon - Fri 9 AM - noon. No admis fee. Estab 1970 to give professional artists one or two-man shows in a lovely gallery space and to expose the congregation and public to fine visual art. The entire sanctuary wall space is like a large gallery and the building is light, airy with a woodsy backdrop. Average Annual Attendance: 10,000
Income: $30,000 (financed by membership)
Collections: Paintings, wall sculptures by local artists
Publications: Bulletin, weekly; newsletter, monthly
Activities: Classes for adults and children; dramatic programs; lect open to the public, 8 vis lectr per yr; concerts; sales shop selling books

ROSEBURG

PASTEL SOCIETY OF OREGON
For further information, see National and Regional Organizations

SAINT BENEDICT

L **MOUNT ANGEL ABBEY LIBRARY,** 97373. Tel 503-845-3317. *Head Librn* Hugh Feiss
Open 8:30 AM - 5 PM (school yr), 10:30 AM - 4:30 PM (summer & holidays). Estab 1882. The library serves Mount Angel Abbey, Mount Angel Seminary & the public. It Sponsors art exhibits in the foyer designed for this purpose & makes the auditorium available for concerts
Library Holdings: Vols 5000; Per subs 10; Micro — Fiche 10; Other — Framed reproductions 30, manuscripts, original art works 100, prints 30
Exhibitions: Local artists; Alvar Aalto

SALEM

A **SALEM ART ASSOCIATION,** 600 Mission St SE, 97302. Tel 503-581-2228. *Exec Dir* Cynthia Addams
Estab 1919 to collect, preserve & interpret history & art. Sales gallery & exhibition galleries featuring contemporary art. Average Annual Attendance: 125,000. Mem: 1300; dues $25; annual meeting in Sept
Income: $335,000 (financed by sales, Salem Art Fair & Festival special fundraisers, admissions, membership and donations)
Exhibitions: 10 exhibits yearly in 2 galleries
Activities: Sponsor competitions
M **Bush Barn Art Center,** 600 Mission St SE, Salem, 97302. Tel 503-581-2228. *Exec Dir* Cynthia Addams; *Gallery Dir* Peter Held
Open Tues - Fri 10 AM - 5 PM, Sat & Sun 1 - 5 PM. No admis fee. Estab 1965 to exhibit the best art of the past & the present. Houses the AN Bush Gallery and Corner Gallery which features 10 exhibitions each year and a sales gallery of Northwest artand crafts. Average Annual Attendance: 20,000
Activities: Docent training; awards; scholarships; individual paintings rented to members only (2-D work only)
M **Bush House,** 600 Mission St SE, Salem, 97302. Tel 503-363-4714. *Bush House Cur* Jennifer Hagloch
Open Summer Tues - Sun noon - 5 PM, Winter Tues - Sun 2 - 5 PM. Admis adults $2, sr citizens & students $1.50, children $.75. Estab 1953 to preserve & interpret the Victorian Era of 1870-1900. Contains 16 room mansion with original furnishings. Average Annual Attendance: 10,000
Collections: Furniture, books, documents & antiques
Activities: Lectures open to public; tours; original objects of art lent to organizations for display; museum shop sells books, post cards & brochures
L **Archives,** 600 Mission St SE, 97302. Tel 503-363-4714. *Cur* Jennifer Hagloch
Library Holdings: Vols 150; AV — A-tapes, cassettes, motion pictures, v-tapes; Other — Clipping files, manuscripts, memorabilia, photographs
Collections: Bush family papers 1840-1950

M **WILLAMETTE UNIVERSITY,** George Putnam University Center, 900 State St, 97301. Tel 503-370-6267, ext 6394. *Dir* Robert Hess
Open Mon - Sun 8 AM - 11 PM. No admis fee. Estab 1970 to enrich the atmosphere of the University Center and to acquaint students, faculty and staff with various forms of art. Two separate areas are used: one area is a paneled wall; the other area is comprised of free standing art panels with surface area of approx 54 x 54 inches. Average Annual Attendance: 45,000
Income: Financed through the University
Exhibitions: China exhibit; Robert Hess; Betty LaDuke; sculptures; several exhibits from Visual Arts Resources (University of Oregon); several local artists and photographers
Activities: Lect; gallery talks

SPRINGFIELD

A **EMERALD EMPIRE ART GALLERY,** 421 N A St, 97477. Tel 503-726-8595. *Pres* Phyllis K Coffin
Open Mon - Fri 11 AM - 4 PM. No admis fee. Estab 1957 to promote cultural arts in Springfield & surrounding areas. Downtown area is 3000 sq ft. Mem: 90; dues $25 contributing members, $60 assoc membership; monthly meetings on the 3rd Tues
Income: Financed by mem dues, commission on sales, fund raisers
Collections: Paintings donated by workshop teachers
Exhibitions: Exhibitions twice a year at local shopping malls & convention centers
Publications: Monthly Art League Bulletin
Activities: Classes for adults, material available to anyone; lectures open to public; picture of the month award; competitions; individual paintings and original objects of art lent; traveling exhibitions organized and circulated; sales shop sells crafts, magazines and original art

PENNSYLVANIA

ALLENTOWN

M **ALLENTOWN ART MUSEUM,** Fifth & Courts Sts, PO Box 388, 18105-0388. Tel 215-432-4333; FAX 215-434-7409. *Pres Board Trustees* Leon C Holt Jr; *Dir* Peter F Blume; *Cur* Sarah A McNear; *Chief Cur* Mimi C Miley; *Business Mgr* David Innes; *Registrar* Patricia Delluva; *Dir Planning & Development* Barbara L Phillips; *Sales Gallery* Sharon Yurkanin
Open Tues - Sat 10 AM - 5 PM, Sun 1 - 5 PM, cl Mon. No admis fee. Estab 1939 to acquire, protect, display and interpret the visual arts from the past and present, world wide. Building and land cover three quarters of a city block; 28,000 sq ft wing was added in 1975 to more than double the space. Average Annual Attendance: 74,000. Mem: 2800; dues $15-$1000
Income: $850,000 (financed by endowment, membership, city, county and state appropriations, and contributions)
Purchases: American & European paintings; textiles; prints & drawings; photography
Collections: †American 18th, 19th & 20th century paintings, sculptures, prints & drawings; Chinese porcelains; English & American silver; Japanese Prints; Samuel H Kress Collection of European paintings & sculpture, c 1350-1750 (Bugiardini, Lotto, de Heem, Rembrandt, Ruisdael, Steen & others); Textile study room; 20th century photographs; Frank Lloyd Wright period room, 1912
Publications: Calendar of events, quarterly; catalogs of major exhibitions; descriptive gallery handouts
Activities: Docent training; lect open to public; gallery talks; tours; competitions; concerts; individual paintings lent to museums; lending collection contains original art works, original prints, paintings and textiles; traveling exhibitions organized and circulated; museum shop sells cards, catalogs, children's books, crafts, jewelry & other art related merchandise; Max Hess Junior Gallery Artspace

M **LEHIGH COUNTY HISTORICAL SOCIETY,** Hamilton at Fifth, 18101. Tel 215-435-9601. *Pres* Kurt Zwill; *Exec Dir* Carol B Wickkiser; *Cur Coll* Andree Mey; *Coll Mgr* Gloria F McFadden; *Librn* June B Griffith; *Educ Cur* Sarah Nelson
Open Mon - Fri 9 AM - 4 PM, Sun 1 - 4 PM. No admis fee. Estab 1904 for collection, preservation & exhibition of Lehigh County history. Lock Ridge Furnace Museum 1868, Frank Buchman House 1892, Haines Mill Museum 1760, Lehigh County Museum 1814, Trout Hall 1770, George Taylor House 1768, Saylor Cement Industry Museum 1868, Troxell-Steckel House 1755. Average Annual Attendance: 53,000. Mem: 1300; annual dues $15-$1000; annual meeting 3rd Wed in Apr
Income: $664,000 (financed by endowment, membership, tax-based support, foundations corporate & business support)
Collections: American Indian items; †decorative arts; †structures; †local artworks
Exhibitions: (1991) The Mansion That Was Muhlenberg: Trout Hall 1847-1991 (1992 - 93) Quillers, Warpers & Weavers: Silk Workers in the Lehigh Valley
Publications: Proceedings, biennial; Town Crier, quarterly newsletter
Activities: Adults & children's classes; films; college internships; docent training; off-site community lectures open to public, 4-8 vis lectrs per yr; concerts; tours; children's art competitions; individual paintings & original objects of art lent to museums; lending collection contains one motion picture, one filmstrip, 100 original art works, 40 original prints, 100 paintings, 3000 photographs, 8000 decorative arts, tools & other objects; book one traveling exhibition per yr
L **Scott Andrew Trexler II Library,** Old Court House, Hamilton at Fifth (Mailing add: PO Box 1548, 18105). Tel 215-435-4664. *Librn* June B Griffiths; *Asst Librn* Carol M Herrity
Open Mon - Sat 10 AM - 4 PM. Estab 1974. For reference only
Income: $45,000
Purchases: $14,000
Library Holdings: Vols 10,000; Per subs 20; Micro — Reels 225; AV — A-tapes 10, cassettes 10, lantern slides 1000; Other — Framed reproductions, manuscripts 1000, memorabilia, original art works, pamphlets, photographs 30,000, prints
Special Subjects: Genealogy, Local & regional history
Collections: Allentown imprints; broadsides; Civil War; early German newspapers; fraktur; Native American materials; photographs
Publications: Proceedings, semi-annual; Town Crier

M **MUHLENBERG COLLEGE CENTER FOR THE ARTS,** Frank Martin Gallery, 2400 Chew St, 18104-5586. Tel 215-821-3466; FAX 215-821-3234. *Acting Gallery Dir* Sandra Ericson
Open Tues - Fri 11 AM - 5 PM, Sat & Sun noon - 5 PM. No admis fee. Estab 1976. The building was designed by architect Philip Johnson; the focal point of its design and function is a 220 ft glass-covered galleria which bisects the structure
Collections: Contemporary art; 1700 master prints; Rembrandt, Durer, Whistler, Goya, Pennell
Exhibitions: Three or more exhibitions each semester; three summer exhibitions
Publications: Exhibition catalogs

AMBLER

A **FUDAN MUSEUM FOUNDATION,** 1522 Schoolhouse Rd, 19002-1936. Tel 215-699-6448 (voice & FAX).
Estab 1988 to exhibit & teach Chinese museology in collaboration with the Shanghai Museum, Shanghai, China. Holds the complete material of the Gao-shan culture & currently building the American collection. Now contains the monoprints of Harry Bertoia
Income: Financed by University
Collections: Permanent collection of Chinese & American archaeology, history, anthropology, ethnography, arts, sciences, technology, industry & business
Activities: Originate traveling exhibitions about Chinese & American achievements in arts, sciences, technology & industry

AUDUBON

M AUDUBON WILDLIFE SANCTUARY, Mill Grove, PO Box 25, 19407. Tel 215-666-5593. *Adminr* D Roger Mower Jr; *Asst to Cur* L Alan Gehret; *Museum Asst* Edward W Graham
Open Tues - Sat 10 AM - 4 PM, Sun 1 - 4 PM. No admis fee. Estab 1951 to display the major artwork of John James Audubon, artist-naturalist, who made Mill Grove his first home in America 1803-06. This is a National Historic Landmark & features two original artworks by Audubon, plus examples of all his major publications. Average Annual Attendance: 25,000 - 30,000
Income: Financed by county appropriation
Collections: Birds of America (double elephant folio, 4 vols, Audubon & Havell); Birds of America (first ed Octavo, 7 vols, Audubon, Lithos by Bowen); Quadrupeds of North America (Imperial size, 2 vols, Audubon & Bachmann); Quadrupeds of North America (Octavo, 3 vols, Audubon, Lithos by Bowen)
Activities: Educ dept for children; lect open to public; gallery talks, tours; museum shop sells books & prints

BETHLEHEM

M KEMERER MUSEUM OF DECORATIVE ARTS, 427 N New St, 18018. Tel 215-868-6868. *Pres* Raymond E Holland; *VPres* Jan Bealer; *Dir* Gerald R Bastoni; *Cur* Sarah W LeCount; *Dir of Development* Linda C Robertson; *Treas* Michael Foster
Open Tues - Sun, noon - 5 PM, cl Mon. Admis adults $3. Estab 1954 for public education. Devoted to the display of antiques and historical and other objects illustrative of the growth of the museum's geographical area. Gallery on second floor of the south wing provides changing exhibits. Average Annual Attendance: 9000. Mem: 400
Income: $180,000 (financed by endowment & membership)
Collections: Bohemian Glass, Early Bethlehem Oil Paintings and Prints, 18th and 19th Century Furniture, Oriental Rugs, Pennsylvania German Frackturs, Victoriana, quilts and coverlets, locally made tall case clocks, and tinware
Exhibitions: Changing gallery exhibitions; changing temporary museum; private collection exhibits
Publications: Newsletter, quarterly
Activities: Docent training; gallery talks; tours; competitions; museum shop sells books, reproductions, prints & decorative arts items

M LEHIGH UNIVERSITY ART GALLERIES, Chandler-Ullman Hall, No 17, 18015. Tel 215-758-3615. *Dir Exhib & Coll* Ricardo Viera; *Asst to Dir* Denise Beslanovits
Open Mon - Fri 9 AM - 10 PM, Sat 9 AM - noon, cl Sun (DuBois Gallery). 9 AM - 5 PM, Sat 9 AM - noon, Sun 2 - 5 PM (Ralph Wilson Gallery). Estab to bring diverse media and understanding to the Lehigh students and general public of the Lehigh Valley area. Collection is maintained in two galleries: DuBois Gallery has four floors of approx 250 running ft of wall hanging space per floor; Ralph Wilson Gallery has two rooms of exhibition space; hall gallery consists of two corridors. Average Annual Attendance: 25,000 (per all galleries)
Income: Financed by endowment and gifts
Collections: Adler Collection of Paintings; Baker Collection of Porcelain; Berman Collection of Paintings & Outdoor Sculpture; Driebe Collection of Paintings; Grace Collection of Paintings; Kempsmith Collection of Sculpture and Graphics; photography collection; Ralph Wilsion Collection of Paintings & Graphics
Exhibitions: Philadelphia, Past & Present; The Deutscher Werkbund; Transformed Houses (sites); Lehigh Valley Artists Biennial (DuBois Gallery)
Publications: Calendar, twice per year; exhibition catalogs
Activities: Classes for adults; lect open to the public, 6 visiting lectrs per year; gallery talks; individual paintings and original objects of art lent to other schools and galleries; originate traveling exhibitions

M MORAVIAN COLLEGE, Payne Gallery, Church St Campus, 18018. Tel 215-861-1675. *Chmn Art Dept* Dr Rudy Ackerman; *Dir* Les Reker; *Asst to Dir* David Leidich
Open Tues - Sun 11 AM - 4 PM. No admis fee. Estab 1982 to present historic & contemporary art to a diverse audience. main floor & mezzanine have a combined total of 200 running ft. Average Annual Attendance: 15,000
Income: Financed by endowment & through the college
Purchases: Collection of paintings by W Elmer Schofield, Susan Eakins & Antonio Martino acquired
Collections: Collection of 18th, 19th & 20th century landscape paintings of Eastern Pennsylvania; Collection of contemporary paintings & prints
Publications: Exhibition catalogues
Activities: Lect open to the public, 8 vis lectr per yr; competitions with awards; scholarships

BLOOMSBURG

M BLOOMSBURG UNIVERSITY OF PENNSYLVANIA, Haas Gallery of Art, Arts Dept All Science Hall, 17815. Tel 717-389-4646. *Dir* Stewart Nagel; *Chmn Dept of Art* Kenneth Wilson
Open Mon - Fri 9 AM - 5 PM. No admis fee. Estab 1966 as an educational and cultural extension of the College's Department of Art. Gallery covers 2350 sq ft with track lighting and three dome skylights. Average Annual Attendance: 16,000
Income: Financed by community activities and grants
Collections: Permanent Collection
Exhibitions: Ten monthly exhibitions in a variety of media
Publications: Exhibition catalogs and brochures, monthly
Activities: Lect open to the public, 6-8 vis lectrs per yr; gallery talks; tours

BOALSBURG

M COLUMBUS CHAPEL & BOAL MANSION MUSEUM, Business Route 322, 16827. Tel 814-466-6210. *Pres* Mathilde Boal Lee; *Dir* Christopher G Lee
Open daily (except Tues) 10 AM - 5 PM June - Labor Day; May, Sept & Oct 2 - 5 PM, weekends in Dec 1:30 - 5 PM. Admis adults $5, children $2. Estab 1952 as a nonprofit educational organization devoted to preservation of this unique American and international heritage and collection. Average Annual Attendance: 25,000
Income: Financed by admissions
Collections: Chapel contains 16th & 17th century Spanish, Italian and Flemish art; furniture, china and glassware; mansion contains 18th and 19th century French, Spanish, Italian, Flemish and American art; weapons: American, French and German (1780-1920)
Activities: Sales shop selling books, slides and postcards

BRYN ATHYN

M ACADEMY OF THE NEW CHURCH, Glencairn Museum, 1001 Cathedral Rd, PO Box 757, 19009. Tel 215-947-9919; FAX 215-938-1056. *Pres* Daniel W Goodenough; *Dir* Stephen H Morley
Open Mon - Fri 9 AM - 5 PM by appointment, Sept - June 2nd Sun 2 - 5 PM. Admis adults $3, children & students free, students $3 for special school program. Estab 1878 to display, study & teach about works of art & artifacts which illustrate the history of world religions. Museum housed in Romanesque style building (1939), former home of Raymond & Mildred Pitcairn
Income: Financed by endowment
Collections: †American Indian; †Ancient Near East; †Egypt; †Greece & Rome; Medieval sculpture, stained glass & treasury objects; †19th & 20th Century art by Swedenborgian artists; oriental rugs
Exhibitions: (1991) Medieval Art: A new installation. (1993) Ancient Faith: Prayer Rugs from the Collection
Activities: Classes for children, docent training; lectures open to the public, 3 vis lectr per year; concerts; gallery talks; tours; individual paintings & original art objects of art lent to institutions which provide satisfactory evidence of adequate security, insurance, fire protection

BRYN MAWR

L BRYN MAWR COLLEGE, Art and Archaeology Library, Thomas Library, 19010. Tel 215-526-5088; FAX 215-526-7480. *Head Librn* Eileen Markson; *Library Asst* Carol Vassallo
Open during academic year Mon - Thurs 9 AM - midnight, Fri 9 AM - 10 PM, Sat 9 AM - 5 PM, Sun 2 PM - midnight, summer Mon - Fri 9 AM - 5 PM. Estab 1931 to serve the needs of the general college program, the undergraduate majors and graduate students through the PhD degree in both history of art and Classical and Near Eastern archeology. Non-circulating
Income: Financed by college funds
Library Holdings: Vols 90,000; Per subs 450; Micro — Fiche, reels; Other — Exhibition catalogs, pamphlets
Special Subjects: Early Christian and Byzantine, Italian Renaissance, Italian Baroque, Impressionism, Greek architecture and sculpture, Near Eastern archaeology, Aegean archaeology

CARLISLE

M DICKINSON COLLEGE, Trout Gallery, High St, 17013-2896. Tel 717-245-1344; FAX 717-245-1899. *Dir* Peter M Lukehart; *Registrar & Exhib Preparator* Dwayne Franklin; *Community Outreach* Martha A Metz
Open Tues - Sat 10 AM - 4 PM. Estab 1983 as display & care facilities for college's art collection, serves college & community. Two floors with exhibition & permanent collection space
Income: $167,564 (financed by endowment, college & special grants)
Purchases: Joseph Stella's Bold Flowers; African Art; Baselitz's Madchen mit Harmonika IV
Collections: Carnegie Collection of prints; Cole Collection of Oriental & decorative arts; Gerofsky Collection of African art; Potamkin Collection of 19th & 20th century work; 5000 Old Master & modern prints
Exhibitions: (1991) Tibetan Tantric Art. (1992) Ordered Chaos: Surrealist Art; Leon Golub Worldwide; Artists of the American West; China Between Revolutions
Publications: Exhibition catalogues, 3 - 5 per year
Activities: Classes for adults & children; lect open to public, 4 - 8 vis lectr per year; book traveling exhibitions 2 - 4 per year; originate traveling exhibitions

CHADDS FORD

M BRANDYWINE RIVER MUSEUM, US 1, PO Box 141, 19317. Tel 215-388-2700; FAX 215-388-1197. *Dir* James H Duff; *Business Mgr* John Anderson; *Assoc Cur* Virginia O'Hara; *Cur Coll* Gene E Harris; *Dir Public Relations* Lucinda Laird; *Registrar* Jean A Gilmore; *Supv Educ* Mary Cronin; *Bookstore Mgr* Sue Coleburn; *Librn* Ruth Bassett
Open daily 9:30 AM - 4:30 PM, cl Christmas. Admis adults $5, sr citizens, students & children $2.50. Estab 1971, devoted to the preservation, documentation and interpretation of art history in the Brandywine Valley, the history of American illustration, American still-life painting, and the relationship of regional art to the natural environment. Four main galleries are housed in a renovated 1864 grist mill with contemporary additions for public services, storage, offices, restaurant & bookstore. Average Annual Attendance: 175,000. Mem: 3700; dues $30 - $2500
Purchases: $64,000
Collections: †American illustration; †art of the Brandywine Valley from early 19th century; †regional artists of the 20th century; †American still-life painting, drawing and sculpture, including a major Wyeth Family Collection

Exhibitions: (1991 - 92) George A Weymouth: A Retrospective; William Tylee Ranney: East of the Mississippi; Portraits & History Paintings of Alonzo Chappel; The Land of the Brandywine; The American Paintings of Herman Herzog; The Helga Pictures: Then & Now American Illustration: Recent Accessions from the Jane Collette Wilcox Collection; A B Frost Retrospective; Eakins at Avondale
Publications: The Catalyst, quarterly; Catalogue of the Collection; exhibition catalogs
Activities: Classes for children; tours; individual paintings and original objects of art lent to other museums for exhibition purposes; traveling exhibitions organized and circulated; museum shop selling books, reproductions, slides, postcards and catalogs
L **Library,** PO Box 141, 19317. Tel 215-388-2700; FAX 215-388-1197. *Librn* Ruth Bassett
Open daily 9:30 AM - 4:30 PM. For reference to staff and volunteers; by appointment to the public
Purchases: $4000
Library Holdings: Vols 6500; Per subs 20; Posters; Other — Clipping files, exhibition catalogs, manuscripts, memorabilia, pamphlets, photographs, reproductions
Special Subjects: The History of American illustration in books and periodicals; The History of Regional Art of the Brandywine Valley
Collections: Howard Pyle's published work; Other collections related to American illustration & American art history; Wyeth family memorabilia
Exhibitions: Illustrated Books From The Museum Library

CHESTER

M **WIDENER UNIVERSITY,** Art Museum, 13th & Potter Sts, 19013. Tel 215-499-1189, 499-4000. *Acting Dir* Patricia Brant; *Asst to Dir* Rebecca Warda
Open Tues - Sat 10 AM - 4PM. Estab 1970
Income: Financed by endowment and University funding
Collections: 18th and 19th century Oriental art objects; 19th century European landscape and genre pictures; 20th century American paintings and sculpture
Exhibitions: (1989) Lee R Chesney III, Printmaker; Deborah Deichler/William Gannotta; Ashbrook in China; Alfred O Deshong Collection; W. Elmer Schofield. (1990) John G Bullock & the Photo-Secession; Alfred O Deshong Collection
Publications: Exhibition catalog
Activities: Lectures; guided tours

CLARION

M **CLARION UNIVERSITY,** Hazel Sandford Gallery, 16214. Tel 814-226-2412; WATS 800-669-2000. *Dir* Joelien Schaffer
Open Mon - Fri 10 AM - 1 PM, Sun 2 - 4 PM. No admis fee. Estab 1970 for aesthic enjoyment and artistic education of students. Gallery is 66 ft long, 17ft 3 inches wide; lit by some 50 adjustable spot lights; one side of gallery is glassed in; other side is fabric-covered panels; and a dozen free standing panels, available for hanging. Average Annual Attendance: 4000. Mem: 85
Income: Financed by university & memberships
Purchases: Lidded basket by Chris Richard; High Country paintings and refrigerator by Norman Scott Quinn
Collections: Original paintings, drawings and prints, purchased from selected artists who have shown at gallery; sculpture and †ceramics; †photographs
Publications: Monthly announcements of shows
Activities: Lectures open to the public, 2 - 3 vis lectr per yr; concerts; gallery talks; tours; competitions; individual paintings and original objects of art lent to departments on campus and other state colleges; lending collection contains original art works, original prints, paintings, photographs and sculpture; book traveling exhibitions

COLLEGEVILLE

M **URSINUS COLLEGE,** Philip & Muriel Berman Museum of Art, Main St, PO Box 1000, 19426-1000. Tel 215-489-4111, Ext 2354; FAX 215-489-0627. *Dir* Lisa Tremper Barnes; *Colls Mgr* Nancy E Fago; *Admins Asst* Jane McLaughlin
No admis fee. Estab 1987 to support the educational goals of Ursinus College & to contribute to the cultural life of the campus & regional community. Main gallery: 3200 sq ft; sculpture court; upper gallery 800 sq ft. Average Annual Attendance: 32,000. Mem: 155; dues minimum $50; meeting in Oct, Feb, June
Income: $150,000 (financed by endowment, mem, Ursinus College, government, foundation & corporate grants)
Purchases: $25,000
Collections: Philip & Muriel Berman Collection; 18th, 19th & 20th century European & American Art (drawings, paintings, prints & sculpture); Lynn Chadwick Sculpture Collection
Exhibitions: Temporary exhibitions, 10 per year; selections from permanent collections on continuous view
Publications: Exhibitions catalogues; Museum newsletter, 4 times a year
Activities: Dramatic programs; docent programs; lect open to public, 4 - 5 vis lectr per year; lending collection contains 1000 paintings; book traveling exhibitions 4 per year; originate annual traveling exhibitions; retail store

DOYLESTOWN

M **BUCKS COUNTY HISTORICAL SOCIETY,** Mercer Museum, 84 S Pine, 18901. Tel 215-345-0210. *Chairperson* W Roy Colb; *Cur Coll* Cory Amsler
Open Tues - Sat 10 AM - 5 PM; Sun 1 - 5 PM; Mar - Dec. Admis adults $3 and students $1.50. Estab 1880. Inside this poured, re-inforced concrete building, four galleries wrap around a towering central court where different hand crafts are exhibited inside small cubicles. Additional artifacts hang from ceilings, walls and railings. A six story tower on each end completes the building. Average Annual Attendance: 40,000. Mem: 2400; dues $20 and up; annual meeting Nov

Collections: Over 40,000 artifacts representing more than 40 early American crafts, their tools and finished products; large American folk art collection; the history and growth of our country as seen through the work of the human hand
Exhibitions: Continuous small changing exhibits. (1993) Developing Bucks County
Publications: Journal, bi-monthly; newsletter, monthly
Activities: Classes for adults and children; lect open to public, 6-7 vis lectr per year; Annual Folk Festival; museum shop selling books, magazines, reproductions and prints
L **Spruance Library,** 84 S Pine, 18901. Tel 215-345-0210; FAX 215-230-0823. *Librn* Terry A McNealy
Open Tues 1 - 9 PM, Wed - Fri 10 AM - 5 PM, cl July 4th, Thanksgiving, Christmas & New Year's Day. No admis fee for BCHS members only. Open to the public for reference only
Library Holdings: Vols 18,000; Per subs 100; Archives; Micro — Reels; Other — Clipping files, manuscripts, pamphlets, photographs
Special Subjects: Folk Art, Crafts and Early Industries of America

M **JAMES A MICHENER ARTS CENTER,** 138 S Pine St, PO Box 2213, 18901. Tel 215-340-9800. *Dir* Bruce Katsiff
Estab 1987
Collections: Drawings; paintings; sculpture
Exhibitions: Fern Coppedge Retrospective; Diversity of Expression, Blake Edwards; American Indians; Edward S Curtis
Activities: Lect open to public

EASTON

M **LAFAYETTE COLLEGE,** Morris R Williams Center for the Arts, Art Gallery, Hamilton & High St, 18042. Tel 215-250-5361, 250-5010. *Gallery Dir* Michiko Okaya; *Center Dir* H Ellis Finger; *Center Adminr* Susan Ellis
Open Tues - Fri 10 AM - 5 PM, Sun 2 - 5 PM & by appointment. No admis fee. Estab 1983 to present a variety of exhibitions for enrichment of campus & community's exposure to visual arts. Versatile space with movable panels & 160 running ft of wall space, climate control & track lighting
Income: Financed by endowment, college program subsidy, government grants
Collections: 19th & 20th century American painting, prints & photographs
Exhibitions: Bill Barrette; PingChong (performance artist): In the Absence of Memory; William King (sculpture) Grace Hartigan (painting); William Tucker. (1991) Robert Watts. (1992) Robert Watts: The Emperors Old Clothes; Ancient Andean Textiles
Publications: Annual exhibit catalogue; brochures; exhibit handouts
Activities: Lectures open to public

EPHRATA

A **HISTORICAL SOCIETY OF THE COCALICO VALLEY,** 249 W Main St, PO Box 193, 17522. Tel 717-733-1616. *Librn* Cynthia Marquet
Open Tues - Fri 9 AM - 5 PM. No admis fee. Estab 1957. Average Annual Attendance: 1200. Mem: 450; dues family $18, individual $10
Income: $35,000 (financed by endowment, mem, publications)
Collections: Pennsylvania German Folk Art
Publications: Journal of the Historical Society of the Cocalico Valley, annual
Activities: Children's classes; lect open to public, 10 vis lectr per yr

ERIE

M **ERIE ART MUSEUM,** 411 State St, 16501. Tel 814-459-5477. *Pres* Michael Victor; *Dir* John Vanco; *Treas* Michael Bergquiste
Open Tues - Sat 11 AM - 5 PM, Sun 1 - 5 PM. Admis $1.50 for non-members. Estab 1898 for the advancement of visual arts. Galleries are located in historic building. Average Annual Attendance: 40,000. Mem: Dues family $35, individual $25
Income: $345,000 (financed through private donations, fundraising, memberships; some grants)
Collections: Indian Bronze & Stone Sculpture; Chinese Porcelains, Jades, Textiles; American Ceramics (historical & contemporary); Graphics (European, American & Oriental); Photography; Paintings & Drawings (predominately 20th century); Contemporary Baskets
Exhibitions: Frederick Hurten Rhead: An English Potter in America; Paperthick: Forms & Images in Cast Paper; The Tactile Vessel - New Basket Forms; TECO - Art Pottery of the Prairie School; Art of India; Early Color Photography; Chicago Works - Art from the Windy City; Annual Spring Show; Art of China & Japan
Publications: Four exhibition catalogues
Activities: Classes for adults and children; docent training; gallery talks; tours; competitions; concerts; individual paintings and original objects of art lent to public buildings, community centers, colleges; lending collection contains original art works; traveling exhibitions organized and circulated; sales shop sells books, gifts etc. Frame shop offers retail framing
L **ERIE COUNTY LIBRARY SYSTEM,** Plavcan Gallery, 27 S Park Row, 16501-1102. Tel 814-451-6900. *Dir* Michele M Ridge
Open Mon & Tues 9 AM - 9 PM, Wed - Fri 9 AM - 8 PM, Sat 9 AM - 5 PM, cl Sun. No admis fee. Estab 1899 to provide public library services to the community. Gallery contains original paintings, drawings and prints and reproductions of paintings and sculpture. Mem: 160,000
Income: Financed by county and state appropriations
Library Holdings: Micro — Cards, fiche, reels; AV — Cassettes 500, motion pictures 800, v-tapes 1000; Other — Clipping files, original art works 45, pamphlets, photographs, sculpture
Activities: Original paintings, prints, drawings and sculpture reproductions lent; lending collection contains color reproductions and photographs

M ERIE HISTORICAL MUSEUM & PLANETARIUM, 356 W Sixth St, 16507.
Tel 814-453-5811. *Dir* June C Pintea
Open Tues - Sun 1 - 5 PM, extended summer hours. Admis adults $1, children
under 18 free. Estab 1899 to display and collect regional and maritime history
and art. Museum is located in a Victorian mansion built in 1891-1892 and
designed by Green & Wicks of Buffalo, NY. Average Annual Attendance: 30,000
Income: $120,000 (financed by Erie School District)
Collections: Moses Billings (paintings); George Ericson-Eugene Iverd (paintings);
genre paintings; Native American pottery; Southwest & Northwest Coast baskets;
Victorian decorative arts; †Marx Toys
Exhibitions: Rotating exhibits of historical and art interest
Publications: Exhibition catalogs
Activities: Docent tours; film programs; lesson tours for students; lectures open
to public, 3 vis lectr per yr; gallery talks; tours; competitions; book traveling
exhibitions; originate traveling exhibitions; museum shop sells books, magazines
and prints

FRANKLIN CENTER

M FRANKLIN MINT MUSEUM, 19091. Tel 215-459-6168. *Mgr* Judie Ashworth
Open Tues - Sat 9:30 AM - 4:30 PM, Sun 1 - 4:30 PM, cl Mon. No admis fee.
Estab 1973 to make available to the general public a location where the
collectibles created by The Franklin Mint can be viewed. Average Annual
Attendance: 55,000
Income: Financed by Franklin Mint funding
Collections: †Etchings & woodblock prints; †foreign coinage - coins minted for
19 foreign governments; †heirloom furniture; †medallic collecitons; †heirloom
dolls; †leather bound books ornamented in 22 karat gold; †porcelain, †crystal,
†bronze & †pewter art; precision dye-cast models
Activities: Franklin Mint Gallery Store selling jewelry, medals, greeting cards
and collectibles

GLENSIDE

M BEAVER COLLEGE ART GALLERY, Church & Easton Rds, 19038. Tel 215-
572-2131. *Gallery Dir* Paula Marincola; *Dept Chmn* Dennis Kuronen
Open Mon - Fri 11 AM - 4:30 PM, June 1 - 4 PM. No admis fee. Estab 1969 to
show contemporary art generally. Gallery dimensions 20 x 50 ft. Average Annual
Attendance: 2000
Collections: Benton Spruance Print Collection
Publications: Brochures for major exhibitions, 3 per year
Activities: Lectures open to public, 4 vis lectr per yr; gallery talks; competitions;
awards

GREENSBURG

L SETON HILL COLLEGE, Reeves Memorial Library, Seton Dr, 15601. Tel 412-
834-2200; FAX 412-834-4611.
For lending & reference. Circ 40,000
Library Holdings: Vols 101,000; Per subs 500; Micro — Cards; AV — A-tapes,
cassettes, fs, motion pictures, rec, slides, v-tapes; Other — Original art works,
pamphlets, sculpture

M WESTMORELAND MUSEUM OF ART, 221 N Main St, 15601-1898. Tel
412-837-1500; FAX 412-837-2921. *CEO & Dir* Dr Paul A Chew; *Admin Dir of
Development* Betty W Hammer; *Executive Asst to Dir* Regina L Narad; *Dir
Educ* Clara Pascoe; *Preparator & Registrar* John A Sakal; *Asst Registrar* Michael
Beam; *Conservator* Christine Daulton; *Mgr Museum Store* Helen F Hartzell;
Membership & Development Secy Janet Carns; *Chief of Security* Eugene
Komives
Open Tues - Sat 10 AM - 5 PM; Sun 1 - 5 PM, cl Mon & holidays. No admis
fee. Estab 1949 to operate & maintain a free public art museum. The museum
houses five galleries for changing exhibitions; six galleries for permanent
collection. Average Annual Attendance: 30,000. Mem: dues $2 - $1000 & up
Income: Financed by endowment, grants & gifts
Collections: †American art (paintings, drawings, sculpture & decorative arts);
†American prints; †antique toys
Exhibitions: (1992) Holiday Exhibition: Antique Toy Collection & Large Gauge
Model Train Display; Selected Works of Art from Southwestern Pennsylvania
Private Collections; A World Observed, The Art of Everett Longley Warner,
1877 - 1963
Publications: Collections, quarterly newsletter
Activities: Classes for children; docent training; lect open to the public; gallery
talks; tours; individual paintings & original objects of art lent to museums; book
traveling exhibitions; originate traveling exhibitions; museum shop sells books,
magazines, original art, reproductions, slides, toys, cards, prints & crafts
L Art Reference Library, 221 N Main St, 15601. Tel 412-837-1500; FAX 412-837-
2921. *Dir* Dr Paul A Chew
Open Tues - Sat 10 AM - 5 PM; Sun 1 - 5 PM, cl Mon & holidays. Estab 1949
for art reference. For reference only. Average Annual Attendance: 18,000
Purchases: $1200
Library Holdings: Vols 8000; Per subs 40; Other — Clipping files, exhibition
catalogs, pamphlets
Special Subjects: American art

GREENVILLE

M THIEL COLLEGE, Sampson Art Gallery, College Ave, 16125. Tel 412-588-
7700, Ext 415. *Dir* Ronald Pivovar; *Dir of Permanent Coll* Bill Mancuso;
Student Dir Sandy Reed
Open Mon - Fri 1 - 9 PM, Sat 11 AM - 5 PM, Sun 11 AM - 9 PM. No admis
fee. Estab 1971 to provide students, faculty, college staff and the community
with a gallery featuring a variety of exhibitions, and give students an opportunity
to show their work. Gallery has white walls, track floodlighting system, linoleum
tile floor, and one window wall. Average Annual Attendance: 1000
Income: $1000 (financed by College budget)
Activities: Lectures open to the public, gallery talks

HARRISBURG

M ART ASSOCIATION OF HARRISBURG, School and Galleries, 21 N Front
St, 17101. Tel 717-236-1432; FAX 717-236-6631. *Pres* Carrie Wissler-Thomas
Open Mon - Thurs 9 AM - 4 PM & 6:30 - 9 PM, Fri 9 AM - 4 PM, Sat 10 AM
- 3 PM. No admis fee. Estab 1926 to act as showcase for member artists and
other professionals; community services offered. Building is historic Brownstone
Building, former Governor's mansion (1817) & holds 2 floors of galleries,
classroom & a garden. Average Annual Attendance: 5000. Mem: 800, dues $30 -
$1000; annual meeting in May
Income: Financed by endowment and membership
Collections: Old area masters; member's work; Lavery & Lebret
Exhibitions: Annual International Juried Exhibition; Art School Annual;
invitational shows; membership shows, 2 times per year; community shows in 9
locations - 36 total per year
Publications: Monthly exhibition announcements; newsletter, 6 times per year;
quarterly school brochure; Poetry Group: Paper Sword, bi-monthly
Activities: Classes for adults and children; lect open to public, competitions open
to all states; monetary awards; concerts; gallery talks; tours; scholarships offered;
sales shop sells original art & prints by member artists

A DOSHI CENTER FOR CONTEMPORARY ART, 441 Market St, 17101. Tel
717-233-6744. *Pres* David G Forney; *VPres* Alice Ann Schwab; *Exec Dir*
Kathleen A Philbin
Open Mon - Fri 11 AM - 4 PM, Sat 2 - 5 PM, cl Sun. No admis fee. Estab 1972
as a non-profit gallery offering exposure to artists and enlightenment to the
community. gallery is on street level. Average Annual Attendance: 6500. Mem:
242; dues benefactor $500, patron $100, donor $50, supporting $25; board
meeting every second Wed every month
Income: $31,000 (financed by grants from Pa Council on the Arts, Allied Fund
for the Arts, memberships & corporate contributions)
Exhibitions: Five 2 person exhibitions; one 3 person exhibition; two juried
competitive exhibitions; one 20th Anniversary retrospective; Annual Holiday
Show
Activities: Student internships; lect open to public; gallery talks; tours; Maya
Schock Educational Fund awarded; invitational cradft show & sale

A PENNSYLVANIA DEPARTMENT OF EDUCATION, Arts in Education
Program, 333 Market St, 8th floor, 17126-0333. Tel 717-783-3958. *Sr Adviser*
Beth Cornell; *Dir Arts in Special Education Project* Lola Kearns; *Dir,
Governor's School for the Arts* Dr Gene Van Dyke
The Arts in Education Program provides leadership & consultative & evaluative
services to all Pennsylvania schools & arts educational agencies in arts program
development & instructional practices. Infusion of arts processes into
differentiated curriculums for all students is a particular thrust. The program
offers assistance in designing aesthetic learning environments & consultation in
identifying & employing regional & community resources for arts education

A STATE MUSEUM OF PENNSYLVANIA, Third & North Sts, PO Box 1026,
17108-1026. Tel 717-787-3362. *Dir* Anita D Blackaby; *Sr Cur Art Coll* N Lee
Stevens
Open Tues - Sat 9 AM - 5 PM, Sun noon - 5 PM, cl Mon. Estab 1945 to
interpret the history & heritage of Pennsylvania. Mem: 3000; dues vary; annual
meeting 2nd Wed in Apr
Income: $13,000,000 for entire commission
Exhibitions: Art of the State, annual spring-summer juried statewide exhibition;
Contemporary Artists Series; changing history exhibits
Publications: Pennsylvania Heritage, quarterly
Activities: Classes for adults & children; docent training; lectures open to the
public; concerts; tours; exhibits; special events
M Pennsylvania Historical & Museum Commission, PO Box 1026, 17108-1026. Tel
717-787-4980; FAX 717-783-1073. *Dir* Anita D Blackaby; *Sr Cur Art* N Lee
Stevens; *Registrar* Susan Hanna
Open Tues - Sat 9 AM - 5 PM, Sun Noon - 5 PM. Offices Mon - Fri 8:30 AM -
5 PM. Mus estab 1905. Average Annual Attendance: 200,000. Mem: 700; dues
$35; annual meeting 2nd Wed in Apr
Income: Financed by state & private funds
Collections: Anthropology; archaeology; ceramics; decorative arts; folk art; glass;
silver; textiles; Indian artifacts; paintings & sculpture 1.2 million objects in all
disciplines relating to Pennsylvania
Exhibitions: (1993) Art of the State, annual juried exhibition; Contemporary
Artists Series; CAPITOLS
Publications: Books, brochures, quarterly calendar, quarterly newsletter
Activities: Classes for adults and children; docent training; lectures open to
public; 12 vis lectr per yr; concerts; gallery talks; tours; awards; individual
paintings & original objects of art lent to qualified & approved institutions; book
traveling exhibitions, 1-2 per yr; originate traveling exhibitions; museum shop
sells books, reproductions, prints & gift items
L Library, PO Box 1026, 17108-1026. Tel 717-783-9898; FAX 717-783-1073.
Librn Carol W Tallman
Open to the public for use on premises only, by appointment
Library Holdings: Vols 27,000; Per subs 200; Micro — Fiche, reels; AV —
Motion pictures, v-tapes; Other — Clipping files, exhibition catalogs
Special Subjects: Archaeology, Decorative Arts, Historical Material, Fine Arts
M Brandywine Battlefield Park, US Route 1, PO Box 202, Chadds Ford, 19317.
Tel 215-459-3342; FAX 215-459-9586. *Admnr* Dennis K McDaniel; *Dir Visitor
Servs* Maurice Patrizio; *Educ Coordr* Lori Dillard
Open 9 AM - 5 PM. Estab 1947 to commemorate Battle of the Brandywine, Sept
11, 1777. 2 historic Quaker farmhouses. Average Annual Attendance: 90,000.
Mem: 85; dues $35; annual meeting in spring
Income: $295,000 (financed by endowment, mem & state appropriation)
Activities: Classes for children
M Railroad Museum of Pennsylvania, Route 741, PO Box 15, Strasburg, 17579. Tel
717-687-8628. *Dir* Robert L Emerson; *Cur* Benjamin F G Kline Jr; *Office Mgr*
Cheri S Ney; *Prog Coordr* Robert McFadden
Open Mon - Sat 9 AM - 5 PM, Sun noon - 5 PM, cl Mon Nov - Apr. Admis
Adults $5, sr citizens $4, children $3. Estab 1975 for preservation of significant

artifacts appropriate to railroading. Average Annual Attendance: 150,000. Mem: 700; annual dues $15 - $100
Income: $750,000 (financed by state appropriation & private fundraising
Purchases: $45,000 (negative collection of the Baldwin Locomotive Works acquired)
Collections: Railroad Rolling Stock; locomotives & related artifacts including tools, maps, manuals, timetables, passes, uniforms, silverware & lanterns
Activities: Children programs; docent programs; lect open to public, 6 vis lectr per yr; lending collection includes paintings & art objects; museum shop sells books, prints & magazines

HAVERFORD

A **MAIN LINE CENTER OF THE ARTS,** Old Buck Rd & Lancaster Ave, 19041. Tel 215-525-0272. *Exec Dir* Judy Herman; *Prog Asst* Rebecca Kootchick; *Registrar* Tonya Weaver
Open Mon - Fri 10 AM - 4 PM, Sat 10 AM - 1 PM. No admis fee. Estab 1937 to develop and encourage the fine arts. Three large, well lit galleries, completely modernized to accommodate exhibits including sculptures, ceramics, paintings, crafts. Mem: 800; dues family $35, adult $25 & children $20; meetings once a month except Aug
Income: Financed by membership, tuition & fund raising
Exhibitions: Juried Exhibitions & Sale; membership exhibitions
Publications: Brochures, five times a year
Activities: Classes for adults, teens & children; gallery talks; trips; tours; competitions with awards; individual paintings & original objects of art lent to banks; lending collection contains original art works by children's & adult classes

HERSHEY

M **HERSHEY MUSEUM,** 170 W Hershey Park Dr, 17033. Tel 717-534-3439. *Dir* David L Parke Jr
Open daily 10 AM - 5 PM, summer daily 10 AM - 6 PM. Admis adults $4, 3 - 15 yrs $1.75, 2 & under free. Estab 1937 to preserve & collect history of Hershey, Central PA hritage (Pennsylvania Germans). Average Annual Attendance: 100,000. Mem: 1000; dues family $30
Collections: History of Hershey (the town, the business, & M S Hershey); 19th C Pennsylvania German Life - American Indian & Alaskan Eskimo
Exhibitions: Hudson River School Painting; M S Hershey; Navajo Images; PA German Life; Treasure of the Conception; PA quilts & coverlets; other traditional crafts; Soup Tureens from the Campbell Museum; American Illustrative Art from Delaware Art Museum; Industries of the Shakers from the Smithsonian; Carowel Art; Craft & Community (Balch INstitute)
Publications: Newsletter, 3 times per year
Activities: Classes for adults and children; docent training; family programs; programs in schools; lect open to public; concerts; gallery talks; tours; museum shop sells books and craft items relating to museum collections; childrens' area

HONESDALE

M **WAYNE COUNTY HISTORICAL SOCIETY,** Museum, 810 Main St, PO Box 446, 18431-0446. Tel 717-253-3240. *Pres* Marjorie Murphy; *VPres* Kurt Reed; *VPres* Dorothy Noble; *Secy* Alma Hames; *Treas* Charles Hames
Admis adults $1, children 12 - 18 $.50, children under 12 free. Estab 1924 as a repository of artifacts, publications, archival & other items relating to Wayne County. Average Annual Attendance: 19,750. Mem: 675; dues $10; 4 meetings per year
Income: $25,000 (financed by dues, donations, sales & grants)
Collections: Artifacts of Wayne County History; Jennie Brownscomb (paintings)
Activities: School group tours; lect open to public, 4 vis lectr per year; tours; sales shop sells books, maps, t-shirts, train memorabilia

INDIANA

M **INDIANA UNIVERSITY OF PENNSYLVANIA,** Kipp Gallery, Sprowls Hall, 15705. Tel 412-357-2530. *Gallery Dir* Mary Ella Marra
Open Mon - Fri noon - 4 PM; Sat & Sun 2 - 4 PM. No admis fee. Estab 1970 to make available a professional gallery program to Western Pennsylvania and to the university community. Versatile space with portable wall system, track lighting, secure, humidity controlled. Average Annual Attendance: 12,000
Income: Financed by Student Coop Assoc
Activities: Lect open to public, 3-5 vis lectr per yr; gallery talks; tours; traveling exhibitions organized and circulated; sales shop selling original art and prints

KUTZTOWN

KUTZTOWN UNIVERSITY

M **Sharadin Art Gallery,** 19530. Tel 215-683-4546, 683-4500; FAX 215-683-4547. *Gallery Dir* Mary Ella Marra
Open Mon - Fri 10 AM - 4 PM; Sat 12 - 5 PM; Sun 2 - 5 PM. No admis fee. Estab 1956 to make the best of the contemporary arts available to the town and college communities
Income: Financed by state & private appropriations
Collections: Approximately 400 works in prints, drawings and paintings
Publications: Brochure listing gallery shows; annual catalog
Activities: Artist-in-residence series; lectures; European travel tours
L **Rohrbach Library,** 19530. Tel 215-683-4480; FAX 215-683-4483. *Dir Library Serv* Margaret Devlin
Open Mon - Thurs 7:45 AM - midnight, Fri 7:45 AM - 5 PM, Sat 10 AM - 4 PM, Sun 2 PM - midnight. Estab 1866. Circ 130,000
Library Holdings: Vols 401,842; Per subs 2022; Micro — Cards 17,331, fiche 861,211, prints 212,908, reels 20,304; AV — A-tapes, cassettes, fs, motion pictures, rec, slides; Other — Exhibition catalogs, pamphlets
Special Subjects: Art Education, Art History, Russian Art
Collections: Curriculum Materials; maps; Russian Culture

A **NEW ARTS PROGRAM INC,** Gallery, 173 W Main St, PO Box 82, 19530-0082. Tel 215-683-6440. *Dir* James F L Carroll
Open Thurs & Fri 1 - 5 PM, Sat 10 AM - 2 PM. Estab 1974 for artists who have counsultation residencies with the program & eastern Pennsylvania artists. 310 sq ft of exhibition space, wall 8 ft high, 65 linear ft. Average Annual Attendance: 3500. Mem: 150; annual dues $25
Income: $50,000 (financed by mem, state appropriation, foundations & sales)
Exhibitions: Eastern Pennsylvania Artists Salon Invitational (small works)
Publications: In & out of Kutztown; 71 Small Works on Paper; Program Journal, annually; Flyers Preview, 3 or 4 per year
Activities: Lect open to the public; awards; Sales shop sells NAP books, prints & posters

LANCASTER

M **COMMUNITY GALLERY OF LANCASTER COUNTY,** 135 N Lime St, 17602. Tel 717-394-3497. *Pres* Nancy Roskos; *Dir* Shirley M Reed
Open Mon - Sat 10 AM - 4 PM; Sun 12 - 4 PM. No admis fee. Estab 1965 to present the best quality in art exhibits. Average Annual Attendance: 17,000. Mem: 1500; dues, various categories
Income: $120,000 (financed by mem, local business and county commissioners)
Exhibitions: Red Groom; Elizabeth Layton; Sinikka Laine & Caroline Rister Lee
Publications: Quarterly newsheet
Activities: Docent training, art appreciation for 4-11 yr old children; lect; gallery talks; bus trips; museum shop

M **HERITAGE CENTER OF LANCASTER COUNTY,** 13 W King St, PO Box 997, 17603. Tel 717-299-6440. *Dir & Cur* Patricia J Keller; *Cur Education* Tricia Meley; *Assoc Cur* Susan Messimer
Open May - Nov 10 AM - 4 PM. No admis fee. Estab 1976 to preserve & exhibit Lancaster County decorative arts. Three major galleries. Average Annual Attendance: 22,000. Mem: 800; dues vary; annual meeting third Wed in May
Income: $300,000 (financed by endowment, mem, city appropriation, grants, fundraising efforts)
Collections: †Lancaster County Decorative Arts & Crafts
Exhibitions: (1991) New Discoveries
Activities: Children's classes; docent programs; retail stores sells books, slides

A **LANCASTER COUNTY ART ASSOCIATION,** 22 E Vine St, 17602. Tel 717-299-2788. *Pres* Richard Ressel; *Office Mgr* Sheryl Brinkman
Open Mon - Fri 9 AM - 1 PM, Sat & Sun 1 - 4 PM during exhibitions. No admis fee. Estab 1936, incorporated 1950, to increase appreciation of & participation in the fine arts. Average Annual Attendance: 250. Mem: 600; dues $20; general mem meeting the second Sunday of the month, Oct - May
Income: Financed by house tours, classes, contributions & volunteer service
Exhibitions: Monthly exhibitions for professional & non-professional members
Publications: Monthly newsletter; annual membership brochure
Activities: Classes for adults & children; lect open to the public; 7 vis lectr per yr; house tours; competitions with awards; scholarships

M **LANDIS VALLEY MUSEUM,** 2451 Kissel Hill Rd, 17601. Tel 717-569-0401; FAX 717-560-2147. *Dir* Robert W Johnson; *Cur & Education* Elizabeth Johnson; *Cur Collections* Vernon S Gunnion
Open Tues - Sat 9 AM - 5 PM, Sun noon - 5 PM, cl some holidays. Admis adults $3, sr citizens $2, children 6-17 $1.50 children under 6 free, group rates available. Estab 1925 to collect, preserve and interpret Pennsylvania rural life and Pennsylvania German culture, circa 1750 to 1900; farm implements, crafts, tools, domestic furnishings and folk art. The outdoor museum has 25 exhibit buildings, including restored 18th and 19th century structures and historical gardins landscapes, as well as historical animal breeds. Average Annual Attendance: 50,000. Mem: 1200; dues $5 and up
Income: Financed by state appropriation and local support group
Collections: Folk art including ceramics, textiles, furniture and decorative ironware, tools, farm implements, baskets, toys
Publications: Newsletter, 4 times per year; Valley Gazette; special exhibit catalogs
Activities: Classes for adults; docent training; lectures open to public, 7-10 vis lectrs per year; tours; traditional crafts programs, special events; individual paintings & original objects of art lent to other museums & historic sites; museum shop sells books, original art, reproductions, prints, crafts items and period reproductions
L **Library,** 2451 Kissel Hill Rd, 17601. Tel 717-569-0401. *Dir* Robert W Johnson
Open to staff, scholars by appointment for reference only
Library Holdings: Vols 12,000; Per subs 25
Special Subjects: Crafts, Decorative Arts, Folk Art, Historical Material, Local & Pennsylvania German culture

M **ROCK FORD FOUNDATION, INC,** Rock Ford Plantation & Kauffman Museum, 881 Rock Ford Rd, PO Box 264, 17603. Tel 717-392-7223. *Exec Dir* Lockett Ford Ballard Jr
Open Apr - Oct Tues - Sat 10 AM - 4 PM, Sun noon - 4 PM, cl Mon. Estab 1959 for preservation of General Edward Hand Mansion. Average Annual Attendance: 6000. Mem: 600; dues $15 - $100; annual meeting 1st Fri in Dec
Income: $120,000 (financed by mem, endowment, shop sales & special events)
Purchases: $10,000
Collections: †American furniture & decorative arts 1780 - 1802; Pennsylvania Folk Arts 1780 - 1850
Publications: Newsletter, semi-annual
Activities: Children's classes; docent programs; retail store sells books & reproductions

LENHARTSVILLE

A PENNSYLVANIA DUTCH FOLK CULTURE SOCIETY INC, Pennsylvania
Dutch Folklife Museum, Folk Culture Center, 19534-0015. Tel 215-562-4803.
Pres Florence Baver; *Secy* George Unangst; *Consultant* Peter Fritsch
Open 10 AM - 5 PM. Admis $3. Estab 1965 for preservation of the heritage of
the people of the area. Average Annual Attendance: 2000. Mem: 400; dues $10;
annual meeting in Nov
Income: $30,000 (financed by endowment, mem, donations & fund raising
events)
Purchases: Genealogical material
Collections: Folklore, Genealogy, Local History Library; Log House Colonial
Period; One Room School Museum
Exhibitions: Turn of the Century Exhibits
Publications: Pennsylvania Dutch News & Views
Activities: Classes for adults & children; lectures open to public, 3 vis lectr per
year; sales shop sells books, slides, souvenirs
L Baver Genealogical Library, 19534-0015
Reference library
Income: Financed by endowment, mem, city appropriation & fund raising
Library Holdings: Vols 4000; Micro — Reels; AV — A-tapes, cassettes, rec,
slides, v-tapes; Other — Clipping files, manuscripts, memorabilia, pamphlets,
photographs, prints
Special Subjects: Calligraphy, Folk Art, Handicrafts, History of Art &
Archaeology, Manuscripts

LEWISBURG

M BUCKNELL UNIVERSITY, Center Gallery, 17837. Tel 717-524-3792. *Dir*
Open; *Asst to Dir* Cynthia Peltier
Open Mon - Fri 11 AM - 4 PM, Sat & Sun 1 - 4 PM. Estab 1979. Gallery
contains a study collection of 20 paintings and one sculpture of the Renaissance
given by the Samuel H Kress Foundation. Average Annual Attendance: 25,000
Income: Financed by endowment, tuition and gifts
Exhibitions: Organic Themes in Islamic Art; Black South African Art; Made in
Pennsylvania: Antique Toys from the Lawrance Wilkinson Collection
Activities: Lectures open to the public, 6 vis lectr per yr; concerts; gallery talks;
tours; competitions; individual paintings & original objects of art lent; originate
traveling exhibitions; sales shop

M FETHERSTON FOUNDATION, Packwood House Museum, 15 N Water St,
17837. Tel 717-524-0323. *Chmn* Theresa Eichhorn; *Acting Museum Adminr*
Ricki Jayne-Walter Kerstetter
Open Tues - Fri 10 AM - 5 PM, Sat 1 - 5 PM, Sun 2 - 5, last tour at 4 PM daily.
Admis adults $4, senior citizens $3.25, students $1.75, under 6 free. Estab 1976
to serve the community as an educational institution. Average Annual
Attendance: 12,000. Mem: 411, dues life-time $1000, benefactor $500, patron
$250, friend $100, family $30, individual $20
Income: Financed by endowment, admissions, memberships and museum shop
Collections: †American Fine Arts; †Paintings by Edith H K Fetherston; †Fine
Period Clothing ranging from 1890's to 1960's; †1800 - 1940 Decorative Arts:
ceramics, furniture, glass, metalwork, textiles
Exhibitions: Holiday Exhibit: Packwood House. (1992) Museum Presents: The
Nutcracker
Publications: Chanticleer, quarterly newsletter for members
Activities: Classes for adults and children; docent training; lectures open to the
public, 3 - 4 vis lectr per yr; tours; competitions with awards; lending collection
contains books, cassettes & slides; book traveling exhibitions; originate traveling
exhibitions; museum shop sells books, original art, reproductions and local
handcrafted items

LORETTO

M SOUTHERN ALLEGHENIES MUSEUM OF ART, Saint Francis College
Mall, PO Box 8, 15940. Tel 814-472-6400; FAX 814-472-4131. *Dir* Michael M
Strueber; *Cur* Paul Binai; *Asst Dir* Mary L Durbin; *Public Relations &
Membership Coordr* Michelle Kline; *Blair Art Extension Coordr* Mary Hollister;
Johnstown Art Extension Coordr Madelon Sheedy
Open Tues - Fri 10 AM - 4 PM, Sat & Sun 1:30 - 4:30 PM. No admis fee. Estab
and dedicated June 1976 to facilitate interest, understanding and the appreciation
of the visual arts of the past, present and future through the exhibition of our
permanent as well as temporary collections. Large open main gallery with flexible
space, second floor graphics gallery. Average Annual Attendance: 45,000. Mem:
750; dues $15 and up
Income: Financed by membership, business, corporate and foundation grants
Purchases: Contemporary American Art especially by living Pennsylvania artists
are purchased for the permanent collection
Collections: †American paintings; 19th & 20th century drawings †graphics and
sculpture; 19th century ceramics and crafts
Exhibitions: Surveys of contemporary American art with emphasis on living
Pennsylvania artists. (1993) Soaphollow Furniture; Photography Exhibit
Publications: Exhibition catalogues
Activities: Intern program in cooperation with area colleges; lect open to public,
5 vis lectr per year; concerts; gallery talks; tours; extension dept serves Altoona,
Johnstown & Hollidaysburg; individual paintings and original objects of art lent
to other institutions on request for special exhibitions; lending collection contains
2000 lantern slides; book traveling exhibitions, 1-3 per year; originate traveling
exhibitions to art galleries
L Library, Saint Frances College Mall, PO Box 8, 15940. Tel 814-472-6400; FAX
814-472-4131.
Library Holdings: Vols 450; Per subs 25; AV — Lantern slides, slides; Other —
Clipping files, exhibition catalogs, pamphlets, photographs
M Blair Art Museum, 314 Allegheny St, 16648. Tel 814-695-0648. *Coordr* Mary
Hollister
Open Mon - Fri 10 AM - 5 PM, Sat 1 - 5 PM
Income: Financed by grants and private donations
Activities: Classes for adults & children; video programs air on local public
access cable; lect open to public, 18 vis lectr per year; classes open to
community; gallery talks; tours; Lunch Ala Art

M Johnstown Art Museum, 430 Main St, 15901. Tel 814-535-1803. *Cur* Madelon
Sheedy
Open Mon - Fri 10 AM - 5 PM, Sat noon - 4 PM. No admis fee. Estab 1982 to
bring regional art to a wider audience & provide educational opportunities. Entry
gallery 54 running ft, foyer gallery 60 running ft, main gallery 130 running ft.
Average Annual Attendance: 10,000
Income: Financed by membership, city appropriation, private & foundation
support, state & federal art agency funding
Exhibitions: Annual Artists Boutique
Activities: Classes for adults & children; dramatic programs; docent programs;
film series; workshops; lectures open to the public, 10 vis lectr per year; book
traveling exhibitions 1 per year; originate traveling exhibitions

MEADVILLE

M ALLEGHENY COLLEGE, Bowman, Megahan and Penelec Galleries, Allegheny
College, Box U, 16335. Tel 814-332-4365; FAX 814-333-8180. *Gallery Dir*
Robert Raczka
Open Tues - Fri 12:30 - 5 PM, Sat 1:30 - 5 PM, Sun 2 - 4 PM, cl Mon. No
admis fee. Estab 1971 as one of the major exhibition spaces in northwest
Pennsylvania; the galleries present exhibits ranging from works of contemporary
artists to displays relevant to other fields of study. Galleries are housed in three
spacious rooms, white walls, terrazzo floor, 10 ft ceilings. Average Annual
Attendance: 8000
Income: Financed by college funds & grants
Collections: †Alleghany College Permanent Collection; †General David M Shoup
Collection of Korean Pottery; Samuel Pees Collection of Contemporary Painting
Publications: Exhibition catalogs, 2 - 3 per year
Activities: Lect open to the public; gallery talks; tours; individual paintings &
original objects of art lent to art gallerie & museums; book traveling exhibitions

M CRAWFORD COUNTY HISTORICAL SOCIETY, Baldwin-Reynolds House
Museum, 848 N Main St, 16335. Tel 814-724-6080. *Cur* Stephanie E Przybylek;
Pres David M Ellis; *1st VPres* P Richard Thomas; *Office Mgr* Barbara Finney
Open Wed, Sat & Sun 1 - 5 PM, Memorial Day - Labor Day and by
appointment. Admis adults $2, students $1. Estab to preserve & interpret the
history of the region. Art is hung in a period mansion. Average Annual
Attendance: 3000. Mem: 700; annual meeting in June
Income: Financed by endowment, membership, city & county appropriation
Collections: Oil paintings - portraits; 1 Gouache 1812 Melling F; Photo portraits;
Printer's proofs
Publications: Crawford County History (newsletter), semi-annually
Activities: Classes for children, docent training; tours

A MEADVILLE COUNCIL ON THE ARTS, Meadville Market House, PO Box
337, 16335. Tel 814-336-5051. *Exec Dir* Gwen Barboni
Open Tues - Fri 9 AM - 4:30 PM, Sat 9 AM - noon. No admis fee. Estab 1975
for local arts information and programming; to create community arts center.
Gallery has 50 ft of wall space. Average Annual Attendance: 2000. Mem: 500;
dues businesses $25 - $250, individual $10 - $50; annual meeting Jan
Income: $50,000 (financed by membership and state appropriation)
Purchases: Yearly piece for permanent collection
Exhibitions: Annual October Evenings Exhibition; annual county wide exhibits;
monthly gallery shows for local artists and crafters exhibits
Publications: Monthly calendar; monthly newsletter
Activities: Classes for adults and children; dramatic programs; lectures open to
the public, 8 - 10 vis lectr per yr; concerts; competitions with awards;
scholarships

MERION STATION

M BARNES FOUNDATION, 300 N Latch's Lane, 19066. Tel 215-667-0290. *Pres
Board of Trustees* Richard H Glanton; *Development Officer* Laura Linton
Open Sept - June only Fri & Sat 9:30 AM - 4:30 PM, Sun 1 - 4:30 PM. Admis
$1. Closing for two years for renovation beginning in spring 1993
Collections: Permanent collection of post-impressionism & eary French modern
art. Includes works by Cezanne, Matisse & Renoir

NAZARETH

M MORAVIAN HISTORICAL SOCIETY, Whitefield House Museum, 214 E
Center St, 18064. Tel 215-759-5070; FAX 215-759-3892. *Exec Dir* Susan
Dreydoppel
Open daily 1 - 4 PM, other times by appointment. Admis $1. Built in 1740 by
George Whitefield, famous preacher, bought by the Moravians in 1741 &
continued in use by various segments of the church. Now the seat of the
Moravian Historical Society (organized on Apr 13, 1857 to elucidate the history
of the Moravian Church in America; not however, to the exclusion of the general
history of the Moravian Church); used as a museum, which houses many unique
& distinctive items pertaining to early Moraviana & colonial life. Average Annual
Attendance: 7500. Mem: 500; dues $10 - $200; annual meeting second Thurs in
Oct
Income: Financed by endowment, membership and donation
Collections: Clothing and textiles; John Valentine Haidt Collection of Paintings;
handwrought and cast bells; Indian and foreign mission artifacts; musical
instruments; pottery and Stiegel glass; rare books; manuscripts
Publications: Transactions, biennial
Activities: Lect open to public, 1-2 vis lectr per year; libr tour; lending collection
contains individual & original objects of art; originate travel exhibitions; museum
shop sells books

NEW BRIGHTON

M MERRICK ART GALLERY, Fifth Ave & 11th St, PO Box 312, 15066. Tel 412-846-1130. *Dir & Educ Dir* Cynthia A Kundar; *Trustee* Robert S Merrick
Open Tues - Sat 10 AM - 4:30 PM; Sun 1 - 4:30 PM; cl Mon & holidays; reduced hours during summer. No admis fee. Estab 1880 to preserve and interpret the collection of paintings and other objects owned by Edward Dempster Merrick, the founder. Also to foster local art through classes and one-man shows. All galleries are on the second floors of two parallel buildings with a connecting bridge; there are three small rooms and one large one. Three rooms have clerestory monitors overhead. Average Annual Attendance: 6000. Mem: 415; dues $25, $15 and $10; annual meeting Jan or Feb
Income: Financed by endowment and membership
Collections: Most paintings date from the 18th & 19th century. American artists Emil Bott; Birge Harrison; Thomas Hill; A F King; Edward and Thomas Moran; E Poole; F K M Rehn; W T Richards; W L Sonntag; Thomas Sully; Charles Curran; John F Kensett; Andrew Melrose; Ralph A Blackelock; Asher B Durand; Worthington Whittredge. European artists Gustave Courbet; Hans Makart; Pierre Paul Prud'hon; Richard Westall; Franz Xavier; Winterhalter; Peter Baumgartner; Leon Herbo; Jaques Bertrand
Publications: Newsletter, bimonthly
Activities: Classes for adults & children; lectures open to public, 6 vis lectr per yr; concerts; gallery talks; tours; E B Merrick Award; scholarships

NEW CASTLE

M HOYT INSTITUTE OF FINE ARTS, 124 E Leasure Ave, 16105. Tel 412-652-2882. *Pres Board of Trustees* Richard E Flannery; *Exec Dir* Susan V Miller
Open Tues - Sat 9 AM - 4 PM. No admis fee. Estab 1968 to encourage the development of the arts within the community. Average Annual Attendance: 27,000. Mem: 850; dues $100, $50, $30, $20
Income: Commission on sales of arts and crafts
Collections: National & regional artists
Exhibitions: Hoyt National Art Show
Publications: Newsletter, monthly
Activities: Classes for adults and children; dramatic programs; lect open to public; concerts; competitions; scholarships

NEWTOWN

M BUCKS COUNTY COMMUNITY COLLEGE, Hicks Art Center, Fine Arts Department, Swamp Rd, 18940. Tel 215-968-8425. *Chmn* Frank Dominguez
Open Mon - Fri 8 AM - 10 PM, Sat 9 AM - 5 PM. No admis fee. Estab 1970 to bring outside artists to the community. Gallery covers 960 sq ft. Average Annual Attendance: 5000
Income: Financed by county and state appropriation
Exhibitions: Six exhibits each academic year, ending with student annual exhibit
Activities: Lectures open to the public, 8 vis lectr per year; competitions; artmobile

NEW WILMINGTON

M WESTMINSTER COLLEGE, Art Gallery, 16172. Tel 412-946-7266. *Dir* P Lynn Cox
Open Mon - Sat 9 AM - 9 PM, Sun 1 - 9 PM. No admis fee. Estab 1854 to organize and present 7 exhibitions per season, to organize traveling exhibitions, publish art catalogs of national interest, and to conduct visiting artists program. Average Annual Attendance: 15,000
Income: Financed by endowment, state and local grants
Collections: 19th and 20th century paintings; 20th century drawings and prints
Publications: Catalogs; Westminster College Art Gallery, annually
Activities: Lectures open to public, 4 vis lectr per year; gallery talks; traveling exhibitions organized and circulated

PAOLI

M WHARTON ESHERICK MUSEUM, Wharton Esherick Studio, Horseshoe Trail, PO Box 595, 19301. Tel 215-644-5822. *Pres* Ruth E Bascom; *Secy* Helen Esherick; *Dir* Robert Leonard
Open Sat 10 AM - 5 PM, Sun 1 - 5 PM, by reservation only, weekdays groups only. Admis adults $5, children under 12 $3. Estab 1971 for the preservation and exhibition of the Studio and collection of sculptor Wharton Esherick (1887-1970), one of America's foremost artist/craftsmen. Esherick worked mostly in wood and is best known for his sculptural furniture. Studio is set high on hillside overlooking the Great Valley, and is one of Wharton Esherick's monumental achievements. He worked forty years building, enlarging and altering it. Average Annual Attendance: 4000. Mem: 450; dues family $40, individual $25
Income: $80,000 (financed by mem, endowment, admis, sales & grants)
Collections: 200 pieces of the artist's work, including furniture, paintings, prints, sculpture in wood, stone and ceramic, utensils and woodcuts
Publications: Brochures; catalog of Studio, collection & exhibit catalogues; Drawings by Wharton Esherick
Activities: Tours; individual paintings and original objects of art lent to museums or exhibitions; museum shop sells books, reproductions, prints and slides

PHILADELPHIA

M AFRO-AMERICAN HISTORICAL & CULTURAL MUSEUM, Seventh & Arch Sts, 19106. Tel 215-574-0380. *Exec Dir* Rowena Stewart; *Exhib Dir* Richard Watson; *Educ Dir* Pearl Robinson; *Pub Relations & Develpment Dir* Anthony Ng
Open Tues - Sat 10 AM - 5 PM, Sun noon - 6 PM, cl New Years, Martin Luther King's Birthday, Memorial Day, July 4, Labor Day, Columbus Day,

Thanksgiving, Christmas. Admis adults $3.50, sr citizens, children & students $1.75; group rates adults $1, children & students $.50. Estab 1976. Average Annual Attendance: 236,000. Mem: Dues patron $1500, friend $600, donor $150, sponsor $60, family $35, individual $25, student $5
Purchases: Bas relief in plaster by Henry O Tanner
Collections: African sculpture & artifacts; Afro-Americana; artifacts relating to Slave Trade, American Revolution, Black Church, Civil War, Reconstruction Period, Westward Movement, Harlem Renaissance, Civil Rights Movement, Black Scientists & Inventors; paintings, prints & sculpture by black artists; †archival documents; Chief Justice Robert N C Nix Sr Collection, legal writings & memorabilia; Negro Baseball Leagues Collection of photographs & documents
Exhibitions: (1990) Let This Be Your Home; Odunde; Contemporary African Artists: Changing Tradition; Collections from Ile Ife Humanitarian Center; Afro-America prints & drawings
Publications: Annual report; brochure; exhibition catalog
Activities: Educ dept; classes for adults and children; docent training; lectures open to the public; concerts; gallery talks; tours; awards; individual paintings & original objects of art lent; museum shop sells books, magazines, original art, reproductions, prints & African crafts

AMERICAN COLOR PRINT SOCIETY
For further information, see National and Regional Organizations

M AMERICAN SWEDISH HISTORICAL FOUNDATION AND MUSEUM, 1900 Pattison Ave, 19145. Tel 215-389-1776; FAX 215-389-7701. *Dir* Ann Barton Brown
Open Tues - Fri 10 AM - 4 PM, Sat & Sun noon - 4 PM, cl Mon & holidays. Admis adults $2, students $1, children under 12 free. Estab 1926 to preserve Swedish heritage in America and to promote continued cultural interchange between Scandinavia & USA. 14 galleries containing materials interpreting over 300 years of Swedish influence on American life. Average Annual Attendance: 15,000. Mem: 700; dues family $40, individual $25; annual meeting in Sept
Collections: †History and culture of Americans of Swedish descent
Exhibitions: Temporary exhibitions of paintings, arts and crafts by Scandinavian and Swedish-American artists; Scandinavian history and culture
Publications: Newsletter, quarterly
Activities: Classes for adults & children; workshops; lectures open to public, 5 vis lectr per year; gallery talks; tours; individual paintings and original objects of art lent to other museums; book traveling exhibitions; museum shop sells books, magazines, folk art & Swedish decorative arts
L Library, 1900 Pattison Ave, 19145. Tel 215-389-1776; FAX 215-389-7701. For general reference
Library Holdings: Vols 15,000; Per subs 5; Micro — Reels; AV — Rec, slides; Other — Clipping files, exhibition catalogs, memorabilia
Special Subjects: Fredrika Bremer, John Ericsson, Jenny Lind, Rambo Research of genealogical and colonial material

L ART INSTITUTE OF PHILADELPHIA LIBRARY, 1622 Chestnut St, 19103. Tel 215-567-7080. *Librn* Paul Patanella
Open daily 9 AM - 9 PM. Estab 1966
Income: $88,000 (annual corporate budget)
Library Holdings: AV — A-tapes, cassettes, fs, Kodachromes, v-tapes; Other — Clipping files, exhibition catalogs, memorabilia, photographs
Special Subjects: Architecture, Art Education, Commercial Art, Fashion Arts, Graphic Arts, Graphic Design, History of Art & Archaeology, Illustration, Interior Design, Lettering, Painting - American, Photography, Posters

M ATHENAEUM OF PHILADELPHIA, 219 S Sixth St, 19106-3794. Tel 215-925-2688; FAX 215-925-3755. *Dir* Roger W Moss Jr; *Program Coordr* Eileen Magee; *Architectural Archivist* Bruce Laverty; *Circulation Librn* Ellen Batty; *Bibliographer* Keith A Kamm
Open Mon - Fri 9 AM - 5 PM. No admis fee. Estab 1814 to collect, preserve & make available original sources on American cultural history, 1814-1914. The fine & decorative arts are arranged in room settings. Average Annual Attendance: 15,000. Mem: 1200; annual meeting first Mon in Apr
Income: Financed by endowments, dues & fees
Collections: †Permanent study collection of American decorative arts, 1810-1850; 19th & 20th century architectural books; architectural drawings; trade catalogues
Publications: Annotations, quarterly newsletter; Athenaeum Architectural Archive; Annual Report; Bookshelf, six per year; Monographs, three to five per year
Activities: Lectures for members only; annual associates symposium open to public; tours; individual paintings lent to museums; sales shop sells books, prints & slides
L Library, 219 S Sixth St, 19106. Tel 215-925-2688; FAX 215-925-3755. *Circulation Librn* Ellen Batty
Open Mon - Fri 9 AM - 5 PM by appointment for reference only
Library Holdings: Vols 75,000; Per subs 50; Architectural drawings and related materials; Micro — Cards, fiche, reels; AV — Cassettes; Other — Manuscripts, original art works
Special Subjects: Architecture, Decorative Arts, Victorian Studies
Collections: Nineteenth century fiction and literary periodicals; trade materials relating to the building arts
Publications: Biographical dictionary of Philadelphia Architects, monograph

M ATWATER KENT MUSEUM, 15 S Seventh St, 19106. Tel 215-922-3031. *Chmn Board Trustees* Marian Mitchell; *Chmn Board Dir* Fred Lindquist; *Cur Coll* Jeffrey Ray; *Cur Coll* Robert Eskend
Open Tues - Sun 9:30 AM - 5 PM, cl holidays. No admis fee. Estab 1938. The museum is dedicated to the history of Philadelphia. The main interpretive gallery covers the growth of Philadelphia from 1680-1880. Smaller galleries on William Penn, his life & times; The History of the city through maps; Municipal services: fire, police, gas & water. Average Annual Attendance: 63,000
Income: $200,000 (financed by endowment & city appropriation)
Collections: Artifacts of the colonial city; costumes; print & painting collection; manufactured & trade goods; maritime artifacts; toys & dolls; ceramics &

glassware; urban archaeology

Exhibitions: Fairmount Park & the Fairmount Waterworks; Fine Art from the Atwater Kent Collections; Poetry of Motion-Eadweard Muybridge & Children's Action Toys; Sights for City Eyes; Travelling Neighborhood Exhibits

Publications: Philadelphia: A City for All Centuries (in conjunction with KYW Newsradio)

Activities: Lect open to public, gallery talks, media events, tours; 500 original art works, 2500 original prints, 100 paintings available on loan to museums with adequate security systems; originate traveling exhibitions to community organizations & schools

A **BRANDYWINE WORKSHOP,** 1520-22 Kater St, 19146. Tel 215-546-3757, 546-3670. *Pres & Exec Dir* Allan L Edmunds
Open 10 AM - 5 PM by appointment. Estab 1972 to develop interest & talent in printmaking & other fine visual arts. 4000 sq ft over two floors in downtown Philadelphia. Facilities include offset lithography presses. Average Annual Attendance: 1500. Mem: Dues friends $100, board only $50; annual meeting in June
Income: Financed by membership, city & state appropriations, private corporations & foundations
Collections: †Contemporary fine art prints, including etchings, woodblocks, offset lithographs, silkscreens
Exhibitions: USA Artworks; Contemporary Print Images
Activities: Visiting artist workshop; intern training; lectures open to the public, 3 vis lectrs per yr; competitions with awards; fels offered; exten dept serves Philadelphia; original objects of art lent; lending collection contains prints; book traveling exhibitions, 6 per yr; originate traveling exhibitions

C **CIGNA CORPORATION,** CIGNA Museum & Art Collection, 1601 Chestnut St-TLP 7, 19192-2078. Tel 215-761-4907. *Dir* Melissa Hough; *Cur* Sue Levy; *Registrar* Nancy Powell
Exhibits available by appointment Mon - Fri 9 AM - 5 PM. Estab 1925. Exhibits on company history, fire fighting history, Maritime history & American fine art
Income: Financed by company
Collections: Historical fire & marine art & artifacts 18th - 20th century American Art, two-dimensional works, ceramics, & sculpture
Exhibitions: Ships and the Sea
Publications: The Historical Collection of the Insurance Company of North America
Activities: Lect open to public; lending collection contains over 9000 pieces of historic fire & marine art & artifacts; 20th century American art & sculpture; loans are processed to qualifying institutions; book traveling exhibitions, 1 - 3 per yr; originate traveling exhibitions

M **CLAY STUDIO,** 139 N Second St, 19106. Tel 215-925-3453; FAX 215-925-7774. *Exec Dir* James Clark; *Gen Mgr* Kathryn Narrow
Open Tues - Fri noon - 6 PM, Sat & Sun noon - 5 PM. Estab 1974. Two galleries with exhibits changing monthly of various ceramic artwork of solo, group & historical shows. Average Annual Attendance: 24,000
Collections: Ceramic Arts
Exhibitions: Annual Fellowship Artist Solo Show; The Forum Exhibition; Annual Resident Artist Group Show; Annual Holiday Show. (1991) Rookwood Ceramics; 1991 - Pueblo Pottery. (1992) Contemporary East European Ceramics (1993) Architectural Clay
Activities: Classes for adults & children; lect open to public, 4 - 6 vis lectr per year; gallery talks; tours; spring jurying for group & solo exhibition & one year residency program; scholarships; exten dept serves Philadelphia & suburbs; sales shop sells books, magazines, original art

M **CLIVEDEN,** 6401 Germantown Ave, 19144. Tel 215-848-1777. *Exec Dir* Jennifer Esler; *Office Mgr* Jean S Mitchell
Open Apr - Dec Tues - Sat 10 AM - 4 PM, Sun 1 PM - 4:30 PM, cl Easter, July 4th, Thanksgiving & Christmas. Admis adults $4, students $3. 18th Century house museum. Average Annual Attendance: 10,000. Mem: 350
Collections: 18th Century house museum with decorative arts, furniture, paintings, collections site related only, no acquisitions
Activities: Educ dept; classes for children; docent training; guided tours for individuals & groups; museum shop sells books, reproductions, prints, gift items

A **THE COMMUNITY EDUCATION CENTER,** 3500 Lancaster Ave, 19104. Tel 215-387-1911. *Executive Dir* Sara Moran; *Exhibition Coordr* Todd Gilens
Open Mon - Fri 9 AM - 5 PM. No admis fee. Estab 1973 to support emerging talent. 35 ft x 60 ft room, 14 ft ceilings. Average Annual Attendance: 1000. Mem: dues single $20, family $30
Income: $180,000 (financed by mem, city & state appropriation, foundation, corporate & private donars)
Activities: Classes for adults & children; lectures open to public, 4 vis lectr per year

A **FAIRMOUNT PARK ART ASSOCIATION,** 1530 Locust St, Suite 3A, 19102. Tel 215-546-7550; FAX 215-546-2363. *Pres* Charles E Mather III; *VPres* William P Wood; *VPres* Henry W Sawyer III; *Exec Dir* Penny Balkin Bach; *Asst Dir* Laura S Griffith; *Treas* Theodore T Newbold
Estab 1872 for the purpose of acquiring sculpture for the City of Philadelphia. Mem: 350; dues $25 - $100; annual meeting May
Income: Financed by membership, grants & endowment

M **FOUNDATION FOR TODAY'S ART,** Nexus Gallery, 137 N Second St, 19106. Tel 215-629-1103. *Gallery Dir* Anne Raman; *Foundation Dir & Trustee* Suzanne Horvitz; *Trustee* Vivian Golden; *Trustee* Alexandra Lerner
Open Tues & Fri noon - 6 PM, Sat & Sun noon - 5 PM. No admis fee. Estab 1975, artist-run space for contemporary art, featuring experimental-emerging artists, new directions-new media; national/international exchanges; cultural outreach programs. Two contemporary galleries, each 750 sq ft. Average Annual Attendance: 5000. Mem: 25; dues $35 per month; monthly meetings; half of exhibits feature member artists selected for experimental & creative approach to both traditional & new media with demonstrated level of consistency &

commitment; the other half feature non-member artists & invited curators
Income: Financed by membership, state, federal, & foundation grants
Activities: Lect open to public, 5 or more visiting lectr per yr; concerts; gallery talks; tours upon request; internship

FREE LIBRARY OF PHILADELPHIA

L **Art Dept,** Logan Square, 19103. Tel 215-686-5403. *Library Pres & Dir* Elliot Shelkrot; *Head Librn, Art Dept* William Lang
Open Mon - Wed 9 AM - 9 PM, Thurs - Fri 9 AM - 6 PM, Sat 9 AM - 5 PM, Sun 1 - 5 PM, cl Sun June - Aug. Estab 1891, art department estab 1896, to serve the citizens of the City of Philadelphia. Non-circulating, reference & research collection
Income: Financed by endowment, city and state appropriations
Purchases: $71,000
Library Holdings: Vols 60,000; Per subs 220; Vertical Files 40,000; Micro — Fiche, reels; Other — Clipping files, exhibition catalogs, pamphlets
Collections: 18th & 19th century architectural pattern books; John Frederick Lewis Collection of books on fine prints & printmaking; 368 original measured drawings of colonial Philadelphia buildings, Philadelphia Chapter, American Institute of Architects
Exhibitions: Rotating exhibitions

L **Print and Picture Dept,** 1901 Vine St, 19103-1189. Tel 215-686-5405. *Head* J B Post
Open 9 AM - 6 PM, Sat 9 AM - 5 PM. Estab 1954 by combining the Print Department and the Picture Collection
Collections: (non-circulating) †Americana (1200); Hampton L Carson Collection of Napoleonic prints (3400); †graphic arts (2000); †greeting and tradesmen's cards (27,000); †John Frederick Lewis Collection of portrait prints (211,000); †Philadelphiana (8000); Rosenthal Collection of American Drawings (900); †Benton Spruance lithographs (450) (circulating) †picture collection of pictures in all media and universal in subject coverage (1,000,000)
Exhibitions: Benton Spruance Prints

L **Rare Book Dept,** Logan Square, 19103. Tel 215-686-5416. *Bibliographer* Frank Helpern; *Senior Cataloger* Cornelia King; *Ref Librn* Karen Lightner; *Cataloger* Laurie Wolfe
Open Mon - Fri 9 AM - 5 PM. No admis fee. Estab 1949. Average Annual Attendance: 3000
Collections: †American Sunday-School Union; †early American children's books including Rosenbach Collection of Early American Children's books (1682-1836); Elisabeth Ball Collection of Horn books; †Borneman and Yoder Collection of Pennsylvania German Fraktur; Hampton L Carson Collection of legal prints; †Frederick R Gardner Collection of Robert Lawson original drawings; Kate Greenaway; early American prints and engravings; †Grace Clark Haskell Collection of Arthur Rackham; John Frederick Lewis Collection of cuneiform tablets and seals, Medieval and Renaissance manuscripts and miniatures, Oriental manuscripts and miniatures (mostly Mughul, Rajput and Persian); Thornton Oakley Collection of †Howard Pyle and His School, books and original drawings; †Beatrix Potter, including H Bacon Collamore Collection of original art; Evan Randolph Collection consisting of angling prints from the 17th to the 20th century, and prints of Philadelphia from 1800-1950; †original drawings, paintings, prints and other illustrative material relating to the works of Dickens, Goldsmith, Poe and Thackeray
Activities: Individual paintings & original objects of art lent to other institutions for exhibition not to exceed 3 months; lending collection contains books, original artworks & paintings

M **GIRARD COLLEGE,** Stephen Girard Collection, Girard & Corinthian Aves, 19121. Tel 215-787-2600; FAX 215-787-2710. *College Pres* Howard Maxwell
Open Thurs 2 - 4 PM. No admis fee. Estab 1848. The basic plan & structured details of Founder's hall were dictated by Girard in his will. America's most outstanding example of Greek Revival architecture, the huge Corinthian temple-form building was designed by a twenty-nine year old Philadelphian, Thomas Ustick Walter, who later planned & drew the wings & dome of the US Capitol at Washington. Average Annual Attendance: 1500
Income: Financed by endowment
Collections: Furniture, silver, porcelain, paintings, marble busts & statues which belonged to Stephen Girard (1750 - 1831) founder of Girard College
Exhibitions: Continuous display in room settings

A **HISTORICAL SOCIETY OF PENNSYLVANIA,** 1300 Locust St, 19107. Tel 215-732-6201; FAX 215-732-2680. *Pres* Susan Stitt; *VPres Coll* Linda Stanley; *Dir Development* Adam Corson-Finnerty; *Cur* Elizabeth Jarvis; *Membership Coordr* Jennifer Peters; *VPres Interpretation* Cynthia Little
Open Tues, Thurs, Fri & Sat 10 AM - 5 PM, Wed 1 - 9 PM, cl Sun & Mon. Admis $5, students $2 to library & manuscript department; $2.50 admis fee to museum, srs & students $1.50. Estab 1824 to collect & preserve records relating primarily to 18th century national US history, 19th century regional Pennsylvania & 20th century Delaware Valley history; also collects various artifacts & paintings of persons relevant to Pennsylvania history. Art gallery comprises three exhibit rooms containing one permanent & changing exhibits from the collections & loans from other institutions. Mem: 2900; dues $35; meeting 5 per yr
Income: Financed by endowment and membership
Collections: Unmatched collection of manuscripts, archives, graphics, paintings, furniture, household & personal effects from pre- Revolution through 1990; more than 1000 paintings & miniatures by early American artists Birch, Copley, Inman, Neagle, Peale, Stuart, Sully, Wright, & others; more than 14 million manuscripts
Exhibitions: Finding Philadelphia's Past; Neighborhood Exhibitions. (1993) Common Ground; The Downtown (1988) Legacies of Genius: A Celebration of Philadelphia Libraries
Publications: Guide to the Manuscript Collection of the Historical Society of Pennsylvania; Magazine of History & Biography, quarterly
Activities: Lessons for children; collaborative projects with schools; curriculum development for schools; workshops for adults; conferences on history & historical research; guided tours; manuscript collections available for loan for exhibit purposes

M INDEPENDENCE NATIONAL HISTORICAL PARK, 313 Walnut St, 19106. Tel 215-597-8974, 626-1666. *Supt* Martha Alkens; *Chief Museum Operations* John C Milley
Open daily 9 AM - 5 PM. No admis fee. Estab 1948 to preserve and protect for the American people, historical structures, properties and other resources of outstanding national significance, and associated with the Revolution and growth of the Nation. Seventeen public buildings with 54 period rooms & 38 on-site exhibits. Average Annual Attendance: 4,500,000. Mem: Dues $85
Collections: †18th century American period furnishings; decorative arts; American portraits from 1740-1840
Exhibitions: (1991) The Founding Fathers
Activities: Dramatic programs; docent training; lectures open to public, 6 vis lectr per yr; tours; individual paintings & original objects or art lent to qualified professional institutions; museum shop selling books, reproductions, prints, slides
L Library, 120 S Third St, 19106. Tel 215-597-8974. *Librn* Shirley Mays
Open to public Mon - Fri 8 AM - 4:30 PM
Library Holdings: Vols 5500; Per subs 23; Research notecard file; Micro — Reels; AV — Motion pictures, slides, v-tapes; Other — Pamphlets, photographs
Collections: Decorative arts of Philadelphia and Pennsylvania for the 18th century

A INSTITUTE OF CONTEMPORARY ART, 118 S 36th St, 19104-3289. Tel 215-898-7108; FAX 215-898-5050. *Dir* Patrick T Murphy; *Asst Dir* Judith Tannenbaum
Open daily (except Mon) 10 AM - 5 PM, Wed evenings until 7 PM, cl holidays. Estab 1963 to provide a continuing forum for the active presentation of advanced development in the visual arts. Gallery space devoted to exhibiting contemporary art in all media. Average Annual Attendance: 80,000. Mem: 600; dues $30, $75, $150, $300 & up
Income: Approx $700,000 (financed by endowment, membership & grants)
Exhibitions: ICA Street Sights 1 & 2; Masks, Tents, Vessels & Talismans; Paul Thek; Processions; Urban Encounters; Art Architecture Audience; Drawings: The Pluralist Decade; Made in Philadelphia 4 & 5; Machineworks; Vito Acconci; Alice Aycock; Dennis Oppenheim; Robert S Zakanitch; Photography: A Sense of Order; The East Village Scene; Laurie Anderson; Siah Armajani; David Salle; Robert Kushner
Publications: Annual newsletter; calendar of events; exhibition catalogs
Activities: Lectures open to the public, 5-10 vis lectr per year; concerts; gallery talks; tours; traveling exhibitions organized & circulated; sales shop sells original art & catalogs

M LA SALLE UNIVERSITY, Art Museum, 20th & Olney Ave, 19141. Tel 215-951-1221. *Dir* Daniel Burke; *Cur* Caroline Wistar
Open Tues - Fri 11 AM - 4 PM, Sun 2 - 4 PM; cl Mon. No admis fee. Estab 1975 for educational purposes and to house the collection begun in 1965, also as support for the art history program and as a service to the community. Average Annual Attendance: 11,000. Mem: 60; dues $5 - $1000
Income: Financed by endowment, university budget, grants, public & private donations
Collections: †15th - 20th century paintings, drawings, watercolors, Old Master & those of 19th & 20th centuries prints; †Western, European & American art, with a few pieces of sculpture & decorative art; †rare illustrated 15th - 20th century Bibles; portrait prints
Exhibitions: Two special exhibitions are held each semester
Publications: La Salle Art Museum Guide to the Collection
Activities: Classes for adults; lectures open to public, 2-3 vis lectr per year; concerts; gallery talks; tours; individual paintings & original objects of art lent to museums

L LIBRARY COMPANY OF PHILADELPHIA, Print Dept, 1314 Locust St, 19107. Tel 215-546-3181, 546-8229. *Librn* John C Van Horne; *Asst Librn* Gordon Marshall; *Cur of Printed Books* James Green; *Cur of Prints* Kenneth Finkel; *Chief of Reference* Mary Anne Hines; *Chief Conservation* Jennifer L Woods
Open Mon - Fri 9 AM - 4:45 PM. No admis fee. Estab 1731 for the purpose of scholarly research. Average Annual Attendance: 2500. Mem: 800; dues $25; annual meeting first Mon May
Income: Financed by endowment, membership, city appropriation, state & federal grants
Library Holdings: Other — Exhibition catalogs, original art works, pamphlets, photographs, prints, sculpture
Collections: †American Printing; †Philadelphia prints, watercolors, drawings and photography; collection of Americana
Exhibitions: Africa & the Africans; Benjamin Henry Latrobe's View of Jeffersonian America; The Larder Invaded: Reflections on Three Centuries of American Food
Publications: Annual Report; Occasional Miscellany, 2-4 times per year; exhibition catalogues
Activities: Lectures open to public; gallery talks; tours; individual and original objects of art lent to museums, libraries and cultural institutions; sale of books and publications

L LUTHERAN THEOLOGICAL SEMINARY, Krauth Memorial Library, 7301 Germantown Ave, 19119-1794. Tel 215-248-4616; FAX 215-248-4577. *Dir Library* David J Wartluft; *Asst Librn* Lillian Scoggins; *Head Technical Servs* Lois Reibach; *Cur Archives* John E Peterson
Open 9 AM - 5 PM. Library estab 1906
Library Holdings: Vols 170,000; Per subs 678; AV — A-tapes, cassettes, fs, Kodachromes, lantern slides, rec, slides, v-tapes; Other — Manuscripts, memorabilia, original art works, reproductions
Collections: Liturgical arts; Modern Prints; Rentschler Coll of Last Supper Art; Schreiber Coll of Numismatic Art on Martin Luther & the Reformation
Exhibitions: (1992) 20 Religious Artists

M MOORE COLLEGE OF ART & DESIGN, Golden Paley Gallery, 20th & the Parkway, 19103. Tel 215-568-4515, Ext 1119; FAX 215-568-8017. *Gallery Dir* Elsa Longhauser
Open Mon - Fri 10 AM - 5 PM, Sat noon - 4 PM. No admis fee. Estab 1831 to offer the Philadelphia community and its students the opportunity to view contemporary artwork that is usually not available locally. Gallery is housed in moderate exhibition space with flexible panels to accommodate current exhibit. Average Annual Attendance: 5000
Income: Financed by endowment
Exhibitions: (1991) Drawings & Objects by Joses Hoffman. (1993) Dan Graham Exhibit; Marlene Dumas, Give the People What They Want
Publications: Bulletins, irregularly; Catalogs for major exhibitions
Activities: Lectures open to public, 10 vis lectr per yr; gallery talks; tours
L Library, 20th & The Parkway, 19103. Tel 215-568-4515; FAX 215-568-8017. *Library Dir* Paula Feid; *Catalog Librn* Kristin Bayrus; *Slide Cur* Helen F McGinnis; *AV Specialist* Rick Fellechner
Open Mon - Thurs 8 AM - 10 PM, Fri 8 AM - 6 PM, Sat 8:30 AM - 5 PM, Sun 1 - 5 PM, for student use; public use Mon - Fri 8:30 AM - 4:30 PM and by appointment. Estab to serve Moore Staff & students. For lending & reference
Purchases: $37,000
Library Holdings: Vols 37,000; Per subs 230; Picture files; Micro — Fiche, reels; AV — A-tapes, cassettes, fs, lantern slides, motion pictures, rec, slides 110,000, v-tapes; Other — Clipping files, exhibition catalogs, manuscripts, memorabilia, reproductions
Special Subjects: Women in the Visual Arts
Collections: Sartain Family Collection; Bookworks Artists Books Collection

M MUSE ART GALLERY, 60 N Second St, 19106. Tel 215-627-5310. *Dir* Sissy Pizzollo
Open Wed - Sun noon - 6 PM. Estab 1970 to make women artists more visible. Average Annual Attendance: 2500. Mem: 15; qualifications: professional exhibiting or emerging artist; annual dues $600; monthly meetings first Sun
Income: Financed by membership, sales commissions, Pennsylvania State Council of the Arts & private contributions
Exhibitions: Members & community oriented exhibitions
Publications: Catalogues; MUSE Gallery and Her Own Space
Activities: Art consultant program; lect open to the public, 2 vis lectrs per yr; poetry readings; competitions; originate international traveling exhibitions; original art for sale

M THE MUSEUM AT DREXEL UNIVERSITY, Chestnut & 32nd Sts, 19104. Tel 215-895-2424, 895-2423. *Dir & Cur* Dr Jean Henry
Open Mon - Fri 10 AM - 4 PM, cl Sat, Sun & holidays. No admis fee. Estab 1891; Picture Gallery 1902. Main Gallery contains the John D Lankenau and the Anthony J Drexel Collections of German and French paintings, sculpture & decorative arts of the 19th century and a changing exhibition gallery. Average Annual Attendance: 10,000
Income: Financed by Drexel University
Collections: 19th century sculpture, academic European painting, decorative arts & costumes; ceramics; hand printed India cottons; decorative arts of China, Europe, India & Japan
Exhibitions: (1988) Images for the Folks Back Home: US Military Photographs of World War II & their Technology
Activities: Lectures open to the public, 8 - 10 vis lectr per yr; concerts; gallery talks; book traveling exhibitions

M PAINTED BRIDE ART CENTER, The Gallery at the Painted Bride, 230 Vine St, 19106. Tel 215-925-9914. *Exec Dir* Gerry Givnish; *Dir* A M Weaver; *Dir Development* Patricia Robinson
Open Wed - Sun noon - 6 PM. No admis fee. Estab 1968, forum for work outside traditional channels to present interdisciplinary work. Average Annual Attendance: 25,000. Mem: 350
Activities: Lect open to public, 2 vis lectrs per yr; gallery talks

M PENNSYLVANIA ACADEMY OF THE FINE ARTS, Galleries, 118 N Broad St, 19102. Tel 215-972-7600; FAX 215-972-5564. *Chmn Bd* Harold A Sorgenti; *Pres* Frank H Goodyear Jr; *Dir Museum* Linda Bantel; *VPres Development* Victor Chira; *VPres Finance Admin* Maureen Brusca; *Dir Annual Giving & Membership* Marni Christian; *Special Events Coordr* Martha Tucker; *Public Information Officer* Sharin Skeel; *Cur* Susan Danly; *Cur* Judith E Stein; *Museum Registrar* Gale Rawson; *Museum Shop Mgr* Fred Kelley; *Paintings Conservator* Mark F Bockrath
Open Tues - Sat 10 AM - 5 PM, Sun 11 AM - 5 PM. Admis adults $5, sr citizens $3, students $2, members & children under 5 free. Estab 1805 by Charles Willson Peale to cultivate collecting, training, and development of the fine arts in America. The Academy building, opened in 1876, was restored for the American Bicentennial. Considered the masterpiece of its architect, Philadelphian Frank Furness, its style is called, alternatively, polychrome picturesque and High or Gothic Victorian. It was designated a Registered National Historic Landmark in 1975. The Morris Gallery is maintained for exhibitions and the School Gallery features faculty and student exhibitions. Average Annual Attendance: 75,000. Mem: 4500; dues $30-$10,000
Income: Financed by endowment, mem, city & state appropriations, contributions & federal grants
Purchases: Shadow by Jennifer Bartlett; Second Small Quarter by Mel Bochner; Pink Chinese Scissors by Jim Dine; Study for Political Prisoner by Sidney Goodman; Vanquished by Bill Jensen; Dream Series No 5, The Library by Jacob Lawrence; Let us Celebrate by Ree Morton; For M W & the Pure Desire by William T Wiley
Collections: American contemporary works; 18th, 19th and early 20th century American paintings, sculpture, drawings and prints, including Allston, West, the Peale Family, Stuart, Sully, Rush, Neagle, Mount, Eakins, Cassatt, Homer, Hopper, Hassam, Carles, Bellows, Henri, Beaux, Pippin
Exhibitions: (1993) Art Exposition: Advanta USArtists '92; Native to Neon; Morris Gallery Exhibition: Louise Fishman, Paintings 1986 - 1992; Main Gallery Exhibition: The Silhouette Selection: Recent Celebrity Photography; 92nd Annual Student Exhibition; Facing the Past: 19th Century Portraits from the

Collection of the Pennsylvania Academy of the Fine Arts; Masterworks of American Art: 1750 - 1950. (1994) Main Gallery Exhibition: I Tell My Heart: The Art of Horace Pippin.
Publications: Annual report; exhibition and school catalogues; Calendar of Events, quarterly
Activities: Classes for adults and children; docent training; lectures open to public, 6 vis lectrs per yr; concerts; gallery talks; tours; competitions with awards; scholarships; exten dept serves senior citizens; original objects of art lent to other institutions, the White House, the Governor of Pennsylvania and embassies abroad; book traveling exhibitions, 2-3 per year; originate traveling exhibitions; museum shop sells books, magazines, reproductions, prints, slides, ceramics, games, stationery, jewelry, toys & pottery

L **Library,** 1301 Cherry St (Mailing add: Broad & Cherry Sts, 19102). Tel 215-972-7600, Ext 3256; FAX 215-569-0153. *Librn* Marietta P Boyer
Open Mon - Fri 9 AM - 7 PM, open to public, cl during school vacations. Estab 1805, the library serves students of painting, sculpture, printmaking & research in American Art. Open to public for reference
Income: Financed by school funds
Library Holdings: Vols 12,000; Per subs 75; Clipping files include biography of American artists; AV — Slides, v-tapes; Other — Clipping files, exhibition catalogs

L **Archives,** Broad & Cherry Sts, 19102. Tel 215-972-7600. *Archivist* Cheryl Leibold
Open weekdays by appointment only; mail inquires welcome
Library Holdings: Artifacts; AV — A-tapes, fs, Kodachromes, lantern slides, slides, v-tapes; Other — Clipping files, exhibition catalogs, manuscripts, memorabilia, pamphlets, photographs
Special Subjects: History of Penn Academy
Collections: Charles Bregler's Thomas Eakins Collection, consisting of more than 1000 art objects and documents
Publications: Brochure about the archives; Index to Annual Exhibitions, 3 vols

A **Fellowship of the Pennsylvania Academy of the Fine Arts,** Hatfield House, 33rd St & Girard Ave, 19130. Tel 215-765-8820. *Pres* Brigitte Rutenberg; *VPres* Margaret Engman; *Treas* Anthony Di Rienzi
Estab 1897 to provide opportunities for creative incentive and sharing in responsibilities for the development of facilities and activities in the field of art for its members and to maintain relations with the students of the Pennsylvania Academy of the Fine Arts. Mem: 1200; dues resident $20, students $10, nonresidents and associate $15; meetings held Sept, Nov, Feb & May
Income: Approx $3000
Collections: Paintings and sculpture
Exhibitions: Annual Fellowship Show
Publications: History of the Fellowship; quarterly newsletter
Activities: Classes; lectures; films; workshops

A **PHILADELPHIA ART ALLIANCE,** 251 S 18th St, 19103. Tel 215-545-4305. *Pres* Thomas J Reilly Jr; *Executive Dir* Marilyn J S Goodman; *VPres Admin* Charles Byer
Open Mon - Fri 11:30 AM - 9 PM, Sat 10:30 AM - 5 PM. No admis fee. Estab 1915, a unique, educational and cultural organization catering to all the arts: music, drama, painting, sculpture, prints, design, literary arts, illustration, architecture, photography. Average Annual Attendance: 80,000. Mem: 1600; both artist & non-artist categories are available; dues $25 - $1000; annual meeting in May
Income: Financed by membership
Collections: †Contemporary paintings; original antique furnishings
Exhibitions: Juried visual exhibitions
Publications: The Art Alliance Bulletin, published 6 times a year, Sept to July;
Activities: Lectures open to public, 24 vis lectr per year; concerts; gallery talks; tours; competitions with awards; individual paintings & original objects of art lent; originate traveling exhibitions

A **PHILADELPHIA ART COMMISSION,** 1600 Arch St, 19102. Tel 215-686-4470, 686-1776. *Pres* Theodore T Newbold; *Exec Dir* Sandra Gross Bressler
Open 8:30 AM - 5 PM. No admis fee. Estab 1911 under Philadelphia Home Rule Charter as the Art Jury, later retitled Art Commission. An Art Ordinance passed in 1959 provides for art work in city buildings and on city owned property. The Art Commission reviews architectural designs and art work covering all media for municipal locations or other locations in which municipal funds are expended. The Art Commission's files are open to inspection by anyone since the information contained therein qualifies as public information. As indicated, the material deals solely with art proposals and architectural designs. Designs cover all buildings, major highways, and bridges. Mem: 9; between 20 and 24 meetings annually
Income: Financed by city appropriation

M **PHILADELPHIA COLLEGE OF TEXTILES AND SCIENCE,** Paley Design Center, 4200 Henry Ave, 19144. Tel 215-951-2860; FAX 215-951-2615. *Dir* Anne R Fabbri; *Cur* Susan Shifrin
Open Tues - Fri 10 AM - 4 PM, Sat & Sun Noon - 4 PM. No admis fee; guided tour $2. Estab 1978 to promote knowledge & appreciation of textiles & their design. Three galleries. Average Annual Attendance: 9000. Mem: 2000; dues $20
Collections: Historic and contemporary textiles 1st - 20th Centuries, International; Fabric Library, 19th and 20th Centuries, American and Western European; manuscripts, records, textile fibers, tools, and related materials
Exhibitions: Works from permanent collection; local artists and designers of international repute
Publications: The Art of the Textile Blockmaker; Florabunda: The Evolution of Floral Design on Fabrics; Flowers of the Yayla, Yoruk Weaving of the Toros Mountains; The Philadelphia System of Textile Manufacture 1884 - 1984
Activities: Classes for adults; lectures; scholarships; sales shop sells books, cards, jewelry, pottery & crafts

M **PHILADELPHIA MARITIME MUSEUM,** 321 Chestnut St, 19106. Tel 215-925-5439. *Dir* John S Carter; *Cur* Jane E Allen; *Librn* E Ann Wilcox; *Educator* William Ward
Open Tues - Sat 10 AM - 5 PM, Sun 1 PM - 5 PM. Admis by donation. Estab 1960 to preserve and interpret the maritime heritage of the Bay and River Delaware, and the Ports of Philadelphia. Gallery 1, Man and the Sea, general maritime history; Gallery 2, The Titanic & Her Era, collection of the Titanic Historical Society; Gallery 3, changing exhibits; Gallery 4, changing exhibits. Average Annual Attendance: 41,5000. Mem: 965; dues $35 minimum; annual meeting May
Income: Financed by endowment, membership and federal, private and corporate gifts
Collections: †Paintings by major American marine artists; Philadelphia Views; †19th-20th century maritime prints; †small craft
Exhibitions: Dr Franklin Set Sails; Preserving the Past
Publications: Annual Report; books and catalogs, intermittently; Spindrift (newsletter), quarterly
Activities: Classes for adults and children; lect for members only, 10 visiting lectr per year; concerts; gallery talks; competitions; individual paintings and original objects of art lent to recognized non-profit museums with adequate facilities and pertinent need, six months only; museum shop selling books, magazines, reproductions, prints, postcards, models and souvenirs

L **Library,** 321 Chestnut St, 19106. Tel 215-925-5439. *Librn* E Ann Wilcox
Open Mon - Fri 9 AM - 4:45 PM by appointment. Open to members and scholars, for reference only
Library Holdings: Vols 10,000; Per subs 100; rare books and maps; Micro — Fiche, reels; AV — Cassettes, Kodachromes, lantern slides, motion pictures, slides; Other — Exhibition catalogs, manuscripts, original art works, pamphlets, photographs, prints
Special Subjects: Traditional Small Craft Plans, Maritime Art and History Reference Works; Shipbuilders of the Delaware River, Maritime History of Philadelphia
Collections: Photographic file of Birch prints; photographic file of ships built by New York Shipbuilding Corp; art reference books on marine artists

M **PHILADELPHIA MUSEUM OF ART,** 26th & Parkway, PO Box 7646, 19101. Tel 215-763-8100; FAX 215-236-4465. *Chmn Board* Philip Berman; *Pres* Robert Montgomery Scott; *The George D Widener Dir* Anne d'Harnoncourt; *VPres Operations* Walter Taylor Jr; *VPres Development* Alexander Q Aldridge; *VPres Finance* John Sergovic; *VPres External Affairs* Cheryl McClemey-Brooker; *McNeil Cur American Art* Darrel Sewell; *Sr Cur Prints, Drawings & Photographs* Innis Shoemaker; *Cur Drawings* Ann Percy; *Cur Educ* Danielle Rice; *Registrar* Irene Taurins; *Public Relations Mgr* Sandra Horrocks; *Special Exhibitions Coordr* Suzanne Wells
Open Tues - Sun 10 AM - 5 PM, Wed 10 AM - 8:45 PM. Admis adults $6, senior citizens, students & children over 5 $3, Sun 10 AM - 1 PM free. Estab 1876 as an art museum and for art education; known as Pennsylvania Museum of Art until the present name was adopted in 1938. Buildings owned by the City, opened 1928; wings 1931 and 1940; fashion galleries 1949, 1951 and 1953; Gallatin and Arensberg Collections 1954; Far Eastern Wing 1957; decorative arts galleries 1958; Charles Patterson Van Pelt Auditorium 1959; Nepalese-Tibetan Gallery 1960; new galleries of Italian and French Renaissance Art 1960; American Wing, galleries of contemporary painting, sculpture, and decorative arts and special exhibitions galleries 1976; Alfred Stieglitz Center of Photography 1978; print and drawing gallery 1979; 19th century decorative arts galleries 1980 and 1981. Museum contains 200 galleries. Average Annual Attendance: 600,000. Mem: 25,000; dues $20-$1000; annual meeting Oct
Income: $26,000,000 (financed by endowment, mem, city & state appropriations, grants, bequests & auxiliary activities)
Collections: †Indian sculpture and miniature painting, and the installation of 16th century South Indian temple; †Chinese and Southwest Asian sculpture, ceramics, and decorative arts from the Crozier, Crofts, Williams, McIlhenny, Thompson, and other collections, with installations of a Ming period Chinese palace hall and temple and a Ch'ing scholar's study; †Japanese scroll paintings, prints, and decorative arts, with installations of a tea house and a 14th century temple; Himalayan sculpture and painting; Middle Eastern tile, miniatures, and decorative arts from the White and other collections; Oriental carpets from the McIlhenny, Williams, and other collections; Pre-Columbian sculpture and artifacts from the Arensberg Collections; †Medieval and Renaissance sculpture, painting, and decorative arts from the Foulc, Barnard, and other collections; installations of a Gothic chapel, Romanesque cloister, French Renaissance choir screen, and period rooms; Barbarini-Kress Foundation tapestry series; Kienbusch Collection of Arms and Armor; †French, Dutch, English, and Italian painting and decorative arts of the 14th - 19th centuries, from the †Wilstach, Elkins, McFadden, Tyson, John G Johnson, McIlhenny, Coxe-Wright and other collections; †Italian, Dutch and French drawings from the Clark and other collections; †French and English 17th and 18th century decorative arts from the Rice, Bloomfield-Moore, and other collections, with period rooms; †French and English art-nouveau decorative arts; †costume and textiles from all periods of western and eastern art, including the Whitman sampler collection; †American collections include painting, sculpture, and decorative arts from the colonial era to the present, with period rooms, Philadelphia furniture and silver, Tucker porcelain, Lorimer Glass Collection, and the Geesey Collection of Pennsylvania German folk art; †20th century painting, sculpture and works on paper from the Gallatin, Arensberg, Tyson, White, Stern, Stieglitz, Zigrosser, Greenfield, Woodward, and other collections; †Ars Medica Collection of prints on the subject of sickness and healing from all periods of western art; †Alfred Stieglitz Center Collection of Photograhy; †20th century decorative arts
Exhibitions: Design 1900-1940; European Sculpture and Decorative Art: Acquisitions by David DuBon, 1958-1985; The Quest for Eternity: Chinese Ceramic Sculpturé from the People's Republic of China; Double You (and X, Y, Z) Videodisc Installation by Peter d'Agostino; Twelve Photographers Look at Us; Claude Monet; Federal Philadelphia, 1785-1825: The Athens of the Western World; Recent Acquisitions of Prints, Drawings and Photographs; Miro; Richard Misrach: The American Desert; Duchamp Centennial Celebration; Paul Klee; The Henry P McIlhenny Collection. (1988) Contemporary American Crafts; From the Collections: The Hague School; Anselm Kiefer; New Art on Paper; Fans from the Collection; Form in Art: Works by Blind and Partially Sighted Adults; Master of 17th-Century Dutch Landscape Painting; The Fairmount Waterworks, 1812-1911; Art Nouveau in Munich: Masters of Jugendstil; Jasper Johns; Work Since 1974; Pietro Testa (1612-1650): Prints and Drawings. (1989)

A Visual Testimony: Judaica from the Vatican Library; Robert Adams: To Make It Home: Photographs of the American West, 1965-1985; Masterpieces of Impressionism and Post-Impressionism: The Annenberg Collection; Perpetual Motif: The Art of Man Ray

Publications: Bulletin, quarterly; exhibitions catalogs; members' magazine, semi-annually; monthly calendar

Activities: Classes for adults, children & families; guide training; symposia; lect open to public; concerts; gallery talks, films; tours; traveling exhibitions organized & circulated; museum shops sells books, magazines, reproductions, prints, slides, jewelry, needlework & postcards; art sales & rental gallery

M **Rodin Museum of Philadelphia,** 22nd & Benjamin Franklin Parkway, 19101. Tel 215-763-8100; Cable PHILMUSE. *Cur of Pre-1900 European Painting & Sculpture* Joseph Rishel; *Assoc Cur* Christopher Riopelle
Open Tues - Sun 10 AM - 5 PM, cl holidays. Admis by donation. Estab 1926. Rodin Museum of Philadelphia houses one of the largest collections outside of Paris of works by the major late 19th Century French sculptor, Auguste Rodin. Average Annual Attendance: 30,000
Collections: Collection includes many of the most famous sculptures created by Rodin, as well as drawings, prints, letters, books & a variety of documentary material
Activities: Classes for adults and children; docent training; concerts; gallery talks; tours; individual sculptures & drawings lent to museums for exhibitions; museum shop sells books, reproductions, slides, cards & memorabilia; audio tour

M **Mount Pleasant,** Fairmount Park, 19101. Tel 215-787-5449. *Cur American Decorative Arts* Jack Lindsey; *Mgr Vol Services* Caroline T Gladstone; *Admin Asst* Deborah W Troemner
Open daily except Mon, cl major holidays. Admis adults $1, children $.50. Historic house built in 1761; an outstanding example of the Georgian style in 18th century building & woodcarving; installed with period furnishings
Collections: †Period furnishings from the Museum represent the elegant way of life in Philadelphia in the 1760's
Activities: Tours

M **Cedar Grove,** Fairmount Park, Lansdowne Dr, 19131. Tel 215-787-5449.
Open Tues - Sun 10 AM - 5 PM, cl Mon. Admis adults $1, children $.50. This Quaker farmhouse built as a country retreat in 1748 was moved stone by stone to Fairmount Park in 1928 and restored with the furnishings of the five generations of Quakers who lived in it
Collections: The furniture was given with the house and reflects changes in styles through the 17th, 18th and 19th centuries
Activities: Tours

M **John G Johnson Collection,** Parkway & 26th, PO Box 7646, 19101-7646. Tel 215-787-5401. *Cur* Joseph Rishel; *Assoc Cur* Lawrence W Nichols; *Adjunct Cur* Carl B Strehlke
Open Tues - Sun 10 AM - 5 PM. Admis to Philadelphia Museum of Art $6. Upon his death in 1917, prominent Philadelphia lawyer, John Graver Johnson left his extensive collection intact to the city of Philadelphia; since 1933 the collection has been housed in the Philadelphia Museum of Art; administration and trusteeship of the collection is maintained separately from the other collections in the museum
Income: Financed by trust established by John G Johnson, contributions city of Philadelphia and Philadelphia Museum of Art
Collections: Early and later Italian Renaissance paintings; French 19th century paintings; northern European schools of Flanders, Holland and Germany in the 15th, 16th and 17th century
Exhibitions: In house exhibitions featuring works from permanent collection
Publications: Several catalogs for various parts of the collection including Catalog of Italian Paintings and Catalog of Flemish and Dutch Paintings
Activities: Special lect and related activities; occasional lending of collection to significant exhibitions

M **Samuel S Fleisher Art Memorial,** 709-721 Catharine St, 19147. Tel 215-922-3456; FAX 215-922-5327. *Pres* James Nelson-Kise; *Dir* Thora E Jacobson
Open during exhibitions Mon - Fri noon - 5 PM, Mon - Thurs 7 - 9:30 PM, Sat 1 - 3 PM. No admis fee. Estab 1898 as a free art school and sanctuary (Museum of Religious Art). Permanent collections are housed in an Italian Romanesque Revival building; Gallery is used for school-related exhibitions & for special shows of contemporary artists. Mem: 2800; membership contribution $15 per term
Income: $580,000 (financed by estate income, membership, materials fees, grants & gifts)
Collections: Medieval and Renaissance religious paintings and sculpture; 18th - 19th century Portuguese liturgical objects; 17th - 20th century Russian icons; some sculpture
Exhibitions: Challenge Series, annual schedule of five exhibitions featuring work by emerging Philadelphia area artists; annual student, faculty, adult & childrens' exhibitions; occasional special subject exhibitions
Activities: Classes for adults and children; lectures open to the public; 12 vis lectrs per year; concerts; gallery talks; competitions with awards; sales shop sells art materials

L **Library,** PO Box 7646, 19101. Tel 215-763-8100, Ext 258; FAX 215-236-4465. *Librn* Anita Gilden; *Research & Reference Librn* Gina Erdreich
Open Wed - Fri 10 AM - 4 PM. Estab 1876, as a research source for Museum staff, and to serve the public three days per week. For reference only
Library Holdings: Vols 127,000; Per subs 500; Micro — Fiche, reels; AV — Slides; Other — Clipping files, exhibition catalogs, pamphlets
Special Subjects: Art History, Decorative Arts, Drawings, Etchings & Engravings, Painting - American, Painting - European, Photography, Prints, Silver, Textiles, 20th century art

L **Slide Library,** 26th St & Benjamin Franklin Pkwy, PO Box 7646, 19101-7646. Tel 215-763-8100, Ext 320. *Slide Librn* Robin Miller
Provides slides to museum staff, not open to public
Library Holdings: AV — Slides 137,000

A **Women's Committee,** PO Box 7646, 19101-7646. Tel 215-763-8100, Ext 448; FAX 215-236-4465. *Pres* Alice B Lonsdorf; *Projects Coordr* Nancy C O'Meara
Office open Mon - Fri 9 AM - 5 PM. Estab 1883, incorporated 1915; takes an active interest in the museum. Organization sponsors Art Sales & Rental Gallery, park houses & museum guides, The Philadelphia Craft Show, classes for blind artists & tours for the deaf
Income: Financed by fund raising events

A **PHILADELPHIA SKETCH CLUB, INC,** 235 S Camac St, 19107. Tel 215-545-9298. *Pres* M Bruce Vieth
Call for hours. No admis fee. Estab 1903 to provide a showcase for artist members and juried and invited shows. Gallery is on 2nd floor of the Club House, 30 ft x 40 ft, skylighted, also used 6 times a week for life and still-life classes. Average Annual Attendance: 3500. Mem: 135; applicants must be proposed by two members & show portfolio of their artwork to Board of Directors; dues $100; meetings 10 times per year
Income: Financed by endowment, and membership
Collections: Permanent collection is from past and present members, oils, watercolors, etchings; fourty-four Thomas Anshutz Portraits; J Pennell Lithographs
Publications: The Portfolio, (bulletin), monthly
Activities: Classes for adults & life classes; lectures open to public, 9 vis lectrs per year; gallery talks; tours; competitions with cash awards; individual paintings and original objects of art lent to art museums who have exhibitions of PSC past members; lending collection contains 100 books, 100 original art works, photographs, sculptures, documents and letters of past members; Philadelphia area Art College Students Scholarship Competition

A **PLASTIC CLUB,** Art Club for Women, 247 S Camac St, 19107. Tel 215-545-9324. *Pres* Martin Davenport; *VPres* Ellen Davenport; *Secy* Mary Reith; *Treas* Elizabeth MacDonald; *House Chmn* Hannah Kohn
Open Mon, Tues & Thurs 10 AM - 2 PM, Wed 10 AM - 3 PM. No admis fee. Estab 1897 to promote wider knowledge of art and to advance its interest among artists. Two historic homes provide space for exhibits & a studio. Average Annual Attendance: 200 at lectures, 400 at exhibits & receptions. Mem: 80; must qualify for membership by submitting three framed paintings or other works of art to be juried; dues $35; association members (non-exhibiting) $25; annual meeting in May
Income: Financed by mem, donations, gifts & money-making projects
Exhibitions: Monthly exhibitions of paintings by members & invited artists. (1993) Open Works on Paper; Open Show All Media
Publications: Calendar of Events, 3 times a year; newsletter, 3 times a year
Activities: Classes for adults; lectures open to public, 20 vis lectrs per yr; gallery talks; competitions with awards; scholarships & fels offered; individual paintings & objects of art lent to hospitals, banks & public buildings; lending collection contains original art works, original prints, paintings, sculpture & crafts, such as jewelry; sales shop sells original art, prints & craft items

M **PLEASE TOUCH MUSEUM,** 210 N 21st St, 19103. Tel 215-963-0667, 567-5551; FAX 215-963-0424. *Exec Dir* Nancy D Kolb; *Cur Educ* Cynthia Chalker; *Dir Exhibits* Aaron Goldblat; *Dir Development & Marketing* Laura Campbell; *Dir Visitors Serv* Renee Henry; *Dir Finance* James Hall
Open Tues - Sun 10 AM - 4:30 PM, Sun 12:30 - 4:30 PM. Admis $4. Estab 1976 & accredited by American Association of Museums (1986) to provide a developmentally appropriate museum for young children, their parents and teachers. Gallery spaces are small-scaled, objects are accessible; two-tiered interpretation for adults coming with children (arts, crafts, ethnic materials and childlife exhibits). Average Annual Attendance: 136,000. Mem: 1100; dues family units $55
Income: $900,000 (financed by earned income: admissions, store receipts, program fees; contributions, memberships, governmental appropriations, foundations, corporate support & individuals)
Collections: Art works by contemporary artists, sculpture, environmental, paintings & crafts; †cultural artifacts from around the world: costumes, playthings, musical instruments, objects from daily life; Materials from the natural sciences; †contemporary American toys, artifacts & archives documenting American childhood
Exhibitions: Happily Ever After: Folklore & Fairy Tales; Future Step Into Art
Publications: Newsletters, quarterly; annual report; thematic exhibition catalogs, bi-annually; follow-through materials for groups and parents
Activities: Workshops for adults and children; theater programs; docent training; work with area colleges, universities and art schools; coop programs; lectures open to public, 3 vis lectr per yr; concerts; competitions with awards; original objects of art lent; lending collection contains art works, sculpture & artifacts concerning childhood; originate traveling exhibitions; museums shop sells books, posters, toys & educational materials

M **PORT OF HISTORY MUSEUM,** Penn's Landing, Delaware Ave at Walnut St, 19106. Tel 215-925-3804. *Dir* Ronald Barber; *Cur Exhibits* Corliss Cavalaieri; *Cur Educ* Jonah Roll; *Design Dir* Zenon Feszczak; *Spec Events Coordr* Joan Seals
Open Wed - Sun 10 AM - 4:30 PM, cl Mon, Tues & legal holidays. Admis adults $2, children $1. Estab 1981 for international exhibitions of design, fine arts & crafts. Museum is 10,000 sq ft. Average Annual Attendance: 100,000
Collections: Textiles; costume & material culture of West Africa, Central & South America, China, Siberia, Philippines, Southeast Asia from 1890-1920
Exhibitions: Israel Art Today; Recherche/Den Flexible; New American Focus. (1992) Art Around he Edges II
Publications: Florence to Philadelphia; exhibition catalogs
Activities: Classes for children; book traveling exhibitions

A **PRESBYTERIAN HISTORICAL SOCIETY,** 425 Lombard St, 19147. Tel 215-627-1852. *Dir* Frederick J Heuser; *Mgr Cataloging Servs* Barbara Schnur
Open Mon - Fri 8:30 AM - 4:30 PM. No admis fee. Estab May 1852 to collect and preserve official records and memorabilia of the Presbyterian Church USA, its predecessors and affiliates. Portraits displayed in the Reading Room, Museum Room, Mackie Room, Board Room & hallways. Six Alexander Stirling Calder statues representing American Presbyterian personalities who played a significant role in the history of the Church are displayed outside in front of the building. Average Annual Attendance: 1900. Mem: 1275; dues $20; annual meeting first Fri Mar
Income: Financed by membership & General Assembly
Collections: †Paintings & sculptures; †church plates; †relics; †silver and pewter communionware
Publications: American Presbyterians: Journal of Presbyterian History, quarterly
Activities: Tours

L Library, 425 Lombard St, 19147. Tel 215-627-1852.
Open to the public for reference
Collections: Jackson Collection; National Council of Churches Collection; Scotch-Irish Society Archives; Shane Collection

PRINT CLUB CENTER FOR PRINTS & PHOTOGRAPHS
For further information, see National and Regional Organizations

A PRINTS IN PROGRESS, 54 N Third St, 19106. Tel 215-928-0206. *Exec Dir* Michele Grant
Open Mon - Fri 9AM - 5 PM. Estab 1960. 300 sq ft with 12 ft ceilings. Average Annual Attendance: 1000 (classes)
Income: $250,000 (financed by endowment, city & state appropriation, businesses, foundations, individual contributions, art sales & classes)
Exhibitions: Animals of East Africa (ceramics, sculptures, prints); Celebration '86 (prints, masks, handmade dolls, banners, drawings); Myths, Legends & Storytelling (paintings, bas relief work, prints); Exhibition of Art Work by Children
Activities: Adult & children's classes; 1-5 day adult workshops; visiting artists programs; lectures open to public; scholarships & fels offered; exten dept serves five Philadelphia neighborhoods; originate traveling exhibitions to libraries, parks, art centers, galleries & other public facilities; sales shops sells original art, various handmade objects made by children

M THE ROSENBACH MUSEUM AND LIBRARY, 2010 DeLancey Place, 19103. Tel 215-732-1600. *Dir* Ellen S Dunlap; *Cur Books & Manuscripts* Leslie A Morris
Open daily 11 AM - 4 PM except Mon, open to scholars Mon - Fri 9 AM - 4:45 PM by appointment; cl Aug & national holidays. Admis adults $3.50, students $2.50, groups of 8 or more $3 per person; exhibits $2.50. Estab 1953 as a nonprofit corporation
Special Subjects: Bookplates & Bindings, Decorative Arts, Drawings, Etchings & Engravings, Furniture, Historical Material, Illustration, Manuscripts, Maps, Miniatures, Painting - American, Painting - British, Silver
Collections: 18th century English antiques and silver, paintings, prints and drawings, porcelain, rugs and objets d'art; rare books and manuscripts, consisting of British and American literature, Americana, and book illustrations; 260,000 manuscripts; 30,000 books, Marianne Moore Archive; Maurice Sendak Archive
Exhibitions: Jean Baptiste Le Prince: Drawings; Marianne Moore: Vision into Verse; Rosenbach Abroad: In persuit of books in private collections
Publications: A Selection from Our Shelves; Fantasy Sketches; The Rosenbach Newsletter; exhibition catalogs
Activities: Lect open to public, 3 vis lectr per yr; gallery talks; tours; individual paintings & original objects of art lent to museum & libraries with proper environmental & security systems; originate traveling exhibitions; museum shop sells books & reproductions

M ROBERT W RYERSS LIBRARY AND MUSEUM, 7370 Central Ave, 19111. Tel 215-745-3061. *Park Historian & Admin Supv* John McIlhenny; *Supv* Mary L Campbell; *Asst Facility Supv* Norma Gentner
Library open Fri - Sun 10 AM - 5 PM, Museum Sat & Sun 1 - 4 PM or by appointment. No admis fee. Estab 1910. House (Historic Register) left to City complete with contents in 1905; three period rooms; three other museum rooms with art objects - predominately Victorian. Average Annual Attendance: 20,000. Mem: 75; dues $5; meeting first Mon every month
Income: Financed by endowment, city appropriation, volunteer fund raising and trust fund
Collections: Static collection; export china, ivory, paintings, period rooms, prints, sculpture, weapons
Activities: Tours; lending collection contains 12,000 books
L Library, 7370 Central Ave, 19111. Tel 215-745-3061. *Librn* Mary L Campbell; *Asst Librn* Norma Gentner
Open Fri - Sun 10 AM - 5 PM. Estab 1910. Victoriana Collection available to scholars by appointment only
Library Holdings: Vols 20,000; Per subs 40; AV — Cassettes, fs, slides; Other — Framed reproductions, memorabilia, original art works, photographs, prints, sculpture
Collections: Victoriana

SOCIETY OF ARCHITECTURAL HISTORIANS
For further information, see National and Regional Organizations

TEMPLE UNIVERSITY
M Tyler School of Art-Galleries, Tyler Gallery, Elkins Park, Beech and Penrose Aves, 19126. Tel 215-782-2776, 787-5041. *Dean* Rochelle Toner; *Dir Exhibs* Don Desmett; *Asst to Dir* Tracy Neal
Open Tues - Sat 10 AM - 5 PM. No admis fee. Track lighting. Average Annual Attendance: 12,000
Income: Financed by state appropriation and grants
Publications: Brochures, posters, announcements or exhibitions catalogs for major shows
Activities: Lectures open to the public, 10-15 vis lectr per yr; gallery talks; special events
L Tyler School of Art Library, Beech & Penrose Aves, 19126. Tel 215-782-2849. *Librn* Andrea Goldstein
Open Mon - Thurs 8:30 AM - 9 PM, Fri 8:30 AM - 6 PM, Sat 9 AM - 5 PM, Sun 1 - 9 PM. Estab 1935 to provide library services to students and faculty. Circ 27,254
Income: $118,368 (financed by appropriation from Central University Library)
Purchases: $32,600
Library Holdings: Vols 30,000; Per subs 83; Auction Sale Catalogs; Micro — Fiche, reels; AV — Cassettes, v-tapes; Other — Exhibition catalogs, pamphlets, prints
—Slide Library, Beech & Penrose Aves, 19126. Tel 215-782-2848. *Slide Cur* Diane Sarachman; *Asst Cur* Del Ramers
Library Holdings: AV — Slides 350,000
Special Subjects: Art History, Ceramics, Decorative Arts, Graphic Design, Photography

M UNIVERSITY OF PENNSYLVANIA, Arthur Ross Gallery, Furness Bldg, 220 S 34th St, 19104-6308. Tel 215-898-4401; FAX 215-573-2045. *Dir* Dilys Winegrad; *Coordr* Lucia I Dorsey, BA
Open Tues - Fri 10 AM - 5 PM, Sat & Sun noon - 5 PM. No Admis fee. Estab 1983 to make art accessable to campus community & the general public. Average Annual Attendance: 7124. Mem: 54; dues $50; annual meeting
Income: $290,000 (financed by endowment, grants, gifts, in-kind contributions)
Collections: University art collection of paintings, prints, photographs, books, mss, textiles & sculpture
Exhibitions: (1991) Frank Furness: The Flowering of an American Architecture; Paintings by Reva Urban; Seeing Women: America Drawings from the Susan & Herbert Adler Collection. (1992) Frederic Church: Under Changing Skies; Sylvia Plachy: The Danube Isn't Blue. (1993) The Parthenon: Restoration, Research & Results; Sculpture by Maury Lowe
Publications: Exhibition catalogues
Activities: Lect open to public, 1 - 2 vis lectr per yr; tours; book traveling exhibitions, 1 per year; originate traveling exhibitions

UNIVERSITY OF PENNSYLVANIA
L Fisher Fine Arts Library - Art Dept, 220 S 34th St 34th & Walnut Sts, 19104-6308. Tel 215-898-8325; FAX 215-573-2066. *Librn* Alan E Morrison
Library Holdings: Vols 100,000
M University Museum of Archaelogy & Anthropology, 33rd & Spruce Sts, 19104. Tel 215-898-4000; FAX 215-898-0657. *Dir & Near East Section Cur* Dr Robert H Dyson; *Assoc Dir* Dr Vincent Pigott; *Am Hist Arch Assoc Cur* Dr Robert L Schuyler; *Am Section Cur* Dr Robert Sharer; *Babylonian Section Tablet Coll Cur* Dr Ake W Sjoberg; *Akkadian Cur* Dr Erle Leichty; *Egyptian Section Cur* Dr David O'Connor; *European Section Assoc Cur* Dr Bernard Wailes; *Mediterranean Section Cur* Dr Donald White; *Physical Anthropology Cur* Dr Francis E Johnston; *African Section Asst Cur* Dr Kris Hardin
Open Tues - Sat 10 AM - 4:30 PM, Sun 1 - 5 PM, cl Mon & Sun from Memorial Day - Labor Day. Admis adults $3 donation, students & sr citizens $1.50 donation, children under 6, members, U of P faculty, staff & students free. Estab 1887 to investigate the origins & varied developments of human cultural achievements in all times & places; to preserve & maintain collections to document these achievements, & to present to the public the results of these investigations by means of permanent exhibits, temporary exhibitions & special events. Average Annual Attendance: 200,000. Mem: 3300; dues individual $35, Loren Eiseley Assoc $1000
Income: $5,000,000 (financed by endowment, membership, state appropriation & University)
Collections: Archaeological & ethnographic artifacts relating to the Old & New World; the classical civilization of the Mediterranean, Egypt, Mesopotamia, Iran, Southeast Asia & the Far East, North, Middle & South America, Oceania; Africa; physical anthropology
Exhibitions: (1993) Tutavoh; Learning the Hopi Way; Symbolic Heat; Gender, Health & Worship among the Tamils of South India & Sri Lanka. (1994) Ancient Greek World
Publications: Expedition Magazine, quarterly; Museum Applied Science Center for Archaeology Journal; Museum Monographs; exhibition catalogues
Activities: Classes for adults & children; docent training; lectures open to the public, 20 vis lectrs per year; concerts; gallery talks; tours; exten dept serving Pennsylvania Commonwealth; objects of art lent to libraries & instructional centers in the state; lending collection contains motion pictures, original art works & slides; traveling exhibitions organized & circulated; museum shop sells books, magazines, reproductions, slides, jewelry & craft items
L Library, 33rd & Spruce Sts, 19104. Tel 215-898-7840; FAX 215-573-2008. *Librn* Jean S Adelman
Library Holdings: Vols 110,000; Per subs 800; microforms 70,000; Micro — Fiche, reels; AV — Fs; Other — Pamphlets

M UNIVERSITY OF THE ARTS, Broad & Pine Sts, 19102. Tel 215-875-1116; FAX 215-875-5467. *Pres* Peter Solmssen; *Provost* Virginia Red; *Dir Exhib* Leah Douglas
Open Sept - May Mon, Tues, Thurs & Fri 10 AM - 5 PM, Wed 10 AM - 9 PM, Sat noon - 5 PM, June - Aug Mon - Fri 10 AM - 5 PM. No admis fee. College contains two galleries: Rosenwald - Wolf Gallery & Haviland - Strickland Building Galleries. Temporary exhibitions which relate to the University's diverse instruction. The galleries present high quality contemporary exhibitions which attract national & international artists to the campus. Major exhibitions are accompanied by catalogs, symposia & lectures
Income: Financed by city, state and federal appropriations, private & corporate support
Exhibitions: Contemporary & 20th century work in visual arts and design
Publications: Catalogs & brochures accompany major gallery exhibitions
Activities: Lectures; opening receptions; tours; slide presentations; gallery talks; workshops
L Albert M Greenfield Library, 320 S Broad St, 19102. Tel 215-875-1111; FAX 215-875-5467. *Library Dir* Stephen Bloom; *Visual Resources Librn* Martha Hall; *Assoc Dir* Carol Homan Graney; *Reference Librn* Sara MacDonald
Open Mon - Thurs 8:30 AM - 9 PM, Fri 8:30 AM - 5 PM, Sat noon - 5 PM (shorter hours during the summer). Estab 1876 to support the academic programs of the School
Library Holdings: Vols 100,000; Per subs 300; Picture files, Reproduction files; Micro — Fiche, prints, reels; AV — A-tapes, cassettes, rec, slides 160,000, v-tapes; Other — Clipping files, exhibition catalogs, photographs, reproductions
Special Subjects: Theatre Arts, Dance, Design, Music, Visual Arts

L WILLET STAINED GLASS STUDIOS, 10 E Moreland Ave, 19118. Tel 215-247-5721; FAX 215-247-2951. *Pres* E Crosby Willet; *General Mgr* William G Stewart; *Librn* Helen H Weis
Open Mon - Fri 8 AM - 4:30 PM by appointment. Estab 1890 as the largest stained glass studio in the United States. For reference only
Activities: Individual paintings and original objects of art lent; lending collection contains photographs, Kodachromes and motion pictures; traveling exhibitions organized and circulated

WOMEN'S CAUCUS FOR ART
For further information, see National and Regional Organizations

M **WOODMERE ART MUSEUM,** 9201 Germantown Ave, 19118. Tel 215-247-0476. *Pres* Robert E May; *VPres* Sedra Schiffman; *VPres* Earle N Barber; *Treas* Joseph Baxter; *Dir* Michael W Schantz
Open Tues - Sat 10 AM - 5 PM, Sun 2 - 5 PM, cl holidays. No admis fee. Estab 1940; founded by Charles Knox Smith, in trust for benefit of the public. A large addition in 1965 provides additional gallery and studio space. Average Annual Attendance: 15,000. Mem: 1200; dues $20 and higher; annual meeting Jan
Income: Financed by endowments, gifts, grants & membership fees
Purchases: Philadelphia art, past & present
Collections: Contemporary American †paintings, †sculpture, and †graphics; European porcelains and furniture; European and American sculpture; Oriental rugs, furniture, porcelains; Smith Collection of European and American paintings
Exhibitions: 8 current exhibitions annually; prizes awarded in Members' Annual Juried and Special Exhibitions
Activities: Classes for adults and children; concerts, lect, gallery tours; field trips
L **Library,** 9201 Germantown Ave, Philadelphia, 19118. Tel 215-247-0476. *Librn* Sandy Drinker
Reference only
Library Holdings: Micro — Cards; Other — Clipping files, exhibition catalogs

PITTSBURGH

A **ASSOCIATED ARTISTS OF PITTSBURGH,** 6300 Fifth Ave, 15232. Tel 412-361-4235. *Pres* Irene Pasinski
Open Tues - Sat 10 AM - 5 PM, Sun 1 - 5 PM, cl Mon. Estab 1910 to give exposure to member artists and for education of the area in the field of art. An art gallery is maintained. Average Annual Attendance: 25,000. Mem: 568 (must be juried into the group); dues $45
Income: Financed by membership
Publications: The First 75 Years
Activities: Lectures open to public; competitions with awards

M **JOHN P BARCLAY MEMORIAL GALLERY,** 526 Penn Ave, 15222. Tel 412-263-6600. *Dir* Steve Frye; *Admin Asst* Susan Moran
Open Mon, Tues & Thurs 9 AM - 8 PM, Wed & Fri 9 AM - 5 PM, Sat 9 AM - 4 PM. No admis fee. Estab 1921 as an art school and proprietary trade school
Exhibitions: Local art group shows; local artists; loan exhibitions; student and faculty members; technical art exhibits
Publications: Brochures; Catalog; School Newspaper
Activities: Classes for adults and teens; lectures open to public, 2-4 visiting lectures per year; Scholarships available
L **Resource Center,** 526 Penn Ave, 15222. Tel 412-263-6600. *Admin Asst* Susan Moran
Open Mon - Fri 7:30 AM - 3 PM, Mon, Tues & Thurs 6 - 10 PM. Estab 1971 to supply our students with readily available reference materials. Circ Approx 2600
Purchases: $1295
Library Holdings: Vols 2840; Per subs 127; Micro — Fiche; AV — Cassettes, fs, rec, slides; Other — Clipping files, exhibition catalogs, framed reproductions, memorabilia, pamphlets
Special Subjects: Architecture, Art History, Commercial Art, Crafts, Fashion Arts, Graphic Arts, Interior Design, Mixed Media, Photography

M **CARNEGIE INSTITUTE,** Carnegie Museum of Art, 4400 Forbes Ave, 15213. Tel 412-622-3200; FAX 412-622-3112. *Dir* Phillip M Johnston; *Asst Dir* Michael J Fahlund; *Cur Contemporary Art* Richard Armstrong; *Cur Educ* Marilyn M Russell; *Conservator* William A Real; *Cur Film and Video* William D Judson; *Registrar* Cheryl A Saunders; *Cur Section Antiquities, Oriental & Decorative Arts* Sarah Nichols; *Dir Marketing* Doris Carson Williams; *Chmn Museum of Art Committee* Milton Fine; *Assoc Cur Contemporary Art* Vicky A Clark; *Head Publications* Marcia Whitehead; *Media Relations Mgr* Elisa Behnk; *Cur Architecture* Christopher Monkhouse
Open Tues - Sat 10 AM - 5 PM, Fri evenings until 9 PM, Sun 1- 5 PM, cl Mon and major holidays. Admis by suggested contribution adults $4; children & students $2.50; members free. Estab 1895, incorporated 1926. Original building 1896-1907. Average Annual Attendance: 700,000. Mem: 23,000; dues $30 & up
Income: Financed by endowment, membership, city, county & state appropriation and other funds
Collections: †American and European paintings & sculpture, especially Impressionist and Post-Impressionist; †Contemporary International Art; Japanese woodblock prints; †American & European decorative arts; antiquities; Asian Art; African Art; †Films; †Video tapes; †Photographs, †Prints and Drawings
Publications: Annual report; Carnegie Magazine, six times per year; catalogue of permanent collection; exhibition catalogs
Activities: Classes for adults and children; lectures open to public; concerts; gallery talks; tours; film & video programs; inter-museum loans; originate traveling exhibitions; museum shop sells books, periodicals, posters, reproductions, slides, textiles, jewelry, ceramics, and postcards
L **Library,** 4400 Forbes Ave, 15213. Tel 412-622-3100. *Dir* Robert B Croneberger
Open to staff and museum docents for reference only
Library Holdings: Vols 2,998,670; Per subs 3830; Micro — Cards; AV — Cassettes, motion pictures, rec, slides, v-tapes; Other — Clipping files, exhibition catalogs, manuscripts, memorabilia, pamphlets, photographs

L **THE CARNEGIE LIBRARY OF PITTSBURGH,** Music and Art Department, 4400 Forbes Ave, 15213. Tel 412-622-3105; FAX 412-621-1267. *Head* Kathryn Logan; *Asst Head* Kirby Dilworth; *Staff Librn* John Forbis; *Staff Librn* Katherine Snovak; *Staff Librn* Catherine Tack
Open Mon, Tues, Wed & Fri 9 AM - 9 PM, Thurs & Sat 9 AM - 5:30 PM, Sun 1 - 5 PM, cl Sun during summer. Estab 1930 to provide reference and circulating materials on all aspects of art
Income: Financed by city, state and county appropriation
Library Holdings: Vols 65,000; Per subs 85; Micro — Reels; AV — Fs, slides, v-tapes; Other — Clipping files, exhibition catalogs, pamphlets, reproductions
Special Subjects: Advertising Design, Afro-American Art, American Western Art, Architecture, Art History, Bronzes, Calligraphy, Carpets & Rugs, Commercial Art, Conceptual Art
Collections: Architecture; costume; Pittsburghiana

CARNEGIE MELLON UNIVERSITY
M **Forbes Gallery,** 5200 Forbes Ave, 15213. Tel 412-268-2081. *Co-Dir* Ted McCann; *Co-Dir* Melissa Thorn
Open Tues & Thurs 7 - 9 PM, Wed & Sun noon - 4 PM. Estab 1969 to offer exhibition space to students, and an opportunity to learn about gallery management through practice. Gallery is approximately 20 x 40 ft plus small back room space. Average Annual Attendance: 750
Income: $1700 (financed by university funding)
Exhibitions: Weekly student exhibitions
L **Hunt Library,** Frew St, 15213-3890. Tel 412-268-2444; FAX 412-268-3890. *Fine Arts Librn* Henry Pisciotta; *University Librn* Charles B Lowrey
Open Mon - Thurs 8 AM - 3 AM, Fri 8 AM - midnight, Sat 9 AM - midnight, Sun noon - 3 AM. Estab 1912. The Fine Arts Library is on the 4th floor of the Hunt Library, supports College of Fine Arts programs & is open to the public
Income: Financed by University Libraries general operating funds & endowments
Library Holdings: Vols 54,900; Per subs 4000; architectural drawings, CDs, electronic datafiles; Micro — Reels; AV — A-tapes, rec, slides 120,700, v-tapes; Other — Clipping files, exhibition catalogs, reproductions
Special Subjects: Architecture, Design, Modern Art
Collections: Architectural Archives, Swiss Poster Collection, Thomas Gonda Poster Collection
Exhibitions: Pittsburgh Architectural Drawings
M **Hunt Institute for Botanical Documentation,** Frew St, 15213-3890. Tel 412-268-2434; FAX 412-268-6944. *Dir* Robert W Kiger; *Asst Dir* Terry D Jacobsen; *Cur of Art* James J White; *Librn* Charlotte Tancin; *Bibliographer* Gavin D R Bridson; *Archivist* Anita L Karg
Open Mon - Fri 9 AM - noon & 1 - 5 PM. No admis fee. Estab 1961 for the study of botany, history of botany, botanical art & illustration
Special Subjects: Art History, Drawings, Historical Material, Illustration, Printmaking, Prints, Watercolors, Woodcuts, Botanical Art & Illustration
Collections: †Botanical Art Collection, Archives, Library
Exhibitions: (1992) 7th International Exhibition of Botanical Art & Illustration
Publications: Huntia, irregular; Bulletin, semi-annually; exhibition catalogues, reference works, monographs
Activities: Retail store sells books, posters & cards

M **CHATHAM COLLEGE,** Art Gallery, Woodland Rd, 15232. Tel 412-365-1100. *Chmn* Dr Lewis Coyner; *Prof* Michael Pestel
Open Tues - Sun 2 - 5 PM, cl Mon. No admis fee. Estab 1960 as an art gallery in a small liberal arts college, serving both the college and community by mounting exhibitions of high quality. Gallery is 100 running ft, is located in Jennie King Mellon Library, and is fitted with track lighting. Average Annual Attendance: 1500
Income: Financed by college
Exhibitions: Linda Benglis; Don Reitz; Idelle Weber; Jerry L Caplan
Activities: Lect open to the public, 2 visiting lectr per year; gallery talks; scholarships; individual paintings & original objects of art lent

C **FISHER SCIENTIFIC COMPANY,** Fisher Collection of Alchemical and Historical Pictures, 711 Forbes Ave, 15219. Tel 412-562-8300; FAX 412-562-2233. *Dir* John Pavlik
Open Mon - Fri 9 AM - 4 PM. Estab 1917 to preserve for scientists a record of their professional ancestors. To maintain paintings and other graphics regarding science history, especially chemistry, for the public. Collection is housed in two small rooms and a hallway with 4000 sq ft of wall space, housed within Fisher Scientific Company's headquarters. Average Annual Attendance: 1000
Collections: Permanent collection consists of 40 oil paintings, engravings and etchings dealing with science history, especially alchemy; works executed by 17th century Dutch and Flemish artists: D Teniers, Hellemont, Wyck and Heerschopp; Louis Pasteur Special Collection, books, artworks, letters

M **THE FRICK ART MUSEUM,** 7227 Reynolds St, 15208. Tel 412-371-0600; FAX 412-241-5393. *Admin Asst* Jeanne Brown; *Admin Asst* Catherine Rudy Kiefer; *Asst Cur & Registrar* Nadine Grabania
Open Tues - Sat 10 AM - 5:30 PM, Sun Noon - 6 PM. No admis fee. Estab 1970 as an art museum for public enjoyment and education. Average Annual Attendance: 24,455
Income: Financed by endowment
Collections: Italian, French Renaissance; bronzes, Chinese porcelains, furniture, sculpture, tapestries
Exhibitions: (1992) Dutch & Flemish 17th Century Paintings - Harold Samuel Collection. (1993) Ottocento: Romanticism & Revolution in 19th Century Italian Painting; Three Centuries of Roman Drawings from the Villa Farnesina Rome; Renaissance & Baroques from the Frick Art Museum Collection. (1994) Florentine Drawings of the 17th & 18th Centuries from the Musee des Beaux-Arts de Lille
Publications: Exhibit catalogues
Activities: Lect open to public; concerts; gallery talks; tours; special programs; sales shop sells books, catalogues, posters, post cards

M **MATTRESS FACTORY,** 500 Sampsonia Way, 15212. Tel 412-231-3169. *Exec Dir* Barbara Luderowski; *Cur* Michael Olijnyk
Open Wed - Sun noon - 4 PM. No admis fee. Estab 1978. Average Annual Attendance: 16,000
Collections: Permanent Collection of James Jurell, Allan Wexler, Bill Woodrow & Jane Highstein

C **MELLON BANK,** Three Mellon Bank Center, 15259. Tel 412-234-4100. *Art Dir* Laura Kintner
Collections: 18th & 19th century British drawings & paintings; American historical prints; 19th century American & Pennsylvanian paintings; contemporary American & British paintings; contemporary works on paper; textiles

A **PITTSBURGH CENTER FOR THE ARTS,** 6300 Fifth Ave, Mellon Park, 15232. Tel 412-361-0873. *Exec Dir* Bob Grote
Open Tues - Sat 10 AM - 5 PM, Sun 1 - 5 PM, cl Mon. No admis fee, suggested donation. Estab 1944, incorporated 1947 to support artists & educate public about & through art. Galleries maintained for monthly contemporary exhibitions, group and one-man shows. Headquarters for non-profit organizations in the creative arts consists of sixteen resident and two affiliated member groups, gallery lodged in old mansion. Average Annual Attendance: 150,000. Mem: 6500; dues vary; patron members; annual meeting in Nov
Income: Financed by school tuition, membership, commission on art sales & contributions
Exhibitions: Viola Frey; Ron Isaacs; New Attitudes; Urban Pulses; contemporary crafts
Publications: The Arts, regional magazine with PCA listings; artists directory; exhibition catalogs; monthly calendar
Activities: Arts and crafts classes for adults and children; dramatic programs; docent training; workshops; vocational & teacher training; summer art camp; lectures open to public, 6 vis lectrs per year; concerts; gallery talks; tours; awards; annual holiday art sales; scholarships & fels offered; exten dept serves western Pennsylvania; originate traveling exhibitions; sales shop sells original art

L **PITTSBURGH HISTORY & LANDMARKS FOUNDATION,** James D Van Trump Library, Landmarks Bldg, Room 450, Station Square, 15219. Tel 412-471-5808. *Pres* Arthur P Ziegler, Jr; *Exec Dir* Louise Sturgess
Open Mon - Fri 9 AM - 5 PM. 1964. Reference for members only. Mem: 2200; annual dues $5
Library Holdings: Vols 3400; Per subs 20; Architectural & engineering drawings; Other — Clipping files, original art works, photographs, prints
Special Subjects: Architecture, Drawings, Landscape Architecture, Allegheny County history & architecture, historic preservation, civil engineering
Collections: Paintings: Otto Kuhler, Daron Gorsou, William C Wall, Edward B Lee

C **PITTSBURGH NATIONAL BANK,** Art Collection, 2300 One Oliver Plaza, 15222. Tel 412-762-2000. *Real Estate Adminr* Nancy Sherman
No admis fee. Estab 1970 to enhance offices. Collection displayed at Pittsburgh National Building
Collections: Eclectic media and periods
Activities: Awards to local groups only; individual objects of art lent

C **ROCKWELL INTERNATIONAL CORPORATION TRUST,** 625 Liberty Ave, 15222. Tel 412-565-2000, ext 7436. *Secy* Thomas J Joyce
Annual amount of contributions and grants $667,800; supports fine and performing arts

A **SILVER EYE CENTER FOR PHOTOGRAPHY,** 1015 E Carson St, 15203. Tel 412-431-1810. *Dir* Jody Guy
Open Tues - Sat noon - 5 PM, Fri evenings until 8 PM. No admis fee
Exhibitions: Rotating exhibits of national & international photography, every 6 weeks. (1993) Encountering Differences; Living with the Enemy, Donna Ferrato's work
Publications: PHOTOpaper, quarterly
Activities: Workshops; lect series

UNIVERSITY OF PITTSBURGH
M **University Art Gallery,** 15260. Tel 412-648-2400; FAX 412-648-2792. *Dir* David G Wilkins; *Admin* Linda Hicks
Open Tues - Sat 10 AM - 4 PM, Sun 2 - 5 PM, cl Mon. No admis fee. Estab 1970 to provide exhibitions for the university community and the community at large and to provide students with gallery experience. Gallery comprised of 350 running ft in five areas. Average Annual Attendance: 4000
Income: Financed through the University
Collections: †Drawings, †paintings, †prints and †sculpture
Publications: Exhibition catalogs, three per year
Activities: Original objects of art lent; lending collection contains 922 original art works, 700 original prints, paintings, 100 photographs, 100 sculptures and drawings; originate traveling exhibitions
L **Henry Clay Frick Fine Arts Library,** Henry Clay Frick Fine Arts Bldg, 15260. Tel 412-648-2410; FAX 412-648-7568. *Librn* Ray Anne Lockard
Open Mon - Thurs 9 AM - 9 PM, Fri & Sat 9 AM - 5 PM, Sun noon - 7 PM. Estab 1928 to support the teaching activities of the Departments of Fine Arts and Studio Arts. For reference only
Library Holdings: Vols 71,000; Per subs 335; Micro — Fiche 13,000, reels; AV — Slides; Other — Clipping files, exhibition catalogs, pamphlets
Special Subjects: Art History, Graphic Arts, Sculpture, Architectural History, Medieval, Renaissance and Modern Art
Collections: Facsimile mss

C **WESTINGHOUSE ELECTRIC CORPORATION,** Art Collection, Gateway Center, Westinghouse Bldg, 15222. Tel 412-642-5904. *Cur & Consultant* Barbara Antel
Open by appointment 8:15 AM - 5:15 PM. Estab 1970 to create pleasant working environment for employees. Collection displayed in headquarters building; a working collection used by the employees
Collections: 1600 pieces: American Contemporary Abstract Paintings & Prints, 1965 to present; American Indian Tapestries; †Poster Classics
Activities: Individual objects of art lent

READING

M **ALBRIGHT COLLEGE,** Freedman Gallery, 13th & Exeter Sts, 19604. Tel 215-921-2381, Ext 7171; FAX 215-921-7530. *Pres* David G Ruffer; *Dean* Eugene S Lubot; *Acting Dir* Janice Schiffman
Open Mon, Wed - Fri Noon - 4 PM, Tues Noon - 8 PM, Sun 2 - 5 PM, also by appointment. No admis fee. Estab 1976 to present primarily contemporary art in a context of teaching. Large Gallery: 40 ft x 50 ft; Small Gallery: 20 ft x 24 ft.

Average Annual Attendance: 18,000. Mem: 220; dues $20, students $5
Income: $150,000 (financed by endowment, college, membership & grants)
Collections: Contemporary Painting, Prints, Sculpture, Photography
Exhibitions: (1988) Ellen Brooks; Life Forms: Contemporary Organic Sculpture; Gregory Botts; Bert Brouwer; Motorized Sculpture; Edward Albee Collection, Cynthia Carlson; The European Avant Garde. (1989) Mark Innerst; Contemporary Hispanic Shrines; Art About Aids; Donald Lipski; Poetic Sculpture; Recent Abstract Painting (1987) Mark Kostabi; Peter Campas, William Baziotes; New Video: Japan; Ron Kuivila; Robert Keyser; Computer Assisted: The Computer in Contemporart Art (1988) Ellen Brooks; Life Forms: Contemporary Organic Sculpture; Gregory Botts; Bert Brouwer; Motorized Sculpture; Edward Albee Collection
Publications: Exhibit catalogues
Activities: Lectures open to public, 4-6 vis lectr per year; gallery talks; tours; Freedman Gallery Student Award; produce video-tapes on exhibitions, these include interviews with artists and commentary, tapes are available for rent; film series; individual paintings and original objects of art lent to galleries and museums; originate traveling exhibitions; sales desk sells catalogues, prints, t-shirts

A **BERKS ART ALLIANCE,** Wyomissing Institute of Art Bldg, Trent & Belmont St, 19610. Tel 215-376-1576. *Pres* Joyce Floreen; *First VPres* Ingrid Hemphill; *Second VPres* Ann Buck
Estab 1941 to maintain active art center in Reading and Berks county. Mem: 150; dues $12; annual meetings 2nd Tues of odd months
Income: Financed by dues; art auction; commisions from members shows
Exhibitions: Three annual membership shows, plus solo or two-persons shows of a two week period each; juried show
Publications: Palette, every other month
Activities: Life or costume drawing workshop Thurs morning; open painting workshop Thurs afternoon; life drawing workshop Thurs evening; three day seminars by professional artists; sponsors annual trip to American Watercolor Society Show in New York

M **READING PUBLIC MUSEUM AND ART GALLERY,** 500 Museum Rd, 19611-1425. Tel 215-371-5850. *Dir* Bruce L Dietrich; *Cur Fine Arts* Jefferson A Gore
Open Mon - Wed 10 AM - 8 PM, Thurs - Sat 10 AM - 4 PM, Sun noon - 4 PM, members only Mon & Tues. Admis suggested adults $3, children $2. Estab 1904 to promote knowledge, pleasure, and cultivation of the arts and sciences. Ground floor: oil painting gallery. First floor: natural and social sciences exhibits. Second floor: permanent and temporary art exhibitions. Average Annual Attendance: 160,000. Mem: 600; dues $30; annual meeting in May
Income: $750,000 (financed by government)
Collections: American & European paintings; Natural Science; 19th Century Paintings; Old Masters Gallery; Pennsylvania-German Room; World History
Exhibitions: American Beauty Photographs by David Graham; Spectrums of Seasons, Jimmie Ernst; Retrospective Exhibits
Publications: Catalogue of selections from Permanent Collection
Activities: Classes for children; docent training; lectures open to public & for members only, 10 vis lect per year; concerts; gallery talks; tours; competitions with purchase awards; individual paintings & original objects of art lent to AAM accredited museums; lending collection contains 6000 original prints, 750 paintings, 100 photographs & 100 sculpture; museum shop sells books, reproductions, gift items, prints & slides
L **Library,** 500 Museum Rd, 19611. Tel 215-371-5850.
Open Mon - Fri 9 AM - 4 PM. For reference only
Library Holdings: Vols 15,000; Per subs 31; Original documents; AV — A-tapes, cassettes, fs, Kodachromes, lantern slides, v-tapes; Other — Clipping files, exhibition catalogs, manuscripts, memorabilia, pamphlets, prints, reproductions
Collections: American Bureau of Ethnology Collection

SCRANTON

M **EVERHART MUSEUM,** Nay Aug Park, 18510. Tel 717-346-7186. *Chmn Trustees* James J Walsh; *Dir* Kevin O'Brien; *Cur Art* Barbara Rothermel
Open Tues - Fri 10 AM - 5 PM, Sat & Sun & summer holidays noon - 5 PM, cl major holidays. No admis fee. Estab and inc 1908, a gift to the city by Dr Isaiah F Everhart; building enlarged 1928-29. Average Annual Attendance: 52,000. Mem: 1400; dues $15 & up
Income: Financed by endowment, city, state & county appropriations, memberships
Collections: African Art; American Folk Art; American Indian objects; European and American painting, prints and sculpture; Dorflinger Glass; Oceanic Art; Oriental Art
Exhibitions: 5-6 exhibitions per year
Publications: Newsletter, 4 times per yr; annual report; exhibition catalogs
Activities: Lectures open to public; gallery talks; tours; educational programs for schools and other groups by appointment; planetarium demonstrations; book traveling exhibitions; originate traveling exhibitions & circulate to other museums; sales shop sells gifts & crafts

SEWICKLEY

M **INTERNATIONAL IMAGES, LTD,** The Flatiron Bldg, 514 Beaver St, 15143. Tel 412-741-3036; FAX 412-741-8606. *Pres* Elena Kornetchuk; *Dir of Exhib* Charles M Wiebe; *Gallery Assoc* Janet Caldarelli; *Gallery Assoc* Dawn Moore
Open Tues - Fri 9:30 AM - 5:30 PM, Sat 10 AM - 4 PM

SHIPPENSBURG

M SHIPPENSBURG UNIVERSITY, Kauffman Gallery, N Prince St, 17257. Tel 717-532-1530; FAX 717-532-1273. *Dir* William Q Hynes; *Secy* Veronica Mowery
Open Mon - Fri 9 AM - 4 PM, Wed evenings 6 - 9 PM. No admis fee. Estab 1972 to bring art to the college community. Average Annual Attendance: 1500
Income: Financed by Student Association funds & university
Exhibitions: Scholastic Art Awards - Area 6; SU Student Art Exhibits; changing exhibitions every month
Activities: Lect open to the public, 4 vis lectr per year; gallery talks

STROUDSBURG

M MONROE COUNTY HISTORICAL ASSOCIATION, Elizabeth D Walters Library, 537 Ann St, 18360. Tel 717-421-7703. *Dir* Janet Mishkin
Open Tues - Fri 10 AM - 4 PM, Sun 1 - 4 PM, cl Sat. Admis fee $1. Estab 1921 for research. Average Annual Attendance: 5000
Income: $80,000 (financed by endowment, mem, state appropriation & county)
Collections: Decorative Arts; Furniture; Indian Artifacts; Textiles
Exhibitions: Period Room; Toy Room
Publications: Fanlight Newsletter, quarterly
Activities: Lect open to public, 5 vis lectr per year; museum shop sells books

SWARTHMORE

L SWARTHMORE COLLEGE, Friends Historical Library, 500 College Ave, 19081. Tel 215-328-8496; FAX 215-328-8673; Elec Mail mchijio1@cc.swarthmore.edu. *Dir* Dr J William Frost; *Cur* Mary Ellen Chijioke; *Cur Peace Collection* Wendy Chmielewski
Open Mon - Fri 8:30 AM - 4:30 PM, Sat 9 AM - Noon; cl Sat when college not in session. Estab 1871 to preserve and make available to the public material by and about Quakers and their concerns, records of non-sectarian peace organizations and papers of peace movement leaders. Circ 4885
Income: $375,000 (financed by endowment & college)
Purchases: $15,000
Library Holdings: Vols 55,000; Per subs 584; charts; maps; original documents; posters; Micro — Reels; AV — A-tapes, cassettes, Kodachromes, lantern slides, motion pictures, rec, slides, v-tapes; Other — Clipping files, manuscripts, memorabilia, original art works, pamphlets, photographs, prints, sculpture
Collections: Quaker paintings; Quakers as subject in art; †Meeting House Picture Collection; †portraits, group pictures, †residence pictures, †silhouettes and sketches of individual Friends; †Swarthmore College pictures; Swarthmore College Peace Collection consists primarily of archival material, records of non-sectarian peace organizations in the United States and 59 foreign countries, papers of peace leaders including Jean Addams, Emily Greene Balch, Elihu Burritt, A J Muste, †Wilhelm Sollmann and others; †1400 peace posters and war posters
Exhibitions: (1992) John Greenleaf Whittier, 1807 - 1892. (1993) Lucretia Mott Bi-centennial: The Nineteenth Struggle for Peace, Racial Justice & Women's Rights
Publications: Collection guides; exhibit catalogs
Activities: Annual Honorary Curators & Lippincott lect

UNIONTOWN

A TOUCHSTONE CENTER FOR CRAFTS, 107 S Beeson Ave, PO Box 2141, 15401. Tel 412-438-2811. *Exec Dir* Marcene R Clark
Open Mon - Fri 9 AM - 5 PM. Estab 1972, dept estab 1983 to promote excellence in the crafts. Average Annual Attendance: 5800. Mem: 300
Income: $170,000 (financed by membership, grants & donations)
Activities: Classes for adults & children; lectures open to the public, 4 vis lectr per yr; scholarships

UNIVERSITY PARK

PENNSYLVANIA STATE UNIVERSITY
M Palmer Museum of Art, 16802. Tel 814-865-7672; FAX 814-863-8608. *Dir* Dr Kahren Jones Arbitman; *Cur* Dr Glenn Williumson; *Registrar* Ok Hi Lee; *Exhib Designer* Ronald Hand; *Asst Dir* Dr Mary F Linda; *Cur Ed* Dr Patrick J McGrady
Open Tues - Fri 10 AM - 4:30 PM, Sat 11 AM - 4:30 PM, Sun noon - 4 PM, cl Mon & major holidays; cl from spring of 1992 to summer of 1993 for renovation. No admis fee. Estab 1972 to promote a program of changing exhibitions; estab 1972 to promote a program of changing exhibitions; a window to the world f or the university community. Museum is now a ten gallery post-modernist structure designed by Charles W Moore renovated & expanded in 1992 to accomodate continuous desplay of the permanent collection as well as changing exhibitions that are national & international in scope. Average Annual Attendance: 60,000
Income: Financed by state appropriation
Collections: American & European painting, drawings, graphics & sculpture with some emphasis on Pennsylvania artists; limited material in Ancient, African & Near Eastern areas; Kehl & Nina Markley Collection of Ancient Peruvian Ceramics; Dr Helen Adolf Collection of Austrian Academic Paintings; Asian paintings, sculpture, prints & decoratives art (ceramics, jade & cloisonne); John C O'Connor & Ralph M Yeager Collection of Pennsylvania Prints from the late 18th to the early 20th Century; Professor Francis E Hyslop Jr Collection of American & European prints; Tonkin Collection of Chinese export porcelain, Chinese jade carvings, paintings & watercolors releated to the Oriental Trade
Exhibitions: (1991-1992) The Permanent Collection: From Floor to Ceiling; Sqissart: In Celebration of the 700th Anniversary of the Swiss Confederation; The Art of American Livestock Breeding The Presence of Absence: New Installations; The Save River: A New History; Florence Putterman: A Twenty Year Survey, 1970- 1990; Abstracting the Landscape: The Work of Landscape

Architect A E Bye
Publications: Brochures; quarterly newsletter; exhibition catalogs; posters
Activities: Lect open to public, 18 vis lectrs per yr; concerts; gallery talks; symposia; museum store sells books, original art and reproductions

L Pattee Library, Arts Library, E 405, 16802. Tel 814-865-6481. *Arts & Architecture Librn* Loanne Snavely; *Music Librn* Kathleen Haefliger
Open Mon - Thurs 8 AM - Midnight, Sat 8 AM - 9 PM, Sun Noon - Midnight. Estab 1957 to support the academic programs of the College of Arts and Architecture and the Division of Art and Music Education; to provide information on the arts to members of the university and community
Income: Financed through University Libraries
Library Holdings: Vols 85,000; Per subs 610; Micro — Fiche; AV — Cassettes, rec; Other — Prints
Special Subjects: Art Education, Asian Art, Prints, Byzantine, Medieval, Baroque and Renaissance art and architecture history, history of printmaking, illuminated manuscripts
Collections: †Fine Print Collection (original prints)

M HUB Galleries, 312 Hub, 16802. Tel 814-863-0611; FAX 814-863-7700. *Dir* Isabel Farrel Del-Ariew
Open Daily 10 AM - 8 PM, cl Mon. No admis fee. Estab 1976 to provide life-enriching visual arts experiences to the University & community. Browsing gallery; Art Alley Panels & Cases; HUB gallery (formal). Average Annual Attendance: 8400
Activities: Book traveling exhibitions, 7 per yr

WARREN

M CRARY ART GALLERY INC, 511 Market St, 16365. Tel 814-723-4523. *Pres & CEO* Ann Lesser; *VPres* Adele Tranter; *Secy* Quinn Smith
Open by appointment. No Admis fee. Estab 1977 for art appreciation & education, & to exhibit the work of Clare J Crary, Gene Alden Walker & guest artists. The gallery was contructed in 1962 as a private dwelling on the general plan of a Roman Villa. There are 6 gallery rooms, one housing a permanent exhibit of Crary photographs. The others will accomodate fine art exhibits of the works of other artists
Income: $28,000 (financed by endowment)
Collections: Photographs by Clare J Crary; Oils by Gene Alden Walker; drawings, etchings, oils, acrylics by various artists; 19th Century Japanese wood-block prints-Ukiyo-E
Exhibitions: (1991) Watercolors by Anne F Fallin, NWS, AWS. (1992) various media by Buffalo NY area women artists of the early 20th century.
Activities: Gallery talks; tours; book traveling exhibitions

WASHINGTON

M WASHINGTON & JEFFERSON COLLEGE, Olin Art Gallery, E Wheeling St, Olin Art Center, 15301. Tel 412-223-6084, 223-6110. *Gallery Dir* Paul B Edwards
Open Mon - Sun noon - 7 PM during school yr. No admis fee. Estab 1980 to provide college & community with art shows. Flexible lighting, air conditioned gallery. Average Annual Attendance: 5000-6000
Income: Financed by college
Purchases: Over $3000 annually during National Painting Show
Collections: Art dept collection; college historical collection; National Painting Show collection
Exhibitions: Monthly exhibits
Publications: Exhibition catalogs
Activities: Lect open to public; concerts; gallery talks; competitions with awards;; individual paintings & original objects of art lent to students, faculty & staff; lending collection contains 200 original art works, 100 original prints, 300 paintings, 200 photographs & 4 sculpture; book traveling exhibitions 1 - 2 per year

WAYNE

A WAYNE ART CENTER, 413 Maplewood Ave, 19087. Tel 215-688-3553. *Dir* Dr Nancy Kimbell
Open Mon - Fri 9:30 AM - 4 PM. No admis fee. Estab 1930 as a community art center. Two galleries offer rotating exhibits of work by local artists. Average Annual Attendance: 2000. Mem: 400; dues $20; annual meeting May
Income: $60,000 (financed by membership, grants, corporations and Pennsylvania Council on the Arts)
Exhibitions: 10-12 changing exhibitions per year
Activities: Classes for adults and children; gallery talks; competitions

WEST CHESTER

A CHESTER COUNTY HISTORICAL SOCIETY, 225 N High St, 19380. Tel 215-692-4800; FAX 215-692-4357. *Exec Dir* Roland H Woodward; *Museum Cur* Margaret Bleecker Blades
Estab 1893 for the acquisition and preservation of property and information of historic value or interest to the people of Chester County. Maintains reference library. Average Annual Attendance: 35,000. Mem: 2500; dues family $35, individual $25
Income: Financed by endowment and membership
Collections: Museum houses regional collections of furniture, from ca 1690 to early 20th century through Victorian; ceramics, needlework, glassware, pewter, textiles, clocks, iron, dolls & costumes
Exhibitions: Chester County Furniture; decorative arts (permanent installation); changing interpretive exhibits on county history, agriculture & industries
Publications: Chester County History, occasionally; Newsletter, bi-monthly
Activities: Docent training; lectures open to the public; tours; individual paintings and original objects of art lent to other museums; museum shop selling books, reproductions and prints

WHITEHALL

NATIONAL SOCIETY OF PAINTERS IN CASEIN & ACRYLIC, INC
For further information, see National and Regional Organizations

WILKES-BARRE

M **WILKES UNIVERSITY,** Sordoni Art Gallery, 150 S River St, 18766. Tel 717-824-4651, Ext 4325. *Dir* Judith H O'Toole; *Asst Dir* Jean C Adams
Open Mon - Wed & Fri - Sun noon - 5 PM, Thurs 5 - 9 PM. No admis fee. Estab 1973 to encourage the fine arts in the Wilkes-Barre and the northeastern Pennsylvania areas. The Gallery has one exhibition space, 30 x 40 ft, with adjustable flats used for hanging. Average Annual Attendance: 20,000. Mem: 600; dues $15 - $1000
Income: Financed by mem, foundation endowment, & Wilkes University
Collections: Nineteenth century European sculpture & paintings; 19th & 20th century American paintings & prints; mining photography collection
Exhibitions: They consist of loan exhibitions from other college galleries, independent galleries, major museums and loan services; group and one-person exhibits feature established modern masters and contemporary artists
Publications: Calendar of Events, bimonthly; scholarly catalogs; illustrated brochures; posters
Activities: Gallery talks; tours; loans to other universities & museums; book traveling exhibitions; originate traveling exhibitions to schools and museums

WILLIAMSPORT

M **LYCOMING COLLEGE GALLERY,** 17701. Tel 717-321-4242, 368-1140. *Coordr* Deborah Caulkins; *Co-Dir* Roger Shipley
Open Mon - Thurs 8 AM - 11 PM, Fri 8 AM - 4:30 PM, Sat 10 AM - 5 PM, Sun 1 - 11 PM. No admis fee. Estab 1980 to bring quality art work to the students and faculty as well as to the interested community. The new gallery, 30 x 60 ft, is located in the College Library. Average Annual Attendance: 5000
Income: Financed by school budget
Collections: †Paintings and prints of 19th and 20th century artists
Exhibitions: One-man shows of regional and area artists and alumni of the Department; traveling exhibitions
Activities: Gallery talks; tours; individual paintings lent; book traveling exhibitions; originate traveling exhibitions

YORK

A **HISTORICAL SOCIETY OF YORK COUNTY,** 250 E Market St, 17403. Tel 717-848-1589. *Exec Dir* Patrick A Foltz; *Cur Museum* Janet Deranian; *Cur Educ* Tamara Funk
Open Mon - Sat 9 AM - 5 PM, Sun 1 - 4 PM, Historic Houses Mon - Sat 10 AM - 4 PM, Sun 1 - 4 PM, cl all major holidays. Admis adults $4.50, children $2.25, senior citizen group rates for Historic Houses. Estab 1895 to record, preserve, collect and interpret the history of York County and Pennsylvania, including music and art of the past and present. Restoration Properties: General Gates House (1751); Golden Plough Tavern (1741) and Log House (1812), 157 W Market; Bonham House (1875), 152 E Market. Average Annual Attendance: 30,000. Mem: 1700; dues $18 and higher; annual meeting in April
Income: $350,000 (financed by endowment, gifts & membership)
Collections: Fraktur & other Pennsylvania decorative arts & furnishings; Works by Lewis Miller & other local artists; James Shettel Collection of theater & circus material; Horace Bonham artworks
Exhibitions: Four gallery shows per year featuring various subjects of regional interest
Publications: The Kentucky Rifle; Lewis Miller Sketches and Chronicles; Monthly Newsletter; The Philadelphia Chair, 1685-1785
Activities: Educ program; classes for adults and children; summer internship program; guided tours; lect; concerts; museum shop sells books, magazines, reproductions, prints and slides
L **Library,** 250 E Market St, 17403. Tel 717-848-1589. *Librn* June Lloyd
Open to the public, cl Sun & Mon. For reference only
Library Holdings: Vols 21,000; Per subs 50; Maps, 156 VF; AV — Slides, v-tapes; Other — Manuscripts, photographs

L **MARTIN MEMORIAL LIBRARY,** 159 E Market St, 17401. Tel 717-846-5300. *Dir* William H Schell; *Adult Servs* Rebecca Shives
Open Mon - Fri 9 AM - 5:30 PM, Sat 9 AM - 5 PM. No admis fee. Estab 1935
Library Holdings: Vols 315,000; Per subs 200; mounted pictures; AV — Cassettes, motion pictures, rec; Other — Pamphlets
Publications: Annual Reports; Bulletin, monthly; Martin Memorial Library Historical Series; occasional bibliographies of special collections
Activities: Programs for adults and children; lect; concerts

RHODE ISLAND

KINGSTON

A **SOUTH COUNTY ART ASSOCIATION,** 2587 Kingstown Rd, 02881. Tel 401-783-2195. *Pres* Stephanie Parker; *VPres* Peg Gregory; *Recording Secy* Gail Ambrose; *Treas* Cheslie Carpenter; *Cur & Caretaker* Jane Auger
Open Wed - Sun 1 - 4 PM during exhibitions. No admis fee. Estab 1929 to promote an interest in art and to encourage artists and to support, in every way, the aesthetic interests of the community. Average Annual Attendance: 400; applicants for membership must submit three paintings and be accepted by a committee; dues lay member & artist $15; annual meeting Oct

Collections: No large permanent collection; paintings by early members, usually not on display
Publications: Newsletter, 3-4 annually
Activities: Classes for adults and children; lectures open to the public, 4 vis lectr per yr; gallery talks; competitions with awards; scholarships; original objects of art lent to other art associations; lending collection contains books, lantern slides, sculpture, original art works and slides

M **UNIVERSITY OF RHODE ISLAND,** Fine Arts Center Galleries, c/o Department of Art, 02881-0820. Tel 401-792-2131; FAX 401-792-2729. *Galleries Dir* Judith Tolnick
Open Main Gallery Tues - Fri noon - 4 PM, 7:30 - 9:30 PM, Sat 1 - 4 PM, Photography Gallery Tues - Fri noon - 4 PM, Sat 1 - 4 PM, Corridor Gallery, Mon - Fri 9 AM - 5 PM. No admis fee. Estab 1970 to expose university & Southern New England communities to contemporary & historical art. Average Annual Attendance: 10,000 - 15,000
Income: Financed through University
Exhibitions: 18-20 ongoing exhibitions per yr
Publications: Catalogs, occasionally; brochures/wall text for each exhibit
Activities: Educ dept; classes for adults; lect open to the public, 20 vis lectr per year; concerts; gallery talks; sponsor competitions; book traveling exhibitions two times a year; originate traveling exhibitions to university museums & galleries nationally

NEWPORT

M **NAVAL WAR COLLEGE MUSEUM,** Coasters Harbor Island, 02841-1270. Tel 401-841-4052; FAX 401-841-3804. *Dir* Anthony S Nicolosi; *Sr Cur* Robert Cembrola
Open Mon - Fri 10 AM - 4 PM, Sat & Sun noon - 4 PM, June - Sept. Estab 1978, Themes: history of naval warfare, history of Navy in Narragansett Bay. 7000 sq ft on two floors of Founder Hall, a National Historic Landmark. Average Annual Attendance: 17,000
Income: Financed by Federal Navy & Naval War College Foundation, Inc
Exhibitions: Sea Power According to Alfred Thayer Mahan; Nav-Newport Articles & Art Exhibit, annual
Publications: Exhibition catalogs
Activities: Staff talks on themes & exhibits; lect open to public, 2 vis lectr per year; gallery talks; tours; retail store sells books, reproductions, prints, clothing, & costume jewelry

M **NEWPORT ART MUSEUM,** 76 Bellevue Ave, 02840. Tel 401-848-8200; FAX 401-848-8205. *Dir* Richard Y West; *Asst Dir* Arnold Cogswell; *Cur Educ* Lora Lee Gibbs; *Dir Development* Paula Sharp
Open summer Mon - Sat 10 AM - 5 PM, Sun & most holidays 1 - 5 PM, winter Tues - Sat 10 AM - 4 PM, Sun & most holidays 1 - 4 PM, cl Christmas, New Year's Day & Thanksgiving. Admis adults $3, sr citizens & students $2, children 12 & under free. The Griswold House, designed by Richard Morris Hunt for John N A Griswold in 1862 - 1863, has been the home of the Art Museum since 1916. Retaining some of the original interior decor of the era, the building is listed in the National Register of Historic Places. Cushing Memorial Gallery was built in 1920, commissioned from the firm of Delano & Aldrich, by friends & associates of Howard Gardiner Cushing. Buildings contain 6 galleries exhibiting contemporary visual arts, historic & regional exhibits. Average Annual Attendance: 20,000. Mem: 1300; dues $35 & up; annual meeting in Sept
Income: Financed by donations, endowment, mem, classes & admissions
Collections: †Drawings, †Paintings, †Photographs, †Prints, †Sculpture
Exhibitions: Changing exhibitions, all media
Publications: News, quarterly members' newsletters
Activities: Day & evening classes for adults & children; docent training; lectures open to the public & some for members only, 25 vis lectrs per year; concerts; gallery talks; tours; awards; scholarships; exten dept serves area schools; individual paintings & original objects of art lent to other museums; book traveling exhibitions, 1 - 2 per year; originate traveling exhibitions
L **Library,** 76 Bellevue Ave, 02840. Tel 401-848-8200; FAX 401-848-8205. *Coordr Library* Nancy Preston Bredbeck
Reference for school & docent use only; archives accessible to staff
Library Holdings: Vols 500; Per subs 6; Other — Exhibition catalogs, memorabilia, pamphlets, photographs
Special Subjects: Aesthetics, Art History, Etchings & Engravings, History of Art & Archaeology, Landscapes, Marine Painting, Painting - American, Period Rooms, Restoration & Conservation, Video

A **NEWPORT HISTORICAL SOCIETY,** 82 Touro St, 02840. Tel 401-846-0813. *Pres* Samuel M C Barker; *VPres* W Ogden Ross; *Secy* Patrick O'Hayes Jr; *Exec Dir* Dr Daniel Snydacker
Open Tues - Fri 9:30 AM - 4 PM, Sat 9:30 AM - noon; summer, Sat 9:30 AM - 4:30 PM, cl Sun. No admis fee. Estab 1853 to collect and preserve items of historical interest pertaining to the city. Maintains a regional art gallery and small marine museum. Also owns and exhibits the first Seventh Day Baptist Church in America (1729); the Wanton-Lyman-Hazard House (1675), the first home to be restored in Newport; the Friends Meeting House (1699), site of the annual New England Quakers Meeting for over 200 years. Average Annual Attendance: 9500. Mem: 1250; dues $20 and up; annual meeting May
Income: Financed by endowment, membership, state appropriation and other contributions
Collections: Artifacts, china, Colonial silver, dolls, glass, furniture, Newport scenes and portraits, pewter and toys
Exhibitions: Numerous changing exhibits
Publications: Newport History, quarterly; Newport Historical Society Newsletter, 6 times per yr
Activities: School programs; lect open to public, 4-6 visiting lectr per year; walking tours of historic Newport; original objects of art lent to museums
L **Library,** 82 Touro St, 02840. Tel 401-846-0813. *Librn* Bertram Lippincott III
Open Tues - Fri 9:30 AM - 4:30 PM, Sat 9 AM - noon; summers, Sat 9:30 AM - 4:30 PM. Estab 1853 to provide resource materials. For reference only
Library Holdings: Vols 14,300; Per subs 32; Micro — Fiche, reels; AV —

Kodachromes, slides; Other — Clipping files, exhibition catalogs, manuscripts, memorabilia, original art works, pamphlets, photographs, prints, sculpture
Special Subjects: Architecture, Art History, Ceramics, Costume Design & Construction, Decorative Arts, Dolls, Furniture, Historical Material, Landscape Architecture, Maps, Painting - American, Period Rooms, Pewter, Restoration & Conservation, Silver, Silversmithing, Stained Glass, Textiles, Genealogy

L **REDWOOD LIBRARY AND ATHENAEUM,** 50 Bellevue Ave, 02840. Tel 401-847-0292. *Librn* Eric Stocker
Open Mon - Sat 9:30 AM - 5:30 PM, 9:30 AM - 5 PM in July & Aug. Estab 1747 as a general library. Art gallery consists of three rooms with 140 paintings. Circ 53,000
Income: Financed by endowment and membership
Library Holdings: Vols 150,000; Per subs 175; AV — Rec
Collections: Portraits by Feke, Healy, Charles Willson Peale, Rembrandt Peale, Stuart, Sully & other early American painters; many paintings by Charles B King; pictures, statues
Activities: Library tours

PAWTUCKET

M **OLD SLATER MILL ASSOCIATION,** Slater Mill Historic Site, 67 Roosevelt Ave, PO Box 727, 02862-0727. Tel 401-725-8638. *Dir* Holly Begley; *Cur* Gail Fowler Mohanty
Open May - Labor Day Tues - Sun 10 AM - 5 PM, Labor Day - Dec 20 & Mar - May Sat & Sun 1 - 5 PM. Estab 1922. Wilkinson Gallery for temporary exhibits including history, art & craft shows. Three permanent galleries in historic buildings. Average Annual Attendance: 17,000. Mem: dues $35; annual meeting in June
Income: $190,000 (financed by endowment, mem & city appropriation)
Collections: Graphic; Machine Tools; Textiles; Textile Machinery
Exhibitions: Tour of site including textile mill, 18th century dwelling & machine shop. Art exhibits in Wilkinson Gallery
Activities: Adult classes; docent programs; lect open to public, 2 - 3 vis lectr per year; traveling educ programs; book traveling exhibitions 4 per year; retail store sells books, prints, slides & photographs

A **RHODE ISLAND WATERCOLOR SOCIETY,** Slater Memorial Park, Armistice Blvd, 02861. Tel 401-726-1876. *Pres* Betty Dunlop; *VPres & Treas* Edward Weber; *Treas* Patricia Sheridan; *Asst Treas* Theresa George
Open Tues - Sat 10 AM - 4 PM, Sun 1 - 5 PM; cl Mon. No admis fee. Estab 1896 to encourage & promote the advancement of watercolor painting. Large carpeted upper & lower tiled gallery. Lower level gallery open for receptions & exhibitions. Mem: 249; dues $50; annual meeting May; must submit work for jurying for membership
Income: Financed by dues, commissions, contributions, & rentals
Collections: Paintings & drawings by early members; prints & paintings by contemporary members
Exhibitions: Annual Exhibition of Member's work; Annual Christmas Exhibition; Annual Open Graphics Show; Annual Open Juried Watermedia Show; Annual New Members Show; 12 or more member exhibitions per year
Activities: Educ dept; classes for adults; 6 lectures & demonstrations per year, open to members & guests; concerts; competitions; sales shop sells wrapped matted paintings from bins

PROVIDENCE

BROWN UNIVERSITY
M **David Winton Bell Gallery,** 64 College St, 02912. Tel 401-863-2932. *Dir* Diana L Johnson; *Adminr* Richard Benefield
Open Sept - May Mon - Fri 11 AM - 4 PM, Sat & Sun 1 - 4 PM, cl major holidays. No admis fee. Estab 1971 to present exhibitions of interest to the university and community. The gallery is modern, covers 2625 sq ft, 14 ft ceilings, and has track lighting. Average Annual Attendance: 12,000
Income: Financed by endowment and university funds
Collections: Substantial print collection of historical & modern masters; selected color field paintings & modern sculpture
Exhibitions: (1992-93) Varujan Boghosian: Myth & Memory; Power in the Blod, The North of Ireland: Photographs by Gilles Peress; Figments of a Landscape: Photographic Monoprints by Denny Moers; The Crawford Bequest: Chinese Objects in the Collection of the Museum of Art, Rhode Island School of Design; Annual Juried Student Exhibition; The Rome Project: Works by Sherman, Prince, West, Vaisman, Kawara, Hume, Lethbridge, Wool, Struth, Weiner & Mucha
Publications: Exhibition catalogs
Activities: Lect open to public; art work lent to exhibitions mounted by museums & galleries; permanent collection contains 5000 original prints & photographs, over 100 modern paintings & sculptures; originates traveling exhibitions
M **Annmary Brown Memorial,** 21 Brown St, PO Box 1905, 02912. Tel 401-863-2429. *Cur* Catherine Denning
Open Mon - Fri 9 AM - 5 PM. Estab 1907 to offer representatives of schools of European and American painting. There are three galleries which house the art collection of the founder & his wife, & portraits of the Brown family. Average Annual Attendance: 3000
Activities: Lectures open to public, 10-20 vis lectr per year; concerts; tours
L **Art Slide Library,** 02912. Tel 401-863-3218. *Cur* Norine D Cashman; *Assoc Cur* Karen Bouchard
Open Mon - Fri 8:30 AM - 5 PM. Circ 35,000
Income: $175,000 (financed by university funds)
Library Holdings: Vols 550; Micro — Fiche; AV — Slides; Other — Exhibition catalogs, photographs, reproductions
Special Subjects: Architecture, Art History, Asian Art, Decorative Arts, Drawings, Etchings & Engravings, Folk Art, Industrial Design, Ivory, Landscapes, Manuscripts, Metalwork, Mosaics, Photography, Portraits, Religious Art, Antiquities, Paintings, Sculpture, Stained Glass, Watercolors

A **PROVIDENCE ART CLUB,** 11 Thomas St, 02903. Tel 401-331-1114. *Pres* Robert P Emlen; *Secy* Alice Teixeira; *Gallery Secy* Majory Dalenius
Open Mon - Fri 10 AM - 4 PM, Sun 3 - 5 PM. No admis fee. Estab 1880 for art culture, and to provide exhibition space for artists. Galleries maintained in two 18th century buildings on historic Thomas street in Providence. Average Annual Attendance: 4000. Mem: 710, to qualify, artists' work must pass a board of artists; personal qualifications for non-artists; dues non-artist $336, artist $240; annual meeting first Wed in June
Income: Financed by endowment and membership
Collections: Small permanent collection of paintings & sculpture by Club members since 1880
Exhibitions: Eighteen shows a season of which two-three are juried open shows
Publications: Newsletter for members
Activities: Lect for members & guests; gallery talks; competitions with awards; scholarships; work in shows usually for sale

M **PROVIDENCE ATHENAEUM,** 251 Benefit St, 02903. Tel 401-421-6970; FAX 401-421-2860. *Exec Dir* Michael Price; *Asst Dir* Juliet Saunders
Open Mon - Fri 8:30 AM - 5:30 PM, Sat 9:30 AM - 5:30 PM; cl Sat mid June - Labor Day; cl Sun. No admis fee. Estab 1753 to provide cultural services, information, rare and current materials in an historic setting. Maintains a rare book library. Mem: Estab 1367; dues $25-$100 annual meeting in the Fall
Income: $303,544 (financed by endowment & memberships)
Purchases: $40,000
Collections: Strength in the 19th century
Exhibitions: Exhibitions vary each month; local artists' works shown. (1993) Reflections of Athenaeum Book Collections
Publications: The Athenaeum Bulletin, summer; Annual Report, Fall
Activities: Dramatic programs; film programs; lectures open to the public; tours; festivals; concerts; day trips; original objects of art lent to bonafide institutions, libraries or societies; lending collection contains books, periodicals, records, videotapes, cassettes; the center sells Audubon prints in limited editions, stationery, t-shirts & Athenaeum cookbooks
L **Library,** 251 Benefit St, 02903. FAX 401-421-2860; *Asst Librn* Juliet Saunders; *Head Adult Servs* Risa Gilpin
Open Mon - Fri 8:30 AM - 5:30 PM, Sat 9:30 AM - 5:30 PM, cl Sun. Estab 1753 to provide cultural services, information rare and current materials in a historic setting. Circ 106,000
Library Holdings: Vols 161,486; Per subs 133; posters; AV — A-tapes, cassettes, rec, v-tapes; Other — Clipping files, exhibition catalogs, manuscripts, memorabilia, original art works, pamphlets, photographs, prints, sculpture
Special Subjects: Art History, Architecture History, Biography, Voyage and Travel, Literature, Fiction and Children's
Collections: 19th century Robert Burns collection; 19th century library - rare book library; Audubon, Old Fiction, Holder Borde Bowen collection
Activities: Docent training; childrens programs; film programs; festivals; readings and lectures; tours; trips

L **PROVIDENCE PUBLIC LIBRARY,** Art & Music Services, 225 Washington St, 02903. Tel 401-455-8036; FAX 401-455-8080. *Coordr* Susan R Waddington; *Specialist* Margaret Chevian
Open Mon 1 - 9 PM, Tues & Thurs 9:30 AM - 6 PM, Fri & Sat 9:30 AM - 5:30 PM, cl Wed; summer hours vary. Estab 1878 to serve needs of the public
Income: $2,700,000 (financed by endowment, city and state appropriations and federal funds)
Purchases: $1500 (circulating art)
Library Holdings: Vols 43,000; Per subs 85; posters; AV — Fs, rec; Other — Clipping files, framed reproductions, original art works, photographs, prints
Special Subjects: Advertising Design, Architecture, Cartoons, Ceramics, Commercial Art, Costume Design & Construction, Crafts, Decorative Arts, Drawings, Furniture, Graphic Design, Handicrafts, Illustration, Interior Design, Landscape Architecture, Painting - American, Painting - British, Photography, Pottery, Sculpture, Silversmithing, design
Collections: †Nickerson Architectural Collection; art & music books

M **RHODE ISLAND COLLEGE,** Edward M Bannister Gallery, 600 Mount Pleasant Ave, 02908. Tel 401-456-8054, 456-9765; FAX 401-456-8379. *Dir* Dennis M O'Malley
Open Mon - Fri 11 AM - 4 PM, Thurs evenings 6 - 9 PM, cl weekends. No admis fee. Estab 1977 to provide the Rhode Island community with a varied and progressive exposure to the visual arts, to offer to the college community, with its liberal arts perspective, access to top quality exhibits, artists and workshops. Gallery consists of one room, 25 x 60 ft separated by supports; a 12 ft ceiling on one side and an 8 ft ceiling on the other, as well as moveable walls and partitions used in two person shows, lighting is incandescent track light, approx 60 track fixtures. Average Annual Attendance: 5000
Income: Financed by state appropriation
Purchases: Works of artists exhibited at the gallery
Collections: Teaching collection of works purchased from exhibiting artists
Publications: Brochures, 2 Calendars per yr

A **RHODE ISLAND HISTORICAL SOCIETY,** 110 Benevolent St, 02906. Tel 401-331-8575. *Dir* Albert T Klyberg; *Ed, Nathanael Green Papers* Richard K Showman; *Museum Cur* Linda Eppich; *Cur Education* L Candace Pezzerd; *Public Relations* Carol Spadaccinni
Admis adults $2, students $1. Estab 1822 to preserve, collect and interpret Rhode Island historical materials, including books, manuscripts, graphics, films, furniture and decorative arts. Mem: 2500; dues $35; annual meeting in Sept
Income: Financed by endowment, membership and city and state appropriation
Exhibitions: Changing exhibitions on Rhode Island history and decorative arts
Publications: American Paintings in the Rhode Island Historical Society, (catalogue); The John Brown House Loan Exhibition of Rhode Island Furniture; Nathanael Green Papers; Rhode Island History, quarterly; Roger Williams Correspondence; occasional monographs; newsletter, bimonthly
Activities: Classes for adults and children; children's tours; film programs; lect open to public, 4-6 visiting lectr per year; concerts; gallery talks; tours; lending collection contains 10,000 prints for reference and copying; traveling exhibitions organized and circulated locally; bookshop

M **John Brown House,** 52 Power St, 02906. Tel 401-331-8575.
Open Tues - Sat 11 AM - 4 PM, Sun 1 - 4 PM, cl weekdays Jan & Feb except by appointment. Estab 1942, the 1786 house carefully restored and furnished with fine examples of Rhode Island heritage. Average Annual Attendance: 11, 500
Collections: Carrington Collection of Chinese export objects; McCrellis Collection of Antique Dolls; †Pieces by Rhode Island Cabinetmakers, some original to the house; †portraits, †china, †glass, †pewter, and †other decorative objects; Rhode Island furniture, silver, porcelain, paintings, textiles
Activities: Classes for children; docent training; lectures open to public, 10 vis lectr per year; tours; museum shop sells books, reproductions, prints and slides
M **Aldrich House,** 110 Benevolent St, 02906. Tel 401-331-8575. *Cur* Linda Eppich
Open Mon - Sat 11 AM - 4 PM, Sun 1 - 4 PM. Admis adults $2, senior citizens & students $1. Estab 1974. Galleries for changing exhibitions of Rhode Island artists & history
Income: Financed by endowment, state & local funds, grants (state & federal) and admission rates
L **Library,** 121 Hope St, 02906. Tel 401-331-8575. *Dir* Madeleine Telseyan
Open Tues - Sat 9 AM - 5 PM, June, July & Aug Mon 1 - 9 PM, Tues - Fri 9 AM - 5 PM. No admis fee. Estab 1822 to collect, preserve and make available materials relating to state's history and development. Small exhibit area at library, also galleries at John Brown and Aldrich houses. Average Annual Attendance: 9000. Mem: 3000; dues individual $30; annual meetings in Sept
Income: $700,000 (financed by endowment, membership & state appropriation)
Library Holdings: Per subs 80
Collections: †5000 manuscripts collections dating from 17th century; †Rhode Island Imprints, 1727-1800; †Rhode Island Broadsides; †Providence Postmaster Provisional Stamps; †Rhode Island Post Office Covers; †genealogical sources, all state newspapers, maps, films, TV news films and movies, graphics, architectural drawings; †150,000 reference volumes; †200,000 photographs; business archives; oral history tapes
Exhibitions: Rhode Island photography
Publications: Rhode Island History, quarterly
Activities: Classes for adults and children; docent training; lectures open to public, 12 vis lectr per year; concerts; gallery talks; tours; awards; individual paintings lent; originate traveling exhibitions to educational and governmental institutions; museum shop sells books and prints

M **RHODE ISLAND SCHOOL OF DESIGN,** Museum of Art, 224 Benefit St, 02903-2723. Tel 401-454-6500; FAX 401-454-6556. *Chmn Museum Committee* Donald Roach; *Cur Decorative Arts* Thomas Michie; *Cur Education* David Stark; *Museum Shop Mgr* Anne Meretta
Open Tues, Wed, Fri, Sat 10:30 AM - 5 PM, Thurs Noon - 8 PM. Admis adults $2, children 5 - 18 $.50, children under 5 free. Estab 1877 to collect & exhibit art for general education of RISD students & the public. Present buildings opened in 1897, 1906 & 1926; new wing projected for fall 1993. Average Annual Attendance: 115,000. Mem: 3500
Income: Financed by endowment, mem, state & federal appropriation, private & corporate contributions
Collections: Lucy Truman Aldrich Collection of European porcelains & Oriental textiles; †Ancient Oriental & ethnographic art; †American painting; †contemporary graphic arts; †Nancy Sayles Day Collection of modern Latin American art; †English watercolors; †15th - 18th century European art; †19th & 20th century French art from Romanticism through Surrealism; †Albert Pilavin Collection of 20th century American Art; Pendleton House collection of 18th century American furniture & decorative arts; Abby Aldrich Rockefeller collection of Japanese prints
Exhibitions: Neoteric Jewelry; Romanticism & Revival: 19th Century American Art from Permanent Collection; Expressionist Visions: Prints & Drawings from the Museum's Collection; Form, Pattern & Function: Design in American Indian Art; Edward W Curtis Photogravures: Selections from the North American Indian
Publications: Calendar of Events, five per year; A Handbook of the Collection
Activities: Classes for adults & children; docent training; field trips; lectures open to the public, 15-20 visiting lecturers per year; gallery talks; concerts; tours; outreach programs serve schools, nursing homes & hospital children's ward in the area; traveling exhibitions organized & circulated; museum shop sells books, original art, reproductions, prints, jewelry, posters & postcards
L **Library,** 2 College St, 02903-2784. Tel 401-454-6100; FAX 401-454-6320. *Dir* Carol Terry
Open to the public for reference
Library Holdings: Vols 77,000; Per subs 375; Artists' books, posters, postcards; Micro — Fiche; AV — Lantern slides 127,595, rec, slides, v-tapes; Other — Clipping files 407,000, exhibition catalogs, framed reproductions 19,174, pamphlets, photographs, reproductions
Special Subjects: Architecture, Fine Arts and Crafts

SAUNDERSTOWN

M **GILBERT STUART MEMORIAL ASSOCIATION, INC,** Museum, Gilbert Stuart Rd, 02874. Tel 401-294-3001. *Cur* Michael Hegarty; *Cur* Marianna Hegarty; *Pres* George Gardiner
Open daily 11 AM - 5 PM; cl Fri & winters. Admis adults $2, children under 12 $1. Estab 1966 as a national historic landmark, the furnished birthplace of America's foremost portrait painter; the home was built 1751. Average Annual Attendance: 10,000. Mem: 180; dues $15 - $25; annual meeting July
Income: Financed by endowment, membership and grants
Activities: Guided tours of the home

WARWICK

M **COMMUNITY COLLEGE OF RHODE ISLAND,** Art Department Gallery, Knight Campus, 400 East Ave, 02886. Tel 401-825-2220; FAX 401-825-2265. *Chmn* Donald F Gray
Open Mon - Fri 8 AM - 9:30 PM. Library maintained
Exhibitions: Exhibitions are changed bi-monthly
Activities: Lect open to public; original objects of art lent; lending collection contains 300 color reproductions, 20 filmstrips, 10,000 Kodachromes, motion pictures & clippings & small prints; book shop

M **Flanagan Valley Campus Art Gallery,** Louisquisset Pike, Lincoln, 02865. Tel 401-333-7154; FAX 401-825-2265. *Dir & Librn* Tom Morrissey
Open Mon - Fri 8 AM - 4 PM
Exhibitions: Exhibitions are changed bi-monthly

WESTERLY

M **WESTERLY PUBLIC LIBRARY,** Hoxie Gallery, PO Box 356, 02891. Tel 401-596-2877; FAX 401-596-5600. *Dir* David J Panciera; *Cur* Webster Terhune; *Head of Graphics* Lorraine Byrne
Open Mon - Wed 8 AM - 9 PM, Thurs & Fri 8 AM - 5 PM, Sat 8 AM - 3 PM, July & Aug cl Sat. Estab 1892 as a memorial to soldiers of the Civil War, and to provide a library and activities center for the community. Art gallery maintained, 30 x 54 ft, 16 ft ceiling, with incandescent track lighting
Income: Financed by endowment, city and state appropriation
Exhibitions: Ten - twelve exhibitions scheduled per year
Publications: First Westerly Coloring Book; Life's Little Pleasures; Westerly Photographys 1890-1910
Activities: Lect open to public; library tours

SOUTH CAROLINA

AIKEN

M **AIKEN COUNTY HISTORICAL MUSEUM,** 433 New Berry St SW, 29801. Tel 803-642-2015.
Open Tues - Fri 9:30 AM - 4:30 PM, 1st Sun of every month 2 - 5 PM. Admis donations requested. Open 1970 to document local history. Average Annual Attendance: 5000. Mem: 300; mem open to residents; dues $10 & up; annual meeting in Oct
Income: $6000 (financed by endowment, mem, County subsidy)
Purchases: All donations
Collections: Agricultural - implements; Dairy - implements; Schools - furniture & winter items; Winter Colony furniture
Exhibitions: Selections from permanent collection
Activities: Children's classes; docent programs; book traveling exhibitions 10 per year; retail store sells books & prints

ANDERSON

A **ANDERSON COUNTY ARTS COUNCIL,** 405 N Main St, 29621. Tel 803-224-8811. *Exec Dir* Diane Lee; *Prog Dir* Kimberly Spears
Open Mon - Fri 9 AM - 5 PM, Sun 2 - 5 PM. No admis fee. Estab 1972 as a non-profit institution, serving as a clearinghouse for individuals and organizations interested in the promotion of visual, literary and performing arts. Gallery rotates exhibits monthly, featuring locally, regionally and nationally known artists. Average Annual Attendance: 10,000. Mem: 550; dues $1000, $500, $100, $50, $25, $18, $10, $5; annual meeting last Tues of Sept
Income: Financed by membership, foundations, donations, county appropriation and grants
Publications: Calendar of events; newsletter, bi-monthly
Activities: Classes for adults and children; gallery talks; tours

CHARLESTON

M **CAROLINA ART ASSOCIATION,** Gibbes Museum of Art, 135 Meeting, 29401. Tel 803-722-2706. *Pres Board* Helen Pruitt; *Dir* Paul C Figueroa; *Cur Coll* Angela D Mack; *Cur Educ* Diane Doeppel-Horn; *Public Information* Cynthia Mappus; *Business Mgr* Sandra Tucker
Open Tues - Sat 10 AM - 5 PM, Sun & Mon 1 - 5 PM; cl national holidays. Admis adults $3, students & senior citizens $2, children under 12 $1. Estab 1858 as an art gallery and museum. Beauz-Arts style building erected in 1905, renovated in 1978; gallery is 31,000 sq ft. Average Annual Attendance: 55,000. Mem: 2000; dues $40 & up; annual meeting 3rd Mon in Oct
Income: $600,000 (financed by endowment, membership, city & county appropriation, grants & contributions)
Purchases: Contemporary paintings, sculpture, prints, drawings & photographs
Collections: Colonial and Federal Portraits; Contemporary American Paintings and Prints; Japanese Woodblock Prints; Miniature Portraits; Oriental Art Objects; American art related to Charleston
Exhibitions: Approx 25 per yr
Publications: Bulletins, quarterly; books; exhibit catalogs
Activities: Classes for adults and children; docent training; lectures open to public, 5 vis lectrs per yr; gallery talks; tours, competitions; exten dept serves tri-county area; individual paintings & original objects of art lent to museums; lending collection includes framed reproductions & original prints; originate traveling exhibitions; museum shop sells books, reproductions, prints, original crafts & jewelry
L **Library,** 135 Meeting, 29401. Tel 803-722-2706.
Open to scholars for reference only, by appointment
Income: Financed by public and private support
Library Holdings: Vols 3609; Per subs 26; AV — Kodachromes, rec, v-tapes; Other — Clipping files, exhibition catalogs, manuscripts, original art works, pamphlets, photographs, sculpture
Special Subjects: Oriental Art, American Art, History of Charleston art & architecture

M CHARLESTON MUSEUM, 360 Meeting St, 29403. Tel 803-722-2996; FAX 803-722-1784. *Dir* Dr John R Brumgardt; *Pres* J Addison Ingle Jr; *Cur Historic Archaeology* Martha Zierden; *Cur History* Christopher Loeblein; *Cur Historic Houses* Karen King; *Cur Natural History* Albert E Sanders; *Registrar* Jan Hiester; *Cur Ornithology* Dr William Post; *Archivist* K Sharon Bennett; *Ed Cur* Karen King
Open daily 9 AM - 5 PM. Admis adults $3, children $1.50. Estab 1773 as a museum and library to diffuse knowledge of history, decorative arts, art, natural history, anthropology and technology; also to preserve houses and monuments. It is the oldest museum in the United States. Average Annual Attendance: 20,000. Mem: 550; dues $15 and up; annual meeting Feb 22
Income: $530,000 (financed by membership, city and county appropriations, admissions and sales)
Collections: Ceramics, decorative arts, furniture, glass, maps, photos, prints and textiles, art of northern BC
Publications: Newsletter, bi-monthly
Activities: Tours for adults and children;; docent training; lectures 8 per year; concerts; sales shop sells books, magazines and prints related to collections
L Library, 350 Meeting St, 29403. Tel 803-722-2996, Ext 57. *Librn* K Sharon Bennett; *Asst Archivist* Mary Giles
Open daily 9 AM - 5 PM by appointment only. Estab 1773 as an educational institution, collects, preserves and uses artifacts of natural history, history, anthropology and decorative arts
Income: Financed by city & county appropriations & memberships
Library Holdings: Vols 5000; Per subs 120; Maps; AV — Rec; Other — Clipping files, exhibition catalogs, manuscripts, memorabilia, pamphlets, photographs, prints
Special Subjects: Decorative Arts, Natural History
Publications: Newsletter, quarterly
M Heyward-Washington House, 87 Church St, 29401. Tel 803-722-0354. *House Adminr* Joann Chrisman
Open daily 10 AM - 5 PM; Sun 1 - 5 PM. Admis adults $3, children $1.50. Built 1772; home of Thomas Heyward, Jr; purchased by the Museum in 1929. Museum is furnished with Charleston-made furniture of the period; a National Historic Landmark
M Joseph Manigault House, 350 Meeting St, 29403. Tel 803-723-2926. *House Adminr* Anne Fox
Open daily 10 AM - 5 PM, Sun 1 - 5 PM. Admis adults $3, students $1.50. Built 1803 as Adam style mansion designed by Gabriel Manigault. Museum contains Charleston-made furniture of the period; a National Historic Landmark
M Aiken-Rhett House, 48 Elizabeth St, 29403. Tel 803-723-1159. *House Adminr* Ernest Shealy

M CITY OF CHARLESTON, City Hall Council Chamber Gallery, 80 Broad St, 29401. Tel 803-724-3799. *Cur* Lynda Heffley
Open Mon - Fri 8:30 AM - 5 PM. No admis fee. Estab 1818 to preserve for the citizens of Charleston a portrait collection of the city's history. A unique collection of American portraits housed in the 2nd oldest city council chamber in continuous use in the US. Average Annual Attendance: 16,000
Collections: Washington Trumbull, 1791; J Monroe Samuel Morse, 1819; A Jackson John Vanderlyn, 1824; Zachary Taylor James Beard, 1848; Pierre Beauregard George Healy,1850; Marquis de Lafayette Charles Fraser, 1825; C Gadsden-R Peale; portraits by Jarvis, Savage, John Blake White, James Earle, G Whiting Flagg
Publications: Catalogue of paintings & sculpture

M COLLEGE OF CHARLESTON, Halsey Gallery, School of the Arts, 66 George St, 29424-0001. Tel 803-792-5680. *Gallery Dir* Rene Paul Barilleaux
Open Mon - Sat 11 AM - 4 PM. No admis fee. Estab 1978 as a college gallery with focus on contemporary art. Two floors in modern building located in Schools of the Arts building, includes director's office & storage space. Average Annual Attendance: 5000
Income: $15,000 (financed by state appropriation)
Exhibitions: (1992) Anne Wilson: The Furs (1985 - 1991). (1993) Regarding Beauty
Publications: Periodic catalogs & gallery guides
Activities: Lect open to public, 6 - 8 vis lectr per year; juried student competitions

M TRADD STREET PRESS, Elizabeth O'Neill Verner Studio Museum, 38 Tradd St, 29401. Tel 803-722-4246. *Pres* David Verner Hamilton; *Secy* Daphne vom Baur
Open 10 AM - 5 PM. No admis fee. Estab 1970 to exhibit works of Elizabeth O'Neill Verner. Average Annual Attendance: 31,200
Income: Financed by endowment
Collections: †Works of Elizabeth O'Neill Verner
Exhibitions: Collected works of Elizabeth O'Neill Verner
Activities: Educ dept provides cultural presence, historic perspective programs; lectures open to public; sales store sells books, prints, original art, reproductions

CLEMSON

CLEMSON UNIVERSITY
M Rudolph E Lee Gallery, College of Architecture, 29634. Tel 803-656-3883; FAX 803-656-0204. *Dir* David Houston
Open Mon - Fri 9 AM - 4:30 PM, Sun 2 - 5 PM, cl Sat. No admis fee. Estab 1956 to provide cultural and educational resources; to collect, preserve, interpret and display items of historical, educational and cultural significance. Average Annual Attendance: 20,000
Income: Financed by state appropriation
Collections: †Clemson Architectural Foundation Collection; Contemporary American Paintings and Graphics
Exhibitions: (1993) From the Outhside In; The National Print & Drawing Exhibitions; National Juried Exhibition
Publications: Exhibition Bulletin, annually; Posters on Exhibits, monthly
Activities: Lect open to public, 12-15 visiting lectr per year; gallery talks; tours; exten dept serving southeast United States; individual paintings and original objects of art lent to museums, universities; lending collection contains original prints, paintings, sculpture; originate traveling exhibitions

L Emery A Gunnin Architectural Library, College of Architecture, 29634-0501. Tel 803-656-3933; FAX 803-656-0204. *Branch Head* Deborah Johnson; *Media Resources Cur* Phyllis Pivorun; *Asst Architecture Librn* Steve Moon
Mon - Thurs 8 AM - 10 PM, Fri 8 AM - 5 PM, Sat 1 - 5 PM, Sun 2 - 10 PM. For reference only. Average Annual Attendance: 74,000
Library Holdings: Vols 30,000; AV — A-tapes, cassettes, motion pictures, slides 71,000, v-tapes; Other — Exhibition catalogs, pamphlets
Special Subjects: Aesthetics, Archaeology, Art History, Ceramics, Conceptual Art, Constructions, Crafts, Decorative Arts, Drafting, Drawings
Collections: Rare Book Collection; South Carolina City & Regional Planning Documents
M Fort Hill, 29634-5605. Tel 803-656-5605, 656-0671; FAX 803-656-2064. *Dir Historic Houses* Susan Cline-Cordonier; *Cur* Will Hoitt
Open Mon - Fri 10 AM - 5 PM, Sat 10 AM - 5 PM, Sun 2 - 5 PM, cl holidays & Christmas week. An historic house museum located in the home of John C Calhoun. Restoration of the house and furnishings are an on-going project of the John C Calhoun Chapter of the United Daughters of the Confederacy and Clemson University
Income: Clemson University
Collections: Flemish paintings; family portraits; period rooms and furnishings of original family heirlooms and memorabilia
Publications: Fort Hill, brochure
Activities: Lect; guided tours; sales shop

COLUMBIA

M COLUMBIA MUSEUM OF ART, 1112 Bull St, 29201. Tel 803-799-2810. *Dir* Salvatore G Cilella; *Pres* Robert S McCoy Jr; *VPres* C Witaker Moore; *VPres* Arlen L Cotter; *Registrar* Cynthia Connor; *Admin Asst* Patsy Martin; *Cur Exhib* Lisa Ray; *Cur Colls* Lin Nelson-Mayson; *Dir External Affairs* Bob Wislinski; *Public Relations* Janna Cotterill; *Dept Public Programming* Christine Minkler
Open Tues - Fri 10 AM - 5 PM, Sat & Sun 12:30 PM - 5 PM. Admis free. Estab 1950 to extend and increase art understanding, to assist in the conservation of a valuable cultural heritage, and to recognize and assist contemporary art expression. Library for reference only. Average Annual Attendance: 100,000. Mem: 2100; dues family $35 and up, single $20; annual meeting Jan
Income: $900,000 (financed by membership, city and county appropriation)
Purchases: Works of art on paper, Southeastern artists & textiles
Collections: Kress Collection of Renaissance Paintings; Scotese Collection of Graphics; European and American paintings and decorative art; South Carolina dispensary bottles; Spanish Colonial Collection; textiles; South Carolina collection of paintings & graphics; †decorative arts & textiles
Exhibitions: Adornment in Africa: Treasures of the Continent; British Watercolors; Chinese Porcelain; White House Photographs
Publications: Annual Report; exhibition folders and catalogues; Member Calendars, monthly; Columbia Museum Magazine, quarterly
Activities: Classes for adults and children, docent training; lectures open to public, 6 vis lect per year; concerts; gallery talks; tours; exten dept serving Metropolitan area; originate traveling exhibitions; museum shop sells books, original art, reproductions, prints, ceramics, glass, jewelry
L Library, 1112 Bull St, 29201. Tel 803-799-2810. *Librn* Libby Rich
Open Tues - Fri 10 AM - 5 PM, Sat - Sun 1 - 5 PM. Open to members and public for reference only
Income: $10,000 (Financed by museum)
Library Holdings: Vols 12,800; Per subs 15; Vertical files; AV — A-tapes, cassettes, v-tapes; Other — Clipping files, exhibition catalogs, memorabilia, pamphlets
Special Subjects: Reference relating to the permanent collection, plus general art sources
A Columbia Art Association, 1112 Bull St, 29201. Tel 803-799-2810. *Pres* Joseph Anderson; *Dir* Salvatore G Cilella
Open Tues - Sat 10 AM - 5 PM, Sun 1 - 5 PM. No admis fee. Estab 1949 to provide exhibitions & education programs to the public. Average Annual Attendance: 110,000. Mem: 3000; dues $15-$140; annual meeting in Jan
Collections: †American fine, decorative & design arts of 16th century to present, †Works on Paper, †Furniture, †Paintings & Sculpture, †Textiles; Kress Collection of Rennaisance & Baraque Art
Activities: Classes for adults & children; docent training; lectures open to the public, 3 vis lectr per year; concerts; gallery talks; tours; exten dept serves central South Carolina; individual paintings & original objects of art lent; book traveling exhibitions 6-8 times per year; museum shop sells books, original art, reproductions & prints

A SOUTH CAROLINA ARTS COMMISSION, 1800 Gervais St, 29201. Tel 803-734-8696. *Dir* Scott Sanders; *Exhibitions Coordr* Susan Leonard; *Visual Arts Dir* David Houston; *Equipment Coordr* Charles Webb
Open 9 AM - 5 PM. No admis fee. Estab 1967 to promote and develop the arts in Southeast
Income: $225,000 (financed by state & federal income)
Purchases: Films, videotapes, video/film equipment
Collections: †State Art Collection
Exhibitions: Film/Video artists exhibitions
Publications: Independent Spirit, media arts newsletter, 3 times a yr
Activities: Educational programming; lectures open to the public, 4 vis lectr per yr; concerts; gallery talks; competitions with awards; artists' workshops; grants-in-aid & fellowships; exten dept serves state; art mobile; individual paintings & original objects of art lent to other galleries & museums; lending collection contains lantern slides, 235 original art works, paintings, photographs, sculpture, slides, 100 books & 125 motion pictures; book traveling exhibitions; originate traveling exhibitions, circulates to 6 sites in the Southeast
L Media Center, 1800 Gervais St, 29201. *Dir* Scott Sanders
Library Holdings: AV — A-tapes, cassettes, motion pictures, slides, v-tapes
Special Subjects: Film

C SOUTH CAROLINA NATIONAL BANK, 1426 Main St, 29226. Tel 803-765-3669. *VPres* Virginia M Grose
Estab 1971 to recognize & promote artists who have or have had a connection with South Carolina. Collection displayed in offices throughout South Carolina
Collections: Contemporary South Carolina art
Activities: Sponsor purchase awards for selected competitions in the state; individual objects of art lent to museums for display; originate traveling exhibitions, have carried-out two statewide tours from collection, work was displayed in a number of cities at museums, libraries, court houses and banks

M SOUTH CAROLINA STATE MUSEUM, 301 Gervais St, PO Box 100107, 29202-3107. Tel 803-737-4921; FAX 803-737-4969. *Exec Dir* Overton G Ganong; *Dir Coll & Interpretation* Rodger Stroup; *Dir Exhibits* Mike Fey; *Dir Public Information & Marketing* Tut Underwood; *Exec VPres* Patty Cooper; *Chief Cur Art* Lise Swensson
Open Mon - Fri 10 AM - 5 PM, Sun 1 - 5 PM. Estab 1973. Four large floors in a renovated textile mill with exhibits in art, history, natural history & science & technology. Average Annual Attendance: 250,000. Mem: 6500; annual meeting in June
Income: Financed by admis, state appropriations, store revenue & supplement state money
Collections: †Art - all media; Cultural History; Natural History; Science & Technology
Exhibitions: Art - South Carolina/Kentucky Exchange; History - The Palmetto State Goes Tower: WW II & South Carolina; Natural History - Fossil Collectors & Collections
Publications: Annual report; Images, quarterly
Activities: Docent programs; lect open to public; lending collection contains 500 paintings; book traveling exhibitions 10 per year; originate traveling exhibitions 4 per year; retail store sells books & slides

M UNIVERSITY OF SOUTH CAROLINA, McKissick Museum, 29208. Tel 803-777-7251. *Dir* Lynn R Myers; *Chief Cur* Catherine W Horne; *Office Administrator* Maria Ballard; *Cur Natural Science* Karin L Willoughby; *Cur Community Servs* Dr Gail Matthews; *Cur Education Museum* Craig Kridel; *State Folk Arts Coordr* Dr Doug De Natale; *Cur of Exhib* Alice R Bauknight
Open Mon - Fri 9 AM - 4 PM, Sat 10 AM - 5 PM, Sun 1 PM - 5 PM, cl July 4th, Labor Day, Thanksgiving & day after, Dec 25, Jan 1. No admis fee. Estab 1976 to centralize the university's museum collections. Contains 4 major gallery areas for temporary & changing exhibitions in art, science & history. Average Annual Attendance: 65,000
Income: Financed by state appropriation & donations
Purchases: Southern Folk Art
Collections: Bernard Baruch Collection of 18th Century Silver; Movietonews News Reels; James F Byrnes Collection; Howard Gemstone Collection; Richard Mandell: Art Nouveau Collection; Colburn Gemstone Collection; university memorabilia; southeastern folk art; minerals, fossils, rocks & meteorites; contemporary art works
Exhibitions: Changing exhibits of permanent collections; War in the Pacific (based on Movietonews Collection); Todd Murphy; Klukert/Black; Student Art Show; Cochran Collection; Jim Stevens; Children Samplers; Florescent Minerals & Mineral Library; Spring Mills annual traveling; Welcome to Planet Earth; Indian Baskets
Publications: Exhibition catalogs; Calendar of events (quarterly)
Activities: Docent training; lect open to public, 4-5 visiting lectr per year; concerts; gallery talks; tours; competitions; slide-tape programs & classes for students & sr citizens; community outreach to sr citizens groups & children's hospital wards; originate traveling exhibitions
L Art Library, Sloan College, Room 202, 29208. Tel 803-777-7260, 777-4236. *Instructional Media Specialist* Linda D Morgan
Open Mon - Fri 8 AM - 4 PM. Estab as a major teaching resource for the Art Department
Library Holdings: Vols 3000; Per subs 17; Slide-tape Programs; AV — Cassettes, motion pictures, slides 96,000, v-tapes; Other — Clipping files, exhibition catalogs, manuscripts, pamphlets, photographs
Special Subjects: Decorative Arts, Museology

FLORENCE

M FLORENCE MUSEUM, 558 Spruce St, 29501. Tel 803-662-3351. *Dir* Susan Leath; *Pres* Rebecca H Crawford; *VPres* William S Dowis, Jr; *Treas* J Banks Scarborough
Open Tues - Sat 10 AM - 5 PM, Sun 2 - 5 PM, cl Mon & major holidays. No admis fee. Estab 1924 (incorporated in 1936) as a general museum of art, natural science, and history of South Carolina, with emphasis on the region know as the Pee Dee, and to acquaint the public with fine art. Two changing art galleries monthly, main galleries. Average Annual Attendance: 75,000. Mem: 350; dues $1000 benefactor, $500 patron, $100 sustaining, $50 sponsor, $25 club, $25 family, $15 individual, $10 student, $7.50 retiree, annual meeting first Thur in May
Income: $40,000 (financed by membership, county & city appropriation, and donations)
Collections: Permanent Collection includes African, Chinese, Japanese, Korean Southwestern American Indians, Catawba Indians Collections; artifacts; works of local Black artists particularly William H Johnson; works of local & regional artists; Museum Permanent Collection, Regional Artists
Exhibitions: Changing exhibitions
Publications: Florence Museum newsletter, quarterly
Activities: Classes for adults and children; docent training; lect open to the public, gallery talks; self-guided tours; too competitions with prizes; Permanent collection includes 1000 framed reproductions, 300 original art works, 50 original prints, 300 paintings and 500 photographs; traveling exhibitions organized and circulated

GREENVILLE

M BOB JONES UNIVERSITY, Museum & Art Gallery, 29614. Tel 803-242-5100. *Chmn of the Board* Bob Jones; *Dir* Joan C Davis; *Staff Supvr* Janice Churdar
Open Tues - Sun 2 - 5 PM, cl Mon, Dec 20 - 25, New Year's Day and July 4. No admis fee. Estab 1951 to show how universal the Word of God is in its appeal to human hearts in every generation. Average Annual Attendance: 23,000
Income: Financed by University and gifts
Collections: Religious art by the Old Masters from the 13th - 19th centuries including Benson, Botticelli, Cranach the Elder, G David, Murillo, Rembrandt, Ribera, Rubens, Solimena del Piombo, Tintoretto, Titian, Van Leyden, Veronese, Zurbaran; Bowen Collection of Biblical antiquities & illustrative material from Palestine, Syria, Lebanon, Egypt & Jordan; Revealed Religion by Benjamin West, 7 paintings; furniture; sculpture; because of the illness of the King, plans for the construction of the Chapel were abandoned & the completed paintings were returned to the painter. The posthumous sale of West's works in 1829 included a number of the pictures on Revealed Religion. Joseph Neeld, MP, was the successful bidder and the pictures hung in his home until 1962. At that time they were offered for sale by Christie's of London. Six were acquired for the Bob Jones University with funds provided for that purpose by an anonymous friend of the University, a seventh painting of this series was also acquired by gift
Publications: Catalogs; illustrated booklets
Activities: Tours for school and adult groups by appointment; individual paintings lent to other galleries in the US and abroad; sales shop sells reproductions, prints & slides

M GREENVILLE COUNTY MUSEUM OF ART, 420 College St, 29601. Tel 803-271-7570; FAX 803-271-7579. *Exec Dir* Thomas W Styron; *Head Collections Management & Security* Claudia Beckwith; *Pub Relations Officer* Paula Hysinger
Open Tues - Sat 10 AM - 5 PM, Sun 1 - 5 PM, cl Mon. No admis fee. Estab 1958 for the collection and preservation of American Art. Four major galleries devoted to permanent collections of American art from the colonial to the contemporary, changing & traveling exhibitions. Average Annual Attendance: 100,000. Mem: 1000; dues $30 - $1000; annual meeting in May
Income: Financed by membership, donations & county appropriation
Purchases: Recent acquisitions include works by Louis Remy Mignot, Gari Melchers & Elaine de Kooning
Collections: Limited to American art with emphasis on Southern-related works before World War II & contemporary American art
Exhibitions: (1993) Telling Tales: 19th-century Narrative Painting From the Collection of the Pennsylvania Academy of the Fine Arts; Messengers of Tyle: Itinerancy & Taste in Southern Portraiture, 1790-1861; Homecome: William H Johnson & Afro-America, 1938-1946
Publications: Museum News, bi-monthly; exhibition catalogs; quarterly events calendars
Activities: Classes for adults & children; docent training; Museum School of Art; lect open to public, 6 - 10 vis lectr per yr; gallery talks; tours; extension dept serves Greenville County schools; lending collection contains slides; museum shop sells books, original art, slides, prints, children educational toys, regional crafts & cards

C LIBERTY LIFE INSURANCE COMPANY, 2000 Wade Hampton Blvd, PO Box 789, 29602. Tel 803-268-8111; FAX 803-292-4211. *Chmn* Francis M Nipp
Open during normal business hrs by appointment. No admis fee. Estab 1978 to collect textile art selections from various cultures & historical periods. Collection displayed throughout corporate headquarters
Collections: Limited edition prints, graphics & silkscreens; textile art works from around the world
Exhibitions: Greenville County Museum of Art; selections from the collection, Winston - Salem, NC, Arts Council, Museum of American Folk Art; traveling exhibition
Publications: The Liberty Textile Collection
Activities: Individual paintings & original objects of art lent to regional & national museums & galleries

GREENWOOD

M THE MUSEUM, 106 Main St, PO Box 3131, 29648. Tel 803-229-7093. *Pres* Estelle M Mauldin; *Admin* Despina Panagakos; *Secy* Holly Brown
Open Tues - Fri 9 AM - 5 PM, Sat & Sun 2 - 5 PM, cl Mon. No admis fee. Estab June 1967 for educational purposes. Average Annual Attendance: 9000. Mem: 220; dues $25; meeting Jan, March, May and Nov
Income: Financed by memberships, contributions & grants
Collections: Frank E Delano Gallery of African animal mounts and rare African works of art by the now extinct Katanga Tribe; bone, wood and ivory carvings; chinaware; crystals; glassware; limited art works; photographs
Exhibitions: Individual artists; Siebozs; Bruce; South Carolina arts & crafts; South Carolina Watercolor Society
Activities: Lectures open to public; book traveling exhibitions; sales shop sells original art

HARTSVILLE

M CECELIA COKER BELL GALLERY, Coker College, Gladys C Fort Art Building, 29550. Tel 803-383-8152. *Dir* Larry Merriman
Open Mon - Fri 10 AM - 4 PM. No admis fee. Estab 1983 to serve campus and community. 30 ft x 40 ft self-contained, movable partitions, track light, security system. Average Annual Attendance: 1500
Income: $2500
Collections: American prints
Exhibitions: Area artists; annual student juried show; senior students show; vis artists; national, international exhibitions
Publications: Collection catalog
Activities: Classes for adults; lectures open to public, 1 vis lectr per year; gallery talks; student juried competitions; awards

MURRELLS INLET

M BROOKGREEN GARDENS, 1931 Brookgreen Gardens Dr, 29576. Tel 803-237-4218. *Pres* Gurdon Tarbox Jr; *VPres Academic Affairs & Cur* Robin Salmon
Open 9:30 AM - 4:45 PM, cl Christmas. Admis adults $5, 6-12 years $2, under six free. Estab 1931 to exhibit the flora and fauna of South Carolina and to exhibit objects of art. The outdoor museum exhibits American sculpture, while smaller pieces are shown in the Small Sculpture Gallery & Visitors Pavilion. Average Annual Attendance: 180,000. Mem: 3000; dues $25-$5000
Income: Financed by endowment, membership, gifts, grants and admission
Special Subjects: American Western Art, Art Education, Art History, Bronzes, Coins & Medals, Film, Landscape Architecture, Photography, Restoration & Conservation, Sculpture
Collections: Collection of American representative, sculpture, 535 pieces by 235 sculptors
Exhibitions: Permanent Collection
Publications: Brookgreen Journal, quarterly; Brookgreen Newsletter, quarterly; Brookgreen Gardens Sculpture, catalogue
Activities: Classes for adults and children; docent training; workshops; lectures open to public, 4 vis lectrs per yr; concerts; gallery talks; tours; awards; museum shop sells books, magazines, postcards, pamphlets, prints & slides
L Library, 1931 Brookgreen Gardens Dr, 29576. Tel 803-237-4218; FAX 803-237-1014. *Pres* Gurdon Tarbox Jr; *VPres & Cur* Robin Salmon
For reference only to staff
Library Holdings: Vols 2200; Per subs 50; maps, architectural and engineering drawings and plans; Micro — Reels; AV — A-tapes, cassettes, fs, Kodachromes, motion pictures, slides, v-tapes; Other — Clipping files, exhibition catalogs, framed reproductions, manuscripts, memorabilia, pamphlets, photographs, prints
Special Subjects: American sculpture, local history, plants & animals of the Southeast
Publications: Brookgreen Journal, quarterly; Brookgreen Newsletter, quarterly; Brookgreen Calendar of Events, three times per year; Brookgreen Gardens Annual Report

ROCK HILL

M MUSEUM OF NEW YORK, 4621 Mount Gallant Rd, 29732-9905. Tel 803-329-2121; FAX 803-329-5249. *Exec Dir* Wayne Clark
Open 9 AM - 5 PM. Admis $2. Estab 1948. Spring, Alternative & Lobby galleries (changing art exhibits). Average Annual Attendance: 50,000. Mem: 1248; dues vary
Income: $1,383,225 (financed by mem, admis & county appropriation)
Collections: African animals - mounted specimens; African art & ethnography; local art; local history & archaeology; local natural history specimens
Exhibitions: Stans African Halls (African peoples & natural history); Hall of Western Hemisphere (natural history of the Americas); Vernon Grant Gallery (changing exhibits); Come See Me, local artist competition; Student Art, local jr & sr high school students competition; Southern Visions, photography - Southeast
Publications: Quarterly, bi-monthly; Teacher's Guide, annual
Activities: Classes for adults & children; docent programs; lect open to public, 10 vis lectrs per year; competitions with purchase awards; exten dept servs county; book traveling exhibitions 5 per year; retail store sells books & prints
L Staff Research Library, 4621 Mount Gallant Rd, 29732-9905
For research
Income: Financed by departmental budgets
Library Holdings: AV — A-tapes, cassettes, v-tapes; Other — Exhibition catalogs, pamphlets
Special Subjects: American Indian Art, Anthropology, Archaeology, Art Education, Crafts, Ethnology, Photography, Primitive Art, Restoration & Conservation, African Art, Museum Studies, Travel & Adventure

M WINTHROP UNIVERSITY GALLERIES, 701 Oakland Ave, 29733. Tel 803-323-2493; FAX 803-323-2333. *Dir* Tom Stanley
Open Mon - Fri 8:30 AM - 4:30 PM. No admis fee. Housed within Rutledge Building, Department of Art & Design of the School of Visual & Performing Arts at Winthrop College. Presents temporary visual art & design exhibitions for the enhancement of academic achievement & understanding within the college community. Gallery is 3500 sq ft. Average Annual Attendance: 15,000
Income: Financed by state appropriation
Exhibitions: Student Exhibitions; South Carolina State Art Collection; Spring Mills Annual Traveling Exhibition; one-person shows; invitational exhibitions in photo, drawing, painting, printmaking, textiles, design, ceramics & glass. (1991) Inaugural Exhibition; A Celebration of Diversity
Activities: Classes for adults; lectures open to the public; concerts; gallery talks; scholarships & fels offered; originate traveling exhibitions

SPARTANBURG

A ARTS COUNCIL OF SPARTANBURG COUNTY, INC, Spartanburg Arts Center, 385 S Spring St, 29306. Tel 803-583-2776; FAX 803-583-2777. *Exec Dir* Cassandra Baker; *Dir Spec Projects* Mrs Danny R Hughes; *Operations Mgr* William C Taylor Jr; *Dir Development* Judy B Bynum
Open Mon - Fri 9 AM - 5 PM, Sat 10 AM - 2 PM, Sun 2 - 5 PM. No admis fee. Estab 1968 to coordinate all cultural activities in the area; to promote its member organizations; maintain an Arts Center with changing and permanent exhibitions. Average Annual Attendance: 200,000. Mem: 68 organizations; dues $100; annual meetings in Jan
Income: $320,000 (financed by private and corporate donations & project grants)
Collections: †Over 150 works in permanent collection, mixed media
Exhibitions: Changing exhibits
Publications: Membership Brochure, annual; Spartanburg Arts Calendar, quarterly
Activities: SHARE-Day tour experiences for all ages; David W Reid Award for Achievement in the Arts; scholarships; individual paintings & original objects of art lent to businesses, community centers, private residences; lending collection includes slides and 50 original art works; book traveling exhibitions, 10 per year; sales shop sells books, original art and prints

M The Gallery, 385 S Spring St, 29306. Tel 803-582-7616. *Cur* Pamela Nienhuis
Open Tues - Fri 10 AM - noon & 2 - 4 PM, Sun & Mon 2 - 4 PM (or by appointment). No admis fee. Estab 1969 to promote the works of contemporary artists in the southeastern United States. Gallery is located in the Spartanburg County Arts Center & contains both a permanent sales section & a changing exhibit area. Average Annual Attendance: 2500. Mem: 450; dues $25 - $500
Income: Financed by endowment & mem
Collections: †Contemporary Southeastern Artists
Exhibitions: Annual Juried Exhibit
Publications: Quarterly newsletter
Activities: Classes for adults & children; lect open to public, 2 vis lectr per yr; gallery talks; tours; competitions with awards; individual paintings & original objects of art lent to local government & qualified businesses; sales shop sells original art & fine crafts

M CONVERSE COLLEGE, Milliken Art Gallery, PO Box 29, 29301. Tel 803-585-6421, Ext 251. *Dir* Mayo Mac Boggs
Open Mon - Fri 11 AM - 4 PM, cl holidays. No admis fee. Estab 1971 for educational purposes. A brick and glass structure of 40 x 60 ft; movable panels 4 x 6 ft for exhibition of work, 16 panels, 12 sculpture stands. Average Annual Attendance: 2400
Income: Financed by endowment
Exhibitions: Invitational exhibits of regional artists; annual juried student show
Activities: Educ dept; Lect open to public, 5 - 6 vis lect per year; gallery talks; tours

M UNIVERSITY OF SOUTH CAROLINA AT SPARTANBURG, Art Gallery, Art Gallery, Horace C Smith Bldg, 800 University Way, 29303. Tel 803-599-2256. *Gallery Dir* John Caputo
Open daily 10 AM - 4 PM. No admis fee. Estab 1982, primarily as a teaching gallery. Contemporary art displayed. 800 sq ft of carpeted wall space with windows along one wall, located across from Performing Art Center
Income: $1200 (financed by Student Affairs Office of University)
Exhibitions: Recent Paintings by Tom Stanley; Annual Student Art Exhibition
Publications: Exhibition announcements
Activities: Lect open to public, 4 - 6 vis lectr per year; competitions; book traveling exhibitions, 5 per year; originate traveling exhibitions 1 per year

M WOFFORD COLLEGE, Sandor Teszler Library Gallery, 29303-3663. Tel 803-597-4300; FAX 803-597-4329. *Dir* Oakley H Coburn
Open daily 8 - noon. Estab 1969 to support educational & cultural activities of the college. Gallery located within college library. Average Annual Attendance: 100,000
Exhibitions: US & regional & international works in all media
Activities: Book traveling exhibitions, 1-2 per year

SUMTER

M SUMTER GALLERY OF ART, 421 N Main St, PO Box 1316, 29151. Tel 803-775-0543. *Exec Dir* Mary Jane Caison
Open Tues - Fri noon - 5 PM, Sat & Sun 2 - 5 PM, cl Easter, Thanksgiving & Christmas. No admis fee. Estab 1970 to bring to area exhibits of works of recognized artists, to provide an outlet for local artists for showing and sale of their work, and to serve as a facility where visual art may become a part of life and education of the people, particularly children of this community. The Gallery is the 1850 home of the late Miss Elizabeth White, well-known artist of Sumter, which was deeded to the gallery in 1977 under the terms of her will. Presently using hall, four downstairs rooms, back studio and rooms upstairs. Average Annual Attendance: 8500. Mem: 460; dues commercial patron $100, patron $100, family $40, individual $25; annual meeting May
Income: $100,000 (financed by membership, earned income, exhibit sponsors, donations, County Council)
Collections: Approximately sixty paintings, etchings and drawings of Elizabeth White given to the gallery by trustees of her estate
Exhibitions: Annual Young People's Exhibit; Individual & group exhibits of paintings, sculpture, collages, photography & crafts by recognized artists primarily from Southeast; Touchable exhibit for the blind & visually impaired
Publications: Newsletter, 3 times a year
Activities: Classes for adults and children; lect open to public; competitions, awards given; gallery gift shop primarily sells works by South Carolinian artists. Also on sale art to wear including jewelry

SOUTH DAKOTA

ABERDEEN

M DACOTAH PRAIRIE MUSEUM, Lamont Gallery, 21 S Main St, PO Box 395, 57401. Tel 605-622-7117; FAX 605-225-6094. *Cur Educ* Sherri Rawstern; *Cur Exhib* Michael Keneally; *Dir* Merry Coleman
Open Tues - Fri 9 AM - 5 PM, Sat 1 - 5 PM. No admis fee. Estab 1969 to preserve the heritage of the peoples of the Dakotas; to maintain and develop exhibits that educate people about the heritage of the Dakotas. Average Annual Attendance: 30,000
Income: Financed by county funds
Collections: Sioux and Arikara Indian artifacts; local and regional artists; photography
Exhibitions: (1993) Lamont Gallery: Mark McGinnis - Lakota & Dakota Animal Wisdom Stories; James Lauver; Sherri Treeby; Lee Leuning; Jerome DeWolfe; Susan Luzier; Darwin Wolf; Gallery Annexes: A Life's Work, Anna Graber; Reach Out Rural Artists Show; Enriching Daily Life, Crafts from Native American Traditions; Southwest Gallery: Enriching Daily Life, Crafts from Euro-American Traditions

Publications: Annual Report; Dacotah Prairie Times, 6 per year
Activities: Classes for adults & children; gallery talks; tours; individual paintings and original objects of art lent to museums, art centers and some materials to schools; book traveling exhibitions, 12 per yr; museum shop sells books, magazines, prints, original art and reproductions

L **Ruth Bunker Memorial Library,** 21 S Main St, PO Box 395, 57402-0395. Tel 605-622-7117; FAX 605-225-6094. *Dir* Merry Coleman; *Cur Coll* Sue Batteen
Open Tues - Fri 9 AM - 5 PM, Sat 1 - 5 PM, cl national holidays. Estab 1980 to store books, archives, maps, blueprints, etc. Reference only
Income: Financed by county funds
Library Holdings: Vols 2300; AV — A-tapes, slides; Other — Clipping files, exhibition catalogs, manuscripts, original art works, pamphlets, photographs, prints, reproductions, sculpture
Exhibitions: Exhibits of regional & national art
Publications: Annual report; quarterly newsletter
Activities: Special classes; lect open to public; gallery talks; tours; book traveling exhibitions; originate traveling exhibitions in midwest

M **NORTHERN STATE UNIVERSITY,** Art Galleries, S Jay St, 57401. Tel 605-622-7762; FAX 605-622-3022. *Gallery Dir* Jim Gibson
Open 8 AM - 5 PM. No admis fee. Estab 1902 to support University program. Four galleries. Lincoln professional secure setting. Union - student area. Two hallway locations. Average Annual Attendance: 3000
Income: $6000 (financed by state appropriation)
Collections: Drawing, Painting, Photography, Prints, Sculpture
Exhibitions: Walter Piehl, paint; Small Works on Paper; Electronic Media

BROOKINGS

M **SOUTH DAKOTA STATE UNIVERSITY,** South Dakota Art Museum, Medary Ave at Harvey Dunn St, 57007. Tel 605-688-5423. *Dir* Joseph Stuart; *Cur of Marghab Collection* Cora Sivers
Open Mon - Fri 8 AM - 5 PM, Sat 10 AM - 5 PM, Sun 1 - 5 PM. No admis fee. Estab 1969 as the state center for visual arts with various programs. The facility was designed by Howard Parezo, AIA, Sioux Falls, and occupies 112 x 90 foot site. There are seven galleries and a 147 seat auditorium. Average Annual Attendance: 140,000. Mem: 3200; annual meeting in April
Income: Financed by state appropriation, endowment, gifts and grants
Collections: Harvey Dunn Paintings; MarghabLinens; Sioux Tribla Art, Oscar How Paintings; Native American Art
Exhibitions: (1989) Art for a New Century; Textiles from Vanishing Cultures, Alchemical Reconnaissance; South Dakota Architectural
Publications: Annual report; bulletin, quarterly; exhibition catalogues; newsletter, monthly
Activities: Docent training; lect; films; tours; competitions; traveling exhibitions; sales shop

L **Jeannette Lusk Library Collection,** Medary Ave at Harvey Dunn St, 57007. Tel 605-688-5423.
Open to the public for lending through the main library
Library Holdings: Vols 1500; Per subs 15; AV — Slides
Special Subjects: Archives of South Dakota Art

CRAZY HORSE

M **CRAZY HORSE MEMORIAL,** Indian Museum of North America, Ave of the Chiefs, 57730-9506. Tel 605-673-4681; FAX 605-673-2185. *Chief Executive Officer & Chmn Board* Ruth Ziolkowski; *Museum Dir* Anne Ziolkowski
Open dawn - dusk. Admis memorial $10 per car, museum free. Memorial estab 1947, museum estab 1974 for preservation of the culture of the North American Indian. Three wings. Average Annual Attendance: 1,100,000
Income: Financed by Crazy Horse Memorial Foundation
Collections: North American Indian Artifacts; Mountain Sculpture/Carving Displays; Pioneer memorabilia; Paintings & Sculptures
Publications: Memorial: Progress; Mus: Indian Museum of North America; Crazy Horse Coloring Book
Activities: Lect open to public; book traveling exhibitions; retail store sells books, prints, magazines, slides, original art, reproductions

CUSTER

M **GLORIDALE PARTNERSHIP,** National Museum of Woodcarving, Hwy 16 W, PO Box 747, 57730. Tel 605-673-4404. *Co-owner* Dale E Schaffer; *Co-owner* Gloria Schaffer
Open May - Oct, Mon - Fri 8 AM - 9 PM, cl Oct - May. Admis adult $5.50, sr citizens $5, children 6 - 14 $3, group rates available. Estab 1972 in order to elevate the art of woodcarving. Average Annual Attendance: 74,000
Income: $200,000 (financed by mus admis)
Purchases: $100,000 for gallery & gift shop
Collections: †Wooden Nickel Theater; †36 scenes by original animator of Disneyland; †carving studio
Exhibitions: Area woodcarvers & artists
Activities: Scholarships & fels offered; exten dept serves Custer Community School; museum & sales shop sells books, original art, reproductions, prints, slides

DEADWOOD

M **HOUSE OF ROSES,** Senator Wilson Home, 15 Forest Ave, 57732. Tel 605-578-1879. *Pres* Harry Lehman; *VPres* Michael Bockwoldt
Open daily 9 AM - 6 PM. Admis by donation. Estab 1976 to offer a Victorian home tour. Twenty-seven rooms open to public. Average Annual Attendance: 1,000,000
Collections: †Antique Victorian furniture; †old prints
Activities: Lects open to the public; tours; museum shop sells antiques; junior museum

FLANDREAU

A **MOODY COUNTY HISTORICAL SOCIETY,** PO Box 25, 57028. Tel 605-997-3191. *Pres* Archy L Lupia; *Dir* Bonnie Marquardt
Open Memorial Day - Labor Day, Sun & holidays 2 - 5 PM. No Admis fee. Estab 1965 to promote understanding of history. Average Annual Attendance: 500. Mem: 400; dues single $3 per year, life $25; couple $5 per year, life $40; annual meeting is on first Sun after Labor Day
Income: $4000 (financed by county appropriation, donations & mem)
Activities: Sales shop sells note papers, silver teaspoons, centennial museum plates

MITCHELL

A **OSCAR HOWE ART CENTER,** 119 W Third Ave, 57301. Tel 605-996-4111. *Dir* Pat Amhert
Open Sept - May Tues - Sat 10 AM - 5 PM, June - Aug Tues - Sat 9 AM - 6 PM, Sun 1 - 5 PM. Admis adult $1 (June - Aug only), children under 12 free. Estab to promote Native American artists, local & regional artists. Center is housed in a former Carnegie Library building constructed in 1902 and designated as a National Historic Site
Income: Financed by private & public funds
Collections: †19 paintings by Sioux artist & South Dakota artist laureate, Oscar Howe
Exhibitions: Young Artists Competition; Formal Images: Photographic Exhibit; Joseph Broghammer & Mark Anderson: Pastel Images & Bronze Sculpture; South Dakota Traditional Folk Art; Wild Life Exhibit; Mitchell Area Juried Art Competition; James Munce; Calligraphy: Diane Grupp; Book Art: Richard Zauft; Native American Art; Red Cloud Indian Art
Activities: Classes for adults & children; docent training; lectures open to public; concerts; gallery talks; tours; competitions with awards; scholarships; individual paintings & original objects of art lent to other galleries; lending collection contains paintings; book traveling exhibitions; Garret Museum Shop sells original art work of regional artists including pottery, watercolors, weavings, oils and acrylics, books, Indian beadwork & reproductions of Oscar Howe paintings, magazines & prints

PINE RIDGE

M **HERITAGE CENTER, INC,** Red Cloud Indian School, PO Box 100, 57770. Tel 605-867-5491. *Pres* C Jumping Bull; *VPres* John Paul; *Dir* C M Simon
Open Mon - Fri 9 AM - 5 PM. Estab 1974 to exhibit Indian art and culture. Museum has four changing galleries of American and Canadian Native American art. Mainly paintings and sculpture. Average Annual Attendance: 9000
Income: Financed by donations and grants
Collections: †Native American paintings and prints; †native American sculpture; †star quilts and tribal arts
Exhibitions: Selections from permanent collection; Eskimo prints; Northwest coast prints; Annual Red Cloud Indian Art Show
Activities: Tours; awards; individual paintings & original objects of art are lent to other museums & art centers; book traveling exhibitions, 4 - 6 per yr; originate traveling exhibitions; museum shop sells books, original art, reproductions

RAPID CITY

M **INDIAN ARTS AND CRAFTS BOARD,** Sioux Indian Museum, PO Box 1504, 57709. Tel 605-348-0557; FAX 605-348-6182. *Cur* Paulette Montileaux
Open June - Sept, Mon - Sat 9 AM - 5 PM, Sun 1 - 5 PM; Oct - May, Tues - Sat 10 AM - 5 PM, Sun 1 - 5 PM; cl New Year's Day, Thanksgiving, Christmas. No admis fee. Estab 1939 to promote the development of contemporary native American arts and crafts of the United States. Average Annual Attendance: 80,000
Income: Financed by federal appropriation
Collections: Contemporary native American arts and crafts of the United States; Historic works by Sioux craftsmen
Exhibitions: Contemporary Sioux Quillwork; continuing series of one-person exhibitions
Publications: One-person exhibition brochure series, monthly
Activities: Gallery talks; tours; sales shop selling books and original arts and crafts

M **RAPID CITY FINE ARTS COUNCIL,** Dahl Fine Arts Center, 713 Seventh St, 57701. Tel 605-394-4101; FAX 605-394-6121. *Exec Dir* Ruth Brennan; *Admin Asst* Diane Bullard
Open Mon - Sat 9 AM - 5 PM, Sun 1 - 5 PM. No admis fee. Estab 1974 to promote, educate & serve the arts. The art center contains 3 galleries: Cyclorama Gallery, a 200 ft oil mural of American history; Central Gallery, touring invitational exhibitions; Dakota Art Gallery for juried original works for sale. Average Annual Attendance: 37,000. Mem: Annual meeting third Mon in July
Income: $81,710 (financed by earned income, city appropriation, rentals, grants & contributions)
Purchases: $151,000
Collections: Grace French, oils & watercolors; †Contemporary original prints; Hazel Schwentker, watercolors, inks & washes
Exhibitions: Black Hill Impressions; Print & Cast Paper Mediums; Dennis Navart, Lloyd Menard, Batiks; By Bob H Miller, Paintings, Watercolor, Callagraphy
Publications: The French Sisters
Activities: Art & Drama classes for adults & children; music series; docent training; workshops for artists & non-profit organizattions; lectures open to public, 2-3 vis lectr per yr; lending collection contains art books books of play scripts, reproductions series & art slides; book traveling exhibition; sales shop sells books, magazines, original art & reproductions

SIOUX FALLS

A AUGUSTANA COLLEGE, Center for Western Studies, PO Box 727, 57197. Tel 605-336-4007. *Exec Dir* Arthur R Huseboe; *Dev Dir* Dean A Schueler; *Secy* Phyllis Harmsen; *Cur & Managing Ed* Harry F Thompson
Open 8 AM - 5 PM. No admis fee. Estab 1970 for collection and preservation of historic material for the promotion of South Dakota and its Western artists. Artists of the Plains Gallery, original oils, watercolors, bronzes and prints by regional artists. Average Annual Attendance: 500-750. Mem: 400; dues $30 & up; annual meeting in Dec
Income: Financed by endowment, mem, gifts, grants & book sales
Collections: South Dakota Art; historical manuscripts; photos; art by regional artists
Exhibitions: 3 - 4 exhibits per year featuring SD Artists
Publications: An Illustrated History of the Arts in South Dakota; Poems & Essays of Herbert Krause; Yanktonai Sioux Water Colors: Cultural Remembrance of John Saul
Activities: Classes for adults; docent training; Lectures open to the public, 10 vis lectr per yr; tours; competitions with awards; individual paintings and original objects of art lent to other offices on campus; six to eight traveling exhibitions booked per year; traveling exhibitions organized and circulated; museum shop sells books, original art, prints and slides, beadwork & silver jewelry
L Center for Western Studies, 57197-0001. Tel 605-336-4007. *Dir* Arthur R Huseboe; *Cur & Managing Ed* Harry F Thompson; *Dev Dir* Dean A Schueler; *Secy* Phyllis Harmsen
Open daily 8 AM - 5 PM. For reference only
Library Holdings: Vols 30,000; Per subs 15; Micro — Reels; AV — A-tapes, slides; Other — Clipping files, memorabilia, original art works, pamphlets, photographs, prints, sculpture
Special Subjects: American Indian Art, American Western Art, Archaeology, Bronzes, Display, Ethnology, Historical Material, Furniture, Historical Material, Manuscripts, Maps, Painting - American, Photography, Prints, Sculpture, Western Americana
Collections: Historical manuscripts, photos art by regional artists
Publications: The Country Railroad Station in America by H Roger Grant & Charles Bohi; other titles in book & catalog, available on request; newsletter; Center for Western Studies Newsletter (bi- annually)

M CIVIC FINE ARTS CENTER, 235 W Tenth St, 57102. Tel 605-336-1167. *Executive Dir* Sheila Agee; *Asst to Dir* Paul Groeneveld
Open Mon - Fri 9 AM - 5 PM, Sat 10 AM - 5 PM. No admis fee. Estab 1961 as a contemporary museum. Four galleries: two permanent & two for special exhibitions. Average Annual Attendance: 60,000. Mem: 1250; dues $15; annual meeting in June
Collections: Historical & contemporary interest, monthly 2D work; National Printmakers collection
Exhibitions: Paul Manship; A New Look: Terry Malkey
Publications: Newsletter, monthly
Activities: Educ dept; classes for adults & children; lect open to the public, 3 vis lectr per yr; concerts; gallery talks; tours; individual paintings & original art lent; museum shop sells books, magazines, original art, prints, reproductions, pottery and cards
L Library, 235 W Tenth St, 57102. Tel 605-336-1167. *Exec Dir* Shelia Agee
Open to members only
Library Holdings: Vols 320; Per subs 2
Publications: Art News

SPEARFISH

M BLACK HILLS STATE COLLEGE, Ruddell Gallery, 1200 University, 57799. Tel 605-642-6104. *Dir* Jim Knutsen
Open Mon - Fri 8 AM - 4 PM, Sat & Sun by appointment. Estab 1936 to encourage art expression and greater appreciation in the Black Hills area. Work of the Art Center is promoted jointly by Black Hills State College Art Department and the Student Union. Average Annual Attendance: 1500. Mem: 500; dues $5 and up
Exhibitions: (1993) Women's History Month Native American Show
Activities: Classes for adults; programs held each semester; summer workshop; lectures open to public, 3 vis lectrs per yr; competitions with awards; individual paintings & original objects of art lent to other colleges & universities; sales shop sells original art
L Library, Ruddell Gallery, 57799
Library Holdings: Vols 300; AV — Motion pictures; Other — Reproductions
Collections: Carnegie gift library containing 1000 prints and 150 books

VERMILLION

M UNIVERSITY OF SOUTH DAKOTA ART GALLERIES, W M Lee Center for the Fine Arts, 57069. Tel 605-677-5481. *Dir* John A Day
Open Mon - Fri 10 AM - 4:30 PM; Sat & Sun 1 - 5 PM. No admis fee. Estab 1965. Primary mission is educational, serving specifically the needs of the college and augmenting the university curriculum as a whole. There are two galleries. One is a changing gallery 50' x 50' located in the Fine Arts Center. The second houses the university collection of Works by Oscar Howe, a native American painter. This facility is approximately 30' x 20'. Average Annual Attendance: 15,000
Income: $30,000 (financed by state appropriation and student fee allotment)
Purchases: $4000
Collections: †60 Works by Oscar Howe; †variety of media by contemporary artists
Exhibitions: Mail Art Invitational Myth America
Publications: Catalogues for major exhibitions
Activities: Lect open to public; gallery talks; tours; competitions, awards given; exten dept serves 150 miles in general region; individual paintings and original objects of art lent to professional museums and galleries; book traveling exhibitions, 2 per year; originate traveling exhibitions

YANKTON

M YANKTON COUNTY HISTORICAL SOCIETY, Dakota Territorial Museum, 610 Summit St, PO Box 1033, 57078. Tel 605-665-3898. *Pres* Frank R Yaggie; *VPres* Harold Tisher; *Dir & Cur* Donald J Binder
Open Memorial Day - Labor Day 1 - 5 PM. No admis fee, contributions accepted. Estab 1961 as an historical museum. Average Annual Attendance: 6000. Mem: 200; dues $5; annual meeting in Jan
Income: $20,000 (financed by city & county appropriation)
Collections: Paintings by Louis Janousek; sculptures by Frank Yaggie

TENNESSEE

CHATTANOOGA

L CHATTANOOGA-HAMILTON COUNTY BICENTENNIAL LIBRARY, Fine Arts & Audio Visuals Department, 1001 Broad St, 37402. Tel 615-757-5316. *Head of Dept* M Keating Griffiss, MA
Open Mon - Sun Sept - May, Mon - Sat June - Aug. No admis fee. Estab 1888, dept estab 1976
Income: Financed by city, county & state appropriation
Library Holdings: AV — A-tapes, cassettes, motion pictures, v-tapes; Other — Clipping files
Special Subjects: Architecture, Art History, Crafts, Decorative Arts, Embroidery, Film, Furniture, Handicrafts, Historical Material, Interior Design, Painting - American, Painting - British, Pre-Columbian Art
Collections: Collection of books, music books, phono records & cassette tapes, CDs, 16mm film & video VHS Tapes

M HOUSTON MUSEUM OF DECORATIVE ARTS, 201 High St, 37403. Tel 615-267-7176. *Dir & Cur* Julia Harman
Open Tues - Sat 10 AM - 4:30 PM; Sun 2 - 4:30 PM; cl Mon & major holidays. Admis donations. Estab 1961, incorporated 1949. Average Annual Attendance: 8000. Mem: 700; dues $500, $250 $100, $50, $25, $15, $10; annual meeting May
Income: Financed by membership, dues, annual grant from Allied Arts, Inc
Collections: Early American furniture; rare collection of glass (5000 pitchers, 600 patterns of pressed glass, all types of art glass, steins and Tiffany glass); ceramics, dolls, porcelains
Publications: The Fabulous Houston; Houston Musuem of Decorative Arts Coverlet Collection
Activities: Classes for adults & children; docent training; lect open to public, 6 - 8 vis lectr per year; tours; originate traveling exhibitions to other museums; sales shop sells books, magazines, slides and antique items

M HUNTER MUSEUM OF ART, 10 Bluff View, 37403. Tel 615-267-0968. *Dir* Cleve K Scarbrough; *Cur Educ* A Talley Rhodes; *Program Coordr* Mary Anne Kaiser; *Chief Preparator* John Hare; *Registrar* Jacquelyn F Casey; *Cur Coll* Ellen Simak
Open Tues - Sat 10 AM - 4:30 PM; Sun 1 - 4:30 PM; cl Mon. Suggested admis adults $2, children $1, under 12 free. Estab 1924, chartered in 1951, to present a visual arts program of high quality, maintain a fine collection of American art, and to carry out a vigorous educational program in the community and the schools. The permanent collection of American art is housed in the George Thomas Hunter Masion constructed in 1904 & a contemporary addition was opened in 1975 with 50,000 sq ft of space in four major gallery areas, a classroom wing & an auditorium. Average Annual Attendance: 55,000. Mem: 2500; dues grand benefactor $5000, benefactor $2500, member $1000, patron $500, sponsor $250, donor $100, advocate $50, general $30, advantage hunter $20, student & sr citizen $15
Collections: American paintings, later 18th century to present, including works by Bierstadt, Benton, Burchfield, Cassatt, Durand, Hassam, Henri, Inness, Marsh, Miller, Twachtman, Whistler & others; contemporary works including Beal, Bechtle, Fish, Frankenthaler, Golub, Goodman, Johns, LeWitt, Park, Pearlstein, Rauschenberg, Schapiro, Stackhouse, Wesselman, Wonner & Youngerman; contemporary American prints; sculpture by Calder, Hunt, Nevelson, Segal, Snelson & others; glass by Chihuly, Littleton, Morris, Zinsky
Exhibitions: (1993) Suzy Frelinghuysen & George L K Morris, American Abstract Artists: Aspects of their Work & Collection; The American West: Legendary Artists of the Frontier, the John F Eulich Collection of American Western Art; Robert Henri: Nebraska's Favorite Son; Charles Burchfield's Spirituality; Clearly Art: Pilchuck's Glass Legacy
Publications: Brochures & announcements; bulletin, bi-monthly; A Catalogue of the American Collection, Hunter Museum of Art, 1985, 300-page illustrated focus on pieces in the permanent collection
Activities: Classes for adults and children; docent training; lect open to public, approximately 7 vis lectr per yr; gallery talks; concerts; tours; individual paintings are lent to other museums; book traveling exhibitions, 18 - 20 per year; originate traveling exhibitions which circulate to qualified galleries & museums; museum shop sells books, reproductions, gift items, jewelry
L Reference Library, 10 Bluff View, 37403. Tel 615-267-0968.
Open Tues - Sat 10 AM - 4:30 PM, Sun 1 - 4:30 PM, cl Mon, open to public by appointment. Estab 1958
Library Holdings: Vols 15,000; Per subs 8; Micro — Cards; AV — Cassettes, motion pictures, slides; Other — Clipping files, exhibition catalogs, memorabilia, original art works, pamphlets, photographs, prints, sculpture
Special Subjects: Architecture, American Art

M UNIVERSITY OF TENNESSEE AT CHATTANOOGA, George Ayres Cress Gallery of Art, Fine Arts Center, 37043. Tel 615-755-4178. *Gallery Coordr* Ron Buffington
Open Mon - Fri 9 AM - 4 PM, cl university holidays. No admis fee. Estab 1952
Collections: Graphics; paintings; students work
Activities: Gallery talks; loan program; temporary and traveling exhibitions

CLARKSVILLE

M **AUSTIN PEAY STATE UNIVERSITY,** Margaret Fort Trahern Gallery, Art Department, PO Box 4677, 37044. Tel 615-648-7348. *Dir* Bettye Holte
Open Mon - Fri 9 AM - 4 PM. No admis fee. Estab 1962 as a university community service to exhibit a variety of visual media from regional professionals and university art majors. Average Annual Attendance: 8000
Income: Financed by university appropriations
Collections: Larson Drawing Collection; †Graphics & sculpture; watercolors
Exhibitions: Average 10-12 per year
Publications: Announcements of shows and artist biographies, monthly
Activities: Lectures open to the public, 12 vis lectrs per yr; gallery talks; tours; competitions with awards; scholarships
L **Art Dept Library,** 37040. Tel 615-648-7333. *Gallery Cur* Bettye Holte-Lucas; *Slide Librn* Dixie Webb
Open Mon - Fri 8:30 AM - 4 PM. Estab 1974. Large single unit space with storage. Average Annual Attendance: 4,000
Library Holdings: AV — Fs, motion pictures, slides; Other — Clipping files, original art works, photographs, prints, reproductions, sculpture
Collections: †Larson Drawing Collection

COOKEVILLE

A **CUMBERLAND ART SOCIETY INC,** Cookeville Art Gallery, 186 S Walnut, 38501. Tel 615-526-2424. *Pres* Ritha R Glass; *VPres* Chris Trella Koczwara
Open Mon - Fri & Sun 1 - 4 PM. No admis fee. Estab 1961 to promote arts in the community and area. A new building with adequate gallery and studio space. The gallery is carpeted and walls are finished with wallscape and track lighting. Average Annual Attendance: 3000. Mem: 100; dues $20, Students $10; meetings twice annually
Income: $5500 (financed by membership, city & state appropriations)
Exhibitions: Changing exhibits, monthly
Activities: Classes for children & adults; lectures open to public, 6 vis lectr per yr; gallery talks; tours; competitions with awards

JOHNSON CITY

EAST TENNESSEE STATE UNIVERSITY

M **Carroll Reece Museum,** 37614. Tel 615-929-4392, 929-4283; FAX 615-461-7026, Ext 5309. *Museum Dir* Helen Roseberry; *Museum Registrar* Margaret S Carr; *Installation Supv* Willie J Ferguson; *Cur* Blair White; *Slide Cur* Nancy Earnest
Open Mon - Sat 9 AM - 4 PM, Sun 1 - 5 PM. No admis fee. Estab 1965 to enhance the cultural & educational advantages of the University & the people of upper East Tennessee. The purpose of Friends of the Reece Museum is to acquire fine arts works for the permanent collection. Average Annual Attendance: 23,500. Mem: 200; dues President's trust $10,000 plus, President's partners $500, Century Club $100-$499, supporting $25, family $15, individual $10, student $1
Income: Financed through the state of Tennessee
Collections: Frontier Exhibit, an exhibit of historical Tennessee household & farming items, includes a log cabin & conestoga wagon; Marks Collection of Pre-Columbian Art; Music From the Past, a collection of early musical instruments; Old Master & contemporary prints; Printshop of the Past; Reece Room, an exhibition of memorabilia of former United States Congressman from Tennessee, B Carroll Reece; John Steele Collection of Contemporary Prints; contemporary paintings; historical material
Publications: CRM Newsletter, quarterly
Activities: Lectures, 6 vis lectr per yr; concerts; gallery talks; tours; competitions with awards; scholarships; individual paintings & original objects of art lent to inner administrative offices on campus; lending collection contains 354 original prints, 25 paintings, 400 original art works, 6 sculpture & 1000 slides; book traveling exhibitions; originate traveling exhibitions; rotating exhibitions at Kingsport University Center
M **Elizabeth Slocumb Galleries,** Art Department, PO Box 70708, 37614-0708. Tel 615-461-7078. *Dir Exhib* Ann Ropp
Open daily 9 AM - 4 PM. No admis fee. Estab 1950 to augment all the programs and areas of instruction within the Art Department and to foster interest in various modes of artistic expression in the campus at large. Average Annual Attendance: 5000
Collections: A small teaching collection of prints, paintings, ceramics, weaving, wood, photographs and graphic designs and a camera collection
Exhibitions: Five Contemporary Illustrators; National Annual Competition: Positive & Negative
Publications: Catalogs; posters
Activities: Classes for adults and children; art education program; seminars and workshops; lect, gallery talks, tours and competitions; scholarships and fellowships; originate traveling exhibitions
L **C C Sherrod Library,** Art Collection, PO Box 70,665, 37614-0665. Tel 615-929-5308. *Dir* F Borchuck
Open Mon - Thurs 8 AM - midnight, Fri 8 AM - 6 PM, Sat 9 AM - 6 PM, Sun 1 PM - midnight
Income: Financed by the state
Library Holdings: Vols 14,799
Special Subjects: Drawings, Photography, Sculpture, Painting
Collections: Appalachian Culture and Arts; photographs archives; videotape archives

KINGSPORT

A **ARTS COUNCIL OF GREATER KINGSPORT,** 1200 E Center St, 37660-4946. Tel 615-392-8420. *Pres* Katherine Singleton; *Dir* Charles Shain
Open Mon - Fri 10 AM - 4 PM. No admis fee, charge for special events. Estab 1968 to promote and present all the arts to all the people in area; this includes performing arts, visual arts & classes. Two galleries with monthly shows. Average

Annual Attendance: 20,000. Mem: 400; dues $20 - $500; annual meeting May
Income: $60,000 (financed by mem)
Publications: Newsletter, bimonthly
Activities: Classes for adults & children; lectures open to public, 3 vis lectrs per yr; concerts; competitions with awards; scholarships; originate traveling exhibitions through Southern Arts Federation

KNOXVILLE

M **BECK CULTURAL EXCHANGE CENTER,** 1927 Dandridge Ave, 37915. Tel 615-524-8461. *Chief Exec Officer* Robert J Booker
Estab 1975 to encourage local Black history research. Average Annual Attendance: 5000. Mem: 400; dues $10; annual meeting in Sept
Income: $90,000 (financed by mem, city, county & state appropriations)
Exhibitions: Federal Judge William H Hastie Room; Library of Books & Recordings; oral histories; weekly newspapers of the local Black experience; Senior Citizens Storywriting Contest
Activities: Classes for adults & children; school & community presentations; docent programs; competitions with cash awards; traveling slide presentations

M **KNOXVILLE MUSEUM OF ART,** 410 Tenth St, 37916. Tel 615-525-6101; FAX 615-546-3635. *Chmn* Tim Keller; *VChmn* Tom Ingram; *Secy* Melinda McCoy; *Treas* Carey Brown; *Dir* Henry Flood Robert
Admis adults $2, students & children free, no admis Sun. Estab 1962 as a nonprofit private corporation. Recently completed $10.5 million capital campaign for a new 53,000 sq ft facility. Grand opening was held in March, 1990. Located on the former World's Fair site downtown. Average Annual Attendance: 75,000. Mem: 4000; dues from $30 - $5000
Income: Financed by membership, contributions, foundations and state and federal grants
Collections: American paintings; Southeast regional art; works from last 20 Dulin National Works on Paper Competitions.
Exhibitions: American Women Artists: The 20th Century; Philip Morris Collection of Contemporary American Art; Soft Covers for Hard Times: Depression Era Quilts, Thonet; Decorative Arts Exhibition; Selections from the Janos Scholz Collection of Italian Old Master Drawings
Publications: Calender, bi-monthly; exhibition catalogs
Activities: Classes for adults and children; docent training; arts to the schools; lect open to public, 1 - 2 vis lectr per yr; tours; competitions with awards; museum store

UNIVERSITY OF TENNESSEE

M **Frank H McClung Museum,** 1327 Circle Park Dr, 37996-3200. Tel 615-974-2144. *Dir* Jefferson Chapman; *Exhib Coordr* Andrew W Hurst; *Cur Coll* Elaine A Evans
Open Mon - Fri 9 AM - 5 PM, Sun 2 - 5 PM. No admis fee. Estab 1961 to collect, maintian and interpret paintings, works of art, items of natural history and historical objects with emphasis placed on the Tennessee area. A major purpose is to provide research materials for students and faculty of the university. Average Annual Attendance: 20,000
Income: Financed by city and state appropriations
Collections: Eleanor Deane Audigier Art Collection; Frederick T Bonham Collection (18th - 20th Century furniture, art objects); Lewis-Kneberg Collection (Tennessee archaeology); Grace Moore Collection (memorabilia of her career 1920's - 1940's); Malacology Collection (marine species & fresh water North American mollusks)
Activities: Lectures open to public; gallery talks; tours; competitions; exten dept serves the Southwest; original objects of art lent to mem of university & educational organizations; lending collection contains prints and photographs
M **Eleanor Dean Audigier Art Collection,** Frank H McClung Museum, Circle Park Dr, 37916. Tel 615-974-2144; FAX 615-974-6435. *Dir* Jefferson Chapman; *Cur* Elaine A Evans; *Exhibits Coordr* Andrew W Hurst
Open Mon - Fri 9 AM - 5 PM, Sat 10 AM - 3 PM, Sun 2 - 5 PM. No admis fee. Estab 1961. Average Annual Attendance: 19,600
Income: Financed by state apropriations, supplemental income from mem sponsorships
Collections: †The Audigier Collection Greco-Roman objects; 19th Century copies of Italian Renaissance paintings, furniture and sculpture; personal jewelry; early 20th century decorative arts objects
Exhibitions: The American Indian in Tennessee; Ancient Egypt: The Eternal Voice
Activities: Lectures open to public; tours; individual and original objects of art lent
M **Ewing Gallery of Art and Architecture,** University of Tennessee, 1715 Volunteer Blvd, 37996-2410. Tel 615-974-3200. *Dir* Sam Yates; *Registrar* Cindy Spangler
Open Mon - Fri 9 AM - 4:30 PM, Mon - Thurs 7 - 9 PM, Sun 1 - 4:30 PM. Estab 1981 to provide quality exhibitions focusing on contemporary art and architecture. Gallery consists of 3500 sq ft exhibition space. Average Annual Attendance: 15,000
Collections: †Contemporary American prints, paintings & drawings; Japanese prints
Exhibitions: Corporation collections, fund raising, professional and student exhibitions
Activities: Lectures open to public, 12 vis lectr per year; gallery talks; tours; sponsor competitions; scholarships offered; lending collection contains individual and original objects of art; originate traveling exhibitions
A **University of Tennessee Exhibits Committee,** 305 University Center, 37996. Tel 615-974-5455. *Prog Advisor* Tracy Augustine
Open Mon - Fri 7:30 AM - 10:30 PM, Sat 7 AM - 10 PM, Sun 1 - 8 M. No admis fee. Estab to provide cultural arts for the students of the university. Two major galleries; Gallery Concourse has 300 running ft & Barton Music Lounge & Gallery has 60 running ft for intimate shows. Average Annual Attendance: 20,000
Income: Financed by student activities fees
Collections: †Dunford Collection; †Marion Heard Collection of Crafts
Exhibitions: 20 exhibits per year - student shows and traveling shows
Activities: Lectures open to public, 3 vis lectr per year; originate traveling exhibitions

MARYVILLE

C FIRST TENNESSEE BANK, 200 S Hall Rd, PO Box 9720, 37802-9720. Tel 615-977-5100; FAX 615-977-5196. *In Charge of Art Coll* Dolores Simerly
Estab to provide community interest in the arts; to aid participating artists; to enhance lobby. Supports local artists and art forms or displays that lend an interest to the community
Activities: Sponsors Wildlife Artist Guy Coheleach

M MARYVILLE COLLEGE, Fine Arts Center Gallery, 37801. Tel 615-981-8150; FAX 615-983-0581. *Chmn* Daniel Taddie
Open Mon - Fri during school year. No admis fee
Library Holdings: Vols 1300
Collections: †Print collection
Activities: Gallery programs in connection with circulating exhibitions; art movies, four times a year; ten to twelve traveling exhibitions during college year

MEMPHIS

AUTOZONE
For further information, see National and Regional Organizations

A CENTER FOR SOUTHERN FOLKLORE, 152 Beale St, 38103. Tel 901-525-3655; FAX 901-525-3945. *Exec Dir* Judy Peiser
Open 9 AM - 5:30 PM. Admis $2. Estab 1972 as a non-profit organization which archives, documents & presents folk art, culture & music through film, photography, exhibits & lectues. Mem: 800; dues $25
Income: $350,000 (financed by mem, state appropriation & national endowment)
Collections: African - American Quilt; Contemporary Slides - Folk Art & Culture; Folk Art; Historical & Contemporary Photographs
Exhibitions: WDIA Radio; Rockabilly; Memphis Music
Activities: Classes for adults & children; cultual tourism; lect open to public; lending collection contains 50 paintings & art objects; retail store sells books, magazines & original art

M THE DIXON GALLERY & GARDENS, 4339 Park Ave, 38117. Tel 901-761-5250; FAX 901-682-0943. *Dir* John Buchanan Jr; *Asst Dir* Katherine Lawrence; *Cur Coll* Sheila K Tabakoff; *Registrar* Lisa Incardona; *Comptroller* Priscilla Campbell; *Vol Coordr* Jane Faquin; *Museum Shop Mgr* Alisa Shoptaw
Open Tues 10 AM - 5 PM, Sun 1 - 5 PM, cl Mon. Admis adults $4, children 2 - 11 years $1, students & sr citizens $3. Estab 1976 as a bequest to the public from the late Margaret & Hugo Dixon. Their Impressionist Art Collection & their Georgian-style home & gardens, situated on 17 acres of landscaped woodland, serve as the museum's foundation. Two wings added in 1977 & 1986 house the developing permanent collection & accommodate loan exhibitions. Formal & informal gardens, a camellia house & greenhouses are located on the site. Average Annual Attendance: 160,000. Mem: 5200; dues corporate patron $1000, patron $500, donor $250, sponsor $100, friend $75, family $45, individual $35, student $15
Income: Financed by endowment; contributions
Collections: French Impressionist painting; Barbizon, Post-Impressionist & related schools; 18th century British paintings; Georgian period furniture & decorative arts; the Warda Stevens Stout Collection of 18th century German porcelain; 18th & 19th centuries works by Pierre Bonnard, Eugene Boudin, A F Cals, Jean-Baptiste Carpeaux, Mary Cassatt, Marc Chagall, William Merritt Chase, John Constable, J B C Corot, Kenyon Cox, Henri-Edmond Cross, Charles Francois Daubigny, Edgar Degas, Julien Dupre, Sir Jacob Epstein, Henri Fantin-Latour, Thomas Gainsborough, Paul Gauguin, Francesco Guardi, Paul Guigou, Armand Guillaumin, Henri Joseph Harpignies, William James, Johan Jongkind, S V E Lepine, Maximilien Luce, Albert Marquet, Paul Mathey, Henri Matisse, Claude Monet, Berthe Morisot, Henriette A Oberteuffer, Ludovic Piette, Camille Pissarro, Sir Henry Raeburn, J F Raffaelli, Auguste Renoir, Sir Joshua Reynolds, Henri Rouart, Paul Signac, Alfred Sisley, Allen Tucker, J M W Turner, Horatio Walker and Richard Wilson
Exhibitions: Bayre Bronzes from the Corcoran Gallery of Art; Delights for the Senses: Dutch & Flemish Still Life Paintings from Budapest; Gold Boxes from the Arthur & Rosalind Gilbert Collection; The World of Toulouse-Lautrec
Publications: Exhibition catalogues; newsletter, bi-monthly
Activities: Classes for adults; workshops; docent training; film series, lect open to the public; concerts; gallery talks; tours; individual paintings and original objects of art lent to museums and galleries; lending collection contains original paintings, prints and sculpture, porcelain, silver and antique furniture; museum shop sells books, magazines, prints & slides
L Library, 4339 Park Ave, 38117. Tel 901-761-5250; FAX 901-682-0943. *Cur Coll* Sheila K Tabakoff; *Registrar* Lisa Incardona
Open to members during museum hours, for reference only
Income: $8000
Library Holdings: Per subs 15; Micro — Cards; Other — Clipping files, exhibition catalogs, pamphlets, photographs
Special Subjects: Ceramics, Decorative Arts, Painting - American, Painting - French, 18th century German Porcelain, 19th century French art; gardens

C FIRST TENNESSEE NATIONAL CORP, First Tennessee Heritage Collection, 165 Madison Ave, 38103. Tel 901-523-4382; FAX 901-523-4354. *Chmn* Ronald Terry; *Public Relations Representative* Kathie Alexander
Open Mon - Thurs 8:30 AM - 4 PM, Fri 8:30 AM - 5 PM. No admis fee. Estab 1979 to depict Tennessee's heritage & history through art. Gallery, with over 150 original works, is located in First Tennessee's corporate headquarters.
Average Annual Attendance: 20,000
Income: Financed by Corporation
Purchases: $75,000
Collections: Engravings, etchings, lithographs, murals, paintings, sculpture, watercolors
Exhibitions: Permanent collection
Activities: Educ dept; scout program; lectures open to public, 100 vis lectrs per yr; individual paintings & original objects of art lent; book traveling exhibitions, 3 per yr

M MEMPHIS BROOKS MUSEUM OF ART, 1914 Poplar Ave, 38104. Tel 901-722-3525, 722-3500; FAX 901-722-3522. *Interim Dir* Patty Bladon; *Admin Asst* Susan McDaniel; *Dir Educ* Mary Scheuner; *Registrar* Kip Peterson; *Shop Mgr & Special Events* Lisa Durkan; *Chief Preparator* Elbert L Sharp III; *Asst Preparator* Paul Tracy; *Development Dir* Roder MaCaulay; *Chief Financial Officer* Kay Dickerson; *Accounting Mgr* Jennifer Long; *Librn* Helen Karpinski; *Education Office Asst* Carola Preston; *Asst Shop Mgr* George Meredith; *Public Relations Dir* Dorothy McClure; *Dir Facility Servs & Security* Charles Beagle
Open Tues - Sat 10 AM - 5 PM; Sun 1 - 5 PM. No admis fee. Estab 1912 to exhibit, preserve & elucidate works of art. The original building was opened in 1916 with additions in 1955 and 1973. Maintained by the city of Memphis, Public Service Department. Average Annual Attendance: 125,000. Mem: 3156; dues $35 & up
Income: $1,000,000 (financed by city appropriation & Friend's Foundation)
Collections: American Paintings and Sculpture, 18th-20th centuries; Dutch and Flemish Paintings, 16th-18th centuries; Eastern and Near-Eastern Decorative Arts Collection (Han, Tang and Ching Dynasty); English Paintings, 17th-19th centuries; French Paintings, 16th-19th centuries; †International Collection of Paintings and Sculpture, 19th & 20th centuries; Kress Collection of Italian Paintings and Sculptures, 13th-18th centuries; Dr Louis Levy Collection of American Prints; Mid-South Collection of 20th century paintings and sculptures; glass, textile and porcelain collection
Publications: Newsletter, bimonthly
Activities: Classes for adults & children; docent training; outreach program & studio art activities for student groups; lect open to public, 9 vis lectrs per year; concerts; gallery talks; tours; competitions; awards; individual paintings & original objects of art lent; book traveling exhibitions, 7 - 10 per yr; originate traveling exhibitions; museum shop sells books, reproductions, prints, slides, museum replicas, jewelry & regional pottery
L Library, 1934 Poplar Ave, 38104. Tel 901-722-3500. *Librn* Helen Karpinski
Open Wed & Fri 10 AM - 4 PM & by appointment. Reference only
Library Holdings: Vols 5166; Per subs 24; Other — Clipping files 2910, exhibition catalogs 1705

MEMPHIS COLLEGE OF ART
L G Pillow Lewis Memorial Library, Overton Park, 38112. Tel 901-726-4085. *Pres* Jeffrey D Nesin; *Dean* Phillip S Morris; *Librn* Paul S Williford
Open Mon - Thurs 8 AM - 9 PM, Fri 8 AM - 6 PM, Sat 9 AM - 4 PM, Sun 1 - 6 PM, summer hrs Mon - Fri 8 AM - 5 PM. No admis fee. Estab 1936 as an adjunct educational program. The Standing Committee on Exhibitions arranges visiting shows
Library Holdings: Vols 14,000; Per subs 100; AV — Slides; Other — Clipping files, exhibition catalogs, prints, reproductions
Collections: Jacob Marks Memorial Collection; works by college graduates
Exhibitions: Juried student shows; one and two-person faculty shows; senior exhibition; summer student show; traveling exhibitions
Publications: Exhibition catalogs
Activities: Classes for adults, children and undergraduate college students; lect; guided tours; films; competitions; book traveling exhibitions
L Library, Overton Park, 38112. Tel 901-726-4085. *Librn* Paul Williford; *Slide Cur* Bette Ray Callow
Open Mon - Thurs 8 AM - 8 PM, Fri 8 AM - 5 PM, Sat 10 AM - 2 PM
Income: Financed by city and county appropriations
Library Holdings: Vols 14,100; Per subs 105; Original prints; AV — Slides 30,000; Other — Reproductions

L MEMPHIS-SHELBY COUNTY PUBLIC LIBRARY AND INFORMATION CENTER, Dept of Art, Music & Films, 1850 Peabody, 38104. Tel 901-725-8837; FAX 901-725-8883. *Dir* Judith Drescher; *Deputy Dir* Sallie Johnson; *Head Art, Music & Films* Lloyd Ostby
Open Mon - Thurs 9 AM - 9 PM, Fri & Sat 9 AM - 6 PM, Sun 1 - 5 PM. Estab 1895 to serve the reference, informational, cultural and recreational needs of residents of Memphis-Shelby County. Turner-Clark Gallery exhibits promising and established local and regional artists of various media
Income: Financed by city and state appropriation
Library Holdings: Vols 63,000; Per subs 245; AV — Cassettes 800, motion pictures 3000, rec 35,000, v-tapes 3000

MEMPHIS STATE UNIVERSITY
M University Gallery, Communication & Fine Arts Bldg, Room 142, 38152. Tel 901-678-2224; FAX 901-678-5118. *Dir* Leslie L Luebbers
Open Tues - Fri 9 AM - 5 PM, Sat & Sun 1 - 5 PM, year round except between changing exhibits. No admis fee. Estab 1981 to sponsor programs & mount temporary exhibitions to expand knowledge about all periods of art with a special emphasis on contemporary art. Gallery has over 6000 sq ft of exhibition space including two permanent exhibits of ancient Egypt & traditional African art. Average Annual Attendance: 30,000. Mem: 200
Income: Financed by state appropriation, public & private support
Collections: Egyptian Hall: antiquities from 3500 BC - 7th century AD; Neil Nokes Collection of African Art, traditional West African masks & sculpture; Print Collection: contemporary prints collection of over 100 prints, an overview
Exhibitions: Changing exhibition schedule
Activities: Classes for adults & children; lectrs open to the public, 5 vis lectrs per year; tours; competitions with awards; scholarships; permanent collections lent to other institutions with proper facilities; lending collections contain 250 original art works, slides & VHS tapes
L Art History Slide Library, Jones Hall, Room 220, 38152. Tel 901-678-2938. *Slide Cur* Joyce E King
Open Mon - Fri 80 AM - 4:30 PM. Estab 1967 to provide slides for Art Faculty, University Faculty, and some outside organizations. Circ 106,000
Income: Financed by University
Library Holdings: Vols 180; Per subs 160; AV — A-tapes, cassettes, fs, lantern slides, motion pictures, rec, slides, v-tapes; Other — Clipping files, exhibition catalogs, original art works, prints, reproductions, sculpture
Collections: †35 mm slides of history of Western art, †photography

M **MISSISSIPPI RIVER MUSEUM AT MUD-ISLAND,** 125 N Front St, 38103. Tel 901-576-7230; FAX 901-576-6666. *General Mgr* Jimmy Ogle; *River Museum Mgr* Susan Elliott
Open 10 AM - 5:30 PM, Memorial Day - Labor Day 10 AM - 7 PM. Admis adults $4, children $3.25. Estab 1978 to interpret the natural and cultural history of the Mississippi River Valley. Average Annual Attendance: 150,000
Income: $350,000 (financed by city appropriation)
Collections: 2-D & 3-D pieces that interpret the natural and cultural history of the lower Mississippi River
Activities: Classes for children; dramatic and docent programs; lect open to the public, 3 - 5 vis lectr per yr; competitions; awards; book traveling exhibitions, 6 - 10 per yr; museum shop sells books, reproductions, prints

M **RHODES COLLEGE,** Jessie L Clough Art Memorial for Teaching, Clough Hall, 2000 N Parkway, 38112. Tel 901-726-3927; FAX 901-726-3917. *Cur* William M Short
Open Mon - Fri 8:30 AM - 5 PM. Estab 1951 for the study of fine & decorative arts
Collections: Japanese & woodblock prints; Asian & European textiles
Exhibitions: Selections from the Jessie L Clough Art Memorial for Teaching

MURFREESBORO

M **MIDDLE TENNESSEE STATE UNIVERSITY,** Photographic Gallery, PO Box 305, 37132. Tel 615-898-2085; FAX 615-898-5682. *Cur* Tom Jimison
Open Mon - Fri 8 AM - 4:30 PM; Sat 9 AM - noon; Sun 1 - 6 PM. No admis fee. Estab 1969 for the exhibition of outstanding photographers and beginners. Gallery has 137.5 running ft of display area. Average Annual Attendance: 8,000-10,000
Income: Financed by the University
Collections: Ansel Adams; Richard Avedon; Harold Baldwin; Harry Callahan; Geri Della Rocea de Candal; Jim Ferguson; Minor White & Others; Jim Norton; Aaron Siskind; Marianne Skogh; H H Smith; Jerry Velsman; Ed Weston by Cole; Kelly Wise
Publications: Lightyear, annually
Activities: Original objects of art lent to responsible organizations; lending collection contains photographs; traveling exhibitions organized and circulated

NASHVILLE

M **BOARD OF PARKS & RECREATION,** The Parthenon, Centennial Park, West End Ave (Mailing add: Metro Postal Service, Centennial Park Office, 37201). Tel 615-862-8431. *Dir* Wesley M Paine; *Asst Dir* Gary Pace; *Pres Board* Dr George Reichardt; *Sr Museum Guide* Timothy Cartmell
Open Tues - Sat 9 AM - 4:30 PM, Apr - Sept Sun 12:30 - 4:30 PM, cl Sun, Mon & legal holidays. Admis adult $2.50, children (4-17) $1.25, sr citizens $1.25. Estab 1897 to offer Nashville residents and tourists quality art for viewing and sale in a historical setting of significance and beauty. Central Gallery, changing exhibit gallery & James M Cowan Gallery of American Art. Average Annual Attendance: 160,000
Income: Financed by city and county taxes and donations
Collections: Cowan Collection, sixty three paintings by 19th and 20th century American artists, donated by James M Cowan; †Century III Collection, sixty two art works, purchased from area artists, juried by John Canaday in celebration of Nashville's bicentennial
Exhibitions: Exhibitions change monthly
Publications: The Cowan Catalog, Century III Catalog
Activities: Co-sponsor, with Tennessee Art League of Annual Central South Exhibition, juried show with awards given; sales shop sells books, magazines, souvenirs, prints and slides

M **CHEEKWOOD-TENNESSEE BOTANICAL GARDENS & MUSEUM OF ART** (Formerly Tennessee Botanical Gardens & Musuem of Art, Inc), 1200 Forrest Park Dr, 37205-4242. Tel 615-356-8000; FAX 615-353-2168. *Dir* John A Cherol; *Cur Coll & Exhib* Christine Kreyling; *Registrar* Elizabeth Cunningham; *Preparator* Windle Morgan; *Public Information* Joan Cirillo; *Educational Specialist* Nancy Cavener
Open Mon - Sat 9 AM - 5 PM, Sun 1 - 5 PM, Thanksgiving, Christmas, New Year's Day. Admis adults $5, children 7 - 17 $2, children under 7 free. Estab 1957 to collect, preserve & interpret American art, with special emphasis on artists of the region. Museum opened to public in 1960 in a Georgian-style mansion built in 1929 by Mr & Mrs Leslie Cheek. Originally adapted for museum use in 1960, the site underwent further renovation & adaptation in 1980. Galleries contain approx 12,000 sq ft of exhibition space, divided almost equally between installation of permanent collection & temporary, special exhibitions. Three galleries are used for temporary exhibitions. Mary Cheek Hill Gallery houses the Thompson Snuff and Medicine Bottle Collection; adjoining gallery houses the Ewers Collection of Worcester Porcelain; other permanent collection gallery installations include: Painters in Middle Tennessee, 1825-1925, An American Gallery & William Edmondson, Sculptor. Average Annual Attendance: 160,000. Mem: 8700; dues patron (family or individual) $35; annual meeting 3rd Wed in June
Income: Financed by membership, admissions, corporate & foundation grants, private gifts, several fundraising events
Collections: †American paintings & sculpture, 1750-1950; †Mid-state Tennessee paintings & sculpture, 1750-1950; †sculpture; †graphic art, all periods & schools; Oriental snuff & medicine bottles; †Worcestor Porcelain, 1750-1825; Shefields Silver, 19th & 20th century Landscape collection; Tennessee Paintings, William Edmundson
Exhibitions: (1993) The Year of the Craft: Gods, Prophets & Heroes: Sculpture by Donald DeLue; Rodin: Sculpture from the Iris & B Gerald Cantor Collections; From the Mountains to the Mississippi: The Middle Tennessee Exhibit; More Than One: Studio Production Now; English Silver: Masterpieces by Omar Ramsden from the Campbell Collection; The Craftsman Aesthetic; Breaking Boundaries: American Puppetry in the 1980s; Cheekwood National Contemporary Painting Competition. (1994) Mourning Becomes Electric: Neon

Sculptures by Lili Lakich; Drawings from the Thomas Hart Benton Trust. (1995) The Biltmore Estate: A Centennial Celebration 1895 - 1995
Publications: Brochures, catalogues, checklists, monographs, monthly newsletter, posters
Activities: Classes for adults & children; dramatic programs; docent training; workshops; poetry readings; lectures open to public, 8 - 10 vis lectrs per year; concerts; gallery talks; tours; competitions; awards; individual paintings & original objects of art lent to museums; lending collection contains original art works, paintings & sculpture; book traveling exhibitions, 10 per yr; traveling exhibitions organized and circulated to museums and cultural institutions; museum shop sells books, slides, posters; junior museum

L **Museum of Art Library,** 1200 Forrest Park Dr, 37205. Tel 615-353-2140; FAX 615-353-2168. *Librn* Virginia Khouri
Open to staff and members for reference
Library Holdings: Vols 5000; Per subs 58
Collections: Extensive snuff bottle collection

L **Botanic Hall Library,** 1200 Forrest Park Dr, 37205. Tel 615-353-2140; FAX 615-353-2168. *Librn* Muriel Connell

M **FISK UNIVERSITY MUSEUM OF ART,** University Galleries, 1000 17th Ave N, 37203. Tel 615-329-8720. *Dir* Kevin Grogan
Open Tues - Fri 10 AM - 5 PM, Sat and Sun 1 - 5 PM; cl Mon. Admis contributions requested. Estab 1949 as an education resource center for the Fisk and Nashville communities and for the promotion of the visual arts. Van Vechten Gallery houses the library, temporary exhibits & art offices; The Aaron Douglas Gallery in the library houses selections from the permanent collection of African & African- American Art. Average Annual Attendance: 24,000
Income: Financed through the University & state appropriations
Collections: Afro-American Collection; Alfred Stieglitz Collection of Modern Art; Traditional African Art Collection; Cyrus Baldridge Drawings; Carl Van Vechten Photographs; European & American Prints & Drawings
Publications: Fisk Art Report, annually
Activities: Lect open to public; gallery talks; tours; individual paintings and original objects of art lent to institutions, organizations, community groups; lending collection contains original prints and paintings; traveling exhibitions organized and circulated; sales shop sells books, catalogs, posters & reproductions

L **Florine Stettheimer Library,** 1000 17th Ave N, 37208. Tel 615-329-8720. Open Tues - Fri 10 AM - 5 PM, Sat & Sun 1 - 5 PM, cl Mon. Estab 1949. Publications are used by students and instructors for research
Library Holdings: Vols 1100; AV — A-tapes, fs, Kodachromes, lantern slides, motion pictures, slides; Other — Clipping files, exhibition catalogs, framed reproductions, original art works, pamphlets, photographs, reproductions

M **GENERAL BOARD OF DISCIPLESHIP, THE UNITED METHODIST CHURCH,** The Upper Room Chapel & Museum, 1908 Grand Ave, PO Box 189, 37202. Tel 615-340-7207; FAX 615-340-7006. *Upper Room Cur* Kathryn Kimball
Open 8 AM - 4:30 PM. No admis fee. Estab 1953 as a religious museum reflecting universal Christianity. Average Annual Attendance: 70,000
Income: Self supporting
Collections: Bibles from 1577; 2/3 Lifesize Woodcarving of da Vinci's Last Supper; †Navtivity Scenes; Ukranian Eggs; Furniture; Illuminated Manuscripts; Oriental rugs; Porcelain
Exhibitions: Woodcarving; Porcelains; Furniture; Manuscripts from 1300-1800s; Paintings-copies from several masterworks of Raphael, da Vinci, Ruebens
Publications: Upper Room Devotional Guide, every 2 months; books; magazines
Activities: Retail store sells books, magazines, slides, post cards of woodcarving

A **TENNESSEE HISTORICAL SOCIETY,** Ground Floor, War Memorial Bldg, 37243. Tel 615-741-8934; FAX 615-741-8937. *Exec Dir* Ann Toplovich
Open Mon - Fri 8 AM - 5 PM, cl national holidays. No admis fee. Estab 1849 to preserve & interpret the history of all Tennesseans. Average Annual Attendance: 700, does not include museum attendance. Mem: 2800; dues John Haywood Society $250, sustaining $50, regular $25; annual meeting in May
Income: Financed by mem dues, grants & gifts
Collections: Art, decorative art & artifacts related to Tennessee culture, history & pre-history The Tennessee State Museum holds the entire collection belonging to the Society in trust
Publications: News in Tennessee History, seasonal, Tennessee Historical Quarterly
Activities: Lect profided, 7 vis lectr per year;; individual painting & original works of art lent; sales shop sells books, magazines & reproductions

M **TENNESSEE STATE MUSEUM,** Polk Cultural Center, 505 Deaderick, 37219. Tel 615-741-2692. *Dir* Lois Riggins; *Admin Asst* Evadine McMahan; *Chief Cur of Collections* Dan Pomeroy; *Chief of Exhibits* Philip Kreger; *Cur of Education* Patricia Rasbury; *Coordr of Museum Information* Paulette Fox; *Coordr of Tennessee State Museum Foundation* Julia Holman
Open Sun 1 - 5 PM; Mon - Sat 10 AM - 5 PM, cl Christmas, Easter, Thanksgiving, New Year's Day. No admis fee. Estab 1937 to preserve and interpret the historical artifacts of Tennessee through museum exhibits and statewide outreach and educational programs. A military history museum in the War Memorial Building depicts Tennessee's involvement in modern wars (Spanish-American to World War II). Exhibits highlight life in Tennessee from early man through 1920. Gallery houses changing art and history exhibits. Maintains small reference library. Average Annual Attendance: 250,000. Mem: 700; dues $20 & up
Income: Financed by state appropriation
Purchases: Tennessee related early 19th century paintings and prints; 19th century Tennessee made silver; 19th century Tennessee made firearms
Collections: The museum collection of objects relating to Tennessee history from pre-historic times to the present. It holds in trust the collection of the Tennessee Historical Society as well as portraits and paintings of and by prominent Tennesseans; contemporary Tennessee related artists works
Exhibitions: (1991) Masterworks: Paintings from Bridgestone Museum of Art. (1993) Alex Haley; Art & Art History of Fire Arms/History of Fire Arms; Anne Frank in the World

Publications: Calendar, guarterly; exhibition catalogues
Activities: Classes for adults and children; docent training; exten dept serving statewide; individual paintings & original objects of art; originate traveling exhibitions; museum shop sells books, Tennessee crafts, items relating to the collection; junior museum

L **Library,** 505 Deaderick, 37219. Tel 615-741-2692. *Chief Cur* Dan Pomeroy
Income: Financed by State Appropriation
Library Holdings: Vols 1700; Per subs 15; AV — Slides, v-tapes; Other — Exhibition catalogs, pamphlets, photographs
Special Subjects: American Indian Art, Ceramics, Coins & Medals, Costume Design & Construction, Crafts, Decorative Arts, Dolls, Flasks & Bottles, Folk Art, Glass, Handicrafts, Historical Material, Jewelry, Laces, Painting - American, Period Rooms, Photography, Portraits, Pottery, Pre-Columbian Art, Prints

C **UNITED STATES TOBACCO MANUFACTURING COMPANY INC,** Museum of Tobacco & History, 800 Harrison St, 37203. Tel 615-271-2349; FAX 615-271-2285. *Museum Cur* David Wright
Open Mon - Sat 9 AM - 4 PM. No admis fee. Estab 1982 to preserve & display art objects related to tobacco history. Outstanding collection of tobacco-related antiques including Meerschaum pipes, tobacco containers, snuff boxes, cigar store figures, advertising art, antique pipes from America, Europe, Africa & Asia. Average Annual Attendance: 15,000
Income: Financed by Corporate Museum
Purchases: Corporate Museum
Collections: †Advertising Art; Antique Pipes; Cigar Store Figures; †Tobacco Containers
Exhibitions: (1991) Meerschaum Masterpieces: The Premiere Art of Pipes
Activities: Tours; original objects of art lent to museums; book traveling exhibitions 1 per yr; sales shop sells books, prints, reproductions

M **VANDERBILT UNIVERSITY,** Fine Arts Gallery, West End Ave at 23rd, PO Box 1801 B, 37235. Tel 615-322-2831. *Dir* Joseph S Mella
Open Mon - Fri 1 - 4 PM; Sat & Sun 1 - 5 PM, cl holidays and some University vacations. No admis fee. Estab collection 1956, gallery 1961, to provide exhibitions for the University and Nashville communities, and original art works for study by Vanderbilt students. The gallery is included in the Old Gym, built in 1880 and listed in the National Register of Historic Places. Mem: 300; dues $10 - $500
Income: Financed by university resources and Art Association dues
Collections: †Vanderbilt Collection of Western, Eastern, Ancient and Modern Cultures; Harold P Stern Collection of Oriental Art; Anna C Hoyt Collection of Old Master Prints; former Peabody College Art Collection including Kress Study Collection of Italian Renaissance Paintings
Activities: Art Association lectures open to members only; biennial art auction to benefit acquisition fund; tours

L **Arts Library,** 419 21st Ave S, 37203. Tel 615-343-7875; Elec Mail Mountsd@vuctravax(Bitnet). *Librn* Sigrid Docken Mount
Library Holdings: Vols 50,000; Per subs 300; Micro — Fiche, reels; AV — Fs, motion pictures; Other — Clipping files, exhibition catalogs, pamphlets, reproductions 6000
Special Subjects: Afro-American Art, American Indian Art, American Western Art, Anthropology, Archaeology, Decorative Arts, Ethnology, Folk Art, History of Art & Archaeology, Landscape Architecture, British 18th & 19th century landscape painting & the Norwich School

A **WATKINS INSTITUTE,** 601 Church St, 37219. Tel 615-242-1851; FAX 615-242-4278. *Dir* Steve Reed; *Art Dir* Madeline Reed
Open Mon - Thurs 9 AM - 9 PM, Fri 9 AM - 1:30 PM, cl Sat & Sun, Christmas, New Years, July 4, Labor Day, Thanksgiving Day. No admis fee. Estab 1885 as an adult education center for art, interior design, adult evening high school & courses of a general nature
Income: Financed by rent from business property
Collections: All-State Artist Collection (oldest collection of Tennessee art in the state); this is a purchase-award collection of oil, pastels, watercolors, graphics and sculpture; several other collections of lesser value
Exhibitions: Six or eight exhibitions per year
Publications: Art brochure; quarterly catalogue listing courses
Activities: Classes for adults and children; lectures open to public, 6-8 visiting lectrs per year; competitions; individual paintings lent to schools; original objects of art lent; traveling exhibitions organized and circulated

L **Library,** 601 Church St, 37219. Tel 615-242-1851; FAX 615-242-4278. *Librn* Sue Coomer
Open 9 AM - 8:30 PM. Estab 1885
Library Holdings: Vols 12,000; Per subs 15; AV — Fs, slides, v-tapes

OAK RIDGE

A **OAK RIDGE ART CENTER,** 201 Badger, PO Box 7005, 37831-7005. Tel 615-482-1441. *Pres* Alice Runtsch; *Dir* Leah Marcum-Estes
Open Tues - Fri 9 AM - 5 PM, Sat - Mon 1 - 4 PM. No admis fee. Estab 1952 to encourage the appreciation & creation of the visual arts. Two galleries house temporary exhibitions & permanent collection exhibitions, one rental gallery, classrooms & library. Average Annual Attendance: 50,000. Mem: 500; dues $25; meetings 2nd Mon of month
Income: $30,000 (financed by membership)
Collections: †The Mary & Alden Gomez Collection; Contemporary Regional Works; European Post World War II
Exhibitions: Open Show, Juried Competition (all media)
Publications: Vison, monthly bulletin
Activities: Classes for adults and children; docent training; forums; workshops; lectures open to public, 6-8 lectrs per year; recorded concerts; gallery talks; tours; competitions with awards; scholarships; individual paintings & original objects of art rented to individuals & businesses on semi-annual basis; lending collection contains 2000 books, 400 original art works, 50 VCR tapes & 1000 slides; sales shop sells original art

L **Library,** 201 Badger Rd, PO Box 7005, 37831-7005. Tel 615-482-1441. *Dir* Leah Marcum-Estes
Open to members for lending & reference
Library Holdings: Vols 2000; AV — A-tapes, fs, slides, v-tapes; Other — Exhibition catalogs, memorabilia, original art works
Special Subjects: Pottery
Publications: Monthly newsletter

SEWANEE

M **UNIVERSITY OF THE SOUTH,** University Gallery, 735 University Ave, 37375. Tel 615-598-1384; FAX 615-598-1145. *Gallery Coordr* Lane Magruder
Open Mon - Fri 10 AM - 12 PM & 1 - 3 PM, Sun 1 - 3 PM, cl holidays & non-university sessions. No admis fee. Estab 1938 to provide exhibits of broad scope to coincide with art classes. One large space with balcony, one main entry door, carpeted walls, trac lighting. Average Annual Attendance: 3000 - 5000
Exhibitions: Monthly exhibitions during school year, 1 per month; changing shows
Activities: Lect open to public, 1 - 3 vis lectr per yr; gallery talks; tours; Individual paintings & original objects of art lent to professors & administration

TEXAS

ABILENE

M **MCMURRY UNIVERSITY,** Ryan Fine Arts Center, Sayles Blvd, PO Box 8, 79697. Tel 915-691-6307. *Dept Chmn & Gallery Dir* Linda Stricklin
Open Mon - Fri 8 AM - 5 PM, cl Sat & Sun. No admis fee. Estab 1970 when building was completed. Large room overlooking larger sculpture garden. Average Annual Attendance: 2500
Income: Financed by college art budget
Collections: Artists represented include Picasso, Adolph Dehn, Frelander
Publications: Art Through the Ages (color reproductions and slides to accompany text)
Activities: Classes for adults; lectures open to the public; gallery talks; competitions; individual paintings and original objects of art lent to college offices

M **MUSEUMS OF ABILENE, INC,** 102 Cypress, 79601. Tel 915-673-4587. *Exec Dir* Terence Keane; *Deputy Dir* Debbie Bolls; *Cur* Greg Tipton; *Cur* Hollye Yates
Open Tues - Sat 10 AM - 5 PM, Sun 1 - 5 PM, clo Mon. Admis adults $2, children $1. Estab 1937 as an art and history education institution. Art, History & Children's museums located in restored 1909 hotel, 4 floors, 50,000 sq ft. Average Annual Attendance: 60,000. Mem: 1200; dues $35 & up; monthly meeting 2nd Mon
Income: Financed by membership, grants, fund-raising events
Collections: †American Paintings & Prints; †Local History; †T&P Railway Collection
Exhibitions: Regular schedule of temporary & long-term exhibitions, including contemporary art
Publications: Annual report; brochures; quarterly newsletter
Activities: Educ dept; classes for adults & children; docent training; lect open to the public, 2 - 5 vis lectr per year; gallery talks; tours; competitions with prizes; scholarships; individual paintings & original works of art lent to other museums; lending collection contains original art works, original prints, paintings, photographs, sculptures, slides; book traveling exhibitions 2 - 3 per year; museum shop sells books, magazines, reproductions, prints, slides, games, toys, crafts

ALBANY

M **OLD JAIL ART CENTER,** Hwy 6 S, Rte 1, PO Box 1, 76430. Tel 915-762-2269. *Chair* Nancy E Green; *VChair* Donald Lucas; *Treas* James H Cotter; *Dir* Ellen G Oppenheim
Open Tues - Sat 10 AM - 5 PM, Sun 2 - 5 PM. No admis fee. Estab 1980 to collect & display contemporary art of US & Europe. Four galleries in old 1877 jail, 3 additional new galleries plus small atrium gallery. Courtyard for outdoor sculpture. Average Annual Attendance: 30,000. Mem: 636; dues $25; annual meetings in Fall
Income: $175,000
Collections: †Antique Furniture & Pre-Columbian; Sculpture; †Paintings & graphics; †Photography; †Oriental pottery & Chinese tomb figures
Exhibitions: Paintings from the permanent collection; Terra Cotta tomb figures - the Tang collection
Publications: Exhibit catalogs
Activities: Classes for adults & children; dramatic programs; docent training; lectures for members only, 2 vis lectrs per yr; individual paintings & original objects of art lent; lending collection contains 400 paintings & some sculpture; book traveling exhibitions, annually; originate traveling exhibitions; sales shop sells books, reproductions & notecards

L **Green Research Library,** Hwy 6 S, Rte 1, PO Box 1, 76430. Tel 915-762-2269. Open Tues - Sat 10 AM - 5 PM, Sun 2 - 5 PM. Estab 1984. For reference only
Library Holdings: Vols 2000; Per subs 4

AMARILLO

AMARILLO ART ASSOCIATION

A **Amarillo Art Center,** 2200 S Van Buren, PO Box 447, 79178. Tel 806-371-5050; FAX 806-371-5370. *Dir & Cur* Patrick McCracken; *Cur Education* Mark Morey; *Admin Asst* Jena McFall; *Registrar* Reba Jones
Open Tues - Fri 10 AM - 5 PM, Thurs until 9:30 PM, Sat & Sun 1 - 5 PM. No admis fee. Estab 1972 for visual arts. Gallery 100, 90 x 30 ft, atrium area 45 ft; Gallery 200 & 203, 90 x 32 ft, 11 ft ceiling; Gallery 305 & 307, each 32 x 28 ft, 10 ft ceiling. Average Annual Attendance: 60,000. Mem: 1800; dues $50-$5000, family $35, single $25
Income: Financed by membership, college, endowment sponsorship program & exhibition underwriting
Special Subjects: Advertising Design, Aesthetics, Afro-American Art, American Indian Art, American Western Art, Antiquities-Byzantine, Antiquities-Egyptian, Antiquities-Greek, Antiquities-Oriental, Antiquities-Roman, Archaeology, Architecture, Art Education, Art History, Asian Art
Collections: †Contemporary American drawings, paintings, prints & sculpture
Exhibitions: (1990) East & West of the Divide; 19th Century Paintings of the American West (1991) Amarillo Competition; Mystic References: 19th Century Visionary Art
Publications: Annual Report; Calendar of Events, bimonthly; catalogs on exhibits; brochures, as needed
Activities: Classes for adults & children; docent training; Lectrs open to public; 2 vis lectr per year; gallery talks; tours; individual paintings & original objects of art lent to qualified institutions; originate traveling exhibitions; museum shop sells books, original art, reproductions, prints, posters, crafts
L **Library,** 2200 S Van Buren, PO Box 447, 79178. Tel 806-371-5050; FAX 806-371-5370. *Librn* Mary Van Dyke
For reference only
Library Holdings: Vols 1500; Per subs 18

ARLINGTON

M **UNIVERSITY OF TEXAS AT ARLINGTON,** Center for Research & Contemporary Arts, 700 W Second St, 76013. Tel 817-273-3110; FAX 817-273-2857. *Dir* Al Harris
Open Mon - Thurs 9 AM - 4 PM, Tues 5 - 9 PM, cl Sat & major holidays. No admis fee. Estab 1975 on completion of Fine Arts Complex. The Gallery serves the entire university; exhibitions are contemporary. Main Gallery is air-cooled, carpeted, fabric wall covered with incandescent light. Average Annual Attendance: 15,000
Income: $56,000 (financed by state appropriation and private gifts)
Collections: Very small collection mainly American and Contemporary
Exhibitions: UTA Art Faculty Exhibit; A Video Invitational, Selected Work by Steiva Vasulka; Bill Viola; & Tom Giebink; A Photo Invitational, Selected Work by Geanna Merola; Gary Monroe; & Lew Thomas; A Small Sculpture Invitational, Selected Work by Nancy Chambers; Thelma Coles; Nick DeVries; Joe Havel; Leslie Leuppe; Randy Long; Marjorie Schick; & Pat Tillman Graduating Art Senior Exhibition
Activities: Undergraduate course on museum techniques; lect open to the public, 3 vis lectr per yr; catalogs on sale

AUSTIN

M **AUSTIN CHILDREN'S MUSEUM,** 1501 W Fifth, 78703. Tel 512-472-2494; FAX 512-472-2499. *Dir* Deborah Edward; *Dir Public Relations* Deidre Strong
Open Wed - Sat 10 AM - 5 PM, Sun noon - 5 PM. Admis adults $2.50, children $1.50, children under 2 free. Estab 1983 to provide hands on exhibits & activities for children & families focusing on everyday science & technology & the human body
Collections: Mexican Folk Art
Exhibitions: (1991) Your Are Here; Wondering through the Solar Systems

M **LAGUNA GLORIA ART MUSEUM,** 3809 W 35th St, PO Box 5568, 78763. Tel 512-458-8192; FAX 512-454-9408. *Dir* Daniel E Stetson; *Dir Prog* Judith Sims; *Dir Development* Darcy Olesen; *Dir Public Information* Teresa Kendrick; *Dir Admin* Jack Nokes; *Interim Dir & Cur* Peter Mears
Open Tues - Sat, 10 AM - 5 PM, Thurs 10 AM - 9 PM, Sun 1 - 5 PM. No admis fee. Three galleries downstairs, one upstairs. Average Annual Attendance: 90,000. Mem: 4000; dues $1000 - $25; annual meeting September
Income: Financed by City of Austin, Fiesta, memberships, annual fund, grants, Art School, corporate donations, special events
Special Subjects: 20th Century American Art
Exhibitions: Changing exhibitions of 20th Century American Art, its roots and antecedents
Publications: Calendar, bi-monthly; Estate-Planning, quarterly
Activities: Art School classes for children and adults; cultural and educational programs in conjunction with exhibitions; museum guides program; art after school; museum shop

A **MEXIC-ARTE MUSEUM,** 419 Congress Ave, PO Box 2632, 78768. Tel 512-480-9373; FAX 512-480-8626. *Co-Dir* Sylvia Orozzo; *Co-Dir* Pio Pulido
Open Tues - Sat 11 AM - 6 PM, Mon by appointment. Estab 1984 to help develop the arts by production & presenting high quality exhibits, performances & programs. Average Annual Attendance: 100,000
Collections: Graphic prints from workshop of popular graphics from Mexico; Contemporary art work in all disciplines with a focus on culturally diverse communities
Activities: Children's hands-on activities; panel discussions; lect open to public; gallery talks; awards; New Forms Regional Initiative Grants Program; original objects of art lent to other arts facilities; lending collection contains 564 photographs; museum shop sells books, magazines, reproductions, folk art

M **ELISABET NEY MUSEUM,** 304 E 44th, 78751. Tel 512-458-2255. *Cur* Mary Collins Blackmon
Open Wed - Sat 10 AM - 5 PM, Sun noon - 5 PM. No admis fee. Estab 1908 to preserve & exhibit the studio & works of Elisabet Ney. Administered by the city of Austin. Eclectic limestone castle, one of four 19th century American sculpture

studios to survive intact with its contents. Average Annual Attendance: 12,000
Income: $70,000 (financed by city appropriation)
Collections: Works of Elizabet Ney in the form of original plaster casts, supplemented by bronze and marble works and tools, furnishings and memorabilia; nineteenth century sculpture
Publications: Sursum (annotated letters of Elizabet Ney)
Activities: Classes for adults; docent training; concerts; gallery talks; tours; original objects of art lent to museums; lending collection contains 300 books, 200 original art works, paintings, photographs, 75 sculpture, 200 slides; museum shop sells books
L **Library,** 304 E 44th, 78751. Tel 512-458-2255.
Open Wed - Sat 10 AM - 5 PM, Sun noon - 5 PM. Estab 1908 to collect background material on subjects relevant to the Museum's history and period. For reference only
Library Holdings: Vols 330; Per subs 7; Letters; AV — Slides; Other — Clipping files, exhibition catalogs, manuscripts, memorabilia, original art works, pamphlets, photographs
Special Subjects: Art Education, Art History, Bronzes, Furniture, Historical Material, Manuscripts, Portraits, Sculpture, 19th Century Sculpture; Elizabet Ney
Exhibitions: A Life in Art; Elizabet Ney in Austin
Publications: SURSUM, collected letters of Elizabet Ney
Activities: Classes for adults and children; dramatic programs; docent training; AV programs; lectures open to public, 3-5 vis lectr per year; concerts; gallery talks; tours; exten dept serves Austin area school systems

M **SAINT EDWARD'S UNIVERSITY,** Fine Arts Exhibit Program, 78704. Tel 512-448-8400; FAX 512-448-8492. *Dir* Connie Cabezas
Open Mon - Fri 8 AM - 6 PM, Sun 1 - 5 PM. No admis fee. Estab 1961 to present for the university population and general public a monthly schedule of exhibits in the visual arts, as a means of orientation toward established and current trends in art styles in terms of their historical-cultural significance and aesthetic value, through teaching exhibitions, art films, public and private collections from distributing and compiling agencies, museums, galleries and artists. Average Annual Attendance: 10,000
Exhibitions: Annual and art student exhibitions
Activities: Classes; lect, one visiting lectr per year; tours; literature

A **TEXAS FINE ARTS ASSOCIATION,** 3809-B W 35th St, 78703. Tel 512-453-5312. *Dir* Sandra Gregor; *Asst to Dir* Emily Horowitz
Open Mon - Fri 8:30 AM - 5:30 PM. Estab 1922. Purpose is to promote the growth, development, & appreciation of contemporary visual arts in Texas. Average Annual Attendance: 20,000. Mem: 1300
Income: $180,000 (financed by endowment, mem, government grants, earned income)
Exhibitions: Two annual national juried survey exhibitions, one of which is always new American talent; an all media exhibition shown at Laguna Gloria Art Museum, Austin's Museum of 20th Century American Art
Publications: Exhibition catalogs; quarterly newsletter
Activities: Lectures open to public, 3 vis lectrs per year; originate traveling exhibitions to tour in Texas

UNIVERSITY OF TEXAS AT AUSTIN
L **Fine Arts Library,** 23rd & Trinity, 78713-7330. Tel 512-495-4480. *Fine Arts Librn* Marcia M Parsons
Open Mon - Thurs 8 AM - 11 PM; Fri 8 AM - 5 PM; Sat 10 AM - 5 PM; Sun 2 - 11 PM. Estab 1948 to support teaching & research in Fine Arts fields including PhD level in art history, & to the master's level in art education & studio art. For lending. Circ 300,000
Income: Financed by state appropriation
Library Holdings: Vols 160,000; Per subs 3500; Micro — Fiche, reels; AV — A-tapes, cassettes, rec, v-tapes; Other — Exhibition catalogs
M **Archer M Huntington Art Gallery,** College of Fine Arts, 23rd & San Jacinto Sts, 78713-7330. Tel 512-471-7324. *Dir* Eric McCready; *Asst Dir* Jessie Higtie; *Asst Dir* Becky Duval Reese; *Cur of Prints and Drawings* Judith Keller; *Educational Coordr* Susan M Mayer; *Educational Cur* J Baber
Open Mon - Sat 9 AM - 5 PM, Sun 1 - 5 PM. No admis fee. Estab 1963 to serve the students and faculty of the university and the general public. Galleries in the art building house temporary exhibitions; galleries in the Harry Ransom Center house the permanent collections. Average Annual Attendance: 125,000. Mem: 650; dues $40 & up
Collections: †Greek and Roman art; †19th & 20th century American paintings, including James and Mari Michener Collection of 20th Century American Art and the C R Smith Collection of Western American Painting; contemporary Australian paintings; †20th century Latin American art; †prints and drawings from all periods
Publications: Exhibition catalogues; children's publications
Activities: Classes for adults; project for gifted and talented children; docent training; lect open to public; concerts; gallery talks; tours; exten dept serves Texas and the region; individual paintings and original objects of art are lent to other museums; originate traveling exhibitions to other university art museums and city museums; museum shop sells books, reproductions
L **Harry Ransom Humanities Research Center,** 21st & Guadalupe, PO Box 7219, 78713. Tel 512-471-8944; FAX 512-471-9646. *Dir* Thomas F Staley, PhD; *Assoc Dir* Sally Leach, MLIS
Open 9 AM - 5 PM. Library estab 1957 for reference only
Income: Financed by endownment, mem, city & state appropriation
Library Holdings: Vols 1,000,000; Other — Manuscripts, photographs, prints
Exhibitions: (1992) The Bebop Revolution; The Imagist Revolution. (1993) The Art of Letters
Publications: The Library Chronicle, quarterly

A **WOMEN AND THEIR WORK,** 1137 W Sixth St, 78703. Tel 512-477-1064; FAX 512-477-1090. *Dir* Chris Cowden; *Operations Mgr* Leslie Wilkes; *Asst Dir* Cindy Noe; *Prog Coordr* Genny Duncan
Open Mon - Fri 9 AM - 5 PM. Estab 1976 to promote recognition & appreciation of women's art. Average Annual Attendance: 7500. Mem: 175; dues $25

Income: $140,000 (financed by endowment, mem, city & state appropriation, private foundations & corporations)
Collections: Ties That Bind: Photography; Cuban Film Posters; Red River Women's Press Posters
Publications: Membership Report, quarterly
Activities: Workshops & symposia; lectures open to public, 3-4 vis lectrs per yr; competitions with awards; book traveling exhibitions; originate traveling exhibitions, circulate to Dallas, Snyder, Houston, Victoria, & San Antonio

BANDERA

M FRONTIER TIMES MUSEUM, PO Box 1918, 78003. Tel 512-796-3864. *Pres* Pat D'Spain; *Cur & Mgr* Wanda Fitzpatrick
Open Mon - Sat 10 AM - 4:30 PM, Sun 1 - 4:30 PM. Admis adults $1.50, children under 12 years $.25 (free when accompanied by teachers). Estab 1933 to preserve records, photographs, and artifacts of the American West with emphasis on the local Texas hill country area. Average Annual Attendance: 12,000. Mem: 25; no dues; Board of Directors meets 4 times a year
Income: $20,000 (financed by endowment, $8000 from F B Doane Foundation)
Collections: F B Doane Collection of Western Paintings; Louisa Gordon Collection of Antiques, including bells from around the world; J Marvin Hunter Collection of Photographs, Artifacts, Memorabilia of American West and the Texas Hill Country; Photograph Collection; many rare items
Exhibitions: Monthly one-man shows by Texas artists whose work coincides with the theme of the museum
Activities: Tours; museum shop sells books, Indian dolls, arrowheads, bolos and wildlife posters

BEAUMONT

M ART MUSEUM OF SOUTHEAST TEXAS, 500 Main St, 77701. Tel 409-832-3432. *Exec Dir* Shelia Stewart; *Asst to Dir* JoNell Chance; *Cur Art* Lynn Castle; *Registrar* Helen Graves; *Cur Education* Suzy Bruce; *Member Secy* Stephen Mayfield; *Museum Secy* Cindy Forbes; *Admin Asst* Patsy Bittain; *Public Relations* Ann Reece
Open Mon - Sat 9 AM - 5 PM, Thurs evening until 8 PM, Sun noon - 5 PM, cl major holidays. No admis fee. Estab 1950 as a non-profit institution to serve the community- through the visual experience and its interpretation as an instrument for education, cultural enrichment and aesthetic enjoyment. The museum has 2400 sq ft of exhibition space, four galleries. Average Annual Attendance: 65,000. Mem: 1223; dues $20 - $10,000; annual meeting May
Income: Financed by endowment, mem, city appropriation, Kaleidoscope, grants, museum shop & contributions
Collections: 19th and 20th century American folk art, painting, sculpture, graphics & photography
Publications: Newsletter, bi-monthly
Activities: Classes for adults & children; docent training; lect open to public, 9 vis lectr per year; slide lect; gallery talks; tours; sponsors competitions with awards; scholarships offered; individual paintings and original objects of art lent to other institutions; traveling exhibitions organized and circulated; museum shop sells books, original art and reproductions
L Library, 500 Main St, 77701. Tel 409-832-8508; FAX 409-832-8508. *Educ Cur* Suzy Bruce; *Librn* Bea Holloway
Open Tues - Fri 10 AM - 5:30 PM, Sat & Sun 2 - 5 PM. Open to staff and docents for reference only
Library Holdings: Vols 3400; AV — Slides; Other — Exhibition catalogs
Publications: Bi-monthly newsletter; exhibition catalogs

A THE ART STUDIO INC, 700 Orleans, 77701. Tel 409-838-5393. *Dir* Greg Busceme; *Admin Asst* Terri Fox
Open Mon - Fri 10 AM - 5 PM, Sat by appointment. No admis fee. Estab 1983 to provide workspace for area artist/community outreach. One gallery 60 x 30 for exhibitions; one sales gallery; 2-D & 3-D work specializing in ceramics. Mem: 1800; dues $15-$250
Income: $70,000 (financed by mem, individual contributions)
Exhibitions: Feet First: Resident Artist Exhibition
Publications: Studio Ink, 3 timea a year; Thoughtcrime, Poetry Magazine, 3 times a year
Activities: Educ dept; classes for adults & children; lect open to public; concerts; competitions with prizes; scholarships & fels; artmobile; retail store sells original art

M BEAUMONT ART LEAGUE, 5775 Regina Lane, 77706. Tel 409-892-6320. *Office Mgr* Maggie Wilkerson; *Pres* Sandra Laurette; *VPres* John Gordon; *Treas* Nancy Fitzpatrick
Open Tues - Fri 10 AM - 4 PM, Sun 2 - 4 PM. No admis fee. Estab 1943 to promote fine art through exhibitions & art education. Two spacious galleries with color corrected lighting & spot lights. Average Annual Attendance: 2500. Mem: 325; dues $10, $20, $30, $35, $60, $100, $500; annual meeting in May
Income: $26,000 (financed by mem, donations & fundraising)
Purchases: Five paintings through purchase awards from juried competition
Collections: Permanent collection of paintings, photography & sculpture (87 pieces)
Exhibitions: (1992) Southeast Texas Woodcarver's Exhibition; Winner of Membership Show 1991 - Brett Barham; Membership Show. (1993) Portrait Show; 3-D Show; Tri-State 1993; Neches River Festival Exhibition; Gulf Coast Educators; Photography 1993 - Juried Competition
Publications: Newletters, 10 per year; class schedules, 4 per year; show entry forms & invitations
Activities: Classes for adult & children; lect open to public, 1 - 2 per year; competitions with awards; fine art sales gallery

A BEAUMONT ARTS COUNCIL, 3360 Beard St, 77703. Tel 409-892-0336. *Chmn* Jeannette Pennell Doiron
Estab 1969 to foster total esthetic involvement in the community and improve communications among cultural organizations
Activities: Sponsored forum for city election candidates to discuss their attitudes toward cultural environment

M MAMIE MCFADDIN WARD HERITAGE HISTORIC FOUNDATION, 1906 McFaddin Ave, 77701. Tel 409-832-1906. *Dir* Gary N Smith; *Cur of Coll* Jessica Foy; *Adminr* Matthew White; *Buildings & Grounds Supv* Kenneth Saunderfer
Open Tues - Sat 10 AM - 4 PM, Sun 1 - 4 PM, cl Mon. Admis adults $3, sr citizens $1.50, children under 12 not admitted. Estab 1982 to preserve, publish, exhibit & present knowledge of the period. Historic house museum with original collections of decorative arts of the period 1890-1950 as left by original owners; 17 rooms, 12,800 sq ft wood frame Beaux Arts Colonial Home with carriage house. Average Annual Attendance: 10,000
Income: $700,000 (financed by endowment)
Collections: American-made furniture; Continental European ceramics; Oriental rugs; period glass; period silver & porcelain
Publications: Brochure; souvenir booklet; Viewpoints, quarterly
Activities: Classes for adults; docent training; lectures open to public, 4-6 vis lectrs per yr; museum shop sells magazines, reproductions, prints & slides
L McFaddin-Ward House, 1906 McFaddin Ave, 77701. Tel 409-832-1906.
Open Tues - Sat 10 AM - 4 PM, Sun 1 PM - 4 PM. Admis adults $3. Estab 1982 for staff & docent study. For reference only. Average Annual Attendance: 10,000
Income: Foundation funded
Library Holdings: Vols 300; Per subs 30; AV — A-tapes, slides, v-tapes; Other — Clipping files, memorabilia, pamphlets, photographs
Special Subjects: Decorative arts, 1890-1950
Collections: Decorative arts
Activities: Classes for adults & children; docent training; lectures open to the public, 3 vis lectrs pr yr; museum shop sells books, magazines, slides

BROWNSVILLE

M BROWNSVILLE ART LEAGUE MUSEUM, 230 Neale Dr, 78520. Tel 210-542-0941. *Dir* May Verkaik; *Librn* Claire Hines
Open Mon - Fri 9:30 AM - 3 PM, occasionally Sun; cl Thanksgiving & Christmas. No admis fee, donations requested. Estab 1935, museum opened 1977 to offer cultural advantages to lower Rio Grande Valley. Permanent collection on rotating basis housed in the Clara Ely Gallery, 90 ft x 14 ft; loan exhibitions and members' work in Octavia Arneson Gallery, a 90 ft x 26 ft gallery; student work in the Ruth Young McGonigle Gallery. Average Annual Attendance: 3000. Mem: 216; dues $15 sustaining, $45 active, $65 family; meetings 1st Thurs of each month
Collections: Paintings by H A DeYoung, M Enagnit, Augustus John, Dale Nichols, Fredric Taubes, Hauward Veal, James McNeil Whistler, N C Wyeth, Milford Zornes, Marc Chagall, William Hogarth, Ted Goe
Exhibitions: RGB arts & crafts
Publications: Brush Strokes, six per year
Activities: Classes for adults & children; workshops by vis artists; lectures open to public; tours; International Art Show competition; purchase & monetary awards; individual paintings lent to schools; originate traveling exhibitions

CANYON

M PANHANDLE-PLAINS HISTOICAL SOCIETY MUSEUM, 2401 Fourth Ave, 79015. Tel 806-656-2244; FAX 806-656-2250. *Dir* Walter R Davis II; *Asst to the Dir* Diane Brake
Open Mon - Sat 9 AM - 5 PM, Sun 2 - 6 PM, cl New Years Day, Thanksgiving, Christmas. No admis fee. Estab 1921 to preserve history of the region, including all phases of history, fine arts and natural sciences. Average Annual Attendance: 125,000. Mem: 1000; dues contributing $1000, life $500, annual $20, student $10; annual meeting May
Income: $500,000 (financed by state)
Collections: Over 1300 paintings by early & contemporary American Painters; 19th century European painters
Exhibitions: (1993) Edward R Roberts: Panhandle Photographer; Archaeology of the Texas Panhandle: 1907 - 1992; New Mexico Art & Panhandle Collection; Women Artists of Texas 1850 - 1950; John Steuart Curry's America; Studer Collection
Publications: Panhandle-Plains Historical Review, annually
Activities: Classes for adults & children; dramatic programs; docent training; outreach programs for public schools; lectures open to the public, 4-6 vis lectrs per yr; gallery talks; tours; individual paintings & original objects of art lent to museums only, lending collection includes 1300 paintings; book traveling exhibitions, 1-2 per yr; museum shop sells books, reproductions, prints, slides
L Library, 2401 Fourth Ave, 79015. Tel 806-656-2261; FAX 806-656-2250. *Archivist & Librn* Claire Kuehn
Reference library
Library Holdings: Vols 20,000; Per subs 250; Other — Photographs

COLLEGE STATION

M TEXAS A & M UNIVERSITY, University Center Galleries, PO Box J-3, 77844. Tel 409-845-8501. *Dir Art Exhib* Open; *Registrar Art* Cathy Hastedt
Open Tues - Fri 9 AM - 8 PM, Sat - Sun noon - 6 PM. No admis fee. Estab 1974 to bring art exhibits of state and national significance to Texas A & M University
Income: Financed by university funds
Collections: Paintings by Texas artists
Activities: Docent training; lectures open to the public, 2 vis lectr per yr; gallery talks; tours; individual paintings and original objects of art lent to qualified exhibitors and to publishers for use in books or catalogues
A Visual Arts Committee, Memorial Student Center, PO Box J-1, 77844-9081. Tel 409-845-9252. *Chmn* Clover Cochran; *Gallery Coordr* Griseloa Campa
Open daily 8 AM - 8 PM. No admis fee. Estab 1989. Gallery is 35 x 35 ft with movable hanging partitions and lighting; two exterior walls are glass for partial viewing after hours. Mem: 94
Income: Financed by student service fees allotment
Purchases: 2-3 works

Exhibitions: Annual Juried Student Competition
Publications: Exhibition brochures
Activities: Educ dept; classes for adults; Lect open to public, 1 vis lectr per year; gallery talks; tours; sponsor competitions; book traveling exhibitions, 1 - 2 per year

COLORADO CITY

M COLORADO CITY HISTORICAL MUSEUM, 183 W Third St, 79512. Tel 915-728-8285. *Pres* Jake Merritt; *Cur* Ruby Cawthron
Open Tues - Sat 2 - 5 PM, cl Mon. No admis fee
Income: Financed by city appropriation

COMMERCE

M EAST TEXAS STATE UNIVERSITY, University Gallery, 75429. Tel 903-886-5207; FAX 903-886-5415. *Dir* Barbara Frey
Open Mon - Fri 9 AM - 5 PM. No admis fee. Estab 1977 to house all student exhibitions; 9-month exhibition calendar of exchange and traveling shows. Gallery 55 x 69 ft
Income: Financed by state appropriation
Collections: Collection of Student Work
Activities: Lect open to the public, 30 vis lectr per yr; gallery talks; tours; competitions; individual paintings and original objects of art lent to regional citizens; traveling exhibitions organized and circulated; sales shop selling original art

CORPUS CHRISTI

M ART COMMUNITY CENTER, Art Center of Corpus Christi, 100 Shoreline, 78401. Tel 512-884-6406. *Dir* Alley Josey; *Admin Asst* Kendall Peterson
Open Tues - Fri 10 AM - 4 PM, Sat & Sun 1 - 5 PM. No admis fee. Estab 1972 to promote & support local artists. Average Annual Attendance: 7500. Mem: 700, dues $10-$15; annual meeting in June
Income: $75,000 (financed by city appropriation, exhibit fees & sales commissions)
Exhibitions: Monthly exhibits by member groups; Annual Dimension Show
Activities: Adult classes; lectures open to public; competitions with awards; retail store sells books, prints, original art

M ART MUSEUM OF SOUTH TEXAS, 1902 N Shoreline Dr, 78401. Tel 512-884-3844. *Cur* Margaret Gillham; *Adminr* Marilyn Smith
Open Tues - Sat 10 AM - 5 PM; Sat & Sun noon - 5 PM, cl Mon, New Year's, Christmas, Thanksgiving. Admis fee. Estab 1960 as a non-profit organization offering a wide range of programs to the South Texas community in an effort to fulfill its stated purpose to stimulate and encourage the fullest possible understanding and appreciation of the fine arts in all forms. A large central area, the Great Hall, and a small gallery. The sky-lighted Upper Gallery on the second floor level has over 1900 sq ft of space. Average Annual Attendance: 100,000. Mem: 1200; dues $10 - $50
Income: $900,000 (financed by membership, city and state appropriations, school district)
Collections: Works on Paper (permanent drawing collection); paintings; sculpture; graphics; photographs, Mexican folk art
Exhibitions: (1992) Of God's & Kings; Annual Christmas Tree Forest. (1993) Audubon's Birds of America; Palmer Hayden & Black Experience; South Texas Show; Contemporary Glass
Publications: Exhibition catalogs
Activities: Classes for adults and children; docent training;; lectures open to public, 8-12 vis lectrs per year; concerts; gallery talks; tours; museum shop sells books, magazines, original art, reproductions, prints, records, clothes, memorabilia
L Library, 1902 N Shoreline Dr, 78401. Tel 512-884-3844.
Open Tues - Fri 10 AM - 5 PM. Estab 1965, to provide reference information for visitors to museum and docent students. For reference only
Income: $2723
Purchases: $2100
Library Holdings: Vols 3000; Per subs 15; AV — A-tapes, cassettes, Kodachromes, slides, v-tapes; Other — Clipping files, exhibition catalogs, pamphlets, photographs, reproductions
Special Subjects: 19th & 20th century American Art History

M CORPUS CHRISTI STATE UNIVERSITY, Weil Art Gallery, Center for the Arts, 6300 Ocean Dr, 78412. Tel 512-994-2314, Ext 314. *Dir* Dr Carey Rote
Open Mon - Fri, cl school holidays. No admis fee. Estab 1979 to provide high quality art exhibitions to the university and the public. Average Annual Attendance: 10,000
Income: Financed by private and state funding
Purchases: Corpus Christi Star, Vernon Fisher
Collections: The Lee Goodman Collection
Exhibitions: Benho Huerta; Faculty Art Exhibit; Student Exhibition; Touched by Man: Landscape Photographs from Around the World; The Oso Bay Biennial VI: The Human Image
Activities: Classes for adults and children; dramatic programs; docent training; lectures open to the public; gallery talks; tours; scholarships; extension dept serves regional and local communities

M DEL MAR COLLEGE, Joseph A Cain Memorial Art Gallery, 101 Baldwin, 78404-3897. Tel 512-886-1216. *Dir* William E Lambert
Open Mon - Thurs 9 AM - 4 PM, Fri 9 AM - noon. No admis fee. Estab 1932 to teach art and provide exhibition showcase for college and community. Gallery consists of 1750 sq ft plus other smaller areas. Average Annual Attendance: 2000
Income: Financed by state appropriation & private donations
Collections: Purchases from Annual National Drawings and Small Sculpture Show
Exhibitions: 27th Annual Exhibition
Activities: Originate traveling exhibitions

M MUSEUM OF ORIENTAL CULTURES, 418 Peoples St, 78401. Tel 512-883-1303. *Exec Dir* Jean Neri; *Education Dir* Catherine LaCroix
Open Tues - Sat 10 AM - 4 PM, also by appointment, cl New Years, Easter, Memorial Day, July 4, Labor Day, Thanksgiving & Christmas. Admis adults $1, sr citizens $.75, student $.50, children $.35. Estab 1973. Maintains 600 vol library for research. Mem: Dues patron $1000, sustaining $500, supporting $100, family $50, individual $25, senior citizen $15
Income: Financed by private donations & grants
Collections: Buddhist decorative arts; oriental & decorative arts including Hakata dolls, porcelains, metal ware, cloisonne and lacquerware; oriental fan collection
Publications: Quarterly newsletter
Activities: Educ dept; lectures; tours; films; culture festivals

DALLAS

M BIBLICAL ARTS CENTER, 7500 Park Lane, PO Box 12727, 75225. Tel 214-691-4661; FAX 214-691-4752. *Dir* Ronnie L Roese
Open Tues - Sat 10 AM - 5 PM, Sun 1 - 5 PM, cl New Years Day, Thanksgiving, Christmas Eve and Christmas Day. Admis adults $3.75, sr citizens $3, children 6-12 $2.00, exhibition free. Estab 1966
Collections: Joseph Boggs Beale's Biblical Illustrations; founder's collection of oriental art; Torger Thompson's Miracle at Pentecost painting & Miracle at Pentecost pilot painting
Publications: Books, Creation of a Masterpiece
Activities: Educ programs; docent training; tours; individual paintings & original objects of art lent; museum shop sells books, reproductions, prints, slides

A DALLAS HISTORICAL SOCIETY, Hall of State, Fair Park, PO Box 150038, 75315. Tel 214-421-4500. *Dir* Dr R Peter Mooz
Open Mon - Sat 9 AM - 5 PM, Sun 1 - 5 PM. No admis fee. Estab 1922 to collect & preserve materials relative to the history of Texas and Dallas. The Hall of State is an example of Art-Deco architecture; exhibition space totals 5000 sq ft. Average Annual Attendance: 130,000. Mem: 2000; dues $50; annual meeting in Apr
Income: Financed by membership and city appropriation
Collections: Texas/Dallas Gallery; Dallas Fashion Gallery
Publications: Dallas Historical Society Register, newsletter quarterly; Dallas Rediscovered: A Photographic Chronicle of Urban Expansion; When Dallas Became a City: Letters of John Milton McCoy, 1870-1881; A Guide to Fair Park, Dallas
Activities: In-class programs; dramatic programs; docent training; summer children's workshops; gallery talks; tours; awards; exten dept; individual & original objects of art lent; book traveling exhibitions, 4 per yr; originate traveling exhibitions
L Research Center Library, Hall of State, Fair Park, PO Box 150038, 75315. Tel 214-421-4500.
For reference only
Library Holdings: Vols 1600; Per subs 20; Archives, pages 2,000,000; Micro — Cards, reels; AV — Cassettes, fs, motion pictures, rec, slides, v-tapes; Other — Clipping files, exhibition catalogs, framed reproductions, memorabilia, original art works, pamphlets, photographs, prints, reproductions, sculpture
Collections: R M Hayes Photographic Collection of Texas Historic Sites; J J Johnson & C E Arnold Photographs of Turn-of-the-Century Dallas; Frank Reaugh Paintings; Allie Tennant Papers; Texas Centennial Papers; WWI & WWII posters; Texas Centennial posters
Exhibitions: All Together; WWI Posters of the Allied Nations; Fair Park Moderne: Art & Architecture of the 1936 Texas Centennial Exposition
Publications: Exhibit catalogs

M DALLAS MUSEUM OF ART, 1717 N Harwood, 75201. Tel 214-922-1200; FAX 214-954-0174. *Dir* Dr Richard Brettell; *Assoc Cur American Art* Eleanor Jones; *Cur Textiles* Carol Robbins; *Cur Decorative Arts* Charles Venable; *Sr Cur Western Art* Susan Barnes; *Sr Cur Non-Western Art* Emily J Sano; *Cur Exhib* Anna McFarland; *Assoc Cur Contemporary Art* Annegreth Nill; *Assoc Cur Ancient Art* Dr Anne R Bromberg; *Publications* Meg Hanlon; *Registrar* Kimberly Bush
Open Tues, Wed & Fri 11 AM - 4 PM, Sat & Sun 11 AM - 5 PM, Thurs 11 AM - 9 PM, cl Mon. No admis fee. Estab 1903 to purchase and borrow works of art from all periods for the aesthetic enjoyment and education of the public. Fifteen galleries for permanent collection; five for temporary exhibition. Average Annual Attendance: 350,000. Mem: 22,000 dues $30 - $10,000; annual meeting May
Income: $7,200,000 (financed by endowment, membership and city appropriation)
Purchases: $1,000,000
Collections: †European and American painting and sculpture; †ancient Mediterranean, Pre-Columbian, African, Oceanic and Japanese art; †decorative arts; †drawings; †prints; American furniture
Publications: Newsletter, bimonthly; annual report; president's newsletter; exhibition catalogs; Dallas Museum of Art Bulletin quarterly
Activities: Classes for adults and children; docent training; lect open to public, 10 vis lectr per year; concerts; gallery talks; tours; exten dept serving Dallas County; artmobile; individual paintings & original objects of art lent to other museums; book traveling exhibitions; originate traveling exhibitions; museum shop sells books, magazines, original art, reproductions, prints and slides
L Library, 1717 N Harwood St, 75201. Tel 214-922-1277. *Librn* Allen Townsend
For reference only
Income: Financed by city and private funds
Library Holdings: Vols 25,000; Per subs 105; Artist File; Other — Exhibition catalogs
Special Subjects: Pre-Columbian Art, African & Contemporary Art

L DALLAS PUBLIC LIBRARY, Fine Arts Division, 1515 Young St, 75201-9987. Tel 214-670-1400. *Division Head* Roger Carroll; *First Asst* Sharon Herfurth; *Music Librn* John Elfers; *Recordings Librn* Donna Mendro; *Theatre Librn* Robert Eason; *Art Librn* Valerie Pinkney
Open Mon - Thurs 9 AM - 9 PM; Fri & Sat 9 AM - 5 PM; Sun 1 AM - 5 PM. Estab 1901 to furnish the citizens of Dallas with materials and information

concerning the arts

Income: Financed by city appropriation, federal & state aid, Friends of the Library, endowment

Purchases: $84,960

Library Holdings: Vols 52,662; Per subs 500; Micro — Fiche, reels; AV — A-tapes, fs, rec, slides; Other — Clipping files, exhibition catalogs, manuscripts, memorabilia, original art works, pamphlets, photographs, prints, reproductions

Collections: W E Hill Collection (history of American theater); Lawrence Kelly Collection of Dallas Civic Opera Set and Costume Designs; Manuscript Archives (music); Margo Jones Theater Collection; original fine print collection; John Rosenfield Collection (art and music critic); Interstate Theatre Collection; USA Film Festival Files; Local Archival Material in Film, Dance, Theatre & Music

M D-ART, A VISUAL ARTS CENTER FOR DALLAS, 2917 Swiss Ave, 75204. Tel 214-821-2522; FAX 214-821-9103. *Exec Dir* Katherine Wagner; *Financial Adminr* Chery Mick

Open Mon - Fri 9:30 AM - 5 PM, Sat noon - 4 PM. No admis fee. Estab 1981 to provide exhibition, educ & information opportunities for visual arts in North Texas. 5 galleries totalling 24,000 sq ft, large windows, natural light; track lighting; third gallery long uninterrupted auditorium walls with no natural light. Average Annual Attendance: 15,000. Mem: 500; dues $35; mem open to artists & art appreciators

Income: Financed by donations, grants, facility use fees, mem & fundraising

Exhibitions: Various Art Exhibitions throughout the year open to the public with both private & public openings

Publications: D-Art Newsletter, monthly; exhibition programs & catalogues

Activities: Classes for adults & children; docent training; lect open to public, 10 vis lectr per year; gallery talks; tours; competitions

A SOCIETY FOR PHOTOGRAPHIC EDUCATION, PO Box 222116, 75222-2116. Tel 214-943-8442; FAX 214-943-8771. *Exec Dir* Lee Hutchins

Estab 1963. Open to all with an interest in photography. Average Annual Attendance: 1000. Mem: 1700; annual dues $55; annual meeting Mar

Income: 180,000 (financed by endowment, membership & federal funds)

Exhibitions: Photograph Exhibitions

Publications: Exposure, 3 per yr; SPE newsletter, 5 per yr; annual membership directory & resource guide

Activities: Eight regional conferences each fall

SOUTHERN METHODIST UNIVERSITY

L Hamon Arts Library, Owen Arts Center, 75275-0356. Tel 214-692-2796. *Art Librn* Thomas P Gates; *Dir* Ginsley Silcox

Open Mon - Thurs 8 AM - 10 PM, Fri 8 AM - 5 PM, Sat 9 AM - 5 PM, Sun 1 - 10 PM. No admis fee. Estab to support educational curriculum of art & art history dept of univ. Open to the public for reference and research

Library Holdings: Vols 80,000; Per subs 120; Music scores; Micro — Fiche, reels; AV — V-tapes; Other — Exhibition catalogs, pamphlets

Special Subjects: Antiquities-Byzantine, Antiquities-Egyptian, Antiquities-Etruscan, Antiquities-Greek, Antiquities-Roman, Archaeology, Art History, Coins & Medals, Drawings, History of Art & Archaeology, Latin American Art, Mexican Art, Painting - American, Painting - British, Painting - European, Painting - Flemish, Painting - French, Painting - German, Painting - Italian, Painting - Spanish, Pre-Columbian Art, Prints, Religious Art, Sculpture

M Meadows Museum, Meadows School of the Arts, Owens Art Center, 75275. Tel 214-692-2516; FAX 214-692-3272. *Dir* Samuel K Heath; *Cur of Educ* Maria Teresa Garcia; *Registrar* R Eric Davis; *Exhib Designer* Anthony Foster; *Admin Asst* Christine Moore; *Coordr of Vol & Membership* Marilyn Spencer

Open Mon, Tues, Fri & Sat 10 AM - 5 PM, Thurs 10 AM - 8 PM, Sun 1 - 5 PM, cl Wed. No admis fee. Estab 1965 to preserve and study the art of Spain. Average Annual Attendance: 44,000

Income: Financed by endowment

Collections: Algur H Meadows Collection of Spanish Paintings from Late Gothic to Modern, including works by Juan de Borgona, Yanez, Velazquez, Murillo, Zurbaran, Ribera, Goya, Miro, Juan Gris & Picasso; Elizabeth Meadows Sculpture Garden; University Art Collection; Paintings: Antonio Tapes, Grand Noir (1973); Miguel Zapata, untitled (Bishop from Astorga Cathedral), 1985; Juan Valdes Leal (1622-90), Joachim and the Angel (ca 1655-60); anonymous, St Ignatius Loyola, polychromed and gilded wood (ca 1609-22); Juan Martin Cabazalero (1633-73), St Jerome (1666); Juan Carreno de Miranda (1614-85) Portrait of the Dwarf Michol (ca 1670-82); Alonso Lopez de Herrera (active before 1609; died Mexico after 1648) St Thomas Aquinas/St Francis of Assisi (1639); Sculpture: Alejo de Vahia (active circa 1480-1510) Pieta (1490-1510) polychrome wood; Anonymous, Saint Anthony of Padua Holding the Christ Child (ca 1700) polychrome wood; Decorative Arts: Hispano-Moresque Charger (ca 1500), copper lustreware

Exhibitions: Frida Kahlo; Churches of Portugal: Photographs by Chester Brummel; Rosa Bonheur: Academic Artist; Zanne Hochberg; Debora Hunter: Portraits of Persons Under the Age of One; A Tribute to Robert Rauschenberg; Jorge Castillo 1979 - 1989; Ceremony of Memory; Private Views: Flemish & Dutch Paintings from Dallas Collections; Images of Reality, Images of Arcadia: 17th Century Netherlandish Paintings from Swiss Collections; Andres Nagel; The Texas Printmakers: 1940 - 1965; Edward G Eisenlohr: Texas Painter

Publications: Exhibition Catalogue

Activities: Classes for children; docent training; outreach program; lect open to public; concerts; tours; internships & apprenticeships; individual paintings and original objects of art lent to other museums and galleries in US and Europe for scholarly exhibitions; traveling exhibitions organized and circulated; sales shop sells slides and catalogs & postcards

C THE SOUTHLAND CORPORATION, Art Collection, 2711 N Haskell, PO Box 711, 75221-0711. Tel 214-828-7434. *Cur* Richard P Fitzgerald

Collections: 19th & 20th Century Paintings, Sculpture, Photography & Works on Paper

DENTON

MIDWEST ART HISTORY SOCIETY

For further information, see National and Regional Organizations

M TEXAS WOMAN'S UNIVERSITY ART GALLERY, TWU Station, PO Box 22995, 76204. Tel 817-898-2530; FAX 817-898-3198. *Dir* Corky Stuckenbruck

Open Mon - Fri 9 AM - 4 PM, Sat & Sun upon request. No admis fee. Fine Arts Building consists of two galleries, each consisting of 3000 sq ft. Average Annual Attendance: 4000

Income: Financed by Art Department and student activities fees

Exhibitions: Departmental galleries have approx twelve exhibits per school year

Activities: Concerts; gallery talks; tours; competitions with awards; scholarships

M UNIVERSITY OF NORTH TEXAS, University Art Gallery, Mulberry and Welch, North Texas PO Box 5098, 76203-5098. Tel 817-565-4005, 565-4316; FAX 817-565-4717. *Gallery Dir* Diana Block

Open Mon & Tues 11 AM - 8 PM, Wed - Sat 11 AM - 4 PM. No admis fee. Estab 1960 as a teaching gallery directed to students of University of North Texas, the Denton Community & Dallas/Fort Worth area. The gallery covers 193 running ft of exhibition wall space, approximately 10 ft high, which may be divided into smaller spaces by the use of semi-permanent portable walls; the floor is carpeted-terrazzo. Average Annual Attendance: 10,000

Income: Financed by state appropriation

Collections: †Voertman Collection (student purchases); †permanent collection; †permanent student collection

Exhibitions: Komar & Melamid, Russians in America; Avant Guard & the Text; Stars over Texas. (1991) Lines of Vision; Contemporary drawings by women; Working with Harry, Harry Geffert & others at his Crowley Texas Foundry; Eye for I: Video Self Portraits. (1992) The New British Sculpture: Selected works from the Patsy R & Raymond D Nasher Collection. (1993) Sandy Skoglund, The Green House

Publications: Exhibition announcements

Activities: Lect open to the public, 4-8 vis lectr per year; tours; competitions; individual paintings and original objects of art lent to the university offices; originate traveling exhibitions to other univs & museums

L Visual Resources Collection, School of Visual Arts, 76203. Tel 817-565-4019. *Slide Cur* Ann Graham

Open during school term Mon - Fri 7:45 AM - 9 PM. Estab to provide art slides for instruction. For reference only

Income: Financed by state taxes

Purchases: $6000

Library Holdings: AV — Cassettes, fs, lantern slides, slides 110,000, v-tapes 114

L Willis Library, PO Box 5188, 76203-5188. Tel 817-565-3245; FAX 817-565-2599. *Dir* Donald Grose; *Fine Arts Subject Specialist & Reference Librn* Deborah Barlow

Open Mon - Thurs 7:30 AM - midnight; Fri 7:30 AM - 9 PM; Sat 9 AM - 9 PM, Sun 1 PM - midnight. Estab 1903 to support the academic programs & faculty & student research

Income: Financed by state appropriation

Library Holdings: Vols 50,000; Per subs 186; AV — Fs, motion pictures, slides; Other — Exhibition catalogs

Special Subjects: Advertising Design, Art Education, Art History, Fashion Design, Medieval - 20th Century Art

Collections: Art auction sales catalogs & information

EDINBURG

M HIDALGO COUNTY HISTORICAL MUSEUM, 121 E McIntrye, 78539. Tel 210-383-6911; FAX 210-381-8518. *Executive Dir* Mrs Shan Rankin; *Asst Dir & Cur Exhibits* Tom Fort; *Cur Archaeology & Coll* David Mycue; *Development* Lynne Beeching; *Educ* Oliver Franklin; *Public Relations* Kathryn Ellison

Open 9 AM - 5 PM. Admis $1, $.25. Estab 1967. Average Annual Attendance: 15,000. Mem: 500; dues $20-$1000

Income: $280,000 (financed by endowment, mem, county & city appropriation, fundraising)

Purchases: $450,000 (building)

Exhibitions: Regional Emphasis: Early Spanish Settlement; Mexican American War; Civil War; Ranching; Steamboat Era; Bandit Wars; Hanging Tower; Early Agriculture

Publications: Exhibition catalogs

Activities: Children's classes; docent programs; lectures open to public, 15-20 vis lectr per year; sales store sells books

EL PASO

M EL PASO MUSEUM OF ART, 1211 Montana, 79902-5588. Tel 915-541-4040; FAX 915-533-5688. *Dir* Becky Duval Reese; *Chief Cur* Stephen Vollmer; *Registrar* Sally Meeks

Open Tues - Sat 10 AM - 5 PM, Sun 1 - 5 PM, cl Mon & national holidays. No admis fee. Estab 1960 as a cultural and educational institution. One gallery houses a permanent display of the Kress Collection; second gallery is used for monthly changing exhibits; Heritage Gallery has decorative arts from 18th, 19th and 20th centuries. Average Annual Attendance: 80,000. Mem: 1036; dues $25 - $10,000; meetings Jan, Mar, Apr, Sept, Nov

Income: Financed by membership and city appropriation

Collections: 19th - 20th Century American art; Kress Collection; Mexican Colonial paintings and sculpture; decorative arts of the 18th, 19th & 20th centuries; graphics

Publications: Artline (newsletter), quarterly

Activities: Classes for adults and children; dramatic programs; docent training; lectures open to the public, 12 vis lectrs per year; concerts; gallery talks; tours; competitions; individual paintings and original objects of art lent to other museums on request; book traveling exhibitions, 16 per yr; museum shop sells books, magazines, original art, reproductions & prints

L Library, 1211 Montana, 79902-5588. Tel 915-541-4040; FAX 915-533-5688. *Dir* Becky Duval Reese
Open to the public and members for reference only
Library Holdings: Vols 1500; Per subs 8

M Wilderness Park Museum, 2000 Transmountain Rd (Mailing add: Two Civic Center Plaza, 79999). Tel 915-755-4332; FAX 915-533-5688. *Cur* Thomas C O'Laughlin
Open Tues - Sun 9 AM - 5 PM. No admis fee. Estab 1977 as an archaeological museum to show man's adaptation to a desert environment. Museum contains replica of Olla Cave and Mogollon cliff dwelling. Average Annual Attendance: 27,000
Income: Financed by city appropriation
Collections: Five dioramas depict life styles and climate changes of Paleo Indians including the hunting and gathering era and the Hueco Tanks site; Pre-Columbian (Casas Grandes) & Mogollon archaeological artifacts; Hopi; Apache, Tarahumara artifact collections
Exhibitions: Nazca Lines, Photos by Marilyn Bridges; Yucatan Landscapes
Activities: Slide lectures & demonstrations at schools & civic organizations; lectures open to public; book traveling exhibitions, annually; sales shop sells books, original art, reproductions, prints & slides

M UNIVERSITY OF TEXAS AT EL PASO, University Ave at Wiggins Rd, 79968. Tel 915-747-5565. *Dir* Florence Schwein
Open Tues - Fri 10 AM - 4:30 PM, Sat 10 AM - 4 PM. No admis fee. University established 1916, Department of Art established 1940. Average Annual Attendance: 50,000
Income: Financed by city and state appropriation
Collections: The permanent collection reflects the nature & culture of the region
Exhibitions: Dark Lady Dreaming: Quilts & Drawings by Amy Cordova; Tejanos
Publications: Exhibition catalogs
Activities: Classes for adults and children; lectures open to the public, 2-4 gallery talks per year; tours; competitions; extension work offered through university extension service to anyone over high school age; fees vary

FORT WORTH

M AMON CARTER MUSEUM, 3501 Camp Bowie Blvd, PO Box 2365, 76113. Tel 817-738-1933. *Pres* Ruth Carter Stevenson; *Dir* Jan Keene Muhlert; *Asst Dir* Irvin Lippman; *Cur of Painting & Sculpture* Doreen Bolger; *Cur Western Paintings* Rick Stewart; *Cur Photographic Coll* Tom Southall; *Registrar* Melissa Thompson; *Public Affairs* Ruth Ann Rugg; *Development Coordr* Judy Gibbs; *Ed* Nancy Stevens
Open Tues - Sat 10 AM - 5 PM; Sun noon - 5 PM; cl Mon. No admis fee. Estab 1961 for the study and documentation of nineteenth and early twentieth century American art through permanent collections, exhibitions and publications. Main gallery plus ten smaller galleries. Average Annual Attendance: 160,000
Income: Financed by endowment, grants & contributions
Collections: American paintings & sculpture; print collection; photographs
Publications: Monthly Calendar of Events, bi-annual Program & active publication program in American art & history
Activities: Classes for adults; docent training; produces films and TV cassettes; lect and symposia open to public; gallery talks; tours; works of art lent to museums; traveling exhibitions organized and circulated; museum shop selling books, magazines, reproductions, prints and slides

L Library, 3501 Camp Bowie Blvd, 76107. Elec Mail *BM.ACC@RLG.BITNET* *Librn* Milan R Hughston; *Asst Librn* Sherman Clarke; *Archivist* Paula Stewart
Open Mon - Fri 10 AM - 5 PM. Estab 1961. By appointment only
Library Holdings: Vols 30,000; Per subs 130; Micro — Fiche 100,000, reels 7000; Other — Clipping files, exhibition catalogs, pamphlets
Collections: Western Americana; exhibition catalogs (including the Knoedler Library on fiche); American art, history & photography; Laura Gilpin Library of photographic books, pamphlets & periodicals; New York Public Library artist files and print files on microfiche

M FORT WORTH ART ASSOCIATION, Modern Art Museum of Fort Worth, 1309 Montgomery, 76107. Tel 817-738-9215; FAX 817-735-1161. *Dir* Marla Price; *Membership & Special Events* Suzanne Woo; *Secy to the Dir* Susan Colegrove; *Receptionist* Katherine Smith; *Cur of Prints and Asst Dir* James L Fisher; *Curatorial Asst* Andrea Karnes; *Registrar* Rachael Blackburn Wright; *Head Design & Installation* Tony Wright; *Design & Installation* Bill LeSueur; *Cur of Educ* Linda Powell; *Tour Coordr* Ann Farmer; *Business Mgr* James B Corser III; *Librn* Laura Martinez; *Bookstore Mgr* Francie Allen; *Asst Bookstore Mgr* Keith Lymon
Open Tues 10 AM - 9 PM, July & Aug 10 AM - 5 PM, Wed - Sat 10 AM - 5 PM, Sun 1 - 5 PM, cl Mon & holidays. No admis fee. Estab 1901 as a museum of 20th century art. Five large galleries on the main floor. Average Annual Attendance: 80,000. Mem: 800; dues $1000, $100, $25
Income: Financed by membership, city appropriations, grants and private donations
Collections: 20th Century Art from all countries - paintings, sculpture, drawings, and prints
Exhibitions: Modern & Contemporary Masters: Selections from the Los Angeles County Museum of Art; Woodcuts from the Permanent Collection; Jackson Pollock: Recent Acquisitions; Morris Louis: Recent Acquisitions; Letters & Numbers (Summer Show for Children); Affinities: Prints by Hayter, Masson, Matta & Pollock; Matisse Prints from the Museum of Modern Art; Irving Penn: Photographs; Letters & Numbers: 20th 20th Century Works; Mark Rothko: Works on Paper; Nancy Graves: A Sculpture Retrospective; Jasper Johns: A Print Retrospective; Ellsworth Kelly: Works on Paper
Publications: Bi-monthly calendar
Activities: Classes for adults and children; docent training; lectures open to the public; traveling exhibitions organized and circulated

L Library, 1309 Montgomery, 76107. Tel 817-738-9215; FAX 817-735-1161. *Librn* Laura Martinez
Estab 1971 as a reference library for museum staff
Income: $4348 (trust)

Purchases: $4348
Library Holdings: Vols 6000; Per subs 25; Other — Clipping files, exhibition catalogs, pamphlets, photographs
Special Subjects: 20th Century Art

L FORT WORTH PUBLIC LIBRARY, Fine Arts Section, 300 Taylor St, 76102. Tel 817-871-7739. *Arts Unit Mgr* Thelma Stone; *Asst* Thomas K Threatt; *Librn* Elmer Sackman
Open Tues - Thurs 9 AM - 9 PM, Fri & Sat 10 Am - 6 PM, cl Sun. No admis fee. Estab 1902
Income: Financed by appropriation
Library Holdings: Books, sheet music, music scores, special files of clipped pictures, articles, pamphlets & programs; Micro — Fiche; AV — Cassettes, rec, v-tapes; Other — Clipping files, original art works, pamphlets, photographs, prints
Special Subjects: Bookplates & Bindings, Cartoons, Sheet Music
Collections: Hal Coffman Collection of original political cartoon art; Nancy Taylor Collection of bookplate; historic picture & photograph collection autographed by various celebrities; rare books
Exhibitions: Antiques, crafts, prints, original photographs & original works
Publications: Bibliographies; catalogs; monthly Focus
Activities: Tours

INTERCULTURA, INC
For further information, see National and Regional Organizations

M KIMBELL ART MUSEUM, 3333 Camp Bowie Blvd, 76107. Tel 817-332-8451; FAX 817-877-1264. *Pres* Kay Fortson; *Dir* Dr Edmund P Pillsbury; *Asst Dir Programs & Academic Servs & Cur Exhibitions* Beverly Louise Brown; *Cur Education* Marilyn Ingram; *Sr Cur* Colin B Bailey; *Assoc Dir Admin* Barbara White; *Public Affairs Asst Dir* Wendy Gottlieb; *Registrar* Anne Adams; *Librn* Chia-Chun Shih
Open Tues - Fri 10 AM - 5 PM, Sat noon - 8 PM, Sun noon - 5 PM, cl Mon, July 4, Thanksgiving, Christmas & New Year's. No admis fee. Open to public 1972 for the collection, preservation, research, publication and public exhibition of art of all periods. Average Annual Attendance: 300,000. Mem: 6000; dues $30 - $250
Income: Financed by endowment
Collections: Highly selective collection of European paintings & sculpture from Renaissance to early 20th century; Mediterranean antiquities; African sculpture; Asian sculpture, paintings & ceramics; Pre-Columbian sculpture & ceramics
Exhibitions: (1992) Guercino Drawings from Windsor Castle; Mantegna to Matisse: Selected Treasures of the Cincinnati Art Museum; Nicolas Lancret 1690 - 1743; Fra Bartolommeo: Master Draughtsman of the High Renaissance; The Loves of the Gods: Mythological Painting from Watteau to David; Egypt's Dazzling Sun: Amenhotep III & His World; Italian Drawings, 1350 - 1800: Masterworks from the Albertina. (1993) Jacopo Bassano: A Quadricentennial Celebration & First American Retrospective; Sir Thomas Lawrence: Portrait of an Age, 1790 - 1830; Degas to Matisse: The Maurice Wertheim Collection; Louis I Kahn: In the Realm of Architecture; Giambattista Tiepolo: Master of the Oil Sketch; The Royal Art of Benin
Publications: Calendar, biannual; Light is the Theme: Louis I Kahn & the Kimbell Art Museum; In Pursuit of Quality: The Kimbell Art Museum/An Illustrated History of the Art & Architecture
Activities: Classes for adults & children, hearing impaired & sight impaired; docent training; lectures open to the public; concerts; gallery talks; tours; film series; original objects of art & individual paintings lent to other museums organizing important international loan exhibitions; book traveling exhibitions, 10 per year; originate traveling exhibitions to other museums; museum shop sells books, magazines, reproductions, slides, art related videotapes, puzzles, posters

L Library, 3333 Camp Bowie Blvd, 76107. Tel 817-332-8451; FAX 817-877-1264. *Librn* Chia-Chun Shih
Open Tues - Fri 10 AM - 5 PM by appointment. Estab 1967 to support museum staff, docents and research in area. For reference use of curatorial staff
Library Holdings: Vols 32,500; Per subs 120; Micro — Fiche 2410, reels; AV — Motion pictures, slides; Other — Exhibition catalogs
Collections: Western art from ancient to early 20th century, Oriental, Pre-Columbian & African art; Witt Library on microfiche

M SID W RICHARDSON FOUNDATION, Collection of Western Art, 309 Main St, 76102. Tel 817-332-6554; FAX 817-332-8671. *Dir* Jan Brenneman
Open Tues & Wed 10 AM - 5 PM, Thurs & Fri 10 AM - 8 PM, Sat 11 AM - 8 PM, Sun 1 - 5 PM, cl Mon & major holidays. No admis fee. Estab 1982 to enable downtown visitors & workers to view the paintings in a metropolitan setting. Average Annual Attendance: 36,000
Income: Financed by the Sid W Richardson Foundation
Collections: Frederic Remington, Charles M Russell & others (over 100 western art paintings)
Exhibitions: Permanent exhibit of 52 paintings by Frederic Remington & Charles M Russell
Publications: Remington & Russell, The Sid Richardson Collection
Activities: Classes for adults & children; outreach program; gallery talks; tours; museum shop sells books, prints, postcards, note cards & posters

C TEAM BANK FORT WORTH, PO Box 2050, 76113. Tel 817-884-4000; FAX 817-870-2454. *Pres* Terry Kelley
Estab 1974 to enhance the public areas of bank lobby and building; to provide art for offices of individual bank officers. Collection displayed throughout bank building, offices and public space
Collections: Alexander Calder sculpture; more than 400 pieces of drawings, graphics, paintings, prints, sculpture and tapestries, focusing on art of the Southwest, including artists throughout the nation and abroad
Activities: Tours for special groups only; sponsor two art shows annually; provide cash prizes; scholarships

M TEXAS CHRISTIAN UNIVERSITY, Moudy Exhibition Hall, Brown-Lupton Student Center, PO Box 30793, 76129. Tel 817-921-7643; FAX 817-921-7070. *Dir* David Conn
Open Mon - Fri 10 AM - 4 PM, Sat & Sun 1 - 4 PM. No admis fee. Estab to present the best art possible to the student body; to show faculty and student work. Gallery consists of one large room, 30 x 40 ft, with additional moveable panels. Average Annual Attendance: 10,000
Income: Financed by college funds
Collections: Japanese 18th Century Prints & Drawings; Contemporary Graphics
Exhibitions: Semi-Annual One-Person Retrospected & student exhibitions
Publications: Exhibition notes, mailers and posters
Activities: Classes for adults; lect open to the public, 15 vis lectr per yr; gallery talks; competitions

GAINESVILLE

L COOKE COUNTY COLLEGE LIBRARY, Art Dept, 1525 W California St, 76240. Tel 817-668-7731, Ext 237. *Dir Library Services* Patsy Wilson
Open Mon - Thur 8 AM - 9:30 PM, Fri 8 AM - 4:30 PM, Sun 2 - 5 PM. Estab 1924 to serve the needs of the administration, faculty and students. Circ 500
Purchases: $1500
Library Holdings: Vols 43,000; Per subs 325; Micro — Cards, fiche; AV — A-tapes, cassettes, fs, Kodachromes, lantern slides, motion pictures, rec, slides, v-tapes; Other — Clipping files, pamphlets, prints, reproductions

GALVESTON

L ROSENBERG LIBRARY, 2310 Sealy Ave, 77550. Tel 409-763-8854; FAX 409-763-2526. *Exec Dir* Nancy M Smith; *Head Special Coll* Lisa Shippee Lambert; *Rare Books Librn* Margaret Schlankey; *Museum Cur* Lise Darst
Open Mon - Sat 9 AM - 5 PM; cl Sun and national holidays. No admis fee. Estab 1904 to provide library services to the people of Galveston, together with lectures, concerts, exhibitions. Library includes the Harris Art Gallery, The James M Lykes Maritime Gallery, The Hutchings Gallery, together with miscellaneous art and historical exhibit galleries and halls. Mem: 800; dues $7.50 - $100; annual meeting in Apr
Income: $1,387,480 (financed by endowment, city and state appropriation)
Purchases: $125,778
Collections: †Contemporary American graphics; †historical artifacts relating to Texas, 15th century to present; Lalique crystal; 19th century American and European paintings and sculptures; 19th century Japanese art; photographic reference collection; †maritime history, maps & charts; incunabula; †Russian icons, 15th - 20th centuries; †works by Texas artists
Exhibitions: Approx 14 per year; numerous one-man shows
Activities: Lectures open to public, 5 vis lectrs per yr; tours; competitions; awards; exten dept serves Galveston County; material available to individuals & organizations; libraries lending collection contains 7071 photographs, 18,527 color reproductions, 708 motion pictures, 311 film strips, 615 framed pictures, 10 sculptures; 3600 items lent in average yr; originate traveling exhibitions; sales shop

HOUSTON

A ART LEAGUE OF HOUSTON, 1953 Montrose Blvd, 77006. Tel 713-523-9530. *Pres of Board* Gary Hernandez; *Exec Dir* Kimberly Zeidan
Open Mon - Fri 10 AM - 4 PM; Sat Noon - 4 PM. No admis fee. Estab 1948 to promote public interest in art and the achievements of Houston area artists. Gallery maintained for monthly exhibits. Average Annual Attendance: 30,000 - 40,000. Mem: 1500; annual dues $20 - $1000; annual meeting May
Income: $300,000 (financed by membership and fund-raising functions)
Exhibitions: Dimension Houston; Membership Exhibits; Student Exhibits; Regional exhibitions
Publications: Newsletter, monthly; year book and membership roster, annually; exhibition catalogs
Activities: Classes for adults & children; lect open to the public 6 - 10 vis lectr per yr; competitions with prizes; workshops; gallery talks; tours; scholarships & fels offered; exten dept for exhibitions & classes for the detainees at Harris County Juvenile Detention Center, individual paintings lent to other art leagues; sales shop sells calendars, craft items, original art, print reproductions

M CONTEMPORARY ARTS MUSEUM, 5216 Montrose, 77006-6598. Tel 713-526-0773; FAX 713-526-6749. *Dir* Suzanne Delchanty; *Asst Cur* Lynn Herbert; *Engelhard Cur* Peter Doroshenko; *Registrar* Jean Story; *Public Information Officer* Susan Schmaeling; *Coordr of Educ Prog* Dana Baldwin
Open Tues - Fri 10 AM - 5 Pm, Sat & Sun noon - 5 PM. Estab 1948 to support & exhibit contemporary arts & to advance the field of contemporary art through scholarly publications & nationally traveling exhibitions. One large gallery of 10,500 sq ft and a smaller gallery of 1500 sq ft. Average Annual Attendance: 60,000. Mem: 1800; dues $30 or more
Income: $1,600,000
Exhibitions: (1992) Gulliermo Kuitea; Ange Leccia: Arrangements; William Wegman: drawings, paintings, photographs, videotapes. (1993) Agnes Martin; Liz Phillipps; Works by Lorna Simpson; Robin Utterback: Paintings 1989-92; Meg Webster: Garden & Sculpture; Krzysztof Wodiczko: Public Address; On The Road: Selections from the Permanent Collection of the Museum of Contemporary Art, San Diego; 3-D Rupture
Publications: Exhibition catalogs; quarterly calendar; annual report
Activities: Educ Dept; lect open to public, 12 vis lectrs per year; gallery talks; sales shop sells books, magazines, original art, reproductions, prints, artist designed jewelry & gifts

M DIVERSE WORKS, 1117 E Freeway, 77002. Tel 713-223-8346; FAX 713-223-4608. *Co-Dir* Caroline Huber; *Co-Dir* Michael Peranteau; *Asst Dir* Deborah Grotfielt
Estab 1983 to present the work of emerging & recognized artists from Texas, as well from across the country & abroad

M HOUSTON BAPTIST UNIVERSITY, Museum of American Architecture and Decorative Arts, 7502 Fondren Rd, 77074. Tel 713-995-3311. *Dir* Lynn Miller
Open Tues - Fri 10 AM - 4 PM & by appointment, cl Easter, June thru mid-Aug & Christmas vacation. No admis fee. Estab 1964. Small reference library maintained
Collections: African art; dolls; furniture and decorative arts; pre-Columbian art; toys
Activities: Lectures; tours; films

A HOUSTON CENTER FOR PHOTOGRAPHY, 1441 W Alabama, 77006. Tel 713-529-4755. *Pres* Joan Morgenstern; *Exec Dir* Jean Caslin; *Admin Dir* Michael G DeVoll; *Coordr Marketing & Development* Sam Lasseter; *Membership Asst* Adele Horne
Open Wed - Fri 11 AM - 5 PM, Sat - Sun Noon - 5 PM. No admis fee. Estab 1981. Mem: 900; dues $35 & up
Income: $175,000 (financed by endowment, mem, city & state appropriation, NEA & private gifts)
Exhibitions: Windows on Houston, juried competition for Houston area photographers with an exhibition at Houston Intercontinental Airport
Publications: Spot, tri-annual; bi-monthly newsletter
Activities: Adult & children's classes; lect open to public; gallery talks; tours; competitions; fels; book traveling exhibitions; originate traveling exhibitions to museums & non-profit galleries

L HOUSTON PUBLIC LIBRARY, Fine Arts and Recreation Department, 500 McKinney, 77002. Tel 713-236-1313, Ext 71624, 71625. *Mgr, Fine Arts & Recreation* John Harvath; *Asst Mgr* Scott Skelton
Open Mon - Fri 9 AM - 9 PM, Sat 9 AM - 6 PM, Sun 2 - 6 PM. Estab 1848 as a private library for the Houston Lyceum and opened to the public in 1895. Monthly exhibits, including art shows are spread throughout the Central Library Building. Circ 134,601
Income: Financed by endowment, city appropriation, federal and state aid (LSA & LSCA), Friends of the Library
Purchases: $177,187
Library Holdings: Vols 138,088; Per subs 373; exhibition posters, portrait file, sheet music collection, auction catalogs; Micro — Reels; AV — Cassettes, fs, rec, slides; Other — Clipping files, exhibition catalogs, framed reproductions, pamphlets, reproductions, sculpture
Special Subjects: Decorative Arts, Oriental Art
Activities: Lect open to public; tours; lending collection contains 20,000 printings, photographs, sculpture, compact discs

M MENIL COLLECTION, 1511 Branard St, 77006. Tel 713-525-9405; FAX 713-525-9444. *Pres* Dominique De Menil; *Acting Dir* Paul Winkler; *Chief Cur* Bertrand Davezac; *Registrar* Julie Bakke; *Registrar* Nancy Swallow
Open Wed - Sun 11 AM - 7 PM. No admis fee. Estab to organize and present art exhibitions. Average Annual Attendance: 38,000
Publications: Exhibition catalogues
Activities: Lectures open to public; originate traveling exhibitions; museum shop sells books and exhibition posters

M MIDTOWN ART CENTER, 3414 La Branch, 77004. Tel 713-524-1079. *Dir* Lindi Yeni
Estab 1982 as a multi-cultural, multi-disciplinary art center serving grassroots artists
Exhibitions: Frank Fajardo's Works

M MUSEUM OF FINE ARTS, HOUSTON, 1001 Bissonnet, PO Box 6826, 77005. Tel 713-526-1361; FAX 713-639-7399; Telex 77-5232; Cable MUFA HOU. *Dir* Peter C Marzio; *Chmn Board* Alfred C Glassell Jr; *Assoc Dir & Sr Cur* David Warren; *Cur Decorative Arts* Katherine Howe; *Assoc Dir Spec Projects* Celeste Adams; *Cur of Photography* Anne Tucker; *Cur Bayou Bend* Michael Brown; *Registrar* Charles Carrol; *Asst Cur Africa, Oceania & the Americas* Anne Louise Schaffer; *Assoc Dir Development* Margaret Skidmore; *Assoc Dir Finance & Admin* Gwen Goffe; *Cur of European Art* George Shackelford; *Assoc Cur of 20th Century Art* Allison Greene; *Eduction Dir* Beth Schneider; *Cur Prints & Drawings* Barry Walker
Open Tues - Sat 10 AM - 5 PM, Thurs evening until 9 PM, Sun 12:15 - 6 PM. Estab 1924 as an art museum containing works from prehistoric times to the present. Exhibition space totals 75,000 sq ft. Average Annual Attendance: 375,000. Mem: 10,000; dues $35; annual meeting May
Collections: †African, Oceanic, Pre-Columbian and American Indian art objects; †American and European graphics, paintings & sculpture; †European and American decorative arts including Bayou Bend Collection of American Decorative Arts; major collection of Impressionist and Post-Impressionist paintings; †Medieval and Early Christian work; †Oriental art; †Western Americana; †antiquities; †photography; Lillie & Hugh Roy Cullen Sculpture Garden
Exhibitions: (1993) Arms & Armor from the State of Syria; Benin: Royal Art of Africa; Imperial Austria: Treasures of Art; The Lure of Italy; Kenneth Noland: The Concentric Circle Paintings; The Royal Tombs of Sipan, Peru; Two Lives: Georgia O'Keefe & Alfred Stieglitz
Publications: Bulletin, semi-annual; calandar of events, bimonthly; catalogs of exhibitions
Activities: Classes for adults & children; docent training; lectures open to public, 25 vis lectr per yr; concerts; gallery talks; tours; individual paintings & original objects of art lent to other art institutions; originate traveling exhibitions; museum shop sells books, magazines, prints & slides

L Hirsch Library, 1001 Bissonnet, PO Box 6826, 77265-6826. Tel 713-639-7326; FAX 713-639-7399; Elec Mail RLIN@bm.mfc. *Librn* Jeannette Dixon; *Archivist* Kathleen Hartt; *Acting Slide Librn* Erin Loftus; *Assoc Librn* Margaret Ford
Open Tues, Wed & Fri 10 AM - 5 PM, Thur 10 AM - 9 PM, Sat noon - 5 PM, cl Sun. For reference only. Average Annual Attendance: 7000
Income: Financed by Hirsch Endowment
Library Holdings: Vols 35,000; Per subs 160; Archival Records; Micro — Fiche, reels; AV — Slides, v-tapes; Other — Clipping files, exhibition catalogs, pamphlets
Special Subjects: Art History, Decorative Arts, Photography, Fine Arts

RICE UNIVERSITY

L **Alice Pratt Brown Library of Art, Architecture & Music,** Fondren Library, PO Box 1892, 77251-1892. Tel 713-527-4832, 527-4800. *Art Librn* Jet M Prendeville
Open Mon - Thurs 8:30 AM - 11 PM, Fri 8:30 AM - 10 PM, Sat 11 AM - 10 PM, Sun 2 - 11 PM. Estab 1964 combined art, architecture, music collections in the Alice Pratt Brown Library established 1986
Income: $130,300 (financed by Rice Univ)
Library Holdings: Vols 83,749; Per subs 470; Scores; AV — Cassettes, rec; Other — Exhibition catalogs 6000
Special Subjects: Architecture, Art History, Film, Photography, Classical Archaeology

M **Sewall Art Gallery,** 6100 S Main (Mailing add: PO Box 1892, 77251-1892). Tel 713-527-8011, Ext 3470, 3502, 527-6069 (Gallery). *Dir* Stella Dobbins; *Coordr* Jaye Locke
Open Tues - Sat noon - 5 PM & Thurs til 9 PM during academic year. No admis fee. Estab 1971 as an extension of the teaching activities in the Dept of Art & Art History. Gallery is administered by a member of the faculty. Average Annual Attendance: 8000
Income: $12,000 (financed by Rice University, gifts & grants)
Purchases: Prints, master & contemporary
Collections: African, †Pre-Columbia, †prints, †photos
Exhibitions: (1992 - 93) Karin Broker: 1980 - 1992; 20th Century Texas Folk Art; recent gifts to the Rice Art Collection; Contemporary Realist Watercolor; 30th Annual Student Exhibition
Publications: Exhibit catalogs
Activities: Lect & panel discussions, symnposia & performances are free & open to public; gallery talks; tours; lending from permanent Rice Art Collection; book traveling exhibitions; originate traveling exhibitions

C **TRANSCO ENERGY COMPANY INC,** Transco Gallery, 77251, PO Box 1396, 77251-1396. Tel 713-439-4401; FAX 713-439-2440. *Admin VPres* T W Spencer; *Art Cur* Sally Sprout
Gallery open Mon - Fri 8 AM - 6 PM. Estab 1974 to enhance atmosphere for employees. Collection displayed within office spaces and hallways; annual amount of art contributions and grants $250,000; supports Museum of Fine Arts, Houston Ballet, Houston Symphony, Grand Opera, Business Committee for the Arts, Public Library, Public Television, Combined Arts Corporation Campaign, Houston Business Committee For The Arts and various Houston Cultural Arts Council projects
Purchases: Financed by art budget
Collections: †2000 original works, mostly on paper by living contemporary artists; †American master watercolors including artists: Homer, Sargent, LaFarge, Demuth, Burchfield, Wyeth & Bricher
Publications: Catalog of American Master Watercolors; exhibit catalogs
Activities: Competitions with awards; loans of original prints, drawings and watercolors to non-profit institutions for exhibition purposes may be arranged; book traveling exhibitions to museums in Transco's marketing areas in United States

M **UNIVERSITY OF HOUSTON,** Sarah Campbell Blaffer Gallery, Entrance 16 off Cullen Blvd, 77204-4891. Tel 713-743-9530; FAX 713-749-1855. *Dir* Marti Mayo; *Registrar* Nancy S Hixson
Open Mon - Fri 10 AM - 5 PM; Sat - Sun 1 - 5 PM; cl major holidays, Aug, and between exhibitions. Estab 1973 to present a broad spectrum of visual arts, utilizing the interdisciplinary framework of the University, to the academic community and to the rapidly increasing diverse population of greater Houston. Main gallery is 7000 sq ft, ceiling height varies from 10-25 ft; Mezzanine gallery is 1500 sq ft. Average Annual Attendance: 30,000
Income: Financed by state appropriation, university, local funds, grants, gifts
Collections: Charles & Katherine Fleetwood and Edward F Heyne Pre-Columbian Collections; Freda and Clara Radoff Mexican Print Collection; †Print Study Collection; Roy Hofheinz Tapestry Collection
Exhibitions: (1992) The Art of Private Devotion: Retablo Painting of Mexico; This Sporting Life, 1878 - 1991. (1993) Darkness & Light; Student Exhibition; Master of Fine Arts Thesis Exhibition
Publications: Exhibition catalogues
Activities: Lect open to public; concerts; gallery talks; tours; competitions; originate traveling exhibitions; sales shop selling books

L **Architecture and Art Library,** 77204-4431. Tel 713-743-2340. *Librn* Margaret Culbertson; *Asst* Lynn Sterba
Open Mon - Thurs 8 AM - 8 PM, Fri 8 AM - 5 PM, Sat 1 - 5 PM. Reference
Income: Financed by state appropriation
Library Holdings: Vols 55,000; Per subs 230; Micro — Fiche, reels; Other — Pamphlets
Special Subjects: Architecture

INGRAM

A **HILL COUNTRY ARTS FOUNDATION,** Hwy 39, PO Box 176, 78025. Tel 512-367-5121. *Exec Dir* Open ; *Art Dir* Betty Vernon; *Theatre Dir* Susan Balentine
Open 10 AM - 4 PM. No admis fee except for special events. Estab 1959 to provide a place for creative activities in the area of visual arts and performing arts; and to provide classes in arts, crafts and drama. Art Gallery maintains small reference library. Average Annual Attendance: 30,000. Mem: 650; annual meeting second Sat in Dec
Income: Financed by endowment, mem, benefit activities & donations
Publications: Spotlight, quarterly newsletter
Activities: Classes for adults & children; national juried competitions with awards; scholarships; sales shop sells original art & original crafts

KERRVILLE

M **COWBOY ARTISTS OF AMERICA MUSEUM FOUNDATION,** 1550 Bandera Hwy, PO Box 1716, 78029. Tel 512-896-2553. *Dir* Byron Fullerton
Open Tues - Sat 9 AM - 5 PM, Sun 1 - 5 PM, open Mon during summer. Admis adults $2.50, children 6-18 $1. Estab 1983 to display contemporary art of American West. Average Annual Attendance: 35,000. Mem: 1000; dues $30-$10,000
Income: $330,000 (financed by membership dues, contributions, entrance fees & sales in museum shop)
Collections: Western American Realism Art by members of The Cowboy Artists of America
Exhibitions: (1991) Ride Like the Wind
Publications: Visions West: History of the Cowboy Artists Museum, newsletter, quarterly
Activities: Classes for young serious art students; docent programs; lectures open to public, 4 vis lectr per yr; original objects of art lent to other museums; book traveling exhibitions, 2 times per yr; originate traveling exhibitions; museum shop sells books, magazines, prints

L **Library,** PO Box 1716, Kerrville, TX 78029. Tel 512-896-2553. *Librn* Mary Meyers
Reference
Income: Financed by donations & memberships
Library Holdings: Other — Clipping files, exhibition catalogs, framed reproductions, manuscripts, memorabilia, original art works, pamphlets, photographs, prints
Special Subjects: American Western Art, Art History, Bronzes, Historical Material, Illustration, Painting - American, Printmaking, Prints, Western Art, History of Range Cattle Industry

KINGSVILLE

M **TEXAS A & I UNIVERSITY,** Art Gallery, Art Department, 78363. Tel 512-595-2619. *Dir* Dr Richard Scherpereel
Open Mon - Fri 9 AM - 4 PM. No admis fee. Estab to exhibit art work of students, as well as visitors. Average Annual Attendance: 3000
Income: Financed by state appropriations

LONGVIEW

M **LONGVIEW MUSEUM AND ARTS CENTER,** 102 W College, 75601. Tel 903-753-8103. *Dir* Millicent Canter
Open Mon - Fri 9 AM - 5 PM; Sun 1 - 3 PM. No admis fee. Estab 1970 for the encouragement of art through a program of exhibition of professional quality work, education & participation of all interested persons. East Gallery 40 x 60 ft, overhead lights; West Gallery smaller but similar; galleries between are rooms that were once a private home, plus two class rooms. Average Annual Attendance: 20,000. Mem: 800; dues patron $500, sponsor $200, contributing $100, family $40; Board of Trustees monthly meetings
Income: Financed by membership and guild projects
Purchases: Contemporary Southwestern artists work
Collections: †Regional Artists Collection formed by purchases from Annual Invitational Exhibitions over the past 20 years; work by contemporary Texas artists
Exhibitions: Permanent collection & 6 - 8 temporary exhibitions of a variety of art styles & periods
Publications: Exhibition catalogs
Activities: Classes for adults and children; docent training; day at museum with artist in residence for all 4th grade students; graduate course, Art for Elementary Teachers, offered by Univ of Texas-Tyler extension department; lectures open to the public, 6 vis lectr per year; talks; tours; competitions with cash awards; individual paintings and original objects of art lent; lending collection contains books, cassettes, film strips; book traveling exhibitions; originate traveling exhibitions

L **Library,** 102 W College, 75601. Tel 903-753-8103. *Dir* Millicent Canter
Open Mon - Sat 10 AM - 4 PM, cl holidays. Estab 1970 for the enjoyment of members and public
Income: Financed by membership, guild fundraising, local & state grants
Library Holdings: Vols 300
Collections: Work by contemporary Texas artists
Exhibitions: Permanent collection & 6 - 8 temporary exhibitions of a variety of art styles & periods
Publications: Exhibit catalogues
Activities: Classes for adults & children; docent training; day at museum; Films & slide shows when available with exhibition

LUBBOCK

A **LUBBOCK ART ASSOCIATION, INC,** Municipal Garden & Art Center, 4215 University Ave, PO Box 93125, 79493-3125. Tel 806-767-3725. *Pres* Charles Freeburg; *VPres* Pricilla Marsh; *Secy* Sharon Beauchamp; *Treas* Beth Pennington
Open Mon - Fri 9 AM - 5 PM, Sat & Sun 1 - 5 PM. No admis fee. Estab 1951 to promote art in Lubbock-South Plains. Located in beautiful Municipal Garden & Art Center near arboretum and is 54 x 64 ft. Average Annual Attendance: 100,000. Mem: 200; dues $18; meeting second Thurs every month
Income: Financed by membership
Collections: Regional and nationally known artists; works representing professional quality in graphics, painting, sculpture and crafts
Exhibitions: Classic; Membership show; permanent collection; special one & three-person exhibitions; state level invitationals
Publications: Bi-monthly newsletter
Activities: Workshops for adults; lectures open to public, 4 vis lectr per yr; gallery talks; competitions with awards; scholarships; lending collection contains 1000 books; book traveling exhibitions; originate traveling exhibitions; studio art and gallery sales

M TEXAS TECH UNIVERSITY, Museum, Fourth & Indiana Aves, PO Box 43191, 79409. Tel 806-742-2442. *Dir* Gary Edson; *Asst Dir Operations* David K Dean; *Dir & Cur Ranching Heritage Center* Dr David Salay; *Registrar* Henry Crawfor; *Cur Anthropology* Dr Eileen Johnson; *Cur Clothing & Textile* Mei Wan Campbell; *Educ Mgr* Patsy Jackson; *Cur Natural Science Research Lab* Dr Robert Baker; *Cur Vertebrate Paleontology* Dr Sankar Chatterjee; *Coll Mgr (Sciences)* Steve Williams; *Coll Mgr (Anthropology)* Nicola Ladkin
Open Main Bldg Tues - Sat 10 AM - 5 PM, Thurs 10 AM - 8:30 PM, Sun 1 - 5 PM, cl Mon; Ranching Heritage Center Mon - Sat 10 AM - 5 PM, Sun 1 - 5 PM; Moody Planetarium Tues - Fri - 2 PM, Thurs 2 PM - 7:30 PM, Sat & Sun 2 - 3:30 PM. Estab 1929 for public service, research and teaching. Museum Complex Theme: collect, preserve and interpret knowledge about the Southwest and other regions as related by natural history, heritage and climate. Two permanent galleries for art; five temporary galleries in Main Bldg. Average Annual Attendance: 200,000. Mem: 2500; dues WTMA $15 & $25, RHA $20; annual meetings WTMA in Feb & RHA in Sept
Income: Financed by state appropriations, West Texas Museum Association, Ranching Heritage Association; private donations; local, regional, national research grants
Collections: Archaeology; ceramics; contemporary paintings; ethnology; graphics; history
Exhibitions: Fourteen Acre Outdoor Museum of 30 Historic Ranch Structures display history of Southwest ranching; changing exhibitions of art, sciences, photography and history; permanent exhibitions of anthropology, archeology and history; Paleo/indian aracheological site, Lubbock Lake Landmark
Publications: Museum Digest, quarterly; Ranch Record, quarterly; Museum Journal; Occasional Papers; MuseNews, semi-annual; Museology, annually
Activities: Classes for adults & children; docent training; lectures open to public, 10 vis lectr per year; concerts; gallery talks; tours; scholarships; individual paintings & original objects of art lent to other museums; book traveling exhibtons, 10 per year; originate traveling exhibitions; two museum shops sell books, magazines, reproductions, prints and slides
L Art Dept Library, PO Box 4720, 79409-2081. Tel 806-742-2887. *Librn & Slide Cur* Bonnie Aycock
Income: $7000 (Financed by State legislature appropriations, private donations, grants)
Library Holdings: Vols 1900; Per subs 47; AV — Fs, slides 62,000, v-tapes; Other — Clipping files, exhibition catalogs, manuscripts, original art works, pamphlets
Special Subjects: Advertising Design, Aesthetics, American Indian Art, American Western Art, Antiquities-Egyptian, Decorative Arts, Furniture, Glass, Graphic Arts, Graphic Design, Illustration, Jewelry, Photography, Printmaking, Sculpture, Southwestern Art, Textiles, Video

LUFKIN

A MUSEUM OF EAST TEXAS, 503 N Second St, 75901. Tel 409-639-4434. *Exec Dir* J P McDonald; *Admin Asst* Cindy Farney; *Cur Exhib & Prog* Judy Ferguson
Open Tues - Fri 10 AM - 5 PM, Sun 1 - 5 PM, cl Thanksgiving & Christmas. No admis fee. Estab 1975 by the Lufkin Service League to bring the fine arts to East Texas & to cultivate an interest in regional history. Average Annual Attendance: 12,000. Mem: 500; dues benefactor $5000, guarantor $1000, patron $500, sustainer $250, sponsor $150, family $60, individual $25 & $20
Exhibitions: East Texas Art
Publications: Bi-monthly newsletter
Activities: Classes for adults & children; docent training; trips; film series; lectures open to public; gallery talks; tours; competitions with awards; book traveling exhibitions

MARSHALL

M HARRISON COUNTY HISTORICAL MUSEUM, Old Courthouse, Peter Whetstone Square, 75670. Tel 903-938-2680. *Pres* Sarah Lentz Sinclair; *Dir* Inez H Hughes
Open Sun & Mon 1:30 - 5:00 PM, Tues - Sat 9 AM - 5 PM, cl wk before Christmas. Admis adults $2, students $1, children under 6 free, groups of 10 or more half price. Estab 1965, housed in a 1901 courthouse. Average Annual Attendance: 3000. Mem: 475; dues couples $15, individual $10
Income: Financed by membership, donations, admissions, & endowment
Collections: Cut & Pressed Glass; 400 BC - 1977 Ceramics; Hand-painted China; Historical Material; Religious Artifacts; etchings; jewelry; paintings; porcelains; portraits; Pioneer implements; transportation
Exhibitions: Caddo-Lake Room
Publications: Historical Newsletter, monthly
Activities: Guided tours; genealogical records researched; competitions with awards

M MICHELSON-REVES MUSEUM OF ART, 216 N Bolivar, PO Box 8290, 75671. Tel 903-935-9480. *Dir* Glenda Knutson; *Educ Coordr* Laurie Krushenisky
Open Tues - Fri noon - 5 PM, Sat & Sun 1 - 4 PM, cl Mon & holidays. Admis adults $2, children & groups $1, members free. Estab 1985 to exhibit works of Leo Michelson & special exhibits. two galleries, one exhibits permanent collection of works by Leo Michelson, second gallery contains traveling exhibits. Average Annual Attendance: 8000. Mem: 400; dues $15 & up
Income: $75,000 (financed by mem, city & state appropriations)
Collections: Leo Michelson, Russian/American 1887 - 1978
Exhibitions: Five Centuries of Italian Painting from Blaffer Foundation
Activities: Classes for adults & children; docent programs; lect open to public, 4 vis lect per year; book traveling exhibitions 4 per year

MCALLEN

M MCALLEN INTERNATIONAL MUSEUM, 1900 Nolana, 78504. Tel 210-682-1564. *Exec Dir* David A Ross; *Exhib Coordr* Leila Kabil; *Education Coordr* Jim Miller; *Public Relations* Berry Fritz; *Cur Colls* Vernon Weckbacher
Open Tues - Sat 9 AM - 5 PM, Sun 1 - 5 PM, cl holidays. Admis adults $1, students $.25. Estab 1969 to exhibit arts & sciences. One folk art gallery, two for traveling exhibits & a science hall. Average Annual Attendance: 65,000. Mem: 800; dues $25 & up
Income: Financed by membership, city appropriation and other funds
Collections: †Local, state & regional artists; †Mexican folk art; 20th century prints - US & European Canton Collection of old European oil paintings; †original prints; natural sciences
Exhibitions: Continuous traveling exhibits for one to two month duration
Publications: Bulletins and brochures periodically; Newsletter, monthly
Activities: Classes for adults and children; docent training; art and craft demonstrations; lect open to the public, 30 vis lectr per year; concerts; gallery talks; tours; competitions; traveling exhibitions organized and circulated; museum shop selling books, reproductions, prints, slides, museum related science kits
L Library, 1900 Nolana, 78504. Tel 210-682-1564, 682-5661; FAX 210-686-1813. *Cur Colls* Vernon Weckbacher
Open to staff, volunteers, and researchers for reference only
Library Holdings: Vols 2100; Per subs 10; AV — Slides; Other — Photographs

MIAMI

M ROBERTS COUNTY MUSEUM, Hwy 60 E, PO Box 306, 79059. Tel 806-868-3291. *Dir* Cecil Gill; *Cur* Jane Bright
Open Tues - Fri 10 AM - 5 PM, Sun 2 - 5 PM, cl Mon, Sat & holidays. No admis fee. Estab 1979. Average Annual Attendance: 3000
Collections: Mead Collection of mammoth bones & fossils; Locke Collection of Indian artifacts; Historical Museum of early Miami
Activities: Lectures open to the public; museum shop sells books, shirts, jewelry, keychains

MIDLAND

M MUSEUM OF THE SOUTHWEST, 1705 W Missouri, 79701-6516. Tel 915-683-2882. *Dir* Wendell Ott; *Asst to Dir* Enid Davis; *Cur Art* Gary A Hood; *Planetarium Dir* Mark Hartman
Open Tues - Sat 10 AM - 5 PM, Sun 2 - 5 PM, cl Mon. No admis fee. Incorporated 1965 as an art and history museum with a separate planetarium providing various science exhibits; children's museum. Average Annual Attendance: 100,000. Mem: 800; dues $20-$1000; board meeting third Wed monthly
Income: Financed by mem, contributions & grants
Collections: †Art & archaelogical materials of the Southwest; European fan collection; †Indian art collection; permanent art collection
Exhibitions: (1989-1990) Photographs by Karsh; Art of New Mexico; Tracings of Light; some permanent collection at all times
Publications: Annual Report; Museum Bulletin, bimonthly
Activities: Classes for adults and children; docent training; arts and crafts classes; video showings; lectures open to public & for members only, 2-4 vis lectrs per yr; concerts; gallery talks; tours; individual paintings lent to other museums; book traveling exhibitions, 6-8 per yr; museum shop sells books, jewelry, gifts and original clothing
L Library, 1705 W Missouri, 79701-6516. Tel 915-683-2882. *Planetarium Dir* Mark Hartman
Open Tues - Sat 10 AM - 5 PM, Sun 2 - 5 PM. No admis fee. Estab 1965. Average Annual Attendance: 20,000. Mem: 795; dues $15-$1000
Income: Financed by foundations, county and private donations
Purchases: Fine arts and cultural anthropology material from the US Southwest
Library Holdings: Vols 400; Per subs 15; Other — Clipping files, exhibition catalogs
Collections: †Southwestern material
Publications: Quarterly bulletin; catalog

NACOGDOCHES

M STEPHEN F AUSTIN STATE UNIVERSITY, SFA Gallery, PO Box 13022, SFA, 75962. Tel 409-568-1131; FAX 409-568-1168. *Dir* Eloise Adams
Open Mon - Sun noon - 5 PM. No admis fee. Estab as a teaching gallery & to bring in art from outside this area for our students & the East Texas community. One room approx 56 x 22 ft, plus storage. Average Annual Attendance: 10,000
Income: Financed by state education funds & private contributions
Collections: Student works; Donation of Prints & Mulitiples from Martin Ackerman Foundation
Exhibitions: (1992) Faculty Exhibition; A Reverent Eye: Photographs by David H Gibson; The Cunningham Connection; Slouching Toward 2000: The Politics of Gender. (1993) Bill Hawes/Recent Work; Texas Clay II; Art Furniture
Activities: Classes for children; workshops; lect open to the public; gallery talks; museum trips; competitions with awards

ODESSA

M ART INSTITUTE FOR THE PERMIAN BASIN, 4909 E University Blvd, 79762-8144. Tel 915-368-7222, 550-3811; FAX 915-368-9226. *Dir* Marily Bassinger; *Asst Cur* Letha Hooper; *Office Mgr* Brenda Wharton
Open Tues - Sat 10 AM - 5 PM, Sun 2 - 5 PM. No admis free. Estab 1985 to increase public awareness & appreciation of art through exposure & education. Average Annual Attendance: 18,000. Mem: 475; dues $25 & up; annual meeting in Apr
Income: $210,000 (financed by mem, grants, donations & fund raisers)
Collections: Jeff Parker Collection of contemporary US paintings & sculpture;

Italian contemporary bronzes from the Meadows Foundation
Exhibitions: (1992) Children's Christman Exhibit; Fabric Concers: The Quilt Renewed; In Focus; The Odessa Needlework Guild; Odessa Quilter's Guild Exhibit; Out of the Ordinary; 3-D Works; Visions of the Night Fires; Wilderness Series. (1993) The Art of the Heart Man; Child's Play '93: The Heart of the Arts; Cocktail Party & Musical Sculpture; Contentment; Ector County Independent School District Secondary Student Art Show; Music in 2 & 3-D; Odessa Art Association Juried Show; Texas Black Arts Alliance Juried Show
Activities: Classes for adults & children; docent training; gallery walks; lectures open to public, 2-3 vis lectr per year; competitions; scholarships offered; exten dept serves lending collection, contains paintings; museum shop sells books, prints & videos

M **PRESIDENTIAL MUSEUM,** 622 N Lee, 79761. Tel 915-332-7123. *Exec Dir* Robe Reese; *Cur Educ* Tim Hewitt
Open Tues - Sat 10 AM - 5 PM. No admis fee. Estab 1965 & dedicated to the study & understanding of constitutional government & the election process culminating in the Presidency. Average Annual Attendance: 23,000. Mem: 244; dues $500 - $25
Income: Financed by Ector County & Presidential Museum board of trustees
Collections: Campaign memorabilia; original signatures; portraits
Exhibitions: Long-term exhibitions on the presidency & first ladies; special temporary exhibitions
Publications: News & Views, 4 times per yr; library newsletter, 4 times per yr
Activities: Classes for children; docent training; lectures open to public, 4 vis lectrs per year; concerts; gallery talks; tours; photography competition with awards; individual paintings & original objects of art lent to qualified museums & other cultural organizations; lending collection includes books, 3-D objects & memorabilia; originate traveling exhibitions to circulate to qualified museums; museum shop sells books, magazines, children's games & toys
L **Library of the Presidents,** 622 N Lee, 79761. Tel 915-332-7123.
For reference only
Library Holdings: Vols 4000; Per subs 15; books relating to the presidency; AV — A-tapes, cassettes, rec, slides, v-tapes; Other — Clipping files, exhibition catalogs, pamphlets
Special Subjects: Cartoons, Coins & Medals, Decorative Arts, Flasks & Bottles, Folk Art, Historical Material, Photography, Restoration & Conservation, Material related to the presidency

ORANGE

M **NELDA C & H J LUTCHER STARK FOUNDATION,** Stark Museum of Art, 712 Green Ave, PO Box 1897, 77630. Tel 409-883-6661; FAX 409-886-3530. *Chmn* Nelda C Stark; *VChmn* Eunice R Benckenstein; *Secy* Clyde V McKee; *Dir* Bruce B Eldredge; *Registrar* Jennifer Stafford; *Curatorial Asst* Janis Ziller; *Gift Shop Mgr* Gina Carline
Open Wed - Sat 10 AM - 5 PM, Sun 1 - 5 PM. No admis fee. Estab 1978 to preserve and display the Stark collection of art and promote interests in subjects relative to the same through exhibitions, publications and educational programs. Five galleries, three corridors & lobby exhibition area. Average Annual Attendance: 10,000
Income: Financed by endowment
Collections: †American Indian art; †Western American Art; art relating to American West 1830 - 1965 porcelain; †crystal, rare books
Publications: Exhibition catalogs
Activities: Lectrs; gallery talks; tours; museum shop sells books, reproductions, posters & postcards

PANHANDLE

M **CARSON COUNTY SQUARE HOUSE MUSEUM,** Fifth and Elsie Sts, PO Box 276, 79068. Tel 806-537-3524. *Exec Dir* Dr Paul Katz; *Office Mgr* Laquita Huret; *Registrar* David Hoover; *Dir of Educ* James Hinkley
Open Mon - Sat 9 AM - 5:30 PM, Sun 1 - 5:30 PM, cl Thanksgiving, Christmas and New Years. No admis fee. Estab 1965 as a general museum with art galleries, area and State and National historical displays; Wildlife building and displays; Historic house, listed in National Register of Historic Places. Two enclosed security controlled art galleries, an education center & art gallery. Average Annual Attendance: 30,000
Income: Financed by endowments, county funds and public contributions
Collections: Paintings of area pioneers by Marlin Adams; Sculpture and bronze by Jim Thomas, Grant Speed and Keith Christi; Kenneth Wyatt paintings; Ben Carlton Mead and Harold Bugbee paintings; †contemporary Native American art, Native American beadwork, Acoma pottery; costumes; antiques
Publications: A Time To Purpose, book; Land of Coronado, coloring book; The Square House Cook Book; Voices of the Square House, poems
Activities: Classes for adults and children; dramatic programs; docent training; lect open to public, 1 vis lectr per yr; concerts; gallery talks; tours; scholarships; museum shop sells books, magazines, reproductions, prints & museum related gift items

SAN ANGELO

M **ANGELO STATE UNIVERSITY,** Houston Harte University Center, PO Box 11027, 76909. Tel 915-942-2062; FAX 915-942-2229. *Chmn Art Committee* Donald White; *Dir* Phil Martin; *Program Dir* Rick E Greig
Open Mon - Fri 8 AM - 7:30 PM, Sat & Sun 2 - 5 PM. No admis fee. Estab 1970 to provide entertainment and informal education for the students, faculty and staff. Gallery is maintained
Income: $3000 (financed by city and state appropriations)
Collections: Wax drawings done by Guy Rowe for illustration of the book In Our Image by Houston Harte
Exhibitions: Historical artifacts; modern drawings; photography; pottery; weaving; children, students and faculty exhibitions
Activities: Lect open to public, 2 vis lectrs per yr; gallery talks, tours; concerts; dramatic programs; competitions

M **SAN ANGELO ART CLUB,** Helen King Kendall Memorial Art Gallery, 119 W First St, 76902. Tel 915-653-4405. *Pres* Glenn Lewallen; *Secy* Rosa Gray
Open Wed 9:30 AM - 3:30 PM, Sat & Sun 2 - 5 PM. No admis fee. Club estab 1928 & gallery estab 1948 to promote the visual fine arts in San Angelo. Average Annual Attendance: 1500. Mem: 100; dues $20; meeting first Mon each month
Income: $8000 (financed by Memorial Endowment Fund)
Collections: Paintings by George Biddle, Gladys Rockmore Davis, Xavier Gonzales, Iver Rose and Frederick Waugh, Hazel Janick Karl Albert, Joseph Sharp, Willard Metcalf, Robert Woods, Dwight Holmes
Exhibitions: Monthly exhibits from area artists
Publications: Splashes, monthly newsletter
Activities: Classes for adults & children; tours; competitions with awards; individual paintings & original objects of art lent to libraries, churches & businesses

M **SAN ANGELO MUSEUM OF FINE ARTS,** 704 Burgess, PO Box 3092, 76902. Tel 915-658-4084; FAX 915-659-2407. *Pres* Joel D Sugg; *VPres* Donna Crisp; *Dir* Howard J Taylor; *Registrar & Prog Coordr* Valerie C Bluthardt; *Educator* Donna Griffin-Hughes; *Development Coordr* Beth Churchwell
Open Tues - Sat 10 AM - 4 PM, Sum 1 - 4 PM, cl Mon & major holidays. Admis adults $.75, students & sr citizens $.25, members & children under 6 free. Estab 1981 to provide quality visual arts exhibits & stimulating programs for educational & cultural growth. Museum housed in 1868 Quartermaster building on grounds of FT Concho. Interior adapted for art museum with 3 lower level galleries & one on the mezzanine. Total exhibition space is 3800 sq ft. Average Annual Attendance: 25,000
Income: $250,000 (financed by endowment, sales, admissions)
Collections: Texas art (1942 - present); American Crafts (1945 - present), particularly ceramic & fiber art; American Paintings & sculpture of all eras; Mexican & Mexican-American art of all eras; Selected European, Oriental & African art
Exhibitions: Monarch Tile National Ceramic Competition; Annual Fiber Art Exhibit; Vistas Series Living Texas artists exhibitions; Architect & the British Country House; Summer for Kids Hands-on exhibit; Narrative Images: Folk & Contemporary Art; Images on Stone: Artists' Lithography; Contemporary Art of Mexico
Publications: Exhibit catalogs; gallery talks
Activities: Classes for adults & children; programs; docent training; lectures open to public; competitions with awards; exten dept serves 14 counties in W Texas; book traveling exhibitions, 15 per yr; originate traveling exhibitions; museum shop sells books, magazines, original art, reproductions, prints, educational toys, paper goods

SAN ANTONIO

A **COPPINI ACADEMY OF FINE ARTS,** 115 Melrose Place, 78212. Tel 210-824-8502. *Pres* Louis Mar; *VPres & Exhib Chmn* Marilyn Lingerfelt; *Gallery Mgr* Sally Gatlin
Open Fri & Sun 1 - 5 PM or by appointment. No admis fee. Estab 1945 to foster a better acquaintance and understanding between artists and patrons; to encourage worthy accomplishment in the field of art and to serve as a means of public exhibition for the work of active members. Upstairs gallery donated by founder Dr Pompeo Coppini to the academy for exhibition of works. Mem: 210; dues $20 per annum; annual meeting third Sun of November
Income: Financed by membership
Collections: Oil paintings by Rolla Taylor; sculpture by Waldine Tauch and Pompeo Coppini; paintings
Exhibitions: Annual May Garden Show. Monthly changing exhibits in upper gallery by members
Publications: Coppini News Bulletin, monthly newsletter distributed to members
Activities: Educ dept; lectures open to the public, 6 vis lectr per yr; gallery talks; tours; competitions; scholarships; individual paintings & original objects of art lent; originate traveling exhibitions
L **Library,** 115 Melrose Place, 78212. Tel 210-824-8502. *Pres* Marilyn Lingerfelt
Library Holdings: Vols 200; Per subs 50; AV — Slides, v-tapes; Other — Clipping files, original art works, photographs, sculpture

A **GUADALUPE CULTURAL ARTS CENTER,** 1300 Guadalupe St, 78207. Tel 210-271-3151. *Exec Dir* Pedro A Rodriguez; *Visual Arts Dir* Kathy Vargas; *Xicano Music Prog Dir* Juan Teieda; *Literature Prog Dir* Ray Gonzalez; *Dance Prog Dir* Belinda Munchaca; *Theater Arts Prog Dir* Jorge Pilia
Estab 1979, non-profit, multi-disciplinary arts organization dedicated to the development, preservation & promotion of Latino arts & to facilitating a deeper understanding & appreciation of Chicano/Latino & Native American cultures. Center manages the beautifully restored, historic Guadalupe Theatre, a 410 seat, handicapped accessible, multi-purpose facility that houses the Theater Gallery, a large auditorium, a proscenium stage & equipment for theatrical & cinematic presentations
Income: $1,500,000
Exhibitions: Annual Tejano Conjunto Festival; Annual Performing Arts Series; Annual San Antonio Inter-Americas Bookfair. (1993) David Zamora Casas (paintings); The Art You Love to Hate (velvet painting by Jennifer Heath); Ninth Annual Juried Women's Art Exhibit; Statewide exhibit in conjunction with Chicano art: Resistance & Affirmation; CARA Exhibit; Attempted Not Known; Student Exhibit; Agnes Chavez; Hecho a Mano/Made by Hand (annual fine arts & crafts market)
Activities: Visual arts program; classes & workshops; creative dramatics classes; dance program; media program

M **MARION KOOGLER MCNAY ART MUSEUM,** 6000 N New Braunfels Ave, PO Box 6069, 78209-6069. Tel 210-824-5368, 824-5369; FAX 210-824-0218. *Pres* Gaines Voigt; *Dir* William J Chiego; *Cur Educ* Rose M Glennon; *Cur Tobin Theatre Coll & Library* Linda Hardberger; *Acting Coll Mgr* Heather Hornbuckle; *Acting Librn* Patricia Blackman; *Development Dir* Ellen Sawyer; *Public Relations* Judson Taylor; *Operations Mgr & Preparator* Edward D Hepner; *Controller* Sheri D Grams; *Museum Store Mgr* Liz Davis; *Dir Emeritus* John P Leeper; *Asst Cur Prints & Drawings* Lyle Williams

Open Tues - Sat 10 AM - 5 PM, Sun noon - 5 PM, cl Mon, Jan 1, July 4, Thanksgiving & Christmas. No admis fee, donations appreciated; occasional charge for temporary exhibits. Estab 1950 for the encouragement & development of modern art. 22,000 vol art history reference library; Robert L B Tobin Theatre Arts Library; 23 acres of gardens; 175-seat auditorium; McNay Museum Store; handicap accessibility. Average Annual Attendance: 92,000. Mem: dues benefactor $5000, corporate patron $2500, patron $500, contributing $250, sustaining $100, family $50, individual $25
Income: Financed by endowment, memberships & private gifts
Collections: Modern art, 19th & 20th century European & American painting, sculpture & graphics; Oppenheimer Collection of late medieval & early Renaissance sculpture & paintings; Southwest religious art & Native American decorative arts; Tobin Theatre Arts Collection related to opera, ballet & musical stage
Exhibitions: Duncan Phillips Collects: Paris Between the Wars; Theatre in Revolution: Russian Avant-Garde Stage Design; Women Photographers in Camera Work; Arch Lauterer, Henry Kurth & John Rothgeb: A Teacher & His Student; The Drawings of Stuart Davis: the Amazing Continuity; Mad Dogs & Englishmen: 20th Century Stage Design; Pochoir to Silk Screen: A Printing Process
Publications: Annual report; exhibition catalogues & brochures; Impressions, quarterly newsletter
Activities: Docent training; lect; gallery talks & school tour program; symposia; chamber concerts; films; co-operative programs with Trinity University, San Antonio Art Institute, University of Texas at San Antonio, Incarnate Word College
L **Reference Library,** 6000 N New Braunfels St, 78209. *Librn* Pat Blackman
Open to the public Tues - Sat 10 AM - 5 PM. Estab 1970 as an adjunct to the museum. For reference only. Circ non-circulating
Income: Financed by endowment and gifts
Library Holdings: Vols 22,000; Per subs 35; Micro — Fiche; AV — V-tapes; Other — Clipping files, exhibition catalogs
Special Subjects: Fine Arts

A **SAN ANTONIO ART LEAGUE,** 130 King Williams St, 78204. Tel 210-223-1140. *Pres* Mrs Pete Hammond; *Executive Secy* Norma Champlin; *Museum Consultant* Mrs Dana Young
Open Mon - Fri 10 AM - 4 PM. No admis fee. Estab 1912 as a public art gallery for San Antonio, and for the promotion of a knowledge and interest in art by means of exhibitons. 4 rooms & large hall capable of hanging 150 paintings. Mem: 700; dues $15 - $300; meetings monthly Oct - May
Income: Financed by membership and fund raising projects
Collections: Crafts, paintings, prints and sculpture
Exhibitions: 63rd Annual Artist Exhibition
Publications: Exhibiton catalogs; monthly calendar of events
Activities: Educ dept; lectures open to public, 3 vis lectrs per yr; gallery talks; tours; paintings and original art objects lent
L **Library,** 130 King Williams St, 78204. Tel 210-223-1140.
For reference only
Library Holdings: Vols 350

A **SAN ANTONIO MUSEUM ASSOCIATION, INC,** PO Box 2601, 78299-2601. Tel 210-829-7262. *Pres* Dr E Laurence Chalmers, Jr
Open 10 AM - 5 PM weekdays, weekends and holidays. Admis adult $2, children under 12 $1. Estab 1981. Consists of Museum of Art, Witte Memorial and Museum of Transportation. Average Annual Attendance: 400,000. Mem: 3500; contributions $25, $50 & $100
Income: $3,000,000 (financed by endowment, membership, city appropriation and other fund raising projects)
Purchases: $300,000
Exhibitions: Regional Juried Exhibition
Publications: Monthly calendar; books
Activities: Educ dept sponsors classes for adults and for children; docent training; dramatic programs; lectures open to public, 10 - 12 vis lectr per yr; concerts; gallery talks & tours; paintings and original art objects lent; museum loans must be approved by the Associations' Board; book traveling exhibitions, 2 per year; originate traveling exhibitions; shop sells books, magazines, original art, prints, reproductions, slides and local crafts
M **San Antonio Museum of Art,** 200 W Jones Ave, 78215. Tel 210-978-8111. *Dir* Douglas Hyland; *Cur Western Antiquities* Gerry Scott III; *Cur Folk Art* Marion Oettinger
Open Summer 10 AM - 6 PM, Sept 1- May 31 Wed - Sun 10 AM - 5 PM, cl Mon. Adults $3; children $1.50; group discount rates available. Estab 1981; a renovation project, the Brewery was originally chartered in 1883. Anheuser-Busch Brewing Asn of St Louis, during the early 1900, replaced the original wooden structures with a castle-like brick complex. Twin towers, housing glass elevators can be seen for miles; 66,000 sq ft of exhibition space. Average Annual Attendance: 127,825
Collections: †Contemporary & Modern Art; †18th & 19th & 20th Century Paintings & Sculpture; †Greek & Roman Antiquities †American Photography since 1920; †Mexican Folk Art; †Pre-Columbian Art; †Paintings & Decorative Arts; †Spanish Colonial Art;
Exhibitions: Zacualpa Pottery: Mexican Village Pottery; Chinese Cloisonne from the Clagne Collection; Homage to Fra Casas; Texas Seen, Texas Made; Con Carino; Art Among Us Mexico, Splenders of Thirty Centuries
M **Witte Museum,** 3801 Broadway, 78209. Tel 210-820-2151. *Dir* Mark Lane
Open Winter Mon - Sun 10 AM - 5 PM, Summer Mon - Sun 10 AM - 6 PM. Admis adults $2, children $1; group discount rates; Sat free until noon. The Witte Museum, a historical building, is located in Brackenridge Park near the old San Pedro Springs and ancient Indian encampment area. Average Annual Attendance: 208,229
Activities: Exten dept sponsors gallery talks, tours and an artmobile; museum shop sells reproductions, art works, folk art, posters, antique picture frames, pottery and ceramics

L **SAN ANTONIO PUBLIC LIBRARY,** Dept of Fine Arts, Art, Music & Films Dept, 203 S Saint Marys St, 78205-2786. Tel 210-299-7790; FAX 210-271-9497. *Acting Dir* Ron Darner; *Asst Dir* Nancy Gandara; *Dept Head* Mary A Wright
Open Mon - Fri 9 AM - 9 PM, Sat 9 AM - 6 PM. Estab to provide art reference and lending materials to the residents of Bexar County. Art gallery is maintained. Also serves as a major resource center to regional libraries in South Texas
Income: Financed by city, state and federal appropriation
Purchases: $250,000
Library Holdings: Micro — Fiche, reels; AV — A-tapes, cassettes, fs, motion pictures, rec, slides, v-tapes; Other — Clipping files, exhibition catalogs, memorabilia, pamphlets, photographs, reproductions
Exhibitions: Monthly exhibit of local artists work
Activities: Classes for children; dramatic programs; lectures open to the public, 2 vis lectr per yr; concerts; gallery talks; tours; competitions with awards; exten dept; lending collection contains 320,000 books, 400 video cassettes, 10,000 audio cassettes, 15,000 motion pictures; book traveling exhibitions

A **SOUTHWEST CRAFT CENTER,** Emily Edwards & Ursuline Sales Gallery, 300 Augusta St, 78205. Tel 210-224-1848; FAX 210-224-9337. *Pres* Rick Collier; *Ursuline Gallery Mgr* Laura Barberio
Open daily 10 AM - 4 PM. Estab 1963, shop estab 1968; an alternative art worksite for children and adults. Ursuline Gallery sells crafts by a variety of local, regional & national artists, Emily Edwards Gallery hosts exhibits of nationally-recognized artists. Average Annual Attendance: 2000. Mem: 100; dues $25 & up; annual meeting in May
Income: Financed by mem, National Endowment for the Arts, Texas Commission on the Arts, City of San Antonio Arts & Cultural Affairs Department
Exhibitions: Eight exhibitions per year. Student show, plus seven one to three person shows by nationally recognized artists. One show by young San Antonio artist during Contemporary Art Month in July
Publications: Opening Invitations; handouts for all exhibitions including photo of artists, curator's essay, exhibition checklist
Activities: Classes for adults and children; arts workshop programs with visiting artists; lectures open to public, 30 vis lectrs per year; tours; performances; scholarships; sales shop sells books & magazines,

M **SPANISH GOVERNOR'S PALACE,** 115 Plaza de Armas, 78205. Tel 210-224-0601. *Cur* Nora Ward; *Museum Asst* Gildardo Lopez
Open Mon - Sat 9 AM - 5 PM, Sun 10 AM - 5 PM. Admis adults $1, children under 14 $.50. Estab 1749. Average Annual Attendance: 62,000
Income: $66,000 (financed by city appropriation)
Collections: Spanish-colonial furnishings, paintings, earthenware, brass & copper pieces from 16th - 17th century
Publications: Spanish Governor's Palace brochure
Activities: Museum shop sells slides & postcards

M **THE UNIVERSITY OF TEXAS,** Institute of Texan Cultures, 801 S Bowie at Durango Blvd, PO Box 1226, 78294. Tel 210-226-7651; FAX 210-222-8564. *Exec Dir* Rex Ball; *Dir Coll* Jim McNutt; *Dir Production* David Haynes; *Dir Information* Carey Deckard; *Dir Educ Prog* Nancy McNaul
Open Tues - Sun 9 AM - 5 PM, cl Mon. Estab 1968. Average Annual Attendance: 400,000. Mem: 900; dues $25
Income: $4,500,000 (financed by endowment, mem, state appropriation, gifts & sales)
Collections: Ethnic Culture including Spanish, Mexican, Filipino, French, LeGanese, Belgian, Dutch, Greek, Italian, Japanese, Chinese, Jewish, Czech, Polish, German, Black, Hungarian, English, Indian, Anglo, Scottish, Danish, Norwegian, Swedish (all Texans); one room school house, barn, windmill, fort & log house
Publications: Texan, quarterly; Texican II, quarterly
Activities: Classes for adults & children; dramatic programs; docent programs; lect open to public, 15 lectr per year; sales shop sells books, prints, magazines & slides, original art, reproductions

SHERMAN

M **AUSTIN COLLEGE,** Ida Green Gallery, PO Box 1177, Suite 61628, 75091. Tel 903-813-2253; FAX 214-813-3199. *Dir* Mark Stephen Smith
Open 9 AM - 5 PM weekdays. No admis fee. Estab 1972 to serve campus and community needs. Selected exhibitions of contemporary art by regional & national artists. Average Annual Attendance: 7000
Income: Financed by endowment
Purchases: Annual purchases of outdoor sculpture
Collections: Prints
Exhibitions: Monthly, except summer
Activities: Classes for adults & children; lectures open to public, 12 vis lectr per year; gallery talks; tours; competitions; scholarships offered; lend paintings & original objects of art; lending collection contains film strips, koda chromes & sculptures; book traveling exhibitions semi-annually; originate traveling exhibitions

TYLER

M **TYLER MUSEUM OF ART,** 1300 S Mahon Ave, 75701. Tel 214-595-1001. *Dir* Ron Gleason; *Cur Educ* Sandy Shepard; *Asst Dir Admin* Sharon Smirl
Open Tues - Sat 10 AM - 5 PM, Sun 1 - 5 PM. No admis fee. Estab 1968 as a museum of 19th & 20th century art. Two galleries are 40 x 60 ft with 20 ft ceilings; one gallery covers 25 x 45 ft. Average Annual Attendance: 18,000. Mem: 720; dues $25 - $10,000
Income: $239,000 (financed by endowment, membership and auction)
Collections: 200 works: large regional photography collection; sculpture; paintings; artists represented: Connell, Allen, Fisher, Blackburn, Munoz & Carter
Activities: Docent training; lect open to public; concerts; gallery talks; tours; musical performances; films; individual paintings and original art objects lent; originate traveling exhibitions; shop sells books

L Reference Library, 1300 S Mahon Ave, 75701. Tel 903-595-1001; FAX 903-595-1092. *Dir* Ron Gleason; *Asst Dir Admin* Sharon Smirl; *Cur Educ* Sandy Shepard
Open Tues - Sat 10 AM - 5 PM, Sun 1 - 5 PM. No admis fee. Open for reference only. Average Annual Attendance: 20,000
Income: $236,000 (financed by private donations, grants & city appropriation)
Library Holdings: Vols 1500; Per subs 6; AV — Slides, v-tapes; Other — Clipping files, exhibition catalogs
Activities: Artists travel to schools for hands on projects with all age groups; book traveling exhibitions 1 per year; originate traveling exhibitions to other museums; sales shop sells books, t-shirts, cards

VERNON

M RED RIVER VALLEY MUSEUM, 4600 College Dr W, PO Box 2004, 76384. Tel 817-553-1848. *Exec Dir* Ann G Huskinson; *Clerical Hostess* Bettye McLaughlin
Open Tues - Sun 1 - 5 PM. No admis fee. Estab 1963 to provide for & perserve local heritage while maintaining national exhibits in the arts, history & science programs. One gallery with one hundred linear feet of hanging space. Average Annual Attendance: 8000
Income: Financed by contributions, local government & donations
Collections: Electra Waggoner Biggs Sculpture Collection; J H Ray Indian Artifacts; Taylor Dabney Mineral Collection Bill Bond Wild Game Trophies
Publications: Museum Newsletter, quarterly
Activities: Classes for children; lect open to the public; gallery talks; tours; book traveling exhibitions; museum shop sells books, brochures, collectors items

WACO

M THE ART CENTER, 1300 College Dr, 76708. Tel 817-752-4371. *Dir* Joseph A Kagle; *Dir Educ* Mary Burke
Open Tues - Sat 10 AM - 5 PM, Sun 1 - 5 PM. No admis fee. Estab 1972 to provide a variety of exhibitions for appreciation, and classes for participation. Former residence of William Cameron, now renovated and contains one large main gallery and a small adjacent gallery, also additional exhibition space on the second floor. Average Annual Attendance: 20,000. Mem: 1100; dues $30-$1500
Income: $200,000 (financed by endowment, membership and grants)
Collections: Contemporary regional art
Exhibitions: (1992) 20th Anniversary Exhibition; Central Texas Competition. (1993) Edmund Kinzinger; Robert Wilson; Art View 1993; Karl Umlauf; Dixie Friend Gay; Leon Lank Leonard; Chelsey Smith
Publications: Catalogs; newsletter; exhibit brochures
Activities: Classes for adults and children; docent training; lect open to the public, 2 - 3 visiting lectr per year; gallery talks; tours; competitions; exten dept serves ethnic minorities and low socio-economic groups; originates traveling exhibitions; museum shop sells books, reproductions and gift items
L Library, 1300 College Dr, 76708. Tel 817-752-4371. *Dir Educ & Library* Mary Burke
Open 10 AM - 5 PM Tues - Sat, 1 - 5 PM Sun. Estab 1976 as a non-circulating reference source for staff, faculty and patrons of the Art Center
Income: $2000
Purchases: $650
Library Holdings: Vols 1000; Per subs 18; Other — Exhibition catalogs
Special Subjects: Architecture, Crafts, Photography, Regional Art

BAYLOR UNIVERSITY
M Martin Museum of Art, 76798-7263. Tel 817-755-1867. *Dir* Dr Heidi Hornik
Open Mon - Fri 10 AM - 5 PM, cl Sat & Sun. No admis fee. Estab 1967 as a teaching arm of the university to serve the area. Gallery contains one large room with storage and preparation room. Average Annual Attendance: 5000
Income: Financed through the art department
Collections: †Contemporary painting & sculpture; graphics; local artists; prints; sculpture from Sepik River area, New Guinea, African
Activities: Lectures open to public, 4 vis lectr per yr; gallery talks
L Armstrong Browning Library, Eighth & Speight Sts, PO Box 97152, 76798-7152. Tel 817-755-3566. *Dir* Roger L Brooks; *Librn* Betty A Coley; *Admin Asst* Rita S Humphrey; *Hostess* Cynthia A Burgess
Open to visitors Mon - Fri 9 AM - Noon and 2 - 4 PM, Sat 9 AM - Noon; open for research Mon - Fri 8 AM - 5 PM, Sat 9 AM - Noon. Estab 1918 to provide a setting for the personal possessions of the Brownings and to have as complete as is possible a collection for the use of Browning scholars. Gallery is maintained. Average Annual Attendance: 16,000. Mem: Dues individual $25
Income: Financed by endowment and private university
Library Holdings: Vols 15,000; Per subs 25; original documents; Micro — Reels; AV — A-tapes, cassettes, fs, motion pictures, rec, slides; Other — Clipping files, manuscripts, memorabilia, original art works, pamphlets, photographs, prints, reproductions, sculpture
Special Subjects: Robert and Elizabeth Barrett Browning, Victorian Era of Literature
Collections: Kress Foundation Gallery Collection of Portraits; Meynell; Pen Browing photograph collection of prints; portraits of Robert Browning and Elizabeth Barrett Browning; portraits of donors; Julia Margaret Cameron, photographs; Forster; Lytton; Armstrong
Exhibitions: (1989) Robert Browning: A Telescopic View, 1812-1889
Publications: Armstrong Browning Library Newsletter, semi-annual; Baylor Browning Interests, irregular; Studies in Browning & His Circle, annual; More Than Friend, The Letters of Robert Browning to Katherine Dekay Bronson; Robert Browning's Flowers; EBB at the Mercy of Her Publishers
Activities: Lect open to the public, 2 vis lectrs per yr; tours; exhibits

M TEXAS RANGER HALL OF FAME AND MUSEUM, Interstate 35 & the Brazos River, Fort Fisher Park (Mailing add: PO Box 2570, 76702-2570). Tel 817-750-5986. *Cur* Tom Burks; *Supt* B G Smith
Open 9 AM - 5 PM daily (winter), 9 AM - 5 PM daily (summer). Admis adults $3.50, children (6 & up) $1.50, 10 or more adults $2.50, 10 or more children $1
Collections: Texas Ranger items; Western history; paintings and sculpture
Exhibitions: Temporary and traveling exhibitions
Activities: Lect; research on Texas Rangers; sales shop

L Library, 76703. *Librn* Janice Reece
For reference only
Library Holdings: Vols 1511; Micro — Reels; AV — Cassettes, v-tapes; Other — Clipping files, manuscripts, memorabilia, photographs
Special Subjects: Texas History, Texas Rangers (law enforcement agency)

WAXAHACHIE

M ELLIS COUNTY MUSEUM INC, 201 S College, PO Box 706, 75165. Tel 214-937-0681. *Cur* Shannon Simpson
Open Tues - Sat 10 AM - 5 PM, Sun 1 - 5 PM, cl Mon. Estab 1969 to collect & maintain artifacts relating to County's history. Average Annual Attendance: 10,000-12,000. Mem: 275; dues business $20, family $20, individual $10, sr citizen $5; annual meeting last Mon in July
Income: $30,000-$40,000 (financed by annual fundraiser)
Collections: Decorative Arts, Clothing, Furniture; Folding Fans; Photographs, Memorabilia; Technological Implements; Weaponry
Activities: Retail store sells books, prints

WICHITA FALLS

M WICHITA FALLS MUSEUM AND ART CENTER, Two Eureka Circle, 76308. Tel 817-692-0923; FAX 817-696-5358. *Dir* Lin Owen
Open Tues - Sat 10 AM - 5 PM, Sun 1 - 5 PM. Admis fee varies with exhibits. Estab 1964 for the purpose of serving the community. Two galleries house art exhibits, 2 galleries house science & history exhibits. Average Annual Attendance: 60,000. Mem: 1000; dues $25 - $1000; annual meeting May
Income: Financed by endowment, membership, city appropriation and schools
Collections: †American prints
Publications: Events calendar, Sept, Jan, May
Activities: Classes for adults and children; docent training; lect open to public, 2 - 5 vis lectr per yr; gallery talks; tours; lending collection has original prints; originate traveling exhibitions; shop sells books, prints, crafts and jewelry

WIMBERLEY

M PIONEER TOWN, Pioneer Museum of Western Art, 7A Ranch Resort, PO Box 259, Route 1, 78676. Tel 512-847-3289. *Dir* Raymond L Czichos
Open Memorial Day - Labor Day 9 AM - 10 PM daily, rest of the year, Sat & Sun afternoons, cl Oct - Feb. No admis fee. Estab 1956 as a village and art museum
Collections: Contemporary Western artists; sculpture and metalwork; Jack Woods, sculpture; Remington Bronze Collections

UTAH

BRIGHAM CITY

M BRIGHAM CITY MUSEUM-GALLERY, 24 N Third W, PO Box 583, 84302. Tel 801-723-6769; FAX 801-723-5011. *Dir* Larry Douglas; *Chmn* Colleen H Bradford
Open Tues - Fri 11 AM - 6 PM, Sat 1 - 5 PM, cl Sun & Mon. No admis fee. Estab 1970 to document local history and serve as a state-wide art collection. Average Annual Attendance: 13,000
Income: Financed by Brigham City Corporation
Collections: Crystal and glass; 19th century clothing, artifacts and furniture folk art; fibers; ceramics; painting; printmaking
Activities: Educ dept for research, & oral histories; lectures open to public; gallery talks; tours; awards; monthly rotating exhibits of art and varied collections

CEDAR CITY

M SOUTHERN UTAH UNIVERSITY, Braithwaite Fine Arts Gallery, Braithwaite Liberal Arts Ctr, 84720. Tel 801-586-5432. *Cur* Valerie A Kidrick
Open Mon - Wed 10 AM - 7 PM, Thurs & Fri 10 AM - 5 PM, Sat 1 - 5 PM. No admis fee. Estab 1976 to provide a quality visual arts forum for artists' work and the viewing public. The gallery has 2000 sq ft of space with 300 lineal ft of display surface; it is equipped with facilities for two and three-dimensional media with electronic security system. Average Annual Attendance: 18,000. Mem: 210; annual dues $50 - $75
Income: Financed by city and state appropriations and private donations
Collections: 18th, 19th & 20th century American art
Exhibitions: Annual Faculty Exhibition; Annual Student Exhibition; Shakespeare: Designed & Realized; Southern Utah Artist Invitational; Recent art gifts to college
Publications: Exhibition announcements, monthly; NOVUS, quarterly newsletter
Activities: Classes for adults & children; docent training; lect open to public, 8-10 vis lectrs per year; gallery talks; tours; individual paintings & original objects of art lent to state school districts & individual campus offices; lending collection contains 500 Kodachromes, 500 original art works, 100 original prints, 300 paintings, 1000 slides; book traveling exhibitions 10 per year

FILLMORE

M UTAH DEPARTMENT OF NATURAL RESOURCES, DIVISION OF PARKS & RECREATION, Territorial Statehouse, 50 W Capital Ave, PO Box 657, 84631. Tel 801-743-5316. *Contact* Matt Sheridan
Open 8 AM - 7 PM June 1 - Sept 1, all other months 8 AM - 5 PM. Admis 6 &

over $.50. Estab 1930, as a museum for pioneer relics. Restored by the state and local Daughters of Utah Pioneers; owned & operated by Utah State Division of Parks & Recreation. Average Annual Attendance: 25,000

Income: Financed by state appropriations

Collections: Charcoal and pencil sketches; paintings by Utah artists; photograph prints collection; pioneer portraits in antique frames; silk screen prints; furniture arranged in household settings

Activities: Educ dept; lectures; gallery talks; tours

LOGAN

M **NORA ECCLES HARRISON MUSEUM OF ART,** Utah State Univ, UMC 4020, 84322-4020. Tel 801-750-1412; FAX 801-750-3423. *Dir & Chief Cur* Steven W Rosen; *Assoc Cur* Rose M Milovich; *Staff Asst* Cheryl E Sampson
Open Tues, Thurs & Fri 10:30 AM - 4:30 PM, Wed 10:30 AM - 9 PM, Sat & Sun 2 - 5 PM. No admis fee. Estab 1983. Over 10,000 sq ft of exhibition area, half devoted to permanent exhibits & half to temporary shows. Average Annual Attendance: 25,000. Mem: 120; dues $10 - $500; annual meeting 2nd Tues of May

Purchases: $120,000

Collections: †Native American art; †20th century American art, with emphasis on Western US artists; †20th century American ceramics

Exhibitions: Harrison Ceramics Collection; Boyden Collection of Native American Art; Life & Land: The FSA Photographers in Utah; A Dozen and One Utah Furniture Makers; Large scale ceramic sculpture

Publications: Exhibition catalogs; Insight, newsletter, three times per yr

Activities: Lectures open to public & to members only, 5 vis lectrs per yr; scholarships & fels offered; book traveling exhibitions, 3-4 per yr; originate traveling exhibitions; musuem shop sells books & magazines

OGDEN

A **ECCLES COMMUNITY ART CENTER,** 2580 Jefferson Ave, 84401. Tel 801-392-6935; FAX 801-392-5295. *Dir* Sandy Havas; *Asst Dir* Karen Poggemeyer; *Gift Shop Mgr* Arlene Muller
Open 9 AM - 5 PM Mon - Fri, 10 AM - 4 PM Sat, cl Sun & holidays. No admis fee. Estab 1959 to serve as focal point for community cultural activities & to promote cultural growth. Maintains an art gallery with monthly exhibits. Average Annual Attendance: 25,000. Mem: 300 dues $25 - $100; annual meeting Nov

Income: $100,000 (financed by mem, state appropriation & fund raising)

Collections: †Utah Artists (historic & contemporaries)

Exhibitions: (1993) Paintings by Carlin, Ji, Leek, Preece, Brown-Wagner, Songer South; Chris Gittins (ceramics); woodcuts & wood engravings from Utah State University; 5th Statewide Black & White Competition; 19th Statewide Competition, Ogden Collects; Utah Quilt Show; Weber School District Student Show; Westcoast Watercolor Society

Publications: Newsletter, quarterly

Activities: Educ dept; classes for adults & children; lect open to public; concerts; competition with awards; gallery talks; tours;; individual paintings & original art works lent to galleries, government offices, hospitals & businesses; book traveling exhibitions; sales shop sells original art, reproductions, prints, ceramics, jewelry & artist produced cards

OGDEN UNION STATION

M **Myra Powell Art Gallery,** 2501 Wall Ave, 84401. Tel 801-629-8444.
Open Mon - Sat 10 AM - 5 PM. No admis fee. Estab 1979 to acquaint more people with the visual arts & to heighten awareness of art. 12.5 ft x 113 ft; 39 panels 6 ft x 4 ft

Income: Financed by endowment

Collections: Non-objective painting, Indian Design, Landscape, Navajo Sand Painting, Alumin Sculpture

Activities: Lectures open to public; competitions with awards; scholarships & fels offered; individual paintings & original objects of art lent

M **Union Station Museums,** 2501 Wall Ave, 84401. Tel 801-629-8444, 629-8533. *Exec Dir* Elizabeth Griffith; *Museum Coordr* Dot Roddom
Open Mon - Sat 10 AM - 6 PM, Sun 1 - 5 PM (Memorial Day - Labor Day). Admis adults $2, sr citizens $1.50, children under 12 $1. Estab 1976 to serve as a cultural & civic center for Ogden, Utah. Average Annual Attendance: 40,000. Mem: Dues $15 - $1000; meetings 1st Tues of month

Income: Financed by endowment, mem, city appropriation

Collections: Railroad memorabilia

Exhibitions: Junction City Festival Exhibit, 1930s & 1940s memorabilia; Browning Firearms; Browning Classic Cars; Wattis-Dumke Model Railroad; Gem & Mineral Display; Myra Powell Gallery

Publications: The Inside Track, annual newsletter

Activities: Shop sells books & reproductions

PARK CITY

A **KIMBALL ART CENTER,** 638 Park Ave, PO Box 1478, 84060. Tel 801-649-8882; FAX 801-649-8892. *Dir* Gary Sanders
Open Mon - Sun 10 AM - 6 PM. Estab 1976 for monthly gallery shows & workshops in arts & crafts, fine arts. Main gallery has movable walls & is 80 x 180 ft, little gallery measures 17 x 20 ft. Average Annual Attendance: 500,000. Mem: 600; dues $35; meetings in June & Jan

Income: $500,000 (financed by endowment, membership & contributions)

Exhibitions: Twenty-four exhibits annually in various styles & mediums

Activities: Classes for adults & children; docent training; lectures open to public; opening receptions with exhibiting artists; annual art festival; book traveling exhibitions; sales shop sells original art & prints

PRICE

M **COLLEGE OF EASTERN UTAH,** Gallery East, 451 E Fourth North, 84501. Tel 801-637-2120, Ext 264; FAX 801-637-4102. *Dir* James L Young; *Chmn* Brent Haddock
Open daily 8:30 AM - 5 PM, open special nights. No admis fee. Estab 1975 to provide an educational and aesthetic tool within the community. Average Annual Attendance: 5000

Income: $1600 (financed by school appropriation)

Collections: Broad collection of contemporary prints & painting

Exhibitions: Changing exhibits

Activities: Lectures open to the public, 9-10 vis lectrs per year; gallery talks; tours; competitions with awards; scholarships; traveling exhibits organized and circulated to colleges

PROVO

BRIGHAM YOUNG UNIVERSITY

M **B F Larsen Gallery,** Harris Fine Arts Center F-303, 84602. Tel 801-378-2881; FAX 801-378-5964. *Gallery Dir* Marcus Vincent; *Art Gallery Secy* Sharon Lyn Heelis
Open 8 AM - 10 PM. No admis fee. Estab 1965 to bring to the University students and faculty a wide range of new experiences in the visual arts. B F Larsen Gallery is a three story atrium shaped gallery with exhibition areas in center floor and upper levels; Gallery 303 is large room with foyer and single entrance-exit; total exhibition space 15,260 sq ft. Average Annual Attendance: 55,000 Gallery 303; 100,000 Larsen

Income: Financed by university

Exhibitions: Invitational exhibits; exhibits by students & faculty, curated exhibits of contemporary artists & circulating exhibits. (1993) Gallery 303: Mexican Religious Art; Art Discussing Life; Computer Art Invitational. (1993) B F Larsen Gallery: Textile Invitational; Celebrating Year of Craft; Alumni 100: An Exhibit Chronicling 100 Years of Alumni Art Work; Drawing 1993

Activities: Lectures open to public; competitions; monetary and certificate awards; individual paintings and original objects of art lent to university executive, faculty and university library; book traveling exhibitons monthly

L **Harold B Lee Library,** 84602. Tel 801-378-4005. *Dir Libraries* Sterling Albrecht; *Fine Arts Librn* Russell T Clement
Open Mon - Sat 7 AM - 12 PM. Estab 1875 to support the university curriculum

Income: Financed by endowment, membership and Latter-day Saints church funds

Library Holdings: Vols 55,000; Per subs 215; Micro — Fiche, reels; AV — A-tapes, cassettes, fs, motion pictures, slides; Other — Memorabilia, pamphlets, photographs 12,000, prints

Collections: George Anderson Collection of early Utah photographs; 15th and 16th century graphic art collection; C R Savage Collection; Vought indexed and mounted art print collection

Activities: Tours

SAINT GEORGE

M **DIXIE COLLEGE,** Southwestern Utah Art Gallery, 84770. Tel 801-673-4811, Ext 297; FAX 801-673-8552. *Dir* Max E Bunnell
Open 8 AM - 6 PM. No admis fee. Estab 1960 to serve southwestern Utah as a visual arts exhibit center. Gallery is located in Fine Arts Center. Average Annual Attendance: 10,000 - 15,000

Income: Financed by state appropriation and 30% of sales from monthly shows

Collections: Early and contemporary Utah painters

Exhibitions: Dixie Annual Invitational (regional)

Activities: Classes for adults; dramatic programs; lect open to public, vis lectrs; gallery talks

SALT LAKE CITY

M **CHURCH OF JESUS CHRIST OF LATTER-DAY SAINTS,** Museum of Church History & Art, 45 N West Temple, 84150. Tel 801-240-2299. *Dir* Glen Leonard; *Operation Mgr* Steven Olsen
Open Mon - Fri 9 AM - 9 PM, Sat, Sun & Holidays 10 AM - 7 PM, cl Easter, Thanksgiving, Christmas & New Year's Day. No admis fee. Estab 1869 to disseminate information and display historical memorabilia, artifacts and art to the visiting public. Assists in restorations and furnishing of Church historic sites. Average Annual Attendance: 300,000

Income: Financed by Church

Collections: †Mostly 19th and 20th century Mormon art and historical artifacts †portraits, paintings, drawings, sculpture, prints, American furniture, china, pottery, glass; †Mormon quilts and handwork; †decorative arts; †clothing and textiles; architectural elements and hardware; †Oceanic and American Indian pottery, basketry, and textiles

Exhibitions: Permanent Installations: Presidents of the Church; Portraits of Church Leaders; Western Themes; Masterworks of Mormon art; Latter-day Saint History

Publications: Exhibition catalogs; brochures

Activities: Docent training; seminars; gallery demonstrations; school outreach; lectures open to the public; gallery talks; tours; individual paintings & original objects of art lent; originate traveling exhibitions; museum shop sells books, reproductions, prints, slides & posters

L **Art Library,** 45 N West Temple, 84150. Tel 801-240-4604.
Reference library

Library Holdings: Vols 2000; Per subs 20; Micro — Fiche, reels; AV — A-tapes, cassettes, motion pictures, slides, v-tapes; Other — Clipping files, exhibition catalogs, memorabilia, original art works, pamphlets, photographs, sculpture

Special Subjects: Latter-day Saints art, artists, history & historic sites

A **SALT LAKE ART CENTER,** 20 S W Temple, 84101. Tel 801-328-4201; FAX 801-322-4323. *Pres* Nancy Holman; *Dir* Sam Gappmayer
Open Tues - Sat 10 AM - 5 PM, Fri 10 AM - 9 PM, Sun 1 - 5 PM, cl Mon. No admis fee. Estab 1931 to educate the community in the visual arts through exhibitions and classes. Center has one large gallery of 5000 sq ft; one small gallery of 2000 sq ft; sales shop of 1000 sq ft, one permanent collection gallery of 2500 sq ft. Average Annual Attendance: 60,000. Mem: 1250; annual dues family $30, individual $20; annual meeting Nov
Income: $400,000 (financed by membership, city & state appropriation, earned income, gifts, & private & corporate contributions)
Purchases: $70,000 Bolotowsky Sculpture
Collections: Utah artists (1930-Present)
Exhibitions: 200 Years of American Art, Santa Barbara Museum of Art Collection; Art of the Muppets; Santa Fe Collection of Southwester Art; Retrospectives of Utah Artists: V Douglas Snow, Bonnie Sucec & Avard Fairbanks; Rembrandt Etchings, Brigham Young University Collection; Lost & Found: An Archaeological Composition
Publications: Bulletin, quarterly
Activities: Classes for adults & children; studio & lecture courses; lect open to public, 20 vis lectr per yr; concerts; gallery talks; tours; competitions with awards; originate traveling exhibitions; sales shop sells books, original art, reproductions & prints

L **SALT LAKE CITY PUBLIC LIBRARY,** Fine Arts/Audiovisual Dept and Atrium Gallery, 209 E Fifth S, 84111. Tel 801-524-8200, Ext 214. *Dir* J Dennis Day; *Head Fine Arts & Audiovisual Dept* Mary Johns
Open Mon - Thurs 9 AM - 9 PM, Fri - Sat 9 AM - 6 PM. Estab 1898. Maintains an art gallery with monthly exhibitions
Income: Financed by endowment and city appropriation
Library Holdings: Picture files; AV — Fs, rec, slides, v-tapes; Other — Clipping files, exhibition catalogs, framed reproductions, original art works, reproductions
Special Subjects: Film, Contemporary art, photography
Collections: Art of Western United States; Utah Artists; American & European Works on Paper
Exhibitions: (1991) Wayne Chubin (photographs); Sharon Alderman (textiles); Susan Harris (ceramics); Portraits & Perspectives; Tom Tessman: Domestic Liturgical Furniture & Objects; Figurative Paintings, Susan Beck, Sam Collett, John Erickson
Publications: Brochures accompanying individual exhibitions; Permanent Art Collection Catalogue
Activities: Films; gallery talks; tours; demonstrations; slide presentations; individual paintings & original objects of art lent to museums & non-profit galleries; originate traveling exhibitions

M **UNIVERSITY OF UTAH,** Utah Museum of Fine Arts, 101 Art & Architectural Center, 84112. Tel 801-581-7332; FAX 801-585-5198. *Dir* E F Sanguinetti; *Cur of Exhibitions* Thomas Southam; *Gallery Supt & Preparator* David Hardy; *Registrar* David Carroll; *Cur Educational Services* Open ; *Asst Dir* Charles Loving; *Membership & Vol Coordr* Kristine E Widner; *Assoc Cur of Education* Ann Stewart
Open Mon - Fri 10 AM - 5 PM, Sat & Sun 2 - 5 PM. No admis fee. Average Annual Attendance: 95,000. Mem: 1,000; dues family $35, single $20
Income: Financed by University & private gifts
Collections: Winifred Kimball Hudnut Collection; Natacha Rambova Egyptian Collection; Marion Sharp Robinson Collection; Trower & Michael Collections of English, American & Peruvian Silver; Bartlett Wicks Collection; English 17th and 18th century furniture and pictures; Egyptian antiquities; French 18th century furnishings and tapestries; graphics, contemporary works; Italian Renaissance paintings and furniture; objects from the Buddhist culture African Art; Indonesian Art; Oceanic Art, Amerian Indian Art; North Western Coastal Art
Activities: Classes for adults; docent training; lect open to public, some members only; concerts; gallery talks; tours; paintings and art objects lent; originate traveling exhibitions

L **Owen Library,** Art and Architecture Center, 84112. Tel 801-581-3840. *Dir* Robert S Olpin; *Librn* Sandra Gray
Open Mon - Fri 10 AM - 5 PM. Estab 1978 as a reference library for art students
Library Holdings: Vols 2000; Per subs 40; AV — Cassettes, Kodachromes, slides, v-tapes; Other — Clipping files, exhibition catalogs, manuscripts, memorabilia, original art works, pamphlets

L **Marriott Library,** 84112. Tel 801-581-8104. *Fine Arts Librn* Myron Patterson; *Sr Libr Specialist* Dorothy Greenland
Open Mon - Thurs 8 AM - 11 PM, Fri 8 AM - 5 PM, Sat 9 AM - 5 PM, Sun 1 - 11 PM. Estab 1967 to serve the students & faculty of the University with research materials & specialized services. For lending & reference
Income: Financed by state appropriation
Purchases: $60,000 per yr for fine arts books
Library Holdings: Vols 2,000,000; Per subs 17,000; AV — Slides; Other — Clipping files, exhibition catalogs, prints, reproductions
Special Subjects: Advertising Design, Aesthetics, Afro-American Art, American Indian Art, American Western Art, Folk Art, Furniture, Glass, Graphic Arts, Graphic Design, Painting - American, Painting - British, Painting - Dutch, Painting - European, Painting - Flemish

M **UTAH ARTS COUNCIL,** Chase Home Museum of Utah Folk Art, 617 E South Temple, 84102. Tel 801-533-5760. *Chmn* Burtch Beall Jr; *Exec Dir* Bonnie Stephens; *Folk Arts Coordr* Carol Edison
Open mid Apr - Oct noon - 5 PM, spring & fall weekends only, daily during the summer. Estab 1986 to showcase folk art in the State Art Collection. Four small galleries, one small reception area & two hallways for display in a 19th century two-story farmhouse. Average Annual Attendance: 20,000
Income: Financed by state and federal appropriations
Library Holdings: Vols 400; Per subs 5; AV — A-tapes, cassettes, motion pictures, rec, slides; Other — Clipping files, pamphlets, photographs, prints
Special Subjects: American Indian Art, Decorative Arts, Folk Art, Furniture, Historical Material, Textiles, Folklore, Folklife of Utah & the American West

Collections: †Familial; †Ethnic; †Occupational; †Religious; †Regional with an emphasis on traditional work by living folk artists
Exhibitions: Annual exhibit of Utah folk art
Activities: Lect open to the public; concerts; group tours; originates traveling exhibitions; sales shop sells books

A **UTAH LAWYERS FOR THE ARTS,** 170 S Main St, Suite 1400, 84101. Tel 801-521-3200; FAX 801-328-0537. *Pres* Randon Wilson
Estab 1983 to provide pro bono legal services. Mem: 36; mem open to attorneys & law students; $30 annual fee, $15 student fee
Income: Financed by membership
Publications: Art/Law News, quarterly newsletter

A **UTAH TRAVEL COUNCIL,** Council Hall, Capitol Hill, 84114. Tel 801-538-1030; FAX 801-538-1399. *Dir* Jay C Woolley; *Deputy Dir* Osamu Hoshino; *Travel Publications Specialist* Janice Carpenter; *Media Dir* Dave Porter; *Travel Development Specialist* Pam Westwood
Open 8 AM - 5 PM; Sat & Sun 10 AM - 5 PM. No admis fee. Constructed in 1866 and served as seat of government for 30 years; reconstructed on Capitol Hill and presented to Utah state in 1963; contains small museum of pioneer and historic items, paintings and furniture
Income: Financed by legislative appropriation
Publications: Brochures; two newsletters
Activities: Lending collection contains motion pictures, photographs, transparencies for public use, videos on travel opportunities in Utah; originate traveling exhibitions

SPRINGVILLE

M **SPRINGVILLE MUSEUM OF ART,** 126 E 400 South, 84663. Tel 801-489-2727. *Dir* Vern G Swanson; *Asst Dir* Dr Sharon R Gray
Open Tues - Sat 10 AM - 5 PM, Wed 10 AM - 9 PM, Sun 2 - 5 PM, cl Mon. No admis fee. Estab 1903 for the collection and exhibition of Utah fine arts, and as educational resource. Built in 1935-1937, is one of the largest museums in the mountain west, it has eleven galleries with 25,000 sq ft of exhibit space; maintains a photographic art reference library for Utah art history. Average Annual Attendance: 115,000. Mem: 400; dues family $25, individual $15; annual meeting in Apr
Income: $200,000 (financed by membership, city and state appropriations)
Purchases: $5000 - $10,000 of fine art
Collections: Artwork by Cyrus Dallin & John Hafen; Utah artists from 1850 to present of all styles
Exhibitions: Annual Spring Salon Utah Invitational Fine Art; June Quilt Show; High Schools of Utah Show; Annual Utah Autumn Exhibit
Publications: Exhibition catalogs, quarterly bulletin
Activities: Classes for adults and children; docent and intern training; guided tours; library research; lectures open to public, 5 vis lectr per year; 6 concerts per year; 5 gallery talks per year; scholarships and fels offered; Individual paintings and original objects of art lent to art institutions; lending collection contains nature artifacts & 7000 sculpture; museum shop sells books, reproductions, catalogues & note cards

VERMONT

BENNINGTON

M **BENNINGTON MUSEUM,** W Main St, 05201. Tel 802-447-1571. *Dir* Laura C Luckey; *Cur Decorative Arts* Kenneth Cogry; *Cur History* Eugene R Kosche; *Registrar* Ruth Levin; *Dir Educ* Elspeth Inglis; *Museum Shop Mgr* Priscilla Hall; *Membership & Public Relations Coordr* Elisa Lanzi
Open March 1 - Nov 30 9 AM - 5 PM daily, cl Thanksgiving Day. Admis adults $4.50, students & sr citizens $3.50, family $10, children under 12 free. Estab 1875 as resource for history and fine and decorative arts of New England. Local historical museum with 10 galleries, Grandma Moses Schoolhouse Museum. Average Annual Attendance: 70,000. Mem: 700; dues $15-$1000; annual meeting May
Income: $486,385
Collections: Bennington pottery; Bennington battle flag; American blown & pressed glass; American painting & sculpture; American furniture & decorative arts; dolls & toys; Grandma Moses paintings; rare documents
Exhibitions: The Country Store in Vermont; American Toys from the Barenholtz Collection; Norman Rockwell Paintings; American Trade Signs; Bennington Photographs; Commemorative Objects from the Bennington Museum Collection; A Good Day's Work: Folk Art from the Bennington Museum Collection; Vermont Workers, Vermont Resources; And Life is What You Make It: Grandma Moses at the Bennington Museum; Vermont in the Victorian Age: 19th Century Birdseye and Panoramic Views; Fine Prints in Colors: The Lithographs of Currier and Ives; Celebrating Vermont, Myths & Realizations
Publications: Exhibition catalogs
Activities: Classes for adults and children; docent training; lectures open to public, 5 vis lectr per year; concerts; gallery talks; tours; individual paintings and original objects of art lent through a rental program; originate traveling exhibitions to other northern New England museums; museum shop sells books, magazines, original art, reproductions, prints and slides

L **Library,** W Main St, 05201. Tel 802-447-1571.
Open by appointment only. For reference only
Library Holdings: Vols 5000; Per subs 10; Micro — Reels; AV — Lantern slides, slides, v-tapes; Other — Clipping files, exhibition catalogs, manuscripts, memorabilia, pamphlets, photographs
Special Subjects: Art History, Ceramics, Coins & Medals, Decorative Arts, Flasks & Bottles, Folk Art, Furniture, Glass, Historical Material, Portraits, Pottery, Sculpture, Silver, Textiles, American Decorative Arts, New England Genealogy

BRATTLEBORO

M BRATTLEBORO MUSEUM & ART CENTER, Union Railroad Station, PO Box 662, 05302-0662. Tel 802-257-0124. *Pres* Roger Miller; *Dir* Mara Williams
Open May 15 - Nov 1 Tues - Sun noon - 6 PM. Admis adults $2, sr & college $1, children & members free. Estab 1972 to present art & historical exhibition programs integrated through an annual theme. The museum is located in a railroad station built in 1915, now a registered historic site. Four galleries with changing exhibitions & one permanent gallery of Estey organs. Average Annual Attendance: 15,000. Mem: 700; dues family $40, individual $25; annual meeting in Mar
Income: $185,000 (financed by membership, donations, town, state and federal appropriations)
Collections: Estey Organ Exhibit
Publications: A Working Heritage; Built Landscapes; Gardens of the Northeast; Workshop Experiments
Activities: Docent training; programs for school groups; week-long artist-in-residence program; lectures open to public, 20 vis lectrs per year; concerts; gallery talks; originate traveling exhibitions

BROOKFIELD

M MUSEUM OF THE AMERICAS, 05036. Tel 802-276-3386. *Dir* Earle W Newton
Open daily 2 - 5 PM. Admis donations requested. Estab 1971 to gather materials in support of Anglo American and Hispanic-American studies. 4000 sq ft gallery
Income: Financed by endowment & gifts
Collections: Anglo-American 16th - 19th century paintings; English mezzotints; Hispanic-American decorative arts; Hogarth prints and paintings; Latin American folk art; maps of the colonies; Pre-Columbian artifacts
Exhibitions: World of William Hogarth: Paintings & Ingravings. (1991) Fielding, Gay & Hogarth: Art, Music & Literature of Georgian England. English Faces: 1500 - 1800
Activities: Classes for adults in prospect; lect open to public; concerts; individuals paintings lent; lending collection contains 5000 books, 1000 video cassettes, 300 paintings; museum shop sells books
L Library, 05036. Tel 802-276-3386. *Dir* Earle W Newton
For reference only
Income: Financed by endowment & gifts
Library Holdings: Vols 5000; Per subs 10; AV — V-tapes; Other — Clipping files, original art works
Special Subjects: Art History, Etchings & Engravings, Maps, Mexican Art, Painting - American, Painting - British, Painting - Spanish, Portraits, Pre-Columbian Art, Prints
Collections: Anglo-American and Latin American art and history

BURLINGTON

M UNIVERSITY OF VERMONT, Robert Hull Fleming Museum, 05405. Tel 802-656-0750, 656-2090; FAX 802-656-8059. *Dir* Ann Porter; *Cur* Janie Cohen; *Business Mgr* Anna Seyller; *Exhibition Designer & Preparator* Merlin Acomb; *Museum Educator* Chris Fearon; *Registrar* Christina Kelly
Call 802-656-2090 for hours. No admis fee. Estab 1873 as a fine arts museum for the area and a teaching facility for the University. Permanent gallery of 18th & 19th century American Art; permanent gallery of European painting; ethnographic gallery of rotating exhibitions. Museum also contains a reference library. Average Annual Attendance: 30,000. Mem: 700; dues Fleming Society $1000, benefactor $500 - $999, patron $250-$499 supporting $100-$249 contributing $50-$99, family $30, individual $20, student $10
Income: Financed membership, university appropriations and grants
Collections: American, European, Pre-Columbian and Oriental art including paintings, sculpture, decorative arts and artifacts; costumes; ethnographic collection, especially native American; prints and drawings of various periods
Exhibitions: American historic and contemporary; Asian; Ethnographic; Medieval and Ancient; European; Egyptian
Publications: Exhibition catalogs; newsletter-calendar, 3 per yr
Activities: Classes for adults & children; docent training; lectures open to public, 20 vis lectr per yr; concerts; gallery talks; tours; community outreach serves all Vermont; individual paintings & original objects of art lent to museum community; book traveling exhibitions; originate traveling exhibitions; museum shop sells books, magazines, reproductions, prints & Vermont crafts
M Francis Colburn Gallery, Williams Hall, 05405. Tel 802-656-2014.
Open Sept - May 9 AM - 5 PM. No admis fee. Estab 1975
Exhibitions: Student, faculty and visiting artist works
L Wilbur Room Library, Robert Hull Fleming Museum, 05405. Tel 802-656-0750; FAX 802-656-8059.
Open Wed 1 - 4 PM. Estab for Museum staff & volunteers & use by University & community. Books & materials related to Fleming Museum collections. For reference only
Library Holdings: Vols 1000; Other — Clipping files, exhibition catalogs, pamphlets
Special Subjects: Asian Art, Decorative Arts, Painting - American

FERRISBURGH

A ROWLAND EVANS ROBINSON MEMORIAL ASSOCIATION, Rokeby Museum, Rural Route 1, PO Box 1540, 05456-9711. Tel 802-877-3406. *Dir* Karen Petersen
Open May - Oct Thurs - Sun 11 AM - 3 PM, open by appointment only remainder of year. Estab 1963 to exhibit & interpret lives & works of the Robinson family. Robinson family (prolific artists) art is displayed throughout the house. Work of Rachael Robinson Elmer (1878 - 1919), student at Art Students League, is most prominent. She & her father, Rowland E Robinson (1833 - 1900), were published artists. Average Annual Attendance: 1300. Mem: 250; dues family $20, individual $10, sr citizen & student $6; annual meeting mid-May
Income: Financed by endowment, mem, contributions & grants
Collections: Art, oils & watercolor sketches; books & manuscripts; 17th - 20th century furnishings; textiles & costumes
Exhibitions: (1992) Toons of the Times, The Political & Satirical Costumes of Rowland Evans Robinson 1858 - 1875
Publications: Messenger
Activities: Classes for adults & children; lect open to public, 2 vis lectr per year; retail store sells books & prints

GLOVER

M BREAD & PUPPET THEATER, Museum, Route 122, RD 2, 05839. Tel 802-525-6972. *Mgr* Elka Schumann; *Artist* Peter Schumann
Open June - Oct daily 10 AM - 5 PM. No Admis fee. Estab 1975 to exhibit & promote the art of puppetry. Average Annual Attendance: 25,000
Income: $10,000 (financed by donationa, sales of publications & art & by the Bread & Puppet Theater
Collections: Puppets; giant puppets; masks; graphics
Publications: Bread & Puppet Museum, The Radicality of Puppetry
Activities: Museum shop sells books, prints, original art, posters & postcards

JERICHO

A JERICHO HISTORICAL SOCIETY, The Old Red Mill, PO Box 35, 05465. Tel 802-899-3225.
Open Mon - Sat 10 AM - 5 PM, cl winter. No admis fee. Estab 1978
Income: Financed by mem & contributions
Collections: Milling Machinery (video tape); Slides of Snow Flakes & Ice Crystals (video tape)
Exhibitions: Machinery, permanent exhibit

LUDLOW

M BLACK RIVER HISTORICAL SOCIETY, Black River Academy Museum, High St, PO Box 73, 05149. Tel 802-228-5050. *Dir* Georgia L Brehm
Open noon - 4 PM, summer only. Estab 1972. 3-story brick building built in 1889. Average Annual Attendance: 1200. Mem: 200, annual dues family $15, single $10
Income: $25,000 (financed by endowment)
Collections: School memorabilia, farming implements, domestic items - 19th century, furnishings, clothing
Publications: History of Ludlow, VT, J Harris (monograph)
Activities: Dramatic programs; concerts; tours on holidays; Traveling exhibitions, 2 per yr; museum shop sells books

MANCHESTER

A SOUTHERN VERMONT ART CENTER, PO Box 617, 05254. Tel 802-362-1405. *Pres* Marshall Peck; *Dir* Christopher Madkour; *Dir Public Relations* Trisha Hayes
Open Tues - Sat 10 AM - 5 PM, Sun noon - 5 PM, cl July 4th. Admis adults $3, students $.50, free admis Sun. Estab 1929 to promote education in the arts and to hold exhibitions of art in its various forms. 10 galleries; sculpture garden. Average Annual Attendance: 20,000. Mem: Dues $30 - $45; annual meeting in Sept
Income: Financed by membership and contributions
Collections: Contemporary American sculptors and painters; loan collection
Exhibitions: Annual exhibitions for members; Fall Show; one-man and special exhibitions
Publications: Annual catalog and brochures
Activities: Classes for adults and children in painting, drawing, graphic arts, photography, sculpture and pottery; concerts; scholarship and fels offered
L Library, PO Box 617, 05254. Tel 802-362-1405.
Library Holdings: Vols 500

MIDDLEBURY

M MIDDLEBURY COLLEGE, Museum of Art, Center for the Arts, 05753. Tel 802-388-3711, Ext 5235. *Dir* Richard H Saunders; *Asst Dir* Emmie Donadio; *Exhib Coordr* Monica McCabe; *Preparator* Ken Pohlmann
Open Tues, Wed & Fri 10 AM - 5 PM, Thurs 10 AM - 8 PM, Sat & Sun noon - 5 PM, cl Mon & holidays. No admis fee. Estab 1968 as a teaching collection. Now also presents loan exhibitions, work by individuals & groups, student exhibits
Income: Financed through College, Friends of Art, grants
Collections: †Drawings; †paintings; photographs; †prints; †sculpture;
Publications: Annual Report; Friends of Art Newsletter, 2 per year; gallery brochure; exhibition catalogues
Activities: Lectures open to public, 4 vis lectrs per year; Book traveling exhibitions, 6-7 per yr; originate traveling exhibitions

M SHELDON MUSEUM, One Park St, 05753. Tel 802-388-2117. *Dir* Virginia H Brown; *Asst Dir* Sandra Olivo
Open June - Oct Mon - Fri 10 AM - 5 PM, Sat 10 AM - 1 PM, winter hours Wed & Fri 1 - 4 PM. Admis adults $3.50, sr citizens & students $3, children $.50. Estab 1882 for the preservation of portraits, decorative arts & artifacts of Middlebury. Twelve rooms arranged as a 19th century Vermont home. Average Annual Attendance: 3500. Mem: 450; dues $10 & up
Collections: China; Glass; Pewter; †Historical material; Portraits; Landscapes; Furniture; Prints
Exhibitions: Changing exhibits in the Cerf Gallery; permanent exhibits of 19th Century home & furnishings
Publications: Annual Report; semi-annual newsletter
Activities: Classes for children; guided tours, lectures; out-reach program to county schools; museum shop sells books, prints, crafts & toys

M VERMONT STATE CRAFT CENTER AT FROG HOLLOW, Mill St, 05753. Tel 802-388-3177. *Exec Dir* Pamela Siers; *Gallery Dir* Anne Majusiak; *Sales Mgr* Maria Kriefal; *Public Relations* Linda Baker
Open Mon - Sat 9:30 AM - 5 PM, Sun afternoon spring - fall. No admis fee. Estab 1971 to provide craft educational, informational and marketing services to school children, adults and professionals. Sales gallery exhibits the work of over 250 juried Vermont crafts people, also hosts yearly exhibition schedule featuring the work of noted crafts people world wide. Average Annual Attendance: 80,000. Mem: 500; dues $25 - $100; annual meeting Sept; exhibiting members are juried into the gallery
Income: $545,000 (financed by membership, federal & state grants, fund raising activities, consignment receipts & tuition)
Collections: †Vermont Crafts
Publications: Information services bulletin; calendar; show announcements; course brochures
Activities: Classes for adults & children; craft demonstrations; professional workshops for crafts people; pottery facility; resident potter studios; lect open to public, 4 vis lectr per yr; tours; scholarships & fels offered; original objects of art lent to Vermont State Senate office in Washington; traveling exhibitions organized and circulated; gallery shop sells books, Vermont crafts

MONTPELIER

M VERMONT HISTORICAL SOCIETY, Museum, 109 State St, 05609-0901. Tel 802-828-2291. *Dir* Michael Sherman, PhD
Open Tues - Fri 9 AM - 4:30 PM, Sun 9 AM - 4 PM, Sun noon - 4 PM, cl Mon; call for holiday hours. Admis donation. Estab 1838 to collect, preserve and make available for study items from Vermont's past. Average Annual Attendance: 22,000. Mem: 2500; dues $25-$500; annual meetings Sept
Income: Financed by endowment, membership, state appropriation and contributions
Special Subjects: Historical Material, Manuscripts, Geneology
Collections: Collection of fine arts, decorative arts, tools & equipment and work of Vermont artists
Exhibitions: (1993) Winning the War at Home: Vermont During WW II
Publications: Vermont History, quarterly; Vermont History News, bi-monthly
Activities: Lect open to the public; fellowships; museum shop sells books
L Library, 109 State St, 05609-0901. Tel 802-828-2291. *Dir* Michael Sherman, PhD
Open 9 AM - 4:40 PM. Admis donation. Estab 1838 as a refrence library
Purchases: $4900
Library Holdings: Micro — Reels; AV — A-tapes, cassettes, motion pictures, rec, slides, v-tapes; Other — Clipping files, manuscripts, memorabilia, pamphlets, photographs
Special Subjects: Advertising Design, Archaeology, Architecture, Bookplates & Bindings, Ceramics, Coins & Medals, Costume Design & Construction, Crafts, Decorative Arts, Dolls, Embroidery, Flasks & Bottles, Folk Art, Furniture, Glass, Handicrafts, Historical Material, Interior Design, Landscape Architecture, Landscapes, Manuscripts

M WOOD ART GALLERY, Vermont College Arts Center, College Hall, Vermont College, 05602. Tel 802-828-8743. *Dir & Cur* Jane Roberts
Open Tues - Sun noon - 4 PM. Admis $2 non-members. Estab 1895 by 19th century genre and portrait artist T W Wood to house and exhibit a portion of his works. Gallery acts as archive for information about T W Wood. 3 gallery spaces: 2700 sq ft, 800 sq ft, 500 sq ft, 15 ft high ceilings; in newly renovated 1870 College Hall on Vermont College campus. Average Annual Attendance: 10,000. Mem: 335; dues $25 - $100; annual meeting Dec
Income: Financed by endowment, city appropriation, grants, mem
Collections: Oil paintings, watercolors, prints by T W Wood, A B Durand, J G Brown, A Wyant, Edward Gay; 100 works from the 1920s & 30s, some by WPA painters Reginald Marsh, Louis Boucher, Paul Sample, Joseph Stella; early 19th century American portraits
Exhibitions: (1991) The People of Vermont (mixed media); Unknown Secrets: Art & The Rosenberg Era; A Celebration of Vermont Crafts (baskets, metalwork, pottery, textiles & woodworking); Two Hundred Years of The Vermont Landscape; The Black Image in The Art of T W Wood; The Rural Worker & His Setting
Publications: Monograph on the Wood Collection
Activities: Children's classes; docent training; lectures open to public, 25 vis lectr per yr; concerts; gallery talks; tours; state-wide competition; individual paintings & original objects of art lent to local organizations, businesses & other museums with appropriate security systems; lending collection includes original prints & photographs; museum shop sells crafts, magazines, reproductions, prints, postcards, & posters

RUTLAND

M NEW ENGLAND MAPLE MUSEUM, Route 7 in Pittsford, PO Box 1615, 05701. Tel 802-483-9414. *Pres* Thomas H Olson; *Cur & Mgr* Dona Olson; *Shop* Jean Lyon
Open daily 8:30 AM - 5:30 PM. Admis adults $1.50, sr citizens $1.25, children between 6 - 12 $.50. Estab 1977 to present the complete history of maple sugaring. Average Annual Attendance: 15,000-20,000
Income: $100,000 - $200,000 (financed by gift shop sales & admissions)
Purchases: $1000 per yr, mainly maple sugaring antiques
Collections: Oil paintings on maple sugaring by Paul Winter; oil murals on early maple sugaring by Vermont artist Grace Brigham
Exhibitions: Permanent collection
Activities: Museum shop sells books, reproductions, slides

A RUTLAND AREA ART ASSOCIATION, INC, Chaffee Art Center, 16 S Main St, 05701. Tel 802-775-0356. *Pres* Barbara Carris
Open daily 10 AM - 5 PM July - Oct, 11 AM - 4 PM Nov - June, cl Tues. No admis fee, donations appreciated. Estab and incorporated 1961 to promote and maintain an educational and cultural center in the central Vermont region for the

area artists, photographers, craftsmen and others in the art field. Average Annual Attendance: 10,000. Mem: 200; juried artists; dues $30; annual meeting in Jan
Income: Financed by memberships, special funding, contributions, grants, foundations and activities
Exhibitions: Annual Members Exhibit, juried; Art-in-the-Park outdoor festivals; one-man and invitational exhibits
Publications: Calendar of events, annually; exhibition posters
Activities: Classes for adults & children; lectrs open to the public, 4 vis lectrs per year; concerts; tours; competition with awards; scholarships; individual printings lent to local banks & corporations; sales shop sells original art & prints

SAINT JOHNSBURY

M FAIRBANKS MUSEUM AND PLANETARIUM, Main and Prospect Sts, 05819. Tel 802-748-2372; FAX 802-748-3347. *Dir* Charles C Browne; *Registrar* Kathy Armstrong
Open Mon - Sat 10 AM - 4 PM, Sun 1 - 5 PM, extended summer hours. Admis families $6, adults $2.50, students & senior citizens $2, children $1.25, group rates available. Estab 1889 as a center for exhibits, special exhibitions & programs; special exhibitions & programs on science, technology, the arts & the humanities. Art gallery for special exhibitions and work of regional artists. Average Annual Attendance: 70,000. Mem: 600; dues $30; monthly meeting
Income: $330,000 (financed by admissions income, grants, endowment, mem & municipal appropriations)
Collections: Hudson River School, primarily oil paintings; 19th century American & European art; Extensive natural science, history & anthropology collections
Exhibitions: Technology & Perception, the Photographic Vision of Nature; Victorian Legacies Swedish Nature Photography; Strong & Spirited: Women of the Northeast Kingdom; Visions, Toil, & Promise: Man in Vermont's Forests
Publications: Exhibit catalogs; quarterly newsletter
Activities: Classes for adults and children; docent training; lectures open to the public; concerts; gallery talks; tours; exten dept serving Northeast Vermont; artmobile; individual paintings and original objects of art lent to other accredited museums; lending collection contains 500 nature artifacts, 50 original art works, 10 paintings & 500 photographs; book traveling exhibitions; museum shop sells books, magazines, original art, reproductions, prints, slides, science kits, kites and crafts; junior museum

M SAINT JOHNSBURY ATHENAEUM, 30 Main St, 05819. Tel 802-748-8291. *Librn, Dir* Gael B Stein; *Cur* Sallee Lawrence
Open Mon - Sat 9:30 AM - 5 PM, during summer, Mon & Wed 9:30 AM - 8 PM, Sat 9:30 AM - 2 PM. No admis fee. Estab 1873 and maintained as a 19th century gallery; given to the townspeople by Horace Fairbanks. It is the oldest art gallery still in its original form in the United States; a one-room addition to the public library building
Income: Financed by endowment and city appropriation
Collections: 19th century American landscape paintings of the Hudson River School (Bierstadt, Colman, Whittredge, Cropsey, Gifford, Hart brothers); copies of masterpieces; sculpture
Exhibitions: Permanent Collection
Publications: Art Gallery Catalogue

SHELBURNE

M SHELBURNE MUSEUM, Route 7, 05482. Tel 802-985-3346. *Dir* Brian Alexander; *Registrar* Pauline Mitchell
Open 10 AM - 5 PM, mid-May - mid-Oct. Admis adults $15, children $6, special group & student rates. Estab 1947 as Museum of the American Spirit to collect, preserve and exhibit American fine, decorative and utilitarian arts, particular emphasis on Vermont. 37 buildings on 45 acres. Average Annual Attendance: 160,000
Income: Financed primarily by admissions and fund raising from members
Collections: American paintings, folk art, decoys, architecture, furniture, quilts and textiles, dolls, sporting art and sculpture, ceramics, tools, sleighs and carriages, toys, farm and home implements; European material: Impressionist and Old Master paintings; English furniture and architectural elements; seven period houses; Native American ethnographic artifacts; Sidewheeler Ticonderoga, railroad memorabilia including steam train, circus material and carousel animals
Activities: Classes for children; docent training; lectures open to public, 5 vis lectr per yr; concerts; gallery talks; tours; exten dept serves Vermont; book traveling exhibitions, annually; originate traveling exhibitions; museum shop sells books, reproductions, prints & slides
L Library, Route 7, 05482. Tel 802-985-3346, Ext 390; FAX 802-985-3346, Ext 137. *Dir* Brian Alexander
Open to public by appointment
Library Holdings: Vols 6000; Per subs 40; AV — A-tapes, cassettes, fs, Kodachromes, motion pictures, rec, slides, v-tapes; Other — Clipping files, exhibition catalogs, manuscripts, memorabilia, pamphlets, photographs, prints

SPRINGFIELD

A SPRINGFIELD ART & HISTORICAL SOCIETY, 9 Elm St, PO Box 313, 05156. Tel 802-885-2743. *Pres* Hubbard Richardson; *Treas* Frederick Richardson; *Dir* Rita Pierce
Open Tues, Wed & Fri 10 AM - 4 PM, Thurs 1 - 5 PM & 7 - 9 PM. No admis fee. Estab 1956 for the purpose of presenting history, art and classes in the arts to the community. Gallery located in a Victorian mansion built in 1867 & is maintained for monthly exhibits. Average Annual Attendance: 1200. Mem: 140; dues $50, $20, and $10 annual meeting in Sept
Income: $15,000 (financed by endowment and membership)
Collections: Primitive portraits by H Bundy, Aaron D Fletcher, and Asahel Powers; Richard Lee, pewter; Bennington pottery; paintings by local artists; toys, costumes, sculpture, crafts
Exhibitions: Historical exhibits: costumes; toys; photography; fine arts

Publications: Annual schedule of events and monthly notices
Activities: Classes for adults and children; lect open to the public, 4 vis lectr per year; concerts; gallery talks; competitions; scholarships & fels offered; individual paintings lent; lending collection contains original art work, paintings, photographs, sculpture, slides; sales shop sells books, original art, slides

VIRGINIA

ALEXANDRIA

L **ALEXANDRIA LIBRARY,** 717 Queen St, 22314-2420. Tel 703-838-4555; FAX 703-838-4524. *Dir* Patrick M O'Brien
Open Mon - Thurs 9 AM - 9 PM, Fri 9 AM - 6 PM, Sat 9 AM - 5 PM, Sun 1 - 5 PM. Estab 1794 as a public library. Circ 1,959,483
Income: $2,155,586 (financed by city & state appropriation, fines, fees & gifts)
Purchases: $344,957
Library Holdings: Vols 342,282; Per subs 450; Micro — Fiche, reels; AV — A-tapes, cassettes, lantern slides, motion pictures, rec, v-tapes; Other — Clipping files, exhibition catalogs, framed reproductions, manuscripts, memorabilia, original art works, pamphlets, photographs, prints, reproductions, sculpture
Activities: Individual paintings lent to registered borrowers

A **ART LEAGUE,** 105 N Union St, 22314. Tel 703-683-2323, 683-1780. *Pres* Kathy O'Day; *VPres* Jamie Brooks; *Exec Dir* Cora Rupp; *Asst Executive Dir* Maria Simonsson; *Asst Dir* Linda Hafer; *Gallery Dir* Nancy Saulnier; *School Dir* Geri Gordon; *Treas* Marge Alderson
Open Mon - Sat 10 AM - 5 PM, Sun noon - 5 PM. No admis fee. Estab 1953 to promote & maintain standards of art through mem juried exhibitions & a large school which teaches all facets of the fine arts & some high skill crafts. Eleven rooms in the Torpedo Factory Art Center in Old Town Alexandria, Virginia; also has four galleries & seven classrooms plus annex. Average Annual Attendance: 500,000. Mem: 950; annual dues $35; meetings in June
Exhibitions: Monthly juried shows for members
Activities: Classes for adults & children; docent training; lectures open to public, 15 vis lectr per year; gallery talks; tours; sponsors competitions with awards; sales shop sells art supplies

ART SERVICES INTERNATIONAL
For further information, see National and Regional Organizations

A **THE ATHENAEUM,** 201 Prince St, 22314. Tel 703-548-0035. *Dir* Mary Gaissert Jackson
Open Wed - Sat 11 AM - 4 PM, Sun 1 - 4 PM, cl Mon, Tues & holidays. No admis fee. Estab 1964 to promote education, appreciation, participation and pursuit of excellence in all forms of art and crafts; to enrich the cultural life of the metropolitan area and Northern Virginia. Main gallery space on main floor, with additional area available. Average Annual Attendance: 15,000. Mem: 990; dues $15 - $25
Income: Financed by membership & fund raisers
Exhibitions: Annual Joint Art League/Athenaeum Multi-media Juried show. (1991) Retrospective: Photographs of Marvin Breckinridge Patterson. (1992) Old Friends-New Works II; Sculpture of Jerome Meadows
Publications: Quarterly newsletter
Activities: Dance classes for children; dramatic programs; docent training; lectures open to public, 4 - 6 vis lectrs per year; gallery talks; tours; competitions with awards; concerts

M **GALLERY WEST LTD,** 205 S Union St, 22314. Tel 703-549-7359. *Dir* Craig Snyder
Open Mon & Wed - Sun 11 AM - 5 PM, cl Tues. Estab 1979 to showcase artists in the Washington DC metro area. Average Annual Attendance: 3100. Mem: 30; dues $720; meeting first Mon night of each month
Income: $45,000 (financed by mem & commission on sales of art)
Collections: All media
Exhibitions: Solo & group shows

ARLINGTON

M **ARLINGTON ARTS CENTER,** 3550 Wilson Blvd, 22201-2348. Tel 703-524-1494. *Dir* Tim Close; *Cur* Andrea Pollan
Open Tues - Fri 11 AM - 5 PM, Sat & Sun 1 - 5 PM. No admis fee. Estab to present new work by emerging & established artists from the region (Virginia, Maryland, Washington DC, West Virginia, Pennsylvania, Delaware)
Exhibitions: (1992) The Trust Piece (group exhibit); Collateral Damage: The Unseen Cost of Gun Damage (public mail art project); The Mighty Hudson (artist Carol Lopatin)

L **ARLINGTON COUNTY DEPARTMENT OF PUBLIC LIBRARIES,** Fine Arts Section, 1015 N Quincy St, 22201. Tel 703-358-5959; FAX 703-358-5962. *Head* Jody Haberland
Open Mon - Thur 9 AM - 10 PM, Fri & Sat 9 AM - 5 PM, Sun 1 - 9 PM. Estab 1935 to serve needs of an urban-suburban population in all general subjects
Income: Financed by county & state appropriatins
Library Holdings: Vols 1800; Total holdings: 20,000
Exhibitions: Local artists, crafts people and photographers have exhibitions at the central library each month in second floor lounge gallery, and first floor display cases. Six branch libraries also have special exhibits of similar nature
Publications: Monthly almanac of programs, library activities & exhibit
Activities: Lectures open to public, 10 vis lectr per year; workshops; film shows; extended learning institute video-tapes from Northern Virginia Community College available

M **ARLINGTON HISTORICAL SOCIETY INC,** Museum, 1805 S Arlington Ridge Rd, PO Box 402, 22210. Tel 703-892-4204. *Pres* Bruce G McCoy; *Museum Dir* Johanna Baker
Open Fri & Sat 11 AM - 3 PM, Sun 2 - 5 PM. Estab 1963 for the research, collection, preservation, discovery, & dissemination of local history. Mem: 500; dues $10
Collections: The Museum includes exhibits, displays, photographs & memorabilia illustrative of Arlington history
Publications: Articles on local history
Activities: Lectures on local history; tours of local historical sites

BLACKSBURG

VIRGINIA POLYTECHNIC INSTITUTE & STATE UNIVERSITY
M **Armory Art Gallery,** 201 Drapper Rd, 24061-0103. Tel 703-231-4859, 231-5547; FAX 703-231-7826. *Head Art Dept* Derek Myers
Open Mon - Fri 10 AM - 5 PM. No admis fee. Estab 1969; new location Sept 1975 to serve needs of Art Department as a teaching gallery as well as to meet community needs in an area where there are few large art centers and museums. Gallery is located in same building as Art Department; exhibition area is approx 30 x 30 ft. Average Annual Attendance: 2000 plus student use
Income: Financed through Departments Operational Budget
Collections: Student print collection
Exhibitions: (1993) Black History Month Artist; Preview Exhibition for Art Extravaganza - 93; Women's Month Artist Exhibit; Departmental Bachelor of Arts Nature Exhibit
Publications: Exhibition calendar; gallery announcements
Activities: Docent training to college students; lect open to the public, 3 vis lectr per yr; gallery talks; individual paintings and original objects of art lent to faculty and staff offices on campus, as well as library and continuing education center; traveling exhibitions organized and circulated
M **Perspective Gallery,** Squires Student Center, Virginia Tech, 24061. Tel 703-231-5431. *Art Dir* Thomas F Butterfield
Estab 1969 to provide exhibits on the local & national level for the students, faculty & the college community. Average Annual Attendance: 50,000
Income: Financed by university unions & student activities
Activities: Lect open to public; competitions
L **Art & Architecture Library,** 301 Cowgill Hall, 24061. Tel 703-231-9271; Elec Mail APBURR@VTVM1.BITNET. *Librn* Annette Burr
Open Mon - Thurs 8 AM - 11 PM, Fri 8 AM - 5 PM, Sat 1 AM - 5 PM, Sun 2 - 11 PM. Estab 1928 to provide service to the College of Architecture and Urban Studies and the other divisions of the University. Circ 55,000
Income: Financed by state appropriation & gifts
Purchases: $69,500
Library Holdings: Vols 60,000; Per subs 380; Micro — Fiche, reels; AV — Cassettes, slides 50,000, v-tapes; Other — Clipping files, exhibition catalogs, pamphlets
Special Subjects: Architecture, Art, Building Construction, Urban Affairs & Planning
Publications: New Acquisitions List - Architecture Library, monthly

BROOKNEAL

M **PATRICK HENRY MEMORIAL FOUNDATION,** Red Hill National Memorial, Route 2, PO Box 127, 24528. Tel 804-376-2044. *Executive Dir* James M Elson; *Admin Asst* Edith C Poindexter
Estab 1944 to preserve & develop a memorial to Patrick Henry. 1 room with Rothermel painting as focal point. Average Annual Attendance: 7000. Mem: dues $10 & up; annual meeting in May
Income: $168,000 (financed by endowment, mem, county & state appropriation)
Exhibitions: Patrick Henry Before the Virginia House of Burgesses by P F Rothermel; Patrick Henry Memorabilia
Publications: Quarterly newsletter
Activities: Classes for adults & children; docent programs; lectures open to public; exten dept provides lending collection; retail store sells books, prints, slides

CHARLES CITY

M **SHIRLEY PLANTATION,** 501 Shirley Plantation Rd, 23030. Tel 804-829-5121. *Owner* Charles Hill Carter Jr
Open daily 9 AM - 5 PM, cl Christmas Day. Admis adults $4.50, students $3.50, sr citizens $4, children $2.50, group rates. Estab 1723 to show the history of one distinguished family from colonial times to the present. Average Annual Attendance: 40,000
Income: $136,000 (maintained by admission fees)
Collections: Original portraits; silver and furniture: English and American
Activities: Individual paintings and original objects of art lent occasionally for exhibitions staged by such organizations as Virginia Museum and Colonial Williamsburg; museum shop sells books, reproductions, prints and slides

M **WESTOVER,** 7000 Westover Rd, 23030. Tel 804-829-2882. *Owner* Mrs B C Fisher; *Mgr* F S Fisher
Grounds and garden open daily 9 AM - 6 PM. Admis $2, children $.50; house interior not open. Built about 1730 by William Byrd II, Founder of Richmond, the house is considered an outstanding example of Georgian architecture in America, with steeply sloping roof, tall chimneys in pairs at both ends, elaborate Westover doorway, a three story central structure with two end wings. The path from the Caretakers House to the house is lined with tulip poplars over 100 years old; former kitchen is a separate small brick building. East of the house (open to vistiors) is the Necessary House, an old icehouse and a dry well with passageways leading under the house to the river. The Westover gates of delicate ironwork incorporate initials WEB; lead eagles on the gateposts, fence columns topped with stone finials cut to resemble pineapples, and other symbolic designs. Long established boxwood garden with tomb of William Byrd II. Members of his family, and Captain William Perry, who died August 1637, are buried in old church cemetery one-fourth mile west of the house

CHARLOTTESVILLE

M **THOMAS JEFFERSON MEMORIAL FOUNDATION,** Monticello, PO Box 316, 22902. Tel 804-293-2158. *Dir* Daniel P Jordan
Open Mar - Oct Mon - Sun 8 AM - 5 PM, Nov - Feb Mon - Sun 9 AM - 4:30 PM, cl Christmas. Admis adults $7, children 6-11 & school groups $2. Monticello is owned and maintained by the Thomas Jefferson Memorial Foundation, a non-profit organization founded in 1923. The home of Thomas Jefferson, designed by him and built 1769-1809, contains many original furnishings and art objects
Collections: †Jeffersonian furniture; †memorabilia; †art objects & manuscripts
Activities: Museum shop sells books, reproductions & slides

M **SECOND STREET GALLERY,** 201 Second St, NW, 22902. Tel 804-977-7284. *Exec Dir* Paige Turner; *Pres Board of Dirs* Jeffrey Dreyfus; *Treas* Beatrice Segal
Open Tues - Sat 10 AM - 5 PM, Sun 1 - 5 PM. No admis fee. Estab 1973 as an alternative arts space to present emerging & accomplished contemporary artists from regional & national localities, to increase the appreciation of contemporary art in Virginia region, & to increase the dialogue between artists & the community. One gallery 24 ft x 32 ft. Average Annual Attendance: 15,000. Mem: 300; dues individual $25, sustaining $50, contributing $100
Income: Financed by individual, corporate & foundation contributions, grants from the Virginia Commision for the Arts, The National Endowment for the Arts & special fund raising activities
Exhibitions: Sally Mann at Twelve; Robert Reed: The Tree for Mime Series; Nicholas Nixon & Shelby Lee Adams: Photographs from the South; In Pursuit of the Human Spirit; Emmet Gowin, Frank Goulke
Publications: Recent American Works on Paper, exhibit catalog, biennially
Activities: Lectures; tours; literary readings; workshops

UNIVERSITY OF VIRGINIA

M **Bayly Art Museum,** Rugby Rd, 22903. Tel 804-924-3592, 924-7458 (Tours); FAX 804-924-6321. *Dir* Anthony Hirschel; *Cur* Suzanne Foley; *Dir of Education* Jane Anne Young; *Registrar* Jean Collier; *Cur Works on Paper* Stephen Margulies; *Admin* Ruth C Cross; *Dir Development* Cecila Mindencupp; *Preparator* Rob Browning
Open Tues - Sun 1 - 5 PM, cl Mon. No admis fee, donations accepted. Estab 1935 to make original works of art available to the University community & to the general public. Average Annual Attendance: 26,000. Mem: 1400; dues: director's circle $2500, benefactor $1000, patron $500, sponsor $250, fellow $100, donor $60, member $35, sr citizens $15, student $5
Income: Financed by membership and state appropriation
Purchases: Attic Black Figure Column Krater (510 - 500 BC); Old Master prints; 17th to 19th century; contemporary photography
Collections: †American art; †European & American Art in the age of Jefferson; †Old Master prints; †East Asian art; †contemporary art; †American Indian art; †Ocean Art; †prints, drawings, photographs, Roman Coins
Exhibitions: (1991 - 92) American Art from the Age of Jefferson; The American Dream: 20th Century Paintings, Prints & Photographs; Masterpieces of Renaissance & Baroque Printmakeing: A Decade of Collecting; George Cooke, 1793 - 1849; Contemporary Sculpture from the Virginia Museum of Fine Arts; John Barber, 1893 - 1963: Paintings, Drawings, Prints; Subjects: Prints & Multiples by Jonathan Borofsky 1982 - 1991; American Indian Art: When Cultures Meet; plus many other varied exhibitions
Publications: Masterpieces of Renaissance & Baroque Printmaking: A Decade of Collecting; Leon Kroll: A Spoken Memoir; John Barber: Selections from the archives; exhibition brochures; Newsletter
Activities: Educ programs for adults, students, children; docent training; lect open to public, 10 vis lectr per year; gallery talks; fellowships; original works of art lent; museum shop sells books, cards

L **Fiske Kimball Fine Arts Library,** Bayly Dr, 22903. Tel 804-924-7024; FAX 804-982-2678. *Librn* Jack Robertson; *Asst Librn & Public Services* Lynda White; *Asst Librn Acquisitions* Christie Stephenson
Open school year Mon - Thurs 8 AM - 11 PM, Fri 8 AM - 6 PM, Sat 9 AM - 6 PM, Sun 1 - 11 PM. Estab 1970; combination of existing Art and Architecture libraries to provide a research facility providing printed, microfilm and audio visual materials for the art, architecture and drama curriculum. Fifty percent of collection is noncirculating. Circ 58,470
Income: $189,400
Purchases: $189,400
Library Holdings: Vols 121,000; Per subs 285; Rare Books; Micro — Fiche, reels; AV — A-tapes, cassettes, fs, Kodachromes, slides; Other — Exhibition catalogs, manuscripts, photographs
Special Subjects: Archaeology, Architecture, Art History, Film, Photography, Drama, Landscape Architecture, Planning and Urban Design
Collections: Francis Benjamin Johnson Photographs of Virgina Architecture; playbills, primarily New York Theatre; Rare books
Publications: Guide to Souices, irregular serial; Notable Additionsto the library collection, quarterly
Activities: Lect; tours

CHRISTIANSBURG

A **BLACKSBURG REGIONAL ART ASSOCIATION,** 302 Rolling Hills Dr, 24073. Tel 703-381-1018. *Pres* Barbara Barlow; *Secy* Jean Nelson; *Membership Chmn* Marie Livermore
Estab 1950, affiliated with the Virginia Museum of Fine Arts, dedicated to the encouragement & the enjoyment of the arts. Mem: Dues including membership to the Virginia Museum, family $12, individual $8
Income: Financed by membership & patron contributions
Collections: †Collection of paintings by contemporary artists who have exhibited in Blacksburg
Activities: Dramatic programs; lectures open to public, 3 - 5 vis lectr per year; concerts; competitions; artmobile; originate traveling exhibitions

COURTLAND

M **WALTER CECIL RAWLS MUSEUM,** PO Box 310, 23837. Tel 804-653-2821; FAX 804-653-9374. *Asst Dir* Beverly Worsham
Open Mon, Wed & Thurs 9 AM - 8:30 PM, Tues & Fri 9 AM - 5 PM, Sat 9 AM - 3 PM. Estab 1958 to promote the arts in the city of Franklin and the counties of Isle of Wight, Southampton, Surry and Sussex. Main gallery is 45 by 50 ft, 12 ft high with track lighting. Average Annual Attendance: 3000. Mem: 248; dues $14, $17, $30; annual meeting in April, Board of Trustees meet monthly
Income: $17,500 (financed by endowment & mem)
Collections: Antique glass & silver; †Southeastern Virginia Artists; drawings, paintings, lithographs
Exhibitions: Annual Regional Photography Exhibition ; Annual Student Art Show; regular; regular group exhibitions by area artists
Publications: R M A Bulletin
Activities: Classes for adults and children; Chamber concert series; sponsor annual 4 county art show; awards; paintings and art objects lent to museums and libraries

DANVILLE

M **DANVILLE MUSEUM OF FINE ARTS & HISTORY,** 975 Main St, 24541. Tel 804-793-5644. *Pres* Samuel A Cushner; *VPres* E L Wright; *Dir* Thomas W Jones; *Chmn Finance Committee* Budge Kent; *Museum Shop Mgr* Jennifer Thomas; *Guild Dir* Doris Jones; *Office Secy* Betty Jones
Open Tues - Fri 10 AM - 5 PM, Sun 2 - 5 PM. No admis fee. Estab 1974. Museum has two galleries: 27 x 35 ft with track lighting; two smaller galleries: 24 x 17 ft with track lighting. Average Annual Attendance: 8000. Mem: 779; meetings March & Sept
Income: Financed by mem, city & state appropriation & grants
Collections: 19th & 20th century decorative arts including furniture, silver, porcelain; Victorian American paintings & works on paper 1932 - present; Emphasis on works by contemporary Southern & Mid Atlantic Artists; American Costume Collection including many locally made crazy quilts; Historic artifacts & documents pertaining to the history of Danville;
Exhibitions: Rotating schedule of art exhibitions concerned with both popular & avant-gard ideas in art; Survey shows highlighting historic & modern artists in movement; Historic exhibit includes restored period rooms, a Victorian parlor, bedroom & library; Civil War artifacts; Artifacts from the wreck of The Old 97. (1993) African American Works on Paper; True Friends of Charity 1870-Time Capsule Exhibit
Publications: Last Capital of the Confederacy, book; Activities Report, quarterly newspaper; Record of Davis' government in Danville, Last week of Civil War
Activities: Classes for adults & children; dramatic programs; docent training; lectures open to the public, 6 vis lectr per year; concerts; gallery talks; tours; original objects of art lent to other museums or galleries; museum shop sells books, original art & reproductions

FAIRFAX

C **MOBIL CORPORATION,** Art Collection, 22037. Tel 212-532-4595. *Art Consultant* Ivan Chermayeff; *Art Consultant* Lori Shepherd
Collections: Primarily works of young artists; paintings, drawings; watercolors; original prints; sculpture

FORT MONROE

M **HEADQUARTERS FORT MONROE, DEPT OF ARMY,** Casemate Museum, Bldg 20, Bernard Rd, PO Box 341, 23651-0341. Tel 804-727-3935; AUTOVON 680-3935. *Dir* Dennis Mroczkowski; *Exhibit Specialist* Bill Matthews; *History Specialist* Kathy Rothrock; *Archivist* David J Johnson; *Secy* Carol Hanson
Open daily 10:30 AM - 4:30 PM. No admis fee. Estab 1951 to depict history of Fort Monroe. Average Annual Attendance: 60,000. Mem: 200; dues one-time-only fee based on plateaus: annual meeting in mid Jan
Income: Financed by mem, federal appropriation
Collections: Jack Clifton Paintings; Remington Drawings; Zogbaum Drawings; Artillery Implements; Military Posters
Exhibitions: Civil War Artifacts; Coast Artillery Guns in Action
Publications: Exhibition catalogs
Activities: Docent programs; outreach programs at schools; originate traveling exhibitions 3 per yr; retail store sells books, prints, slides, reproductions, postcards, games, models, toys

FREDERICKSBURG

M **MARY WASHINGTON COLLEGE,** The Gari Melchers Estate & Memorial Gallery, 224 Washington St, 22405. Tel 703-899-4860. *Dir* David Berreth; *Cur* Joanna D Catron
Open Apr - Sept, daily 10 AM - 5 PM, Sun 1 - 5 PM, Oct - Mar, daily 10 AM - 4 PM, Sun 1 - 4 PM. Admis adults $3, adult groups, sr citizens & groups 2.40, children between 6 & 18 $1, school & scout groups free. Estab 1975 to exhibit, preserve and interpret the works of art and memorabilia of the late American artist Gari Melchers, in his former estate and studio. Studio consists of three gallery rooms, a work room, and storage rooms. Average Annual Attendance: 10,000
Income: $200,000 (financed by endowment & state appropriation)
Collections: †Over six hundred works of art, paintings, drawings, & etchings by Gari Melchers; †Over 1000 sketches & studies by Gari Melchers; †Paintings & drawings by Berthe Morisot, Franz Snyders, Puvis de Chavannes and others; †Furnishings from Europe & America
Publications: Gari Melchers: His Works in the Belmont Collection (1984); Gari Melchers: A Retrospective Exhibition (1989)
Activities: Docent training; aesthetics tours for school groups; outreach programs for school & nursing homes; lect open to the public; gallery talks; tours; individual paintings & original objects of art lent

M JAMES MONROE MUSEUM, 908 Charles St, 22401. Tel 703-899-4559. *Cur* Lee Langston-Harrison

Open Mar 1 - Oct 31 daily 9 AM - 5 PM, Nov 1 - Feb 28 daily 10 AM - 4 PM, cl Thanksgiving, Dec 24, 25, 31 & Jan 1. Admis adults $3, children 6 - 18 $1. Estab 1927 to keep in memory the life and service of James Monroe and of his contribution to the principles of government, to preserve his treasured possessions for present and future generations. Open to the public in 1928; owned by Commonwealth of Virginia and under the control of Mary Washington College; a National Historic Landmark. Average Annual Attendance: 25,000

Collections: Louis XVI furniture purchased by the Monroes in France in 1794 and later used by them in the White House; portraits; sculpture; silver; china; jewelry; books; documents

Exhibitions: (1993) Images of a President: Portraits of James Monroe; Time Pieces: Monroe's Fascination with Clocks & Watches; From Washington to Carter: Presidential Paraphanelia at the J M Museum

Publications: Images of a President: Portraits of James Monroe, catalog Library of James Monroe, catalog

Activities: Docent training, workshops; lectures open to public; gallery talks; tours; scholarships offered; exten dept serves Mary Washington College—University of VA area; museum shop sells books, magazines, reproductions, prints, slides, history related objects & exclusive items from local crafts people

L Library, 908 Charles St, 22401. Tel 703-899-4559. *Cur* Lee Langston-Harrison; *Dir of Planning & Prog* John N Pearce

Open daily 9 AM - 5 PM. Estab 1927 as a presidential museum & library. Open to public; archival resources available by appointment only. Average Annual Attendance, 20,000

Income: Financed by state allocations & revenues

Library Holdings: Vols 10,000; letters; documents; Other — Manuscripts 27,000

Special Subjects: Monroe, Jefferson, Carter, Minor, Hoes, Virginia manuscripts

GLEN ALLEN

M COUNTY OF HENRICO, Meadow Farm Museum, Courtney & Mountain Rds (Mailing add: PO Box 27032, Richmond, 23273). Tel 804-672-5106. *Historic Preservation Supv* Susan Hanson; *Asst Historic Preservation Supv* Christopher Gregson; *Coll Mgr* Kimberly Sicola

Open Tues - Sun Noon - 4 PM. Admis adults $1,·children under 12 $.50. Estab 1981 to exhibit works of 20th century American folk artists. 20 ft by 20 ft, AV room. Average Annual Attendance: 50,000

Income: Financed by Henrico County

Collections: 19th & 20th Century folk art

Publications: Exhibition flyers, annually

Activities: Children's classes; lectures open to public, 4 vis lectr per year; tours; individual paintings & original objects of art lent to Valentine Museum, Museum of the Confederary, Univ of Richmond; lending collection contains original art works, paintings & sculptures

GREAT FALLS

INDUSTRIAL DESIGNERS SOCIETY OF AMERICA
For further information, see National and Regional Organizations

HAMPTON

A CITY OF HAMPTON (Formerly Hampton Center for Arts & Humanities), Hampton Arts Commission, 4205 Victoria Blvd, 23669. Tel 804-723-2787. *Dir* Michael P Curry; *Marketing Dir* Mark S Watson; *Admin Asst* Tricia Waldon

Open year round Tues - Fri 10 AM - 6 PM, Sat - Sun 1 - 5, cl major holidays. No admis fee. Created in December, 1987, housed in the Charles H Taylor Arts Center

Income: Financed by municipal funds & contributions

Exhibitions: Regional artists presented at Charles H Taylor Arts Center, monthly; special events art shows; performances by international artists presented at Ogden Hall

Activities: Classes for adults & children; dramatic programs; workshops; demonstrations; lect open to public; concerts; gallery talks; tours; competitions with awards

M HAMPTON UNIVERSITY, University Museum, 23668. Tel 804-727-5308. *Dir* Jeanne Zeidler

Open Sept - May, Mon - Fri 8 AM - 5 PM, Sat & Sun noon - 4 PM. No admis fee. Estab 1868 as a museum of traditional art & artifacts from African, Asian, Oceanic & American Indian cultures & contemporary & traditional Afro-American Art. Average Annual Attendance: 36,000

Income: Financed by college funds

Collections: African, Asian, Oceanic & American Indian Art; Contemporary & traditional Afro-American Art

Activities: Educ dept; lect open to public; gallery talks; group tours by appointment; individual paintings and original objects of art lent to other museums and art galleries with appropriate security; lending collection includes 900 paintings & 800 sculptures; sales shop

HARRISONBURG

M JAMES MADISON UNIVERSITY, Sawhill Gallery, Duke Hall, 22807. Tel 703-568-6407. *Gallery Dir* Stuart C Downs

Open Sept - Apr, Mon - Fri 10:30 AM - 4:30 PM, Sat & Sun 1:30 - 4:30 PM, May - Aug call for summer schedule & hours. No admis fee. Estab 1967 to schedule changing exhibitions for the benefit of students and citizens of this area. One-room gallery of 1040 sq ft with movable panels. Average Annual Attendance: 10,000-12,000

Income: Financed by state appropriation, and is part of operation in Art Department budget

Collections: Sawhill Collection, mainly artifacts from classical civilizations; Staples Collection of Indonesian Art; small group of modern works

Exhibitions: One person exhibitions. Holography by D E Tyler; Philip Pearlstein: Personal Selections, Faith Ringgold, Alan Shields, Ken Tyler, Jerry Vellsmann

Activities: Competitions

LEESBURG

M OATLANDS, INC, Route 2, PO Box 352, 22075. Tel 703-777-3174. *Mgr* Kaye Napolitano

Open Mar - Dec, Mon - Sat 10 AM - 5 PM, Sun 1 - 5 PM, cl Thanksgiving Day. Admis adults $5, sr citizens & youth (7-18) $4, under 12 free; special events at special rates, group rates by arrangement, free to National Trust members except during special events. Oatlands is a Classical Revival Mansion constructed by George Carter, son of Robert (Councillor) Carter (circa 1800-06). It was partially remodeled in 1827 when the front portico with hand carved Corinthian capitals was added. Confederate troops were billeted here during part of the Civil War. The home remained in possession of the Carters until 1897. In 1903 Mr & Mrs William Corcoran Eustis, of Washington DC, bought Oatlands. Their daughters gave the property to the National Trust for Historic Preservation; the property is protected by preservation easements which help insure the estates continuing role as a center for equestrian sports & cultural events which are produced by Oatlands and various groups. Average Annual Attendance: $50,000

Income: $600,000 (financed by grants, endowments, admis, fund raising events & shop sales)

Collections: Carter and Eustis Collection of Furniture; Greek-Revival ornaments adorn interior

Exhibitions: Annual needlework Show; Christmas at Oatlands

Publications: Oatlands Column, quarterly newsletter

Activities: Special events

LEXINGTON

WASHINGTON & LEE UNIVERSITY
M Gallery of DuPont Hall, 24450. Tel 703-463-8861.

Open Mon - Fri 9 AM - 5 PM, Sat 11 AM - 3 PM, Sun 2 - 4 PM. No admis fee. Estab 1929 in separate gallery as teaching resource of art. One room, 30 x 60 ft, is maintained for temporary exhibits; also maintained one storeroom. Average Annual Attendance: 40,000

Income: Financed through the university

Exhibitions: Annual faculty show; annual student show; monthly exhibitions; traveling exhibitions

Publications: Exhibition catalogs

Activities: Lectures open to public, 5 vis lectrs per year; gallery talks; tours; book traveling exhibitions, 3 per year

L University Library, 24450. Tel 703-463-8644, 463-8662. *Head Librn* Barbara J Brown; *Art Librn* Yolanda Warren

Open for reference to students, scholars, public; this library is part of the main University library

Library Holdings: Vols 350,000; Per subs 35; AV — Slides 40,000; Other — Sculpture 4000

Special Subjects: Oriental Art, American Art of 18th & 19th centuries

Collections: Rare books, 17th - early 20th centuries

Activities: Lectures open to public, 2 vis lectrs per year; gallery talks

M Lee Chapel and Museum, 24450. Tel 703-463-8768. *Dir* Robert C Peniston; *Dir* Robert C Peniston

Open mid-Apr to mid-Oct Mon - Sat 9 AM - 5 PM, Sun 2 - 5 PM, mid-Oct to mid-Apr Mon - Sat 9 AM - 4 PM, Sun 2 - 5 PM. No admis fee. Estab 1868 as a part of the University. It is used for concerts, speeches and other events. Museum is used also to display the paintings, collections and personal items of the Washington and Lee families. The Lee Chapel is a National Historic Landmark. Average Annual Attendance: 55,00

Income: Financed through the University

Collections: Custis-Washington-Lee Art Collection; Lee archives; Lee family crypt; Lee's office; recumbent statute of General Lee by Valentine

Publications: Brochure

Activities: Sales shop sells books, prints, souvenirs

LORTON

M GUNSTON HALL PLANTATION, 10709 Gunston Rd, 22079. Tel 703-550-9220; FAX 703-550-9480. *Dir* Thomas A Lainhoff; *Asst Dir* Mary L Allen

Open daily 9:30 AM - 5 PM, cl Thanksgiving, Christmas, New Years Day. Admis adults $5, students (6 - 15) $1.50. Estab 1950 to acquaint the public with George Mason, colonial patriot & his 18th century house & gardens, covering 555 acres. Owned and operated by the Commonwealth of Virginia. Average Annual Attendance: 50,000

Income: Financed by state appropriation and admis fee

Collections: 18th century English and American decorative arts, furniture and paintings; 18th and 19th century family pieces

Activities: Docent training; tours; individual paintings and original objects of art lent to other museums; sales shop sells books, reproductions; Childrens Touch Museum located in basement

L Library, 10709 Gunston Rd, 22079. Tel 703-550-9220; FAX 703-550-9480. *Librn* Anne Baker; *Cur* Susan Borchardt

Open Mon - Fri 9:30 AM - 5 PM by appointment. Estab 1974 to recreate an 18th Century Virginia gentlemen's library as a research source plus acquiring a working reference collection on George Mason and the decorative arts

Income: Financed by endowment

Library Holdings: Vols 11,000; Per subs 50; original documents; Micro — Fiche, reels; AV — Cassettes, fs, motion pictures; Other — Exhibition catalogs, manuscripts, memorabilia, pamphlets, photographs, reproductions

Special Subjects: Decorative Arts, Mason family, Early Virginiana

Collections: Robert Carter Collection; Pamela C Copeland Collection; Elizabeth L Frelinghuysen Collection; Mason-Mercer Rare Book Collection

LYNCHBURG

L JONES MEMORIAL LIBRARY, Jones Memorial Library, 2311 Memorial Ave, 24501. Tel 804-846-0501. *Dir* Edward Gibson
No admis fee. Estab 1907. For reference
Income: $180,000 (financed by endowment & donations)
Purchases: $5000
Library Holdings: Vols 30,000; Per subs 45; Architectural drawings; Other — Clipping files, exhibition catalogs, manuscripts, memorabilia, original art works, photographs, sculpture
Special Subjects: Architecture, Historical Material, Manuscripts, Painting - American, Photography
Collections: †Lynchburg Architectural Archives

A LYNCHBURG FINE ARTS CENTER INC, 1815 Thomson Dr, 24501. Tel 804-846-8451. *Exec Dir* Mary Brumbaugh
Open Mon - Fri 9 AM - 5 PM, Sun 1 - 5 PM; other hours depending upon programs. No admis. Estab 1958 to promote interest in and appreciation and talent for art, music, dramatic literature and other fine arts. Mem: 850; dues $25 - $75; annual meeting in June
Income: Financed by mem, corporate & private donation, earned income from programs & performances
Exhibitions: Eighteen per year including Annual Crafts Show
Publications: Facets, (newspaper), monthly except July
Activities: Classes for adults & children; dramatic programs; docent training; dance, theatre, music & visual arts workshops; lect open to public, 2 - 3 vis lectr per yr; concerts; gallery talks; tours; competitions with cash awards; scholarships; exten dept serving youth; concerts for youth & theatre classics in public schools; book traveling exhibitions; originate traveling exhibitions; sales shop sells original art

M RANDOLPH-MACON WOMAN'S COLLEGE, Maier Museum of Art, One Quinlan St, 24503. Tel 804-947-8136; FAX 804-948-1632. *Dir* Ellen Schall Agnew; *Registrar* Barbara Jastrebsky; *Educ Outreach Coordr* Betsy Jaxtheimer
Open Sept - May Tues - Sun 1 - 5 PM, cl Mon. No admis fee. American Art Collection established 1920 to promote scholarship through temporary exhibitions and a permanent collection. Building currently housing collection built in 1952. 5 galleries contain more than 75 paintings from the permanent collection by American artists. One gallery is used for the 6 to 8 temporary exhibitions displayed each academic year
Income: Financed by endowment
Purchases: Joseph Cornell (collage), Wayne Higby & Paul Soldner (cermic), Jamie Wyeth (watercolor); John Frederick Peto (oil), Michiko Itatani (oil), Dorothy Hood (oil)
Collections: Extensive collection of 19th & 20th Century American paintings European and American graphics
Exhibitions: Abstract Art in the 80's Quilts & Collages: American Art in Pieces; The Figure in Contemporary American Art; The Creative Spirit: A Celebration of Contemporary Craft; The Art of Queena Storall: Genre Paintings of the Blue Ridge Piedmont; Realism in a Post-Modern World: Selections from the Sydney & Frances Lewis Collection; Jennifer Bartlett
Publications: Annual exhibition catalogue; biannual newsletter
Activities: Dramatic programs; lectures open to public, 5 vis lectr per year; concerts; gallery talks; tours; objects of art lent; originate traveling exhibitions

MIDDLETOWN

M BELLE GROVE PLANTATION, PO Box 137, 22645. Tel 703-869-2028; FAX 703-869-9638. *Pres* Kay S Whitworth; *Exec Dir* Michael Gore
Open April - Oct Mon - Sat 10 AM - 4 PM, Sun 1 - 5 PM, Nov - March by appointment. Admis adults $2.50 sr citizens $2, students $1.25, special rates. Open to the public in 1967, it is preserved as an historic house and is the property of the National Trust for Historic Preservation and managed by Belle Grove, Inc, an independent local nonprofit organization. It serves as a local preservation center and resource for the interpretation of regional culture in the Shenandoah Valley. Built in 1794 for Major Isaac Hite, Jr, a Revolutionary War officer and brother-in-law of James Madison, Belle Grove was designed with the help of Thomas Jefferson. During the Battle of Cedar Creek in 1864, the house served as headquarters to General Phillip Sheridan. The property is a working farm, and Belle Grove maintains an active program of events for the visiting public
Exhibitions: Four Portraits by Charles Peal Polk: Colonel James Madison, Nelly Conway Madison, Major Isaac Hite, Mrs Isaac Hite
Activities: Seminars on various subjects in museum field offered through the year; gift shop open all year

MOUNT VERNON

M MOUNT VERNON LADIES' ASSOCIATION OF THE UNION, 22121. Tel 703-780-2000. *Regent* Mrs Clarence M Bishop; *Resident Dir* Neil W Horstman; *Asst Dir* James C Rees; *Cur* Christine Meadows; *Librn* Barbara McMillan
Open to the public every day in the year from 9 AM: entrance gate closes Mar 1 - Oct 1 at 5 PM, Oct 1 - Mar 1 at 4 PM. Admis $5, $4.50 for groups of 12 or more children or groups of 20 or more adults, adults over 62 $4, $2 for children 6-11, children under 6 no admis fee. The home of George Washington, purchased in 1858 from his great-grand-nephew by the Mount Vernon Ladies Association of the Union, which maintains it. The estate includes spinning house, coach house, various quarters, restored flower and kitchen gardens; also the tomb of George and Martha Washington. Average Annual Attendance: 1,000,000. Mem: Semi-annual meeting Oct & May
Income: Financed by admission fees & donations
Collections: Mansion is fully furnished with original and period furniture, silver, portraits and prints; large collection of original Washington memorabilia, manuscripts & books
Publications: Annual Report; The Gardens & Grounds at Mount Vernon; George

Washington, A Brief Biography; The Last Will & Testament of George Washington; The Maxims of Washington; Mount Vernon; The Mount Vernon Coloring Book; The Mount Vernon Cookbook; The Mount Vernon Gardens; Mount Vernon Handbook; Nothing More Agreeable: Music in George Washington's Family; George Washington: Citizen - Soldier
Activities: Sales shop sells books, reproductions, prints & slides

M WOODLAWN PLANTATION, PO Box 37, 22121. Tel 703-780-4000; FAX 703-780-8509. *Dir* Linda Goldstein
Open 9:30 AM - 4:30 PM, except Thanksgiving Day, Christmas Day, and New Years Day. Admis adults $5, sr citizens & students $3.50, group rates by arrangement. Land originally part of Mount Vernon. Built in 1800-05 for George Washington's foster daughter upon her marriage to Lawrence Lewis, Washington's nephew. It was designed with central pavilion and flanking wings by Dr William Thornton, winner of the architectural competition for the design of the United States Capitol. A group of Quakers, a pioneer anthropologist, a playwright and Senator Oscar W Underwood of Alabama were among Woodlawns residents after the Lewises. In 1951 the foundation's trustees decided that the visiting public would be better served if Woodlawn was administered by the National Trust. The mansion furnishings are largely from the Federal and early Empire periods and include Lewis family furniture, memorabilia and gifts from the Robert Woods Bliss and Colonel Garbish Collection. Average Annual Attendance: 60,000. Mem: 305; dues family $35, individual $25
Exhibitions: Needlework exhibit; A Woodlawn Christmas in December; Fall Festival of Needlework, seminar in October; Fall Quilt Show; Needlework Exhibit each March, antiques & crafts fair in June
Publications: Friends of Woodlawn Newsletter, quarterly; Welcome to Woodlawn, booklet
Activities: Classes for children; docent training; lectures; concerts; tours; competitions with awards; museum shop sells books, slides, gifts & craft items

M FRANK LLOYD WRIGHT POPE-LEIGHEY HOUSE, PO Box 37, 22121. Tel 703-780-3264; FAX 703-780-8509. *Dir* Linda Goldstein
Open Mar - Dec, daily 9:30 AM - 4:30 PM. Frank Lloyd Wright's Pope-Leighey House is a property of the National Trust for Historic Preservation, located on the grounds of Woodlawn Planation. This residence was designed in 1939 by Frank Lloyd Wright for his clients, the Loren Pope Family. Built of cypress, brick and glass, the Usonian structure contains such features as a flat roof, radiant heat, indirect lighting, carport & custom furniture, all designed by Frank Lloyd Wright, as an example of architecture for the average-income family. Threatened by construction of an interstate highway in 1964, Mrs Marjorie Folsom Leighey, second owner, presented the property to the National Trust for Historic Preservation. It was then moved to the Woodlawn grounds
Publications: Brochure and paperback history of house
Activities: Classes for adults & children; docent training; lect open to public, 6 vis lectr per yr; tours

NEWPORT NEWS

M THE MARINERS' MUSEUM, 100 Museum Dr, 23606-3759. Tel 804-595-0368. *Pres* John Jamison; *Dir* William D Wilkinson; *Dir of Finance & Admin* Larry Dobrinsky; *Deputy Dir* Linda D Kelsey; *Dir External Relations* Karen Wible; *Dir Facilities Management* John Cannup
Open Mon - Sat 9 AM - 5 PM, Sat & Sun noon - 5 PM. Admis adults $5, students (all ages) $1, children under 6 free. Estab 1930, the museum is devoted to the culture of the sea and its tributaries, its conquest by man and its influence on civilization. Museum has twelve galleries, including Age of Exploration & Chesapeake Bay galleries; two paintings & decorative arts galleries; Miniature Ship Models; collection of International Small Craft; Great Hall of Steam; William F Gibbs: Naval Architect Gallery. Average Annual Attendance: 100,000. Mem: 1300
Collections: Crabtree Collection of miniature ships; thousands of marine artifacts; over 1000 paintings; over 1000 ship models; ceramics, scrimshaw, small craft
Exhibitions: (1992) Engage the Enemy More Closely: Admiral Horation Nelson
Activities: Classes for adults and children; docent training; lect open to members, 6 vis lectr per year; concerts; gallery talks; tours; competitions with awards; individual paintings & original objects of art lent to museums; collection contains 120 motion pictures, 2000 original art works, 8000 original prints, 1000 paintings; museum gift gallery sells books, magazines, reproductions, prints, slides, jewelry & other maritime related items

L Library, 100 Museum Dr, 23606. Tel 804-595-0368; FAX 804-591-8212. *Librn* Benjamin Trask; *Asst to Librn* Kathryn B Braig; *Archivist* Roger T Crew Jr
Open Mon - Sat 9 AM - 5 PM. Estab 1930. For reference only
Income: Financed by endowment
Library Holdings: Vols 70,000; Per subs 155; original documents; Micro — Reels; AV — A-tapes, fs, rec; Other — Clipping files, exhibition catalogs, manuscripts, memorabilia, pamphlets, photographs 300,000
Special Subjects: Maritime and Naval history

A PENINSULA FINE ARTS CENTER, 101 Museum Dr, 23606. Tel 804-596-8175; FAX 804-596-2936. *Pres* Leroy Thompson; *VPres* Judy Rauch; *VPres* Robert O H Mitchell; *VPres* Harry Fagan; *Exec Dir* Constance O'Sullivan
Open Tues - Sat 10 AM - 4 PM, Sun 1 - 4 PM. No admis fee. Estab 1962 to promote an appreciation of the fine arts through changing monthly exhibitions with works from the Virginia Museum, other institutions & outstanding artists, both emerging & established. Three galleries maintained with changing exhibitions. Mem: 850; dues family (incl membership) $30, individual $25
Income: Financed by membership
Exhibitions: Juried exhibition
Publications: Art class schedules; newsletter to members, quarterly; notification of special events
Activities: Classes for adults and children; lect open to public, 8 vis lectr per yr; gallery talks; competitions; cash awards & certificates of distinction; gallery shop sells books, original art and crafts

NORFOLK

M **CHRYSLER MUSEUM,** 245 W Olney Rd, 23510-1587. Tel 804-622-1211; FAX 804-623-5282. *Dir* Robert H Frankel; *Activities Coordr* Shirley Beafore; *Chief Cur* Roger D Clisby; *Cur Glass* Gary Baker; *Cur American Art* B Clark; *Cur Decorative Arts* Mark A Clark; *Cur of Photography* Brooks Johnson; *Dir Education* Ann D Vernon; *Public Information Officer* Donna Sawyer; *Pres of Board of Trustees* Roy B Martin Jr; *Cur Contemporary Art* Trinkett Clark; *Registrar* Catherine Jordan; *Head Librn* Rena Hudgins; *Cur European Art* Jeff Harrison
Open Tues - Sat 10 AM - 4 PM, Sun 1 - 5 PM, cl Mon. No admis fee. Museum originates from a memorial association established in 1901 to house a collection of tapestries and paintings donated in memory of and by Irene Leache. The Norfolk Society of Arts was founded in 1917, which raised funds throughout the 1920's to erect a building to permanently hold the collection. A Florentine Renaissance style building, named the Norfolk Museum of Arts & Sciences, opened to the public in 1933. The Houston Wing, housing the Museum Theatre and Lounge, was added in 1956, the Centennial Wing in 1976, & another wing to house the library & additional galleries was opened in 1989. The building has been designated the Chrysler Museum since 1971, when a large portion of the collection of Walter P Chrysler, Jr was given to Norfolk. Museum contains 140, 000 sq ft. Average Annual Attendance: 200,000. Mem: 3500; dues benefactor $10,000, fellow $5000, sponsor $2500, director's circle $1000, patron $500, friend $250, sustaining $100, associate $60, family $35, individual $25, student & sr citizen $20, corporate memberships also available
Income: Financed by municipal appropriation and state appropriations as well as federal grants
Collections: African artists; American art from 18th century primitives - 20th century Pop Art; Bernini's Bust of the Savior; Francoise Boucher, The Vegetable Vendor; Mary Cassatt, The Family; Thomas Cole, The Angel Appearing to the Shepherds; Decorative arts including furniture, silver, gold, enameled objects and Worcester porcelain; 18th century English paintings; 14th-18th century Italian paintings; 15th-18th century Netherlandish and German works; Gauguin's Loss of Virginity; Bernice Chrysler Garbisch and Edgar William Garbish Naive American paintings; Institute of Glass; Matisse, Bowl of Apples on a Table; Near and Far East Artists; Oriental artists; photography collection including Alezander Gardner, Lewis W Hine, Walker Evans, Ansel Adams, W Eugene Smith & contemporaries Joel Meyerowitz & Sheila Metzner; Pre-Columbian artists; Reni, The Meeting of David & Abigail; 16th - 20th century French paintings; works from Spanish school
Exhibitions: The Ricau Collection (neoclassic sculpture); Mirror of an Era: The Daguerreotype in Virginia; Home of the Brave (photography); Treasures for the Table: Silver from the Chrysler Museum; The Paris Universal Exposition of 1889; Prophets & Translators: Four Black Artists; American Modernist Painters from the Phillips Collection; A Golden Age: Art and Society in Hungary 1896-1914; The Art of Babar; Alexander Gardner (photography); Master Drawings from the Chrysler Museum; Images of Childhood: the World of Children in the Chrysler Museum; Frank Lloyd Wright; Daguerrean Masters; Light Images 1990 (photography); Fantasy in Fabric: The Artist as Couturier; 30th Irene Leach Memorial Exhibition
Publications: Monthly members' newsletter; exhibition catalogues; Annual Report
Activities: Educ program; family programs; docent training; teacher workshops; outreach information packages; lectures open to public, 20 vis lectr per year; concerts; gallery talks; tours; competitions (juried); exten dept operates three historic homes; individual paintings and original objects of art lent to accredited museums; book traveling exhibitions; traveling exhibitions organized and circulated; museum shop sells books, original art, reproductions, prints, slides, glass, gold & silver jewelry, ceramics, stationary, postcards and toys

L **Jean Outland Chrysler Library,** 245 W Olney Rd, 23510-1587. Tel 804-622-1211; FAX 804-623-5282. *Chief Librn* Rena Hudgins; *Cataloger* Lynda W Wright
Open by appointment only. Estab 1918 to collect materials in support of the collections of the Chrysler Museum. Reference only
Income: Financed by city appropriation
Library Holdings: Vols 60,000; Per subs 200; Auction catalogs; Micro — Fiche; Other — Clipping files, exhibition catalogs
Special Subjects: American Indian Art, American Western Art, Architecture, Art History, Costume Design & Construction, Decorative Arts, Fashion Arts, Furniture, Glass, Painting - American, Painting - British, Painting - Dutch, Painting - European, Painting - Flemish, Painting - French, Painting - German, Painting - Italian, Period Rooms, Photography, Porcelain, Pre-Columbian Art, Primitive Art, American Art, Art Nouveau, Western European Art
Collections: M Knoedler & Co, London Library: Western European painting, monographs, auction & exhibition catalogues; M Knoedler & Co, New York, microfiche, auction & exhibition catalogues, international, 18th century-1970
Activities: Lectures open to public

M **HERMITAGE FOUNDATION MUSEUM,** 7637 N Shore Rd, 23505. Tel 804-423-2052; FAX 804-423-1604. *Dir* Philip R Morrison; *Asst to Dir* Patricia Kirby; *Pres of Bd* W Marshall Jr; *Admin Asst* Jean Turmel
Open daily 10 AM - 5 PM, Sun 1 - 5 PM, cl New Years Day, Thanksgiving Day, Christmas Day. Admis adults $4, children 6 - 18 $1. Estab 1937 to disseminate information concerning arts, and maintain a collection of fine art materials. Mansion on 12 acre site houses major collections as well as two small changing exhibition galleries. Average Annual Attendance: 20,000. Mem: 400; dues $30; meeting four times per yr
Income: $110,000 (financed by endowment and membership)
Collections: English oak and teakwood woodcarvings; Major collection of decorative arts from various periods and countries; Oriental collection of Chinese bronzes and ceramic tomb figures, lacquer ware, jades and Persian rugs; Spanish and English furniture; 20th century paintings
Exhibitions: American Illustrator; Art on Paper; Isabel Bishop; Bernard Chaet (paintings); Contemporary American Graphics; Currier and Ives; Export Porcelain from a Private Collection; Freshwork (Virginia photographers); Alexandra Georges (photographs); The Photographs of Wright Morris; Henry Pitz (one man show); student exhibitions from summer workshops
Activities: Classes for adults and children; dramatic programs; lectures open to public and auxiliary lect for members only, 10 - 12 vis lectr per yr; concerts; tours; scholarships offered; individual paintings & original objects of art lent to institutions; lending collection contains 750 original art works, 300 paintings, 150 records & 50 sculpture; book traveling exhibitions; originate traveling exhibitions

L **Library,** 7637 N Shore Rd, 23505. Tel 804-423-2052; FAX 804-423-1604. *Dir* Philip R Morrison
Open to students for reference only
Library Holdings: Vols 800; Per subs 6

M **MACARTHUR MEMORIAL,** MacArthur Square, 23510. Tel 804-441-2965. *Dir* Edward M Condra III; *Admin Asst* Janice Stafford Dudley; *Cur* Jeffrey Acosta
Open Mon - Sat 10 AM - 5 PM, Sun 11 AM - 5 PM, cl Thanksgiving, Christmas, New Years Day. No admis fee. Estab 1964 to memorialize General Douglas MacArthur. Located in the 1850 Court House which was rebuilt in 1962; eleven galleries contain memorabilia. Average Annual Attendance: 75,000
Income: $390,892 (financed by city appropriation & the General Douglas MacArthur Foundation)
Collections: Objects d'art, murals, portraits, photographs
Activities: Concerts; gallery talks; tours; research assistance grants & fellowships offered; individual paintings and original objects of art lent to museums; sales shop created by General Douglas MacArthur Foundation sells books, reproductions, prints, slides

L **Library & Archives,** MacArthur Square, 23510. Tel 804-441-2965. *Archivist* Edward J Boone
Library Holdings: Vols 4000; original documents; Micro — Fiche, reels; AV — A-tapes, cassettes, motion pictures, rec, slides, v-tapes; Other — Clipping files, framed reproductions, manuscripts
Special Subjects: Life and Times of General of the Army Douglas MacArthur
Activities: Lect open to the public, 2-3 vis lectr per yr; tours; scholarships offered

L **NORFOLK PUBLIC LIBRARY,** Feldman Fine Arts & Audio Visual Dept, 301 E City Hall Ave, 23510. Tel 804-441-2426. *Head Librn* Audrey Hays
Open Mon - Thurs 9 AM - 9 PM, Fri 9 AM - 5:30 PM, Sat 9 AM - 5 PM. Estab 1972 to offer free use of all types of materials in the performing, audio and visual arts. Circ 52,816
Income: Financed by city and state appropriation
Purchases: $56,000
Library Holdings: Vols 880,854; Per subs 923; Micro — Fiche, reels; AV — Cassettes, fs, motion pictures, rec, slides, v-tapes; Other — Clipping files, exhibition catalogs, framed reproductions, manuscripts, memorabilia, original art works, pamphlets, photographs, prints, reproductions, sculpture
Collections: Original Art by Local Artists; Postcard Collection

M **OLD DOMINION UNIVERSITY,** Gallery, 765 Granbe St, 23510. Tel 804-683-4047, 683-2843; FAX 804-683-5457. *Dir* Fred Bayersdorfer; *Art Chmn* Carol S Hines
Open Mon - Sun 1 - 5 PM. No admis fee. Estab 1972 for the exhibition of contemporary work; also established as a public forum for contemporary artists, with student exposure. Average Annual Attendance: 3000
Income: Financed by endowment and city appropriation
Library Holdings: Vols 7000; Per subs 40
Exhibitions: Monthly exhibitions during academic year
Activities: Lectures open to public, 10 vis lectr per year; gallery talks; tours; competitions; exten dept

L **Elise N Hofheimer Art Library,** Fine & Performing Arts Center, Room 109, 23529. Tel 804-683-4059; Elec Mail ME200U@ODUVM.BITNET. *Art Librn Asst* Margaret Chatfield
Open Mon - Thurs 8 AM - 9 PM, Fri 8 AM - 5 PM, Sat 1 - 5 PM, Sun 1 - 6 PM. Open to students and faculty; open to the public for reference
Income: Financed by state, gifts and grants
Library Holdings: Vols 7000; Per subs 40; Micro — Cards, fiche, prints, reels; AV — A-tapes, fs, rec, slides, v-tapes; Other — Clipping files, exhibition catalogs, framed reproductions, manuscripts, memorabilia, original art works, pamphlets, photographs, prints, reproductions

PETERSBURG

M **THE CITY OF PETERSBURG MUSEUMS,** 15 W Bank St, 23803. Tel 804-733-2401. *Dir* William J Martin; *Cur* Suzanne Savery
Open Mon - Sat 9 AM - 5 PM, Sun 12:30 - 5 PM, cl holidays. Admis adults $2, sr citizens, children & groups $1. Estab 1972 as a system of historic house museums. Seven historic sites dating from 1770-1839. Average Annual Attendance: 85,000
Collections: †Decorative arts of the 19th century; †Military - Civil War; †Photos & manuscripts - City of Petersburg
Activities: Classes for adults & children, dramatic programs; docent training; lect open to public, 8 vis lectr per yr; concerts; gallery talks; tours; individual paintings & original objects of art lent to other museums; book traveling exhibitions, four per yr; museum shop sells books, reproductions, prints & slides

PORTSMOUTH

M **PORTSMOUTH MUSEUMS,** Arts Center, 420 High St, PO Box 850, VA 23705. Tel 804-393-8543, 393-8983; FAX 804-393-5107. *Dir* M E Burnell; *Museum Coordr* Albert Harris; *Sr Curatorial Asst* Shelley Brooks
Open Tues - Sat 10 AM - 5 PM, Sun 1 - 5 PM, cl Mon. Admis fee $1.50 to tour four municipal museums. Estab 1974 to offer a wide variety of the visual arts to the citizens of Tidewater area & beyond. Average Annual Attendance: 60,000. Mem: 850; individual $20, family $25, sponsoring $50, contributing $100
Income: $400,000 (financed by city appropriation)
Purchases: $3000
Collections: Contemporary drawings & paintings, primarily by American artists
Exhibitions: (1992) New Work by J Robert Burnell. (1993) Fear & Confidence; Work by Geoff Smith; Big Al Carter. (1994) Presswork: The Art of Women

Printmakers
Publications: Quarterly newsletter
Activities: Classes for adults & children; workshops; lect open to public, 4 vis lectr per yr; concerts; gallery talks; tours; outreach program; book traveling exhibitions, 6 per year; museum shop

PULASKI

M **FINE ARTS CENTER FOR THE NEW RIVER VALLEY,** 21 W Main St, 24301. Tel 703-980-7363. *Exec Dir* Mary Goodwin; *Secy* Ellen Mitchellrgrast
Open 10 AM - 5 PM. No admis fee. Estab 1978 to foster & furnish activities, programs & facilities to increase understanding of the arts. Gallery area 800 sq ft, classroom area 1800 sq ft. Average Annual Attendance: 14,000. Mem: 550; dues $10-$550; annual meeting in Sept
Income: $72,900 (financed by mem, city & state appropriation & business sponsorship)
Purchases: $80,000 (building in 1988)
Collections: Permanent collection established by donated pieces of art, sculpture & original paintings
Exhibitions: Monthly exhibits of regional artists work
Publications: Centerpiece, monthly newsletter; Rainbow of Arts, childrens quarterly newsletter
Activities: Classes for adults & children; dramatic programs; docent programs; scholarships & fels offered; artmobile serves New River Valley; lending collection; retail store sells books, prints, original art, local craft items

RESTON

NATIONAL ART EDUCATION ASSOCIATION
For further information, see National and Regional Organizations

NATIONAL ASSOCIATION OF SCHOOLS OF ART & DESIGN
For further information, see National and Regional Organizations

RICHMOND

A **AGECROFT ASSOCIATION,** Agecroft Hall, 4305 Sulgrave Rd, 23221. Tel 804-353-4241. *Dir* Richard Moxley; *Coordr Educ* Alice Young; *Cur* Elizabeth Schmidt
Open Tues - Fri 10 AM - 4 PM, Sat & Sun 2 - 5 PM. Admis adults $2, students $1, group rates by prior arrangements. Estab 1968 to exhibit 15th century Tudor Manor House brought over from Lancashire, England in 1925-26 and rebuilt in Richmond. Furnished with period objects of art. Average Annual Attendance: 18,000
Income: Financed by endowment and admission
Purchases: 1560 portrait of William Dauntesey
Collections: 16th & early 17th century furniture & objects of art depicting Elizabethan lifestyle, when Agecroft Hall was at its pinnacle
Exhibitions: Permanent exhibit of British memorabilia 1890 - present
Activities: Classes for adults; docent training; lectures open to public; concerts; gallery talks; specialized tours
L **Library,** Agecroft Hall, 4305 Sulgrave Rd, 23221. Tel 804-353-4241.
Open Tues - Fri 10 AM - 4 PM, Sat & Sun 2 - 5 PM. Estab to interpret !6th Century English lifestyle
Library Holdings: Vols 100; Other — Original art works

A **ARTS COUNCIL OF RICHMOND, INC,** 1435 W Main St, 23220. Tel 804-355-7200; FAX 804-643-5006. *Pres* Charles Chambliss; *Exec Dir* Adrienne G Hines
Open Mon - Fri 9 AM - 5 PM. Estab 1949 to promote and support the arts and to provide arts programs and services to enhance the quality of city living
Income: Financed by grants, contributions, and city appropriation
Publications: Arts Spectrum Directory, annually
Activities: Management seminars; downtown arts festival, children's festival for the arts; outreach program to hospitals, senior centers & prisons; Public Art Program including art at airport

A **ASSOCIATION FOR THE PRESERVATION OF VIRGINIA ANTIQUITIES,** 2300 E Grace St, 23223. Tel 804-648-1889; FAX 804-648-1894. *Pres* Mrs VanLandingham
Estab 1889 to acquire and preserve historic buildings, grounds and monuments in Virginia. APVA owns and administers 36 properties in Virginia. Among the properties: Jamestown Island; Walter Reed Birthplace, Gloucester County; Bacon's Castle and Smith's Fort Plantation, Surry County; John Marshall House, Richmond; Scotchtown, Hanover County; Mary Washington House, Hugh Mercer Apothecary Shoe and Rising Sun Tavern, St James Cottage, Fredericksburg; Smithfield Plantation, Blacksburg; Farmers Bank, Petersburg; Cape Henry Lighthouse and Lynnhaven House, Virginia Beach; Dora Armistead House, Williamsburg; Holly Brook, Eastville. Hours and admissions vary according to location. Mem: 6000; dues individual $20; annual meeting in Spring
Income: Financed by membership, endowment fund donations, & grants
Collections: Decorative arts; 17th - 19th century furniture, glass, ceramics, metalwork and textiles
Exhibitions: (1989) Centennial Exhibit
Publications: Discovery (magazine) annually; newsletter, quarterly
Activities: Lectures open to public; individual paintings & objects of art lent to other non-profit preservation organizations' exhibits; sales shop sells books, reproductions, prints and slides, magazines, gifts, Virginia handicrafts
L **Library,** 2300 E Grace St, 23223. FAX 804-648-1894; *Cur & Librn* Open
For reference use only
Library Holdings: Vols 3000; Per subs 12; AV — Slides; Other — Clipping files, exhibition catalogs, pamphlets, photographs
Special Subjects: Architecture, Decorative Arts, Historical Material, Restoration Technology & archaeology

M **John Marshall House,** 818 E Marshall St, 23219. Tel 804-648-7998. *Site Coordr* Melissa J Haines
Open 10 AM - 5 PM. Admis fee $1.25 - $3. Estab 1790 to represent John Marshall's life in Richmond & hist contribution to the nation. Historical house museum depicting the 1790 - 1835 period in which John Marshall lived here. Average Annual Attendance: 8000
Collections: Decorative arts, porcelain; period furniture 1790 - 1835
Exhibitions: Marshall family pieces including his judicial robes
Activities: Classes for children; dramatic programs; scholarships; Retail store sells books, prints & slides

C **CRESTAR BANK,** Art Collection, 919 E Main St, 23219. Tel 804-782-5737. *In Charge* Rae Rothweile
Estab 1970. Collection displayed in banks and offices; separate gallery used for new exhibit each month
Collections: Contemporary Art
Activities: Competitions with awards

C **FEDERAL RESERVE BANK OF RICHMOND,** 701 E Byrd St, 23219. Tel 804-697-8000. *Cur & Asst VPres* Jackson L Blanton
Open to public by appointment only. No admis fee. Estab 1978 to provide enjoyment, education and a stimulating work environment for employees and visitors; to give encouragement and support to artists of the Fifth Federal Reserve District. Collection displayed throughout building
Collections: Primarily a regional collection, representing artists who live or who formerly lived in the Fifth Federal Reserve District
Exhibitions: Occasional rotating cameo exhibits in lobby
Activities: Tours

A **HAND WORKSHOP,** Virginia Center for the Craft Arts, 1812 W Main St, 23220. Tel 804-353-0094; FAX 804-353-8018. *Dir* Paula Owen; *Dir Instructional Prog* Barbara Hill
Open Mon - Sat 10 AM - 4 PM. No admis fee. Estab 1963 as a non-profit center for the visual arts committed to preservation of craft traditions & to promote artistic excellence through educational programs, gallery exhibitions & artists services
Exhibitions: (1993) Touch: Beyond the Visual; Lilian Tyrell - Tapestries; Contemporary Taiwanese Ceramics; Work from the New York Experimental Glass Workshop

M **NATIONAL SOCIETY OF THE COLONIAL DAMES,** Wilton House Museum, 215 S Wilton Rd, PO Box 8225, 23226. Tel 804-282-5936. *Adminr* Karen Steele
Open Tues - Sat 10 AM - 4:30 Pm, Sun 1:30 AM - 4:30 AM, cl Mon. Admis $3.50. Estab 1935. Average Annual Attendance: 3500
Collections: †18th & 19th century furniture; †18th century decorative arts
Activities: Educ dept; classes for children; docent training; lect open to public, 5 - 7 vis lectr per year; tours

C **NATIONS BANK** (Formerly Sovran Bank NA), Art Collection, Sovran Center, PO Box 27025, 23261. Tel 804-788-2387; FAX 804-788-2804. *In Charge* Constance Cann Hancock
Certain areas open to public 9 AM - 5 PM, or by appointment with tour guides. Estab 1974 to support the arts (mostly Virgina artists), to enhance bank surroundings and as an investment. Collection displayed on 2nd floor (monthly exhibits); permanent collection in reception areas and offices throughout 24 floors
Collections: Contemporary works of art in different media, mostly local and Va artists, and some known artists
Activities: Tours by appointment; sponsored employee art exhibit; individual objects of art lent; monthly exhibits by local, employee and Virginia artists; paintings on loan by local gallery

M **1708 EAST MAIN GALLERY,** 1708 E Main, 23223. Tel 804-643-7829. *Dir* Julyen Norman
Open Sept - June, Tues - Sun 1 - 5 PM. No admis fee. Estab 1978 to offer an alternative presentation space to emerging & professional artists. Two ground floor, artist-run galleries are devoted to the presentation of contemporary art. Average Annual Attendance: 10,000. Mem: 24; mem open to professional artists; dues 1st & 2nd yr $25, 3rd & 4th yr $20, 5th yr pledge; monthly meetings
Income: $85,000 (financed by endowment, mem, state appropriation, grants, gifts from corporations & foundations)
Exhibitions: One & two-person & group shows in drawing, painting, photography & sculpture by local, regional & national artists
Activities: Lect open to public, 9 vis lectrs per yr; performance art series, 6 events per season; poetry & fiction readings, monthly; originate traveling exhibitions

M **VALENTINE MUSEUM,** 1015 E Clay St, 23219-1590. Tel 804-649-0711. *Dir* Frank Jewell; *Deputy Dir* Judy Lankford
Open Mon - Sat 10 AM - 5 PM, Sun noon - 5 PM. Admis adults $3.50, students $2.75, children 7-12 $1.50. Estab 1892 as a museum of the life & history of Richmond. Average Annual Attendance: 94,000. Mem: 1500; dues individual $35
Income: Financed by endowment, mem, city & state appropriation & gifts
Collections: Conrad Wise Chapman (oils, almost entire life works); William Ludwell Sheppard (drawings & watercolors); Edward Virginius Valentine (sculpture); outstanding collection of Southern photographs; candlesticks, ceramics, costumes, glass, jewelry, lace, paintings, photographs, prints, sculpture, local history, regional art and decorative arts; neo classical wall paintings
Publications: Valentine Newsletter, bimonthly
Activities: Classes for adults and children; docent training; dramatic programs; lect open to the public; concerts; tours; exten dept serving city and area counties; originate traveling exhibitions; museum & sales shops sell books, original art, reproductions, prints, slides & silver; Family Activity Center

L **Library,** 1015 E Clay St, 23219-1590. Tel 804-649-0711; FAX 804-643-3510. *Cur of Books* Gregg Kimball; *Librn* Teresa Roane
Open to the public by appointment only; non-lending, reference library
Library Holdings: Vols 10,000; Per subs 20; Other — Clipping files, exhibition catalogs, manuscripts, memorabilia, original art works, pamphlets, photographs 50,000, prints 600, reproductions
Special Subjects: Photography, Local history, tobacco, Virginia's art

VIRGINIA COMMONWEALTH UNIVERSITY

M **Anderson Gallery,** 907 1/2 W Franklin St, 23824-2514. Tel 804-067-1522; FAX 804-367-0102. *Dir* Steven High; *Admin* Kathryn Emerson; *Mgr* Leon Roger; *Store Mgr* Kathy Messick; *Registrar* Leslie Brothers
Open Tues - Fri 10 AM - 5 PM, Sat & Sun 1 - 5 PM, cl Mon except by appointment. Estab 1930, re-opened 1970 as the showcase for the contemporary arts in Richmond; to expose the university and community to a wide variety of current artistic ideas and expressions. Gallery is situated on campus in a four-story converted stable. There are seven galleries with a variety of exhibition spaces. Average Annual Attendance: 20,000
Collections: †Contemporary prints & paintings; cross section of prints from the 15th to 20th century covering most periods; vintage & contemporary photography
Exhibitions: Messages: words & images; Jud Fine; Paul Rotterdam; Future Histories; Larry Miller; Masters of Contemporary Drawing; Francesc Torres; Rita Myers Suzan Etkin; Thomas Florschuetz; Clemens Weiss. Abstraction in Contemporary Photography. (1991) Alfred Jaar; Terry Adkins. (1992) Alfredo Ceibal; Lynn Cohen
Publications: Catalogs;newsletters; posters & brochures; periodically; quarterly
Activities: Lectures open to public, 10 vis lectr per yr; concerts; gallery talks; competitions; lending collection contains 100 original art works, 100 original paintings & photographs; originate traveling exhibitions

L **School of The Arts Library,** 325 N Harrison St, 23284-2519. Tel 804-367-1683. *Dir* Jeanne Boone-Bradley
Open Mon - Thurs 9 AM - 6 PM, Fri 9 AM - 5 PM. Estab 1926 to support the teaching program of the eleven departments of the School of the Arts
Income: Financed by state appropriation
Library Holdings: Micro — Fiche; AV — Slides 450,000; Other — Exhibition catalogs 20,000
Collections: †Transparencies (2 x 2 inch) of works of art; †Exhibition Catalogs, worldwide in scope

L **VIRGINIA DEPT HISTORIC RESOURCES,** Research Library, 221 Governor St, 23219. Tel 804-786-3143. *Archivist* Joseph S White III
Open daily 8:30 AM - 4:30 PM. Estab 1966
Library Holdings: Vols 3000; Per subs 20; Other — Clipping files, manuscripts, photographs
Special Subjects: Archaeology, Architecture, Decorative Arts, Ethnology, Furniture, Historical Material, History of Art & Archaeology, Landscape Architecture, Landscapes, Maps
Collections: Archaeology; Architecture; Ethnography; History

A **VIRGINIA HISTORICAL SOCIETY,** 428 North Blvd, PO Box 7311, 23221. Tel 804-358-4901; FAX 804-355-2399. *Dir* Dr Charles Bryon; *Assoc Dir* Robert Strohm; *Cur Spec Coll* James Kelly
Open Mon - Sat 10 AM - 5 PM, Museum Sun 1 - 5 PM. Admis $3, students $2, members free. Estab 1831 for collecting, preserving and making available to scholars research material relating to the history of Virginia, its collections include extensive holdings of historical portraiture. Seven galleries feature changing & permanent exhibits drawn from public & private collections throughout Virginia. Average Annual Attendance: 5600. Mem: 5000; dues $35
Income: Financed by endowment and membership
Collections: †Books; †Manuscripts; Museum Collection; †Portraits
Exhibitions: (1991) Fevers, Aques & Cures: Medical Exhibit
Publications: Virginia Magazine of History and Biography, quarterly; bulletin, quarterly
Activities: Classes for adults & children; docent training; teacher recertification; lect open to public 15 per year; gallery talks; William Rachel Award; individual paintings & original objects of art lent consisting of 125,000 books, 800 paintings, 100's original prints, 100,000 photographs, 100 sculptures; Museum shop sells books, prints

L **Library,** 428 North Blvd, PO Box 7311, 23221-0311. Tel 804-358-4901; FAX 804-355-2399. *Dir* Charles F Bryan
Open Mon - Sat 9 AM - 4:45 PM. Estab 1831 for the study of Virginia history. For reference only
Income: Financed by endowment, membership, state appropriation and private donations
Library Holdings: Vols 125,000; Per subs 300; Micro — Fiche, reels; AV — Fs; Other — Clipping files, exhibition catalogs, manuscripts, memorabilia, original art works, pamphlets, photographs 100,000, prints, reproductions, sculpture
Special Subjects: 17th & 18th century English architecture
Publications: Bulletin, quarterly; Virginia Magazine of History and Biography, quarterly
Activities: Lectures open to members, 3 vis lectrs per yr

M **VIRGINIA MUSEUM OF FINE ARTS,** 2800 Grove Ave, 23221-2466. Tel 804-367-0844; FAX 804-367-9393. *Pres* Dr Herbert A Claiborne Jr; *Dir* Katharine C Lee; *Deputy Dir* William Rowland; *Assoc Dir Exhib/Prog Div* Richard Woodward; *Education Dir* Mary W Fritzsche; *Registrar* Lisa Hancock; *Development Dir* David Bradley; *Deputy Dir Coll* David Park Curry
Open Tues - Sat 11 AM - 5 PM, Sun 1 - 5 PM, cl Mon. Estab 1934; theatre opened 1955; South Wing added 1970. Participating in the museum's programs are the Fellows of Virginia Museum, who meet yearly to counsel the museum on its future plans; the Women's Council, which sponsors and originates special programs; the Collector's Circle, a group of Virginia art lovers which meets four times a year to discuss various aspects of collecting; the Corporate Patrons, state and local business firms who lend financial support to museum programs; Virginia Museum Youth Guild; and the Institute for Contemporary Art, which presents exhibitions of works by state, nationally and internationally known contemporary artists. Average Annual Attendance: 1,250,000. Mem: 16,500; dues $15 and higher; annual meeting in May
Collections: Lady Nancy Astor Collection of English China; Branch Collection of Italian Renaissance Paintings, Sculpture and Furniture; Ailsa Mellon Bruce Collection of 18th Century Furniture and Decorative Arts; Mrs Arthur Kelly Evans Collection of Pottery and Porcelain; †Arthur and Margaret Glasgow Collection of Flemish and Italian Renaissance Paintings, Sculpture and Decorative Arts; Nasli and Alice Heeramaneck Collection of Art of India, Nepal, Kashmir and Tibet; T Catesby Jones Collection of 20th Century European Paintings and Drawings; Dr and Mrs Arthur Mourot Collection of Meissen Porcelain; The John Barton Payne Collection of Paintings, Prints and Portuguese Furniture; Lillian Thomas Pratt Collection of Czarist Jewels by Peter Carl Faberge; †Adolph D and Wilkins C Williams Collection of Paintings, Tapestries, China and Silver; archaic Chinese bronzes; archaic Chinese jades; comprehensive collections of early Greek vases (8th century to 4th century BC); representative examples of the arts from early Egypt to the present time, including paintings, sculpture, furniture and objects d'art
Exhibitions: Painting in the South; Wealth of the Ancient World; Paintings from the Royal Academy
Publications: Arts in Virginia, 3 times per year; Virginia Museum Bulletin, monthly; brochures; bulletins, nine per year; catalogues for special exhibitions and collections; programs
Activities: Classes for adults and children in painting, drawing, graphics, ceramics and weaving; workshops; demonstrations; lectures; concerts; drama productions; fels offered (10 - 15 per year) to Virginia artists; art mobile; originate traveling exhibitions throughout the state of Virginia

L **Library,** 2800 Grove Ave, 23221. Tel 804-367-0827; FAX 804-367-9393. *Librn* Betty Stacy
Open Tues - Fri 9 AM - 5 PM. Estab 1954 for art history research. For reference only
Income: Financed by private funds
Library Holdings: Vols 61,000; Per subs 215; Micro — Prints, reels; Other — Clipping files, exhibition catalogs, pamphlets
Special Subjects: Art History, Crafts, Decorative Arts, Painting - American, Sculpture, Art Nouveau, Art Deco, Classical Art
Collections: Weedon Collection; Hayes Collections; Strauss Collection; Oriental art

ROANOKE

M **ARI MUSEUM OF WESTERN VIRGINIA** (Formerly Roanoke Museum of Fine Arts), Center in the Square, One Market Square, 2nd Floor, 24011-1436. Tel 703-342-5760; FAX 703-224-1238. *Exec Dir* Dr Ruth Stevens Appelhof; *Dir Development* Jeff Roberts; *Asst Cur Colls & Exhibit* Carissa South; *Registrar* Mary LaGue; *Dir Community Relations* Rebekah Woodie; *Dir Education* Mark Scala
Open Tues - Sat 10 AM - 5 PM. Admis $2 non-members, $1.50 sr citizens, $.50 children, members & Fri free. Estab 1951. Museum is located in a downtown cultural complex called Center in the Square. There are three major rotating galleries, one permanent collection gallery, studio classrooms, educational gallery & lecture hall. Average Annual Attendance: 50,000. Mem: 1500; dues $25 & up; annual meeting in May
Income: Financed by membership, earned income, donations & endowment
Collections: African Sculpture; Contemporary American Paintings, Sculpture & Graphic Arts; Folk Art; Japanese Prints & Decorative Arts; 19th Century American Paintings; Regional Art
Exhibitions: (1992)Land Ho
The Mythical World of Rodney Alan; Beth Shively, In the Garden; William Dunlap, Re-constructed Re-Collections. (1993) Hunt Slonem, In the Realm of the Spirit; Gari Melchers (portraits & landscapes); William Eggleston (photographs); Gregory Henry (paintings & sculpture); Art in Bloom; Roanoke City Art Show; Steven Bickley (sculpture); Cartoon Magic; Ray Kass (watercolors); Edward Beyer (painting & prints). (1994) Brian Sieveking (paintings); Roanoke City Art Show; Fritz Bultman; Martin Johnson; Donna Essig; Children's Regional Juried Exhibition
Publications: Annual Report; Docent Guild newsletter; exhibition catalogs; quarterly newsletter
Activities: Classes for adults and children; docent training; lect open to the public; gallery talks; tours; individual paintings lent to qualified museums; museum store selling books, original art, prints, reproductions, handmade crafts including jewelry & children's items

STAUNTON

A **STAUNTON FINE ARTS ASSOCIATION,** Staunton Augusta Art Center, One Gypsy Hill Park, 24401. Tel 703-885-2028. *Exec Dir* Clair C Bell
Open Mon - Fri 9 AM - 5 PM, Sat 10 AM - 2 PM. No admis fee. Estab 1961 for art exposure & education to area residents. Average Annual Attendance: 5000. Mem: 550; dues $50
Income: $106,000 (financed by mem, city & state appropriations)
Exhibitions: Christmas Art for Gifts; Youth Art Month; Virginia Museum Teams Exhibit; Virginia Artist Craft Invitational
Activities: Classes for adults & children; lect open to public; book traveling exhibitions 8 per year; retail store

M **WOODROW WILSON BIRTHPLACE FOUNDATION,** 20 N Coalter St, PO Box 24, 24402-0024. Tel 703-885-0897. *Dir* Susan E Klaffky
Open daily 9 AM - 5 PM, cl Sun of Dec, Jan & Feb, Thanksgiving, Christmas and New Year's Day. Admis adults $5, senior citizens $4, children 6-16 $1. Estab 1938 for the interpretation & collection of life & times of Woodrow Wilson. Collection is housed in the 1846 Presbyterian Manse which was the birthplace of Woodrow Wilson. Mem: 900; dues $15-$25, annual meeting Oct/Nov
Collections: Historical Material pertinent to the Wilson family; decorative arts, furniture, manuscripts, musical instruments, paintings, photographs, prints and drawings, rare books, textiles

Exhibitions: (1993) Ellen Wilson Original Paintings
Publications: Brochures; guides; Newsletter, semi-annually; pamphlets
Activities: Classes for children; dramatic programs; lectures open to public, 4 vis lectr per yr; concerts; tours; competitions with awards; scholarships; original objects of art lent to museums & libraries; lending collection contains original art work & sculpture; sales shop sells books, magazines, reproductions, prints & slides
L **Library,** 20 N Coalter St, PO Box 24, 24402-0024. Tel 703-885-0897. *Librn* Jean Smith
Income: Financed by endowment, admissions, members, grants
Library Holdings: Vols 2000; Other — Pamphlets, photographs
Special Subjects: Wilsoniana; World War I; diplomatic history
Exhibitions: Women's History; Black History; Wedding Customs
Publications: Wilson Newsletters, quarterly

STRASBURG

M **STRASBURG MUSEUM,** E King St, 22657. Tel 703-465-3428. *Pres* David Nelson
Open May to Oct, daily 10 AM - 4 PM. Admis adults $1, children $.50. Estab 1970 to present the past of a Shenandoah Valley community and to preserve the pottery-making tradition of Strasburg. The museum is housed in the former Southern Railway Depot, which was orginally built as a steam pottery. Average Annual Attendance: 4000. Mem: 133; dues $3; annual meeting in March
Income: Financed by membership, admission fees and gifts
Collections: Indian Artifacts; pottery
Activities: Classes for adults and children in pottery making; museum shop selling books, original art, pottery and other local crafts

SWEET BRIAR

L **SWEET BRIAR COLLEGE,** Martin C Shallenberger Art Library, 24595. Tel 804-381-6138; FAX 804-381-6173. *Dir* John G Jaffe; *Asst Dir* Patricia Wright; *Public Service* Kathleen A Lance; *Bibliographic Instruction & Branch Librn* Lisa N Johnston
Estab 1961, when it was separated from the main library, the library serves an undergraduate community. The Art Library is now located in the Pannell Fine Arts Center
Income: Financed by college funds
Library Holdings: Vols 11,500; Per subs 55; Micro — Fiche; AV — Cassettes, Kodachromes, lantern slides; Other — Exhibition catalogs, original art works, pamphlets, prints
Special Subjects: Aesthetics, Afro-American Art, American Indian Art, American Western Art, Antiquities-Assyrian, Folk Art, Furniture, Glass, Gold, Graphic Arts, Painting - American, Painting - Australian, Painting - British, Painting - Canadian, Painting - Dutch
M **Art Gallery,** 24595. Tel 804-381-6248; FAX 804-381-6173. *Dir* Rebecca Massie-Lane
Open Tues - Sun noon - 5 PM, Tues - Thurs 7:30 PM - 9:30 PM. Estab 1985 to support the educational mission at Sweet Briar College through its exhibits, collections & educational programs. Average Annual Attendance: 4000. Mem: 215; annual dues $25; annual meeting in Apr
Collections: American & European drawings & prints; Japanese Woodblock prints, 18th & 19th century
Exhibitions: Rotating exhibits from permanent collection plus traveling exhibits
Activities: Docent training; lect open to the public, 4 vis lectr per year; concerts; gallery talks; tours; individual paintings are lent to other museums; originate traveling exhibitions; bookshop sells books, magazines & reproductions

VIRGINIA BEACH

A **VIRGINIA BEACH CENTER FOR THE ARTS,** 2200 Parks Ave, 23451. Tel 804-425-0000; FAX 804-425-8186. *Pres* Helen Snow; *Dir Educ* Betsy Gough-DiJulio; *Museum Shop Mgr* Gray Dodson
Open Mon - Sat 10 AM - 5 PM, Sun 1 PM - 5 PM. Admis adults $2, children $1. Estab 1952, as a non-profit organization serving citizens of the greater Hampton Roads area with exhibits & programming in the visual arts. Exhibition space 800 sq ft student gallery & 5600 sq ft main gallery. Average Annual Attendance: 50,000. Mem: 1500, dues family $50 and up, single $30; annual meeting in Sept
Income: Financed by memberships, public grants, private donations, various fund raising events
Collections: Best-in-Show winners from Boardwalk Art Show
Exhibitions: 15 exhibitions per year covering all media
Publications: ArtLetter, monthly; exhibition catalogues
Activities: Educ dept; classes & workshops for adults & children; dramatic programs; docent training; film series; performing arts; lect open to public; 15 vis lectr per yr; concerts; gallery talks; tours; scholarships & fels offered; exten dept serves municipal employees; museum shop sells books, original art, reproductions, prints, crafts, jewelry, wearable art

WILLIAMSBURG

M **COLLEGE OF WILLIAM AND MARY,** Joseph & Margaret Muscarelle Museum of Art, 23185. Tel 804-221-2710. *Dir* Mark M Johnson; *Cur* Ann Madonia; *Registrar* Louise Kale; *Educator* Lisa Leek; *Spec Prog Admin* Ursula McLaughlin; *Preparator* Steven Riffee; *Business Mgr* Cindy Lucas
Open Mon - Fri 10 AM - 4:45 PM, Sat - Sun Noon - 4 PM. Estab 1983. Average Annual Attendance: 60,000. Mem: 600; dues $10 & up
Income: Financed by endowments, state appropriations & donations
Collections: 17th - 20th century drawings, prints & paintings
Exhibitions: Sponsors changing exhibitions of art in the museum
Publications: Calendar, twice a year; exhibition catalogues
Activities: Educ dept; member seminars; classes for children; docent training;

music series; college program; lect open to public; 8 - 12 vis lectrs per year; concerts; gallery talks; tours; individual paintings & original objects of art lent to special exhibitions organized by other museums; loans are from permanent collection; originate traveling exhibitions that circulate to other museums, art centers, colleges; sales shop sells books & gifts

M **COLONIAL WILLIAMSBURG FOUNDATION,** PO Box 1776, 23187-1776. Tel 804-229-1000. *Pres* Robert Wilburne; *Dir Media Relations* Albert O Louer; *VPres Media & Government Relations* Norman G Beatty; *Dir & Cur Coll* Graham S Hood; *VPres Museums* Beatrix T Rumford; *Dir Editorial Services* Wayne Barrett
Open 9 AM - 5 PM, Folk Art Center re-opens fall 1991; DeWitt Wallace Decorative Art Gallery open 10 AM - 6 PM. Estab 1927 the worlds' largest outdoor museum, providing first hand history of 18th-century English colony during period of subjects becoming Americans. The colonial area of this 18th-century capital of Virginia, encompassing 173 acres with nearly 500 homes, shops, taverns, public buildings, dependencies, has been carefully restored to its original appearance. Included are 90 acres of gardens and greens. The work was initiated by the late John D Rockefeller, Jr. There are more than 40 exhibition homes, public buildings and craft shops where guides and craftsmen in colonial costume show visitors the arts and decoration as well as the way of life of pre-Revolutionary Virginia. Included are the historic Bruton Parish Church, the Governors Palace, Capitol, the Courthouse of 1770, Bassett Hall (local residence of the Rockefellers), the Wallace Gallery and Carter's Grove plantation. The exhibition properties include 225 furnished rooms. Average Annual Attendance: 1,300,000
Income: Financed by admis, gifts & grants, real estate, products, restaurants & hotels
Collections: †18th-Century English and American Painting; †English Pottery and Porcelains; †English and Early American Silver; †Collections of American and English furnishings, with frequent additions, include representative pieces, rare English pieces in the palace; †exceptionally fine textiles and rugs; extensive collection of primary & secondary materials relating to British North America, the Colonial Period & the early National Period
Exhibitions: Brush-Everard House (small well-appointed home, typical of a comfortable but not wealthy colonial); The Capitol (one of colonial America's most important buildings, scene of Patrick Henry's oration against the Stamp Act); Craft Shops (the trades and crafts of 200 years ago are carried on in 20 authentically furnished craft shops where artisans use the tools and methods of the 18th century); The Gaol (where debtors, criminals and Blackbeard's pirates were imprisoned); James Geddy House (original dwelling and workshop of a well-known colonial silversmith and businessman); Governor's Palace and Gardens (residence of seven royal governors; outstanding English and American 18th century furnishing and extensive formal colonial gardens); Public Magazine (arsenal of the Virginia colony, now exhibiting colonial arms); Raleigh Tavern (one of the most famous taverns of colonial times, where Virginia patriots plotted Revolutionary action, and social center of the capital); Peyton Randolph House (original residence of the first president of the Continental Congress); Wetherburn's Tavern (among the most famous of the 18th century Virginia hostelries, over 200 years old); Wren Building of the College of William and Mary (the oldest academic building in British America in continuous use with six rooms open to the public and the remainder still in use for college classes and faculty offices); Wythe House (home of George Wythe, signer of Declaration of Independence and teacher of Jefferson and John Marshall)
Publications: The foundation publishes many books on a wide range of subjects; Colonial Williamsburg, quarterly journal
Activities: Classes & tours for adults & children; lectures open to public, 30 vis lectr per yr; concerts; gallery talks; special focus tours; individual paintings & original objects of art lent; museum shop sells books, magazines, original art, reproductions, prints & slides
A **Visitor Center,** PO Box 1776, 23187-1776. Tel 804-220-7645. *Dir* Rob Weir
Outside the historic area this modern center houses graphic exhibits of the restoration and colonial life. Continuous showings of a full-color, vista vision film, Williamsburg: The Story of a Patriot
Publications: Books and brochures on Williamsburg and colonial life; gallery book of the Folk Art Collection
Activities: Limited grant-in-aid program for researchers; Annual events including Antiques Forum; Garden Symposium; regular performance of 18th century dramas, organ recitals and concerts; slide lectures
L **Library,** 415 N Boundary St, PO Box 1776, 23187-1776. Tel 804-220-7422. *Dir* Susan Berg
Library Holdings: Vols 55,000; Per subs 500; Drawings 65,000; AV — Slides 250,000; Other — Manuscripts 45,000, photographs 250,000
Special Subjects: Crafts, Architecture, Archaeology, Fine Arts, Clothing
Collections: History of the Restoration of Colonial Williamsburg; Historical Preservation in America
M **Abby Aldrich Rockefeller Folk Art Center,** 307 S England St, PO Box 1776, 23187-1776. Tel 804-220-7670. *Cur* Carolyn Weekley
Open Mon - Sun 10 AM - 6 PM. Admis $4. Estab 1939 for research, education and the exhibition of one of the country's leading collections of American folk art of the 18th, 19th & 20th centuries. Nine galleries of American folk art, including a craft gallery. Average Annual Attendance: 150,000
Collections: Decorative usefulwares, decoys, needlework, painted furniture, paintings, sculptures & signs
Publications: Exhibition Catalogs
Activities: Learning Weekend on American Folk Art (every other yr); lectures open to public, 1-2 vis lectrs per yr; paintings & sculpture lent to other museums; book traveling exhibitions
—**Abby Aldrich Rockefeller Folk Art Center Library,** 307 S England St, PO Box 1776, 23187-1776. Tel 804-220-8934. *Registrar & Librn* Anne E Watkins
Open to serious scholars of folk art for reference
Library Holdings: Vols 5000; Per subs 7; Micro — Fiche; AV — Rec, slides; Other — Clipping files, exhibition catalogs, manuscripts, memorabilia, pamphlets, photographs, prints
Special Subjects: Folk Art

M **DeWitt Wallace Decorative Arts Gallery,** 325 Francis St, PO Box 1776, 23187-1776. Tel 804-229-1000.
Open daily 10 AM - 6 PM. Admis adults $8.50. Estab 1985. The Wallace Gallery is a contemporary bi-level museum featuring an introductory gallery, an upper level balcony of the central court which presents works from the permanent collection, study galleries which are organized by specific media, and changing special exhibition galleries
Collections: English and American decorative arts from 1600-1830
Exhibitions: Permanent: Selected Masterworks from the Colonial Williamsburg Collection; study galleries present English & American furniture, ceramics, metals, prints & textiles. (1993) Special exhibitions include Patron & Tradesman: Forces that Fashioned Objects, 1660 - 1800; Images of Nature, Creations of Man: Natural History & the Decorative Arts
Activities: Lectures open to public; tours; slide & video presentations; musical events

YORKTOWN

M **JAMESTOWN-YORKTOWN FOUNDATION,** Route 1020 & Colonial Parkway, PO Box 1976, 23690. Tel 804-887-1776. *Dir* Nancy S Perry; *Cur* Lucinda P Cockrell
Open daily 9 AM - 5 PM, cl Christmas & New Year's. Admis adults $5.75, children $2.75, sr & group discounts. Estab 1976 to interpret the history of the American Revolution. Average Annual Attendance: 100,000. Mem: 260; dues $25 - $5000; annual meeting in Apr
Income: $700,000 (financed by admissions & state appropriation)
Purchases: $20,000
Collections: Gen John Steele collection of furniture, silver, paintings; †paintings by Oscar DeMejo; †varied series of prints, paintings & art works on theme of Revolution; 18th century Revolutionary War artifacts
Exhibitions: (1991-1992) The Town of York; Yorktown's Sunken Fleet; The Road to Revolution, Witnesses to Revolution
Publications: Series of biographies of Revolutionary Virginia leaders
Activities: Classes for adults & children; dramatic programs; school programs; lectures open to public, 2-5 per yr; craft shows; book traveling exhibitions, 1-2 per yr; sales shop sells books, magazines, original art, reproductions, prints, slides & craft items

WASHINGTON

BELLEVUE

M **BELLEVUE ART MUSEUM** (Formerly Pacific Northwest Arts & Crafts Association), 301 Bellevue Square, 98004. Tel 206-454-3322. *Dir & Cur* Diane Douglas; *Chief Finance Officer* Linda Krouse; *Public Relations & Marketing Coordr* Abigail Ehrlich; *Operations Coordr* Anne Gray; *Development Coordr* Sharon Rose; *Development Asst* Stacey Sterm; *Development Officer* Susan Anderson; *Assoc Cur* Susan Sagawa; *Vol Coordr* Lisa Yeager; *Store Mgr* Liza Halvorsen; *Educ Coordr* Beverly Silver
Open Mon & Tues 10 AM - 8 PM, Wed - Sat 10 AM - 6 PM, Sun 11 AM - 6 PM. Admis adults $3, senior citizens & students $2, children under 12 free; free every Tues. Estab 1975 to bring visual arts to Bellevue East King County area. Maintains 6000 sq ft for changing and temporary exhibitions. Average Annual Attendance: 48,000 - 60,000. Mem: 1450; dues $40 per family
Income: $850,000 (financed by mem, private contributions, store sales, grants, fundraising events, arts & crafts fair)
Collections: Contemporary Northwest art & crafts
Exhibitions: Exhibitions of local, regional & national significance, with an emphasis on Northwest art & crafts; Annual Pacific Northwest Art & Crafts Fair
Publications: Annual report; quarterly newsletter; exhibition catalogs; posters; membership brochures
Activities: Workshops for adults & children; docent training; lectures open to public, 8-12 vis lect pr year; films; symposia; hands-on activities for children; awards through art & craft juries; museum store sells books, prints, jewelry, reproductions, cards & papers

BELLINGHAM

M **WESTERN WASHINGTON UNIVERSITY,** Viking Union Gallery, High St (Mailing add: 202 Viking Union, 98225-9106). Tel 206-738-6534. *Gallery Dir* Susan Musi; *Asst Gallery Dir* Mark Shetabi; *Advisor* Lisa Rosenberg
Open Mon - Sat 10 AM - 4 PM. No admis fee. Estab 1899 to provide a wide variety of gallery exhibits in a visible campus gallery. Average Annual Attendance: 5000
Income: $7000 (financed by student activity fees)
Exhibitions: Exhibitions change every month
Activities: Book traveling exhibitions 2 per year
M **Western Gallery,** Fine Arts Complex, 98225. Tel 206-676-3963; FAX 206-647-6878. *Dir* Sarah Clark-Langager
Open Mon - Fri 10 AM - 4 PM, Sat noon - 4 PM. No admis fee. Old gallery estab 1949, new gallery estab 1989 to exhibit contemporary art. Rotating exhibitions on contemporary art, 7 per year. Average Annual Attendance: 15,000. Mem: dues Friends of Gallery Group $25
Income: Financed by state appropriation
Collections: Outdoor Sculpture Collection WWU (contemporary art since 1960)
Exhibitions: (1992) African-American Art 1880 - 1987 (Smithsonian Institution). (1993) Elaine Reichek: Native Intelligence
Publications: Outdoor Sculpture Collection brochures
Activities: Wed noon hour discussions; lect open to public; audio tour of outdoor sculpture collection; book traveling exhibitions 7 per year; originate traveling exhibitions 3 per year

M **WHATCOM MUSEUM OF HISTORY AND ART,** 121 Prospect St, 98225. Tel 206-676-6981. *Dir* George Thomas; *Deputy Dir* John Olbrantz; *Education Coordr* Richard Vanderway; *Cur of Collections* Janis Olson; *Public Relations* Michael Vouri; *Business Mgr* Gladys Fullford
Open Tues - Sun noon - 5 PM, cl Mon and holidays. No admis fee. Estab 1940 to collect, preserve and use, through exhibits, interpretation and research, objects of historic or artistic value, and to act as a multi-purpose cultural center for the Northwest Washington area providing presentations in all aspects of the arts. Eight galleries plus a permanent history exhibit space. Average Annual Attendance: 60,000. Mem: 750; dues family $50, individual $25; annual meeting in February; open to public
Income: Financed by private and public funds
Collections: Contemporary Northwest Arts; Darius Kinsey and Wilbur Sandison Historic Photograph Collection; Northwest Native American Artifacts; Regional Historic Photographs and Artifacts; H C Hanson Naval Architecture Collection
Exhibitions: (1989) Gaylen Hansen: Paintings; Environments: Gale Bard & Heather Ramsey; Norman Lundin; Vietnam: The Artists Perspective; Randy Hayes; Marsha Burns: Polaroids; The Raven Speaks
Publications: Art and Events Calendar, bi-monthly; Exhibit catalogs; History texts
Activities: Classes for adults and programs for children; docent training; lectures open to the public; concerts; gallery talks; tours; competitions; awards; individual paintings and original objects of art lent to other museums and galleries; originate traveling exhibitions; museum shop selling books, craftwork from around the world, original art, prints, toys, jewelry, pottery & ethnic clothing
L **Library,** 121 Prospect St, 98225
Open to public by appointment only. For reference only
Library Holdings: Vols 500

CHEHALIS

M **LEWIS COUNTY HISTORICAL MUSEUM,** 599 NW Front St, 98532. Tel 206-748-0831. *Dir* Brenda A O'Connor, MA
Open Tues - Sat 9 AM - 5 PM, Sun 1 - 5 PM. Donations. Estab 1979 to preserve Lewis County history. Displays of a parlor, kitchen, logging displays. Average Annual Attendance: 14,000. Mem: 600; annual meeting Jan
Income: $55,000 (financed by endowment, membership & county funds)
Collections: Local Indian History; Photographic Collection of Lewis County; Obits of County Residents; Oral History
Exhibitions: Ethnic Heritage, Pioneer Heritage; Pioneer Clothing
Publications: The Log
Activities: Classes for adults, docent training; lectures open to public, 3-5 vis lectr per yr; traveling exhibitions, 6 per yr; originate traveling exhibitions, 10 per yr; museum shop sells books, prints, magazines, reproductions
L **Library,** 599 NW Front St, 98532. *Dir* Brenda A O'Connor, MA
Library Holdings: Vols 150; Other — Clipping files, manuscripts, memorabilia, pamphlets, reproductions
Special Subjects: Dioramas, Display, Dolls, Fashion Arts, Flasks & Bottles, Furniture, Historical Material, Manuscripts, Maps, Period Rooms, Photography, Pottery, Restoration & Conservation, Textiles

CLARKSTON

A **VALLEY ART CENTER INC,** 842 Sixth St, PO Box 65, 99403. Tel 509-758-8331. *Executive Dir* Pat Rosenberger; *Co-Chmn & Secy* Gloria Teats; *Treas* Richard Schutte
Open Mon - Fri 9 AM - 4 PM, & by appointment. No admis fee, donations accepted. Estab 1968 to encourage and instruct in all forms of the visual arts and to promote the cause of art in the community. A portion of the Center serves as the gallery; wall space for display of paintings or other art; showcases for collections & artifacts. Average Annual Attendance: 5000-7000. Mem: 175; dues $10; annual meeting Jan 20
Income: Financed by membership and class fees
Exhibitions: Annual Heritate Show; Annual Western Bronze Show; Lewis-Clark Art Association Show; Kaleidoscope of Prize Winning Art
Publications: Newsletter, semi-annually
Activities: Classes for sr citizens, adults & children; lectures open to the public, 4 vis lectrs per yr; gallery talks; tours; competitions with awards; scholarships offered; individual paintings and original objects of art lent to local businesses & individuals, including artists; lending collection contains books, original prints, paintings, records & photographs; sales shop sells books, original art, prints, pottery & soft goods

ELLENSBURG

M **CENTRAL WASHINGTON UNIVERSITY,** Sarah Spurgeon Gallery, 98926. Tel 509-963-2665. *Dir Art Gallery* James Sahlstrand
Open Mon - Fri 8 AM - 5 PM. No admis fee. Estab 1970 to serve as university gallery and hold regional and national exhibits. The gallery is a large, single unit. Average Annual Attendance: 20,000
Income: Financed by state appropriations
Exhibitions: (1991) Handmade paper exhibits; Seattle Glass Exhibit. (1992) Richard Fairbanks: An American Potter Exhibit
Publications: Catalogs for all National shows
Activities: Lect open to the public; competitions

GOLDENDALE

M **MARYHILL MUSEUM OF ART,** 35 Maryhill Museum Dr, 98620. Tel 509-773-3733; FAX 509-773-6138. *Dir* Josie E DeFalla; *Registrar* Betty Long; *Cur Education* Colleen Schafroth; *Business Mgr* Patricia Perry; *Public Relations Officer* William Lamarche; *Development Officer* Ross Randall
Open daily 9 AM - 5 PM Mar 15 - Nov 15. Admis adults $3.50, students (6-16) $1.50, under six free. Estab 1923 as a museum of art. Chateau-style mansion with

3 stories of galleries on 7 acres of parklands plus full scale Stonehenge nearby; cafe & museum shop. Average Annual Attendance: 80,000. Mem: 600; dues $20 individual, $35 family
Collections: American Indian artifacts; antique & modern chessmen; Columbia River Basin prehistoric arts; European & American paintings; Rodin sculpture & drawings; royal furniture designed by Marie, Queen of Romania & memorabilia; World Warr II costumed French fashion mannequins, decorative arts; regional historic photographics; Russian icons
Publications: Brochure, souvenir & exhibition booklets;
Activities: Classes for adults & children, performing arts programs, docent training; lectr open to public, 4 vis lectr per year; concerts; gallery talks; tours; competitions with awards; lending collection contains individual paintings & original objects of art; book traveling exhibitions, 4 annually; originate traveling exhibitions to national & international museums; museum shop sells gift items & publications on collections

KENNEWICK

A **ARTS COUNCIL OF THE MID-COLUMBIA REGION,** 895 Columbia Center (Mailing add: PO Box 730, Richland, 99352). Tel 509-735-4612. *Exec Dir* Barbara Gurth
Open Mon - Fri 10:30 AM - 5 PM, Sat 11 AM - 4 PM. Estab Apr 1968 to advocate the arts in the Mid-Columbia Region. Average Annual Attendance: 17,000. Mem: 300; dues $25 - $15
Income: $100,00 (finance by mem)
Publications: Calendar and Newsletter, monthly
Activities: Educ programs; lect open to the public, 5 vis lectr per year; gallery talks; tours; scholarships; book traveling exhibitions 1 per year

OLYMPIA

M **EVERGREEN STATE COLLEGE,** Evergreen Galleries, 98505. Tel 206-866-6000, Ext 6488. *Dir* Peter Ramsey
Exhibitions: Contemporary West Coast art; functional & sculptured ceramics

M **STATE CAPITOL MUSEUM,** 211 W 21st Ave, 98501. Tel 206-753-2580; FAX 206-586-8322. *Dir* Derek R Valley; *Cur Exhib* Susan Torntore
Open Tues - Fri 10 AM - 4 PM, Sat & Sun noon - 4 PM, cl Mon. No admis fee. Estab 1941 to interpret history of the State of Washington and of the capital city. The one-room gallery presents changing monthly shows. Average Annual Attendance: 40,000. Mem: 400; dues family $12, individual $6; annual meeting in June
Income: Financed by city and state appropriation and local funds
Collections: Etchings by Thomas Handforth; Winslow Homer Woodcuts; Northwest Indian serigraphs; small collection of paintings by Washington artists
Publications: Museum Newsletter, bi-monthly; Museum Calender; every other month: lists all scheduled events
Activities: Classes for adults and children; dramatic programs; docent training; lect open to the public; concerts; gallery talks; tours; individual paintings and original objects of art lent to State offices; lending collection contains original prints, paintings; originate traveling exhibitions; sales shop selling books and slides

PULLMAN

M **WASHINGTON STATE UNIVERSITY,** Museum of Art, 99164-7460. Tel 509-335-1910. *Dir* Patricia Watkinson; *Cur* Barbara Coddington
Open Mon - Fri 10 AM - 4 PM, Tues evening 7 - 10 PM, Sat & Sun 1 - 5 PM. No admis fee. Estab 1973 to contribute to the humanistic and artistic educational purpose and goal of the university for the direct benefit of the students, faculty and surrounding communities. Gallery covers 5000 sq ft and is centrally located on campus. Average Annual Attendance: 25,000. Mem: 400; dues $25 - $1000; annual meeting in the spring
Income: Financed by the state of Washington and private and public grants and contributions
Collections: Late 19th century to present-day American art, with particular strength in the areas of the Ash Can School and Northwest regional art; contemporary American and British prints
Exhibitions: The American Eight from permanent collection; Americans in Glass; Diverse Directions: The Fiber Arts; Drawing 1900-47, A Survey of American Works; Earthworks; Canaletto Etchings; Form and Figure; Historic Visions: Early Photography as Document; Imperial Robes from the Ch'ing Dynasty; Young Photographers in the Northwest; Regionalism: Northwest Artists; Richard Smith: Recent Work 1972-77; Spectrum - New Directions in Color Photography; Contemporary American Potter; Swords of the Samurai; British Landscape Photography; Contemporary Metals; Arts of Kenya; British Prints; Noritake Art Deco Porcelains; Living With the Volcano: Artists of Mt St Helens; Philip Pearlstein: Paintings to Watercolor; annual faculty and student exhibitions; Fabric Traditions of Indonesia; Gaylen Hansen: The Paintings of a Decade; 1975 - 1985 The Master Weavers; Milton Avery: Progressive Images; Outside Japan; A Different War: Vietnam in Art; Arnulf Raines: Drawing on Death; British Printmakers & Some Literary Sources
Publications: Annual special exhibition catalog
Activities: Docent training; lectures open to the public, 4 vis lectr per year; gallery talks; tours; competitions; originate traveling exhibitions

SEATTLE

A **ALLIED ARTS OF SEATTLE, INC,** 105 S Main St, 98104. Tel 206-624-0432. *Admin Dir* Richard Mann
Open Mon - Fri 9 AM - 4 PM. No admis fee. Estab 1954 to promote and support the arts and artists of the Northwest and to help create the kind of city that will attract the kind of people who support the arts. Mem: 1000; dues $10 - $250 depending on category; annual meeting Jan
Income: $70,000 (financed by membership and fund raising events)
Exhibitions: Access Book Cover for Disabled Artists; Competition for Art a La Carte
Publications: Allied Arts Newsletter, 10 times per year; Access: The Lively Arts, directory of arts organizations in Puget Sound, biannual; Art Deco Seattle; Image of Imagination: Terra-Cotta Seattle
Activities: Self-guided tours; tour of artists' studios; competitions; awards; scholarships

A **CENTER ON CONTEMPORARY ART,** 1309 First Ave, PO Box 1277, 98111. Tel 206-682-4568. *Dir* Katherine Marczuk
Open Tues - Sat 1 - 6 PM. Estab 1980 to serve as a catalyst & forum for the advancement & understanding of contemporary art. Average Annual Attendance: 5000
Exhibitions: (1991) Exhibition by Christy Rupp; Natural Selection Night; Gallery

M **CORNISH COLLEGE OF THE ARTS,** Cornish Galleries, 710 E Roy St, 98102. Tel 206-323-1400; FAX 206-323-1400. *Dir* Greg Skinner; *Admin Asst* Amalia Fisch
Open Tues - Fri 10 AM - 6 PM, Sat Noon - 4 PM. No admis fee. Estab 1975 to support and enhance the visual arts curricula and reflect current trends in art. Gallery is 36 x 22 ft and has a lite-trak system, double door entry, 120 ft of free wall space, 10 ft ceilings, and tile floor
Income: Financed through institution
Exhibitions: Temporary one-person & group exhibitions
Publications: Gallery mailers
Activities: Classes for adults interested in part-time study; dramatic programs; lect open to public; gallery talks; competitions; traveling exhibitions organized and circulated
L **Cornish Library,** 710 E Roy St, 98102. Tel 206-323-1400, Ext 302, 305; FAX 206-323-1574. *Librn* Ronald G McComb
Open to students & faculty; primarily for lending
Library Holdings: Vols 12,000; Per subs 90; AV — Rec 9000, slides 20,000, v-tapes; Other — Exhibition catalogs 1000
Special Subjects: Design
Activities: Lending collection contains 1500 books, 2000 phono records, 20,000 slides, 150 video tapes & 1100 compact discs

A **CORPORATE COUNCIL FOR THE ARTS,** 1420 Fifth Ave, 98111. Tel 206-682-9270; FAX 206-447-0954. *Pres* Peter Donnelly
Open 8:30 AM - 5 PM. Estab 1968 as a clearinghouse for corporate contributions to the arts, to monitor budgeting of art agencies and assess ability of business to provide funding assistance. Gallery not maintained. Mem: 300; minimum contribution of $500 to qualify for membership; annual meeting in Sept
Income: $1,012,000 (financed by membership)
Publications: Annual Report; brochures; periodic membership reports
Activities: Annual fund-raising event and campaign

M **CHARLES AND EMMA FRYE ART MUSEUM,** 704 Terry Ave, PO Box 3005, 98114. Tel 206-622-9250. *Pres & Dir* Mrs W S Greathouse
Open weekdays 10 AM - 5 PM, Sun noon - 5 PM. No admis fee. Estab 1952 to display and preserve the Frye Art Collection. Three galleries cover 30 x 60 ft and four galleries cover 30 x 30 ft, plus foyer; Alaskan Wing for showing art work, small auditorium with stage, space for sculpture & two studios on balcony for art work shops. Average Annual Attendance: 60,000
Income: Financed by endowment
Collections: Charles and Emma Frye Collection represents 13 nationalities and includes Baer, Boudin, Carlsen, Corrodi, Dahl, Diaz, Defregger, Grubner, Hoch, Jongkind, Kaulbach, Koester, Lenbach, Leibl, Liebermann, Lier, Llermitte, Manet, Gabriel Max, Monticelli, Slevogt, Soren, Stuck, Thoma, Willroider, Winterhalter, Uhde, Ziem, Zugel, Zumbusch
Exhibitions: Alaskan Collection (Alaska's 4 principal painters); Nicolai Fechin, Russian; 19th Century American Watercolors; Handmade Glass; Joseph Scayled (photographs); Tim Holmes (sculpture); Norman Nelson (porcelains); Arts for the Parks; Russian Art
Publications: Frye Vues, monthly
Activities: Lectures open to the public; gallery talks; tours; one competition yearly with awards
L **Library,** Po Box 3005, 98114. Tel 206-622-9250; FAX 206-223-1707. *Pres* W S Greathouse
Open Mon - Sat 10 AM - 5 PM, Sun noon - 5 PM. No admis fee. Estab 1950. For reference only. Average Annual Attendance: 100,000
Income: Financed by private funds
Purchases: American 19th Century and Alaskan Paintings; Russian Collection of Paintings
Activities: Classes for adults & children; lect open to public; concerts; gallery talks; tours; awards

A **KING COUNTY ARTS COMMISSION,** 1115 Smith Tower, 506 Second Ave, 98104-2311. Tel 206-296-7580; FAX 206-296-8686. *Exec Dir* Mayumi Tsutakawa; *Arts Coordr* Vicky Lee; *Arts Coordr* Rob Roth; *Arts Coordr* Peggy Weiss; *Public Arts Coordr* Glenn Weiss
Open Mon - Fri 8:30 AM - 4:30 PM. Estab 1967 to provide cultural arts opportunities to the citizens of King County. The Arts Commission purchases & commissions many works of art for public buildings; annual grant program for organizations & artists in all artistic disciplines, also multi-cultural & disabled arts population; operates touring program of performing arts events in county locations. Mem: 16; 1 meeting per mon
Income: $1.3 million (financed by county government, plus one percent for commissioned art in county construction projects)
Purchases: Occasional works commissioned for public art
Collections: †King County art collection
Publications: The ARTS, bimonthly newsletter; The Touring Arts Booklet biennially; public art brochure; guide to programs, annually
Activities: Workshops; performances

A 911 ARTS MEDIA CENTER, 117 Yale Ave N, 98109. Tel 206-682-6552; FAX 206-682-7422. *Dir* Robin Reidy
Open Tues - Fri 10 AM - 5 PM. No admis fee. Estab 1981 as a film & video post-production center. Exhibition space. Average Annual Attendance: 15,000. Mem: 350; annual dues $25
Income: Financed by National Endowment for the Arts and locally matched funds
Collections: †Artists' video tapes
Publications: film & video calendar, quarterly
Activities: Workshops in film video making, video editing & grant writing

C SAFECO INSURANCE COMPANY, Art Collection, Safeco Plaza, T-12, 98185. Tel 206-545-6100; FAX 206-545-5730. *Art Cur* Julia Anderson
Gallery open Mon - Fri 8 AM - 4:30 PM for employees & invited guests. Estab to support the work of both established & emerging Northwest artists through purchase. Gallery is located in mezzanine space
Income: $100,000 (financed by Company)
Purchases: Northwest Artists & glass artists associated with Dilchuck Glass School
Collections: Works in all media by artists of the Pacific Northwest
Activities: Lectures open to public; individual paintings & original objects of art lent to non-profit museums

M SEATTLE ART MUSEUM, 100 University St, PO Box 22000, 98122-9700. Tel 206-625-8900. *Chmn* Malcolm Stamper; *Pres Board* Faye Sarkowski; *Dir* Jay Gates; *Asst Dir Finance & Admin* Jeff Eby; *Public Relations Mgr* Jacki Thompson-Dodd
Open Tues - Sat 10 AM - 5 PM, Thurs 10 AM - 9 PM, Sun noon - 5 PM. Admis adults $2, students & senior citizens $1, children under 6 with adult, members & Thurs free. Estab 1906, incorporated 1917, building opened 1933; gift to the city from Mrs Eugene Fuller and Richard Eugene Fuller, for recreation, education and inspiration of its citizens. Average Annual Attendance: 300,000. Mem: 10,000; dues $12 and up
Collections: LeRoy M Backus Collection of Drawings and Paintings; Manson F Backus Collection of Prints; Norman Davis Collection (with emphasis on classical art); Eugene Fuller Memorial Collection of Chinese Jades from Archaic through 18th Century; Eugene Fuller Memorial Collection (with special emphasis on Japan, China, India, and including Egypt, Ancient Greece and Rome, European, Near Eastern, primitive and contemporary Northwest art); Alice Heeramaneck Collection of Primitive Art; Henry and Marth Issacson Collection of 18th Century European porcelain; H Kress Collection of 14th - 18th Century European Paintings; Thomas D Stimson Memorial Collection (with special emphasis on Far Eastern art); Extensive Chinese and Indian Collection; 18th Century Drawing Room (furnished by the National Society of Colonial Dames of American in the State of Washington); major holdings in Northwest art, including Tobey, Callahan, Graves as well as all contemporary art, especially American artists Gorky, Pollock, Warhol and Lichtenstein; selected highlights on Asian collection on permanent display (with special emphasis on on Japanese screens, paintings, sculpture and lacquers); Katherine C White Collection of African Art
Publications: Annual Report; Japanese Paintings from the Sanso Collection; Johsel Namking: An Artist's View of Nature; Newsletter, 10 per year; Northwest Traditions; Song of the Brush
Activities: Docent service; film programs; double lecture course under the Museum Guild; adult art history classes; lect open to the public, 12 visiting lectr per year; tours; Program for senior citizens; museum store sells books, gifts and jewelry
L Library, 100 University St, PO Box 22000, Seattle, 98122-9700. Tel 206-625-8900. *Librn* Elizabeth de Fato
For reference only
Library Holdings: Vols 15,000; Per subs 50; AV — Slides 75,000; Other — Exhibition catalogs 3000

M SHORELINE HISTORICAL MUSEUM, 749 No 175th, PO Box 7171, 98133. Tel 206-542-7111. *Pres* Miriam Yates; *VPres* M L Burke; *Secy* Barbara Berg; *Treas* Margaret Boyce
Open Tues - Sat 10 AM - 4 PM. Admis by donation. Estab 1976 to preserve local history. Average Annual Attendance: 5000. Mem: 360; dues family $25, annual $10, pioneer $5; annual meeting first Sun in Nov
Income: $35,000 (financed by mem, donations, room rentals & fundraising)
Exhibitions: School room; home room; vintage radios; vintage clothing; blacksmith shop; railroad exhibit; post office; country store; other rotating exhibits
Publications: Newsletter, 5 times a year
Activities: Classes for children; docent training; lectr open to public; tours; original objects of art lent; sales shop sells books, prints, postcards & area photo cards

C US WEST, 1600 Seventh Ave, Room 1503, 98191. Tel 206-345-4999. *Art Cur* Jeff Davis
Open Mon - Fri 8:30 AM - 5 PM. No admis fee. Estab 1977 to display the varying cultural traditions which have contributed to Pacific Northwest Art. Collection displayed throughout 32 floors of Bell Plaza
Collections: Reflects the Pacific Northwesterner's eye and shows the influence of the region (restricted to include only artists who live in Washington, Oregon and Idaho)

UNIVERSITY OF WASHINGTON

M Henry Art Gallery, 15th Ave NE & NE 41st St, 98195. Tel 206-543-2281; FAX 206-685-3123. *Dir* Richard Andrews; *Asst Dir* Joan Caine; *Sr Cur* Chris Bruce; *Cur of Coll* Judy Sourakli; *Public Information Dir* Claudia Bach; *Asst Dir* Nancy Duncan; *Bookstore Mgr* Paul Cabarga; *Cur of Education* Tamara Moats
Open Tues - Fri 10 AM - 5 PM, Sat & Sun 11 AM - 5 PM, Thurs evenings 5 - 7 PM, cl Mon. Estab 1923. 8 galleries, 6000 sq ft of exhibition space. Average Annual Attendance: 100,000. Mem: 1250; dues $15 & up
Collections: 19th century American landscape painting; contemporary West Coast ceramics; works on paper, prints, drawings & photographs; 20th century

Japanese folk pottery; Elizabeth Bayley Willis Collection of Textiles from India; western & ethnic textiles; 19th & 20th century western dress (formerly Costume & Textile Study Center)
Publications: Books, exhibition catalogues; monographs
Activities: Symposia; lect; originate traveling exhibitions; museum shop sells books and posters

L Architecture & Urban Planning Library, 334 Gould Hall, JO-30, 98195. Tel 206-543-4067. *Librn* Betty L Wagner
Estab 1923
Library Holdings: Vols 45,000; Per subs 300; Micro — Fiche 5246; Other — Exhibition catalogs, memorabilia, pamphlets 1684
Special Subjects: Architecture, Landscape Architecture, Building Construction, Urban Planning

L Suzzallo Library, Arch History Collection, 98195-0001. Tel 206-543-1929. *Librn* Gary Menges
Library Holdings: Architectural plans, drawings & renderings 100,000

L Art Library, 101 Art Bldg, DM 10, 98195. Tel 206-543-0648. *Librn* Connie Okada
Open Mon - Thurs 8 AM - 9 PM, Fri 8 AM - 5 PM, Sat 1 - 5 PM, Sun 1 - 5 PM. Estab 1940 primarily to provide resources for the courses, degree and research programs of the School of Art; and serves as the Art Library for the university community as a whole. Circ 60,055
Income: Financed by state appropriation
Library Holdings: Vols 40,316; Per subs 402; Other — Clipping files, exhibition catalogs, photographs, reproductions
Special Subjects: Art History, Ceramics, Graphic Design, Industrial Design, Photography, Printmaking, Sculpture, Fiber Arts, General Art, Metal Design
Activities: Library tours
—**Art Slide Collection,** 120 Art Bldg, DM-10, 98195. Tel 206-543-0649. *Dir Visual Servs* Joan H Nilsson
Library Holdings: AV — Slides 250,000
Collections: Tribal & Asian Works
Costume and Textile Study Center
For collection see Henry Art Gallery

M Thomas Burke Memorial Washington State Museum, 98195. Tel 206-543-5590. *Dir* Dr Karl Hutterer; *Cur Asian & Pacific Ethnology* Miriam Kahn; *Cur Native American Art* Robin Wright; *Asst Dir* Roxana Augusztiny; *Cur Vertebrate Paleontology* John Rensberger; *Cur Birds* Sievert Rohwer; *Public Servs Mgr* Sally Erickson; *Cur Invertebrate Paleontology* Peter Ward; *Cur Archaeology* Julie Stein; *Dir Public Prog* Scott Freeman
Open 10 AM - 5 PM, Thurs 10 AM - 8 PM. Admis general $3, sr citizens & students $2, children 6 - 18 $1.50. Estab 1885 for research and exhibitions. Average Annual Attendance: 170,000. Mem: 800; dues $15 - $500 & up
Income: Financed by state, endowment, self-generated revenues
Collections: Natural & cultural history of Washington State, the Pacific Northwest & the Pacific Rim
Publications: Contributions and Monograph series
Activities: Classes for adults & children; docent training; lectures open to the public, 4-8 vis lectr per yr; tours; circulates study collection; museum store sells books, native art, jewelry & cards

A WASHINGTON LAWYERS FOR THE ARTS, New England Bldg, No 315A, 219 First Ave S, 98104. Tel 206-292-9171. *Exec Dir* Consuelo Underwood
Open Mon - Wed 10 AM - 2 PM. Estab 1976 to provide free & low cost legal assistance for artists
Income: $20,000 (financed by mem, city, corporate & individual contributions)
Publications: A Guide to Washington Artist/Dealer Consignment Law; A Musician's Guide to Select Legal Issues; Art that Angers: Artistic Expression & the Law; Artists' Live/Work Space; Contracts, The Art of Negotiation; Publishing Contracts: Negotiating Your Own; Copyright Basics; Copyright Basics & Specific Copyright Issues for Photographers; Copyright Trademark & Patent Basics; Formation & Maintenance of Non-Profit Organizations; Legal Issues for Filmmakers; Liability Concerns for the Theater Owner & Operator; Private/Public Restraints on Free Speech & the Arts; The Fine Art of Filing
Activities: Classes for adults; lect open to the public

M WIND LUKE ASIAN MUSEUM MEMORIAL FOUNDATION, INC, 407 Seventh Ave S, 98104. Tel 206-623-5124. *Dir* Ron Chew; *Pres* Patricia Akiyama; *VPres* Elizabeth Willis; *VPres* Heng-pin Kiang; *Treas* Frank Kiuchi; *Secy* Nina Ventura; *Registrar & Colls Mgr* Ruth Vincent; *Educ Coordr* Charlene Mano
Open Tues - Fri 11 AM - 4:30 PM, Sat Noon - 4 PM, Sun noon - 4 PM. Estab 1966 to promote Asian folk art & history of Asian-American immigration. Permanent Asian-American immigration history gallery & changing exhibit gallery used for Asian folk art & traveling exhibitions. Average Annual Attendance: 27,000. Mem: 781; annual dues $35; annual meeting in Jan
Income: $200,000 (financed by endowment, mem, annual art auction, local & state commiss ions & grants for exhibits)
Collections: †Asian folk art; Asian-American historical artifacts & photographs
Exhibitions: Changing exhibits of Asian folk art, comtemporary art & Asian American history
Publications: Chinese Medicine on the Gold Mountain
Activities: Adult & children's classes; docent programs; lectures open to public, 20 vis lectrs per yr; gallery talks; tours; awards; annual Asian American artists award; Exten dept serves teacher educ; artifacts lent to accredited scholars & institutions for study, research, publishing & exhibition; lending collection contains 2800 pieces; book one traveling exhibition per yr; originate traveling exhibitions that circulate to community colleges, libraries, & museums; museum shop sells books, magazines, original art, reproductions, prints, slides, card, clothing, folk art, items, Asian imports & antiques
L Library, 407 Seventh Ave S, 98104. *Librn* Scott Ductiweicz
Library Holdings: Vols 5000; AV — Slides 150, v-tapes; Other — Clipping files, photographs

SPOKANE

M EASTERN WASHINGTON STATE HISTORICAL SOCIETY, Cheney
Cowles Museum, 2316 W First Ave, 99204. Tel 509-456-3931; FAX 509-456-
7690. *Dir* Glenn Mason; *Cur Art* Beth Sellars
Open Tues - Sat 10 AM - 5 PM, Sun 1 - 5 PM. Admis adult $2; sr citizens &
children $1; members free. Estab 1959 as a museum of regional history,
American Indian cultures & visual art. Fine arts gallery with regular monthly art
exhibitions. Average Annual Attendance: 80,000. Mem: 1300; dues $25 & up;
annual meeting in Oct
Income: Financed by membership, state appropriations & private sector support
Collections: Regional history; major collection of American Indian material
culture; historic house of 1898 by architect Kirtland K Cutter, interior designed
and decorated with period furnishings; 19th & 20th century American &
European art; representative works of Pacific Northwest artists
Publications: Museum Notes, six per year; exhibition catalogs
Activities: Docent training; lectures open to public weekly Wednesday night,
program series; concerts; gallery talks; tours; competitions; individual paintings &
original objects of art lent to qualified institutions; Art at Work Program rents
regional art work to businesses; book traveling exhibitions; traveling exhibitions
organized and circulated; museum shop sells books, original art and gift items
L Library, 2316 W First Ave, 99204. Tel 509-456-3931. *Cur Spec Coll & Archives*
Laura Arksey
For reference & research only by staff
Library Holdings: Vols 3000; Per subs 18; Manuscripts for library use only,
limited copies available upon request; Other — Clipping files, exhibition catalogs,
manuscripts, pamphlets, photographs
Special Subjects: Architecture, Historical Material, Manuscripts, Photography
Collections: Inland Empire history

M GONZAGA UNIVERSITY, Ad Art Gallery, 502 E Boone Ave, 99258-0001. Tel
509-328-4220, Ext 3211; FAX 509-484-2818. *Dir* J Scott Patnode
Open Mon - Fri 10 AM - 4 PM. No admis. Estab 1971 to service the
Spokane Community & art department at Gonzaga University. One room 24 ft x
40 ft, with moveable trac lighting. Average Annual Attendance: 25,000
Income: Financed by parent institution
Purchases: Jacob Lawrence, Wayne Thieband & Robert Gwathmey prints
Collections: Student art collection; †Contemporary and old master print
collection; †Rodin Scupture Collection
Activities: Classes for adults; lectures open to public, 2 vis lectr per yr; gallery
talks

L SPOKANE PUBLIC LIBRARY GALLERY, 906 W Main St, 99201. Tel 509-
838-3361. *Dir* Daniel Walters; *Mgr Community Relations* Lisa Wolfe
Open Mon, Tues & Thurs 9 AM - 9 PM, Wed 1 - 6 PM, Fri & Sat 9 AM - 6
PM. Estab 1894 basically to meet citizens education, information, recreation and
cultural lifelong learning needs through a variety of programs and facilities.
Gallery maintained to exhibit local work and changed monthly
Library Holdings: Original documents; Micro — Fiche, prints, reels; AV — A-
tapes, cassettes, fs, Kodachromes, motion pictures, rec, slides, v-tapes; Other —
Clipping files, exhibition catalogs, framed reproductions, manuscripts,
memorabilia, original art works, pamphlets, photographs, reproductions, sculpture
Collections: Rare books
Exhibitions: One each month in picture gallery
Publications: Previews, monthly
Activities: Classes for adults and children; dramatic programs; lectures open to
the public; concerts

TACOMA

M TACOMA ART MUSEUM, 1123 Pacific Ave, 98402. Tel 206-272-4258. *Sr Cur
& Cur Exhib* Barbara Johns; *Cur Educ* Halinka Wodzicki
Open Sun noon - 5 PM. Admis general $3, students & sr citizens $2, children 6 -
12 years $1, under 6 free, Tues free. Estab 1895 to perpetuate the finest in the
visual Fine Arts. Museum features galleries for permanent collection, traveling
exhibitions and an interactive art center. Average Annual Attendance: 65,000.
Mem: 1300; dues $7 - $1000 plus; annual meetings in June
Income: $525,000 (financed by gifts, grants & membership)
Purchases: Lois Peterson, Untitled Vessel, 1987; Richard Mahaffey, Clay 1988;
Carol Berry, Lizzie's House: Lizzie's Myths; Peter Juvonen, Easy Travel to
Other Planets
Collections: †American & French paintings; American sculpture; European &
Asian works of art
Exhibitions: (1992) Deborah Small: 1492; Beauty from the Earth: Pueblo Indian
Pottery from the University Museum of Archaeology & Anthropology; Viva la
Vida: Paintings by Alfredo Arreguin; In Search of Sunsets: Images of the
American West 1850 to the Present; Mary Henry; Faith Ringgold: A Twenty-
Five Year Restrospective. (1993) Weegee; New Faces (Northwest Juried
Competition)
Publications: Annual Report; Quarterly Bulletin; exhibit catalogs
Activities: Classes for adults & children; docent training; lectures open to the
public, 10 vis lectr per yr; gallery talks; tours; competitions with awards;
individual paintings and original objects of art lent to other professional
museums; lending collection contains paintings, photographs & sculpture;
museum shop sells books, magazines, original art, reproductions, prints, cards,
jewely
L Reference Library, 1123 Pacific Ave, 98402. Tel 206-272-4258. *Librn* Sadie
Uglow
Open to the public for reference only
Income: Financed by membership, donations and grants
Library Holdings: Vols 1884; Per subs 37; Other — Clipping files, exhibition
catalogs, pamphlets, reproductions
Special Subjects: Japanese woodcuts
Collections: Unique collection of research material on Japanese woodcut
Publications: Monthly bulletins

L TACOMA PUBLIC LIBRARY, Handforth Gallery, 1102 Tacoma Ave S, 98402.
Tel 206-591-5666. *Dir* Kevin Hegarty; *Dir Handforth Gallery* David Domkoski
Open Mon - Thurs 9 AM - 9 PM, Fri & Sat 9 AM - 6 PM. Estab 1952 to extend
library services to include exhibits in all media in the Thomas S Handforth
Gallery. Circ 1,237,000
Income: Financed by city appropriation
Library Holdings: Vols 800,000; Per subs 1600; Audio compact discs; Micro —
Reels; AV — A-tapes, cassettes, motion pictures, rec, slides, v-tapes; Other —
Clipping files, exhibition catalogs, framed reproductions, memorabilia, original art
works, pamphlets, photographs, prints
Special Subjects: Genealogy, manuscripts, Northwest Collection, photographs of
local and regional subjects
Collections: Kaiser Collection; Lincoln Collection; city, county, federal and state
documents; rare books; art books
Exhibitions: Monthly changing exhibits
Activities: Classes for children; dramatic programs; lect open to public, 3 - 4 vis
lectr per yr; originate traveling exhibitions

M UNIVERSITY OF PUGET SOUND, Kittredge Art Gallery, 15th and
Lawrence, 98416. Tel 206-756-3348; FAX 206-756-3500. *Dir* Greg Bell
Open Mon - Fri 10 AM - 4 PM, Sun 2 - 4 PM. No admis fee. Estab 1961 for
showing of student & professional works. Exhibition space consists of 2 galleries:
Fireplace Gallery with 100 ft of running wall space & Kittredge Gallery with 160
ft of running wall space; track lighting; security alarms. Average Annual
Attendance: 6200
Collections: †Abby Williams Hill, painter of Northwest scenes from 1880s to
1930s
Exhibitions: (1991) Jennifer McLerran & Tom Patin (painting); Jeffrey Mitchell
(sculpture); Suzanne Larmon (painting); Irv McArthur (bird carvings); Student's
Senior Exhibits
Publications: Monthly show bulletins
Activities: Classes for adults & children; lectures open to public, 8 vis lectrs per
year; gallery talks; scholarships; individual paintings & original works of art lent
to professional art museums & historical museums; lending collection contains
165 original prints, 120 paintings; book traveling exhibitions, 4 per year; originate
traveling exhibitions circulated to art museums, university galleries, historical
museums

M WASHINGTON STATE HISTORICAL SOCIETY, 315 N Stadium Way,
98403. Tel 206-593-2830. *Dir* David Nicandri
Open Mon - Fri 10 AM - 4 PM, Sat & Sun noon - 4 PM; cl holidays. Admis
adults $2, sr citizens $1.50, students $1, members and children under 6 free.
Estab 1891 to research, preserve & display the heritage of Washington State.
Society owns three buildings; art gallery under the direction of the Society; two
floors of exhibits (Washington State, Native American Artifacts, temporary
special exhibits). Average Annual Attendance: 300,000. Mem: 3000; dues $25 &
up; annual meeting in August
Income: Financed by membership, state appropriations & gifts
Collections: Pre-historic relics; †Indian and Eskimo artifacts, baskets, clothing,
utensils; Oriental items; †Washington-Northwest pioneer relics; archives
Publications: History Highlights (newsletter), quarterly; Columbia (popular
historical journal), quarterly
Activities: Classes for adults and children; docent training; lect open to public, 15
vis lectr per yr; tours; interpretative programs; concerts; dramatic programs
awards; scholarships offered; individual paintings & original objects of art lent to
comparable museums & cultural institutions; lending collection contains natural
artifacts, photographs & sculpture; traveling exhibitions organized and circulated;
museum shop sells books, magazines, reproductions, prints, postcards &
stationery
L Hewitt Memorial Library, 315 N Stadium Way, 98403. Tel 206-593-2830. *Librn*
Ed Nolan; *Asst Librn Photos* Elaine Miller; *Asst Librn Manuscripts* Joy Werlink
Admis same as to museum with provision for continuing research. Estab 1941 for
research in Pacific Northwest history. For reference only. Average Annual
Attendance: 40,000
Income: Financed by membership, state appropriations and gifts
Library Holdings: Vols 20,000; Micro — Reels; Other — Clipping files,
manuscripts, memorabilia, pamphlets, photographs, prints
Special Subjects: Railroads, lumber, fishing, Indians, missions, labor
Collections: Asahel Curtis Photograph Collection

WALLA WALLA

A CARNEGIE ART CENTER, 109 S Palouse, 99362. Tel 509-525-4270. *Dir*
Christine Bishop
Open Tues - Sat 11 AM - 4:30 PM, June - Aug 11 AM - 3 PM. No admis fee.
Estab 1970 in 1905 Carnegie Library, built of Kansas brick and paneled with oak,
inc 1971 as a non-profit educational organization. Average Annual Attendance:
12,000. Mem: 500; dues from individual $15 to life $1500 or more
Income: Financed by endowments, dues, contributions, art sales and rentals, and
gift shop
Exhibitions: 10 exhibitions annually
Activities: Classes for adults and children; docent training; lectures open to the
public; gallery talks; tours; competitions with awards; scholarships; individual
paintings lent; book traveling exhibitions; sales shop sells books, original art,
reproductions, prints, pottery & handcrafted gifts

WENATCHEE

M CHELAN COUNTY PUBLIC UTILITY DISTRICT, Rocky Reach Dam, US
97A Chelan Hwy, PO Box 1231, 98807-1231. Tel 509-663-8121; FAX 509-664-
2874; 509-663-7522 (Visitor Center). *CEO & General Mgr* Sonny Smart
Open 8 AM - dusk. No admis fee. Estab 1971 as a landscape ground & exhibit
galleries. History of Electricity & Edisonia, Geology, Anthopology - Local Indian
& Pioneer History. Average Annual Attendance: 100,000
Income: Financed from Hydro Electric revenue
Collections: Electrical artifacts; Indian Artifacts (Central Columbia River
Region); Nez Perce Indian Portraits
Exhibitions: 30th Local Artists Show Multi-Media

M **NORTH CENTRAL WASHINGTON MUSEUM,** Art Gallery, 127 S Mission, 98801. Tel 509-664-5989. *Pres* Lloyd Berry; *Dir* Keith Williams; *Cur* Mark Behler; *Dir Public Relations* Mary Tomsen; *Art Gallery Coordr* Terri White
Open Mon - Fri 10 AM - 4 PM, Sat & Sun 1 - 4 PM, cl holidays. Admis by donation. Estab 1939 to preserve & present history & the arts. Gallery program offers exhibits of regional, national & international importance. Average Annual Attendance: 32,000. Mem: 1055; dues $15; annual meeting in April
Collections: International Ceramics Collection; 19th Century Japanese Woodblock Prints; local historical collections
Exhibitions: Contemporary Wood Design; rotating historical exhibits; permanent history exhibits, including Pioneer Living & Apple Industry Exhibit
Publications: The Confluence, quarterly
Activities: Docent training; lectures open to public, 70 vis lectrs per yr; exten dept serves local public schools; original objects of art lent; book traveling exhibitions annually; originate traveling exhibitions; museum shop sells books, magazines, original art, slides

M **WENATCHEE VALLEY COLLEGE,** Gallery 76, 1300 Fifth St, 98801. Tel 509-664-2521. *Coordr* Corine Schmidt
Open Mon - Fri 1 - 4 PM, Mon and Thurs Eve 7 - 9 PM. Donation accepted. Estab 1976 to serve a rural, scattered population in North Central Washington State, which without Gallery 76, would not have access to a non-sales gallery. Non-profit community art gallery housed in Sexton Hall on Wenatchee Valley College Campus. Average Annual Attendance: 3150. Mem: 235; dues $15-$100; annual meeting February
Income: $18,000 (financed by membership, grants, donations, fund raising events, art auction, Casino Night)
Collections: Oil Painting, Stephen Tse
Publications: Annual Brochure
Activities: Lectures open to the public; one or two vis lectrs per year; gallery talks; tours; Invitational Exhibit for North Central Washington Artists; Juried art exhibit (national); sales shop, located in another building, sells and rents original art

YAKIMA

A **ALLIED ARTSGALLERY OF THE YAKIMA VALLEY,** 5000 W Lincoln Ave, 98908. Tel 509-966-0930. *Pres* Barbara Greenberg; *Exec Dir* George W Loundon
Open Mon - Fri 9 AM - 5 PM. No admis fee. Estab 1962 to encourage, promote and coordinate the practice and appreciation of the arts among the people of Yakima Valley. General gallery shows changing monthly exhibits. Average Annual Attendance: 20,000. Mem: 600; dues $25 - $500; annual meeting in Sept
Income: Financed by membership
Exhibitions: Monthly exhibits by local and area artists; annual juried exhibit
Publications: Artscope (arts calendar) monthly
Activities: Classes for adults & children; dramatic programs; lectures open to public, 1-3 vis lectrs per yr; concerts; gallery talks; tours; competitions with awards; sales shop sells original art
L **Library,** 5000 W Lincoln Ave, 98908. Tel 509-966-0930.
Library Holdings: Vols 100

WEST VIRGINIA

CHARLESTON

M **SUNRISE MUSEUM, INC,** Sunrise Art Museum, Sunrise Children's Museum & Planatarium, 746 Myrtle Rd, 25314. Tel 304-344-8035; FAX 304-344-8038. *Dir* Ross McGire; *Business Mgr* Debbie Jewel; *Assoc Cur Fine Arts* Geraldine Markovitz; *Planetarium Dir* Greg Rawlings; *Pub Information Dir* Guy Young
Open Tues - Sat 10 AM - 5 PM, Sun 2 - 5 PM, cl Mon & national holidays. Admis adults $2, students, teachers & senior citizens $1, children under 3 free. Estab 1960. Sunrise is located on a 16 acre estate containing two stone mansions & a carriage/nature trail. The Colonial Revival Sunrise Mansion, built in 1905, houses a children's museum, planetarium & nature center. The Georgian Torquilstone Mansion, built in 1928, houses the art museum. Average Annual Attendance: 70,000. Mem: 1500; dues Benefactors' Circle $1000, patron $500, supporting $250, contributing $100, participating $50, family $35, double $30, individual $20; annual meeting mid-April
Income: $500,000 (financed by endowment, membership & Memorials)
Collections: Botany; †native American, African and Oceanic artifacts; †natural history specimens in geology, mineralogy; †19th and 20th century American paintings, prints, decorative arts and sculpture
Exhibitions: Numerous exhibits held throughout the year; annual invitational exhibits
Publications: Art Museum Bulletin, monthly newsletter
Activities: Classes for adults & children; docent training; guided tours; planetarium programs; individual and original objects of art lent to other museums and public institutions; museum shop sells books, prints & variety of scientific, educational & decorative gift items including jewelry

HUNTINGTON

M **HUNTINGTON MUSEUM OF ART,** 2033 McCoy Rd, 25701. Tel 304-529-2701; FAX 304-529-7447. *Dir* Charles T Butler; *Chief Cur* G Eason Eige; *Adminr* James C Lawhorn; *Cur Exhib* Louise Polan; *Cur Education* Marian Owens; *Development Officer* Charles Evans; *Registrar* Daniel Silosky; *Public Relations* Julie Brown Marsh; *Comptroller* Kathy Saunders
Open Tues - Sat 10 AM - 5 PM, Sun Noon - 5 PM; cl Mon. No admis fee. Estab 1952 to own, operate and maintain an art museum for the collection of paintings, prints, bronzes, porcelains and all kinds of art and utility objects; to permit the study of arts and crafts and to foster an interest in the arts. Three building

complex on 52-acre site includes ten galleries, two sculpture courts, seven studio workshops, a 10,000 volume capacity library, 300 seat auditorium, two & one-half miles of nature trails, an observatory with Celestron-14 telescope & an amphitheatre. Average Annual Attendance: 75,000. Mem: Membership dues vary; annual meeting June
Income: Financed by endowment, membership, city, state and county appropriations
Collections: American and European Paintings and Prints; American Decorative Arts; Georgian silver; firearms; historical and contemporary glass; Turkish prayer rugs
Exhibitions: (1991) Selection from Campbell Collections; Agent of Change: Railroads in West Virginia; Ten American Painters
Publications: Bulletin, bi-monthly; catalogues for exhibitions
Activities: Classes and workshops for adults and children; docent training; public lectures; concerts; theatre productions; gallery talks; tours; individual paintings and original objects of art lent to museums; traveling exhibitions organized and circulated; museum shop sells books, original art, reproductions, prints and crafts; Junior Art Museum

MORGANTOWN

WEST VIRGINIA UNIVERSITY
M **Art Galleries,** Creative Arts Center, 26506-6111. Tel 304-293-2140, 293-3140. *Cur* Kristina Olson
Open 1 - 5 PM. Estab 1968 primarily as teaching galleries for WVU students, public & campus community. Two galleries, 22 x 42 ft, flexible arrangements, approximately 600 running ft. Average Annual Attendance: 30,000
Income: Financed by state appropriation and funds from the private sector
Collections: Ceramics, drawings, paintings, prints, sculpture
Exhibitions: Graduate Thesis Exhibits of ceramics, paintings, and prints produced by candidates for the degree of Fine Arts in the Division of Art; Contemporary Photography; Watercolorist; undergraduate exhibits of ceramics, drawings and prints; exhibits by art faculty; WVU permanent art collection and visiting artists
Activities: Originate traveling exhibitions
L **Evansdale Library,** PO Box 6105, 26506-6105. Tel 304-293-5039. *Head Librn* Dana Sally; *Head Ref Librn* Natalie Rutledge
Library Holdings: Vols 220,000; Per subs 1000
Special Subjects: Art Education, Art History, Landscape Architecture
M **Creative Arts Center and Gallery,** Evansdale Campus, PO Box 6111, 26506-6111. Tel 304-293-2140; FAX 304-293-3550. *Cur* Kristina Olson
Open Mon - Fri 1 - 4 PM, cl national holidays. No admis fee. Estab 1867
Collections: Costumes; music; paintings; theatre
Activities: Lectures; gallery talks; tours; concerts; drama; competitions; temporary traveling exhibitions

PARKERSBURG

A **PARKERSBURG ART CENTER,** 220 Eighth Street, PO Box 131, 26101. Tel 304-485-3859. *Dir & Exhib Coordr* Jeff Martin; *Cur of Education* Peery Elswick
Open Tues - Fri 10 AM - 4 PM, Sat & Sun 1 - 4 PM, Mon evenings 7 - 9 PM. No admis fee. Estab 1938 for the operation and maintenance of an art center and museum facility for the appreciation and enjoyment of art, both visual and decorative, as well as art history, crafts, and other related educational or cultural activities. Main gallery 43 x 27 ft and upper gallery 38 x 27 ft, completely carpeted, airconditioned and climate controlled. Average Annual Attendance: 25,000. Mem: 500; dues individual $15, family $25, sustaining $75, corporate or patron $125; annual meeting June
Income: $160,000 (financed by endowment, membership and state appropriation)
Collections: Advice of Dreams (oil by Beveridge Moore); Amish: African Artifacts; Patrick Henry Land Grant Document; The Hinge (watercolor by Rudolph Ohrning); Parmenides (sculpture by Beverly Pepper)
Exhibitions: West Virginia Watercolor Society; David Hostetler; Artists & Models-Portraits from the Hirschorn; Architecture-Wright, Sullivan, Fuller; Symbols of Faith/Islamic Prayer Rugs; American Impressionism
Publications: Calendar of events, bimonthly; annual report; exhibition catalogs
Activities: Classes for adults and children; docent training; workshops; outreach program, Arts-in-the-parks; lectures open to public; concerts; gallery talks; tours; competition with awards; book traveling exhibitions, up to 8 vis lect per yr; originate traveling exhibitions
L **Art Center,** 220 Eighth St, 26101. Tel 304-485-3859. *Exec Dir* Jeffry Martin; *Educ Coordr* Peery Elswick
Open Tues - Fri 10 AM - 4 PM, Sat - Sun 1 - 4 PM, cl Mon. Estab 1938, main gallery 2000 sq ft, upper gallery 1400 sq ft. Open to the public. Average Annual Attendance: 20,000. Mem: 400; $30; meetings: every June
Income: Financed by grants, memberships, united arts fund drive, fundraising
Library Holdings: Vols 500; Per subs 3; AV — Slides, v-tapes; Other — Clipping files, exhibition catalogs, reproductions
Collections: Collection of Amish items: Buggy, Clothes, Quilts, Photo Essay
Activities: Outreach: Art in the parks, Video Library; Vis lectr per yr 5; American Realistim: A Nation Competition (painting; cash/purchase); qualified museums who request: Books 20, prints 15, Natural Artifacts 125, Original 3, Original prints 15, phonorecords 30

ROMNEY

L **HAMPSHIRE COUNTY PUBLIC LIBRARY,** 153 Main St, 26757. Tel 304-822-3185. *Librn* Brenda Riffle; *Children's Prog Specialist* Evelyn Smith
Open Mon - Sat 10 AM - 5 PM. No admis fee. Estab 1942. 7 Display cases changed every month. Average Annual Attendance: 25,000-30,000. Mem: 8469
Income: $57,000
Purchases: $8000
Library Holdings: Vols 28,000; Per subs 9; Micro — Reels; AV — Cassettes, fs, motion pictures, rec, v-tapes; Other — Clipping files, exhibition catalogs, framed reproductions, memorabilia, original art works, pamphlets, photographs, prints

Exhibitions: Children's art; private collections of rocks, antiques, displays of items of other countries; various local artists collection; weaving
Activities: Lectures open to public; concerts; tours; competitions with awards; individual paintings lent

WHEELING

M **OGLEBAY INSTITUTE,** Mansion Museum, Oglebay Park, 26003. Tel 304-242-7272; FAX 304-242-4203. *Exec Dir* Dr Fredrick A Lambert; *Dir* John A Artzberger; *Cur of Collections* Gerald I Reilly; *Cur of Educ* Holly McCluskey
Open Mon - Sat 9:30 AM - 5 PM, Sun & holidays 1 - 5 PM. Admis $3.50, 55 & over $3, students $2.50, children under 12 free with paying adults. Estab and incorporated 1930 to promote educational, cultural and recreational activities in Wheeling Tri-State area. Building & grounds are the property of the city; an exhibition wing adjoins the main house; annual Christmas decorations. Average Annual Attendance: 83,394. Mem: 1430; dues $15 and above
Collections: †Early 19th century china; †early glass made in Wheeling & the Midwest; period rooms; †pewter
Exhibitions: Current exhibits of art and other allied subjects change periodically
Activities: Antique show & sales; antique classes; gallery talks; self-guided & prearranged group tours
L **Library,** Oglebay Park, 26003 FAX 304-242-4203
Open by appointment only. Founded 1934. Highly specialized on the early history of the area
Library Holdings: Vols 750; Documents bound 100, Maps, VF 4; Micro — Prints 20; AV — Slides
Special Subjects: Decorative Arts, local history
Collections: Brown Collection of Wheeling History, photographs; Wheeling City Directories; Wheeling & Belmont Bridge Company Papers

WISCONSIN

APPLETON

M **LAWRENCE UNIVERSITY,** Wriston Art Center Galleries, PO Box 599, 54912. Tel 414-832-6621. *Cur* Timothy R Rodgers; *Gallery Coordr* Edward Holgate
Open Tues - Fri 10 AM - 4 PM, Sat & Sun 1 - 4 PM, cl Mon. Estab 1950 for teaching & community exhibitions. Wriston Art Center opened Spring 1989. Three exhibitions galleries for changing exhibits of contemporary & historical shows
Collections: Ohilia Buerger Collection of Ancient Coins; Pohl Collection-German Expressionism; American regionalist art; graphics; Japanese prints & drawings
Exhibitions: (1991) Putting Pottery in Prospective; Past, Present & Future, Academic Drawings of the late 19th & 20th Century; Carl Von Marr (drawings); Prof Emeritus Author Thrall; One Man Show; Senior Students Show
Activities: Lect open to public, 3-6 vis lectrs per yr; individual paintings & original works of art lent for exhibitions in other museums

BELOIT

M **BELOIT COLLEGE,** Wright Museum of Art, 700 College St, 53511. Tel 608-363-2677; FAX 608-363-2718. *Dir* Henry Moy; *Registrar* Carol Simon
Open Mon - Fri 9 AM - 5 PM, Sat & Sun 11 AM - 4 PM. No admis fee. Estab 1893; Wright Art Hall built 1930 to house the collection for the enrichment of the college & community through exhibition of permanent collection & traveling & temporary art exhibitions of cultural & aesthetic value. A Georgian building architecturally styled after The Fogg Museum in Cambridge, Mass. Three galleries on main floor, on a large center court; Art Department shares other floors in which two student galleries are included. Average Annual Attendance: 10,000 - 20,000
Purchases: 17th - 20th century graphics; Asian decorative arts
Collections: European & American (paintings, sculpture & decorative arts); Fisher Memorial Collection of Greek Casts; graphics, emphasis on German Expressionist & contemporary works; Gurley Collection of Korean Pottery, Japanese Sword Guards, Chinese Snuff Bottles & Jades; Morse Collection of Paintings & Other Art Objects; Neese Fund Collection of Contemporary Art; Oriental; Pitkin Collection of Oriental Art; Prints by Durer, Rembrandt, Whistler and others; sculpture of various periods; 19th century photography
Exhibitions: 35th Annual Beloit & Vicinity Exhibition. (1991) Art Directors Club (NY) Award Winners; Contemporary Australian Graphics; Photography of Chuck Savage; Richard Olson: New Works; The Art of the Snapshot; A Sense of Place (Photography); The Samuel & Ileen Campbell Collection of Western Art. (1992) Annual Beloit & Vicinity Exhibition; Outsider Art 1991/92; master graphics from the permanent collection; Art Faculty Exhibition; Rookwood Ceramics; Art of the Americas Before Columbus; Barney Jensen, Wildlife Artist; Costa Rican Gold & Jade; master drawings from the permanent collection
Publications: Exhibition catalogs
Activities: Classes; supportive programs; docent training; lectures open to public; gallery talks; tours; traveling exhibitions organized and circulated
A **Friends of the Beloit College Museums,** 700 College St, 53511. Tel 608-363-2677; FAX 804-381-6173.
Estab 1972, to support the Beloit College Museums. Mem: 200; dues $10; annual meetings in Sept
Publications: Friends of the Beloit College Museums newsletter, quarterly
Activities: Lect open to the public, 10 vis lectr per year

CEDARBURG

A **WISCONSIN FINE ARTS ASSOCIATION, INC,** Ozaukee Art Center, W62 N718 Riveredge Dr, 53012. Tel 414-377-8230. *Pres* Lon Horton
Open Tues - Sun 1 - 4 PM. No admis fee. Estab 1971. Historical landmark with cathedral ceiling. Average Annual Attendance: 5000-10,000. Mem: 600; dues business patron $500, patron $200, sustaining $100, associate sustaining $50, family $30, individual $22, student $10; annual meeting in Oct
Collections: Paintings, sculpture, prints, ceramics
Exhibitions: Ozaukee County Show; Harvest Festival of Arts
Publications: Monthly newsletter
Activities: Classes for adults and children; docent training; lectures open to public, 2 vis lectr per year; concerts; gallery talks; tours; competitions with awards; arts festivals

EAU CLAIRE

M **UNIVERSITY OF WISCONSIN-EAU CLAIRE,** Foster Gallery, Fine Arts Center, 54702-5008. Tel 715-836-2328. *Dir* Eugene Hood
Open Mon - Fri 10 AM - 4:30 PM, Sat & Sun 1 - 4:30 PM. No admis fee. Estab 1970 to show finest contemporary art in all media. State University Gallery in Fine Arts Center. Average Annual Attendance: 23,000
Income: Funded by state appropriation
Purchases: Lia Cook: Shimmer Curtain II
Collections: Eau Claire Premanent Art Collection
Exhibitions: Fendrick at Foster; Cypis/Hanson/Charlesworth: 3 Photo-Artists; Drawing on Tradition; New Light Metals; Art Moderne; Annual Juried Student Art Show
Activities: Lect open to public, 10-12 vis lectr per yearr; competition with awards; book traveling exhibits 2-3 per year

GREEN BAY

M **NEVILLE PUBLIC MUSEUM,** 210 Museum Place, 54303. Tel 414-448-4460; FAX 414-448-4458. *Dir* Ann L Koski
Open Tues - Sat 9 AM - 5 PM, Sun & Mon noon - 5 PM. No admis fee. Estab 1915 as Green Bay Public Museum; names changed 1926. Average Annual Attendance: 150,000. Mem: 1630; dues family $25, individual $15; annual meeting in the spring
Income: Financed by county appropriation & private donations
Collections: David Belasco Collection of Victoriana antique furniture, †china, †glass, †silver, fans, lace, costumes and †accessories; †contemporary and historical paintings; †drawings; Neville family portraits; †prints and sculpture
Exhibitions: (1993 - 94) Walter Gallery: Winslow Homer the Illustrator: His Wood Engravings; The 51st Art Annual; The Midwest Watercolor Society Annual Exhibition; Textiles & Paintings by Sue Benner; Formed & Fired: Ceramics from Northeastern Wisconsin. (1993 - 94) West Gallery: Bears: Imagination & Reality; Phil Austin: A Retrospective; Drawing on the Issues: Joe Heller; Green Bay Art Colony Annual Exhibition; Contemporary Photography II; Willion Jauquet, Sculptor; Two From Door County. (1993 - 94) East Gallery: Bears: Imagination & Reality; Tomorrow's Artists; Heroes; Barbie. (1993 - 94) Frankenthal Gallery: Bears, Baskets & Berries; Shavings: Folk Art from the Permanent Collection; Alydia Brasskamp World War I Collection; Breath of Fresh Air; Trees of Giving; Permanent Exhibition: On the Edge of the Inland Sea. (1993 - 95) Science Gallery: Bears: Imagination & Reality; Gardens; Water Quality
Publications: Musepaper, 6 times per yr
Activities: Classes for adults and children; dramatic programs; docent training; lectures open to the public, some for members only; concerts; gallery talks; tours; competitions; individual paintings and original objects of art lent to other museums or galleries; traveling exhibitions organized and circulated; gallery shop sells books, magazines, original art, reproductions & prints
L **Library,** 210 Museum Pl, 54303. Tel 414-448-4460; FAX 414-448-4458. *In Charge* Louise Pfotenhauer
Open to the public for reference by appt only
Library Holdings: Vols 3000; Per subs 100

M **UNIVERSITY OF WISCONSIN, GREEN BAY,** Lawton Gallery, 2420 Nicolet Dr, 54311. Tel 414-465-2271. *Cur Art* Karon Winzenz
Open Tues - Sun Noon - 4 PM, cl Mon. No admis fee. Estab 1974 to show changing exhibitions of contemporary & 20th century art & recent ethnic art. Gallery is 2000 sq ft. Average Annual Attendance: 5000
Income: $5000
Publications: Exhibition catalogs
Activities: Lectures open to public, 2-3 vis lectr per yr; competitions; book traveling exhibitions; originates traveling exhibitions

GREENBUSH

M **WADE HOUSE & WESLEY W JUNG CARRIAGE MUSEUM,** Historic House & Carriage Museum, W 7747 Plank Rd, PO Box 34, 53026. Tel 414-526-3271; FAX 414-526-3626. *Dir* Jeffrey Schultz; *Cur Interpretation* Sally Wood
Open May 1 - Oct 31 9 AM - 5 PM. Admis adult $5, sr citizen $4.50, child $2. Estab 1953 to educate public concerning 1850s Wisconsin Yankee town life. Average Annual Attendance: 25,000-30,000
Income: $125,000 (financed by state appropriation, admission fees)
Collections: Wisconsin made Carriages; 1850-1870 Household Furnishings
Exhibitions: 1850s Historic House Tour
Activities: Educ dept; classes for adults & children; docent training; lect open to public, 5 - 8 vis lectr per year; tours; museum shop sells books, reproductions & prints

KENOSHA

M KENOSHA PUBLIC MUSEUM, 5608 Tenth Ave, 53140. Tel 414-656-8026. *Dir* Paula Touhey; *Cur Education* Nancy Evans; *Cur Ex & Coll* Daniel Joyce
Open Mon - Fri 9 AM - 5 PM; Nov - Apr Sat 9 AM - noon; Sun 1 - 4 PM, May - Oct Sat 9 AM - 4 PM. No admis fee. Estab 1935 to promote interest in general natural history and regional art. The gallery has 8000 sq ft of permanent exhibition space and 1000 sq ft for temporary exhibits. Average Annual Attendance: 50,000. Mem: 1500; dues $10; annual meeting April
Income: $300,000 (financed by city appropriation)
Purchases: $2200
Collections: †African Art; †Historic Wisconsin Pottery; Ivory Carvings: Oriental Art; Regional Artists; Regional Natural History
Exhibitions: (1991) Murals in Kenosha; Catching Fish; Carolyn Galiardi Art; Viewing Nature. (1993) Wooly Mammoth found in Kenosha County
Publications: Newsletter, bi-monthly; Wisconsin Folk Pottery Book
Activities: Classes for adults and children; dramatic programs; docent training; lectures open to public, 12 vis lectr per yr; gallery talks, tours; competitions; individual paintings lent on yearly basis to municipal & county offices to be displayed in public areas; lending collection contains cassettes, color reproductions, filmstrips, 30 framed reproductions, 280 motion pictures, nature artifacts & slides; museum shop sells crafts, ethnic jewelry, earrings, Oriental boxes, toys;

KOHLER

C KOHLER COMPANY, Art Collection, 444 Highland Dr, 53044. Tel 414-457-4441. *Archivist* Leah Weisse
Estab 1973. Collection displayed in Kohler Company general office
Collections: Original ceramic art pieces created in Kohler Company facilities by resident artists in the Art Industry Program
Activities: Individual objects of art lent

LA CROSSE

M VITERBO COLLEGE ART GALLERY, 815 S Ninth St, 54601. Tel 608-791-0330; FAX 608-791-0367. *Dir* Tim Crane
Open Mon - Fri 10 AM - 5 PM. Estab 1964 to exhibit arts and crafts which will be a valuable supplement to courses offered. Gallery is located in the center of the Art Department; 100 running feet; soft walls; good light
Income: Financed by school appropriation
Collections: Mrs Lynn Anna Louise Miller, Collection of the contemporary United State primitive; Peter Whitebird Collection of WPA project paintings
Activities: Classes for adults; dramatic programs; lect open to public; gallery talks

MADISON

M STEPHEN BREW GALLERY (Formerly A-Space Gallery), 544 State St, 53703. Tel 608-238-1654. *Dir* Dean Olsen
Open Mon - Thurs 8 AM - 10 PM, Fri & Sat 9 AM - 11 PM, Sun 11 AM - 8 PM. Estab 1985 as a gallery showing emerging & experimental local artists. Store front street level gallery with 1700 sq ft of space
Income: $4000 (financed by exhibition fees & commission on sales)
Purchases: Ray Esparsen, Theron Caldwell Ris, Randy Arnold
Exhibitions: Ray Esparsen, Theron Caldwell Ris, David Auquirre, Doris Litzer, Terry Gottesfeld, Douglas Isaac Busch, Mark Duerr, Anita Jungi, Dennis Carroll, Woody Holliman
Activities: Concerts; gallery talks

M EDGEWOOD COLLEGE, DeRicci Gallery, 855 Woodrow, 53711. Tel 608-257-4861; FAX 608-257-1455. *Pres* Dr James Ebben; *Art Department Chmn* Robert Tarrell; *Art Lecturer* David Smith
Open Mon - Fri 9 AM - 5 PM. Estab 1965 to serve local artists, and provide educational opportunity for students. Large room; carpeted walls. Average Annual Attendance: 5000
Collections: Edgewood College Collection
Exhibitions: Old Bergen Art Guild; Local Artists

M MADISON ART CENTER, 211 State St, 53703. Tel 608-257-0158; FAX 608-257-5722. *Dir* Stephen Fleischman; *Registrar* Marilyn Sohi; *Business Mgr* Michael Paggie; *Dir Development & Community Relations* Kathy Paul; *Membership & Program Liaison* Barbara Banks; *Technical Services Supvr* Mark Verstegen; *Cur Exhibitions* Tina Yapelli; *Gallery Shop Mgr* Leslie Genszler; *Cur Educ & Public Programming* Sheri Castelnuovo; *Publicist* Jonathan Zarov; *Gallery Operations Mgr* Jim Kramer
Open Tues - Thurs 11 AM - 5 PM, Fri 11 AM - 9 PM, Sat 10 AM - 5 PM, Sun 1 - 5 PM. No admis fee, donations accepted. Estab 1969 to promote the visual arts. Galleries on 3 levels in civic center complex. Average Annual Attendance: 100,000. Mem: 1800; dues $20 and up; annual meeting May
Income: $850,000 (financed by mem, grants, gifts, earned revenue)
Purchases: $41,790
Collections: Emphasis on contemporary Americans; large print and drawing collection (Japanese, European, Mexican and American); paintings; sculpture
Exhibitions: (1992) Frank Lloyd Wright: In the Realm of Ideas; Fred Stonehouse. (1993) Jim Dine: Drawing from the Glyptothek; Kristin Jones/Andrew Ginzel; Wisconsin Triennial
Publications: Catalogs; posters and announcements usually accompany each exhibition
Activities: Docent training; lectures open to the public, 10 vis lectr per yr; concerts; tours; competitions; films; originate traveling exhibitions; sales shop sells books, magazines, original art, reproductions and prints

M STATE HISTORICAL SOCIETY OF WISCONSIN, State Historical Museum, 30 N Carroll St, 53703-2707. Tel 608-264-6555; FAX 608-262-5554. *Dir* Nicholas Muller III; *Assoc Dir* Robert Thomasgard; *Dir Museum* William Crowley; *State Historian* Michael Stevens; *Dir Visual & Sound Archives* Christine Schelshorn
Open Tues - Sat 10 AM - 5 PM, Sun noon - 5 PM, cl Mon. No admis fee. Estab 1846, museum added 1854; organized to promote a wider appreciation of the American heritage, with particular emphasis on the collection, advancement and dissemination of knowledge of the history of Wisconsin and of the Middle West. Average Annual Attendance: 100,000. Mem: 7000; dues $20 & up
Income: Financed by state appropriation, earnings, gifts and federal grants
Collections: Historical material; iconographic collection; ceramics, coins, costume dolls, furniture, paintings, prints, photographs and slides
Exhibitions: Frequent special exhibitions; four annual gallery changes
Publications: Wisconsin Magazine of History, quarterly
Activities: Docent training; lectures open to public; individual paintings & original objects of art lent to other museums & individuals for educational purposes; book traveling exhibitions; originate traveling exhibitions; sales shop sells books, magazines, reproductions, slides & post cards
L Archives, 816 State St, 53706. Tel 608-264-6460. *Archivist* Peter Gottlieb
Open Mon - Fri 8 AM - 5 PM, Sat 9 AM - 4 PM
Library Holdings: Original documents, maps; AV — Motion pictures; Other — Photographs, prints

UNIVERSITY OF WISCONSIN-MADISON

M Wisconsin Union Galleries, 800 Langdon St, 53706. Tel 608-262-2214. *Dir & Secy* Ted Crabb; *Art Coordr* Margaret Tennessen
Open 10 AM - 6 PM. No admis fee. Estab 1907 to provide a cultural program for the members of the university community. Owns three fireproof buildings with three galleries: Memorial Union, 800 Langdon; Union South, 227 N Randall Ave. Average Annual Attendance: 193,000. Mem: 50,000 faculty, alumni & townspeople, plus 45,000 students; dues $45; annual meeting Nov
Purchases: $1500
Collections: Oil and watercolor paintings, prints and sculptures, mostly by contemporary American artists
Publications: A Reflection of Time: The WI Union Art Collection
Activities: Informal classes in arts and crafts; films; gallery talks; loan collection available on rental to students and members

M Elvehjem Museum of Art, 800 University Ave, 53706. Tel 608-263-2246; FAX 608-263-8188. *Dir* Russell Panczenko; *Assoc Dir* Corinne Magnoni; *Ed* Patricia Powell; *Registrar* Lucille Stiger; *Cur Education* Anne Lambert
Open Mon - Sun 9 AM - 5 PM, clo holidays. No admis fee. Estab 1962, building opened 1970 to display, preserve and build a general art collection of high quality for the study and enjoyment of students, community and state. Three levels, 12 galleries covering 25,000 sq ft of exhibition space. Average Annual Attendance: 100,000. Mem: 1800; dues $20 - $1000
Income: Financed by endowment, membership, state appropriation and private sources
Purchases: Vary according to income
Collections: Ancient Egyptian and Greek pottery, sculpture, glass and coins; Joseph E Davies Collection of Russian Icons, Russian and Soviet Paintings; Vernon Hall Collection of European Medals; Indian sculpture; Medieval painting and sculpture; Renaissance painting and sculpture; Edward Burr Van Vleck Collection of Japanese Prints; Ernest C and Jane Werner Watson Collection of Indian Miniatures; 16th - 20th century prints - †general collection; 17th - 20th century European painting, sculpture, furniture and decorative arts; 18th, 19th and 20th century American painting, sculpture and furniture
Exhibitions: Six to eight temporary exhibitons per year in all media from varied periods of art history
Publications: Annual bulletin; calendar, bimonthly; special exhibition catalogs
Activities: Docent training; lect open to the public; concerts; gallery talks; tours; individual paintings & original objects of art lent to other museums; book traveling exhibitions, 2 - 4 per year; originate traveling exhibitions; sales shop sells books, magazines & reproductions
L Kohler Art Library, 800 University Ave, 53706. Tel 608-263-2256; Elec Mail BUNCE@MACC.WISC.EDU. *Dir* William Bunce
Open Mon - Thurs 8 AM - 9:45 PM, Fri 8 AM - 4:45 PM, Sat & Sun 1 - 4:45 PM. Estab 1970 to support the teaching and research needs of the Art and Art History Departments and the Elvehjem Museum of Art. For lending. Circ 34, 000. Average Annual Attendance: 69,000
Income: Financed by state appropriation and private funding
Library Holdings: Vols 110,000; Per subs 300; Micro — Fiche 19,000, reels; AV — Cassettes, v-tapes; Other — Clipping files, exhibition catalogs
Activities: Tours

MANITOWOC

M RAHR-WEST ART MUSEUM, Park St at N Eighth, 54220. Tel 414-683-4501; FAX 414-683-4424. *Dir* Richard Quick; *Asst Dir* Daniel Juchniewich
Open Mon - Fri 9 AM - 4:30 PM, Sat & Sun 1 - 4 PM, cl holidays. No admis fee. Estab 1950 as an art center to serve the city of Manitowoc. Transitional gallery in new wing built 1975; period rooms in Victorian Rahr Mansion built c 1981; a Registered Historic home; American art wing built in 1986. Average Annual Attendance: 25,000. Mem: 500; dues $10-$500
Income: $170,000 (financed by membership and city appropriation)
Collections: 19th and 20th Century American Paintings and Prints; Schwartz Collection of Chinese Ivories; contemporary art glass; porcelain; works by Francis, Johns & Lichtenstein
Exhibitions: Monthly changing exhibitions
Activities: Classes for adults and children; docent training; lectures open to the public, 4-5 vis lectr per yr; gallery talks; tours
L Library, Park St at N Eighth, 54220. Tel 414-683-4501; FAX 414-683-4424. *Dir* Richard Quick
Open to the public for reference only
Library Holdings: Vols 1500; Per subs 6
Special Subjects: Art reference

MARSHFIELD

M **NEW VISIONS GALLERY, INC,** 1000 N Oak, Marshfield Clinic, 54449. Tel 715-387-5562. *Dir* Ann Waisbrot, BS
Open Mon - Fri 9 AM - 5:30 PM, Sat 10 AM - 4 PM. No admis fee. Estab 1975 for the education, awareness & appreciation of visual arts. 1500 sq ft exhibition space, track lighting, moveable display panels, sculpture stands. Average Annual Attendance: 75,000. Mem: 250; annual dues $10 - over $1000
Income: $62,000 (financed by mem, earned income, fundraising & gifts)
Exhibitions: (1993) African Sculpture/Haitian oils; Alchemic Emporium of Davis Holmes; Culture & Agriculture 1993; Emerging Talents; Lee Weiss Watercolors; Sticks; Marshfield Art Fair
Publications: Brochures, every 6 wks; catalogs
Activities: Adult & children classes; lect open to public, 5-6 vis lectrs per year; gallery talks; tours; competitions with awards; book traveling exhibitions, 1-3 annually; museum shop sells gifts produced by artists or craft studios, jewelry, pottery & cards

MENOMONIE

M **UNIVERSITY OF WISCONSIN-STOUT,** J Furlong Gallery, 54751. Tel 715-232-2261, 223-1287. *Cur* Gene Bloedhorn
Open Mon - Fri 10 AM - 5 PM. No admis fee. Estab 1966 to serve university and local community with exhibits of art. A single room gallery; track lighting. Average Annual Attendance: 9500. Mem: Financed by state appropriation
Collections: African Art; paintings including works by Warrington Colescott, Roy Deforest, Walter Quirt, George Roualt and Raphael Soyer; drawings; prints; sculpture
Exhibitions: Changing exhibits
Activities: Classes for children; lect, 2-3 vis lectr per yr; gallery talks

MEQUON

M **CONCORDIA UNIVERSITY WISCONSIN,** Fine Art Gallery, 12800 N Lake Shore Dr, 53092. Tel 414-243-5700. *Academic Dean* Dr David Eggebrecht; *Gallery Dir* Prof Gaylund Stone
Open Sun Tues, Wed, Thurs 1 - 4 PM, Tues 7 - 9 PM. No admis fee. Estab 1972 to exhibit work of area and national artists as an educational arm of the college. Average Annual Attendance: 1000
Income: Financed through college budget
Collections: Russian bronzes and paintings; graphics include Roualt, Altman and local artists; John Wiley Collection; American landscape; religious art

MILWAUKEE

M **CHARLES ALLIS ART MUSEUM,** 1801 N Prospect Ave (Mailing add: 1630 E Royall Place, 53202). Tel 414-278-8295. *Cur Artistic Prog* Richard Morgan; *Acting Admin Dir* Susan Modder
Open Wed - Sun 1 - 5 PM, Wed evenings 7 - 9 PM. Estab 1947 as a house-museum with 850 art objects from around the world & spanning 2500 years, collected by Charles Allis, first president of the Allis-Chalmers Company & bequeathed to the people of Milwaukee. The Museum is part of the Milwaukee County War Memorial Complex. Average Annual Attendance: 40,000. Mem: 700; dues $5 - $100; annual meetings in Oct
Income: $170,000 (financed by endowment & Milwaukee County appropriation)
Collections: Chinese, Japanese and Persian ceramics; Greek and Roman antiques; 19th century French and American paintings; Renaissance bronzes
Publications: Exhibition catalogs
Activities: Docent training; lectures open to public, vis lectr; concerts; gallery talks; tours; film series

M **ALVERNO COLLEGE GALLERY,** 3401 S 39th St, 53215. Tel 414-382-6000; FAX 414-382-6354. *Fine Arts Mgr* Bonnie Gendel
Open Mon - Fri 11 AM - 3 PM, Sun 1 - 3 PM, by appointment. No admis fee. Estab 1954 for the aesthetic enrichment of community and the aesthetic education of students
Income: $2000
Activities: Docent training; lectures open to the public, 4 vis lectr per year; concerts; gallery talks; tours; competitions with awards; book traveling exhibitions, 1-2 per year

C **BANC ONE WISCONSIN CORP,** 111 E Wisconsin Ave, PO Box 481, 53201. Tel 414-765-3000; FAX 414-765-0553. *In Charge Art Coll* Cathy Voss; *Gallery Coordr* Kelly Skinezelewski
Estab to encourage Wisconsin art and artists; to enhance the environment of Marine personnel. Collection displayed in offices, conference rooms and corridors of headquarters of bank holding company
Collections: Acrylics, batik, bronze sculpture, lithographs, oils, wall sculpture, watercolors by Wisconsin artists
Activities: Invitational competitions in 1965, Wisconsin Renaissance in 1976; cash and purchase awards sponsored for college university and community art exchange; individual ojbects of art lent

M **CARDINAL STRITCH COLLEGE,** Layton Honor Gallery, 6801 N Yates Rd, 53217. Tel 414-352-5400. *Chmn* Gary Rosine
Open daily 10 AM - 4 PM. No admis fee. Estab 1947 to encourage creative art in each individual
Income: Financed by endowment, city and state appropriations and tuition
Collections: Folk Crafts; paintings
Exhibitions: Acquisitions from distant lands, children's art, professor's works, senior graduating exhibitions, well-known area artists. (1992) Clay, an exhibit of ten of Wisconsin's outstanding ceramic artists; Concerning the Narrative, prints, painting & sculpture; Two Views, photography. (1993) Student Exhibit; Global Awareness Exhibit; Ray Gloeckler, Wisconsin woodblock artist; Joanna Poehlmann, book artist; Student Show
Activities: Classes for adults & children; lect open to public, 2-4 vis lectr per yr; gallery talks; tours; individual paintings & original objects of art lent to galleries, libraries & educational institutions

M **MARQUETTE UNIVERSITY,** Haggerty Museum of Art, 13th & Clybourn St, 53233. Tel 414-288-7290; FAX 414-288-5415. *Dir* Curtis L Carter; *Registrar* Xiuqin Zhou; *Preparator* Jim Mazur; *Cur* Johann J K Reusch; *Cur of Education and Public Prog* Kit Basquin; *Secy* Irene Juckem; *Communications Asst* Marilyn Meissner; *Asst Dir of Administration* Marcia Eidel
Open Mon - Wed & Fri 10 AM - 4:30 PM, Thurs 10 AM - 8 PM, Sat 10 AM - 4:30 PM, Sun noon - 5 PM. No admis fee. Estab 1955 to house the University's permanent collection of art & sponsor fine arts museum programs. Modern building with security and climate control. Average Annual Attendance: 40,000. Mem: 400
Income: Financed through private contributions & the university
Collections: Old Master, Modern, Contemporary paintings; prints, photography; decorative arts; tribal arts
Exhibitions: (1991 - 92) Five Centuries of Italian Painting 1300 - 1800 from the Collection of the Sarah Blaffer Foundation; Twentieth Century Masters of American Glass; Collaborative Photography by Patrick Nagatani & Andree Tracey; Art & the Law: Sixteenth Annual Exhibition; Rouault: Miserere; Contemporary Folk Art. (1992 - 93) Facing the future; Francesco Spicuzza: Wisconsin Impressionist; Franta: Contemporary Art in Southern France; Prairie Rings: Environmental Site Sculpture by Roy Staab; Rufino Tamayo: Recent Prints; Contemporary American & European Prints; Contemporary Paintings from the Solovy Collection; Leonaert Bramer (1596 - 1674): Painter of the Night; The Black Family; Dolls in Contemporary Art; American Design; Songs of My People
Publications: Antique & Amish Quilts; exhibit catalogs
Activities: Docent training; lectures open to the public, 6 - 10 vis lectrs per year; concerts; gallery talks; tours; awards; individual paintings and original objects of art lent to museums; originate traveling exhibitions; museum shop sells artifacts, books, magazines, reproductions and prints

M **MILWAUKEE ART MUSEUM,** 750 N Lincoln Memorial Dr, 53202. Tel 414-224-3200; FAX 414-271-7588. *Pres Bd Trustees* Susan Jennings; *Dir* Russell Bowman; *Admin Dir* Christopher Goldsmith; *Cur Educ & Actg Cur Decorative Arts* Barbara Brown-Lee; *Dir Marketing & Communications* Fran Serlin-Cobb; *Registrar* Leigh Albritton; *Dir Communications* Nancy McDonald
Open Tue, Wed, Fri & Sat 10 AM - 5 PM, Thurs noon - 9 PM, Sun 12 - 5 PM, cl Mon. Admis adults $3, students, handicapped & sr citizens $1.50, children under 12 with adult free. Estab 1888 to create an environment for the arts that will serve the people of the greater Milwaukee community. Large, airy, flexible galleries, including a sculpture court and outdoor display areas. Fine arts and decorative arts are mixed to create an overview of a period, especially in the fine American Wings; small galleries provided for specific or unique collections. Average Annual Attendance: 150,000. Mem: 9000, dues $40, senior citizens & students $20; annual meeting May
Income: Financed by endowment, membership, county and state appropriations and fund drive
Collections: 19th and 20th Century American and European Art, including the Bradley and Layton Collections: The American Ash Can School and German Expressionism are emphasized; All media from Ancient Egypt to Modern America; The Flagg Collection of Haitian Art; a study collection of Midwest Architecture—The Prairie Archives; The von Schleinitz Collection of 19th Century German Painting, Mettlach Steins, and Meissen Porcelain
Exhibitions: 100 Years of Wisconsin Art; Second Benefit Art Auction Exhibition; Early Needlework from Milwaukee Collection; William Wegman; The Centennial Collection; Jennifer Barlett: Recent Work; Richard Misrach: The American Desert; Focus: American Folk Art from the Permanent Collection; The Velvet Line: Drypoint Prints from Milwaukee Collections; The Detective's Eye: Investigating the Old Masters; Objects of Bright Pride: Northwest Coast Indian Art from The American Museum of Natural History; Currents 14: Ross Bleckner; Joseph Albers Photographs; The Modern Poster: Sellections from The Museum of Modern Art; Really Big Prints; Currents 15; Sounding the Depths: 150 Years of American Seascape; Renaissance and Baroque Bronzes; recent acquisitions
Publications: Exhibitions and program brochure, tri-yearly; numbers calendar, bi-monthly
Activities: Classes for adults and children; docent training; lectures open to public, 5 vis lectr per yr; concerts; gallery talks; tours; competitions; films; originate traveling exhibitions; museum shop sells books, magazines, original art, reproductions, slides and cards

L **Library,** 750 N Lincoln Memorial Dr, 53202. Tel 414-224-3200; FAX 414-271-7588. *Librn* Suzy Weisman
For reference Tues, Wed & Thurs 10 AM - 4 PM
Library Holdings: Vols 19,000; Per subs 31; Vertical files, 60 drawers
Special Subjects: 19th Century German painting
Collections: Prairie Archives material (architecture and decorative arts of the Frank Lloyd Wright period) gift of Jacobson; von Schleinitz bequest of material on Meissen porcelain and 19th Century German painting

L **MILWAUKEE INSTITUTE OF ART DESIGN** (Formerly Institute of Art & Design), Library, 273 E Erie St, 53202. Tel 414-276-7889. *Librn* Terry Marcus
Open Mon & Thurs 7:45 AM - 10 PM, Fri 7:45 AM - 4 PM, Sat 11 AM - 3 PM. Estab 1974 as an Art & Design Library for the art school
Income: Financed by institution & private grants
Library Holdings: Vols 17,000; Per subs 50; Post cards 2300; AV — Motion pictures 01, slides 32,000, v-tapes 45; Other — Clipping files, exhibition catalogs 3000, pamphlets, reproductions
Special Subjects: Decorative Arts, Graphic Design, Industrial Design, Fine Art, Photography
Publications: MIAD Acquisitions List, quarterly

L **MILWAUKEE PUBLIC LIBRARY,** Art, Music & Recreation Dept, 814 W Wisconsin Ave, 53233. Tel 414-286-3000; FAX 414-286-2137. *City Librn* Kathleen Huston; *Supvr Central Servs* Sandra B Lockett; *Coordr Fine Arts* Ruth Ruege
Open Mon - Thurs, 8:30 AM - 9 PM, Fri & Sat 8:30 AM - 5:30 PM. No admis fee. Estab 1897. Circ 60,000
Income: $47,000 (financed by budgeted funds and endowments)

Library Holdings: Vols 138,712; auction catalogs, original documents, theatre programs, compact discs; Micro — Fiche, reels; AV — Cassettes, rec, v-tapes; Other — Clipping files, exhibition catalogs, framed reproductions, manuscripts, memorabilia, original art works, pamphlets, photographs, prints, reproductions, sculpture
Special Subjects: Architecture, Art History, Coins & Medals, Costume Design & Construction, Crafts, Decorative Arts, Landscape Architecture, Photography, City Planning, Philately, Recreation
Collections: Record Collection; Historic Popular Song Collection
Exhibitions: Bi-monthly changing exhibits in Wehr-McLenegan Gallery

M **MILWAUKEE PUBLIC MUSEUM,** 800 W Wells St, 53233. Tel 414-278-2702; FAX 414-278-6100. *Dir* Dr Barry H Rosen; *Deputy Operations Dir* James Krivitz; *Marketing Coordr* Debra Zindler; *Museum Librn* Judy Turner; *Dir Audio-Visual* Sharon Kayne Chaplock
Open Mon noon - 8 PM, Tues - Sun 9 AM - 5 PM. Admis family $10, adults $4, sr citizens with county ID & children 4-17 $2. Estab 1883 as a natural history museum. Vihlein Hall & Gromme Hall are two rooms used to display traveling, temporary & in-house collections. Average Annual Attendance: 413,000. Mem: 7400
Collections: All major sub-disciplines of anthropology, including botany, geology-paleontology; invertebrate & vertebrate zoology; decorative, fine & folk arts; film, photographs & specimen collection
Activities: Classes for children (school groups only); lect open to public & members; vis lectrs annually; sales shop sells pottery, jewelry, stationery, ornaments, models, games, dolls

M **MOUNT MARY COLLEGE,** Tower Gallery, 2900 Menomonee River Parkway, 53222. Tel 414-258-4810. *Chmn* Sr Angele Fuchs
Open Mon - Fri 8 AM - 4:30 PM, Sat & Sun 1 - 4 PM. No admis fee. Estab 1940 to provide both students and local community with exposure to art experiences and to provide artists, both estab professionals and aspirants with a showplace for their work
Income: Financed by private funds
Collections: Antique furniture, 16th Century and Victorian period; contemporary print collection; watercolors by Wisconsin artists
Exhibitions: (1991) Art Faculty Show; Bob Merline; Sculpture Works; Art Students

UNIVERSITY OF WISCONSIN
M **University Art Museum,** 3253 N Downer Ave, PO Box 413, 53201. Tel 414-229-6509. *Dir* Michael Flanagan; *Assoc Cur* Michal Ann Carley
Open Tues - Fri 10 AM - 4 PM, Wed 10 AM - 8 PM, Sat & Sun 1 - 4 PM, cl holidays& Sun. No admis fee. Estab 1982 to function as university museum; also oversees operations of art history gallery & fine arts galleries
Income: Financed by state appropriation
Collections: †Large graphic collection, primarily 20th century; †19th & 20th century painting, sculpture, drawings and photography; Oriental art; Ethiopian Art & Artifacts; 18th & 19th Century English Regency Prints; Greek & Russian icons & religious objects; Renaissance through 18th century sculptures, paintings & drawings
Exhibitions: Permanent, temporary & traveling exhibitions. (1992) Richard Haas: Drawings, Paintings, & Prints; Michiko Itatani: Recent Paintings. (1993) Narratives of Loss: The Body Displaced
Publications: Catalogs; checklists; handouts
Activities: Classes for children; lect open to public, 4 - 5 vis lectr per year; gallery talks; concerts; tours; inter-museum loans; paintings & original works of art lent; book traveling exhibitions 2 - 3 per year; originate traveling exhibitions 1 - 2 per year
M **Union Art Gallery,** 2200 E Kenwood Blvd, 53211. Tel 414-229-6310. *Dir* Patricia Kozik
Open Mon, Tues, Wed 11 AM - 4 PM, Thurs 11 AM - 7 PM, cl Sat & Sun. No admis fee. Estab 1971 to provide space for student art, primarily undergraduate, to be shown in group exhibits established by peer selection and apart from faculty selection. Average Annual Attendance: 13,000
Activities: Concerts; competitions with awards; sale shop sells original art

A **WISCONSIN PAINTERS & SCULPTORS, INC,** 341 N Milwaukee St, 53202. Tel 414-276-0605. *Chmn* Maggie Beal; *VPres* Jim Chism; *Treas* Erv Norwicki
Estab 1914 to support Wisconsin artists. Mem: 150; dues $25; meeting 2nd Wed of each month; mem open to professional artists exhibiting in juried shows represented by gallery
Income: Financed by member fees patron contributions
Exhibitions: Annual Membership Show; Wisconsin Artists Biennial, 1989/1991
Publications: Art in Wisconsin, bimonthly
Activities: Lect open to public, numerous vis lectrs per yr; competitions with awards; Endowment Trust Fund; originate traveling exhibitions

NEENAH

M **BERGSTROM MAHLER MUSEUM,** 165 N Park Ave, 54956. Tel 414-751-4658. *Executive Dir* Alex Vance; *Cur* Jan Smith; *Secy* Kathy Smits; *Membership Secy* Barbara Anderson
Open Tues - Fri 10 AM - 4:30 PM, Sat & Sun 1 - 4:30 PM. No admis fee. Estab 1959 to provide cultural and educational benefits to the public. Average Annual Attendance: 29,000
Income: $200,000 (financed by endowment, state and county appropriations and gifts)
Collections: Over 1900 contemporary & antique paperweights; Victorian Glass Baskets; Mahler Collection of Germanic Glass; paintings; sculpture
Exhibitions: Monthly exhibitions in varied media
Publications: Museum Quarterly; Glass Paperweights of Bergstrom - Mahler Museum Collection Catalogue; Paul J Stankard: Poetry in Glass
Activities: Classes for adults and children; docent training; lect open to public; concerts; gallery talks; tours; individual paintings and original objects of art lent to museums; Museum shop sells glass paperweights & glass items, original art

L **Library,** 165 N Park Ave, 54956. Tel 414-751-4658. *Membership Secy* Barbara Anderson
Open to the public for reference only
Library Holdings: Vols 2000; Per subs 10; AV — Slides
Special Subjects: Art History, Glass

NEW GLARUS

M **CHALET OF THE GOLDEN FLEECE,** 618 Second, 53574. Tel 608-527-2614. *Cur* Phyllis Richert
Open May - Oct 9 AM - 4:30 PM. Admis adults $2.50, students 6 - 17 $1. Estab 1955. Authentic Swiss style chalet which was once a private residence; collection from around the world. Average Annual Attendance: 7000
Income: Financed by admission fees
Collections: Swiss wood carvings and furniture; antique silver and pewter samplers; prints; exceptional glass and china
Activities: Lectures open to public; tours

OSHKOSH

M **OSHKOSH PUBLIC MUSEUM,** 1331 Algoma Blvd, 54901. Tel 414-424-4731. *Pres of Board* Laureen Heinenman; *Dir* Bradley Larson; *Prog Coordr* Paul Poeschl; *Registrar* Brenda Acker; *Cur* Debra Daubert; *Chief Cur* Martha Frankel; *Staff Artist* Don Oberweiser
Open Tues - Sat 9 AM - 5 PM; Sun 1 - 5 PM; cl Mon. No admis fee. Estab 1924 to collect and exhibit historical, Indian and natural history material relating to the area and fine and decorative and folk arts. 1908 converted home with new wing, Steiger Memorial Wing, opened in 1983 for additional exhibition space. Museum housed in city owned mansion near University campus. Average Annual Attendance: 50,000. Mem: 200; dues $10
Income: Financed by city appropriation
Collections: †American Artists: archeology; firearms; †Indian Artifacts; †Local & Wisconsin History; †Natural History; Pressed Glass; period textiles
Exhibitions: Monthly changing exhibits; permanent exhibits; Annual Art Fair
Publications: Introductions to the Art & Artists Exhibited
Activities: Classes for adults and children; offers museology & graduate history internship; lectures open to public; competitions with purchase awards; individual paintings and original objects of art lent to museums; originate traveling exhibitions; museum shop sells books, reproductions, postcards
L **Library,** 1331 Algoma Blvd, 54901. Tel 414-424-4732. *Archivist* Kitty A Hobson
Open Tues - Sat 9 AM - 5 PM; Sun 1 - 5 PM. Estab 1923. Research for museum exhibits and general public. For reference only
Income: Financed by city & county appropriations
Purchases: $2000
Library Holdings: Vols 10,000; Per subs 25; Maps; AV — Slides; Other — Clipping files, exhibition catalogs, manuscripts, memorabilia, original art works, pamphlets, photographs, prints, sculpture
Special Subjects: Archaeology, Art Reference, Wisconsin, Upper Midwest
Publications: Exhibition catalogs
Activities: Classes for adults & children; lectures open to public, 2-4 vis lectr per year; competitons

A **PAINE ART CENTER AND ARBORETUM,** 1410 Algoma Blvd, 54901. Tel 414-235-4530; FAX 414-235-6303. *Exec Dir* William C Landwehr; *Business Mgr* Nancee Boettcher; *Cur & Registrar* Celeste N Lopina; *Cur Horticulture* Thomas Jensen; *Cur Educ* Jane Nicholson; *Gift Shop Mgr* Pat Schwalenberg; *Exec Secy* Diana Lock
Open Tues - Fri 11 AM - 4:30 PM, Sat & Sun 1 - 4:30 PM; cl national holidays. Admis $3. Estab 1948 as a non-profit corporation to serve the needs of the upper midwest by showing fine and decorative arts and horticulture. Average Annual Attendance: 30,000. Mem: 900; dues contributing $50, general $35, sr citizens $15
Income: Financed by endowment, membership and donations
Collections: American glass; †decorative arts; icons; †19th & 20th century American paintings & sculpture; †19th century English & French paintings; period rooms; oriental rugs; American silver; †arboretum contains displays of native & exotic trees, shrubs & herbacious plants
Exhibitions: Temporary exhibitions drawn from sources, coast to coast
Publications: Exhibition catalogues; bi-monthly newsletter; class schedules
Activities: Classes for adults and children; docent training; lect open to public, 3-6 vis lectr per yr; concerts; gallery talks; tours; individual paintings and original objects of art lent to other museums and institutions; traveling exhibitions organized & circulated; sales shop sells books, reproductions and jewelry
L **George P Nevitt Library,** 1410 Algoma Blvd, 54901. Tel 414-235-4530. *Librn* Corinne H Spoo
Open Mon - Fri 10 AM - 4:30 PM upon request. Estab primarily for staff use as an art reference but also open to public by appointment. For reference only
Library Holdings: Vols 4000; Per subs 8; AV — Slides; Other — Exhibition catalogs, pamphlets
Special Subjects: Architecture, Art History, Asian Art, Ceramics, Decorative Arts, Drawings, Etchings & Engravings, Goldsmithing, History of Art & Archaeology, Interior Design, Oriental Art, Painting - American, Period Rooms, Photography, Sculpture, English furniture
Exhibitions: (1993 - 94) American Realism: The Urban Scene; Creative Plays; American Pottery from New Orleans Museum of Art; Romar Bearden as Printmaker

M **UNIVERSITY OF WISCONSIN OSHKOSH,** Allen R Priebe Gallery, 800 Algoma Blvd, 54901. Tel 414-424-2222. *Dir* T C Farley
Open Mon - Fri 10 AM - 3 PM, Mon - Thurs 7 - 9 PM, Sat & Sun 1 - 4 PM. No admis fee. Estab 1971 for the purpose of offering exhibits which appeal to a wide range of people. Gallery is 60 x 40 with additional wall space added with partitions, a skylight along back ceiling. Average Annual Attendance: 15,000
Income: Financed by student allocated monies & Dept of Art
Purchases: $1500
Collections: Works Progress Administration Collection; †prints and drawings

Exhibitions: (1991) Paul Pratchenko (paintings); High School Student Art Show; National Graduate Drawing Exhibit
Activities: Classes for adults and children; lectures open to the public, 2 - 4 vis lectrs per year; gallery talks; tours; competitions with awards; individual paintings and original objects of art lent to University staff, and area museums

PLATTEVILLE

M **UNIVERSITY OF WISCONSIN - PLATTEVILLE,** Harry Nohr Art Gallery, 1 University Plaza, 53818. Tel 608-342-1398. *Dir* John Mominee
Open Mon - Fri 11 AM - 4 PM, Mon - Wed evenings 6 - 8 PM, Sat & Sun Noon - 4 PM. No admis fee. Estab 1978. Average Annual Attendance: 9000
Income: Financed by state appropriation
Purchases: $3000
Activities: Lectures open to the public, 4 vis lectr per yr; gallery talks; tours; competitions with awards; individual paintings & original objects of art lent; lending collection contains color reproductions, framed reproductions, original art works, original prints, paintings, photographs, sculpture & ceramics; book traveling exhibitions

PORT WASHINGTON

COALITION OF WOMEN'S ART ORGANIZATIONS
For further information, see National and Regional Organizations

RACINE

A **WUSTUM MUSEUM ART ASSOCIATION,** 2519 Northwestern Ave, 53404. Tel 414-636-9177; FAX 414-636-9231. *Pres* Serge E Logan; *VPres* Roger Hoff; *Treas* Neil Vail; *Dir* Bruce W Pepich
Open Sun - Sat 1 - 5 PM and 1 - 9 PM Mon & Thurs. Estab 1941 to foster and aid the establishment and development of public art galleries and museums, programs of education and training in the fine arts, and to develop public appreciation and enjoyment of the fine arts. Maintains an art gallery with six galleries. Average Annual Attendance: 50,000. Mem: 650; dues $20 and up; annual meeting May
Income: $500,000 (financed by mem, grants & fundraising)
Collections: 20th century American works on paper & crafts
Exhibitions: Watercolor Wisconsin (annual); Wisconsin Photography (biennial); Annual Nationwide Thematic Show (summer)
Publications: Exhibit brochures & catalogs; Vue, quarterly newsletter
Activities: Classes for adults & children; docent training; lectures open to public, 6-10 vis lectrs pr yr; gallery talks; tours; competitions with awards; individual paintings & original art objects lent to museums; lending collection contains books, nature artifacts, original art works; original prints & paintings; book traveling exhibitions 2-4 times pr yr; originate traveling exhibitions; museum shop sells books & original art

M **Charles A Wustum Museum of Fine Arts,** 53404. Tel 414-636-9177. *Dir* Bruce W Pepich
Open Sun - Sat 1 - 5 PM & Mon & Thurs 5 - 9 PM. No admis fee. Estab 1940 to serve as cultural center for greater Racine community. Museum contains six galleries located in 1856 Wustum homestead & 1966 addition. Average Annual Attendance: 40,000
Income: $300,000 (financed by endowment, city and county appropriations, private gifts and programs)
Purchases: $500 - $1000
Collections: Contemporary Wisconsin Watercolors; WPA Project paintings and prints; †contemporary graphics; †works on paper, †ceramic sculpture, †glass sculpture, all post-1850 & primarily American
Exhibitions: Ruth Kao: Silk Tapestries; Robert Burkert: 30 Years; Claire Prussian: A Survey of Painting & Works on Paper; Watercolor Wisconsin; Joseph Hlavacek: A Retrospective
Activities: Classes for adults and children; docent training; lect open to public, 2-3 vis lectrs per yr; gallery talks; tours; competitions with awards; film programs; individual paintings and original objects of art lent to other institutions; lending collection contains 1500 original art works, 500 original prints, 350 paintings, 200 photographs & 250 sculptures; book traveling exhibitions; originate traveling exhibitions; museum shop sells books, original art, stationery, arts & crafts

L **Wustum Art Library,** 2519 Northwestern Ave, 53404. Tel 414-636-9177. *Dir* Bruce W Pepich
Open Sun - Sat 1 - 5 PM, Mon & Thurs 5 - 9 PM. Estab 1941 to provide museum visitors and students with exposure to art history and instructional books. For reference only to public, members may check out books
Income: $2500
Library Holdings: Vols 1500; Per subs 12; Other — Clipping files, exhibition catalogs
Special Subjects: 20th Century Art & Architecture

RIPON

M **RIPON COLLEGE ART GALLERY,** 300 Seward St, 54971. Tel 414-748-8110. *Chmn* Evelyn Kain
Open Mon - Fri 9 AM - 4 PM. No admis fee. Estab 1965 to provide student body with changing exhibits. Average Annual Attendance: 4000
Collections: Paintings, print, sculpture, multi-media
Activities: Individual paintings lent to schools

RIVER FALLS

M **UNIVERSITY OF WISCONSIN,** Gallery 101, Cascade St, 54022. Tel 715-425-3236. *Gallery Dir* Michael Padgett
Open Mon - Fri 9 AM - 5 PM & 7 - 9 PM; Sat & Sun 1 - 5 PM. No admis fee. Estab 1973 to exhibit artists of regional and national prominence and for educational purposes. Maintains one gallery. Average Annual Attendance: 21,000
Income: $5000 (financed by state appropriation and student activities funds)
Collections: †National and International Artists; †Regional Artists; WPA Artists
Activities: Lect open to public; gallery talks; originate traveling exhibitions

SHEBOYGAN

A **SHEBOYGAN ARTS FOUNDATION, INC,** John Michael Kohler Arts Center, 608 New York Ave, 53082-0489. Tel 414-458-6144; FAX 414-458-4473. *Dir* Ruth DeYoung Kohler; *Mgr of Admin Svcs* Mary Jo Ballschmider
Open daily Noon - 5 PM, Mon 7 - 9 PM. No admis fee. Estab 1967 as a visual & performing arts center focusing on contemporary American crafts & works which break barriers between art forms. Contains five exhibition galleries, the largest being 60 ft x 45 ft, theatre, four studio-classrooms, library, sales gallery. Average Annual Attendance: 135,000. Mem: 1132; dues family $25, individual $20, student $15; contributing mem
Income: Financed by mem, grants, corporate-foundation donations, sales gallery, ticket sales
Collections: †Contemporary Ceramics; †Contemporary Visionary Art; Historical Decorative Arts; Prehistoric Wisconsin Indian Artifacts
Publications: Biennial Report; Exhibition Checklist 6-10 annually; Exhibition Catalogues, 2-4 annually; Newsletter, bi-monthly
Activities: Classes for adults and children; dramatic programs; docent training; artists-in-residence programs; demonstrations; lectures open to the public, 18-20 vis lectrs per year; concerts; gallery talks; tours; competitions with awards; scholarships & fels; individual paintings & original objects of art lent to other arts institutions which meet the loan requirements, lending collection includes 6000 original art works & 100 paintings; book traveling exhibitions; originate traveling exhibitions which circulate to museums & artists organizations; sales shop sells magazines, original art, slides, postcards & notecards

STEVENS POINT

M **UNIVERSITY OF WISCONSIN-STEVENS POINT,** Carlsten Art Gallery, Fine Arts Center, 54481-3897. Tel 715-346-4797. *Dir* Stanley I Grand
Open Mon - Fri 10 AM - 4 PM, Sat & Sun 1 - 4 PM, Thurs evening 7:30 - 9:30 PM. No admis fee
Exhibitions: (1992) Faculty Exhibition; Wisconsin 92; 31 Contemporary Native American Artists; We, the Human Beings. (1993) Tom Bamberger; Juried Student Exhibition; Drawing on the Figure; BFA Exhibition

STURGEON BAY

M **DOOR COUNTY,** Miller Art Center, 107 S Fourth Ave, 54235. Tel 414-743-6578. *Adminr* Bonnie Oehlert Smith
Open Mon - Sat 10 AM - 5 PM, Mon - Thurs evenings 7 - 9 PM. No admis fee. Estab 1975. Gallery is 30 x 50 ft, plus mezzanine. Average Annual Attendance: 14,000. Mem: 220; dues associate $20, active $5; annual meeting second Thurs in Nov
Income: Financed by endowment, mem & county funds
Collections: †Permanent collection contains over 250 paintings
Exhibitions: (1993) 4 Phtographers from Lake Michigan's Shores; Jack Anderson & Phil Austin; Salon of High School Art; Wildlife Biennial Invitational exhibit VI; Wearable Art Invitational Exhibit; 18th Juried Annual; Very Special Arts Wisconsin
Activities: Lect open to public; concerts; gallery talks; tours; competitions; individual paintings lent to other museums & art centers; lending collection contains 250 original art works

SUPERIOR

M **DOUGLAS COUNTY HISTORICAL SOCIETY,** Fairlawn Mansion & Museum, 906 E Second St, 54880. Tel 715-394-5712. *Exec Dir* Rachael E Martin; *Secy & Bookkeeper* Grace Hebb; *Dir Vol Servs* Phyllis Gerber
Estab 1854 to promote education of religious history. 1890's historic house, period rooms. Average Annual Attendance: 16,000. Mem: 200; dues corporation $100, family $20, individual $10; annual meeting in Apr
Income: $105,000 (financed by endowment, mem, city & county appropriations, grants, catering & gift shop)
Purchases: 1847 sideboard originally used in historic house
Collections: David Barry Photography Collection; †Chippewa Indian Artifacts; Railroad, Shipping, Logging, Farming & Mining Tools (from area); †1890's Period Furniture & Furnishings
Exhibitions: David Barry Photographs; Chippewa Indian Artifacts; Railroad, Shipping, Logging, Farming & Mining in Area; Children's Photo Contest
Activities: Classes for adults & children; dramatic programs; docent programs; lect open to public, 6 vis lectr per year; competitions with awards; book traveling exhibits 4 per year; retail store sells books

L **Archives,** 906 E Second St, 54880
For reference
Income: $105,000 (financed by endowment, mem, city & county appropriations, gift shop, catering & grants)
Library Holdings: Documents, Maps, Scrapbooks; AV — A-tapes, cassettes, fs, motion pictures, rec, slides, v-tapes; Other — Clipping files, framed reproductions, manuscripts, memorabilia, original art works, pamphlets, photographs, prints
Special Subjects: American Indian Art, Historical Material, Maps, Period Rooms, Photography, Portraits, Religious Art, Restoration & Conservation, Tapestries

WAUSAU

M LEIGH YAWKEY WOODSON ART MUSEUM, INC, 700 N 12th St, Franklin and Twelfth Sts, 54401. Tel 715-845-7010; FAX 715-845-7103. *Pres* John W Ullrich; *VPres* Alice Forester; *Cur of Exhib* Andrew J McGivern; *Assoc Cur* Jane Weinke; *Interim Dir* Marica M Theel
Tues - Fri 9 AM - 4 PM, Sat & Sun Noon - 5 PM. No admis fee. Estab 1973 for acquisition of a creditable permanent collection of wildlife art; program of changing exhibits; art education. 775 net square feet of exhibition space; galleries on three floo rs; parquet and carpeted floors; 628 running feet in galleries. Average Annual Attendance: 45,000. Mem: 275; membership $250
Income: $735,000 (financed by membership and private foundation)
Collections: Wildlife theme paintings and sculptures with birds as the main subject; Historical period pieces of Royal Worcester porcelain; 19th and 20th century art glass
Exhibitions: (1993) Maintain the Right; Paintings from the Potlatch Mounty Collection; '93 Sticks
Publications: Birds in Art, annually; Delights for the senses: Dutch & Flemish Still - life paintings from Budapest (1989); Wildlife in Art; Wildlife: The Artist's View
Activities: Docent programs; lectures open to the public; gallery talks; tours; competitions for participation in exhibitions; student competitions; scholarships; individual paintings and original objects of art lent to recognized museums and art centers; book 6 - 8 traveling exhibitions per year; originate traveling exhibitions, circulation to established museums, art centers, galleries & libraries
L Art Library, 700 N 12th St, 54401. *Educ Asst* Doris Kamradt
Open by appointment. Estab 1976. For reference only
Income: $1500
Purchases: $1500
Library Holdings: Vols 2500; Per subs 20; AV — A-tapes, cassettes, fs, motion pictures, slides 5000, v-tapes 50; Other — Exhibition catalogs 1000, pamphlets
Special Subjects: Aesthetics, Architecture, Art Education, Art History, Decorative Arts, Glass, Painting - American, Porcelain, Birds, Wildlife art

WEST BEND

M WEST BEND GALLERY OF FINE ARTS, 300 S Sixth Ave, PO Box 426, 53095. Tel 414-334-9638, 334-1151. *Pres* Edward G Kocher; *Exec Dir* Thomas D Lidtke; *Asst Dir* Cheryl Ann Parker; *Librn* Linda Goetz
Open Wed - Sat 10 AM - 4:30 PM, Sun 1 - 4:30 PM, cl Mon & Tues. No admis fee. Estab 1961 as an art museum & exhibition space for regional & national shows. The large colonial style building contains eight gallery exhibit rooms and three basement art classrooms. Average Annual Attendance: 12,000. Mem: 585; annual meeting first Tues in Apr
Income: Financed by endowment, membership and donations
Purchases: $10,000
Collections: Carl von Marr Collection; Wisconsin Art History 1850-1950
Exhibitions: Monthly exhibitions, 10 - 12 per yr
Publications: Carl Von Marr, American-German Artist (1858-1936); Bulletin, monthly
Activities: Classes for adults and children; docent training; lect open to public; travelogues; tours; Art Aware an eductional outreach (art appreciation) service to local schools; book traveling exhibits, 1-3 per yr; originate traveling exhibitions; museum shop sells books, reproductions, prints
L Library, 300 S Sixth Ave, 53095. Tel 414-334-9638. *Exec Dir* Thomas D Lidtke
Open Wed - Sat 10 AM - 4:30 PM, Sun 1 - 4:30 PM. Estab 1986 for the purpose of providing art reference. Open to public. Average Annual Attendance: 12,000. Mem: 600; dues $10 - $25; annual meeting April
Library Holdings: Vols 2000; Per subs 6; AV — Cassettes, slides, v-tapes; Other — Clipping files, exhibition catalogs, original art works, photographs
Special Subjects: Architecture, Art Education, Art History, Decorative Arts, Drawings, Folk Art, Photography, Printmaking, Textiles, Woodcarvings
Collections: WI Art History
Publications: Carl Von Marr (catalogue)
Activities: Classes for adults and children; docent training, educational out-reach to public schools, art history; lect open to public; concerts; tours; Enten dept serves local public schools; art history

WHITEWATER

M UNIVERSITY OF WISCONSIN-WHITEWATER, Crossman Gallery, Center of the Arts, 800 W Main St, 53190. Tel 414-472-1207, 472-5708. *Dir* Susan Walsh
Open Mon - Fri 10 AM - 5 PM & 7 - 9 PM, Sun 1 - 5 PM, cl Sat. No admis fee. Estab 1965 to provide professional exhibits. 47 ft x 51 ft, 3 walls gray carpeted. Average Annual Attendance: 5000
Income: $7000 (financed by segregated student fee appropriation)
Exhibitions: (1991) Drawing on Art Installation; Picture Peace Professional Illustrators Exhibition. (1992) Bindley Ceramic Collection; Color Photo Invitational Exhibition; Presswork National Women Printmakers
Activities: Classes for adults & children; student training in gallery management

WYOMING

BIG HORN

M BRADFORD BRINTON MEMORIAL MUSEUM & HISTORIC RANCH, 239 Brinton Rd, PO Box 460, 82833. Tel 307-672-3173. *Dir* Kenneth L Schuster; *Office & Sales Mgr* Tessa Dalton; *Ranch Foreman* Andy Kukuchka; *Cur* Dorothy Savage; *Asst Cur* Charles B Faust
Open May 15 - Labor Day daily 9:30 AM - 5 PM. Admis adults $3, students over 6 & sr citizens over 62 $2. Estab 1961 to show a typical well-to-do ranch of the area of northern Wyoming as established in the late 19th century. Two galleries and house museum are maintained. Average Annual Attendance: 13,000
Income: $150,000 (financed by endowment)
Collections: Plains Indians Artifacts; Western American Art by Frederic Remington and Charles M Russell; American art and a few pieces of European art, largely of the 19th and 20th century; china; furniture; silver
Exhibitions: American Quilts; Art of Bill Gollings; Art of Winold Reiss; Etchings of Ed Borein; (1993) Bob Barlow & Gerald Anthony Shippen; Walter Ufer
Publications: Monographs on artists in the collection from time to time
Activities: Educ dept; lectures open to public, 4 vis lectr per yr; tours; museum shop sells books, original art, reproductions, prints, slides, American Indian jewelry & crafts

CASPER

M NICOLAYSEN ART MUSEUM AND DISCOVERY CENTER, Childrens Discovery Center, 400 E Collins Dr, 82601. Tel 307-235-5247; FAX 307-235-0923. *Interim Dir* Alex Efinoff; *Coordr* Kathy Shiroki; *Registrar* Michael Monroe
Open Tues - Sun 10 AM - 5 PM, Thurs till 8 PM. Admis fee adults $2, children $1, family $5, members free. Estab 1967 to exhibit permanent collection, nationwide traveling exhibits and provide school art classes and workshops. Two galleries, 2500 sq ft and 500 sq ft. Average Annual Attendance: 6000. Mem: 250; annual meeting third Tues in May
Income: $200,000 (financed by membership, Wyoming Council for the Arts, fundraising events)
Collections: Carl Link Drawings; †Robert Lyn Nelson Graphics Collection †Artists of the Region
Exhibitions: Twenty per year. (1993) Frank Werner; Marc Vischer; Jean Goedicke
Publications: Historic Ranches of Wyoming
Activities: Classes for adults and children; docent training; dramatic programs; lectures open to the public, 5-10 vis lectr per yr; concerts; gallery talks; competitions with cash awards; individual paintings & original objects of art lent to qualified educational institutions; lending collection contains 2500 original art works; book traveling exhibitions; originate traveling exhibitions; children's museum
L Museum, 400 E Collins Dr, 82601. Tel 410-235-5247; FAX 410-235-0923. *Interim Dir* Alex Efinoff; *Discovery Center Coordr* Kathy Shiroki; *Registrar* Michael Monroe
Open Tues - Sun 10 AM - 5 PM, Thurs till 8 PM. Admis fee family $5, adults $2, children under 12 $1, members free. Estab 1967 to collect and exhibit regional Contemporary Art. 8000 sq ft including 6 small and 1 large gallery. Computer controlled temerature & humidity. Hands on discovery center for children. Average Annual Attendance: 60,000. Mem: 700; dues $60; annual meeting May 8
Income: $300,000 (financed by donations and fundraising events)
Library Holdings: Vols 66; Per subs 8; AV — Slides; Other — Exhibition catalogs, pamphlets
Collections: Carl Link Collection; Regional Contemporary Pottery
Activities: Classes for children; dramatic programs; lectures open to public, 2000 lectr per year; gallery talks; tours; juried regional competitions; book traveling exhibitions, 1-2 per yr; museum shop sells books, original art, prints, pottery, glass, jewelry & cards

CHEYENNE

M WYOMING STATE MUSEUM, State Art Gallery, 2301 Central Ave, 82002. Tel 307-777-7022; FAX 307-777-6005. *Dir Wyo State Archives, Museum & Hist Dept* Dr Dona Bachman; *Cur of Art* Terry Kreuzer
Open Mon - Fri 8:30 AM - 5 PM, Sat noon - 4 PM. No admis fee. Estab 1969 to collect, preserve and exhibit the work of Wyoming and Western artists. Average Annual Attendance: 50,000
Income: Financed by state appropriation
Collections: Wyoming artists, historical & contemporary including Historical Hans Kleiber, William Gollings, M D Houghton, Cyrenius Hall, William H Jackson, J H Sharp
Exhibitions: Regional & Wyoming contemporary art, western art
Activities: Educ dept; lect open to public, 9 vis lectr per year; gallery talks; tours; individual paintings & original objects of art lent to institutions belonging to AAM, Colo-Wyo Association of Museums (CWAM) & Mount Plains Museums Association; museum shop sells books, original art, reproductions, prints & gift merchandise

CODY

A BUFFALO BILL MEMORIAL ASSOCIATION, Buffalo Bill Historical Center, PO Box 1000, 82414. Tel 307-587-4771; FAX 307-587-5714. *Chmn* Mrs Henry H R Coe; *Dir* Peter H Hassrick; *Cur Whitney Gallery* Sarah Boehme; *Cur Plains Indian Museum* Emma Hanson; *Cur Cody Firearms Museum* Howard M Madaus; *Dir Buffalo Bill Museum* Paul Fees; *Dir Education* Joy Comstock; *Dir Public Relations* Richard Wentz; *Registrar* Joanne Kudla; *Asst Dir* Wally Reber
Open May & Sept 8 AM - 8 PM, Oct & Apr 8 AM - 5 PM, March & Nov 10 AM - 3 PM, June - Aug 7 AM - 10 PM. Admis adults $5, sr citizens $4.25, family $14, & special group rate. Estab 1917 to preserve & exhibit art, artifacts and memorabilia of the Old West; to operate Buffalo Bill Museum, Plains Indian Museum, Whitney Gallery of Western Art and Cody Firearms Museum
Income: Financed by admissions & private funds
Exhibitions: Interior West: The Craft of Thomas Molesworth; The Plateau: The Doris Bounds Collection; Yellowstone's Faithful; The New West; Rendezvous to Roundup; Wyoming by the Book; Wounded Knee
Publications: Annual exhibition catalogues
Activities: Educ dept; docent training; lectures open to public; scholarships; originate traveling exhibitions around the US; museum shop sells books, original art, reproductions, prints, slides, jewelry, collectible items, Indian crafts & Kachina dolls

M **Buffalo Bill Historical Center,** 720 Sheridan Ave, PO Box 1000, 82414. Tel 307-587-4771; FAX 307-587-5714.
Open June-Aug 7 AM - 10 PM, May & Sept 8 AM - 8 PM, Oct-Apr 8 AM - 5 PM. Admis adults $7, sr citizens $6, students 13 & over $4, youth 6 - 12 $2, under 5 free. Estab 1927, is one of the largest western heritage centers. four museums in one complex; Buffalo Bill Museum, Whitney Gallery of Western Art, Cody Firearms Museum, Plains Indian Museum. Average Annual Attendance: 260,000. Mem: 1500
Collections: Western American art includes Catlin, Bierstadt, Miller, Remington, Russell & others
Exhibitions: (1993) Art of the American Indian Frontier: The Chandler-Pobrt Collection; Retrospective of the works of Contemporary Western Artists & designer Buckeye Blake; Artistry in Arms: The Guns of Smith & Wesson; Art of the American Indian Frontier: The Chandler-Pobrt Collection; 17th Annual Plains Indian Seminar
Publications: Exhibition catalogs
Activities: Classes for adults & children; dramatic programs; docent training; art & ethnology programs; lectures open to public, 10 vis lectr per year; gallery talks; tours; scholarships; individual paintings & original objects of art lent to other recognized museums; museum shop sells books, magazines, original art, reproductions & prints
L **Harold McCracken Research Library,** PO Box 1000, 82414. Tel 307-587-4771. *Librn & Archivist* Tina Stopka
Open 9 AM - 4 PM. Estab 1980 for research in Western history. Open to the public for reference only
Library Holdings: Vols 15,000; Per subs 45; Micro — Fiche, reels; AV — Cassettes, fs, Kodachromes, motion pictures, slides, v-tapes; Other — Clipping files, exhibition catalogs, manuscripts, memorabilia, original art works, pamphlets, photographs, prints, reproductions
Special Subjects: Firearms, Plains Indians, Western Art & History
Collections: WHD Koerner Archives; Buffalo Bill Cody Archives; Photo Collections; Rare Books
Publications: American West Magazine
Activities: Classes for children; docent training; lectures open to public, 10 vis lectr per year; gallery talks; tours

A **CODY COUNTRY ART LEAGUE,** 836 Sheridan Ave, 82414. Tel 307-587-3597. *Pres* Elizabeth Ruhl
Open noon - 8 PM. No admis fee. Estab 1964 for promotion of artistic endeavor among local and area artists; also established for exhibits, displays and sales. Average Annual Attendance: 15,000. Mem: 115; dues $10; annual meeting Dec
Income: Financed by endowment, membership, grants from Wyoming Council on the Arts, yearly auction, and sponsors
Activities: Classes for adults and children; dramatic programs; films; workshops; lect open to public, 2-3 vis lectrs per year; competitions

JACKSON

WILDLIFE OF THE AMERICAN WEST ART MUSEUM, 110 Center St, PO Box 2984, 83001. Tel 307-733-5771; FAX 307-733-5787. *Dir* Daniel Provo, MA; *Cur* Maria Hajic; *Marketing Dir* Patti Boyd
Open 10 AM - 6 PM. Admis $3. Estab 1986 devoted to North American Wildlife Art; collection spans 150 years. Three galleries: one gallery is devoted to the work of Carl Rungius, the lower and middle galleries host special exhibitions and our permanent collection. Average Annual Attendance: 7500. Mem: Annual dues $25 individual
Income: Financed by endowment & membership
Publications: WAW newsletter, quarterly
Activities: Lectures open to public, 3-4 vis lectr per yr; museum shop sells books, prints, magazines
L **Library,** 110 Center St, PO Box 2984, 83001. Tel 307-733-5771; FAX 307-733-5787.
Library Holdings: Vols 1000; AV — A-tapes, motion pictures, v-tapes; Other — Pamphlets

LARAMIE

M **UNIVERSITY OF WYOMING,** Art Museum, Corner of 21st & Willet St, PO Box 3807, University Station, 82071. Tel 307-766-6622. *Dir* Charles Allan Guerin; *Cur of Education* Barbara Westerfield; *Registrar* E K Kim; *Cur Museum & Progs* Susan Moldenhauer
Open Tues - Fri 10 AM - 5 PM, Sat - Sun noon - 5 PM. Estab 1968 to serve as an art resource center for faculty, students & the general public. Exhibition space consists of two galleries & outdoor sculpture court. Average Annual Attendance: 120,000. Mem: 500; dues $20 & up
Income: $50,000 (financed by state appropriation & friends organization)
Purchases: $7000
Collections: 19th & 20th Century American & European paintings, prints, sculpture & drawings
Exhibitions: Special exhibits from the permanent collections as well as traveling exhibitions on a regular basis during the year; faculty shows; student shows
Publications: Exhibition catalogs
Activities: Lect open to the public, 6 vis lectr per yr; gallery talks; tours; individual paintings and original objects of art lent to other museums; lending collection contains 5000 original art works, 3000 original prints and 2000 paintings; originates traveling exhibitions

MOOSE

A **GRAND TETON NATIONAL PARK SERVICE,** Colter Bay Indian Arts Museum, PO Drawer 170, 83013. Tel 307-543-2484. *Cur* C J Brafford
Open June - Sept 8 AM - 8 PM, cl Oct - May. No admis fee. Estab 1972
Collections: David T Vernon Indian Arts Collection
Exhibitions: David T Vernon Indian Arts Collection; Native American Guest Artist's Demonstration Program

ROCK SPRINGS

A **SWEETWATER COMMUNITY FINE ARTS CENTER,** 400 C St, 82901. Tel 307-362-6520; FAX 307-382-4640. *Dir* Gregory Gaylor
Open Mon & Thurs Noon - 9 PM, Tues, Wed & Fri 10 AM - 5 PM, Sat Noon - 5 PM. No admis fee. Estab 1966 to house permanent art collection and hold various exhibits during the year; Halseth Gallery houses permanent art collection. Average Annual Attendance: Approx 5000
Income: Financed by endowment, city appropriation, county funds & school district No 1
Collections: Own 408 pieces of original art including Norman Rockwell, Grandma Moses, Raphael Soyer among others
Exhibitions: Sweetwater County Art Guild National Exhibit and Competition; Western Winds Photography Expo
Publications: Calendar of events, two or three a year
Activities: Classes for adults; dramatic programs; art painting workshops for children and students; concerts; tours; competitions; Best of Show, Peoples Choice Guild and Photo Awards

SUNDANCE

M **CROOK COUNTY MUSEUM AND ART GALLERY,** PO Box 63, 82729. Tel 307-283-3666. *Chmn Board* Mary S Garman; *Dir* Jan Galloway
Open Mon - Fri 8 AM - 5 PM, cl holidays. No admis fee. Estab to preserve & display Crook County history, display County artists & provide a showcase for county residents' collections
Income: Financed by County appropriation
Collections: Furniture, pictures, Western historical items
Publications: Brochure
Activities: Tours for school children

PACIFIC ISLANDS

PAGO PAGO, AMERICAN SAMOA

M **JEAN P HAYDON MUSEUM,** PO Box 1540, 96799. FAX 011-684-633-2059; Tel 011-684-633-4347. *Chmn Board of Trustees* Moaali'itele Tuusuli; *Exec Dir* Leala Pili; *Cur* Fa'ailoilo Lauvao
Open Mon - Fri 10 AM - 4 PM, Sat 10 AM - noon. No admis fee. Estab 1971 to establish, maintain, acquire and supervise the collection, study preservation, interpretation and exhibition of fine arts objects and such relics, documents, paintings, artifacts and other historical and related materials as will evidence and illustrate the history of the Samoan Islands and the culture of their inhabitants, particularly of American Samoa. New extension of the museum is an Art Gallery displaying local artists work and student arts. Average Annual Attendance: 42,000
Income: Financed by city or state appropriations and grants from NEA
Collections: Natural Sciences; Polynesian Artifacts; Samoan Village Life; US Navy History; †painting, drawing, slides, †photographs, †artifacts
Exhibitions: (1992) Traditional Tattoos
Activities: Classes for adults and children; dramatic programs; museum & sales shop sell books, original art

PUERTO RICO

PONCE

M **MUSEO DE ARTE DE PONCE,** Ponce Art Museum, The Luis Ferre Foundation (Mailing add: Avenida de las Americas, PO Box 1492, 00733). Tel 809-848-0505, 840-1510; FAX 809-841-7309. *Dir* Dr Carmen Fischler; *Emeritus Dir* Dr Rene Taylor; *Registrar* Hiromi Shiba; *Conservator* Lidia Quigley
Open Mon, Wed, Thurs, Fri & Sat 10 AM - 4 PM, Sun 10 AM - 5 PM, cl everyday noon - 1 PM for lunch except Sun. Admis adults & children $1.50. Estab 1959 to exhibit a representative collection of European paintings & sculpture; Puerto Rican art. Seven hexagonal galleries on upper floor; three rectangular galleries on lower floor. Average Annual Attendance: 80,000. Mem: 700; dues single $30, double $50
Income: Financed by endowment, mem & government
Collections: African, Latin American, Pre-Columbian & Puerto Rican Santos Art; 19th century art, contemporary art, 14th - 18th century paintings & sculpture
Exhibitions: El Paisaje Puertorriqueno; Arquitectura Barroca y Moderna; Ceramica del Grupo Manos Auspiciador; Grabados de Jose Luis Cuevas y Actualidad Grafica Panamericana; Colectiva Juan Ramon Velazquez, Carmelo Sobrino y Joaquin Reyes; El Puerto Rico que nunca fue; Artistas Puertorriquenos residentes en NY; Juan Ramon Jimenez y los ninos; Francisco Oller: A Realist Impressionist; Diaspora Puertorriquena; Fashion in Puerto Rico XV to XIX Century; Jaime Suarez; 25 Years of Puerto Rican Painting; Fernando Botero; Actos Compulsivos: Arnaldo Roche; Ponce Carnival Masks
Activities: Lectures open to public, 10 vis lectrs per year; concerts; gallery talks; individual paintings & original objects of art lent to other museums & government offices; book traveling exhibitions, 1-2 per year; originate traveling exhibitions; museum shops sells books, magazines, reproductions, prints, slides & crafts
L **Library,** Avenida de las Americas, PO Box 1492, 00733. Tel 809-848-0505, 840-1510. *Librn* Open
Closed for reference with the exception of special permission
Library Holdings: Vols 4000; Per subs 4; Other — Exhibition catalogs

RIO PIEDRAS

M UNIVERSITY OF PUERTO RICO, Museum of Anthropology, History & Art, PO Box 21908, 00931. Tel 809-764-0000. *Dir* Annie Santiago de Curet; *Cur Archaeology* Diana Lopez; *Cur Art* Flavia Marichal; *Archaeologist* Luis A Chanlatte; *Admin Asst* Ruth Rodriguez
Open Mon - Fri 9 AM - 9 PM, Sat & Sun 8 AM - 3:30 PM, cl national holidays. No admis fee. Estab 1940
Purchases: Puerto Rican graphics; paintings of past & contemporary Puerto Rican artists
Collections: Archaeology; Puerto Rican paintings of the past and present; sculpture
Exhibitions: Temporary exhibitions from the collection and from museum loans
Activities: Provide concerts; gallery talks; tours; individual paintings and original objects of art lent to organizations and museums; originate traveling exhibitions; sales shop sells books and reproductions

SAN JUAN

M ATENEO PUERTORRIQUENO, Apartado 11-80, 00902. Tel 809-722-4839; FAX 809-725-3873. *Pres* Eduardo Morales-Coll
Open Mon - Fri 9 AM - 5 PM, cl Sun & holidays. No admis fee. Estab 1876 and is the oldest cultural institution in Puerto Rico. Mem: dues $25; annual meeting in June
Collections: Decorative arts; drawings; historical material; prints; Puerto Rican paintings; sculpture
Exhibitions: Temporary exhibitions
Publications: Cuadernos (publications on general topics); Revista Ateneo, every 4 months
Activities: Classes for adults; dramatic programs; lect; gallery talks; guided tours; films; concerts; recitals; competitions with prizes; dramas; individual paintings & original objects of art lent to other cultural institutions; book traveling exhibitions 1 per year; book shop
L Library, Ponce de Leon, Stop Two, 00902. Tel 809-722-4839; FAX 809-725-3873. *Pres* Eduardo Morales-Coll
Library Holdings: Vols 15,000

INSTITUTE OF PUERTO RICAN CULTURE

M Escuela de Artes Plasticas Galleria, 00905. Tel 809-724-5477; FAX 809-725-5608. *Dir* Jose Bartelo
Open daily 8 AM - 4 PM. Exposition of drawing, painting and art work of the students of visual school
Collections: †Permanent collection of student art work
—Library, PO Box 4184, 00905. Tel 809-721-6866; FAX 724-8393.
Reference only
Library Holdings: Micro — Fiche; AV — Slides; Other — Exhibition catalogs, manuscripts, original art works, pamphlets, reproductions, sculpture
A Instituto de Cultura Puertorriquena, Calle Norzgaray 98, Apartado 4184, 00905. Tel 809-724-0680. *Dir* Agustin Echevarria
Open Mon - Sun 8 AM - noon & 1 - 5 PM. No admis fee. Estab 1955 to stimulate, promote, divulge and enrich Puerto Rico's cultural and historical heritage. The institute has created 16 museums around the island and has five more in preparation, including museums of historical collections, art museums and archaeological museums
Income: Financed by endowment, and state appropriation
Collections: Puerto Rican art, archaeology and historical collections
Publications: Revista del Institute de Cultura Puertorriquena, quarterly
Activities: Educ dept; lectures open to public; gallery talks; tours; competitions; exten dept serving cultural centers around the Island; artmobile; individual paintings and original objects of art lent to Government agencies, universities and cultural centers; lending collection contains motion pictures, original art works; original prints, paintings, photographs; originates traveling exhibition; sales shop sells books, records and craft items; junior museum
M Museo de Bellas Artes, Cave Cristo 253, PO Box 4184, 00905. Tel 809-722-0621; FAX 809-725-5608. *Dir* Jose Bartelo
Open 9 AM - 4:30 PM. No admis fee. Estab 1977 for the exhibition of paintings and sculpture of Puerto Rican artists in a chronological way from 18th - 20th centuries. Show the techniques and trends in fine arts development in Puerto Rico
Income: Financed by state appropriation
Collections: Campeche-Oller Halle-religious & profane paintings of these two painters; Ramon Frade & Miguel Pou; Primitive Paintings Hall - works of Manuel Hernandez Acevdeo; documental & folklorical painting of the history of Puerto Rico; contemporary artists
Exhibitions: Program of contemporary exhibitions
Activities: Lectures open to public; gallery talks; tours; exten dept; individual paintings and original objects of art lent to educational and cultural orgainzations and government offices; lending collection contains original art works, original prints, paintings; originate traveling exhibitions
M Dr Jose C Barbosa Museum and Library, 00905. Tel 809-786-8115; FAX 809-725-5608. *Dir* Jose Bartelo
Open 9 AM - 5 PM. No admis fee. The house where patriot Jose Celso Barbosa was born and raised, restored to its original status as representative of a typical Puertorrican family home of the 19th century. Contains a small library geared to children's books
Income: Financed by state appropriations
Collections: Furniture, personal objects and documents belonging to Dr Barbosa, including medical instruments, manuscripts and books
M Centro Ceremonial de Caguana, 00905. Tel 809-894-7325; FAX 809-725-5608. *Dir* Angel Perez
Open daily 8:30 AM - 5 PM. No admis fee. Caguana Indian Ceremonial Park and Museum includes the ceremonial center of the Taino Indians in Caguana, Utuado, a small town in the center of the Island, constituting the most important archeological find of the Caribbean and the most outstanding exposition of Indian primitive engineering. The plazas and walks where the Indians held their ceremonies, celebrations and games were restored and excavated to form an archeological park. Numerous petrogliphs are exhibited in the monoliths bordering the plazas, and a museum exhibits Indian objects found during the excavations at the site
Income: Financed by state appropriations
M Casa Blanca Museum, PO Box 4184, 00905. Tel 809-724-4102, 724-5477.
Open 9 AM - 4:30 PM. No admis fee. This magnificent restored building constructed in 1521 by the sons of Juan Ponce de Leon and inhabited by their descendents until mid 18th century. The Museum present domestic life in San Juan during the first three centuries of Spanish colonization. The furniture and decorations correspond to the 16th and 17th centuries, with the architectural details recreating the interior of a typical 16th century home. Average Annual Attendance: 110,000
Collections: 16th and 17th century furniture; Ponce de Leon II, office, throne hall; kitchen, library paintings
Activities: Lectures open to the public; concerts; guided tours; museum shop
M Colonial Architecture Museum, 00905. Tel 809-725-5250; FAX 809-725-5608.
Cl for renovation, re-opening 1994. No admis fee. A typical San Juan house of the 18th century has been restored to present not only its original structural splendor but also, plans, drawings, photos, maquettes and other details of San Juan colonial architecture. The exposition also includes ceramic tiles, iron works and stone masonry decorative items
Income: Financed by state appropriations
Collections: Colonial architecture
M Dominican Convent Museum, Calle Norzgaray 98, PO Box 4184, 00905. Tel 809-724-5477; FAX 809-725-5608. *Dir* Jose Bartelo
Cl for renovation, re-opening 1994. No admis fee. Restored building constructed in 1523 to serve as a convent for Order of Dominican Monks. Use primarily as the main offices of the Institute of Puerto Rican Culture, the chapel and library have been restored to their original splendor. Average Annual Attendance: 52,000
Income: Financed by state appropriations
Collections: Manuscripts, books, religious objects and paintings; Magnificent 18th century ornate altar
Activities: Lectures open to the public; concerts; gallery talks; tours
M Museo de Arte Religioso Porta Coeli, 00905. Tel 809-892-5845; FAX 809-725-5608. *Dir* Jose Bartelo
Open 8:30 AM - 5 PM. No admis fee. In the first years of the 17th century the Dominican monks constructed a convent in the townof San German, with a chapel they called Porta Coeli, the convent has now disappeared, but the chapel has been restored as a valuable example of missionary architecture in America
Income: Financed by state appropriations
Collections: Paintings and sculptures from between the 11th and 19th century obtained from different churches in the island
M Museo de Historia Naval y Militar de Puerto Rico, 00905. Tel 809-724-5477; FAX 809-725-5608. *Dir* Jose Bartelo
Open 8:30 AM - 4:30 PM. No admis fee. The Museum of Naval and Military History is the historic fort of San Jeronimo del Boqueron at the entrance to the Condado lagoon, whose origins date to the second half of the 16th century, now restored to present a collection of weapons, flags and uniforms used by the Spaniards in the island. The major attacks and invasions to Puerto Rico are also illustrated
Income: Financed by state appropriations
Collections: Naval and Military canons, pistols, flags
M Museo de la Familia Puertorriquena del Siglo XIX, 00905. Tel 809-724-5477; FAX 809-725-5608. *Dir* Jose Bartelo
Cl for renovation, re-opening 1994. No admis fee. This museum presents furniture and decoration that illustrate the ambiance and lifestyle characteristic of Puerto Rico in the 19th century. All the rooms in this museum are furnished with artistic as well as historic furniture of the epoch
Income: Financed by state appropriations
Collections: Paintings, piano, complete furnishings
M Museo de la Farmacia Puertorriquena, 00905. Tel 809-724-5477; FAX 809-725-5608. *Dir* Jose Bartelo
Open 8:30 AM - 4:30 PM. No admis fee. The Museum of the Puerto Rican Pharmacy contains a rare and valuable collection of porcelain and crystal pharmacy jars, as well as objects and furnishings characteristic of 19th century Puerto Rican pharmacies
Income: Financed by state appropriations
Collections: Pharmacy jars
M Museo del Grabado Latinoamericano, Calle San Sebastian, Plaza San Jose, PO Box 4184, 00905. Tel 809-724-5477; FAX 809-725-5608.
Open 8:30 AM - 4:30 PM. No admis fee. A magnificent collection is presented in the Museum of Latin American Graphics which houses representative samples of graphic art of past and contemporary Puerto Rican artists along with outstanding works of Latin American graphic engravers. This collection of prized works from the San Juan Biennial of Latin American Graphics also forms part of this museum
Income: Financed by state appropriations
Collections: Grafics; works from Orozco, Matta, Tamayo, Martorell, Alicea, Cardillo, Nevarez, Hernandez Acevedo
M Museo y Parque Historico de Caparra, Carretera 2, PO Box 4184, 00905. Tel 809-782-4795. *Dir* Jose Bartelo
Open 8:30 AM - 4:30 PM. No admis fee. The Caparra Museum and Historic Park contain ruins of Caparra, first nucleus of colonization in Puerto Rico, founded by Ponce de Leon in 1508 and 1509, now excavated and transformed into a park memorial plaques indicating the historic significance. While the restoration and excavation were being conducted, numerous objects related to the period were discovered, which are now exhibited at this museum
Income: Financed by state appropriations
Collections: Cannons, flags, pistols, ceramics
L Library, Avenida Ponce de Leon 500, 00905. Tel 809-725-7405. *Librn* Gloria A Vegavega
Open for reference to public, investigators & students
Library Holdings: Vols 120,000; AV — A-tapes, cassettes, fs, Kodachromes, lantern slides, motion pictures, slides, v-tapes; Other — Clipping files, exhibition catalogs, framed reproductions, manuscripts, memorabilia, original art works, pamphlets, photographs, prints, reproductions, sculpture
Collections: Pre-Columbian Archaeological Collection

M LA CASA DEL LIBRO MUSEUM, Calle del Cristo 255, PO Box S-2265, 00902. Tel 809-723-0354. *Dir* Maria Teresa Arraras
Open Tues - Sat 11 AM - 4:30 PM. No admis fee. Estab 1955 as a museum-library devoted to the history and arts of the book and related graphic arts.
Average Annual Attendance: 14,000. Mem: 350; dues $25 & up
Income: Financed by donations & state appropriation
Collections: Bibliography of graphic arts; binding; book illustration; calligraphy; early printing, especially 15th and 16th Century Spanish; modern fine printing; papermaking
Exhibitions: Gallery has displays on the first floor relating to printing and other arts of the book, such as: Editions of the Quixote, Spanish Incunables, Sevilla y El Libro Sevillano, Espana 1492, Homenajea Nebrija, Conversosy Sefarditas
Activities: Visits from school groups; students of library science and workers in graphic arts; material available, no fees; gallery talks; original objects of printing arts, material must be used on premises; originate traveling exhibitions; museum shop sells books, posters & cards

National and Regional Organizations In Canada

O **AMERICAN SOCIETY FOR AESTHETICS,** 4-108 Humanities Centre, University of Alberta, Edmonton, AB T6G 2E5. Tel 403-492-4102. *Pres* Peter Kivy; *Journal Ed* Phillip Alperson; *Secy-Treas* Roger A Shiner
Estab 1942 for the advancement of philosophical and scientific study of the arts and related fields
Income: Financed by dues and subscriptions
Publications: Journal of Aesthetics & Art Criticism, quarterly; ASA Newsletter, 3 times per year

O **CANADIAN CONFERENCE OF THE ARTS,** 189 Laurier Ave E, Ottawa, ON K1N 6P1. Tel 613-238-3561; FAX 613-238-4849. *National Dir* Keith Kelly; *Dir, Cultural Human Resources* Susan Annis; *Librn* Jody L Humble
Estab 1945 as a national non-profit association to strenghten public & private support to the arts & enhance the awareness of the role & value of the arts.
Mem: 1223: dues individuals $25 & GST organizations based on budget; annual meeting in May
Income: Financed by membership and grants
Publications: Handbook Series: Directory of the Arts, Who Teaches What, policy papers & reports; Proscenium, quarterly
Activities: Awards-Diplome d'Honneur to persons who have contributed outstanding service to the arts in Canada; Financial Post Awards: in collaboration with The Council for Business and the Arts in Canada, encourages the corporate sector's involvement with the visual and performing arts in Canada and recognizes those corporations whose involvement is already at a high and productive level; Imperial Oil reward for Excellence in Arts Journalism; Rogers Communications Inc Media Award

O **CANADIAN CRAFTS COUNCIL,** Conseil Canadien de l'Artisanat, 189 Laurier Ave E, Ottawa, ON K1N 6P1. Tel 613-235-8200. *Pres* Claudette Hardy-Pilon; *VPres* Jean Kares; *VPres* Ross Bradley; *VPres* Megan Broner; *Exec Dir* Peter H Weinrich
Open Mon - Fri 8:30 AM - 4:30 PM. Estab 1974 to encourage the highest quality Canadian crafts and improve standards of craftsmen through education and information. Mem: 31 associations; annual meeting Sept
Income: $350,000 (financed by membership and federal appropriation)
Collections: Cooperating with National Museum of Civilization
Publications: Bulletin, members only
Activities: Educ dept; lect open to public; originate traveling exhibitions

O **CANADIAN MUSEUMS ASSOCIATION,** Association des Musees Canadiens, 306 Metcalfe St, Suite 400, Ottawa, ON K2P 1S2. Tel 613-567-0099; FAX 613-233-5438. *Pres* Morris Flewwelling; *Exec Dir* John G McAvity
Estab 1947 to advance public museum services in Canada, to promote the welfare and better administration of museums, and to foster a continuing improvement in the qualifications and practices of museum professions. Mem: 2300; dues $50 - $2000; annual meeting May/June
Income: Financed by membership, and government grants
Publications: Muse, quarterly; Museogramme, monthly; Official directory of Canadian Museums, occasional CMA Bibliography of museum literature bi-annual
Activities: Correspondence course in introductory museology; bursary program; travel grants; book sales

O **CANADIAN SOCIETY FOR EDUCATION THROUGH ART,** 1487 Parish Lane, Oakville, ON L6M 2Z6. Tel 416-847-0975; FAX 416-847-0975. *Secy General* Dr A Wilson
Estab 1955 to promote art education in Canada. Average Annual Attendance: 400. Mem: 700; dues professional $55 (Can)
Income: Financed by membership
Collections: Historical Canadian Art; Children's Art
Publications: Canadian Review of Art Education, 1-2 times per yr; Journal, 1-2 times per yr; Newsletter, 4 times a yr
Activities: Workshops; research; lect open to public; gallery talks; tours; awards; scholarships offered

O **CANADIAN SOCIETY OF PAINTERS IN WATERCOLOUR,** c/o Visual Arts Ontario, 439 Wellington St W, 3rd Floor, Toronto, ON M5V 1E7. Tel 416-591-8883. *Pres* Mark Critoph; *Admnr* Shirley Barrie
Estab 1926 to promote watercolor painting in Canada. AIRD Gallery, MacDonald Block, Queen's Park - shared on a rotating basis with five other societies. Average Annual Attendance: 30,000. Mem: 142 & 130 associates; annual dues $90, annual meeting Apr. Membership qualifications: recommendation by members &/or chosen for annual open exhibition plus election at annual meeting
Income: $12,000 (financed by members dues, associates, commissions on sale of work, book sales)
Collections: Diploma Collection at Rodman Hall Art Gallery, St Catharines, Ontario

Exhibitions: Annual Open Juried Exhibition; Members' Exhibitions; International Exchanges (1991 - 93) International Waters with AWS & RWS
Publications: Aquarelle; Tri-annual newsletter
Activities: Lectures member; competitions with awards; originate traveling exhibitions across Canada to galleries; internationally to fellow arts organizations; national watercolor weekend of demonstrations & discussions

O **ORGANIZATION OF SASKATCHEWAN ARTS COUNCILS (OSAC),** 1102 Eighth Ave, Regina, SK S4R 1C9. Tel 306-586-1250; FAX 306-586-1250. *Exec Dir* Dennis Garreck; *Visual Arts Coordr* Sheila Archer; *Performing Arts Coordr* Nan Carson
Estab 1969 to tour exhibitions of Saskatchewan artists work and tour performers from acros Canada. Mem: 69; annual meeting in June & Oct
Library Holdings: Vols 175; Per subs 10; AV — A-tapes, cassettes, Kodachromes, rec, slides, v-tapes; Other — Clipping files, exhibition catalogs, manuscripts, pamphlets, reproductions
Activities: Classes for adults & children; deramatic programs; docent training; lectures open to public; extn dept serves lending collection

O **PROFESSIONAL ART DEALERS ASSOCIATION OF CANADA,** 296 Richmond St W, Suite 502, Toronto, ON M5V 1X2. Tel 416-979-1276. *Pres* Susan Whitney; *VPres* David Tuck; *Treas* Ian Muncaster; *Exec Admnr* Donald Bracket
Estab 1966 for the promotion of art and artists of merit in Canada. Mem: 59, members must have five years in operation plus approved reputation, general exhibitions, financial integrity; dues $500; annual meeting May
Income: Financed by membership and appraisal fees
Publications: Benefits of donation brochure; general information brochure; membership directory; print brochure
Activities: Scholarships

O **QUICKDRAW ANIMATION SOCIETY,** 209 Eighth Ave SW, Suite 300, Calgary, AB T2P 1B8. Tel 403-261-5767. *Pres* Kevin Kurytnik
Open Mon - Fri 9 AM - 9 PM. Estab 1984 to promote study of animation & provide equipment for the production of independent animated film. Mem: 30; dues $20; annual meeting April 1st
Income: $50,000 (financed by endowment, membership & state appropriation)
Purchases: $5000
Exhibitions: Animated film festivals
Publications: Pegbar, quarterly
Activities: Classes for adults & children; lectures open to public, 1 vis lectr per yr; competitions; awards; lending collection contains books, videotapes, equipment for use in animated film

O **ROYAL ARCHITECTURAL INSTITUTE OF CANADA,** 55 Murray St, Suite 330, Ottawa, ON K1N 5M3. Tel 613-232-7165; FAX 613-232-7559. *Chief Admin Officer* William Shields
Open 9 AM - 5 PM. Estab 1908 to promote a knowledge and appreciation of architecture and of the architectural profession in Canada and to represent the interests of Canadian architects
Publications: RAIC Directory, annually
L **Library,** 55 Murray St, Ottawa, K1N 5M3. Tel 613-232-7165.
Library Holdings: Vols 200
Special Subjects: Architecture, building and construction

O **ROYAL CANADIAN ACADEMY OF ARTS,** 900 Dufferin St, Suite 201, Toronto, ON M6H 4B1. Tel 416-588-8770; FAX 416-363-0920. *Pres* Bruce Le Dain; *VPres* Jan Kuypers; *Sec* Blanche Lemco van Ginkel
Estab 1880 to better the visual arts field in Canada through exhibitions. Mem: 550; membership open to visual artists concerned with excellence in their own medium; dues $200; annual meeting late Nov
Income: Non-profit association financed by membership & donations
Exhibitions: Special exhibitions of the History of the Royal Canadian Academy 1880-1980; national, multi-disciplined, juried exhibition
Publications: Passionate Spirits: A History of the Royal Canadian Academy of Arts 1880-1980; limited edition of original prints
Activities: Originate traveling exhibitions

O **SASKATCHEWAN ARTS BOARD,** 2550 Broad St, Regina, SK S4P 3V7. Tel 306-787-4056; FAX 306-787-4199. *Exec Dir* Valerie Creighton Wells
Open 8 AM - 4:30 PM. Estab 1948 as an autonomous agency for promotion and development of the arts in Saskatchewan; Board is composed of 7-15 appointed members whose major concern at the present time is the support and development of professionals and professional standards within the province
Income: Financed by annual provincial government grant
Collections: †Permanent collection containing over 1000 works by Saskatchewan artists and artisans only, dating from 1950 to present; part of collection hangs in the Saskatchewan Centre of the Arts, Regina

Publications: Annual Report; brochures for Saskatchewan School of the Arts classes; services and programs brochure
Activities: Programs include individual & group assistance grants; workshop assistance; aid for exhibitions; community assistance for the performing arts; script reading service; play-script duplication subsidy; community artists program; consultative services; operates Saskatchewan School of the Arts at Echo Valley Centre, summer classes for young people are offered in a wide variety of crafts, visual & performing arts

O **SCULPTOR'S SOCIETY OF CANADA,** 62 Wells Hill Rd, Toronto, ON M5R 3A8. Tel 416-883-3075. *Pres* Andrew Pawlowski; *Treas* Herman Falke
Estab 1928 to promote the art of sculpture, to present exhibitions (some to travel internationally), to educate the public about sculpture. Mem: 108; to qualify for mem, sculptors must submit photos of work for jury approval; dues $45; 2 general meetings per yr, exec committee meetings, 6 per yr
Income: $10,000 (financed by membership, provincial appropriation and sales commission)
Collections: 150 pieces representing all sculpture media
Exhibitions: Sculptures for the Eighties; McMichael Canadian Collection; Member Show; Canadian National Exhibition
Publications: Exhibition catalogues
Activities: Workshops

O **SIAS INTERNATIONAL ART SOCIETY,** 253-52152 Range Rd 210 (Mailing add: PO Box 3039, Sherwood Park, AB T8A 2A6). Tel 403-922-5463. *Managing Dir* Dr Klaus Bous; *Assoc Dir* Horacio Venancio; *Assoc Dir* Doria Venancio
Admis fee $25. Estab 1986 to promote unity of art, science and humanity, and to promote interrealism

Collections: †Prem Bio chemistry of Canada; †SIAS International Art Society; Ernst Fuchs, Wolfgang Hutter, Rud Hausner (engravings); Claus Cumpel (oil paintings)
Publications: Creativity from the Sub conscious; The Art of Claus Cumpel (monograph)
L **Library,** T8G 1A5
Income: $56,000 (financed by membership, sponsors)
Library Holdings: Vols 981; Per subs 11; AV — Cassettes, motion pictures, rec, slides, v-tapes; Other — Manuscripts, original art works, photographs, prints, reproductions
Special Subjects: American Indian Art, Art Education, Etchings & Engravings, Film, Graphic Arts, Manuscripts, Mixed Media, Painting - European, Painting - German, Photography, Portraits, Religious Art, Reproductions, Woodcuts

O **SOCIETY OF CANADIAN ARTISTS,** 500 Lawrence Ave W, PO Box 54029, Toronto, ON M6A 3B7. Tel 416-769-4886. *Pres* Elizabeth Crammond; *Shows* Elizabeth Elliott; *Treas* Margaret Nurse
Estab in 1957 as the Society of Cooperative Artists and operated the first cooperative gallery in Toronto. In 1967 the name was changed to the Society of Canadian Artists and the gallery moved to larger premises. In 1968 the members elected to give up the gallery and concentrate on organizing group art shows for members in galleries across Canada. Mem: 120, membership by jury, open to artists throughout Canada
Income: Financed by membership, community fundraisings and commissions
Publications: Two Decades, members' biographical catalog; quarterly newsletter
Activities: Sponsorship of art conferences and workshops; promotion of Canadian artists; originate traveling exhibitions

Museums, Libraries and Associations In Canada

ALBERTA

BANFF

M BANFF CENTRE, Walter Phillips Gallery, PO Box 1020, Station 14, T0L 0C0.
Tel 403-762-6281; FAX 403-762-6659. *Chief Cur* Daina Augaitis
Open noon - 5 PM, cl Mon. No admis fee. Estab 1977 to serve the community
and artists in the visual arts program at The Banff Centre, School of Fine Arts.
Contemporary exhibits are presented. Gallery is 15.24 x 21.34 m with 60.96 m of
running space. Average Annual Attendance: 15,000
Income: Financed by provincial and public funding
Collections: Walter J Phillips Collection; permanent collection of artwork in
various media by artists making a significant contribution to contemporary art
Exhibitions: (1992) Radio Rethink: Art, Sound & Transmission; Queues,
Rendezvous, Riots: Questioning the Public; As Public as Race: Performance by
Margo Kane, James Luna & Paul Wong; Refleksija: Contemporary Art from
Estonia, Latvia & Lithuania; Much Sense: Erotics & Life; Between Views &
Points of Views, series of projects on traveling & territories
Publications: Exhibition catalogs
Activities: Lectures open to public; concerts; gallery talks; individual works lent
to art institutions; book traveling exhibitions, 1 - 2 per year; originate traveling
exhibitions to Canadian & international galleries
L Centre for the Arts Library, PO Box 1020, Station 14, T0L 0C0. Tel 403-762-
6265. *Head Librn* Bob Foley; *Music Librn* Patrick Lawless
For reference only
Library Holdings: Vols 32,000; Per subs 200; Micro — Fiche; AV — Cassettes,
rec 7000, slides 27,000, v-tapes 650; Other — Exhibition catalogs
Special Subjects: Aesthetics, Architecture, Art Education, Conceptual Art,
Costume Design & Construction, Film, Furniture, Intermedia, Painting -
American, Painting - Canadian, Photography, Pottery, Primitive Art

M PETER AND CATHARINE WHYTE FOUNDATION, Whyte Museum of the
Canadian Rockies, 111 Bear St, Po Box 160, T0L 0C0. Tel 403-762-2291. *Pres*
Cliff White; *Dir* E J Hart; *Art Cur* Katherine Lipsett; *Archives* Donald Borden
Open winter Mon - Wed, Fri - Sun 1 - 5 PM, Thurs 1 - 9 PM, summer 10 AM -
6 PM. Admis adults $2, students & senior $1, children under 12 free. Estab 1968
to preserve and collect materials of importance in the Canadian Rocky Mountain
regions; to exhibit, publish and make material available for research, study and
appreciation. Gallery consists of three main areas: the large main gallery and the
Swiss Guides' Room downstairs and the George Browne and Belmore Browne
Room upstairs. Average Annual Attendance: 75,000
Income: Financed by endowment, federal & provincial special activities grants,
private fundings, admissions, sales
Collections: †Historical & contemporary art by artists of the Canadian Rockies;
art relating to or influenced by the region
Exhibitions: Approximately 30 per year: local, regional and national interest;
ceramics, paintings, photographs, sculpture, textiles both historic and
contemporary
Publications: The Cairn, quarterly; gallery calendars, tri-annual
Activities: Educ dept; classes for adults & children; dramatic programs; docent
training; lectures open to public, 10 vis lectrs per year; concerts; gallery talks;
tours; films; exten dept; book traveling exhibitions; originate traveling exhibitions;
sales shop sells books, reproductions, note cards
L Gallery Library, 111 Bear St, PO Box 160, T0L 0C0. Tel 403-762-2291; FAX
403-762-8919. *Archives* Donald Borden
Open winter (Oct 16 - May 31) Tues, Wed & Fri - Sun 1 - 5 PM, Thurs 1 - 9
PM, summer daily 10 AM - 6 PM. For reference only
Library Holdings: Vols 5000; AV — Fs, Kodachromes; Other — Clipping files
2000, exhibition catalogs 3000, pamphlets, photographs, prints
Special Subjects: Canadian National Parks, Rocky Mountains, wildlife, national,
regional & local artists
Collections: Archives, Heritage & Art
Exhibitions: Semi-permanent heritage exhibition & rotating art exhibitions in
three gallery spaces
Publications: The Cairn, newsletter; exhibit posters & catalogs
Activities: Heritage Homes Tours during summer months

CALGARY

M ALBERTA COLLEGE OF ART, Illingworth Kerr Gallery, 1407 14th Ave NW,
T2N 4R3. Tel 403-284-7632; FAX 403-289-6682. *Dir & Cur* Ron Moppett;
Gallery Display Artist Charles Cousins; *Asst Cur* Richard Gordon; *Technician*
Kevin Bird
No admis fee. Estab 1958 as an academic-didactic function plus general visual art
exhibition service to public. Two galleries: 425 sq meters of floor space; 125
meters running wall space; full atmospheric & security controls

Collections: †Permanent collection of ceramics, graphics, paintings, photography,
student honors work
Exhibitions: Contemporary art in all media by regional, national & international
artists
Publications: Exhibition catalogs; posters
Activities: Lectures open to public, 20 vis lectr per year; book traveling
exhibitions
L Luke Lindoe Library, 1407 14th Ave NW, T2N 4R3. Tel 403-284-7631, 284-
7630; FAX 403-284-3355. *Library Dir* Christine E Sammon
Open Mon - Thurs 8 AM - 10 PM, Fri 8 AM - 5 PM, Sat 10 AM - 5 PM. Estab
1972 to support both college academic and studio programs. Circ 45,000. Mem:
$15 annual fee for community borrowers
Purchases: $50,000
Library Holdings: Vols 15,000; Per subs 80; AV — Cassettes, fs, lantern slides,
motion pictures, slides 95,000, v-tapes; Other — Clipping files, exhibition
catalogs, reproductions
Activities: Lect open to public, 25 vis lectr per year; concerts; gallery talks;
competitions; individual and original objects of art lent to galleries

A ALBERTA SOCIETY OF ARTISTS, 147, 5151 Third St SE, T2H 2X6. Tel
403-640-4542. *Pres* Geoffrey Jamieson
Estab 1926 as an association of professional artists designed to foster and
promote the development of visual and plastic fine arts primarily within the
province. Mem: Approx 100; dues $15; annual meeting May
Publications: Highlights (newsletter), bimonthly

M CALGARY CONTEMPORARY ARTS SOCIETY, Triangle Gallery of Visual
Arts, 800 Macleod Trail SE, T2G 2M3. Tel 403-262-1737; FAX 403-262-1764.
Gallery Admin Inese Birstins; *Gallery Asst* Celia Meade
Open Mon - Fri 11 AM - 5 PM, Sat noon - 4 PM. Estab 1988 to exhibit
contemporary art in all media & provide extension programs for public. 3500 sq
ft adjacent to municipal hall. Average Annual Attendance: 17,000. Mem: 500;
dues $15; annual meeting in Nov
Income: $150,000 (financed by membership, city & state appropriation, corporate
& private donations, fundraising events)
Collections: Artist circle, donated works
Exhibitions: Contemporary Canadian Drawing; Alberta Craft; John Snow,
retrospective; Childrens Art; Quebec Abstract Artists
Publications: Update, monthly newsletter; exhibition brochures & catalogs
Activities: Docent training; workshops; lectures open to public, 20-30 vis lectr
per yr; performances; exten servs provides paintings & art rentals; book traveling
exhibitions 3-6 times a year

L CALGARY PUBLIC LIBRARY, Arts & Recreation Dept, 616 Macleod Trail
SE, T2G 2M2. Tel 403-260-2648. *Head Arts & Recreation* Gail Anderson
Open Mon - Thurs 9 AM - 9 PM, Fri & Sat 9 AM - 5 PM. Estab to provide
information & recreational materials for the general public
Purchases: $80,000
Library Holdings: Vols 60,000; Per subs 250; AV — Motion pictures, rec;
Other — Clipping files, exhibition catalogs
Special Subjects: American Indian Art, American Western Art, Architecture,
Art History, Crafts, Fashion Arts, Film, Graphic Arts, Painting - Canadian,
Photography, Theatre Arts, Video
Collections: Clipping files on local artists

M GLENBOW MUSEUM, 130 Ninth Ave SE, T2G 0P3. Tel 403-286-4100; FAX
403-265-9769; Telex 03-825523. *Chmn Board* Fred Abbott; *Dir* Dr R Janes;
Acting Chief Cur Patricia Ainslie; *Cur Art* Patricia Ainslie; *Cur Cultural History*
Sandra Morton Weizman; *Cur Ethnology* Gerald Konaty; *Head Extension &
Education* Open; *Mgr Museum Shop* Anthony Cooney; *Public Relations* John
Gilchrist
Open Tues - Sun 10 AM - 6 PM, cl Mon. Admis adults $3, student $2, senior
citizen $1, children under 12 with adult free. Estab 1966 for art, books,
documents, Indian & pioneer artifacts that lead to the preservation & better
understanding of the history of Western Canada. Museum has three exhibition
floors; 100,000 sq ft of exhibition space. Average Annual Attendance: 200,000.
Mem: 5000; dues family $35, individual $25, senior citizen $15, student $10
Income: $9,000,000 (financed by endowment, provincial & federal appropriation)
Purchases: $100,000
Collections: †Art: Representative collections of Canadian historical &
contemporary art, Indian & Inuit. Large collection of natural history illustration
& works of art on paper; †Ethnology: Large collection of material relating to
Plains Indians; representative holdings from Africa, Australia, Oceania, Central &
South America, Inuit & Northwest Coast; †Library & Archives: Western
Canadian historical books, manuscripts & photographs
Exhibitions: (1993) Ronald L Bloore: Not Without Design; Rita McKeough: An
Excavation; In Our Times: The World as seen by Magnum Photographers;
Morrice, A Gift to The Nation: The Blair Laing Collection; Matisse: The Inuit

Face; Wyndham Lewis: The Canadian Years 1940 - 1945; The Crisis of Abstraction in Canada: The Fifties; New Acquisitions; John Hammond. (1994) Max Beck Mann; Janice Gurney: Ten Years; The Tiger General & The Beautiful Lady; Ana Mendieta: A Retrospective. (1995) The Urban Image in Prairie Art; The Art of Alex Janvier: His First Thirty Years; Fluffs & Feathers: An Exhibit on the Symbols of Indianness; Jacques Villon

Publications: Chautauqua in Canada; Max Ernst; Four Modern Masters; exhibition catalogs

Activities: Classes for children; docent training; lectures open to public; gallery talks; tours; exten dept; individual paintings & original objects of art lent to public museums & galleries; lending collection contains 15,000 works on paper, 5000 paintings, sculpture & 5000 items of decorative art; book traveling exhibitions 25 per year; originate traveling exhibitions; museum shop sells books, magazines, reproductions & prints; Luxton Museum, Banff, Alberta

L   **Library,** 130 Ninth Ave SE, T2G 0P3. Tel 403-264-8300. *Archivist* Tony Rees; *Librn* Len Gottselig
Open for reference
Income: Financed by endowment and government of Alberta
Library Holdings: Vols 80,000; Per subs 500; Micro — Cards, fiche, reels; Other — Clipping files, exhibition catalogs, pamphlets
Collections: †Western Canadian Art

M   **MUSEUM OF MOVIE ART,** 3600 21st St NE, No 9, T2E 6B6. Tel 403-250-7588. *General Mgr* Sol Candel
Open Tues - Fri 9:30 AM - 5:30 PM, Sat 11 AM - 5 PM. Admis $1. Estab 1950. Average Annual Attendance: 3000
Purchases: $58,000
Collections: Consolidated Theatre Services; Federal Estate (Gaiety Theatre)
Publications: Catalogue
Activities: Retail store sells prints & original movie posters

M   **MUTTART ART GALLERY,** 1221 Second St SW, T2R 0W5. Tel 403-266-2764, 233-7337. *Pres* Gean Shaw; *Dir & Cur* Richard L White; *Treas* Cathleen McFarlan; *Cur* Franklyn Heislar
Open winter Tues - Sun noon - 5 PM, Thurs 1 - 9 PM, summer Tues - Sat noon - 5 PM, Thurs 1 - 9 PM. No admis fee. Estab 1978 to exhibit the works of amateur and emerging professional artists and to provide artists information for the following communities: Calgary, Alberta, Saskatchewan, Manitoba and British Columbia. Top floor of the restored Memorial Park Library (old Carnegie Library). Average Annual Attendance: 35,000. Mem: 1000; dues $15; annual meeting Mar
Income: $140,950 (financed by membership, city and state appropriation, private donations and corporate funds)
Exhibitions: Deb Brown-Ridley (cartoons); Alberta College of Art (jewelry). (1986-87) A Sense of Space (sculpture); Brenda Hemsing/David Collins (photographs); Isabell Hunt-Johnson (drawings/watercolors); Prairie Spaces; Robert Dalton (paintings); Marja de Zwart (paintings); Studio Ceramics in Alberta III (1964-1984); Lesley Beaupre (paintings); The Group (paintings); School Art Exhibition (mix-media art works); William Bushell (drawings); Bow Valley Group (paintings); Phil Mix; Courtney Andersen; Janusz Malinowski; Carolyn Christenson-Qualle/Eileen Oxendale; Karen Christensen; Coleen Anderson-Millard; Calgary Sketch Club; The Group; Bow Valley Group; Steve Burger/Masami Takahashi; Janet Morgan; Calgary Artists Society; Alex Jadah; Ruth Syme; Alberta Potters Association; Robert Benn; Barbara Amos; Marilyn Sagert, Janice Wong, Amy Gogarty; Calgary Public School Board; Calgary Separate School Board; Jean Biccum, Jane Pawson, Ilse Salkauskas; Marcia Perkins; Peter Raabe; Alberta Society of Artists; Hilda Fast; Jacques Rioux; Esso Resources Collection; Civic Collection of the Calgary Allied Arts Foundation; Art & the Handicapped Exhibition; Jeff Stellick; Jill Percival; Jim Davis; Calgary Community Painters; Alberta Porcelain Artists of Calgary; Paul Shykora; Frances Chapman
Publications: Annual Report (One and One Third); Visual Arts Information Project
Activities: Classes for children; lect open to public, 2-3 vis lectr per year; gallery talks; tours; competitions; book traveling exhibitions three per year

C   **NOVA CORPORATION OF ALBERTA,** NOVA Garden Court Gallery, 801 Seventh Ave SW, T2P 2N6. Tel 403-290-5936; Telex 038-21503. *Art Coordr* Pat Morton
Open Mon - Fri 8 AM - 6 PM. No admis fee. Estab 1982 to provide employees & general public exposure to a variety of art
Collections: †Mostly contemporary art prints & paintings, with emphasis on Canadian artists
Exhibitions: Canadian Association of Photographers & Illustrators in Communication Show; John Snow Exhibition
Activities: Individual paintings lent; book traveling exhibitions

C   **PETRO-CANADA INC,** Corporate Art Programme, PO Box 2844, T2P 3E3. Tel 403-296-8949; FAX 403-296-3030. *Art Cur* Pauline Lindland
Open noon - 2 PM. No admis fee. Estab 1984 for encouragement of Canadian art. 1130 sq ft, two external display cases, lighting & humidity controls, excellent security. Average Annual Attendance: 2300
Collections: †Two-dimensional works in all media by contemporary Canadian artists
Activities: Educ dept; lect open to public, 2 vis lectr per yr; gallery talks; tours; individual paintings & original objects of art lent to cultural institutions & artists for exhibition purposes; book traveling exhibitions, quarterly

QUICKDRAW ANIMATION SOCIETY
For further information, see National and Regional Organizations

C   **SHELL CANADA LTD,** 400 Fourth Ave SW, PO Box 100 Sta M, T2P 2H5. Tel 403-691-3111; FAX 403-691-4183.
Collections: Works of contemporary Canadian artists with media concentrations in painting, sculpture, graphics, photography, mixed media & works on paper

M   **UNIVERSITY OF CALGARY,** The Nickle Arts Museum, 2500 University Dr NW, T2N 1N4. Tel 403-220-7234; FAX 403-282-7298. *Dir* Ann Davis; *Cur Art* Katherine Ylitalo; *Cur Numismatics* Mary Walbank
Open Tues - Fri 10 AM - 5 PM, Sat & Sun 1 - 5 PM, cl Mon & holidays. Admis adults $2, children, students & sr citizens $1, students of institutions of higher learning & children under 6 free; Tues free. In 1970 an Alberta pioneer, Mr Samuel C Nickle, gave the University a gift of one million dollars and the museum was opened in 1979. His son, Carl O Nickle, presented the University with an immensely valuable collection of some 10,000 ancient coins, covering over 1500 years of human history which is housed in the Numismatics department of the museum. Museum houses the permanent collection of the University; exhibitions are presented on a continuous basis in the gallery on the main floor (15,000 sq ft). A smaller numismatic gallery displays rotating collections. The smaller Gallery II on the second floor (1500 sq ft) is used for small exhibitions lectures, films & seminars. Average Annual Attendance: 25,000
Income: Financed by state appropriation through the University
Purchases: $15,000
Collections: Ceramics; †contemporary paintings; †drawings; †photography, †prints; sculpture; †watercolors
Exhibitions: Local, national & international exhibitions are presented on a continuous basis
Publications: Exhibition catalogs
Activities: Educ dept; lectures open to public; gallery talks; tours; individual paintings & original objects of art lent to other museums & art galleries; book 10-16 traveling exhibitions pr year; originate traveling exhibitions; sales shop sells catalogs, posters, note cards & books

L   **Faculty of Environmental Design,** 2500 University Dr, ES 951, T2N 1N4. Tel 403-220-6815. *Resource Coordr* Nancy Donovan
Open Mon - Fri 9:30 AM - 4:30 PM. Estab 1973 as a resource facility for students & faculty in 4 program areas: architecture, urban planning, industrial design & environmental science. Small gallery for display of student works & traveling exhibitions; workshop; photo lab facilities
Library Holdings: Vols 500; Per subs 30; Models, drawings; AV — A-tapes, cassettes, slides, v-tapes; Other — Manuscripts, memorabilia
Special Subjects: Architecture, Interior Design, Industrial Design

CZAR

M   **SHORNCLIFFE PARK IMPROVEMENT ASSOC,** Prairie Panorama Museum, PO Box 60, T0B 0Z0. Tel 403-857-2155. *Cur* Helena Lawrason; *Cur* Irene Brown
Open Sun 2 - 6 PM, other days by appointment. Estab 1963 for the enjoyment of the public. Average Annual Attendance: 580
Income: Finances by government grant &donations
Collections: Salt & Pepper Collection
Activities: Classes for children

EDMONTON

A   **ALBERTA FOUNDATION FOR THE ARTS,** Beaver House, 5th floor, 10158 103rd St, T5J 0X6. Tel 403-427-9968; FAX 403-422-0398. *Chmn* R C Jarvis; *Exec Dir* W Tin Ng
Open Mon - Fri 8:15 AM - 4:30 PM. No admis fee. Estab 1972 to collect & to exhibit art works produced by Alberta artists; to provide financial assistance to Alberta public, institutional & commercial art galleries, art groups & organizations for programs & special projects
Income: Financed by the Province of Alberta & Alberta Lotteries
Collections: Alberta Art Foundation Collection
Exhibitions: Spaces & Places Little by Little
Publications: Annual Report; exhibition catalogs
Activities: Acquisition of art works by Alberta artists; exhibition program in and outside Canada; individual paintings & original objects of art lent to public government buildings

AMERICAN SOCIETY FOR AESTHETICS
For further information, see National and Regional Organizations

DEPARTMENT OF CULTURE & MULTI-CULTURALISM
L   **Arts Branch Resource Center,** 10158 103rd St, T5J 0X6. Tel 403-427-6315. *Dir Arts Branch* Dr Clive Padfield
Reference materials
Library Holdings: Vols 1620; Per subs 34; Other — Clipping files, exhibition catalogs, pamphlets
M   **Provincial Museum of Alberta,** 12845 102nd Ave, T5N 0M6. Tel 403-453-9100; FAX 403-454-6629. *Dir* Dr Philip H R Stepney; *Asst Dir Exhibits & Visitor Servs* Don Clevett; *Asst Dir Natural History & Coll Admin* Dr Bruce McGillivray; *Asst Dir Archaelogy & Ethnology* Dr Jack Ives
Open summer 9 AM - 8 PM, winter Tues - Sun 9 AM - 5 PM. cl Mon. Admis fee. Estab 1967 to preserve and interpret the human and natural history of the province of Alberta. Four major exhibit areas divided equally into human & natural history under broad themes of settlement history, archaelogy & anthropology, natural history & habitats. Average Annual Attendance: 325,000. Mem: 800; dues $12 - $19; annual meeting in June
Income: $4,714,000 (financed by provincial government)
Purchases: $54,000
Collections: Archaeological; ethnographical; fine & decorative arts; folk life; geology; historical; invertebrate zoology; mammalogy; palaeontology; ornithology; vascular & non vascular plants
Exhibitions: Approx 10 feature exhibits
Publications: Ocassional papers; occasioinal series; Publication series; exhibit catalogs; teacher guides
Activities: Classes for children; lectures open to public; competitions; gallery talks; individual artifacts lent; originate traveling exhibitions; museum gift shop

L **Provincial Archives of Alberta,** 12845 102nd Ave, T5N 0M6. Tel 403-427-1750; FAX 403-454-6629. *Provincial Archivist* David Leonard; *Chief A-V Archivist* Brock Silversides
Open Mon - Fri 9 AM - 4:30 PM, Wed evening until 9 PM, Sat 9 AM - 1 PM. Estab 1967 to identify, evaluate, acquire, preserve, arrange and describe and subsequently make available for public research, reference and display those diversified primary and secondary sources that document and relate to the overall history and development of Alberta
Income: Financed by provincial appropriation
Purchases: $73,000
Library Holdings: Vols 100; Original documents; Micro — Fiche, reels; AV — A-tapes, cassettes, motion pictures, rec, slides; Other — Clipping files, manuscripts, original art works, pamphlets, photographs, prints
Special Subjects: Ethno-cultural groups and activities, genealogy, immigration and land settlement, local histories, religious archives
Exhibitions: Several small displays each year highlighting recent accessions or historical themes; periodic major exhibitions
Publications: Guides to collections; information leaflets; occasional papers; exhibition catalogues

M **EDMONTON ART GALLERY,** 2 Sir Winston Churchill Square, T5J 2C1. Tel 403-422-6223. *Exec Dir* Alf Bogusky
Open Mon, Tues & Sat 10:30 AM - 5 PM, Wed - Fri 10:30 AM - 8 PM, Sun & holidays 11 AM - 5 PM, cl New Year's & Christmas. Admis adults $2, senior citizens & students $1, members & children 12 & under free. Estab 1924 to collect and exhibit paintings, sculptures, photographs and other works of visual art and to teach art appreciation. Gallery covers 45,000 sq ft; exhibition area 20,000 sq ft. Average Annual Attendance: 180,000. Mem: 2000; dues $40
Income: $2,000,000 (financed by donations, fees, membership, municipal, provincial & federal grants)
Purchases: $119,000
Collections: †Contemporary Canadian art; †contemporary & historical photography; †contemporary international art; †historical Canadian art; historical European and American art
Exhibitions: 29 in-house exhibitions and 23 extension shows
Publications: Outlook magazine, quarterly; exhibition catalogues
Activities: Classes for adults and children; docent training; workshops; lectures open to public & members only; gallery talks; tours; individual paintings & original objects of art lent to other institutions; traveling exhibitions organized and circulated; gallery shop sells books, magazines, original art, reproductions, prints, jewelry, novelties & craft items; junior museum maintained, Margaret Brian Gallery

L **Library,** 2 Sir Winston Churchill Square, T5J 2C1. Tel 403-422-6223; FAX 403-426-3105. *Dir* Alf Bogusky; *Chief Cur* Elizabeth Kidd
Open Tues. Estab 1924. Maintained by volunteer staff
Library Holdings: Vols 10,000; Per subs 38; Micro — Fiche, reels; AV — Cassettes, slides 17,000, v-tapes 150; Other — Clipping files, exhibition catalogs, sculpture 70,000
Special Subjects: Painting - Canadian, Photography, Sculpture
Publications: Outlook, the magazine of the Edmonton Art Gallery, quarterly
Activities: Classes for adults & children; docent training; lectures open to public; concerts; gallery talks; tours; original objects of art lent to members & non-members; originate traveling exhibitions circulating to Alberta and other Canadian areas; museum shop sells books, magazines, prints, jewelry, toys, handicrafts

L **EDMONTON PUBLIC LIBRARY,** Foyer Gallery, 7 Sir Winston Churchill Sq, T5J 2V4. Tel 403-423-2331. *Coordr* Sherri Ritchie
Open Mon - Fri 9 AM - 9 PM, Sat 9 AM - 6 PM, Sun 1 - 5 PM. Foyer Gallery has 120 running ft with 420 sq ft of floor space
Exhibitions: Twelve exhibitions per year

A **LATITUDE 53 SOCIETY OF ARTISTS,** 10137 104th St, T5J 0Z9. Tel 403-423-5353. *Pres* Mark Siegner; *Gallery Adminr* Allen Boyle
Open Mon - Fri 10 AM - 6 PM, Sat noon - 6 PM. Estab 1973 to encourage & promote the artistic endeavors of contemporary artists & to build a public awareness of current & experimental cultural developments. Average Annual Attendance: 2000. Mem: 100; dues $20; annual meeting first Wed in June
Income: $125,000 (financed by grants, donations, public & private funding, membership & fund raising events)
Exhibitions: Peggy Taylor Reid; Miriam Fabijam; Lynda Gammon; Frances Robson; Politically Speaking; Mary Scott; Luc Bergen; Kevin Kelly; Issues of Censorship; Evergon; Quebec Documentary Photography; Gerry Dotto; Sophie Doorzsak; Kenneth Housego; Heather Spears; Group Show: D Genier, D Albert, L Hoff & M Turner
Publications: Exhibition catalogues
Activities: Lectures open to the public, 15 vis lectrs per yr; concerts; gallery talks; tours; book traveling exhibitions, 10 per yr; originate traveling exhibitions for other art centers

M **UKRAINIAN CANADIAN ARCHIVES & MUSEUM OF ALBERTA,** 9543 110th Ave, T5H 1B3. Tel 403-424-7580. *Pres* M Shmiliar; *Cur* Christine Jendyk
Open by appointment, July & Aug Sun 2 - 5 PM. No admis fee. Estab 1941
Collections: Drawings, historical material, national costumes, paintings, prints, sculpture and textiles
Exhibitions: (1993) Graphics; Professor Getz
Activities: TV and radio programs; study clubs; lect; guided tours; films; loan service

FORT SASKATCHEWAN

L **FORT SASKATCHEWAN MUNICIPAL LIBRARY,** Exhibit Room, 10011-10 Second St, T8L 2C5. Tel 403-998-4275. *Dir* Marcia Redford
Open winter Mon, Tues & Thurs noon - 9 PM, Wed & Fri 10 AM - 6 PM, Sat & Sun 1 - 5 PM, cl Sat & Sun in summer. Estab 1980 as a gallery available for local artists & for interested citizens. Exhibit Room has 78 running feet of exhibition space and a floor space of approximately 731 square feet
Income: Financed by town grant, provincial grant, fees & fines
Library Holdings: Vols 46,000; Per subs 100
Exhibitions: Monthly exhibitions

GRANDE PRAIRIE

M **PRAIRIE GALLERY,** 10209 99 St, T8V 2H3. Tel 403-532-8111; FAX 403-539-1991. *Dir* Elizabeth Ginn; *Cur & Educator* Chris Carson, MFA; *Curatorial Asst* Fiona Portwood, BFA; *Admin Asst* Cindy Guary
Open Mon - Thurs 10 AM - 6 PM, Fri 10 AM - 9 PM, Sat, Sun & state holidays 1 - 5 PM. No admis fee. Estab 1975 for exhibitions. Average Annual Attendance: 36,000. Mem: 285; dues individual $20, family $35, supporter $50-$99, patron $399, presidents council $400; annual meeting on March 30th
Income: $360,000 (financed by mem, city appropriation, provincial & federal government grants)
Collections: Alberta Art; Contemporary Western Canadian Art
Exhibitions: Glenn Gould
Activities: Classes for adults & children; docent training; exten dept provides lending collection of 350 paintings & art objects; book traveling exhibitions; originate traveling exhibitions

LETHBRIDGE

A **ALLIED ARTS COUNCIL OF LETHBRIDGE,** Bowman Arts Center, 811 Fifth Ave S, T1J 0V2. Tel 403-327-2813. *Pres* Birthe Perry; *Exec Mgr* Shirley Hamilton
Open Mon - Fri 10 AM - 9 PM, Sat & Sun 1 - 5 PM. No admis fee. Estab 1958 to encourage and foster cultural activities in Lethbridge, to provide facilities for such cultural activities, and to promote the work of Alberta and Western Canadian artists. Average Annual Attendance: 20,000. Mem: 300; dues $15; annual meeting Feb
Income: $67,000 (financed by membership and city appropriation, Alberta Culture granting & fund raising)
Exhibitions: Local & regional exhibitions: Children's art, fabric makers, painters, potters; one-man shows: Paintings, photography, prints, sculpture, silversmithing; provincial government traveling exhibits
Publications: Calendar of Arts, weekly
Activities: Classes for adults and children; dramatic programs; concerts; competitions; scholarships; traveling exhibitions organized and circulated; sales shop selling original art

M **CITY OF LETHBRIDGE,** Sir Alexander Galt Museum, c/o City of Lethbridge, 910 Fourth Ave S, T1J 0P6. Tel 403-320-3898 (museum); 329-7302 (archives). *Museum Supv* M Cecile McCleary; *City Archivist* Greg Ellis; *Display Artist* Brad Brown; *Museum Technician* Richard Shockley
Open daily July & Aug, cl statutory holidays Sept - June. No admis fee. Estab 1964 to promote the study of human history in Southern Alberta. Five Galleries; One gallery is for community use; 800 sq ft & 100 ft running wall space. Average Annual Attendance: 25,000
Income: $247,000
Collections: Historical artifact collection; Archives Collection--photos, manuscripts, books, tapes, films
Exhibitions: Urbane Urbanization (photos); Fusion (mixed media); Lethbridge Numismatic Club; Festival of Quilts
Activities: Children's classes; docent programs; Lectrs open to public, 10 vis lectr per year; tours; book traveling exhibitions, 8 per yr; originate traveling exhibitions to area schools, institutions, fairs; museum shop sells books & locally handcrafted items

M **LETHBRIDGE COMMUNITY COLLEGE,** Buchanan Gallery, 3000 College Dr S, T1K 1L6. Tel 403-320-3352; FAX 403-320-1461. *Mgr Library Servs* Kathy Lea; *Public Servs Librn* Wayne Briscoe
Open Mon - Thurs 8 AM - 10 PM, Fri 8 AM - 5 PM, Sat 1 - 5 PM, Sun 1 - 6:30 PM. No admis fee. Estab 1978 in memory of the Hon W A Buchanan & Mrs Buchanan. Gallery consists of 183.41 running ft of wall space in the Buchanan Library
Collections: Canadian Perspectives Collection

L **LETHBRIDGE PUBLIC LIBRARY,** Art Gallery, 810 Fifth Ave, S, T1J 4C4. Tel 403-380-7330; FAX 403-329-1478. *Cur* Janet Walters; *Librn* Duncan Rand
Estab 1974 to expand human experience, to encourage people to look at art as well as read and attend library programs
Activities: Originates traveling exhibitions

M **SOUTHERN ALBERTA ART GALLERY,** 601 Third Ave S, T1J 0H4. Tel 403-327-8770; FAX 403-328-3913. *Pres* George Virtue; *VPres* Cindy Kenwood; *Dir & Cur* Joan Stebbins; *Public Prog Cur* Anine Vonkeman
Open Tues - Sat 10 AM - 5 PM, Thurs & Fri 6:30 - 9 PM, Sun 1 - 5 PM. No admis fee. Estab 1975 to present historical & contemporary art programs designed to further the process of art appreciation. Three gallery spaces contained in historical Lethbridge building remodelled as art gallery. Average Annual Attendance: 30,000. Mem: 500; dues $25 family, $15 single; meeting Feb 15
Income: Financed by membership, city, provincial and federal appropriation
Collections: Buchanan Collection of City of Lethbridge containing mid-20th Century Canadian work and various international pieces
Exhibitions: Historical and contemporary art changing monthly
Publications: Exhibition catalogues; quarterly newsletter
Activities: Lectures open to the public, numerous vis lectr per yr; concerts; gallery talks; tours; artmobile; book traveling exhibitions, 12 per yr; originate traveling exhibitions

L **Library,** 601 Third Ave S, T1J 0H4. Tel 403-327-8770. *Librn* David A Clearwater
Reference library by appointment only
Library Holdings: Vols 520; Per subs 43; AV — A-tapes, cassettes, fs, slides, v-

tapes; Other — Clipping files, exhibition catalogs, manuscripts, pamphlets 3200, reproductions
Activities: Classes for children; lect open to public, 25 - 30 vis lectr per year; concerts; gallery talks; tours; video competitions; exten dept serves southern & central Alberta; lending collection contains 520 books, 22 cassettes, film strips, 56 videos (in house viewing only)

M **UNIVERSITY OF LETHBRIDGE,** Art Gallery, 4401 University Dr, T1K 3M4. Tel 403-329-2690; FAX 403-382-7127. *Gallery Dir & Cur* Jeffrey Spalding; *Asst Dir Adminstration* Carol A Demers; *Asst Cur* Victoria V Baster; *Chief Preparator* Adrian G Cooke; *Registrar* Lucie E Linhart; *Gift Adminr* Pam Clark
Open Mon - Fri noon - 4:30 PM. No admis fee. Estab 1968 for public service and the teaching mechanism. 29 ft x 42 ft gallery; Visual Arts Study Centre, open same hours as the Gallery, where any work from the collection will be made available for viewing
Income: Financed by university & government appropriations
Collections: †Permanent Collection consists of 19th century art (primarily Canadian), 20th century international art; Inuit
Exhibitions: Exhibitions with exception of the Annual BFA show are curated from the permanent collection; Faculty & Staff Exhibitions; approximately 10 shows per yr
Activities: Lect open to public, 10 - 15 vis lectr per yr; tours; individual paintings & original objects of art lent to public & commercial galleries & corporations

A **WESTERN CANADA ART ASSOCIATION INC,** 601 Third Ave S, T1J 0H4. Tel 403-327-8770; FAX 403-328-3913. *Secy & Treas* Janet Walters
Estab 1970 as art lobby & support association. Mem: 100
Income: Financed by membership
Publications: Wagon, annual
Activities: Seminars; competitions with awards

MEDICINE HAT

M **MEDICINE HAT MUSEUM & ART GALLERY,** 1302 Bomford Crescent, SW, T1A 5E6. Tel 403-527-6266 (museum), 526-0486 (gallery); FAX 403-528-2464. *Dir* Tom Willock
Open June - Aug Mon - Fri 9 AM - 5 PM, winter hours Mon - Fri 10:30 AM - noon, 1 - 5 PM, cl New Year's, Good Friday & Christmas. Admis donations are welcomed. Estab 1951. Gallery has 2425 sq ft on main floor. Average Annual Attendance: 13,000
Collections: Pioneer artifacts of city & the district; Indian artifacts
Activities: School programs; films; gallery talks

L **MEDICINE HAT PUBLIC LIBRARY,** 414 First St SE, T1A 0A8. Tel 403-527-5528; FAX 403-527-4595. *Chief Librn* Bruce Evans; *Asst Chief Librn* Erin T Boyle
Open Mon - Thurs 10 AM - 9 PM, Fri & Sat 10 AM - 5:30 PM, Sun 1 - 5:30 PM. $6 mem fee. Library has a display area for traveling and local art shows. 600 sq ft room with track lighting and alarm system
Library Holdings: Vols 128,270; Per subs 297; Phono Disc 2844; Micro — Reels 18; AV — Cassettes 3189, motion pictures 476, rec, v-tapes 820; Other — Clipping files, original art works, pamphlets 22, prints, sculpture
Activities: Dramatic programs; lect open to public, 10 vis lectr per year; concerts

MUNDARE

A **BASILIAN FATHERS,** PO Box 379, T0B 3H0. Tel 403-764-3860. *Dir* Myron Chimy
Open May - Oct, Mon - Sat 10 AM - 6 PM. Donations accepted. Estab 1902 to serve the people in their church
Income: Financed by donations, government grants
Collections: Ukrainian Folk Art, Arts and Crafts; Historical Church Books
L **Library,** PO Box 379, T0B 3H0. Tel 403-764-3860. *Dir* Larry Huculak
Library Holdings: Vols 650

RED DEER

M **NORMANDEAU CULTURAL & NATURAL HISTORY SOCIETY,** Red Deer & District Museum & Archives, 4525 47A Ave, PO Box 800, T4N 5H2. Tel 403-343-6844; FAX 403-342-6644. *Dir* Morris Flewwelling; *Prog Coordr* Doris Northey
Open daily 1 - 5 PM, Mon - Thurs evenings 7 - 10 PM, summer Mon - Thurs 10 AM - 9 PM, Fri 10 AM - 5 PM. No admis fee. Estab 1978 to present the human history of the region through an on-going series of exhibitions & interpretive programs. Stewart Rooms has 50 - 60 running ft of exhibition space; Volunteer's Gallery has 50 - 60 running ft of exhibition space; 3500 sq ft total area. Average Annual Attendance: 60,000. Mem: 1000; dues individual $2, family $5
Income: Financed by municipal, provincial & federal grants
Collections: Bower Collection of archaeological specimens from Central Alberta; Inuit carving, prints & related material; Central Alberta human history; Swallow Collection of Inuit & Indian Art
Exhibitions: Programs featuring local international, national & provincial artist; Artists Proof: An Exhibition of Contemporary Japanese Prints; Red Deer College Student Show; Alberta Community Art Clubs Association, Alberta Wide Juried Exhibition
Activities: Educ dept; museo-kits; concerts; gallery talks; tours; museum shop sells books, coloring books, learning tools, souvenirs, postcards, stationery
M **Red Deer & District Museum Exhibition Centre,** 4525 47A Ave, PO Box 800, T4N 5H2. Tel 403-343-6844; FAX 403-342-6644. *Dir* Morris Flewwelling
Open Mon - Thurs 1 - 5 PM, 7 - 10 PM, Fri - Sun 1 - 5 PM. Admis free. Estab 1978. The exhibition centre Donor's Gallery presents an on-going series of temporary exhibits featuring art, science, history & crafts from local, regional & national sources. It contains 1016 sq ft exhibition space. Average Annual Attendance: 40,000. Mem: 600; dues $5, annual meeting in May
Activities: Classes for adults and children, docent training; lectures open to the public; gallery talks and tours; book traveling exhibitions 6-12 per year; originate traveling exhibitions

SHERWOOD PARK

SIAS INTERNATIONAL ART SOCIETY
For further information, see National and Regional Organizations

STONY PLAIN

M **MULTICULTURAL HERITAGE CENTRE,** 5411 51st St, T0E 2G0. Tel 403-963-2777. *Exec Dir* Judy Unterschultz; *Cur Oppertshauser House* Jenny Woods
Open Mon - Sat 10 AM - 4 PM, Sun 10 AM - 6:30 PM. No admis fee. Estab 1974 to provide exposure to high quality art with priority given to local Alberta artists, to develop an appreciation for good art, to provide exposure for upcoming artists. Gallery has 1200 sq ft of exhibition space; Multicultural Heritage Centre also consists of Opertshauser Gallery on same site. Average Annual Attendance: 102,000. Mem: 300; dues individual $20, family $30; annual meeting Jan
Income: Financed by Government grants, fees for children & adult programs, commissions from handicraft sales, art rental fees, Homesteaders Kitchen & bingos
Collections: Area history; family histories; photographs
Exhibitions: 14 exhibitions per yr
Publications: Monthly newsletter
Activities: Classes for adults & children; gallery talks; tours; competitions; sales shop sells handicrafts; Homesteader's Kitchen serves ethnic fare

BRITISH COLUMBIA

BURNABY

M **BURNABY ART GALLERY,** 6344 Deer Lake Ave, V5G 2J3. Tel 604-291-9441; FAX 604-291-6776. *Pres Board of Trustees* Anne Houseman; *Dir & Cur* Karen Henry; *Asst Cur* Todd Davis; *Preparator* Mark B Stevens
Open Tues - Fri 9 AM - 5 PM, weekends & holidays noon - 5 PM, cl Christmas. Admis $2. Estab 1967 to collect & exhibit Canadian art, with continually changing exhibitions of prints, paintings, sculpture & other art forms. Gallery is housed in Ceperley Mansion in Deer Lake Park. Average Annual Attendance: 25,000. Mem: 350; dues sponsor $100, sustaining $50, family $40, single $25, sr citizen & student $10; annual meeting June
Income: Financed by municipal, provincial & federal grants, public & private donations
Collections: 20th Century prints including contemporary artists; Works on paper
Exhibitions: (1993) New Acquisitions; Drawings: The Ethics of Gesture; Michael De Courcy: Board with Painting; Art in the Schools: Burnaby Students; Straight From the Pile: Contemporary Rococo Sculpture; Collection: The Created Image: Collage from the Permanent Collection; Grant McConnell: Tales of Dominion; Glenn Lewis: Utopiary Selected Works 1967 - 1993; Karen Kazmer: A Short History of An Idea, Home; Ceramics as Art: Four members of the Burnaby Potter's Guild; Collections: Portraits: Self & Others; Construction Identity
Publications: Catalogues & brochures to accompany exhibitions; quarterly members bulletin
Activities: Docent training; film series; workshops for schools; lect open to public; concerts; gallery talks; tours; exten dept serves BC; individual paintings & original objects of art lent to other exhibition centers; lending collection contains 600 original prints, 50 paintings, 25 sculpture & drawings; museum shop sells books, magazines, original art, prints, crafts & pottery by local and other artists

M **SIMON FRASER UNIVERSITY,** Simon Fraser Gallery, V5A 1S6. Tel 604-291-4266. *Dir* Dr E M Gibson; *Registrar* Janet Menzies
Open Mon 1 - 7 PM, Tues - Fri 10 AM - 4 PM, cl Sat & Sun. No admis fee. Estab 1971 to collect, conserve and display original works of art, principally contemporary Canadian. Gallery is 150 to 310 running ft, 1200 sq ft. Permanent works are installed throughout the university campus. Average Annual Attendance: 10,000
Income: Financed by public university appropriations, government grants and corporate donations
Collections: Simon Fraser Collection, including contemporary and Inuit graphics; international graphics
Exhibitions: (1992) Severino Trica. (1993) Bident Bigelow; Alistair Bell, Woodcut; Visual Arts Student Show; Recent Works by Patricia Kushner; British Columbia Glass Show; Faculty, Staff & Students at Simon Fraser, Photography; Patricia Johnston
Publications: Bi-annual report
Activities: Individual paintings & original objects of art loaned to University faculty & staff on campus; exhibiting artists' works occasionally available for sale
L **Library,** V5A 1S6. Tel 604-291-3869; FAX 604-291-4455. *Librn* Theodore C Dobb
Reference material available in Fine Arts Room & University Archives
Library Holdings: Vols 1,000,000; Per subs 11,500; CD-ROM, Compact Discs; Micro — Cards, fiche, reels; AV — A-tapes, fs, rec, slides, v-tapes; Other — Clipping files, exhibition catalogs, manuscripts, pamphlets

CHILLIWACK

A **CHILLIWACK COMMUNITY ARTS COUNCIL,** 45899 Henderson Ave, V2P 2X6. Tel 604-792-2069; FAX 604-792-2640. *General Mgr* Anita Lloyd
Open 9 AM - 4 PM. Estab 1959 as Arts Council, Arts Centre estab 1973 to encourage all forms of art in the community. Mem: 5000; dues organizational $7.50, individual $5; annual meeting September
Income: Financed by endowment, membership and grants
Collections: Twenty-six Salish Weavings
Exhibitions: Local artists' exhibitions, including oils, pottery, prints, weavings, wood carving and other fabric arts
Publications: Arts Council Newsletter, 11 per year
Activities: Classes for adults and children; dramatic programs; concerts; scholarships

COQUITLAM

A **PLACE DES ARTS,** 1120 Brunette Ave, V3K 1G2. Tel 604-526-2891. *Dir* Gillian Elliot
Open Mon - Thurs 9 AM - 10 PM, Fri 3 - 10 PM, Sat 9 AM - 4 PM. No admis fee. Estab Sept 1, 1972 as a cultural, community crafts and resource center, an art school and gallery. Average Annual Attendance: 3000
Income: Financed by municipal grant
Exhibitions: Bi-weekly shows of artists and craftsmen throughout the year
Publications: Program (12 weeks), every three months
Activities: Special Educ Dept serving retarded young adults, school children, senior citizens and women's groups; satellite courses within the school of the district on request; classes for adults and children; dramatic programs; music program; lect open to public; concerts; gallery talks; scholarships

DAWSON CREEK

M **SOUTH PEACE ART SOCIETY,** Dawson Creek Art Gallery, 101-816 Alaska Ave, V1G 4T6. Tel 604-782-2601. *Pres* Lyne Powell; *Dir* Elizabeth Hillman; *Treas* Edna McPhail
Open winter Mon - Sat 10 AM - 5 PM, summer daily 8 AM - 8 PM. Estab 1961 to promote art appreciation in community. Art Gallery in elevator annex in NAR Park. NAR Park includes museum & Tourist Information Office. Average Annual Attendance: 65,000. Mem: 100; dues $15; annual meeting third Thurs of Mar
Income: $130,000 (financed by municipal building & annual sponsorship, commission from sales, provincial cultural grant, federal grant Canada council)
Exhibitions: Approximately 15 - 18 per year, local and traveling
Activities: Classes for adults & children; docent training; lect open to public, 4 vis lectr per yr; gallery talks; tours; individual paintings lent to members, businesses, private homes; lending colleciton contains color reproductions, slides, 145 books & 350 original prints; book traveling exhibitions, 4 per year; sales shop sells original art, magazines, books, prints, slides, jewelry, souvenirs, pottery

GRAND FORKS

M **MOUNTAIN VIEW DOUKHOBOR MUSEUM,** PO Box 1235, V0H 1H0. Tel 604-442-8855. *Dir* Peter Gritcher
Estab 1972
Collections: Collection of authentic artifacts, hand-made household articles such as tables, chairs, beds, looms, linen & wool carders, spinning wheels; collection of hand-made tools & implements, antique lamps & stoves, handicrafts, hand-woven linen & wool fabrics & clothing; needlework; embroidery on traditional head shawls; collection of historical materials and photographs

KAMLOOPS

M **KAMLOOPS ART GALLERY,** 207 Seymour St, V2C 2E7. Tel 604-828-3543; FAX 604-828-0662. *Dir* Jann L M Bailey; *Admin Asst* Shelley Whittaker
Open Mon - Sat 10 AM - 5 PM, Sun 1 - 5 PM, summer Mon - Sat 10 AM - 7 PM, cl Sun. Admis fee $1.25. Estab 1978. Two exhibition galleries, 200 running ft & 100 running ft, also children's gallery. Average Annual Attendance: 40,000. Mem: 400; membership fee $100; dues family $40, individual $25, senior citizens $15; annual meeting in Mar & Apr
Income: $450,000 (financed by mem, city & province appropriation, government & fund raising)
Purchases: $20,000
Collections: †Contemporary Canadian Art; †Canadian Prints & Drawings
Exhibitions: Monthly National & International Exhibitions
Publications: Newsletter, 5 times a year; exhibition catalogs
Activities: Classes for adults & children; lectures open to public, 12-15 vis lectr per year; lending collection of 100 paintings; sale shop sells books, magazines, prints & regional crafts

KELOWNA

M **KELOWNA CENTENNIAL MUSEUM AND NATIONAL EXHIBIT CENTRE,** 470 Queensway Ave, V1Y 6S7. Tel 604-763-2417. *Pres* James Baker; *Dir & Cur* Ursula Surtees; *Asst Cur* Dan Bruce; *Asst Cur* Wayne Wilson
Open summer Mon - Sat 10 AM - 5 PM, Sun 2 - 5 PM, winter Tues - Sat 10 AM - 5 PM. No admis fee. Estab 1936 as a community museum, a national exhibit center where traveling exhibits are received and circulated. 12,000 sq ft of display plus storage, workshop & archives; permanent galleries: Natural History, Local History, Ethnography, two exhibit galleries. Average Annual Attendance: 35,000. Mem: 200; dues $7; annual meeting in March
Income: Financed by membership, city and state appropriation
Collections: †Coins & metals; †decorative arts; †enthnography; †general history; †Kelowna History; †natural history
Exhibitions: Changing exhibitions every 4 - 6 weeks
Publications: A Short History of Early Fruit Ranching Kelowna; Lak-La-Hai-Ee Volume III Fishing; Nan, A Childs Eye View of the Okanagan; Sunshine and Butterflies; The Games Grandpa Played, Early Sports in BC
Activities: Classes for adults and children; lect open to public, 6 vis lectr per year; tours; gallery talks; individual paintings & original objects of art lent to qualified museums; book traveling exhibitions, 7 - 8 per yr; originate traveling exhibitions; museum shop sells books, original art, reproductions, prints
L **Library,** 470 Queensway Ave, V1Y 6S7. Tel 604-763-2417.
Library Holdings: Micro — Fiche, prints; AV — Cassettes, motion pictures, slides, v-tapes; Other — Clipping files, manuscripts, original art works, photographs, prints
Collections: Photograph Collection

NANAIMO

M **MALASPINA COLLEGE,** Nanaimo Art Gallery & Exhibition Centre, 900 Fifth St, V9R 5S5. Tel 604-755-8790; FAX 604-755-8725. *Cur* John Charnefski; *Adminr* Linda Martin; *Educ Office* Cathy GIbson
Open 10 AM - 5 PM. No admis fee. Estab 1976 for art, cultural, historical & scientific exhibits, events & educational programs. Two galleries: gallery I is 1300 sq ft with 11 ft ceilings; gallery II is 775 sq ft with 10 ft ceilings
Income: Financed by mem, earned gallery shop, city & state appropriations; schools & school districts
Exhibitions: Art, Cultural, Historical & Scientific exhibits; Street Banner Painting Competition
Publications: Madrona, newsletter, 6 per year
Activities: Children's classes; docent programs; lect open to public, 2 - 3 vis lectr per year; competitions with awards; book traveling exhibitions 10 - 12 per year; retail sells books & prints

PRINCE GEORGE

M **PRINCE GEORGE ART GALLERY,** 2820 15th Ave, V2M 1T1. Tel 604-563-6447. *Pres* Anne Wylie; *VPres* Judy Weninger; *Dir & Cur* Anna Pickett; *Treas* Linda Bishop
Open Tues - Sat 10 AM - 5 PM, Sun 1 - 4 PM, cl Mon. No admis fee. Estab 1970 to foster development of arts and crafts in the community; to foster and promote artists. Old Forestry Building, 2 floors, art rental section; two 1000 sq ft galleries, offices, storages space & small foyer. Average Annual Attendance: 10,000. Mem: 385; dues business $50, family $15, single $10; annual meeting Feb
Income: Financed by provincial & municipal grants, private donations
Collections: Original paintings by British Columbia artists
Exhibitions: Exhibitions held every 4-6 wks, primarily Canadian Artists; Annual Art Auction
Publications: Bi-monthly newsletter
Activities: Lectures open to public; gallery talks; tours for school children; individual paintings and original objects of art rented to members; book traveling exhibitions, 5 per year; sales shop sells original paintings, drawings, pottery, handicrafts, prints, cards

PRINCE RUPERT

M **MUSEUM OF NORTHERN BRITISH COLUMBIA,** Ruth Harvey Art Gallery, McBride St & First Ave, PO Box 669, V8J 3S1. Tel 604-624-3207; FAX 604-627-8009. *Pres* Robert Punnett; *Dir & Cur* Elaine Moore
Open Sept - May Mon - Sat 10 AM - 5 PM, June - Aug Mon - Sat 9 AM - 9 PM, Sun 9 AM - 5 PM. Estab 1924, new building opened 1958, to collect, maintain and display the history of the north coast, particularly of the Prince Rupert area. One main hall has two small side galleries, and a third gallery is the museum art gallery. Average Annual Attendance: 60,000. Mem: 200; dues family $10, individual $6, annual meeting May
Income: $250,000 (financed primarily by municipality and province)
Collections: †Contemporary North Coast Indian art; †historical collections; †native Indian collections; natural history; †photographs
Exhibitions: A continually changing display program; fine arts exhibitions from large galleries; local artists shows
Activities: Classes for adults and children; lect open to public, 3 - 4 vis lectr per yr; gallery talks; tours; harbor tours; demonstrations; native Indian carving shed; museum shop sells books, original art, reproductions, prints, Northwest coast native art (contemporary)
L **Library,** McBride St and First Ave, PO Box 669, V8J 3E7. Tel 604-624-3207. *Dir* Elaine Moore; *Asst Dir* Robin Weber
Open June - Aug Mon - Sat 9 AM - 9 PM, Sun 9 AM - 5 PM, Sept - May Mon - Sat 10 AM - 5 PM, cl Sun. No admis fee. Small reference library for staff
Income: $180,000 (financed by city, province & gift shop)
Library Holdings: Vols 100; Per subs 3; Some archival materials
Special Subjects: Concentration on British Columbia pre-modern history
Exhibitions: Monthly exhibitions
Publications: Newsletter, quarterly
Activities: Educ dept

REVELSTOKE

A **REVELSTOKE ART GROUP,** 315 W First St West, V0E 2S0. Tel 604-837-3067. *Pres & Dir* Bud Stovel; *VPres* Lorna Duncan; *Treas* Valerie Munroe; *Dir* Georgina Gaetz; *Dir* Donna Ony; *Dir* Mary Kwong
Open May - Aug Tues - Sat 10 AM - 8 PM. Estab 1949 to promote and stimulate interest in art by studying art, artists methods and work, developing local interest and interchanging ideas. Average Annual Attendance: 2500. Mem: 30; dues $5; annual meeting in April
Income: $2200 (financed by art show commissions, donations and raffles)
Purchases: $460
Collections: Centennial collection contains 50 watercolours, acrylics and oils by Sophie Atkinson, Art Phillips, Mel Abbott, Mary Wells
Exhibitions: Landscapes by Jack Davis; Weaving & Pottery by Local Artisans; Sr Citizens' Paintings; Snowflake Porcelain Painters; Works by members of the Revelstoke Art Group; Annual fall art show
Activities: Education dept; classes for adults & children; lectures open to public, 3 vis lectr per yr; competitions; original objects of art lent to Selkirk Health Clinic, Moberly Manor and Royal Bank; sales shop sells original art

RICHMOND

A RICHMOND ARTS CENTRE, 7700 Minoru Gate, V6Y 1R9. Tel 604-276-4012. *Coordr* Jane Wheeler
Open Mon - Fri 9 AM - 9 PM, Sat 10 AM - 5 PM, Sun 10 AM - 5 PM. No admis fee. Estab 1967 to provide stimulation and nourishment to the arts in the community
Income: Financed by city appropriation
Publications: Newsletter, monthly
Activities: Classes for adults & children in visual & dramatic arts, ballet & jazz; special events and festivals

SOOKE

M SOOKE REGION MUSEUM & ART GALLERY, PO Box 774, V0S 1N0. Tel 604-642-6351; FAX 604-642-7089. *Dir & Cur* Lee Boyko
Open Tues - Sun 9 AM - 5 PM. Admis donation. Estab 1977 to advance local history & art. Exhibit changes monthly featuring a different local artist or artist group, or segment of museum collection. Average Annual Attendance: 30,000
Collections: Fishing, Logging & Mining Artifacts; Native Indian Crafts (post & pre-contact); Pioneer Implements
Exhibitions: Polemaker's Shack; Moss Cottage; Wreck of Lord Western
Activities: Children classes; docent programs; retail store sells books & prints

SURREY

M SURREY ART GALLERY, 13750 88th Ave, V3W 3L1. Tel 604-596-7461; FAX 604-597-2588. *Cur* Liane Davison; *Dir* Karen Hasselfelt; *Asst Cur* Carol Prokof; *Public Progs Coordr* Ingrid Kolt
Open Fri 9 AM - 5 PM, Tues - Thurs 9 AM - 9 PM, Sat & Sun 1 - 5 PM, cl statutory holidays. No admis fee. Estab 1975. Average Annual Attendance: 32,000
Income: $264,000 (financed by city and provincial appropriation, special private foundations grants, and federal grants per project application)
Purchases: $4200
Collections: Contemporary Canadian Art, mostly works on paper
Exhibitions: (1993) Personal Histories
Publications: Exhibition catalogues; Surrey Arts Center, bi-monthly calendars
Activities: Workshops for school and community groups; docent training; lect open to public, 6 visiting lectr per year; concerts; gallery talks; tours; lending collection contains cassettes, slides and packaged workshop kits; book traveling exhibitions 2 or 3 per year; originates traveling exhibitions
L Library, Surrey Centennial Arts Centre, 13750 88th Ave, V3W 3L1. Tel 604-596-7461; FAX 604-597-2588.
Estab 1975, reference for staff and docents only
Purchases: $300
Library Holdings: Vols 550; Per subs 20; Micro — Cards; AV — Slides; Other — Clipping files, exhibition catalogs

VANCOUVER

M THE CANADIAN CRAFT MUSEUM, 639 Hornby St, V6C 2G3. Tel 604-687-8266; FAX 604-687-7174. *Cur* Lloyd Herman; *Cur Asst* Rachelle Geneau; *Public Relations Asst* Gillian Schick; *Admin Asst* Wendy Rogers
Open Mon - Sat 9:30 AM - 5:30 PM, Sun & holidays noon - 5 PM. Admis Adults $2.50, students & sr citizens $1.50, mem & children under 12 free. Estab 1981 dedicated to public recognition & appreciatoin of excellence in contemporary & historical craft. Main floor 4000 sq ft, Mezzanine has 5 display cases & small pedistal area. Average Annual Attendance: 30,000. Mem: 850; dues individual $37.50, group & family $53.50, annual meeting in May
Income: $203,636 (financed by membership, city & state appropriation & fundraising)
Purchases: $12,000
Collections: †Permanent collection
Exhibitions: Made by Hand: Felt & Paper
Publications: Exhibition catalogues; CCM Communique newsletter, quarterly
Activities: Classes for adults & children; demonstration workshops; lect open to public, 12 - 20 lectr per year; gallery talks; tours; book traveling exhibitions 3 per year; originate traveling exhibitions 3 per year; museum shop sells books, magazines, original art & Canadian craft

A COMMUNITY ARTS COUNCIL OF VANCOUVER, 837 Davie St, V6Z 1B7. Tel 604-683-4358. *Exec Dir* Ingrid Alderson; *Admin Asst* Lisa Sorokan
Open 9 AM - 5 PM. No admis fee. Estab 1946 as a society dedicated to the support of arts, with a wide range of interest in the arts; to promote standards in all art fields including civic arts; also serves as a liaison centre. Exhibition Gallery shows works of semi-professional and emerging artists; 2200 sq ft on two levels, street level entrance. Mem: 500; dues $15; annual meeting in Sept
Income: Financed by British Columbia Cultural and Lotteries Fund, City of Vancouver, membership and donations
Exhibitions: Two shows per month
Publications: Arts Vancouver Magazine, 4 issues per year
Activities: Lectures open to public; performances; workshops; concerts; gallery talks; competitions; scholarships & fels offered; museum shop

M CONTEMPORARY ART GALLERY SOCIETY OF BRITISH COLUMBIA, 555 Hamilton St, V6B 2R1. Tel 604-681-2700; FAX 604-683-2710. *Dir* Linda Milrod; *Admin* Ann Hepper; *Cur* Keith Wallace
Open Tues - Sat 11 AM - 5 PM. No admis fee. Estab 1971 as an exhibition space for contemporary Canadian art; as a non-profit gallery for the City of Vancouver Art Collection and Loan program. The Gallery has a medium sized exhibition area with collection storage and framing area. Average Annual Attendance: 20,000. Mem: 400; dues $15
Income: Financed by Federal Government, consulting fees, British Columbia Cultural Fund, city of Vancouver, and Federal Tax Exemption status under the name of the Greater Vancouver Artists Gallery Society
Collections: †City of Vancouver Art Collection; †Contemporary Gallery Society of B C Art Collection
Exhibitions: (1993) Lorna Brown - Once Removed; After Virtue, Miguel Angel Beneyto; Roy Arden, Photographs; Rebecca Belmore; Nan Groldin; The Ballad of Sexual Dependency, Noel Harding
Publications: Exhibition catalogues
Activities: Lectures open to the public, 10 vis lectr per yr; gallery talks; individual paintings & original objects of art lent to civic agencies; lending collection contains 3400 works
L Art Library Service, 555 Hamilton St, V6B 2R1. Tel 604-681-2700; FAX 604-683-2710. *Dir* Linda Milrod
Open Tues - Sat 11 AM - 5 PM. Estab 1971 for public enhancement, the Gallery provides this service to public agencies for free, commercial agencies pay a fee. Circ 3000
Income: Financed by British Columbia Cultural Fund, Vancouver Civic Cultural Grant, federal grant, consulting, sales
Library Holdings: AV — Slides; Other — Pamphlets
Publications: Brochures; exhibit catalogs

M EMILY CARR COLLEGE OF ART & DESIGN, The Charles H Scott Gallery, 1399 Johnston St, V6H 3R9. Tel 604-844-3800. *Cur* Greg Bellerby; *Admin Asst* Kate Miller
Open Sun - Tues & Thurs - Sat Noon - 5 PM, Wed 9 AM - 1 PM & 4 - 9 PM. No admis fee. Estab 1980 to provide museum quality exhibitions & publications of critically significant visual art. 3000 sq ft gallery with all environmental & security safeguards. Average Annual Attendance: 30,000
Income: $95,000 (financed by provincial appropriation)
Exhibitions: (1991) Adventures on Table Mountain. (1993) Graphic Design; Sunnybrook Installation by Persimmon Blackbridge
Publications: Exhibition catalogues
Activities: Three-year Curatorial Studies Program; tours upon request; book traveling exhibitions, 1-2 per year; originate traveling exhibitions; sales shop sells exhibition catalogues
L Library, 1399 Johnston St, V6H 3R9. Tel 604-844-3800; FAX 604-844-3801. *Acting Library Dir* Donna Zwierciadlowski; *Sr Library Asst* Michael Clark
Open May - Aug Mon - Fri 9 AM - 5 PM, Sept - Apr Mon - Thurs 8:30 AM - 8 PM, Fri 8:30 - 5 PM
Income: Financed by government funding
Library Holdings: Vols 11,792; Per subs 195; Micro — Fiche; AV — A-tapes, rec, slides, v-tapes; Other — Clipping files, exhibition catalogs
Special Subjects: Film, Painting - American, Painting - Canadian, Painting - European, Painting - French, Printmaking, Photography, Posters, Pottery, Pre-Columbian Art, Primitive Art, Prints, Sculpture, Video, Woodcarvings, Electronic Communication Design

UNIVERSITY OF BRITISH COLUMBIA

M Fine Arts Gallery, 1956 Main Mall, V6T 1Z1. Tel 604-822-2759; FAX 604-822-6689. *Cur* Scott Watson; *Prog Asst* Mary Williams
Open Sept - Apr Tues - Fri 10 AM - 5 PM, Sat noon - 5 PM. No admis fee. Estab 1948, The gallery has a mandate to encourage projects conceived for its special content. Our programming emphasizes contemporary art & also projects which serve to further understanding of the history of Avant-Garde. Gallery covers 27,000 sq ft. Average Annual Attendance: 15,000
Income: Financed by departmental funds
Exhibitions: Rotating exhibitions
Publications: Exhibition catalogues; announcements
Activities: Lect open to public, 2 vis lectr per year; gallery talks; originate traveling exhibitions
L Fine Arts Library, 1956 Main Mall, V6T 1Z1. Tel 604-822-2720; Telex 04-53296. *Head Librn* Hans Burndorfer; *Reference Librn* Diana Cooper; *Reference Librn* Peggy McBride
Open Mon - Thurs 8 AM - 11 PM, Fri 8 AM - 5 PM, Sat noon - 5 PM, Sun noon - 8 PM. Estab 1948 to serve students & faculty in all courses related to fine arts, architecture, planning, dance, costume & design
Library Holdings: Vols 150,000; Marburg Index; Dial Iconographic Index; Micro — Fiche, prints, reels; Other — Clipping files, exhibition catalogs, pamphlets, reproductions
Special Subjects: Architecture, fashion design & planning (emphasized in clipping files), Canadian art
Publications: Fine Masters Theses, updated annually; Starts Here (short introductory bibliographies), produced as needed
Activities: Lectures; tours
M Museum of Anthropology, 6393 NW Marine Dr, V6T 1Z2. Tel 604-822-5087; FAX 604-822-2974. *Dir* M M Ames; *Cur Ethnology* Marjorie M Halpin; *Cur Art & Public Prog* Rosa Ho; *Public Information Officer* Kersti Krug; *Cur Documentation* Elizabeth Johnson; *Cur Collections* Carol Mayer; *Graphic Designer, Photographer* Bill McLennan; *Designer* David Cunningham
Open Tues 11 AM - 9 PM, Wed - Sun 11 AM - 5 PM. Admis adults $4, senior citizens & students $2, children $2, family $10, group rates for 20 or more, Tues free. Estab 1976 to develop a high quality institution that maximizes public access & involvement while also conducting active programs of teaching, research & experimentation. Average Annual Attendance: 126,000. Mem: 1000; dues family $30, individual $20, student & senior citizens $15
Collections: Ethnographic tribal areas around the world; oriental art and history; museum journals
Activities: Classes for adults & children; dramatic programs; docent training; field trips; lectures open to public, some for members only, 10 vis lectr per yr; gallery talks; tours; exten dept; original objects of art lent to institutions for special exhibits; book traveling exhibitions; originate traveling exhibitions; museum shop sells books, original art, reproductions, prints, slides & jewelery

M VANCOUVER ART GALLERY, 750 Hornby St, V6Z 2H7. Tel 604-682-4668; FAX 604-682-1086. *Pres* Colin Dobell; *Dir* Willard Holmes; *Senior Cur* Gary Dufour; *Senior Cur* Ian Thom; *Head Public Progs* Judith Mastai; *Head Marketing Development* Janet Meredith; *Head of Exhib* Nancy Kirkpatrick; *Conservator* Monica Smith; *Registrar* Helle Viirlaid

Open Mon, Wed, Fri & Sat 10 AM - 5 PM, Thurs 10 AM - 9 PM, Sun noon - 5 PM, cl Tues, Christmas & New Year's Day. Admis adults $4.25, students with cards & sr citizens $2.50, children under 12 free, Thurs evening pay-what-you-can. Estab 1931 to foster the cultural development of the community and a public interest in the arts. Gallery moved in 1983 into a reconstructed 1907 classical courthouse which had been designed by Francis Rattenbury. The building contains 41,400 net sq ft of gallery space. Complex contains a total gross area of 164,805 sq ft. Average Annual Attendance: 200,000. Mem: 3500; dues family $55, individual $39, sr family $27, student & sr citizen $22
Income: Financed by city, provincial & federal government grants, private & corporate donations
Collections: Emily Carr; 5000 works, including drawings, film, objects, paintings, photographs, prints, sculpture, videotape & watercolors, mostly 20th century Canadian works
Activities: Classes for adults & children; docent training; lectures open to the public; gallery talks; tours; individual paintings and original objects of art lent to museums who comply with security and climate control standards; originate traveling exhibitions; gallery shop sells books, magazines, reproductions, postcards, posters, native Indian art, jewelry, goods in leather, paper & wood by local artisans

L **Library,** 750 Hornby St, V6Z 2H7. Tel 604-682-4668; FAX 604-682-1086. *Librn* Cheryl A Siegel
Open Mon, Wed & Thurs 1 - 5 PM. Estab 1931 to serve staff, docents, students & the public. For reference only
Library Holdings: Vols 9500; Per subs 135; Micro — Fiche; Other — Clipping files, exhibition catalogs 15,000, memorabilia, pamphlets, photographs
Special Subjects: Fine arts specializing in Canadian and contemporary art

L **VANCOUVER CITY ARCHIVES,** 1150 Chestnut St, V6J 3J9. Tel 604-736-8561. *Dir* Sue M Baptie; *Deputy Dir* John K Chang
Open Mon - Fri 9:30 AM - 5:30 PM, other times by appointment, cl weekends and legal holidays. No admis fee. Estab 1933
Income: Financed by city appropriation
Library Holdings: Charts, Civic Records, Drawings, Maps, Paintings; Other — Manuscripts, prints
Exhibitions: Temporary exhibitions
Activities: Lect open to public; tours

M **VANCOUVER MUSEUM ASSOCIATION,** Vancouver Museum, 1100 Chestnut St, V6J 3J9. Tel 604-736-4431; FAX 604-736-5417.
Estab 1894 as a civic museum reflecting the history & natural history of the area & its peoples. Mem: dues family $30, adult $20
Activities: Children's classes; docent programs; lect open to public; retail store

L **Vancouver Museum Library,** 1100 Chestnut St, V6J 3J9
For reference
Library Holdings: Vols 9000; Per subs 30; AV — A-tapes, cassettes, v-tapes; Other — Clipping files, exhibition catalogs, pamphlets
Special Subjects: American Indian Art, Anthropology, Archaeology, Asian Art, Decorative Arts, Eskimo Art, Folk Art, Historical Material, Mexican Art, Oriental Art

M **VANCOUVER PUBLIC LIBRARY,** Fine Arts & Music Div, 750 Burrard St, Fine Arts Div, V6Z 1X5. Tel 604-665-3388; FAX 604-665-2265. *Librn* Musa Tryon; *Visual Materials Librn* Susan Bridgman
Open Mon - Thurs 9:30 AM - 9:30 PM, Fri & Sat 9:30 AM - 6 PM, cl Sun. Estab 1960; Library estab 1903
Library Holdings: Vols 100,000; Per subs 500; AV — Cassettes, lantern slides, slides, v-tapes; Other — Clipping files, exhibition catalogs, pamphlets, photographs, prints
Collections: Negatives & Prints of early Vancouver & the Yukon

VERNON

M **VERNON ART GALLERY** (Formerly Topham Brown Public Art Gallery), 206-3203 30th St, V1T 9G9. Tel 604-545-3173. *Dir* Susan Brandoli; *Admin Asst* June Bender; *Art Educ* Jude Clarke; *Gift Shop Coordr* Pamela Burns-Resch
Open Mon - Fri 10 AM - 5 PM, Sat noon - 4 PM. No admis fee. Estab 1967 for the collection & exhibition of art work by Okanagan, national & international artists. Two gallery spaces professionally designed & measures 2200 sq ft, also reception area, gift shop & administrative/kitchen area. Average Annual Attendance: 24,000. Mem: 350; dues family $20, individual $15, sr citizen & student $10
Income: Financed by membership, city appropriation and grants
Collections: Permanent collection consists of ceramics, paintings, prints, sculpture and serigraphs
Exhibitions: 14 exhibits annually
Publications: Art Quarterly
Activities: Classes for adults & children; docent training; lect, 3 vis lectr per year; gallery talks; concerts; tours; performances; competitions; fels; book traveling exhibitions, 3 - 4 per year; originate traveling exhibitions; museum shop sells books, magazines, original art, reproductions & local crafts

VICTORIA

M **ART GALLERY OF GREATER VICTORIA,** 1040 Moss St, V8V 4P1. Tel 604-384-4101; FAX 604-361-3995. *Pres* Robert Gull; *Dir* Patricia A Bovey; *Asst Dir & Chief Cur* Nicholas Tuele; *Cur Asian Art* Barry Till; *Educ Officer* Nancy Klazek; *Financial Officer* Linda Mary Giles
Open Mon, Tues, Wed, Fri, Sat 10 AM - 5 PM, Thurs 10 AM - 9 PM, Sun 1 - 5 PM. Admis nonmembers $4, students $2, children under 12 free. Estab 1949. Six modern galleries adjoin 19th Century Spencer Mansion-Japanese Garden. Average Annual Attendance: 56,500. Mem: 3000; dues family $30, individual $20, student & non-resident $10; annual meeting 2nd wk of June
Income: $700,000 (financed by membership, city, federal and provincial grants)
Collections: Chinese, Indian, Persian and Tibetan Art; Contemporary Canadian, American and European; European Painting and Decorative Arts from 16th -

19th Centuries; Japanese Art from Kamakura to Contemporary; Primitive Arts
Exhibitions: Approx 35 exhibitions in 6 exhibition halls, changing every 6 weeks
Publications: Membership newsletter, 6 times a year
Activities: Classes for adults & children; docent training; gallery in the schools program; workshops; lectures open to public, 12 vis lectr per year; concerts; tours; exten dept serves BC; individual paintings and original objects of art lent to museums and local public buildings; lending collection contains 4800 books, 20 cassettes, original art works, 5000 original prints, 400 sculpture, 2000 slides, 300 scrolls; book traveling exhibitions, 5-20 per yr; originate traveling exhibitions; sales shop sells books, magazines, reproductions, stationery, jewelry, pottery, ornaments, glass & prints

L **Library,** 1040 Moss St, V8V 4P1. Tel 604-384-4101; FAX 604-361-3995. *Librn* Mrs J M Paige
Open Mon 11:30 AM - 1 PM by appt only. Estab 1951. For reference only
Income: $1000
Purchases: $1000
Library Holdings: Vols 4800; Per subs 46; Micro — Fiche; AV — Slides; Other — Clipping files, exhibition catalogs, pamphlets, reproductions
Special Subjects: Asian Art, Canadian Art

L **BRITISH COLUMBIA ARCHIVES & RECORDS SERVICE,** 655 Belleville St, V8V 1X4. Tel 604-387-5885; FAX 604-387-2072. *Dir* John A Bovey; *Head, Visual Records Unit* J R Davison
Open Mon - Fri 8:45 AM - 4:45 PM. Estab 1893 to collect and preserve all records relating to the historical development of British Columbia
Income: Financed by provincial appropriation
Library Holdings: Vols 51,000; Per subs 300; original documents; maps; Micro — Reels; AV — A-tapes; Other — Clipping files, exhibition catalogs, manuscripts, original art works, pamphlets, photographs
Special Subjects: British Columbia history
Publications: Art reproductions

A **BRITISH COLUMBIA MUSEUMS ASSOCIATION,** 514 Government St, V8V 4X4. Tel 604-387-3315. *Exec Dir* David A E Spalding
Open Mon - Fri 8:30 AM - 4:30 PM. Estab 1956 supports museums & art galleries of British Columbia
Activities: Training in museum methods

M **CRAIGDARROCH CASTLE HISTORICAL MUSEUM SOCIETY,** 1050 Joan Crescent, Station B, V8S 3L5. Tel 604-592-5323. *Exec Dir* Bruce W Davies; *Regisgtrar & Technician* Dalphine Castle; *Vol Coordr* Bill Blore
Open daily. Admis $3. Estab 1959 for conservation & restoration of house. Average Annual Attendance: 120,000. Mem: 500; annual dues $10, annual meeting spring
Income: $300,000 (financed by visitation)
Activities: Docent training; lect open to public; museum shop sells books, magazines, original art, reproductions, souvenirs

M **EMILY CARR GALLERY ARCHIVES,** Parliament Bldg, 1107 Wharf St, V8V 1X4. Tel 604-384-3130. *Cur* Linda McNayr
Open Tues - Sat 10 AM - 4:30 PM. Estab 1977. Average Annual Attendance: 25,000
Collections: Art by Emily Carr; historical documents & records
Activities: Lectures open to the public; tours; paintings & original objects of art are lent ot accredited institutions; sales shop sells art reproductions

A **OPEN SPACE,** 510 Fort St, V8W 1E6. Tel 604-383-8833. *Dir* Sue Donaldson
Open Tues - Sat 12 - 5 PM, cl Mon & Sun. No admis fee. Estab 1975 for the encouragement and promotion of photography as a fine art and of those photographers, particularly in Western Canada, who are engaged in making photographs as art. The program emphasis is on new forms of photography. Gallery has 3000 sq ft, 220 running ft with full light grid controlled to level for works of art on paper. Average Annual Attendance: 10,000. Mem: 230; dues $10
Income: $110,000 (financed by federal & provincial appropriations, city grants, donations & mem fees)
Exhibitions: 10 - 12 contemporary visual art exhibitions per year
Publications: B C Photos 1978, Photos 1979; Secession Excerpts from the Literature of Photography, periodic; Stereo Bookwork
Activities: Lect; gallery talks; tours; performance productions; music concerts; literary readings; book traveling exhibitions, 2-3 per year; originate traveling exhibitions

M **UNIVERSITY OF VICTORIA,** Maltwood Art Museum and Gallery, PO Box 3025, V8W 3P2. Tel 604-721-8298; FAX 604-721-8997. *Dir & Cur* Martin Segger; *Pres* Dr H Petch; *VPres* T Matthews; *Chmn of Board* Dr S Scully; *Secy-Registrar* B Jackson
Open Mon - Fri 10 AM - 4 PM, Sun Noon - 4 PM. No admis fee. Estab 1968 to collect, preserve and exhibit the decorative arts. Gallery has 3000 sq ft of environmentally controlled exhibition space. Average Annual Attendance: 150,000
Income: $200,000 (financed by endowment & state appropriation)
Purchases: $25,000
Collections: †Maltwood Collection of Decorative Art; †contemporary art (Canadian)
Exhibitions: Permanent collections, continuing and rotating
Activities: Lect open to public, 3 visiting lectr per year; gallery talks; tours; individual paintings lent to offices & public spaces on campus; lending collection contains 1500 original prints, 1000 paintings & sculpture; book traveling exhibitions 5 per year; originate traveling exhibitions

MANITOBA

BRANDON

A **THE ART GALLERY OF SOUTHWESTERN MANITOBA,** 638 Princess Ave, R7A 0P3. Tel 204-727-1036; FAX 204-726-8139. *Dir* Glenn Allison
Open Mon - Sat 9 AM - 5 PM, Sun 2 - 5 PM. No admis fee. Estab 1960 to promote and foster cultural activities in Western Manitoba. Average Annual Attendance: 2400. Mem: 700; dues $6 - $20; annual meeting May
Income: Financed by membership, city and provincial appropriations and federal grants
Exhibitions: Exhibitions of regional, national & international significance
Publications: Bulletin, every 2 months
Activities: Classes for adults and children; lect open to public, 2 visiting lectrs per year; gallery talks; tours; competitions; individual paintings and original objects of art lent to members; lending collection contains original art works, original prints, paintings, weavings

L **Centennial Library - Arts Complex,** R7A 0P3. Tel 204-727-6648. *Chief Librn* Kathy Thornborough
Open to members
Library Holdings: Vols 10,000

CHURCHILL

M **ESKIMO MUSEUM,** 242 La Verendrye, PO Box 10, R0B 0E0. Tel 204-675-2030. *Dir* Bishop Reynald Rouleau; *Cur* Lorraine Brandson
Open Mon - Sat 9 AM - noon & 1 - 5 PM, Sun 1 - 4 PM. No admis fee. Estab 1944 to depict the Eskimo way of life through the display of artifacts. Museum has large single display room. Average Annual Attendance: 10,000
Income: Administered and funded by the Roman Catholic Episcopal Corporation of Churchill Hudson Bay
Collections: †Contemporary Inuit carvings; ethnographic collections; prehistoric artifacts; wildlife specimens
Publications: The Churchill Eskimo Museum by Jeannine Veisse
Activities: Films and slide shows for school groups upon request; tours upon request; original objects of art lent to special exhibits and galleries; sales shop sells books, magazines, and original art

L **Library,** 242 La Verendrye, PO Box 10, R0B 0E0. Tel 204-675-2030. *Cur* Lorraine Brandson
Estab mainly for Arctic Canada material
Purchases: $200
Library Holdings: Vols 500; Other — Clipping files, exhibition catalogs, photographs
Special Subjects: Archaeology, Crafts, Eskimo Art, Ethnology, Restoration & Conservation, European exploration of Arctic Canada

DAUPHIN

M **DAUPHIN & DISTRICT ALLIED ARTS COUNCIL,** 104 First Ave NW, R7N 1G9. Tel 204-638-6231. *Admınr* Bernice Einarson
Open noon - 5 PM. Estab 1973 to provide a home for the arts in the Dauphin District. Average Annual Attendance: 20,000. Mem: dues association $25, family $15, individual $5; annual meeting in Mar
Income: $100,000 (financed by membership, town appropriation, provincial appropriation, donations)
Publications: Arts council newsletter, quarterly
Activities: Classes for adults & children; dramatic programs; lending collection contains paintings & art objects; book traveling exhibitions 12 per yr; originate traveling exhibitions

PORTAGE LA PRAIRIE

A **PORTAGE AND DISTRICT ARTS COUNCIL,** 160 Saskatchewan Ave W, R1N 0M1. Tel 204-239-6029. *Exec Dir* Karen Braden; *Exec Asst* Nettie Fletcher; *Office Coordr* Ilene Jackson
Open Mon - Fri 9 AM - 5 PM, Sat 10 AM - 5 PM. Financed by donations. Estab 1976 to coordinate body of art groups. 1240 sq ft (146 running ft) exhibition area, hanging system - chain & hook, sculpture stands, display stands, shelves & cases. Average Annual Attendance: 5000. Mem: 420; dues $10; annual meeting in June
Income: Financed by commission on sale of art, mem, fees, government grants, ticket sales & fundraising events
Exhibitions: (1992) 15th Anniversary of Portage & District Arts Council; Contrasts. (1993) Country Vision; Exhibition from Winnipeg Art Gallery; Sold To the Highest Bidder; Mennonite Artists; Music & Arts Festival - Visual Arts; Hosting Central Region Juried Art Show at Portage Community Centre; For the Love of It; Habitual Perfection; Central Region Juried Art Show Tour; Lovers & Friends; Dufresne - Watercolors; Mauws - Photography; Rural Manitoba - Winnipeg Art Gallery; Smith - Mixed Media; Hart - Papier-mache
Publications: Newsletter, Sept - June
Activities: Classes for adults & children; dramatic programs; lect open to public, 6 vis lectr per year; concerts; gallery talks; tours; competitions with awards; individual paintings & original objects of art lent to members, private individuals & businesses; lending collection contains books, color reproductions, original artworks & paintings; sales shop sells handcrafted pottery, stained glass, jewelry, stationery, books, original art, reproductions, prints, photo cards

WINNIPEG

L **CRAFTS GUILD OF MANITOBA, INC,** Library, 183 Kennedy St, R3C 1S6. Tel 204-943-1190. *Librn* Moira Wilson
Open to members only. For lending & reference
Income: $1500 (financed by mem)
Library Holdings: Vols 1500; Per subs 22
Special Subjects: Carpets & Rugs, Ceramics, Crafts, Dolls, Embroidery, Eskimo Art, Glass, Handicrafts, Pottery, Textiles
Collections: Crafts

A **MANITOBA ASSOCIATION OF ARCHITECTS,** 137 Bannatyne Ave, 2nd Fl, R3B 0R3. Tel 204-925-4620. *Pres* R Eastwood
Open Mon - Fri 9 AM - 5 PM. Established 1906 as a Provincial Architectural Registration Board and professional governing body. Mem: 350; dues $375; annual meeting Feb
Income: Financed by annual membership dues
Publications: Newsletter, 4 times a yr
Activities: The Manitoba Association of Architects has established a joint lectureship fund with the School of Architecture at the University of Manitoba, & has established a practice of bringing three or more outstanding lecturers to Winnipeg each yr for university & public lectures

M **MANITOBA HISTORICAL SOCIETY,** Dalnavert Museum, 61 Carlton St, R3C 1N7. Tel 204-943-2835. *Pres Manitoba Historical Society* Doug Taylor; *Secy* Betty Summers; *Chmn Management Committee* John White; *Cur* Timothy Worth; *Cur Asst* Nancy Anderson
Open summer 10 AM - 6 PM, winter noon - 5 PM. Admis adults $3, senior citizens and students $2, children $1. Estab 1975 to preserve and display the way of life of the 1895 well-to-do family. Average Annual Attendance: 9000
Income: $40,000 (financed by membership, city and state appropriation and private donation)
Collections: Home furnishings of the 1895 period: clothing, decorative arts material, furniture, household items, paintings and original family memorabilia
Activities: Classes for children; docent training; lectures open to the public, 6 vis lectr per yr; sales shop sells books, postcards and tourist material

A **MANITOBA SOCIETY OF ARTISTS,** 504 Daer Blvd, R3K 1C5. Tel 204-837-1754. *Pres* Tony Kuluk
Estab 1901 to further the work of the artist at the local and community levels. Mem: 60; dues $20; annual meeting Oct
Income: Financed by membership and commission on sales
Exhibitions: Annual competition & exhibition open to all residents of Manitoba
Activities: Educ aspects include teaching by members in rural areas and artist-in-residence work in public schools; workshops; lect open to public; gallery talks; tours; competitions with awards; scholarships; originate traveling exhibitions

L **PROVINCIAL ARCHIVES OF MANITOBA,** 200 Vaughan St, R3C 1T5. Tel 204-945-3971. *Provincial Archivist* Peter Bower
Open June - Labour Day Mon - Fri 9 AM - 4 PM, mid-Sept - May Tues - Sat 9 AM - 4 PM. No admis fee. Estab 1952 to gain access to Manitoba's documentary heritage; to preserve the recorded memory of Manitoba
Income: Financed by provincial appropriation through the Minister of Culture, Heritage & Recreation
Collections: Documentary & archival paintings, drawings, prints & photographs relating to Manitoba
Activities: Individual paintings & original objects of art lent to public institutions with proper security; book traveling exhibitions

M **UKRAINIAN CULTURAL AND EDUCATIONAL CENTRE,** 184 Alexander Ave E, R3B 0L6. Tel 204-942-0218; FAX 204-943-2857. *Exec Dir* Eugene Cherwick; *Cur* Shawna Balas; *Archivist* Zenon Hluszok; *Educ Exten Coordr* Katrusia Stolar; *Exec Asst* Phyllis Hawryliuk; *Secy* Judy Kapty
Open Tues - Sat 10 AM - 4 PM; Sun 2 - 5 PM, cl Mon. No admis fee. Estab as the largest Ukrainian cultural resource centre and repository of Ukrainian historical and cultural artifacts in North America. Mem: 2000; dues $15, annual meeting June
Income: $216,328 (financed by province of Manitoba, federal government, donations, memberships, trust fund, fund raising events)
Collections: Ukrainian Folk Art; †folk costumes; †embroidery; †weaving; †pysanky (Easter eggs); †woodcarving; †ceramics; coins, postage stamps and documents of the Ukrainian National Republic of 1918-1921; works of art by Ukrainian, Ukrainian Canadian and Ukrainian American artists: †prints, †paintings, †sculpture; archives: †Ukrainian immigration to Canada, †music collections
Publications: Visti Oseredok/News from Oseredok, members' bulletin, 2-3 times per yr
Activities: Classes for adults and children; workshops; lectures open to the public; gallery talks; tours; competitions; scholarships; individual paintings and original objects of art lent to educational institutions, galleries and museums; lending collection contains color reproductions, framed reproductions, motion pictures, phonorecords, 40,000 photographs, 2000 slides; book traveling exhibitions, annually; originate traveling exhibitions; sales shop sells books, original art, reproductions, prints, folk art, phonorecords, cassettes

M **Gallery,** 184 Alexander Ave E, R3B 0L6. Tel 204-942-0218; FAX 204-943-2857. *Gallery Cur* Shawna Balas
Mem: Dues family & organization $25, individual $15, student & senior citizen $5
Collections: 18th Century Icons; Contemporary Graphics (Archipenko, Gritchenko, Trutoffsky, Krycevsky, Hluschenko, Pavlos, Kholodny, Hnizdovsky, Mol, Levytsky, Shostak, Kuch); Contemporary Ukrainian; †Canadian Collection
Exhibitions: Works by visiting Ukrainian, Canadian, American and European artists; permanent collection

L **Library and Archives,** 184 Alexander Ave E, R3B 0L6. Tel 204-942-0218; FAX 204-943-2857. *Librn* Tamara L Opar
For reference only
Library Holdings: Vols 30,000; Newspapers and periodicals in the Ukrainian

language; AV — Cassettes, motion pictures, rec, slides, v-tapes; Other — Clipping files, exhibition catalogs, pamphlets, photographs
Special Subjects: Ukrainian Studies
Publications: Visti, newsletter

M **UNIVERSITY OF MANITOBA,** Gallery III, School of Art, R3T 2N2. Tel 204-474-9322; FAX 204-269-6629. *Dir* Dale Amundson
Open Mon - Fri noon - 4 PM. No admis fee. Estab 1965. Gallery III estab 1965 to provide exhibitions of contempory art & activities on the university campus; exhibitions open to the public. Average Annual Attendance: 20,000
Collections: †Contemporary Canadian and American painting, prints and sculpture; Fitzgerald Study Collection
Exhibitions: Exhibitions of Canadian, European and American Art, both contemporary and historical; special exhibitions from other categories; annual exhibitions by the graduating students of the School of Art
Publications: Exhibition catalogues
Activities: Discussion groups; workshops; lectures open to the public, 3 - 6 vis lectr per yr; gallery talks; individual paintings & original objects of art lent; book traveling exhibitions, 2 - 4 per yr; originate traveling exhibitions
M **Faculty of Architecture Exhibition Centre,** Architecture II Bldg, R3T 2N2. Tel 204-474-9558. *Dir Exhib* Alf Simon
Open Mon - Fri 9 AM - 10:30 PM, Sat 9 AM - 5 PM. Estab 1959 with the opening of the new Faculty of Architecture Building to provide architectural and related exhibitions for students and faculty on the University campus and particularly for architecture students. Exhibitions also open to the public. Average Annual Attendance: 15,000
Exhibitions: Exhibitions from National Gallery of Canada, Smithsonian Institution, American Federation of Arts, Museum of Modern Art and from other private and public sources; annual exhibitions by the students in the Faculty of Architecture
Activities: Lect; gallery talks; symposia
L **Architecture & Fine Arts Library,** 206 Russell, MB R3T 2N2. Tel 204-474-9216; FAX 204-269-8357; Telex 07-587721. *Head Librn* Mary Lochead; *Reference Librn* Love Negrych
Open Mon - Thurs 8:30 AM - 9 PM, Fri 8:30 AM - 5 PM, Sat 10:30 AM - 5 PM, Sun 1 - 5 PM. Estab 1916 to serve the needs of students and faculty in the areas of architecture, fine arts, landscape architecture, environmental studies, city and regional planning, graphic design, interior design and photography. Circ 100,000
Income: Financed primarily by provincial government
Library Holdings: Vols 60,000; Per subs 300; Product catalogs 1130; Micro — Fiche 560, reels 210; AV — A-tapes 75; Other — Clipping files, pamphlets, photographs, reproductions 776
Special Subjects: Architecture, Interior Design, Landscape Architecture, Photography, City & Regional Planning, Design, Environmental Studies, Fine Arts, Sculpture

M **WINNIPEG ART GALLERY,** 300 Memorial Blvd, R3C 1V1. Tel 204-786-6641; FAX 204-788-4998. *Assoc Dir, Operations* Mary Lou McGurran; *Assoc Dir, Development & Communications* James August; *Assoc Dir, Interpretive Servs* Claudette Lagimodiere; *Assoc Dir, Curatorial Servs* Jon Tupper; *Public Relations Mgr* Terry Aseltine; *Cur of Contemporary Art* Shirley Madill; *Assoc Cur of Decorative Art* Kathleen Campbell; *Assoc Cur of Historical Art* Gary Essar; *Assoc Cur of Inuit Art* Darlene Wight; *Photographer* Ernest Mayer; *Designer* Tiana Karras; *Art Educator* Donna Bolster; *Art Educator* Liz Coffman; *Registrar* Karen Kislow; *Personnel Mgr* Mary Ann Stayner
Open Tues, Fri, Sat 11 AM - 5 PM, Wed & Thurs 11 AM - 9 PM, Sun Noon - 5 PM. Admis family $5, adult $3, sr citizen & student $2, children under 12 free. Estab 1912, incorporated 1963. Rebuilt and relocated 1968, opened 1972, to present a diversified, quality level program of art in all media, representing various cultures, past and present. Building includes 9 galleries as well as displays on mezzanine level, sculpture court and main foyer. Average Annual Attendance: 250,000. Mem: 4400; dues family $50, individual $35, student & sr citizen $20, sr citizen couple $30; annual meeting in Aug
Income: $3,500,000 (financed by endowment, membership, city, state and federal appropriation)
Collections: Canadian art; contemporary Canada; contemporary Manitoba; decorative arts; Inuit art; European art; Gort Collection; Master prints & drawings; modern European art; †photography
Exhibitions: The changing exhibition includes contemporary and historical works of art by Canadian, European & American artists
Publications: Tableau (calendar of events), monthly; exhibition catalogs
Activities: Classes for adults and children; docent training; lectures open to public, 20-30 vis lectr per yr; concerts; gallery talks; tours; exten dept serves Manitoba, Canada, United States & Europe; individual paintings & original objects of art lent to centres & museums; originate traveling exhibitions; sales shop sells books, gift items, prints, reproductions and slides
L **Clara Lander Library,** 300 Memorial Blvd, R3C 1V1. Tel 204-786-6641, Ext 237. *Chief Librn* Tamara L Opar
Open Tues - Fri 11 AM - 5 PM. Estab 1954 to serve as a source of informational and general interest materials for members and staff of the Winnipeg Art Gallery and to art history students. Circ 1500
Income: Financed by membership, city and provincial appropriations
Purchases: $10,000
Library Holdings: Vols 19,500; Per subs 40; original documents; Micro — Fiche, reels; AV — Slides; Other — Clipping files, exhibition catalogs, manuscripts, memorabilia, pamphlets, photographs, prints, reproductions
Special Subjects: Eskimo Art, Canadian Art, George Swinton Collection
Collections: Archival material pertaining to Winnipeg Art Gallery; Rare Books on Canadian and European Art; George Swinton Collection on Eskimo and North American Indian art and culture

NEW BRUNSWICK

CAMPBELLTON

M **GALERIE RESTIGOUCHE GALLERY,** 39 Andrew St, PO Box 674, E3N 3H1. Tel 506-753-5750; FAX 506-759-9601. *Dir & Cur* Colette Bourgoin
Open Mon - Fri 9 AM - 5 PM, Tues - Thurs evenings 7 - 9 PM, Sat 2 - 5 PM. No admis fee. Estab 1975 for exhibitions and activities. Building has 4800 sq ft; the Exhibition Hall is 1500 sq ft, small gallery 400 sq ft; 230 running feet. Average Annual Attendance: 20,000-25,000. Mem: 185; dues $15
Income: $100,000 (financed by federal, provincial & city appropriations, by Friends of the Gallery & by private donations)
Publications: Exhibitions catalogues; Restigouche Gallery brochure
Activities: Classes for adults and children; art and craft workshops; lectures open to public, 10 vis lectr per year; concerts; gallery talks; tours; traveling exhibitions exten service; originate traveling exhibitions

FREDERICTON

M **BEAVERBROOK ART GALLERY,** 703 Queen St, PO Box 605, E3B 5A6. Tel 506-459-7450; FAX 506-459-7450. *Dir* Ian G Lumsden; *Financial Adminr* Angela Flynn; *Education & Communications Officer* Caroline Walker; *Cur* Tom Smart
Open Tues - Sat 10 AM - 5 PM, Sun - Mon noon - 5 PM. Admis adults $3, srs $2, students $1, children under 6 free. Estab 1959 to foster & promote the study & the public enjoyment & appreciation of the arts. Major galleries upstairs: British, Canadian & High Galleries & Pillow Porcelain Room. East wing galleries: Hosmer, Pillow-Vaughan Gallery, Sir Max Aitken Gallery & Vaulted Corridor Gallery. Downstairs galleries: exhibition gallery & Foyer Gallery. Average Annual Attendance: 30,000. Mem: 800; dues couple $25, single, firms & organizations $15
Income: $670,000 (financed by endowment & private foundation)
Purchases: $330,000
Collections: Works by Dali, Reynolds, Gainsborough, Hogarth, Sutherland, Constable, Turner & Cornelius Krieghoff; 16th-20th century English paintings; 18th & early 19th century English porcelain; 19th & 20th century Canadian paintings; Hosmer-Pillow-Vaughan collection of Continental European fine & decorative arts from the 14th to 19th century
Exhibitions: (1991) Printmaking in Quebec: 1900-1950; Ernest Cormier (architect); Gainsborough in Canada; The Marion McCain Juried Exhibition. (1992) Daniel Solomon; John Boyle Retrospective; Jonathan Kenworthy (sculpture); The Architecture of Edward and William S Maxwell; Immolation: Graham Metson. (1993) William Blake & his Contemporaries: Prints & Drawings from the National Gallery of Canada; The Nan Gregg Gift; Fallout: Chernobyl Through the Eyes of Soviet Children; Light, Air & Colour: American Impressionist Paintings from the Collection of the Pennsylvania Academy of the Fine Arts; Studio Watch: Sarah Petit - Modern Times; Chris Cran: Ileads; Tauromaquia: Goya - Picasso; Studio Watch: Terry Graff - Ectopia; Fred Ross & the Tradition of Figurative Painting in Saint John; Dan Steeves; Through the Looking Glass: Self Portraits of Leslie Poole
Publications: The New Brunswick Landscape Print: 1760-1880; The Murray & Marguerite Vaughan Inuit Print Collection; The Beaverbrook Art Gallery; exhibition catalogs; Tableau announcing gallery's program; annual report
Activities: Classes for adults & children; docent training; lect open to the public, 6 vis lectr per year; gallery talks; tours; films; competitions with cash awards; exten dept serves New Brunswick as well as the rest of Canada; individual paintings lent to recognized art galleries and museums which operate as educational institutions; collection contains 1575 original art works, sculpture; book traveling exhibitions; originate traveling exhibitions; sales shop sells books, magazines, reproductions, exhibition catalogs, Christmas cards, postcards & hasty-notes
L **Library,** 703 Queen St, E3B 5A6. Tel 506-458-8545; FAX 506-459-7450. *Librn* Barry Henderson
Open to gallery personnel only, for reference
Library Holdings: AV — V-tapes; Other — Exhibition catalogs
Special Subjects: Painting - British, Painting - Canadian, Painting - European
Publications: Auction Catalogs

M **FREDERICTON NATIONAL EXHIBITION CENTRE,** Queen St, PO Box 6000, E3B 5H1. Tel 506-453-3747; FAX 506-459-0481. *Exhib Dir* Carolyn Cole
Open summer Mon - Thurs & Sat 10 AM - 5 PM, Fri 10 AM - 9 PM, Sun 1 - 5 PM. No admis fee. Estab 1976. Gallery deals with traveling & local exhibitions. Average Annual Attendance: 18,000
Income: Financed by federal and provincial appropriation
Activities: Classes for adults and children; lectures open to public; concerts; gallery talks; tours; book traveling exhibitions 10 - 12 per year

A **NEW BRUNSWICK COLLEGE OF CRAFT & DESIGN,** PO Box 6000, E3B 5H1. Tel 506-457-7352; FAX 506-457-7352. *Dir* George Fry
Open Mon - Fri 8:30 AM - 4:30 PM. Estab 1947 as a training school for professional craftspeople. Small gallery, craft related shows monthly. Average Annual Attendance: 1800
Income: Financed by provincial government
Exhibitions: Student & staff juried shows; periodic vis exhibitions
Publications: Provincial Craft Directory
Activities: Classes for adults; lectures open to public, 12 vis lectr per year; concerts; competition with award; scholarships; original objects of art lent; craft objects lent; originate traveling exhibitions
L **Library,** PO Box 6000, E3B 5H1. Tel 506-453-2305; FAX 506-457-7352.
A very small but growing library which is primarily for students & craftsmen
Income: Financed by government & book donations
Library Holdings: Vols 3500; Per subs 35; AV — Fs, Kodachromes, motion pictures; Other — Exhibition catalogs, memorabilia, pamphlets, photographs
Special Subjects: Advertising Design, Aesthetics, American Indian Art, Antiquities-Egyptian, Antiquities-Greek, Antiquities-Oriental, Antiquities-Roman, Architecture, Art Education, Art History, Asian Art, Calligraphy, Carpets & Rugs, Ceramics, Commercial Art
Publications: Computerized catalogue

M UNIVERSITY OF NEW BRUNSWICK, Art Centre, University Ave, PO Box 4400, E3B 5A3. Tel 506-453-4623; FAX 506-453-4599; Telex 014-46202. *Dir* Marie Maltais
Open Mon - Fri 10 AM - 5 PM, Sun 2 - 4 PM, cl Sat. No admis fee. Estab 1940 to broaden the experience of the university students and serve the city and province. Two galleries, each with approx 100 running ft of wall space; display case. Average Annual Attendance: 23,000
Income: Financed by provincial university and grants for special projects
Purchases: $7000
Collections: Chiefly New Brunswick Artists; some Canadian (chiefly printmakers)
Publications: Chiefly New Brunswick Artists; Canadian artists
Activities: Classes for adults; lect open to public, 2 visiting lectr per year; gallery talks; tours; individual paintings & original objects of art lent to public but secure areas on this campus & the university campus in Saint John, & reproductions to students; lending collection contains 200 framed reproductions, 400 original prints, 700 paintings, photographs, 10 sculptures & 1000 slides; book traveling exhibitions 4 per year; originate traveling exhibitions

HAMPTON

M KINGS COUNTY HISTORICAL SOCIETY AND MUSEUM, General Delivery, Sussex Corner, E0G 1Z0. Tel 506-832-6009, 534-2576. *Pres* Mary Powers; *Cur* John J Corey; *Treas* Nancy Meech
Open Mon - Sat 10 AM - 5 PM, Sun 2 - 5 PM. Admis adult $1, children 5 & under free. Estab 1968 to preserve loyalist history and artifacts. Maintains small reference library. Average Annual Attendance: 1400. Mem: annual dues $10
Income: $2250 (financed by provincial & student grants, dues, fairs & book sales)
Collections: Coin; dairy; glass; 1854 brass measures; jewelry; quilts
Exhibitions: School exhibitions; Women's Institute; Special Quilt Fair
Publications: Newsletters
Activities: Tours for children; lect open to public; 7 vis lectr per yr; tours; sales shop sells books

MONCTON

M GALERIE D'ART DE L'UNIVERSITE DE MONCTON, 85th Ed Ficfclment Corter, E1A 3E9. Tel 506-858-4088. *Dir* Luc Charette; *Secy* Necol LaBlanc; *Technician* Paul Bourque
Open Mon - Fri 10 AM - 5 PM, Sat - Sun 1 - 5 PM. No admis fee. Estab 1965 to offer outstanding shows to the university students and to the public. 400 linear ft wall space, 3500 sq ft vinyl plywood walls, controlled light, temperature, humidity systems, security system. Average Annual Attendance: 13,000
Income: $100,000 (financed through university)
Collections: Artists represented in permanent collection: Bruno Bobak; Alex Colville; Francis Coutellier; Tom Forrestall; Georges Goguen; Hurtubise; Hilda Lavoie; Fernand Leduc; Rita Letendre; Toni Onley; Claude Roussel; Romeo Savoie; Pavel Skalnik; Gordon Smith
Exhibitions: (1986) Etudiants finissants '86; Porter; Redgrave; Portraits and Dreams; Claver-Fournier; Exposition--concours de metiers d'art '86; Artistes de la region; Etudiants du secondaire; Vautour; Chopra; Belliveau; Savoie; Arsenault; Chisel and Brush; Estamps contemporaines de Provinces de l'Ouet; Vies deracinees; Latino-Americaines et des Caribes; Coutellier; Gouguen; Cantieni; Maguire; Flewelling; Van Ginhoven; Rolfe; Bourgois-Horne
Activities: Classes for children, dramatic programs; lectures open to public, 10 vis lectr per yr; concerts; gallery talks; tours; individual paintings & original objects of art lent to university personnel & art galleries & museums; lending collection contains 500 reproductions, 300 original art works, 180 original prints, 30 paintings, 20 sculpture

SACKVILLE

M MOUNT ALLISON UNIVERSITY, Owens Art Gallery, York St, E0A 3C0. Tel 506-364-2574; FAX 506-364-2575; Telex 014-2266. *Dir* Gemey Kelly; *Asst to Dir* Mrs M Hofland; *Fine Arts Conservator* J Cheney; *Fine Arts Technician* R Ibbitson
Open Mon - Fri 10 AM - 5 PM, Thurs evenings 7 - 10 PM, Sat & Sun 2 - 5 PM, cl university holidays. No admis fee. Estab 1895, rebuilt 1972. Building includes five gallery areas; conservation laboratory. Average Annual Attendance: 11,000
Income: Financed by Mount Allison University, Government, Corporate and Private Assistance
Collections: Broad collection of graphics, paintings, works on paper; parts of collection on display throughout the campus; 19th & 20th century Canadian, European and American Art
Publications: Exhibition catalogs
Activities: Lect open to the public, 20 vis lectr per yr; concerts; gallery talks; tours; individual paintings lent to other galleries and museums; book traveling exhibitions, 10 - 12 per yr; originate traveling exhibitions

SAINT ANDREWS

M HENRY PHIPPS ROSS & SARAH JULIETTE ROSS MEMORIAL MUSEUM, 188 Montague St (Mailing add: PO Box 603, E0G 2X0). Tel 506-529-3906; FAX 506-529-3383. *Cur* Irene R Ritch
Open Late May - early Oct Mon - Sat 10 AM - 4:30 PM, Sun from July 1:30 - 4:30 PM. Estab 1980. 1 small gallery. Average Annual Attendance: 8000
Purchases: $500
Collections: Jacqueline Davis China Collection; Mowat Loyalist Collection; Ross Decorative Art Collection
Exhibitions: (1991) Chinese Export Porcelain in Canada. (1992) Expressions of an Eastern Tradition - Oriental Rugs from the Ross Collection
Activities: Classes for children; lectures open to public, 1 vis lectr per year; exten dept provides lending collection of paintings

A SUNBURY SHORES ARTS AND NATURE CENTRE, INC, Gallery, 139 Water St, PO Box 100, E0G 2X0. Tel 506-529-3386. *Pres* Barbara McQueen; *Dir* Margaret Peterson
Open Tues - Fri 9 AM - 4:30 PM, Sat & Sun 2 - 4 PM. No admis fee. Estab 1964, to function as a link for, and harmonize views of scientists, artists and industrialists. Gallery maintained, 200 running ft, fire and burglar protection, security during hours, controllable lighting and street frontage. Average Annual Attendance: 5000. Mem: 500; dues family $20, individual $12, students & sr citizens $6; annual meeting Aug
Income: Financed by endowment, membership, grants, revenue from courses & activities, including special projects
Exhibitions: Exhibits change frequently throughout the year
Publications: Brochure, summer annually; Sunbury Notes, quarterly
Activities: Lect open to public, 10 - 15 visiting lectr per year; gallery talks; scholarships; museum shop sells books, original art, reproductions & prints
L 139 Water St, Saint Andrews, E0G 2X0. Tel 506-529-3386. *Dir* Margaret Ray Peterson
Open to public; primarily for reference
Income: Financed by mem
Library Holdings: Vols 600; Per subs 10; Other — Exhibition catalogs

SAINT JOHN

M NEW BRUNSWICK MUSEUM, 277 Douglas Ave, E2K 1E5. Tel 506-658-1842; FAX 506-635-5360. *Dir* Dr Frank Milligan; *Business Mgr* Art Robinson; *Chief Cur* Gary Hughes; *Cur Art* Regina Mantin; *Technology* Robert Elliot; *Head Natural Sciences* D McAlpine; *Educ Officer Natural Science* Ellen Melvin; *Educ Officer Humanities* Anne Baker
Open May - Aug 10 AM - 5 PM daily, Sept - Apr Tues - Sun 10 AM - 5 PM, cl Mon. Admis adults $2, students $.50, families $4, senior citizens & children under 6 free. Estab 1842 to collect, conserve, exhibit & interpret the Human & Natural history of New Brunswick in relation to itself & to the outside world. Six major galleries for permanent exhibits, three galleries for changing temporary exhibits. Average Annual Attendance: 60,000. Mem: 375; dues $20 - $100; annual meeting June
Income: $900,000 (financed by mem, federal & provincial appropriations)
Collections: African art; Contemporary Prints; decorative arts; dolls; European art; Japanese prints; maps; New Brunswick & Maritime artists of 19th & 20th centuries; Oriental arts; Russian Silver (Faberge pre-Revolution); social history
Publications: Journal of the New Brunswick Museum, yearly; bi-monthly newsletter
Activities: Classes for children; docent training; lectures open to the public; gallery talks; tours; competitions sponsored in schools; individual paintings & original objects of art lent to museums & galleries; book traveling exhibitions, 6 per yr; traveling exhibitions organized & circulated nationally & internationally; museum shop sells books
L Library, 277 Douglas Ave, E2K 1E5. FAX 701-635-5360; *Head* Carol Rosevear
Open to the public for reference only
Library Holdings: Vols 10,000; Per subs 150; Micro — Cards, reels; Other — Clipping files, exhibition catalogs, manuscripts, memorabilia, photographs

NEWFOUNDLAND

CORNER BROOK

M CLYDE FARNELL FOLK ART PARK, Sticks & Stones House, 7 Farnell's Lane, A2H 1J6. Tel 709-783-2455; FAX 709-634-8011. *Owner* Ruby MacDonald
Admis $2. Estab 1986. Average Annual Attendance: 3000. Mem: annual meeting in Apr
Income: $10,000 (financed by federal government & providence grants
Collections: Folk Art; pictures (mixed media); wall decorations

SAINT JOHN'S

M MEMORIAL UNIVERSITY OF NEWFOUNDLAND, Art Gallery, Arts & Culture Centre, A1C 5S7. Tel 709-737-8209; FAX 709-737-2007. *Dir* Patricia Grattan; *Supv of Operations* Edward Cadigan; *Educ & Exhib Cur* Caroline Stone; *Secy* Judy Tucker; *Registrar* Brian Murphy; *Admin Staff Specialist* Wanda Mooney
Open Tues - Sun noon - 5 PM, Thurs & Fri evenings 7 - 10 PM, cl Mon. No admis fee. Estab 1961 to display contemporary Canadian art, with an emphasis on Newfoundland work, & to provide visual art educational programs. Four galleries with 130 running ft each. Average Annual Attendance: 30,000
Income: Financed through the university & federal funding
Collections: Post 1960 Canadian art
Exhibitions: Contemporary art
Publications: Catalogs of in-house exhibitions
Activities: Classes for children; workshops; lectures open to public; concerts; gallery talks; tours; individual paintings & original objects of art lent to other institutions; lending collection contains books, catalogs & 1500 slides; book traveling exhibitions; originate traveling exhibitions

M NEWFOUNDLAND MUSEUM, 285 Duckworth St, A1C 1G9. Tel 709-576-2329. *Dir* David Mills; *Exhib Officer* Allan Clarke
No admis fee. Estab 1878 as the Athenaeum for the preservation of Provincial Heritage. The Newfoundland Museum now houses collections & exhibitions reflecting the 7000 year history of Newfoundland & Labrador. Branches at The Murray Premises Museum, St John's & The Newfoundland Seamen's Museum at Grand Bank & The Mary March Museum at Grand Falls. Average Annual Attendance: 80,000

Income: Financed by federal and provincial appropriations
Collections: Beothuk, Thule, Maritime Archaic, pre-Dorset, Dorset, Naskapi, Montagnais and Micmac artifacts; history material; maps; naval and military; 19th century Newfoundland domestic artifacts, maritime, natural history, mercantile; 18th - 20th century Newfoundland material, outport furniture, textiles, navigational instruments, ship portraits, watercolors, prints, drawings
Exhibitions: (1993) Women of Invention; Bringing Research to Life; Modelers Association Exhibition; St Lawrence River Valley
Publications: Museum Notes; exhibition catalogues; technical bulletins; Archeology in Newfoundland and Labrador, Natural History Curatorial Reports; annual report
Activities: Classes for children; docent training; lectures open to public, 12 visiting lecturers per year; tours; book traveling exhibitions; originate traveling exhibitions

M **Newfoundland Museum at the Murray Premises,** c/o 283 Duckworth St, Saint John's, A1C 1G9. Tel 709-729-5044; FAX 709-729-2179. *Head Public Programming* Allan Clarke
Open Mon - Fri 9 AM - noon & 1 - 4:45 PM, Sat & Sun 2 - 5 PM. No admis fee. Estab 1887 to collect & interpret the heritage of the province of Newfoundland & Labrador. This branch displays the marine history, natural history & military history components of the Newfoundland Museum collection. Average Annual Attendance: 55,000
Income: Financed by provincial government
Exhibitions: Periodic exhibitions
Publications: Archaeology in Newfoundland & Labrador, irregular; Newfoundland Museum Note Series, irregular
Activities: Classes for children; docent training; lectures open to public; gallery talks; tours; exten dept serves province; original objects lent to museums of the province

L **Library,** 283 Duckworth St, A1C 1G9. Tel 709-729-2460; FAX 709-729-2179. *Public Programming Asst* Karen Walsh
Open to researchers for reference
Special Subjects: Military history
Collections: Mercury Series of National Museums in Archaeology, Ethnology, Restoration; National Historic Parks and Sites Reports

NOVA SCOTIA

DARTMOUTH

M **DARTMOUTH HERITAGE MUSEUM,** 100 Wyse Rd, B3A 1M1. Tel 902-464-2300; FAX 902-464-8210. *Dir* Dr Richard Henning Field; *Cur* Betty Ann Aaboe-Milligan
Open summer Mon - Fri 9 AM - 4 PM, Sat & Sun 1 - 4:30 PM, winter Mon - Sat 1 - 4:30 PM, Sun 2 - 5 PM. No admis fee. Estab 1968 to collect & preserve the history & heritage of the City of Dartmouth. Average Annual Attendance: 45,000
Income: Financed by city appropriation & provincial funds
Exhibitions: Twenty-four exhibitions scheduled per year
Activities: Classes for adults and children; gallery talks; tours; exten dept serves historic houses; book traveling exhibitions

HALIFAX

M **ART GALLERY OF NOVA SCOTIA,** 1741 Hollis at Cheapside, PO Box 2262, B3J 3C8. Tel 902-424-7542; FAX 902-424-7359. *Dir* Bernard Riordon; *Educ Cur* Virginia Stephen; *Registrar* Judy Dietz; *Exhib Cur* Susan Foshay
Open Mon - Wed, Fri, Sat 10 AM - 5:30 PM, Thurs 10 AM - 9 PM, Sun Noon - 5:30 PM, cl Mon. Admis adult $5, adults $2, students & seniors $1, children under 12 & members free, Tues free. Estab 1975 to replace the Nova Scotia Museum of Fine Arts; dedicated to the collection, preservation, display and interpretation of art. Seventeen galleries, for permanent collection & temporary exhibitions. Average Annual Attendance: 50,000. Mem: 2000; dues family $30, individual $20, student $15; annual meeting June
Income: Financed by provincial and federal agencies, donations
Collections: †Nova Scotia Folk Art; †Nova Scotian, Canadian Collection (both historical and contemporary); drawings, paintings, prints and sculpture
Activities: Classes for adults & children; docent training; lect open to the public, 20 vis lectr per yr; gallery talks; tours; exten dept serves Canada; artmobile; individual paintings and original objects of art lent to Province and Government House; lending collection contains original art works, framed reproductions, original prints, paintings & sculpture; book traveling exhibitions, 6 - 8 per yr; originate traveling exhibitions, 10 - 15 per yr; museum & sales shop sells books, jewelry, magazines, original art, pottery, prints, reproductions, slides, crafts & also rental service

M **DALHOUSIE UNIVERSITY,** Art Gallery, 6101 University Ave, B3H 3J5. Tel 902-494-2403, 494-2195. *Dir* Mern O'Brien; *Registrar & Preparator* Michele Gallant; *Cur* Susan Gibson Garvey; *Office Mgr* Denise Hoskin
Open Tues - Fri 11 AM - 5 PM, Tues 7 - 10 PM, Sat & Sun 1 - 5 PM, cl Mon. No admis fee. Estab 1970 to collect, preserve, interpret & display works of art, primarily of Canadian origin. Dalhousie Art Gallery is located in the Dalhousie Arts Centre and open to university community and local area; it contains 400 running ft of wall space & 4000 sq ft floor space. Average Annual Attendance: 16,000
Income: Financed by university supplemented by government grants
Collections: †Canadian works on paper
Publications: Annual Report; Calendar of Events, 3 times per yr
Activities: Classes for children; docent training; lectures open to public, 12 vis lectr per yr; concerts; gallery talks; tours; exten dept serves regional & national area; individual paintings & original objects of art lent to professional galleries & campus areas; book traveling exhibitions; originate traveling exhibitions; sales shop sells gallery publications

M **MOUNT SAINT VINCENT UNIVERSITY,** Art Gallery, B3M 2J6. Tel 902-443-4450, Ext 160; FAX 902-445-3960. *Dir Art Gallery* Mary Sparling; *Exhib Officer* John Kennedy; *Office Mgr* Jan Anthony
Open Mon - Fri 9 AM - 5 PM, Sat, Sun & holidays 1 - 5 PM, Tues until 9 PM. No admis fee. Estab 1970 and operating throughout the year with continuously-changing exhibitions of local, regional, national and international origin in the area of fine arts and crafts. Gallery situated on the main floor and mezzanine. Average Annual Attendance: 15,000
Income: Financed by university funds
Purchases: Judith Mann; Peter Barss; Susanne MacKay, Herself; Felicity Redgrave, Peggy's Rocks; Carol Fraser, Nocturne
Collections: The Art Gallery is custodian of a collection of pictures, ceramics and pottery of the late Alice Egan Hagen of Mahone Bay, noted Nova Scotia potter and ceramist; †works by regional artists; women artists
Publications: Gallery News, 4 times per yr; exhibition catalogs
Activities: Classes for adults and children; workshops; lect open to public, 12 visiting lectr per year; concerts; gallery talks; tours; competitions; individual paintings and original objects of art lent to other galleries; lending collection contains videotapes; book traveling exhibitions, 6 per year; originate traveling exhibitions

A **NOVA SCOTIA ASSOCIATION OF ARCHITECTS,** 1361 Barrington St, B3J 1Y9. Tel 902-423-7607; FAX 902-425-7024. *Exec Dir* Diane Scott-Stewart
Estab 1932. Mem: 200; annual meeting Feb
Publications: Newsletter, monthly

M **NOVA SCOTIA COLLEGE OF ART AND DESIGN,** Anna Leonowens Gallery, 5163 Duke St, B3J 3J6. Tel 902-422-7381. *Pres* Ian Christie Clark; *Dir* Jessica Kerrin
Open Tues - Sat 11 AM - 5 PM, Mon evenings 6 - 8 PM. Estab for educational purposes. One small and two large galleries
Income: Financed by state appropriations & tuition
Exhibitions: 100 exhibitions per yer
Publications: Ten books; exhibition catalogs, occasionally
Activities: Lectures open to public; gallery talks

L **Library,** 5163 Duke St, B3J 3J6. Tel 902-422-7381; FAX 902-425-2420. *Dir* Ilga Leja; *Dir of Non-Print Coll* Mary Snyder
Open Mon - Fri 8:30 AM - 10 PM, Sat & Sun noon - 5 PM. Circ 30,000
Income: $239,000 (financed by state appropriation and student fees)
Purchases: $57,500
Library Holdings: Vols 26,000; Per subs 300; Micro — Fiche, reels; AV — A-tapes, cassettes, fs, rec, slides, v-tapes; Other — Exhibition catalogs, pamphlets
Special Subjects: Contemporary art

M **NOVA SCOTIA MUSEUM,** Maritime Museum of the Atlantic, 1675 Lower Water St, B3J 1S3. Tel 902-429-8210; FAX 902-424-0612.
Open May 15 - Oct 15 9:30 AM - 5:30 PM, Sun 1 - 5:30 PM. No admis fee. Estab 1948 to interpret maritime history of eastern coast of Canada. Average Annual Attendance: 140,000
Income: Financed by state appropriations
Collections: Historical Marine Painting display; Lawrence Family memorabilia; small craft, ship models, ship portraits, uniforms, marine artifacts
Activities: Lect open to public, 20 lectr per yr; gallery talks; individual paintings & original objects of art lent to other institutions; sales shop sells books

M **ST MARY'S UNIVERSITY,** Art Gallery, Robie St, B3H 3C3. Tel 902-420-5445; FAX 902-420-5561. *Dir & Cur* J R Leighton Davis; *Asst Dir & Cur* Gordon Laurin; *Performing Arts Coordr* Sheila Lane
Open Tues - Thurs 1- 7 PM, Fri 1 - 5 PM, Sat & Sun noon - 4 PM, cl Mon. Estab 1970 to present a variety of exhibitions and performances of both regional and national interest and by contemporary artists. Average Annual Attendance: 12,000
Income: Financed by provincial appropriation
Collections: Works on paper by contemporary Canadian artists
Publications: Exhibit catalogues, 1 - 2 times per year
Activities: Adult drawing classes; lectures open to the public, 3 - 4 vis lectr per yr; concerts; gallery talks; tours; individual paintings & original objects of art lent; exten dept serves university; book traveling exhibitions, 2 - 3 per year; originate travelling exhibitions; circulated to the Atlantic Provinces of Canada

WOLFVILLE

M **ACADIA UNIVERSITY ART GALLERY,** c/o Beveridge Arts Centre, B0P 1X0. Tel 902-542-2201; FAX 902-542-4727. *Dir* Franziska Kruschen Leiter; *Secy* Marjorie Gee Baird
Estab 1978, art dept 1928, to exhibit contemporary & historical art particularly from the Atlantic region. Average Annual Attendance: 15,000
Income: $65,000 (financed by endowment & University funds)
Purchases: $15,000 (works by Atlantic region artists)
Collections: Contemporary & Historical Paintings, Drawings & Prints
Activities: Lectures open to public; 4 vis lectr per year; book traveling exhibitons 8 per year; originate travel exhibitions 4 per year

YARMOUTH

M **YARMOUTH COUNTY HISTORICAL SOCIETY,** Yarmouth County Museum, 22 Collins St, B5A 3C8. Tel 902-742-5539. *Pres* Marshall Moses; *Cur* Eric Ruff; *Archivist* Laura Bradley
Open Jun 1 - Oct 15 9 AM - 5 PM, Sun 1 - 5 PM, Oct 10 - May 31 2 - 5 PM, cl Mon. Admis adults $1, students $.50, children $.25. Estab 1958 to display artifacts and paintings relating to Yarmouth's past. Located in former Congregational Church built in 1893. Average Annual Attendance: 14,000. Mem: 400; dues $12; meetings Second Fri each month
Income: $100,000 (financed by membership, admis & state appropriation)
Purchases: $500
Collections: General historical collection; paintings of an by Yarmouthians;

collection of ship portraits of Yarmouth vessels and vessels commanded by Yarmouthians; general & marine artifacts; marine drawings & portraits
Publications: Newsletter, monthly
Activities: Lect open to public, 12 vis lectr per yr; concerts; gallery talks; tours; Heritage Awards; museum shop sells books, prints

ONTARIO

ALMONTE

M MISSISSIPPI VALLEY CONSERVATION AUTHORITY, Mill of Kintail Museum, RR 1 (Mailing add: PO Box 268, Lanark, K0G 1K0). Tel 613-256-3610. *Community Relations Coordr* Pamela McGrath; *Cur* Carol Munden
Open May 15 - Oct 15 Wed - Sun & holidays 11:30 AM - 4:30 PM. Admis family $2.50, adults $1, senior citizens & children $.50. Estab 1952 as a private museum, publicly owned since 1973 by Mississippi Valley Conservation Authority as a memorial to Dr R Tait McKenzie, Canadian sculptor, physical educator, surgeon and humanitarian. Average Annual Attendance: 7500
Income: Financed by provincial government grant
Collections: 70 Original Athletic, Memorial and Monumental Sculptures, nearly all in plaster; 600 Pioneer Artifacts, mostly collected by Dr McKenzie
Activities: Classes for children; gallery talks, tours; sales shop sells books, reproductions, postcards and gift notes

BANCROFT

M ALGONQUIN ARTS COUNCIL, Bancroft Art Gallery, PO Box 1360, K0L 1C0. Tel 613-332-1542; FAX 613-332-2119. *Dir* Richard Capener; *Cur* Bill Tomlinson; *Exec Dir* Heather Rennie; *Secy* Deanna Powell
Open June & July daily noon - 5 PM, May, June & Sept Wed - Sun noon - 5 PM. Donation box. Estab 1980 to foster the fine arts in the area. Gallery is located in an historic railway station. Average Annual Attendance: 7000. Mem: 15; dues $15; annual meeting in June
Income: $15,000 (financed by mem, grants from the Ontario Arts Council & fundraising)
Collections: Murray Schafer: Sound Sculptures; miscellaneous, glass, fabric, paintings
Publications: The News BAG, newsletter monthly
Activities: Classes for children; lectures open to public, 3 vis lectr per year; lending collection contains 20 paintings; sales shop sells books, prints, original art, crafts, pottery blown & stained glass, wood carvings & photographs

BELLEVILLE

M HASTINGS COUNTY MUSEUM, 257 Bridge St E, K8N 1P4. Tel 613-962-2329, 962-6340. *Cur* Rona Rustige; *Education* Jane Lambe
Open summer Tues - Sun 10 AM - 4:30 PM, winter Tues - Sun 1 - 4:30 PM. Admis $3. Estab 1973 to collect & interpret history of Hastings County & 1890's historic home. Historic House with art gallery dedicated to local artist Manley McDonald, also extensive collection of Victorian paintings, notably Horatio Henry Couldery, copies of Gainsborough, Constable, Uens & Wilkie. Average Annual Attendance: 11,500
Income: Financed by city and county appropriation
Exhibitions: Permanent collection of Manley McDonald Originals and Beverley McDonald Originals; artists, photographers. (1992) Belleville's Marine Heritage. (1993) The Furtrade - Parks Canada Exhibit
Activities: Classes for adults & children; docent training; education kits lent to schools & groups; lect open to public; tours; exten dept serves Hastings County; individual paintings & original objects of art lent to museums, galleries & City Hall; lending collection contains history artifacts & slides; book traveling exhibitions, annually; museum shop sells books & reproductions artifacts

BRACEBRIDGE

M MUSKOKA ARTS & CRAFTS INC, Chapel Gallery, 45 Muskoka Rd S, PO Box 376, P1L 1S5. Tel 705-645-5501. *Cur* Elene J Freer
Open 10 AM - 5 PM. Admis donations accepted. Estab 1963, museum estab 1989. Average Annual Attendance: 10,000. Mem: 340; dues $15 - $20; annual meeting in Oct
Publications: Newsletter, 12 per year

BRAMPTON

M ART GALLERY OF PEEL, Peel Heritage Complex, Nine Wellington St E, L6W 1Y1. Tel 416-454-5441. *Cur* David Somers
Open Tues - Fri 10 AM - 4:30 PM, Thurs 6 - 9 PM, Sat & Sun noon - 4:30 PM. Estab 1968 to collect works relevant to Region of Peel & to promote visual art & artists. Average Annual Attendance: 18,000. Mem: 200; dues corporate $100, family $25, individual $20; annual meeting in Feb
Collections: Permanent art collection of Canadian Artists; Caroline & Frank Armington print collection
Exhibitions: Eight exhibits per year (all mediums); Annual Open Juried Show; Regional Artists
Publications: Caroline & Frank Armington: Canadian Painter - Etchers in Paris
Activities: Classes for children; docent training; lectures open to the public, 1 - 2 vis lectrs per yr; gallery talks; tours; competitions with prizes; exten dept serves Southern Ontario; individual paintings & original objects of art lent to public buildings & other institutions; originate traveling exhibitions to libraries & other galleries; sales shop sells books, reproductions & prints

L Library, Nine Wellington St E, L6W 1Y1. Tel 416-454-5441; FAX 416-451-4931. *Cur* David Somers; *Asst Cur* Judy Daley
Reference only
Library Holdings: Vols 500; Per subs 3; Other — Clipping files, exhibition catalogs

L BRAMPTON PUBLIC LIBRARY, Art Gallery, 250 Central Park Dr (Mailing add: 150 Central Park Dr, L6T 1B4). Tel 416-793-4636. *Dir* G C Burgis
Open Mon - Thurs 10 AM - 9 PM, Fri 10 AM - 6 PM, Sat 10 AM - 5 PM, Sun 1 - 5 PM. No admis fee. Estab 1972 to encourage an interest in and knowledge of the arts through exhibits and related activities. Gallery is 1400 sq ft, 165 running ft and walls are stretch fabric over wood. Average Annual Attendance: 542,894 (library & art gallery combined)
Income: Financed by city & state appropriation
Collections: Small permanent collection
Activities: Classes for children; dramatic programs; lect open to public; concerts; gallery talks; book traveling exhibitions, 2 per year

BRANTFORD

M BRANT HISTORICAL SOCIETY, Brant County Museum, 57 Charlotte St, N3T 2W6. Tel 519-752-2483. *Dir* Susan Twist; *Asst Cur* Joan de Kat
Open Sept - Apr Tues - Fri 9 AM - 5 PM, Sat 1 - 4 PM, July - Aug Tues - Fri 9 AM - 5 PM, Sat & Sun 1 - 4 PM. Admis adults $1.50, students & seniors $1, children $.75, under 6 free. Estab 1908 to preserve, interpret & display Brant County history. Average Annual Attendance: 8000. Mem: 150; dues patron $25, family $15, single $10
Income: Financed by memberships, provincial, county & city grants & fundraising
Collections: Early Indian history; historical figures; portraits & paintings; Brant County history
Publications: Annual brochure; A Glimpse of the Past, Brant County, the Story of its People, vol I & II
Activities: Classes for children; docent training; lectures open to public; tours; museum shop sells books, reproductions & prints

L Library, 57 Charlotte St, N3T 2W6. Tel 519-752-2483.
Library Holdings: Vols 500
Collections: First editions of history and archaeology; old Bibles available for research on premises under supervision of curator; rare books

M GLENHYRST ART GALLERY OF BRANT, 20 Ava Rd, N3T 5G9. Tel 519-756-5932. *Dir* Carolyn Vesely
Open Tues - Fri 10 AM - 5 PM, Sat & Sun 1 - 5 PM. No admis fee. Estab 1956 as a non-profit public arts center serving the citizens of Brantford & Brant County. Four gallery rooms located inside the house, on a 15 & one-half acre estate. Average Annual Attendance: 20,000. Mem: 620; dues benefactors $250 & up, patrons $100-$250, family $25, individual $15, student & senior citizen $10; annual meeting in Mar
Income: Financed by membership, municipal, provincial & federal appropriations & local foundations
Collections: Contemporary Canadian graphics/works on paper; historical works by R R Whale & descendants
Activities: Classes for adults and children; lectures open to public, 8 vis lectr per year; gallery talks; competitions; Art rental & sales service; originate traveling exhibitions

L Library, 20 Ava Rd, N3T 5G9. Tel 519-756-5932.
Open to public for reference
Library Holdings: Vols 140
Special Subjects: Art Education, Art History, Folk Art, History of Art & Archaeology, Painting - Canadian, Primitive Art, Printmaking, Prints, Tapestries, Textiles
Activities: Lect open to public, 8 vis lectr per year; gallery talks; juried shows; art rental and sales service; works from permanent collection are circulated

CAMBRIDGE

L CAMBRIDGE PUBLIC LIBRARY AND GALLERY, 20 Grand Ave N, N1S 2K6. Tel 519-621-0460. *Chief Librn* Greg Hayton; *Coordr Cultural Servs* Mary Misner
Open Mon - Thurs 9:30 AM - 8:30 PM, Fri & Sat 9:30 AM - 5:30 PM; Sept - May open Sun 1 - 5 PM. No admis fee. Estab 1969. Gallery on second floor with 2000 sq ft, 250 linear ft. Average Annual Attendance: 25,000
Income: Financed by provincial appropriation, federal and private
Collections: Regional Artists
Publications: Bi-monthly newsletter
Activities: Classes for adults and children; lect open to public, 10 visiting lectr per year; concerts; gallery talks; tours; competitions; awards; individual paintings and original objects of art lent; originate traveling exhibitions

CHATHAM

A CHATHAM CULTURAL CENTRE, Thames Art Gallery, 75 William St N, N7M 4L4. Tel 519-354-8338; FAX 519-436-3237. *Dir* Doug Jackson; *Marketing Coord* Marie Lloyd; *Gallery Cur* Sheelagh Carroll-de Sousa; *Museum Cur* Kathryn Schwenger
Open Tues - Sun 1 - 5 PM. No admis fee. Estab 1963 to operate as a regional arts centre, to advance knowledge and appreciation of, and to encourage, stimulate and promote interest in the study of culture and the visual and performing arts. Gallery maintained; designated National Exhibition Centre for the presentation of visual art works and museum related events to the public of this country. Average Annual Attendance: 25,000. Mem: 600; dues family $18, single $10
Income: Financed by membership, city and state appropriation, and National Museum Grants
Collections: Local Artists; Historical Photographs

Publications: Chatham-Kent Events, quarterly; bi-monthly bulletin
Activities: Classes for adults & children; dramatic programs; docent training; lect open to the public, 5 vis lectrs per yr; concerts; gallery talks; tours; juried fine art & craft shows; individual and original objects of art lent to accredited galleries and museums; lending collection contains 2100 slides

DON MILLS

C ROTHMANS, BENSON & HEDGES, Art Collection, 1500 Don Mills Rd, M3B 3L1. Tel 416-449-5525; FAX 416-449-4486. *Dir Corp Affairs* John MacDonald
Open to public. No admis fee. Estab 1967. Collection displayed at head office
Collections: Contemporary Canadian art from last decade
Activities: Awards for Toronto Outdoor Art Exhibition each year; individual objects of art lent to traveling or special exhibitions; originate traveling exhibitions to all major public galleries in Canada

GANANOQUE

M GANANOQUE HISTORICAL MUSEUM, 10 King St, E, PO Box 158, K7G 2T8. Tel 613-382-4024. *Pres* Cliff Weir; *Cur* Lynette McClellan
Open Mon - Sat 11 AM - 5 PM. Admis adults $1, children under 12 $.50. Estab 1964 to preserve local history. Average Annual Attendance: 2500
Collections: China Collection; Military and Indian Artifacts; Victorian Dining Room, Parlour and Bedroom; glass; portraits and photographs pertaining to local history; Victorian kitchen
Activities: Book traveling exhibitions

GLOUCESTER

M CANADIANA SPORT ART COLLECTION, Canadian Sport and Fitness Centre, 1600 Prom James Naismith Dr, K1B 5N4. Tel 613-746-0060; FAX 613-748-5706. *Dir Sales & Marketing* John P Restivo
Open Mon - Fri 8:30 AM - 4:30 PM. Estab 1970 to provide a vehicle through which recognition could be passed on to the many fine amateur athletes of Canada, by Canadian artists
Exhibitions: Jack Bush: The Pass (painting); Ken Danby - Skates (and other watercolors); Louis Phillipe Hebert (bronze sculpture); Allan de la Plante (photographs); Siggy Puchta Bronze Sculptures: Decisive Moment, Karate Player and Touchdown; Joe Rosenthal's Struggle with Time (bronze sculpture); Hanni Rothschild: Hockey Player, Ball Game (ceramics); Alan Sapp: Playing Hockey (painting); Esther Wertheimer: The Olympics (metal sculpture); William Winter's Street Hockey
Activities: Tours; individual paintings and original objects of art lent to Canada's Sport Hall of Fame, Canada Games Society and Olympic Association; originate traveling exhibition

GUELPH

M MACDONALD STEWART ART CENTRE ART CENTER, 358 Gordon St, N1G 1Y1. Tel 519-837-0010; FAX 519-767-2261. *Dir* Judith Nasby; *Cur* Nancy Campbell; *Prog Coordr* Steve Robinson
Open Tues - Sun noon - 5 PM, Thurs 5 - 9 PM. No admis fee. Estab 1978 by Univ of Guelph, city, county and board of education to collect and exhibit works of art; maintain and operate a gallery; and related facilities for this purpose fulfilling a public role in city and county. 30,000 sq ft building comprising galleries, lecture room, studio, meeting rooms, resource centre, gift shop and rental service. Restored and renovated in 1980. Average Annual Attendance: 25,000. Mem: 600; dues family $30, individual $20, sr & student $10; annual meeting Sept - Oct
Income: Financed by university, city, county, board of education, provincial and federal grants, memberships and donations
Purchases: Canadian art
Special Subjects: Donald Forster Sculpture Park
Collections: †Historical & contemporary Canadian art; historical & contemporary international prints; †Inuit Collection; †contemporary sculpture; outdoor sculpture (Donald Forster Sculpture Park)
Publications: Catalogue of permanent collection of University of Guelph 1980; exhibition catalogues, 6 per yr; newsletter (4 per year)
Activities: Classes for adults & children; docent training; parent/child workshops; lectures open to public; gallery talks; school & group tours; competitions; awards; exten dept serves Wellington County and other Canadian public galleries, also have circulated in US & Europe; individual paintings lent to institutions and public galleries; art rental to gallery members; lending collection contains 500 original paintings, 400 prints, photographs & 50 sculptures; book traveling exhibitions 4-6 per year; originate traveling exhibitions, 1 -2 per year for museums in Canada & abroad; sales shop sells books, magazines, reproductions, toys, pottery, textiles, jewelry and catalogues

HAILEYBURY

M TEMISKAMING ART GALLERY, PO Box 1090, P0J 1K0. Tel 705-672-3706; FAX 705-672-3200. *Office Mgr* Anne Leblanc
Open daily 2 - 8 PM. Admis free. Estab 1980 to educate. Average Annual Attendance: Annual meeting Jan
Income: Financed by mem & city appropriation
Activities: Classes for adults & children; lectures open to public, 5 vis lectr per year

HAMILTON

M ART GALLERY OF HAMILTON, 123 King St W, L8P 4S8. Tel 416-527-6610; FAX 416-577-6940. *Dir* Ted Pietrzak; *Education & Extension Officer* Wendy Woon; *Community Relations* Alexandra Harrison; *Preparator* Greg Dawe; *Membership Development* Terry McDougall
Open Tues - Sat 10 AM - 5 PM, Thurs 7 - 9 PM, Sun 1 - 5 PM. Estab Jan 1914 to develop & maintain a centre for the study & enjoyment of the visual arts; new gallery opened Oct 1977. Building is 76,000 sq ft, 24,000 sq ft of exhibition space. Average Annual Attendance: 70,000. Mem: 1500; dues family $35, single $25; annual meeting last Thurs in May
Income: Financed by endowment, mem, city & provincial appropriation & federal grants
Collections: Complete graphics of Karel Appel; Canadian fine arts; American, British & European fine arts
Exhibitions: Twenty-seven exhibitions scheduled per year
Publications: Art Gallery of Hamilton Bulletin, bimonthly
Activities: Classes for adults & children; docent training; lect open to public, 18 visiting lectr per year; concerts; gallery talks; tours; exten dept; individual paintings & original objects of art lent to other galleries & museums; lending collection contains 2458 original prints, 1717 paintings, 285 sculpture, 669 drawings; originate traveling exhibitions; museum shop sells books, magazines & reproductions
L Muriel Isabel Bostwick Library, 123 King St W, Hamilton, L8P 4S8. Tel 416-527-6610; FAX 416-577-6940. *Contemporary Cur* Ihor Holubizky; *Librn* Helen Hadden
Open to gallery members and researchers for reference
Library Holdings: Vols 3000; Per subs 14; Other — Clipping files, exhibition catalogs, photographs
Special Subjects: Art History, Mixed Media, Oriental Art, Painting - American, Painting - European, Portraits, Printmaking, Prints, Restoration & Conservation, Sculpture, Good references on Canadian art history and large holding of exhibition catalogues relating to this field

M DUNDURN CASTLE, Dundurn Park, York Blvd, L8R 3H1. Tel 416-522-5313; FAX 416-522-4535. *Cur* Bill Nesbitt; *Head Historical Interpreter* David Adames
Open mid-June to Labor Day daily 11 AM - 4 PM, evening appointments for groups of 25 or more, Labor Day to mid-June booked tours mornings and evenings, open to public 1 - 4 PM, cl Christmas and New Year's Day. Admis adults $2.75, senior citizen $2, students $1.55, children $.90, family $6.75, discounts on group rates for over 25 people. Dundurn, the home of Sir Allan Napier MacNab; Hamilton's Centennial Project was the restoration of this historic house; built in 1832-35, it was tenured by MacNab until his death in 1862. The terminal date of the furnishings is 1855. Approximately 35 rooms are shown; two-room on-site exhibit area. Average Annual Attendance: 70,000
Income: Financed by city of Hamilton, owner & operator
Collections: Regency & mid-Victorian furnishings depicting the lifestyle of an upper class gentleman living in upper Canada in the 1850's; restored servants quarters
Exhibitions: (1991) Historical Crafts Fair
Activities: Classes for adults & children; docent training; lectures open to the public; concerts; gallery talks; tours; individual paintings & original objects of art lent; museum shop sells books, reproductions, prints & slides

M MCMASTER UNIVERSITY, Art Gallery, Togo Salmon Hall 114, L8S 4M2. Tel 416-525-9140, Ext 3924, 3081; FAX 416-527-4548. *Dir* Kim G Ness; *Registrar* Geraldine Loveys; *Preparator* Jennifer Petterplace
Open (Sept - May) Mon - Fri 10 AM - 5 PM, Tues evening 7 - 9 PM, Sun 1 - 5 PM; (summer) Mon - Fri noon - 5 PM. No admis fee. Estab 1967 to provide the university and public with exhibitions of historical and contemporary art from Canada and other countries. Two galleries 2136 sq ft & 150 sq ft; incandescent lighting throughout; display cases; sculpture stands. Average Annual Attendance: 15,000
Income: $12,400 (financed by university and private endowment, corporate & individual support)
Purchases: $15,000
Collections: †American and †Canadian Art; †European paintings, prints and drawings; †German Expressionist Prints
Exhibitions: (1992) September '67 Revisited; Faculty Show: Galloway, Maddison, Major-Girardin, Todd; Hannah Hoch: 1889 - 1978/Collagen. (1993) Canadian Artists in Paris; In the Name of Art, In the Name of Science; Bruce Johnson, Making the News; Student Show; Twenty-Five Years After
Publications: The Art Collection of McMaster University
Activities: Classroom facilities; lect open to public; concerts; gallery talks; individual paintings and original objects of art lent to National Gallery of Canada, Art Gallery of Ontario & other Canadian institutions
L Library, 1280 Main St W, L8S 4P5. Tel 416-525-9140, Ext 4256; FAX 416-522-1277, 546-0625. *Librn* G A Hill
Open Mon - Thurs 10 AM - 5 PM, Thurs evenings 7 - 9 PM, Sun 1 - 5 PM. Houses reference materials on art gallery management, exhibition and sales catalogues
Library Holdings: Vols 1,613,971; Serial titles

HULL

M CANADIAN MUSEUM OF CIVILIZATION, Victoria Memorial Museum Bldg, 100 Laurier, J8X 4H2. Tel 613-776-8261; FAX 613-954-1016. *Dir* Dr George MacDonald; *Managing Dir* Jacque Ovellet; *Dir Exhib* Sylvie Morel
Open Tues - Sun 10 AM - 5 PM, Summer 10 AM - 5 PM daily. No admis fee. Estab 1968 as one of four components of the National Museums of Canada; to trace the development of Man from prehistoric times to the present, particularly Canadian development. The Victoria Memorial Museum Building, located at Metcalfe and McLeod Streets, houses on the first floor the development of early man and the technology of Canada's indigenous peoples and archaeological method of recovering such past; on the second floor an overview of the Plains Indians and Iroquois; on the third floor an overview of contemporary and

traditional native art; on the fourth floor Canadian history to present and tracing the contribution made by ethnic peoples in Canada. The Canadian War Museum, located at 330 Sussex Drive, displays historical material relating to the military history of Canada and of other countries. Average Annual Attendance: Victoria Memorial Museum Building 493,470
Collections: Archaeological Collection; Ethnological Collection; Folk Culture Collections; Historical Collection; Military History Collection
Publications: Several series of publications and periodicals, 500 titles published in-house in last six years
Activities: Classes for adults and children; dramatic programs; docent training; lect open to the public, several vis lectr per year; extension department; original artifacts lent to museums and other institutions meeting specifications regarding security, environment, etc; originate traveling exhibitions; museum shop sells books, reproductions, magazines, prints

JORDAN

M **JORDAN HISTORICAL MUSEUM OF THE TWENTY,** PO Box 39, L0R 1S0. Tel 416-562-5242. *Acting Cur* Marie Troup
Open May - Oct daily 1 - 5 PM. Admis $1. Estab 1953 to preserve the material and folklore of the area known as The Twenty, Mile Creek vicinity. Average Annual Attendance: 10,000. Mem: 100; dues $5; annual meeting Feb
Income: Financed by admissions, provincial grants, municipal grants, internal fund raising activities & donations
Collections: Archives; furniture; historical material & textiles
Exhibitions: Special annual exhibits
Activities: Classes for children; Special displays as requested by the community; Pioneer Day first Sat after Canadian Thanksgiving holiday; lectures open to public, 1 vis lectr per yr; individual paintings & original objects of art lent; sales shop sells books, original art, prints, pottery, textiles & local craft items

KINGSTON

M **QUEEN'S UNIVERSITY,** Agnes Etherington Art Centre, K7L 3N6. Tel 613-545-2190; FAX 613-545-6765. *Dir* Dr David McTavish; *Cur* Dorothy Farr; *Assoc Cur* Jan Allen; *Assoc Cur* Bruce Millen; *Assoc Cur* Mary Jo Hughes; *Educ Officer* Jeri Harmsen; *Communications Officer* Betty Clark
Open year round Tues - Fri 10 AM - 5 PM, Sat & Sun 1 - 5 PM. Admis adult $2, student & sr citizen $1, members & children under 12 free, free admis Thurs evening July - Aug. Estab 1957 to provide the services of a public art gallery and museum for the community and region. Gallery has approximately 8000 sq ft of display space, in four separate areas, showing a balanced program of exhibitions of contemporary & historical, national, international & regional art. Average Annual Attendance: 30,000. Mem: 870; dues $12 - $150; annual meeting in May (Gallery Association)
Income: $1,081,000 (financed by endowment, city & provincial appropriation, University & Canada Council funds)
Purchases: $100,000
Collections: African Art; Canadian Dress Collection; †Canadian Paintings, Prints, Sculpture, Historical & Contemporary; Decorative Objects; †Ethnological Collection; †European Graphics; †Old Master Paintings; Quilts; Silver
Exhibitions: About 30 exhibitions mounted each year
Publications: Currents, bimonthly; exhibition publications and catalogues; studies
Activities: Docent training regarding tours for school & other groups;; lectures open to public, 10 vis lectr per yr; gallery talks; tours; individual paintings rented by Gallery Association Art Rental to private individuals & businesses; rental collection contains original prints & paintings; originate traveling exhibitions
L **Art Library,** Ontario Hall, Kingston, K7L 3L6. Tel 613-545-2841; FAX 613-545-6819; Elec Mail vanwerin@qucdn.queensu.ca. *Librn* Reinolde van Weringh
Open to students, faculty & staff; open to public for reference only
Purchases: $41,000
Library Holdings: Vols 42,000; Per subs 140; reference books; Micro — Fiche 1400, reels 300; Other — Exhibition catalogs 12,000, photographs
Special Subjects: Art History, Art Conservation, British, Canadian & European Art

M **ST LAWRENCE COLLEGE,** Art Gallery, King & Portsmouth, K7L 5A6. Tel 613-544-5400. *Gallery Dir* David Gordon; *Dept Coordr* Terry Pfliger
Open noon - 4 PM. No admis fee. College estab 1968, mus estab 1973 to augment the creative art program with shows, visiting artists. Average Annual Attendance: 4000
Exhibitions: (1990) Kate Wilson; Ann Clarke; Mary-Louise Schppiticciolajoc. (1991) Arlene Stamp; Josephine Wren

KITCHENER

M **KITCHENER-WATERLOO ART GALLERY,** 101 Queen St N, N2H 6P7. Tel 519-579-5860; FAX 519-578-9230. *Pres* Open; *Dir* Brad Blain
Open Tues - Sat 10 AM - 5 PM, 1 hr before Center performances, Sun 1 - 5 PM, cl Mon. Admis contribution adults $2, students & sr citizens $1, members free. Estab 1956, the Kitchener-Waterloo Art Gallery is a public institution interested in stimulating an appreciation of the visual arts and dedicated to bringing to the community exhibitions, art classes, lectures, workshops and special events. Average Annual Attendance: 75,492. Mem: 756; dues business $100, family $40, individual $30, sr citizens & students $15
Income: Financed by government grants, foundation grants, corporate and individual donations, special events, membership dues, voluntary admissions & sales of publications
Collections: Canadian; Homer Watson Collection
Publications: Calendar, quarterly; exhibition catalogs, quarterly
Activities: Art classes for adults and children; lectures open to public; tours;; scholarships; extension dept serves Waterloo region; book traveling exhibitions; sales shop sells books, original art, reproductions

L **Eleanor Calvert Memorial Library,** 101 Queen St N, Kitchener, ON N2H 6P7. Tel 519-579-5860. *Dir* Brad Blain
Estab 1972 for public art reference & lending to members
Library Holdings: Vols 4500; Per subs 25; AV — Cassettes, slides; Other — Clipping files, exhibition catalogs, pamphlets
Special Subjects: Canadian artists biographical material

KLEINBURG

M **MCMICHAEL CANADIAN ART COLLECTION,** 10365 Islington Ave, L0J 1C0. Tel 416-893-1121; FAX 416-893-2588. *Chmn Bd Trustees* H Michael Burns; *Dir & CEO* Barbara Tyler
Open Nov 1 - Mar 31 Tues - Sun 11 AM - 4:30 PM, Apr 1 - Oct 31 daily 10 AM - 5 PM. Admis family $8, adults $4, students & sr citizens $2, children under 5 free, Wed free
Collections: Focus of the collection is the works of art created by Indian, Inuit and Metis artists, the artists of the Group of Seven and their contemporaries and other artists who have made or make a contribution to the development of Canadian Art
Exhibitions: Temporary exhibitions lasting from 1 to 3 months
Publications: Permanet collection catalogue; exhibition catalogues; quarterly newsletters
Activities: Comprehensive education programme at the elementary and secondary school levels; guided group tours by appointment; extension programme and temporary exhibition programme; programmes for kindergarten and special interest groups
L **Library,** L0J 1C0. Tel 416-893-1121; FAX 416-893-2588. *Librn & Archivist* Linda Morita
Open by appointment
Library Holdings: Vols 5000; Per subs 30; Archival material; AV — Slides; Other — Clipping files, exhibition catalogs, manuscripts, memorabilia, pamphlets, photographs
Special Subjects: American Indian Art, Art History, Eskimo Art, Landscapes, Painting - Canadian, Printmaking, Prints, Canadian Art, Inuit & Canadian Native Art & Culture

LINSAY

M **THE LINDSAY GALLERY,** 8 Victoria Ave N, K9V 4E5. Tel 705-324-1780; FAX 705-324-2051. *Cur* Chuck Burns
Open Mon - Fri 10 AM - 5 PM, Sat 1 - 5 PM. Estab 1976. 600 sq ft of converted house for main gallery & separate room 100 sq ft. Average Annual Attendance: 10,500. Mem: 400; family $20, individual $15, sr citizens $10, student $5; annual meeting in February
Income: $76,000 (financed by membership, city & province appropriation, corporate sponsorship)
Purchases: $50,000 (200 drawings by Ernest Thompson Seton)
Collections: †Historical & contemporary Canadian; †Ernest Thompson Seton Collection
Publications: Quarterly bulletin
Activities: Classes for adults & children; lect open to the public, 10 vis lectr per yr; book traveling exhibitions, 1 - 2 times per yr

LONDON

M **LONDON REGIONAL ART & HISTORICAL MUSEUMS,** 421 Ridout St N, N6A 5H4. Tel 519-672-4580; FAX 519-660-8397. *Exec Dir* Nancy Poole; *Chief Cur Gallery* Judith Rodger; *Cur Contemporary Art* James Patten; *Registrar & Cur Historical Art* Barry Fair; *Dir Finance & Personnel* Shelagh Parg; *Chief Cur Museums* Lynne DiStefano; *Asst Cur Museums* Michael Baker; *Chief Cur of Museums* Lynne Distefano; *Dir of Conservation* Jane Holland; *Exec Asst* Gloria Kerr; *Technican Museums Coll & Exhib* Linda Berks; *Coordr Public Progs* Bonnie Morgan; *Publicity & Promotion Coordr* Ruth Anne Murray; *Graphic Designer* Robert Ballantine; *Accounts Receivable & Donations Clerk* Colleen Ross; *Bookkeeper* Chen Hwon Yeh; *Membership Clerk* Elaine Laszlo; *Tour Coordr & Secy* Heidi Sara; *Information Receptionist* Janet Hartshom; *Dir Development* Sarah Israels
Open Tues - Sun & holidays noon - 5 PM. No admis fee. Estab 1940. New bldg open 1980 containing 26,500 sq ft of exhibition space, 150 seat auditorium. Mem: 3310; family $50, individual $30, sr citizens & students $15; annual meeting in Jan
Income: $1,201,900 (financed by city, province, mem & donations, community)
Collections: Permanent Collection stresses regional & local artists, who have become internationally & nationally recognized such as Jack Chambers, Greg Curnoe, F M Bell-Smith & Paul Peel; Hamilton King Meek Memorial Collection; F B Housser Memorial Collection; The Moore Collection; a collection of historical art & artifacts, primarily of London & region
Exhibitions: Works of art - international, national & regional; programs of multi-media nature, including performing arts, exhibitions of historical artifacts & art
Publications: Exhibition catalogues
Activities: Classes for adults & children; docent training; lect open to public, some for members only; concerts; gallery talks; tours; individual paintings & objects of art lent; book traveling exhibitions; originate traveling exhibitions; gallery shop sells books, jewelery magazines, original art, prints and reproductions

M **UNIVERSITY OF WESTERN ONTARIO,** McIntosh Art Gallery, N6A 3K7. Tel 519-661-3181; FAX 519-661-3292. *Dir* Arlene Kennedy; *Cur* Catherine Elliot Shaw; *Installations Officer & Registrar* David Falls
Open Tues - Thurs noon - 7 PM, Fri - Sun noon - 4 PM, cl Mon. No admis fee. Estab 1942. Three galleries with a total of 2960 sq ft. Average Annual Attendance: 14,000. Mem: 155
Income: Financed by endowment, membership, provincial appropriation, special grants and University funds
Collections: Canadian Art

Publications: Newsletter, bimonthly; exhibition catalogues
Activities: Lect open to public, 4 - 6 visiting lectr per year; concerts; gallery talks; tours; individual paintings and original objects lent to galleries; originate traveling exhibitions

L **D B Weldon Library,** 1151 Richmond St, N6A 3K7. Tel 519-679-2111. *Dir* Catherine Quinlan
Open to all university staff, faculty, and students for research and borrowing. Open to the public for in-house research
Library Holdings: Vols 59,900; Per subs 129; Micro — Fiche, reels; Other — Exhibition catalogs, pamphlets
Special Subjects: Applied Art, Canadian Art, Medieval & Byzantine Art, Western Art

MIDLAND

M **HURONIA MUSEUM,** Little Lake Park, L4R 4P4. Tel 705-526-2844; FAX 705-526-8757. *Dir* James Hunter; *Photographer & Cur* Bill Smith; *Educ* Natalie Quealey
Open Mon - Sat 9 AM - 5 PM, Sun 10 AM - 5 PM. Admis adult $4, student $3. Estab 1947 to collect art of Historic Huronia. Several large galleries dealing with local contemporary artists, historical regional artists, design exhibit on Thor Hansen & other designers. Average Annual Attendance: 20,000. Mem: dues $25; annual meeting last Thurs in May
Income: $2000,000 (financed by endowment, mem, admissions, sales, fund raising, grants)
Purchases: $10,000 (Ted Lord Art Collection)
Collections: †Mary Holln Collection (watercolors); †Franz Johnson Collection (oils, watercolors); †Ted Lord Collection (paintings, prints, watercolors); †Bill Wood Collection (etchings, oils, watercolors); General Collection (carvings, oil, watercolors)
Exhibitions: A Photographic History of the Georgian Bay Lumber Co 1871-1942
Publications: Exhibition catalogues, annual
Activities: Children's classes; docent programs; lectures open to public, 3 vis lectr per yr; competitions; lending collection contains paintings & art objects; book traveling exhibitions 5 per yr; originate traveling exhibitions 5 per yr; retail store sells books, prints, magazines, slides, original art, reproductions

MISSISSAUGA

L **MISSISSAUGA LIBRARY SYSTEM,** 301 Burnhamthorpe Rd W, L5B 3Y3. Tel 416-615-3600; FAX 416-615-3615. *Chief Librn* Don Mills
Open: hours vary according to branch. No admis fee. Outlet for local artists at branch galleries; present more widely recognised artists at Central and Burnhamthorpe Galleries. Total of eleven galleries in system, 90 running ft each, often multi-purpose rooms
Collections: Permanent collection of 135 paintings and prints by Canadian artists, emphasis on prints (all framed)
Exhibitions: Annual Juried Art Show Open
Publications: Link News Tabloid Format, quarterly
Activities: Lectures open to public; competitions with cash prizes; lending collection contains books and 150 motion pictures; book traveling exhibitions

L **Central Library, Art Department,** 301 Burnhamthorpe Rd W, L5B 1H3. Tel 416-615-3600; FAX 416-615-3615. *Dir Public Serv* Barbara Quinlan
Open Mon - Fri 9 AM - 9 PM, Sat 9 AM - 5 PM, Sept - June Sun 1 - 5 PM
Income: $7,000,000 (financed by Municipal & Provincial funds)
Library Holdings: Vols 22,700; Per subs 29; AV — Cassettes, fs, lantern slides, motion pictures, slides, v-tapes; Other — Clipping files, exhibition catalogs, original art works, pamphlets, prints
Special Subjects: Canadian prints
Activities: Lectures open to public; competitions with awards

M **UNIVERSITY OF TORONTO,** Blackwood Gallery, Mississauga Rd, L5L 1C6. Tel 416-828-3789; FAX 416-825-5474. *Cur* Nancy Hazelgrove
Open Mon - Fri noon - 2 PM & 3 - 5 PM, other times by appointment. No admis fee. Estab 1973 to educate the public & display artists works. Gallery has four walls with various dividers & floor space of 36 x 60 ft. Average Annual Attendance: 2000
Collections: Acrylics, drawings, oils, pen sketches & prints, sculpture, water colour
Exhibitions: Sally Glanville, drawings; Lorraine Phillips, constructions; Bert Weir, paintings
Publications: Blackwood Bulletin, bi-annual
Activities: Classes for children; lect open to public; competitions with awards; individual paintings & original objects of art lent; book traveling exhibitions

NORTH YORK

M **JEWISH COMMUNITY CENTRE OF TORONTO,** The Koffler Gallery, 4588 Bathurst St, M2R 1W6. Tel 416-636-2145; FAX 416-636-1536. *Dir* Jane Mahut; *Admin Asst* Rose Brinder; *Asst Cur* John Massier
Open Sun - Thurs 10 AM - 4 PM, Tues & Wed 6 - 9 PM, Fri 9 AM - noon. Estab 1976. Average Annual Attendance: 12,000. Mem: 250
Income: $35,000 (financed by membership)
Collections: Clay, Glass
Publications: Catalogues & exhibitions brochures
Activities: Classes for adults & children; docent training; lectures open to public, 3 vis lectr per yr; traveling exhibitions, 3-5 per yr; originate traveling exhibitions, 1-3 per yr; gallery shop sells original glass, ceramics & jewelry produced by Canadian artisans

M **YORK UNIVERSITY,** Art Gallery of York University, 4700 Keele St, Ross Bldg N145, M3J 1P3. Tel 416-736-5169; FAX 416-736-5461. *Dir & Cur* Loretta Yarlow; *Asst Cur* Catherine Crowston; *Admin Asst* Jeanette SilverThorne
Open Tues - Fri 10 AM - 4 PM, Wed 10 AM - 8 PM, Sun noon - 5 PM, cl June, July & Aug. Admis donations welcomed. Estab 1970 to maintain a program of

exhibitions covering a broad spectrum of the contemporary visual arts. Gallery is 3600 sq ft, exhibition space only 2800 sq ft, including program space & support space 750 sq ft. Average Annual Attendance: 15,000
Income: Financed by university, federal, provincial & municipal grants & private donations
Collections: Approx 750 works including ethnographical items and artifacts, approx 550 of the works are by Canadian artists
Exhibitions: (1992) Crossroads: Genevieve Cadieux, Robin Collyer, Isa Genzken, Rodney Grahm, Bernie Miller, Maria Norman, Cristina Iglesias
Publications: Exhibit catalogs
Activities: Lectures open to public, 3 - 4 vis lectrs per yr; gallery talks; tour; individual paintings and original objects of art lent for major shows or retrospectives to other members of the University and faculty for their offices; book traveling exhibitions; originate traveling exhibitions

L **Fine Arts Phase II Slide Library,** 4700 Keele St, M3J 1P3. Tel 416-736-5534; FAX 416-736-5534. *Cur* M Metraux; *Slide Librn* Marie Holubec; *Slide Librn* Lillian Heinson
Income: Financed through university
Library Holdings: AV — Slides 250,000
Collections: Bazin Library; T A Heinrich Collection; Rare Books Library

OAKVILLE

CANADIAN SOCIETY FOR EDUCATION THROUGH ART
For further information, see National and Regional Organizations

OAKVILLE GALLERIES
M **Centennial Gallery and Gairloch Gallery,** 1306 Lakeshore Rd E, L6J 1L6. Tel 416-844-4402; FAX 416-844-7968. *Pres of Board* G McIntyre; *Dir* Francine Perinet; *Cur Contemporary Art* Marnie Fleming; *Installations & Registrar* Rod Demerling; *Public Programmes Coordr* Rebecca Diederichs; *Office Mgr* Marilyn Barnes
Centennial Gallery open Tues - Thurs noon - 9 PM, Fri & Sat noon - 5 PM, Sun 1 - 5 PM; Gairloch Gallery open Tues - Sun 1 - 5 PM. Estab Centennial 1967, Gairloch 1972, to exhibit contemporary visual arts. Average Annual Attendance: 48,000. Mem: 500
Special Subjects: Contemporary Canadian Art
Collections: Contemporary Canadian painting, sculpture, photographs, drawing and prints; contemporary outdoor sculpture
Exhibitions: Monthly exhibits
Publications: Exhibition catalogues
Activities: Classes for children; docent training, volunteer committee; Lect open to public; gallery talks; tours; originate traveling exhibitions

L **SHERIDAN COLLEGE OF APPLIED ARTS AND TECHNOLOGY,** Visual Arts & Crafts Library, 1430 Trafalgar Rd, L6H 2L1. Tel 416-845-9430, Ext 2488. *Library Technician* M LaPointe; *Library Technician* I Sillius
Open daily 8 AM - 5 PM. Estab 1970 to serve the students and faculty of the School of Visual Arts
Library Holdings: Vols 9000; Per subs 116; Micro — Fiche; AV — Slides 27,000; Other — Clipping files, exhibition catalogs
Special Subjects: Art History, Crafts, Graphic Design, Illustration, Photography, Computer Animation Design, Computer Graphics

OSHAWA

M **THE ROBERT MCLAUGHLIN GALLERY,** Civic Centre, L1H 3Z3. Tel 416-576-3000. *Dir* Joan Murray; *Chief Adminr* Sally Bowers
Open Mon - Fri 10 AM - 6 PM, Tues evenings 7 - 9 PM, Sat noon - 5 PM, Sun 2 - 5 PM. No admis fee. Estab Feb 1967 as The Art Gallery of Oshawa, in May 1969 as the Robert McLaughlin Gallery. R S McLaughlin Gallery 77 x 38 x 15 ft; Isabel McLaughlin Gallery 77 x 38 x 13 ft; Alexandra Luke Gallery (no 1) 62 x 48 x 9 1/2 ft; Alexandra Luke Gallery (no 2) 46 x 27 x 13 ft; E P Taylor Gallery 23 x 37 x 9 ft; General Motors Gallery 25 x 37 x 9 ft; Corridor Ramp (Isabel McLaughlin Gallery) 48 x 8 x 10 ft; Corridor (Alexandra Luke) 68 x 5 1/2 x 8 ft with Foyer & Director's Office. Average Annual Attendance: 27,000. Mem: 700; dues family $20, single $15, student & Sr citizen $5; annual meeting Feb
Income: Financed by membership, city appropriation, Canada Council, Ministry Culture & Recreation, Wintario & Ontario Arts Council
Collections: Canadian 19th & 20th century drawings, paintings, prints & sculpture; †major collection of works by Painters Eleven
Exhibitions: (1993) Richard Toms: Lithographs-Series I; William Blair Bruce: Perfect Reality - 1890; Stephanie Ravner: The Skin of God; Decade of Voices: Photographs by Thelma Pepper; The Three R's; John Bartosik: A Vision in Retrospect; Roman Catholic Separate School Board; John McGregor: Time; Barbara Astman: Fruit Series; Grant McConnel: Tales of Dominion; Fire Fire
; Georges Loranger; Firefighters Anniversary; The Great Effect of the Imagination on the World: Brenda Pelkey; Oshawa Art Association; Immolation: Recent Figurative Paintings by Graham Metson; Painters Eleven; Family Studies: Photographs & Text by Avanti Apple; The Circus is Coming
; Dorothy Cameron: Reflections of the Inner Eve; Ralph Price: Crucifixes; Doris McCarthy: Feast of Incarnation, Paintings: 1929 - 1989; Michael Forster: Order Out of Chaos, Sixty Years of a Canadian Artist; Today's Three R's; Hugh Michaelson: Paintings; Art Mart. (1994) Painters Eleven; Richard Sturm; Mead Art Gallery Exchange; Cornerstones & Cobblestones; Barbara Elizabeth Mercer: Dreams of the Night
Publications: Annual Report; Bulletin, monthly; Calendar of Events, annually, Exhibition catalogs
Activities: Classes for adults and children; docent training; lect open to public, 6 visiting lectr per year; concerts; gallery talks; tours; competitions; exten dept; individual paintings and original objects of art lent to schools, institutions and industries; lending collection contains 300 cassettes, 300 color reproductions, framed reproductions, 10 original art works, 10,000 slides, 2000 books; originate traveling exhibitions; sales shop sells books, original art and local crafts

L Library, Civic Centre, L1H 3Z3. Tel 416-576-3000; FAX 416-576-9774. *Librn* Patricia Claxton-Oldfield
Open Tues & Thurs 10 AM - 9 PM, Wed & Fri 10 AM - 6 PM, Sat & Sun noon - 5 PM. Admis donations accepted. Open to gallery members
Library Holdings: Vols 3000; AV — A-tapes, cassettes, slides, v-tapes; Other — Clipping files, exhibition catalogs, manuscripts, pamphlets, photographs
Special Subjects: Research of Painters Eleven and 19th and 20th Century works
Collections: †Canadian contemporary art books

OTTAWA

A CANADIAN ARTISTS' REPRESENTATION-LE FRONT DES ARTISTES CANADIENS, 189 Laurier E, K1N 6P1. Tel 613-235-6277; FAX 613-235-7425. *Dir* Greg Graham; *Admin Asst* Flora Kallies
Open daily 9 AM - 4 PM. Estab 1968, Canadian Artists' Representation-Le Front des Artistes Canadiens is an association of professional artists whose mandate is the improvement of the financial & professional status of all Canadian artists through research & public education. CARFAC is a national organization run by artists for artists, membership works on three levels: local, provincial & national. Mem: 1200; open to practicing professional artists; dues $20 - $250; annual meeting in May
Income: Financed by endowment and membership
Publications: ArtAction, 3 issues per year; Canadian Visual Artist; Taxation Information for Canadian Visual Arts
Activities: Lect open to the public, 1 vis lectr per yr

CANADIAN CONFERENCE OF THE ARTS
For further information, see National and Regional Organizations

CANADIAN CRAFTS COUNCIL, Canadien de l'Artisanat
For further information, see National and Regional Organizations

M CANADIAN MUSEUM OF CONTEMPORARY PHOTOGRAPHY
(Formerly National Gallery of Canada), PO Box 465, Station A, K1N 9N6. Tel 613-990-8257; FAX 613-990-6542. *Dir Museum* Martha Langford; *Asst Cur* Martha Hanna; *Asst Cur* Pierre Dessureault; *Prog Mgr* Maureen McEvoy
Estab 1939 to initiate & promote the production & distribution of still photographs designed to interpret Canada to Canadians & to other nations; mandate expanded in early 70's to include photography as a more expressive & subjective form of communication
Income: Financed by federal government agency
Library Holdings: Per subs 500; Monographs, 100,000 vols
Collections: Collection of works by Contemporary Canadian Photographers
Exhibitions: Philip Bergerson; Robert Bourdeau; Randy Bradley; Corinne Bronfman; Edward Burtynsky; Michel Campeau; Fred Cattroll; Lawrence Chrismas; Donigan Cumming; Doug Curran; Walter Curtin; Nigel Dickson; Pierre Gaudard; Richard Holden; Stephen Livick; Chris Lund; David Miller; Pat Morrow; David McMillan; Claude Palardy; John Paskievich; Denis Plain; Michael Schreier; Volker Seding; Orest Semchishen; Tom Skudra; James Stadnick; Shin Sugin; Kryn Taconis; Sam Tata; Jeremy Taylor; Gary Wilson; Evergon; Cheryl Sourkes, Lynne Cohen, Michael Mitchell; John Flanders; Alain Chagnon; Justin Wonnacott; Pierre Guimond; Susan McEachern
Publications: Walter Curtin: A Retrospective - Walter Curtin; Reality & Motive in Documentary Photography - Donigan Cumming; Evergon; The Tata Era - Sam Tata
Activities: Gallery talks on request; originate traveling exhibitions, across Canada & outside the country

M CANADIAN MUSEUM OF NATURE (Formerly National Museum of Natural Sciences), Musee Canadien de la Nature, Metcalfe & McLeod Sts, PO Box 3443, Station D, K1P 6P4. Tel 613-998-3923; FAX 613-998-1065. *Head Library & Archives* Arch W L Stewart; *Project Leader Temporary Exhib* Helene Arsenault-Desfosses
Open Sept - Apr daily 10 AM - 5 PM & Thurs 10 AM - 8 PM, May - Sept daily 9:30 AM - 5 PM & Sun, Mon & Thurs 9:30 AM - 8 PM, cl Christmas. Admis family $12, adult $4, students $3, sr citizens & children 6 - 16 $2, children under 6 free. Estab 1842 to disseminate knowledge about the natural sciences, with particular but not exclusive reference to Canada. Average Annual Attendance: 300,000
Collections: †Prints; †Paintings, †Sculpture
Exhibitions: (1992) Evergreen (Natiional nature-related exhibition, annual); 15 exhibitions by various artists
Activities: Lectures; film series; demonstrations & workshops dealing with natural history subjects; exten dept; individual paintings & original objects of art lent to other museums on the traveling exhibition circuit; lending collection contains 600 original prints & paintings, 150 photographs, 400 sculputres; book traveling exhibitions; originate traveling exhibitions

CANADIAN MUSEUMS ASSOCIATION, Association des Musees Canadiens
For further information, see National and Regional Organizations

M CANADIAN WAR MUSEUM, 330 Sussex Dr, K1A 0M8. Tel 613-992-2774; 613-954-1016. *Dir* V J H Suthren
Open daily, cl Christmas. Estab 1880 to collect, classify, preserve & display objects relevant to Canadian military history. Average Annual Attendance: 225,000
Income: Financed by government funds
Collections: Uniforms & accoutrements; medals & insignia; equipment; vehicles; art; archives; photographs; weapons
Exhibitions: (1990-1991) Armored Warriors
Activities: Educ dept; lectures & film presentations open to public; tours; artwork lent to other museums & galleries, educational institutions, national exhibition centers; Lending Collection contains 13,000 books; sales shop sells books, reproductions, prints, slides, shirts, caps, spoons, plastic models, films & postcards

M CANADIAN WILDLIFE & WILDERNESS ART MUSEUM, 150 MacLaren St, K2P 0L2. Tel 613-237-1581; FAX 613-235-5027. *Dir* Gary Slimon
Open Mon - Sun 10 AM - 5 PM. Admis $3. Estab 1987. Mem: dues $50-$1000; annual meeting in Jan
Income: Financed by endowment, membership, state appropriation, museum proceeds
Collections: Wildlife & wilderness paintings, sculpture, carvings & decoys
Publications: newsletter & brochure
Activities: Classes for children; 'how-to' seminars; lectures open to the public, 4 vis lectr per yr; book traveling exhibitions, 1 per yr; originate traveling exhibitions; museum shop sells books, magazines, prints, slides

L Library, 150 MacLaren St, K2P 0L2. *Dir* Gary Slimon
Library mainly for research for member artists
Library Holdings: magazines; AV — Slides; Other — Exhibition catalogs

A ENVIRONMENT CANADA - CANADIAN PARKS SERVICE, Laurier House, 335 Laurier Ave E, K1N 6R4. Tel 613-692-2581, 992-8142; FAX 613-692-3457. *Area Mgr* Peter Minnelli
Open Oct - Mar Tues - Sat 10 AM - 5 PM, Sun 2 - 5 PM; Apr - Sept Tues - Sat 9 AM - 5 PM, Sun 2 - 5 PM. No admis fee. Estab 1951. This is a historic house and former residence of two Prime Ministers, Sir Wilfrid Laurier and the Rt Honorable William Lyon Mackenzie King, and contains furniture and memorabilia belonging to a third Prime Minister, Lester Pearson. The house is primarily furnished in the style of its last occupant, the Rt Honorable William Lyon Mackenzie King, with space given to the Laurier Collection. The Lester Pearson study was installed in 1974. Average Annual Attendance: 30,000
Income: Financed by federal government and trust fund
Publications: Main Park Brochure provided to visitors
Activities: Guided tours

NATIONAL ARCHIVES OF CANADA
L Documentary Art and Photography, 395 Wellington St, K1A 0N3. Tel 613-995-1300, 992-3884; FAX 613-995-6226. *National Archivist* Jean-Pierre Wallot; *Dir* Lilly Koltun; *Collections Mgr* Brian Carey; *Consultation of Coll* Sylvie Gervais; *Documentary Art Acquisition* Jim Burant; *Information Services Section* Gerald Stone; *Photography Acquisition* Joan M Schwartz
Open daily 9 AM - 4:45 PM. Estab 1905 to acquire and preserve significant Canadian archival material in the area of visual media, including paintings, watercolours, drawings, prints, medals, heraldry and posters, and photography relating to all aspects of Canadian life and to the development of the country, and to provide suitable research services and facilities to make this documentation available to the public by means of exhibititions, publications and public catalogue
Income: Financed by federal appropriation
Purchases: $80,000
Library Holdings: Vols 4000
Special Subjects: Art History, Coins & Medals, Etchings & Engravings, Miniatures, Photography, Printmaking, 18th & 19th century paintings, prints & drawings of Canadian views & subjects; 19th & 20th century Canadian photography
Collections: †1200 paintings; †18,000 watercolours & drawings; †80,000 prints; †13,000 posters; †10,000 medals; †7000 heraldic design & seals; 14,000 caricatures; 12 million photographs
Publications: Catalog of publications available on request

M NATIONAL GALLERY OF CANADA, 380 Sussex Dr, PO Box 427, Station A, K1N 9N4. Tel 613-990-1985; FAX 613-990-9824. *Dir* Dr Shirley L Thomson; *Deputy Dir Business* Mr Yves Dagenais; *Asst Dir Coll & Research* Brydon Smith; *Asst Dir Public Prog* Gyde Shepherd; *Asst Dir Communications & Marketing* Helen Murphy; *Asst Dir Museum Servs* Robert Kaszanits; *Cur Canadian Art* Charles Hill; *Asst Cur Later Canadian Art* Denise Leclerc; *Asst Cur Later Canadian Art* Pierre Landry; *Asst Cur Early Canadian Art* Victoria Baker; *Asst Cur Early Canadian Art* Rene Villeneuve; *Assoc Cur Canadian Prints & Drawings* Rosemarie Tovell; *Asst Cur Inuit Art* Marie Routledge; *Assoc Cur Contemporary Art* Diane Nemiroff; *Asst Cur Film & Video* Open; *Acting Asst Cur Contemporary Art* Janice Seline; *Cur European Art* Catherine Johnston; *Assoc Cur European Art* Michael Pantazzi; *Curatorial Asst European Art* Open; *Cur Prints & Drawings* Mimi Cazort; *Assoc Cur European & American Prints & Drawings* Douglas Schoenherr; *Curatorial Asst Prints & Drawings* Julie Hodgson; *Cur Photography Coll* James Borcoman; *Asst Cur Photography Coll* Ann Thomas; *Coordr Colls, Prints, Drawings & Photographs* Michael Gribbon
Open Sept - May, Tues - Sat 10 AM - 5 PM, Wed - Fri 10 AM - 8 PM. No admis fee. Founded 1880 under the patronage of the Governor-General, the Marquess of Lorne, & his wife the Princess Louise; first incorporated 1913 & charged with the development & care of the National Collections & the promotion of art in Canada. Since 1968, the National Gallery has been part of the National Museums of Canada, reporting to a Board of Trustees estab for the Corporation. The Gallery is housed (since 1960) in the Lorne Building with 8 floors devoted to exhibition space, auditorium, workshops, offices, laboratories & cafeteria; a new building is under construction & will open in 1988. Average Annual Attendance: 350,000
Purchases: $3,000,000
Collections: More than 40,000 works; including paintings, sculpture, prints, drawings, photographs, silver, decorative arts, video & film; Canadian, American, European & Asian art from the 14th-20th century prints & drawings of the five principal art schools; American painting & sculpture, including Calder (Jacaranda), Newman (the Way I); Canadian works by Brymner, Carr-Harris, Max Dean, Edson, Fitzgerald, Fraser, Goodwin, Jacobi, Bill Jones, Lyman, Magor, Massey, Peel, D & R Rabinowitch, Snow, A Y Jackson, Homer Watson, John Hammond, George Reid, Louis-Philippe Hebert, Claude Tousignant, Charles Gagnon, William Ronald, Michael Snow, Robin Collyer, Joe Fafard, Betty Goodwin, Ulysse Comtois, Louise Gadbois, Dennis Burton, William von Mott Berczy, Paul-Emile Borduas, Daniel Gowler, Lucius O'Brien, Joyce Weiland, Adolph Vogt, Cornelius Krieghoff, J W Beatty, Otto Jacobi, Emanuel Hahn, Elizabeth Wyn Wood, John Lyman, Maurice Cullen, Henry Sandham, Charles Comfort, Paterson Ewen, David Bolduc, David Craven, Roland Poulin, Shirley Wutasalo, Paraskeva Clark, Graham Coughtry, Jack Humphrey, Greg

Curnoe, J W G MacDonald, Carl Schaefer, Jean-Baptiste Cote, William Sawyer, Denis Juneau, Pierre Boogaerts; European painting and sculpture including Jan Both, Annibale Caracci, Courbet, A Cuyp, Philippe de Champaigne, Jean-Germain Drouais, Baron Gros, Klee Jean-Francois Millet, Murillo, Preti, Theodore Rousseau, Vernet, Carriera, James Ensor, Giovanni Battista, Foggini, Braque, Salvator Rosa, Bernardo Cavallino; prints and drawings by Cezanne, Degas, Fragonard, M Gandolfi, Kandinsky, Le Prince, A Milani, Pissaro, Rembrandt, Redon, Paul Klee, Edouard Manet, Honore Daumier, Henri Fantin-Latour, Edvard Munch, Mauro Gandoffi, Annibule Carracci, Jean-Baptiste Oudry, Salvador Dali, Camille Pissaro, Edgar Degas, J B C Corot, Mary Cassatt, Paul Signac, Baron Gros (Bacchus and Ariadne), Klee (Angst), Jean-Francois Millet (The Pig Slaughter), Murillo (Portrait of a Vacalier), Preti (The Feast of Absalom), Theodore Rousseau (The Old Park at St Cloud)
Exhibitions: Exhibitions from permanent collections, private & public sources are organized & circulated in Canada & abroad
Publications: Annual Bulletin (incorporating Annual Review, with current acquisition lists); catalogs of permanent collections (beginning Nov 1988); Documents in the History of Canadian Art; exhibition-related books & catalogs; Masterpieces in the National Gallery of Canada
Activities: Lectures; films; gallery talks; guided tours at Gallery & lect tours throughout Canada; rents transparencies & colour separations & sells slides, catalogs & black & white prints, through sub-section Reproduction Rights & Sales; originate traveling exhibitions; specialized art bookstore with reproductions, postcards, etc
L Library, 380 Sussex Dr, K1N 9N4. Tel 613-998-8949; FAX 613-998-9818. *Chief Librn* Murray Waddington; *Reference Librn* M Vilcins; *Head Reader Serv* Marsia Sweet
Open Mon - Fri noon - 6 PM. Estab 1918 to support the research and information requirements of gallery personnel; to make its collections of resource materials in the fine arts available to Canadian libraries and scholars; to serve as a source of information about Canadian art and art activities in Canada
Library Holdings: Vols 87,000; Per subs 1000; Micro — Fiche, reels; Other — Clipping files, exhibition catalogs, pamphlets
Special Subjects: Canadian art, post-medieval Western art with special emphasis on drawings, painting, prints, photography and sculpture
Collections: Art Documentation; Canadiana
Publications: Artists in Canada; Files in National Gallery Library; Files of Fiche: Canadian Art Microdocuments
Activities: Library tours

M NATIONAL MUSEUM OF SCIENCE & TECHNOLOGY, 1867 St Laurent Blvd, PO Box 9724, Ottawa Terminal, K1G 5A3. Tel 613-991-3044; FAX 613-990-3636. *Dir* Dr G Sainte-Marie
Open daily 9 AM - 5 PM, Thurs to 8 PM, cl Mon during winter. Admis adults $4, senior citizens & students $3, children 6-15 $1. Estab 1967 to foster scientific & technological literacy throughout Canada by establishing & maintaining a collection of scientific & technological objects
Activities: Educ Dept

M NATIONAL MUSEUM OF SCIENCE & TECHNOLOGY CORPORATION, National Aviation Museum, Rockcliffe Airport, K1G 5A3. Tel 613-993-2010; FAX 613-990-3655; 800-463-2038 (Canada). *Dir* C Terry; *Cur* A J (Fred) Shortt
Open daily 9 AM - 5 PM, Thurs to 9 PM, cl Mon, Labor Day to May 1. Admis adults $4.28, srs & students $3.50, children $1.50. Estab 1960 to illustrate the evolution of the flying machine & the important role aircraft played in Canada's development. Average Annual Attendance: 250,000. Mem: 700; dues $25 - $60
Collections: 115 aircraft plus thousands of aviation related artifacts
Exhibitions: (1992) Artflight 92. (1993) Artflight 93, annual nation-wide competition & exposition of aviation art
Activities: Educ Dept; sales shop sells books, magazines & prints

L OTTAWA PUBLIC LIBRARY, Fine Arts Dept, 120 Metcalfe St, K1P 5M2. Tel 613-236-0301; FAX 613-567-4013. *Dir* Gilles Frappier; *Admin Dir* Jean Martel
Open Mon - Thurs 10 AM - 9 PM, Fri 10 AM - 6 PM, Sat 9:30 AM - 5 PM, Sun 1 - 5 PM (winters). Estab 1906 to serve the community as a centre for general & reliable information; to select, preserve & administer books & related materials in organized collections; to provide opportunity for citizens of all ages to educate themselves continuously
Income: $8,808,600 (financed by city, province, other)
Library Holdings: Vols 9000; Per subs 65; Micro — Fiche, reels; AV — Cassettes, fs; Other — Clipping files, pamphlets
Exhibitions: Monthly exhibits highlighting local artists, craftsmen, photographers and collectors
Activities: Lect open to public; library tours

ROYAL ARCHITECTURAL INSTITUTE OF CANADA
For further information, see National and Regional Organizations

OWEN SOUND

M TOM THOMSON MEMORIAL ART GALLERY, 840 First Ave W, N4K 4K4. Tel 519-376-1932; FAX 519-371-0511. *Dir* Maggie Mitchell
Open Sept - June, Tues - Sat 10 AM - 5 PM, Wed 7 - 9 PM, Sun noon - 5 PM; July & Aug, daily 10 AM - 5 PM, Sun noon - 5 PM. No admis fee. Estab 1967 to collect & display paintings by Tom Thomson, a native son & Canada's foremost landscape artist; to educate the public. Two galleries: paintings by Tom Thomson on permanent display; changing exhibitions in both galleries. Average Annual Attendance: 20,000. Mem: 550; dues family $25, individual $15; senior citizens & students $10
Income: Financed by city appropriation & provincial grants & fundraising
Collections: Tom Thomson; Historic & Contemporary Canadian Artists; Group of Seven
Exhibitions: (1993) John Boyle; Jim Thomson; Calendar in Pottery; Catherine Widgery; Sculpture
Publications: Bulletin, six per year; four exhibition catalogs per year
Activities: Classes for adults & children; docent training; lectures open to public; gallery talks; tours; films; competitions with awards; concerts; exten dept serves city buildings; art rental & sales library; museum shop sells books, reproductions, prints & postcards

L Library, 840 First Ave W, N4K 4K4. Tel 519-376-1932; FAX 519-371-0511. *Dir* Maggie Mitchell
Open for lending & reference of Canadian Art only
Library Holdings: Vols 2000; Per subs 300; Other — Exhibition catalogs
Collections: Files on Tom Thomson

PETERBOROUGH

M ART GALLERY OF PETERBOROUGH, 2 Crescent St, K9J 2G1. Tel 705-743-9179. *Dir* Illi-Maria Tamplin; *Prog Asst* Dominick Hardy; *Secy* Vera Novacek
Open Tues - Sun 1 - 5 PM, Thurs 1 - 9 PM. No admis fee. Estab 1973. Gallery situated along a lake and in a park; new extension added and completed June 1979. Average Annual Attendance: 18,600. Mem: 1000; dues sustaining $25, family $20, individual $15, sr citizens $12, student $8; annual meeting June
Income: Financed by membership, fund raising & provincial, federal, municipal grants
Collections: European and Canadian works of art
Publications: Catalogues on some exhibitions; Bulletin of Events, monthly; pamphlets on artists in exhibitions
Activities: Classes for adults and children; dramatic programs; docent training; workshops; art program to public schools; lectures open to public; gallery talks; tours; individual paintings & original objects of art lent to other galleries; lending collection contains 250 original art works; sales shop sells books, magazines, crafts

SAINT CATHARINES

A RODMAN HALL ARTS CENTRE, 109 St Paul Crescent, L2S 1M3. Tel 416-684-2925. *Pres* E Boyagian; *VPres* D Nazar; *Secy* M Zuberec; *Dir* A Peter Harris; *Executive Secy* Susan Dickinson; *Cur of Education* Debra Attenborough
Open Tues, Thurs, Fri 9 AM - 5 PM, Wed 9 AM - 5 PM & 7 - 10 PM, Sat & Sun 1 - 5 PM, cl Mon. No admis fee. Estab 1960, art gallery, cultural centre and visual arts exhibitions. Four galleries in an 1853, 1960 and 1975 addition. 1975 - A1 - National Museums of Canada. Average Annual Attendance: 35,000. Mem: 850; dues $50, $25, $15, & $5; annual meeting in Sept
Income: Financed by membership, city, state and national appropriation
Collections: American graphics & drawings; †Canadian drawings, †paintings, †sculpture & †watercolours; international graphics & sculpture
Exhibitions: Monthly exhibitions featuring painting, photographs, sculpture & other art
Publications: Catalogue - Lord and Lady Head Watercolours; monthly calendar; Rodmon Hall Arts Center (1960-1981)
Activities: Classes for adults and children; dramatic programs; docent training; lectures open to public, 5 vis lectr per year; concerts; gallery talks; tours; jury show competitions; jury and public awards given for best three works in exhibition; exten dept serves city of St Catharines; individual paintings and original objects of art lent to schools and gallery at City Hall; lending collection contains 10 original art works and 200 original prints; book traveling exhibitions, 16 per year; originate traveling exhibitions; sales shop sells books, crafts, magazines, paper things, prints, reproductions and weaving
L Library, 109 St Paul Crescent, Saint Catharines, L2S 1M3. Tel 416-684-2925. *Librn* Debra Attenborough
Open Tues - Fri 9 AM - 5 PM. Estab 1960. Reference library
Library Holdings: Vols 1500; Per subs 4; Micro — Prints; AV — Lantern slides, slides; Other — Clipping files, exhibition catalogs, memorabilia, pamphlets, photographs, reproductions

SAINT THOMAS

M ST THOMAS ELGIN ART GALLERY, 301 Talbot St (Mailing add: PO Box 224, N5P 3T9). Tel 519-631-4040; FAX 519-633-1371. *Exec Dir* Jim Buckingham; *Public Prog Officer* Patti Moore; *Admin Asst* Diane Dobson
Open Tues - Sat 10 AM - 5 PM, Sun noon - 5 PM, cl Mon. No admis fee. Estab 1969. Mem: 658; dues senior citizens $10, family $20; single $15; annual meeting in May
Income: $120,000 (financed by endowment, mem, province appropriation & earned revenues)
Purchases: $20,000
Collections: †Fine Art Works by Canadian Artists
Publications: Exhibition catalogues, semi-annually; gallery newsletter 6 per year
Activities: Classes for adults & children; docent training; school programs; lectures open to public, 10 vis lectr per year; scholarships offered; exten servs provide lending collection of 500 paintings & art objects; book traveling exhibitions 5 per year; originate traveling exhibitions; sales shop sells books & original art

SARNIA

L GALLERY LAMBTON (Formerly Sarnia Public Library & Art Gallery), 124 Christina St S, N7T 2M6. Tel 519-337-3291; FAX 519-337-8164. *Dir & Cur* Howard Ford
Open Mon - Fri 9 AM - 9 PM, Sat 9 AM - 5:30 PM, Sun Oct - May 2 - 5 PM. No admis fee. Estab 1961, a collection of Canadian paintings instituted in 1919 and administered by the Women's Conservation Art Association of Sarnia. The Collection was turned over to the Sarnia Library Board in 1956 and additions are being made from time to time. 3500 sq ft; also small display area of 300 sq ft in newly renovated Lawrence House, a Victorian home. Average Annual Attendance: 35,000
Income: Financed by municipal & provincial appropriations
Purchases: Canadian works of art
Collections: †Canadian Paintings; Eskimo Carvings; a Collection of Old Photographs of Sarnia and Lambton County; sculpture
Exhibitions: Twelve to fifteen shows a year, either traveling from other galleries or initiated by the Sarnia Art Gallery

Publications: Exhibition catalogues
Activities: Classes for adults and children; lectures open to the public; gallery talks; tours; competitions with awards; films; bus trips; workshops; individual paintings & original objects of art lent; book traveling exhibitions, 6 - 7 per yr; junior museum located at Lawrence House

SCARBOROUGH

M CITY OF SCARBOROUGH, Cedar Ridge Creative Centre, 225 Confederation Dr, M1G 1B2. Tel 416-396-4026; FAX 416-396-5399. *Mgr* Todd Davidson
Open 9 AM - 9 PM. No admis fee. Estab 1985 as a gallery & teaching studio. 3-interconnecting rooms & solarium with oak panelling, 18' x 22', 18' x 28', 16' x 26'. Average Annual Attendance: 1300. Mem: Annual dues $10 (it entitles member to rent gallery for one week for $39)
Activities: Classes for adults & children; one day workshops in arts & crafts; lect open to public, 2 vis lectr per yr

SIMCOE

M EVA BROOK DONLY MUSEUM, 109 Norfolk St S, N3Y 2W3. Tel 519-426-1583. *Cur* William Yeager; *Secy* Susan Reid
Open Sept - May Wed - Sun 1 - 5 PM, May - Sept Mon - Fri 10 AM - 5 PM, Sat & Sun 1 - 5 PM. Admis general $1. Estab 1946 to display and aid research in the history of Norfolk County. Average Annual Attendance: 7000. Mem: 600; dues $15 - $25; annual meeting in Jan
Income: Financed by endowment, membership, city and provincial appropriation
Collections: Large Collection of important Early Documents and Newspapers, 370 Paintings of Historic Norfolk by W E Cantelon; Display of Artifacts of the 19th Century Norfolk County; Historical Material
Exhibitions: Concerned mainly with focusing new light on some aspects of the permanent collection; 1860's Victorian Home; Glorious Old Norfolk: 300 years of Norfolk History; Changing Exhibitions
Activities: Lectures open to the public, 15 vis lectrs per yr; tours; book traveling exhibitions, 3 per yr; museum shop sells books, crafts & candy
L Library, 109 Norfolk St S, N3Y 2W3. Tel 519-426-1583. *Cur* William Yeager
Reference and a photograph collection for display
Library Holdings: Vols 2000; Per subs 2; Micro — Fiche, reels; AV — Cassettes, slides; Other — Clipping files, manuscripts, memorabilia, original art works, photographs, prints

A LYNNWOOD ARTS CENTRE, 21 Lynnwood Ave, PO Box 67, N3Y 4K8. Tel 519-428-0540. *Chmn* Hazel Andrews; *Dir* Ellen McIntosh; *Office Mgr* Bettianne Engell
Open Tues - Fri 9 AM - 5 PM, Sat & Sun 1 - 5 PM. No admis fee. Estab 1973 to provide a focal point for the visual arts in the community. Built in 1851 - Greek Revival Architecture; orange brick with ionic columns; and is a National Historic Site. Average Annual Attendance: 20,000. Mem: 800; dues family $15, individual $10, student & sr citizen $5; annual meeting in Jan
Income: $140,000 (financed by membership, patrons - private and commercial, Ministry of Citizenship and Culture, Ontario Arts Council, Town of Simcoe, Regional Municipality of Haldimand-Norfolk)
Collections: †Contemporary Canadian Art
Exhibitions: Changing monthly exhibitions
Publications: Bi-monthly Newsletter
Activities: Classes for adults and children; docent training; lect open to public, 15 lectr per year; concerts; gallery talks; tours; seminars; juried art exhibitions (every two years) with purchase awards; individual paintings and original objects of art lent to members; museum shop sells books, hand-crafted items, prints & reproductions

STRATFORD

M STRATFORD ART ASSOCIATION, The Gallery Stratford, 54 Romeo St N, PO Box 129, N5A 6S8. Tel 519-271-5271; FAX 519-271-1642. *Dir* Robert Freeman; *Pres Bd Trustees* John Banks
Open Sept - May Sun, Tues - Fri 1 - 5 PM, Sat 10 AM - 5 PM; summer hours June - Sept Tues - Sun 9 AM - 6 PM; business hours weekdays 9 AM - 5 PM. Admis $3.50, seniors $2.50, children under 12 free. Estab 1967 as a non-profit permanent establishment open to the public and administered in the public interest for the purpose of studying, interpreting, assembling and exhibiting to the public. Average Annual Attendance: 25,000. Mem: 700; annual meeting March
Income: $348,743 (financed by mem, city appropriation, provincial & federal grants & fundraising)
Collections: †Works of art on paper
Exhibitions: Changing exhibits, monthly geared to create interest for visitors to Stratford Shakespearean Festival; during winter months geared to local municipality
Publications: Catalogs; calendar of events
Activities: Classes for adults and children; docent training; lect open to the public; gallery talks; tours; scholarships; traveling exhibitions organized and circulated; sales shop sells books, glass, Inuit, jewelry, Northwest Indian, pottery & silk

SUDBURY

LAURENTIAN UNIVERSITY
M Museum & Art Centre, c/o Department Cultural Affairs, Laurentian University, P3E 2C6. Tel 705-675-1151, Ext 1400,1402; FAX 705-674-3065. *Dir* Pamela Krueger
Open Tues - Sun noon - 5 PM, cl Mon, mornings by appointment. Admis fee voluntary. Estab 1968 to present a continuous program of exhibitions, concerts and events for the people of Sudbury and the district. Gallery has two floors of space: 124 running ft in one and 131 running ft in the second gallery and 68.5

running feet in third gallery. Average Annual Attendance: 23,000. Mem: 400; dues family $26.75, single $16.05, student & sr citizen $8.56; annual meeting in June
Income: Financed by endowment, membership, city and provincial appropriation, government and local organizations
Collections: Canadian collection dating from the late 1800's & early 1900's to contemporary. The Group of Seven, Eskimo sculptures & prints as well as works of historical Canadian artists comprise the collection; Indian works from Northern Ontario
Exhibitions: (1991) Leda Watson, Confrontations of Form; Bruno Cavallo, Impressionism & Its Context; London Life Young Contemporaries; Contemporary Artists from the Permanent Collection; Jocko Chartrand: Landscapes; Janice Gurney, Landscapes from the Permanent Collection; Doug Donley: Adam & Eve; Memory & Subjectivity; Changers: A Spiritual Renaissance; The Works of William Morris 1834 - 1896; Dennis Castellan; Pre-Raphaelite Works from area collections; Victorian Magazine Illustrations. (1992) Barbara Astman: The Fruit Series; Jean Eng: Grey Scales; Animals in Art - Works from the Permanent Collection; Dennis Geden: New Works from Canada; Frederick Hagan: Ontario North Works 1938 - 1991; Ray Laporte: Field Sketches; A Living Tradition: Selections from American Abstract Artists; Secondary School Art; Portraits in the Permanent Collection
Publications: Communique, every six weeks
Activities: Lect open to public, 10 vis lectr per year; concerts; gallery talks; tours; lending collection contains 1194 original art works & 8300 slides; museum shop sells magazines, catalogues, postcards, posters, prints & gift items
L Art Centre Library, Department Cultural Affairs, Laurentian University, P3E 2C6. Tel 705-675-1151, Ext 1400; FAX 705-674-3065. *Dir* Pamela Krueger
Open Winter daily 9 AM - 4:30 PM, Summer daily 8:30 AM - 4 PM. Estab 1977 for reference
Library Holdings: Vols 5000; Per subs 78; Micro — Cards; AV — Cassettes, lantern slides, slides 8300, v-tapes; Other — Clipping files, exhibition catalogs, pamphlets, photographs

TORONTO

M ART GALLERY OF ONTARIO, 317 Dundas St W, M5T 1G4. Tel 416-977-0414. *Dir* Glen Lowry; *Chief Cur* Dr Roald Nasgaard; *Depty Chief Admin* Sharilyn J Ingram; *Controller* Tom Lewis; *Head Educ Servs* Sheila Greenspan; *Mgr Marketing* Frank Comella; *Head Development* David Fieldman; *Dir External Affairs* Elizabeth Addison
Open Tues - Sun 11 AM - 5:30 PM, Wed evening until 9 PM, cl Mon. Admis adults $3.50, students $1.50, sr citizens $1.50 & free on Fri, members & accompanied children under 12 free, Wed evenings free. Estab 1900 to cultivate and advance the cause of the visual arts in Ontario; to conduct programmes of education in the origin, development, appreciation and techniques of the visual arts; to collect and exhibit works of art and displays and to maintain and operate a gallery and related facilities as required for this purpose; to stimulate the interest of the public in matters undertaken by the Gallery. Average Annual Attendance: 400,000. Mem: 28,000; dues supporting $100, family $60, individual $45; annual meeting June
Income: Financed by membership, provincial, city and federal appropriations and earned income
Purchases: $1,000,000
Collections: American and European Art (16th century to present); Canadian Historical and Contemporary Art; Henry Moore Sculpture Center, Prints and Drawings
Publications: Ago News, eleven times per year; annual report; exhibition catalogs
Activities: Classes for adults & children; docent training; lectures open to public; 35 vis lectr per year; concerts; gallery talks; tours; exten dept organizes traveling exhibitions, circulated throughout the Province, Canada and United States; individual paintings and original objects of art loaned; lending collection includes 60 cassettes, 80 film strips, 100,000 slides, 40 educational video tapes; originate traveling exhibitions; sales shop sells books, magazines, reproductions, prints, slides and jewelry; art rental shop for members to rent original works of art
L Edward P Taylor Research Library & Archives, 317 Dundas St W, M5T 1G4. Tel 416-979-6642; FAX 416-979-6646. *Chief Librn* Karen McKenzie; *Deputy Librn* Larry Pfaff; *Reference Librn* Randall Speller
Open Tues - Fri 1:30 - 4:45 PM. Estab 1933 to collect printed material for the documentation and interpretation of the works of art in the Gallery's collection; to provide research and informational support for the Gallery's programmes and activities; to document the art and artists of Ontario, Toronto, and Canada
Income: Financed by parent institution, donations, grants
Library Holdings: Vols 100,000; Per subs 650; Auction catalogs; Micro — Fiche, reels; Other — Clipping files, exhibition catalogs, manuscripts, pamphlets, photographs, reproductions
Special Subjects: Canadian, American and European Art from the Renaissance to the present, concentrating mainly on drawing, engraving, painting and sculpture
Collections: †Canadian Illustrated Books; Alan Garrow Collection of British Illustrated Books and Wood Engravings of the 1860's; Canadian Book-Plates; †International Guide Books; Robert D McIntosh Collection of Books on Sepulchral Monuments
L Edward P Taylor Audio-Visual Centre, 317 Dundas St W, M5T 1G4. Tel 416-977-0414, Ext 258; FAX 416-979-6646. *Head* Margaret Brennan
Media collection contains both circulating and archive material
Income: Financed by minimal fees, institutional support
Library Holdings: Media kits circulating coll 116, archive coll; AV — A-tapes 825, fs 3, lantern slides 2000, motion pictures 231, rec 5, slides 137,311, v-tapes 822
Special Subjects: Canada, Henry Moore

L ART METROPOLE ARCHIVES, 788 King St W, M5V 1N6. Tel 416-367-2304; FAX 416-365-9208. *Dir* Stella Kyriakakis; *Distribution Coordr* Margaret Brunet; *Coll Coordr* Amy Maggiacomo
Open Tues - Sat noon - 5 PM. Estab 1974 to document work by artists internationally working in non-conventional & multiple media. For reference only
Library Holdings: AV — A-tapes, rec, v-tapes; Other — Exhibition catalogs, manuscripts, memorabilia, original art works, pamphlets, photographs, prints
Collections: Books, video & performances by artists

A **ARTS AND LETTERS CLUB OF TORONTO,** 14 Elm St, M5G 1G7. Tel 416-597-0223. *Pres* Lyman Henderson
Admis by appointment. Estab 1908 to foster arts & letters in Toronto. Mem: 550; annual meeting May
Collections: Club Collection - art by members and others; Heritage Collection - art by members now deceased
L **Library,** 14 Elm St, M5G 1G7. Tel 416-597-0223. *Librn* David Skene Melvin
Open to club members and researchers for reference
Library Holdings: Vols 2500; Per subs 40; AV — A-tapes, cassettes, Kodachromes, motion pictures, slides, v-tapes; Other — Clipping files, exhibition catalogs, manuscripts, memorabilia, original art works, prints, sculpture
Special Subjects: Architecture, Sculpture, Theatre Arts, Literature, Music, Paintings, Canadian Art

CANADIAN SOCIETY OF PAINTERS IN WATERCOLOUR
For further information, see National and Regional Organizations

M **GEORGE R GARDINER MUSEUM OF CERAMIC ART,** 111 Queen's Park, M5S 2C7. Tel 416-586-5551; FAX 416-586-8085. *Cur* Meredith Chilton
Open Tues - Sun 10 AM - 5 PM. Admis adults $6, sr citizens, students & children $3.25. Estab 1984 as the only specialized museum of ceramics in North America. Museum houses one of the world's greatest collections of European ceramic art from the early 15th century to the turn of the 19th century. The earlier museum merged operations with the Royal Ontario Museum in 1984 & visitors now pay one fee to visit both facilities
Collections: English delftware; European porcelain; Italian maiolica; Pre-Columbian pottery
Activities: Classes for adults & children; docent programs; lect open to public; book traveling exhibitions 2 per year; retail store sells books, original art & modern ceramics

A **LYCEUM CLUB AND WOMEN'S ART ASSOCIATION OF CANADA,** 23 Prince Arthur Ave, M5R 1B2. Tel 416-922-2060. *Pres* R B Cumine
Open Mon - Fri 8:30 AM - 2:30 PM, cl Sat & Sun. Estab 1885 to encourage women in the arts; branches in Ontario, Hamilton, Owen Sound, St Thomas & Peterborough. Mem: 250; annual meeting April
Activities: Special exhibitions; drawing, painting; study groups; awards Founder's memorial scholarships to art students annually; scholarships given to Ontario College of Art, Royal Conservatory of Music, National Ballet
L **Library,** 23 Prince Arthur Ave, M5R 1B2. Tel 416-922-2060. *Librn* D M Johnston
Library Holdings: Vols 800
Special Subjects: Extensive Canadiana

M **THE MARKET GALLERY OF THE CITY OF TORONTO ARCHIVES,** 95 Front St E, M5E 1C2. Tel 416-392-7604; FAX 416-392-6990. *Cur* Pamela Wachna; *Cur* Gillian Reddyhoff
Open Wed - Fri 10 AM - 4 PM, Sat 9 AM - 4 PM, Sun noon - 4 PM, cl Mon & Tues. Admis free. Estab 1979 to bring the art & history of Toronto to the public. Average Annual Attendance: 25,000
Collections: †City of Toronto Fine Art Collection (oil, watercolor, prints & sculpture)
Exhibitions: (1993) Toronto Impressions: Historical & Contemporary Prints From the City's Collection; City Maps 1834 - 1900; A Canadian Art Legacy: The Toronto Board of Education Heritage Collection
Publications: Exhibit catalogs
Activities: Tours; exten dept servs other institutions; paintings lent

METROPOLITAN TORONTO LIBRARY BOARD
L **Arts Dept,** 789 Yonge St, M4W 2G8. Tel 416-393-7077; FAX 416-393-7229. *Libr Bd Dir* Frances Schwenger; *Asst Dir Reference Div* Dora Dempster; *Mgr of Arts Dept* Isabel Rose
Open Mon - Thur 9 AM - 9 PM, Fri 9 AM - 6 PM, Sat 9 AM - 5 PM, Sun Oct 15 - end of April 1:30 - 5 PM. Estab 1959 for public reference
Income: Financed by city appropriation
Library Holdings: Vols 50,000; Per subs 450; Micro — Fiche, reels; Other — Clipping files, exhibition catalogs
Special Subjects: Costume Design & Construction, Decorative Arts, Canadian fine arts, printing and printing design
Collections: Postcards, scenic & greeting; †printed ephemera; †private presses with emphasis on Canadian; 834,000 picture clippings; theatre arts & stage design
L **History Dept,** 789 Yonge St, M4W 2G8. Tel 416-393-7155; FAX 416-393-7229; Telex 06-22232. *Mgr History Dept* David B Kotin
Open Mon - Thurs 9 AM - 9 PM, Fri 9 AM - 6 PM, Sat 9 AM - 5 PM, Sun mid Oct - Apr 30 1:30 - 5 PM. Estab 1960 to house rare Canadiana and to support Canadian historical research
Library Holdings: Other — Original art works, photographs, prints
Collections: †65,000 paintings, prints & photographs

A **ONTARIO ASSOCIATION OF ART GALLERIES,** 489 King St W, Suite 306, M5V 1K4. Tel 416-598-0714; FAX 416-598-4128. *Pres* Megan Bice; *VPres* Rob Freeman; *Exec Dir* Anne Kolisnyk
Open 9 AM - 5 PM. Estab in 1968 as the provincial nonprofit organization representing public art galleries in the province of Ontario. Institutional membership includes approximately 84 public art galleries, exhibition spaces & arts related organizations. Membership is also available to individuals. Gallery not maintained. Mem: 83; annual meeting June
Income: Financed by mem, Ontario Arts Council, Ontario Ministry of Culture & Communications, Dept of Communications & the Canada Council
Publications: Dateline, bimonthly newsletter
Activities: Professional development seminars & workshops; annual awards; active job file & job hot-line

M **ONTARIO COLLEGE OF ART,** Gallery 76, 76 McCaul St, M5T 1W1. Tel 416-977-8530; FAX 416-977-0235. *Cur* Christine Swiderski; *Cur* Robert Windrum
Open Tues - Sat 11 AM - 5 PM. Estab 1970 for faculty and student exhibitions

and to exhibit outside work to benefit the college. Average Annual Attendance: 15,000
Income: Financed by College
Collections: Small print collection
Publications: Invitations; small scale catalogs
Activities: Dramatic programs; Concerts; competitions; individual paintings and original objects of art lent; traveling exhibitions organized and circulated
L **Dorothy H Hoover Library,** 100 McCaul St, M5T 1W1. Tel 416-977-5311, Ext 255; FAX 416-977-0235. *Dir* Jill Patrick
Open Mon - Thurs 8:30 AM - 7:45 PM, Fri 8:30 AM - 5 PM. Estab to support the curriculum
Income: Financed through the College
Purchases: $70,000
Library Holdings: Vols 22,000; Per subs 250; VF 43,000; Micro — Fiche, reels; AV — A-tapes 600, cassettes 500, fs, Kodachromes, lantern slides, motion pictures, rec, slides 70,000, v-tapes 500; Other — Clipping files, exhibition catalogs, pamphlets
Special Subjects: Advertising Design, Art History, Commercial Art, Conceptual Art, Decorative Arts, Drawings, Graphic Arts, Graphic Design, Jewelry, Mixed Media, Contemporary Art & Design

A **ONTARIO CRAFTS COUNCIL,** Chalmers Bldg, 35 McCaul St, M5T 1V7. Tel 416-977-3551; FAX 416-977-3552. *Pres* Ann Mortimer; *Exec Dir* Alan Elder; *Mgr Resource Centre* Sandra Dunn
Open Tues - Sat 10 AM - 5 PM. No admis fee. Estab 1976 to foster crafts & crafts people in Ontario & is the largest craft organization in Canada. Has over 100 affiliated groups. Maintains an art gallery. Average Annual Attendance: 15,000. Mem: 6200; dues $30; annual meeting in June
Income: Financed by mem & provincial appropriation, The Guild Shop, fundraising & publications
Collections: †Canadian Contemporary Crafts
Exhibitions: Ontario Crafts Regional Juried Exhibition; travelling exhibitions; monthly exhibitions in craft gallery
Publications: Craftnews, 4 times a year; Ontario Craft, quarterly magazine; shows list, annual
Activities: Lectures open to public; gallery talks; competitions with awards; scholarships; exten dept serves Ontario; original objects of art lent to galleries, libraries & alternate exhibition spaces; book traveling exhibitions; originate traveling exhibitions; sales shop sells books, original craft, prints, Inuit art, sculpture & prints
L **Craft Resource Centre,** 35 McCaul St, M5T 1V7. Tel 416-977-3551; FAX 416-977-3552. *Mgr* Kathleen Morris
Open Mon - Sat 10 AM - 5 PM. No admis fee. Estab 1976. A comprehensive, special library devoted exclusively to the field of crafts. It is a partly government-funded non-profit organization & is available as an information service to the general public & Ontario Crafts Council members. Has an extensive portfolio registry featuring Canadian craftspeople. Average Annual Attendance: 6000. Mem: 5000; dues $30; annual meeting in June
Library Holdings: Vols 3000; Per subs 350; Portfolios of craftspeople 530; AV — Slides 100,000, v-tapes; Other — Exhibition catalogs
Special Subjects: Enamels, Glass, Metalwork, Pottery, Fibre, Leather, Wood
Publications: Directory of Suppliers of Craft Materials; The Photography of Crafts; Annual Craft Fairs in Ontario; Crafts in Ontario; Shops and Galleries; The Trials of Jurying: A Guide for Exhibition Organizers and Jurors; Starting your own Craft Business; Business Bibliography
Activities: Educ dept; lectures open to public; tours; competitions with awards; scholarships & fels offered; exten dept serves Ontario & other Canadian areas; slide rental; consultation services; publishing; originate traveling exhibitions; sales shop sells books, magazines, contemporary Canadian crafts

PROFESSIONAL ART DEALERS ASSOCIATION OF CANADA
For further information, see National and Regional Organizations

ROYAL CANADIAN ACADEMY OF ARTS
For further information, see National and Regional Organizations

M **ROYAL ONTARIO MUSEUM,** 100 Queen's Park, M5S 2W2. Tel 416-586-5549; FAX 416-586-5863. *Chmn Board of Trustees* Kenneth W Harrigan; *Secy Board of Trustees* Robert Barnett; *Dir* Dr John McNeill; *Acting Assoc Dir Curatorial* Dr Joseph Mandarino; *Assoc Dir Public Communication* Jean Lavery; *Assoc Dir Adminr & Finance* Mike Shoreman; *Assoc Dir Human Resources* Donald Mitchell; *Assoc Dir Project Management* Dr David Barr
Open daily 10 AM - 6 PM, Tues & Thurs evenings until 8 PM, cl Labor Day in Sept to Victoria Day in May. Admis families $13, adults $6, senior citizens, students & children $3.25. Estab 1912 & includes 20 curatorial departments in the fields of fine & decorative arts, archaeology & the natural & earth sciences. Average Annual Attendance: 1,000,000. Mem: 35,000; dues individual $65
Income: $25,000,000 (financed by federal grants, provincial grants, museum income, mem, bequests & donations)
Collections: Extensive Far Eastern collection
Exhibitions: (1992) Fluffs & Feathers, an Exhibition on the Symbols of Indianness (1993) Sharks
Facts & Fantasy; Feathers of the Rainbird: Design Images on Painted Pottery of the Southwest
Publications: Rotunda, quarterly magazine; numerous academic publications; gallery guides; exhibition catalogs; publications in print
Activities: Classes for adults & children; throughout the school year, prebooked classes receive lessons in the Museum. Unconducted classes can also be arranged with the Museum at a cost of $3 per student; lect open to public with visiting lectr, special lect for members only; concerts; gallery talks; tours; competitions; outreach dept serves Ontario; individual paintings and original objects of art lent to museums and galleries; originate traveling exhibitions; museum shop sells books, magazines, reproductions, prints and slides
L **Library & Archives,** 100 Queen's Park, M5S 2W2. Tel 416-586-5595; FAX 416-586-5863. *Head Librn* Julia Matthews
Estab 1960 for curatorial research
Library Holdings: Vols 60,000; Per subs 550; Micro — Fiche, reels; Other — Exhibition catalogs
Special Subjects: Archaeology, Decorative Arts, Furniture, Textiles, Antiquities, Canadiana, Museology

M Canadian Decorative Arts Department, 100 Queen's Park, M5S 2W2. Tel 416-586-5524; FAX 416-586-5516. *Cur-in-Charge* Mrs M Allodi; *Cur* Donald B Webster; *Departmental Asst* K Smith; *Cur Asst* J Holmes
Open Mon - Sat 10 AM - 5 PM, Sun 1 - 5 PM. No admis fee. Estab 1951 to collect, exhibit & publish material on Canadian historical paintings & Canadian decorative arts. Canadiana Gallery has three galleries: first gallery has six rooms showing English Colonial, French, Maritime, Ontario & German-Ontario furniture, also silver, glass, woodenware; second gallery has ceramics, toys, weathervanes, religious carving, early 19th century Quebec panelled room; third is a picture gallery for changing exhibitions. Average Annual Attendance: 35,000
Collections: Candian 18th & 19th century decorative arts - ceramics, coins & medals books, †furniture, †glass, guns, silver, woodenware; 16th-18th exploration; †portraits of Canadians & military & administrative people connected with Canada; 18th & 19th century topographic & historical Canadian views; 19th century travels
Exhibitions: Passionate Pursuit
Publications: William Berczy; D B Webster Brantford Pottery; Canadian Watercolors & Drawings; The William Eby Pottery, Conestogo, Ontario 1855 - 1970; English Canadian Furniture of the Georgian Period; An Engraver's Pilgrimage: James Smillie Jr in Quebec, 1821-1830; Georgian Canada: Conflict & Culture, 1745 - 1820; Printmaking in Canada: The Earliest Views & Portraits
Activities: Classes for children; lectures; gallery talks; exten dept serves Ontario; original objects of art lent to institutions

L RYERSON POLYTECHNICAL INSTITUTE, Library, 350 Victoria St, M5B 2K3. Tel 416-979-5031; FAX 416-979-5215. *Chief Librn* Richard M Malinski
Open Mon - Thurs 8:30 AM - 10:30 PM, Fri 8:30 AM - 5 PM, Sat 9 AM - 5 PM, Sun 10 AM - 6 PM. Estab 1948 to meet the needs of the students
Income: Financed by provincial appropriation & student fees
Purchases: $27,200
Library Holdings: Vols 16,070; Per subs 160; Micro — Fiche, prints, reels; AV — A-tapes, cassettes, fs, motion pictures, rec, slides, v-tapes; Other — Clipping files, pamphlets
Special Subjects: Architecture, Fashion Arts, Interior Design, Photography, Film, Theatre Arts, Graphic Arts, Media Arts

SCULPTOR'S SOCIETY OF CANADA
For further information, see National and Regional Organizations

SOCIETY OF CANADIAN ARTISTS
For further information, see National and Regional Organizations

C TORONTO DOMINION BANK, Toronto Dominion Center, PO Box 1, M5K 1A2. Tel 416-982-8222; FAX 416-982-6335. *Mgr* Barry Webster; *Art Admin* Natalie Ribkoff
Contemporary Art Collection is available for viewing by appointment only. The Inuit Gallery is open Mon - Fri 8 AM - 6 PM, Sat & Sun 10 AM - 4 PM. The Contemporary Art Collection is shown throughout branch offices in Canada & internationally; the Inuit Art Collection has its own gallery in the Toronto-Dominion Centre
Collections: The Inuit Collection consists of a selection of prints, as well as stone, bone & ivory carvings; the Contemporary Collection is an ongoing project focusing on the art of emerging and mature Canadian artists, including original prints, paintings, sculpture & works on paper

A TORONTO HISTORICAL BOARD, Historic Fort York, 100 Garrison Rd (Mailing add: Stanley Barracks Exhibition Place, M6K 3C3). Tel 416-392-6907; FAX 416-392-6917. *Cur* Carl Benn; *Asst Cur* Mike LiPowski
Open daily 9:30 AM - 5 PM. Admis fee adults $4, senior citizens & children $2, family $10. Estab 1934 to tell the story of the founding of Toronto & the British Army in the 19th century. Average Annual Attendance: 55,000
Income: Financed by city appropriation
Collections: 19th century British Military; Original War of 1812 Buildings; Original War of 1812 Uniforms; Original War of 1812 Weapons
Activities: Classes for adults & children; docent training; lectures open to public, 10 vis lectr per year; Sales shop sells books, prints & reproductions

UNIVERSITY OF TORONTO
M Justina M Barnicke Gallery, 7 Hart House Circle, M5S 1A1. Tel 416-978-2453, 978-8398; FAX 416-978-8387. *Dir* Judith Schwartz
Open Mon - Fri 11 AM - 7 PM, Sat & Sun 1 - 4 PM. No admis fee. Estab 1919 to promote young Canadian artists, as well as present a historical outlook on Canadian art. Gallery has modern setting and total wall space of 350 running ft; outdoor quadrangle is available for summer sculpture shows. Average Annual Attendance: 12,000
Income: Financed by Hart House
Purchases: Canadian art
Collections: †Canadian Art (historical and contemporary)
Exhibitions: Temporary exhibitions of historical & contemporary Canadian art
Publications: The Hart House Collection of Canadian Paintings by Jeremy Adamson
Activities: Classes for adults; docent training; lectures, 8 vis lectr per year; concerts; gallery talks; tours; individual paintings and original objects of art lent; originate traveling exhibitions
L Fine Art Library, Sidney Smith Hall, 100 St George St, M5S 1A1. Tel 416-978-5006; FAX 416-978-1491. *Librn* A Retfalvi
Open Mon - Fri 10 AM - 5 PM. Estab 1936 for reference only
Income: Financed by state appropriation and Department of Fine Art
Library Holdings: Vols 20,000; Other — Exhibition catalogs 19,000, photographs 90,000
Special Subjects: Archaeology, Art History
Collections: Catalog materials including †temporary, †permanent, †dealer catalogs; †photographic archives in various fields of Western art
Publications: Canadian Illustrated News (Montreal); Index to Illustrations, quarterly

A VISUAL ARTS ONTARIO, 439 Wellington St W, 2nd Floor, M5V 1E7. Tel 416-591-8883. *Exec Dir* Hennie L Wolff; *Coordr Art Placement* Andrew Cripps; *Projects Officer* Len Pendercast; *Reprography Coordr* Ian Smith-Rubenzahl; *Reprography Coordr* Andrienne Trent; *Membership Coordr & Admin Asst* Suzanne Luke; *Bookkeeper* Frima Yolleck; *Asst Art Placement* Gary Ponzo
Open Mon - Fri 9 AM - 5 PM. Estab 1974. Visual Arts Ontario is a non-profit organization dedicated to furthering the awareness and appreciation of the visual arts. Mem: 3000; dues 2 year $35, 1 year $20
Income: Financed by membership, fundraising, municipal, provincial & federal grants, attendance at events
Collections: Resource Center; Slide Registry of Ontario artists
Publications: Agenda, quarterly newsletter; Art in Architecture: Art for the Built Environment in the Province of Ontario; The Guidebook to Competitions & Commissions; Visual Arts Handbook
Activities: Workshops for professional artists; lectures open to public; seminars & conferences, special projects; individual paintings & original objects of art lent to Ontario Government Ministries & corporations; art rental programme; colour reprography programmes; originate traveling exhibitions
L Library, 439 Wellington St W, 2nd Floor, M5V 1E7. Tel 416-591-8883. *Exec Dir* Hennie Wolff
Resource library open to public for reference
Income: Financed by government, private funds, membership fees and programme revenues
Library Holdings: Archival material and current art periodicals

WATERLOO

M ENOOK GALLERIES, 78 Euclid Ave, PO Box 335, N2J 4A4. Tel 519-884-3221, 744-6740 (evenings/answering machine). *Dir* H Norman Socha; *Cur* Laura Napran
Open daily 10:30 AM - 5:30 PM. No admis fee. Estab 1981 to promote awareness of Native art
Income: Financed by sales
Collections: Native American, Indian & Eskimo/Inuit Art; Papua New Guinea artifacts; graphics, paintings & sculptures; †David General; †Kiaksahu, C O; †Doug Maracle; Wayne Yerxa
Exhibitions: (1992) Cape Dorset Graphics; Aspects of the Feminine; Aspects of the Masculine
Publications: Vision of Rare Spirit
Activities: Classes for adults & children; research programs; lect open to public, 2 vis lectr per year; lending collection contains 150 paintings & art objects; book traveling exhibitions 2 per year; originate exhibitions for international art galleries & universities on contemporary Native art, 4 per year; retail store sells books, prints, original art & reproductions

M THE SEAGRAM MUSEUM, 57 Erb St W, N2L 6C2. Tel 519-885-1857; FAX 519-746-1673. *Exec Dir* T G Tyssen
Open Tues - Fri 11 AM - 8 PM, Sat & Sun 11 AM - 5 PM. Estab 1980. Permanent and temporary exhibitions, decorative and fine art related to wines and spirits on mezzanine gallery space; Restaurant; provincially-operated liquor store. Average Annual Attendance: 120,000
Income: Financed by annual donation
Collections: Historic glass, vessels, acessories for liquor service
Exhibitions: History & technology of spirits, wines, related trades; decorative arts
Activities: Programs on feature exhibitions; lectures open to public; tours; museum shop sells books, reproductions
L Library, 57 Erb St W, N2L 6C2. FAX 519-746-1673; *Archivist Librn* Sandra Lowman; *Asst Archivist Librn* Sean Thomas
Estab 1971
Library Holdings: Vols 6000; Per subs 30; AV — Motion pictures, slides, v-tapes; Other — Clipping files, manuscripts, memorabilia, original art works, pamphlets, photographs, prints, sculpture
Special Subjects: Advertising Design, Decorative Arts, Drawings, Etchings & Engravings, Flasks & Bottles, Glass, Porcelain, Prints, Restoration & Conservation, engravings, industrial artefacts, tools

UNIVERSITY OF WATERLOO
M Art Gallery, N2L 3G1. Tel 519-885-1211, Ext 2439. *Cur* Joseph Wyatt
Open Mon - Fri 11 AM - 4 PM, Sun 2 - 5 PM, cl Sun July & Aug. No admis fee. Estab 1962
Collections: Contemporary Canadian Art
Exhibitions: Independent Variations; St Michael's Printshop: 1972 - 1987; Threads of Survival: Chilean Arpilleras; Elders of the Anishnabe (1991) Vision and Invention: Drawings and Paintings by Robert Marchessault; Virgil Burnett, 1960-1990; Gathering Forces; Handwriting on the Wall-Jewel Goodwyn; Selections from the Permanent Collection
L Dana Porter Library, University Ave, N2L 3G1. Tel 519-885-1211, Ext 2282; FAX 519-747-4606; Telex 069-5259. *University Librn* Murray Shepherd; *Special Coll Librn* Susan Bellingham; *Reference & Coll Development Librn - Fine Arts & Architecture* Michele Sawchuk
Open Mon - Thurs 8 AM - 11 PM, Fri 8 AM - 10 PM, Sat 11 AM - 10 PM, Sun 11 AM - 11 PM. Estab 1958 to provide access to information appropriate to the needs of the academic community
Income: $244,311
Library Holdings: Vols 26,770; Per subs 160; Micro — Fiche, reels; AV — Rec; Other — Clipping files, exhibition catalogs
Special Subjects: Etchings & Engravings, Printmaking
Collections: The Dance Collection (monographs, periodicals and pamphlets from 1535 to date relating to the history of dance-ballet); B R Davis Southy Collection; Eric Gill Collection; Lady Aberdeen Library of Women; George Santayana Collection; Private Press Collection; Rosa Breithaupt Clark Architectural History Collection; Euclid's Elements and History of Mathematics
Publications: Library publishes four bibliographic series: Bibliography, Technical Paper, Titles & How To
Activities: Undergraduate curriculum in architecture, art history and studio

M **WILFRID LAURIER UNIVER2ITY,** Art Gallery, N2L 3C5. Tel 519-884-1970. *Pres* Dr Lorna Marsden; *Chmn Art Committee* Ira Ashcroft
Open Mon - Sat 10 AM - 7 PM. No admis fee. Estab 1969 to exhibit for the students, staff & faculty. The gallery has its own space in the John Aird Building & has 18 x 50 rectangular space including various modular mounts. Average Annual Attendance: 50,000
Purchases: $16,000
Collections: 331 pieces of original art works & prints
Exhibitions: The gallery mounts from 12-14 exhibitions each year, mostly shows by artists in local area
Publications: Buried Treasure (75th Anniversary of WLU 1986)
Activities: Lectures open to public; sponsors faculty-student exhibition annually

WINDSOR

M **ART GALLERY OF WINDSOR,** 445 Riverside Dr W, N9A 6T8. Tel 519-258-7111; FAX 519-256-8071. *Pres* Dennis Staudt; *VPres* Ronald W Ianni; *Dir* Alf Bogusky; *Business Mgr* Ken Ferguson; *Cur* Vincent J Varga; *Cur* Catharine Mastin; *Information Coordr* Dee Douglas; *Registrar* Betty Wilkinson; *Admin Asst* Diane Lane
Open Tues, Wed, Sat 11 AM - 5 PM, Thurs - Fri 11 AM - 9 PM, Sun 11:30 AM - 5 PM, cl Mon. No admis fee. Estab 1943 for collection and exhibition of works of art, primarily Canadian, for the study and enjoyment of the Windsor-Detroit area. Gallery contains 56,000 sq ft of space on three floors; it is environmentally-controlled and highly fire resistant; AGW Restaurant. Average Annual Attendance: 50,000. Mem: 1800; president's club $1000 and up, director's circle $500- $999, advocate $250-$499, supporter $100-$249, gallery friend $50-$99, family $45, single $25, student $20; annual meeting Mar
Income: $1,300,000 (financed by membership, city appropriation & federal & provincial grants)
Collections: †Primarily Canadian drawings, paintings, prints and sculpture 18th century to present; †Inuit prints and sculpture; non-Canadian paintings and sculpture
Exhibitions: Approx 30 exhibitions a year, besides installation of permanent collection, of mostly Canadian historic & contemporary art works, paintings & graphics
Publications: Monthly calendar and catalogues for exhibitions organized by this gallery, 10 times a year
Activities: Docent training; lectures open to public, 20 vis lectr per yr; tours; individual paintings and original objects of art lent; book traveling exhibitions approximately 20 per year; originate traveling exhibitions; museum shop sells Canadian handicrafts, original art, reproductions and prints; Education Gallery

L **Reference Library,** 445 Riverside Dr W, N9A 6T8. Tel 519-258-7111; FAX 519-256-8071. *Librn* Betty F Wilkinson
Open Tues, Wed, Fri & Sun 1 - 4 PM, Thurs 1 - 8 PM. Estab 1966. Reference for staff, members and public
Income: 4000
Library Holdings: Vols 4000; Per subs 35; Catalogs and museum bulletins; Other — Clipping files, exhibition catalogs
Special Subjects: Painting - Canadian

WOODSTOCK

M **WOODSTOCK PUBLIC LIBRARY,** Art Gallery, Woodstock Public Art Gallery, 447 Hunter St, N4S 4G7. Tel 519-539-6761. *Acting Cur* Brenda Irvine; *Chief Librn* Atephen Nelson
Open Mon - Fri 11 AM - 5 PM, Sat 10 AM - 5 PM, Sun 1 - 4:30 PM, cl Sun May - Oct. No admis fee. Estab 1967 as a community art gallery. Moved into neo-Georgian building (c1913) in 1983. Four gallery spaces: Carlyle Gallery (313 sq ft); Verne T Ross Gallery (464 sq ft); Nancy Rowell Jackman Gallery (323 sq ft): East Gallery (1303.75 sq ft). Average Annual Attendance: 11,000. Mem: 350; dues, family $20, individual $15, sr citizen $8, children & students $6
Income: Financed by City of Woodstock, Ministry of Citizenship & Culture, Ontario Arts Council, mem & donations
Collections: 150 works collection of Canadian Art, concentrating on Florence Carlyle contemporary Canadian regional artists
Exhibitions: (1992) David Ferguson, Pierre Guimond Photo Show; Student Photo Show; Selection of recent donations & acquisitions from the Permanent Collection; Art Beat '92, Kindergarten to OAC; Works by Basketmakers from the Northwest coast; 34th Annual Oxford County Juried Show; From First to Last: The Public Trust; Titanic Exhibit; Christina Luck: Realboro; Mother & Child - Leslie Sorochan; Ellen Bitz; Anne Walk. (1993) Patterns in Light; Victorian glass from the Royal Ontario Museum
Publications: Newsletter 6 times per yr; educational handouts on current exhibitions; monthly bulletin for vol com
Activities: Classes for children & adults; lect open to public, 4 - 6 vis lectr per year; concerts; gallery talks; tours; scholarships; individual paintings are lent to residents of Oxford County and business firms; lending collection contains 125 paintings; originate traveling exhibitions to circulate Southwestern Ontario & Toronto vicinity; gift shop sells cards, wrapping & writing paper, pottery, jewelry, weaving

PRINCE EDWARD ISLAND

CHARLOTTETOWN

M **CONFEDERATION CENTRE ART GALLERY AND MUSEUM,** PO Box 848, C1A 7L9. Tel 902-628-6111; FAX 902-566-4648. *Dir* Ted Fraser; *Ed* Joseph Sherman; *Registrar* Kevin Rice
Open Tues - Sat 10 AM - 5 PM, Sun 2 - 5 PM, Mid June - Sept 10 AM - 8 PM, cl Mon. Admis fee, Sun free. Estab 1964 as a national collection devoted to Canadian art and fine crafts. Average Annual Attendance: 100,000. Mem: 500, group $25, family $25, individual $15
Income: Financed by federal, provincial, city and the private sector
Collections: 19th & 20th century Canadian paintings, drawings and decorative arts; paintings and drawings by Robert Harris
Exhibitions: Twenty-five exhibitions including special exhibition each July and August to coincide with summer festival
Publications: ArtsAtlantic, quarterly subscription
Activities: Lect open to public; tours; concerts; lending collection contains paintings, 7000 kodachromes, 50 film strips, slides; originate traveling exhibitions; junior museum

L **Library,** PO Box 848, Charlottetown, C1A 7L9. Tel 902-628-6111; FAX 902-566-4648. *Dir* Ted Fraser; *Registrar* Kevin Rice
Open for reference
Library Holdings: Vols 3500; Per subs 20; AV — A-tapes 30, fs 60, slides 5000; Other — Photographs

L **HOLLAND COLLEGE,** Centre of Creative Arts Library & Gallery, 50 Burns Ave, C1E 1H7. Tel 902-566-9310. *Dir* Henry Purdy
Open Mon - Fri 8:30 AM - 5 PM and 6:30 - 10 PM, Sat & Sun 10 AM - 6 PM. Average Annual Attendance: 5000
Library Holdings: Vols 3000; Per subs 35; Micro — Cards; AV — A-tapes, cassettes; Other — Clipping files, exhibition catalogs, photographs
Special Subjects: Carpets & Rugs, Ceramics, Crafts, Decorative Arts, Display, Dolls, Drafting, Drawings, Embroidery, Enamels, Eskimo Art, Folk Art, Furniture, Glass, Goldsmithing, Handicrafts, History of Art & Archaeology, Illustration, Industrial Design, Interior Design, Jewelry, Leather, Lettering, Metalwork, Mixed Media, Pewter, Photography, Porcelain, Pottery
Exhibitions: Emerald Visions; On A Roll; Beginnings; A Christmas Show; Bruno Bobak - The Classical Period; Ron Arvidson & Daphne Irving; Annual Staff Exhibition; Annual Studen Exhibition; Island Visual Artists '91
Activities: Classes for adults and children; workshops; summer courses; lect open to the public; gallery talks; tours; competitions; scholarships; book travelling exhibitions, 3 - 6 per yr; originate traveling exhibitions; sales shop sells craft supplies

QUEBEC

DORVAL

A **DORVAL CULTURAL CENTRE,** 1401 Lakeshore Dr, H9S 2E5. Tel 514-633-4170; FAX 514-633-4177. *Coordr* Danyelle Brodeur
Open Tues - Thurs 2 - 5 PM & 7 - 9 PM, Fri - Sun 2 - 5 PM. No admis fee. Estab 1967 to promote culture and art. Maintains an art gallery
Income: Financed by city appropriation
Publications: Calendar, biannually
Activities: Classes for adults and children; dramatic programs; lect open to public; gallery talks; tours

HULL

M **LA GALERIE MONTCALM LA GALERIE D'ART DE LA VILLEDE HULL,** 25 rue, Laurier Maison du Citoyen, J8X 4C8. Tel 819-595-7488; FAX 819-595-7425. *Admin Secy* Claudette Bergeron; *Technician* Louise Gravel; *Dir* Jacqueline Tardif
No admis fee. Estab 1981, to present the art of local artists & national exhibitions, multi-disciplinary. one gallery, 2505 sq ft, three other secondary areas. Average Annual Attendance: 25,000
Income: $145,500 (financed by public & private enterprises)
Purchases: $37,000
Collections: City of Hull (permanent collection); heritage artifacts; paintings; photographs; prints; sculpture
Exhibitions: Hull & His Area in Paintings; Exhibition of the Permanent Collection
Publications: Exhibition catalogs
Activities: Classes for children; workshops; lect open to public, 1560 vis lectr per year; concerts; gallery talks; tours of the permanent collection; competitions with awards; retail store sells books, prints, original art

JOLIETTE

M **MUSEE D'ART DE JOLIETTE,** 145 Wilfrid-Corbeil St, PO Box 132, J6E 3Z3. Tel 514-756-0311; FAX 514-756-6511. *Pres* Anamd Swaminadhan; *VPres* Me Serge Joyal; *VPres* Antoine Blanchette; *Dir* Michell Perron
Open Tues - Sun noon - 6 PM July & Aug, Wed - Sun noon - 5 PM Winter. Admis adults $1, students $.25. Estab 1961 for educational purposes; preservation of the collections; save local patrimony. Gallery Six - Contemporary Gallery, temporary exhibitions; Sacred Art Gallery; European Medieval Renaissance Gallery; Canadian Art Gallery; Permanent Collection. Average Annual Attendance: 15,000. Mem: 200; dues $10; annual meeting Sept
Income: $170,000 (financed by endowment, municipal & provincial government grants)
Collections: †Canadian art; European art; sacred art of Quebec; painting & sculpture
Exhibitions: 10 exhibitions per year
Publications: Catalog and pamphlet entitled Le Musee d'Art de Joliette
Activities: Classes for children; lectures open to public; concerts; gallery talks; tours; films; sales shop sells books, magazines, postcards & reproductions

L Library, 145 Wilfrid-Corbeil St, PO Box 132, J6E 3Z3. Tel 514-756-0311. *Librn* Open
Estab 1976. Open with reservations only for art reference
Purchases: $200-$250
Library Holdings: Vols 1000; Per subs 5; AV — Slides; Other — Exhibition catalogs, photographs, sculpture
Special Subjects: History of art, well-known artists
Collections: Art Journal; Great Masters; History of Painting; Larousse Mensuel

JONQUIERE

M INSTITUT DES ARTS AU SAGUENAY, Centre National D'Exposition A Jonquiere, 4160 Du Vieux Pont, CP 605, Succursale A, G7X 7W4. Tel 418-542-4516. *Dir* Jacqueline Caron; *Animateur Technician* Steven Renald; *Secy* Lucie Corneau
Estab 1979 as an art exposition. Four galleries. Average Annual Attendance: 15,000. Mem: 40; open to all interested in Au Milieu Des Arts; dues $15; annual meeting in June
Income: $139,000 (financed by endowment, mem, city & state appropriation)
Exhibitions: Prix Sculpture Alcan
Activities: Classes for adults & children; competitions with awards;; book traveling exhibitions 3-5 per year

KAHNAWAKE

M KATERI TEKAKWITHA SHRINE, Musee Kateri Tekakwitha, CP 70, J0L 1B0. Tel 514-632-6030. *Dir* Louis Cyr
Open daily 9 AM - noon and 1 - 5 PM. No admis fee. Estab as a mission in 1667
Collections: Archives, Canadian church silver, historic chapel, old paintings
Publications: Kateri

LAVAL

M GALERIE DE L'ATELIER, 74 av due Pacifique, H7N 3X7. Tel 514-662-1513. *Pres* Roxanne Brunet
No admis fee. Estab 1983. Mem: 45; mem open to printers & others; annual meeting in May
Income: $2000 (financed by mem, city & state appropriation)
Purchases: A press machine
Exhibitions: Engraving exhibits
Publications: Newsletter, bi-annual
Activities: Classes for adults & children; lect open to members only; approx 40 vis lectr per year; book traveling exhibitions; originate traveling exhibitions

MONTREAL

C ALCAN ALUMINIUM LTD, 1188 Sherbrooke St W, H3A 3G2. Tel 514-848-8000; FAX 514-848-8115. *Cur* Joanne Meade
Estab 1979 to enhance the offices in which they are installed and enrich the lives of those who work there. Collection displayed in reception areas and private offices
Purchases: $250,000
Collections: Contemporary International Art
Activities: Lect; individual objects of art lent for special exhibits upon request

L ARTEXTE INFORMATION CENTRE, 3575, boul St-Laurent, Suite 303, H2X 2T7. Tel 514-845-2759; FAX 514-845-4345. *Librn* Danielle Leger; *Coordr* Michel Des Jardins
Open Tues - Sat 12 AM - 5:30 PM & by appointment, cl Sun & Mon. Institution estab 1980, libr estab 1982. Documentation of contemporary visual arts, from 1965 - present with particular emphasis on Canadian art, for reference only.
Mem: 125; annual dues $15 & up
Income: $336,500 (financed by membership, city & state appropriation, donations)
Purchases: $25,000 ($15,000 in donated documents)
Library Holdings: Vols 1200; Per subs 100; Other — Clipping files 5200, exhibition catalogs 4500, memorabilia, pamphlets, photographs
Special Subjects: Ceramics, Collages, Conceptual Art, Drawings, Eskimo Art, Mixed Media, Painting - Canadian, Photography, Printmaking, Sculpture, Artist Books, Copy Art, Installation, Performance, Public Art
Publications: Bibliography of Canadian exhibition catalogues, 1965 - 1990; Catalogue of catalogues, annual
Activities: Shop sells exhibition catalogues, books, magazines

A SAIDYE BRONFMAN CENTRE, 5170 Cote Ste Catherine Rd, H3W 1M7. Tel 514-739-2301. *Exec Dir* Cecil Rabinovitch; *Asst Dir* Alain Danciger; *Cur* Regine Basha
Open Mon - Thurs 9 AM - 9 PM, Fri 9 AM - 3:30 PM, Sun 9 AM - 5 PM, cl Sat. No admis fee. Estab 1967 as a non-profit cultural centre for the promotion and dissemination of the arts. 3000 sq ft gallery. Average Annual Attendance: 90,000
Income: Financed by membership and government grant
Exhibitions: Ten plus major exhibitions per year, special interest in contemporary art, local, national & international
Publications: Exhibition catalogs
Activities: Classes for adults & children; lectures open to public, 12 vis lectr per yr; gallery talks; tours; competitions with awards; book traveling exhibitions; originate traveling exhibitions; sales shop sells books & magazines

M CHATEAU RAMEZAY MUSEUM, 280 Notre-Dame E, H2Y 1C5. Tel 514-861-7182; FAX 514-861-8317. *Dir* Pierre Brouillard
Open Tues - Sun 10 AM - 4 PM, cl Mon. Admis adults $1, students $.50. Estab 1895 in residence of Claude de Ramezay (1705), governor of Montreal. Average

Annual Attendance: 60,000. Mem: 300; dues life $500, individual $10
Collections: Canadian drawings, furniture, paintings, prints & sculpters; 18th, 19th & 20th century collections; Indian collections
Activities: Classes for children; docent training; lectures open to public & some for members only, 6 vis lectr per yr; gallery talks; tours; sales shop sells books, reproductions, prints & slides

L Library, 280 Notre-Dame E, H2Y 1C5. *Librn* Judith Berlyn
Library Holdings: Vols 2200
Special Subjects: Canadian history

M CONCORDIA UNIVERSITY, Leonard & Bina Ellen Art Gallery, 1400 de Maisonneuve Blvd W, H3G 1M8. Tel 514-848-4750; FAX 514-848-3494. *Acting Cur* Karen Antaki; *Curatorial Asst* Kristina Huneault
Open Mon - Fri 10 AM - 8 PM, Sat 10 AM - 5 PM. No admis fee. Estab 1962 for exhibitions of Canadian art, to provide a venue for a variety of significant touring exhibitions chosen from within the region and across Canada; to display the permanent collection, all with the idea of providing an important cultural arena both for the university & public alike. One gallery, 3500 sq ft with 328 running ft, located in University Library Pavillian. Average Annual Attendance: 66,000
Income: Financed by university & governmental funds
Purchases: Historic, modern & contemporary Canadian art
Collections: †Modern and Contemporary Canadian art
Exhibitions: Edge & Image; ChromaZone; John MacGregor: A Survey; The Photographs of Professor Oliver Buell (1844-1910); Goodridge Roberts: The Figure Works; Figure Painting in Montreal 1935-1955; Sickert, Orpen, John & their Contemporaries at the New English Art Club; Robert Bordo: New York + Montreal; Conservation: To Care for Art; Undergraduate Student Exhibition; Recent Acquisitions to the Collection: Selections from the Concordia Collection of Art; Michael Jolliffe: Paintings; Phillip Guston: Prints; John Arthur Fraser: Watercolours; Brian Wood: Drawings & Photographs; Barbara Astman: Floor pieces; K M Graham: Paintings & Drawings 1971-1984; Robert Flaherty: Photographs; Work by Selected Fine Art Graduates: A 10th Anniversary Celebration; Joyce Wieland: A Decade of Painting; Francois Baillarge (1759-1830): A Portfolio of academic drawings; Faculty of Fine Arts Biennial; Murray MacDonald & R Holland Murray: Recent Sculptures; Jean Paul Lemieux: Honoured by the University; The Figurative Tradition In Quebec; Contemporary Works on Paper; Undergraduate Student Exhibition; Selections from the Concordia Collection of Art; Canadian Pacific Poster Art 1881-1955; Shelagh Keeley: Drawings; Bernard Gamoy: Paintings; Harold Klunder:Paintings; Marcel Bovis: Photographs; Neerland Art Quebec: an exhibition by artists of Dutch descent in Quebec; Canada in the Nineteenth Century: The Bert & Barbara Stitt Family Collection; Posters from Nicaragua; Betty Goodwin: Passages; Ron Shuebrook: Recent Work; Louis Muhlstock: New Themes & Variations 1980 - 1985; John Herbert Caddy 1801 - 1887; Expressions of Will: The Art of Prudence Heward; Riduan Tomkins: Recent Paintings; Undergraduate Student Exhibition; Selections from the Concordia Collection of Art; Concordia: The Early Years of Loyola & Sir George Williams; Porcelain: Traditions of Excellence; Francois Houde: Glass Work; Shelley Reeves: Relics; Pre-Columbian Art from the Permanent Collection; Josef Albers: Interaction of Color; Brian McNeil: Ironworks; Robert Ayre: The Critic & the Collection; Claude-Philppe Benoit: Interieur, jour
Publications: Exhibition catalogues
Activities: Lect open to public, 3 visiting lectr per year; originate traveling exhibitions

A GUILDE CANADIENNE DES METIERS D'ART, QUEBEC, Canadian Guild of Crafts, Quebec, 2025 Peel St, H3A 1T6. Tel 514-849-6091. *Adminr* Nairy Kalemkerian
Open Tues - Fri 9 AM - 5:30 PM, Sat 10 AM - 5 PM. Estab 1906 to promote, encourage & preserve arts & crafts of Canada. Permanent Collection Gallery of Eskimo & Indian Art; Exhibition Gallery. Average Annual Attendance: 30,000. Mem: 172; dues $25 & up; annual meeting Mar/Apr
Collections: †Permanent collection of Eskimo and Indian Arts and Crafts; Audio Video tapes
Exhibitions: Fine craft exhibitions every 5 weeks except Jan & Feb
Activities: Educ dept; lectures open to public; gallery talks; tours; awards; individual paintings & original objects of art lent to accredited institutions; lending collection includes prints; sales shop sells books, original art, reproductions, prints & Canadian crafts

M INTERNATIONAL MUSEUM OF CARTOON ART, 5788 Notre Dame de Grace Ave, H4A 1M4. Tel 514-489-0527. *Pres* Peter Adamakos; *VPres* Mark Scott
Estab 1988 to foster public appreciation of cartoon arts & research. Mounts exhibitions & screenings in museums & universities across North America. Special events vary
Income: Financed by government & corporate sponsorships
Collections: Artifacts, Novelties, Posters & Publicity, Toys, Clippings; Films & Tapes; Original Artwork; Publications of all types relating to the Cartoon Arts
Exhibitions: The Hollywood Cartoons
Activities: Retrospective screenings; lect open to public, vis lectr varies per year; book traveling exhibitions; originate traveling exhibitions

L JARDIN BOTANIQUE DE MONTREAL, Bibliotheque, 4101 Sherbrooke St E, H1X 2B2. Tel 514-872-1824; FAX 514-872-3765. *Botanist & Librn* Celine Arseneault
Estab 1931. For reference
Library Holdings: Vols 14,000; Per subs 400; Posters 300; AV — Cassettes 100, slides 100,000, v-tapes 75; Other — Photographs
Special Subjects: Asian Art, Landscape Architecture, Botany, Garden History, Horticulture, Japanese Art

M LA CENTRALE POWERHOUSE GALLERY, 279 rue Sherbrooke, Suite 311-D, H2X 1Y2. Tel 514-844-3489. *Coordr* Carol Brouillette; *Coordr* Susanne Paquette
Open Wed - Sun Noon - 5 PM. No admis fee. Estab 1973 to promote and

broadcast the work of women artists in all domains. Gallery has 1500 sq ft. Mem: 35; dues $20; annual meeting in June
Income: $120,000 (financed by mem, grants from federal, provincial & city governments, corporate & private donations)
Exhibitions: Twelve exhibitions per year; a mixture of local & other parts of the country, occasionally American
Publications: Exhibit catalogues
Activities: Lectures open to public, 2-3 vis lectr per year; book traveling exhibitions, 8 per year; concerts; gallery talks; originate traveling exhibitions; sales shop sells catalogues & t-shirts

A LA SOCIETE DES DECORATEURS-ENSEMBLIERS DU QUEBEC, Interior Designers Society of Quebec, 20 Elmera, Floor E/Place de Bonaventure, H5A 1G4. Tel 514-397-1770; FAX 314-288-7090. *Pres* Denise Chouinard; *Dir* Louise Caement
Open 9 AM - 5 PM. Estab 1935 as a nonprofit professional association. Mem: 483; dues $320
Exhibitions: Traveling exhibitions in the Province of Quebec
Publications: Journal magazine, monthly; News Bulletin, 10 issues per year
Activities: Education Committee to improve the level of teaching in interior design; lect for members only, 5 - 8 vis lectr per yr; book traveling exhibitions

M MCCORD MUSEUM OF CANADIAN HISTORY, 690 Sherbrooks St W, H3A 1E9. Tel 514-398-7100. *Chief Cur* France Gascon; *Cur Photography* Stanley Triggs; *Cur Costume* Jacqueline Beaudoin-Ross; *Head Exhib* Elizabeth Kennell; *Registrar* Nicole Vallieres; *Cur Ethnology* Morra McCaffrey; *Cur Decorative Arts* Conrad Graham; *Archivist* Pamela Miller; *Librn* JoAnne Turnbull; *Exec Dir* Luke Romboul
Open Tues - Sun 10 AM - 5 PM, Thurs to 9 PM, cl Mon. Admis family $8, adults $5, sr citizens $3, student $2, children under 12 free. Estab 1919 as a museum of Canadian Ethnology & Social History
Publications: Exhibition catalogs & monographs; guides to collections for children
Activities: Book traveling exhibitions 2 per year; originate traveling exhibitions to other museological institutions in Canada

MCGILL UNIVERSITY
L Blackader-Lauterman Library of Architecture and Art, 3459 McTavish St, H3A 1Y1. Tel 514-398-4742; FAX 514-398-6695; Elec Mail CZTD@MUSICA. MCGill.CA. *Librn* Mrs I Murray; *Ref Librn* Mrs M Berger; *Curatorial Asst* F Roux
Open winter 9 AM - 8 PM, summer 9 AM - 5 PM. Estab 1922 to establish a special collection of architectural material. Circ 68,000
Library Holdings: Vols 79,300; Per subs 348; Drawings 80,000; Other — Exhibition catalogs, pamphlets, photographs 20,211
Special Subjects: Baroque, Byzantine Art, Dutch Art Renaissance & Northern Renaissance, Medieval Art, 19th & 20th century Canadian architecture
Collections: †Canadian Architecture Collection
Exhibitions: (1992) Mansions of McGill
Publications: The Libraries of Edward & W S Maxwell in the Collection of the Blackader-Lauterman Library; exhibition catalogs; bibliographies; study guides

M MAISON SAINT-GABRIEL MUSEUM, 2146 place Dublin, H3K 2A2. Tel 514-935-8136. *Dir* Therese Cloutier
Group tours Tue - Fri 1:30 & 3 PM, Sun 1:30, 2:30 & 3:30 PM. No admis fee. Estab 1966
Collections: †Antique Tools, Embroidery, Paintings & Sculpture; †Furniture, Craft & †Upholstery of 19th Century located in a 17th Century House

M MONTREAL MUSEUM OF FINE ARTS, 3400 Ave du Musee, PO Box 300, Station H, H3G 2T9. Tel 514-285-1600; FAX 514-844-6042. *Dir* Pierre Theberge; *Chief Conservator* John R Porter; *Cur Non-Canadian Decorative Arts* Robert Little; *Cur Prints & Drawings* Dr Micheline Moisan; *Cur Contemporary Art* Louise Dery; *Cur Old Masters* Didier Paul; *Dir Communications* Danielle Sauvage; *Dir Admin* Paul Lavallee; *Registrar* Elaine Tolmatch; *Cur European Art* Louise d'Argencourt; *Cur Early Canadian Art* Yves Lacasse; *Cur Canadian Decorative Arts* Rosalinci Pepail
Open Tues - Sun 10 AM - 5 PM, cl Mon. Admis adults $4, students $2, students 12-16, children under 12 $1, handicapped, sr citizens & members free. Estab 1860 as an art association for the exhibition of paintings; museum estab 1916. Average Annual Attendance: 275,000. Mem: 15,000; dues $30 & up; annual meeting Sept
Income: Financed by endowment, membership and provincial appropriation
Collections: Collection of African art by Fr Gagnon; Chinese, Near Eastern, Peruvian, Inuit primitive art; Saidye and Samuel Bronfman Collection of Contemporary Canadian art; European decorative arts; French, Spanish, Dutch, British, Canadian and other schools; Japanese incense boxes; The Parker Lace Collection; Harry T Norton Collection of ancient glass; Lucile Pillow Collection of porcelain; decorative arts, painting, sculpture from 3000 BC to the present
Exhibitions: (1992) A Fresh Look at Canadian Art. (1993) Pop-Art; Painting in Quebec 1820 - 1850: New Views, New Perspectives; Grand Siecle, 17th Century French Painting in French Public Collections; Living in Style: Fine Furniture in Victorian Quebec; Bacon-Picasso; Pictures for the Sky: Art Kites; Jean Paul Lemieux; Design 1935 - 1965: What Modern Was; The Art of Building; Figures through Time & Place; Touch Wood
Publications: Collage (a calendar of events)
Activities: Docent training; lectures open to public; concerts; gallery talks; tours; exten dept serving Quebec and other provinces; individual paintings and original objects of art lent to art galleries and cultural centers; museum shop sells books, original art, reproductions, prints, slides
L Library, 3400 Ave du Musee, H3G 1K3. Tel 514-285-1600; FAX 514-285-5655. *Librn* Joanne Dery
Open 11 AM - 4:45 PM, cl Mon. Estab 1882 for a reference and research centre for art students, specialists and visitors. Open for reference to students, scholars, teachers, researchers & general public
Income: Financed by endowment and membership
Library Holdings: Vols 64,000; Per subs 650; Art sales catalogs 45,570; Vertical

files 11,951; Institutional Archives 8552; Micro — Fiche; AV — A-tapes, slides; Other — Clipping files, exhibition catalogs, manuscripts, pamphlets, photographs
Collections: Canadiana; costumes
Publications: Collage, bi-monthly; Annual report

M MUSEE D'ART CONTEMPORAIN DE MONTREAL, 185 Saint Catherine St W, H2X 1Z8. Tel 514-847-6226; FAX 514-847-6292. *Dir* Marcel Brisebois; *Cur* Paulette Gagnon; *Dir of Traveling Exhib* Real Lussier
Open Tues, Thurs - Sun 11 AM - 6 PM, Wed 11 AM - 9 PM. Admis adults $4. 75. Estab 1964. Conservation and information about contemporary art are the most important aspects of the museum; also to present contemporary artists to the general public. Building is a medium-sized four-story art museum, with an exhibition area of 2200 sq meters divided in eight galleries & a foyer. Average Annual Attendance: 100,000
Income: Financed by provincial grants
Collections: Contemporary Art - †Canadian, international and †Quebecois: drawings, engravings, paintings, photographs and sculptures
Publications: Catalogs of exhibitions
Activities: Lect open to public, 15 visiting lectr per year; concerts; gallery talks; tours; competitions; exten dept serving Quebec province; originate traveling exhibitions; sales shop sells books & magazines
L Mediatheque, 185 Saint Catherine St W, H2X 1Z8. Tel 514-847-6906. *Librn* Michelle Gauchier
Open Tues, Thurs & Fri 11 AM - 4:30 PM, Wed 11 AM - 9 PM, Sat noon - 6 PM. Estab 1965. For reference only
Income: Financed by Quebec Government
Purchases: $22,000
Library Holdings: Vols 5700; Per subs 189; Micro — Fiche 3498; AV — A-tapes 250, slides 40,000, v-tapes 325; Other — Clipping files 8332, exhibition catalogs 25,644
Special Subjects: Contemporary art
Collections: Archives of Paul-Emile Borduas (Painter 1905-1960); about 12,500 items including writings, correspondence, exhibition catalogs, etc

M MUSEE DE LA BASILIQUE NOTRE-DAME, 424 St Sulpice St, H2Y 2V5. Tel 514-842-2925. *Pastor & Dir* Ivanhoe Poirier
Open Sat, Sun & Holidays 9 AM - 4:30 PM. Admis adults $1, students and adults over 65 $.50. Estab 1937 as an historical and religious museum. Average Annual Attendance: 10,000 - 15,000
Activities: Concerts; tours; individual paintings & original objects of art lent to other museums; lending collection contains cassettes, film strips, framed reproductions, nature artifacts, original art works, original prints & paintings; sales shop sells religious artifacts

M SAINT JOSEPH'S ORATORY, Museum, 3800 Queen Mary Rd, H3V 1H6. Tel 514-733-8211. *Dir* Marcel Taillefert; *Artistic Cur* Andre Bergeron
Open daily 10 AM - 5 PM. Admis contributions welcomed. Shrine founded 1904, estab 1953 as art museum. St Joseph's Oratory is also a Montreal landmark, the highest point in this city (856 ft above sea level), a piece of art - architecture - with a history, style, etc of its own
Collections: Ancient & Contemporary Art; Nativity Scenes from around the world
Exhibitions: Christmas Exhibition; Sacred Art Exhibition
Activities: Concerts; films
L Library, 3800 Queen Mary Rd, H3V 1H6. Tel 514-733-8211, Ext 234. Open to public for use on the premises, and for inter-library loan
Library Holdings: Vols 80,000; Other — Photographs

A SOCIETE DES MUSEES QUEBECOIS, 870 Boulevard de Mainsonueuve E St, T-4410 (Mailing add: CP8888, SUCC A, UQAM, 870 Boulevard de Mainsonnuuve E, H3C 3P8). Tel 514-987-3264; FAX 514-987-8210. *Dir* Sylvie Gagnon
Open daily 9 AM - noon & 1 PM - 5 PM. Estab 1958. Mem: 735; annaul meeting Oct
Income: $900,000 (finaced by public grants & sponsorships)
Publications: Musees 4 times a year; bulletin 10 times a year
Activities: Classes for museum works; lect open to public; museum shop sells books & magazines
L Library, 870 Boulevard de Mainsonneuve Est (Mailing add: CP8888, SUCC A, UQAM, H3C 3P8). Tel 514-987-3264.
Library Holdings: Per subs 20; AV — Fs; Other — Pamphlets

M DAVID M STEWART MUSEUM, The Old Fort, St Helen's Island, PO Box 12,000, Station A, H3C 3P3. Tel 514-861-6701; FAX 514-284-0123. *Dir* Bruce D Bolton; *Mgr* Guy P E Duchesneau; *Cur* Guy Vadeboncoeur
Open summer daily 10 AM - 6 PM, cl Tues. Estab 1955 to exhibit artifacts relating to Canada's history. Located in an old British Arsenal, built between 1820-24; galleries cover theme chronologically and by collection. Average Annual Attendance: 75,000. Mem: 100; dues $5; annual meeting May
Collections: Firearms; Kitchen & Fireplace, dating from 16th century; prints; maps, navigation & scientific instruments
Exhibitions: Mission Montreal, 1992
Publications: Exhibition catalogs
Activities: Classes for children; during summer months 18th century military parades by La Compagne Franche de la Marine and the 78th Fraser Highlanders; museum shop sells books, reproductions, prints and sells
L Library, The Old Fort, St Helen's Island, PO Box 12000, Station A, H3C 3P3. Tel 514-861-6701; FAX 514-284-0123. *Librn* Eileen Meillon
Open Mon - Fri 9 AM - 5 PM. Estab 1955 as an 18th century administrator's library. Library of rare books open to researchers and members for reference
Library Holdings: Vols 8083; Per subs 50; Maps 704; AV — Slides; Other — Original art works, photographs, prints 3501, reproductions
Special Subjects: Cookbooks, Exploration, History pre 1763, Military, New France, Science
Exhibitions: The Discovery of the World 1985 - 1990
Publications: Exhibition catalogs

C UNITED WESTURNE INC, Art Collection, 6333 Decarie Blvd, Suite 400, H3W 3E1. Tel 514-342-5181; FAX 514-342-5181.
Estab 1977. Mem: 250; annual dues $15
Collections: Sculptures, mixed media, works on canvas, works on paper
Publications: Selections from the Westburne Collection
Activities: Individual paintings & original objects of art lent

L UNIVERSITE DE MONTREAL, Bibliotheque d'Amenagement, 5620 Darlington No 1004, CP 6128, H3C 3J7. Tel 514-343-6009, 343-7177; FAX 514-343-2183. *Chef de Bibliotheque* Vesna Blazina
Estab 1964
Purchases: $100,000
Library Holdings: Vols 31,963; Per subs 626; Micro — Fiche; AV — A-tapes, fs, rec, slides 44,000, v-tapes; Other — Clipping files, exhibition catalogs, photographs
Special Subjects: Architecture, Industrial Design, Landscape Architecture, urban studies
Collections: †Rare books; †History of Landscape Architecture

L UNIVERSITE DU QUEBEC, Library, Bibliotheque des Arts, CP 8889 Succ A, H3C 3P3. Tel 514-987-6134; FAX 514-987-4070.
Library Holdings: Vols 60,000; Per subs 350; AV — Slides; Other — Clipping files, exhibition catalogs
Special Subjects: Advertising Design, Architecture, Art Education, Eskimo Art, Painting - American, Pre-Columbian Art, Primitive Art, Religious Art, Restoration & Conservation, Textiles

POINTE CLAIRE

A POINTE CLAIRE CULTURAL CENTRE, Stewart Hall Art Gallery, Stewart Hall, 176 Bord Du Lac, H9S 4J7. Tel 514-630-1254; FAX 514-630-1227. *Dir Cultural Serv* Claire Cote; *Art Gallery Dir* Ingeborg Hiscox; *Prog Dir* Nicole Pesold
Open Mon & Wed 2 - 5 PM & 7 - 9 PM, Tues, Thurs & Fri 2 - 5 PM, Sat & Sun 1 - 5 PM, cl Sat after June 24 & Sun after June 1 for summer. No admis fee. Estab 1963. Gallery is 25 x 80 ft. Average Annual Attendance: 10,000. Mem: Policy and Planning Board meets ten times per year
Income: Financed by endowment and city appropriation
Collections: Permanent collection of contemporary Canadian art
Exhibitions: Approximately ten per year, local, provincial, national and international content
Publications: Bulletins; schedules of classes, study series, social events, approximately 30 per year
Activities: Classes for adults and children; dramatic programs; resident workshops in pottery, weaving and photography; lect open to the public, 4 vis lectr per yr; gallery talks; lending collection contains framed reproductions, original prints & paintings; sells framed reproductions for young people and adults in Art Lending Service

QUEBEC

M L'UNIVERSITE LAVAL, Ecole des Arts Visuels, Bureau 3412, Pavillon Louis-Jacques-Casault, Cite Universitaire, G1K 7P4. Tel 418-656-7631; FAX 418-656-7807. *Dir* David Taylor
Open Mon - Fri 8:30 AM - 7 PM. No admis fee. Estab 1970
Collections: Art color slides, decorative arts, graphics, paintings, sculpture
Exhibitions: Temporary exhibitions, changing monthly
Activities: Traveling exhibitions organized and circulated
L Library, Jean Charles Bonentant, G1K 7P4. Tel 418-656-3344; FAX 418-656-7897. *Dir General Library System* Claude Bonnelly; *Dir Art* Madeleine Robin
Open to the public for use on the premises; original prints and works of art available for study
Library Holdings: Vols 25,000

M MUSEE DES AUGUSTINES DE L'HOTEL DIEU OF QUEBEC, 32 rue Charlevoix, G1R 5C4. Tel 418-692-2492. *Dir Museum* Sr Alvine Bouille; *Guide* Jacques St-Arnaud
Open daily 9 - 11 AM & 2 - 5 PM, Sun 2 - 5 PM, other times by appointment, cl carnival time. No admis fee. Estab 1639 in the Monastere des Augustines (1695). The Hotel Dieu relives three centuries of history of the French Canadian people
Collections: Archives; domestic artifacts; medical history; paintings; sculpture; silver
L Library, 32 rue Charlevoix, G1R 5C4. Tel 418-692-2492, Ext 247. *Archivist* Sr Marie-Paule Couchon; *Dir of Museum* Sr Alvine Bouille
Religious and medical books available for research upon special request
Library Holdings: Vols 4000

M MUSEE DU QUEBEC, Parc des Champs-de-Bataille, 1 Ave Wolfe-Montcalm, G1R 5H3. Tel 418-643-2150. *Dir* A Laliberte-Bourque; *Secy-General* Gaetan Chouinard; *Conservator Early Art* Mario Beland; *Conservator Modern Art* Pierre L'Allier; *Conservator Contemporary Art* Michel Martin; *Conservator Art Now* Louise Dery; *Dean Communication & Head Educative Serv* Andre Marchand; *Public Relations* Lise Boyer; *Publications* Pierre Murgia; *Dir Admin* Jean-Noel Tremblay
Open daily 10 AM - 6 PM. Admis $4.75. Estab 1933 under Government of Province of Quebec. Average Annual Attendance: 150,000 - 200,000
Income: Financed by Quebec government appropriation
Purchases: $60,000
Collections: Drawings, goldsmith's work, paintings, sculpture, tapestry works
Exhibitions: Rotating exhibitions
Publications: Exhibit catalogs
Activities: Classes for adults & children; lectures open to public; concerts; gallery talks; tours; individual paintings lent to the government; museum shop sells books, magazines, reproductions, postcards

L Bibliotheque des Arts, Parc des Champs-de-Bataille, 1 Ave Wolfe-Montcalm, G1R 5H3. Tel 418-643-7134. *Chief Librn* L Allard; *Asst Librn* N Gastonguay; *Asst Librn* Luce Gariepy; *Asst Librn* L Belley; *Asst Librn* M Audet; *Asst Librn* R St Gelais
Open 9 AM - noon, 1:30 - 5 PM. Estab 1933
Income: $150,000 (financed by Quebec government appropriation)
Purchases: $35,000
Library Holdings: Vols 35,000; Per subs 200; Micro — Fiche, reels; AV — Slides 58,000, v-tapes; Other — Clipping files, exhibition catalogs, photographs 18,000
Special Subjects: Quebecois art; Canadian art; American art; English art; French art

M MUSEE DU SEMINAIRE DE QUEBEC, 9 rue de l'Universite, CP 460 Haute-Ville, G1R 4R7. Tel 418-692-2843; FAX 418-692-5206. *Dir* Andre Juneau; *Registrar* Mme Sonia Mimeault; *Cur* Yves Bergeron; *Asst to Cur* Jean-Pierre Pare
Open daily from June 1 - Sept 30 10 AM - 5:30 PM, Oct 1 - May 31 Tues - Sun 10 AM - 5 PM, free on Tues. Admis family $6, adult $3, sr $2, student $1.50, under 16 $1. Mem: dues $25
Income: Financed by Ministere des Affaires Culturelles, Gouvernement du Quebec, Gouvernement Federal
Collections: †18th & 19th Centuries Canadian paintings; †17th & 18th Centuries European paintings; †Ethnology; †Gold & Silver Objects; †Scientific Instruments; †Sketches & Prints; †Sculpture; †Coins & Medals; †Zoology
Activities: Classes for adults & children; lectures open to public; concerts; gallery talks; tours; scholarships & fels offered; sales shop sells books, magazines, prints & slides

M VU CENTRE D'ANIMATION ET DE DIFFUSION DE LA PHOTOGRAPHIE, 95 rue Dalhousie (Mailing add: CP 126, Sta B, G1K 7A1). Tel 418-692-1322. *Dir* Gaetan Gosselin; *Coordr* Alain Belanger
Open Thurs - Sun 1 - 5 PM. Estab 1982. Gallery contains exhibition area, studio & darkroom. Average Annual Attendance: 15,000. Mem: 200
Income: $200 (financed by endowment, mem, city appropriation & special events)
Activities: Classes for adults; workshop; lectures open to public, 5 vis lectr per year; book traveling exhibitions annually; originate traveling exhibitions

RIMOUSKI

M LE MUSEE REGIONAL DE RIMOUSKI, Centre National d' Exposition, 35 W St Germain, G5L 4B4. Tel 418-724-2272; FAX 418-725-4433. *Dir Museum* Francois Lachapelle; *Animatrice* Monique Michaud; *Conservatrice en Art Contemporain* Claire Gravel
Open Wed - Sun 10 AM - 6 PM. Admis $2, students & sr citizens $1. Estab 1972 for the diffusion of contemporary art, historic and scientific exhibitions; to present local, national and international exhibitions and organize itinerant exhibitions. An old church, built in 1823, now historical monument, completely restored inside with three floors of exhibitions. Average Annual Attendance: 15,000. Mem: 400; dues $20; annual meeting in May or June
Income: $270,000 (financed by federal, provincial & municipal appropriation)
Publications: L'Esprit des lieux; L'Artiste au jardin; Messac; Opera, Les Nuits de Vitre; Cozic; exhibit catalogs
Activities: Classes for children; school programs; lectures open to public, 5 vis lectrs per yr; concerts; gallery talks; tours; originate traveling exhibitions; museum shop sells magazines
L Library, 35 W St Germain, G5L 4B4. Tel 418-724-2272; FAX 418-724-2272. Open to public for reference
Library Holdings: Vols 2000; Documents 600; Other — Exhibition catalogs, pamphlets, reproductions, sculpture

SAINT-LAURENT

M MUSEE D'ART DE SAINT-LAURENT, 615 Blvd Sainte-Croix, H4L 3X6. Tel 514-747-7367; FAX 514-747-8892. *Pres* Jean Royer; *VPres* Louise Vander Abeepe
Open Sun & Tues - Fri 12:30 - 5 PM. No admis fee. Estab 1962 to didactic exhibitions of traditional arts and crafts of Quebec. Museum situated in a Gothic chapel of the Victorian period, built in 1867 in Montreal & moved in Saint-Laurent in 1930. Besides its permanent collection, the Museum presents periodical modern art exhibitions
Collections: European and African prehistoric stones; Indian Artifacts: artifacts, ceramics, costumes, prehistoric stones; traditional and folk art of French Canada from 17th - 19th century: artifacts, ceramics, furniture, metalworks, sculpture, silver, textiles, tools, wood-carving
Exhibitions: Album: Email au Quebec: 1949 - 1989; La dentelle au fil des ans; Album: Un musee dans une eglise
Publications: Album: Images Taillees du Quebec; Album: Les eglises et le tresor de Saint Laurent; Album: Les cahiers du musee: Hommage a Jean Palardy; Les cahiers du musee: Premier biennale de la reliure du Quebec; La main et l'outil; monthly calendar
Activities: Lect open to public; concerts; gallery talks; tours

SHAWINIGAN

A SHAWINIGAN ART CENTER (Formerly Centre Cultural de Shawinigan), 2100 rue Dessaules, CP 400, G9N 6V3. Tel 819-539-1888; FAX 819-536-7255. *Dir* Robert Y Desjardins
Open Thurs - Sun 2:30 - 4:30 PM & 7 - 9:30 PM. No admis fee. Estab 1967. Gallery is maintained. Average Annual Attendance: 50,000
Income: Financed by city appropriation
Collections: Oils; pastels; watercolors; polyesters; reproductions; copper enameling; inks; sculpture; tapestries
Activities: Classes for adults and children; dramatic programs; concerts; lending collection contains original art works, original prints, paintings, sculpture, slides; sales shop selling original art

SHERBROOKE

M UNIVERSITY OF SHERBROOKE, Art Gallery, J1K 2R1. Tel 819-821-7748; FAX 819-820-1361. *Dir* Johanne Brouillet
Open Mon - Fri 12:30 - 4:30 PM, Sat & Sun 1 - 5 PM. No admis fee. Estab 1964 to introduce public to the best art work being done in Canada and to place this work in an historical (European) and geographical (American) context. Gallery has three exhibition areas totalling 12,800 sq ft on university campus & serves the community. Average Annual Attendance: 30,000
Income: $300,000 (financed by state & city appropriation & university funds)
Collections: 90 per cent Contemporary Graphics & Paintings Quebec & 10 per cent international
Publications: Monthly bulletin; catalogue
Activities: Lect open to public, 20 vis lectr per yr; gallery talks; lending collection contains books, cassettes, color reproductions, Kodachromes, original prints, paintings, photographs, sculpture, slides and videos

SUTTON

M EBERDT MUSEUM OF COMMUNICATIONS, Heritage Sutton, 30 A Main St, J0E 2K0. Tel 514-538-2649, 538-2646. *Cur* Edmund Eberdt
Admis $1.50. Estab 1965 to educate. Average Annual Attendance: 2000. Mem: 160; dues $10
Income: $20,000 (financed by membership, city & state appropriation)
Collections: †History, art & †communications collection
Activities: Lect open to the public; museum shop sells books & prints

TROIS RIVIERES

A CENTRE CULTUREL DE TROIS RIVIERES, 376 Ire Des Soijrs, CPC 368, G9A 5H3. Tel 819-372-4614; FAX 819-372-4632. *Dir* Francois Lahaye
Open 9 AM - Noon, 1:30 - 5 PM and 7 - 10 PM. Estab 1967
Income: Financed by city appropriation
Activities: Classes for adults and children; dramatic programs

VAUDREUIL

M MUSEE REGIONAL DE VAUDREUIL-SOULANGES, 431 Blvd Roche, J7V 2N3. Tel 514-455-2092. *Dir* Daniel Bissonnette
Open Mon - Fri 10 AM - 5 PM, Sat & Sun 1 - 5 PM. Admis adults $3, children $1.50. Estab 1953, non-profit organization subsidized by the Direction des Musees et Centres d'Exposition du Ministere des Affaires culturelles du Quebec. The collection consists of artifacts and artists production that have and still illustrate the traditional way of life in the counties of Vaudreuil and Soulanges, the surroundings and the Province of Quebec. Museum has four rooms for permanent collection and one for temporary and traveling exhibitions. A documentation centre is open for searchers and students and an animator will receive groups on reservation for a commented tour. Average Annual Attendance: 10,000. Mem: 300; dues $20; annual meeting in Apr
Income: Financed by endowment
Collections: Edison Gramophone 1915; antique pottery; historic documents and material; farming; furniture, paintings, portraits, sculpture and woodworking
Publications: Musee de Vaudreuil Catalog (selectif); Vaudreuil Soulanges, Western Gateway of Quebec
Activities: Classes for children; concerts; original objects of art lent; book shop
L Library, 431 Blvd Roche, J7V 2N3. Tel 514-455-2092.
Reference only
Library Holdings: Vols 2000; AV cylinders 600; Other — Photographs

SASKATCHEWAN

ESTEVAN

M ESTEVAN NATIONAL EXHIBITION CENTRE INC, 118 Fourth St, S4A 0T4. Tel 306-634-7644. *Dir* Sallie Pierson; *Admin Asst* Marni McKnight; *Educ Coordr* Scott Nicholson
Open Mon - Fri 9 AM - 5 PM, Sat & Sun 1 - 3:30 PM. No admis fee. Estab 1978 to receive, display and interpret objects and collections, that would increase the communities access to culture. Two galleries; one 16 x 30, the other 26 x 65. Average Annual Attendance: 16,000
Income: $150,000 (financed by federal, state & city appropriation & private sector fundraising)
Collections: Saskatchewan artists print series; Saskatchewan painting collection
Exhibitions: (1991) Nuclear Visions; Quilt Exhibition
Publications: Annual Report; newsletter, 6 times per year
Activities: Classes for adults and children; lectures open to public, 4 vis lectr per yr; children's and regional art show competitions; awards of merit; exten dept serves area within a 30 mile radius; book traveling exhibitions, 13-18 per yr; originate traveling exhibitions; sales shop sells souvenirs

LLOYDMINSTER

A BARR COLONY HERITAGE CULTURAL CENTRE, c/o City of Lloydminster, 5011 49th Ave, S9V 0T8. Tel 306-825-6184, 825-5655; FAX 403-825-7170. *Chmn* Richard Larsen; *Cur* Kathy Classen
Open daily May - Sept 10 AM - 8 PM, Sept - May Wed - Sun 1 - 6 PM. Admis family $5.75, adults $2.75, sr citizens & students $2, children 12 & under $1.50, school tours $.50. Estab 1963 to promote & support appreciation for & education about local history & the arts. The center is comprised of 4 exhibit galleries

(1000 sq ft), a museum bldg (24,000 sq ft) & classroom teaching space
Income: Financed by donations & city appropriations
Collections: Antique Museum; Fuchs' Wildlife; Imhoff Paintings; Berghammer Art Collection; over 5000 artifacts related to the Barr Colonists, the first settlers of the area
Activities: Gallery talks; tours; traveling exhibitions

M IMHOFF ART GALLERY, Weaver Park, S9V 0X5. Tel 403-825-3726. *Cur* Kathy Classen
Open 8 AM - 6 PM. Admis adults $2.75, students $2, children $1.50. Estab to exhibit 200 paintings done by Berthold Imhoff, who died in 1939
Exhibitions: (1991) Storm Warnings; Power for Prespective; Students Show; Alberta Flora; Still Life: Saskatchewan; Chris Frazier (pottery); Alberta Natural Photography; Weavers Guild

MOOSE JAW

M MOOSE JAW ART MUSEUM AND NATIONAL EXHIBITION CENTRE, Art & History Museum, Crescent Park, S6H 0X6. Tel 306-692-4471; FAX 306-692-3368. *Dir* Norma Lang; *Admin Asst to Dir* Liz Ellis; *Caretaker & Installation Technician* Gordon Ambrose
Open summer noon - 5 PM & 7 - 9 PM, cl Mon; winter Tues - Sun noon - 5 PM, Thurs & Fri 7 - 9 PM, cl Mon. No admis fee. Gallery has 4304 sq ft with movable walls, Museum has 3970 sq ft, Discovery Centre has 1010 sq ft. Average Annual Attendance: 23,000. Mem: 100; dues family $25, individual $15
Income: $160,000 (financed by city, state and national appropriation)
Collections: †Canadian Traditional & Contemporary; †Local & District Historical Artifacts 3,000; Sioux & Cree Beadwork, Native Weapons & Tools; †Art Collection of Canadiana; †Historical Collection; †Government Extended Loan
Publications: Annual catalogs; bi-annual newsletter
Activities: Classes for adults; classes for children; dramatic programs; docent training; lectures open to public, 22-25 vis lectr per year; gallery talks; tours; individual paintings & original objects of art lent; lending collection contains books, cassettes, film strips, 100 original prints, 250 paintings, photographs, sculpture, 20,000 slides; book traveling exhibitions 20 per year; originate traveling exhibitions

NORTH BATTLEFORD

M ALLEN SAPP GALLERY, 1091 100th SE, PO Box 460, S9A 2Y6. Tel 306-445-3304; FAX 306-445-0411. *Cur* Dean Bauche
Open daily 1 - 5 PM. Estab 1989. 8000 sq ft gallery built in 1916 contains state of the art equipment incl high tech audiovisual presentation equipment. Average Annual Attendance: 12,000. Mem: 100
Income: $10,000
Collections: The Gonor Collection, paintings, photos, slides
Exhibitions: Two Spirits Soar: The Art of Allen Sapp & The Inspiration of Allan Gonor (1991) Without Women. (1992) Beyond Art
Publications: gallery catalog, biennially
Activities: Lectures open to the public, 5 vis lectr per yr; sales shop sells books, original art, prints

PRINCE ALBERT

M JOHN M CUELENAERE LIBRARY, Grace Campbell Gallery, 125 12th St E, S6V 1B7. Tel 306-763-8496; FAX 306-763-3816. *Head Librn* Eleanor Acorn
Open Mon - Fri 9 AM - 9 PM, Sat 9 AM - 5:30 PM, Sun 1 - 5 PM. No admis fee. Estab 1973. Gallery is 100 linear ft
Income: Financed by city appropriation

REGINA

M NORMAN MACKENZIE ART GALLERY, 3475 Albert St, S4S 6X6. Tel 306-522-4242; FAX 306-569-8191. *Dir* Andrew Oko; *Business Mgr* Sudeep Bhargava; *Cur Exhib* Cindy Richmond; *Coordr Communications* Bonnie Schaffer; *Coordr Educ* Mary Mahon Jones
Open Mon, Tues, Fri, Sat & Sun 11 AM - 6 PM, Wed & Thurs 11 AM - 10 PM. No admis fee. Estab 1953 to preserve & expand the collection left to the gallery by Norman MacKenzie & to offer exhibitions to the city of Regina; to offer works of art to rural areas through the outreach program. Eight discreet galleries totalling approx 1500 running ft of exhibition space. Average Annual Attendance: 98,000
Income: $1,000,000 (financed by federal and provincial governments, University of Regina and city of Regina and private funds)
Collections: Contemporary Canadian and American work; contemporary Saskatchewan work; 19th and early 20th century works on paper; a part of the collection is early 20th century replicas of Eastern and Oriental artifacts and art
Exhibitions: Changing exhibitions from the permanent collection and traveling exhibitions
Publications: Exhibition catalogues; staff publications of a professional nature; Vista, quarterly
Activities: Docent training; community programme of touring exhib in Saskatchewan; interpretive programs; lect open to public, 8 - 10 visiting lectr per year; concerts; gallery talks; tours; films; exten dept serves entire province; originate traveling exhibitions nation-wide; gallery shop sells cards and catalogues
L Resource Centre, 3475 Albert St, S4S 6X6. Tel 306-522-4242; FAX 306-569-8191.
Open Mon, Tues, Fri, Sat & Sun 11 AM - 7 PM, Wed & Thurs 11 AM - 10 PM. Estab 1970 to offer the community a resource for art information, both historical and current. For reference only
Library Holdings: Vols 1500; Per subs 32; Artists' files; AV — Slides; Other — Clipping files, exhibition catalogs, pamphlets
Special Subjects: Saskatchewan art, historical & contemporary

Collections: Regional press clippings from 1925
Exhibitions: Between Abstraction & Representation, George Glenn; Jana Sterbak; Jan Gerrit Wyels 1888 - 1973; The Asymmetric Vision; Philosophical Intuition & Original Experience in the Art of Yves Gaucher; Peace Able Kingdom, Jack Severson; Artists With Their Work: Ryan Arnott; Grant McConnell: Memory in Place
Publications: Exhibition catalog
Activities: Film program, twice a month
L **Fine Arts Library,** College Ave, S4S 0A2. Tel 306-779-4826; FAX 306-779-4825. *Library Supv* M Fielden
Open Mon - Fri 8:30 AM - 5 PM & 7 AM - 10 PM, Sat - Sun 1 - 5 PM. Estab 1969 to service the students of music and the visual arts. For both lending & reference
Library Holdings: Vols 14,000; Per subs 55; Micro — Fiche, reels; AV — A-tapes, cassettes, rec; Other — Clipping files, exhibition catalogs, pamphlets
L **Slide Library,** Visual Arts Department, S4S 0A2. Tel 306-779-4879. *Cur* Susan Tlosker
Estab for the instruction of art history
Library Holdings: AV — Slides 90,000, v-tapes
Special Subjects: 20th century art
Collections: †Prehistoric - contemporary, Eastern & Western art

ORGANIZATION OF SASKATCHEWAN ARTS COUNCILS (OSAC)
For further information, see National and Regional Organizations

L **REGINA PUBLIC LIBRARY,** Art Dept, PO Box 2311, S4P 3Z5. Tel 306-777-6070; FAX 306-352-5550. *Chief Librn* Ken Jensen
Open Mon - Fri 9:30 AM - 9 PM, Sat 9:30 AM - 6 PM, Sun 1:30 - 5 PM, cl holidays. No admis fee. Estab 1947. Also operate: Glen Elm Branch Gallery and Sherwood Village Branch Gallery
Library Holdings: Vols 10,230; Per subs 60; Micro — Fiche; AV — A-tapes, cassettes, fs, motion pictures, slides, v-tapes; Other — Clipping files, exhibition catalogs 4000, original art works, pamphlets, photographs, prints
Special Subjects: Saskatchewan Art and Artists; Folk Art
M **Dunlop Art Gallery,** 2311 12th Ave, PO Box 2311, S4P 3Z5. Tel 306-777-6040; FAX 306-352-5550. *Dir & Cur* Helen Marzolf; *Asst Cur* Ingrid Jenkner; *Asst Cur* Suzanne Probe; *Cur Asst* Joyce Clark; *Technician* Jane Sather
No admis fee. Estab 1947. Average Annual Attendance: 120,000
Income: Financed by city appropriation, provincial & federal grants
Purchases: $10,000
Collections: †Permanent collection of Saskatchewan art; Inglis Sheldon-Williams Collection; †Art Rental Collection
Exhibitions: About 30 per year; local, regional, provincial, national and international art, artists, and themes in all media, both as loan exhibitions and self-organized
Publications: At the Dunlop, quarterly; exhibition catalogs
Activities: Classes for adults and children; lectures open to the public, 6 vis lectr per yr; gallery talks; tours; competitions; individual paintings & original objects of art lent through an art rental collection available to the public and works from permanent collection lent to other galleries; lending collection contains original art works, original print and drawings; book traveling exhibitions; originate traveling exhibitions; sales shop sells books, magazines, cards, catalogues & posters

SASKATCHEWAN ARTS BOARD
For further information, see National and Regional Organizations

C **SASKPOWER,** Gallery on the Roof, 2025 Victoria Ave, S4P 0S1. Tel 306-566-3176; FAX 306-566-2548. *Graphics Supv* Dale Kilbride; *Commercial Artist* Shirley Fehr
Open Mon - Fri 1 PM - 9 PM, Sun & holidays 1 PM - 5 PM. No admis fee. Estab 1963 to give local artists and art groups exposure. Gallery approx 100 ft of wall space adjoining the observation deck that overlooks the city. Average Annual Attendance: 100,000
Exhibitions: Changing monthly
Publications: Brochure, monthly; exhibition brochures

SASKATOON

M **MENDEL ART GALLERY AND CIVIC CONSERVATORY,** 950 Spadina Crescent E, PO Box 569, S7K 3L6. Tel 306-975-7610; FAX 306-975-7670. *Pres* Henry Kloppenburg; *Acting Dir & Business Mgr* Richard Moldenhauer; *Cur* Bruce Grenville; *Admin Asst* Judy Koutecky; *Asst Cur* George Moppett; *Educ Coordr* Cheryl Meszaros; *Extension Coordr* Dan Ring; *Gallery Store Supvr* Michael Gibson; *Communications Coordr* Helen B Coleman; *Registrar* Sylvia Tritthardt
Open daily 10 AM - 9 PM, cl Christmas Day & Good Friday. No admis fee. Estab 1964 to exhibit, preserve, collect and interpret works of art; to encourage the development of the visual arts in Saskatoon; to provide the opportunity for citizens to enjoy and understand and to gain a greater appreciation of the fine arts. Average Annual Attendance: 250,000. Mem: 850; dues $30, sr citizens & students $10
Income: $2,000,000 (financed by grants, gift shop, mem, donations & other sources)
Collections: Regional, National and International Art
Exhibitions: (1991) The Object as Subject: Still-Life Art in Saskatchewan; Guido Molinari 1951 - 1961: The Black & White Paintings; The Griffiths Brothers; Studio Visit - Ruth Cuthand; William G R Hind: The Pictou Sketchbook; The Green Show: Moscow Art of the 1980s; From Regionalism to Abstraction: Mashel Teitelbaum & Saskatchewan Art in the 1940s; Portraits: Self & Other; Changers: A Spiritual Renaissance: School Art '91; Janet Werner; Graphothek; Douglas Bentham/Robert Christie; Frances Robson; The River in Prairie Art 1880 - 1990; Annette Messager: Making Up Stories; Work, Weather & the Grid: Agriculture in Saskatchewan; Ruth Welsh; J E H MacDonald: Logs on the Gatineau; Joanne Tod; Murals from a Great Canadian Train; New Tapes by Saskatchewan Artists. (1992) Clint Hunker: Paintings & Pastels; Jack Goldstein;

Terry Atkinson; Studio Visit - Marilyn Bain; Molly Lenhardt Retrospective; Grant McConnell: Tales of Dominion; Gretchen Bender; Marie Lannoo: The Academy; School Art '92; Douglas Walker: A Future in Ruins; Laughing Matters; Pictorial Incidents: The Photography of William Gordon Shields; Doris Wall Larson: Home Truths; Sam Spencer; Saskatchewan Open '92; Margaret Vanderhaeghe: What the Moon Saw; Mary Scott; El Corazon Sangrante/The Bleeding Heart; The Great Effect of the Imagination on the World: Brenda Pelkey; Good Stories, Well Told: Video Art for Young Audiences; Studio Visit - Laureen Marchand
Publications: Exhibition catalogues; Folio, gallery newsmagazine
Activities: Classes for children; docent training; lectures open to public; concerts; gallery talks; tours; exten dept; individual paintings & original objects of art lent to other galleries; book traveling exhibitions; originate traveling exhibitions; gallery shop sells books, magazines, original Inuit art, reproductions, prints & craft items, all with an emphasis on Canadian handcrafts
L **Reference Library,** 950 Spadina Crescent E, PO Box 569, S7K 3L6. Tel 306-975-7610; FAX 306-975-2891.
For staff use
Library Holdings: Vols 10,057; Per subs 52; AV — A-tapes, cassettes, fs, rec, slides, v-tapes; Other — Clipping files, exhibition catalogs, pamphlets, photographs
Special Subjects: Canadian art, Saskatchewan art

L **NUTANA COLLEGIATE INSTITUTE,** Memorial Library and Art Gallery, 411 11th St E, S7N 0E9. Tel 306-653-1677; FAX 306-242-0196. *Principal* Ron Hunter; *VPrincipal* George Rathwell
Open daily 8 AM - 4 PM, summer 9 AM - 3 PM. No admis fee. Estab 1919 to promote an appreciation for art; a memorial to students who lost their lives in the two world wars. Maintains an art gallery
Library Holdings: Vols 12,000; Per subs 100; Micro — Reels; AV — A-tapes, cassettes, fs, Kodachromes, motion pictures, rec, slides, v-tapes; Other — Clipping files, exhibition catalogs, original art works, pamphlets
Collections: Paintings & wood cuts by Canadian artists

M **PHOTOGRAPHERS GALLERY,** 12 23rd St E Saskatoon, 2nd floor, S7K 0H5. Tel 306-244-8018; FAX 306-665-6568. *Dir* Monte Greenshields; *Program Coordr* Ulike Veith; *Admin Coordr* Brenda Pelkey
Open Sept - June 30 Tues - Sun noon - 5 PM. No admis fee. Estab 1970, incorporated 1973 to encourage the development of photography as a creative visual art. Main gallery is 650 sq ft, and workshop gallery is 250 sq ft. Average Annual Attendance: 8000. Mem: 100; dues $25; annual meeting first Sun in May
Income: $196,000 (financed by mem, province appropriation, federal grants & fundraising)
Collections: Permanent Collection of 901 Contemporary Canadian photographs
Exhibitions: 8 main gallery exhibitions per year; 8 workshop gallery exhibitions per year
Publications: Backflash, quarterly magazine; members monthly newsletter
Activities: Lect open to public, 12 vis lectr per year; tours; exten dept; worshops throughout the province; portable darkrooms travel with instructors; book traveling exhibitions; originate traveling exhibitions to public galleries in Canada; sales shop sells books, postcards, tee shirts
L **Library,** 12 23rd E Saskatoon, 2nd Floor, S7K 0H5. *Dir* Monte Greenshields
Open Tues - Sun noon - 5 PM. Estab 1970. Reference
Library Holdings: Vols 1500; Per subs 10; AV — A-tapes, cassettes, slides; Other — Clipping files, exhibition catalogs, manuscripts, pamphlets, reproductions

A **SASKATCHEWAN ASSOCIATION OF ARCHITECTS,** Marr Residence, 326 - 11th St E, S7N 0E7. Tel 306-242-0733; FAX 306-664-2598. *Exec Secy* Pennie Bainbridge
Estab 1911. Mem: 111; dues $350; annual meeting Feb
Publications: Newsletter, monthly
Activities: Book prize given to architectural technology student at Saskatchewan Technical Institute, Moose Jaw (4 twice a yr); scholarships & fels offered

M **SASKATCHEWAN CRAFT GALLERY,** 813 Broadway Ave, S7N 1B5. Tel 306-653-3616. *Exhib Coordr* Marigold Cribb; *Dir* Terry Schwalm
Estab 1975 to exhibit Saskatchewan craft. 900 sq ft. Average Annual Attendance: 13,000. Mem: dues $40; annual meeting in June
Income: $429,000 (financed by mem, city appropriation, provincial grants)
Exhibitions: 10 exhibitions yearly (1992) The Eccentric Vessel. (1993) Dimensions '93
Publications: The Craft Factor, 3 per year
Activities: Classes for adults; lectures open to the public, 10 vis lectr per yr; open juried competition with award for residents; book traveling exhibitions, 2 per yr; originate traveling exhibitions

M **UNIVERSITY OF SASKATCHEWAN,** Gordon Snelgrove Art Gallery, S7N 0W0. Tel 306-966-4196, 966-4208. *Gallery Cur* Don Foulos
Open Mon - Fri 9 AM - 4:30 PM. No admis fee. Estab approx 1960 for the education of students and local families. Gallery covers approx 3000 sq ft of floor space, 300 running ft of wall space. Average Annual Attendance: 12,000
Income: Financed by provincial and federal government appropriations and university funds
Collections: Contemporary art from western & midwestern Canada
Exhibitions: Constantly changing exhibitions of art works; internationally organized and traveling shows
Publications: Show announcements, every three weeks; catalogues for selected exhibits
Activities: Individual paintings and individual objects of art lent to recognized regional exhibition centres for one time presentation or tour; lending collection contains 150 original art works, 75 original prints, 150 paintings, 100,000 slides; originate traveling exhibitions on a limited basis
M **John G Diefenbaker Centre,** University of Saskatchewan, S7N 0W0. Tel 306-966-8382; FAX 306-966-8706. *Dir* Stan Hanon; *Archivist* Open; *Educ Liaison* Frann Harris; *Technician* G Burke
Open 9:30 AM - 4:30 PM. No admis fee. Estab 1979 to promote interest and life

of John Diefenbaker. Average Annual Attendance: 25,000

Income: $400,000 (financed by fed & prov governments)

Collections: †Diefenbaker Archives; †Diefenbaker Memorabilia

Exhibitions: Diefenbaker (permanent); traveling exhibits on historical, social and anthropological subjects

Activities: Classes for adults & children; docent programs; lectures open to public; book traveling exhibitions, 30 plus per year; retail store sells books, prints, slides, jewelry, scarfs, gifts

SWIFT CURRENT

M **SWIFT CURRENT NATIONAL EXHIBITION CENTRE,** 411 Herbert St E, S9H 1M5. Tel 306-778-2736; FAX 306-778-2194. *Dir & Cur* Dave Humphries; *Education Coordr* Hugh Henry; *Admin Asst* Wendy Muri

Open 2 - 5 PM & 7 - 9 PM. No admis fee. Estab 1974 to exhibit temporary art exhibitions. 1876 sq ft. Average Annual Attendance: 18,000

Income: $120,000 (financed by city & state appropriation & federal grant)

Exhibitions: Ima Uhtoff; Swift Current Photo Works; Nuclear Visions

Activities: Classes for adults & children; docent training; film series; lectures open to public, 3-6 vis lectrs per year; book traveling exhibitions; originate traveling exhibitions

YUKON TERRITORY

DAWSON CITY

M **DAWSON CITY MUSEUM & HISTORICAL SOCIETY,** PO Box 303, Y0B 1G0. Tel 403-993-5291; FAX 403-993-5389. *Dir* Heather Smith; *Registrar* Leslie Peircy; *Exhib Coordr* Sally Robinson

Open 10 AM - 6 PM. Admis $3.25. Estab 1959 to collect, preserve & interpret the history of the Dawson City area. Average Annual Attendance: 20,000. Mem: 250; dues $15 - $250; annual meeting in Mar or Apr

Income: $300,000 (financed by mem, state appropriation, grants)

Collections: 30,000 piece collection including archives, cultural, enthnographic, household, industrial, paleontology, photographs

Exhibitions: Gold Rush; Railway; natural history; mining; Han People

Publications: Newsletter, quarterly

Activities: Docent programs; lect open to public, 600 vis lectr per year; originate traveling exhibitions 2 per year; retail store sells books

L **Resource Room Library,** PO Box 303, Y0B 1G0

For reference

Library Holdings: AV — Cassettes, lantern slides, slides; Other — Clipping files, photographs

Special Subjects: Ethnology, Historical Material, Gold Rush, Han People, Klondike, Mining

WHITEHORSE

A **YUKON HISTORICAL & MUSEUMS ASSOCIATION,** PO Box 4357, Y1A 3T5. Tel 403-667-4704.

Open Wed - Fri 9:30 - 3:30 PM. No admis fee. Estab 1977 as a national organization to preserve & interpret history. Mem: 180; dues individual $20, annual meeting in Oct

Income: Financed by mem, donations & fundraising

Publications: Newsletters, tour booklet, Yukon Exploration by G Dawson

Activities: Lect open to public, 4 or more vis lectr per year; tours; competitions with awards; lending collection contains books, photographs, audio equipment (oral history taping); originate traveling photo exhibitions to Yukon communities; sales shop sells books, t-shirts & heritage pins

II ART SCHOOLS

Arrangement and Abbreviations

Art Schools in the U.S.

Art Schools in Canada

ARRANGEMENT AND ABBREVIATIONS
KEY TO ART ORGANIZATIONS

ARRANGEMENT OF DATA

Name and address of institution; telephone number, including area code.

Names and titles of key personnel.

Hours open; admission fees; date established and purpose; average annual attendance; membership.

Annual figures on income and purchases.

Collections with enlarging collections indicated.

Exhibitions scheduled from 1991 onward.

Activities sponsored, including classes for adults and children, dramatic programs and docent training; lectures, concerts, gallery talks and tours; competitions, awards, scholarships and fellowships; lending programs; museum or sales shops.

Libraries also list number of book volumes, periodical subscriptions, and audiovisual and micro holdings; subject covered by name of special collections

ABBREVIATIONS AND SYMBOLS

Acad—Academic
Admin—Administration, Administrative
Adminr—Administrator
Admis—Admission
A-tapes—Audio-tapes
Adv—Advisory
AM—Morning
Ann—Annual
Approx—Approximate, Approximately
Asn—Association
Assoc—Associate
Asst—Assistant
AV—Audiovisual
Ave—Avenue
Bldg—Building
Blvd—Boulevard
Bro—Brother
C—circa
Cert—Certificate
Chap—Chapter
Chmn—Chairman
Circ—Circulation
Cl—Closed
Col—College
Coll—Collection
Comt—Committee
Coordr—Coordinator
Corresp—Corresponding
Cr—Credit
Cur—Curator
D—Day
Den—Denominational
Dept—Department
Dipl—Diploma
Dir—Director
Dist—District
Div—Division
Dorm—Dormitory
Dr—Doctor, Drive
E—East, Evening
Ed—Editor

Educ—Education
Elec Mail—Electronic Mail
Enrl—Enrollment
Ent—Entrance
Ent Req—Entrance Requirements
Est, Estab—Established
Exec—Executive
Exhib—Exhibition
Exten—Extension
Fel(s)—Fellowships
Fri—Friday
Fs—Filmstrips
Ft—Feet
FT—Full Time Instructor
GC—Graduate Course
Gen—General
Grad—Graduate
Hon—Honorary
Hr—Hour
HS—High School
Hwy—Highway
Inc—Incorporated
Incl—Including
Jr—Junior
Lect—Lecture(s)
Lectr—Lecturer
Librn—Librarian
M—Men
Maj—Major in Art
Mem—Membership
Mgr—Manager
Mon—Monday
Mss—Manuscripts
Mus—Museums
N—North
Nat—National
Nonres—Nonresident
Per subs—Period subscriptions
PM—Afternoon
Pres—President
Prin—Principal

Prof—Professor
Prog—Program
PT—Part Time Instructor
Pts—Points
Pub—Public
Publ—Publication
Pvt—Private
Qtr—Quarter
Rd—Road
Rec—Records
Reg—Registration
Req—Requirements
Res—Residence, Resident
S—South
Sat—Saturday
Schol—Scholarship
Secy—Secretary
Sem—Semester
Soc—Society
Sq—Square
Sr—Senior, Sister
St—Street
Sun—Sunday
Supt—Superintendent
Supv—Supervisor
Thurs—Thursday
Treas—Treasurer
Tues—Tuesday
Tui—Tuition
TV—Television
Undergrad—Undergraduate
Univ—University
Vol—Volunteer
Vols—Volumes
VPres—Vice President
V-tapes—Videotapes
W—West, Women
Wed—Wednesday
Wk—Week
Yr—Year(s)

* No response to questionnnaire
† Denotes collection currently being enlarged
A Association
C Corporate Art Holding
L Library
M Museum
O Organization

Art Schools In The United States

ALABAMA

AUBURN

AUBURN UNIVERSITY, Dept of Art, School of Fine Arts, 36849-5125. Tel 205-844-4373. *Head* Joseph W Gluhman; *Dean* Gordon C Bond
Estab 1928; pub; D; scholarships; enrl 300
Ent Req: HS dipl, ACT, SAT
Degrees: BFA 4 yr, MFA 2 yr
Tuition: Res—$585 per quarter; nonres—$1755 per quarter
Courses: †Ceramics, †Drawing, †Graphic Design, †Illustration, †Painting, †Printmaking, †Sculpture
Summer School: Complete 10 wk program

BAY MINETTE

JAMES H FAULKNER COMMUNITY COLLEGE, 1900 US Hwy 31 S, 36507. Tel 205-937-9581. *Div Chmn of Music* Milton Jackson, MM; *Instr* Walter Allen, MFA
Estab 1965; pub; D & E; scholarships; SC 4, LC 3; enrl D 35, E 40, non-maj 57, maj 18
Ent Req: HS dipl
Degrees: AA 2 yrs
Tuition: Res—undergrad $150 per quarter; nonres $300 per quarter; campus res—room & board $1215
Courses: †Art History, †Drawing, History of Art & Archaeology, †Painting, †Printmaking, †Sculpture, †Commercial Design
Summer School: Dir, Milton Jackson. Courses—Art Appreciation

BIRMINGHAM

BIRMINGHAM-SOUTHERN COLLEGE, Art Dept, 900 Arkadelphia Rd, PO Box A-21, 35254. Tel 205-226-4928. *Chmn Div Fine & Performing Arts* Dr James Cook. Instrs: FT 5
Estab 1946; den; D; financial aid awarded, some leadership scholarships available on variable basis; SC 22, LC 8, interim term courses of 4 or 8 wk, 4 req of each student in 4 yr period; enrl 500, maj 50
Ent Req: HS dipl, ACT, SAT scores, C average
Degrees: AB, BS, BFA, BM and BME 4 yr
Tuition: $2800 per term
Courses: Art Education, Art History, Drawing, Graphic Design, Painting, Printmaking, Sculpture
Adult Hobby Classes: Enrl 50; 8 wk term. Courses—Art History, Basic Drawing, Basic Painting
Children's Classes: Enrl approx 20. Laboratory for training teachers
Summer School: Enrl 50; 8 wk beginning June 11 and Aug 10. Courses—Same as regular session

SAMFORD UNIVERSITY, Art Dept, 800 Lakeshore Dr, 35229. Tel 205-870-2849. *Chmn* Dr Lowell C Vann. Instrs: FT 3, PT 8
Estab 1841; pvt; D; scholarships; SC 24, LC 4
Ent Req: HS dipl, ent exam, ACT, SAT
Degrees: BA and BS Educ 4 yrs
Tuition: $3000 per sem
Courses: Advertising Design, Art Education, Ceramics, Commercial Art, Costume Design & Construction, Drawing, Graphic Arts, Graphic Design, Handicrafts, History of Art & Archaeology, Interior Design, Painting, Photography, Sculpture, Stage Design, Teacher Training, Theatre Arts
Adult Hobby Classes: Enrl 45; tuition $381 for 3 cr hr. Courses—Appreciation, Studio Arts
Children's Classes: Enrl 10; 2 wk summer session. Courses—Introduction to Art
Summer School: Dir, Lowell Vann. Enrl 30, 2 five week terms.
Courses—Appreciation, Studio Arts

UNIVERSITY OF ALABAMA IN BIRMINGHAM, Dept of Art, University Station, 35294. Tel 205-934-4741; FAX 205-934-4941. *Chmn Dept* Sonja Rieger; *Prof* John W Dillen; *Assoc Prof* James Alexander, MFA; *Asst Prof* Janice Kluge, MFA; *Asst Prof* Gary Chapman; *Asst Prof* Heather McPherson, PhD; *Asst Prof* Marie Weaver; *Instr* Danille Baptista, MEd. Instrs: FT 9, PT 2
Estab 1966, dept estab 1974; pub; D & E; SC 27, LC 34, GC 10; enrl D 212, E 78, maj 100, grad 18
Ent Req: HS dipl, ACT, SAT
Degrees: BA
Tuition: Res—undergrad $58 per sem hr, grad $116 per sem hr; nonres—undergrad $63 per sem hr, grad $126 per sem hr

Courses: Aesthetics, Art History, Ceramics, Drawing, Graphic Design, Painting, Photography, Printmaking, Sculpture, †Teacher Training, Theatre Arts, †Art Studio
Adult Hobby Classes: Enrl 208; tuition $35-$60. Courses—Calligraphy, Drawing & Sketching, Experience of Art, Painting
Children's Classes: Enrl 60; tuition $20-$30. Courses—Drawing & Sketching, Painting, Sculpture
Summer School: Enrl 107; tuition as above for term of 11 wks beginning June 7. Courses—range over all fields and are about one half regular offerings

BREWTON

JEFFERSON DAVIS COMMUNITY COLLEGE, Art Dept, 220 Alco Dr, 36426. Tel 205-867-4832. *Instructor* Larry Manning
Estab 1965; pub; D & E; SC 10, LC 1; enrl D 700, E 332, maj 25
Ent Req: HS dipl or equiv
Degrees: AA & AS
Tuition: Res—$200 per yr; nonres—$400 per yr
Courses: Art History, Ceramics, Drawing, Handicrafts, Painting, Photography, Basic Design, Introduction to Art
Summer School: Enrl 200. Courses—Ceramics, Drawing, Introduction to Art

DECATUR

JOHN C CALHOUN STATE COMMUNITY COLLEGE, Division of Fine Arts, Hwy 31 N, PO Box 2216, 35609. Tel 205-353-3102; FAX 205-350-1379. *Div Chair* Arthur Bond, PhD; *Instr* Helen C Austin, PhD; *Instr* Janice Gibbons, MFA; *Instr* Robert Stephens, MA; *Instr* William Godsey, MA; *Instr* Jimmy Cantrell, EDS; *Instr* Joan Goree, MA; *Instr* Joyce Lowman, MA; *Instr* Frances Moss, EdD; *Instr* William Provine, MBA
Estab 1963, dept estab 1963; pub; D & E; scholarships; SC 46, LC 8; enrl D 80, E 22, non-maj 29, maj 70, others 3
Ent Req: HS dipl, GED
Degrees: AS, AA and AAS 2 yrs
Tuition: $600 per yr, $200 per qtr
Courses: Advertising Design, Art Education, Art History, Ceramics, †Commercial Art, †Drawing, †Film, †Graphic Design, Illustration, Lettering, Museum Staff Training, †Painting, †Photography, Printmaking, Sculpture, †Video
Summer School: Courses are selected from regular course offerings

FLORENCE

UNIVERSITY OF NORTH ALABAMA, Dept of Art, PO Box 5006, 35632-0001. Tel 205-760-4384; FAX 205-760-4329. *Prof* Fred Owen Hensley, MFA; *Prof* Elizabeth M Walter, PhD; *Asst Prof* Chiong-Yiao Chen, MFA; *Asst Prof* John D Turner, MFA; *Asst Prof* Duane L Phillips, MFA; *Asst Prof* Ronald Shady, MFA; *Asst Prof* Wayne Sides, MFA; *Instr* Michele Fabiano, MA. Instrs: FT 8
Estab 1830, dept estab approx 1930; pub; D; scholarships; SC 39, LC 10; enrl D 5380, non-maj 550, maj 125
Ent Req: HS dipl, or GED, ACT
Degrees: BFA, BS & BA 4 yr
Tuition: $720 per sem in state, $1020 out of state; campus res—room & board $1590
Courses: Advertising Design, Art Appreciation, Art Education, Art History, Ceramics, Design, Drawing, Graphic Arts, Graphic Design, History of Art & Archaeology, Illustration, Lettering, Painting, Photography, Printmaking, Sculpture
Summer School: Dir, Dr Elizabeth Walter. Enrl 50; tuition $343 for 8 wk term beginning June 6. Courses—Computer Graphics, Painting

HUNTSVILLE

UNIVERSITY OF ALABAMA IN HUNTSVILLE, Dept of Art & Art History, Roberts Hall, Room 313, 35899. Tel 205-895-6114. *Chmn Art & Art History Dept* Glenn T Dasher, MFA; *Prof* Michael G Crouse; *Asst Prof* Mark Marchlinski, MFA; *Asst Prof* David Stewart, PhD; *Asst Prof* Jerry Counselman, MFA; *Asst Prof* Carol Farr, PhD
Estab 1969 (as independent, autonomous campus), dept estab 1965; pub; D & E; scholarships; SC 46, LC 14; enrl D 150
Ent Req: HS dipl, ACT
Degrees: BA 4 yr
Courses: Advertising Design, Art Education, Art History, Commercial Art, Drawing, Graphic Arts, Illustration, Mixed Media, Painting, Photography, Printmaking, Sculpture, Commercial Design, Screen Printing, Typography
Adult Hobby Classes: Tuition $411 per 3 hr course. Courses—Computer Graphics, other miscellaneous workshops offered through Division of Continuing Education
Summer School: Dir, Glenn T Dasher. Tuition $411 for 3 hr for term of 10 wks beginning mid-June. Courses—Vary from summer to summer, part of the 46 studio classes & some art history offered

JACKSONVILLE

JACKSONVILLE STATE UNIVERSITY, Art Dept, 36265. Tel 205-782-5626.
Head Charles Groover
Estab 1883; pub; D & E; scholarships; SC 22, LC 8, GC 4; enrl D 8000, E 24, non-maj 70, maj 100, grad 11, others 15
Ent Req: HS dipl, ACT
Degrees: BFA, BA 4 yr
Tuition: $660 per sem

LIVINGSTON

LIVINGSTON UNIVERSITY, Division of Fine Arts, 35470. Tel 205-652-9661.
Chmn Dennis P Kudlawiec
Estab 1835; pub; scholarships; enrl 1800
Degrees: BA, BS, BMus, MEd, MSc
Tuition: $270 per qtr
Courses: Art Education, Art History, Ceramics, Display, Drawing, Graphic Arts, Industrial Design, Painting, Art Appreciation, Art for the Teacher, Crafts, Design, Mechanical Drawing, Metal Work, Woodworking

MARION

JUDSON COLLEGE, Division of Fine Arts, 36756. Tel 205-683-6161. *Chmn* Wade Peoples
Estab 1838; den, W; D & E; scholarships, loans, grants; SC 23, LC 6; enrl 450
Ent Req: HS grad, adequate HS grades and ACT scores
Degrees: BA 3-4 yr
Tuition: $3175 per yr
Courses: Commercial Art, Drawing, Painting, Sculpture, Design, Watercolor, Special Courses, Elementary Art, Pottery, Perspective Drafting
Adult Hobby Classes: Enrl 5. Courses—Studio Drawing, Painting
Children's Classes: Courses—Painting, Drawing

MOBILE

SPRING HILL COLLEGE, Fine Arts Dept, 4000 Dauphin St, 36608. Tel 205-460-2392. *Chmn* Ruth Belasco, MFA; *Asst Prof* Barbara Patten, MA; *Asst Prof* Thomas Loehr, MFA
Estab 1830, dept estab 1965; den; D & E; SC 21, LC 3; enrl D 163, non-maj 128, maj 35
Ent Req: HS dipl, ACT, CEEB, SAT
Degrees: BA
Tuition: Undergrad $5000 per sem; campus res—room $950 - $1200, board $700 - $825 per sem
Courses: Advertising Design, Aesthetics, Art Appreciation, Art Education, Art History, Ceramics, Commercial Art, Costume Design & Construction, Design, Drawing, †Art Business, †Therapy, †Studio Art, Textile Printing
Adult Hobby Classes: Enrl 15. Courses—wide variety
Summer School: Enrl 15. Courses—wide variety

UNIVERSITY OF SOUTH ALABAMA, Dept of Art, 307 University Blvd, 36688. Tel 205-460-6335. *Chmn* James E Kennedy, MAT; *Photography & Graphics* Paul Romejko; *Printmaker* John Cleverdon; *Printmaker* Sumi Putman; *Art Historian* Robert Bantens; *Art Historian* Janice Gandy; *Art Historian* Philipe Oszuscik; *Painting & Design* Lee Hoffman; *Ceramisist* Lloyd Pattern; *Sculptor* James Conlon
Estab 1963, dept estab 1964; pub; D & E; SC 32, LC 25; enrl maj & 150
Ent Req: HS dipl, ACT
Degrees: BA, BFA and BA(Art History) 4 yrs
Courses: Advertising Design, Aesthetics, Architecture, Art Education, Art History, Ceramics, Commercial Art, Drawing, Graphic Arts, Painting, Photography, Printmaking, Sculpture
Summer School: Chmn, James E Kennedy. Courses—Drawing, Painting, 3-D Design

MONROEVILLE

ALABAMA SOUTHERN COMMUNITY COLLEGE (Formerly Patrick Henry State Junior College), Art Dept, PO Box 200, 36461. Tel 205-575-3156. *Chmn* Dr Margaret H Murphy
Sch estab 1965, dept estab 1971; pub; D & E; SC 6, LC 1; enrl D 25, E 8, non-maj 23, maj 3
Ent Req: HS dipl, GED
Degrees: AA & AS 2 yrs
Tuition: Res—undergrad $600 per yr
Courses: Art Appreciation, Drafting, †Drawing, †Painting, Stage Design, Theatre Arts

MONTEVALLO

UNIVERSITY OF MONTEVALLO, College of Fine Arts, Art Department, 35115. Tel 205-665-2521, Ext 6400. *Dean* L Frank McCoy; *Chmn* Sandra Jordan
Estab 1896; pub; D & E; scholarships, Work Study; SC 35, LC 10, GC 7; enrl Maj 120, others 2800
Ent Req: ACT
Degrees: BA, BS, BFA, BM, MA, MM
Tuition: $490 per sem
Courses: Advertising Design, Art Appreciation, Art Education, Art History, Ceramics, Commercial Art, Design, †Drawing, †Graphic Arts, †Graphic Design, †Painting, †Photography, †Printmaking, †Sculpture
Children's Classes: Enrl 20; tuition $30 per 10 wk term. Courses—General Studio
Summer School: Dir, Sandra Jordan. Enrl 1000; two 5 wk sessions beginning June 5 & July 5

MONTGOMERY

ALABAMA STATE UNIVERSITY, Art Dept, 915 S Jackson, 36195. Tel 205-293-4473. *Dept Chmn* Ellen C Larkins
Degrees: BA, BS
Tuition: Res—undergrad $1044 per yr
Courses: Advertising Design, Art Appreciation, Art History, Calligraphy, Ceramics, Design, Drawing, Handicrafts, Printmaking, Photography, Printmaking, Stage Design, Graphics

AUBURN UNIVERSITY AT MONTGOMERY, Dept of Fine Arts, 36193. Tel 205-244-3377. *Head Dept* Joseph Schwarz, PhD; *Dean School Liberal Arts* Marion Michaels; *Prof* Philip Coley, MFA; *Prof* Richard Mills, MFA; *Asst Prof* Mark Benson, PhD; *Asst Prof* Sue Jensen, MFA; *Asst Prof* Peter Thompson, MFA
Estab 1972; pub; D & E; SC 18, LC 5, GC 4; enrl D 400, non-maj 200, maj 125
Ent Req: HS dipl
Degrees: BA
Tuition: Res—$533 per qtr; non res—$1599 per qtr
Courses: Art Education, Art History, Ceramics, Drawing, Graphic Arts, Painting, Photography, Sculpture
Adult Hobby Classes: Courses—Ceramics, Painting
Summer School: Head, Joseph Schwartz. Tuition $533. Courses—same as above

HUNTINGDON COLLEGE, Dept of Art, 1500 E Fairview Ave, 36106-2148. Tel 205-265-0511, Ext 454. *Chmn* L Dennis Sears; *Asst Prof* Christopher Payne, MFA
Estab 1973; E; enrl 119
Tuition: $5800 per yr
Courses: Art Appreciation, Art History, Ceramics, Drawing, Painting, Photography, Printmaking, Sculpture, Advanced Studio Class, Fine Arts Photography, Graphics, 2-D Design, 3-D Design
Adult Hobby Classes: Courses—non-credit offered through continuous educational programs

NORMAL

ALABAMA A & M UNIVERSITY, Art and Art Education, PO Box 26, 35762. Tel 205-851-5516. *Head Dept* Clifton Pearson, EdD; *Prof* Robert Adams, PhD; *Assoc Prof* Jimmie Dawkins, MFA; *Assoc Prof* William W Nance, MFA; *Assoc Prof* William L Boyd, MA; *Assoc Prof* Oscar Logan, PhD
Estab 1875, dept estab 1966; pub; D & E; scholarships; SC 18, LC 3; enrl non-maj 430, maj 35, grad 10
Ent Req: HS dipl
Degrees: BS (Commercial Art & Art Education), MS, MEd (Art Educ)
Courses: †Advertising Design, Art Appreciation, †Art Education, †Commercial Art, Drawing, Graphic Arts, Jewelry, Painting, Photography, Printmaking, Sculpture, Weaving, Fibers, Glass Blowing
Adult Hobby Classes: Enrl 10 - 15; tuition $89 per sem. Courses offered in all areas
Children's Classes: Enrl 15 - 20; tuition $89 per sem. Courses offered in all areas
Summer School: Dir, Dr Clifton Pearson. Enrl 50; tuition $426 for 8 wk sem. Courses—Art Education, Art History, Ceramics

TROY

TROY STATE UNIVERSITY, School of Art & Classics, 36082. Tel 205-566-8112. *Dean School of Fine Arts* Dr John M Long. Instrs: FT 7
Estab 1957. University has 2 other campuses; pub; schol and fel; SC 23, LC 11
Ent Req: HS grad, ent exam
Degrees: BA and BS (Arts & Sciences), MS
Tuition: Res—undergrad $20 per cr hr, grad $22.50 per cr hr; in- state $465 12-18 cr hrs; out-of-state $690 12-18 cr hrs
Courses: Art History, †Art History, Commercial Art, Drawing, Graphic Arts, Handicrafts, Jewelry, Lettering, Painting, Photography, Silversmithing, Teacher Training, Museology, Pottery
Adult Hobby Classes: Courses—Basketry, Crafts, Matting & Framing
Children's Classes: Enrl 30. Courses—Summer Workshop
Summer School: Dir, Earl P Smith. Tuition same as regular session for 8 wk term. Courses—Art History, Studio

TUSCALOOSA

STILLMAN COLLEGE, Stillman Art Gallery and Art Dept, 3601 15th St, PO Box 1430, 35403. Tel 205-349-4240, Ext 560. *Prof* Raymond L Guffin, MFA; *Asst Prof* Keyser Wilson, MFA
Estab 1876, dept estab 1951; pvt den; D; SC 8, LC 2; enrl D 73, non-maj 73
Ent Req: HS dipl, ent exam
Tuition: $3050 per yr; campus res—room & board $2450 per yr
Courses: Art Education, Art History, Ceramics, Commercial Art, Design, Drawing, Mixed Media, Painting, Sculpture, Afro-American Art History

UNIVERSITY OF ALABAMA, Art Dept, PO Box 870270, 35487-0270. Tel 205-348-5967. *Chmn Dept* W Lowell Baker
Estab 1831, dept estab 1919; pub; D & E; scholarships; SC 43, LC 12, GC 18; enrl D 750, maj 200, grad 30
Ent Req: HS dipl, ACT
Degrees: BA and BFA 4 yr, MFA 3 yr, MA (art) 2 yr
Tuition: Res—undergrad & grad $905 per sem; nonres—undergrad & grad $2243 per sem; campus res available
Courses: †Art Education, †Art History, †Ceramics, †Graphic Design, †Painting, †Photography, †Printmaking, †Sculpture, Drawing and Design
Children's Classes: Enrl 70; tuition $52-$70 for 5 wk term. Courses—Discoveries, Drawing, Explorations, Photography, 3-D Design
Summer School: Tuition $358.31 per term for two 5 wk terms. Courses—Art History, Ceramics, Foundation, Graphic Design, Painting, Photography, Printmaking, Sculpture

TUSKEGEE INSTITUTE

TUSKEGEE UNIVERSITY, College of Arts & Sciences, Art Dept, 36088. Tel 205-727-8913. *Dept Chmn* Open; *Prof* William Gay. Instrs: PT 1
Estab 1881; pvt
Degrees: 4 yr
Courses: Art Appreciation, Art Education, Textile Design, Applied Art

ALASKA

ANCHORAGE

UNIVERSITY OF ALASKA ANCHORAGE, Dept of Art, College of Arts and Sciences, 3211 Providence Dr, 99508. Tel 907-786-1783; FAX 907-786-1783. *Chmn* Cole H Welter. Instrs: FT 10, PT 15
Pub; D & E; schol; SC 43, LC 7-9; enrl College of Arts & Sciences FT 1310
Ent Req: Open enrl
Degrees: BA in art, BFA 4 yr
Tuition: Res—$55 per cr, $660 for 12 or more cr; nonres—$55 per 3 cr, $1980, 9 or more cr
Courses: †Art Education, †Ceramics, †Drawing, Graphic Design, Illustration, †Painting, †Photography, †Printmaking, †Sculpture
Adult Hobby Classes: Same as regular prog
Summer School: Dir, Cole H Welter. One term of 10 wks beginning May or two 5 wk sessions. Courses—Native Art History, Art Appreciation, Photography, Art Education & various studio courses

FAIRBANKS

UNIVERSITY OF ALASKA, Dept of Art, Fine Arts Complex, 99775-0200. Tel 907-474-7530. *Dept Head* Dwain Naragon; *Prof* Glen C Simpson; *Prof* Arthur W Brody; *Asst Prof* Todd Sherman; *Asst Prof* Wendy Erntz; *Asst Prof* Barbara Alexander; *Asst Prof* Kessler Woodward; *Asst Prof* Larry Dienneau; *Instr* James Behlke; *Instr* David Mollett; *Lectr* Harry Calkins
Estab 1963; pub; D & E; scholarships; SC 28, LC 4; enrl D 293, E 50, maj 45
Ent Req: HS dipl
Degrees: BA, BFA
Tuition: Res—$200 per sem; nonres $780 per sem
Courses: Ceramics, Drawing, Graphic Arts, History of Art & Archaeology, Jewelry, Lettering, Painting, Sculpture, Textile Design
Adult Hobby Classes: Enrl 30; courses—Crafts, Drawing, Painting, under the direction of the community college
Children's Classes: Enrl 40; courses—Ceramics, Drawing & Painting, Sculpture, under the direction of the community college
Summer School: Dean, Donald R Theophilus. Term of 3 or 6 wk. Courses—Drawing, Painting, Printmaking, Sculpture, Watercolor

ARIZONA

DOUGLAS

COCHISE COLLEGE, Art Dept, 85607. Tel 602-364-7943, Ext 225. *Instr* Monte Surratt; *Instr* Manual Martinez. Instrs: PT 11
Estab 1965, department estab 1965; pub; D & E; scholarships; SC 12, LC 2; enrl D 280, E 225, maj 20
Ent Req: HS dipl, GED
Degrees: AA 2 yrs
Tuition: Res—$23 per unit per sem; nonres—$35 per unit per sem; campus res available
Courses: Art History, Ceramics, Drawing, Jewelry, Painting, Photography, Printmaking, Sculpture, Commercial Design, Art in Elementary School, Color & Design, Special Topics in Art
Adult Hobby Classes: Courses—Painting

FLAGSTAFF

NORTHERN ARIZONA UNIVERSITY, School of Art & Design, 86011. Tel 602-523-4612. *Dir* C Hiers; *Prof* Dr D Bendel, EdD; *Prof* Dr Ronald Piotrowski, EdD; *Assoc Prof* J Cornett, MFA; *Assoc Prof* W Williams, MFA; *Assoc Prof* C Caldwell, MFA; *Assoc Prof* P Veinus, PhD; *Assoc Prof* T Knights, MFA; *Assoc Prof* G Balzer; *Assoc Prof* J O'Hara, MFA; *Assoc Prof* B Horn, MFA; *Assoc Prof* J Everett; *Assoc Prof* C Everett; *Assoc Prof* T Micco; *Assoc Prof* C Peterson; *Assoc Prof* C Piotrowski; *Asst Prof* A Bakovych, MA
Estab 1899; pub; D & E; scholarships; SC 56, LC 19, GC 8-10; enrl D 400, E 100, non-maj 342, maj 300, grad 30
Ent Req: HS dipl, ACT
Degrees: BFA, BA & BS 4 yr, MA (Art Education), MA (Studio) 1-2 yr
Tuition: Res—undergrad & grad $739 per sem; nonres—undergrad & grad $244 per cr hr, $2683 per 11 cr hrs; campus res available
Courses: †Art History, †Ceramics, †Interior Design, †Jewelry, †Painting, †Photography, †Printmaking, †Sculpture, †Construction Management, †Fashion Merchandizing, †Fine Arts, †Metalsmithing
Adult Hobby Classes: Most of the above studio areas
Children's Classes: Enrl 80; tuition $5 for 5 Sat. Courses—Ceramics, Drawing, Painting, Puppetry
Summer School: Dir, Richard Beasley. Enrl 150; tuition $46 per cr. Courses—Most regular courses

HOLBROOK

NORTHLAND PIONEER COLLEGE, Art Dept, 1200 E Hermosa Dr, PO Box 610, 86025. Tel 602-524-6111; FAX 602-524-2772. *Dir* Pat Wolf, MS. Instrs: FT 2, PT 60
Estab 1974; pub; D & E; SC 28, LC 2
Degrees: AA, Assoc of Applied Sci 2 yr
Tuition: Res—$20 per sem, nonres—$1125 per sem
Courses: Art History, Calligraphy, Ceramics, Commercial Art, Drawing, Graphic Arts, Art Appreciation, Design, Painting, Photography, Lettering, Printmaking, Sculpture, Textile Design, Weaving, Crafts
Adult Hobby Classes: Courses—Same as above
Summer School: 4 wk session in June

MESA

MESA COMMUNITY COLLEGE, Dept of Art & Art History, 1833 W Southern Ave, 85202. Tel 602-461-7524. *Chmn Dept Art* Robert Galloway; *Instr* Carole Drachler, PhD; *Instr* Jim Garrison, MA; *Instr* Ned Tuhey, MA; *Instr* Darlene Swain, MFA; *Instr* Sara Capawana, MFA
Estab 1965; pub; D & E; schol; SC 10, LC 8; enrl D 667, E 394
Ent Req: HS dipl or GED
Degrees: AA 2 yrs
Tuition: Res—$26 per cr hr, nonres—out of state $152 per cr hr, out of county $121 per cr hr, audit $25 per hr
Courses: †Advertising Design, †Art Appreciation, †Art History, †Ceramics, †Drawing, Film, Interior Design, Jewelry, †Painting, †Photography, Weaving, Crafts

PHOENIX

GRAND CANYON UNIVERSITY, Art Dept, 3300 W Camelback Rd, 85017. Tel 602-249-3300, Ext 2840. *Art Dept Chair* Kathy Rivers, MFA; *Res Artist* Esmeralda Delaney, MFA; *Res Artist* Kay Emig, MFA; *Instr* Arlene Foti, BFA; *Instr* Greg Osterman, BS
Estab 1949; den; D & E; scholarships; SC 23, LC 10; enrl D 106, E 25, non-maj 75, maj 30
Ent Req: HS dipl
Degrees: BA and BS
Tuition: Res—undergrad $4752 per yr, $2376 per sem, $198 per hr; nonres—undergrad $4752 per yr, $2376 per sem, $198 per hr; campus res available
Courses: Aesthetics, Art History, Ceramics, †Drawing, †Jewelry, †Graphic Design, †Mixed Media, †Painting, †Photography, †Printmaking, †Sculpture, †Teacher Training, Professional Artist Workshop
Children's Classes: Enrl 31; tuition $25. Courses—Ceramics, Composition, Drawing, Sculpture

PHOENIX COLLEGE, Dept of Art & Photography, 1202 W Thomas Rd, 85013. Tel 602-285-7276. *Chmn* John Mercer. Instrs: FT 5, PT 22
Estab 1920; pub; scholarships
Ent Req: HS dipl
Degrees: AA & AG 2 yrs
Tuition: Res—undergrad $26 per cr hr
Courses: Art Appreciation, Ceramics, Commercial Art, Drawing, Painting, Photography, Sculpture, Basic Design, Computer Design, Computer Graphics, Oil Painting, Watercolor
Adult Hobby Classes: Enrl 500; tuition $22.50 for 16 wks. Courses—Full range incl Computer Art
Summer School: Dir, John Mercer. Enrl 100; two 5 wk sessions. Courses—Intro to Art, Western Art

PRESCOTT

YAVAPAI COLLEGE, Visual & Performing Arts Division, 1100 E Sheldon, 86301. Tel 602-776-2243. *Chmn* Vincent N Kelly, MA; *Instr* Edward V Branson, MFA; *Instr* Beth LaCour, MFA; *Instr* Glen L Peterson, EdD; *Instr* Richard B Marcusen, MFA
Estab 1966, dept estab 1969; pub; D & E; scholarships; SC 50, LC 50; enrl D 1650, E 1563
Ent Req: HS dipl
Degrees: AA 2 yr
Courses: Advertising Design, Art History, Ceramics, Drawing, Sculpture, Glass, Handicrafts (batik, crafts, dyeing, macrame, spinning, stitchery, weaving, wood), Indian art survey, Stained Glass, Watercolor, Welded Metal
Adult Hobby Classes: Enrl open; tuition per course. Courses offered through Retirement College
Children's Classes: Enrl open; tuition $15 per course. Courses—Ceramics, Drawing, Painting
Summer School: Dir, Donald D Hiserodt. Enrl open; tuition $12 per sem hr for term of 6 wks beginning June 4. Courses—Ceramics, Drawing, Jewelry, Painting, Photography, Printmaking

TEMPE

ARIZONA STATE UNIVERSITY
—**School of Art,** 85287-1505. Tel 602-965-3468; FAX 602-965-8338. *Dir* Julie Codell, PhD
Estab 1885; pub; D & E; SC 88, LC 70, GC 116; enrl D 44,500, maj 960, grad 175
Ent Req: HS dipl, ACT
Degrees: BA and BFA 4 yrs, MFA 3 yrs, MA 2 yrs, EdD 3 yrs
Tuition: Res—undergrad & grad $764 per sem; nonres—undergrad & grad $3467 per sem; campus res—room & board $4110
Courses: Art Education, Art History, Ceramics, Drawing, Graphic Design, Intermedia, Jewelry, Painting, Photography, Sculpture, Art Criticism, Fibers, Intaglio, Lithography, Papermaking, Silkscreen, Wood Art, Computer Art, Video Art
Children's Classes: Tuition $40 for 5 wk term. Courses—Studio Art
Summer School: Enrl 150; tuition $60 per sem hr for two 5 wk sessions June through Aug. Courses—Same as regular session

—**College of Architecture & Environmental Design**, 85287. Tel 602-965-3216. *Dean* John Meunier; *Dir Archit* Michael Underhill, McPUD; *Dir Design* Robert L Wolf, MFA; *Chmn Planning* Frederick Steiner
Estab 1885, college estab 1949; pub; D & E; enrl lower div 212, upper div 466, grad 135
Ent Req: HS dipl, SAT
Degrees: MArchit 2 yrs, MS (Building Design & Design) 2 yrs, MEP 2 yrs, BS (Planning) 4 yrs, BS (Design) 4-5 yrs
Tuition: Res—undergrad & grad $764 per sem; nonres—undergrad & grad $3467 per sem; PT $80 per hr; campus res—room & board $3680 per yr
Courses: †Architecture, †Design, Drafting, Drawing, Graphic Design, †Industrial Design, †Interior Design, †Landscape Architecture, Mixed Media, Photography, Architectural History, †Housing and Urban Development, †Urban Planning
Summer School: Courses—lower & upper div courses primarily in Design, Graphics, History, Sketching and Rendering

THATCHER

EASTERN ARIZONA COLLEGE, Art Dept, 85552. Tel 602-428-8322. *Instr* James Gentry; *Instr* Richard Green, PhD. Instrs: PT 14
Estab 1888, dept estab 1946; pub; D & E; scholarships; SC 25, LC 3; enrl D 105, E 202, maj 30
Ent Req: HS dipl or GED
Degrees: AA & AAS 2 yrs
Tuition: Res—$300 per sem; nonres—$1562 per sem
Courses: Art Appreciation, Art History, Calligraphy, Ceramics, Design, Drawing, Photography, Printmaking, Sculpture, Silversmithing, Stage Design, Weaving, Airbrush, Fibers, Gem Faceting, Lapidary, Life Drawing, Stained Glass, Wood Carving

TUCSON

TUCSON MUSEUM OF ART SCHOOL, 140 N Main Ave, 85701. Tel 602-624-2333; FAX 602-624-7202. *Dir* Bob Kuegel. Instrs: PT 30
Estab 1924; pvt; D & E; scholarships; SC 42, LC 2; enrl D & E 1139
Ent Req: None
Tuition: Varies per course; no campus res
Courses: Art Appreciation, Art History, Ceramics, Drawing, Painting, Photography, Printmaking, Sculpture, Papermaking, Stained Glass
Adult Hobby Classes: Courses—Same as above
Children's Classes: Courses—Ceramics, Drawing, Painting, Photography, Primary art
Summer School: Enrl 650

UNIVERSITY OF ARIZONA, Dept of Art, Art Bldg, Room 108, 85721. Tel 602-621-1251, 621-7570. *Dept Head* Jon Meyer, MFA; *Prof* Robert Colescott, MA; *Prof Jewelry & Metalsmithing* Michael Croft, MFA; *Prof* Peggy Bailey Doagan, MA; *Prof Sculpture* Moira Geoffrion, MFA; *Prof Photography* Judith Golden, MFA; *Prof Art Educ* Dwaine Greer, PhD; *Prof Painting & Drawing* Harmony Hammond, MA; *Prof Painting & Drawing* Chuck Hitner, MFA; *Prof Sculpture* Dennis Jones, MFA; *Prof Art History* Keith McElroy, PhD; *Prof Painting & Drawing* Bruce McGraw, MFA; *Prof Art History* Lee Parry, PhD; *Prof Painting & Drawing* Barbara Rogers, MA; *Prof* Gayle Wimmer, MFA; *Assoc Prof Painting & Drawing* Rosemarie Bernardi, MFA; *Assoc Prof Graphic Illustration* Jerold Bishop, MFA; *Assoc Prof Graphic Design-Illustration* Jackson Boelts, MFA; *Assoc Prof Ceramics* Aurore Chabot, MFA; *Assoc Prof Sculpture* John Heric, MFA; *Assoc Prof* Bart Morse, MFA; *Assoc Prof Painting & Drawing* Barbara Penn, MFA; *Assoc Prof Printmaking* Andrew Polk, MFA; *Assoc Prof Photography* Ken Shorr, MFA; *Asst Prof Art Educ* Jeanne Carrigan, PhD; *Asst Prof Art History* Pia Cuneo, PhD; *Asst Prof Art Educ* Lynn Galbraith, PhD; *Asst Prof Art History* Paul Ivey, PhD; *Asst Prof Gallery Management* Sheila Pitt, MFA; *Asst Prof Art History* Julie Plax, PhD; *Asst Prof Painting & Drawing* Alfred Quiros, MFA; *Asst Prof New Genre* Joyan Saunders, MFA; *Asst Prof Art History* Stacie Widdifield, PhD; *Asst Prof Art History* Jane Williams, PhD
Estab 1891, dept estab 1893; pub; D; scholarships; SC 30, LC 21, GC 32; enrl D 3094, maj 535, grad 70
Ent Req: HS dipl, ACT
Degrees: BFA(Studio), BFA(Art Educ) and BA(Art History) 4 yrs, MFA(Studio) and MA(Art History or Art Educ) 2-3 yrs
Tuition: Res—undergrad $770 per 7 units, 1-6 units $80 per sem hr; grad $1922 per 7 units per sem; campus res—available
Courses: Art Education, Art History, Ceramics, Drawing, Graphic Design, Illustration, Painting, Photography, Printmaking, Sculpture, Fibers, New Genre
Summer School: Presession & two sessions offered. Request catalog (available in April) by writing to: Summer Session Office, Univ of Arizona, Tucson, AZ 85721

ARKANSAS

ARKADELPHIA

OUACHITA BAPTIST UNIVERSITY, Dept of Art, OBU Box 3785, 71998-0001. Tel 501-245-5000. *Chmn* Betty Berry, MA; *Dean School Arts & Science* Michael Arrington; *Instr* Ed Rhodes
Estab 1886, dept estab 1934; den; D; scholarship; SC 11, LC 2
Ent Req: HS dipl, ACT
Degrees: BA, BSE, BS and BME 4 yr
Tuition: $3495 per sem
Courses: Art Education, Art History, Ceramics, Commercial Art, Drawing, Handicrafts, History of Art & Archaeology, Illustration, Jewelry, Painting, Sculpture, Teacher Training, †Theatre Arts, Public School Arts
Summer School: Dir, Jim Berryman. Enrl 550; tui $50 sem hr; two terms of 5 wks beginning June 1

CLARKSVILLE

UNIVERSITY OF THE OZARKS, Dept of Art, 115 College Ave, 72830. Tel 501-754-3839. *Prof* Blaine Caldwell; *Asst Prof* Nancy Farrell
Estab 1836, dept estab 1952; den; D; schol; SC 9, LC 2; enrl D 83, non-maj 8, maj 17
Ent Req: HS dipl, ACT
Degrees: BA and BS 4 yr
Tuition: Res—undergrad $2300 per sem
Courses: Design, Sculpture, Art Appreciation
Summer School: Courses—Drawing, History of Contemporary Art, Sculpture, Watercolor

COLLEGE CITY

WILLIAMS BAPTIST COLLEGE, Dept of Art, 72476. Tel 501-886-6741. *Chmn of Humanities Div* Jerry Gibbons, MS
Den; D & E; scholarships
Tuition: Res—$1850 per yr; campus residence available
Courses: Art Education, Ceramics, Conceptual Art, Drawing, Graphic Design, Painting, Theatre Arts
Summer School: Dir, Dr Jerrol Swaim. Tuition $925 for 12-16 hrs, $59 for less than 12 hrs, $59 for each additional hr over 16 hrs

CONWAY

UNIVERSITY OF CENTRAL ARKANSAS, Art Dept, 72032. Tel 501-450-3113. *Chair* Dr Kenneth Burchett; *Prof* Patrick Larsen; *Prof* Robert C Thompson; *Prof* Helen Phillips; *Assoc Prof* Gayle Seymour; *Assoc Prof* Roger Bowman; *Asst Prof* Andrew Cohen; *Asst Prof* Cathy Caldwell; *Asst Prof* Bryan Massey; *Asst Prof* Lyn Brands. Instrs: FT 10, PT 6
Estab 1908; pub; SC 26, LC 16
Ent Req: HS dipl
Degrees: BFA, BA & BSE 4 yr
Tuition: Res $710 12 hrs & up; nonres—additional fee $710, summer term res— $64 per cr hr; nonres—$128 per cr hr
Courses: Art Appreciation, Art Education, Art History, †Ceramics, Design, †Drawing, †Graphic Design, †Painting, Printmaking, Sculpture, Advanced Studio, Color, Crafts, Figure, †Watercolor
Summer School: Dir, Kenneth Burchett. Tuition $64 per sem hr. Courses—various

FAYETTEVILLE

UNIVERSITY OF ARKANSAS, Art Dept, 116 Fine Arts Bldg, 72701. Tel 501-575-5202; FAX 501-575-2642. *Dept Chairperson* Michael Peven; *Prof Emeritus* Lothar Krueger, MS; *Prof Emeritus* Neppie Conner, MFA; *Prof* Myron Brody, MFA; *Prof* Thomas D Turpin, MFA; *Assoc Prof* Donald Harington, MA; *Assoc Prof* John W Smith EdD; *Assoc Prof* Robert Ross, MFA; *Assoc Prof* Ken Stout, MFA; *Asst Prof* Lynn Jacobs, PhD; *Asst Prof* Walter D Curtis, MFA; *Asst Prof* Kristin Musgnug, MFA; *Asst Prof* John Newman, MFA; *Vis Asst Prof* Jackie Golden, MFA; *Vis Asst Prof* Sarah Rogers, CFA. Instrs: FT 13
Estab 1871; pub; D & E; scholarships; SC 34, LC 16, GC 20; enrl D 14,000, non-maj 950, maj 115, grad 15
Ent Req: HS dipl, ent exam, GED
Degrees: MFA 60 cr hours & BA 4 yrs
Tuition: Res—$774 per sem; nonres—$1950 per sem; campus res—available
Courses: †Art Education, †Art History, †Ceramics, †Graphic Design, †Jewelry, †Painting, †Photography, †Printmaking, †Sculpture
Adult Hobby Classes: Enrl 100; tuition res $500 & nonres $1256 per sem. Courses—Ceramics, Painting, Sculpture
Summer School: Dir, M Peven. Enrl 150; 6 wk session. Courses—Ceramics, Drawing, Painting, Photography, 2-D Design, 3-D Design

HARRISON

NORTH ARKANSAS COMMUNITY COLLEGE, Art Dept, Pioneer Ridge, 72601. Tel 501-743-3000, Ext 311. *Chmn Div of Communications & Arts* Bill Skinner
Estab 1974, dept estab 1975; pub; D & E; SC 7, LC 1; enrl in art dept D 80, E 30-40, non-maj 45, maj 35
Ent Req: HS dipl
Degrees: AA 2 yrs
Tuition: County res—$210 per sem; non-county res—$270 per sem; nonres—$402 per sem
Courses: Advertising Design, Aesthetics, Architecture, Art Education, Art History, Calligraphy, Ceramics, Collages, Commercial Art, Constructions, Costume Design & Construction, Display, Drafting, Drawing, Fashion Arts, Film, Graphic Arts, Graphic Design, Handicrafts, History of Art & Archaeology
Adult Hobby Classes: Various courses offered each sem through Continuing Education Program
Summer School: Enrl 20-30; tuition $30-$35 for term of 6-8 wks beginning June 1. Courses—open; Art Workshop on Buffalo National River

HELENA

PHILLIPS COUNTY COMMUNITY COLLEGE, Dept of English and Fine Arts, PO Box 785, 72342. Tel 501-338-6474. *Artist in Residence* Larry Spakes
Estab 1966; pub; D & E; scholarships; SC 8, LC 1; enrl 55
Ent Req: HS dipl, ent exam, GED
Degrees: AA and AAS 2 yr
Tuition: County res—$264 per sem, $528 per yr; non-county res—$672 per yr; nonres—$984 per yr
Courses: Calligraphy, Ceramics, Design, Drafting, Drawing, History of Art & Archaeology, Painting, Sculpture, History of Western Art, Pottery, Stained Glass, Watercolor, Watercolor Elements & Principles
Summer School: Tuition same. 5 wk term beginning May 28

JONESBORO

ARKANSAS STATE UNIVERSITY, Dept of Art, PO Box 1920, 72467. Tel 501-972-3050. *Chmn* Curtis Steele, MFA; *Prof* Evan Lindquist, MFA; *Prof* William Allen, PhD; *Prof* Steven L Mayes, MFA; *Assoc Prof* Tom Chaffee, MFA; *Assoc Prof* John Keech, MFA; *Assoc Prof* Roger Carlisle, MFA; *Assoc Prof* William Rowe, MFA; *Asst Prof* Debra Satterfield, MFA; *Asst Prof* Bonnie Black, EdD; *Asst Prof* Dr Valerie Hutchinson, PhD; *Asst Prof* Dr Paul Hickman, PhD; *Asst Prof* John J Salvest, MFA; *Temporary Asst Prof* Gayle Ross, MFA. Instrs: FT 13
Estab 1909, dept estab 1938; pub; D & E; scholarships; SC 33, LC 10, GC 34; enrl D 300, E 100, non-maj 800, maj 192, grad 10
Ent Req: HS dipl
Degrees: BFA, BSE and BS 4 yrs, MA
Tuition: Res—$700 per sem, $59 per sem hr; nonres—$1325 per sem, $112 per sem hr; campus res—room & board $1045 per sem
Courses: †Art Education, Art History, †Ceramics, †Graphic Design, Illustration, †Painting, Photography, †Printmaking, †Sculpture
Adult Hobby Classes: Enrl 20; tuition $59 per sem hr. Courses—Art History, Ceramics, Drawing, Painting
Summer School: Dir, Curtis Steele. Enrl 100; tuition res—$345; nonres—$635 per 5 wk term. Courses—Art History, Drawing, Painting, Photography, Sculpture

LITTLE ROCK

THE ARKANSAS ARTS CENTER, Museum School, PO Box 2137, 72203. Tel 501-372-4000; FAX 501-375-8053. *Chief Cur* Townsend Wolfe; *Dir Museum School* David Bailin, MA; *Instr* Sam Horn; *Instr* Hilda Roddy; *Instr* Rebeca Whitfield; *Instr* Fred Schmidt; *Instr* Betty Borg-Russell; *Instr* Ron Mynatt; *Instr* Jil Smith; *Instr* Harvey Luber, BS; *Instr* Sharon Struthers; *Instr* Debra Moseley, BFA; *Instr* Brenda Scrimager; *Instr* Sheila Parsons, MA; *Instr* Laura Phillips; *Instr* Dale Seal; *Instr* Aj Smith, MFA; *Instr* Selma Blackburn; *Instr* Barbara Bennett; *Instr* Mary Brown; *Instr* Nancy Wilson, MA; *Instr* Jean Mross; *Instr* Jerry Colburn; *Instr* Jan Copeland; *Instr* Rick Hall; *Instr* Gary Hufford; *Instr* Amy Hill; *Instr* Thomas Harding; *Instr* Bridget Kresse; *Instr* Kevin Kresse; *Instr* Cynthia Kresse; *Instr* Evalyn Kirkwood; *Instr* Martha Jordon; *Instr* Kathy Lindsey; *Instr* Joyce Olds; *Instr* Cecil Persons. Instrs: FT 4, PT 27
Estab 1960, dept estab 1965; pub; D & E; scholarships; SC 62, LC 3; enrl D 350, E 300 children & adults
Ent Req: Open to anyone age 2 through adult
Tuition: 10 wk course for adults $104; 10 wk course for children $65
Courses: Art History, Calligraphy, Drawing, Jewelry, Painting, Photography, Printmaking, Sculpture, Theatre Arts, Enameling, Fabric & Flower Art, Glassblowing, Pottery, Stained Glass, Woodworking
Adult Hobby Classes: Enrl 1200; tuition $104. Courses—same as regular
Children's Classes: Enrl 2435; tuition $65 per 10 wks. Courses—same as regular
Summer School: Dir of Museum School, David Bailin. Enrl 719; tuition adult $104 for 10 wk term, child $55 for 8 wk term. Courses—same as regular

UNIVERSITY OF ARKANSAS AT LITTLE ROCK, Dept of Art, 2801 S University, 72204. Tel 501-569-3182; FAX 501-569-8775. *Chmn* Don Van Horn. Instrs: FT 13, PT 5
Estab 1928; pub; D & E; schol; SC, LC; enrl 5200
Ent Req: HS grad
Degrees: BA 4 yr, MA(studio), MA(art history)
Tuition: $785 per yr
Courses: Art Appreciation, Art Education, †Art History, Ceramics, †Commercial Art, †Drawing, Graphic Design, Illustration, †Painting, †Photography, †Printmaking, †Sculpture, †Design, †Pottery, Studio Art
Summer School: Dean, Lloyd W Benjamin III. Enrl 250; tuition $475 per yr. Courses—Art Appreciation, Art Education, Art History, Studio Art, Watercolor

MAGNOLIA

SOUTHERN ARKANSAS UNIVERSITY, Dept of Art, Magnolia Branch, N Jackson & University, 71753. Tel 501-235-4242. *Chmn* Jerry Johnson, MFA; *Asst Prof* Dianne O'Hern, MA; *Asst Prof* Steven Ochs
Estab 1909; pub; D & E; scholarships; SC 18, LC 4; enrl D 240, non-maj 260, maj 40
Ent Req: HS dipl
Degrees: BA & BSE 4 yr
Tuition: Res—undergrad $1080 per yr; nonres—undergrad $1250 per yr
Courses: Advertising Design, Art Appreciation, Art Education, Art History, †Ceramics, Commercial Art, Design, Drafting, Drawing, Graphic Arts, †Graphic Design, †Painting, †Printmaking, †Sculpture
Adult Hobby Classes: Classes & courses open to all at regular tuition rates
Children's Classes: Enrl 30; tuition $30. Courses—Kinder Art
Summer School: Dir, Jerry Johnson. Enrl 60. Courses—Art, Fine Arts

MONTICELLO

UNIVERSITY OF ARKANSAS AT MONTICELLO, Fine Arts Dept, PO Box 3607, 71655. Tel 501-460-1060. *Chmn* Annette Hall
Degrees: BA
Tuition: Res—undergrad $705 per sem, $82.75 per cr hr; waiver from MI, LA, TX
Courses: Art Education, Art History, Ceramics, Design, Drawing, Jewelry, Painting, Printmaking

PINE BLUFF

UNIVERSITY OF ARKANSAS AT PINE BLUFF, Art Dept, N University Dr, 71601. Tel 501-543-8236, 543-8238. *Dept Chmn* Henri Linton
Scholarships offered
Degrees: BS
Tuition: Undergrad—$540 per sem
Courses: Art Appreciation, Art Education, Art History, Calligraphy, Ceramics, Design, Drawing, Handicrafts, Painting, Photography, Printmaking, Sculpture, Textile Design, Weaving

RUSSELLVILLE

ARKANSAS TECH UNIVERSITY, Dept of Art, 72801. Tel 501-968-0244. *Head Dept* Ron Reynolds, MA; *Assoc Prof* Gary Barnes, MFA; *Asst Prof* John Mori, MFA; *Assoc Prof* John Sullivan, MFA
Estab 1909; pub; D & E; scholarships; SC 28, LC 5, GC 1; enrl D 200, non-maj 130, maj 88
Ent Req: Ent req HS dipl, ACT, SAT
Degrees: BA 4 yr
Tuition: Res—undergrad $750 per sem, $66 per cr hr, grad $68 per cr hr; nonres—undergrad $1500 per sem, $132 per cr hr, grad $136 per cr hr; no campus res
Courses: Advertising Design, Architecture, Art Education, Art History, Ceramics, Display, Drawing, Graphic Arts, Illustration, Industrial Design, Lettering, Painting, Printmaking, Teacher Training, †Fine Arts, Intro to Art, Packaging Design
Adult Hobby Classes: Drawing, Oil Painting, Watercolor
Summer School: Head Dept, Ron Reynolds. Enrl 30-50; tuition res $66 per cr hr, nonres $132 per cr hr; terms of 6 wk beginning June 8 & July 12. Courses—Art Education, Art History, Design, Drawing, Painting, Ceramics

SEARCY

HARDING UNIVERSITY, Dept of Art, PO Box 2253, 72149. Tel 501-279-4000, Ext 4426. *Chmn Dept* Don D Robinson, MA; *Prof* Faye Doran, EdD; *Prof* Paul Pitt, MFA; *Assoc Prof* John Keller, PhD; *Assoc Prof* Greg Clayton, MFA; *Asst Prof* Daniel Adams, MFA; *Assoc Instr* Susan Knight, MA
Estab 1924; pvt; D; schol; SC 27, LC 9, GC 7; enrl D 103, non-maj 25, maj 103
Ent Req: HS dipl, ACT
Degrees: BA, BS and BFA 4 yrs, MEd 5-6 yrs
Tuition: $154 per sem hr; campus res—room & board $3184 per yr
Courses: Advertising Design, Aesthetics, Art Education, Art History, Ceramics, Constructions, Drafting, Drawing, Graphic Design, Graphic Arts, Handicrafts, History of Art & Archaeology, Illustration, Interior Design, Jewelry, Lettering, Mixed Media, Painting, Printmaking, Sculpture, Silversmithing, Weaving, 2-D Design, Color Theory, Computer Graphics
Adult Hobby Classes: Enrl 45; tuition $138 per sem hr. Courses—Art in Elementary School, Teaching Art
Summer School: Dir, Dr Dean Priest. Enrl 1000; tuition $138 pr sem hr for two 5 wk sessions beginning June 9. Courses—vary depending upon the demand, usually Art Education, Art History, Ceramics, Drawing, Painting

SILOAM SPRINGS

JOHN BROWN UNIVERSITY, Art Dept, 72761. Tel 501-524-3131, Ext 182. *Head Dept* Charles Peer
Estab 1919; pvt; D; SC 9, LC 3
Ent Req: HS grad
Degrees: AS(Art)
Tuition: $2700 yr, $1350 per sem, $112.50 per sem hr; campus res—room & board $2100
Courses: Art Appreciation, Art Education, Drawing, Painting, Composition, Design & Color, Crafts (copper tooling, enameling, jewelry, macrame, mosaic, pottery, weaving)

CALIFORNIA

ANGWIN

PACIFIC UNION COLLEGE, Art Dept, 94508. Tel 707-965-6311. *Chmn* Jon Carstens
Degrees: AS, BA, BS, cert
Courses: Advertising Design, Art History, Ceramics, Design, Illustration, Painting, Photography, Printmaking, Sculpture, Stained Glass

APTOS

CABRILLO COLLEGE, Visual Arts Division, 6500 Soquel Dr, 95003. Tel 408-479-6464. *Chmn* Millard Irwin. Instrs: FT 12, PT 22
Estab 1959; pub; D & E; SC 46, LC 7
Ent Req: HS dipl
Degrees: AA 2 yr
Tuition: $50 for 6 or more units
Courses: Art History, Ceramics, Design, Drawing, Handicrafts, Jewelry, Painting, Photography, Sculpture, Textile Design, Color

ARCATA

HUMBOLDT STATE UNIVERSITY, College of Arts & Humanities, 95521. Tel 707-826-3624. *Chmn* James Crawford; *Instr* M D Benson; *Instr* M Bravo; *Instr* C DiCostanza; *Instr* M Isaacson; *Instr* R Johnson; *Instr* E Land-Weber; *Instr* D M LaPlantz; *Instr* L B Marak; *Instr* D Mitsanas; *Instr* J Crawford; *Instr* L Price; *Instr* S Ross; *Instr* E S Sundet; *Instr* W H Thonson; *Instr* M Morgan; *Instr* W Anderson; *Instr* A M Scott; *Instr* D Anton; *Instr* T Stanley
Estab 1913; pub; D & E; scholarships; SC 35, LC 11, GC 11
Degrees: MA 2 yr, BA 4 yr, BA with credential 5 yr
Tuition: Res—$4200 per yr; campus residence available
Courses: Ceramics, Drawing, Graphic Design, Jewelry, Painting, Photography, Printmaking, Sculpture, Teacher Training
Children's Classes: Children's Art Academy
Summer School: Dir, Dick Swanson. Enrl 24; tuition $75 per unit for 6 weeks

AZUSA

AZUSA PACIFIC UNIVERSITY, College of Liberal Arts, Art Dept, 901 E Alosta, PO Box 7000, 91702-7000. Tel 818-969-3434; FAX 818-969-7180. *Chmn Dept* Susan Ney, MA; *Assoc Prof* James Thompson, EdD; *Asst Prof* William Catling, MA; *Lectr* Robert S Bullock, MA
Estab 1915, dept estab 1974; den; D & E; scholarships; SC 16, LC 3; enrl maj 26
Ent Req: HS dipl, state test
Degrees: BA(Art) 4 yrs
Tuition: $4996 per sem
Courses: Advertising Design, Art Education, Art History, Ceramics, Drawing, Graphic Arts, Illustration, Painting, Printmaking, Teacher Training

BAKERSFIELD

BAKERSFIELD COLLEGE, Art Dept, 1801 Panorama Dr, 93305. Tel 805-395-4011. *Chmn* Albert Naso
Estab 1913; pub; D & E; SC 16, LC 4; enrl D 6000, maj 150-200
Ent Req: Ent exam, open door policy
Degrees: AA 2 yr
Tuition: Calif res—$5 per unit (max 5 and a half); 6 or more units $50; nonres—$85 per unit (max 15); no charge for units in excess of maximum
Courses: Ceramics, Art History, Art Appreciation, Photography, Printmaking, Graphic Arts, Drawing, Painting, Jewelry, Sculpture, Glassblowing
Adult Hobby Classes: Enrl 100-150. Courses—Ceramics, Painting, Photography
Summer School: Dir, Ron McMasters. For term of 6 wks beginning June. Courses—Ceramics, Design, Drawing, Figure Drawing, Photography

CALIFORNIA STATE UNIVERSITY, BAKERSFIELD, Fine Arts Dept, 9001 Stockdale Hwy, 93311. Tel 805-664-3093; FAX 805-664-3194. *Chmn* Dr Jeffrey Mason. Instrs: FT 13
Scholarships offered
Degrees: BA
Tuition: Res—$304 per qtr; nonres $2055 per qtr
Courses: Art Education, Art History, Design, Drawing, Painting, Photography, Printmaking

BELMONT

COLLEGE OF NOTRE DAME, Dept of Art, 1500 Ralston Ave, 94002. Tel 415-595-3595. *Head Dept* Terry St John. Instrs: FT 2, PT 6
Estab 1951; den; D & E; scholarships; SC 18, LC 12; enrl D 200, E 70, maj 50
Ent Req: HS dipl, ent exam
Degrees: BA 3 1/2 - 4 yrs, BFA
Courses: Advertising Design, Art Education, Art History, Drawing, Interior Design, Painting, Photography, Sculpture, Color, Composition, Etching, Gallery Techniques, Lithography, Silk Screen, 2-D & 3-D Design
Summer School: Dir, Lisa Baker. Upper division courses as in regular program plus special art education workshops; 6 wk term

BERKELEY

UNIVERSITY OF CALIFORNIA, BERKELEY
—College of Letters & Sciences-Art Dept, 238 Kroeber Hall, 94720. Tel 510-642-2582. *Chmn* Anne Healy; *Prof* Jerrold Ballaine, MFA; *Prof* Christopher Brown, MFA; *Prof* James Melchert, MFA; *Prof* George Miyasaki, MFA; *Prof* Mary O'Neal, MFA; *Prof* Richard Shaw, MFA; *Prof* Brian Wall; *Prof* Katherine Sherwood, MFA; *Prof* Wendy Sussman, MFA
Estab 1915; pub; D; scholarships
Degrees: BA, MFA, PhD (History of Art)
Courses: Ceramics, Drawing, Painting, Printmaking, Sculpture
—College of Environmental Design, Wurster Hall, 94720. Tel 510-642-5577. *Dean Environmental Design* Roger Montgomery; *Chmn Architecture* Jean-Pierre Protzen; *Chmn City & Regional Planning* Edward Blakely; *Chmn Landscape Archit* Randolf Hester
College encompasses Schools of Architecture, Landscape Architecture & City & Regional Planning. Maintains reference library of 150,000 vols; pub; D & E; scholarships
Degrees: AB, AB(Archit, Landscape), MArch, MCP, PhD
Courses: Design, Landscape Architecture, Photography, Environmental Design, History of Environment, Urban Planning

BURBANK

WOODBURY UNIVERSITY, Dept of Graphic Design, 7500 Glen Oaks Blvd, 91510-7846. Tel 818-767-0888. *Chmn Graphic Design* Bill Keeney; *Chmn Interior Design* Mark Bielski; *Chmn Fashion Design* Rosalie Utterbach
Estab 1884; pvt; D & E; SC 56, LC 18
Ent Req: HS dipl
Degrees: BS 4 yrs, MRA 2 yrs, BArc 5 yrs
Tuition: $3150 per quarter
Courses: Graphic Design, †Interior Design, †Fashion Design
Summer School: Regular session

CARSON

CALIFORNIA STATE UNIVERSITY, DOMINGUEZ HILLS, Art Dept, School of Humanities & Fine Arts, 1000 E Victoria St, 90747. Tel 310-516-3696. *Chairwoman* Louise H Ivers
Estab 1960; pub; D & E; scholarships; SC 35, LC 25; enrl maj 130
Ent Req: 2.0 GPA
Degrees: BA 4 yr
Tuition: Res—undergrad $198 per sem for 5.9 units or less, $342 per sem for 6 units

or more; nonres—undergrad $156 per unit
Courses: Art History, Design, Studio Art
Children's Classes: Tuition $36 - $55 per unit for 4 - 8 wk term. Courses—Crafts
Summer School: Dir, Dr Louise H Ivers. Enrl 40; tuition $36 - $55 per unit for 4 - 8 wk term. Courses—Crafts, Experiencing Creative Art

CHICO

CALIFORNIA STATE UNIVERSITY, CHICO, Art Dept, First & Normal, 95929-0820. Tel 916-898-5331. *Chmn* Vernon Patrick; *Graduate Advisor* Marion Epting; *Instr* Sheri Simons; *Instr* Michael Bishop, EdD; *Instr* Marion Epting, MFA; *Instr* Paul Feldhaus, MA; *Instr* David Hoppe, MFA; *Instr* Richard Hornaday, MFA; *Instr* James Kuiper, MFA; *Instr* Yoshio Kusaba, PhD; *Instr* Jean Gallagher, BA; *Instr* Fred Lucero, MA; *Instr* James McManus, MFA; *Instr* Winston Megorden, MA; *Instr* Dolores Mitchell, PhD; *Instr* Michael Monahan, MFA; *Instr* Lisa Reinertson, MFA; *Instr* Vernon Patrick, MFA; *Instr* Ann Pierce, MFA; *Instr* Michael Simmons, EdD; *Instr* Sharon Smith, EdD; *Instr* Karen VanDerpool, MFA; *Instr* Stephen Wilson, MFA
Estab 1887; pub; D & E; scholarships; SC 39, LC 29, GC 29; enrl non-maj & maj 1704, grad 59
Ent Req: Ent exam and test scores
Degrees: BA 4 yr, BFA 4 yr, MA 1 1/2 yr minimum
Tuition: Res—$280 per sem for less than 6 cr hrs, $439 per sem for over 6 cr hrs; nonres— $189 per unit
Courses: Art History, Ceramics, Drawing, Painting, Printmaking, Sculpture, Weaving, Glass
Summer School: Chmn, James Kuiper. Courses—same as above

CLAREMONT

CLAREMONT GRADUATE SCHOOL, Dept of Fine Arts, 251 E Tenth St, 91711. Tel 909-621-8071. *Chmn* Roland Reiss, MA; *Prof* Karl Benjamin, MA; *Assoc Prof* Michael Brewster, MFA; *Assoc Prof* Connie Zehr, BFA; *Vis Instr* Coleen Sterritt, MFA; *Vis Instr* Karen Carson, MFA; *Vis Instr* Ann Bray, MFA; *Vis Instr* John Mille, MFA; *Vis Instr* robert Storr PhD
Estab 1925; priv; D; scholarships; SC 43 LC 7 GC50; enrl non-maj 1, maj 52, grad 53
Ent Req: BA, BFA or Equivalent, GRE
Degrees: MA 1 yr, MFA 2 yr
Tuition: Grad $15,000 per yr; $600 per unit fewer than 12; campus res available
Courses: Aesthetics, Art History, †Drawing, †Film, Graphic Arts, Intermedia, Mixed Media, †Painting, †Photography, †Printmaking, †Sculpture, Performance

PITZER COLLEGE, Dept of Art, 1050 N Mills Ave, 91711. Tel 909-621-8000, Ext 3176. *Prof Art* C H Hertel; *Prof Ceramics & Pottery* David Furman; *Prof Drawing & Painting* Michael Woodcock
Estab 1964; pvt; D; scholarships; SC 8, LC 6; enrl Sept-June maj 19, grad 10 (Claremont Grad School)
Ent Req: HS dipl, various criteria, apply Dir of Admis
Degrees: BA 4 yr
Tuition: Res—$15,784 (including campus res)
Courses: Aesthetics, Ceramics, Drawing, History of Art & Archaeology, Painting, Photography, Printmaking, Sculpture, Video, Environments, Weaving

POMONA COLLEGE, Art Dept, 333 N College Way, 91711-6322. Tel 909-621-8000, Ext 2221; FAX 909-621-8403. *Chmn Art Dept* George Gorse, PhD; *Prof* Karl Benjamin, MFA; *Prof* Norman Hines, MFA; *Assoc Prof* Sheila Pinkel, MFA; *Assoc Prof* Judson Emerick, PhD; *Assoc Prof* Frances Pohl, PhD; *Asst Prof* Phyllis McGibbon, MFA
Estab 1889; pvt; D; schol; SC 15, LC 25; enrl D 330 maj 37
Ent Req: HS dipl
Degrees: BA 4 yrs
Tuition: Res—undergrad $7850 per sem. $22,455 with room & board
Courses: †Art History, Ceramics, Drawing, Graphic Design, Painting, Photography, Sculpture, Art Studio

SCRIPPS COLLEGE, Art Dept, Lang Art Bldg, 1030 Columbia, 91711. Tel 909-621-8000, Ext 2973. *Chmn Dept* Arthur Stevens
Estab 1928, dept estab 1933; pub; D; scholarships; enrl D 580, non-maj 480, maj 100
Ent Req: HS dipl
Degrees: BA
Courses: Architecture, Art History, Ceramics, Drawing, Film, Mixed Media, Painting, Printmaking, †Sculpture, Fiber Arts, Typography

COALINGA

WEST HILLS COMMUNITY COLLEGE, Fine Arts Dept, 300 Cherry Lane, 93210. Tel 209-935-0801, Ext 328. *Chmn* Dorothy Ash
Estab 1935; pub; D & E; SC 15, LC 2; enrl D 625, E 1250, non-maj 25, maj 10
Degrees: AA 2 yrs
Tuition: Res—undergrad $100 per yr; campus res—available
Courses: Art History, †Ceramics, Design, †Drawing, Fashion Arts, †Illustration, Lettering, †Museum Staff Training, †Painting, Printmaking, Sculpture

COLUMBIA

COLUMBIA COLLEGE, Fine Arts, PO Box 1849, 95310. Tel 209-533-5115, 533-5290. *Area Coordr* Terry Hoff
Estab 1968; pub; D & E; SC 50, LC 4; enrl D 100, E 75, non-maj 90, maj 10
Ent Req: HS dipl or over 18 yrs old
Degrees: AA 2 yrs
Tuition: Nonres—$58 per unit; no campus res
Courses: Art History, Calligraphy, Ceramics, Costume Design & Construction, Design, Drawing, Jewelry, Lettering, Painting, Photography, Printmaking, Sculpture, Silversmithing
Summer School: Dir, C H Palmer. Courses—Ceramics, Watercolor

COMPTON

COMPTON COMMUNITY COLLEGE, Art Department, 1111 E Artesia Blvd, 90221. Tel 310-637-2660. *Chmn* David Cobbs; *Prof* Verneal De Silvo. Instrs: FT 1
Estab 1929; pub; D & E; schol; SC 16, LC 6; enrl D 3500, E 2000, maj 18
Ent Req: HS dipl, 18 yrs of age
Degrees: AA 2 yr
Tuition: None for state residents
Courses: Advertising Design, Drafting, Drawing, History of Art & Archaeology, Lettering, Painting, Photography, Theatre Arts, Afro-American Art, Art Appreciation, Showcard Writing
Summer School: Courses—Art Appreciation

CORONADO

CORONADO SCHOOL OF FINE ARTS, 176 C Ave, PO Box 156, 92178. Tel 619-435-8541. *Dir* Monty Lewis
Estab 1944; pvt; SC, LC; enrl D 50, E 25
Degrees: Dipl 3-4 yr
Tuition: Full-time $275 for 4 wks, part-time $125-$200 for 4 wks
Courses: Advertising Design, Art History, Commercial Art, Graphic Arts, Illustration, Painting, Sculpture, Fine Arts, Mural Decoration
Children's Classes: Enrl 15; tuition $25 for Sat morning classes
Summer School: Dir, Monty Lewis. Enrl 75; tuition $160 per 4 wk; watercolor seminar $95 per 4 wk, $160 per 8 wk

COSTA MESA

ORANGE COAST COLLEGE, Division of Fine Arts, 2701 Fairview, 92628. Tel 714-432-0202. *Division Dean* Edward R Baker. Instrs: FT 35, Adjunct 80
Estab 1946; pub; D & E; scholarships; SC 225, LC 25; enrl D 4000, E 3500, maj 750
Ent Req: Ent exam
Degrees: AA 2 yr
Courses: †Advertising Design, Architecture, Art Appreciation, †Art History, †Ceramics, †Commercial Art, Conceptual Art, Design, †Display, Drafting, Drawing, Drawing, †Film, Goldsmithing, Graphic Arts, Graphic Design, †History of Art & Archaeology, †Illustration, †Interior Design, Jewelry, †Lettering, Mixed Media, Painting, †Photography, Printmaking, †Sculpture, Silversmithing, Stage Design, †Theatre Arts, Video, †Art, †Music, †Broadcasting, †Computer Graphics, Advertising Design, †Display & Visual Presentation
Summer School: Eight wk session. Courses—same as regular session

CUPERTINO

DE ANZA COLLEGE, Creative Arts Div, 95014. Tel 408-996-4832. *Acting Dean Creative Arts* Duane Kubo; *Instr* Gerald Eknoian; *Instr* William Geisinger; *Instr* Sal Pecoraro; *Instr* Michael Cole; *Instr* Lee Tacang; *Instr* Charles Walker; *Instr* Michael Cooper
Estab 1967, dept estab 1967; pub; D & E; scholarships
Ent Req: 16 yrs of age
Degrees: Certificates of Proficiency, AA 2 yr
Courses: Aesthetics, Art History, Ceramics, Drafting, Drawing, Film, Graphic Arts, Graphic Design, Lettering, Painting, Photography, Printmaking, Sculpture, Theatre Arts, Video, Stage Design
Adult Hobby Classes: Tuition varies per class. Courses—Bronze Casting, Calligraphy, Museum Tours,
Children's Classes: Computer art camp
Summer School: Courses—Drawing, Painting, Printmaking

CYPRESS

CYPRESS COLLEGE, Fine Arts Division, 9200 Valley View St, 90630. Tel 714-826-2220, Ext 139. *Chairperson* Charlene Felos
Estab 1966; pub; D & E; scholarships; enrl D 13,200
Ent Req: HS dipl
Degrees: AA 2 yrs
Tuition: $10 per unit up to 5 units, $50 per unit with BA; no campus res
Courses: Advertising Design, Art Appreciation, Art History, Ceramics, Commercial Art, Design, Drawing, Goldsmithing, Graphic Arts, Graphic Design, Instrumental Music, Vocal Music
Adult Hobby Classes: Adults may take any classes offered both day and extended; also offer adult education classes
Summer School: Extended Day Coordinator, Dr Evelyn Maddox

DAVIS

UNIVERSITY OF CALIFORNIA, DAVIS, Art Dept, 95616. Tel 916-752-0105; FAX 916-752-0795. *Dept Chmn* Open. Instrs: FT 17
Estab 1952; pub; D; scholarships; SC 28, LC 35; enrl maj 130, others 1000
Degrees: BA 4 yrs, MA(Art History), MFA(Art Studio)
Tuition: Res—$993; nonres—$1088 per quarter
Courses: Art History, Drawing, Painting, Photography, Printmaking, Sculpture, Ceramic Sculpture, Criticism Drawing

EL CAJON

GROSSMONT COLLEGE, Art Dept, Div of Communications & Fine Arts, 8800 Grossmont College Dr, 92020. Tel 619-465-1700. *Head Dept* Harry Lum. Instrs: FT 7, PT 16
Estab 1961; pub; D & E; schol; SC 22, LC 5; enrl total 1000
Ent Req: None
Degrees: AA

Tuition: Res—$10 per unit
Courses: Art History, Ceramics, Drawing, Painting, Photography, Sculpture, Art History
Summer School: Dir, Suda House. Enrl 100; tuition res $10 per unit for 6 - 8 wks. Courses—Art History, Drawing, Photography

EUREKA

COLLEGE OF THE REDWOODS, Arts, Humanities & Social Sciences Division, 7351 Tompkins Hill Rd, 95501. Tel 707-443-8411; FAX 707-445-6990. *Chmn* Bob Benson; *Dir* Lea Mills. Instrs: FT 4, PT 8
Estab 1964; pub; D & E; scholarships; SC 15, LC 3 per sem; enrl 8330, maj 160
Ent Req: HS grad
Degrees: AA & AS 2 yrs
Tuition: Nonres—$102 per unit plus $20 unit fee
Courses: Art Fundamentals, Fabrics
Summer School: Tuition $20 per unit

FRESNO

CALIFORNIA STATE UNIVERSITY, FRESNO, Art Dept, 5225 N Backer Ave, 93740-0065. Tel 209-278-4240, 278-2516. *Chmn* Richard Delaney. Instrs: FT 18
Estab 1911, dept estab 1915; pub; D; schol; SC 45, LC 9, GC 4; enrl 1000
Ent Req: HS dipl, SAT or ACT
Degrees: BA 4 yrs, MA 2 yrs
Tuition: Res—undergrad $748 per sem; nonres—$4438 per sem; campus res available
Courses: Art Education, Art History, Ceramics, Drawing, Film, Painting, Photography, Printmaking, Sculpture, Teacher Training, Crafts, Metalsmithing
Adult Hobby Classes: Tuition $35 unit. Courses—various
Summer School: Courses—Ceramics

FRESNO CITY COLLEGE, Art Dept, 1101 E University Ave, 93741. Tel 209-442-4600. *Dean* Carl Waddle, PhD
Estab 1910, dept estab 1955; pub; D & E; SC 13, LC 3; enrl D 14,000, E 2000
Ent Req: None, open door policy
Degrees: AA 2 yrs
Tuition: Res—$5 reg fee per unit up to maximum of $50; nonres—$96 per unit
Courses: Art Appreciation, Art History, Ceramics, Drawing, Painting, Printmaking, Sculpture, Fiber Art, Gallery Practices, Interaction of Color
Adult Hobby Classes: Ceramics, Design, Drawing, Painting, Sculpture
Summer School: Art Appreciation, Art History, Ceramics

FULLERTON

CALIFORNIA STATE UNIVERSITY, FULLERTON, Art Dept, 92634-9480. Tel 714-773-3471; FAX 714-773-3005. *Dean School of Arts* Jerry Samuelson, MA; *Chmn Dept* Darryl J Curran
Estab 1957, dept estab 1959; pub; D & E; scholarships; SC 62, LC 27, GC 12; enrl grad 140, undergrad 700
Ent Req: HS dipl, SAT or ACT
Degrees: BA, BFA, MA, MFA
Tuition: Res—undergrad & grad $356 for 0 - 6 units, $554 for 7 or more units; nonres—undergrad & grad $246 per unit plus $356 or $554; no campus res
Courses: Art Education, Art History, Ceramics, Design, Drawing, Graphic Design, Illustration, Jewelry, Painting, Photography, Printmaking, Sculpture, Environmental Design, Fibers, Glass, Museum Studies, Wood
Summer School: Enrl 60; tuition $125 per unit. Courses—Art History, Printmaking

FULLERTON COLLEGE, Division of Fine Arts, Art Dept, 321 E Chapman Ave, 92634. Tel 714-992-7000. *Chmn Division Fine Arts* Terrence Blackley
Estab 1913; pub; D & E; scholarships
Ent Req: HS dipl, ent exam
Degrees: AA 2 yr
Tuition: Nonres—$104 per unit; no campus res
Courses: Art History, Ceramics, Display, Drawing, Graphic Arts, Graphic Design, Illustration, Jewelry, Museum Staff Training, Painting, Photography, Printmaking, Sculpture, Textile Design, Weaving, Computer Graphics, Woodworking

GILROY

GAVILAN COLLEGE, Art Dept, 5055 Santa Teresa Blvd, 95020. Tel 408-847-1400. *Chmn* Art Juncker; *Prof* John Porter; *Prof* Silva Riof-Metcalf; *Prof* Jane Rekedael; *Prof* Richard Young; *Prof* Morrie Roison. Instrs: FT 2, PT 3
Estab 1919; pub; D & E; SC 12, LC 2; enrl D 150, E 75, maj 30
Ent Req: HS dipl or 18 yrs of age
Degrees: AA 2 yrs
Tuition: None to res; no campus res
Courses: Ceramics, Drafting, Drawing, Painting, Photography, Sculpture, Teacher Training, Theatre Arts, Art of the American, History of Art & Architecture
Summer School: Courses—Ceramics, Drawing, Painting

GLENDALE

GLENDALE COMMUNITY COLLEGE, Dept of Fine Arts, 1500 N Verdugo Rd, 91208. Tel 818-240-1000. *Chmn Division* Kathy Burke-Kelly; *Prof* Leonard de Grassi, MA; *Prof* Martin Mondrus, MFA; *Prof* Joan Watanabe; *Prof* Andrew Georgias, MFA; *Assoc Prof* Robert Kibler, MA; *Instr* Susan Sing, MA
Estab 1927; pub; D & E; SC 25, LC 7; enrl D 4100, E 3900, nonmaj 800, maj 200
Ent Req: HS dipl, ent exam
Degrees: AA 2 yrs
Tuition: None
Courses: Advertising Design, Architecture, Art History, Ceramics, Commercial Art,

Design, Drawing, Graphic Arts, Graphic Design, Lettering, Painting, Photography, Printmaking, Sculpture, Crafts, Serigraphy
Summer School: Dir, Dr John Davitt. Term of 8 wk beginning end of June.
Courses—Art History, Ceramics, Design, Drawing, Photography

GLENDORA

CITRUS COLLEGE, Art Dept, 1000 W Foothill, 91740. Tel 818-914-8862. *Art Dept Chmn* Tom Tefft
Estab 1915; pub; D & E; scholarships; SC 26, LC 7; enrl D 400, E 175, non-maj 400, maj 175
Ent Req: HS dipl
Degrees: AA and AS 2 yrs
Tuition: Nonres—$76 per unit
Courses: Advertising Design, Art History, Calligraphy, Ceramics, Collages, Commercial Art, Drawing, Graphic Arts, History of Art & Archaeology, Interior Design, Jewelry, Lettering, Mixed Media, Painting, Photography, Printmaking
Children's Classes: Courses—Ceramics, Painting
Summer School: Dir, Robert Hallet. Enrl 150; Term of 6 wks beginning June 20.
Courses—Art History, Ceramics, Drawing, Painting

HAYWARD

CALIFORNIA STATE UNIVERSITY, HAYWARD, Art Dept, 94542. Tel 510-881-3111. *Chmn* Gregory MacGregor
Estab 1957; pub; D & E; SC 30, LC 12; enrl 9900
Ent Req: HS dipl, ent exam, ACT
Degrees: BA 4 yr
Tuition: Res—undergrad $865.50 per yr; nonres—undergrad $3024 per yr
Courses: Art History, Calligraphy, Ceramics, Collages, Drawing, History of Art & Archaeology, Intermedia, Mixed Media, Museum Staff Training, Painting, Computer Graphics
Adult Hobby Classes: Courses offered through Continuing Education Dept

CHABOT COLLEGE, Humanities Division, 25555 Hesperian Blvd, 94545. Tel 510-786-6600. *Chmn* Elliott Charnow. Instrs: FT 21, PT 50
Estab 1961; pub; D & E; schol; SC 27, LC 5
Ent Req: HS dipl
Degrees: AA 2 yr
Tuition: None to res; nonres—$24.49 per quarter unit, 15 units or more, $367.35 per yr; no campus res
Courses: Advertising Design, Ceramics, Costume Design & Construction, Drafting, Drawing, History of Art & Archaeology, Illustration, Lettering, Painting, Sculpture, Stage Design, Theatre Arts, Cartooning
Summer School: Dir, Robert Hunter. Enrl 72-100; tuition $2-$100 per 6 wks.
Courses—Art History, Drawing, Introduction to Art, Sculpture, Watercolor

HOLLYWOOD

HOLLYWOOD ART CENTER SCHOOL, 2027 N Highland Ave, 90068. Tel 213-851-1103. *Dir* Mona Lovins
Estab 1912; pvt; D & E; SC 6; enrl D 40, E 12
Ent Req: HS dipl, submission of art work
Degrees: 3 yr cert
Courses: Commercial Art, Illustration, Interior Design, Fashion Design, Fine Art

HUNTINGTON BEACH

GOLDEN WEST COLLEGE, Visual Art Dept, 15744 Golden West St, 92647. Tel 714-895-8358. *Dean* David Anthony; *Chmn* B Conley, MA; *Instr* R Camp, MFA; *Instr* H Clemans, MA; *Instr* P Donaldson, MFA; *Instr* D Ebert, MA; *Instr* C Glassford; *Instr* J Heard, MA; *Instr* A Jackson; *Instr* K Hauser Mortenson; *Instr* N Tornheim
Estab 1966; pub; D & E; SC 12, LC 6; enrl D 13,820, E 9339
Ent Req: HS dipl
Degrees: AA 2 yrs
Tuition: Nonres—undergrad $104 per unit
Courses: †Advertising Design, Art History, Calligraphy, Ceramics, Costume Design & Construction, Display, †Drafting, Drawing, Illustration, Interior Design, Jewelry, Lettering, Mixed Media, Painting, Photography, Printmaking, Sculpture, Silversmithing, Stage Design, Textile Design, †Theatre Arts, Video
Summer School: Classes offered

IDYLLWILD

IDYLLWILD SCHOOL OF MUSIC AND THE ARTS, PO Box 38, 92549. Tel 909-659-2171. *Chmn Dance* Jean-Marie Martz; *Chmn Theater* Jude Levinson; *Visual Arts Chmn* Greg Kennedy; *Chmn Music* Susan Lim; *Humanities Chmn* Rob Pafco; *Chmn Math & Science* Jerry McCampbell
Estab 1950; pvt; Idyllwild School of Music and the Arts is a 14 wk summer program beginning in mid-June with courses in the arts for all ages; schol
Degrees: Not granted by the Idyllwild Campus, university credits earned through USC-LA Campus; documentation provided to high schools for credit
Tuition: Ranges from $145-170 wk; campus res—available
Courses: Ceramics, Painting, Photography, Printmaking, Sculpture, Fiber, Papermaking
Adult Hobby Classes: Enrl open; tui $165 per wk
Children's Classes: Enrl open; tui $90 - $120 per wk, $65 for half day program. Day and Residential Children's Arts Program; also Youth Ceramics

IMPERIAL

IMPERIAL VALLEY COLLEGE, Art Dept, PO Box 158, 92251. Tel 619-352-8320. *Chmn Dept Humanities* Carolyn Fordan; *Asst Prof Art* Mitjl Capet
Scholarships
Degrees: AA
Courses: Art Appreciation, Art History, Commercial Art, Design, Display, Drawing, History of Art & Archaeology, Interior Design, Painting, Sculpture, Theatre Arts

IRVINE

CITY OF IRVINE, Fine Arts Center, 14321 Yale Ave, 92714. Tel 714-522-1018. *Supv* Amy Aspell, MA; *Educ Coordr* Tim Jahns, MA; *Cur* Dori Fitzgerald, BA; *Resources Coordr* Lisa Cone. Instrs: FT 3
Estab 1980; pub; D & E; SC 35; enrl D 600, E 600
Tuition: Res—undergrad $20 - $150 per course
Courses: Art Appreciation, Calligraphy, Ceramics, Drawing, Handicrafts, Jewelry, Mixed Media, Painting, Sculpture, Teacher Training
Children's Classes: Enrl 400. Tuition varies. Courses—Arts
Summer School: Enrl 40. Tuition varies. Courses—Arts

UNIVERSITY OF CALIFORNIA, IRVINE, Studio Art Dept, School of Fine Arts, 92717. Tel 714-856-6648; FAX 714-725-2450. *Dean* Dr Robert Hickok; *Chmn* Catherine Lord
Estab 1965; pub; D; scholarships; SC 24, LC 2, GC 4
Ent Req: HS dipl
Degrees: BA(Studio Art) 4 yr, MFA(Art)
Tuition: Nonres—$1972 per qtr, $67 per unit less than 12 units
Courses: Architecture, Ceramics, Costume Design & Construction, Design, Drawing, Film, History of Art & Archaeology, Painting, Printmaking, Sculpture, Stage Design, Theatre Arts
Summer School: Ceramics, Drawing, Painting, Printmaking

KENTFIELD

COLLEGE OF MARIN, Dept of Art, 94904. Tel 415-485-9480. *Chmn* Deborah Loft
Estab 1926; pub; D & E; SC 48, LC 8; enrl D 5000
Ent Req: HS dipl, ent exam
Degrees: AA, AS 2 yrs
Courses: Architecture, Art History, Ceramics, Commercial Art, Drawing, Interior Design, Jewelry, Museum Staff Training, Painting, Photography, Printmaking, Sculpture, Textile Design, Architectural Design, Color Theory, History of Art & Architecture
Adult Hobby Classes: Enrl 400. Courses—Calligraphy, Drawing, Illustration, Jewelry, Painting, Printing
Children's Classes: College for Kids
Summer School: Courses—Ceramics, Drawing, Painting, Sculpture

LAGUNA BEACH

ART INSTITUTE OF SOUTHERN CALIFORNIA, 2222 Laguna Canyon Rd, 92651. Tel 714-497-3309. *Pres* John W Lottes
Estab 1962; pvt; D & E
Courses: Art History, †Ceramics, Collages, Drawing, †Graphic Arts, †Graphic Design, Jewelry, †Painting, Photography, †Printmaking, Sculpture, Fine Arts, Visual Communication
Adult Hobby Classes: 15 wk semesters. Courses—Studio & Lecture courses
Children's Classes: 15 wk semesters. Courses—Studio & Lecture courses
Summer School: Pres, Patricia Caldwell. Two 5 wk sessions. Courses—Studio & Lecture courses

LA JOLLA

UNIVERSITY OF CALIFORNIA, SAN DIEGO, Visual Arts Dept, 9500 Gilman Dr, 92093-0327. Tel 619-534-2860. *Dept Chmn* Jerome Rothenberg
Estab 1967; pub; D & E; scholarships; SC 55, LC 30, GC 15; enrl Maj 350, grad 40
Ent Req: HS dipl
Degrees: BA(Studio Art, Art History/Criticism, & Media) 4 yrs, MFA(Studio or Art Criticism) 2-3 yrs
Courses: Art Criticism/Film Criticism
Summer School: Dir, Mary Walshok

LA MIRADA

BIOLA UNIVERSITY, Art Dept, 13800 Biola Ave, 90639. Tel 310-944-0351. *Chmn Dept* Barry A Krammes; *Assoc Prof* Dan Callis; *Assoc Prof* Roger Feldman
Estab 1908, dept estab 1971; pvt; D & E; scholarships; SC 17, LC 4; enrl D 55, maj 55
Ent Req: HS dipl, SAT or ACT
Degrees: BA 4 yrs
Tuition: $3634 per yr, $1817 per sem, part-time $152; campus res—room & board $2148 per yr
Courses: †Advertising Design, †Art History, †Ceramics, Design, †Drawing, Lettering, †Painting, †Printmaking, †Sculpture
Summer School: Dir, Craig Stekette. Six week courses. Courses—vary

LANCASTER

ANTELOPE VALLEY COLLEGE, Art Dept, Division of Fine Arts, 3041 W Ave K, 93536. Tel 805-943-3241. *Dean Fine Arts Div* Dr Dennis White; *Prof* Robert McMahan, MFA; *Prof* Richard Sim, MFA; *Prof* Pat Hinds, MFA; *Asst Prof* Cynthia Minet
Estab 1929; pub; D & E
Degrees: AA 2 yrs
Tuition: Nonres—undergrad $1170 yr;
Courses: Art History, Ceramics, Drawing, Graphic Arts, Jewelry, Painting, Photography, Sculpture, Color & Design, Computer Graphics

LA VERNE

UNIVERSITY OF LA VERNE, Dept of Art, 1950 Third St, 91750. Tel 909-593-3511, Ext 4274. *Chmn* Ruth Trotter
Estab 1891; pvt; D & E; scholarships; SC 12, LC 4; enrl D 125, E 60, maj 12
Ent Req: HS dipl
Degrees: BA(Art) 4 yrs
Tuition: $2775 per sem; campus res—room and board $1375 per sem
Courses: Ceramics, Drawing, History of Art & Archaeology, Painting, Photography, Sculpture, Theatre Arts, Contemporary Art Seminar
Summer School: Terms of 3 and 4 wks

LONG BEACH

CALIFORNIA STATE UNIVERSITY, LONG BEACH
—Art Dept, 1250 Bellflower Blvd, 90840. Tel 310-985-4376. *Chmn* Patricia J Clark. Instrs: FT 40, PT 36
Estab 1949; pub; scholarships; SC 164, LC 26, GC 23, for both locations; enrl 5356 for both locations
Ent Req: HS grad, ent exam
Degrees: BA, BFA 4 yrs, MA, MFA
Tuition: Res—$436.50 per sem for 6 units; nonres—$1666.50 per sem for 6 units; campus res available
Courses: †Art Education, †Art History, †Ceramics, †Drawing, Graphic Design, †Illustration, †Painting, †Printmaking, †Sculpture, †Textile Design, Bio Medical Art, †Crafts (furniture), †General Art, †Jewelry-Metalsmithing, Museum Studies
Children's Classes: Ceramics, Design, Painting
Summer School: Dean, Dr Donna George. Tuition $77 per unit for sessions beginning June 7 & 23. Courses—Art History, Ceramics, Drawing, Painting, Special Topics
—Design Dept, 1250 Bellflower Blvd, 90840. Tel 310-985-5089. *Chmn* Michael Kammermeyer. Instrs: FT 10, PT 9
Estab 1949; pub; SC 164, LC 26, GC 23 for both locations; enrl 5356 for both locations
Ent Req: HS grad, ent exam
Degrees: BA, BFA 4 yrs, MA, MFA
Tuition: Res—$436.50 per sem for 6 units; nonres—$1666.50 per sem for 6 units; campus res available
Courses: †Display, †Industrial Design, †Interior Design
Summer School: Dean, Dr Donna George

LONG BEACH CITY COLLEGE, Dept of Art, 4901 E Carson St, 90808. Tel 310-420-4319. *Head Dept Art* Larry White; *Instr* Joseph Hooten, MA; *Instr* Marcia Lewis, MFA; *Instr* Larry White, MA; *Instr* Linda King, MFA; *Instr* Carol Roemer, PhD; *Instr* Rodney Tsukashima, MA; *Instr* Harvey Stupler, MA; *Instr* Mike Daniel, MFA
Pub; D & E; Scholarships; SC 13, LC 2; enrl D 400, E 200, non-maj 450, maj 150
Ent Req: HS dipl, ent exam
Degrees: AA and cert 2 yrs
Tuition: $10 per unit
Courses: Art History, Ceramics, Commercial Art, Drawing, Illustration, Jewelry, Lettering, Mixed Media, Painting, Photography, Printmaking, Sculpture, Studio Crafts, Weaving, Computer Art & Design
Adult Hobby Classes: Enrl 800; tui none. Courses—Crafts, Drawing, Painting
Summer School: Courses—same as above

LOS ALTOS HILLS

FOOTHILL COLLEGE, Fine Arts and Communications Div, 12345 El Monte Rd, 94022. Tel 415-949-1431. *Dean* Terry Summa
College has three campuses; scholarships
Degrees: AA, cert
Courses: Advertising Design, Art Appreciation, Art History, Ceramics, Design, Drawing, Photography, Film, Illustration, Interior Design, Painting, Printmaking, Sculpture, Stage Design, Textile Design, Weaving, Computer Graphics

LOS ANGELES

ART IN ARCHITECTURE, 7917 1/2 W Norton Ave, 90046. Tel 213-654-0990, 656-2286. *Dir* Dr Joseph L Young
Estab 1955; pvt; D; scholarships; SC 4, LC 4, GC 4; enrl D 6, E 7, non-maj 2, maj 8, grad 3
Ent Req: Art school diploma, ent exam
Tuition: $4000 for annual nine month program
Courses: †Architecture, Art History, Drawing, Mixed Media, Painting, Sculpture, †History of Art in Architecture

BRENTWOOD ART CENTER, 13031 Montana Ave, 90049. Tel 310-451-5657. *Dir* Edward Buttwinick, BA. Instrs: 23
Estab 1971; D & E; SC 40; enrl D 400, E 100
Tuition: $95 - $175 per month per class
Courses: Design, Drawing, Mixed Media, Painting, Sculpture

Adult Hobby Classes: Enrl 300; tuition $150 - $175 per month. Courses—Life Drawing, Basic Drawing, Design, Mixed Media, Painting, Sculpture
Children's Classes: Enrl 200; tuition $95 - $150 per month. Courses—Drawing, Mixed Media, Painting
Summer School: Ten wk program

CALIFORNIA STATE UNIVERSITY, LOS ANGELES, Art Dept, 5151 State University Dr, 90032. Tel 213-343-4010; FAX 213-343-4045. *Acting Chmn* Barbara Boyer; *Assoc Chmn* Joseph Soldate, MFA
Estab 1947; pub; D & E; scholarships; SC 85, LC 12, GC 9; enrl D 2500 (Art), non-maj 150, maj 324, grad 47 (per quarter)
Ent Req: HS dipl, ent exam
Degrees: BA(Art), MA(Art), MFA(Art)
Tuition: Res-undergrad & grad $474 per quarter; nonres-undergrad & grad $164 per unit; campus res available
Courses: Advertising Design, Architecture, †Art Appreciation, Art Education, Art History, Calligraphy, †Ceramics, †Commercial Art, Costume Design & Construction, Design, Display, †Drawing, Graphic Arts, History of Art & Archaeology, †Illustration, †Interior Design, Jewelry, Lettering, Painting, †Photography, Printmaking, Sculpture, Silversmithing, †Teacher Training, †Textile Design, Weaving, †Art Therapy, Costume Design, †Design Theory, Enameling, Exhibition Design, Fashion Illustration, Textiles, Weaving, †Computer Graphics

LOS ANGELES CITY COLLEGE, Dept of Art, 855 N Vermont Ave, 90029-9990. Tel 213-953-4240. *Chmn* Phyllis Muldavin-Smirle, MFA; *Prof* Dennis Elmore, MA; *Prof* Kaz Higa, MA; *Prof* Gloria Bohanon, MFA; *Prof* Lee Whitten, MA; *Assoc Prof* Gay Johnson. Instrs: PT 9
Estab 1929; pub; D & E; schol; SC 48, LC 8; enrl D 450, E 150, non-maj approx 2/3, maj approx 1/3
Ent Req: HS dipl and over 18 yrs of age
Degrees: AA 2 yr
Tuition: Res—undergrad $10 per unit, 10 or more units $100; nonres—$123 per unit
Courses: †Advertising Design, †Art History, Ceramics, †Commercial Art, Display, Drawing, †Graphic Design, †Painting, Printmaking, Sculpture, Life Drawing
Adult Hobby Classes: Enrl 2090; tuition approx $20 per class of 8 wks. Courses—Ceramics, Design, Drawing, Painting, Perspective, Printmaking, Sculpture
Summer School: Chmn, Phyllis Muldavin. Enrl 250; tuition $50 for term of 6 wks beginning July. Courses—basic courses only

LOYOLA MARYMOUNT UNIVERSITY, Art & Art History Dept, Communications & Fine Arts, Loyola Blvd & W 80th St, 90045. Tel 310-338-2700, 338-3054. *Chmn* Teresa Munoz, MFA; *Prof* Rudolf Fleck, MFA; *Assoc Prof* Michael Brodsky, MFA; *Prof* Susan Robinson, PhD; *Assoc Prof* Carm Goode, MFA; *Assoc Prof* Katherine Harper, PhD; *Vis Asst Prof* Craig Antrim, MFA. Instrs: FT 8, PT 9
Estab as Marymount Col in 1940, merged with Loyola Univ 1968; pvt; D; scholarships; SC 37, LC 21
Ent Req: HS dipl
Degrees: BA 4 yrs
Tuition: $8580 annual tuition; campus res available
Courses: Advertising Design, Art History, Ceramics, Design, Drawing, Graphic Arts, Illustration, Mixed Media, Painting, Photography, Sculpture, Computer Graphics, Stained Glass
Adult Hobby Classes: Animation, Ceramics, Computer Graphics, Jewelry, Sculpture, Stained Glass
Summer School: Dir, Dr Joanne Fisher. Courses— Ceramics, Computer Graphics, Drawing, Jewelry, Mixed Media, Photography

MOUNT SAINT MARY'S COLLEGE, Art Dept, 12001 Chalon Rd, 90049. Tel 310-476-2237, Ext 250. *Chmn & Prof* Norman Schwab
Chalon Campus estab 1925, also maintains Doheny Campus estab 1962; den; D & E; scholarships; enrl D 60, non-maj 31, maj 29
Ent Req: HS dipl
Degrees: BA and BFA 4 yrs
Tuition: $9250 per yr; $350 per cr hr; campus res—room & board available
Courses: †Art Education, †Art History, Ceramics, †Collages, †Conceptual Art, †Constructions, Drawing, †Graphic Arts, †Graphic Design, †Illustration, †Intermedia, †Mixed Media, Painting, Photography, †Printmaking, Sculpture, †Textile Design, Fiber Design

OCCIDENTAL COLLEGE, Dept of Art History & Visual Arts, 1600 Campus Rd, 90041. Tel 213-259-2749. *Chmn* Linda Lyke. Instrs: FT 7, PT 2
Estab 1887; pvt; D; scholarships & grants according to need; SC 19, LC 25, GC 5; enrl maj 40, others 300
Ent Req: HS dipl, col transcript, SAT, recommendations
Degrees: BA 4 yr
Tuition: $4565 campus res—room & board $1700 per term
Courses: †Art Education, †Art History, †Drawing, †Painting, †Sculpture, †Graphics, †Theory & Criticism
Adult Hobby Classes: Fundamentals

OTIS SCHOOL OF ART & DESIGN, Fine Arts, 2401 Wilshire Blvd, 90057. Tel 213-251-0500; FAX 213-480-0059. *Pres* Roger Workman
Estab 1918; pvt; scholarships; SC 150, LC 48, GC 9; enrl D 820, E 209, maj 600, grad 20
Degrees: BFA 4 yrs, MFA 2 yrs
Tuition: $11,850
Courses: Ceramics, Graphic Design, Illustration, Photography, †Architecture Design, †Communication Design, Environmental Art, †Environmental Design, Fashion Design, †Fashion Design, Fine Arts, †Glass, Metal & Surface Design
Adult Hobby Classes: Enrl 820; tuition $234 per cr
Children's Classes: Enrl 200; tuition $500 4 wks
Summer School: Continuing education and pre-college programs

SOUTHERN CALIFORNIA INSTITUTE OF ARCHITECTURE, 5454 Beethoven St, 90066. Tel 310-574-1123; FAX 310-829-7518. *Dir* Michael Rotondi
Degrees: BArch, MArch
Tuition: Undergrad—$4700 person
Courses: Architecture
Adult Hobby Classes: Dir, Rose Marie Rabin. Summer term only
Summer School: Dir, Gary Paige. Enrl 30; tuition $1000 for 12-15 wk term beginning July. Courses—Foundation Program in Architecture

UNIVERSITY OF CALIFORNIA, LOS ANGELES
—Dept of Art, 1300 Dickson Art Center, 405 Hilgard Ave, 90024. Tel 310-825-3281; FAX 310-206-6676. *Chmn* Henry T Hopkins
Scholarships & fels
Degrees: BA, MA, MFA
Tuition: Res—$1152 quarterly; nonres—$2566 quarterly
Courses: Collages, Conceptual Art, Drawing, Film, Intermedia, Mixed Media, Video, New Genre
—Dept of Design, 1200 Dickson Art Center, 405 Hilgard Ave, 90024-1456. Tel 310-825-9007; FAX 310-206-6676. *Acting Chmn* William Hutchinson
Degrees: BA, MA, MFA
Tuition: Res—undergrad $968 per quarter, grad $1152 per quarter; nonres—undergrad $3535 per quarter, grad $3719 per quarter
Courses: Ceramics, Graphic Design, Industrial Design, Interior Design, Video, Computer Imagery, Fiber Textile
—Dept Art History, 3209 Dickson Art Center, 405 Hilgard Ave, 90024-1417. Tel 310-206-6905. *Dept Chmn* Susan B Downey
Scholarships & fels
Degrees: BA, MA, PhD
Tuition: Res—undergrad $1152 per quarter, nonres—$2566 per quarter
Courses: †Art History

UNIVERSITY OF JUDAISM, Dept of Continuing Education, 15600 Mulholland Dr, 90077. Tel 213-879-4114; FAX 213-471-1278. *Dir* Jack Shechter, MA
Sch estab 1947; den; SC 14, LC 6
Degrees: Units in continuing education only
Tuition: $144 per sem, reg fee $9
Courses: Art History, Calligraphy, Drawing, Interior Design, Painting, Photography, Sculpture, Book Illustration, History of Jewish Art, Picture Book Making for Children, Tile Painting
Adult Hobby Classes: Enrl 8; tuition $127 per sem
Summer School: Courses offered

UNIVERSITY OF SOUTHERN CALIFORNIA, School of Fine Arts, Watt Hall 104, University Park, 90089-0292. Tel 213-940-2787; FAX 213-749-9703. *Dean* Dr Lynn Matteson; *Prof* Jud Fine; *Prof* Robbert Flick; *Prof* Ron Rizk; *Prof* Ruth Weisberg; *Prof* Jay Willis; *Prof* Dr Susan Larsen-Martin; *Prof* Dr John Pollini; *Assoc Prof* Dr Eunice Howe; *Assoc Prof* Margaret Lazzari; *Assoc Prof* Dr Carolyn Malone; *Assoc Prof* Bob Alderette; *Assoc Prof* Margit Omar; *Assoc Prof* David Bunn; *Asst Prof* Dr Glenn Hartcourt; *Adjunct Prof* Dr John Bowlt; *Adjunct Assoc Prof* Dr Selma Holo; *Adjunct Asst Prof* Hisako Asano; *Adjunct Asst Prof* Dr Shelley Bennett; *Adjunct Asst Prof* Leslie Bowman; *Adjunct Asst Prof* Dr Kenneth Hamma; *Adjunct Asst Prof* Edward Maeder; *Adjunct Asst Prof* Dr Marion True
Estab 1887, school estab 1979; pvt; D & E; scholarships; SC 78, LC 11, GC 23; enrl non-maj 600, maj 250, grad 50
Ent Req: HS dipl, SAT, GRE
Degrees: BA and BFA 4 yrs, MFA 2-3 yrs, MA 2 yrs, MA with Museum Studies Option 3 yrs, PhD 4 yrs minimum
Tuition: $529 per unit
Courses: Architecture, Art Appreciation, Art Education, †Art History, Ceramics, Conceptual Art, Costume Design & Construction, Design, Fashion Arts, Graphic Design, †History of Art & Archaeology, Intermedia, Interior Design, †Museum Staff Training, †Painting, †Photography, †Printmaking, †Sculpture, Teacher Training
Summer School: Dir, Lynn R Matteson. Enrl 150; tuition $529 per unit for 7 wks. Courses—Art History, Drawing, Painting

MALIBU

PEPPERDINE UNIVERSITY, SEAVER COLLEGE, Dept of Art, Culture Art Center, 90263. Tel 310-456-4155. *Instr* Avery Falkner; *Instr* Bob Privitt; *Instr* Joe Piesentin; *Instr* Susan Shutt; *Instr* Stephany de Lange; *Instr* Nora Halpern; *Instr* Sonya Sorrell
Scholarships
Tuition: $235 per unit; campus res—room & board per trimester $2015
Courses: Art Appreciation, Art Education, Art History, Ceramics, Design, Drawing, Graphic Arts, Jewelry, Painting, Sculpture, Monotypes
Summer School: Enrl 20; tuition $235 per unit. Courses—Jewelry, Monotypes, Mixed Media, Painting

MARYSVILLE

YUBA COLLEGE, Fine Arts Division, 2088 N Beale Rd at Linda Ave, 95901. Tel 916-741-6829. Instrs: FT 2
Estab 1927; pub; D & E; scholarships; SC 23, LC 2; enrl total 1437, maj 493
Ent Req: HS grad or 18 yrs of age
Degrees: AA 2 yr
Tuition: Res—$50 per sem; nonres—$72 per unit
Summer School: Dean & Assoc Dean Community Educ, Cal Gower. Courses—Ceramics, Drawing

MENDOCINO

MENDOCINO ART CENTER, 45200 Little Lake St, PO Box 765, 95460. Tel 707-937-5818; WATS 800-653-3328. *Prog Coordr* James Maxwell, MFA; *Ceramics Coordr* Peter Von Wilken Zook
Estab & inc 1959; pvt; D & E; SC 24, LC 6; enrl D 24
Ent Req: Mutual interview, ceramics ROP 2 yr program
Courses: Calligraphy, †Ceramics, Drawing, Graphic Design, Jewelry, Lettering, Painting, Printmaking, Sculpture, Silversmithing, Textile Design, Weaving, Silkscreen
Children's Classes: Enrl 12 - 20; $15 per session, duration is on-going, 1 day a wk. Courses—Teen Jewelry
Summer School: Dir, Robert Avery. Tuition $95 - $150 per each one wk workshop offered between June 14 & Aug 27. Courses—over 65 wk long classes in all media

MERCED

MERCED COLLEGE, Arts Division, 3600 M St, 95348. Tel 209-384-6000. *Head* Jan Moser; *Chmn* Robert Harvey
Estab 1964; pub; D & E; scholarships; SC 50, LC 10; enrl D 4741, E 3187, non-maj 3700, maj 4228
Ent Req: 18 yrs & older
Degrees: AA & AS 2 yr
Tuition: Res—undergrad $13 per sem; nonres—undergrad $75 per hr
Courses: Art History, Calligraphy, Ceramics, Drawing, Illustration, Painting, Photography, Sculpture, Theatre Arts
Summer School: Dir, Dr Ron Williams, Dean of Arts & Sciences. Tuition res—undergrad $13 for 7 wk term beginning June 21

MODESTO

MODESTO JUNIOR COLLEGE, Arts Humanities and Speech Division, 435 College Ave, 95350. Tel 209-575-6067. *Division Dean* Robert Gauvreau; *Instr* Richard Serroes; *Instr* Doug Smith; *Instr* Terry L Hartman, MA; *Instr* Daniel W Petersen, MA; *Instr* Jerry M Reilly, MFA; *Instr* J Gary Remsing, MA. Instrs: FT 259, PT 385
Estab 1921, div estab 1964; pub; D & E; schol; enrl 16,024 total
Ent Req: Grad of accredited high school, minor with California High School Proficiency Cert and parental permission, 11th and 12th graders with principal's permission, persons 18 or older who are able to profit from the instruction
Degrees: AA and AS 2 yrs
Tuition: Res—$6 health fee; nonres—$87 per sem unit to maximum of $1044 per sem plus health fee; no campus res
Courses: Advertising Design, Architecture, Art History, Ceramics, Display, Drafting, Drawing, Film, Jewelry, Lettering, Painting, †Photography, Printmaking, Sculpture, Silversmithing, Theatre Arts, Enameling, Lapidary
Adult Hobby Classes: Courses—Arts & Crafts, Lapidary
Summer School: Dir, Dudley Roach. Tuition $6 health fee. Courses—a wide variety offered

MONTEREY

MONTEREY PENINSULA COLLEGE, Art Dept, Div of Creative Arts, 980 Fremont St, 93940. Tel 408-646-4200. *Chairperson Div Creative Arts* Don S Chamber, MA; *Chairperson Dept Art* Pat Boles; *Instr* Karen Nagano; *Instr* Richard Janick, MA; *Instr* Gary Quinonez; *Instr* Jane Miller; *Instr* Robynn Smith; *Instr* Peter Pilat, MA; *Instr* Anita Benson; *Instr* Bonnie Britton; *Instr* Skip Kadish; *Instr* Cathy Hendig; *Instr* Martha Manson, MA
Estab 1947; pub; D & E; schol; SC 17, LC 8; enrl D 1343, E 623, maj 160
Ent Req: HS dipl, 18 yrs or older
Degrees: AA and AS 2 yrs
Tuition: Res—$50; nonres—$28 per unit; no campus res
Courses: †Art History, Design, †Drawing, Painting, Photography, Weaving, †Commercial Graphics, †Studio Art
Summer School: Dir, Thorne Hacker. Term of 6 wks beginning June. Courses are limited

MONTEREY PARK

EAST LOS ANGELES COLLEGE, Art Dept, 1301 Brooklyn Ave, 91754. Tel 213-265-8650, 265-8842. *Dept Chmn* June L Smith. Instrs: FT 5
Estab 1949; pub; D & E; SC 43, LC 10; enrl D 486, E 160, maj 646
Degrees: AA 2 yr
Tuition: $10 per unit, $150 per sem
Courses: †Advertising Design, †Art History, †Ceramics, Design, Display, †Drawing, Graphic Arts, Graphic Design, Lettering, Mixed Media, †Painting, †Art Fundamentals, †Art Graphic Communications, †Computer Graphics, †Electronic Publishing, †Life Drawing
Children's Classes: Enrl 60. Courses—Ceramics, Direct Printing Methods, Drawing, Painting
Summer School: Dept Chmn, June Smith. Enrl 50; tuition $10 per unit for 6 wk term. Courses—Art 201, Beginning Drawing, Beginning 2-D Design

NAPA

NAPA VALLEY COLLEGE, Art Dept, 2277 Napa Vallejo Highway, 94558. Tel 707-253-3201 (Div), 253-3203, 253-3205 (Dept). *Dir* Jan Molen; *Prof* Jay Golik; *Prof* Carolyn Broodwell
Tuition: $5 per unit up to 5 units, $50 for 6 units
Courses: Art Appreciation, Art History, Ceramics, Design, Drawing, Painting, Photography, Printmaking, Sculpture
Adult Hobby Classes: Courses offered
Children's Classes: Courses offered
Summer School: Courses—Painting, Ceramics, Drawing

NORTHRIDGE

CALIFORNIA STATE UNIVERSITY, NORTHRIDGE, Dept of Art-Two
Dimensional Media, School of the Arts, 18111 Nordhoff St, 91330. Tel 818-885-
1200. *Dept Chmn* Art Weiss, MFA; *Chmn General Studies* Anne Heath; *Chmn Art
History* Donald Strong; *Chmn Art 3-D Media* Joe Arimitsu. Instrs: 48
Estab 1956; pub; D & E; SC 13, GC 5; enrl D & E 2231, grad 101
Ent Req: HS dipl, GRE, SAT
Degrees: BA 4-5 yrs, MA
Tuition: Nonres—$189 per unit
Courses: Art Education, †Calligraphy, Ceramics, Design, Drawing, †Graphic Design,
History of Art & Archaeology, Industrial Design, Interior Design, Jewelry,
Lettering, Painting, Photography, Printmaking, Sculpture, Textile Design, Video,
Airbrush, Animation, Typography, Packaging Graphics, Reproduction Graphics,
Computer Graphics
Summer School: Dir, Art Weiss. Tuition $92 per unit for 6 wks beginning June 1.
Courses—Beginning Design, Drawing, Graphic Design, Illustration, Painting
—Art History Dept, 18111 Nordhoff St, 91330. Tel 818-885-2192. *Chmn* Donald S
Strong
Estab 1958, dept estab 1971; pub; D & E; scholarships & fels; SC 1, LC 30, grad 10;
enrl grad 50, undergrad 75
Ent Req: HS dipl, SAT, subject to GPA
Degrees: BA(Art) 4 yrs, MA(Art History) 5 yrs
Tuition: $936 annually
Courses: Art History, Survey of Non-Western Arts, Western Arts
Adult Hobby Classes: Courses available through Continuing Educ Extension Prog

NORWALK

CERRITOS COMMUNITY CENTER, Art Dept, 11110 Alondra Blvd, 90650. Tel
310-860-2451. *Instructional Dean Fine Arts & Communication* Michael Coppenger
Estab 1956; pub; D & E; scholarships; SC 36, LC 6
Ent Req: HS dipl or 18 yrs of age
Degrees: AA 2 yrs
Tuition: Res—$5 unit; nonres—$72 per unit
Courses: Calligraphy, Ceramics, Commercial Art, Display, Drawing, Graphic Arts,
Graphic Design, History of Art & Archaeology, Jewelry, Museum Staff Training,
Printmaking, Sculpture, 2-D & 3-D Design
Summer School: Drawing, Painting, History, Design, Ceramics, Calligraphy

OAKLAND

CALIFORNIA COLLEGE OF ARTS AND CRAFTS, 5212 Broadway, 94618. Tel
510-653-8118. *Pres* Neil J Hoffman, MS; *Interior Architecture Design* Keith Wilson;
Woodwork & Furniture Design Janice Sandeen; *Textiles* Lia Cook; *Photography*
Larry Sultan; *Ceramics* Viola Frey; *Printmaking* Charles Gill; *General Studies*
Sandra Roos; *Film-Video* Donald Day; *Sculpture* Linda Fleming; *Graduate Studies*
Stephen Goldstine; *Glass* Mark McDonnell; *Drawing* Larry McClary; *Art History*
Marc LeSueur; *Graphic Design* Steve Reoutt; *Jewelry & Metal Arts* Marilyn
DaSilva; *Painting* Mary Snowden; *Ethnic Art Studies* James Garrett
Estab 1907; pvt; D & E; scholarships; SC 24, LC 58, GC 5; enrl D 1100, non-maj
70, maj 955, grad 75
Ent Req: HS dipl, Portfolio, SAT or ACT recommended, C grade-point average, 2
letters of recommendation
Degrees: BARCH 5 yrs, BFA 4 yrs, MFA 3 yrs
Tuition: $5990 per sem: campus res available
Courses: Aesthetics, Architecture, Art History, †Ceramics, Drawing, †Film, Graphic
Arts, Graphic Design, Handicrafts, Illustration, †Interior Design, †Jewelry, Mixed
Media, †Painting, †Photography, †Printmaking, †Sculpture, Textile Design, †Video,
†Ethnic Studies, †Fine Arts, †General Crafts, †Glass, †Interior Architectural Design,
†Metal Arts, †Textiles, †Woodwork & Furniture Design
Summer School: Enrl 150 per session; tuition $500 per unit for term of 6 wks
beginning mid-June. Courses—Limited

HOLY NAMES COLLEGE, Art Dept, 3500 Mountain Blvd, 94619. Tel 510-436-
0111, Ext 1458. *Chmn Dept* Rick Patrick. Instrs: FT 2, PT 4
Estab 1917; pvt; D & E; school; SC 24, LC 4
Ent Req: HS dipl
Degrees: BA and BFA 4 yrs
Tuition: $255 per unit; $3650 per sem
Courses: Art History, Calligraphy, Ceramics, Drawing, Jewelry, Painting,
Photography, Printmaking, Sculpture, Weaving, Stained Glass,

LANEY COLLEGE, Art Dept, 900 Fallon St, 94607. Tel 510-464-3221; FAX 510-
464-3240. *Chmn* David Bradford; *Asst Dean* Fran White. Instrs: FT 8, PT 9
Estab 1962; pub; D & E; SC 52, LC 8; enrl D 1400, E 450
Ent Req: HS dipl
Degrees: AA 2 yrs
Tuition: Res—undergrad $10 per unit, grad $50 per unit
Courses: †Ceramics, †Commercial Art, Design, Drawing, †Graphic Arts, Graphic
Design, Handicrafts, History of Art & Archaeology, Lettering, †Painting, †Sculpture,
Illustration, Cartooning, Color & Design, Etching, Lithography, Portraiture, Relief
Printing, Silkscreen, Advertising Design and Architectural Design Courses available
through the Architectural Design Dept; Photography Courses available through the
Photography Dept
Summer School: Chmn, David Bradford. Enrl 250; tuition $10 per unit for 6 wk
term

MERRITT COLLEGE, Art Dept, 12500 Campus Dr, 94619. Tel 510-436-2511. *Dir*
Helmut Schmitt
Degrees: AA
Courses: Art History, Ceramics, Design, Illustration, Painting, Sculpture, Life
Drawing
Adult Hobby Classes: Dir, Helmut Schmitt
Summer School: Dir, Helmut Schmitt. Enrol 120; tuition $5 per unit; six week
courses. Courses—Life Drawing, Painting

MILLS COLLEGE, Art Dept, 5000 MacArthur Blvd, PO Box 9975, 94613. Tel
510-430-2117; FAX 510-430-3314. *Prof Studio Art & Chmn* Catherine F Wagner,
MA; *Prof Hist* Joanne Bernstein, PhD; *Prof Art Hist* Moira Roth, BA; *Prof* Ron
Nagle, BA; *Prof Hist* Mary-Ann Lutzker, PhD; *Asst Prof* Hung Liu, MFA; *Asst
Prof* Anna Valentina Murch, MFA
Estab 1852; pvt; D; scholarships; SC 23, LC 22, GC 20; enrl grad 16-20
Ent Req: HS dipl, SAT, Advanced Placement Exam
Degrees: BA 4 yrs, MFA 2 yrs
Tuition: $14,100 per yr; campus res—room & board $6700
Courses: Aesthetics, Art History, Ceramics, Drawing, Mixed Media, Painting,
Photography, Sculpture, 3-D Design

OCEANSIDE

MIRACOSTA COLLEGE, Art Dept, 1 Barnard Dr, 92056. Tel 619-757-2121. *Dir*
Kristina Nugent, MA; *Instr* Michael Portera; *Instr* Erik Growborg, MA; *Instr*
Howard Ganz, MA; *Instr* Susan Delaney
Estab 1934; pub; D & E; scholarships; SC 12, LC 4; enrl maj 200
Ent Req: HS dipl
Degrees: AA and AS normally 2 yrs
Tuition: Res—no fee; nonres—$1272 per yr; no campus res
Courses: Art History, Ceramics, Design, Drawing, Painting, Photography,
Printmaking, Sculpture, Computer Art, Woodworking and Furniture Design
Summer School: Enrl 250; 6 wk session. Courses—Ceramics, Painting, Photography,
Drawing

ORANGE

CHAPMAN UNIVERSITY, Art Dept, 333 N Glassell, 92666. Tel 714-997-6729.
Chmn Wendy Salmond, PhD; *Prof* Jane Sinclair, MFA; *Prof* Richard Turner, MFA
Estab 1918, branch estab 1954; den; D & E; scholarships; SC 20, LC 15; enrl D 245,
non-maj 200, maj 50
Ent Req: HS dipl, ACT, SAT or CLEP
Tuition: $460 per unit; campus res—room & board $5346 per yr
Courses: Advertising Design, Art History, Ceramics, Drawing, Film, Graphic Arts,
Illustration, Interior Design, Painting, Photography, Printmaking, Sculpture, Teacher
Training, Computer Graphics
Children's Classes: Courses—workshops in connection with art education classes
Summer School: Courses—Introductory Art, Ceramics

OROVILLE

BUTTE COLLEGE
—Dept of Fine Arts, 3536 Butte Campus Dr, 95965. Tel 916-895-2404. *Dean
Instruction* Frederick E Allen, MFA; *Chmn* David Cooper; *Ceramic Coordr* Idie
Adams; *Prof* John R Wilson, MA; *Vis Prof* Ruben Heredia; *Prof* Will Stule; *Prof*
Geoff Fricker
Estab 1968; pub; D & E; scholarships; SC 21, LC 4; enrl D 3988, E 4194
Ent Req: HS dipl or 18 yrs or older
Degrees: AA 2 yrs
Tuition: Nonres—$102 per unit; no campus res
Courses: Graphic Design, Ceramics, Painting, Photography, Printmaking, Sculpture,
Gallery Production
—Dept of Performing Arts, 3536 Butte Campus Dr, 95965. Tel 916-895-2581.
Assoc Dean Roger Ekins
Degrees: AA 2 yrs
Tuition: Res—undergrad $102 per unit
Courses: Music, Music Theory

PALM DESERT

COLLEGE OF THE DESERT, Art Dept, 43-500 Monterey Ave, 92260. Tel 619-
773-2574. *Chmn* John Norman. Instrs: FT 4, PT 10
Estab 1962; pub; D & E; schol; SC 10, LC 3; enrl D 150, E 150, maj 15
Ent Req: HS dipl, ent exam
Degrees: AA 2 yrs
Tuition: $50 gen fee; no campus res
Courses: Art History, Ceramics, Design, Drawing, Painting, Photography,
Printmaking, Sculpture, Advertising Art, Introduction to Art, Oriental Brush
Painting
Summer School: Six wk session. Courses—Art History, Ceramics, Painting,
Sculpture

PASADENA

ART CENTER COLLEGE OF DESIGN, 1700 Lida St, PO Box 7197, 91109. Tel
818-584-5000; FAX 818-405-9104. *Pres* David R Brown, MA; *Communication
Design Chmn* James Miho, BFA; *Fine Arts Dept Chmn* Laurence Drieband, MFA;
Film Dept Chmn Robert Peterson, BFA; *Photography Dept Chmn* Tim Bradley,
BFA; *Transportation Design Chmn* Ron Hill, BS; *Liberal Arts, Sciences & Graduate
Studies Chmn* Richard Hertz, PhD; *Computer Graphics Chmn* Robert Hennigar,
MFA; *Illustration Chmn* Philip Hayes, BFA; *Product Design Chmn* C Martin Smith,
BFA; *Environmental Design Chmn* Patricia Oliver, MArch
Estab 1930; pvt; D & E; scholarships; SC 168, LC 82, GC 22; enrl D 1200, E 200,
non-maj 200, maj 1200, grad 60
Ent Req: HS dipl, ACT, SAT if no col background, portfolio required, at least 12
samples of work in proposed maj
Degrees: BFA, BS, MFA, MS
Courses: †Advertising Design, Aesthetics, Architecture, Art History, Calligraphy,
Collages, Commercial Art, Conceptual Art, Design, Drafting, Drawing, Fashion
Arts, †Film, Graphic Arts, †Graphic Design, History of Art & Archaeology,
†Illustration, †Industrial Design, Intermedia, Interior Design, Lettering, Mixed
Media, †Painting, †Photography, Printmaking, Video, †Advertising Illustration,

†Environmental Design, †Fashion Illustration, †Graphic Packaging, †Product Design, †Transportation Design
Adult Hobby Classes: Enrl 550, tuition $255 per cr for 14 wk term.
Courses—Advertising, Computer Graphics, Film, Fine Arts, Graphics, Illustration, Industrial Design, Liberal Arts & Sciences, Photography
Children's Classes: Enrl 230; tuition $125 per class for 10 wks; Sat classes for high school

PASADENA CITY COLLEGE, Art Dept, 1570 E Colorado Blvd, 91106. Tel 818-578-7238. *Chmn Dept* Linda Malm; *Acting Area Head Design* Bob Rahm, MA; *Acting Area Head Art* Suzanne Bravender, MA; *Acting Area Head Photography* Michael Mims, MA; *Acting Area Head History* Sandra Haynes, MA; *Acting Area Head Apparel Arts* Karlene Cunningham, MA; *Acting Area Head Jewelry* Kay Yee, MA; *Acting Area Head Ceramics* Phil Cornelius, MA
Estab 1902, dept estab 1916; pub; D & E; scholarships; SC 50; enrl D 2000, E 1200, non-maj 3200, maj 400
Ent Req: HS dipl
Degrees: AA 2 yrs
Tuition: $5 per unit
Courses: Advertising Design, Art History, Ceramics, Commercial Art, Costume Design & Construction, Drawing, Fashion Arts, Graphic Arts, Graphic Design, Illustration, Interior Design, Jewelry, Lettering, Painting, Photography, Printmaking, Sculpture, Video, Electronic Filmmaking, Film Art, Product Design
Adult Hobby Classes: Enrl 3000; tuition $10 per unit, BA $50 per unit
Summer School: Dir, Linda Malm. Enrl 500; two 6 wk sessions. Courses—Art, Ceramics, Design, Photography

POMONA

CALIFORNIA STATE POLYTECHNIC UNIVERSITY, POMONA, Art Dept, College of Environmental Design, 3801 W Temple Blvd, 91768. Tel 909-869-3508. *Chair* Charles Fredrick; *Prof* Walter Glaser, MFA; *Prof* Stanley Wilson, MFA; *Prof* Yoram Makow, MA; *Prof* Dr Maren Henderson, MA; *Prof* Joe Hannibal, MFA; *Prof* Eileen Fears, MFA; *Asst Prof* Babette Mayor; *Prof* Diane Divelbess; *Asst Prof* Sandra Rowe, MFA
Estab 1966; pub; D & E; SC 66, LC 15; enrl D approx 300, E approx 50, non-maj 470, maj 300
Ent Req: HS dipl, plus testing
Degrees: BA 4 yrs
Tuition: $297 per qtr 6 or more units, $187 per qtr 5 units or less; campus res $4245 per yr
Courses: †Advertising Design, †Art Education, †Art History, †Ceramics, †Drafting, †Drawing, †Graphic Arts, †History of Art & Archaeology, †Illustration, †Lettering, Museum Staff Training, †Painting, †Teacher Training, Textile Design, †Studio Crafts
Adult Hobby Classes: Courses offered through Office of Continuing Education
Summer School: Tuition same as above for regular 10 wk quarter. Courses—usually lower division

PORTERVILLE

PORTERVILLE COLLEGE, Dept of Fine Arts, 100 E College, 93257. Tel 209-781-3130, Ext 257, 323. *Chmn* Tom Howell. Instrs: FT 2, PT 6
Estab 1927; pub; D & E; SC 18, LC 3; enrl D 300, E 78, non-maj 320, maj 58
Ent Req: HS dipl or over 18 yrs of age
Degrees: AA and AS 2 yrs
Tuition: Nonres—$1080 per sem
Courses: Art History, Ceramics, Drawing, Design, Handicrafts, Jewelry, Painting, Photography, Sculpture, Textile Design, Theatre Arts, Airbrush, color, weaving
Adult Hobby Classes: Courses—Jewelry, Weaving
Summer School: Dir, Nero Pruitt. Enrl 700 Term of 6 wks beginning June 13. Courses—Ceramics, Jewelry, Weaving

QUINCY

FEATHER RIVER COMMUNITY COLLEGE, Art Dept, PO Box 1110, 95971. Tel 916-283-0202. *Chmn* Ray Evans
Scholarships
Courses: Art Appreciation, Art History, Ceramics, Design, Drawing, Painting, Sculpture, Textile Design, Weaving

RANCHO CUCAMONGA

CHAFFEY COMMUNITY COLLEGE, Art Dept, 5885 Haven Ave, 91737. Tel 909-987-1737. *Dept Chmn* Jan Raithel
E; scholarships offered
Degrees: AA
Tuition: Nonres—$55 per unit
Courses: †Art History, †Ceramics, Design, †Drawing, †Illustration, Industrial Design, Interior Design, Painting, Photography, Sculpture, Stage Design, Weaving
Summer School: Dir, Andon Alger. Enrl 200; tuition out-of-state non res $55 per unit for 12 wk courses - Photography, Illustrator, Painting, Drawing, Design, Ceramics, Art History

REDDING

SHASTA COLLEGE, Art Dept, Fine Arts Division, PO Box 496006, 96049. Tel 916-225-4761. *Art Dept Chmn* Richard Wilson; *Dir Division Fine Arts* Kathleen Kistler
Estab 1950; pub; D & E
Ent Req: HS dipl
Degrees: AA 2 yr
Tuition: Res—$68 per sem; nonres—$73 per cr hr
Courses: Art History, Ceramics, Commercial Art, Drawing, Jewelry, Painting, Printmaking, Sculpture, Watercolor
Summer School: Dir, Dean Summer Prog. Enrl 150; tuition same as regular sem

REDLANDS

UNIVERSITY OF REDLANDS, Dept of Art, 1200 E Colton Ave, 92373. Tel 909-793-2121. *Chmn* John Brownfield
Estab 1909; pvt; D & E; scholarships and fels; SC 18, LC 12; enrl 1500
Ent Req: HS grad, ent exam
Degrees: BA and BS 4 yr, MA, ME, MAT
Tuition: $10,910 per yr; campus res available
Courses: Art History, Ceramics, Drawing, Graphic Arts, Painting, Teacher Training, Ethnic Art

RIVERSIDE

CALIFORNIA BAPTIST COLLEGE, Art Dept, 8432 Magnolia Ave, 92504. Tel 909-689-5771, Ext 270. *Chmn* Mack Branden
Scholarships
Degrees: BA
Tuition: $1515 per sem
Courses: Art Appreciation, Art History, Ceramics, Design, Drawing, Painting, Printmaking, Sculpture

LA SIERRA UNIVERSITY (Formerly Loma Linda University, La Sierra Campus), Art Dept, 4700 Pierce, 92515. Tel 909-785-2170. *Chmn & Prof* Luis Ramirez; *Prof* Susan Patt; *Prof* Roger Churches; *Instr* Jan Inman; *Instr* Richard McMillan
Estab 1905; den; D & E; SC 29, LC 8, GC 1; enrl D 2354
Ent Req: HS dipl, SAT
Degrees: BA, BS 4 yrs
Tuition: Res—$3580 per quarter; nonres—$3580 per quarter; campus res—room & board $1195
Courses: Art History, Calligraphy, †Ceramics, Drawing, †Graphic Design, Illustration, Lettering, Occupational Therapy, †Painting, †Photography, †Printmaking, †Sculpture, Computer Graphics
Adult Hobby Classes: Enrl 35 per wk; tuition $330 per wk for 4 wk term. Courses—Watercolor Workshop
Summer School: Chmn, Roger Churches. 6 wk, 2-4 units. Courses—Art in the Elementary & Secondary School

RIVERSIDE COMMUNITY COLLEGE, Dept of Art & Mass Media, 4800 Magnolia Ave, 92506. Tel 909-684-3010, 684-3240; FAX 909-275-0651. *Div Dean* Gary Schultz
Estab 1917; pub; D & E; SC 20, LC 3; enrl D 910, E 175
Ent Req: HS dipl or over 18 yrs of age
Degrees: AA 2 yrs
Tuition: Res—undergrad $10 per unit, nonres— $104 per unit
Courses: Advertising Design, Art Appreciation, Art History, Ceramics, Design, Drawing, Painting, Printmaking, Sculpture, Teacher Training, 3-D Design
Summer School: Term of 6 wks beginning June 21. Courses—Art for Elementary Teachers, Art History, Ceramics, Drawing, Painting, Sculpture

UNIVERSITY OF CALIFORNIA, RIVERSIDE
—Dept of the History of Art, 900 University Ave, 92521. Tel 909-787-1012. *Chmn* Conrad Rudolph; *Prof* Dericksen M Brinkerhoff, PhD; *Prof* Francoise Forster-Hahn, PhD; *Assoc Prof* Thomas O Pelzel, PhD
Estab 1954; pub; D; LC 18, GC 5; enrl maj 13, grad 13
Ent Req: HS dipl, res grad-point average 3.1, nonres grade-point average 3.4
Degrees: BA 4 yrs, MA 2 yrs
Courses: Art History, History of Photography
—Dept of Art, 92521. Tel 909-787-4634. *Chmn* John Divola; *Prof* James S Strombotne, MFA; *Assoc Prof* Erika Sudeburg; *Asst Prof* Uta Barth; *Lectr* Gordon L Thorpe, MA
Estab 1954; pub; D; SC 14, LC 2; enrl maj 48
Ent Req: HS dipl
Degrees: BA 4 yrs
Tuition: Nonres—$1120 per qtr
Courses: Drawing, Painting, Photography, Printmaking, Video

ROCKLIN

SIERRA COLLEGE, Art Dept, Humanities Division, 5000 Rocklin Rd, 95677. Tel 916-624-3333. *Dean Humanities* Dr Robert Meyer; *Instr* Jim Adamson, MA; *Instr* Pam Johnson; *Instr* Dottie Brown; *Instr* Sheldon Hocking
Estab 1914; pub; D & E; SC 18, LC 4; enrl D & E approx 9000
Ent Req: English Placement Test
Degrees: AA
Tuition: Res—undergrad $10 per unit, with BA $50 per unit; nonres—$104 per unit
Courses: Art Education, Art History, Ceramics, Drawing, Painting, Photography, Printmaking, Sculpture
Summer School: Courses—Ceramics, Painting

ROHNERT PARK

SONOMA STATE UNIVERSITY, Art Dept, 1801 E Cotati Ave, 94928. Tel 707-664-2151, 664-2364; FAX 707-664-2505. *Art Chmn* Shane Weare
Estab 1961, dept estab 1961; pub; D & E; SC 38, LC 17; enrl D 6000
Ent Req: HS dipl, SAT, eligibility req must be met
Degrees: BA & BFA
Tuition: Res—$581 regular fee; nonres—$581 regular fee plus $246 per unit; regular campus res available
Courses: Art Education, Art History, Ceramics, Drawing, Painting, Photography, Printmaking, Sculpture, Teacher Training, Papermaking
Adult Hobby Classes: Various classes offered through Extended Education
Summer School: Various classes offered through Extended Education

SACRAMENTO

AMERICAN RIVER COLLEGE, Dept of Art, 4700 College Oak Dr, 95841. Tel 916-484-8011. *Chmn* Joe Patitucci; *Instr* Ken Magri; *Instr* Betty Nelsen, MA; *Instr* Gary L Pruner, MA; *Instr* Pam Maddock; *Instr* Tom J Brozovich, MA
Estab 1954; pub; D & E; scholarships; SC 50, LC 12; enrl D 10,000, E 10,000, non-maj 5000, maj 5000
Ent Req: HS dipl
Degrees: AA 2 yrs or more
Tuition: Nonres—$600 per sem or $40 per unit
Courses: Advertising Design, Art Education, Art History, Calligraphy, Ceramics, Commercial Art, Conceptual Art, Drawing, Fashion Arts, Film, Graphic Arts, Graphic Design, Handicrafts, History of Art & Archaeology, Interior Design, Jewelry, Lettering, Mixed Media, Painting, Photography, Printmaking, Sculpture, Silversmithing, Teacher Training, Textile Design, Computer Graphics
Summer School: Dir, Jeff Tucker. Enrl 80; tuition none. Courses—Art History, Drawing & Photography, held June-Aug

CALIFORNIA STATE UNIVERSITY, SACRAMENTO, Dept of Art, 6000 J St, 95819-6061. Tel 916-278-6166; FAX 916-278-6664. *Chmn* Lita Whitesel. Instrs: FT 23
Estab 1950; pub; D; schol; SC 40, LC 18, GC 12; enrl major 606
Ent Req: HS dipl, ent exam
Degrees: BA 4 yr, MA
Tuition: Res—$269 (0-6 units), $428 (7 plus units); nonres—$458 per unit
Courses: Art Education, Art History, Ceramics, Drawing, Jewelry, Painting, Printmaking, Sculpture, Arts with Metals, Computer Graphics
Summer School: Enrl 225; 1 wk pre-session, 6 wks

SACRAMENTO CITY COLLEGE, Art Dept, 3835 Freeport Blvd, 95822. Tel 916-558-2551. *Dir Humanities & Fine Arts* Larry Hendricks; *Instructor* Al Byrd, MFA; *Instr* Laureen Landau, MFA; *Instr* F Dalkey; *Instr* Darrell Forney; *Instr* George A Esquibel, MA; *Instr* B Palisin; *Instr* I Shaskan
Estab 1927, dept estab 1929; pub; D & E; SC 17, LC 9; enrl D 880, E 389
Ent Req: HS dipl
Degrees: AA 2 yr
Tuition: None; no campus res
Courses: Art Education, Art History, Ceramics, Commercial Art, Drafting, Drawing, Film, Jewelry, Painting, Photography, Printmaking, Sculpture, Stage Design, Video
Summer School: Dir, George A Esquibel. Courses—Art History, Design, Drawing, Oil-Acrylic, Watercolor

SALINAS

HARTNELL COLLEGE, Art and Photography Dept, 156 Homestead Ave, 93901. Tel 408-755-6905; FAX 408-755-6751. *Chmn Fine Arts* Dr Daniel A Ipson. Instrs: FT 3, PT 10
Estab 1922; pub; D & E; SC 14, LC 3; enrl D 350 E 160, major 30
Ent Req: HS dipl
Degrees: AA 2 yr
Tuition: None; no campus res
Courses: Ceramics, Drafting, Drawing, Graphic Arts, History of Art & Archaeology, Painting, Photography, Sculpture, Stage Design, Theatre Arts, Video, Weaving, Foundry, Gallery Management, Metalsmithing
Summer School: Enrl 150; tuition free; begins approx June 15. Courses—Art Appreciation, Ceramics, Drawing, Film Making, Photography

SAN BERNARDINO

CALIFORNIA STATE UNIVERSITY, SAN BERNARDINO, Art Dept, 5500 University Parkway, 92407. Tel 909-880-5802. *Chmn Dept* Richard M Johnston; *Instr* Leo Doyle, MFA; *Instr* Roger Lintault, MFA; *Instr* Joe Moran, MFA; *Instr* Don Woodford, MFA; *Instr* Matthew Gaynor, MFA; *Instr* Julius Kaplan, PhD; *Instr* George McGinnis; *Instr* Sant Khalsa, MFA; *Instr* Shwu Ting Lee, MFA; *Instr* Mary Goodwin, PhD; *Instr* Bill Warehall, MFA; *Instr* Peter Holliday, PhD
Estab 1965; pub; D & E; schol; enrl D 10,000, maj 150
Ent Req: HS dipl, SAT
Degrees: BA 4 yrs
Tuition: Res—undergrad $299 per 15 units; nonres—undergrad $126 per unit; campus res—room & board $3195 per yr
Courses: †Advertising Design, Art Education, †Art History, †Ceramics, Drawing, †Painting, †Photography, †Printmaking, †Sculpture, †Furniture Design, †Glassblowing

SAN BERNARDINO VALLEY COLLEGE, Art Dept, 701 S Mount Vernon Ave, 92410. Tel 909-888-6511. *Head Dept* David Lawrence. Instrs: FT 5, PT 7
Estab 1926; pub; D & E; schol; enrl D 750, E 400, maj 230
Ent Req: HS dipl or 18 yrs of age
Degrees: AA and AS 2 yrs
Tuition: Res—undergrad $91 per unit; nonres—$93 per unit
Courses: Architecture, Art History, Ceramics, Commercial Art, Drafting, Drawing, Film, Lettering, Painting, Photography, Sculpture, Theatre Arts, Advertising Art, Basic Design, Computer Graphics, Designs in Glass, Glass Blowing, Life Drawing

SAN DIEGO

LELA HARTY SCHOOL OF ART, 903 K St, 92101. Tel 619-234-7356. *Dir* Lela Harty
Courses: Art Education, Drawing, Painting
Adult Hobby Classes: Tuition $100 per 8 lesson series. Courses—Acrylic, Life Drawing, Oil Painting, Pastel

SAN DIEGO MESA COLLEGE, Fine Arts Dept, 7250 Mesa College Dr, 92111. Tel 619-627-2829. *Chmn* John Conrad, PhD; *Instr* Barbara Blackmun, PhD; *Instr* Ross Stockwell, MA; *Instr* Anita Brynolf, MA; *Instr* Hiroshi Miyazaki, MA; *Instr* Georgia Laris, MA; *Instr* Kathleen Stoughton, MA; *Inst* Charles Lee, MA; *Instr* Beate Bermann, PhD
Estab 1964; pub; D & E; scholarships; SC 29, LC 7; enrl D 10,000, E 29,000, maj 300
Ent Req: HS dipl or age 18
Degrees: AA 2 yrs
Tuition: Res—$10 per unit; nonres—$75 per unit; no campus res
Courses: Art History, Ceramics, Drawing, Handicrafts, Jewelry, Art Education, Painting, Photography, Sculpture, Crafts, Graphic Communications, Gallery Studies
Summer School: Dir, John Conrad. Enrl 200; tuition & courses same as regular sem

SAN DIEGO STATE UNIVERSITY, Dept of Art, 92182-0214. Tel 619-594-6511. *Chmn* Fredrick Orth, MFA; *Studio Grad Coordr* Gail Roberts, MFA; *Art History Grad Coordr* Eda K Rigby, PhD
Estab 1897; pub; D & E; schol; SC 140, LC 35, GC 30; enrl maj 1044
Ent Req: HS dipl
Degrees: BA 4 yrs, MA, MFA
Tuition: Campus res—room & board
Courses: Advertising Design, Aesthetics, Architecture, Art Education, Art History, Ceramics, Commercial Art, Conceptual Art, †Drawing, Fashion Arts, Goldsmithing, †Graphic Design, Handicrafts, History of Art & Archaeology, Intermedia, †Interior Design, †Jewelry, Mixed Media, †Painting, †Printmaking, †Sculpture, †Silversmithing, †Teacher Training, †Textile Design, †Environmental Design, †Furniture Design †Gallery Design, †Weaving

UNITED STATES INTERNATIONAL UNIVERSITY, School of Performing and Visual Arts, 10455 Pomerado Rd, 92131. Tel 619-271-4300. *Dean* Dr Jeanett Lauer
Estab 1966; pvt; D; scholarships; SC 27, LC 4; enrl D 300
Ent Req: HS dipl, interview, portfolio, letters of recommendation
Degrees: BA(Comprehensive Design), BA(Art Teaching), BFA(Advertising Design), BFA(Design for Stage), BFA(TV & TV Production) 4 yrs, MFA(Advertising Design), MFA(Design for Stage & TV) 2 yrs
Tuition: $2925 per 15 units, $119 per unit; campus res available
Courses: Advertising Design, Art Education, Ceramics, Commercial Art, Costume Design & Construction, Drafting, Drawing, Graphic Arts, Graphic Design, History of Art & Archaeology, Illustration, Interior Design, Painting, Photography, Printmaking, Stage Design, Teacher Training, Theatre Arts, †Fine Arts, Lighting Design, †Scenic & Lighting, †Technical Direction, †Television Production
Children's Classes: Conservatory of the Arts for children
Summer School: Two 5 wk terms

UNIVERSITY OF SAN DIEGO, Art Dept, 5998 Alcala Park, 92110. Tel 619-260-4600; FAX 619-260-4619, Ext 4486. *Chmn* Sally Yard. Instrs: FT 4
Estab 1952; pvt; D & E; scholarships; SC 19, LC 7; enrl univ 5300, maj 50
Ent Req: HS dipl, SAT
Degrees: BA 4 yrs
Tuition: $3630 per sem; campus res—room and board $1625-$2550 per sem
Courses: †Art History, †Ceramics, †Drawing, †Painting, †Photography, †Printmaking, †Sculpture, †Art in Elementary Education, †Art Management, †Design, †Enameling, †Exhibition Design, †Museum Internship, †Weaving
Summer School: Tui $230 per unit for terms of 3 wk, 6 wk beginning June 1; 2 courses offered

SAN FRANCISCO

ACADEMY OF ART COLLEGE, Fine Arts Dept, 540 Powell, 94108. Tel 415-765-4200, Ext 269. *Pres* Elisa Stephens; *Dir Advertising* Jacques Bailhe; *Dir Illustration* Barbara Bradley, BFA; *Co Chair Fine Art* Craig Nelson; *Co Chair Fine Art* William Maughan; *Dir Photography* Lynn Ingersoll; *Co Chair Interior Design* Shirley Goldberg; *Co Chair Interior Design* David Davis. Instrs: FT 2, PT 8
Estab 1929; pvt; D & E; scholarships; SC 200, LC 100; enrl D 2000, E 150, grad 20
Ent Req: HS dipl
Degrees: BFA 4 yrs, MFA 2 yrs
Tuition: Res—undergrad $6000 per yr, $250 per unit, grad $6600 per yr, $275 per unit; campus res available
Courses: Advertising Design, Art Education, Art History, Calligraphy, Ceramics, Collages, Commercial Art, Conceptual Art, Display, †Drawing, †Fashion Arts, Film, Goldsmithing, †Graphic Arts, †Graphic Design, Handicrafts, †Illustration, †Interior Design, Jewelry, Lettering, †Painting, †Photography, †Printmaking, †Sculpture, Theatre Arts
Adult Hobby Classes: Enrl 75; tuition $175 per unit. Courses—Basic Painting, Ceramics, Portrait Painting, Pottery
Summer School: Tuition $1050 for term of 6 wks beginning June 23. Courses—Commercial & Fine Art

CITY COLLEGE OF SAN FRANCISCO, Art Dept, 50 Phelan Ave, 94112. Tel 415-239-3157. *Chairperson* Mike Ruiz
Estab 1935; pub; D & E; SC 45, LC 10; enrl col D 15,000, E 11,000
Degrees: AA 2 yrs
Tuition: None
Courses: Art History, Ceramics, Drawing, Graphic Design, Illustration, Industrial Design, Jewelry, Lettering, Painting, Sculpture, Basic Design, Metal Arts, Visual Communication
Summer School: Courses—same as regular yr

SAN FRANCISCO ART INSTITUTE, Admissions Office, 800 Chestnut St, 94133. Tel 415-771-7020. *Dir Admissions* Tim Robison; *Chmn Painting Dept* Pat Klein; *Chmn Printmaking Dept* Larry Thomas; *Chmn Photography Dept* Henry Wessell; *Chmn Sculpture Dept* Richard Berger; *Chmn Performance & Video Dept* Ton Labat
Estab 1871; pvt; D & E; schol; SC 80, LC 22, GC 11; enrl non-maj 44, maj 4538 grad 143
Ent Req: HS dipl or GED
Degrees: BFA 4 yrs, MFA 2 yrs

Tuition: $12,400 per yr, $6200 per sem; no campus res
Courses: †Ceramics, Film, Painting, Photography, Printmaking, Sculpture, †Performance/Video
Adult Hobby Classes: tuition $210 for 6 wk term (per course). Courses—Ceramic Sculpture, Drawing, Film, Painting, Photography, Printmaking
Children's Classes: Young Artists program, 6-week summer session $210 per course for 6-wk term
Summer School: Tuition $560 per course for term of 10 wks

SAN FRANCISCO STATE UNIVERSITY, Art Dept, 1600 Holloway, 94132. Tel 415-338-2176. *Chmn* Sylvia Walters; *Dean* Warren Rasmussen, PhD. Instrs: FT 25, PT 10
Estab 1899; pub; D; SC 80, LC 20, GC 15; enrl D 450, maj 450, grad 80
Ent Req: HS dipl
Degrees: BA 4 yrs, MFA 3 yrs, MA 2 yrs
Tuition: Nonres—$189 per unit; campus res available
Courses: Art Education, Art History, Ceramics, Painting, Photography, Printmaking, Sculpture, Textile Design, Conceptual Design, Mixed Emphasis
Summer School: Not regular session. Self-supporting classes in Art History, Ceramics, Photography, Printmaking

SAN JACINTO

MOUNT SAN JACINTO COLLEGE, Art Dept, 1499 N State St, 92583. Tel 909-654-8011, Ext 1531. *Instr* John Seed, MA; *Instr* Carolyn Kaneshiro, MA; *Instr* Max DeMoss; *Instr* Gary Cominotto; *Instr* Sandra Robinson; *Instr* Anita Rodriguez
Estab 1964; pub; D & E; SC 8, LC 2; enrl D 250, E 420, non-maj 400, maj 50
Ent Req: HS dipl
Degrees: AA & AS
Tuition: $12 per unit
Courses: Art History, Ceramics, Painting, Sculpture, Basic Design
Children's Classes: Studio courses
Summer School: Courses—Drawing

SAN JOSE

SAN JOSE CITY COLLEGE, School of Fine Arts, 2100 Moorpark Ave, 95128. Tel 408-298-2181, Ext 3815. *Asst Dean Humanities & Social Science* William Kester; *Instr* Luis Gutierrez
Estab 1921; pub; D & E; SC 7, LC 2; enrl D 320, E 65
Ent Req: HS dipl or 18 yrs of age or older
Degrees: AA 2 yrs
Tuition: Res—$10 per unit; nonres—$57 per unit
Courses: Art History, Ceramics, Design, Drawing, Graphic Arts, Painting, Photography, Printmaking, Theatre Arts, Color, Figure Drawing

SAN JOSE STATE UNIVERSITY, School of Art & Design, 1 Washington Sq, 95192-0089. Tel 408-924-4320; FAX 408-924-4326. *Dir* Robert Milnes, PhD; *Art Educ Coordn* Adrienne Kraut, DED; *Art Educ Coordr* Pamela Sharp, PhD; *Assoc Chair, Art History* Kathleen Cohen, PhD; *Assoc Chair, Studio* Linda Walsh, MFA; *Assoc Chair, Design* Lanning Stern, MFA; *Graduate Program Coordr* Paul Staiger, MFA
Estab 1857, dept estab 1911; pub; D & E; scholarships; SC 90, LC 28, GC 25; enrl D 4529, maj 1400, grad 94
Ent Req: ACT and grade point average, SAT
Degrees: BA(Art), BA(Art History) 4 yrs, BS(Graphic Design), BS(Industrial Design), BS(Interior Design) & BFA(Art) 4 1/2 yrs, MA(Art), MA(Art History), MA(Design), MA(Multimedia) & MA(Computers in Fine Arts) 1 yr, MFA(Pictorial Arts), MFA(Photography), MFA(Spatial Arts) & MFA(Computers in Fine Arts) 2 yrs
Tuition: Res—$502 - $778 per sem; non-res—$502 - $778 per sem plus $246 per unit
Courses: †Art Education, †Art History, Ceramics, Drawing, †Graphic Design, Illustration, †Industrial Design, †Interior Design, Jewelry, Photography, Printmaking, Sculpture, Teacher Training, †Crafts (Jewelry, Textiles)
Summer School: Dean Continuing Educ, Ralph C Bohn. Tuition $105 per unit for three summer sessions of 3 & 6 wks; 3 wk Jan session. Courses—vary according to professors available & projected demand

SAN LUIS OBISPO

CALIFORNIA POLYTECHNIC STATE UNIVERSITY AT SAN LUIS OBISPO, Dept of Art and Design, 93407. Tel 805-756-1148. *Prof* C W Jennings, MFA; *Prof* Robert Reynolds, MAE; *Prof* Robert Densham, MFA; *Prof* Clarissa Hewitt, MFA; *Prof* Robert D Howell, MA; *Prof* John Mendenhall, MA; *Prof* Keith Dills, PhD; *Prof* Eric Johnson, MFA; *Prof* Henry Wessels, MFA; *Prof* Joanne Ruggles, MFA; *Assoc Prof* Mary La Porte, MFA; *Assoc Prof* George Jercich, MFA; *Assoc Prof* Norman Lerner, MA. Instrs: FT 15
Estab 1901, dept estab 1969; pub; D & E; SC 40, LC 12; enrl D 1000, E 100, non-maj 1100, maj 220
Ent Req: HS dipl, portfolio review
Degrees: BS(Applied Art & Design) 4 yrs
Tuition: Res—undergrad $675 per yr; nonres—undergrad $4029 per yr; campus res—room & board $3120 per yr
Courses: Advertising Design, Art History, Ceramics, Drawing, Graphic Arts, Graphic Design, Photography, Printmaking, Sculpture, Design History, Metalsmithing
Summer School: Dir, Charles Jennings. Enrl 90; tuition $200 for term June 20-Sept 2. Courses—Fundamentals of Drawing, Basic b/w Photography, Intermediate Drawing, Ceramics

CUESTA COLLEGE, Art Dept, PO Box 8106, 93403-8106. Tel 805-546-3199. *Chmn Fine Arts Div* Barry Frantz, MA; *Instr* Chet Amyx, MA; *Instr* Robert Pelfrey, MA; *Instr* Guyla Call Amyx; *Instr* Marian Galczenski
Estab 1964; pub; D & E; scholarships; enrl in col D 3200, E 3082

Ent Req: HS dipl or Calif HS Proficiency Exam
Degrees: AA and AS
Tuition: Nonres—$85 per unit
Courses: Art History, Ceramics, Display, Drawing, Graphic Design, Painting, Printmaking, Sculpture, Video, Camera Art
Summer School: Chmn Div Fine Arts, Barry Frantz. Courses—Drawing, Art History

SAN MARCOS

PALOMAR COMMUNITY COLLEGE, Art Dept, 1140 W Mission Rd, 92069. Tel 619-744-1150, Ext 2302. *Chmn* Val Sanders, MA; *Assoc Prof* Harry E Bliss, MFA; *Assoc Prof* G D Durrant, MA; *Assoc Prof* Jay Shultz; *Assoc Prof* Frank Jones, MFA; *Assoc Prof* Anthony J Lugo, MA; *Assoc Prof* Barry C Reed, MFA; *Assoc Prof* James T Saw, MA; *Assoc Prof* Louise Kirtland Boehm, MA; *Assoc Prof* Michael Steirnagle; *Assoc Prof* Steve Miller
Estab 1950; pub; D & E; schol; SC 31, LC 4; enrl D 775, E 200
Ent Req: Ent exam
Degrees: AA 2 yr
Tuition: None; no campus res
Courses: Art History, †Ceramics, Collages, †Commercial Art, †Drawing, Graphic Arts, Graphic Design, Handicrafts, Illustration, †Jewelry, Lettering, †Painting, †Printmaking, Sculpture, †Silversmithing, Design Composition, Glassblowing, Life Drawing, Stained Glass
Summer School: Courses—basic courses except commercial art and graphic design

SAN MATEO

COLLEGE OF SAN MATEO, Creative Arts Dept, 1700 W Hillsdale Blvd, 94402. Tel 415-574-6288. *Dir Fine Arts* Leo N Bardes
Pub; D & E
Degrees: AA 2 yr
Tuition: Res $5 per unit, maximum of $50; nonres $77 per unit; no campus res
Courses: †Architecture, Art History, Ceramics, †Commercial Art, Drafting, Drawing, †Film, History of Art & Archaeology, †Interior Design, Lettering, Painting, Photography, Printmaking, Sculpture, †General Art

SAN PABLO

CONTRA COSTA COMMUNITY COLLEGE, Dept of Art, 2600 Mission Bell Dr, 94806. Tel 510-235-7800. *Dept Head* Paul Pernish
Estab 1950; pub; D & E; SC 10, LC 16; enrl D 468, E 200
Ent Req: HS dipl or 18 yrs old
Degrees: Cert of Achievement 1 yr, AA and AS 2 yrs
Tuition: Res—$5 per unit; nonres—$76 per unit; no campus res
Courses: Art History, Ceramics, Drawing, Painting, Photography, Sculpture, Silkscreen
Summer School: Assoc Dean Continuing Educ, William Vega. Enrl 50; tuition free for term of 8 wks beginning June 26. Courses—Art, Art Appreciation

SAN RAFAEL

DOMINICAN COLLEGE OF SAN RAFAEL, Art Dept, 50 Acacia Ave, 94901. Tel 415-457-4440. *Chmn* Edith Bresnahan
Scholarships
Degrees: BA, MA 4 yr
Tuition: Undergrad—$4650 per sem
Courses: Advertising Design, Art Appreciation, Art Education, Art History, Calligraphy, Ceramics, Design, Drawing, Handicrafts, Painting, Photography, Printmaking, Sculpture, Stage Design, Textile Design, Theatre Arts, Weaving, Pottery

SANTA ANA

RANCHO SANTIAGO COLLEGE, Art Dept, 17th at Bristol, 92706. Tel 714-667-3000, 564-6000, 564-5600. *Dean of Fine & Performing Arts* Thom Hill, MA; *Instr* Gene Isaacson; *Instr* Estelle Orr, MFA; *Instr* George E Geyer, MA; *Instr* Patrick Crabb, MA; *Instr* Frank Molner, MA; *Instr* Mayde Herberg; *Instr* Sharon Ford, MA; *Instr* Carol Miura; *Instr* Shifra Goldman; *Instr* Jim Nemsik
Estab 1915, dept estab 1960; pub; D & E; scholarships; SC 21, LC 5; enrl D 280, E 160, maj 57
Ent Req: HS dipl
Degrees: AA 2 yrs
Tuition: Res—$5 per unit; nonres—$72 per unit
Courses: Advertising Design, Architecture, Art History, Ceramics, Commercial Art, Display, Drawing, Graphic Arts, Graphic Design, Handicrafts, Interior Design, Jewelry, Museum Staff Training, Painting, Sculpture, Computer Graphics, Glass Blowing
Adult Hobby Classes: Ceramics, Stained Glass
Summer School: Dir, Dean Thom Hill. Enrl 3000; tuition free for term of 6-8 wks beginning early June. Courses—Art Concepts, Ceramics, Design, Drawing, Painting

SANTA BARBARA

SANTA BARBARA CITY COLLEGE, Fine Arts Dept, 721 Cliff Dr, 93109-2394. Tel 805-965-0581. *Chmn* Linda Benet
Scholarships
Degrees: AA
Tuition: Res—undergrad $100 per yr
Courses: Advertising Design, Architecture, Art Appreciation, Art History, Calligraphy, Ceramics, Design, Drawing, Fashion Arts, Film, Handicrafts, Industrial Design, Interior Design, Jewelry, Painting, Printmaking, Sculpture, Stage Design, Textile Design, Weaving, Cartooning, Glassblowing

UNIVERSITY OF CALIFORNIA, SANTA BARBARA, Dept of Art Studio, 93106. Tel 805-893-3138. *Chmn Dept* Richard Bolton
Estab 1868, dept estab 1950; pub; D; schol; SC 32, LC 17, GC 7; enrl D 431, grad 60
Ent Req: HS dipl
Degrees: BA 4 yrs, MFA 2 yrs, PhD 7 yrs
Courses: Art Education, Ceramics, Drawing, Painting, Photography, Printmaking, Sculpture

SANTA CLARA

SANTA CLARA UNIVERSITY, Art Dept, Alameda & Bellomy, 95053. Tel 408-554-4594; FAX 408-554-2700. *Chmn* Brigid Barton, PhD; *Assoc Prof* Kelly Detweiler, MFA; *Assoc Prof* Susan Felter, MFA; *Assoc Prof* Sam Hernandez, MFA; *Sr Lect* Gerald P Sullivan, SJ; *Asst Prof* Eric Apfelstadt, PhD; *Lectr* Kathleen Maxwell, PhD; *Lectr* Jan Thompson, PhD
Estab 1851, dept estab 1972; pvt; D; SC 9, LC 14; enrl D 700, non-maj 650, maj 50
Ent Req: HS dipl
Degrees: BA(Fine Arts)
Tuition: $4050 per quarter; campus—res room & board $1866 per quarter
Courses: †Art History, Ceramics, Drawing, Painting, Photography, Printmaking, Sculpture, Computer Art, Etching, Intro to Studio Art
Summer School: Dir, Dr Philip Boo Riley. Enrl 15 per class; 5 & 10 wk terms. Courses—Ceramics, Intro to Art History, Painting, Watercolor

SANTA CRUZ

UNIVERSITY OF CALIFORNIA, SANTA CRUZ, Board of Studies in Art, Performing Arts Bldg, 95064. Tel 408-459-2171. *Chmn* Douglas McClellan
Pub; D; SC per quarter 11, LC per quarter 3; enrl D approx 7000, maj 80
Ent Req: HS dipl
Degrees: BA 4 yrs
Tuition: Res—$726 per qtr; nonres—$1972 per qtr
Courses: Aesthetics, Ceramics, Drawing, Graphic Arts, History of Art & Archaeology, Painting, Photography, Sculpture, Stage Design, Theatre Arts, Book Arts, Intaglio Printmaking, Lithography, Metal Sculpture, Watercolor, Women Artists

SANTA MARIA

ALLAN HANCOCK COLLEGE, Fine Arts Dept, 800 S College Dr, 93454. Tel 805-922-6966, Ext 3252. *Head* Edward Harvey. Instrs: FT 3, PT 6
Estab 1920. College has three other locations; pub; D & E; SC 24, LC 4; enrl D 800, E 220, maj 115
Ent Req: HS dipl, over 18 and educable
Degrees: AA 2 yrs
Tuition: Nonres—$91 per unit
Courses: Art History, Ceramics, Drawing, Film, Graphic Design, Handicrafts, Lettering, Painting, Photography, Sculpture, Theatre Arts, Air Brush Watercolor, Art Appreciation, Design, Life Drawing, Silk Screen
Adult Hobby Classes: Tuition varied; classes offered upon need
Summer School: Enrl 230; term of 6 - 8 wks beginning June. Courses—Ceramics, Crafts, Drawing, Opera Workshop, Repertory Theatre, Watercolor

SANTA ROSA

SANTA ROSA JUNIOR COLLEGE, Art Dept, 1501 Mendocino Ave, 95401. Tel 707-527-4011. *Chmn* John Watrous; *Instr* Will Collier, MA
Estab 1918, dept estab 1935; pub; D & E; schol; SC 40, LC 8; enrl D approx 800, E approx 1000
Ent Req: HS dipl
Degrees: AA 2 yrs
Tuition: Res—undergrad none; nonres—undergrad $510 per sem, $73 per unit; campus res available
Courses: Art Appreciation, Art History, Ceramics, Drawing, Graphic Design, Jewelry, Lettering, Painting, Photography, Printmaking, Sculpture, Bronze Casting, Etching, Layout, Poster Design, Pottery, Principles of Color, Silkscreen, 3-D Design, Watercolor
Summer School: Chmn Dept, Maurice Lapp. Term of 6 wks beginning June 20. Courses—Art History, Ceramics, Design, Drawing, Jewelry, Painting, Printmaking, Sculpture, Watercolor

SARATOGA

WEST VALLEY COLLEGE, Art Dept, 14000 Fruitvale Ave, 95070. Tel 408-867-2200, Ext 7411. *Chmn* Kathy Westly. Instrs: FT 8, PT 5
Estab 1964; pub; D & E; SC 51, LC 12; enrl D 1260, E 801
Ent Req: HS dipl or 18 yrs of age
Degrees: 8, 2 yrs
Tuition: Res fee under $50; no campus res
Courses: Aesthetics, †Ceramics, Commercial Art, Costume Design & Construction, †Design, †Drawing, †Graphic Arts, †History of Art & Archaeology, †Jewelry, Museum Staff Training, †Painting, †Sculpture, Theatre Arts, Weaving, †Etching, †Furniture Design, †Lithography, †Metal Casting, †Occupational Work Experience, †Papermaking, Stained Glass
Adult Hobby Classes: Tuition varies. Courses—many classes offered by Community Development Dept
Summer School: Tuition $6 per unit, under $10 depending on load, for terms of 4 wks beginning June 1 & 6 wks beginning mid-June. Courses—Ceramics, Design, Drawing, Jewelry, Sculpture

SOUTH LAKE TAHOE

LAKE TAHOE COMMUNITY COLLEGE, Art Dept, PO Box 14445, 96150. Tel 916-541-4660, Ext 228. *Chmn Art Dept* David Foster, MA
Estab 1975; pub; D & E; schol; SC 22, LC 6; enrl D 375, E 150, non-maj 300, maj 75
Ent Req: HS dipl
Degrees: AA 2 yrs
Tuition: Undergrad $7 per unit, grad $33 per unit
Courses: Art History, Ceramics, Design, Drawing, Graphic Arts, Photography, Painting, Printmaking, Sculpture, Color, Design, Wartercolor Painting
Summer School: Dir David Foster. Enrl 100; tuition undergrad $7 per unit, grad $33 per unit. Courses—Drawing, Intro to Art, Raku Pottery, Watercolor

STANFORD

STANFORD UNIVERSITY, Dept of Art, Cummings Art Bldg, 94305-2018. Tel 415-723-3404. *Chmn Dept Art* Paul V Turner. Instrs: FT 19
Estab 1891; pvt; D; scholarships; SC 48, LC 63, GC 37 (seminars); enrl 3200, maj 70, grad 40
Ent Req: HS dipl
Degrees: BA 4 yrs, MA 1 yr, MFA 2 yrs, PhD 5 yrs
Tuition: $16,056 per yr; campus res—room & board $4570 per yr
Courses: Art History, Drawing, Painting, Photography, Printmaking, Sculpture
Adult Hobby Classes: Offered through Stanford Continuing Education
Children's Classes: Enrl 250. Courses—Offered through Museum
Summer School: Dir, Paul V Turner. Enrl 100; eight wk term. Courses—Art History, Drawing, Painting, Photography, Printmaking

STOCKTON

SAN JOAQUIN DELTA COLLEGE, Art Dept, 5151 Pacific Ave, 95207. Tel 209-474-5209. *Chmn* Dr Don Bennett
Estab 1935; pub; D & E; SC 12, LC 2; enrl D 7000, E 6000, Maj 100
Ent Req: HS dipl
Degrees: AA 2 yrs
Tuition: Res—undergrad $10 per unit, with BA $50 per unit; nonres—$115 per unit; no campus res
Courses: Art History, Ceramics, Drafting, Drawing, Graphic Arts, Painting, Photography, Sculpture, Stage Design, Theatre Arts
Summer School: Dir, Dr Merrilee R Lewis. Enrl 8000; five week session. Courses—Same as regular sessions

UNIVERSITY OF THE PACIFIC, College of the Pacific, Dept of Art, 3601 Pacific Ave, 95211. Tel 209-946-2241. *Chmn* J Ronald Pecchenino. Instrs: FT 8
Estab 1851; pvt; scholarships; 37 (3 unit) courses & 14 (4 unit) courses available over 4 yrs, independent study; enrl maj 85-90
Ent Req: HS grad with 20 sem grades of recommending quality earned in the 10th, 11th and 12th years in traditional subjects, twelve of these grades must be in acad subj
Degrees: BA & BFA
Tuition: $14,160 per yr, $616 per unit (9 - 11 units), $485 per unit (1/2 - 8 1/2 units); campus res—$5100
Courses: Art Education, †Art History, Ceramics, Design, †Graphic Design, †Painting, Photography, Sculpture, †Arts Administration, Commercial Design, Computer Art, †Studio Art
Summer School: Two 5 wk sessions

SUISUN CITY

SOLANO COMMUNITY COLLEGE, Division of Fine & Applied Art, 4000 Suisun Valley Rd, 94585. Tel 707-864-7000. *Div Chmn Fine & Applied Art* Carol Bishop; *Instr* Jan Eldridge; *Instr* Kate Delos; *Instr* Marc Lancet; *Instr* Marilyn Tannebaum; *Instr* Ray Salmon; *Instr* Alden Erickson; *Instr* Jake Lovejoy; *Instr* Brice Bowman; *Instr* Marc Pondone; *Instr* Debra Bloomfield; *Instr* Vern Grosowsky; *Instr* Christine Rydell; *Instr* Al Zidek; *Instr* Art Bawin; *Instr* Bruce Blondin
Estab 1945; pub; D & E; SC 16, LC 5; enrl D 255, E 174, maj 429
Ent Req: HS dipl
Degrees: AA 2 yrs
Tuition: Res—$10 per unit; nonres—$91 per unit
Courses: Art History, Ceramics, Commercial Art, Drawing, Illustration, Lettering, Painting, Photography, Printmaking, Sculpture, Fashion Illustration, Form & Composition, Fundamentals of Art, Papermaking, Raku, Silkscreen, Survey of Modern Art, †3-D Art, Watercolor
Adult Hobby Classes: Tuition varies per class. Courses—Cartooning, Jewelry Design, Stained Glass
Summer School: Dean summer session, Dr Don Kirkorian

TAFT

TAFT COLLEGE, Division of Performing Arts, 29 Emmons Park Dr, 93268. Tel 805-763-4282. *Chmn* Sonja Swenson
Estab 1922; pub; D & E; scholarships; SC 67, LC 6; enrl 1500 total
Ent Req: HS grad or 18 yrs old
Degrees: AA 2 yrs
Tuition: Nonres—$72 per unit under 7, 7 - 14 units $1080
Courses: Architecture, †Art History, Ceramics, Commercial Art, Conceptual Art, †Drafting, Drawing, Fashion Arts, Graphic Arts, Graphic Design, Handicrafts, †History of Art & Archaeology, Illustration, Interior Design, Jewelry, Painting, †Photography, Sculpture, Textile Design, †Theatre Arts, Basic Design
Adult Hobby Classes: Courses—Ceramics, Graphic Arts, Jewelry, Painting, Photography
Summer School: Dean, Don Zumbro. Term of 6-8 wks. Courses—vary

THOUSAND OAKS

CALIFORNIA LUTHERAN UNIVERSITY, Art Dept, 60 W Olson Rd, 91360.
Tel 805-493-3315. *Chmn* John Solem; *Instr* Larkin Higgins; *Lectr* John Galloway
Estab 1961; pvt; D & E; scholarships; SC 12, LC 7; enrl D 110, non-maj 46, maj 40
Ent Req: HS dipl, SAT or ACT, portfolio suggested
Degrees: BA 4 yr; MA(Educ) 1 - 2 yr
Tuition: Res—undergrad $7500 per yr, $3750 per sem, $230 per unit; campus
res—room & board $2900 per year
Courses: Advertising Design, Art Education, Art History, Ceramics, Commercial
Art, Drawing, Graphic Arts, Graphic Design, Illustration, Painting, Photography,
Printmaking, Sculpture, Stage Design, Teacher Training, Theatre Arts, Medical
Illustration
Summer School: Dir, Pam Jolicoeur. Tuition $210 per unit for term June-July, July-
Aug. Courses—Art Education, Design, Drawing, Painting, Pottery, Sculpture

TORRANCE

EL CAMINO COLLEGE, Division of Fine Arts, 16007 Crenshaw Blvd, 90506. Tel
310-715-7715; FAX 310-715-7734. *Dean Div* Dr Roger Quadhamer. Instrs: FT 35,
PT 61
Estab 1947; pub; D & E; scholarships; SC 46, LC 6; enrl D 1700, E 900, non-maj
2378, maj 222
Ent Req: HS dipl
Degrees: AA 2 yrs
Tuition: None; no campus res
Courses: †Advertising Design, Architecture, Art History, Calligraphy, Ceramics,
Costume Design & Construction, Display, Stage Design, Textile Design, †Theatre
Arts
Children's Classes: Enrl 30. Courses—Exploration of Children's Art

TUJUNGA

MCGROARTY CULTURAL ART CENTER, Cultural Affairs Dept, City of Los
Angeles, 7570 McGroarty Terrace, 91042. Tel 818-352-5285, 352-6275. *Dir* Joan de
Bruin. Instrs: PT 24
Estab 1953; pub; D & E; scholarships; SC 40, LC 1; enrl D 600, E 200
Tuition: Fees for adults $20-$50 per 10 wk session; fees for children and teens $15
per 10 wk session
Courses: Art History, Calligraphy, Ceramics, Collages, Costume Design &
Construction, Drawing, Graphic Arts, Handicrafts, Sculpture, Mixed Media,
Painting, Textile Design, Chinese Brush Painting, Drama, Lace Making &
Embroidery, Piano, Stained Glass, Tai Chi Chuan, Water Colors
Children's Classes: Arts & Crafts, Ceramics, Dance, Guitar, Maskmaking, Painting,
Piano, Vocal Techniques

TURLOCK

CALIFORNIA STATE UNIVERSITY, Art Dept, 801 W Monte Vista Ave, 95380.
Tel 209-667-3431. *Chmn Dept* Martin Camarata, MA; *Prof* Hope Werness, PhD;
Prof C Roxanne Robbin; *Prof* James Piskoti, MFA; *Prof* John Barnett; *Vis Prof*
Richard Savini, MFA
Estab 1963; pub; D & E; scholarships; SC 27, LC 6, GC 4; enrl D
400, E 50, non-maj 350, maj 85, grad 20
Ent Req: HS dipl
Degrees: BA 4 yrs; Printmaking Cert Prog, Special Masters Degree Prog
Tuition: Res—undergrad & grad $741 per yr, $57 winter terms; nonres—undergrad
& grad are same as res plus $141 per unit; limited campus residence
Courses: †Art History, †Ceramics, †Drawing, †Film, †Graphic Arts, †Painting,
†Photography, †Printmaking, †Sculpture, Teacher Training, †Gallery Management
Summer School: Enrl 50. Courses—Ceramics

VALENCIA

CALIFORNIA INSTITUTE OF THE ARTS, School of Art, 24700 McBean Pkwy,
91355. Tel 805-255-1050; FAX 805-254-8352. *Pres* Dr Steven D Lavine; *Dean*
Thomas Lawson. Instrs: FT 28
Estab 1970; pvt; scholarships; enrl D 230
Ent Req: Portfolio
Degrees: BFA 4 yrs, MFA
Tuition: $13,000 per yr; campus res available
Courses: Art History, †Conceptual Art, Design, Drawing, †Graphic Design,
†Intermedia, †Painting, †Photography, †Sculpture, †Video, Post Studio, Visual
Communication, Critical Theory

COLLEGE OF THE CANYONS, Art Dept, 26455 N Rockwell Canyon Rd, 91355.
Tel 805-259-7800, Ext 392. *Head Dept* Joanne Julian, MFA; *Instr* Robert Walker,
MFA; *Instr* Deborah Horewitz, MFA; *Instr* Philip Morrison, MFA; *Instr* Janice
Metz, BA
Estab 1970; dept estab 1974; pub; D & E; SC 11, LC 4; enrl D 300, E 300, maj 50
Ent Req: Must be 18 yrs of age
Degrees: AA and AS 2 yrs
Tuition: $50, student fee $10
Courses: Advertising Design, Art History, Drafting, Drawing, Painting, Photography,
Printmaking, Sculpture, 3-D Design
Adult Hobby Classes: Tuition $10 plus lab fees usually another $10 per sem
Children's Classes: Classes offered in continuing education under child development

VAN NUYS

LOS ANGELES VALLEY COLLEGE, Art Dept, 5800 Fulton Ave, 91401-4096.
Tel 818-781-1200, Ext 358, 431; FAX 818-785-4672. *Chmn* Henry Klein
Degrees: AA, cert
Tuition: undergrad—$12 per unit, grad—$50 per unit
Courses: Advertising Design, Art History, Ceramics, Design, Drawing, Painting,
Photography, Printmaking, Sculpture
Summer School: Drawing, Beginning Design I

VENICE

VENICE PLACE SCULPTURE GARDENS, 1031 Abbot Kinney Blvd, 90291. Tel
310-392-6695; FAX 310-476-6618. *Owner* Dr Jerry Rowitch
Estab 1976; pvt; D & E; SC 22; enrl D 50, E 50
Ent Req: Portfolio
Degrees: None
Tuition: Various
Courses: Ceramics, Sculpture, Landscape Design
Adult Hobby Classes: Courses offered
Children's Classes: Coarses—Art Appreciation
Summer School: Dir, Howard Kiefer. Individual tutoring. Courses—same as regular
offerings

VENICE BEACH

EASTERN COMMUNITY COLLEGE, Dept of Art, 101 Clubhouse, Suite 2,
90291. Tel 213-826-5696. *Head Dept* Ginger Kerns; *Instr* Donald Bumper
Estab 1955; dept 1970; pub; D & E; scholarships; SC 12, LC4; enrl D 130, E 222,
non-maj 317, maj 35
Ent Req: HS dipl, Non-res Act
Degrees: AA 2 yrs
Tuition: Res - undergrad $317 per sem
Courses: Advertising Design, Art Education, Leather
Adult Hobby Classes: Enrl 100; tuition $2 per sem cr hr. Courses vary

VENTURA

VENTURA COLLEGE, Fine Arts Dept, 4667 Telegraph Rd, 93003. Tel 805-642-
3211, Ext 1280. *Chmn* Tom Roe. Instrs: FT 13, PT 15
Estab 1925; pub; D & E; SC 50, LC 15; enrl D 500, E 500, maj 300
Ent Req: HS dipl or 18 yrs of age
Degrees: AA and AS
Tuition: $10 per unit to 90 units, 90 units & above $50 per unit; no campus
residence
Courses: Advertising Design, Art Appreciation, Art History, †Ceramics,
†Commercial Art, Drawing, Fashion Arts, Graphic Arts, Graphic Design,
Illustration, Painting, †Photography, Sculpture, Textile Design, Fiber Design
Adult Hobby Classes: Enrl 500; tuition same as regular session. Courses—Art,
Ceramisc, Photography
Summer School: Dir, Tom Roe. Enrl 200; tuition same as regular courses, 6 - 8 wk
term. Courses—Ceramics, Color & Design, Drawing, Life Drawing, Photography

VICTORVILLE

VICTOR VALLEY COLLEGE, Art Dept, 18422 Bear Valley Rd, 92392. Tel 619-
245-4271. *Chmn* Gene Kleinsmith; *Instr Photo & Art* John Foster; *instructional
Aide* Brian Youmans
Estab 1961, dept estab 1971; pub; D & E; scholarships; SC 20, LC 5; enrl D 125, E
125, non-maj 200, maj 50
Ent Req: HS dipl
Degrees: AA 2 yrs
Courses: Advertising Design, Aesthetics, Art History, Calligraphy, Ceramics,
Commercial Art, Conceptual Art, Drawing, Graphic Arts, Graphic Design, History
of Art & Archaeology, Interior Design, Painting, Photography, Printmaking,
Sculpture
Adult Hobby Classes: Enrl 100; tuition $10 per 6 wks. Courses - Interior Design
Summer School: Enrl 60. Courses—Art History, Art Concepts

VISALIA

COLLEGE OF THE SEQUOIAS, Art Dept, Fine Arts Division, 915 S Mooney
Blvd, 93277. Tel 209-730-3700. *Chmn* Marlene Taber; *Instructor* Ralph Homan,
MA; *Instr* Ralph Gomas; *Instr* Gene Maddox. Instrs: PT 12
Estab 1925; dept estab 1940; pub; D & E; scholarships; SC 12, LC 4; enrl D 60,
E37, maj 10
Ent Req: HS dipl, must be 18 yr of age
Degrees: AA 2 yr
Tuition: None; no campus res
Courses: Aesthetics, Art Education, Art History, Ceramics, Commercial Art,
Drawing, Graphic Arts, History of Art & Archaeology, Lettering, Museum Staff
Training, Painting, Printmaking, Sculpture, Stage Design, Theatre Arts
Adult Hobby Classes: Ceramics, China Painting, Jewelry, Stained Glass
Summer School: Dir, George C Pappas. Courses—Drawing, Painting, Stained Glass

WALNUT

MOUNT SAN ANTONIO COLLEGE, Art Dept, 1100 N Grand Ave, 91789. Tel
909-594-5611. *Chmn* Ronald B Ownbey. Instrs: FT 14, PT 10
Estab 1945; pub; D & E; SC 24, LC 5; enrl D 2254, E 852, maj 500
Ent Req: Over 18 yrs of age
Degrees: AA and AS 2 yrs

Tuition: Non-district res—$95 per unit
Courses: Advertising Design, Ceramics, Commercial Art, Drafting, Drawing, Graphic Arts, Art History, Illustration, Lettering, Painting, Photography, Printmaking, Sculpture, Theatre Arts, Fibers, Life Drawing, Metals & Enamels, Watercolor, Woodworking
Summer School: Enrl art 50; term of 6 wks beginning June 16. Courses—Ceramics, Drawing

WEED

COLLEGE OF THE SISKIYOUS, Art Dept, 800 College Ave, 96094. Tel 916-938-4463. *Area Dir* James Witherell
Estab 1957; pub; D & E; scholarships; SC 15, LC 2; enrl D 1200, maj 20
Ent Req: HS dipl
Degrees: AA 2 yrs
Tuition: None to res; campus residence available
Courses: Art History, Ceramics, Collages, Constructions, Drafting, Drawing, Graphic Arts, History of Art & Archaeology, Painting, Photography, Printmaking, Sculpture, Life Drawing

WHITTIER

RIO HONDO COLLEGE, Fine Arts - Humanitites Division, 3600 Workman Mill Rd, 90608. Tel 310-908-3428. *Dean* Lance Carlson. Instrs: FT 28, PT 13
Estab 1962; pub; D & E; SC 18, LC 3; enrl D & E 19,000, non-maj 2100, maj 200
Ent Req: HS dipl
Degrees: AA 2 yrs
Tuition: $50; no campus residence
Courses: Advertising Design, Art History, Ceramics, †Commercial Art, Display, Drawing, Graphic Arts, History of Art & Archaeology, Illustration, Lettering, Painting, Photography, Printmaking, Sculpture, Stage Design, Theatre Arts, Video
Adult Hobby Classes: Courses—Calligraphy, Printmaking, Oriental Brush Painting, Tole & Decorative Painting
Summer School: Enrl 3468; tuition $5 per unit for term of 6 wks beginning June 23

WHITTIER COLLEGE, Dept of Art, 13406 Philadelphia St, 90608. Tel 310-693-0771. *Chmn* Dr John Sloan. Instrs: FT 2, PT 2
Estab 1901; pvt; D & E; scholarships and fels; SC 12, LC 12; enrl 552-560 per sem
Ent Req: HS dipl, accept credit by exam CLEP, CEEBA
Degrees: BA 4 yrs
Tuition: $6675; $7165 total per year live off campus, $9871 total per year live on campus
Courses: Art Education, Art History, Ceramics, Drawing, Painting, Printmaking, Adult and children's classes for special students; tui $5
Summer School: Dir, Robert W Speier. Enrl 25; tui $140 per credit 1-7 credits, $125 per credit 7-up credits, May 31-June 17, June 20-July 29, Aug 1-Aug 19. Courses—Water Soluble Painting, Color & Basic Drawing

WILMINGTON

LOS ANGELES HARBOR COLLEGE, Art Dept, 1111 Figueroa Place, 90744. Tel 310-522-8200; FAX 213-834-1882. *Chmn Humanities & Fine Arts* Robert H Billings, MA; *Assoc Prof* John Cassone, MA; *Asst Prof* Nancy E Webber, MFA; *Instructor* DeAnn Jennings, MA; *Instructor* Jay McCafferty, MA
Estab 1949; pub; D & E; SC 48, LC 11; enrl D 10,000, E 4200
Ent Req: HS dipl
Degrees: AA 2 yrs
Tuition: Non-res—$1116 per yr
Courses: Architecture, Art History, Ceramics, Drawing, Fashion Arts, Painting, Photography, Printmaking, Stage Design, Theatre Arts
Summer School: Art Dept Chmn, DeAnn Jennings. Courses—Art Fundamentals, Art History and Photography

WOODLAND HILLS

PIERCE COLLEGE, Art Dept, 6201 Winnetka, 91371. Tel 818-347-0551, Ext 475, 719-6475. *Art Dept Chmn* John D Kuczynski; *Prof* Milton Hirschl, MFA; *Prof* Walter Smith, MFA; *Assoc Prof* Roberta Barrager, MFA; *Assoc Prof* Constance Moffatt, PhD; *Asst Prof* A Nancy Snooks, MFA; *Instr* Paul C Nordberg, AA
Estab 1947, dept estab 1956; pub; D & E; scholarships; SC 35, LC 3; enrl D & E 23,000
Ent Req: HS dipl 18 yrs and over
Degrees: AA 60 units
Tuition: Res—$5 per unit up to 5 units, $50 for 6 or more units; non-res—$97 per unit plus enrl fee
Courses: Art History, Ceramics, Display, Drawing, Film, Illustration, Interior Design, Jewelry, Painting, †Photography, Printmaking, Sculpture, Fine Art
Adult Hobby Classes: Offered through Community Services Dept
Children's Classes: Offered through Community Services Dept
Summer School: Dir, Paul Whelan

COLORADO

ALAMOSA

ADAMS STATE COLLEGE, Dept of Visual Arts, 81102. Tel 719-589-7823. *Head Dept* Roberta Kaserman, MFA; *Prof* Edwin L Clemmer, MFA; *Adjunct Prof* Mary Lavey, MA; *Asst Prof of Art* Grace Norman; *Asst Prof Art* Marty Mitchell; *Vis Asst Prof* Judy Angus, MFA

Estab 1924; pub; D & E; scholarships; SC 43, LC 6, GC 5; enrl D 450, non-maj 200, maj 40, grad 7
Ent Req: HS dipl, ACT & SAT
Degrees: BA 4 yrs, MA 1-1/2 yrs
Tuition: Res—undergrad $675 per sem, grad $779 per sem; nonres—$1755 per sem, grad $2075 per sem; campus res—room & board $375 - $1120
Courses: Art Education, Art History, Ceramics, Drawing, Jewelry, Painting, Photography, Printmaking, Sculpture, Teacher Training
Adult Hobby Classes: Enrl 60; tuition $36 per sem hr. Courses—Drawing, Photography, Stained Glass
Summer School: Dir, Gary Peer. Tuition res—$38 per cr hr, nonres—$91 per cr hr. Courses—Art Education, Ceramics, Metals, Painting, Photography

BOULDER

UNIVERSITY OF COLORADO, BOULDER, Dept of Fine Arts, Sibell-Wolle Fine Arts Bldg N196A, Campus Box 318, 80309. Tel 303-492-6504. *Chmn* Jerry W Kunkel; *Assoc Chmn* Eugene Matthews. Instrs: FT 28, PT 15
Estab 1861; pub; D & E; scholarships; SC 55, LC 53, GC 67; enrl D 2000, E 90, non-maj 1340, maj 380, grad 84, others 100
Ent Req: HS dipl
Degrees: BA or BFA (Art Educ, Art History and Studio Arts) 4 yrs, MA (Art History) 3-5 yrs, MFA (Studio Arts) 2-3 yrs
Tuition: Res—undergrad $666 per sem plus $133 fees; grad $756 per sem for 9-15 hrs plus $133 fees; nonres—undergrad $2835 per sem plus $133 fees; grad $2637 per sem plus $133 fees; campus res—room & board $1350-$1559 per sem, $2700-$3118 per yr
Courses: Art Education, Art History, Ceramics, Drawing, Painting, Photography, Printmaking, Sculpture, Video, Integrated Media Art, Watermedia
Summer School: Enrl 20-25 per course; tuition $540 res, $1920 nonres for term of 5 weeks beginning in June. Courses—Art History, Drawing, Painting, Photography, Printmaking, Sculpture, Special Topics, Watermedia

COLORADO SPRINGS

COLORADO COLLEGE, Dept of Art, 80903. Tel 719-389-6000. *Chmn* Bougdon Swider; *Prof* James Trissel, MFA; *Assoc Prof* Louise LaFond, MFA; *Assoc Prof* Gale Murray, PhD; *Assoc Prof* Carl Reed; *Assoc Prof* Edith Kirsch, PhD
Estab 1874; pvt; D; schol; SC 20, LC 20; enrl D 1800, maj 40
Ent Req: HS dipl or equivalent and selection by admissions committee
Degrees: BA and MAT 4 yr
Tuition: Res—undergrad $16,000 per yr; campus res—room and board $2400
Courses: Art History, Drawing, Graphic Design, Painting, Photography, Printmaking, Sculpture, 3-D Design, Art Studio
Summer School: Dean, Elmer R Peterson. Tuition $260 per unit for term of 8 wks beginning June 19. Courses—Architecture, Art Education, Photography

UNIVERSITY OF COLORADO-COLORADO SPRINGS, Fine Arts Dept, Austin Bluffs Pkwy, PO Box 7150, 80933-7150. Tel 719-593-3563. *Chmn* Louis Cicotello, MFA; *Prof* Lin Fife, MFA; *Assoc Prof* Julia Hoerner, MFA; *Asst Prof* Kathryn Andrus-Walck, PhD
Estab 1965, dept estab 1970; pub; D & E; SC 18 LC 16; enrl maj 63
Ent Req: HS dipl, res-ACT 23 SAT 1000, non-res ACT 24 SAT 1050
Degrees: BA Studio 4 yr, BA (Art History) 4 Yr
Tuition: Res—undergrad $67 per sem hr; nonres—undergrad $215 per sem hr
Courses: Aesthetics, Art History, Constructions, Drawing, Mixed Media, Painting, Photography, Printmaking, Sculpture, Textile Design, Weaving, Computer Graphics, Papermaking

DENVER

COLORADO INSTITUTE OF ART, 200 E Ninth Ave, 80203. Tel 303-837-0825; FAX 303-837-0825. *Pres* Bill Bottoms; *Dir of Educ* James Graft
Estab 1952; pvt; D & E; schol; SC all; enrl D 1200, non-maj 600, maj 600
Ent Req: HS dipl
Degrees: Assoc 2 yr
Tuition: Undergrad—$1950 per quarter; photography $2050; campus res $1190 - $1475 per quarter
Courses: Interior Design, Photography, Video, †Fashion Illustration, †Fashion Merchandising, Music & Video Business
Adult Hobby Classes: Evening career training; 1 yr diploma. Courses—Nine week avocational workshops in fine arts & photography
Summer School: Commercial art prep school for post-secondary students only

METROPOLITAN STATE COLLEGE OF DENVER, Art Dept, Box 59, PO Box 173362, 80217-3362. Tel 303-556-3090. *Chmn* Susan Josepher, PhD
Estab 1963, dept estab 1963; pub; D & E; SC 52, LC 8; enrl D 650, E 325, maj 400
Ent Req: HS dipl or GED
Degrees: BFA 4 yrs
Courses: Advertising Design, Art Education, Art History, Ceramics, Commercial Art, Drawing, Graphic Arts, Graphic Design, Industrial Design, Jewelry, Painting, Photography, Printmaking, Sculpture, Product Design
Summer School: Same as regular session

REGIS COLLEGE, Fine Arts Dept, W 50th Low, 80221. Tel 303-458-4100. *Head Div* Richard Stepheson. Instrs: FT 4, PT 10
Estab 1880; pvt; D & E; SC 8, LC 4
Ent Req: HS dipl, ent exam
Degrees: BA, BS & BFA 4 yrs
Courses: Art Education, Drawing, Graphic Arts, History of Art & Archaeology, Jewelry, Lettering, Painting, Sculpture, Theatre Arts, †Music, †Studio Art, Weaving
Summer School: Courses—Ceramics, Glass, Jewelry, Printmaking, Weaving

ROCKY MOUNTAIN COLLEGE OF ART & DESIGN, 6875 E Evans Ave, 80224. Tel 303-753-6046. *Dir* Steven M Steele; *Financial Aid* Kari Aurino-Martel; *Academic Dean* Lisa Steele; *Adminr* Rex Whisman. Instrs: FT 6, PT 40
Estab 1963; pvt; D & E; scholarships; enrl D 350
Ent Req: Portfolio
Degrees: AA & BA
Tuition: $2805 per trimester for all full time students; $187 per cr for all part-time students; no campus res
Courses: †Advertising Design, Art History, Drawing, †Graphic Design, †Illustration, Lettering, †Painting, Graphic Arts, History of Art & Archaeology, Illustration, Intermedia, †Interior Design, †Sculpture, Mixed Media, Photography, Textile Design
Adult Hobby Classes: Enrl 350, tuition $2805 for 15 wk term. Courses—Same as regular semester
Summer School: Enrl 350; tuition $2805 for 15 wk term; Courses—Same as regular semester

UNIVERSITY OF COLORADO AT DENVER, Dept of Fine Arts, Campus Box 177, PO Box 173364, 80217-3364. Tel 303-556-4891. *Chmn* Judith Thorpe, MFA; *Prof* Jerry Johnson, MFA; *Prof* John Fudge; *Prof* Ernest O Porps, MFA; *Asst Prof* Lorre Hoffman, MFA; *Asst Prof* Stephanie Grilli; *Sr Instr* Jane Comstock
Estab 1876, dept estab 1955; pub; D & E; schol; SC 21, LC 13, GC 11; enrl maj 114
Ent Req: HS dipl, ACT or SAT, previous academic ability and accomplishment
Degrees: BA and BFA 4 yrs
Tuition: Res—undergrad $742 per sem, $89 per cr hr; grad $1030 per sem, $124 per cr hr; nonres—undergrad $3278 per sem; grad $3451 per sem; no campus res available
Courses: †Art History, †Drawing, Film, †Painting, †Photography, †Sculpture, †Creative Arts, †Studio Arts
Summer School: Tuition same as regular sem, term of 10 wk beginning June 12. Courses—Art History, Studio Workshops

UNIVERSITY OF DENVER, School of Art, 2121 E Asbury, 80210. Tel 303-871-2846; FAX 303-871-4112. *Dir* Maynard Tischler, MFA
Estab 1880; pvt; D; scholarships; SC 44, LC 33, GC 50; enrl D 450, non-maj 170-200, maj 176, grad 40
Ent Req: HS dipl
Degrees: BA & BFA 4 yrs, MFA 2 yrs, MA 4 quarters; honors program
Tuition: $332 per cr hr; campus res available
Courses: Ceramics, Drawing, Graphic Design, Painting, Photography, Sculpture, †Graphic Communications Design
Summer School: Enrl 100; tuition $268 per quarter hr for sem of 9 wks beginning June 11. Courses—Art History, Ceramics, Drawing, Graphic Design, Painting, Photography, Workshop-Seminar in conjunction with Aspen Design Conference & with Anderson Ranch in Snowmass

DURANGO

FORT LEWIS COLLEGE, Art Dept, College Heights, 81301-3999. Tel 303-247-7010. *Chmn* Ellen Cargile; *Prof* Stanton Englehart, MFA; *Prof* Gerald Wells, MFA; *Assoc Prof* Laurel Covington-Vogl, MFA; *Assoc Prof* David Hunt, MA; *Prof* Mick Reber; *Artist in Residence* Bruce Lowney
Estab 1956; pub; D & E; scholarships; SC 30, LC 6; enrl D 600, non-maj 450, maj 150
Ent Req: HS dipl, SAT
Degrees: BA & BS
Tuition: Campus res available
Courses: Advertising Design, Aesthetics, Art Education, Art History, Ceramics, Commercial Art, Drawing, Handicrafts, Illustration, Industrial Design, Intermedia, Jewelry, Mixed Media, Painting, Photography, Printmaking, Sculpture, Silversmithing, Teacher Training, Art Seminars, Southwest Art
Summer School: Dean, Ed Angus. Enrl 1000. Courses—Art Education, Ceramics, Drawing, Mural Design, Painting

FORT COLLINS

COLORADO STATE UNIVERSITY, Dept of Art, 80523. Tel 303-491-6774. *Chmn* James T Dormer. Instrs: 34
Estab 1870, dept estab 1956; pub; D; scholarships; SC 55, LC 13, GC 5; enrl D 547, non-maj 860, maj 547, grad 22
Ent Req: HS dipl, portfolio if by transfer
Degrees: BA(Art History & Art Education) and BFA 4 yr, MFA 60 hrs
Tuition: Res—undergrad $2511 per yr, $1255.50 per sem, $83 per cr; grad $2813 per yr, $1406 per sem; nonres—undergrad $7677 per yr, $3838.50 per sem; grad $7985 per yr, $3992.50 per sem
Courses: †Art Education, †Art History, †Ceramics, †Drawing, †Graphic Design, Painting, Photography, Printmaking, Sculpture, †Fibers, Metalsmithing, Pottery
Children's Classes: Continuing education art offerings not on regular basis
Summer School: Dir, James T Dormer. Enrl 700; tuition $77 per cr. Courses—most regular session courses

GOLDEN

FOOTHILLS ART CENTER, INC, 809 15th St, 80401. Tel 303-279-3922. *Exec Dir* Carol Dickinson, MA. Instrs: PT 10
Estab 1968; pvt; D & E (winter and spring)
Ent Req: None
Tuition: $100 & up for 6-10 wk class
Courses: Drawing, Painting, Sculpture, Marketing One's Art
Adult Hobby Classes: Enrl limited; tuition $30-$45 for 8-10 wk class. Courses—Pottery, Printmaking
Summer School: Exec Dir, Marian J Metsopoulos. Workshops for adults and classes for children beginning in June

GRAND JUNCTION

MESA COLLEGE, Art Dept, PO Box 2647, 81502. Tel 303-248-1020. *Dean* Laurence W Madzeno
Estab 1925; pub; D & E; scholarships; SC 23, LC 5; enrl D 538, E 103
Ent Req: HS dipl, GED
Degrees: AA, BA
Courses: Art Education, Art History, Ceramics, Drawing, Painting, Printmaking, Sculpture, Exhibitions & Management, Metalsmithing

GREELEY

AIMS COMMUNITY COLLEGE, Design & Creative Studies Dept, PO Box 69, 80632. Tel 303-330-8008. *Chmn Div Communications & Humanities* Christa Frost; *Design & Creative Studies Dept Coordr* Tedd Runge
Tuition: Res—$12 per cr hr; $20 per cr hr for in-state, out of district; nonres—$60 per cr hr
Courses: Art Appreciation, Art History, Ceramics, Design, Drawing, Fashion Arts, Interior Design, Jewelry, Painting, Photography, Sculpture, Textile Design, Weaving
Children's Classes: Courses offered
Summer School: Courses offered

UNIVERSITY OF NORTHERN COLORADO, Dept of Visual Arts, 80639. Tel 303-351-2143. *Chmn* Richard Munson. Instrs: FT 12
Estab 1889; pub; D & E
Ent Req: HS dipl
Degrees: BA 4 yr
Tuition: Res—undergrad $853.50 per sem, grad $1010 per sem; nonres—undergrad $3284 per sem, grad $3495 per sem; campus—room & board $1837 - $1906 per sem
Courses: Art Education, Art History, Ceramics, Drawing, Graphic Design, Graphic Arts, Jewelry, Painting, Photography, Printmaking, Sculpture, Fiber Art, Papermaking, Photo Communications
Summer School: Courses—Comparative Arts Program in Florence, Italy, Study of the Indian Arts of Mesa Verde, Mesa Verde workshop and on campus courses, Workshops in Weaving & Ceramics in Steamboat Springs, Colorado

GUNNISON

WESTERN STATE COLLEGE OF COLORADO, Dept of Art & Industrial Technology, 81231. Tel 303-943-0120. *Chmn* Charles Tutor. Instrs: FT 7, PT 3
Estab 1911; pub; D & E; SC 29, LC 7, GC 8; enrl 850
Ent Req: HS dipl, special exam
Degrees: 4 yr
Tuition: Res—$704 per sem; nonres—$1818 per sem
Courses: Art Education, Calligraphy, Ceramics, Drawing, Jewelry, Painting, Printmaking, Sculpture, Design, Indian Art, Introduction to Art, Studio Art, Weaving
Summer School: Dir, Dr Edwin H Randall. 2, 4 and 8 wks courses

LA JUNTA

OTERO JUNIOR COLLEGE, Dept of Arts, 18th & Colorado Ave, 81050. Tel 719-384-8721. *Head Dept* Timothy F Walsh
Estab 1941; pub; D & E; scholarships; SC 12, LC 3; enrl 776
Ent Req: HS grad
Degrees: AA and AAS 2 yr
Courses: Art History, Ceramics, Drawing, Painting, Creative Design, Metal Sculpture, Watercolor
Adult Hobby Classes: Enrl 60; tuition $47.50 per cr, non-credit courses vary. Courses—Art, Drawing, Painting

LAKEWOOD

RED ROCKS COMMUNITY COLLEGE, Arts & Humanities Department, 13300 W Sixth Ave, 80401. Tel 303-988-6160. *Instr Pottery* Thomas L Nielsen; *Art Instr* Susan Arndt; *Art Instr* Don Coen
Tuition: $33 per sem cr hr
Courses: Art Appreciation, Art History, Ceramics, Design, Drawing, Painting, Photography, Printmaking, Sculpture, Electronic Studio
Summer School: Enrl 80; tuition $99 per 3 cr course per 10 wks. Courses—Ceramics, Drawing, Design, Watercolor

PUEBLO

UNIVERSITY OF SOUTHERN COLORADO, BELMONT CAMPUS, Dept of Art, 2200 Bonforte Blvd, 81001. Tel 719-549-2816. *Chmn* Carl Jensen; *Assoc Prof* Robert Hench, MA; *Assoc Prof* Charles Marino; *Asst Prof* Carl Jensen, MFA; *Asst Prof* Robert Wands, MA; *Asst Prof* Nick Latka, MFA; *Instr* Laura Audrey
Estab 1933; pub; D & E; scholarships; SC 66, LC 19, GC 2; enrl D 700, E 50, non-maj 600, maj 150
Ent Req: HS dipl, GED, Open Door Policy
Degrees: BA and BS 4 yrs
Tuition: Res—undergrad & grad $662 18 hr sem; nonres—$2624 18 hr sem; campus res—available
Courses: Advertising Design, Art History, Ceramics, Collages, Commercial Art, Drawing, Film, Graphic Design, Illustration, Museum Staff Training, Painting, Photography, Printmaking, Sculpture, Teacher Training
Summer School: Dir, Ed Sajbel. Enrl 125; tuition resident $40 per cr hr, nonres $150 per cr hr. Courses—Art Education, Art History, Ceramics, Introduction to Art, Painting

STERLING

NORTHEASTERN JUNIOR COLLEGE, Dept of Art, 80751. Tel 303-522-6600, Ext 671. *Instructional Dir, General Studies* Peter L Youngers, MFA
Estab 1941; pub; D & E; schol; SC 16, LC 2; enrl D 103, E 23, non-maj 73, maj 30, others 23
Ent Req: HS dipl, GED
Degrees: AA 2 yr
Tuition: Res—$783 per yr; nonres—$1998 per yr
Courses: Art Education, Art History, Ceramics, Display, Drawing, Handicrafts, Lettering, Mixed Media, Painting, Printmaking, Sculpture, Teacher Training
Adult Hobby Classes: Enrl 100; tuition $8 per cr hr. Courses—Basic Crafts, Ceramics, Drawing, Macrame, Painting, Stained Glass
Summer School: Dir, Dick Gritz. Courses—vary each yr

VALE

COLORADO MOUNTAIN COLLEGE, Visual & Performing Arts, 1310 W Haven Dr, 1402 Blake Ave, 81657. Tel 303-476-4040. *Dir* Katherine Schmidt
Estab 1971 for summers only; enrl 1500 per summer
Tuition: Res—$25 per cr hr; nonres—$150 per cr hr; res room & board $150 per week
Courses: Ceramics, Drawing, Painting, Photography, Children's Art, Enameling, Foundry Fibers & Surface Design, Watercolor

CONNECTICUT

BRIDGEPORT

HOUSATONIC COMMUNITY COLLEGE, Art Dept, 510 Barnum Ave, 06608. Tel 203-579-6443, 579-6400. *Prog Coordr* Ronald Abby, MFA; *Faculty* David Kintzler, MFA; *Faculty* Burt Chernow, MA; *Faculty* Michael Stein, MFA
Estab 1967, dept estab 1968; pub; D & E; SC 15, LC 5; enrl maj 100
Ent Req: HS dipl
Degrees: AA 2 yr
Tuition: Res—$165 per sem; nonres—$625 per sem
Courses: Art Education, Art History, Ceramics, Collages, Constructions, Drafting, Drawing, Film, †Graphic Design, Mixed Media, Painting, Photography, Sculpture, Teacher Training
Adult Hobby Classes: Varied
Summer School: Dir, Dr Joseph Shive. Courses—Same as regular session

UNIVERSITY OF BRIDGEPORT, Art Dept, College of Arts & Sciences, University and Iranistan Ave, 06602. Tel 203-576-4436. *Chmn* Ketti Kupper; *Prof* Merrillee Byron, MFA; *Prof* Bruce Glaser, MA; *Prof* Donal J O'Hara, MA; *Prof* Paul Vazquez, MFA; *Assoc Prof* Arthur Nager, MFA; *Assoc Prof* Robert Cuneo, MFA; *Assoc Prof* Susan Reinhart, MFA; *Assoc Prof* Peter Schier, MA; *Assoc Prof* Adele Shtern, MFA; *Assoc Prof* Gabor Gergo, MFA
Estab 1927, dept estab 1947; pvt; D & E; scholarships; SC 38, LC 24, GC 15; enrl D 1150, E 200, non-maj 1070, maj 260, GS 22
Ent Req: Portfolio for BFA candidates only, college boards
Degrees: Certificate 1 yr, AA 2 yr, BA, BS and BFA 4 yr, MS 1 yr
Tuition: Res—$5565 per sem, undergrad $260 per cr hr; nonres—undergrad $235 per cr hr, grad $260 per cr hr; campus res available
Courses: Advertising Design, Architecture, Art History, Ceramics, Graphic Design, Illustration, Industrial Design, Interior Design, Painting, Photography, Printmaking, Sculpture, Theatre Arts, †Art Education, †Art Therapy, †Pre-Architecture, Weaving
Adult Hobby Classes: Enrl open; Courses—most crafts
Summer School: Chmn, Peter Schier. Tuition $235 per hr for term of 5-6 wks beginning May. Courses—Computer Graphics, Drawing, Painting, Photography, Photo Graphics

DANBURY

WESTERN CONNECTICUT STATE UNIVERSITY, School of Arts & Sciences, 181 White St, 06810. Tel 203-797-4305. *Dean* Carol Hawkes; *Dept Chmn* J E Wallace. Instrs: FT 7
Estab 1903; pub; D & E; scholarships; SC 30, LC 3-6, GC 5; enrl D 100
Ent Req: HS dipl
Degrees: BA (graphic communications) 4 yr
Tuition: Res—$1060 per yr; nonres—$3430 per yr
Summer School: Courses—same as regular session

FAIRFIELD

FAIRFIELD UNIVERSITY, Fine Arts Dept, N Benson Rd, 06430. Tel 203-254-4000. *Chmn* Dr Orin Grossman
Scholarships offered
Tuition: $2500 per sem
Courses: Art History, Design, Drawing, Video, Painting, Photography, Printmaking, Sculpture, Film Production, History of Film, Visual Design
Adult Hobby Classes: Enrl 2000; tuition $330 per 3 cr. Courses—Full Fine Arts curriculum
Summer School: Dir, Dr Vilma Allen. Enrl 2000. Semester June - August

SACRED HEART UNIVERSITY, Dept of Art, 5151 Park Ave, 06432-1000. Tel 203-371-7737. *Coordr* Virginia F Zic, MFA. Instrs: 13
Estab 1963, dept estab 1977; pvt; D & E; scholarships; SC 26, LC 5; enrl D 300, E 100, non-maj 225, maj 70
Ent Req: HS dipl

Degrees: BA 4 yrs
Tuition: $4750 per sem; campus res—available
Courses: Art History, Drawing, †Graphic Design, †Illustration, †Painting, Design
Summer School: Dir, Virginia Zic. Tuition $675 per 5 wk term. Courses—Art History, Design, Drawing

FARMINGTON

TUNXIS COMMUNITY COLLEGE, Graphic Design Dept, Junction Route 6 & 177, 06032. Tel 203-677-7701. *Acting Acad Dean* Dr John Carey; *Graphic Design Coordr* Stephen A Klema, MFA; *Instr* William Kluba, MFA
Estab 1970, dept estab 1973; pub; D & E; SC 15, LC 4; enrl non-maj 40, maj 90
Ent Req: HS dipl
Degrees: AS, AA(Graphic Design, Visual Fine Arts)
Tuition: $300 per sem
Courses: Drawing, Graphic Design, Illustration, Painting, Photography, Color, Computer Graphics, Typography, 2-D & 3-D Design
Summer School: Dir Community Services, Dr Kyle. Courses—Computer Graphics, Drawing, Painting, Photography

GREENWICH

CONNECTICUT INSTITUTE OF ART, 581 W Putnam Ave, 06830. Tel 203-869-4430. *Chmn Dept* Dan Loizeaux; *VPres* Joann Propersi; *Dir* August Propersi; *Asst Dir* Linda Propersi; *Adminr* Michael Propersi
Estab 1954; pvt; D & E; scholarships; SC 7, LC 2; enrl D 60, E 40
Ent Req: HS dipl, portfolio, interview
Degrees: Dipl, 2 yrs
Tuition: $5400 per yr; no campus res
Courses: Advertising Design, Commercial Art, Conceptual Art, Drawing, Graphic Design, Illustration, Lettering, Painting, Airbrushing, Fine Art, Production, Studio Skills

HAMDEN

PAIER COLLEGE OF ART, INC, 6 Prospect Court, 06517. Tel 203-777-3851; FAX 203-287-3021. *Pres* Edward T Paier. Instrs: FT 36, PT 11
Estab 1946; pvt; D & E; scholarships; SC 10, LC 6 GC 1; enrl D 185, E 130
Ent Req: HS grad, presentation of portfolio, transcript of records, recommendation
Degrees: BFA & AFA programs offered
Tuition: Res—undergrad $8610 per yr
Courses: Graphic Design, Illustration, Interior Design, Painting, Photography, Fine Arts
Summer School: Dir E T Paier. Enrl 100; $199 per sem hr, one 5 wk term beginning July. Courses—Fine Arts, Graphic Design, Illustration, Photography

HARTFORD

GREATER HARTFORD COMMUNITY COLLEGE, Humanities Division & Art Dept, 61 Woodland St, 06105. Tel 203-520-7800. *Prof* Ronald Buksbaum; *Prof* Thomas Werle
Degrees: AA & AS 2 yr
Tuition: $708 per yr
Courses: Art History, Ceramics, Design, Drawing, Painting, Printmaking, Sculpture, Figure Drawing
Summer School: Courses offered

TRINITY COLLEGE, Dept of Fine Arts, Summit St, 06106. Tel 203-297-2330. *Chmn* Michael R T Mahoney, PhD; *Prof* George Chaplin, MFA; *Assoc Prof* Alden R Gordon, PhD; *Assoc Prof* Jean Cadogan, PhD; *Asst Prof* Michael Fitzgerald; *Asst Prof* Robert Kirschbaum, MFA; *Asst Prof* Kathleen Curren, PhD; *Vis Asst Prof* Bridget Kennedy, MFA; *Vis Asst Prof* Gwen Kerber, MFA; *Vis Asst Prof* Mary Lewis, PhD; *Vis Asst Prof* Ann Norton, PhD; *Vis Asst Lecturer* Michael Grillo, MA; *Austin Fellow* Paul Rogers, MA; *Graduate Mentor* Johann Reusch, MA
Estab 1823, dept estab 1939; pvt; D; scholarships; SC 20, LC 22; enrl D 400, non-maj 350, major 50
Ent Req: HS dipl
Degrees: MA
Tuition: Res—undergrad $15,120 per yr; campus res—room $2710, board $1760
Courses: Aesthetics, Architecture, †Art History, Drawing, Painting, Printmaking, Sculpture, †Studio Arts

MANCHESTER

MANCHESTER COMMUNITY COLLEGE, Fine Arts Dept, 60 Bidwell St, PO Box 1046, 06040. Tel 203-647-6272. *Prof* John Stevens. Instrs: PT 4
Estab 1963, dept estab 1968; pub; D & E; enrl D & E 300, non-maj 240, maj 60
Ent Req: HS dipl, portfolio for visual fine arts prog
Degrees: AA and AS 2 yrs
Tuition: 3 credit courses $106.50 per credit hr
Courses: Art History, Calligraphy, Ceramics, Drawing, Film, Graphic Arts, Lettering, Painting, Photography, Printmaking, Sculpture, Basic Design, History of Film, Sign Painting

MIDDLETOWN

MIDDLESEX COMMUNITY COLLEGE, Fine Arts Div, 100 Training Hill Rd, 06457. Tel 203-344-3077. *Head of Dept* Charles Eckert
Degrees: AS
Tuition: Res—$396 per sem; nonres—$1287 per sem
Courses: Art History, Ceramics, Design, Drawing, Painting, Sculpture

WESLEYAN UNIVERSITY, Art Dept, Center for the Arts, Wesleyan Station, 06459-0442. Tel 203-347-9411, Ext 2253. *Chmn* Clark Maines; *Prof* John T Paoletti, PhD; *Prof* David Schorr, MFA; *Prof* Jeanine Basinger; *Prof* Clark Maines, PhD; *Prof* J Seeley, MFA; *Prof* Jonathan Best, PhD; *Prof* John Frazer, MFA; *Adjunct Prof* Ellen D'Oench, PhD; *Assoc Prof* Joseph Siry, PhD; *Assoc Prof* Peter Mark, PhD; *Asst Prof* Ben Ledbetter; *Asst Prof* Jeffrey Schiff; *Asst Prof* Tula Telfair; *Asst Prof* Elizabeth Milroy, PhD; *Adjunct Asst Prof* Phillip Wagoner, PhD; *Adjunct Assoc Prof* Mary Risley, MFA
Estab 1831, dept estab 1928; pvt; D; SC 30, LC 25; enrl in school D 3604, maj 94, undergrad 2667
Ent Req: HS dipl, SAT
Degrees: BA 4 yrs
Tuition: Campus res available
Courses: Ceramics, Drawing, History of Art & Archaeology, Mixed Media, Painting, Photography, Printmaking, Sculpture, Silversmithing, Film History, Film Production, History of Prints, Printroom Methods & Techniques, Typography
Summer School: Dir, Barbara MacEachern. Enrl 576; Term of 6 wks beginning July 5. Courses—grad courses in all areas

NEW BRITAIN

CENTRAL CONNECTICUT STATE UNIVERSITY, Dept of Art, 1615 Stanley St, 06050. Tel 203-827-7204; FAX 203-827-7963. *Chmn Dept* Dr M Cipriano. Instrs: FT 14, PT 15
Estab 1849; pub; D & E; SC 36, LC 8, GC 20; enrl D 200, E 150, non-maj 1000, maj 200, grad 500
Ent Req: HS dipl
Degrees: BA(Graphic Design), BA(Fine Arts) & BS(Art Educ) 4 yrs
Courses: Art Education, Art History, Ceramics, Display, Drawing, Graphic Arts, Graphic Design, Handicrafts, Jewelry, Lettering, Painting, Photography, Printmaking, Sculpture, Teacher Training, Ceramic Sculpture, Color Theory, Fibre Sculpture, Fine Arts, Serigraphy (Silk Screen), Stained Glass
Children's Classes: Enrl 30, 5-17 yr olds; tuition $30 per 30 wks. Courses—Crafts, Fine Arts
Summer School: Dean Continuing Educ, J Zulick. Tuition $48 per cr hr for term of 5 wks. Enrl 200; Courses—Crafts, Design, Drawing, Fine Arts

NEW CANAAN

GUILD ART CENTER, 1037 Silvermine Rd, 06840. Tel 203-866-0411, 966-6668. *Dir* Michael J Costello
Estab 1949; pvt; D & E; SC 60, LC 1; enrl 560
Ent Req: None
Degrees: None
Tuition: No campus res
Courses: Advertising Design, Art History, Ceramics, Drawing, Illustration, Painting, Photography, Printmaking, Sculpture, Sogetsu Ikebana, Youth Programs in Art
Adult Hobby Classes: Enrl 550-600; tuition $6 per studio hr for sem of 14 wks. Courses offered
Children's Classes: Enrl 80-100; tuition $6 per studio hr for sem of 14 wks. Courses offered
Summer School: Dir, Michael J Costello. Tuition $6 for 8 wk prog. Courses—same as above

NEW HAVEN

ALBERTUS MAGNUS COLLEGE, Art Dept, 700 Prospect St, 06511. Tel 203-773-8546. *Chmn* Jerry Nevins, MFA; *Prof* Jerome Nevins, MFA; *Instr* Beverly Chieffo, MA
Estab 1925, dept estab 1970; pvt; D & E; schol; SC 20, LC 9; enrl D 120, non-maj 60, maj 40
Ent Req: HS dipl, SAT, CEEB
Degrees: BA, BFA 8 sem
Tuition: Res—undergrad $7095 per yr, part-time $314 per cr; campus res—room & board $4930 per yr
Courses: Aesthetics, Art Education, Art History, Ceramics, Collages, Design, Drawing, History of Art & Archaeology, Mixed Media, Painting, Photography, Printmaking, Sculpture, Teacher Training, Art Therapy, Fabric Design & Construction, Weaving
Adult Hobby Classes: Courses offered
Summer School: Dir, Elaine Lewis. Courses—vary

SOUTHERN CONNECTICUT STATE UNIVERSITY, Dept of Art, 501 Crescent St, 06515. Tel 203-397-4279; FAX 203-397-4649. *Dept Head* Keith Hatcher. Instrs: FT 18, PT 12
Estab 1893; pub; D & E; SC 40, LC 18, GC 20; enrl D 350, GS 100
Ent Req: HS dipl, SAT
Degrees: BS, MS(Art Educ), BA(Art History) & BA, BS(Studio Art) 4 yrs
Tuition: Res—$1594 per yr, $113 per cr hr, nonres—$3501 per yr, $81 per cr hr; out-of-state $5162 per yr; campus res—available
Courses: Art Education, Art History, Ceramics, Drawing, Graphic Design, Handicrafts, Illustration, Jewelry, Painting, Photography, Printmaking, Sculpture, Teacher Training, Metalsmithing
Summer School: Dir, Keith Hatcher. Enrl 320; tuition undergrad $133 per cr hr, grad 144 per cr hr for 2 - 5 wk terms. Courses—Art History, Crafts, Drawing, Graphic Design, Painting, Photography, Printmaking, Sculpture, Stained Glass

YALE UNIVERSITY
—**School of Art,** 180 York St 1605A Yale Station, 06520. Tel 203-432-2600; FAX 203-432-7158. *Dean* David Pease, MFA; *Prof* Andrew Forge, MA; *Prof* Alice Aycock, MA; *Prof* Tod Papageorge, MA; *Prof* William Bailey, MFA; *Prof* Richard Lytle, MFA; *Prof* Sheila de Bretteville, MFA; *Prof* Richard Benson; *Prof* Robert Reed, MFA
#Estab 1869; pvt; D; scholarships; GC 118
Ent Req: BFA, BA, BS or dipl from four year professional art school and portfolio

Degrees: MFA 2 yrs
Tuition: $13,100 per yr
Courses: Drawing, Film, †Graphic Design, †Painting, †Photography, †Printmaking, †Sculpture
Summer School: Tuition $1060. Courses—Drawing, Graphic Design, Painting, Photography. Four undergrad 8 wk courses in New Haven, 3 cr each; 5 wk Graphic Design Program in Brissago, Switzerland; 8 wk Fellowship Program in Norfolk, Connecticut
—**Dept of the History of Art,** PO Box 2009, Yale Station, 06520-2009. Tel 203-432-2668; FAX 203-432-2667. *Chmn* Mary Miller; *Dir Grad Studies* Judith J Colton; *Dir Undergrad Studies* Mimi Yiengpruksawan. Instrs: FT 27, PT 2
Estab 1940; pvt; D; scholarships, fels and assistantships
Ent Req: For grad prog—BA and foreign language
Degrees: BA 4 yrs, PhD 6 yrs
Tuition: $15,920 per yr
Courses: †Art History
—**School of Architecture,** 06520. Tel 203-432-2296; FAX 203-432-7175. *Dean* Fred Koetter
Estab 1869; pvt; scholarships; enrl 142 maximum
Ent Req: Bachelor's degree, grad record exam
Degrees: MArchit 3 yrs, MEnviron Design 2 yrs
Tuition: $15,900 per yr
Courses: Aesthetics, Architecture, Art History, Design, Drawing, Landscape Architecture, Photography

NEW LONDON

CONNECTICUT COLLEGE
—**Dept of Art,** 270 Mohegan Ave, 06320-4196. Tel 203-439-2740, 439-2741; FAX 203-439-2700. *Chmn* Peter Leibert; *Prof* David Smalley; *Prof* Barkley L Hendricks; *Prof* Maureen McCabe; *Assoc Prof* Tim McDowell; *Asst Prof* Ted Hendrickson
Estab 1911; pvt; D; scholarships; SC 20, LC 34
Ent Req: HS dipl, ent exam
Degrees: BA 4 yrs
Tuition: $15,175 per yr; campus res—room & board $4800
Courses: Art History, Ceramics, Collages, Conceptual Art, Design, Drawing, Graphic Arts, Graphic Design, History of Art & Archaeology, Illustration, Mixed Media, Painting, Photography, Printmaking, Sculpture, Video
Adult Hobby Classes: Chmn, Lee Kneerim
Summer School: Dir, Lee Kneerim. Courses—varies
—**Dept of Art History,** 270 Mohegan Ave, 06320. Tel 203-439-2740; FAX 203-439-2700. *Chmn* Nancy Rash; *Instr* Barbara Zabel; *Instr* Robert Baldwin
Estab 1911, dept estab 1972; pvt; D & E
Ent Req: HS dipl, SAT
Degrees: BA 4 yrs
Tuition: $17,000 per yr
Courses: Art History
Adult Hobby Classes: Film History
Summer School: Dir, Lee Kneerim. Courses—Film History

STORRS

UNIVERSITY OF CONNECTICUT, Art Dept, U-99, 875 Coventry Rd, 06269-1099. Tel 203-486-3930; FAX 203-486-5845. *Head Dept* David C Kelly. Instrs: FT 24, PT 10
Estab 1882, dept estab 1950; pub; D; SC 43, LC 32, GC 15; enrl D 1600, maj 280
Ent Req: HS dipl, SAT
Degrees: BA(Art History), BFA(Studio) 4 yrs, MFA 2 yrs
Tuition: Res—undergrad $1580, grad $1944, nonres—undergrad $4816, grad $5053; campus res available
Courses: Architecture, †Art History, †Ceramics, Drawing, †Graphic Design, Illustration, †Painting, †Photography, †Printmaking, †Sculpture
Summer School: Dir, Matthew McLoughlin. Enrl 100; tuition $92 per cr hr; 3 wk studio sessions. Courses—Computer Graphics, Drawing, Painting, Photography

VOLUNTOWN

FOSTER CADDELL'S ART SCHOOL, Northlight, Route 49, RFD 2, 06384. Tel 201-376-9583. *Head Dept* Foster Caddell
Estab 1958; D & E; enrl D 75, E 50
Tuition: $750 per course; no campus res
Courses: †Drawing, †Painting, †Teacher Training, †Pastel

WEST HARTFORD

SAINT JOSEPH COLLEGE, Dept of Fine Arts, 1678 Asylum Ave, 06117. Tel 203-232-4571; FAX 203-233-5695. *Chmn Dept* Dorothy Bosch Keller. Instrs: FT 2, PT 1
Estab 1932; pvt; W; D & E; scholarships & fels; SC 5, LC 7; enrl D 104
Ent Req: HS dipl, CEEB
Degrees: BA, BS and MA 4 yr
Tuition: $10,400 (24 - 36 cr) incoming freshman
Courses: Drawing, †Art History, Painting, Creative Crafts, Fundamental of Design, Egyptian Art, Greek Art, Art of Ireland, History of American Antiques, American Architecture, History of American art, History of Women Artists, Victorian Antiques, Impressionism, Pre-Art Therapy, Renaissance
Summer School: Dir, D Keller. Enrl 20; tuition $200 per cr hr. Some courses in art history offered

UNIVERSITY OF HARTFORD, Hartford Art School, 200 Bloomfield Ave, 06117. Tel 203-243-4391, 243-4393. *Dean* Stuart Schar, MFA; *Asst Dean* Stephen Keller, MA; *Prof* Lloyd Glasson, MFA; *Prof* Frederick Wessell, MFA; *Assoc Prof* Gilles Giuntini,MFA; *Assoc Prof* Christopher Horton, MAT; *Assoc Prof* Peter McLean, MFA; *Assoc Prof* Walter Hall, MFA; *Asst Prof* Douglas Anderson, MA; *Asst Prof*

Dennis Nolan, MFA; *Asst Prof* Stephen Brown, MFA; *Asst Prof* Patricia Sutton, MA; *Asst Prof* Ellen Carey, MFA; *Asst Prof* John Rohlfing, MFA; *Asst Prof* Mary Frey; *Asst Prof* Jan Kubasiewicz; *Asst Prof* Robert Jessup, MFA; *Asst Prof* Lisa Lindholm, MFA; *Asst Prof* Alex White, MFA
Estab 1877; pvt; D & E; scholarships; SC 70, LC 5, GC 32; enrl D 275, E 100, non-maj 125, maj 300, grad 20
Ent Req: HS dipl, SAT
Degrees: BFA 4 yr
Tuition: Undergrad $11,900 yr, $4120 per sem, $175 per cr hr; $175 evenings; campus res—room $2423 & board $1710
Courses: Ceramics, Design, Drawing, Film, Painting, Photography, Printmaking, Sculpture, Video
Adult Hobby Classes: Day and evening classes
Children's Classes: Summer only
Summer School: Tuition same for 2 terms of 6 wks beginning May

WEST HAVEN

UNIVERSITY OF NEW HAVEN, Dept of Visual & Performing Arts & Philosophy, 300 Orange Ave, 06516. Tel 203-932-7000. *Chmn* Michael G Kaloyamides; *Coordr of Arts* Jerry Zinser. Instrs: FT 2, PT 8
Estab 1927, dept estab 1972; pvt; D & E; SC 30, LC 5; enrl D 350, E 110
Ent Req: HS dipl
Degrees: BA & BS 4 yrs, AS 2 yrs
Courses: †Advertising Design, Art History, Calligraphy, Ceramics, Commercial Art, Constructions, Drawing, Graphic Arts, Graphic Design, History of Art & Archaeology, Illustration, Interior Design, Mixed Media, Painting, Photography, Printmaking, Sculpture, Dimensional Design, Film Animation, Interaction of Color
Summer School: June 12th - July 20th. Courses—Ceramics, Drawing, History of Art, Painting, Photography, Sculpture

WILLIMANTIC

EASTERN CONNECTICUT STATE UNIVERSITY, Fine Arts Dept, 83 Windham St, 06226. Tel 203-456-5325; FAX 203-456-5508. *Chmn* Imna Arrowo; *Asst Prof* Lula Blocton. Instrs: FT 4, PT 4
Estab 1881; pub; D & E; scholarships; enrl D 300, E 75, maj 40
Ent Req: HS dipl
Degrees: BA(Fine Arts) & BS(Art) 4 yrs
Tuition: Res—$445 per sem; nonres—$1435 per sem
Courses: Art History, Ceramics, Drawing, Graphic Arts, Interior Design, Jewelry, Painting, Sculpture, Enameling, Weaving
Summer School: Dir, Owen Peagler. Courses—Art & Craft Workshop

WINSTED

NORTHWESTERN CONNECTICUT COMMUNITY COLLEGE, Fine Arts Dept, Park Place, 06098. Tel 203-738-6373; FAX 203-379-4995. *Prof* Michael Christiana; *Prof* Charles Dmytria; *Prof* Richard Finman
Courses: Advertising Design, Art Appreciation, Art History, Ceramics, Design, Drawing, Graphic Arts, Painting, Photography, Printmaking, Sculpture, Video

DELAWARE

DOVER

DELAWARE STATE COLLEGE, Dept of Art and Art Education, 19901-2275. Tel 302-739-5182; FAX 302-739-3533. *Art Dept Chmn* Kathleen Berhalter, PhD. Instrs: FT 4
Estab 1960; pub; D & E; scholarships; SC 13, LC 9; enrl 50-60 maj
Ent Req: HS dipl or GED, SAT or ACT
Degrees: BS(Art Educ), BS(General Art) & BS(Art Business)
Tuition: Boarding: in state $1513 sem, out of state $2101 sem; commuter $447.50 per sem in state, commuter $2032.50 out of sta te
Courses: Art Appreciation, Art History, Jewelry, †Art Education, Ceramics, Commercial Art, Drawing, Interior Design, Lettering, Painting, Photography, Printmaking, Sculpture, Teacher Training, Design, Fibers, Independent Study, Senior Exhibition (one man show & research)
Adult Hobby Classes: Courses—same as above
Summer School: Courses—same as above

NEWARK

UNIVERSITY OF DELAWARE, Dept of Art, 19716. Tel 302-831-2244. *Chmn* Larry Holmes, MFA; *Coordr Sculpture* Joe Moss, MA; *Coordr Photography* John Weiss, MFA; *Coordr Ceramics* Victor Spinski, MFA; *Coordr Printmaking* Rosemary Lane, MFA; *Coordr Jewelry* Anne Graham, MFA; *Coordr Drawing & Painting* Steven Tanis, MFA; *Coordr Foundations* Robert Straight, MFA; *Coordr Fibers* Vera Kaminsky, MFA; *Coordr Illustration* Charles Rowe
Estab 1833; pub; D & E; SC 62, LC 2, GC 12, non-maj 600, maj 400, grad 30
Ent Req: Portfolio, BFA prog and graphic design prog (both sophomore yr)
Degrees: BA, BS and BFA 4 yrs, MFA 2 yrs, MA 1 yr
Tuition: Res—undergrad $1590 per yr, grad $89 per cr hr, res—grad $795 per sem; nonres—undergrad $3900, grad $217 per cr hr, nonres—grad $1950 per sem; campus res—room & board $2254, nonres—room & board $2354
Courses: †Art Education, †Ceramics, †Drawing, †Graphic Design, †Illustration, †Jewelry, †Painting, †Photography, †Printmaking, †Sculpture, Fibers
Adult Hobby Classes: Courses—various

REHOBOTH BEACH

REHOBOTH ART LEAGUE, INC, 12 Dodds Ln, 19971. Tel 302-227-8408. *Dir* Charles Palmer
Estab 1938; pvt; D; SC 7; enrl D 400, others 400
Ent Req: Interest in art
Courses: Ceramics, Drawing, Graphic Arts, Painting, Printmaking
Adult Hobby Classes: Enrl 150. Courses—Ceramics, Drawing, Painting, Printmaking, Pottery, Weaving
Children's Classes: Courses—Art Forms

DISTRICT OF COLUMBIA

WASHINGTON

AMERICAN UNIVERSITY, Dept of Art, 4400 Massachusetts Ave NW, 20016. Tel 202-885-1670; FAX 202-686-2828. *Chmn Dept* Don Kimes; *Prof* C Stanley Lewis; *Prof* Mary Carrard; *Prof* Norma Broude, PHD; *Assoc Prof* M Hirano; *Assoc Prof* M Oxman; *Assoc Prof* C Ravenal; *Full Prof* T Turak; *Assoc Prof* Ron Haynie; *Asst Prof* Charlotte Story; *Asst Prof* Debora Kahn
Estab 1893, dept estab 1945; pvt; D & E; scholarships; SC 19, LC 14, GC 26; enrl D & E 1520, maj 191, grad 65
Ent Req: HS dipl
Degrees: BA, BFA(Studio Art), BA(Design), BA(Art History) 4 yrs, MA(Art History) 18 months, MFA(Painting, Sculpture, Printmaking) 2 yrs
Tuition: $4467 per sem
Courses: †Art History, Drawing, †Graphic Design, †Painting, †Printmaking, Sculpture
Summer School: Dir, Ben L Summerford. Tuition $299 per cr hr. Courses—Design, Studio & Art History

CATHOLIC UNIVERSITY OF AMERICA
—School of Architecture & Planning, 20064. Tel 202-319-5188. *Dean* Stanley I Hallet; *Assoc Dean* James O'Hear III, MArchit; *Dir Grad Studies* Joseph Miller, BArchit; *Prof* Seymour Auerbach, MArchit; *Prof* Ernest Forest Wilson, PhD; *Prof* W Dodd Ramberg, BArchit; *Assoc Prof* Julius S Levine, MCP; *Prof* George T Marcou, MArchit; *Assoc Prof* Theodore Naos, MArchit; *Assoc Prof* Thomas Walton; *Assoc Prof* John V Yanik; *Vis Asst Prof* Ann Cederna; *Vis Asst Prof* Neal Payton; *Asst Prof* J Ronald Kabriel, MArchit; *Asst Prof* Richard Loosle
Estab 1887, dept estab 1930; den; D & E; SC 6, LC 4 per sem, GC 15 per sem; enrl D 240, maj 240, grad 95
Ent Req: HS dipl and SAT for undergrad, BS or BA in Archit or equivalent plus GPA of 2.5 in undergrad studies for grad
Degrees: BS(Archit) 4 yrs, BArchit 1 yr, MArchit 2 yrs, MArchit 1 yr
Tuition: Undergrad $6332 per sem, PT $480 per cr hr; campus res—room $1525 - $2013 per sem, board $569 - $1300 per sem
Courses: Architecture, Drafting, Landscape Architecture, Photography, Graphics, History and Theory of Architecture, Urban Design, Planning, Technology, Practice
Children's Classes: Session of 3 wks. Courses—High School Program
Summer School: Dir, Richard Loosle. Enrl 100, term of 5-9 wks May-Aug. Courses—Design Studio, Graphics, Computers, History & Theory of Architecture, Photography, Structures, Environmental Systems, Construction & Documents
—Dept of Art, 20064. Tel 202-319-5282. *Chmn Dept* John Winslow; *Assoc Prof* Thomas Rooney; *Assoc Prof* Thomas Nakashima; *Asst Prof* Robert Ross
Estab 1930; den; D & E; scholarships; SC 17, LC 9, GC 20; enrl D 48, maj 38, grad 10
Ent Req: HS dipl and SAT for undergrad, BA-BFA; MAT, GRE for grad
Degrees: MFA(Painting) 2 yrs
Tuition: FT $6278 per sem; PT $480 per cr hr
Courses: †Art History, †Ceramics, †Painting, †Printmaking, †Sculpture
Summer School: Chmn, Jack R Leibowitz. Term of 8 wks beginning June. Courses—Drawing, Jewelry, Painting, Special Independent Courses, Ceramics, Sculpture

CORCORAN SCHOOL OF ART, 500 17th St NW, 20006-4899. Tel 202-628-9484; FAX 202-628-3186. *Dean* Samuel Hoi; *Assoc Dean of Faculty* Rona Slade, BA; *Chmn Fine Arts* Tom Green, MFA; *Chmn Academic Studies* Beth Joselow; *Chmn Ceramics* Robert Epstein, MFA; *Chmn Printmaking* Dennis O'Neil, MFA; *Chmn Sculpture* Berthold Schmutzhart; *Chmn Photography* Claudia Smigrod, MA; *Chmn Graphic Design* Johan Severtson, BFA
Estab 1890; pvt; D & E; scholarships; SC 84, LC 42; enrl D 300 maj, E 750 non-maj
Ent Req: HS dipl, SAT or ACT, portfolio and interview
Degrees: BFA 4 yrs
Tuition: $9980 per yr, $425 per 3 cr hr course; campus—res dorm $2700 per yr
Courses: Advertising Design, Art History, Aesthetics, Calligraphy, Ceramics, Commercial Art, Design, Drawing, †Graphic Design, Illustration, Mixed Media, Painting, †Photography, Printmaking, Sculpture, Textile Design, Airbrush, Animation, Business & Law for the Artist, Computer Art, †Fine Arts, Furniture, History of Photography, Philosophy, Typography, Watercolor
Adult Hobby Classes: Enrl 750 per sem; tuition $360 - $910 for 15 wks. Courses—Art History, Ceramics, Color & Design, Computer Graphics, Drawing, Furniture, Interior Design, Landscape Design, Painting, Photography, Printmaking, Sculpture
Children's Classes: Enrl 70, tuition $100 per 5 wk session, Saturday ages 6 - 10; $310 - $345 per 13 wk session, Saturday ages 10 -15. Courses—General Studio ages 15 - 18. Courses—Ceramics, Computer Art, Drawing, Painting, Photography, Portfolio Prep Workshop, Screenprinting
Summer School: Dean, Samuel Hoi. Enrl 400; Adult—tuition $310 - $860 for 6 wks beginning June. Courses—Art History, Ceramics, Computer Graphics, Drawing, Illustration, Interior Design, Landscape Design, Painting, Photography, Printmaking, Sculpture, Watercolor. HS (ages 15 - 18)—tuition $225 - $450 for 5 wks beginning June. Courses—Ceramics, Drawing, Painting, Photography, Portfolio Prep, Pre-College. Children's Workshops (ages 6 -10)—tuition $100 for 5 day session beginning June

GEORGETOWN UNIVERSITY, Dept of Fine Arts, 20057. Tel 202-625-4085. *Prof* Clifford Chieffo; *Prof* Donn Murphy, PhD; *Instr* Peter Charles, MFA; *Instr* Alison Hilton, PhD; *Instr* B G Muhn, MFA; *Instr* Carra Ferguson, PhD; *Instr* Cynthia Schneider, PhD; *Instr* Elizabeth Prelinger, PhD; *Instr* John Morrell, MFA; *Instr* Paul McCarren
Estab 1789, dept estab 1967; pvt; D; SC 8, LC 6; enrl D 600 (includes non-maj), maj 12 per yr
Ent Req: HS dipl
Degrees: BA 4 yrs
Tuition: campus res available
Courses: †Art History, †Drawing, Graphic Arts, †Painting, †Printmaking, †Sculpture, Theatre Arts, Music History
Adult Hobby Classes: Continuing Education Dir, Phyllis O'Callaghan
Summer School: Dir, Michael Collins. Courses offered

GEORGE WASHINGTON UNIVERSITY, Dept of Art, Smith Hall of Art, 20052. Tel 202-994-6085; FAX 202-994-0458. *Chmn* Lilien Robinson; *Prof* Douglas H Teller, MFA; *Prof* J Franklin Wright Jr, MFA; *Prof* Arthur Hall-Smith, MFA; *Prof* Constance C Costigan, MFA; *Prof* Jerry L Lake, MFA; *Prof* Turker Ozdogan, MFA; *Assoc Prof* H I Gates, MFA; *Assoc Prof* Barbara Von Barghahn, PhD; *Assoc Prof* Jeffrey C Anderson, PhD; *Assoc Prof* D Michael Hitchcock, PhD; *Assoc Prof* W T Woodward, MFA; *Assoc Prof* Samuel B Molina, MFA; *Assoc Prof* Jeffrey L Stephanic, MFA; *Assoc Prof* Kim Hartswick, PhD; *Asst Prof* Fuller O Griffith, MFA; *Asst Prof* David Bjelajac,PhD
Estab 1821, dept estab 1893; pvt; D & E; scholarships; SC 103, LC 74, GC 68; enrl D 1350, GS 196
Ent Req: HS dipl, ent exam
Degrees: BA 4 yr, MA 2-2 1/2 yr, MFA 2 yr, PhD 4 yr
Tuition: Res—$13,560 per yr; campus res—room & board $4200- $5800
Courses: †Art History, †Ceramics, †Drawing, †Design, †Graphic Arts, †Painting, †Photography, †Sculpture, †American Art, †Classical Art & Archaeology, †Contemporary Art, †Medieval Art, †Renaissance & Baroque Art, †Visual Communications
Summer School: Chmn, Melvin P Lader. Enrl 150; tuition $403 per cr hr for two 6 wk sessions. Courses— Art History, Ceramics, Drawing, Painting, Photography, Sculpture, Visual Communications

MOUNT VERNON COLLEGE, Art Dept, 2100 Foxhall Rd NW, 20007. Tel 202-625-4541. *Dept Chmn* Jim Hull
Estab 1875; pvt; D & E; scholarships; SC 16
Degrees: AA and BA
Tuition: $7992
Courses: Interior Design, Teacher Training, Theatre Arts, Video, Arts & Humanities, Historical Perspective, Interior Design, Studio Art
Adult Hobby Classes: Interior Design, Studio Art
Summer School: Enrl 20; 8 weeks, June - July

TRINITY COLLEGE, Art Dept, 20017. Tel 202-939-5178. *Head Dept* Dr Yvonne Dixon; *Asst Prof* Dr Rebecca Easby; *Adjunct Prof* Gordon Kray; *Adjunct Prof* Gene Markowski; *Lectr* Sara Stout; *Lectr* Ann Betts Burton; *Lectr* Kenneth Conley; *lectr* Constance Vieiva da Cunha
Estab 1897; den; D & E; scholarships; SC 8, LC 2-3; enrl D 120, maj 34
Ent Req: HS dipl, SAT or ACT, recommendation
Degrees: BA & BFA 4 yrs
Tuition: $11,080 per yr, $363 per cr hr; campus res—room & board $17,510
Courses: Art History, Design, Drawing, Film, Graphic Design, History of Art & Archaeology, Lettering, Painting, Photography, Printmaking, Sculpture, Theatre Arts, Documentary Photography, Photojournalism, Techniques of Etching, Serigraphy, Typography
Summer School: Dir, Ellie Fedor-Alford. Courses—Vary

UNIVERSITY OF THE DISTRICT OF COLUMBIA, Art Dept, 4200 Connecticut Ave NW, MB-10-01, 20008. Tel 202-727-2662. *Chairperson* Charles A Young; *Prof* Meredith Rode, MFA; *Prof* Manon Cleary, MFA; *Prof* David Lanier, MFA; *Prof* Charles A Young, MA; *Prof* Yvonne Carter, MFA; *Asst Prof* Walter Lattimore, BFA; *Asst Prof* George Smith, MS; *Asst Prof* Rufus Wells, BFA
Estab 1969, dept estab 1969; pub; D & E; SC 65, LC 21; enrl D 616, E 99, non-maj 405, maj 112
Ent Req: HS dipl, GED
Degrees: AA(Advertising Design) 2 yrs, BA(Studio Art) and BA(Art Educ) 4 yrs
Tuition: Res—undergrad $300 per sem; non-res—undergrad $1200 per sem; no campus res
Courses: †Advertising Design, †Art Education, Art History, Ceramics, Conceptual Art, Drawing, Graphic Arts, Graphic Design, Handicrafts, Illustration, Lettering, Mixed Media, Museum Staff Training, †Painting, Photography, †Printmaking, Sculpture
Summer School: Chmn Art Dept, C A Young. Enrl 200. Courses—Art History, Ceramics, Drawings, Painting, Photography

FLORIDA

BELLEAIR

FLORIDA GULF COAST ART CENTER, INC, 222 Ponce de Leon Blvd, 34616. Tel 813-584-8634; FAX 813-586-0782. *Exec Dir* Open ; *Ed Coordr* Barbara Hill
Estab 1949; pvt; D & E; enrl D 315
Ent Req: None
Degrees: None
Courses: Art History, Ceramics, Drawing, Painting, Photography, Sculpture, Metalsmithing
Children's Classes: After school & summer programs

BOCA RATON

COLLEGE OF BOCA RATON, Art & Design Dept, 3601 N Military Trail, 33431. Tel 407-994-0770, Ext 101. *Instr* Ernest Ranspach, MFA; *Instr* Joan Savage-Hutchinson
Scholarships offered
Degrees: AA
Tuition: $6350 per yr
Courses: Advertising Design, Art Appreciation, Art History, Design, Drafting, Drawing, Fashion Arts, Interior Design, Painting, Photography, Stage Design, Textile Design, Corporate Identity Rendering Techniques, Environmental Design, Graphics, Portfolio & Exhibition

FLORIDA ATLANTIC UNIVERSITY, Art Dept, 33431. Tel 407-367-3870. *Chmn* Dr Kathleen Russo. Instrs: FT 8
Estab 1964; pub; D & E; scholarships; SC 25, LC 8, GC 6; enrl D 1600, maj 220, grad 7, special students 7
Degrees: BFA & BA 4 yrs
Tuition: Res—$57.77 per cr hr; nonres—$216.42 per cr hr; grad res—$108.18 per cr hr; nonres—$361.20 per cr hr
Courses: Art History, Ceramics, Drawing, Graphic Design, Jewelry, Painting, Photography, Sculpture, Applied Art, History of Architecture, Silkscreen & Etching, Studio Crafts, Weaving
Adult Hobby Classes: Courses offered through continuing education
Summer School: Courses offered

BRADENTON

MANATEE COMMUNITY COLLEGE, Dept of Art & Humanities, PO Box 1849, 34206. Tel 813-755-1511, Ext 4251. *Chmn* Cortez Francis, MA; *Prof* Edward Camp, MFA; *Prof* James McMahon, MFA; *Prof* Priscilla Stewart, MA; *Prof* Joe Loccisano. Instrs: FT 5, PT 4
Estab 1958; pub; D & E; scholarships; SC 22, LC 5; enrl D 310, E 90, maj 75
Ent Req: HS dipl, SAT
Degrees: AA & AS 2 yrs
Tuition: Res—undergrad $24 per cr hr; nonres—undergrad $52 per cr hr
Courses: Art History, Ceramics, Drawing, Graphic Design, Interior Design, Painting, Photography, Printmaking, Sculpture, Art Appreciation, 2-D & 3-D Design, Color Fundamentals, Figure Drawing
Adult Hobby Classes: Enrl 200; average tuition $30 per class. Courses—Ceramics, Drawing, Oil Painting, Photography, Watercolor
Summer School: Pres, Cortez Francis. Enrl 100; tuition $20.50 per cr hr for term of 6 wks. Courses—Art Appreciation, Ceramics, Photography, Intro Art Studio

CORAL GABLES

UNIVERSITY OF MIAMI, Dept of Art & Art History, PO Box 248106, 33124. Tel 305-284-2542; FAX 305-284-4686. *Chmn* Darby Bannard; *Prof* Christine Federighi, MFA; *Prof* Ken Uyemura, MS; *Prof* Bill Ward, MFA; *Prof* Gerald G Winter, MFA; *Assoc Prof* Paula Harper, PhD; *Assoc Prof* Edward Ghannam, MFA; *Assoc Prof* Peter Zorn, MFA; *Assoc Prof* Ron Fondaw; *Asst Prof* William Betsch, PhD; *Asst Prof* Brian Curtis, MFA; *Asst Prof* Perri Lee Roberts, PhD
Estab 1925, dept estab 1960; pvt; D; scholarships; SC 81, LC 15, GC 25; enrl D 975, non-maj 800, maj 140, grad 20
Ent Req: HS dipl, SAT
Degrees: BA and BFA 4 yrs, MA (Art History) & MFA 4 yrs
Tuition: Res & nonres—undergrad $8740 per yr, $4370 per sem, $285 per cr hr
Courses: †Art History, †Ceramics, †Graphic Arts, Illustration, †Painting, †Photography, †Printmaking, †Sculpture, †Weaving
Summer School: Dir, Dr Marcilene K Wittmer. Enrl 75; tuition $232 per cr hr for 2 six wk sessions. Courses—Airbrush, Art History, Photography, Silkscreen

DANIA

SOUTH FLORIDA ART INSTITUTE OF HOLLYWOOD, 35 SW First Ave, 33004. Tel 305-920-2961. *Dir* Elwin Porter
Estab 1958; pvt; D & E; scholarships; SC 30, LC 2, GC 2; enrl D 230, E 20
Ent Req: Portfolio
Degrees: Cert fine arts and cert graphic art 2 and 4 yrs
Tuition: $1180 per yr, $640 per sem; no campus res
Courses: Design, Drawing, Graphic Design, Painting, Sculpture, Abstraction, Anatomy, Clay Modeling, Color Theory, Composition, Life Sketching
Adult Hobby Classes: Enrl 100. Courses—Fine Arts, Graphic Design
Children's Classes: Enrl 30; tuition $45 per 8 wks. Courses—Painting, Drawing, Sculpture
Summer School: Dir, Elwin Porter. Courses—Most of above

DAYTONA BEACH

DAYTONA BEACH COMMUNITY COLLEGE, Dept of Fine Arts & Visual Arts, 1200 Volusia Ave, PO Box 2811, 32115-2811. Tel 904-255-8131, 362-3011. *Dean* Norman Wills, PhD; *Prog Mgr* Stephen Marsh, MA; *Prof* Denis Deegan, MFA; *Prof* Pamela Griesinger, MFA; *Prof* Allan Maxwell, MFA; *Prof* Gary Monroe, MFA; *Prof* Don Brueing, MBA; *Prof* Eric Breitenbach, MS; *Prof* Patrick Van Dueben, BS; *Prof* Dan Biferie, MFA; *Prof* Bobbie Clementi; *Prof* Jacques A Dellavalle; *Prof* John Wilton;
Estab 1958; pub; D & E; scholarships; SC 15, LC 3; enrl D 250, E 50, maj 30
Ent Req: HS dipl or GED
Degrees: 2 year program offered
Tuition: Res—$25.35 per sem hr; nonres—$52.50 per sem hr
Courses: Ceramics, Design, Drawing, Painting, Printmaking, Sculpture, Cinematography, Papermaking
Summer School: Courses offered

DE LAND

STETSON UNIVERSITY, Art Dept, 32720. Tel 904-822-7260. *Head Dept*
Roberta Favis. Instrs: FT 3
Estab 1880; den; scholarships; SC 5, LC 5; enrl 200
Ent Req: Col boards
Degrees: 4 yr
Courses: Art Education, Ceramics, Drawing, Drawing, Graphic Arts, Painting,
Sculpture
Summer School: Dir, Roberta Favis

DUNEDIN

DUNEDIN FINE ARTS AND CULTURAL CENTER, 1143 Michigan Blvd,
34698. Tel 813-738-1892; FAX 813-738-1871. *Dir* Nancy McIntire; *Instr* Chris Still;
Instr Kitty Johnson; *Instr* Susan Huskey; *Instr* Mary Lowe; *Instr* Brooke Allison;
Instr Ira Burhans
Estab 1975; pub; D & E and weekends; scholarships; SC 20-25, LC 5-10; enrl
approx 900
Tuition: Members $38-$75 per class; nonmembers $48-$85 per class; no campus res
Courses: Art History, Ceramics, Collages, Drawing, Handicrafts, Painting,
Photography, Printmaking, Sculpture, Textile Design, Theatre Arts, Arts for the
Handicapped, Batik, Children's Art, Etching, Exhibits for Emerging & Mid Career
Florida Artists, Fine Crafts, Papermaking, Performing Arts, Watercolor Pastel
Pottery, Weaving, Workshops Art Education
Children's Classes: Tuition $25-$35 per quarter. Courses—Fine Arts, Drama
Summer School: Dir, Carla Crook. Enrl approx 250; tuition $15-$45 for two 5 wk
sessions beginning June. Courses—Visual Arts

FORT LAUDERDALE

ART INSTITUTE OF FORT LAUDERDALE, 1799 SE 17th St, 33316. Tel 305-
527-1799; WATS 800-327-7603. *Pres* David P Higley; *Dir Admissions* Eileen
Northrop; *Dir Educ* Frank Raia, MA; *Dir Advertising Design & Fashion Illustration*
Mary Good; *Dir Photography* Sterling Clarke; *Dir Interior Design* Bill Kobrynich,
AA; *Dir Fashion Illustration* John Miele; *Asst Chmn Advertising Design* Jim
Radford; *Dir Music & Video Business* John Mann; *Dir Fashion Design* Susan
Phillips; *Dir Photography* M Gilizee
Estab 1968; pvt; D & E; scholarships; enrl D 1900, maj 1900
Ent Req: HS dipl
Degrees: AS(technology)
Tuition: Res—undergrad $2395 per quarter
Courses: Advertising Design, Art History, Conceptual Art, Display, Drafting,
Drawing, †Fashion Arts, Graphic Arts, Graphic Design, Illustration, †Interior
Design, Lettering, Mixed Media, Painting, †Photography, Video, Fashion Design
Summer School: Same as regular semester

FORT MYERS

EDISON COMMUNITY COLLEGE, Dept of Fine and Performing Arts, 8099
College Pkwy, 33907. Tel 813-489-9300. *Head Dept Fine & Performing Arts* Dr
James Peterson; *Instr of Art* Robert York; *Music Instr* Dr Dennis Hill; *Music Instr*
Dr Glenn Cornish; *Music Instr* Dr T Defoor; *Theatre Arts Instr* Richard Westlake.
Instrs: FT 1, PT 5
Estab 1962; pub; D & E; scholarships
Ent Req: HS dipl
Degrees: AA & AS 2 yrs
Tuition: Res—$19 per cr hr; nonres—$34 per cr hr
Courses: Art History, Ceramics, Commercial Art, Design, Drawing, Jewelry,
Painting, Photography, Printmaking, Sculpture, Design
Adult Hobby Classes: Enrl 20. Courses—any non-cr activity of interest for which a
teacher is available

FORT PIERCE

INDIAN RIVER COMMUNITY COLLEGE, Fine Arts Dept, Virginia Ave,
33450. Tel 407-478-1388, 468-4769. *Chmn Fine Arts* Anthony Allo; *Dean of Arts &
Sciences* Dr Charles R Lunceford; *Dir* Open ; *Div Dir of Art & Science* Ray C
Lunceford, EDDS; *Asst Prof* Jack Biedenham, MA
Estab 1960; pub; D & E; scholarships; SC 10, LC 10
Ent Req: HS dipl
Degrees: AA & AS 2 yrs
Tuition: Res—$22 per unit; nonres—$44 per unit
Courses: Advertising Design, Art Education, Art History, Ceramics, Display,
Drafting, Drawing, Graphic Arts, Painting, Printmaking, Sculpture, General Art,
Landscape, Portrait
Summer School: Dir, Jane Howard. Enrl 80. Courses—Gifted students in the arts

GAINESVILLE

UNIVERSITY OF FLORIDA, Dept of Art, 302, FAC Complex, 32611. Tel 904-
392-0211; FAX 904-392-8453. *Chmn* John E Catterall; *Prof* Kenneth A Kerslake,
MFA; *Prof* Jack C Nicholson, MFA; *Prof* Robert C Skelley, MFA; *Prof* Roy
Craven; *Prof* Joseph Sabatella; *Prof* John A O'Connor, MFA; *Prof* Evon Streetman,
MFA; *Prof* John L Ward, MFA; *Prof* Wallace Wilson, MFA; *Assoc Prof* Barbara
Barletta, PhD; *Assoc Prof* Jerry Cutler, MFA; *Assoc Prof* Richard Heipp, MFA;
Assoc Prof Marcia Isaacson, MFA; *Assoc Prof* David Kremgold, MFA; *Assoc Prof*
Robin Poynor, PhD; *Assoc Prof* John Scott, PhD; *Assoc Prof* Nan Smith, MFA;
Assoc Prof David Stanley, PhD; *Assoc Prof* Ray Ferguson; *Assoc Prof* Merle
Flannery; *Assoc Prof* Karen Valdes; *Asst Prof* Jan Schall; *Asst Prof* Sam Losario;
Asst Prof George Lowe; *Asst Prof* Robert Mueller; *Asst Prof* Simon Penny; *Asst
Prof* Craig Roland; *Asst Prof* Brian Slawson; *Asst Prof* Louise Rothman. Instrs: FT
22

Estab 1925; pub; D & E; scholarships; SC 40, LC 26, GC 11; enrl maj 200 upper
div, grad 16
Ent Req: HS dipl, SAT, ACT, TOEFL, SCAT or AA degree (transfers must have
2.0 average) GRE
Degrees: BAA and BFA 4 yrs, MFA 2 yrs
Tuition: Res—undergrad $37.29 per cr hr, grad $64.58 per cr hr; nonres—undergrad
$124.44 per cr hr, grad $189.53 per cr hr; campus res—$800 per yr with air
conditioning
Courses: †Art Education, †Art History, †Ceramics, †Drawing, †Graphic Design,
Lettering, †Painting, †Photography, †Printmaking, †Sculpture, Typography
Summer School: Limited classes

JACKSONVILLE

FLORIDA COMMUNITY COLLEGE AT JACKSONVILLE, SOUTH CAMPUS,
Art Dept, 11901 Beach Blvd, 32216. Tel 904-646-2023; FAX 904-646-2209. *Dir
Fine Arts* Larry Davis; *Prof* Eleanor Allen; *Prof* Mary Joan Hinson; *Prof* Derby
Ulloa; *Prof* Ron Wetherell. Instrs: FT 5
Estab 1966; pub; D & E; scholarships; SC 14, LC 6; enrl D 150, E 75
Ent Req: HS dipl
Degrees: AA & AS 2 yrs
Tuition: Res—$18 per cr hr; nonres—$26 per cr hr; no campus res
Courses: Ceramics, Drawing, Graphic Design, Handicrafts, History of Art &
Archaeology, Painting, Photography, Sculpture, Batik, Blockprinting, Computer
Graphics, Glaze Techniques, Macrame, Serigraphy, Weaving
Adult Hobby Classes: Enrl 75-80; for term of 6 wks beginning June. Courses—Art
Appreciation, Crafts, Drawing, Painting, Photography
Summer School: Courses—Ceramics, Design, Drawing, Painting, Printmaking,
Sculpture

JACKSONVILLE UNIVERSITY, Dept of Art, College of Fine Arts, 2800
University Blvd N, 32211. Tel 904-744-3950. *Dean* Dr Thomas G Owen; *Chmn Div*
Betty Swenson; *Art Chair* Dr S Barre Barrett
Estab 1932; pvt; D & E; scholarships; SC 47, LC 13; enrl D 403, maj 80
Ent Req: HS dipl, ent exam
Degrees: BFA, BA, BS & BAEd, 4 yr; MAT
Tuition: $3780 per sem
Courses: †Art Education, †Art History, Ceramics, Drawing, Painting, Photography,
Sculpture, †Computer Art & Design, †Studio Art, †Visual Communication, Hotglass
Adult Hobby Classes: Enrl 10. Courses vary
Children's Classes: Courses offered June-July
Summer School: Tuition $180 per sem hr. Courses—Basic Art

UNIVERSITY OF NORTH FLORIDA, Dept of Communications & Visual Arts,
4567 St Johns Bluff Rd S, 32216. Tel 904-646-2650. *Chmn* Kenneth L McMillian,
MFA; *Prof* Louise Freshman Brown, MFA; *Assoc Prof* Dr Shirley S Carter; *Assoc
Prof* David S Porter, MFA; *Assoc Prof* Robert L Cocaougher, MFA; *Assoc Prof*
Charles Charles MA; *Assoc Prof* Paul Ladnier, MFA; *Asst Prof* Debra E Murphy
Estab 1970; pub; D & E; enrl maj 385
Ent Req: AA
Degrees: BA 2 yr, BFA
Tuition: Res—undergrad $16.50 per sem hr, grad $22 per qtr hr; nonres—undergrad
$51.50 per qtr hr, grad $62 per qtr hr
Courses: Advertising Design, Aesthetics, Art Appreciation, †Art History,
Calligraphy, Ceramics, †Commercial Art, Conceptual Art, Design, †Drawing,
Aesthetics, Computer Images, TV Broadcasting
Summer School: Various courses offered on demand

KEY WEST

FLORIDA KEYS COMMUNITY COLLEGE, Art Dept, 33040. Tel 305-296-9081.
Chmn Fine Arts Div Malcolm C Ross
Scholarships offered
Degrees: AA, AS
Tuition: Res—$23 per cr hr; nonres—$46 per cr hr
Courses: Art Appreciation, Art Education, Art History, Calligraphy, Ceramics,
Design, Drawing, Handicrafts, Painting, Photography, Printmaking, Sculpture, Stage
Design, Jewelry Making
Adult Hobby Classes: Enrl 150; Sept - Apr. Courses - Varied

LAKE CITY

LAKE CITY COMMUNITY COLLEGE, Art Dept, 32055. Tel 904-752-1822, Ext
256. Instrs: FT 1, PT 2
Estab 1962; pub; D & E; SC 9, LC 2; enrl D 160, maj 10
Ent Req: HS dipl
Degrees: AA 2 yrs
Courses: Ceramics, Drawing, Handicrafts, Jewelry, Painting, Sculpture, Composition,
Weaving

LAKELAND

FLORIDA SOUTHERN COLLEGE, Art Dept, 33801. Tel 813-680-4224. *Chmn
Dept* Downing Barnitz, MFA; *Asst Prof* Gale L Doak, MA; *Asst Prof* Allyson
Sheckler, PhD; *Asst Prof* Beth M Ford, MA
Estab 1885; den; D; scholarships; SC 20, LC 6, maj 34
Ent Req: HS dipl
Degrees: AB & BS 128 hr
Courses: †Art Education, Art History, Ceramics, Drawing, Graphic Arts,
Handicrafts, Lettering, Painting, Photography, Sculpture, Teacher Training, Theatre
Arts, Advertising Design, Ancient & Medieval Art, †Art Communication, Design
(19th & 20th century art), Graphic Illustration, Renaissance & Baroque Art, †Studio
Art, Watercolor
Adult Hobby Classes: Courses—Graphics, Oil Painting
Summer School: Dean, Dr Ben F Wade. Tuition $126 per hr, two terms of 4 wks
beginning June and July. Courses—Art Humanities, Drawing, Painting

LAKE WORTH

PALM BEACH COMMUNITY COLLEGE, Dept of Art, 4200 S Congress Ave, 33461. Tel 407-439-8000; Cable FLASUNCOM. *Chmn* Richard Holcomb
Estab 1935; pub; D & E; scholarships; SC 20, LC 5; enrl D 15,000 maj 400
Ent Req: HS dipl or over 25
Degrees: AA and AS 2 yr
Tuition: $24.50 per cr hr
Courses: Advertising Design, Ceramics, Commercial Art, Drawing, Film, †Graphic Design, †Handicrafts, History of Art & Archaeology, Illustration, Intermedia, Interior Design, Jewelry, Lettering, Printmaking, †Architectural Drawing, †Basic Design, Enameling, †Etching, †Lithography, †Screen Printing, †Technical Photo Courses, †Typography
Adult Hobby Classes: Courses—Floral Design, Jewelry, Picture Frame Making, Weaving, Photography, Painting, Printmaking
Summer School: Dir, Richard Holcomb. Ernl 300; tuition $24.50 per cr hr.
Courses—Art Appreciation, Design, Drawing, History of Art, Photography

MADISON

NORTH FLORIDA JUNIOR COLLEGE, Dept Humanities & Art, 100 Turner Davis Dr, 32340. Tel 904-973-2288. *Chmn* William F Gardner Jr
Scholarships
Degrees: AA
Tuition: Res—$25.75 per sem hr; nonres—$100 per sem hr
Courses: Art History, Ceramics, Design, Drawing, Painting, Sculpture

MARIANNA

CHIPOLA JUNIOR COLLEGE, Division of Fine Arts and Humanities, College St, 32446. Tel 904-526-2761, Ext 225. *Chmn Fine Arts Division* Sara Clemmons
Estab 1947; pub; D & E; scholarships; SC 14, LC 2; enrl D 60
Ent Req: HS dipl
Degrees: AA 2 yr
Tuition: Res—$18 per sem hr; nonres—$39 per sem hr
Courses: Art History, Ceramics, Drawing, Painting, Sculpture, Stage Design, Theatre Arts, 2-D & 3-D Design
Summer School: Dir, Dr Donald A Dellow. Enrl 300; tuition res—$18 per sem hr, nonres—$39 per sem hr. Courses—varied

MIAMI

FLORIDA INTERNATIONAL UNIVERSITY, Visual Arts Dept, University Park Campus Bldg DM-382, 33199. Tel 305-348-2897. *Chmn* Clive King; *Prof* William Maguire; *Prof* James M Couper; *Prof* Ellen Jacobs; *Assoc Prof* Richard Duncan; *Assoc Prof* William J Burke; *Assoc Prof* R F Buckley; *Assoc Prof* Manuel Torres; *Assoc Prof* Ed del Valle; *Assoc Prof* Mirta Gomez; *Assoc Prof* Sandra Winters; *Asst Prof* Barbara Watts; *Gallery Dir & Lecturer* Dahlia Morgan; *Instr & Art Historian* Juan Martinez; *Instr & Art Historian* Carol Damiam
Estab 1972, dept estab 1972; pub; D & E; scholarships; SC 20, LC 12, GC 18; enrl D 320, E 100, non-maj 225, maj 175, grad 20
Ent Req: 1000 on SAT, 3.0 HS grade point average
Degrees: BFA
Tuition: Res—undergrad $1400 per yr; nonres—undergrad $4700 per yr
Courses: Art History, Ceramics, Drawing, Jewelry, Painting, Photography, Printmaking, Sculpture, Glass Blowing
Summer School: Dir, Clive King. Enrl 160; tuition $55 per sem hr for term of 6.5 wks beginning May 13 & June 28

INTERNATIONAL FINE ARTS COLLEGE, 1737 N Bayshore Dr, 33132. Tel 305-373-4684. *Dir* Jenny Smith; *Pres College* Edward Porter; *Dean* Danial M Stack
Estab 1965, dept estab 1966; pvt; D; SC 6; enrl D 180, maj 110
Ent Req: HS dipl
Degrees: AA
Tuition: $6585
Courses: Art History, Costume Design & Construction, Display, Drawing, Fashion Arts, History of Art & Archaeology, Illustration, Interior Design, Painting

MIAMI-DADE COMMUNITY COLLEGE, Visual Arts Dept, 11011 SW 104 St, 33176. Tel 305-237-2281. *Chmn Dept Kendall Campus* Robert Huff
Estab 1960, dept estab 1967; pub; D & E; scholarships; SC 14, LC 4; enrl E 300, non-maj 150, maj 150
Ent Req: Open door
Degrees: AA and AS 2 yr
Tuition: Res—$30.65 per cr; nonres—$109.15 per cr
Courses: Ceramics, Commercial Art, Design, Drawing, Jewelry, Painting, Photography, Printmaking, Sculpture, Metals
Adult Hobby Classes: Courses by demand
Summer School: Dir, Robert Huff. Courses vary

MIAMI SHORES

BARRY UNIVERSITY, Dept of Fine Arts, 11300 NE Second Ave, 33161. Tel 305-899-3426. *Chmn Fine Arts Dept* Derna Ford; *Dean* Dr Shirley Paolini. Instrs: FT 4
Estab 1940; pvt; D & E; scholarships; SC 33, LC 12; enrl D 300, E 60, maj 30
Ent Req: HS dipl, portfolio for BFA
Degrees: BA, BFA, BFA(Educ) 4 yrs
Tuition: $3545 per sem
Courses: Advertising Design, Art Appreciation, Art Education, Art History, Ceramics, Collages, Commercial Art, History of Art & Archaeology, Mixed Media, †Photography, Sculpture, Theatre Arts, Video, Costume Design & Construction, Design, Drawing, Graphic Design, Jewelry, Painting, Photography, Stage Design, Teacher Training
Summer School: Dir, Dr Shirley Paolini. Tuition $155 per cr hr for 6 wk terms.
Courses—Drawing, Ceramics, Photography, Watercolor

NICEVILLE

OKALOOSA-WALTON JUNIOR COLLEGE, Dept of Fine and Performing Arts, 100 College Blvd, 32578. Tel 904-678-5111. *Chmn* Cliff Herron; *Instr* Walter B Shipley, MA; *Instr* Arnold Hart; *Instr* David Owens
Estab 1964, dept estab 1964; pub; D & E; scholarships; SC 26, LC 3; enrl D 2000, E 1000, maj 80
Ent Req: HS dipl
Degrees: AA 2 yrs
Tuition: Res—$20 per cr hr; nonres—$40 per cr hr; campus res available
Courses: Architecture, Art History, Ceramics, Costume Design & Construction, Drafting, Drawing, Graphic Arts, Handicrafts, Interior Design, Jewelry, Painting, Photography, Printmaking, Sculpture, Silversmithing, Stage Design, Teacher Training, Theatre Arts, Weaving
Adult Hobby Classes: Enrl 15 per class. Courses—Antiques, Interior Decorating, Painting, Photography, Pottery, Vase Painting, others as needed
Summer School: Dir, Dr James Durham. Term of 6 or 12 wks beginning May 2 and June 18. Courses—same as regular sessions

OCALA

CENTRAL FLORIDA COMMUNITY COLLEGE, Humanities Dept, 3001 SW College Rd, PO Box 1388, 32678. Tel 904-237-2111, Ext 293. *Chmn* Ira Holmes
Estab 1957; pub; D & E; SC 5, LC 1; enrl enrl 3500, non-maj 85, maj 15
Ent Req: HS dipl
Degrees: AA and AS 2 yr
Tuition: Res-$22 per cr hr; nonres-$45 per cr hr
Courses: Art History, Ceramics, Design, Drawing, Painting, Printmaking, Sculpture
Adult Hobby Classes: Ceramics, Drawing, Painting, Commercial Art; Design
Summer School: Two 6 week terms

ORLANDO

UNIVERSITY OF CENTRAL FLORIDA, Art Dept, PO Box 25000, 32816. Tel 407-823-2676. *Acting Chmn* Dr Francis Martin Jr
Scholarships
Degrees: BA, BFA, cert
Tuition: Res—undergrad $40.85 per sem hr; nonres—undergrad $132.82 per sem hr
Courses: Art History, Ceramics, Design, Drawing, Graphic Design, Painting, Photography, Printmaking, Sculpture, Fibers & Fabrics
Summer School: Tuition same as above. Courses—vary

VALENCIA COMMUNITY COLLEGE - WEST CAMPUS, Art Dept, 1800 S Kirkman Rd, PO Box 3028, 32811. Tel 407-299-5000; FAX 407-293-8839. *Chmn* Rosita Martinez
Estab 1967, dept estab 1974; pub; D & E; scholarships; SC 16, LC 5; enrl D 6858
Ent Req: HS dipl
Degrees: AA and AS 2 yrs
Courses: Art History, Ceramics, Design, Drawing, History of Art & Archaeology, Painting, Photography, Printmaking, Sculpture, Visual Arts Today
Summer School: Same as for regular academic yr

PALATKA

FLORIDA SCHOOL OF THE ARTS, Visual Arts, 5001 Saint Johns Ave, 32177-3897. Tel 904-328-1571. *Dean* Gayle Kassing, PhD; *Coordr Fine Art* Gene Roberds, MFA; *Coordr Graphic Design* Phil Parker, BFA; *Dir Galleries* David Ouellette, MFA
Estab 1974, dept estab 1974; pub; D; scholarships; SC 35, LC 10; enrl D 85, maj 85
Ent Req: HS dipl, recommendation, review, interview
Degrees: AA 2 yrs, AS 2 1/2 yrs
Tuition: Res—$29 per hr; nonres—$116 per hr
Courses: Advertising Design, Art History, Commercial Art, Display, Drafting, Drawing, Graphic Arts, †Graphic Design, Illustration, Lettering, Mixed Media, †Painting, Photography, †Printmaking, †Stage Design, †Theatre Arts

PANAMA CITY

GULF COAST COMMUNITY COLLEGE, Division of Fine Arts, 5230 W Hwy 98, 32401. Tel 904-769-1551. *Chmn* Norman J Hair, MM; *Assoc Prof* Sharron Barnes, MA; *Assoc Prof* Roland L Hockett, MS
Estab 1957; pub; D & E; SC 5, LC 2; enrl D 300, E 70, non-maj 330, maj 40
Ent Req: HS dipl
Degrees: AA 2 yrs
Tuition: Res—undergrad $26 per cr hr; nonres—undergrad $105 per cr hr
Courses: Art History, Ceramics, Design, Drawing, Illustration, Lettering, Photography
Adult Hobby Classes: Courses—Macrame, Painting, Weaving

PENSACOLA

PENSACOLA JUNIOR COLLEGE, Dept of Visual Arts, 1000 College Blvd, 32504. Tel 904-484-2550; FAX 905-484-1826. *Head Dept* Allan Peterson. Instrs: FT 9, PT 6
Estab 1948; pub; D & E; scholarships; enrl maj 180
Ent Req: HS dipl
Degrees: AS & AA 2 yrs
Tuition: Res—$30.30 per cr hr; nonres—$129.10 per cr hr; no campus res
Courses: Advertising Design, Art History, Ceramics, Drawing, Graphic Arts, Illustration, Mixed Media, Painting, Photography, Printmaking, Sculpture, †Art Studio, Crafts, Design, Pottery
Adult Hobby Classes: Enrl 600. Courses—Drawing, Painting
Summer School: Dir, Allan Peterson. Enrl 300; tuition $30.30 per cr.
Courses—same as regular session

UNIVERSITY OF WEST FLORIDA, Dept of Art, 11000 University Pkwy, 32514. Tel 904-474-2045; FAX 904-474-3247. *Chmn* Jim Jipson, MFA; *Prof* William A Silhan, EdD; *Assoc Prof* Henry J Heuler, MFA; *Assoc Prof* Robert Marshman, MFA; *Assoc Prof* Duncan E Stewart, MA; *Asst Prof* Deb Davis, MFA; *Asst Prof* Stephen K Haworth, MFA; *Asst Prof* Suzette J Doyon-Bernard, PhD
Estab 1967; pub; D & E; scholarships; SC 20, LC 10; enrl D 600, E 300, non-maj 500, maj 175
Ent Req: AA degree or 60 sem hrs credit
Degrees: BA & BFA 4 yr
Tuition: Res—undergrad $48.76 per sem hr; nonres—undergrad $186.71 per sem hr, grad $86.38 per sem hr; campus res—room $1760 two sem
Courses: Aesthetics, †Art Education, †Art History, Calligraphy, Design, Drawing, †History of Art & Archaeology, †Jewelry, †Lettering, Painting, Photography, Printmaking, Sculpture, Weaving
Summer School: Dir, Jim Jipson. Enrl 400; 2 sessions. Courses—Ceramics, Drawing, Painting, Photography, Printmaking, Sculpture

SAINT AUGUSTINE

FLAGLER COLLEGE, Visual Arts Dept, 74 King St, 32084. Tel 904-829-6481. *Chmn* Robert Hall; *Prof* Enzo Torcoletti,MFA; *Assoc Prof* Don Martin
Estab 1968; pvt; D & E; scholarships; SC 29, LC 7; enrl 1000, maj 100
Ent Req: HS dipl
Degrees: BA 4 yr
Tuition: $4750 for 2 sem
Courses: Advertising Design, Art Education, Art History, †Commercial Art, Drawing, Graphic Design, Illustration, Jewelry, Painting, Photography, Sculpture, Teacher Training, Air Brush, †Visual Arts
Summer School: Academic Affairs, William Abare. Tuition $100 per hr for terms of 7 wks beginning May. Courses—Airbrush, Art, Ceramics, Computer Illustration

SAINT PETERSBURG

ECKERD COLLEGE, Art Dept, PO Box 12560, 4200 54th Ave S, 33711. Tel 813-867-1166; FAX 813-866-2304. *Chmn* Dr Claire Stiles; *Prof* James Crane; *Assoc Prof* Margaret Rigg; *Asst Prof* Arthur Skinner
Scholarships
Degrees: BA
Tuition: $4325 full time per sem
Courses: Art Education, Art History, Calligraphy, Ceramics, Design, Drawing, Painting, Photography, Printmaking
Adult Hobby Classes: Enrl 25. Courses—Ceramics, Drawing, Painting
Summer School: Dir, Cheryl Gold. Enrl 150

SAINT PETERSBURG JUNIOR COLLEGE, Humanities Dept, 6605 Fifth Ave N, PO Box 13489, 33710. Tel 813-341-4360. *Acting Dir* Helen Gilbart
Estab 1927. College has four campuses; pub; D & E; scholarships; SC 13, LC 3; enrl D 7031, E 2478
Ent Req: HS dipl
Degrees: AA and AS 2 yr
Tuition: Res—$22.75 per cr hr; nonres—$44.75 per cr hr; no campus residence
Courses: Advertising Design, Ceramics, Design, Drawing, Painting, Photography, Theatre Arts, Art History Survey, Survey in Crafts
Summer School: Courses—Same as regular session

SARASOTA

FRIENDS OF THE ARTS AND SCIENCES, HILTON LEECH STUDIO, Leech Studio Workshops, PO Box 15766, 34277-1766. Tel 813-924-5770. *Coordr* Jerrine Grim
Estab 1946; dept estab 1963; pvt; SC 16; enrl D 200, E 10
Courses: Drawing, Painting, Photography
Adult Hobby Classes: Enrl 200. Courses—Drawing, Painting, Photography
Summer School: Dir, Katherine L Rowland. Enrl 80. Courses—Photography, Watercolor

NEW COLLEGE OF THE UNIVERSITY OF SOUTH FLORIDA, Fine Arts Dept, Humanities Division, 5700 N Tamiami Trail, 34243. Tel 813-359-4360. *Chmn Humanities Division* Arthur Miller. Instrs: FT 4
Estab 1963; D; SC 6, LC 5; enrl D 150-200, maj 15
Ent Req: Ent exam, SAT
Degrees: BA(Fine Arts) 3 yrs
Tuition: Res—$391 per sem; non-res—$1047 per sem
Courses: †Aesthetics, †Art History, Ceramics, †Drawing, †Painting, †Printmaking, †Sculpture, †Color Theory, Design, Life Drawing, Stained Glass

RINGLING SCHOOL OF ART AND DESIGN, 2700 N Tamiami Trail, 34234. Tel 813-351-4614; FAX 813-359-7517. *Pres* Arland F Christ-Janer; *Dir Admissions* Jim Dean. Instrs: 31
Estab 1931; pvt; scholarships; enrl 430
Ent Req: HS dipl or equivalency, portfolio
Degrees: 3-year certificate, BFA, 4 yrs
Tuition: $4068 per sem; campus res—room & board $2500
Courses: Graphic Design, †Illustration, Photography, Painting, Photography, Sculpture, Computer Graphics, †Fine Arts
Adult Hobby Classes: Enrl 150; tuition $40 per 7 wk session

TALLAHASSEE

FLORIDA A & M UNIVERSITY, Dept of Visual Arts, Humanities & Theatre, 32307. Tel 904-599-3831. *Dir* Ronald O Davis; *Prof* Ronald F Yarbedra; *Prof* Kenneth Falana; *Assoc Prof* Yvonne Tucker; *Asst Prof* Jan DeCosmo
Estab 1887; pub; D & E; scholarships; enrl D 5887, non-maj 5800, maj 87
Ent Req: HS dipl, ent exam

Degrees: BS and BA with Fine Arts Cert; BA with Teacher Cert
Tuition: Res—$25 per sem hr; nonres—$66 per sem hr
Courses: Art Education, Art History, Ceramics, Design, Drawing, Textile Design, Metals, Plastic, Wood
Summer School: Enrl 125; tui same as regular session for term of 9 and 7 wks beginning June. Courses—Ceramics, Design, Drawing, Arts, Textile Design, Wood, Metal & Plastics

FLORIDA STATE UNIVERSITY
—Art Dept, 220 Fine Arts Bldg, 32306. Tel 904-644-6474. *Chairperson Studio Art* Gail Rubini; *Prof* Trevor Bell; *Prof* James Roche, MFA; *Prof* Ed Love, MFA; *Prof* George C Blakely, MFA; *Prof* Robert Fichter, MFA; *Assoc Prof* Ray Burggraf, MFA; *Assoc Prof* George Bocz, MEd; *Assoc Prof* Janice E Hartwell, MFA; *Assoc Prof* Charles E Hook, MFA; *Assoc Prof* Mark Messersmith, MFA; *Asst Prof* Anne Bush; *Asst Prof* Paul Rutkovsky , MFA; *Asst Prof* Susan Cannell, MFA; *Asst Prof* Charles Cohan; *Asst Prof* Terri Lindbloom
Estab 1857, dept estab 1911; pub; D & E; scholarships & fels
Ent Req: HS dipl, C average and upper 40 percent of graduating class, SAT
Degrees: BA, BFA, BS, MFA
Courses: Drawing, Graphic Design, Illustration, Painting, Photography, Printmaking, Sculpture, †Studio Art
Summer School: Term of 13 wks; two terms of six & a half wks
—Art Education Dept, 32306. Tel 904-644-5473. *Chmn* Tom Anderson, PhD; *Prof* Jessie Lovano-Kerr, PhD; *Assoc Prof* Betty J Troeger, PhD; *Asst Prof* June Eyestone, PhD
Estab 1857, dept estab 1948; pub; D & E; scholarships
Ent Req: HS dipl
Degrees: BS, BA, MA, MS, EdD, PhD
Courses: †Art Education, Teacher Training, Arts Administration, Art Therapy, Special Population
Summer School: Studio Art and Art History Emphasis
—Art History Dept (R133B), 220D Fine Arts Bldg, 32306. Tel 904-644-1250. *Chmn* Patricia Rose, PhD; *Dean School Visual Arts* Jerry L Draper, PhD; *Prof* Francois Bucher, PhD; *Assoc Prof* Penelope E Mason, PhD; *Assoc Prof* Robert M Neuman, PhD; *Assoc Prof* Cynthia J Hahn, PhD; *Assoc Prof* Lauren Weingarden, PhD; *Asst Prof* Karen Bearor, PhD; *Asst Prof* Jack Freiberg, PhD
Estab 1857, dept estab 1948; pub; D & E; scholarships
Ent Req: HS dipl
Degrees: BA, MA & PhD (all in art history)
Tuition: Res—undergrad $55 per sem hr, grad $93 per sem hr; nonres—undergrad $197 per sem hr, grad $302 per sem hr
Courses: Art Appreciation, †Art History, History of Art & Archaeology, Arts Administration

TALLAHASSEE COMMUNITY COLLEGE, Art Dept, 444 Appleyard Dr, 32304. Tel 904-422-9200. *Chmn Art Prog* Ruth Dryden Deshaies, MA. Instrs: PT 4
Estab 1966; pub; D & E; scholarships; SC 13, LC 2; enrl D 350 per sem, E 150 per sem
Ent Req: HS dipl
Degrees: AA 2 yrs
Tuition: $16 per sem hr
Courses: Art History, Design, Drawing, Painting, Photography, Color Theory, History & Appreciation of Cinema, Silk Screen, Art Appreciation
Summer School: Chmn Art Program, Ruth Dryden Deshales, MA. Enrl 150; 10 wk term. Courses—Art History, Drawing Techniques, Photo I, Silkscreen

TAMPA

HILLSBOROUGH COMMUNITY COLLEGE, Fine Arts Dept, Ybor Campus, PO Box 5096, 33675-5096. Tel 813-253-7601. *Chmn* James Bull; *Assoc Prof* David Dye; *Assoc Prof* Jerry Meatyard
Scholarships
Degrees: AA
Tuition: Res—$22.50 per cr hr; nonres—$49 per cr hr
Courses: Art Appreciation, Art History, Ceramics, Design, Drawing, Painting, Photography, Printmaking, Sculpture, Weaving

UNIVERSITY OF SOUTH FLORIDA, Art Dept, College of Fine Arts, 4202 Fowler Ave, 33620. Tel 813-974-2360; FAX 813-974-2091. *Chmn* Dr Janet Marquardt-Cherry. Instrs: FT D 26
Estab 1956; pub
Ent Req: HS grad, 14 units cert by HS, ent exam
Degrees: BA(Art) minimum 120 sem hrs, MFA 60 sem hrs, MA(Art History) 40 sem hrs
Tuition: Res—undergrad $29 per cr hr, grad $47 per cr hr; nonres—undergrad $80 per cr hr, grad $137 per cr hr
Courses: Art History, Ceramics, Drawing, Painting, Photography, Sculpture, Printmaking, Cinematography
Adult Hobby Classes: Chmn, Alan Eaker
Summer School: 7 - 14 wks

UNIVERSITY OF TAMPA, Dept of Art, Fine Arts Division, 401 W Kennedy Blvd, 33606. Tel 813-253-3333, Ext 217. *Division Chmn* Lou Harris. Instrs: FT 5
Estab 1930; pvt; D & E; SC 17, LC 8
Degrees: 4 yrs
Tuition: $205 per cr hr
Courses: Art Education, Art History, Ceramics, Drawing, Painting, Photography, Printmaking, Sculpture, Design, Arts Management
Adult Hobby Classes: Enrl 35; tuition $50 per 8 wks. Courses—Jewelry Making, Silver Smithing, Fabric Dyeing
Summer School: Courses offered

TEMPLE TERRACE

FLORIDA COLLEGE, Division of Art, 33617. Tel 813-988-5131. *Faculty* Julia Bryant
Scholarships offered
Degrees: BA
Tuition: $1850 per sem
Courses: Art Appreciation, Art Education, Art History, Design, Drawing, Painting, Photography, Sculpture

WINTER HAVEN

POLK COMMUNITY COLLEGE, Art, Letters & Social Sciences, 999 Ave H NE, 33881. Tel 813-297-1025. *Dir* Hugh B Anderson; *Prof* Gary Baker, MFA; *Prof* Jane Jaskevich, MEd; *Prof* Bob Morrisey, MFA
Estab 1964; pub; D & E; scholarships; SC 10, LC 1; enrl D 175, E 50
Ent Req: HS dipl
Degrees: AA & AS 2 yrs
Tuition: Res—undergrad $34.82 per cr hr; nonres—undergrad $130.46 per cr hr, no campus res
Courses: Advertising Design, Art Appreciation, Ceramics, Design, Drawing, Film, Interior Design, Painting, Photography, Printmaking, Sculpture, Theatre Arts, Watercolor
Adult Hobby Classes: Enrl 60; tuition $1.60 per class hr. Courses—Calligraphy, Ceramics, Christmas Crafts, Drawing, Interior Design, Jewelry, Painting

WINTER PARK

ROLLINS COLLEGE, Dept of Art, Main Campus, 32789. Tel 407-646-2498; FAX 407-646-1500. *Chmn & Prof* Ron Larned
Estab 1885; pvt; D & E; scholarships; SC 11, LC 10; enrl D & E 250
Degrees: 4 yrs
Tuition: Res—$10,881
Courses: Aesthetics, Art History, Drawing, Painting, Sculpture, Art History Survey, Design, Humanities Foundation, Principles of Art
Adult Hobby Classes: Courses—selected studio and history courses
Summer School: Courses—selected art history and appreciation courses

GEORGIA

AMERICUS

GEORGIA SOUTHWESTERN COLLEGE, Dept of Fine Arts, Wheatley St, 31709. Tel 912-928-1357, 928-1555; FAX 912-928-1630. *Chmn* Dr Duke Jackson
Scholarships
Degrees: BA, BSEd, cert
Tuition: Res—$278 per quarter; nonres—$708 per quarter
Courses: Ceramics, Drawing, Graphic Design, Jewelry, Painting, Photography, Printmaking, Sculpture, Textile Design, Glassblowing, Woodworking

ATHENS

UNIVERSITY OF GEORGIA, FRANKLIN COLLEGE OF ARTS & SCIENCES, Dept of Art, Visual Arts Bldg, Jackson St, 30602-4102. Tel 706-542-1511. *Interim Dean* Wyatt Anderson; *Head Dept* Evan R Firestone; *Undergrad Coordr* Andra Johnson; *Grad Coordr* Tom Hammond; *Art Appreciation* William Squires; *Art Education* W Robert Nix; *Art History* Dr Tom Polk; *Ceramics* Andy Nasisse; *Drawing & Painting* Arthur Rosenbaum; *Drawing & Painting* Bill Johansen; *Fabric Design* Glen Kaufman; *Foundation* William Marriott; *Graphic Design* Kenneth Williams; *Interior Design* John Huff; *Jewelry & Metalwork* Gary Noffke; *Photographic Design* Stephen Scheer; *Printmaking* Tom Hammond; *Sculpture* Horace Farlowe
Opened 1801, chartered 1875; scholarships & grad assistantships
Ent Req: HS dipl, SAT
Degrees: BA, BFA, BSEd, MA, MFA, MAE, EdS, EdD, PhD
Tuition: Res—undergrad $692 per quarter, grad $692 per quarter; nonres—undergrad $1840 per quarter, grad $1840 per quarter
Courses: Art Appreciation, Art Education, Art History, Ceramics, Drawing, Graphic Design, Interior Design, Jewelry, Painting, Printmaking, Sculpture, Fabric Design, Foundation, Metalwork, Photographic Design, Scientific Illustration
Summer School: Dept Head, Evan R Firestone

ATLANTA

ART INSTITUTE OF ATLANTA, 3376 Peachtree Rd NE, 30326. Tel 404-266-1341. *Head Visual Communications & Graphic Arts* Ann Critchfield
The Institute has the following departments: Visual Communications, Photography, Interior Design & Fashion Merchandising; scholarships offered
Degrees: AA
Courses: Advertising Design, Commercial Art, Design, Display, Drawing, Graphic Arts, Interior Design, Lettering, Mixed Media, Painting, Photography, Video, Cartooning, Fashion, Photo Design, Portrait

ATLANTA AREA TECHNICAL SCHOOL, Dept of Commercial Art, 1560 Stewart Ave SW, 30310. Tel 404-756-3700; FAX 404-756-0932. *Head Dept* Don M Ballentine
Estab 1967; pub; D; SC 13; enrl D 25, E 25
Ent Req: HS dipl, ent exam
Degrees: AA in conjunction with the Atlanta Metro Col
Tuition: $168 per quarter
Courses: Advertising Design, Commercial Art, Graphic Arts, Photography, Video, Print Production Art

ATLANTA COLLEGE OF ART, 1280 Peachtree St NE, 30309. Tel 404-898-1164; FAX 404-898-9577. *Pres* Ellen Meyer, MFA; *Academic Dean* Mark Salmon, PhD; *Dir of Student Life* Zach Zuehlke, MA; *Visual Studies Chmn* William Nolan, MFA; *Electronic Arts Chmn (computer)* Evelyn Hirata, MFA; *Electronic Arts Chmn (Video)* Scott Vogel, MFA; *Drawing Chmn* Larry Anderson, MFA; *Sculpture Chmn* Scott Gilliam, MFA; *Printmaking Chmn* Norman Wagner, MA; *Acting Communication Design Chmn* Mark Rokfalusi; *Photography Chmn* Elizabeth Turk, MFA; *Painting Chmn* Tom Francis, MFA; *Interior Design Chmn* Allan Hing, MFA; *Prof* Anthony Greco, MFA; *Assoc Prof* Michael Brekke, MFA; *Assoc Prof* Curtis Patterson, MFA; *Assoc Prof* Fred Gregory, MFA; *Assoc Prof* Corrine Colarusso, MFA; *Prof* Marcia R Cohen, MA; *Prof* Martin Emanuel, MFA; *Assoc Prof* Daniel Zins, PhD; *Asst Prof* Harriette Gressom, PhD; *Asst Prof* J Mark Rokfalusi; *Assoc Prof* Robert Stewart; *Instr* Kay Klein Kallos, MA; *Vis Prof* Cynthia Graham, PhD; *Vis Instr* Patti Hastings, BFA
Estab 1928; pvt; D & E; scholarships; SC 168, LC 46; enrl D 422, E 450, non-maj 450, maj 422
Ent Req: HS dipl, ent exam, SAT, portfolio of art work
Degrees: BFA 4 yrs
Tuition: $3542 per 12 cr hr; $4098 per 15 cr hr
Courses: †Advertising Design, †Drawing, †Graphic Design, †Illustration, †Intermedia, †Interior Design, †Sculpture, †Video, Mixed Media, †Painting, †Photography, †Printmaking, †Sculpture, †Video, †Communication Designs, †Computer Arts & Graphics
Adult Hobby Classes: Dir, Rick Fisher. MA. Enrl 400 - 500; tuition $130 per course for 10 wk term
Children's Classes: Enrl 30 - 50; tuition $90 for 10 wk term. High School (15 - 18) - Enrl 40; tuition $110 for 10 wk term
Summer School: Dir, Rick Fisher. Enrl 400; tuition $130 for 2 five wk terms. Children's Classes—Enrl 50; tuition $100 for 5 wks. Courses—Drawing, Painting, Art & Theatre Camp. Summer Visual Studies Program for High School students enrl 30 - 50; tuition $1175 for 3 wk term. BFA Program: Dir Xena Zed. Enrl 95; tuition $775 per course for 7 wk term. Courses—Curriculum Courses

CLARK-ATLANTA UNIVERSITY, School of Arts & Sciences, 240 James P Brawley Dr SW, 30314. Tel 404-880-8730. *Chmn Dept* Christopher Hickey
Estab 1869, dept estab 1964; pvt; D; SC 8, LC 8; enrl D 198, non-maj 240, maj 30
Ent Req: HS dipl
Degrees: BA (Art, Art Educ, Fashion Design) 4 yrs, Honors Program
Tuition: Res—undergrad $6545 yr; nonres—undergrad $4465 yr
Courses: Art Education, Art History, Design, Drawing, Graphic Design, Illustration, Painting, Photography, Printmaking, Sculpture, Fashion Design

EMORY UNIVERSITY, Art History Dept, 30322. Tel 404-727-6282. *Chmn* Dorinda Evans, PhD; *Prof* Clark V Poling, PhD; *Prof* John Howett, PhD; *Assoc Prof* Walter S Melion, PhD; *Assoc Prof* Bonna D Wescoat, PhD; *Asst Prof* Judith Rohrer, PhD; *Asst Prof* Sidney L Kasfir, PhD; *Asst Prof* Rosemary Gay Robins, PhD; *Asst Prof* David H Brown, PhD; *Asst Prof* Rebecca Stone-Miller, PhD; *Asst Prof* Marc J Gotlieb, PhD; *Adjunct Prof* Maxwell L Anderson; *Lectr* Eycke Strickland; *Lectr* Stan Sharshal, MFA; *Lectr* Nancy Marshall, BA; *Lectr* Katherine Mitchell, MFA; *Lectr* Dorothy Fletcher, MA; *Lectr* William A Brown, MFA; *Lectr* Mollie Michala, MFA
Estab 1847; pvt; D; scholarships; SC 4, LC 29, GC 18; enrl non-maj 700, maj 80, grad 30
Ent Req: HS dipl, ent exam, SAT
Degrees: BA(Art History) & PhD(Art History) & Interdisciplinary PhD through Institute of Liberal Arts
Tuition: $15,820 per yr; campus residency available
Courses: †Art History, Ceramics, Drawing, Film, History of Art & Archaeology, Painting, Photography, Sculpture, Video
Summer School: Dir, Clark V Poling. Tuition $1832 per course (4 cr hrs) for 6 wk terms beginning May 19 & June 30. Courses—History of Art, Studio Art, various seminars in Europe (variable) 8 cr hrs

GEORGIA INSTITUTE OF TECHNOLOGY, College of Architecture, 225 North Ave NW, 30332. Tel 404-894-4887. *Dean* Thomas D Galloway, PhD
Estab 1885, dept estab 1908; pub; D; schol; SC 41; enrl D 904, maj 904, grad 165
Ent Req: HS dipl, CEEB
Degrees: BS(Architecture), BS(Industrial Design) and BS(Building Construction) 4 yr, M(Architecture) and MCP 2 yr
Tuition: Res—$726 per quarter; nonres—$2106 per quarter
Courses: Architecture, Industrial Design, Building Construction, City Planning
Summer School: Dir, R Roark. Enrl 100; tuition same. Courses—vary

GEORGIA STATE UNIVERSITY, School of Art & Design, University Plaza, 30303. Tel 404-651-2257; FAX 404-651-2013. *Dir School* Larry Walker. Instrs: FT 28, PT 8
Estab 1914; pub; scholarships; SC 80, LC 16; enrl maj 450, others 300
Ent Req: HS dipl, ent exam, college board, interview
Degrees: BFA, BA(Art) and BA(Art History) 4 yrs, MA(Art History), MAEd (Art Education), MFA (Studio), MFA
Tuition: Res—$36.40 per cr hr; nonres—$124.80 per cr hr
Courses: Art Education, Art History, Ceramics, Drawing, Graphic Design, Illustration, Interior Design, Jewelry, Painting, Photography, Printmaking, Sculpture, Textile Design, Weaving, Metalsmithing
Children's Classes: Enrl 10-15, 8-10 wk term
Summer School: Dir, Larry Walker. Enrl 350-400; tuition $36.40 per cr hr for 6-8 wk term. Courses—Art Education, Art History, Studio

AUGUSTA

AUGUSTA COLLEGE, Dept of Fine Arts, 2500 Walton Way, 30904. Tel 706-737-1453. *Head Dept* John Schaffer; *Asst Prof* Eugenia Comer; *Asst Prof* Janice Williams, MFA; *Asst Prof* James Rosen, MFA; *Asst Prof* Michael Schwartz; *Instr* Brian Rust, MFA; *Scholar in Art* Morris Eminent
Estab 1925, dept estab 1965; pub; D & E; scholarships; SC 46, LC 4, GC 1; enrl D 150, E 30, non-maj 10, maj 140, GS 5
Ent Req: HS dipl, SAT

Degrees: AA, BA & BFA
Tuition: Res—undergrad $247 per quarter, $21 per quarter hr; nonres—undergrad $742 per quarter, $62 per quarter hr; no campus res
Courses: †Ceramics, †Drawing, †Photography, †Mixed Media, †Painting, †Printmaking, †Sculpture
Adult Hobby Classes: Enrl 25; tuition $30-$60 per 10 sessions. Courses—Painting

BARNESVILLE

GORDON COLLEGE, Dept of Fine Arts, 419 College Dr, 30204. Tel 706-358-1700. *Acting Dir* Mary Jean Simmons
Scholarships offered
Degrees: AA
Tuition: Res—$313 per quarter; nonres—$906 per quarter
Courses: Art Appreciation, Ceramics, Design, Drawing, Graphic Design, Illustration, Painting, Photography, Printmaking, Introduction to Art, Survey Art History

CARROLLTON

WEST GEORGIA COLLEGE, Art Dept, 30018. Tel 706-836-6521. *Chmn* Bruce Bobick
Estab 1906; pub; D; scholarships; SC 36, LC 12, GC 16; enrl maj 124
Ent Req: HS dipl, ent exam
Degrees: BFA, AB(Studio, Art Educ), MEd 4 yrs
Tuition: Res—$1704 per yr, PT $37 per quarter hr; nonres—$1462 per quarter, PT $112 per quarter hr; campus res—$400 - $440 per quarter
Courses: †Advertising Design, Art Appreciation, †Art Education, Art History, Calligraphy, †Ceramics, Commercial Art, Conceptual Art, Constructions, Design, Display, Drafting, †Drawing, Illustration, †Interior Design, Lettering, †Painting, †Photography, †Printmaking, †Sculpture, Textile Design, Art Appreciation
Children's Classes: Enrl 10-20; Sat school. Creative studio experiences in fine arts & crafts
Summer School: Dir, B Bobick. 8 wk sem. Courses - Art Education, Art History, Art Appreciation, Art Education, Ceramics, Design, Drawing, Painting, Papermaking, Printmaking, Sculpture

CLEVELAND

TRUETT-MCCONNELL COLLEGE, Arts Dept, 30528. Tel 706-865-2134; FAX 706-865-0975. *Prof* Dr David N George
Estab 1946; den; D & E; SC 10, LC 2; enrl D 700, non-maj 98, maj 15
Ent Req: HS dipl, SAT
Degrees: AA and AS 2 yr
Tuition: $670 per quarter
Courses: Aesthetics, Art History, Ceramics, Drawing, Graphic Design, Handicrafts, Painting, Sculpture, Three Dimensional Design
Children's Classes: Enrl 21; tuition $20. Courses—Children's Art

COCHRAN

MIDDLE GEORGIA COLLEGE, Dept of Art, 31014. Tel 912-934-3088, 934-3085. *Chmn* W Hal Lunsford. Instrs: FT 2
Estab as Junior College Unit of University of Georgia; Pub; D & E; SC 6; enrl D 270, E 45
Ent Req: HS dipl, GED
Degrees: AA 2 yr
Tuition: $301 per quarter; campus res—$300 per quarter; board (5 day) $380, (7 day) $405 per quarter
Courses: Art Education, Commercial Art, Drawing, Lettering, Painting, Fine Art

COLUMBUS

COLUMBUS COLLEGE, Dept of Art, Fine Arts Hall, 3600 Algonquin Dr, 31907-2079. Tel 706-568-2047; FAX 706-568-2084. *Chmn* Jarrell Hethcox
Estab 1958; pub; D & E; scholarships; SC 30, LC 7, GC 28; enrl D 300, E 50, maj 130, grad 20
Ent Req: HS dipl, ent exam
Degrees: BS (Art Educ), BA (Art) and MEd (Art Educ) 4 yr
Tuition: Res—$515 per qtr; nonres—$1409 per qtr
Courses: Art Appreciation, Art Education, Art History, Ceramics, Drawing, History of Art & Archaeology, Jewelry, Painting, Photography, Printmaking, Sculpture, Teacher Training, Textile Design, Critical Analysis, Intaglio, Watercolor
Adult Hobby Classes: Enrl 200. Courses—various subjects
Children's Classes: Enrl 200. Courses—various subjects
Summer School: Enrl 200; term of one quarter. Courses—various

DAHLONEGA

NORTH GEORGIA COLLEGE, Fine Arts Dept, 30597. Tel 706-864-1423; FAX 706-864-1462. *Chmn* Robert L Owens
Scholarships
Degrees: BA, BS, MEd
Tuition: $382
Courses: Art Appreciation, †Art Education, Art History, Calligraphy, †Ceramics, Design, †Drawing, Handicrafts, Painting, †Photography, Printmaking, †Sculpture, Textile Design, Weaving
Adult Hobby Classes: Enrl 15; tuition $30. Courses—Weaving, Watercolor
Children's Classes: Enrl 10; tuition $30. Courses—Children's Art
Summer School: Dir, Robert L Owens. Enrl 20. Courses—Art Appreciation

DECATUR

AGNES SCOTT COLLEGE, Dept of Art, E College Ave, 30030. Tel 404-371-6000. *Chmn* Terry McGehee
Estab 1889; pvt; D; scholarships; SC 13, LC 15; enrl non-maj 200, maj 23
Degrees: BA 4 yr
Tuition: Res—undergrad $5500 yr; nonres—undergrad $5500 yr; room & board $2250 per yr
Courses: Aesthetics, Art History, Ceramics, Drawing, Graphic Arts, History of Art & Archaeology, Painting, Printmaking, History of Architecture

DEMOREST

PIEDMONT COLLEGE, Art Dept, 30535. Tel 706-778-3000. *Dept Head* Cheryl Goldsleger
Scholarships offered
Degrees: BA
Tuition: Res—undergrad $250 per cr
Courses: Art Appreciation, Art Education, Art History, Ceramics, Design, Drawing, Handicrafts, Jewelry, Painting, Photography, Printmaking

GAINESVILLE

BRENAU COLLEGE, Art Dept, 204 Boulevard, 30501. Tel 706-534-6110, Ext 6240. *Dir* Mary Jane Taylor, MAEd; *Asst Prof* Neal Smith-Willow; *Asst Prof* Lynn Jones
Estab 1878; pvt; D & E; Schol; enrl maj 75
Ent Req: HS dipl
Degrees: BA & BS 4 yrs
Courses: Advertising Design, Art History, Ceramics, Commercial Art, Drawing, Graphic Design, †Interior Design, Jewelry, Lettering, Painting, Photography, Printmaking, Sculpture, Textile Design, Silkscreen, †Studio
Summer School: Dir, Dr John Upchurch. Enrl 150; Tuition $575 for 2 wks. Courses—Visual Art, Theatre, Music, Dance

LA GRANGE

LA GRANGE COLLEGE, Lamar Dodd Art Center Museum, 30240. Tel 706-882-2911, ext 211. *Dept Head* John D Lawrence. Instrs: FT 3, PT 1
Estab 1831; pvt; D & E; scholarships; SC 11, LC 2; enrl maj 40
Ent Req: HS dipl, ent exam
Degrees: BA 4 yr
Tuition: Undergrad $1649 per qtr; room & board $2709 per qtr
Courses: Art Education, Art History, Ceramics, Commercial Art, Drawing, Graphic Design, Painting, Photography, Printmaking, Sculpture, Textile Design, Art History Survey, Batik, Weaving
Summer School: Dir, Luke Gill. Enrl 200; tuition $250 per course. Courses—Art History, Ceramics, Drawing, Photography

MACON

MERCER UNIVERSITY, Art Dept, 1400 Coleman Ave, 31207. Tel 912-752-2591. *Chmn* Roger A Jamison. Instrs: FT 4
Estab 1945; den; D; SC 9, LC 7, GC 2; enrl maj 25
Ent Req: HS dipl
Degrees: BA 4 yr
Tuition: Res—$2805 per qtr; nonres—$3387 per qtr; campus res—room and board $2196
Courses: Art Education, Art History, Ceramics, Drawing, Photography, Printmaking, Sculpture
Adult Hobby Classes: Chmn, Roger A Jamison. Evening classes
Summer School: Dir, JoAnna Watson. 2 terms, 5 wks each beginning June 15. Courses—Art Education, Ceramics, Crafts, Drawing, Painting, Photography, Sculpture

WESLEYAN COLLEGE, Art Dept, 4760 Forsyth Rd, 31297. Tel 912-477-1110. *Acting Chmn* Art Werger, MFA; *Assoc Prof* Scott Duce, MFA; *Lectr in Art* Lebe Bailey
Estab 1836; den; D & E; schol; SC 38, LC 10; enrl D 159, non-maj 13, maj 45, others 12
Ent Req: HS dipl, SAT, GPA
Degrees: BFA 4 yrs
Tuition: $8100 per yr; $13,500 per yr incl room & board
Courses: Advertising Design, Art Education, Art History, Ceramics, Commercial Art, Drawing, Graphic Arts, Graphic Design, Illustration, Painting, Printmaking, Sculpture, Stage Design, Teacher Training, Theatre Arts, Elementary School Arts & Crafts, Special Topics in Art, Visual Arts, Watercolor
Summer School: Dir, Dr Karyon McMinn. Courses—Art Appreciation, Ceramics, Graphic Design, Illustration, Photography, Printmaking, Watercolor

MILLEDGEVILLE

GEORGIA COLLEGE, Art Dept, 31061. Tel 912-453-4572. *Chmn* Dorothy D Brown
Scholarships
Courses: Art Appreciation, †Art Education, Art History, Ceramics, Design, Drawing, Handicrafts, Jewelry, Printmaking, Sculpture, Textile Design, Weaving, Watercolor
Adult Hobby Classes: Courses offered
Summer School: Courses offered

MOUNT BERRY

BERRY COLLEGE, Art Dept, 30149. Tel 706-232-5374, Ext 2219. *Chmn* T J Mew, PhD; *Asst Prof* Jere Lykins, MEd
Estab 1902, dept estab 1942; pvt; D & E; scholarships; SC 24, LC 9; enrl D 122, non-maj 38, maj 84, others 7
Ent Req: HS dipl, SAT, CEEB, ACT
Degrees: BA, BS 4 yrs
Tuition: Res—undergrad $6500 yr; nonres—undergrad $6600 yr; campus res—available
Courses: Aesthetics, Art Education, Art History, Calligraphy, †Ceramics, Collages, Conceptual Art, Constructions, Drawing, Film, Graphic Arts, History of Art & Archaeology, Printmaking, Sculpture, Teacher Training, Video, Ecological Art
Summer School: Dir, Dr T J Mew. Courses—Same as above

MOUNT VERNON

BREWTON-PARKER COLLEGE, Visual Arts, Hwy 280, 30445. Tel 912-583-2241, Ext 306. *Dir* E W Addison, MFA
Estab 1906, dept re-estab 1976; pvt, den; D & E; SC 10, LC 4; enrl in dept D 19, non-maj 4, maj 15
Ent Req: HS dipl
Degrees: AA(Visual Arts) 2 yrs
Tuition: $1050, 12-16 units
Courses: Art History, Drawing, Painting, Photography, Printmaking, Sculpture, Art Media & Theory, 2-D & 3-D Design, Art for Teachers
Adult Hobby Classes: Same courses as above, on and off campus classes
Summer School: Same courses as above

ROME

SHORTER COLLEGE, Art Dept, Shorter Ave, 30161. Tel 706-291-2121. *Asst Prof* Paulette Zeller; *Asst Prof* Matthew Bohler, MFA; *Asst Prof* Jim Gibbons
Estab 1873, dept estab 1900; den; D; scholarships; SC 5; enrl D 250, non-maj 230, maj 20
Ent Req: HS dipl
Degrees: AB(Art) and BS(Art Ed) 4 yr
Tuition: $5300 per quarter
Courses: †Art Education, Art History, Ceramics, Commercial Art, Drawing, Handicrafts, Interior Design, Jewelry, Painting, Photography, Printmaking, Sculpture, Teacher Training, Textile Design, Color Theory
Children's Classes: Enrl 20; tuition varies

SAVANNAH

ARMSTRONG STATE COLLEGE, Art & Music Dept, 11935 Abercorn St, 31406. Tel 912-927-5325; FAX 912-927-5391. *Chmn* Dr Jim Anderson
Scholarships
Tuition: Res—$474 per quarter
Courses: Art Appreciation, Art Education, Art History, Ceramics, Design, Drawing, Handicrafts, Jewelry, Painting, Photography, Printmaking, Sculpture, Weaving
Adult Hobby Classes: Courses—Ceramics, Painting, Watercolors

SAVANNAH STATE COLLEGE, Dept of Fine Arts, PO Box 20059, 31404. Tel 912-356-2248. *Dir* Terrance A Anderson; *Asst Prof* Farnese Lumpkin, MA; *Asst Prof* Clara Aquero, MA
Estab 1880s, dept estab 1950s; pub; D; SC 13, LC 3
Ent Req: HS dipl
Tuition: Res—$540, nonres—$238; campus residence—available
Courses: Art History, Ceramics, Calligraphy, Photography, Sculpture, Basic Design
Summer School: Dir, Dr Luetta Milledge. Enrl 60; tuition $180. Courses—on demand

STATESBORO

GEORGIA SOUTHERN UNIVERSITY, Dept of Art, 30460. Tel 912-681-5918, 681-5358. *Head Dept* Richard Tichich, MFA; *Prof* Stephen Bayless, MFA; *Prof* Henry Iler, MFA; *Prof* Joseph Olson Jr, EdD; *Assoc Prof* Bernard Solomon, MFA; *Asst Prof* Pat Walker, MFA; *Asst Prof* Thomas Steadman, MFA; *Asst Prof* Roy Sonnema, MFA; *Asst Prof* Jessica Hines, MFA; *Asst Prof* Bruce Little, MFA; *Instr* Marie Cochran, MFA; *Instr* Laura Hale, MFA
Pub; D & E
Ent Req: HS dipl
Degrees: AB and BSEd 4 yr
Tuition: Res—undergrad $488 per quarter; nonres—undergrad $763 per quarter; campus res—room & board $315
Courses: Art Education, Art History, Ceramics, Commercial Art, Constructions, Drawing, Graphic Arts, Graphic Design, Lettering, Mixed Media, Painting, Photography, Printmaking, Sculpture, Teacher Training
Adult Hobby Classes: Enrl 40; tuition $35 per 10 wks. Courses—Painting, Photography
Children's Classes: Offered in Laboratory School & Sat Program

THOMASVILLE

THOMAS COLLEGE, Humanities Division, 31792. Tel 912-226-1621. *Div Chmn* Douglas Haydel, PhD; *Asst Prof of Art* John Cone
Scholarships offered
Degrees: AA
Tuition: $60 per quarter cr hr
Courses: Art Appreciation, Art Education, Drawing, Painting
Adult Hobby Classes: Enrl 30; 2 terms (quarters) per yr. Courses—Art Structure
Children's Classes: Courses offered on demand
Summer School: Enrl 60; summer quarter. Courses—same as regular yr

TIFTON

ABRAHAM BALDWIN AGRICULTURAL COLLEGE, Art & Humanities Dept, ABAC Sta, 31794-2693. Tel 912-386-3236, 386-3250. *Chmn* Lew S Akin
Degrees: Certificate
Courses: Art Appreciation, Art History, Design, Drawing, Painting

VALDOSTA

VALDOSTA STATE COLLEGE, Dept of Art, Patterson St, 31698. Tel 912-333-5835; FAX 912-333-7408. *Head Dept* L Milbrandt. Instrs: FT 8
Estab 1911; pub; D; scholarships; SC 25, LC 10, GC 9; enrl 400, maj 95, total 7500
Ent Req: SAT
Degrees: BA, BFA & BFA (Art Ed) 4 yr
Tuition: Res—$447 12 hrs or more per quarter, $37 per hr; nonres—$1341 12 hrs or more, $112 per hr; plus other fees
Courses: †Art Education, Art History, Ceramics, Design, Drawing, Graphic Design, Illustration, Painting, Photography, Printmaking, Sculpture, Air Brush, Computer Aided Graphic Design, Hand Made Paper, Package Design, Weaving
Summer School: Dir, L Milbrandt. Enrl 91; tuition res—$37 per hr for 4 wk terms. Courses—Art Appreciation, Art Education, Design, Graphic Design

YOUNG HARRIS

YOUNG HARRIS COLLEGE, Dept of Art, 30582. Tel 706-379-3112. *Chmn* Richard Aunspaugh; *Instr* Tena Magher. Instrs: FT 2
Estab 1886; den; D; schol; SC 6, LC 4; enrl D 450, maj 25
Ent Req: HS dipl
Degrees: AFA 2 yr
Tuition: $2500 per yr
Courses: Art History, †Drawing, †Painting, †Sculpture, Design

HAWAII

HONOLULU

HONOLULU ACADEMY OF ARTS, The Art Center at Linekona, 1111 Victoria St, 96814. Tel 808-532-8742; FAX 808-532-8787. *Cur* Carol Khewhok. Instrs: FT 3, PT 1
Estab 1946; pvt
Ent Req: 16 yrs of age with talent
Courses: Drawing, Painting, Printmaking, Etching, Lithography
Adult Hobby Classes: Tuition $130 per sem. Courses—Ceramics, Drawing, Jewelry, Painting, Printmaking, Watercolors, Weaving
Children's Classes: tuition $95 for 11 wks. Courses—Drawing, Exploring Art, Painting

HONOLULU COMMUNITY COLLEGE, 874 Dillingham Blvd, 96817. Tel 808-845-9211. *Dept Head* Maria Robert-Deutsch; *Instr Commercial Art* Jerome Hock; *Instr Commercial Art* Michael Kaiser; *Instr Graphic Arts* Romolo Valencia, BA
College maintains three art departments: Commercial Art, Art & Graphic Arts; pub; D & E; SC 20, LC 2; enrl D 150 majors
Ent Req: 18 yrs of age, English & math requirements, motivation, interest in learning, willingness to work
Degrees: AS 2 yr
Tuition: Res—$95 plus $15 per cr hr; nonres—$1030 fee plus $5 for 12 cr hr or more
Courses: Advertising Design, Commercial Art, Drafting, Drawing, Graphic Arts, Graphic Design, Illustration, Lettering, Painting, Photography, Printmaking, Textile Design

UNIVERSITY OF HAWAII, Kapiolani Community College, 4303 Diamond Head Rd, 96816. Tel 808-734-9776. *Chmn* Caroline Nakamura. Instrs: FT 4, PT 4
Estab 1965; pub; D & E; scholarships; SC 11, LC 5; enrl D 4800, E 500
Ent Req: Ent exam
Degrees: AA and AS 1-2 yr
Tuition: No campus res
Courses: Art Appreciation, Art History, Ceramics, Design, Drawing, Painting, Photography, Printmaking, Sculpture, Crafts, Light and Color, Perception, Screen Printing, 3-D Design, Visual Arts
Adult Hobby Classes: Enrl 25 per class; tuition depends on number of units. Courses—Art Business, Drawing, Intro to Visual Arts, Painting
Summer School: Enrl 700; tuition depends on number of units taken for term of 6 wks. Courses—vary each summer

UNIVERSITY OF HAWAII AT MANOA, Dept of Art, 2535 The Mall, 96822. Tel 808-956-8251; FAX 808-956-9043. *Chmn* Robert Jay. Instrs: FT 26, PT 25
Estab 1907; pub; D & E; scholarships; SC 64, LC 34; enrl maj 450, grad 40
Ent Req: HS dipl or GED and SAT or ACT
Degrees: BA(Art History), BA(Studio) and BFA 4 yr
Tuition: Res—undergrad $615 per sem, $52 per cr hr; grad $730 sem, $61 per cr hr; nonres—undergrad $1840 per sem, $154 per cr hr; grad $2190 per sem, $183 per cr hr, plus fees; campus res limited
Courses: Art History, Ceramics, Drawing, Graphic Design, Illustration, Jewelry, Painting, Photography, Printmaking, Sculpture, Weaving, †Graphic Design, †Illustration, †Fiber Arts, Glass
Adult Hobby Classes: Evenings only. Courses - Drawing, Painting, Sculpture
Summer School: Dean, Victor Kobayashi. Tuition res $55 per cr hr, nonres $110 per cr hr, plus fees. Courses—Art History (Western & Pacific), Ceramics, Drawing, Design, Glass Painting, Printmaking, Sculpture

KAHULUI

MAUI COMMUNITY COLLEGE, Art Dept, 310 Kaahumanu Ave, 96732. Tel 808-244-9181. *Chmn* Barbara Miller. Instrs: FT 1, PT 3
Estab 1967; pub; D & E; scholarships; SC 8, LC 2; enrl D 2000, E 400
Ent Req: Ent exam
Degrees: AS 2 yr
Tuition: Res—$150; nonres—$800
Courses: Advertising Design, Architecture, †Ceramics, Display, †Drawing, Graphic Arts, Graphic Design, †History of Art & Archaeology, Jewelry, †Painting, †Photography, Sculpture, †Textile Design, †Weaving, †Batik, Copper Enameling, History of Architecture, Welding
Adult Hobby Classes: Enrl 1600; tuition $10.50-$45. Courses—Batik, Jewelry, Silk Screen, Beginning Drawing

LAIE

BRIGHAM YOUNG UNIVERSITY, HAWAII CAMPUS, Division of Fine Arts, 55 220 Kulanui, 96762. Tel 808-293-3900; FAX 808-293-3645. *Chmn* Dr Preston K Larson
Scholarships
Degrees: BA
Tuition: Church mem $760 per sem; non church mem $1140 per sem
Courses: †Ceramics, †Painting, †Printmaking, †Sculpture, Polynesian Handicrafts
Summer School: Dir, V Napua Tengaio. Tuition $60 per cr, 2 four wk blocks. Courses—Ceramics, Polynesian Handicrafts

LIHUE

KAUAI COMMUNITY COLLEGE, Dept of Art, 3-1901 Kaumualii, 96766. Tel 808-245-8284. *Faculty* Wayne A Miyata, MFA; *Faculty* Waihang Lai, MA. Instrs: FT 2, PT 1
Estab 1965; pub; D & E; scholarships; SC 6, LC 2; enrl D 965, E 468
Ent Req: HS dipl
Degrees: AA and AS 2 yr
Tuition: Res—$17 per cr hr; nonres—$104 per cr hr
Courses: Art History, Ceramics, Drawing, Painting, Photography, Oriental Brush Painting, Watercolor
Summer School: Term of 6 wk beginning June and July

PAHOA

**A
KALANI HONUA INSTITUTE FOR CULTURAL STUDIES,** Conference Center, RR2 Box 4500, 96778-9724. Tel 808-965-7828; FAX 808-965-9613. *Exec Dir* Richard Koob, MFA; *Registrar* Delton Johnson, BA; *Arts Instr* Arthur Johnson, BA; *Personnel Mgr* Michael Fleck, BA
Estab 1980, sch estab 1982; pvt; D & E; scholarships offered; SC 3; enrl D 4000, E 4000, all non-maj
Tuition: $6 - $15 per 1 - 1 1/2 hr class; campus res—$15 - $80 per night
Courses: Costume Design & Construction, Design, Drawing, History of Art & Archaeology, Illustration, Painting, Photography, Textile Design, Theatre Arts, Weaving
Adult Hobby Classes: Enrl 3500; tuition approx $300 per wk. Courses—Dance, Drawing, Music, Yoga
Children's Classes: Enrl 500; tuition approx $200 per wk

PEARL CITY

LEEWARD COMMUNITY COLLEGE, Arts and Humanities Division, 96-045 Ala Ike, 96782. Tel 808-455-0228. *Dean* Gerald St James
Estab 1968; pub; D & E; schol; SC 11, LC 3; enrl D 400, E 100
Ent Req: Over 18 yrs of age
Degrees: AA and AS 2 yrs
Tuition: Res—$19 per cr hr; nonres—$112 per cr hr
Courses: Art History, Ceramics, Costume Design & Construction, Drawing, Graphic Arts, Painting, Photography, Printmaking, Sculpture, Theatre Arts, Aspects of Asian Art, Two Dimensional Design, Three Dimensional Design
Summer School: Enrl 100; Term of 7 wks beginning June 12th. Courses—vary

IDAHO

BOISE

BOISE STATE UNIVERSITY, Art Dept, 1910 University Dr, 83725. Tel 208-385-1230. *Chmn* Dave Oravez
Estab 1932; pub; D & E; scholarships; SC 51, LC 8, GC 4; enrl D 2539, maj 550, GS 14
Ent Req: HS dipl
Degrees: BA, BFA, BA(Educ), BFA(Educ), BA(Graphic Design), BFA(Graphic Design) 4 yr, MA(Art Educ) 4 yr
Courses: Art Education, Art History, Ceramics, Drawing, Graphic Design, Painting, Photography, Printmaking, Sculpture, Metals, Watercolor

COEUR D'ALENE

NORTH IDAHO COLLEGE, Art Dept, 1000 W Garden Ave, 83814. Tel 208-769-3300. *Dept Chmn* Joe Jonas; *Instr* Lisa Lynes, MA; *Instr* Allie Vogt
Tuition: Res—$402 per sem; nonres—$900 per sem
Courses: Advertising Design, Art Education, Art History, Calligraphy, Ceramics, Design, Drawing, Fashion Arts, Graphic Design, Illustration, Interior Design, Painting, Photography, Printmaking, Sculpture, Stage Design, Weaving, Animation, Cartooning, Fashion Design, Portfolio, Professional Advertising

LEWISTON

LEWIS-CLARK STATE COLLEGE, Art Dept, 83501. Tel 208-746-2341. *Discipline Coordr* Robert Almquist, MFA. Instrs: FT 1
Estab 1893; pub; D & E; schol; SC 10, LC 1; enrl D 89, E 43
Ent Req: HS dipl or GED, ACT
Degrees: BA and BS 4 yrs
Tuition: Res—undergrad $600 per yr; nonres—undergrad $2300 per yr; PT (up to 7 cr) $40 per cr; campus res—room and board $1870 double room, $2070 single room
Courses: Art Education, Drawing, Graphic Arts, Painting, Stage Design, Teacher Training, Theatre Arts, Video, Composition, Independent Study, Watercolor
Adult Hobby Classes: Discipline Coordr, Robert Almquist, MFA

MOSCOW

UNIVERSITY OF IDAHO, College of Art & Architecture, 83843. Tel 208-885-6111. *Dept Chmn* David Giese; *Prof* George T Wray
Estab 1923; pub; D & E; scholarships; SC 30, LC 6, GC 8; enrl D 450 (Art and Architecture), non-maj 345 (Architecture), maj 85 (Art), GS 18 (Art)
Ent Req: HS dipl
Degrees: BA, BS, BFA, MFA, MA, MAT
Tuition: Campus res—available
Summer School: Dir, Frank Cronk. Enrl 40; tuition $43 per cr hr per 8 wks. Courses—vary

NAMPA

NORTHWEST NAZARENE COLLEGE, Art Dept, Holly at Dewey, 83651. Tel 208-467-8412. *Art Head* Dr Mary Shaffer. Instrs: FT 3
Den; D & E; schol; SC 12, LC 5; enrl D 200, E 40, maj 24
Ent Req: HS dipl
Degrees: AA and AB 4 yrs
Courses: Art Education, Ceramics, Drawing, Graphic Design, History of Art & Archaeology, Illustration, Painting, Printmaking, Sculpture, Teacher Training, Crafts for Teachers
Adult Hobby Classes: Crafts, Painting
Summer School: Courses—Art Education

POCATELLO

IDAHO STATE UNIVERSITY, Dept of Art, 1010 S Fifth, PO Box 8004, 83209. Tel 208-236-2361, 236-2484. *Chmn* Gail Dial; *Faculty* Don Brown, MFA; *Faculty* Dr Miles E Friend, PhD; *Faculty* Scott Evans, MFA; *Faculty* Tony Martin, MFA; *Faculty* Rudy Kovacs, MFA; *Faculty* Robert Granger, MFA
Estab 1901; pub; D & E; scholarships; SC 32, LC 6, GS 22; enrl maj 75, GS 15, total 500
Ent Req: HS dipl, GED, ACT
Degrees: BA, BFA and MFA 4 yr
Tuition: Nonres—$850 per yr; campus res—$1260 per yr
Courses: Art Education, Art History, Ceramics, Drawing, Painting, Printmaking, Sculpture, Design, Metals, Weaving
Adult Hobby Classes: Enrl 400; tuition $750 per sem. Courses—Studio, Art History
Children's Classes: Enrl 15; tuition $35 for 6 wks. Courses—Children's Art
Summer School: Dir, Gail Dial. Enrl 100. Courses—Art History, Art Appreciation, Studio Art

REXBURG

RICKS COLLEGE, Dept of Art, 83460. Tel 208-356-2913. *Chmn* Robert Powell; *Instr* Richard Bird; *Instr* Kelly Burgner; *Instr* Vince Bodily; *Instr* Gerald Griffin; *Instr* Mathew Geddes; *Instr* Leon Parson; *Instr* Gary Pierson
Estab 1888; pvt; D & E; schol; SC 23, LC 1; enrl D 123, maj 123
Ent Req: HS dipl
Degrees: AAS, AAdv Design and AFA 2 yrs
Tuition: $660
Courses: †Advertising Design, Art Education, Art History, Ceramics, †Commercial Art, †Drawing, †Graphic Design, History of Art & Archaeology, †Illustration, Interior Design, Lettering, †Painting, †Photography, †Sculpture, Teacher Training
Summer School: Dir, Jim Gee. Enrl 100; tuition $60 per cr hr. Courses - Art History, Drawing, Sculpture, Photography

SUN VALLEY

SUN VALLEY CENTER FOR THE ARTS AND HUMANITIES, Dept of Fine Art, PO Box 656, 83353. Tel 208-726-9491. *Dir* Julie Gorton; *Visual Arts & Community Programs Dir* Roberta Heinrich; *Performing Arts* Kate Wright
Estab 1971
Adult Hobby Classes: Courses - Calligraphy, Ceramics, UFE Drawing
Children's Classes: Enrl vary per sem; courses - Ceramics, Musical Theatre Workshop
Summer School: Dir, Roberta Heinrich. Tuition $100 - $200 per wk. Courses - Ceramics, Mixed Media, Painting from Nature, Photography, Water Color

TWIN FALLS

COLLEGE OF SOUTHERN IDAHO, Art Dept, PO Box 1238, 83301. Tel 208-733-9554, Ext 344; FAX 208-736-3014. *Chmn* LaVar Steel, MS; *Assoc Prof* Michael Green, MFA; *Assoc Prof* Russell Hepworth
Estab 1965; pub; D & E; schol; SC 26, LC 2; enrl D 3000, E 2000, non-maj 50, maj 45
Ent Req: HS dipl, ACT
Degrees: Dipl or AA
Tuition: Res—undergrad $500 per yr, $200 per sem, $50 per sem hr; nonres—undergrad $1200 per yr, $600 per sem, $65 per cr hr; campus res—room & board
Courses: Art History, Ceramics, Design, Drawing, Lettering, Mixed Media, Painting, Photography, Printmaking, Sculpture, Theatre Arts, Papermaking
Adult Hobby Classes: Enrl 100; tuition $35 per class. Courses—Photography, Pottery, Printmaking
Children's Classes: Enrl 50; tuition $20 per class. Courses—Crafts, Drawing, Photography, Pottery
Summer School: Dir Jerry Beck. Courses—Art General, Crafts, Drawing, Papermaking, Pottery

ILLINOIS

AURORA

AURORA UNIVERSITY, Art Dept, 347 S Gladstone Ave, 60506. Tel 708-844-5519. *Assoc Prof* Stephen Lowery, MFA
Estab 1893, dept estab 1979; pvt; D & E; SC 7, LC 3; enrl D 116, E 55, non-maj 171
Ent Req: HS dipl
Degrees: BA 4 yrs
Tuition: $8150 per yr; campus res—$3175 per yr
Courses: Art Appreciation, Art Education, Drawing, Graphic Design, Painting, Sculpture, Teacher Training, Theatre Arts, 2-D Design, 3-D Design
Summer School: Courses—2-D Design

BELLEVILLE

BELLEVILLE AREA COLLEGE, Art Dept, 2500 Carlyle Rd, 62221. Tel 618-235-2700. *Dept Head* Wayne Shaw
Estab 1948; pub; D & E; scholarships; SC 36, LC 9; enrl D 4000, E 3500, maj 200
Ent Req: HS dipl
Degrees: AA and AS 2 yrs
Tuition: $450 per sem
Courses: Advertising Design, Art Appreciation, Art Education, Art History, Calligraphy, Ceramics, Commercial Art, Design, Drawing, Film, Graphic Arts, Graphic Design, History of Art & Archaeology, Jewelry, Lettering, Painting, Photography, Printmaking, Sculpture, Theatre Arts, Video
Summer School: Dir, Wayne Shaw. Tuition $30 per hr for 8 wks. Courses—Art History, Ceramics, Drawing, Photography

BLOOMINGTON

ILLINOIS WESLEYAN UNIVERSITY, School of Art, PO Box 2900, 61702. Tel 309-556-1000. *Instr* Miles Bair, MA; *Instr* Ann Taulbee, MFA; *Instr* Rimas VisGirda, MFA; *Instr* Timothy Garvey, PhD; *Instr* Kevin Strandberg, MFA; *Instr* Sherri McElroy
Estab 1855, school estab 1946; pvt; D; scholarships; enrl non-maj 150, maj 60
Ent Req: HS dipl, SAT or ACT
Degrees: BA, BFA and BFA with Teaching Cert 4 yrs
Courses: Art Education, Art History, Ceramics, Conceptual Art, Drawing, Film, Graphic Arts, History of Art & Archaeology, Painting, Photography, Printmaking, Sculpture, Teacher Training

CANTON

SPOON RIVER COLLEGE, Art Dept, 61520. Tel 309-647-4645. *Dir* Janet Gardner, PhD; *Instr* Tracy Snowman
College maintains three campuses; scholarships offered
Degrees: AA
Tuition: $14 per cr hr
Courses: Ceramics, Design, Drawing, Painting, Sculpture

CARBONDALE

SOUTHERN ILLINOIS UNIVERSITY, School of Art & Design, 62901-4301. Tel 618-453-4315; FAX 618-453-3000. *Dir* L Brent Kington, MFA; *Undergrad Admissions* Joyce Jolliff; *Grad Studies* Michael O Onken, MA; *Two-Dimensional Area Head* Robert Paulson; *Sculpture Area Head* Thomas Walsh, MFA; *Crafts Area Head* Bill H Boysen, MFA; *Academic Area Head* Roy E Abrahamson, EdD; *Design Area Head* Larry S Briggs, BFA; *Prof* Harris Deller, MFA; *Prof* Sylvia R Greenfield, MFA; *Prof* M Joan Lintault, MFA; *Prof* Richard Mawdsley, MFA; *Prof* Robert Paulson, MFA; *Assoc Prof* Aldon Addington, MFA; *Assoc Prof* Lawrence A Bernstein, MFA; *Assoc Prof* W Larry Busch, MS; *Assoc Prof* Joel B Feldman, MFA; *Assoc Prof* Gretel Chapman, PhD; *Assoc Prof* Michael S Youngblood, PhD; *Assoc Prof* George Mavigliano, MA; *Assoc Prof* James E Sullivan, MA; *Assoc Prof* Ann O Saunders, MFA; *Assoc Prof* Larry S Briggs, BFA; *Assoc Prof* Robert B Croston, MS; *Asst Prof* Richard Archer, MS; *Asst Prof* Jed Jackson; *Asst Prof* Sunand Bhattacharya

Estab 1874; pub; D & E; scholarships; SC 100, LC 24, GC 28; enrl D 1304, E 338, non-maj 400, maj 350, grad 60, others 400
Ent Req: HS dipl, upper 50 percent of class, ACT
Degrees: BA, BFA & BS 4 yrs, MFA 3 yrs
Tuition: Res—undergrad & grad $1125 per sem, $75 per cr hr; nonres—undergrad & grad $3375 per sem, $225 per cr hr; campus res—available
Courses: Advertising Design, Aesthetics, Architecture, †Art History, †Art Education, †Ceramics, Collages, †Commercial Art, Conceptual Art, Constructions, Drafting, Drawing, Fashion Arts, Goldsmithing, Graphic Arts, Graphic Design, Industrial Design, Jewelry, Lettering, Mixed Media, Museum Staff Training, Painting, Printmaking, Sculpture, Silversmithing, †Teacher Training, Textile Design, †Art for Elementary Education, †Blacksmithing, †Fibers, †Foundry, †Glassblowing, †Weaving
Adult Hobby Classes: Courses—Drawing, Jewelry, Painting
Children's Classes: Enrl 150; tuition $30 per 4-6 wk term. Courses—Drawing, Painting, Ceramics, 3-D Design, Fibers, Mask-Making, Soft Sculpture, Jewelry, Printing, Papermaking
Summer School: Enrl 500; tuition $75 per hr for term of 4-8 wks beginning June. Courses—selection from regular courses
—College of Technical Careers, 62901. Tel 618-453-8863. *Coordr* John L Yack, MFA. Instrs: 5
Art Dept Estab 1960; pub; D; enrl D 65, maj 65
Ent Req: HS dipl, ent exam
Degrees: AAS 2 yr, BS 4 yr
Tuition: Res—undergrad$75.00 per cr hr; nonres—undergrad $225.00 per cr hr
Courses: Drawing, Graphic Design, Air Brush & Photo Retouching

CARLINVILLE

BLACKBURN COLLEGE, Dept of Art, 300 College Ave, 62626. Tel 217-854-3231, Ext 235. *Chmn* James M Clark, MFA; *Prof* Peter J Slavish, MFA. Instrs: FT 2, PT 2
Estab 1837; pvt; D & E; scholarships; SC 14, LC 7; enrl maj 15
Ent Req: HS grad
Degrees: BA 4 yrs
Tuition: $5700 per yr; room & board $2800
Courses: †Art History, Ceramics, Drawing, Painting, Printmaking, †Teacher Training, Theatre Arts, Art Studio

CHAMPAIGN

UNIVERSITY OF ILLINOIS, URBANA-CHAMPAIGN, College of Fine and Applied Arts, 61820. Tel 217-333-1661. *Dean* Kathryn Martin. Instrs: FT 268, PT 150
Estab 1931; pub; D; scholarships, fels and assistantships; enrl underg 2000, grad 750
Ent Req: HS grad, ent exam
Degrees: Bachelors 4 yrs, Masters, Doctorate
Tuition: Res—undergrad $1674 per sem, grad $1994 per sem; nonres—undergrad $3800 per sem, grad $4760 per sem
Adult Hobby Classes: Scheduled through University Extension
Children's Classes: Sat; summer youth classes
Summer School: courses offered
—School of Art and Design, 143 Art and Design Bldg, 408 E Peabody Dr, Urbana, 61820. Tel 217-333-0855. *DirSchool* Theodore Zernich; *In Charge Art Educ* George W Hardiman, EdD; *In Charge Art History* Katherine Manthorne; *In Charge Ceramics, Glass & Metal* William Carlson, MFA; *In Charge Graphic Design* Thomas Kovacs, MFA; *In Charge Industrial Design* Andrzej Wroblewski; *In Charge Painting* Jerome Savage, MFA; *In Charge Photography* Bea Nettles, MFA; *In Charge Printmaking* Dan Socha, MFA; *In Charge Sculpture* Frank Gallo, MFA
Estab 1867, dept estab 1877; pub; D & E; scholarships; SC 119, LC 72, GC 77; enrl maj 563, grad 137, others 15
Ent Req: HS dipl, ACT, SAT, CLEP
Degrees: BFA 4 yrs, MA 1 yr, MFA 2 yrs, EdD and PhD 5 yrs
Tuition: Res—undergrad $2,130 per yr, $1,065 per sem, part time $375 per sem, grad $2,700 per yr, $1,350 per sem, part time $470 per sem; nonres—undergrad $5,670 per yr, $2,835 per sem, part time $985 per sem, grad $7,380 per yr, $3,690 per sem, part time $1,270 per sem; campus res—room & board $1,826 for double for undergrad per sem
Courses: †Art Education, †Art History, †Ceramics, Design, †Display, Drawing, Film, †Graphic Arts, †Graphic Design, Industrial Design, Museum Staff Training, †Painting, †Photography, †Printmaking, †Sculpture, Silversmithing, Video, †Cinematography, Glassmaking
Adult Hobby Classes: Enrl 150; tuition varies. Courses—Art History, Art Education, Studio
Children's Classes: Enrl 220; tuition $40 per sem. Courses—Creative Arts for Children
Summer School: Dir, Donald W Pilcher. Courses— foundation and lower division courses with some limited offerings and independent study at upper division and graduate levels

CHARLESTON

EASTERN ILLINOIS UNIVERSITY, Art Dept, FAA 216, 61920. Tel 217-581-3410, 581-2311. *Dean* Vaughn Jaenike, EdD; *Asst Dean* Beverly Garten, EdD; *Dept Chmn* James K Johnson, MFA; *Prof* Suzan Braun, MFA; *Prof* Garret DeRuiter, MFA; *Prof* Hannah Eads, DEd; *Prof* Carl Emmerich, EdD; *Prof* Bill Heyduck, EdD; *Prof* Dick Moldroski, MA; *Prof* Walter Sorge, EdD; *Prof* Carl Wilen, MFA; *Assoc Prof* Paul Bodine, MA; *Assoc Prof* Jerry McRoberts, PhD; *Assoc Prof* Glen Hild, MFA; *Asst Prof* Melinda Hegarty, MA; *Assoc Prof* Mary Leonard-Cravens, MFA; *Assoc Prof* Janet Marquardt-Cherry, PhD; *Assoc Prof* Charles Nivens, MFA; *Assoc Prof* Denise Rehm-Mott, MFA; *Asst Prof* Jeff Boshart; *Asst Prof* Kathleen Browne, MFA; *Asst Prof* Robert Troxell, PhD. Instrs: FT 20, PT 4
Estab 1895, dept estab 1930; pub; D & E; scholarships; SC 45, LC 24, GC 29; enrl non-maj 1700, maj 225, grad 15
Ent Req: HS dipl, ACT, grad - MAT or GRE

Degrees: BA 4 yrs, MA 1 yr, Specialist Educ 2 yrs
Tuition: Res—undergrad $786-$798 per sem, $1572-$1596 per yr, $65.60-$66.50 per hr, grad $840 per sem, $1680 per yr, $70 per sem hr; nonres—undergrad $2358.50-$2394 per sem, $4716-$4788 per yr, $196.50-$199.50 per hr, grad $2520 per sem, $5040 per yr, $210 per sem hr; campus res—available
Courses: Art Education, Art History, Ceramics, Design, Drawing, Graphic Design, Weaving, Painting, Printmaking, Sculpture, Silversmithing, Watercolor
Summer School: Dept Chmn, James K Johnson. Enrl 180; tuition undergrad $524.30-$532.30 per sem, grad $560; nonres—undergrad $1572-$1596 per sem, grad $1680 per sem. Courses—Same as regular session

CHICAGO

AMERICAN ACADEMY OF ART, 122 S Michigan Ave, 60603. Tel 312-939-3883; FAX 312-939-5429. *Chmn* John Balester. Instrs: FT 17, PT 22
Estab 1923; pvt; D & E; scholarships; SC 13; enrl D 396, E 462
Ent Req: HS dipl, portfolio
Degrees: AA 2-3 yrs
Tuition: Days $6800 per yr, evenings & Sat $170 per 10 wks
Courses: Advertising Design, Aesthetics, Art Appreciation, Art History, Calligraphy, Commercial Art, Design, Display, Drawing, Graphic Arts, Graphic Design, Illustration, Lettering, Mixed Media, Painting, Photography, Computer Graphic Arts & Design, Commercial Illustration, Advertising Market Rendering, Life Drawing, Advanced Fundamentals of Art
Adult Hobby Classes: Enrl 460; tuition $2464 per semester, $4928 per school year. Courses—Commercial Art, Fine Art
Children's Classes: Enrl 20; tuition $104 for 10 Saturdays. Courses—General Art
Summer School: Dir, Kitty R McCannon. Enrl 150; tuition $100-1000 for term of 8 wks beginning the end of June. Courses—Commercial Art, Fine Art

CITY COLLEGES OF CHICAGO
—**Daley College,** Art and Architecture Dept, 7500 S Pulaski Rd, 60652. Tel 312-735-3000. *Chmn Art* V Bodnaruk; *Prof* A Lerner; *Prof* T Palazzolo; *Prof* C Grenda; *Prof* M Rosen; *Prof* D Wiedemann
Estab 1960; enrl 5500
Tuition: Undergrad—$600
Courses: Weaving
—**Kennedy-King College,** Art and Humanities Dept, 6800 S Wentworth Ave, 60621. Tel 312-962-3200. *Chmn* Dr Thomas Roby
Estab 1935; enrl 9010
Tuition: Undergrad—$31.50 per ch hr
Courses: Art Education, Drafting, Drawing, History of Art & Archaeology, Industrial Design, Painting, Photography, Theatre Arts
—**Harold Washington College,** Art and Humanities Dept, 30 E Lake St, 60601. Tel 312-984-2807. *Chmn Humanities* James Mack
Estab 1962; enrl 8000
Tuition: Undergrad—$390
Courses: Drawing, Painting, Commercial Art, Photography, Printmaking
—**Malcolm X College,** Art and Humanities Dept, 1900 W Van Buren St, 60612. Tel 312-850-7324. *Chmn Humanities* Claudette Burchett; *Asst Prof* Barbara J Hogu; *Asst Prof* Robert Witter
Estab 1911; enrl 5000
Tuition: Res—undergrad $21.50 per cr hr
Courses: Art Appreciation, Art Education, Art History, Ceramics, Design, Drawing, Painting, Sculpture, Theatre Arts, Photography, Radio-TV
—**Olive-Harvey College,** Art and Humanities Dept, 10001 S Woodlawn Ave, 60628. Tel 312-568-3700. *Chmn Humanities* Judith Cieslak
Estab 1957; enrl 4700
Tuition: Res—undergrad$31.50 per cr hr
Courses: Art Education, Drafting, Drawing, History of Art & Archaeology, Industrial Design, Painting, Theatre Arts
—**Truman College,** Art and Humanities Dept, 1145 W Wilson Ave, 60640. Tel 312-878-1700. *Chmn Humanities* Edmund Dehnert
Estab 1956; enrl 3800
Tuition: Res—undergrad$31.50 per cr hr
Courses: Art Education, Ceramics, Drafting, Drawing, History of Art & Archaeology, Industrial Design, Painting, Photography, Theatre Arts
—**Wright College,** Art Dept, 3400 N Austin Ave, 60634. Tel 312-481-8650. *Chmn* Daniel Lackowski. Instrs: FT 3
Estab 1934; pub; D & E; SC 15, LC 8; enrl D 3000, E 2500
Ent Req: HS dipl
Degrees: AA & AAS 2 yrs
Tuition: Res—$31.50 per cr hr; nonres out of district $66.73 per cr hr; nonres out of state $141.53 per cr hr
Courses: Advertising Design, †Architecture, Art Appreciation, Drafting, Drawing, †Graphic Design, History of Art & Archaeology, Lettering, Painting, Computer Art, Multi-Image
Adult Hobby Classes: Enrl 400; tuition $15 per course for 6 or 7 wks. Courses—Drawing, Fashion, Painting, Watercolor
Summer School: Dir, Roy LeFevour. Enrl 24; 8 wk session. Courses—Vary

COLUMBIA COLLEGE, Art Dept, 600 S Michigan Ave, 60605. Tel 312-663-1600. *Chairperson Art & Photography Depts* John Mulvany, MFA; *Coordr Graphics* Marlene Lipinski, MFA; *Coordr Interior Design* Tony Patano, BFA; *Coordr Fine Arts* Tom Taylor, BFA; *Coordr Illustration* Fred Nelson; *Coordr Fashion Design* Dennis Brozynski
Estab 1893; pvt; D & E; scholarships; SC 43, LC 17
Ent Req: HS dipl
Degrees: BA 4 yrs, MA (photog)
Tuition: Res—undergrad $2914 per sem, $198 per cr hr; no campus res
Courses: Advertising Design, Architecture, Art Education, Art History, Calligraphy, Ceramics, Commercial Art, Drafting, Drawing, Fashion Arts, Film, Graphic Arts, Graphic Design, Handicrafts, Illustration, Industrial Design, Interior Design, Jewelry, Mixed Media, Painting, Printmaking, Sculpture, Silk Screen, Typography
Summer School: Dir, John Mulvany

CONTEMPORARY ART WORKSHOP, 542 W Grant Place, 60614. Tel 312-472-4004. *Dir* Lynn Kearney, BA; *Sculpture* Paul Zakoian, MA
Estab 1950. Twenty artists studios are available to artists for a modest fee on a month to month basis; D & E
Ent Req: None, studio artists are juried
Degrees: None, we offer an apprentice program in sculpture
Tuition: $110 for 10 wks
Courses: Sculpture
Adult Hobby Classes: Tuition $110 for 10 wks. Courses—Sculpture, Painting
Summer School: Dir, Paul Zakoian. Tuition $110 for 10 wks. Summer courses—Sculpture

DEPAUL UNIVERSITY, Dept of Art, College of Liberal Arts and Sciences, 2323 N Seminary, 60614. Tel 312-362-8194; FAX 312-362-5684. *Chmn Dept* Robert Donley, MFA; *Prof* Jenny Morlan, MFA; *Prof* Sally Kitt Chappell, PhD; *Assoc Prof* Simone Zurawski, PhD; *Assoc Prof* Stephen Luecking, MFA; *Asst Prof* Bibiana Swarez; *Asst Prof* Elizabeth Lillehoj; *Instr* William Seiger
Estab 1897, dept estab 1965; pvt; D; scholarships; SC 20, LC 12; enrl D 30 art maj
Ent Req: HS dipl, SAT or ACT
Degrees: BA(Art) 4 yrs
Tuition: All tuition fees are subject to change, contact admissions office for current fees; campus res available
Courses: †Art History, Design, Drawing, Painting, Photography, Printmaking, Sculpture, Studio Art
Summer School: Chmn, Robert M Donley

HARRINGTON INSTITUTE OF INTERIOR DESIGN, 410 S Michigan, 60605. Tel 312-939-4975; FAX 312-939-8005. *Dean* Robert C Marks
Estab 1931; pvt; D & E; scholarships; enrl D 220, E 209
Ent Req: HS dipl, interview
Degrees: AA & BA(interior design)
Tuition: $7980 per yr, $3990 per sem; campus res—room & board $4420
Courses: Interior Design
Adult Hobby Classes: Enrl 209; tuition $1864 per sem, 3-yr part-time prog. Courses—Interior Design

ILLINOIS INSTITUTE OF TECHNOLOGY
—**College of Architecture,** Crown Hall Bldg, 3360 S State St, 60616. Tel 312-567-3262; FAX 312-567-8871. *Chmn Architecture* Gene Summers; *Asst Dean* Bernadette Ivers; *Asst Dean* Dirk Denison. Instrs: FT 23
Estab 1895 as Armour Institute, consolidated with Lewis Institute of Arts and Sciences 1940; pvt; enrl 345
Degrees: BA 5 yrs, MSA 2 - 3 yrs, MSC 2 - 3 yrs
Tuition: Res—undergrad $6535 per sem, $410 per cr hr; res—grad $6730 per sem, $448 per cr hr
Courses: Architecture
Summer School: Term June 15 through August 8
—**Institute of Design,** 10 W 35th St, 60616. Tel 312-567-3250. *Dir* Patrick Whitney. Instrs: FT 12, PT 5
Estab 1937; pvt; D; scholarships; enrl D 150
Degrees: BS(Design) 4 yrs, Master of Design(Communication Design, Product Design, Photography, Design Planning & Human Centered Design), Phd(Design)
Tuition: Res—undergrad & grad $13,000 per yr
Courses: Industrial Design, Photography, Visual Communications

LOYOLA UNIVERSITY OF CHICAGO, Fine Arts Dept, 6525 N Sheridan Rd, 60626. Tel 312-508-2820; FAX 312-508-2282. *Chmn Fine Arts Dept* James Jansen; *Prof* Ralph Arnold, MFA; *Prof* Juliet Rago, MFA; *Assoc Prof* Justine Wantz, MFA; *Asst Prof* James Jensen, MFA; *Asst Prof* Eugene Geimzer, MFA. Instrs: PT 20
Estab 1870, dept estab 1970; den; D & E; SC 25, LC 17
Degrees: BA & BS 4 yrs
Tuition: Res—undergrad $4620 per yr, $2310 per sem, $123 per hr; campus res—room & board $1460-$1540 per sem
Courses: Art Education, Art History, Calligraphy, Ceramics, Drawing, Jewelry, Painting, Photography, Printmaking, Sculpture, Art Therapy, Medical Illustration, Visual Communications
Summer School: Dir, Dr Mark Wolff. Courses—Art Appreciation, Art History, Ceramics, Drawing, Painting, Photography

MONTAY COLLEGE, Art Dept, 3750 W Peterson Ave, 60659. Tel 312-539-1919. *Art Dir* Irene Maloney
Estab 1953; pvt; D & E; enrl D 167, E 240
Ent Req: HS dipl
Degrees: AA 2 yrs
Tuition: $2000 per yr, $1000 per sem
Courses: Art Appreciation, Art Education, Calligraphy, Design, Drawing, Painting, Photography, Sculpture
Adult Hobby Classes: Enrl 30; tuition $55 for 15 sessions. Courses - Calligraphy
Children's Classes: Enrl 30; tuition $50 for 3 weeks. Courses—Adventures in Art

NORTHEASTERN ILLINOIS UNIVERSITY, Art Dept, 5500 N St Louis, 60625. Tel 312-583-4050, Ext 3324. *Chmn* La Verne Ornelas
Estab 1869; pub; D & E; scholarships; SC 44, LC 22; enrl total 10,200, maj 175, grad 1583, others 798
Ent Req: HS dipl, GED, upper half high school class or higher ACT
Degrees: BA 4 yrs
Courses: Art Education, Art History, Ceramics, Commercial Art, Drawing, Graphic Arts, Jewelry, Painting, Photography, Printmaking, Sculpture, Teacher Training

NORTH PARK COLLEGE, Art Dept, 3225 W Foster, 60625. Tel 312-583-2700, Ext 4301. *Chmn Dept* Neale Murray, MA; *Prof* Gayle V Bradley-Johnson, MA; *Prof* Luis Ramirez, MA; *Prof* Carrie Notari
Estab 1957; den; D & E; scholarships; SC 18, LC 5; enrl D 40
Ent Req: HS dipl
Degrees: BA 4 yrs
Tuition: Res—undergrad $9930 per yr; nonres—undergrad $7500; campus res—room & board $3765

Courses: Advertising Design, Aesthetics, Art Education, Art History, Calligraphy, Ceramics, Commercial Art, Drawing, Illustration, Painting, Photography, Printmaking, Sculpture, Teacher Training
Summer School: Enrl 25; tuition $200 course for term of 8 wks beginning June 12. Courses—Ceramics, Drawing, Painting, Sculpture

RAY COLLEGE OF DESIGN, 401 N Wabash Ave, 60611. Tel 312-280-3500; FAX 312-280-3528. *Pres* Wade Ray; *Dept Head* Veronica Chin; *Dept Head* Ann Rosen; *Dept Head* John Goehlich; *Dept Head* James Fraher; *Dept Head* Charlyn Fuchsen; *Dept Head* David Ray; *Dept Head* Cheryl Zuhn; *Dept Head* Carolyn Buchach; *Dept Head* Madeleine Slutsky; *Dept Head* Wayne Hanna
Estab 1916; pvt; D; SC 7; enrl D 450
Ent Req: HS dipl, portfolio review
Degrees: BA, AAS
Tuition: $7260 per yr, $3630 per sem; no campus res
Courses: †Advertising Design, Architecture, Art History, Commercial Art, Costume Design & Construction, Design, Display, Drafting, Drawing, Fashion Arts, Graphic Arts, Graphic Design, †Illustration, †Interior Design, Jewelry, Landscape Architecture, Painting, †Photography, †Fashion Design, Fashion Illustration, †Fashion Merchandising
Adult Hobby Classes: Enrl 150; tuition $190 per cr hr for 15 wk courses. Courses—Advertising Design, Fashion Design, Fashion Merchandising, Interior Design
Summer School: Pres, Wade Ray. Enrl 125; tuition $110 per cr for 8 wks beginning 4th wk of June. Courses—Advertising Design, Fashion Design, Fashion Merchandising, Illustration, Interior Design, Photography, Display

SAINT XAVIER UNIVERSITY, Dept of Art, 3700 W 103rd St, 60655. Tel 312-779-3300; FAX 312-779-9061. *Chmn* Jayne Hileman, MFA; *Assoc Prof* Mary Ann Bergfeld, MFA; *Assoc Prof* Brent Wall, MFA; *Assoc Prof* Michael Rabe, PhD; *Assoc Prof* Cathie Ruggie Saunders, MFA; *Assoc Prof* Monte Gerlach, MS
Estab 1847, dept estab 1917; pvt; D & E; scholarships; SC 35, LC 15; enrl D 50, E 5, maj 55, others 250
Ent Req: HS dipl
Degrees: BA & BS 4 yrs
Tuition: Undergrad—$318 per cr hr; campus res—room & board $4056 per yr
Courses: Art Education, Art History, Ceramics, Drawing, Film, Graphic Design, Illustration, Painting, Photography, Printmaking, Sculpture, Teacher Training, Video, Art Business
Adult Hobby Classes: Enrl 15-20; tuition $20-$40 per course. Courses—Drawing, Calligraphy, Painting, Photography
Summer School: Dir, Richard Venneri. Tuition $242 per cr hr for term of 6 wks beginning June 1. Courses—Various studio courses

SCHOOL OF THE ART INSTITUTE OF CHICAGO, 37 S Wabash, 60603. Tel 312-899-5100; FAX 312-263-0141. *Acting Pres* Peter Brown; *Undergrad Division Chmn* Martin Prekop; *Grad Division Chair* Carol Becker; *Dir of Admissions* Elizabeth Hoover; *Prof* Leah Bowman; *Prof* Barbara Crane; *Prof* Theodore Halkin; *Prof* Ken Josephson; *Prof* Richard Keane; *Prof* Robert Loescher; *Prof* Richard Loving; *Prof* Ray Martin; *Prof* Bill Farrell; *Prof* Ray Yoshida; *Prof* John Kurtich; *Prof* Frank Barsotti; *Prof* Catherine Bock; *Prof* Joseph Cavalier; *Prof* Tom Jaremba; *Prof* Michael Miller; *Prof* Joyce Neimanas; *Prof* Angela Paterakis; *Prof* Anthony Phillips; *Prof* Don Seiden; *Prof* Robert Skaggs; *Prof* Robert Snyder. Instrs: FT 80, PT 160
Estab 1866; pvt; D 1600; E 600; scholarships; SC 280, LC 90, GC 50; enrl maj 1400, non-maj 800
Ent Req: Portfolio; recommendations
Degrees: BFA 4 yrs, MFA 2 yrs, Grad Certificate in Art History 1 yr, MA in Art Therapy 1 yr, MA in Modern Art History, Theory, and Criticism 2 yr
Tuition: Res—undergrad $5250 per sem, grad $5400 per sem
Courses: †Art Education, Art History, †Ceramics, †Drawing, †Film, †Painting, †Photography, †Printmaking, †Sculpture, †Video, †Art & Technology, Art Therapy, †Fashion Design, †Fiber, †Interior Architecture† Time Arts, †Visual Communication, Scientific Illustration, Holography-Laser Sculpture, Computer Graphics
Adult Hobby Classes: Enrl 600; tuition $720 per 15 wk 3 cr course. Courses—various
Children's Classes: Tuition $160 per 14 wk sem or 6 wk summer course. Courses—Visual Arts, Studio Courses
Summer School: Dean, Roger Gilmore. Enrl 500; tuition $555 per 8 wk 3 cr course. Courses—Visual Art Studio Areas, Art Education, Art History, Art Therapy

UNIVERSITY OF CHICAGO, Dept of Art History and Committee on Art and Design, 5540 S Greenwood, 60637. Tel 312-753-3879. *Chmn* Robert Nelson
Estab 1892; pvt; D; scholarships; SC, LC and GC vary; enrl maj 11, grad 104, others 3
Ent Req: Through college of admissions
Degrees: BA 4 yrs, MA 1 yr, PhD 4-6 yrs
Tuition: $15,210

UNIVERSITY OF ILLINOIS AT CHICAGO, College of Architecture, Art and Urban Planning, PO Box 4348, 60680. Tel 312-996-3351, Art & Design 996-3337; FAX 312-996-5378. *Dean* Dr Ellen Baird; *Dir School Architecture* Stanly Tigerman; *Dir School Art & Design* Judith Kirshner; *Chmn Dept Hist of Architecture & Art* Victor Margolin; *Dir School Urban Planning* Charles Orlebeke. Instrs: FT 80, PT 28
Estab 1946; pub; D; scholarships; SC 79, LC 10, GC 3; enrl D 579, non-maj 325, maj 579, grad 17
Ent Req: 3 units of English plus 13 additional units, rank in top one-half of HS class for beginning freshman, transfer students 3.25 grad point average
Degrees: BA(Design), BA(Studio Arts), BA(Art Educ), BA(History of Archit and Art), BArchit, MFA(Studio Art or Design), MArchit
Tuition: Res—freshmen & sophomores $930, jrs & srs $1012, grad $1154 per qtr; nonres—freshmen & sophomores $2110, jrs & srs $2356, grad $2714 per qtr; no campus res
Courses: †Architecture, †Art History, †Art Education, Ceramics, Drawing, †Film, †Industrial Design, †Painting, †Photography, †Printmaking, †Sculpture, †Video, †Communications Design, †Comprehensive Design, †Studio Arts, †Urban Planning

& Policy
Children's Classes: Enrl 50; tuition $5. Courses—Saturday school in connection with art education classes
Summer School: Dir, Morris Barazani. Tuition res undergad $229, nonres undergrad $547 for term of 8 wks beginning June

UNIVERSITY OF ILLINOIS, CHICAGO, HEALTH SCIENCE CENTER, Biomedical Visualizations, College of Associated Health Professions, Room 211, 1919 Taylor St, 60612. Tel 312-996-7337. *Head* Louis Sadler; *Prof* Leon Lebeau, PhD; *Assoc Prof* Alfred Teoli, MFA; *Assoc Prof* Robert Parshall, BS; *Asst Prof* Deirdre McConathy, MA
Estab 1963; pub; D
Ent Req: Bachelors degree
Degrees: Master of Associated Medical Sciences in Biocommunication Arts
Tuition: Res—$1154 per quarter; nonres— $2714 per quarter
Courses: Medical Illustration

CHICAGO HEIGHTS

PRAIRIE STATE COLLEGE, Art Dept, 202 S Halsted, 60411. Tel 312-756-3110. *Dept Chmn* John Bowman. Instrs: FT 4, PT 30
Estab 1958; pub; D & E; SC 24, LC 6; enrl dept 600, maj 200
Ent Req: HS dipl, ACT
Degrees: AA 2 yrs
Tuition: $48 per cr hr, out of district $109 per cr hr, out of state $145 per cr hr
Courses: Art History, Design, Drawing, †Graphic Design, Illustration, †Interior Design, Painting, †Photography, Printmaking, Airbrush, Computer Graphics, Life Drawing, Materials Workshop, Package Design, Production Processes, Sign Painting, Stained Glass, Typography, Video Graphics, Watercolor
Summer School: Dir, John Bowman. Tuition $48 per cr hr for term of 8 wks. Courses—Art History, Drawing, Graphic Design, Interior Design, Painting, Photography

DECATUR

MILLIKIN UNIVERSITY, Art Dept, 1184 W Main St, 62522. Tel 217-424-6227. *Chmn Art Dept* Marvin L Klaven, MFA. Instrs: FT 3, PT 3
Estab 1901, dept estab 1904; pvt; D & E; scholarships; SC 47, LC 3; enrl D 1700, non-maj 25, maj 110
Ent Req: HS dipl, ACT
Degrees: BA & BFA 4 yrs
Tuition: $9200 per yr; campus res—room & board $2600 yr
Courses: Art Education, Commercial Art, Graphic Arts, History of Art & Archaeology, Mixed Media, Painting, Printmaking, Sculpture, Theatre Arts, Art Management, Art Therapy, Computer Graphics
Summer School: Dir Special Prog, Gerald Redford. Enrl 400; tuition $164 per cr hr for 7 wk term beginning June 13. Courses—Ceramics, Drawing, Painting

DE KALB

NORTHERN ILLINOIS UNIVERSITY, School of Art, 60115. Tel 815-753-1473. *Chmn, School of Art* Richard M Carp, PhD; *Asst Chmn* Jerry D Meyer, PhD; *Grad Coordr* Robert Bornhuetter, MFA; *Div Coordr* David McKay, EdD; *Div Coordr* Gordon Dorn, MFA; *Div Coordr* Norman Magden, PhD; *Div Coordr* Ron Mazanowski V, MFA; *Div Coordr* J Dimitri Liakos
Estab 1895; pub; D & E; scholarships; SC 127, LC 59, GC 98, other 15; enrl D 5000, maj 1000, grad 160
Ent Req: HS dipl, ACT, SAT
Degrees: BA, BFA, BSEd 4 yrs, MA, MS 2 yrs, MFA 3 yrs, EdD 3 yrs
Tuition: Res—$2828 per yr; nonres—$6792 per yr; campus res available
Courses: Advertising Design, Art Education, Art History, Ceramics, Design, Drawing, Graphic Arts, Graphic Design, Illustration, Interior Design, Painting, Photography, Sculpture, Teacher Training, Art Gallery Studies, †Art Therapy, Cinematography, †Computer Graphics/Design, †Jewelry/Metalwork, †On-Loom/Off-Loom Construction, Television Graphics, †Visual Communications, Watercolor
Summer School: Dir, Richard M Carp. Tuition res—$117 per cr hr, nonres—$283 per cr hr. Courses—Vary

DES PLAINES

OAKTON COMMUNITY COLLEGE, Art & Architecture Dept, 1600 E Golf Rd, 60016. Tel 708-635-1600; FAX 708-635-1987. *Chmn & Prof* James A Krauss, MA; *Prof* Robert A Stanley, MS; *Assoc Prof* Bernard K Krule, MS; *Assoc Prof* Peter Hessemer, MFA
Degrees: AA
Tuition: Res district—$17 per sm hr; nonres district—$55 per sem hr; nonres—$75 per sem hr
Courses: Architecture, Art Appreciation, Art History, Ceramics, Design, Drawing, Painting, Photography, Printmaking, Sculpture, Weaving
Summer School: Dir, James A Krauss. Enrl 90; tuition $17 cr for 8 wk term. Courses—Design I, Photography, Ceramics, Field Study, Painting

EAST PEORIA

ILLINOIS CENTRAL COLLEGE, Dept of Fine Arts, 61635. Tel 309-694-5011. *Chmn* Dr Kenneth Camp; *Instr* Wayne Forbes, MFA; *Instr* Fred Hentchel, MFA; *Instr* Robert Majeske, MFA; *Instr* Marlene Miller, MFA; *Instr* Stan Adams, MA; *Instr* Christie Cirone, BA
Estab 1967, dept estab 1967; pub; D & E; SC 27, LC 3; enrl D 800, E 400, maj 272
Ent Req: HS dipl
Degrees: Associate in Arts and Science 2 yrs, Associate in Applied Science
Tuition: $16 per sem hr; no campus res
Courses: †Advertising Design, Art Education, Art History, Ceramics, †Commercial

Art, Drawing, †Graphic Arts, †Graphic Design, Illustration, Interior Design, Jewelry, Lettering, Painting, Photography, Printmaking, Sculpture, Color, Design
Adult Hobby Classes: Tuition $28 per cr hr. Courses - Drawing & Painting
Summer School: Chmn Fine Arts, Kenneth Camp. Tuition $28 per cr hr. Courses - Photography, Introduction to Art, Drawing, Sculpture

EDWARDSVILLE

SOUTHERN ILLINOIS UNIVERSITY AT EDWARDSVILLE, Dept of Art & Design, PO Box 1764, 62026-1764. Tel 618-692-3071; FAX 618-692-3096. *Chmn Dept* Robin Brown; *Asst Chmn Dept* Pamela Decoteau; *Head Art History* John A Richardson, EdD; *Head Printmaking* Robert R Malone, MFA; *Head Drawing* Dennis L Ringering; *Head Fiber & Fabric* Paulette Myers; *Head Ceramic* Daniel J Anderson; *Art Education* Joseph A Weber, PhD; *Photography & Graphic Design* Robin Brown; *Head Painting* Michael J Smith, MFA; *Head Sculpture* Thomas D Gide
Estab 1869, dept estab 1959; pub; D & E; scholarships; SC 65, LC 26, GC 45; enrl D 250, E 75, maj 200, grad 50
Ent Req: HS dipl, ACT, portfolio req for BFA and MFA
Degrees: BA, BS and BFA 4 yrs, MFA 3 yrs, MS 2 yrs
Tuition: Res—undergrad & grad $1245 per yr, $415 per quarter, $197 for 5 hrs, $295 for 6-11 hrs, $415 for 12 hrs or more; nonres—for 12-up hours undergrad & grad $3129 per yr, $1041 per quarter, $458 for 5 hrs, $713 for 6-11 hrs, $1041 for 12 hrs or more; campus res available
Courses: Aesthetics, †Art Education, Art History, †Ceramics, †Drawing, †Graphic Design, History of Art & Archaeology, Jewelry, Mixed Media, †Painting, Photography, †Printmaking, †Sculpture, Silversmithing, †Teacher Training, Fiber Art
Summer School: Chmn, Don F Davis. Term of 8 weeks beginning June 21. Courses—full curriculum

ELGIN

ELGIN COMMUNITY COLLEGE, Fine Arts Dept, 1700 Spartan Dr, 60123. Tel 708-697-1000. *Dean* Holly Nash-Wright; *Instr* Roger Gustafson; *Instr* Steven Lebeck
Scholarships offered
Degrees: AA
Tuition: In district—$29 per cr hr; res—$76.51 per cr hr; nonres—$100.86 per cr hr
Courses: Advertising Design, Art Appreciation, Art Education, Art History, Ceramics, Design, Drawing, Jewelry, Painting, Photography, Printmaking, Sculpture

JUDSON COLLEGE, Division of Fine Arts, 1151 N State, 60123. Tel 708-695-2500. *Chmn* Dr Paul Satre
Pvt; D; scholarships; SC 15, LC 10; enrl D 481
Ent Req: HS dipl, ent exam, ACT, or SAT
Degrees: BA 4 yrs
Tuition: $2745 per sem; campus res—room & board $2940 per yr
Courses: Aesthetics, Art Education, Art History, Ceramics, Drawing, Graphic Arts, Graphic Design, History of Art & Archaeology, Painting, Printmaking, Stage Design, Textile Design, Photography

ELMHURST

ELMHURST COLLEGE, Art Dept, 190 Prospect, 60126. Tel 708-617-3542. *Prof* Sandra Jorgensen, MFA; *Prof* John Weber, MFA; *Chmn* Richard Paulsen, MFA; *Instr* Fern Logan, MFA
Estab 1871; den; D & E; scholarships; enrl D 1927, E 1500, maj 33
Ent Req: HS dipl, ACT or SAT
Degrees: BS, BA and BM 4 yrs
Tuition: $6300 per yr including room and board, $4040 per yr without room and board
Courses: †Painting, †Photography, †Printmaking, †Sculpture, †Art-business, †Time Arts, †Visual Communications
Summer School: Dir, Joan Lund. Enrl 1379; tuition $160 per cr hr for courses of 4, 6 & 8 weeks. Courses in selected program

EVANSTON

NORTHWESTERN UNIVERSITY, EVANSTON
—Dept of Art Theory & Practice, 1859 Sheridan Rd, 60208-2207. Tel 708-491-7346; FAX 708-491-5090. *Chmn Art Dept* William Conger. Instrs: FT 4, PT 3
Estab 1851; pvt; assistantships; SC 15, LC 8, GC 5; enrl 300-500
Degrees: AB 4 yrs, MFA
Tuition: $11,475
Courses: Practice of Art
Summer School: Courses—Introductory & graduate level independent study
—Dept of Art History, 254 Kresge Hall, 60208-2208. Tel 708-491-3230. *Chmn Dept* David Van Zanten; *Prof* Larry Silver, PhD; *Mary Jane Crowe Distinguished Prof* Otto-Karl Werckmeister; *Prof* Nancy J Troy; *Prof* Sandra Hindman; *Assoc Prof* Hollis Clayson, PhD; *Assoc Prof* Whitney Davis, PhD; *Asst Prof* Olan A Rand Jr, PhD; *Asst Prof* Michael Leja; *Lectr* Ikem Okoye
Estab 1851; pvt; D; scholarships; LC 36, GC 15; enrl maj 60, grad 40
Ent Req: HS dipl, SAT or ACT
Degrees: BA 4 yrs, MA 1 yr, PhD 3 yrs
Tuition: $15,075 per yr, $5025 per quarter; PT $1788 per course; campus res available
Courses: Architecture, †Art History, †Art Theory and Practice
Summer School: Dir Louise Love. Courses—vary in Western Art History

FREEPORT

HIGHLAND COMMUNITY COLLEGE, 2998 Pearl City Rd, 61032. Tel 815-235-6121. *Dir* Robert Apollini. Instrs: FT 1, PT 5
Estab 1962; pub; D & E; scholarships; SC 6, LC 1; enrl 126
Ent Req: HS dipl, ent exam
Degrees: AS, AA, ABA, AAS 2 yrs
Tuition: $18 per cr hr
Courses: Art History, Design, Drawing, Graphic Design, Painting, Printmaking, Sculpture, Art Materials & Processes, Fabrics, History of Modern Art, Introduction to Art, Pottery, Metals & Jewelry
Adult Hobby Classes: Enrl 278. Courses—Basic Drawing, Oil, Charcoal, Printmaking, Sculpture, Pottery, Handweaving & Related Crafts, Rosemaking, Macrame, Needlepoint
Children's Classes: Occasional summer workshops for high school and elementary school students
Summer School: Courses same as above

GALESBURG

KNOX COLLEGE, Dept of Art, 61401. Tel 309-343-0112. *Chmn* Frederick Ortner, MFA; *Prof* Henry Joe, MFA; *Asst Prof* Lynette Lombard
Scholarships
Degrees: BA 4yrs
Tuition: $12,609 per yr
Courses: Art History, Ceramics, Design, Drawing, History of Art & Archaeology, Painting, Photography, Printmaking, Sculpture

GLEN ELLYN

COLLEGE OF DUPAGE, Humanities Division, Lambert Rd at 22nd St, 60137. Tel 708-858-2800. *Assoc Dean Fine Arts* Jack Weiseman, MA; *Prof* Patricia Kurriger, PhD; *Asst Prof* Charles Boone, MFA; *Prof* Pamela B Lowrie, MS-MA; *Prof* Richard Lund, MFA; *Prof* Willard Smith, MS; *Prof* John A Wantz, MA; *Coordr Commercial Art* Peter Bagnuolo, AAS; *Asst Prof* Anita Dickson, AAS; *Asst Prof* Lynn Mackenzie, MA
Estab 1966; pub; D & E; SC 24, LC 5
Ent Req: Completion of application
Degrees: AA(Art) & AAS(Interior Design, Fashion Design, Commercial Art) 2 yrs
Tuition: DuPage Co res—$18 per cr hr, other Illinois res—$57 per cr hr, out of state res—$82 per cr hr; no campus res
Courses: Aesthetics, Architecture, Art History, Ceramics, Commercial Art, Costume Design & Construction, Design, Drafting, Drawing, Fashion Arts, Graphic Arts, Illustration, Interior Design, Jewelry, Landscape Architecture, Painting, Photography, Printmaking, Sculpture, Textile Design, Theatre Arts
Children's Classes: Courses—Ceramics
Summer School: Tuition $17 per hr for term of 3, 5 or 10 wks. Courses vary

GODFREY

LEWIS AND CLARK COMMUNITY COLLEGE, Art Dept, 5800 Godfrey Rd, 62035. Tel 618-466-3411, Ext 279. *Chmn Div Communications & Humanities* William Gardner; *Coordr* Mary Griesell. Instrs: FT 2, PT 3
Estab 1970, formerly Monticello College; pub; D & E; scholarships; SC 13, LC 2; enrl D 1800, E 600, maj 40
Ent Req: HS dipl, ent exam, open door policy
Degrees: AA 2 yrs
Tuition: $20 per sem hr; no campus res
Courses: Art History, Ceramics, Drafting, Drawing, Handicrafts, Painting, Sculpture, Basic Design, Weaving, Watercolor
Adult Hobby Classes: Enrl 30; tuition variable. Courses—Antiques, Interior Design, Introduction to Drawing & Painting
Summer School: Enrl 15; tuition $17 per sem hr for 8 wks. Courses—Introduction to Visual Arts

GRAYSLAKE

COLLEGE OF LAKE COUNTY, Art Dept, 19351 W Washington St, 60030. Tel 708-223-6601, Ext 377. *Dean of Curriculum & Adult Educ* Russell O Peterson; *Assoc Dean* Sandria Rodriguiz
Estab 1969, dept estab 1969; pub; D & E; SC 22, LC 5; enrl D 250, E 250, non-maj 500, maj 100
Ent Req: HS dipl, SAT
Degrees: AA and AS 2 yrs
Tuition: In-district—$17.25 per sem hr; out-of-district—$56.27 per sem hr; nonres—$83.23 per sem hr
Courses: Art Education, Art History, Ceramics, Costume Design & Construction, Drafting, Drawing, Fashion Arts, Landscape Architecture, Mixed Media, Painting, Photography, Printmaking, Sculpture, Stage Design, Theatre Arts
Adult Hobby Classes: Advertising, Ceramics, Drawing, Lettering, Mixed Media, Portrait, Stained Glass
Summer School: Dir, Russ Hamm. Courses—same as above

GREENVILLE

GREENVILLE COLLEGE, Division of Language, Literature & Fine Arts, Dept of Art, 315 E College Ave, 62246. Tel 618-664-1840, Ext 311. *Dept Head* Guy M Chase, MFA; *Asst Prof* Susan I Crotchett, MA
Estab 1892, dept estab 1965; pvt; D & E; SC 16, LC 4; enrl D 135, non-maj 105, maj 30
Ent Req: HS dipl
Degrees: BA 4 yrs, BS 4 1/2 yrs
Tuition: $5742 per yr; campus res—room & board $2734 per yr

Courses: †Art Education, Art History, Calligraphy, †Ceramics, †Drawing, †Graphic Arts, †Graphic Design, Handicrafts, History of Art & Archaeology, Lettering, †Painting, Photography, †Sculpture, †Teacher Training
Summer School: Registrar, Tom Morgan. Tuition $424 or $848 for term of 8 wks beginning June. Courses—Introduction to Fine Arts

JACKSONVILLE

MACMURRAY COLLEGE, Art Dept, 447 E College, 62650. Tel 217-245-6151. *Chmn Art Dept* Larry Calhoun
Estab 1846; den; scholarships; SC 29, LC 6
Degrees: 4 yr degrees
Courses: Advertising Design, Ceramics, Drawing, Painting, Teacher Training, Photography, Sculpture

JOLIET

COLLEGE OF SAINT FRANCIS, Fine Arts Dept, Division of Humanities and Fine Arts, 500 N Wilcox St, 60435. Tel 815-740-3360. *Dept Head* Dr K M Kietzman
Estab 1950; pvt; D & E; SC 6, LC 3; enrl D 150, maj 25
Ent Req: HS grad, ent exam
Degrees: BA(Creative Arts with Art Specialization or Art Educ)
Courses: Ceramics, Photography, Silversmithing, Advanced Drawing & Painting, Applied Studio, Basic Design, Fabrics, Special Topics, Textiles
Children's Classes: Courses—Art in variety of media
Summer School: Term of 6 wks beginning June

JOLIET JUNIOR COLLEGE, Fine Arts Dept, 1216 Houbolt Ave, 60436. Tel 815-729-9020, Ext 223. *Chmn Dept* Jerry Lewis, MM; *Instr* James Dugdale, MA; *Instr* Joe Milosevich, MFA; *Instr* William Fabrycki, MA
Estab 1901, dept estab 1920; pub; D & E; scholarships; SC 15, LC 4; enrl D 10,000, maj 120
Ent Req: HS dipl, ent exam
Degrees: AA 2 yrs
Tuition: $31 per sem cr for res of Ill Dist 525; $113.86 per sem cr for res outside Ill Dist 525; no campus res
Courses: Art Appreciation, Art History, Ceramics, Drawing, Graphic Arts, Interior Design, Jewelry, Painting, Silversmithing, Weaving, 2-D & 3-D Design
Summer School: Dir, Jerry Lewis, MM. Courses—Same as winter school

KANKAKEE

OLIVET NAZARENE UNIVERSITY, Dept of Art, 60901. Tel 815-939-5229, 939-5172. *Chmn Dept* Dr Don Royal; *Asst Prof* William Greiner. Instrs: PT 2
Estab 1907, dept estab 1953; den; D & E; scholarships; SC 14, LC 4; enrl D 100, non-maj 80, maj 21
Ent Req: HS dipl
Degrees: MBA, BS & BA 4 yrs, MEd & MTheol 2 yrs
Tuition: $1940 per yr, $970 per sem, $81 per sem hr; campus res—room & board
Courses: †Art Education, Art History, †Ceramics, Drawing, Film, Graphic Arts, Graphic Design, Lettering, †Painting, Photography, Printmaking, Sculpture, Teacher Training, Textile Design
Summer School: Dean, Dr Don Royal. Courses — Ceramics, Drawing, Harpbuilding, Intro to Fine Arts

LAKE FOREST

BARAT COLLEGE, Dept of Art, 700 E Westleigh Rd, 60045. Tel 708-234-3000, Ext 353. *Chmn Art Dept* Sharon Booko. Instrs: FT 6, PT 4
Estab 1858; den; W; D; scholarships; SC 32, LC 16; enrl maj 58
Ent Req: HS dipl, ent exam
Degrees: BA & BFA 4 yrs
Tuition: $3161 per sem; campus res—housing $1489
Courses: Ceramics, Drawing, History of Art & Archaeology, Illustration, Painting, Photography, Printmaking, Sculpture, Theatre Arts, Fibers, Three Dimensional Design, Weaving
Summer School: Courses—Ceramics, Fibers, History of Art, Painting, Photography, Two Dimensional Design

LAKE FOREST COLLEGE, Dept of Art, 555 N Sheridan Rd, 60045. Tel 708-735-5181; FAX 708-735-6291. *Chmn* Michael Croydon, ARCA; *Prof* Alex F Mitchell, MA; *Prof Emeritus* Franz Schulze, MFA; *Asst Prof* Lynne Pudles, PhD; *Asst Prof* Douglas MacLean, PhD; *Lectr* Ramona Mitchell; *Lectr* Irmfrieda Hogan, MFA; *Lectr* Colleen McNally, MFA; *Lectr* Arthur Lazar, MFA
Estab 1857; pvt; D & E; SC 8, LC 21; enrl D 1050 (sch total), maj 38
Ent Req: HS dipl, SAT, CEEB or ACT
Degrees: BA 4 yrs
Tuition: Res—undergrad $17,072 per yr, $8395-$8677 per sem; nonres—undergrad $13,895 per yr, $6855-$7040 per sem; $1715 per course; campus res—room & board $3362 per yr
Courses: Aesthetics, Architecture, Art Education, Art History, Design, Drawing, Painting, Photography, Sculpture, Monoprint
Adult Hobby Classes: Enrl 5-15. Courses—Photography
Summer School: Dir, Arthur Zilversmit. Enrl 200; tuition $990 per 4 sem hrs for 7 wks. Courses—Photography

LINCOLN

LINCOLN COLLEGE, Art Dept, 300 Keokuk St, 62656. Tel 217-732-3155. *Assoc Prof* E J Miley; *Assoc Prof* Marty Hargett, EdD
Estab 1865; pvt; D & E; scholarships; SC 35, LC 5; enrl maj 200
Ent Req: HS dipl
Degrees: AA
Tuition: $4000 per yr; campus res—$3000 per yr
Courses: Art History, Ceramics, Drawing, Illustration, Painting, Photography, Stage Design, Textile Design, Theatre Arts
Children's Classes: Courses offered through summer
Summer School: Dir, Dr Joe DiLillo. Courses—Art of France, Theatre of England, Introduction to Fine Arts (New York)

LISLE

ILLINOIS BENEDICTINE COLLEGE, Fine Arts Dept, 5700 College Rd, 60532. Tel 708-960-1500; FAX 708-960-1126. *Head* Michael E Komechak, MA
Estab 1887, dept estab 1978; den; D & E; enrl Full time 1150, grad 915
Ent Req: HS dipl, ACT, SAT
Degrees: BA, BS, MS & MBA 4 yrs
Tuition: Undergrad $9300 per yr; campus res available
Courses: Art Appreciation, Art History, Calligraphy, Design, Drawing, Lettering, Painting, Printmaking
Summer School: Dir, Philip Bean, PhD

MACOMB

WESTERN ILLINOIS UNIVERSITY, Art Dept, 32 Garwood Hall, 61455-1396. Tel 309-298-1549. *Dean College Fine Arts* James M Butterworth; *Chmn Art Dept* Edmond Gettinger, MFA; *Instr* F G Jones, MFA; *Instr* T M Karlowicz, PhD; *Instr* D J Kelly, MFA; *Instr* W L Moffett, MFA; *Instr* A G Mullin, MFA; *Instr* J E Neumann, MFA; *Instr* S M Parker, MFA; *Instr* G W Potter, MFA; *Instr* D F Scharfenberg, EdD; *Instr* A Schindle, MFA; *Instr* L C Schwartz, PhD; *Instr* J Smith, MA; *Instr* E V Solot, MFA; *Instr* D E Crouch, MFA
Estab 1900, dept estab 1968; pub; D & E; scholarships; SC 40, LC 30, GC 50; enrl maj 200
Ent Req: HS dipl
Degrees: BA 4 yrs, BFA
Tuition: Res—undergrad $1576 per yr
Courses: Advertising Design, Art Education, Art History, Ceramics, Commercial Art, Conceptual Art, Drafting, Drawing, Graphic Design, Illustration, Jewelry, Painting, Printmaking, Sculpture, Foundry Casting, Metal Working
Children's Classes: Dir, D Scharfenberg, EdD. HS Summer Arts Prog

MOLINE

BLACK HAWK COLLEGE, Art Dept, 6600 34th Ave, 61265. Tel 309-796-1311, Ext 3218. *Chmn Dept* Philip H Johnson, MS; *Asst Prof* Jeanne Tamisiea; *Assoc Prof* William Hannan
Estab 1962; pub; D & E; scholarships; SC 17, LC 4; enrl D 300, E 100, non-maj 300, maj 60
Ent Req: HS dipl
Degrees: AA & AAS(Commercial Art) 2 yrs
Tuition: Res—undergrad $45 per cr hr; nonres—undergrad $178 per cr hr; outside dist res—undergrad $103 per cr hr; no campus res
Courses: Advertising Design, Art History, Calligraphy, Ceramics, Drawing, Graphic Design, Jewelry, Painting, Photography, Printmaking, Sculpture, Art Appreciation
Adult Hobby Classes: Courses—Calligraphy, Drawing, Painting, Stained Glass, Photography
Summer School: Chmn, Philip H Johnson. Enrl 20; tuition $45 per cr hr for term of 6 wks beginning June 7. Courses—Art Appreciation, Photography

MONMOUTH

MONMOUTH COLLEGE, Dept of Art, McMichael Academic Hall, 61462. Tel 309-457-2311. *Chmn Dept* George L Waltershausen. Instrs: FT 2, PT 1
College estab 1853; pvt; D; scholarships, grants; SC 16, LC 4
Ent Req: 15 units incl English, history, social science, foreign language, mathematics & science, SAT or ACT
Degrees: BA
Tuition: $11,450 per yr
Courses: Art History, Drawing, Painting, Photography, Printmaking, Sculpture, Ceramics, Advanced Special Topics, Contemporary Art, Independent Study, Secondary Art Methods, Senior Art Seminar, Open Studio

NAPERVILLE

NORTH CENTRAL COLLEGE, Dept of Art, 30 N Brainard St, 60566. Tel 708-420-3429. *Chmn* Barry Skurkis, MA; *Prof Emeritus* Diane Duvigneaud, MFA; *Assoc Prof* Vytas Virkau, MFA; *Vis Lectrurer* Linda Johnsen, MFA; *Vis Lectr* Joseph Pinder, BA; *Vis Lectr* Dale Wisniewski, MA; *Vis Lectr* Edward Herbeck, MFA; *Vis Lectr* Joan Bredendick, MFA
Estab 1861; pvt; D & E; scholarships; SC 16, LC 5; enrl non-maj 3000, maj 35
Ent Req: HS dipl, SAT or ACT
Degrees: BA 4 yrs
Tuition: Res & nonres—undergrad $9096 per yr, $3032 per term, $160-$1890 part time per term; non-degree—$135-$2394 per term; campus res—room & board $3528 per yr
Courses: Art Education, Art History, Ceramics, Drawing, Mixed Media, Painting, Photography, Printmaking, Sculpture, Teacher Training, Figure Drawing, Studio Survey, Advanced Studio
Adult Hobby Classes: Courses offered through Continuing Education

Children's Classes: Enrl 48; tuition $45-$50 per term of 8 wks. Courses—Art, Beginning Art, Ceramics, Drawing
Summer School: Dir, Carol Brown. Enrl 50; tuition $679 per course. Courses—Ceramics, Drawing, Painting

NORMAL

ILLINOIS STATE UNIVERSITY, Art Dept, CVA 119, 61761. Tel 309-438-5621. *Chmn* Ron Mottram. Instrs: FT 50; 6 vis profs pr yr
Estab 1857; pub; D & E; scholarships; SC 50, LC 35, GC 40; enrl D 23,000, non-maj 100, maj 500, grad 50
Ent Req: HS dipl, SAT or ACT
Degrees: BA & BS 4 yrs, BFA 5 yrs, MA, MS, MFA, EdD
Tuition: Res—undergrad & grad $2430 per yr, $1215 per sem, $75 per hr; nonres—undergrad $6030 per yr, $3015 per sem, $225 per hr, grad $2454 per yr, $1227 per sem
Courses: †Art Education, †Art History, †Ceramics, †Drawing, Film, †Graphic Design, Mixed Media, †Painting, Photography, †Sculpture, Art Foundations, Art Therapy, †Fibers, †Glass, †Intaglio, †Lithography, †Metalwork & Jewelry Design
Summer School: 8 wk term beginning in June

OGLESBY

ILLINOIS VALLEY COMMUNITY COLLEGE, Div of Humanities and Fine Arts, RR No 1, 61348. Tel 815-224-2720, Ext 491. *Chmn* Samuel J Rogal, MA; *Instr* David Bergsieker, MFA; *Instr* Dana Collins, MFA
Estab 1924; pub; D & E; scholarships offered; SC 14, LC 2; enrl D 120, E 44, non-maj 156, maj 8
Degrees: AA 2 yrs
Tuition: $17 per sem hr
Courses: Art Education, Art History, Ceramics, Drawing, Graphic Design, Painting, Photography, Sculpture, Weaving
Summer School: Dir, Samuel J Rogal. Tuition $17 per hr

PEORIA

BRADLEY UNIVERSITY, Division of Art, Heuser Art Center, 61625. Tel 309-677-2967. *Dir* Robert Reedy. Instrs: FT 9, PT 4
Pvt; undergrad scholarships, grad assistantships & grad scholarships; enrl maj 121, others 500
Ent Req: HS grad
Degrees: BA, BA, BS, BFA 4 yrs, MA, MFA
Tuition: $7990 per yr
Courses: †Art History, †Ceramics, †Drawing, †Graphic Design, Art Appreciation, Commercial Art, Film, †Graphic Arts, †Jewelry, Lettering, †Art Metal
Summer School: Dir, Robert Reedy. Enrl 39; tuition $217 per cr hr for courses June - Aug. Courses—Ceramics, Drawing, Independent Study, Painting

QUINCY

QUINCY UNIVERSITY, Dept of Art, 1800 College Ave, 62301-2699. Tel 217-222-8020, Ext 5371; FAX 217-228-5354. *Prof Art* Robert Lee Mejer. Instrs: FT 3, PT 2
Estab 1860, dept estab 1953; SC 21, LC 13; enrl maj 25, total enrl 1715, E 150
Ent Req: HS grad, ACT or SAT ent exam
Degrees: BA, BS & BFA 4 yrs
Tuition: $4475 per sem; campus res—$773 - $865 per sem
Courses: Aesthetics, Art Appreciation, Art Education, Art History, Ceramics, Commercial Art, Design, Drawing, Teacher Training, Weaving, Illustration, Jewelry, Mixed Media, Painting, Photography, Printmaking, Sculpture, Art Seminars, Modern Art, Non-Western Art, 2-D & 3-D Design, Watercolor, Weaving
Summer School: Dir, Robert Lee Mejer. Tuition $190 per sem hr, optional junior year abroad

RIVER GROVE

TRITON COLLEGE, School of Arts & Sciences, 2000 Fifth Ave, 60171. Tel 708-456-0300. *Chmn* Norman Weigo. Instrs: FT 5, PT 6
Estab 1965; pub; D & E; SC 17, LC 3; enrl D 650, E 150, maj 138, adults and non-cr courses
Ent Req: HS dipl, some adult students are admitted without HS dipl, but with test scores indicating promise
Degrees: AA 2 yrs
Tuition: No campus res
Courses: Advertising Design, Art History, Ceramics, Commercial Art, Drawing, Graphic Arts, Graphic Design, Illustration, Lettering, Painting, Printmaking, Sculpture, Theatre Arts, Recreational Arts & Crafts
Adult Hobby Classes: Enrl 550. Courses—Candle Making, Continuing Education Classes, Crafts, Drawing, Ceramics, Jewelry, Quilting, Painting, Plastics, Stained Glass, Sculpture, Theatre Arts
Summer School: Dir, Norm Wiegel. Enrl 100; tuition $27 per cr hr. Courses—Selection from regular classes offered

ROCKFORD

ROCKFORD COLLEGE, Dept of Fine Arts, Clark Arts Center, 5050 E State St, 61108. Tel 815-226-4000. *Chmn Dept Fine Arts* Robert N McCauley. Instrs: FT 4, PT 2
Estab 1847, dept estab 1848; pvt; D & E; scholarships; SC 20, LC 3-4; enrl D 750, E 700, non-maj 135, maj 45
Ent Req: HS dipl, SAT or ACT
Degrees: BA, BFA and BS 4 yrs, MAT 2 yrs

Tuition: $8630 per yr
Courses: Art History, Ceramics, Drawing, Painting, Photography, Printmaking, Sculpture, Papermaking
Summer School: Dir, Dr Winston McKean. Courses—Art History, Fine Arts (Studio), Stage Design

ROCK VALLEY COLLEGE, Dept of Art, 3301 N Mulford Rd, 61111. Tel 815-654-4250. *Pres* Lester Salberg; *Prof* Cheri Rittenhouse. Instrs: FT 2, PT 1
Estab 1964, dept estab 1965; pub; D & E; SC 10, LC 4; enrl D 158, non-maj 70, maj 27
Degrees: AA, AS & AAS 2 yrs
Courses: Art Education, Art History, Commercial Art, Drawing, Painting, Printmaking, Color Theory, Design

ROCK ISLAND

AUGUSTANA COLLEGE, Art & Art History Dept, 61201. Tel 309-794-7231. *Chmn Dept* M E Kirn. Instrs: FT 6, PT 2
Estab 1860; den; D & E; scholarships & fels; SC 8, LC 9, LabC 3; enrl 2000
Ent Req: HS grad plus exam
Degrees: 4 yr degree
Tuition: $3984 per term
Courses: Art Education, Art History, Ceramics, Design, Drawing, Painting, Photography, Printmaking, Sculpture, Computer Art, Fibers
Children's Classes: Enrl 130-150; tuition $30 for 8 wk term. Courses—Drawing, Painting, Sculpture, Multi-media
Summer School: Dir, Douglas Nelson. Enrl 300; tuition $298 per sem hr for 5 wk term. Courses—Drawing, Fibers, Painting, Photography

SOUTH HOLLAND

SOUTH SUBURBAN COLLEGE, Art Dept, 15800 S State St, 60473. Tel 708-596-2000. *Chmn* Open ; *Assoc Dean* Linda Uzureau
Degrees: AA, AAS
Tuition: $32 per cr hr
Courses: †Advertising Design, Art Appreciation, Art History, Calligraphy, Ceramics, Design, Drawing, Illustration, Jewelry, Painting, Printmaking, Sculpture, Illustration
Summer School: Dir, Dr Fred Hanzelin. Enrl 65; tuition $32 per academic hr. Courses - Art History, Ceramics, Design, Drawing, Nature of Art

SPRINGFIELD

SANGAMON STATE UNIVERSITY, Visual Arts Program, Shepherd Rd, 62794-9243. Tel 217-786-6790; FAX 217-786-7280. *Assoc Prof* Bob Dixon, MFA & MS; *Asst Prof* Mauri Formigoni, MFA
Estab 1969, dept estab 1974; pub; D & E; scholarships; SC 24, LC 10
Ent Req: 2 yrs col educ
Degrees: BA(Creative Arts) 2 yrs
Tuition: Res—$537 per sem, $44.75 per hr PT; nonres—undergrad $1611 per sem, $134.25 per hr PT; campus res
Courses: †Advertising Design, Aesthetics, Art History, †Ceramics, Constructions, †Drawing, †Painting, †Photography, †Printmaking, †Sculpture, Theatre Arts, Video

SPRINGFIELD COLLEGE IN ILLINOIS, Dept of Art, 1500 N Fifth, 62702. Tel 217-525-1420. *Head Dept* Regina Marie Fronmuller, MA; *Instr* Marianne Stremsterfer, BA; *Instr* John Seiz, MA; *Instr* Tom Roth, BA; *Instr* Jim Allen, MA; *Instr* Lisa Manuele, BA
Estab 1929, dept estab 1968; pvt; D & E; SC 12, LC 4; enrl D 27, E 6, non-maj 11, maj 16
Ent Req: HS dipl, ACT
Degrees: AA 2 yrs
Tuition: $2420 per sem
Courses: Art History, Ceramics, Design, Drawing, History of Art & Archaeology, Painting, Photography, Printmaking, Two & Three Dimensional Design, Weaving
Adult Hobby Classes: Enrl 125; tuition $125 per cr hr. Courses—Art History, Ceramics, Design, Drawing, Photography
Children's Classes: Enrl 20; tuition $30 for 2 wks in summer. Courses—Art for Children 6 - 9 yrs, 10 - 14 yrs
Summer School: Dir, Dorothy Shiffer. Tuition $125 per cr hr

SUGAR GROVE

WAUBONSEE COMMUNITY COLLEGE, Art Dept, Route 47 at Harter Rd, 60554. Tel 708-466-4811. *Chmn* Robert Gage
Estab 1967; pub; D & E; scholarships; SC 8, LC 3; enrl D approx 275, E approx 200, maj 25
Ent Req: HS dipl, open door policy for adults without HS dipl
Degrees: AA, AS and AAS 2 yrs
Tuition: $33 per sem hr
Courses: Art Education, Art History, Ceramics, Drawing, Jewelry, Painting, Teacher Training, Theatre Arts, Video
Adult Hobby Classes: Enrl 250; tuition $33 per sem hr. Courses—Ceramics, Interior Design, Oil Painting
Children's Classes: Enrl 50; tuition $30 per course. Courses—Dramatics, Experience in Art, Photography
Summer School: Dean External Services, Dr Ken Allen. Enrl 50; tuition $20.50 per sem hr for term of 8 wks beginning June 6. Courses—as per regular session

UNIVERSITY PARK

GOVERNORS STATE UNIVERSITY, College of Arts & Science, Art Dept, 60466. Tel 708-534-5000. *Div Chmn* Dr Arthur P Bourgeois
Scholarships offered
Degrees: BA, MA
Tuition: Res—$453; nonres—$1359
Courses: Art History, Ceramics, Drawing, Painting, Photography, Printmaking, Sculpture

VILLA PARK

SCHOOL OF AIRBRUSH ARTS, 1330 S Villa Ave, 60181-1098. Tel 708-834-7333; FAX 708-832-0897. *Dir* Dennis D Goncher, MFA
Estab 1982; priv; D & E
Ent Req: For vocational status HS dipl or portfolio or professional status, no entrance requirements for avocational status
Degrees: Dipl in Airbrush painting 120 hrs, photo-retouching 160 hrs, photorestoration 160-200 hrs
Tuition: $450 per class
Courses: Airbrush Painting, Photo-Retouching, Photo Restoration
Summer School: Dir, Dennis D Goncher. Enrl 16 per class; tuition $450 for 40 hrs per class. Courses—Airbrush Painting, Photo-Retouching, Photo-Restoration

WHEATON

WHEATON COLLEGE, Dept of Art, 501 E Seminary, 60187. Tel 708-752-5000. *Chmn* Dr E John Walford. Instrs: FT 5
Estab 1861; pvt; D & E; scholarships; SC 24, LC 13; enrl 2250, maj 38, grad 350
Ent Req: HS dipl
Degrees: BA 4 yrs
Tuition: $4418 per sem; room & board $1820 per sem
Courses: Advertising Design, Aesthetics, Art Education, Ceramics, Drawing, Film, Graphic Arts, Graphic Design, History of Art & Archaeology, Painting, Photography, Printmaking, Sculpture, Video, Television Production, Theory & Techniques

WINNETKA

NORTH SHORE ART LEAGUE, 620 Lincoln, 60093. Tel 708-446-2870. *Pres* Pam Elesh
Estab 1924; pvt; D & E; SC 28; enrl D 310, E 84
Tuition: 16 wks, 3 hrs a session; no campus res
Courses: Drawing, Graphic Arts, Graphic Design, Jewelry, Painting, Critique, Stitchery

INDIANA

ANDERSON

ANDERSON UNIVERSITY, Art Dept, Fifth & College, 46012. Tel 317-641-4320; FAX 317-641-3851. *Chmn* M Jason Knapp
Estab 1928; pvt; D & E; scholarships; SC 30, LC 3; enrl non-maj 15, maj 60
Ent Req: HS dipl, ent exam plus recommendation
Degrees: BA 4 yrs
Tuition: Undergrad $7330 per yr
Courses: Advertising Design, Art Education, †Art History, Ceramics, Commercial Art, Drawing, †Graphic Arts, Graphic Design, History of Art & Archaeology, Illustration, Jewelry, Lettering, Museum Staff Training, †Painting, †Photography, Printmaking, Sculpture, †Stage Design, Teacher Training, †Air Brush & Watercolor Painting, Glass
Summer School: Dir, Robert Smith

BLOOMINGTON

INDIANA UNIVERSITY, BLOOMINGTON, Henry Radford Hope School of Fine Arts, 47405. Tel 812-855-7766. *Dir* John Goodheart; *Prof* Robert Barnes; *Prof* Bruce Cole; *Prof* Thomas Coleman; *Prof* Molly Faries; *Prof* Louis Hawes; *Prof* William Itter; *Prof* Jerry Jacquard; *Prof* Eugene Kleinbauer; *Prof* Marvin Lowe; *Prof* Ronald Markman; *Prof* Rudy Pozzatti; *Prof* Roy Sieber; *Prof* Bonnie Sklarski; *Prof* Budd Stalnaker; *Prof* Joan Sterrenburg; *Prof* Barry Gealt; *Assoc Prof* Sarah Burns; *Assoc Prof* Randy Long; *Assoc Prof* Jean-Paul Darriau; *Assoc Prof* Wendy Calman; *Assoc Prof* Reginald Heron; *Assoc Prof* Patrick McNaughton; *Assoc Prof* Wolf Rudolph; *Assoc Prof* Shehira Davezac; *Assoc Prof* Janet Kennedy; *Assoc Prof* Jeffrey Wolin; *Assoc Prof* Georgia Strange; *Assoc Prof* Susan Nelson; *Assoc Prof* James Reidhaar; *Assoc Prof* Ed Bernstein; *Asst Prof* Elizabeth Pastan; *Asst Prof* Dora Natella
Estab 1911; pub; D; scholarships; SC 55, LC 100, GC 110; enrl maj undergrad 300, grad 135 (45 Art History, 90 Studio), others 5600
Ent Req: Admis to the Univ
Degrees: AB, BFA, 4 yrs, MA, MFA, PhD
Tuition: Res—undergrad $2100 per yr, grad $2400 per yr; nonres—undergrad $6600 per yr, grad $6600 per yr
Courses: Art History, Ceramics, Graphic Design, Jewelry, Photography, Printmaking, Sculpture, Painting & Drawing, Printed Textiles, Woven Textiles
Summer School: Dir, John Goodheart. Tuition res—undergrad $71 per cr hr, grad $93 per cr hr; nonres—undergrad $222.15 per cr hr, grad $266.60 per cr hr. Courses—Art History, Ceramics, Drawing, Painting, Photography

CRAWFORDSVILLE

WABASH COLLEGE, Art Dept, 301 W Wabash Ave, 47933. Tel 317-362-1400, Ext 386. *Chmn* Douglas Calisch, MFA; *Prof* Gregory Huebner, MFA
Estab 1832, dept estab 1950; pvt; D; scholarships; SC 16, LC 7; enrl D 80, non-maj 70, maj 10
Ent Req: HS dipl, SAT
Degrees: BA 4 yrs
Tuition: $8450 per yr; campus res—room & board $3025
Courses: Aesthetics, Art History, †Ceramics, Display, †Drawing, †History of Art & Archaeology, †Painting, †Photography, Printmaking, †Sculpture, 2-D & 3-D Design

DONALDSON

ANCILLA COLLEGE, Art Dept, PO Box One, 46513. Tel 219-936-8898; FAX 219-935-1773. *Head Dept* Sr M Angelene Bilicke, MA
Estab 1936, dept estab 1965; pvt; D & E; SC 9-12, LC 2
Ent Req: HS dipl
Degrees: AA, AAA(Applied Arts) 2 yrs
Tuition: $65 per sem hr, $15 applied fee
Courses: Aesthetics, Art Appreciation, Calligraphy, Ceramics, Design, Drawing, Lettering, Graphic Design, Enameling, Watercolor
Children's Classes: Enrl 12; tui $40 for 6 sessions; Courses—Crafts for Children, Drawing and Painting for Children. Classes on Saturday

EVANSVILLE

UNIVERSITY OF EVANSVILLE, Art Dept, 1800 Lincoln Ave, 47722. Tel 812-479-2043. *Dept Head* Les Miley; *Prof* Les Miley, MFA; *Asst Prof* William Richmond, MFA; *Asst Prof* William Brown, MFA; *Asst Prof* Michelle Bollinger, MFA; *Instr* Jeffrey Bender, MFA; *Instr* Suzanne Aiken, MA; *Instr* Janice Greene, MA; *Instr* James Goodridge, MA
Estab 1854; pvt; D & E; scholarships; SC 22, LC 11, GC 11; enrl D 800, E 400, maj 72, grad 21
Ent Req: HS dipl
Degrees: BA(Educ, Art History), BS(Art, Art Therapy), BFA 4 yrs
Tuition: Campus res available
Courses: †Art Education, †Art History, †Ceramics, †Commercial Art, †Graphic Design, †History of Art & Archaeology, †Painting, †Printmaking, †Sculpture, Graphic Design
Summer School: 5 wk sessions. Courses—Painting, Ceramics, Art Education

UNIVERSITY OF SOUTHERN INDIANA (Formerly Indiana State University, Evansville), Art Dept, 8600 University Blvd, 47712. Tel 812-464-8600; FAX 812-464-1960. *Chmn* Kathryn M Waters; *Prof* James W McNaughton, MFA; *Asst Prof* Michael Aakhus, MFA; *Asst Prof* Leonard Dowhie Jr, MFA. Instrs: FT 5, PT 1
Estab 1969; pub; D & E; scholarships; SC 27, LC 4; enrl D 150, E 30, maj 90
Ent Req: HS dipl
Degrees: BS (Art Educ), BA (Art) 4 yrs
Tuition: Res—$50.75 per cr hr; nonres—$124 per cr hr
Courses: Art History, Graphic Design, Painting, Ceramics, Photography, Printmaking, Sculpture, Contemporary Art
Adult Hobby Classes: Enrl 25. Courses—Silkscreen

FORT WAYNE

INDIANA-PURDUE UNIVERSITY, Dept of Fine Arts, 2101 Coliseum Blvd E, 46805-1499. Tel 219-481-6705. *Chmn* Leslie P Motz; *Prof* Russell L Oettel, MFA; *Assoc Prof* Hector Garcia, MFA; *Assoc Prof* Donald Kruse, BS; *Assoc Prof* Anne-Marie LeBlanc, MFA; *Assoc Prof* Norman Bradley, MFA; *Assoc Prof* Audrey Ushenko, PhD; *Asst Prof* Dennis Krist, BFA; *Asst Prof* John Hrehov, MFA; *Asst Prof* Nancy McCroskey, MFA
Estab 1920, dept estab 1976; pub; D & E; scholarships; SC 96, LC 5; enrl non-maj 60, maj 235
Degrees: AB, AS, BFA 4 yrs
Tuition: Res—$69.45 per cr hr; nonres—$172.05 per cr hr; no campus res
Courses: Art History, †Ceramics, †Drawing, †Graphic Arts, Illustration, †Painting, †Photography, †Printmaking, †Sculpture, †Crafts, †Computer Design, †Metalsmithing
Children's Classes: Enrl 75; tuition $60 for 11 wks. Courses—Ceramics, Drawing, Painting, Sculpture

SAINT FRANCIS COLLEGE, Art Dept, 2701 Spring St, 46808. Tel 219-434-3100; FAX 219-434-3194. *Head Dept* Maurice A Papier, MS; *Assoc Prof* Sufi Ahmad, MFA; *Asst Prof* Rick Cartwright, MFA; *Instr* Lawrence Endress, MAT; *Instr* Karen Thompson, BFA; *Instr* Jenny Sanders, MS; *Instr* Tony Bouillon, MFA; *Instr* Audrey Riley, BA; *Instr* Alan Nauts, BA
Estab 1890; den; D & E; scholarships; SC 22, LC 6, GC 14; enrl D 100, maj 100
Ent Req: HS dipl, class rank in HS, SAT
Degrees: AA(Commercial Art) 2 yrs, BA and BS(Art or Art Educ) 4 yrs, MA(Art Educ) 1 yr
Tuition: Undergrad $250 per sem hr, grad $250 per sem hr; campus res—room & board $3000 per yr
Courses: Advertising Design, †Art Education, Art History, Calligraphy, Ceramics, †Commercial Art, Display, Drawing, Fashion Arts, Graphic Arts, Graphic Design, Illustration, Lettering, Painting, Photography, Printmaking, Sculpture, †Teacher Training, Computer Graphics
Children's Classes: Enrl 60; tuition $65 per sem. Courses—General Art Instruction grades K - 8
Summer School: Dir, M Papier. Enrl 150; two 6 wk sessions. Courses—Art Appreciation, Computer Graphics, Drawing, Painting

FRANKLIN

FRANKLIN COLLEGE, Art Dept, 501 E Monroe, 46131. Tel 317-738-8279; FAX 317-736-6030. *Chmn Dept* Thomas Fellner; *Instr* Luigi Crispino. Instrs: FT 2, PT 2
Estab 1834; D; scholarships; SC 9, LC 4; enrl 900
Ent Req: HS grad
Degrees: BA 4 yrs
Tuition: $13,200 per yr
Courses: Art History, Drawing, Painting, Sculpture, Basic Design

GOSHEN

GOSHEN COLLEGE, Art Dept, 1700 S Main St, 46526. Tel 219-535-7400, Ext 354; WATS 800-348-7422. *Chmn* Abner Hershberger, MFA; *Prof* Marvin Bartel, EdD; *Assoc Prof* Judy Wenig-Horswell, MFA; *Asst Prof* John Mishler, MFA; *Asst Prof* Rebekah Short, MA
Estab 1950; den; D & E; scholarships; enrl D 145, E 25, non-maj 60, maj 50
Ent Req: HS dipl, top half of class
Degrees: AB(Art) and AB(Art) with Indiana Teaching Cert
Tuition: $8310 per yr, $3760 per trimester, $295 per hr, campus res—room & board $3180 yr
Courses: Aesthetics, Art Appreciation, Art Education, Art History, Ceramics, Design, Drafting, Drawing, Graphic Design, Jewelry, Painting, Photography, Printmaking, Sculpture, Teacher Training, Architectural Drawing
Summer School: Acad Dean, John Eby. Tuition $520 for term of 3 1/2 wks beginning end of Apr, ending in late July. Courses—Drawing, Raku, Screenprinting, Watercolor; Florence, Italy Tour

GREENCASTLE

DEPAUW UNIVERSITY, Art Dept, 46135. Tel 317-658-4340. *Chmn* Robert Kingsley; *Asst Prof* David Herrold; *Asst Prof* Catherine Fruhan, PhD
Estab 1837, dept estab 1877; pvt den; D; SC 14, LC 9, GC 18; enrl D 300, E 20 (Art Dept), non-maj 25%, maj 75%, grad 20
Ent Req: HS dipl, upper half of high school graduating class
Degrees: BA & BM 4 yrs, MAEd, MAT
Tuition: $4100 per sem; campus res—room & board $1607.50
Courses: Art Education, †Art History, Ceramics, Commercial Art, Drawing, Graphic Arts, Illustration, Painting, Photography, Printmaking, Studio Arts

HAMMOND

PURDUE UNIVERSIRY CALUMET, Dept of Communication & Creative Arts, 2233 171st St, 46323. Tel 219-989-2393; FAX 219-989-2581. *Acting Head* William Robinson
Estab 1946; pub; D & E; scholarships; SC 1-4, LC 1-2, GC 1
Ent Req: HS dipl
Tuition: Res—$60 per cr hr; nonres—$160 per cr hr
Courses: Architecture, Art Education, Ceramics, Drawing, Film, Painting, Teacher Training, Theatre Arts, Video, Photography, Watercolor
Summer School: Dir, Michael R Moore. Enrl 60; tuition $60 per cr hr for res; $166 nonres. Courses—vary

HANOVER

HANOVER COLLEGE, Dept of Art, PO Box 108, 47243. Tel 812-866-7000; FAX 812-866-7114. *Chmn Dept* James W Shaffstall, MFA; *Prof* John Thomas, MFA
Estab 1827, dept estab 1967; pvt; D; schol; SC 16, LC 4; enrl D 960
Ent Req: HS dipl
Degrees: BS and BA 4 yrs
Tuition: $5300 per yr
Courses: Advertising Design, Aesthetics, Art Education, Art History, Ceramics, Collages, Commercial Art, Constructions, Drawing, Film, Graphic Arts, Graphic Design, Jewelry, Painting, Photography, Printmaking, Sculpture, Stage Design, Teacher Training, Theatre Arts, Video, Fiber, Glass Blowing, Stained Glass

HUNTINGTON

HUNTINGTON COLLEGE, Art Dept, 2303 College Ave, 46750. Tel 219-356-6000; FAX 219-356-9448. *Dean* Gerald D Smith; *Instr* W Kenneth Hopper
Estab 1897; den; D & E; SC 5, LC 3
Ent Req: HS dipl, SAT & two recomendations
Tuition: $7280 per year; campus res available
Courses: Art Appreciation, †Art Education, Art History, Ceramics, Drawing, †Graphic Design, Painting, Painting, Photography, †Printmaking, Arts & Crafts, Computer Graphics
Summer School: Dean, Dr G D Smith. Tuition $180 per sem hr beginning May 21. Courses—same as above

INDIANAPOLIS

INDIANA UNIVERSITY-PURDUE UNIVERSITY, INDIANAPOLIS, Herron School of Art, 1701 N Pennsylvania St, 46202. Tel 317-920-2416. *Dean* William J Voos; *Asst Dean* John Werenko; *Coordr Fine Arts* Robert Eagerton; *Coordr Visual Communications* Aaron Law; *Coordr Art History* Edward Kelley; *Coordr Foundation* Adolfo Doddoli; *Coordr Art Educ* Lance Baber
Estab 1902; pub; D & E; scholarships; SC 112, LC 16, GC 20; enrl D 415, non-maj 395, grad 20
Ent Req: Portfolio
Degrees: BFA and BAE 4 yrs, MAE 5 yrs
Tuition: Res—undergrad $80.50 per cr hr, grad $107.85 per cr hr; nonres—undergrad $242.60 per cr hr; grad $311.05 per cr hr; no campus res

Courses: Art Education, Art History, Ceramics, Drawing, Graphic Arts, Graphic Design, Illustration, Mixed Media, Painting, Photography, †Printmaking, †Sculpture, Teacher Training, †Fine Arts, Furniture Design, †Visual Communications, Computer Graphics
Children's Classes: Enrl 150; tuition $125 (partial scholarships) for 10 wk term, Saturday art classes for jr & sr HS students
Summer School: Dir, William Voos. Enrl 450; tuition res—$80.50, nonres—$242.60 per cr hr, two 6 wk sessions. Courses—Art Appreciation, Art History, Ceramics, Drawing, Painting, Printmaking, sr HS workshop

MARIAN COLLEGE, Art Dept, 3200 Cold Spring Rd, 46222. Tel 317-929-0298; FAX 317-929-0263. *Chmn & Instr* Megan Rohn; *Instr* Mark Hall, MFA; *Instr* Richard Patterson, MFA; *Instr* Sam Smith; *Instr* Mary Ellen Reed, BFA; *Instr* Roberta Williams, MA
Estab 1851, dept estab 1938; den; D & E; scholarships; SC 21, LC 6; enrl D 60, E 30, non-maj 20, maj 30
Ent Req: HS dipl, SAT
Degrees: AA 2 yrs, BA 4 yrs
Tuition: Undergrad—$6448 per yr; campus res—room & board $2450 per yr
Courses: Art History, Ceramics, Design, Drawing, Graphic Design, Interior Design, Painting, Photography, Sculpture, Stage Design, Theatre Arts, Art Therapy, Crafts

UNIVERSITY OF INDIANAPOLIS, Art Dept, 1400 E Hanna Ave, 46227. Tel 317-788-3253. *Chmn Dept* Ronald D Rarick, PhD; *Prof* Earl Snellenberger, MFA; *Prof* Dee Schaad, MFA
Estab 1902; den; D & E; scholarships; SC 24, LC 7, GC 7; enrl D 400, E 160, maj 70, grad 5
Ent Req: HS dipl, SAT, upper half of HS class
Degrees: BA and BS 4 yrs
Tuition: Commuter $9820 pr yr; campus res—room & board $3700 per yr
Courses: †Art Education, Art History, Ceramics, †Commercial Art, Drawing, Graphic Arts, Lettering, Painting, Photography, Printmaking, Sculpture, Textile Design, †Art Therapy
Adult Hobby Classes: Enrl 20; tuition $126 for 6 wks. Courses—Calligraphy, Ceramics, History, Photography, Watercolor
Summer School: Dir, Ronald D Rarick. Enrl 60; $104 per cr hr. Courses—Art History, Photography

MARION

INDIANA WESLEYAN UNIVERSITY, Art Dept, 4201 S Washington, 46953. Tel 317-674-6901; FAX 317-677-2333. *Head Dept* Ardelia Williams, MA; *Asst Prof* Robert Curfman, MA; *Instr* Rodney Crossman, BS Ed
Estab 1890, dept estab 1969; den; D & E; SC 32, LC 11; enrl D 35, non-maj 5, maj 30
Ent Req: HS dipl
Degrees: BS(Art Educ)
Tuition: $9350 per yr; campus res—available
Courses: †Art Education, Art History, Ceramics, Commercial Art, Drawing, Graphic Design, Jewelry, Painting, Photography, Printmaking, Sculpture, Silversmithing, †Teacher Training, Weaving, Batik, Stained Glass, Studio Administration, Studio Practicum, †Visual Arts Education
Summer School: Dir, Ardelia Williams. Enrl 8; tuition $375 for 5 wk 3 cr hr. Courses—Weaving

MUNCIE

BALL STATE UNIVERSITY, Dept of Art, 2000 University Ave, 47306. Tel 317-285-5838; FAX 317-285-3790. *Chmn* Thomas Spoerner, EdD. Instrs: FT 22
Estab 1918; pub; D & E; scholarships; SC 60, LC 25, GC 30; enrl non-Maj 800, maj 700, grad 40
Ent Req: HS dipl
Degrees: BS & BFA 4 yrs, MA 1 yr
Tuition: Res—undergrad $996 per sem, grad $800 per sem; nonres—undergrad $2295 per sem, grad $1740; campus res—available
Courses: †Art Education, Art History, †Ceramics, †Drawing, †Graphic Design, †Interior Design, †Painting, †Photography, †Printmaking, †Sculpture, †Metals
Adult Hobby Classes: Enrl 15; tuition $79 per cr hr
Children's Classes: Enrl 75; tuition $25 per child. Courses—General Art Activities
Summer School: Enrl 5000; tuition $996 for term of 5 wks beginning May

NEW ALBANY

INDIANA UNIVERSITY-SOUTHEAST, Fine Arts Dept, 4201 Grant Line Rd, 47150. Tel 812-945-2731, Ext 2342. *Coordr & Assoc Prof* Brian H Jones, MFA; *Assoc Prof* John R Guenthler, MFA; *Prof* Jonas A Howard; *Assoc Prof* Susan M Matthias, MFA
Estab 1945, dept estab 1966; pub; D & E; SC 25, LC 2; enrl D 150, E 35, non-maj 100, maj 50
Ent Req: HS dipl
Degrees: BA 4 yrs
Tuition: $1200 per yr, $600 per sem; no campus res
Courses: Advertising Design, Art Appreciation, Art Education, Art History, Ceramics, Drawing, Painting, Printmaking
Adult Hobby Classes: Enrl 35; tuition $25 per sem. Courses—Crafts, Watercolor
Summer School: Enrl 60; term of two 6 wk sessions beginning May 15 and July 5. Courses—same as above

NORTH MANCHESTER

MANCHESTER COLLEGE, Art Dept, 604 College Ave, 46962. Tel 219-982-5000; FAX 219-982-6868. *Chmn Dept* James R C Adams, MFA; *Assoc Prof* Stephen Batzka, BA
Estab 1889; den; D & E; scholarships; SC 15, LC 3; enrl D 45, maj 15
Ent Req: HS dipl
Degrees: AA 2 yrs, BA and BS 4 yrs
Tuition: Res—undergrad $10,766 per yr, including room & board
Courses: Advertising Design, Art Education, †Art History, Ceramics, Drawing, Film, Graphic Arts, Handicrafts, History of Art & Archaeology, Lettering, Painting, Photography, Printmaking, Sculpture, Teacher Training, Textile Design, Camera Techniques
Adult Hobby Classes: Tuition $38 per sem. Courses—Camera Techniques, Sculpture

NOTRE DAME

SAINT MARY'S COLLEGE, Dept of Art, 46556. Tel 219-284-4000, Ext 4631. *Chmn* Douglas E Tyler
Estab 1855; pvt, W; D & E; scholarships, fels; SC 21, LC 10; enrl maj 117, others 418
Ent Req: CEEB, standing, recommendations, others
Degrees: BA and BFA 3 1/2-5 yrs
Tuition: $2735 per sem
Courses: Art Education, Ceramics, Drawing, Jewelry, Painting, Photography, Printmaking, Sculpture, Design, Photo Silkscreen, Weaving. Rome Program: Courses—Art History, Design, Drawing
Summer School: Dir, Bill Tourtillotte. Enrl 40; tuition $459 (includes room & board) for 2 wk session. Courses—Ceramics, Drawing, Painting, Photography, Printmaking

UNIVERSITY OF NOTRE DAME, Dept of Art, Art History & Design, 132 O'Shaughnessy Hall, 46556. Tel 219-239-7602; FAX 219-239-8209. *Chmn* William Kremer. Instrs: FT 15, PT 8
Estab 1855; pvt; D; fels; SC 38, LC 8, GC 20; enrl maj 100
Ent Req: Upper third HS class, ent exam
Degrees: BA, BFA 4 yrs, MA, MFA
Tuition: Undergrad $12,390, grad $12,270 per yr; campus res—available
Courses: Drawing, †Art History, †Ceramics, †Graphic Design, †Industrial Design, †Painting, †Photography, †Printmaking, †Sculpture, Fibers
Summer School: Enrl 30-50; $93 per cr hr plus general fee for 7 wk term. Courses—Art History, Studio Workshops, Photography, Ceramics

OAKLAND CITY

OAKLAND CITY COLLEGE, Division of Fine Arts, 47660. Tel 812-749-4781, Ext 274; FAX 812-749-1233. *Div Chair Arts & Science* Margaret Harper; *Assoc Prof* Joseph E Smith, MFA; *Assoc Prof* Carol Spitler; *Assoc Prof* Jean Cox; *Asst Prof* Donna Hazelwood. Instrs: FT 4, PT 1
Estab 1961; den; D & E; scholarships; SC 10, LC 5; enrl maj 35
Ent Req: HS dipl, SAT
Degrees: AA 2 yrs, BA and BS 4 yrs
Courses: Art Appreciation, Art Education, Art History, Ceramics, Design, Drawing, Painting, Sculpture, Teacher Training, Weaving, Crafts
Summer School: Two 5 wk terms. Courses—Ceramics, Painting, plus others

RICHMOND

EARLHAM COLLEGE, Art Dept, PO Box 148, 47374. Tel 317-983-1200, 983-1410. *Chmn Dept* Dick Rodgers
Estab 1847; den; D; scholarships; SC 10, LC 7; enrl maj 10
Ent Req: HS dipl
Degrees: BA 4 yrs
Tuition: Res—undergrad $1600 per yr
Courses: Art History, Ceramics, Drawing, Film, Painting, Photography, Printmaking, Theatre Arts

INDIANA UNIVERSITY-EAST, Humanities Dept, 2325 Chester Blvd, 47374. Tel 317-973-8200; FAX 317-973-8237. *Chmn* Dr Ron Carter
Tuition: Res—$37.25 per cr hr; nonres—$91 per cr hr
Courses: Art Appreciation, Art Education, Art History, Drawing, Handicrafts, Painting, Photography, Sculpture

SAINT MARY-OF-THE-WOODS

SAINT MARY-OF-THE-WOODS COLLEGE, Art Dept, 47876. Tel 812-535-5151, 535-5279. *Chmn* Donna Foy. Instrs: FT 2, PT 1
Estab 1840; den; D; scholarships; SC 15, LC 4; enrl maj 14
Ent Req: HS dipl, SAT or ACT
Degrees: BA and BS 4 yrs
Tuition: Campus res available
Courses: †Art Education, Art History, †Ceramics, Drawing, †Graphic Design, †Painting, Photography, Printmaking, Teacher Training, Fiber Arts

SAINT MEINRAD

SAINT MEINRAD COLLEGE, Humanities Dept, 47577. Tel 812-357-6501. *Chmn* Steven S Scheer, PhD; *Assoc Prof* Donald Walpole, MFA
Estab 1854; pvt; D & E; SC 3, LC 3; enrl D 36, E 30
Ent Req: Admis and reg in the school
Tuition: $1456 per sem
Courses: Advertising Design, Aesthetics, Ceramics, Drawing, Graphic Design, History of Art & Archaeology, Painting, Theatre Arts
Adult Hobby Classes: Enrl 30. Courses—Ceramics, Painting

SOUTH BEND

INDIANA UNIVERSITY SOUTH BEND, Fine Arts Dept, 1700 Mishawaka Ave, 46615. Tel 219-237-4134. *Chmn* Robert W Demaree, Jr; *Prof* Harold Langland, MFA; *Assoc Prof* Alan Larkin, MFA; *Asst Prof* Susan Hood, PhD; *Adjunct Asst Prof* Linda Crimson, MFA; *Adjunct Asst Prof* Anthony Droega
Estab 1964; pub; D & E; SC 18, LC 6; enrl non-maj 300, maj 40
Ent Req: HS dipl
Degrees: BA(Fine Arts) 4 yrs
Tuition: Res—undergrad $68.95 per cr hr, grad $90.40 per cr hr; nonres—undewgrad $175.45 per cr hr, grad $204 per cr hr
Courses: Art Education, Art History, Drawing, Graphic Design, Painting, Printmaking, Sculpture
Summer School: Chmn, Anthony Droege. Tuition same as regular session; two 6 wk summer sessions. Courses—Art Appreciation, Drawing, Painting

TERRE HAUTE

INDIANA STATE UNIVERSITY
—Dept of Art, Fine Arts 108, 47809. Tel 812-237-3697. *Chmn* Wayne Enstice. Instrs: FT 19, PT 3
Estab 1870; pub; D & E; SC 66, LC 45, GC 61; enrl D 2432, E 311, maj 180, grad 40
Ent Req: HS dipl, top 50% of class with C average
Degrees: BS, BA & BFA 4 yrs, MS & MA 1 yr, MFA 3 yrs
Tuition: Res—undergrad $88 per cr hr, grad $105 per cr hr; nonres—undergrad $209 per cr hr, grad $235 per cr hr; campus res—room & board $3451 per yr
Courses: Art Education, Art History, Ceramics, Drawing, Graphic Design, Mixed Media, Painting, Photography, Printmaking, Sculpture, Metalry, Papermaking, Studio Furniture, Wood Sculpture
Summer School: Dir, Dr Louis Jensen. Tuition res—undergrad $88, grad $105 per cr hr; nonres—undergrad $209, grad $235 per cr hr for term of two 5 wks beginning June. Courses—variety of studio & lecture courses

UPLAND

TAYLOR UNIVERSITY, Art Dept, 46989. Tel 317-998-2751, Ext 5322. *Chmn* Craig Moore, MFA
Estab 1846, dept estab 1968; pvt; D & E; SC 12, LC 7; enrl D 175, E 10, non-maj 125, maj 25
Ent Req: HS dipl, SAT, recommendations
Degrees: BA and BS 4 yrs
Tuition: Campus res—room & board $8640 per yr
Courses: Advertising Design, Aesthetics, †Art Education, Art History, Ceramics, Collages, Drawing, Graphic Arts, †Jewelry, Lettering, Mixed Media, Painting, Photography, Printmaking, Sculpture, Silversmithing, Stage Design, †Teacher Training
Summer School: Dir, Dr Ray E Bullock. Courses—Photography, Survey of Fine Arts, Art for Teachers

VINCENNES

VINCENNES UNIVERSITY JUNIOR COLLEGE, Art Dept, 1002 N First St, 47591. Tel 812-885-4318; FAX 812-885-5868. *Chmn* Andrew Jendrzejewski; *Instr* Amy DeLap; *Instr* Steve Black; *Instr* Jim Pearson; *Instr* Deborah Hagedorn; *Instr* Priscilla Hollingsworth; *Instr* John Puffer; *Instr* Susan Baker; *Instr* Bernard Hagedorn; *Instr* Kevin Hughes
Scholarships offered
Degrees: AA, AS
Tuition: Knox county res—$63.20 per cr hr; other Ind & nearby Ill counties—$99.70 per cr hr, state nonres—$172.20 per cr hr; campus res—$3120 - $3480 per yr
Courses: Art Appreciation, †Art Education, Art History, Ceramics, †Design, Drawing, Graphic Design, Painting, Photography, Printmaking, Sculpture, Design & Materials, Portfolio Development & Review, Typographic Design
Adult Hobby Classes: Enrl 30, tuition $63.20 per cr hr for 15 wks. Courses—vary
Summer School: Dir Andrew Jendrzejewski. Enrl 6, tuition $63.20 per cr hr for 5 wks. Courses—Ceramics

WEST LAFAYETTE

PURDUE UNIVERSITY, WEST LAFAYETTE, Dept of Visual & Performaing Arts, Div of Art & Design, 1352 CA-1 Bldg, 47907-1352. Tel 317-494-3058. *Chmn Div* S Hagaman; *Head Dept* G R Sudano. Instrs: FT 32
Estab 1869; pub; D & E; scholarships; SC 50, LC 22, GC 22; enrl maj 523, other 2390
Degrees: BA 4 yrs, MA
Tuition: Res—$1260 per sem; nonres—$4095 per sem
Courses: †Art History, †Ceramics, †Industrial Design, †Interior Design, †Art Education, †Painting, †Photography, †Printmaking, †Sculpture, †Visual Communications Design, †Metals, †Textiles
Summer School: Courses offered

WINONA LAKE

GRACE COLLEGE, Dept of Art, 200 Seminary Dr, 46590. Tel 219-372-5267. *Head Dept* Art Davis, MA; *Assoc Prof* Bruce Johnson, MFA
Estab 1952, dept estab 1971; pvt; D & E; SC 12, LC 3; enrl maj 45, non-maj 80
Ent Req: HS dipl, SAT
Degrees: 4 yr Art Major, 4 yr Art Educ Major, 4 yr Graphic Art and 2 yr assoc
Tuition: $205 per cr hr; campus res—available
Courses: †Art Education, Art History, Ceramics, Drawing, †Graphic Design, Illustration, Painting, Photography, Printmaking, Teacher Training, Typography, 2-D Design, 3-D Design
Children's Classes: Sponsors competitions with awards
Summer School: Scholarships

IOWA

AMES

IOWA STATE UNIVERSITY, Dept of Art and Design, 158 College of Design Bldg, 50011. Tel 515-294-6724; FAX 515-294-9755. *Chmn Dept & Coordr Interior Design* Nancy Polster; *Coordr Drawing & Painting* Katherine Gibbs, MFA; *Coordr Crafts* Timothy J McIlrath, MS; *Coordr Graphic Design* Roger Baer, MFA; *Coordr Art Educ* Dennis Dake, MA; *Coordr Visual Studies* Donna Friedman, MFA; *Coordr Art History* Gary Tartakov, PhD
Estab 1858, dept estab 1920; pub; D & E; scholarships; SC 45, LC 15, GC 6; enrl non-maj 1500, maj 960, grad 30
Ent Req: HS dipl
Degrees: BA, BFA(Graphic Design, Craft Design, Interior Design, Drawing, Painting, Printmaking & Visual Studies), MA(Art & Design & Art Education), MFA(Graphic & Interior Design)
Tuition: Res—undergrad $940 per sem; nonres—undergrad $3080 per sem; campus res—available
Courses: Art Education, Art History, Calligraphy, †Ceramics, †Design, †Drawing, †Graphic Design, †Interior Design, †Jewelry, †Painting, †Mixed Media, Photography, †Printmaking, Sculpture, †Weaving, Fashion Illustration, †Surface Design, †Wood Design
Summer School: Dir, Prof Nancy Polster. Term of 8 wks. Courses—Art History, Design, Drawing, Painting; Workshops: Art Education, Ceramics, Fiber Art

BOONE

DES MOINES AREA COMMUNITY COLLEGE, Art Dept, Boone Campus, 1125 Hancock Dr, 50036. Tel 515-432-7203; FAX 515-432-6311. *Chmn* Lee McNair
Estab 1927, dept estab 1970; pub; D & E; SC 3, LC 2; enrl D 100, E 60
Ent Req: HS dipl
Degrees: AA 2 yrs
Tuition: Res—$39.45 per cr hr; nonres—$78.90 per cr hr
Courses: Art Appreciation, Art History, Drawing, Painting, Stage Design, Teacher Training, Theatre Arts, Life Drawing

CEDAR FALLS

UNIVERSITY OF NORTHERN IOWA, Dept of Art, Col of Humanities and Fine Arts, 50614-0362. Tel 319-273-2077; FAX 319-273-2731. *Head Dept* William W Lew, PhD; *Prof* Steve Bigler, MFA; *Prof* Felipe Echeverria, MFA; *Prof* Vera Jo Siddons, MA; *Prof* Roy Behrnes, MA; *Assoc Prof* Charles Adelman, PhD; *Assoc Prof* Crit Streed, MFA; *Assoc Prof* Allan Shickman, MA; *Assoc Prof* Matthew Sugarman, MFA; *Assoc Prof* Richard Colburn, MFA; *Asst Prof* Thomas Stancliffe, MFA; *Asst Prof* Cynthia Bickley-Green, PhD; *Asst Prof* Jeff Byrd, MFA; *Asst Prof* Philip Fass, MFA; *Asst Prof* Anna Martin, EdD; *Asst Prof* JoAnn Schnabel, MFA; *Asst Prof* Kee-Ho Yuen, MFA; *Asst Prof* Deborah Zlotsky, MFA
Estab 1876, dept estab 1945; pub; D & E; scholarships; SC 65, LC 20, GC 31; enrl 13,045, non-maj 150, maj 250, grad 7
Ent Req: HS dipl, ACT
Degrees: BA and BFA 4 yrs, MA 1 yr
Tuition: Res—undergrad $1044 per sem, grad $1173 per sem; nonres—undergrad $2715 per sem, grad $2993 per sem; campus res—room & board $2620 per yr
Courses: Art Education, Art History, Ceramics, Drawing, Graphic Design, Jewelry, Painting, Photography, Printmaking, Sculpture, Metalwork, papermaking
Summer School: Head Dept, William Lew, PhD. Enrl 100; tuition $696 for term of 8 wks beginning June 4

CEDAR RAPIDS

COE COLLEGE, Dept of Art, 52402. Tel 319-399-8564. *Prof* Robert Kocher, MA; *Chmn & Assoc Prof* John Beckelman, MFA; *Assoc Prof* David Goodwin, MFA; *Asst Prof* Lucy Goodson, MFA; *Asst Prof* Steve Whitney; *Lectr* Kahleen Carracio
Estab 1851; pvt; D & E; scholarships; SC 15, LC 8; enrl D 1200
Ent Req: HS dipl, SAT, ACT or portfolio
Degrees: BA 4 yr
Tuition: $8000; campus res—room & board $7920 per yr
Courses: Advertising Design, Aesthetics, Architecture, Art Appreciation, †Art Education, †Art History, †Ceramics, Collages, Commercial Art, Conceptual Art, Constructions, †Costume Design & Construction, Design, Display, Drafting, †Drawing, †Fashion Arts, Film, Graphic Arts, Graphic Design, History of Art & Archaeology, Illustration, Lettering, Mixed Media, Museum Staff Training, †Painting, †Photography, †Printmaking, †Sculpture, †Stage Design, †Teacher Training, †Textile Design, †Theatre Arts

KIRKWOOD COMMUNITY COLLEGE, Dept of Fine Arts, 6301 Kirkwood Blvd SW, 52406. Tel 319-398-5537. *Head Dept* Rhonda Kekke; *Prof* Doug Hall, MFA; *Prof* Rick Hintze, MFA; *Asst Prof* Helen Gruenwald, MA
Estab 1966; pub; D & E; SC 18, LC 6; enrl D 180, E 50
Ent Req: HS dipl
Degrees: AA 2 yr
Tuition: $35 per cr hr; no campus res
Summer School: Tuition $35 per cr hr. Courses—Art History, Art Appreciation, Ceramics, Design, Drawing, Lettering, Painting, Photography, Printmaking, Sculpture

MOUNT MERCY COLLEGE, Art Dept, 1330 Elmhurst Dr NE, 52402. Tel 319-363-8213, Ext 256. *Chmn Dept* Robert Naujoks, MFA; *Prof* Charles Barth, PhD
Estab 1928, dept estab 1960; pvt; D & E; scholarships; SC 20, LC 6; enrl D 150, E 35, non-maj 150, maj 35
Ent Req: HS dipl, ACT
Degrees: BA 4 yr

Tuition: $5200 per yr, $2600 per sem, $150 per cr hr; campus res—room & board $1300
Courses: Art Education, Art History, Drawing, Graphic Design, Painting, Photography, Printmaking, Sculpture, Textile Design, Multi-Media, †Studio Art
Summer School: Dir, Dr Jean Sweat. Enrl 500, tuition $420 for 3 hr course, two 5 wk sessions. Courses—Art Appreciation, Ceramics, Drawing, Painting, Photography

CENTERVILLE

INDIAN HILLS COMMUNITY COLLEGE, Dept of Art, Centerville Campus, N First St, 52544. Tel 515-856-2143, Ext 27. *Head Dept* Richard H Dutton, MA; *Instructor* Mark McWhorter, MA
Estab 1932, dept estab 1967; pub; D & E; scholarships; SC 10; enrl D 70, E 30, non-maj 50, maj 14
Ent Req: HS dipl or equal, open door
Degrees: AA 2 yr
Tuition: Res—$45 per cr hr; nonres—$60 per cr hr
Courses: Art History, Ceramics, Drawing, Painting, Sculpture, Art Appreciation, Arts & Crafts, Design, Watercolor
Adult Hobby Classes: Enrl 20; tuition $90 for 12 wks. Courses—Ceramics, Design, Drawing, Painting, Watercolor
Summer School: Dir, Dick Sharp. Courses—Art Appreciation, Ceramics, Design, European Art Tours, Painting

CLINTON

EASTERN IOWA COMMUNITY COLLEGE, Art Dept, 1000 Lincoln Blvd, 52732. Tel 319-242-6841; FAX 319-242-7868. *Instr* Curt Pefferman
Scholarships
Degrees: AA
Tuition: Res—$46 per sem hr; nonres—$68.50 per sem hr (includes fees)
Courses: Art Appreciation, Art History, Design, Drawing, Painting, Photography, Printmaking

MOUNT SAINT CLARE COLLEGE, Art Dept, 400 N Bluff, 52732. Tel 319-242-4023. *Head Dept* Dr Arthur P Dyck
Estab 1928, dept estab 1940; den; D & E; scholarships; SC 5, LC 1; enrl non-maj 80, maj 8
Ent Req: HS dipl
Degrees: AA 2 yr
Tuition: Res—undergrad $8330 per yr
Courses: Art Appreciation, Calligraphy, Ceramics, Design, Drawing, Computer Art, Computer Graphics, Desk Top Publishing, Fiber Art, Fiber Sculpture, 2-D & 3-D Design
Summer School: Courses—Art Appreciation, Calligraphy, Painting

COUNCIL BLUFFS

IOWA WESTERN COMMUNITY COLLEGE, Art Dept, 2700 College Rd, PO Box 4C, 51502. Tel 712-325-3200; FAX 712-325-3424. *Chmn* Bonnie Miley; *Prof Art* Nick J Chiburis
Enrl 2000
Courses: Art Appreciation, Art History, Ceramics, Design, Drawing, Painting, Photography, Sculpture

CRESTON

SOUTHWESTERN COMMUNITY COLLEGE, Art Dept, 1501 W Townline Rd, 50801. Tel 515-782-7081. *Dir Art Dept* Dale Jackson
Estab 1966; pub; D & E; scholarships; SC 6, LC 3; enrl D 550, E 200, non-maj 40, maj 15, others 15
Ent Req: HS dipl
Degrees: AA 2 yrs
Courses: Art Appreciation, Art Education, Art History, Ceramics, Design, Drawing, Graphic Design, Painting, Photography, Teacher Training, Computer Graphics
Adult Hobby Classes: Enrl 10-30; tuition $30 per sem. Courses—Per regular session
Summer School: Workshops in arts science

DAVENPORT

SAINT AMBROSE UNIVERSITY, Art Dept, 518 W Locust St, 52803. Tel 319-383-8800; FAX 319-383-8791. *Chmn* John W Schmits, BA; *Assoc Prof* Kristin Quinn, MFA; *Faculty* Janet Seiz, MA
Estab 1892; den; D & E; scholarships; SC 17, LC 12; enrl D 450, E 40, maj 55
Ent Req: HS dipl
Degrees: BA 4 yrs
Tuition: $244 per cr hr; campus res—available
Courses: Advertising Design, Art Education, Calligraphy, Ceramics, Commercial Art, Drawing, Graphic Arts, Graphic Design, History of Art & Archaeology, Illustration, Lettering, Painting, Photography, Printmaking, Sculpture, Teacher Training
Summer School: Tuition $244 per sem hr. Courses—vary

TEIKYO MARYCREST UNIVERSITY (Formerly Marycrest College), Art and Computer Graphics Dept, 1607 W 12th St, 52804. Tel 319-326-9532; FAX 319-326-9250. *Chmn* Dr Alan Garfield; *Assoc Prof* Bruce Walters; *Asst Prof* Lane Hall
Estab 1939; den; D & E; scholarships; SC 35, LC 15, GC 13; enrl D 446, E 129, maj 68, grad 56
Ent Req: HS dipl
Degrees: BA 3-4 yrs, MA
Tuition: Tuition $2070 per sem; campus res—room & board $995 per sem
Courses: Advertising Design, Aesthetics, Art Education, Ceramics, Commercial Art, Drafting, Drawing, Fashion Arts, Graphic Design, History of Art & Archaeology,

Museum Staff Training, Painting, Photography, Sculpture, Stage Design, Teacher Training, Theatre Arts, †Computer Graphics, Computer Art & Design
Adult Hobby Classes: Tuition $125 per cr hr; Weekend College Courses—Art Appreciation, Drawing, Composition, Masterpieces of Art, Painting
Summer School: Dir, Dr A Garfield. Courses - Independent Study, Painting, Readings, Computer Graphics

DECORAH

LUTHER COLLEGE, Art Dept, 52101. Tel 319-387-1113; FAX 319-387-2158.
Head Dept Dale Raddatz Lackore. Instrs: FT 3, PT 2
Estab 1861; den; D; scholarships; SC 13, LC 5; enrl D 160
Ent Req: HS dipl or ent exam
Degrees: BA 4 yr
Courses: †Aesthetics, †Art Education, †Ceramics, †Drawing, Graphic Arts, †History of Art & Archaeology, †Lettering, †Painting, †Printmaking, †Stage Design, †Teacher Training, †Theatre Arts, Art Management, Fibers, Spinning, Hand Made Paper, Computer Art
Children's Classes: Enrl 50; Courses offered spring & fall
Summer School: Academic Dean, A Thomas Kraalsel. Enrl 200 June & July. Courses—Drawing, Invitation to Art

DES MOINES

DRAKE UNIVERSITY, Art Dept, 25th & University Ave, 50311. Tel 515-271-2863. *Chmn Dept* Jules Kirschenbaum. Instrs: FT 10, PT 8
Estab 1881; pvt; D & E; scholarships; SC 64, LC 15, GC 33; enrl D 140, maj 140, grad 10
Ent Req: 2 pt average in HS or previous col
Degrees: BA, BFA, MFA
Tuition: $5145 per sem
Courses: †Advertising Design, †Art Education, †Art History, †Commercial Art, †Drawing, †Graphic Arts, †Graphic Design, Illustration, †Interior Design, Jewelry, Lettering, †Painting, †Printmaking, †Sculpture, Stage Design, Teacher Training
Summer School: Tuition $525. Courses—Art History, Drawing, Painting, 2-D & 3-D Design, Textiles, Sculpture

GRAND VIEW COLLEGE, Art Dept, 1200 Grandview Ave, 50316. Tel 515-263-2800. *Dept Head* Dana Shaeffer
Scholarships offered
Degrees: BA, cert
Tuition: Res—$2270 per sem
Courses: Drawing, Jewelry, Painting, Photography, Printmaking, Textile Design, Theatre Arts, Art Therapy, Computer Graphics

DUBUQUE

CLARKE COLLEGE, Dept of Art, 1550 Clarke Dr, 52001. Tel 319-588-6300; FAX 319-588-6789. *Chmn* Carmelle Zserdin, BVM
Estab 1843; den; D & E; scholarships; SC 15, LC 4; enrl maj 50, others 900
Ent Req: HS grad, 16 units and Col Ent Board
Degrees: BFA(studio) & BA(studio & art history)
Tuition: $9560
Courses: Aesthetics, Art Education, Art History, Calligraphy, Ceramics, Conceptual Art, Design, Drawing, Graphic Design, Lettering, Mixed Media, Painting, Photography, †Printmaking, †Sculpture, †Teacher Training, †Adult Continuing Educ Program: D & E
Adult Hobby Classes: Enrl varies; 3, 4, 7 & 15 wk terms
Children's Classes: Enrl 95; tuition $55 per wk, summers
Summer School: Dir, Ann Siegrist. 3-4 wk term

LORAS COLLEGE, Dept of Art, 1450 Alta Vista, 52004-0178. Tel 319-588-7117. *Chmn* John Hoffman; *Prof* Roy Haught; *Instr* Barbara Sedler; *Instr* Dina Morelli; *Assoc Prof* Thomas Jewell Vitale; *Instr* Tom Gibbs
Degrees: MA (Art Educ &Studio Arts), BA
Tuition: $3912 per sem
Courses: Art Appreciation, †Art Education, †Art History, Design, Drawing, Painting, Printmaking, Sculpture, †Fibers, †Studio Art
Summer School: Dir, John Hess. Enrl $170 per course

ESTHERVILLE

IOWA LAKES COMMUNITY COLLEGE, Dept of Art, 300 S 18th St, 51334. Tel 712-362-2604; FAX 712-362-7649. *Dept Head* Dennis Hageman; *Instr* Wayne Hollis, MA; *Instr* David Goughnour, MA; *Instr* Dick Williams, MA
Estab 1967; pub; D & E; scholarships; SC 26, LC 1
Ent Req: HS dipl
Degrees: AA, AS(Commercial Art) 2 yrs
Tuition: Res—undergrad $510 per sem
Courses: Advertising Design, Art History, Calligraphy, Ceramics, Commercial Art, Drawing, Graphic Arts, Graphic Design, Illustration, Mixed Media, Painting, Photography, Computer Graphics, Commercial Studio Portfolio Preparation
Summer School: Courses—Internships in Commercial Art

FOREST CITY

WALDORF COLLEGE, Art Dept, 50436. Tel 515-582-2450; FAX 515-582-8111.
Chmn Dept Ruth Ann Kovach. Instrs: FT 1, PT 1
Estab 1903; den; D; scholarships; SC 4; enrl D 80, maj 15
Ent Req: HS dipl, ACT or SAT
Degrees: AA, AC and AAS 2 yr
Tuition: $1995 per sem
Courses: Design, Photography, Printmaking, Art History, Ceramics, Drafting, Drawing, Painting

FORT DODGE

IOWA CENTRAL COMMUNITY COLLEGE, Dept of Art, 330 Ave M, 50501.
Tel 515-576-7201; WATS 800-362-2793. *Assoc Prof* Maureen Seamonds; *Instr* Rusty Farrington
Pub; D & E; scholarships; SC 4, LC 2; enrl D 120, E 15, non-maj 153, maj 20
Ent Req: HS dipl
Degrees: AA 2 yr
Tuition: Res—$410 per sem, $41.50 per hr; nonres—$565 per sem, $56.25 per hr; campus res—room & board $1995 per yr
Courses: Art History, Painting, Studio Art
Adult Hobby Classes: Enrl 50; tuition $25 for 6 wk session. Courses—Cartooning, Drawing, Printmaking
Summer School: Dir Rusty Farrington. Enrl 45; tuition $53 per cr hr

GRINNELL

GRINNELL COLLEGE, Dept of Art, Fine Arts Center, PO Box 805, 50112-0806.
Tel 515-269-3064, 269-3085; FAX 515-269-3408. *Chmn Dept* Robert McKibbin; *Instr* Susan Strauber; *Instr* Merle W Zirkle; *Instr* J Anthony Crowley
Estab 1846, dept estab 1930; pvt; D; scholarships; SC 9, LC 9; enrl D 150, non-maj 125, maj 25
Ent Req: HS dipl, SAT or ACT
Degrees: BA 4 yr
Tuition: Res—undergrad $16,150 per yr; campus res—room & board
Courses: Art Education, Art History, Ceramics, Design, Drawing, Jewelry, Painting, Printmaking, Sculpture

INDIANOLA

SIMPSON COLLEGE, Art Dept, 701 N C, 50125. Tel 515-961-1561; FAX 515-961-1498. *Chairperson Dept* Janet Heinicke
Estab 1860, dept estab 1965; pvt; D & E; scholarships; SC 3, LC 3; enrl D 120, maj 20
Ent Req: HS dipl, ACT or SAT
Degrees: BA and BM 4 yrs
Tuition: Res—undergrad $8815 per yr; campus res—room $1380 and board $1695
Courses: Art Education, Art History, Ceramics, Drawing, History of Art & Archaeology, Painting, Photography, Printmaking, Sculpture, Teacher Training, Art Management, Fundamentals of Design & Color Theory, 3-D Design
Adult Hobby Classes: Enrl 500; tuition $130 per sem hr. Courses—Art Education, Art Methods
Summer School: Dir, Dr Jill Rossiter

IOWA CITY

UNIVERSITY OF IOWA, School of Art and Art History, N Riverside Dr, 52242.
Tel 319-335-1771; FAX 319-335-2951. *Dir* Wallace J Tomasini, PhD. Instrs: FT 38, PT 3
Estab 1847, school estab 1911; pub; D & E; scholarships; SC 60, LC 55, GC 55; enrl D 681, maj 508, grad 173
Ent Req: HS dipl, ACT or SAT, upper rank in HS
Degrees: BA and BFA 4 yr, MA, MFA, PhD
Tuition: Res—undergrad $940 per sem, grad $1113 per sem; nonres—$3110 per sem, grad $3242 per sem; campus res—room and board $2769 per yr
Courses: Aesthetics, Art Education, Art History, Ceramics, Conceptual Art, Design, Drawing, Graphic Design, Industrial Design, Intermedia, †Interior Design, †Jewelry, Lettering, †Painting, †Photography, †Printmaking, †Sculpture, †Silversmithing, †Teacher Training, †Video, †Multimedia
Summer School: Dir, Wallace J Tomasini. Enrl undergrad 195, grad 115; tuition res—undergrad $940, grad $1113; nonres—undergrad $3110, grad $3242 for term of 8 wks, beginning June 10. Courses —full range of Art Education, Art History & Studio Courses

IOWA FALLS

ELLSWORTH COMMUNITY COLLEGE, Dept of Fine Arts, 1100 College Ave, 50126. Tel 515-648-4611; FAX 515-648-3128. *Chmn* Bill Phelps; *Instr* Patricia McLoone
Estab 1890, dept estab 1890; pub; D & E; SC 10, LC 1; enrl in dept D 20-25
Ent Req: HS dipl, ACT
Degrees: AA 2 yrs
Tuition: Res $900 per yr; nonres undergrad $1800; campus res—room & board $1900
Courses: †Advertising Design, Art Education, Art History, Calligraphy, Ceramics, Commercial Art, Conceptual Art, Drawing, Handicrafts, Illustration, Lettering, Mixed Media, Painting, Photography, Sculpture, Teacher Training, Theatre Arts, Weaving
Adult Hobby Classes: Enrl 12; tuition $20 per 20 hrs. Courses—Pottery
Summer School: Dir, Dr Del Shepard. Enrl 14; tuition $40 per sem hr for 4 weeks. Courses—Art Interpretation

LAMONI

GRACELAND COLLEGE, Fine Arts Dept, 700 College Ave, 50140. Tel 515-784-5000. *Chmn Fine Arts* Richard I Clothier; *Instr* Craig L Warner; *Instr* Bette J Sellars
Estab 1895, dept estab 1961; pvt den; D; scholarships; SC 30, LC 10; enrl D 180, maj 52, others 4
Ent Req: HS dipl
Degrees: BA and BS 4 yrs
Tuition: $2205 per sem
Courses: Advertising Design, †Art Education, Art History, Ceramics, Commercial Art, Constructions, Drawing, Graphic Arts, History of Art & Archaeology, Intermedia, Lettering, Painting, Photography, Printmaking, Sculpture, Teacher Training
Summer School: Dir, Dr Velma Ruch

LEMARS

TEIKYO WESTMAR UNIVERSITY, Art Dept, 1002 Third Ave SE, 51031. Tel 712-546-7081, Ext 2570. *Art Prog Dir* Randy Strathman-Becker; *Instr* Anne Lubben. Instrs: FT 1
Estab 1890; pvt; D; enrl 700, maj 22
Ent Req: ACT, SAT or PSAT
Degrees: BA, BMEd and BAS 4 yr
Tuition: $4060 per yr
Courses: Aesthetics, Architecture, Art Appreciation, Art Education, Art History, Ceramics, Design, Drawing, Graphic Arts, History of Art & Archaeology, Mixed Media, Painting, Printmaking, Sculpture, Art Philosophy & Criticism, Business World of Art, Design, Foundations of Art, Synthetic Media & Color, Watercolor
Adult Hobby Classes: JANUS Continuing Education for Retired Persons
Summer School: Dir, Randy Strathman-Becker. Tuition $600-$700 for 4-6 wk term. Courses—Painting, Printmaking, Sculpture

MASON CITY

NORTH IOWA AREA COMMUNITY COLLEGE, Dept of Art, 500 College Dr, 50401. Tel 515-423-1264, Ext 242, 307. *Instr* Peggy L Bang; *Instr* Carol Faber
Estab 1964; pub; D & E; scholarships; SC 4, LC 2; enrl D 240, E 100, maj 30
Ent Req: HS dipl
Degrees: AA 2 yr
Tuition: $766 per sem
Courses: Art Education, Art History, Ceramics, Drawing, Painting, Photography, Computer Graphic Design, 2-D Design
Adult Hobby Classes: Enrl 30. Courses—Crafts, Painting
Summer School: Dir, Carol Faber. Enrl 30; tuition $46 per cr for 6 wk term. Courses—Essence of Art, Drawing

MOUNT PLEASANT

IOWA WESLEYAN COLLEGE, Art Dept, 601 N Main, 52641. Tel 319-385-8021. *Chmn* Don R Jones; *Asst Prof* Ann Klingensmith
Estab 1842; den; scholarships; SC 10, LC 4; enrl maj 32
Degrees: BA 4 yr
Tuition: Res—undergrad $12,400 per yr including room & board
Courses: Art Education, Art History, Ceramics, Design, Drawing, Graphic Arts, Painting, Photography, Printmaking, Introduction to Art, Secondary Art, Special Problems, Twentieth Century Art History

MOUNT VERNON

CORNELL COLLEGE, Art Dept, Armstrong Hall, Fine Arts, 52314. Tel 319-895-4000; FAX 319-895-4492. *Head Dept* Doug Hanson. Instrs: FT 3
Estab 1853; den; D; scholarships; SC 30, LC 3; enrl 900
Ent Req: HS dipl
Degrees: BA, BSS and BPhil 4 yr
Tuition: $5710
Courses: Art History, Ceramics, Drawing, Painting, Photography, Sculpture, Batik, Design, Metal & Fiber Design, Weaving

ORANGE CITY

NORTHWESTERN COLLEGE, Art Dept, 51041. Tel 712-737-4821, Ext 156. *Chmn* John Kaericher, MFA; *Asst Prof* Rein Vanderhill, MFA; *Prof* Nella Kennedy, MA
Estab 1882; dept estab 1965; den; D & E; scholarships; SC 25, LC 3-4; enrl D 200, non-maj 175, maj 23-25
Ent Req: HS dipl
Degrees: BA 4 yr
Tuition: Campus residency available
Courses: Art Education, Art History, Ceramics, Design, Drawing, Painting, Photography, Printmaking, Sculpture

OSKALOOSA

WILLIAM PENN COLLEGE, Art Dept, 201 Trueblood Ave, 52577. Tel 515-673-1001; FAX 515-673-1396. *Chmn* Ron Lofgren
Estab 1876; pvt; D & E; scholarships; SC 5, LC 5; enrl D 120
Ent Req: HS dipl, ACT, PSAT or SAT
Degrees: BA
Courses: Art Education, Ceramics, Costume Design & Construction, Drafting, Drawing, History of Art & Archaeology, Industrial Design, Interior Design, Teacher Training
Adult Hobby Classes: Enrl 500; tuition $120 per hr. Courses—Crafts
Summer School: Dir, Dr Howard Reitz. Tuition $120. Courses—Ceramics, Elementary Art Methods

OTTUMWA

INDIAN HILLS COMMUNITY COLLEGE, OTTUMWA CAMPUS, Dept of Art, 525 Grandview, 52501. Tel 515-683-5111, 683-5149. *Dept Head* Richard Dutton; *Dir of Arts & Sciences* Bob Thomas; *Instr* Mark McWhorter
Estab 1932; pub; D & E; scholarships; SC 3, LC 2; enrl D 73, E 5
Ent Req: HS dipl, GED, ACT or SAT
Degrees: AA, AAS and AAA 2 yrs
Tuition: Res—$45 per sem cr hr; nonres—$75 per sem cr hr (res acquired after 90 days)
Courses: Art History, Ceramics, Design, Drawing, Painting, Crafts, Watercolors
Adult Hobby Classes: Enrl 10-20; tuition $30 per sem cr hr. Courses—Ceramics, Painting, Watercolor
Children's Classes: Enrl 15-20. Courses—General Workshops, Painting, Ceramics
Summer School: Dir, Bob Thomas. Enrl 120; six wk session. Courses—Liberal Arts

PELLA

CENTRAL UNIVERSITY OF IOWA, Art Dept, 812 University, 50219. Tel 515-628-5261. *Chmn* J Vruwink, MFA; *Assoc Prof* Lawrence Mills, PhD; *Asst Prof* J D DeJong, MA
Estab 1853; pvt; D & E; scholarships; SC 20, LC 6; enrl D 180, non-maj 140, maj 40
Ent Req: HS dipl, ACT
Degrees: BA 4 yrs
Tuition: $8517 per yr; campus res—room & board $3285
Courses: Art History, Ceramics, Drawing, Painting, Glassblowing, Modern Art, Primitive Art, Studio Art
Children's Classes: Enrl 40; part of Elementary School Art Program

SIOUX CITY

BRIAR CLIFF COLLEGE, Art Dept, 3303 Rebecca St, 51104. Tel 712-279-5321, Ext 5452. *Chairperson* William J Welu, MFA; *Instructor* Mary Ann Lonergan, MA
Estab 1930; den; D & E; scholarships; SC 7, LC 7; enrl D 250, non-maj 150, maj 30
Ent Req: HS dipl, ACT
Degrees: BA and BS 4 yr
Tuition: $2920 per term, $292 per hr; campus res—room & board $3237 per yr
Courses: Aesthetics, Architecture, Art Education, Ceramics, †Drawing, History of Art & Archaeology, Intermedia, †Mixed Media, †Painting, †Sculpture, †Teacher Training, Art 1, 2, 3 & 4 (major studio areas & independent study), Critical Seminar, Design
Summer School: Dir, William Welu. Enrl 30; tuition $185 per cr hr for 5 wk term. Courses—Contemporary Art History, Elementary Art Education, Pottery

MORNINGSIDE COLLEGE, Art Dept, 1501 Morningside Ave, 51106. Tel 712-274-5212. *Chmn* Frank Breneisen. Instrs: FT 3
Pvt; D & E; SC 17, LC 4; enrl D 161, maj 40
Ent Req: HS dipl
Degrees: BA and BS (Art Educ) 4 yr
Tuition: $6036 per yr; campus res—$2150 per yr
Courses: Art Appreciation, Art Education, Art History, Ceramics, Drawing, Graphic Design, Painting, Photography, Sculpture, Teacher Training, Textile Design, Jewelry, Printmaking
Children's Classes: Enrl 40; tuition $25 for 5 wk summer term. Courses—Ceramics, Photography
Summer School: Dir, Frank Breneisen. Enrl 50; tuition $120 per cr, May, June, July. Courses—Photography, Drawing, Teaching Methods

SIOUX CITY ART CENTER, 513 Nebraska St, 51101. Tel 712-279-6272. *Dir* Jim L Zimmer; *Instr* Open
Estab 1938; pvt; D & E; scholarships; SC 14-20, LC 1-2; enrl D 100, E 400
Tuition: $20.50 members, $27.50 non-members
Courses: †Art Education, †Art History, †Ceramics, †Drawing, †Mixed Media, †Painting, †Photography
Adult Hobby Classes: Enrl 60, tuition $25-$30 for 3-6 wk terms. Courses—Drawing, Painting, Pottery, Studio, Printmaking
Children's Classes: Enrl 900; tuition $25-$27 for 6 wk term. Courses—Clay, Drawing, Mixed Media, Painting, Photography

WAVERLY

WARTBURG COLLEGE, Dept of Art, 222 Ninth St NW, 50677. Tel 319-352-1200; WATS 800-553-1797. *Dept Head* Arthur C Frick, MS; *Prof* Maynard Anderson, PhD; *Asst Prof* Aida Frick, MA; *Asst Prof* John Quirk, MA; *Instr* Heidi Peterson
Estab 1852; den; D & E; scholarships; SC 18, LC 4; enrl D 135, non-maj 110, maj 25
Ent Req: HS dipl, PSAT, ACT & SAT, foreign students TOEFL and upper 50 percent of class
Degrees: BA(Art), BA(Art Education) 4 yrs
Tuition: Res—undergrad $10,250 per yr, $550 PT; campus res—room $1410 - $1550, board $1770; general fee $110
Courses: Art Appreciation, †Art Education, Art History, Ceramics, Commercial Art, Design, Drawing, Jewelry, Painting, Photography, Printmaking, Sculpture, Teacher Training, Computer Design, Field Experience, Gallery Techniques, Independent Study, †Pre-Architecture, Studio-Art, 2-D & 3-D Design
Summer School: Dir, Dr Edith Waldstein. Enrl 20; tuition $550 per course for 3 wk term. Courses—Drawing, Independent Study, Painting

KANSAS

ATCHISON

BENEDICTINE COLLEGE, Art Dept, 1020 N Second St, 66002. Tel 913-367-5340; FAX 913-367-6102. *Chmn* George Renault. Instrs: FT 1
Estab 1971; den; D; SC 15, LC 3; enrl D 145, non-maj 123, maj 22
Ent Req: HS dipl, ent exam
Tuition: Campus res—room and board $3800
Courses: Art Education, Art History, Calligraphy, Ceramics, Drawing, Graphic Arts, Painting, Photography, Printmaking, Sculpture, Teacher Training

BALDWIN CITY

BAKER UNIVERSITY, Dept of Art, 606 Eighth St, 66006. Tel 913-594-6451; FAX 913-594-2522. *Chmn* Walter J Bailey; *Assoc Prof* Inge Balch; *Assoc Prof* Collene Z Gregoire
Estab 1858; pvt; D; scholarships; SC 11, LC 3; enrl D 105, maj 28
Ent Req: HS dipl, provision made for entrance without HS dipl by interview and committee action
Degrees: AB (Art) 4 yrs
Tuition: $33 annual tuition
Courses: Art Education, Ceramics, Drawing, Graphic Arts, History of Art & Archaeology, Painting, Printmaking, Sculpture, Teacher Training, Textile Design

COFFEYVILLE

COFFEYVILLE COMMUNITY COLLEGE, Art Dept, 11th & Willow, 67337. Tel 316-251-7700, Ext 2091; FAX 316-251-7798. *Head Dept* Harold Koerth
Estab 1923, dept estab 1969; pub; D & E; scholarships; SC 8, LC 2; enrl D 75, E 60, non-maj 25, maj 110
Ent Req: HS dipl
Degrees: AA
Tuition: Res—undergrad $224 per yr (incl $41.50 fees); nonres—undergrad $52.80 per cr hr (incl $41.50 fees); campus res $1100
Courses: Art History, Art Appreciation, Art Education, Ceramics, Drawing, Handicrafts, Painting, Photography, Printmaking, Sculpture
Adult Hobby Classes: Crafts

COLBY

COLBY COMMUNITY COLLEGE, Visual Arts Dept, 1255 S Range, 67701. Tel 913-462-3984; FAX 913-462-8135. *Dir* Kathy Gordon
Estab 1965, dept estab 1966; pub; D & E; scholarships; SC 18, LC 8; enrl D 141, E 210, maj 18
Ent Req: HS dipl
Degrees: AA 2 yrs
Tuition: Res—$26 per cr hr; nonres—$62 per cr hr
Courses: Color Structure and Design, Figure Drawing: Advanced, Problems in Drawing, Problems in Painting, Watercolor I & II
Adult Hobby Classes: Enrl 10-20; tui $15 per hr
Summer School: Enrl 5-20; Term of 4 wks beginning June 1. Courses—Drawing, Jewelry, Watercolor

EL DORADO

BUTLER COUNTY COMMUNITY COLLEGE, Art Dept, 901 S Haverhill Rd, 67042. Tel 316-321-2222; FAX 316-322-3318. *Chmn* Larry Patton; *Instr* Peter Johnson, MFA
Estab 1927, dept estab 1964; pub; D & E; scholarships; SC 13, LC 1; enrl D 168, E 57
Ent Req: HS dipl, ACT, EED
Degrees: AA 2 yr
Tuition: Res—$28.50 per cr hr; nonres—$69 per cr hr
Courses: Art History, Ceramics, Drawing, Interior Design, Painting, Printmaking, Silversmithing

EMPORIA

EMPORIA STATE UNIVERSITY, Division of Art, 66801. Tel 316-341-5246. *Chmn* Donald Perry
Estab 1863, dept estab early 1900's; pub; D & E; scholarships; SC 42, LC 15, GC 30; enrl D 700, E 25, maj 120, grad 25
Ent Req: HS dipl, HS seniors may enroll in regular classes
Degrees: BFA, BSE, BS(Art Therapy) 4 yr, MS(Art Therapy)
Tuition: Red-undergrad $800 per sem, grad $950 per sem; nonres—undergrad $2250 per sem, grad $2400 per sem; campus res—room & board $1565 per sem
Courses: Art Education, Art History, Ceramics, Commercial Art, Display, Drawing, Graphic Arts, History of Art & Archaeology, Illustration, Interior Design, Jewelry, Mixed Media, Painting, Photography, Printmaking, Sculpture, Silversmithing, Teacher Training, Weaving, Introduction to Graphic Design, Metals
Summer School: Acting Chair, Donald Perry. Enrl 150; tuition res $55 per hr, nonres $140 per hr for term beginning June 11. Courses—most of the regular classes

GARDEN CITY

GARDEN CITY COMMUNITY COLLEGE, Art Dept, 801 Campus Dr, PO Box 977, 67846. Tel 316-276-7611; FAX 316-276-9630. *Chmn Human & Fine Arts* Larry Walker
Degrees: AA
Tuition: Res—undergrad $620 per yr, $20 per cr hr
Courses: Art Appreciation, Art History, Ceramics, Design, Drawing, Handicrafts, Interior Design, Jewelry, Painting, Photography, Printmaking, Stage Design, Stained Glass

GREAT BEND

BARTON COUNTY COMMUNITY COLLEGE, Fine Arts Dept, R R No 3, 67530. Tel 316-792-2701. *Instr* Steve Dudek, MFA; *Instr* Linda Ganstrom, MA
Estab 1965, dept estab 1969; pub; D & E; scholarships
Ent Req: HS dipl or GED
Degrees: AA
Tuition: Res—undergrad $28 per cr hr; campus residence available
Courses: Art Appreciation, Art Education, Art History, Ceramics, Commercial Art, Design, Drawing, Painting, Photography, Printmaking, Sculpture, Silversmithing

HAYS

FORT HAYS STATE UNIVERSITY, Dept of Art, Visual Arts Center, 600 Park St, 67601. Tel 913-628-4247. *Chmn* Gary Coulter; *Prof* Jim Hinkhouse, MFA; *Prof* Kathleen Kuchar; *Prof* Darrell McGinnis, MA; *Prof* Frank Nichols, MFA; *Assoc Prof* Joanne Harwick, MFA; *Assoc Prof* Zoran Stevanov, PhD; *Asst Prof* Martha Holmes, MA; *Assoc Prof* Michael Jilg, MFA; *Asst Prof* Chaiwat Thumsujarit, MFA
Estab 1902, dept estab 1930; pub; D & E; scholarships; SC 66, LC 19, GC 28; enrl D 742, non-maj 555, maj 164, grad 23, others 7
Ent Req: HS dipl
Degrees: BA & BFA 4 yrs, AA & MFA 2 - 3 yrs
Tuition: Res—undergrad $44.50 & grad $51.25 per cr hr; nonres—undergrad $100. 52 & grad $107.25 per cr hr; campus res—room & board: double $600, single $839 (20 meals included)
Courses: Art Education, Art History, Ceramics, Commercial Art, Drawing, Graphic Design, Handicrafts, History of Art & Archaeology, Illustration, †Jewelry, †Mixed Media, †Painting, †Photography, †Printmaking, †Sculpture, †Silversmithing, †Teacher Training, †Art Therapy
Summer School: Enrl 157; tuition res—undergrad $41.75 per cr hr, grad $45; nonres—undergrad $91.25 per cr hr, grad $94.75 per cr hr for term of 8 wks beginning June 6. Courses—Studio Courses & Workshops

HESSTON

HESSTON COLLEGE, PO Box 3000, 67062-3000. Tel 316-327-4221; FAX 316-327-8300. *Head Dept* John Blosser, MA
Estab 1915; den; D & E; SC 9, SC 1; enrl non-maj 50, maj 5
Ent Req: HS dipl
Degrees: AA 2 yr
Tuition: $4600 annual tuition; campus res available
Courses: Art History, Ceramics, Drafting, Drawing, Painting, Photography, Sculpture, Design

HUTCHINSON

HUTCHINSON COMMUNITY JUNIOR COLLEGE, Visual Arts Dept, 600 E 11th St, 67501. Tel 316-665-3500, Ext 3503. *Prof* Dee Connett; *Prof* Roy Swanson; *Color & Graphic Instr* Nancy Masterson; *Ceramics & Sculpture Instr* Jerri Griffin; *Art History Instr* Teresa Hess
Estab 1928; pub; D & E; scholarships; SC 17, LC 4; enrl D 215, E 41, non-maj 180, maj 81
Ent Req: HS dipl
Degrees: AA 2 yrs
Tuition: $27 per cr hr; campus res—room & board $2300 per yr
Courses: †Art Education, †Art History, †Ceramics, †Drawing, †Graphic Design, †History of Art & Archaeology, †Jewelry, †Painting, †Printmaking, †Sculpture, †Silversmithing, †Theatre Arts, Computer Graphics Design
Summer School: tuition $23 per hr

IOLA

ALLEN COUNTY COMMUNITY COLLEGE, Art Dept, 1801 N Cottonwood, 66749. Tel 316-365-5116. *Dept Head* Steven R Greenwall, MFA
Estab 1965; pub; D & E; scholarships; SC 5, LC 2; enrl D 700, E 1000, non-maj 40, maj 10
Ent Req: HS dipl or GED
Degrees: AA, AS & AAS 2 yr
Tuition: Res—$22 per cr hr; nonres—$67.50 per cr hr
Courses: Ceramics, Commercial Art, Drawing, Painting, Photography, Sculpture, Art Appreciation, Art Fundamentals, 2-D & 3-D Design
Summer School: Courses—all courses

LAWRENCE

HASKELL INDIAN JUNIOR COLLEGE, Art Dept, 155 Indian Ave, 66046. Tel 913-749-8458. *Instr* B J Wahnee, MA
Estab 1884, dept estab 1970; pub; D; SC 14, LC 1; enrl in dept D, non-maj 90, maj 10
Ent Req: HS dipl or GED, at least 1/4 Indian, Eskimo or Aleut and receive agency approval
Degrees: AA and AAS 2 yrs
Tuition: Campus residence available
Courses: Art Appreciation, Art History, Ceramics, Design, Drawing, Jewelry, Painting, Sculpture, Textile Design

UNIVERSITY OF KANSAS, School of Fine Arts, 66045. Tel 913-864-3421; FAX 913-864-5387. *Dean* Peter G Thompson; *Assoc Dean* Jerry C Moore; *Assoc Dean Grad Studies* Carole Ross
Pub; scholarships and fels; enrl 1300
Degrees: BA, BFA, BAE, BS, MFA 4-5 yrs
—Dept of Art, 66045. Tel 913-864-4401. *Chmn* Robert Brawley. Instrs: FT 19
Estab 1885; SC 50, GC 25; enrl maj 150
Tuition: Res—undergrad $899 per sem, grad $1088 per sem; nonres— $2985 per sem
Courses: †Drawing, †Painting, †Printmaking, †Sculpture
Summer School: Dir Robert Brawley. Enrl 60; Tuition $57 for 8 wks. Courses—Life Drawing, Intro to Drawing I & II, Painting I-IV
—Dept of Design, 66045. Tel 913-864-4401. *Chmn* Joe Zeller. Instrs: FT 25, PT 5
Estab 1921; SC 83, LC 32, GC 26; enrl maj 550, grad 30
Tuition: Res—undergrad $899 per sem, grad $1088 per sem; nonres—undergrad $2985 per sem, grad $3198 per sem
Courses: Art Education, Art History, Ceramics, Industrial Design, Interior Design, Jewelry, Teacher Training, Textile Design, Design, Weaving, Textile Printing & Dyeing, Visual Communications
Summer School: Term of 4-8 wks beginning June

—**Kress Foundation Dept of Art History,** Spencer Museum of Art, 66045. Tel 913-864-4713. *Chairperson* Edmund Eglinski; *Prof Emeritus* Chu-tsing Li PhD; *Prof* Charles Eldredge, PhD; *Prof* Marilyn Stokstad, PhD; *Prof* Timothy Mitchell, PhD; *Assoc Prof* Marsha Weidner, PhD; *Assoc Prof* Nancy Corwin, PhD; *Grad Advisory & Assoc Prof* Linda Stone-Ferrier, PhD; *Assoc Prof* Stephen Goddard; *Asst Prof* David Cateforts, PhD; *Asst Prof* John Teramoto; *Asst Prof* Marie Aquilino, PhD; *Asst Prof* Amy McNair, PhD; *Lectr* Deborah Emont-Scott; *Lectr* Roger Ward; *Lectr* Wai-Kam Ho
Estab 1866, dept estab 1953; pub; D & E; scholarships; LC 30, GC 10; enrl D 900, E 40, maj 50, grad 70
Ent Req: HS dipl
Degrees: BA, BGS, MA, PhD
Tuition: Res—undergrad $899, grad $1088; nonres—undergrad $2985, grad $3198
Courses: Art History, Chinese Art, Japanese Art, Western European Art
Summer School: Enrl 80; tuition varies. Courses—Art History, History, Literature. Classes in Great Britain

—**Dept of Art & Music Education & Music Therapy,** 311 Bailey Hall, 66045. Tel 913-864-4784; FAX 913-864-5076. *Chmn Dept* George L Duerksen, PhD; *Asst Prof* Denise Stone, PhD; *Asst Prof* Patricia Villanueve
Estab 1865, dept estab 1969; pub; D & E; scholarships; GC 12; enrl D 535, maj 123, grad 123, others 289
Ent Req: HS dipl, ent exam
Degrees: BAE 5 yrs, MA 1-6 yrs, PhD 3-6 yrs
Tuition: Res—undergrad $899 per sem, $74 per cr hr, grad $1088 per sem, $86 per cr hr; non res—undergrad $2985 per sem, $213 per cr hr, grad$3198 per sem, $227 per cr hr
Courses: Visual Arts Education
Summer School: Term of 8 wks beginning June

LEAVENWORTH

SAINT MARY COLLEGE, Art Dept, 4100 S Forth St Trafficway, 66048-5082. Tel 913-682-5151; FAX 913-682-2406. *Dept Chmn* Mary Rebecca Conner, MA; *Instr* Susan Nelson
Estab 1923; pvt; D & E; scholarships; SC 25, LC 5; enrl non-maj 80, maj 10
Ent Req: HS dipl
Degrees: BA, BS, BM and BME 4 yr
Courses: Art Education, Art History, Calligraphy, Ceramics, Commercial Art, Drawing, Graphic Arts, Handicrafts, History of Art & Archaeology, Jewelry, Lettering, Mixed Media, Painting, Photography, Printmaking, Sculpture, Teacher Training, Stitchery, Weaving
Children's Classes: Enrl 30; Courses—Crafts Camp; Painting (Saturday)
Summer School: Courses—variable 3 wk workshop

LIBERAL

SEWARD COUNTY COMMUNITY COLLEGE, Art Dept, N Hwy 83, PO Box 1137, 67905. Tel 316-624-1951; FAX 316-624-0637. *Chmn Humanities* John Loucks
Estab 1969; pub; D & E; scholarships; SC 23, LC 5; enrl D 650, E 900
Ent Req: HS dipl
Degrees: AA 2 yrs
Tuition: Res—$590 per yr; nonres—$2126 per yr
Courses: Art Education, Art History, Ceramics, Costume Design & Construction, Drawing, History of Art & Archaeology, Painting, Photography, Sculpture, Stage Design
Summer School: Dir, Jon Ulm. Term of 6 wks beginning June 1. Courses varied & subject to change

LINDSBORG

BETHANY COLLEGE, Art Dept, 421 N First St, 67456. Tel 913-227-3311, Ext 146 & 147; FAX 913-227-2860. *Head Art Dept* Caroline Kahler, MA; *Prof* Mary Kay, MFA
Den; D; scholarships; SC 19, LC 3; enrl D 195, non-maj 200, maj 40
Ent Req: HS dipl
Degrees: BA 3-4 yr
Courses: Art Education, Ceramics, Drawing, Painting, Photography, Printmaking, Sculpture, Art Therapy, Studio Concentration
Summer School: Acad Dean, Dr Richard Torgerson

MANHATTAN

KANSAS STATE UNIVERSITY
—**Art Dept,** Art Bldg, 66506. Tel 913-532-6605. *Head Dept* Garr Woodard; *Prof* Yoshiro Ikedo, MFA; *Prof* Oscar V Larmer, MFA; *Prof* Elliott Pujol, MFA; *Prof* Ed Sturr; *Assoc Prof* Rex Replogle, MFA; *Assoc Prof* John Vogt, MFA; *Assoc Prof* Gary Woodward, MFA; *Assoc Prof* Lou Ann Culley, PhD; *Assoc Prof* Ed Sturr, DEd; *Assoc Prof* James C Munce; *Assoc Prof* Duane Noblett, MFA; *Assoc Prof* Margo Kren, MFA. Instrs: FT 23, PT 3, 13 Area Coordrs
Estab 1863, dept estab 1965; pub; D & E; scholarships; SC 45, LC 19, GC 7; enrl D 1940, E 60, non-maj 1800, maj 200, grad 15
Ent Req: HS dipl
Degrees: BS(Art Educ) jointly with Col Educ, BA and BFA 4 yrs, MFA 60 sem cr
Tuition: Res—undergrad $775 per sem, grad $800 per sem; nonres—undergrad $2200 per sem; grad $2015 per sem; campus res available, out-of-state tuition waived plus reduction of fees with GRA & GTA appointments
Courses: †Art Education, †Art History, †Ceramics, †Drawing, †Graphic Design, †Jewelry, Lettering, †Painting, †Printmaking, †Sculpture, Fibers, Pre-Art Therapy
Summer School: Dir, Charles Stroh. Enrl 150; tuition res $37 per cr hr, nonres $118 per cr hr for term of 4 to 8 wks beginning June 5. Courses—most of above, varies from summer to summer

—**College of Architecture and Design,** Seaton Hall, 66506. Tel 913-532-5950; FAX 913-532-6722. *Dean* Lane L Marshall; *Assoc Dean* Ray Weisenburger. Instrs: FT 53
Estab 1904; enrl 800
Degrees: BArchit, BInterior Archit and BLandscape Archit 5 yrs, MArchit, MLandscape Archit, MRegional and Community Planning
Tuition: Res—undergrad $920 per sem, grad $1109; nonres—undergrad $3006 per sem, grad $3219
Courses: Architecture, Art History, Landscape Architecture, †Interior Architecture, †Regional and Community Planning
Adult Hobby Classes: Dean, Lane L Marshall. Courses—Graphic Delineation, Preservation
Children's Classes: Courses—Special Design Program in June
Summer School: Dean, Lane L Marshall. 8 wks from June 4. Courses—Design Discovery Program, Design Studio

MCPHERSON

MCPHERSON COLLEGE, Art Dept, 1600 E Euclid, PO Box 1402, 67460. Tel 316-241-0731, Ext 234. *Chmn* Susan Dodson, MA; *Asst Prof* Wayne Conyers, MA
Estab 1887; den; D & E; scholarships; SC 14, LC 5; enrl D 150, maj 10, others 140
Ent Req: HS dipl, ACT
Degrees: AB 4 yr
Tuition: Res—undergrad $8190 per yr, $125 per cr hr; campus res—room & board $2100
Courses: †Art Education, Art History, Ceramics, Drawing, †Interior Design, Lettering, Museum Staff Training, Painting, Printmaking, Teacher Training, Textile Design
Adult Hobby Classes: Offered in summer
Children's Classes: Offered in summer
Summer School: Dir, Dr Constance Nichols. Term of 10 wks beginning end of May. Courses—Varied Liberal Arts

NORTH NEWTON

BETHEL COLLEGE, Dept of Art, 67117. Tel 316-283-2500; FAX 316-284-5286. *Chmn* Merrill Kraball; *Assoc Prof* Gail Lutsch, MFA
Estab 1888, dept estab 1959; den; D; scholarships; SC 11, LC 3; enrl D 240, non-maj 215, maj 25
Ent Req: HS, ACT
Degrees: BA(Art) 4 yrs
Tuition: $4610 per yr, $2305 per sem, $164 per hr; campus res—room & board $2524 per yr
Courses: Art Education, Art History, Ceramics, Drawing, Graphic Arts, Graphic Design, Painting, Photography, Printmaking, Sculpture, Crafts
Adult Hobby Classes: Enrl 15; tuition $40 per 6 wk session. Courses—Ceramics, Drawing, Painting
Summer School: Courses—Drawing, Painting

OTTAWA

OTTAWA UNIVERSITY, Dept of Art, 1001 S Cedar, 66067-3399. Tel 913-242-5200; FAX 913-242-7429. *Chmn* Frank J Lemp. Instrs: FT 1
Estab 1865; pvt; D; scholarships; SC 16, LC 5; enrl D 35, maj 5
Ent Req: HS grad, SAT, ACT
Degrees: BA 4 yrs
Courses: Art Education, Art History, Ceramics, Drawing, Graphic Arts, Painting, Photography, Arts Management
Children's Classes: Enrl 15. Courses—Art Foundation, Ceramics
Summer School: Dir, Dr Ed Morrissey. Tuition $89 per cr hr for 8 wk session. Courses—Life Drawing, Painting

OVERLAND PARK

JOHNSON COUNTY COMMUNITY COLLEGE, Visual Arts Program, 12345 College Blvd, 66210. Tel 913-469-3856; FAX 913-469-4409. *Dir* George Thompson; *Instr* Stuart Beals, BA; *Instr* Judy Brazil, MA; *Instr* Ron Hicks, MS; *Instr* John Larry; *Instr* Karen Schory, MFA; *Instr* Thomas Tarnowski, MFA; *Instr* Dorothy Wadsworth, MFA; *Instr* Zigmunds Priede, MFA; *Instr* Nancy Schneider-Wilson, MFA; *Dir Art Gallery* Bruce Hartman, MFA
Estab 1969; pub; D & E; scholarships; SC 30, LC 4; enrl D 200, E 100
Ent Req: HS dipl or equivalent
Degrees: AA 2 yr
Tuition: Res—$28 per sem cr hr; nonres—$93.50 per sem cr hr; no campus res
Courses: Art Education, Art History, Ceramics, Commercial Art, Drawing, Illustration, Lettering, Painting, Photography, Printmaking, Sculpture, Silversmithing, Design (2-dimensional, 3-dimensional & color), Layout, Preparation of Portfolio, Silkscreen, Weaving, Visual Communications, Visual Technology, Life Drawing, Watercolor
Adult Hobby Classes: All fine arts areas
Children's Classes: Accelerated fine arts for gifted children
Summer School: Dir, Dr Landon Kirchner. Enrl 95; tuition $25.50 per cr hr for term of 8 wks beginning June 5. Courses—Ceramics, Design, Drawing, Painting, Photogrpahy, Sculpture, Silversmithing

PITTSBURG

PITTSBURG STATE UNIVERSITY, Art Dept, 1701 S Broadway St, 66762. Tel 316-235-4302; FAX 316-232-7515. *Chairperson* Harry E Krug, MS; *Prof* Robert Russell, MFA; *Prof* Marjorie Schick, MFA; *Assoc Prof* Alex Barde, MFA; *Asst Prof* Sandra Belfield, MH; *Asst Prof* Malcolm Kucharski, MFA; *Asst Prof* Larrie Moody, PhD
Estab 1903, dept estab 1921; pub; D & E; scholarships; SC 50, LC 24, GC 22; enrl D 600, E 50, non-maj 300, maj 80, grad 30

Ent Req: HS dipl
Degrees: BFA & BSed 4 yr, MA 36 hr
Tuition: Res—undergrad $679 & grad $811 per sem, $44 per sem hr; nonres—undergrad $1740 & grad $1878 per sem, undergrad $114 per sem hr, grad $124 per sem hr; campus res—room & board available
Courses: Art Education, Ceramics, Commercial Art, Design, Drawing, Jewelry, Occupational Therapy, Painting, Photography, Printmaking, Sculpture, Teacher Training, Weaving, †Art Therapy
Adult Hobby Classes: Enrl 20; Courses—Printing
Children's Classes: Enrl 40; tuition varies for 6 wk term
Summer School: Dir, Harry Krug. Enrl 200; tuition res—undergrad $44 per cr hr; grad $52 per cr hr; nonres—undergrad, $114 per cr hr, grad $124 per cr hr, for term of 8 wks beginning June 4th. Courses—Ceramics, Crafts, Painting

PRATT

PRATT COMMUNITY COLLEGE, Art Dept, Hwy 61, 67124. Tel 316-672-5641, Ext 228. Chmn Gene Wineland, MFA
D & E; scholarships; SC 12, LC 1
Ent Req: HS dipl
Degrees: AA and AS
Tuition: Res—$30 per cr hr; nonres $825 per sem
Courses: Ceramics, Commercial Art, Drawing, Painting, Photography, Printmaking, Elementary School Arts, Introduction to Art
Adult Hobby Classes: Enrl 6 - 10 per class; tuition $20 per cr hr plus fees.
Courses—Cast Paper, Ceramics, Drawing, Painting, Textiles
Summer School: Small selection of courses

SALINA

KANSAS WESLEYAN UNIVERSITY, Art Dept, 100 E Claflin, 67401. Tel 913-827-5541; FAX 913-827-0927. Chmn Dr Jack Faver
Estab 1886; den; scholarships; SC 8, LC 3; enrl maj 15, others 500 for two sem
Degrees: AB 4 yr
Courses: †Art Education, Art History, †Advertising Art, †Arts Management, †Art Studio
Summer School: Enrl 125; for term of 8 wks beginning June

STERLING

STERLING COLLEGE, Art Dept, Eighth & Washington, 67579. Tel 316-278-2173. Head Dept Donna Brownlee; Instr George William Forst; Instr Lori Martin
Estab 1876; den; D & E; scholarships; SC 16, LC 2; enrl D 410
Ent Req: HS dipl
Degrees: AB and BS
Tuition: $3350 per sem
Courses: Ceramics, Costume Design & Construction, Drawing, Graphic Arts, Graphic Design, Painting, Fibers, 2-D Color Design, 3-D Design
Adult Hobby Classes: Enrl 25; tuition $20. Courses—all areas
Children's Classes: Courses—Art Education

TOPEKA

WASHBURN UNIVERSITY OF TOPEKA, Dept of Art & Theatre Arts, 1700 SW College, 66621. Tel 913-231-1010; FAX 913-231-1089. Art & Theatre Arts Chmn John Hunter. Instrs: FT 4, PT 5
Estab 1900; pub; SC 11, LC 5; enrl maj 60, others 280
Ent Req: HS dipl
Degrees: AB and BFA 4 yr
Tuition: Res—$1272 per yr, $75 per cr hr; nonres—$1872 per yr
Courses: Art Appreciation, Art History, Ceramics, Design, Drawing, Painting, Photography, Printmaking, Sculpture, Computers, Computer Graphic Design, Etching, Lithography, Silkscreen
Children's Classes: Tuition $35 for ten 1 1/2 hr sessions

WICHITA

FRIENDS UNIVERSITY, Art Dept, 2100 University Ave, 67213. Tel 316-261-5800. Chmn Ted Krone
Estab 1898; den; D & E; scholarships; SC 18, LC 4; enrl D 329, E 37
Ent Req: HS dipl
Degrees: MA 6 yrs, BA & BS 4 yrs
Tuition: Res—undergrad $2960 per sem, $225 per cr hr; campus res—room & board $1140-$1386 per sem
Courses: †Art Education, Photography, Printmaking, Sculpture, Silversmithing, Teacher Training, †Computer Graphics, †Fine Arts 2 & 3-D
Adult Hobby Classes: Courses—Drawing, Jewelry, Painting
Summer School: Courses of 6 wks beginning June 5th

WICHITA CENTER FOR THE ARTS (Formerly Wichita Art Association), 9112 E Central, 67206. Tel 316-634-2787; FAX 316-634-0593. Pres Dr William G Atton; Admin Asst Linda Johnson; Dir Educ Annie Lowrey; Div Performing Arts Kathy Hauptman. Instrs: 35
Estab 1920; pvt; D & E; scholarships; enrl 300
Tuition: $45 - $180 per class
Courses: Art Education, Art History, Ceramics, Drawing, Mixed Media, Painting, Photography, Printmaking, Sculpture, Teacher Training, Enameling, Pottery, 3-D Design, Weaving
Adult Hobby Classes: Enrl 150; tuition $40 for 6 wk term. Courses—Performing Arts, 2-D & 3-D Design
Children's Classes: Enrl 150; tuition $40. Courses—Performing Arts, 2-D & 3-D Design
Summer School: Dir, Glenice L Matthews. Enrl 300; tuition $45-$55 for 6 wk term. Courses—same as regular sessions

WICHITA STATE UNIVERSITY, Division of Art, College of Fine Arts, 67208. Tel 316-689-3555. Acting Chmn Liz Sowards; Graduate Coordr Ray Olivero
Estab 1895; dept estab 1901; pub; D & E; scholarships; enrl D 1149, E 194, non-maj 78, maj 351, others 2
Ent Req: HS dipl
Degrees: BAE and BFA 4 yr, MFA 2 yr, MA 1 yr
Tuition: Res—undergrad $937.50 per sem, grad $1126.50 per sem, 15-18 hrs; nonres—undergrad $62.50 per cr hr, grad $75.10 per cr hr; no campus res
Courses: †Art Education, †Art History, †Ceramics, Drawing, †Graphic Design, Illustration, Lettering, †Painting, Photography, †Printmaking, †Sculpture, Teacher Training
Summer School: Tuition as above for term of 8 wks

WINFIELD

SOUTHWESTERN COLLEGE, Art Dept, 100 College St, 67156. Tel 316-221-4150, Ext 270. Dept Head Rick L Peters; Prof Michael Wilder, PhD; Adjunct Instr Art Educ Teresa Bevis, BAEd
Estab 1885; pvt & den; D & E; scholarships; SC 12, LC 4
Ent Req: HS dipl
Degrees: BA 4 yr
Tuition: $2300 per sem
Courses: Art Education
Adult Hobby Classes: Design, History of Art, Life Drawing, Painting
Summer School: Dir, Rick L Peters. Enrl 15-20; term May 27-June 20. Courses—Art History, Design, Drawing, Painting, Sculpture

KENTUCKY

BARBOURVILLE

UNION COLLEGE, Art Dept, 310 College St, 40906. Tel 606-546-4151; FAX 606-546-2215. Dept Head Dr Betty Stroud
Den; D & E
Ent Req: HS dipl
Degrees: BA, BS and MA (Educ) 4 yr
Tuition: $1950 per sem
Courses: Art Education, Art History, Drawing, Painting, Teacher Training, Theatre Arts, Art Appreciation, Art Fundamentals, Recreational Arts and Crafts

BEREA

BEREA COLLEGE, Art Dept, 40404. Tel 606-986-9341, Ext 5530. Chmn Walter Hyleck, MFA; Prof Neil DiTeresa, MA; Assoc Prof William Morningstar, MFA; Assoc Prof Robert Boyce, PhD; Asst Prof Christopher Pierce, MFA; Asst Prof Ann Schumacher, MFA; Asst Prof David Wang, PhD
Estab 1855, dept estab 1936; pvt; D; scholarships; SC 14, LC 8; enrl C 1500, D 324, maj 71
Ent Req: HS dipl (preference given to students from Southern Appalachian region)
Degrees: BA 4 yr
Tuition: None; campus res—room and board $1812
Courses: †Art Education, †Art History, †Ceramics, †Drawing, †Painting, †Printmaking, †Sculpture, †Textile Design

BOWLING GREEN

WESTERN KENTUCKY UNIVERSITY, Art Dept, Ivan Wilson Center for Fine Arts, Room 441, 42101. Tel 502-745-3944. Chmn Leo Fernandez. Instrs: FT 13
Pub; D; SC 49, LC 21; enrl maj 187
Ent Req: HS dipl
Degrees: BA and BFA 4 yrs, MA(Art Educ)
Tuition: $772 per sem; nonres—$2112; campus res—$555 - $680 per sem
Courses: †Art Education, Art History, †Ceramics, Drawing, Graphic Design, †Painting, Photography, †Printmaking, †Sculpture, Design, †Weaving
Summer School: Dir, Leo Fernandez. Enrl 100; tuition res $61 per cr hr, nonres $172 per cr hr. Courses—Lecture & Studio Art Courses

CAMPBELLSVILLE

CAMPBELLSVILLE COLLEGE, Fine Arts Division, 200 W College St, 42718. Tel 502-465-8158, Ext 6268. Div Head Robert Gaddis; Asst Prof Tommy Clark; Asst Prof Linda Cundiff; Instr Russell Mobley; Instr Dr Wesley Roberts; Instr Dr Jim Moore; Instr Nevalyn Moore; Instr Dr Kenneth Martin; Instr Dr Mark Bradley
Estab 1906, dept estab 1967; den; D & E; scholarships; SC 26, LC 5; enrl D 35, E 10, non-maj 12, maj 22, others 8 minors
Ent Req: HS dipl, ACT
Degrees: BA, BS, BM & BChM 4 yr, AA, AS & ASSW 2 yr
Courses: Art Appreciation, Art Education, Art History, Ceramics, Collages, Commercial Art, Constructions, Design, Drawing, Graphic Design, Jewelry, Lettering, Painting, Photography, Printmaking, Sculpture, Stage Design, Teacher Training, Theatre Arts, Elementary School Art, Secondary School Art
Adult Hobby Classes: Enrl 15; tuition $50 per audit hr. Courses - Understanding Art, courses above as auditors
Summer School: Term of 8 wks. Courses—Art Education, Art Appreciation, Drawing, Painting

CRESTVIEW HILLS

THOMAS MORE COLLEGE, Art Dept, 233 Thomas More, 41017. Tel 606-341-5800, Ext 3420; FAX 606-344-3345. *Chmn* Darrell W Brothers, MFA; *Assoc Prof* Barbara Rauf, MFA
Estab 1921; pvt; D & E; SC 12, LC 4; enrl D 12, E 5, maj 17
Ent Req: HS dipl
Degrees: BA, BES, BS, AA and AES
Tuition: $158 per sem hr, $2590 per sem; campus res—room & board $1375 per sem
Courses: Aesthetics, Art Education, Art History, Ceramics, Design, Drawing, Painting, Photography, Printmaking, Sculpture, Teacher Training, Theatre Arts, Arts Management, Figure Drawing, Anatomy, Perspective, Color
Summer School: Dir, Dr Raymond Hebert. Courses—various

GEORGETOWN

GEORGETOWN COLLEGE, Art Dept, Mulberry St, PO Box 201, 40324. Tel 502-863-8106; FAX 502-863-8888. *Chmn* Charles James McCormick. Instrs: FT 2
Estab 1829; den; D; scholarships and grants; SC 14, LC 6; enrl 1150
Ent Req: HS transcript, ACT
Degrees: BA 4 yrs
Tuition: Res—$1480 per term; nonres—$1525 per term; sem curriculum; May interterm
Courses: Art History, Ceramics, Graphic Arts, Painting, Photography, Sculpture, Art Appreciation, Art Careers, Art Survey, Graphic Design Internship, Public School Art, Secondary Art, Three-Dimensional Design, Travel Classes, Two-Dimensional Design
Summer School: Two 4 1/2 wk sem 6-7 hrs each. Courses—Art Education, Art Humanities, Studio Classes

HIGHLAND HEIGHTS

NORTHERN KENTUCKY UNIVERSITY, Art Dept, 41099. Tel 606-572-5421; FAX 606-572-5566. *Chmn* Barbara Houghton. Instrs: FT 8, PT 12
Estab 1968; pub; D & E; scholarships; SC 31, LC 10
Ent Req: HS grad, ACT scores
Degrees: BA(Art Educ), BFA(Studio Art), BA(Graphic Design)
Tuition: Res—$55 per sem hr; nonres—$153 per sem hr
Courses: Art Appreciation, †Art Education, Art History, Ceramics, Drawing, †Graphic Design, Painting, Photography, Printmaking, Sculpture
Adult Hobby Classes: Enrl 350; tuition $50-$100 for a period of 5-10 wks. Courses — Various Art & Crafts
Summer School: Dir, Howard Storm. Enrl 90; tuition $47 per sem hr for sessions. Courses — Art Appreciation, Drawing

LEXINGTON

TRANSYLVANIA UNIVERSITY, Studio Arts Dept, 300 N Broadway, 40508. Tel 606-233-8246, 233-8115. *Prog Dir* Jack Girard, MFA; *Prof* Dan S Selter, MFA; *Asst Prof* Florence Thorne, MFA; *Instr* Nancy Wolsk, MA
Estab 1780; pvt; D & E; scholarships; SC 20, LC 3; enrl D 105, E 14, maj 18
Ent Req: HS dipl
Degrees: BA
Tuition: $10,000
Adult Hobby Classes: Enrl 5 - 10; tuition $40 - $80 per 3 - 5 wk sessions
Children's Classes: Enrl 5 - 10; tuition $40 - $60 per 3 - 5 wk sessions
Summer School: Dir, Jack Girard. Enrl 5 - 20; tuition $625 per course. Courses—Black & White Photographics, Ceramics, Painting, Survey

UNIVERSITY OF KENTUCKY, Dept of Art, College of Fine Arts, 207 Fine Arts Bldg, 40506-0022. Tel 606-257-8151; FAX 606-257-3042. *Dean* Rhoda-Gale Pollack; *Chair* Robert James Foose. Instrs: FT 20, PT 20
Estab 1918; pub; scholarships and grad assistantships; SC 23, LC 19, GC 6; enrl maj 200, others 1500
Degrees: BA, BFA, MA & MFA 3 yr
Tuition: Res—undergrad $840, grad $920; nonres—undergrad $2520, grad $2760
Courses: †Art Education, †Art History, Ceramics, Drawing, Graphic Design, Painting, Photography, Printmaking, Sculpture, Film, Video, †Studio Art, Fibers
Children's Classes: Saturday classes for children
Summer School: Dir, Robert James Foose. Tuition res—$70 per cr hr, nonres—$210 per cr hr. Courses—varied

LOUISVILLE

JEFFERSON COMMUNITY COLLEGE, Fine Arts, 109 E Broadway, 40202. Tel 502-584-0181, Ext 289. *Coordr Fine Arts & Prof* R M Crask; *Assoc Prof* Ann Hemdahl-Owen; *Asst Prof* J Barry Motes. Instrs: PT 6
Estab 1968; pub; D & E; scholarships; SC 11, LC 6; enrl D 4774, E 4172
Ent Req: HS dipl
Degrees: AA & Assoc in Photography 2 yrs
Tuition: $350 per sem
Courses: †Advertising Design, Aesthetics, Art Education, Art History, †Commercial Art, Display, Drawing, Graphic Arts, Graphic Design, Mixed Media, Painting, †Photography, Sculpture, †Theatre Arts
Summer School: Dean, Dr Pat Ecker. Tuition $30 per cr hr. Courses—Art Appreciation, Drawing, Photography

UNIVERSITY OF LOUISVILLE, Allen R Hite Art Institute, Department of Fine Arts, Belknap Campus, 40292. Tel 502-588-6794. *Chmn* John Whitsell; *Prof* Henry J Chodkowski, MFA. Instrs: FT 21, PT 10
Estab 1846, dept estab 1935; pub; D & E; scholarships; SC 35, LC 71, GC 26; enrl D 1000, E 90, non-maj 800, maj 400, grad 29
Ent Req: HS dipl, CEEB
Degrees: MA 1 to 2 yrs, PhD 3 yrs, BA & BS 4 yrs, BFA 5 yrs

Tuition: Res—undergrad $77.50 per cr hr, grad $112 per cr hr; nonres—undergrad $217.50 per cr hr, grad $316.50 per cr hr
Courses: Art Education, Art History, Ceramics, Drawing, Graphic Design, Interior Design, Painting, Photography, Printmaking, Sculpture, Teacher Training, †Fiber
Summer School: Tuition res—$77.50 per hr, nonres—$217.50 per hr for term of 5 wks, beginning early June. Courses—3 or 4 of above courses

MIDWAY

MIDWAY COLLEGE, Art Dept, 512 E Stephens St, 40347-1120. Tel 606-846-4421, Ext 5415; FAX 606-846-5349. *Instr* Kate Davis-Rosenbaum; *Instr* Wayne Gebb; *Instr* Steve Davis-Rosenbaum. Instrs: FT 2
Den, W; D; scholarships; SC 7, LC 3; enrl 55
Ent Req: HS dipl, ACT
Degrees: 2 yr
Tuition: $2750 per sem
Courses: Art Education, Ceramics, Drawing, Painting, Sculpture, Textile Design, Basic Design, Historical Furniture, Art in the Child's World

MOREHEAD

MOREHEAD STATE UNIVERSITY, Art Dept, Claypool-Young Art Bldg 211, 40351. Tel 606-783-2221, 783-2193. *Chmn* Tom Sternal
Estab 1922; pub; D & E; scholarships; SC 40, LC 16, GC 28; enrl D 900, E 20, non-maj 800, maj 180, GS 55, others 145
Ent Req: HS dipl, ACT
Degrees: BA 4 yr, MA 1 yr
Tuition: Res—undergrad $760 per sem, grad $830 per sem; nonres—undergrad $2100 per sem, grad $2310 per sem
Courses: Art Education, Art History, Ceramics, Commercial Art, Drawing, Painting, Photography, Printmaking, Sculpture, Computer Art
Adult Hobby Classes: Courses—Ceramics, Crafts, Oil Painting, Watercolor Painting, Weaving
Summer School: Courses—same as above on demand

MURRAY

MURRAY STATE UNIVERSITY, Art Dept, College of Fine Arts and Communication, One Murray St, 42071-3303. Tel 502-762-3784. *Chmn* Richard Dougherty; *Prof* Karen W Boyd, MFA; *Prof* Fred Shepard, MFA; *Prof* Robert W Head, MFA; *Prof* Dale Leys, MFA; *Assoc Prof* Harry Furches, MFA; *Assoc Prof* Michael Johnson, MFA; *Assoc Prof* Paul Sasso, MFA; *Assoc Prof* Jerry Speight, MFA; *Assoc Prof* Camille Douglas, PhD; *Assoc Prof* Steve Bishop, MFA; *Asst Prof* Mary Jane Timmerman, MA; *Asst Prof* David Jackson; *Asst Prof* Peggy Schrock; *Gallery Dir* Albert Sperath
Estab 1925, dept estab 1931; pub; D & E; scholarships; SC 117, LC 15, GS 48; enrl non-maj 475, maj 200, grad 13
Ent Req: HS dipl, ACT, portfolio required for grad students
Degrees: BA, BS & BFA 4 yr, MA(Studio) 1 1/2 - 2 yrs
Tuition: Res—undergrad $1600 per yr, $800 per sem, $60 per hr, grad $1740 per yr, $870 per sem, $89 per hr; nonres—undergrad $4280 per yr, $2140 per sem, $173 per cr hr, grad $4700 per yr, $2350 per sem, $252 per hr; campus res—room & board $1170 per yr
Courses: Art Appreciation, Art Education, †Art History, †Ceramics, Drawing, Graphic Design, Jewelry, †Painting, †Photography, †Printmaking, †Sculpture, †Weaving, Computer Graphics, †Functional Design, †Surface Design
Children's Classes: After school art enrichment program, grades 1-8; summer art workshops for HS students
Summer School: Tuition res—undergrad $60 per hr, grad $89 per hr; nonres—undergrad $173 per hr, grad $252 per hr for short sessions of 5 wk 7 1/2 wk or 10 wk terms

OWENSBORO

BRESCIA COLLEGE, Dept of Art, 717 Frederica St, 42301. Tel 502-685-3131; FAX 502-686-4266. *Chmn* Sr Mary Diane Taylor. Instrs: FT 4
Estab 1950; den; D & E; scholarships; SC 47, LC 10; enrl 960, maj 30
Ent Req: HS dipl, placement exam, ACT, GED
Degrees: AA(Photograph) 2 yr, BA in art and art education 4 yr
Tuition: $4000 per yr; campus res—$575 per yr room, $1400 yr board
Courses: Art Education, Art History, Calligraphy, †Ceramics, Drawing, †Graphic Design, Painting, Printmaking, †Black & White Photography, †Color Photography, 2-D & 3-D Design, Museology
Adult Hobby Classes: Tuition $110 per cr hr, sr citizens free. All regular courses offered
Summer School: Dir, Sr Mary Diane Taylor. Tuition $110 per cr hr for 6 wk term. Courses according to demand

KENTUCKY WESLEYAN COLLEGE, Dept Art, 3000 Frederica St, 42302. Tel 502-926-3111, Ext 250; FAX 502-926-3196. *Chmn* William Kolok, MFA; *Asst Prof* Kimble Bromley
Dept estab 1950; den; scholarships; SC 11, LC 4; enrl maj 40
Degrees: BA 4 yr
Tuition: Res—$5950 per yr, $185 per cr hr
Courses: Art Appreciation, Arts and Crafts, Design, Watercolor
Summer School: Enrl 60. Courses—Art for the Elementary Schools, Art Survey

PIKEVILLE

PIKEVILLE COLLEGE, Humanities Division, Sycamore St, 41501. Tel 606-432-9200; FAX 606-432-9372. *Chmn* Dr Frank Jacks; *Gallery Dir* Janice Ford
Estab 1889; pvt den; D & E; SC 16, LC 5
Ent Req: SAT, ACT
Degrees: BA and BS 4 yrs
Tuition: $2825 annual tuition
Courses: †Art Education, Art History, Ceramics, Drawing, History of Art & Archaeology, Painting, Printmaking, Sculpture, †Teacher Training
Summer School: Courses—vary

PIPPA PASSES

ALICE LLOYD COLLEGE, Art Dept, 41844. Tel 606-368-2101, Ext 5606. *Instr* Mike Ware. Instrs: FT 1, PT 1
Estab 1922; pvt; D & E; scholarships; SC 6, LC 1
Ent Req: HS dipl, ent exam
Degrees: BS & BA 4 yrs
Tuition: $1750 per sem; no tuition for 76 mountain counties
Courses: Art Appreciation, †Art for Elementary Education, Art History Survey No 2, Pottery
Children's Classes: Enrl 10-20; tui free. Courses—Drawing, Painting, Sculpture

RICHMOND

EASTERN KENTUCKY UNIVERSITY, Art Dept, Campbell 309, 40475. Tel 606-622-1629. *Chmn* Tim Glotzbach
Estab 1910; pub; D; SC 30, LC 6, GC 6
Ent Req: HS grad
Degrees: BA, BFA and MA (Educ) 4 yrs
Tuition: Res—$626 per yr; nonres—$1780 per yr
Courses: Art Appreciation, Art History, †Ceramics, †Design, Drawing, †Painting, †Sculpture, †Metals
Adult Hobby Classes: Non-credit courses offered
Summer School: Dir, Richard Adams. Tuition same as regular sem

WILLIAMSBURG

CUMBERLAND COLLEGE, Dept of Art, College Station, PO Box 7523, 40769. Tel 606-549-2200, Ext 4265 & 4416. *Chmn* Kenneth R Weedman
Estab 1889; den; D & E; scholarships; SC 20, LC 10; enrl D 720, E 60, maj 30
Ent Req: HS dipl, ACT test
Degrees: BA and BS 4 yr
Tuition: $1732 per sem
Courses: Aesthetics, Art Appreciation, Art Education, Art History, Design, Drawing, Painting, Printmaking, Sculpture, Stage Design, Teacher Training, Theatre Arts, Video

WILMORE

ASBURY COLLEGE, Art Dept, One Macklem Dr, 40390. Tel 606-858-3511, Ext 239. *Art Dept Head* Rudy Medlock; *Div Head Music & Art* Dr Ronald W Holz; *Instr* Clifford Davis. Instrs: FT 13
Estab 1892; pvt; D & E; scholarships; SC 30, LC 6; enrl D 1150, maj 65, others 250
Ent Req: HS dipl
Degrees: AB & BS 4 yr
Tuition: $2135 per quarter
Courses: Aesthetics, †Art Education, Art History, Ceramics, Drawing, Graphic Design, Handicrafts, Lettering, †Mixed Media, †Painting, †Photography, †Printmaking, †Sculpture, Teacher Training, Batik, †Weaving
Summer School: Dir, Rudy Medlock. Enrl 8 - 12; tuition $650.50 for term June 9 - July 9. Courses—Art Appreciation, Ceramics, Drawing, Painting, Stained Glass

LOUISIANA

BATON ROUGE

LOUISIANA STATE UNIVERSITY, School of Art, 123 Design Center, 70803. Tel 504-388-5411. *Dir* Michael Crespo, MFA; *Prof* Richard Cox, PhD; *Prof* James Burke, MFA; *Prof* Sidney Garrett, MA; *Prof* Ann Harding, MFA; *Prof* Michael Daugherty, MFA; *Prof* Mark Zucker, PhD; *Prof* Patricia Lawrence, PhD; *Prof* Melody Guichet, MFA; *Prof* A J Meek, MFA; *Prof* Christopher Hentz, MFA; *Prof* Ed Pramuk, MA; *Prof* Walter Rutkowski, EdD; *Prof* Robert Warrens, MFA; *Prof* Kimberly Arp, MFA; *Prof* Robert Lyon, MFA; *Prof* Robert Hausey, MFA; *Prof* Gerald Bower, MFA; *Prof* Marchita Mauck, PhD; *Assoc Prof* Michael Book, MFA; *Asst Prof* Gregory Elliot, MFA; *Asst Prof* Paul Dean; *Asst Prof* Herb Goodman, MFA; *Asst Prof* John Carambat, MFA; *Asst Prof* Erin Wright, MFA
Estab 1874, dept estab 1935; pub; D & E; scholarships
Ent Req: HS dipl, ACT scores
Degrees: BFA 4 yr, MFA 3
Tuition: Res—undergrad and grad $1020 per sem; nonres—undergrad $2620 per sem, grad $2620 per sem; campus res—room $420-$930, board $380-$550 per sem
Courses: †Art History, †Ceramics, Drawing, †Graphic Design, †Painting, †Printmaking, †Sculpture
Summer School: Tuition res—$273, nonres—$653 for 8 wk course

SOUTHERN UNIVERSITY A & M COLLEGE, School of Architecture, Southern Branch PO, 70813. Tel 504-771-2011; FAX 504-771-2495. *Dean* Henry L Thurman
Estab 1956; pub; D & E; scholarships; SC 14; enrl D 250, non-maj 7, maj 162
Ent Req: HS dipl
Degrees: BA 5 yrs
Tuition: $788 per sem
Courses: Architecture, Art Education
Summer School: Dir, Arthur L Symes. Tuition $164 for term of 8 wks beginning June. Courses—Architectural Design, Construction Materials & Systems, Graphic Presentation, Structures

GRAMBLING

GRAMBLING STATE UNIVERSITY, Art Dept, PO Box 4206, 71245-3090. Tel 318-274-2274. *Chmn* Thomas O Smith
Tuition: Res—$234 per sem; nonres—$549 per sem
Courses: Art Appreciation, †Art Education, Art History, Ceramics, Design, Drawing, Handicrafts, Illustration, Painting, Printmaking, Sculpture, Teacher Training

HAMMOND

SOUTHEASTERN LOUISIANA UNIVERSITY, Dept of Visual Arts, PO Box 765, 70402. Tel 504-549-2193. *Chmn* C Roy Blackwood, MFA; *Prof* Ronald Kennedy, MFA; *Assoc Prof* Barbara Tardo, MA; *Assoc Prof* Gail Hood, MFA; *Instr* Lynda Katz, MFA; *Instr* Sunjata Gopalan, MFA; *Instr* Lyna Pitts, MFA; *Instr* Paul Ryan, MFA
Estab 1925; pub; D & E; scholarships; SC 25, LC 4, GC 2; enrl D 109, E 75, maj 122
Ent Req: HS dipl, ACT
Degrees: BA(Educ), BA(Humanities), BA(Cultural Resource Management) 4 yrs
Tuition: $598 per 12 hr load
Courses: Art Education, Art History, Ceramics, Drawing, Painting, Photography, Printmaking, Sculpture, Teacher Training
Summer School: Dir, C Roy Blackwood. Enrl 150; 8 wk term. Courses—Art Education, Art Survey for Elementary Teachers

LAFAYETTE

UNIVERSITY OF SOUTHWESTERN LOUISIANA, School of Art and Architecture, USL Box 43850, 70504. Tel 318-231-6224; FAX 318-231-5907. *Dir* Gordon Brooks. Instrs: FT 40, PT 5
Estab 1900; pub; enrl univ 16,000
Degrees: BArchit & BFA 4-5 yrs
Tuition: $700 per sem
Courses: †Advertising Design, †Architecture, †Art Education, †Ceramics, †Photography, †Choreographic Design, †Fine Arts, †Interior Architecture
Children's Classes: Courses for gifted children—Design, Drawing, Photography
Summer School: Study abroad program in Toulon, France. Courses—Ceramics, Design, Drawing, Painting, Photography

LAKE CHARLES

MCNEESE STATE UNIVERSITY, Dept of Visual Arts, Ryan St, MSU Box 92295, 70609. Tel 318-475-5060. *Chmn* Bill R Iles. Instrs: FT 9
Estab 1950, dept estab 1953; pub; D & E; scholarships; SC 24, LC 4, GC 1; enrl D 85, E 15, non-maj 215, maj 85
Ent Req: HS dipl
Degrees: BA (Art Educ) and BA (Studio Arts) 4 yrs
Tuition: $679 per sem
Courses: Advertising Design, Art Education, Art History, Ceramics, Drawing, Painting, Printmaking, Survey crafts course
Adult Hobby Classes: Enrl 50; tuition $254 per sem (3 hrs). Courses—Art History & Ceramics
Summer School: Dir, Bill Iles. Enrl 100; tuition $254 per 3 hrs. Courses—Basic Design, Beginning Drawing, Ceramics, Printmaking, Photography

MONROE

NORTHEAST LOUISIANA UNIVERSITY, Dept of Art, 700 University Ave, Stubbs 141, 71209. Tel 318-342-1375. *Head Dept* Ronald J Alexander, MFA
Estab 1931, dept estab 1956; pub; D & E; scholarships; SC 28, LC 4, GC 9; enrl non-maj 300, maj 125, GS 3
Ent Req: HS dipl
Degrees: BFA 4 yrs, MEd
Tuition: Res—$168 per unit
Courses: Advertising Design, Ceramics, Drawing, Painting, Photography, Printmaking, Sculpture
Adult Hobby Classes: Enrl 20. May 31 - July 2. Courses—Art 411
Summer School: Dir, Ronald J Alexander. Enrl 30; tuition $168 from May 25 - July 3 & July 5 - Aug 11. Courses—Art Appreciation, Art Education, Drawing, Painting

NATCHITOCHES

NORTHWESTERN STATE UNIVERSITY OF LOUISIANA, Dept of Art, 71497. Tel 318-357-4476; FAX 318-357-5567. *Head Dept* Rivers Murphy, MFA; *Asst Prof* Nolan Bailey, MA
Estab 1885; pub; D & E; SC 67, LC 17, GC 36; enrl maj 93, grad 16
Degrees: BA & BS 4 yrs, MA 2 yrs, special prog for advanced students MA in Art
Courses: †Advertising Design, †Art Education, Art History, Ceramics, Commercial Art, Drawing, Painting, Printmaking, Sculpture, Fiber Arts, Professional Photography, Stained Glass, Stringed Instrument Construction
Adult Hobby Classes: Courses—most of above

NEW ORLEANS

DELGADO COLLEGE, Dept of Fine Arts, 615 City Park Ave, 70119. Tel 504-483-4511. *Chmn Fine Arts* Margaret Wirstrom
Dept estab 1967. College has 2 campuses; pub; D & E; scholarships; SC 12-20, LC 12-20; enrl D 150, E 65, maj 60
Ent Req: HS dipl, 18 yr old
Degrees: AA and AS 2 yrs
Tuition: Res—$485 per sem; nonres—$1085 per sem
Courses: Art History, Ceramics, Drawing, History of Art & Archaeology, Painting, Sculpture, Jewelry, Art Appreciation, Watercolor

LOYOLA UNIVERSITY OF NEW ORLEANS, Dept of Visual Arts, 6363 Saint Charles Ave, 70118. Tel 504-865-2011, 861-5456. *Chmn* William M Grote
Den; D & E; scholarships; SC 9, LC 3; enrl D 150, E 45, maj 28
Ent Req: HS dipl, ent exam
Degrees: BSA 4 yrs
Tuition: $4785 per yr, 12 - 20 hrs
Courses: Art History, Ceramics, Design, Drawing, Painting, Photography, Printmaking, Sculpture, Teacher Training, Computer Graphics
Summer School: Chmn, John Sears. Enrl 40; term of 6 wks beginning in June. Courses—Drawing, Painting, Printmaking, Sculpture

SOUTHERN UNIVERSITY IN NEW ORLEANS, Art Dept, 6400 Press Dr, 70126. Tel 504-286-5000, 286-5267. *Chmn* Dr Sara Hollis, MA; *Prof* Eddie J Jordan, EdD; *Asst Prof* Gary Oaks, MFA; *Asst Prof* Ron Bechet, MFA
Estab 1951, dept estab 1960; pub; D & E; BA 4 yrs; enrl D 21, E 26, non-maj 700, maj 47
Ent Req: HS dipl
Degrees: BA 4 yrs, BS(Art Education) 4 yrs, BS(Music Education) 4 yrs
Tuition: Res—undergrad $728 per 12 cr hrs, grad $735.50 per 12 cr hrs
Courses: Art Education, Art History, Ceramics, Commercial Art, Drawing, Painting, Photography, Printmaking, Sculpture, Teacher Training, Video, African Art, African & American Art, Crafts
Adult Hobby Classes: Courses offered
Summer School: Courses offered

TULANE UNIVERSITY
—School of Architecture, 6823 Saint Charles Ave, 70118. Tel 504-865-5389; FAX 504-862-8798. *Dean* Donna Robertson; *Assoc Dean* John Klingman; *Asst Dean* Wendy Sack. Instrs: FT 24, PT 12
School estab 1907; pvt; enrl 320
Degrees: BArchit 3 yrs & 5 yrs, MArchit 1 yr & 3 1/2 yr
Tuition: $8750 per sem
Courses: †Architecture
—Sophie H Newcomb Memorial College, Art Department, 119 Newcomb Art Bldg, 70118. Tel 504-865-5327; FAX 504-862-8710. *Chmn* Richard Tuttle; *Prof* Arthur Okazaki; *Prof* Caecilia W Davis; *Prof* Arthur E Kern; *Prof* Mary E Smith; *Assoc Prof* Gene H Koss; *Assoc Prof* Marilyn R Brown; *Asst Prof* Ronna Harris; *Asst Prof* Jeremy Jerenigan; *Asst Prof* Barry Bailey
Estab 1886; pvt; D & E; scholarships; SC 33, LC 25, GC 29; enrl D 817 per sem, E 37 per sem
Ent Req: HS dipl, CEEB, interview, review of work by chairman and/or faculty (optional)
Degrees: BA and BFA 4 yrs, MA, MFA and MAT 2 yrs
Tuition: Res—undergrad $705 per cr hr, grad $965 per cr hr
Courses: †Art History, †Ceramics, †Drawing, †Painting, †Photography, †Printmaking, †Sculpture, †Glass
Adult Hobby Classes: Courses—Ceramics, Drawing, Painting, Photography, Printmaking, Sculpture, Glass, Art History
Children's Classes: Offered through the Dept of Education
Summer School: Dean, Richard Marksbury. Courses—Art History, Ceramics, Drawing, Glass, Painting, Sculpture, Photography

UNIVERSITY OF NEW ORLEANS-LAKE FRONT, Dept of Fine Arts, 70148. Tel 504-286-6493. *Chmn* Peggy P McDowell, MFA; *Prof* Doyle J Gertjejansen, MFA; *Prof* Richard A Johnson, MFA; *Prof* Joseph Howard Jones, MFA; *Prof* Carolyn J Kolb, PhD; *Prof* Harold James Richard, MFA; *Assoc Prof* George Rowan, MFA; *Assoc Prof* George H Rowan, MFA; *Assoc Prof* Marcia E Vetroco, PhD; *Assoc Prof* Thomas C Whitworth, MFA; *Assoc Prof* Annette E Fournet, MFA; *Asst Prof* Cheryl A Hayes, MFA; *Asst Prof* Christopher Saucedo, MFA
Estab 1958, dept estab 1968; pub; D & E; SC 29, LC 24, GC 34; enrl D 16,000 (university), non-maj 3000, maj 150, grad 20
Ent Req: HS dipl
Degrees: BA 4 yrs, MFA 60 hrs
Tuition: Res—undergrad & grad $2062 yr, $1031 per sem FT, $326 - $962 PT; nonres—undergrad $2427 per sem FT, $530 - $1227 PT, grad $2427 per sem FT, $856 - $1770 PT; campus res available
Courses: †Art History, Drawing, †Graphic Arts, Graphic Design, †Printmaking, †Sculpture
Adult Hobby Classes: Ceramics, Design, Drawing, Painting, Photography
Children's Classes: Design, Drawing, Painting, Sculpture
Summer School: Tuition $600 for term of 6 wks beginning June > Courses—Art Fundamentals, Art History, Drawing, Graphic Design, Graphics, Painting, Photography, Sculpture

XAVIER UNIVERSITY OF LOUISIANA, Dept of Fine Arts, 7325 Palmetto St, 70125. Tel 504-486-7411. *Chmn* Charles E Graves; *Prof* John T Scott, MFA; *Assoc Prof* Lloyd Bennett; *Asst Prof* Claire Paige
Estab 1926, dept estab 1935; den; D & E; scholarships; SC 48, LC 10; enrl D 50, E 12, non-maj 10, maj 52
Ent Req: HS dipl, SAT or ACT, health cert, C average at least
Degrees: BA, BA (Art Ed), BFA, BS & MA
Tuition: $1500 per sem
Adult Hobby Classes: Courses—Creative Crafts

PINEVILLE

LOUISIANA COLLEGE, Dept of Art, 71359. Tel 318-487-7262. *Chmn* John T Suddith; *Asst Prof* Ted Barnes
Den; scholarships; LC, Lab C; enrl maj 20
Ent Req: HS grad
Degrees: BA 4 yrs, 49 hrs of art req plus 78 hrs acad for degree
Tuition: Res—$149 per sem hr
Courses: Advertising Design, Art Appreciation, Art Education, Art History, Ceramics, Design, Drawing, Illustration, Lettering, Painting, Photography, Printmaking, Studio Arts
Adult Hobby Classes: Courses offered through Continuing Education
Summer School: Limited courses

RUSTON

LOUISIANA TECH UNIVERSITY, School of Art and Architecture, 3175 Tech Station, 71272. Tel 318-257-3909; FAX 318-257-4687. *Dir* Joseph W Strother. Instrs: FT 28, PT 14
Estab 1904; pub; D; scholarships; SC 98, LC 8, GC 87; enrl maj 652, others 538
Ent Req: HS dipl
Degrees: Degrees BA & MA 4 yrs, BArchit 5 yrs
Courses: †Architecture, †Ceramics, †Drawing, †Graphic Design, †Interior Design, †Painting, †Photography, †Printmaking, †Sculpture, †Studio Art
Summer School: Summer program in Rome & on campus

SHREVEPORT

CENTENARY COLLEGE OF LOUISIANA, Dept of Art, Centenary Blvd, 71104. Tel 318-869-5261. *Chmn Dept & Assoc Prof* Bruce Allen, MFA; *Lectr* Neil Johnson, BA; *Lectr* Donna Service, MFA; *Lectr* Ann Roberts, MLA; *Lectr* Carolyn Nelson, MA
Estab 1825, dept estab 1935; den; D & E; scholarships; SC 22, LC 8; enrl D 125 per sem
Ent Req: HS dipl, SAT or ACT
Degrees: BA 4 yrs
Tuition: $3775 per sem, $270 per hr; campus res—room & board $3200 per yr
Courses: Aesthetics, Art Education, Art History, Ceramics, Drafting, Drawing, Graphic Arts, Painting, Printmaking, Sculpture, Teacher Training

THIBODAUX

NICHOLLS STATE UNIVERSITY, Dept of Art, 70310. Tel 504-446-8111. *Art Dept Head* Dennis Sipiorski. Instrs: FT 5
Estab 1948; pub; D & E; scholarships; SC 73, LC 6; enrl D 100, non-maj 20, maj 80, others 20
Ent Req: HS dipl, ACT
Degrees: BA 4 yrs
Tuition: $824.55 for 12 hrs or more per sem
Courses: †Advertising Design, Art Education, Art History, †Ceramics, Commercial Art, Conceptual Art, †Drawing, Graphic Arts, Graphic Design, Illustration, Mixed Media, †Painting, Photography, †Printmaking, †Sculpture, Teacher Training, Applied Design, Rendering, Water Media

MAINE

AUGUSTA

UNIVERSITY OF MAINE AT AUGUSTA, Division of Fine & Performing Arts, University Heights, 04330. Tel 207-621-3000. *Prof* Joshua Nadel, MFA; *Prof* Philip Paratore, MFA; *Prof* Robert Katz, MFA; *Prof* Karen Gilg, MFA; *Assoc Prof* Brooks Stoddard, PhD; *Asst Prof* Liz Libby; *Asst Prof* R Richmond
Estab 1965, dept estab 1970; pub; D & E; SC 20, LC 8; enrl D 50, E 40, non-maj 40, maj 60
Ent Req: HS dipl
Degrees: AA(Architural Studies) 2 yrs
Tuition: Res—$3840 per yr, $64 per cr hr; nonres—$9000 per yr, $150 per cr hr
Courses: Advertising Design, Art History, Ceramics, Drawing, Graphic Arts, Mixed Media, Painting, Photography, Sculpture, Paper Making
Summer School: Provost, Richard Randall. Enrl 30-50; tuition $52 per cr hr for term of 7 wks beginning last wk in June. Courses - Drawing, Painting, Sculpture

BRUNSWICK

BOWDOIN COLLEGE, Art Dept, Visual Arts Center, 04011. Tel 207-725-3697; FAX 207-725-3123. *Chmn* Mark C Wethli, MFA; *Dir Art History* Susan Wegner; *Emeritus Prof* Philip C Beam, PhD; *Prof* Clifton C Olds, PhD; *Prof* Larry D Lutchmansingh, PhD; *Prof* Thomas B Cornell, AB; *Prof* Ann Lofquist; *Prof* Linda Docherty, PhD; *Lectr* John McKee, MA; *Vis Instr* Christopher Glass, PhD
Estab 1794; pvt; D & E; scholarships; SC 15, LC 18; enrl maj 54
Ent Req: HS dipl
Degrees: AB 4 yrs
Tuition: $9325 per yr, campus res—room & board $3375
Courses: Art History, Visual Arts

DEER ISLE

HAYSTACK MOUNTAIN SCHOOL OF CRAFTS, 04627-0518. Tel 207-348-2306. *Dir* Stuart J Kestenbaum. Instrs: FT 36
Estab 1951; pvt; D, Summer school; scholarships; enrl D 75
Tuition: $180 per wk plus shop fees
Courses: Ceramics, Graphic Arts, Basketry, Blacksmithing, Fabric, Glassblowing, Metalsmithing, Papermaking, Quiltmaking, Stained Glass, Woodworking, Weaving
Summer School: Dir, Stu Kestenbaum. Enrl 80; tuition $450 for 3 wks. Courses - Basketry, Blacksmithing, Fabric Arts, Glassblowing, Graphics, Metalsmithing, Papermaking, Quiltmaking, Woodmaking

GORHAM

UNIVERSITY OF SOUTHERN MAINE, Art Dept, 37 College Ave, 04038. Tel 207-780-5460. *Chmn* Rose Marasco, MFA
Estab 1878, dept estab 1956; pub; D & E; SC 9, LC 2; enrl maj 200
Ent Req: HS dipl, portfolio
Degrees: BA, BFA
Tuition: Res—undergrad $69 per cr hr; nonres—undergrad $155 per cr hr; New England Prog $90 per cr hr; campus res available
Courses: Art Education, Art History, Ceramics, Design, Drawing, Film, Museum Staff Training, Painting, Photography, †Printmaking, †Sculpture, Philosophy of Art; Problems in Art
Summer School: Dir, Rosa Redonnet. Enrl 125. Courses—Art History, Ceramics, Design, Drawing, Painting, Photography, Sculpture

LEWISTON

BATES COLLEGE, Art Dept, Liberal Arts College, 04240. Tel 207-786-6258. *Chmn* Rebecca Corrie. Instrs: FT 4, PT 4
Estab 1864, dept estab 1964; pvt; D; scholarships; SC 13, LC 19; enrl 1450 total
Degrees: BA 4 yrs
Tuition: $22,850 per yr (comprehensive fee)
Courses: Aesthetics, Art History, Ceramics, Drawing, History of Art & Archaeology, Painting, Printmaking, †Studio Art

ORONO

UNIVERSITY OF MAINE, Art Dept, 04469-5712. Tel 207-581-3245. *Chmn & Prof* Michael H Lewis, MFA; *Prof* James Linehan, MFA; *Prof* Susan Groce, MFA; *Prof* Deborah DeMoulpied, MFA; *Assoc Prof* Ronald Ghiz, MFA; *Asst Prof* Laurie Hicks, PhD; *Asst Prof* Owen Smith, PhD; *Asst Prof* Charles Shepard, MA; *Asst Prof* Michael Grillo, PhD
Estab 1862, dept estab 1946; pub; D & E; scholarships; SC 24, LC 24; enrl D 135, maj 135
Ent Req: HS dipl, 3 CEEB tests
Degrees: BA and BS 4 yrs
Tuition: Red—undergrad $89 per cr hr; nonres—undergrad $252 per cr hr; campus res—room & board $4362 per yr
Courses: †Art Education, †Art History, †Drawing, †Painting, †Printmaking, †Sculpture, †Teacher Training
Children's Classes: Chmn, Michael Lewis, MFA
Summer School: Dir, Robert White. Tuition $89 per cr hr. Courses—Basic Drawing, Basic Painting, Fundamentals of Painting, Independent Study in Art, Art Education, Photography

PORTLAND

PORTLAND SCHOOL OF ART, 97 Spring St, 04101. Tel 207-775-3052. *Pres* Roger Gilmore; *Dean* Ray Allen; *Instr* Edwin P Douglas, MFA; *Instr* John Eide, MFA; *Instr* Allen R Gardiner; *Instr* John T Ventimiglia, MFA; *Instr* Mark Johnson, MFA; *Instr* Tim McCreight, MFA; *Instr* Richard Mehl, MFA; *Instr* Johnnie Ross, MFA; *Instr* Gan Xu, Ph; *Instr* Joan Uraneck, MFA; *Instr* Jonathan Aldrich, MA
Estab 1882; pvt; D & E; scholarships; SC 37, LC 9; enrl D 300, E 200, maj 300, others 140 HS
Ent Req: HS dipl, portfolio
Degrees: BFA 4 yr (under Maine law, an academically advanced high school senior may take the freshman yr at Portland School of Art for both HS and Portland School of Art credit)
Tuition: $9960 per yr; no campus res
Courses: Art History, †Ceramics, Drawing, †Graphic Design, †Jewelry, †Painting, †Photography, Aesthetics, Architecture, Art Appreciation, Design, Drafting, Goldsmithing, Graphic Arts, History of Art & Archaeology, Landscape Architecture, †Printmaking, †Sculpture, Textile Design, †Metalsmithing, Art in Service
Adult Hobby Classes: Enrl 200, tuition $190 per 1 credit course plus lab fee $10-$25. Courses—Apparel Design, Ceramics, Design, Drawing, Graphic Design, Illustration, Jewelry, Landscape Design, Metalsmithing, Painting, Photography, Printmaking, Sculpture, Textile Design
Children's Classes: Enrl 150; tuition $135 per class. Courses—Ceramics, Drawing, Graphic Design, Photography, Printmaking, Sculpture, Metalsmithing
Summer School: Enrl 200; tuition $190 per cr for term of 1-6 wks beginning June 17, 1991. Courses—Art History, Ceramics, Drawing, Graphic Design, Jewelry & Metalsmithing, Painting, Photography, Printmaking, Sculpture, 2 & 3-D Design, Watercolor

ROCKPORT

MAINE PHOTOGRAPHIC WORKSHOPS, 2 Central St, 04856. Tel 207-236-8581; FAX 207-236-2558. *Founder & Dir* David H Lyman
Enrl 1200
Degrees: AA
Tuition: Workshops $600
Courses: Film, Editorial, Fine Art & Commercial Photography, Television & Video, Writing
Adult Hobby Classes: Enrl 1000
Summer School: Dir, David H Lyman. Enrl 1000; tuition $250 - $600 for 1 & 2 wk workshops & masterclasses

SKOWHEGAN

SKOWHEGAN SCHOOL OF PAINTING AND SCULPTURE, PO Box 449, 04976. Tel 212-529-0505; FAX 212-473-1342. *Exec Dir Admin* Constance Evans; *Exec Dir Prog* Barbara Lapcek. Instrs: 12 prominent res & visiting artists
Estab 1946; nine wk summer residency program for independent work; fels; enrl 65
Ent Req: Proficient in English, 19 years of age & slide portfolio
Degrees: Credits recognized for transfer, no degrees
Tuition: $4700 includes room & board
Courses: No academic work; individual critiques only
Summer School: Enrl 65; 9 wk summer residency program in Maine for independent work. Contact admin office at 200 Park Ave S, No 116, New York, NY 10003

WATERVILLE

COLBY COLLEGE, Art Dept, 04901. Tel 207-872-3233. *Prof* Harriett Matthews, MFA; *Prof* David Simon; *Assoc Prof* Michael Marlais, PhD; *Assoc Prof* Sonia Simon; *Assoc Prof* David Lubin, PhD; *Assoc Prof* Abbott Meader; *Asst Prof* Nancy Goetz, MFA; *Asst Prof* Sonia Simon; *Instr* Scott Reed
Estab 1813, dept estab 1944; pvt; D & E; scholarships; SC 12, LC 17; enrl D 500, non-maj 425, maj 75
Ent Req: HS dipl
Degrees: BA 4 yrs
Tuition: $20,400 per yr incl room & board
Courses: Drawing, History of Art & Archaeology, Painting, Printmaking, Sculpture

MARYLAND

BALTIMORE

COLLEGE OF NOTRE DAME OF MARYLAND, Art Dept, 4701 N Charles St, 21210. Tel 410-435-0100; WATS (Md) 800-435-0200; all other 800-435-0300. *Chairperson* Kevin Raines; *Prof* Linelle LaBonte; *Prof* Kevin Raines, MFA; *Asst Prof* Domenico Firmani, PhD; *Asst Prof* Ruth Watkins, ME
Pvt; D & E; scholarships; SC 32, LC 13; enrl D 680, non-maj 480, maj 45
Ent Req: HS dipl, SAT
Degrees: BA 4 yrs
Tuition: Res—undergrad $9450 yr, $4725 per sem; nonres—undergrad $6050 per yr, $3025 per sem; campus res—room & board $3400 per yr
Courses: Aesthetics, Art History, Calligraphy, Ceramics, Design, Drawing, Graphic Design, Illustration, Painting, Photography, Printmaking, Sculpture, Teacher Training, Fiber/Sculpture, History & Aesthetics of Photography, Pre Museum Studies, Slidemaking, Studio Art for Education Majors, 3-D Design, Typography
Adult Hobby Classes: Enrl 55; tuition $95 per cr (1-9 cr). Courses offered in Weekend College & Continuing Education Programs
Summer School: Dir, Suzanne Brafman. Enrl 35; tuition $95 per cr. Courses—Calligraphy, Drawing, Painting, Photography, Printmaking, Sculpture, Teacher Training

COPPIN STATE COLLEGE, Dept Fine & Communication Arts, 2500 W North Ave, 21216. Tel 410-383-5828. *Acting Chmn* Dr Judith Willner. Instrs: FT 1, PT 2
Scholarships; SC 6, LC 7; enrl D 350, E 45
Degrees: BS, MA & Doc in Art Education
Tuition: Res—$1896 per yr; nonres—$3364 per yr
Courses: Advertising Design, Art Education, Art History, Calligraphy, Ceramics, Drawing, Film, Graphic Design, Lettering, Painting, Photography, Printmaking, Sculpture, Teacher Training, Theatre Arts

JOHNS HOPKINS UNIVERSITY
—Dept of the History of Art, 3400 N Charles St, 21218. Tel 410-516-7117; FAX 410-338-5188. *Chmn* Charles Dempsey. Instrs: FT 5, PT 3
Estab 1947; pvt; D & E; scholarships; LC; enrl 10-20 in advanced courses, 80-100 in introductory courses
Degrees: BA, MA & PhD
Tuition: $16,750 per yr
Courses: Art History
—School of Medicine, Dept of Art as Applied to Medicine, 1830 E Monument St, Suite 7000, 21205. Tel 410-955-3213. *Dir Dept & Assoc Prof* Gary P Lees, MS; *Dir Emeritus & Assoc Prof* Ranice W Crosby, MLA; *Assoc Prof* Marjorie Gregerman, MS; *Assoc Prof* Timothy H Phelps, MS; *Assoc Prof* Leon Schlossberg; *Asst Prof* Howard C Bartner, MA; *Asst Prof* Brent A Bauer, MA; *Asst Prof* Elizabeth Blumenthal; *Asst Prof* Emeritus J Lindsey Burch; *Asst Prof* Neil Hardy, BFA; *Asst Prof* Dale R Levitz, MS; *Asst Prof* Raymond Lund; *Asst Prof* Corrine Sandone, MA; *Instr* Norman Barker; *Instr* Paul S Calhoun; *Lectr* Anne R Altemus; *Lectr* Joseph Dieter Jr; *Lectr* Nancy L Held
Univ estab 1876, School Medicine estab 1893, dept estab 1911; pvt; D; scholarships; SC 13, LC 5, GC 18
Ent Req: Baccalaureate degree

Degrees: MA 2 yrs
Tuition: $16,750 per yr; campus res—room $1890 per yr
Courses: Display, Drawing, Graphic Design, Illustration, Intermedia, Mixed Media, Painting, Photography, Sculpture, Video, Computer Graphics, †Medical, Biological Illustration

MARYLAND INSTITUTE, College of Art, 1300 W Mt Royal Ave, 21217. Tel 410-669-9200. *Pres* Fred Lazarus IV. Instrs: FT 45, PT 55
Estab 1826; pvt; D & E; scholarships; enrl D 1107, E 554, Sat 280
Ent Req: HS grad, exam
Degrees: BFA and MFA 4 yrs
Tuition: $12,300 per yr; campus res—$3700
Courses: Ceramics, Drawing, Graphic Design, Illustration, Interior Design, Painting, Photography, Printmaking, Sculpture, Teacher Training, Computer Graphics, Fibers & Wood
Adult Hobby Classes: Evenings and Saturdays, credit-non credit classes
Children's Classes: Saturdays and Summer classes
Summer School: Dir Continuing Studies, M A Marsalek. Enrl 1066; tuition $400 per sem per class for Continuing Studies
—**Hoffberger School of Painting,** 1300 W Mt Royal Ave, 21217. Tel 410-225-2255; FAX 310-669-9206. *Dir* Grace Hartigan
Fel awarded annually for study at the grad level; enrl limited to 14
Tuition: $12,400
—**Rinehart School of Sculpture,** 1300 W Mt Royal Ave, 21217. Tel 410-225-2255; FAX 301-669-9206. *Dir* Norman Carlberg
Tuition: $12,400
Adult Hobby Classes: Enrl 748; tuition $200 per cr
Children's Classes: Enrl 174; tuition $170 per class
—**Mount Royal School of Art,** 21217. Tel 410-225-2255. *Faculty* Babe Shapiro; *Faculty* Salvatore Scarpitta
Enrl 79
Degrees: MAT 2 yrs
Tuition: $12,400 per yr
Courses: Aesthetics, Art Education, Art History, Calligraphy, †Ceramics, †Drawing, History of Art & Archaeology, Intermedia, †Mixed Media, Painting, Photography, †Sculpture, Teacher Training, Video, Studio Art
—**Graduate Photography,** 1300 W Mount Royal Ave, 21217. Tel 410-225-2306. *Dir* Will Larson
Degrees: MFA 2 yrs
Tuition: Res—grad $12,400 per yr
Courses: History of Photography
—**Art Education Graduate Studies,** 1300 W Mount Royal Ave, 21217. Tel 410-225-2306. *Dir* Karen Carroll
Degrees: MFA 2 yrs
Tuition: Res—grad $12,400 per yr
Courses: Art Education, Teacher Training

MORGAN STATE UNIVERSITY, Dept of Art, Hillen Rd at Coldspring Lane, 21239. Tel 410-319-3020, 319-3021. *Dept Chmn* Dr Nathan Carter. Instrs: FT 7
Estab 1867, dept estab 1950; pub; D & E; scholarships; SC 28, LC 11, GC 17; enrl D 340, E 50, non-maj 250, maj 140, GS 11
Ent Req: HS dipl
Degrees: BA(Art) and BS(Art Educ) 4 yr
Tuition: Res—$372.50 per sem; nonres—$890 per sem
Courses: Architecture, Art Education, Art History, Ceramics, Design, Drawing, Graphic Arts, Graphic Design, Illustration, Painting, Photography, Sculpture, †Theatre Arts, 3-D Design
Children's Classes: Enrl 20; tuition $10 per sem. Courses—Painting, Printmaking, Sculpture
Summer School: Dir, Dr Beryl W Williams. Term of 6 wks beginning June and July. Courses—Art Appreciation, Art Education, Basic Design, Photography

NEW COMMUNITY COLLEGE OF BALTIMORE, Dept of Fine Arts, 2901 Liberty Heights Ave, 21215. Tel 410-333-5555, Ext 5449. *Coordr* Carlton Leverette, MFA; *Prof* Allyn O Harris, MFA; *Prof* Bill Webber; *Assoc Prof* David Bahr, MFA; *Asst Prof* Sally De Marcos, MEd. Instrs: FT 7, PT 20
Estab 1947; pub; D & E; scholarships; enrl D & E 9800, non-maj 505, maj 388
Ent Req: HS dipl or HS equivalency, ent exam
Degrees: AA 2 yrs
Tuition: City res—$810 per yr, $405 per sem, $27 per cr hr; state res—$1620 per yr, $810 per sem, $54 per cr hr; non-res—$2430 per yr, $1215 per sem; no campus res
Courses: Advertising Design, Art Education, Art History, Ceramics, Commercial Art, Drawing, Graphic Arts, †Graphic Design, Jewelry, Painting, †Photography, Printmaking, Sculpture, Textile Design, †Fashion Design, Fashion Illustration, †Fashion Merchandising
Adult Hobby Classes: Tuition county res $54 per cr; state res $54 per cr; nonres $81 per cr. Courses—same as above
Summer School: Dir, Dr Stephen Millman. Enrl 2655. Courses - Ceramics, Crafts, Design, Drawing, Fashion Design, Painting

SCHULER SCHOOL OF FINE ARTS, 5 E Lafayette Ave, 21202. Tel 410-685-3568. *Dir* Hans C Schuler
Estab 1959; pvt; D & E; SC 9, GC 3; enrl D 50, E 30, grad 2
Degrees: 4 yrs
Tuition: $2600 per yr, part-time students pay by schedule for sem
Courses: Drawing, Painting, Sculpture
Children's Classes: Tuition $400-$550 (summer - ages 14 and over). Courses—Drawing, Painting, Sculpture
Summer School: Dir, Hans C Schuler. Enrl 30; tuition $400 for term of 6 wks beginning June, $550 for 6 hrs per day, 6 wks. Courses—Drawing, Oil Painting, Sculpture, Watercolor

TOWSON STATE UNIVERSITY, Dept of Art, 21204. Tel 410-830-2142. *Dept Chmn* James W Flood. Instrs: FT 20, PT 19
Estab 1866; pub; D & E
Ent Req: HS grad
Degrees: BA, BS, MEd(Art Educ) 4 yr & MFA; spring sem Florence, Italy, Feb-

May
Courses: Art Education, Art History, Ceramics, Drawing, Graphic Arts, Jewelry, Painting, Sculpture, Textile Design, Enameling, Weaving, Wood & Metal
Adult Hobby Classes: Enrl 60
Summer School: Dir, Jim Flood. Enrl 25; 2 five wk sessions. Courses—Art History, Studio

UNIVERSITY OF MARYLAND, BALTIMORE COUNTY, Visual Arts Dept, 5401 Wilkens Ave, Room 111, 21228. Tel 410-455-2150; FAX 410-455-1070. *Chmn* David Yager; *Assoc Prof* Carol Fastuca; *Assoc Prof* Jerry Stephany; *Asst Prof* Harvey Kirstel; *Assoc Prof* Daniel Bailey; *Assoc Prof* Ruth Leavitt; *Assoc Prof* Vin Grabill; *Assoc Prof* Ron Petrochuz
Estab 1966, dept estab 1966; pub; D & E; SC 27, LC 12, GC 4; enrl in dept D 485, non-maj 375, maj 110
Ent Req: HS dipl, SAT
Degrees: BA 4 yrs
Tuition: Res—$681 per sem; nonres—$1879 per sem
Courses: Advertising Design, Aesthetics, †Art History, Calligraphy, Ceramics, Collages, Commercial Art, Conceptual Art, †Drawing, †Film, Graphic Arts, †Graphic Design, †History of Art & Archaeology, Intermedia, Lettering, Mixed Media, †Painting, †Photography, Printmaking, †Video
Summer School: Dir, David Yager. Six wk term. Courses—Drawing, Film, History, Photography, Video

BEL AIR

HARFORD COMMUNITY COLLEGE, Fine & Applied Arts Dept, Div of Arts & Sciences, 401 Thomas Run Rd, 21015. Tel 410-836-4000; FAX 410-836-4198. *Prof* Paul Labe. Instrs: FT 4, PT 5
Estab 1957; pub; D & E; SC 17, LC 4; enrl FT 1000, PT 1000
Ent Req: HS dipl
Degrees: AA 2 yrs
Tuition: No campus res
Courses: Art History, Ceramics, Commercial Art, Design, Drawing, Graphic Arts, Graphic Design, History of Art & Archaeology, Interior Design, Painting, †Photography, Sculpture, Architectural Drawing, Design
Summer School: Dept Chair, Paul Labe

BOWIE

BOWIE STATE UNIVERSITY, Fine Arts Dept, MLK Bldg, Room 236, Jericho Park Rd, 20715. Tel 301-464-3000, 464-7286. *Chmn* Dr Amos White IV; *Coordr* Robert Ward; *Gallery Dir* Clark Mester. Instrs: FT 12
Estab 1865, dept estab 1968; pub; D; SC 7, LC 3; enrl D 1600, E 350, non-maj 180, maj 45
Ent Req: HS dipl
Degrees: BA(Art) & BS(Art Educ) 4 yrs
Tuition: Res—undergrad $1257 per sem, grad $111 per cr hr; nonres—$2344.50 per sem
Courses: †Art Education, Art History, Ceramics, Design, Drawing, Painting, Photography, Sculpture, African & American History, Cinematography, Crafts, †Fine Arts, Graphics, Museum & Gallery Study, Computer Graphics
Summer School: Dir, Dr Ida Brandon. Courses—Ceramics, Media Workshop

CATONSVILLE

CATONSVILLE COMMUNITY COLLEGE, Art Dept, 800 S Rolling Rd, 21228. Tel 410-455-4429. *Chmn Dept* Dr W C Zwingelberg
Estab 1957; pub; D & E; scholarships; SC 26, LC 6; enrl D 600, E 400, non-maj 200, maj 300, applied arts maj 350
Ent Req: HS dipl
Degrees: Cert & AA 2 yrs
Tuition: $37 per cr hr
Courses: †Advertising Design, Art Education, Art History, Ceramics, Commercial Art, Drawing, Graphic Design, Illustration, Interior Design, Painting, †Photography, Sculpture
Adult Hobby Classes: Chmn Dept, Dr Dian Fetter
Summer School: Same as above

COLLEGE PARK

UNIVERSITY OF MARYLAND
—Dept of Art History, 1211-E Art-Sociology Bldg, 20742. Tel 301-405-1479. *Chmn* James Douglas Farquhar. Instrs: FT 15, PT 1
Estab 1944; pub; D; scholarships; SC 39, LC 37, GC 22; enrl 2000 per sem, maj 100, grad 20
Ent Req: 3.0 grade average
Degrees: BA, MA, PhD 4 yrs
Tuition: Res—undergrad $125 per cr hr, grad $164 - $294 per cr hr
Courses: Architecture, †Art History, †History of Art & Archaeology, Restoration & Conservation
Adult Hobby Classes: Enrl 500 per yr. Courses—Art History
Summer School: Dir, Dr Melvin Bernstein. Enrl 350; tuition $56 per cr hr for term of 6 wks. Courses—Art History
—Department of Art, 1211 - E Art-Sociology Bldg, 20742-1311. Tel 301-405-1442. *Chmn* Keith Morrison. Instrs: FT 20, PT 3
Estab 1944; pub; D; scholarships; SC 39, LC 37, GC 22; enrl 850 per sem, maj 170, grad 20
Ent Req: 3.0 grade average
Degrees: BA, MFA
Tuition: Res—undergrad $267 per cr hr, grad $170 per cr hr; grad nonres—grad$300 per cr hr
Courses: Design, Drawing, Painting, Photography, Printmaking, Sculpture
Summer School: Dir, Dr Melvin Bernstein. Two six-week sessions. Courses—Painting, Drawing, Design, Printmaking, Sculpture

CUMBERLAND

ALLEGANY COMMUNITY COLLEGE, Art Dept, Willow Brook Rd, 21502. Tel 301-724-7700; FAX 301-724-6892. *Chmn* James D Zamagias
Estab 1966; pub; D & E; scholarship; SC 6, LC 1; enrl Enrl D 30, E 9
Ent Req: HS dipl
Degrees: AA 2 yrs
Courses: Ceramics, Drawing, Painting, Survey of Art History, Two & Three Dimensional Design
Adult Hobby Classes: Courses offered
Summer School: Dir, James D Zamagias. Term of 6 wks beginning July. Courses—Painting, Two-D Design

EMMITSBURG

MOUNT SAINT MARY'S COLLEGE, Visual & Performing Arts Dept, 21727. Tel 301-447-6122; FAX 301-447-5755. *Chmn* Daniel C Nusbaum, PhD; *Prof* Walter Nichols, MA; *Prof* Kurt E Blaugher, PhD; *Prof* Robert Terentieff, MS; *Prof* Carolyn J Fraley, PhD; *Prof* Pamela Crockett, MFA
Estab 1808; pvt; D & E; scholarships; SC 9, LC 10; enrl D 1200, maj 12
Ent Req: HS dipl, SAT
Degrees: BA and BS 4 yrs
Tuition: $14,400 per yr, $7200 pr sem; campus res available
Courses: Art History, Drawing, Painting, Sculpture, Theatre Arts

FREDERICK

HOOD COLLEGE, Dept of Art, 401 Rosemont Ave, 21701. Tel 301-663-3131; FAX 301-694-7653. *Chairperson* Dr Anne Derbes; *Assoc Prof* Elaine Gates, MFA; *Assoc Prof* Fred Bohrer; *Assoc Prof* Harry St Hours
Estab 1893; pvt, W; D; SC 18, LC 16; enrl D 700, maj 60
Ent Req: HS dipl
Degrees: BA 4 yrs
Tuition: $11,395 per yr; campus res—room & board $5600
Courses: Five Areas of Concentration: Studio Arts, Art History, Art Therapy, Secondary Art Eduction, Visual Communications
Summer School: Dir, Dr Patricia Bartlett. Tuition by course for term of 6 wks, June-Aug. Courses—Internships and Independent Studies, Photography, Watercolor and Sketching, Woodcut

FROSTBURG

FROSTBURG STATE UNIVERSITY, Dept of Visual Arts, E College Ave, 21532-1099. Tel 301-689-4797; FAX 301-689-4737; WATS 800-689-8677. *Head Dept* Nancy P Rosnow
Estab 1898; pub; D; SC 25, LC 5; enrl D 230, maj 150, GS 13
Ent Req: HS dipl
Degrees: BA (Art, Art Educ), BS and MEd (Art Educ) 4 yrs
Tuition: Res—$781 per sem; nonres—$1441 per sem; campus res—room & board $1386 - $1608 per yr
Courses: Advertising Design, Art Education, Art History, Ceramics, Drawing, Graphic Design, Painting, Photography, Printmaking, Sculpture, Teacher Training, Textile Design, Art Criticism, Art Therapy, Art Awareness, Crafts, 2-D & 3- D Design, Visual Imagery

HAGERSTOWN

HAGERSTOWN JUNIOR COLLEGE, Art Dept, 11400 Robinwood Dr, 21742. Tel 301-790-2800, Ext 221; FAX 301-739-0737. *Coordr* Roz Rutstein, MA
Sch estab 1946; pub; D & E; SC 10, LC 4; enrl D 110, E 66
Degrees: AA, 2 yrs
Tuition: Washington County Res—$21 per cr hr; out of county—$45 per cr hr; nonres—$70 per cr hr
Courses: Art Appreciation, Art History, Ceramics, Drawing, Painting, Photography, Sculpture, Video, Art Methods, Basic Design
Summer School: Courses - Art & Culture, Basic Drawing, Painting, Photography, Special Studies in Ceramics, Parent & Child Art Studio

LARGO

PRINCE GEORGE'S COMMUNITY COLLEGE, Art Dept, English & Humanities Div, 301 Largo Rd, 20772. Tel 301-322-0966. *Chmn* Judith Andraka
Estab 1958, dept estab 1967; pub; D & E; scholarships; SC 18, LC 2; enrl D 220, E 140, maj 11
Ent Req: HS dipl, CGP test
Degrees: AA
Courses: Advertising Design, Art Appreciation, Art History, Ceramics, Design, Drawing, Graphic Arts, Graphic Design, Illustration, Jewelry, Lettering, Mixed Media, Painting, Photography, Printmaking, Sculpture, Advertising Illustration, Art Survey, Computer Graphics
Summer School: Dean, Dr Robert Barshay. Courses—Drawing, Intro to Art, Painting, Photography

PRINCESS ANNE

UNIVERSITY OF MARYLAND EASTERN SHORE, Art & Technology Dept, 21853. Tel 410-651-6488. *Coordr Art Education* Ernest R Satchell
Tuition: $1128
Courses: Art Appreciation, Art Education, Art History, Calligraphy, Ceramics, Drawing, Handicrafts, Jewelry, Painting, Photography, Printmaking, Sculpture

ROCKVILLE

MONTGOMERY COLLEGE, Dept of Art, 51 Manakee St, 20850. Tel 301-279-5115; FAX 301-251-7134. *Chmn* Ed Ashlstrom; *Prof* Orest S Poliszczuk
Estab 1946, dept estab 1966; pub; D & E; scholarships; SC 25, LC 7
Ent Req: HS dipl
Degrees: AA 2 yrs
Tuition: Res—$660 per sem, $44 per sem hr; nonres—$1245 per sem, $90 per sem hr; out-of-state $1710 per sem, $114 per sem hr
Courses: †Advertising Design, †Architecture, Art Appreciation, †Art Education, †Art History, Ceramics, †Commercial Art, Design, Drawing, Film, Goldsmithing, †Illustration, †Interior Design, Jewelry, Lettering, Painting, †Photography, Printmaking, Sculpture, Video, Color, Crafts, Computer Graphics, Enameling, Metalsmith, Printing
Summer School: Dir Robert S Cohen. Tuition $35 per sem hr. Courses—Ceramics, Color, Crafts, Design, Drawing, Painting, Printmaking

SAINT MARY'S CITY

SAINT MARY'S COLLEGE OF MARYLAND, Arts and Letters Division, 20686. Tel 301-862-0200, 862-0225; FAX 301-862-0958. *Head* Bruce Wilson; *Assoc Prof* Jonathan Ingersoll, MS; *Assoc Prof* Jeffery Carr; *Assoc Prof* Sandra L Underwood, PhD; *Asst Prof* Lisa Scheer, MFA
Estab 1964; pub; D & E; scholarships; SC 14, LC 16; enrl D 155, E 43, non-maj 128, maj 70
Ent Req: HS dipl, SAT scores
Degrees: BA
Tuition: Res—undergrad $2200 per yr; nonres—undergrad $3800 per yr; campus res—room & board $3500
Courses: Art History, Drawing, Painting, Photography, Printmaking, Sculpture
Adult Hobby Classes: Courses—Drawing, Ceramics, Painting, Sculpture
Summer School: Tuition $65 per cr. Courses—Drawing, Painting, Photography

SALISBURY

SALISBURY STATE UNIVERSITY, Art Dept, College & Camden Ave, 21801. Tel 410-543-6270; FAX 410-543-6068. *Chmn* James L Burgess, MA; *Prof* Kent N Kimmel, PhD; *Assoc Prof* Marie A Cavallaro, MA; *Assoc Prof* John R Cleary, MFA; *Asst Prof* Ursula M Ehrhardt, MA; *Asst Prof* Dean A Peterson
Estab 1925, dept estab 1970; pub; D & E; scholarships; SC 26, LC 7, GC 1; enrl non-maj 500, maj 111, grad 2
Ent Req: HS dipl, SAT verbal & math, ACT
Degrees: BA & BFA 4 yrs,
Tuition: Res—undergrad $6220 per yr (incl room & board); nonres—undergrad $7886 per yr (incl room & board); part-time res—undergrad $59 per sem cr hr, grad $82 per sem cr hr; part-time nonres—undergrad $64 per sem cr hr, grad $86 per sem cr hr
Courses: †Advertising Design, Art Appreciation, Art Education, Art History, Ceramics, Commercial Art, Design, History of Art & Archaeology, Painting, Photography, Sculpture, †European Field Study, †Independent Study, †Principles of Color, †Visual Communications
Summer School: Dean, Dr Darrel Hagar. Courses—various art education & studio courses

SILVER SPRING

MARYLAND COLLEGE OF ART AND DESIGN, 10500 Georgia Ave, 20902. Tel 301-649-4454. *Pres* Dr Danish; *Dean* Edward Glynn; *Prof* Christopher Bartlett, MFA; *Asst Prof* Lewis Hawkins, MFA
Estab 1955; pvt; D & E; scholarships; enrl Degree Prog 83, Enrichment & Special Students 175
Ent Req: HS dipl, SAT verbal scores, letter of recommendation, portfolio interview
Degrees: AA 2 yrs
Tuition: $5751 per yr, $1917 per quarter, $145 per cr hr; no campus res
Courses: Advertising Design, Art History, †Commercial Art, Design, †Drawing, Graphic Arts, Mixed Media, †Graphic Design, †Painting, Photography, Printmaking, †Sculpture, †Fine Art
Adult Hobby Classes: Enrl 300; tuition $150 per course for 10 wks. Courses—Animation, Illustration, Studio Painting, Watercolor
Children's Classes: Enrl 300; tuition $150 for 4-10 wks. Courses—Art Discovery, Drawing, Painting, Pastel, Art Explorations
Summer School: Dir, Eileen Hawes. Enrl 200; tuition $65-$170 - 2-6 wks

TOWSON

GOUCHER COLLEGE, Art Dept, 1021 Dulaney Valley Rd, 21204. Tel 410-337-6000, 337-6235; FAX 410-337-6405. *Chmn* Karen Acker
Estab 1885; pvt; D; scholarships; SC 38, LC 18; enrl D 970, non-maj 558, maj (art) 29
Ent Req: HS dipl, SAT, achievement tests (CEEB), American College Testing Program
Degrees: MA 4 yrs, MA (Dance Movement Therapy) 2 yrs
Tuition: $4987.50 per sem
Summer School: Dir, Fontaine M Belford. Enrl 160; Term of 4 wks beginning June 12 and July 10. Courses—(Art) Dance, Fibers Workshop, Nature Drawing Workshop, Photography, Pottery Workshop, Theatre

WESTMINSTER

WESTERN MARYLAND COLLEGE, Art Dept, 21157. Tel 410-857-2598. *Head Dept* Dr Julie Badiee; *Prof* Wasyl Palijczuk; *Asst Prof* Sue Bloom; *Asst Prof* Michael Losch. Instrs: FT 3, PT 2
Estab 1867; independent; D & E; SC 15, LC 12, GC 6; enrl D 1213, maj 40-60, grad 15
Ent Req: HS dipl, ent exam, SAT
Degrees: BA, BS & MEd 4 yrs
Tuition: $7275 per yr; campus res $1590
Courses: †Art Education, Ceramics, Drawing, Graphic Design, †History of Art & Archaeology, Jewelry, Lettering, Painting, Photography, Printmaking, Sculpture, †Teacher Training, Computer Graphics, Design, Watercolor
Children's Classes: Enrl over 120 Sat AM conducted by col students
Summer School: Two 5 wk terms beginning June 21. Courses—Art History, Ceramics, Painting, Printmaking, Sculpture, Weaving

MASSACHUSETTS

AMHERST

AMHERST COLLEGE, Dept of Fine Arts, Fayerweather Hall, 01002. Tel 413-542-2365; FAX 413-542-7917. *Chmn* Robert Sweeney. Instrs: FT 9
Estab 1822; pvt; D; scholarships; SC 15, LC 15
Ent Req: HS dipl
Degrees: BA 4 yrs
Tuition: $22,700 comprehensive fee for yr
Courses: Aesthetics, Art History, Drawing, Painting, Printmaking, Sculpture, Anatomy, 3-D Design

UNIVERSITY OF MASSACHUSETTS, AMHERST
—College of Arts and Sciences, Department of Art-FAC, 01003. Tel 413-545-1902. *Chmn Dept* Hanlyn Davies. Instrs: FT 36
Dept estab 1958; pub; SC 50, LC 19, GC 20; enrl maj undergrad 430, grad 85
Ent Req: HS grad, portfolio & SAT required, 16 units HS
Degrees: BA (Studio, Art History) & BFA (Studio, Computer Graphics, Interior Design, Art Educ) 4 yrs, MA (Art History), MFA (Ceramics, Computer Graphics, Painting, Printmaking, Sculpture), MS (Interior Design), MAT
Tuition: Res—undergrad $1067 per sem, grad $1335 per sem; nonres—undergrad $4118 per sem, grad $4118 per sem
Courses: Computer Graphics, 2-D Design, 3-D Design
Summer School: Dir, Angel Ramirez. Enrl 150-250; tuition $175 per 3 cr course, 2 six wk sessions. Courses—Architectural Drawing, Design, Drawing, Painting, Photography
—Art History Program, 317 Bartlett Hall, 01003. Tel 413-545-3595; FAX 413-545-3880. *Emeritus Prof* Jack Benson, PhD; *Prof* Iris Cheney, PhD; *Prof* Paul Norton, PhD; *Prof* Mark Roskill, PhD; *Prof* Walter B Denny, PhD; *Assoc Prof* Kristine Edmondson-Haney, PhD; *Prof* Craig Harbison, PhD; *Asst Prof* William Oedel, PhD; *Assoc Prof* Anne Mochon, PhD; *Asst Prof* Laetitia La Follette, PhD
Estab 1947, prog estab 1958; pub; D & E; scholarships & fels; LC 36, GC 16; enrl D 1735, non-maj 1369, maj 105, grad 40
Ent Req: HS dipl and transcript, SAT
Degrees: BA(Art History) 4 yrs, MA(Art History) 2 yrs
Tuition: Res—$4860 per yr; nonres—$10,730 per yr; room & board available
Courses: Aesthetics, Architecture, †Art History, History of Art & Archaeology, Museum Staff Training
Adult Hobby Classes: All courses available through Continuing Education
Summer School: Enrl 15 per course. Tuition $30 per cr & $42 service fee for term of 6 wks beginning June 2 & July 14. Courses—Introduction to Art, Modern Art
—Dept of Landscape Architecture & Regional Planning, 109 Hills N, 01003. Tel 413-545-2255. *Dept Head* John R Mullin; *Asst Dept Head* Merle Willman, PhD
Estab 1903; pub; D; SC 6, LC 5; enrl 35
Ent Req: Res-undergrad $702 per sem, graduate $73.25 pr cr hr up to $879
Degrees: AS (Arboriculture & Park Management, Landscape Operations) 2 yrs, BS (Landscape Architecture, Environmental Design, Leisure Studies & Resources) 4 yrs, MRP 2 yrs, MLA 2-3 yrs, PhD (Planning)
Tuition: Res—$1067 per sem, grad $1335 per sem; nonres—$4118 per sem
Courses: Drafting, Drawing, Landscape Architecture
Summer School: Planning and design short courses

AUBURNDALE

LASELL COLLEGE, Art & Interior Design Program, 1844 Commonwealth Ave, 02166. Tel 617-243-2000. *Dir* Andre S Van De Putte
Estab 1851; pvt, W; D & E; scholarships
Ent Req: HS dipl
Degrees: AA and AS 2 & 4 yrs
Tuition: Res—undergrad $8575 per yr
Courses: Ceramics, Drawing, Interior Design, Jewelry, Painting, Photography, Art for Child Study, Design & Color, Three-Dimensional Design, Portfolio

BEVERLY

ENDICOTT COLLEGE, Art Dept, 376 Hale St, 01915. Tel 508-927-0585; WATS 800-325-1114. *Head Dept* J David Broudo, EdM
Estab 1939; pvt, W; D; scholarships; enrl 250, non-maj 15, maj 235
Ent Req: HS dipl
Degrees: BS 4 yr, AA & AAS 2 yrs
Tuition: Res—$16,200 per yr (incl tuition, room & board); non—$7200 per yr
Courses: Advertising Design, Art History, †Ceramics, †Commercial Art, Drafting, Drawing, Fashion Arts, Graphic Arts, Illustration, †Interior Design, Jewelry,

Painting, †Photography, Printmaking, Sculpture, Silversmithing, Weaving, †Apparel Design, †Fibers, †Metal, †Fine Arts Management
Adult Hobby Classes: Enrl 100. Tuition $90 per cr. Courses— majority of day courses
Summer School: Dir, Ralph Carrivono. Tuition $90 per cr. Courses—Majority of day courses

MONSERRAT COLLEGE OF ART, Dunham Rd, PO Box 26, 01915. Tel 508-922-8222. *Pres* Arthur Greenblatt; *Dean* Barbara Moody; *Foundation Dept* George Creamer; *Painting* Kathy Speranza; *Printmaking* Ethan Berry; *Illustration* Elissa Della-Piana; *Sculpture* George Creamer; *Graphic Design* Pricilla Serafin; *Gallery Dir* B A O'Conner
Estab 1970; pvt; D & E; scholarships; SC 58, LC 13; enrl D 225, E 250
Ent Req: Personal interview and portfolio review
Degrees: BFA 4 yr dipl granted
Tuition: $7900 per yr, $3950 per sem, $990 per yr per course; no campus res
Courses: Art History, Conceptual Art, Design, Drawing, †Graphic Design, †Illustration, Graphic Design, Mixed Media, †Painting, †Photography, †Printmaking, †Sculpture, Video
Adult Hobby Classes: Enrl 200; tuition $135 per 8 wks. Courses—Drawing, Graphic Design, Illustration, Painting, Photography, Printmaking
Children's Classes: Enrl 50; tuition $115 per 8 wks. Courses—Painting & Drawing
Summer School: Dir, Robert Roy. Enrl 200; tuition $135 per cr for 4 wks beginning July, $405 FT for 3 cr courses beginning June. Courses—same as above

BOSTON

ART INSTITUTE OF BOSTON, 700 Beacon St, 02215. Tel 617-262-1223; FAX 617-437-1226. *Pres* Stan Trecker, MA; *Chmn Design Dept* Sue Morrison, MFA; *Chmn Illustration Dept* David Schuster,; *Chmn Fine Arts Dept* Anthony Apesos, MFA; *Chmn Photography Dept* Christopher James, MFA; *Chmn Found Dept* Nathan Goldstein, MFA; *Chmn Liberal Arts* Robert Wauhkonen
Estab 1912; pvt; D & E; scholarships; SC 80, LC 20; enrl D 400, E 250
Ent Req: HS dipl, portfolio and interview
Degrees: BFA
Tuition: Res—$7150 per yr, $3575 per sem
Courses: Advertising Design, Art Appreciation, Art History, Ceramics, Collages, Commercial Art, Conceptual Art, Constructions, Design, Drawing, Film, Graphic Arts, †Graphic Design, History of Art & Archaeology, †Illustration, Lettering, †Painting, †Photography, †Printmaking, †Sculpture, Video, Computer Graphics, Typography
Adult Hobby Classes: Enrl 200; tuition $180 per cr. Courses—Continuing education offers most of the above typically 2-3 cr each
Summer School: Enrl 250; tuition $180 per cr term of 8 wks beginning June 15. Courses—most of above

BOSTON CENTER FOR ADULT EDUCATION, 5 Commonwealth Ave, 02116. Tel 617-267-4430; FAX 617-247-3606. *Exec Dir* Paul Fishman
Estab 1933; pvt; D & E; scholarships; SC 26, LC 2; enrl D 2300, E 20,000
Ent Req: Open to all over 17
Tuition: $57 for 2 hr art or craft studio course; no campus res
Courses: Advertising Design, Architecture, Art Appreciation, Art History, Calligraphy, Ceramics, Drawing, Graphic Design, Interior Design, Painting, Photography, Printmaking, Video, Weaving, Sculpture, Theatre Arts, Clay Sculpture, Crafts, Studio Crafts, Stained Glass, Wood Carving
Summer School: Same as winter program

BOSTON UNIVERSITY, School of Visual Arts, 855 Commonwealth Ave, 02215. Tel 617-353-3371. *Dir* Stuart Baron; *Prof* Joseph Ablow; *Prof* Lloyd Lillie; *Prof* John Moore; *Assoc Prof* Alston Purvis; *Assoc Prof* Edward Leary; *Assoc Prof* Nicolas Edmonds; *Assoc Prof* Isabel McIlvan Shedd
Estab 1869, school estab 1954; pvt; D; scholarships; SC 38, LC 12, GC 15; enrl 395, non-maj 75, maj 260, grad 60
Ent Req: Ent req HS dipl, portfolio
Degrees: BFA 4 yrs, MFA 2 yrs
Tuition: $16,950 per yr, $518 per cr; campus res—room & board $4700 per yr
Courses: Art Education, Art History, Design, Drawing, Graphic Design, Painting, Photography, Printmaking, Sculpture, Teacher Training, Studio Teaching (grad level), Typographic Design
Adult Hobby Classes: Enrl 215; tuition $2072 (4 cr) 15 wk term.
Courses—Drawing, Graphic Design, Painting, Sculpture

BUTERA SCHOOL OF ART, 111 Beacon St, 02116. Tel 617-536-4623. *Pres* Joseph L Butera, MFA; *Dir* Charles Banks; *Head Commercial Art* Hal Trafford; *Head Sign Painting* Jim Garballey
Estab 1932; pvt; D & E; enrl D 100, E 60
Ent Req: HS dipl, portfolio
Degrees: 2 yr and 3 yr dipl progs
Tuition: $7400-$7550 per yr; independent dormitories available
Courses: Advertising Design, Art Education, Art History, Calligraphy, Commercial Art, Drawing, Fashion Arts, Graphic Arts, Graphic Design, Illustration, Lettering, Painting, Sign Painting

EMMANUEL COLLEGE, Art Dept, 400 The Fenway, 02115. Tel 617-735-9794; FAX 617-735-9877. *Chmn Art Dept* Ellen M Glavin, SND; *Prof* Theresa Monaco, MFA; *Assoc Prof* C David Thomas, MFA; *Asst Prof* Kathleen A Soles, MFA; *Adjunct Instr* Karen Saltalamacchia, MA
Estab 1919, dept estab 1950; pvt; D & E; scholarships; SC 30, LC 11; enrl D 300, E 50, non-maj 200, maj 80
Ent Req: HS dipl, SAT
Degrees: BA & BFA 4 yrs
Tuition: $10,966 full time or $1372 per course; campus res—room & board $5528 per yr
Courses: †Art Education, †Art History, Ceramics, Drawing, †Graphic Arts, Graphic Design, Mixed Media, †Painting, †Printmaking, Sculpture, Teacher Training, †Art Therapy

Adult Hobby Classes: Enrl 300; tuition $174 per cr. Courses—Art Educ, Art History, Art Theory, In Studio Art
Summer School: Dir, Dr Jacquelyn Armitage. Enrl 230; tuition $174 per cr hr for term of 6 wks in June - Aug

MASSACHUSETTS COLLEGE OF ART, 621 Huntington Ave, 02115. Tel 617-232-1555; FAX 617-566-4034. *Pres* William O'Neil, PhD; *Sr VPres* Betty Bachsbaum, PhD; *Dean Grad & Continuing Educ* Pat Doran; *Chmn Fine Arts, 2D Dean* Nimmer, MFA; *Chmn Fine Arts, 3-D* Marilyn Pappas; *Chmn Design* Margaret Hickey, BArch; *Chmn Art* Christy Park; *Chmn Media* Abelardo Morell; *Chmn Critical Studies* Virginia Allen; *Co-Chmn Design* Marilyn Gabarro
Estab 1873; pub; D & E; SC 400, LC 250, GC 50; enrl D 1100, E 1000, grad 100
Ent Req: HS transcript, college transcript, SAT, statement of purpose, portfolio
Degrees: BFA 4 yrs, MFA 2 yrs, MSAE 2 yrs
Tuition: Res—$1295 per yr; nonres—$5079 per yr; no campus res
Courses: Art Education, Art History, Ceramics, Film, Graphic Design, Illustration, Industrial Design, Intermedia, Painting, Photography, Printmaking, Sculpture, Video, Architectural Design, Fashion Design, Fibers, Film Making, Freshman Artistic Seminars, Glass, Metals
Adult Hobby Classes: Enrl 1000; tuition $65 per cr hr. Courses—All areas
Children's Classes: Enrl 150; tuition $45 for 10 wks. Courses—All areas
Summer School: Dir Continuing Educ. Enrl 900; tuition $65 per cr hr. Courses—all areas

MOUNT IDA COLLEGE
—**Chamberlayne School of Design & Merchandising,** 777 Dedham St, 02159. Tel 617-969-7000, Ext 236. *School Dir* Samuel L Guiffre; *Lectr* M Crowe, MFA
Estab 1892, dept estab 1952; pvt; D & E; enrl D 253, E 38, maj 253
Ent Req: HS dipl
Degrees: AAS 2 yrs, Interior Design 2 & 4 yrs, BS 4 yrs
Tuition: $3660 per yr; campus res—room & board $2750
Courses: Architecture, Art History, Commercial Art, Costume Design & Construction, Drafting, Drawing, Fashion Arts, Graphic Arts, Illustration, Interior Design, Jewelry, Painting, Sculpture, Textile Design
Summer School: Dir Susan Holton. 12 wks beginning June 1. Courses—same as regular academic yr

NEW ENGLAND SCHOOL OF ART & DESIGN, 28 Newbury St, 02116. Tel 617-536-0383; FAX 617-536-0461. *Pres* Christy R Rufo; *VPres* W M Davis; *Chmn Dept of Graphic Design* Jean Hammond; *Chmn Dept of Interior Design* Heidi Richards; *Chmn Fine Arts* Audrey Goldstein
Estab 1923; pvt; D & E; scholarships; enrl D 200, E 250, maj 200
Ent Req: HS dipl, portfolio
Degrees: Dipl, BFA
Tuition: $8850 per yr, $4425 per sem, $398 per cr PT
Courses: Advertising Design, Art History, Calligraphy, Commercial Art, Drafting, Drawing, Graphic Arts, †Graphic Design, Illustration, †Interior Design, Lettering, Painting, Photography, Printmaking, †Fine Arts, Computer Graphics
Adult Hobby Classes: Enrl 275; tuition $366 per cr for 10 wk term. Courses—Fine Arts, Interior Design, Graphic Design, Computer Graphics
Summer School: Dir, Felicia Onksen. Enrl 275; tuition $366 per cr for 10 wk term. Courses—those above

NORTHEASTERN UNIVERSITY, Dept of Art & Architecture, 360 Huntington Ave, 02115. Tel 617-437-2347; FAX 617-437-2942. *Chmn* Peter Serenyi, PhD; *Prof* Mardges Bacon, PhD; *Assoc Prof* Samuel Bishop, MFA; *Assoc Prof* T Neal Rantoul, MFA; *Asst Prof* Mira Cantor, MFA; *Asst Prof* Dianne Pitman, PhD; *Asst Prof* Edwin Andrews, MFA
Estab 1898, dept estab 1952; pvt; scholarships; enrl D 1200, E 1200, non-maj 1500, maj 380
Ent Req: HS dipl
Degrees: BA & BS 4 yrs
Tuition: Freshmen $9450 per academic yr; upperclassmen $4360 per academic quarter, $1363 per course; campus res—available
Courses: Advertising Design, Aesthetics, Architecture, Art History, Design, Drafting, Drawing, Film, Graphic Arts, Graphic Design, Illustration, Mixed Media, Painting, Photography, Video, †History of Art & Architecture, Architectural Design, Computer Aided Design, Media Design
Adult Hobby Classes: Enrl 180; tuition $116 per 12 wk quarter cr. Courses—same as full-time program
Summer School: Chmn, Peter Serenyi. Enrl 240. Tuition & courses—same as above

THE SCHOOL OF FASHION DESIGN, 136 Newbury St, 02116. Tel 617-536-9343. *Head Art Dept* Richard Vyse
Estab 1934; pvt; D & E; scholarships; enrl D approx 100, E approx 200
Ent Req: HS dipl
Degrees: No degrees, 2 yr cert or 3 yr dipl
Tuition: Res—$4950 per yr; school approved res
Courses: Costume Design & Construction, Drawing, Fashion Arts, Illustration, Textile Design, Theatre Arts
Adult Hobby Classes: Enrl 100; tuition $400 per 3 cr course. Courses—Fashion Design
Summer School: Dir, R F Alartosky. Enrl 100; tuition $400 per 3 cr course of 15 wks. Courses—Fashion Design

SCHOOL OF THE MUSEUM OF FINE ARTS, 230 The Fenway, 02115. Tel 617-267-6100, 267-1219; FAX 617-267-0280. *Dean* Bruce K MacDonald, PhD
Estab 1876; pvt; D & E; scholarships; SC 139, LC 16; enrl D 700, E 1000, grad 50, others 24
Ent Req: HS dipl, HS and col transcripts, portfolio
Degrees: Dipl, BFA, BFA plus BA or BS, BSEd, MFA, MAT (all degrees in affiliation with Tufts University)
Tuition: Dipl $12,250 per yr; BFA varies on ratio of academics & studies taken in any given year; MFA $23,000 for the degree
Courses: Art Education, Art History, Ceramics, Collages, Constructions, Design, Drawing, Film, Goldsmithing, Graphic Arts, Graphic Design, Illustration, Jewelry, Mixed Media, Painting, Photography, Printmaking, Sculpture, Silversmithing,

Teacher Training, Textile Design, Video, Metalsmithing, Stained Glass
Adult Hobby Classes: Evening classes; enrl 1000; tuition $555 per 15 wk sem, 3 cr per course; Saturday classes; tuition $210 per course. Courses—Ceramics, Drawing, Graphic Design, Video, Jewelry, Painting, Photography, Printmaking, Sculpture, Film
Summer School: Dir, Donald Grey. Enrl 264; term of 6 wks beginning last wk in June. Courses—same as adult education courses

UNIVERSITY OF MASSACHUSETTS AT BOSTON, Art Dept, 100 Morrissey Blvd, Harbor Campus, 02125. Tel 617-287-5730; FAX 617-265-7173. *Co-Chmn* Ronald Polito; *Co-Chmn* Ruth Butler, PhD; *Assoc Prof* Robert Risse, PhD; *Assoc Prof* Wilfredo Chiesa; *Assoc Prof* Melissa Shook; *Asst Prof* John Gianvito; *Asst Prof* Ann McCauley; *Asst Prof* Nancy Stieber; *Asst Prof* Pamela Jones; *Instr* Paul Tucker
Sch estab 1965, dept estab 1966; pub; D & E; SC 18, LC 32; enrl D 900, E 100, maj 200
Ent Req: Entrance exam
Degrees: BA
Tuition: Res—$1300 per sem; nonres—$3600 per sem
Courses: Art History, Constructions, Drawing, Film, Intermedia, Painting, Photography, Printmaking, Video, Film History

BRADFORD

BRADFORD COLLEGE, Creative Arts Division, 320 S Main St, 01830. Tel 508-372-7161. *Chmn* Richard Newman, MFA; *Asst Prof* Mary Lee Karlins; *Asst Prof* Marc Mannheimer, MFA; *Asst Prof* Richard Lewis, MFA; *Asst Prof* Fred Evers, MFA; *Asst Prof* Rita Berkowitz, BA; *Asst Prof* Marvin Sweet, MFA; *Asst Prof* Dr Frederick Schvetze; *Asst Prof* Scott Stroot, MFA; *Asst Prof* Peter Waldron, MFA
Estab 1803; pvt; D & E; scholarships; SC 20, LC 12; enrl D 300
Ent Req: HS dipl
Degrees: BA(Creative Arts) 4 yrs
Tuition: Res—$12,415 per yr; nonres—$425 per cr; campus res—room $5950 per yr
Courses: Advertising Design, Aesthetics, Art Appreciation, Art History, Ceramics, Collages, Costume Design & Construction, Design, Drawing, Film, Painting, Theatre Arts, Color & Composition, 2-D & 3-D Design, Psychology of Art, Weaving

BRIDGEWATER

BRIDGEWATER STATE COLLEGE, Art Dept, School and Summer Sts, 02325. Tel 508-697-1359; FAX 508-697-1707. *Chmn* Dorothy Pulsifer, MA; *Prof* John Droege, MFA; *Prof* John Heller, MFA; *Prof* Joan Hausrath, MFA; *Prof* William Kendall, MFA; *Prof* Stephen Smalley, EdD; *Prof* Roger Dunn, PhD; *Prof* John Crowe, MA; *Prof* Robert Ward
Estab 1840, dept estab 1840; pub; D & E; SC 35, LC 10, GC 35; enrl D 500, E 100, non-maj 440, maj 100, grad 10
Ent Req: HS dipl, SAT
Degrees: BA 4 yrs
Tuition: $37 per cr, $950 per yr; campus residence available
Courses: Art Education, Art History, Ceramics, Drawing, Goldsmithing, Graphic Arts, Graphic Design, Handicrafts, Jewelry, Painting, Printmaking, Sculpture, Silversmithing, Theatre Arts, †Studio Art
Adult Hobby Classes: Enrl 100; tuition $75 per sem hr. Courses—same as day course; rotational
Summer School: Dir, Dorothy Pulsifer. Enrl 40, tuition $75 per sem hr. Courses—same as above

CAMBRIDGE

HARVARD UNIVERSITY, Dept of Fine Arts, Sackler Museum, 485 Broadway, 02138. Tel 617-495-2377; FAX 617-495-1769. *Chmn Dept* John Shearman. Instrs: FT 24
Estab 1874; pvt; scholarships; LC 26 incl GC 12; enrl undergrad 88, grad 100
Courses: Art History

LESLEY COLLEGE, Arts Institute, 29 Everett St, 02238. Tel 617-868-9600; FAX 617-349-8717; WATS 800-999-1959. *Prog Dir* Peter J Rowan
Scholarships
Tuition: $5400 annual tuition
Courses: Art Appreciation, Art Education, Art History, Ceramics, Design, Drawing, Handicrafts, Painting, Photography, Printmaking, †Art Therapy
Summer School: Dir, Paolo J Knill. Enrl 80; 6 wk

MASSACHUSETTS INSTITUTE OF TECHNOLOGY
—**School of Architecture and Planning,** 77 Massachusetts Ave, 02139. Tel 617-253-4401. *Dean* William J Mitchell; *Assoc Dean* Lois A Craig; *Head Dept* Stanford Anderson; *Urban Studies & Planning* Phillip L Clay. Instrs: FT 62
Estab 1865; pvt; scholarships; SC, LC, GC; enrl 600
Degrees: SB(Art & Design), SB(Urban Studies), MArchit, MS(Archit Studies), MS(Building Technology), MS(Media Arts & Sciences), MS(Real Estate Development), MS(Visual Studies), MCP, PhD(Urban Studies), PhD(Archit, Art, Environmental Studies), PhD(Media Arts & Sciences) 2, 4 & 6 yrs
Tuition: $18,000 per yr
—**Center for Advanced Visual Studies,** 40 Massachusetts Ave, W11, 02139. Tel 617-253-4415; FAX 617-253-1660. *Dir* Otto Piene
Estab dept 1967; pvt; D & E; SC 9, LC 1, GC 5; enrl D & E 250, non-maj 240, grad 10
Ent Req: BA degree
Degrees: MS 2 yrs
Tuition: $16,500 per yr
Courses: †Video, †Celebrations, †Concepts, †Developmental Media, †Environmental Art, †Holography, †Laser
Summer School: Art Workshop

CHESTNUT HILL

PINE MANOR COLLEGE, Visual Arts Dept, 400 Heath St, 02167. Tel 617-731-7158; FAX 617-731-7199. *Div Chmn* Robert Owczarek
Estab 1911; pvt; D; SC 25, LC 25; enrl D 80
Ent Req: HS dipl
Degrees: AA & AS 2 yrs, BA 4 yrs
Tuition: Res—undergrad $10,200 per academic yr; campus res—room & board $5400 per academic yr
Courses: Architecture, †Art History, Costume Design & Construction, Drafting, Drawing, Graphic Arts, Interior Design, Museum Staff Training, Painting, Printmaking, Sculpture, Stage Design, Theatre Arts, Visual Arts
Adult Hobby Classes: Studio courses 25, lecture courses 25
Summer School: Dir, Dr Eva I Kampits

CHICOPEE

OUR LADY OF ELMS COLLEGE, Dept of Fine Arts, 291 Springfield St, 01013. Tel 413-594-2761; FAX 413-592-4871. *Chmn Dept* Nancy Costanzo
Estab 1928, dept estab 1950; pvt; D & E; scholarships; SC 14, LC 6; enrl D 210, non-maj 193, maj 17
Ent Req: HS dipl, Col Ent Exam (Verbal and Math)
Degrees: BA 4 yrs
Tuition: Res—$6850 per yr; nonres—$4350 per yr
Courses: Art Education, Photography, Art History, Calligraphy, Ceramics, Drawing, Painting, Printmaking, Sculpture

DOVER

CHARLES RIVER SCHOOL, Creative Arts Program, 56 Centre St, PO Box 339, 02030. Tel 508-785-0068, 785-1260. *Dir* Talbot Dewey Jr
Estab 1969; pvt summer school; D
Ent Req: None
Tuition: $860 per 4 wks
Courses: Ceramics, Costume Design & Construction, Drawing, Film, Mixed Media, Painting, Photography, Printmaking, Stage Design, Theatre Arts, Video
Children's Classes: Enrl 210; tuition $565 for 4 weeks
Summer School: Dir, Talbot Dewey Jr.

FRAMINGHAM

DANFORTH MUSEUM OF ART SCHOOL, 123 Union Ave, 01701. Tel 508-620-0050. *Dir* Marcia Rosenberg
Pvt; scholarships
Ent Req: None
Tuition: Varies per course; museum members receive a tuition reduction
Courses: Art History, Calligraphy, Ceramics, Drawing, Graphic Arts, Interior Design, Jewelry, Painting, Photography, Printmaking, Sculpture, Weaving, Watercolor
Adult Hobby Classes: Enrl 100 - 200; tuition varies per 9 wk sessions. Courses—Arts, Crafts, Photography
Children's Classes: Enrl 100 - 200; tuition varies per 8 wk session. Courses—Art Multi-Media, Ceramics
Summer School: Enrl 100-150; tuition varies per 2 wk courses. Courses—Same as above

FRAMINGHAM STATE COLLEGE, Art Dept, State St, 01701. Tel 617-620-1220. *Chmn* James Eng; *Prof* Dr Brucia Witthoft, PhD; *Prof* Leah Lipton; *Prof* Eugene Sullivan; *Assoc Prof* John Anderson; *Asst Prof* Sachiko Beck; *Asst Prof* Barbara Milot; *Asst Prof* Marc Cote
Estab 1839, dept estab 1920; pub; D & E; scholarships; SC 20, LC 10, GC 10; enrl D 3000, E 2500, maj 124
Ent Req: HS dipl, portfolio review
Degrees: BA 4 yrs
Tuition: Res $845 per yr, nonres $2957; campus res—room & board $1800 per yr
Courses: †Art History, Museum Studies, †Studio Art
Adult Hobby Classes: Art History, Studio Art
Summer School: Dir, James Brown. Tuition $170 per course for term of 8 wks. Courses—Art History, Studio

FRANKLIN

DEAN JUNIOR COLLEGE, Visual and Performing Art Dept, 99 Main St, 02038. Tel 508-528-9100. *Coordr Visual Arts* Richard Dean, MFA; *Asst Prof* Lyn Stangland-Cameron, MFA; *Instr* Marcia Kola; *Instr* Alexandra Broches, MA; *Instr* John Takacs, MFA; *Instr* Randy LeSage, MFA; *Instr* Kitty Wales, MFA
Estab 1865, dept estab 1960; pvt; D & E; scholarships; SC 10, LC 4; enrl D 220, E 30, non-maj 180, maj 30
Ent Req: HS dipl
Degrees: AA, AS 2 yrs
Tuition: $9155 per yr; campus res—room & board $5700
Courses: Ceramics, †Drawing, †Painting, †Photography, Fundamentals of Color, †Graphics, †Introduction to Visual Art, †Survey of Art - Greek through Renaissance, †Survey of Modern Art & Architecture, †2-D Design, †3-D Design
Adult Hobby Classes: Tuition $90 cr. Courses—Color Communication, Fundamental Drawing, Introduction to Visual Art, Photography I
Summer School: Courses—Introduction to Visual Art, Fundamental Drawing, Photography I

GREAT BARRINGTON

SIMON'S ROCK OF BARD COLLEGE, Visual Arts Dept, Alford Rd, 01230. Tel 413-528-0771; FAX 413-528-7365. *Chmn Studio Arts Dept* Arthur Hillman, MFA; *Instr* Arthur Hillman, MFA; *Instr* William Jackson, MFA. Instrs: PT 2
Estab 1966; pvt; D & E; scholarships; SC 14, LC 4
Ent Req: Personal interview
Degrees: AA 2-3 yrs, BA 4 yrs
Tuition: $12,990 per yr, room & board $4800
Courses: Aesthetics, Art History, Ceramics, Drawing, Graphic Design, Illustration, Jewelry, Painting, Photography, Printmaking, Sculpture, Artist & the Book, Introduction to the Arts, Microcomputer Graphics, 2-D Design, 3-D Design

GREENFIELD

GREENFIELD COMMUNITY COLLEGE, Art, Graphic Design & Media Communication Dept, One College Dr, 01301. Tel 413-774-3131. *Head Art Dept* T Budge Hyde, MFA; *Instr* John Bross, MFA; *Instr* Peter Dudley, MFA; *Instr* Pamela Sacher, MA; *Instr* Penne Krol, MFA; *Instr* Tom Young, MFA; *Art Historian* Keith Hollingworth; *Instr* Ron Kim; *Instr* Tom Boisvert; *Art Historian* Keith Hollingworth
Estab 1962; maintains a small gallery; pub; D & E; scholarships; SC 16; enrl in school D 1400, E 400, maj 110
Ent Req: HS dipl
Degrees: AA, AS 2 yrs
Tuition: Res—$708 per yr, $354 per sem; nonres—$1200 per yr, $600 per sem
Courses: †Advertising Design, †Art History, Commercial Art, Display, †Drawing, Graphic Arts, Graphic Design, Illustration, †Painting, †Photography, †Printmaking, Video, Media Communication
Adult Hobby Classes: Enrl 85; tuition $38 per cr. Courses—Design, Drawing, Photography & Non-credit workshops
Children's Classes: Enrl 50; no tuition during Spring & Fall. Courses—Talented & Gifted Program
Summer School: Dir, Bob Keir. Tuition $38 per cr for a 7 wk term. Courses—Color, Design, Drawing Workshop, Photography

HOLYOKE

HOLYOKE COMMUNITY COLLEGE, Dept of Art, 303 Homestead Ave, 01040. Tel 413-538-7000; FAX 413-534-8975. *Chmn* Frank Cressotti
Estab 1946; pub; D & E; scholarships; SC 7, LC 4; enrl D 115, E 20, maj 50
Ent Req: HS dipl, portfolio
Degrees: AA 2 yrs
Tuition: Res—$600.50 per sem; nonres— $1344 per sem plus $198 student fee
Courses: Art Education, Drawing, Graphic Arts, Graphic Design, History of Art & Archaeology, Painting, Photography
Summer School: Dir, William Murphy. Courses—Per regular session, on demand

LONGMEADOW

BAY PATH COLLEGE, Dept of Art, 588 Longmeadow St, 01106. Tel 413-567-0621; FAX 413-567-9324. *Dir Humanities* Dr Nancy Eaton; *Instr* Carole Guthrie
Estab 1947; pvt, W; D & E; SC 18, LC 2; enrl D 660, E 400, maj 10
Ent Req: HS dipl
Degrees: AFA 2 yr
Tuition: $152 per cr, $8600 comprehensive tuition, room & board
Courses: Ceramics, Drawing, Graphic Arts, Handicrafts, History of Art & Archaeology, Painting
Adult Hobby Classes: Enrl 300; tuition $80 per 8 wk course. Courses - Drawing, Painting, Watercolor

LOWELL

UNIVERSITY OF MASSACHUSETTS AT LOWELL, Dept of Art, 01854. Tel 508-934-3851, 934-3494. *Chairperson Dept* Dr Liana Cheney; *Prof* Brenda Pinardi, MFA; *Prof* Fred Faudie, MFA; *Assoc Prof* James Veatch, EdM; *Assoc Prof* Robert Griffith, MFA; *Assoc Prof* James Coates, MFA; *Assoc Prof* Arno Minkkinen; *Asst Prof* Carol Pendergast
Estab 1975 (merger of Lowell State College and Lowell Technological Institute); pub; D & E; enrl D 1200, E 25, non-maj 450, maj 150
Ent Req: HS dipl, SAT
Degrees: BA(Art), BFA 4 yrs
Tuition: Res—undergrad $4000 per yr, $2000 per sem; nonres—undergrad $10,000 per yr, $5000 per sem; campus res—room & board $2366 per yr
Courses: †Art History, †Studio Art
Adult Hobby Classes: Enrl 15 - 20 per course; tuition $135. Courses—Art Appreciation, Drawing, Painting, Survey of Art
Summer School: Dir, Fred Yalouris. Enrl 10 - 15; tuition $135 per cr for 3 weeks. Courses—Art Appreciation, Drawing, Photography, Survey of Art I & II, Seminars in Italy, Finland, France

MEDFORD

TUFTS UNIVERSITY, Dept of Art & Art History, 11 Talbot Ave, 02155. Tel 617-628-5000, Ext 3567; FAX 617-627-3890. *Chmn Art & Art History* Judith Wechsler; *Prof* Miriam Balmuth, PhD; *Prof* Madeline H Caviness, PhD; *Assoc Prof* Margaret H Floyd, PhD; *Asst Prof* Elizabeth Honig, PhD; *Asst Prof* Eric Rosenberg, PhD; *Asst Prof* Eva Hoffman, PhD; *Asst Prof* Jodie Magness, PhD; *Adjunct Prof* Barbara E White, PhD; *Adjunct Prof* Lucy Der Manuelina, PhD
Pvt; D
Ent Req: HS dipl
Degrees: BA, BS, BFA, MA, MFA; certificate in museum studies
Tuition: $17,970 per yr, room, board & fees
Courses: Architecture, †Art History, Calligraphy, Ceramics, Design, Drawing, Film,

Graphic Arts, Graphic Design, History of Art & Archaeology, Illustration, Jewelry, Lettering, Mixed Media, Museum Staff Training, History of Architecture, Studio, Museum Studies, Metal Working, Interdisciplinary Studio Art
Adult Hobby Classes: Courses offered
Summer School: Dir, Judith Wechsler. Enrl 55; tuition $850 for 12 wks.
Courses—African Art, Boston Architecture, Modern Art, Survey

NEWTON

BOSTON COLLEGE, Fine Arts Dept, 885 Centre St, 02159. Tel 617-552-4295. *Chmn* Jeffery Howe. Instrs: FT 11, PT 20
Degrees: BA offered
Courses: Art History, Ceramics, Drawing, Film, Painting, Photography, Sculpture, Studio Art

NORTHAMPTON

SMITH COLLEGE, Art Dept, Hillyer Hall, Room 112, 01063. Tel 413-584-2700. *Chmn Art Dept* Susan Heideman; *Prof* Marylin Rhei, PhD; *Prof* Helen Searing; *Prof* Elliot Offner, MFA; *Assoc Prof* Craig Felton, PhD; *Assoc Prof* A Lee Burns, MFA; *Assoc Prof* Caroline Houser; *Assoc Prof* Dwight Pogue, MFA; *Asst Prof* Brigitte Buettner; *Asst Prof* N C Christopher Couch; *Asst Prof* Barbara Kellum; *Asst Prof* Marylin Rhie, PhD; *Asst Prof* John Moore; *Lecturer* Richard Joslin, MArchit; *Lectr* Ruth Mortimer, MS. Instrs: FT 17
Estab 1875, dept estab 1877; pvt, W; D; scholarships; SC 24, LC 34; enrl maj 170
Ent Req: HS dipl, col board exam
Degrees: BA 4 yrs
Tuition: $20,000 per yr incl room & board
Courses: Architecture, Art History, Calligraphy, Drafting, Drawing, Graphic Arts, Graphic Design, History of Art & Archaeology, Landscape Architecture, Painting, Photography, Printmaking, Sculpture, Color, Design with Computer, Woodcut

NORTH DARTMOUTH

UNIVERSITY OF MASSACHUSETTS DARTMOUTH (Formerly Southeastern Massachusetts University), College of Visual and Performing Arts, Old Westport Rd, 02747. Tel 508-999-8564; FAX 508-999-8901. *Dean Col* Michael D Taylor, PhD; *Chmn Music Dept* Eleanor Carlson, DMA; *Chmn Art Educ* Dante Vena, PhD; *Chmn Fine Art* Anthony J Miraglia, MFA; *Chmn Design* Elaine Fisher; *Chmn Art History* Magali Carrera, PhD; *Coordr Gallery* Lasse Antonsen, MA. Instrs: FT 50, PT 6
Estab 1895, col estab 1948; pub; D & E; SC 75, LC 41, GC 7; enrl D 700
Ent Req: HS dipl, SAT, open admis to qualified freshmen
Degrees: BFA and BA 4 yr, MFA and MAE 2-5 yrs
Tuition: Res—undergrad $1600 per yr, grad $1825 per yr; nonres—undergrad $5485 per yr, grad $5850 per yr; campus res room & board $4128 per yr
Courses: †Art Education, †Art History, Calligraphy, †Ceramics, †Design, Drawing, Graphic Arts, Illustration, Intermedia, Mixed Media, Painting, Photography, Printmaking, Sculpture, Textile Design, Theatre Arts, Video, †Wood, Furniture Design
Summer School: Dean, Armand Desmaris

NORTON

WHEATON COLLEGE, Art Dept, 02766. Tel 508-285-7722; FAX 508-285-2908. *Chmn Dept* Roberta J M Olson. Instrs: FT 6, PT 3
Estab 1834; pvt; scholarships; SC 6, LC 18; enrl 1307
Degrees: AB 4 yr
Tuition: $19,000 incl room and board
Courses: †Art History, Drawing, Painting, Photography, Printmaking, Sculpture, 2-D & 3-D Design

PAXTON

ANNA MARIA COLLEGE, Dept of Art, Sunset Lane, 01612. Tel 508-849-3441. *Chmn Dept* Ralph Parente. Instrs: FT 2, PT 3
Estab 1948; pvt; D & E; scholarships; SC 15, LC 12; enrl D 397, maj 32
Ent Req: HS dipl, ent exam
Degrees: 4 yr
Tuition: $2625 per sem
Courses: †Advertising Design, Aesthetics, †Art Education, Art History, Ceramics, Drawing, Lettering, Painting, Photography, Sculpture, †Teacher Training, Weaving, †Art Therapy, Enameling, Macrame, Modeling, Rug Design, Silk Screen, Stitchery, †Studio Art
Summer School: Dir, Ann McMorrow. Two sessions beginning May.

PITTSFIELD

BERKSHIRE COMMUNITY COLLEGE, Dept of Fine Arts, West St, 01201. Tel 413-499-4660; FAX 413-448-2700. *Chmn Dept* Mark Milloff; *Instr* Benigna Chilla, MFA
Estab 1960, dept estab 1961; pub; D & E; scholarships; SC 16, LC 4; enrl D 72, E 75, non-maj 12, maj 72
Ent Req: HS dipl
Degrees: AA 2 yrs
Tuition: Res—$288 per sem; nonres—$1008 per sem; no campus res
Courses: Art History, Drawing, Mixed Media, Painting, Photography, Printmaking, Applied Graphics, 2-D Design, 3-D Design, Primitive Art, 20th Century Art
Adult Hobby Classes: Continuing education evening classes, some may be applied to degree program
Summer School: Enrl 75; tuition $35 per cr hr for term of 7 wks beginning June. Courses—Design, Drawing, Painting, Photography

PROVINCETOWN

CAPE COD SCHOOL OF ART (Formerly Cape School of Art), 48 Pearl St, 02657. Tel 508-487-0101. *Dir* Lois Griffel
Estab 1899; pvt summer school; D
Ent Req: None
Courses: Drawing, Painting, Plein Air Painting in Landscape, Still Life, Portraits

QUINCY

QUINCY JUNIOR COLLEGE, Fine Arts Dept, 34 Coddington St, 02169. Tel 617-984-1600; FAX 617-984-1779. *Chmn Humanities Div* Ed White
Degrees: AA, AS and Certificate offered
Tuition: $850 per sem
Courses: Drawing, Painting, Photography, Development to American Film

SALEM

SALEM STATE COLLEGE, Art Dept, 352 LaFayette St, 01970. Tel 508-741-6222; FAX 508-741-6126. *Chmn Dept* Dr Patricia Johnston; *Prof* Elissa Ananian, MAT; *Prof* N E Wagman, ME; *Prof* Ingrida Raudzens; *Prof* John Voltacchio; *Prof* Frank Quimby, MEd
Estab 1854; pub; D & E; scholarships; SC 19, LC 8, GC 5; enrl maj 102
Ent Req: HS dipl
Degrees: BA 4 yrs
Tuition: Res—$645 per yr; nonres—$1465 per yr; campus res available
Courses: Art Education, Art History, Calligraphy, Ceramics, Drawing, Film, Graphic Design, Illustration, Jewelry, Painting, Photography, Printmaking, Sculpture, Stage Design, Teacher Training, Crafts, Computer Aided Graphic Design, History of Photography, Women, Art & Ideology, Portrait
Adult Hobby Classes: Enrl 80; tuition $150 per 15 wks. Courses—varied
Summer School: Dir, Dr Nancy D Harrington. Enrl 120; tuition $137.50 per two 5 wk sessions. Courses—varied

SOUTH HADLEY

MOUNT HOLYOKE COLLEGE, Art Dept, 01075. Tel 413-538-2200. *Chmn* Nancy Campbell
Estab 1858; pvt; W; D & E; scholarships; SC 13, LC 32; enrl D 409, maj 52
Ent Req: SAT, college boards
Degrees: BA
Tuition: Res—undergrad $12,100 per yr
Courses: Drawing, Painting, Printmaking, Sculpture
Adult Hobby Classes: Continuing education program leading to BA

SPRINGFIELD

SPRINGFIELD COLLEGE, Dept of Visual and Performing Arts, 263 Alden St, 01109. Tel 413-748-3540; FAX 413-748-3764. *Chmn Dept* William Blizard, MA; *Adjunct Prof* Emil Schnorr, MA; *Prof* Carroll Britch, MA; *Asst Prof* Ron Maggio, MFA; *Asst Prof* Simone Alter-Muri, Ed; *Asst Prof* Cynthia Noble, MA; *Asst Prof* Eugene Vinyard, MA; *Instr* Paula Hodecker, MA; *Instr* Brendan Stecchini, MFA; *Instr* Holly Murray, MFA; *Instr* Ruth West, MFA
Estab 1885, dept estab 1971; pvt; D & E; scholarships; SC 30, LC 6; enrl D 335, E 10, non-maj 300, maj 50
Ent Req: HS dipl, SAT, portfolio
Degrees: BA, BS 4 yr, MS(Art Therapy) 2 yr
Tuition: $9441 per yr, $273 per hr; campus res—room & board $4376
Courses: Advertising Design, Aesthetics, Art Appreciation, Art Education, Art History, Ceramics, Collages, Conceptual Art, Constructions, Costume Design & Construction, Design, Drawing, Graphic Arts, Graphic Design, History of Art & Archaeology, Illustration, Intermedia, Teacher Training, Mixed Media, Museum Staff Training, Painting, Photography, Printmaking, Restoration & Conservation, Sculpture, Stage Design, Theatre Arts, Video, †Art Therapy, †Computer Graphics, Computer Graphics Animation, Arts Management
Adult Hobby Classes: Enrl 25; tuition $217 per credit hour for 15 weeks.
Summer School: Dir, Dr Roland Holstead. Enrl 200; tuition $274 per hr for term of 3 or 6 wks beginning May 30. Courses—Drawing, Painting, Photography, Pottery

TRURO

TRURO CENTER FOR THE ARTS AT CASTLE HILL, INC, Castle Rd, PO Box 756, 02666. Tel 508-349-7511. *Dir* Mary Stackhouse; *Instr* Tony Vevers; *Instr* E J Kahn, Jr; *Instr* Paul Bowen; *Instr* Sally S Fine. Instrs: over 45 other nationally known instructors
Estab 1972; pvt summer school; D & E; scholarships; SC 50, LC 3, GC 30; enrl 590
Ent Req: None
Tuition: $72 for one wk; no campus res
Courses: Ceramics, Collages, Conceptual Art, Drawing, Painting, Printmaking, Photography, Sculpture, Bronze Foundry, Literature, Writing
Summer School: Dir Mary Stackhouse. Enro 590; tuition $25.30 per session, varies from 1 - 17 sessions

WALTHAM

BRANDEIS UNIVERSITY, Dept of Fine Arts, PO Box 9110, 02254-9110. Tel 617-736-2655. *Chmn* Robert Maeda. Instrs: FT 12
Estab 1948; pvt; D; scholarships; SC 10, LC 28; enrl 2800
Ent Req: HS dipl, college board ent exam
Degrees: BS 4 yr
Tuition: Campus res available
Courses: Art History, Drawing, Painting, Sculpture, Design
Summer School: Dir, Sanford Lotlor. Enrl 10-12 per course; tuition $585 per course for 4 week term. Courses—Introduction to History of Art II, Survey of Western Architecture

WELLESLEY

WELLESLEY COLLEGE, Art Dept, 02181. Tel 617-283-2042; FAX 617-283-3647. *Chmn* Lilian Armstrong; *Prof* Peter J Fergusson, PhD; *Prof* James F O'Gorman, PhD; *Prof* James W Rayen, MFA; *Prof* Richard W Wallace, PhD; *Prof* Miranola Marvin, PhD; *Prof* Anne Clapp, PhD; *Assoc Prof* Bunny Harvey, MFA; *Assoc Prof* Alice T Friedman, PhD; *Asst Prof* Margaret D Carroll, PhD; *Asst Prof* Carlos Dorrien
Estab 1875, dept estab 1886; pvt; D; SC 19, LC 46; enrl D 1233
Ent Req: HS dipl
Degrees: BA
Tuition: $16,690 per yr; campus res—room $2860 & board $3025
Courses: †Architecture, †Art History, Drawing, Graphic Arts, Painting, Photography, Printmaking, Sculpture, †Studio Art

WEST BARNSTABLE

CAPE COD COMMUNITY COLLEGE, Art Dept, Humanities Division, 02668. Tel 508-362-2131; FAX 508-362-8638. *Coordr Art* Robert McDonald, MFA; *Prof* Mary Kelsey, MFA; *Prof* Marie Canaves
Estab 1963, dept estab 1973; pub; D & E; SC 14, LC 7; enrl in school D 2000, E 3000, maj 60
Ent Req: HS dipl
Degrees: AA and AS 2 yrs
Tuition: Res—$950 per yr, nonres—$5052 per yr
Courses: Art History, Drafting, Drawing, Graphic Design, Illustration, Mixed Media, Painting, Stage Design, Theatre Arts, Video, Life Drawing, Visual Fundamentals
Adult Hobby Classes: Enrl 100 - 150; tuition $225 per 3 cr. Courses—Art History, Drawing, Graphic Design, Watercolor
Summer School: Dir, Dean Peter Birkel. Enrl 100 - 200; tuition $225 per 3 cr for 8 wk term beginning June 23. Courses—Art History, Drawing, Graphic Design, Visual Fundamentals

WESTFIELD

WESTFIELD STATE COLLEGE, Art Dept, Western Ave, 01086. Tel 413-568-3311, Ext 300. *Chmn* Pat Conant
Estab 1972; pub; D & E; scholarships
Ent Req: HS dipl & portfolio review
Degrees: BA (Fine Arts) 4 yrs
Courses: Art Appreciation, Art Education, Ceramics, Drawing, Graphic Design, Lettering, Painting, Printmaking, Sculpture, Anatomy, Practicum, Computer Graphics
Summer School: Dept Chmn, P Conant. Courses—Watercolor, Paintings, Design Fundamentals, Art Survey & other courses

WESTON

REGIS COLLEGE, Dept of Art, 235 Wellesley St, 02193. Tel 617-893-1820; FAX 617-899-4725. *Chmn* Sr Marie de Sales Dinneen
Estab 1927, dept estab 1944; den; D & E; scholarships; SC 12, LC 12; enrl D 250, non-maj 200, maj 50
Ent Req: HS dipl, SAT, various tests
Degrees: AB 4 yr
Tuition: $11,410 annual tuition
Courses: †Art History, Ceramics, Drawing, Illustration, Painting, Art Therapy, Computer Design, Coordinating Seminars, Enameling, Etching, †Introduction to Art, Silk Screen, Stained Glass, Weaving, Woodcut, Graphic Techniques

WILLIAMSTOWN

WILLIAMS COLLEGE, Dept of Art, 01267. Tel 413-597-2377. *Chmn Art History* Carol Ockman, PhD; *Chmn Studio Art* Barbara Takenaga, MFA; *Dir Grad Progam* Samuel Y Edgerton, PhD. Instrs: FT 12, PT 12
Estab 1793, dept estab 1903; pvt; D; scholarships; SC 14, LC 40, GC 10; enrl 2000, maj 85, grad 29
Ent Req: HS dipl
Degrees: BA 4 yrs, MA(History of Art) 2 yrs
Tuition: $17,685 per yr; campus res—room & board $5410 per yr
Courses: Architecture, Art History, Drawing, History of Art & Archaeology, Painting, Photography, Printmaking, Sculpture, Video

WORCESTER

ASSUMPTION COLLEGE, Dept of Art & Music, 500 Salisbury St, 01615-0005. Tel 508-752-5615, Ext 206. *Chmn* Michelle Graveline, DMA; *Instr* Mary Ann Powers; *Asst Prof* Mary Ann Powers; *Asst Prof* Nancy Flanagan, MFA
Estab 1904, dept estab 1976; den; D & E; scholarships; enrl D 600, E 25
Ent Req: HS dipl
Degrees: BA 4 yr
Tuition: $10,210 per yr; campus res available
Courses: Aesthetics, Architecture, Art Education, Art History, Drawing, Graphic Arts, History of Art & Archaeology, Painting, Printmaking, Theatre Arts

CLARK UNIVERSITY, Dept of Visual & Performing Arts, 950 Main St, 01610. Tel 508-793-7113. *Chmn* Gerald Castonguay; *Dir Studio Art Prog* Donald W Krueger, MFA; *Dean Admissions* Richard Pierson. Instrs: FT 4, PT 10
University estab 1887; pvt; D & E; scholarships; SC 50, LC 24; enrl Maj 100, non-maj 450, other 20
Ent Req: HS dipl, portfolio, CEEB, achievement tests, SAT & ACH
Tuition: BFA & BA $7906 per yr, diploma $4000 per yr; campus res room & board $2610 per yr

Courses: Aesthetics, Ceramics, Drawing, †Graphic Design, †Illustration, †Painting, †Photography, Printmaking, Arts Management, Art Therapy, Environmental Art, †History of Art & Architecture, Visual Design, Visual Studies
Adult Hobby Classes: Offered through Clark University College of Professional and Continuing Education
Summer School: Offered through Clark University College of Professional and Continuing Education

COLLEGE OF THE HOLY CROSS, Dept of Visual Arts, 01610. Tel 508-793-2237. *Chair* John P Reboli, PhD; *Prof* Virginia C Raguin, PhD; *Assoc Prof* J N Italiano, MFA; *Assoc Prof* Terri Priest, MFA; *Assoc Prof* J E Ziegler, PhD; *Assoc Prof* Susan S Schmidt, MFA; *Asst Prof* Marion Schouten, MFA; *Vis Lectr* Ellen Lawrence
Estab 1843, dept estab 1954; pvt; D; SC 12, LC 15; enrl D 485, maj 25
Ent Req: HS dipl, SAT, ATS
Degrees: BA 4 yr
Courses: Aesthetics, Architecture, †Art History, Drawing, Graphic Arts, Graphic Design, History of Art & Archaeology, Painting, Photography, Printmaking, Sculpture, †Studio

WORCESTER CENTER FOR CRAFTS, 25 Sagamore Rd, 01605. Tel 508-753-8183. *Exec Dir* Cyrus D Lipsitt, BFA
Estab 1856; pvt; D & E; scholarships; SC 33, LC varies; enrl D & E 280, non-maj 30, maj 12
Ent Req: Portfolio review for two year professional prog, no req for adult educ
Tuition: $4,300 per yr, 2 year program; adult educ $105 per 10 wk session; no campus res
Courses: Calligraphy, †Ceramics, Goldsmithing, †Jewelry, Photography, †Silversmithing, Textile Design, Weaving, Enameling, †Fibre, Furniture Restoration, Stained Glass, †Wood Working
Adult Hobby Classes: Enrl 12-14 per class; four 10 wk sessions, Courses—Ceramics, Enamel, Furniture Refinishing, Photography, Stained Glass, Weaving & Fibre, Wood Working, Metal Working
Children's Classes: Enrl 10-14 per class; tuition $100 per 12 wks. Courses—Clay, Wood, Photography, Enameling, Baskets
Summer School: Exec Dir, Cyrus D Lipsitt. Enrl 150 adults & children, also childrens summer camp

WORCESTER STATE COLLEGE, Media, Arts, and Philosophy, 486 Chandler, 01602. Tel 508-793-8000; FAX 508-793-8191. *Chmn* Donald F Bullens
Estab 1874; pub; D & E; SC 18, LC 9; enrl D & E 725
Ent Req: HS dipl, col board exams, completion of systems application form
Degrees: BA and BS 4 yrs
Courses: Art Education, Art History, Collages, Drafting, Drawing, Graphic Design, Handicrafts, Intermedia, Mixed Media, Painting, Printmaking, Sculpture, Environmental Design, History of Urban Form
Summer School: Usually 5-8 courses and workshops

MICHIGAN

ADRIAN

ADRIAN COLLEGE, Art Dept, 110 S Madison, 49221. Tel 517-265-5161, Ext 454. *Chmn Art Dept* Pauleve Benio, MFA; *Prof* Michael Cassino, MFA; *Prof* Norman Knutson, MFA; *Instr* Barbara Lock, MA; *Instr* Nancy Van Over, MA; *Instr* Louise Kleinsmith, MA
Estab 1859, dept estab 1962; den; D & E; scholarships; SC 27, LC 6; enrl in dept D 250, E 50, non-maj 200, maj 70
Ent Req: HS dipl
Degrees: BA, BA with teaching cert & BFA
Tuition: $3126 per sem, $145 per sem hr; $854 per yr for room, $1260 per yr for board
Courses: Art Education, Art History, †Ceramics, Drawing, †Interior Design, †Painting, Photography, †Printmaking, Silversmithing, Textile Design, †Fashion Design, Fibers, 2-D & 3-D Design, Weaving
Children's Classes: Enrl 30; 6 wks May - July. Courses—Mixed Media
Summer School: Dir, Pi Benio. Enrl 15; May term, summer term June - July. Courses—Advanced Study, Art Education, Interior Design

SIENA HEIGHTS COLLEGE, Studio Angelico-Art Dept, 1247 Siena Heights Dr, 49221. Tel 517-263-0731, Ext 272; FAX 517-265-3380. *Chairperson Dept* Thomas Venner, MFA; *Assoc Prof* David Van Horn, MFA; *Assoc Prof* Joseph Bergman, MFA; *Assoc Prof* John Wittershiem, MFA; *Assoc Prof* Christine Reising, MFA; *Asst Prof* Deborah Danielson, MFA; *Instr* Rosemary Bathurst, MFA; *Instr* Lois DeMots, MA
Estab 1919; pvt; D & E; scholarships; SC 56; enrl D 200, maj 96, grad 25
Ent Req: HS dipl
Degrees: AFA 2 yrs, BFA and BA 4 yrs
Tuition: Undergrad $270 per cr hr, grad $270 per cr hr; campus res—room & board $2100 per yr
Courses: Art Education, Art History, Ceramics, Design, Drawing, Graphic Arts, Painting, Photography, Printmaking, Sculpture, Fibers, Metalsmithing, 2-D & 3-D Design
Summer School: Dir, Thomas Venner. Enrl 20 - 40; tuition $270 cr hr, May 15 - June 15. Courses—Ceramics, Photography, Sculpture

ALBION

ALBION COLLEGE, Dept of Visual Arts, 49224. Tel 517-629-0246. *Chmn Dept Visual Arts* Douglas Goering; *Prof* Richard Brunkus, MFA; *Assoc Prof* Douglas Goering, MFA; *Asst Prof* Lynne Chytilo, MFA; *Asst Prof* Thelma Rohrer, MA
Estab 1835; den; D & E; scholarships; SC 32, LC 8
Ent Req: HS dipl
Degrees: BA and BFA 4 yrs
Tuition: $4327 per sem; campus res - room & board $1841 per sem
Courses: Art History, Ceramics, Drawing, Film, Painting, Photography, Printmaking, Sculpture, Stage Design, Teacher Training, Theatre Arts
Summer School: Acad Dean, Dr Daniel Poteet. Tuition $131 per sem hr for term of 7 wks beginning May 15

ALLENDALE

GRAND VALLEY STATE UNIVERSITY, Art & Design Dept, 49401. Tel 616-895-3486; FAX 616-895-3106. *Chmn* J David McGee PhD; *Prof* Chester Alkema; *Prof* Donald Kerr; *Assoc Prof* Daleene Menning; *Assoc Prof* Beverly Seley; *Assoc Prof* Rosalyn Muskovitz; *Assoc Prof* Dellas Henke; *Asst Prof* Lorelle Thomas; *Asst Prof* Richard Weis; *Asst Prof* Gary Sampson
Estab 1960; pub; D & E; SC 15, LC 12, GC 1; enrl D 80, E 40
Ent Req: HS dipl or equivalent, ent exam
Degrees: BA(Studio), BS(Studio), BFA 4 yrs
Tuition: Res—undergrad $1093 per sem, $96 per cr hr; nonres—undergrad $2420 per sem, $220 per cr hr; campus res—room & board $3500 - $3970
Courses: Art Education, Art History, Ceramics, Drawing, Sculpture, Jewelry, Graphic Design, Painting, Printmaking, Teacher Training
Summer School: Courses—Introduction to Art, Art for the Classroom Teacher, Workshops; Drawing and Painting at Aix-en-Provence, France

ALMA

ALMA COLLEGE, Clack Art Center, 614 W Superior, 48801. Tel 517-463-7220, 463-7111; FAX 517-463-7277. *Chmn* Robert Rozier, MFA; *Assoc Prof* Carie Parks-Kirby, MFA; *Instr* Jan White Arvanetes, MA
Estab 1886; pvt; D & E; SC 10, LC 3; enrl D 200, maj 32
Degrees: BA, BFA
Tuition: $9030; campus res—room & board $3390
Courses: Ceramics, Drawing, Graphic Design, History of Art & Archaeology, Jewelry, Museum Staff Training, Painting, Photography, Printmaking, Sculpture, Weaving, Advertising Design, Aesthetics, Art Education, Art History, Film, Illustration, Mixed Media, Computer Graphics, Foreign Study, History of Film, Scientific/Medical Illustration

ANN ARBOR

UNIVERSITY OF MICHIGAN, ANN ARBOR
—School of Art, 2000 Bonisteel Blvd, 48109. Tel 313-764-0397. *Interim Dean* John H Stephenson, MFA. Instrs: Instrs: FT 35, PT 13
Estab 1817, school estab 1974; pub; D & E; scholarships; SC 50, LC 6, GC 15; enrl non-maj 533, maj 490, grad 50
Ent Req: HS dipl, portfolio exam
Degrees: Degrees BFA 4 yrs, MA 1 1/2 yrs, MFA 2 1/2 yrs
Tuition: Res—undergrad lower level $2095, upper level $2314 per sem, grad $3608 per sem; nonres—undergrad lower level $6947, upper level $7449 per sem, grad $7424 per sem; campus res available
Courses: Ceramics, Drawing, Graphic Design, Illustration, Industrial Design, Interior Design, Jewelry, Mixed Media, Painting, Photography, Printmaking, Sculpture, Silversmithing, Textile Design
Summer School: Interim Dean, John H Stephenson. Enrl varies; tuition res $799, nonres $3000 for term of spring & summer, spring May 1 to June 30, summer July 1 to Aug 30. Courses—2 & 3 wk intensive workshops offered
—Dept of History of Art, 48109. Tel 313-764-5400. *Chmn* Diane Kirkpatrick; *Dir Kelsey Museum* Elaine K Gazda; *Adjunct Prof* Milo Beach; *Cur* Marshall Wu; *Dir Museum Art* William Hennessey; *Prof* Ilene H Forsyth; *Prof Emeritus* Richard Edwards; *Prof Emeritus* Marvin Eisenberg; *Prof* Graham Smith; *Prof* R Ward Bissell; *Prof Emeritus* Nathan T Whitman; *Prof* Joel Isaacson; *Prof* Victor H Miesel; *Prof* John G Pedley; *Prof* Walter M Spink; *Prof* Margaret Root; *Prof* Leonard Barkan; *Assoc Prof* Virginia C Kane; *Assoc Prof* Martin Powers; *Assoc Prof* Patricia Simons; *Assoc Prof* John Humphrey; *Asst Prof* Yasser Tabbaa; *Assoc Prof* Sharon Patton; *Assoc Prof* Celeste Brusati; *Asst Prof* Thelma Thomas; *Asst Prof* Anatole Sonkevitch; *Asst Prof* Rebecca Zurier; *Asst Prof* Nil Quarcoopome; *Asst Prof* Jonathan Reynolds; *Asst Prof* Elizabeth Sears; *Instr* Eleanor Mannikka. Instrs: FT 16
Dept estab 1910; pub; scholarships and fels; enrl maj 75, grad 60
Degrees: BA, MA, PhD
Tuition: Res—undergrad $2095 per term, grad $3608 per term; nonres—undergrad $6947, grad $7424
Courses: †Art History, Museology
Summer School: Chairman, Diane Kirkpatrick. Enrl 77; tuition res $379 per cr, nonres $803 per cr

BATTLE CREEK

KELLOGG COMMUNITY COLLEGE, Visual & Performing Arts Dept, 450 North Ave, 49017. Tel 616-965-3931, Ext 2555; FAX 616-965-4133. Instrs: FT 9, PT 18
Estab 1962; pub; D & E; scholarships; enrl D 2200, E 2000, maj 60
Ent Req: None
Degrees: AA 2-4 yr
Courses: Advertising Design, †Architecture, †Art Education, †Art History, †Ceramics, †Commercial Art, Drafting, †Drawing, Graphic Arts, Graphic Design, Illustration, Industrial Design, Painting, Photography, Sculpture, Teacher Training
Adult Hobby Classes: Courses—all areas
Summer School: Courses—Basic Art & Appreciation

BENTON HARBOR

LAKE MICHIGAN COLLEGE, Dept of Art, 2755 E Napier Ave, 49022. Tel 616-927-3571. *Instr* Ken Schaber, MFA
Estab 1943; pub; D & E; scholarships; SC 10, LC 5; enrl 3377 total
Ent Req: Open door policy
Degrees: AA 2 yrs
Tuition: Res—$32 per sem hr; nonres—out of district $42 per sem hr, out of state $52 per sem hr; no campus res
Courses: Art Appreciation, Art Education, Art History, Ceramics, Design, Drawing, Occupational Therapy, Painting, Photography, Printmaking, Sculpture, Weaving, 2-D & 3-D Design

BERRIEN SPRINGS

ANDREWS UNIVERSITY, Dept of Art, Art History & Design, 49104. Tel 616-471-3279. *Prof* Peter Erhard; *Prof* Gregory Constantine; *Instr* Charyl Jetter; *Instr* D L May; *Instr* Steve Hansen. Instrs: FT 4
Estab 1952; den; D & E; SC 18, LC 5; enrl enrl 130, maj 20
Ent Req: HS grad
Degrees: BS(Art Educ), BA 4 yrs, BFA 4 yrs
Tuition: Tuition, room & board $2540 per quarter
Courses: Art Education, Art History, Ceramics, Drawing, Graphic Design, Painting, Photography, Printmaking, Sculpture, European Study
Summer School: Classes June 14-Aug 6

BIG RAPIDS

FERRIS STATE UNIVERSITY, Visual Communication Dept, 901 S State St, 49307. Tel 616-592-2000. Instrs: 10
Scholarships offered
Degrees: AAS and BS offered
Tuition: $800 per qtr
Courses: Art History, Design, Design, Graphic Design, Illustration, Photography, Air Brush, Concept Development, Creative Writing, Figure Drawing, Production Art, Rendering, Typography
Adult Hobby Classes: Enrl 400; tuition $46.50 per cr hr
Summer School: Dir, Karl Walker. Enrl 3195, tuition $557 per qtr

BIRMINGHAM

BIRMINGHAM-BLOOMFIELD ART ASSOCIATION, 1516 S Cranbrook Rd, 48009. Tel 313-644-0866. *Executive Dir* Kenneth R Gross, MFA. Instrs: PT 75
Estab 1956; pub; D & E; SC 90-100, LC 4; enrl 3000 total
Tuition: $0-$300 per term, no campus res
Courses: Advertising Design, Aesthetics, Architecture, Art Appreciation, Art History, Calligraphy, Ceramics, Collages, Commercial Art, Design, Drawing, Fashion Arts, Goldsmithing, Graphic Arts, Graphic Design, Handicrafts, History of Art & Archaeology, Illustration, Intermedia, Jewelry, Lettering, Mixed Media, Painting, Printmaking, Sculpture, Silversmithing, Textile Design, Weaving, Design, Glass, Surface Design
Adult Hobby Classes: Enrl 3000-3500; tuition $0-$300 for 3-39 hrs.
Courses—Crafts, Drawing, Painting, Pottery, Sketching
Children's Classes: Enrl 500; tuition $75-$100.
Summer School: Dir, K R Gross. Enrl 4-500; 6 wk term. Program on abbreviated basis

BLOOMFIELD HILLS

CRANBROOK ACADEMY OF ART, 500 Lone Pine Rd, PO Box 801, 48303-0801. Tel 313-645-3300; FAX 313-646-0046. *Pres* Roy Slade; *Co-Head Design Dept* Michael McCoy; *Co-Head Design Dept* Katherine McCoy; *Head Fiber Dept* Gerhardt Knodel; *Head Metalsmithing Dept* Gary Griffin; *Head Painting Dept* Beverly Fishman; *Head Photography Dept* Carl Toth; *Head Ceramics Dept* Graham Marks; *Head Architecture Dept* Dan Hoffman; *Head Printmaking Dept* Steve Murakishi; *Head Sculpture Dept* Heather McGill
Estab 1932; pvt; scholarships; enrl 140
Ent Req: Portfolio
Degrees: MFA & MArchit 2 yrs
Tuition: $8100 per yr, campus res—room & board $2000 (single), $1200 (double)
Courses: Architecture, Ceramics, Painting, Photography, Printmaking, Sculpture, Design, Fiber, Metalsmithing

DEARBORN

HENRY FORD COMMUNITY COLLEGE, Art Dept, 5101 Evergreen Rd, 48128. Tel 313-845-9634. *Chmn Dept* Kirk McLendon. Instrs: FT 6, PT 40
Estab 1938; pub; D & E; scholarships; SC 25, LC 9; enrl D 3500, E 7500, maj 600
Ent Req: HS dipl
Degrees: AA 2 yrs
Tuition: Res—$30 per cr hr; nonres—$42 per cr hr, plus lab fees; drive in campus
Courses: Art Appreciation, Art History, †Ceramics, Drawing, †Graphic Design, †Interior Design, Jewelry, †Painting, Photography, Printmaking, Sculpture, Textile Design, 2-D Design, 3-D Design
Children's Classes: Ceramics, Jewelry, Painting/Drawing, Sculpture
Summer School: Dir, Martin W Anderson. Tuition res-$30 per cr hr, nonres $42. Courses—Art Appreciation, Art History, Ceramics, Color Photography, Directed Study, Drawing, Black & White Photography, 2-D Design

DETROIT

CENTER FOR CREATIVE STUDIES, College of Art & Design, 201 E Kirby, 48202. Tel 313-872-3118. *Pres* Dr Josephine Kelsey; *Chmn Graphic Design* Lothar Hoffman; *Chmn Industrial Design* William House; *Chmn Photography* Robert Vigiletti; *Chmn Fine Arts* Aris Koutroulis; *Chmn Crafts* Herb Babcock; *Chmn General Studies* Harry Smallenberg; *Chmn Illustration* Mike Mikos; *Chmn Art Direction* Larry Fleming
Estab 1926; pvt; D & E; scholarships; enrl D 950, E 250, others 200
Ent Req: HS dipl & portfolio
Degrees: BFA 4 yrs
Tuition: $8900 yr, $4450 per sem
Courses: Advertising Design, Art History, Ceramics, Graphic Design, Illustration, Industrial Design, Interior Design, Jewelry, Painting, Photography, Printmaking, Sculpture, †Printmaking, Sculpture, Textile Design, †Art Direction, Art Therapy, Computer Graphics, †Crafts, Environmental/Interior Design, †Fiber Design, Design, †Glass, †Metals/Jewelry, †Product Design
Adult Hobby Classes: Tuition $225 per cr hr. Courses—Most of the above
Children's Classes: Youth, high school and pre-college programs
Summer School: Dean, Arthur Greenblatt. Enrl 250; tuition $225 per cr hr for term of 8 wks beginning June 15. Courses—Advertising Design, Crafts, Fine Arts, Industrial Design, Photography

MARYGROVE COLLEGE, Visual & Performing Arts Div, 8425 W McNichols Rd, 48221. Tel 313-862-8000, Ext 290. *Chmn Div* David Vandegrift, MFA; *Prof* Rose DeSloover; *Assoc Prof* Sr John Louise Leahy, DEd; *Assoc Prof* David Vandegrift, MFA; *Assoc Prof* James Lutomski, MFA
Estab 1910; pvt; D & E; SC 37, LC 20, GC 5; enrl D 150, E 25, non-maj 60, maj 50, grad 5
Ent Req: Interview with portfolio
Degrees: BA & BFA 4 yrs
Tuition: Res—undergrad $250 per cr hr, grad $262 per cr hr; campus res available
Courses: Advertising Design, Art Education, Art History, †Ceramics, Commercial Art, Constructions, †Drawing, †Graphic Arts, Graphic Design, Lettering, Mixed Media, †Painting, Photography, †Printmaking, †Teacher Training
Adult Hobby Classes: Enrl 65; tuition $35-$90 per course. Courses—Drawing, Painting, Photography
Children's Classes: Enrl 100; tuition $20-$50 per course. Courses—Ceramics, Painting, Photography
Summer School: Dean Continuing Educ, Sr Andrea Lee, PhD. Enrl 40, tuition $86 per cr hr for term of two 6 wk terms. Courses—Basic courses, graduate and undergraduate

MERCY COLLEGE OF DETROIT, Art Dept, 8200 W Outer Dr, PO Box 19900, 48219. Tel 313-993-6000, Ext 36085. *Chmn* Lloyd Radell; *VPres Acad Affairs* Daniel Hoeber; *Dean Arts & Science* Dr Jacqlyn Zeff
Scholarships offered
Tuition: $211 per cr hr
Courses: Art Education, Art History, Calligraphy, Ceramics, Commercial Art, Drawing, Painting, Sculpture, Modern Art, Pottery

UNIVERSITY OF DETROIT MERCY, School of Architecture, 4001 W McNichols, PO Box 19900, 48219-0900. Tel 313-993-1532; FAX 313-993-1011. *Prof* John C Mueller
Univ estab 1877, school estab 1964; pvt; D & E; scholarships; SC 14, LC 36; enrl D 200, maj 200
Ent Req: HS dipl, B average
Degrees: B Arch 5 years
Tuition: $5712 per sem, $336 per cr hr; campus res—room $760 - $1712, board $400 - $992 per trm
Courses: Architecture, Design

WAYNE STATE UNIVERSITY, Dept of Art and Art History, School of Fine, Performing & Communication Arts, 150 Community Arts Bldg, 48202. Tel 313-577-2980. *Chmn* Jeffrey Abt. Instrs: FT 25, PT 20
Tuition: Res—undergrad $971 for 12 cr hrs, grad $944 for 8 cr hrs; nonres—undergrad $2105 for 12 cr hrs, grad $1990 for 8 cr hrs
Courses: Advertising Design, Art History, Ceramics, Design, Drawing, Industrial Design, Painting, Photography, Printmaking, Sculpture, Fibers, Interiors, Metals
Summer School: Tuition same as regular sem for 7 wks. Courses—Art History, Ceramics, Design, Drawing, Fibers, Painting, Photography, Sculpture

DOWAGIAC

SOUTHWESTERN MICHIGAN COLLEGE, Fine & Performing Arts Dept, 58900 Cherry Grove Rd, 49047. Tel 616-782-5113. *Chmn* William Skoog, DA; *Instr* David R Baker, MFA; *Instr* Camille Riner, MFA; *Instr* Patty Bunner, MFA; *Instr* Jonathan Korzun, MA; *Instr* Wendy Willis, MM
Estab 1964; pub; D & E; scholarships; SC 13, LC 3; enrl D 200, E 100, non-maj 200, maj 100
Ent Req: HS dipl
Degrees: AA & AS
Tuition: Res—undergrad $36 per hr; nonres—undergrad $46 per hr; out of state $54 per hr
Courses: Advertising Design, Architecture, Ceramics, Commercial Art, Drafting, Drawing, Graphic Arts, Lettering, Painting, Photography, Printmaking
Adult Hobby Classes: Art Appreciation, Ceramics, Painting, Photography
Summer School: Dir, Marshall Bishop. Enrl 1000; 7 wk terms

EAST LANSING

MICHIGAN STATE UNIVERSITY, Dept of Art, 113 Kresge Art Center, 48824-1119. Tel 517-355-7610; FAX 517-355-6577. *Chmn* Linda O Stanford. Instrs: FT 30
Estab 1855; pub; D & E; scholarships; SC 77, LC 45, GC 25; enrl D 2500, non-maj 1500, maj 450, grad 60

Ent Req: HS dipl
Degrees: BA & BFA 4 yrs, MA 1 yr, MFA 2 yrs
Tuition: Res—undergrad $105 - $115 per cr hr, grad $157 per cr hr; nonres—undergrad $279 - $289 per cr hr, grad $318 per cr hr; campus res—room & board $1651 - $1687
Courses: †Art Education, †Art History, †Ceramics, †Graphic Design, †History of Art & Archaeology, †Painting, †Photography, †Printmaking, †Sculpture, †Teacher Training
Adult Hobby Classes: Tui $30-$40 per class, these meet once per wk. Courses—Ceramics, Drawing, Painting, Photography, Sculpture
Children's Classes: Saturday Art Program $15 per sem. Courses—Drawing, Fabrics & Fibers, Painting, Photography

ESCANABA

BAY DE NOC COMMUNITY COLLEGE, Art Dept, 2001 N Lincoln Rd, 49829. Tel 906-786-5802. *Chmn* Larry Leffel
Scholarships offered
Tuition: County res—$37.75 per sem cr hr; non-county res—$52 per sem cr hr; non-state res—$84 per sem cr hr
Courses: Art History, Design, Drawing, Painting, Sculpture

FARMINGTON HILLS

OAKLAND COMMUNITY COLLEGE, Art Dept, Orchard Ridge Campus, 27055 Orchard Lake Rd, 48334-4579. Tel 313-471-7500. *Chmn* Kegham Tazian
Degrees: AA and ASA offered
Tuition: District res—$37 per cr hr; non-district—$61 per cr hr; non-state—$88 per cr hr
Courses: Advertising Design, Art Appreciation, Art History, Calligraphy, Ceramics, Design, Drawing, Fashion Arts, Handicrafts, Photography, Sculpture

FLINT

CHARLES STEWART MOTT COMMUNITY COLLEGE, Art Area, School of Arts & Humanities, 1401 E Court St, 48502. Tel 313-762-0443. *Coordr* Thomas Bohnert, MFA; *Instr* Jessie Sirna, MA; *Instr* Samuel E Morello, MFA; *Instr* Catherine Smith, MFA; *Instr* Thomas Nuzum, MFA; *Instr* William O'Malley, MAEd
Estab 1923; pub; D & E; enrl D & E 250, maj 250
Ent Req: HS dipl or 19 yrs old
Degrees: AA 2 yrs
Tuition: Dist res—$46 per cr hr; state res—$65 per cr hr; nonres—$87 per cr hr; no campus res
Courses: Art Education, Art History, Ceramics, Drafting, Drawing, Film, Graphic Design, Jewelry, Painting, Printmaking, Sculpture, Teacher Training
Adult Hobby Classes: Classes offered through cont education division
Summer School: Coordr, Thomas Bohnert. Tuition same as above; 7.5 wk sessions, first May 15 - July 1, second July 1 - Aug 15. Courses—vary

GRAND RAPIDS

AQUINAS COLLEGE, Art Dept, 1607 Robinson Rd SE, 49506. Tel 616-459-8281, Ext 3401; WATS 800-678-9593. *Chmn Dept* Steve Schousen; *Prof* Sr Marie Celeste Miller, MA, PhD; *Assoc Prof* James Karsina, MFA; *Prof* Larry Blovits, MFA; *Sr Lectr* Claudia Liberatore
Estab 1940, dept estab 1965; pvt; D & E; scholarships; SC 28, LC 9; enrl D 250, non-maj 210, maj 40
Ent Req: HS dipl
Degrees: BA and BFA 4 yrs
Tuition: $4790 per yr; campus res—room & board $2436 per yr
Courses: Art History, Ceramics, †Drawing, †Painting, †Printmaking, †Sculpture, Photography
Adult Hobby Classes: Courses - Art History, Ceramics, Color, Design, Drawing, Painting, Photography, Printmaking, Sculpture

CALVIN COLLEGE, Art Dept, 3201 Burton SE, 49506. Tel 616-957-6326. *Chmn Dept* Robin Jensen; *Prof* Chris Stoffel Overvoorde, MFA; *Prof* Carl J Huisman, MFA; *Prof* Robert A Jensen, MFA; *Prof* Helen Bonzelaar, PhD; *Assoc Prof* Charles Young, PhD; *Assoc Prof* Franklin Spevers, MS; *Asst Prof* Anna Greidanus Probes, MFA; *Assoc Prof* James Mellick MFA
Estab 1876, dept estab 1965; den; D & E; scholarships; SC 16, LC 4, GC 5; enrl maj 130, grad 4, others 4
Ent Req: HS dipl, SAT or ACT
Degrees: BA(Art, Art Educ, Art History) & BFA(Art), MAT
Tuition: $3090 per sem, $790 per class; campus res - room & board $2620 per yr
Courses: Aesthetics, Architecture, Ceramics, Collages, Conceptual Art, Drawing, Film, Graphic Arts, Jewelry, Painting, Photography, Printmaking, Sculpture, †Teacher Training, Art Therapy
Summer School: Chmn Art Dept, Edgar Boeve. Enrl varies; tuition $565 for term of 3 1/2 wks beginning May. Courses vary

GRAND RAPIDS JUNIOR COLLEGE, Art Dept, 143 Bostwick NE, 49503. Tel 616-771-3942. *Chmn* Lynn Asper; *Instr* Nancy Close. Instrs: FT 6, PT 4
Estab c 1920; pub; D & E; scholarships; SC 17, LC 2; enrl D 250, E 75, maj 60
Ent Req: HS dipl or ent exam
Degrees: AA 2 yrs
Tuition: $732 per yr; no campus res
Courses: Art Appreciation, Art Education, Art History, Ceramics, Drawing, Graphic Design, Painting, Printmaking, Teacher Training, Architecture Rendering, Color & Design, Life Drawing, 20th Century Art, Watercolor
Summer School: Term of 8 wks beginning June. Courses—Art History & Appreciation, Drawing, Pottery

KENDALL COLLEGE OF ART & DESIGN, 111 Division Ave N, 49503-3194.
Tel 616-451-2787. *Pres* Charles L Deihl, EdD; *Chmn Foundation Fine Arts*
Margaret Vega, MFA; *Chmn Design Studies* Ed Wong-Ligda, MFA; *Chmn Art
History & Liberal Arts* Robert Sheardy, MA; *Dean of Student Affairs* Susanne
Hamady, MA. Instrs: FT 42, PT 14
Estab 1928; pvt; D&E; scholarships; SC 64, LC 27, AH 9; enrl 700
Ent Req: HS dipl, ACT, SAT
Degrees: BFA 4 yrs
Tuition: $3525 per sem
Courses: †Advertising Design, Art History, Design, Drafting, Drawing, Graphic
Design, †Illustration, †Industrial Design, †Interior Design, Lettering, Painting,
Photography, Printmaking, Sculpture, Textile Design, Video, Weaving, Mixed
Media, †Broadcast Video, †Environmental Design, †Furniture Design, †Fine Arts
Adult Hobby Classes: Courses—Drawing, Painting, Calligraphy, Photography
(Airbrush), Interiors, Advertising, Furniture Detailing
Children's Classes: Enrl 200; tuition $50 per class. Courses—Calligraphy,
Commercial Art, Drawing, Painting
Summer School: Full semester, May - July; same program as regular session

HANCOCK

SUOMI COLLEGE, Fine Arts Dept, Quincy St, 49930. Tel 906-482-5300.
Chairperson Dept Jon Brookhouse, MA; *Instr* Elizabeth Leifer, MA; *Instr* Katie
Knight MA
Estab 1896, dept estab 1974; pvt; D & E; SC 5; enrl D 24, E 30, non-maj 18, maj 12
Ent Req: HS dipl, open door policy
Degrees: AA 2 yrs
Tuition: $8330 per yr; campus res—$3140 per yr
Courses: Ceramics, Design, Drawing, Graphic Arts, Painting, Photography,
Printmaking, Sculpture, Weaving

HILLSDALE

HILLSDALE COLLEGE, Art Dept, College St, 49242. Tel 517-437-7341, Ext
2371; FAX 517-437-3923. *Dir* Samuel Knecht, MFA; *Asst Prof* Tony Frudakis,
MFA
Estab 1844; pvt; scholarships; SC 12, LC 5; enrl D 1000, non-maj 150, maj 15
Ent Req: HS dipl, SAT
Degrees: BA & BS 4 yrs
Tuition: $7960 per yr, $3980 per sem; campus res available
Courses: Art Education, Art History, Ceramics, Drawing, Painting, Photography,
Sculpture, Teacher Training
Summer School: Dir, Dr Jerome Fallon. Courses vary

HOLLAND

HOPE COLLEGE, Art Dept, 49423. Tel 616-394-7500; FAX 616-394-7922. *Chmn*
William Mayer, MFA; *Prof* Delbert Michel, MFA; *Prof* John M Wilson, PhD;
Assoc Prof Bruce McCombs, MFA; *Asst Prof* Carol Anne Mahsun, PhD; *Instr* Judy
Hillman, BS
Estab 1866, dept estab 1962; den; D & E; scholarships; SC 18, LC 12; enrl D 185, E
61, non-maj 488, maj 26
Ent Req: HS dipl, CEEB-SAT or ACT
Degrees: BA and BM 4 yrs
Tuition: $5361 per sem
Courses: †Art Education, †Art History, Ceramics, Design, †Drawing, †Painting,
†Photography, †Printmaking, †Sculpture, 2-D & 3-D Design
Summer School: Registrar, John Haskens. Tuition $55 per cr hr. Courses—Vary
from year to year

INTERLOCHEN

INTERLOCHEN ARTS ACADEMY, Dept of Visual Art, 49643. Tel 616-276-
9221, Ext 407. *Chmn Dept* Jean Parsons; *Instr* Lary Lien, MFA; *Instr* Wayne Brill,
BS; *Instr* John Church, MFA; *Instr* Jean Parsons, MFA
Pvt; D; scholarships; enrl 440, non-maj 30, maj 40
Ent Req: Portfolio, HS dipl
Tuition: $12,750 per yr, includes room and board
Courses: Art History, Ceramics, Drawing, Jewelry, Painting, Photography,
Printmaking, Sculpture, Fibers, Metalsmithing, Screen-printing, Weaving
Summer School: Dir Carlene Perebrine. Enrl 1300; Interlochen Arts Camp, formerly
National Music Camp Courses—same as above

IRONWOOD

GOGEBIC COMMUNITY COLLEGE, Fine Arts Dept, E 4946 Jackson Rd,
49938. Tel 906-932-4231, Ext 283. *Chmn* Jeannie Milakovich
Estab 1932; pub; D & E; scholarships; SC 14, LC 3; enrl D 37, E 32, non-maj 65,
maj 4
Ent Req: HS dipl or equivalent
Degrees: AA 2 yrs
Tuition: $360
Adult Hobby Classes: Courses—Painting
Summer School: Dean Instruction, Dale Johnson. Courses—Ceramics, Ceramic
Sculpture, Drawing, Painting

KALAMAZOO

KALAMAZOO COLLEGE, Art Dept, 1200 Academy St, 49006. Tel 616-337-7047.
Chmn Dept Billie Fischer, PhD; *Prof* Marcia J Wood, MFA; *Prof* Bernard Palchick,
MFA; *Prof* David Curl, EdD
Estab 1833, dept estab approx 1940; pvt; D; scholarships; SC 14, LC 10; enrl
(school) 1200, non-maj 250 (dept), maj 20, others 5
Ent Req: HS dipl, SAT, ACT, class rank
Degrees: BA 4 yrs
Tuition: $13,800 per yr; campus res available
Courses: †Art Education, †Art History, Ceramics, Design, Drawing, History of Art
& Archaeology, Painting, Photography, Printmaking, Sculpture, Stage Design,
†Theatre Arts, Video

KALAMAZOO INSTITUTE OF ARTS, KIA School, 314 S Park St, 49007. Tel
616-349-7775. *Dir KIA School* Thomas Kendall, MA; *Head Sculpture Dept* Dora
Natella, MFA; *Head Photography Dept* James Riegel; *Head of Painting & Drawing
Dept* Denise Lisiecki Freed, MA; *Head Weaving Dept* Nancy Crampton, MA; *Head
Jewelry Dept* Tom Turner, BFA; *Head Paper Making* Eve Reid, MFA; *Head
Children's Prog* Maryjo Lemanski, MA
Estab 1924; pvt; D & E; SC 29; enrl D 530, E 490
Tuition: $75-$90 depending upon membership; no campus res
Courses: Ceramics, Design, Drawing, Jewelry, Painting, Photography, Sculpture,
Courses for the Handicapped, Weaving
Adult Hobby Classes: Enrl 275; tuition $75-$90 per 12 wks. Courses—Painting,
Sculpture, Drawing, Printmaking, Ceramics, Design, Jewelry, Courses for the
Handicapped, Studio classes in media photography
Children's Classes: Enrl 120; tuition $50-$65 per 12 wks. Courses—Ceramics,
Drawing, Painting, Photography
Summer School: Dir, Tom Kendall. Enrl 130; tuition $45-$50 per 12 sessions per 6
wks. Courses—same as adult & children

KALAMAZOO VALLEY COMMUNITY COLLEGE, Humanities Development
Center, 6767 W O Ave, 49009. Tel 616-372-5000, Ext 505. *Instr* Arleigh Smyrnios,
MA
Estab 1968; pub; E; SC 12; enrl D & E 500
Degrees: AA and AS
Tuition: In-county—$21 per cr hr; out-of-county—$41 per cr hr; nonres—$61 per cr
hr
Courses: Ceramics, Drafting, Drawing, Graphic Design, Painting, Photography,
Sculpture, 2-D Design
Adult Hobby Classes: Courses—Same as regular session
Children's Classes: Courses—Ceramics
Summer School: Dir Arleigh Smyrnios. Enrl 1125; tuition $21 per cr hr for 8 wk
term. Courses—Ceramics, Design, Drawing, Watercolor

WESTERN MICHIGAN UNIVERSITY, Dept of Art, 49008. Tel 616-387-2436.
Chairperson Dept Phillip VanderWeg. Instrs: FT 22
Estab 1904, dept estab 1939; pub; D & E; scholarships; SC 60, LC 9, GC 8; enrl
non-maj 200, maj 500, grad 20
Ent Req: HS dipl, ACT
Degrees: BA, BS & BFA 4 yrs, MA 1 yr, MFA 2 yrs
Tuition: Res—undergrad $77.50 - $87.25 per cr hr, grad $111.50 per cr hr;
nonres—undergrad $250 per cr hr, grad $276 per cr hr; campus res—room & board
$3827
Courses: †Art Education, Art History, †Ceramics, Drawing, †Graphic Design,
†Jewelry, †Painting, †Photography, †Printmaking, †Sculpture, †Metalsmithing
Adult Hobby Classes: Chairperson Dept
Summer School: Chairperson dept. Enrl 250; tuition same per hr as academic yr for
one 8 wk term beginning May. Courses—same as above

LANSING

LANSING COMMUNITY COLLEGE, Media Dept, 315 N Grand Ave, PO Box
40010, 48901-7210. Tel 517-483-1957; FAX 517-483-9781. *Prog Dir Art* Nancy
Lombardi; *Asst Prof* Jack Bergeron, MA; *Asst Prof* John Hutton, BFA; *Asst Prof*
Lily Liu, BFA; *Assoc Prof* Sharon Wood, MFA; *Asst Prof* Francia Trosty, MFA;
Inst John Washington, BS. Instrs: FT & PT 60
Pub; D & E; scholarships; SC 80, LC 10; enrl D 758, E 506, non-maj 400, maj 560,
others 304
Ent Req: HS dipl
Degrees: AA 2 yrs
Tuition: Res—$26 per cr hr; nonres—$42 per cr hr; out-of-state- $58 per cr hr; no
campus res; $59 International
Courses: Art History, Calligraphy, Commercial Art, Design, Drawing, Graphic
Design, Illustration, Lettering, Painting, Printmaking, Computer Graphics
Adult Hobby Classes: Enrl 60; duration 11 wks. Courses - Handmade Paper,
Watercolor, Sketching
Summer School: Prog Dir Art, Nancy Lombardi. Enrl 250; 8 wks sem

LIVONIA

MADONNA COLLEGE, Art Dept, 36600 Schoolcraft Rd, 48150. Tel 313-591-
5187. *Chmn Art Dept* Ralph F Glenn; *Prof* Sr M Angeline, PhD; *Instr* Anthony
Balogh, MA; *Instr* Gerry Panyard; *Instr* Douglas Semiven; *Instr* Marjorie Chellstrop;
Commercial Art George Toth; *Sculptor* Donald Gheen
Estab 1947; pvt; D & E; SC 17, LC 3; enrl D 43, E 22, maj 17
Ent Req: HS dipl, portfolio
Degrees: AA 2 yrs, AB 4 yrs
Tuition: $103 per sem hr
Courses: Advertising Design, Art History, Calligraphy, Ceramics, Commercial Art,
Drawing, Lettering, Painting, Photography, Printmaking, Sculpture, Teacher
Training
Adult Hobby Classes: Enrl 50; tuition $60 per 10 wk course. Courses—Painting
Summer School: Dir, Sr Mary Angeline

SCHOOLCRAFT COLLEGE, Dept of Art and Design, 18600 Haggerty Rd, 48152. Tel 313-462-4400. *Chairperson Dept of Art & Design & Prof* Lincoln Lao, MFA; *Prof* James R Black, MFA; *Prof* Robert DuFort, MFA; *Prof* Stephen Wroble, MA Estab 1964; pub; D & E; scholarships & fels; SC 13, LC 4; enrl D 300, E 150, maj 100
Ent Req: Ent exam
Degrees: AAS & AA 2 yrs
Tuition: Res—In District $1050 per yr, In State $1590 per yr; nonres—$2340 per yr; no campus res
Courses: Ceramics, Design, Drawing, Film, Graphic Arts, Jewelry, Painting, Photography, Printmaking, Sculpture, Computer Aided Art & Design, History of Art & Design
Adult Hobby Classes: Enrl 200; tuition res—$35 per cr, non-res—$53 per cr, out of state res—$78 per cr. Courses—Acrylic Painting, Ceramics, Drawing, Jewelry, Macrame, Photography, Stained Glass
Children's Classes: Enrl 40; tuition same as above. Courses—Talented & Gifted Program
Summer School: Courses—Drawing, Design, Printmaking, Watercolor

MARQUETTE

NORTHERN MICHIGAN UNIVERSITY, Dept of Art and Design, 49855. Tel 906-227-2194, 227-2279. *Head Dept* Michael J Cinelli; *Prof* Thomas Cappuccio; *Prof* John D Hubbard; *Prof* Marvin Zehnder; *Prof* William C Leete; *Prof* James Quirk; *Prof* Diane D Kordich; *Prof* Dennis Staffne; *Assoc Prof* Dale Wedig; *Assoc Prof* Eileen Roberts
Estab 1899, dept estab 1964; pub; D & E; scholarships; SC 30, LC 20, GC 18
Ent Req: HS dipl, ACT
Degrees: BS, BFA, BA 4 yrs, MAE
Tuition: Res—undergrad $65.20 per cr hr, grad $84.70 per cr hr; nonres—undergrad $125.20 per cr hr, grad $125.20 per cr hr; campus res—room & board $3326 per yr
Courses: †Art Education, †Art History, †Ceramics, †Drawing, †Film, †Graphic Design, †Illustration, †Industrial Design, †Jewelry, †Painting, Video, †Photography, †Printmaking, †Sculpture, Blacksmithing, †Fibers, †Furniture & Package Design, †Metalworking
Summer School: Dir, Michael J Cinelli. Enrl 40; 2 wk terms. Courses—Studio Workshops

MIDLAND

MIDLAND CENTER FOR THE ARTS, Midland Art Council, 1801 W St Andrews, 48640. Tel 517-631-3250. *Interim Dir Midland Art Council* Bruce Winslow. Instrs: FT 15
Estab 1971; pvt; D & E; SC 12-20, LC 2; enrl D & E 250
Tuition: $35-$80 member-nonmember status
Courses: Calligraphy, Ceramics, Mixed Media, Painting, Photography, Printmaking, Sculpture, Design, Metalsmithing, Papermaking, Stained Glass, Weaving
Adult Hobby Classes: Enrl 200; tuition $35-$80 per sem
Children's Classes: Enrl 50; tuition $25-$30 per sem

NORTHWOOD INSTITUTE, Alden B Dow Creativity Center, 48640-2398. Tel 517-837-4478. *Exec Dir* Carol B Coppage
Available to those with innovative ideas or specific projects

MONROE

MONROE COUNTY COMMUNITY COLLEGE, Humanities Division, 1555 S Raisinville Rd, 48161. Tel 313-242-7300. *Secy* Peggy Faunt. Instrs: FT 4
Degrees: AFA offered
Tuition: Res—$25 per sem cr hr; nonres—$37 per sem cr hr
Courses: Illustration, Art Appreciation, Art History, Ceramics, Design, Drawing, Painting, Printmaking, †Art for Elementary Teachers

MOUNT PLEASANT

CENTRAL MICHIGAN UNIVERSITY, Dept of Art, 48859. Tel 517-774-3025. *Chmn Dept* Sari Khoury, MFA. Instrs: FT 17, PT 2
Estab 1892; pub; D & E; scholarships & fels; SC 50, LC 9; enrl for univ 17,000
Ent Req: HS dipl
Degrees: BA, BFA & BAA 4 yrs, MA, MFA
Tuition: Res—undergrad $70.50 per cr hr, grad $96.50 per cr hr; nonres—undergrad $183 per cr hr, grad $210.50 per cr hr
Courses: Aesthetics, Art Education, Art History, Ceramics, Drawing, Graphic Design, Jewelry, Painting, Photography, Printmaking, Sculpture, Art Appreciation, Art Criticism, Fiber Design, Metalsmithing

MUSKEGON

MUSKEGON COMMUNITY COLLEGE, Dept of Creative and Performing Arts, 221 S Quarterline Rd, 49442. Tel 616-773-9131, Ext 324. *Chmn* Judith Brooky
Estab 1926; pub; D & E; scholarships; SC 18, LC 6; enrl D 280, E 60
Ent Req: HS dipl
Degrees: AA 2 yrs
Tuition: County res—$31 per cr hr; state res—$43 per cr hr; nonres—$56 per cr hr
Courses: Art Education, Art History, Ceramics, Costume Design & Construction, Drawing, Film, Interior Design, Painting, Printmaking, Sculpture, Stage Design, Teacher Training, Theatre Arts
Adult Hobby Classes: Enrl 50; tuition variable, 6 wk term. Courses—Cartooning, Interior Design, Stained Glass, Watercolor
Children's Classes: Enrl 30; 6 wk term, 6 sessions. Courses—Beginning Art, Pottery

OLIVET

OLIVET COLLEGE, Art Dept, 320 S Main, 49076. Tel 616-749-7000. *Chmn* Gary Wertheimer; *Prof* Donald Rowe; *Instructor* Susan Rowe, MFA
Estab 1844, dept estab 1870; pvt; D & E; scholarships; SC 17, LC 8, GC 10; enrl D 610, non-maj 50, maj 20, grad 2
Ent Req: HS dipl
Degrees: BS and BM 4 yrs, MA 1 yr
Tuition: $6060 per yr, part-time $215 per hr; campus res—room & board $2565 per yr
Courses: Art History, †Commercial Art, †Design, †Drawing, †Painting, †Printmaking, †Sculpture

PETOSKEY

NORTH CENTRAL MICHIGAN COLLEGE, Art Dept, 1515 Howard St, 49770. Tel 616-348-6651. *Chmn* Douglas Melvin, MA
Degrees: AA offered
Tuition: Res—$24 per cr hr; nonres—$30 per cr hr
Courses: Art Education, Art History, Drawing, Painting, Photography, Printmaking, Sculpture, Stained Glass
Adult Hobby Classes: Courses offered
Summer School: Courses offered

PONTIAC

CREATIVE ART CENTER, 47 Williams St, 48341. Tel 313-333-7849. *Interim Dir* Angela Petroff
Estab 1968; pub; D & E; scholarships; SC 15; enrl 200
Ent Req: Open enrollment
Tuition: Varies; no campus res
Courses: Ceramics, Drawing, Painting, Photography, Sculpture, Watercolor
Children's Classes: Courses—Dance, Drawing, Music, Painting, Sculpture
Summer School: Three wk session. Courses—Creative Writing, Dance, Drama, Visual Arts

PORT HURON

SAINT CLAIR COUNTY COMMUNITY COLLEGE, Art Dept, 323 Erie St, PO Box 5015, 48061-5015. Tel 313-984-3881. *Dean* Patrick Bourke
Estab 1923; pub; D & E; scholarships; SC 30, LC 5; enrl D 60
Ent Req: HS dipl
Degrees: AA and AAS 2 yrs
Tuition: In-county—$40 per cr hr; out-of-county—$63 per cr hr; nonres—$87 per cr hr
Courses: †Advertising Design, †Drawing, †Graphic Arts, Graphic Design, †Illustration, †Interior Design, †Lettering, †Painting, †Photography, †Sculpture, †Theatre Arts, †Pottery
Adult Hobby Classes: Courses—Drawing, Painting, Pottery

ROCHESTER

OAKLAND UNIVERSITY, Dept of Art and Art History, 48309-4401. Tel 313-370-3375. *Chmn Dept* Charlotte Stokes, PhD; *Prof* John Beardman, MFA; *Prof* John B Cameron, PhD; *Prof* Carl F Barnes Jr; *Assoc Prof* Janice C Schimmelman, PhD; *Assoc Prof* Susan Wood, PhD; *Asst Prof* Bonnie Abiko, PhD; *Lectr* Lisa Ngote, MA; *Lectr* Andrea Eis, MFA; *Lectr* Paul Webster, MFA; *Lectr* Monica Molinaro, MFA
Estab 1957, dept estab 1960; pub; D & E; scholarships; SC 3, LC 9
Ent Req: HS dipl
Degrees: BA 4 yrs
Tuition: Res—on Campus $65.25 Freshman & Sophomore, $74.75 Jr & Sr; Grad on Campus $122; nonres—$192.50 Freshman & Sophomore, $210 Jr & Sr, $270 Grad
Courses: †Art History, Studio Art

SCOTTVILLE

WEST SHORE COMMUNITY COLLEGE, Division of Humanities and Fine Arts, 3000 N Stiles Rd, 49454. Tel 616-845-6211. *Chmn* Sharon Bloom; *Instr* Paul Flickenger; *Instr* Todd Reed, BA; *Instr* Norman Vandersluys, BA. Instrs: PT 3
Pub; D & E; scholarships; SC 18, LC 10; enrl non-maj 250, maj 10
Ent Req: HS dipl
Degrees: AA 2 yrs
Tuition: Res—$445 per sem, $29 per cr hr; nonres—$670 per sem, $44 per cr hr; no campus res
Courses: †Art History, Ceramics, Drafting, Drawing, Graphic Design, Mixed Media, Painting, Photography, Printmaking, Sculpture, Stage Design, †Theatre Arts
Adult Hobby Classes: Enrl 20 per class; tuition $16 for 5 wk classes; directed by Community Services. Classes—Art Workshops & Studio, Crafts, Photography

SOUTHFIELD

LAWRENCE INSTITUTE OF TECHNOLOGY, School of Architecture, 21000 W Ten Mile Rd, 48075-1058. Tel 313-356-0200, Ext 2800. *Dean* Neville Clouten
Degrees: BArchit, BS(Archit), BS(Interior Archit)
Tuition: $98 per cr hr freshman & sophomore, $102 per cr hr Jr & Sr, $115 per cr hr for BA Architecture
Courses: †Architecture, †Interior Architecture
Children's Classes: Enrl 50; tuition $150 for 10 wk term. Courses—Design Discovery
Summer School: Dir, Harold Linton. Enrl 75; tuition $150. Courses—Pre-College Architecture

SPRING ARBOR

SPRING ARBOR COLLEGE, Art Dept, 106 E Main, 49283. Tel 517-750-1200, Ext 496. *Dir* Paul Wolber, MA; *Division Dir Music Arts* Bill Bippes, MFA
Estab 1873, dept estab 1971; pvt den; D & E; scholarships; SC 17, LC 6; enrl D 200, E 20, non-maj 20, maj 32
Ent Req: HS dipl
Degrees: AA(Commercial) 2 yrs, BA 4 yrs
Tuition: $7000-$7500 per yr, $3500-$3750 per sem, $140 per hr; campus res—room & board $3200-$3500
Courses: †Advertising Design, Commercial Art, †Drawing, †Graphic Arts, †Illustration, †Painting, †Printmaking, †Sculpture, †Teacher Training
Children's Classes: Summer programs. Enrl 15-20; tuition $25
Summer School: Dir, Dr Charles Campbell. Courses—Crafts, Drawing, Ceramics

TRAVERSE CITY

NORTHWESTERN MICHIGAN COLLEGE, Art Dept, 1701 E Front St, 49684. Tel 616-922-1325. *Chmn Dept* Stephen Ballance, MA; *Instr* Norman Averill, MA; *Instr* Doug Domine, BFA; *Instr* Jill Hinds
Estab 1951, dept estab 1957; pub; D & E; scholarships; SC 40, LC 4; enrl non-maj 400, maj 75
Ent Req: HS dipl
Degrees: AA 2 yrs
Tuition: $28.25 per cr hr per term in-dist, $46.75 per cr hr per term in-state, $52.25 per cr hr per term out-of-state; maritime classes $46.75 per cr hr instate, $61 per cr hr out-of-state; campus res room & board
Courses: Advertising Design, Art Education, Art History, Commercial Art, Drawing, Goldsmithing, Graphic Arts, Graphic Design, Illustration, Jewelry, Lettering, Painting, Photography, Printmaking, Silversmithing, Textile Design, Life Drawing, Perspective, Pottery, Publication Design, Reproduction Techniques; Typography, Watercolor
Adult Hobby Classes: Enrl 50; tuition $23. Courses - Drawing, Life Drawing, Painting, Pottery, Printmaking
Summer School: Dir, Stephen Ballance. Enrl 100; tuition $23 per cr hr in -dist, $37 per cr hr other for 5, 8 10 wk terms. Courses - Design, Drawing, Photography, Pottery

TWIN LAKE

BLUE LAKE FINE ARTS CAMP, Art Dept, Route 2, 49457. Tel 616-894-1966; FAX 616-894-8849. *Chmn* Angelina Davis
Tuition: $495 for 2 wk session & camp res
Courses: Drawing, Illustration, Painting, Photography

UNIVERSITY CENTER

DELTA COLLEGE, Art Dept, Humanities Division, 48710. Tel 517-686-9000. *Chmn Dept* Linda Menger, MA; *Assoc Prof* John McCormick, MFA; *Assoc Prof* Larry Butcher, MA; *Assoc Prof* Russel Thayer, MA; *Instr* Suzanne Settle
Estab 1960; pub; D & E; scholarships; SC 21, LC 5; enrl D 550, E 100, maj 190
Ent Req: Open door policy
Degrees: AA 2 yrs
Tuition: Res—in district $43 per cr hr, out of district $61 per cr hr; nonres—$90 per cr hr; campus res—room and board $1067.50 per sem
Courses: Art Education, Art History, Ceramics, Commercial Art, Drawing, Graphic Design, Interior Design, Painting, Photography, Printmaking, Sculpture

SAGINAW VALLEY STATE UNIVERSITY, Dept of Art and Design, 2250 Pierce Rd, 48710. Tel 517-790-4390. *Chmn Dept* Matthew Zivich, MFA; *Prof* Barron Hirsch, MFA; *Assoc Prof* Hideki Kihata, MFA; *Adjunct Instr* Bruce Winslow, MFA; *Adjunct Instr* David Littell, MFA; *Adjunct Instr* Karen Egan; *Adjunct Instr* Marlene Pellerito; *Adjunct Instr* Curtis Leece, BFA; *Adjunct Instr* Paul Kowaski; *Staff Asst* Sara B Clark, MFA
Estab 1960, dept estab 1968; pub; D & E; scholarships; SC approx 20, LC approx 15; enrl D 200, E 50, maj 65
Ent Req: HS dipl
Degrees: BA(Art) 4 yrs or less
Tuition: $62.50 per cr hr; campus res available
Courses: †Advertising Design, Art Education, Art History, Ceramics, Collages, †Commercial Art, Constructions, †Drawing, †Graphic Arts, †Graphic Design, †Illustration, †Intermedia, †Painting, †Photography, †Printmaking, †Sculpture, †Teacher Training
Summer School: Courses vary

WARREN

MACOMB COMMUNITY COLLEGE, Art Dept, Division of Humanities, 14500 Twelve Mile Rd, 48093. Tel 313-445-7000. *Prof* David Barr, MA; *Prof* Al Hebert, MA; *Prof* James Johnston, MA; *Prof* James Pallas, MFA
Estab 1960, dept estab 1965; pub; D & E; scholarships; SC 14, LC 6
Ent Req: HS dipl, ent exam
Degrees: AA 2 yrs
Tuition: Res—in county $38 per hr, in state $61 per hr; nonres—$74 per hr
Courses: Art History, Ceramics, Design, Drawing, Painting, Photography, Sculpture

YPSILANTI

EASTERN MICHIGAN UNIVERSITY, Dept of Art, 114 Ford, 48197. Tel 313-487-1268. *Head Dept* John E Van Haren, MS
Estab 1849; dept estab 1901; pub; D & E; scholarships; SC 55, LC 18; enrl undergrad maj 420, non-maj 800, grad 100
Ent Req: HS dipl

Degrees: BA, BS & BA(Art Educ) 4 yrs, MA(Art Educ), MA(Studio) & MFA 2 yrs
Courses: Art Education, Art History, Ceramics, Drawing, Graphic Design, Illustration, Jewelry, Photography, †Printmaking, †Sculpture, †Textile Design, Watercolor Painting
Children's Classes: Enrl 40; tuition $35 for 8-10 classes offered on Sat for Art talented & gifted
Summer School: Term of 6 wks, major & non-major courses

MINNESOTA

BEMIDJI

BEMIDJI STATE UNIVERSITY, Visual Arts Dept, 1500 Birchmont Dr, 56601. Tel 218-755-3735. *Chmn* Marley Kaul; *Prof* Kyle Crocker, PhD; *Assoc Prof* William Kelly, MFA; *Asst Prof* John Holden, MFA; *Asst Prof* Sally James
Estab 1918; pub; D & E; SC 54, LC 17, GC individual study
Ent Req: HS dipl, ACT, SAT, PSAT, or SCAT
Degrees: BA, BS(Teaching) and BS(Tech Illustration, Commercial Design), BFA
Tuition: Res—undergrad $36.30 per quarter hr, grad $52 per quarter hr; nonres—undergrad $62.30 per quarter hr, grad $75 per quarter hr; campus residency available
Courses: †Art Education, Art History, †Ceramics, †Commercial Art, Conceptual Art, Design, †Drawing, †Graphic Arts, †Graphic Design, Illustration, Industrial Design, Jewelry, Painting, Printmaking, Sculpture, †Teacher Training, Textile Design, Crafts
Adult Hobby Classes: Tuition res—$29.25 per quarter hr. Courses—Curriculum Design, Early Childhood Art, Elementary Art Concepts & Methods, Secondary Art Concepts & Methods
Children's Classes: Enrl 20; tuition free. Courses—Art, preschool classes offered each fall
Summer School: Dir, Sally James. Tuition res—undergrad $30.45 per quarter hr, nonres—$49 per quarter hr. Courses—vary, mostly studio courses

BLOOMINGTON

NORMANDALE COMMUNITY COLLEGE, 9700 France Ave S, 55431. Tel 612-832-6000. *Instr* E L Gleeman, MA; *Instr* D R Peterson, BFA; *Instr* Marilyn Wood, MFA
Tuition: $30.75 per cr
Courses: Art Appreciation, Art History, Ceramics, Design, Drawing, Jewelry, Painting, Photography, Sculpture
Adult Hobby Classes: Courses offered
Summer School: Courses offered

COLLEGEVILLE

SAINT JOHN'S UNIVERSITY, Art Dept, 56321. Tel 612-363-2011 *Prof* Bela Petheo, MFA; *Assoc Prof* James Hendershot, MFA; *Assoc Prof* Bro Alan Reed, MFA; *Asst Prof* Hugh Witzmann, MFA
Estab 1856; pvt; scholarships; SC 20, LC 15
Ent Req: HS dipl
Degrees: BA, BS
Tuition: Approx $10,000 for all 4 yrs; campus res—room & board $4000
Courses: Art History, Ceramics, Drawing, Jewelry, Painting, Photography, Printmaking, Sculpture
Adult Hobby Classes: Occasional adult education classes

COON RAPIDS

ANOKA RAMSEY COMMUNITY COLLEGE, Art Dept, 11200 Mississippi Blvd NW, 55433. Tel 612-422-3522; FAX 612-422-3341. *Dean* Rose Ann Findlen; *Instr* Robert E Toensing, MFA; *Instr* Laura Migliovino, MFA
Scholarships
Degrees: AA offered
Tuition: $32.75 per cr hr
Courses: Advertising Design, Art Appreciation, Art Education, Ceramics, Design, Drawing, Film, Jewelry, Painting, Photography, Sculpture, Glassblowing

DULUTH

UNIVERSITY OF MINNESOTA, DULUTH, Art Dept, 317 Humanities Bldg, 10 University Dr, 55812. Tel 218-726-8225; 800-232-1339, Ext 8225 (Admissions). *Head Dept* Gloria D Brush, MFA; *Prof* Rudolph Schauer, MS; *Prof* Thomas Kerrigan, MFA; *Prof* Thomas F Hedin, PhD; *Prof* Leif Brush, MFA; *Assoc Prof* Phillip Meany, MFA; *Assoc Prof* Dean R Lettenstrom, MFA; *Assoc Prof* James H Brutger, MFA; *Assoc Prof* Cheng-Khee Chee, MA; *Asst Prof* Robyn Roslak, PhD; *Asst Prof* James Klueg, MFA; *Asst Prof* Nancy Lettenstrom, MFA; *Teaching Specialist* Jon Tofte, MIS
Pub; D & E; scholarships; SC 30, LC 6, GC 10; enrl D 200, E 50, maj 200, grad 12
Ent Req: HS dipl
Degrees: BFA, BA 4 yrs, MA
Tuition: Averages $50 per cr hr; campus res available
Courses: Advertising Design, Art Appreciation, Art Education, Art History, Calligraphy, Ceramics, Commercial Art, Constructions, Design, Drawing, Film, Graphic Arts, Graphic Design, History of Art & Archaeology, Illustration, Intermedia, Jewelry, Lettering, Mixed Media, Museum Staff Training, Painting, Photography, Printmaking, Sculpture, Silversmithing, Teacher Training, Weaving, Fibers, †Studio Major
Adult Hobby Classes: 10 wk courses. Courses—Studio Arts, Graphic Design
Summer School: Dir, Gloria D Brush. 5 wk terms. Courses—Painting, Drawing, Art Education, Photography, Prints, Jewelry & Metals, Ceramics

ELY

VERMILION COMMUNITY COLLEGE, Art Dept, 1900 E Camp St, 55731. Tel 218-365-7273; WATS 800-657-3608. *Instr* Harlan Tjader
Estab 1922, dept estab 1964; pub; D & E; SC 13, LC 5; enrl D 63, E 15, non-maj 65, maj 13
Ent Req: HS dipl
Degrees: AA 2 yr
Tuition: $32.50 per cr
Adult Hobby Classes: Tuition $26 per cr. Courses—Drawing, Introduction, Painting

FERGUS FALLS

LUTHERAN BRETHREN SCHOOLS, Art Dept, 815 W Vernon Ave, 56537. Tel 218-739-3371, 739-3376. *Head Dept* Gaylen Peterson
Estab 1900; den; D & E; SC 1, LC 1; enrl D 20
Ent Req: HS dipl, questionnaire
Tuition: $1100 per sem; campus res—room & board $850 per sem
Courses: Drawing

GRAND MARAIS

GRAND MARAIS ART COLONY, 55604. Tel 218-387-2737. *Adminr* Jay Andersen; *Faculty* Elizabeth Erickson; *Faculty* Hazel Belvo; *Instr* George Morrison; *Faculty* Gerald Korte; *Faculty* Howard Sivertson; *Instr* Jim Northrup Jr
Estab 1947; D & E; scholarships; SC 4; enrl D 200
Ent Req: Open
Tuition: $200 per wk
Courses: Drawing, Painting, Pastels,Personal Creativity, Watercolor
Adult Hobby Classes: Enrl 200; tuition same as above; 15 wks of 1 - 2 wk workshops. Courses—Drawing, Painting
Children's Classes: Enrl 50; tuition $70 for 1 full wk. Courses—Drawing, Mixed Media, Painting
Summer School: Dir, Jay Andersen. Courses—Drawing, Painting, Watercolor

HIBBING

HIBBING COMMUNITY COLLEGE, Art Dept, 1515 E 25th St, 55746. Tel 218-262-6700. *Instr* Bill Goodman
Scholarships offered
Degrees: AA & AAS 2 yrs
Tuition: Res—undergrad $37.50 per cr hr; nonres—$75.00 per cr hr
Courses: Art Appreciation, Ceramics, Design, Drawing, Painting, Photography, Sculpture, Stage Craft, Introduction to Theatre

MANKATO

BETHANY LUTHERAN COLLEGE, Art Dept, 734 Marsh St, 56001. Tel 507-625-2977. *Head of Dept* William Bukowski
Estab 1927; dept estab 1960; den; D; scholarships; SC 2, LC 2; enrl D 36, non-maj 40, maj 18
Ent Req: HS dipl, ACT
Degrees: AA 2 yr, dipl
Tuition: $4890 per sem
Courses: Art History, Ceramics, Design, Drawing, Painting, Art Appreciation, Art Structure
Adult Hobby Classes: Enrl 20; tuition $60 per sem cr. Courses—Drawing
Summer School: Dir, William Bukowski. Enrl 20; tuition $130 for 2 wk - 1 1/2 days

MANKATO STATE UNIVERSITY, Art Dept, PO Box 8400, 56001-8400. Tel 507-389-6412. *Chmn* Robert Finkler, MFA. Instrs: FT 15
Estab 1868, dept estab 1938; pub; D & E; SC 42, LC 28, GC 54; enrl D 3000 (total), E 500, non-maj 1000, maj 250, grad 50
Ent Req: HS dipl
Degrees: BA, BFA and BS 4 yr, MA and MS 1-1 1/2 yr
Tuition: Res—undergrad $1742 per yr, $36 per quarter hr, grad $2115 per yr, $47 per quarter hr; nonres—grad $3060 per yr, $68 per quarter hr
Courses: Advertising Design, Art Education, Art History, Ceramics, Commercial Art, Drawing, Graphic Arts, Graphic Design, Illustration, Jewelry, Lettering, Painting, Photography, Printmaking, Sculpture
Summer School: Tuition same as above

MINNEAPOLIS

ART INSTRUCTION SCHOOLS, Education Dept, 500 S Fourth St, 55415. Tel 612-339-8721; FAX 612-339-3307. *Dir* Glen Hoyle, PhD
Estab 1914; pvt
Courses: Fundamentals of Art and Specialized Art
Adult Hobby Classes: Enrl 5000; tuition $1495 - $2000. Courses—Fundamentals of Art, Specialized Art

AUGSBURG COLLEGE, Art Dept, 731 21st Ave W, 55454. Tel 612-330-1000. *Chmn* Kristin Anderson. Instrs: FT 3, PT 4
Estab 1869, dept estab 1960; den; D & E; scholarships; SC 15, LC 6; enrl D 200, maj 60, others 1500
Ent Req: HS dipl
Degrees: BA 4 yrs
Tuition: $10,853 per yr; campus res—room & board $4022
Courses: Art Education, Art History, Calligraphy, Ceramics, Drawing, Handicrafts, History of Art & Archaeology, Painting, Photography, Sculpture, Stage Design, Teacher Training, Theatre Arts, Communications Design, Environmental Design
Adult Hobby Classes: Enrl 1200; tuition $780 per course. Courses—Art History, Calligraphy, Ceramics, Communications Design, Drawing, Environmental Design, Painting, Publication Design
Summer School: Enrl 350; term of six or four wks beginning end of May

MINNEAPOLIS COLLEGE OF ART AND DESIGN, 2501 Stevens Ave S, 55404. Tel 612-874-3700; FAX 612-874-3704. *Pres* John S Slorp, MFA; *Chmn Fine Arts* Hazel Belvo, MFA; *Acting Visual Studies* Aribert Munzner; *Liberal Arts* Anedith Nash; *Chmn Media Arts* Thomas De Biaso; *Dir Continuing Studies* Brian Szott. Instrs: FT 58 PT 20
Estab 1886; pvt; D & E; scholarships; SC 78, LC 23; enrl D 585, E 490
Ent Req: HS dipl or GED
Degrees: BFA 4 yr
Tuition: $11,090 annual tuition; campus res—available
Courses: Advertising Design, Art History, Drawing, Film, Graphic Arts, Illustration, Painting, Photography, Printmaking, Sculpture, Video, Computer Graphics, Critical Studies, Design Theory & Methods, Liberal Arts, Packaging & Product Design, Performance Arts
Adult Hobby Classes: Continuing Studies
Children's Classes: Courses offered
Summer School: Dir of Continuing Studies & the Gallery, Brian Scott. Courses—Drawing, Graphic Design, History of Art & Design, Liberal Arts, Painting, Papermaking, Photography, Printmaking, Sculpture, Video

NORTH HENNEPIN COMMUNITY COLLEGE, Art Dept, 7411 85th Ave N, 55445. Tel 612-424-0775. *Asst Dean* Gayla Shoemake. Instrs: FT 6
Estab 1964; pub; D & E; scholarships; SC 15, LC 4; enrl D 500, E 100, maj 200, others 100
Ent Req: HS dipl. ent exam
Degrees: AA & AAS 2 yr
Tuition: In-state $32 per hr; out-of-state $48 per hr
Courses: Art History, Drawing, Graphic Design, Illustration, Jewelry, Painting, Photography, Printmaking, Contemporary Crafts, Exhibition Design, Introduction to Art, Metalsmithing, 2-D & 3-D Design, Typography, Visual Communications
Adult Hobby Classes: Enrl 30-100. Courses—Painting, Photography, Video
Summer School: Two 5 week sessions. Enrl 700; Courses—Drawing, Introduction of Art, Photography, Fundamentals of Color, Painting

UNIVERSITY OF MINNESOTA, MINNEAPOLIS

—Art History, 27 Pleasant St SE, 108 Jones Hall, 55455. Tel 612-624-4500. *Chmn* Frederick Asher, PhD; *Prof* Norman Canedy, PhD; *Prof* Karal Ann Marling, PhD; *Prof* Marion Nelson, PhD; *Prof* Robert Poor, PhD; *Assoc Prof* John Steyaert, PhD; *Assoc Prof* Michael Stoughton, PhD; *Assoc Prof* Charles Haxthausen, PhD; *Assoc Prof* Robert Silberman, PhD; *Asst Prof* Catherine Asher, PhD
Pub; D & E; scholarships & fels; LC 28, GC 59; enrl res 108 per quarter, nonres 216 per quarter, maj 68, grad 52
Ent Req: HS dipl, ent exam, GRE required for grad school
Degrees: BA 4 yrs, MA 2 yrs
Tuition: Res—$58.93 per cr, nonres—$173.84 per cr
Courses: †Art History
Adult Hobby Classes: Enrl 200; qtr system. Courses—Ancient & Modern Art History
Summer School: Dir, Frederick Asher. Enrl 270; tuition $46 per cr for terms June 11 - July 16 & July 18 - Aug 21
—Dept of Studio Art, 216 21st Ave S, 55455. Tel 612-625-8096; FAX 612-625-7881. *Chmn Dept* Wayne Potratz, MA; *Prof* Karl Bethke, MFA; *Prof* Curtis Hoard, MFA; *Prof Emeritus* Warren MacKenzie; *Prof Emeritus* Malcolm Myers, MFA; *Prof* Thomas Rose, MA; *Prof* Herman Rowan, MFA; *Prof* Mary Diane Katsiaficas, MFA; *Assoc Prof* Victor Caglioti, BS; *Assoc Prof* Thomas Cowette, BFA; *Assoc Prof* David Feinberg, MFA; *Assoc Prof* Gary Hallman, MFA; *Assoc Prof* Lynn Gray, MFA; *Assoc Prof* James Henkel, MFA; *Assoc Prof* Guy Baldwin, MFA; *Assoc Prof* Jerald Krepps, MFA; *Assoc Prof* Thomas Lane, MFA; *Assoc Prof* Susan Lucey, MFA; *Assoc Prof* William Roode, MFA; *Assoc Prof* Joyce Lyon, MFA; *Assoc Prof* Clarence Morgan, MFA
Estab 1851, fine arts estab 1939; pub; D & E; scholarships; SC 39, LC 7; enrl D 1000, E 560, maj 325, grad 55
Ent Req: HS dipl, PSAT, ACT
Degrees: BA and BFA 4 yrs, MFA 2-3 yrs
Tuition: Res—undergrad approx $1000 per quarter, grad $1127 per quarter; nonres—undergrad approx $3000 per quarter, grad $2254 per quarter
Courses: †Ceramics, †Drawing, †Painting, †Photography, †Printmaking, †Sculpture, Computer & Electronic Media, Papermaking, Performance Art
Adult Hobby Classes: Tuition $160-$166 for 4 cr for 10 wk term. Courses—same as above
Children's Classes: Summers Honors College for HS students
Summer School: Dir, Carol Ann Dickinson. Enrl 20; tuition $500 for June 16 - July 2 term. Courses—same as above

MOORHEAD

CONCORDIA COLLEGE, Art Dept, 901 S Eighth, 56562. Tel 218-299-4623; FAX 218-299-3947. *Chmn* David Boggs, MFA; *Assoc Prof* Orland Rourke, MA; *Assoc Prof* Jean Gumpper, MFA; *Asst Prof* Robert Meadows-Rogers, MA; *Asst Prof* Duane Mickelson, MFA; *Instr* Barbara Anderson, MA; *Instr* Susan Pierson Ellingson, PhD; *Instr* John Borge, BA; *Instr* Suzanne Smemo; *Instr* John Borge
Estab 1891; pvt; D; scholarships; SC 10, LC 5; enrl D 300, maj 80, total 2900
Ent Req: HS dipl, character references
Degrees: BA and BM 4 yrs, independent studio work, work-study prog and special studies
Tuition: $10,200 per yr, $5250 per sem, student association dues $80; campus res—room $1500 & board $2025
Courses: †Art Education, †Art History, Ceramics, Drawing, Painting, Printmaking, Figure Drawing, 2-D Foundations, 3-D Foundations, Macintosh Computer Design Lab, Senior Project, †Studio Art
Summer School: Dir, Donald Dale. Enrl 40; tuition $1100 for term of 4 wks beginning May 15 & June 12. Courses—Art History, Travel Seminar, Drawing, Graphic Design, Painting, Printmaking, 2-D Foundations

MOORHEAD STATE UNIVERSITY, Dept of Art, 1104 Seventh Ave S, 56560. Tel 218-236-2011. *Chmn* Timothy Ray, MFA; *Prof* Lyle Laske, MFA; *Prof Dr* John Boyd Hollad, PhD; *Prof* P J Mousseau, MFA; *Prof* Donald B McRaven Jr, MFA; *Prof* P R Szeitz, MFA; *Prof* Carl Oltvedt, MFA; *Assoc Prof* Allen Sheets, MFA; *Assoc*

Prof Deborah Broad, MFA; *Asst Prof* Robert Tom, MFA; *Asst Prof* Christine Degraeve, PhD
Estab 1887; pub; D & E; scholarships; SC 47, LC 20, GC 11; enrl D 4520, maj 175, grad 2
Ent Req: HS dipl
Degrees: BA, BS 4 yr, BFA 5 yr, MS additional 1 1/4 yr
Courses: Advertising Design, Art Education, Art History, Ceramics, Collages, Constructions, Drawing, Graphic Arts, Graphic Design, Illustration, Mixed Media, Painting, Photography, Printmaking, Sculpture, Teacher Training, Theatre Arts
Summer School: Tuition per cr hr for term of 5 wks beginning June. Courses—Basic Drawing, Ceramics, Elements of Art Design, Graphic Design, Painting, Photography, Printmaking

MORRIS

UNIVERSITY OF MINNESOTA, MORRIS, Humanities Division, 600 E Fourth St, 56267. Tel 612-589-2211. *Chmn* C F Farrell Jr; *Coordr* Lois Hodgell, MFA; *Coordr* Frederick Peterson, PhD
Estab 1960, dept estab 1963; pub; D; scholarships; SC 16, LC 8; enrl D 195, non-maj 150, maj 45
Ent Req: Top 50% in HS, ACT or PSAT
Degrees: BA 4 yrs
Tuition: Res—undergrad $721 per quarter; nonres—undergrad $1803.67 per quarter; campus res—room and board $945 per quarter
Courses: †Art History, Teacher Training, †Studio Art

NORTHFIELD

CARLETON COLLEGE, Dept of Art & Art History, 55057. Tel 507-663-4341. *Chmn* Alison Kettering
Estab 1921; pvt; scholarships; SC 30, LC 20; enrl maj 42, others 550
Degrees: 4 yr
Tuition: $17,360; campus res—room & board $3540
Courses: †Art History, †Studio Art

SAINT OLAF COLLEGE, Art Dept, 1520 Saint Olaf Dr, 55057-1098. Tel 507-646-3248. *Chmn* Jan Shoger; *Prof* John Maakestad, MFA; *Prof* Reidar Dittman, PhD; *Prof* Malcolm Gimse, MFA; *Prof* Arch Leean, MA; *Assoc Prof* Jan Shoger, MFA; *Asst Prof* Irve Dell; *Asst Prof* Meg Ojala; *Asst Prof* Ron Gallas; *Asst Prof* Jil Evans Taliaferro; *Asst Prof* Steve Edwins; *Instr* Sharon Sudman
Estab 1875, dept estab 1932; den; D & E; scholarships
Ent Req: HS dipl, SAT
Degrees: BA 4 yr
Tuition: Campus residency available
Courses: Aesthetics, Architecture, †Art Education, †Art History, Calligraphy, Ceramics, Commercial Art, Drafting, Drawing, Film, Graphic Arts, Graphic Design, History of Art & Archaeology, Interior Design, Lettering, Painting, Photography, Printmaking, Sculpture, Stage Design, Teacher Training, Theatre Arts, Video, †Art Studio
Adult Hobby Classes: Dir, Lydia Quanbeck
Summer School: Dir, Lydia Quanbeck. Courses—Ceramics, Landscape Painting, 20th Century Art

NORTH MANKATO

ALBERT LEA - MANKATO TECHNICAL COLLEGE (Formerly Mankato Area Vocational-Technical Institute), Commercial and Technical Art Dept, 1920 Lee Blvd, 56001. Tel 507-625-3441. *Instr* Robert Williams; *Instr* Kevin McLaughlin
Estab 1969; pub; D; scholarships; enrl D 20
Ent Req: Portfolio
Degrees: AA 2 yr
Courses: Advertising Design, Calligraphy, Commercial Art, Conceptual Art, Drafting, Drawing, Fashion Arts, Graphic Arts, Graphic Design, Illustration, Lettering, Mixed Media, Desktop Publishing
Adult Hobby Classes: Enrl 200; tuition $36.35 per cr. Courses—Adobe Illustrator, Photoshop, Quark XPress

ROCHESTER

ROCHESTER COMMUNITY COLLEGE, Art Dept, 55904-4999. Tel 507-285-7215. *Instr* James Prom, MS; *Instr* Pat Kraemer, MS; *Instr* Randy Johnston; *Instr* Terry Richardson, MA
Estab 1920s; pub; D & E; scholarships; SC 17, LC 4; enrl D & E 4000, maj 50
Ent Req: State req
Degrees: AAS, AA
Tuition: Res— $32.75 pr cr; nonres—$49.25 except in reciprocal states
Courses: Advertising Design, Art Appreciation, Art History, †Ceramics, Design, †Drawing, †Graphic Design, Interior Design, Jewelry, †Painting, Photography, Printmaking, Sculpture, Stage Design, Theatre Arts, Weaving, Craft Design Series, Fibers
Adult Hobby Classes: All areas, cr and non cr for variable tuition. Courses—Cartooning, & others on less regular basis
Summer School: Dir, A Olson. Art workshops are offered for at least one session each summer

SAINT CLOUD

SAINT CLOUD STATE UNIVERSITY, Dept of Art, 720 Fourth Ave S, KVAC, Room 111, 56301. Tel 612-255-4283, 255-0121. *Chmn* Dr James Roy. Instrs: FT 13, PT 6
Pub; D & E; SC 65, LC 15, GC 20; enrl maj 300, grad 30
Ent Req: HS dipl
Degrees: BA, BFA, BS, MA(Studio Art) 4 yrs

Tuition: Res—undergrad $42.55 per cr hr, grad $58.25 per cr hr; nonres—undergrad $68.55 per cr hr, grad $81.25 per cr hr
Courses: Art Education, Ceramics, Drawing, Design, Graphic Design, Art History, Jewelry, Painting, Photography, Sculpture, Teacher Training, Textile Design, Printmaking, Weaving
Summer School: Two terms

SAINT JOSEPH

COLLEGE OF SAINT BENEDICT, Art Dept, 56374. Tel 612-363-5036. *Chmn* Bela Petheo, MFA; *Prof* Gordon Goetemann, MFA; *Assoc Prof* Sr Baulu Kuan, MA; *Asst Prof* Sr Dennis Frandrup, MFA
Estab 1913; joint studies with St John's University, Collegeville, MN; pvt; D & E; scholarships; SC 21, LC 15; enrl D 1726, maj 70
Ent Req: HS dipl, SAT, PSAT, ACT
Degrees: BA(Art) & BA(Art History) 4 yr, internships & open studio
Tuition: $10,000 per yr; campus res—room & board $4000 per yr
Courses: †Art History, †Ceramics, †Drawing, Jewelry, Mixed Media, †Painting, †Photography, †Printmaking, †Sculpture

SAINT PAUL

BETHEL COLLEGE, Dept of Art, 3900 Bethel Dr, 55112. Tel 612-638-6400. *Assoc Prof* Wayne L Roosa, PhD; *Prof* Stewart Luckman, MFA; *Prof* George Robinson, BFA; *Asst Prof* Karen Berg-Johnson, MFA; *Assoc Prof* Kirk Freeman; *Prof* Dale R Johnson, MFA
Estab 1871; den; D & E; scholarships; SC 30, LC 7; enrl non-maj 100, maj 75
Ent Req: HS dipl, SAT, ACT, PSAT or NMSQT, evidence of a standard of faith and practice that is compatible to Bethel lifestyle
Degrees: BA(Art Educ), BA(Art History) and BA(Studio Arts) 4 yr
Tuition: $5270 per sem; campus res—room $1045 & board $850
Courses: †Art Education, †Art History, †Ceramics, †Drawing, †Graphic Design, †Painting, †Photography, †Printmaking, †Sculpture, Three Dimensional Design, Two Dimensional Design

COLLEGE OF ASSOCIATED ARTS, 344 Summit Ave, 55102. Tel 612-224-3416; FAX 612-224-8854. *Pres* Robert E Hankey, MEd; *Assoc Prof* Maria Junnila, MFA; *Assoc Prof* Philip Ogle, MFA; *Assoc Prof* Glenn Biegon, MFA; *Asst Prof* Peter Martin, BFA
Estab 1924; pvt; D; scholarships; SC 30, LC 8; enrl D 134, maj 134
Ent Req: HS dipl
Degrees: BFA 4 yr
Tuition: $6250 per yr
Courses: †Advertising Design, Art History, Commercial Art, Commercial Art, Conceptual Art, Design, †Drawing, Graphic Arts, Graphic Design, †Illustration, Intermedia, Lettering, †Painting, Photography, Printmaking, †Sculpture, Mass Communications

COLLEGE OF SAINT CATHERINE, Visual Arts Dept, 2004 Randolph, 55105. Tel 612-690-6636. *Chmn* M Wilson. Instrs: FT 4, PT 8
Pvt; W; D; scholarships
Ent Req: HS dipl
Degrees: BA(Art) 4 yr
Courses: †Art Education, †Art History, Calligraphy, Ceramics, Drawing, Jewelry, Lettering, Painting, Printmaking, Photography, Sculpture, Pottery, Publication Design, Typography, †Studio Art
Adult Hobby Classes: Special Workshops
Summer School: Summer high school workshop

CONCORDIA COLLEGE, Art Dept, Fine Arts Division, 275 N Syndicate St, 55104. Tel 612-641-8494. *Chmn* Win Bruhl; *Prof* Robert E Rickels, MA
Estab 1897, dept estab 1967; den; D & E; scholarships; SC 14, LC 3; enrl D 84, E 20, others 35
Ent Req: HS dipl
Degrees: BS and BA 4 yrs
Tuition: $1150 per qtr
Courses: Aesthetics, Art Education, Art History, Ceramics, Drawing, Jewelry, Painting, Photography, Printmaking, Sculpture, Teacher Training, Theatre Arts
Summer School: Courses—Art Educ Methods, Art Fundamentals

HAMLINE UNIVERSITY, Art Dept, 55104. Tel 612-641-2296, Ext 2415. *Head Dept* Michael Price, MFA; *Prof* James Conaway, MFA; *Prof* Leonardo Lasansky, MFA; *Prof* Michelle Madsen; *Prof* Clifford Garten, MFA; *Prof* Barbara Kreft
Estab 1854; pvt; D & E; scholarships; SC 13, LC 13; enrl non-maj 70, maj 35
Ent Req: HS dipl
Degrees: BA 4 yrs
Tuition: $12,190 per yr; campus res—room & board $3895 per yr
Courses: Art Education, †Art History, †Ceramics, Drawing, Museum Staff Training, †Painting, †Printmaking, †Sculpture, Design
Summer School: Dir, Deirdre Kramer

MACALESTER COLLEGE, Dept of Art, 1600 Grand Ave, 55105. Tel 612-696-6279. *Head Dept* Jerry Rudquist
Estab 1946; den; D; scholarships; SC 9, LC 8; enrl 20
Degrees: BA(Art) 4 yr
Tuition: Res—undergrad $14,000 per yr; campus res—room & board $4200 per yr
Courses: Art History, Ceramics, Design, Drawing, Painting, Printmaking, Sculpture, American Art, Art of the Last Ten Years, Classical Art, Far Eastern Art, Fibers, Medieval Art, Principles Art, Renaissance Art, Tribal Art, Senior Seminar, Women in Art
Summer School: Dir, W Harley Henry. Two 4 wk sessions June & July

UNIVERSITY OF MINNESOTA, Dept of Design, Housing & Apparel, 1985 Buford Ave (Mailing add: 240 McNeal Hall, 55108-6136). Tel 612-624-9700; FAX 612-624-2750. *Head Dept* Earl W Morris
Pub; D & E; SC 57, LC 54, GC 25; enrl D 877 (spring quarter 92), grad 75

Ent Req: HS dipl; math requirement
Degrees: BS, MS, MA & PhD 4 yr
Tuition: Res—undergrad lower division $66 per cr, upper division $76 per cr, grad $1127 for 7 - 15 cr; nonres—undergrad lower division $194.70 per cr, upper division $224.20 per cr
Courses: Art History, †Costume Design & Construction, Drawing, Handicrafts, †Interior Design, Textile Design, †Applied Design, Costume History, Decorative Arts, †Housing, †Textiles Clothing, Weaving Off-Loom, †Retail Merchandising
Summer School: Courses—vary each yr

UNIVERSITY OF SAINT THOMAS, Dept of Art History, 2115 Summit Ave, Loras Mall, Mail LOR 301, 55105-1096. Tel 612-962-5560. *Chmn* Dr Mary T Swanson
Estab 1885, dept estab 1978; den; D & E; scholarships; SC 25, LC 8; enrl D 2847, E 275, maj 40
Ent Req: HS dipl
Degrees: BA 4 yrs
Courses: Art Education, †Art History, Calligraphy, Ceramics, Drawing, Graphic Arts, Graphic Design, Jewelry, Painting, Photography, Printmaking, Sculpture, Teacher Training
Summer School: Dir, Dr Verome Halverson. Courses—Introduction to Art History

SAINT PETER

GUSTAVUS ADOLPHUS COLLEGE, Art & Art History Dept, Schaefer Fine Arts Center, 800 W College Ave, 56082-1498. Tel 507-931-7019. *Chmn* Bruce McClain. *Instrs:* FT 5, PT 2
Estab 1876; den; D; scholarships; SC 27; enrl 2300 total, 750 art, maj 50
Ent Req: HS grad, ent exam
Degrees: BA 4 yr
Tuition: $15,825 per yr (comprehensive fee); PT $1400 per course
Courses: †Art Education, †Art History, Ceramics, Drawing, Painting, Photography, Printmaking, Sculpture, Theatre Arts, Basic Design, Bronze Casting, †Studio Art
Summer School: Independent Study prog for three 4 wk periods during June, July or Aug

WHITE BEAR LAKE

LAKEWOOD COMMUNITY COLLEGE, Humanities Dept, 3401 Century Ave, 55110. Tel 612-779-3200; FAX 612-779-3417. *Instr* Kenneth Maeckelbergh; *Instr* Lew Schnellman; *Instr* Mel Sundby; *Instr* Karin McGinness; *Instr* Frank Zeller; *Instr* Lois Gelbman; *Instr* Harold Stone; *Instr* Ken Kulhawy
Tuition: Res—$37.50 per quarter cr; nonres $75 per cr hr
Courses: Art Appreciation, Art History, Calligraphy, Ceramics, Design, Drawing, Painting, Photography, Printmaking, Sculpture, Stage Design, American Art, Art Therapy
Summer School: Dir, Rosina Fieno. Tuition $37.50 quarter cr, two 5 wk sessions

WILLMAR

WILLMAR COMMUNITY COLLEGE, 2021 15th Ave NW, PO Box 797, 56201. Tel 612-231-5102; FAX 612-231-6602. *Staff* Robert Mattson. Instrs: FT 1, PT 1
Estab 1962-63; pub; D & E; SC 8, LC 3; enrl D 50, maj 15
Ent Req: HS dipl
Degrees: AA and AS 2 yrs
Tuition: Res—$32.75 per cr hr; nonres—$49.25 per cr hr
Courses: Art Education, Ceramics, Display, Drawing, Graphic Arts, Graphic Design, History of Art & Archaeology, Painting, Teacher Training, Introduction to Studio Practices, Structure
Adult Hobby Classes: Courses—Ceramics, Design, History of Art, Painting

WINONA

SAINT MARY'S COLLEGE OF MINNESOTA, Art Dept No 18, 700 Terrace Heights, 55987. Tel 507-457-1593; FAX 507-457-1633. *Head Dept* Roderick Robertson, MFA; *Prof* Helen Galloway, PhD; *Assoc Prof* Margaret Mear, MFA; *Assoc Prof* Karen Kryszko, MFA; *Asst Prof* Bill Kitt, MFA
Estab 1912, dept estab 1970; den; D; scholarships; SC 20, LC 6; enrl in school D 1240
Ent Req: HS dipl
Degrees: BA 4 yrs
Tuition: $9630 per yr; campus res—room & board $3250 per yr
Courses: Aesthetics, Art History, Ceramics, Drawing, Graphic Design, Painting, Photography, Printmaking, Sculpture

WINONA STATE UNIVERSITY, Dept of Art, 55987. Tel 507-457-5395; FAX 507-457-5086. *Chmn* Dominic Ricciotti; *Prof* Judy Schlawin, MS; *Asst Prof* Seho Park, PhD; *Asst Prof* Ann Plummer, MFA; *Asst Prof* Paul Burmeister, MFA; *Assoc Prof* Don Schmidlapp, MFA
Estab 1860; pub; D & E; scholarships
Degrees: BA and BS
Tuition: Res—undergrad $35 per cr hr; nonres—undergrad $83 per cr hr; plus student fees; campus res—room & board $2500 per yr single occupancy, double occupancy $2032
Courses: Art Education, Art History, Ceramics, Drawing, Graphic Design, Interior Design, Lettering, Painting, Printmaking, Sculpture, Weaving
Summer School: Courses offered

MISSISSIPPI

BLUE MOUNTAIN

BLUE MOUNTAIN COLLEGE, Art Dept, Box 338, 38610. Tel 601-685-4771, Ext 62. *Chmn Dept* William Dowdy, MA
Estab 1873, dept estab 1875; den; D & E; scholarships; SC 16, LC 2; enrl D 28, E 12, non-maj 20, maj 8, others 12
Ent Req: HS dipl
Degrees: BA and BS(Educ) 4 yr
Tuition: $3248 per yr, plus fees
Courses: Art History, Commercial Art, Drawing, Painting
Adult Hobby Classes: Enrl 12; tuition $42 per sem hr. Courses—Drawing, Painting
Summer School: Dir, William Dowdy. Enrl 20

BOONEVILLE

NORTHEAST MISSISSIPPI JUNIOR COLLEGE, Art Dept, 38829. Tel 601-728-7751, Ext 229. *Chmn* Marty McLendon; *Instr* Terry Anderson; *Instr* Judy Tucci. Instrs: FT 2, PT 1
Estab 1948; pub; D & E; scholarships; SC 6, LC 3; enrl D 2800, maj 30
Ent Req: HS dipl, ent exam
Degrees: 2 yr Associate degrees in art educ, fine arts and interior design
Tuition: res—$435 per sem; nonres—$830 per sem; foreign countries—$2385 per sem
Courses: Advertising Design, Aesthetics, Art Education, Art History, Ceramics, Design, Drafting, Drawing, Painting, Teacher Training, Theatre Arts
Adult Hobby Classes: Watercolor

CLARKSDALE

COAHOMA COMMUNITY COLLEGE, Art Education & Fine Arts Dept, Rte 1, PO Box 616, 38614. Tel 601-627-2571. *Chmn* Henry Dorsey
Degrees: AA
Tuition: In district—$700 per yr; res—$2511.70 per yr; outside district $1100 per yr; outside state $2100 per yr; out of district boarding $2911.70 per yr, out of state boarding $3911.70 per yr
Courses: Art Appreciation, Art Education, Art History, Drawing, Handicrafts, Intro to Art
Adult Hobby Classes: Enrl 15-32; tuition $27.50 per sem hr. Courses—Art & Music Appreciation

CLEVELAND

DELTA STATE UNIVERSITY, Dept of Art, PO Box D-2, 38733. Tel 518-846-4720. *Chmn* Collier B Parker; *Prof* Dr Carolyn Rea Stone, Ph D; *Prof* Sam Glenn Britt, MFA; *Prof* William Carey Lester Jr, MFA; *Assoc Prof* Terry K Simmons, MA; *Assoc Prof* Ron Koehler, MFA; *Assoc Prof* Mary Anne Ross, BFA; *Assoc Prof* Kim Rushing; *Instr* Joe Abide; *Instr* Marcella Small; *Instr* Patricia L Brown; *Instr* Catherine Koehler
Estab 1924; pub; D & E; scholarships; SC 42, LC 10, GC 30; enrl maj 116
Ent Req: HS dipl
Degrees: BA & BFA
Tuition: Res—undergrad & grad $1845 per yr, $1000 per sem; nonres—undergrad & grad $3307 per yr, $1731 per sem
Courses: †Advertising Design, Aesthetics, †Art Education, Art History, Calligraphy, Ceramics, †Commercial Art, Costume Design & Construction, Drawing, Fashion Arts, Graphic Arts, †Graphic Design, Handicrafts, Illustration, †Interior Design, Lettering, Mixed Media, †Painting, Printmaking, †Sculpture, Teacher Training, Textile Design, Clay, Computer Graphics, Fibers
Summer School: Tuition & living expenses $488 per term, June 2 - July 3 or July 7 - August 8. Courses—Art for Elementary, Ceramics, Drawing, Internship in Commercial Design, Introduction to Art, Painting, Sculpture

CLINTON

MISSISSIPPI COLLEGE, Art Dept, PO Box 4205, 39058. Tel 601-925-3231. *Head Dept* Dr Sam Gore. Instrs: FT 4, PT 2
Estab 1825, dept estab 1950; den; HS grad; scholarships and student assistantships; SC 22, LC 3; enrl maj 80, others 300
Ent Req: BA, BE(Art), MA(Art) and ME(Art) 4 yr, Freshman Art merit
Tuition: Undergrad $147 per cr hr, grad $165 per cr hr
Courses: †Art Education, Art History, Ceramics, Drawing, †Graphic Design, †Interior Design, †Painting, †Sculpture, Foundry Casting
Adult Hobby Classes: Enrl 50; tuition $35 for 5 weeks. Courses—Calligraphy, Drawing, Flower Arranging, Painting
Summer School: Dir, Dr Sam Gore. Tuition $1200 for two 6-wk terms. Courses—Ceramics, Drawing, Painting, Printmaking

COLUMBUS

MISSISSIPPI UNIVERSITY FOR WOMEN, Division of Fine & Performing Arts, PO Box W-70 MUW, 39701. Tel 601-329-7341. *Head Dept* Dr Sue S Coates; *Prof* Mary Evelyn Stringer, PhD; *Prof* David Frank; *Prof* Thomas Nawrocki, MFA; *Prof* Lawrence Feeny, MFA; *Asst Prof* Robert Gibson; *Instr* John Alford
Estab 1884; pub; D & E; scholarships; SC 49, LC 8; enrl D 263, E 39, non-maj 45, maj 72
Ent Req: HS dipl, ACT, SAT
Degrees: BA, BS and BFA 4 yrs
Tuition: Res—undergrad $1119.50 per sem; nonres—undergrad $2228 per sem
Courses: †Art Education, Art History, Calligraphy, Ceramics, Commercial Art,

Conceptual Art, Graphic Design, †Interior Design, Illustration, Lettering, Mixed Media, †Painting, Photography, †Printmaking, Sculpture, Stage Design, Teacher Training, †Theatre Arts, Weaving, Architectual Construction & Materials
Adult Hobby Classes: Enrl 45; tuition $25 per hr. Courses—Drawing, Painting, Weaving
Summer School: Tuition $66 per hr for term of 5 wks beginning June 1 & July 6. Courses—Vary according to demand

DECATUR

EAST CENTRAL COMMUNITY COLLEGE, Art Dept, PO Box 27, 39327. Tel 601-635-2121. *Head Dept* J Bruce Guraedy, MEd
Estab 1928, dept estab 1965; pub; D & E; scholarships; SC 10, LC 8; enrl in dept D 120, E 52, non-maj 58, maj 10
Ent Req: HS dipl, GED
Degrees: AA and AS 2 yrs
Tuition: Res—$2500 per yr, $1250 per sem; nonres—$3700 per yr, $1850 per sem; campus residence available
Courses: Advertising Design, Art Appreciation, Art Education, Art History, Ceramics, Collages, Design, Drafting, Drawing, Fashion Arts, Handicrafts, Illustration, Industrial Design, Interior Design, Landscape Architecture, Mixed Media, Painting, Printmaking, Sculpture, Stage Design, Theatre Arts
Adult Hobby Classes: Enrl 15; tuition $75 per sem for 10 wks. Courses—Beginning Painting, Drawing, Painting
Children's Classes: Kid's College & pvt lessons available
Summer School: Acad Dean, Dr Phil Sutphin. Enrl 300 - 400; tuition $50 per sem hr for term of 10 wks. Courses—vary according to student demand

ELLISVILLE

JONES COUNTY JUNIOR COLLEGE, Art Dept, College Dr, 39437. Tel 601-477-4148. *Chmn Fine Arts* Jeff Brown
Estab 1927; pub; D; scholarships; SC 12, LC 4; enrl D 100, E 12, maj 15, others 12
Ent Req: HS dipl
Degrees: AA 2 yrs
Tuition: Res—$303 per sem; $33 per cr hr; nonres—$788 per sem; $42 per cr hr
Adult Hobby Classes: Enrl 20. Courses—Painting
Summer School: Dir, B F Ogletree. Term of 4 wks beginning June. Courses—same as regular session

GAUTIER

MISSISSIPPI GULF COAST COMMUNITY COLLEGE-JACKSON COUNTY CAMPUS, Art Dept, PO Box 100, 39553. Tel 601-497-9602. *Chmn Fine Arts Dept* Martha Richardson, MA; *Instr* Patt Odom, MA
Pub; D & E; scholarships; SC 9, LC 2; enrl D 90, E 8, non-maj 62, maj 28
Degrees: AA, 2 yrs
Tuition: $130 per 3 hrs
Courses: Aesthetics, Art Appreciation, Art Education, Ceramics, Design, Display, Drafting, Drawing, Fashion Arts, Lettering, Mixed Media, Painting, Photography, Sculpture, Theatre Arts, Allied Art, Introduction Art, Pottery
Adult Hobby Classes: Courses—Ceramics, Art Appreciation, Drawing, Painting
Children's Classes: Enrl 50. Courses—Drawing, Painting, Ceramics
Summer School: Dir, Patt Odom. Courses—Art Appreciation, Ceramics, Introductory Art, Art Educ

HATTIESBURG

UNIVERSITY OF SOUTHERN MISSISSIPPI, Dept of Art, College of the Arts, 39406. Tel 601-266-4972. *Chmn* Jerry Walden. Instrs: FT 11, PT 3
Estab 1910; pub; D & E; scholarships; SC 64, LC 41, GC 34; enrl non-maj 35, maj 120, grad 5
Ent Req: HS dipl
Degrees: BA, BFA, MAE
Tuition: Res—undergrad $1188 per sem; nonres—$980 fee; res—grad $127 per sem hr; campus residency available
Courses: Advertising Design, Aesthetics, Art Appreciation, Art Education, Art History, Calligraphy, Ceramics, Commercial Art, Conceptual Art, Design, Drawing, Graphic Arts, Graphic Design, Handicrafts, Illustration, Interior Design, Jewelry, Lettering, Mixed Media, Painting, Photography, Printmaking, Sculpture, Teacher Training, Textile Design, Weaving
Adult Hobby Classes: Enrl 20-50; 16 wk sem. Courses—Ceramics, Crafts, Drawing, Painting
Children's Classes: Classes offered by Office of Lifelong Learning. Courses—Crafts, Painting
Summer School: Dir, Jerry Walden. Enrl 60; 5 & 10 wk sessions. Courses—as above

ITTA BENA

MISSISSIPPI VALLEY STATE UNIVERSITY, Fine Arts Dept, PO Box 1301, MVSU, 38941. Tel 601-254-9041, Ext 6261. *Head* Sandra Scott
Estab 1952; pub; D & E
Ent Req: HS dipl
Degrees: BA & BS
Tuition: Res—undergrad $1825 per sem
Courses: Art History, Ceramics, Drawing, Graphic Arts, Illustration, Painting, Photography, Printmaking, Art Appreciation, Arts & Crafts, Color Fundamentals, Public School Art, 2 & 3-D Design, Typography, Visual Communications
Summer School: Courses—Art Appreciation, Public School Art

JACKSON

BELHAVEN COLLEGE, Art Dept, 1500 Peachtree, 39202. Tel 601-968-5950. *Chmn* Jon Whittington, MA
Estab 1883, dept estab 1889; den; D & E; scholarships; LC 3; enrl D 650, E 200, maj 30
Ent Req: HS dipl
Degrees: BA
Courses: Art History, Drawing, Graphic Arts, Painting, Photography, Printmaking
Summer School: Dir, Dr Dewey Buckley

JACKSON STATE UNIVERSITY, Dept of Art, Lynch at Dalton St, 39217. Tel 601-968-2040. *Chmn* Dr A D Macklin
Estab 1949; pub; D; scholarships; SC 16, LC 7, GC 1; enrl D 486, maj 57
Ent Req: HS dipl
Degrees: BA & BS(maj in Art) 4 yrs
Tuition: $72 per cr hr 1 - 11 hrs; $863 per sem 12 -19 hrs; campus res available
Courses: Art Education, Art History, Ceramics, Commercial Art, Drawing, Graphic Arts, Painting, Studio Crafts
Adult Hobby Classes: Athenian Art Club activities
Summer School: Dir, Dr A D Macklin. Course - same as regular session

MILLSAPS COLLEGE, Dept of Art, 1700 N State St, PO Box 15429, 39210. Tel 601-974-1000. *Chmn* Jack Agricoa, PhD; *Assoc Prof* Lucy Millsaps, MA; *Asst Prof* Elsie Smith; *Instr* Skip Allen, BFA
Estab 1913, dept estab 1970; priv; D & E; scholarships; LC 4; enrl non maj 100, maj 20
Ent Req: HS dipl, SAT combined 1100 average
Degrees: BA 4 yr
Tuition: Res—undergrad $5,200 per yr, $165 per cr hr; campus residence available
Courses: Aesthetics, Architecture, Art History, Calligraphy, Ceramics, Design, Drawing, History of Art & Archaeology, Lettering, Museum Staff Training, Painting, Photography, Printmaking, Sculpture, Stage Design, Teacher Training, Textile Design, Theatre Arts, Weaving
Adult Hobby Classes: Tuition $35 per class
Children's Classes: Tuition $50 per class

LORMAN

ALCORN STATE UNIVERSITY, Dept of Fine Arts, 39096. Tel 601-877-6271. *Chmn* Joyce Bolden, PhD; *Assoc Prof* Constance Alford, MFA
Estab 1871, dept estab 1973; pub; D & E; SC 9, LC 3
Ent Req: HS dipl, ACT
Tuition: In-state $875 per yr; out-of-state $1466
Courses: Art Appreciation, Art Education, Ceramics, Drawing, Painting
Adult Hobby Classes: Enrl 20. Courses—Drawing, Painting, Graduate Level Art Education
Summer School: Enrl 40 for term of 10 wks beginning May 28. Courses—Art Education, Fine Arts

MISSISSIPPI STATE

MISSISSIPPI STATE UNIVERSITY, Art Dept, PO Box 5182, 39762. Tel 601-325-2970. *Head* Larry Jan Webber, BFA; *Prof* Paul Brown; *Assoc Prof* Paul Grootkerk, PhD; *Assoc Prof* Robie Scucchi, MFA; *Assoc Prof* Jack Bartlett, MFA; *Assoc Prof* Linda Seckinger, MFA; *Assoc Prof* Brent Funderburk, MFA; *Asst Prof* Marita Gootee, MFA; *Asst Prof* Robert Long, MFA; *Asst Prof* Jamie Mixon
Estab 1879, dept estab 1971; pub; D; scholarships; SC 23, LC 6; enrl D 750, non-maj 650, maj 150
Ent Req: HS dipl
Degrees: BFA 4 yrs
Tuition: Campus res—room & board $1700 per yr
Courses: Art History, Ceramics, Commercial Art, Drawing, Painting, Photography, Printmaking, Sculpture
Adult Hobby Classes: Enrl 40; tuition $1700 per yr. Courses—Drawing, Fundamentals, Painting

MOORHEAD

MISSISSIPPI DELTA COMMUNITY COLLEGE, Dept of Fine Arts, PO Box 668, 38761. Tel 601-246-5631, Ext 121. *Chmn* Joseph R Abrams III; *Coordr* Jean Abrams; *Instr* Evelyn Kiker
Estab 1926; pub; D & E; SC 11, LC 2; enrl D 68, E 29, maj 28
Ent Req: HS dipl, ent exam
Degrees: AA and AS(Commercial Art) 2 yrs
Tuition: Res—undergrad $750 per yr
Courses: Advertising Design, Ceramics, Commercial Art, Drawing, Graphic Arts, Painting, Art Appreciation
Adult Hobby Classes: Enrl 29. Courses—Ceramics, Painting

POPLARVILLE

PEARL RIVER COMMUNITY COLLEGE, Art Dept, Division of Fine Arts, Station A, PO Box 5007, 101 Highway 11 N, 39470. Tel 601-795-6801, Ext 230; FAX 601-795-6815. *Chmn* James A Rawls; *Instr* Kim R Du Boise. Instrs: FT 1, PT 2
Estab 1921; pub; D & E; enrl D 85 - 100, non-maj 65 - 75, maj 20 - 25, E 20 - 40, non-maj 20 - 30, maj 10 - 20
Ent Req: HS dipl or ACT Score & GED
Tuition: res—$425 per sem; out of state $925; campus res available
Courses: Art Appreciation, Art Education, Design, Drafting, Drawing, Handicrafts, Interior Design, Painting, Teacher Training, Elementary Art Education, Introduction to Art

RAYMOND

HINDS COMMUNITY COLLEGE, Dept of Art, 39154. Tel 601-854-3275, 857-3274; FAX 601-857-3293. *Chmn* Russell Schneider. Instrs: FT 4
Estab 1917; pub; D & E; scholarships; SC 5, LC 2; enrl D 400, E 75, maj 60
Degrees: AA 2 yr
Tuition: Res—$510 per sem (12-19 hrs), nonres—$1613 per sem (12-19 hrs); cmapus res available
Courses: Advertising Design, Ceramics, Commercial Art, Display, Drawing, Graphic Design, Painting
Adult Hobby Classes: Courses offered
Children's Classes: Courses offered
Summer School: Dir, Russell F Schneider. Enrl 24; tuition $165 for 8 wk term. Course—Art Appreciation

TOUGALOO

TOUGALOO COLLEGE, Art Dept, 39174. Tel 601-977-7700. *Pres* Johnnie Mae Gilbert; *Chmn Dept* Ronald Schnell, MFA; *Assoc Prof* Bruce O'Hara, MFA
Estab 1869, dept estab 1968; pvt; D; scholarships; SC 14, LC 4; enrl D 650, non-maj 420, maj 10
Ent Req: HS dipl
Degrees: BA and BS 4 yrs
Tuition: Res—undergrad average $5158 per yr
Courses: Art Appreciation, Art Education, Art History, Commercial Art, Drawing, Graphic Arts, Handicrafts, History of Art & Archaeology, Painting, Photography, Printmaking, Sculpture, American & Contemporary

UNIVERSITY

UNIVERSITY OF MISSISSIPPI, Dept of Art, 38677. Tel 601-232-7193; FAX 601-232-7010. *Chmn* Margaret Gorove, MFA; *Prof* Robert L Tettleton, MEd; *Prof* Charles M Gross, MFA; *Prof* J Leslie Wyatt, MFA; *Prof* Jere H Allen, MFA; *Assoc Prof* John L Winters, MFA; *Assoc Prof* Tom Dewey II, PhD; *Assoc Prof* Tom Rankin, MFA; *Assoc Prof* Paula Temple, MFA; *Assoc Prof* Ron Dale, MFA; *Asst Prof* Betty Crouther, PhD; *Asst Prof* Gregory Shelnutt; *Asst Prof* John Hull, MFA. Instrs: FT 13, PT 6
Dept estab 1949; pub; D; merit scholarships and out-of-state tuition waivers; SC 470, LC 265, GC 48; enrl D 735, non-maj 350, maj 260, grad 15
Ent Req: HS dipl
Degrees: BA 4 yr, BFA 4 yr, MFA 2 yr, MA 1 yr
Tuition: Res—undergrad $998 per sem, $83 per cr hr, grad $998 per sem;, $111 per cr hr; nonres—undergrad $1979 per sem $165 per cr hr, grad $1979 per sem, $192 per cr hr; campus res—room $644 - $700
Courses: Advertising Design, Aesthetics, †Art Education, †Art History, †Ceramics, Drawing, Graphic Arts, †Graphic Design, Illustration, †Interior Design, †Painting, †Printmaking, †Sculpture, Watercolor
Summer School: Dir, G Walton. Two 5 wk sessions beginning June. Courses—Art Education, Art History, Ceramics, Design, Drawing, Painting, Printmaking, Sculpture

MISSOURI

BOLIVAR

SOUTHWEST BAPTIST UNIVERSITY, Art Dept, 1601 S Springfield, 65613. Tel 417-326-1651. *Chmn* Wesley A Gott, MFA; *Assoc Prof* Sandra Brown, MFA; *Asst Prof* Diane Callahan, BFA
Sch estab 1876, dept estab 1974; den; D & E; scholarships offered; SC 30, LC 3; enrl D 150, E 20, maj 35
Ent Req: HS dipl
Degrees: BS & BA
Tuition: Res—undergrad $75 per hr; nonres—undergrad $3500; campus res—room & board $2400 per academic yr
Courses: †Art Education, Art History, †Ceramics, †Commercial Art, Costume Design & Construction, †Drawing, †Graphic Arts, Graphic Design, Interior Design, †Painting, †Photography, †Printmaking, †Sculpture, Stage Design, †Teacher Training, Theatre Arts
Adult Hobby Classes: Enrl 10; tuition $35 per hr for 15 weeks. Courses—Drawing, Painting, Photography
Children's Classes: Drawing, Painting
Summer School: Enrl 600; tuition $75 per hour for 4 wk term beginning in June, also a 4 wk term beginning in July. Courses—Drawing, Painting, Photography

CANTON

CULVER-STOCKTON COLLEGE, Division of Fine Arts, 63435-1299. Tel 314-288-5221; FAX 314-288-3984. *Gallery Dir* Dr Wm R Detmers; *Prof* Albert Beck; *Technical Theater & Visual Arts* Joe Harris
Estab 1853; pvt; D; scholarships; SC 16, LC 6; enrl 844, maj 30
Ent Req: HS dipl, ACT or Col Board Ent Exam
Degrees: BFA & BA(Visual Arts), BS(Art Educ) & BS(Arts Management) 4 yrs
Tuition: Campus Res—room & board $8000 per yr
Courses: Aesthetics, Art Education, Ceramics, Costume Design & Construction, Drawing, Film, Graphic Arts, History of Art & Archaeology, Illustration, Jewelry, Museum Staff Training, Painting, Photography, Sculpture, Stage Design, Teacher Training, Theatre Arts
Summer School: Reg, Peggy King. Tuition $124 per cr hr for 5 wks. Courses—Art Appreciation, Art Education & various studio

CAPE GIRARDEAU

SOUTHEAST MISSOURI STATE UNIVERSITY, Dept of Art, One University Plaza, 63701. Tel 314-651-2143. *Chmn* Bill Chamberlain
Estab 1873, dept estab 1920; pub; D & E; scholarships; SC 28, LC 10, GC 18; enrl D 1300
Ent Req: HS dipl
Degrees: BS, BS(Educ) and BA 4 yrs, MAT
Tuition: Res—$745 per sem; nonres—$1445 per sem
Courses: Advertising Design, Art History, Ceramics, Commercial Art, Drawing, Graphic Design, Illustration, Lettering, Painting, Printmaking, Sculpture, Silversmithing, Color Composition, Design Foundation, Fiber, Perceptive Art, Screen Printing, 3-D Design, Typography, Video Art Graphic
Summer School: Chairperson, Bill Needle. Enrl 164 undergrad, 60 grad; tuition $160 for res, $375 for nonres

COLUMBIA

COLUMBIA COLLEGE, Art Dept, 1001 Rogers, 65216. Tel 314-875-8700, 875-7520. *Chmn* Ed Collings; *Instr* Sidney Larson, MA; *Instr* Ben Cameron; *Instr* Thomas Watson, MFA; *Instr* Richard Baumann; *Instr* Michael Sledd. Instrs: FT 5, PT 2
Estab 1851; den; D; scholarships; SC 55, LC 13; enrl D 180, non-maj 80, maj 115
Ent Req: HS dipl or equivalent, ACT or SAT, also accept transfer students
Degrees: AA 2 yrs, BA, BS and BFA 4 yrs
Tuition: Res—$3583 per sem; nonres—$5201
Courses: Art History, Ceramics, Drawing, Fashion Arts, Graphic Arts, Graphic Design, Illustration, Painting, Photography
Adult Hobby Classes: Enrl 15; tui $75 per cr. Courses—Arts & Crafts, Photography
Summer School: Evening Studies Dir, Dr John Hendricks. Enrl 20; tui $75 per cr hr

STEPHENS COLLEGE, Art & Fashion Dept, PO Box 2012, 65215. Tel 314-442-2211, Ext 173. *Instr* Robert Friedman; *Instr* Sara Riley-Land; *Instr* Rosalind Kimball-Moulton; *Instr* Deborah Porter
Estab 1833, dept estab 1850; pvt; D & E; scholarships; SC 25, LC 6; enrl D 800, maj 3, others 10
Ent Req: SAT or ACT, recommendations, interview
Degrees: BA 3-4 yrs, BFA 3 1/2-4 yrs
Tuition: $9000 Per yr; campus res—room & board $3300
Courses: Advertising Design, Art Education, Art History, Ceramics, Commercial Art, Costume Design & Construction, Drawing, †Fashion Arts, Film, Graphic Arts, Graphic Design, Illustration, Occupational Therapy, †Painting, †Photography, †Printmaking, †Sculpture, Stage Design, Teacher Training, †Theatre Arts, †Video
Children's Classes: Tui $900 per yr; Stephens Child Study Center, grades K-3, preschool; includes special creative arts emphasis

UNIVERSITY OF MISSOURI
—Art Dept, A 126 Fine Arts, 65211. Tel 314-882-3555. *Chmn* Oliver A Schuchard. Instrs: FT 12, PT 3
Estab 1901, dept estab 1912; pub; D & E; SC 76, LC 1, GC 53; enrl non-maj 1600 per sem, maj 180, grad 34
Ent Req: HS dipl
Degrees: BFA, AB(Art Educ), BS(Art Educ), MFA(Art), MEd, DEd, PhD & Educ Specialist
Tuition: Res—$1275 - $1350 per sem; nonres—$3219 - $3713
Courses: Art Education, Calligraphy, Ceramics, Drawing, Graphic Design, Illustration, Jewelry, Painting, Photography, Printmaking, Sculpture, Fibers, Serigraphy, Watercolor
Summer School: Chmn, Oliver A Schuchard. Enrl 175; tuition $161 for term of 8 wks beginning June 12. Courses—Art Education, Ceramics, Design, Drawing, Fibers, Intro to Art, Jewelry, Painting, Photography, Printmaking, Sculpture, Watercolor
—Art History and Archaeology Dept, 109 Pickard Hall, 65211. Tel 314-882-6711; FAX 314-884-4039. *Chmn* Kathleen Warner Slane; *Prof* Osmund Overby, PhD; *Prof* Norman Land, PhD; *Prof* William R Biers, PhD; *Prof* Howard Marshall, PhD; *Assoc Prof* Marcus Rautman, PhD; *Assoc Prof* Patricia Crown, PhD; *Assoc Prof* Edward Baumann, PhD; *Asst Prof* John Klein, PhD
Estab 1839, dept estab 1892; pub; D; scholarships; LC 42, GC 18; enrl maj 48, grad 39
Ent Req: HS dipl, SAT, GRE for grad students
Degrees: BA 4 yrs, MA 2-3 yrs, PhD 4 yrs
Tuition: Res—grad $103 per cr hr; nonres—grad $288 per cr hr; campus res available
Courses: Art History, Museum Staff Training, Classical Archaeology, Historic Preservation
Summer School: Courses offered

FERGUSON

SAINT LOUIS COMMUNITY COLLEGE AT FLORISSANT VALLEY, Division of Communications & Arts, 3400 Pershall Rd, 63135. Tel 314-595-4375. *Chmn Div* Larry Byers
Estab 1962; pub; D & E; SC 36, LC 4; enrl maj 70
Ent Req: HS dipl, ent exam
Degrees: AA, AAS 2 yr
Tuition: District res—$31, non district res—$41, non state res—$52
Courses: Advertising Design, Art History, Ceramics, Commercial Art, Drawing, Illustration, Lettering, Painting, Photography, Printmaking, Sculpture, Air Brush, Electronic Certificate, Transfer Art, Typography
Summer School: Dir, Richard Buckman. Enrl 270; tuition $20.50 per cr hr for term of 8 wks beginning June 9. Courses—Design, Drawing, Figure Drawing, Lettering, Painting

FULTON

WILLIAM WOODS-WESTMINSTER COLLEGES, Art Dept, 200 W 12th, 65251. Tel 314-592-4372. *Chmn Div Fine Arts & Head Art Dept* George E Tutt, MA; *Assoc Prof* Paul Clervi, MFA; *Instr* Terry Martin, MA; *Emeritus Prof* George Latta, MFA; *Instr* Jeff Ball, MA; *Instr* Tina Mann, MA; *Instr* Bob Elliott, MA; *Instr* Sharon Kilfoyle; *Instr* Ken Greene, BA
Estab 1870; pvt; D; scholarships; SC 54, LC 6; enrl maj 71
Ent Req: HS dipl, SAT or ACT
Degrees: BA, BS and BFA 4 yr
Tuition: Res—$6100 per yr (incl room and board); nonres—$4160 per yr; campus res—room and board $1790
Courses: Aesthetics, Art Education, Art History, Ceramics, Collages, Commercial Art, Costume Design & Construction, Drawing, Handicrafts, History of Art & Archaeology, Illustration, Interior Design, Jewelry, Painting, Photography, Printmaking, Sculpture, Silversmithing, Stage Design, Teacher Training, Theatre Arts, Weaving, Art Therapy

HANNIBAL

HANNIBAL LA GRANGE COLLEGE, Art Dept, 2800 Palmyra, 63401. Tel 314-221-3675. *Chmn* James Stone; *Instr* Richard Cerretti; *Instr* Richard Griffen
Scholarships
Degrees: AA, BA(Art)
Tuition: $2215 per sem (12-17 hrs)
Courses: Advertising Design, Art Appreciation, Art Education, Art History, Calligraphy, Ceramics, Commercial Art, Design, Drawing, Handicrafts, Lettering, Mixed Media, Painting, Photography, Printmaking, Sculpture, Textile Design, Cartooning
Summer School: Dean, Dr Woodrow Burt. Term 2-4 wk & one 8 wk. Courses—vary

JEFFERSON CITY

LINCOLN UNIVERSITY, Dept Fine Arts, 820 Chestnut St, 65102-0029. Tel 314-681-5280. *Chmn* James Tatum; *Instr* Jane Carol. Instrs: FT 2, PT 1
Estab 1927; pub; enrl maj 35, others 100
Degrees: BS(Art) and BS(Art Educ) 4 yr
Tuition: Res—undergrad $1200 per yr
Courses: Art Education, Art History, Teacher Training, Applied Art, Studio Art
Summer School: Courses—same as above

JOPLIN

MISSOURI SOUTHERN STATE COLLEGE, Dept of Art, 3950 Newman Rd, 64801. Tel 417-625-9563. *Dir Dept* Jim Bray
Estab 1937; pub; D & E; scholarships; SC 22, LC 3; enrl D 425, E 83, non-maj 360, maj 105, others 10
Ent Req: HS dipl
Degrees: BA & BSE 4 yrs
Tuition: Res—undergrad $48 per cr hr
Courses: Art Education, Graphic Design, Jewelry, Painting, Printmaking, Sculpture, Studio Crafts
Adult Hobby Classes: Enrl approx 30; tui $1 per hr. Courses—Photography, Tole, plus others. Offered by Continuing Educ Div
Summer School: Dir Dept, C Robert Schwieger. Enrl 15-20 per workshop; tuition res—$17 per cr hr, nonres—$27 per cr hr for term of 2 wks beginning June. Courses—Arts & Crafts, Drawing, Jewelry, Pottery, Printmaking, Watercolor, and others

KANSAS CITY

AVILA COLLEGE, Art Division, Dept of Performing and Visual Art, 11901 Wornall Rd, 64145. Tel 816-942-8400. *Chmn* Daniel Larson; *Coordr* Daniel Keegan; *Instr* George Christman; *Instr* Henry Dixson; *Instr* Laura Bogue; *Instr* Sharyl Wright; *Artist in Res* Sr Margaret Renehart
Estab 1963; den; D & E; scholarships; SC 35, LC 4; enrl D 140, E 20, non-maj 120, maj 40
Ent Req: HS dipl, SAT and PSAT
Degrees: BA 4 yrs
Tuition: $2975 per sem
Courses: Art History, Art Education, Ceramics, Commercial Art, Drawing, Painting, Photography, Sculpture
Adult Hobby Classes: Courses offered

KANSAS CITY ART INSTITUTE, 4415 Warwick Blvd, 64111. Tel 816-561-4852; FAX 816-561-6404. *Pres* Beatrice Rivas Sanchez, MFA; *Chmn Ceramics* Kenneth Ferguson, MFA; *Chmn Design* Jack Lew; *Chmn Painting & Printmaking* Warren Rosser, MFA; *Chmn Photography* Patrick Clancy, MFA; *Chmn Sculpture* Dale Eldred, MFA; *Chmn Found* Steve Whitacre, MFA; *Chmn Liberal Arts* Milton Katz, PhD; *Chmn Fiber* Jane Lackey, MFA
Estab 1885; D & E; scholarships; maj areas 7, LC 104 in liberal arts; enrl D 517, maj 517
Ent Req: HS dipl, portfolio interview
Degrees: BFA 4 yrs
Tuition: $11,138 per yr, $5694 per sem, $475 per cr hr; campus res—room $3960 per yr (double occupancy)
Courses: Art History, †Ceramics, Commercial Art, †Design, †Graphic Design, †Illustration, †Industrial Design, Drawing, Film, Graphic Arts, Graphic Design, Illustration, Industrial Design, Interior Design, Mixed Media, †Painting, †Photography, †Printmaking, †Sculpture, †Video, †Textile
Adult Hobby Classes: Enrl 250; tuition $400 per cr hr for 12 wk term. Courses—Ceramics, Design, Fiber, Liberal Arts, Painting, Printmaking, Photography, Video
Summer School: Enrl 25; 8 wk term. Courses—Liberal Arts, Studio

MAPLE WOODS COMMUNITY COLLEGE, Dept of Art and Art History, 2601 NE Barry Rd, 64156. Tel 816-436-6500, Ext 179; FAX 816-734-2963. *Head Dept* Helen Mary Turner, MSecEd. Instrs: PT 6
Estab 1969; pub; D & E; scholarships; SC 12, LC 2; enrl D 125, E & Sat 80
Ent Req: HS dipl or GED
Degrees: AA 2 yrs
Tuition: Distric res—$30 per cr hr; nonres district—$54 per cr hr; nonres state—$54 per cr hr
Courses: Art Education, Art History, Ceramics, Commercial Art, Drawing, Painting, Photography, Printmaking, Sculpture, Art Fundamentals
Adult Hobby Classes: Enrl 30; tuition same as above. Courses same as above
Children's Classes: Summer classes; enrl 30; tuition $30 for 6 wks
Summer School: Dir, Helen Mary Turner. Tuition same as above for 8 wks beginning June 1. Courses—Drawing, Painting, Ceramics

PENN VALLEY COMMUNITY COLLEGE, Art Dept, 3201 SW Trafficway, 64111. Tel 816-759-4326. *Chmn* Judith Flynn; *Head Art Dept* Robert L Morris
Scholarships offered
Degrees: AA
Tuition: District res—$31 per sem hr; non-district res—$50 per sem hr; non-state res—$75 per sem hr
Courses: Advertising Design, Art History, Calligraphy, Ceramics, Design, Drawing, Fashion Arts, Film, Painting, Photography, Printmaking, Sculpture, Video, Animation, Art Fundamentals, Cartooning, Computer Graphics

UNIVERSITY OF MISSOURI-KANSAS CITY, Dept of Art and Art History, 5100 Rockhill Rd, 64110. Tel 816-235-1501; FAX 816-235-5191. *Chmn* Dr Burton Dunbar. Instrs: FT 10, PT 7
Estab 1933; pub; D & E; enrl maj 138
Ent Req: Contact Admis Office
Tuition: Res—freshman & sophomore $68.10 per cr hr, jr & sr $74.40, grad $88.40; nonres—freshman & sophomore $187.80 per cr hr, jr & sr $206.90, grad $226
Courses: Architecture, Drawing, Graphic Design, Painting, Photography, Printmaking, Sculpture, Computer Art
Summer School: Chmn, Dr Geraldine E Fowle

KIRKSVILLE

NORTHEAST MISSOURI STATE UNIVERSITY, Art Dept, Division of Fine Arts, 63501. Tel 816-785-4417. *Head Div Fine Arts* Dr John M Lee
Estab 1867; pub; D & E; scholarships; SC 27, LC 8; enrl D 220, non-maj 45, maj 155
Ent Req: HS dipl
Degrees: BFA(Visual Comminications, Studio) 4 yrs, BA(Liberal Arts) 4 yrs, BA(Art History) 4 yrs
Tuition: Res—undergrad $93 per sem hr, grad $99 per sem hr; nonres—undergrad $164 per sem hr, grad $176 per sem hr
Courses: †Art History, †Ceramics, †Painting, †Photography, †Printmaking, †Sculpture, Visual Communications, Fibers
Summer School: Enrl 80-100; term of two 5 wk sessions beginning June & July

LIBERTY

WILLIAM JEWELL COLLEGE, Art Dept, College Hill, 64068. Tel 816-781-7700, Ext 5414. *Chmn* David B Johnson, MFA; *Instr* Nano Nore Lueders, MFA; *Instr* Rebecca Koop, BFA
Estab 1849; dept estab 1966; pvt (cooperates with the Missouri Baptist Convention); D & E; scholarships; enrl D 120, E 35-40, maj 30
Degrees: BA & BS 4 yrs
Tuition: 11,270 (incl room & board)
Courses: Art Appreciation, Art History, Calligraphy, Ceramics, Design, Drawing, Painting, Photography, Printmaking, Sculpture, Computer Graphic
Adult Hobby Classes: Enrl 10 - 15; tuition $120 per 14 wk sem. Courses—Calligraphy, Drawing, Illustration, Painting, Photography
Children's Classes: Enrl 10 - 15; tuition $30 - $40 for a 6 wk session. Courses—Ceramics, Drawing, Painting, Photography
Summer School: Dir, Dr Steve Schwegler. Enrl 10 - 15; tuition $120 per cr hr for 8 wk term. Courses—Calligraphy, Drawing, Painting ,

MARYVILLE

NORTHWEST MISSOURI STATE UNIVERSITY, Dept of Art, 64468. Tel 816-562-1314. *Chmn* Lee Hageman, MFA; *Assoc Prof* Philip Laber, MFA; *Assoc Prof* George Rose, MFA; *Assoc Prof* Robert Sunkel, MFA; *Assoc Prof* Kenneth Nelsen, MFA; *Asst Prof* Russell Schmaljohn, MS; *Asst Prof* Kim Spradling, PhD; *Asst Prof* Paul Falcone, MFA
Estab 1905; dept estab 1915; pub; D & E; scholarships; SC 74, LC 19; enrl D 475, E 25, non-maj 350, maj 150
Ent Req: HS dipl
Degrees: BFA, BSE & BA 4 yrs
Tuition: Res—$50 per hr; nonres—$90.50 per hr; campus res—room & board $1200 per sem
Courses: Art Appreciation, Art Education, Art History, Ceramics, Commercial Art, Drawing, Graphic Design, Jewelry, Painting, Photography, Printmaking, Sculpture, Computer Graphics, Metalsmithing
Summer School: Chmn Dept Art, Lee Hageman. Two week short courses varying from summer to summer; cost is hourly rate listed above. Courses—Ceramics, Photography, Watercolor, Jewelry, Painting, Art Education

NEOSHO

CROWDER COLLEGE, Art & Design, 601 La Clede, 64850. Tel 417-451-4700, Ext 306. *Dept Chmn* Janie Lantz. Instrs: FT 1, PT 5
Estab 1964; Pub; D & E; scholarships; enrl D 1000, E 300, maj 20, others 250
Ent Req: HS grad or equivalent
Degrees: AA & AAS 2 yrs
Courses: Art History, Design, Drawing, Graphic Design, Jewelry, Painting, Sculpture, Ceramic Design, Fibers Design
Summer School: Dean of Col, Dr Hansen. Term of 8 wks beginning in June. Courses—Varied academic courses

NEVADA

COTTEY COLLEGE, Art Dept, 1000 W Austin, 64772. Tel 417-667-8181. *Dean* Harold Ross; *Instr* L Bruce Holman, PhD; *Instr* Cameron Crawford, MFA; *Instr* Donna Lynde, MFA. Instrs: FT 3
Estab 1884; pvt, W; D; scholarships; SC 15, LC 4; enrl maj 12-15, total 369
Ent Req: HS grad, AC Board
Degrees: AA 2 yrs
Tuition: $6100 comprehensive fee (includes room & board)
Courses: Art History, Ceramics, Drawing, Graphic Arts, Handicrafts, Jewelry, Painting, Photography, Printmaking, Design, Metals, Weaving

PARKVILLE

PARK COLLEGE, Dept of Art, 8700 River Park Dr, 64152. Tel 816-741-2000, Ext 457. *Chmn* Donna Bachmann
Estab 1875; pvt; D & E; scholarships; SC 13, LC 4; enrl D 50, non-maj 40, maj 20
Ent Req: HS dipl, ACT
Degrees: BA, 4 yrs
Tuition: Res—undergrad $84 per hr; campus res—room & board available
Courses: Advertising Design, Art Education, Art History, Ceramics, Drawing, Graphic Design, History of Art & Archaeology, Painting, Photography, Sculpture, Teacher Training, 3-D Design
Adult Hobby Classes: Tuition $60 per hr
Summer School: Chmn, Donna Bachmann. Tuition $84 per hr for 8 wk term. Courses—Ceramics, Printmaking, varied curriculum

POINT LOOKOUT

COLLEGE OF THE OZARKS, Dept of Art, 65726. Tel 417-334-6411, Ext 253. *Assoc Prof* Anne Allman, PhD; *Assoc Prof* Donald Barr, MA; *Prof* Jayme Burchett, MFA; *Assoc Prof* Jeff Johnston, MFA
Estab 1906, dept estab 1962; pvt; D & E; scholarships; SC 22, LC 4; enrl D 200, E 25, non-maj 180, maj 40
Ent Req: HS dipl, ACT
Degrees: BA & BS 4 yr
Tuition: No fees are charged; each student works 960 hrs in on-campus employment
Courses: †Art Education, †Ceramics, †Drawing, †Painting, Graphic Design, Fibers

SAINT CHARLES

LINDENWOOD COLLEGE, Art Dept, 209 S Kings Hwy, 63301. Tel 314-949-4862. *Chmn Dept* W Dean Eckert. Instrs: FT 3, PT 4
Estab 1827; pvt; D & E; scholarships; SC 24, LC 16; enrl D 200, E 30, maj 40
Ent Req: HS dipl, ent exam
Degrees: BA, BS, BFA 4 yrs, MA
Tuition: Res—undergrad $7600 per yr
Courses: Art Education, Art History, Ceramics, Design, Drawing, Painting, Photography, Printmaking, Teacher Training

SAINT JOSEPH

MISSOURI WESTERN STATE COLLEGE, Art Dept, 4525 Downs Dr, 64507-2294. Tel 816-271-4200, Ext 422. *Chmn Dept* William Eickhorst, EdD; *Prof* Jim Estes, MFA; *Assoc Prof* John Hughes, MFA; *Assoc Prof* Jean Harmon, MFA; *Asst Prof* Martin Grohlinghorst, ABD
Estab 1969; pub; D & E; scholarships; SC 25, LC 8; enrl D 355, E 100, non-maj 120, maj 130
Ent Req: HS dipl, GED, ACT
Degrees: BS(Art Educ), BA & BS(Commercial Art) 4 yrs
Tuition: Res—$465 per sem; nonres—$875 per sem; campus residence available
Courses: Advertising Design, Aesthetics, Art Appreciation, Art Education, Art History, Ceramics, Commercial Art, Design, Drawing, Graphic Arts, Graphic Design, History of Art & Archaeology, Illustration, Painting, Photography, Printmaking, Sculpture, Commercial Art, Teacher Training, Computer Art, Tools & Techniques
Summer School: Chmn, Art Dept, William S Eickhorst. Tuition res—$130 for 5 or more cr hrs, nonres—$240 for 5 or more cr hrs; term of 8 wks beginning June 1. Courses—Art Education, Ceramics, Introduction to Art, Photomedia, Painting

SAINT LOUIS

FONTBONNE COLLEGE, Art Dept, 6800 Wydown Blvd, 63105. Tel 314-889-1431. *Chmn Dept* Rudolph E Torrini, MFA
Estab 1923; pvt; D & E; scholarships; SC 10, LC 2, GC 6; enrl non-maj 10, maj 46, grad 12, others 5
Ent Req: HS dipl, portfolio
Degrees: BA and BFA 4 yrs, MA 1 yr, MFA 2 yrs
Courses: Aesthetics, †Art Education, Art History, †Ceramics, Drawing, Interior Design, Mixed Media, †Painting, Photography, Printmaking, †Sculpture

Adult Hobby Classes: Tuition $180 per cr. Courses—Art History, Ceramics, Drawing, Painting, Photography, Sculpture
Summer School: Dir, C Connor. Tuition $80 per cr hr. Courses—same as for adult education

MARYVILLE UNIVERSITY OF SAINT LOUIS, Art Division, 13550 Conway Rd, 63141-7299. Tel 314-576-9300, Ext 413; FAX 314-542-9085. *Art Division Chmn* Steven Teczar, MFA; *Prof* B Kent Addison, MA; *Prof* Nancy Rice, MFA; *Asst Prof* John Baltrushunas, MFA; *Adjunct Instr* Jeanne Merson; *Adjunct Instr* Michael Lyss; *Adjunct Instr* Geof Wheeler; *Adjunct Instr* Dayne Sislen; *Adjunct Instr* Clay Pursell; *Adjunct Instr* Peggy Carothers; *Adjunct Instr* Mark Weber; *Adjunct Instr* Esley Hamilton; *Adjunct Instr* Elizabeth Metcalfe; *Adjunct Instr* Nancy Bridwell; *Adjunct Instr* Carol A Felberbaum, IES; *Adjunct Instr* Ken Worley; *Adjunct Instr* Frank McGuire; *Adjunct Instr* Carole Lasky, PhD; *Adjunct Instr* Robert Acree, BA; *Adjunct Instr* Beth Baile, MA; *Adjunct Instr* Ken Mohr; *Adjunct Instr* Bob Moskowitz, MFA; *Adjunct Instr* Ron Nuetzel, BFA; *Adjunct Instr* Evann Richards, BFA; *Adjunct Instr* Bettina Braun, MA; *Instr* Les Addison, MA
Estab 1872, dept estab 1961; pvt; D & E; scholarships; SC 74, LC 6; enrl D 140, E 30, non-maj 60, maj 110
Ent Req: HS dipl, ACT or SAT
Degrees: BA, BFA, cert(Interior Design)
Tuition: $8200 per yr, $4100 per sem;, $235 per cr hr; campus res—room & board $3990 per yr
Courses: Advertising Design, †Aesthetics, Architecture, †Art Appreciation, †Art Education, †Art History, †Calligraphy, †Ceramics, †Commercial Art, Conceptual Art, Constructions, †Design, †Drafting, Drawing, Film, †Graphic Arts, †Graphic Design, History of Art & Archaeology, Illustration, †Interior Design, †Mixed Media, †Painting, †Photography, †Printmaking, †Sculpture, †Teacher Training, †Art Studio, †Auto CAD, †Color Theory, †Fibers & Soft Sculpture, Furniture Design, †2-D & 3-D Design, †Handmade Book, †Painting the Figure, †Stone - Carving
Adult Hobby Classes: Enrl & tuition vary. Courses—Art & Architectural History, Art in St Louis, Drawing, Interior Design, Painting, Photography
Children's Classes: Enrl 115; tuition $150 (1 cr) & 100 (no cr) for 10 wk session. Courses—Ceramics, Cartooning, Drawing, Painting, Photography, Printmaking, Watercolor
Summer School: Dir, Dan Ray. Enrl 60; tuition same as regular year. Courses—Photography, Art Appreciation, Art History, Auto CAD, Drawing, Painting

SAINT LOUIS COMMUNITY COLLEGE AT FOREST PARK, Art Dept, 5600 Oakland, 63110-1393. Tel 314-644-9350. *Chmn* Carol Niederlander; *Assoc Prof* Leon Anderson, MFA; *Asst Prof* Evann Richards, BA; *Instr* Joe C Angert, MA; *Instr* Allen Arpadi, BA. Instrs: PT 14
Estab 1962, dept estab 1963. College maintains three campuses; pub; D & E; scholarships; SC 36, LC 6; enrl D 200, E 100, non-maj 75, maj 75
Ent Req: HS dipl
Degrees: AA & AAS 2 yrs
Tuition: College area—$31 per cr hr; out of area—$38.50 per cr hr; nonres—$49.50 per cr hr
Courses: Advertising Design, Art Appreciation, Art Education, †Art History, Ceramics, Commercial Art, Design, Drawing, Film, †Graphic Design, Illustration, Lettering, †Painting, †Photography, Color, Commercial Photography, Computer-Assisted Publishing
Adult Hobby Classes: Courses—Drawing, Painting, Photography, Printmaking, Sculpture, Video
Summer School: Dir, Carol Niederlander. Enrl 100; tuition $31.50 per cr hr. Courses—Same as those above

SAINT LOUIS COMMUNITY COLLEGE AT MERAMEC, Art Dept, 11333 Big Bend Blvd, 63122. Tel 314-966-7632. *Chmn Dept* David Durham, BFA; *Instructor* F Robert Allen, MFA; *Instructor* John Ferguson; *Instructor* Kay Hagan, MA; *Instructor* Ruth Hensler, MFA; *Instructor* Peter Hoell, BFA; *Instructor* John Nagel, BA; *Instructor* Patrick Shuck, MFA; *Instructor* Mary Sprague, MA; *Instructor* Ronald Thomas, MFA; *Instructor* Sam Wayne, MA; *Instructor* Yvette Woods, BFA
Estab 1964; D & E; scholarships; SC 15, LC 2
Ent Req: HS dipl
Degrees: AA 2 yrs
Tuition: Res—$31 per cr hr; no campus res
Courses: Advertising Design, Art History, Ceramics, Commercial Art, Drawing, Illustration, Interior Design, Painting, Photography, Printmaking, Sculpture
Summer School: Chmn Dept, David Durham. Tuition $22.50 per cr hr for term of 8 wks beginning June 11. Courses—Art Appreciation, Ceramics, Drawing, Design, Photography

SAINT LOUIS UNIVERSITY, Fine & Performing Arts Dept, 221 N Grand, 63103. Tel 314-658-3030. *Chmn* Theodore T Wood
Degrees: BA
Tuition: Undergrad $4240 full-time per term, $315 part-time per hr
Courses: Art History, Design, Drawing, Painting, Photography, Sculpture, Approaching the Arts, †Studio Art
Summer School: Courses—Studio Art, Drawings, Painting

UNIVERSITY OF MISSOURI-SAINT LOUIS, Art Dept, 8001 Natural Bridge, 63121. Tel 314-553-5975. *Chmn* Thomas Patton; *Assoc Prof* Ken Anderson, MFA; *Prof* Janet Berlo; *Asst Prof* Ruth Bohan, PhD; *Asst Prof* Yael Evan; *Lectr* Juliana Wuan Burch; *Lectr* Thomas Kochheiser, MA
Estab 1963; pub; D & E; Scholarships; SC 7, LC 20; enrl maj 40
Ent Req: HS dipl
Degrees: BA(Art Hist)
Tuition: Undergrad $60 per cr hr; upper division $66 per cr hr
Courses: Art History, Graphic Design, History of Art & Archaeology, Painting, Photography
Adult Hobby Classes: Courses—Photography
Summer School: Courses—Introduction to Art, Primitive Art

WASHINGTON UNIVERSITY
—**School of Fine Arts**, One Brookings Dr, Campus Box 1031, 63130. Tel 314-935-6500; FAX 314-935-4862. *Dean School* Joe Deal, MFA, *Assoc Dean School* Ronald A Leax, MFA
Estab 1853; pvt; D; scholarships; SC 62, LC 10, GC 31; enrl 390, non-maj 50, maj 300, grad 40
Ent Req: HS dipl, SAT or ACT, portfolio
Degrees: BFA 4 yrs, MFA 2 yrs
Tuition: $16,750 per yr, $8375 per sem, $700 per cr hr; campus res—room & board available
Courses: †Advertising Design, †Ceramics, †Graphic Design, History of Art & Archaeology, †Illustration, †Painting, †Photography, †Printmaking, †Sculpture, †Silversmithing, †Fashion Design, †Glass Blowing
Adult Hobby Classes: Enrl 120; tuition $185 per cr hr. Courses—Calligraphy, Design, Drawing, Fashion, Graphic Communications, Painting, Printmaking, Wood Furniture & Workshops
Summer School: Dir, Libby Reuter. Enrl 80; tuition $185 - $285 per cr for term beginning June 9 - Aug 1. Courses—Computer Graphics, Drawing, Fashion Design, Graphic Design, High School Workshop, Photography. Santa Reparata, Florence, Italy, enrl 32; tuition $855 June 2 - June 25. Courses—On-site Drawing, Photography, Printmaking
—**School of Architecture**, One Brookings Dr, PO Box 1079, 63130. Tel 314-935-6200; FAX 314-935-8520. *Dean School* C Michaelides, MArch
Estab 1910; pvt; D; scholarships; SC 28, LC 58, GC 42; enrl 300, maj 200, grad 100
Degrees: BA(Arch), MArch, MA(UD)
Tuition: $16,750 per yr, $700 per cr hr
Courses: †Architecture, Design, Drawing, Interior Design, Landscape Architecture, Photography
Adult Hobby Classes: Enrl 43; tuition $175 per unit. Certificate degree program, Bachelor of Technology in Architecture
Summer School: Tuition varies. Courses—Advanced Architectural Design, Fundamentals of Design, Structural Principles

SPRINGFIELD

DRURY COLLEGE, Art and Art History Dept, 900 N Benton Ave, 65802. Tel 417-865-8731, Ext 263. *Chmn Dept* Thomas Parker. Instrs: FT 6, PT 9
Estab 1873; den; scholarships; SC 12, LC 5; enrl 2246
Degrees: 4 yrs
Tuition: Res—undergrad $85 per cr hr
Courses: Architecture, Art History, Ceramics, Commercial Art, Photography, Teacher Training, Weaving, Studio Arts
Adult Hobby Classes: Enrl 25-35; tuition $74 per cr hr. Courses—Studio Art & History of Art
Children's Classes: Summer Scape, gifted children. Courses—Architecture, Design, Photography
Summer School: Dir, Sue Rollins. Enrl 292; tuition $69 per cr hr June - Aug for 9 wk term. Courses—Art History, Ceramics, Drawing, Painting, Photography

SOUTHWEST MISSOURI STATE UNIVERSITY, Dept of Art & Design, 901 S National, 65804-0089. Tel 417-836-5110. *Head Dept* Dr James K Hill. Instrs: FT 25, PT 5
Estab 1901; D & E; scholarships; SC 31, LC 10; enrl maj 400, others 2100
Ent Req: HS dipl, ent exam
Degrees: BFA, BS(Educ, Educ Comprehensive) & BA 4 yrs
Tuition: Res—$876; nonres—$1692; campus res—$1315 or $1512 per sem
Courses: Art Education, Art History, Ceramics, Drawing, Graphic Design, Jewelry, Printmaking, Sculpture, Silversmithing, Bronze Casting, Computer Graphics, Fibers, Metals/Jewelry, Watercolor
Adult Hobby Classes: Tuition $68 per cr hr for 1 & 2 wk sessions. Courses—Computer Graphics, Photography, Watercolor
Summer School: Dir, Robert Scott. Enrl 3000; special workshops available during summer session; tuition $68 per cr hr for 5 & 8 wk sessions. Courses—Selected from above curriculum

UNION

EAST CENTRAL COLLEGE, Art Dept, PO Box 529, 63084. Tel 314-583-5195, Ext 225. *Chmn* Larry Pogue, BFA & MS. Instrs: FT 2, PT 1
Estab 1968; pub; D & E; scholarships; SC 8, LC 8; enrl D 370, E 120, maj 40
Ent Req: HS dipl, ent exam
Degrees: AA & AAS 2 yrs
Tuition: In-district—$21 per cr hr; out-of-district—$26 per cr hr; nonres—$38 per cr hr
Courses: Art Appreciation, Art Education, Art History, Design, Drawing, Handicrafts, History of Art & Archaeology, Lettering, Painting, Photography, Printmaking, Sculpture, Teacher Training, Art Appreciation, Business of Art, Figure Drawing
Adult Hobby Classes: Enrl 121; tuition $21-$38 per semester. Courses—Painting
Children's Classes: Tuition $25 for 4 wk summer term. Courses—Art, Drawing, Sculpture, Painting
Summer School: Tuition $21 per cr hr for 8 wk term. Courses—Art Appreciation, Art History

WARRENSBURG

CENTRAL MISSOURI STATE UNIVERSITY, Art Dept, 64093. Tel 816-543-4481. *Chair Dept* Jerry Miller, EdD; *Prof* Richard Luehrman, EdD; *Prof* Richard D Monson, MFA; *Assoc Prof* Margaret Peterson, MFA; *Assoc Prof* John R Haydu, MFA; *Asst Prof* Harold M Reynolds, EdD; *Asst Prof* George Sample, MSEd; *Asst Prof* Andrew Katsourides, MFA; *Asst Prof* Chris Willey, MFA; *Asst Prof* John W Lynch, MFA; *Asst Prof* LeRoy McDermott, PhD
Estab 1871; pub; D & E; scholarships; SC 40, LC 14, GC 10; enrl D 300, maj 300
Ent Req: HS dipl, Missouri School & Col Ability Test, ACT
Degrees: BA, BSE, & BFA 4 yrs, MA 1 yr

Tuition: Res—$210 per quarter; nonres—$435 per quarter; campus res—room & board $582
Courses: †Art Education, Art History, †Commercial Art, Drawing, Graphic Arts, Illustration, †Interior Design, Painting, Teacher Training, Sculpture, Teacher Training, †Studio Art
Summer School: Chair Dept, Jerry L Miller. Term of 8 wks beginning first wk in June. Courses—Ceramics, Drawing, Grad Studio Courses, Painting

WEBSTER GROVES

WEBSTER UNIVERSITY, Art Dept, 470 E Lockwood Blvd, 63119. Tel 314-968-7171. *Chmn* Tom Lang; *Prof* Jack Canepa, MA; *Assoc Prof* Leon Hicks, MFA; *Asst Prof* Carol Hodson; *Asst Prof* Jeffrey Hughes, PhD; *Asst Prof* Bert VanderMark; *Asst Prof* Lynda Rockwood, MFA; *Asst Prof* Jeri Au; *Lectr* Bill Kreplin, MFA; *Artist-in-Residence* Gary Passanise
Estab 1915, dept estab 1946; pvt; D & E; scholarships; SC 60, LC 15; enrl 1100, maj 100
Ent Req: HS dipl, SAT or ACT
Degrees: BA & BFA 4 yrs
Tuition: $6700 per yr; campus res available
Courses: †Art Education, †Art History, †Ceramics, Collages, Conceptual Art, †Drawing, Film, †Graphic Design, †Painting, †Photography, †Printmaking, †Sculpture, †Teacher Training, †Papermaking
Adult Hobby Classes: Tuition $175 per cr hr for 16 wk sem. Courses—Art, Photography, Watercolor
Summer School: Assoc Dean Fine Arts, Peter Sargent. Tuition $175 per cr hr for term of 6 or 8 wks beginning June. Courses—Introductory Photography, Sculpture Workshop: Bronze

MONTANA

BILLINGS

EASTERN MONTANA COLLEGE, Art Dept, 1500 N 30th St, 59101-0298. Tel 406-657-2324. *Head* Peter W Warren. Instrs: FT 7, PT 11
Estab 1927; pub
Ent Req: HS dipl
Degrees: AA, BS(Educ), BSEd(Art), BA(Lib Arts)
Tuition: Res—$40.50 - $133.50 per cr hr; nonres—$118.50 - $211.50 per cr hr
Courses: Art Appreciation, Art Education, Art History, Ceramics, Design, Drawing, Painting, Photography, Printmaking, Sculpture, Teacher Training, Crafts, Design, Fibers, Metalwork
Summer School: Tuition res $40.50 - $133.50 per cr, nonres $88.50 - $181.50 per cr for two 6 wk sessions from May 18 - June 11 & June 25 - July 31. Courses—Art Appreciation, Ceramics, Drawing, Painting, Sculpture, Ceramics

ROCKY MOUNTAIN COLLEGE, Art Dept, 1511 Poly Dr, 59102. Tel 406-657-1094. *Chmn Dept* Mark Moak, MA; *Asst Prof* James Baken
Estab 1878, dept estab 1957; pvt; D; scholarships; SC 12, LC 5; enrl 112, non-maj 40, maj 30, others 5
Ent Req: HS dipl, ACT
Degrees: BA & BS 4 yrs
Tuition: $7975 per yr, $3987.50 per sem, $332 per sem hr; campus res—room & board $1664 per yr for double
Courses: Art Education, Art History, Ceramics, Drawing, Graphic Design, Painting, Photography, Sculpture, Teacher Training
Adult Hobby Classes: Enrl 100; tuition $20 for 5 wks. Courses—Crafts, Painting, Picture Framing

BOZEMAN

MONTANA STATE UNIVERSITY
—**School of Art**, Haynes Hall, 59717. Tel 406-994-4501. *Dir Art* Richard Helzer. Instrs: 14
Estab 1893; pub; D; scholarships; SC 38, LC 19, GC 13; enrl maj 250, grad 15
Ent Req: HS dipl 2.5 GPA or ACT score of 20
Degrees: BA 4 yrs, MA/MFA 2 yrs
Tuition: Res—$920 per sem; nonres—$2782 per sem
Courses: †Art Education, Art History, †Ceramics, †Drawing, †Graphic Design, †Jewelry, †Painting, †Printmaking, †Sculpture, †Metalsmithing
Summer School: Dir, Richard Helzer. Enrl 65; tuition res—$760, nonres—$1178 for 12 wk term. Courses—Art History, Ceramics, Drawing, Graphic Design, Metals, Painting, Printmaking, Sculpture, Special Workshops
—**School of Architecture**, Cheever Hall, Room 160, 59717. Tel 406-994-4255. *Dir Architecture* Thomas R Wood. Instrs: FT 13, PT 1
Pub; scholarships; LabC 31, LC 39; enrl maj 400
Degrees: BArchit 5 yrs, BA (Interior Design) 4 yrs
Tuition: Res—$1500 per sem; nonres—$3015 per sem; campus res available
Courses: Architecture, Interior Design
Summer School: Dir, Thomas R Wood. Enrl 35; tuition $358 for 4 wks, $381.75 for 8 wks

DILLON

WESTERN MONTANA COLLEGE, Art Dept, 710 S Atlantic, 59725. Tel 406-683-7342; FAX 406-683-7493. *Chmn Dept* Barney Brienza. Instrs: FT 3
Estab 1897; pub; D & E; scholarships; SC 15, LC 6, GC 21
Ent Req: HS dipl
Degrees: BS 4 yrs, MA
Courses: Art Education, Art History, Ceramics, Commercial Art, Drawing, Graphic

Arts, Handicrafts, Jewelry, Lettering, Painting, Blacksmithing, Design, Glass Blowing, Stained Glass, Weaving
Adult Hobby Classes: Enrl 100; fees & duration vary. Courses—Blacksmithing, Jewelry, Oil Painting, Stained Glass, Watercolor
Summer School: Dir, Sue Jones. Enrl 350; 15 wk term. Courses—Art Methods, Blacksmithing, Ceramics, Drawing, Glassblowing, Graphics, Oil Painting, Watercolor

GREAT FALLS

COLLEGE OF GREAT FALLS, Humanities Div, 1301 20th St S, 59405. Tel 406-761-8210. *Div Chmn & Prof* William J Furdell. Instrs: FT 1, PT 2
Estab 1933; den; D & E; SC, Lab C, LC; enrl approx 1250
Degrees: 4 yrs
Tuition: $3900 per yr
Courses: Art Education, Ceramics, Drawing, Design
Summer School: Dir, Richard Gretch; 6 wks

HAVRE

MONTANA UNIVERSITY SYSTEM-NORTHERN MONTANA COLLEGE, Humanities & Social Sciences, PO Box 7751, 59501. Tel 406-265-3751. *Art Dept Chmn* Steve Sylvester
Estab 1929; pub; D & E; scholarships; SC 15, LC 5, GC 9; enrl D 425, grad 7
Ent Req: HS dipl
Degrees: AA 2 yrs, BS(Educ) and BA 4 yrs, MSc(Educ)
Tuition: Res—$399 per quarter; nonres—$915 per quarter
Courses: Art Education, Ceramics, Commercial Art, Drafting, Drawing, Graphic Arts, Painting, Sculpture
Adult Hobby Classes: Enrl 60. Courses—Classroom and Recreational Art, Watercolor Workshop
Summer School: Dir, Dr Gus Korb. Enrl 1390; two 5 wk sessions. Courses—Art Education, Art Methods K-12, Art Therapy

MILES CITY

MILES COMMUNITY COLLEGE, Dept of Fine Arts and Humanities, 2715 Dickinson St, 59301. Tel 406-232-3031. *Head Dept* Sydney R Sonneborn; *Instr* Fred McKee, MFA
Estab 1937, dept estab 1967; pub; D & E; scholarships; SC 17, LC 1; enrl D 36, E 23, non-maj 55, maj 4
Ent Req: HS dipl, ACT
Degrees: AA 2 yrs, cert
Tuition: Res—$531 per yr; nonres—$981 per yr; campus res available
Courses: Advertising Design, Art Appreciation, Ceramics, Design, Drawing, Graphic Design, Jewelry, Painting, Photography, Teacher Training
Adult Hobby Classes: Enrl 39; tuition $33 per cr hr. Courses—Crafts, Jewelry Making, Painting, Photography, Pottery

MISSOULA

UNIVERSITY OF MONTANA, Dept of Art, 59812. Tel 406-243-4181; FAX 406-243-2327. *Interim Chmn* Thomas Rippon, MFA; *Prof* Don Bunse, MFA; *Prof* James Todd, MFA; *Assoc Prof* Stephen Connell, MA; *Assoc Prof* Marilyn Bruya, MFA; *Assoc Prof* Beth Lo, MFA; *Assoc Prof* David James, MFA; *Asst Prof* Barbara Tilton; *Asst Prof* Norman Nilsen
Pub; D & E; scholarships; SC 28, LC 20, GC 10; enrl D 850, E 30
Ent Req: HS dipl
Degrees: BA & BFA 4 yrs, MA & MFA
Tuition: Res—$483 per quarter (12-18 cr hrs); nonres—$1173 per quarter (12-18 cr hrs)
Courses: Art Education, Art History, †Ceramics, †Drawing, †Painting, Photography, †Printmaking, †Sculpture, Art Criticism and Social History of Art
Summer School: Tuition same as above for 2 - 4 wk term. Courses—Art Education, Art History, Ceramics, Drawing, Painting, Photography, Sculpture

NEBRASKA

BELLEVUE

BELLEVUE COLLEGE, Art Dept, Galvin Rd at Harvell Dr, 68005. Tel 402-291-8100. *Chmn* Dr Joyce Wilson, PhD
Scholarships offered
Degrees: BA, BFA, BTS(Commercial Art)
Tuition: $95 per cr hr
Courses: Advertising Design, Aesthetics, Art History, Ceramics, Commercial Art, Design, Drawing, History of Art & Archaeology, Painting, Photography, Printmaking, Sculpture, Art Management, Life Drawing, Papermaking

BLAIR

DANA COLLEGE, Art Dept, 2848 College Dr, 68008. Tel 402-426-7206. *Dept Head* Jim Olsen; *Prof* Milton Heinrich
Scholarships offered
Degrees: BA, BS
Tuition: $3290 per sem
Courses: Advertising Design, Art Appreciation, Art Education, Art History, Ceramics, Commercial Art, Drawing, Jewelry, Painting, Photography, Printmaking, Sculpture, Teacher Training, Theatre Arts

CHADRON

CHADRON STATE COLLEGE, Dept of Art, Speech & Theatre, Tenth & Main Sts, 69337. Tel 308-432-6317; FAX 308-432-3561. *Prof* Noel Gray; *Assoc Prof* Richard Bird, MFA; *Asst Prof* John Dillon, MA
Estab 1911, dept estab 1935; pub; D & E; scholarships; SC 20, LC 6, GC 2; enrl 4000, D 3000, off-campus 1000, non-maj 200, maj 35
Ent Req: HS dipl
Degrees: BSE & BA 4 yrs
Tuition: Res—undergrad $45.50 per hr, grad $57 per hr; nonres—undergrad $82 per hr, grad $102.50 per hr; campus res—room & board $1233
Courses: Art Education, Art History, Ceramics, Drawing, Graphic Arts, Jewelry, Painting, Photography, Sculpture, †Teacher Training, Weaving
Adult Hobby Classes: Enrl 30. Tuition varies. Courses vary
Summer School: Dir, Donald Green, PhD. Enrl 30; tuition same as above. Courses—usually 2 - 4 courses on semi-rotation basis

COLUMBUS

CENTRAL COMMUNITY COLLEGE - PLATTE CAMPUS, Business & Arts Cluster, PO Box 1027, 68602-1027. Tel 402-564-7132. *Head Dept* Ellen Lake; *Instr* Richard Abraham, MA
Estab 1969, dept estab 1971; pub; D & E; scholarships; SC 8, LC 1; enrl D 100, E 20, non-maj 77, maj 43
Ent Req: HS dipl
Degrees: AA 2 yrs
Tuition: Res—$36 per cr hr; nonres—$42 per cr hr; campus res
Courses: Art History, Ceramics, Commercial Art, Design, Drafting, Drawing, Graphic Arts, Handicrafts, Interior Design, Mixed Media, Photography, Stage Design, Textile Design, Theatre Arts, Oil, Acrylic & Watercolor Painting
Summer School: Dir, Richard D Abraham. Enrl 40; tuition $36 per hr for term of 7 wks beginning June. Courses—Drawing, Painting

CRETE

DOANE COLLEGE, Dept of Art, 1014 Boswell, 68333. Tel 402-826-2161, Ext 273. *Head Dept* Richard Terrell
Estab 1872, dept estab 1958; pvt; D; scholarships; SC 6, LC 5; enrl 150, non-maj 140, maj 10
Ent Req: HS dipl
Degrees: BA 4 yrs
Tuition: $10,295 per yr, includes room & board
Courses: Art Education, Art History, Ceramics, Drawing, Film, Graphic Design, Painting, Printmaking, Sculpture, Stage Design

HASTINGS

HASTINGS COLLEGE, Art Dept, Seventh & Turner, 68902-0269. Tel 402-463-2402; FAX 402-463-3002. *Chmn Dept* Gilbert L Neal; *Dir Pub Relations* Joyce Ore. Instrs: FT 3, PT 2
Estab 1925; den; scholarships; SC 16, LC 5; enrl maj 50, others 350
Ent Req: HS grad
Degrees: BA 4 yrs
Tuition: $3585 per sem; campus res—room & board $1380 per sem
Courses: Art Education, Art History, Ceramics, Design, Drawing, Painting, Printmaking, Sculpture, Color, Glass Blowing
Summer School: Dean, Dwayne Strasheim. Enrl 25; tuition $235 per cr hr for 6 weeks beginning June

KEARNEY

UNIVERSITY OF NEBRASKA, KEARNEY (Formerly Kearney State College), Dept of Art & Art History, 68849. Tel 308-234-8353. *Chmn Dept* Jack Karraker, MFA; *Prof* Keith Lowry, MFA; *Prof* Larry D Peterson, EdD; *Prof* Raymond W Schultze, MFA; *Prof* Gary E Zaruba, EdD; *Prof* John N Dinsmore, EdD; *Prof* Bill Campton, PhD; *Assoc Prof* Jake Jacobson; *Assoc Prof* Al Kraning, MFA; *Asst Prof* James M May, MA; *Asst Prof* Kent Smith, MFA; *Asst Prof* Tom Dennis; *Asst Prof* John McKirahan. Instrs: FT 15, PT 12
Estab 1905; pub; D & E; scholarships; SC 20, LC 12, GC 18; enrl D 870, E 22, non-maj 1400, maj 200, grad 25
Ent Req: HS dipl, SAT or ACT recommended
Degrees: Degrees BFA, BA, BA(Art History),BA(Educ), BFA(Educ) 4 yrs, MA(Educ-Art)
Tuition: Res—$30.50 per cr hr; nonres—$51 per cr hr; campus res—$873 per sem
Courses: Aesthetics, Art Education, Art History, Ceramics, Commercial Art, †Drawing, †Painting, Photography, †Printmaking, †Sculpture, †Teacher Training, †Textile Design, Glass blowing
Adult Hobby Classes: Enrl 3000; tuition $40 per hr for 2 sem. Courses—College Art Courses undergrad & grad
Summer School: Dir, Chmn Jack Karraker. Enrl 496, tuition $40 per hr. Courses—undergrad & grad

LINCOLN

NEBRASKA WESLEYAN UNIVERSITY, Art Dept, 5000 St Paul, 68504. Tel 402-465-2273. *Head Dept* Dr Clifford Fall; *Vis Prof* Lisa Lockman; *Vis Prof* Susan Horn; *Vis Prof* P J Peters; *Vis Prof* Brad Krieger; *Vis Prof* Willy Sapp
Estab 1888, dept estab 1890; pvt; D & E; scholarships; SC 22, LC 4; enrl non-maj 300, maj 50
Ent Req: HS dipl, ent exam
Degrees: AA 2 yrs, BA & BS 4 yrs
Tuition: $2500 per sem
Courses: Advertising Design, Art Education, Art History, Ceramics, Commercial

Art, Drawing, Jewelry, Museum Staff Training, Painting, Photography, Printmaking, Sculpture, Silversmithing, Design
Adult Hobby Classes: Enrl 30; tuition $95 per sem hr. Degree Program
Children's Classes: Enrl 20; tuition $25 per 4 wks. Courses—Ceramics, Sculpture, Drawing, Painting
Summer School: Head, John Clabaugh. Enrl 30; tuition $95 per sem hr per 8 wks. Courses—Painting, Paste-up, Special Projects

UNIVERSITY OF NEBRASKA-LINCOLN, Dept of Art & Art History, 207 Nelle Cochrane Woods Hall, 68588. Tel 402-472-2631. *Chmn Dept* Joseph M Ruffo, MFA; *Chmn Graduate Committee* David Routen. Instrs: FT 20, PT 15
Estab 1869, dept 1912; pub; D & E; scholarships; SC 71, LC 27, GC 45; enrl D 1950, E 175, non-maj 600, maj 400, grad 25
Ent Req: HS dipl
Degrees: BA, BFA and BFA(Educ) 4 yrs, MFA 2-3 yrs
Tuition: Res—undergrad $53.50 per cr hr, grad $67.75; nonres—$145.50 per cr hr
Courses: Art Education, Art History, Ceramics, Commercial Art, Drawing, Film, Graphic Design, Illustration, Painting, Photography, Printmaking, Sculpture, Teacher Training, Weaving, Book Art, Papermaking, †2-D & 3-D Design
Summer School: Dir Herbert Smail. Enrl 250; two 5 wk sessions beginning June and Aug. Courses—Art History, Ceramics, Drawing, Painting, Photography, Printmaking, Special Problems & Topics

NORFOLK

NORTHEAST COMMUNITY COLLEGE, Dept of Liberal Arts, 801 E Benjamin Ave, PO Box 469, 68702-0469. Tel 402-371-2020, Ext 417. *Chmn Dept* Larry Godel; *Instr* Julie Noyes, MA; *Instr* Harry Lindner, MA
Estab 1928; pub; D & E; scholarships; SC 5, LC 5; enrl D 150, E 50, non-maj 100, maj 50
Ent Req: HS dipl
Degrees: AA 2 yrs
Tuition: Res—$442 per sem, $26 per cr hr; non-res—30.50 per cr hr; campus res—room & board $1800 per yr
Courses: Art Education, Art History, Drawing, Graphic Design, Painting, Photography
Adult Hobby Classes: Oil Painting
Summer School: Chmn Dept, Patrick Keating. Tuition same as regular yr. Courses—Photography

OMAHA

COLLEGE OF SAINT MARY, Art Dept, 1901 S 72nd St, 68124. Tel 402-399-2400. *Chmn Dept* Tom Schlosser
Estab 1923; pvt, W; D & E; scholarships; SC 11, LC 5; enrl D 620, maj 18, special 2
Ent Req: HS dipl
Degrees: BA and BS 4 yrs
Tuition: $200 per cr hr
Courses: Art History, Ceramics, Painting, Photography, Sculpture, Teacher Training, Computer Graphics, Design, Women in Art
Adult Hobby Classes: Enrl 587; tuition $133 per cr hr. Evening & weekend college offer full range of general education classes
Summer School: Dir, Dr Vernon Lestrud. Enrl 572; tuition $133 per cr hr. Full range of studio & history general education classes

CREIGHTON UNIVERSITY, Fine and Performing Arts Dept, 2500 California St, 68178. Tel 402-280-2509. *Chmn Dept* Jerome Horning; *Asst Prof* Michael Flecky, MFA; *Instr* Roger Aikin, PhD; *Instr* Alan Klem, MFA; *Instr* Lynn Banka; *Instr* Tracy Dunn; *Instr* Valerie Roche, ARAD; *Instr* John Thein, MFA; *Instr* Gail Dunning; *Instr* Carole Bean, B Mus Ed; *Instr* Bob Bosco, MFA; *Instr* Nancy Samogis; *Instr* Bill Hutson; *Instr* Elaine Majors; *Instr* Bill Vandest; *Instr* Kathy Vouk; *Artist-in-Res* Mary Beth Fogarty, MFA; *Artist-in-Res* Littleton Alston
Estab 1878, dept estab 1966; den; D & E; scholarships; SC 87, LC 16; enrl 888, non-maj 850, maj 38, cert prog 24
Ent Req: HS dipl, regular col admis exam
Degrees: BA and BFA 4 yrs
Tuition: $600 average per yr; campus res available
Courses: Advertising Design, Art Appreciation, Art Education, Art History, Ceramics, Drawing, History of Art & Archaeology, Painting, Photography, Printmaking, Sculpture, Teacher Training, †Theatre Arts, Color Theory, Design, Intaglio, Lithography, Studio Fundamentals, 3-D Design
Adult Hobby Classes: Life Drawing, Photography, Ceramics, Art History, Advertising Design, Painting

UNIVERSAL TECHNICAL INSTITUTE, Commercial Art Division, 902 Capitol Ave, 68102. Tel 402-345-2422.
Scholarships
Degrees: Dipl offered
Courses: Commercial Art, Computer Graphics
Adult Hobby Classes: Enrl 60; tuition $7950. Courses—Commercial Art

UNIVERSITY OF NEBRASKA AT OMAHA, Dept of Art, 60th & Dodge Sts, 68182. Tel 402-554-2420. *Chmn Dept* Thomas Majeski; *Prof Emeritus* Dr J V Blackwell; *Prof* Sidney Buchanan, MA; *Prof* Peter Hill, MFA; *Prof* Frances T Keut, MA; *Assoc Prof* Henry Serenco, MFA; *Assoc Prof* Gary Day, MFA; *Assoc Prof* Dr Martin Rosenberg; *Assoc Prof* James Czarnecki; *Asst Prof* Bonnie O'Connell
Estab 1908, dept estab 1910; pub; D & E; scholarships; SC 32, LC 22, GC 10; enrl D 550, E 100
Ent Req: HS dipl
Degrees: BA & BFA 4 yrs
Tuition: Res—undergrad $57.50 per cr hr, grad $64.50 per cr hr; nonres—undergrad $140.75 per cr hr, grad $156.75 per cr hr; no campus res
Courses: †Art Education, †Art History, †Ceramics, †Drawing, †Painting, †Printmaking, †Sculpture
Summer School: Chmn Dept, Thomas Majeski. Tuition same as above for term of 5 wks. Courses vary

PERU

PERU STATE COLLEGE, Art Dept, PO Box 106, 68421. Tel 402-872-2271. *Prof* Leland Sherwood; *Asst Prof* Ken Anderson
Scholarships offered
Degrees: BA, BAEd, BS, MA
Tuition: Res—$375 per sem; nonres—$630 per sem
Courses: Art Appreciation, Art Education, Art History, Ceramics, Design, Drawing, Lettering, Painting, Photography, Printmaking, Sculpture, Stage Design, Figure Drawing, Independent Art Study, Watercolor

SCOTTSBLUFF

WESTERN NEBRASKA COMMUNITY COLLEGE (Formerly Nebraska Western College), Division of Language and Arts, 1601 E 27th St, 69361. Tel 308-635-3606. *Chairperson Div Language & Arts* Paul Jacobson; *Instr* Ziya Sever, MA
Estab 1926; pub; D & E; scholarships; SC 8, LC 3; enrl D 60, E 150, non-maj 50, maj 10
Ent Req: HS dipl
Degrees: AA & AS 2 yrs
Tuition: Res—$35.50 per cr hr; nonres—$36.50 per cr hr; campus res available
Courses: Art Education, Art History, Drawing, Painting, Photography, Theatre Arts, Music Education, History of Film
Adult Hobby Classes: Enrl 150; tui $15 per course. Courses—Carving, Drawing, Macrame, Pottery, Sculpture, Stained Glass, Watercolor & Oil Painting, Weaving

SEWARD

CONCORDIA COLLEGE, Art Dept, 800 N Columbia, 68434. Tel 402-643-3651. *Head Dept* William R Wolfram, MFA; *Prof* Donald Dynneson, MFA; *Prof* Reinhold P Marxhausen, MFA; *Prof* Richard Wiegmann, MFA; *Prof* Lynn Soloway, MFA
Estab 1894; den; D & E; scholarships; SC 8, LC 4; enrl non-maj 30, maj 40
Ent Req: HS dipl
Degrees: BS, BA 4 yr
Tuition: $150 per cr hr; campus res available
Courses: Art Education, Art History, Ceramics, Drawing, Handicrafts, History of Art & Archaeology, Painting, Photography, Printmaking, Sculpture, Teacher Training, Commercial Art
Summer School: Tuition $90 per cr hr for term of 2 1/2 wks beginning June 6

WAYNE

WAYNE STATE COLLEGE, Art Dept, 68787. Tel 402-375-7359. *Div Chmn* Dr Jay O'Leary; *Prof* Ray Replogle; *Prof* Pearl Hansen; *Assoc Prof* Wayne Anderson; *Assoc Prof* Marlene Mueller; *Assoc Prof* Vic Reynolds
Estab 1910; pub; scholarships; SC 21, LC 8; enrl maj 65, others 700, total 4000
Ent Req: HS grad
Degrees: BA, BFA, MA & MS
Tuition: Res—$33 per cr hr; nonres—$54 per cr hr
Courses: Art History, Commercial Art, Drafting, Drawing, Graphic Arts, Handicrafts, Jewelry, Painting, Sculpture, †Teacher Training, Design
Summer School: Three sessions

YORK

YORK COLLEGE, Art Dept, Ninth & Kiplinger St, PO Box 442, 68467. Tel 402-362-4441, Ext 218; WATS 800-228-4342. *Asst Prof* Paul M Shields
Sch estab 1956, dept estab 1962; pvt; D; scholarships; SC 6, LC 1; enrl D 26, non-maj 20, maj 10
Ent Req: HS dipl, ACT
Degrees: AA 2 yrs
Tuition: Res—undergrad $1950 per sem
Courses: Art Appreciation, Art History, Drawing, Painting, Commercial Design, 2-D & 3-D Design

NEVADA

INCLINE VILLAGE

SIERRA NEVADA COLLEGE, Art Dept, 800 College Dr (Mailing add: PO Box 4269, 89450). Tel 702-831-1314. *Chmn* Anne Shipley, MA; *Dir, Gallery* Julie LaCroix, MFA; *Dir, Summer Art Prog* Carol Sphar, BS
Estab 1969; pvt; D & E; scholarships; SC 75, LC 8; enrl D 260, E 40, maj 26
Ent Req: HS dipl, 2.5 grade point avg
Degrees: BA & BFA 4 yr
Tuition: res—undergrad $250 per sem, $70 per cr hr; nonres—undergrad $250 per sem, $70 per cr hr; campus res—room & board $2000 per yr
Courses: Art Appreciation, Art Education, Art History, †Ceramics, Design, †Drawing, Goldsmithing, Graphic Arts, Jewelry, Mixed Media, †Painting, Photography, Printmaking, Sculpture, Silversmithing, Teacher Training
Adult Hobby Classes: Enrl 80; tuition $60 per cr. Courses—Calligraphy, watercolor
Children's Classes: Enrl 60. Courses—Ceramics, painting
Summer School: Dir, Carol Sphar, PhD. Enrl 220; tuition $250 per cr, $60 per unit non credit. Courses—Studio Arts

LAS VEGAS

UNIVERSITY OF NEVADA, LAS VEGAS, Dept of Art, 4505 S Maryland Parkway, 89154-5002. Tel 702-895-3237, 895-3112. *Chmn Dept* Robert Tracy; *Assoc Prof* Lee T Sido; *Asst Prof* Cathie Kelly; *Instr* Mary Bonjorni; *Instr* Thomas J Holder; *Instr* Ed Inks; *Instr* Bill Leaf; *Instr* Jim Pink; *Instr* Pasha Rafat
Estab 1955; pub; D & E; scholarships; SC 32, LC 18; enrl all courses 551, maj 95
Ent Req: HS dipl, ACT
Degrees: BA and BFA 4 yrs, MFA
Tuition: Res—$46 per cr hr; nonres—$60 per cr hr; campus res—room & board $1000-$1200 per sem
Courses: Art History, Ceramics, Conceptual Art, Drawing, Film, Intermedia, Painting, Photography, Printmaking, Sculpture
Adult Hobby Classes: Courses—Drawing, Fiber, Painting, Photography
Summer School: Dir, Thomas Holder. Enrl varies; tuition $41 per cr hr for 5 wk session. Courses—Ceramics, Drawing, Fiber, Painting, Printmaking

RENO

UNIVERSITY OF NEVADA, RENO, Art Dept, 89557-0007. Tel 702-784-6682. *Chmn Dept* Ed W Martinez. Instrs: FT 10
Estab 1940; pub; scholarship; SC 20, LC 6, GC 5; enrl maj 120, others 800
Ent Req: HS grad and 16 units
Degrees: BA 4 yr
Courses: †Art Education, †Art History, †Ceramics, †Drawing, Graphic Design, †Painting, †Photography, †Printmaking, †Sculpture
Adult Hobby Classes: Evening division in all areas
Summer School: Courses in all studio areas

NEW HAMPSHIRE

DURHAM

UNIVERSITY OF NEW HAMPSHIRE, Dept of the Arts, Paul Creative Arts Center, 03824. Tel 603-862-2190. *Chmn* Dan Valenza; *Prof* Sigmund Abeles, MFA; *Prof* Melvin Zabarsky, MFA; *Prof* Michael McConnell; *Assoc Prof* Margot Clark, PhD; *Assoc Prof* David Smith, PhD; *Assoc Prof* Maryse Searls-McConnel, MFA; *Assoc Prof* Mara Witzling, PhD; *Prof* Carol Aronson, MFA; *Asst Prof* Chris Enos, MFA; *Asst Prof* Craig Hood, MFA; *Asst Prof* Scott Schnepf, MFA; *Asst Prof* Jennifer Moses; *Asst Prof* Grant Drumheller
Estab 1928, dept estab 1941; pub; D & E; scholarships; SC 60, LC 20; enrl non-maj 1000, maj 175, grad 5, others 60
Ent Req: HS dipl, portfolio
Degrees: BA, BFA and BA(Art History) 4 yrs, MAT 5 yrs
Tuition: Campus res available
Courses: Architecture, Art Education, Art History, Ceramics, Drawing, Painting, Photography, Printmaking, Sculpture
Summer School: Dir, Edward J Durnall. Courses—varied

HANOVER

DARTMOUTH COLLEGE, Dept of Art History, 03755-3570. Tel 603-646-2306. *Chmn* Joy Kenseth. Instrs: FT 7
Estab 1906; pvt; SC 16, LC 26; enrl in col 4000, maj 46
Degrees: AB 4 yr
Tuition: $5743 per term; operating 4 terms on yr-round basis
Courses: Art History, 3-D Design

HENNIKER

NEW ENGLAND COLLEGE, Art & Art History, 03242. Tel 603-428-2211; FAX 603-428-7230. *Assoc Prof* David F MacEachran, MFA; *Prof* Farid A Haddad, MFA; *Prof* Doris A Birmingham; *Assoc Prof* Marguerite Walsh, MFA; *Lectr* Virginia Reynolds; *Lectr* Peter Sabin; *Lectr* Emile Birch
Also has campuses in Arundel, West Sussex England; scholarships
Degrees: BA
Courses: Aesthetics, †Art History, Ceramics, Design, Drawing, Graphic Arts, Graphic Design, Mixed Media, †Painting, †Photography, Printmaking, Sculpture, Stage Design, Theatre Arts, Video
Summer School: Prof, Farid A Haddad. Enrl 10 -14; 5 - 6 wk prog in Arundel, West Sussex, England. Courses—Drawing & Painting

MANCHESTER

MANCHESTER INSTITUTE OF ARTS AND SCIENCES, 148 Concord St, 03104. Tel 603-623-0313. *Exec Dir* Angelo Randazzo
Estab 1898; pvt; credit and adult educ courses; SC 16; enrl 1000
Ent Req: None
Courses: Calligraphy, Ceramics, Drawing, Graphic Design, Jewelry, Painting, Photography, Silversmithing, Stained Glass, Weaving
Adult Hobby Classes: Enrl 400; tui $80-$240, 12-15 wks; Courses—Same as in Fall & Spring
Summer School: Dir, Angelo Randazzo. Enrl 260; tui $40-$110, May-June. Courses—Same as in Fall & Spring

NOTRE DAME COLLEGE, Art Dept, 2321 Elm St, 03104. Tel 603-669-4298. *Chmn* Sr Blanche Lamarre, MFA; *Asst Prof* Frank Oehlschlaeger, MA; *Assoc Prof* Jean Landry; *Asst Prof* Harry Umen, MFA; *Lectr* Lisa Vaal; *Lectr* William Canter; *Lectr* Lisa Cyr; *Lectr* Caire Mowbray; *Lectr* Al Jaeger; *Lectr* Ruthanne Harrington,

MEd; *Lectr* Richard Carlson. Instrs: 2
Estab 1950, dept estab 1965; pvt; D & E; scholarship; SC 20, LC 6; enrl non-maj 15, maj 125
Ent Req: HS dipl
Degrees: BA(Fine Arts), BA(Commercial Art & Art Educ) 4 yr
Tuition: Undergrad $7470; campus res—room & board $4290
Courses: Advertising Design, Architecture, Art Education, Ceramics, Commercial Art, Drawing, Graphic Design, Illustration, Painting, Photography, Printmaking, Sculpture, Teacher Training, Visual Arts, Women in Art, Primitive Art, History of Modern Art, American Art, 19th Century Art, Western Art and Culture, Basic Design
Adult Hobby Classes: Enrl 110; tuition $109 per cr
Summer School: Dir, Janet Clark. Tuition $109 per cr. Courses—Art History, Ceramics, Computer Graphics, Drawing, Sculpture

SAINT ANSELM COLLEGE, Dept of Fine Arts, 03102-1310. Tel 603-641-7370. *Chmn* Katherine Hoffman. Instrs: FT 3
Estab 1889; pvt; D & E; SC 2, LC 9; enrl 1500
Ent Req: HS dipl, relative standing, SAT, interview
Degrees: BA 4 yr
Tuition: $2600 annual tuition
Courses: Aesthetics, Architecture, Art History, Design, Drawing, Graphic Arts, History of Art & Archaeology, Painting, Photography, Printmaking, Sculpture, Teacher Training, Studio Art
Summer School: Courses—Art, Art History, History of American Art Seminar, Still Photography

NASHUA

NASHUA CENTER FOR ARTS, 14 Court St, 03060. Tel 603-883-1506. *Dir* Steven Jones. Instrs: PT 25-30
Estab 1958; pub; D & E; SC, LC
Ent Req: None
Degrees: None, nonaccredited
Courses: Ceramics, Drawing, Painting, Photography, Sculpture, Theatre Arts
Adult Hobby Classes: Tuition varied. Courses—all of the above
Children's Classes: Tuition varied. Courses—Drawing, Jewelry, Painting, Pottery, Preschool Art, Puppet Making, Sculpture
Summer School: Tuition varied; 5 wk terms from June to July

RIVIER COLLEGE, Art Dept, S Main St, 03060. Tel 603-888-1311, Ext 276. *Co-Chmn* Sr Marie Couture, MA; *Co-Chmn* Sr Theresa Couture, MFA
Estab 1933, dept estab 1940; pvt; D & E; scholarships; SC 100, LC 25; enrl D 50, E 40, non-maj 20, maj 70
Ent Req: HS dipl, SAT, certain HS equivalencies, preliminary evidence of artistic ability, slide portfolio
Degrees: AA 2 yrs, BA, and BFA 4 yrs
Tuition: $3990 per sem, $266 per cr; campus res—available
Courses: Aesthetics, †Art Education, Art History, Calligraphy, Ceramics, Conceptual Art, Constructions, Display, Drawing, Film, †Graphic Design, Illustration, Jewelry, Lettering, Mixed Media, †Painting, Photography, Printmaking, Sculpture, Teacher Training, Textile Design, Art Therapy, Computer Graphics, Design History, Design Internship, Design Portfolio, Film Graphics, Loom Weaving, Stitchery
Adult Hobby Classes: Enrl 60; tuition $132 per cr for 15 wk term. Courses—variety of fine arts & design studio courses
Children's Classes: Enrl 24; tuition $200 for 6 wk term. Courses—Pre-college summer art program
Summer School: Dir, Rose Arthur, PhD. Tuition $132 per cr for 6 wks. Courses—Master Workshops in Basic Design, Drawing, Etching, Graphic Design, Painting, Sculpture

NEW LONDON

COLBY-SAWYER COLLEGE, Dept of Fine & Performing Arts, 03257. Tel 603-526-2010, Ext 500. *Prof* Loretta Barnett, MFA; *Prof* Jon Keenan, MFA; *Assoc Prof* John Bott, MFA; *Assoc Prof* Martha Andrea, MFA; *Adj Asst Prof* Jerry Bliss, MFA. Instrs: FT 5
Estab 1837; pvt; W; D; scholarships; SC 10, LC 25; enrl 500
Degrees: BA, BFA(Art & Graphic Design) & BS (Arts Management) 4 yrs
Tuition: Res—undergrad $13,900 per yr, $4900 per sem; nonres—undergrad $9980 per yr
Courses: Advertising Design, Aesthetics, Art Appreciation, Art History, †Ceramics, Painting, Design, Drawing, Graphic Arts, Graphic Design, Illustration, Museum Staff Training, Painting, †Photography, †Printmaking, †Sculpture, Stage Design, Theatre Arts, Acting, American Art, Contemporary Art since 1945, Creative Expression, Dance, European Trips to France & Italy, Life Drawing, Music, Origins of Modern Art, Stage Craft, Theatre Design, Theatre History, Women in Art
Adult Hobby Classes: Assoc Provost, Jean Wyld, PhD. Continuing education classes

PLYMOUTH

PLYMOUTH STATE COLLEGE, Art Dept, 03264. Tel 603-535-5000. *Head Dept* Robert Morton. Instrs: FT 10
Estab 1871; pub; D & E; scholarships; SC 17, LC 8; enrl D 3050, maj 90
Ent Req: HS grad, references, health record, transcript, SAT, CEEB, ACT
Degrees: BS, BFA & BA 4 yrs
Tuition: Res—$2040 per sem; nonres—$5900 per sem; room & board $1295
Courses: †Art Education, †Art History, †Ceramics, †Drawing, †Graphic Design, †Painting, Photography, †Printmaking, †Sculpture, Design
Adult Hobby Classes: Dir, Doris Salis. Enrl 50; tuition res—$102 per cr, nonres—$295 per cr hr for sessions beginning May-June, June-Aug. Courses vary
Children's Classes: Courses available
Summer School: Dir, Dr Doris Salis. Enrl 50; tuition res $82 per cr, nonres $102 per cr for sem of 8 wks. Courses—varied

RINDGE

FRANKLIN PIERCE COLLEGE, Dept of Fine Arts & Graphic Communications, College Rd, PO Box 60, 03461. Tel 603-899-4201; FAX 603-899-4308.
Estab 1962; pvt; D & E; scholarships; SC 20, LC 2
Ent Req: HS dipl
Degrees: BA(Fine Arts), BA(Graphic Design)
Tuition: $12,000; campus res—room & board $4400
Courses: Art Education, Art History, Ceramics, Commercial Art, Design, Drawing, Graphic Design, Illustration, Painting, Photography, Printmaking, Sculpture, Stage Design, Teacher Training, Color Photography
Summer School: Courses—Landscape Painting, Color Photography

SHARON

SHARON ARTS CENTER, RFD 2, Box 361, 03458. Tel 603-924-7256. *Dir* Marilyn Ash. Instrs: PT 30
Estab 1947; pvt; D & E; scholarship; SC 20; classes yr round
Ent Req: None
Tuition: $60 members, $75 non-members
Courses: Calligraphy, Ceramics, Drawing, Graphic Arts, Jewelry, Lettering, Painting, Photography, Printmaking, Textile Design, Basketry, Batik, Patchwork & Applique, Pottery, Stained Glass, Sumi-E, Weaving
Adult Hobby Classes: Enrl 600. Courses—Visual & Tactile Arts
Children's Classes: Enrl 100. Courses—Visual & Tactile Arts
Summer School: Dir, Anne D Lunt. Enrl 200; tuition $60 per 8 wks.
Courses—Visual & Tactile Arts

NEW JERSEY

BLACKWOOD

CAMDEN COUNTY COLLEGE, Dept of Art, College Dr, PO Box 200, 08012. Tel 609-227-7200. *Academic Dean* Michael Donahue; *Prof* L Dell'Olio; *Prof* J Conrey; *Prof* W Marlin
Estab 1966; SC 12, LC 10; enrl 100
Ent Req: HS dipl or equivalent
Degrees: AA 2 yrs
Tuition: In county—$17 per cr hr; res—$19 per cr hr; nonres—$65 per cr hr
Courses: Art History, Ceramics, Drawing, Painting, Sculpture, Art Therapy, Computer Graphics, Design
Adult Hobby Classes: Special sessions
Children's Classes: Special sessions
Summer School: Courses available

CALDWELL

CALDWELL COLLEGE, Art Dept, 9 Ryerson Ave, 07006-6195. Tel 201-228-4424, Ext 254. *Chmn* Judith Croce. Instrs: FT 3, PT 6
Estab 1964; pvt, W; D; scholarship; SC 24, LC 12; enrl maj 76, dept 90
Ent Req: HS grad, ent exam, art portfolio
Degrees: BA 3-4 yr, BFA 4-5 yr
Tuition: $179 per cr hr
Courses: Advertising Design, Aesthetics, Art Education, Ceramics, Commercial Art, Drawing, Graphic Arts, Handicrafts, History of Art & Archaeology, Jewelry, Lettering, Painting, Printmaking, Sculpture, Teacher Training, Stain Glass, Computer Graphics, Enameling, Leather Carving, Metal Workshop, Weaving
Summer School: Dir, Sr Mary Daniel. Three terms of 3 wks each beginning June. Courses—Crafts, Drawing, Painting, Sculpture

CAMDEN

RUTGERS UNIVERSITY, CAMDEN, Art Dept, Fine Arts Center, 311 N Fifth St, 08102. Tel 609-757-6243. *Chmn* William M Hoffman Jr. Instrs: FT 6, PT 8
Pub; D; SC 24, LC 13; enrl D 450, maj 75
Ent Req: HS dipl, must qualify for regular col admis, portfolio
Degrees: BA(Art) 4 yrs
Tuition: Res—$1200 per sem; nonres—$2600 per sem
Courses: Art History, Graphic Arts, Graphic Design, Painting, Printmaking, Sculpture, Computer Graphics, Museum Studies
Summer School: Dir, Helen Weber. Three sessions beginning May 20.
Courses—Photography

DOVER

JOE KUBERT SCHOOL OF CARTOON & GRAPHIC ART, INC, 37 Myrtle Ave, 07801. Tel 201-361-1327; FAX 201-361-1844. *Pres* Joe Kubert; *Instr* Hal Campagna; *Instr* Phillip Blaisdell; *Instr* Hy Eisman; *Instr* Irwin Hasen; *Instr* Douglas Compton; *Instr* Ben Ruiz; *Instr* Michael Chen; *Instr* Jose Delbo; *Instr* Dennis Corrigan; *Instr* Kum Demulder; *Instr* Jim McWeeney; *Instr* Carl Paolini; *Instr* Judy Mates; *Instr* Art Raveson; *Instr* Greg Webb; *Instr* George Pratt; *Instr* John Troy; *Instr* Ronald Wagner; *Instr* Rowena Moorill
Estab 1976; pvt; D & E; scholarships; SC all, LC all; enrl D 200, E 100
Ent Req: HS dipl, interview, portfolio
Degrees: 3 yr dipl
Tuition: $6290 per yr; campus res—room $2625 per yr
Courses: Commercial Art, Design, Graphic Arts, Illustration, Lettering, Painting, Video, Cartoon Graphics, Cinematic Animation
Adult Hobby Classes: 100; tuition $225 per 8 wks. Courses—Basic and Advanced Paste-Ups and Mechanicals, Cartoon Workshop, Computer Graphic/Animation Workshop
Children's Classes: Enrl 20, tuition $10.50 per class. Courses—Saturday Cartoon Sketch Class
Summer School: Courses—same as regular session

EAST ORANGE

ART CENTRE OF NEW JERSEY, Upsala College, Puder Hall Room B-13, 07019. Tel 201-675-7411. *Pres* Neil Fogarty; *First VPres* James Marchese; *Recording Secy* Lillian Reese
Estab 1924 as an art school and as a venue for art events, lectures, etc;
Adult Hobby Classes: Workshops

EDISON

MIDDLESEX COUNTY COLLEGE, Visual Arts Dept, 155 Mill Rd, PO Box 3050, 08818. Tel 908-906-2589. *Chmn* Jay Siegfried
Degrees: AA
Tuition: County res—$640 per sem; out-of-county $1280 per sem; out-of-state—$2560 per sem
Courses: Art Appreciation, Art Education, Art History, Ceramics, Drawing, Painting, Printmaking, Sculpture, Stage Design, Video, Weaving, Art Foundation, Art Industry & Communication
Adult Hobby Classes: Courses offered
Summer School: Dir, Warren Kelerme. Courses—Art History, Ceramics, Drawing, Painting

GLASSBORO

ROWAN COLLEGE OF NEW JERSEY (Formerly Glassboro State College), Dept of Art, 201 Mullica Hill Rd, 08028-1701. Tel 609-863-7081; FAX 609-863-6553. *Chmn Dept* George Neff
Estab 1925; pub; D & E; enrl D 6100, E 5000, maj 300, grad 5-
Ent Req: HS dipl, ent exam, portfolio and SAT
Degrees: BA 4 yrs, MA
Tuition: Res—$70 per cr hr; nonres—$105 per cr hr
Courses: Advertising Design, Art Appreciation, Art Education, Ceramics, Drawing, Illustration, Jewelry, Sculpture, Theatre Arts, Art History Survey, Batik, Computer Art, Enameling, Fiber Arts, Metalry, Puppetry, Theatrical Design
Children's Classes: Enrl 30. Courses—Drawing, Painting, Mixed Media, Crafts
Summer School: Dir, Dr George Neff. Enrl 100; tuition $107 per cr hr res grad & $67 per cr hr res undergrad for 8 wk term. Courses—Art History, Computer Art, Drawing, Jewelry, Painting, Printing, Print Making

HACKETTSTOWN

CENTENARY COLLEGE, Div of Fine Arts, 400 Jefferson St, 07840. Tel 201-852-1400, Ext 265. *Chmn Div* Carol Yoshimine-Webster; *Asst Prof* David Wang; *Instr, Interior Design* Elena Kays. Instrs: FT 7, PT 1
Estab 1874; pvt; scholarships; SC 11, LC 2; enrl maj 70, others 367, total 678
Degrees: BFA(Art & Design), AA(Interior Design), BFA(Interior Design), BS(Communications)
Tuition: Res—$1455; nonres—$9480
Adult Hobby Classes: Tuition $98 per cr. Courses—Interior Design, Graphic Arts
Summer School: Dir, Larry Friedman. Tuition $98 per cr. Courses—Graphic Art, Interior Design

JERSEY CITY

JERSEY CITY STATE COLLEGE, Art Dept, 2039 Kennedy Blvd, 07305. Tel 201-547-3214, Ext 3241 or 3242; FAX 201-200-2352. *Chmn* Dr Esther Barish, EdD; *Prof* Dr Elaine Foster, EdD; *Prof* Harold Lemmerman, EdD; *Prof* Anneke Prins Simons, PhD; *Prof* Ben Jones, MFA; *Prof* Dr Eleanor Campulli, EdD; *Assoc Prof* Marguarite LaBelle, MA; *Assoc Prof* Denise Mullen, MFA; *Assoc Prof* Charles Plosky, MFA; *Assoc Prof* Herbert Rosenberg, MFA; *Assoc Prof* Raymond Statlander, MFA; *Asst Prof* Sr Joan Steans, MFA; *Asst Prof* Mary Campbell, MFA; *Asst Prof* Peter Fikaris, MFA. Instrs: PT 12
Estab 1927, dept estab 1961; pub; D & E; scholarships; SC 61, LC 19, GC 31; enrl D 350, E 60, GS 60
Ent Req: HS dipl or equivalent
Degrees: BA & BFA 128 sem hrs, MA
Tuition: Res—undergrad $80 per cr, grad $146 per cr; nonres—undergrad $106 per cr; grad $172 per cr; campus res available
Courses: Advertising Design, Art Education, Commercial Art, Drawing, Graphic Design, Handicrafts, Painting, Photography, Stage Design, Teacher Training, Textile Design, Art Therapy, †Communications Design & Technology, †Crafts, †Fine Arts, †Teacher Certification

SAINT PETER'S COLLEGE, Fine Arts Dept, 2641 Kennedy Blvd, 07306. Tel 201-915-9238. *Chmn* Jon D Boshart, PhD
Estab 1872, dept estab 1963; D & E; scholarships; SC 4, LC 13; enrl D 2000, E 900, maj 10
Ent Req: HS dipl
Degrees: BA, BA in Cursu Classico, BS 4 yrs
Tuition: $272 per cr hr
Courses: Advertising Design, Architecture, †Art History, Commercial Art, Design, Drawing, Film, History of Art & Archaeology, Mixed Media, †Painting, Photography, Sculpture, Teacher Training
Adult Hobby Classes: tuition $272 per sem. Coures—Art History, Dance, Studio
Summer School: Dir, Dr Boshart. Tuition $816 per 3 cr, one 3 wk session & two 5 wk sessions. Courses—Art History, Electives, Dance, Drawing, Film History, Introduction to Visual Arts, Painting

LAKEWOOD

GEORGIAN COURT COLLEGE, Dept of Art, 900 Lakewood Ave, 08701. Tel 908-364-2200, Ext 348. *Head Dept* Sr Mary Christina Geis, MFA; *Prof* Geraldine Velasque, EdD; *Prof* Sr Mary Phyllis Breimayer, MA; *Asst Prof* Suzanne Pilgram, MFA; *Asst Prof* Sr Joyce Jacobs, MA; *Lectr* Vincent Hart; *Lectr* Nicholas Caivano, MFA; *Lectr* Connie Bracci-McInode, MA
Estab 1908, dept estab 1924; pvt; D & E; scholarships; SC 18, LC 11; enrl 240, non-maj 150, maj 90
Ent Req: HS dipl, col board scores, portfolio
Degrees: BA 4 yr
Tuition: Undergrad $7750, $215 per cr; campus res—room & board 7 day $3750, 5 day $3600
Courses: Advertising Design, †Art Education, †Art History, Calligraphy, Ceramics, Commercial Art, Drafting, Drawing, Fashion Arts, Handicrafts, Illustration, Jewelry, Lettering, Painting, Photography, Printmaking, Sculpture, Teacher Training, Textile Design, Weaving, †Art (studio & art history), Color & Design, Computer Graphics
Summer School: Dir, Sr Madeline McCarthy. Tuition $215 per cr for term of 12 wks beginning May 17. Courses—Art History, Ceramics, Watercolor

LAWRENCEVILLE

RIDER COLLEGE, Dept of Fine Arts, 2083 Lawrenceville Rd, 08648. Tel 609-896-5168. *Chmn* Patrick Chmel. Instrs: FT 3
Estab 1966; pvt; D & E; SC 9, LC 4; enrl D 3500, E 5169, maj 35
Ent Req: HS dipl
Degrees: BA(Fine Arts) 4 yrs
Tuition: $10,000 per yr; campus res available
Courses: Drawing, Graphic Arts, Graphic Design, Painting
Summer School: Dir John Carpenter. Tuition $123 per cr. Courses—Drawing, Art & Society

LINCROFT

BROOKDALE COMMUNITY COLLEGE, Art Dept, 765 Newman Springs Rd, 07738. Tel 908-842-1900. *Chmn* Ed Stein
Degrees: AA
Tuition: County res—$52.05 per cr hr; non-county res—$104.10 per cr hr; non-state res—$156.15 per cr hr
Courses: Ceramics, Design, Drawing, Jewelry, Painting, Printmaking

MADISON

DREW UNIVERSITY, Art Dept, College of Liberal Arts, 36 Madison Ave, 07940. Tel 201-408-3553. *Chmn Dept* Livio Saganic, MFA; *Prof* Martyvonne Dehoney, EdD; *Prof* Sara Henry, PhD; *Adjunct Asst Prof* Michael Peglau, PhD; *Adjunct Asst Prof* Adele Starensier, PhD
Estab 1928; pvt; D & E; SC 17, LC 10; enrl D 275, E 12, maj 35, minors 6
Ent Req: HS dipl
Degrees: BA 4 yrs
Tuition: $10,860 per yr
Courses: Aesthetics, †Art History, Ceramics, Drawing, History of Art & Archaeology, Painting, Photography, Printmaking, Sculpture, New York Semester on Contemporary Art, †Studio Art
Summer School: Dir, Johanna Glazewsky. Term of 6 wks beginning June. Courses—Studios

MAHWAH

RAMAPO COLLEGE OF NEW JERSEY, School of Contemporary Arts, 505 Ramapo Valley Rd, 07430-1680. Tel 201-529-7368. *Dir* Shalom Gorewitz; *Prof Art History* Carol Duncan, PhD; *Prof* Judith Peck, EdD; *Prof Painting* Warner W Wade, MFA; *Prof* Jay Wholley, MFA; *Assoc Prof Architecture* Newton LeVine, MCRP; *Assoc Prof Photography* David Freund, MFA
Estab 1968; pub; D & E; SC 53, LC 15; enrl D 800, E 50, non-maj 750, maj 100
Ent Req: HS dipl, SAT
Degrees: BA
Tuition: Res—undergrad $32 per cr hr; nonres—undergrad $50 per cr hr; campus res available
Courses: Architecture, Art Appreciation, Art History, Commercial Art, Conceptual Art, Design, Drawing, Film, Graphic Arts, Graphic Design, Intermedia, Painting, Photography, Printmaking, Sculpture, Stage Design, Video, Computer Art
Summer School: Dir, Shalom Gorewitz. Tuition $71.50 cr hr, $91.50 out of state. Courses—Computer Graphics, Photography

MERCERVILLE

JOHNSON ATELIER TECHNICAL INSTITUTE OF SCULPTURE, 60 Ward Ave Extension, 08619. Tel 609-890-7777; FAX 609-890-1816. *Pres* James Barton, MFA; *Acad Dir* Brooke Barrie, MFA; *Dir of Production* Dona Warner
Estab 1974; pvt; D & E; scholarships; SC 12; enrl D 30, maj 25, grad 5
Ent Req: BFA or MFA in sculpture
Degrees: The Atelier is a non degree granting institution with a two year apprenticeship program in sculpture
Tuition: $4800 per academic yr, $400 monthly
Courses: †Sculpture, Ceramic Shell, Foundry, Metal Chasing, Modeling & Enlarging, Moldmaking, Patina, Sand Foundry, Structures, Wax Working & Casting

MONTCLAIR

MONTCLAIR ART MUSEUM, Art School, Education Dept, 3 S Mountain Ave, 07042. Tel 201-746-5555. *Dir* Ellen Harris; *Registrar* Ronald Lomas; *Cur of Coll* Marilyn S Kushner; *Cur of Education* Marion Grzesiak; *Prog Coordr* Catherine Fazekas; *Instr* Miriam Beerman; *Instr* Bill Grah; *Instr* Edwin Havas; *Children's Instr* Roberta Klein; *Instr* Mary Louise Long; *Children's Instr* Elizabeth Seaton
Art school estab 1924; pvt; D & E; scholarships; SC 17; enrl D 300 per term, E 100 per term
Tuition: Children $85-$100 for 11 sessions; adults $120-$175 for 11 sessions
Courses: Art Education, Collages, Drawing, Mixed Media, Painting, Printmaking, Portraiture, Watercolor
Adult Hobby Classes: Enrl 300; tuition $120-$175, duration 11 wks.
Courses—Anatomy, Drawing, Painting, Pastels, Portraiture, Still Life, Watercolor
Children's Classes: Enrl 90; tuition $85-$100 per 11 wk sem. Courses—Mixed Media

YARD SCHOOL OF ART, 99 S Fullerton Ave, 07042. Tel 201-746-6106. *Dir* William J Senior
Estab 1927; pvt; D & E; scholarships; enrl D 130, E 6
Tuition: Adults & children $4 per cr hr
Courses: Drawing, Painting, Sculpture, Multi-media, Oil Painting, Portraiture, Watercolor
Adult Hobby Classes: Enrl 80; tuition $125 for 12 wk term. Courses - Drawing, Multi-media, Painting, Portraiture, Sculpture, Watercolor
Children's Classes: Enrl 80; tuition $100 per 12 wk term. Courses - Acrylic, Drawing, Painting, Pastel, Watercolor
Summer School: Dir, Gretchen Prater. Tuition $50 per wk. Courses - Childrens Art, Drawing, Painting, Portraiture, Sculpture

MORRISTOWN

COLLEGE OF SAINT ELIZABETH, Art Dept, 2 Convent Rd, 07960-6989. Tel 201-539-1600. *Chmn Dept* Sr Ann Haarer
Estab 1899, dept 1956; den, W; D & E; scholarships; SC 17, LC 4; enrl D 250, maj 27
Ent Req: HS dipl, ent exam
Degrees: BA 4 yrs
Tuition: $8500 per yr; campus res available
Courses: Sculpture, Teacher Training, Color and Design, Leather Work, Sand Casting, Stitchery
Summer School: Dir, Sr Mary Kathleen. Courses—Art Education, Painting

NEWARK

NEWARK SCHOOL OF FINE AND INDUSTRIAL ART, 550 M L King Blvd, 07102. Tel 201-733-7390. *Dir* Elaine C Sopka. Instrs: D PT 42, E PT 28
Estab 1882; pub; scholarships; enrl D 300, E 300
Tuition: City res—$300 per yr; nonres—$900 per yr
Courses: Advertising Design, Illustration, Interior Design, Painting, Sculpture, Textile Design, Fashion
Adult Hobby Classes: Enrl D 150, E 75; tuition res $300, nonres $800; Sept - Apr. Courses - Advertising, Fashion, Fine Arts, Illustration, Interior Design, Textile Design
Children's Classes: Ages 10-18

RUTGERS UNIVERSITY, NEWARK, Newark Col Arts & Sciences, University Heights, 360 Dr Martin Luther King Blvd, 07102. Tel 201-648-5600. *Chmn* Frank D'Astolfo. Instrs: FT 6
Pub; D; scholarship; enrl D 486, maj 100
Ent Req: HS dipl, or as specified by col and univ
Degrees: BA 4 yr, BFA(Design)
Courses: Art Education, Drawing, Graphic Design, Illustration, Painting, Photography, Printmaking, Sculpture, Computer Graphics
Children's Classes: Enrl 50. Courses—Art & Design, Graphic Design
Summer School: Dir, Hildreth York. Courses—Drawing, Photography

NEW BRUNSWICK

RUTGERS, THE STATE UNIVERSITY OF NEW JERSEY
—**Mason Gross School of the Arts,** Visual Arts Dept, Downtown Arts Bldg, 125 New St, 08901. Tel 908-932-9078, 932-9093. *Dean* Marilyn Sombille; *Dir Visual Arts* Mark Berger, MA; *Assoc Dean* Charles Woolfolk; *Dir Graduate Prog* Martha Rosler; *Dir Undergrad Prog* Paul Bruner, MFA; *Prof* Judith Brodsky; *Prof* Geoffrey Hendricks; *Prof* Rafael Ortiz, EdD; *Prof* Melvin Edwards; *Prof* John Goodyear, MDesign; *Prof* Gary Kuehn, MFA; *Prof* Emma Amos, MA; *Assoc Prof* Lloyd McNeill, MFA; *Prof* Joan Semmel, MFA; *Assoc Prof* Toby MacLennan; *Assoc Prof* Robert T Cooke, MFA; *Assoc Prof* Lauren Ewing, MFA; *Asst Prof* Stephen Cagen; *Asst Prof* Diane Neumaiere; *Asst Prof* Michael Eisenmenger; *Asst Prof* Ardele Lister; *Asst Prof* Sheena Calvert; *Asst Prof* Martin Ball; *Asst Prof* Lynne Allen
Estab 1766, school estab 1976; pub; D; scholarships; SC 24, LC 9, GC 33; enrl MFA program 60, BFA program 450
Ent Req: HS dipl, portfolio
Degrees: BFA, MFA
Tuition: Res—grad $6500 per yr
Courses: Ceramics, Film, Mixed Media, Painting, Photography, Printmaking, Sculpture, Video, Computer Arts, Critical Studies, Event and Performance, Seminars and Museum Internship
Summer School: Dir, Mark Berger. Four week courses. Courses—Computer Art, Drawing Fundamentals, Figure Drawing, Painting Studio, Seminar on Contemporary Art, Studio Fundamentals

—**Graduate Program in Art History,** Voorhees Hall, Hamilton St, 08903. Tel 908-932-7041, 932-7819; FAX 908-932-1261. *Dir Prog* Dr Archer St Claire; *Prof* Matthew Baigell; *Prof* Sarah McHam; *Prof* Jack J Spector, PhD; *Prof* Rona Goffen; *Prof* Martin Eidelberg, PhD; *Prof* Joan Marter; *Prof* Jocelyn Small; *Assoc Prof* John F Kenfield, PhD; *Assoc Prof* Hildreth York, PhD; *Assoc Prof* Tod Marder, PhD; *Assoc Prof* Catherine Puglisi, PhD; *Assoc Prof* Elizabeth McLachlan, PhD; *Asst Prof* David Underwood, PhD; *Asst Prof* Sara Brett-Smith, PhD; *Asst Prof* Angela Howard, PhD; *Asst Prof* Dr James Small
Estab 1766, grad prog estab 1971; pub; D; scholarships; grad courses 15; enrl grad students 97
Ent Req: BA
Degrees: MA 2 yrs, PhD 4 yrs
Tuition: Res—undergrad $191 per cr hr, grad $2315 per sem; nonres—$282 per cr hr, grad $3394 per sem
Courses: †Art History
Summer School: Dir, Albert A Austen. Courses—Intro to Art Hist, 19th & 20th century Art

OCEAN CITY

OCEAN CITY ART CENTER, 1735 Simpson Ave, 08226. Tel 609-399-7628. *Instr* William Hopkins; *Instr* Edward Wismer; *Instr* Cheryl Crews-Lynch; *Instr* Lance Balderson, BA; *Instr* Susan Hopkins, BA; *Instr* Lorraine Watson; *Instr* Susan Brooks, BAED; *Instr* Sherry Mirakian; *Instr* Ruth Veasey; *Instr* Scott Griswold; *Instr* Robin Conover; *Instr* Anthony Frudakis; *Instr* Betsy Young; *Instr* Bethany Bonner; *Instr* Monica Goldberg; *Instr* Bruce Hippel
Estab 1974; pvt; D & E; scholarship; SC 14, LC 1; enrl D 1, E 8
Ent Req: None
Tuition: Varies
Courses: Calligraphy, Ceramics, Drawing, Mixed Media, Painting, Photography, Sculpture, Dance, Pottery
Summer School: Courses—Same classes offered during summer plus workshops and demonstrations

PARAMUS

BERGEN COMMUNITY COLLEGE, Visual Art Dept, 400 Paramus Rd, 07652. Tel 201-447-7100. *Dean Humanities* Amparo Codding
Scholarships offered
Degrees: AA
Tuition: In county—$600 per yr; res—$1200 per yr; nonres—$2400 per yr
Courses: Art Appreciation, Art History, Ceramics, Design, Drawing, Graphic Design, Handicrafts, Interior Design, Lettering, Painting, Photography, Printmaking, Sculpture, Animation, Art Anatomy, Color Theory, Commercial Illustration, Craft Design, Fundamentals Art

PATERSON

PASSAIC COUNTY COMMUNITY COLLEGE, Division of Humanities, College Blvd, 07505-1179. Tel 201-684-6800. *VPres* H Edwin Titus; *Prof* Mark G Bialy
Estab 1969, dept estab 1969; pub; D & E; SC 4, LC 3; enrl D 100, E 25
Ent Req: HS dipl, New Jersey basic skills exam
Degrees: AA 2 yrs
Tuition: $920 per yr
Courses: Advertising Design, Aesthetics, Art Appreciation, Art History, Commercial Art, Design, Drawing

PEMBERTON

BURLINGTON COUNTY COLLEGE, Humanities & Fine Art Div, Route 530, Pemberton & Browns Mills Rd, 08068. Tel 609-894-9311, Ext 617. *Division Chmn* Dr Shirley Hughes
Degrees: AA
Tuition: County res—$29 per cr hr; non-county res—$31 per cr hr; non-state res—$77 per cr hr
Courses: Art Appreciation, Art Education, Art History, Calligraphy, Ceramics, Design, Drawing, Film, Handicrafts, Painting, Photography, Sculpture, Theatre Arts, Video

PRINCETON

PRINCETON UNIVERSITY
—**Dept of Art and Archaeology,** 104 McCormick Hall, 08544-1018. Tel 609-452-3782; FAX 609-258-0103. *Chmn Dept* John Wilmerding; *Chmn Prog Chinese and Japanese Art and Archaeology* Wen Fong, PhD; *Chmn Prog in Classical Archaelogy* William A P Childs, PhD; *Prof* T Leslie Shear Jr, PhD; *Prof* Yoshiaki Shimizu, PhD; *Prof* John Wilmerding, PhD; *Prof* Peter Bunnell, MFA; *Prof* R J Clark, PhD; *Prof* Slobodan Curcic, PhD; *Prof* Dorothea Dietrich, PhD; *Prof* Robert Bagley; *Prof* John Pinto, PhD; *Prof* Hugo Meyer, PhD; *Prof* Thomas Kaufmann, PhD; *Prof* Pat Brown, PhD; *Prof* Deborah Kahn, PhD; *Prof* Mary Vidal, PhD; *Prof* James Marrow, PhD
Estab 1783; pvt; scholarships; LC 16, GC 9; enrl 761, maj 70, grad 50
Degrees: AB, MA, MFA, PhD
Courses: Art History, History of Art & Archaeology, Architectural History, History of Photography, Visual Arts
—**School of Architecture,** 08544. Tel 609-258-3737. *Dean* Open. Instrs: FT 16
Estab 1919; pvt; D; scholarships and fels; SC 6, LC 13, GC 6, seminars 17; enrl undergrad 120, grad 50
Ent Req: HS dipl
Degrees: AB 4 yr, MArchit, PhD (Archit)
Tuition: $17,850 annual tuition

RANDOLPH

COUNTY COLLEGE OF MORRIS, Art Dept, 214 Center Grove Rd, 07869. Tel 201-328-5000. *Chmn & Prof* Charles Luce
Estab 1970; pub; D & E; SC 15, LC 3; enrl maj 263
Ent Req: HS dipl
Degrees: AA(Humanities/Art) 2 yrs, AAS(Photography Technology) 2 yrs
Tuition: $990 per sem, $50 student fee; $1980 per yr
Courses: Advertising Design, Art History, Ceramics, Drawing, Painting, Photography, Printmaking, Sculpture, Color & Design, Major Styles & Historical Periods, Modern Art
Summer School: Two 5 week day sessions, one evening session

RUTHERFORD

FAIRLEIGH DICKINSON UNIVERSITY, Fine Arts Dept, Becton Hall, 223 Montross Ave, 07070. Tel 201-460-5215. *Chmn* David A Hanson; *Asst Prof* Marie Roberts, MFA; *Prof* A Wm Clark, MEd; *Prof* Robert Nunnelley, MA; *Assoc Prof* Joan Taylor, MA
Estab 1942, dept estab 1965; pvt; D & E; scholarships offered; SC 37, LC 9
Ent Req: HS dipl, SAT
Degrees: Degrees BA (Art & Fine Arts)
Tuition: Res—undergrad $16,000 per yr room & board; nonres—undergrad $328 per cr hr; campus res available
Courses: Advertising Design, Art Appreciation, Art History, Calligraphy, Ceramics, Commercial Art, Design, Drawing, History of Art & Archaeology, Illustration, †Graphic Design, Lettering, Mixed Media, Painting, Photography, Printmaking, Sculpture, Bio & Wildlife Illus, Computer Graphics, Desktop Publishing

SEWELL

GLOUCESTER COUNTY COLLEGE, Liberal Arts Dept, Tanyard Rd, Rural Route 4, Box 203, 08080. Tel 609-468-5000. *Head* Dr Ross Beitzel
Estab 1967; pub; D & E; scholarships; SC 6, LC 6
Ent Req: HS dipl
Tuition: In-county—$550 per yr; in-state—$19 per cr hr; nonres—$2560 per yr
Courses: Art History, Ceramics, Drawing, Graphic Arts, Jewelry, Mixed Media, Painting, Sculpture, Arts & Crafts for Handicapped, General Design
Summer School: Dir, Dr Mossman

SHREWSBURY

GUILD OF CREATIVE ART, 620 Broad St, Rte 35, 07702. Tel 908-741-1441. *Pres* Caroline Klein
Tuition: $75-$225 per 10 wks
Courses: Design, †Drawing, Handicrafts, Painting, Stage Design
Adult Hobby Classes: Enrl 185; tuition $75-$115 for 10 wk term. Courses—Design, Drawing, Painting
Children's Classes: Enrl 100; tuition $55-$105 for 10 wk term. Courses—Design, Life Drawing, Painting
Summer School: Dir, Madlyn Ann Woolwich. Enrl 100; tuition $90-$105. Courses—Drawing, Oil & Acrylic Painting, Watercolor

SOUTH ORANGE

SETON HALL UNIVERSITY, College of Arts & Sciences, 400 S Orange Ave, 07079. Tel 201-761-9022. *Chmn* Petra Chu; *Prof* Julius Zsako, PhD; *Assoc Prof* F Ming Chang, MA; *Assoc Prof* Barbara Kaufman, MA; *Asst Prof* Edwin Havas; *Assoc Prof* Peter Rosenblum, MA; *Asst Prof* William K Burns, MA; *Assoc Prof* Jeanette Hile, MA; *Asst Prof* Alison Wenz, MFA; *Asst Prof* Anthony Triano; *Asst Prof* Charlotte Nichols, PhD. Instrs: FT 10, PT 9
Estab dept 1968; pvt; D & E; scholarships & fels; SC 8
Degrees: BA 4 yr
Tuition: $2048 per sem
Courses: Art Education, Art History, Commercial Art, Design, Drawing, Illustration, Mixed Media, Painting, Printmaking, Sculpture, Advertising, Chinese Brush Painting, Fine Art, Music Art
Summer School: Enrl 200; May-July. Courses—Art, Art History

TOMS RIVER

OCEAN COUNTY COLLEGE, Humanities Dept, College Dr, 08753. Tel 908-255-4000, Ext 375. *Chmn Dept* Dr Martin Novelli; *Asst Dean of Humanities* Dr Judith A Longo; *Coordr* Joseph Conrey; *Prof* Tom Funk, MFA; *Prof* William Schoenfeld, MA; *Prof* Howard Unger, EdD; *Prof* John R Gowen; *Prof* Charles Reed; *Prof* Arthur Waldman
Estab 1964, dept estab 1964; pub; D & E; SC 19, LC 3; enrl D 1500, E 1500, maj 67
Ent Req: HS dipl
Degrees: AA in Liberal Arts with concentration in Fine Art & AAS(Visual Communication Technology) 2 yrs
Tuition: Res—undergrad $1066 per yr, PT $41; nonres—undergrad $1196 per yr, PT $46; no campus res
Courses: Advertising Design, Aesthetics, †Art History, Calligraphy, †Ceramics, †Commercial Art, †Conceptual Art, Costume Design & Construction, †Drawing, †Film, †Graphic Arts, †Graphic Design, †Handicrafts, †Lettering, †Painting, †Photography, †Printmaking, †Sculpture, †Stage Design, †Theatre Arts
Summer School: Dir, Dr James Doran. Enrl 175; tuition $34 for term or 5 wks or 6 wks beginning June. Courses—Arts and Humanities, Basic Drawing, Ceramics, Crafts

TRENTON

MERCER COUNTY COMMUNITY COLLEGE, Arts & Communications, 1200 Old Trenton Rd, PO Box B, 08690. Tel 609-586-4800, Ext 350; FAX 609-587-4666. *Dean* David S Levin, PhD; *Prof* Mel Leipzig, MFA; *Prof* Frank Rivera, MFA; *Asst Prof* James Colavita, MFA; *Cur* Henry Hose. Instrs: FT 10, PT 13
Estab 1902, dept estab 1967; pub; D & E; scholarships; SC 44, LC 6; enrl E 350, maj 261
Ent Req: HS dipl
Degrees: AA & AAS 2 yrs
Tuition: Res—grad $40 pr hr
Courses: †Advertising Design, †Architecture, Art Appreciation, Art Education, Art History, †Ceramics, Commercial Art, Design, Drawing, Film, Graphic Arts, Graphic Design, History of Art & Archaeology, Illustration, †Painting, †Photography, Printmaking, †Sculpture, †Theatre Arts, Video
Adult Hobby Classes: Enrl 448. Tuition varies. Courses—Caligraphy, Ceramics, Drawing, Painting, Photography, Stained Glass
Children's Classes: Enrl 1000. Tuition varies. Courses—Drawing, Maskmaking, Painting, Printmaking, Soft Sculpture
Summer School: Dir, R Serofkin. Enrl 712 (camp college); 2 - 4 wk sessions. Dir, M Dietrich. Enrl 22; 4 wks. Courses—Architecture. Dir, M K Gitlick. Enrl 160; Arts Camp 2 - 4 wk sessions. Also regular cr courses

TRENTON STATE COLLEGE, Art Dept, Pennington Rd, 08625. Tel 609-771-2652. *Chmn Dept* Dr Howard Goldstein; *Prof* Bruce Rigby, MFA; *Prof* Joseph Shannon, EdD; *Assoc Prof* Kenneth Kaplowitz, MFA; *Assoc Prof* Ruane Miller, MFA; *Assoc Prof* Lois Fichner-Rathus, PhD; *Assoc Prof* Marcia Taylor, PhD, MAATR; *Asst Prof* Wendell Brooks, MFA; *Asst Prof* Christina Craig, EdD; *Asst Prof* Tom Klinkowstein, MA; *Asst Prof* Charles Kumnick, MFA; *Asst Prof* Mark Lehman, MFA; *Asst Prof* Elizabeth Mackie, MFA; *Asst Prof* Charles McVicker, BPA; *Asst Prof* Guy Norman, BS; *Asst Prof* William Nyman, MFA; *Asst Prof* Steve Hirsch, MFA; *Instr* Diane Laird, BA. Instrs: FT 17, PT 18
Estab 1855; pub; D & E; scholarship; SC 40, LC 10, GC 11; enrl non-maj 300, maj 400
Ent Req: HS dipl
Degrees: BA & BFA 4 yr
Tuition: Res—$1233; nonres—$1683
Courses: †Art Education, Art History, Calligraphy, Ceramics, Drawing, Fashion Arts, Graphic Arts, †Graphic Design, Illustration, †Interior Design, Jewelry, Lettering, Painting, Photography, Printmaking, Sculpture, Silversmithing, Teacher Training, Textile Design, Crafts, †Fine Arts
Summer School: June & July five wk sessions, Governor's School of the Arts (July)

UNION

KEAN COLLEGE OF NEW JERSEY, Fine Arts Dept, Morris Ave, 07083. Tel 908-527-2307. *Chmn* Lenny Pierro; *Coordr Interior Design* Asher Derman, PhD; *Coordr Art Educ* Pearl Greenberg, EdD; *Coordr Visual Communications* Robin Landa, MFA; *Coordr Art History* Virginia Stotz, MA; *Coordr Studio Prog* Michael Metzger, MFA. Instrs: FT 31
Estab 1855; pub; D & E; scholarships; SC 58, LC 37, GC 24; enrl FT 383, PT 236, maj 656, grad 37
Ent Req: HS dipl, portfolio interview for art maj
Degrees: BA 4 yrs, BFA 4, MA(Art Educ)
Tuition: Res—undergrad $70.75 per cr hr, grad $121 per cr hr; nonres—undergrad $93.75 per cr hr, grad $145 per cr hr
Courses: Advertising Design, Aesthetics, †Art Education, †Art History, Ceramics, †Commercial Art, Display, Drafting, Drawing, Film, Graphic Arts, Graphic Design, Illustration, †Interior Design, Jewelry, Lettering, Museum Staff Training, Occupational Therapy, Painting, Photography, Printmaking, Sculpture, Textile Design, Furniture Making
Summer School: Asst Dir, George Sisko. Tuition $43 per cr for term of 6 wks beginning June 26. Courses—Art History, Art in Education, Ceramics, Drawing, Introduction to Art, Introduction to Interior Design, Jewelry, Life Drawing, Painting, Printmaking, Sculpture, Watercolor

UPPER MONTCLAIR

MONTCLAIR STATE COLLEGE, Fine Arts Dept, Normal Ave, 07043. Tel 201-893-7295. *Dean* Geoffrey Newman; *Chmn* Dr Anne Betty Weinshenker. Instrs: FT 18, PT 4
Estab 1908; pub; scholarship; SC 35, LC 18; enrl maj 250, grad maj 200
Ent Req: HS grad and exam, interview, portfolio
Degrees: BA 4 yr, BFA 4 yr, MA
Courses: Art Education, Art History, Ceramics, Drawing, Film, Graphic Design, Illustration, Jewelry, Painting, Photography, Printmaking, Sculpture, Textile Design, Metalwork, TV as Art
Summer School: Courses—Life drawing, painting, photography, sculpture

VINELAND

CUMBERLAND COUNTY COLLEGE, Humanities Div, College Dr, PO Box 517, 08360. Tel 609-691-8600. *Coordr* John M Adair.
Tuition: County res—$532.50 per sem; out of county res—$1065 per sem; out of state res—$2130 per sem
Courses: Art Appreciation, Art History, Drawing, Painting, Photography, Video, Multi-media

WAYNE

WILLIAM PATERSON COLLEGE, Art Dept, Div of Fine and Performing Arts, 300 Pompton Rd, 07470. Tel 201-595-2401. *Chmn* Alan H Lazarus. Instrs: FT 24, PT 8
Dept estab 1958; pub; scholarships; SC 9, LC 9; enrl maj 420, grad 105, E non-maj 170
Degrees: BA 4 yr, BFA, MA
Tuition: Res—undergrad $73, grad $131
Courses: Art History, Graphic Design, Painting, Photography, Printmaking, Sculpture, Arts Management, Computer Graphics, Enameling, Fibers, Furniture Design, Gallery Workshop & Design
Summer School: Dir, Alan Lazarus. Enrl 150; tuition $65 per cr, $90 out of state. Courses—Art History, Drawing, Painting, Photography

WEST LONG BRANCH

MONMOUTH COLLEGE, Dept of Art, Norwood & Cedar Aves, 07764. Tel 908-571-3428. *Chmn* Vincent Dimattio; *Assoc Prof* Arie van Everdingen, MFA; *Assoc Prof* Martin Ryan, MA; *Assoc Prof* Alfred Provencher; *Asst Prof* Edward Jankowski, MFA
Estab 1933; pvt; D & E; scholarship; SC 25, LC 8; enrl in dept D 108, E 6, non-maj 80, maj 108, audits 6
Ent Req: HS dipl, portfolio for transfer students
Degrees: BA(Art), BFA and BA(Art Educ) 4 yr
Tuition: Undergrad $4570 per sem, grad $4000 per sem; campus res—room & board $2060
Courses: †Art Education, Art History, †Ceramics, Drawing, Graphic Arts, Handicrafts, History of Art & Archaeology, †Painting, Photography, Printmaking, †Sculpture, Teacher Training, Appreciation of Art, Metalsmithing
Adult Hobby Classes: Courses—Painting
Summer School: Dean, Kenneth C Stunkel. Enrl 80; tuition $89 per cr hr for 3 or 6 wk courses beginning June 2. Courses—Art Appreciation, Ceramics, Independent Study, Painting, Sculpture

NEW MEXICO

ALBUQUERQUE

AMERICAN CLASSICAL COLLEGE, PO Box 4526, 87196-4526. Tel 505-296-2320. *Dir* Dr C M Flumiani. Instrs: FT 2
Estab 1970; pvt; D; scholarship
Ent Req: Ent exam
Degrees: None
Tuition: FT $100 per month
Courses: Advertising Design, Aesthetics, Art Education, Commercial Art, Drawing, History of Art & Archaeology, Painting, Sculpture

UNIVERSITY OF NEW MEXICO
—College of Fine Arts, Fine Arts Ctr, 87131. Tel 505-277-2111. *Dean Colls* Dr Thomas A Dodson
Estab 1935; pub
Tuition: Res—$828 per sem; nonres—$2940 per sem
Adult Hobby Classes: Wide variety of courses offered
Summer School: Arts of the Americas Program, wide variety of courses offered
—Dept of Art & Art History, 87131. Tel 505-277-5861. *Chmn* Christopher Mead, PhD
Estab 1889; pub; D & E; scholarships; SC 190, LC 43, GC 73; enrl E 511, non-maj 230, maj 227, grad 116
Ent Req: HS dipl
Degrees: BA and BFA 4 yrs, MA 2 yrs, MFA 3 yrs, PhD 3 yrs
Tuition: Res—undergrad $1554 per yr, $777 per sem, grad $1684 per yr, $842 per sem; nonres—undergrad $5520 per yr, $2760 per sem, grad $5656 per yr, $2828 per sem
Courses: Art History, Ceramics, Drawing, Jewelry, Painting, Photography, Printmaking, Sculpture, Teacher Training, Theatre Arts, Metalwork
Children's Classes: Offered through Art Educ Dept
Summer School: Tuition res $64.50 per cr hr, 6 - 9 hrs $388.50. Two 4 wk terms & one 8 wk term beginning June 11.
—Tamarind Institute, 108 Cornell Dr SE, 87106. Tel 505-277-3901; FAX 505-277-3920. *Dir* Marjorie Devon; *Tamarind Master Printer & Studio Mgr* Bill Lagatutta; *Educ Dir* Jeffrey Sippel
Fellowships offered
Degrees: Cert as Tamarind Master Printer 2 yrs
Tuition: $60.75 per cr hr
Courses: †Lithography
Summer School: 4 wk prog; campus res available. Courses—Various lithographic techniques

FARMINGTON

SAN JUAN COLLEGE, Art Dept, 4601 College Blvd, 87402. Tel 505-326-3311, Ext 281. *Dept Head* Bill Hatch. Instrs: FT 1, PT 3
Scholarships offered
Degrees: AA
Tuition: Res—$180; nonres—$504
Courses: Art Appreciation, Art Education, Art History, Calligraphy, Ceramics, Design, Drawing, Film, Graphic Design, Jewelry, Painting, Photography, Printmaking, Sculpture
Summer School: Dir, Jay B Zeiger. Enrl 180; tuition $15 per cr hr. Courses—Motion Picture as art, Painting, Drawing, Ceramics

HOBBS

NEW MEXICO JUNIOR COLLEGE, Arts & Sciences, 5317 Lovington Hwy, 88240. Tel 505-392-4510. *Dean* Steve McCleery; *Instr* Terry Bumpass, MFA; *Instr* Lawrence Wilcox, MFA
Estab 1965, dept estab 1965; pub; D & E; scholarships; SC 5, LC 1; enrl D 75, E 25, non-maj 95, maj 5
Ent Req: HS dipl, GED or special approval
Degrees: AA 2 yrs
Courses: Advertising Design, Ceramics, Drawing, Goldsmithing, Interior Design, Jewelry, Painting, Photography, Printmaking, Collage, Color & Design
Adult Hobby Classes: Drawing, Painting, Portraiture, Watercolor
Children's Classes: Drawing, Painting
Summer School: Dean, Gerald Martin. Enrl 30; term of 8 wks beginning June 10.
Courses—Ceramics, Printmaking

LAS CRUCES

NEW MEXICO STATE UNIVERSITY, Art Dept, PO Box 30001, 88003. Tel 505-646-1705. *Dept Head & Prof* Louis Ocepek, MFA; *Prof* Joshua Rose, MFA; *Prof* Dale Newkirk, MFA; *Prof* Spencer Fidler, MFA; *Prof* John Moffitt, PhD; *Prof* Amamda Jaffe, MFA; *Asst Prof* Doug DuBois; *Asst Prof* William Green
Estab 1975; pub; D & E; scholarships & fels; SC 52, LC 25, GC 53; enrl maj 150, grad 28
Ent Req: HS dipl
Degrees: BA & BFA 4 yrs, MFA 3 yrs, MA(Studio) & MA(Art Hist) 2 yrs
Tuition: Res—$854 per sem; nonres—$2819 per sem
Courses: Art Appreciation, Art History, Ceramics, Design, Drawing, Graphic Design, Jewelry, Painting, Photography, Sculpture, †Metal Arts
Summer School: Tuition $186 for term of 6 wks. Courses—Art Appreciation, Drawing, Painting

LAS VEGAS

NEW MEXICO HIGHLANDS UNIVERSITY, School of Liberal & Fine Arts, National Ave, 87701. Tel 505-454-3238. *Dean* Dr Roy Lujan; *Prof* Gary Coulter, MA; *Asst Prof* Dorothy McSherry
Estab 1898; pub; D & E; scholarships; SC 24, LC 8, GC 12; enrl non-maj 55, maj 51, grad 4
Ent Req: HS dipl, ACT, Early Admis Prog, GED
Degrees: BA 4 yrs, MA 1 yr
Tuition: Res—$587 per sem; nonres—$2063 per sem; campus res available
Courses: Art Education, Art History, Calligraphy, Ceramics, Drawing, Graphic Arts, Jewelry, Lettering, Painting, Photography, Printmaking, Sculpture, Silversmithing, Stage Design, Teacher Training, Theatre Arts
Adult Hobby Classes: Courses—Ceramics, Painting, Weaving
Summer School: VPAA, Gilbert D. Riveva. Tuition sames as winter school. Courses—Mainly studio plus core curriculum, depending upon staffing

PILAR

PLUM TREE FINE ARTS PROGRAM, PO Box 1-A, 87531. Tel 505-758-4696; WATS 800-678-7586. *Dir* Rich Thibodeau, BFA
Estab 1982; pvt; D; scholarships; SC 26; enrl D 140
Tuition: Campus res available
Courses: Ceramics, Drawing, Graphic Arts, Jewelry, Mixed Media, Painting, Photography, Printmaking, Sculpture, Weaving, Monet Gardening, Oil Marbling, Papermaking, Stoneware
Adult Hobby Classes: Enrl 120. Courses—same as above
Children's Classes: Enrl 120. Courses—same as above
Summer School: Dir, Rich Thibodeau. Tuition $250 - $350 for 1 wk, $100 - $150 weekend. Courses—Ceramics, Drawing, Oil Marbling, Painting, Papermaking, Photography, Sculpture, Watercolor

PORTALES

EASTERN NEW MEXICO UNIVERSITY, Dept of Art, 88130. Tel 505-562-2778. *Chmn* Greg Erf; *Asst Prof* Greg Senn, MFA; *Asst Prof* Greg Deming, MFA; *Asst Prof* Mary Finneran, MFA
Estab 1932; pub; D & E; scholarships; SC 44, LC 6, GC 25; enrl D 507, E 150, maj 110
Ent Req: HS dipl, GED, ACT
Degrees: AA 2 yrs, BS, BA & BFA 4 yrs
Tuition: Res—$615 per sem; nonres—$2124 per sem
Courses: †Advertising Design, Art Education, Art History, Calligraphy, †Ceramics, †Commercial Art, †Drawing, †Graphic Arts, Graphic Design, Illustration, †Jewelry, Lettering, †Painting, Photography, †Sculpture, †Teacher Training, Theatre Arts, Video
Summer School: Chmn, David Noblett. Terms of 8 & 16 wks beginning June 4. Courses—Ceramics, Commercial Art, Crafts, Drawing, Lettering, Photography

RUIDOSO

CARRIZO ART AND CRAFT WORKSHOPS, PO Drawer A, 88345. Tel 505-257-9131. *Dir* Barbara Theodore. Instrs: PT 75
Estab 1956; pvt; D; SC 150; enrl 300 summer school; 200 fall school; 200 spring school
Ent Req: Art interest
Tuition: $185 to $220 for 1 wk workshop; campus res—room & board $200-500 for 1 wk
Courses: Calligraphy, Collages, Jewelry, Mixed Media, Painting, Photography, Sculpture, Weaving, Creative Writing, Stained Glass

SANTA FE

COLLEGE OF SANTA FE, Visual Arts Dept, Saint Michael's Dr, 87501. Tel 505-473-6500. *Chmn* Richard L Cook; *Prof* Ronald Picco, MFA; *Asst Prof* Robert Sorrell, MFA; *Asst Prof* David Schienbaum, MFA; *Instr* Ralph Pardington, MFA; *Asst Prof* Richard Fisher, *Adjunct Assoc* Edna Glenn; *Gallery Dir* Patrick Harris, MFA; *Artist-in-Res* Willa Shalit
Estab 1947, dept estab 1984; pvt; D & E; scholarships; SC 35, LC 10; enrl D 350, non-maj 250, maj 95, non-degree 30
Ent Req: HS dipl or GED
Degrees: BA & BFA (Visual Arts)
Tuition: $2625 per sem, $250 per sem hr; campus res—room & board $2200 per yr
Courses: Ceramics, Drawing, Graphic Design, Painting, Photography, Printmaking, Sculpture, Video, Gallery Practices, Southwestern Art History, 2-D Design, 3-D Design
Children's Classes: Enrl 20-25. Courses—General Studio Art & Design
Summer School: Dir, Richard Cook. Tuition $250 per sem hr for term of 4-12 wks beginning May 13. Courses—Art History, Drawing, Outdoor Sketching, Landscape Painting, Lifecasting, Photography, Printmaking, Primitive Pottery

INSTITUTE OF AMERICAN INDIAN ARTS MUSEUM, 108 Cathedral Place, 87501. Tel 505-988-6281. *Dir* Paul Gonzales; *Cur Coll* Manuelita Lovato
Estab 1962; pvt; D; scholarships; SC 18, LC 11; enrl 263
Ent Req: HS dipl
Degrees: AA (Fine Arts) 2 yrs
Tuition: $75 per hr non-Indian, free to native Americans
Courses: Art Appreciation, Art History, Costume Design & Construction, Drawing, History of Art & Archaeology, Lettering, Museum Staff Training, Painting, Photography, Printmaking, Restoration & Conservation, Sculpture, Silversmithing, Traditional Indian Techniques, Two & Three-Dimensional Design
Summer School: Dir, Jon Wade. Enrl 150; tuition $60 per cr hr, free to Native Americans. Courses—Arts, Creative Writing, Museum Training

SANTA FE INSTITUTE OF FINE ARTS, 1807 Second St, No 42, 87501-9608. Tel 505-983-6157. *Pres* Bobbie Webb Thomas
Estab 1985; pvt; D & E; scholarships; SC 12
Ent Req: Portfolio review
Tuition: $1000 per session
Courses: Painting, Sculpture
Adult Hobby Classes: Enrl 10 per session; $100 per session. Courses—Master classes in Printing, Sculpture

SOUTHWEST ART LEAGUE SEMINARS, Art Horizons Ltd, 812 Camino Acoma, 87505. Tel 505-982-9981, 983-4825. *Dir* Maurice Loriaux, PhD
Estab 1971; D & E; enrl all seminars are limited to 21 delegates
Ent Req: Intermediate proficiency in painting—watercolor, oil, acrylics, all styles
Tuition: $519 per 6 day seminar includes room & board
Courses: All media

SILVER CITY

WESTERN NEW MEXICO UNIVERSITY, Dept of Expressive Arts, 88062. Tel 505-538-6614. *Chmn* Claude Smith; *Prof* Gloria Maya, MFA; *Prof* Anthony Howell, MFA; *Prof* Cecil Howard, MFA; *Artist-in-Residence* Ruben Gonzalez
Pub; D & E; scholarships; SC 10, LC 7; enrl D 211, non-maj 196, maj 15
Ent Req: HS dipl
Degrees: BA & MA, 4 yrs
Tuition: Res— $40 per cr hr; $483 for 12-18 cr hrs; nonres—$2050 for 12-18 cr hrs; campus res available
Courses: Art Education, Art History, †Ceramics, Collages, Constructions, Drawing, Graphic Design, †Jewelry, Mixed Media, †Painting, †Printmaking, †Sculpture, Silversmithing, Teacher Training, Textile Design, Fiber Arts
Adult Hobby Classes: Courses—Ceramics, Lapidary, Silversmithing, Stained Glass, Fiber
Summer School: Enrl 44; tuition $163 for 4-6 cr hr more credits from June 9 - July 11 or July 14 - Aug 15. Courses—Photography, Elementary Art Methods, Clay Workshop, Painting & Drawing Workshop, Printmaking, Art Appreciation, Ceramics, Special Art Tours in New Mexico & Europe

NEW YORK

ALBANY

COLLEGE OF SAINT ROSE, Dept of Art, 432 Western Ave, 12203. Tel 518-454-5111; FAX 518-438-3293. *Chairperson* Karene Faul, MFA; *Prof* Patricia Clahassey, EdD; *Assoc Prof* Paul Mauren; *Asst Prof* Scott Brodie, MFA; *Asst Prof* Kristine Herrick, MFA; *Instr* Jessica Loy; *Asst Prof* Leslie Stewart Curtis, PhD; *Lectr* Thomas Santelli, MFA
Estab 1920, dept estab 1970; pvt; D & E; scholarships; SC 21, LC 7, GC 8; enrl non-maj 200, maj 120, GS 20
Ent Req: HS dipl, SAT or ACT, rank in top 2/5 of class
Degrees: BS(Art, Art Educ, Graphic Design, Studio Art), MS(Art Educ)
Tuition: Res—undergrad $3915 per sem, grad $208 per cr hr
Courses: Aesthetics, Art Education, Art History, Ceramics, Drawing, Graphic Arts, Graphic Design, Illustration, Jewelry, Painting, Photography, Printmaking, Sculpture, Teacher Training, Studio Art, Typography
Adult Hobby Classes: Enrl 20; tui $135 per cr hr. Courses —Some continuing education courses each semester
Summer School: Dir Karene Faul. Enrl 80; two 5 wk courses begin from May 19 - June 27 & June 30 - Aug 8. Courses—Photo I & II, Ceramics I & II, Graduate Screenprint Fibers

JUNIOR COLLEGE OF ALBANY, Fine Arts Division, 12208. Tel 518-445-1778. *Chairperson* Terrance Tiernan
Estab 1957, dept estab 1970; pvt; D & E; scholarships; SC 43, LC 16 (Art); enrl D 700 (total), 200 (art), E 823 (total)
Ent Req: HS dipl, references, records, SAT
Degrees: AAS 2 yrs
Tuition: $5700 per yr
Courses: Art History, Ceramics, Commercial Art, Drawing, Graphic Arts, Graphic Design, Illustration, †Interior Design, Mixed Media, Painting, †Photography, Printmaking, Sculpture
Children's Classes: Summer courses for High School students
Summer School: Dir, Robert Pennock. Courses—vary

STATE UNIVERSITY OF NEW YORK AT ALBANY, Art Dept, 1400 Washington Ave, 12222. Tel 518-442-4020. *Chair Dept* Thom O'Connor, MFA; *Prof* Edward Mayer, MFA; *Prof* Mojmir Frinta, PhD; *Prof* Thom O'Connor, MFA; *Assoc Prof* Mark Greenwold; *Assoc Prof* Arthur Lennig; *Assoc Prof* Robert Cartmell, MFA; *Assoc Prof* Phyllis Galembo; *Asst Prof* Roberta Bernstein, PhD; *Asst Prof* Marja Vallila, MFA; *Asst Prof* Joann Carsen; *Asst Prof* James Buchman; *Asst Prof* Sarah Cohen
Estab 1848; pub; D & E; scholarships; SC 43, LC 20, GC 33; enrl D 750, E 400, non-maj 600, maj 150, grad 45
Ent Req: HS dipl and portfolio
Degrees: BA 4 yr, MA 1.5 yr, MFA 2 yr
Tuition: Res—undergrad $1325 per sem, $105 per cr hr, grad $2000 per sem, $168 per cr hr; nonres undergrad $3275 per sem; $274 per cr hr, grad $3658 per sem, $308 per cr hr; campus res—room & board $1930 per sem
Courses: Aesthetics, Art History, Calligraphy, Collages, Constructions, †Drafting, History of Art & Archaeology, Intermedia, Mixed Media, †Painting, †Photography, †Printmaking, †Sculpture, Theatre Arts, Plastics
Adult Hobby Classes: Courses in all studio areas
Summer School: Asst Dean Grad Studies, Paul Saimond. Enrl 350; term of 3 - 6 wks beginning July 1

ALFRED

NEW YORK STATE COLLEGE OF CERAMICS AT ALFRED UNIVERSITY, School of Art & Design, 14802. Tel 607-871-2412. *Dean* Kathleen Collins. Instrs: FT 25
Estab 1900; enrl maj undergrad 280, grad 25, others 300. Two yrs of foundation study & two yrs of upper level study
Degrees: BFA and MFA 4 yrs
Tuition: Res—undergrad $5585 per yr, grad $8900 per yr; nonres—undergrad $7985
Courses: Art Education, Ceramics, Graphic Design, Painting, Photography, Printmaking, Sculpture, Video, Glass Arts, Wood
Summer School: Dr Jim Curl. Tuition 4 cr $1100, 6 cr $1650 for two 6 wk terms. Courses—Ceramics, Sculpture

AMHERST

DAEMEN COLLEGE, Art Dept, 14226. Tel 716-839-3600, Ext 241. *Chmn Dept* Dennis Barraclough, MFA; *Prof* Sr M Jeanne File, PhD; *Prof* James K Y Kuo, MA; *Asst Prof* John Davis, BFA; *Asst Prof* Donald Bied, MFA
Estab 1947; pvt; D & E; scholarships; SC 50; enrl D 1200, non-maj 1135, maj 65
Ent Req: HS dipl, art portfolio
Degrees: BFA(Drawing, Graphic Design, Illustration, Painting, Printmaking, Sculpture), BA(Art), & BS(Art Educ) 4 yrs
Tuition: Undergrad—$3625 per sem, $240 per cr hr; campus res—room & board $1875
Courses: Aesthetics, Art Education, Art History, Ceramics, Drawing, Graphic Design, Illustration, Painting, Photography, †Printmaking, †Sculpture, Silversmithing, Theatre Arts, Computer Art
Summer School: Dean, Karin Kovach-Allen

ANNANDALE-ON-HUDSON

BARD COLLEGE, Milton Avery Graduate School of the Arts, 12504. Tel 914-758-4105. *Dir Program* Arthur Gibbons; *Instr* Lydia Davis; *Instr* Robert Kelly; *Instr* Alan Cote; *Instr* Adolfas Mekas; *Instr* Elie Yarden; *Instr* Nicholas Maw; *Instr* Perry Bard; *Instr* Jean Feinberg; *Instr* Regina Granne; *Instr* Stephen Scheer; *Instr* Ann Turyn; *Instr* Archie Rand; *Instr* Tom McDonough
Estab 1981; pvt; scholarships; enrl 70
Degrees: MFA
Tuition: $4250
Courses: Film, Painting, Photography, Sculpture, Music, Writing
Summer School: A student will normally be in residence for three summers terms, earning 13 credits per term; eight credits are awarded for the Master's project, for a total of 60; 13 independent study credits are awarded towards a degree

AURORA

WELLS COLLEGE, Dept of Art, 13026. Tel 315-364-3237. *Division Chmn* Suzanne Hecht
Estab 1868; pvt; W; D; scholarships; SC 19, LC 20; enrl D 500 (total), non-maj 122, maj 18
Ent Req: HS dipl, credit by examination programs
Degrees: BA 4 yrs
Tuition: Res—undergrad $11,400 per yr; campus res available
Courses: Aesthetics, †Art History, †Ceramics, †Drawing, †Painting, Photography, Printmaking, Teacher Training, †Theatre Arts

BAYSIDE

QUEENSBOROUGH COMMUNITY COLLEGE, Dept of Art and Photography, 222-05 56th Ave, 11364. Tel 718-631-6395. *Chmn* Lola B Gellman, PhD; *Prof* John Hawkins, MFA; *Prof* Paul Tschinkel, MFA; *Prof* Kenneth Walpuck, PhD; *Assoc Prof* Robert Rogers, MFA; *Asst Prof* Heinz Wipfler, MA; *Asst Prof* Jules Allen
Estab 1958, dept estab 1968; pub; D & E; scholarships; SC 21, LC 14; enrl D 9000, E 4000
Ent Req: HS dipl, placement exams
Degrees: AA, AS and AAS
Tuition: Res—undergrad $1050 per sem, $85 per cr; nonres—undergrad $1338 per sem, $104 per cr; no campus res
Courses: Advertising Design, Art History, Ceramics, Drawing, Painting, Photography, Printmaking, Sculpture, Video, Artist Apprenticeships, Arts Internships, Arts for Teachers of Children, Color Theory, Design
Adult Hobby Classes: Enrl 18; tuition $90 - $190 per course. Courses—Antiques, Calligraphy, Interior Design, Jewelry, Photography, Stained Glass, Ceramics, Cabinetmaking, Drawing Techniques
Summer School: Dir, Bob Rogers. Tuition $40 per cr for term of 7 wks beginning mid-June. Courses—Art History, Drawing, Photography, Sculpture

BINGHAMTON

STATE UNIVERSITY OF NEW YORK AT BINGHAMTON, Dept of Art & Art History, University Center, 13902. Tel 607-777-2605. *Chmn Dept* Donald Bell
Estab 1950; pub; D; scholarships; SC 18, LC 32, GC 63; enrl 679, non-maj 400, maj 82, grad 45
Ent Req: HS dipl, Regents Scholarship, ACT or SAT
Degrees: BA 4 yrs, BFA 4 yrs, MA 1-2 yrs, PhD varies
Tuition: Res—undergrad $55 per cr hr, grad $105 per cr hr; nonres—undergrad $167 per cr hr, grad $240 per cr hr
Courses: †Art History, Drawing, Film, Graphic Design, Painting, Printmaking, Video, †Cinema, †Studio Art
Summer School: Dir, Donald Bell. Tuition same as academic yr, 3 separate sessions during summer. Courses—Art History, Drawing Workshop, Sculpture Foundry

BROCKPORT

STATE UNIVERSITY OF NEW YORK COLLEGE AT BROCKPORT, Dept of Art & Art History, Tower Fine Arts, 14420. Tel 716-395-2209; FAX 716-395-KEYS. *Chmn* Tom Markusen; *Assoc Prof* Wolodymry Pylyshenko; *Assoc Prof* Anna Holcombe; *Asst Prof* Jill Gussow; *Asst Prof* Jennifer Hecker; *Asst Prof* Leopoldo Fuentes; *Asst Prof* Dr Hafez Chehab; *Lectr* Nancy Leslie. Instrs: FT 9, PT 10
Pub; D; scholarships; SC 33, LC 29(Art History); enrl 8188, maj 100, grad 2000, grad 30
Ent Req: HS dipl, ent exam
Degrees: BA, BS & BFA 4 yrs
Tuition: Res—$2650; nonres—$3600, grad $4000
Courses: Art History, Ceramics, Drawing, Jewelry, Painting, Photography, Printmaking, Video, Artists Books
Summer School: Four 5 wk sesssions per yr

BRONX

BRONX COMMUNITY COLLEGE, Music & Art Dept, 181 St & University Ave, 10453. Tel 718-220-6213, 220-6240. *Chmn* Valerie Capers; *Deputy Chmn* Peter Schira
Degrees: Cert, AS, AAS
Tuition: $1050 per sem
Courses: Art Appreciation, Art History, Ceramics, Commercial Art, Design, Drawing, Painting, Photography, Printmaking, Modern Art
Adult Hobby Classes: Enrl 25; tuition $45 for 7 weeks. Courses—Calligraphy, Drawing

HERBERT H LEHMAN COLLEGE, Art Dept, Bedford Park Blvd, 10468. Tel 718-960-8256. *Chmn* George Corbin, PhD; *Prof* Richard Ziemann, MFA; *Prof Emeritus* Ursula Meyer, MA; *Assoc Prof* Arvn Bose; *Asst Prof* Salvatore Romano; *Asst Prof* Herbert Broderick, PhD; *Asst Prof* David Gillison, MFA
Dept estab 1968; pub; D & E; scholarship; SC 18, LC 29, GC 31; enrl non-maj 100, major 50, grad 15
Ent Req: HS dipl, ent exam
Degrees: BA & BFA 4 yrs, MA, MFA & MA 2 yrs
Tuition: Res—undergrad $462.50 per sem, $35 & $40 per cr, grad $750 per sem, $75 per cr; nonres—undergrad $712.50 per sem, $55 per cr, grad $1000 per sem, $95 per cr; no campus res available
Courses: †Art History, †Graphic Arts, †Painting, †Sculpture
Summer School: Dean, Chester Robinson. Enrl 45; tuition $35 & $40 per cr for 6 wk term beginning June 28. Courses—Art History, Drawing, Painting

MANHATTAN COLLEGE, School of Arts and Sciences, Manhattan College Parkway, 10471. Tel 718-920-0345. *Chmn Fine Arts Dept* George L McGeary, EdD; *Asst Prof* John F Omelia, PhD
Estab 1853; pvt den; D; scholarships; LC 8; enrl D 3000
Ent Req: HS dipl
Degrees: BA 4 yrs
Tuition: Res—undergrad $14,890 per yr, $275 per cr; nonres—undergrad $9640 per yr; campus res—room & board $2500 per yr
Courses: Art History, Ceramics, Drawing, Film, Graphic Arts, Graphic Design, History of Art & Archaeology, Painting, Photography, Printmaking, Sculpture

BRONXVILLE

CONCORDIA COLLEGE, 171 White Plains Rd, 10708. Tel 914-337-9300. *Assoc Prof* Dr Ann Franco; *Asst Prof* Ellen F Halter, MA
Estab 1881; pvt; D; scholarships; SC 4, LC 2
Ent Req: HS dipl, SAT or ACT
Degrees: BA and BS 4 yrs
Tuition: $3870 per sem
Courses: Art Education, Art History, Ceramics, Drawing, Handicrafts, History of Art & Archaeology, Painting, Photography, Sculpture, Teacher Training
Adult Hobby Classes: Courses—Painting

SARAH LAWRENCE COLLEGE, Dept of Art History, 10708. Tel 914-337-0700. *Instr* Abigail Child, MFA; *Instr* Nancy Bowen, MFA; *Instr* Dave Gearey, BA; *Instr* Gary Burnley, MFA; *Instr* Mary Delahoyd, MA; *Instr* Joseph C Forte, PhD; *Instr* David Castriota, PhD; *Instr* U Schneider, MFA; *Instr* Kris Phillips, MFA; *Instr* Susanna Heller, BFA; *Instr* Joel Sternfeld, BA; *Instr* Marsha Pels, MFA; *Instr* Mira Schor, MFA; *Instr* Terry Koshel, MFA; *Instr* Mary Patierno, BA; *Instr* Patricia Karetzky, PhD; *Instr* Suzanne Boorsch, MA; *Instr* Mac Griswold, BA; *Instr* Sandra Sider, PhD. Instrs: FT 1, PT 9
Estab 1926; pvt; D; scholarships
Ent Req: HS dipl
Degrees: BA 4 yrs
Tuition: $17,280 per yr
Courses: Drawing, Painting, Printmaking, Art History, Photography, Sculpture, Filmmaking, Visual Fundamentals
Summer School: Center for Continuing Education

BROOKLYN

BROOKLYN COLLEGE, Art Dept, Bedford Ave & Ave H, 11210. Tel 718-951-5181. *Acting Chmn* Michael Mallory
Scholarships offered
Degrees: BA, BFA, MA, MFA
Tuition: Res—undergrad $92 - $100 per cr hr, grad $145 per cr hr; non res—grad $250 per cr hr
Courses: Architecture, Art Appreciation, Art History, Ceramics, Collages, Design, Graphic Arts, Graphic Design, History of Art & Archaeology, Painting, Photography, Printmaking, Sculpture
Summer School: Enrl 100; 6 weeks. Courses—Survey

KINGSBOROUGH COMMUNITY COLLEGE, Dept of Art, 2001 Oriental Blvd, 11235. Tel 708-368-5000. *Chmn* Thomas I Nonn, PhD
Estab 1965, dept estab 1972; pub; D & E; SC 10, LC 8; enrl maj 135
Ent Req: HS dipl
Degrees: AS 2 yrs
Courses: Art History, Ceramics, Design, Drawing, Graphic Arts, Graphic Design, Illustration, Jewelry, Mixed Media, Painting, Printmaking, Sculpture, Communication Design
Adult Hobby Classes: Overseas travel courses
Summer School: Courses—Art

LONG ISLAND UNIVERSITY, BROOKLYN CENTER, Art Dept, University Plaza, 11201. Tel 718-488-1051. *Chmn* Liz Rudey. Instrs: FT 3, PT 15
Pvt; D & E; scholarships; SC 5, LC 3
Ent Req: HS dipl, ent exam
Degrees: BA & BS 4 yrs
Tuition: $270 per cr
Courses: Art History, Calligraphy, Ceramics, Drawing, Painting, Printmaking, Sculpture, Arts Management, Media Arts, Medical-Scientific Illustration, Teaching Art to Children, Visual Experience
Adult Hobby Classes: Courses—Teaching Art to Children
Summer School: Dir, Liz Audey. Term of two 6 wk sessions. Courses—Ceramics, Drawing, Painting

NEW YORK CITY TECHNICAL COLLEGE OF THE CITY UNIVERSITY OF NEW YORK, Dept of Art and Advertising Design, 300 Jay St, 11201. Tel 718-260-5000. *Chmn* Joel Mason
Estab 1949; pub; D & E; SC 16, LC 3; enrl D 350, E 125
Ent Req: HS dipl
Degrees: AAS 2 yrs
Tuition: $705 per sem
Courses: †Advertising Design, Commercial Art, Drawing, Graphic Design, Illustration, Lettering, Painting, Printmaking, Packaging, Paste-ups, Type Specing
Summer School: Dir, B Pearlstein. Enrl 50. Courses—Design, Lettering, Life Drawing, Paste-up

PRATT INSTITUTE
—School of Art and Design, 200 Willoughby Ave, 11205. Tel 718-636-3600, 636-3619. *Dean* William Fasolino
Pub; enrl 3700
Tuition: Res—undergrad $11,744 per yr, $372 per cr hr, grad $425 per cr hr
Courses: †Art Education, †Art History, †Ceramics, †Drawing, †Film, †Graphic Design, †Illustration, †Industrial Design, †Interior Design, †Painting, †Photography, †Printmaking, †Sculpture, †Video, †Computer Graphics
Adult Hobby Classes: Enrl 195. Various courses offered
Children's Classes: Morning classes
Summer School: Dean, Vieri Salvadori. Enrl for high school students only; tuition $400 per 4 cr. Courses—Computer Graphics, Fine Arts, Foundation Art
—School of Architecture, 200 Willoughby Ave, 11205. Tel 718-636-3405. *Dean* Frances Halsband; *Assoc Dean* Mark Haber
Degrees: BS and BProf Studies 4 yrs, BArchit 5 yrs, MArchit, MS(Urban Design), MS(Planning), BArchit/MS(Urban Design) and BArchit/MS(Planning)
Tuition: Res—undergrad $355 per cr, grad $405 per cr
Courses: Architecture, Art History, Landscape Architecture, Design, History of Architecture, Materials, Structures, Construction documents in professional practice

BUFFALO

STATE UNIVERSITY COLLEGE AT BUFFALO, Fine Arts Dept, 1300 Elmwood Ave, 14222. Tel 716-878-6014. *Chmn* Peter Sowiski. Instrs: FT 16
Estab 1875, dept estab 1969; pub; D & E; SC 34, LC 17, GC 6; enrl maj 300 (art) 50 (BFA) 12 (art history)
Ent Req: HS dipl
Degrees: BA(Art), BA(Art History) & BFA 4 yrs
Tuition: Res—undergrad $1325 per sem, $105 per cr hr; nonres undergrad—$3125 per sem, $274 per cr hr; campus res available
Courses: †Art History, †Drawing, †Painting, †Photography, †Printmaking, †Sculpture, †Papermaking
Summer School: Dir, Gerald Accurso. Tuition res—$45 per cr hr, nonres—$107 per cr hr for 10 wk term beginning June 2. Courses—Art History, Studio

UNIVERSITY AT BUFFALO, STATE UNIVERSITY OF NEW YORK, Dept of Art, 2917 Main St, 14214. Tel 716-829-3477; FAX 716-831-2392. *Chmn* Tyrone Georgiou
Estab 1846; pub; D & E; scholarships, fels; SC, LC, GC; enrl D 400, E 150, grad 35
Ent Req: HS dipl for all undergraduate students
Degrees: BA & BFA 4 yrs, MFA 2 yrs
Tuition: Res—undergrad $1325 per sem, $105 per cr hr, grad $2000 per sem, $168 per cr hr; nonres—undergrad $3275 per sem, $274 per cr hr, grad $3658 per sem, $308 per cr hr; campus res—single $1565 per sem, double $1263 per sem, three-person $1113 per sem (rates vary depending on campus location)
Courses: Drawing, †Illustration, †Painting, †Photography, †Printmaking, †Sculpture, †Communications Design
Summer School: Dean, Eric Streiff. Courses—Drawing, Painting, Photo Workshop, Printmaking & Linotype Workshops, Sculpture, Illustration Workshop & Papermaking Workshop

VILLA MARIA COLLEGE OF BUFFALO, Art Dept, 240 Pine Ridge Rd, 14225. Tel 716-896-0700, Ext 324. *Chmn* Brian R Duffy, MFA; *Assoc Prof* Carol B Wells, MS; *Instr* Carole C Gates, MS; *Instr* Roberley Bell, MFA; *Instr* Daniel V Calleri; *Instr* Barbara P Wojciechowski; *Instr* Bonnie Scheller
Estab 1961; pvt; D & E; scholarships; SC 27, LC 3; enrl D 450, E 100, maj 170
Ent Req: HS dipl of equivalency
Degrees: AA, AAS & AS 2 yrs
Tuition: $2350 per sem
Courses: Advertising Design, Art History, Design, Drafting, Drawing, Graphic Arts, Graphic Design, Interior Design, Lettering, Painting, Photography, Printmaking, †Graphic Design, †Interior Design, Lettering, Painting, †Photography, Printmaking, Sculpture, Textile Design, Advertising Graphics, Color Photo, Commercial Design, Computer-aided Design, Etching, History of Interior Design, History of Photography, Mechanical Systems & Building Materials, Rendering & Presentation, Serigraphy, Studio Lighting, 3-D Design, View Camera Techniques
Adult Hobby Classes: Courses - Drawing, Painting, Photography
Summer School: Enrl 10-20. courses—a variety of interest courses, including drawing, painting and photography

CANANDAIGUA

FINGER LAKES COMMUNITY COLLEGE (Formerly Community College of the Finger Lakes), Visual & Performing Arts Dept, Lincoln Hill Campus, 14424. Tel 716-394-3500; FAX 716-394-5005. *Chmn* Elaine Lomber; *Prof* Thomas F Insalaco, MFA; *Prof* Wayne Williams; *Asst Prof* John Fox, MFA. Instrs: FT 5
Estab 1966; pub; D & E; SC 14, LC 2; enrl D 60, non-maj 700, maj 50
Ent Req: HS dipl
Degrees: AA & AAS 2 yrs
Tuition: Res—$890 per sem; nonres—$1780 per sem
Courses: Advertising Design, Art History, Ceramics, Commercial Art, Drawing, Graphic Arts, Graphic Design, Illustration, Painting, Photography, Printmaking, Sculpture, Stage Design, Theatre Arts
Summer School: Courses—Per regular session

CANTON

ST LAWRENCE UNIVERSITY, Dept of Fine Arts, 13617. Tel 315-379-5192. *Chmn* Guy Berard, MFA; *Prof* J Michael Lowe, MFA; *Prof* Roger Bailey, MFA; *Assoc Prof* Elizabeth Kahn, PhD; *Asst Prof* Dr Dorothy LiMouze
Estab 1856; pvt; D; SC 16, LC 13; enrl maj 48
Ent Req: HS dipl
Degrees: BA
Tuition: $16,700 per yr; campus res—room & board $5300
Courses: Art History, Ceramics, Drawing, Painting, Photography, Printmaking, Sculpture, Teacher Training

CAZENOVIA

CAZENOVIA COLLEGE, Center for Art & Design Studies, 13035. Tel 315-655-9446, Ext 162; FAX 315-655-2190. *Chmn* John Aistars, MFA; *Assoc Prof* Constance Roy, MA; *Assoc Prof* Josef Ritter, MFA; *Assoc Prof* Jeanne King, MFA; *Assoc Prof* Anita Fitzgerald, MS; *Assoc Prof* Scotty Ottaviano, MFA; *Assoc Prof* Jo Buffalo; *Asst* Charles Goss, MFA; *Instr* Kim Waale, MFA; *Instr* Anita Welych, MFA; *Instr* Karen Steen, MFA
Estab 1824; pvt; D & E; scholarships; SC 21, LC 3
Ent Req: HS dipl
Degrees: AA, AS, AAS, BS, & BPS 2 yr & 4 yr progs
Tuition: Res—$8592 per yr, $187 per cr hr; campus res—room & board $4388
Courses: †Advertising Design, Ceramics, Drawing, Drafting, †Illustration, †Interior Design, Lettering, Painting, Photography, Printmaking, Advertising Layout, †Advanced Studio Art, Basic Desing, Fashion Desing, Typography, Rendering, Residential Interiors, Office & Mercantile Interiors
Adult Hobby Classes: Enrl 159; tuition $210 per 3 sem course. Courses—large variety

CHAUTAUQUA

CHAUTAUQUA INSTITUTION, School of Art, PO Box 1098, 14722. Tel 716-357-6233. *Dir Art School* Don Kimes; *Instr* Stanley Lewis; *Instr* William Daley; *Instr* Frank Martin; *Instr* Polly Martin; *Instr* Chris Semergieff; *Instr* Barbara Goodstein; *Instr* Josette Urso; *Instr* Barbara Grossman; *Instr* Jackie Hayden; *Instr* George Rose; *Instr* Libby Kowalski; *Instr* Shari Mendelson; *Instr* David Lund; *Instr* Ed Smith; *Instr* Steffi Franks; *Instr* Piper Shepard
Estab 1874; pub; D (summers only); scholarships; SC 40, LC 20; enrl D 500
Tuition: $2425 full cost for 8 wk term
Courses: Ceramics, Drawing, Painting, Photography, Sculpture, †Fiber Arts, †Art Metals
Adult Hobby Classes: Enrl 300; tuition $75 per wk; Courses—same as above
Children's Classes: Young artists programs, ages 6 - 17
Summer School: Dir, Don Kimes. Enrl 55; tuition $2200 beginning June 26 - Aug 18

CLAYTON

THOUSAND ISLANDS CRAFT SCHOOL & TEXTILE MUSEUM, 314 John St, 13624. Tel 315-686-4123. *Dir* Margaret Rood. Instrs: PT 27
Estab 1964; D & E; scholarships; SC 21; enrl D 210, E 10
Degrees: No degrees but transfer credit
Tuition: $140 plus $20 registration fee for 1 wk course
Courses: Drawing, Weaving, Basketry, Bird Carving, Country Painting, Decoy Carving, Pottery, Quilt Making, Spinning, Watercolor
Children's Classes: Courses—Drawing, Pottery, Weaving
Summer School: July 3 - August 25. Courses—Country Painting, Creative Stitchery, Decoy Carving, Painting on Silk, Pottery, Quilting, Watercolor Painting, Weaving

CLINTON

HAMILTON COLLEGE, Art Dept, 13323. Tel 315-859-4269; FAX 315-859-4632. *Chmn* John McEnroe, PhD; *Instr* Deborah Pokinski, PhD; *Instr* Steven Liebman, MFA; *Instr* Robert Palusky, MFA; *Instr* William Salzillo, MFA; *Instr* Robert Muirhead, MFA; *Instr* John McEnroe, PhD; *Instr* Scott MacDonald, PhD; *Instr* Ella Gant, MFA; *Instr* Louanne Getty, MFA
Pvt; D; enrl non-maj 850, maj 50
Ent Req: HS dipl, SAT
Degrees: AB
Tuition: $20,000 per yr
Courses: †Art History, Ceramics, Mixed Media, Painting, Photography, Sculpture, Video

COBLESKILL

STATE UNIVERSITY OF NEW YORK, AGRICULTURAL AND TECHNICAL COLLEGE, Art Dept, PO Box 4, 12043. Tel 518-234-5011. *Chmn Art Dept* Charles C Matteson, MA
Estab 1950; pub; D & E; SC 2, LC 2; enrl D 95
Ent Req: HS dipl
Degrees: AA and AS 2 yrs
Tuition: Res—undergrad $675 per sem; nonres—undergrad $600 per sem; campus res—room & board $1260 per yr
Courses: Art Education, Art History, Drawing, Painting, Sculpture, Teacher Training, Theatre Arts
Adult Hobby Classes: Enrl 4000 per yr; tuition $9 per course. Courses—large variety of mini-courses

CORNING

CORNING COMMUNITY COLLEGE, Division of Humanities, 14830. Tel 607-962-9238. *Prof* John M Runyon, MFA; *Prof* Margaret Brill, MA; *Assoc Prof* Horst Werk, MFA. Instrs: FT 3
Estab 1958, dept estab 1963; pub; D & E; SC 8, LC 6
Ent Req: HS dipl, SAT
Degrees: AA, AS, AAS 2 yrs
Tuition: $1100 per sem
Courses: Art History, Lettering, Ceramics, Drawing, Painting, Airbrush, 2-D & 3-D Design, Layout, Silkscreen
Adult Hobby Classes: Enrl 18; $73 sem
Summer School: Dir, Ms Clarke

CORTLAND

STATE UNIVERSITY OF NEW YORK, COLLEGE AT CORTLAND, Art Dept, PO Box 2000, 13045. Tel 607-753-4316. *Chmn* Fred Zimmerman; *Prof* Steven Barbash, MFA; *Prof* John Jessiman, MFA; *Assoc Prof* Libby Kowalski; *Prof* George Dugan, MFA; *Assoc Prof* James Thorpe, MFA; *Assoc Prof* Charles Heasley; *Asst Prof* Allen Mooney, MFA
Estab 1868, dept estab 1948; pub; D & E; scholarships; SC 40, LC 10; enrl D 5600 (total), 1200 (art), maj 80
Ent Req: HS dipl, all college admissions standards based on high school average or scores from SAT, ACTP or Regent's tests
Degrees: BA 4 yrs
Tuition: Res—undergrad $1450 per yr; nonres—undergrad $3100 per yr; other college fee & activity assessment $87 per yr; campus res—$1400 per yr(room) and $972 per yr(board)
Courses: Aesthetics, Art Education, Art History, Ceramics, Drawing, Film, Graphic Arts, History of Art & Archaeology, Painting, Photography, Printmaking, Sculpture, Textile Design, Arts Management, Design, Lithography, Weaving
Summer School: Dir, Frank Navia. Enrl 40; 2 terms of 5 wks beginning June 26. Courses—Art History, Studio

ELMIRA

ELMIRA COLLEGE, Art Dept, 14901. Tel 607-735-1800. *Chmn* Douglas Holtgrewe; *Asst Prof* Peter Chamberlain, MFA; *Asst Prof* Edwin Christenson; *Asst Prof* Leslie Kramer, MFA
Estab 1855; pvt; D & E; scholarships; SC 26, LC 15, GC 8; enrl D 250, E 125, maj 35, grad 6
Ent Req: HS dipl
Degrees: AA, AS, BA, BS and MEduc
Tuition: $12,450 per yr; campus res—available
Courses: †Art Education, †Art History, †Ceramics, †Drawing, †Painting, †Photography, †Printmaking, †Sculpture, †Video
Adult Hobby Classes: Tuition $180 - $265 per cr hr. Courses—Art History, Ceramics, Drawing, Landscape Painting & Drawing, Painting, Photography, Video
Summer School: Dir, Lois Webster. Tuition undergrad $180 cr hr, grad $265 per cr hr. Courses—Art History, Ceramics, Drawing, Landscape Painting & Drawing, Painting

FARMINGDALE

STATE UNIVERSITY OF NEW YORK AT FARMINGDALE, Advertising Art Design Dept, Melville Rd, 11735. Tel 516-420-2181. *Dept Chmn* Francis N Pellegrini
Degrees: AAS
Tuition: $1800 per yr
Courses: †Advertising Design, Design, Drawing, Illustration, Lettering, Painting, Photography, Printmaking, Airbrush, Computer Art, Computer Graphics, Electronic Publishing, Layout, TV Graphics
Adult Hobby Classes: Tuition $45 per credit hr. Courses same as above
Summer School: Dir, Francis N Pellegrini. Tuition $45 per cr; June-Aug. Courses—Advertising, Production, Art History, Design, Drawing, Lettering, Mechanical Art

FLUSHING

QUEENS COLLEGE, Art Dept, 65-30 Kissena Blvd, 11367. Tel 718-997-5770. *Chmn* Barbara G Lane
Degrees: BA, BFA, MA, MFA, MSEd
Tuition: Res—undergrad $49 per cr hr, grad $84 per cr hr; nonres—$202.50 per cr hr
Courses: Advertising Design, Architecture, Art Appreciation, Art Education, Art History, Calligraphy, Ceramics, Design, Drawing, Illustration, Painting, Photography, Printmaking, Sculpture
Summer School: Courses held at Caumsett State Park

FOREST HILLS

FOREST HILLS ADULT CENTER, 6701 110th St, 11375. Tel 718-263-8066. *Admin Asst* Gertrude Schaller
Degrees: Cert
Tuition: $70 plus materials for 8 wk course
Courses: Art Appreciation, Art History, Calligraphy, Ceramics, Drawing, Handicrafts, Painting, Photography, Cartooning

FREDONIA

STATE UNIVERSITY COLLEGE, Dept of Art, 14063. Tel 716-673-3537. *Chmn* Robert Booth
Estab 1867, dept estab 1948; pub; D & E; scholarships; SC 30, LC 18; enrl D 650, E 70, non-maj 610, major 140
Ent Req: Ent req HS dipl, GRE, SAT, portfolio review all students
Degrees: BA 4 yrs, BFA 4 yrs
Courses: Art History, †Ceramics, Drawing, †Painting, †Photography, Printmaking, †Sculpture, Video, †Printmaking, †Sculpture, Video

GARDEN CITY

ADELPHI UNIVERSITY, Dept of Art and Art History, 11530. Tel 516-877-4460. *Chmn & Prof* Harry Davies; *Prof* Richard Vaux, MFA; *Prof* Yvonne Korshak; *Asst Prof* Thomas MacNulty; *Asst Prof* Dale Flashner. Instrs: FT 8, PT 18
Estab 1896; pvt; D & E; scholarships; SC 40, LC 20, GC 20; enrl D 700, E 100, maj 130, grad 60
Ent Req: HS dipl; portfolio required for undergrad admission, required for grad
Degrees: BA 4 yrs, MA 1 1/2 yrs
Tuition: $4650 per sem; campus res available
Courses: Advertising Design, †Art Education, †Art History, Ceramics, †Costume Design & Construction, †Design, Drawing, Graphic Design, †History of Art & Archaeology, Jewelry, †Painting, †Photography, †Printmaking, †Sculpture, Weaving
Summer School: Tuition—same as regular session; two 4 wk summer terms also 2 wk courses. Courses—Crafts, Drawing, Painting, Photography

NASSAU COMMUNITY COLLEGE, Art Dept, Stewart Ave, 11530. Tel 516-222-7162. *Chmn* Dr Leon Frankston; *Prof* John Fink; *Prof* Dr Russell Housman; *Prof* Stanley Kaplan; *Adjunct Prof* Charles Reina; *Prof* Salli Zimmerman; *Prof* Robert Carter; *Prof* Robert Lawn; *Prof* Edward Fox; *Prof* Susan Kravitz
Estab 1959, dept estab 1960; pub; D & E; scholarships; SC 22, LC 5; enrl D & E 20, 000
Ent Req: HS dipl
Degrees: AA 2 yrs, certificate in photography & advertising design 1 yr
Tuition: $56 per cr hr
Courses: Advertising Design, Art History, Ceramics, Costume Design & Construction, Painting, Drawing, Fashion Arts, Graphic Design, History of Art & Archaeology, Painting, Photography, Printmaking, Sculpture, Arts & Crafts
Summer School: Two 5 wk terms

GENESEO

STATE UNIVERSITY OF NEW YORK COLLEGE AT GENESEO, Dept of Art, College of Arts & Science, 14454. Tel 716-245-5814. *Chmn* Paul H Hepler. Instrs: FT 8, PT 3
Estab 1871; pub; D & E; Scholarships; SC 35, LC 7; enrl D 1000, E 1150, maj 115
Ent Req: HS dipl, ent exam
Degrees: BA(Art) 3-4 yrs
Tuition: $1375 per yr
Courses: Art Education, Art History, Ceramics, Drawing, Graphic Arts, Jewelry, Painting, Photography, Sculpture, Textile Design, Computer Art, 2-D & 3-D Design, Photolithography, Watercolor, Wood Design
Summer School: Enrl 180; tuition undergrad $45.85 per hr, grad $90.85 per hr for two 5 wk sessions & a 3 wk session. Courses vary

GENEVA

HOBART AND WILLIAM SMITH COLLEGES, Art Dept, Houghton House, 14456-3397. Tel 315-781-3487; FAX 315-781-3560. *Chmn* M Bogin. Instrs: FT 7
Estab 1822; pvt; D; scholarships; SC 15, LC 8; enrl D 1800
Ent Req: HS dipl, ent exam
Degrees: BA and BS 4 yrs
Tuition: $16,992
Courses: †Architecture, †Art History, Drawing, Mixed Media, Painting, Photography, Printmaking, Sculpture, †Studio Art

GREENVALE

C W POST CENTER OF LONG ISLAND UNIVERSITY, School of Visual & Performing Arts, Northern Blvd, 11548. Tel 516-299-0200. *Chmn* Prof Howard LaMarcz; *Dean Visual & Performing Arts* Lynn Croton; *Prof* Marilyn Goldstein; *Prof* Stephen Soreff; *Prof* Robert Yasuda; *Prof* Jerome Zimmerman; *Assoc Prof* Stern Einzig; *Assoc Prof* Joan Harrison; *Assoc Prof* Frank Ott; *Assoc Prof* JoAnn Powers; *Asst Prof* John Fekner; *Asst Prof* Richard Mills; *Asst Prof* Jeffrey Silverthorne
Dept estab 1957; pvt; D & E; scholarships; SC 70, LC 15, GC 40; enrl D 2000, E 450, non-maj 2000, maj 250, grad 150, others 50
Ent Req: HS dipl, portfolio
Degrees: BA(Art Educ), BA(Art Hist), BA(Studio), BS(Art Therapy) & BFA(Graphic Design) 4 yrs, MA(Photography), MA(Studio), MS(Art Educ) & MFA(Art, Design or Photography) 2 yrs
Tuition: $10,810 per yr; campus res—available
Courses: †Advertising Design, Aesthetics, †Art Education, †Art History, Ceramics, Collages, Commercial Art, Conceptual Art, Constructions, Drawing, Film, Graphic Arts, Graphic Design, Handicrafts, Illustration, Intermedia, Jewelry, Lettering, Mixed Media, Painting, Photography, Printmaking, Sculpture, Stage Design, Teacher Training, Theatre Arts, Video, Computer Graphics, Fine Arts, Weaving
Adult Hobby Classes: Courses—Varied
Summer School: Prof, Howard LaMarcz. Duration 3-5 wk sessions. Courses—varied

HAMILTON

COLGATE UNIVERSITY, Dept of Art & Art History, 13346. Tel 315-824-1000, Ext 633; FAX 315-824-1000, Ext 292. *Chmn* Robert McVaugh, PhD; *Prof* Jim Loveless, MFA; *Prof* Jim Loveless, MFA; *Asso Prof* John Knecht, MFA; *Assoc Prof* Judith Oliver, PhD; *Asst Prof* Gail S White, MFA; *Asst Prof* Priscilla Smith, MFA; *Asst Prof* Lynn Schwarzer, MFA; *Asst Prof* Padma Kaimal, MA
Estab 1819, dept estab 1905; pvt; D; scholarships; SC 22, LC 23; enrl D 941, maj 50
Ent Req: HS dipl, CEEB or ACT
Degrees: BA 4 yrs
Tuition: $13,595 per yr; campus res—room & board $4540
Courses: Art History, Drawing, Mixed Media, Painting, Photography, Printmaking, Sculpture, Combined Media, Motion Picture Productions

HEMPSTEAD

HOFSTRA UNIVERSITY
—**Department of Fine Arts,** Calkins Hall, Room 218, 107 Hofstra University, 11550-1090. Tel 516-463-5474. *Chmn* Donald Booth. Instrs: FT 11
Estab 1935, dept estab 1945; pvt; D & E; scholarships; LC 20, GC 16; enrl D 1610, maj 100, grad 10
Ent Req: HS dipl
Degrees: BA 4 yrs, MA 1 - 2 yrs, BS 4 yrs
Tuition: Res—undergrad $4920 per sem, grad $339 per cr
Courses: †Advertising Design, †Art Education, †Art History, †Ceramics, †Jewelry, †Painting, †Photography, †Sculpture, Appraisal of Art and Antiques
Summer School: Dean, Deanna Chitayat. Courses—Art History, Fine Arts

HERKIMER

HERKIMER COUNTY COMMUNITY COLLEGE, Social Sciences & Humanities Division, Reservoir Rd, 13350. Tel 315-866-0300, Ext 200. *Chmn* Dr Joseph DeLorenzo; *Prof* Guido Correro, MA; *Instr* James Bruce Schwabach, MFA
Estab 1966; pub; D & E; SC 8, LC 4; enrl D 329 (total), maj 16
Ent Req: HS dipl, SAT or ACT
Degrees: AA, AS & AAS 2 yrs
Tuition: Res—undergrad $675 per sem, $50 per cr hr; nonres—undergrad $1285 per sem; no campus res
Courses: Art Appreciation, Art History, Drawing, Museum Staff Training, Painting, Photography, Theatre Arts, Video
Adult Hobby Classes: Enrl 40 credit, 100 non-credit; tuition $33 per cr hr. Courses—Art Appreciation, Calligraphy, Pastels, Portraits, Photography
Children's Classes: Enrl 40; tuition varies. Courses—Cartooning Workshop, Introduction to Drawing
Summer School: Dir, John Ribnikac. Enrl 40. Courses—Same as regular session

HOUGHTON

HOUGHTON COLLEGE, Art Dept, One Willard Ave, 14744. Tel 716-567-2211. *Head Art Dept* Scott Bennett
Estab 1883; den; D & E; scholarship; SC 8, LC 6
Degrees: BA & BS 4 yrs
Tuition: $2085 per sem
Courses: Ceramics, Drawing, Graphic Design, Painting, Photography, Printmaking, Sculpture

ITHACA

CORNELL UNIVERSITY
—**Dept of Art,** College of Architecture, Art and Planning, 14853. Tel 607-255-3558. *Dean College* William McMinn; *Chmn Dept* Victor Kord, MFA; *Prof* Steve Poleskie, BS; *Prof* Jack L Squier, MFA; *Assoc Prof* Zevi Blum, BArchit; *Assoc Prof* Eleanore Mikus, MA; *Assoc Prof* Stanley J Bowman; *Assoc Prof* Jean Locey, MFA; *Assoc Prof* Greg Page, MFA; *Assoc Prof* Elisabeth Meyer, MFA; *Assoc Prof* Roberto Bertoia; *Assoc Prof* Barry Perlus; *Asst Prof* W Stanley Taft; *Asst Prof* Kay Walking Stick; *Asst Prof* Gail Scott White
Estab 1868, dept estab 1921; pvt; D; scholarships; SC 25, LC 1, GC 4; enrl maj 118, grad 13
Ent Req: HS dipl, HS transcript, SAT
Degrees: BFA 4 yrs, MFA 2 yrs
Tuition: $17,220 per yr; campus res available
Courses: Aesthetics, Drawing, †Painting, †Photography, †Printmaking, †Sculpture
Summer School: Dir, Stanley Taft. Tuition $375 per cr for term of 3 & 6 wks beginning June 27
—**Dept of the History of Art,** College of Arts and Sciences, 35 Goldwin Smith Hall, 14853. Tel 607-255-4905. *Prof* Robert G Calkins, PhD; *Prof* Stanley J O'Connor, PhD; *Prof* Andrew Ramage, PhD; *Prof* Martie W Young, PhD; *Assoc Prof* Judith E Bernstock, PhD; *Assoc Prof* Hal Foster, PhD; *Assoc Prof* Peter I Kuniholm, PhD; *Assoc Prof* Claudia Lazzaro, PhD; *Assoc Prof* Laura L Meixner, PhD; *Asst Prof* Karen-edis Barzman, PhD; *Prof Emeritus* Esther G Dotson, PhD
Estab 1939; pvt; D; scholarships; LC 64, GC 12; enrl D 1300, maj 40, grad 18, others 5
Ent Req: HS dipl, SAT, grad admission requires GRE
Degrees: BA & PhD
Tuition: $17,220 per yr; campus res available
Courses: Architecture, Art History, History of Art & Archaeology, Archaeology, Art Criticism
Summer School: Dean, Glenn Altschuler. Tuition $410 per cr hr. Courses—Introductory
—**New York State College of Human Ecology,** Dept of Design and Environmental Analysis, 14853-4401. Tel 607-255-2168; FAX 607-255-0305. *Chmn Dept* William R Sims. Instrs: FT 12
Scholarships
Degrees: BS, MA, MS
Tuition: Res—$5944; nonres—$10,884
Courses: Design, Drafting, Drawing, Graphic Design, †Interior Design, Facility Planning & Management, Human Factors/Ergonomics

ITHACA COLLEGE, Fine Art Dept, Danby Rd, 14850-7277. Tel 607-274-3011, Ext 3330. *Chmn* Harry McCue, MFA; *Prof* Raymond Ghirrardo; *Asst Prof* Carl Johnson; *Asst Prof* Susan Pickens; *Asst Prof* Joy Adams
Estab 1892, dept estab 1968; pvt; D & E; scholarships; SC 10; enrl non-maj 200, maj 40
Ent Req: HS dipl, SAT scores, review of portfolio
Degrees: BA and BFA 4 yrs
Tuition: $18,547 per yr; campus res—available
Courses: Drawing, Painting, Printmaking, Sculpture, Stage Design, Theatre Arts, Video, Book Design, Computer Art

JAMAICA

SAINT JOHN'S UNIVERSITY, Dept of Fine Arts, Grand Central & Utopia Parkways, 11439. Tel 718-990-6161. *Chmn* William Ronalds
Pvt; D; scholarships; SC 24, LC 9; enrl D 1300, maj 100
Ent Req: HS dipl, ent exam, portfolio review
Degrees: BFA and BS 4 yrs
Tuition: $260 per cr hr, $3925 per sem (12 - 18 cr)
Courses: †Graphic Design, †Photography, Saturday Scholarship Program, †Fine Arts
Adult Hobby Classes: Enrl 100; tuition $0 senior citizens. Courses—Drawing, Painting, Figure
Children's Classes: Enrl 300; tuition $0 advanced placement art. Courses—Airbrush, Cartoon
Summer School: Dir, Joyce Lawlor. Enrl 150-200; Courses—Drawing, Painting, Watercolor

YORK COLLEGE OF THE CITY UNIVERSITY OF NEW YORK, Fine and Performing Arts, 94-20 Guy Brewer Blvd, 11451. Tel 718-262-2400. *Coordr Fine Arts* Elena Borstein; *Prof* Jane Schuler, PhD; *Assoc Prof* Phillips Simkin, MFA; *Assoc Prof* Ernest Garthwaite, MA; *Assoc Prof* Arthur Anderson, MFA
Estab 1968; pub; D & E; enrl 4303
Ent Req: HS dipl
Degrees: BA 4 yrs
Tuition: Nonres—$170 per cr, $2025 per sem; no campus res
Courses: Art Education, Art History, Drawing, Graphic Arts, Painting, Photography, Printmaking, Sculpture, Computer Graphics
Summer School: Dean, Wallace Schoenberg. Enrl $20 per course; tuition $47 per cr for term of 6 wks beginning late June. Courses—Art History, Drawing, Painting

JAMESTOWN

JAMESTOWN COMMUNITY COLLEGE, Visual & Performing Arts Division, 525 Falconer St, 14701. Tel 716-665-5220, Ext 241; FAX 716-665-3498. *Div Chmn* Dr Robert A Hagstrom. Instrs: FT 7, PT 12
Estab 1950, dept estab 1970; pub; D & E; SC 11, LC 1; enrl D 310, E 254
Ent Req: Open
Degrees: AA 60 cr hrs
Tuition: Res—$70 per cr hr; non res—$140 per cr hr
Courses: Ceramics, Drawing, Painting, Photography, Sculpture, Stage Design, Theatre Arts, Video, Computer Graphics, Design, Introduction to Visual Art, Survey of Visual Arts
Summer School: Dir, Dr Robert A Hagstorm. Enrl 50 - 75; tuition res $70 per cr hr; non res $140 per cr hr, 2 terms of 6 wks beginning in May. Courses—Ceramics, Drawing, Painting, Photography

LARCHMONT

ADAMY'S CONCRETE AND CAST PAPER WORKSHOPS, 10538. Tel 914-941-1157. *Dir* George E Adamy, MBA. Instrs: FT 1, PT 1
Estab 1968; pvt; D & E; SC 13, LC 2, GC 13; enrl D 20, E 30
Tuition: From $30 per hr (open-ended sessions) to $225 for 10 sessions of advanced courses. Individual arrangements for special projects or commissions, & for lect & demonstrations at other schools, museums, art organizations; no campus res
Courses: Collages, Museum Staff Training, †Sculpture, †Teacher Training, Plastics, Polyadam Concrete & H-M (Hand-Made) Paper Casting & Construction
Adult Hobby Classes: Courses offered
Children's Classes: Courses offered
Summer School: Courses offered

LOCH SHELDRAKE

SULLIVAN COUNTY COMMUNITY COLLEGE, Division of Commercial Art and Photography, Leroy Rd, 12759. Tel 914-434-5750, Ext 215. *Prof* Joe Hopkins, MFA; *Prof* L Jack Agnew, MEd; *Assoc Prof* Earl Wertheim, BS; *Prof* Thomas Ambrosino, BPS; *Instructional Asst* Bernie Kroop, BPS
Estab 1962, dept estab 1965; pub; D & E; SC 24; enrl D 200, maj 180
Ent Req: HS dipl or equivalent
Degrees: AAS 2 yrs
Tuition: Res—undergrad $675 per sem, $56 per cr; nonres—undergrad $1500 per sem, $125 per cr
Courses: Advertising Design, Aesthetics, Art Appreciation, †Art History, Commercial Art, Design, Drawing, Graphic Arts, Graphic Design, History of Art & Archaeology, Photography, Sculpture, Video
Summer School: Assoc Dean of Faculty for Community Services, Allan Dampman

LOUDONVILLE

SIENA COLLEGE, Fine Arts Dept, 12211. Tel 518-783-2300. *Chmn* Gregory Zoltowski
Tuition: $160 per cr hr
Courses: Art Appreciation, Art History, Design, Drawing, Printmaking
Adult Hobby Classes: Enrl 35; tuition $315 per cr hr for 15 wks.
Courses—Introduction to Visual Arts
Summer School: Dir Mark A Heckler. Enrl 35; tuition $315 per cr hr for 7 wk term. Courses—Intro to Visual Arts

MALDEN BRIDGE

MALDEN BRIDGE SCHOOL OF ART, 12115. Tel 518-766-3616. *Dir* Betty Warren; *Instr* Lillian Longley; *Instr* Peter Guest. Instrs: FT 2, PT 5
Estab 1965; pvt; D; scholarships; SC 6; enrl D 55
Ent Req: Students who are seriously interested in developing their skills and knowledge
Courses: Drawing, Sculpture, Figure, Landscape, Portrait, Still Life
Summer School: Dir, Betty Warren. Four 2 wk workshops, one week workshop, 3 weekend courses. Courses—Drawing, Landscape, Oil Painting, Pastel

MIDDLETOWN

ORANGE COUNTY COMMUNITY COLLEGE, Art Dept, 115 South St, 10940. Tel 914-343-1121. *Chmn Dept* Patrick Kennedy, BFA
Estab 1950, dept estab 1950; pub; D & E; scholarships; SC 12, LC 5; enrl D 135, maj 60
Ent Req: HS dipl
Degrees: AA 2 yrs
Tuition: $875; no campus res
Courses: Art History, Ceramics, Design, Drawing, Painting, Photography, Sculpture, Color, Design

NEW PALTZ

STATE UNIVERSITY OF NEW YORK COLLEGE AT NEW PALTZ
—Art Studio Dept, SAB 106, 12561. Tel 914-257-3830; FAX 914-257-3859. *Chmn Art Studio & Art Educ* Patricia C Phillips. Instrs: 33
Pub
Degrees: BFA, BA, BS, MA & MFA, BSArt Ed, MSArt Ed
Tuition: Res—undergrad $90 per cr, grad $134 per cr; nonres—undergrad $240 per cr, grad $274 per cr
Courses: †Ceramics, †Graphic Design, †Painting, †Photography, †Printmaking, †Sculpture, Metal
Summer School: Dir, Patricia C Phillips. Courses—Art Education

—Art Education Dept, SAB 108-B, 12561. Tel 914-257-3850. *Chmn* Helen Gaige. Instrs: 3
Degrees: BS(Art Educ) and MS(Art Educ)
Summer School: Dir, Robert Davidson. 8 wk sem

NEW ROCHELLE

COLLEGE OF NEW ROCHELLE SCHOOL OF ARTS AND SCIENCES, Art Dept, School of Arts and Sciences, 10805. Tel 914-654-5274. *Chmn* William C Maxwell, EdD; *Assoc Prof* Mary Jane Robertshaw, MFA; *Assoc Prof* Steve Bradley, MFA; *Assoc Prof* Susan Canning, PhD
Estab 1904, dept estab 1929; pvt; scholarships; SC 52, LC 14, GC 21; enrl D 150, non-maj 45, maj 105, grad 98
Ent Req: HS dipl, SAT or ACT scores, college preparatory program in high school
Degrees: BA, BFA and BS 4 yrs
Tuition: $9300 per yr; campus res— room and board $4320 per yr
Courses: Art Education, Art History, Ceramics, Design, Drawing, Graphic Design, Jewelry, Painting, Photography, Printmaking, Sculpture, †Art Therapy, Computer Graphics, Fiber Arts, Metalwork, †Studio Arts
Summer School: Dir, Ann Raia. Enrl 400; tuition $180-255 per cr for two terms of 5 wks beginning June. Courses - Computer Graphics, Drawing, Painting, Photography & special workshops

NEW YORK

AESTHETIC REALISM FOUNDATION, 141 Greene St, 10012. Tel 212-777-4490; FAX 212-777-4426. *Class Chmn Aesthetic Realism* Ellen Reiss; *Exec Dir* Margot Carpenter
Estab 1973, incorporated 1975 as a not for profit educational foundation for teaching & philosophy of Aesthetic Realism founded by American poet & critic Eli Siegel (1902 - 1978)
Courses: Art History, Drawing
Adult Hobby Classes: Music, Poetry, Singing; Art History & Criticism, Drawing
Children's Classes: Learning to Like the World

AMERICAN ACADEMY IN ROME, 41 E 65th St, 10021. Tel 212-517-4200; FAX 212-517-4893. *Chmn* John W Hyland Jr; *Pres* Adele Chatfield Taylor; *Exec VPres* Wayne Linker
Estab 1894, chartered by Congress 1905; consolidated with School of Classical Studies 1913; Dept of Musical Composition estab 1921; scholarships
Summer School: 28 fellowships

ARTIST STUDIO CENTERS, INC, 1651 Third Ave, 10128. Tel 212-348-3102. *Head Dept* James E Youngman
Estab 1956; pvt; D & E
Tuition: $3700 per yr
Courses: Constructions, Drawing, Painting, Sculpture, Crafts all Media, Moldmaking, Sculpture Installation & Mounting, Sculpturing of Clay-Stone-Wax & Wood
Adult Hobby Classes: Enrl 70; tuition $4200 per yr for full time. Part time available. Courses—Moldmaking, Painting, Sculpture
Summer School: Dir, Jim Youngman. Courses—Painting, Sculpture

ART STUDENTS LEAGUE OF NEW YORK, 215 W 57th St, 10019. Tel 212-247-4510. *Exec Dir* R A Florio. Instrs: FT 65
Estab 1875; pvt; schol; LC; enrl D 1200, E 600, Sat 500 (adults and children)
Ent Req: None
Tuition: $115
Courses: Drawing, Graphic Arts, Illustration, Painting, Sculpture
Children's Classes: Classes on Saturday
Summer School: Enrl 800, beginning June

BERNARD M BARUCH COLLEGE OF THE CITY UNIVERSITY OF NEW YORK, Art Dept, 46 E 26th St (Mailing add: 17 Lexington Ave, PO Box 281, 10010). Tel 212-447-3340. *Chmn* Elsbeth Woody
Estab 1968, dept estab 1968; pub; D & E; SC 26, LC 16; enrl D 2000, E 500
Ent Req: HS dipl
Degrees: BA, BBA and BSEd 4 yrs, MBA 5 yrs, PhD
Courses: Advertising Design, Art History, Ceramics, Drawing, Graphic Arts, Graphic Design, History of Art & Archaeology, Illustration, Painting, Photography, Sculpture
Summer School: Courses - Art History Survey, Ceramics, Crafts, Drawing, Painting, Photography

THE CHILDREN'S AID SOCIETY, Visual Arts Program of the Greenwich Village Center, Visual Arts Program, 219 Sullivan St, 10012. Tel 212-254-3074. *Dir* Judy Mensch
Estab 1854, dept estab 1968; D & E; scholarships; SC 7; enrl D 200, E 175
Tuition: Adults $135 per sem; children $100 per sem; no campus res
Courses: Aesthetics, Art Education, Art History, Ceramics, Collages, Constructions, Drawing, Handicrafts, Jewelry, Mixed Media, Painting, Photography, Silversmithing, Teacher Training, Cabinet Making, Enameling, Pottery, Puppet Making
Adult Hobby Classes: Enrl 95; tuition $60-$75 per sem. Courses—Cabinetmaking, Ceramics, Drawing, Enameling, Painting, Photography, Pottery
Children's Classes: Enrl 325; tuition $32-$42 per sem. Courses—Dance, Drawing, Enameling, Mixed Media, Painting, Photography, Puppet Making, Woodwork, Theatre & Mime
Summer School: Dir, H Zaremben & Allen M Hart

CITY COLLEGE OF NEW YORK, Art Dept, 138th St & Convent Ave, 10031. Tel 212-690-4201. *Deputy Chair* Harriette Senie; *Dir Grad Studies* Shen Hong; *Supervisor Art Education* Joan Price, EdD; *Dir Evening Session* Al Loving
Estab 1847; pub; D & E; scholarships; SC 45, LC 29; enrl D 1043, E 133, maj 100, grad 122
Ent Req: HS dipl, entrance placement exams
Degrees: BA, MA, MFA
Tuition: Res—undergrad $650 per sem, $46 per cr hr, grad $950 per sem, $81 per cr

hr; nonres—undergrad $937.50 per sem, $76 per cr hr, grad $1337.50 per sem, $116 per cr hr
Courses: †Advertising Design, Art Appreciation, †Art Education, †Art History, Calligraphy, †Ceramics, Collages, Constructions, †Design, Drawing, †Graphic Arts, Illustration, †Interior Design, Mixed Media, Museum Staff Training, †Painting, †Photography, †Printmaking, †Sculpture, Teacher Training
Adult Hobby Classes: Courses—Drawing, Painting, Photography, Sculpture, Textile Design
Summer School: Dir, Stanley Wyatt. Courses—Introduction to Studio, Principles of Art, Drawing, Design, Painting, Photography, Art Education

CITY UNIVERSITY OF NEW YORK, PhD Program in Art History, Grad School & University Center, 33 West 42nd St, 10036. Tel 212-642-2865. *Chmn Exec Committee* Rose-Carol Washton Long, PhD; *Distinguished Prof Emeritus* John Rewald, PhD; *Distinguished Prof* Rosalind Krauss, PhD; *Assoc Prof* Mona Hadler, PhD; *Prof* Diane Kelder, PhD; *Prof* Rosalind Krauss, PhD; *Prof* William H Gerdts, PhD; *Prof* Marlene Park, PhD; *Res Prof* Milton W Brown, PhD; *Assoc Prof* H Barbara Weinberg, PhD; *Assoc Prof* Eugene A Santomasso, PhD; *Assoc Prof* Patricia Mainardi, PhD
Estab 1961, prog estab 1971; pub; D; scholarships; LC 6, GC 6; enrl D 95, grad 150
Ent Req: BA or MA in Art History
Degrees: PhD
Courses: Art History, †European Art & American Art, from c 1750-present, Criticism & Theory

COLUMBIA UNIVERSITY
—Graduate School of Architecture, Planning & Preservation, 400 Avery Hall, Broadway & 116th St, 10027. Tel 212-854-3414. *Dean Architectural Planning* Bernard Tschumi; *Chmn Div Architecture* Robert McCarter; *Chmn Div Urban Design* Stan Allen; *Chmn Div Urban Planning* Sig Guava. Instrs: FT 31, PT 32
Estab 1881; pvt; scholarships and fels; enrl 400
Ent Req: Bachelor's degree in appropriate area of study
Degrees: MArchit 3 yrs, MSArchit & Urban Design 1 yr, MSBuilding Design, MSPlanning 2 yrs, MSReal Estate Development, MSHistoric Preservation 1 1/2 yrs
Tuition: $16,140 per yr; campus res available
Courses: Architecture, Architecture and Urban Design, Historic Preservation, Urban Planning
—Dept of Art History and Archaeology, 826 Schermerhorn Hall, 10027. Tel 212-854-4505; FAX 212-854-7329; Telex 749-0397. *Chmn* David Rosand; *Dir Grad Studies* Suzanne Preston Blier
Pvt
Degrees: MA 2 yrs, MPhil 4 yrs, PhD 7 yrs
Tuition: $8810 per term
Courses: Aesthetics, Architecture, Art Appreciation, Art History, History of Art & Archaeology, Classical Art & Archaeology, Far Eastern Art & Archaeology, History of Architecture, History of Western Art, Near Eastern Art & Archaeology, Primitive & Pre-Columbian Art & Archaeology, History & Theory of Art History
—Columbia College, 212 Hamilton Hall, 10027. Tel 212-854-1754. *Dean* Kathryn Yatrakis
Pvt, M; scholarships and fels
Degrees: BA 4 yrs
Tuition: $8257 per sem; $170 (PT under 15 cr)
Courses: Art and Archaeology of South Eastern Asia, Asian Art and Archaeology, Classical Art and Archaeology, History of Western Art, Near Eastern Art and Archaeology, Primitive and Pre-Columbian Art and Archaeology
—School of the Arts, Division of Painting & Sculpture, 617 Dodge Hall, 116th St & Broadway, 10027. Tel 212-854-2829, 854-4065; FAX 212-854-1309. *Chmn* Alan Hacklin; *Admin Asst* Grace Pushkin; *Instr* Tony Harrison; *Instr* Archie Rand; *Instr* Reeva Potoft; *Instr* Stuart Diamond; *Instr* Donald Hazlitt; *Faculty* Donald Hazlitt; *Instr* William Norton; *Instr* Judy Pfzff; *Instr* David Chow; *Instr* Suzanne Joelson; *Instr* Elke Solomon; *Instr* Pier Conragra; *Instr* Suzanne Winkler
Estab 1754, div estab 1945; pvt; D & E; scholarships
Ent Req: Special students required to have studied at the college level in an institution of higher learning, non-degreed students are permitted to register for one or more courses in the division
Degrees: BA(Visual Arts) offered through the School of General Studies, Columbia College
Tuition: Campus res available
Courses: Drawing, Painting, Printmaking, Sculpture
Summer School: Enrl 25. Two sessions per summer. Courses—Drawing & Painting
—Barnard College, Dept of Art History, 3009 Broadway, 10027. Tel 212-854-2014, 854-2118. *Chmn* Keith Moxey
Estab 1923; pvt, W; scholarships; enrl maj 29, total 1930
Degrees: AB 4 yrs
Tuition: $16,228 per yr; campus res available
Courses: Art History, Painting
—Teachers Col Program in Art & Art Education, Teachers College, 525-W 120th St, 10027. Tel 212-678-3360, 678-3361; FAX 212-678-4048. *Dean* Judith Brandenburg; *Dir* Judith Burton
Estab 1888; pvt; scholarships, assistantships & fels; GC; enrl 225
Ent Req: Bachelor's degree & Portfolio review
Degrees: MA, MA with certification, EdM, supervisor/administrator license, EdD
Tuition: $460 per cr
Courses: Ceramics, Drawing, Painting, Photography, Printmaking, Sculpture, Art Education, Art Appreciation, Artistic-Aesthetic Development, Crafts, Curriculm Design, Design, Historical Foundations, Museum Studies, Painting Crafts, Philosophy of Art, Teacher Education
Adult Hobby Classes: Enrl 35; tuition $150 per 10 wk session

COOPER UNION SCHOOL OF ART, Cooper Square, 10003. Tel 212-353-4200. *Dean* Lee Anne Miller, MFA
Estab 1859; pvt; D & E; scholarships
Ent Req: HS dipl, ent exam
Degrees: BFA 4 yr

EDUCATION ALLIANCE, Art School, 197 E Broadway, 10002. Tel 212-475-6200, 475-4595. *Dir* Michael Rubin
Scholarships offered
Degrees: Cert
Tuition: Varies per course
Courses: Ceramics, Drawing, Mixed Media, Painting, Photography, Sculpture, Metal Sculpture
Adult Hobby Classes: Enrl 150; 15 wk term; Courses—Painting, Drawing, Sculpture, Metal Sculpture, Ceramics, Photography, Photo Silk Screen
Children's Classes: Enrl 20; 30 wk term. Courses—Mixed Media
Summer School: Dir Clare J Kagel. Enrl 60; tuition by the course for 10 wk term. Courses—Painting, Sculpture

FASHION INSTITUTE OF TECHNOLOGY, Art & Design Division, 227 W 27th St, 10001. Tel 212-760-7665. *Dean* Susan Rietman; *Asst Dean* Steven Bleicher; *Chmn Interior Design* James Vaughan; *Chmn Fashion Design* D Gioello, BFA; *Chmn Advertising Design* R Friedland, BFA; *Chmn Fine Arts* R Schechke, MFA; *Chmn Illustration* Elinore Brandon, BFA; *Chmn Photography* J Gollier; *Chmn Display Design* G Murray; *Chmn Jewelry Design* S Beizer, BA
Estab 1951; pub; D & E; scholarships; SC 317, LC 26; enrl D 4011, E 7004
Ent Req: HS dipl, ent exam
Degrees: AAS 2 yr, BFA 4 yr
Tuition: Res—undergrad $675 per sem; nonres—undergrad $1350 per sem; campus res—room and board $3270 per yr
Courses: †Advertising Design, Aesthetics, Art History, Calligraphy, †Costume Design & Construction, †Display, Drafting, Drawing, Fashion Arts, Goldsmithing, Graphic Arts, Graphic Design, History of Art & Archaeology, Illustration, †Interior Design, †Jewelry, Lettering, Mixed Media, Painting, †Photography, Printmaking, Restoration & Conservation, Sculpture, Silversmithing, Stage Design, †Textile Design, Theatre Arts, Video, Accessories Design, Computer Graphics, Design & Production, †Fur Design & Marketing, Toy Design
Adult Hobby Classes: Courses offered by Division of Continuing Education
Children's Classes: Courses offered by Division of Continuing Education
Summer School: Dean, Richard Meagher. Enrl 4589; tuition $60 - $120 per course for term of 3, 5 & 7 wks beginning June. Courses—as above

HARRIET FEBLAND ART WORKSHOP, 245 E 63rd St, Suite 1803, 10021. Tel 212-759-2215. *Dir* Harriet FeBland; *Instructor* Bernard Kassoy
Estab 1962; pvt; D & E; SC 4, LC 1, GC 2; enrl D 55, others 15
Ent Req: Review of previous work, paintings or sculpture
Tuition: $325 per 15 wk class, $150 for 5 wk 1 hr critique session
Courses: Collages, Constructions, Drawing, Painting
Adult Hobby Classes: Tuition $325, duration 15 wks. Courses—(all advanced) Assemblage, Drawing, Painting

FORDHAM UNIVERSITY, Art Dept, Arts Division, Lincoln Center, 10023. Tel 212-841-5269. *Division Chmn* Andree Hayum. Instrs: FT 7
Estab 1968; pvt; D & E; scholarships; SC 18, LC 25; enrl D 900, E 1750, maj 56
Ent Req: HS dipl
Degrees: BA 4 yr
Tuition: $285 per cr hr; campus res—available
Courses: Aesthetics, Costume Design & Construction, Drawing, Graphic Arts, History of Art & Archaeology, Painting, Photography, Sculpture, Stage Design, Teacher Training, Theatre Arts
Summer School: Dir, Dr Levak. Four terms per summer for 5 wks each

GREENWICH HOUSE POTTERY, 16 Jones St, 10014. Tel 212-242-4106. *Acting Dir* JoAnne Ruggeri. Instrs: 26
Estab 1902, dept estab 1948; pvt; D & E; scholarships; SC 32; enrl D 200, E 94
Ent Req: None
Degrees: None
Tuition: $200 per sem; no campus res
Courses: Ceramics, Sculpture, Glazing Chemistry
Adult Hobby Classes: Enrl 200; tuition $170 per 12 wk term. Courses—Pottery Wheel, Handbuilding, Sculpture
Children's Classes: Enrl 50; tuition $55 and $65 for 12 wk term. Creative technique instruction
Summer School: Dir, Susan B Wood. Enrl 40; tuition $160 per 4 wk term

HENRY STREET SETTLEMENT ARTS FOR LIVING CENTER, 466 Grand St, 10002. Tel 212-598-0400. *Dir* Barbara Tate
Estab 1895; pvt; D; scholarships; enrl D 60, E 60
Ent Req: None
Tuition: $30-$120 per course
Courses: Calligraphy, Ceramics, Drawing, Graphic Arts, Mixed Media, Painting, Printmaking, Sculpture
Adult Hobby Classes: Courses—Crafts, Drawing, Painting, Pottery
Children's Classes: Courses—Arts & Crafts, Cartooning, Drawing, Experimental Art, Painting, Pottery, Printmaking

HUNTER COLLEGE, Art Dept, 695 Park Ave, 10021. Tel 212-772-4000. *Chmn Art Dept* Sanford Wurmfeld; *Dean* Carlos Hortas. Instrs: FT 29
Estab 1890, dept estab 1935; pub; D & E; SC 20-25, LC 10, GC 14-20; enrl D 250 (including evening), maj 250, GS 250
Ent Req: HS dipl
Degrees: BA and BFA 4 yrs
Tuition: Res—$635 per sem, $100 per cr hr; nonres—$2025 per sem, $225 per cr hr
Courses: Art History, Drawing, Painting

JOHN JAY COLLEGE OF CRIMINAL JUSTICE, Dept of Art, Music and Philosophy, 10019. Tel 212-237-8325. *Chmn* Timothy Stroup; *Prof* Marlene Park, PhD; *Prof* Laurie Schneider, PhD; *Assoc Prof* John Dobbs, BFA; *Assoc Prof* Helen Ramsaran, MFA; *Lectr* Irene Gordon, AB; *Lectr* John I Russell, BFA. Instrs: FT 6, PT 4
Estab 1964, dept estab 1971; pub; D & E; SC 5, LC 6; enrl D 180, E 180
Ent Req: HS dipl
Degrees: BA and BS 4 yr
Tuition: Res—undergrad $625 per sem, $47 per cr; nonres—undergrad $2025 per sem, $170 per cr
Courses: Art History, Drawing, Painting, Sculpture

MARYMOUNT MANHATTAN COLLEGE, Fine & Performing Arts Dept, 221 E 71st St, 10021. Tel 212-517-0400. *Chmn* Mary Fleischer; *Prof* Bill Bordeau. Instrs: FT 12
Degrees: BA & BFA
Tuition: $4320 per term
Courses: Advertising Design, Art Appreciation, Ceramics, Design, Drawing, Illustration, Museum Staff Training, Painting, Photography, Printmaking, Conservation-Restoration

NATIONAL ACADEMY SCHOOL OF FINE ARTS, 5 E 89th St, 10128. Tel 212-996-1908; FAX 212-360-6795. *Dir* Edward P Gallagher; *Adminr* Ellen Lee Klein. Instrs: 35
Estab 1826; pvt; D, E & weekends; scholarships; SC 16; enrl 500
Ent Req: None
Tuition: $2700
Courses: Drawing, Painting, Printmaking, Sculpture, Anatomy, Composition-Portraiture, Drawing the Classical Orders, Life Sketch Class, Methods & Techniques, Painting Materials, Perspective
Adult Hobby Classes: Enrl 500; tuition $180 per class, $740 per sem $1350 per yr. Courses—Drawing, Painting, Printmaking, Sculpture & related subjects
Children's Classes: Enrl 25; tuition $70 per workshop. Courses ages 9 - 16—Drawing & Painting
Summer School: Dir, Edward P Gallagher, Adminr, Ellen Lee Klein. Enrl 150.Courses—Drawing, Painting, Printmaking, Sculpture

NEW SCHOOL FOR SOCIAL RESEARCH, Adult Education Division, 66 W 12th St, 10011. Tel 212-229-5600. *Dean* Gerald A Heeger
Tuition: $285 per course
Courses: Advertising Design, Art Appreciation, Art History, Calligraphy, Ceramics, Design, Drawing, Fashion Arts, Film, Jewelry, Painting, Photography, Printmaking, Sculpture, Textile Design, Fine Art, Cartooning, Glassblowing
Adult Hobby Classes: Enrl 1500; tuition $220 per course. Courses—All fine arts
Children's Classes: Summer Program for Young Adults
Summer School: Dir, Wallis Osterholz. Enrl 500; 6 wk term. Courses—All fine arts

NEW YORK ACADEMY OF ART, Graduate School of Figurative Art, 419 Lafayette St, 10003. Tel 212-505-5300; FAX 212-777-1160. *Dean* Albert W Landa; *Assoc Dean* David Davidson; *Chmn* James Lecky; *Instr* Edward Schmidt; *Instr* Joseph Groell; *Instr* Harvey Citron; *Instr* Xavier de Callatay
Scholarships
Degrees: MFA 2 yrs, part-time MFA 4 yrs
Tuition: $11,000 per yr
Courses: Art History, †Drawing, Painting, Sculpture, Anatomy
Adult Hobby Classes: Enrl 300; tuition $300 - $450 per course for 12 wk term. Courses—Anatomy, Art History, Drawing, Painting, Sculpture
Summer School: Dir, Albert W Lands. Enrl 40; 6 - 8 wk term. Courses—Anatomy, Art History, Drawing, Painting, Sculpture

NEW YORK INSTITUTE OF PHOTOGRAPHY, 211 E 43rd St, 10017. Tel 212-867-8260. *Dean* Charles DeLaney; *Dir* Donald Sheff
Estab 1910; Correspondence course in photography approved by New York State and approved for veterans; enrl 10,000
Degrees: Cert of graduation
Tuition: $798
Courses: Photography

NEW YORK SCHOOL OF INTERIOR DESIGN, 155 E 56th St, 10022. Tel 212-753-5365. *Pres* Paul Heyer
Estab 1916; pvt; D & E; schol; SC 25, LC 8; enrl D 700, E 300, non-maj 865, maj 135
Ent Req: HS dipl, portfolio and interview
Degrees: 3 yr design program, AAS, BFA
Tuition: $315 per cr; no campus res
Courses: Architecture, Art History, Drafting, Drawing, Graphic Design, Interior Design, Color, Space Planning, Design Materials
Adult Hobby Classes: Enrl 300; tuition $160 per cr. Courses—lower division courses offered
Summer School: Dean, Kerwin Katler. Enrl 400; tuition $160 per cr per 6 wks. Courses—various

NEW YORK STUDIO SCHOOL OF DRAWING, PAINTING AND SCULPTURE, 8 W Eighth St, 10011. Tel 212-673-6466; FAX 212-777-0996. *Dean* Graham Nickson; *Prog Dir* Ro Lohin; *Instr* Robert Bordo; *Instr* Garth Evans; *Instr* Bruce Gagnier; *Instr* Elena Sisto; *Instr* Charles Cajori; *Instr* Riley Brewster; *Instr* Ruth Miller; *Instr* Mercedes Matter; *Instr* Glenn Goldberg; *Instr* Jake Berthol; *Instr* Carole Robb; *Instr* Hugh O'Donnell
Estab 1964; pvt; D; scholarships; SC 13, LC 2; enrl D 80
Ent Req: HS dipl, portfolio of recent work
Tuition: $2900 per sem; campus res—available
Courses: Drawing, Painting, Sculpture
Adult Hobby Classes: Enrl 40; tuition $185 per 16 wks. Courses—Drawing (from the model)
Summer School: Program Dir, Ofra Shemesh. Enrl 60; tuition $1200 for term of 8 wks beginning June. Courses— Drawing, Painting, Sculpture

NEW YORK UNIVERSITY, Institute of Fine Arts, One E 78th St, 10021. Tel 212-772-5800; FAX 212-772-5807. *Dir* James R McCredie
Pvt; D & E; scholarships and fels offered; enrl grad 400
Tuition: $1700 per course
Courses: History of Art & Archaeology, Conservation and Technology of Works of Art; Curatorial Staff Training
—**Dept of Art & Art Professions,** 34 Stuyvesant St, 10003. Tel 212-998-5700; FAX 212-505-9092. *Chmn* Leonard Lehrer; *Dir Undergraduate Studies* Judith S Schwartz; *Prof* Angiola R Churchill, EdD; *Prof* David W Ecker, EdD; *Prof* Marilynn G P Karp, PhD; *Prof* Laurie Wilson; *Assoc Prof* Peter Campus, BS; *Assoc Prof* Judith Reiter Weissman, PhD; *Artist-in-Residence* N Krishna Reddy; *Artist-in-Residence* Gerald Pryor. Instrs: FT 10, PT 72

Pvt; D & E; scholarships and fels; undergrad SC 26, LC 13, grad SC 40, LC 25; enrl maj undergrad 115, grad 230
Ent Req: Col board ent exam, 85 HS average, portfolio, interview
Degrees: BS, MA, EdD, DA, PhD
Tuition: $484 per cr
Courses: Aesthetics, Art History, Design, †Drawing, †Graphic Arts, Painting, Photography, Printmaking, Sculpture, Teacher Training, Video, Arts Administration, Art Management, Art Theory & Criticism, Art Therapy, Computer Art, Costume History and Design, Crafts, Folk Art Studies, Interdisciplinary Arts, International Center for Advanced Studies, Internships, Lithography, Museum Education
Adult Hobby Classes: Tuition $125-$235. Courses—Art Therapy, Color Printmaking, Fiber Arts, Typographic Art of Letterform
Summer School: Chairperson, Angiola Churchill. Tuition $270 per cr. Four summer sessions 3-wk period, four days a wk; International Overseas Prog in Studio Arts in Venice, Italy; three summer prog, two summers abroad & one in New York (8 wks each summer) - Arts Administration in Paris, France and Art Therapy in Turin, Italy

PACE UNIVERSITY, Theatre & Fine Arts Dept, Pace Plaza, 10038. Tel 212-346-1352.
Estab 1950; pvt; D & E; scholarships; SC 4, LC 20; enrl D 200, E 150, 700-800 per yr art only
Ent Req: HS dipl, ent exam
Degrees: 4 yr, Art History Major
Tuition: $7228 per sem, $291 per cr hr; campus res—available
Courses: Art History, Drawing, Graphic Design, Modern Art, Oriental Art, Studio Art
Adult Hobby Classes: Courses same as above
Summer School: Two summer sessions. Courses—Studio Art

PARSONS SCHOOL OF DESIGN, 66 Fifth Ave, 10011. Tel 212-741-8910. *Dean* Charles S Olton, PhD
Estab 1896; pvt (see also Otis Art Institute of Parsons School of Design, Los Angeles, California); D & E; scholarships; SC 200, LC 400, GC 25; enrl D 1800, E 4000, GS 25, other 40
Ent Req: HS dipl, portfolio
Degrees: AAS, BFA, BBA, MA, MFA & MArch
Tuition: $11,050 per yr, $374 per cr; campus res—room & board $6200
Courses: †Advertising Design, Aesthetics, Architecture, †Art Education, Art History, Calligraphy, †Ceramics, †Commercial Art, Fashion Arts, Graphic Design, History of Art & Archaeology, Illustration, Industrial Design, Interior Design, Jewelry, Painting, Photography, Sculpture, Silversmithing, †Textile Design, Criticism, †Environmental Design, †Fine Arts, †History of Decorative Arts, Lighting Design, Marketing & Fashion Merchandising, Product Design
Adult Hobby Classes: Enrl 4200; tuition $374 per cr for term of 12 wks. Courses—Advertising, Computer Graphics, Fashion Design, Fine Arts, Floral Design, Illustration, Interior Design, Lighting Design, Marketing & Merchandising, Product Design, Surface Decoration, Theatre Design
Summer School: Dir, Francine Goldenhar. Tuition $4000 for term of 4-6 wks. Courses—Art, Art History, Design

PRATT INSTITUTE, Pratt Manhattan, 295 Lafayette St, 10012. Tel 212-925-8481; FAX 212-941-6397. *Dean* Elliott Gordon
Estab 1892; pvt; D; scholarships
Ent Req: HS dipl, portfolio, interview
Degrees: AOS, 2 yrs
Tuition: $336 per cr; campus res—available
Courses: †Graphic Design, †Illustration

SCHOOL OF VISUAL ARTS, 209 E 23rd St, 10010. Tel 212-679-7350, Div Continuing Educ 683-0600; FAX 212-725-3587. *Chmn* Silas H Rhodes; *Pres* David Rhodes
Estab 1947; pvt; scholarships; enrl FT 2035, PT 2684
Ent Req: HS transcript, portfolio review, SAT or ACT test results, interview, 2 letters of recommendation
Degrees: BFA, MFA, teachers' cert (K-12) in Art Educ
Tuition: $9900 plus fees per yr
Courses: †Advertising Design, †Film, †Graphic Design, †Illustration, Interior Design, Photography, Video, Art History & Criticism, Art Therapy, †Cartooning, Computer Graphics, †Fine Arts, †Art Education
Adult Hobby Classes: Enrl 2684; tuition $120 per cr; 12 wk term. Courses—Same as above
Summer School: Courses—Fine Arts, Design & Photography in Tangier, Morocco, other courses same as above

SCULPTURE CENTER GALLERY & SCHOOL, 167 E 69th St, 10021. Tel 212-737-9870, 879-3500. *Dir* Michael Cochran; *Gallery Dir* Marion Griffith
Estab 1933; pvt; D & E; scholarships
Tuition: Varies according to course
Courses: Drawing, Sculpture (stone, wood, welding, plaster molds, bronze casting)
Adult Hobby Classes: Enrl 102; tuition $50-$300 per month during June - Aug. Courses same as regular sem
Children's Classes: Enrl 16; tuition $45 per month. Courses—Sculpture (clay, wood, stone & plaster)
Summer School: Dir, G L Sussman. Enrl 100; tuition $50 - $300. Courses—Same as reg session plus special seminars

SKOWHEGAN SCHOOL OF PAINTING AND SCULPTURE, 200 Park Ave S, Suite 1116, 10003. Tel 212-529-0505; FAX 212-473-1342. *Dir* Barbara Lapcek
Estab 1946; pvt; schol & fel
Ent Req: Proficient in English, 18 years of age & slide portfolio review
Tuition: $4400, campus res avail
Courses: Painting, Sculpture, Fresco
Summer School: Enrl 65; 9 wk term

TOBE-COBURN SCHOOL, Eight E 40th St, 10016. Tel 212-686-9040; FAX 212-686-9171. *Pres* Rosemary Duggan. *Instrs:* FT 7, PT 10
Estab 1937; pvt; D; scholarships; 2 yr course, 16 months, for HS grad; 1 yr course, 9-12 months, for those with 15 or more transferable college sem cr, classroom study alternates with periods of work in stores or projects in fashion field; enrl 250
Degrees: AOS(Occupational Studies)
Tuition: $8395 per yr
Courses: Display, Fashion Arts, Fabrics, Fashion Design, Fashion Merchandising, Marketing & Management

NIAGARA FALLS

NIAGARA UNIVERSITY, Fine Arts Dept, De Veaux Campus, 14109. Tel 716-285-2090. *Chmn* Louis M Centofanti
Tuition: $2805 per sem
Courses: Art Appreciation, Art History, Ceramics, Drawing, Painting
Adult Hobby Classes: Enrl 150; tuition $85 per sem. Courses—Ceramics, Painting
Summer School: Dir, L Centofanti. Enrl 25; tuition $185 per sem hr. Courses—Ceramics

OAKDALE

DOWLING COLLEGE, Dept of Visual Arts, Idle Hour Blvd, 11769. Tel 516-244-3099. *Div Coordr* Dr Stephen Lamia; *Instr* Filomena Romano; *Instr* Loretta Lorance; *Instr* Ronald Baron; *Instr* Pascale Garrow; *Instr* David Carter; *Instr* Eric Furubotn; *Instr* Alan Brodsky; *Instr* Mary Abell; *Instr* Cosmo Prete; *Instr* Ellen Goldin; *Instr* Seung Lee; *Instr* Colin Lee; *Instr* Susan Dunkerley; *Instr* Charissa Baker; *Instr* Woody Hughes; *Instr* Kathy Levine; *Instr* Ginger Levant; *Instr* Christina Staudt
Pvt; D & E; enrl D 1100, E 500
Ent Req: HS dipl
Degrees: BA(Visual Art), BS and BBA 4 yrs
Tuition: $145 per cr hr
Courses: Advertising Design, Art History, Ceramics, Design, Drawing, Graphic Arts, Graphic Design, Illustration, Jewelry, Lettering, Painting, Photography, Printmaking, Sculpture

OLD WESTBURY

NEW YORK INSTITUTE OF TECHNOLOGY, Fine Arts Dept, Wheatley Rd, 11507. Tel 516-686-7543. *Chmn* John Murray, MFA; *Prof* Marvin Horowitz; *Prof* Valdis Kupris, MFA; *Prof* Shirley Marein, MFA; *Assoc Prof* Peter Voci; *Assoc Prof* Janet de Cecilia, MA; *Assoc Prof* Thomas Martin, MFA; *Asst Prof* Anthony Clementi, MA; *Adjunct Asst Prof* Steven Woodburn, MFA; *Adjunct Asst Prof* Krystov Wodiczko; *Asst Prof* Domenic Alfano; *Master Printer* Roni Henning
Estab 1910, dept estab 1963; pvt; D; scholarships; SC 11, LC 85; enrl D 427, non-maj 100, maj 327
Ent Req: HS dipl, portfolio review
Degrees: BFA 4 yr
Tuition: $4700 per yr, $190 per cr; no campus res
Courses: Art History, Calligraphy, Drawing, Graphic Arts, †Graphic Design, Illustration, †Interior Design, Lettering, †Painting, †Photography, †Printmaking, †Sculpture, †Teacher Training, Textile Design, Computer Graphics
Summer School: Tuition $80 per cr for term of 8 wks. Courses—Drawing, Interior Design, Painting, Sculpture

STATE UNIVERSITY OF NEW YORK COLLEGE AT OLD WESTBURY, Visual Arts Department, PO Box 210, 11568. Tel 516-876-3000, 876-3056. *Chmn* Mac Adams
Estab 1968, Dept estab 1969; pub; D & E; SC 10, LC 10; enrl D & E 277
Ent Req: HS dipl, skills proficiency exam, GED, special exception - inquire through admissions
Degrees: BA & BS(Visual Arts) 4 yr
Tuition: Res—$705 per sem
Courses: Collages, Conceptual Art, History of Art & Archaeology, Mixed Media, Painting, Photography, Printmaking, Sculpture, Video, TV Production/Editing

ONEONTA

HARTWICK COLLEGE, Art Dept, 13820. Tel 607-431-4825. *Chmn* Katharine Kreisher, MFA; *Prof* C Philip Young; *Prof* Roberta Griffith; *Asst Prof* Elizabeth Ayer; *Asst Prof* Terry Slade; *Asst Prof* Fiona Dejardin; *Asst Prof* Gloria Escobar. Instrs: FT 7, PT 8
Estab 1797; pvt; D; scholarships; enrl 1480, non-maj 1428, maj 52
Ent Req: HS dipl, SAT or ACT, recommendation from teacher or counselor & personal essay, $35 fee
Degrees: BA 4 yr
Tuition: $14,350 per yr; campus res—$4450
Courses: Art History, Ceramics, Drawing, Graphic Design, Painting, Photography, Printmaking, Sculpture, Teacher Training, Fiber, Glassblowing, Papermaking, Weaving
Summer School: High schhol arts workshop, 3 wks in July

STATE UNIVERSITY OF NEW YORK COLLEGE AT ONEONTA, Dept of Art, 13820. Tel 607-431-3717, 431-3718. *Chmn* James Mullen; *Instr* Nancy Callahan; *Instr* William Hubschmitt, MA; *Instr* Ernest Mahlke, MFA; *Instr* Andrea Modica, MFA; *Instr* Daniel Young; *Instr* Yolanda Sharpe
Estab 1889; pub; D & E; SC 31, LC 22; enrl D 660, E 35, maj 123, 25-30 at Cooperstown Center
Ent Req: HS dipl, regents scholarship exam, SAT and ACT
Degrees: BA(Studio Art, Art History) other programs include: one leading to MA(Museum History, Folk Art) in conjunction with the New York State Historical Association at Cooperstown, NY 13326 (Daniel R Porter III, SUNY Dir); a 3-1 program in conjunction with the Fashion Institute of Technology in New York City,

with 3 years at Oneonta as a Studio Art major leading to a BS degree and/or 1 year at FIT leading to a AAS (Advertising & Communications, Advertising Design, Apparel Production and Management, Fashion Buying & Merchandising, Fashion Design, Textile Design, and/or Textile Technology)
Courses: Art History, Ceramics, Drawing, Painting, Computer Art, Images of Women in Western Art, 2-D Design, 3- D Design, Visual Arts
Adult Hobby Classes: Offered only on a subscription basis at normal tuition rates through the Office of Continuing Education
Summer School: Dir, Dr Robert Nichols. Enrl 40-50. Tuition same as in regular session for two 4 & 5 wk terms beginning June and July. Courses—Studio

ORANGEBURG

DOMINICAN COLLEGE OF BLAUVELT, Art Dept, Western Hwy, 10962. Tel 914-359-7800. *Chmn* Sr Margaret J Gillis; *Dir Dept Arts & Science* Leigh Holt
Tuition: $230 per cr
Courses: Art Education, Art History, Drawing, Painting
Adult Hobby Classes: Enrl 40; tuition $117 per cr. Courses—Art History, Painting
Summer School: Dir, S Florence Dwyer. Enrl 35; tuition $117 per cr. Courses—History of Art, Watercolor

OSWEGO

STATE UNIVERSITY OF NEW YORK COLLEGE AT OSWEGO, Art Dept, Tyler Hall, 13126. Tel 315-341-2111. *Chmn* Allen Bremmer. Instrs: FT 18
Estab 1861; pub; D & E; SC 31, LC 9; enrl maj 150, grad 10
Ent Req: HS dipl, SAT or NYS regents scholarship exam
Degrees: BA 4 yr, BFA 4 yr, MA 2 yr
Tuition: Res—$675 per sem; nonres—$1600 per sem; campus res—room $775 per sem and board $555 per sem
Courses: Aesthetics, †Art History, †Ceramics, †Drawing, †Graphic Arts, †Graphic Design, Museum Staff Training, †Painting, †Photography, †Printmaking, Jewelry/Metalsmithing
Summer School: Dir, Lewis C Popham III. Tuition state grad res $90.85 per cr hr, non-grad res $45.85 per cr hr, grad nonres $156.85 per cr hr, non-grad nonres $107. 85 per cr hr

PLATTSBURGH

CLINTON COMMUNITY COLLEGE, Art Dept, Bluff Point, 12901. Tel 518-562-4200. *Assoc Prof* Ellen H Heyman
Courses: Art Appreciation, Design, Drawing, Painting, Photography, Sculpture

STATE UNIVERSITY OF NEW YORK AT PLATTSBURGH, Art Dept, Myers Fine Arts Bldg, 12901. Tel 518-564-2464, 564-2474. *Chmn* Rick Mikkelson, MFA. Instrs: FT 9, PT 4
Estab 1789, dept estab 1930; pub; D & E; scholarships; SC 30, LC 10; enrl D 700, Maj 90
Ent Req: HS dipl, EOP
Degrees: BA & BS 4 yrs
Tuition: $2650 per yr; campus res available
Courses: Art Appreciation, Art History, †Ceramics, †Design, †Drawing, †Graphic Design, Museum Staff Training, †Painting, †Photography, †Printmaking, †Sculpture, †Computer Graphics

PLEASANTVILLE

PACE UNIVERSITY, Dyson College of Arts & Sciences, Fine Arts Dept, Bedford Rd, 10570. Tel 914-773-3675. *Dean Arts & Science* Ruth Ann Thompson; *Chmn* John Mulgrew, MA; *Prof* Barbara Friedman, MFA; *Prof* Janetta Benton, PhD; *Prof* Martha Bartsch, BFA; *Prof* Ruis Woertendyke, MA. Instrs: FT 5, PT 20
Pvt; D & E; SC 4, LC 4
Ent Req: HS dipl
Degrees: AA & BS
Tuition: Full-time—$4237 per sem; part-time—$268 per credit hr; campus res—available
Courses: Art Education, Ceramics, Drawing, Graphic Arts, History of Art & Archaeology, Illustration, Interior Design, Painting, Photography, Printmaking, Sculpture, Stage Design, Theatre Arts, Typography
Summer School: Dir, Prof John Mulgrew. Courses—Art History, Ceramics, Drawing, Painting

POTSDAM

STATE UNIVERSITY OF NEW YORK COLLEGE AT POTSDAM, Dept of Fine Arts, 13676. Tel 315-267-2251. *Chmn* Joseph Hildreth MFA; *Prof* Arthur Sennett, MFA; *Prof* John Riordan; *Prof* James Sutter, MFA; *Prof* Michelle Van Parys, MFA; *Asst Prof* Tracy Watts, PhD; *Asst Prof* Sarah Gutwirth, MFA
Estab 1948; pub; D & E
Ent Req: HS dipl, SAT, portfolio review recommended
Degrees: BA 4 yrs, special program Empire State studio sem in New York City
Tuition: Res undergrad lower div $1155 per yr, $525 per sem, $35.85 per cr hr; nonres—undergrad lower div $1855 per yr; no grad students; campus res—$550 room & $470 (10 meals per wk) per sem
Courses: †Art History, †Ceramics, Drawing, †Painting, Photography, †Printmaking, †Sculpture
Adult Hobby Classes: Enrl 15; tuition $30 for 10 weeks. Courses—Pottery
Children's Classes: Enrl 30; tuition $20 for 6 weeks. Courses—General Art Workshop
Summer School: Dir, Joe Hildreth. Enrl 50-60; tuition $180 for 4 cr class of 5 weeks. Courses—Ceramic Survey, Intro to Studio Art

POUGHKEEPSIE

DUTCHESS COMMUNITY COLLEGE, Dept of Visual Arts, 53 Pendell Rd, 12601. Tel 914-471-4500; FAX 914-471-8467. *Dir* Eric Somers
Estab 1957; pub; D & E; scholarships; SC 24, LC 22; enrl D 660, E 340, maj 100
Ent Req: HS dipl
Degrees: AAS (Commercial Art)
Tuition: Res—$825 per yr; nonres—$3300 per yr
Courses: Painting, Photography, Glass, Leather, Metal, Plastic, Weaving, Wood

VASSAR COLLEGE, Art Dept, Raymond Ave, 12601. Tel 914-437-7000; FAX 914-437-7187. *Chmn* Peter Huenink; *Prof* U A Carroll; *Prof* E A Carroll; *Prof* Susan D Kuretsky; *Prof* Nicholas Adams. Instrs: FT 10, PT 7
Estab 1861; pvt; D; scholarships; SC 8, LC; enrl maj 90, others 2400
Ent Req: HS grad, ent exam
Degrees: BA(Art History) 4 yr
Courses: Architecture, †Art History, Drafting, Drawing, Painting, Printmaking, Sculpture

PURCHASE

MANHATTANVILLE COLLEGE, Art Dept, 2900 Purchase St, 10577. Tel 914-694-2200, Ext 331. *Head Dept* Louis Trakis
Estab 1841; pvt; D & E; scholarships; SC 25, LC 10, GC 7; enrl D 180, non-maj 90, maj 90, grad 10
Ent Req: HS dipl, portfolio, interview
Degrees: BA and BFA 4 yrs, MAT 1 yr, special prog MATA (Masters of Art in Teaching Art)
Tuition: $13,125 per yr; room & board $6200
Courses: Advertising Design, Art Education, Art History, Ceramics, Commercial Art, Conceptual Art, Constructions, Design, Drawing, Graphic Arts, Graphic Design, Illustration, Lettering, Painting, Photography, Printmaking, Sculpture, Teacher Training, Book Design, Design, Metal Sculpture
Summer School: Dir, Donna Messina. Two sessions June & July. Courses—Art History, Ceramics, Computer Graphics, Drawing, Painting, Sculpture

STATE UNIVERSITY OF NEW YORK COLLEGE AT PURCHASE
—Division of Visual Arts, 735 Anderson Hill RD, 10577-1400. Tel 914-251-6750. *Dean* George Parrino. Instrs: FT 18, PT 18
Estab 1974; pub; scholarships; enrl 3600, maj 400
Degrees: BFA(Visual Arts)
Tuition: Res—undergrad $2650 per yr; nonres—undergrad $6550 per yr; campus res—room $2430 per yr, board $1720 per yr
Courses: Art History, Drawing, Graphic Design, Painting, Printmaking, Photography, Art of the Book, Design in Wood, Media, 3-D Design
Adult Hobby Classes: Enrl 450-500
Children's Classes: Enrl 50; summer session art program
Summer School: Dir, Laura Evans. Enrl 400; 6 wk sessions
—Art History Board of Study, 735 Anderson Hill RD, 10577-1400. Tel 914-251-6550. *Coordr* Paul Kaplan, PhD; *Prof* Eric Carlson, PhD; *Prof* Irving Sandler, PhD; *Asst Prof* Jane Kromm, PhD
Estab 1971, dept estab 1977; pub; D & E; scholarships; enrl 2500, maj 50
Ent Req: HS dipl, essay on application, grades, test scores
Degrees: BA and BALA 4 yrs
Tuition: Res—$2650 per yr; nonres—$6550 per yr
Courses: Art History

RIVERDALE

COLLEGE OF MOUNT SAINT VINCENT, Fine Arts Dept, 6301 Riverdale Ave, 10471. Tel 718-549-8000. *Prof* Enrico Giordana, BFA; *Prof* Richard Barnett
Estab 1911; pvt; D & E; scholarships; SC 22, LC 10; enrl D 950, E 50
Ent Req: HS dipl and SAT
Degrees: BA, BS and BS(Art Educ) 4 yrs
Tuition: $5200 per sem
Courses: Design
Summer School: Dir Continuing Education, Dr Marjorie Connelly. Courses—vary each summer

ROCHESTER

MONROE COMMUNITY COLLEGE, Art Dept, 1000 E Henrietta Rd, 14623. Tel 716-292-2000. *Prof* George C McDade, MA; *Assoc Prof* Bruce R Brown, MFA; *Assoc Prof* Joe Hendrick; *Assoc Prof* Juliana F Williams; *Asst Prof* Charles W Haas, MFA
Estab 1961; pub; D & E; SC 16, LC 4
Ent Req: HS dipl
Degrees: Assoc in Arts 2 yrs, Assoc in Science 2 yrs, Assoc in Applied Science 2 yrs
Tuition: $1150 per nine months
Courses: Art History, Ceramics, †Commercial Art, Drafting, Drawing, Graphic Arts, Graphic Design, Handicrafts, Illustration, Jewelry, Lettering, Painting, Printmaking, Sculpture, Textile Design, Theatre Arts, Video, Weaving
Adult Hobby Classes: Tuition $36 per hr. Courses—Batik, Ceramics, Jewelry, Leatherwork, Macrame, Rugmaking, Soft Sculpture, Weaving
Summer School: Dir, George C McDade

NAZARETH COLLEGE OF ROCHESTER, Art Dept, 4245 East Ave, 14610. Tel 716-586-2525, Ext 521. *Head Dept* Ron Netsky; *Assoc Prof* Kathy Calderwood, BFA; *Assoc Prof* Roger J Adams; *Assoc Prof* Lynn Duggan, MFA; *Asst Prof* Maureen Brilla, MFA; *Asst Prof* Karen Trickey, MSEd; *Asst Prof* Mitchell Messina
Estab 1926, dept estab 1936; pvt; D & E; scholarships; SC 40, LC 15, GC 6; enrl D 180, E 74, non-maj 50, maj 200, grad 48
Ent Req: HS dipl
Degrees: BA and BS 4 yrs

Tuition: Undergrad $3335 per sem, $150 per cr hr; nonres—grad $121 per cr hr; campus res—room & board $3520 per yr
Courses: †Art Education, †Art History, Ceramics, Drawing, †Graphic Arts, Jewelry, Painting, Photography, Printmaking, Sculpture, Textile Design, Art Therapy
Summer School: Dir, Elaine Hayden. Enrl 60; tuition $150 per cr hr for term of 6 wks beginning July 5th. Courses—Grad & undergrad

ROBERTS WESLEYAN COLLEGE, Art Dept, 2301 West Side Dr, 14624. Tel 716-594-9471. *Dir* Loren Baker; *Prof* Willard Peterson; *Assoc Prof* Douglas Giebel Scholarships
Degrees: BA(Fine Art), BA(Studio Art), BS(Studio Art), BS(Art Education)
Tuition: $4511 per sem
Courses: Art Appreciation, Art History, Ceramics, Design, Drawing, Art Education, Graphic Design, Jewelry, Lettering, Painting, Photography, Printmaking, Sculpture, Weaving

ROCHESTER INSTITUTE OF TECHNOLOGY
—College of Imaging Arts & Sciences, One Lomb Memorial Dr, 14623. Tel 716-475-2646; FAX 716-475-6447. *Dean* Col Dr Margaret Lucas; *Assoc Dean* Col Carol Sack; *Asst Dean* Steve Loar; *Asst Dean Admin* Becky Eddy; *Dir* Dr Rodney Shaw
Tuition: Res—undergrad $18,000 per yr, grad $18,912 per yr
Courses: †Ceramics, †Graphic Arts, †Industrial Design, †Interior Design, †Jewelry, †Painting, †Sculpture, †Textile Design, †Weaving, Metalcrafts, Furniture Design, Medical Illustration, Computer Graphics Design
Adult Hobby Classes: Courses offered
Children's Classes: One wk summer workshop for juniors in HS
Summer School: 5 wk sessions, 2 1/2 wk sessions, & special one wk workshops
—School of Art and Design, College of Fine & Applied Arts, One Lomb Memorial Dr, 14623. Tel 716-475-2646. *Chmn Fine Arts* David Dickinson, MFA; *Chmn Graphic Design* Bernadette Merkel, MFA; *Chmn Industrial, Interior & Packaging Design* Toby Thompson; *Chmn Foundation Studies* Norman Williams, MS; *Chmn Crafts* Don Bujnowski, MFA; *Prof* Kener E Bond Jr, BEd; *Prof* Frederick Lipp, MFA; *Prof* R Roger Remington, MS; *Prof* Joanne Szabla, PhD; *Prof* James E Thomas, MFA; *Prof* Lawrence Williams, MFA; *Prof* Philip W Bornarth, MFA; *Prof* Barbara Hodik, PhD; *Prof* James Ver Hague; *Prof* Robert Kerr, MFA; *Prof* Robert A Cole, MS; *Prof* Robert Heischman, UCFA; *Prof* Craig McArt, MFA; *Prof* William Keyser, MFA; *Prof* Doug Sigler, MFA; *Prof* Robert Schmitz, MFA; *Prof* Richard Hirsch, MFA; *Prof* Richard Tanner, MS; *Prof* Michael Taylor, MFA; *Prof* Mark Stanitz, MA; *Prof* Len Urso, MFA; *Prof* Max Lenderman; *Prof* Albert Poley, MFA; *Prof* Wendell Castle, MFA; *Prof* Robert C Morgan, PhD; *Prof* James H Sias, MA; *Prof* Robert Wabnitz, Dipl & Cert; *Assoc Prof* Edward C Miller, MFA; *Assoc Prof* Bruce Sodervick, MFA; *Assoc Prof* Joseph A Watson, MFA; *Assoc Prof* Robert M Kahute, MFA; *Assoc Prof* Mary Ann Begland, MFA; *Assoc Prof* Steve Loar, MA; *Assoc Prof* Joyce Shikowitz, MFA; *Assoc Prof* Luvon Sheppard, MST; *Asst Prof* Heinz Klinkon, BFA; *Asst Prof* Doug Cleminshaw, MFA; *Asst Prof* Elizabeth Fomin, MFA; *Asst Prof* Glen Hintz, MFA; *Asst Prof* Thomas Lightfoot, PhD. Instrs: FT 47, PT 19
Estab 1829; pvt; enrl 1000
Ent Req: HS grad, ent exam, portfolio
Degrees: AAS, BS, BFA, MFA, MST
Tuition: Undergrad $10,950 per yr, grad $11,600 per yr
Courses: †Advertising Design, †Art History, †Ceramics, †Commercial Art, Design, Drawing, Graphic Arts, †Handicrafts, History of Art & Archaeology, †Illustration, †Industrial Design, †Interior Design, †Jewelry, Sculpture, †Silversmithing, †Textile Design, †Weaving, †Computer Graphics Design, †Glass, †Interior Design, †Medical Illustrations, †Printmaking Illustration, †Woodworking and Furniture Design
Adult Hobby Classes: Crafts, Design, Painting
Summer School: Enrl 250; tuition undergrad $260 per cr, grad $330 per cr for 8 wk term beginning June. Courses—Ceramics, Computer Graphics, Glass, Graphic Design, Metal, Painting, Printmaking, Textiles, Wood, Industrial, Interior, Packaging Design, Art History, 2-D and 3-D Design
—School of Photographic Arts & Sciences, College of Graphic Arts & Photography, One Lomb Memorial Dr, Rochester, 14623. Tel 716-475-2716. *Dir* Elaine O'Neil, MS; *Chmn Applied Photography* Nancy Stuart, AB; *Chmn Imaging & Photographic Technology* Andrew Davidhazy, MEd; *Chmn Fine Arts Photography* Ken White; *Chmn Film/Video* Malcom Spaull, BS; *Chmn Biomedical Photography Communications* Michael Peres; *Chmn American Video Institute* John Ciampa, JD; *Chmn Photographic Processing & Finishing Management* James Rice, BS; *Prof* John E Karpen, MFA; *Prof* Weston D Kemp, MFA; *Prof* Lothar K Engelmann, PhD; *Prof* Russell C Kraus, EdD; *Prof* David J Robertson, BFA; *Assoc Prof* Owen Butler, BFA; *Assoc Prof* Kerry Coppin; *Assoc Prof* Jeff Weiss; *Assoc Prof* Patti Ambroge; *Assoc Prof* Bradley T Hindson, BA; *Assoc Prof* Alan Vogel; *Assoc Prof* Robert Kayser, BS; *Assoc Prof* James Reilly, MA; *Assoc Prof* Guenther Cartwright, BA; *Assoc Prof* Howard Lester, MFA; *Assoc Prof* Howard LeVant, BS; *Assoc Prof* Elliott Rubenstein, MA; *Assoc Prof* Erik Timmerman, BS; *Assoc Prof* Douglas F Rea, MFA; *Assoc Prof* Steve Diehl, BS; *Assoc Prof* Mark Haven, BA; *Assoc Prof* John Retallack, BA; *Assoc Prof* Nancy Stuart, MS; *Assoc Prof* Ken White; *Asst Prof* Tom Lopez; *Asst Prof* Stephanie Maxwell; *Asst Prof* Bruce Lane; *Asst Prof* Adrianne Carrageorge; *Asst Prof* Lorett Falkner; *Asst Prof* Deni Defenbaugh; *Asst Prof* Sabrine Susstrink; *Asst Prof* Kaleen Moriority; *Asst Prof* Jack Holm; *Asst Prof* Glen Miller; *Asst Prof* William Osterman, MFA; *Asst Prof* Martha Leinroth, MFA; *Lectr* Dan Larken
Enrl 900
Degrees: BS, MS, MFA
Tuition: Res—undergrad $12,000 per yr, grad $12,000 per yr
Courses: Film, Photography, Video, †Biomedical Photographic Communication; †Photographic Illustration; Photographic Processing & Finishing; †Fine Art Photography, Imaging & Photographic Technology
Summer School: Courses—Photography, Film/Video, Motion Picture Workshops, Narrative/Documentary/Editorial workshop, Nature Photography
—School of Printing, College of Graphic Arts & Photography, One Lomb Memorial Dr, Rochester, 14623. Tel 716-475-2728. *Dir* George Ryan, PhD; *Chmn Management Division* W Frederick Craig, BS & MEd; *Chmn Photography Plates & Press Division* Walter G Horne, BS & MEd; *Chmn Design Composition Division* Emery E Schneider, BS & MEd; *Coordr Grad Program* Joseph L Noga, MS; *Paul & Louise Miller Prof* Robert G Hacker, BS; *Prof* Barbara Birkett, BS; *Prof* Walter A Campbell, BA; *Prof* Julius L Silver, BA; *Prof* Miles F Southworth, BS; *Assoc Prof*

Bekir E Arpag, BS; *Assoc Prof* William H Birkett, BS; *Assoc Prof* Joseph E Brown, BS; *Assoc Prof* Clifton T Frazier, BS; *Assoc Prof* Alfred F Horton, AAS; *Assoc Prof* Herbert H Johnson, BS; *Assoc Prof* Archibald D Provan, BS; *Assoc Prof* Werner Rebsamen, dipl; *Assoc Prof* Robert J Webster, BS; *Assoc Prof* Charles J Weigand, BS, MS & SUC; *Asst Prof* Robert Y Chung, BA; *Asst Prof* Hugh R Fox, AB & JD; *Asst Prof* David P Pankow, BA & MA; *Asst Prof* Harry Rab, BSME & MSME; *Asst Prof* Robert S Tompkins
School has 25 laboratories, occupying 125,000 sq ft. More than 70 courses are offered; enrl 700
Degrees: BS, MS, MST
Tuition: Res—undergrad $9075 per year, grad $9618 per year
Courses: Printmaking, †Printing Technology, †Newspaper Production Management, †Printing Systems & Engineering, †Printing & Applied Computer Science
Summer School: Graphic Arts, Layout & Printing, Reproduction Photography, Ink & Color, Newspaper & Magazine Design, Hand Papermaking, Web Offset, Gravure, Lithography, Printing Plates, Typography, Bookbinding
—**College of Graphic Arts & Photography,** One Lomb Memorial Dr, PO Box 9887, 14623. Tel 716-475-2732, 475-2733, 475-2743. *Dean* Dr Robert M Desmond; *Dir* Elaine O'Neil
Tuition: Undergrad $9075 per yr; grad $9618 per yr
Adult Hobby Classes: Extensive seminar schedule
Summer School: scholarships

UNIVERSITY OF ROCHESTER, Dept of Art & Art History, Morey Hall, 424, 14627. Tel 716-275-9249. *Chmn* Michael Ann Holly. *Instrs:* FT 10, PT 5
Estab 1902; scholarships; SC 25, LC 25; enrl maj 15, others 600
Degrees: MA, PhDComarative Arts
Tuition: $14,210 per yr
Courses: Art History, Painting, Photography, Sculpture
Summer School: Enrl 40; tuition & duration vary. Courses—Beginning Photography

SANBORN

NIAGARA COUNTY COMMUNITY COLLEGE, Fine Arts Div, 3111 Saunders Settlement Rd, 14132. Tel 716-731-3271, 731-4101, Ext 480. *Chmn* Rosemary Sweetman. *Instrs:* FT 17, PT 21
Estab 1965; pub; D & E; SC 12, LC 4; enrl D 400, E 120, maj 140
Ent Req: HS dipl
Degrees: AS(Fine Arts) 2 yrs
Tuition: In state $800 per sem; out of state $1600 per sem
Courses: Art Education, †Drawing, †Graphic Design, Illustration, †Painting, Photography, Sculpture, Art Therapy, Visual Art

SARATOGA SPRINGS

SKIDMORE COLLEGE, Dept of Art & Art History, 12866. Tel 518-584-5000. *Chmn* Doretta M Miller. *Instrs:* FT 22
Estab 1911; pvt; scholarships; SC 32, LC 18; enrl maj 350, 2000 total
Ent Req: HS grad, 16 cr, ent exam, portfolio
Degrees: BA and BS 4 yrs
Tuition: $8050 per yr
Courses: Art Education, Art History, Drawing, Graphic Design, Painting, Photography, Printmaking, Sculpture, Computer Imaging, Design, Jewelry/Metalsmithing, Pottery, Weaving
Summer School: Dir, Regis Brodie. Enrl 194 for two 6 wk sessions. Courses—Advanced Studio & Independent Study, Art History, Ceramics, Drawing, Etching, Jewelry, Lettering, Painting, Photography, Sculpture, 2-D Design, Vidio, Watercolor, Weaving

SCHENECTADY

UNION COLLEGE, Dept of the Arts, Arts Bldg, 12308. Tel 518-370-6201. *Chmn Visual Arts* Martin Benjamin. *Instrs:* FT 10
Estab 1795; pvt; D; schol; SC 14, LC 4; enrl maj 35
Ent Req: HS dipl, ent exam
Degrees: BA with emphasis in music, art or theatre arts 4 yr
Tuition: $13,500 per yr
Courses: Art History, Drawing, Intermedia, Painting, Photography, Printmaking, Sculpture, Stage Design, Theatre Arts, History of Architecture, Improvisation, 2-D Design, 3-D Design
Summer School: Courses—Theatre Improvisation, Intermedia

SEA CLIFF

STEVENSON ACADEMY OF TRADITIONAL PAINTING, 361 Glen Ave, 11579. Tel 516-676-6611. *Head Dept* Alma Gallanos Stevenson. *Instrs:* FT 2
Estab 1960; pvt; E; SC 3, LC 5; enrl 95
Ent Req: Interview
Tuition: $275 per 10 wk sem, one evening per wk; $1100 per 10 wk sem, four evenings per wk; no campus res
Courses: Drawing, Illustration, Painting, Artistic Anatomy, Basic Form
Summer School: Enrl 57; tuition $250 per term of 8 wks beginning June-July. Courses—Artistic Anatomy, Drawing, Painting

SELDEN

SUFFOLK COUNTY COMMUNITY COLLEGE, Art Dept, 533 College Rd, 11784. Tel 516-451-4110. *Dean* Maurice Flecker. *Instrs:* FT 6, PT 6
Degrees: AFA
Tuition: Res—$39 per cr; nonres—$78 per cr
Courses: Art Appreciation, Art History, Ceramics, Design, Drawing, Painting, Printmaking
Adult Hobby Classes: Enrl 200; tuition $15 per hr. Courses—Photography, Interior Design
Summer School: Dir, Maurice Flecker. Tuition res $60 per cr for 6-8 wk sessions. Courses—Painting, Sculpture, 2-D Design, Life Drawing, Printmaking & Ceramics

SOUTHAMPTON

SOUTHAMPTON CAMPUS OF LONG ISLAND UNIVERSITY, Fine Arts Division, 11968. Tel 516-283-4000, Ext 427 & 428. *Div Dir* Jon Fraser; *Prof* Robert Shaughnessy; *Prof* Robert Skinner, PhD; *Prof* Yosh Higa, MGA; *Assoc Prof* Roy Nicholson; *Asst Prof* P Kudder-Sullivan; *Asst Prof* Marc Fasanella; *Asst Prof* Jennifer Cross; *Asst Prof* Gary Washington
Estab 1963; pvt; D & E; scholarships; SC 36, LC 17, GC 11; enrl D 398, E 20, non-maj 100, maj 280, grad 20, others 18
Ent Req: HS dipl and portfolio review
Degrees: BFA, BS(Art Educ), BA(Fine Arts), 4 yrs, MA Educ
Tuition: $5150 per sem; campus res—room & board $2340 per sem
Courses: †Advertising Design, †Art Education, †Art History, Calligraphy, †Ceramics, Collages, †Commercial Art, Constructions, Drafting, †Drawing, †Graphic Arts, Handicrafts, History of Art & Archaeology, †Illustration, Jewelry, Lettering, Museum Staff Training, †Painting, †Photography, †Printmaking, †Sculpture, Stage Design, †Teacher Training, Theatre Arts, Music Art Therapy, Basketry, Enameling, †Weaving
Adult Hobby Classes: Courses—Drawing, Painting, Photography, Various Crafts
Children's Classes: 8 wk summer children's prog
Summer School: Dir, Jon Fraser. Tuition $325 per cr hr for term of 5 wks beginning in July. Courses—Master Workshop in Art & various other courses

SPARKHILL

SAINT THOMAS AQUINAS COLLEGE, Art Dept, Route 340, 10976. Tel 914-359-9500, Ext 211. *Prof* Carl Rattner, MFA; *Assoc Prof* George Jones; *Instr* Sr Adele Myers, MFA; *Instr* Sr Elizabeth Slenker, MFA
Estab 1952, dept estab 1969; pvt; D & E; scholarships; enrl D 1100, maj 50
Ent Req: HS dipl
Degrees: BA and BS 4 yrs
Tuition: $6000 per yr; campus res—available
Courses: Advertising Design, Art Education, Art History, Ceramics, Commercial Art, Drawing, Handicrafts, Jewelry, Painting, Photography, Printmaking, Sculpture, Teacher Training, Textile Design, Theatre Arts, Video, Art Therapy
Summer School: Dir, Dr Joseph Keane. Tuition $210 for 3 cr course. Courses—Varies 3-6 art courses including Ceramics, Painting, Photography

STATEN ISLAND

COLLEGE OF STATEN ISLAND, Performing & Creative Arts Dept, 120 Stuyvesant Pl, 10301. Tel 718-390-7992. *Chmn* Dr George Custen
Degrees: BA & MA(Cinema Studies), BS(Art), BS(Photography)
Tuition: Res—undergrad $1100 per sem, grad $1675 per sem
Courses: Advertising Design, †Architecture, †Art Appreciation, Art Education, †Art History, †Design, †Drawing, †Film, †Museum Staff Training, †Painting, †Photography, †Printmaking, Sculpture, Video
Summer School: Courses offered

WAGNER COLLEGE, Performing & Visual Arts Dept, Howard & Campus Rd, 10301. Tel 718-390-3192; FAX 718-390-3467. *Chmn* Richard W Gaffney
Estab 1948; den; D & E; SC 20, LC 6; enrl maj 35, others 2000
Ent Req: HS grad
Degrees: BA(Art), BS(Art Admin)
Tuition: Res—undergrad campus res $10,500 per yr
Courses: Advertising Design, Art History, Ceramics, Drawing, Mixed Media, Painting, Photography, Printmaking, Sculpture, Crafts Design, 3-D Design, 2-D Design
Summer School: Two sessions of 4 wks

STONE RIDGE

ULSTER COUNTY COMMUNITY COLLEGE, Dept of Visual Arts, 12484. Tel 914-687-5066. *Head Dept* Allan Cohen, MFA; *Prof* John A Locke III, MFA; *Prof* Peter Correia, MS; *Instr Asst* Susan Jeffers, BFA. *Instrs:* PT 5
Estab 1963; pub; D & E; SC 17, LC 6; enrl D 540, E 120, non-maj 590, maj 70
Ent Req: HS dipl
Degrees: AA 2 yrs, AS 2 yrs
Tuition: Res—undergrad $1750 per yr; nonres—undergrad $3500 per yr; no campus res
Courses: Advertising Design, Aesthetics, Art History, Drawing, †Graphic Design, Painting, Photography, Theatre Arts, Computer Art, Computer Assisted Graphic Design, Desk-Top Publishing, Life Drawing & Anatomy, 3-D Design, 2-D Design
Summer School: Dir, Allen Cohen. Enrl 30 - 50; tuition $198 per 3 sem hrs for 6 wks. Courses—Computer Art, Drawing, Painting, Photography

STONY BROOK

STATE UNIVERSITY OF NEW YORK AT STONY BROOK, Art Dept, 11794-5400. Tel 516-632-7250. *Chmn* James Rubin; *Prof* Jacques Guilmain, PhD; *Prof* George Koras; *Prof* Donald B Kuspit, PhD; *Prof* Nina Mallory, PhD; *Prof* Howardena Pindell, MFA; *Prof* Toby Buonagurio, MA; *Assoc Prof* Michael Edelson; *Assoc Prof* Michele H Bogart; *Assoc Prof* Anita Moskowitz, PhD; *Asst Prof* Barbara Frank; *Asst Prof* Kay Walking Stick; *Asst Prof* Michele H Bogart, PhD; *Asst Prof* Martin Levine, MFA; *Asst Prof* Molly Mason, MFA
Estab 1957; pub; D; SC 33, LC 39; enrl D 1850
Ent Req: HS dipl, SAT
Degrees: BA(Art History) & BA(Studio Art), MA(Art History & Criticism), MFA(Studio Art)
Tuition: Res—undergrad $1350 per yr, $675 per sem, $45 per cr hr; nonres—undergrad $3200 per yr, $1600 per sem, $407 per cr hr; campus res—room $1550 per yr
Courses: †Art History, Ceramics, Drawing, Painting, Photography, Printmaking, Sculpture, Ceramic Sculpture, 2-D Design, 3-D Design

Summer School: Tuition res—undergrad $45 per cr hr, grad $90 per cr hr; nonres—undergrad $107 per cr hr, grad $156 per cr hr for term of 6 wks (two sessions). Courses vary in areas of Art Education, Art History & Criticism, Studio Art

SUFFERN

ROCKLAND COMMUNITY COLLEGE, Graphic Arts & Advertising Tech Dept, 145 College Rd, 10901. Tel 914-574-4251; FAX 914-356-1529. *Chmn* Emily Harvey
Estab 1965; pub; D & E; SC plus apprenticeships; enrl D 900, E 300, maj 200
Ent Req: Open
Degrees: AAS 2 yrs
Tuition: Res—$81.50 per sem hr; nonres—$163 per sem hr
Courses: Advertising Design, Art History, Drawing, Graphic Arts, Graphic Design, Lettering, Painting, Photography, Sculpture, Art Appreciation, Art Therapy, Color Production, Electric Art
Adult Hobby Classes: Enrl 528; tuition varies. Courses—Ceramics, Crafts
Summer School: Dir, Emily Harvey. Enrl 180; June - Aug. Courses—Computer Graphics, Drawing, Overseas Program, Painting, Sculpture

SYRACUSE

LE MOYNE COLLEGE, Fine Arts Dept, Le Moyne Heights, 13214. Tel 315-445-4100. *Chmn & Prof* Jacqueline Belfort-Chalat; *Adjunct Asst Prof* Barry Darling; *Adjunct Asst Prof* Charles Wollowitz; *Adjunct Instr* Charles Aho, MA; *Adjunct Instr* William West
Pvt; D; SC 4, LC 1; enrl non-maj 350
Ent Req: HS dipl, SAT or ACT
Degrees: BS and BA 4 yrs
Tuition: $9620 per yr, $224 per cr hr; campus res—room & board $4260 per yr
Courses: Art History, Drawing, Graphic Arts, Painting, Sculpture
Adult Hobby Classes: Dir Continuing Learning, Norbert Henry
Summer School: Dir Continuing Learning, Norbert Henry

SYRACUSE UNIVERSITY
—College of Visual and Performing Arts, School of Art & Design, 203 Crouse College, 13244-1010. Tel 315-443-2507; FAX 315-443-1935. *Dean* Donald M Lantzy, MFA; *Dir* Tom Sherman. Instrs: FT 60, PT 52
Estab 1873; D & E; scholarships; SC 200, LC 25, GC 100; enrl D 1200
Ent Req: HS dipl, portfolio review
Degrees: BID 5 yrs, BFA 4 yrs, MFA, MID & MA(Museum Studies) 2 yrs
Tuition: Undergrad $13,480 per yr; grad $406 per cr; campus res available
Courses: †Advertising Design, Art Education, †Art History, †Ceramics, Drawing, †Film, †Illustration, †Industrial Design, †Interior Design, †Painting, †Printmaking, †Sculpture, †Video, †Art Photography, †Computer Graphics, †Communications Design, †Metalsmithing, Papermaking, †Surface Pattern Design, †Museum Studies Program
Adult Hobby Classes: Vice Pres, Thomas Cummings. Enrl 155; tuition undergrad $350 per cr. Courses—same as above
Children's Classes: Enrl 80, tuition $50 per sem. Courses—general art
Summer School: Dean, Thomas O'Shea. Tuition undergrad $400 per cr, grad $450 per cr. Courses—same as above
—Dept of Fine Arts (Art History), 441 Hall of Languages, 13213. Tel 315-443-4184. *Prof* Gary Radke, PhD; *Prof* David Tatham, PhD; *Prof* Meredith Lillich, PhD; *Prof* Ellen Oppler, PhD; *Prof* Wayne Franits PhD; *Prof* Laurinda Dixon, PhD; *Prof* Mary Marien, PhD; *Prof* Peg Weiss, PhD
Estab 1870, dept estab 1946; pvt; D & E; scholarships; LC 25, GC 15; enrl non-maj 900, maj 82, grad 46
Ent Req: HS dipl, SAT
Degrees: BA 4 yrs, MA 1-2 yrs, PhD 3-6 yrs
Tuition: Res—undergrad $21,140 per yr, $10,570 per sem, grad $406 per cr; campus res available
Courses: Art History

TARRYTOWN

MARYMOUNT COLLEGE, Art Dept, Neperhan Rd, 10591. Tel 914-631-3200. *Chmn* Maria Chamberlin-Hellman; *Prof* Bianca Haglich, RSHM; *Assoc Prof* Robert J Lee; *Asst Prof* Scott Ageloff; *Asst Prof* David Holt
Estab 1918; pvt; D & E; schol; SC 42, LC 15; enrl D 806, Weekends 337
Ent Req: HS dipl, CEEB
Degrees: BA and BS 4 yrs
Tuition: Res—undergrad $10,350 per yr; nonres—undergrad $10,350 per yr; PT student $325 per hr; campus res—room board $5990 per yr
Courses: Advertising Design, Art Education, Art History, Ceramics, Drawing, Fashion Arts, Film, Handicrafts, Illustration, Interior Design, Mixed Media, Painting, Photography, Printmaking, Sculpture, Stage Design, Teacher Training, Textile Design, Theatre Arts, Weaving, Stitchery
Adult Hobby Classes: Changing lect series - continuing education
Summer School: Dir, Dr Vilma Allen. Tuition $165 per cr. Courses—Changing Studio & Art History courses

TROY

EMMA WILLARD SCHOOL, Arts Division, 285 Pawling Ave, 12180. Tel 518-274-4440, Ext 231. *Div Chmn* Christine Leith
Estab 1814, dept estab 1969; pvt; D & E; scholarships
Tuition: $11,900 plus $550 escrow
Courses: Art Appreciation, Art History, Ceramics, Drawing, Jewelry, Photography, Printmaking, Theatre Arts, Advanced Studio Art, Dance, Music, Visual Arts Foundation, Weaving

RENSSELAER POLYTECHNIC INSTITUTE
—School of Architecture, 110 Eighth St, 12180-3590. Tel 518-276-6466; FAX 518-276-2999. *Dean* Donald Watson. Instrs: FT 18, PT 18
EStab 1929; pvt; D; scholarships; enrl 275
Degrees: BArchit, BS, MArchit & MS 3 - 4 yrs
Tuition: $15,900 per yr; campus res
Courses: †Architecture, Aesthetics, Art Appreciation, Art Education, Museum Staff Training, Teacher Training, †Building Science, Computer Graphics
Summer School: Architectural Design
—Dept of Art, School of Humanities and Social Science, 12180-3590. Tel 518-276-4778. *Chmn* Larry Kagan, MFA; *Dir of Graduate Programs* Neil Rolnick, PhD Scholarships & fels
Degrees: MFA (Electronic Arts) 2 1/2 - 3 yrs
Tuition: $12,250 annual tuition
Courses: Drawing, Painting, Sculpture, Video, Animation, Computer Music, Computer Graphics, Installation, Performance

RUSSELL SAGE COLLEGE, Visual and Performing Arts Dept, Schacht Fine Arts Center, 12180. Tel 518-270-2000. *Chmn* Dr Richard Jones; *Dir Creative Arts* Marion Terenzio
Pvt, W; enrl 20-40 per class
Ent Req: HS grad
Degrees: Fine arts and divisional maj in Music, Art and Drama 4 yrs
Tuition: Res—undergrad $9500 per yr; campus res—room & board $3500
Courses: †Arts Management, †Creative Arts Therapy, 2-D Design

UTICA

MOHAWK VALLEY COMMUNITY COLLEGE, Advertising Design and Production, 1101 Sherman Dr, 13510. Tel 212-797-9530. *Pres* Michael L Schafer, PhD; *Head Dept* Ronald Labuz, MA; *Prof* Virginia Juergensen, MFA; *Assoc Prof* James O'Looney, MS; *Assoc Prof* Henry Godlewski, BS; *Asst Prof* Larry Migliori; *Asst Prof* E Duane Isenberg, MA; *Asst Prof* Jerome Lalonde; *Asst Prof* Don Dempsey; *Asst Prof* Robert Duffek, BA; *Asst Prof* Robert Clarke, BFA; *Instr* Thomas Maneen; *Instr* Alex Piejko, BFA; *Instr* Kathleen Partridge, BFA; *Instr* Kenneth Murphy, BA; *Instr* Cindy Doolittle, BFA; *Instr* Douglas Hyldelund, BFA. Instrs: FT 16, ADJ 14
Estab 1947, dept estab 1955; pub; D & E; scholarships; SC 18 (over 2 yr period), LC 6 (over 2 yr period); enrl D 450, E varies, maj 450
Ent Req: HS dipl
Degrees: AAS 2 yrs
Tuition: $2000 per yr; campus res—available
Courses: Advertising Design, Aesthetics, Art Appreciation, Art History, Calligraphy, Commercial Art, Conceptual Art, Design, Drawing, Graphic Arts, Graphic Design, Handicrafts, History of Art & Archaeology, Illustration, Lettering, Painting, Photography, Weaving, Computer Graphics
Adult Hobby Classes: Enrl 440; tuition $1000 per 15 wks sem. Courses—Air Brush, Design, Illustration, Painting, Photography, Sketching, Watercolor
Summer School: Dir, Ronald Labuz. Enrl 40; tuition $200 per course. Courses—Drawing, Design, Photography

MUNSON-WILLIAMS-PROCTOR INSTITUTE, School of Art, 310 Genesee St, 13502. Tel 315-797-0000. *Dir* Clyde E McCulley, EdD; *Instr* Everett Adelman, MFA; *Instr* Bryan McGrath, MFA; *Instr* James McDermid, MFA; *Instr* Francis Fiorentino, MFA; *Instr* John Loy, MFA; *Instr* Marjorie Salzillo, MFA; *Instr* Keith Sandman, MFA; *Instr* Lisa Wightman, MA; *Instr* Alfred Wardle, BS. Instrs: FT 12, PT 15
Estab 1941; pvt; scholarships; enrl adults 1900, children 533
Degrees: Dipl 2 yrs
Tuition: Nonres—undergrad $2200 per sem
Courses: Ceramics, Drawing, Painting, Photography, Printmaking, Sculpture, Dance, Metal Arts, Pottery, Humanities, 2-D & 3-D Design, Color Theory
Adult Hobby Classes: Enrl 805. Courses—Dance, Design, Drawing, Jewelry, Painting, Photography, Pottery, Printmaking, Sculpture
Children's Classes: Enrl 423. Courses - Dance, Drama, Drawing, Painting, Pottery
Summer School: Dir, Clyde E McCulley. Enrl 413, tuition $65 - $110 for 4 wk term. Courses—Dance Drawing, Jewelry Making, Painting, Photogrphy, Pottery

UTICA COLLEGE OF SYRACUSE UNIVERSITY, Division of Humanities, Burrstone Rd, 13502. Tel 315-792-3057. *Assoc Dean Humanities* Frank Bergmann
Estab 1946, school of art estab 1973; pvt; D; scholarships; SC 20, LC 7; enrl School of Art D 94, Utica College maj 14
Degrees: BA(Fine Arts) 4 yrs
Tuition: $11,140 per yr
Courses: Art History, †Ceramics, Drafting, Drawing, Film, Graphic Arts, Occupational Therapy, †Painting, Photography, †Sculpture, Stage Design, Theatre Arts, Video, Design

WATERTOWN

JEFFERSON COMMUNITY COLLEGE, Art Dept, Outer Coffeen St, 13601. Tel 315-786-2200. *Pres* John T Henderson; *Prof* Klaus Ebeling. Instrs: FT 1
Estab 1963; pub; D & E; SC 2, LC 1; enrl 850 college total
Degrees: 2 yr
Tuition: $675 per sem
Courses: Art Appreciation, Art History, Photography, Sculpture, Computer-Aided Art & Design, Film Appreciation, Snow Sculpture, Two-Dimensional Studio
Summer School: Pres, John T Henderson

WEST NYACK

ROCKLAND CENTER FOR THE ARTS, 27 S Greenbush Rd, 10021. Tel 914-358-0877; FAX 914-358-0971. *School Dir* Lucy Brody, MFA; *Exec Dir* Julianne Ramos, MFA
Estab 1947; pub; D & E; scholarships; SC 100; enrl D 1000, E 500
Courses: Calligraphy, Ceramics, Drawing, Graphic Arts, Jewelry, Painting, Photography, Printmaking, Theatre Arts, Weaving, Fencing, Writing
Adult Hobby Classes: Enrl 300; tuition $170 - $200 for twelve 3 hr sessions. Courses—Ceramics, Fine Arts & Crafts, Writing
Children's Classes: Enrl 300; tuition $110 for ten 1 1/2 hr sessions. Courses—same as above
Summer School: Dir, Lucy Brody. Enrl 100 children & 200 adults; tuition average $120 per 6 wks. Courses—same as above

WHITE PLAINS

WESTCHESTER COMMUNITY COLLEGE, Westchester Art Workshop, County Center, 10607. Tel 914-684-0094. *Dir* Wayne Kartzinel
Estab 1926; pub; D & E; scholarships; SC 90 per sem, 5 sem per yr; enrl D 650, E 550, others 700 (credits given for most courses)
Ent Req: No special req
Degrees: AAS
Tuition: $73 per cr; no campus res
Courses: Art Appreciation, Calligraphy, Drawing, Graphic Design, Jewelry, Mixed Media, Painting, Photography, Printmaking, Sculpture, Weaving, Art Foundation, Art Therapy, Faux Finishes, Lost Wax Casting, Portrait Painting, Quilting, Stained Glass
Adult Hobby Classes: Enrl 1000; $56 per cr Sept - May
Children's Classes: Enrl 200; tuition $3 per hr Sept - Aug. Courses—Ceramics, Jewelry, Mixed Media, Painting, Photography
Summer School: Enrl 700; tuition $56 per cr. Courses—same as above

WOODSTOCK

WOODSTOCK SCHOOL OF ART, INC, PO Box 338W, 12498. Tel 914-679-2388. *Dir* Paula Nelson; *Instr* Mary Anna Goetz; *Instr* Deane Keller; *Instr* Anna Contes; *Instr* Karen O'Neil; *Instr* Mary James; *Instr* Eduardo Chavez; *Instr* Richard Pantell; *Instr* Richard Segalman; *Instr* Chester Dewitt Rose; *Instr* Zhang Hong Nian; *Instr* Richard McDaniel; *Instr* Ric Pike Dragon; *Instr* Elizabeth Mowry; *Instr* Nancy Summers; *Instr* Robert Angeloch
Estab 1968, dept estab 1981; pvt; D & E; Cert & fels; SC 19, LC 8; enrl D 110, E 15
Tuition: $85 - $230 per month
Courses: Drawing, Painting, Printmaking, Sculpture
Children's Classes: Instr, Nancy Summers. Enrl 10; tuition $150 per month
Summer School: Dir, Paula Nelson. Enrl 110; tuition $220 per wk. Courses—Drawing, Etching, Landscape, Lithography, Monotype, Painting, Pastel, Sculpture, Watercolor

YONKERS

IONA COLLEGE, Seton School of Associate Degree Studies, Art Dept, 1061 N Broadway, 10701. Tel 914-969-4000. *Chmn* William Lovell, MFA
Estab 1960; pvt; D, E & weekends; schol; SC 15, LC 3; enrl D 30, E 20, maj 25
Ent Req: HS dipl
Degrees: AS, AAS and AOS
Tuition: $5760 per yr; campus res—available
Courses: †Advertising Design, Art History, Calligraphy, Ceramics, Drawing, Graphic Design, Illustration, Interior Design, Jewelry, Lettering, †Painting, Photography, Sculpture, Video, †Art Therapy, Computer Art, Paste-up/Mechanical Art
Adult Hobby Classes: Enrl 60. Cources—Art History, Calligraphy, Chinese Painting, Painting, Photography
Summer School: Dir, Mary Egan. Courses in Fine and Commercial Art

NORTH CAROLINA

ASHEVILLE

UNIVERSITY OF NORTH CAROLINA AT ASHEVILLE, Dept of Art, University Heights, 28801. Tel 704-251-6559. *Chmn* S Tucker Cooke, MFA
Estab 1927, dept estab 1965; pub; D & E; scholarships; SC 20, LC 5; enrl 3277, maj 69
Ent Req: HS dipl, ent exam
Degrees: BA, BFA 4-5 yrs
Tuition: Res—$636 per sem; nonres—$3097 per sem; campus res—available
Courses: Art Education, Art History, Ceramics, Drawing, Intermedia, Mixed Media, Painting, Photography, Printmaking, Sculpture, Life Drawing, 2-D & 3-D Design
Summer School: Dir, S Tucker Cooke. Courses vary

BOONE

APPALACHIAN STATE UNIVERSITY, Dept of Art, 28608. Tel 704-262-2000. *Chmn* Marianne Stevens Suggs
Estab 1960; pub; D; scholarships; SC 38, LC 10, GC 12; enrl D 1000, maj 350, grad 45
Ent Req: HS dipl, ent exam
Degrees: BA, BS & BFA (graphic design, art educ, studio art, art marketing & production) 4 yrs

Tuition: Res—$628 per sem; nonres—$2893 per sem
Courses: Art Appreciation, Fibers
Summer School: Dir, L F Edwards. Enrl 300; term of 2, 4 & 6 wks beginning May-Aug. Courses—per regular session

BREVARD

BREVARD COLLEGE, Division of Fine Arts, 28712. Tel 704-883-8292. *Acting Chmn* Dr Stephanie Blanelli; *Prof* Timothy G Murray, MACA; *Prof* Virginia Tilotson. Instrs: PT 2
Estab 1853; den; D & E; scholarships; SC 12, LC 2
Ent Req: HS dipl
Degrees: AFA 2 yrs
Tuition: Res—undergrad $6980 per yr
Courses: Art History, Ceramics, Drawing, Film, Graphic Arts, Graphic Design, Painting, Photography, Printmaking, Sculpture, Theatre Arts, 2-D Design, 3-D Design
Summer School: Courses vary

CHAPEL HILL

UNIVERSITY OF NORTH CAROLINA AT CHAPEL HILL, Art Dept, Hanes Art Center, 27599-3405. Tel 919-962-2015. *Chmn* Arthur S Marks, PhD; *Asst Chmn Art Hist* Mary Pardo, PhD; *Asst Chmn Studio Art* Jerry Noe, PhD; *Prof* Jaroslav Folda, PhD; *Prof* Marvin Saltzman, MA; *Prof* R Kinnaird; *Prof* Mary Sturgeon, PhD; *Prof* Dennis Zaborowski; *Assoc Prof* James Gadson, MFA; *Prof* Jerry Noe, MFA; *Assoc Prof* Mary Sheriff, PhD; *Asst Prof* Beth Grabowski, MFA; *Assoc Prof* Xavier Toubes, MFA; *Asst Prof* Jim Hirschfield, MFA; *Asst Prof* Carol Mavor
Estab 1793, dept estab 1936; pub; D; scholarships; SC 15, LC 15, GC 10; enrl D 200 undergrad, 65 grad
Ent Req: HS dipl, SAT
Degrees: BA & BFA 4 yrs, MFA & MA(Art History) 2 yrs, PhD(Art History) to 8 yrs
Tuition: Res—undergrad $604 per sem, grad $604 per sem; nonres—undergrad $5106 per sem, grad $5106; campus res—available
Courses: Art History, Ceramics, Drawing, History of Art & Archaeology, Painting, Printmaking, Sculpture
Summer School: 2 terms of 5 wks beginning May & July. Courses—various art history & studio courses

CHARLOTTE

CENTRAL PIEDMONT COMMUNITY COLLEGE, Visual & Performing Arts, PO Box 35009, 28235. Tel 704-342-6956. *Chmn* Gene Bryant
Degrees: AS 2 yrs
Tuition: Res—undergrad $13.25 per cr hr; nonres—$81.75 per cr hr
Courses: Advertising Design, Architecture, Art Appreciation, Art History, Calligraphy, Ceramics, Design, Drawing, Fashion Arts, Handicrafts, Interior Design, Jewelry, Painting, Photography, Printmaking, Sculpture, Stage Design, Weaving, Cartooning, Stained Glass

QUEENS COLLEGE, Fine Arts Dept, 1900 Selwyn Ave, 28274-0001. Tel 704-337-2213. *Fine Arts Chmn* Dr E Lammers. Instrs: FT 3, PT 1
Estab 1857; den; scholarships; SC 19, LC 7
Degrees: Granted
Tuition: $9850 annual tuition
Courses: Art History, Ceramics, Commercial Art

UNIVERSITY OF NORTH CAROLINA AT CHARLOTTE, Dept of Visual Arts, 137 Rowe Arts Bldg, 28223. Tel 704-547-2473. *Chmn* Dr Sally Kovach, PhD; *Instr* Eric Anderson; *Instr* Edwina Bringle; *Instr* Dean Butchovitz; *Instr* Michael Kampen; *Instr* Rod MacKillop; *Instr* Rita Schumaker; *Instr* Martha Strawn; *Instr* Ron Taylor; *Instr* Winston Tite; *Instr* Joan Tweedy; *Instr* Eldred Hudson; *Instr* Donald R Byrum; *Instr* Linda Kroff; *Instr* Linda Brown; *Instr* Heather Hoover; *Instr* Carol Cooke; *Instr* Sister Aguilo; *Instr* Robert Kaufman; *Instr* Betsy Bilger; *Instr* William Wylie; *Instr* Leslie Malone; *Instr* Tony Swider
Estab 1965, dept estab 1971; pub; D & E; SC 54, LC 26; enrl D 785, non-maj 500, maj 430
Ent Req: HS dipl, SAT, Col Boards
Degrees: BCA 4 yrs, K - 12 Art Educ Cert 4 yrs
Tuition: res—$574.50; nonres—$3101.50; room & board per sem $1216 - $1720.52
Courses: Advertising Design, Aesthetics, Art Appreciation, †Art Education, Art History, †Ceramics, Design, †Drawing, †Graphic Design, †Illustration, Jewelry, Mixed Media, †Painting, †Photography, †Printmaking, †Sculpture, †Weaving, Computer-Aided Design, Fibers, Visual Communications & Design
Summer School: Dir, Dr Sally Kovach. Enrl 120; tuition res—$384, nonres—$2912; two 5 wk sessions, one 3 wk session. Courses—Art Appreciation, Art History, Freshman Foundation Program

CULLOWHEE

WESTERN CAROLINA UNIVERSITY, Dept of Art, Belk Bldg, 28723. Tel 704-227-7210. *Head Dept* Robert Godfrey; *Assoc Prof* Lee P Budahl, PhD; *Prof* James E Smythe, MFA; *Assoc Prof* Joan Byrd; *Assoc Prof* Jon Jicha, MFA; *Asst Prof* William C Buchanan, MFA; *Asst Prof* Cathryn Griffin, MFA; *Asst Prof* James Thompson; *Asst Prof* Rich Borge, MA; *Asst Prof* Lois Petrovich-Mwaniki
Estab 1889, dept estab 1968; pub; D & E; scholarships; SC 51, LC 12; enrl non-maj 1200 day, maj 150
Ent Req: HS dipl, SAT & C average in HS
Degrees: BFA, BA & BSE 4 yrs, MA, art honors studio
Tuition: Res—undergrad and grad $830 per yr, $425 per sem; nonres—undergrad and grad $3697 per yr, $1848.50 per sem; campus res—room & board $1600 per yr
Courses: Art Education, Art History, Ceramics, Drawing, Graphic Design, Illustration, Painting, Photography, Printmaking, Sculpture, Teacher Training,

Glassblowing
Summary School: Dir, Dr Diana Henshaw. Tuition $14 per sem hr for summer beginning June 2. Courses—Glassblowing, Introductory Studio Courses, Workshops in Primitive Pottery, Wheel Throwing & Techniques & Raku

DALLAS

GASTON COLLEGE, Art Dept, 201 Hwy 321 S, 28034. Tel 704-922-6343, 922-6344. *Dept Chmn* D Keith Lambert
Estab 1965; pub; D & E; SC 22, LC 3; enrl D 140, E 50, maj 50
Ent Req: HS dipl
Degrees: AA & AFA 2 yrs, certificate 1 yr, program for Commercial Art
Tuition: Res—$3.25 per quarter cr hr; nonres—$16.50 per quarter cr hr
Courses: Drawing, Illustration, Jewelry, Painting, Printmaking, Sculpture, 2-D & 3-D Design, Color Design, Computer Graphics, Commercial Art Fundamentals, Fabrication & Casting, Pottery
Adult Hobby Classes: Courses—Ceramics, Jewelry, Macrame, Weaving
Summer School: Dir, Franklin U Creech. Enrl 20; term of 11 wks beginning June. Courses—Design, Drawing, Painting, Pottery, Sculpture

DAVIDSON

DAVIDSON COLLEGE, Art Dept, Main St, 28036. Tel 704-892-2000; FAX 704-892-2005. *Chmn* Herb Jackson, MFA; *Prof* Larry L Ligo, PhD; *Prof* Russell Warren, MFA; *Assoc Prof* Shaw Smith, PhD; *Asst Prof* Nina Serebrennikov; *Asst Prof* Cort Savage
Estab 1837, dept estab 1950; pvt & den; D; scholarships; SC 12, LC 9; enrl non-maj 300, maj 18
Ent Req: Col Boards, HS transcripts
Degrees: BA & BS 4 yrs
Tuition: $19,500 per yr (comprehensive fee); campus res—room & board fee included in tuition
Courses: Aesthetics, Art History, Collages, Conceptual Art, Drawing, Graphic Design, History of Art & Archaeology, Painting, Printmaking, Sculpture, Theatre Arts

DOBSON

SURRY COMMUNITY COLLEGE, Art Dept, PO Box 304, 27017. Tel 919-386-8121. *Dir* James Reeves; *Instr* Archie Bennett; *Instr* William Sanders; *Instr* Abbe Rose Cox
Tuition: Res—$13.25 per cr hr; nonres—$99.25 per cr hr
Courses: Art Appreciation, Art History, Commercial Art, Design, Drawing, Handicrafts, Painting, Printmaking, Sculpture

DURHAM

DUKE UNIVERSITY, Dept of Art and Art History, 112 E Duke Bldg, 27708. Tel 919-684-2224; FAX 919-684-3200. *Chmn* Caroline Bruzelius; *Prof* John Spencer, PhD; *Assoc Prof* Vernon Pratt, MFA; *Assoc Prof* Annabel Wharton, PhD; *Asst Prof* Claude Cernuschi, PhD; *Asst Prof* Richard Powell, PhD; *Adjunct Asst Prof* Dorie Reents-Budet, PhD; *Asst Prof* Kristine Stiles, PhD; *Asst Prof* Judy Sund, PhD; *Asst Prof* Hans Van Miegroet, Phd; *Artist in Residence* Merrill Shatzman, MFA; *Instr* Helen Smith, MFA
Pvt; D; SC 19, LC 41, GC 12; enrl D 1850, maj 134
Ent Req: HS dipl & ent exam
Degrees: MA 4 yrs
Tuition: Campus res—available
Courses: Art History, Design, Drawing, Painting, Printmaking, Sculpture
Summer School: Dir, Calvin Ward. Two wk sessions offered

NORTH CAROLINA CENTRAL UNIVERSITY, Art Dept, 1801 Fayetteville St, PO Box 19555, 27707. Tel 919-560-6391, 6012; FAX 919-560-6413. *Chmn* Melvin Carver, MPD; *Prof* Lana Henderson, Phd; *Prof* Acha Debla; *Prof* Rosie Thompson; *Prof* Isabell Levitt, MFA; *Prof* Norman Pendergraft, MA; *Prof* John Hughley, MA; *Prof* Michelle Patterson
Estab 1910, dept estab 1944; pub; D & E; SC 30, LC 11; enrl D 120, E 30, non-maj 1678, maj 120
Ent Req: HS dipl, SAT
Degrees: In Art Educ, Visual Communications & Studio Art 4 yrs
Tuition: Res—undergrad $421.50 yr; nonres—undergrad $1800 yr; campus res—$2041.50-$2854.50 per yr
Courses: †Advertising Design, †Art Education, Art History, Calligraphy, Ceramics, Commercial Art, Drawing, Graphic Arts, Handicrafts, Illustration, Jewelry, Lettering, Painting, Printmaking, Sculpture, Teacher Training, Engineering Graphics, Stained Glass, Studio Arts
Children's Classes: Saturday school
Summer School: Dir, Dr Eugene Eaves. Tuition $225 for term of 9 wks. Courses—Art Appreciation, Design

ELIZABETH CITY

ELIZABETH CITY STATE UNIVERSITY, Dept of Art, 1704 Weeksville Rd, 27909. Tel 919-335-3632, 335-3347. *Chmn* Jenny C McIntosh, PhD
Estab 1891, dept estab 1961; pub; D & E; Scholarships; SC 27, LC 18, advance courses in Studio and History of Art; enrl D 2003, E 455, non-maj 1928, maj 75
Ent Req: HS dipl, portfolio
Degrees: BA 4 yrs
Tuition: Res—$368 per yr; nonres—$3740 per yr
Courses: Art History, Painting, Photography, Sculpture, Teacher Training, Art Studio general
Summer School: Dir, James Townes. Enrl 950. Courses—same as regular session

FAYETTEVILLE

FAYETTEVILLE STATE UNIVERSITY, Fine Arts & Communications, Newbold Station, 28301. Tel 919-486-1111. *Head Div Humanities & Fine Arts* Richard Hadley; *Dept Head* Dr Robert Owens
Estab 1877; pub; D & E; enrl D 60, E 20
Ent Req: HS dipl, ent exam
Tuition: Res—$616; nonres—$2198
Courses: Advertising Design, Aesthetics, Art Education, Ceramics, Drawing, Graphic Arts, Handicrafts, History of Art & Archaeology, Lettering, Painting, Photography, Sculpture, Weaving, Leather Craft
Summer School: Dir, Dr Beeman C Patterson. Courses—Art in Childhood Education, Arts & Crafts, Drawing, Photography, Survey of Art

METHODIST COLLEGE, Art Dept, 5400 Ramsey St, 28311-1499. Tel 919-630-7000; FAX 919-822-1289. *Chmn* Silvana Foti-Soublet, MFA. *Instrs:* FT 2, PT 1
Estab 1960; den; D & E; scholarships; SC 6, LC 4; enrl D 650, maj 22
Ent Req: HS dipl, SAT
Degrees: BA & BS 4 yrs
Tuition: Res—undergrad $10,200 per yr
Courses: Art Education, Art History, Design, Drawing, Painting, Photography, Printmaking, Sculpture, Papermaking
Summer School: 3 terms, 3 wk early session, 5 wk main session, 6 wk directed study. Courses—Art Appreciation, Painting, Sculpture, others as needed

GOLDSBORO

GOLDSBORO ART CENTER, Community Arts Council, 901 E Ash St, 27530. Tel 919-736-3335, 736-3300. *Exec Dir* Alice Strickland
Estab 1971; pub; D & E; scholarships; SC 25; enrl D 150, E 60, others 210
Courses: Drawing, Painting, Pottery, Spinning, Watercolor
Adult Hobby Classes: Enrl 75; tuition $19 for 11 wk term. Courses— Calligraphy, Oil Painting, Pottery, Watercolors
Children's Classes: Enrl 50; tuition $15 for 6 wk term. Courses—Discovering Art, Drawing, Painting, Pottery

WAYNE COMMUNITY COLLEGE, Liberal Arts Dept, Caller Box 8002, 27533. Tel 919-735-5151. *Chmn* Marion Wessell; *Instr* Bea Balkcum
Degrees: AA
Tuition: Res—$194.50 per quarter; nonres—$1514 per quarter
Courses: Art Appreciation, Art History, Design, Drawing
Adult Hobby Classes: Courses offered
Children's Classes: Courses offered in conjunction with Arts Council

GREENSBORO

GREENSBORO COLLEGE, Dept of Art, Division of Fine Arts, 815 W Market St, 27401. Tel 919-272-7102. *Assoc Prof* Robert Kowski, MFA
Estab 1838; pvt den; D; scholarships; SC 15, LC 4; enrl D 50, non-maj 30, maj 15
Ent Req: HS dipl
Degrees: BA 4 yrs
Tuition: Res and nonres—undergrad $4290 per yr; campus res—room & board $2260 per yr
Courses: Art Education, Art History, Ceramics, Drawing, †Painting, Photography, †Sculpture
Adult Hobby Classes: Enrl 40; tuition $120 per cr hr. Courses—Art History
Summer School: Dir, Dr Daniel Moury. Tuition $85 per cr hr for two 5 wk sessions. Courses—Art Appreciation, Art History

GUILFORD COLLEGE, Art Dept, 5800 W Friendly Ave, 27410. Tel 919-292-5511. *Chmn* George Lorio, MFA
Estab 1837, dept estab 1970; den; D & E; scholarships; enrl 35 maj
Ent Req: HS dipl, entrance examination
Degrees: BA 4 yr, BFA 4 yr
Courses: Art Appreciation, Art History, Ceramics, Design, Drawing, History of Art & Archaeology, Painting, Photography, Printmaking, Sculpture

NORTH CAROLINA AGRICULTURAL AND TECHNICAL STATE UNIVERSITY, Art Dept, 312 N Dudley St, 27411. Tel 919-334-7993. *Chmn* LeRoy F Holmes. *Instrs:* FT 4, PT 1
Estab 1930; pub; SC 29, LC 7; enrl maj 100
Courses: Art Education, Art History, Ceramics, Commercial Art, Drawing, Graphic Arts, Painting, †Art Design, Crafts, 3-D Desigh, 2-D Design
Summer School: Dir, Dr Ronald Smith. Courses—Crafts, Public School Art, Art History, Art Appreciation

UNIVERSITY OF NORTH CAROLINA AT GREENSBORO, Art Dept, 162 McIver Bldg, 27412. Tel 919-334-5248. *Head* K Porter Aichele. *Instrs:* FT 22
Dept estab 1935; pub; SC 22, LC 6, GC 8; enrl D 1000, non-maj 750, maj 200, grad 63
Ent Req: HS grad, ent exam
Degrees: BA, BFA, MEd & MFA 4 yrs
Tuition: Res—undergrad $681.75; non res $3015
Courses: Art History, Ceramics, Drawing, Painting, Photography, Printmaking, Sculpture, Teacher Training, Fibers
Summer School: Dir, Dr John Young. Enrl 225; beginning May - June and July - Aug. Courses—Art History, Drawing, Etching, Fibers, Jewelry, Moldmaking-Metal Casting, Painting, Photography, Picture Composition, Sculpture, Watercolor

GREENVILLE

EAST CAROLINA UNIVERSITY, School of Art, E Fifth St, 27858-4353. Tel 919-757-6665. *Acting Dean* Michael Dorsey. Instrs: FT 38, PT 3
Estab 1907; pub; scholarships; SC 155, LC 28, GC 142; enrl maj 608
Ent Req: HS dipl, 20 units, Col Board Exam
Degrees: BA, BFA, MA & MFA, MAEd
Tuition: Campus res—available
Courses: Design, Drawing, †Art History, †Printmaking, †Painting, †Graphic Design, †Illustration, Video, †Sculpture, †Weaving, †Art Education, Intermedia, †Illustration, Intermedia, Interior Design, †Jewelry, Landscape Architecture, Lettering, Mixed Media, Museum Staff Training, †Painting, Photography, †Printmaking, Restoration & Conservation, Sculpture, Silversmithing, Teacher Training, †Textile Design, †Theatre Arts, Video, †Weaving, Color & Design, †Community Arts Management, †Fabric Design, Computer-Aided Art & Design, †Wood Design, †Metal Design, †Environmental Design, Interdisciplinary 3-D Design, Work Experience in the Visual Arts & Design, Independent Study
Children's Classes: Enrl 60; no tuition for 10 wk term. Courses—General Art Class
Summer School: Dir, James McGee, Art Dir, Dr Phil Phillips. Enrl 400; tuition res—$141 for 5 sem hrs & $206 for 6-8 sem hrs, nonres—$1299 for 5 sem hrs in a 5 wk term

HICKORY

LENOIR RHYNE COLLEGE, Dept of Art, Seventh Ave & Eighth St NW, 28603. Tel 704-328-1741. *Chmn Dept* Dr Art Barnes; *Asst Prof* Douglas Burton, MA; *Asst Prof* Robert Winter, PhD
Estab 1892, dept estab 1976; den; D & E; scholarships; SC 5; enrl D 1200, E 350
Ent Req: HS dipl
Degrees: AB and BS 4 yrs
Tuition: Res—undergrad $13,165 per yr; campus res—room & board $3085 per yr
Courses: Aesthetics, Art Appreciation, Art Education, Art History, Ceramics, Drawing, Painting, Photography, Printmaking, Sculpture
Adult Hobby Classes: Courses on Tues & Thurs evenings
Children's Classes: Summer courses for gifted & talented
Summer School: Dir, Dr James Lichtenstein. Enrl 900; tuition 70 per sem hr for 2-5 wk terms beginning June. Courses—Art Appreciation, Art Education, Ceramics, Painting

HIGH POINT

HIGH POINT COLLEGE, Fine Arts Dept, 933 Montlieu Ave, 27262. Tel 919-841-9000. *Chmn* Cheryl Harrison
Estab 1924, dept estab 1956; pvt den; D & E; scholarships; SC 16, LC 6; enrl non-maj 950, maj 10
Ent Req: HS dipl, SAT
Degrees: AB and BS 4 yrs
Tuition: Res—undergrad $3800 per yr, $1900 per sem; nonres—undergrad $3800 per yr, $1900 per sem; campus res—available
Courses: Advertising Design, Aesthetics, †Art Education, Art History, Ceramics, Drawing, History of Art & Archaeology, Interior Design, Painting, Printmaking, Sculpture, Stage Design, Teacher Training, †Theatre Arts, Crafts
Summer School: Dean, W H Bearce. Enrl 200; two 5 wk sessions. Courses—Art Education, Crafts, Design, Interior Design

JAMESTOWN

GUILFORD TECHNICAL COMMUNITY COLLEGE, Commercial Art Dept, PO Box 309, 27260. Tel 919-454-1126, Ext 224. *Head* Norman D Faircloth, MA; *Instr* Ralph E Calhoun, MEd Art; *Instr* Jerry E Painter, BA; *Instr* F Eugene Stafford, BFA; *Instr* Matilda Kirby-Smith, MA; *Instr* Margaret Reid
Estab 1964; pub; D & E; scholarships; SC 20, LC 4; enrl D 130, E 60
Ent Req: HS dipl, English & math placement
Degrees: AAS 2 yrs
Tuition: Res—undergrad $8.75 per hr up to $105 per quarter; nonres—undergrad up to $981 per quarter; no campus res available
Courses: †Advertising Design, Art History, Commercial Art, Drafting, Drawing, Graphic Arts, Illustration, Lettering, Photography, Computer Graphics
Adult Hobby Classes: Tuition $.75 per contact hr. Courses—Variety of subjects
Summer School: Tuition $.75 per contact hr per 9 wk term. Courses—Various

KINSTON

LENOIR COMMUNITY COLLEGE, Dept of Visual Art, PO Box 188, 28501. Tel 919-527-6223. *Dept Head* Gerald A Elliott
Degrees: AFA
Tuition: Res—$51
Courses: Art Appreciation, Art History, Calligraphy, Ceramics, Design, Drawing, Illustration, Painting, Photography, Printmaking
Summer School: Dir, Gerald A Elliott. Enrl 32; tuition $51 for 12 cr hrs. Courses—Lecture & Studio Art

LAURINBURG

SAINT ANDREWS PRESBYTERIAN COLLEGE, Art Program, 28352. Tel 919-276-3652, Ext 5264. *Chmn Dept Humanities & Fine Arts* Mel Bringle; *Chmn Art Dept* Robert Carter; *Instr* Stephanie McDavid. Instrs: FT 2
Estab 1960; den; D; scholarships; SC 14, LC 2; enrl D 852, maj 20 - 30
Ent Req: HS dipl, SAT, 2.6 grade point average, 12 academic units
Degrees: BA, MS & BM 4 yrs or 32 courses
Tuition: $6100 per yr
Courses: Aesthetics, Art Education, Art History, Drawing, Painting, Sculpture, Computer Graphics
Summer School: Studio courses offered

LEXINGTON

DAVIDSON COUNTY COMMUNITY COLLEGE, Fine Arts & Humanities Div, Old Greensboro Rd, PO Box 1287, 27293-1287. Tel 704-249-8186, Ext 247. *Chmn* Camille Lawrence, MA; *Instr* Katherine Montgomery, MFA. Instrs: FT 2, PT 3
Estab 1963, dept estab 1966; pub; D & E; scholarships; SC 14, LC 4; enrl D 100, E 30, non-maj 195, maj 30
Ent Req: HS dipl
Degrees: AFA & AA 2 yrs
Tuition: Res—undergrad $53 per quarter; no campus res—available
Courses: Art Education, Art History, Drafting, Handicrafts, Painting, Photography, Printmaking, Sculpture, Design, Independent Studio
Adult Hobby Classes: Courses—Variety taught through continuing education

MARS HILL

MARS HILL COLLEGE, Art Dept, 28754. Tel 704-689-1200. *Chmn* Gordon Mahy, MFA; *Assoc Prof* Richard Cary, PhD
Estab 1856, dept estab 1932; pvt and den; D & E; scholarships; SC 9, LC 6; enrl D 120, non-maj 100, maj 20
Ent Req: HS dipl, ent exam
Degrees: BA 4 yrs
Tuition: Undergrad $5900 per yr, $9100 per yr incl room & board
Courses: †Advertising Design, Aesthetics, †Art Education, †Art History, Ceramics, †Graphic Arts, †Painting, Photography, †Printmaking, Sculpture, †Teacher Training, †Theatre Arts
Summer School: Enrl. 450; tuition $65 per cr hr for 5 wk term. Courses—Introduction to the Arts & Photography

MISENHEIMER

PFEIFFER COLLEGE, Art Program, 28109. Tel 704-463-7343, Ext 2667. *Dir* James Haymaker. Instrs: FT 1
Estab 1965; den; D; scholarships; SC 4, LC 4; enrl D 100
Ent Req: HS dipl
Courses: Art Education, Art History, Ceramics, Drawing, Painting, Sculpture

MOUNT OLIVE

MOUNT OLIVE COLLEGE, Dept of Art, 209 N Breazeale Ave, 28365. Tel 919-658-2502. *Chmn* Larry Lean
Estab 1951; den; D & E; scholarships; SC 5, LC 3
Degrees: AA and AS
Tuition: Res—undergrad $6550 per yr; campus res—available
Courses: Art History, Ceramics, Drawing, Painting, Art Appreciation, American Art, Arts & Crafts, Design
Summer School: Tuition $180 for session beginning May 19. Courses—Art Appreciation

MURFREESBORO

CHOWAN COLLEGE, Division of Art, Jones Dr, 27855. Tel 919-398-4101, Ext 267. *Head Div* Douglas E Eubank, MHE; *Prof* Elizabeth Vick, MFA; *Prof* Stanley A Mitchell, MA; *Prof* Susan Fecho, MFA
Estab 1848, dept estab 1970; den; scholarships; SC 18, LC 3; enrl maj 64
Ent Req: HS dipl, SAT recommended
Degrees: AA 2 yrs
Tuition: Room & board $9500 per yr; commuter—$4950 per yr, $2475 per sem
Courses: Advertising Design, Art Appreciation, Art Education, Art History, Ceramics, Commercial Art, Drawing, Illustration, Lettering, Painting, Figure Drawing
Summer School: Dir, Doug Eubank. Enrl 10; tuition $165 per sem hr for term of 6 wks beginning June 8. Courses—Art Appreciation, Ceramics, Drawing, Painting

PEMBROKE

PEMBROKE STATE UNIVERSITY, Art Dept, PO Box 5064, 28372. Tel 919-521-6000, Ext 6216. *Chmn Dept* Paul VanZandt. Instrs: FT 4, PT 3
Estab 1887; pub; Scholarships; SC 30, LC 12; enrl maj 60
Ent Req: CEEB scores, HS record, scholastic standing in HS grad class, recommendation of HS guidance counselor & principal
Degrees: BA & BS 4 yrs
Tuition: $474 per sem
Courses: †Art Education, Art History, †Ceramics, Commercial Art, Design, Drawing, Handicrafts, Jewelry, †Painting, Photography, †Printmaking, †Sculpture
Summer School: Variety of courses

PENLAND

PENLAND SCHOOL OF CRAFTS, Penland Rd, 28765. Tel 704-765-2359. *Dir* Connie Sedberry
Estab 1929; pvt; D (summer, spring & fall classes); scholarships; SC 10-20; enrl D approx 100
Ent Req: Age 18, special fall and spring sessions require portfolio and resume
Degrees: None granted but credit may be obtained through agreement with East Tennessee State Univ & Western Carolina Univ
Tuition: $225 - $275 per wk for term of 2 - 3 wks; campus res—room & board $130 - $330 per wk
Courses: Ceramics, Graphic Design, Jewelry, Photography, Printmaking, Sculpture, Weaving, Basketry, Blacksmithing, Book Arts, Clothing Construction, Crochet, Dyeing, Enameling, Felting, Fibers, Glass, Marbling, Metalsmithing, Papermaking, Quilting, Spinning, Woodworking

Summer School: Dir, Verne Stanford. Tuition varies for 1, 2 & 3 wk courses between June & Sept. Courses—Basketry, Book Arts, Clay, Clothing Construction, Crochet, Dyeing, Enameling, Felting, Fiber, Glass, Graphics, Jewelry, Marbling, Metal, Paper, Photography, Printmaking, Quilting, Sculpture, Spinning, Surface Design, Weaving, Wood

RALEIGH

MEREDITH COLLEGE, Art Dept, Gaddy-Hamrick Art Center, Hillsborough St, 27607-5298. Tel 919-829-8332. *Chmn* J Craig Greene
Estab 1898; den, W; D & E; scholarships; SC 15, LC 5; enrl D 490, E 130, maj 85, others 30
Ent Req: HS dipl
Degrees: AB 4 yrs
Tuition: Res—undergrad $5310 per yr; campus res—room & board $2310 per yr
Courses: Advertising Design, Art Appreciation, Art Education, Art History, Calligraphy, Ceramics, Costume Design & Construction, Design, Drawing, Graphic Design, Handicrafts, Computer Graphics
Adult Hobby Classes: Courses—Art History, Ceramics, Drawing, Fibers, Graphic Design, Painting, Photography, Sculpture
Summer School: Dir, John Hiott. Courses—vary

NORTH CAROLINA STATE UNIVERSITY AT RALEIGH, School of Design, PO Box 7701, 27695-7701. Tel 919-515-2011. *Dean* J Thomas Ragan; *Head Landscape Architecture Dept* Arthur Rice; *Head Architecture Dept* Robert P Burns; *Head Product & Visual Design Dept* Haig Khachatoorian; *Head Design Dept* Charles Joyner. Instrs: FT 38, PT 5
Estab 1948; pub; enrl Architecture 303, Landscape Architecture 119, Product Design 174
Ent Req: Col board, ent exam
Degrees: BEnvDesign (in Architecture, Design, Landscape Architecture, Product Design & Visual Design), MArch, MLandscape Arch, MProduct Design 4-6 yrs
Tuition: Res—$563; non-res—$2896
Courses: Architecture, Design, Landscape Architecture, Product Design, Visual Design
Summer School: Courses—Undergrad: Architecture, Visual & Product Design

PEACE COLLEGE, Art Dept, 15 E Peace St, 27604. Tel 919-832-2881. *Head Dept* C J Parker, MFA; *Chmn Division Fine Arts, Language, Literature* Dr E P DeLuca; *Instr* M M Baird
Estab 1857; pvt; D; SC 8, LC 2; enrl D 500
Ent Req: HS dipl, SAT
Degrees: AA and AFA 2 yrs
Tuition: Res—$1950 per yr; nonres—$4850 per yr
Courses: Art Education, Art History, Drawing, Fashion Arts, History of Art & Archaeology, Painting, Theatre Arts, Color & Design

SAINT MARY'S COLLEGE, Art Dept, 900 Hillsborough St, 27603. Tel 919-828-2521. *Chmn Dept* Betty B Adams; *Assoc Prof* Ellen Anderson
Estab 1842; pvt den; D; scholarships; SC 11, LC 2; enrl D 150
Ent Req: HS dipl, SAT or PSAT
Degrees: AA
Tuition: Res—undergrad $3830 per yr; campus res available
Courses: Art History, Ceramics, Drawing, Graphic Arts, Painting, Printmaking, Stage Design, Theatre Arts
Adult Hobby Classes: Tuition $25-$50 for 6 week courses. Courses - Drawing, Painting
Summer School: Dean of the College, Robert J Miller. Enrl varies; tui $250 for term of 3-5 wks beginning May or June

ROCKY MOUNT

NORTH CAROLINA WESLEYAN COLLEGE, Dept of Visual & Performing Arts, 3400 N Wesleyan Blvd, 27804-8630. Tel 919-985-5100; FAX 919-977-3701. *Chmn Dept* Michael McAllister; *Instr* Everett Mayo Adelman; *Instr* Michele A Cruz
Scholarships
Tuition: Grad $7250 per yr
Courses: Advertising Design, Architecture, Art Appreciation, Art Education, Visual Communication
Adult Hobby Classes: Enrl 1055; tuition $125 per sem hr. Courses—Art Appreciation, American Architecture

STATESVILLE

MITCHELL COMMUNITY COLLEGE, Visual Art Dept, E Broad St, 28677. Tel 704-878-3200, Ext 202. *Acting Chmn* Donald Everett Moore, MA. Instrs: FT 2, PT 1
Estab 1852, dept estab 1974; pub; D & E; scholarships; SC 12-15, LC 5; enrl D 85, E 40, non-maj 100, maj 25
Ent Req: HS dipl, HS transcripts, placement test
Degrees: AA & AFA 2 yrs
Tuition: Nonres—undergrad in state $315 yr; $75 per quarter, $19 per course part-time, out of state $2943 yr; no campus res—available
Courses: Art History, †Ceramics, Drawing, Intermedia, †Painting, Printmaking, †Sculpture, Color Theory
Adult Hobby Classes: Enrl 100; tuition $20 per 10 wks. Courses - Continuing education courses in art & crafts available

SYLVA

SOUTHWESTERN COMMUNITY COLLEGE, Commercial Art and Advertising Design Dept, 275 Webster Rd, 28779. Tel 704-586-4091, Ext 233. *Head Dept* Bob Clark, MS; *Instr* Roger Stephens, MA. Instrs: FT 2, PT 2
Estab 1964, dept estab 1967; pub; D; scholarships; SC 19, LC 14; enrl D 40, maj 40
Ent Req: HS dipl
Degrees: AAS
Tuition: Res—undergrad $185.50 quarterly; nonres—undergrad $1505 quarterly; no campus res
Courses: †Advertising Design, Art History, Calligraphy, †Commercial Art, Display, Drafting, Drawing, Fashion Arts, Graphic Arts, Graphic Design, Illustration, Lettering, Painting, Photography, Computer Graphics
Adult Hobby Classes: Enrl 30, tuition $35 per class hr

WHITEVILLE

SOUTHEASTERN COMMUNITY COLLEGE, Dept of Art, PO Box 151, 28472. Tel 919-642-7141, Ext 237; FAX 919-642-5658. *Instr* Christa Balogh, MFA
Estab 1965; pub; D & E; scholarships offered; SC 18, LC 7
Ent Req: HS dipl or 18 yrs old
Degrees: AFA 2 yrs
Tuition: Res—undergrad $104.50 per qtr, part time $8.75 per hr; nonres—undergrad $899.25 per quarter, part time $81.25 per hr
Courses: Art History, Ceramics, Drawing, Painting, Printmaking, Sculpture, Pottery
Adult Hobby Classes: Tuition res—$25 per course
Summer School: Dir, Christa Balogh

WILKESBORO

WILKES COMMUNITY COLLEGE, Arts and Science Division, PO Box 120, 28697. Tel 919-667-7136. *Dir* Bud Mayes; *Instr* William Moffett
Estab 1965, dept estab 1967; pub; D & E; scholarships; SC 2, LC 2; enrl D 1600, E 800
Ent Req: HS dipl
Degrees: AA, AFA
Tuition: Res—$60 per quarter, nonres—$985 per quarter; no campus res
Courses: Art History, Costume Design & Construction, Drafting, Drawing, Painting, Sculpture, †Theatre Arts, Art Travel Courses
Summer School: Dir, Bud Mayes

WILMINGTON

UNIVERSITY OF NORTH CAROLINA AT WILMINGTON, Dept of Fine Arts - Division of Art, 601 S College Rd, 28403-3297. Tel 919-395-3415; FAX 919-395-3550. *Chmn* John Myers; *Assoc Prof* Ann Louise Conner, MFA; *Assoc Prof* John Myers, PhD; *Assoc Prof* Stephen Lequire, MFA; *Asst Prof* Kemille Moore, PhD; *Asst Prof* Donald Furst, MFA; *Asst Prof* Heidi Chretien, PhD; *Lectr* Margart Worthington
Estab 1789, dept estab 1952; pub; D & E
Ent Req: HS dipl, ent exam
Degrees: BCA 4 yrs
Tuition: $267 per sem
Courses: †Art History, †Ceramics, †Drawing, †Painting, Printmaking, †Sculpture
Adult Hobby Classes: Courses—Drawing, Painting
Summer School: Two sessions. Courses—varied

WILSON

BARTON COLLEGE (Formerly Atlantic Christian College), Communication, Performaing & Visual Arts, 27893. Tel 919-237-3161. *Chmn* Thomas Marshall, MAT; *Prof* Edward Brown, MFA; *Prof* Chris Wilson, MFA; *Assoc Prof* Jennifer Reitmeyer, MFA; *Asst Prof* John Hancock, BFA; *Instr* Lora Stutts, MFA
Estab 1903, dept estab 1950; pvt; D & E; scholarships; SC 15, LC 8; enrl D 60, E 5, non-maj 68, others 8 (PT)
Ent Req: HS dipl, ent exam
Degrees: BS, BA & BFA 4 yrs
Tuition: Undergrad—$5730 yr, $2866 per sem; campus res—room & board $2000 yr
Courses: Advertising Design, Art Education, Art History, †Ceramics, †Commercial Art, Display, †Drawing, †Graphic Design, †Illustration, Museum Staff Training, †Painting, Photography, †Printmaking, †Sculpture, †Teacher Training, Textile Design, Theatre Arts
Adult Hobby Classes: Tuition $120 per sem hr. Courses—any adult can audit any studio class
Summer School: Dir, Thomas Marshall. Enrl 30; 2 four-week sessions. Courses—Art Appreciation, Drawing, Crafts (stained glass, paper making, wearing, ceramics)

WINGATE

WINGATE COLLEGE, Division of Fine Arts, 28174. Tel 704-233-8000; Telex 75-3023; WATS 800-277-9996. *Chmn Div* Kenneth Murray
Estab 1896, dept estab 1958; den; D & E; scholarships; enrl D & E 1500
Ent Req: HS grad
Degrees: BA(Art), BA(Art Education) 4 yrs
Tuition: $2880 average per sem, campus res—available
Courses: Art History, Ceramics, Drawing, Film, Painting, Photography, Printmaking, Sculpture, Art Appreciation, Art Methods, Composition, Gallery Tours, Metalsmithing, Sketching, 3-D Design
Summer School: Pres, Dr Jerry McGee. Term of 4 wks beginning first wk in June. Courses—all regular class work available if demand warrants

WINSTON-SALEM

SALEM COLLEGE, Art Dept, PO Box 10548, 27108. Tel 919-721-2600, 721-2683. *Asst Prof* James G Austin; *Asst Prof* Geoff Bates; *Asst Prof* Penny Griffin; *Instr* John Hutton; *Instr* Carann Graham
Den, W; D; scholarships; enrl D 642, maj 44
Ent Req: HS Dipl
Degrees: BA 4 yrs
Tuition: Res—$15,060 per yr includes room & board; nonres—$9270 per yr includes room & board
Courses: Art Education, Art History, Ceramics, Drawing, Graphic Arts, Painting, Sculpture

SAWTOOTH CENTER FOR VISUAL ART, 226 N Marshall St, 27101. Tel 919-723-7395. *Executive Dir* James H Sanders III. Instrs: PT 75
Estab 1943
Tuition: $25 - $125 per 10 wk course
Courses: Ceramics, Graphic Arts, Painting, Photography, Printmaking, all visual arts media including advertising, fibers, metals, stained glass
Adult Hobby Classes: Enrl 2000; tuition $38-72 for 5-10 wk term. Courses—All visual arts & craft mediums
Children's Classes: Enrl 2000; tuition $19-35, for 5 wks. Courses—35 different media oriented courses
Summer School: Courses offered

WAKE FOREST UNIVERSITY, Dept of Art, PO Box 7232, 27109. Tel 919-759-5310. *Chmn* Harry B Titus; *Gallery Dir* Victor Faccinto; *Prof* Robert Knott, PhD; *Prof* Margaret Supplee Smith; *Assoc Prof* David Faber; *Asst Prof* Page Laughlin; *Asst Prof* Bernadine Barnes; *Vis Asst Prof* David Helm; *Instr* Alix Hitchcock
Estab 1834, dept estab 1968; pvt; D; scholarships; SC 14, LC 28; enrl D 350, non-maj 300, maj 50
Ent Req: HS dipl, SAT
Degrees: BA 4 yrs
Tuition: Undergrad—$8000 yr, $4000 per sem, $220 per cr; campus res—room & board $1260
Courses: Art History, Drawing, Painting, Printmaking, Sculpture, Theatre Arts
Summer School: Dir, Lu Leake. Enrl 25; tuition $125 per cr

WINSTON-SALEM STATE UNIVERSITY, Art Dept, 27110. Tel 919-750-2000. *Chmn* Roland S Watts, MFA
Estab, 1892, dept estab 1970; pub; D & E; SC 10, LC 7; enrl D 65, nonmaj 275, maj 65
Ent Req: HS Dipl
Degrees: BA 4 yr
Tuition: Campus res—available
Courses: Art Education, Art History, Drawing, Graphic Arts, Painting, Sculpture
Summer School: Courses offered

NORTH DAKOTA

BISMARCK

BISMARCK JUNIOR COLLEGE, Fine Arts Dept, 58501. Tel 701-224-5446, 223-5422. *Chmn* Barbara Cichy; *Instr* Richard Sammons; *Instr* Sheryl Monkelien; *Instr* Ervin Ely; *Instr* Michelle Lindblom; *Instr* Dan Rogers
Degrees: AA 2 yrs
Tuition: Res—undergrad $807.60 per sem; nonres—undergrad $2019 per sem
Courses: Art Appreciation, Ceramics, Drawing, Design, Handicrafts, Jewelry, Painting, Photography, Printmaking, Sculpture, Elementary Art, Gallery Management, Introduction to Understanding Art, Lettering

DICKINSON

DICKINSON STATE UNIVERSITY, Dept of Art, Div of Fine Arts and Humanities, 58601. Tel 701-227-2312. *Chmn* David Solheim; *Prof* Katrina Callahan-Dolcater, MFA; *Asst Prof* Lily Pomeroy, MA; *Asst Instr* Mary Huether, BA
Estab 1918, dept estab 1959; pub; D & E; scholarship; SC 36, LC 8; enrl D approx 150 per quarter, non-maj 130, maj 20
Ent Req: HS dipl, out-of-state, ACT, minimum score 18 or upper-half of class
Degrees: BA, BS and BCS 4 yr
Tuition: Res—undergrad $1300 per yr, $741 per sem, $54.13 per sem hr, $69 extension per sem hr; nonres—undergrad $2917 per yr, $1977 per sem, $1417 per yr for the following states MN, SD, MT, MB & SK, $879 per sem hr; campus res—room & board $1750 double occupancy per yr
Courses: Advertising Design, †Art Education, Art History, †Ceramics, Costume Design & Construction, Display, Drawing, Graphic Design, Display, Drawing, Graphic Design, Handicrafts, Intermedia, Jewelry, Lettering, Painting, Photography, Printmaking, Sculpture, Stage Design, Teacher Training, Theatre Arts, Color
Adult Hobby Classes: Enrl 15 - 25; tuition $213.40 & up for 16 wks. Courses—Photography

FARGO

NORTH DAKOTA STATE UNIVERSITY, Div of Fine Arts, State University Station, PO Box 5691, 58105. Tel 701-237-7932. *Dir* Don Stowell Jr, PhD; *Dept Coordr* Vince Pitelka, MFA; *Assoc Prof* Wayne Tollefson, MFA; *Lectr* Catherine Mulligan, MFA; *Lectr* Jaime Penuel, BFA; *Lectr* Kent Kapplinger
Estab 1889, dept estab 1964; pub; D & E; scholarships; SC 21; enrl D 225, E 60, non-maj 250, maj 30
Ent Req: HS dipl
Degrees: BA & BS 4 yr

Tuition: Res—undergrad $77.50 per cr hr; nonres—$207 per cr hr; campus res available
Courses: †Architecture, Art Appreciation, Art History, †Ceramics, †Painting, †Photography, †Printmaking, †Sculpture, †Theatre Arts

GRAND FORKS

UNIVERSITY OF NORTH DAKOTA, Visual Arts Dept, PO Box 8134, 58202. Tel 701-777-2257. *Chmn* J McElroy-Edwards. Instrs: D FT 11
Estab 1883; pub; scholarships; SC 30, LC 4, GC 14; enrl maj 90, others 1000
Degrees: BFA, BA, BSEd, MFA
Tuition: Campus res—available
Courses: Art Appreciation, †Art Education, Art History, †Ceramics, Design, †Drawing, †Jewelry, Lettering, †Painting, †Photography, †Printmaking, †Sculpture, †Fibers, †Metalsmithing
Adult Hobby Classes: Enrl 20; 2-8 wk term beginning mid-June. Courses—Vary annually
Children's Classes: Enrl 20-30. Courses—Varied
Summer School: Dir, J McElroy Edwards. 1-4 wk terms beginning mid-June. Courses—Varies each sem

JAMESTOWN

JAMESTOWN COLLEGE, Art Dept, 58401. Tel 701-252-3467. *Chmn* Sharon Cox. Instrs: FT 21
Pvt; D; scholarship; SC 13, LC 4; enrl 146, maj 14
Ent Req: HS dipl
Degrees: BA and BS 4 yr, directed study and individual study in advanced studio areas, private studios
Tuition: $6000 per yr; campus res—available
Courses: Art Appreciation, Art Education, Art History, Ceramics, Commercial Art, Drawing, Graphic Arts, History of Art & Archaeology, Painting, Printmaking, Sculpture, Theatre Arts, †2-D Design; Art Business; Fine Arts
Summer School: Term of 6 wks beginning June

MINOT

MINOT STATE UNIVERSITY, Dept of Art, Division of Humanities, 58701. Tel 701-857-3108. *Chmn Div Humanities* Dr George Slanger; *Instr* Walter Piehl. Instrs: FT 3, PT 1
Estab 1913; pub; scholarships; SC 30; enrl per quarter 200, maj 40
Degrees: BA and BS 4 yr
Tuition: Res—undergrad $551 per quarter, grad $721 per quarter; nonres—under grad $1375 per quarter, grad $1851 per quarter; campus res—available
Courses: Advertising Design, Art History, Ceramics, Drawing, Handicrafts, Jewelry, Painting, Photography, Printmaking, Sculpture, Design, Silk Screen, Weaving
Summer School: Courses—same as above

VALLEY CITY

VALLEY CITY STATE COLLEGE, Art Dept, College St, 58072. Tel 701-845-7598. *Art Dept Chmn* Lila Hauge. Instrs: FT 2, PT 3
Estab 1890, dept estab 1921; pub; D & E; scholarship; SC 20, LC 3; enrl D 1300, E 200, non-maj 120, maj 30
Ent Req: HS dipl, ACT
Degrees: AA 2yr, BS and BA 4 yr
Courses: Art Education, Art History, Ceramics, Commercial Art, Drawing, Painting, Printmaking, Sculpture, Teacher Training
Adult Hobby Classes: Enrl 20; tuition $21 per quarter. Courses—Drawing

WAHPETON

NORTH DAKOTA STATE SCHOOL OF SCIENCE, Dept of Graphic Arts, 800 N Sixth St, 58075. Tel 701-671-1130. *Dept Head* Bruce Gard
Estab 1903, dept estab 1970; pub; D & E
Tuition: Res—$520 per quarter; nonres—$1328 per quarter
Courses: Drawing, Graphic Design, Lettering, Painting, Layout Design & Image Assembly
Adult Hobby Classes: Enrl 15; tuition $30. Courses—Calligraphy, Drawing, Painting
Summer School: Dir, Mary Sand. 2 wk term, 3 hrs per day. Courses—Teacher's Art Workshop

WILLISTON

UNIVERSITY OF NORTH DAKOTA-WILLISTON CENTER, Interior Design Dept, PO Box 1326, 58801. Tel 701-774-4200.
Scholarships offered
Degrees: AA 2 yrs, 9 month cert
Tuition: $900 per sem
Courses: Advertising Design, Architecture, Art Appreciation, Art History, Calligraphy, Design, Fashion Arts, Textile Design, Color Theory, 3-D Drawing Techniques, Rendering Techniques
Adult Hobby Classes: Enrl 18; tuition $1000 per yr. Courses—Interior Design Program

OHIO

ADA

OHIO NORTHERN UNIVERSITY, Dept of Art, 500 S Main St, 45810. Tel 419-772-2000. *Chmn* Bruce Chesser
Pvt; D; scholarships; SC 30, LC 8; enrl maj 30
Ent Req: HS dipl, ent exam
Degrees: BA and BFA 4 yrs
Tuition: $10,000
Courses: Art Education, Art History, Ceramics, Drawing, Graphic Arts, Jewelry, Lettering, Painting, Sculpture, Teacher Training
Adult Hobby Classes: Enrl 10-15; tuition $48 for 6 wks. Courses—Ceramics, Watercolor Painting
Summer School: Dir, Bruce Chesser. Enrl 10. Courses - Ceramics, Drawing, Watercolor Painting

AKRON

UNIVERSITY OF AKRON, School of Art, 44325. Tel 216-972-8257; FAX 216-972-5960. *Dept Head* Andrew Borowiec
Estab 1926; pub; D & E; scholarships; SC 25, LC 7, GC 8; enrl D 943, E 129, non-maj 493, maj 450
Ent Req: HS dipl
Degrees: AA 2 yr, BA, BS and BFA 4 yr
Tuition: Res—undergrad $1328 per yr, grad $110 per cr; nonres—undergrad $108 per cr, grad $110 per cr; campus res—available
Courses: †Art History, †Ceramics, †Commercial Art, †Drawing, †Graphic Design, Illustration, †Interior Design, †Jewelry, †Painting, †Photography, †Printmaking, †Sculpture, Textile Design, Weaving, †Art Studio, Computer, †Metalsmithing
Adult Hobby Classes: Tuition $45 - $75 for 5 - 6 wks. Courses—Art History, Ceramics, Drawing, Painting, Photography
Children's Classes: Tuition $354 for 2 wks. Courses—Visual Literacy (high school students)
Summer School: Dir, Bud Houston. Enrl 400; tuition $354 per course for term of 5 wks. Courses—Art History, Computer, Drawing, Graphics, Photography, Painting

ALLIANCE

MOUNT UNION COLLEGE, Dept of Art, 44601. Tel 216-821-5320. *Chmn* James Hopper, MFA; *Prof* Joel Collins, MFA
Estab 1846; pvt; D; scholarships; SC 27, LC 6; enrl D 150, non-maj 125, maj 25
Ent Req: HS dipl, SAT
Degrees: BA
Tuition: Res—undergrad $6000 per yr; campus res—available
Courses: Aesthetics, Art Education, Art History, Drawing, Lettering, Painting, Printmaking, Sculpture, Teacher Training

ASHLAND

ASHLAND UNIVERSITY, Art Dept, College Ave, 44805. Tel 419-289-5130. *Chmn* Albert W Goad. Instrs: FT 4
Estab 1878; den; D & E; scholarship; enrl D 1460, maj 32, minors 12
Ent Req: HS dipl
Degrees: BA, BS 4 yr
Tuition: $9067 per yr
Courses: †Advertising Design, Art Appreciation, Art Education, †Ceramics, †Commercial Art, Constructions, Costume Design & Construction, Design, Drawing, Fashion Arts, Computer Art, available through affiliation with the Art Institue of Pittsburgh: Fashion Illustration, Interior Design, Photography/Multi-media, Visual Communication

ATHENS

OHIO UNIVERSITY, School of Art, College of Fine Arts, 45701. Tel 614-593-4288. *Dean* Dora Wilson; *Assoc Dean* James Stewart. Instrs: FT 32, PT 5
Estab 1936; pub; D & E; scholarships and fel; SC 88, LC 30, LGC 29, SGC 50; enrl maj 573, others 1718
Ent Req: Secondary school dipl, portfolio
Degrees: BFA, MA and MFA 4-5 yr
Tuition: Res—undergrad $1083 per quarter, grad $1118 per quarter; nonres—undergrad $1935 per quarter, grad $2040 per quarter
Courses: †Art Education, †Art History, †Ceramics, Drawing, †Graphic Design, †Illustration, †Painting, †Photography, †Printmaking, †Sculpture, †Art Therapy, Fibers, Glass, †Studio Arts, †Visual Communication
Summer School: Two - 5 wk sessions June-July and July-August; 8 quarter hr maximum per session; SC, LC, GC

BEREA

BALDWIN-WALLACE COLLEGE, Dept of Art, 95 E Bagley Rd, 44017. Tel 216-826-2900. *Chmn Div* Harold D Cole; *Head Dept* Dean Drahos
Estab 1845; den; D & E; SC 23, LC 12; enrl 1900, maj 65
Degrees: AB 4 yrs
Tuition: $6153 per yr; campus res—available
Courses: Art Education, Art History, Ceramics, Drawing, Painting, Photography, Printmaking, Sculpture, Design & Color
Summer School: Tuition $89 per cr hr

BOWLING GREEN

BOWLING GREEN STATE UNIVERSITY, School of Art, Fine Arts Bldg, 43403. Tel 419-372-2786; FAX 419-372-2300. *Dir* Thomas Hilty; *Assoc Dir* Adrian Tio; *Dir Grad Studies* Dennis Wojtkiewicz; *Chmn Design Studies* Ronald Jacomini; *Chmn 3-D Studies* Robert Hurlstone; *Chmn 2-D Studies* Robert Mazur; *Chmn Art Educ* Karen Kakas; *Chmn Art History* Willard Misfeldt, PhD; *Gallery Dir* Jacqueline Nathan
Estab 1910, dept estab 1946; pub; D & E; scholarships and fels; SC 53, LC 14, GC 33; enrl D 2460, E 150, non-maj 995, maj 629, grad 33, others 40
Ent Req: ACT (undergrad), GRE (grad)
Degrees: BA, BS & BFA 4 yrs, MA 1 yr, MFA 2 yrs
Tuition: Res—undergrad $1404 per sem, grad $171 per cr hr, FT $1825 per sem; nonres—undergrad $3500 per sem
Courses: Art Education, Art History, Ceramics, Drawing, Graphic Design, †Jewelry, †Mixed Media, †Painting, †Photography, †Printmaking, †Sculpture, †Art Therapy, Computer Art, †Fibers, †Glass Working
Children's Classes: Enrl 120; tuition $40 per 10 wk sem of Sat mornings
Summer School: Dir, Thomas Hilty. Enrl 300; tuition $1192 for 8 wk & 5 wk session. Couses—Art History, Drawing, Jewelry, Photography, Printmaking, Sculpture, Special Workshops, Watercolor

CANTON

CANTON ART INSTITUTE, 1001 Market Ave N, 44702. Tel 216-453-7666. *Dir* Manuel J Albacete; *Cur Exhibits* Joseph R Hertzi; *Cur Educ* Laura Kolinski; *Business Mgr* Bebo Adams; *Registrar* Lynnda Arrasmith
Pub; D & E; scholarships; SC 28; enrl D 322, E 984, others 1306
Tuition: Children $35; Adults $48
Adult Hobby Classes: Enrl 150 - 200; tuition $60 for 12 wks. Courses—Drawing, Jewelry, Photography, Pottery
Children's Classes: Enrl 100; tuition $25 - $45 for 6 - 12 wks. Courses—Clay, Drawing, Mask Making, Mixed Media, Painting, Puppetry
Summer School: Enrl $100; tuition $25 - $45 for 6 - 12 wks. Courses—Clay, Drawing, Mask Making, Mixed Media, Painting, Puppetry

KENT STATE UNIVERSITY, STARK CAMPUS, School of Art, 6000 Frank Ave NW, 44720. Tel 216-499-9600; FAX 216-494-6121. *Coordr* Emily Bokovec, MA. Instrs: FT 2, PT 3
Estab 1946; dept estab 1967; pub; D & E; scholarships; SC 20, LC 6; enrl D 174, E 13, non-maj 50, maj 40
Ent Req: HS dipl, ACT
Degrees: AA
Tuition: Res—undergrad $1153.50 per sem, $96.25 per hr
Courses: †Art Education, †Art History, Ceramics, Conceptual Art, Drawing, Film, †Graphic Design, †Industrial Design, †Painting, †Printmaking, †Sculpture, Weaving, Stained Glass
Adult Hobby Classes: Enrl varies; tuition $175 per course for 16 wks sem. Courses—same as regular classes
Summer School: 6 & 8 wk sessions. Courses—same as regular classes

MALONE COLLEGE, Dept of Art, Division of Fine Arts, 515 25th St NW, 44709. Tel 216-489-0800. *Chmn Fine Arts* Sandra Carnes; *Assoc Prof* Barbara Drennen; *Assoc Prof* Timothy Young; *Asst Prof* Dr Susan Armstrong
Estab 1956; den; D & E; scholarships; SC 20, LC 2; enrl D 75, maj 30
Ent Req: HS dipl, ent exam
Degrees: BA and BS(Educ) 4 yrs
Tuition: $270 per hr; campus res—available
Courses: †Art Education, †Ceramics, †Drawing, Lettering, †Painting, Printmaking, †Photography, †Printmaking, †Sculpture, Teacher Training, Applied Design, Graphic Communications, History and Criticism of Art
Summer School: Enrl 400; tui $124 cr for term of 5 wks beginning June 15 and July 15

CHILLICOTHE

OHIO UNIVERSITY-CHILLICOTHE CAMPUS, Fine Arts & Humanities Division, 571 W Fifth St, PO Box 629, 45601. Tel 614-774-7200, 774-7251. *Assoc Prof* Dennis Deane, MFA; *Asst Prof* Margaret McAdams, MFA
Estab 1946; D & E; scholarships
Ent Req: HS dipl, ACT or SAT
Tuition: Res—$52 per hr; nonres—$114 per hr
Courses: Art Appreciation, Art Education, Art History, Ceramics, Design, Drawing, Film, Graphic Design, History of Art & Archaeology, Painting, Photography, Teacher Training

CINCINNATI

ACA COLLEGE OF DESIGN, 2528 Kemper Lane, 45206. Tel 513-751-1206; FAX 513-751-1209. *Pres* Marion Allman; *Instr* Roy Waits; *Instr* Dan Devlin; *Instr* Dan Rodgers; *Instr* Cyndi Mendell; *Instr* Tom Greene
Estab 1976; priv; D; scholarships
Ent Req: HS dipl, portfolio, interview
Degrees: Commercial Art AD 2 yr
Tuition: $5980 per yr, additional $2000 second yr for computer graphics major
Courses: Advertising Design, Commercial Art, Design, Graphic Design
Adult Hobby Classes: Enrl 4 - 6. Courses—Computer Graphics, Design
Summer School: Dir, Ennis Jones. Enrl 4 - 6. Courses—Computer Graphics for professional artists

ANTONELLI INSTITUTE OF ART & PHOTOGRAPHY, 124 E Seventh St, 45202. Tel 513-241-4338. *Dir* Dr Robert M Resnick; *Dir Educ* Jim Slouffman; *Dir Student Services* Christy Connelly; *Instr* Connie Motsinger; *Instr* Kelly Tow; *Instr* Bob Wilson; *Instr* Martin Williams; *Instr* Teresa Eichhold. Instrs: FT 5, PT 12
Estab 1947; pvt; D & E; enrl D 200

Ent Req: HS dipl, review of portfolio
Tuition: Undergrad— # 3495 Commercial Art & Interior Design, $3995 Photography
Courses: †Commercial Art, †Interior Design, †Photography, †Fashion Merchandise
Adult Hobby Classes: Courses offered
Summer School: Courses offered

ART ACADEMY OF CINCINNATI, Eden Park, 45202. Tel 513-721-5205. *Chmn* Mark Thomas; *Chmn* Anthony Batchelor; *Chmn* Stewart Goldman, BFA; *Dir* Roger Williams, MFA; *Chmn* Gary Gaffney, MFA; *Instr* Lawrence W Goodridge, MFA; *Instr* Kenn Knowlton, MS; *Instr* Calvin Kowal, MS; *Instr* Larry May, MFA; *Instr* Diane Smith-Hurd, MA; *Instr* Mark Barensfeld, BFA; *Instr* Jay Zumeta, MA; *Instr* April Foster, MFA; *Instr* Rebecca Seeman, MFA
Estab 1887; pvt; D & E; scholarships; enrl 220
Ent Req: HS grad
Degrees: Cert, BS collaboration with Univ of Cincinnati, BFA offered at the Academy, 4-5 yr
Tuition: $8450 per yr, $290 per cr hr
Courses: Art History, Drawing, Graphic Arts, Graphic Design, Illustration, †Painting, †Photography, †Printmaking, †Sculpture, †Communication Design
Adult Hobby Classes: Six wk term; Courses—Ceramics, Drawing, Painting, Sculpture, Photography, Watercolor
Children's Classes: Drawing, Introductory Studies Experience
Summer School: Supvr, Roger Williams. Enrl 64; tuition $90 per cr hr for term of 6 wks beginning June 17

CINCINNATI ACADEMY OF DESIGN (Formerly Central Academy of Commercial Art), 2368 Victory Parkway, 45206. Tel 513-961-2484. *Dean Educ* Michael C McGuire; *Instr* Dan Hogan; *Registrar* Darleen McGuire
Tuition: $3900 per yr, $1950 per sem
Courses: Advertising Design, Calligraphy, Commercial Art, Drawing, Fashion Arts, Illustration, Lettering, Painting, Color Composition, Finished Art, Keyline, Layout, Letterhead, Life Class Mediums, Logotype, Magic Marker, Mediums, Package Design, Perspective, TV Storyboard, others
Adult Hobby Classes: Enrl 65; tuition $3900 per yr

COLLEGE OF MOUNT SAINT JOSEPH, Art Dept, 5701 Delhi Rd, 45233-1670. Tel 513-244-4420; WATS 800-654-9314. *Chmn* Daniel Mader, MA; *Asst* Beth Belknap, MDES; *Prof* Sharon Kesterson-Bollen, EdD; *Asst Prof* Loyola Walter, MFA; *Asst Prof* Gerry Bellas, MFA; *Instr* Laurie Woliung, BA
Estab 1920; den; D & E; scholarships; SC 35, LC 4; enrl 203 maj
Ent Req: HS dipl, national testing scores
Degrees: AA 2 yr, BA and BFA 4 yr
Tuition: Res—undergra $8740 per yr; campus res—room & board $2020 per sem
Courses: †Art Education, Art History, †Ceramics, †Drawing, †Graphic Design, †Interior Design, †Jewelry, Lettering, †Painting, †Photography, †Printmaking, †Sculpture, Enameling, †Fabrics Design, †Pre-Art Therapy
Adult Hobby Classes: Enrl 1000; tuition $228 per cr hr
Summer School: Chairperson, Daniel Mader, MA. Tuition $228 per cr hr

UNIVERSITY OF CINCINNATI, School of Art, 839c DAAP, ML 16, 45221. Tel 513-556-2962; FAX 513-556-2887. *Dir* Derrick Woodham; *Chmn Art History* Jonathan Reeves; *Chmn Art Educ* Robert Russell; *Dir MFA Prog* Kimberly Burleigh; *Prof Art History* Lloyd Engelbrecht, PhD; *Prof Fine Arts* Frank Hermann, MFA; *Prof Art History* George Stricevic, PhD; *Prof Fine Arts* John Stewart, MFA; *Prof Fine Arts* Martin Tucker, MFA; *Prof Fine Arts* Pat Renick, MFA; *Prof Fine Arts* Roy Cartwright, MFA; *Prof Art Educ* Ron Sylva, PhD
Estab 1819, dept estab 1946; pub; D & E; scholarships
Ent Req: HS dipl, transfers to Fine Arts & MFA , portfolio required
Degrees: BA(Art History) 4 yr, 5 yr with teaching certification, BFA(Fine Arts) 4 yr, 5 yr with teaching certification, MA(Art History) 2 yr, MA(Art Educ) 2 yr, MFA 2 yr
Tuition: Res—undergrad $1977, $78 per cr hr, grad $3093, $121 per cr hr; nonres—undergrad $4764, $187 per cr hr, grad $6117, $240 per cr hr; campus res—available
Courses: †Art Education, †Art History, †Ceramics, †Drawing, †Painting, †Photography, †Printmaking, †Sculpture, Teacher Training, Textile Design, Video, Weaving, Fiber Arts

XAVIER UNIVERSITY, Dept of Art, 2220 Victory Parkway, 45207. Tel 513-745-3811. *Chmn* Bernard L Schmidt, MFA; *Prof* Marsha Karagheus-Murphy, MFA; *Prof* Suzanne Chauteau, MFA; *Prof* Jerome Pryor, DEd; *Prof* Ann Beiersdorfer, MA
Estab 1831, dept estab 1935; priv; D & E; scholarships; SC 17, LC 20; enrl D 403, E 349, non-maj 349, maj 54
Ent Req: HS dipl, SAT or ACT
Degrees: BA 4 yr, BFA 4 yr
Tuition: Res—undergrad $10,450 per yr; nonres—$335 cr hr
Courses: Aesthetics, †Art Education, †Ceramics, †Design, †Drawing, †Graphic Design, †Painting, †Printmaking, †Sculpture, Weaving, Art Therapy, History of Art, Humanities

CLEVELAND

CASE WESTERN RESERVE UNIVERSITY, Dept of Art History & Art, Mather House, 44106-7110. Tel 216-368-4118; FAX 216-368-4681. *Chmn* Jenifer Neils, PhD; *Prof* Walter Gibson, PhD; *Prof* Edward J Olszewski, PhD; *Assoc Prof* Ellen G Landau, PhD; *Asst Prof* David Steinberg, PhD; *Asst Prof* Tim Shuckerow, MA; *Asst Prof* Michelle Facos, PhD
Estab 1875; pvt; D; scholarships; SC 24, LC 55, GC 73; enrl D 644, grad 75
Ent Req: HS transcript, SAT or ACT, TOEFL for foreign students
Degrees: BA, BS, MA and PhD
Tuition: $7250 per sem; campus res available
Courses: Architecture, †Art Education, †Art History, †Ceramics, Drawing, Jewelry, †Museum Staff Training, Painting, Photography, Restoration & Conservation, Teacher Training, Textile Design, Weaving, Enameling, Medical Illustration
Summer School: An occasional introductory course in Art History

CLEVELAND INSTITUTE OF ART, 11141 E Blvd, 44106. Tel 216-421-4322. *Pres* Robert A Mayer; *Prof* Tina Cassara; *Prof* Carroll Cassill; *Prof* Francis Taft; *Prof* Hugh Greenlee; *Prof* Julian Stanczak; *Prof* Robert Jergens; *Prof* Lawrence Krause; *Assoc Prof* Robert Palmer; *Assoc Prof* Brent Young; *Assoc Prof* Judith Salomon; *Vis Prof* Kenneth Dingwall
Estab 1882; pvt; D & E; scholarships; SC 90, LC 38; enrl D 507, E 266, non-maj 216, maj 291, others 33
Ent Req: HS dipl SAT, ACT and transcript, portfolio
Degrees: BFA 5 yrs, BS & MEd (educ with Case Western Reserve Univ) 4 yrs
Courses: Aesthetics, Art Education, Art History, Calligraphy, †Ceramics, †Drawing, Film, †Graphic Arts, †Illustration, †Industrial Design, †Jewelry, †Painting, †Photography, †Printmaking, †Sculpture, †Silversmithing, †Enameling, †Fiber, †Glass, †Medical Illustration, †Surface Design
Adult Hobby Classes: Enrl 266; tuition $175 per course. Courses—Calligraphy, Ceramic, Crafts, Design, Drawing, Fiber and Surface Design, Graphic Design, Painting, Printmaking, Sculpture, Silversmithing, Watercolor
Children's Classes: Enrl 210; tuition $49 per course. Courses—Art Basics, Ceramic Sculpture, Crafts, Design, Drawing, Painting, Portfolio Preparation, Printmaking, Photography
Summer School: Dean of Faculty, Robert D Weitzel, Jr. Courses—Ceramics, Design, Drawing, Jewelry and Metalsmithing, Photography, Printmaking, Sculpture, Watercolor

CLEVELAND STATE UNIVERSITY, Art Dept, 2307 Chester Ave (Mailing add: 1983 E 24th St, 44115). Tel 216-687-2040. *Chmn* Thomas E Donaldson, PhD; *Prof* Gene Kangas, MFA; *Prof* Jan Vandermeuen; *Prof* Marvin H Jones, MFA; *Prof* John Hunter, PhD; *Prof* Kenneth Nevadomi, MFA; *Assoc Prof* Masumi Hayashi, MFA; *Assoc Prof* George Mauersberger; *Asst Prof* David Gariff; *Asst Prof* Laurel Lampela, DEd
Dept estab 1972; pub; D & E; scholarships; SC 26, LC 32
Ent Req: HS dipl
Degrees: BA 4 yr
Tuition: 1 - 11 hrs $83 per quarter per cr hr; 12 - 18 hrs $992 per quarter
Courses: †Art Education, †Art History, †Ceramics, †Drawing, †Painting, †Photography, †Printmaking, †Sculpture, Introduction of Art & Design
Summer School: Chmn, John Hunter. Tuition & courses same as regular schedule

CUYAHOGA COMMUNITY COLLEGE, Dept of Art, 2900 Community College Ave, 44115. Tel 216-987-4525. *Prof* David Haberman, MFA; *Prof* Gerald Kramer, MFA; *Instr* Marilyn Fzalay; *Instr* Megan Sweeney
Estab 1963. College maintains four campuses; pub; D & E; scholarships; SC 15, LC 4; enrl D 150, E 80, maj 50
Ent Req: HS dipl
Degrees: AA yrs
Tuition: County res—$31.50 per cr hr; out-of-county—$41.75 per cr hr; nonres—$83.50 per cr hr
Courses: Art Appreciation, Art Education, Art History, Calligraphy, Ceramics, Graphic Design, Occupational Therapy, Painting, Photography, Printmaking, Sculpture, Stage Design, Teacher Training, Theatre Arts, Video
Summer School: Courses—various

JOHN CARROLL UNIVERSITY, Dept of Art History & Humanities, University Heights, 44118. Tel 216-397-1886. *Chmn* Dr Charles Scillia
Sch estab 1886, dept estab 1965; pvt; D & E; SC 3, LC 30; enrl D 400, non-maj 350, maj-humanities 30, art hist 14
Ent Req: HS dipl, SAT
Degrees: BA Art History 4 yrs, BA Humanities 4 yrs
Tuition: Res—undergrad $266 per cr hr, grad $277 per cr hr; campus res—available
Courses: Art History, Modern History
Summer School: Dir, Dr Roger A Welchans. Tuition $111 per credit hr for 5 wk term beginning June 15. Courses—Art History, Musicology

COLUMBUS

CAPITAL UNIVERSITY, Fine Arts Dept, 2199 E Main St, 43209. Tel 614-236-6011. *Chmn* Richard Phipps. Instrs: FT 3
Degrees: BA, BFA
Tuition: $5870 per yr
Courses: Advertising Design, Art Education, Art History, Ceramics, Design, Drawing, Jewelry, Painting, Photography, Sculpture, Theatre Arts, Weaving, Stained Glass

COLUMBUS COLLEGE OF ART AND DESIGN, Fine Arts Dept, 107 N Ninth St, 43215. Tel 614-224-9101. *Dean* Lowell Tolstedt. Instrs: 68
Estab 1879; pvt; approved for Veterans; D & E; scholarships
Ent Req: HS grad, art portfolio
Degrees: BFA 4 yr
Courses: Advertising Design, Fashion Arts, Graphic Arts, Illustration, Industrial Design, Interior Design, Painting, Sculpture, Fine Arts, Packaging Design, Retail Advertising
Children's Classes: Saturday sessions 9 - 11:30 AM
Summer School: Dean, Mary T Kinney

OHIO DOMINICAN COLLEGE, Art Dept, 1216 Sunbury Rd, 43219. Tel 614-253-2741. *Dept Chmn* Dr Larry Cepek
Estab 1911; den; D & E; scholarships; SC and LC 709 per sem; enrl D 139, E 105, maj 17
Ent Req: HS dipl
Degrees: BA 4 yrs, also secondary educ cert or special training cert, K-12
Tuition: $5900 per yr
Courses: Textile Design, Theatre Arts, Video
Summer School: Dir, Joe Stotski. Term of 7 wks beginning June

OHIO STATE UNIVERSITY

—**School of Architecture,** 190 W 17th Ave, 43210. Tel 614-292-1012; FAX 614-292-7106. *Dir* Jerrold Voss, AIP. Instrs: FT 43, PT 23
Estab 1899; pub; scholarships; enrl Archit 450, Landscape Archit 170, City and Regional Planning 65
Degrees: BSArchit, BSLand Archit, MArchit, MLA, MCRP, PhDCRP
Tuition: Res—undergrad $993 per quarter, grad $1322 per quarter; nonres—undergrad $2764 per quarter, grad $3426 per quarter
Courses: Architecture, Landscape Architecture, City and Regional Planning
Adult Hobby Classes: Enrl limited; Tuition $170-$469.
Summer School: Dir, Robert Liveson. Enrl 50-70; tui $170-$469 for 10 weeks.
Couses - Architecture 200, 202, 341, 441, 844
—**College of the Arts,** 304 Mershon Auditorium, 1871 N High St, 43210. Tel 614-292-5171. *Dean Col* Donald Harris
Univ estab 1870, col estab 1968; pub; D & E; scholarships; SC 106, LC 192, GC 208; enrl D 3678, E varies, non-maj 2300, maj 893, grad 150
Ent Req: HS dipl
Degrees: BA, BAEd, BFA, BSID 4 yrs, MA, MFA, PhD
Tuition: Res—undergrad $2064 per yr, $688 per quarter, grad $3135 per yr, $1045 per quarter; nonres—undergrad $5040 per yr, $1680 per quarter, grad $5790 per yr, $1930 per quarter; campus res—room & board $4800 per yr
Courses: †Art Education, †Art History, †Ceramics, †Drawing, †History of Art & Archaeology, †Industrial Design, Mixed Media, †Painting, †Printmaking, †Sculpture, †Stage Design, †Teacher Training, †Theatre Arts, †Weaving, †Glass, Graphics of Communication, Interior Space Design, Product Design
Adult Hobby Classes: Courses—art experiences in all media for local adults
Children's Classes: Enrl 300 per quarter; fees $36 per quarter; Sat School. Courses—art experiences in all media for local children
Summer School: Same as regular session
—**Dept of Art,** 146 Hopkins Hall, 128 N Oval Mall, 43210. Tel 614-292-5072. *Actg Chmn* Robert Shea. Instrs: FT 36, PT 34
SC 56, LC 6, GC 30
Degrees: BA, BFA, MFA
Tuition: Res—undergrad $993 per quarter, grad $1322 per quarter; nonres—undergrad $2764 per quarter, grad $3426 per quarter
Courses: †Ceramics, †Drawing, †Painting, †Sculpture, †Fine Arts, †Glass
Adult Hobby Classes: Offered through CAP (Creative Art Program)
—**Dept of Art Education,** Hopkins Hall 340, 43210-1363. Tel 614-292-7183. *Chmn Dept* Michael J Parsons, PhD; *Prof* Arthur Efland; *Assoc Prof* Judith Koroscik, PhD; *Assoc Prof* Louis Lankford, PhD; *Assoc Prof* Terry Barrett, PhD; *Asst Prof* Pat Stuhr, PhD
Estab 1907; pub; D & E; scholarships; SC 6, LC 10, GC 16; enrl maj 95, grad 115
Ent Req: HS dipl
Degrees: BAEd, MA, PhD
Tuition: Res—undergrad $993 per quarter, grad $1322 per quarter; nonres—undergrad $2764 per quarter, grad $3462 per quarter
Courses: †Art Appreciation, †Art Education, †Teacher Training, †Art Administration, †Art Criticism, †Art for Special Audiences, †Arts of the Books, †Computer Graphics, †Multi- Cultural, †Photo Criticism
Children's Classes: Enrl 1000; tuition $25 for 7 wks; Courses—Variety of studio activities
Summer School: Chmn Dept, Michael J Parsons, PhD
—**Dept of Industrial Design,** 380 Hopkins Hall, 128 N Oval Mall, 43210. Tel 614-292-6746; FAX 614-292-7641. *Chmn* Jim Kaufman. Instrs: FT 11, PT 5
Scholarships; SC 35, LC 10, GC 10
Degrees: BSID, MA
Tuition: Res—undergrad $993 per quarter, grad $1322 per quarter; nonres—undergrad $2764 per quarter, grad $3462 per quarter
Courses: †Interior Space Design, †Product Design, †Visual Communication Design, †Design Development, †Design Education, †Design Management
Summer School: Advanced Typography
—**Dept of the History of Art,** 100 Hayes Hall, 108 N Oval Mall, 43210. Tel 614-292-7481. *Chmn Dept* Christine Verzar, PhD
Estab 1871, dept estab 1968; pub; D & E; scholarships; LC 56, GC 29; enrl D 854, non-maj 700, maj 71, grad 73
Ent Req: HS dipl
Degrees: BA, MA 2 yrs, PhD 4-6 yrs
Courses: †Art History, History of Art & Archaeology
Summer School: Enrl 250; tuition same as regular session for term of ten wks beginning June. Courses—vary each yr

CUYAHOGA FALLS

CUYAHOGA VALLEY ART CENTER, 2131 Front St, 44221. Tel 216-928-8092. *Pres* Bill Bryant; *Instr* Eugene Bell; *Instr* Robert Putka; *Instr* Jean Deemer; *Instr* Dino Massaroni; *Instr* Jack Lieberman; *Instr* Beth Lindenberger; *Instr* Tony Cross; *Instr* Pat Selby; *Instr* Donna Schoommaker
Estab 1942; pub; D & E; SC 23; enrl 200
Ent Req: None, interest in art
Degrees: None
Tuition: $75 members for 10 wks, $90 nonmembers; no campus res
Courses: Ceramics, Collages, Drawing, Acrylic Painting, Oil Painting, Watercolor, Special Workshops
Adult Hobby Classes: Enrl 100. Courses—Drawing, Painting, Pottery
Children's Classes: Enrl 25; tuition $50 for members, $60 for nonmembers per 10 wks. Courses—Ceramics, Painting
Summer School: Courses—same as regular session

STUDIOS OF JACK RICHARD CREATIVE SCHOOL OF DESIGN, 2250 Front St, 44221. Tel 216-929-1575. *Dir* Jack Richard. Instrs: FT 3
Estab 1960; pvt; D & E; scholarships; SC 4, LC 10; enrl D 50-60, E 50-60
Courses: Aesthetics, Art Education, Drawing, Illustration, Occupational Therapy, Painting, Photography, Sculpture, Color, Design, Mural
Adult Hobby Classes: Enrl 200 - 300 per session; tuition $11 per class. Courses—Drawing, Painting, Design
Children's Classes: Saturday mornings
Summer School: Dir, Jane Williams. Enrl 90; tuition $10 - $12 per class for term of 8 wks beginning June. Courses—Design, Drawing, Painting

DAYTON

SINCLAIR COMMUNITY COLLEGE, Div of Performing & Fine Arts, 444 W Third St, 45402. Tel 513-226-2540. *Chmn Fine Arts* Annamary Bierley
Estab 1973; pub; D & E
Ent Req: HS dipl, ent exam
Degrees: AA 2 yrs
Tuition: County res—$29 per cr hr; non-county res—$39 per cr hr; out of state—$59 per cr hr; no campus res
Courses: Advertising Design, Ceramics, Commercial Art, Drawing, Graphic Arts, Painting, Sculpture, Theatre Arts
Summer School: Ten week term

UNIVERSITY OF DAYTON, Visual Arts Dept, 300 College Park, 45469. Tel 513-229-3237. *Acting Chmn* Sean Wilkinson, MFA; *Assoc Prof* Louis Weber, MA; *Assoc Prof* Fred Niles, MFA; *Asst Prof* Mary Zahner, PhD; *Asst Prof* Joann E Swanson, MFA; *Asst Prof* Tammy Sparks, MFA; *Asst Prof* Beth Edwards, MFA; *Asst Prof* Tim Wilbers, MFA; *Asst Prof* Peter Gooch, MFA; *Asst Prof* Terri Hitt, MFA
Estab 1850; pvt; D & E; SC 15, LC 8; enrl D 225, E 75-100, non-maj 100, maj 200
Ent Req: HS dipl
Degrees: BA, BFA
Tuition: $4110 per term; campus res— available
Courses: †Art Education, Art History, Calligraphy, Ceramics, Drawing, Illustration, Jewelry, Mixed Media, †Painting, †Photography, †Printmaking, †Sculpture, Teacher Training, Weaving, †Visual Communication Design
Summer School: Dir, Jon Meyer. Tuition $230 per cr hr

WRIGHT STATE UNIVERSITY, Dept of Art & Art History, Colonel Glenn Hwy, 45435. Tel 513-873-2896. *Chmn* Linda Caron; *Prof* Thomas Macaulay, MFA; *Prof* Jerry McDowell, MA; *Prof* Ron Geibert, MFA; *Assoc Prof* David Leach, MFA; *Assoc Prof* Raymond Must, MA; *Assoc Prof* Carol Nathanson, PhD; *Assoc Prof* Diane Fitch, MFA; *Assoc Prof* Ernest Koerlin, MFA; *Assoc Prof* Ron Geibert, MFA; *Assoc Prof* Kimmerly Kiser, MFA
Estab 1964, dept estab 1965; pub; D & E; scholarships; SC 67, LC 16, GC 8; enrl D 516, E 43, non-maj 80, maj 150
Ent Req: HS dipl
Degrees: BA(Studio Art), BA(Art History), BFA 4 yr
Tuition: Res—undergrad $961 per quarter; nonres—undergrad $1922 per quarter
Courses: Art History, Drawing, Painting, Photography, Printmaking, Sculpture
Summer School: Dir, Linda Caron. Enrl 65; tuition res $961, nonres $1922 per 5 - 10 wk sessions. Courses—Painting, Drawing, Photography

DELAWARE

OHIO WESLEYAN UNIVERSITY, Fine Arts Dept, 60 S Sandusky St, 43015. Tel 614-368-3600; FAX 614-368-3299. *Chmn* Justin Kronewetter, MFA; *Prof* Marty J Kalb, MA; *Assoc Prof* Carol Neuman de Vegvar, PhD; *Assoc Prof* James Krehbiel, MFA; *Assoc Prof* Rinda Metz, MFA; *Asst Prof* Cynthia Cetlin, MFA; *Instr* Joh Quick; *Instr* Wendy Peters
Estab 1841, dept estab 1864; pvt; D & E; scholarships & fels; enrl D 1925, non-maj 1805, maj 120
Ent Req: HS dipl, SAT or ACT
Degrees: BA and BFA 4 yrs
Tuition: Res—$14,644 per yr; campus res—room & board $5130 per yr
Courses: Aesthetics, Art Education, Art History, Ceramics, Drawing, Graphic Design, Jewelry, Painting, Photography, Printmaking, Sculpture, Teacher Training, Computer Graphics
Children's Classes: Various media courses
Summer School: Dean, W Louthan. Tuition $975 per unit, 6 & 8 wk courses offered. Courses—Varied

ELYRIA

LORAIN COUNTY COMMUNITY COLLEGE, Art Dept, 1005 N Abbe Rd, 44035. Tel 216-365-4191.
Courses: Art Appreciation, Ceramics, Design, Drawing, Painting, Photography, Printmaking, Sculpture, Textile Design

FINDLAY

UNIVERSITY OF FINDLAY, Art Dept, 1000 N Main St, 45840. Tel 419-422-8313, Ext 4577. Instrs: FT 2, PT 6
Estab 1882; pvt; D & E; scholarships; SC 21, LC 4; enrl maj 30
Ent Req: HS dipl
Degrees: AA 2 yr, BA and BS 4 yr
Tuition: $3658 per sem (12-17 sem hrs)
Courses: Advertising Design, Aesthetics, Art Education, Art History, Ceramics, Collages, Drawing, Graphic Design, Painting, Photography, Printmaking, Sculpture, Teacher Training
Adult Hobby Classes: Enrl 10-20. Courses—Ceramics
Children's Classes: Courses—Ceramics, Drawing
Summer School: Dir, Ed Erner

GAMBIER

KENYON COLLEGE, Art Dept, 43022. Tel 614-427-5459. *Chmn* Claudia J H Esslinger, MA; *Prof* Martin Garhart; *Assoc Prof* Barry Gunderson, MFA; *Assoc Prof* Eugene J Dwyer, PhD; *Assoc Prof* Gregory P Spaid, MFA; *Asst Prof* Melissa Dabakis; *Asst Prof* Kay Willens
Estab 1824, dept estab 1965; pvt; D; scholarships; SC 15, LC 10; enrl D 450, non-maj 250, maj 60
Ent Req: HS dipl
Degrees: BA and BFA
Tuition: Res—undergrad $14,865 per yr; campus res required
Courses: †Art History, Drawing, Painting, Photography, Printmaking, Sculpture

GRANVILLE

DENISON UNIVERSITY, Dept of Art, PO Box M, 43023. Tel 614-587-0810. *Chmn Dept* L Joy Sperling, PhD; *Prof* George Bogdanovitch, MFA; *Prof* Michael Jung, MFA; *Asst Prof* Karl Sandin, PhD; *Asst Prof* David Jokinen, MFA; *Asst Prof* Debra Fisher, MFA
Estab 1831, dept estab 1931; pvt; D; scholarships; SC 24, LC 16; enrl D 800, maj 65, double maj 35
Ent Req: HS
Degrees: BA, BFA, BS 4 yr
Tuition: Res—undergrad $14,900 per yr; campus res—double room & board $4220 per yr
Courses: Aesthetics, Architecture, †Art History, †Ceramics, Drawing, Graphic Arts, Graphic Design, History of Art & Archaeology, Mixed Media, Museum Staff Training, †Painting, Photography, †Printmaking, Restoration & Conservation, †Sculpture

HAMILTON

MIAMI UNIVERSITY, Dept Fine Arts, 1601 Peck Blvd, 45011. Tel 513-529-6026. *Art Coordr* Phil Joseph; *Prof* Edward Montgomery
Scholarships offered
Tuition: $73 per cr hr
Courses: Advertising Design, Art Appreciation, Art Education, Art History, Calligraphy, Drawing, Painting, Printmaking, Sculpture
Adult Hobby Classes: Enrl 25-30. Courses—Painting, Printmaking
Summer School: Courses—Drawing

HIRAM

HIRAM COLLEGE, Art Dept, Dean St, 44234. Tel 216-569-5304. *Chmn* George Schroeder. Instrs: FT 3, PT 2
Estab 1850; pvt; D; scholarships; SC 20, LC 14; enrl D 400
Ent Req: HS dipl
Degrees: AB 4 yr
Tuition: $12,627 per acad yr, $4209 per 10 wk term
Courses: Aesthetics, Art Education, Art History, Ceramics, Drawing, Handicrafts, Painting, Photography, Printmaking, Sculpture, Teacher Training, †Studio Art

HURON

BOWLING GREEN STATE UNIVERSITY, Art Dept, Firelands Col, Div of Humanities, 901 Rye Beach Rd, 44839. Tel 419-433-5560. *Assoc Prof* Julius T Kosan, MFA. Instrs: FT 1, PT 3
Estab 1907, col estab 1966; pub; D & E; scholarships; SC 12, LC 3; enrl D 1200
Ent Req: HS dipl, SAT
Degrees: AA 2 yr
Tuition: Res—undergrad $1083 per sem, $108 per cr hr
Courses: Art Education, Art History, Drawing, History of Art & Archaeology, Painting, Photography, Teacher Training, Theatre Arts, Enameling
Summer School: Term of 5 wks beginning June 18. Courses—Art Education, Studio Courses

KENT

KENT STATE UNIVERSITY, School of Art, 44242. Tel 216-672-2192. *Dir* William Quinn; *Div Coordr Design* J Charles Walker, MFA; *Div Coordr Painting* Paul O'Keefe; *Div Coordr Art History* Fred T Smith; *Div Coordr Crafts* Janice Lessman-Moss; *Grad Coordr* Frank Susi; *Div Coordr Art Educ* Frank Susi. Instrs: FT 43, PT 6
Estab 1910; pub; D & E; scholarships; SC 105, LC 35, GC 50; enrl non-maj 600, maj 600, grad 100
Ent Req: HS dipl, ACT
Degrees: BFA, BA 4 yrs, MA 1 - 2 yrs, MFA 2 - 3 yrs
Tuition: Res—undergrad $1650 per sem, grad $1915 per sem; nonres—undergrad $3285 per sem, grad $3713 per sem, $309.82 per cr hr; campus res—room & board $1601 per sem
Courses: †Art Education, †Art History, Calligraphy, †Ceramics, †Drawing, †Film, †Graphic Design, †Illustration, †Jewelry, Lettering, Mixed Media, Museum Staff Training, †Painting, †Printmaking, †Sculpture, Textile Design, Arts Therapy, Enameling
Children's Classes: Enrl 150; tuition $15 per 6 wk session, two 6 wk sessions, fall & spring
Summer School: Dir, William Quinn. Enrl 500; tuition $137.50 per cr hr, 5 or 10 wk term. Courses—approx 30 - 35

MARIETTA

MARIETTA COLLEGE, Art Dept, 45750. Tel 614-374-4696. *Assoc Prof* Valdis Garoza; *Assoc Prof* William H Gerhold. Instrs: FT 2
Estab 1835; pvt; grants in aid and student loans; SC 20, LC 7; enrl maj 75, total col 1600
Degrees: BA(Studio, Art History, Art Education), BFA 4 yr
Tuition: $6185 per sem
Courses: Advertising Design, Art Appreciation, Art Education, Art History, Calligraphy, Ceramics, Commercial Art, Design, Drawing, Painting, Printmaking, Carving in Wood & Stone, Life Drawing, Lithography & Silkscreen, Modeling & Casting, Stained Glass

MENTOR

LAKELAND COMMUNITY COLLEGE, Visual Arts Dept, Rt 306 at I-90, 44060. Tel 216-953-7028. *Chmn & Dir of Humanities Div* Dr Larry Aufderheide; *Prof* Thomas W Betts, MA; *Prof* Richard Parsons, MA; *Prof* Walter Swyrydenko, MA; *Prof* George Somogyi, MA; *Instr* John Merchant, BA
Sch estab 1967, dept estab 1968; D & E; scholarships; enrl D & E 350
Ent Req: HS dipl
Degrees: AA with concentration in Art 2 yrs, AA Technology degree in Graphic Arts
Tuition: Res—undergrad $1500 per academic yr
Courses: Advertising Design, Art Appreciation, Art History, Calligraphy, Ceramics, Commercial Art, Conceptual Art, Drawing, †Graphic Arts, Graphic Design, Illustration, Intermedia, Jewelry, Lettering, Painting, Photography, Printmaking, Sculpture
Summer School: Courses—Ceramics, Drawing, Jewelry, Painting, Sculpture

MOUNT VERNON

MOUNT VERNON NAZARENE COLLEGE, Art Dept, Martinsburg Rd, 43050. Tel 614-397-1244. *Chmn* Stephen Self; *Assoc Prof* Gim Hendrikx, MFA; *Instr* John Donnelly
Estab 1968, dept estab 1970; den; D & E; scholarships; SC 20, LC 5; enrl D 1052, non-maj 1032, maj 20
Ent Req: HS dipl and grad of upper 2/3, ACT
Degrees: BA; Sr project required for graduation
Tuition: Res, nonres, undergrad $2597 per term
Courses: Aesthetics, Art Education, Art History, Ceramics, Design, Drafting, Drawing, Painting, Photography, Printmaking, Sculpture, Art in the Western World, Design Fundamentals, Graphic Communication, Selected Topics, Senior Project

NEW CONCORD

MUSKINGUM COLLEGE, Art Department, Johnson Hall, 43762. Tel 614-826-8315. *Chmn* Gaile Gallatin; *Asst Prof* Keith J Williams; *Asst Prof* Martha Mitchell; *Instr* Carole Jordan; *Instr* Mike Seiler. Instrs: FT 2
Estab 1837; pvt; D; scholarships; SC 13, LC 6; enrl D 300, maj 15
Ent Req: HS dipl, ent exam, specific school standards
Degrees: BA and BS 4 yı
Tuition: $14,000 per yr
Courses: Art History, †Art Education, Ceramics, Design, Drawing, Graphic Arts, Painting, Photography, Sculpture, Teacher Training
Adult Hobby Classes: Enrl 60. Courses—Art Educ
Children's Classes: Enrl 10. Courses—Ceramics
Summer School: Dir, Keith J Williams. Enrl 15; tuition $300 for 5 wk term. Courses—Ceramics I, Drawing I

OBERLIN

OBERLIN COLLEGE, Dept of Art, 44074. Tel 216-775-8181; FAX 216-775-8886. *Chmn* Susan Kane; *Prof* Richard Spear, PhD; *Prof* John Pearson, MFA; *Prof* Athena Tacha, PhD; *Prof* William Hood, PhD; *Assoc Prof* Susan Kane, PhD; *Assoc Prof* Patricia Mathews, PhD; *Assoc Prof* Jeffrey Hamburger; *Asst Prof* Robert Harrist, PhD; *Asst Prof* Sarah Schuster, MFA; *Asst Prof* Ellen Garvens, MFA; *Asst Prof* Michael Rees, MFA
Estab 1833, dept estab 1917; pvt; D; scholarships; SC 28, LC 38, advanced undergrad and grad courses 13; enrl D approx 1200, non-maj 500, maj 100, grad 5
Ent Req: HS dipl, SAT
Degrees: BA 4 yr, MA(Art Hist) 2 yr
Tuition: Undergrad and grad $15,600 per yr; campus res—room and board $4890
Courses: Art History, Drawing, History of Art & Archaeology, Painting, Photography, Printmaking, Sculpture, Computer Imaging

OXFORD

MIAMI UNIVERSITY, Art Dept, New Art Bldg, 45056. Tel 513-529-2900. *Dean School Fine Arts* Hayden B May; *Chmn* Linnea S Dietrich
Estab 1809, dept estab 1929; pub; D & E; scholarships; SC 49, LC 35, GC 20; enrl D 2309, non-maj 1890, maj 419, grad 32
Ent Req: HS dipl, class rank, ACT or SAT
Degrees: BFA and BS(Art) 4 yrs, MFA 2 yrs, MA(Art or Art Educ) and MEd(Art Educ) 1 yr
Tuition: Res—$2040 per sem, with room & board $1445; nonres—$3220 per sem, with room & board $4650
Courses: Advertising Design, Architecture, †Art Education, Art History, Calligraphy, †Ceramics, Collages, Commercial Art, Display, †Drawing, Graphic Arts, †Graphic Design, History of Art & Archaeology, Illustration, †Jewelry, Lettering, Museum Staff Training, †Painting, Photography, †Printmaking, †Sculpture, †Silversmithing, †Teacher Training, †Textile Design, Stitchery, Weaving
Children's Classes: Enrl 70; tuition $5 per sem. Courses—General Art
Summer School: Dir, Peter Dahoda. Courses—varied workshops

PAINESVILLE

LAKE ERIE COLLEGE-GARFIELD SENIOR COLLEGE, Fine Arts Dept, 44077. Tel 216-352-3361, Ext 416. *Prof* Bonnie Selip; *Prof* Michael Demeter. Instrs: FT 2, PT 1
Estab 1856; pvt; SC 20, LC 7; enrl 800 total
Ent Req: Col board exam
Degrees: BA and BFA 4 yrs
Tuition: Res—undergrad $245 per cr hr
Courses: Art Education, Art History, †Ceramics, Drawing, †Painting, †Photography, †Printmaking, Sculpture, Design, Introductory Art
Summer School: Courses vary

SAINT CLAIRSVILLE

OHIO UNIVERSITY-BELMONT COUNTY CAMPUS, Dept Comparative Arts, 43950. Tel 614-695-1720. *Prof* David Miles
Degrees: BA & BS 4 yrs
Tuition: Res—undergrad $733 per qtr, grad $1012 per qtr; nonres—undergrad $1761 per qtr, grad $2040 per qtr
Courses: Art Appreciation, Art Education, Design, Drawing, Photography

SPRINGFIELD

SPRINGFIELD MUSEUM OF ART, 107 Cliff Park Rd, 45501. Tel 513-325-4673. *Dir* Mark Chepp. Instrs: PT 20
Estab 1951; pvt; D & E; scholarships; D 600
Tuition: No campus res
Courses: Ceramics, Drawing, Jewelry, Painting, Photography, Sculpture
Adult Hobby Classes: Enrl 287; tuition $79 per quarter
Children's Classes: Enrl 286; tuition $39 per quarter. Courses—Art Experiences, Drawing, Pottery & Sculpture

WITTENBERG UNIVERSITY, Art Dept, Koch Hall, N Wittenberg Ave, 45501. Tel 513-327-6231. *Chmn* Jack Osbun, MFA; *Prof* Don Dunifon, MFA; *Assoc Prof* Jack Mann; *Assoc Prof* Ann Terry, MFA; *Prof* George Ramsay
Estab 1842; pvt den; D & E; scholarships; SC 30, LC 17; enrl D 350, non-maj 270, maj 80
Ent Req: HS dipl, class rank, transcript, SAT or ACT test results, recommendations and if possible, a personal interview
Degrees: AB and BFA 4 yr
Tuition: Nonres—undergrad $18,000 per yr; campus res—room & board $4900
Courses: †Art Education, †Art History, †Ceramics, Drawing, Graphic Arts, Graphic Design, †Illustration, Interior Design, Jewelry, †Painting, Photography, †Printmaking, †Sculpture, †Teacher Training
Summer School: Provost, William Wiebenga. Enrl 400; tuition $250 for term of 7 wks beginning June 14. Courses—Art in the Elementary School, Fundamental of Art, Painting

SYLVANIA

LOURDES COLLEGE, Art Dept, 6832 Convent Blvd, 43560. Tel 419-885-3211; FAX 419-882-3987. *Chmn Fine Arts* Sr Sharon Havelak
Estab 1958; pvt, den; D & E; SC 12, LC 9; enrl D 70, E 30, non-maj 60, maj 35
Ent Req: HS dipl, ACT or SAT
Degrees: AA, BA, BIS
Tuition: $197 per sem; no campus res available
Courses: Art History, Calligraphy, Ceramics, Design, †Drawing, Graphic Design, †Painting, Printmaking, Sculpture, Weaving, Art Therapy, Copper Enameling, Fiber Arts, Weaving, Watercolor
Adult Hobby Classes: Enrl 40; tuition $3-$35 per 1-5 classes. Courses - Same as above & others through Life-Long Learning Center
Children's Classes: Enrl 95; tuition $50 for 10 wks. Courses—Ceramics, Drawing, Painting
Summer School: Dir, Sr Sharon Havelak. Enrl 17; tuition $197 per cr for 5 wk term. Courses—Chinese Art History, Drawing, Watercolor

TIFFIN

HEIDELBERG COLLEGE, Dept of Art, 44883. Tel 419-448-2202. *Chmn* Jim Hagemeyer
Estab 1850; pvt; D; scholarships; SC 22, LC 9; enrl 200, maj 24
Ent Req: HS dipl, each applicant's qualifications are considered individually
Degrees: AB 4 yrs, independent study, honors work available
Tuition: $10,910 per yr
Courses: Advertising Design, Aesthetics, Art Education, Ceramics, Commercial Art, Display, Drawing, Graphic Arts, Graphic Design, History of Art & Archaeology, Illustration, Jewelry, Lettering, Museum Staff Training, Painting, Sculpture, Stage Design, Teacher Training, Textile Design, Chip Carving, Copper Enameling, Metal Tooling, Mosaic
Summer School: Dir, Dr Roy M Bacon. Term of 6 wks beginning June. Courses—Materials and Methods in Teaching, Practical Arts

TOLEDO

UNIVERSITY OF TOLEDO, Dept of Art, University Art Bldg, 620 Grove Place, 43620. Tel 419-537-3434; FAX 419-255-5638. *Chmn* Elizabeth S Cole; *Prof* Duane Bastian, PhD; *Prof* David Guip, PhD; *Prof* Diana Attie, MS; *Prof* Linda Ames-Bell, MFA; *Prof* Peter Elloian, MFA; *Assoc Prof* Elizabeth Cole, PhD; *Assoc Prof* Carolyn Autry, MFA; *Assoc Prof* Marc Gerstein, PhD; *Assoc Prof* Rex Fogt, MFA; *Assoc Prof* Alan Melis, MFA; *Assoc Prof* Thomas Lingeman, MFA. Instrs: FT 13, PT 12
Estab 1919; D & E; scholarships; Same as regular session
Ent Req: HS dipl
Degrees: BA, BFA, BEd 4 yr; MEd (Art Educ) 2 yr
Tuition: Res—undergrad $929.33 per quarter or $77.43 per cr hr, grad $1269 per quarter or $105.83 per cr hr; nonres—undergrad $2177 per quarter or $181.43 per cr hr, grad $2517 per quarter or $209 per cr hr
Courses: Advertising Design, Art Education, †Art History, †Ceramics, Design, †Drawing, †Painting, †Photography, †Printmaking, †Sculpture, †Metalsmithing
Summer School: Courses offered from those above

WESTERVILLE

OTTERBEIN COLLEGE, Dept of Visual Arts, 43081. Tel 614-898-1508. *Chmn* Joseph Ansell
Pvt; scholarships; SC 11, LC 4; enrl D 1400, maj 32
Ent Req: HS dipl
Degrees: BA 4 yrs
Tuition: Res—undergrad $11,502 per yr; campus res—room & board $4107
Courses: Art Education, Ceramics, Drawing, Graphic Design, Art History, Painting, Photography

WILBERFORCE

CENTRAL STATE UNIVERSITY, Dept of Art, 45384. Tel 513-376-6610. *Chmn* Willis Davis. Instrs: FT 6
Estab 1856; D; SC 20, LC 8; enrl D 175, maj 50, others 130
Ent Req: HS dipl
Degrees: BA and BS 4 yr
Courses: Advertising Design, Art Education, Art History, Ceramics, Drawing, Graphic Arts, Lettering, Painting, Sculpture, Teacher Training, Studio
Summer School: Chmn, Willis Bing Davis. Enrl maj 50, others 200; term of 12 wks beginning June 16, two sessions. Courses—Art for the Elementary Teacher, Art History, Black Artists, Ceramics, Introduction to Art, Painting, Sculpture

WILBERFORCE UNIVERSITY, Art Dept, 45384. Tel 513-376-2911. *Advisor* James Padgett, MFA
Estab 1856, dept estab 1973; pvt; D; scholarships; SC 22, LC 5
Ent Req: HS dipl
Degrees: BA, BS and BS(Educ) 4 yrs
Tuition: $5877 per yr
Courses: Commercial Art, Printmaking, Sculpture, Teacher Training, Fine Arts
Summer School: Courses offered

WILLOUGHBY

SCHOOL OF FINE ARTS, Visual Arts Dept, 38660 Mentor Ave, 44094. Tel 216-951-7500. *Dir* Charles M Frank; *Visual Arts Coordr* Robert Raack
Estab 1957; pvt; D & E; scholarships; enrl D 85, E 195
Tuition: $54-$89 per class; no campus res
Courses: Ceramics, Drawing, Intermedia, Mixed Media, Painting, Photography
Adult Hobby Classes: Enrl 147; tuition $60-$89 for one 6 wk & two 16 wk sessions. Courses—Ceramics, Drawing, Painting, Photography
Children's Classes: Enrl 240; tuition $30-$54 for one 6 wk session & two 16 wk sessions. Courses—Ceramics, Drawing, Painting
Summer School: Dir, Doris Foster. Enrl 210; tuition $25-$71 for term of 6 wks beginning mid-June. Courses—same as above

WILMINGTON

WILMINGTON COLLEGE, Art Dept, 45177. Tel 513-386-6661. *Prof* Terry Inlow; *Asst Prof* Hal Shunk
Scholarships offered
Degrees: BA
Tuition: $7900 per yr
Courses: Art Education, Art History, Ceramics, Design, Drawing, Handicrafts, Painting, Photography, Printmaking, Sculpture, Stage Design

WOOSTER

COLLEGE OF WOOSTER, Dept of Art, University St, 44691. Tel 216-263-2388; WATS 800-321-9885. *Chmn* Arnold Lewis, PhD; *Prof* Walter Zurko, MFA; *Prof* George Olson, MFA; *Prof* Thalia Gouma-Pederson, PhD; *Assoc Prof* Linda Hults, PhD; *Asst Prof* Susan Hanson, MFA
Estab 1866; pvt; D & E; SC 13, LC 19; enrl D 1800, maj 40
Ent Req: HS dipl
Degrees: BA 4 yr
Tuition: $18,680 per yr (board & room included)
Courses: Architecture, Art Education, Art History, Ceramics, Drawing, Graphic Arts, History of Art & Archaeology, Painting, Photography, Printmaking, Sculpture, African Art, Women Artists in America
Adult Hobby Classes: Available through student activities board. Enrl 12-20; tuition varies
Summer School: Dir, Dr Thomas Falkner

YELLOW SPRINGS

ANTIOCH COLLEGE, Visual Arts Institute, 45387. Tel 513-767-7331, Ext 467. *Chmn* David Lapalombara, MFA; *Prof* Gary Bower, MFA; *Prof* Karen Shirley, MFA
Estab 1853; pvt; D & E; SC 48, LC 10; enrl D 665 per quarter, non-maj 100, maj 50
Ent Req: HS dipl
Degrees: BA
Tuition: 13,000 per yr (tuition, fees, room and board)
Courses: Ceramics, †Drawing, Painting, Printmaking, †Sculpture

YOUNGSTOWN

YOUNGSTOWN STATE UNIVERSITY, Art Dept, 410 Wick Ave, 44555. Tel 216-742-3000. *Chmn* Michael Walusis
Estab 1908, dept estab 1952; pub; D & E; SC 44, LC 26, GC 8; enrl D & E 1250, maj 300, grad 15
Ent Req: HS dipl

Degrees: AB, BFA and BS 4 yrs
Tuition: $890 per quarter
Courses: †Art Education, †Art History, †Ceramics, †Commercial Art, Drawing, Graphic Arts, †Graphic Design, Illustration, Interior Design, Jewelry, Lettering, Museum Staff Training, †Painting, Photography, †Printmaking, †Sculpture, †Teacher Training
Adult Hobby Classes: Courses—Calligraphy, Ceramics, Drawing, Painting, Photography, Weaving
Summer School: Two 5 wk sessions beginning June. Courses—same as above

OKLAHOMA

ADA

EAST CENTRAL UNIVERSITY, Art Dept, 74820. Tel 405-332-8000, Ext 353. *Chmn* Robert Sieg, MFA; *Prof* Grant Thorp, MFA; *Instr* Marc Etier, MFA; *Instr* Brad Jessop
Estab 1909; pub; D & E; scholarships; SC 22, LC 10, GC 8; enrl D 222, E 105, non-maj 103, maj 80, grad 3, others 36
Ent Req: HS dipl, ATC
Degrees: BA and BA(Educ) 4 yr, MEd 33 hrs, post graduate work, public service program
Tuition: Res—1000-2000 level courses $39.50, 3000-4000 level courses $41, 5000 level courses $51.45; nonres—1000-2000 level courses $98.20, 3000-4000 level courses $107.25, 5000 level courses $121.45
Courses: †Art Education, Art History, †Ceramics, Conceptual Art, †Drawing, Film, Graphic Arts, Jewelry, Mixed Media, †Painting, Photography, †Printmaking, †Sculpture, Silversmithing, †Teacher Training, Wood Design
Adult Hobby Classes: Enrl 25 average. Courses—Drawing, Painting, Silk Screen
Summer School: Dir, E Gettinger. Enrl 90; tuition $34 per cr hr for res, $83.50 for nonres. Courses—Art Education, Fundamentals, Painting

ALTUS

WESTERN OKLAHOMA STATE COLLEGE, Art Dept, 2801 N Main, 73521. Tel 405-477-2000; FAX 405-521-6154. *Chmn* Lloyd C English
Scholarships offered
Degrees: AA, AS, AT
Tuition: Res—undergrad $27.80 per hr; nonres—undergrad $49.25 hr
Courses: Advertising Design, Art Appreciation, Art History, Ceramics, Design, Drawing, Handicrafts, Jewelry, Painting, Photography, Printmaking, Sculpture, Stage Design, Video, Weaving

BETHANY

SOUTHERN NAZARENE UNIVERSITY, Art Dept, 6729 NW 39th Expressway, 73008. Tel 405-789-6400. *Head Dept* Nila West Murrow
Estab 1920; den; D & E; scholarships; SC 13, LC 7; enrl D 51, E 6, non-maj 38, maj 13
Ent Req: HS dipl, ACT
Tuition: Res—undergrad $158 per hr, grad $171 per hr; campus res available
Courses: Aesthetics, Art Education, Art History, Commercial Art, Drawing, Painting, Printmaking, Sculpture, †Teacher Training, Crafts, Pottery
Children's Classes: Enrl 55; tuition $115 one wk summer art camp (grades 3 - 12). Courses—Drawing, Pottery, Watercolor & various crafts
Summer School: Dir, Nila Murrow. Same as children's classes

CHICKASHA

UNIVERSITY OF SCIENCE AND ARTS OF OKLAHOMA, Arts Dept, 73018. Tel 405-224-3140, Ext 301. *Prof* Kent Lamar. Instrs: FT 3, PT 2
Estab 1909; pub; D; scholarship; SC 26, LC 3; enrl maj 84, others 180
Degrees: 124 hr req for grad
Tuition: Res—undergrad $40.90 per hr, grad $41.75 per hr; nonres—undergrad $99.45 per hr, grad $108.50 per hr
Courses: Ceramics, Design, Drawing, Jewelry, Painting, Photography, Printmaking, Sculpture, Teacher Training, Pottery & Modeling, Watercolor
Adult Hobby Classes: Enrl 30; tuition $15 per hr. Courses—Ceramics, Stained Glass, Graphics Design, Drawing
Summer School: Enrl 60; tuition $15 per hr for 10 wk course. Courses—Painting, Sculpture, Ceramics

CLAREMORE

ROGERS STATE COLLEGE, Art Dept, Will Rogers & College Hill, 74017-3252. Tel 918-341-7510. *Dir* Gary E Moeller, MFA
Estab 1971; pub; D & E; scholarships; SC 12, LC 3; enrl D 126, E 60, non-maj 146, maj 82
Ent Req: HS dipl, ACT
Degrees: AA and AS 2 yr
Tuition: Res—$30.55 per hr; nonres—$79.80 per hr; campus res available
Courses: Art History, Ceramics, Drawing, Lettering, Painting, Photography, Printmaking, Sculpture, †Fine Arts, †Graphic Technology
Children's Classes: Tui $16.35 per hr. Courses—Children's Art
Summer School: Tui $16.35 per hr for term of 8 wks beginning June 5th. Courses—Advanced Ceramics, Art Appreciation, Drawing, Graphic Technology, Painting

DURANT

SOUTHEASTERN OKLAHOMA STATE UNIVERSITY, Art Dept, Station A, 74701. Tel 405-924-0121; FAX 405-924-7313. *Chmn* Brad Cushman; *Asst Prof* Paul Pfrehm
Estab 1909; pub; scholarships; enrl 330
Ent Req: HS dipl, col exam
Degrees: BA & BAEduc 4-5 yrs, MEd
Tuition: Res—lower div $35.15 per hr, upper div $36 per hr, grad div $46.85 per hr; nonres—lower div $93.70 per hr, upper div $102.75 per hr, grad div $122.95 per hr
Courses: Art Appreciation, Art Education, Art History, Ceramics, Design, Drawing, Graphic Arts, Jewelry, Painting, Printmaking, Sculpture, Applied Design, Crafts
Adult Hobby Classes: Enrl 20; 12 wk term. Courses—Ceramics, Drawing, Jewelry, Painting
Summer School: Dir, Susan H Allen. Enrl 130; tuition same as above. Courses—Art Appreciation, Ceramics, Drawing, Design, Fundamentals, Painting, Printmaking, Special Studies

EDMOND

UNIVERSITY OF CENTRAL OKLAHOMA (Formerly Central State University), Dept of Visual Arts & Design, 100 N University Dr, 73034-0180. Tel 405-341-2980, Ext 5201; FAX 405-341-4964. *Chmn* William L Hommel, PhD
Estab 1890; pub; D & E; scholarships; enrl maj 280, grad 20, dept 1168, school 13, 086
Ent Req: HS dipl, health exams, IQ test, scholarship tests
Degrees: BA, BS and MEduc 3-4 yrs
Courses: Art Education, Art History, Ceramics, Commercial Art, Graphic Design, Jewelry, Museum Staff Training, Painting, Photography, Sculpture, African Art, Art in America, Arts & Crafts, Design, Etching & Lithography, Figure Drawing, Metal Design, Studio Art, Watercolor, Weaving
Summer School: Chmn, William L Hommel PhD. Enrl 185; tuition $39.50 per cr hr lower division, $40 per cr hr upper division. Courses——Art Appreciation, Art History, Computer Graphics, Design, Drawing, European Study Tour, Figure Drawing, Painting

ENID

PHILLIPS UNIVERSITY, Dept of Art, University Station, 73702. Tel 405-237-4433. *Chmn* Paul Denny Jr, DFA; *Assoc Prof* Mary Phillips, MFA
Estab 1907, dept estab 1909; den; D & E; scholarships; SC 20, LC 6; enrl D 45, E 18, non-maj 20, maj 25, others 18
Ent Req: HS dipl
Degrees: MBA and ME 5 yrs, BA, BS and BFA 4 yrs
Tuition: Res & nonres—undergrad $247 per hr; campus res—room & board $3000
Courses: †Advertising Design, Art Appreciation, †Art Education, Art History, Calligraphy, †Ceramics, Commercial Art, Design, Drawing, Graphic Arts, History of Art & Archaeology, Lettering, Painting, Photography, Sculpture, Teacher Training, Pre-Art Therapy
Adult Hobby Classes: Enrl 18; tuition $125 per course. Course—Ceramics
Summer School: Enrl 15; tuition $227 for term of one cr hr. Courses vary

LAWTON

CAMERON UNIVERSITY, Art Dept, 2800 W Gore Blvd, 73505. Tel 405-581-2450. *Chmn* Jack Bryan
Estab 1970; pub; D & E; scholarships; SC 22, LC 5; enrl D 417, E 90, maj 60
Ent Req: HS dipl
Degrees: BA 4 yrs
Tuition: Res—undergrad $46.65 per hr, grad $58.65 per hr; nonres—undergrad $117.65 per hr, grad $141.40 per hr; campus res—room & board $643 per sem
Courses: Art Appreciation, Art Education, †Art History, Ceramics, Drawing, Design, Graphic Arts, Graphic Design, †Mixed Media, Painting, Photography, †Printmaking, †Sculpture, Color, Crafts
Summer School: Courses—Art Education, Ceramics, Drawing, Graphics, Mixed Media, Painting, Photography, Printmaking

MIAMI

NORTHEASTERN OKLAHOMA A & M COLLEGE, Art Dept, 74354. Tel 918-542-8441, Ext 263; FAX 918-542-9759. *Chmn* Nancy Blackwood. Instrs: FT 2, PT 1
Estab 1919; pub; D & E; scholarships; SC 12, LC 3
Ent Req: HS dipl
Degrees: AA 2 yr
Tuition: Res—$27.30 per hr; nonres—$76.55; campus res available
Courses: Advertising Design, Art Appreciation, Art Education, Calligraphy, Ceramics, Commercial Art, Costume Design & Construction, Design, Display, Drawing, Fashion Arts, Graphic Arts, Lettering, Painting, Photography, Sculpture, Stage Design, Theatre Arts, Video

NORMAN

UNIVERSITY OF OKLAHOMA, School of Art, 520 Parrington Oval, Room 202, 73019. Tel 405-325-2691. *Dir* Dr Phelam
Estab 1911; pub; scholarships; SC 27, LC 22, GC 12; enrl maj 400, others 1200
Degrees: BFA, MA(Art History) and MFA
Courses: Advertising Design, Art History, Ceramics, Drawing, Film, Graphic Arts, Painting, Photography, Video, Metal Design, Product Design

OKLAHOMA CITY

OKLAHOMA CHRISTIAN UNIVERSITY OF SCIENCE & ARTS, Department of Art & Design, PO Box 11000, 73136-1100. Tel 405-425-5000; FAX 405-425-5316. *Chmn* Michael J O'Keefe, MFA
Scholarships
Tuition: $2125 per trimester (12-16 hrs)
Courses: †Advertising Design, †Art Education, Art History, Drawing, Illustration, †Interior Design, Painting, Photography, Printmaking, Stage Design, Art

OKLAHOMA CITY UNIVERSITY, Norick Art Center, 2501 N Blackwelder, 73106. Tel 405-521-5226. *Chmn* Jack R Davis. Instrs: FT 3, PT 13
Estab 1904; den; D & E; scholarships offered; SC 44, LC 26; enrl maj 62
Degrees: 4 yr
Tuition: $2700 per sem
Courses: †Art History, Ceramics, Drawing, Graphic Arts, Graphic Design, Illustration, Jewelry, Painting, Sculpture, Teacher Training, Airbursh, Art Marketing, Design, Computer Graphics, Native American Art, Watercolor
Adult Hobby Classes: Summer workshops & weekend classes
Children's Classes: Enrl 120; tuition $90 for 2 wks in summer. Courses—Drawing, Painting, Printmaking, Sculpture
Summer School: Chmn, Jack Davis, Enrl 15; tuition $175 per cr hr for two 6 wk sessions June to July, July to August. Courses—Drawing, Painting, Sculpture, Ceramics

OKMULGEE

OKLAHOMA STATE UNIVERSITY, Graphic Arts Dept, 1801 E Fourth, 74447. Tel 918-756-6211. *Head Dept* Gary Borchert; *Instructor* Paul A Gresham, MFA; *Instructor* H Allen Shaw Jr, BFA; *Instructor* Bill Welch, BS. Instrs: FT 5, PT 1
Estab 1946, dept estab 1970; pub; D & E; scholarships; SC 12, LC 1; enrl D 130, E 18
Ent Req: HS dipl or 18 yrs of age
Degrees: 2 yr Associate, degree granting technical school
Tuition: Res—undergrad $160 per hr, grad $180 per hr; $2500 per sem; campus res—$1100 per yr
Courses: Advertising Design, †Art History, Commercial Art, Drafting, Drawing, Graphic Arts, †Graphic Design, Illustration, Jewelry, Lettering, Photography, †Studio
Summer School: Tuition same as above per trimester beginning June 1st to last of Sept

SHAWNEE

OKLAHOMA BAPTIST UNIVERSITY, Art Dept, 500 W University, 74801. Tel 405-275-2850, Ext 2345. *Chmn* Steve Hicks, MFA; *Asst Prof* Janie Wester, MA; *Asst Prof* Nelle Agee, MEd; *Instr* Gloria Duncan, MA
Estab 1910; den; D; scholarships offered; SC 7, LC 3, grad 2; enrl D 100, non-maj 75, maj 25, grad 2
Ent Req: HS dipl, SAT-ACT
Degrees: BA & BFA 4 yrs
Tuition: Res—undergrad $1615 per sem, $110 per hr; nonres—undergrad $1300; campus res—room & board $1000 per academic yr
Courses: Art Appreciation, Art Education, Art History, Calligraphy, Ceramics, Design, Drawing, History of Art & Archaeology, Painting, Photography, Printmaking, Teacher Training, Weaving, Fibers

SAINT GREGORY'S COLLEGE, Dept of Art, 1900 W MacArthur Dr, 74801. Tel 405-273-9870. *Chmn* Shirlie Bowers Wilcoxson, BFA
Estab 1898, dept estab 1960; den; D & E; SC 6; enrl D 325
Ent Req: HS dipl, ACT or SAT
Degrees: AA 2 yrs
Tuition: $1710 per sem
Courses: Art History, Ceramics, Commercial Art, Drawing, Mixed Media, Sculpture
Adult Hobby Classes: Courses—Ceramics, Drawing, Sculpture

STILLWATER

OKLAHOMA STATE UNIVERSITY, Art Dept, 108 Bartlett Center for the Studio Arts, 74078. Tel 405-744-6016; FAX 405-744-7074. *Dept Head* Nancy B Wilkinson, PhD
Estab 1890, dept estab 1928; pub; D & E; scholarships; SC 20, LC 4; enrl D 850, E 60, non-maj 810, maj 210
Ent Req: HS dipl
Degrees: BA, BA(Art Hist), BFA, 4 yr
Courses: †Art History, Ceramics, Drawing, Graphic Design, Jewelry, Lettering, Painting, Printmaking, Sculpture
Summer School: Dept Head, Nancy B Wilkinson, PhD

TAHLEQUAH

NORTHEASTERN OKLAHOMA STATE UNIVERSITY, 74464. Tel 918-456-5511, Ext 2705. *Dean Arts & Letters* Dr Thomas Cottrill, EdD; *Instructor* Jerry Choate, MFA; *Instructor* R C Coones, MFA; *Instructor* Dr Kathleen Schmidt, EdD
Estab 1889; pub; D & E; scholarships; enrl non-maj 50, maj 30, grad 10
Ent Req: HS dipl
Degrees: BA and BA(Educ) 4 yr
Tuition: Res—undergrad $39.65 per hr, grad $40.50 per hr; nonres—undergrad $58.55 per hr, grad $66.75; campus res available
Courses: Art Education, Art History, Ceramics, Commercial Art, Costume Design & Construction, Drafting, Drawing, Graphic Arts, Lettering, Painting, Photography, Printmaking, Sculpture, Stage Design, Teacher Training, Theatre Arts
Adult Hobby Classes: Enrl 20; tuition $20.85 per cr hr for 1 semester. Courses—Indian Art
Summer School: Dir, Tom Cottrill. Enrl 20; tuition $20.85 - $22.30 per cr hr for 8 wk term. Courses—Art Education, Fundamentals of Art

TULSA

ORAL ROBERTS UNIVERSITY, Fine Arts Dept, 7777 S Lewis, 74171. Tel 918-495-6611; FAX 918-495-6033. *Chmn* Stu Branston; *Vis Prof* Dorothea Heit, photography; *Vis Prof* Will Tate, computer graphics; *Vis Prof* Don Wilson, photography; *Asst Prof* Stuart Branston, MFA; *Asst Prof* Douglas Latta, MFA; *Instr* Greg Stiver
Estab 1965; pvt; D & E; scholarships; SC 22, LC 3; enrl D 287, maj 100, others 87
Ent Req: HS dipl, SAT
Degrees: BA(Art Educ), BA & BS(Commercial Art), BA(Studio Art) & BS(Broadcast Design) 4 yrs
Tuition: Res & nonres—undergrad $280 per hr, $2975 per sem 12 - 18.5 hrs; campus res—room & board $1658
Courses: Advertising Design, Art Appreciation, Art Education, Art History, Calligraphy, Ceramics, Commercial Art, Design, Constructions, Drawing, Graphic Arts, Graphic Design, Handicrafts, Art History, Illustration, Intermedia, Interior Design, Jewelry, Lettering, Mixed Media, Painting, Photography, Printmaking, Sculpture, Teacher Training, †Studio Art, †Broadcast Design

TULSA JUNIOR COLLEGE, Art Dept, 909 S Boston, 74119. Tel 918-587-6561. *Instr* William Derrevere, MA; *Instr* Dwayne Pass, MFA. Instrs: PT 8
Estab 1970; pub; D & E; scholarships; SC 16, LC 7; enrl non-maj 40, maj 160
Ent Req: HS dipl
Degrees: AA 2 yrs
Tuition: Campus residency available
Courses: Art History, Drawing, Goldsmithing, Jewelry, Painting, Printmaking, Silversmithing, Art Appreciation, 2-D & 3-D Design, Health & Safety in the Arts & Crafts, Life Drawing
Adult Hobby Classes: Special prog of art courses and crafts courses
Summer School: Courses—Art Appreciation, Drawing, Color & Design, Painting

UNIVERSITY OF TULSA, Dept of Art, 600 S College Ave, 74104. Tel 918-631-2000, Ext 2202. *Acting Chmn* Stephen Sumner
Estab 1898; pvt; scholarships; SC 20, LC 13, GC 22; enrl maj 160, others 400
Degrees: BA, BFA, MA, MFA and MTA 4 yrs
Tuition: Res—$5200 per yr; campus res available
Courses: †Art Education, †Ceramics, †Commercial Art, †Painting, †Printmaking, †Sculpture
Adult Hobby Classes: Courses offered through Continuing Education
Summer School: Dir, Tom Manhart. Enrl 50; tuition $185 per sem hr. Courses—Art Education, Painting

WEATHERFORD

SOUTHWESTERN OKLAHOMA STATE UNIVERSITY, Art Dept, 100 Campus Dr, 73096. Tel 405-772-6611, Ext 5000; FAX 405-772-5447. *Chmn* G Patrick Riley
Estab 1901, dept estab 1941; pub; D & E; scholarships; SC 35, LC 8, GC 43; enrl D 5000
Ent Req: HS dipl
Degrees: BA(Art), BA(Art Educ) and BA(Commercial Art) 4 yr
Tuition: Res—undergrad $38.65 per hr, grad $39.50 per hr; nonres—undergrad $97.20 per hr; grad $106.25; campus res available
Courses: Advertising Design, Art Education, Art History, Ceramics, Commercial Art, Drawing, Graphic Arts, Graphic Design, Illustration, Jewelry, Lettering, Mixed Media, Painting, Sculpture, Teacher Training
Adult Hobby Classes: Tuition $40.30 for 16 wk term. Courses—Native American Art, Painting, Stained Glass
Summer School: Courses—Ceramics, Drawing, Elements of Art, Fundamentals of Art, Introduction to Clay, Jewelry, Metal, Painting

OREGON

ALBANY

LINN BENTON COMMUNITY COLLEGE, Fine & Applied Art Dept, 6500 SW Pacific Blvd, 97321. Tel 503-928-2361; FAX 503-967-6550. *Chmn Dept* James A Tolbert; *Instr* John Aikman; *Instr* Rich Bergeman; *Instr* Judith Rogers; *Instr* Doris Litzer; *Instr* Jason Widmer; *Instr* Sandra Zimmer
Estab 1968; pub; D & E; SC 14, LC 2; enrl D 2000, E 4000
Ent Req: Open entry
Degrees: AA, AS & AAS 2 yrs
Tuition: Res—$700 per yr
Courses: †Advertising Design, Art History, Ceramics, Display, Drafting, Drawing, †Graphic Arts, †Graphic Design, Handicrafts, Illustration, Lettering, Painting, Photography, Sculpture, Textile Design, Theatre Arts
Adult Hobby Classes: Courses—Painting, Tole Painting, Watercolor

ASHLAND

SOUTHERN OREGON STATE COLLEGE, Dept of Art, 1250 Siskiyou Blvd, 97520. Tel 503-552-6386. *Chmn Dept Art* Margaret Sjogren
Estab 1926; pub; D & E; scholarships; SC 53, LC 17, GC 18; enrl D 120, E 30, non-maj 700, maj 100
Ent Req: HS dipl, SAT or ACT
Degrees: BFA, BA and BS(Art) 4 yrs
Tuition: Res—undergrad $2487 per yr; nonres—undergrad $5988 per yr; campus res available
Courses: Advertising Design, Art Appreciation, †Art History, †Ceramics, †Drawing, Graphic Design, †Painting, Photography, †Printmaking, †Sculpture, Fibers
Adult Hobby Classes: Various courses
Children's Classes: Summer classes
Summer School: Dir, Kevin Talbert. Enrl 210; 4 - 8 wk term. Courses—various

BEND

CENTRAL OREGON COMMUNITY COLLEGE, Dept of Art, 2600 NW College Way, 97701. Tel 503-382-6112; FAX 503-385-5978. *Prof* Douglas Campbell-Smith, MA
Estab 1949; pub; D & E; scholarships; enrl in col D 2025, E 2000
Ent Req: HS dipl
Degrees: AA, AS, Cert
Tuition: In-district—$200 per term; out-of-district—$330 per term; out-of-state—$1082 per term; campus res—available
Courses: Calligraphy, Ceramics, Drawing, Painting, Photography, Printmaking, Stage Design, Theatre Arts
Adult Hobby Classes: Enrl 1500-2000; tuition, duration & courses offered vary
Summer School: Dir, John Weber. Enrl 300-400; tuition $200 for a term of 8 wks beginning June 23. Courses—general courses

COOS BAY

COOS ART MUSEUM, 235 Anderson Ave, 97420. Tel 503-267-3901. *Dir* Larry Watson
Estab 1966; pvt; D & E; SC 7; enrl D 15, E 100
Tuition: Members—$30-$60 per class; nonmembers—$45-$60 per class
Courses: Painting, Rose Maling
Adult Hobby Classes: Enrl 100; tuition for 10 wks, non-mem $23, mem $20
Children's Classes: Tuition $18 - $38 depending on course and membership status
Summer School: Tuition same as above

SOUTHWESTERN OREGON COMMUNITY COLLEGE, Visual Arts Dept, 1988 Newmark, 97420. Tel 503-888-2525, Ext 291. *Div Chmn* Bob Bower; *Instr* Melanie Schwartz, MA; *Instr* Carol Vernon, MA
Estab 1962, dept estab 1964; pub; D & E; scholarships; SC 11, LC 1; enrl D 420, E 300, non-maj 250, maj 170
Degrees: AA 2 yrs
Tuition: Res—undergrad $324 per quarter; nonres—undergrad $972 per quarter; no campus res
Courses: Art Education, Art History, Calligraphy, Ceramics, Commercial Art, Drawing, Graphic Design, Painting, Photography, Printmaking, Sculpture, Theatre Arts, Video
Adult Hobby Classes: Tuition $150 per quarter. Courses—Art Appreciation, Ceramics, Painting, Tole Painting, Wood Carving
Children's Classes: Only as occasional workshops
Summer School: Dean Instruction, Phill Anderson. Tuition varies. Courses—Ceramics, Painting & Composition, Watercolor

CORVALLIS

OREGON STATE UNIVERSITY, Dept of Art, 97331-3702. Tel 503-737-4745. *Chmn* David Hardesty, MFA; *Prof* Harrison Branch, MFA; *Prof* Clinton Brown, MFA; *Prof* Berkley Chappell, MFA; *Prof* Thomas Morandi, MFA; *Prof* Alan Munro, MFA; *Prof* Theodore Wiprud, MFA; *Assoc Prof* Henry Sayre, PhD; *Assoc Prof* Yuji Hiratsuka, MFA; *Assoc Prof* Shelley Jordon, MFA; *Assoc Prof* Barbara Loeb, PhD; *Assoc Prof* Andrea Marks, MFA; *Assoc Prof* Edward McDonald, MFA; *Asst Prof* Thomas Morandi; *Instr* Deborah Kadas, BFA; *Sr Resident Asst* Douglas Russell, BA
School estab 1868, dept 1908; pub; D & E; scholarships; SC 63, LC 16, GC 271; enrl non-maj 2000, maj 275, grad 10
Ent Req: HS dipl
Degrees: BA, BS, BFA & MAIS
Tuition: Res—undergrad $875 per quarter; res—grad $1200 per quarter; nonres—undergrad $2302 per quarter; nonres—grad $1922 per quarter; campus res available
Courses: Art History, Ceramics, Drawing, Graphic Design, Illustration, Painting, Photography, Printmaking, Sculpture, 2-D & 3-D Design, Visual Appreciation
Summer School: 8 wk session beginning 3rd wk in June. Courses—various studio & art history

EUGENE

MAUDE I KERNS ART CENTER SCHOOL, 1910 E 15th Ave, 97403. Tel 503-345-1571. *Artistic Dir* Nancy Frey
Estab 1951; pvt; D & E; scholarships; SC 45; enrl D & E 450
Tuition: $38-$45 per class per quarter
Courses: Calligraphy, Ceramics, Design, Drawing, Graphic Design, Handicrafts, Jewelry, Photography, Printmaking, Sculpture, Textile Design, Weaving
Adult Hobby Classes: Enrl 100. Courses—Per regular session
Children's Classes: Enrl 200; tuition $75. Courses—Ceramics, Drawing & other special workshops
Summer School: Courses varied

LANE COMMUNITY COLLEGE, Art and Applied Design Dept, 4000 E 30th Ave, 97405. Tel 503-747-4501, Ext 2409. *Div Chmn* Richard Reid, PhD
Estab 1964, dept estab 1967; pub; D & E; SC 42, LC 4; enrl D 300, E 75, non-maj 240, maj 60
Ent Req: HS dipl
Degrees: AA, AS 2 yrs
Tuition: Res—$264 per term; out-of-state $1012 per term
Courses: Art Appreciation, Art History, Ceramics, Design, Drawing, †Graphic Design, Illustration, Jewelry, Lettering, Painting, Photography, Printmaking, Sculpture, Textile Design, Weaving, Metal Casting, 2-D & 3-D Design, Air Brush
Adult Hobby Classes: Varied courses
Summer School: Div Chmn, Richard Reid. Enrl 198; tuition $72 per class for 8 wks. Courses—Design, Drawing, Painting, Watercolor

UNIVERSITY OF OREGON, Dept of Fine & Applied Arts, School of Architecture and Allied Arts, 97403. Tel 503-346-3610; FAX 503-346-3660. *Prof* Kenneth R O'Connell, MFA. Instrs: FT 20, PT 10
Pub; D; scholarships; enrl D 1475, non-maj 350, maj 1050
Degrees: BA, BS 4 yrs, BFA 5 yrs, MFA 2 yrs minimum after BFA or equivalent
Tuition: Res—undergrad $595 per term; nonres—undergrad $854 per term; grad $1681 per term; grad $1388; campus res available
Courses: Ceramics, Drawing, Painting, Photography, Printmaking, Sculpture, Metalsmithing, Visual Design, Computer Graphics, Fibers
Summer School: Dir, Ron Trebon. Tuition grad $1020, undergrad $606 for term of 8 wks beginning June. Courses—Ceramics, Computer Graphics, Painting, Photography, Printmaking, Sculpture, Weaving, Metalsmithing, Jewelry

FOREST GROVE

PACIFIC UNIVERSITY IN OREGON, Arts Division, 2043 College Way, 97116. Tel 503-359-2216. *Chmn* Garry Mueller, MFA; *Assoc Prof* Jan Shield, MFA
Estab 1849; D & E; scholarships
Ent Req: HS dipl, SAT or ACT, counselor recommendation, transcript of acad work
Degrees: BA, MA(Teaching)
Tuition: $9832 per yr; campus res—room & board $3200
Courses: Advertising Design, Art History, Ceramics, Design, Drawing, Graphic Design, Illustration, Jewelry, Painting, Photography, Printmaking, Sculpture, Art for Contemporary Life
Summer School: Dir, John L Parker

GRESHAM

MOUNT HOOD COMMUNITY COLLEGE, Visual Arts Center, 26000 SE Stark St, 97030. Tel 503-667-7309; FAX 503-667-7389. *Chmn* Eric Sankey Scholarships
Degrees: AA
Courses: Art Education, Art History, Calligraphy, Ceramics, Design, Drawing, Film, Graphic Design, Illustration, Jewelry, Painting, Printmaking, Sculpture
Adult Hobby Classes: Tuition $30 per cr. Courses—All studio courses
Summer School: Dir, Eric Sankey. Enrl 60 - 90; two 5 wk sessions. Courses—Calligraphy, Ceramics, Drawing, Watercolor

LA GRANDE

EASTERN OREGON STATE COLLEGE, Arts & Humanities Dept, Division of Humanities and Fine Arts, 1410 L Ave, 97850-2899. Tel 503-962-3672; FAX 503-962-3335. *Dean Art* G E Young; *Assoc Prof Art* Judd R Koehn, MFA; *Asst Prof Art* Thomas Dimond, MFA; *Asst Prof* Terry Gloeckler
Estab 1929; pub; D & E; SC 32, LC 8, GC 2
Ent Req: HS dipl
Degrees: BA & BS in Art, BA & BS in Secondary Educ with Endorsement in Art, BA & BS in Elementary Educ with Specialization in Art 4 yrs
Tuition: Res—$588 per term; campus res available
Courses: Aesthetics, Art Education, Art History, Calligraphy, Ceramics, Design, Drawing, Lettering, Painting, Photography, Drawing, Jewelry, Lettering, Painting, Photography, Glassblowing, Life Drawings
Adult Hobby Classes: Dir, Dr Werner Bruecher
Summer School: Dir, Dixie Lund. Enrl 400. Term of 4-8 wks. Courses—Two or three per summer, beginning level

MARYLHURST

MARYLHURST COLLEGE, Art Dept, 97036. Tel 503-636-8141. *Chairperson* Kay Slusarenko; *Asst Chairperson* Paul Sutinen; *Instr* Stephen Hayes; *Instr* Rodd Ambrson; *Instr* Kelcy Beardsley; *Instr* David Gobel; *Instr* Christopher Rauschenberg; *Instr* Dennis Cunningham; *Instr* Margaret Shirley; *Instr* Sr Patricia Stebinger; *Instr* Bonnie Bruce; *Instr* Fernanda D'Agostino; *Instr* Ken Butler; *Instr* Michael Bowley; *Instr* Karen O'Malley; *Instr* Barbara Eiswerth; *Instr* Rich Rollins; *Instr* Terri Hopkins; *Instr* Lisa Marecha; *Instr* Martha Pfanschmidt; *Instr* Denise Roy; *Instr* JoAnn Thomas
Scholarships; enrl 110
Ent Req: HS dipl or equivalent
Degrees: BA, BFA, MA (Art Therapy)
Tuition: $159 per cr
Courses: Art History, Design, Drawing, Interior Design, Mixed Media, Museum Staff Training, Painting, Photography, Printmaking, Sculpture, Art Therapy Program, History of Photography
Summer School: Chairperson, Kay Slusarenko. Tuition $159 per cr for 8 wk term. Courses—Drawing, Independent Studies, Interior Design, Painting, Photography, Printmaking

MCMINNVILLE

LINFIELD COLLEGE, Art Dept, 97128. Tel 503-472-4121, Ext 275. *Chmn Dept* Ron Mills
Estab 1849, dept estab 1964; pvt; D; scholarships; SC 16, LC 2; enrl non-maj 250, maj 35
Ent Req: HS dipl
Degrees: BA 4 yr, ME 2 yr
Tuition: $8600 per yr
Courses: Art Education, Art History, Ceramics, Drawing, Mixed Media, Painting, Photography, Printmaking, Sculpture, Teacher Training

MONMOUTH

WESTERN OREGON STATE COLLEGE, Creative Arts Division, Visual Arts, 97361. Tel 503-838-8000; FAX 503-838-8144. *Chmn Creative Arts* Richard Davis; *Assoc Prof* Kim Hoffman. Instrs: FT 8, PT 1
Estab 1856; pub; D & E; SC 72, LC 21, GC 27; enrl total 3600
Degrees: BA and BS 4 yr
Tuition: Res—undergrad $604 per term, grad $887 per term; nonres—undergrad $1662 per term, grad $1510 per term
Courses: Art Education, Art History, Ceramics, Drawing, Graphic Arts, Jewelry, Lettering, Mixed Media, Painting, Photography, Printmaking, Sculpture, Art Theory, Design, Individual Studies, The Art Idea: Visual Thinking, Watercolor
Summer School: Tuition res—undergrad $37 per cr hr, grad $64 per cr hr, plus a one time charge of $34 in incidental fees. Courses as above

ONTARIO

TREASURE VALLEY COMMUNITY COLLEGE, Art Dept, 650 College Blvd, 97914. Tel 503-889-6493, Ext 270. *Chmn* Robin Jackson; *Instr* Mike Lundstrom; *Instr* Carson Legree
Estab 1961; pub; D & E; scholarships; SC 14, LC 1; enrl D 50, E 35, non-maj 10, maj 15
Ent Req: Placement testing
Degrees: AS & AA 2 yrs
Tuition: Res—$312 per quarter; nonres—$380 per quarter; out-of-country—$900 per quarter; campus res available
Courses: Art History, Drawing, Painting, Sculpture
Summer School: Chmn, Robert M Jackson. Tuition $190 for term of 8 wks beginning June 22. Courses—Ceramics, Drawing, Painting

OREGON CITY

CLACKAMAS COMMUNITY COLLEGE, Art Dept, 19600 S Molalla, 97045. Tel 503-657-8400 Ext 386. *Chmn* Leland John
Tuition: Res—$20 per cr hr, nonres—$73 per cr hr
Courses: Advertising Design, Art History, Calligraphy, Ceramics, Design, Drawing, Jewelry, Painting, Sculpture

PENDLETON

BLUE MOUNTAIN COMMUNITY COLLEGE, Fine Arts Dept, 2411 NW Carden Ave, PO Box 100, 97801. Tel 503-276-1260. *Chmn* Michael Booth
Estab 1962, dept estab 1964; pub; D & E; SC 8, LC 2; enrl D 255, E 72
Degrees: AA, 2 yrs
Tuition: Res—undergrad $540 per yr; nonres—undergrad $792 per yr
Courses: Art History, Ceramics, Drawing, Jewelry, Lettering, Painting

PORTLAND

LEWIS & CLARK COLLEGE, Dept of Art, 0615 SW Palatine Hill Rd, 97219. Tel 503-768-7390. *Chmn Dept* Michael Taylor; *Prof* Ken Shores, MFA; *Assoc Prof* Phyllis A Yes; *Lectr* Bruce West
Dept estab 1946; pvt; D; scholarships; SC 10, LC 2
Ent Req: HS dipl
Degrees: BS and BA 4 yr
Tuition: Res—undergrad $12,588 per yr, grad $155 per quarter hr
Courses: Art History, Ceramics, Drawing, Graphic Arts, History of Art & Archaeology, Jewelry, Painting, Printmaking, Sculpture, Weaving
Summer School: Dir, Richard Steiner

OREGON SCHOOL OF ARTS AND CRAFTS, 8245 SW Barnes Rd, 97225. Tel 503-297-5544. *Pres* Paul Magnusson, PhD; *Dean Admissions* Jean Malarkey. Instrs: Ft 10, PT 13
Estab 1906; pvt; D & E; scholarships; SC & LC 60; enrl D 225, E 250
Ent Req: Portfolio review
Degrees: Certif in Art, 3 yr
Tuition: $6960 full-time certificate program; classes vary in laboratory fees; no campus res
Courses: Aesthetics, Art History, Calligraphy, †Ceramics, Design, †Drawing, Goldsmithing, Jewelry, Lettering, Mixed Media, Painting, Photography, Printmaking, Arts & Crafts History, †Book Arts, Criticism, †Fibers, Fine Cabinetry, Furniture Design, Furniture Making, †Metals, †Wood
Adult Hobby Classes: Enrl 1300; tuition $195 noncredit hr $245 per 1.5 cr hrs for 10 wk term. Courses—Aesthetics, Book Arts, Ceramics, Design, Drawing, Fibers, Metals, Photography, Writing, Wood
Summer School: Dir, Valorie Hadley. Enrl 215; tuition $225 for 1 wk workshop. Courses—same as above

PACIFIC NORTHWEST COLLEGE OF ART, 1219 SW Park Ave, 97205. Tel 503-226-4391, 226-0462. *Dir* Sally Lawrence; *Dir of Admissions* Colin Page; *Instr* Terry Toedetemeir; *Instr* Manuel Izquierdo; *Instr* Robert Hanson; *Instr* Betsy Lindsay; *Instr* Harry Widman; *Instr* Frank Irby; *Instr* Anne Johnson; *Instr* Jim Hicks; *Instr* Bill Moore; *Instr* Tom Fawkes; *Instr* Gordon Gilkey; *Instr* Paul Missal. Instrs: FT 19, PT 24
Estab 1909; pvt; D & E; scholarships; SC 24, LC 9; enrl D 192, PT 27, E 249
Ent Req: HS dipl, portfolio
Degrees: BFA 4 yr
Tuition: $6750 per yr, $3375 per sem; no campus res
Courses: †Ceramics, †Drawing, †Graphic Design, †Illustration, †Painting, †Photography, †Printmaking, †Sculpture, †Crafts
Adult Hobby Classes: Enrl 500, Tuition $195 per course. Courses—Calligraphy, Ceramics, Graphic Design, Illustration, Life Drawing, Painting, Photography, Printmaking, Sculpture & other art-related courses
Children's Classes: Enrl 250; tuition $115 per course. Courses—Ceramics, Drawing, Painting, Printmaking, Sculpture
Summer School: Dir, Greg Ware. Enrl 500; tuition $195 per course. Courses—Wide range of Visual Arts

PORTLAND COMMUNITY COLLEGE, Visual & Performing Arts Division, PO Box 19000, 97219-0990. Tel 503-244-6111, Ext 4263. *Dept Chmn* Owen Chamberlain, MFA
Estab 1961, dept estab 1963; pub; D & E; SC 40, LC 5; enrl D 864, E 282
Ent Req: None
Degrees: AA 2 yrs
Tuition: $28 per cr hr, 1 - 12 hrs; $364 per cr hr, 13 - 19 hrs
Courses: Art History, Calligraphy, Ceramics, Drawing, Graphic Design, Painting, Photography, Sculpture, Stage Design, Theatre Arts, Printing Tech
Adult Hobby Classes: Tuition varies per quarter. Courses—various
Children's Classes: Courses offered
Summer School: Dept Chmn, Owen Chamberlain. Enrl 400; Term of 8 wks beginning June. Courses—same as regular session

PORTLAND STATE UNIVERSITY, Dept of Art, PO Box 751, 97207. Tel 503-725-3515; FAX 503-725-4882. *Dept Head* Barbara Sesteak; *Prof* James Hibbard, MFA; *Prof* Mary Constans, MA; *Prof* Melvin Katz, Cert; *Prof* Michihiro Kosuge, MFA; *Prof* Leonard B Kimbrell, PhD; *Prof* Craig Cheshire, MFA; *Prof* Richard Muller, MFA; *Assoc Prof* Claire Kelly-Zimmers, MA; *Assoc Prof* Jane Kristof, PhD; *Assoc Prof* Lisa Audrus, PhD; *Assoc Prof* Barbara Sestac
Estab 1955; pub; D & E; scholarships; enrl E 2000, non-maj 1300, maj 600, grad 30, others 70
Ent Req: HS dipl
Degrees: BS and BA(Art) 4 yr, MFA(Painting, Ceramics, Sculpture) 2 yr
Tuition: Res—undergrad $639 per quarter; nonres—undergrad $1892 per quarter; campus res available
Courses: Architecture, Art History, †Ceramics, †Drawing, †Graphic Design, †Painting, Printmaking, †Sculpture, †Applied Design
Summer School: Enrl 4-500; term of 8-12 wks beginning June 28. Courses—vary. Two centers, one in Portland and one at Cannon Beach: The Haystack Program

REED COLLEGE, Dept of Art, 3203 S E Woodstock Blvd, 97202. Tel 503-771-1112; FAX 503-777-7269. Instrs: FT 5
Estab 1911; pvt; D; scholarships; SC 7, LC 5; enrl D 1150, E 15
Degrees: BA 3-5 yr
Tuition: $14,520 annual tuition; campus res—available
Courses: Aesthetics, Drawing, Painting, Printmaking, Sculpture, History of Art & Architecture, Humanities, Theory
Adult Hobby Classes: Courses offered & MA degree
Summer School: Courses offered

ROSEBURG

UMPQUA COMMUNITY COLLEGE, Fine & Performing Arts Dept, PO Box 967, 97470. Tel 503-440-4600, Ext 692. *Chmn Fine & Performing Arts* Marie Rasmussen; *Instr* Ted Isto; *Instr* Florence Jacoby; *Instr* Robert Bell; *Instr* Walt O'Brien
Estab 1964; pub; D & E; scholarships; SC 5, LC 2; enrl D 190, E 90, maj 18
Ent Req: HS dipl
Degrees: AA 2 yr
Tuition: Res—$300 per term (12 hrs); out of district $1500
Courses: Art History, Calligraphy, Ceramics, Drawing, Painting, Photography, Printmaking, Sculpture, Theatre Arts, Basic Design
Adult Hobby Classes: Enrl 195; tuition $35 & lab fee for 10 weeks. Courses—Calligraphy, Ceramics, Drawing, Painting, Photography, Printmaking, Sculpture

SALEM

CHEMEKETA COMMUNITY COLLEGE, Dept of Humanities & Communications, 4000 Lancaster Dr NE, 97309. Tel 503-399-5184; FAX 503-399-5038. *Dir* Bernie Knab; *Instr* Robert Bibler, MFA; *Instr* Lee Jacobson, MFA; *Instr* Donna Reid, PhD
Estab 1969, dept estab 1975; pub; D & E; scholarships; SC 9, LC 3; enrl D 125, E 75
Ent Req: None
Degrees: AA 2 yr
Tuition: Res—$23 per cr hr, $210 per quarter; nonres—$83 per cr hr
Courses: Art History, Calligraphy, Ceramics, Drawing, Film, Painting, Photography, Printmaking, Sculpture, Theatre Arts, Stained Glass
Adult Hobby Classes: Enrl 150-200; tuition $1.25 per contact hr
Summer School: Dir, Alan Koch. Term of 8 wks

SHERIDAN

DELPHIAN SCHOOL, 20950 SW Rock Creek Rd, 97378. Tel 503-843-3521; FAX 503-843-4158. *Headmaster* Greg Ott; *Dir Educ Consulting* Bruce Wiggins
Degrees: Cert
Courses: Art Education, Calligraphy, Drawing, Handicrafts, Painting, Sculpture

PENNSYLVANIA

ALLENTOWN

CEDAR CREST COLLEGE, Art Dept, 100 College Dr, 18104-6196. Tel 215-437-4471. *Chmn* Nelson R Maniscalco, MFA; *Prof* Ryland W Greene; *Asst Prof* Pat Badt; *Asst Prof* William Clark; *Instr* Andrew Hall. Instrs: FT 3, PT 2
Estab 1867; pvt; D & E; scholarships; SC 11, LC 4; enrl 750
Ent Req: HS dipl, CEEB
Degrees: BA, BS, Interdisciplinary Fine Arts Maj (art, theatre, music, dance,

creative writing), 4 yr
Tuition: Res—$14,000 per yr
Courses: Aesthetics, Art Education, Art History, Ceramics, Drawing, Jewelry, Painting, Sculpture, Theatre Arts, Comparative Study of Art, Metal Forming
Summer School: Courses—Ceramics, Jewelry-Metalsmithing

MUHLENBERG COLLEGE, Dept of Art, 2400 Chew St, 18104. Tel 215-821-3243. *Assoc Prof* Scott Sherk, MFA; *Assoc Prof* Jadviga Da Costa Nunes, PhD; *Asst Prof* Raymond S Barnes, MFA; *Asst Prof* Joseph Elliott, MFA
Estab 1848; den; D & E; SC 16, LC 12; enrl D 320, non-maj 284, maj 36
Ent Req: HS dipl, SAT, 3 achievement tests and English Composition Achievement required
Degrees: BA 4 yrs
Tuition: Res—$13,900 per yr; campus res—room & board 7 days $1910, 5 days $1820
Courses: Art Education, †Art History, Ceramics, Drawing, Graphic Arts, History of Art & Archaeology, Painting, Photography, Printmaking, Sculpture, †Studio Arts
Adult Hobby Classes: Courses—Art History, Drawing, Painting, Photography, Photo-Journalism
Summer School: Courses—same as adult education courses

BETHLEHEM

LEHIGH UNIVERSITY, Dept of Art and Architecture, Chandler-Ullmann Hall, Bldg 17, 18015. Tel 215-758-3610. *Chmn* Ivan Zacnic; *Prof* Ricardo Viera, MFA; *Prof* Thomas Peters, PhD; *Prof* Lucy Gans, MFA; *Adjunct Prof* Anne Priester, PhD; *Assoc Prof* Richard Redd, MFA; *Assoc Prof* Berresford Boothe, MFA; *Asst Prof* Bruce Thomas, PhD. Instrs: FT 10, PT 4
Estab 1925; pvt; D & E; SC 22, LC 16; enrl D & E 100
Ent Req: HS dipl, SAT, CEEB
Degrees: BA 4 yrs
Tuition: $8350 per sem; campus res available
Courses: †Architecture, Art History, Drawing, Graphic Design, Painting, Photography, Printmaking, Sculpture, Computer Aided Design
Summer School: Dir, James Brown. Courses—Architectural Design, Art History, Graphic Design Workshop, Coloı

MORAVIAN COLLEGE, Dept of Art, Church Street Campus, 18018. Tel 215-861-1480. *Chmn Dept* Rudy S Ackerman, DEd; *Asst Prof* Les Reker, MFA; *Photographer in Residence* Jeffrey Huvwitz; *Instr* James Franki, MFA; *Ceramist-in-Residence* Renzo Faggioli, Master Craftsman
Estab 1807, dept estab 1963; pvt; D & E; scholarships; SC 15, LC 8; enrl D 350, E 15, non-maj 1200, maj 100
Ent Req: HS dipl
Degrees: BA and BS 4 yrs
Tuition: $7575 per yr
Courses: †Art History, †Ceramics, Design, †Drawing, Film, Jewelry, †Painting, †Photography, Printmaking, Sculpture, Silversmithing, †Graphic Advertising
Adult Hobby Classes: Enrl 240; tuition $410 for two 15 wk terms.
Courses—Ceramics, Drawing, Graphic Design, History of Art, Painting, Photography
Summer School: Dir, Dr Susan Schuehler. Enrl 110; tuition $410 per course beginning June. Courses—Same as adult

NORTHAMPTON COMMUNITY COLLEGE, Art Dept, 3835 Green Pond Rd, 18017. Tel 215-861-5300, Ext 5485; FAX 215-861-5373. *Prog Coordr* Gerald Rowan; *Asst Prof* Andrew Szoke
Estab 1967; pub; D & E; scholarships; SC 12, LC 8; enrl D 100, E 350
Ent Req: HS dipl, portfolio
Degrees: AAS(Advertising), cert in photography
Tuition: Res—$52 per cr hr; nonres—$107 per cr hr
Courses: Advertising Design, Architecture, Art History, Ceramics, Drafting, Drawing, Fashion Arts, Graphic Arts, Graphic Design, Handicrafts, History of Art & Archaeology, Illustration, Interior Design, Lettering, Painting, Photography, Printmaking, Sculpture, Color & Spacial Concepts, Computer Graphics, Pottery, 3-D Materials
Adult Hobby Classes: Courses—Art, Photography

BLOOMSBURG

BLOOMSBURG UNIVERSITY, Dept of Art, Bakeless Center for the Humanities, Old Science Hall, 17815. Tel 717-389-4646. *Chmn* Kenneth Wilson; *Assoc Prof* Barbara J Strohman, MFA; *Prof* Stewart Nagel, MFA; *Prof* Robert Koslosky, PhD; *Assoc Prof* Karl Beamer, MFA; *Asst Prof* Carol Burns; *Asst Prof* Gary F Clark, MA; *Asst Prof* Vera Ziditz-Ward; *Asst Prof* Charles Thomas Walter, PhD; *Asst Prof* Christine Sperling, PhD
Estab 1839, dept estab 1940; pub; D & E; scholarships; SC 7, LC 12; enrl D 1800, E 200, maj 75
Ent Req: HS dipl
Degrees: BA(Art Studio) and BA(Art History) 4 yrs, MA(Art Studio), MA(Art Hist)
Tuition: Res—tuition & campus res—room & board $5978; nonres—tuition & campus res—room & board $7868
Courses: Aesthetics, Ceramics, Drawing, History of Art & Archaeology, Painting, Photography, Printmaking, Sculpture, Textile Design, Computer Graphics, Crafts, General Design, Weaving
Adult Hobby Classes: Creative arts & crafts mini-courses offered
Children's Classes: Enrl 20; tuition $30 per 8 sessions
Summer School: Dean, Michael Vavrek. Enrl 200 - 300; tuition $95 per cr hr. Courses—vary

BLUE BELL

MONTGOMERY COUNTY COMMUNITY COLLEGE, Art Dept, 340 De Kalb Pike, 19422. Tel 215-641-6328. *Chmn* Frank Short; *Assoc Prof* Roger Cairns, MFA; *Assoc Prof* Michael Smyser. Instrs: FT 6, PT 8
Pub; D & E; scholarships; LC 3; enrl D 250
Ent Req: HS dipl
Degrees: AA Fine Arts, AAS Commercial Art
Tuition: County res—undergrad $494 per sem, $41 per credit hr; nonres—undergrad $988 per sem, $82 per credit hr
Courses: Advertising Design, Art Education, Art History, Ceramics, †Commercial Art, Drawing, Film, Graphic Design, Illustration, Painting, Photography, Printmaking, Sculpture, Teacher Training, Theatre Arts, Video, †Fine Art, Typography
Summer School: Dir, Michael Smyser. Enrl 66; tuition $35 per cr.
Courses—Ceramics, Drawing, Painting, Photography

BRYN MAWR

BRYN MAWR COLLEGE, Dept of the History of Art, 19010. Tel 215-526-5000; FAX 215-525-4739. *Chmn Dept* Dale Kinney; *Prof* Steven Levine; *Prof* Phyllis B Bober, PhD; *Prof* Gridley McKim-Smith, PhD; *Asst Prof* Christiane Hertel. Instrs: FT 5, PT 1
Estab 1913; pvt, W (men in grad school); scholarships and fel; LC 10, GC 8; enrl maj 15, grad 30, others 250
Degrees: BA 4 yr, MA, PhD
Tuition: $9700 per yr; campus res available
Courses: Art History

HARCUM JUNIOR COLLEGE, Dept of Fine Arts, 19010. Tel 215-525-4100, Ext 215. *Instr* Lane Heise; *Prof* Katherine Little. Instrs: FT 1, PT 5
Estab 1915; pvt; W; D & E; scholarships; SC 7, LC 1; enrl D 40, E 8, maj 10
Ent Req: HS dipl
Degrees: AA 2 yr
Tuition: $4708 per yr
Courses: Commercial Art, Drawing, Fashion Arts, Graphic Design, History of Art & Archaeology, Lettering, Painting, Sculpture

CALIFORNIA

CALIFORNIA UNIVERSITY OF PENNSYLVANIA, Dept of Art, 15419. Tel 412-938-4000, 938-4182. *Dept Chmn* Richard Grinstead
Estab 1852, dept estab 1968; pub; D & E; SC 20, LC 5; enrl maj 137
Ent Req: SAT
Degrees: Cert(Art Educ), BA 4 yrs
Courses: Advertising Design, Architecture, Art History, Calligraphy, Ceramics, Drafting, Drawing, Graphic Arts, Graphic Design, Industrial Design, Intermedia, Jewelry, Painting, Photography, Printmaking, Sculpture, Teacher Training, Stained Glass
Adult Hobby Classes: Enrl 25 per class. Courses—Pottery, Stained Glass
Summer School: Chmn, Richard Grinstead. Term of 5 or 10 wks beginning June

CARLISLE

DICKINSON COLLEGE, Fine Arts Dept, Weiss Center for the Arts, 17013. Tel 717-245-1344; FAX 717-245-1899. *Prof* Sharon Hirsh, PhD; *Assoc Prof* Barbara Diduk, MFA; *Asst Prof* Ward Davenny, MFA; *Asst Prof* Melinda Schlitt, PhD; *Asst Prof* Peter Lukehart, PhD; *Instr* Robin Reisenfeld, MA
Estab 1773, dept estab 1940; pvt; D; SC 7, LC 11; enrl 550, non-maj 500, maj 50
Ent Req: HS dipl, SAT
Degrees: BA and BS 4 yrs
Tuition: Res—undergrad $16,645 per yr, campus res available
Courses: Architecture, Art Appreciation, †Art History, Ceramics, Design, Drawing, History of Art & Archaeology, Mixed Media, Museum Staff Training, Painting, Photography, Printmaking, Sculpture, †Studio Major
Summer School: Dir, Stephen MacDonald. Tuition $835 per course for term of 6 wks beginning May. Courses—per regular session

CHELTENHAM

CHELTENHAM CENTER FOR THE ARTS, 439 Ashbourne Rd, 19012. Tel 215-379-4660. *Acting Exec Dir* Mary Cope
Estab 1940; enrl 3600
Courses: Drawing, Jewelry, Mixed Media, Painting, Photography, Sculpture, Pottery, Stained Glass, Theater Classes

CHEYNEY

CHEYNEY UNIVERSITY OF PENNSYLVANIA, Dept of Art, 19319. Tel 215-399-2286. *Chmn* Dr William Cunninghan
Estab 1937; pub; D & E; scholarships; SC 16, LC 4
Ent Req: HS dipl, ent exam
Degrees: BA 4 yrs
Tuition: Res—$3289 per sem; nonres—$4936 per sem
Courses: Drawing, Handicrafts, Painting, Sculpture

CLARION

CLARION UNIVERSITY OF PENNSYLVANIA, Dept of Art, 16214. Tel 814-226-2291. *Chmn* April Katz; *Prof* Cathie Joselyn, MFA; *Asst Prof* Charles H Dugan, MFA; *Asst Prof* Emily Williams; *Asst Prof* James Flahaven; *Asst Prof* Gary Greenberg; *Asst Prof* Christopher Lambl; *Instr* Sherry L Best; *Instr* Joeliene Schaffer
Estab 1867; pub; D & E; scholarships; SC 13, LC 7; enrl D & E 925 per sem, maj 25
Ent Req: HS dipl
Degrees: BFA(Art)
Tuition: Res—undergrad $915 per sem, $76 per cr; nonres—undergrad $1633 per sem, $136 per cr
Courses: Art Appreciation, Art Education, Art History, †Ceramics, Design, Drawing, Graphic Arts, Graphic Design, Handicrafts, History of Art & Archaeology, Jewelry, †Painting, Photography, †Sculpture, Textile Design, Weaving, †Fabric, Fiber, 3-D Design, Commercial Design
Adult Hobby Classes: Enrl 20; tuition $55-$65 for 9-12 wk course.
Courses—Calligraphy, Ceramics, Drawing, Painting
Summer School: Dir, Dr Randall Potter. Tuition $76 per cr hr for 2-5 wk sessions.
Courses—various

EASTON

LAFAYETTE COLLEGE, Dept of Art, Williams Center for the Arts, 18042-1768. Tel 215-250-5356, 5357, 5358, 5359 & 5360. *Dept Head* Robert S Mattison. Instrs: FT 4, PT 4
Estab 1827; pvt; D & E; SC 8, LC 12; enrl D 300, E 250, non-maj 1, maj 17
Ent Req: HS dipl, ent exam, selective admis
Degrees: BS and AB 4 yr
Tuition: $9950 per yr
Courses: Art History, Drawing, Painting, Printmaking, Sculpture, History of Architecture, Two & Three-Dimensional Design
Summer School: Courses—Graphic Design, Photography

EAST STROUDSBURG

EAST STROUDSBURG UNIVERSITY, Art Dept, Fine Arts Bldg, 18301. Tel 717-424-3759. *Chmn* Dr Daniel Luongo; *Acting Chair* Dr Larry Fisher; *Asst Prof* Dr Herb Weigand
Estab 1894; pub; D & E; scholarships offered; SC 17, LC 6, grad 1; enrl D 45
Ent Req: HS dipl, HS equivalency
Degrees: BA in Fine Arts
Tuition: Res—$1089 per sem; nonres—$2017 per sem; campus res available
Courses: Aesthetics, Art Education, Art History, Calligraphy, Ceramics, Design, Drawing, Handicrafts, Lettering, Painting, Printmaking, Sculpture, American Art Communication Graphics, Graphics
Summer School: Dir, Quintin Currie. Tuition res—undergrad $68 per cr hr, grad $89 per cr hr; nonres—undergrad $102 per cr hr, grad $89 per cr hr for 3 wk pre & post session & 6 wk main session

EDINBORO

EDINBORO UNIVERSITY OF PENNSYLVANIA, Art Dept, Doucette Hall, 16444. Tel 814-732-2406. *Chmn Art Dept* Dr George Shoemaker; *Chmn Crafts* Bernard Maas; *Art Education* Connie Mullineaux; *Fine Arts Representative* Ben Gibson; *Gallery Dir* William Cox. Instrs: FT 31, PT 3
Estab 1857; pub; D & E; scholarships; SC 86, LC 30, GC 20; enrl D 400 art maj, non-maj 6000, grad 30
Ent Req: HS dipl, SAT
Degrees: BSEd, BFA and BA 4 yrs, MA 1 yr, MFA 2 yrs
Tuition: Res—$5512; nonres—$7546
Courses: Advertising Design, †Art Education, †Art History, †Ceramics, Commercial Art, Film, Goldsmithing, Handicrafts, History of Art & Archaeology, †Jewelry, Mixed Media, †Painting, †Photography, †Printmaking, †Sculpture, †Silversmithing, †Teacher Training, †Textile Design, Video, Weaving, †Communications Graphics, †Weaving
Adult Hobby Classes: Enrl 200; tuition $89 per cr, $2130 per yr
Summer School: Dir, Dr George Shoemaker. Enrl 200, tuition $89 per cr for two 5 wk sessions

ERIE

MERCYHURST COLLEGE, Dept of Art, Glenwood Hills, 16546. Tel 814-824-2000; FAX 814-825-0438. *Dept Chmn* Thomas Hubert. Instrs: FT 4, PT 4
Estab 1926, dept estab 1950; pvt; D & E; scholarships; SC 45, LC 12; enrl D 50, E 30, maj 50
Ent Req: HS dipl, col boards, portfolio review
Degrees: BA 4 yr
Courses: Advertising Design, Aesthetics, Art Education, Art History, Ceramics, Drawing, Graphic Design, Jewelry, Painting, Photography, Printmaking, Sculpture, Airbrush Design, Art Foundations, Art Therapy, Child Art, Contemporary Art Theories, Creative Arts for Adolescents & Childrren, Fabrics, Fibers, Internship, Independent Study, Individualized Studio, Senior Seminar, Teaching Internship
Adult Hobby Classes: 6-8 wks. Courses—Crafts, Drawing, Painting
Summer School: Dir, Thomas Hubert. Term of 5 - 6 wks beginning June/July.
Courses—vary

FACTORYVILLE

KEYSTONE JUNIOR COLLEGE, Fine Arts Dept, College Avenue (Mailing add: PO Box 50, LaPlume, PA 18440-0200). Tel 717-945-5141. *Chmn Fine Arts* Karl O Neuroth, MEd; *Prof* William Tersteeg; *Assoc Prof* Clifton A Prokop, MFA; *Instr* Rochelle Campbell; *Instr* Mark Webber, MFA
Estab 1868, dept estab 1965; pvt; D & weekends; scholarships; SC 15, LC 2; enrl D 155, weekenders 15, non-maj 100, maj 55
Ent Req: HS dipl, SAT
Degrees: AFA 2 yrs
Tuition: Res—$6200 per yr; campus res—room & board $4080
Courses: Art History, Ceramics, Drawing, Painting, Photography, Printmaking, Sculpture, Color, Intro to Commercial Design, Life Drawing, Three-Dimensional Design, Two-Dimensional Design
Adult Hobby Classes: Enrl 15; Weekend Program, trimester. Course—Art History
Summer School: Dir, Joanna Naylor. Enrl limited to 18; tuition $110 per cr for term of 5 wks beginning June. Courses—Ceramics, Photography

GETTYSBURG

GETTYSBURG COLLEGE, Dept of Art, PO Box 2452, 17325. Tel 717-337-6000. *Chmn* Dr Amelia Trevelyan; *Prof* Norman Annis; *Prof* Alan Paulson; *Assoc Prof* James Agard; *Instr* Carol Small; *Instr* Jim Ramos; *Instr* Brent Blair; *Instr* Lynn Hanley; *Instr* John Winship; *Instr* Leslie Przybylek
Estab 1832, dept estab 1956; pvt; D; scholarships; SC 10, LC 15; enrl D 300
Ent Req: HS dipl, ent exam
Degrees: BA 4 yrs
Tuition: $21,000 annual tuition; campus res available
Courses: Architecture, Art Appreciation, Art History, Ceramics, Design, Drawing, Film, Graphic Design, History of Art & Archaeology, Painting, Photography, Printmaking, Sculpture, America Indian Art, Art of Cinema, 2-D & 3-D Design

GLENSIDE

BEAVER COLLEGE, Dept of Fine Arts, Easton & Church Rds, 19038. Tel 215-572-2900. *Chmn* Dennis Kuronen, MFA; *Asst Prof* Bonnie Hayes, MA, ABD; *Assoc Prof* Robert Mauro, MFA; *Asst Prof* Rebecca Michaels, MFA. Instrs: PT 7
Estab 1853; pvt; D & E; scholarships; SC 43, LC 14; enrl in Col D FT 625, PT 115, non-maj in dept 30, maj in dept 140
Ent Req: HS dipl, SAT, ACT, optional portfolio review
Degrees: BA and BFA 4 yrs, MA(Educ) 1 yr
Tuition: $7000 per year, $3500 per sem, $760 per 4 cr course; campus res—room & board $3200
Courses: Advertising Design, Aesthetics, †Art Education, †Art History, †Ceramics, †Commercial Art, Drawing, †Graphic Design, †Illustration, †Interior Design, †Jewelry, †Painting, †Photography, †Printmaking, Teacher Training, †Art Therapy
Summer School: Chmn, Dennis Kuronen. Enrl approx 200; tuition $120 per cr hr for term of 7 wks beginning June 8. Courses—Painting, Printmaking

GREENSBURG

SETON HILL COLLEGE, Dept of Art, 15601. Tel 412-834-2200, Ext 399. *Chairperson* Maureen Vissat, MA; *Prof* Josefa Filkosky, MFA; *Prof* Stuart Thompson, PhD; *Assoc Prof* Suzanne Harding, PhD; *Assoc Prof* Raymond DeFazio; *Dir Gallery & Instr* Carol Brode
Estab 1918, dept estab 1950; den; D & E; scholarships; SC 40, LC 8; enrl D 300, maj 100, minor 15, pt 10
Ent Req: HS dipl, review portfolio
Degrees: BA, BFA 4 yr
Tuition: $8100 per yr; campus res—room and board $3400 per yr
Courses: †Art Education, Art History, Calligraphy, †Ceramics, †Drawing, †Graphic Design, †Painting, †Photography, †Printmaking, †Sculpture, Fabrics, 3-D Design, Metalsmithing
Adult Hobby Classes: Enrl 25; tuition $208 per cr for 14 wk sem. Courses— Art History, Photography, Design
Summer School: Dean Martha Raak. Enrl 20; tuition $208 per cr. Courses—Art in Elementary Educ, Photography, Design

GREENVILLE

THIEL COLLEGE, Dept of Art, 75 College Ave, 16125. Tel 412-589-2094. *Chmn Dept* Ronald A Pivovar, MFA
Estab 1866, dept estab 1965; pvt; D & E; scholarships; SC 14, LC 11; enrl D 105, non-maj 65, maj 40
Ent Req: HS dipl, interviews
Degrees: BA 4 yrs
Courses: Art History, Ceramics, Drawing, Graphic Arts, Jewelry, Painting, Printmaking, Sculpture, Stage Design, Theatre Arts
Adult Hobby Classes: Classes offered
Summer School: Asst Acad Dean, Richard Houpt. Term of 4 wks beginning June 3. Courses—Art History, Extended Studies, Drawing

HARRISBURG

HARRISBURG AREA COMMUNITY COLLEGE, Division of Communication and the Arts, 3300 Cameron Street Rd, 17110. Tel 717-780-2420. *Chmn* Michael Dockery, PhD; *Instr* Ronald Talbott, MFA; *Art Coordr* Robert Troxell
Estab 1964; pub; D & E; SC 15, LC 5; enrl D 500, E 100, maj 100
Ent Req: HS dipl
Degrees: AA 2 yrs
Tuition: Res—undergrad $890 per yr, $445 per sem, $35 per cr hr; out of district—undergrad $1780 per yr, $890 per sem, $70 per cr hr; out-of-state $2670 per yr, $1335 per sem, $105 per cr hr; no campus res
Courses: Art History, Ceramics, Commercial Art, Drafting, Drawing, Film, Graphic Arts, Handicrafts, Jewelry, Painting, Photography, Printmaking, Sculpture, Stage Design, Theatre Arts
Adult Hobby Classes: Courses—Calligraphy, Drawing, Painting, Photography, Pottery
Children's Classes: Courses—Creative Dramatics, Calligraphy
Summer School: Dir, Michael Dockery. Courses vary

HAVERFORD

HAVERFORD COLLEGE, Fine Arts Dept, 19041. Tel 215-896-1266. *Chmn & Prof* Charles Stegeman; *Prof* R Christopher Cairns; *Prof* William E Williams, MFA
Estab 1833, dept estab 1969; pvt; D, M; scholarships; enrl maj 12
Ent Req: HS dipl, programs in cooperation with Bryn Mawr College, Fine Arts Program
Degrees: BA 4 yrs
Tuition: $16,960 annual yr; campus res—$5700 room & board
Courses: Drawing, Graphic Arts, History of Art & Archaeology, Painting, Photography, Sculpture

MAIN LINE CENTER FOR THE ARTS, Old Buck Rd & Lancaster Ave, 19041. Tel 215-525-0272. *Admin Exec Dir* Judy S Herman; *Instr* Jeanne Adams, BS; *Instr* Marc Castelli, BFA; *Instr* John Devlieger; *Instr* Catherine Allen, BFA; *Instr* Carol Cole, BA; *Instr* Meg Fish, BFA; *Instr* Robert Finch, BFA; *Instr* Penelope Fleming, MFA; *Instr* Ginny Kendall; *Instr* Deborah Deichler, BFA; *Instr* Carol Kardon; *Instr* Sandra Elicker, BA; *Instr* Francine Shore, BFA; *Instr* Carson Fox; *Instr* Sallee Rush, BFA; *Instr* Chris Fox, MA; *Instr* Elissa Glassgald, MFA; *Instr* Janet Grau, BFA; *Instr* Reda Scher; *Instr* Amy Sarner, BA; *Instr* Martha Martin, BFA; *Instr* Linda Carroll, BFA; *Instr* Debbie Kaplan; *Instr* Diane Lachman, MFA; *Instr* Karen Kolkka; *Instr* Lydia Lehr, MFA; *Instr* Diane Lachman, BFA; *Instr* Lydia Lehr, MFA; *Instr* Kathy Logue, BFA; *Instr* Martha Kent Martin; *Instr* Bill Scott; *Instr* Emily Paulmier, BFA; *Instr* Ann Simon; *Instr* Kathie Regan, BA; *Instr* Shelly Rosen, BFA; *Instr* Aurelia Viguers, BFA; *Instr* Amy Sarner; *Instr* Nury Vicens Weinmann, MFA; *Instr* Susanna T Saunders, BA; *Instr* Kathryn Meyers, BA; *Instr* Mark McCullen, MFA
Estab 1937; pvt; D & E; SC 45; enrl D 300, E 250
Ent Req: Must be member of the Arts Center
Courses: Calligraphy, Ceramics, Collages, Conceptual Art, Drawing, Jewelry, Mixed Media, Printmaking, Sculpture, Silversmithing, Sculpture, Batik, Tie-dyeing
Children's Classes: Enrl 1500, Courses—General Arts, Pottery
Summer School: Admin Dir, Judy S Herman. Tuition varies, classes begin mid-June. Courses—same as above

HUNTINGDON

JUNIATA COLLEGE, Dept of Art, Moore St, 16652. Tel 814-643-4310. *Chmn Dept* Karen Rosell. Instrs: FT 2, PT 1
Estab 1876; pvt; D; scholarships; SC 12, LC 3; enrl 1100, maj 40
Ent Req: HS dipl
Degrees: BA 4 yrs
Tuition: Campus res
Courses: Aesthetics, Ceramics, Drawing, Graphic Arts, History of Art & Archaeology, Painting, Photography, Theatre Arts
Summer School: Dir, Jill Pfrogner, Courses —Art History, Ceramics, Studio Art

INDIANA

INDIANA UNIVERSITY OF PENNSYLVANIA, Dept of Art and Art Education, 114 Sprowls Hall, 15705. Tel 412-357-2530. *Chairperson* Dr A G DeFurio; *Instr* Paul Ben'zvi; *Instr* Sandra Burwell; *Instr* Ronald Ali; *Instr* Charles Battaglini; *Instr* Vaughn Clay; *Instr* George Johnson; *Instr* P Parker Doerner; *Instr* Donn Hedman; *Instr* Robin Clark; *Instr* Thomas Lacey; *Instr* Chris Weiland; *Instr* Robert Hamilton; *Instr* Robert Slenker; *Instr* Jean Slenker; *Instr* James Nestor; *Instr* Nevin Mercede
Estab 1875, dept estab 1875; pub; D & E; scholarships & assistantships; SC 26, LC 21, GC 30; enrl D 250, non-maj 1700, maj 270, grad 30
Ent Req: HS dipl, SAT, portfolio review
Degrees: BS(Art Educ), BA(Humanities with Art Concentration), BFA(Studio Art Concentration) 4 yr, MA 2 yr & MFA
Tuition: Res undergrad $2478 per yr, grad $2478 per yr; nonres—undergrad $4512 per yr, grad $4512 per yr; campus res—room & board $1340 per yr
Courses: Art Appreciation, Art Education, Art History, Ceramics, Design, Drawing, Goldsmithing, Graphic Design, Jewelry, Painting, Printmaking, Sculpture, Silversmithing, Weaving, Art studio, Fiber Arts, Papermaking, Woodworking
Adult Hobby Classes: 60; Courses—Ceramics, Drawing
Summer School: Dir, Anthony G DeFurio. Enrl 140; tuition regular acad sem cr cost. Courses—Studios, Art History, Art Appreciation, Special Workshops

JOHNSTOWN

UNIVERSITY OF PITTSBURGH AT JOHNSTOWN, Dept of Fine Arts, 15904. Tel 814-266-9661; FAX 814-269-2096. *Chmn* Carroll Grimes
Estab 1968; pub, pvt; D & E; SC 4, LC 10; enrl D 120, maj 3
Ent Req: HS dipl, SAT
Degrees: BA 4 yrs
Tuition: Campus res available
Courses: Aesthetics, Art Education, Art History, †Commercial Art, Drawing, Film, History of Art & Archaeology, Painting, Photography, Stage Design, Theatre Arts
Summer School: Enrl 30. Courses—Contemporary Art

KUTZTOWN

KUTZTOWN UNIVERSITY, College of Visual & Performing Arts, 19530. Tel 215-683-4500; FAX 215-683-4547. *Dean* Arthur W Bloom, PhD
Institution estab 1860, art dept estab 1929; pub; D & E; scholarships; SC 284, LC 40, GC 8; enrl D 943, maj 10
Ent Req: HS dipl
Degrees: BFA, 4 yr, BS (Art Educ 4 yr), MA (Educ)
Tuition: Res—undergrad & grad $1830; nonres—undergrad $3266, grad $2040; campus res—$2447 per yr
Courses: †Advertising Design, Aesthetics, Art Appreciation, †Art Education, †Art History, †Ceramics, †Commercial Art, Design, Drafting, †Drawing, Graphic Arts, †Graphic Design, History of Art & Archaeology, Illustration, †Jewelry, Mixed

Media, †Painting, Photography, †Printmaking, Sculpture, Silversmithing, Textile Design, Weaving
Adult Hobby Classes: Courses—Stage Costume Design
Children's Classes: Courses—Young at Art
Summer School: Regular sessions 5 wks. Courses—Art Ed, Studio

LANCASTER

FRANKLIN AND MARSHALL COLLEGE, Art Dept, PO Box 3003, 17604. Tel 717-291-4199. *Chmn Dept* Linda Cunningham, MFA; *Asst Prof* James Peterson, MFA; *Asst Prof* Linda Aleci; *Instr* Carol Hickey
Estab 1966; pvt; D & E; scholarships; SC 10, LC 17; enrl in col D 1900, E 580
Ent Req: HS dipl, SAT
Degrees: BA 4 yr
Tuition: Res—$9150 per yr
Courses: Architecture, Art History, Drawing, History of Art & Archaeology, Painting, Printmaking, Sculpture, Basic Design
Summer School: Dir, Russ Burke. Tuition $580 for course, two 5 wk sessions beginning June 7. Courses—Drawing, Painting, Photography

LEWISBURG

BUCKNELL UNIVERSITY, Dept of Art, 17837. Tel 717-524-1307. *Head Dept* Gerald Eager, PhD; *Prof* Neil Anderson, MFA; *Prof* James Turnure, PhD; *Prof* Rosalyn Richards, MFA; *Prof* William Lasansky, MFA; *Prof* Jody Blake, PhD; *Prof* Laura Spitzer, PhD
Estab 1846; pvt; D; scholarships; SC 19, LC 20, GC 30; enrl D 500, non-maj 450, maj 50, grad 2
Ent Req: HS dipl
Degrees: BA 4 yrs
Tuition: $16,560 per yr; campus res—room $2170, board $1940
Courses: Art History, Drawing, Graphic Arts, History of Art & Archaeology, Painting, Printmaking, Sculpture
Summer School: Dir, Lois Huffines. Enrl 426; term of 3 or 6 wks beginning June 14. Courses—Lectures, Studio

LOCK HAVEN

LOCK HAVEN UNIVERSITY, Art Dept, 17745. Tel 717-893-2130; FAX 717-893-2432. *Chmn* E May Dyer. Instrs: FT 4
Scholarships offered
Degrees: BA
Tuition: Res—$2278 2 sem; nonres—$4312 2 sem
Courses: Art Appreciation, Art Education, Art History, Ceramics, Drawing, Jewelry, Painting, Photography, Printmaking, Sculpture, Stage Design, Textile Design, Weaving, Arts & Crafts, 2-D Design, 3-D design
Summer School: Courses offered

LORETTO

ST FRANCIS COLLEGE, Fine Arts Dept, 15940. Tel 814-472-3216; FAX 814-472-3044. *Chmn* Charles Olsen, MFA
Scholarships offered
Tuition: $8192 per yr; campus res—room & board $4120
Courses: Art Appreciation, Art History, Design, Drawing, Museum Staff Training, Painting, Photography, Weaving, Culture & Values, Exploration of Arts, Independent Study, Modern Art

MANSFIELD

MANSFIELD UNIVERSITY, Art Dept, Allen Hall, 16933. Tel 717-662-4500; FAX 717-662-4114. *Chmn Dept* James G Cecere, DEd; *Assoc Prof* Dr Harold Carter; *Assoc Prof* Dale Witherow, MFA; *Assoc Prof* Tom Loomis, MA; *Assoc Prof* Sam Thomas, MEd; *Asst Prof* Stan Zujkowski, MS; *Instr* Dr Bonnie Kutbay
Estab 1857; pub; D; scholarships; SC 26, LC 18; enrl D 700, maj 90
Ent Req: HS dipl, SAT, portfolio and interview
Degrees: BA(Studio Art), BA(Art History) and BSE(Art Educ) 4 yr, MEd(Art Educ)
Tuition: Res—$800 per sem, $1600 per yr; nonres—$2868 per yr, $1434 per sem; campus residency available
Courses: Architecture, †Art Education, †Art History, Ceramics, Display, Drawing, History of Art & Archaeology, Illustration, Mixed Media, Painting, Printmaking, Sculpture, Color & Design, Computer Art, Fibers, Studio Crafts, Visual Studies in Aesthetic Experiences
Adult Hobby Classes: Enrl 10. Courses—Art History, Studio Art, Graduate Level Art Education
Children's Classes: Instr, Dr Harold Carter. Enrl 100, tuition $10 for 10 wks, fall sem. Courses—Elementary Art Education
Summer School: Term of 5-6 wks beginning May 27. Courses—Ceramics, Drawing, Fibers, Graduate Courses, Painting, Printmaking, Sculpture, Studio Courses

MEADVILLE

ALLEGHENY COLLEGE, Art Dept, 16335. Tel 814-332-3100. *Head Dept* Richard Kleeman, MFA
Estab 1815, dept estab 1930; pvt; D; scholarships; SC 17, LC 7; enrl 550, maj 30
Ent Req: HS dipl, ent exam
Degrees: BA and BS 4 yr
Tuition: Tuition $13,760; tuition, room & board $17,890
Courses: Art History, Ceramics, Drawing, Graphic Arts, Lettering, Painting, Photography, Printmaking, Sculpture
Summer School: Dir, R Kleeman. Enrl 40. Courses—Art History, Studio Art

MEDIA

DELAWARE COUNTY COMMUNITY COLLEGE, Communications and Humanities House, Route 252 & Media Line Rd, 19063. Tel 215-359-5000 Ext 5391. *Asst Dean* Clifford Brock; *Prof* John Botkin, MFA; *Prof* Al DeProspero, EdM; *Instr* Judith Wisniewfki, BFA; *Instr* Lisa Woollman; *Instr* Gail Fox
Estab 1967; pub; D & E
Degrees: AS, AA and AAS 2 yrs
Tuition: Distric res—$348 per sem, $46 per hr; non-district res—$696 per sem, $96 per hr; non-state res—$1044 per sem; no campus res
Courses: Art Education, Art History, Drawing, Graphic Design, Illustration, Painting, Photography, Printmaking, Theatre Arts, Advertising, Cmputer Graphics, Desk Top Publishing, 2-D & 3- D Design, Production Techniques, Typography
Adult Hobby Classes: Enrl varies; tuition varies. Courses—Calligraphy, Crafts, Drawing, Graphic Design, Interior Design, Needlepoint, Photography, Stained Glass, Sketching, Woodcarving
Summer School: Tuition res $27 per cr hr, nonres $81 per cr hr for term of 6 wks. Courses—Drawing, Painting

MIDDLETOWN

PENN STATE HARRISBURG, Humanities Division, 777 W Harrisburg Pike, 17057. Tel 717-948-6189; FAX 717-948-6008. *Prof* Irwin Richman, PhD; *Asst Prof* Troy Thomas, MFA & PhD; *Head Humanities* William J Mahar. Instrs: PT 10
Estab 1965; pub; D & E; scholarships; SC 7, LC 15; enrl D & E 60, grad 40
Ent Req: 2 yrs of col or CLEP
Degrees: BHumanities 2 yrs, MA
Tuition: Res—undergrad 12 or more crs per sem $2166, undergrad 11 or fewer crs $179 per cr, grad 12 or more crs per sem $2423, grad ll or fewer crs $203 per cr; nonres—undergrad 12 or more crs per sem $4559, undergrad 11 or fewer crs $381 per cr, grad 12 or more crs per sem $4846, grad 11 or fewer crs $403 per cr
Courses: Aesthetics, Architecture, Art Education, Art History, Drawing, Graphic Design, History of Art & Archaeology, Mixed Media, Painting, Photography, Theatre Arts, Video

MILLERSVILLE

MILLERSVILLE UNIVERSITY, Art Dept, Breidenstine Hall, 17551. Tel 717-872-3298. *Chmn* R Gordon Wise, EdD
Estab 1855, dept estab 1930; pub; D & E; SC 65, LC 10, GC 64; enrl maj 326, grad 20
Ent Req: HS dipl
Degrees: BA(Art), BS(Art Educ), BFA 4 yr, MEd(Art Educ) 1 yr
Tuition: res—$1314 per sem; nonres—$3061 per sem
Courses: †Art Education, †Art History, †Ceramics, †Design, †Drawing, †Graphic Arts, Illustration, †Jewelry, Lettering, †Painting, †Photography, †Printmaking, †Sculpture, †Teacher Training, Art Crafts, Computer Art, †Visual Communication
Summer School: Dir, Gordon Wise. Enrl 300; terms of 5 wks, two sessions beginning June and July. Studio courses offered

MONROEVILLE

COMMUNITY COLLEGE OF ALLEGHENY COUNTY, BOYCE CAMPUS, Art Dept, 595 Beatty Rd, 15146. Tel 412-733-4342. *Prof* Bruno Sorento, MFA; *Prof* Jeanne Moffatt Connors, MEd
Pub; D & E; SC 13, LC 1; enrl D 200, E 40, non-maj 140, maj 60
Ent Req: HS dipl
Degrees: AS 2 yrs
Tuition: In County—$672 per sem; out of county—$1344 per sem; out of state & foriegn—$2016 sem
Courses: Art History, Ceramics, Collages, Constructions, Drawing, Graphic Arts, Mixed Media, Painting, Photography, Printmaking, Sculpture, Color & Design
Adult Hobby Classes: Courses—Calligraphy, Drawing, Painting, Photography
Children's Classes: Enrl varies. Courses—Drawing, Painting
Summer School: Tuition $50 per cr. Courses—vary

NANTICOKE

LUZERNE COUNTY COMMUNITY COLLEGE, Commercial Art Dept, Prospect St & Middle Rd, 18634. Tel 717-735-8300, 829-7319. *Coordr* Susan Sponenberg, BFA; *Instr* Mike Molnar; *Instr* George Schelling; *Instr* Sam Cramer
Estab 1967; pub; D & E; SC 20, LC 7; enrl D 65, E 10, non-maj 5, maj 60
Ent Req: HS dipl
Degrees: 2 year programs offered
Courses: Art History, Drawing, Graphic Arts, †Graphic Design, Illustration, Lettering, Mixed Media, †Painting, †Photography, Airbrush, Color & Design, Color Photography, †Computer Graphics, Life Drawing, Phototypesetting
Adult Hobby Classes: Enrl 10; tuition $48 per cr for 15 wk term. Courses—selected from above offerings
Summer School: Dir, Susan Sponenberg. Enrl 10; tuition $48 per cr for 15 wk term. Courses—Selected from above offerings

NEW KENSINGTON

PENNSYLVANIA STATE UNIVERSITY AT NEW KENSINGTON, Depts of Art & Architecture, 3550 Seventh St Rd, 15068. Tel 412-339-5466. *Acting Chief Exec Officer* Roy Myers. Instrs: FT 2
Estab 1968; pub; D; scholarships; SC 3-4, LC 1 per sem
Ent Req: Col boards
Degrees: 2 yr (option for 4 yr at main campus at University Park)
Tuition: No campus res
Courses: Art Education, Art History, Ceramics, Drawing, Painting, Theatre Arts, Design, Music, Watercolor

Adult Hobby Classes: Enrl 250; tuition $75 per cr hr. Courses—Theater for Children, Ceramics, Painting
Children's Classes: Enrl 100; tuition $75 per cr hr. Courses—Drama, Art, Music Workshops
Summer School: Dir, Joseph Ferrino. Enrl 100; 8 wk term. Courses—Drama, Art, Music Workshops

NEWTOWN

BUCKS COUNTY COMMUNITY COLLEGE, Fine Arts Dept, Swamp Rd, 18940. Tel 215-968-8421. *Chmn Dept* Frank Dominguez; *Instr* Jon Alley; *Instr* Robert Dodge; *Instr* Jack Gevins; *Instr* Alan Goldstein; *Instr* Catherine Jansen; *Instr* Diane Lindenheim; *Instr* Marlene Miller; *Instr* Charlotte Schatz; *Instr* Helen Weisz; *Instr* Mark Sfirri; *Instr* Milt Sigel; *Instr* Gwen Kerber; *Instr* John Mathews
Estab 1965; pub; D & E; enrl D & E 9200 (school)
Ent Req: HS dipl
Degrees: AA
Courses: Art History, Ceramics, Drawing, Graphic Design, Jewelry, Painting, Photography, Printmaking, Sculpture, Design, Glass, Woodworking

NEW WILMINGTON

WESTMINSTER COLLEGE, Art Dept, 16172. Tel 412-946-8761, Ext 7267. *Head Dept* Kathy Koop. Instrs: 3
Estab 1852; den; D; scholarships; enrl maj 30, total 1100
Degrees: BS and BA(Fine Arts, Educ) 4 yrs
Adult Hobby Classes: Enrl 25; tuition $90 for 6 wk term. Courses—Ceramics
Children's Classes: Enrl 20; tuition $20 for 6 wk term. Courses— Mixed Media

PHILADELPHIA

ART INSTITUTE OF PHILADELPHIA, 1622 Chestnut St, 19103. Tel 215-567-7080; TWX 222-2787; WATS 800-235-2787. *Interim Pres & Dir Educ* Phillip Juska; *Dir Admissions* James Palermo; *Registrar* Dianne Runyon. Instrs· FT 40, PT 65
Estab 1966; pvt; D & E; scholarships; SC 30, LC 8; enrl D 1125, E 72
Ent Req: HS dipl, portfolio
Degrees: AST 2 yr
Tuition: $2225 per qtr hr
Courses: Advertising Design, Art History, Design, Graphic Design, Illustration, †Interior Design, Lettering, Mixed Media, †Photography, Weaving, Computer Graphics, †Fashion Merchandising, †Fashion Illustration

DREXEL UNIVERSITY, Nesbitt College of Design Arts, Nesbitt Hall, 33rd & Market Sts, 19104. Tel 215-895-2386; FAX 215-895-4917. *Dean* J Michael Adams; *Head Dept Interiors & Graphic Studies* Sylvia Clark; *Head Dept Fashion & Visual Studies* David Raizman; *Head Dept Architecture* Paul Hirschorn, MArch. Instrs: FT 19, PT 38
Estab 1891; pvt; scholarships; SC 39, LC 9; enrl undergrad $550, grad 50
Ent Req: Col board exam
Degrees: BS 4 yr (cooperative plan for BS), BArch 2 yr undergrad & 4 yr part time program, MS
Tuition: Freshmen $11,000; Sophmore - Sr $13,100 plus $560 general fee
Courses: †Architecture, †Graphic Design, †Interior Design, Photography, Design & Merchandising, †Fashion Design
Summer School: Dir, J Michael Adams. Enrl 220; term of 11 wks

SAMUEL S FLEISHER ART MEMORIAL, 709-721 Catharine St, 19147. Tel 215-922-3456; FAX 215-922-5327. *Dir* Thora E Jacobson; *Asst Dir* Nancy Wright; *Instr* Mac Fisher; *Instr* Frank Gasparro; *Instr* Tom Gaughan; *Instr* Anthony Gorny; *Instr* Louise Clement
Estab 1898; administered by the Philadelphia Museum of Art; pvt; E; LC 1; enrl E 2000
Ent Req: None
Degrees: None
Courses: Ceramics, Drawing, Painting, Photography, Printmaking, Sculpture
Adult Hobby Classes: Enrl 2900; tuition free. Courses—Ceramics, Drawing, Painting, Photography, Printmaking, Sculpture
Children's Classes: Enrl 1350; tuition free Oct - June, Sat only. Courses—Drawing, Painting, Sculpture
Summer School: Courses—Ceramics, Drawing, Landscape Painting, Painting, Photography, Printmaking, Sculpture

HUSSIAN SCHOOL OF ART, INC, Commercial Art Dept, 1010 Arch St, 19107. Tel 215-238-9000. *Pres* Ronald Dove. Instrs: FT 4, PT 28
Estab 1946; pvt; D; enrl 200
Ent Req: HS dipl, portfolio interview
Degrees: AST
Tuition: No campus res
Courses: †Advertising Design, Commercial Art, Drawing, Graphic Design, Illustration, Lettering, Painting, Photography, Printmaking, Airbrush, Computer Graphics, Fine Art
Adult Hobby Classes: Courses offered
Summer School: Five week summer workshop in Advertising Design, Drawing & Painting, Illustration

LA SALLE UNIVERSITY, Dept of Art, 20th St & Olney Ave, 19141. Tel 215-951-1126. *Chmn Dept Fine Arts* George Diehl, PhD; *Prof* James Lang, MFA; *Asst Prof* Beverly Marchant
Estab 1865; dept estab 1972; den; D & E; SC 2; enrl D 4, maj 2
Ent Req: HS dipl
Degrees: BA 4 yr
Tuition: $10,000 per yr; campus res—available
Courses: Art History, Painting, Printmaking
Summer School: Selected courses offered

MOORE COLLEGE OF ART & DESIGN, 20th & The Parkway, 19103-1179. Tel 215-568-4515; FAX 215-568-8017. *Pres* Mary-Linda Merriam; *Dean* Deborah Warner; *Chmn 2-D Fine Arts* Wayne Morris; *Chmn 3-D Fine Arts* Charles Fahlen; *Chmn Fashion Design* Janet Lewis; *Chmn Fashion Illustration* Mildred Ivins, Dipl; *Chmn Liberal Arts* Janet Kaplan; *Chmn Illustration* Bill Ternay; *Chmn Interior Design* Mark Karlen, BS; *Chmn Photography* Jack Sal; *Chmn Textile Design* Michael Olszewski, MFA; *Chmn Basic Arts* Charles Kaprelian, MFA
Estab 1844; pvt; D; scholarships; enrl D 400, non-maj 25, maj 375
Ent Req: HS dipl, portfolio, SAT
Degrees: BFA 4 yr, Certification in Art Education
Tuition: Res—$12,594 per yr; PT students $530 per cr; campus res—room & board $4864 per yr
Courses: Ceramics, Drawing, Graphic Design, †Illustration, Interior Design, Mixed Media, Painting, Photography, Printmaking, Textile Design, 2-D & 3-D Fine Arts
Adult Hobby Classes: Tuition $250 per 3 hr class, 1 cr each, once per wk; 10 wk term. Courses—Art Carpentry, Computer Seminars, Desktop Publishing, Drawing, Fashion Design Studio, Jewelry Making, Life Drawing, Oil Painting, Print Design
Children's Classes: Enrl 500; tutition $30, registration $165 per class; Oct - Dec & Feb - Apr on Sat. Courses—General Art
Summer School: Dir, Hilda Schoenwetter. Enrl 470; tuition $30, registration $320 1st class, $200 2nd class

PENNSYLVANIA ACADEMY OF THE FINE ARTS, 118 N Broad St, 19102. Tel 215-972-7625; FAX 215-569-0153. *Dir* Frederick S Osborne
Estab 1805; pvt; D & E; scholarships; SC 15, LC 4
Ent Req: HS dipl, portfolio & recommendations
Degrees: Cert, 4 yrs; BFA coordinated program with Univ of Pennsylvania or Univ of the Arts, 5 yr, MFA(Painting), MFA(Printmaking) & MFA(Sculpture) 2 yrs
Tuition: Nonres—undergrad $1600 per sem; no campus res
Courses: Drawing, Painting, Printmaking, Sculpture, Anatomy, Perspective
Adult Hobby Classes: Courses—Clay Modeling, Wood & Stone Carving, Life Drawing & Painting, Portrait, Still Life, Anatomy, Pastel, Materials & Technique, Watercolor
Summer School: Dir, Angela G Walker. Term of 7 wks. Courses—Anatomy, Cast Drawing, Life Drawing & Painting, Lithography, Pastel, Portrait, Sculpture, Silkscreen, Still Life & Drawing, Watercolor

PHILADELPHIA COLLEGE OF TEXTILES & SCIENCE, School of Textiles, School House Lane & Henry Ave, 19144. Tel 215-951-2751. *Pres* James Gallagher
Estab 1884; pvt; scholarships; enrl D 1600, E 1100
Degrees: BS 4 yrs
Tuition: $10,844 per yr
Courses: Interior Design, Chemistry & Dyeing, Fashion Apparel Management, Fashion Design, Fashion Merchandising, Knitted Design, Print Design, Textile Engineering, Textile Quality Control & Testing, Weaving Design
Summer School: Dir, Maxine Lentz

PHILADELPHIA COMMUNITY COLLEGE, Dept of Art, 1700 Spring Garden St, 19130. Tel 215-751-8771. *Dir Div Liberal Arts* Aram Terzian; *Prof* Diane Burko, MFA; *Prof* Robert Paige, MFA; *Assoc Prof* Valerie Seligsohn, MFA; *Assoc Prof* Wallace Peters, MA; *Assoc Prof* Madeline Cohen, PhD; *Assoc Prof* Dan Evans, MA; *Asst Prof* Meiling Hom, MFA; *Asst Prof* Bill Woods, MFA; *Asst Prof* Karen Aumann, BFA; *Asst Prof* Michael Saluato, MA
Estab 1967; pub; D & E; SC 10, LC 6; enrl D 80 art maj
Ent Req: HS dipl, portfolio
Degrees: AA 2 yr
Tuition: Approx $1500 per yr; no campus res
Courses: Art History, Ceramics, Drawing, Graphic Design, Painting, Photography, Design, 2-D Design, 3-D Design, Transfer Foundation Program
Summer School: Dir, Bob Paige. Tuition $61 per cr. Courses—Art History, Ceramics, Design, Drawing, Painting

SAINT JOSEPH'S UNIVERSITY, Dept of Fine & Performing Arts, 5600 City Ave, 19131. Tel 215-660-1000, 660-1840. *Chmn* Dennis McNally, PhD; *Assoc Prof* Dennis Weeks, MFA; *Assoc Head Music* Lewis Gordon, DMA; *Lectr* Peg Schofield, MFA; *Lectr* Jeff Blake; *Lectr* Betsy Anderson, MA
Estab 1851, prog estab 1975; den; D & E; Scholarships; SC 15, LC 4; enrl D 200, E 20
Ent Req: HS dipl
Tuition: $7786 per yr; campus res available
Courses: Aesthetics, Art Education, Architecture, Art Appreciation, Art Education, Art History, Ceramics, Drawing, Film, History of Art & Archaeology, Painting, Photography, Stage Design, Theatre Arts, Advertising Design, Aesthetics, Architecture, Art Appreciation, Art Education, Art History, Ceramics, Drawing, History of Art & Archaeology, Stage Design, Painting, Photography, Stage Design, Theatre Arts, Music History
Adult Hobby Classes: Enrl 30 per sem; tuition $175 per cr hr. Courses—same as above
Children's Classes: Chmn, Rev Dennis McNally, SJ, PhD. Enrl 60; tuition $175 per cr hr, 3 cr for 6 wk term. Courses—Art History, Drawing, Photography

TEMPLE UNIVERSITY, Tyler School of Art, Beech & Penrose Aves, Elkins Park, 19126. Tel 215-782-2715. *Dean* Rochelle Toner, MFA; *Chmn Painting, Drawing, & Sculpture* Susan Moore, MFA; *Chmn Graphic Design* Allen Koss, MFA; *Chmn Crafts* Jon Clark, MFA; *Chmn Art History* Philip Betancourt, PhD; *Chmn Univ Art & Art Educ* Marilyn Holsing
Dept estab 1935; pvt; D & E; scholarships; enrl 700
Ent Req: HS dipl, SAT, portfolio
Degrees: BA(Art History & Studio Art), BS(Art Educ), BFA, MA(Art History), MEd(Art Educ), MFA & PhD(Art History)
Tuition: Res—undergrad $5624 per yr, grad $7110 per yr; nonres—undergrad $9860 per yr, grad $9000 per yr
Courses: †Art Education, †Art History, †Ceramics, Drawing, Film, †Graphic Design, †History of Art & Archaeology, Illustration, †Painting, †Photography, †Printmaking, Sculpture, Video, Weaving, Computers, †Fibers/Fabric Design, Foundry, Handmade Cameras, Metals, Papermaking, Performance Art, †Glass, Animation,
Children's Classes: Courses—Computer & Studio, also programs for HS students

TRACEY-WARNER SCHOOL, 401 N Broad St, 19108. Tel 215-574-0402. *Pres* Maxine Friedman
Estab 1956; pvt; D; enrl D 125
Ent Req: HS dipl
Degrees: AA 2 yrs, dipl or cert
Tuition: $9385 per Program (1800 clock hrs), $5385 per Program (900 clock hours)
Courses: Advertising Design, Art Education, Art History, †Costume Design & Construction, Fashion Arts, Handicrafts, †Illustration, Jewelry, Textile Design, †Draping Design, Pattern Drafting, Pattern Grading
Adult Hobby Classes: Enrl 75; tuition $4950 per 2 yr course. Courses—Fashion Technology, Fashion Merchandising & Retailing, Men"s & Women"s Tailoring

UNIVERSITY OF PENNSYLVANIA, Graduate School of Fine Arts, 19104-6311. Tel 215-898-8321; FAX 215-898-9215. *Dean* Patricia Conway, MA
Estab 1874; pvt; scholarships and fels; GC
Ent Req: Ent exam
Tuition: Grad $8792 per sem; campus res available
Courses: Landscape Architecture, Architectural Design, Fine Arts
Summer School: Dir, Adele Santos. Tuition $2500 per 6 wks. Studio courses in Paris, Venice & India
—Dept of Architecture, 110 Meyerson Hall, 19104-6311. Tel 215-898-5728; FAX 215-898-9215. *Chmn* David Leatherbarrow; *Chmn Grad Group* Joseph Rykwert. Instrs: FT 7, PT 25
Enrl 180
Degrees: MA 3 yrs, PhD 4 - 5 yrs
Tuition: $16,546 per yr
Courses: Architectural Design and Construction
Summer School: Chmn, Adele Santos. Enrl 70; tuition $1200 per 3 cr course (4-6 wks duration). Courses—Summer studios (only upper level students)
—Dept of Landscape Architecture & Regional Planning, Room 119 Meyerson, 19104-6311. Tel 215-898-6591; FAX 215-898-5756. *Chairperson* Anne Whiston Spirn. Instrs: FT 8, PT 5
Scholarships; LC 7, Design Courses 4; enrl 113
Degrees: MLA 2 - 3 yrs, MRP 2 yrs, Cert & joint degrees available
Tuition: Res—grad $8273 per sem
Courses: Construction, Ecological Design, Field Ecology, Garden Studio, Housing Studio, Plants & Design, Regional Planning Studio, Studio
Summer School: Dir, James/Thoere, Enrl 18 - 20; Tuition $1400 for 6 wk sem—Courses Field Ecology
—Graduate School of Fine Arts, Dept of Fine Arts, 205 S 34th St, Rm 100 Morgan/6312, 19104-6311. Tel 215-898 8374; FAX 215-898-2915. *Chmn* Leonard Stokes; *Assoc Prof* Maurice C Lowe; *Lectr* Arlene Gostin; *Asst Prof* Hitoshi Nakazato; *Lectr* Sewell Sillman; *Lectr* Diane Keller; *Lectr* Susan Leites; *Lectr* Nick Vidnovic; *Lectr* Becky Young. Instrs: FT 7, PT 3
SC 21, LC 5, GC; enrl 65
Degrees: BFA 4 yrs, MFA 3 yrs
Tuition: $16,546 per yr
Courses: Painting, Printmaking, Sculpture, Color

UNIVERSITY OF THE ARTS, Philadelphia College of Art & Design, Broad & Pine Sts, 19102. Tel 215-875-4800; FAX 215-875-5467. *Pres* Peter Solmssen, JD; *Provost* Virginia Red, MM; *Dean, College of Art & Design* Stephen Tarantal, MFA; *Dean, College of Performing Arts* Stephen Jay, MM; *Dir of Admis* Barbara Elliot; *Chmn Crafts* Lizbeth Stewart, BA; *Chmn Graphic Design* Chris Myers, MFA; *Chmn Illustration* Phyllis Purves-Smith, MFA; *Chmn Industrial Design* Charles Burnette, PhD Arch; *Chmn Fine Arts Dept* Barry Parker, MFA; *Chmn Photography & Film* Alida Fish, MFA; *Chmn Printmaking* Patricia Smith, MAEd; *Co-Chmn Foundation Prog* Niles Lewandoswki, MFA; *Co-Chmn Foundation Program* Karen Saler, MFA; *Chmn Educ* Janis Norman, PhD; *Interim Dir Continuing Studies* Barbara Lippman, BA
Estab 1876; pvt; D & E; scholarships; enrl undergrad 1269, grad 90
Ent Req: HS dipl, portfolio, SAT
Degrees: BFA 4 yrs, BS, MA, MFA, Mat certificates
Tuition: $11,200 per yr; campus res—room $3750 per yr
Courses: †Architecture, †Art Education, Art History, Calligraphy, †Ceramics, Design, Drawing, †Film, Goldsmithing, Graphic Arts, †Graphic Design, Handicrafts, History of Art & Archaeology, †Illustration, †Industrial Design, Lettering, Museum Staff Training, †Painting, †Photography, †Printmaking, †Sculpture, Silversmithing, †Teacher Training, †Theatre Arts, Video, †Art Therapy, Environmental Design, Fibers, Glassblowing, Liberal Arts, Metals, Typography, †Woodworking
Adult Hobby Classes: Evening program; Tuition $280 per cr. Courses—Computer Studies, Crafts, Design, Fine Arts, Illustration, Photography
Children's Classes: Saturday school; enrl 267; ;tuition $130 per course & materials. Courses—Cartooning, Ceramics, Drawing, Illustration & Graphic Design, Jewelry of Metals, Painting
Summer School: Pre-College Program: Enrl 356; tuition $150 - $1309; term of 1 - 6 wks beginning July

PITTSBURGH

ART INSTITUTE OF PITTSBURGH, 526 Penn Ave, 15222. Tel 412-263-6600. *Pres* Sandra Van Dyke
Estab 1921; pvt; scholarships; enrl D 1900, E 200
Ent Req: HS grad
Degrees: AA 2 yrs, dipl
Tuition: $2250 per quarter
Courses: †Interior Design, Photography, Airbrush Technique, †Fashion Illustration, †Photography-Audiovisual-Multimedia, †Visual Communications
Adult Hobby Classes: Enrl 200; tuition $790 per qtr (4 qtrs). Courses—Layout & Production Art, Photography Technician, Retailing, Residential Planning

CARLOW COLLEGE, Art Dept, 3333 Fifth Ave, 15213. Tel 412-578-6000. *Chmn Dept* Richard Devlin; *Assoc Chmn* Suzanne Steiner. Instrs: FT 1, PT 3
Estab 1945; den; D & E; scholarships; SC 17, LC 6; enrl 800, maj 35
Ent Req: HS dipl and transcript, col boards
Degrees: BA, Certificate Art Education
Tuition: Res—undegrad $259 per cr hr, grad $279 per cr hr

Courses: Art Education, Ceramics, Drawing, Painting, Printmaking, Sculpture, Teacher Training, American Art, Art Therapy, Fiber Arts, Survey of Art, Twentieth Century Art, 2-D Design
Summer School: Acad Dean, Sr Elizabeth McMillan. Enrl approx 40; two summer sessions 4 wks each. Courses—Fiber Arts, Ceramics

CARNEGIE MELLON UNIVERSITY, College of Fine Arts, 5000 Forbes Ave, 15213. Tel 412-268-2000. Dean Lowry Burgess; Assoc Dean Lynn Holden
Estab 1905; pvt; scholarships and fels
Ent Req: Col board ent exam plus auditions or portfolio
Degrees: 4-5 yr, MFA in Stage Design available in Dept of Drama
Tuition: Undergrad $12,000 per yr, grad $167 per unit; campus res available
Summer School: Term of 6 wks. Courses—includes some pre-college courses
—Dept of Architecture, 15213. Tel 412-268-2354. Head John Eberhard. Instrs: FT 22, PT 20
Enrl 295
Degrees: BArch, MS, PhD
Tuition: Undergrad $16,500 per sem, grad $181 per unit
Courses: Architecture
Summer School: Dir, John Papinchak. tuition $2094 per 6 wks
—Dept of Design, MMCH 110, 15213. Tel 412-268-2828. Head Richard Buchanan. Instrs: FT 14, PT 4
Enrl 200
Degrees: BFA 4 yrs
Tuition: Res—undergrad $6000 per sem, grad $167 per unit
Courses: Graphic Design, Industrial Design
Adult Hobby Classes: Courses—Calligraphy
Summer School: Courses—Design Studio
—Dept of Art, 15213. Tel 412-268-2409; FAX 412-268-7817. Head Byran Rogers. Instrs: FT 22, PT 5
Scholarships; enrl 235
Degrees: BFA & MFA
Tuition: Undergrad $16,000 per yr, grad $12,000 per yr
Courses: Drawing, Painting, Printmaking, Sculpture, Video, †Art, Computer
Children's Classes: Enrl 100; tuition $400 for 9 months. Courses—same as undergrad prog
Summer School: Enrl 50; tuition $2300 for 6 wks. Courses—same as undergrad prog

CHATHAM COLLEGE, Fine & Performing Arts, Woodland Rd, 15232. Tel 412-365-1100. Chmn Dr Louis Coyner; Asst Prof Michael Pestel. Instrs: FT 2, PT 2
Estab 1869; pvt; W; SC 17, LC 7
Ent Req: HS grad
Degrees: BA 4 yrs
Tuition: $12,190 (incl res fees)
Courses: Aesthetics, Art Appreciation, Art Education, †Art History, Conceptual Art, Constructions, Design, Drawing, Film, History of Art & Archaeology, Mixed Media, †Painting, Photography, Printmaking, †Sculpture, Independent Study, Introduction to Art, Tutorial

LA ROCHE COLLEGE, Division of Graphics, Design & Communication, 9000 Babcock Blvd, 15237. Tel 412-367-9300. Chairperson Martha Fairchild-Shepler, MFA; Prof Tom Bates; Prof Martha Fairchild MFA; Assoc Prof George Founds; Instr Diane Foltz, PhD; Instr Wendy Bechwith, MArchit; Instr Grant Dismore, MFA; Instr Devvrat Nagar, BArchit. Instrs: PT 15
Estab 1963, dept estab 1965; pvt; D & E; SC 25, LC 15; enrl D & E 200, non-maj 20, maj 180
Ent Req: HS dipl
Degrees: BA and BS 4 yr
Tuition: Res—Undergrad $231 per cr, grad $237 per cr; campus res available
Courses: Advertising Design, Aesthetics, Art History, Ceramics, Commercial Art, Display, Drawing, †Graphic Arts, †Graphic Design, Illustration, Industrial Design, †Interior Design, Lettering, Painting, Photography, Sculpture, Airbrush Illustration, Communication, Computer Graphics, Fashion Design, †Multimedia Design, Package Design, 3-D Design
Summer School: Dir of Admissions, Marianne Shertzer. Tuition $170 per cr

POINT PARK COLLEGE, Performing Arts Dept, Wood St & Blvd of Allies, 15222. Tel 412-392-3450; FAX 412-391-1980. Chmn Alan Forino
Degrees: BA & BFA
Tuition: $4300 per sem
Courses: Architecture, Art Appreciation, Art History, †Film, †Interior Design, †Photography, †Stage Design, †Fashion Illustration, †Visual Arts

UNIVERSITY OF PITTSBURGH, 15260
—Henry Clay Frick Fine Arts Dept, 15260. Tel 412-648-2400. Chmn Anne Weis
Estab 1787, dept estab 1927; pvt; D & E; scholarships; LC 35, GC 20; enrl D 750, E 250, grad 50
Ent Req: HS dipl, BA, GRE for grad work
Degrees: BA 4 yrs, MA 2 yrs, PhD
Tuition: Res—grad $3095; nonres—grad $6190
Courses: †Art History
Summer School: Dir, Anne Weis. Enrl 150; 7 wks, 2 sessions
—Dept of Studio Arts, 104 Frick Fine Arts Bldg, 15260. Tel 412-648-2430. Chmn Kenneth Batista. Instrs: FT 6, PT 4-7
Estab 1968; pub; D; SC 29; enrl 1500
Degrees: BA, undergrad maj in Studio Arts
Tuition: Res—$1675 per term; nonres—$3350 per term
Courses: Drawing, Graphic Arts, Painting, Sculpture
Adult Hobby Classes: Enrl 120; tuition res—$113 per cr, nonres—$226 per cr for 15 wk term . Courses—Design, Color, Drawing, Sculpture
Summer School: Dir, Kenneth Batista. Enrl 60; tuition res $113 per cr, nonres—$226 per cr, 7 1/2 wks each. Courses—Design, Color, Drawing, Sculpture

PLYMOUTH MEETING

ANTONELLI INSTITUTE, Professional Photography, Commercial Art & Interior Design, 2910 Jolly Rd, PO Box 570, 19462. Tel 215-275-3040; FAX 215-275-5630. Pres Joseph B Thompson; VPres Harry W Hollingsworth; Dir Thomas D Treacy, EdD; Instr James Donato, MBA
Estab 1938; pvt; D & E; enrl D 350, E 75
Ent Req: HS dipl
Tuition: $4182 per sem (photography), $3425 per sem (all others); campus res—room & board $1925 per sem
Courses: Commercial Art, Interior Design
Adult Hobby Classes: Workshops as scheduled

RADNOR

CABRINI COLLEGE, Dept of Fine Arts, 610 King of Prussia Rd, 19087-3699. Tel 215-971-8380; FAX 215-971-8539. Chmn Dept Adeline Bethany, EdD. Instrs: FT 2, PT 3
Estab 1957; den; D & E; scholarships; SC 11, LC 4
Ent Req: HS dipl, satisfactory average and rank in secondary school class, SAT, recommendations
Degrees: BA(Fine Arts), BA Arts Administration), BS & BSED
Tuition: $9020 per yr; campus res—room & board $5790
Courses: Art Education, Ceramics, Drawing, Graphic Design, History of Art & Archaeology, Painting, Teacher Training, Computer Publication Design, Design & Composition
Adult Hobby Classes: Courses offered
Summer School: Dir, Dr Midge Leahy. Term of 6 wks beginning May & July. Courses—Color Theory, Drawing, Elem Art Methods, Mixed Media, Painting

READING

ALBRIGHT COLLEGE, Dept of Art, 13th & Exeter Sts, PO Box 15234, 19612-5234. Tel 215-921-2381, Ext 7715; FAX 215-921-7530. Chmn Bert Brouwer, MFA
Estab 1856, dept estab 1964; SC 14, LC 7; enrl D 322, E 41, non-maj 340, maj 14, others 20
Ent Req: HS dipl, SAT
Degrees: BA 4 yrs
Tuition: $11,800 per yr; campus res—room $1970, board $1650
Courses: Art History, Ceramics, Constructions, Drawing, Fashion Arts, Film, History of Art & Archaeology, Interior Design, Mixed Media, †Painting, Photography, Printmaking, †Sculpture, Theatre Arts
Adult Hobby Classes: Enrl 40; tuition $110 per cr. Courses—Drawing, Photography
Children's Classes: Enrl 25-35; tuition $35-$50 per course. Courses—Crafts, Drawing
Summer School: Chmn, Bert Brouwer. Enrl 30 - 50; 2 terms of 4 wks beginning in June & July. Courses—Art History, Drawing, Painting

ROSEMONT

ROSEMONT COLLEGE, Division of the Arts, 19010. Tel 215-527-0200. Chmn Div Tina Walduier Bizzarro; Assoc Prof Patricia Nugent, MFA; Assoc Prof Michael Willse, MFA; Asst Prof Amy Orr, MFA; Lectr Peter Lister; Lectr Janice Merendino, BFA; Lectr David Tafler, MFA; Lectr James Victor. Instrs: FT 4, PT 7
Estab 1921; pvt; W (exchange with Villanova Univ, Cabrini College, Eastern College, The Design Schools); D; scholarships; enrl total col 600, art 200, grad approx 17
Ent Req: HS dipl, SAT
Degrees: BFA (Studio Art), BA (Art History, Studio Art), Teacher certificate in Art K-12
Tuition: $8350 annual tuition; campus res available
Courses: Aesthetics, Art Education, Ceramics, Drawing, Graphic Arts, Painting, Photography, Printmaking, Sculpture, Teacher Training, American Indian Art, Art Criticism, Creativity & the Marketplace, Fibres History, Studio Art, Watercolor
Summer School: Dir, Tina Walduicr Bizzarro

SCRANTON

INTERNATIONAL CORRESPONDENCE SCHOOLS
—School of Interior Design, 925 Oak St, Scranton, 18515. Tel 717-342-7701, Ext 341. VPres Educ Svcs Gerald Burns, PhD; Instr Rachel Michaels. Instrs: FT 1
Estab 1890, dept estab 1969; pvt; enrl 4200
Ent Req: 8th grade
Tuition: $689
Courses: Interior Decorating
—School of Art, 925 Oak St, Scranton, 18515. Tel 717-342-7701, Ext 341. VPres Educ Gerald Burns PhD; Chief Instr Rachel Michaels. Instrs: FT 1, PT 2
Estab 1890; pvt; enrl 4900
Ent Req: 8th grade
Tuition: $499
Courses: Drawing, Painting

LACKAWANNA JUNIOR COLLEGE, Art Dept, 901 Prospect Ave, 18505. Tel 717-961-7827. Chmn John De Nunzio
Degrees: AA
Courses: Art Appreciation, Art History, Calligraphy, Photography, Printmaking

MARYWOOD COLLEGE, Art Dept, 2300 Adams Ave, 18509. Tel 717-348-6211. Chairperson Dept Sr Cor Immaculatum. Instrs: FT 12, PT 15
Estab 1926; pvt; D & E; scholarships; SC 28, LC 7, GC 12; enrl maj 240, grad 80
Ent Req: HS dipl, portfolio and interview
Degrees: BA(Art Educ), BA(Arts Admin), BS(Educ with concentration in Art), BFA(Drawing & Painting, Illustration, Advertising Graphics, Photography, Ceramics, Sculpture, Interior Design), MA(Studio Art, Art Educ, Art Therapy),

MFA(Painting, Ceramics, Weaving)
Tuition: Grad MA $305, MFA $315 per cr, undergrad $300 per cr
Courses: †Advertising Design, †Art Education, Art History, Calligraphy, †Ceramics, Drawing, Fashion Arts, †Graphic Arts, †Illustration, †Interior Design, Jewelry, Mixed Media, †Painting, †Photography, Printmaking, †Sculpture, Textile Design, Theatre Arts, †Weaving, †Art Therapy, Contemporary Learning Theories, Fabrics, Metalcraft, Serigraphy, Tapestry
Adult Hobby Classes: Enrl 50; tuition varies for non-cr 10 wk term.
Courses—Ceramics, Drawing, Painting, Photography
Children's Classes: College for Kids, enrl 50. Courses—Computer Graphics, Drawing, Painting, Sculpture
Summer School: Graduate degree programs only

SHIPPENSBURG

SHIPPENSBURG UNIVERSITY, Art Dept, Huber Art Center, 17257. Tel 717-532-1530; FAX 717-532-1273. *Chmn Art Dept* William Hynes; *Asst Prof* Bill Davis, MFA; *Asst Prof* George Waricher, MEd; *Asst Prof* Michael Campbell, MFA
Estab 1871, dept estab 1920; pub; D & E; scholarships; SC 17, LC 6; enrl D 400, E 100, non-maj 600, grad 15, continuing educ 20
Ent Req: HS dipl, Portfolio review
Degrees: BA(Art)
Tuition: Res—$1314 per sem, nonres—$2446 per sem; campus res—room & board $1451 per sem
Courses: Art History, Ceramics, Drawing, Painting, Printmaking, Sculpture, Arts & Crafts, Enamelling
Adult Hobby Classes: Sr citizen tuition waived in regular classes if space is available
Summer School: Dir, William Hynes. Tuition $110 per cr hr for terms of 3 - 5 wks beginning May 18. Lectr & Studio courses

SLIPPERY ROCK

SLIPPERY ROCK UNIVERSITY OF PENNSYLVANIA, Dept of Art, 16057. Tel 412-738-0512; FAX 412-738-2098. *Chmn Dept* James Myford. Instrs: FT 9
Pub; D & E; SC 27, LC 3; enrl maj 70
Ent Req: HS dipl
Degrees: BA(Art), BFA(Art) 4 yr
Tuition: In state res—$1139 per sem (12-18 hrs); out of state—$2156 per sem
Courses: Art History, Ceramics, Drawing, Painting, Photography, Printmaking, Sculpture, Textile Design, Art Synthesis, Metalsmithing
Summer School: Tui $52 per cr hr

SWARTHMORE

SWARTHMORE COLLEGE, Dept of Art, 500 College Ave, 19081-1397. Tel 215-328-8116. *Chairperson Dept Art* Michael Cothren, PhD; *Prof* T Kaori Kitao, PhD; *Prof* Constance Cain Hungerford, PhD; *Assoc Prof* Randall L Exon, MFA; *Assoc Prof* Brian A Meunier, MFA; *Assoc Prof* Maribeth Graybill; *Asst Prof* Syd Carpenter
Estab 1864, dept estab 1925; pvt; D; scholarships; SC 14, LC 33; enrl non-maj 500, maj 25
Ent Req: HS dipl, SAT, CEEB
Degrees: BA 4 yrs
Tuition: $14,380 per yr; campus res—room & Board $4920 per yr
Courses: Aesthetics, Architecture, Art History, Ceramics, Drawing, History of Art & Archaeology, Landscape Architecture, Mixed Media, Painting, Photography, Printmaking, Sculpture, Stage Design, Theatre Arts, Art, History, History of Architecture, History of Cinema, Philosophy, Theatre Program, Urban History

UNIONTOWN

TOUCHSTONE CENTER FOR CRAFTS, 107 S Beeson Ave, PO Box 2141, 15401. Tel 412-438-2811; WATS 800-753-2723. *Exec Dir* Marcene R Clark
Estab 1983; D; scholarships; enrl D 500
Tuition: $100-$250 per wk; campus housing available
Courses: Ceramics, Design, Fashion Arts, Handicrafts, Illustration, Jewelry, Painting, Photography, Printmaking, Sculpture, Silversmithing, Textile Design, Video, Weaving
Adult Hobby Classes: Enrl 400; tuition $100 - $250 per wk. Courses—Clay, Fibre, Glass, Metal, Painting, Photography, Printmaking, Wood
Children's Classes: Enrl 100. Courses—Art

UNIVERSITY PARK

PENNSYLVANIA STATE UNIVERSITY, UNIVERSITY PARK
—School of Visual Arts, 102 Visual Arts Bldg, 16802. Tel 814-865-0444; FAX 814-865-7140. *Dir School of Visual Arts* James Stephenson, MA
Estab 1855, col estab 1963; pub; D & E; SC 282, LC 99, GC 104
Ent Req: HS dipl and GPA, SAT
Degrees: BA, BS & BFA 4 yrs, MS, MFA, MA, MEd, DEd, PhD
Tuition: Res—undergrad $4332 per yr, $2166 per sem, $179 per cr, grad $4846 per yr, $2423 per sem, $203 per cr; nonres—undergrad $9118 per yr, $4559 per sem, $381 per cr, grad $9692 per yr, $4846 per sem, $403 per cr; campus res—room & board $1765 (undergrads use double rooms per sem)
Courses: †Art Education, Ceramics, Drawing, Graphic Design, Painting, Photography, Printmaking, Sculpture, Metal Arts
Adult Hobby Classes: Tuition varies. Courses—informal, vary with demand
Summer School: Enrl 1565; tuition same. Courses—regular session
—Dept of Art History, 229 Arts II Bldg, 16802. Tel 814-865-6326. *Dept Head* Hellmut Hager; *Adjunct Assoc Prof* Robert Berger; *Prof* Roland E Fleischer, PhD; *Prof* George L Mauner, PhD; *Prof* Heinz Henisch, PhD; *Assoc Prof* Jeanne Chenault Porter, PhD; *Assoc Prof* Elizabeth B Smith, PhD; *Assoc Prof* Elizabeth J Walters, PhD; *Assoc Prof* Craig Zabel, PhD; *Graduate Officer* Roland E Fleischer

Estab 1855, dept estab 1963; pub; D & E; scholarships; LC 50, GC 36; enrl D 56, maj 51, grad 27, others 10
Ent Req: HS dipl
Degrees: BA 4 yrs, MA 2-3 yrs, PhD approx 4 yrs
Tuition: Res—undergrad $4548 two sem, grad $4548 two sem; nonres—undergrad $9574 two sem, grad $9574 two sem; campus res-room & board $3790
Courses: Aesthetics, †Art History, History of Art & Archaeology, Connoisseurship, History of Photography, Historiography
Adult Hobby Classes: Classes offered through Continuing Education
Summer School: Courses same as regular session, but limited

VILLANOVA

VILLANOVA UNIVERSITY, Dept of Art and Art History, 19085. Tel 215-645-4610. *Prof* George Radan; *Prof* Br Richard Cannuli; *Asst Prof* Dr Mark Sullivan
Estab 1842, dept estab 1971; pvt; D & E; SC 25, LC 6; enrl D 35, maj 35
Ent Req: HS dipl, SAT
Degrees: BFA 4 yrs; courses taught in conjunction with Rosemont College
Tuition: Res—undergrad $3500 per yr; campus res—room & board $2200 per yr
Courses: †Aesthetics, Art Education, Art History, Drawing, Painting, Theatre Arts, Archaeology, Conservation
Adult Hobby Classes: Enrl 20-30; tuition $336 per course in 14 wk sem.
Courses—Drawing, Calligraphy
Summer School: Held in Siena, Italy. Courses—Art History, Studio Art, Language

WASHINGTON

WASHINGTON AND JEFFERSON COLLEGE, Art Dept, Olin Art Center, 15301. Tel 412-222-4400, 223-6110. *Chmn Art Dept* Paul B Edwards, MA; *Prof* Hugh H Taylor, MA; *Asst Prof* Patricia Maloney, MFA; *Adj Prof* John Yothers, MA; *Adj Prof* James McNutt; *Adj Prof* Kathleen Madigan
Estab 1787, dept estab 1959; pvt; D & E; scholarships; SC 14, LC 8; enrl D 162, E 18, non-maj 139, maj 23, others 15
Ent Req: HS dipl, SAT, achievement tests
Degrees: BA 4 yr, MA
Tuition: $13,360 per yr; campus res—room & board $3490 per yr
Courses: Architecture, Art Appreciation, †Art Education, Art History, Calligraphy, Ceramics, Design, Drawing, Fashion Arts, Lettering, Painting, Photography, Printmaking, Restoration & Conservation, Sculpture, Teacher Training, Gallery Management, Photography
Adult Hobby Classes: Enrl 24, tuition $675 per course for term of 13 wks. Courses—Art Education, Drawing, Matting & Framing, Stained Glass, Photography
Summer School: Dir, Dir Karen Bush. Enrl 300; tuision $225 per cr hr for 2 - 4 wk sessions., Courses—Ceramics, Painting, Photography

WAYNE

WAYNE ART CENTER, 413 Maplewood Ave, 19087. Tel 215-688-3553. *Pres* Patricia Fish; *Exec Dir* Nancy Campell; *Instr* Lucy Edwards; *Instr* Edward Lis; *Instr* Carolyn Howard; *Instr* Marianne Tebbens; *Instr* Maevernon Varnum; *Instr* Paul Gorka; *Instr* Zhe-Zhou Jiang; *Instr* Diane Ippoldo; *Instr* Candace Stringer; *Instr* Nancy Barch; *Instr* Jill Rupinski
Estab 1930; pvt; D & E; SC 25; enrl D 200, E 50, others 40
Ent Req: None; free program for senior citizens
Tuition: $84 for 12 wk session
Courses: Mixed Media, Painting, Sculpture, Pottery, Woodcarving
Adult Hobby Classes: Tuition $84 for 12 wk sem, yearly dues $20. Courses—as above
Children's Classes: Tuition $35 for 10 wk sem, yearly dues $6. Courses—Drawing, Painting, Sculpture
Summer School: Exec Dir, Meg Miller. Courses—same as above plus Landscape Painting

WAYNESBURG

WAYNESBURG COLLEGE, Dept of Fine Arts, 51 W College St, 15370. Tel 412-627-8191; FAX 412-627-6416. *Chmn* Daniel Morris, MA; *Asst Prof* Susan Howsare, MFA; *Instr* Robert Gay, BSJ
Estab 1849, dept estab 1971; pvt; D & E; scholarships; SC 25, LC 6; enrl D 131, E 3, maj 17
Ent Req: HS dipl
Degrees: BA(Visual Communication) 4 yrs, MBA
Tuition: res—$7030 per yr; nonres—$7220 per yr; campus res—room & board $10, 120 per yr
Courses: Art Education, Art History, Ceramics, Design, Drawing, Graphic Arts, Painting, Photography, Printmaking, Sculpture, Theatre Arts, Computer Applications for Visual Communication, Computer Graphics, Desk Top Publishing, Layout & Photography for Media, Photo-Journalism, Media Presentation, Television, Typography, †Visual Art, †Visual Communication, †Visual Communication-Print Media
Adult Hobby Classes: Courses—Art History, Graphic Design, Photography
Summer School: Dept Chmn, Daniel Morris. Tuition $270 for term of 5 wks beginning June 2 and July 7

WEST MIFFLIN

COMMUNITY COLLEGE OF ALLEGHENY COUNTY, Fine Arts Dept, 1750 Clairton Rd, 15122. Tel 412-469-1100; FAX 412-469-6370. *Chmn Arts Dept* Micheal Stefanko
Degrees: AA, AS
Tuition: $600 per yr
Courses: Advertising Design, Art Appreciation, Calligraphy, Commercial Art, Ceramics, Design, Drawing, Handicrafts, Painting, Photography

WILKES-BARRE

WILKES UNIVERSITY, Dept of Art, Bedford Hall, 18766. Tel 717-824-4651, Ext 4240. *Chmn & Prof* Richard A Fuller, MA; *Assoc Prof* William Sterling, PhD; *Asst Prof* Sharon Bower; *Adjunct Prof* Mark Cohen, BA; *Adjunct Prof* Judith O'Toole, MA; *Adjunct Prof* Michael Stanford, MFA; *Adjunct Prof* Kevin O'Toole, MFA; *Adjunct Prof* Jean Adames, BA
Estab 1947; pvt; D & E; scholarships; SC 20, LC 7; enrl D 170, E 23, non-maj 120, maj 35
Ent Req: HS dipl, SAT
Degrees: BA & BFA 4 yr
Tuition: Undergrad $8950 per yr, $4475 per sem, PT $250 per cr hr; campus res—room & board $3700 per yr
Courses: †Art Education, †Art History, †Ceramics, Drawing, Painting, †Photography, †Printmaking, †Sculpture, Teacher Training, Textile Design, Weaving, †Art Management, †Communication Design, †Fiber Design, Surface Design
Adult Hobby Classes: Courses variable
Summer School: Dir, Dr Paul Adams. Enrl variable; tuition $250 per cr hr for term of 5 - 8 wks beginning June 12. Courses—variable

WILLIAMSPORT

LYCOMING COLLEGE, Art Dept, 17701. Tel 717-321-4000, 321-4002, 321-4240. *Prof* Jon Robert Bogle, MFA; *Prof* Roger Douglas Shipley, MFA; *Chmn Dept Asst Prof* Amy Golahny, PhD; *Asst Prof* Dierdre Monks
Estab 1812; pvt; D & E; scholarships; SC 20, LC 7; enrl College 1200, Dept 500, maj 40
Ent Req: HS dipl, ACT or SAT
Degrees: BA 4 yr, BFA(Sculpture) 4 yrs
Tuition: $12,000 per yr; campus res—room & board $4100 per yr
Courses: †Advertising Design, †Art Education, Art History, Ceramics, Design, Drawing, †Graphic Arts, †Painting, †Photography, †Printmaking, †Sculpture, †Theatre Arts
Summer School: Tuition $460 for 6 wks course. Courses—Photography

PENNSYLVANIA COLLEGE OF TECHNOLOGY, Dept of Design & Communication Arts, 1 College Ave, 17701. Tel 717-326-3761; FAX 717-327-4503. *Prof* Dale Straub, MEd; *Prof* Ralph Horne, EdD; *Assoc Prof* Dale Metzker, AA; *Assoc Prof* Patrick Murphy, MSEd; *Asst Prof* William Ealer, BS; *Asst Prof* Fred Schaefer Jr, AAS; *Asst Prof* Steven Hirsch, MFA; *Instr* Jackie Welliver, CET; *Instr* Joseph Mark, BArch; *Instr* Harold Newton
Estab 1965; pub; D & E; scholarships; enrl D 2903, E 2909
Ent Req: HS dipl, placement test
Degrees: AA 2 yr
Tuition: Res—$156.20 per hr; nonres—$238.60 per hr
Courses: †Advertising Design, Art History, Design, Drawing, Graphic Arts, Graphic Design, Lettering, Mixed Media, Painting, Photography, Technical Illustration

YORK

YORK COLLEGE OF PENNSYLVANIA, Dept of English & Humanities, Country Club Rd, 17405. Tel 717-846-7788. *Chmn Fine Arts* Dr Thomas Hall
Estab 1941; pvt; D & E; SC 17, LC 7
Ent Req: HS dipl, SAT or ACT
Degrees: BA 4 yrs and AA 2 yrs
Tuition: $2098 per yr; campus res available
Courses: Art Education, Art History, Commercial Art, Drawing, Painting, Photography, Sculpture
Adult Hobby Classes: Enrl 40; Courses—per regular session
Summer School: Dir, Thomas Michalski. Enrl 15; Term of three weeks beginning May 19 and two 5 week sessions beginning June and July

RHODE ISLAND

BRISTOL

ROGER WILLIAMS COLLEGE, Art Dept, One Old Ferry Rd, 02809. Tel 401-253-1040. *Coordr* Ronald Wilczek; *Instr* Carol J Hathaway; *Instr* Thomas Russell, MFA; *Instr* Kathleen Hancock
Estab 1948; dept estab 1967; pvt; D & E; SC 18, LC 8; enrl D 1800, E 1500, maj 42
Ent Req: HS dipl
Degrees: AA 2 yr, BA 4 yr, apprenticeship and senior teaching
Tuition: Res—$16,290 per yr; nonres—$10,960 per yr; campus res—room & board $3130 per yr
Courses: Architecture, Art History, Drawing, Film, Graphic Design, Painting, Photography, Printmaking, Restoration & Conservation, Sculpture, Teacher Training, Theatre Arts, Weaving, Gallery Mgmt, 2-D & 3-D Design
Summer School: Dean, Bart Schiaro. Courses—Ceramics, Design, Drawing, Painting, Weaving

KINGSTON

UNIVERSITY OF RHODE ISLAND, Dept of Art, Fine Arts Center, 02881. Tel 401-792-2131, 792-5821; FAX 401-792-2729. *Chmn* Ronald J Onorato, PhD; *Prof* William Klenk, PhD; *Prof* William Leete, MFA; *Prof* Bart Parker, MFA; *Prof* Robert H Rohm, MFA; *Prof* Richard Calabro, MFA; *Prof* Marjorie Keller, PhD; *Prof* Wendy Roworth, PhD; *Prof* Wendy Holmes, PhD; *Prof* Gary Richman, MFA; *Asst Prof* Barbara Pagh, MFA; *Asst Prof* Mary Hollinshead. Instrs: Ft 12, PT 6
Estab 1892; pub; D & E; scholarships; SC 21, studio seminars 24, LC 23; enrl D 900, E 30, non-maj 725, maj 200, other 10 - 20
Ent Req: Same as required for Col of Arts & Sciences
Degrees: BA(Studio), BA(Art History) and BFA(Art Studio) 4 yrs
Tuition: Res—undergrad $3643 per yr, $2011 per sem, $1358 PT, $148 per cr hr; nonres—undergrad $9597 per yr, $4983 per sem, $4075 PT, $395 per cr hr; campus res—available
Courses: Aesthetics, Architecture, Art History, Conceptual Art, Drawing, Film, Graphic Arts, History of Art & Archaeology, Painting, Photography, Sculpture, Theatre Arts, Studio Art
Adult Hobby Classes: Art History, Drawing, Painting, Sculpture
Summer School: Chairperson Dept Art, Ronald Onorato, Enrl 45 - 50; tuition in-state—undergrad $121 per cr, out-of-state—undergrad $388 per cr for 5 wk terms beginning May 24 - June 25 & June 28 - July 30. Courses— Art History, Drawing, Photography

NEWPORT

NEWPORT ART MUSEUM SCHOOL, 76 Bellevue Ave, 02840. Tel 401-848-8200; FAX 401-848-8205. *Dir* Richard V West
Estab 1912; D & E; scholarships; SC 25, LC 3; enrl D 300 (total)
Ent Req: None
Degrees: None
Courses: Art History, Ceramics, Collages, Drawing, Jewelry, Painting, Photography, Printmaking, Sculpture, Etching, Multimedia, Pastels
Adult Hobby Classes: Enrl 200; tuition varies; 6, 8 or 10 wk courses
Children's Classes: Enrl 100 per term; tuition varies per 6, 8, or 10 wk session
Summer School: Enrl 160; tuition varies. Courses—Painting, Drawing, Workshops, Children's Multimedia

SALVE REGINA COLLEGE, Art Dept, Ochre Point Ave, 02840. Tel 401-847-6650. *Chmn* Barbara Shamblin, MFA; *Assoc Prof* Sr Arlene Woods, MFA; *Asst Prof* Ralph Bucci, MFA; *Asst Prof* Gabrielle Bleek-Byrne, PhD; *Asst Prof* Daniel Ludwig, MFA
Estab 1947; den; D & E; SC 28, LC 8; enrl D 270 per sem (dept), non-maj 95, maj 72
Ent Req: HS dipl, ent exam
Degrees: BA 4 yr
Tuition: Res—undergrad $3450 per sem, $215 per sem hr, $130 per cr (night), grad $215 per cr
Courses: Aesthetics, Art Appreciation, Art Education, Art History, Calligraphy, Ceramics, Commercial Art, Design, Drawing, Graphic Design, Illustration, Painting, Photography, Printmaking, Sculpture, Teacher Training, Aesthetics, Anatomy, Environmental Design, 2 & 3-D Design
Summer School: Dir, Jay Lacouture

PROVIDENCE

BROWN UNIVERSITY
—Dept History of Art & Architecture, PO Box 1855, 02912. Tel 401-863-1174. Pvt; D; scholarships; LC 13-15, GC 10-12; enrl maj 59, grad 47
Degrees: BA 4 yrs, MA & PhD in Art History
Tuition: Res—undergrad $16,256 per yr, $8178 per sem, $2032 per unit
Courses: Art History, History of Art & Archaeology
Summer School: Dean, Karen Sibley. Courses—limited
—Dept of Visual Art, PO Box 1861, 02912. Tel 401-863-2423; FAX 401-863-1680. *Chmn* Roger Mayer
Pvt; D; SC 19-21, LC 13-15, GC 10-12; enrl maj 140
Degrees: BA 4 yrs
Tuition: $18,015 per yr; room & board $5488
Courses: Drawing, Painting, Printmaking, Sculpture, Papermaking

PROVIDENCE COLLEGE, Art and Art History Dept, River Ave & Eaton St, 02918. Tel 401-865-2401, 865-1000. *Chmn* John DiCicco, MFA Ed; *Assoc Prof* Richard N Elkington, MFA; *Assoc Prof* Adrian G Dabash, MFA; *Assoc Prof* Richard A McAlister, MFA; *Prof* James Baker, MFA; *Assoc Prof* Alice Beckwith, PhD; *Asst Prof* Suzanne II D'Avanzo; *Asst Prof* James Janecek, MFA; *Asst Prof* Dr David Gillerman, PhD; *Asst Prof* Deborah Johnson, PhD; *Slide Librn* Marie Woodard
Estab 1917; dept estab 1969; pvt; D & E; SC 49, LC 8; enrl D 254, E 250, non-maj 209, maj 45
Ent Req: HS dipl, portfolio needed for transfer students
Degrees: BA 4 yr
Tuition: Res & nonres—undergrad $10,935 per yr; campus res—room & board $4700 per yr
Courses: †Art History, †Ceramics, †Drawing, †Painting, †Photography, †Printmaking, †Sculpture
Adult Hobby Classes: Dean, Dr O'Hara. Courses—History of Architecture, Art History, Calligraphy, Ceramics, Drafting, Drawing, Painting, Photography, Sculpture, Studio Art, Watercolor
Summer School: Dir, James M Murphy. Tuition $180 & $50 lab fee for three credit courses beginning mid-June through July. Courses—Art History, Calligraphy, Ceramics, Drawing, Painting, Photography, Printmaking, Soft and Hard Crafts. A summer program is offered at Pietrasanta, Italy: Dir, Richard A McAlister, MFA. Courses—Art History, Languages, Literature, Religious Studies, Studio Art, Drawing, Painting, Sculpture

RHODE ISLAND COLLEGE, Art Dept, 600 Mt Pleasant, 02908. Tel 401-456-8054. *Prof* Ronald M Steinberg, PhD; *Prof* John DeMelim, MFA; *Prof* Curtis K LaFollette, MFA; *Prof* Donald C Smith, MA; *Prof* Krisjohn O Horvat, MFA; *Prof* Lawrence F Sykes, MS; *Prof* David M Hysell, PhD; *Chmn* Samuel B Ames, MFA; *Prof* Harriet Brissan, MFA; *Prof* Ronald M Steinberg, PhD; *Assoc Prof* Mary Ball Howkins, PhD; *Asst Prof* Heemong Kim, MFA; *Asst Prof* Stephen Fisher, MFA
Estab 1854; dept estab 1969; pub; D & E; SC 31, LC 10, GC 5; enrl D 443, E approx 50, non-maj approx 228, maj 357, grad 30
Ent Req: HS dipl, CEEB and SAT
Degrees: BA(Art History), BA & MA(Studio), BS(Art Educ) & BFA(Studio Art) 4

yr, MAT 1 yr
Tuition: Res—$910 plus fees $160, grad $60 per cr; nonres—$3174 plus fees $160, grad $125 per cr; campus res—room & board $1345 - $1396
Courses: †Art Education, †Art History, Ceramics, Drawing, Graphic Design, Painting, Photography, Printmaking, Sculpture, Teacher Training, Metals, Fibers
Adult Hobby Classes: Visual Arts in Society, Drawing, Design, Photography
Children's Classes: Enrl 165; tuition $175 per 20 wks. Courses—Ceramics, Drawing, Life Drawing, Painting, Printmaking
Summer School: Dir, W Swigert. Enrl 150; tuition $75 per cr, nonres—$135 per cr for term of 6 wks beginning June 26th. Courses—Ceramics, Drawing, Painting, Photography, Relief Printing

RHODE ISLAND SCHOOL OF DESIGN, Two College St, 02903. Tel 401-454-6100. *Pres* Thomas F Schutte; *Public Relations* Melinda M Hill
Estab 1877; pvt; endowed; scholarships, grants-in-aid to res, student loans, fels; enrl D 1960
Ent Req: HS grad, SAT, visual work
Degrees: BFA, BArch, BID, BLA, BIntArch, BGD, MFA, MID, MLA, MAE, MAT
Tuition: $14,036
Courses: †Architecture, †Ceramics, †Film, †Graphic Design, †Illustration, †Industrial Design, †Jewelry, †Landscape Architecture, †Painting, †Photography, †Printmaking, †Sculpture, †Teacher Training, †Textile Design, †Apparel Design, †Glass, †Interior Architecture, †Metalsmithing, †Television Studies, †Wood & Furniture Design
Adult Hobby Classes: Enrl 2800; tuition $270 non cr, $310 for 1.5 cr of 13 wks. Courses—Advertising Design, Fine & Applied Arts, Interior Design, Scientific & Technical Illustration
Children's Classes: Enrl 850. Courses—vary
Summer School: Enrl 630; tuition varies. Courses—vary. Summer studies for adults & pre-college students

WARWICK

COMMUNITY COLLEGE OF RHODE ISLAND, Dept of Art, 400 East Ave, 02886. Tel 401-825-2220; FAX 401-825-2365. *Chmn* Donald Gray; *Instr* R Clark; *Instr* T Aitken; *Instr* R Judge; *Instr* F Robertson; *Instr* M Kelman; *Instr* C Smith; *Instr* S Hunnibell; *Instr* T Morrissey. Instrs: FT 10, PT 15
Estab 1964; pub; D & E; scholarships; SC 16, LC 3, seminar 1; enrl D 4600
Ent Req: HS dipl, ent exam, equivalency exam
Degrees: AA, AFA, AS & AAS 2 yr
Tuition: Res—$600 per sem
Courses: Ceramics, Commercial Art, Drawing, Graphic Arts, Graphic Design, Handicrafts, History of Art & Archaeology, Interior Design, Painting, Photography, Sculpture

SOUTH CAROLINA

AIKEN

UNIVERSITY OF SOUTH CAROLINA AT AIKEN, Dept of Fine Arts, 171 University Parkway, 29801. Tel 803-648-6851. *Head Dept* Al Beyer
Estab 1961, dept estab 1985; pub; D & E; SC 31, LC 6; enrl D 180, E 60
Ent Req: HS dipl, GED, SAT
Tuition: $850 per sem
Courses: Advertising Design, Art Education, Art History, Ceramics, Commercial Art, Drawing, Graphic Arts, Graphic Design, History of Art & Archaeology, Illustration, Painting, Photography, Sculpture, Theatre Arts
Adult Hobby Classes: Tuition $850 per sem. Courses—vary
Summer School: Dir, Al Beyer. Tuition $75 per hr. Courses—vary

CHARLESTON

CHARLESTON SOUTHERN UNIVERSITY (Formerly Baptist College at Charleston), Dept of Language & Visual Art, PO Box 10087, 29411. Tel 803-797-4226. *Chmn* Dr Harold Overton
Estab 1960; den; D & E; scholarships; SC 14, LC 2; enrl D 80, E 71, maj 15
Ent Req: GED or HS dipl
Degrees: BA and BS 4 yrs
Tuition: $1975 per sem; campus res available
Courses: Art Education, Ceramics, Drawing, Graphic Arts, History of Art & Archaeology, Painting, Sculpture, Teacher Training
Summer School: Enrl 1500; tui $45 per sem hr; campus res—room and board $240 per sem; two 5 wk sessions beginning June. Courses—same as regular session

COLLEGE OF CHARLESTON, School of the Arts, 29424. Tel 803-792-5600. *Dean* Edward McQuire; *Chmn Music Dept* Steve Rosenberg; *Chmn Theatre Dept* Allen Lyndrup; *Chmn Studio Art* Michael Tyzack; *Chmn Art History* Diane Johnson
Estab 1966; pub; D & E; SC 36, LC 24
Ent Req: HS dipl
Degrees: BA(Fine Arts) 4 yrs
Tuition: Res—$1470 per yr; nonres—$2670 per yr
Courses: Art History, Drawing, †Painting, †Sculpture, †Stage Design, †Theatre Arts

GIBBES MUSEUM SCHOOL, Gibbes Museum Studio, 76 Queen St, 29401. Tel 803-577-7275. *Studio Admin* Jean Smith. Instrs: PT 20
Estab 1969; pub; D & E; scholarships; SC 18; enrl D 150, E 150
Ent Req: None
Tuition: $55 per course, materials fee $10
Courses: Calligraphy, Drawing, Graphic Design, Handicrafts, Interior Design, Photography, Printmaking, Sculpture, Weaving, Air Brush, Book Binding, Pottery
Children's Classes: Enrl 15 per course; tuition $37 per course per sem. Courses—Mixed Media (ages 4-7)
Summer School: Dir, Valerie Miller. Courses—same as regular session

CLEMSON

CLEMSON UNIVERSITY, College of Architecture, Lee Hall, 29634-0509. Tel 803-656-3881. *Head Dept* John Acorn
Estab 1967; pub; D; GC 24, SC 40, LC 29 (undergrad courses for service to pre-architecture and other Univ requirements); enrl approx 1500 annually, grad maj 10
Ent Req: Available on request
Degrees: MFA 60 hrs
Tuition: Res—$1200 per sem
Courses: Architecture, Art History, Ceramics, Drawing, Painting, Photography, Printmaking, Sculpture

CLINTON

PRESBYTERIAN COLLEGE, Fine Arts Dept, Broad St, 29325. Tel 803-833-2820, Ext 8295. *Chmn* D O Raines; *Prof* C T Gaines; *Prof* Mark Anderson
Estab 1880, Dept estab 1966; den; D & E; scholarships; SC 8, LC 5; enrl D 200, non-maj 190, maj 10
Ent Req: HS dipl with C average, SAT
Degrees: BA & BS 4 yr
Tuition: $8000 annual tuition; campus res—available
Courses: Art Education, Art History, Drawing, Painting
Summer School: Dean, J W Moncrief. Enrl 150; tuition $120 per sem. Courses—Art Appreciation, Painting

COLUMBIA

BENEDICT COLLEGE, Art Department, Harden & Blanding Sts, 29204. Tel 803-253-5290; FAX 803-253-5065. *Chmn Humanities Div* Lynne De Bauche
Estab 1870; pvt; D; scholarships; SC 11, LC 6
Ent Req: HS dipl
Degrees: BA(Teaching of Art), BA(Commercial Art)
Courses: Commercial Art, Teacher Training
Summer School: Term of two 5 wk sessions beginning June. Courses—Art Appreciation, Arts & Crafts

COLUMBIA COLLEGE, Dept of Art, 1301 Columbia College Dr, 29203. Tel 803-786-3012; FAX 803-786-3647. *Chmn* Steve Nevitt
Scholarships
Degrees: BA, cert
Tuition: $7950 per yr
Courses: Advertising Design, Art Appreciation, Art History, Ceramics, Design, Drawing, Painting, Photography, Printmaking, Crafts, 3-D Design
Adult Hobby Classes: Enrl 20 per class. Courses—Art Appreciation, Art History, Drawing, Photography
Summer School: Dir, Becky Hulion. Enrl 20 per class. Courses—Art Appreciation, Art History, Art Education, Drawing, Photography, Printmaking

COLUMBIA MUSEUM SCHOOL, 1112 Bull St, 29201. Tel 803-799-2810; FAX 803-343-2150. *Executive Dir* Sal Cilella
Estab 1950 (operates as service of the Columbia Museum of Art); D & E
Ent Req: None; classes for youths and adults
Tuition: Varies according to courses
Courses: Calligraphy, Ceramics, Drawing, Graphic Design, Painting, Acrylic, Egg Tempera, Portraiture, Pottery, Stained Glass
Adult Hobby Classes: Enrl 250; tuition $65 for 10 wk term. Courses—Acrylic, Calligraphy, Ceramics, Oils, Pottery, Stained Glass, Watercolor
Children's Classes: Enrl 250; tuition $40 for 13 wks. Courses—Multi-media
Summer School: Dir, Judy Kennedy. Enrl 200; tuition $40 for four 2 wk sessions. Courses—Batik, Collage, Collograph, Papermaking, Sculpting, Tye Dyeing

UNIVERSITY OF SOUTH CAROLINA, Dept of Art, Sloan College, 29208. Tel 803-777-4236. *Chmn* John O'Neil, PhD; *Chmn Studio* Jim Edwards, MFA; *Chmn Art Educ* Cynthia Colbert, EdD; *Chmn Art History* Brad Collins, PhD; *Prof* Philip Mullen, PhD; *Prof* Howard Woody, MA
Estab 1801, dept estab 1924; pub; D & E; scholarships; SC 89, LC 57, GC 73; enrl D 1620, E 174, non-maj 1000, maj 620, grad 82
Ent Req: HS dipl
Degrees: BA, BFA and BS 4 yrs, MA and MAT 1 yr, MFA 2 yrs
Tuition: Res—undergrad $3810 pr yr; $1905 per sem, PT $127 per cr, grad $4230 per yr, $2115 per sem, PT $127 per cr; nonres—undergrad $9240 per sem, PT undergrad $308 per cr, grad $282; Campus res—room $1800 per yr
Courses: †Advertising Design, †Art Education, †Art History, †Ceramics, †Commercial Art, †Drawing, †Graphic Arts, †Graphic Design, Illustration, †Interior Design, Jewelry, Museum Staff Training, Painting, Photography, Printmaking, Restoration & Conservation
Adult Hobby Classes: Enrl 125; tuition $127 per hr for 16 wk term. Courses—Art for Elementary School, Basic Drawing, Ceramics, Fiber Arts, Fundamentals of Art, Interior Design, Intro to Art
Children's Classes: Enrl 100; tuition $30 for 9 wk term. Courses—Children's Art
Summer School: Dir, John O'Neil. Enrl 400; tuition undergrad $127 per hr, grad $141 per hr. Courses—Same as academic yr

FLORENCE

FRANCIS MARION UNIVERSITY, Fine Arts Dept, PO Box 100547, 29501-0547. Tel 803-661-1385; FAX 803-661-1219. *Chmn* Dennis C Sanderson
Scholarships offered
Degrees: BA
Tuition: Res—$1800 per yr; nonres—$3600 per yr
Courses: Art Appreciation, †Art Education, Art History, †Ceramics, Costume Design & Construction, Design, Drafting, Drawing, Film, †Painting, †Photography, Sculpture, †Stage Design, †Theatre Arts, Video
Summer School: Dir, Dennis Sanderson. Enrl 50; 6 wk term. Courses—Art Appreciation, Art Education, Photography

GAFFNEY

LIMESTONE COLLEGE, Art Dept, Division of Fine Arts, 29340. Tel 803-489-7151. *Chmn* Dr Joe Parker
Estab 1845; pvt; D & E; scholarships; SC 19, LC 9; enrl D 112, maj 42, others 3
Ent Req: HS dipl, ent exam
Degrees: BS(Educ, Studio) 4 yrs
Courses: Silk-Screen, Wood-Block

GREENVILLE

BOB JONES UNIVERSITY, School of Fine Arts, 29614. Tel 803-242-5011, Ext 2700. *Dean* Dwight Gustafson, DMus; *Chmn Division of Art* Emery Bopp, MFA; *Instr* David Appleman, MA; *Instr* Kathy Bell, MA; *Instr* Carl Blair, MFA; *Instr* James Brooks, BA; *Instr* Karen Brinson, BA; *Instr* Darrel Koons, MA; *Instr* Harrell Whittington, MA; *Instr* Michael Slattery
Estab 1927, dept estab 1945; pvt; D; scholarships; SC 29, LC 12, GC 10; enrl M 59, W 57
Ent Req: HS dipl, letters of recommendation
Degrees: BA & BS 4 yrs, MA 1-2 yrs
Tuition: $3780 per yr, $1890 per sem; campus res—room & board $3420 per yr
Courses: Aesthetics, Art Education, Art History, Calligraphy, Ceramics, Costume Design & Construction, †Graphic Design, Photography, Printmaking, Restoration & Conservation, Sculpture, Stage Design, †Teacher Training

FURMAN UNIVERSITY, Dept of Art, 29613. Tel 803-294-2074. *Chmn* Dr R O Sorensen
Estab 1826; pvt den; D & E; scholarships; SC 21, LC 8; enrl D 245, non-maj 205, maj 40
Ent Req: HS dipl, SAT
Degrees: BA 4 yr
Courses: Advertising Design, Aesthetics, Art Education, Art History, Calligraphy, Ceramics, Drawing, Graphic Design, Handicrafts, History of Art & Archaeology, Lettering, Painting, Printmaking, Sculpture, Teacher Training

GREENVILLE COUNTY MUSEUM OF ART, Museum School of Art, 420 College St, 29601. Tel 803-271-7570; FAX 803-271-7579. *Coordr* Robert A Strother. *Instrs* PT 35
Estab 1960; pub; D & E; scholarships; SC 12, LC 2, GC 6; enrl D 250, E 170
Degrees: AAA and AFA 2-3 yr
Tuition: $50 regis fee, cost on per class basis
Courses: †Advertising Design, Art History, †Drawing, †Painting, †Photography, †Printmaking, Sculpture, Museology, Philosophy of Art, †Pottery, Weaving
Adult Hobby Classes: Classes offered each semester
Children's Classes: Enrl 15 per course, ages 4 - 16. Courses—Clay, Drawing, Mixed Media, Painting
Summer School: Enrl approx 300 per sem; 5 or 8 wk term. Courses—same as regular sem

GREENVILLE TECHNICAL COLLEGE, Art History Dept, Station B, PO Box 5616, 29606. Tel 803-250-8197. *Acad Dean Educ* Dr Edward Opper
Degrees: AA
Tuition: $185
Courses: Art Appreciation, Art History, Film
Adult Hobby Classes: Courses offered
Summer School: Dir, Dr David S Trask. Enrl 35. Courses—Art Appreciation

GREENWOOD

LANDER UNIVERSITY, Dept of Art, Stanley Ave, 29649. Tel 803-229-8323. *Chmn* Alan MacTaggart. *Instrs:* FT 5, PT 3
Estab 1872; pub; D & E; scholarships; SC 25, LC 5; enrl D 250, E 60, maj 91
Ent Req: HS dipl
Degrees: BA(Art) 4 yrs
Tuition: $1200 per yr; nonres—$1700 per yr; campus res—$1300 - $1500
Courses: Advertising Design, Aesthetics, Art Education, Ceramics, Commercial Art, Drawing, Graphic Arts, Graphic Design, History of Art & Archaeology, Illustration, Painting, Photography, Sculpture, Teacher Training
Adult Hobby Classes: Ceramics, Enameling
Children's Classes: General Studio Skills
Summer School: Art Appreciation, Art Education, Ceramics, Photography, Printmaking

HARTSVILLE

COKER COLLEGE, Art Dept, 29550. Tel 803-383-8150. *Chmn* J Kim Chalmers. *Instrs:* FT 3
Estab 1908; pvt; D & E; scholarships; SC 26, LC 9; enrl 416, art maj 25
Ent Req: HS dipl, ent exam
Degrees: AB and BS 4 yrs
Tuition: $8736 per yr; campus res—room & board $4076 per yr
Courses: Art Appreciation, Art Education, Art History, Ceramics, Design, Drawing, Graphic Design, Illustration, Painting, Photography, Printmaking, Sculpture
Summer School: Tuition $100 per sem hr for 8 wk term. Courses—Introduction level art

NEWBERRY

NEWBERRY COLLEGE, Dept of Art, 2100 College St, 29108. Tel 803-276-5010. *Head Dept* Bruce Nell-Smith
Estab 1856, dept estab 1973; den; D & E; SC 35, LC 2; enrl D 114, non-maj 106, maj 15
Ent Req: HS dipl, SAT
Degrees: AB(Art) 4 yrs, BS(Arts Mgt), two courses in independent study, financial aid available
Courses: Art History, Drawing, Mixed Media, Painting, Printmaking, Stage Design, Theatre Arts

ORANGEBURG

CLAFLIN COLLEGE, Dept of Art, 400 College Ave, 29115. Tel 803-534-2710. *Chmn* Dr Kod Igwe; *Assoc Prof* Donna Bratcher; *Instr* Dan Smith
School estab 1869, dept estab 1888; pvt; D; scholarships; SC 10, LC 2; enrl D 20
Ent Req: HS dipl, SAT
Degrees: BA 4 years, BA Teacher Educ 4 years
Tuition: Res—undergrad $6510 including room & board; nonres—$4230
Courses: †Advertising Design, †Art Education, Ceramics, Drawing, Film, Graphic Arts, Lettering, Painting, Photography, Printmaking, Sculpture, Theatre Arts, Video, Afro-American Art History, Advanced Studio
Summer School: Dir, Karen Woodfaulk. Enrl 10-12, 6 wk term beginning June. Courses—Art Appreciation, Art-Elem School Crafts, Advertising Art, Textile Design

SOUTH CAROLINA STATE UNIVERSITY, Art Dept, 200 College St NE, 29117. Tel 803-536-7174, 8119. *Chmn* Leo F Twiggs, EdD; *Assoc Prof* Henry G Michaux, EdD; *Asst Prof* James L McFadden, MA; *Instr* Terry K Hunter, MFA, PhD; *Cur Colls & Exhib* Frank Martin, II
Dept estab 1972; D & E; SC 15, LC 7; enrl D 73, nonmaj 8, maj 73
Ent Req: HS dipl
Degrees: BA & BS 4 yrs, MA & MS approx 2 yrs
Tuition: Res—$975 per sem, nonres—$1500 per sem; campus res available
Courses: Art Education, Printmaking
Adult Hobby Classes: Courses—Ceramics, Sculpture
Summer School: Dir, Dr Leroy Davis. Tuition $90 per cr hr. Courses—Art Appreciation, Arts & Crafts for Children

ROCK HILL

WINTHROP COLLEGE, Dept of Art & Design, 29733. Tel 803-323-2126. *Chmn & Prof* Alfred Ward; *Asst Chmn & Prof* Curt Sherman; *Prof* E Wade Hobgood, MFA; *Prof* Mary Mintich, MFA; *Prof* John Olvera; *Prof* David Freeman; *Prof* Jean McFarland; *Assoc Prof* Alan Huston; *Assoc Prof* Paul Martyka, MFA; *Asst Prof* Jim Connell; *Asst Prof* Quentin Currie; *Asst Prof* Laura Dufresne; *Asst Prof* Jean Edwards; *Asst Prof* Charles Harmon; *Asst Prof* Carol Ivory; *Asst Prof* Margaret Johnson; *Asst Prof* Lynn Smith; *Asst Prof* David Stokes; *Asst Prof* Dr Eli Bentor; *Asst Prof* Dr Peg Delamater
Estab 1886; pub; D & E; SC 42, LC 10; enrl in college D 4983, non-maj 360, maj 147, grad 6
Ent Req: HS dipl, SAT, CEEB
Degrees: BA and BFA 4 yrs
Tuition: Res—undergrad $2568 per yr, $1284 per sem, grad $1284; nonres—undergrad $4612 per yr, $2306 per sem, grad $2306 campus res—available
Courses: †Advertising Design, †Art Education, Art History, Calligraphy, †Ceramics, Collages, †Commercial Art, Conceptual Art, †Drawing, Fashion Arts, †Graphic Arts, †Graphic Design, Handicrafts, †Illustration, †Interior Design, †Jewelry, Lettering, Mixed Media, †Painting, †Photography, Art Appreciation, Design, Display, Drafting, History of Art & Archaeology, Industrial Design, Museum Staff Training, Printmaking, Sculpture, Silversmithing, Teacher Training, Textile Design, Weaving
Summer School: Dir, Wade Hobgood. Enrl 120. Courses—Art Appreciation, Art for Classroom Teacher, Creative Art for Children, Drawing, Painting, Photography

SPARTANBURG

ART ASSOCIATION SCHOOL, 385 S Spring St, 29306. Tel 803-582-7616. *Dir* Bert Howard
Estab 1970; D & E; SC 25; enrl 300-400
Ent Req: None
Tuition: $75 - $90 for 10 wks
Courses: Calligraphy, Commercial Art, Drawing, Interior Design, Mixed Media, Painting, Photography, Sculpture, Weaving, Pottery, Stained Glass
Children's Classes: Tuition $60 for 8 - 10 wk term. Courses—Drawing, Painting, Pottery

CONVERSE COLLEGE, Art Dept, PO Box 29, 29302. Tel 803-569-9180, 596-9178, 596-9181. *Chmn Dept* Teresa Prater; *Assoc Prof* Mayo McBoggs, MFA; *Assoc Prof* Judy Voss Jones, MFA; *Assoc Prof* Fraz Pajak, MA Arch; *Asst Prof* David Zacharias, MFA; *Asst Prof* Donn Britt Ping; *Asst Prof* Dr Suzanne Schuweiler-Daab; *Vis Asst Prof* Douglas White
Col estab 1889; pvt; D; scholarships; SC 40, LC 17; enrl D 290, non-maj 240, maj 90, others 12, double major available
Ent Req: HS dipl, SAT, CEEB, ACT, Advanced placement in Art & Art History
Degrees: BA & BFA 4 yrs
Tuition: $9600 incl room & board
Courses: Art Education, †Art History, Ceramics, †Drawing, Film, †Interior Design, Museum Staff Training, †Painting, Photography, †Printmaking, †Sculpture, Teacher Training
Adult Hobby Classes: Adult classes; tuition reduced for women over 25. Courses—all areas
Summer School: Dir, Joe Dunn

SOUTH DAKOTA

ABERDEEN

NORTHERN STATE UNIVERSITY, Art Dept, 57401. Tel 605-622-2514. *Chmn* Mark Shekore, MFA; *Prof* Jim Gibson, MFA; *Prof* Mark McGinnis, MFA; *Asst Prof* Carlene Roters, PhD; *Assoc Prof* Bill Hoar, PhD; *Asst Prof* Lynn Carlsgaard, MA. *Instrs:* Estab 1901, dept estab 1920
Pub; D & E; scholarships; SC 40, LC 14, GC 6; enrl D 385, non-maj 300, maj 85

Ent Req: HS dipl
Degrees: AA 2 yrs, BA, BS, BSEd 4 yrs
Tuition: Res—undergrad $38.05 per cr, grad $57.35 per cr; nonres—undergrad $80.50 per cr, grad $105.85 per cr; campus res—room $477 per sem
Courses: Advertising Design, †Art Education, Art History, †Ceramics, †Commercial Art, †Drawing, Illustration, Mixed Media, Painting, Photography, Printmaking, Sculpture, Teacher Training, Video, Computer Graphics, Fiber Arts
Adult Hobby Classes: Enrl 30; tuition $34.50 per cr
Summer School: Dir, Mark Shekore. Enrl 35; $38.05 Per cr for term of 4 wks beginning June 4

BROOKINGS

SOUTH DAKOTA STATE UNIVERSITY, Dept of Visual Arts, PO Box 2223, 57007. Tel 605-688-4103; FAX 605-688-5014. *Head Dept* Norman Gambill, PhD; *Prof* Helen Morgan; *Prof* Joseph Stuart, MA; *Prof* Signey Stuart, MA; *Assoc Prof* Melvin Spinar, MFA; *Assoc Prof* Gerald Kruse, MFA; *Assoc Prof* Tim Steele, MFA; *Asst Prof* John J Miller; *Asst Prof* Jeannie French
Estab 1881; pub; D & E; scholarships; SC 26, LC 10
Ent Req: HS dipl, ent ACT
Degrees: BA & BS 128 sem cr
Tuition: Res—$39.20 per cr hr; nonres—$89.30 per cr hr; tuition reciprocity agreements with Minnesota & Wyoming residents, in- state tuition with Minnesota only
Courses: Art Education, Calligraphy, Ceramics, Design, Drawing, Graphic Design, Intermedia, Museum Staff Training, †Painting, †Printmaking, †Sculpture, Textile Design, Weaving, General Art, History of Art & Design
Summer School: Head Dept, Norman Gambill. Regular tuition per cr hr.
Courses—Design, Drawing

HURON

HURON UNIVERSITY, Arts & Sciences Division, 333 Ninth St SW, 57350. Tel 605-352-8721. *Head Div* Dr Alice Frantz
Pvt; scholarships; enrl 510
Ent Req: HS dipl or GED
Degrees: BA and BS 4 yrs
Tuition: $5775 per yr
Courses: Art Appreciation, Manual & Public School Art

MADISON

DAKOTA STATE UNIVERSITY, College of Liberal Arts, 57042. Tel 605-256-5270. *Dean* Eric Johnson. Instrs: FT 1, PT 1
Estab 1881; pub; D; scholarships; SC 16, LC 5; enrl D 120, maj 20
Ent Req: HS dipl, ACT
Degrees: BS 4 yrs
Tuition: Res—undergrad $1502 per yr
Courses: Art Education, Art History, Ceramics, Drawing, Jewelry, Painting, Sculpture, Teacher Training
Summer School: Term of 8 wks beginning June

SIOUX FALLS

AUGUSTANA COLLEGE, Art Dept, 57197. Tel 605-336-5516. *Chmn* Carl A Grupp, MFA; *Asst Prof* Steve Thomas, MFA; *Asst Prof* Tom Shields, MFA; *Asst Prof* Adrien Happus, PhD; *Asst Prof* Robert Aldern, BFA; *Asst Prof* Endre Gastony, PhD; *Instr* Gerry Punt, BA
Estab 1860; den; D & E; scholarships; SC 14, LC 3; enrl total 1861
Ent Req: HS dipl, ent exam
Degrees: BA and MAT
Tuition: $8640 annual tuition; campus res available
Courses: †Architecture, †Art Education, †Drawing, †Graphic Design, History of Art & Archaeology, Museum Staff Training, †Painting, †Sculpture, Etching, Lithography
Summer School: Dir, Dr Gary D Olson. Term of 7 wks beginning June.
Courses—Arts, Crafts, Drawing

SIOUX FALLS COLLEGE, Dept of Art, Division of Fine Arts/Music, 1501 S Prairie Ave, 57105-1649. Tel 605-331-6671. *Chmn* David Thye
Estab 1883; pub; scholarships; SC, LC; enrl 1000
Degrees: BA with maj in Art or Art Educ 4 yrs
Tuition: $6900 per yr
Courses: Art Education, Art History, Ceramics, Drawing, Handicrafts, Painting, Photography, Printmaking, Sculpture, Design & Illustration
Summer School: Terms one 3 wk session, two 4 wk sessions. Courses—Crafts, Design, Drawing, Education

SPEARFISH

BLACK HILLS STATE UNIVERSITY, Art Dept, 57799. Tel 605-642-6011, 642-6420. Instrs: FT 13
Estab 1883; pub; D; scholarships; SC 15, LC 4; enrl maj 50
Ent Req: HS dipl, transcripts, ACT, physical exam
Degrees: BA 4 yrs
Tuition: Res—$38.05 per cr hr; nonres—$80.05 per cr hr
Courses: Art Education, Calligraphy, Ceramics, Commercial Art, Drafting, Drawing, Painting, Photography, Sculpture
Summer School: Courses—Art in our Lives, Ceramics, Drawing, Painting, School Arts & Crafts

VERMILLION

UNIVERSITY OF SOUTH DAKOTA, Dept of Art, 414 Clark St, 57069. Tel 605-677-5636. *Dean* John A Day, MFA; *Chmn* Dennis Navrat, MFA; *Prof* Daniel Packard, MFA; *Prof* Kenneth Grizzell, MFA; *Prof* Lloyd Menard, MFA; *Assoc Prof* William Wold, MA; *Assoc Prof* Martin Wanserski, MFA; *Assoc Prof* Jeff Freeman, MFA; *Assoc Prof* John Banasiak, MFA; *Asst Prof* Ann Balakier, PhD
Estab 1862, dept estab 1931; pub; D & E; scholarships; SC 32, LC 9, GC 9; enrl non-maj 200, maj 100, grad 10
Ent Req: HS dipl, ACT
Degrees: BFA, BS, BFA with Teacher Cert, MFA
Tuition: Res—undergrad $37.30 per cr hr, grad $55.65 per cr hr; nonres—undergrad $85.05 per cr hr, grad $109.20 per cr hr; campus res—room & board $1948
Courses: Aesthetics, †Art Education, Calligraphy, †Ceramics, Drawing, †Graphic Arts, Graphic Design, History of Art & Archaeology, Museum Staff Training, †Painting, †Photography, †Printmaking, †Sculpture, Weaving
Summer School: Chmn, Dennis Navrat. Tuition $37.30 per cr hr for term of 8 wks. Courses—Drawing, Graphics, Painting, Sculpture

YANKTON

MOUNT MARTY COLLEGE, Art Dept, 1105 W Eighth, 57078. Tel 605-668-1011, 668-1574. *Dept Head* David Kahle; *Lectr* Sr Kathleen Courtney, MA; *Lectr* Virgil Petrik
Estab 1936; den; D; SC 17, LC 5; enrl 9
Ent Req: HS dipl
Degrees: BA 4 yrs, MA(Anesthesia)
Tuition: $4950 two sem & interim; $195 per cr hr; campus res available
Courses: Art Appreciation, Calligraphy, Ceramics, Collages, Design, Drawing, Handicrafts, Mixed Media, Printmaking, Teacher Training, 2-D & 3-D Design
Adult Hobby Classes: Enrl 146. Courses—Art Appreciation, Calligraphy, Ceramics, Crafts, Design, Painting & Drawing, Photography, Printmaking
Summer School: Dir, Sr Pierre Roberts. Tuition $100 per cr hr for term of 4 wks beginning June and July

TENNESSEE

CHATTANOOGA

CHATTANOOGA STATE TECHNICAL COMMUNITY COLLEGE, Advertising Arts Dept, 4501 Amnicola Hwy, 37406. Tel 615-697-4400, 697-4441. *Dir Fine Arts* Denise Frank; *Instr* Ralph Sanders; *Instr* Alan Wallace
Pub; D & E; scholarships; SC 30, LC 5; enrl D 3000, E 2000
Ent Req: HS dipl
Degrees: Certificate, AA(Advertising Art)
Tuition: Res—$420 per sem; nonres—$1635 per sem
Courses: Advertising Design, Art Education, Art History, Ceramics, Commercial Art, Display, Drafting, Drawing, Graphic Arts, Graphic Design, Illustration, Lettering, Painting, Photography, Printmaking, Sculpture, Teacher Training, Advertising Concepts, Air Brush, Internships, Production Art, Typography
Adult Hobby Classes: Tuition $45 per course. Courses—Painting, Photography
Children's Classes: Tuition $20 per course. Courses—Arts & Crafts, Ceramics & Sculpture
Summer School: Tuition $140 per term of 10 wks

UNIVERSITY OF TENNESSEE AT CHATTANOOGA, Dept of Art, 615 McCallie Ave, 37403. Tel 615-755-4178. *Head* E Alan White; *Assoc Prof* Anne Lindsey, MFA; *Assoc Prof* Bruce Wallace, MFA; *Assoc Prof* Maggie McMahon, MFA; *Asst Prof* Stephen S LeWinter, MA; *Asst Prof* Gavin Townsend, PhD; *Asst Prof* Jeffrey Morin, MFA; *Asst Prof* Barry Roseman, MFA
Estab 1886; pub; D & E; SC 11, LC 13, GC 1; enrl D 420, E 80, non-maj 500, maj 130, grad 6, others 14
Ent Req: HS dipl, ACT or SAT, health exam
Degrees: BA and BFA 4 yrs
Tuition: Res—undergrad $746 per sem, grad $974 per sem; nonres—undergrad $2428 per sem, grad $2656 per sem; campus res—room available
Courses: Art Education, Art History, Ceramics, Commercial Art, Drawing, Graphic Design, Painting, Printmaking, Sculpture
Summer School: Tuition $72 per sem hr

CLARKSVILLE

AUSTIN PEAY STATE UNIVERSITY, Dept of Art, PO Box 4677, 37044. Tel 615-648-7333. *Chmn* Max Hochstetler; *Prof* Charles Young, EdD; *Prof* James T Diehr; *Assoc Prof* Bruce Childs, MFA; *Assoc Prof* Susan Bryant, MFA; *Asst Prof* W Renkl; *Asst Prof* Bettye Holte; *Asst Prof* Gregg Schlanger, MFA; *Asst Prof* Dixie Webb, PhD
Estab 1927, dept estab 1930; pub; D & E; scholarships; GC 3; enrl D 740, E 75, non-maj 590, maj 150
Ent Req: HS dipl
Degrees: BFA, BA & BS 4 yrs
Tuition: Res—undergrad $761 per sem; nonres—$2363 per sem; campus residence available
Courses: †Art Education, Art History, †Ceramics, Drawing, †Graphic Design, Illustration, Lettering, †Painting, †Photography, †Printmaking, †Sculpture
Adult Hobby Classes: Enrol 15; tuition $332. Courses--Photography, Printmaking, Ceramics, Drawing, Painting
Summer School: Dir Max Hochstetler. Enrol 150; tuition $761 for 5 wks. Courses—Art Appreciation, Art Education, Sculpture

CLEVELAND

CLEVELAND STATE COMMUNITY COLLEGE, Dept of Art, Adkisson Dr, PO Box 3570, 37320-3570. Tel 615-472-7141; WATS 800-826-0023. *Assoc Prof* Jere Chumley, MA
Estab 1967; pub; D & E; scholarships; SC 6, LC 5; enrl D 95, E 20, non-maj 60, maj 35
Ent Req: HS dipl or GED
Degrees: AA and AS 2 yrs
Tuition: Res—$420 per sem; nonres—$1635 per sem
Courses: Advertising Design, Art Appreciation, Art Education, Art History, Ceramics, Design, Drawing, Painting, Sculpture, Art Appreciation, Design

LEE COLLEGE, Dept of Music & Fine Arts, 1120 N Ocoee St, 37311. Tel 615-472-2111; FAX 615-478-7041. *Chmn* Lonnie McCalister
Tuition: Res—$1850 per sem
Courses: Art Appreciation

COLLEGEDALE

SOUTHERN COLLEGE OF SEVENTH-DAY ADVENTISTS, Art Dept, PO Box 370, 37315. Tel 615-238-2732. *Chmn* Robert F Garren
Estab 1969; den; D & E; LC 4; enrl maj 12
Ent Req: HS dipl, ent exam
Degrees: BA(Art) and BA(Art Educ) 4 yrs
Tuition: $6650 per yr

COLUMBIA

COLUMBIA STATE COMMUNITY COLLEGE, Dept of Art, 412 Hwy W, PO Box 1315, 38401. Tel 615-388-0120. *Head Dept* Fred Behrens, MFA
Estab 1966; pub; D & E; scholarships; SC 17, LC 4; enrl D 230, non-maj 215, maj 12-15
Ent Req: Open door institution
Degrees: AA & AS 2 yrs
Tuition: Res—$420 per sem; nonres—$1600 per sem
Courses: Art History, Design, Drawing, Film, Painting, Photography, Printmaking, †Art Studio, Visual Arts
Children's Classes: Enrl 18-20, tuition $30 per session

GATLINBURG

ARROWMONT SCHOOL OF ARTS AND CRAFTS, 556 Parkway, PO Box 567, 37738. Tel 615-436-5860. *Dir* Sandra J Blain; *Asst Dir* Bill Griffith
Estab 1945; pvt; D & E (operate mostly in spring & summer with special programs for fall & winter); scholarships; SC 44-50, GC 30; enrl D 1000
Degrees: None granted, though credit is offered for courses through the Univ of Tennessee, Knoxville
Tuition: $185 per wk, 1 & 2 wk sessions; campus res—room & board $135-$225 per wk
Courses: Ceramics, Drawing, Weaving, Jewelry, Painting, Photography, Textile Design, Basketry, Bookbinding, Enamel, Papermaking, Quilting Stained Glass, Woodturning

GOODLETTSVILLE

NOSSI SCHOOL OF ART, 907 2 Mile Parkway E6, 37072. Tel 615-851-1088. *Exec Dir* Nossi Vatandoost, BA; *Instr* William H Nussle, BA
Priv; D & E; SC 1, LC 4
Ent Req: HS dipl or GED
Degrees: Dipl in Fine Arts 2 yr; Dipl in Commercial Art 3 yr; degrees Dipl in Fashion Merchandising 2 yr
Tuition: $3000 per yr
Courses: Advertising Design, Architecture, Art Appreciation, Art Education, Art History, Calligraphy, Collages, Conceptual Art, Design, Display, Drawing, Graphic Arts, Graphic Design, Illustration, Mixed Media, Textile Design, Interior Design, Lettering, Painting, Photography, History of Art & Archaeology
Adult Hobby Classes: Enrl 120; tuition $3600 per yr. Courses—Commercial Art (3 yrs), Fashion Merchandising (2 yrs), Fine Arts (2 yrs)
Summer School: Dir, Nossi Vantandoost, BA. Enrol 40; $1200 tuition for 12 wks sem. Courses—Airbrush, Drawing, Painting, Photography, Watercolor

GREENEVILLE

TUSCULUM COLLEGE, Fine Arts Dept, Division of Arts & Humanities, PO Box 5084, 37743. Tel 615-636-7300. *Div Head* Clement Allison, MFA
Estab 1794; den; D; scholarships; SC 25, LC 3; enrl D 445, maj 18
Ent Req: HS dipl
Degrees: BA and BS 4 yrs
Tuition: $8000 per yr
Courses: Art Education, Ceramics, Design, Drawing, History of Art & Archaeology, Painting, Printmaking, Sculpture, 2-D & 3-D Design
Adult Hobby Classes: Enrl 14. Courses—Painting

HARROGATE

LINCOLN MEMORIAL UNIVERSITY, Division of Humanities, Kimberland Gap Parkway, PO Box 670, 37752. Tel 615-869-3611. *Chmn Humanities* Dr David McDonald; *Assoc Prof Art* Bebe DeBord; *Instr* Alex Buckland
Estab 1897; dept estab 1974; pvt; D & E; SC 30, LC 3; enrl D 120, E 75, non-maj 97, maj 98
Ent Req: HS dipl

Degrees: BA 4 yrs
Tuition: Res—$2125 per sem; campus res—room & board $1175
Courses: Aesthetics, Art Education, Art History, Ceramics, Commercial Art, Drawing, Film, Goldsmithing, †Graphic Arts, Jewelry, Lettering, Museum Staff Training, †Painting, †Photography, †Sculpture, Silversmithing, †Teacher Training, †Textile Design, †Theatre Arts, Weaving

JACKSON

LAMBUTH UNIVERSITY, Dept of Human Ecology & Visual Arts, 705 Lambuth Blvd, PO Box 431, 38301. Tel 901-425-3275, 425-2500; FAX 901-423-1990. *Chmn* Lawrence A Ray, PhD; *Assoc Prof* June Creasy, MS; *Asst Prof* Lendon H Noe, MS; *Lectr* Susan Foote, MEd; *Lectr* Belinda A Patterson, BS; *Lectr* Glynn Weatherley, BS; *Lectr* Rosemary Carroway, BA
Estab 1843, dept estab 1950; den; D & E; scholarships; SC 21, LC 10
Ent Req: HS dipl
Degrees: BA, BS, B(Mus) & B(Bus Ad) 4 yrs
Tuition: $2317 per sem
Courses: Advertising Design, Aesthetics, †Art Education, †Art History, †Commercial Art, †Drawing, †Graphic Design, †Interior Design, †Painting, †Photography, †Printmaking, †Sculpture, Stage Design, Crafts, Fiber Crafts, Human Ecology, †Stained Glass, Visual Art
Adult Hobby Classes: Adult Evening Prog. $1800 per term
Children's Classes: Enrl 45-50; tuition $50 for 5 wk term. Courses—Elementary art classes
Summer School: Dir, William Shutowski. Courses—Art Appreciation, Art Education, Basic ID, Painting, Printmaking

UNION UNIVERSITY, Dept of Art, Hwy 45 Bypass, 38305. Tel 901-668-1818; FAX 901-664-7476. *Chmn* Michael Mallard
Estab 1824, dept estab 1958; den; D & E; scholarships; SC 20, LC 5; enrl D 200, E 40, maj 28
Ent Req: HS dipl, portfolio, ACT
Degrees: BA and BS 4 yrs
Tuition: $2125 per sem
Courses: Art Appreciation, Art Education, Art History, †Ceramics, Commercial Art, Drawing, Jewelry, †Painting, Photography, Printmaking, †Sculpture, Teacher Training, Art Appreciation, Metalsmithing
Adult Hobby Classes: Enrl 20; tuition $125 per cr hr. Courses—Painting, Drawing, Art History, Ceramics, Sculpture, Metalsmithing
Children's Classes: Enrl 10; 5 wks. Courses—Drawing
Summer School: Dir, Reid Parish. Tuition $125 per cr hr for 4 wks. Courses—Art History, Ceramics

JEFFERSON CITY

CARSON-NEWMAN COLLEGE, Art Dept, 37760. Tel 615-475-9061; FAX 615-475-7956. *Chmn Dept* H T Niceley. Instrs: FT 3
Col estab 1851; den; D & E; scholarships; SC 26, LC 7; enrl maj 36
Ent Req: HS dipl
Degrees: BA(Art & Photography) 4 yrs
Tuition: Res—$5980 per yr; nonres—$6080 per yr; campus res $1800
Courses: Aesthetics, Art Education, Art History, Drawing, Handicrafts, Interior Design, Lettering, Painting, Photography, Printmaking, Sculpture, Stage Design, Teacher Training, Theatre Arts, Advertising Art, Computer Graphics
Summer School: Dir, R Earl Cleveland. Enrl 25; tuition $80 per sem hr. Courses—Art Appreciation, Photography

JOHNSON CITY

EAST TENNESSEE STATE UNIVERSITY, Fine Arts Dept, PO Box 23740A, 70708. Tel 615-929-4247. *Chmn Dept* John E Schrader, MFA; *Asst Prof* Peter Pawlowicz, PhD; *Assoc Prof* Gerald Edmundson, MA; *Prof* David Logan, MFA; *Prof* James Mills, PhD; *Asst Prof* Ralph Slatton, MFA; *Assoc Prof* John Steele, MA; *Assoc Prof* Charles Thompson, MFA; *Asst Prof* Lynn Whitehead, MFA; *Asst Prof* David Dixon, MFA; *Assoc Prof* Michael Smith, MFA; *Assoc Prof* M Wayne Dyer, MFA; *Asst Prof* Dr Vida Hull, PhD; *Asst Prof* Jean Murakami, MFA
Estab 1909, dept estab 1949; pub; D & E; scholarships; SC 102, LC 30, GC 46; enrl D approx 1400
Ent Req: HS dipl, ACT or SAT
Degrees: BA, BS & BFA 4 yrs, MA, MFA
Tuition: Res—undergrad $62 per sem hr, $691 per sem, grad $91 per sem hr, $898 per sem; nonres—undergrad $202 per sem hr, $2297 per sem; campus res—room & board $1000 per sem hr
Courses: Art Education, Art History, Ceramics, Drawing, †Graphic Design, †Jewelry, †Painting, †Photography, Printmaking, †Sculpture, †Metalsmithing, †Weaving/Fibers
Adult Hobby Classes: Credit/no credit classes at night. Courses—Art History, Drawing, Photography, painting
Children's Classes: Saturdays
Summer School: Dir, John Schrader. Enrl 300; tuition $300 May - Aug. Courses—Art Educ, Drawing, Graphic Design, Painting, Sculpture

KNOXVILLE

UNIVERSITY OF TENNESSEE, KNOXVILLE, Dept of Art, 1715 Volunteer Blvd, 37996-2410. Tel 615-974-3408; FAX 615-974-3198. *Head Art Dept* Donald F Kurka, PhD. Instrs: FT 29, PT 6
Estab 1794, dept estab 1951; pub; D & E; scholarships; SC 51, LC 23, GC 50; enrl D 1600, E 250, non-maj 300, maj 400, grad 40
Ent Req: HS dipl
Degrees: BA & BFA, MFA; both undergraduate & graduate credit may be earned through the affiliated program at Arrowmont School of Arts & Crafts, Gatlinburg, TN

Tuition: Res—undergrad $783 per sem. grad $975 per sem; nonres—undergrad $1682 per sem, grad $1682 per sem; campus res—room & board $3166 per yr
Courses: †Advertising Design, †Art History, †Ceramics, †Drawing, †Graphic Design, †Painting, Photography, †Printmaking, †Sculpture, Video, Computer Graphics, Fiber-Fabric, †Watercolor
Adult Hobby Classes: Enrl 150. Courses - Ceramics, Drawing, Graphic Design, Photography
Children's Classes: Tuition none. Courses - pre-college high school Sat workshops
Summer School: Dir, Prof William Kennedy. Enrl 400; term of 2 sessions beginning June & Aug. Courses—Art History, Design, Drawing

MARYVILLE

MARYVILLE COLLEGE, Dept of Fine Arts, 37801. Tel 615-982-6414. *Chmn* Dan Taddie. Instrs: FT 2, PT 1
Estab 1937; den; scholarships; SC 10, LC 6
Degrees: 4 yr
Tuition: $1920 per term
Courses: Art Education, Art History, Ceramics, Drawing, Graphic Design, Painting, Photography, Printmaking, Weaving, Computer Graphics, Fabric Design, Visual Theory & Design
Adult Hobby Classes: Courses offered
Children's Classes: Art Education, Crafts

MEMPHIS

MEMPHIS COLLEGE OF ART, Overton Park, 38112. Tel 901-726-4085. *Exec VPres* Phillip S Morris, MFA. Instrs: FT 14, PT 10
Estab 1936; pvt; D & E; scholarships; enrl D 200, E 300
Ent Req: HS dipl
Degrees: BFA 4 yrs, MFA 2 yrs
Tuition: $3755 per sem; women's campus res
Courses: †Advertising Design, Aesthetics, Art History, Calligraphy, Ceramics, Collages, †Commercial Art, Drawing, †Graphic Arts, †Graphic Design, †Illustration, Jewelry, Design, Lettering, †Painting, Photography, †Printmaking, †Sculpture, †Textile Design, †Video, Computer Design, Computer Loom, Enameling, †Surface Design
Adult Hobby Classes: Enrl 300; tuition $195 for 16 wk term. Courses—Same as above
Children's Classes: Enrl 300, tuition $25-$100 for 10 wk term. Courses—Computer Graphics, Drawing, Jewelry, Painting, Papermaking, Photography, Pottery, Sculpture
Summer School: Dir, Frieda Hamm. Enrl 250; tuition $130 per cr hr for term of 6 wks beginning early June. Courses—same as above

MEMPHIS STATE UNIVERSITY, Dept of Art, 38152. Tel 901-678-2216; FAX 901-678-3299. *Chmn Dept* Robert E Lewis
Estab 1912; pub; D & E; scholarships; SC 100, LC 40, GC 30; enrl D 2200, maj 400, grad 80
Ent Req: HS dipl, SAT
Degrees: BA & BFA 4 yrs, MA & MAT 1 yr, MFA 2 yrs
Tuition: Campus residence available
Courses: Art Education, Ceramics, Drawing, Graphic Design, History of Art & Archaeology, Illustration, Interior Design, Museum Staff Training, Painting, Photography, Printmaking, Sculpture, Teacher Training
Adult Hobby Classes: Courses offered
Summer School: Dir, Carol Crown

RHODES COLLEGE, Dept of Art, 2000 N Parkway, 38112. Tel 901-726-3825; FAX 901-726-3718. *Chmn* James Clifton; *Prof* Lawrence Anthony; *Asst Prof* James C Thompson; *Instr* Betty Gilow, BFA; *Instr* Martha Christian, BFA; *Instr* James S Williamson; *Lectr* Julia Graham, BFA
Estab 1848, dept estab 1940; pvt; D & E; SC 17, LC 12; enrl D 250, non-maj 240, maj 10
Ent Req: SAT or ACT, 13 acad credits, 16 overall
Degrees: BA 4 yrs
Tuition: $11,470 per yr; campus res—room & board $2712 per yr
Courses: Aesthetics, Architecture, Art History, Calligraphy, Drawing, History of Art & Archaeology, Museum Staff Training, Painting, Photography, Printmaking, Sculpture, Theatre Arts, Fiber Design

MURFREESBORO

MIDDLE TENNESSEE STATE UNIVERSITY, Art Dept, PO Box 25, 37132. Tel 615-898-2455; FAX 615-898-2254. *Chmn Art Dept* Carlyle Johnson
Estab 1911, dept estab 1952; pub; D & E; scholarships; SC 62, LC 10, GC 35; enrl non-maj 900, maj 200, grad 5
Ent Req: HS dipl
Degrees: BS(Art Educ), & BFA 4 yrs
Courses: †Art Education, †Ceramics, †Commercial Art, Drawing, Graphic Design, Goldsmithing, †Jewelry, †Painting, †Printmaking, †Sculpture, †Silversmithing, Textile Design
Adult Hobby Classes: Courses Offered
Children's Classes: Creative Art Clinic for Children; enrl 45; tuition $25 per term
Summer School: Courses Offered

NASHVILLE

CHEEKWOOD-TENNESSEE BOTANICAL GARDEN MUSEUM OF ART
(Formerly Tennessee Botanical Gardens & Fine Arts Center), Education Dept, 1200 Forrest Park Dr, 37205. Tel 615-353-2140; FAX 615-353-2162. *Pres* John Cherol; *Dir Educ* Nancy Cavener; *Cur Coll* Christine Kreyling; *Dir Botanical Gardens* Richard C Page; *Registrar* Beth Cunningham
Estab 1960; pvt; D & E; SC 10-15, LC 5-10
Tuition: $60-$70 for 8 wk term

Courses: Art Appreciation, Art History, Ceramics, Commercial Art, Drawing, Graphic Arts, Jewelry, Painting, Printmaking, Sculpture, Textile Design, Weaving, Landscape Design, Papermaking
Adult Hobby Classes: Courses—Calligraphy, Design, Life Drawing, Painting, Photography, Watercolor
Children's Classes: Jr Studio Courses—Art Start, Exploring Art

FISK UNIVERSITY, Art Dept, 37208-3051. Tel 615-329-8673, 329-8674, 329-8500. *Chmn* Earl J Hooks; *Instr* LiFran Fort, MA
Estab 1867, dept estab 1937; pvt; D; scholarships; SC 10, LC 3; enrl 65, non-maj 40, maj 15
Ent Req: HS dipl, SAT
Degrees: BS & BA 4 yrs
Tuition: $2157.50 per sem; campus res & tuition $3200 per sem
Courses: Aesthetics, Art History, Drawing, Painting, Sculpture, African Art, Afro-American Art

VANDERBILT UNIVERSITY, Dept of Fine Arts, 23rd Ave S at West End Ave, PO Box 1801 Station B, 37235. Tel 615-322-2831. *Chmn* Robert L Mode, PhD; *Prof* F Hamilton Hazlehurst, PhD; *Assoc Prof* Robert A Baldwin, MFA; *Assoc Prof* Donald H Evans, MFA; *Assoc Prof* Leonard Folgarait, PhD; *Assoc Prof* Milan Mihal, PhD; *Assoc Prof* Robert L Mode, PhD; *Assoc Prof* Ljubica D Popovich, PhD; *Asst Prof* Barbara Tsakirgis, PhD; *Assoc Prof* Marilyn Murphy, MFA; *Assoc Prof* Michael Aurbach, MFA; *Asst Prof* Vivien G Fryd, PhD; *Asst Prof* Ellen Konowitz; *Sr Lectr* Amy Kirschke, PhD; *Lectr* Susan DeMay, MFA; *Lectr* Carlton Wilkinson, MFA
Estab 1873, dept estab 1944; pvt; D; scholarships; SC 19, LC 29, GC 2; enrl non-maj 367,, maj 47, grad 10
Ent Req: HS dipl, ent exam
Degrees: BA 4 yrs, MA(Art Hist) 1-2 yrs
Tuition: $15,975 per yr, $7987.50 per sem; campus res—room & board $5764 per yr
Courses: Architecture, Art Appreciation, Ceramics, Design, Film, Printmaking, Sculpture, Video, Painting, Photography, Multimedia Design
Summer School: Dean, John Venable. Tuition $666 per sem for two 4 wk terms beginning early June. Courses—Vary

WATKINS INSTITUTE, School of Art, 601 Church, 37219-2390. Tel 615-242-1851. *Dir* Madeline Reed. Instrs: 50
Estab 1885; pvt; D & E; SC 30, LC 5; enrl D 1000, E 1000
Ent Req: Noncredit adult educ program, must be 17 yrs of age or older
Degrees: AA in Art, approved by Tennessee Higher Education Commission, 2 yr
Tuition: $90 - $135 per course
Courses: Art History, Drawing, †Commercial Art, Painting, Photography, Printmaking, Sculpture, Composition & Design, Crafts, Figure Structure, Introduction to Art
Adult Hobby Classes: Enrl 2000; tuition $90-$120 per course. Lecture & Studio courses. Courses—Commercial Art, Fine Arts, Interior Design
Children's Classes: Enrl 500; tuition $150-$200 for 12 wks. Courses—Fine Arts
Summer School: Enrl 400; tuition $90 - $135 per course for 10 wks. Summer Art Camp for children, 2 wk sessions. Courses—Commercial Art, Fine Arts, Interior Design

SEWANEE

UNIVERSITY OF THE SOUTH, Dept of Fine Arts, Carnegie Hall, 37375. Tel 615-598-1000, Ext 493, 256, 344. *Chmn Dept* Pradip Malde. Instrs: FT 4
Pvt, den; D; scholarships; SC 20, LC 20; enrl D 250, non-maj 225, maj 30
Degrees: BS & BA, MDivinity
Tuition: $9100 per yr
Courses: Aesthetics, Art Education, Drawing, Film, History of Art & Archaeology, Painting, Photography, Printmaking, Sculpture, Stage Design, Theatre Arts
Summer School: Dir, Dr Peggy Hart. Enrl 150 for term of 6 wks beginning June. Courses—Regular university curriculum

TULLAHOMA

MOTLOW STATE COMMUNITY COLLEGE, Art Dept, PO Box 88100, 37388-8100. Tel 615-455-8511; WATS 800-654-4877. *Dir Division Liberal Arts* Dr Mary McLemore; *Art Teacher* Jack Moore; *Art Teacher* Ann Smotherman
Scholarships offered
Tuition: Res—$387 per sem; nonres—$1602 sem
Courses: Art Appreciation, Ceramics, Commercial Art, Design, Drawing, Painting, Photography, Arts & Crafts
Adult Hobby Classes: Enrl 200
Children's Classes: Enrl 40

TEXAS

ABILENE

ABILENE CHRISTIAN UNIVERSITY, Dept of Art, ACU Station Box 7987, 79699. Tel 915-674-2085; FAX 915-674-2202. *Head Dept* Brent Green, PhD. Instrs: FT 6, PT 1
Estab 1906; den; D & E; SC 29, LC 8; enrl maj 79
Ent Req: Upper 3/4 HS grad class or at 19 standard score ACT composite
Degrees: BA, BA(Educ) & BFA 4 yrs
Tuition: $230 per sem hr
Courses: Art History, Drawing, Art Education, Ceramics, Graphic Design, Painting, Sculpture, Printmaking, Jewelry, Design, Pottery
Summer School: Dir, Dr Brent Green. Enrl 10; tuition $230 for 3 & 6 wk blocks. Courses— ceramics, Drawing, Introduction to Art History

HARDIN-SIMMONS UNIVERSITY, Art Dept, Hickory at Ambler St, PO Box 1151 Univ Station, 79698. Tel 915-670-1246. *Chmn* Linda D Fawcett, MFA; *Prof* Ira M Taylor, MFA; *Prof* Bob Howell, MFA; *Instr* Martha Kiel, MEd
Univ estab 1891; den; D & E; scholarships; SC 27, LC 5; enrl D 130, E 25, non-maj 65, maj 65
Ent Req: HS dipl, SAT, ACT
Degrees: BS & BA 4 yrs
Tuition: $190 per cr hr; campus res—room & board $1195
Courses: †Art Education, Art History, Ceramics, Painting, Printmaking, Sculpture, †Teacher Training, †Teacher Training, †Theatre Arts
Summer School: Dir, Linda D Fawcett. Enrl 50; tuition $190 per cr hr for term of 15 wks beginning June 2. Courses—vary

MCMURRY UNIVERSITY, Art Dept, PO Box 308 McMurry Station, 79697. Tel 915-691-6200. *Head Dept* Don Ellis, MFA; *Prof* Sherwood Suter, MFA; *Lectr* J Robert Miller, BS; *Lectr* Emily Jennings
Estab 1923; pvt; D & E; scholarships; SC 19, LC 1; enrl D 80, E 8, non-maj 18, maj 15
Ent Req: HS dipl
Degrees: BA, BFA & BS 4 yrs
Tuition: Res—undergrad $6790 per yr, $3345 per sem (incl room, board, & books) $120 per sem hr; nonres—same as res fees
Courses: Art Education, Art History, Ceramics, Drawing, Jewelry, Lettering, Painting, Teacher Training, Design, Stone Sculpture, Assemblage Sculpture
Adult Hobby Classes: Enrl 24; tuition $360 fall, spring & summer terms. Courses—Art Education I & II
Summer School: Dir, Bob Maniss. Two summer terms. Coursses—Exploring the Visual Arts, Art Education I

ALPINE

SUL ROSS STATE UNIVERSITY, Dept of Fine Arts & Communications, C-90, 79832. Tel 915-837-8130; FAX 915-837-8046. *Prof* Charles R Hext; *Prof* Dr Roy Dodson
Estab 1920, dept estab 1922; pub; D & E; scholarships; SC 21, LC 3, GC 19; enrl D 183, E 32, non-maj 170, maj 25-30, GS 15
Ent Req: HS dipl, ACT or SAT
Degrees: BFA 4 yrs, MEd(Art) 1 1/2 yrs
Tuition: Res—12 hr $578 pr sem, nonres—12 hr $2210 per sem
Courses: Art History, Ceramics, Conceptual Art, Drawing, Jewelry, Mixed Media, Painting, Printmaking, Sculpture, Teacher Training, Advertising Art
Summer School: tuition 6 hr $309 per term; nonres 6 hr $1125 per term

ALVIN

ALVIN COMMUNITY COLLEGE, Art Dept, 3110 Mustang Rd, 77511. Tel 713-388-4792; FAX 713-331-2064. *Chmn* Doris Burbank
Estab 1949; D & E
Ent Req: HS dipl
Degrees: AA 2 yrs
Tuition: In district—$90; res—$105; nonres—$245
Courses: Art Appreciation, Art History, Ceramics, Drawing, Graphic Design, Painting, Sculpture, Design Communication
Summer School: Dir, Bruce Turner. 6 - 12 wk term. Courses vary

AMARILLO

AMARILLO COLLEGE, Art Dept, 2200 S Washington, PO Box 447, 79178. Tel 806-371-5000, Ext 5084. *Chmn* Denny Fraze, MFA; *Prof* David Cale, MFA; *Prof* William Burrell, MFA; *Instr* Dennis Olson
Estab 1926; pub; D & E; scholarships; SC 18, LC 2; enrl D 142, E 60
Ent Req: HS dipl, CEEB
Degrees: AA 2 yrs
Tuition: Res—undergrad $236.25 per sem, lab fee $8; nonres—undergrad $360 per sem; no campus res
Courses: Art History, Ceramics, †Commercial Art, Drawing, Graphic Design, Illustration, Jewelry, †Painting, †Sculpture, †Fine Art, Layout, Typographics
Summer School: Chmn, Denny Fraze, MFA

TEXAS STATE TECHNICAL COLLEGE, Commercial Art in Advertising, PO Box 11197, 79111. Tel 806-335-2316, Ext 405, 425. *Prog Chmn* Karen Atkins
Estab 1970; pub; D; scholarships; SC 32, LC 2; enrl D 42, non-maj 1, maj 47
Ent Req: HS dipl, GED
Degrees: AA(Applied Science)
Tuition: Res—$14 per quarter cr, nonres—$140 per quarter cr
Courses: Advertising Design, Art History, Commercial Art, Drafting, Graphic Design, Illustration, Interior Design, Mixed Media, Painting, Photography, Air Brush, Computer Graphic, Corporate Design, Drawing, Production, Figure Drawing, Layout, Mass Media Advertising, Screen Printing, Typography
Adult Hobby Classes: Enrl 10; tuition $1 per contact hr for 12 wk term. Courses—regular curriculum courses
Summer School: Same as regular session

ARLINGTON

UNIVERSITY OF TEXAS AT ARLINGTON, Dept of Art & Art History, 335 Fine Arts Bldg, PO Box 19089, 76019. Tel 817-273-2891. *Chmn* Kenda North
Estab 1895, dept estab 1937; pub; D & E; scholarships; SC 46, LC 39, maj 400
Ent Req: HS dipl, SAT or ACT
Degrees: BFA 4 yrs
Tuition: Res—$497 for 15 cr hrs; nonres—$2057 for 15 cr hrs
Courses: †Art Education, †Art History, †Ceramics, †Drawing, †Graphic Design, †Painting, †Video, †Photography, †Printmaking, †Sculpture, †Video, †Metalsmithing
Adult Hobby Classes: Continuing Education division of university
Children's Classes: Continuing Education division of university
Summer School: Chmn, Jack Plummer

AUSTIN

AUSTIN COMMUNITY COLLEGE, Dept of Commercial Art, North Ridge Campus, 11928 Stonehollow Dr, 78758. Tel 512-832-4801. *Head Dept* Daniel Traverso, MFA. Instrs: FT 1, PT 20
Estab 1974; pub; D & E; enrl 386 per sem
Ent Req: HS dipl or GED
Degrees: AAS 2 yr
Tuition: Res—undergrad $21.50 per cr hr; nonres—undergrad $105.50 per cr hr
Courses: †Calligraphy, †Commercial Art, †Drawing, †Graphic Design, †Illustration, †Photography, †Film, †Graphic Arts, †Mixed Media, †Painting, †Photography, †Printmaking, †Sculpture, †Video, Animation, Commercial Art History, Environmental Graphics, Figure Drawing, Illustrative Techniques, Production Art, Advertising, Desktop Publishing, Elementary Design, Graphics Practicum, Sign Painting, Silkscreening, Special Problems, Typography Design

CONCORDIA LUTHERAN COLLEGE, Dept of Fine Arts, 3400 I-35 N, 78705. Tel 512-452-7661; FAX 512-459-8517. *Chmn* Dr Milton Riemer. Instrs: FT 1
Estab 1925; den; D; scholarships; SC 1, LC 1; enrl D 350
Ent Req: HS dipl
Degrees: AA 2 yr
Tuition: $175 per sem hr; campus res available
Courses: Design, Drawing, Painting, Art Fundamentals, Drawing Media, Experience of Drama

UNIVERSITY OF TEXAS
—School of Architecture, Goldsmith Hall, 78712. Tel 512-471-1922. *Acting Dean* Lawrence Speck. Instrs: FT 38, PT 9
Estab 1909; pub; scholarships; enrl undergrad 450, grad 210
Ent Req: Reasonable HS scholastic achievement, SAT, ACT
Degrees: BS 4 yr, BArch 5 yr, BS(archit eng) 6 yr; MArch 1-3.5 yr
Tuition: Res—undergrad $584 per sem, grad $682 per sem; nonres—undergrad $2240 per sem, grad $1798 per sem
Courses: †Architecture, Community & Regional Planning
Adult Hobby Classes: Courses through Division of Continuing Education
Children's Classes: Six week summer program for high school
Summer School: Dir, Harold Box
—Dept of Art & Art History, 78712. Tel 512-471-3365; FAX 512-471-7801. *Dean* David L Deming. Instrs: FT & PT 80
Estab 1938; scholarships; enrl grad 127, 900 undergraduate maj
Degrees: BA 4yrs, BFA 4 yrs, MA 2 yrs, MFA 2 yrs, PhD
Tuition: Res—undergrad $584 per sem, grad $574 per sem; nonres—undergrad $2240 per sem, grad $1798 per sem
Courses: Art Education, Art History, Ceramics, Drawing, Graphic Arts, Illustration, †Painting, †Photography, †Printmaking, †Sculpture, †Criticism of Art, Installation Film Art, Metals, †Teacher Certificatoin, Trans Media, †Visual Communications
Summer School: Two 6 wk terms

BEAUMONT

LAMAR UNIVERSITY, Art Dept, PO Box 10027, LU Station, 77710. Tel 409-880-8141. *Head Dept* Robert G O'Neill; *Prof* J Robert Madden, MFA; *Prof* Jerry Newman, MFA; *Assoc Prof* Meredith M Jack MFA; *Assoc Prof* Philip Fitzpatrick, MFA; *Asst Prof* Lynn Lokensgard, PhD; *Adjunct Instr* Kieth Carter
Estab 1923, dept estab 1951; pub; D & E; scholarships; SC 50, LC 10; enrl D 607, E 62, non-maj 214, maj 192
Ent Req: HS dipl
Degrees: BA, BFA, BS & MA, 4 yr
Tuition: Res—undergrad $215 for 3 sem hrs; nonres—undergrad $445 for 3 sem hrs; campus res available
Courses: †Advertising Design, †Art Education, Art History, Ceramics, Commercial Art, Drawing, Film, Graphic Arts, †Graphic Design, History of Art & Archaeology, Handicrafts, Illustration, Jewelry, †Painting, Photography, Printmaking, †Sculpture, Weaving, History of Art & Architecture, Weaving
Summer School: Dir, Robert O'Neill. Tuition in state $72, out of state $384 per 3 sem hrs for two 5 wk sessions. Courses—Art Appreciation, Art History, Free Drawing, Oil & Watercolor Painting

BELTON

UNIVERSITY OF MARY HARDIN-BAYLOR, Dept of Fine Arts, 76513. Tel 817-939-4678. *Chmn* George Stansbury
Estab 1845; den; D & E; scholarships; SC 6, LC 1 and one independent learning course per sem
Ent Req: Upper half of HS grad class
Degrees: BA, BFA and BS 4 yrs
Tuition: $3000 per yr
Courses: Art Education, Art History, Ceramics, Drawing, Graphic Arts, Jewelry, Painting, Design
Children's Classes: Summer Art Camp
Summer School: Sem of 5 wks, from 1 to 4 cr hrs. Courses—Crafts, Independent Learning

BIG SPRING

HOWARD COUNTY JUNIOR COLLEGE, Art Dept, Division of Fine Arts, 1001 Birdwell Lane, 79720. Tel 915-264-5000; FAX 915-264-5082. *Chmn* Dr Mary Bailey
Estab 1948, dept estab 1972; pub; D & E; scholarships; SC 5, LC 1; enrl D 70, E 20, non-maj 60, maj 10
Ent Req: HS dipl, ACT
Degrees: AA
Tuition: Res—$4 per sem cr hr; nonres—$20 per sem cr hr

BORGER

FRANK PHILLIPS COLLEGE, Art Dept, Fine Arts Division, PO Box 5118, 79008. Tel 806-274-5311. *Chmn Div* Marlin C Adams, MFA
Estab 1948; pub; D & E; scholarships; SC 14, LC 3; enrl D 60, E 10, non-maj 20, maj 40
Ent Req: HS dipl, GED or transfer from another college
Degrees: AA, AS and AAS 2 yrs
Courses: Advertising Design, Art Appreciation, Art Education, Art History, Calligraphy, Ceramics, Commercial Art, Design, Drawing, Graphic Arts, Painting, Photography, Sculpture, Pottery
Adult Hobby Classes: Enrl 100; tuition $30 & up. Courses—Community Services classes, Calligraphy, Ceramics, Drawing, Painting, Photography, others on demand
Children's Classes: Enrl 90; tuition $10 & up. Courses—Drawing, Painting
Summer School: Dir, Marlin Adams. Courses—Painting, others on demand

BROWNSVILLE

TEXAS SOUTHMOST COLLEGE, Fine Arts Dept, 80 Fort Brown, 78520. Tel 210-544-8283. *Chmn Fine Arts* Terry Tomlin
Estab 1973; pub; D & E; scholarships; SC 10, LC 10; enrl D 300, E 100
Ent Req: HS dipl
Degrees: AA(Fine Arts) 2-3 yrs
Tuition: Res—undergrad $386, grad $506 for 12 hrs or more; nonres—undergrad $1346, grad $2162 for 12 hrs or more
Courses: Art Education, Ceramics, Drawing, Graphic Design, History of Art & Archaeology, Painting, Photography, Sculpture, Design I and II
Adult Hobby Classes: Courses—Ceramics, Drawing
Summer School: Term of 16 wks. Courses—Art Appreciation

BROWNWOOD

HOWARD PAYNE UNIVERSITY, Dept of Art, School of Fine and Applied Arts, Howard Payne Station, 76801. *Dean* Donal Bird, PhD; *Chmn Dept Art* Eloise Trigg, MA. Instrs: FT 2, PT2
Estab 1889; den; D & E; SC 18, LC 8; enrl D 120, E 25, maj 2
Ent Req: HS dipl, ent exam
Degrees: BA and BS 4 yrs
Tuition: $118 per sem hr
Courses: †Advertising Design, Art Appreciation, †Art Education, Art History, Ceramics, Commercial Art, Constructions, Design, Drawing, Film, Graphic Arts, Graphic Design, Handicrafts, History of Art & Archaeology, †Painting, Photography, Sculpture, Stage Design, Teacher Training, Theatre Arts, Video, Studio
Adult Hobby Classes: Enrl 30; tuition $50 per course. Courses—Crafts, Painting, Travel Seminars
Children's Classes: tuition $20-$50 per 2 wk course
Summer School: Enrl 75; tuition term of 6 wks beginning June. Courses—Crafts, Drawing, Painting, Photography

CANYON

WEST TEXAS STATE UNIVERSITY, Art, Communication & Theatre Dept, PO Box 747, WT Station, 79016. Tel 806-656-2799. *Head Dept* Dr Bob Vartabedian; *Prof* Robert Caruthers, MFA; *Prof* Darold Smith, MFA; *Assoc Prof* David Rindlisbacher, MFA; *Assoc Prof* Mary Ann Petry, PhD; *Asst Prof* Sven Anderson, MFA; *Instr* Bill Green
Estab 1910; pub; D & E; scholarships; SC 70, LC 23, GC 50; enrl maj 120, grad 23
Ent Req: HS dipl
Degrees: BA, BS, BFA, MA and MFA
Tuition: Res—$192 per sem, $100 PT; non-res—$1440 per sem, $720 PT; foreign students $1140 per sem; campus res—$1154
Courses: †Advertising Design, Aesthetics, †Art Education, Art History, †Ceramics, Commercial Art, †Drawing, †Goldsmithing, Graphic Arts, †Graphic Design, Handicrafts, Illustration, †Jewelry, †Painting, †Printmaking, †Sculpture, †Silversmithing, Teacher Training
Children's Classes: Summer session offered by Gifted & Talented Dept
Summer School: Dir, Steven Mayes. Tuition res $108 per session, nonres $1080 per session; Session I from June 2 - July 8, Session II July 9 - Aug 20. All art courses offered

COLLEGE STATION

TEXAS A & M UNIVERSITY, College of Architecture, 77843-3137. Tel 409-845-1221; FAX 409-845-4491. *Dean* Walter V Wendler. Instrs: FT 92
Estab 1905; pub; D; scholarships; enrl maj Ed 800, total 1750
Ent Req: SAT; Achievement, HS rank
Degrees: BEenviron Design, BS(Building Construction), BLandscape Arch, MArch, MLandscape, MUrban Planning, MS(Urban Science) 4 yr, MS(Construction Mgmt), MS(Land Development), MS(Architecture), PhD(Architecture), MS(Visualization) (Computer Animation)
Tuition: Res—$24 per sem cr hr; nonres—$162 per sem cr hr; fees $700
Courses: Architecture, Art History, Constructions, Design, Drafting, Drawing, History of Art & Archaeology, Illustration, Landscape Architecture, Photography, Restoration & Conservation, Video, Computer Animation
Adult Hobby Classes: Enrl 30; tuition $375 for one wk term. Courses—Career Horizons
Summer School: Dir, Rodney Hill. Enrl 1000; tuition same as above for 2 wk sessions. Courses—Construction Science, Arch Design, Drawing, Arch History, Planning

COMMERCE

EAST TEXAS STATE UNIVERSITY, Dept of Art, East Texas Station, 75429. Tel 903-886-5208; FAX 214-886-5415. *Head* William Wadley; *Chmn Ceramics* Barbara Frey, MFA; *Chmn Printmaking* Lee Baxter Davis, MFA; *Chmn Sculpture* Jerry Dodd, MFA; *Chmn Art Ed* Dr James Allumbaugh; *Coordr Grad Programs* Gerard Huber, MFA; *Chmn Painting* Michael Miller; *Chmn Art History* Ivana Spalatin; *Prof* James Newberry; *Asst Prof* Stan Godwin; *Instr at Interim* Terry Falke
Pub; D & E; scholarships; SC 64, LC 29, GC 19; enrl maj 300, GS 30
Ent Req: HS dipl, ACT or SAT
Degrees: BA, BS and BFA 4 yrs, MFA 2 yrs, MA and MS 1 1/2 yrs. There is a special program called the Post Masters-MFA which is worked out on an individual basis
Tuition: campus res available
Courses: †Advertising Design, Aesthetics, †Art Education, Art History, †Ceramics, Collages, †Commercial Art, Constructions, Drafting, †Drawing, †Graphic Arts, †Graphic Design, History of Art & Archaeology, †Illustration, †Intermedia, Industrial Design, †Jewelry, Lettering, †Mixed Media, †Painting, †Photography, †Printmaking, †Sculpture, Silversmithing, †Teacher Training, Video, Intaglio Printmaking, Lithography, Papermaking and Casting
Adult Hobby Classes: Enrl 15; tuition $77 per sem. Courses—Bonzai, Ceramics, Drawing, Painting, Watercolor
Summer School: Enrl 15; tuition res—$64.75-$393; nonres—$134.75-$2121, for 2 terms of 2 to 6 wks beginning June. Courses—Art Education, Ceramics, Design, Drawing, Painting, Printmaking

CORPUS CHRISTI

DEL MAR COLLEGE, Art Dept, 101 Baldwin, 78404-3897. Tel 512-886-1216. *Chmn* William E Lambert, MFA; *Prof* Jan R Ward; *Prof* Ronald Dee Sullivan, MA; *Assoc Prof* Randolph Flowers; *Assoc Prof* Kitty Dudics MFA; *Asst Prof* Ken Rosier, MFA
Estab 1941, dept estab 1965; pub; D & E; scholarships; SC 21, LC 3; enrl D 500, E 100, non-maj 400, maj 139
Ent Req: HS dipl, SAT score or any accepted test including GED
Degrees: AA 2 yr in studio, art educ
Tuition: Res—$10 per sem hr, $50 minimum; nonres—$120 per sem hr, $200 minimum; foreign students $120 per sem hr, $200 minimum; plus other fees; no campus res
Courses: Graphic Design, History of Art & Archaeology, Painting, Photography, Printmaking, Sculpture
Adult Hobby Classes: Tuition varies according to classes. Courses—as above
Summer School: Chmn, W E Lambert, MFA. Enrl 60; tuition $10 per sem hr, $50 minimum, for 6 wks. Courses—Design, Drawing, Principles of Art

CORSICANA

NAVARRO COLLEGE, Art Dept, 3200 W Hwy 31, 75110. Tel 214-874-6501; WATS: 800-NAVARRO. *Dir* Sandra Dowd. Instrs: FT2, PT2
Estab 1946; pub; D & E; scholarships; SC 11, LC 1; enrl D 300, maj 30
Ent Req: HS dipl, ent exam, special permission
Degrees: AA, AS, A Gen Educ and A Appl Sci 60 sem hr
Tuition: $350 per sem
Courses: Advertising Design, Art Appreciation, Calligraphy, Ceramics, Commercial Art, Design, Drafting, Drawing, Graphic Arts, Illustration, Painting, Photography, Sculpture, Video, 2-D & 3-D Design, †Computer Art
Adult Hobby Classes: Enrl 200; tuition $30-150 for sem of 6-12 wks. Courses—Drawing, Design, Crafts, Art Appreciation, Photography, Painting, Sculpture
Summer School: Dir, Evans David. Enrl 30; Courses—Art Appreciation

DALLAS

THE ART INSTITUTE OF DALLAS, 2 N Park East, 8080 Park Lane, 75231-9959. Tel 214-692-8080; FAX 214-692-6541; WATS 800-441-1577.
Scholarships offered
Degrees: AA
Tuition: $2050 per quarter
Courses: †Advertising Design, Architecture, Art Appreciation, Art Education, Art History, Calligraphy, Commercial Art, Design, Display, Drafting, Drawing, Fashion Arts, Graphic Arts, Graphic Design, Illustration, Interior Design, Jewelry, Landscape Architecture, Lettering, Painting, Photography, Theatre Arts, Video, Animation, Bookbinding, Cartooning, Glassblowing
Adult Hobby Classes: Enrl 850; tuition $2050 per quarter. Courses—Commercial Art, Fashion Merchandising, Interior Design, Music Business, Photography, Video

DALLAS BAPTIST UNIVERSITY, Dept of Art, 3000 Mountain Creek Parkway, 75211-9299. Tel 214-333-5300, 331-8311; FAX 214-333-5293. *Asst Prof* Dawna Hamm Walsh, PhD; *Asst Prof* Jim Colley, MFA; *Asst Prof* Rosalie Lemme; *Artist-in-Residence* Jack Hamm
Estab 1965; pvt den; D & E; scholarships; enrl D 75, E 25, non-maj 75, maj 25
Ent Req: HS dipl
Degrees: BA & BS 4 yrs, Bachelor of Applied Studies 2 - 4 yrs, Graduate Art Degree: MLA
Tuition: $200 per sem hr
Courses: Art Education, Art History, Ceramics, Commercial Art, Drawing, Graphic Design, Interior Design, Painting, Photography, Sculpture, Teacher Training, Theatre Arts, Crafts, Fine Arts
Adult Hobby Classes: Art Education, Art History, Ceramics, Commercial Art, Crafts, Drawing, Fine Arts, Graphic Design, Interior Design, Painting, Photography, Sculpture, Teacher Training, Theatre Arts
Children's Classes: Contact PBU Lab School
Summer School: Dir, Dr Dawna Walsh. Tuition $200 per cr hr. Courses—varies each summer. Art Travel Program for cr available

SOUTHERN METHODIST UNIVERSITY, Art Div, 75275-0356. Tel 214-692-2489. *Chair* Mary Vernon
Estab 1911, Meadows School of Arts estab 1964; pvt; D & E; scholarships; enrl maj 142, grad 41
Ent Req: Selective admission
Degrees: BFA(Art), BFA(Art Histroy), BA(Art History) 4 yr, MFA(Art) 2 yr, MA(Art History) 1 1/2 yr
Tuition: $400 per cr hr; campus res—room & board $4688
Courses: †Art History, †Ceramics, †Drawing, †Painting, †Photography, †Printmaking, †Sculpture
Summer School: Tuition $570 per course for term of 5 wks beginning June 4. Selected courses in art & art history at Taos, NM

DENISON

GRAYSON COUNTY COLLEGE, Art Dept, 6101 Grayson Dr, 75020. Tel 903-465-6030. *Dean Arts & Science* Cliff Wood; *Instr* Mary Lou Underwood; *Media Instr* Tim Ard; *Instr* Terri Blair
Estab 1965; pub; D & E; scholarships; LC 3; enrl D 63, E 35
Ent Req: HS dipl
Degrees: AA 2 yrs
Courses: Art Education, Art History, Drawing, Graphic Design, Painting, Appreciation, Watercolor
Adult Hobby Classes: Courses—Ceramics, Crafts, Drawing, Painting
Summer School: Dir, Mary Lois O'Neal. Courses—Drawing, Painting, Watercolor

DENTON

TEXAS WOMAN'S UNIVERSITY, Dept of Visual Arts, PO Box 22995, TWU Station, 76204. Tel 817-898-2530. *Chmn* Betty D Copeland, EdD; *Prof* Alfred E Green, MFA; *Prof* John B Miller; *Prof* Linda Stuckenbruck, MFA; *Assoc Prof* John A Calabrese, PhD; *Assoc Prof* Susan K Grant, MFA; *Asst Prof* Jeanne Broussard; *Asst Prof* Gary Washmon; *Adjunct Asst Prof* Don Radke; *Adjunct Asst Prof* Laurie Weller; *Adjunct Asst Prof* Millie Giles; *Lectr* Chris Morgan; *Lectr* James Watral
Estab 1901; pub; D & E; scholarships; SC 21, LC 34, GC 17; enrl non-maj 400, maj 110, undergrad 150, total 750
Ent Req: HS dipl, MA and MFA portfolio review required
Degrees: BA, BS and BFA 4 yrs, MA 1 yr, MFA 2 yrs
Tuition: Res—$16 per sem hr, $100 minimum; nonres—$120 per sem hr; campus res—$590 - $1180 for room only, meal plan available at extra charge
Courses: Art Education, Art History, Interior Design, Jewelry, Painting, Photography, Sculpture, Textile Design, Advertising Art, Bookmaking-Typography, Clay, Fibers, Fashion Illustration, Handmade Paper, Metalsmithing, Premedical Illustration
Adult Hobby Classes: Art History, Children's Art, Studio Courses
Children's Classes: Courses through Office of Continuing Education
Summer School: Dir, Dr Betty D Copeland. Enrl 150; tuition same as above. Courses—as above

UNIVERSITY OF NORTH TEXAS, School of Visual Arts, PO Box 5098, 76203. Tel 817-565-2855; FAX 817-565-4717. *Acting Dean* Scott Sullivan, PhD; *Grad Studies Coordr* Jerry Austin, MFA; *Undergrad Coordr* Mickey McCarter, MFA; *Interior Design Coordr* Bruce Nacke, MA; *Advertising Design Coordr* Jack Sprague, MFA; *Printmaking Coordr* Judy Youngblood, MFA; *Photography Coordr* Brent Phelps, MFA; *Painting and Drawing Coordr* Vincent Falsetta, MFA; *Sculpture Coordr* Richard Davis, MFA; *Art History Coordr* Larry Gleeson, PhD; *Fashion Design Coordr* Kay Selle, MA; *Ceramics Coordr* Jerry Austin, MFA; *Jewelry & Metalsmithing Coordr* Harlan Butt, MFA; *Basic Drawing Coordr* Robert Jessup, MFA
Estab 1897, dept estab 1901; pub; D & E; scholarships; SC 92, LC 54, GC 83; enrl non-maj 500, maj 1500, grad 100, others 25
Ent Req: HS dipl, SAT, GRE, portfolio for MFA, letters of recommendation for PhD
Degrees: BFA 4 yrs, MFA, MA, PhD
Tuition: Res—undergrad & grad $24 per sem hr, minimum of $100 plus fees; nonres—undergrad, grad & foreign $162 per sem hr; campus res—room & board $1486.70 - $1984.70 per sem
Courses: †Advertising Design, Aesthetics, †Art Education, †Art History, †Ceramics, Commercial Art, Conceptual Art, Drafting, †Drawing, †Fashion Arts, Graphic Arts, Graphic Design, †Handicrafts, †Interior Design, †Jewelry, Museum Staff Training, †Painting, †Photography, †Printmaking, Restoration & Conservation, †Sculpture, †Silversmithing, Teacher Training, †Textile Design, Video, †Weaving
Adult Hobby Classes: Tuition determined by class. Courses—Mini-classes in arts and craft related areas
Children's Classes: Courses—Mini-classes in arts and crafts related areas; special prog for advanced students
Summer School: Dir, Scott Sullivan. Enrl 500 per session; tuition $24 per sem hr for term of 6 wks; 2 summer sessions. Courses—All studio & lect courses as needed

EDINBURG

UNIVERSITY OF TEXAS PAN AMERICAN, Art Dept, 1201 W University Dr, 78539. Tel 210-381-3480. *Chmn Dept* Richard Hyslin, MA
Estab 1927, dept estab 1972; pub; D & E; scholarships; SC 43, LC 14; enrl D 1200, E 150, non-maj 650, maj 209
Ent Req: Open, immunization
Degrees: BA and BFA 4 yrs
Tuition: Res—$148 per 3 cr hr, $483 per 15 cr hr; nonres—$414 per 3 cr hr, $2147 per 15 cr hr
Courses: †Advertising Design, †Art Education, Art History, †Ceramics, Drawing, Graphic Arts, Graphic Design, Illustration, †Jewelry, Lettering, †Painting, Photography, †Printmaking, †Sculpture, †Silversmithing, Computer Graphic
Summer School: Dir, Richard Hyslin. Enrl 23 per class; tuition $31-$78 for term of 5 wks beginning June 2 and July 9. Courses—Art Education, Art Appreciation, Beginning & Advanced Painting, Ceramics, Drawing, Elementary Art Educ, Metals, Photography, Sculpture

EL PASO

UNIVERSITY OF TEXAS AT EL PASO, Dept of Art, 79968. Tel 915-747-5181. *Head Dept* W Ray Parish. Instrs: FT 12
Estab 1939; pub; D & E; scholarships; SC 24, GC 8; enrl 200
Degrees: BA & BFA 4 yrs, MA (Studio & Art Ed)
Tuition: $300 per sem
Courses: Art Education, Art History, Ceramics, Design, Drawing, Graphic Design, Painting, Printmaking, Sculpture, Metals
Adult Hobby Classes: Enrl 9; tuition varies from class to class. Courses—offered through Extension Division
Children's Classes: Enrl 25; tuition $25 for 6 week class. Courses—Kidzart
Summer School: Chmn, Charles Fensch. Enrl 150; tuition $80 for 3 hr course. Courses—Art Education, Intro to Art, Life Drawing, Painting, Printmaking

FORT WORTH

TEXAS CHRISTIAN UNIVERSITY, Art & Art History Dept, College of Fine Arts & Communication, PO Box 30793, 76129. Tel 817-921-7643. *Dean of Fine Arts* Robert Garwell; *Chmn of Art & Art History* David Cohen, MFA; *Prof* Margie Adkins, MFA; *Prof* Babette Bohn, PhD; *Prof* Thad Duhigg; *Prof* Linda Guy, MFA; *Prof* Lewis Glaser, MFA; *Prof* Susan Harrington, MFA; *Prof* Jim Woodson, MFA; *Prof* Mark Thistlethwaite, PhD; *Prof* Luther Smith, MFA. Instrs: FT 11, PT 9
Estab 1909; pvt; scholarships and grad fels; SC 35, LC 10, GC; enrl maj 150, others 450
Degrees: BA, BFA & BFA Art Ed, MFA 2 yrs
Tuition: $230 per sem hr
Courses: Art Education, Art History, Drawing, Painting, †Photography, †Printmaking, †Sculpture, †Communication Graphics
Summer School: Dir, Kathi Robinson. Enrl 200; tuition $195 per sem hr. Courses—ARA Camp

TEXAS WESLEYAN UNIVERSITY, Dept of Art, 1201 Wesleyan St, 76105-1536. Tel 817-531-4444; FAX 817-531-4814. *Dean* Joe Brown; *Chmn Dept* Mary Apple McConnell
Den; D & E; scholarships; SC, LC
Ent Req: HS dipl
Degrees: BA 4 yrs
Tuition: $2650 per sem
Courses: Art Education, Ceramics, Drawing, History of Art & Archaeology, Painting, Printmaking, Teacher Training

GAINESVILLE

COOKE COUNTY COLLEGE, Div of Communications & Fine Arts, 1525 W California, 76240. Tel 817-668-7731; FAX 817-668-6049. *Chairperson* Dr Ona Wright
Estab 1924; pub; D & E; scholarships; SC 14, LC 1; enrl D 50
Ent Req: HS dipl, SAT or ACT, individual approval
Degrees: AA and AFA 2 yrs
Courses: Ceramics, Drafting, Drawing, Graphic Design, Jewelry, Painting, Sculpture, Figure Drawing, Foundation of Art
Adult Hobby Classes: Enrl 120; tuition $10 - $20. Courses—Basketry, Country Art, Drawing, Flower Arrangement, Painting, Weaving
Children's Classes: Enrl 20; tuition $15. Courses - Art

GEORGETOWN

SOUTHWESTERN UNIVERSITY, Art Dept, 78626. Tel 512-863-6511. *Chmn* Thomas Howe, PhD; *Assoc Prof* Patrick Veerkamp; *Assoc Prof* Mary Visser, MFA; *Asst Prof* Victoria Star Varner
Estab 1840, dept estab 1940; pvt; D; scholarships; SC 28, LC 9; enrl D 160, maj 43
Ent Req: HS dipl, SAT, portfolio
Degrees: BA and BFA 4 yrs
Tuition: $6900 per yr
Courses: †Architecture, Art Appreciation, Art Education, Art History, †Ceramics, †Design, Drawing, †Painting, †Photography, †Printmaking, Sculpture
Summer School: Courses—various

HILLSBORO

HILL COLLEGE, Fine Arts Dept, PO Box 619, 76645. Tel 817-582-2555; FAX 817-582-7591. *Music Prog Coordr* Phillip Lowe; *Art Prog Coordr* Dottie Allen
Scholarships offered
Degrees: AA, cert
Tuition: In district—$30.50 per sem hr; res—$33 per sem hr; nonres—$76 per sem hr
Courses: Art Appreciation, Art Education, Art History, Ceramics, Design, Drawing, Painting, Weaving
Adult Hobby Classes: Enrl 15; tuition $33 per sem hr for 8 wks. Courses—Art Appreciation, Art History, Design, Drawing, Painting, Weaving
Summer School: Dir, Edith Clinkscales. Enrl 20 for 2 wks. Courses—Camp Rebel-various activities

HOUSTON

ART INSTITUTE OF HOUSTON, 1900 Yorktown, 77056. Tel 713-623-2040; WATS 800-231-6093. *Dir Educ* Michael Maki; *Dept Head Interior Design* Shannon Nelson; *Dept Head, Photography* Jim Estes; *Dept Head, Advertising Design* David Bennett; *Dept Head Fashion Marketing* Donna Sullivan; *Dir CE* Michael McClure. Instrs: FT 25, PT 15
Estab 1964; pvt; D & E; scholarships; enrl D 800, E 145
Ent Req: HS transcripts and graduation or GED, interview
Tuition: $1990 per quarter
Courses: Advertising Design, Interior Design, Photography, Fashion Merchandising
Adult Hobby Classes: Applied Photography, Interior Planning, Layout & Production

GLASSELL SCHOOL OF ART, The Museum of Fine Arts, 5101 Montrose, 77006. Tel 713-639-7500. *Dir* Daniel Gorski; *Assoc Dir* Joseph Navel; *Dean Jr School & Community Outreach Prog* Norma R Ory
Estab 1926. Under the auspices of the Museum of Fine Arts; pvt; D & E; fels; SC 34, LC 5; enrl studio 1552, Jr 2597
Ent Req: Ent req portfolio review, transfer students
Degrees: 4 yr cert
Tuition: $780 FT, $240 each SC, $160 each Art History; no campus res
Courses: Art History, Ceramics, Drawing, Jewelry, Painting, Photography, †Printmaking, †Sculpture, Visual Fundamentals
Children's Classes: Enrl 2597; tuition $85-$100 per class (4-17 yrs)

HOUSTON BAPTIST UNIVERSITY, Dept of Art, 7502 Fondren Rd, 77074. Tel 713-271-7213, 271-0461; FAX 713-995-3489. *Dean Fine Arts* Robert Linder; *Chmn* James Busby; *Instr* Erik Mandaville
Estab 1963; den; D & E; scholarships; SC 7, LC 9; enrl D 2500, maj 35
Ent Req: HS dipl, ent exam
Degrees: BA & BS
Tuition: $155 per sem hr
Courses: Art Appreciation, Art Education, Ceramics, Design, Drawing, History of Art & Archaeology, Painting, Printmaking, Sculpture, Elementary Art with Teacher Certification

RICE UNIVERSITY, Dept of Art and Art History, PO Box 1892, 77251. Tel 713-527-4815; FAX 713-285-5207. *Chmn* Basilios N Poulos; *Dir Sewall Art Gallery* Stella Douglas; *Prof* William A Camfield, PhD; *Prof* C A Boterf, MFA; *Prof* Neil Havens, MA; *Prof* W M Widrig, PhD; *Assoc Prof* George Smith, MFA; *Prof* Geoffrey Winningham; *Assoc Prof* Karin Broker, MFA; *Asst Prof* John Sparagana; *Assoc Prof* Brian Huberman; *Lectr* Bren DuBay; *Lectr* Stella Dobbins, MFA; *Vis Lectr* Thomas McEvilley, PhD; *Asst Prof* Richard Wilson, PhD; *Dir Sewall Art Gallery* Judith Steinhoff Morrison, PhD
Estab 1912, dept estab 1966-67; pvt; D; scholarships; SC 27, LC 31, GC (BFA) 7; enrl D 125, non-maj 75, maj 50, grad 2 (BFA)
Ent Req: HS dipl, CEEB, evaluations of HS counselors and teachers, interview
Degrees: BA 4 yrs, BFA 5 yrs, MA(Art History, Classical Archaeology)
Tuition: $8500 per yr, $3450 per sem, grad $9300 for first six sem; PT 370 per hr; campus res—room & board $5200
Courses: †Art History, Design, Drawing, Film, History of Art & Archaeology, Museum Staff Training, Photography, Printmaking, Sculpture, Theatre Arts, Video
Adult Hobby Classes: Tuition $300 per class. Courses—Photography

SAN JACINTO COLLEGE-NORTH, Art Dept, 5800 Uvalde, 77049. Tel 713-458-4050. *Chmn* Dr Timothy Fleming; *Instr* Robert Hume; *Instr* Bill Frazier; *Instr* Ken Luce
Estab 1972; pub; D & E; scholarships; SC 16, LC 3; enrl D 56, E 21, non-maj 50, maj 27
Ent Req: HS dipl
Degrees: AA 2 yrs
Tuition: Res—undergrad $318 per yr, $136 per 12 hrs, $80 for 6 hrs; nonres—undergrad $1286 per yr, $643 per sem, $270 per 6 hrs; no campus res
Courses: Art Appreciation, Art History, Drawing, Fashion Arts, Illustration, Interior Design, Lettering, Painting, Photography, Sculpture, Textile Design, 2-D Design, 3-D Design, †Studio Art
Adult Hobby Classes: Enrl 50; tuition $15 - $40 per 6-18 hrs. Courses—Calligraphy, Ceramics, Origami, Pastel Art, Photography, Stained Glass
Children's Classes: Enrl 15, tuition $30 per 6 wks. Courses—Pastel Art
Summer School: Dir, Kenneth A Luce. Enrl 10 - 25; tuition $78 - $96. Courses—vary beginning May

TEXAS SOUTHERN UNIVERSITY, Dept of Fine Arts, 3100 Cleburne Ave, 77004. Tel 713-527-7337. *Chmn* Fennoyee Thomas
Estab 1949; pub; D & E; scholarships; SC 31, LC 12, GC 4; enrl maj 85, other 100
Ent Req: HS dipl
Degrees: BFA and B(Art Educ) 5 yrs
Tuition: $412 annual tuition
Courses: Art Education, Ceramics, Design, Drawing, Weaving, Painting, Sculpture, Hot Print Making, Silk Screen Painting
Summer School: Dir, Joseph Jones, Jr. Enrl 100; for a term of 6 wks beginning June. Courses—Art Appreciation in Educational Program, Advanced crafts for Teachers, Basic Art for Elementary Teachers, Exhibition: Mural Painting in School, Problems in Art Education, Problems in Secondary Art Education, Research Projects

UNIVERSITY OF HOUSTON, Dept of Art, 4800 Calhoun Rd, 77204-4893. Tel 713-743-3001; FAX 713-743-2823. *Chmn* Dr David L Jacobs. Instrs: FT 29, PT 7
Estab 1927; pub; D & E; scholarships; enrl D 600 maj
Ent Req: HS dipl, SAT
Degrees: BA, BFA, MFA
Tuition: Res—$4 per sem cr hr; nonres—$40 per sem cr hr; campus res available
Courses: Art History, Ceramics, Interior Design, Painting, Photography, †Printmaking, †Sculpture, Silversmithing, Video, †Graphic Communications, †Jewelry/Metals, †Paint/Drawing, †Photography/Video

UNIVERSITY OF SAINT THOMAS, Art Dept, 3800 Montrose Blvd, 77006. Tel 713-522-7911. *Chmn* Nancy L Jircik, MA
Den; D & E; scholarships; SC 15, LC 7; enrl E 30, maj 44
Ent Req: HS dipl
Degrees: BFA
Tuition: $250 per cr hr PT, $3000 per sem FT; campus res available
Courses: Art History

HUNTSVILLE

SAM HOUSTON STATE UNIVERSITY, Art Dept, 77341. Tel 409-294-1315. *Dept Head* Jimmy H Barker, MFA; *Prof* Gene M Eastman, MFA; *Prof* Charles A Pebworth, MA; *Prof* Harry J Ahysen, MFA; *Prof* William J Breitenbach, MFA; *Assoc Prof* Darry Patrick, PhD; *Assoc Prof* Kenneth L Zonker, MA; *Asst Prof*

Patric K Lawler; *Asst Prof* Leah Hardy
Estab 1879, dept estab 1936; pub; D; SC 26, LC 7, GC 12; enrl D 844, non-maj 100, maj 170, grad 15
Ent Req: HS dipl, ACT or SAT
Degrees: BA, BFA 4 yrs, MFA 2 yrs, MA 1 1/2 yrs
Tuition: Res—$548 per 16 hrs; nonres—$2212 per 16 hrs; campus res—room $1040 per yr, board $1310 (7-day plan), $1210 (5-day plan)
Courses: †Advertising Design, †Sculpture, Studio Art
Summer School: Chmn, Jimmy H Barker. Enrl 100; tuition 232 per term of 6 wks beginning June 5 & July 11. Courses—Art History, Crafts, Drawing, Watercolor, 2-D Design

HURST

TARRANT COUNTY JUNIOR COLLEGE, Art Dept, Northeast Campus, 76054. Tel 817-281-7860. *Chmn* Arnold Leondar, MA; *Asst Prof* Richard Hlad, MA; *Asst Prof* Martha Gordon, MFA; *Assoc Prof* Karmien Bowman, MA
Estab 1967, dept estab 1968; pub; D & E; SC 19, LC 3; enrl D 200, E 150, non-maj 150, maj 200
Ent Req: HS dipl, GED, admission by individual approval
Degrees: AA and AAS 2 yrs
Tuition: Res—$14 per hr, minimum $70 per sem; nonres—of county $8 per sem hr added to res fee, others $120 per sem hr with $200 minimum fee, aliens $120 per sem hr with $200 minimum fee; no campus res
Courses: Advertising Design, Art Appreciation, Art Education, Art History, Ceramics, Collages, Constructions, Drawing, Jewelry, Mixed Media, Painting, Photography, Printmaking, Sculpture
Adult Hobby Classes: Enrl 50; for 7 wks. Courses—Drawing, Oil-Acrylic, Tole Painting, Ceramics
Children's Classes: Enrl 100; 7 wks. Courses—Cartooning, Ceramics, College for Kids, Drawing, Painting
Summer School: Dir, Dr Jane Harper. Enrl 100; tuition as above for term of 6 wks beginning June. Courses—Art Appreciation

KILGORE

KILGORE COLLEGE, Art Dept, Fine Arts, 1100 Broadway, 75662-3299. Tel 903-984-8531. *Chmn* Frank Herbert; *Instr* John Hillier
Estab 1935; D & E; scholarships; SC 11, LC 3; enrl D 75, E 25, non-maj 25, maj 50
Ent Req: HS dipl
Degrees: AFA & AA
Tuition: District res— $11 per sem hr; non-district res—$27 per sem hr; non-state res—$39 per sem hr
Courses: †Art Education, †Art History, Commercial Art, †Drawing, Painting, Photography, †Sculpture

KINGSVILLE

TEXAS A & I UNIVERSITY, Art Dept, W Santa Gertrudis Ave, 78363. Tel 512-595-2619. *Chmn* Dr Richard Scherpereel
Estab 1925, dept estab 1930; pub; D & E; SC 21, LC 5, GC 2; enrl D 700, non-maj 300, maj 400, art maj 150, grad 20
Ent Req: HS dipl
Degrees: BFA and BA 4 yr
Tuition: Res $500; nonres $1400 per sem
Courses: Advertising Design, Art Education, Art History, Ceramics, Drawing, Graphic Arts, Painting, Printmaking, Sculpture, Teacher Training
Adult Hobby Classes: Courses offered
Summer School: Courses—full schedule

LAKE JACKSON

BRAZOSPORT COLLEGE, Art Dept, 500 College Dr, 77566. Tel 409-265-6131; FAX 409-265-2944. *Fine Arts Dept Chmn* Richard Wilcher; *Instr* Sandra Baker
Estab 1968; pub; D & E; scholarships; SC 10, LC 3; enrl D 50
Ent Req: HS dipl or GED
Degrees: AA 2 yrs
Tuition: In district—$39 per 3 cr hr; out-of-district—$45 per cr hr; nonres—$214 per 3 cr hr
Courses: Art Appreciation, Art History, Ceramics, Drawing, Mixed Media, Painting, Sculpture, Theatre Arts, Design & Watercolor
Adult Hobby Classes: Courses—Ceramics, Painting, Weaving

LEVELLAND

SOUTH PLAINS COLLEGE, Fine Arts Dept, College Ave, 79336. Tel 806-894-9611, Ext. 263. *Chmn* Jon Johnson. Instrs: FT 2, PT 1
Estab 1958; pub; D & E; SC 8, LC 5; enrl D 252, E 76, maj 52
Ent Req: HS dipl
Degrees: AA 2 yrs
Tuition: Res—$10 per sem hr; nonres—$14 per sem hr
Courses: Advertising Design, Art History, Ceramics, Commercial Art, Drafting, Drawing, Graphic Arts, Graphic Design, Painting, Photography, Sculpture, Teacher Training
Adult Hobby Classes: Enrl 62; tuition & duration vary. Courses—Drawing, Painting, Photography, Sculpture
Children's Classes: Enrl 116; tuition & duration vary. Courses—Crafts, Drawing, Painting
Summer School: Dir, Lynette Watkins. Ernl 66; tuition same as regular sem for 4 wk term. Courses—Art for Elementary Teachers, Art History, Photography

LUBBOCK

LUBBOCK CHRISTIAN UNIVERSITY, Art Dept, 5601 19th St, 79407-2099. Tel 806-796-8800. *Chmn* Karen Randolph, MFA
Scholarships offered
Degrees: BA
Tuition: $2500 - $3000 annual tuition
Courses: Advertising Design, Art Appreciation, Art Education, Art History, Calligraphy, Ceramics, Design, Drawing, Graphic Arts, Graphic Design, Handicrafts, Weaving, Jewelry, Painting, Printmaking, Sculpture, Textile Design, †Fine Arts

TEXAS TECH UNIVERSITY, Dept of Art, 79409. Tel 806-742-3825. *Chmn* Melody Weiler, MFA; *Prof* Ken Dixon, MFA; *Prof* Frank Cheatham, MFA; *Prof* Don Durland, MA; *Prof* Verne Funk, MFA; *Prof* Hugh Gibbons, MA; *Prof* Paul Hanna, MFA; *Prof* Jim Howze, MS; *Prof* Terry Morrow, MS; *Prof* Lynwood Kreneck, MFA; *Prof* Gene Mittler, PhD; *Prof* Sara Waters, MFA; *Assoc Prof* Bill Bagley, MFA; *Assoc Prof* Jane Cheatham, MFA; *Assoc Prof* Tina Fuentes, MFA; *Assoc Prof* Marvin Moon, MFA; *Assoc Prof* Nancy Reed, PhD; *Assoc Prof* Betty Street, MS; *Assoc Prof* James Hanna, MA; *Assoc Prof* Rick Dingus, MFA; *Asst Prof* Glen Brown, PhD; *Asst Prof* Nancy Slagle, MFA; *Asst Prof* Brian Steele, PhD; *Asst Prof* Rob Glover, MFA; *Asst Prof* John Stinespring PhD; *Instr* Dan Johnson, BFA; *Instr* Charlotte Funk, MFA; *Instr* Linda Kennedy, PhD; *Instr* Cornelia Johnson, MAE; *Instr* Kathy Whiteside, MFA
Estab 1925, dept estab 1967; pub; D & E; scholarships; SC 80 undergrad, 23 grad, LC 27 undergrad, 17 grad; enrl D 920, non-maj 500, maj 420, grad 60
Ent Req: HS dipl, SAT or ACT test
Degrees: BFA & BA(Art History), MAE 36 hrs, MFA 60 hrs minimum, PhD 54 hrs beyond MA minimum
Tuition: Variable for res and nonres; campus residence available
Courses: †Art Education, †Art History, †Ceramics, †Drawing, †Illustration, †Jewelry, Mixed Media, †Painting, †Photography, †Printmaking, †Textile Design, Weaving, †Design Communication, Glass, †Metals
Adult Hobby Classes: Art History, Studio
Children's Classes: Art Project for talented high school students, Artery classes for elementary & middle school students
Summer School: Dir, Betty Street. Courses—Art Education, Art History, Studio

MARSHALL

WILEY COLLEGE, Dept of Fine Arts, 711 Wiley Ave, 75670. Tel 903-938-8341. *Head Dept* Mary P Trenkle
Estab 1873; den; D & E; scholarships; SC 16, LC 2; enrl D 56
Ent Req: HS dipl
Degrees: No art major
Tuition: $50 per hr, plus special fees; campus res—$500-$794 per yr
Courses: Advertising Design, Art Education, Art History, Ceramics, Commercial Art, Drawing, Fashion Arts, Graphic Arts, Graphic Design, Painting, Theatre Arts, Decoupage, Enameling
Summer School: Dir, Dr David R Houston. Tuition $50 per hr for term of 8 wks beginning June. Courses—as required

MESQUITE

EASTFIELD COLLEGE, Humanities Division, Art Dept, 3737 Motley, 75150. Tel 214-324-7132. *Chmn* John Stewart
Degrees: AA
Tuition: $36 per 3 cr hr
Courses: Art Appreciation, Art History, Ceramics, Design, Drawing, Jewelry, Painting, Sculpture

MIDLAND

MIDLAND COLLEGE, Allison Fine Arts Dept, 3600 N Garfield, 79705. Tel 915-685-4500. *Chmn* Stan Jacobs, PhD; *Instr* Warren Taylor, MFA
Estab 1972; pub; D & E; scholarships; SC 28, LC 4; enrl D 70, E 80, non-maj 125, maj 25
Ent Req: HS dipl
Degrees: AA and AAA 2 yrs
Tuition: Res—undergrad $158 per 12 hrs plus $36 fee; nonres—undergrad $362 per 12 hrs plus $36 fee; no campus res
Courses: †Advertising Design, Aesthetics, Art Education, Art History, †Ceramics, Collages, †Commercial Art, Constructions, Drafting, †Drawing, Fashion Arts, Film, Graphic Arts, Graphic Design, Handicrafts, Illustration, Interior Design, †Jewelry, Lettering, Mixed Media, †Painting, †Photography, †Printmaking, †Sculpture, †Silversmithing, Stage Design, Teacher Training
Adult Hobby Classes: Tuition $25 per 6 wks. Courses—Ceramics, Drawing, Painting
Children's Classes: Ceramics, Drawing, Painting, Sculpture
Summer School: Same as regular term

NACOGDOCHES

STEPHEN F AUSTIN STATE UNIVERSITY, Art Dept, PO Box 13001, 75962. Tel 409-568-4804. *Chmn* Jon D Wink, MFA
Estab 1923; pub; D & E; SC 28, LC 11, GC 11; enrl D 461, non-maj 150, maj 200, grad 20
Ent Req: HS dipl, ACT score 18
Degrees: BA & BFA 4 yrs, MFA 2 yrs, MA 1 yr
Tuition: Res—undergrad $360 per 15 hr, grad $288 per 12 hr; nonres—undergrad $2430 per 15 hr, grad $1944 per 12 hr; campus res available
Courses: Advertising Design, Art Appreciation, Art Education, Art History, Calligraphy, Ceramics, Commercial Art, Design, Drawing, Film, Graphic Design, Illustration, Jewelry, Lettering, Mixed Media, Painting, Photography, Printmaking, Sculpture, Silversmithing, Teacher Training, Cinematography

ODESSA

UNIVERSITY OF TEXAS OF PERMIAN BASIN, Dept of Art, 79762. Tel 915-367-2011. *Chmn* Pam Price, MFA
Estab 1972; pub; D; scholarships; SC 45, LC 10; enrl non-maj 10, maj 30
Degrees: BA
Tuition: Campus residency available
Courses: Ceramics, Commercial Art, Painting, Printmaking, Sculpture
Summer School: Courses—varied

PARIS

PARIS JUNIOR COLLEGE, Art Dept, 2400 Clarksville St, 75460. Tel 214-785-7661, Ext 460; 800-441-1398 (TX), 800-232-5804 (US). *Chmn* Cathie Tyler
Estab 1924; pub; D & E; scholarships; SC 11, LC 2; enrl D 60-70, E 50-60, non-maj 60-65, maj 15-20
Ent Req: None
Degrees: AA in Art 2 yrs
Tuition: $13 - $20 per hr plus $40 fee
Courses: Art Appreciation, Art History, Ceramics, Design, Painting, Photography, Sculpture, Jewelry Fabrication & Design (General Art Preparatory Program)
Adult Hobby Classes: Enrl 20. Courses—Painting, Drawing, Photography, Art Appreciation
Children's Classes: Classes offered summer only. Courses—Painting, Drawing, Ceramics, Drawing, Sculpture
Summer School: Dir, Cathie Tyler. 2-5 wk sessions June-Aug. Courses—Photography, Painting, Art Appreciation

PASADENA

SAN JACINTO JUNIOR COLLEGE, Div of Fine Arts, 8060 Spencer Hwy, PO Box 2007, 77501-2007. Tel 713-476-1501. *Division Chmn Fine Arts* Jerry Callahan
Estab 1961; pub; D & E; SC 5, LC 1; enrl D 230, E 45, non-maj 120, maj 155
Ent Req: HS dipl, GED or individual approval
Degrees: AA and AS 2 yrs
Tuition: In district—$50 per 6 hr; out of district—$240 per 6 hr; out of state & non-citizens—$240 per 6 hr
Courses: Advertising Design, Art Appreciation, Art History, Ceramics, Commercial Art, Design, Drawing, Lettering, Painting, Photography, Sculpture, Advertising Art, Free Illustration
Summer School: Enrl 25; tuition $25 for term of 6 wks beginning June 5th. Courses—Design, Painting Workshop

PLAINVIEW

WAYLAND BAPTIST UNIVERSITY, Dept of Art, Division of Christian Communication Arts, PO Box 249, 1900 W Seventh, 79072. Tel 806-296-5521. *Assoc Prof* Candace Keller
Den; D & E; scholarships; SC 15, LC 2; enrl D 81, E 24, maj 10
Ent Req: HS dipl, ent exam
Degrees: BA and BS 4 yrs
Tuition: $98 per sem hr
Adult Hobby Classes: Enrl 90 - 100; 16 wk term. Courses—Art Appreciation, Ceramics, Design, Drawing, Painting, Sculpture, Watercolor
Children's Classes: Enrl 25-35; tuition $60 for 2 wk term. Courses offered through Llano Estarado Museum on Campus
Summer School: Dir, Candace Keller. Enrl 30 - 40; 3 wk term. Courses—Ceramics, Crafts, Teacher Art Education, Watercolor

ROCKPORT

SIMON MICHAEL SCHOOL OF FINE ARTS, PO Box 1283, 78382. Tel 512-729-6233. *Head Dept* Simon Michael. Instrs: FT 1
Estab 1947; pvt; enrl professionals & intermediates
Ent Req: None
Degrees: None
Courses: Drawing, Landscape Architecture, Mixed Media, Painting, Sculpture
Summer School: Enrl varies; tuition varies for each 1 wk workshop. Courses—Travel Art Workshop in USA and Europe

SAN ANGELO

ANGELO STATE UNIVERSITY, Art and Music Dept, ASU Station, PO Box 10906, 76909. Tel 915-942-2085. *Coordr* Dr Robert Prestiano; *Chmn Art & Music* Koste Belcheff
Estab 1963, dept estab 1976; pub; D & E; SC 15, LC 9; enrl D 400 (art), E 50, non-maj 320, maj 80
Ent Req: HS dipl
Degrees: BA(Art) and BA(Art) and Teaching Certification
Tuition: Res—$18 per sem hr; nonres—$120 per sem hr; campus res— room & board $892-1640
Courses: Art Education, †Art History, †Ceramics, Drawing, †Painting, †Printmaking, †Sculpture, Creative Design, †Graphic Illustration, History of Contemporary Art, History of Italian Renaissance, Greek and Roman Art, Intaglio Processes
Summer School: Tuition as above for term of 10 wks beginning June 1. Courses—Art History, Introduction to Art, Studio Courses incl Design and Drawing, Art Education, Ceramics, Sculpture

SAN ANTONIO

INCARNATE WORD COLLEGE, Art Dept, 4301 Broadway, 78209. Tel 210-829-6022. *Prof* William A Reily, MFA; *Prof* E Stoker, MA; *Prof* Sr Martha Ann Kirk, PhD; *Asst Prof* Taylor Mitchell, PhD; *Lectr* Nancy Pawel, MA; *Lectr* Don Ewers, MA
Estab 1881, dept estab 1948; den; D; scholarships; SC 14, LC 9; enrl D 195, non-maj 120, maj 30
Ent Req: HS dipl, ent exam
Degrees: BA 4 yrs
Courses: †Art Education, Art History, Ceramics, Design, History of Art & Archaeology, Museum Staff Training, Painting, Photography, Sculpture, Stage Design, Weaving

OUR LADY OF THE LAKE UNIVERSITY, Dept of Art, 411 SW 24 St, 78207-4689. Tel 210-434-6711. *Dean* Sr Isabel Ball, PhD; *Asst Prof* Jody Cariolano, MFA; *Asst Prof* Sr Jule Adele Espey, PhD; *Instr* Alfred Cruz, MA. Instrs: FT 2, PT 1
Estab 1911, dept estab 1920; den; D & E; scholarships; SC 12, LC 3; enrl non-maj 62, maj 8
Ent Req: HS dipl, completion of GED tests, 35 on each test or average of 45 on tests
Degrees: BA(Art)
Tuition: Res—undergrad $2996 per sem; res—grad $201 per sem hr; campus res—room & board $1430-$1675 per yr
Courses: Art Education, Art History, Design, Drawing, Graphic Arts, Painting, Photography, Printmaking, Sculpture, Cinema
Adult Hobby Classes: Courses offered

SAINT MARY'S UNIVERSITY OF SAN ANTONIO, Dept of Fine Arts, 78228. Tel 210-436-3797. *Chairperson* Sharon McMahon. Instrs: FT 6, PT 8
Estab 1852; pvt; D & E; SC 10, LC 20; enrl D 60, maj 58
Ent Req: HS dipl or GED, ent exam
Degrees: BA 4-5 yrs
Tuition: Res—$3220 per 12 cr hr, $210 per cr hr; campus res—room & board $1350-$1620 per sem
Courses: Art Education, Drawing, Film, Graphic Design, History of Art & Archaeology, Painting, Photography, Printmaking, Sculpture, Teacher Training, Theatre Arts, 3-D Design
Adult Hobby Classes: Enrl 75-100; tuition $25. Courses—vary
Summer School: Courses—vary

SAN ANTONIO ART INSTITUTE, 6000 N New Braunfels, 78209. Tel 210-824-7224; FAX 210-824-6622. *Exec Dir* Brooke F Dudley; *Registrar* Patty Beck
D & E; scholarships
Ent Req: None
Courses: Art History, Ceramics, Design, Drawing, Graphic Design, Painting, Printmaking, Sculpture, Life Drawing, 2-D & 3-D Design
Adult Hobby Classes: Enrl 1000 per sem; tuition $215 for 15 wks
Children's Classes: Tuition $65 for 6 wk term. Courses—Cartooning, Ceramics, Computer Art, Drawing, Jewelry, Painting, Sculpture, 2-D Design
Summer School: Enrl 400; 8 wk term; fall/spring program also available.
Courses—Ceramics, Design, Drawing, Painting, Printmaking, Sculpture

SAN ANTONIO COLLEGE, Visual Arts & Technology, 1300 San Pedro Ave, 78284. Tel 210-733-2894; FAX 210-733-2338. *Chmn* Thomas Willome. Instrs: FT 17, PT 20
Estab 1955; pub; D & E; SC 75, LC 4; enrl D 1000-1300, E 250-450
Ent Req: Ent req HS dipl, GED, TASP, ent exam
Degrees: AA and AS 2 yrs
Tuition: $298 per 12 sem hrs; no campus res
Courses: Advertising Design, Drawing, History of Art & Archaeology, Illustration, Lettering, Painting, Photography, Sculpture, Electronic Graphics, Jewelry Repair & Design, Production Pottery
Summer School: Dir, Thomas Willome. Enrl 400; tuition $150 per 6 sem hrs.
Courses—Same as for regular school yr

TRINITY UNIVERSITY, Dept of Art, 715 Stadium Dr, 78212. Tel 210-736-7216. *Chmn* Jim Stoker, MA; *Prof* Robert E Tiemann, MFA; *Prof* Kate Ritson, MFA; *Prof* William A Bristow, MFA
Estab 1869; pvt; D & E; SC 39, LC 20; enrl D 144, E 30, non-maj 50, maj 90
Ent Req: HS dipl, CEEB, SAT, 3 achievement tests
Degrees: BA 4 yrs
Tuition: $348 per sem hr; campus res available
Courses: Art Education, Drawing, Graphic Arts, Painting, Photography, Printmaking, Sculpture, †Studio Art
Adult Hobby Classes: Courses offered by Department of Continuing Educ
Summer School: Dir, Dept of Continuing Educ. Tuition $114 per hr. Courses vary

UNIVERSITY OF TEXAS AT SAN ANTONIO, Division of Art & Architecture, 6900 N Loop 1604 W, 78249. Tel 210-691-4352. *Div Dir* James Broderick, MA; *Prof* Ronald Binks, MFA; *Prof* Charles Field, MFA; *Prof* Jacinto Quirarte, PhD; *Prof* Stephen Reynolds, MFA; *Prof* Judith Sobre, PhD; *Assoc Prof* Ken Little; *Assoc Prof* Kent Rush, MFA; *Assoc Prof* Dennis Olsen, MA; *Assoc Prof* Neil Maurer, MFA; *Asst Prof* Frances Colpitt; *Asst Prof* Constance Lowe, MFA
Pub; D & E; scholarships; SC 31, LC 25, GC 17; enrl maj 200, grad 35
Ent Req: HS dipl, ACT, grad
Degrees: BFA 4 yrs, MFA 2 yrs
Tuition: $240 per sem (12 hrs or under)
Courses: Art History, †Ceramics, †Drawing, †Painting, †Photography, †Printmaking, †Sculpture
Summer School: Tuition $50 per sem. Courses—Art History, Ceramics, Drawing, Painting, Photography, Printmaking, Sculpture

SAN MARCOS

SOUTHWEST TEXAS STATE UNIVERSITY, Dept of Art, 78666. Tel 512-245-2611. *Dean* Richard Cheatham; *Chmn* Brian G Row, MFA; *Dir Works on Paper Exhib* Charles Meng, MFA; *Prof* Mark Todd; *Prof* Jean Laman, MFA; *Prof* Marshall Wortham; *Prof* Erik Nielsen, PhD; *Prof* Eric Weller, MFA; *Prof* Neal Wilson, MFA; *Assoc Prof* Michel Conroy, MFA; *Assoc Prof* Carole Greer, MFA; *Assoc Prof* Tom Williams, PhD; *Asst Prof* Francine Carraro, PhD; *Asst Prof* Roger Colombik, MFA; *Asst Prof* Beverly Penn, MFA; *Asst Prof* Sandra McCallister, MFA; *Asst Prof* Randall Reid, MFA; *Asst Prof* Diane Gregory, PhD; *Asst Prof* David Shields; *Lectr* Gail Fischer, MFA; *Lectr* Chris Hill, BS; *Lectr* Kim Iberg, BFA; *Lectr* Brad Lawton; *Lectr* Roger Christian; *Lectr* Jill Bedgood, MFA; *Lectr* Dana Holland; *Lectr* Pat Taylor; *Instr* Joseph Biel; *Instr* David Olivant
Estab 1903, dept estab 1916; pub; D & E; scholarships; SC 31, LC 7, GC 6; enrl D 1600, E 100, non-maj 1350, maj 360
Ent Req: HS dipl, ACT, SAT
Degrees: BFA(Commercial & Studio), BFA Art Ed all-level & secondary, BA secondary, BA 4 yrs
Courses: Advertising Design, Art Appreciation, Art Education, †Art History, Ceramics, †Commercial Art, Design, †Drawing, Film, Goldsmithing, Graphic Arts, Graphic Design, †Illustration, †Photography, Silversmithing, Design, Video †Weaving, Illustration, †Jewelry, Lettering, †Painting, †Printmaking, †Sculpture, Teacher Training, †Textile Design, Video
Summer School: Chmn, Brian Row. Two 6 week terms

SEGUIN

TEXAS LUTHERAN COLLEGE, Dept of Visual Arts, 1000 W Court St, 78155. Tel 512-372-8000, Ext 6016. *Chmn* Dr John Nellermoe. Instrs: FT 2
Estab 1923; D; SC 18, LC 3; enrl 1000, maj 10
Ent Req: HS dipl
Degrees: BA(Art) 4 yrs
Tuition: Campus residency available
Courses: Advertising Design, Art Appreciation, Art Education, Art History, Ceramics, Drawing, Painting, Printmaking, Sculpture, Watercolor
Adult Hobby Classes: Enrl 12; tuition $72 for 6 wk term. Courses—Art Appreciation, Sketching
Summer School: Instr, John Nellermoe. Enrl 12; tuition $75 for 6 wk term.
Courses—Ceramics, Painting

SHERMAN

AUSTIN COLLEGE, Art Dept, PO Box 1177, 75091-1177. Tel 214-813-2000. *Chmn* Mark Smith, MFA; *Prof* Joseph Havel; *Assoc Prof* Tim Tracz, MFA
Estab 1848; pvt; D; scholarships; SC 9, LC 5, GC 8; enrl D 350, maj 55, grad 2
Ent Req: Ent exam plus acceptance by admission committee
Degrees: BA 4 yrs, MA 5 yrs
Tuition: $7250 per yr, campus res—room & board $2260
Courses: Art History, Ceramics, Drawing, Photography, Printmaking, Sculpture

TEMPLE

TEMPLE JUNIOR COLLEGE, Art Dept, 2600 S First, 76504. Tel 817-773-9961. *Chmn* Michael Donahue, MFA
Estab 1926; pub; D & E; SC 4, LC 2; enrl D 100, E 15, non-maj 85, maj 15
Ent Req: HS dipl, ACT or SAT
Degrees: AA 2 yrs
Tuition: District res—$44 per sem hr; non-district res—$55 per sem hr; non-state res—$230 per sem hr; campus res available
Courses: Art Appreciation, Art History, Ceramics, Design, Drawing, Painting, Printmaking, Sculpture, Figure Drawing
Adult Hobby Classes: Enrl 15 per class; tuition $19 per 8 sessions. Courses—Arts & Crafts, Calligraphy, Drawing

TEXARKANA

TEXARKANA COLLEGE, Art Dept, 2500 N Robison Rd, 75599. Tel 903-838-4541. *Chmn* Dr Rolfe Wylie; *Prof* Mary Long
Estab 1927; D & E; scholarships
Ent Req: HS dipl
Tuition: District res—$280 for 15 cr hrs; out of district res—$300 for 15 cr hrs
Courses: Art Education, Ceramics, Drafting, Drawing, Painting, Printmaking, Sculpture, Teacher Training, Weaving, Watercolor
Summer School: Dir, Rolfe Wylie. Enrl 20; tuition $200. Courses—Drawing & Ceramics

TYLER

TYLER JUNIOR COLLEGE, Art Program, PO Box 9020, 75711. Tel 903-510-2200, 510-2234. *Prog Dir* Charline Wallis
Scholarships offered
Degrees: AA
Tuition: Res—undergrad $578 per yr
Courses: Art Appreciation, Art Education, Art History, Ceramics, Design, Weaving, Drawing, Painting, Sculpture, Weaving
Adult Hobby Classes: Courses—offered
Children's Classes: Courses—Offered for ages 5-8 & 9-12
Summer School: Courses—Offered

UNIVERSITY OF TEXAS AT TYLER, Dept of Art, 3900 University Blvd, 75701. Tel 214-566-7250. *Chmn* Donald Paoletta, PhD; *Prof* William B Stephens, EdD; *Assoc Prof* James Pace, MFA; *Asst Prof* Karen Roberson, MFA; *Instr* Rosalie Loggin, MA

Estab 1973; pub; D & E; scholarships; SC 28, LC 6, GC 11
Ent Req: AA degree or 60 hrs of college study
Degrees: BA and BFA
Tuition: Res—$173 per sem; nonres—$323 per sem
Courses: Aesthetics, †Art Education, †Art History, Ceramics, Drawing, Graphic Arts, Graphic Design, History of Art & Archaeology, Interior Design, Mixed Media, Painting, Photography, Printmaking, Sculpture, Teacher Training, †Studio Art
Summer School: Dir, Donald Van Horn. Tuition res $76, nonres $151.
Courses—vary

VICTORIA

VICTORIA COLLEGE, 2200 E Red River, 77901. Tel 512-573-3291; FAX 512-572-3850. *Head Dept* Larry Shook, MA; *Prof* Nancy Bandy
Estab 1925; pub; D & E; SC 9, LC 3; enrl D 100, E 40, non-maj 40, maj 100
Ent Req: HS dipl
Tuition: Res—$100 per sem; nonres—$200 per sem; no campus res
Courses: Art Education, Art History, Commercial Art, Display, Drafting, Drawing, Graphic Design, Printmaking, Sculpture, Teacher Training
Summer School: Courses—as above

WACO

BAYLOR UNIVERSITY, Dept of Art, 76798-7263. Tel 817-755-1867. *Chmn & Prof* John D McClanahan; *Prof* Paul Z Kemp, MFA; *Prof* William M Jensen, PhD; *Prof* Berry J Klingman, MFA; *Assoc Prof* Terry M Roller, MFA; *Asst Prof* Paul A McCoy, MFA; *Assoc Prof* Charles J Isoline, EdD; *Asst Prof* Janice McCullagh, PhD; *Asst Prof* Heidi J Hornik, PhD; *Asst Prof* Bob Cromer, EdD; *Prof* Karl Umlauf, MFA; *Asst Prof* Mark W Moran, MFA
Estab 1845, dept estab 1870; den; D & E; scholarships; SC 65, LC 24, GC 12; enrl D 1600, E60, non-maj 1300, maj 150
Ent Req: HS dipl, ent exam, SAT/ACT tests
Degrees: BA, BFA(Art Educ) & BFA(Studio) 4 yrs
Tuition: $3200 per yr, $200 per sem hr; campus res—room & board $3640
Courses: †Art Education, †Art History, †Ceramics, Drawing, Graphic Arts, Handicrafts, †Jewelry, †Painting, Photography, Sculpture, †Advertising Design, 2-D & 3-D Design, Fibers, Metalsmithing
Summer School: Prof, John McClanahan. Enrl 200, tuition $200 per cr hr for terms of 5 wks each beginning May 29 & July 3. Courses—Advertising Design, Art Education, Art History, Ceramics, Drawing, Fibers, Jewelry Design, Painting, Printmaking

MCLENNAN COMMUNITY COLLEGE, Fine Arts Dept, 1400 College Dr, 76708. Tel 817-756-6551. *Chmn* Dr Don Balmos
Estab 1965; pub; D & E; SC 8, LC 3; enrl D 35, non-maj 20, maj 40
Ent Req: HS dipl
Degrees: AA 2 yrs
Tuition: Res—$168 per yr; nonres—$900 per yr; no campus res
Courses: Art History, Drawing, Painting, Photography, Sculpture, Art Appreciation, Color, Design, Problems in Contemporary Art
Adult Hobby Classes: Tuition depends on the class. Courses—Ceramics, Drawing, Jewelry, Painting, Sculpture, Stained Glass
Summer School: Tuition $42. Courses—Design, Drawing, Watercolor

WEATHERFORD

WEATHERFORD COLLEGE, Dept of Humanities and Art, 308 E Park Ave, 76086. Tel 817-594-5471, Ext 32. *Head Dept of Art* Myrlan Coleman, MA & MFA
Estab 1856, dept estab 1959; pub; D & E; SC 10, LC 4; enrl D 58, non-maj 30, maj 16, others 12
Ent Req: HS dipl
Degrees: AA
Courses: Art History, Intermedia, Mixed Media, Painting
Summer School: Term May 24 and July 10

WHARTON

WHARTON COUNTY JUNIOR COLLEGE, Art Dept, 911 Boling Hwy, 77488. Tel 409-532-4560, Ext 285. *Chmn* Morna Nation, MFA
Pub; D & E; SC 8, LC 2; enrl D 90, E 15
Ent Req: HS dipl, GED
Degrees: 2 yrs
Tuition: District res—$24 per sem hr; non-district—$43 per sem hr; non-state res—$69 per sem hr
Courses: Art Education, Art History, Ceramics, Drawing, History of Art & Archaeology, Painting, Sculpture, Teacher Training
Summer School: Dir Morna Nation. Enrl 10; 6 wk term. Courses—Ceramics

WICHITA FALLS

MIDWESTERN STATE UNIVERSITY, Div of Fine Arts, 3400 Taft Blvd, 76308. Tel 817-689-4264, Ext 4264. *Art Coordr* Richard Ash
Estab 1926; pub; D & E; scholarships; SC 20-30, LC 406; enrl D 300 per sem, E 30-50 per sem, non-maj 60, maj 125, others 10
Ent Req: HS dipl, ACT, SAT
Degrees: BA, BFA and BSE 4 yrs
Tuition: In-state $131.50 per cr hr
Courses: Advertising Design, Art Education, Art History, Ceramics, Commercial Art, Drawing, Graphic Arts, Graphic Design, Jewelry, Painting, Photography, Printmaking, Sculpture, Silversmithing

UTAH

CEDAR CITY

SOUTHERN UTAH STATE UNIVERSITY, Dept of Art, 351 W Center, 84720. Tel 801-586-7962. *Chmn* Mark Talbert. Instrs: FT 4, PT 2
Estab 1897; pub; D & E; scholarships; SC 29, LC 6; enrl D 300, E 80, maj 60, minors 45
Ent Req: HS dipl ent exam
Degrees: BA and BS 4 yrs
Tuition: $1350 - 10-20 cr hrs
Courses: Ceramics, Commercial Art, Drawing, Graphic Arts, Graphic Design, History of Art & Archaeology, Illustration, Painting, Sculpture, Teacher Training
Summer School: Dir, Arlene Braithwaite. Tuition same as regular school.
Courses—Drawing, Ceramics, Art Methods for Elementary School, Art Appreciation

EPHRAIM

SNOW COLLEGE, Art Dept, 150 E College Ave, 84627. Tel 801-283-4021, Ext 356. *Chmn* Osral Allred
Scholarships offered
Degrees: AA, AAS
Tuition: Res—$720 per yr; nonres— $1500 per yr
Courses: Art Appreciation, Ceramics, Design, Drawing, Interior Design, Jewelry, Painting, Photography, Printmaking, Sculpture

LOGAN

UTAH STATE UNIVERSITY
—Dept of Landscape Architecture Environmental Planning, 84322-4005. Tel 801-750-3471. *Head* Richard E Toth. Instrs: FT 6, PT 3
Degrees: BLA 4 yrs, MLA 2 - 3 yrs
Tuition: Res—$518 per quarter; nonres—$1388 per quarter
Courses: †Landscape Architecture, †Town & Regional Planning
—Dept of Art, UMC 4000, 84322. Tel 801-750-3460. *Head* Marion R Hyde; *Prof* Glen Edwards; *Prof* Jon Anderson; *Prof* Moishe Smith; *Prof* Adrian Van Suchtelen; *Prof* Ray Hellberg; *Assoc Prof* Craig Law; *Assoc Prof* John Neely; *Asst Prof* Thomas Toone; *Asst Prof* Alan Hashimoto; *Asst Prof* Christopher Terry; *Asst Prof* Susanne Warma; *Asst Prof* Sara Northerner; *Asst Prof* Greg Schulte; *Asst Prof* Janet Shapero
Estab 1890; D & E; scholarships; enrl D 300, maj 300, grad 35
Ent Req: HS dipl, HS transcript, ACT
Degrees: BS, BA, BFA, MFA and MA
Tuition: Res—$1821 per 15 cr hrs in 3 quarters; nonres—$4983 per 15 cr hrs in 3 quarters; campus res available
Courses: †Advertising Design, †Art Education, †Art History, †Ceramics, †Drawing, †Graphic Arts, †Illustration, †Painting, †Photography, †Printmaking, †Sculpture
Summer School: Head, Prof Marion R Hyde. 4 wk session. Courses—Ceramics, Ceramic Handbuilding, Ceramic Wheelthrow, Individual Projects, Photography

OGDEN

WEBER STATE UNIVERSITY, Dept of Visual Arts, 84408-2001. Tel 801-626-6762. *Chmn* James R McBeth, MFA; *Prof* Arthur R Adelmann, MFA; *Prof* Dale W Bryner, MFA; *Prof* David N Cox, MFA; *Prof* Richard J VanWagoner, MFA; *Prof* Mark Biddle, MFA; *Prof* Susan Makov, MFA; *Assoc Prof* James Jacobs, MFA; *Assoc Prof* Angelika Pagel, PhD; *Assoc Prof* Drex Brooks, MFA; *Asst Prof* Miguel Almanza, EdD
Estab 1933, dept estab 1937; pub; D & E; scholarships; SC 66, LC 17; enrl D 2464, E 694, non-maj 700, maj 200
Ent Req: HS dipl, ACT
Degrees: BA, BS 4 yr
Tuition: Res—$1542 per yr; nonres— $4332 per yr; campus res available
Courses: Advertising Design, Art Education, Art History, Ceramics, Commercial Art, Drawing, Graphic Arts, †Graphic Design, †Illustration, Jewelry, Lettering, Painting, †Photography, Printmaking, Sculpture, Silversmithing, Teacher Training, Textile Design, †2-D, †3-D
Summer School: Dir James R McBeth. Tuition $514 for term of 8 wks beginning June 24

PROVO

BRIGHAM YOUNG UNIVERSITY, Dept of Art, C-502 HFAC, 84602. Tel 801-378-4266. *Chmn* Robert Marshall. Instrs: FT 19, PT 5
Estab 1875, dept estab 1893; den; D & E; scholarships; SC 50; enrl E 1975, maj 352, grad 30
Ent Req: HS dipl or ACT
Degrees: BA and BFA 4 yrs, MFA 2 yrs and MA 1 1/2 yrs
Tuition: Undergrad $2000 per yr, $1000 per sem, PT $97 per cr hr; grad $2220 per yr $1110 per sem, PT $123 per cr hr; non-church member—undergrad $2320 per yr, $1160 per sem, PT $120 per cr hr, grad $2700 per yr, $1350 per sem, PT $150 per cr hr; campus res—room & board $2420
Courses: †Art Education, †Art History, †Ceramics, †Drawing, †Painting, †Printmaking, †Sculpture, Teacher Training
Summer School: Courses same as regular session

SAINT GEORGE

DIXIE COLLEGE, Art Dept, 84770. Tel 801-673-4811, Ext 297. *Dean Div Fine & Performing Arts* C Paul Anderson; *Head Art Dept* Max Bunnell; *Prof* Glen Blakely; *Asst Prof* Del Parson
Estab 1911; pub; D & E; scholarships; SC 24, LC 7, GC 1; enrl D 400, maj 30
Ent Req: HS dipl, ACT
Degrees: AA and AS 2 yrs
Tuition: Res—$406 per quarter; nonres—$1097 per quarter
Courses: Advertising Design, Art Education, Art History, Ceramics, Commercial Art, Costume Design & Construction, Drafting, Drawing, Film, Illustration, Interior Design, Painting, Photography, Printmaking, Sculpture, Teacher Training, Textile Design, Theatre Arts, Video, Weaving, Life Drawing, Portrait Drawing, Three Dimensional Design
Adult Hobby Classes: Enrl 14-16; tuition res—$355.43, nonres—$956.98; 10 wk term. Courses offered—Art Educ, Ceramics, Design, Drawing, Painting, Photography, Weaving
Children's Classes: Enrl 10-12; tuition res $103.96, nonres $257.87; 10 wk session
Summer School: Dir, Prof Glen Blakely. Enrl 100; tuition res $160.43, nonres $414.09; 8 wk session. Courses—Ceramics, Design, Drawing

SALT LAKE CITY

SALT LAKE COMMUNITY COLLEGE, Graphic Design Dept, 4600 S Redwood Rd, PO Box 30808, 84130. Tel 801-967-4111. *Chmn* Don Merrill; *Dean* Elwood Zaugg; *Prof* Allen Reinhold, MA; *Asst Prof* Douglas Jordan, BA; *Prof* Grant Hulet, MA; *Asst Prof* Fred Van Dyke, BA; *Instr* Lana Hall; *Instr* Richard Graham; *Instr* Terry Martin. Instrs: FT 3, PT 3
Pub; D & E; scholarships; SC 44, LC 7; enrl D 123, E 10, non-maj 81, maj 42
Ent Req: HS dipl or equivalent, aptitude test
Degrees: Cert, Dipl, AAS(Design), AAS(Computer Graphics), AAS(Illustration)
Tuition: Res—$75 per cr hr, $380 per 12 cr hr; nonres—$194 per cr hr, $1040 per 12 cr hr;
Courses: Advertising Design, Drawing, Illustration, Photography, †Graphic Design, †Illustration, †Lettering, Photography, Art Principles, Computer Graphics
Summer School: Dean, James Schnirel. Enrl 30; tuition $145 for term of 10 wks beginning June. Courses—Aesthetics, Drawing, Lettering, Media and Techniques

UNIVERSITY OF UTAH, Art Dept, AAC 161, 84112. Tel 801-581-8677. *Chmn* Joseph Marotta, MFA; *Dean* Robert S Olpin, PhD; *Prof* Dorothy Bearnson, MA; *Prof* Paul H Davis MFA; *Prof* Frank Anthony Smith, MFA; *Prof* Lennox Tierney; *Prof* McRay Magleby, BA; *Prof* Robert W Kleinschmidt, MFA; *Prof* Nathan Winters, PhD; *Assoc Prof* Sheila Muller, MA; *Assoc Prof* Brian Patrick, MFA; *Assoc Prof* David Pendell, MFA; *Assoc Prof* Raymond Morales, BA; *Asst Prof* Mary F Francey, PhD; *Asst Prof* Roger D (Sam) Wilson, MFA
Estab 1850, dept estab 1888; pub; D & E; scholarships; SC 79, LC 57, GC 27; enrl D 3624, E 465, non-maj 1347, maj 350, grad 10
Ent Req: HS dipl
Degrees: BA and BFA 4 yrs, MA and MFA 2 yrs
Tuition: Res—$660.50 for 16 hrs per quarter, $816 for 21 hrs per quarter; nonres—$1865 for 16 hrs per quarter, $2333 for 21 hrs per quarter; campus res available
Courses: Art Education, †Art History, †Ceramics, †Film, †Graphic Design, †Illustration, †Painting, †Photography, †Printmaking, †Sculpture, Teacher Training

WESTMINSTER COLLEGE OF SALT LAKE CITY, Dept of Arts, 1840 S 13th East, 84105. Tel 801-484-7651, Ext 217. *Chmn Fine Arts Program* Catherine Kuzminski; *Prof* Don Doxey. Instrs: FT 2, PT 5
Estab 1875; pvt; D; scholarships; SC 25, LC 2; enrl D 900-1000, maj 25
Ent Req: HS dipl, ent exam acceptable, HS grade point average
Degrees: BA and BS 4 yrs
Tuition: $6000 per yr
Courses: Art Education, Art History, Ceramics, Drawing, Painting, Photography, Sculpture, Teacher Training, Weaving

VERMONT

BENNINGTON

BENNINGTON COLLEGE, Visual Arts Division, 05201. Tel 802-442-5401; FAX 802-442-6164. *Pres* Elizabeth Coleman. Instrs: FT E 70
Estab 1932; pvt; scholarships
Degrees: AB 4 yrs & MA 2 yrs
Tuition: $17,790 per yr; no campus res
Courses: Architecture, Art History, Ceramics, Drawing, Painting, Photography, Sculpture, †Graphics, †Visual Arts

BURLINGTON

UNIVERSITY OF VERMONT, Dept of Art, College of Arts & Sciences, 304 Williams Hall, 05405. Tel 802-656-2045; FAX 802-656-8429. *Chmn* Christie Fengler-Stephany. Instrs: 24
Pub; D & E; enrl D 25
Degrees: BA and BS 4 yrs
Tuition: Res—$176 per cr hr; nonres—$536 per cr hr
Courses: Art Education, Art History, Ceramics, Design, Drawing, Painting, Photography, Printmaking, Sculpture, Teacher Training, Video, Design, Fine Metals
Adult Hobby Classes: College of Continuing Education
Summer School: Dir, Lynne Ballard. Two 9 wk sessions beginning in May

CASTLETON

CASTLETON STATE COLLEGE, Art Dept, 05735. Tel 802-468-5611. *Head Dept* Rita Bernatowicz; *Asst Prof* Bob Gershon, PhD; *Coordr* Julianna Lovell
Estab 1787; Pub; D & E; SC 31, LC 3, GC varies; enrl D 1900, E 1000, non-maj 300, maj 52, grad 5
Ent Req: HS dipl, ACT, SAT, CEEB
Degrees: BA(Art) & BA Art(2nd major Education) 4 yrs
Tuition: Res—undergrad & grad $2328 per yr, $1164 per sem, $97 per cr; nonres—undergrad & grad $5376 per yr, $2688 per sem, $224 per cr; campus res—room & board $2658
Courses: Advertising Design, Art History, Calligraphy, Drawing, Graphic Design, Lettering, Painting, Photography, Printmaking, Sculpture, Video, Computer Graphics, Education, Professional Studio Arts, Typography
Summer School: Dir, Terry Whalen. Courses—Art History, Advertising Design, Drawing, Introduction to Art, Graphic Design

COLCHESTER

ST MICHAEL'S COLLEGE, Fine Arts Dept, Winooski Park, 05439. Tel 802-655-3680. *Chmn* Donald A Rathgeb, MFA; *Asst Prof* Gregg Blasdel; *Asst Prof* Lance Richbourg, MFA
Estab 1903, dept estab 1965; den; D & E; SC 8, LC 3
Ent Req: HS dipl
Degrees: BA 4 yrs
Tuition: Res—undergrad $11,800 per yr, campus res—available
Courses: Art History, Calligraphy, Drawing, Graphic Arts, Painting, Sculpture, Stage Design, Theatre Arts, Art Theory
Summer School: Dir, Jim Jackson. Session 1, 5 wks beginning mid May, session 2, 6 wks beginning last wk in June. Courses—Drawing, Painting, Calligraphy

JOHNSON

JOHNSON STATE COLLEGE, Dept Fine Arts, Dibden Gallery, 05656. Tel 802-635-2356. *Chmn* Lisa Jablow; *Dir* Victoria Patrick; *Photography Dept Head* Peter Moriarty; *Sculpture Instr* Susan Calza
Estab 1828; pub; D & E; SC 30, LC 6; enrl D 325, non-maj 200, maj 140
Ent Req: HS dipl
Degrees: BA and BFA 4 yrs, K-12 teaching cert
Tuition: Res—undergrad $2520 per yr; nonres—undergrad $5832 per yr; campus res—room & board $4086 per yr
Courses: Art Education, Art History, Ceramics, Drawing, Painting, Photography, Sculpture, †Studio Art
Children's Classes: Gifted and talented prog for high school students
Summer School: Enrl 40; tuition res—$75 per cr hr, nonres—$105 per cr hr for term of 6 wks beginning June. Courses—Mixed Media, Painting, Sculpture

VERMONT STUDIO CENTER, PO Box 613, 05656. Tel 802-635-2727. *Dir* Jonathan Gregg. Instrs: Prominent resident & visiting artists & university faculty Scholarships
Courses: Painting, Sculpture, Writing
Adult Hobby Classes: 2 & 4 wk sessions year-round for painters, sculptors & writers. Summer/Fall program provides interaction with major American artists & critics & independent work. Winter Program focuses on independent work & 2 wk interactive sessions for writers

MIDDLEBURY

MIDDLEBURY COLLEGE, Dept of Art, Johnson Memorial Bldg, 05753. Tel 802-388-3711, Ext 5234; FAX 802-388-9646. *Chmn* Christopher Wilson. Instrs: FT 9, PT 2
Estab 1800; pvt; D; SC 7, LC 30; enrl maj 77, others 500 per term
Ent Req: Exam and cert
Degrees: AB
Courses: Art History, Design, Drawing, Painting, Photography, Printmaking, Sculpture

NORTHFIELD

NORWICH UNIVERSITY, Dept of Philosophy, Religion and Fine Arts, S Main St, 05663. Tel 802-485-2580; FAX 802-485-2580. *Assoc Prof* Earl Fechter, MFA; *Assoc Prof* Dean Perkins, PhD; *Assoc Prof* Robert McKay, PhD; *Assoc Prof* James Bennett; *Asst Prof* Benjamin Pfingstaff
Pvt; D & E; enrl D 65 (studio art), E 8, non-maj 126
Ent Req: HS dipl
Degrees: AA
Tuition: Campus residency available
Courses: Architecture, Art Education, Art History, Drawing, Painting, Photography, Printmaking, Design
Adult Hobby Classes: Chairperson, Harold Krauth, PhD

PLAINFIELD

GODDARD COLLEGE, Visual Arts Dept, 05667. Tel 802-454-8311. *Instr* Jon Batdorff; *Instr* Cynthia Ross; *Instr* David Hale
Estab 1938; pvt; D & E
Degrees: BA 4 yr, MA 1-2 yr
Tuition: Res—undergrad $8750 (comprehensive) per sem, $6500 (tuition only) per sem; nonres—undergrad $3350 per sem, grad $3840 per sem; campus res available
Courses: Art Education, Art History, Ceramics, Drawing, Painting, Photography, Printmaking, Sculpture, Video, Weaving, Holography

POULTNEY

GREEN MOUNTAIN COLLEGE, Dept of Art, 05764. Tel 802-287-9313, Ext 251; FAX 802-287-9313, Ext 340. *Chairperson* Susan Smith-Hunter
Estab 1834; enrl maj 60
Ent Req: Scholarships
Degrees: BFA 4 yrs
Tuition: Res—$13,120 per yr; nonres—$10,250 per yr
Courses: Art History, Ceramics, Design, Drawing, Graphic Design, Illustration, Painting, Photography, Printmaking, Sculpture, Graphic Design Studio, Fine Art Studio

STOWE

WRIGHT SCHOOL OF ART, 11 Moss Glen Falls, 03672. Tel 802-253-4305. *Dir* Stanley Marc Wright. Instrs: FT 2
Estab 1949; SC 5, LC 4; enrl 50
Tuition: $60 per wk
Courses: Painting
Children's Classes: Four Mon PM $5 per lesson, June to Sept. Courses—Drawing, Painting
Summer School: June - Sept

VIRGINIA

ANNANDALE

NORTHERN VIRGINIA COMMUNITY COLLEGE, Art Dept, 8333 Little River Turnpike, 22003. Tel 703-323-3107. *Chmn* Dr Jonathan Yoder
Pub; D & E; scholarships; enrl D 589, E 200
Ent Req: Open admis
Degrees: AA(Art Educ), AA(Art History) AAS(Commercial Art), AA(Fine Arts), AAS(Interior Design), & AA(Photography) 2 yrs
Tuition: Res—undergrad $33 per cr hr; nonres—undergrad $145 per cr hr; no campus res
Courses: Aesthetics, †Art Education, †Art History, Drafting, Drawing, Graphic Design, Interior Design, Painting, Printmaking, Sculpture, Stage Design, Theatre Arts, Computer Graphics, †Fine Arts
Summer School: Chmn Humanities Div, Dr Jonathan Yoder. Tuition same as regular session; 2 five wk D sessions and 1 ten wk E session during Summer. Courses—varied, incl study abroad

ARLINGTON

MARYMOUNT UNIVERSITY OF VIRGINIA, School of Arts & Sciences Division, 2807 N Glebe Rd, 22207. Tel 703-522-5600; FAX 703-284-1693. *Dean* Robert Draghi, PhD; *Prof* Pamela Stoessell, MFA; *Asst Prof* Andrew Monje
Estab 1950; pvt; D & E; SC 14, LC 20
Ent Req: HS dipl, SAT results, letter of recommendation
Degrees: BA 4 yrs, AA 2 yrs
Tuition: Res—undergrad $4536 per sem, grad $285 per cr hr; campus res available
Courses: Advertising Design, Art History, Ceramics, Design, Drafting, Drawing, Fashion Arts, Graphic Design, Handicrafts, †Industrial Design, Painting, Sculpture, Textile Design, Clothing Design & Construction, †Studio Arts
Adult Hobby Classes: Courses—any course in fine arts
Summer School: Dir, Alice S Mandanis. Tuition $1600 per summer sem, for term of 5 wks beginning May

ASHLAND

RANDOLPH-MACON COLLEGE, Dept of the Arts, 23005-1698. Tel 804-798-8375, 798-8372; FAX 804-752-7231. *Chmn* E Raymond Berry; *Prof* R D Ward; *Assoc Prof* Joe Mattys; *Asst Prof* Michael Kissane; *Asst Prof* Karen Wacksmith
Sch estab 1830; dept estab 1953; pvt; D; SC 4, LC 4; enrl D 200, non-maj 200
Degrees: BA & BS 4 yrs
Tuition: Res—undergrad $9905 per yr; campus res available
Courses: †Art History, Drawing, Painting, †Art Management, †Drama, †Music, †Studio Art

BLACKSBURG

VIRGINIA POLYTECHNIC INSTITUTE & STATE UNIVERSITY, Dept of Art & Art History, 201 Draper Rd, 24061-0103. Tel 703-231-5547. *Head Dept* Derek Myers, PhD; *Prof* Jane Aiken, PhD; *Prof* Steve Bickley, MFA; *Prof* David Crane, MFA; *Prof* Thomas Carpenter, PhD; *Prof* Robert Fields, MFA; *Prof* Maryann Harman, MFA; *Prof* Robert Graham, MFA; *Prof* Ray Kass, MFA; *Prof* L Bailey Van Hook, PhD; *Prof* Victor Huggins, MFA. Instrs: FT 13
Estab 1969; pub; SC 25, LC 12
Degrees: BA 4 yrs, BFA 5 yrs
Tuition: In state $1176; out of state $2664
Courses: Art History, Ceramics, Design, Drawing, Graphic Design, Jewelry, Painting, Printmaking, Sculpture, Art Education, †Studio Art, Watercolor
Summer School: Dir, Derek Myers. Enrl 100; tuition proportional to academic yr for 2 five-week sessions. Courses—Art History, Design, Drawing, Ceramics, Painting, Sculpture, Watercolor

BRIDGEWATER

BRIDGEWATER COLLEGE, Art Dept, 402 E College St, 22812. Tel 703-828-2501; FAX 703-828-2160. *Chmn* David Cook, MFA; *Dept Head* Dr Paul Kline
Scholarships
Degrees: BA 4 yr
Courses: Art Appreciation, Art History, Design, Drawing, Painting, Photography, Printmaking, Sculpture

BRISTOL

VIRGINIA INTERMONT COLLEGE, Fine Arts Division, Moore St, 24201. Tel 703-669-6101; FAX 703-669-5763. *Chmn* Dr Marvin Tadlock; *Instr* Tedd Blevins, MFA; *Instr* Chris Anderson
Estab 1884; den; D & E; scholarships; SC 15, LC 4; enrl D 35, non-maj 110
Ent Req: HS dipl, review of work
Degrees: BA(Art) and BA(Art Educ) 4 yrs, AA 2 yrs
Tuition: $3487.50 per sem (incl board)

BUENA VISTA

SOUTHERN SEMINARY COLLEGE, 24416. Tel 703-261-8400. *Chmn* Rober Bedell, MA
Estab 1867; pvt; D; SC 10, LC 5; enrl D 185, non-maj 175, maj 2
Ent Req: HS dipl, SAT or ACT
Degrees: AA & AS 2 yrs
Tuition: Res—undergrad $11,400 per yr; nonres—undergrad $7400 per yr
Courses: Architecture, Art Education, Art History, Design, Interior Design, Painting, Photography, Teacher Training, Architectural Drafting & Design, Commercial Design Studio, Furniture History & Design, Introduction to Interior Design, Introduction to Studio Art, Residential Design Studio, Study Abroad, Italian Renaissance, 2-D & 3-D Design, Textiles
Summer School: Dir M. Worth. Enrl 30; tuition $135 per cr hr for 4 wk trm beginning May 17 - June 16. Courses—Art History, Photography

CHARLOTTESVILLE

UNIVERSITY OF VIRGINIA, McIntire Dept of Art, Fayerweather Hall, 22903. Tel 804-924-6123; FAX 804-924-3647. *Chmn* David Summers. Instrs: FT 21
Estab 1819; dept estab 1951; pub; D; scholarships; SC 21, LC 21, GC 14; enrl D 1500, maj 150, grad 40 res, 18 nonres
Ent Req: HS dipl
Degrees: BA(Studio and Art History), MA(Art History) and PhD(Art History)
Courses: Art History, Drawing, Painting, Photography, Printmaking, Sculpture, Computer Graphics
Summer School: Enrl 15; tuition varies. Courses—Art History, Studio Art

DANVILLE

AVERETT COLLEGE, Art Dept, 420 W Main St, 24541. Tel 804-791-5600, 791-5797. *Coordr* Diane Kendrick; *Prof* Robert Marsh, MFA; *Prof* Maud F Gatewood
Estab 1859; dept estab 1930; pvt; D & E; scholarships; SC 13, LC 5; enrl D 1000, non-maj 250, maj 25
Ent Req: HS dipl
Degrees: AB
Tuition: $100 per sem hr, $1725 per term; campus res available
Courses: Advertising Design, Art Education, Art History, Ceramics, Commercial Art, Drawing, Fashion Arts, History of Art & Archaeology, Illustration, Jewelry, Lettering, Painting, Printmaking, Sculpture, Teacher Training, Textile Design
Summer School: Two 4 wk sessions

FAIRFAX

GEORGE MASON UNIVERSITY, Dept of Art & Art History, 4400 University Dr, 22030. Tel 703-323-2076; FAX 703-323-3849. *Chmn* Shelia Sfollite; *Prof* Carol C Mattusch, PhD. Instrs: FT 11, PT 4
Estab 1948, dept estab 1981; pub; D & E; SC 16, LC 15; enrl non-maj 200, maj 130
Ent Req: HS dipl, SAT or CEEB
Degrees: BA
Tuition: Res—$1248 per 12-17 sem hrs; nonres—$2976 per 12-17 sem hrs
Courses: †Art History, Drawing, Graphic Arts, Photography, Painting, Printmaking, Sculpture, Computer Graphics, †Studio Art
Summer School: Courses—Art Appreciation, Art Education, Studio Arts

FARMVILLE

LONGWOOD COLLEGE, Dept of Art, Pine St, 23901. Tel 804-395-2284. *Head Dept* Mark Baldridge
Estab 1839; dept estab 1932; pub; D & E; scholarships; SC 59, LC 15; enrl non-maj 450 per sem maj 110 per sem
Ent Req: HS dipl
Degrees: BFA (Art Educ, Art History, Studio) 4 yr
Courses: Advertising Design, Art Education, Art History, Ceramics, Drawing, Goldsmithing, Illustration, Jewelry, Lettering, Museum Staff Training, Photography, †Printmaking, †Teacher Training, Basic Design, †Crafts, Fibers, Stained Glass, 3-D Design, Design, Wood Design
Summer School: Dir, Mark Baldridge. Tuition varies for one 3-wk & two 4-wk sessions. Couses—Varied

FREDERICKSBURG

MARY WASHINGTON COLLEGE, Art Dept, 22401. Tel 703-899-4357. *Chmn & Prof* Joseph DiBella; *Prof* Paul C Muick, PhD; *Prof* Cornelia Oliver, PhD; *Prof* Joseph Dreiss, PhD; *Assoc Prof* Stephen L Griffin; *Assoc Prof* Lorene Nickel, MFA
Estab 1904; pub; D & E; scholarships; SC 18, LC 20; enrl maj 50
Ent Req: HS dipl, ent exam
Degrees: BA and BS 4 yrs
Tuition: Res—undergrad $95 per cr hr, grad $146 per cr hr; nonres—undergrad $220 per cr hr, grad $275 per cr hr; campus res available
Courses: †Art History, Ceramics, Drawing, Graphic Arts, Painting, Photography, Printmaking, Sculpture, †Studio Art

HAMPTON

HAMPTON UNIVERSITY, Art Dept, 23668. Tel 804-727-5416. *Chmn* Sharon G Beachum. Instrs: FT 6, PT 1
Estab 1869; pvt; D; SC 22, LC 7, GC 9; enrl maj 80, others 300, grad 7
Ent Req: HS grad
Degrees: BA, BS
Tuition: $8600 annual tuition; campus res available
Courses: Ceramics, Interior Design, Painting, Photography
Summer School: Dir, Sheila May. Courses—Advanced Workshop in Ceramics, Art Educ Methods, Art Methods for the Elementary School, Basic Design, Ceramics, Commercial Art, Design, Drawing & Composition, Graphics, Metalwork & Jewelry, Painting, Understanding the Arts

HARRISONBURG

JAMES MADISON UNIVERSITY, Dept of Art, 22807. Tel 703-568-6216. *Head Dept* Philip James; *Prof* Martha B Caldwell, PhD; *Prof* Jerry L Coulter, MFA; *Prof* J David Diller, PhD; *Prof* Rebecca Humphrey, MFA; *Prof* James Crable, MFA; *Prof* Jay Kain, PhD; *Prof* Steve Zapton, MFA; *Prof* Barbara Lewis, MFA; *Prof* Ronald Wyancko, MFA; *Prof* Kathleen Arthur, PhD; *Prof* Gary Chatelain, MFA; *Prof* Jack McCaslin, MFA; *Prof* Masako Miyata, MFA; *Assoc Prof* Alan Tschudi, MFA; *Assoc Prof* Kenneth J Beer, MA; *Assoc Prof* Robert Bersson, PhD; *Assoc Prof* Kenneth Szmagaj, MFA; *Asst Prof* Linda Halpern, ABD; *Asst Prof* Peter Ratner, MFA; *Instr* Linda Cabe, ABD; *Asst Prof* Sang Yoon, MFA; *Instr* Stuart Downs, MA
Estab 1908; pub; D & E; scholarships; SC 31, LC 21, GC 22; enrl D & E 1254, maj 184, GS 12
Ent Req: HS dipl, graduates must submit portfolio, undergrads selected on portfolio & academic merit
Degrees: BA(Art History), BS & BFA(Studio) 4 yrs, MA(Studio, Art History, Art Educ) 1 1/2 to 2 yrs, MFA 60 cr hrs
Tuition: Res—undergrad $1508 per sem, grad $94 per cr; nonres—undergrad $3002 per sem, grad $255 per cr; campus res—room & board $1954 per sem
Courses: Advertising Design, Aesthetics, †Art Education, †Art History, †Ceramics, Drafting, †Drawing, Goldsmithing, †Graphic Design, †Jewelry, Interior Design, Museum Staff Training, Painting, Photography, Printmaking, Sculpture, Silversmithing, Textile Design, Weaving, Art Therapy, Computer Graphics, Design, Papermaking, Stained Glass, Typography, Watercolor
Adult Hobby Classes: Tuition res—$154, nonres—$337 for 1-3 cr hr.
Courses—Summer workshop, all beginning courses
Children's Classes: Enrl 260; tuition $35 for 8 sessions
Summer School: Dir, Gary Smith. Enrl 150; tuition res—undergrad $37 per cr hr, grad $70 per cr hr, nonres—undergrad $85 per cr hr, grad $122 per cr hr

LEXINGTON

WASHINGTON AND LEE UNIVERSITY, Division of Art, Dupont Hall, 24450. Tel 703-463-8400, 463-8861 (Art Dept); FAX 703-463-8945. *Head of Art Div* Pamela H Simpson, PhD; *Prof* Herman W Taylor Jr, PhD; *Prof* Valerie Hedquist; *Asst Prof* Kathleen Olson-Janjic; *Asst Prof* Larry M Stene, MFA
Estab 1742; dept 1920; pvt; D; scholarships; SC 14, LC 26; enrl D 1200 (in col) non-maj 200, maj 4-6
Ent Req: HS dipl, SAT, 3 CEEB, one English CEEB plus essay on skills in English, English composition test; entrance requirements most rigorous in English; required of all, including art majors
Degrees: BA 4 yrs
Tuition: Res—undergrad $10,850 per yr, grad $11,200 per yr; campus res—room & board available
Courses: Art History, Drawing, Graphic Arts, History of Art & Archaeology, Museum Staff Training, Painting, Printmaking, Painting, Printmaking, Sculpture, Stage Design, Theatre Arts, Study Art Abroad (Taiwan, Greece)

LYNCHBURG

LYNCHBURG COLLEGE, Art Dept, 1501 Lakeside Dr, 24501. Tel 804-522-8100; FAX 804-522-8499. *Chmn* Richard G Pumphrey, MFA; *Asst Prof* May Carter; *Dir* Virginia Irby Davis, MEd; *Asst Prof* Pat Kiblinger; *Asst Prof* John Roark; *Asst Prof* Robert Garbee; *Asst Prof* Aubrey Wiley
Estab 1903, dept estab 1948; pvt; D & E; SC 26, LC 16, GC 2; enrl D 400, E 50, non-maj 410, maj 45
Ent Req: HS dipl
Degrees: BA and BS 4 yrs
Tuition: Res—undergrad $15,380 per yr; nonres—undergrad $9000; campus res available
Courses: Art Education, Art History, Ceramics, Design, Drawing, Graphic Arts, Graphic Design, Painting, Photography, Printmaking, Sculpture, Art for Therapy, Art for Communication, Crafts, Figure Drawing, History of Architecture
Summer School: Courses—Art Education, Art History & Introductions, Photography

---

RANDOLPH-MACON WOMAN'S COLLEGE, Dept of Art, 24503. Tel 804-947-8486; FAX 804-846-9699. *Chmn* Gina S Werfel. Instrs: FT 4
Estab 1891; pvt; W; D; scholarships; SC 18, LC 15; enrl maj 35, others 305
Degrees: BA 4 yrs
Tuition: $17,950 incl room & board
Courses: Art History, Ceramics, Drawing, Painting, Printmaking, Sculpture, American Art, Art Survey
Summer School: Dir, Dr John Justice. Enrl 30; 4 wk term. Courses—various

MCLEAN

MCLEAN ARTS CENTER, Art Dept, 1437 Emerson Ave, 22101. Tel 703-790-0861 (Art Dept), 356-3048. *Head Dept* John Bryans
Estab 1955; pvt; D & E; SC 1; enrl D 60, E 12
Tuition: Adults $110 for ten lessons; children $75 for ten lessons
Courses: Drawing, Painting
Adult Hobby Classes: Enrl 26; tuition $100 per 10 lessons. Courses—Drawing, Painting (emphasis on watercolor)
Children's Classes: Enrl 40; tuition $75 per 10 lessons. Courses - Drawing, Painting. Summer classes from June to July

NEWPORT NEWS

CHRISTOPHER NEWPORT COLLEGE, Arts & Communications, 50 Shoe Lane, 23606. Tel 804-594-7089. *Head Dept* Rita Hubbard, PhD; *Prof* Jon Petruchyk, MFA; *Prof* B Anglin, MA; *Prof* James Hines, PhD; *Prof* Bruno Koch, PhD; *Prof* David Balthrope, MA; *Faculty* David Alexick, PhD; *Prof* C Brockett, PhD; *Prof* Carol Callaway, PhD; *Prof* Carol Pierce, PhD; *Prof* Henry Sparks, MFA
Estab 1974; pub; D & E; SC 19, LC 4; enrl D 250, E 60, non-maj 200, maj 100
Ent Req: HS dipl, admis committee approval
Degrees: BA and BS 4 yrs
Tuition: Res—undergrad $1830 per yr, $76 per cr hr; nonres—undergrad $3560 per yr, $148 per cr hr; no campus res
Courses: Art Education, Art History, Ceramics, Collages, Costume Design & Construction, Drawing, Graphic Arts, Painting, Photography, Sculpture, Stage Design, Theatre Arts, †Art, †Theatre, †Music (BM)
Summer School: Dir, Dr Barry Woods. Enrl 25; tuition $300. Courses—Ceramics, Drawing, Painting

NORFOLK

NORFOLK STATE UNIVERSITY, Fine Arts Dept, 23504. Tel 804-683-8844. *Head Dept* Rod A Taylor, PhD
Estab 1935; pub; D & E; SC 50, LC 7; enrl D 355, E 18, non-maj 200, maj 155
Ent Req: HS dipl
Degrees: BA(Art Educ), BA(Fine Arts) and BA(Graphic Design) 4 yrs, MA and MFA in Visual Studies
Tuition: Res—undergrad $92 per sem hr, grad $147 per sem hr; nonres—students $193 per sem hr
Courses: History of Art & Archaeology, Jewelry, Lettering, Mixed Media, †Painting, Photography, Printmaking, Sculpture, Teacher Training
Adult Hobby Classes: Enrl 30. Courses—Ceramics, Crafts
Children's Classes: Enrl 45; tuition none. Courses—all areas

OLD DOMINION UNIVERSITY, Art Dept, 23529. Tel 804-683-4047. *Chmn* Carol Hines; *Grad Prog Dir* Dianne DeBeixedon; *Gallery Dir* Fred Bayersdorfer; *Prof Emeriti* Ernest Mauer; *Prof* Victor Pickett; *Assoc Prof* Linda McGreevy; *Assoc Prof* Ronald Snapp; *Assoc Prof* William Wagner; *Assoc Prof* Dianne Debeixedon; *Assoc Prof* Carol Hines; *Asst Prof* Michael Fanizza; *Asst Prof* Robert Wotojwicz; *Asst Prof* Elizabeth Lipsmeyer; *Asst Prof* Elliott Jones; *Adjunct Instr* Wallace E Dreyer; *Adjunct Instr* Rita Marlier
Scholarships, fellowships & assistantships
Ent Req: HS, dipl, SAT
Degrees: BA(Art History, Art Education or Studio Art), BFA, MA & MFA
Tuition: Res—$1231 per sem; nonres—$2491 per sem
Courses: †Art Education, †Art History, Design, Drawing, Graphic Design, Painting, Photography, Printmaking, Sculpture, Clay, Computer Imaging, Crafts, Metals, †Studio Art
Adult Hobby Classes: Enrl 75; tuition $60-$90 per 8 wk course. Courses—Clay, Drawing, Graphics, Mixed Media, Painting, Photography, Stained-Glass
Children's Classes: Enrl 25; tuition $60 - $90 per 6 - 8 wk course. Courses—Design, Drawing, Painting, Governor's Magnet School classes
Summer School: Dir, Carol Hines. Enrl 125; tuition res—$100 per cr hr; nonres—$205 per cr hr

VIRGINIA WESLEYAN COLLEGE, Art Dept of the Humanities Division, Wesleyan Dr, 23502. Tel 804-455-3200; FAX 804-466-8526. *Dir* Barclay Sheaks; *Prof* R E Neil Britton, MFA; *Adjunct Asst Prof* Robert Karl, MFA; *Asst Prof* Joyce B Howell, PhD
Pvt, den; D & E; scholarships; SC 21, LC 8; enrl E 20
Ent Req: HS dipl, SAT
Degrees: BA(Liberal Arts) 4 yrs
Tuition: $8100 per yr; campus res available
Courses: Aesthetics, Art Appreciation, Art Education, Art History, Ceramics, Collages, Conceptual Art, Constructions, Drawing, Graphic Arts, Graphic Design, Handicrafts, History of Art & Archaeology, Jewelry, Mixed Media, Painting, Photography, Printmaking, Sculpture, Silversmithing, Stage Design, Teacher Training, Theatre Arts, Weaving, Fabric Enrichment
Adult Hobby Classes: Enrl 20; tuition $140 per hr
Summer School: Dir, Dot Hinnman. Enrl 20; tuition $140 per hr

PETERSBURG

RICHARD BLAND COLLEGE, Art Dept, Route 1, Box 77A, 23805. Tel 804-862-6272, 862-6100. *Pres* Clarence Maze Jr, PhD; *Art Prof* Susan Brown
Estab 1960, dept estab 1963; pub; D & E; SC 3, LC 3; enrl D 73
Ent Req: HS dipl, SAT, recommendation of HS counselor
Degrees: AA(Fine Arts) 2 yrs
Tuition: Res—undergrad $860 per sem; nonres—$2475 per sem
Courses: Art History, Drawing, Painting, Sculpture, Art Appreciation, Basic Design
Adult Hobby Classes: Courses—Interior Design, Yoga

VIRGINIA STATE UNIVERSITY, Fine & Commercial Art, PO Box 9026, 23806. Tel 804-524-5000. *Chmn* Eugene R Vango; *Assoc Prof* Leonard Jones; *Asst Prof* Eugene Vango, MFA; *Asst Prof* Doris Woodson, MFA; *Asst Prof* Valery Gates, MFA; *Instructor* Charles Flynn, MA
Estab 1882, dept estab 1935; pub; D & E; SC 16, LC 6, GC 2; enrl D 400, E 60, non-maj 302, maj 98
Ent Req: HS dipl
Degrees: BFA(Art Educ) and BFA(Commercial Art and Design) 4 yrs
Tuition: Res—undergrad $6160 per yr incl room & board; nonres—undergrad $6660 per yr
Courses: Advertising Design, Aesthetics, Art Education, Art History, Ceramics, Drawing, Jewelry, Lettering, Jewelry, Lettering, Painting, Photography, Printmaking, Sculpture, Computer
Adult Hobby Classes: Enrl 20; tuition $165 per course. Courses—Batik, Ceramics, Jewelry, Macrame, Painting, Printmaking, Sculpture, Crafts
Summer School: Dir, Dr M McCall. Enrl 20; tuition $55 per cr for term of 12 wks, beginning May 21. Courses—Basic Art, Ceramics, Crafts, Jewelry

PORTSMOUTH

TIDEWATER COMMUNITY COLLEGE, Art Dept, 7000 College Dr, 23703. Tel 804-484-2121; FAX 804-483-9169. *Chmn* Harriette C F Laskin
Estab 1968; pub; D & E; SC 12, LC 3; enrl D 120, E 180, non-maj 190, maj 110
Ent Req: HS dipl
Degrees: AA(Fine Arts), AAS(Media Arts) 2 yrs
Tuition: Res—$43 per cr hr; nonres—$144 per cr hr; no campus res
Courses: †Advertising Design, Art Appreciation, Art History, Ceramics, Design, Drawing, Illustration, Lettering, Painting
Adult Hobby Classes: Offered through Continuing Educ Div
Summer School: Assoc Dir, H Laskin. Enrl 15 per course; tuition per course beginning May. Courses—Art History, Ceramics, Design, Drawing, Painting

RADFORD

RADFORD UNIVERSITY, Art Dept, PO Box 6965, 24142. Tel 703-831-5475. *Chmn* James Knipe, MFA; *Prof* Dr Paul W Frets, DA; *Prof* Dr Noel G Lawson, PhD; *Prof* Lynn Gordon, DEd; *Prof* Halide Salam; *Assoc Prof* Jerry Krebs, MFA; *Asst Prof* Pam F Lawson; *Asst Prof* Ed LeShock; *Asst Prof* Jennifer Spoon, MA; *Asst Prof* Dr Dorothy Mercer; *Asst Prof* Charles Brouwer, MFA; *Instr* Stephen Arbury; *Instr* Kendall Kessler, MFA
Estab 1910, dept estab 1936; pub; D & E; scholarships; enrl D 1250, E 80, non-maj 1086, maj 164, grad 18
Ent Req: HS dipl, SAT
Degrees: BA, BFA, BS & BS (teaching) 4 yrs, MFA 2 yrs, MS 1 yr
Tuition: In-state undergrad $2076 per yr, grad $2174 per yr; out-of-state undergrad $2076 plus $1398 fee per yr, grad $2174 plus $342 fee per yr; campus res—room & board $3370 per yr
Courses: Art Appreciation, Art Education, Art History, Ceramics, Drawing, Graphic Arts, Graphic Design, Handicrafts, Jewelry, Lettering, Painting, Photography, Printmaking, Sculpture, Teacher Training, Art Safety, Art Foundations, Baroque & Rococo Art, Contemporary Art, Fiber Design, Visual Arts
Summer School: Dir, James Knipe. Enrl 50; two 5 wk sessions each based on sem-hr charge. Courses—Art Appreciation, Studio Art

RICHMOND

J SARGEANT REYNOLDS COMMUNITY COLLEGE, Humanities & Social Science Division, PO Box 85622, 23285-5622. Tel 804-371-3263. *Chmn* Arthur L Dixon
Tuition: Res—$41 per sem hr; nonres—$142 per sem hr
Courses: Art Appreciation, Art History, Design, Drawing, Graphic Design, Handicrafts, Interior Design, Painting, Photography, Sculpture

UNIVERSITY OF RICHMOND, Dept of Art & Art History, 23173. Tel 804-289-8272; FAX 804-287-6006. *Chmn* Charles W Johnson Jr, PhD; *Prof* Robert Palmer; *Asst Prof* Margaret Smith; *Asst Prof* T Ephraim Rubenstein; *Asst Prof* Mark Rhoades
Pvt; D & E; SC 29, LC 15
Ent Req: HS dipl, CEEB
Degrees: BA and BS 4 yrs
Tuition: Res—$1200 per yr
Courses: Art History, Ceramics, Drawing, Graphic Design, Painting, Printmaking, Sculpture, Color & Design, Museum Studies
Summer School: Dir, Dr Max Graeber

VIRGINIA COMMONWEALTH UNIVERSITY
—**Art History Department,** PO Box 3046, 23284-3046. Tel 804-367-1064. *Acting Chmn* Bruce M Koplin; *Prof* Dr Charles Brownell; *Prof* Dr Ann G Crowe; *Prof* Dr James Farmer; *Prof* Dr Lawal; *Assoc Prof* Howard Risatti; *Assoc Prof* Sharon Jones Hill; *Asst Prof* Ann G Crowe; *Asst Prof* Fredrika H Jacobs
—**School of the Arts,** 325 N Harrison St, 23284. Tel 804-367-1700. *Dean* Murray N DePillars; *Dir Summer School* Sue F Murro. Instrs: FT 146, PT 24
Estab 1838; pub; D & E; scholarships, fels and grad assistantships; enrl 2699
Ent Req: Ent req portfoli

Degrees: Degrees BA, BFA, BM and BME 4yrs, MA, MFA, MAE, MM and MME 2 yrs
Tuition: Res—under grad $1359.50 per sem, grad $1537.50 per sem; nonres—undergrad $3349.50 per sem, grad $3342.50 per sem; res—rm & board $1400
Courses: Art Education, Art History, Ceramics, Fashion Arts, Interior Design, Jewelry, Printmaking, Sculpture, Theatre Arts, Communication Arts and Design, Fabric design, Furniture Design
Summer School: Dir, Sue F Murro. Courses 3 - 8 wks, most art disciplines; $105 per cr hr

ROANOKE

HOLLINS COLLEGE, Art Dept, 7916 Williamson Rd, 24020. Tel 703-362-6000; FAX 703-362-6642. *Chmn* Robert Sulkin
Estab 1842; pvt; D; scholarships; SC 13; enrl D 380, maj 35
Ent Req: HS dipl
Degrees: BA 4 yrs
Tuition: $14,100
Courses: Architecture, Art Appreciation, Art Education, Art History, Drawing, Graphic Arts, History of Art & Archaeology, Painting, Photography, Printmaking, Sculpture, Teacher Training, Video, †Studio

VIRGINIA WESTERN COMMUNITY COLLEGE, Commercial Art, Fine Art & Photography, 3095 Colonial Ave SW, PO Box 14007, 24038. Tel 703-857-7271, 857-7255. *Chmn Div Human* Dr Clarence C Mays Jr, EdD; *Dept Head* David Curtis, MFA; *Assoc Prof* Rudolph H Hotheinz, MAE; *Assoc Prof* Sherrye Lantz, MFA
Pub; D & E; SC 11, LC 2
Ent Req: HS dipl
Degrees: AA(Fine Art), AAS(Commercial Art)
Tuition: Res—$41 per sem hr; nonres—$142 per sem hr
Adult Hobby Classes: Courses—Oil Painting, Papermaking, Watercolor

SALEM

ROANOKE COLLEGE, Fine Arts Dept-Art, Olin Hall, High St, 24153. Tel 703-375-2276. *Chmn* Bruce Partin; *Assoc Prof* John Brust; *Assoc Prof* Scott Hardwig, MFA; *Asst Prof* Elizabeth Heil, MFA; *Asst Prof* Dr Mary Fitzgerald
Estab 1842, dept estab 1930; den; D; SC 16, LC 8; enrl D 130, non-maj 120, maj 40
Ent Req: HS dipl, SAT or ACT, 13 academic credits - 2 English, 3 social sciences, 3 humanities, 2 math, 2 science, 1 interdisciplinary
Degrees: BA 4 yrs
Tuition: Res—$14,000 per yr incl room & board; nonres—$10,200 per yr
Courses: Advertising Design, Art Education, †Art History, Ceramics, Drawing, Graphic Design, Painting, Photography, Printmaking, Sculpture, Stage Design, Theatre Arts, †Communication Sciences, Costume Design, †Studio Arts
Adult Hobby Classes: Enrl 25; tuition $75 per sem. Courses—Painting, Watercolor
Children's Classes: Courses—Ceramics
Summer School: Dir, Dr Art Puotinen. Courses—Art History

STAUNTON

MARY BALDWIN COLLEGE, Dept of Art, Frederick and New Streets, 24401. Tel 703-887-7197. *Sr Member* Marlena Hobson; *Prof* Frank Hobbs; *Assoc Prof* Janet Wilkins; *Asst Prof* Pauline Dixson
Estab 1842; pvt; D & E; scholarships; SC 16, LC 18; enrl D 173, E 32, non-maj 172, maj 33, others 4 non-credit
Ent Req: HS dipl
Degrees: BA 4 yrs
Tuition: $1200 annual tuition
Courses: Ceramics, Drawing, Film, Graphic Arts, Graphic Design, Handicrafts, History of Art & Archaeology, Illustration, Interior Design, Lettering, Mixed Media, Museum Staff Training, Painting, Photography, Printmaking, Sculpture, Stage Design, Teacher Training, Theatre Arts, Video, Art for the Exceptional Child, Art Therapy, Fabric Arts, Historical Preservation, Weaving

SWEET BRIAR

SWEET BRIAR COLLEGE, Art History Dept, 24595. Tel 804-381-6125 (Art History Dept), 381-6100. *Chmn* Diane D Moran, PhD; *Prof* Aileen H Laing, PhD; *Asst Prof* Christopher Witcombe, PhD
Estab 1901, dept estab 1930; pvt; D; scholarships; SC 19, LC 19; enrl D 375 per term, maj 32
Ent Req: HS dipl, col boards
Degrees: BA 4 yrs
Tuition: $14,890 incl room and board
Courses: Architecture, †Art History, Ceramics, Drawing, Graphic Arts, History of Art & Archaeology, Mixed Media, Painting, Photography, Printmaking, Sculpture, Teacher Training, †Theatre Arts, Decorative Arts, †Studio Art
Adult Hobby Classes: Courses—Modern Art, Fibre Art History, Graphic Design

WILLIAMSBURG

COLLEGE OF WILLIAM AND MARY, Dept of Fine Arts, PO Box 8795, 23187. Tel 804-221-2520. *Chmn* Barbara Watkinson, PhD; *Prof* Miles Chappell, PhD; *Prof* James D Kornwolf, PhD; *Prof* Miles Chappell, PhD; *Prof* Edwin Pease; *Prof* Dr Alan Wallach; *Assoc Prof* Marlene Jack, MFA; *Assoc Prof* Paul Helfrich MFA; *Assoc Prof* William Barnes, MFA; *Asst Prof* Lewis Cohen, MFA; *Lectr* Muriel Christison; *Lectr* David Parson
Estab 1693, dept estab 1936; pub; D; SC 20, LC 22; enrl D 5000, non-maj 825, maj 64
Ent Req: HS dipl
Degrees: BA 4 yrs

Tuition: Res—$1483 per sem; nonres—$3906 per sem; campus res available
Courses: †Architecture, †Art History, †Ceramics, †Drawing, †Painting, †Printmaking, †Sculpture
Summer School: Dir, Nell Jones. Courses—Art History, Design, Painting, Drawing

WISE

CLINCH VALLEY COLLEGE OF THE UNIVERSITY OF VIRGINIA, Visual & Performing Arts Dept, 24293. Tel 703-328-0100; FAX 703-328-0115. *Dept Chmn* Leander Canady; *Prof Theatre* Dr Charles Lewis, PhD; *Assoc Prof Music* Dr Michael Donathan, PhD
Estab 1954, dept estab 1980; pub; D & E; scholarships; SC 9, LC 4
Ent Req: HS dipl, SAT or ACT
Degrees: BA and BS 4 yrs
Tuition: Res—$1028 per sem; nonres—$1858 per sem
Courses: Art Education, Art History, Ceramics, Costume Design & Construction, Drawing, Film, History of Art & Archaeology, Painting, Sculpture, Stage Design, Teacher Training, Theatre Arts, Applied Music, Music History & Literature, Music Theory, Performance
Adult Hobby Classes: Dir, Dr Winston Ely
Summer School: Dir, Dr Winston Ely. Enrl 15 per course. Courses - Same as above

WASHINGTON

AUBURN

GREEN RIVER COMMUNITY COLLEGE, Art Dept, 12401 SE 320th, 98002. Tel 206-833-9111; FAX 206-939-5135. *Chmn & Instr* Dr Bernie Bleha, EdD; *Instr* Robert Short, MFA; *Instr* Ed Brannan, MFA; *Instr* Elayne Levensky-Vogel; *Instr* Patrick Navin
Estab 1965; pub; D & E; SC 31, LC 4; enrl D 330, E 120
Ent Req: HS dipl or 18 yrs old
Degrees: AA 2 yr
Tuition: Res—undergrad $298 per quarter; nonres—undergrad $1143 per quarter
Courses: Art History, Ceramics, Drawing, Design, Painting, Photography, Weaving, Computer Enhanced Design, Craft, Papermaking
Summer School: Dir, Bruce Haulman. Tuition $193.66. Courses—Ceramics, Drawing, Painting, Photography

BELLEVUE

BELLEVUE COMMUNITY COLLEGE, Art Dept, 3000 Landerholme Circle SE, 98007. Tel 206-641-2341; FAX 206-453-3029. *Dept Chmn* John Wesley
Estab 1966; pub; D & E; SC 15, LC 5; enrl 300, maj 50
Ent Req: No ent req
Degrees: AA 2 yrs
Tuition: Varies according to courses taken
Courses: Art History, Design, Drawing, Interior Design, Painting, Photography, Sculpture, Textile Design
Adult Hobby Classes: Enrl 600. Courses—Ceramics, Design, Drawing, Jewelry, Painting, Photography, Sculpture

BELLINGHAM

WESTERN WASHINGTON UNIVERSITY, Art Dept, Fine Arts Complex, Room 116, 98225-9068. Tel 206-676-3660; FAX 206-647-6878. *Chmn* Gene Vike, MFA. Instrs: FT 15, PT 6
Estab 1899; pub; D & E; scholarships; enrl D 1500, E 200
Ent Req: HS dipl, ent exam
Degrees: BA, BA(Educ), BFA and MEd 4 yrs
Tuition: Res—undergrad $537 per quarter; nonres—undergrad $1883 per quarter
Courses: †Art History, †Ceramics, †Drawing, †Graphic Design, †Painting, †Sculpture, †Fibers, †Metals
Adult Hobby Classes: Enrl 200; tuition $43 per cr continuing education; Courses—Ceramics, Drawing, Fibers, Paintings, Sculpture
Children's Classes: Enrl 100; tuition $125 one wk session; Courses—Adventures in Science/Arts
Summer School: Dir, Shirley Ennons. Tuition $404, six & nine week sessions; Courses—Art Education, Art History, Ceramics, Drawing, Fibers, Painting, Sculpture

BREMERTON

OLYMPIC COLLEGE, Social Sciences & Humanities Division, 1600 Chester Ave, 98310-1699. Tel 206-478-4866; FAX 206-478-7161. *Asst Dean* Lee Brock, MA; *Instr* Don Anton, MA; *Instr* Imy Klett, MA; *Instr* Mel R Wallis, MA
Estab 1946; pub; D & E; scholarships; LC 3; enrl D 125, E 75
Ent Req: HS dipl
Degrees: AA, AS and ATA 2 yrs, cert
Tuition: Res—undergrad $298 per quarter; nonres—undergrad $1134 per quarter; no campus res
Courses: Art Appreciation, Art History, Ceramics, Drawing, Jewelry, Painting, Photography, Printmaking, Sculpture, Life Drawing, Papermaking, Stained Glass
Adult Hobby Classes: Courses—Calligraphy, Painting

CHENEY

EASTERN WASHINGTON UNIVERSITY, Dept of Art, 99004. Tel 509-359-2493. *Chmn* Barbara S Miller
Estab 1886; pub; D; scholarships; SC 58, LC 21, GC 18; enrl D 600, non-maj 200, maj 200, GS 20
Degrees: BA, BEd and BFA 4 yrs, MA and MEd 1 to 2 yrs
Tuition: Res—undergrad $45 per cr hr, grad $78 per cr hr; nonres—undergrad $180 per cr hr, grad $255 per cr hr
Summer School: Dir Barbara Miller. Enrl 100; tuition $120 per cr undergrad, $190 per cr grad. Courses—Varied

ELLENSBURG

CENTRAL WASHINGTON UNIVERSITY, Dept of Art, 98926. Tel 509-963-2665. *Chmn* Constance W Speth. Instrs: 12
Estab 1891; pub; D; enrl maj 250, others 7134
Ent Req: GPA 2
Degrees: BA, MA and MFA 4-5 yrs
Tuition: Res—undergrad $595 per quarter, grad $948 per quarter; nonres—undergrad $2099 per yr, grad $2880 per yr, campus res available
Courses: †Jewelry, †Painting, †Photography, †Printmaking, †Sculpture, †Pottery
Summer School: Courses offered

EVERETT

EVERETT COMMUNITY COLLEGE, Art Dept, 801 Wetmore Ave, 98201. Tel 206-388-9378 (Art Dept), 388-9100. *Chmn* Lowell Hanson
Degrees: AA
Tuition: $28.80 per cr hr
Courses: Art Appreciation, Art History, Ceramics, Design, Drawing, Graphic Arts, Interior Design, Painting, Photography, Stained Glass
Summer School: Dir, Nicki Haynes. Enrl 15-20; tuition $23.30 per cr hr (2 hr minimum) for 8 wk term. Courses—Ceramics, Design, Drawing, Photography

LACEY

ST MARTINS COLLEGE, Humanities Dept, 5300 Pacific Ave SE, 98503-1297. Tel 206-491-4700; FAX 206-459-4124. *Dean* Dr David Suter
Degrees: BFA
Courses: Art Appreciation, Art History, Ceramics, Design, Drawing, Painting, Printmaking

LONGVIEW

LOWER COLUMBIA COLLEGE, 1600 Maple, PO Box 3010, 98632. Tel 206-577-3414. *Art Instr* Rosemary Powelson, MFA; *Instr* Yvette O'Neill, MA
Estab 1934; pub; D & E; scholarships; SC 36, LC 8; enrl D 200, E 100
Ent Req: Open admis
Degrees: AAS 2 yrs
Tuition: Res—undergrad $1200 per yr, $67.80 per hr; nonres—undergrad $4000 per yr, $263.80 per hr; no campus res
Courses: Art History, Calligraphy, Ceramics, Drawing, Graphic Arts, Painting, Printmaking, Sculpture, Photography, Design
Adult Hobby Classes: Courses—Matting & Framing, Relief Woodcuts, Recreational Photography

MOSES LAKE

BIG BEND COMMUNITY COLLEGE, Art Dept, 98857. Tel 509-762-6269. *Chmn* Stephen Tse, MFA
Estab 1962; pub; D & E; SC 8, LC 1; enrl D 325, E 60, maj 10-15
Ent Req: HS dipl
Degrees: AA 2 yrs
Tuition: Res—undergrad $999 per yr; nonres—undergrad $3939 per yr; campus res available
Courses: Art Appreciation, Ceramics, Drawing, Lettering, Painting, Photography, Sculpture, Basic Design, Poster Art, Pottery
Adult Hobby Classes: Enrl 15. Courses—Drawing
Summer School: Dir, Harrell Guard. Enrl 180; tuition $31.50 per cr hr. Courses—Drawing, Painting, Pottery, Photography, Sculpture

MOUNT VERNON

SKAGIT VALLEY COLLEGE, Dept of Art, 2405 E College Way, 98273. Tel 206-428-1213 (Dept Art), 428-1261. *Chmn* Greg Tate. Instrs: FT 2, PT 6
Estab 1926; pub; D & E; scholarships; SC 32, LC 1; enrl D 2500, E 3500
Ent Req: Open
Degrees: AA 2 yrs
Tuition: Res—$278 per quarter full time; nonres—$1025 per quarter full time
Courses: Ceramics, Drawing, Handicrafts, Jewelry, Painting, Photography, Printmaking, Art Appreciation, Design
Adult Hobby Classes: Four nights a week
Summer School: Dir, Bert Williamson

PASCO

COLUMBIA BASIN COLLEGE, Art Dept, 2600 N 20th Ave, 99301. Tel 509-547-0511. *Chmn Performing Arts Div* Ted Neth, MFA; *Instr* Morse Clary, MFA; *Instr* Janette Hopper
Scholarships offered
Degrees: AA and AS offered
Tuition: Res—$178.50; nonres—$684.50
Courses: Advertising Design, Art Appreciation, Art History, Calligraphy, Ceramics, Design, Drawing, Interior Design, Jewelry, Painting, Photography, Printmaking, Sculpture, Stage Design, Video, Stained Glass
Adult Hobby Classes: Enrl 3000; tuition $250 per quarter. Courses—Art Appreciaiton, Fine Arts, Graphic Design
Summer School: Dir, Ted Neth. Enrl 1500; tuition $250

PULLMAN

WASHINGTON STATE UNIVERSITY, Fine Arts Dept, 99164-7450. Tel 509-335-8686. *Chmn* Christopher Watts. Instrs: FT 11
Estab 1890, dept estab 1925; pub; D & E; scholarships; SC 29, LC 13, GC 25; enrl D 1593, E 131, maj 220, GS 25
Ent Req: HS dipl
Degrees: BA(Fine Arts) 4 yrs, BFA 4 yrs, MFA 2 yrs
Tuition: Res—$977; nonres— $2717
Courses: Ceramics, Drawing, Graphic Design, Painting, Photography, Printmaking, Sculpture

SEATTLE

THE ART INSTITUTES INTERNATIONAL, The Art Institute of Seattle, 2323 Elliot Ave, 98121-1622. Tel 206-448-0900; FAX 206-448-2501. *Pres* David Pauldine; *Instructor* William Cumming; *Instructor* Fred Griffin, BFA; *Dir of Education* Daniel Lafferty, MS; *Instructor* James Scott, BFA; *Instructor* Nan Cooper; *Instructor* Jim Richardson, BA; *Instructor* John Hansen; *Instructor* David Mercer; *Instructor* Anita Griffin; *Instructor* John Hillding; *Instructor* David Danioth; *Instructor* Sam Dimico
Estab 1946; pvt; D; scholarships; SC 2; enrl D 1300
Ent Req: HS dipl, portfolio approval recommemded but not required
Degrees: Prof dipl
Tuition: $2250 per quarter for 8 quarters; photography $2395 per quarter
Courses: Advertising Design, Commercial Art, Fashion Arts, Film, Graphic Arts, Graphic Design, Illustration, Lettering, Video, Interior Design, Photography, Fashion Merchandising, Layout & Production, Commercial Art Technician
Summer School: Enrl 975; tuition $2250 per term of 11 wks beginning July 7

CITY ART WORKS, Pratt Fine Arts Center, 1902 S Main St, 98144-2206. Tel 206-328-2200; FAX 206-328-1260. *Exec Dir* Risa Morgan, MA; *Prog Dir* Mary Slowinski, BFA; *Development Dir* Kelly Sanderbeck, MA
Estab 1979; pub; D & E; scholarships & fels; SC 80; enrl 2000
Ent Req: Open enrollment
Degrees: No degree prog
Tuition: $55 - $500 per class
Courses: Collages, Conceptual Art, Constructions, Drawing, Handicrafts, Industrial Design, Mixed Media, Painting, Printmaking, Sculpture, Glass blowing & casting
Adult Hobby Classes: Enrl 2000; tuition $55 - $5000 per workshop or class. Classes—Glass, Jewelry, Printmaking, 2-D Design, Sculpture
Children's Classes: Enrl 200. Classes—Drawing, Painting, Sculpture
Summer School: Enrl 150; tuition $0 - $250 per class. Classes—Glass, Jewelry, Printmaking, Sculpture, 2-D Design

CORNISH COLLEGE OF THE ARTS, Art Dept, 710 E Roy, 98102. Tel 206-323-1400. *Pres* Robert Funk. Instrs: FT 32, PT 93
Estab 1914; pvt; D & E; scholarships; SC 57, LC 6; enrl non-maj 124 PT, maj 423 FT
Ent Req: HS dipl, portfolio review, fine arts, design, personal interview
Degrees: BAA, BFA
Tuition: $8650 per yr
Courses: Advertising Design, Art History, Calligraphy, Commercial Art, Conceptual Art, †Costume Design & Construction, Design, Display, Drafting, Drawing, Graphic Arts, Graphic Design, †Illustration, Industrial Design, Interior Design, Lettering, Mixed Media, Painting, Photography, Printmaking, Sculpture, Stage Design, Theatre Arts, Video, Furniture Design
Summer School: Dir, Greg Skinner. Enrl 50; tuition $329 per cr for 8 wk term. Courses—Drawing, Painting, Photography, Print, Sculpture, Video

NORTH SEATTLE COMMUNITY COLLEGE, Art Dept, Humanities Division, 9600 College Way N, 98103. Tel 206-527-3709; FAX 206-527-3635. *Head Dept* Elroy Christenson, MFA; *Instr* John Constantine, MFA; *Instr* David J Harris, MFA
Estab 1970; pub; D & E; scholarships; SC 27, LC 7; enrl D 150, E 65
Ent Req: HS dipl
Degrees: AA 2 yr, AFA, CFA 2 yr
Tuition: Res—undergrad $326 per quarter, $32.70 per cr, nonres—$1306 per quarter; no campus res
Courses: Art History, Drawing, History of Art & Archaeology, Jewelry, Painting, Sculpture
Adult Hobby Classes: Drawing, Painting
Summer School: Tuition $326 for term of 8 wks beginning June 20. Courses—Drawing, Introduction to Art

PILCHUCK GLASS SCHOOL, 107 S Main St, No 324, 98104-2580. Tel 206-621-8422; FAX 206-621-0713. *Dir* Marjorie Levy; *Asst Dir* John Reed. Instrs: FT 5, PT 30
Estab 1971; summer location: 1201 316th St NW, Stanwood, WA 98292-9600, Tel: 206-445-3111, Fax: 206-445-5515; pvt; D & E; scholarships; SC 25; enrl D & E 250
Ent Req: 18 years or older

Tuition: $1570 - $2020 per class; campus res available
Summer School: Tuition $1570 - $2020 per course. Courses—Casting, Flameworking, Glassblowing, Glass Engraving, Hot Glass Sculpture, Mixed-media Sculpture, Neon Painting, Slumping & Fusing

SEATTLE CENTRAL COMMUNITY COLLEGE, Humanities - Social Sciences Division, 1701 Broadway, 98122. Tel 206-587-3800; FAX 206-587-3878. *Chmn* Rosetta Hunter; *Prof* Ileana Leavenn
Estab 1970; pub; D & E; scholarships; SC 15, LC 5; enrl D 70, E 50
Ent Req: HS dipl, ent exam
Degrees: AA 2 yrs
Tuition: Res—$1148 per yr; nonres—$4528 per yr; no campus res
Courses: Art History, Painting
Summer School: Courses—Art History, Painting, Sculpture

SEATTLE PACIFIC UNIVERSITY, Art Dept, Three W Cremond, 98119. Tel 206-281-2079. *Chmn* Michael Caldwell
Scholarships & fellowships
Courses: Art Appreciation, †Art Education, Ceramics, Design, Drawing, Fashion Arts, Handicrafts, Industrial Design, Interior Design, Jewelry, Painting, Printmaking, Sculpture, Textile Design, Weaving
Children's Classes: Tuition $23 for 8 wk session. Courses - General Art for Children
Summer School: Dir, Larry Metcalf. Two 4 wk sessions. Courses - Elementary Art Education Workshops, Fabrics, Monoprinting, Painting, Papermaking, Silkscreening

SEATTLE UNIVERSITY, Fine Arts Dept, Division of Art, Broadway & Madison, 98122-4460. Tel 206-296-5360 (Fine Arts Dept), 296-6000. *Chmn* William Dore; *Prof* Rebecca Bruckner; *Prof* Marvin T Herard, MFA; *Prof* Marjorie Masel
D; scholarships
Ent Req: HS dipl and entrance exam
Degrees: BA program offered
Tuition: $222 per cr hr
Courses: Art History, Design, Drawing, Painting, Printmaking, Sculpture, Art Ideas, Studio Art
Summer School: Chmn, Kate Duncan. Courses—same as regular session

SHORELINE COMMUNITY COLLEGE, Humanities Division, 16101 Greenwood Ave N, 98133. Tel 206-546-4741; FAX 206-546-4599. *Chmn* Diane Gould; *Prof* Mike Larson, MA; *Prof* Chris Simons, MFA; *Prof* Willy Clark, PhD; *Prof* Morry Hendrickson, MA; *Prof* Brian Edwards, MA; *Assoc Prof* K C Maxwell, MA
Estab 1964; pub; D & E; scholarships; SC 9, LC Art History Survey; enrl D 5500
Ent Req: HS dipl, col ent exam
Degrees: AA and AFA
Tuition: Res—undergrad $286 per qtr, $57.20 per qtr hr; nonres—undergrad $1131 per qtr, $226.20 per qtr hr; no campus res
Courses: Advertising Design, Art Appreciation, Art History, Ceramics, Commercial Art, Costume Design & Construction, Design, Display, Drafting, Fashion Arts, Fashion Arts, Film, Graphic Arts, Graphic Design, Lettering, Painting, Photography, Sculpture, Video, †Visual Communications Technology
Summer School: Dir, Marie Rosenwasser. Enrl 45 maximum; two 4 wk terms. Courses—Ceramics, Design, Design Appreciation, Drawing, Painting, Photography, Sculpture

UNIVERSITY OF WASHINGTON, School of Art, DM-10, 98195. Tel 206-543-0970. *Dir* Constantine Christofides
Estab 1878; pub; D & E; scholarships; SC 113, LC 84, GC 30; enrl D & E 2459, maj 790, grad 99
Ent Req: Must meet university admission req
Degrees: BFA 4 yrs, BA 4 yrs, MA, PhD and MFA
Tuition: Res—undergrad $647, grad $1007, nonres—undergrad $1807, grad $2522, campus res—room & board $3510 for double
Courses: Art Appreciation, Art History, Ceramics, Conceptual Art, Design, Drawing, Goldsmithing, Graphic Design, History of Art & Archaeology, Industrial Design, Jewelry, Painting, Photography, Printmaking, Sculpture, Silversmithing, Textile Design, Video, Weaving, †Fiber Arts, †General Art, †Metal Design
Summer School: Dir, C Christofides. Enrl 897; tuition $647 for two-month term. Various courses offered

SPOKANE

GONZAGA UNIVERSITY, Dept of Art, School of Arts and Sciences, 99258-0001. Tel 509-328-4220, Ext 3214. *Chmn* Terry Gieber; *Prof* J Scott Patnode; *Prof* R Gilmore. Instrs: FT 3, PT 4
Estab 1962; pvt; D & E; SC 20, LC 5, GC 12; enrl D 250 incl maj 50, grad 8, others 80
Ent Req: HS dipl
Degrees: BA 4 yrs, grad cert in art
Tuition: $5000 per sem; campus res available
Courses: Art Education, Ceramics, Drawing, History of Art & Archaeology, Painting, Printmaking, Sculpture, Teacher Training
Adult Hobby Classes: Courses offered
Summer School: Dir, Jerry Tucker. Term of 8 wks beginning June. Courses—Ceramics, Drawing, Painting

SPOKANE FALLS COMMUNITY COLLEGE, Fine & Applied Arts Div, W 3410 Fort George Wright Dr, 99204. Tel 509-459-3720. *Supvr* Dr Ronald C Smith; *Dept Chmn* Jo Fyfe
Estab 1963; pub; D & E; scholarships; SC 41, LC 5; enrl D 600, E 200
Ent Req: HS dipl, GED
Degrees: AAA 3 yrs, and AA 2 yrs
Tuition: Res—$298 per quarter; nonres—$1134 per quarter; no campus res
Courses: Architecture, Art History, Calligraphy, Ceramics, †Display, Drawing, †Graphic Design, Illustration, †Interior Design, Jewelry, Lettering, Mixed Media, Painting, †Photography, Printmaking, Sculpture, Weaving, †Custom Saddle Making, †Electronic Graphics & Publishing, Intro to Art

Adult Hobby Classes: Enrl 35; tuition $25.60 for 6 week term. Courses—Drawing, Watercolor, Weaving
Summer School: Dir, Dr Ron Smith. Enrl 200; 9 wk term. Courses—Airbrush, Ceramics, Drawing, Figure Drawing, Intro to Art, Printmaking, Watercolor

WHITWORTH COLLEGE, Art Dept, 99251. Tel 509-466-1000, 466-3258 (Art Dept). *Chmn* Barbara Filo, MA; *Assoc Prof* Walter Grosvenor, MAT; *Assoc Prof* Gordon Wilson, MFA; *Instr* James Neupert
Pvt; D & E; scholarships; SC 18, LC 6
Ent Req: HS dipl
Degrees: BA and BS 4 yrs, MA, MAT & MEd 2 yrs
Tuition: $1100 per yr
Courses: Art Education, Art History, Ceramics, Drawing, Graphic Design, Mixed Media, Painting, Printmaking, Art Administration, Leaded Glass

TACOMA

FORT STEILACOOM COMMUNITY COLLEGE, Fine Arts Dept, 9401 Farwest Dr SW, 98498. Tel 206-964-6500, 964-6717. *Dept Head* Bill Rades. Instrs: FT 2, PT 2
Estab 1966, dept estab 1972; pub; D & E; SC 20, LC 5; enrl D 3500
Ent Req: Ent exam
Degrees: AA 2yrs
Tuition: $343 per term; nonres—$1323 per term; no campus res
Courses: Drawing, Painting, Photography, Printmaking, Figure Drawing
Adult Hobby Classes: Courses vary
Summer School: Dir, Walt Boyden. Tuition $19 per cr hr. Courses—Ceramics, Drawing, Painting. Tour Italy June 20 - July 15, 1984

PACIFIC LUTHERAN UNIVERSITY, Dept of Art, School of the Arts, 98447. Tel 206-535-7573; FAX 206-535-8320. *Chmn* John Hallam, PhD; *Prof* David Keyes, Ma; *Assoc Prof* Dennis Cox, MFA; *Assoc Prof* Beatrice Geller, MFA; *Assoc Prof* Lawrence Gold, MFA; *Assoc Prof* Walt Tomsic, MFA
Estab 1890, dept estab 1960; den; D & E; scholarships; SC 29, LC 8; enrl D 800, E 75, maj 60
Ent Req: HS dipl, SAT
Degrees: BA, BAEd and BFA 4 yrs
Tuition: $11,968 per yr; PT students $374 per sem hr; campus res—room & board $3470 per yr
Courses: †Advertising Design, Aesthetics, Art Appreciation, Art Education, Art History, †Ceramics, †Commercial Art, †Constructions, †Design, †Drawing, †Graphic Arts, †Graphic Design, Illustration, Jewelry, †Mixed Media, †Painting, †Photography, †Printmaking, †Sculpture, †Teacher Training, Stained Glass
Summer School: Dean, Dr Richard Moe. Enrl 2000; tuition $190 per sem hr; $297 per grad cr, 3 - 4 wk sessions. Courses—Ceramics, Drawing, Jewelry, Photography

TACOMA COMMUNITY COLLEGE, Art Dept, 5900 S 12th St, 98465. Tel 206-566-5000, 566-5300 (Art Dept). *Art Dept Chmn* Frank Dippolito, MFA; *Instr* Richard Rhea, MA
Estab 1965; pub; D & E; scholarships; SC 35, LC 1; enrl D & E 1500
Degrees: AAS & Associate in Liberal Arts 2 yrs
Tuition: Res—undergrad $292 per quarter, grad $1137 per quarter
Courses: Art History, Jewelry, Painting, Photography, Printmaking, Sculpture, 2-D & 3-D Design, Figure Drawing, Pottery

UNIVERSITY OF PUGET SOUND, Art Dept, 1500 N Warner St, 98416. Tel 206-756-3348. *Chmn* Ken Stevens. Instrs: FT 7, PT 2
Estab 1935; den; D & E; scholarships; SC 41, LC 11; enrl maj 65, undergrad 455
Ent Req: HS grad
Degrees: BA 4 yrs
Tuition: $11,300 per yr, $5650 per sem; campus res—room & board $3800 per yr
Courses: Art History, Ceramics, Design, Drawing, Painting, Photography, Printmaking, Sculpture, Oriental Art, Studio Design, Watercolor
Summer School: Dir, Ken Stevens. Enrl 15 per class; tuition $925 per unit for 4 wk course. Courses—Art Education, Art History, Ceramics, Drawing, Painting, Watercolor

VANCOUVER

CLARK COLLEGE, Art Dept, 1800 E McLoughlin Blvd, 98663. Tel 206-694-6521. *Dept Coordr* Warren Dunn; *Instr* Roger Baker; *Instr* Jim Archer, MFA
Estab 1933, dept estab 1947; pub; D & E; scholarships; SC 87, LC 3; enrl D 300, E 400
Ent Req: Open door
Degrees: Assoc of Arts and Science, Assoc of Applied Science, and Assoc of General Studies 2 yrs
Tuition: Res—$27.50 per cr hr, $247.50 (9 cr), $275 (10 cr); nonres—$104 per cr, $936 (9 cr), $1040 (10 cr)
Courses: Art History, Calligraphy, Ceramics, Drawing, Graphic Design, Handicrafts, Jewelry, Lettering, Painting, Photography, Sculpture
Adult Hobby Classes: Enrl 40 FTE; tuition $55 per 2 cr course. Courses—Air Brush, Art History, Calligraphy, Ceramics, Drawing, Photography
Summer School: Enrl 40 FTE; tuition $27.50 per cr. Courses—Art Appreciation, Art History, Calligraphy, Ceramics, Drawing, Photography, Watercolor

WALLA WALLA

WALLA WALLA COMMUNITY COLLEGE, Art Dept, 500 Tausick Way, 99362. Tel 509-527-4212, 527-4600. *Instr* Bill Piper; *Instr* Melissa Webster
Scholarships offered
Degrees: AA offered
Tuition: Res—$298 per quarter; nonres—$1134 per quarter
Courses: Art Appreciation, Ceramics, Design, Drawing, Handicrafts, Photography, Printmaking, Sculpture, Pottery
Summer School: Dir, Don Adams. Tuition same as regular quarter

WHITMAN COLLEGE, Art Dept, Olin Hall, 99362. Tel 509-527-5248. *Chmn* Paul Dewey
Pvt; D; SC 15, LC 8; enrl D 250, maj 15
Ent Req: HS dipl, ent exam
Degrees: BA 4 yrs
Tuition: $6380 per yr
Courses: Aesthetics, Art History, Ceramics, Design, Drawing, History of Art & Archaeology, Painting, Printmaking, Sculpture

WENATCHEE

WENATCHEE VALLEY COLLEGE, Art Dept, 1300 Fifth St, 98801. Tel 509-662-1651. *Prof* Robert Graves, MFA; *Prof* James Mai, MFA; *Instr* Ruth Allan, MFA
Estab 1939; pub; D & E; scholarships; LC 6; enrl D 550, E 200, maj 45
Ent Req: HS dipl, open door policy
Degrees: AA 2 yrs
Tuition: Res—undergrad $780 per yr, $260 per quarter, $26 per cr hr; nonres—undergrad $3075 per yr, $1025 per quarter, $102.50 per cr; campus res available
Courses: Art History, Ceramics, Collages, Design, Drawing, Graphic Arts, Lettering, Painting, Printmaking
Summer School: Dir, Dr Neil Solder

YAKIMA

YAKIMA VALLEY COMMUNITY COLLEGE, Art Dept, S 16th Ave & Nob Hill Blvd, PO Box 1647, 98907. Tel 509-575-2418. *Dir* Robert A Fisher; *Faculty* Herb Blisard. Instrs: PT 5
Scholarships
Degrees: AA & AS offered
Tuition: Res—$333 per quarter, PT $29.25 per cr, nonres—$1313 per quarter
Courses: Advertising Design, Art Appreciation, Art History, Ceramics, Design, Drawing, Jewelry, Painting, Photography, Sculpture
Summer School: Dir, Robert A Fisher. Tuition $333 per quarter, FT

WEST VIRGINIA

ATHENS

CONCORD COLLEGE, Fine Art Division, PO Box 50, 24712-1000. Tel 304-384-5275. *Prof* Maynard R Coiner, MFA; *Prof* Gerald C Arrington, MFA; *Asst Prof* Sheila M Chipley, EdD; *Asst Prof* Steve Glazer
Estab 1872, dept estab 1925; pub; D & E; scholarships; SC 32, LC 3; enrl non-maj 200, maj 75, D 75
Ent Req: HS dipl
Degrees: BA and BS 4 yrs
Tuition: Res—$570 per sem; nonres—$1320 per sem; campus res— room & board available
Courses: †Advertising Design, †Art Education, †Art History, Calligraphy, †Ceramics, Collages, †Commercial Art, Constructions, Drawing, Graphic Arts, Graphic Design, Handicrafts, History of Art & Archaeology, Illustration, Jewelry, Lettering, †Painting, Printmaking, Sculpture, Teacher Training, †Advertising
Adult Hobby Classes: Enrl varies; tuition based on part-time rates. Courses—Vary
Children's Classes: Enrl varies; tuition none for 4 week sessions. Courses vary
Summer School: Tuition res—$420; nonres—$1150 for term of 5 wks beginning June. Courses—varied

BETHANY

BETHANY COLLEGE, Dept of Fine Arts, 26032. Tel 304-829-7000; FAX 304-829-7223, 829-7108. *Dean* Dr Richard M Bernard; *Head Dept* David J Judy; *Asst Prof* Wesley Wagner; *Asst Prof Art History* Piri Halasz; *Asst Prof Studio Art* Kenneth Morgan
Estab 1840, dept estab 1958; den; D; scholarships; SC 27, LC 7; enrl D 136, non-maj 106, maj 30
Ent Req: HS dipl
Degrees: BA and BS 4 yrs
Tuition: $10,695 per yr; campus res available
Courses: Art History, Calligraphy, Ceramics, Drawing, Graphic Design, Illustration, Painting, Photography, Sculpture
Summer School: Dir, Joseph M Kurey. Tuition $160 per hr for two 5 wk summer terms and an 11 wk independent study period. Courses—Independent Studies, Seminars, Tutorials

BLUEFIELD

BLUEFIELD STATE COLLEGE, Art Dept, 24701. Tel 304-327-4171. *Prof* Allen Jonas, MFA
Estab 1895; pub; D & E; scholarships & fels; SC 14, LC 4; enrl D 125, E 40, non-maj 150, minor 10, other 5
Ent Req: HS dipl, 18 yrs old
Degrees: BA, BA(Humanities), BS, BS(Educ) & BS(Engineering Technology) 4 yrs
Tuition: Res—$620 per term; nonres—$1998 per term
Courses: Art Education, Art History, Ceramics, Drawing, Painting, Photography, Printmaking, Sculpture, Computer Art
Adult Hobby Classes: Enrl 10 -15. Courses—Photography, Television, Art in Western World, Woodcarving
Children's Classes: Enrl varies. Courses—Drawing, Ceramics
Summer School: Dir, Dwight Moore. Enrl 15-20; term of 5 wks beginning June/ July. Courses—Art Educ & Appreciation (workshops on occasion)

BUCKHANNON

WEST VIRGINIA WESLEYAN COLLEGE, Dept of Fine Arts, College Ave, 26201. Tel 304-473-8000, 473-8067. *Chmn* Dan Keegan; *Instr* William Oldaker
Estab 1890; den; D & E; SC 16, LC 6; enrl non-maj 120, maj 20, grad 2
Ent Req: HS dipl, ent exam
Degrees: BA and MA(Teaching)
Tuition: $6965 per sem
Courses: Art Education, Theatre Arts
Adult Hobby Classes: Tuition $50 per cr for 12-13 wks
Summer School: Dir, Dr Kenneth B Welliver. Enrl 25; tuition $130 per cr hr for three 4 wk terms. Courses—Art History, Basic & Intermediate Stained Glass, Studio Arts

CHARLESTON

UNIVERSITY OF CHARLESTON, Carleton Varney Dept of Art & Design, 2300 MacCorkle Ave SE, 25304. Tel 304-357-4725. *Dir* Joellen Kerr; *Coordr* Steve Watts; *Instr* Becky Guetzko. Instrs: FT 2, PT 4
Estab 1888; pvt; D & E; Scholarships; enrl maj 55
Ent Req: Usual col req
Degrees: 4 yr
Tuition: $4275 per sem
Courses: Art Education, Art History, Design, Drafting, Drawing, Graphic Design, Interior Design, Lettering, Painting, Photography, Printmaking, Teacher Training, Advanced Studio, Art Appreciation, Color Theory
Children's Classes: Enrl 30; tuition by the wk. Courses—Summer Art Camp Program
Summer School: Tuition $150 per sem hr for sessions of 5 wks beginning May 12, June 9, July 14

ELKINS

DAVIS AND ELKINS COLLEGE, Dept of Art, 100 Campus Dr, 26241. Tel 304-636-1900, Ext 254. *Chmn* Jesse F Reed; *Lectr* Margo Blebin; *Lectr* Scottie Wiest; *Lectr* Donna Morgam. Instrs: FT 1, PT 3
Den; D; scholarships; SC 15, LC 5; enrl maj 3
Ent Req: HS dipl
Degrees: AA & AS 2 yrs, BA 2 yrs
Tuition: $3550 per sem; campus res available
Courses: Art Education, Art History, Drawing, Graphic Arts, Painting, Sculpture, Teacher Training, Weaving, †Computer Art, Pottery
Adult Hobby Classes: Enrl 90
Summer School: Augusta Heritage Arts Workshop. Courses—Appalachian crafts, Folkcarving, Treenware, Woodworking, Coopering, Basketry, Chairbottoming, Toymaking, Musical Instrument Construction & Repair, Bushcraft, Pottery, Clay Prospecting, Calligraphy, Papermaking, Stained Glass, Music, Dance, Folklore

FAIRMONT

FAIRMONT STATE COLLEGE, Div of Fine Arts, 26554. Tel 304-367-4000. *Chmn* Suzanne Snyder; *Prof* Lynn Boggess; *Prof* Dr Stephen Smigocki, PhD; *Prof* Barry Snyder, MFA; *Assoc Prof* John Clovis, MFA
Pub; D & E; scholarships; enrl D maj 35, non-maj 15
Ent Req: HS dipl
Degrees: BA(Art Educ) and BS(Graphics, Fine Arts) 4 yrs
Tuition: $750 per sem
Courses: †Art Education, Art History, Ceramics, Design, Drawing, Graphic Arts, Painting, Photography, Printmaking, Sculpture, Commercial Design
Adult Hobby Classes: Two - three times a wk for 16 wks. Courses—same as above
Children's Classes: Enrl 20; tuition $25 per 6 wk term. Courses—Art for children ages 5 - 12, 2 - D & 3 - D Design
Summer School: Dir Dr S Snyder. Enrl 50; 4 wks per sessions. Courses—Art Education, Drawing, Design, Painting, Art Appreciation

GLENVILLE

GLENVILLE STATE COLLEGE, Dept of Fine Arts, 200 High St, 26351. Tel 304-462-7361, Ext 215. *Chmn* Gary Gillespie, PhD; *Prof* Charles C Scott, MFA; *Prof* James W Rogers, MFA; *Asst Prof* George D Harper, MFA
Estab 1872, dept estab 1952; pub; D & E; scholarships; SC 25, LC 3; enrl D 128, E 42, non-maj 14, maj 55
Ent Req: HS dipl
Degrees: AB 4 yrs
Tuition: Res—undergrad $840 per yr, $420 per sem; nonres—undergrad $2300 per yr, $1150 per sem; campus residency available
Courses: †Art Education, Art History, †Ceramics, Drawing, Graphic Arts, Jewelry, Lettering, †Painting, Photography, Printmaking, Sculpture, Textile Design, Weaving
Summer School: Chmn, Gary Gillespie

HUNTINGTON

MARSHALL UNIVERSITY, Dept of Art, 400 Hal Greer Blvd, 25755. Tel 304-696-6760; FAX 304-696-3333. *Chmn* Michael Cornfeld; *Dean* Dr Paul Balshaw; *Prof* Earlene Allen; *Prof* John Dolin; *Prof* Robert Hutton; *Prof* Susan Jackson; *Prof* Peter Massing; *Prof* Robert Rowe; *Prof* Stan Sporny; *Prof* Laurel Lampela; *Prof* Shahnaz Shahriar; *Office Mgr* Opal Turner. Instrs: FT 10
Estab 1903; pub; enrl maj incl grad 108
Ent Req: HS grad
Degrees: BFA and MA in art educ and studio 4 yrs
Tuition: Res—$480 per sem; nonres—$1300; campus res available
Courses: Art Education, Ceramics, Painting, Printmaking, Sculpture, Weaving
Children's Classes: Enrl 60; tuition $25 per student for 8 wks. Courses—Ceramics, Drawing, Painting
Summer School: Tuition $427.10 for 6 sem hrs, nonres $1247.10 for 5 wk terms

INSTITUTE

WEST VIRGINIA STATE COLLEGE, Art Dept, Campus Box 4, 25112. Tel 304-766-3196, 766-3198; FAX 304-768-9842. *Chmn* Dr Paul Nuchims; *Asst Prof* Molly Erlandson; *Asst Prof* Toni-Maria Kilgore; *Instr* Karen Shriver
D & E; scholarships; SC 26, LC 11
Ent Req: HS dipl
Degrees: AB(Art) and BSEd(Art) 4 yrs
Tuition: Res—$1700 per sem; nonres—$1711 per sem
Courses: Art Education, Art History, Ceramics, Design, Drawing, Graphic Design, Painting, Photography, Printmaking, Sculpture, Teacher Training, Fibers, Computer Graphics, Figure Drawing, Appalachian Art
Summer School: Dir, Dr Paul Nuchims. Enrl 50. Courses—Art Education, Basic Studios, Art Appreciation

KEYSER

POTOMAC STATE COLLEGE, Dept of Art, Mineral St at Fort Ave, 26726. Tel 304-788-6981. *Chmn* Edward M Wade, MA; *Div Chmn* Anthony Whitmore
College estab 1953, dept estab 1974; pub; D & E; SC 8, LC 2; enrl D 160, non-maj 150, others 10
Ent Req: HS dipl
Degrees: AA 2 yrs, AAS 2 yrs
Tuition: Res—undergrad $2311 per yr including room & board; nonres—$3714 per yr including room & board
Courses: Drawing, Painting, Sculpture, Visual Foundation
Summer School: Dir, Edward Wade. Enrl 10-20; tuition res—undergrad $77.25 per 3 hrs, nonres—undergrad $236.25 per 3 hrs for 5 wk term beginning June 1. Courses—Art Appreciation, Drawing, Painting

MONTGOMERY

WEST VIRGINIA INSTITUTE OF TECHNOLOGY, Creative Arts Dept, 405 Fayette Pike, 25136. Tel 304-442-3192 (Dept), 442-3071. *Head Dept* Fred Meyer; *Assoc Prof* Robert Simile
Estab 1896; pub; scholarships; enrl 3500 (total)
Ent Req: HS grad
Degrees: AS, BA and BS 2-4 yrs
Tuition: Res—$765 per sem; nonres—$1800 per sem
Courses: Ceramics, Graphic Design, Painting, Art Appreciation, Design

MORGANTOWN

WEST VIRGINIA UNIVERSITY, College of Creative Arts, Division of Art, PO Box 6111, 26506-6111. Tel 304-293-3140; FAX 304-293-3550. *Chmn* Bernard Schultz, PhD; *Prof* Robert Anderson, MFA; *Prof* Carmon Colangelo, MFA; *Prof* Urban Couch, MFA; *Prof* Victoria Fergus, PhD; *Prof* Margaret Lucas, DEd; *Prof* Ben Freedman, MA; *Prof* Clifford Harvey, BFA; *Prof* Alison Helm, MFA; *Prof* Margaret Rajam, PhD; *Prof* Ed Petrosky, MFA; *Prof* Eve Faulkes, MFA; *Prof* William Thomas, PhD; *Prof* Paul Krainak, MFA; *Prof* Christopher Hocking, MFA; *Prof* Sergio Soave, MFA
Estab 1867, div estab 1897; pub; D & E; enrl D 250, maj 180, grad 28
Ent Req: HS dipl
Degrees: BA(Art Educ) and BFA 4 yrs, MA(Art) and MFA(Art) 2-4 yrs; grad degrees
Tuition: Res—undergrad $888.50 per sem, grad $935.50 per sem; nonres—undergrad $2322.50 per sem, grad $2432.50; campus residency available
Courses: †Art Education, Art History, †Ceramics, Drawing, †Graphic Design, †Painting, †Printmaking, Sculpture, Basic Design
Children's Classes: Enrl 75; tuition $45-$55 for 10 weeks. Courses—Primary & Intermediate Studio
Summer School: Dir, Bernard Schultz. Enrl 100; tuition $49 per cr hr res undergrad, $70 per cr hr res grad, $154 per cr hr nonres undergrad, $217 per cr hr non res grad. Courses—Art History, Drawing, Painting, Ceramics, Printmaking

PARKERSBURG

WEST VIRGINIA UNIVERSITY AT PARKERSBURG, Art Dept, Route 5 Box 167-A, 26101-9577. Tel 304-424-8000. *Chmn* Roger Allen; *Asst Prof* Henry Aglio, MFA
Estab 1961, dept estab 1973; pub; D & E; scholarships; enrl D 120, E 80, non-maj 125, maj 8
Ent Req: HS dipl plus diagnostic tests in reading, math and English
Degrees: AA 2 yrs
Tuition: Res—undergrad $360 per sem, $30 per cr hr
Courses: Art History, Ceramics, Drawing, Painting, Photography, Printmaking, Bronze Castings, Wood Carvings
Adult Hobby Classes: Enrl 20; tuition $15 for 2 wks. Courses—Painting, Photography, Wood Carving
Children's Classes: Enrl 40; tuition $15 for 2 wks. Courses—Ceramics, Painting
Summer School: Dir, Roger Allen. Tuition $60 for 2 four wk sessions. Courses—Painting

SHEPHERDSTOWN

SHEPHERD COLLEGE, Art Dept, 25443. Tel 304-876-2511, Ext 393, 224; WATS 800-826-6807. *Chmn* Dr R L Jones. Instrs: FT 6, PT 3
Estab 1872; pub; D; scholarships; SC 16, LC 7; enrl maj 160
Ent Req: HS dipl
Degrees: AA and BFA, BA(Educ) and BS 4 yrs
Tuition: $930 per yr; campus res $2766.50 per yr
Courses: Art Education, Art History, Drawing, Graphic Design, Painting, Photography, Printmaking, Sculpture, Teacher Training, Aesthetic Criticism, Art

Therapy, Design
Adult Hobby Classes: Enrl 30; tuition $25 per hr. Courses—Drawing, Painting, Sculpture
Children's Classes: Enrl 35; tuition $20 per course. Courses—Crafts, Drawing
Summer School: Dir, R L Jones. Enrl 60; tuition $25 per hr. Courses—Drawing

WEST LIBERTY

WEST LIBERTY STATE COLLEGE, Art Dept, 26074. Tel 304-336-8006. *Chmn* Alfred R DeJaager, MusB; *Prof* Bernie K Peace, MFA; *Prof* Karen Rychlewski, MFA; *Assoc Prof* R Paul Padgett, MFA
Estab 1836; pub; D & E; scholarships; SC 40, LC 6; enrl D 855, E 140, non-maj 900, maj 90, others 12
Ent Req: HS dipl, score of 17 or higher on ACT test or cumulative HS GPA of at least 2.0 or a combined verbal/math score of 680 on the SAT
Degrees: BA and BS 4 yrs
Tuition: Res—undergrad $1590 per yr, $795 per sem, $101 per cr hr; nonres—undergrad $3630 per yr, $1830 per sem, $188 cr hr; campus res—available
Courses: Advertising Design, †Art Education, Art History, Ceramics, Drawing, Film, Graphic Arts, †Graphic Design, History of Art & Archaeology, Illustration, Jewelry, Lettering, Painting, Photography, Printmaking, Sculpture, Stage Design, Theatre Arts, Weaving, Computer Graphics, Studio Crafts
Summer School: Dir, David T Jauersak. Tuition res $100 per sem hr, nonres $190 per sem hr. Courses—Art Education, Special Education

WISCONSIN

APPLETON

LAWRENCE UNIVERSITY, Dept of Art, Wriston Art Center, 54912. Tel 414-832-6621, 832-6643; FAX 414-832-6606. *Chmn* Carol Lawton. Instrs: FT 6
Estab 1847; SC 8, LC 17
Ent Req: HS performance, CEEB scores, recommendation
Degrees: BA 4 yrs
Tuition: $13,641 includes room & board per 3 term yr
Courses: †Art Education, Photography, †Art History, Drawing, Painting, Photography, Printmaking, Metalwork, Studio Ceramics, 3D Design

BELOIT

BELOIT COLLEGE, Dept of Art, 700 College St, 53511. Tel 608-363-2679, 363-2633, 363-2634; FAX 608-363-2718. *Chmn* Michael Simon; *Dir Art Museum* Henry Moy, BA; *Prof* Richard W P Olson, MA; *Assoc Prof* Debra Mancoff, PhD; *Asst Prof* Michael Weber; *Vis Instr* Ralph Knasinski. Instrs: FT 3, PT 2
Estab 1847; pvt; D & E; SC 14, LC 10; enrl maj 30, gen col enrl 1026
Ent Req: Top third of class, 3 yrs foreign language, 4 yrs English, SAT or ACT
Degrees: BA, BS & MAT 4 yrs
Courses: †Art History, Ceramics, Drawing, †Museum Staff Training, Painting, Photography, Printmaking, Sculpture, Modern Architecture, 19th & 20th Century Art, Renaissance Art, †Studio Art
Summer School: Dir, Mike Weber. Enrl 50; Courses—Ceramics

DE PERE

SAINT NORBERT COLLEGE, Div of Humanities & Fine Arts, 334 Boyle Hall, 100 Grant St, 54115. Tel 414-337-3181, 337-3105. *Head Dept* Dr R H Boyer. Instrs: FT 4
Estab 1898; pvt den; D; SC 19, LC 5; enrl D 60, maj 60
Ent Req: HS dipl, ent exam
Degrees: BA 4 yrs
Tuition: $9440 per yr; campus res—$2255-$3100 includes room & board
Courses: Aesthetics, Art Education, Art History, Ceramics, Drawing, Graphic Arts, Graphic Design, Illustration, Jewelry, Painting, Photography, Sculpture, Teacher Training
Summer School: Dir, John Giovannini. Terms of 3 or 5 wks beginning June. Courses—Art Education, Ceramics, Drawing, History of Art, Painting, Sculpture

EAU CLAIRE

UNIVERSITY OF WISCONSIN-EAU CLAIRE, Dept of Art, Park & Garfield Ave, 54702. Tel 715-836-3277; FAX 715-836-2380. *Chmn* Scott Robertson. Instrs: PT 1
Estab 1916; pub; D & E; scholarships; SC 31, LC 12; enrl maj 260
Ent Req: HS dipl, ent exam
Degrees: BA, BS & BFA 4 yrs
Tuition: Res—$819 per sem, nonres—$2360 per sem
Courses: Advertising Design, Art Education, Art History, Ceramics, Drawing, Painting, Photography, Printmaking, Sculpture, Fibers, Metalsmithing
Adult Hobby Classes: Ceramics, Painting
Summer School: Dir, Charles Campbell. Enrl 100; tuition res—$545, nonres—$1573 for 8 wk, 8 cr term. Courses—Art Methods for Teachers, Drawing, Painting

FOND DU LAC

MARIAN COLLEGE, Art Dept, 45 S National Ave, 54935. Tel 414-923-7602, Ext 7622; FAX 414-923-7154. *Coordr* Sr Mary Neff, MA; *Chmn Arts & Humanities* Dr Gary Boelhauer; *Asst Prof* Frank Scotello; *Instr* Kris Krumenauer; *Instr* Cal Jones
Estab 1936; pvt; E; scholarships; SC 20, LC 12; enrl D 107, E 35, maj 6

Ent Req: HS dipl, ACT or SAT
Degrees: BA and BA(Art Educ) 4 yrs
Tuition: $3500 per yr, $300 per cr; campus res available
Courses: Advertising Design, Art Appreciation, Art History, Ceramics, Drawing, Graphic Arts, †Art Education, Illustration, Mixed Media, Painting, Photography, Fiber Arts, Puppetry
Adult Hobby Classes: Workshops, summer sessions, continuing education
Children's Classes: In Relationship with Art Education
Summer School: Workshops, credit art courses

GREEN BAY

UNIVERSITY OF WISCONSIN-GREEN BAY, Art-Communication & the Arts, 2420 Nicolet, 54311-7001. Tel 414-465-2348; FAX 414-465-2718. *Head Dept* David Damkoehler; *Concentration Chmn* Curt Heuer. Instrs: FT 6, PT 2
EStab 1970; pub; D & E; SC 29, LC 3; enrl D 5500
Ent Req: HS dipl, ent exam
Degrees: BA and BS 4 yrs
Tuition: Res—$775 per sem; nonres—$2334.90 per sem
Courses: Aesthetics, Art Education, Ceramics, Drawing, Graphic Design, Intermedia, Jewelry, Mixed Media, Painting, Photography, Printmaking, Sculpture, Stage Design, Textile Design, Theatre Arts, Acting & Directing, Costume & Makeup Design, Environmental Design, Graphic Communications, Styles
Children's Classes: Saturday gifted program
Summer School: Courses—vary

KENOSHA

CARTHAGE COLLEGE, Art Dept, 2001 Alfred Dr, 53140-1994. Tel 414-551-5859; FAX 414-551-6208. *Chmn* Phillip Powell
Scholarships offered
Degrees: BA
Tuition: Res—undergrad $4775 per term
Courses: Advertising Design, Art Education, Art History, Ceramics, Design, Drawing

UNIVERSITY OF WISCONSIN-PARKSIDE, Art Dept, 900 Wood Rd, PO Box 2000, 53141. Tel 414-595-2581; FAX 414-595-2265. *Prof* David Holmes, MFA; *Assoc Prof* Douglas DeVinny, MFA; *Assoc Prof* Dennis Bayuzick, MFA; *Assoc Prof* John Satre Murphy; *Assoc Prof* Rollin Jansky, MS
Estab 1965; pub; D & E; scholarships; SC 25, LC 6
Ent Req: Ent req HS dipl, upper 50%
Degrees: BA and BS 4 yrs
Tuition: Res—undergrad $849 per sem; nonres—undergrad $2529.50 per sem; campus res—available
Courses: Aesthetics, Art Education, Art History, Ceramics, Drawing, Film, †Jewelry, Painting, Printmaking, Sculpture, Teacher Training, Textile Design, Art Metals, Life Modeling
Summer School: Tuition $82.25 res hr for term of 8 wks beginning mid June. Courses—Vary from summer to summer

LA CROSSE

UNIVERSITY OF WISCONSIN-LA CROSSE, Art Dept, 1725 State St, 54601. Tel 608-785-8230; FAX 608-785-8885. *Chmn* Erwin Erickson
Estab 1905; pub; D & E; scholarships; SC 25, LC 5; enrl (univ) 7600
Ent Req: HS dipl
Degrees: BA and BS 4 yrs
Tuition: Res—$929 per sem; nonres—$2752.50 per sem
Courses: Art Education, Ceramics, Drawing, Graphic Arts, Painting, Printmaking, Sculpture, Ancient Art of the Western World, Medieval Art of the Western World, Renaissance Art of the Western World, Modern Art of the Western World, History of American Art, Aesthetics in Art Criticism in the Visual Arts, Art Metals, Blacksmithing, Crafts, Figure Design, History of Animated Film, 2-D Design, 3-D Design
Adult Hobby Classes: Courses—Blacksmithing, Ceramics, Outreach Jewelry
Summer School: Courses—vary

VITERBO COLLEGE, Art Dept, 815 S Ninth, 54601. Tel 608-791-0040, Ext 330; FAX 608-791-0367. *Assoc Prof* Sr Carlene Unser, MA; *Chmn* Tim Crane, MFA; *Instr* Diane Crane; *Assoc Prof* Peter Fletcher
Estab 1890; pvt; D & E; scholarships; SC 10-12, LC 6; enrl D 55, maj 55
Degrees: BA, BAEd & BS 4 yrs
Tuition: $3600 per yr; campus res—room & board $2800 per yr
Courses: Advertising Design, Art Education, Art History, Ceramics, Commercial Art, Drawing, Graphic Arts, Illustration, Painting, Photography, Printmaking, Sculpture, Teacher Training, Weaving, Fibers
Summer School: Tuition $40 per sem hr. Summer catalog sent on request

WESTERN WISCONSIN TECHNICAL COLLEGE, Graphics Division, 304 N Sixth St, PO Box 0908, 54602-0908. Tel 608-785-9178; FAX 608-785-9407. *Chmn* Richard Westpfahl
Estab 1911, dept estab 1964; pub; D & E; scholarships; SC & LC 16; enrl D 130, E 145, non-maj 132, maj 143
Ent Req: HS dipl or GED
Degrees: AAS 2 yrs
Courses: Advertising Design, †Commercial Art, Display, Film, †Graphic Arts, Graphic Design, Illustration, Lettering, Mixed Media, Painting, Photography, Stage Design, Video, Media
Adult Hobby Classes: Enrl 264; tuition $13 per cr. Courses—Color Photo Printing, Home Movie Making, Painting, Photography
Summer School: Dir, T E Hendrickson. Courses—varied

MADISON

EDGEWOOD COLLEGE, Art Dept, 855 Woodrow St, 53711. Tel 608-257-4861, Ext 2307. *Chmn* Robert Tarrell; *Faculty* David Smith; *Faculty* Mary Lybarger
Estab 1941; den; D & E; institutional grants based on financial needs; SC 20, LC 4; enrl D & E 500 (total), non-maj 70, maj 20
Ent Req: HS dipl, ACT
Degrees: BA or BS 4 yrs
Tuition: $5330 annual tuition; campus res available
Courses: †Art Education, Art History, Calligraphy, Ceramics, Design, Drawing, Graphic Design, Painting, Photography, Printmaking, Sculpture, †Teacher Training, Textile Design, Art Therapy
Summer School: Dir, Dr Joseph Schmiedicke. Tuition $110 per cr. Courses—vary

MADISON AREA TECHNICAL COLLEGE, Art Dept, 3550 Anderson St, 53704. Tel 608-246-6058. *Chmn* Jerry E Butler, PhD
Estab 1911; pub; D & E; scholarships; SC 45, LC 12; enrl D 5300, E 23,000 (part-time)
Ent Req: HS dipl
Degrees: AA 2 yrs commercial art, photography & visual communications
Courses: Advertising Design, Art History, Calligraphy, Ceramics, †Commercial Art, Design, Display, Drawing, Handicrafts, Illustration, Jewelry, Lettering, Painting, †Photography, Printmaking, Visual Communications
Adult Hobby Classes: Enrl 1000. Courses—same as regular session

UNIVERSITY OF WISCONSIN, MADISON

—Dept of Art, 6241 Humanities Bldg, 455 N Park, 53706. Tel 608-262-1660. *Chmn* Trumman Lowe; *Prof* Melvin Butor; *Prof* Jack Damer; *Prof* Fred Fenster; *Prof* Raymond Gloeckler; *Prof* Walter Hamady; *Prof* Philip Hamilton; *Prof* Larry Junkins; *Prof* Cavaliere Ketchum; *Prof* Richard Lazzaro; *Prof* Richard Long; *Prof* Eleanor Moty; *Prof* Ronald Neperud; *Prof* R Kenneth Ray; *Prof* Richard Reese; *Prof* N Wayne Taylor; *Prof* William Weege; *Prof* David Becker; *Assoc Prof* George Cramer; *Assoc Prof* Truman Lowe; *Assoc Prof* Laurie Beth Clark; *Assoc Prof* Patricia Fennell; *Assoc Prof* Steve Feren; *Assoc Prof* Doug Marschlek; *Assoc Prof* Edward Pope; *Assoc Prof* Frances Meyers; *Assoc Prof* Carol Pylant; *Asst Prof* Elaine Scheer; *Asst Prof* John Rieben; *Asst Prof* Tom Loeser. Instrs: FT 32, PT 3
Estab 1911; pub; scholarships and fels; SC 68, LC 2, GC 19; enrl maj 500, grad 120
Degrees: BFA, BS(Art, Art Educ), MA(Art, Art Educ), MFA(Art), PhD(Art Educ)
Courses: Art Appreciation, Art Education, Calligraphy, Ceramics, Design, Drawing, Goldsmithing, Graphic Arts, Graphic Design, Handicrafts, Illustration, Intermedia, Jewelry, Lettering, Mixed Media, Computer Art, Serigraphy, Stage Design and Lighting, Typography, Woodworking
Summer School: Three wk intersession, 8 wk session
—Dept of Art History, 302 Elvehjem Museum of Art, 800 University Ave, 53706. Tel 608-263-2340. *Art History Dept Chmn* Jane C Hutchison; *Prof* Henry J Drewal; *Prof* James M Dennis; *Prof* Frank R Horlbeck; *Prof* Narcisco G Menocal; *Assoc Prof* Barbara C Buenger; *Assoc Prof* Gail L Geiger; *Asst Prof* Nicholas D Mirzoeff; *Asst Prof* Julia K Murray; *Asst Prof* Quitman E Phillips; *Dept Secy* Debbie Ganser
Estab 1848, dept estab 1925; pub; D; scholarships & fels; enrl 1500, maj 75, grad 69
Ent Req: HS dipl
Degrees: BA, MA, PhD
Tuition: Res—undergrad $97.75 per cr, nonres—$326.75 per cr; res—grad $202.25 per cr, nonres $614 per cr
Courses: †Art History
—Graduate School of Business, Center for Arts Administration, 1155 Observatory Dr, 53706. Tel 608-263-4161. *Dir* E Arthur Prieve
Estab 1969
Tuition: Res—undergrad $1175 per sem, grad $1619 per sem; nonres—undergrad $3920 per sem, grad $4912 per sem; Minnesota res—undergrad $1625 per sem, grad $1825 per sem
Courses: Arts Administration Seminars, Colloquium in Arts Administration

MANITOWOC

SILVER LAKE COLLEGE, Art Dept, 2406 S Alverno Rd, 54220. Tel 414-684-6691, Ext 181; FAX 414-684-7082. *Assoc Prof* Sr Mariella Erdmann, MA; *Instr* Donna Dart, MA
Estab 1936, dept estab 1959; pvt; D & E; SC 21, LC 6; enrl D 50, E 10, non-maj 25, maj 25
Ent Req: HS dipl, ACT or SAT
Degrees: AA(Commercial Art) 2 yrs, BS or BA(Studio Art) and BS or BA(Art Educ) 4 yrs
Tuition: Res & nonres—undergrad $6500 per yr
Courses: †Art Education, Art History, Calligraphy, Ceramics, †Commercial Art, Drawing, Graphic Arts, Graphic Design, Jewelry, Lettering, Mixed Media, Painting, Photography, Printmaking, Sculpture, Teacher Training, Textile Design, †Studio Art
Children's Classes: Enrl 100; tuition $10-$25 per 6 wk term. Courses—Clay, Drawing, Fibers, Photography, Sculpture, Painting, Graphics
Summer School: Dir, Sr Catherine Gilles. Enrl 350; tuition $90 per cr per 6 wk terms beginning June 18. Courses—vary

MARINETTE

UNIVERSITY OF WISCONSIN CENTER-MARINETTE COUNTY, Art Dept, Bay Shore, 54143. Tel 715-735-7477. *Head Dept* James La Malfa, MFA
Estab 1850, dept estab 1946; pub; D & E; scholarships
Ent Req: HS dipl
Degrees: AAS 2 yrs
Tuition: Res—undergrad $749 per sem; nonres—undergrad $2490 per sem
Courses: Art History, Drawing, Painting, Photography, Sculpture, Survey of Art, 2-D Design
Summer School: Dir, William A Schmidtke. Tuition $52 per cr for term of 8 wks beginning June 7. Courses—Beginning & Advanced Photography plus courses in other disciplines

MENOMONIE

UNIVERSITY OF WISCONSIN-STOUT, Dept of Art & Design, 54751. Tel 715-232-1141; FAX 715-232-1669. *Head Dept* Glen Bloedorn, MFA; *Prof* Gene Bloedorn, MFA; *Prof* Todd Boppel, MFA; *Prof* Doug Cumming, MFA; *Prof* John Perri, MFA; *Prof* Eddie Wong, MFA; *Prof* Ron Verdon, MFA; *Prof* Dr Claudia Smith, PhD; *Prof* Susan Hunt, MFA; *Assoc Prof* William Schulman, ABD; *Assoc Prof* Robb Wilson, MFA; *Assoc Prof* Rob Price, MFA; *Assoc Prof* Alan Gamache, MFA; *Assoc Prof* Humphrey Gilbert, MFA; *Assoc Prof* Paul De Long, MFA; *Assoc Prof* Claudia Smith, PhD; *Asst Prof* Susan Hunt, MFA; *Asst Prof* Dion Manriquez, MFA; *Asst Prof* Rob Price, MFA; *Asst Prof* Paul DeLong, MFA; *Lectr* William De Hoff, MFA; *Lectr* John Du Fresne, MA; *Lectr* Tim Eaton, BFA; *Lectr* Edward Stevens, BA; *Lectr* Richard Caker, MA; *Lectr* Magdalena Laszkiewicz, BFA; *Specialist* Mary Hovind, BS; *Lectr* Scott Wallace, MFA; *Lectr* Justin Wilwerding, MA
Estab 1893, dept estab 1965; pub; E; SC 60, LC 6; enrl D 24, non-maj 1200, maj 630
Ent Req: HS dipl
Degrees: BS(Art), BFA(Art) 4 yrs
Tuition: Res—undergrad $933 per sem, $78 per cr hr, grad $1115 per sem, $120 per cr hr; nonres—undergrad $2757 per sem, grad $3309 per sem; campus res—room & board $2158 per yr
Courses: †Art Education, Art History, Ceramics, Design, Drawing, †Graphic Design, †Industrial Design, †Interior Design, Painting, Printmaking, Sculpture, Silversmithing, Art Period Courses, Art Metals, Blacksmithing, Fashion Illustration
Children's Classes: Courses—Sat classes in Art (Media changes and Drama)
Summer School: Dir, Gene Bloedorn. Enrl varies with class; tuition res—undergrad $452, grad $587; nonres—undergrad $1303, grad $1717 for term of 8 wks beginning June 1 - Aug 6. Courses—Advanced Graphic Design, Ceramics, Drawing, Design, Life Drawing, Painting, Printmaking

MEQUON

CONCORDIA UNIVERSITY, Division of Arts & Sciences, 12800 N Lake Shore Dr, 9 W, 53092. Tel 414-243-5700, Ext 250; FAX 414-243-4351. *Div Dir* Dr Gene Edward Veith
Estab 1881, dept estab 1971; den; D & E; SC 6, LC 1; enrl non-maj 100, maj 5
Ent Req: HS dipl
Degrees: AA 2 yrs, BA 2 yrs
Tuition: $4900 per sem; campus res—room & board $1550 per sem
Courses: Art History, Drawing, Graphic Design, Handicrafts, Painting, Sculpture, Design
Adult Hobby Classes: Courses available in art and other areas
Summer School: Terms of 5 wks. Courses—Drawing & Painting (outdoors)

MILWAUKEE

ALVERNO COLLEGE, Art Dept, 3401 S 39 St, PO Box 343922, 53234-3922. Tel 414-382-6000, 382-6131; FAX 414-382-6354. *Dir* Bonnie Gendel
Estab 1948; pvt, W only in degree program; D & E; scholarships; SC 20, LC 5; enrl D 200, E 50, maj 35
Ent Req: GPA, class rank and ACT or SAT
Degrees: BA 4 yrs (or 128 cr)
Tuition: $3195 per sem; campus res—room & board available
Courses: Art Education, Art History, Ceramics, Drawing, Painting, Printmaking, Sculpture, Stage Design, Teacher Training, Art Therapy, Computer Graphics, Enameling (Cloisonne), General Crafts, Introduction to Visual Art, Metal Working, Weaving
Summer School: Term June to August. Courses—Art Education, Studio Art

CARDINAL STRITCH COLLEGE, Art Dept, 6801 N Yates Rd, 53217. Tel 414-352-5400, Ext 331. *Prof* Gary Rosine, PhD; *Asst Prof* Timothy Abler; *Assoc Prof* Mildred Tryba, MA; *Instr* William Carman; *Instr* Muneer Bahauddeen; *Lectr* Sr Jeanne Moynihan; *Lectr* Claire Pfleger; *Lectr* Estherly Allen; *Lectr* Michael Boyle; *Lectr* James Komas; *Lectr* Barbara Manger; *Lectr* John Michaels-Paque
Estab 1937; den; D & E; scholarships; SC 29, LC 17; enrl maj 98
Ent Req: HS dipl, ent exam
Degrees: AA, BA, BFA, BA(Commercial Art), BA(Education)
Tuition: Undergrad $2586.50 per sem, $125 per cr hr; grad $125 per cr hr; campus res—room & board $1075-$1150 per sem
Courses: Aesthetics, Art Education, Art History, Ceramics, Drawing, Graphic Design, Illustration, Lettering, Mixed Media, Painting, Photography, Printmaking, Sculpture, Computer Graphics, Fibers, Metalsmithing
Adult Hobby Classes: Enrl 200; tuition $40 - $60 per 8 - 12 wk session.
Courses—Basic Drawing, Chinese Brush Painting, Enameling & Jewelry Design, Mixed Media, Painting, Photography, Watercolor, Wood carving
Children's Classes: Enrl 100; tuition $50 per child per 12 classes.
Courses—traditional media plus various crafts

MILWAUKEE AREA TECHNICAL COLLEGE, Graphic Arts Dept, 700 W State St, 53233. Tel 414-278-6252; FAX 414-271-2195. *Head Dept* Michael Walsh; *Instructor* Howard Austin, MS; *Instructor* William Bonifay, BS; *Instructor* Mary Anna Petrick, MFA; *Instructor* William Crandall, MA; *Instructor* Joseph D'Lugosz, BFA; *Instructor* Geraldine Geischer, MFA; *Instructor* Chris Hansen, BFA; *Instructor* Hans Krommenhoek, MFA; *Instructor* Donald O'Connell, BFA; *Instructor* John Strachota, MS
Estab 1912, dept estab 1958; pub; D & E; financial aid; enrl D 240, E 150
Ent Req: HS dipl
Degrees: AA 2 yrs
Tuition: res—$35.25 per cr hr; $564 per sem; $1128 per yr; nonres—$235.80 per cr hr; no campus res
Courses: Advertising Design, Calligraphy, Ceramics, †Commercial Art, Display, Drawing, Graphic Design, Illustration, †Jewelry, Lettering, †Photography, Silversmithing, †Video, Printing & Publishing
Adult Hobby Classes: Tuition $12 per cr
Summer School: One advanced & two beginner courses

MILWAUKEE INSTITUTE OF ART AND DESIGN, 273 E Eric St, 53202. Tel 414-276-7889; FAX 414-291-8077. *Pres* Terrence J Coffman, BFA; *VPres Academic Affairs* John E Spurgin; *Chmn Fine Arts* Alvin Balinsky; *Chmn Design Dept* Becky Balistreri; *Chmn Liberal Arts & Art History* Steve Kapelke; *Chmn Foundations Dept* Bruce Grudzinski. Instrs: FT 25, PT 50
Estab 1974; pvt; D; scholarships; enrl D 400, maj 472
Ent Req: HS dipl, portfolio
Degrees: BFA 4 yrs
Tuition: $7000 per yr
Courses: Advertising Design, Art History, Design, Display, Drafting, Drawing, Graphic Design, Illustration, Industrial Design, Interior Design, Painting, Photography, Printmaking, Silversmithing
Summer School: Dir, John E Spurgin. Enrl, 25; tuition $256 per cr for 12 wk term. Courses—Art History, Basic Design, Drawing, English

MOUNT MARY COLLEGE, Art Dept, 2900 N Menomonee River Parkway, 53222. Tel 414-258-4810. *Chmn* Sr Angelee Fuchs, MA; *Prof* Sr Remy Revor, MFA; *Prof* Charles Kaiser, MFA; *Prof* Joseph Rozman, MFA; *Assoc Prof* Sandra Keiser; *Assoc Prof* Sr Aloyse Hessburg, MA; *Assoc Prof* Elaine Zarse, MA; *Asst Prof* Pamela Steffen, MBS; *Asst Prof* Lynn Kapitan, MPS; *Asst Prof* Catherine Leonard, PhD; *Asst Prof* Jane Febock, MA; *Asst Prof* Geraldine Wind; *Asst Prof* Sr Carla Huebner, MS; *Asst Prof* Lori Vance, MA; *Asst Prof* Dennis Klopfer; *Instr* Greg Miller, MS; *Instr* Karen Olsen, MA; *Instr* Ralph Cavan; *Instr* J Michael Tucci; *Instr* Martha Bolles, MA; *Instr* John Larner, MFA; *Instr* Sue Loesl, MA; *Instr* Virginia Minar, MA; *Instr* Cheryl Mantz; *Instr* Marcia Moriarty, BA; *Instr* Anne Kustner, BA; *Instr* Sonji Yarbrough, MFA; *Instr* Erin Holmgren, MA; *Instr* Mary Elliott, BA; *Instr* Barbara Borgwardt, BA; *Instr* Dawn Oertel; *Instr* Kathy Kubiak, BA; *Instr* Bruce Zamjahn, BA
Estab 1913, dept estab 1929; den; D & E; scholarships; SC 22, LC 12; enrl D 200, E 30, non-maj 50, maj 200
Ent Req: HS dipl
Degrees: BA 4 yrs
Tuition: $7300 per yr, $3650 per sem; campus res—available; board $750 - $1000 per sem
Courses: Advertising Design, Aesthetics, Architecture, Art Appreciation, †Art Education, Art History, Calligraphy, Ceramics, Costume Design & Construction, Design, Display, Drafting, Drawing, †Fashion Arts, Film, Graphic Arts, †Graphic Design, Handicrafts, Illustration, Intermedia, †Interior Design, Jewelry, Lettering, Mixed Media, Occupational Therapy, Painting, Photography, Printmaking, Sculpture, Silversmithing, Stage Design, Teacher Training, Textile Design, Video, Weaving, Art Internship, †Art Therapy, Enameling, Fiber Arts
Adult Hobby Classes: Enrl 1000; tuition variable, on going year round. Courses non-cr—varied, self-interest
Children's Classes: Enrl 165; tuition $45 2 wk term, summer only. Courses—Arts & Crafts
Summer School: Dir, Sr Pamela Moehring. Enrl 710; tuition undergrad $135, grad $230 for 6 wk term. Courses—large selection

UNIVERSITY OF WISCONSIN-MILWAUKEE, Dept of Art, School of Fine Arts, PO Box 413, 53201. Tel 414-229-4200; FAX 414-229-6154. *Dean* Will Rockett. Instrs: FT 30, PT 29
Scholarships; enrl maj 860
Degrees: BFA(Art), BFA with teachers cert, MA(Art), MS(Art Educ), MFA(Art), MFA with teachers cert
Tuition: Res—undergrad $1078.25 per sem
Courses: Art Education, Ceramics, Drawing, Painting, Photography, Printmaking, Sculpture, Graphic Design, Metals
Summer School: Dir, Frank Lutz. 4 & 8 wk sessions offered. Courses—Art Education, Design, Drawing, Fibers, Metals, Painting, Photography, Sculpture

OSHKOSH

UNIVERSITY OF WISCONSIN-OSHKOSH, Dept of Art, 54901. Tel 414-424-2222. *Chmn* Jeff Lipschutz. Instrs: FT 24
Estab 1871; pub; D & E; scholarships for grad students; SC 56, LC 14, GC 31; enrl D 10,5000, E 2500, maj 350, minors 50
Ent Req: HS dipl
Degrees: BA, BAE and BS(Art) 4 yrs, BFA 82 cr
Courses: Advertising Design, Art Education, Art History, Ceramics, Commercial Art, Drawing, Graphic Arts, Jewelry, Lettering, Painting, Photography, Printmaking, Sculpture, Teacher Training, Textile Design, Woodcraft

PLATTEVILLE

UNIVERSITY OF WISCONSIN-PLATTEVILLE, Dept of Fine Art, Art Bldg 212B, 53818. Tel 608-342-1781. *Chmn* Roger Gottschalk. Instrs: FT 8
Estab 1866; pub; D & E; SC 30, LC 5, GC 3; enrl maj 105
Ent Req: HS dipl, ent exam
Degrees: BA and BS 4 yrs
Tuition: Res—undergrad $1043, grad $1268; nonres—undergrad $3135, grad $3732
Courses: Ceramics, Drawing, Graphic Design, Illustration, Painting, Photography, Printmaking, Art Survey, Ethnic Art, Fiber & Fabrics, Lettering & Typographic, Art in Elementary Education
Summer School: Dir, Harold Hutchinson. Enrl 2200; term of 8 wks beginning June. Courses—same as regular session

RICE LAKE

UNIVERSITY OF WISCONSIN, Center-Barron County, Dept of Art, College Dr, 54868. Tel 715-234-8176, Ext 5408; FAX 715-234-1975. *Assoc Prof* Don Ruedy, MFA
Pub; D & E; scholarships; SC 8, LC 2; enrl D 63, E 10, non-maj 57, maj 16
Ent Req: HS dipl
Degrees: AA & AS 2 yrs
Tuition: $710.50 per sem; no campus res

Courses: Art History, Calligraphy, Drawing, Jewelry, Lettering, Painting, Printmaking, Stage Design, Theatre Arts, Oil Painting, Water Color
Adult Hobby Classes: Enrl 20, 2 night 3 hrs. Courses - Art History, Design, Drawing, Painting
Children's Classes: Enrl 30; tuition $40 for 2 weeks in summer
Summer School: Dean, Mary Sommers. Enrl 80, 8 wk sem

RIPON

RIPON COLLEGE, Art Dept, PO Box 248, 54971. Tel 414-748-8110. *Chmn* Evelyn Kain. Instrs: FT 2, PT 1
Estab 1851; pvt; D; scholarships and financial aid; SC 13, LC 8; enrl maj 20
Ent Req: Grad from accredited secondary school, SAT or ACT is recommended, but not required
Degrees: AB 4 yrs
Tuition: $11,936 per yr
Courses: †Art History, Design, Drawing, Mixed Media, Painting, Studio Art

RIVER FALLS

UNIVERSITY OF WISCONSIN-RIVER FALLS, Art Dept, 54022. Tel 715-425-3266; FAX 715-425-4487. *Chmn* Michael Padgett
Estab 1874, major estab 1958; pub; D; scholarships; SC 26, LC 18; enrl non-maj 400, maj 170
Ent Req: HS dipl
Degrees: BA, BS(Educ), BFA and BS(Liberal Arts) 4 yrs
Courses: Aesthetics, †Art Education, Art History, Ceramics, Costume Design & Construction, Drawing, Film, Graphic Design, History of Art & Archaeology, Jewelry, Painting, Photography, Printmaking, Sculpture, Silversmithing, Textile Design, Glass Blowing, Fibers, Stained Glass
Summer School: Dir, Dr Roger Swanson. Enrl 1600; 4 wk sessions. Courses—Clay, Fibers, Glass, Painting, Printmaking, Sculpture

STEVENS POINT

UNIVERSITY OF WISCONSIN-STEVENS POINT, Dept of Art & Design, College of Fine Arts, 1801 Franklin St, 54481. Tel 715-346-2669. *Head Dept* Rex Dorethy; *Prof* Norman Kedts, MFA; *Prof* Daniel Fabiano; *Assoc Prof* Robert Stowers; *Assoc Prof* Gary Hagen, MFA; *Assoc Prof* David L Smith, PhD; *Asst Prof* Robert Erickson; *Asst Prof* Catherine Angel; *Asst Prof* Wayne Halverson, MA; *Asst Prof* Anne-Bridget Gary; *Asst Prof* Patricia Koopman; *Asst Prof* Rebecca Weichinger; *Asst Prof* Diane Bywaters; *Asst Prof* Dennis Angel; *Lectr* Mark Pohlkamp
Estab 1894; pub; D & E; enrl D 866, non-maj 666, maj 200
Ent Req: HS dipl
Degrees: BA(Fine Arts), BS(Art Educ), BS(Fine Arts) & BFA(Art-Professional)
Tuition: Campus res—available
Courses: Architecture, Art Education, †Art History, Ceramics, Drawing, Goldsmithing, Graphic Arts, Graphic Design, Painting, Photography, Printmaking, Sculpture, Silversmithing, Teacher Training, Computer Graphics, Environmental Design, Fiber Arts, Leather, †Studio Art, Wood
Children's Classes: Art Workshop
Summer School: Dir, O E Radke. Term of 8 wks beginning June 14. Courses—Art Education, Design, Drawing, Layout & Lettering, Papermaking

SUPERIOR

UNIVERSITY OF WISCONSIN-SUPERIOR, Programs in the Visual Arts, 54880. Tel 715-394-8391. *Chmn* James Grittner, MFA; *Prof* Mel Olsen, MFA; *Prof* William Morgan, MFA; *Prof* Leonard Petersen, MFA; *Assoc Prof* Laurel Scott, PhD; *Asst Prof* Susan Loonsk, MFA; *Lectr* Kim Borst, MFA; *Lectr* Pope Wright, MA
Estab 1896, dept estab 1930; pub; D & E; scholarships; enrl D 250, E 100-125, non-maj 250, maj 100, grad 30
Ent Req: HS dipl
Degrees: BS, BS(Photography), BS(Art Therapy), BFA & BFA(Photography) 4 yrs, BFA with cert 5 yrs, MA 5 - 6 yrs
Tuition: Res—undergrad $900 per sem, grad $1100; nonres—undergrad $2600 per sem, grad $3100 per qtr; campus res available
Courses: Advertising Design, Art Education, Art History, Ceramics, Collages, Conceptual Art, Drawing, †Jewelry, †Mixed Media, Painting, †Photography, †Printmaking, †Sculpture, Teacher Training, †Art Therapy
Adult Hobby Classes: Courses—Ceramics, Crafts, Drawing, Fibers, Metalwork, Painting, Photography, Spinning
Children's Classes: Summer session only
Summer School: Dir, James Grittner. Enrl 100; tuition varies for term of 3 & 4 wks beginning June 12th. Courses—Art History, Ceramics, Drawing, Painting, Photography

WAUKESHA

CARROLL COLLEGE, Art Dept, 100 N East Ave, 53186. Tel 414-547-1211, 524-7191. *Chairperson* Marceil Pultorak, MA; *Assoc Prof* Philip Krejcarek, MFA; *Asst Prof* Thomas Selle, MFA; *Asst Prof* Brian Mesun, MFA
Estab 1846; pvt; D & E; scholarships; SC 21, LC 4; enrl D 1100, E 350
Ent Req: HS dipl, SAT or ACT
Degrees: BA
Tuition: $9820 annual full-time tuition
Courses: Museum Staff Training, Sculpture, †Stage Design, †Teacher Training, Textile Design, †Theatre Arts, †Video, †Pre-Architecture; †Commercial Art; Weaving
Adult Hobby Classes: Enrl 20 per sess. Courses—Photographing Your Own Work
Children's Classes: New program
Summer School: Dir, Jan Schoeben. Enrl varies; tuition $130 for term of 6 wks. Courses—Drawing, Graphics, Photography

WHITEWATER

UNIVERSITY OF WISCONSIN-WHITEWATER, Dept of Art, Ctr of the Arts 2073, 53190. Tel 414-472-1324; FAX 414-472-2808. *Chmn* Amy E Arntson. Instrs: FT 17, PT 1
Estab 1868; pub; D & E; SC 41, LC 18; enrl D 270, maj 200
Ent Req: HS dipl
Degrees: BA & BS(Art, Art Educ, Art History, Graphic Design), BFA 4 yrs
Tuition: Res—$825 per sem; nonres—$2366 per sem; campus res $994 per sem
Courses: Advertising Design, †Art Education, †Art History, Ceramics, Commercial Art, Drawing, Graphic Arts, Graphic Design, Illustration, Jewelry, Painting, Photography, Sculpture, Teacher Training, Textile Design
Summer School: Tuition res—$68.79 per cr, nonres $197.29 per cr for term of 4 & 8 wks beginning June. Courses—Art History, Ceramics, Drawing, Jewelry, Metal, Painting

WYOMING

CASPER

CASPER COLLEGE, Dept of Visual Arts, 125 College Dr, 82601. Tel 307-268-2110. *Div Head* Lynn R Munns; *Instr* Richard Jacobi, MFA; *Instr* Linda Lee Ryan, MFA; *Instr* Nancy Madura, MFA; *Instr* James L Gaither, MED; *Instr* Michael Keogh, MFA; *Instr* Dorothy Hitchcock, MFA
Pub; D & E; scholarships; LC 2; enrl D 3870
Ent Req: HS dipl
Degrees: AA 2 yrs
Tuition: Res—undergrad $372 per sem; nonres—undergrad $996 per sem; campus res—room & board $1075 - $1275
Courses: Advertising Design, Art History, Ceramics, Collages, Commercial Art, Drafting, Drawing, Handicrafts, Illustration, Jewelry, Painting, Photography, Sculpture, Silversmithing, Textile Design, Theatre Arts
Adult Hobby Classes: Tuition $32 per cr hr. Courses—Air Brush, Ceramics, Drawing, Fiber Art, Jewelry, Painting, Photography, Watercolor
Summer School: Dir, Kathy Anderson. Enrl 100; tuition $126 for summer sem or $21 per hr. Courses—Air Brush, Ceramics, Drawing, Jewelry, Painting, Photography

CHEYENNE

LARAMIE COUNTY COMMUNITY COLLEGE, Division of Arts & Humanities, 1400 E College Dr, 82007. Tel 307-778-1158. *Dir* Chuck Thompson, MA; *Instr* Matt West, MFA; *Instr* Joan Fullerton, MFA
Estab 1969; pub; D & E; scholarships; SC 19, LC 3; enrl D 125, E 100, non-maj 150, maj 20
Ent Req: HS dipl
Degrees: AA
Tuition: Res—$396 per sem; nonres—$1020 per sem
Courses: Ceramics, Drawing, Painting, Photography, Sculpture, Theatre Arts, Computer Graphics, Designs & Welded Sculpture, Metals, Stained Glass
Summer School: Dir, Chuck Thompson. Enrl 40; tuition $34 per cr hr for 8 wk term. Courses—Ceramics, Computer Gaphics, Drawing, Metals

LARAMIE

UNIVERSITY OF WYOMING, Dept of Art, PO Box 3138, 82071-3138. Tel 307-766-3269; FAX 307-766-3520. *Head Dept* Mary Jane Edwards. Instrs: FT 8
Estab 1886, dept estab 1946; pub; D; scholarships; SC 23, LC 6, GC 13; enrl D 80, non-maj 600, maj 120, grad 16
Ent Req: HS dipl
Degrees: BA, BS and BFA 4 yrs, MFA 2 yrs, MA and MAT 1 yr
Tuition: Res—$713 per sem; nonres—$2249 per sem
Courses: Art Education, Art History, Ceramics, Commercial Art, Design, Drawing, Graphic Design, Painting, Printmaking, Sculpture
Adult Hobby Classes: Courses offered
Summer School: Dir, Mary Jane Edwards. Enrl 100; tuition $32 per cr hr 1 - 12, 4 wk & 8 wk sessions. Courses&dsArt Appreciation, Art History, Ceramics, Drawing, Forging, Painting, Printmaking, Sculpture, Watercolor

POWELL

NORTHWEST COMMUNITY COLLEGE, Dept of Art, 231 W Sixth St, 82435. Tel 307-754-6111. *Chmn* Lynn Thorpe; *Instr* Ken Fulton; *Instr* John Giarrizzo; *Instr* Elisa Rausch
Estab 1946, dept estab 1952; pub; D & E; scholarships; SC 12, LC 4; enrl D 130, E 222, non-maj 317, maj 35
Ent Req: HS dipl, nonres ACT
Degrees: AA 2 yrs
Tuition: Res—undergrad $317 per sem, $25 per cr; nonres—undergrad $680 per sem, WUE 150% res tuition
Courses: Advertising Design, Art Education, Ceramics, Commercial Art, Drawing, Graphic Arts, Handicrafts, Lettering, Painting, Photography, Printmaking, Sculpture, Leather
Adult Hobby Classes: Enrl 100; tuition $25 per sem cr hr. Courses—vary each sem

RIVERTON

CENTRAL WYOMING COLLEGE, Art Center, 2660 Peck Ave, 82501. Tel 307-856-9291. *Head Dept* Willis R Patterson, MFA; *Prof* Sallie Wesaw, MFA; *Instr* Jon Cox, MFA; *Instr* Gerald Shippen, MFA
Estab 1966; pub; D & E; scholarships; SC 20, LC 2; enrl D 1500, E 500, non-maj 100, maj 20, others 20
Ent Req: HS dipl, GED
Degrees: AA 2 yrs
Tuition: Res $312 per sem; nonres—$936 per sem; sr citizen free of charge; campus res—room & board $1138
Courses: Art Appreciation, Art Education, Art History, Ceramics, Drawing, Graphic Arts, Mixed Media, Painting, Photography, Printmaking, Sculpture, Stage Design, Teacher Training, Theatre Arts, Bronze Casting, Fiber Arts, Lapidary, Moldmaking, Stained Glass, Stone/Wood Carving, Weaving
Adult Hobby Classes: Enrl 12-20; tuition $15-$50. Courses—Varied Art & General Curriculum
Children's Classes: Enrl 200; classes for a day, wk or sem. Courses—varied
Summer School: Limited Art offerings

ROCK SPRINGS

WESTERN WYOMING COMMUNITY COLLEGE, Art Dept, PO Box 428, 82901. Tel 307-382-1600, Ext 723. *Head Dept* Dr Florence McEwin. Instrs: FT 3, PT 4
Estab 1959; pub; D & E; scholarships; SC 12, LC 1; enrl D 675, E 600, maj 20
Ent Req: HS dipl
Degrees: AA 2 yrs
Tuition: $32 per cr hr
Courses: Art History, Ceramics, Commercial Art, Design, Drawing, Graphic Arts, Painting, Photography, Life Drawing
Adult Hobby Classes: Enrl 100. Courses—Crafts, Drawing, Painting, Pottery
Children's Classes: Dance
Summer School: Dir, Florence McEwin. Courses—Landscape Painting, Photography, Pottery

SHERIDAN

SHERIDAN COLLEGE, Art Dept, PO Box 1500, 82801. Tel 307-674-6446, Ext 123. *Head Dept* Jim Lawson; *Instr* Danna Hildebrand. Instrs: PT 3
Estab 1951; pub; D & E; scholarships; enrl maj 10
Ent Req: HS grad
Degrees: AA, AS & AAS 2 yrs
Tuition: In state res—$296 per sem; out of state res—$659 per sem
Courses: Art Appreciation, Ceramics, Design, Drawing, Jewelry, Painting, Photography, Sculpture, Etching, Lithography, Pottery, Silk Screen
Adult Hobby Classes: Enrl 40-60; tuition varies. Courses—Drawing, Painting, Pottery, Stained Glass
Children's Classes: Enrl 10-15; tuition varies. Courses—Pottery
Summer School: Enrl 10-15; tuition varies. Courses—Painting, Pottery

TORRINGTON

EASTERN WYOMING COLLEGE, Art Dept, 3200 W C St, 82240. Tel 307-532-8291; FAX 307-532-8225. *Head Dept* Sue Milner. Instrs: FT 1, PT 2
Estab 1948; pub; D & E; scholarships; SC 9, LC 1; enrl D 60, 50, maj 6
Ent Req: Varied
Degrees: AA and AAS 2 yrs
Tuition: Res—$312 per sem; nonres—$936 per sem
Courses: Ceramics, Commercial Art, Drawing, Graphic Arts, History of Art & Archaeology, Painting, Sculpture, General Art, Design I
Adult Hobby Classes: Painting Workshops
Summer School: Courses—Ceramics & various subjects

PUERTO RICO

MAYAGUEZ

UNIVERSITY OF PUERTO RICO, MAYAGUEZ, Dept of Humanities, College of Arts & Sciences, PO Box 5000, 00681. Tel 809-832-4040, Ext 3160, 265-3846; FAX 809-265-1225. *Dir* Hector J Huyke. Instrs: FT 40
Estab 1970; pub; D; SC 20, LC 15; enrl 402, maj 90
Ent Req: HS dipl
Degrees: BA(Art Theory) and BA(Plastic Arts) 4 yrs
Adult Hobby Classes: Enrl 40

PONCE

CATHOLIC UNIVERSITY OF PUERTO RICO, Dept of Fine Arts, PO Box 7186, 00732. Tel 809-844-2000, Ext 276. *Head Dept* Alfonso Santiago; *Prof* Ana Basso Bruno, MFA; *Prof* Mahir Laracuente, MM; *Prof* Adrian N Ramirez, MA; *Prof* Julio Micheli, MFA
Estab 1948, dept estab 1964; den; D; scholarships; SC 22, LC 4; enrl D 50 maj
Ent Req: HS dipl
Degrees: BA 4 yrs
Tuition: Res—undergrad $75 per cr hr, grad $85 per cr hr
Courses: Advertising Design, Aesthetics, Art Appreciation, Art Education, Art History, Ceramics, Conceptual Art, Constructions, Design, Drawing, Graphic Design, Painting, Photography, Printmaking, Sculpture, History in Art in Puerto Rico, Contemporary Form

RIO PIEDRAS

UNIVERSITY OF PUERTO RICO, Dept of Fine Arts, Ponce de Leon Ave (Mailing add: PO Box 21A49 UPR Station, San Juan, 00931). Tel 809-764-0000. *Head Dept* Frederico Barreda Ynonge; *Prof* Luis Hernandez-Cruz, MA; *Prof* Arturo Davila, PhD; *Prof* Rafael Rivera-Garcia, MA; *Assoc Prof* Enrique Garcia-Gutierrez, MA; *Assoc Prof* Carola Colom, MA; *Assoc Prof* Susana Herrero, MA; *Assoc Prof* Carmen A Rivera de Figueroa; *Asst Prof* Maria L Moreno, MA; *Asst Prof* Carmen T Ruiz de Fischler, MA; *Asst Prof* Pablo Rubio, MA; *Asst Prof* Jaime Romano, MA; *Asst Prof* Rene Torres-Delgado, MA; *Instr* Nelson Millan, MFA; *Instr* Guy Paizy
Estab 1902, dept estab 1950; pub; D; scholarships; enrl D 200, maj 45
Ent Req: HS dipl
Degrees: BA 4 yrs
Tuition: Res—undergrad $15 per cr; grad $45 per cr; campus res available
Courses: Architecture, Art Appreciation, Art History, Commercial Art, Design, Drawing, Graphic Arts, Painting, Photography, Sculpture, Video, Art in Puerto Rico, Michelangelo: Artist & Poet, Color Theory, General Theory of Art, Pre-Hispanic Art of Antilles
Adult Hobby Classes: Tuition $15 per sem cr (Aug - Dec & Jan - May).
Courses—Art History, Design, Drawing, Painting, Printmaking
Summer School: Dir, Dr Juan Barragan. Tuition $15 per cr for 2 month session.
Courses—Art Appreciation, Art History, Design, Drawing

SAN GERMAN

INTER AMERICAN UNIVERSITY OF PUERTO RICO, Dept of Art, Call Box 5100, 00753. Tel 809-892-1095. *Dir* Jaime Carrero, MS; *Auxiliary Prof* Fernando Santiago, MA; *Auxiliary Prof* Maria Garcia Vera, MFA; *Assoc Prof* Paul Vivoni, EdD; *Instr* Jose B Alvarez, BA
Estab 1912, dept estab 1947; pvt; D; SC 20, LC 12; enrl D 135, maj 135
Ent Req: HS dipl, college board, presentation of portfolio
Degrees: BA 4 yrs
Tuition: Res—undergrad $75 per cr, grad $110 per cr; campus res available
Courses: †Art Education, Art History, Calligraphy, †Ceramics, Drawing, †Graphic Arts, Handicrafts, †Painting, †Photography, †Sculpture, Experimental Design in Native Media, Leather, Macrame, Metals
Summer School: Dir, Jaime Carrero. Enrl 10; tuition $75 per cr hr for 5 wk term.
Courses—Art Appreciation

SAN JUAN

INSTITUTE OF PUERTO RICAN CULTURE, Escuela de Artes Plasticas, School of Fine Arts, El Morro Grounds (Mailing add: Institute of Puerto Rican Culture, PO Box 1112, San Juan, PR 00905-1112). Tel 809-725-1522. *Dir Fine Arts* Jose Balado
Estab 1971; pub; D; scholarships; SC 38, LC 12, GC 10; enrl D 160
Ent Req: HS dipl, ent exam
Degrees: BA 4 yrs
Tuition: None
Courses: †Sculpture, Teacher Training
Adult Hobby Classes: Enrl 137; tuition $3 per cr. Courses—Sculpture, Graphic, Painting
Summer School: Courses—Basic Drawing, Painting, Sculpture

Art Schools In Canada

ALBERTA

BANFF

BANFF CENTRE FOR THE ARTS, PO Box 1020, T0L 0C0. Tel 403-762-6180; FAX 403-762-6345; Cable ARTSBANFF. *VPres Educ* Carol Phillips; *Head Art Studio* Lorne Falk; *Head Ceramics Studio* Les Manning; *Head Photography Studio* Richard Baillargeon
Estab 1933 for summer study, winter cycle prog began 1979; scholarships; enrl winter 78, summer 39
Ent Req: Resume, slides of work, post-secondary art training at a university or art school and/or professional experience in field
Tuition: Res—$2520 per prog
Courses: Ceramics, Photography, Art Studio, Media Arts
Adult Hobby Classes: Enrl 20; tuition $58 - $72. Courses—Ceramics, Drawing

CALGARY

ALBERTA COLLEGE OF ART, 1407 - 14th Ave NW, T2N 4R3. Tel 403-284-7600; FAX 403-289-6682. *Pres* Robin Mayor; *Academic Dean Fine Arts* Helen Sevelius; *Asst Academic Dean* Hanne Weis; *Comptroller* Tom Anderson; *Prog Coordr Foundation* Bill Rodgers; *Prog Coordr Textiles* Jane Kidd; *Prog Coordr Ceramics* Sally Barbier; *Prog Coordr Glass* Norman Faulkner; *Prog Coordr Jewelry* Sarabeth Carnat; *Prog Coordr Sculpture* Wally May; *Prog Coordr Painting* Nancy Earl; *Prog Coordr Printmaking* Gary Olson; *Prog Coordr Visual Communications* Eugene Ouchie; *Prog Coordr Photography* Dan Gordon; *Prog Coordr Drawing* Richard Halliday
Estab 1926; pub; D & E; scholarships; SC approx 250, LC 14; enrl D 650, E 500, non-maj 200, maj 390, others 60
Ent Req: HS dipl, portfolio
Degrees: 4 yr dipl
Tuition: $852 per yr plus course costs
Courses: Ceramics, Drawing, Jewelry, Painting, Photography, Printmaking, Sculpture, Glass, Textiles, Visual Communications
Adult Hobby Classes: Enrl 1000; tuition varies per course. Courses—Ceramics, Art Fundamentals, Drawing, Jewelry, Painting, Printmaking, Sculpture, Glass, Textiles, Watercolor, Photography
Children's Classes: Enrl 560; tuition $75 for 20 hrs. Courses—Painting for Teenagers, Ceramics, Mixed Media, Painting, Puppetry, Sculpture, Jewelry, Pre-College Studio

MOUNT ROYAL COLLEGE, Dept of Interior Design, 4825 Richard Rd SW, T3E 6K6. Tel 403-240-6100. *Chmn* Henri Garand. Instrs: FT 5, PT 10
Estab 1910; pub; D & E; scholarships; SC 12, LC 17
Ent Req: HS dipl
Degrees: 2 yr dipl
Tuition: $450 per sem
Courses: Design, †Interior Design, Sculpture, Stage Design, Business Principles & Practices, Graphic Presentation, History of Art & Architecture, History of Furniture, Technical Design & Drafting

UNIVERSITY OF CALGARY, Dept of Art, 2500 University Dr, AB605, T2N 1N4. Tel 403-220-5252; FAX 403-282-7298. *Dean of Faculty Fine Arts* J P L Roberts; *Head* E Cameron. Instrs: FT 25, PT 16
Estab 1965; pub; D & E; SC 56, LC 19, GC 8; enrl D 263, E 31, all maj
Ent Req: HS dipl
Degrees: BA(Art History), BFA(School Art, Art), MFA(Studio)
Tuition: $1018.25 fall or winter sem
Courses: Art Education, Art History, Drawing, Painting, Photography, Sculpture, Printmaking, Art Fundamentals, Art Theory
Summer School: Two terms of 6 wks, May-July. Courses—Art History, Drawing, Printmaking, Painting, Art Fundamentals, Art Education, Sculpture

EDMONTON

UNIVERSITY OF ALBERTA, Dept of Art and Design, 112 St & 88 Ave, T6G 2C9. Tel 403-492-3261; FAX 403-492-7870. *Chmn* Dr Desmond Rochfort
Estab 1908, dept estab 1946; pub; D & E; scholarships; SC 51, LC 42, grad 23; enrl D 151, grad 15-20
Ent Req: HS dipl, portfolio
Degrees: BFA 4 yrs, MA & MVA 2 yrs
Tuition: Res—undergrad $800 per yr, grad $1000 per yr; nonres—grad $250 per course; campus res available
Courses: †Art History, †Graphic Design, †Industrial Design, †Painting, †Printmaking, †Sculpture

Adult Hobby Classes: Enrl 200; tuition $1300 per yr. Courses—Art History, Drawing, Painting, Printmaking Sculpture
Summer School: Dir, Rick Chenier. Enrl 150; tuition $300 per course. Courses—Art History, Drawing, Painting, Printmaking, Sculpture

LETHBRIDGE

UNIVERSITY OF LETHBRIDGE, Dept of Art, 4401 University Dr, T1K 3M4. Tel 403-329-2691; FAX 403-382-7127. *Chmn* B J McCarroll, MA; *Assoc Prof* Herbert A Hicks, MFA; *Assoc Prof* Carl Granzow, MFA; *Assoc Prof* Larry E Weaver, MFA; *Assoc Prof* Jeffrey Spalding, MFA; *Asst Prof* Janet Cardiff, MFA; *Asst Prof* Leslie Dawn; *Asst Prof* Jennifer Gordon
Estab 1967; pub; D & E; scholarships; SC 26, LC 9
Ent Req: HS dipl
Degrees: BA and BFA 4 yrs
Courses: Aesthetics, Architecture, Art Appreciation, Art Education, Art History, Ceramics, Collages, Conceptual Art, Constructions, Costume Design & Construction, Design, Drawing, Graphic Design, History of Art & Archaeology, Intermedia, Mixed Media, Museum Staff Training, Painting, Photography, Printmaking, Sculpture, Stage Design, Teacher Training, Theatre Arts, Video

RED DEER

RED DEER COLLEGE, Dept of Art and Design, 56 Ave & 32 St, T4N 5H5. Tel 403-342-3300; FAX 403-340-8940. *Chmn* Ian Cook. Instrs: FT 6, PT 2
Estab 1973; pub; D & E; scholarships; enrl max 50 first yr students, 30 second yr
Ent Req: HS dipl, portfolio
Degrees: Dipl, BFA 2 yrs
Courses: Art History, Ceramics, Drawing, Painting, Sculpture, Fundamentals of Visual Communication
Adult Hobby Classes: Enrl 300; tuition $74 - $100 per course. Courses—Ceramics, Drawing, Glass Blowing
Children's Classes: Enrl 80; tuition $350 per week. Courses—Drawing, Painting, Sculpture
Summer School: Dir, Ann Brodie. Enrl 500; tuition $200 per week. Courses—Applied Arts, Drawing, Glass Blowing, Painting, Printmaking

BRITISH COLUMBIA

VANCOUVER

EMILY CARR COLLEGE OF ART & DESIGN, 1399 Johnston St, V6H 3R9. Tel 604-687-2345; FAX 604-844-3801. *Pres* Alan Barkley; *Dir Student Services* Alan C McMillan; *Assoc Dean Studio* Terence Johnson; *Assoc Dean Design* Kenneth Hughes; *Assoc Dean Media* Ian Wallace; *Assoc Dean Foundation* John Wertschek
Estab 1925; pub; D & E; scholarships; SC 20, LC 8; enrl 1500
Ent Req: HS dipl plus presentation of folio of art work
Degrees: 4 yr dipl, 5 yr degree
Tuition: $1030 per yr
Courses: Art History, Ceramics, Conceptual Art, Design, Drawing, Film, Graphic Design, Photography, Printmaking, Sculpture, Video, Animation, Interdisciplinary Studies
Adult Hobby Classes: Enrl 1500-2000; tuition $45 - $758 per yr. Courses—Fine Arts, Design
Children's Classes: Enrl 100
Summer School: Dir, Isabel Spalding. Enrl 500; tuition $170 per course. Courses—Fine Arts, Design

UNIVERSITY OF BRITISH COLUMBIA
—Dept of Fine Arts, 6333 Memorial Rd, V6T 1Z2. Tel 604-822-2757; FAX 604-822-9003. *Head* James O Caswell, PhD; *Prof* Serge Guilbaut, PhD; *Prof* Rhodri Windsor-Liscome, PhD; *Prof* Jeff Wall, MA; *Assoc Prof* Richard Prince, BA; *Assoc Prof* Debra Pincus, PhD; *Assoc Prof* Rose Marie San Juan, PhD; *Assoc Prof* Marvin Cohodas, PhD; *Assoc Prof* Moritaka Matsumoto; *Assoc Prof* John O Brian, PhD; *Assoc Prof* Barbara Z Sungur, MFA; *Asst Prof* Wendy Dobereiner, MA; *Asst Prof* Maureen Ryan, PhD; *Asst Prof* Judith Williams, BA; *Asst Prof* Robert Young, BA; *Asst Prof* Katherine Hacker, MA; *Asst Prof* Carol Knicely, PhD; *Sr Instr* I Marc Pessin, MA
Scholarships & fels
Courses: †Art History, †Drawing, †Painting, †Photography, †Printmaking, †Sculpture, †Western, †Asian, †Indigenous Arts of the Americas

—**School of Architecture,** 6333 Memorial Rd, V6T 1Z2. Tel 604-822-2779; FAX 604-822-3808. *Dir* Sanford Hirshen. Instrs: FT 14
Estab 1946; pub; scholarships & fels
Degrees: BArchit, MAdv Studies in Arch, 3 yrs
Tuition: $2448 per 36 crs
Courses: Architecture
Adult Hobby Classes: Enrl 170; tuition $2448 per yr for 3 yr program

VANCOUVER COMMUNITY COLLEGE, LANGARA CAMPUS, Dept of Fine Arts, 100 W 49th Ave, V5Y 2Z6. Tel 604-324-5511. *Chmn Dept* Scott Plear, BFA; *Instr* Gordan Trick, MFA; *Instr* Gerald Formosa, Dipl Art; *Instr* Don Hutchinson, Dipl Art; *Instr* Barry Holmes, Nat Dipl; *Instr* Catherine Broderick-Lockhart, MFA; *Instr* Judith Brackman Sharp, MTA; *Instr* Daryl Plater, MFA; *Instr* Lesley Finlayson, MFA
Estab 1970; pub; D & E; SC 7, LC 1; enrl D 160
Ent Req: HS dipl, portfolio
Degrees: 2 yr Fine Arts Dipl
Tuition: $565 per sem
Courses: Ceramics, Design, Drawing, Painting, Printmaking, Sculpture
Adult Hobby Classes: Enrl 20 per class; tuition $100 per sem. Courses—Design, Drawing

VICTORIA

UNIVERSITY OF VICTORIA
—**Dept of Visual Arts,** PO Box 1700, V8W 2Y2. Tel 604-721-8011; FAX 604-721-7212. *Chmn* M Baden; *Prof* P Martin Bates, Dipl Royale, RCA; *Prof* D Harvey, ATD, RCA; *Prof* R Brener, Post Dipl, AD; *Assoc Prof* G Tiessen, MFA; *Assoc Prof* G Curry, MFA; *Assoc Prof* F Douglas; *Assoc Prof* Lynda Gammon, MFA; *Asst Prof* Vikky Alexander, BFA; *Asst Prof* Robert Youds, MFA
Estab 1963; pub; D; enrl 210, maj 30, hons 20
Ent Req: HS dipl
Degrees: BFA 4 yrs, MFA 2 yrs
Tuition: Res—undergrad $500 per year
Courses: †Drawing, †Painting, †Photography, †Printmaking, †Sculpture
Summer School: Courses—Drawing, Painting, Printmaking
—**Dept of History in Art,** V8W 2Y2. Tel 604-721-7942. *Chmn* Elizabeth Tumasonis; *Dean* S Anthony Welch, PhD; *Prof* #John L Osborne, PhD; *Asst Prof* Kathlyn Liscomb, PhD; *Asst Prof* Elizabeth Tumasonis, PhD; *Assoc Prof* Victoria Wyatt, PhD; *Asst Prof* Catherine Harding, PhD; *Asst Prof* Nancy Micklewright, PhD; *Asst Prof* Astri Wright, PhD; *Asst Prof* Carol Gibson-Wood, PhD; *Visiting Asst Prof* Christopher Thomas, PhD
LC 52, grad 20
Degrees: BA 4 yrs, MA 2 yrs, PhD 2 yrs
Tuition: Undergrad $118 per unit (15 units), grad $875 per term
Courses: Native American Art; South & Southeast Asia; The Far East; Introduction to World History & Art; Canadian Architecture; Modern History & Art; European Art; Medieval Art
Summer School: July 5 - Aug 17

MANITOBA

WINNIPEG

UNIVERSITY OF MANITOBA
—**School of Art,** R3T 2N2. Tel 204-474-9303. *Dir* Robert C Sakowski, MFA; *Chmn Drawing* Sharon Alward; *Co-Chmn Painting* Steven Higgins, MFA; *Co-Chmn Paintings* Diane Whitehouse, MFA; *Chmn Sculpture* Gordon Reeve, MFA; *Chmn Photography* David McMillan, MFA; *Chmn Graphic Design* Robert Peters; *Chmn Printmaking* William Pura, MFA; *Chmn Art History* Marilyn Baker, PhD; *Chmn Foundations* Charlotte Werner; *Chmn Ceramics* Charles Scott, MFA
Estab 1950; pub; D; SC 35, LC 16; enrl D 420
Ent Req: HS dipl and portfolio
Degrees: BFA 3 yrs, BFA (Art History) 3 yrs, BFA Honors 4 yrs, BFA Honors (Art History) 4 yrs, Dipl in Art 4 yrs
Tuition: Varies per yr; campus res available
Courses: †Art History, †Ceramics, †Drawing, †Graphic Design, †Painting, †Photography, †Printmaking, †Sculpture
Adult Hobby Classes: Courses offered
Summer School: Dir, Robert C Sakowski. Term of 6 wks. Courses—Studio & Art History
—**Faculty of Architecture,** R3T 2N2. Tel 204-474-6433. *Dean* Michael Cox; *Assoc Dean* Mario Carvahio; *Head Environmental Studies* Ian Mcdonald; *Head Landscape Archit* Alexander Rattray; *Head Dept Interior Design* Grant Marshall; *Head Dept City Planning* Christine McKee; *Prof* Thomas Hodne
Estab 1913; pub; scholarships; enrl Environmental Studies 218, Archit 110, Interior Design 284, City Planning 72, Landscape 60
Ent Req: Senior matriculation or Bachelor for particular subject
Degrees: BA Interior Design 4 yrs, MA(Archit), (Landscape Archit), (City Planning) 3 yrs
Tuition: Res—undergran $2100 per yr; grad $4500 per 2 yrs
Courses: Architecture, Interior Design, Landscape Architecture, City Planning, Environmental Studies

NEW BRUNSWICK

EDMUNDSTON

SAINT-LOUIS-MAILLET, Dept of Visual Arts, 165 Blvd Hebert, E3V 2S8. Tel 506-737-5050. *Chief* Marie Elisa Ferrar
Estab 1946, dept estab 1968; pub; D & E; scholarships; SC 12, LC 1; enrl D 20, E 11, non-maj 25, maj 6
Ent Req: HS dipl
Degrees: BA(Fine Arts) 4 yrs
Tuition: $2050 per yr; campus res—room & board $1545 per yr
Courses: Art History, Drawing, Graphic Design, Painting, Sculpture

FREDERICTON

NEW BRUNSWICK COLLEGE OF CRAFT & DESIGN, PO Box 6000, E3B 5H1. Tel 506-453-2305; FAX 506-457-7352. *Dir of Craft School* George F Fry
Estab 1946; pub; D; enrl 70 plus PT
Ent Req: HS dipl, transcript, questionnaire and interview
Degrees: 3 yr dipl
Tuition: $700; no campus res
Courses: Advertising Design, Art History, Ceramics, Design, Drawing, Fashion Arts, Graphic Arts, Illustration, Jewelry, Photography, Silversmithing, Textile Design, Weaving, †Clothing Design & Construction, Colour, †Creative Graphics, †Native Arts Studies
Adult Hobby Classes: Courses—Weekend workshops

UNIVERSITY OF NEW BRUNSWICK, Art Education Section, Faculty of Education, PO Box 4400, E3B 5A3. Tel 506-453-3500; FAX 506-453-4599. *Head Art Educ* Don Soucy
Tuition: Res—$1975 per yr
Courses: Art History, Art Education for Elementary Teachers, Art Media for Schools, Children's Art for Teachers, Art Seminar
Children's Classes: Enrl 70; tuition $15 for 6 weeks, one afternoon per week

MONCTON

UNIVERSITE DE MONCTON, Department of Visual Arts, E1A 3E9. Tel 506-858-4033; FAX 506-858-4166. *Chmn* Francis Coutellier. Instrs: 7
Estab 1967; pub; D & E; SC 7, LC 3; enrl D 80, E 40, grad 10
Ent Req: HS dipl
Degrees: BA(Fine Arts) 4 yrs
Courses: Aesthetics, Art Education, †Ceramics, Drawing, Graphic Arts, †Graphic Design, †History of Art & Archaeology, †Painting, †Photography, †Printmaking, Sculpture, †Teacher Training
Adult Hobby Classes: Evening only

SACKVILLE

MOUNT ALLISON UNIVERSITY, Fine Arts Dept, E0A 3C0. Tel 506-364-2490; FAX 506-364-2575. *Head Dept* Rebecca Burke, MFA; *Prof* Virgil Hammock, MFA; *Prof* David Silverberg, BA; *Prof* Thaddeus Holownia, BFA; *Assoc Prof* John Asimakos; *Assoc Prof* Thomas Henderson, MFA; *Assoc Prof* M J A Crooker, MA; *Assoc Prof* David Bobier, MFA; *Lectr* Kelly Cemey, BFA
Estab 1858; pub; D & E; scholarships; SC 17, LC 5; enrl 85
Ent Req: HS dipl
Degrees: BFA 4 yrs
Tuition: $2625; campus residence available
Courses: †Art History, †Drawing, †Painting, †Photography, †Printmaking, †Sculpture
Adult Hobby Classes: Enrl 20; 12 wk term. Courses—Drawing, Painting
Summer School: Dir, Rebecca Burke, MFA. Enrl 20; 5 day term. Courses—Accomodation Drawing, Painting, Sculpture

NEWFOUNDLAND

CORNER BROOK

MEMORIAL UNIVERSITY OF NEWFOUNDLAND, School of Fine Arts, Visual Arts Dept, University Dr, A2H 6P9. Tel 709-637-6333; FAX 709-637-6383. *Head Dept Visual Arts* Kent Jones, HDFA
Estab 1975, dept estab 1988; pub; D; scholarships; enrl D 50
Tuition: Res—undergrad $1344 yr; non-res—undergrad $1344 yr; campus res—room & board $2740 yr
Courses: Aesthetics, Art Appreciation, Art History, Design, Drawing, Mixed Media, Painting, Photography, Printmaking, Sculpture

NOVA SCOTIA

ANTIGONISH

ST FRANCIS XAVIER UNIVERSITY, Fine Arts Dept, B2G 1C0. Tel 902-867-2172. *Assoc Prof* T Roach. Instrs: PT 4
Scholarships
Courses: Art History, Drawing, Painting, Composition & Painting, General Studios I & II
Adult Hobby Classes: Courses - Drawing, General Studio, Painting
Children's Classes: Courses - Drawing, Painting, Printmaking
Summer School: Dir, Angus Braid. Enrl 15; 5 wk sem beginning July-Aug.
Courses—General Studio

HALIFAX

NOVA SCOTIA COLLEGE OF ART AND DESIGN, 5163 Duke St, B3J 3J6. Tel 902-422-7381; FAX 902-425-2420. *Pres* Ian Christie Clark; *Dean & Chmn Craft Div* Scott MacDougall; *Chmn Art Educ Div* Nick Webb, PhD; *Chmn Art History* M McKay, PhD; *Chmn Design Div* Hanno Ehses; *Coordr MFA Prog* Jan Peacock
Estab 1887; pvt; D & E; SC 67, LC 31, GC 8 each sem; enrl 500, grad 17
Ent Req: HS dipl, portfolio or project
Degrees: BFA, BD(Environmental Planning or Graphic Design) and BA(Art Educ), MFA and MA(Art Educ)
Tuition: $1246 per sem; visa students $2096 per sem; no campus res
Courses: Art Education, Art History, Ceramics, Design, Drawing, Graphic Arts, Graphic Design, Jewelry, Mixed Media, Painting, Photography, Printmaking, Sculpture, Textile Design, Video, Computer Art
Adult Hobby Classes: Enrl 300; tuition $80 - $175. Courses—Art History, Craft, Computer Art, Drawing, Graphic Technology, Painting, Photography, Sculpture
Children's Classes: Enrl 125; tuition, materials fee. Courses—Art
Summer School: Dean, Scott MacDougall. Tuition $803 (1246 Visa students) for term of 14 wks beinning May 15. Half sessions offered

TECHNICAL UNIVERSITY OF NOVA SCOTIA, Faculty of Architecture, 5410 Spring Garden Rd, PO Box 1000, B3J 2X4. Tel 902-420-7692; FAX 902-423-6672. *Dean* E Baniassad, PhD; *Asst Dean* K Hurley; *Instr* S Parcell; *Instr* F Eppell; *Instr* A Frost; *Instr* T Emodi; *Instr* T Cavanagh; *Instr* A Jackson; *Instr* F Palermo; *Instr* M Macalik; *Instr* P McAleer; *Instr* A Penny; *Instr* D Procos; *Instr* M Poulton; *Instr* M Rubinger; *Instr* G Wanzel; *Instr* B MacKay-Lyons
Estab 1911, faculty estab 1961; pvt; D; scholarships; enrl approx 200, maj 200, grad 2
Ent Req: Previous 2 yrs at univ
Degrees: MArchit 4 yrs, Post-professional MArchit 1 yr minimum
Tuition: $2000 per year; differential for foreign students
Courses: Art Education, Art History, Constructions, Drafting, Photography
Summer School: Three terms per yr

WOLFVILLE

ACADIA UNIVERSITY, Art Dept, B0P 1X0. Tel 902-542-2201; FAX 902-542-4727. *Chmn & Prof* Wayne Staples
Scholarships
Tuition: $1970 per yr
Courses: Art History, Drawing, Painting
Summer School: Dir, Prof Kirk Marlow. Enrl 30; tuition $213 for 6 wk term. Courses—Art History, Drawing, Painting

ONTARIO

CORNWALL

ST LAWRENCE COLLEGE, Dept of Visual & Creative Arts, Windmill Point, K6H 4Z1. Tel 613-933-6080, Ext 2234; FAX 613-937-1523. *Chmn* Robert Blair, AOCA; *Instr* Wendy Grant; *Instr* Kathy Roth; *Instr* Linda Smyth; *Instr* Alex Taylor; *Instr* Karen Carriere; *Instr* Joanne Lanoriauct; *Instr* Lucia Deniarinis; *Instr* Regent Menard
Estab 1967, dept estab 1969; pub; D & E
Ent Req: Hs dipl & portfolio
Degrees: Diploma (Visual & Creative Arts, Graphic Design) 3 yrs, Certificate (Basic Photography, Certificate Graphic Design)
Tuition: Res—grad $836; campus res—room $1300
Courses: Art History, Commercial Art, Drawing, †Graphic Design, Illustration, Mixed Media, Painting, Photography, Printmaking, Marketing, Communications, Computer Graphics

DUNDAS

DUNDAS VALLEY SCHOOL OF ART, 21 Ogilvie St, L9H 2S1. Tel 416-628-6357. *Dir* J Trevor Hodgson; *Coordr* J Wilkinson; *Registrar* J Drury
Estab 1964; pvt; D & E; scholarships; SC 56, LC 2, GC 3; enrl D 500, E 2500, maj 20, grad 4
Ent Req: Part time no-req, full time interview with portfolio
Courses: Art Appreciation, Art History, Ceramics, Collages, Commercial Art, Conceptual Art, Constructions, Design, Drawing, Graphic Arts, Graphic Design, Mixed Media, Painting, Photography, Printmaking, Sculpture
Adult Hobby Classes: Enrl 2500; tuition $90 for 10 wk term. Courses— same as above
Children's Classes: Enrl 500; tuition $50 for 10 wk term. Courses—Drawing, Painting, Pottery
Summer School: Enrl 300; tuition 90 10 sessions

ETOBICOKE

HUMBER COLLEGE OF APPLIED ARTS AND TECHNOLOGY, Applied & Creative Arts Division, 205 Humber College Blvd, M9W 5L7. Tel 416-675-3111, Ext 4470. *Dean* Carl Eriksen
Estab 1967; pub; D & E; SC 300, LC 75, GC 6; enrl grad 50, PT 25
Ent Req: HS dipl, mature student status, one yr of employment plus 19 yrs of age
Degrees: None, 2 & 3 yr dipl courses
Tuition: Canadian res—$839 per yr
Courses: Art History, Drafting, Drawing, Film, Graphic Arts, †Graphic Design, †Industrial Design, †Interior Design, Photography, Furniture Design, †Landscape Technology, †Packaging Design, TV Production
Adult Hobby Classes: Enrl 4042; tuition & duration vary. Beginning classes in most regular courses
Children's Classes: Nature studies

GUELPH

UNIVERSITY OF GUELPH, Fine Art Dept, Zavitz Hall, N1G 2W1. Tel 519-824-4120, Ext 6106. *Chmn* Ronald L Shuebrook
Estab 1966; pub; D; scholarships; SC 30, LC 30; enrl 959, maj 300
Ent Req: HS dipl
Degrees: BA 3 yrs, BA(Hons) 4 yrs
Tuition: Res—undergrad $759 per sem; nonres—undergrad $2605 per sem; campus res available
Courses: Aesthetics, †Art History, Collages, †Conceptual Art, †Drawing, History of Art & Archaeology, †Intermedia, †Painting, †Photography, †Printmaking, †Sculpture, Video, Alternative Media
Summer School: Chair, Ron Shuebrook. Enrl 20; tuition res—$179 for 13 wk sem, non-res—$2605. Courses—Studio, Art History

HAMILTON

MCMASTER UNIVERSITY, Dept of Art and Art History, 1280 Main St W, L8S 4M2. Tel 416-525-9140, Ext 3082. *Chmn* Dr Hugh Galloway. Instrs: FT 9
Estab 1934; SC 12, LC 29; enrl 85
Degrees: BA(Art History), Hons BA(Studio & Art History) 3-4 yrs
Tuition: $1322.50 per yr; campus res available
Courses: †Art History, †Studio Art Program

KINGSTON

QUEEN'S UNIVERSITY, Dept of Art, K7L 3N6. Tel 613-545-6166. *Academic Dean* Dr William McCready. Instrs: FT 13, PT 1
Estab 1932; pub; D & E; SC 16, LC 25
Ent Req: Grade XIII
Degrees: BA 3 yrs, BA(Hons) and BFA 4 yrs, MA(Conservation), MA(Art History)
Tuition: $398 per course, campus res available
Courses: Art History, Drawing, Painting, Printmaking, Sculpture
Adult Hobby Classes: Evening classes available
Summer School: Courses offered

LONDON

UNIVERSITY OF WESTERN ONTARIO, Dept of Visual Arts, N6A 5B7. Tel 519-661-3440; FAX 519-661-2020. *Chmn* A Mansell. Instrs: FT 11, PT 10
Estab 1967; pub; D & E; SC 23, LC 31; enrl maj 235
Ent Req: HS dipl, portfolio and/or interview
Degrees: BA 3 yrs, BA(Hons) and BFA 4 yrs
Tuition: $1200
Courses: Drawing, †History of Art & Archaeology, Museum Staff Training, †Painting, †Photography, †Printmaking, †Sculpture
Summer School: Enrl limited; term of 6 wks beginning July. Courses—Visual Arts

NORTH YORK

KOFFLER GALLERY SCHOOL OF VISUAL ART, 4588 Bathurst St, M2R 1W6. Tel 416-636-2145; FAX 416-636-1536. *Dir* Rose Brinder
Pub; D & E; enrl D 400, E 98
Ent Req: SC 35
Courses: Ceramics, Design, Drawing, Mixed Media, Painting, Sculpture, Cartooning, Clay, Stone Sculpture
Adult Hobby Classes: Enrl 350-400; tuition $3.50 per hr. Courses—Cartooning, Ceramics, Design, Drawing, Painting, Sculpture
Children's Classes: Enrl 90; tuition $4.75 per hr. Courses—Ceramics, Mixed Media Art
Summer School: Dir, Rose Brinder. Enrl 100; tuition $70 for 5 wk term & $100 for session term. Courses—Ceramics, Drawing, Painting

YORK UNIVERSITY, Dept of Visual Arts, Center for Fine Arts, 4700 Keele St, M3J 1P3. Tel 416-736-5187; FAX 416-736-5447. *Chmn* Hugh Leroy. Instrs: FT 26, PT 13
Estab 1969; pub; D & E; scholarships; SC 53, LC 17; enrl D over 400, maj 400, others 120
Ent Req: HS dipl, interview and portfolio evaluation
Degrees: BA(Hons), BFA(Hons) 4 yrs, MA in Art History, MFA in Visual Arts
Tuition: Res—$1480; nonres—$4877
Courses: Design, Drawing, Graphic Arts, Painting, Photography, Sculpture, Interdisciplinary Studio
Children's Classes: Enrl 30; tuition $5 from Oct - Dec; Studio Course
Summer School: Chmn, Andrew M Tomzik. Enrl 100; 6 wk course. Courses—vary

OAKVILLE

SHERIDAN COLLEGE, Faculty of Visual Arts, 1430 Trafalgar Rd, L6H 2L1. Tel 416-845-9430, Ext 2610; FAX 416-815-4041. *Dean* S Scott Turner
Estab 1967; pub; D & E; enrl D 1250
Ent Req: HS dipl, ent exam
Degrees: Dip 3 yr
Tuition: Non-res—undergrad $780 pr yr
Courses: Art History, Ceramics, Graphic Design, Illustration, Interior Design, Painting, Photography, Printmaking, Sculpture, Textile Design, Film-Animation, Glass
Summer School: All undergraduate disciplines

OTTAWA

CARLETON UNIVERSITY, Dept of Art History, Colonel By Dr, K1S 5B6. Tel 613-788-2342. *Chmn* Angela Carr. Instrs: FT 8, PT 2
Estab 1964; D & E; scholarships; SC 2, LC 25, GC 3; enrl D over 700, maj 135
Ent Req: HS dipl
Degrees: BA 6 Hons 3-4 yrs
Tuition: $4584
Courses: Art History
Summer School: Chmn, Roger Mesley. Courses— Art History

SOUTHAMPTON

SOUTHAMPTON ART SCHOOL, 20 Albert St S, N0H 2L0. Tel 519-797-5068. *Dir* Open ; *Instr* Gabor P Mezei; *Instr* Guttorn Otto; *Instr* Roly Fenivick
Estab 1958 as a summer school; pub; D, July and Aug
Tuition: Adults $125 per wk; students (14-18) $85 per wk; children (10-13) $35 per wk, half days only; no campus res
Courses: Art Education, Drawing, Mixed Media, Painting
Children's Classes: Tuition $30 per wk, summer only
Summer School: Tuition $75-$100 per wk. Courses—Acrylic, Drawing, Oil, Watercolor

THUNDER BAY

LAKEHEAD UNIVERSITY, Dept of Visual Arts, 955 Oliver Rd, P7B 5E1. Tel 807-343-8787; FAX 807-345-2394; Telex 073-4594. *Dean Faculty of Arts & Sciences* Dr J Gellert, PhD; *Chmn* Patricia Vervoort, MA; *Prof* Oliver Tiura, MFA; *Prof* Mark Nisenholt, MFA; *Prof* Ann Clarke, MFA. Instrs: FT 4, PT 5
Div Estab 1976, dept estab 1988; pub; D & E; scholarships
Ent Req: HS dipl, portfolio
Degrees: HBFA, Dipl in Arts Administration
Tuition: Res—undergrad $1893 per yr, $390 per course, $195 per 1/2 cr; campus res—rooms & board $3109 - $4283
Courses: Art History, †Ceramics, Drawing, †Painting, †Printmaking, †Sculpture
Adult Hobby Classes: Studio and art history courses
Summer School: Dir, Dan Pakulak. Tuition $390 per course for 6 wks

TORONTO

GEORGE BROWN COLLEGE OF APPLIED ARTS AND TECHNOLOGY, Dept of Visual Arts, PO Box 1015, Station B, M5T 2T9. Tel 416-867-2000, 867-2011; FAX 416-867-2600. *Chmn* Earl Walker. Instrs: FT 30, PT 60
Estab 1970; D & E; enrl D 900, E 2000
Ent Req: HS grade 12 dipl, entr exam
Degrees: 3 yr dipl
Courses: †Advertising Design, Calligraphy, †Commercial Art, Graphic Arts, Graphic Design, Illustration, †Lettering, Painting, Photography, Video, Air Brush Techniques, Cartooning, Computer Graphics, Marker Rendering Techniques, Watercolor

ONTARIO COLLEGE OF ART, 100 McCaul St, M5T 1W1. Tel 416-977-5311; FAX 416-977-0235. *Pres* Timothy Porteous; *Registrar* Tom Kowall; *Acad Dean* Michael Harmes; *Business Adminr* John Stewart, MPA; *Financial Aid Officer* Josephine Polera; *Chair Foundation Studies* Jack Dixon, AOCA; *Chair Commun & Design* Jan Van Kampen, AOCA; *Chair Industrial Design* Vello Hubel, AOCA; *Co-Chair Drawing & Painting* Greg Murphy, MA; *Co-Chair Drawing & Painting* Dan Solmon, BSC; *Acting Chair New Media* Johanna Householder, BFA; *Acting Chair Lib Arts Studies* Paul Baker, PhD; *Acting Chair Technol Studies* John Coull; *Dir Student Services* Nora McCardell PhD; *Co-Chair Env Design* Lenore Richards, MD; *Chair Env Design* Jerry Bowes, MArch; *Chair Applied Art & Design* Angelo diPetta, AOCA; *Coordr General Studies* Sheila Lamb,AOCA
Estab 1876; pub; D & E; scholarships; SC approx 450; enrl D 1300, E 2000, grad 25, summer 900
Ent Req: HS dipl, English requirement, interview
Degrees: Diploma AOCA 4 yrs
Tuition: $2041 per yr; yearly fees for applicants outside Canada $7288; no campus res
Courses: †Advertising Design, Art History, †Ceramics, Collages, †Commercial Art, Conceptual Art, Display, †Drawing, Film, †Graphic Arts, †Graphic Design, History of Art & Archaeology, †Illustration, †Industrial Design, †Jewelry, Mixed Media, †Painting, †Photography, †Printmaking, Silversmithing, Stage Design, Video, †Weaving, Animation, Batik, Color, Composition, †Corporate Design, Design Management, †Editorial Design, †Environmental Design, †Experimental Arts, †Fibre, Foundry, †Glass, Holography, Light, Materials & Processes, Metal Work, Moldmaking, †New Media, AOCA, *Coordr* Env Design & Print
Adult Hobby Classes: Enro 2000; tuition $272 per course for 3 hrs per wk for 30 wks. Courses—Advertising Design, Art History, Ceramics, Color, Corporate Design, Drawing, Editorial Design, Environmental Design, Fibre/Weaving, Glasss, Graphics, History of Ceramics & Glass History of Furniture, Illustration, Industrial Design, Painting, Photography, Printmaking, Sculpture, Surface Design/Print, Typography, Watercolor, Woodworking

Summer School: Registrar, Tom Kowall. Enrl 900; tuition $272 per course for term of 3 wks (5 days a wk) or 15 wks (2 evenings a wk) beginning May.
Courses—Advertising Design, Art History, Ceramics, Color, Corporate Design, Drawing, Editorial Design, Environmental, Fibre/Weaving, Glass, Graphics, History of Ceramics & Glass, History of Furniture, Illustration, Industrial Design, Painting, Photography, Printmaking, Sculpture, Surface Design/Print, Typography, Watercolor, Woodworking

TORONTO ART THERAPY INSTITUTE, 216 St Clair Ave W, M4V 1R2. Tel 416-924-6221. *Executive Dir* Martin Fischer, MD & DPsych; *Senior Art Therapist* Gilda S Grossman, DTATI; *Chmn Educ Committee* Morton Manilla, PhD; *Lectr* Ruth Epstein, DTATI & EdD; *Lectr* Mercedes Chacin de Fuchs, DChS & DTATI; *Instr* Temmi Ungerman, MA & ATR; *Thesis Dir* Ken Morrison, PhD
Estab 1968; D & E
Degrees: Dipl, BA and MA(Art Therapy) through affiliation with other US colleges; graduate level certificate program in art therapy
Tuition: $6000
Adult Hobby Classes: Enrl 6-12; fee $40 per session. Courses—workshops
Children's Classes: Enrl 6-12; fee $20 per session. Courses—workshops

TORONTO SCHOOL OF ART, 110 Spadina Ave, Suite 700, M5V 2K4. Tel 416-588-3193. *Chmn* Arline Hebert; *Instr* Susan Beniston; *Instr* Brian Burnett; *Instr* Tom Campbell; *Instr* Moira Clark; *Instr* Denis Cliff; *Instr* Michael Earle; *Instr* Andy Fabo; *Instr* Frances Gage; *Instr* Simon Glass; *Instr* Jean Maddison; *Instr* Carl Skelton; *Instr* Mark Thurman; *Instr* Megan Williams
Estab 1969; pvt; D & E; scholarships; enrl 959, maj 300
Ent Req: Portfolio
Tuition: $1675 full-time, $3200 foreign students, $2400 foreign students returning; no campus res
Courses: Drawing, Graphic Arts, Illustration, Mixed Media, Painting, Photography, Printmaking, Sculpture
Adult Hobby Classes: Enrl 246. Courses—Colour & Design, Drawing, History, Illustration, Painting, Photography, Printing, Sculpture

UNIVERSITY OF TORONTO
—Dept of Fine Art, Sidney Smith Hall, 6th floor, M5S 1A1. Tel 416-978-6272; FAX 416-978-1491. *Chmn* J W Shaw. Instrs: FT 14, PT 4
Estab 1934; pub; LC, GC
Degrees: BA 4 yrs, MA 2 yrs, PhD 5 yrs
Tuition: Nonres—undergrad $12,024; campus res available
Courses: Art Appreciation, Art History, Drawing, Painting, Printmaking, Sculpture, Art Studio
—School of Architecture & Landscape Architecture, 230 College St, M5S 1A1. Tel 416-978-5038. *Dean* Anthony Eardley
Estab 1948; pub; D; scholarships; SC 5, LC 33, GC 11; enrl 299, non-maj 6, maj 293, grad 13
Ent Req: HS dipl, portfolio of work and interview
Degrees: BArch, BLA 5 yrs
Tuition: Campus res available
Courses: Architecture, Drawing, Photography
—Programme in Landscape Architecture, 230 College St, M5S 1A1. Tel 416-978-6788; FAX 416-971-2094. *Chmn* Edward Fife, MLA; *Assoc Prof* Gerald Englar, MLA; *Assoc Prof* John Consolati, BSLA; *Assoc Prof* Rob Wright, BSRec, MLA; *Asst Prof* John Danahy, BLA; *Adjunct Prof* Robert Allsopp, DipArch
Estab 1827, dept estab 1965; pub; D; scholarships; enrl maj 100
Ent Req: Grad 13 dipl
Degrees: BLA 5 yr
Tuition: Nonres—undergrad $12,024; campus res available
Courses: Aesthetics, Architecture, Art History, Constructions, Drafting, Drawing, Film, Graphic Arts, Landscape Architecture, Landscape Architecture Technology, Landscape Planning, Planting Design
Summer School: Contact, Prof Gerald Englar. Enrl 20; tuition $1200 for 4 wks non-degree. Courses—Career initiation program for Architecture & Landscape Architecture

WATERLOO

UNIVERSITY OF WATERLOO, Fine Arts Dept, 200 University Ave W, N2L 3G1. Tel 519-885-1211, Ext 2442; FAX 519-888-4521. *Dean* B Hendley; *Chmn Dept* Don MacKay, MFA; *Prof* Virgil Burnett, MA; *Prof* Ann Roberts, MFA; *Prof* A M Urquhart, BFA; *Assoc Prof* Jan Uhde, PhD; *Assoc Prof* Art Green, BFA; *Assoc Prof* Eve Kliman, PhD; *Asst Prof* Jane Buyers, BA; *Asst Prof* Bruce Taylor, MFA
Estab 1958, dept estab 1968; pub; D & E; scholarships; SC 32, LC 27; enrl maj 100
Ent Req: HS dipl
Degrees: BA 3 yrs, BA(Hons) 4 yrs
Tuition: $2136 per yr; campus res available
Courses: †Art History, †Drawing, Illustration, †Painting, Photography, †Printmaking, †Sculpture, Ceramic Sculpture, †Film Theory & History, Computer Imaging, Applied Graphics
Summer School: Enrl 30. Courses—Drawing

WINDSOR

UNIVERSITY OF WINDSOR, School of Visual Arts, Huron Church Rd at College, N9B 3P4. Tel 519-253-4232, Ext 2828; FAX 519-973-7050. *Dir* John K Pufahl. Instrs: FT 12, PT 5
Estab 1960; pub; D & E; scholarships & assistantships; SC 33, LC 21; enrl D 265, E approx 75, maj 340
Ent Req: Ontario Secondary School Graduation Dipl (OSSD) plus 6 Ontario Academic Courses (OAC) or equivalent
Degrees: BA 3 yrs, BA(Hons) and BFA 4 yrs, MFA 2 yrs
Tuition: Undergrad $1113.70 per sem, grad $917.30 per sem
Courses: †Art History, †Drawing, †Painting, Photography, †Printmaking, †Sculpture, Multi Media

PRINCE EDWARD ISLAND

CHARLOTTETOWN

HOLLAND COLLEGE, Centre of Creative Arts, 50 Burns Ave, W Royalty, C1E 1H7. Tel 902-566-9310. *Dir* Henry Purdy
Estab 1977; scholarships; enrl D 100
Tuition: $1315 per yr
Courses: Photography, †Commercial Design, Woodworking
Adult Hobby Classes: Enrl 100; tuition $1315 per yr. Courses—Commercial Design, Photography, Wood
Children's Classes: Enrl 15; tuition $70 for 8 wks. Courses—Art Activities

QUEBEC

MONTREAL

CONCORDIA UNIVERSITY, Faculty of Fine Arts, 1395 Rene Levesque Blvd, H3G 2M5. Tel 514-848-4600; FAX 514-848-8627. *Dean Faculty Fine Arts* Robert J Parker, PhD
D & E; scholarships
Ent Req: HS dipl, CEGEP dipl Prov of Quebec
Degrees: BFA, post-BFA Dipl in Art Educ & Art Therapy, full-time leading to teaching cert, MA(Art Educ), MA(Art History), MA(Art Therapy), PhD(Art Educ)
Courses: †Art Education, †Art History, †Ceramics, †Drawing, †Painting, †Photography, †Printmaking, †Sculpture, †Theatre Arts, †Art Therapy, †Contemporary Dance, †Design Art, †Fibers, †Film Studies †Music Studies, †Theatre Design, Women & the Fine Arts
Adult Hobby Classes: Courses offered
Children's Classes: Enrl 75; tuition $95 for 8 wk term
Summer School: Courses offered

MCGILL UNIVERSITY
—Department of Art History, 853 Sherbrooke St W, H3A 2T6. Tel 514-398-6541; FAX 514-398-7247. *Chmn* Hans Boker, PhD; *Prof* G Galavaris, PhD; *Assoc Prof* R Bertos, PhD; *Assoc Prof* T Glenn, Phd; *Asst Prof* D Stiebeling, Phd; *Faculty Lectr* R Meyer; *Asst Prof* C Solomon-Kiefer, PhD
Pvt; D; teaching assistantships; SC 2, LC 7, GC 12
Ent Req: HS dipl or CEGEP Dipl
Degrees: BA 3 yrs, MA 2 yrs, PhD 2 yrs
Tuition: Res—$1500 per yr, nonres—$7000 per yr
Courses: †History of Art & Archaeology, Ancient Greek Art, Baroque Art, Medieval Art, Modern Art, Renaissance Art
—School of Architecture, 815 Sherbrooke St W, H3A 2K6. Tel 514-398-6704; FAX 514-398-7372. *Prof* Derek Drummond. Instrs: FT 12, PT 21, FTE 9
Estab 1896; fels; SC 8, LC 32
Ent Req: Ent exam
Degrees: BArchit 4 yrs
Tuition: res—$1500 per yr, nonres—$7000 per yr
Courses: Art History, Drawing, Architectural Design, History of Architecture

UNIVERSITE DE MONTREAL, Dept of Art History, PO Box 6128, Succursale A, H3C 3J7. Tel 514-343-6182; FAX 514-343-2483. *Dir Dept Art History* Luis de Moura Sobral; *Instr* Yves Deschamps; *Instr* Nicole Dubreuil-Blondin; *Instr* Francois Marc Gagnon; *Instr* Pierre Granche; *Instr* Chantal Hardy; *Instr* Alain Laframboise; *Instr* Lise Lamarche; *Instr* Johanne Lamoureux; *Instr* Michel Larouche; *Instr* Gilles Marsolais; *Instr* Constance Naubert-Riser; *Instr* Serge Tousignant; *Instr* Jean Trudel; *Instr* Dominique Auzel; *Instr* David W Booth; *Instr* Andre Gaudreault; *Instr* Jean-Francois Lhote
Dept estab 1961; pvt; D & E; SC 20, LC 70, GC 10; enrl D 270, non-maj 113, maj 106, grad 80, others 151
Ent Req: HS dipl
Degrees: BA & MA
Tuition: Campus res available

UNIVERSITE DU QUEBEC A MONTREAL, Famille des Arts, CP 8888, succursale A, H3C 3P8. Tel 514-987-4545. *Dept Head* Rosemarie Arbour
Estab 1969
Ent Req: 2 yrs after HS
Degrees: Baccalaureat specialise 3 yrs; Master Degrees in Visual Arts; programs in Environmental Design, Graphic Design, History of Art, Visual Arts (engraving, sculpture, painting); MA(Musicology)

Courses: Drawing, Museum Staff Training, Painting, Teacher Training, Architectural Drafting, Ceramic Sculpture, Design, Etching and Engraving, Graphic Techniques, Modeling, Mural Painting, Scenography
Adult Hobby Classes: Certificate in visual arts available
Children's Classes: Saturday courses

QUEBEC

UNIVERSITE LAVAL CITE UNIVERSITAIRE, School of Visual Arts, Pavillon Louis-Jacques-Casault, G1K 7P4. Tel 418-656-7631; FAX 418-656-7807. *Dir Visual Arts* David Naylor; *Faculty Dean of Arts* Francois Demers
Estab 1970; pub; D; enrl 550
Ent Req: 2 yrs col
Degrees: BA(Arts Plastiques, Communication Graphique, Enseignement des Arts Plastiques); cert(arts plastiques)
Tuition: Res—undergrad $675 per yr, $337 per quarter
Courses: Drawing, Film, Graphic Arts, Graphic Design, Illustration, Painting, Photography, Sculpture, Engraving, Lithography, Silk Screen

TROIS RIVIERES

UNIVERSITY OF QUEBEC, TROIS RIVIERES, Fine Arts Section, 3351 boul des Forges, PO Box 500, G9A 5H7. Tel 817-376-5136. *Section Head* Graham Cantieni
Estab 1969; pub; D & E; SC 12, LC 8, GC 28; enrl D 150, E 100
Ent Req: Ent exam or DEC
Degrees: BA(Fine Arts) & BA(Art Education)
Tuition: $50 per course
Courses: Art Education, Art History, †Drawing, †Painting, †Printmaking, †Sculpture, †Glass, †Paper
Adult Hobby Classes: Enrl 100. Courses—Art History, Painting, Printmaking

SASKATCHEWAN

REGINA

UNIVERSITY OF REGINA
—Dept of Visual Arts, S4S 0A2. Tel 306-779-4872; FAX 779-4825. *Head* Roger Lee. Instrs: FT 9
Pub; enrl 450
Ent Req: HS grad
Degrees: 2 yr cert, BA 3 yrs, BA 4 yrs, BFA 4 yrs, MFA 2 yrs
Tuition: $284 per class
Courses: Art History, Ceramics, Drawing, Painting, Printmaking, Sculpture
Summer School: Introductory courses offered
—Dept of Art Education, Faculty of Education, S4S 0A2. Tel 306-585-4519. *Dean of Art* Dr Michael Tymchak; *Dean Faculty Fine Arts* Dr Mary Blackstone. Instrs: FT 9
Estab 1965; pub; D & E; scholarships; LC 6; enrl D 160, E 20, maj 10
Ent Req: HS dipl, matriculation or degree for maj in art
Degrees: BEd(Art Education) 5 yrs, BA(Art Education) 5 - 6 yrs
Tuition: $67 per cr hr
Courses: Aesthetics, Art Education
Children's Classes: Sat
Summer School: Exten Courses, H Kindred; Dean Educ, Dr Toombs. Term of 3 to 6 wks beginning May

SASKATOON

UNIVERSITY OF SASKATCHEWAN, Dept of Art & Art History, S7N 0W0. Tel 306-966-4222. *Head* Hans S Dommasch. Instrs: FT 13, PT 4
Estab 1936; pub; D; scholarships; SC, LC, GC; enrl approx 880, BFA prog 130, grad 9
Ent Req: HS grad
Degrees: BA 3 yrs, BAHons(Art History), BA(Advanced) 4 yrs, BFA 4 yrs, MFA(Studio Art), BEd(Art)
Tuition: $366 per class; 4 classes per acad yr
Courses: †Art History, †Drawing, †Painting, †Photography, †Printmaking, †Sculpture, Structurist Art
Summer School: Dir, A Wong. Enrl 200; tuition $366 per 6 wk term. Courses—Art History, Art Educ, Drawing, Painting, Photography, Printmaking, Sculpture

III ART INFORMATION

Major Museums Abroad

Major Art Schools Abroad

State Arts Councils

State Directors and Supervisors of Art Education

Art Magazines

Newspaper Art Editors and Critics

Scholarships and Fellowships

Open Exhibitions

Traveling Exhibition Booking Agencies

Major Museums Abroad

AFGHANISTAN

KABUL

M **KABUL MUSEUM,** Darul Aman. Tel 42656. *Dir* Ahamad Ali Motamedi
Collections: Kushan art; archaeology of prehistoric, Greco-Roman, Islamic periods; ethnological collections

ALGERIA

ALGIERS

M **MUSEE NATIONAL DES ANTIQUITES,** Parc de la Liberte. Tel 74-66-86. *Dir* Drias Lakhdar; *Cur* Mohammed Temmam
Collections: Algerian antiquities & Islamic art

M **MUSEE NATIONAL DES BEAUX ARTS D'ALGER,** National Museum of Algiers, El Hamma. Tel 66-49-16. *Dir* Malika Bosabdellah
Collections: Contemporary Algerian art; paintings; drawings; bronze reliefs

ARGENTINA

BUENOS AIRES

M **CENTRO DE ARTE Y COMMUNICACION (CAYC),** Center of Art and Communication, Elpidio Gonzalez 4070, 1407. Tel 01-566-8046. *Dir* Jorge Glusberg
Collections: Catalogs and bulletins on every art exhibition and seminar held by the Center in Argentina and abroad; motion pictures on art, architecture; photograph collection of Latin American art works; collections of slides; video-tapes

M **MUSEO DE ARTE MODERNO,** Museum of Modern Art, Teatro General San Martin, Corrientes 1530 y San Juan 350, 1042. Tel 46-9426. *Dir* Ines Perez Suarez
Collections: Latin American paintings, especially Argentine, and contemporary schools

M **MUSEO DE BELLAS ARTES DE LA BOCA,** Fine Arts Museum, Pedro de Mendoza 1835, 1169. Tel 21-1080. *Dir* Dr Guillermo C De La Canal
Collections: Painting, sculpture, engravings, and maritime museum

M **MUSEO MUNICIPAL DE ARTE ESPANOL ENRIQUE LARRETA,** Municipal Museum of Spanish Art, Juramento 2291 y Obligado 2139, 1428. Tel 784-4040. *Dir* Mercedes di Paala de Picot
Collections: 13th - 16th century wood carvings, gilt objects and painted panels, paintings of Spanish School of 16th and 17th centuries, tapestries, furniture

M **MUSEO MUNICIPAL DE ARTES PLASTICAS EDUARDO SIVORI,** Corrientes 1530-7, 1042. Tel 469-680. *Dir* Hugo E Monzon
Collections: 19th & 20th century Argentine painting & sculpture

M **MUSEO NACIONAL DE ARTE DECORATIVO,** National Museum of Decorative Art, Avda del Libertador 1902, 1425. Tel 802-6606. *Dir* Alberto Guillermo Bellucci
Collections: European and South American works; furniture, sculptures and tapestries

M **MUSEO NACIONAL DE BELLAS ARTES,** National Museum of Fine Arts, Avda del Libertador 1473, 1425. Tel 803-8817. *Dir* Dr Jorge A Lorenzutti
Collections: Argentine, American and European art, both modern and classical

CORDOBA

M **MUSEO PROVINCIAL DE BELLAS ARTES EMILIO A CARAFFA,** Provincial Museum of Fine Arts, Avenida Hipolito Irigoyen 651, 5000. Tel 66426. *Dir Lic* Graciela Elizabeth Palela
Collections: Provincial art center, including art library and archives; Argentine and foreign paintings, sculptures, drawings and engravings

ROSARIO

M **MUSEO MUNICIPAL DE ARTE DECORATIVO FIRMA Y ODILO ESTEVEZ,** Municipal Decorative Arts Museum, Santa Fe 748, 2000. Tel 041-62544. *Cur* P A Sinopoli
Collections: Antique glass; paintings by Goya, El Greco; 16th - 18th century furniture & silver ceramics; antique glass; ivories; silver; 19th century English tapestry; 20th century crystal

M **MUSEO MUNICIPAL DE BELLAS ARTES JUAN B CASTAGNINO,** Municipal Museum of Fine Arts, Parque Independencia, 2000. Tel 041-21-73-10. *Dir* Ruben Echague
Library with 3000 vols
Collections: Works by Jose de Ribera, Goya, El Greco, Valdes Leal and Titian; complete collection of Argentine art from 19th century to present

SANTA FE

M **MUSEO PROVINCIAL DE BELLAS ARTES ROSA GALISTEO DE RODRIGUEZ,** Provincial Museum of Fine Arts, 4 de Enero 1510, 3000. Tel (042) 22142. *Dir SRA* Nydia Pereyra Salva de Impini
Library with 4000 vols
Collections: Contemporary Argentine and modern art

TANDIL

M **MUSEO MUNICIPAL DE BELLAS ARTES DE TANDIL,** Municipal Museum of Fine Arts, Chacabuco 357, 7000. Tel 2000. *Dir* E Valor
Collections: Paintings of classical, impressionist, cubist and modern schools

AUSTRALIA

ADELAIDE

M **ART GALLERY OF SOUTH AUSTRALIA,** North Terrace, 5000. Tel (08) 223-7200. *Dir* Ron Radford
Collections: Representative selection of Australian, British and European paintings, prints, drawings and sculpture; large collection of ceramics, glass and silver; extensive South Australian Historical Collection; SE Asian ceramics; furniture

CANBERRA

M **AUSTRALIAN NATIONAL GALLERY,** PO Box 1150, ACT 2601. Telex 6-1500; Tel 062-71-21-11. *Dir* James Mollison
Collections: Extensive Australian collection includes fine and decorative arts, folk art, commercial art, architecture and design; International collection contains arts from Asia, Southeast Asia, Oceania, Africa, Pre-Columbian America and Europe
L **Library,** PO Box 1150, ACT 2601. Tel 62-1111.
Library Holdings: Monographs 70,000, Serials 3000, other materials 200,000; Micro — Fiche 35,000; Other — Exhibition catalogs 12,000

HOBART

M **TASMANIAN MUSEUM AND ART GALLERY,** 40 Macquarie St, GPO Box 1164M, Tasmania 7001. Tel 002-23-14-22. *Dir* D R Gregg
Collections: Australian and Tasmanian art;

LAUNCESTON

M **QUEEN VICTORIA MUSEUM AND ART GALLERY,** Wellington St, Tasmania 7250. Tel 003-31-6777. *Dir* C B Tassell
Collections: Pure and applied art; Tasmanian history: Tasmanian and general anthropology; Tasmanian botany, geology, paleontology and zoology

MELBOURNE

M **NATIONAL GALLERY OF VICTORIA,** 180 St Kilda Rd, Victoria 3004. Tel 618-0222. *Dir* James Mallison
Library with 20,000 vols
Collections: Asian art; Australian art; pre-Columbian art; modern European art; antiquities, costumes, textiles, old master and modern drawings, paintings, photography, prints and sculpture

PERTH

M **ART GALLERY OF WESTERN AUSTRALIA,** 47 James St, Perth Cultural Centre, WA 6000. Telex 9-4988; Tel (09) 328-7233. *Dir* Paula Latos-Valier
Collections: Australian aboriginal artifacts; British, European and Australian paintings, prints, drawings, sculptures and crafts

SOUTH BRISBANE

M **QUEENSLAND ART GALLERY,** POB 686, Queensland 4101. Tel (07) 840-7333. *Dir* Douglas Hall
Collections: Predominantly Australian art, ceramics, decorative arts, paintings and drawings; British and European paintings and sculpture

SYDNEY

M **ART GALLERY OF NEW SOUTH WALES,** Domain, New South Wales 2000. Tel (02) 221-2100 *Dir* Edmund Capon
Collections: Australian Aboriginal and Melanesian art; Australian art; collections of British and European painting and sculpture; Asian art, including Japanese ceramics and painting and Chinese ceramics

M **NICHOLSON MUSEUM OF ANTIQUITIES,** University of Sydney, New South Wales 2006. Tel 02-692-2812. *Cur* Prof A Cambitoglou
Collections: Antiquities of Egypt, Near East, Europe, Greece, Rome

M **POWERHOUSE MUSEUM OF APPLIED ARTS & SCIENCES** (Formerly Museum of Applied Arts & Sciences), 500 Harris St, Ultimo, New South Wales 2007. Tel 217-0111. *Dir* Terence Measham; *Dir* L G Sharp
Library with 20,000 vols
Collections: Scientific Instruments; Numismatics; Philately; Astronomy

AUSTRIA

INNSBRUCK

M **TIROLER LANDESMUSEUM FERDINANDEUM,** Tyrolese Provincial Museum, Museumst 15, 6020. Tel (0512) 59489. *Dir* Gert Ammann
Collections: Historical artifacts, sculptures, baroque & 19th century art

LINZ

M **NEUE GALERIE DER STADT LINZ-WOLFGANG GURLITT MUSEUM,** Lentia 2000, Blutenstrasse 15, 4040. Tel 0732-2393/3600. *Dir* Peter Baum
Collections: 19th and 20th century paintings, drawings, sculptures and prints

SALZBURG

M **RESIDENZGALERIE SALZBURG** (Formerly Salzburger Landessammlungen-Residenzgalerie), Residenzplatz 1, A-5010. Tel (0662) 8042/2070. *Dir* Dr Roswitha Juffinger
Collections: European paintings, 16th - 20th centuries

M **SALZBURGER MUSEUM CAROLINO-AUGUSTEUM,** Salzburg Museum, Museumsplatz 6, Postfach 525, A-5020. Tel 841134. *Dir* A Rohrmoser
Library with 100,000 vols
Collections: Art, coins, musical instruments, costumes, peasant art; Prehistoric and Roman archaeology

VIENNA

M **GEMALDEGALERIE DER AKADEMIE DER BILDENDEN KUNSTE,** Art Gallery of the Academy of Fine Arts, Schillerplatz 3, 1010. Tel (0222) 58816/225. *Dir* Dr Heribert R Hutter
Collections: Prince Liechtenstein; Paintings of the 14th - 20th centuries - Hieronymus Bosch, Hans Baldung Grien; 17th century Dutch (Rembrandt, Ruisdael, van Goyen, Jan Both and others); Flemish, (Rubens, Jordaens, van Dyck), Guardi, Magnasco, Tiepolo, W von Wurzbach

M **GRAPHISCHE SAMMLUNG ALBERTINA,** Albertina Graphic Art Collection, Augustinerstrasse 1, 1010. Tel 0222-534-830. *Dir* Konrud Oberhuber Estab 1796. Average Annual Attendance: 40,000
Collections: Drawings (44,000); sketchbooks, miniatures and posters. This is one of the largest (over one million) and best print collections in Europe

M **KUNSTHISTORISCHES MUSEUM,** Museum of Fine Arts, Burgring 5 & Neue Burg, 1010. Tel (0222) 93-06-20. *Chief Dir* Dr Wilfried Seipel
Collections: Egyptian Collection; antiquities, ceramics, historical carriages and costumes, jewelry, old musical instruments, paintings, tapestries, weapons; collection of secular and ecclesiastical treasures of Holy Roman Empire and Hapsburg dynasty

MUSEUM MODERNER KUNST
M **Palais Liechtenstein,** Furstengasse 1, 1090. Tel 34-12-59. *Dir* Dieter Ronte
Collections: Modern classics & modern art
M **Museum des 20 Jahrunderts,** Schweizergarten, 1030. Tel 78-25-50.
Collections: Works of the 20th century and a sculpture garden; artists represented include: Archipenko, Arp, Barlach, Beckman, Boeckl, Bonnard, Delaunay, Ernst, Gleizes, Hofer, Hoflehner, Jawlensky, Kandinsky, Kirchner, Klee, Kokoschka, Laurens, Leger, Marc, Matisse, Miro, Moore, Munch, Nolde, Picasso, Rodin, Rosso, Wotruba and others

M **OSTERREICHISCHE GALERIE,** Austrian Gallery, Oberes & Unteres Belvedere, Prinz Eugenstrasse 27, Postfach 134, A 1037. Tel 78-41-21. *Dir* Dr Hubert Adolph
Collections: Austrian Gallery of 19th and 20th Century Art; Museum of Austrian Baroque Art; Museum of Austrian Medieval Art; Ambrosi Museum; Branch of the Austrian Gallery at Schloss Halbturn
M **Museum mittelalterlicher osterreichischer Kunst,** Orangerie des Belvedere, Rennweg 6A, Vienna III
Collections: Austrian medieval paintings and sculptures, especially 14th - 16th century
M **Osterreichisches Barockmuseum,** Unteres Belvedere, Rennweg 6A, Vienna III
Collections: Austrian Baroque art (paintings and sculptures)
M **Osterreichische Galerie des XIX und XX Jahrunderts,** Oberes Belvedere, Prinz Eugenstr 27, Vienna III
Collections: 19th - 20th century Austrian paintings and sculptures
M **Gustinus Ambrosi-Museum,** Scherzergasse 1A, Vienna II
Collections: Sculpture by G Ambrosi (1893-1975)
M **Expositur der Osterreichischen Galerie auf Schloss Halbturn,** Burgenland, Halbturn, A-7131. Tel (02172) 3307.
Collections: 20th century Austrian paintings and sculptures
M **Internationale Kunst des XIX und XX Jahrunderts (International Art of the 19th & 20th Centuries),** Stallburg, Vienna
Collections: International painting & sculpture

M **OSTERREICHISCHES MUSEUM FUR ANGEWANDTE KUNST,** Austrian Museum of Applied Art, Stubenring 5, 1010. Tel (0222) 71136-0. *Dir* Peter Noever
Library with 100,000 vols & 250,000 prints
Collections: Applied arts from Roman to modern age

BELGIUM

ANTWERP

M **INTERNATIONAAL CULTUREEL CENTTRUM,** International Cultural Centre, Meir 50, 2000. Tel 03-226-03-06. *Dir* Willy Juwet

M **KONINKLIJK MUSEUM VOOR SCHONE KUNSTEN,** Royal Museum of Fine Arts, Leopold de Waelplein, 2000. Tel (03) 238-78-09. *Deputy Dir* L M A Schoonbaert
Library with 35,000 vols
Collections: Five Centuries of Flemish Painting: Flemish Primitifs, early foreign schools, 16th-17th century Antwerp School, 17th century Dutch School, 19th and 20th century Belgian artists; works of De Braekeleer, Ensor, Leys, Permeke, Smits and Wouters

M **KUNSTHISTORISCHE MUSEA,** Art History Museum, Museum Mayer van den Bergh, Lange Gasthuisstraat 19, 2000. Tel (03) 232-42-37. *Dir* Hans Nieuwdorp
M **Rubenshuis,** Wapper 9-11, 2000. Tel (03) 232-47-51. *Cur* Hans Nieuwdorp
Collections: Reconstruction of Rubens' house and studio; paintings by P P Rubens, his collaborators and pupils
L **Rubenianum,** Kolveniersstraat 20, 2000. Tel (03) 232-39-20. *Cur* Hans Nieuwdorp
Center for the study of 16th and 17th century Flemish art; library and photo archives
Publications: Corpus Rubenianum Ludwig Burchard
M **Open-air Museum of Sculpture,** Middelheimlaan 61, 2020. Tel)03) 827-15-34. *Cur* Hans Nieuwdorp
Collections: Contemporary sculpture of Rodin, Maillol, Zadkine, Marini, Manzu, Gargallo, Moore, biennial exhibitions of modern sculpture
M **Museum Smidt van Gelder,** Belgielei 91, 2000. Tel (03) 239-06-52. *Asst Keeper* Clara Vanderhenst
Collections: Collections of Chinese and European porcelains, 17th century Dutch paintings, 18th century French furniture
M **Museum Mayer van den Bergh,** Lange Gasthuisstraat 19, 2000. Tel (03) 232-42-37. *Cur* Hans Nieuwdorp
Collections: Collection of paintings, including Breughel, Metsys, Aertsen, Mostaert, Bronzino, Heda, de Vos, and medieval sculpture

M **MUSEUM PLANTIN-MORETUS,** Plantin-Moretus Museum, Vrijdagmarkt 22, 2000. Tel (03) 233-02-94. *Dir* Dr Francine de Nave
Library of 30,000 books of 15th - 18th centuries
Collections: Designs, copper and wood engravings, printing presses, typography

M **STEDELIJK PRENTENKABINET,** Municipal Gallery of Graphic Arts, Vrijdagmarkt 23, 2000. Tel 03-232-24-55. *Keeper* Dr Francine de Nave
Collections: Antwerp iconographic collection; modern drawings: J Ensor, F Jespers, H Leys, W Vaes, Rik Wouters; modern engravings: Cantre, Ensor, Masereel, J Minne, W Vaes; old drawings: Jordaens, E and A Quellin, Rubens, Schut, Van Dyck; old engravings: Galle, Goltzius, Hogenbergh, W Hollar, Jegher, Wiericx, etc

BRUGES

M **GROENINGEMUSEM,** Municipal Art Gallery, Dyver, 12, 8000. Tel (050) 33-99-11. *Chief Cur* Dr Valentin Vermeersch
Collections: Ancient & modern paintings, including works by Hieronymus Bosch, Gerard David, Hugo vanderGoes, Jan van Eyck, R van de Weyden & Hans Memling

M **STEDELIJK MUSEUM VOOR VOLKSKUNDE,** Municipal Museum of Folklore, Rolweg 40, 8000. Tel 050-33-00-44. *Cur* W P Dezutter
Collections: Collections including folklore, sculpture, applied arts, ancient and modern paintings, trades and crafts of 19th century, popular art

BRUSSELS

L **BIBLIOTHEQUE ROYALE ALBERT I,** The Belgiam National Library, 4 blvd de l'Empereur, 1000. Tel (02) 519-53-11. *Dir* Denise De Weerdt
Collections: Coins, medals, maps, manuscripts, prints, rare printed books housed in Belgian National Library

M **MUSEE HORTA,** 25 rue Americaine, 1050. Tel 537-16-92. *Dir* Francoise Dierkens-Aubry
Collections: Paintings and works of art by V Horta

M **MUSEES ROYAUX D'ART ET D'HISTOIRE,** Royal Museums of Art and History, 10 Parc du Cinquantenaire, 1040. Tel 02-733-96-11. *Dir* F Van Noten
Collections: Pre-Columbian art; Belgian, Egyptian, Japanese, Greek, Roman and classical art; Medieval, Renaissance and modern art - ceramics, furniture, glass, lace, silver, tapestries, textiles; ethnography; folklore

M **MUSEES ROYAUX DES BEAUX-ARTS DE BELGIQUE,** Royal Museums of Fine Arts of Belgium, 9 rue de Musee, 1000. Tel (02) 513-96-30. *Dir* Henri Pauwels
Collections: Medieval, Renaissance and modern paintings, drawings and sculpture
M **Musee d'Art Ancien,** 3 rue de la Regence, 1000. Tel 02-513-96-30. *Dept Head* Henri Pauwels
Collections: Painting and drawings (15th - 19th centuries) and old and modern sculpture
M **Musee d'Art Moderne,** 1-2 Place Royale, Brussels, 1000. Tel 02-513-96-30. *Dept Head* Phil Mertens
Collections: temporary exhibitions; 20th century paintings, drawings and sculpture
M **Musee Constantin Meunier,** 59 rue de l'Abbaye, 1000. Tel 02-648-44-49.
Collections: Paintings, drawings and sculptures by Constanin Meunier, the artist's house and studio
M **Musee Wiertz,** 62 rue Vautier, Brussels, 1000. Tel 02-648-17-18. *Head Cur* Philippe Roberts-Jones
Collections: Paintings by Antoine Wiertz

M **MUSEUM ERASMUS,** 31 Rue du Chapitre, 1070. Tel 521-13-83. *Cur* Jean-Pierre Van den Branden
Collections: Documents, paintings, manuscripts relating to Erasmus and other humanists of the 16th century

LIEGE

M **MUSEES D'ARCHEOLOGIE ET DES ARTS DECORATIFS,** Liege Museums of Archeology and Decorative Arts, 13 quai de Maastricht, 4000. 041-23-20-68. *Cur* Luc Engen
Collections: Musee Ansembourg - 18th century decorative arts of Liege, housed in a mansion of the same period; Musee Curtius - archaeology; decorative arts from prehistory to 18th century; Musee du Verre - history and art of glass
M **Musee Curtius,** 13 quai de Maastricht, 4000
The museum is the headquarters of the Archaeological Institute of Liege
Collections: Prehistory, Romano-Belgian and Frankish; Liege coins, decorative arts from the Middle Ages to the 19th century; Annex: lapidary collection in Palais de Justice
M **Musee d'Ansembourg,** 114 Feronstree, 4000
Collections: 18th century decorative arts of Liege; reconstituted interiors
M **Musee du Verre,** 13 quai de Maastricht, 4000
Headquarters of the Association Internationale pour l'Histoire du Verre
Collections: Main centers of production, from the earliest times to the present, are represented
Publications: Annales, bulletin

MARIEMONT

M **MUSEE ROYALE ET DOMAINE DE MARIEMONT,** Morlanwelz, 6510. Tel (064) 22-12-43. *Cur* Prof G Donnay
Maintains library with 70,000 volumes
Collections: Belgian archaeology; porcelain from Tournai; Egyptian, Grecian, Roman, Chinese & Japanese antiquities

VERVIERS

M **MUSEES COMMUNAUX DE VERVIERS: BEAUX-ARTS,** Community Museum of Fine Arts, Rue Renier 17, 4800. Tel 087-33-16-95. *Cur* V Bronowski
Collections: European & Asian painting and sculpture, ceramics, & folk arts

BOLIVIA

LA PAZ

M **MUSEO NACIONAL DE ARQUEOLOGIA,** National Museum, Calle Tihuanaco 93, Casilla oficial. Tel 29624. *Dir* Max Portugal Ortiz
Collections: Anthropology, archaeology, ethnology, folklore, Lake Titicaca district exhibitions, traditional native arts and crafts

M **MUSEO NACIONAL DE ARTE,** Calle Socabaya 485, Casilla 7038. Tel 371177. *Dir* Pedro Querejazu
Collections: Colonial and local modern art

BOTSWANA

GABORONE

M **NATIONAL MUSEUM AND ART GALLERY,** Independence Ave, Private Bag 00114. Tel 374616. *Dir* T L Mpulubusi
Collections: Art of all races of Africa south of the Sahara; scientific collections relating to Botswana

BRAZIL

OURO PRETO

M **MUSEU DA INCONFIDENCIA,** History of Democratic Ideals and Culture, Praca Tiradentes, 139, 35400. Tel 031-551-1121. *Dir* Rui Mourao
Collections: Objects & documents related to the 1789 Revolutionaries of Minas Gerais (the Inconfidentes)

RIO DE JANEIRO

M **MUSEU DE ARTE MODERNA DO RIO DE JANIERO,** Museum of Modern Art, Av Infante Dom Henrique 85, C P 44, 20021. Tel 021-240-6351. *Pres* M F Nascimento Brito; *Exec Dir* Gustavo A Capanema
Collections: Collections representing different countries

M **MUSEU NACIONAL DE BELAS ARTES,** National Museum of Fine Arts, Ave Rio Branco 199, 20040. Tel 240-9869. *Dir* Prof Heliosa A Lustosa
Library with 12,000 vols
Collections: 19th and 20th century Brazilian art, works by outstanding painters; European paintings & sculptures - works by Dutch, English, French, German, Italian, Portuguese and Spanish masters; masterpieces of foreign collection: Dutch school - eight Brazilian landscapes by Frans Post; French school - 20 Paintings by Eugene Boudin; Ventania (Storm) by Alfred Sisley; Italian School Portrait of the Cardinal Amadei by Giovanni Battista Gaulli, Baciccia; Sao Caetano (circa 1730) by Giambattista Tiepolo. Graphic art department: Prints and drawings by Annibale Carracci, Chagall, Daumier, Durer, Toulouse Lautrec, Picasso, Guido Reni, Renoir, Tiepolo, etc

SALVADOR

M **MUSEO DE ARTE ANTIGA: INSTITUTO FEMENINO DA BAHIA,** Early Art Museum: Bahia Women's College, Rua Monsenhor Flaviano 2. *Dir* Henriqueta Martins Catharino
Collections: Religious art; Brazilian art; women's apparel, jewelry, gold, silver

SAO PAULO

M **MUSEU DE ARTE CONTEMPORANEA DA UNIVERSIDADE DE SAO PAULO,** Modern Art Museum of Sao Paulo University, CP22031, Parque Ibirapuera, Pavilhao da Bienal, 01499. Tel 571-9610. *Dir* Dr Ana Mae Tavares Bastos Barbosa
Collections: International and Brazilian plastic arts

M MUSEU DE ARTE DE SAO PAULO, Sao Paulo Art Museum, Ave Paulista 1578, 01310. Tel 251-5644. *Dir* P M Bardi
Collections: Representative works by Portinari & Lasar Segall; ancient & modern paintings & sculptures: American, 19th - 20th Centuries; Brazilian, 17th - 20th Centuries; British, 18th - 20th Centuries; Dutch, Flemish & German, 15th - 20th Centuries; French, 16th - 20th Centuries; Italian, 13th - 20th Centuries; Spanish & Portuguese, 16th - 19th Centuries

BULGARIA

PAZARDZIK

M STANISLAV DOSPEVSKY MUSEUM, Bul Georgi Dimitrov 50, 4400. Tel 2-50-30. *Dir* Ganka Radulova
Collections: House where the painter lived and worked; exhibition of paintings, icons, personal effects and documents

PLOVDIV

M REGIONAL MUSEUM OF ARCHAEOLOGY, Pl Saedinenie 1, 4000. Tel 22-43-39. *Dir* Zdravko Karov
Collections: Prehistory; classical and medieval archaeology; numismatics

SOFIA

M NATSIONALNA HUDOZHESTVENA GALERIJA, National Art Gallery, Moskovska 6, 1000. Tel 044-88-35-59. *Dir* Svetlin Rusev
Collections: National and foreign art

CHILE

SANTIAGO

M MUSEO DE ARTE COLONIAL DE SAN FRANCISCO, Alameda Bernardo O'Higgins 834, PO Box 122D. Tel 398737. *Dir* Paul Frings
Collections: 16th - 19th century art; important collection of 17th century paintings in Chile; the life of St Francis depicted in 53 pictures; other religious works of art, furniture

M MUSEO DE ARTE POPULAR AMERICANO, Museum of American Folk Art, Parque Forestal S/N, Casilla 2100, Univ of Chile. Tel 396-488. *Dir* Julio Tobar Urzua
Collections: Araucanian silver; American folk arts of pottery, basketware, metal & wood

M MUSEO NACIONAL DE BELLAS ARTES, National Museum of Fine Arts, Parque Forestal, Casilla 3209. Tel 330655. *Dir* Nemesio Antunez
Collections: Baroque, Chilean and Spanish paintings; sculpture; engravings

CHINA, REPUBLIC OF

TAIPEI

M NATIONAL PALACE MUSEUM, Shih-Lin, Wai-Shuang-Hsi. Tel 02-882-1230. *Dir* Chin Hsiao-yi
Collections: Bronzes, calligraphy, carved lacquer, embroidery, enamelware, jades, miniature crafts, oracle bones, paintings, porcelain, pottery, rare and old books & documents from Shang Dynasty to Ch'ing Dynasty, tapestry, writing implements
L Library, Shih-Lin, Wai-Shuang-Hsi
Library Holdings: Vols 48,000; Per subs 683; Rare books 191,000, Documents 395,000

COLOMBIA

BOGOTA

M MUSEO COLONIAL, Museum of the Colonial Period, Carrera 6, No 9-77. Tel 2-41-60-17. *Dir* Teresa Morales de Gomez
Collections: Spanish colonial period art work: paintings, sculpture, furniture, gold and silver work, drawing

COSTA RICA

SAN JOSE

M MUSEO DE ARTE COSTARRICENSE, La Sabana, 1009. Tel 22-77-34. *Dir* Carlos G Montero
Collections: Representative Costa Rican art

M MUSEO NACIONAL DE COSTA RICA, Calle 17, Avda Central y 2, Apdo 749, 1000. Tel 57-14-33. *Dir* Lorena San Roman Johanning
Collections: Pre-Columbian and colonial religious art; natural history

CROATIA

ZAGREB

M GALERIJE GRADA ZAGREBA, City Art Galleries, Habdeliceva 2, 41000. Tel 041-431-343. *Dir* Marijan Susovski
Collections: Five galleries exhibiting contemporary art, antique and Renaissance works, primitive art, Ivan Mestrovic's sculpture and photography

M STROSSMAYEROVA GALERIJA STARIH MAJSTORA, Strossmayer's Gallery of Old Masters, Trg Nikole Subica Zrinskog 11, 41000. Tel 041-433-504. *Dir* Prof Duro Vandura
Collections: Paintings and sculpture, 13th to 19th century

CUBA

HAVANA

M MUSEO NACIONAL DE BELLAS ARTES, National Museum, Animas entre Zulueta y Monserate, CP 10200. Tel 613915. *Dir* Lucilla Villegas Oria
Collections: Renaissance and other European art; Cuban art from colonial times to the present

CYPRUS

NICOSIA

M CYPRUS MUSEUM, PO Box 2024. Tel (02) 30-2189. *Dir of Antiquities* Athanasios Papugeorghiou; *Cur* M C Loulloupis
Collections: Bronze cauldron from Salamis; middle and late Bronze-age Geometric, Archaic, Classical, Hellenistic and Graeco-Roman pottery; Mycenaean vases; Neolithic stone tools and vessels; sculpture from Archaic to Greco-Roman Age, including the Fine Arsos Head, the Aphrodite of Soli, and the bronze statue of Septimus Sevarus; silver trays from Lambousa

CZECH REPUBLIC

BRNO

M MORAVSKA GALERIE V BRNE, Moravian Gallery in Brno, Husova 14, 662 26. Tel 25339. *Dir* Dr Jaroslav Kacer
Collections: European Art Collection - ceramics, furniture, glass, graphic design, jewelry, photography, textiles; Fine Art Collection - graphic art, painting, sculpture, 14th century to present; Oriental Art Collection

LITOMERICE

M GALERIE VYTVARNEHO UMENI, North Bohemian Gallery of Fine Arts, Michalska 7, 412-47. Tel 4127. *Dir* Libuse Sumichrastova
Collections: Art of the 19th century; Baroque Art of the 17th - 18th centuries; contemporary art; Gothic art of the 13th - 16th centuries; special collections of naive paintings and sculpture; Renaissance paintings and sculptures of the 15th - 16th centuries

PRAGUE

M NARODNI GALERIE V PRAGUE, National Gallery of Prague, Hradcanske Nam 15, 119 04. Tel 538-964. *Pres* Dr Jiri Kotalik
Collections: Czech sculpture of the 19th and 20th century; French and European art of the 19th and 20th century; old Czech art; Old European Art; graphic art, modern art; Oriental art

M STATNI ZIDOVSKE MUZEUM, State Jewish Museum, Jachymova 3, 110 01. Tel 231-078-5. *Dir* Dr Ludmila Kybalova
Collections: Historical archival materials of Bohemian & Moravian Jewish religious communities; library of ancient books with a collection of Hebrew manuscripts; children's drawings & works of painters from the concentration camp Terezin; silver liturgical objects; textiles from synagogues of historic interest

M UMELECKOPRUMYSLOVE MUZEUM, Ulice 17 listopadu 2, 110 01. Tel 232-00-51. *Dir* Dr Helena Koenigsmorkova
Collections: Collections of glass, ceramics, china, furniture, textiles, tapestries, gold and silver work, iron, ivory, clocks, prints, posters, photography, contemporary design

DENMARK

AALBORG

M NORDJYLLANDS KUNSTMUSEUM, Art Museum of Northern Jutland, Kong Christians Alle 50, 9000. Tel 98-13-80-88. *Dir* Nina Hobolth
Collections: Collection of graphics, painting and sculpture from 20th century, Danish and international

AARHUS

M AARHUS KUNSTMUSEUM, Aarhus Art Museum, Vennelystparken, 8000. Tel 86-13-52-55. *Dir* Jens Erik Sorensen
Collections: Danish and European art

CHARLOTTENLUND

M ORDRUPGAARDSAMLINGEN, Vilvordevej 110, 2920. Tel 31-64-11-83. *Dir* Hanne Finsen
Collections: Wilhelm Hansen Collection; paintings by Cezanne, Corot, Courbet, Degas, Delacroix, Degas, Gauguin, Manet, Pissarro, Renoir, Sisley, and other French and Danish artists from the 19th century and the beginning of the 20th century

COPENHAGEN

L DET KONGELIGE DANSKE KUNSTAKADEMI BIBLIOTEK, Library of the Royal Danish Academy of Fine Arts, 1 Kongens Nytoru, K 1050. Tel 33-12-86-59. *Dir* Hakon Lund
Library Holdings: Vols 115,000; Architectural Drawings 110,000; AV — Slides 100,000; Other — Photographs 300,000

M KUNSTINDUSTRIMUSEET, The Danish Museum of Decorative Art, Bredgade 68, 1260. Tel 33-14-94-52. *Pres* Olav Grue; *Dir* Kristian Jakobsen
Library with 60,000 vols
Collections: Chinese and Japanese art and handicrafts; European decorative and applied art from the Middle Ages to present - bookbindings, carpets and tapestries, furniture, jewelry, porcelain and pottery, silverware and textiles

M NATIONALMUSEET, National Museum, Prinsens Palae, Frederiksholms Kanal 12, 1220. Tel 33-13-44-11. *Dir* Dr Olaf Olsen
Collections: Museum has 5 divisions, including Danish historical collection, folk museum, ethnographic collection, classical antiquities collection, royal coin & medal collection

COPENHAGEN K

M ROSENBORG SLOT, Rosenborg Palace, Oster Voldgade 4A, 1350. Tel 33-15-76-19. *Dir* Mogens Bencard; *Dir Chamberlain* Niels Eilschou Holm
Collections: Crown Jewels; arms, apparel, jewelry and furniture from period 1470-1863

M STATENS MUSEUM FOR KUNST, Royal Museum of Fine Arts, Solvgade 48-50, DK 1307. Tel 33-91-21-26. *Dir* Villads Villadsen
Collections: Danish paintings and sculpture; various other works by 19th and 20th century Scandinavian artists; old masters of Italian, Flemish, Dutch and German Schools; modern French art
M Konigliche Gemalde- und Skulpturensammlung, Solvgade 48-50. Tel 01-11 21 26. *Dir* Dr Bente Skovgaard
Collections: Contains the main collection of Danish paintings and sculpture
M Konigliche Kupferstichsammlung, Department of Prints and Drawings, Solvgade 48-50. Tel 01-11 21 26. *Dir* Erik Fischer

M THORVALDSENS MUSEUM, Porthusgade 2, 1213. Tel 33-32-15-32. *Dir* Stig Miss; *Cur* Bjarne Jornas
Collections: 19th century European paintings & drawings; sculpture & drawings by Bertel Thorvaldsen (1770 - 1844) & his collections of contemporary paintings, drawings & prints

COPENHAGEN V

M KOBENHAVNS BYMUSEUM, Copenhagen City Museum, Absalonsgade 3, POB 3004, 1507. Tel 31-21-07-72. *Dir* Torben Ejlersen
Collections: Photographs 1850 to present; architecture; models; Kierkegaard relics

M NY CARLSBERG GLYPTOTEK, Carlsberg Gallery, Dantes Plads 7, 1556. Tel 33-91-10-65. *Pres* Torben Holck Colding; *Dir* Flemming Johansen
Collections: Danish and French paintings and sculptures from 19th and 20th centuries; Egyptian, Etruscan, Greek and Roman sculpture

HUMLEBAEK

M LOUISIANA MUSEUM OF MODERN ART, Gammel Strandvej 13, 3050. Tel 42-19-07-19. *Dir* Knud W Jensen
Collections: Danish, International & Modern art from 1950, including sculpture & paintings
Activities: Concerts; cinema; theatre

SKORPING

M THINGBAEK KALKMINER BUNDGAARDS MUSEUM, Rode Mollerej 4, 9520. Tel 37-51-12. *Dir* Ole Nielsen
Collections: Sculptures by Danish artists A J Bundgard and C J Bonnesen; cement sculptures by Anton Laier

DOMINICAN REPUBLIC

SANTO DOMINGO

M GALERIA NACIONAL DE BELLAS ARTES, National Fine Arts Gallery, Avenida Independencia esq Maximo Gomez. Tel 687-3300. *Dir* Dr Jose de J Alvarez Valverde
Collections: Paintings and sculptures previously exhibited in the Museo Nacional

ECUADOR

QUITO

M MUSEO DE ARTE COLONIAL, Cuenca St & Mejia St, Apdo 2555. Tel 212-297. *Dir* Carlos A Rodriguez
Collections: Art from the Escuela Quitena of the Colonial epoch - 17th, 18th and 19th century art and some contemporary art

M MUSEO DE ARTE E HISTORIA DE LA CIUDAD, Civic Museum of Arts and History, Calle Espejo 1147, Apdo 399. *Dir* Hugo Monacayo
Collections: Sculptures; paintings; documents

EGYPT

ALEXANDRIA

M GRECO-ROMAN MUSEUM, Museum St. *Dir* Doreya Said
Library with 15,000 vols
Collections: Exhibits from the Byzantine, Greek and Roman eras

CAIRO

M COPTIC MUSEUM, Old Cairo. *Dir* Maher Sahib
Library with 6500 vols
Collections: Architecture, bone, ebony, frescos, glass, icons, ivory, manuscripts, metalwork, pottery, sculpture, textiles, woodcarvings

M EGYPTIAN NATIONAL MUSEUM, Midan-el-Tahrir Kasr El-Nil. Tel 754-310. *Dir* Mohammed Mohsen
Library with 39,000 vols
Collections: Ancient Egyptian art from prehistoric times through 6th century AD (excluding Coptic and Islamic periods); houses the Department of Antiquities

M MUSEUM OF ISLAMIC ART, Ahmed Maher Sq, Bab al-Khalq, 11638. Tel 90-19-30. *Dir-Gen* Abd al-Rauf Ali Yousuf
Museum maintains library with 14,000 volumes
Collections: Works of art showing evolution of Islamic art up to 1879

ENGLAND

BATH

M **AMERICAN MUSEUM IN BRITAIN,** Claverton Manor, BA2 7BD. Tel (0225) 460503. *Dir* William McNaught
Collections: American decorative arts from 17th to 19th centuries

M **HOLBURNE MUSEUM & CRAFTS STUDY CENTRE,** Great Pulteney St, Avon BA2 4DB. Tel (0225) 466669. *Cur* Barley Roscoe
Collections: Pictures, furniture, miniatures, silver & other decorative arts exhibited in 18th century building

M **VICTORIA ART GALLERY,** Bridge St, BA2 4AT. Tel 46-11-11. *Cur* Stephen Bird
Collections: British 20th century paintings; English pottery, porcelain, antique glass; 17th to 19th century paintings

BIRMINGHAM

M **BIRMINGHAM MUSEUMS AND ART GALLERY,** Chamberlain Square, B3 3DH. Tel (021) 235-2834. *Dir* Michael Diamond
Collections: Fine and applied art, including English works since 17th century, foreign schools from Renaissance, Pre-Raphaelite works; silver, ceramics, coin, textile collections; Old and New World archeology, ethnography and local history collections; branch museums house furniture, machinery and applied arts

BRIGHTON

M **ROYAL PAVILION, ART GALLERY AND MUSEUMS,** Church St, Sussex BN1 1UE. Tel 0273-603-005. *Dir* Richard Marks
M **Brighton Art Gallery and Museum,** Church St, Brighton. Tel (0273) 603005.
Collections: Early and modern paintings, watercolors, prints and drawings; English pottery and porcelain, including the Willett Collection; decorative art and furniture of Art Nouveau and Art Deco periods; ethnography and archaeology; musical instruments; Brighton history
M **Royal Pavilion,** Brighton. Tel (0273) 603005.
Collections: Once the marine palace of King George IV (1787-1846); interior decorations restored and original furniture
M **Preston Manor,** Preston Park. Tel (0273) 603005.
Collections: Home of the Stanford family for nearly 200 years, this fully furnished Gregorian Era house illustrates the life of the wealthy preceeding the First World War; rebuilt 1738; remodelled 1905
M **Grange Art Gallery and Museum,** Rottingdean. Tel (0273) 301004.
Collections: Toys, Sussex folk-life, Rudyard Kiplingiana

BRISTOL

M **CITY OF BRISTOL MUSEUM AND ART GALLERY,** Queen's Rd, BS8 1RL. Tel (0272) 223571. *Dir Arts* Martyn Heighton
Collections: Fine and applied arts of Great Britain; archaeological and ethnological collection; Oriental Art

CAMBRIDGE

M **UNIVERSITY OF CAMBRIDGE,** Fitzwilliam Museum, Trumpington St, CB2 1RB. Tel (0223) 332900. *Dir* S S Jervis
Collections: European ceramics; Greek, Roman, western Asiatic and Egyptian antiquities; arms and armor, coins, drawings, furniture, illuminated manuscripts, manuscripts, paintings, prints, sculpture, textiles

CARDIFF

M **NATIONAL MUSEUM OF WALES,** Amgueddfa Genedlaethol Cymru, Main Bldg, Cathays Park, CF1 3NP. Tel (0222) 397951. *Pres* Hon Jonathon Davies; *Dir* Alistair Wilson
Collections: Art, natural sciences, archaeology and industry of Wales

DONCASTER

M **DONCASTER MUSEUM AND ART GALLERY,** Chequer Rd, Yorks DN1 2AE. Tel 0302-73-42-87. *Cur* T G Manby
Collections: European painting, ceramics and glass, silver and jewelry; The King's Own Yorkshire Light Infantry Regimental Collection

EAST MOLESEY

M **HAMPTON COURT PALACE,** Surrey KT8 9AU. Tel (081) 977-8441. *Palace Adminr* Crawford McDonald; *Supt Royal Coll* J Cowell; *Surveyor* Sir Oliver Millar
Collections: Paintings & tapestries, including Andrea Mantegna's 9 paintings of The Triumph of Julius Caesar

KENDAL

M **ABBOT HALL ART GALLERY & MUSEUM OF LAKELAND LIFE & INDUSTRY,** Cumbria LA9 5AL. Tel (0539) 722464. *Dir* V A J Slowe; *Cur* J Dugdale
Collections: Gallery provides changing exhibitions of local and international interest; houses permanent collections of 18th century furniture, paintings and objects d'art; modern paintings; sculpture; drawings; museum features working and social life of the area

LEEDS

M **TEMPLE NEWSAM HOUSE,** LS15 0AE. Tel 0532-647-321. *Dir* Christopher Gilbert
Collections: Decorative arts; old master and Ingram family paintings
M **Leeds City Art Gallery,** Municipal Bldg, The Headrow, LS1 3AA. Tel 0532-462-495.
Collections: Early English Watercolors; English & European paintings of 19th century; modern paintings & sculpture; Henry Moore Centre for the Study of Sculpture
M **Lotherton Hall,** Aberford. Tel 0532-813-259.
Collections: Gascoigne Collection of 17th to 19th century paintings, ceramics, silver, furniture; Oriental gallery; modern crafts

LEICESTER

M **LEICESTERSHIRE MUSEUMS, ARTS & RECORDS SERVICE,** 96 New Walk, LE1 6TD. Tel (0533) 554100. *Dir* Dr Patrick J Boylan
Collections: Major special collections include 18th, 19th and 20th century British Art, German Expressionists (largest public collection in Britain); European Art from Renaissance to present; contemporary art

LINCOLN

M **LINCOLNSHIRE MUSEUMS,** County Offices, Newland, LN1 1YL. Tel (0522) 552222. *Asst Dir Museums* Open
Oversees 7 museums
M **Museum of Lincolnshire Life,** Burton Rd, LN1 1YL. Tel (0522) 528448. *Keeper of Social History* P R Cousins
Collections: Displays illustrating the social, agricultural and industrial history of Lincolnshire over the last three centuries
M **Usher Gallery,** Lindum Rd. Tel (0522) 527980. *Keeper* R H Wood
Collections: Exhibits the Usher collection of watches, miniatures, porcelain; special collection of works by Peter De Wint; a general collection of paintings, sculpture and decorative art; collection of coins and tokens from Lincolnshire
M **Lincoln City and County Museum,** Broadgate. Tel (0522) 530401. *Keeper of Archaeology* Antony Page
Collections: Natural history, archaeological and historical collections relating to Lincolnshire; large collection of Roman antiquities from Lincoln

LIVERPOOL

M **WALKER ART GALLERY,** William Brown St, L3 8EL. Tel 2070-001. *Cur* Edward Morris
Collections: English and European drawings, paintings, prints, sculpture, watercolors, including notable collections of Italian and Netherlandish primitives; pop art

LONDON

M **BRITISH MUSEUM,** Great Russell St, WC1B 3DG. Tel (071) 636-1555. *Dir* Dr Robert G W Anderson
Collections: Egyptian, Assyrian, Greek and Roman Prehistoric, Romano-British, Western Asiatic and other arts; coins and medals; prints and drawings

M **DULWICH PICTURE GALLERY,** College Rd, SE21 7AD. Tel (081) 693-5254. *Dir* G A Waterfield
Collections: Collections of Old Masters from 1626 onwards, including Claude, Cuyp, Gainsborough, Murillo, Poussin, Raphael, Rembrandt, Rubens, Teniers, Tiepolo, Van Dyck, Watteau and others

M **NATIONAL GALLERY,** Trafalgar Square, WC2N 5DN. Tel (071) 839-3321. *Chair* Jacob Rothschild; *Dir* Neil MacGregor
Collections: Principal schools, British, Dutch, Early Netherlandish, French, German, Italian; Western European painting up to early 20th century

M **NATIONAL PORTRAIT GALLERY,** 2 St Martin's Place, WC2H 0HE. Tel (071) 306-0055. *Chmn Trustees* Rev Owen Chadwick; *Dir* John T Hayes
Collections: National Collection of portraits spanning last 500 years, including sculpture and photographs; caricatures, drawings, photographs; printings, watercolors

M **QUEEN'S GALLERY,** Buckingham Palace Rd, SW1A 1AA. Tel 799-2331.

M **ROYAL ACADEMY OF ARTS,** Burlington House, Piccadilly, W1V 0DS. Tel 734-9052. *Pres* Sir Hugh Casson
Collections: Paintings, prints, architectural collection
L **Library,** W1V 0DS. Tel (071) 439-7438. *Libr* Mary Anne Stevens
Library Holdings: Vols 15,000; 20,000 books on the fine arts; original drawings, manuscripts, engravings; Other — Manuscripts

M SOUTH LONDON ART GALLERY, 65 Peckham Rd, SE5 8UH. Tel (071) 703-6120. *Keeper* K Sharpe
Collections: Contemporary British art; 20th century original prints; paintings of the Victorian period; topographical paintings and drawings of local subjects
Permanent Collection Exhibited Periodicely
Exhibitions: Exhibitions from permanent collection

M TATE GALLERY, Millbank, SW1P 4RG. Tel (071) 821-1313. *Dir* Nicholas Serota
Collections: Works of Blake, Constable, Hogarth, Turner and the Pre-Raphaelites; British painting from the 16th century to present; modern foreign painting from Impressionism onward; modern sculpture; collection totals 12,000, including 5500 prints; Largest public collection of British Art of 20th Century

M UNIVERSITY OF LONDON, Courtauld Institute Galleries, Somerset House, Strand, WC2R 0RN. Tel (071) 873-2526. *Dir* Dr Dennis Farr
Collections: Samuel Courtauld Collection of French Impressionist and Post-Impressionist Paintings; other collections include old masters, early 20th century French and English paintings, modern British art, English landscape paintings and drawings

M VICTORIA AND ALBERT MUSEUM, Cromwell Rd, South Kensington, SW7 2RL. Tel (071) 938-8500. *Dir* Elizabeth Esteve-Coll
Collections: Collections of fine and applied arts of all countries, periods and styles, including Oriental art. European collections are mostly post-classical, architectural details, art of the book, bronzes, calligraphs, carpets, ceramics, clocks, costumes, cutlery, drawings, embroideries, enamels, engravings, fabrics, furniture, glass, gold and silversmiths' work, ironwork, ivories, jewelry, lace, lithographs, manuscripts, metalwork, miniatures, musical instruments, oil paintings, posters, pottery and porcelain, prints, sculpture, stained glass, tapestries, theatre art, vestments, watches, watercolors, woodwork
M Apsley House (Wellington Museum), 149 Piccadilly, W1V 9FA. Tel (071) 499-5676. *Cur* Jonathan Voak
Opened to the public 1952
Collections: Paintings, silver, porcelain, orders and decorations, and personal relics of the first Duke of Wellington
M Bethnal Green Museum of Childhood, Cambridge Heath Rd, E2 9PA. Tel (081) 980-2415. *Cur* Anthony Burton
Collections: Dolls, ceramics, costumes, textiles, furniture and toys; articles related to childhood
M Ham House, Richmond, Surrey. Tel 01-940-1950. *Adminr* J Juak
Collections: Country house built in 1610 and enlarged by Elizabeth, Duchess of Lauderdale; contains much of the original furniture and interior ornament
M Osterley Park House, Osterley, Middlesex. Tel (081) 560-3918. *Adminr* Barry Williams
Collections: 16th century house remodelled by Robert Adam

M WALLACE COLLECTION, Hertford House, Manchester Square, W1M 6BN. Tel (071) 935-0687. *Dir* J A S Ingamells
Collections: Arms and Armour; French Furniture; Sevres Porcelain; paintings and works of art of all European schools; miniatures; sculpture

M WHITECHAPEL ART GALLERY, 80/82 Whitechapel High St, E1 7QX. Tel (071) 377-0107. *Dir* Catherine Lampert
Collections: Changing exhibitions, primarily of modern & contemporary art

M WILLIAM MORRIS GALLERY, Water House, Lloyd Park, Forest Rd, E17 4PP. Tel 527-5544, Ext 4390. *Dir* Norah Gillow
Publications: Works of William Morris, pre-Raphaelites & the arts & crafts movement; sculpture by late 19th century artistss; works by Frank Brangwyn

MANCHESTER

M MANCHESTER CITY ART GALLERIES, Corner of Mosley St & Princess St, M2 3JL. Tel (061) 236-5244. *Dir* Richard Gray
Collections: British art; English costume, enamels, silver and decorative arts; Old Master and Dutch 17th century painting; pre-Raphaelite painting

M UNIVERSITY OF MANCHESTER, Whitworth Art Gallery, Whitworth Park, Oxford Rd, M15 6ER. Tel 061-275-4865. *Dir* C Reginald Dodwell
Collections: British drawings and watercolors; contemporary British paintings and sculpture; Old Master and modern prints; textiles, wallpapers

NEWCASTLE

M TYNE AND WEAR COUNTY COUNCIL MUSEUMS, Laing Art Gallery and Museum, Higham Place, NE1 8AG. Tel 091-232-6789. *Dir of County Museums* J M A Thompson
Collections: British oil paintings since 1700 (with works by Burne-Jones, Gainsborough, Lansleer, Reynolds, Turner); British prints and watercolors; British (especially local) ceramics, costume, glass, pewter, silver of all periods; British textiles

NEWPORT

M BOROUGH OF NEWPORT MUSEUM AND ART GALLERY, John Frost Square, Gwent NP9 1HZ. Tel (0633) 840064. *Cur* Robert Trett
Collections: Early English watercolors; oil paintings by British artists; local archeology (especially Roman); natural and social history

OXFORD

M MUSEUM OF MODERN ART OXFORD, 30 Pembroke St, OX1 1BP. Telex 8-3147; Tel (0865) 722733. *Dir* David Elliott
Exhibitions: Features changing international exhibitions of 20th century painting, photography, prints, sculpture, drawing and film

M OXFORD UNIVERSITY, Ashmolean Museum, Beaumont St, OX1 2PH. Tel (0865) 278000. *Dir* Dr C J White
Collections: British, European, Egyptian, Mediterranean & Near Eastern archaeology; Chinese Bronzes; Chinese & Japanese porcelain, painting & lacquer; Dutch, English, Flemish, French & Italian oil paintings; Indian sculpture & painting; Hope Collection of engraved portraits Tibetan, Indian and Islamic art objects; Extensive collection of coins from various countries and times; Old Master and modern drawings, prints and watercolors

PLYMOUTH

M PLYMOUTH CITY MUSEUM AND ART GALLERY, Drake Circus, Plymouth, Devon PL4 8AJ. Tel (0752) 668000. *Cur* Tristram P Besterman
Estab to illustrate arts of the West Country
Collections: The Clarendon Collection of Portraits of 16th and 17th Century English worthies; Collection of Cookworthy's Plymouth and Bristol Porcelain; The Cottonian Collection of early printed and illuminated books

SHEFFIELD

M SHEFFIELD CITY MUSEUM, Weston Park, Yorks S10 2TP. Tel (0742) 768588. *Dir* Philip Broomhead
Estab 1875
Collections: Sheffield silver, Old Sheffield Plate, British and European cutlery, coins and medals, ceramics
M Abbeydale Hamlet, Abbeydale Rd S, Sheffield, S7 2QW. Tel (0742) 3677-31. *Dir* Philip Broomhead
Collections: An 18th century scytheworks with Huntsman type crucible steel furnace, tilt-hammers, grinding-shop and hand forges
M Bishop's House, Meersbrook Park, Sheffield, S8 9BE. Tel (0742) 557701. *Dir* Philip Broomhead
Collections: A late 15th century timber-framed domestic building with 16th - 17th century additions
M Graves Art Gallery, Surrey St, Sheffield, S1 1XZ. Tel 0742-734-781. *Dir* D N C Patmore
Collections: English, Italian Renaissance and Netherlands paintings

SOUTHAMPTON

M SOUTHAMPTON CITY ART GALLERY (Formerly Civic Art Gallery), Civic Centre, Hampshire S09 4XF. Tel (0703) 832769. *Cur* Adrian B Rance; *Principal Officer Arts* Elizabeth Goodall
Collections: Continental Old Masters; French 19th and 20th century school; British painting from the 18th century to present; contemporary sculpture and painting

SOUTHPORT

M ATKINSON ART GALLERY, Lord St, Merseyside PR8 No 1DH. Tel (0704) 533133, Ext 2110. *Keeper of Art Galleries & Museums* Anthony K Wray
Collections: British art - local, contemporary and historic; British 18th, 19th and 20th century oils; drawings, prints, sculpture and watercolors

STOKE ON TRENT

M STOKE-ON-TRENT CITY MUSEUM AND ART GALLERY, Hanley, Staffs ST1 3DW. Tel (0782) 202173. *Dir* P F Vigurs
Collections: One of the finest collections of English ceramics in the world, pre-eminent in Staffordshire ware; fine and decorative arts

WOLVERHAMPTON

M WOLVERHAMPTON ART GALLERY AND MUSEUM, Lichfield St, West Midlands WV1 1DU. Tel (0902) 312032. *Art Galleries & Museums Officer* Yvonne Jones
Collections: Contemporary British art; 18th century British paintings; 19th and 20th century British paintings and watercolors; branch museums have English enamels, japanning and porcelain

YORK

M YORK CITY ART GALLERY, Exhibition Square, Y01 2EW. Tel (0904) 623839. *Cur* Richard Green
Collections: British and European paintings, including the Lycett Green Collection of Old Masters; modern stoneware pottery; paintings and drawings by York artists, notably William Etty; watercolors, drawings and prints, mostly local topography

ETHIOPIA

ADDIS ABABA

M **MUSEUM OF THE INSTITUTE OF ETHIOPIAN STUDIES,** University of
Addis Ababa, PO Box 1176. Tel 559469. *Cur* Dr Girma Kidane
Collections: Ethiopian cultural artifacts, ethnology collections, cultural history
documents; religious art from 14th century to present

FINLAND

HELSINKI

M **SUOMEN KANSALLISMUSEO,** National Museum of Finland,
Mannerheimintie 34, 00101. Tel 90-40251. *Dir* Osmo Vuoristo
Numerous branch galleries throughout Finland
Collections: Ethnographical Department with Finnish, Finno-Ugrian and
Comparative Ethnographical Collections; Finnish Historical Department with a
Collection of Coins and Medals; Prehistoric Department with Finnish and
Comparative Collections

M **SUOMEN RAKENNUSTAITEEN MUSEO,** Kasarmikatu 24, 00130. Tel 66-
19-18. *Dir* Marja-Riitta Novi
Collections: Finnish architecture collection includes 60,000 photographs, 10,000
slides & original drawings

TURKU

M **TURUN TAIDEMUSEO,** Turku Art Museum, Puolalanpuisto, 20100. Tel (921)
330-960. *Dir* Berndt Arell
Collections: 19th and 20th century Finnish and Scandinavian art, drawings,
paintings, prints and sculpture; 19th and 20th centuries international print
collection

FRANCE

ALENCON

M **MUSEE DES BEAUX-ARTS ET DE LA DENTELLE,** Rue Charles Aveline,
61000. Tel 33-32-40-07. *Dir* Aude Pessey-Lux
Collections: 17th - 19th century French, Dutch and Flemish paintings; 16th -
19th century French, Italian and Dutch drawings; 16th - 20th century Alencon,
Flemish, Italian and Eastern European lace

ANGERS

M **MUSEE DES BEAUX-ARTS,** Museum of Fine Arts, 10 rue du Musee, 49100.
Tel 41-88-64-65. *Cur* Viviane Huchard
Collections: Paintings of the 17th & 18th centuries; Dutch, Flemish & French
schools; sculpture, including busts by Houdon

ANTIBES

M **MUSEE PICASSO,** Chateau Grimaldi, 06600. Tel 93-34-91-91. *Dir* Daniele
Giraudy
Collections: Modern and contemporary art; 230 works by Picasso

AVIGNON

M **MUSEE DU PETIT PALAIS,** Place du Palais des Papes, 84000. Tel 90-86-44-
58. *Dir* M P Foissy-Aufrere; *Cur* Esther Moench-Scherer
Collections: Italian paintings covering the period from 14th - 16th century;
Medieval sculpture from Avignon from 12th - 15th century; paintings of the
Avignon School of 14th - 15th centuries

CHANTILLY CEDEX

M **MUSEE ET CHATEAU DE CHANTILLY (MUSEE CONDE),** BP 243,
60631. Tel 44-57-08-00. *Cur* Amelie Lefebure
Collections: Ceramics, manuscripts and paintingsq

DIJON

M **MUSEE DES BEAUX-ARTS DE DIJON,** Museum of Fine Arts, Place de la
Sainte-Chapelle, 21000. Tel 80-74-52-70. *Chief Cur* Emmanuel Starcky
Collections: Furniture, objects of art, paintings of French & foreign schools,
sculpture; Granville Collection

FONTAINEBLEAU

M **MUSEE NATIONAL DE FONTAINEBLEAU,** National Museum of
Fontainebleau, Chateau de Fountainebleau, 77300. Tel 64-22-27-40. *Cur*
Jean-Pierre Samoyault; *Cur* Colombe Samoyault-Yerlet; *Cur* Daniele Denise
Collections: Paintings, furniture and interiors of 1st Empire and 17th, 18th and
19th centuries

GRENOBLE

M **MUSEE DES BEAUX-ARTS,** Place de Verdun, 38000. Tel 76-54-09-82. *Chief
Cur* Serge Lemoine
Collections: 16th, 17th and 18th century paintings; French, Italian, Spanish,
Flemish schools; modern collection; Egyptology collection

LILLE

M **MUSEE DES BEAUX-ARTS DE LILLE,** Museum of Fine Arts, Place de la
Republique, 59000. Tel 20-57-01-84. *Chief Cur* Arnauld Brejon de Lavergnee
Collections: Western European paintings from 15th - 20th centuries; collection of
ceramics, objects of art and sculptures

LYON

M **MUSEE DES BEAUX-ARTS,** Museum of Fine Arts, Plais Saint Pierre, 20 Place
des Terreaux, 69001. Tel 78-28-07-66. *Chief Cur* Philippe Durey
Collections: Ancient, Medieval and Modern sculpture; Egyptian, Greek and
Roman antiquities; French art since the Middle Ages; French, Hispano-Moorish,
Italian and Oriental ceramics; Gothic and Renaissance art; Islamic art; modern
art and murals by Purvis de Chavannes; painting of the French, Flemish, Dutch,
Italian and Spanish Schools

M **MUSEE HISTORIQUE DES TISSUS, MUSEE LYONNAIS DES ARTS
DECORATIFS,** 30-34 rue de la Charite, 69002. Tel 78-37-15-05. *Cur* Pierre
Arizzoli Clementel
Collections: Re-created French 18th century salons with furniture, objets d'art &
decorative pieces; 15th & 16th century Italian majolicas; enamels, ivories &
tapestries of Middle Ages & Renaissance; European drawings from 16th to 19th
century

ORLEANS

M **MUSEE DES BEAUX-ARTS D'ORLEANS,** Museum of Fine Arts, Place
Sainte-Croix, 45000. Tel 38-53-39-22. *Cur* E Moynet
Collections: Dutch, French, Flemish, German, Italian and Spanish paintings and
drawings, primarily from 17th and 18th century; sculpture

PARIS

M **CENTRE NATIONAL D'ART ET DE CULTURE GEORGES POMPIDOU,**
Musee National d'Art Moderne, 31 rue Saint-Merri, 75191. Telex 21-2726; Tel
42-77-12-33. *Pres* Helene Ahrweiler; *Pres* Jean Maheu
Collections: Collections of twentieth century paintings, prints, drawings and
sculpture; art films and photographs

L **ECOLE NATIONALE SUPERIEURE DES BEAUX-ARTS,** La Bibliotheque,
17, quai Malaquais, 75006. Tel (1) 42-60-34-57. *Dir of School* Francois Wehrlin
120,000 vol library for school with 2000 students and 75 instructors

M **MUSEE CARNAVALET,** 23 rue de Sevigne, 75003. Tel (1) 42-72-21-13. *Chief
Cur* Bernard De Montgolfier
Collections: History and archaeology of Paris; prints and drawings

M **MUSEE COGNACQ-JAY,** Cognacq-Jay Museum, 8 rue Elzevir, 75003. Tel 40-
27-07-21. *Cur* Pascal de la Vaissiere
Collections: 18th century works of art; English and French furniture, pastels,
paintings, porcelain, sculpture

M **MUSEE D'ART MODERNE DE LA VILLE DE PARIS,** 11 ave du President
Wilson, Post 9 Rue Gaston de St Paul, 75016. Tel 47-23-61-27. *Cur* Suzanne
Page
Collections: Modern painting and sculpture

M **MUSEE DES THERMES ET DE L'HOTEL DE CLUNY,** 6 Place Paul
Painleve, 75005. Tel 43-25-62-00. *Cur* F Joubert
Collections: Enamels, furniture, ivories, sculptures and tapestries of the Middle
Ages

M **MUSEE DU LOUVRE,** Louvre Museum, Palais du Louvre, 34 quai du Louvrel,
75001. Telex 21-4670; Tel 40-20-50-50. *Dir* Michel Laclotte
Collections: Islamic art; The Edmond de Rothschild Collection; Oriental, Greek,
Roman and Egyptian antiquities; decorative arts, drawings, paintings; Medieval,
Renaissance and modern sculpture

M **Musee du Jeu de Paume,** Place de la Concorde, 75001. Tel 42-60-12-07. *Chief
Cur* Michel Laclotte
Collections: Impressionists

M **MUSEE DU PETIT PALAIS,** Municipal Museum, Ave Winston Churchill,
75008. Tel 42-65-12-73. *Cur* Therese Burollet
Collections: Egyptian, Etruscan and Greek antiquities; paintings, sculpture and
other works of art to 19th century

M **MUSEE GUIMET,** 6 place d'Iena, 19 Ave d'Iena, 75116. Tel 47-23-61-65. *Chief Cur* Jean-Francois Jarrige
Maintains library with 100,000 volumes
Collections: Art, archaeology, religions, history of India, Afghanistan, Central Asia, China, Korea, Japan, Khmer, Tibet, Thailand and Indonesia

M **MUSEE MARMOTTAN,** 2 rue Louis Boilly, 75016. Tel 42-24-07-02. *Cur* Arnaud D'Hauterives
Collections: Collection of Primitives, Renaissance, Empire and Impressionist works; medieval miniatures in Wildenstein collection

M **MUSEE NATIONAL DES MONUMENTS FRANCAIS,** Palais de Chaillot, Place du Trocadero, 75116. Tel 47-27-35-74. *Cur* Philippe Chapu
Library with 10,000 works on art history
Collections: Full scale casts of the principal French monuments and sculpture from the beginning of Christianity to the 19th century; full scale reproductions of Medieval murals

M **UNION DES ARTS DECORATIFS,** Central Union of Decorative Arts, 107 rue de Rivoli, 75001. Tel 42-60-32-14. *Pres* Atoine Riboud; *Dir-Gen* Thierry Bondoux
Collections: Housed in four museums: Musee des Arts Decoratifs - decorative arts collection from Middle Ages to present; Western & Oriental Art; includes national arts information & documentation center; library with 100,000 vols; Musee Nissim de Camondo - unique 18th century objects bequeathed by Count Moise de Camondo; Musee de la Publicite - advertising museum with 2 galleries & advertising film library; Musee des Arts de la Mode - costumes & textiles

RENNES

M **MUSEE DES BEAUX-ARTS ET D'ARCHEOLOGIE,** 20, quai Emile Zola, 35000. Tel 99-28-55-85. *Cur* Jean Aubert
Collections: Egyptian, Greek and Roman archeology; drawings, paintings and sculptures from 15th - 20th centuries

STRASBOURG

M **MUSEE DES BEAUX-ARTS,** Museum of Fine Arts, Chateau des Rohan, 2 Place du Chateau, 67000. Tel 88-32-48-95. *Cur* Jean-Louis Faure
Collections: Old Masters; 17th to 19th century French schools; Italian schools

TOULOUSE

M **MUSEE DES AUGUSTINS,** 21 rue de Metz, 31000. Tel 61-22-21-82. *Cur* Denis Milhau
Collections: Medieval sculptures and paintings housed in former Augustine Convent

TOURS

M **MUSEE DES BEAUX-ARTS,** Museum of Fine Arts, 18 Place Francois Sicard, 37000. Tel 47-05-68-73. *Cur* Jacques Nicourt
Collections: Ancient and Modern Tapestries; Furniture; French School of 18th Century, including Boucher and Lancret; Italian Paintings of 13th to 16th Century, including Mantegna and primitives; 17th Century Paintings, including Rembrandt and Rubens; 19th Century Paintings, including Degas, Delacroix and Monet; Sculptures: Bourdelle, Houdon, Lemoyne

VERSAILLES

M **MUSEE NATIONAL DU CHATEAU DE VERSAILLES,** National Museum of the Chateau of Versailles, Chateau de Versailles, 78000. Tel 30-84-74-00. *Chief Cur* Jean-Pierre Babelon
Collections: Furniture from 17th to 19th centuries; painting and sculpture from 16th to 20th centuries

GERMANY

AACHEN

M **SUERMONDT-LUDWIG-MUSEUM,** Wilhelmstrasse 18, 5100. Telex 2-9166; Tel (0241) 432-4000. *Dir* Open
Collections: Paintings from the Middle Ages to the Baroque; portraits from Middle Ages to present; sculpture from the Middle Ages; graphic art (ceramics, textiles)

BERLIN

M **BRUCKE MUSEUM,** Bussardsteig 9, 1000. Tel 831-20-29. *Dir* Dr Magdalena Moeller
Collections: German expressionism, paintings, sculptures & graphic art of the Brucke group

M **STAATLICHE MUSEEN PREUSSISCHER KULTURBESITZ,** State Museums, Foundation for Prussian Cultural Treasures, Stauffenbergstrasse 41, 1000. Tel 220-03-81. *Gen Dir* Dr Wolf-Dieter Dube
Collections: Supervises 13 museums and departments, in addition to an art library and a museum library
—**Skulpturengalerie, Dept of Sculpture,** Tel 8301. *Dir* Dr Wolf-Dieter Dube

—**Kupferstichkabinett, Dept of Prints & Drawings,** Arnimallee 23-27, 1000. Tel 8301-228. *Dir* Dr Alexander Duckers
Collections: Drawings, prints and illustrated books of all epochs of European art
—**Museum fur Volkerkunde, Ethnographical Museum,** Arminallee 27, 1000. Tel 8301-226. *Dir* Dr Klaus Helfrich
Collections: Items of different cultures: Africa, East Asia (China, Tibet), Europe and North America
—**Museum fur Indische Kunst, Museum of Indian Art,** Takustrasse 40, 1000. Tel 8301-361. *Dir* Dr Marianne Yaldiz
Collections: Indian Art
—**Museum fur Ostasiatische Kunst, Museum of Far Eastern Art,** Takustrasse 40, 1000. Tel 8301-381. *Dir* Dr Willibald Veit
Collections: Paintings and ceramics of China and Japan
—**Museum fur Islamische Kunst, Museum of Islamic Art,** Takustrasse 40, 1000. Tel 8301-392. *Dir* Dr Michael Meinecke
—**Museum fur Deutsche Volkskunde, Museum of German Ethnology,** Im Winkel 6/8. Tel 83901-01. *Dir* Dr Theodor Kohlmann
Collections: Folklore objects from German speaking population in Europe
—**Agyptisches Museum, Egyptian Museum,** Schlosstrasse 70, 1000. Tel 32091-261. *Dir* Dr Dietrich Wildung
—**Antikenmuseum, Greek & Roman Antiquities,** Schlosstrasse 1. Tel 32091-216. *Dir* Dr Wolf-Dieter Heilmeyer
Collections: Greek & Roman antiquities
—**Gemaldegalerie, Picture Gallery,** Arnimallee 23-27, 1000. Tel 8301-217. *Dir* Dr Henning Bock
—**Kunstgewerbemuseum, Museum of Arts & Crafts,** Tiergartenstrasse 6, 1000. Tel 266-29-02. *Dir* Dr Barbara Mundt
Collections: Arts & Crafts
—**Museum fur Vor- und Fruhgeschichte, Museum of Pre- & Proto-History,** Schloss Charlottenburg, 1000. Tel 32091-233. *Dir* Dr Wilfried Menghin
—**Nationalgalerie, National Gallery,** Potsdamerstrasse 50, 1000. Tel 266-26-62. *Dir* Dr Dieter Honisch
Collections: 19th & 20th century works

M **STAATLICHE MUSEEN ZU BERLIN,** Bodestrasse 1-3, 1020. Tel 220-03-81. *Gen Dir* Dr G Schade
Collections: Consists of 15 museums & collections, including Nationalgalerie-paintings & sculptures from end of 18th century to present; Ostasiatische Sammlung - art of East Asia; Skulpturensammlung - sculpture

BIELEFELD

M **KUNSTHALLE BIELEFELD,** Artur-Ladebeck-Strasse 5, 4800. Tel 51-24-79. *Dir* Dr Ulrich Weisner
Collections: 20th century art

BONN

M **RHEINISCHES LANDESMUSEUM BONN,** Rhineland Museum in Bonn, Colmantstrasse 14-16, 5300. Tel 72941. *Dir* Open
Collections: Rhenish sculpture, painting & applied arts from the Middle Ages up to the present; Frankish & Roman antiquities of Rhineland

M **STADTISCHES KUNSTMUSEUM BONN,** Art Museum of the City of Bonn, Rathausgasse 7, 5300. Tel (0228) 773686. *Dir* Dr Katharina Schmidt
Collections: Art of the 20th century, especially August Macke and the Rhenish expressionists; German Art since 1945; contemporary international graphic arts

BREMEN

M **KUNSTHALLE BREMEN,** Bremen Art Gallery, Am Wall 207, 2800. Tel 0421-32-47-85. *Dir* Dr Siegfried Salzmann
Collections: Japanese drawings and prints; European paintings, Middle Ages to modern, especially French and German Art of the 19th century; 17th - 20th century sculpture; illustrated books

BRUNSWICK

M **HERZOG ANTON ULRICH-MUSEUM,** Museumsstrasse 1, 3300. Tel (0531) 4842400. *Dir* Dr J Luckhardt
Library with 40,000 vols
Collections: European Renaissance and Baroque decorative art, including bronzes, clocks, French 16th century enamels, furniture, glass, ivory and wood carvings, laces; Medieval art; prints and drawings from the 15th century to present

COLOGNE

M **MUSEEN DER STADT KOLN,** Cologne City Museums, Roncalliplatz 4, 5000. Tel 221-2301. *Dir* Dr Hugo Borger
M **Kunstgewerbemuseum der Stadt Koln,** Eigelsteintorburg, 5000. Tel 0221-22138-60. *Dir* Prof Brigitte Klesse
Collections: Handicrafts
M **Wallraf-Richartz-Museum,** Bischofsgartenstrasse 1, 5000. Tel 221-23-72.
Collections: Painting from 13th century to 1900; 19th century sculpture
M **Romisch-Germanisches Museum,** Roncalliplatz 4, 5000. Tel 221-44-38. *Dir* Dr Hansgerd Hellenkemper; *Dir* Prof Dr Hugo Borger
Collections: Early and pre-historic discoveries; gold ornaments; glass and industrial arts
L **Romisch-Germanisches Museum Bibliothek,** Roncalliplatz 4
Library Holdings: Vols 11,000
M **Rautenstrauch-Joest-Museum,** Ubierring 45, 5000. Tel 31-10-65. *Dir* Dr Gisela Volger
Collections: Ethnological museum; folk culture
L **Rautenstrauch-Joest-Museum Bibliothek,** Ubierring 45
Library Holdings: Vols 30,000

M **Kolnisches Stadtmuseum,** Zeughausstrasse 1-3, 5000. Tel 221-23-52. *Dir* Dr Werner Schafke
Collections: Graphic Arts of Cologne and the Rhineland; photograph collection of the Rhineland; industrial arts of Cologne; religious and rural art and culture

M **Museum fur Ostasiatische Kunst,** Universitatstrasse 100, 5000. Tel 405-038. *Dir* Open
Collections: Art of China, Korea and Japan

M **Schnutgen-Museum,** Cacilienstrasse 29, 5000. Tel 0221-221-23-10. *Dir* Open
Collections: Art of the early Middle Ages to Baroque

M **Josef-Haubrich-Kunsthalle,** Josef-Haubrich-Hof, 5000. Tel 221-23-35. *Dir* Klaus Flemming

M **Museum Ludwig,** Bischofsgartenstrass 1, 5000. Tel 221-2370. *Dir* Dr Siegfried Gohr
Collections: Painting & sculpture from 1900 to present

DRESDEN

M **STAATLICHE KUNSTSAMMLUNGEN DRESDEN,** Postfach 450, Georg-Treu-Platz 1, Albertinum, 8012. Tel 4953056. *Gen Dir* Dr Werner Schmidt
Collections: Consists of 12 galleries & collections

M **Gemaldegalerie Alte Meister,** Sophienstrasse, 8010. Tel 4840. *Dir* Dr Harald Marx

M **Gemaldegalerie Neue Meister,** Georg-Treu-Platz 1, Albertinum, 8010. Tel 4953056. *Dir* Dr Horst Zimmerman

M **Skulpturensammlung,** Georg-Treu-Platz 1, Albertinum, 8010. Tel 953056. *Dir* Martin Raumschussel

M **Historisches Museum,** Sophienstrasse, 8010. Tel 4840. *Dir* Dr Dieter Schaal

DUSSELDORF

L **KUNSTAKADEMIE DUSSELDORF, HOCHSCHULE FUR BILDENDE KUNSTE - BIBLIOTHEK,** State Academy of Art - Library, Eiskellerstrasse 1, 4000. Tel (0211) 329334. *Librn* Helmut Kleinenbroich
Library of 90,000 vols, serves 550 students & 50 teachers

M **KUNSTMUSEUM DUSSELDORF,** Ehrenhof 5, 4000. Tel (0211) 899-2460. *Dir* Dr Hans Albert Peters
Collections: Collections of European & applied art from middle ages to 1800, prints & drawings, & contemporary art at 5 museum locations

M **STADTISCHE KUNSTHALLE DUSSELDORF,** Grabbeplatz 4, Postfach 1120, 4000. Tel (0211) 899-6241. *Dir* Jurgen Harten
Exhibitions: Contemporary art exhibitions

FRANKFURT

M **LIEBIEGHAUS, MUSEUM ALTER PLASTIK,** Museum of Sculpture, Schaumainkai 71, 6000. Tel 2123-38617. *Dir* Dr Herbert Beck
Collections: Sculpture of Egypt, Greece, Rome Medieval period, East Asia, Rococo style and baroque period

M **MUSEUM FUR KUNSTHANDWERK,** Museum of Arts and Crafts, Schaumainkai 17, 6000. Tel (069) 2123-40-37. *Dir* Dr Arnulf Herbst
Collections: European applied art, from Gothic to art nouveau; Far Eastern and Islamic works of art

M **STADELSCHES KUNSTINSTITUT UND STADTISCHE GALERIE,** Durerstrasse 2, 6000. Tel (069) 605098-0. *Dir* Dr Klaus Gallwitz
Library with 50,000 vols
Collections: Paintings, sculptures, prints, drawings

HAMBURG

M **HAMBURGER KUNSTHALLE,** Hamburg Art Museum, Glockengiesserwall, 2000. Tel (040) 24862612. *Dir* Dr Werner Hoffman
Library with 110,000 vols
Collections: Ancient coins; medals, drawings, engravings and masterworks of painting from 14th century to present; sculpture from 19th and 20th centuries

M **MUSEUM FUR KUNST UND GEWERBE HAMBURG,** Steintorplatz 1, 2000. Tel (040) 2486-2631. *Dir* Dr Wilhelm Hornbostel
Collections: European art & sculpture from Middle Ages to present; Near & Far East art; European popular art

HANOVER

M **KESTNER-MUSEUM,** Trammplatz 3, 3000. Tel (0511) 1682120. *Dir* Dr Ulrich Gehrig; *Cur* Helga Hilschenz-Mlynek
Collections: Ancient, medieval and modern coins and medals; Egyptian, Greek, Etruscan and Roman art objects and medieval art; handicrafts, illuminated manuscripts and incunabula of the 15th - 20th centuries

KARLSHRUHE

M **STAATLICHE KUNSTHALLE,** State Art Gallery, Hans-Thoma-Strasse 2-6, 7500. Tel 135-33-55. *Dir* Dr Horst Vey
Collections: 15th - 20th century German painting and graphics; 16th - 20th century Dutch, Flemish and French paintings and graphics; 50,000 prints and drawings

KARLSRUHE

M **BADISCHES LANDESMUSEUM,** Schlossplatz 1, 7500. Tel 135-6514. *Dir* Dr Volker Himmelein
Maintains library with 47,000 vols
Collections: Antiquities of Egypt, Greece & Rome; art from middle ages to present; medieval, Renaissance & baroque sculpture; coins, weapons & folklore

KASSEL

M **STAATLICHE KUNSTSAMMLUNGEN KASSEL,** State Art Collections, Schloss Wilhelmshohe, 3500. Tel (0561) 36011. *Dir* Dr Ulrich Schmidt
Library with 60,000 vols
Collections: Department of classical antiquities gallery of 15th - 18th century old master paintings, collection of drawings and engravings

KLEVE

M **STADTISCHES MUSEUM HAUS KOEKKOEK,** Kavariner Strasse 33, 4190. Tel 84302. *Dir* Dr Guido De Werd
Collections: Painting & sculpture of the Lower Rhine from the 12th century to the present

MUNICH

M **BAYERISCHES NATIONALMUSEUM,** Bavarian National Museum, Prinzregentenstrasse 3, 8000. Tel (089) 21-68-1. *Gen Dir* Dr Johann Georg Prinz Von Hohenzollern
Library with 70,000 vols
Collections: European fine arts: decorative arts, paintings, folk art, sculpture

A **BAYERISCHE STAATSGEMALDESAMMLUNGEN,** Bavarian State Art Galleries, Barerstrasse 29, 8000. Tel (089) 238050. *Dir* Bruno Heimberg
Consists of 5 galleries
Collections: Flemish, Spanish, Italian, German and other European paintings and sculpture; 20th century sculpture and art

M **STAATLICHE GRAPHISCHE SAMMLUNG,** National Graphic Collection, Meiserstrasse 10, 8000. Tel (089) 5591490. *Dir* Dr Tilman Falk
Collections: French, 15th to 20th century German, Italian & Dutch prints & drawings

M **STAATLICHE MUNZSAMMLUNG,** State Coin Collection, Residenzstrasse 1, 8000. Tel (089) 227221. *Dir* Dr Bernhard Overbeck
Library has 14,000 volumes
Collections: Coins from different countries & centuries; medals; precious stones from antiquity, Middle Ages & Renaissance

M **STAATLICHE SAMMLUNG AEGYPTISCHER KUNST,** State Collection of Egyptian Art, Hofgartenstrasse 1, Meiserstrasse 10, 8000. Tel (089) 5591486. *Dir* Dr Sylvia Schoske

M **STADTISCHE GALERIE IM LENBACHHAUS,** Luisenstrasse 33, 8000. Tel (089) 521041. *Dir* Dr Armin Zweite
Collections: Art Nouveau; The Blue Rider and Kandinsky and Klee; paintings by Munich artists

NUREMBERG

M **GERMANISCHES NATIONALMUSEUM,** Kornmarkt 1, 8500. Tel (0911) 1331-0. *Chief Dir* Dr Gerhard Bott
Collections: Ancient historical objects, archives, furniture, folk art, musical instruments, paintings, sculpture, textiles, toys, weapons

RECKLINGHAUSEN

M **STADISCHE KUNSTHALLE RECKLINGHAUSEN,** Recklinghausen City Art Gallery, Perdekamp - Str 25-27, 4350. Tel (02361) 501931. *Dir* Dr Anneliese Schroder
Collections: Paintings, sculpture, drawings & prints by contemporary artists

STUTTGART

M **STAATSGALERIE STUTTGART,** Konrad-Adenauer-Strasse 30-32, 7000. Tel (0711) 212-5050. *Dir* Peter Beye
Collections: European Art 14th - 20th Century; international art of the 20th century; graphic art

WITTEN

M **MARKISCHES MUSEUM DER STADT WITTEN,** Husemannstrasse 12, 5810. Tel 1560/1569. *Dir* Dr Wolfgang Zemter
Collections: 20th century German paintings, drawings & graphics

GHANA

ACCRA

M **GHANA NATIONAL MUSEUM,** Barnes Rd, PO Box 3343. Tel 21633. *Actg Dir* E A Asante
Collections: Art, archeological and ethnological collections for Ghana and West Africa

GREECE

ATHENS

M **BENAKI MUSEUM,** Odos Koumbari 1, 106 74. Tel 361-16-17. *Dir* Dr Angelos Delivorrias
Library, historical archives and photographic archives are maintained
Collections: Ancient Greek art, chiefly jewelry; Byzantine and post-Byzantine art, icons and crafts; collections of Islamic art and Chinese porcelain; Greek popular art and historical relics; textiles from Far East and Western Europe

M **BYZANTINE MUSEUM,** 22 Vasilissis Sophias Ave, 106 75. Tel 7211027. *Dir* Myrtali Acheimastou-Potamianou
Library and photo archives are maintained
Collections: Byzantine and Post-Byzantine icons, ceramics, marbles, metalwork; Christian and Byzantine sculpture and pottery; liturgical items; Greek manuscripts

M **NATIONAL ARCHAEOLOGICAL MUSEUM,** Odos Patisson 44, 10682. Tel 8217724. *Dir* Olga Tzahou-Alexandri
Collections: Original Greek sculptures; Roman period sculptures; Bronze Age relics; Mycenaean treasures; Greek vases, terracottas; jewels; Egyptian antiquities

M **NATIONAL ART GALLERY & ALEXANDER SOUTZOS MUSEUM,** 50 Vassileos Konstantinou Ave, 116 10. Tel 7211010. *Dir* Dr Dimitris Papastamos
Collections: Engravings; 14th - 20th century European painting; 17th - 20th century Greek engravings, paintings and sculpture; impressionist, post-impressionist and contemporary drawings

DELPHI

M **ARCHAEOLOGICAL MUSEUM,** 330 54. Tel (0265) 82313. *Dir* Evangelos Pentazos
Collections: Delphic archaeology

THESSALONIKI

M **ARCHAEOLOGICAL MUSEUM OF THESSALONIKI,** YMCA Sq, 546 21. Tel 830538. *Dir* J Vokotopoulou
Collections: Macedonian archaeology, mainly from Thessaloniki, Chalkidiki and Kilkis

GUATEMALA

GUATEMALA CITY

M **MUSEO NACIONAL DE ARTE MODERNO,** Edificio No 6, Finca La Aurora, Zona 13. Tel 310-403. *Dir* J Oscar Barrientos
Collections: Paintings, sculpture, engravings, drawings

HAITI

PORT AU PRINCE

M **CENTRE D'ART,** 58 rue Roy. Tel 2-2018. *Dir* Francine Murat
Collections: Haitian art

HONDURAS

COMAYAGUA

M **MUSEO ARQUEOLOGIA Y HISTORICO DE COMAYAGUA,** Ciudad de Comayagua. *Dir* Hector Valladares
Collections: Archaelogy dating back to 1000 BC; colonial collections

HONG KONG

EDINBURGH PLACE

M **HONG KONG MUSEUM OF ART,** 7 Edinburgh Place, City Hall, High Block. Tel 224-127. *Cur* Laurence Tam
Collections: Chinese antiquities; Chinese paintings & calligraphy with a specialization of Cantonese artists; historical collection of paintings, prints & drawings of Hong Kong, Macau & China; local & contemporary art

HUNGARY

BUDAPEST

M **MAGYAR NEMZETI GALERIA,** Hungarian National Gallery, Szent Gzorgz Ter 2, Budavari Palota PF 31, 1250. Tel 1757-533. *Dir* Dr Lorand Bereczky
Collections: Ancient and Modern Hungarian paintings and sculpture; medal cabinet; panel paintings

M **SZEPMUVESZETI MUZEUM,** Museum of Fine Arts, Dozsa Gyorgy ut 41, 1146. Tel 1429-759. *Dir* Dr Miklos Mojzer
Collections: Egyptian, Greek and Roman antiquities; paintings and sculpture

ESZTERGOM

M **KERESZTENY MUZEUM,** Christian Museum, Berenyi ZS U2, PF 25, 2501. Tel (36-33) 13-880. *Pres* Pal Csefalvay
Publications: Hungarian, Austrian, Dutch, French, German and Italian medieval panels, pictures, gold & silver artwork, miniatures, porcelain, statues, and tapestries

KECSKEMET

M **MAGYAR NAIV MUVESZEK MUZEUMA,** Museum of Hungarian Native Art, Gaspar A U 11, 6000. Tel 24767.
Collections: Works of Hungarian primitive painters and sculptors

PECS

M **JANUS PANNONIUS MUZEUM,** Kulich Gyula U 5, PF 158, 7601. Tel (72) 10-172. *Dir* Jeno Ujvari
Library with 20,000 vols
Collections: Modern Hungarian art; archaeology, ethnology, local history

SZENTENDRE

M **FERENCZY MUZEUM,** Foter 6, PF 49, 2001. Tel (26) 10-244. *Dir* Jozsef Bihari
Museum maintains library with 22,000 vols
Collections: Paintings, sculptures, drawings; archaeological, ethnographic & local history collections; Gobelin tapestries

ICELAND

REYKJAVIK

M **LISTASAFN EINARS JONSSONAR,** National Einar Jonsson Art Gallery, PO Box 1051. Tel 91-13797. *Dir* Olafur Kvaran
Collections: Sculpture and paintings by Einar Jonsson

M **THJODMINJASAFN,** National Museum, Sudurgata 41, PO Box 1489, 121. Tel 1-28888. *Dir* Thor Magnusson
Collections: Archaeological and ethnological artifacts, Icelandic antiquities, portraits, folk art

INDIA

BARODA

M **BARODA MUSEUM AND PICTURE GALLERY,** Sayaji Park, Gujarat 390005. Tel 64605. *Dir* S K Bhowmik
Library with 19,000 vols
Collections: Indian archeology & art, numismatic collections; Asiatic & Egyptian Collections; Greek, Roman, European civilizations & art; European paintings

BOMBAY

M **HERAS INSTITUTE OF INDIAN HISTORY AND CULTURE,** St Xavier College, Mahapalika Marg, 400001. Tel 262-0661. *Dir* Rev J V Velinkar
Collections: Indian stone sculptures, woodwork, paintings; old rare maps & books

M **PRINCE OF WALES MUSEUM OF WESTERN INDIA,** 159-61 Mahatma Gandhi Rd, Fort, 400023. Tel 244484. *Dir* S V Gorakshkar
Library with 11,000 vols
Collections: Paintings; archaeology; natural history

CALCUTTA

M **INDIAN MUSEUM,** 27 Jawaharlal Nehru Rd, 700016. Tel 29-5699. *Dir* R C Sharma
Collections: Bronzes and bronze figures, ceramic, coins, copper and stone implements of prehistoric and proto-historic origin; geology, botany and zoology collections

JUNAGADH

M **JUNAGADH MUSEUM,** Sakkar Bag. Tel 745. *Dir* P V Dholakia
Collections: Archaeology, miniature paintings, manuscripts, sculptures, decorative & applied arts

MADRAS

M **GOVERNMENT MUSEUM & NATIONAL ART GALLERY,** Pantheon Rd, Egmore, 600008. Tel 89638. *Dir* N Harinarayana
Collections: Ancient & modern Indian art; Buddhist sculptures; bronzes; archaeology; natural sciences collection

NEW DELHI

M **CRAFTS MUSEUM,** All India Handicrafts Board, Bhairon Rd, Pragati Maidan, 110001. Tel 3317641. *Dir* Dr Jyotindra Jain
Collections: Indian traditional crafts, folk & tribal arts; folk crafts

M **NATIONAL GALLERY OF MODERN ART,** Jaipur House India Gate, Sher Shah Rd, 110003. Tel 382835. *Dir* Dr Anis Farooqi
Collections: Indian contemporary paintings, sculptures, graphics, drawings, architecture, industrial design, prints and minor arts

M **NATIONAL MUSEUM OF INDIA,** Janpath, 110011. Tel 3018159. *Dir-Gen* Dr L P Sihare
Library with 30,000 vols
Collections: Arabic, Indian, Persian, Sanskrit language manuscripts; Central Asian antiquities and murals; decorative arts

M **RABINDRA BHAVAN ART GALLERY,** Lalit Kala Akademi (National Academy of Art), 35 Ferozeshah Rd. Tel 38-72-41. *Chmn* Anand Dev
Collections: Permanent collection of graphics, paintings and sculpture

IRAN

ISFAHAN

M **ARMENIAN ALL SAVIOUR'S CATHEDRAL MUSEUM,** Julfa, PB 81735-115. Tel 43471. *Dir* Levon Minassian
Collections: 450 paintings, miniatures & tomb portraits; 700 ancient books

TEHERAN

M **TEHERAN MUSEUM OF MODERN ART,** Karegar Ave, Laleh Park, PO Box 41-3669. *Dir* Kamran Diba
Museum maintains library
Collections: Modern Western art works

IRAQ

BABYLON

M **BABYLON MUSEUM**
Collections: Models, pictures and paintings of the remains at Babylon

BAGHDAD

M **IRAQI MUSEUM,** Salhiya Quarter. Tel 36121-5. *Dir* Abdul Kadir Al-Tikriti
Collections: Antiquities from the Stone Age to the 17th century, including Islamic objects

IRELAND

DUBLIN

M **HUGH LANE MUNICIPAL GALLERY OF MODERN ART,** Charlemont House, Parnell Square, 1. Tel 74-19-03. *Dir* Barbara Dawson
Collections: Works of Irish, English and European artists; sculptures; Sir Hugh Lane collection

M **NATIONAL GALLERY OF IRELAND,** Merrion Square W, 2. Tel 615133. *Dir* Raymond Keaveney
Collections: American, British, Dutch, Flemish, French, German, Greek, Italian, Irish, Russian, and Spanish masters since 1250; oil paintings, sculptures, drawings, watercolors

M **NATIONAL MUSEUM OF IRELAND,** Kildare St, 2. Tel 765521. *Dir* Patrick F Wallace
Collections: Art and Industrial Division; Irish Antiquities Division; Irish Folklife Division; Natural History Division

ISRAEL

HAIFA

M **HAIFA MUSEUM OF MODERN ART,** 26 Shabbetai Levi St. Tel (04) 523255. *Cur* Joanna Nicolau
Library with 10,000 vols
Collections: Israeli paintings, sculpture, drawings and prints; modern American, French, German and English paintings; art posters

M **MUSEUM OF ANCIENT ART,** 26 Shabbetai Levi St. Tel (972-4) 523255. *Cur* Zemer Avshalom
Collections: Ancient Haifa; ancient coins from Israel; antiquities from the excavations of Shikmona from the Bronze Age to Byzantine period; Biblical, Cypriot and Greek pottery and sculpture; Near Eastern figurines

M **MUSEUM OF JAPANESE ART,** 89, Hanassi Ave, 34-642. Tel (04) 383554. *Dir* Eli Lancman
Collections: Ceramics, folk art, drawings, metalwork, netsuke, prints, paintings

JERUSALEM

M **ALEXANDER MONASTERY MUSEUM,** Russian Orthodox Mission, Muristan, 91000. Tel 2845-80.
Collections: Roman Antiquities

M **BEIT HA'OMANIM,** Jerusalem Artists' House, 12 Shmuel Hanagid St. Tel (972-2) 252-636.
Collections: Artwork of Jerusalem citizens

M **ISRAEL MUSEUM,** PO Box 1299, 91012. Tel (972-2) 698211. *Dir* Dr Martin Weyl
Collections: Consists of 6 collections
M **Bezalel National Art Museum,** *Chief Cur* Yigal Zalmona
Lending library of reproductions and slides
Collections: Jewish ceremonial art, ethnological objects, paintings, sculptures, drawings and prints
M **Billy Rose Art Garden,** *Cur* Dr Martin Weyl
Collections: Modern European, American and Israeli sculpture and Reuven Lipchitz collection of Jacques Lipchitz's bronze sketches
M **Bronfman Biblical and Archaeological Museum,** *Chief Cur* Yael Israeli
Collections: Collection of archaeology of Israel from earliest times to Islamic and Crusader periods; material found in excavations since 1948
M **Rockefeller Museum,** *Cur* Tally Ornan
L **Shrine of the Book,** *Cur* Magen Broshi
D Samuel and Jeanne H Gottesman Center for Biblical MSS
Collections: Houses the Dead Sea Scrolls (discovered in Qumran) and manuscripts from adjacent sites on western shore of the Dead Sea, Masada and Nahal Hever
L **Library,** *Librn* Elisheva Rechtman
Library Holdings: Vols 65,000; Other — Exhibition catalogs

TEL AVIV

M ERETZ-ISRAEL, 2 Chaim Levanon St, PO Box 17068, 61 170. Tel (972-3) 415244. *General Mgr* Shild Sasson
Collections: Consists of 15 museums and collections; ancient glass; historical documents of Tel Aviv-Yafo; Jewish ritual and secular art objects; ceramics, coins, prehistoric finds, scientific and technical apparatus, traditional work tools and methods
L Central Library, Ramat Aviv, PO Box 17068
Library Holdings: Vols 40,000
M Alphabet Museum, *Dir* Mrs Z Suchowolski
Collections: Exhibit on the development of the alphabets
M Ceramics Museum, Tel 03-41-52-44. *Cur* Mrs Yael Olenik
Collections: Pottery throughout history
M Museum of Antiquities of Tel-Aviv-Yafo, 10 Mifratz Shlomo St, Jaffa, 680 38. *Dir* Dr Ivan Ordentlich
Collections: Archaeological findings from Tel Aviv-Yafo area, covering Neolithic to Byzantine Periods
M Museum of Ethnography and Folklore, *Dir* D Davidowitz
Collections: Jewish popular art and costumes

M TEL AVIV MUSEUM OF ART, 27 Shaul Hamelech Blvd, POB 33288, 61332. Tel (972-3) 257361. *Dir* Dr Michael Levin
Library with 39,000 vols
Collections: Works from 17th century to present; Israeli art

ITALY

BARI

M PINACOTECA PROVINCIALE, Via Spalato 19, 70121. Tel (080) 392-421. *Dir* Dr Clara Gelao
Collections: Apulian, Venetian and Neapolitan paintings and sculpture from 11th - 19th century

BERGAMO

M GALLERIA DELL' ACCADEMIA CARRARA, Piazza Giacomo Carrara 82/A, 24100. Tel (035) 399425. *Dir* Dr F Rossi
Collections: Paintings by: Bellini, Raffaello, Pisanello, Mantegna, Botticelli, Beato Angelico, Previtali, Tiepolo, Durer, Brueghel, Van Dyck

BOLOGNA

M PINACOTECA NAZIONALE, Via Belle Arti 56, 40100. Tel (051) 243-249. *Dir* Prof Andrea Emiliani
Collections: 14th - 18th century Bolognese paintings; German and Italian engravings

FLORENCE

M GALLERIA D'ARTE MODERNA DI PALAZZO PITTI, Palazzo Pitti, Piazza Pitti 1, 50125. Tel 287096. *Dir* Ettore Spalletti
Collections: Paintings and sculptures of the 19th and 20th centuries

M GALLERIA DEGLI UFFIZI, Uffizi Gallery, Piazzale degli Uffizi, 50122. Tel (055) 218341. *Dir* Annamaria Petrioli Tofani
Collections: Florentine Renaissance painting

M GALLERIA DELL' ACCADEMIA, Via Ricasoli 60, 50122. Tel (055) 214375. *Dir* Giorgio Bonsanti
Collections: Michelangelo's statues in Florence and works of art of 13th -19th century masters, mostly Tuscan

M GALLERIA PALATINA, Palazzo Pitti, Piazza Pitti, 50100. Tel (055) 216673. *Dir* Dr Marco Chiarini
Collections: Paintings from 16th and 17th centuries

M MUSEO DEGLI ARGENTI, Palazzo Pitti, 50100. Tel 2125-57. *Dir* Dr Kirsten Piacenti
Collections: Summer state apartments of the Medici Grand Dukes; gold, silver, enamel, objets d'art, hardstones, ivory, amber, cameos and jewels, principally from the 15th to the 18th centuries; period costumes exhibited in Galleria del Costume on premises

M MUSEO DELLA CASA BUONARROTI, Via Ghibellina 70, 50100. Tel (055) 241-752. *Dir* Pina Ragionieri
Collections: Works by Michelangelo & others; items from the Buonarroti family collections

M MUSEO DI SAN MARCO O DELL' ANGELICO, Piazza San Marco 1, 50100. Tel (055) 218341. *Dir* Antonio Paolucci
Collections: Fra Angelico frescoes, paintings and panels

GENOA

M GALLERIA DI PALAZZO BIANCO, White Palace Gallery, Via Garibaldi 11, 16124. Tel 29-18-03.
This museum is under the control of Servizio Beni Culturali
Collections: Paintings by Genoese and Flemish Masters and other schools; sculpture and tapestries

LUCCA

M MUSEO DI VILLA GUINIGI, Villa Guinigi, Via della Quarquonia, 55100. Tel (0583) 46033. *Dir* Maria Teresa Filieri
Collections: Roman and late Roman sculptures and mosaics; Romanesque, Gothic, Renaissance and Neoclassical sculpture; paintings from 12th to 18th century

M MUSEO E PINACOTECA NAZIONALE DI PALAZZO MANSI, National Museum and Picture Gallery of the Palazzo Mansi, Via Galli Tassi 43, 55100. Tel (0583) 55570. *Dir* Dr Maria Teresa Filieri
Collections: Works of Tuscan, Venetian, French and Flemish Schools; paintings by such masters as Titian and Tintoretto

MANTUA

M GALLERIA E MUSEO DI PALAZZO DUCALE, Gallery and Museum of the Palazzo Ducale, Piazza Sordello 39, 46100. Tel (0376) 369167. *Dir* Dr Aldo Cicinelli
Collections: Classical Antiquities and Sculpture; picture gallery

MILAN

M DIREZIONE CIVICHE RACCOLTE D'ARTE, Castello Sforzesco, 20121. Tel 021-6236-3943. *Dir* Dr Mercedes Garberi
Governs several museums and collections
M Civiche Raccolte di Arte Applicata, Castello Sforzesco, 21022. Tel 869-30-71. *Dir* Dr Claudio Salsi
Collections: Armor, bronzes, ceramics, coins, ironworks, ivories, porcelains, sculpture, textiles
M Raccolte delle Stampe Achille Bertarelli, Castello Sforzesco, 20121. Tel 869-30-71. *Dir* Dr Claudio Salsi
M Civiche Raccolte Archaeologiche e Numismatiche, Via B Luini 2, 20123. Tel 805-3972. *Dir* Dr Ermanno Arslan
Collections: Ancient Egyptian, antique and modern coins; Etruscan, Greek and Roman Collections
M Museo d'Arte Antica, Castello Sforzesco, 20121. *Dir* Dr Mercedes Garberi
Maintains library
Collections: Paintings, including works by Bellini, Guardi, Lippi, Lotto, Mantegna, Tiepolo, Tintoretto and others; sculpture from early Middle Ages to 17th century, including masterpieces like Michelangelo's Pieta-Rondanini; furniture; silver, bronzes, tapestries
M Galleria d'Arte Moderna, Villa Reale, Via Palestro 16, 20121. Tel 76-00-28-19. *Dir* Dr Mercedes Garberi
Collections: Painting and sculpture from Neo-Classical period to present day; includes the Grassi Collection and Museo Marino Marini (approx 200 sculptures, portraits, paintings, drawings and etchings by Marini)

M MUSEO POLDI PEZZOLI, Via A Manzoni 12, 20121. Tel (02) 796-334. *Dir* Dr Alessandra Mottola Molfino
Collections: Paintings from 14th - 18th centuries; armor, tapestries, rugs, jewelry, porcelain, glass, textiles, furniture, clocks and watches

M PINACOTECA AMBROSIANA, Piazza Pio XI, 2, 20123. Tel (02) 800146. *Dir* Dr Gianfranco Ravasi
Collections: Botticelli, Caravaggio, Luini, Raphael, Titian; drawings, miniatures, ceramics and enamels

M PINACOTECA DI BRERA, Via Brera 28, 20121. Tel 86463501. *Dir* Rosalba Tardito
Collections: Pictures of all schools, especially Lombard and Venetian; paintings by Mantegna, Bellini, Crivelli, Lotto, Titian, Veronese, Tintoretto, Tiepolo, Foppa, Bergognone, Luini, Piero della Francesca, Bramante, Raphael, Caravaggio, Rembrandt, Van Dyck, Rubens; also Italian 20th century works

MODENA

M GALLERIA, MUSEO E MEDAGLIERE ESTENSE, Este Gallery, Museum and Coin Collection, Palazzo dei Musei, Piazza S Agostino 109, 41100. Tel 22-21-45. *Dir* Jadranka Bentini
Collections: Bronzes, coins, drawings, medals, minor arts, paintings, prints and sculptures, most from the Este family

NAPLES

M MUSEO CIVICO GAETANO FILANGIERI, Via Duomo 288, 80100. Tel (081) 203175. *Dir* Francesco Acton di Leporano
Collections: Paintings, furniture, archives, photographs

M MUSEO E GALLERIE NAZIONALI DI CAPODIMONTE, Palazzodi Capodimonte, 80100. Tel (081) 7410801. *Dir* Dr Nicola Spinosa
Library with 50,000 vols
Collections: Paintings from 13th to 18th centuries; paintings and sculptures of 19th century; arms and armor; medals and bronzes of the Renaissance; porcelain

M **MUSEO NAZIONALE DI SAN MARTINO,** National Museum of San Martino, Largo San Martino 5, 80129. Tel 377005. *Dir* Dr T Fittipaldi
Collections: 16th to 18th century pictures and paintings; 13th - 19th century sculpture, majolicas and porcelains; section of modern prints, paintings and engravings; Neapolitan historical collection

PADUA

M **MUSEI CIVICI DI PADOVA,** Municipal Museum, Piazza Eremitani 8, 35138. Tel (049) 8750975. *Dir* Dr Gian Franco Martinoni
Collections: Archaeological Museum; Art Gallery - bronzes, ceramics, industrial arts, painting, sculpture; Bottacin Museum - Greco-Roman, Italian, Paduan, Venetian, Napoleonic coins and medals; Renaissance gallery

PARMA

M **GALLERIA NAZIONALE,** Palazzo della Pilotta 15, 43100. Tel (0521) 33309. *Dir* Lucia Fornari Schianchi
Collections: Paintings from 13th to 19th centuries, including works by Correggio, Parmigianino, Cima, El Greco, Piazzetta, Tiepolo, Holbein, Van Dyck, Mor, Nattier & several painters of the school of Parma; modern art

PERUGIA

M **GALLERIA NAZIONALE DELL'UMBRIA,** Umbrian National Gallery, Corso Vannucci, Palazzo dei Priori, 06100. Tel (075) 20316. *Dir* Vittoria Garibaldi
Collections: Jewels; paintings from the Umbrian School from the 13th - 18th centuries; 13th, 14th and 15th century sculpture

PISA

M **MUSEO NAZIONALE DI SAN MATTEO,** Convento di San Matteo, Lungarno Mediceo, 56100. Tel (050) 23750. *Dir* Dr Mariagiulia Burresi
Collections: Sculptures by the Pisanos and their school; important collection of the Pisan school of the 13th and 14th centuries, and paintings of the 15th, 16th, and 17th centuries; ceramics; important collection of coins and medals

ROME

M **GALLERIA BORGHESE,** Borghese Gallery, Villa Borghese, 00197. Tel 06-85-85-77. *Dir* Sara Staccioli
Collections: Baroque and Classical sculptures; paintings

M **GALLERIA DORIA PAMPHILJ,** Piazza del Collegio Romano l/a, 00186. Tel 679-43-65. *Dir* Dr Eduard A Safarik
Collections: Paintings by Caravaggio, Carracci, Correggio, Filippo Lippi, Lorrain, del Piombo, Titian, Velazquez

M **GALLERIA NAZIONALE DI ROMA,** National Gallery of Rome, Palazzo Barberini, Via Quattro Fontane 13, 00184. Tel (06) 4750184. *Dir* Dr Dante Bernini
Collections: Italian & European paintings from the 12th - 18th century; Baroque architecture

M **ISTITUTO NAZIONALE PER LA GRAFICA,** National Institute for Graphic Arts, Farnesina, Via Della Lungara, 230, 00165. Tel (06) 6540565. *Dir* Dr Michele Cordaro
Collections: Italian & foreign prints & drawings from the 14th century to the present

M **MUSEI CAPITOLINI,** Piazza del Campidoglio 1471, 00186. Tel (06) 67103067. *Dir* Carlo G Pietrangeli
Collections: Ancient sculptures

M **MUSEO NAZIONALE ROMANO,** National Museum of Rome, Piazza del Cinquecento 79, 00185. Tel (06) 483617. *Dir* Prof Adriano La Regina
Collections: Archaeological collection; Roman bronzes and sculpture; numismatics

SASSARI

M **MUSEO NAZIONALE G A SANNA,** G A Sanna National Museum, Via Roma 64, 07100. Tel 272-203. *Dir* Dr F Lo Schiavo
Collections: Archeological Collections; Picture Gallery with Medieval and Modern Art; Collection of Sardinian Ethnography

TURIN

M **ARMERIA REALE,** Royal Armory, Piazza Castello 191, 10122. Tel (011) 543889. *Dir* Paolo Venturoli
Collections: Archaeological Arms; Arms and Armours from 13th - 18th Century; Arms of the 19th and 20th Century; Oriental Arms; equestrian arms; engravings of Monaco de Baviera School

M **GALLERIA SABAUDA,** Via Accademia delle Scienze 6, 10123. Tel 54-74-40. *Dir* Giovanna Galante Garrone
Collections: Flemish Masters; French Masters; Italian Masters; Dutch & early Italian collections; Piedmontese Masters; furniture, sculpture, jewelry

M **MUSEO CIVICO DI TORINO,** Municipal Museum, Via Avellino 6, 10144. Tel 011-54-18-22. *Cur Ancient Art* Silvana Pettenati; *Cur Modern Art* Rosanna Maggio Serra
Collections: Antique and modern art; coins, paintings; sculpture

VATICAN CITY

M **MONUMENTI, MUSEI E GALLERIE PONTIFICIE,** Vatican Museums and Galleries, 00120. Tel (06) 6983333. *Dir General* Carlo Pietrangeli
Collections: Twelve Museum sections with Byzantine, medieval and modern art; Classical sculpture; liturgical art; minor arts
Publications: For all except Missionary Museum: Bollettino dei Monumenti, Musei, Gallerie Pontificie

M **Museo Pio Clementino,** *Cur* Paolo Liverani
Founded by Pope Clement XIV (1770-74), and enlarged by his successor, Pius VI; exhibits include the Apollo of Belvedere, the Apoxyomenos by Lysippus, the Laocoon Group, the Meleager of Skopas, the Apollo Sauroktonous by Praxiteles

M **Museo Sacro,** *Cur* Dr Giovanni Morello
Founded in 1756 by Pope Benedict XIV; administered by the Apostolic Vatican Library
Collections: Objects of liturgical art, historical relics and curios from the Lateran, objects of palaeolithic, medieval and Renaissance minor arts, paintings of the Roman era

M **Museo Profano,** *Cur* Dr Giovanni Morello
Founded in 1767 by Pope Clement XIII; administered by the Vatican Apostolic Library
Collections: Bronze sculpture and minor art of the classical era

M **Museo Chiaramonti e Braccio Nuovo,** *Cur* Paolo Liverani
Founded by Pope Pius VII at the beginning of the 19th century, to house the many new findings excavated in that period
Collections: Statues of the Nile, of Demosthenes and of the Augustus of Prima Porta

M **Museo Gregoriano Etrusco,** *Cur* Francesco Buranelli
Founded by Pope Gregory XVI in 1837
Collections: Objects from the Tomba Regolini Galassi of Cerveteri, the bronzes, terracottas & jewelry, & Greek vases from Etruscan tombs

M **Museo Gregoriano Egizio,** *Consultant* Prof Jean-Claude Grenier
Inaugurated by Pope Gregory XVI in 1839
Collections: Egyptian papyri, mummies, sarcophagi and statues, including statue of Queen Tuia (1300 BC)

M **Museo Gregoriano Profano,** *Cur* Paolo Liverani
Founded by Gregory XVI in 1844 and housed in the Lateran Palace, it was transferred to a new building in the Vatican and opened to the public in 1970
Collections: Roman sculptures from the Pontifical States; Portrait-statue of Sophocles, the Marsyas of the Myronian group of Athena and Marsyas, the Flavian reliefs from the Palace of the Apostolic Chancery

M **Museo Pio Cristiano,** *Cur* Open
Founded by Pius IX in 1854 and housed in the Lateran Palace; transferred to a new building in the Vatican and opened to the public in 1970
Collections: Sarcophagi; Latin and Greek inscriptions from Christian cemeteries and basilicas; the Good Shepherd

M **Museo Missionario Etnologico,** *Cur* Rev P J Penkowski
Founded by Pius XI in 1926 and housed in the Lateran Palace; transferred to a new building in the Vatican and opened to the public in 1973
Collections: Ethnographical collections from all over the world
Publications: Annali

M **Pinacoteca Vaticana,** *Cur* Dr Fabrizio Mancinelli
Inaugurated by Pope Pius XI in 1932
Collections: Paintings by Fra Angelico, Raphael, Leonardo da Vinci, Titian and Caravaggio, and the Raphael Tapestries

M **Collezione d'Arte Religiosa Moderna,** *Cur* Dr Mario Ferrazza
Founded in 1973 by Pope Paul VI; paintings, sculptures and drawings offered to the Pope by artists and donors

M **Cappelle, Sale e Gallerie Affrescate,** Tel 698-33-32. *Cur* Dr Fabrizio Mancinelli
Chapel of Beato Angelico (or Niccolo V, 1448-1450); Sistine Chapel constructed for Sixtus IV (1471-1484); Borgia Apartment decorated by Pinturicchio; Chapel of Urbano VIII (1631-1635); rooms and loggias decorated by Raphael; Gallery of the Maps (1580-83)

VENICE

M **BIENNALE DI VENEZIA,** S Marco, Ca' Giustinian, 30100. Tel 5200311. *Pres* Paolo Portoghesi
Collections: Visual arts, architecture, cinema, theatre, music. Owns historical archives of contemporary art

M **CIVICI MUSEI VENE ZIANI D'ARTE E DI STORIA,** S Marco St 52, 30100. Tel (041) 522625. *Dir* Prof Giandomenico Romanelli
M **Museo Correr,** Piazza San Marco, 30100
Collections: 13th - 16th Century Venetian Art, Renaissance coins & ceramics
M **La'Rezzonico,** S Barnaba-Fondamenta Rezzonico, Canal Grande, 30100
Collections: 18th century Venetian art, sculpture, etc
M **Museo Vetario di Murano,** Fondamenta Giustiniani 8, Murano, 30121
Collections: Venetian Glass from middle ages to the present
M **Palazzo Mocenigo** 30100
Collections: Palace of the Doges; collection of fabrics & costumes; library on history of fashion

M **GALLERIA DELL'ACCADEMIA,** Campo della Carita 1059A, 30100. Tel 22247. *Dir* Giovanna Scire Nepi
Collections: Venetian painting, 1310-1700

M **GALLERIA G FRANCHETTI,** Calle Ca d'Oro, Canal Grande, 30100. Tel 387-90. *Dir* Dr Giovanna Nepi Scire
Collections: Sculpture & paintings

M **GALLERIA QUERINI-STAMPALIA**, Palazzo Querini-Stampalia, Castello 4778, 30122. Tel (041) 5203433. *Dir* Dr Giorgio Busetto
Collections: 14th - 19th century Italian paintings

M **MUSEO ARCHEOLOGICO**, Piazza S Marco 17, 30100. Tel (041) 5225978. *Dir* Prof Bianca Maria Scarfi
Collections: Greek & Roman sculpture, jewels, coins & mosiacs

M **MUSEO D'ARTE MODERNA**, Ca' Pesaro, Canal Grande, 30100. Tel (041) 24127. *Dir* Prof Giandomenico Romanelli
Collections: 19th & 20th century works of art

M **MUSEO D'ARTE ORIENTALE**, Ca' Pesaro, Canal Grande, 30100. Tel 27681. *Dir* Dr Adriana Ruggeri

M **PINACOTECA MANFREDINIANA**, Campo della Salute, 30123. Tel 041-25558. *Dir* A Niero
Collections: Paintings & sculpture of the Roman, Gothic, Renaissance & Neo-classical period

IVORY COAST

ABIDJAN

M **MUSEE DE LA COTE D'IVOIRE**, BP 1600. Tel 22-20-56. *Dir* Dr B Holas
Collections: Art, ethnographic, scientific & sociological exhibits

JAPAN

ATAMI

M **MOA BIJUTSUKAN**, MOA Museum of Art, 26-2 Momoyama-Cho, Shizuoka 413. Tel 84-2511. *Dir* Yoji Yoshioka
Library with 20,000 vols
Collections: Oriental fine arts; paintings, ceramics, lacquers and sculptures

HIROSHIMA

M **ITSUKUSHIMA JINJA HOMOTSUKAN**, Treasure Hall of the Isukushima Shinto Shrine, Miyajima-cho, Saeki-gun. *Cur & Chief Priest* Motoyoshi Nozaka
Collections: Paintings, calligraphy, sutras, swords, and other ancient weapons

KURASHIKI

M **OHARA BIJITSUKAN**, Ohara Museum of Art, 1-1-15 Chuo, 710. Tel 22-0005. *Cur* Shinichiro Fujita
Collections: Ancient Egyptian, Persian and Turkish ceramics and sculpture; 19th & 20th century European paintings and sculpture; modern Japanese oil paintings, pottery, sculpture and textiles

KYOTO

M **KYOTO KOKURITSU HAKUBUTSUKAN**, Kyoto National Museum, 527 Chayamachi, Higashiyama-ku, 605. Tel (075) 541-1151. *Dir* Norio Fujisawa
Collections: Fine art; handicrafts & historical collections of Asia, chiefly Japan; over 65,000 research photographs

M **KYOTO KOKURITSU KINDAI BIJUTSUKAN**, National Museum of Modern Art, Enshoji-cho, Okazaki, Sakyo-ku, 606. Tel (075) 761-4111. *Dir* Tadao Ogura; *Chief Cur* Takeo Uchiyama
Collections: Contemporary print works in Japan & Japanese artists who are active abroad, contemporary sculpture, handicrafts works by contemporary artists, paintings by the artists who have been active in Kyoto mainly

M **KYOTO-SHI BIJUTSUKAN**, Kyoto City Art Museum, Okazaki Park, Sakyo-ku. Tel (075) 771-4107. *Dir* Mitsugu Uehira
Collections: Contemporary fine arts objects, including Japanese pictures, sculptures, decorative arts exhibits and prints

NAGOYA

M **TOKUGAWA REIMEIKAI FOUNDATION**, Tokugawa Art Museum, 1017 Tokugawa-cho, Higashi-ku, 461. Tel 935-6262. *Dir* Yoshinobu Tokugawa
Collections: Tokugawa family collection of 12,000 treasures, including scrolls, swords, calligraphy & pottery

NARA

M **HORYUJI**, Horyuji Temple, Aza Horyuji, Ikaruga-cho, Ikoma-gun
Collections: Buddhist images and paintings; the buildings date from the Asuka, Nara, Heian, Kamakura, Ashikaga, Tokugawa periods

M **NARA KOKURITSU HAKUBUTSU-KAN**, Nara National Museum, 50 Nabori-oji-Cho, 630. Tel (0742) 22-7771. *Dir* Kyotaro Niskikawa
Collections: Art objects of Buddhist art, mainly of Japan, including applied arts and archaeological relics, calligraphy, paintings, sculptures

OSAKA

M **FUJITA BIJUTSUKAN**, Fujita Art Museum, 10-32 Amijima-cho, Miyakojima-ku. Tel 351-0582. *Dir* Masaka Fujita
Collections: Scroll paintings

M **OSAKA-SHIRITSU HAKUBUTSUKAN**, Osaka Municipal Museum of Art, 1-82 Chausuyama-Cho, Tennoji-ku, 543. Tel (06) 771-4874. *Dir* Kohyama Noboru
Collections: Art of China, Korea & Japan

TOKYO

M **BRIDGESTONE BIJUTSUKAN**, Bridgestone Museum of Art, 10-1, Kyobashi 1-chome, Chuo-ku, 104. Tel (03) 3563-0241. *Executive Dir* Yasuo Kamon
Collections: Foreign paintings, mainly Impressionism and after; western style paintings late 19th century to present

M **IDEMITSU MUSEUM OF ARTS**, 3-1-1 Marumouchi, Chiyoda-ku, 100. Tel 213-9402. *Dir* Shosuke Idemitsu
Collections: Oriental art & ceramics; Japanese paintings; calligraphy; Chinese bronzes; lacquer wares

M **KOKURITSU SEIYO BIJUTSUKAN**, National Museum of Western Art, Ueno-Koen 7-7, Taito-ku, 110. Tel 828-5131. *Dir* Tetsuo Misumi
Collections: Many works of European art from the 14th - 20th century; Matsukata Collection of 19th century French art, European paintings & sculpture; Old Master paintings

M **NEZU BIJUSUKAN**, Nezu Institute of Fine Arts, 6-5 Minami-aoyama, Minato-ku, 107. Tel 400-2536. *Dir* Hisao Sugahara
Collections: Kaichiro Nezu's private collection, including 7,195 paintings, calligraphy, sculpture, swords, ceramics, lacquer-ware, archeological exhibits; 184 items designated as national treasures

M **NIPPON MINGEI-KAN**, Japanese Folk Art Museum, 4-3-33 Komaba, Meguro-ku, 153. Tel 467-4527. *Dir* Sori Yanagi
Collections: Folk-craft art objects from all parts of the world

M **TOKYO KOKURITSU HAKUBUTSUKAN**, Tokyo National Museum, 13-9 Ueno Koen, Taito-ku, 110. Tel (03) 3822-1111. *Dir Gen* Keijiro Inai
Collections: Largest art museum in Japan; Eastern fine arts, including paintings, calligraphy, sculpture, metal work, ceramic art, textiles, lacquer ware, archaelogical exhibits

M **TOKYO KOKURITSU KINDAI BUJUTSUKAN**, National Museum of Modern Art, Tokyo, 3 Kitanomaru Koen, Chiyoda-ku, 102. Tel (03) 3214-2561. *Dir* Hiroshi Veki
Collections: Calligraphy, drawings, paintings, prints, sculptures, watercolors
M **Crafts Gallery**, 1 Kitanomaru Koen, Chiyoda-ku. *Chief Cur* Mitsuhiki Hasebe
Collections: Ceramics, laquer ware, metalworks

M **TOKYO NATIONAL UNIVERSITY OF FINE ARTS & MUSIC ART MUSEUM**, Ueno Park, Taito-ku. Tel (03) 3828-6111.
Collections: Paintings, sculptures & industrial art of Japan, China & Korea

M **TOKYO-TO BIJUTSUKAN**, Tokyo Metropolitan Art Museum, Ueno Park 8-36, Taito-ku, 110. Tel (03) 3823-6921. *Dir* Yasuyuki Aoyami
Library with 47,500 vols
Collections: Contemporary crafts, paintings and sculptures

WAKAYAMA

M **KOYASAN REIHOKAN**, Museum of Buddhist Art on Mount Koya, Koyasan Koya-cho, Ito-gun. *Cur* Dr Chikyo Yamamoto
Collections: Buddhist paintings and images, sutras and old documents, some of them registered National Treasures and Important Cultural Properties

KOREA, REPUBLIC OF

SEOUL

M **NATIONAL MUSEUM OF KOREA**, 1 Sejong-ro, Chongno-ku, 110. Tel 738-0400. *Dir Gen* Byong-Sam Han
Seven branch museums & library with 20,000 vols
Collections: Korean archaeology, culture & folklore

LATVIA

KAUNAS

M **KAUNAS M K CIURLIONIS STATE ART MUSEUM,** Vlado Putvinskio G 55, Lithuanian SSR 233000. Tel 22-97-38. *Dir* M Sakalauskas
Collections: Lithuanian, Russian, French and Italian art; 8 related galleries and museumns in Kaunas, Druskininkai and Jurbarkas

LEBANON

BEIRUT

M **ARCHAELOGICAL MUSEUM OF THE AMERICAN UNIVERSITY OF BEIRUT,** Bliss. Tel 350000, Ext 2523. *Dir* Dr Leila Badre
Collections: Bronze and Iron Age Near Eastern pottery collections; bronze figurines, weapons and implements of the Bronze Age Near East; Graeco-Roman imports of pottery from Near East sites; Palaeolithic-Neolithic flint collection; Phoenician glass collection; pottery collection of Islamic periods; substantial coin collection

M **DAHESHITE MUSEUM AND LIBRARY,** PO Box 202. *Dir* Dr A S M Dahesh
Library with 30,000 vols
Collections: Aquarelles, gouaches, original paintings, engravings, sculptures in marble, bronze, ivory and wood carvings

M **MUSEE NATIONAL,** National Museum of Lebanon, rue de Damas. Tel 4-01-00/4-40. *Dir* Camille Asmar
Collections: Anthropological sarcophagi of the Greco-Persian period; Byzantine mosaics; royal arms, jewels and statues of the Phoenician epoch; Dr C Ford Collection of 25 sarcophagi of the Greek and Helenistic epoch; goblets, mosaics, relief and sarcophagi of the Greco-Roman period; Arabic woods and ceramics

LIBYA

TRIPOLI

M **ARCHAEOLOGICAL, NATURAL HISTORY, EPIGRAPHY, PREHISTORY AND ETHNOGRAPHY MUSEUMS,** Assarai al-Hamra. Tel 38116/7. *Pres* Dr Abdullah Shaiboub
Administered by Department of Antiquities
Collections: Archaeology from Libyan sites

LIECHTENSTEIN

VADUZ

M **LIECHTENSTEINISCHE STAATLICHE KUNSTSAMMLUNG,** Englander-Bau, Stadtle 37, 9490. Tel 22341. *Dir* Dr George Malin
Collections: Collection features paintings of Rubens

LITHUANIA

VILNIUS

M **ART MUSEUM OF THE LITHUANIAN SSR,** Ul Gorkio 55, Lithuanian SSR 232024. Tel 62-80-30. *Dir* Romualdas Budrys
Collections: Lithuanian art; English, Flemish, French, German & Italian art from 16th-19th century

MALAYSIA

KUALA LUMPUR

M **MUZIUM NEGARA,** National Museum of Malaysia, Jalan Damansara, 50566. Tel (03) 2380255. *Dir-Gen* Haji Mohamed Zulkifli Bin Haji A Bdul Aziz
Collections: Oriental and Islamic arts, ethnographical, archaeological & zoological collections

MALTA

VALLETTA

M **MUSEUMS DEPARTMENT,** Auberge de Provence, Republic St. Tel 25293. *Dir* Marius J Zerafa
Collections: Fine arts; archaeology and natural history

MEXICO

GUADALAJARA

M **MUSEO DEL ESTADO DE JALISCO** Jalisco
Collections: Archaeological discoveries; early Mexican objects; folk art and costumes

M **MUSEO-TALLER JOSE CLEMENTE OROZCO,** Calle Aurelio Aceves 27, Sector Juarez, Jalisco 44100. *Dir* Margarita V de Orozco
Collections: Paintings and sketches by the artist

MEXICO CITY

M **MUSEO DE ARTE MODERNO,** Museum of Modern Art, Bosque de Chapultepec, Paseo de la Reforma y Gandhi, 11560. Tel 553-63-13. *Dir* Teresa del Conde
Collections: International and Mexican collection of modern art

M **MUSEO DE SAN CARLOS,** Puente de Alvarado 50, 06030. Tel 592-37-21. *Dir* Mtra Leonor Cortina
Collections: English, Flemish, French, German, Hungarian, Italian, Polish, Netherlandish and Spanish paintings from 14th - 19th centuries
L **Library,** Puente de Alvarado No 50, 06030
Library Holdings: Vols 2000

M **MUSEO NACIONAL DE ANTROPOLOGIA,** National Museum of Anthropology, Paseo de la Reforma y Gandhi, 11550. Tel 5-53-62-66. *Dir* Sonia Lombardo de Ruiz
Collections: Anthropological, archaeological and ethnographical collections

M **MUSEO NACIONAL DE ARTES E INDUSTRIAS POPULARES DEL INSTITUTO NACIONAL INDIGENISTA,** National Museum of Popular Arts and Crafts, Avda Juarez 44, 06050. Tel 510-34-04. *Dir* Maria Teresa Pomar
Collections: Major permanent collections of Mexican popular arts and crafts

M **MUSEO NACIONAL DE HISTORIA,** National Historical Museum, Castillo de Chapultepec, 5. Tel 553-62-02. *Dir* Amelia Lara Tamburrino
Collections: The history of Mexico from the Spanish Conquest to the 1917 Constitution, through collections of ceramics, costumes, documents, flags and banners, furniture, jewelry & personal objects

M **PINACOTECA NACIONAL DE SAN DIEGO,** San Diego National Art Gallery, Dr Mora 7, Alameda Central, 06050. Tel 5-10-27-93. *Dir* Mercedes Meade de Angulo
Collections: Under auspices of Instituto Nacional de Bellas Artes; paintings of the colonial era in Mexico

PUEBLA

M **MUSEO DE ARTE JOSE LUIS BELLO Y GONZALEZ,** Avenida 3 Poniente 302. Tel 32-94-75. *Dir* Alicia Torres de Araujo
Collections: Ivories; porcelain; wrought iron; furniture; clocks; watches; musical instruments; Mexican, Chinese and European paintings sculptures, pottery, vestments, tapestries, ceramics, miniatures

TOLUCA

M **MUSEO DE LAS BELLAS ARTES,** Museum of Fine Arts, Calle de Santos Degollado 102. *Dir* Prof Jose M Caballero-Barnard
Collections: Paintings; sculptures; Mexican colonial art

MONGOLIAN PEOPLE'S REPUBLIC

ULAN BATOR

M **FINE ARTS MUSEUM**
Collections: Paintings & sculpture

MYAHMAR (BURMA)

YANGON

M **NATIONAL MUSEUM OF ART AND ARCHAEOLOGY,** Jubilee Hall, Pagoda Rd. *Dir* U Tha Myat
Collections: Antiquities; paintings; replica of King Mindon's Mandalay Palace

NEPAL

KATHMANDU

M **NATIONAL MUSEUM OF NEPAL,** Museum Rd, Chhauni. Tel 211504. *Chief* Sanu Nani Kansakar
Collections: Art, history, culture, ethnology & natural history collections

NETHERLANDS

ALKMAAR

M **STEDELIJK MUSEUM ALKMAAR,** Alkmaar Municipal Museum, Nieuwe Doelen, Doelenstraat 3-9, 1811 KX. Tel 11-07-37. *Dir* M E A de Vries
Collections: Collection from Alkmaar region, including archaeological items, dolls and other toys, modern sculpture, paintings, silver tiles; works by Honthorst, van Everdingen, van de Velde the Elder

AMSTERDAM

M **REMBRANDT-HUIS MUSEUM,** Rembrandthouse Museum, Jodenbreestraat 4-6, 1011 NK. Tel 020-624-9486. *Dir* E de Heer
Collections: Rembrandt's etchings and drawings; drawings and paintings by Rembrandt's pupils

M **RIJKSMUSEUM,** State Museum, Stadhouderskade 42, PO Box 50673, 1007 DD. Tel 020-673-2121. *Dir Gen* Dr H W van Os
Library with 80,000 vols
Collections: Asiatic art; Dutch history and paintings; prints and drawings from all parts of the world; sculpture and applied art

M **RIJKSMUSEUM VINCENT VAN GOGH,** Vincent Van Gogh National Museum, Paulus Potterstraat 7, PO Box 75366, 1007 AJ. Tel (020) 570-5200. *Dir* Ronald de Leeuw
Collections: 550 drawings & 200 paintings by Vincent Van Gogh; Van Gogh's personal collection of English & French prints & Japanese woodcuts

M **STEDLIJK MUSEUM,** Municipal Museum, Paulus Potterstraat 13, PO Box 5082, 1007 AB. Tel (020) 5732911. *Dir* W A L Beeren
Library with 20,000 vols and 90,000 catalogs
Collections: Applied art and design; European and American trends after 1960 in paintings and sculptures

ARNHEM

M **GEMEENTEMUSEUM ARNHEM,** Municipal Museum of Arnhem, Utrechtseweg 87, Gelderland 6812 AA. Tel (085) 512431. *Dir* Dr L Brandt Corstius
Collections: Chinese porcelain; Delftware; Dutch paintings, drawings and prints; provincial archaeology and history; silverware; topographical and historical maps of the Province of Gelderland

DELFT

M **STEDELIJK MUSEUM HET PRINSENHOF,** Het Prinsenhof State Museum, St Agathaplein 1, 2611 HR. Tel (015) 602-357. *Dir* Dr D H A C Lokin
Library with 6000 vols
Collections: Delft silver, tapestries and ware; paintings of the Delft School; modern art

DORDRECHT

M **DORDRECHTS MUSEUM,** Museumstraat 40, 3311 XP. Tel 13-41-00. *Dir* Dr J M De Groot
Collections: Dutch paintings, prints, drawings & sculpture

EINDHOVEN

M **MUNICIPAL VAN ABBEMUSEUM INN EINDHOVEN** (Formerly Stedelijk Museum Alkmaar), Eindhoven Municipal Museum, Bilderdijklaan 10, PO Box 235, 5600 AE. Tel (040) 389730. *Dir* J Debbaut
Library with 100,000 vols
Collections: Modern and contemporary art; Lissitzky Collection

ENSCHEDE

M **RIJKSMUSEUM TWENTHE TE ENSCHEDE,** Lasondersingel 129, 7514 BP. Tel (053) 358675. *Dir* Dr D A S Cannegieter
Library with 24,000 vols
Collections: Eastern Netherlands prehistory, local history and paintings, collection of art from middle ages to 1930

GRONINGEN

M **GRONINGER MUSEUM,** Groningen Museum, Praediniussingel 59, 9711 AG. Tel (050) 183343. *Dir* Dr F Haks
Collections: Paintings and drawings from the 16th - 20th Century, mainly Dutch, including Averkamp, Cuyp, Fabritius, Jordaens, Rembrandt, Rubens, Teniers; Oriental ceramics; local archaeology and history

HAARLEM

M **FRANS HALSMUSEUM,** Groot Heiligland 62, 2011 ES. Tel 023-319-180. *Dir* D P Snoep
Collections: Works by Frans Hals & Haarlem school; antique furniture; modern art collection

M **TEYLERS MUSEUM,** Spaarne 16, 2011 CH. Tel (023) 319010. *Dir* E Ebbinge
Library with 125,000 vols
Collections: Drawings; paintings; historical physical instruments, minerals and fossils

THE HAGUE

M **HAAGS GEMEENTEMUSEUM,** Municipal Museum of The Hague, Stadhouderslaan 41, 2517 HV. Telex 3-6990; Tel (070) 3381111. *Dir* Dr R H Fuchs
Collections: Decorative Arts Collection includes ceramics, furniture, glass, silver; modern art of 19th and 20th century; musical instruments; history of The Hague

M **KONINKLIJK KABINET VAN SCHILDERIJEN MAURITSHUIS,** Royal Picture Gallery, Korte Vijverberg 8, 2513 AB. Tel (070) 346-9244. *Dir* F J Duparc
Collections: Paintings of the Dutch and Flemish Masters of the 15th, 16th, 17th and 18th centuries, including G David, Holbein, Hals, Rembrandt, Van Dyck, Vermeer

HERTOGENBOSCH

M **NOORDBRABANTS MUSEUM,** Verwersstraat 41, PO Box 1004, 5200 BA. Tel 073-133834. *Dir* Dr M M A van Boven
Collections: All collections have an emphasis on local history: archaeology, arts and crafts, coins and medals, painting and sculpture

HOORN

M **WESTFRIES MUSEUM,** Rode Steen 1, Acherom 2, 1621 KV. Tel (02290) 15748. *Dir* R J Spruit
Collections: 17th & 18th century paintings, prints, oak panelling, glass, pottery, furniture, costumes, interiors; folk art; historical objects from Hoorn & West Friesland; West Friesland native painting; prehistoric finds

LEERDAM

M **STICHTING NATIONAAL GLASMUSEUM,** National Glass Museum, Lingedijk 28, 4142 LD. Tel (03451) 13141. *Cur* Mrs A Van der Kleij-Blekxtoon
Collections: Antique, machine-made and packaging glass; art glass; unique pieces; contemporary Dutch collection and works from America and Europe

LEEUWARDEN

M **FRIES MUSEUM,** Turfmarkt 24, 8911 KT. Tel 058-123001. *Dir* R Vos
Collections: Archaeology, ceramics, costumes, folk art, historical items, painting, prints and drawings, sculpture

LEIDEN

M **STEDELIJK MUSEUM DE LAKENHAL,** Leiden Municipal Museum, Oude Singel 28-32, PO Box 2044, 2301 CA. Tel 25-46-20. *Dir* Dr H Bolten-Rempt
Collections: Altar pieces by Lucas van Leyden; paintings by Rembrandt, Steen, van Goyen; pictures of Leiden School and modern Leiden School; arms, ceramics, furniture, glass, period rooms, pewter, silver

MUIDEN

M **MUIDERSLOT RIJKSMUSEUM,** State Museum at Muiden, 1398 AA. Tel 02942-1325. *Cur* G Heuff
Collections: 13th century castle furnished in early 17th century style; paintings, tapestries, furniture and armory

NIJMEGEN

M **NIJMEEGS MUSEUM COMMANDERIE VAN ST JAN,** Franse Plaats 3,
6511 VS. Tel 080-22-91-93. *Dir* Dr G T M Lemmens
Collections: Art and history of Nijmegen and region: Middle Ages - 20th
Century; modern international art

OTTERLO

M **RIJKSMUSEUM KROLLER-MULLER,** Kroller-Muller State Museum,
Nationale Park de Hoge Veluwe, Houtkampweg 6, 6731 AW. Tel 08382-1241.
Dir Dr E van Straaten
Library with 5000 vols
Collections: Van Gogh Collection; 19th and 20th century art - drawings,
paintings, sculpture garden, ceramics, graphic arts

ROTTERDAM

M **MUSEUM BOYMANS-VAN BEUNINGEN,** Mathenesserlaan 18-20, 3015 CK.
Tel 010-441-9400. *Dir* W H Crouwel
Collections: Dutch school paintings including Bosch, Hals, Rembrandt, Van
Eyck; 15th - 20th century Dutch, Flemish, French, German, Italian and Spanish
works; Baroque School; Impressionists; old, modern and contemporary sculpture;
Dutch, Italian, Persian and Spanish pottery and tiles

NEW ZEALAND

AUCKLAND

M **AUCKLAND CITY ART GALLERY,** 5 Kitchener St, PO Box 5449, 1. Tel (09)
792-020. *Dir* Christopher Johnstone
Library with 33,000 vols
Collections: American and Australian paintings; general collection of European
paintings and sculpture from 12th century on; historical and contemporary New
Zealand painting, sculpture and prints

L **UNIVERSITY OF AUCKLAND,** Elam School of Fine Arts Library, School of
Fine Arts, Whitaker Place. Tel 31 897. *Dean of Elam School of Fine Arts* Jolyon
D Saunders
Library with 30,000 vols

DUNEDIN

M **DUNEDIN PUBLIC ART GALLERY,** Logan Park, PO Box 566. Tel (03)
4778-770. *Dir* Cheryll Sotheran
Collections: 15th - 19th century European paintings; New Zealand paintings
since 1876; Australian paintings 1900-60; British watercolors, portraits and
landscapes; ancillary collections of furniture, ceramics, glass, silver, oriental rugs;
De Beer collection of Old Masters, including Monet

INVERCARGILL

M **ANDERSON PARK ART GALLERY,** PO Box 755. *Pres* F K Khoy
Collections: Contemporary New Zealand art

NAPIER

M **HAWKES BAY ART GALLERY AND MUSEUM,** 9 Herschell St, PO Box
429. Tel 35-77-81. *Deputy Dir* R B McGregor
Collections: Antiques; Maori and Pacific artifacts; New Zealand painting and
sculpture

WANGANUI

M **SARJEANT GALLERY,** Queen's Park, Box 637. Tel 064-570-52.
Collections: European and English watercolors, 18th century to present; local
works; New Zealand collection of paintings; First World War cartoons

WELLINGTON

M **NATIONAL ART GALLERY OF NEW ZEALAND,** Buckle St. Tel (04) 859-
609. *Dir* Jenny Harper
Library with 20,000 vols
Collections: Australian, British, European and New Zealand art; Sir Harold
Beauchamp Collection of early English drawings, illustrations and watercolors;
Sir John Ilott Collection of prints; Nan Kivell Collection of British original prints;
Monrad Collection of early European graphics; collection of Old Master
drawings

NIGERIA

IFE

M **MUSEUM OF THE IFE ANTIQUITIES,** Tel 21-50. *Dir* Frank Willett
Collections: Western Nigeria Archeology

NORWAY

BERGEN

M **VESTLANDSKE KUNSTINDUSTRIMUSEUM,** Western Norway Museum of
Applied Art, Nordahl Brunsgate 9, 5014. Tel (05) 32-51-08. *Museum Dir* Peter
M Anker
Library with 20,000 vols
Collections: Contemporary Norwegian and European ceramics, furniture, textiles;
The General Munthe Collection of Chinese Art; collections of old European arts
and crafts; The Anna B and William H Singer Collection of art and antiquities

LILLEHAMMER

M **LILLEHAMMER BYS MALERISAMLING,** Lillehammer Municipal Art
Gallery, Kirkegaten 69, PO Box 338, 2600. Tel (062) 51944. *Dir* Per Bjarne
Boym
Collections: Norwegian paintings, sculpture and graphic art from 19th and 20th
centuries

OSLO

M **KUNSTINDUSTRIMUSEET I OSLO,** Oslo Museum of Applied Art, St Olavs
Gate 1, 0165. Tel (02) 203578. *Dir* Anniken Thue
Library with 40,000 vols
Collections: Collection from 1200 to present of applied arts, with ceramics,
furniture, glass, silver, textiles from Norway, Europe and Far East

M **NASJONALGALLERIET,** Universitetsgaten 13, PO Box 8157, 0033. Tel (02)
200404. *Dir* Knut Berg
Library with 25,000 vols
Collections: Norwegian paintings and sculpture; Old European paintings; icon
collection; especially of modern French, Danish and Swedish art; a collection of
prints and drawings; a small collection of Greek and Roman sculptures

M **NORSK FOLKEMUSEUM,** Norwegian Folk Museum, Bygdoy, Museum Veien
10, 2. Tel 39-67-01. *Dir* Halvard Bjorkvik
Collections: The Lappish section provides an insight into the ancient culture of
the Lapps. The Open Air Museum totals about 170 old buildings, all original.
Among them are the 13th century Gol stave church; farmsteads from different
districts of the country; single buildings of particular interest; The Old Town -
17th, 18th and 19th century town houses. Urban Collections; Henrik Ibsen's
study; other collections include peasant art and church history

M **NORSK SJOFARTSMUSEUM,** Norwegian Maritime Museum,
Bygdoynesveien 37, 0286. Tel 02-55-27-00. *Dir* Bard Kolltveit
Library with 25,000 vols
Collections: Amundsen's Gjoa; archives pertaining to maritime history;
instruments, paintings, photographs of ships, ship models, tools and other items
pertaining to maritime collections

M **OSLO KOMMUNES KUNSTSAMLINGER,** Munch museet, Toyengata 53,
0608. Tel (02) 673774. *Dir* Alf Boe; *Chief Cur* Arne Eggum
Collections: Paintings, prints and drawings of Edvard Munch

L **STATENS KUNSTAKADEMI BIBLIOTEKET,** National Academy of Fine
Arts Library, St Olavs Gate 32, 0166. Tel 02-20-01-50. *Rector of Academy* Boge
Berg
Library with 6000 volumes to support training by 14 teachers of 130 students

M **UNIVERSITETETS SAMLING AV NORDISKE OLDSAKER,** University
Museum of National Antiquities, Frederiksgate 2, 1. Tel 02-41-63-00. *Dir* Dr
Egil Mikkelsen
Collections: 70,000 exhibits from prehistoric and Viking times, including Middle
Ages

PAKISTAN

KARACHI

M **NATIONAL MUSEUM OF PAKISTAN,** Burns Garden. Tel 211341. *Supt* Ali
Muhammed Khan Lundkhwar
Collections: Antiquities dating from 2800 to 1500, large collection of coins and
miniature paintings spreading from 6th century BC to present; ethnological
material from the various regions of Pakistan; Buddhist and Hindu sculptures;
paleolithic implements; handicrafts and manuscripts of the Muslim period

LAHORE

M LAHORE FORT MUSEUM, 54000. Tel 56747. *Dir Archaeology* Dr Rafique Mughal
Collections: Mughal Gallery: Mughal paintings, coins, calligraphy, manuscripts, faience, carving, Sikh Gallery: arms and armor, paintings and art of Sikh period; Sikh Painting Gallery: oil paintings from the Princess Bamba Collection

M LAHORE MUSEUM, Sharah-i-Quaid-i-Azam. Tel 322835. *Dir* Dr Saifur Rahman Dar
Library with 35,000 vols
Collections: Greco-Buddhist sculpture; Indo-Pakistan coins; miniature paintings; local arts; armor; stamps; Oriental porcelain & manuscripts; Islamic calligraphy

PESHAWAR

M PESHAWAR MUSEUM, Tel 7-44-52. *Dir* Aurangzeb Khan
Collections: Architectural pieces and minor antiquities; mainly sculptures of the Gandhara School containing images of Buddha, Bodhisattvas, Buddhist deities, reliefs illustrating the life of the Buddha and Jataka stories; Koranic manuscripts

TAXILA

M ARCHAEOLOGICAL MUSEUM, Rawalpindi. *Custodian* Gulzar Mohammed Khan
Collections: Antiquities from Taxila Sites ranging from 6th Century BC to 5th Century AD; gold and silver ornaments; pottery; sculptures of stone and stucco of Gandhara School

PERU

LIMA

M MUSEO DE ARTE, Museum of Art, Paseo Colon 125. Tel 23-4732. *Dir* Cecilia Alayza
Collections: Peruvian art throughout history; Colonial painting; carvings, ceramics, furniture, metals, modern paintings, religious art, sculpture, textiles; modern furniture & paintings

M MUSEO NACIONAL DE LA CULTURA PERUANA, National Museum of Peruvian Culture, Avenida Alfonso Ugarte 650, Apdo 3048. Tel 235892. *Dir* Dr Rosalia Avalos de Matos
Collections: Ethnology, folklore, popular art

PHILIPPINES

MANILA

M NATIONAL MUSEUM OF THE PHILIPPINES, POB 2659, Padre Burgos St, 1000. Tel 48-14-27. *Dir* Gabriel S Casal
Collections: Fine arts, cultural, archaeological, sciences collections

M SANTO TOMAS MUSEUM (Formerly University of Santo Tomas), Museum of Arts & Sciences, Main Bldg, University of Santo Tomas, Calle Espana, 2806. Tel 7313101. *Dir* Fr Angel Aparicio
Collections: Archaeology, cultural and historical items; Chinese trade pottery; ethnology of the Philippines; medals; Philippine art; popular Philippines religious art; stamps

POLAND

CRACOW

L BIBLIOTEKA GLOWNA AKADEMII SZTUK PIEKNYCH, Central Library of the Academy of Fine Arts, ul Smolensk 9, 31-108. Tel 22-15-46. *Dir* Elzbieta Warchalowska
Collections: Over 71,000 vols, 30,000 other items in collection

M MUZEUM NARODOWE W KRAKOWIE, National Museum in Cracow, Ul J Pilsudskiego 12, 31-109. Tel 22-54-34. *Dir* Tadeusz Chruscicki
Collections: National Museum in Cracow consists of several departments with various collections: 3 galleries exhibit Polish painting and sculpture from 14th to 20th centuries; Emeryk Hutten-Czapski Dept has graphic, numismatic and old book collection; Jan Matejko's House exhibits relics and paintings of the eminent Polish painter; Czartoryski Collection contains national relics, armory, Polish and foreign crafts and paintings; Czartoryski Library and Archives holds collections of documents, codices, books and incunabula; Stanislaw Wyspianski Museum exhibits works by the Polish Modernist artist, handicrafts, architecture and town planning; Karol Szymanowski Museum contains exhibits relating to the life of the eminent composer

M PANSTWOWE ZBIORY SZTUKI NA WAWELU, Wawel State Collections of Art, Wawel 5, 31-001. Tel 22-51-55. *Dir* Jan Ostrowski
Collections: Italian Renaissance furniture; King Sigismund Augustus 16th Century Collection of Flemish Tapestries; Oriental art objects; Polish, Western-European Oriental weapons; Western-European and Oriental pottery; Western European painting; royal treasury of crown jewels, gold objects, historical relics

KIELCE

M MUZEUM NARODOWE W KIELCACH, National Museum in Kielce, Pl Zamkowy 1, 25-010. Tel 440-14. *Dir* Alojzy Oborny
Collections: Polish paintings from 17th to 20th century; Polish baroque interiors

LODZ

M MUSEUM SZTUKI W LODZI, Art Museum, Ul Wieckowskiego 36, 90-734. Tel (42) 33-97-90. *Dir* Ryszard Stanislawski
Collections: Gothic art; 15th to 19th century foreign paintings; 18th to 20th century Polish paintings; international modern art

LOWICZ

M MUZEUM W LOWICZU, Rynek Kosciuszki 4, 99-400. Tel 3928. *Dir* Walerian Warchalowski
Collections: Polish baroque art; regional ethnography; Lowicz county architecture; works of J Chelmonski & S Noakowski

POZNAN

M MUZEUM NARODOWE, National Museum, Al Marcinkowskiego 9, 61-745. Tel 52-80-11. *Dir* Dr Konstanty Kalinowski
Library has 85,000 vols; 8 branch museums
Collections: Polish paintings from 15th to 20th century; prints, drawings, sculpture; medieval art; European paintings from 14th to 19th century; modern art; numismatics; 8 branch museums

WARSAW

M BIBLIOTEKA UNIWERSYTECKA W WARSZAWIE (Formerly Gabinet Rycin Biblioteki Uniwersyteckiej), Library of the University of Warsaw, ul Krakowskie Przedmiescie 32, 00-927. Tel 264-155. *Dir* Dr Jadwiga Krajewski
Collections: Prints & drawings from 15th-20th century; various memorial collections

M PANSTWOWE MUZEUM ETNOGRAFICZNE W WARSZAWIE, State Ethnographic Museum in Warsaw, Ul Kredytowa 1, 00-056. Tel 27-76-41. *Dir* Dr Jan Witold Suliga
Library has 23,000 vols
Collections: Polish & non-European ethnography collection

WROCLAW

M MUZEUM ARCHITEKTURY, Museum of Architecture, Ul Bernardynska 5, 50-156. Tel 336-75. *Dir* Prof Olgierd Czerner
Collections: Polish & other architecture; modern art

M MUZEUM NARODOWE WE WROCLAWIU, National Museum in Wroclaw, Pl Powstancow Warszawy 5, 50-153. Tel 388-30. *Dir* Mariusz Hermansdorfer
Library with 77,000 vols
Collections: Medieval art; Polish painting of the 17th, 18th, 19th and 20th centuries; European painting, decorative arts, prints, ethnography and history relating to Silesia; numismatics

PORTUGAL

EVORA

M MUSEU DE EVORA, Largo do Conde de Vila Flor, 7000. Tel 22604. *Dir* Jose Teixeira
Collections: Paintings: 16th century Flemish and Portuguese works; local prehistoric tools and Roman art and archaelogy; sculpture from middle ages to the 19th century; 18th century Portuguese furniture and silver

LAMEGO

M MUSEU DE LAMEGO, 5100. Tel (054) 62008. *Dir* Dr Abel Montenegro-Florido
Collections: 16th century Brussels tapestries; Portuguese painting of 16th and 18th centuries; sculpture; religious ornaments

LISBON

M **MUSEU CALOUSTE GULBENKIAN,** Av de Berne 45 A, 1093. Tel 76-50-61. *Dir* Maria Teresa Gomes-Ferreira
Collections: Gulbenkian art collection covering the period 2800 BC to present; classical, Oriental, European art; manuscripts, furniture, gold and silver; medals; tapestries

M **MUSEU NACIONAL DE ARTE ANTIGA,** National Museum of Ancient Art, Rua das Janelas Verdes, 1293. Tel 672-725. *Dir* Dra Ana Brandao
Library with 16,500 vols
Collections: Portuguese and foreign plastic and ornamental art from 12th to 19th centuries

M **MUSEU NACIONAL DE ARTE CONTEMPORANEA,** National Museum of Contemporary Art, Rua de Serpa Pinto 6. Tel 36-8028. *Dir* Maria de Lourdes Bartholo
Collections: Contemporary painting and sculpture

PORTO

M **MUSEU NACIONAL DE SOARES DOS REIS,** National Museum of Soares Dos Reis, Palacio dos Carrancas, Rua de D Manuel II, 4000. Tel 38-19-56. *Dir* Dr Monica Baldaque
Collections: Furniture, glass, jewelry, old and modern paintings, porcelain, pottery, sculpture

VISEU

M **MUSEU DE GRAO VASCO,** Paco dos Tres Escaloes. Tel 26249. *Dir* Dr Alberto Correia
Collections: Flemish & Portuguese paintings; furniture, tapestries, ceramics & glassware

ROMANIA

BUCHAREST

L **BIBLIOTECA ACADEMIEI REPUBLICII SOCIALISTE ROMANIA,** Calea Victoriei 125, 71102. Tel 50-30-43. *Dir* Prof Victor Sahini
Library Holdings: Over 9 million items in collection; national depository for Romanian and United Nations publications
Collections: Romania, Latin, Greek, Oriental & Slavonic manuscripts, engravings, documents, maps, medals & coins

M **MUZEUL DE ARTA AL RSR,** Str Stirbei Voda 1, 70731. Tel 15-51-93. *Dir* Dr Theodor Enescu
Collections: Medieval Romanian art (9th - 18th century); National Gallery: National, Old Romanian, modern & contemporary works of art; Universal Gallery: paintings, sculptures, European decorative arts & Oriental art; graphic art & prints
M **Sectia de arta brincoveneasca,** Str Donca Simo 18, Mogosoaia, 78911. Tel 10145. *Dir* Alexandru Cebuc
Collections: Old Romanian art
M **Sectia de arta feudala D Minovici,** Str Dr N Minovici 3, 71557. Tel 17-15-05. *Dir* Alexandru Cebuc
Collections: Foreign decorative art collection
M **Muzeul Colectiilor de Arta,** Calea Victoriei 111. Tel 50-61-32.
Collections: Romanian folk art; decorative arts; paintings, sculpture, graphic arts
M **Muzeul Muzicii Romanesti,** Calea Victoriei 141. Tel 50-28-25.
Collections: Musical history of Romania

CLUJ-NAPOCA

M **MUZEUL DE ARTA CLUJ-NAPOCA,** Museum of Art, Piata Libertatii 30, 3400. Tel (95) 11-69-52. *Dir* Anna Maria Baltaru
Collections: Decorative arts; European and Romanian art, including graphics, paintings and sculpture of the 16th - 20th centuries

M **MUZEUL ETNOGRAFIC AL TRANSILVANIEI,** Transylvanian Museum of Ethnography, Str Memorandumului 21, 3400. Tel (95) 11-23-44. *Dir* Tiberiu Graur
Collections: Exhibits of Transylvanian traditional occupations; primitive people; Ethnographical Park, the first open-air museum in Romania

CONSTANTA

M **MUZEUL DE ARTA CONSTANTA,** Bd Tomis 84, 8700. Tel (916) 17012. *Dir* Simona Rusu
Collections: Modern & contemporary Romanian art

M **MUZEUL DE ISTORIE NATIONALA SI ARHEOLOGIE DIN CONSTANTA,** National History & Archaeology Museum, Piata Ovidiu 12, 8700. Tel (917) 13925. *Dir* Dr M Irimia
Library with 22,000 volumes
Collections: Prehistory, history & archaeology of the region; statues, coins, neolithic vessels

RUSSIA

LENINGRAD

M **MUSEUM OF SCULPTURE,** Pl A Nevskogo 1. *Dir* N H Belova
Collections: Collection of Russian sculpture; architectural drawings

M **STATE HERMITAGE MUSEUM,** M Dvortsovaya naberezhnaya 34. Tel 212-95-45. *Dir* Open
Collections: Collection of the arts of prehistoric, ancient Eastern, Graeco - Roman and medieval times; preserves over 2,600,000 objects d'art, including 40,000 drawings, 500,000 engravings; works by Leonardo da Vinci, Raphael, Titian, Rubens and Rembrandt; coins; weapons; applied art

M **SUMMER GARDEN AND MUSEUM PALACE OF PETER THE GREAT,** *Dir* K M Egorova
Collections: 18th century sculpture & architecture

MOSCOW

M **KREMLIN MUSEUMS,** Kremlin, 103073. Tel 928-44-56. *Dir* I A Rodimtseva
Collections: Collections housed in Armoury & various Kremlin cathedrals
M **Armoury**
Collections: Applied decorative art 12th century to the Revolution
M **Kremlin Cathedrals,** Cathedral Square
Collections: Icons, tombs & applied arts found in Cathedral of the Assumption, Cathedral of the Annunciation, Archangel Cathedral, Rizpolozhensky Cathedral & Cathedral of the Twelve Apostles

M **STATE MUSEUM OF ORIENTAL ART,** Suvorovskii bul 12A, 107120. Tel 291-03-41. *Dir* V A Nabachikov
Collections: Art of the Republics of Soviet Central Asia; Chinese art; monuments of art of Japan, India, Vietnam, Korea, Mongolia, Iran and other countries of the Middle and Far East

M **STATE PUSHKIN MUSEUM OF FINE ARTS,** Volkhonka 12, 121019. Tel 203-69-74. *Dir* I A Antonova
Collections: Ancient Byzantine, Greek, Roman and European art; American art

M **STATE TRETYAKOV GALLERY,** Krymskii val 10-14, 117049. Tel 231-13-62. *Dir* P I Lebedev
Collections: 40,000 Russian icons, Russian & Soviet paintings, sculpture & graphic arts from 11th century to present

SCOTLAND

ABERDEEN

M **ABERDEEN ART GALLERY & MUSEUMS,** Aberdeen Art Gallery, Schoolhill, AB9 1FQ. Telex 7-3366; Tel (0224) 646333. *Dir* Ian McKenzie Smith
Collections: 20th century British art; fine & decorative arts; James McBey print room

DUNDEE

M **DUNDEE ART GALLERIES & MUSEUMS,** McManus Galleries, Albert Square, DD1 1DA. Tel (0382) 23141. *Dir* A B Ritchie
Collections: 18th, 19th and 20th Century Scottish and English paintings; 17th Century Venetian and Flemish works; varied selection of watercolors and prints from the 18th - 20th Century; regional archaeology

EDINBURGH

M **NATIONAL GALLERIES OF SCOTLAND,** The Mound, EH2 2EL. Tel (031) 556-8921. *Dir* Timothy Clifford; *Keeper* Michael Clarke
Collections: European and Scottish drawings, paintings, prints and sculpture, 14th - 19th centuries

M **ROYAL MUSEUM OF SCOTLAND,** Chambers St, EH1 1JF. Tel 2257534. *Dir* Dr Robert Anderson
Collections: Collections of the Decorative Arts of the World; archaeology and ethnography

GLASGOW

M **GLASGOW MUSEUMS AND ART GALLERIES,** Kelvingrove, G3 8AG. Tel (041) 357-3929. *Dir* Julian Spalding
Library with 50,000 vols
Collections: Archaeology; British and Scottish art; Decorative Art Collection of ceramics, glass, jewelry, silver (especially Scottish); ethnography; Fine Art Collection representing the Dutch, Flemish, French and Italian schools; history; natural history

M **GLASGOW UNIVERSITY,** Hunterian Museum, Glasgow University, Main Building, Gl2 8QQ. Tel (041) 330-4221. *Dir* Malcolm McLeod
Collections: Prehistoric, Roman, ethnographical & coin collections
M **Art Gallery,** Hillhead St, G12 8QQ. Tel (041) 330-5431. *Dir* Malcolm McLeod
Collections: J M Whistler & C R Mackintosh collections; Scottish painting from the 18th century to the present; Old Master & modern prints

SENEGAL

DAKAR

M **MUSEE D'ART AFRICAIN DE DAKAR,** Musees de l'Institut Fondamental d'Afrique Noire, BP 206. *Cur* Dr Massamba Ng Lame
Collections: African art; ethnography

SINGAPORE, REPUBLIC OF

SINGAPORE

M **NATIONAL MUSEUM,** Stamford Rd, 0617. Tel 3377355. *Dir* Kwa Chong Guan
Houses the National Museum Art Gallery & the Children's Discovery Gallery
Collections: Paintings & sculpture by artists of Singapore & Southeast Asia ethnology and history collections

SLOVAK REPUBLIC

BRATISLAVA

M **GALERIA HALVNEHO MESTA SLOVENSKEJ REPUBLIKY BRATISLAVY,** Gallery of the Slovak Republic, Bratislava, Mirbachov palac, Dibrovovo nam 11, 81535. Tel 33-26-11. *Dir* Milan Jankovsky
Collections: Ancient European art; 18th - 20th century art; Gothic painting and sculpture; Permanent Baroque Art Exhibition

M **SLOVENSKA NARODNA GALERIA,** Slovak National Gallery, Riecna 1, 815 13. Tel 332-081. *Dir* Dr Stefan Mruskovic
Collections: Applied arts; European and Slovak painting; Dutch, Flemish and Italian works of art; graphics and drawings; sculpture

SLOVENIA

LJUBLJANA

M **MODERNA GALERIJA,** Modern Art Gallery, Tomsiceva 14, 61000. Tel 038-61-214-120. *Dir* Jure Mikuz
Library with 38,000 vols
Collections: Slovene art from Impressionists to present

M **NARODNA GALERIJA,** National Art Gallery, Prezihova 1, 61000. Tel 061-219-740. *Dir* Dr Anica Cevc
Library with 19,000 vols
Collections: Copies of medieval frescoes; Foreign Masters from the 14th Century to the beginning of the 20th Century; Slovenian sculptures and paintings from the 13th to the beginning of the 20th Century; Slovenian graphic arts

SOUTH AFRICA, REPUBLIC OF

CAPE TOWN

M **MICHAELIS COLLECTION,** Old Town House, Greenmarket Square. Tel (021) 246367. *Dir* Dr H Fransen
Collections: Dutch and Flemish graphic art and paintings of the 16th - 18th centuries

M **SOUTH AFRICAN NATIONAL GALLERY,** Government Ave, Gardens, PO Box 2420, 8000. Tel (021) 45-1628. *Dir* M Martin
Collections: 19th and 20th century South African art; 15th - 20th century, European art, including drawings, paintings, prints, sculptures and watercolors; traditional African art; 20th century American Art

DURBAN

M **DURBAN ART MUSEUM,** City Hall, Smith St, PO Box 4085, 4000. Tel (031) 3006911. *Dir* W J Oberholzer
Collections: Archaeology, paintings, graphic art, porcelain, sculptures, local history

JOHANNESBURG

M **JOHANNESBURG ART GALLERY,** Joubert Park, PO Box 23561, 2044. Tel (011) 725-3130. *Dir* Christopher Till
Collections: South African and international painting and sculpture; print collection; small collection of ceramics and textiles

KIMBERLEY

M **WILLIAM HUMPHREYS ART GALLERY,** Civic Centre, Cape Province 8300. Tel 81-17-24. *Dir* Mrs R J Holloway
Collections: Representative collection of Old Masters; collection of South African works of art

PIETERMARITZBURG

M **TATHAM ART GALLERY,** Opp City Hall, Commercial Rd. Tel (0331) 421804. *Cur* Lorna Ferguson
Collections: 19th and 20th Century English and French paintings and sculpture; 19th and 20th Century English graphics; modern European graphics; South African painting and sculpture

PORT ELIZABETH

M **KING GEORGE VI ART GALLERY,** One Park Dr, 6001. Tel (041) 561030. *Dir* Melanie Hillebrand
Collections: English painting; international graphics; Oriental ceramics and miniatures; South African art

PRETORIA

M **PRETORIA ART MUSEUM,** Arcadia Park, 0083. Tel (012) 344-1807. *Dir* Dr A J Werth
Collections: European graphics; 17th century Dutch Art; 19th & 20th century South African Art

SPAIN

BARCELONA

M **MUSEO PICASSO,** Calle Montcada 15-19, 08003. Tel 3196310. *Dir* Maria Teresa Ocana
Collections: Pablo Picasso, 1890-1972: paintings, sculpture, drawings and engravings, including the series Las Meninas and the artist's donation, in 1970, of 940 works of art

M **MUSEU D'ART DE CATALUNYA,** Museum of Art, Parc de Montjuic, Palacio Nacional, 08038. Tel (93) 4233031. *Dir* Joan Sureda I Pons
Collections: Baroque and Renaissance paintings; Catalan Gothic and Romanesque paintings and sculpture

M **MUSEU D'ART MODERN DE BARCELONA,** Museum of Modern Art, Parc de la Ciutadella, 08003. Tel 93-319-5732. *Dir* Cristina Mendoza Garriga
Library with 50,000 vols
Collections: Modern art

BILBAO

M **MUSEO DE BELLAS ARTES,** Museum of Fine Arts, Plaza del Museo 2, 48009. Tel 441-95-36. *Dir* Jorge De Barandiaran
Collections: Paintings, sculpture; famous works by El Greco, Goya, Gauguin, Velazquez; general contemporary art; early Spanish paintings

MADRID

M **MUSEO CERRALBO,** Ventura Rodriguez 17, 28008. Tel 247-36-46. *Dir* Manuel Jorge Aragoneses
Library with 12,000 vols
Collections: Paintings; drawings; engravings; porcelain arms; carpets; coins; furniture; includes paintings by: El Greco, Ribera, Titian, Van Dyck and Tintoretto

M **MUSEO LAZARO GALDIANO,** Calle Serrano 122, 28006. Tel 2616084. *Dir* Don Enrique Pardo Canalis
Collections: Italian, Spanish and Flemish Renaissance paintings; primitives; Golden Age 18th - 19th century Spanish paintings; 17th century Dutch paintings; English 18th century collection ivories, enamels, furniture, manuscripts, tapestries

M **MUSEO NACIONAL DEL PRADO** (Formerly Nacional Museo del Prado), National Museum of Paintings and Sculpture, Paseo del Prado. Tel 420-28-36. *Dir* Filipe Vicente Garin Llombart
Collections: Paintings by: Botticelli, Rembrandt, Velazquez, El Greco, Goya, Murillo, Raphael, Bosch, Van der Weyden, Zurbaran, Van Dyck, Tiepolo, Ribalta, Rubens, Titian, Veronese, Tintoretto, Moro, Juanes, Menendez, Poussin, Ribera; classical and Renaissance sculpture; jewels and medals

M **MUSEO ROMANTICO,** Museum of the Romantic Period, Calle de San Mateo 13, 28004. Tel 448-10-45. *Dir* Maria Rosa Donoso Guerrero
Collections: Books, decorations, furniture and paintings of the Spanish Romantic period

M **PATRIMONIO NACIONAL,** Calle de Bailen, 28071. Tel 248-74-04. *Dir* Julio de la Guardi Garcia
Estab 1940 to administer former Crown property; it is responsible for all the museums situated in Royal Palaces & properties & is governed by an administrative council
Publications: Guides to all the Museums

M **Palacio Real de Madrid,** Calle Bailen s/n, 28071. Tel 248-74-04.
Also maintains armoury, coach museum & 350,000 volume library
Collections: Special room devoted to 16th-18th century tapestries, clocks, paintings & porcelain from the Royal Palaces & Pharmacy

M **Palacio Real de Aranjuez,** Aranjuez, 28300. Tel 891-07-40.
Collections: Royal Palace of 18th century art

M **Monasterio de San Lorenzo de El Escorial,** San Lorenzo de El Escorial, El Escorial, 28200. Tel 890-59-03.
Built by Juan de Herrera & contains many famous works by international artists of the 16th & 18th century from royal residences
Collections: Royal Collection of famous international work by artists of 16th & 18th century

M **Alcazar de Sevilla,** Seville
Collections: Royal residence

M **Museo-Monasterio de la Huelgas,** Burgos, 09001. Tel (947) 20-16-30.
Founded by Alfonso VIII in the 9th century

M **Museo-Monasterio de Tordesillas,** Valladolid
Collections: 14th century art

M **Museo de la Encarnacion,** Madrid, 28013. Tel 248-74-04, Ext 309.
Collections: Monastic life in the 16th & 17th centuries

M **Museo de las Descalzas Reales,** Madrid, 28013. Tel 248-74-04, Ext 309.
Collections: Showing monastic life in the 16th & 17th centuries

M **Palacio de Riofrio,** Segovia
18th century rural castle
Collections: Notable furniture & paintings of Spanish romantic movement

M **Palacios de la Granja y Riofrio,** La Granja de San Ildefonso, Segovia, 40100. Tel (911) 47-00-19.
Collections: Gardens & fountains in imitation of Versailles, tapestry museum

M **Museo de Pedralbes,** Barcelona, 08034. Tel (93) 203-75-01.
Collections: 19th century royal residence; tapestries, furniture

M **Palacio de la Almudaina,** Palma de Mallorca, Balearic Is, 07001. Tel (971) 72-71-45.
Arab-Gothic palace

TOLEDO

M **CASA Y MUSEO DEL GRECO: FUNDACIONES VEGA INCLAN,** El Greco's House, Calle Samuel Levi. Tel (925) 22-40-46. *Dir* Maria Elena Gomez-Moreno
Collections: Artist's paintings and those of his followers; 16th century furniture

M **Museo del Greco**
Collections: El Greco's paintings, including portraits of Christ and the apostles and other 16th and 17th century paintings

SRI LANKA

ANURADHAPURA

M **ARCHAEOLOGICAL MUSEUM,** Tel 411. *Keeper* J S A Uduwara
Collections: Stone sculptures, mural paintings & frescoes, coins, bronzes, pottery

COLOMBO

M **COLOMBO NATIONAL MUSEUM,** Sir Marcus Fernando Mawatha, PO Box 854, 7. Tel 94767. *Dir* W Thelma T P Gunawardane
Collections: Art, folk culture and antiquities of Sri Lanka

SWEDEN

GOTEBORG

M **ROHSSKA KONSTSLOJDMUSEET,** Rohss Museum of Arts and Crafts, 37-39 Vasagatan, PO Box 53178, 411 32. Tel 031-20-06-05. *Dir* Christian Axel-Nilssoh
The arts and crafts section of the Goteborgs Museer (Museums of the City of Gothenburg)

GOTHENBURG

M **GOTEBORGS KONSTMUSEUM,** Goteborg Art Gallery, Gotaplatsen, 41256. Tel (031) 61-10-00. *Dir* Folke Edwards
Collections: French art from 1820 to present; Old Masters, especially Dutch and Flemish; Scandinavian art

LANDSKRONA

M **LANDSKRONA MUSEUM,** Slottsgatan, 26131. Tel 0418-79000. *Dir* Margareta Alin
Collections: Swedish paintings since 1900; modern Swiss art; Nell Walden paintings & ethnological collection

LINKOPING

M **OSTERGOTLANDS OCH LINKOPINGS STADTS MUSEUM,** PO Box 232, 58102. Tel (013) 13-23-03-00. *Dir* Gunnar Lindqvist
Collections: Dutch, Flemish & Swedish art; Swedish archaeology; furniture, tapestries; Egyptian collection

STOCKHOLM

M **NATIONALMUSEUM,** Sodra Blasieholmshamnen, PO Box 16176, 103 24. Tel (08) 666-42-50. *Dir* Olle Granath
Collections: 6672 paintings, icons & miniatures; 4492 sculptures, including antiquities; 202,000 drawings & prints; 29,000 items of applied art; collections of several royal castles with 7440 works of art

M **NORDISKA MUSEET,** Scandinavian Museum, Djurgardsvagen 6-16, Box 27820, S-115 21. Tel (08) 666-46-00. *Dir* Sten Rentzhog
Collections: Costumes, industrial art, handcrafts, period furnishings; over one million exhibits

M **OSTASIATISKA MUSEET,** Museum of Far Eastern Antiquities, Skeppsholmen, PO Box 163 81, S-103 27. Tel (08) 666-42-50. *Dir* Dr Jan Wirgin
Collections: Chinese archaeology, Buddhist sculpture, bronzes, painting and porcelain, Stone-age pottery; Indian, Japanese and Korean art

M **RIKSANTIKVARIEAMBETET OCH STATENS HISTORISKA MUSEER,** Central Board of National Antiquities and National Historical Museums, PO Box 5405, S-114 84
Oversees 3 museums and supervises historic monuments

M **Royal Coin Cabinet, National Musem of Monetary History,** PO Box 5405, 114 84. Tel 08-783-94-00. *Dir* Lars Lagerqvist
Collections: The collections range over the entire world and all periods

M **Museum of Mediterranean and Near Eastern Antiquities,** Fredsgatcn 2, PO Box 5405, 114 84. Tel 08-783-94-00. *Dir* Lars Olof Sjoberg

Museum of National Antiquities, PO Box 5405, S-114 84. *Dir* Ulf Erik Hagberg

M **STOCKHOLMS STADSMUSEUM,** City Museum, Peter Myndes Backe 6, S-11646. Tel (08) 70-00-500. *Dir* Bjorn Hallerdt
Collections: The Lohe Treasure, naive 19th century paintings of Josabeth Sjoberg and armed 15th century vessel; photographs; paintings; drawings, sketches and engravings

SWITZERLAND

AARAU

M **AARGAUER KUNSTHAUS,** Aargauer Platz, CH-5001. Tel (064) 21-21-30. *Dir* Beat Wismer
Collections: Swiss painting and sculpture from 1750 to the present day; Caspar Wolf paintings (1735-1783) - art of the first painter of the Alps; landscape painter Adolf Staebli and Auberjonois, Bruhlmann, Amiet, G Giacometti, Hodler, Meyer-Amden, Louis Soutter, Vallotton

ARENENBERG AM UNTERSEE

M **NAPOLEONMUSEUM ARENENBERG,** Salenstein, 8268. Tel 072-64-18-66. *Dir* Hans Peter Mathis
Collections: Works in the 19th century monumental style of Napoleon I

BASEL

M **HISTORISCHES MUSEUM BASEL,** Verwaltung, Steinenberg 4, 4051. Tel (061) 271-05-05. *Dir* Open
Collections: Collection of objects from prehistory to 19th century contained in 4 branches: Barfusserkirche, Haus zum Kirschgarten, Sammlung alter Musikinstrumente, Kutschen- und Schlittensammlung

M **MUSEUM FUR VOLKERKUNDE UND SCHWEIZERISCHES MUSEUM FUR VOLKSKUNDE BASEL,** Augustinergasse 2, PO Box 1048, 4001. Tel (061) 266-56-05. *Dir* Dr Gerhard Baer
Library with 58,000 vols
Collections: Ethnological collections from Indonesia, Europe, Oceania and South America

M **OEFFENTLICHE KUNSTSAMMLUNG BASEL KUNSTMUSEUM** (Formerly Kunstmuseum Basel), St Alben-Graben 16, 4010. Tel (061) 271-08-28. *Dir* Dr Christian Geelhaar
Library with 100,000 vols
Collections: Pictures from 15th century to present day, notably by Witz, Holbein and contemporary painters; collection includes Grunewald, Greco, Rembrandt; 16th - 17th century Netherlandish painting, Cezanne, Gauguin and Van Gogh; large collection of cubist art; sculptures by Rodin and 20th century artists; American art since 1945; German and Swiss masters

BERN

M KUNSTMUSEUM BERN, Musee des Beaux-Arts de Berne, Hodlerstrasse 8-12, 3000. Tel 031-220944. *Dir* Dr C Von Tavel
Collections: Dutch and contemporary artists; French and other European Masters of the 19th and 20th Centuries; Italian Masters; collection of Paul Klee works of 2600 items; Niklaus Manuel; Hermann and Margrit Rupf Foundation, Adolf Wolfli Foundation; Swiss Baroque Masters; Swiss 19th and 20th Century Masters; 38,000 drawings and engravings; illustrations; works by Sophie Taeuber-Arp

CHUR

M BUNDNER KUNSTMUSEUM, Postfach 107, 7002. Tel (081) 22-17-63. *Dir* Dr Beat Stutzer
Collections: Augusto, Alberto, Augusto & Giovanni Giacometti, Angelika Kauffmann, E L Kirchner; Swiss painting

GENEVA

M MUSEE D'ART ET D'HISTOIRE, 2 rue Charles Galland, Case Postale 516, 1211. Tel (022) 29-00-11. *Dir* Claude Lapaire
Collections: Swiss art works; primitive Italian, French, German and Flemish art; modern art; archaeology; European sculpture and decorative arts; six attached museums

LA CHAUX DE FONDS

M MUSEE DES BEAUX-ARTS, Museum of Fine Arts, 33 rue des Musees, 2300. Tel (039) 23-04-44. *Dir* Edmond Charriere
Collections: Works of local artists; Swiss works of the 19th and 20th centuries; modern European painting, sculpture and tapestries

LAUSANNE

M MUSEE CANTONAL DES BEAUX-ARTS, Palais de Rumine, Place de la Riponne, 1014. Tel (021) 312-83-33. *Dir* Dr J Zutter
Collections: Works by Swiss artists & artists of other European countries; works of Vaudois artists from 15th century to present

LIGORNETTO

M MUSEO VELA, 6853. Tel 091-47-32-68. *Cur* Giorgio Lazzeri
Collections: Works of art by Vela family; paintings from old and modern Italian schools

LUCERNE

M KUNSTMUSEUM LUZERN, Robert - Zundstrasse 1, Postfach 3570, 6002. Tel (041) 23-10-24. *Dir* Martin Schwander
Collections: Swiss art from ancient times to 20th century; European expressionism and contemporary works

RIGGISBERG

M ABEGG-STIFTUNG, Werner-Abegg-Str 67, 3132. Tel 031 80-12-01. *Dir* Dr Alain Gruber
Collections: Renaissance, Near East and European Middle Ages applied arts; sculpture, painting, gold, textiles & other artifacts

SANKT GALLEN

M HISTORISCHES MUSEUM, Historical Museum, Museumstrasse 50, CH-9000. Tel 071-24-78-32. *Cur* Dr Louis Specker
Collections: Furniture, glass and glass painting, graphics, period rooms, pewter, porcelain, stoves, weapons

SCHAFFHAUSEN

M MUSEUM ZU ALLERHEILIGEN, klostergasse 1, CH-8200. Tel (053) 25-43-77. *Dir* Dr Gerard Seiterle
Collections: Prehistory, history and art of the region

SOLOTHURN

M KUNSTMUSEUM SOLOTHURN, Solothurn Art Museum, Werkhofstrasse 30, 4500. Tel (065) 22-23-07. *Cur* Andre Kamber
Collections: Swiss art from 1850 to 1980, including Amiet, Berger, Buscher, Frolicher, Hodler, Trachsel; small old master collection; private art section

WINTERTHUR

M KUNSTMUSEUM WINTERTHUR, Museumstrasse 52, POB 378, 8402. Tel (052) 84-51-62. *Pres* Urs Widmer; *Cur* Dr Dieter Schwarz
Collections: Swiss painting and sculpture from 18th century to present day; French, Italian and German painting and sculpture of 19th and 20th centuries, including Monet, Degas, Picasso, Gris, Leger, Klee, Schlemmer, Schwitters, Arp, Kandinsky, Renoir, Bonnard, Maillol, Van Gogh, Rodin, Brancusi, Morandi, Giacometti, de Stael; drawings and prints

M MUSEUM STIFTUNG OSKAR REINHART, Am Romerholz, Stadthausstrasse 6, 8400. Tel (052) 84-51-72. *Cur* Dr Peter Wegmann
Collections: Pictures & drawings of Old Masters; French paintings and sculptures of the 19th century

ZURICH

M KUNSTHAUS ZURICH, Museum of Fine Arts, Heimplatz 1, 8024. Tel 01-251-67-65. *Dir* Dr Felix Baumann
Library with 55,000 vols
Collections: Alberto Giacometti works; medieval and modern sculptures; paintings; graphic arts, 16th - 20th centuries, mainly 19th and 20th

M MUSEUM RIETBERG ZURICH, Gablerstrasse 15, 8002. Tel (01) 202-45-28. *Dir* Dr Eberhard Fischer
Collections: Asiatic, Oceania and African art; Chinese bronzes; Baron von der Heydt Collection

M SCHWEIZERISCHES LANDESMUSEUM-MUSEE NATIONAL SUISSSE, Swiss National Museum, Museumstrasse 2, CH-8023. Tel 01-221-10-10. *Dir* Dr Andres Fuger
Library with 85,000 vols
Collections: History and cultural development of Switzerland since prehistoric times

SYRIA

DAMASCUS

M MUSEE NATIONAL DE DAMAS, National Museum, Syrian University St, 4. Tel 214-854. *General Dir* Dr Ali Abu Assaf
Collections: Ancient, Byzantine, Greek, Islamic, Modern, Oriental, Prehistoric and Roman art

TANZANIA

DAR ES SALAAM

M NATIONAL MUSEUM OF TANZANIA, PO Box 511. Tel 31365. *Dir* M L Mbago
Collections: Archaeology from Stone Age sites; ethnography & history collections

THAILAND

BANGKOK

M NATIONAL MUSEUM, Na Phra-dhart Rd, Amphoe Phda Nakhon, 10200. Tel 2217815. *Dir* Mrs Chira Chongkol
Collections: Bronze & stone sculptures, prehistoric artifacts, textiles, weapons, wood-carvings, royal regalia, theatrical masks, marionettes, shadow-play figures

TRINIDAD AND TOBAGO

PORT OF SPAIN

M NATIONAL MUSEUM AND ART GALLERY, 117 Frederick St. Tel 62-35941. *Dir* M P Alladin; *Cur* Claire Broadbridge
Collections: Fine art, archaeology, history & natural history collections

TUNISIA

TUNIS

M MUSEE NATIONAL DU BARDO, Bardo National Museum, Le Bardo. Tel 51-36-50. *Dir* Aicha Ben Abed
Collections: Ancient and modern Islamic art; Greek and Roman antiquities; Roman mosaics

TURKEY

ISTANBUL

M **ISTANBUL ARKEOLOJI MUZELERI,** Archaeological Museums of Istanbul, Gulhane, 34400. Tel 5207740. *Dir* Alpay Pasinli
Library with 80,000 vols
Collections: Architectural pieces; Turkish tiles; Akkadian, Assyrian, Byzantine, Egyptian, Greek, Hittite, Roman, Sumerian and Urartu works of art

M **TOPKAPI SARAYI MUZESI,** Topkapi Palace Museum, Sultanahmed. Tel 28-35-47. *Dir* Sabahattin Turkoglu
Library with 18,000 manuscripts and 23,000 archival documents
Collections: Chinese and Japanese porcelains; miniatures and portraits of Sultans; private collections of Kenan Ozbel; Sami Ozgiritli's collection of furniture; Islamic relics; Sultan's costumes; Turkish embroideries; armor; tiles; applied arts; paintings

M **TURK VE ISLAM ESERLERI MUZESI,** Museum of Turkish and Islamic Art, Ibrahim Pasa Sarayi, Sultanahmet. Tel 528-5158. *Dir* Nazan Tapan Olcer
Collections: Illuminated manuscripts; monuments of Islamic art; metalwork and ceramics; Turkish and Islamic carpets; sculpture in stone and stucco; wood carvings; traditional crafts gathered from Turkish mosques and tombs

UKRAINE

KIEV

M **KIEV STATE MUSEUM OF RUSSIAN ART,** Ul Repina 9, Ukrainian SSR. Tel 224-82-88. *Dir* M N Soldatova
Collections: 10,000 art objects

M **KIEV STATE MUSEUM OF UKRAINIAN ART,** Ul Kirova 6, Ukrainian SSR 252004. *Dir* V F Yatsenko
Collections: Portraits, icons, wood carvings & paintings from the Middle Ages; exhibits covering 8 centuries

M **KIEV STATE MUSEUM OF WESTERN & ORIENTAL ART,** Ul Repina 15, Ukrainian SSR. *Dir* V F Ovchinikov
Collections: 16,000 items of artistic interest

M **UKRAINIAN MUSEUM OF FOLK AND DECORATIVE ART,** Ul Yanvarskogo Vosstaniya 21, Ukrainian SSR. *Dir* V G Nagai
Collections: Wood carvings, ceramics, weaving & applied arts from 16th century to present

ODESSA

M **ODESSA MUSEUM OF WESTERN AND EASTERN ART,** Ul Pushkinshaya 9, Ukrainian SSR. Tel 22-48-15. *Dir* N G Lutzkevich
Collections: Over 8000 art objects

URUGUAY

MONTEVIDEO

M **MUSEO MUNICIPAL DE BELLAS ARTES,** Avda Millan 4015. Tel 38-54-20. *Dir* Mario C Tempone
Collections: Paintings, sculptures, drawings, wood-carvings

M **MUSEO NACIONAL DE BELLAS ARTES,** National Museum of Fine Arts, Tomas Giribaldi 2283, Parque Rodo. Tel 438-00. *Dir* Angel Kalenberg
Collections: 4217 ceramics, drawings, engravings, paintings and sculptures

VENEZUELA

CARACAS

M **GALERIA DE ARTE NACIONAL,** Plaza Morelos-Los Caobos, Apartado 6729, 1010. Tel 571-26-53. *Dir* Michelle Arias Bernard
Collections: Visual arts of Venezuela throughout history

M **MUSEO DE BELLAS ARTES,** Museum of Fine Arts, Plaza Morelos, Los Caobos, 105. Tel 571-01-69. *Dir* Maria Elena Ramos
Collections: Latin American and foreign paintings and sculpture

VIETNAM

HANOI

M **NATIONAL ART GALLERY,** 66 Nguyen Thai Hoc St. Tel 52830. *Dir* Nguyen Van Chung
Collections: Ancient and modern ceramics, fine arts and handicrafts; Vietnamese cultural heritage; specialized library of over 1100 volumes

YUGOSLAVIA

BELGRADE

M **MUSEUM OF CONTEMPORARY ART,** Usce Save bb, 11071. Tel 011-145-900. *Dir* Zoran Gavric
Collections: Yugoslav and foreign art

ZAIRE

KINSHASA

M **INSTITUT DES MUSEES NATIONAUX DU ZAIRE,** BP 4249, 2. Tel 59536. *Pres* Del-Gen Lema Gwete
Collections: Art, archaeology, traditional music & contemporary art

ZIMBABWE

CAUSEWAY HARARE

M **NATIONAL GALLERY OF ZIMBABWE,** 20 Julius Nyerere Way, PO Box 8155. Tel 704666. *Dir* Prof C A Rogers
Collections: African traditional and local contemporary sculpture and paintings; ancient and modern European paintings and sculpture, including works by Bellini, Caracciolo, Gainsborough, Murillo, Reynolds, Rodin

Major Art Schools Abroad

ARGENTINA

BUENOS AIRES

ESCUELA NACIONAL DE BELLAS ARTES MANUEL BELGRANO, National School of Fine Arts Manuel Belgrano, Venceslao Villafane 1342. Tel 362-3101. *Dir* Isolina G De Oliver

ESCUELA SUPERIOR DE BELLAS ARTES DE LA NACION ERNESTO DE LA CARCOVA, Tristan Aehaval Rodriguez 1701, 1107. Tel 31-5144. *Rector* Mario Vanarelli

AUSTRALIA

DARLINGHURST

SCHOOL OF ART & DESIGN, Forbes St, 2010. Tel 339-0266. *Head* Dr Don Mitchell

GLEBE

SYDNEY COLLEGE OF THE ARTS, 266 Glebe Point Rd, PO Box 226, New South 2037. Tel 02-692-0266. *Dir* R Dunn

HOBART

UNIVERSITY OF TASMANIA, Tasmanian School of Art, GPO Box 252C, Tasmania 7001. Tel (002) 202101. *Dean* R H Ewins

MELBOURNE

VICTORIAN COLLEGE OF THE ARTS, School of Art, 234 St Kilda Rd, Victoria 3004. Tel (03) 616-9300. *Dir* Dr Alwynne Mackie

RED HILL

ROYAL AUSTRALIAN INSTITUTE OF ARCHITECTS, 2A Mugga Way, ACT 2603. Telex 6-2428; Tel (062) 73-1548. *Executive Dir* D C R Bailey

SYDNEY

UNIVERSITY OF SYDNEY, Department of Archaeology, NSW 2006. Telex 20056; Tel 02-692-2222. *Chancellor* Dame Leonie Kramer

AUSTRIA

SALZBURG

INTERNATIONALE SOMMERAKADEMIE FUR BILDENDE KUNST, International Summer Academy of Fine Arts, PO Box 18, 5010. Tel 84-21-13. *Pres* Dr Wieland Schmied

VIENNA

HOCHSCHULE FUR ANGEWANDTE KUNST IN WIEN, University of Applied Arts in Vienna, Stubenring 3, Oskar Kokoschkaplatz 2, 1010. Tel (01) 71111. *Rector* Oswald Oberhuber

BELGIUM

ANTWERP

NATIONAAL HOGER INSTITUUT EN KONINKLIJKE ACADEMIE VOOR SCHONE KUNSTEN, National Higher Institute and Royal Academy of Fine Arts, 31 Mutsaertstraat, 2000. Tel 03-232-41-61. *Dir* Garard Gaudaen

NATIONAAL HOGER INSTITUUT VOOR BOUWKUNST EN STEDEBOUW, National Higher Institute of Architecture and Town Planning, Mutsaertstraat 31, 2000. Tel 31-70-84. *Dir* J de Mol

BRUSSELS

ACADEMIE ROYALE DES BEAUX-ARTS DE BRUXELLES, Brussels Royal Academy of Fine Arts, 144 rue du Midi, B-1000. Tel 02-511-04-91. *Dir* D Vienne

ECOLE NATIONALE SUPERIEURE DES ARTS VISUELS DE LA CAMBRE, 21 Abbaye de la Cambre, 1050. Tel 02-648-96-19. *Dir* Joseph Noiret

NAMUR

ECOLE DES BEAUX-ARTS DE NAMUR, 20 rue du Lombard, 5000. Tel 22-32-90. *Dir* M Evrard

BRAZIL

RIO DE JANEIRO

ESCOLA DE ARTES VISUAIS, School of Visual Arts, 414 Rua Jardim Botanico, Parque Lage, 22461. *Dir* Frederico de Moraes

BULGARIA

SOFIA

NIKOLAJ PAVLOVIC HIGHER INSTITUTE OF FINE ARTS, Shipkal, 1000. Tel 88-17-01. *Rector* B Gondov

CHINA, REPUBLIC OF

TAIPEI

NATIONAL TAIWAN ACADEMY OF ARTS, Pan-chiao Park, 22055. Tel 967-6414. *Pres* S L Ling

COLOMBIA

BOGOTA

PONTIFICIA UNIVERSIDAD JAVERIANA, Carrera 7, No 40-76, Apdo Aereo 56710. Tel 287-57-91. *Dean Faculty of Architecture* Arq Billy Escobar

CROATIA

ZAGREB

AKADEMIJA IIKOVNIJ UMJETNOSTI, Academy of Fine Arts, 85 Ilica, 41000. Tel 577-300. *Dir* Arte Kuduz

CZECH REPUBLIC

PRAGUE

AKADEMIE VYTVARNYCH UMENI, Academy of Fine Arts, Ul v Akademie 4, 17022. Tel 37-36-41. *Rector* Milan Knizak

VYSOKA SKOLA UMELECKOPRUMYSLOVA, Academy of Applied Arts, Nam Jana Palacha 80, 116 93. Tel 231-95-12. *Rector* Jiri Harcuba

DENMARK

AARHUS C

ARKITEKTSKOLEN I AARHUS, Aarhus School of Architecture, Norreport 20, 8000. Tel 86-13-08-22. *Rector* Gosta Knudsen

COPENHAGEN

KONGELIGE DANSKE KUNSTAKADEMI, The Royal Danish Academy of Fine Arts, Charlottenborg, Kongens Nytorv 1, 1050. Tel 33-12-68-60. *Rector School of Fine Arts* Helge Brinch Madsen

DOMINICAN REPUBLIC

SANTO DOMINGO

DIRECCION GENERAL DE BELLAS ARTES, Fine Arts Council, *Dir* Jose Delmonte Peguero

ENGLAND

BIRMINGHAM

BIRMINGHAM POLYTECHNIC, Faculty of Art & Design, Perry Barr, B42 2SU. Tel (021) 331-5000. *Dean Art & Design* J E C Price

BRIGHTON

BRIGHTON POLYTECHNIC, Faculty of Art & Design, Lewes Rd, BN2 4AT. Tel (0273) 600-900. *Dean Art, Design & Humanities* D Brown

EXETER

EXETER COLLEGE OF ART & DESIGN, Earl Richards Rd N, EX2 6AS. Tel 77977. *Head* Dr D Jaremiah

FARNHAM

WEST SURREY COLLEGE OF ART & DESIGN, Falkner Rd, Surrey, GU9 7DS. Tel 0252-722441. *Dir* N J Taylor

GLOUCESTER

GLOUCESTERSHIRE COLLEGE OF ARTS & TECHNOLOGY, The Park. *Dir* J Trotter

IPSWICH

SUFFOLK COLLEGE OF HIGHER & FURTHER EDUCATION, Department of Art & Design, Rope Walk, IP4 1LT. Tel 0473-55885. *Head* J Roger Lowe

LEICESTER

LEICESTER POLYTECHNIC, Faculty of Art and Design, PO Box 143, LE1 9BH. Tel (0533) 551551. *Dean Art & Design* N Witts

LIVERPOOL

LIVERPOOL POLYTECHNIC, Faculty of Art and Design, Rodney House, 70 Mount Pleasant, L3 5UX. Tel (051) 207-3581. *Dean* G Breakwell

LONDON

CAMBERWELL SCHOOL OF ART AND CRAFTS, Peckham Rd, SE5 8UF. Tel (071) 703-0987.

CHELSEA SCHOOL OF ART & DESIGN, Manresa Rd, SW3 6LS. Tel (071) 351-3844. *Principal* William Callaway

CITY AND GUILDS OF LONDON ART SCHOOL, 124 Kennington Park Rd, SE11 4DJ. *Principal* Roger De Grey

LONDON INSTITUTE, Central School of Art & Design, 388-960 Oxford St, W1R 1FE. Tel (071) 491-8533. *Rector* John McKenzie

ROYAL ACADEMY SCHOOLS, Burlington House, Piccadilly, W1V ODS. Tel 01-734-9052, Sch Ext 40. *Keeper Prof* Norman Adams

ROYAL COLLEGE OF ART, Kensington Gore, SW7 2EU. Tel (071) 584-5020. *Rector* Jocelyn Stevens

SAINT MARTIN'S SCHOOL OF ART, 107 Charing Cross Rd, WC2H 0DU. Tel 437-0611. *Principal* Ian Simpson

SLADE SCHOOL OF FINE ART, University College, Gower St, WC1. Tel (071) 387-7050. *Dir* Bernard Cohen

UNIVERSITY OF LONDON, Goldsmiths' College, Lewisham Way, New Cross, SE14 6NW. Tel 081-692-7171. *Warden Prof* Andrew Rutherford

WIMBLEDON SCHOOL OF ART, Merton Hall Rd, SW19 3QA. Tel 081-540-0231; FAX 081-543-1750. *Principal* Colin Painter
—**Department of Foundation Studies,** Palmerston Rd, London, England SW19 1PB. Tel 081-540-0231; Student Tel 081-540-7504; FAX 081-543-1750. *Dept Head* Yvonne Crossley
—**Department of Theatre,** Merton Hall Rd, London, England SW19 3QA. Tel 081-540-0231; FAX 081-543-1750. *Dept Head* Malcolm Pride
—**Department of Fine Arts,** Merton Hall Rd, London, England SW19 3QA. Tel 081-540-0231; FAX 081-543-1750. *Dept Head* Michael Ginsborg
—**Department of History of Art & Contextual Studies,** Merton Hall Rd, London, England SW19 3QA. Tel 081-540-0231; FAX 081-543-1750. *Dept Head* Keith Matthews

MANCHESTER

MANCHESTER POLYTECHNIC, Faculty of Art and Design, All Saints Bldg, All Saints, M15 GBH. Tel (061) 247-2000. *Dean Art & Design* R Wilson

NOTTINGHAM

NOTTINGHAM TRENT POLYTECHNIC, School of Art and Design, Burton Street, NG1 4BU. Telex 37-7534; Tel (0602) 418418. *Dean* E W Newton

OXFORD

UNIVERSITY OF OXFORD, Ruskin School of Drawing and Fine Art, 74 High St, OX1 4BG. Tel 08-65-24-78-25. *Principal* Stephen Farthing

ESTONIA

TALLINN

ESTONIAN SOVIET SOCIALIST REPUBLIC STATE ART INSTITUTE, Tartu Maantee 1. Tel 43-26-64. *Rector* J Kangilaski

FINLAND

HELSINKI

KUVATAIDEAKATEMIA, Academy of Fine Arts, Yrjonkatu 18, 00120. *Rector* Lauri Anttila

FRANCE

FONTAINEBLEAU

ECOLES D'ART AMERICAINES DE FONTAINEBLEAU, Fontainebleau Schools of Fine Arts, Palace of Fontainebleau, 77300. Tel 64-22-25-39.

PARIS

ECOLE DU LOUVRE, School of the Louvre, 34 quai du Louvre, 75001. Tel 42-60-39-26. *Principal* D Ponnau

ECOLE NATIONALE SUPERIEURE DES ARTS DECORATIFS, National College of Decorative Arts, 31 rue d'Ulm, 75005. Tel 43-29-86-79. *Dir* Richard Peduzzi

ECOLE NATIONALE SUPERIEURE DES BEAUX-ARTS, National College of Fine Arts, 17, quai Malaquais, 75006. Tel 42-60-34-57. *Dir* Y Michaud

ECOLE SPECIALE D'ARCHITECTURE, 254 blvd Raspail, 75014. Tel 43-22-83-70. *Dir* Michel Denes

UNIVERSITE DE PARIS I, PANTHEON-SORBONNE, UFR d'Art et d'Archeologie, 12 Place du Pantheon, 75231. Tel 1-46-34-97-00. *Actg Dir Art & Archaeology* L Pressouyre

VILLENEUVE D'ASCQ

UNITED PEDAGOGIQUE D' ARCHITECTURE, rue Verte, Quartier de l'Hotel de Ville, 59650. Tel 20-05-48-91. *Dir* Gerard Engrand

GERMANY

BERLIN

HOCHSCHULE DER KUNSTE BERLIN, 10 Ernst-Reuter-Platz 10, Postfac 126720, 1000. Tel 030-31-85-0.

BRUNSWICK

HOCHSCHULE FUR BILDENDE KUNSTE, Johannes-Selenka-Platz 1, 3300. Tel 391-9122. *Rector* Dr Dieter Welzel

DRESDEN

HOCHSCHULE FUR BILDENE KUNSTE, Guntzstrasse 34, 8019. Tel 4590112. *Rector* Ingo Sandner

DUSSELDORF

STAATLICHE KUNSTAKADEMIE DUSSELDORF, Hochschule fur Bildende Kunste, State Academy of Art, Eiskellerstrasse 1, 4000. Tel 32-93-34. *Dir* Markus Lupentz

FRANKFURT

STADELSCHULE, STEATLICHE HOCHSCHULE FUR BILDENE KUNSTE, Durerstrasse 10, 6000. Tel 069-605-008-0. *Rector* Kasper Konig

HAMBURG

HOCHSCHULE FUR BILDENDE KUNSTE, College of Fine Arts, Lerchenfeld 2, 2000. Tel 040-29188. *Pres* Adrienne Goehler

KARLSRUHE

STAATLICHE AKADEMIE DER BILDENDEN KUNSTE, State Academy of Fine Arts, Reinhold-Frank-Strasse 81-83, 7500. Tel 0721-843038. *Rector* Dr Andreas Franzke

LEIPZIG

HOCHSCHULE FUR GRAFIK UND BUCHKUNST, State Academy of Graphic Arts and Book Production, Dimitroffstrasse 11, Postfach 68, 7010. Tel 391-32-11. *Rector* Arno Rink

MUNICH

AKADEMIE DER BILDENDEN KUNSTE, Academy of Fine Arts, Akademiestr 2, 8000. Tel 089-3852-0. *Pres* Dr Wieland Schmied

NUREMBERG

AKADEMIE DER BILDENDEN KUNSTE IN NURNBERG, Academy of Fine Arts in Nuremberg, Bingstrasse 60, 8500. Tel 0911-40-50-61. *Pres* Dr Rainer Beck

STUTTGART

STAATLICHE AKADEMIE DER BILDENDEN KUNSTE, State Academy of Fine Arts, Am Weissenhof 1, 7000. Tel 0711-2575-0. *Rector* Dr Paul Uwe Dreyer

GREECE

ATHENS

ECOLE FRANCAISE D'ATHENES, French Archeological School, 6 Ave Didotou, 16080. Tel 01-3612518. *Dir* Oliver Picard

HUNGARY

BUDAPEST

MAGYAR KEPZOMUVESZETI FOISKOLA, Hungarian Academy of Fine Arts, Andrassy vt 69-71, 1062. Tel 1421-738. *Rector* Lajos Svaby

INDIA

BARODA

MAHARAJA SAYAJIRAO UNIVERSITY OF BARODA, Faculty of Fine Arts, University Rd, Gujarat 390002. Tel 64721. *Dean Faculty Fine Arts* S G Kantawala

BOMBAY

ACADEMY OF ARCHITECTURE, Plot 278, Shankar Ghaneker Marg, Prabhadevi, 400025. *Principal* C K Gumaste

LUCKNOW

UNIVERSITY OF LUCKNOW, College of Arts and Crafts, Faculty of Fine Arts, Badshah Bagh, 226007. Tel 43138. *Dean* Gopala Singh

MYSORE

SRI VARALAKSHMI ACADEMIES OF FINE ARTS, Chamaraja Double Rd, Ramvilas, Kasphipathy Agarahar, 4. *Principal* C V Srivatsa

IRELAND

DUBLIN

COLAISTE NAISIUNTA EALAINE IS DEARTHA, National College of Art & Design, 100 Thomas St, 8. Tel 01-711-377. *Dir* John Turpin

ISRAEL

JERUSALEM

BEZALEL ACADEMY OF ARTS & DESIGN, Mount Scopus, POB 24046, 91240. Tel 02-89-33-33. *Dir* Ran Sapoznik

ITALY

BOLOGNA

ACCADEMIA DI BELLE ARTI, Academy of Fine Arts, via Belle Arti 54, 40126. Tel 051-243 064. *Dir* A Baccilieri

FLORENCE

ACCADEMIA DI BELLE ARTI, Academy of Fine Arts, via Ricasoli 66, 50122. Tel 055-215-449. *Dir* D Viggiano

MILAN

ACCADEMIA DI BELLE ARTI, Academy of Fine Arts, Palazzo di Brera, via Brera 28, 20121. Tel 02-86-46-19-29. *Pres* Walter Fontana

NAPLES

ACCADEMIA DI BELLE ARTI E LICEO ARTISTICO, Academy of Fine Arts, via Bellini 36, 80135. *Dir* Constanza Lorenzetti

PERUGIA

ACCADEMIA DI BELLE ARTI, Academy of Fine Arts, Piazza San Francesco al Prato 5, 06100. Tel 075-29106. *Dir* Edgardo Abbozzo

RAVENNA

ACCADEMIA DI BELLE ARTI, Academy of Fine Arts, Loggetta Lombardesca, Via di Roma 13, 48100. Tel 30178. *Dir* Adriano Baccilieri

ROME

ACCADEMIA DI BELLE ARTI, Academy of Fine Arts, via di Ripetta 222, 00186. Tel 06-679-88-61. *Dir* Guido Strazza

AMERICAN ACADEMY IN ROME, Via Angelo Masina 5, 00153. Tel 06-58461. *Dir* Joseph Connors

BRITISH SCHOOL AT ROME, Piazzale Winston Churchill 5, 00197. Tel 06-32-30-743. *Dir* R A Hodges

ISTITUTO CENTRALE DEL RESTAURO, Central Institute for the Restoration of Works of Art, Piazza San Francesco di Paola 9, 00184. Tel 48-27-142-5. *Dir* Dott M d'Elia

TURIN

ACCADEMIA ALBESTINA DI BELLE ARTI, via Accademia Albestina 6, 10123. Tel 011-8397008. *Pres* P Delle Roncole

VENICE

ACCADEMIA DI BELLE ARTI, Academy of Fine Arts, Campo della Carita 1050, 30123. Tel 041-27104. *Dir* Nedo Fiorentin

JAMAICA

KINGSTON

EDNA MANLEY SCHOOL FOR THE VISUAL ARTS, Cultural Training Center, One Arthur Wint Dr, Kingston 5. Tel: 92-92350-3. *Librn* Jessica McCurdy

JAPAN

KANAZAWA CITY

KANAZAWA COLLEGE OF ART, 5-11-1 Kodatsuno, Kanazawa-shi, Ishikawa 920, 920. Tel (0762) 62-3531. *Pres* Fujio Kitade

KYOTO

KYOTO CITY UNIVERSITY OF ARTS, 13-6 Kutsukake-Cho, Oheda, Nishikyo-Ku, 610-11. Tel 075-332-0701. *Head* Takeshi Umehasa

TOKYO

TAMA BIJUTSU DAIGATU, Tama Art University, 3-15-34 Kaminoge, Setagaya-Ku, 158. Tel (03) 3702-1141. *Pres* K Goto

TOKYO GRIJUTSO DAIGAKU, Tokyo National University of Fine Arts & Music, 12-8 Ueno Park, Taito-Ku, 110. Tel 828-61-11. *Pres* Masao Yamamoto

KOREA, REPUBLIC OF

SEOUL

SEOUL NATIONAL UNIVERSITY, College of Fine Arts, Sinlim-dong, Kwanak-gu, 151. Tel 877-1601. *Dean* Se-ok Suh

LEBANON

BEIRUT

ACADEMIE LIBANAISE DES BEAUX-ARTS, PO Box 55251, Sin-El-Fil. Tel 480-056. *Chair* Georges Khodr

LITHUANIA

RIGA

VALST MAKSLAS AKADEMIJA, Latvian Soviet Socialist Republic State Academy of Arts, Bulvar Kommunarov 13, 226185. Tel 33-22-02. *Rector* Edgars Iltners

MEXICO

MEXICO CITY

ESCUELA NACIONAL DE ARTES PLASTICAS, National School of Plastic Arts, Calle Academia 22. Tel 522-06-30. *Dir* Roberto Garibay Sida
Courses: Engraving

INSTITUTO NACIONAL DE BELLAS ARTES, Avda Juarez 1. Tel 520-9060. *Dir* Vicgor Sandoval de Leon

PUEBLA

UNIVERSIDAD DE LAS AMERICAS, Artes Graficas y Diseno, Apartado Postal 100, Santa Catarina Martir, 72820. Tel 47-00-00. *Dean* Mtra Maria Gonzalez

MOROCCO

TETOUAN

ECOLE NATIONALE DES BEAUX ARTS, Ave Mohamed V, Cite Scolaire BP 89. *Dir* Mohammed M Serghini

NETHERLANDS

AMSTERDAM

ACADEMIE VAN BOUWKUNST, Academy of Architecture, Waterlooplein 211, 1011 PG. Tel 020-622-0188. *Dir* N Stam

GERRIT RIETVELD ACADEMIE, Lutmastraat 191, 1076 ED, 1000. Tel 73-47-77. *Dir* W H van Schothorst

RIJKSAKADEMIE VAN BEELDENDE KUNSTEN, State Academy of Fine Arts, Stadhouderskade 86, 1073 AT. Tel 020-679-7811. *Dir* J Schrofer

BREDA

ACADEMIE VOOR BEELDENDE KUNSTEN ST JOOST, St Joost Academy of Art and Design, 18 St Janstraat, 4811 ZM. Tel 13-57-86. *Dir* J Peeters

GRONINGEN

AKADEMIE VOOR BEELDENDE KUNSTEN AKADEMIE MINERVA, Minerva Academy of Fine Arts, Gedempte Zuiderdiep 158, 9711 HN. Tel 18-54-54. *Dir* A van Hijum

THE HAGUE

KONINKLIJKE ACADEMIE VAN BEELDENDE KUNSTEN, Royal Academy of Fine and Applied Arts, Prinsessegracht 4, 2514 AN. Tel 070-364-3835. *Dir* C M Rehorst

STICHTING DE VRIJE ACADEMIE VOOR BEELDENDE KUNSTEN, De Gheijnstraat 129, PO Box 61390, 2506 AJ. Tel 63-89-68. *Dir* Frans A M Zwartjes

HERTOGENBOSCH

KONINKLIJKE AKADEMIE VOOR KUNST EN VORMGEVING, Royal Academy of Art and Design, Sportlaan 56, 5223 AZ. Tel 21-47-25. *Dir* C Veldman

ROTTERDAM

ACADEMIE VAN BEELDENDE KUNSTEN ROTTERDAM, Rotterdam Academy of Art, Blaak 10, 3011 TA. Tel 010-411-2853. *Dir* P V D Broek

NEW ZEALAND

AUCKLAND

UNIVERSITY OF AUCKLAND, Elam School of Fine Arts, Whitaker Place. Tel 737-999. *Dean* Jolyon D Saunders

NORWAY

OSLO

STATENS HANDVERKS-OG KUNSTINDUSTRISKOLE, National College of Art, Crafts and Design, Ullevalsveien 5, 0165. Tel 02-201-235. *Rector* Roar Hoyland

STATENS KUNSTAKADEMI, National Academy of Fine Art, St Olavs Gate 32, 0166. Tel 02-20-01-50. *Rector* Zdenka Rusova

PERU

LIMA

ESCUELA NACIONAL SUPERIOR DE BELLAS ARTES, National School of Fine Arts, 681 Jiron Ancash. *Dir* Juan Manuel Ugarte Elespupu

POLAND

CRACOW

AKADEMIA SZTUK PIEKNYCH IM JANA MATEJKI W KRAKOWIE, Academy of Fine Arts in Cracow, Pl Matekji 13, 31-157. Tel 22-24-50. *Rector* Jan Szancenbach

GDANSK

PANSTWOWA WYZSZA SZKOLA SZTUK PLASTYCZNYCH, Higher School of Fine Arts, Ul Targ Weglowy 6, 80-836. Tel 31-28-01. *Rector* Stanislaw Radwanski

LODZ

PANSTWOWA WYZSZA SZKOLA SZTUK PLASTYCZNYCH, Higher School of Applied Arts, Ul Wojska Polskiego 121, 91-726. Tel 56-97-56. *Rector* Ryszard Hunger

WARSAW

AKADEMIA SZTUK PIEKNYCH, Academy of Fine Arts, Ul Krakowskie Przedmiescie 5, 00-068. Tel 26-19-72. *Rector* Jan Tarasin

WROCLAW

PANSTWOWA WYZSZA SZKOLA SZTUK PLASTYCZYNCH, Higher School of Fine Arts, Pl Polski 3/4, 50-156. Tel 315-58. *Rector* Andrzej Klimczak-Dobrazaniecki

PORTUGAL

LISBON

ESCOLA SUPERIOR DE BELAS ARTES, School of Fine Arts, Largo da Academia Nacional de Belas-Artes, 1200. Tel 36-81-74. *Pres* Augusto Pereira Brandao

OPORTO

ESCOLA SUPERIOR DE BELAS ARTES, School of Fine Arts, Av Rodrigues de Freitas 265. Tel 228-77. *Dir* Carlos Ramos

RUSSIA

LENINGRAD

LENINGRAD I E REPIN INSTITUTE OF ARTS, Universitetskaya Naberezhnaya 17, 199034. Tel 213-61-89. *Rector* P T Fomin

MOSCOW

V I SURIKOV STATE ARTS INSTITUTE, 30 Tovarishcheskii Pereulok. Tel 272-73-23. *Dir* N V Tomsky

SCOTLAND

DUNDEE

DUNCAN OF JORDANSTONE COLLEGE OF ART, Perth Rd. Tel (0382) 23261. *Principal* R Miller-Smith

EDINBURGH

EDINBURGH COLLEGE OF ART, Lauriston Place, EH3 9DF. Tel 031-229-9311. *Principal* Alistair Rowan

GLASGOW

GLASGOW SCHOOL OF ART, 167 Renfrew St, G3 6RQ. Tel 041-332-9797. *Dir* Dr J Whiteman

SLOVAK REPUBLIC

BRATISLAVA

VYSOKA SKOLA VYTVARNYCH UMENI, Academy of Fine Arts, Hviezdoslavovo 18, 814 37. Tel 332-431. *Rector* Jozef Jankovic

SOUTH AFRICA, REPUBLIC OF

CAPE TOWN

UNIVERSITY OF CAPE TOWN, Michaelis School of Fine Art, 31 Orange St. Tel 650911. *Dean* J W Rabie

JOHANNESBURG

TECHNIKON WITWATERSRAND, School of Art and Design, PO Box 3293, 2000. Tel 011-406-2911. *Chmn Art* P J Coetzee

SPAIN

BARCELONA

REAL ACADEMIA CATALANA DE BELLAS ARTES DE SANT JORDI, Royal Academy of Fine Arts, Casa Lonja, Paseo de Isabel II, 08003. Tel 319-24-32. *Prés* Joan Bassegoda Nonell

MADRID

CENTRO DE ESTUDIOS HISTORICOS, Departamento de Historia del Arte, Diego Velazquez, CSIC, Duque de Medinaceli 4, 28014. Tel 429-20-17. *Chief of Dept* Enrique Arias Angles

SEVILLE

ESCUELA SUPERIOR DE BELLAS ARTES DE SANTA ISABEL DE HUNGRIA DE SEVILLE, Calle Gonzalo Bilbao 7-13, 41001. Tel 22-11-98. *Dir* Dr Antonio Sancho

VALENCIA

ESCUELA SUPERIOR DE BELLAS ARTES DE SAN CARLOS, Valencia School of Fine Arts, Calle del Museo 2. *Dir* Daniel de Nueda Llisiona

SWEDEN

STOCKHOLM

KONSTFACKSKOLAN, National College of Art & Design, Valhallavagan 191, PO Box 27116, 102 52. Tel 08-667-95-50. *Principal* Inez Svensson

KONSTHOGSKOLAN, College of Fine Arts, Fredsgatan 12, Box 16 317, 103 26. Tel 08-24-63-00. *Principal* Olle Kaks

SWITZERLAND

GENEVA

ECOLES D'ART DE GENEVE, Geneva Schools of Art, 9 blvd Helvetique, 1205. Tel 022-29-05-10. *Dir* Michel Rappo
—**Ecole Superieure D'Art Visuel,** Higher School of Visual Arts, 9, bd Helvetique, Geneva, Switzerland 1205. Tel 022-29-05-10. *Dir* Michel Rappo
—**Ecole des Arts Decoratifs,** School of Decorative Arts, Rue Jacques-Necker 2, Geneva, Switzerland 1201. Tel 022-732-04-39. *Dir* Roger Fallet

LAUSANNE

ECOLE CANTONALE D'ART DE LAUSANNE, Lausanne College of Art, Ave de l'Elysee 4, 1006. Tel 021-617-75-23. *Dir* J Monnier-Raball

VENEZUELA

CARACAS

ESCUELA DE ARTES VISUALES CRISTOBAL ROJAS, Cristobal Rojas School of Visual Arts, Avda Lecund-Este 10 bis, El Conde. *Dir* Carmen Julia Negron de Valery

NATIONAL ENDOWMENT FOR THE ARTS

Dorothy Lewis
1100 Pennsylbania Ave, NW
Washington, DC 20506-0001
Tel 202-682-5400

REGIONAL ORGANIZATIONS

Arts Midwest

David Fraher, Exec Dir
528 Hennepin Ave, Suite 310
Minneapolis, MN 55403
Tel 612-341-0755
(IA, IL, IN, MI, MN, OH, ND, SD, WI)

Mid-America Arts Alliance/Exhibits USA

Henry Moran, Exec. Dir
912 Baltimore Ave, Suite 700
Kansas City, MO 64105
Tel 816-421-1388; FAX 816-421-3918
(AR, KS, MO, NE, OK, TX)

Mid-Atlantic Arts Foundation

Michael E Braun, Exec Dir
11 E Chase St, Suite 2A
Baltimore, MD 21202
Tel 301-539-6656
(DC, DE, MD, NJ, NY, PA, VA, VI, WV)

New England Foundation for the Arts

Michael P. Moore, Exec Dir
678 Massachusetts Ave, Suite 801
Cambridge, MA 02139
Tel 617-492-2914
(CT, MA, ME, NH, RI, VT)

Southern Arts Federation

Jeffrey A. Kesper, Exec Dir
1293 Peachtree St NE, Suite 500
Atlanta, GA 30309
Tel 404-874-7244; FAX 404-873-2148
(AL, FL, GA, KY, LA, MS, NC, SC, TN)

Western States Arts Federation

Donald A Mayer, Exec Dir
236 Montezuma Ave
Santa Fe, NM 87501-2641
Tel 505-988-1166
(AK, AZ, CA, CO, HI, ID, MT, NV, NM, OR, UT, WA, WY)

STATE ART AGENCIES

Alabama State Council on the Arts and Humanities

Joe McInnes, Chairman
P.O. Box 949
Montgomery, AL 36192
Tel 205-244-4348

Albert B Head, Exec Dir
1 Dexter Ave
Montgomery, AL 36130-5801
Tel 205-242-4076

Alaska State Council on the Arts

Carol Heyman, Chmn
411 W 4th Ave, Suite 1E
Anchorage, AK 99501-2343
Tel 907-279-1558

Christine D'Arcy, Exec Dir
411 W 4th Ave, Suite 1E
Anchorage, AK 99501-2343
Tel 907-279-1558; FAX 907-279-4330

Arizona Commission on the Arts

Gordon Murphy, Chmn
417 W Roosevelt Ave
Phoenix, AZ 85003
Tel 602-255-5882

Shelly M. Cohn, Exec Dir
417 W. Roosevelt Ave
Phoenix, AZ 85003
Tel 602-255-5882

Arkansas Arts Council

Betty Jo Hays, Chmn
419 S. Spruce
Hope, AR 71801
Tel 501-324-9766

Bill Puppione, Exec Dir
1500 Tower Bldg
323 Center St
Little Rock, AR 72201
Tel 501-324-9150; FAX 501-324-9154

California Arts Council

Whitey Littlefield, Chmn
2411 Alhambra Blvd
Sacramento, CA 95817
Tel 916-739-3186

Joanne Kozberg, Exec Dir
2411 Alhambra Blvd
Sacramento, CA 95817
Tel 916-739-3186

Colorado Council on the Arts

Jerome Wartgow, Chmn
c/o CCCOES
1391 Speer Blvd
Denver, CO 80204
Tel 303-620-4000

Barbara Neal, Exec Dir
750 Pennsylvania St
Denver, CO 80203-3699
Tel 303-894-2617; FAX 303-894-2615

Connecticut Commission on the Arts

Sherry Banks-Cohn, Chmn
227 Lawrence St
Hartford, CT 06106
Tel 203-566-4770

John Ostrout, Exec Dir
227 Lawrence St
Hartford, CT 06106
Tel 203-566-4770

Delaware Division of the Arts

Stuart B Young, Chmn
Box 391
Wilmington, DE 19899-0391
Tel 302-571-6633

Cecelia Fitzgibbon, Dir
820 N French St
Wilmington, DE 19801
Tel 302-577-3540; FAX 302-577-6561

DC Commission on the Arts and Humanities

Abel Lopez, Chmn
410 8th St, NW, Suite 500
Washington, DC 20004
Tel 202-724-5613

Pamela G. Holt, Exec Dir
410 8th St, NW, Suite 500
Washington, DC 20004
Tel 202-724-5613

Florida Arts Council

W. Kent Barclay, Chmn
Dept of State, Div of Cultural Affairs
Florida Arts Council
The Capitol
Tallahassee, FL 32399-0250
Tel 904-487-2980

Peyton Fearington, Dir
Division of Cultural Affairs,
Florida Dept of State, The Capitol
Tallahassee, FL 32399-0250
Tel 904-487-2980; FAX 904-922-5259

Georgia Council for the Arts

Esther Silver-Parker, Chmn
530 Means St. NW, Suite 115
Atlanta, GA 30318
Tel 404-651-7920

Martha E Evans, Public Information Officer
530 Means St., NW, Suite 115
Atlanta, GA 30318
Tel 404-651-7920; FAX 404-651-7922

Hawaii State Foundation on Culture and the Arts

Millicent Kim, Chmn
335 Merchant St, Rm 202
Honolulu, HI 96825
Tel 808-548-4145

Wendell P K Silva, Exec Dir
355 Merchant St, Suite 202
Honolulu, HI 96825
Tel 808-548-0300; FAX 808-586-0308

Idaho Commission on the Arts

William A. Jackson, Chmn
304 W State St
Boise, ID 83720
Tel 208-334-2119

Margot H Knight, Exec Dir
304 W State St
Boise, ID 83720
Tel 208-334-2119

Illinois Arts Council

Shirley R Madigan, Chmn
100 W Randolph, Suite 10-500
Chicago, IL 60601-3298
Tel 312-814-6750

Richard E Huff, Exec Dir
100 W Randolph, Suite 10-500
Chicago, IL 60601-3298
Tel 312-814-6750; FAX 312-814-1471

Indiana Arts Commission

Peter Jacobi, Chmn
402 W. Washington St, Room 072
Indianapolis, IN 46204
Tel 317-232-1268

Thomas B Schorgl, Exec Dir
402 W. Washington St, Room 072
Indianapolis, IN 46204
Tel 317-232-1268

Iowa Arts Council

Joanne Fetner, Chmn
1223 E Court
Des Moines, IA 50319
Tel 515-281-4451

William Jackson, Exec Dir
1223 E Court
Des Moines, IA 50319
Tel 515-281-4451

Kansas Arts Commission

Rose Mary Mong, Pres
700 Jackson, Suite 1004
Topeka, KS 66603
Tel 913-296-3335

Dorothy L Ilgen, Exec Dir
700 Jackson, Suite 1004
Topeka, KS 66603-3852
Tel 913-296-3335

Kentucky Arts Council

Marilyn Moosnick, Chmn
755 Brook Hill Dr
Lexington, KY 40502
Tel 606-277-3040

Martin Newell, Exec Dir
31 Fountain Place
Frankfort, KY 40601
Tel 502-564-3757

Louisiana State Arts Council

Penne Mobley Holbrook
PO Box 44247
Baton Rouge, LA 70804
Tel 504-342-8180

Emma Burnett, Exec Dir, Div of the Arts
PO Box 44247
Baton Rouge, LA 70804
Tel 504-342-8180

Maine Arts Commission

Peter Plumb, Chmn
55 Capital St
State House Station 25
Augusta, ME 04333
Tel 207-289-2724

Alden C. Wilson, Dir
55 Capital St
State House Station 25
Augusta, ME 04333
Tel 207-289-2724

Maryland State Arts Council

Shirley Giarritta, Chmn
55 N. Centre St.
Cumberland, MD 21502
Tel 301-777-9234; FAX 301-777-9072

James Backas, Exec Dir
601 N Howard St
Baltimore, MD 21201
Tel 410-333-8232

Massachusetts Cultural Council

Josiah Spaulding, Chmn
80 Boylston St, Suite 1000
Boston, MA 02116
Tel 617-727-3668

Rose Austin, Exec Dir
80 Boylston St, Suite 1000
Boston, MA 02116
Tel 617-727-3668

Michigan Council for the Arts & Cultural Affairs

Judith Ann Rapanof, Chmn
1200 Sixth St
Detroit, MI 48226
Tel 313-256-3735

Betty Boone, Interim Dir
1200 Sixth St, Suite 1180
Detroit, MI 48226
Tel 313-256-3735; FAX 313-256-3781

Minnesota State Arts Board

James Nardone, Chmn
432 Summit Ave
Saint Paul, MN 55102
Tel 612-297-2603

Sam W Grabarski, Exec Dir
432 Summit Ave
Saint Paul, MN 55120
Tel 612-297-2603; FAX 612-297-4304

Mississippi Arts Commission

Edwin Downer, Chmn
239 N LaMar St, Suite 207
Jackson, MS 39202
Tel 601-359-6030; FAX 601-359-6008

Missouri Arts Council

Christopher Abele, Chmn
111 N Seventh St, Suite 105
St Louis, MO 63101
Tel 314-340-6845

Anthony J Radich, Exec Dir
111 N Seventh St, Suite 105
St Louis, MO 63101
Tel 314-340-6845

Montana Arts Council

Larry Williams, Chmn
316 N Park Ave, Room 252
Helena, MT 59620
Tel 406-444-6430; FAX 406-444-6548

Carleen Layne, Acting Dir
316 N Park Ave, Room 252
Helena, MT 59620
Tel 406-444-6430; FAX 406-444-6548

Nebraska Arts Council

J. Robert Duncan, Chmn
1313 Farnam-on-the-Mall
Omaha, NE 68102-1873
Tel 402-595-2122

Nevada State Council on the Arts

Robin Greenspun, Chmn
108 Quail Run Rd
Henderson, NV 88014
Tel 702-688-1225

William L Fox, Exec Dir
329 Flint St
Reno, NV 89501
Tel 702-688-1225

New Hampshire State Council on the Arts

Edith Grodin, Chmn
Phoenix Hall
40 N Main St
Concord, NH 03301
Tel 603-271-2789

New Jersey State Council on the Arts

Sharon A Harrington
4 North Broad
Trenton, NJ 08625
Tel 609-292-6130

Barbara S. Russo
4 North Broad
Trenton, NJ 08625
Tel 609-292-6130

Mew Mexico Arts Division

Gary Morton, Chmn
PO Box 84
Lincoln, MN 88338
Tel 505-653-4032

Lara C Morrow, Dir
New Mexico Arts Division
228 E Palace Ave
Santa Fe, NM 87501
Tel 505-827-6490; FAX 505-827-7308

New York State Council on the Arts

Kitty Carlisle Hart, Chmn
915 Broadway
New York, NY 10010
Tel 212-387-7003; FAX 212-387-7164

Mary Hays, Exec Dir
915 Broadway
New York, NY 10010
Tel 212-387-7000

North Carolina Arts Council

Harley F Shuford, Jr, Chmn
PO Box 608
Hickory, NC 28603
Tel 704-328-1851

Mary Regan, Exec Dir
Dept of Cultural Resources
Raleigh, NC 27601-2807
Tel 919-733-2821

North Dakota Council on the Arts

Richard Weber, Chmn
1707 Pinto Place
Bismarck, ND 58501
Tel 701-258-1187

Vern Goodin, Exec Dir
Black Bldg. Suite 606
Fargo, ND 58102
Tel 701-239-7150; FAX 701-239-7153

Ohio Arts Council

Barbara Robinson, Chmn
727 E Main St
Columbus, OH 43205
Tel 614-466-2613

Wayne Lawson, Exec Dir
727 E Main St
Columbus, OH 43205
Tel 614-466-2613

State Arts Council of Oklahoma

Dr. Kay Goebel
Jim Thorpe Bldg, Room 640
Oklahoma City, OK 73105
Tel 405-521-2931; FAX 405-521-6418

Betty Price, Exec Dir
Jim Thorpe Bldg, Room 640
Oklahoma City, OK 73105
Tel 405-521-2931; FAX 405-521-6418

Oregon Arts Commission

Eloise MacMurray, Chmn
550 Airport Rd, SE
Salem, OR 97310
Tel 503-378-3625

Leslie Tuomi, Exec Dir
550 Airport Rd, SE
Salem, OR 97310
Tel 503-378-3625

Pennsylvania Council on the Arts

Carol Brown, Chmn
Rm 216, Finance Bldg
Harrisburg, PA 17120
Tel 717-787-6883

Randall Rosenbaum, Actg Exec Dir
Rm 216, Finance Bldg
Harrisburg, PA 17120
Tel 717-787-6883

Rhode Island State Council on the Arts

Karen Mensel, Chmn
95 Cedar Street, Suite 103
Providence, RI 02903

Iona B Dobbins, Exec Dir
95 Cedar St, Suite 103
Providence, RI 02903
Tel 401-277-3880

South Carolina Arts Commission

Betsy S Terry, Chmn
1800 Gervais St
Columbia, SC 29201
Tel 803-734-8696

Scott Sanders, Exec Dir
1800 Gervais St
Columbia, SC 29201
Tel 803-734-8696

South Dakota Arts Council

Michael Pangburn, Chmn
1314 Cardinal Ct
Spearfish, SD 57783
Tel 605-642-5890; FAX 605-892-2035

Dennis Holub, Exec Dir
230 Phillips Ave, Suite 204
Sioux Falls, SD 57102-0720
Tel 605-339-6646; FAX 605-332-7965

Tennessee Arts Commission

Ron McMahan, Chmn
320 6th Ave N, Suite 100
Nashville, TN 37243-0780
Tel 615-741-1701

Bennett Tarleton, Exec Dir
320 6th Ave N, Suite 100
Nashville, TN 37243-0780
Tel 615-741-1701

Texas Commission on the Arts

Adair Margo, Chmn
PO Box 13406
Austin, TX 78711
Tel 512-463-5535

John Paul Batiste, Exec Dir
PO Box 13406
Austin, TX 78711-3406
Tel 512-463-5535; FAX 512-475-2699

Utah Arts Council

Burtch W Beall, Jr, Chmn Bd
617 E South Temple
Salt Lake City, UT 84102
Tel 801-533-5895

Bonnie H. Stephens, Dir
617 East South Temple
Salt Lake City, UT 84102
Tel 801-533-5895; FAX 801-533-6196

Vermont Council on the Arts

Maxine Brandenburg, Chmn
136 State St
Montpelier, VT 05602
Tel 802-828-3291

Nicolette B. Clarke, Exec Dir
136 State St
Montpelier, VT 05602
Tel 802-828-3291

Virginia Commmissiom on the Arts

Cassandra O. Stoddart, Chmn
208 N Allen Ave
Richmond, VA 23220
Tel 804-225-3132

Peggy Baggett, Exec Dir
Lewis House
223 Governor St
Richmond, VA 23219-2010
Tel 804-225-3132

Washington State Arts Commission

Dennis Couch, Chmn
PO Box 42675
Olympia, WA 98504-2675
Tel 206-753-3860

John Firman, Exec Dir
PO Box 42675
Olympia, WA 98504-2675
Tel 206-753-3860; FAX 206-586-5351

West Virginia Arts and Humanities Division

Pam Parziale, Chmn
Dept of Culture & History
Capitol Complex
Charleston, WV 25305
Tel 304-558-0240

Lakin Ray Cook, Exec Dir
Div. of Culture & History
Capitol Complex
Charleston, WV 25305
Tel 304-558-0240

Wisconsin Arts Board

Kathryn M. Burke, Chmn
101 E Wilson St, First Fl
Madison, WI 53702
Tel 608-266-0190

Dean Amhaus, Exec Dir
101 E Wilson St, First Fl
Madison, WI 53702
Tel 608-266-0190

Wyoming Arts Council

Jo Campbell, Chmn
2320 Capitol Ave
Cheyenne, WY 82002
Tel 307-777-7742

John Coe, Dir
2320 Capitol Ave
Cheyenne, WY 82002
Tel 307-777-7742

American Samoa Council on Arts, Culture and Humanities

Moaali'itele Tu'ufuli, Chmn
Territory of American Samoa
PO Box 1540
Pago Pago, American Samoa 96799
Tel 684-633-5613

Le'Ala E Pili, Actg Exec Dir
Territory of American Samoa
PO Box 1540
Pago Pago, American Samoa 96799
Tel 684-633-5613

Guam Council on the Arts & Humanities Agency

Alberto A Lamorena, Exec Dir
PO Box 2950
Agana, GU 96910
Tel 671-477-7413

Commonwealth Council for Arts and Culture

Crispin Kaipat, Chmn
Dept of Community & Cultural Affairs
PO Box 553, CHRB
Saipan, CM 96950
Tel 670-322-9982, 670-322-9983

Margarita Wonenberg, Exec Dir
Dept of Commmunity & Cultural Affairs
PO Box 553, CHRB
Saipan, CM 96950
Tel 670-322-9982, 670-322-9983

Institute of Puerto Rican Culture

Dr Francisco O'Neill, Chmn
Apartado Postal 4184
San Juan, PR 00902
Tel 809-722-5881; FAX 809-724-8393

Augustin Echevarria, Exec Dir
Apartado Postal 4184
San Juan, PR 00902
Tel 809-722-5881; FAX 809-724-8393

Virgin Islands Council on the Arts

Mark Brooks
41-42 Norre Gade
St. Thomas, VI 00802
Tel 809-774-5984

John M Jowers, Exec Dir
41-42 Norre Gade
St. Thomas, VI 00802
Tel 809-774-5984; FAX 809-774-6206

State Directors and Supervisors of Art Education

ALABAMA

Ms. Betty Purdue
Art Education Specialist
State Department of Education
50 N. Ripley St., Room 3345
Montgomery, AL 36130
Tel 205-242-8082

ALASKA

Judith Entwife
Language Arts/Fine Arts Curriculum Specialist
Alaska Department of Education
801 W. 10th., Ste 200
Juneau, AK 99801-1894
Tel 907-465-2841

ARIZONA

Jeanne Belcheff
Fine Arts Specialist-Performing Arts
Arizona Department of Education
1535 W. Jefferson Street
Phoenix, AZ 85007
Tel 602-542-3052

ARKANSAS

Ms. Brenda Turner
Specialist, Art Education
State Department of Education
Education Building Room 107A
Little Rock, AR 72201
Tel 501-682-4397

CALIFORNIA

Miguel Muto, Consultant
Arts and Humanities Education
California State Department of Education
721 Capitol Mall
Sacramento, CA 95814
Tel 916-322-4015

COLORADO

Charles Cassio
Arts Consultant
Colorado Department of Education
201 E. Colfax Ave.
Denver, CO 80203
Tel 303-866-6790

CONNECTICUT

Vacant
Art Education Consultant
State Department of Education
P.O.Box 2219
Hartford, CT 06145
Tel 203-566-4565

DELAWARE

Vacant
Department of Public Instruction
Townsend Building
P.O.Box 1402
Dover, DE 19903
Tel 302-739-4887; FAX 302-739-3092

DISTRICT OF COLUMBIA

Rena Watson
Supervising Director of Art Curriculum and Instruction
Lingdon Elementary School
20th & Evarts Streets, NE
Washington, DC 20018
Tel 202-576-7813; FAX 202-576-7041

FLORIDA

Dr. Sandy Dilger, Art Specialist
Bureau of School Improvement and Instruction
Florida Department of Education
Tallahassee, FL 32399
Tel 904-487-8826

GEORGIA

Ruth Gassett
Coordinator, Arts Education
1958 Twin Towers East
Atlanta, GA 30334
Tel 404-656-7520

HAWAII

Wendie Liu
Educational Specialist
189 Lunalilo Home Road
Room A-17
Honolulu, HI 96825
Tel 808-396-2534

IDAHO

Mr. Gale Maxey
Fine Arts Representative
Len B. Jordan Office Building
State Department of Education
650 West State Street
Boise, ID 83720
Tel 208-334-2113

ILLINOIS

Lynn Morris
Educational Consultant
Illinois State Board of Education
100 North First Street
Springfield, IL 62777
Tel 217-782-5728

INDIANA

N. Carlotta Parr
Fine Arts Consultant
Indiana Department of Education
Center for School Improvement
Room 229, State House
Indianapolis, IN 46204-2798
Tel 317-232-9156

IOWA

Mary Beth Schroeder
Consultant, Arts Education
Department of Education
Grimes State Office Building
Des Moines, IA 50319-0146
Tel 515-281-3160

KANSAS

Ray Linder
Education Program Specialist
State Department of Education
120 E. Tenth Avenue
Topeka, KS 66612
Tel 913-296-4932

KENTUCKY

Louis Deluca, Consultant
Unit for Arts Social Studies & Humanities
Kentucky Department of Education
Capitol Plaza Tower 1832
Frankfort, KY 40601
Tel 502-564-2106

LOUISIANA

Myrtle Kerr
State Supervisor of Fine Art
P.O. Box 94064
Baton Rouge, LA 70804
Tel 504-342-3393 or 3396

MAINE

Sandra T. Long
Educational Consultant
Maine Department of Education
Station 23
Augusta, ME O4333
Tel 207-287-6315

MARYLAND

James L. Tucker, Jr.
Chief, Arts and Humanities Section
Maryland State Department of Education
200 West Baltimore Street
Baltimore, MD 21201
Tel 410-333-2323

MASSACHUSETTS

Carole Thomson
Exec. Director, Division of School Programs

Before May, 1993
1385 Hancock Street
Quincy, MA 02169
Tel 617-770-7540

After May, 1993
130 Main Street
Malden, MA 02148

MICHIGAN

Vacant
Michigan Department of Education
Box 30008
Lansing, MI 48909
Tel 517-373-3982

MINNESOTA

Susan Vaughan
Art Education Specialist
Minnesota Department of Education
648 Capitol Square Building
St. Paul, MN 55101
Tel 612-296-4075

MISSISSIPPI

Donna A. Lander
Director, Curriculum
Mississippi State Department of Education
P.O. Box 711
Jackson, MS 39205
Tel 601-359-3778

MISOURI

Larry N. Peeno, Ed.D.
Supervisor, Fine Arts
Missouri State Department of Elementary & Secondary Education
P.O. Box 480
Jefferson City, MO 65102
Tel 314-751-2625

MONTANA

M. Christine Pena
Arts Education Specialist
Office of Public Instruction
Helena, MT 59620
Tel 406-444-4442

NEBRASKA

Sheila Brown
Fine Arts Coordinator
Department of Education
301 Centennial Mall South
Lincoln, NE 68509
Tel 402-471-4337

NEVADA

Dr. Bill Abrams
Nevada Department of Education
Capitol Complex,400 West King Street
Carson City, NV 89710
Tel 702-687-3136

NEW HAMPSHIRE

Ms. Rachel Hopkins
Art Consultant
New Hampshire Department of Education
101 Pleasant Street
Concord, NH 03301
Tel 603-271-2632

NEW JERSEY

Roberta Carol
Arts Education
New Jersey Department of Education
Division of General Academic Education
225 West State Street, CN500
Trenton, NJ 08625
Tel 609-984-7454

NEW MEXICO

Vicki Breen
Director of Visual Arts
New Mexico State Department of Education
Education Building, 300 Don Gasper
Santa Fe, NM 87503
Tel 505-827-6562

NEW YORK

Roger E. Hyndman
Associate in Art Education
Bureau of Arts, Music & Humanities Education
State Department of Education
Room 681EBA
Albany, NY 12234
Tel 518-474-5932

NORTH CAROLINA

Norbert W. Irvine
Visual Art Consultant
Section of Arts Education
State Dept. of Public Instruction
Raleigh, NC 27601-2825
Tel 919-733-7467

NORTH DAKOTA

Charles DeRemer
Director of Curriculum
Department of Public Instruction
600 E. Blvd. Ave.
Bismarck, ND 58505-0440
Tel 701-224-2514

OHIO

Jerry Tollifson, Art Education Consultant
Division of Curriculum Instruction and Professional Development
Ohio Departments Building
Room 1005, 65 South Front Street
Columbus, OH 43266-0308
Tel 614-466-5795

OKLAHOMA

Paulette Black, Director
Arts in Education Program
State Department of Education
2500 North Lincoln Blvd.
Oklahoma City, OK 73105
Tel 405-521-3034

OREGON

Richard M. LaTour, Ph.D.
Coordinator of Curriculum
Fed. Programs Fine Arts
Oregon Department of Education
700 Pringle Parkway, SE
Salem, OR 97310-0290
Tel 503-378-3602

PENNSYLVANIA

Dr. Gene Vandyke, Chief
Division of Arts & Sciences
Department of Education, 333 Market Street
Harrisburg, PA 17126-0333
Tel 717-783-6746

Ms. Beth Cornell
Fine Arts Adviser
Division of Arts and Sciences
Department of Education, 333 Market Street
Harrisburg, PA 17126-0333
Tel 717-787-5317

RHODE ISLAND

Richard Lathan, Consultant
Rhode Island Department of Education
Roger Williams Building
22 Hayes Street
Providence, RI 02908
Tel 401-277-2617

SOUTH CAROLINA

MacArthur Goodwin
State Art Consultant
Office of General Education
State Department of Education
801 Rutledge Building
Columbia, SC 29201
Tel 803-734-8384

SOUTH DAKOTA

Jeff Holcomb
Program Representative
Division of Education, 700 Governors Drive
Pierre, SD 57501
Tel 605-773-3395

TENNESSEE

Joe Giles
Arts Specialist
Tennessee Department of Education
Cordell Hull Bldg, 4th Fl.
Nashville, TN 37210
Tel 615-741-0878

TEXAS

Jeanne Rollins
Art Education Consultant
Division of Curriculum Development
Texas Education Agency, 1701 N. Congress Avenue
Austin, TX 78701-1494
Tel 512-463-9556

UTAH

Charles B. Stubbs
State Specialist in Art Education
Utah State Office of Education
250 East 5th South
Salt Lake City, UT 84111
Tel 801-538-7790

VERMONT

Don Hirsch
Arts Education Consultant
Department of Education, 120 State Street
Montpelier, VT 05602
Tel 802-828-3111

VIRGINIA

Cheryle C. Gardner
Associate Director of Fine Arts
Department of Education
P.O. Box 6Q
Richmond, VA 23216-2060
Tel 804-225-2053

WASHINGTON

Gina May, Supervisor
Visual and Performing Arts
Old Capitol Building
P.O. Box 47200
Olympia, WA 98504

WEST VIRGINIA

Dr. Jeanne Moore
Coordinator of Fine Arts
West Virginia Department of Education
Capitol Complex, Building 6 Room 330
1900 Kanawha Blvd., East
Charleston, WV 25305
Tel 304-558-7805

WISCONSIN

Dr. Martin Rayala
Wisconsin Department of Public Instruction
P.O. Box 7841
Madison,WI 53707
Tel 608-267-7461

WYOMING

Judy Minier
Director, School Improvement Unit
Hathaway Building
Cheyenne, WY 82002
Tel 307-777-6238

Art Magazines

A for Annuals; Bi-M for Bi-Monthlies; M for Monthlies;
Q for Quarterlies; Semi-A for Semi-Annually; W for Weeklies

ACA Update (M)—Doug Rose, Ed; American Council for the Arts, 1285 Ave of the Americas, 3rd Fl, New York, NY 10019. Tel 212-245-4510. $50.00

African Arts (Q)—John Povey, Ed; African Studies Center, University of California, 405 Hilgard Ave, Los Angeles, CA 90024. Tel 310-825-1218. Yearly $38.00

Afterimage (10 Issues)—Nathan Lyons, Ed; Visual Studies Workshop Inc, 31 Prince St, Rochester, NY 14607. Tel 716-442-8676. Yearly $30.00

Aha! Hispanic Arts News (9 Issues)—Dolores Prida, Ed; Association of Hispanic Arts, 173 E 116th St, 2nd Fl, New York, NY 10029. Tel 212-860-5445. Yearly $20.00 to individuals, $40.00 to institutions

American Artist (M)—M Stephen Doherty, Ed; BPI Communications Inc, 1515 Broadway, New York, NY 10036. Tel 212-764-7300. Yearly $24.95

American Art Journal (Q)—Jane Van Norman Turano, Ed; Kennedy Galleries, 40 W 57th St, Fifth Floor, New York, NY 10019. Tel 212-541-9600. Yearly $35.00

American Craft (Bi-M)—Lois Moran, Ed; American Craft Council, 72 Spring St, New York, NY 10012. Tel 212-274-0630. Yearly $50.00

American Folk Art (Q)—Rosemary Gabriel, Ed; Museum of American Folk Art, 61 W 62nd St, New York, NY 10023. Tel 212-977-7170. Membership

American Indian Art Magazine (Q)—Roanne Goldfein, Ed; American Indian Art Inc, 7314 E Osborn Dr, Scottsdale, AZ 85251. Tel 602-994-5445. Yearly $20.00

American Journal of Archaeology (Q)—Fred S Kleiner, Ed; 675 Commonwealth Ave, Boston, MA 02215. Tel 617-353-9364. Yearly $50.00 to individuals, $100.00 to institutions.

American Watercolor Society Newsletter (2 Issues)—Kent Coes, Ed; American Watercolor Society, 47 Fifth Ave, New York, NY 10003. Tel 212-206-8986. Membership

Antiquarian (10 Issues)—Allan Everest, Ed; Clinton County Historical Association, PO Box 332, Plattsburgh, NY 12901. Tel 518-561-0340. Yearly $25.00

Aperture (Q)—Charles Hagan, Ed; Aperture Foundation, 20 E 23rd St, New York, NY 10010. Tel 212-505-5555. Yearly $36.00

Archaeology (Bi-M)—Peter Young, Ed; Archaeological Institute of America, 15 Park Row, New York, NY 10038. Tel 212-732-5154. Yearly $20.00

Architectural Digest (M)—Paige Rense, Ed; Knapp Communications Corp, 5900 Wilshire Blvd, Los Angeles, CA 90036. Tel 213-965-3700. Yearly $40.00

Archives of American Art (Q)—Virginia Field, Ed; Smithsonian Institution, 1285 Ave of the Americas, New York, NY 10019. Tel 212-826-5722. Yearly $35.00

Art & Antiques (10 Issues)—Jeffrey Schaire, Ed; Art & Antiques Association, 633 Third Ave, New York, NY 10017. Tel 212-922-9250. Yearly $24.00

Art & Auction (11 Issues)—Lin Smith, Ed; Auction Guild, 250 W 57th St, New York, NY 10019. Tel 212-582-5633. Yearly $42.00

Art and Design News (Bi-M)—John E Grady, Jr, Ed; Boyd Publishing Co Inc, PO Box 50110, Indianapolis, IN 46250. Tel 317-849-6110. Yearly $15.00

Art Bulletin (Q)—Richard Brilliant, Ed; College Art Association of America, 275 Seventh Ave, New York, NY 10001. Tel 212-691-1051. Membership

Art Business News (M)—Jo Yanow-Schwartz, Ed; Myers Publishing Co Inc, Box 3837, Stamford, CT 06905. Tel 203-356-1745. Yearly $25.00

Art Com (Art Contemporary/la Mamelle) (Q)—Anna Couey, Ed; Contemporary Arts Press, PO Box 193123, Rincon Annex, San Francisco, CA 94119. Tel 415-431-7524. Yearly $96.00. Electronically available

Art Direction (M)—Dan Barron, Ed; Advertising Trade Publications Inc, 10 E 39th St, 6th Fl, New York, NY 10016. Tel 212-889-6500. Yearly $28.00

Art Documentation (Q)—Beryl K Smith & Kathryn Vaughn, Eds; Art Libraries Society of North America, 3900 E Timrod St, Tucson, AZ 85711. Tel 602-881-8479. Yearly $55.00 to individuals, $75.00 to institutions

Art Education (Bi-M)—Jerome Hausman, Ed; National Art Education Association, 1916 Association Dr, Reston, VA 22091. Tel 703-860-8000. Yearly $50.00 to non-members

Artforum (10 Issues)—Ingrid Sischy, Ed; Artforum International Magazine Inc, 65 Bleecker St, New York, NY 10012. Tel 212-475-4000. Yearly $46.00

Art Hazards News (10 Issues)—Michael McCann, Ed; Center for Safety in the Arts, 5 Beekman St, New York, NY 10038. Tel 212-227-6220. Yearly $19.00

Artibus Asiae (Q)—Alexander C Soper, Ed; Institute of Fine Art, New York University, 1 E 78th St, New York, NY 10021-0178. Tel 212-988-5500. Yearly $60.00

Art in America (M)—Elizabeth C Baker, Ed; Brant Publications, 980 Madison Ave, New York, NY 10021. Tel 212-734-9797. Yearly $40.00

Artist's Magazine (M)—Michael Ward, Ed; F & W Publications Inc, 1507 Dana Ave, Cincinnati, OH 45207. Tel 513-531-2222. Yearly $24.00

Art Journal (Q)—Lenore Malen, Ed; College Art Association of America Inc, 275 Seventh Ave, 5th Fl, New York, NY 10011-6708. Tel 212-691-1051. Yearly $30.00 (non-members)

Art Material Trade News (M)—Tom C Cooper, Ed; Communication Channels Inc, 6255 Barfield Rd, Atlanta, GA 30328-4369. Tel 404-256-9800. Yearly $38.00

Art New England (10 Issues)—Carla Munsat, Ed; 353 Washington St, Brighton, MA 02135. Tel 617-782-3008. Yearly $18.00

Artnews (10 Issues)—Milton Esterow, Ed; Artnews Associates, 48 W 38th St, New York, NY 10018. Tel 212-398-1690. Yearly $33.00

Artnewsletter (Bi-W)—Bonnie Barrett Stretch, Ed; Artnews Associates, 48 W 38th St, New York, NY 10018. Tel 212-398-1690. Yearly $229.00

Art of California ((Bi-M)—Greg Saffell Communications, 1125 Jefferson St, Napa, CA 94559. Tel 707-226-1776. Yearly $30.00

Art of the West (Bi-M)—Vicki Stavig, Ed; Duerr and Tierney Ltd, 15612 Hwy 7, Suite 235, Minnetonka, MN 55345. Tel 612-935-5850. Yearly $21.00

Art Papers (Bi-M)—Glenn Harper, Ed; Atlanta Art Papers, Inc, PO Box 77348, Atlanta, GA 30357. Tel 404-588-1837. Yearly $20.00

Artpost Magazine (Q)—Art Post Productions Inc, 80 Spadina Ave, Suite 302, Toronto, ON M5V 2J4 Canada. Tel 416-364-5541. Yearly $20.00

Arts (M)—Minneapolis Institute of Arts, 2400 Third Ave S, Minneapolis, MN 55404. Tel 612-870-3046. Yearly free

Arts Magazine (10 Issues)—Art Communications Group, 561 Broadway, New York, NY 10012. Tel 212-431-4410. Yearly $30.00

Artspace (Bi-M)—William Peterson, Ed; Artspace Inc, PO Box 36C69, Los Angeles, CA 90036. Tel 213-931-1433. Yearly $24.95

Arts Quarterly (Q)—Wanda O'Shello, Ed; New Orleans Museum of Art, PO Box 19123, New Orleans, LA 70179. Tel 504-488-2631. Yearly $10.00

Art Students League News (Q)—Lawrence Campbell, Ed; 215 W 57th St, New York, NY 10019. Tel 212-247-4510. Membership

Art Therapy (3 Issues)—Gary Barlow, Ed; American Art Therapy Association, 1202 Allanson Rd, Mundelein, IL 60060-2419. Tel 708-949-6064. Yearly $35.00

ArToday (Q)—William E Bales, Ed; Web Publications Inc, Box 12830, Wichita, KS 67277. Tel 316-946-0600. Yearly $16.00

Artweek ((Bi-M)—Bruce Nixon, Ed; 12 S First St, Suite 520, San Jose, CA 95113. Tel 408-279-2293. Yearly $28.00; $32.00 to institutions

Art/World (10 Issues)—Bruce Duff Hooton, Ed; Arts Review Inc, 55 Wheatley Rd, Glen Head, NY 11545. Tel 516-427-2897. Yearly $20.00

Aviso (M)—Bill Anderson, Ed; American Association of Museums, 1225 Eye ST NW, Suite 200, Washington, DC 20005. Tel 202-289-1818. Yearly $30.00

Bomb (4 Issues)—Betsy Sussler, Ed; PO Box 2003, New York, NY 10013. Tel 212-431-3943. Yearly $18.00

Bulletin of the Cleveland Museum of Art (10 Issues)—Jo Zuppan, Ed; Publications Dept, 11150 East Blvd, Cleveland, OH 44106. Tel 216-421-7340. Yearly $25.00 to non-members

Bulletin of the Detroit Institute of Arts (3 Issues)—Judith A Ruskin, Ed; 5200 Woodward Ave, Detroit, MI 48202. Tel 313-833-7960. Yearly $16.00

Calligraphy Review (Q)—Karyn L Gilman, Ed; 1624 25th Ave SW, Norman, OK 73072-5709. Tel 405-364-8794. Yearly $36.00

Canadian Art (Q)—Jocelyn Laurence, Ed; Key Publishers Co Ltd, 70 The Esplanade, 4th Floor, Toronto, ON M5E 1R2, Canada. Tel 416-360-0044. Yearly $24.00 Canadian

Ceramics Monthly (M)—William Hunt, Ed; Professional Publications Inc, PO Box 12448, Columbus, OH 43212. Tel 614-488-8236. Yearly $20.00

C Magazine (Q)—Joyce Mason, Ed; Box 5, Station B, Toronto, ON M5T 2T2, Canada. Tel 416-539-9495. Yearly $18.00 Canadian to individuals, $28.00 Canadian to institutions

Classical Realism Quarterly (Q)—Kurt Anderson, Ed; Atelier Lack, Inc, 2908 Hennepin Ave, Minneapolis, MN 55408. Yearly $12.00

Columbia-VLA Journal of Law & the Arts (Q)—Brian Robinson, Ed; Volunteer Lawyers for the Arts, 1285 Ave of the Americas, 3rd Fl, New York, NY 10019-6021. Tel 212-977-9270. Yearly $35.00

Communication Arts (8 Issues)—Patrick S Coyne, Ed; Coyne & Blanchard Inc, 410 Sherman AVe, PO Box 10300, Palo Alto, CA 94303. Tel 415-326-6040. Yearly $50.00

Connoisseur (M)—Thomas Hoving, Ed; Hearst Corp, 224 W 57th St, New York, NY 10019. Tel 212-262-6518. Yearly $20.00

Contemporanea (M)—Gabreila Fanning, Ed; Contemporanea Ltd, 260 W Broadway, New York, NY 10013.

Corporate ARTnews (M)—Richard W Walker, Ed; Artnews Associates 48 W 38th St, New York, NY 10018. Tel 212-398-1690. Yearly $110.00

Dialogue (Bi-M)—Ann Slaughter, Ed; Dialogue Inc, Box 2572, Columbus, OH 43216-2572. Tel 614-621-3704. Yearly $16.00 to individuals, $20.00 to institutions

Drawing (Bi-M)—Paul Cummings, Ed; Drawing Society Inc. 15 Penn Plaza, Box 66, New York, NY 10001-2050. Tel 212-563-4822. Yearly $35.00

Evaluator (Q)—Elizabeth Carr, Ed; International Society of Fine Arts Appraisers, PO Box 280, River Forest, IL 60305. Tel 312-848-3340. Membership

Fiberarts (5 Issues)—Ann Batchelder, Ed; Nine Press Inc, 50 College St, Asheville, NC 28801. Tel 704-253-0468. Yearly $18.00

Frame/Work (3 Issues)—Box Muffoletto, Ed; Los Angeles Center for Photographic Studies, 1048 W Sixth St, Suite 424, Los Angeles, CA 90017-2059. Tel 213-482-3566. Yearly $18.00 to individuals, $25.00 to insititutions

Gesta (2 Issues)—William W Clark, Ed; International Center of Medieval Art, The Cloisters, Fort Tryon Park, New York, NY 10040. Tel 212-928-1146. Yearly $30.00 to individuals, $50.00 to institutions

Graphic Design: USA (M)—Susan Benson, Ed; Kaye Publishing Corp, 120 E 56th St, New York, NY 10022. Tel 212-759-8813. Yearly $50.00

Graphiti (Q)—R Biggs, Ed; Artists in Print Inc, 665 Third St, San Francisco, CA 94107. Tel 415-243-8244. Membership

Heresies (2 Issues)—Heresies Collective Inc, Box 1306, Canal Street Station, New York, NY 10013. Tel 212-227-2108. Four issues $23.00 to individuals, $33.00 to institutions

High Performance (Q)—Steven Durland, Ed; 240 S Broadway, Los Angeles, CA 90012. Tel 213-687-7362. Yearly $20.00 to individuals, $24.00 to institutions

ID: Industrial Design Magazine (Bi-M)—C Pearlman, Ed; Design Publications Inc, 250 W 57th St, New York, NY 10107. Tel 212-956-0535. Yearly $55.00

IFAR Reports (10 Issues)—Margaret I O'Brien, Ed; International Foundation for Art Research, 46 E 70th St, New York, NY 10021. Yearly $50.00 to individuals, $65.00 to institutions

Illustrator (2 Issues)—Dr Don L Jardine, Ed; Art Instruction Schools, Bureau of Engraving, 500 S Fourth St, Minneapolis, MN 55415. Tel 612-339-8721. Yearly $8.00

Indianapolis Museum of Art Previews Magazine (Bi-M)—Judith M Fries, Ed; 1200 W 38th St, Indianapolis, IN 46208. Tel 317-923-1331. Membership

International Review of African American Art (Q)—Samella Lewis, Ed; 3000 Biscayne Blvd, Miami, FL 33137. Tel 305-573-2343. Yearly $20.00

Journal of Aesthetics & Art Criticism (Q)—Donald Crawford, Ed; American Society for Aesthetics, University of Wisconsin Press, 114 N Murray St, Madison, WI 53715. Tel 608-262-5839. Yearly $45.00 to institutions

Journal of Canadian Art History (Semi-A)—Concordia University, 1455 blvd de Maissoneuve Ouest, Montreal, PQ H3G 1M8, Canada. Tel 514-848-4699. Yearly $16.00

Journal of Decorative and Propaganda Arts (Q)—Cathy Left, Ed; Wolfson Foundation of Decorative and Propaganda Arts, 2399 NE Second Ave, Miami, FL 33137. Tel 305-573-9170. Yearly $30.00 to individuals, $50.00 to institutions

Journal of the American Institute for Conservation of Historic & Artistic Works (2 Issues)—Elisabeth West Fitzhugh, Ed; 1400 16th St NW, Suite 340, Washington, DC 20036. Tel 202-232-6636. Yearly $28.00

Latin American Art (Q)—PO Box 9888 Scottsdale, AZ 85252. Tel 602-947-8422. Yearly $24.00 to individuals, $36.00 to institutions

Leonardo: Art, Science & Technology (Q) —Roger Malina, Ed; Pergamon Press Inc, Journals Division, Maxwell House, Fairview Park, Elmsford, NY 10523. Tel 914-592-7700. Yearly $225.00

Lightworks Magazine (2 Issues)—Charlton Burch, Ed; PO Box 1202, Birmingham, MI 48012-1203. Tel 313-626-8026. Yearly $20.00 to individuals, $25.00 to institutions

Master Drawings (Q)—Ann Marie Logan, Ed; Master Drawings Association Inc, 29 E 36th St, New York, NY 10016. Tel 212-685-0008. Yearly $45.00

Metropolitan Museum of Art Bulletin (Q)—Joan Holt, Ed; 6 E 82nd St, New York, NY 10028. Yearly $18.00

Museum News (Bi-M)—Bill Anderson, Ed; American Association of Museums, 1225 Eye St NW, Suite 200, Washington, DC 20004. Tel 202-289-1818. Yearly $34.00

Museum of Fine Arts Bulletin (3 Issues)—Celeste Adams, Ed; Museum of Fine Arts, Houston, 1001 Bissonnet, PO Box 6826, Houston, TX 77265. Tel 713-526-1361. Yearly $12.00

Museum Studies of the Art Institute of Chicago (2 Issues)—Susan F Rossen & Rachel A Dressle, Eds; Michigan Ave at Adams St, Chicago, IL 60603. Tel 312-753-3347. Yearly $20.00 to individuals, $32.00 to institutions

New Art Examiner (11 Issues)—Derek Guthrie, Publisher; Chicago New Art Association, 20 W Hubbard, Suite 2W, Chicago, IL 60610. Tel 312-836-0330. Yearly $27.00

New Observations (8 Issues)—Diane Karp, Ed; New Observations Ltd, 142 Greene St, New York, NY 10012. Tel 212-966-6071. Yearly $22.00

October (Q)—MIT Press, 55 Hayward St, Cambridge, MA 02142. Tel 617-258-6779. Yearly $30.00 to individuals, $75.00 to institutions

Ornament (Q)—Robert Liu, Ed; Ornament Inc, 1221 S La Cienega, PO Box 35029, Los Angeles, CA 90035-0029. Tel 213-652-9914. Yearly $25.00

Parachute (Q)—Chantal Pontbriand, Ed; Editions Parachute, 4060 Blvd St Laurent, Suite 501, Montreal, PQ H2W 1Y9, Canada. Tel 514-842-9805. Yearly $40.00 Canadian

Philadelphia Museum of Art Bulletin (Q)—George H Marcus, Ed; PO Box 7646, Philadelphia, PA 19101. Tel 215-763-8100. Yearly $12.00

Primitive Art Newsletter (M)—Irwin Hersey, Ed; Irwin Hersey Associates, PO Box 536, Ansonia Station, New York, NY 10023. Tel 212-877-5328. Yearly $45.00

Princeton University Art Museum Record (2 Issues)—Jill Guthrie, Ed; Princeton University Art Museum, Princeton, NJ 08544. Tel 609-452-4341. Yearly $7.00

Print (Bi-M)—Martin Fox, Ed; RC Publications Inc, 104 Fifth Ave, 9th Fl, New York, NY 10011. Tel 212-463-0600. Yearly $46.00

Print Collector's Newsletter (Bi-M)—Jacqueline Brody, Ed; Print Collector's Newsletter Inc, 72 Spring St, New York, NY 10012. Tel 212-219-9722. Yearly $42.00

Progressive Architecture (M)—John Morris Dixon, Ed; Penton Publishing, Reinhold Division, 600 Summer St, PO Box 1361, Stamford, CT 06904. Tel 203-348-7531. Yearly $36.00

Re: View (M)—David Featherstone, Ed; Friends of Photography, 250 Fourth St, San Francisco, CA 94103. Tel 415-495-7000. Membership

School Arts (9 Issues)—David Baker, Ed; Davis Publicatioins Inc, 50 Portland St, Printers Bldg, Worcester, MA 01608. Tel 617-754-7201. Yearly $20.00

Sculpture (Bi-M)—Penelope Walker, Ed; International Sculpture Center, 1050 Potomac St NW, Washington, DC 20007. Tel 202-965-6066. Yearly $40.00

Sculpture Review (Q)—Theodora Morgan, Ed; National Sculpture Society, 15 E 26th St, Rm 1906, New York, NY 10010-1575. Tel 212-889-6960. Yearly $20.00 to non-members

Smithsonian Studies in American Art (4 Issues)—Lisa Siequist, Ed; Oxford University Press, Journals Division, 200 Madison Ave, New York, NY 10016. Tel 212-679-7300. Yearly $35.00 to individuals, $60.00 to institutions

Society of Architectural Historians Journal (Q)—Patricia Waddy, Ed; 1232 Pine St, Philadelphia, PA 19107-5944. Yearly $55.00

Source: Notes in the History of Art (Q)—Laurie Schneider, Ed; Ars Brevis Inc, 1 E 87th St, Suite 8A, New York, NY 10128. Tel 212-369-1881. Yearly $20.00

Southwest Art (M)—Susan Hallsten McGarry, Ed; PO Box 460535, Houston, TX 77056-8535. Tel 713-850-0990. Yearly $28.00

Stained Glass (Q)—Richard Hoover, Ed; Stained Glass Association of America, 6 SW Second St, #7, Lees Summit, MO 64063. Tel 816-333-6690. Yearly $24.00

Studies in Art Education (4 Issues)—Georgia Collins, Ed; National Art Education Association, 1916 Association Dr, Reston, VA 22091. Tel 703-860-8000. Yearly $25.00 to non-members

Studio Potter (Semi-A)—Gerry Williams, Ed; Box 70, Goffstown, NH 03045. Yearly $20.00

Sunshine Artists USA (M)—J L Wahl, Ed; Sun Country Enterprises Inc, 1700 Sunset Dr, Longwood, FL 32750-9697. Tel 305-323-5927. Yearly $20.00

Tamarind Papers (A)—Clinton Adams, Ed; University of New Mexico, Tamarind Institute, 108 Cornell Ave SE, Albuquerque, NM 87106. Tel 505-277-3901. Yearly $18.00

Technology & Conservation (Q)—S E Schur, Ed; Technology Organization Inc. 1 Emerson Pl, 16M, Boston, MA 02114. Tel 617-227-8581. Yearly $15.00

Tole World (Bi-M)—Zachary Shatz, Ed; EGW Publishing Co, 1320 Galaxy Way, Concord, CA 94520. Tel 415-671-9852. Yearly $15.00

Traveling Exhibition Information Service Newsletter (Bi-M)—S R Howarth, Ed; Humanities Exchange Inc, PO Box 1608, Largo, FL 34649. Tel 813-581-7328. Yearly $30.00

Umbrella (Irreg)—Judith A Hoffberg, Ed; Umbrella Associates, PO Box 40100, Pasadena, CA 91104. Tel 818-797-0514. Yearly $15.00 to individuals, $25.00 to institutions

Vie des Arts (Q)—Jean-Claude LeBlond, Ed; 200 Saint Jacques St, Montreal, PQ H2Y 1M1, Canada. Tel 514-282-0235. Yearly $39.00 Canadian

Views (3 Issues)—Dan Younger, Ed; Photographic Resource Center, Boston University, 602 Commonwealth Ave, Boston, MA 02215. Tel 617-353-0700. Yearly $25.00

Walters Art Gallery Bulletin (10 Issues)—Amy Freese, Ed; 600 N Charles St, Baltimore, MD 21201. Tel 301-547-9000. Yearly $12.00

Washington Internaional Arts Letter (6 Issues)—James S Duncan, Ed; PO Box 12010, Des Moines, IA 50312. Tel 515-243-8961. Yearly $40.00 to individuals, $58.00 to institutions

WestArt (24 Issues)—Martha Garcia, Ed; WestArt Publications, PO Box 6868, Auburn, CA 95604. Tel 916-885-0969. Yearly $16.00

White Walls (3 Issues)—Susan Snodgrass, Ed; PO Box 8204, Chicago, IL 60680. Tel 312-528-5533. Yearly $15.00

Winslow Homer: An Annual (A)—Gene Teitelbaum, Ed; PO Box 86, New Albany, IN 47151-0086. Tel 812-944-9386. Yearly $15.00

Woman's Art Journal (2 Issues)—Elsa Honig Fine, Ed; Woman's Art Inc, 1711 Harris Rd, Laverock, PA 19118. Tel 215-233-0639. Yearly $14.00 to individual, $18.00 to institutions

Women Artists News (4 Issues)—Judy Siegel, Ed; Midmarch Associates, PO Box 3304, Grand Central Station, New York, NY 10163. Tel 212-666-6990. Yearly $12.00 to individuals, $16.00 to institutions

Newspaper Art Editors and Critics

Cities for newspapers that do not start with city name
will have city name in parentheses as part of the listing

ALABAMA

Birmingham News—Fred Kaimann
Birmingham Post-Herald—Suzanne Dent
Florence Times—Terry Pace
Gadsden Times—Deidre Coakley
Huntsville Times—Ann Marie Martin
Lanett Valley Times-News—Johnny Kuy Kendall
Mobile Press Register—Gordon Tatum
Montgomery Advertiser—M.P. Wilkerson

ALASKA

Anchorage Daily News—Thomas Harrison

ARIZONA

Bisbee Daily Review—Jean King
(Flagstaff) Arizona Daily Sun—Tom McLean
Mesa Tribune—Liz Belanger
(Phoenix) Arizona Republic—Richard Nilsen
Phoenix Gazette—Lynn Pyne
Scottsdale Daily Progress—Joan McKenna
(Tucson) Arizona Daily Star—Robert Cauthorn
Tucson Citizen—Charlotte Lowe

ARKANSAS

Batesville Guard—Jeff Porter
Fort Smith Southwest Times-Record—Nancy Steel
(Little Rock) Arkansas Democratic Gazette—John Deering
Paragould Daily Press—Ellen Seay
(Rogers) Northwest Arkansas Morning News—Alan Long

CALIFORNIA

(Antioch) Daily Ledger-Post Dispatch—Lisa Amand
(Bakersfield) Californian—Rick Heredia
Beverly Hills Courier—Ed Gallagher
Chico News & Review—Elizabeth Kieszkowski
Corning Observer—Walter H. Dodd & Shanna Phillips
(Covina) San Gabriel Valley Tribune—Cathie Porelli
Davis Enterprise—Judy Duffy
(El Centro) Imperial Valley Press—Margaret Chairez
Fairfield Daily Republic—Mary Ann Murdoch
Fresno Bee—David Hale
Fullerton News Tribune—Tim Dermody
Hanford Sentinel—Ruth Gomes
(Long Beach) Press-Telegram Todd Cunningham
Los Angeles Daily News—Meg Sullivan
(Los Angeles) La Opinion—Dario Mora
Los Angeles Times—William Wilson
Madera Tribune—Robert Phipps
Martinez News Gazette—Robert V. Osmond
Modesto Bee—Leo Stutzin
(Monterey) Herald—Warren Sharp
Napa Valley Register—L. Pierce Carson
Novato Advance—Mary Connell
Oakland Tribune—Tom Faupl
Ojai Valley News—Kip Allen
(Pacific Palisades) Palisadian-Post—Juliet Schoen
(Palm Springs) Desert Sun—Bruce Fessier
(Palo Alto) Peninsula Times Tribune—Chris Preimesberger
Palos Verdes Peninsula News—Daryl Lubinsky
Porterville Recorder—Harriette Queen
(Riverside) Press-Enterprise—Loretta Scott
Sacramento Bee—Cynthis Davis

Sacramento Union—Holly Johnson
San Bernardino Sun—Betts Griffone
San Diego Daily Transcript—Priscilla Lister
San Diego Union Tribune—Lee Grant
San Francisco Chronicle—Kenneth Baker
San Francisco Examiner—Kelly Frankeny
(San Jose) Mercury News—Dorothy Burkhart
San Mateo Times—Mary Helen McAllister
(Santa Ana) Orange County Register—Laura Bleiberg
Santa Barbara News-Press—Gary Robb
Santa Rosa Press Democrat—Dan Taylor
Stockton Record—Joe Franco
Torrance Daily Breeze—Don Lechman
Turlock Journal—Robin Sheppard
Vallejo Times-Herald—Gene Silverman
Ventura County Star-Free Press—Rita Moran
(Walnut Creek) Contra Costa Times—Carol Fowler
(Weaverville) Trinity Journal—Russell McGrath
(Woodland Hills) Daily News—Meg Sullivan

COLORADO

Boulder Daily Camera—John Lehndorff
Colorado Springs Gazette Telegraph—David Okamoto
Denver Post—Steve Rosen
(Denver) Rocky Mountain News—M. S. Mason
Fort Morgan Times—Bill Spencer
Pueblo Chieftain—Margie Wood

CONNECTICUT

(Bridgeport) Connecticut Post—Patrick Quinn
Bristol Press—Maureen Hamel
Danbury News-Times—Jean Buoy
Greenwich Time—Dorothy Friedman
Hartford Courant—Nancy LaRoche
Lakeville Journal—Anne Longley & Cathryn Boughton
New Britain Herald—Judith Brown
New Haven Register—Hayne Bayless
Stamford Advocate—Geoff O'Connell
Waterbury American & Republican—Collen Collins

DELAWARE

Wilmington News-Journal—Gary Mullinax

DISTRICT OF COLUMBIA

Washington Post—Paul Richard
Washington Times—Janet Addams Allen

FLORIDA

Daytona Beach News Journal—John Wirt
Fort Lauderdale Sun-Sentinel—Roger Hurlburt
Fort Myers News-Press—Heidi Rinella
Fort Walton Northwest Florida Daily News—Brenda Shossner
Gainesville Sun—Bill De Young
(Jacksonville) Florida Times-Union—Scott Simpson
Lakeland Ledger—Lynne Cooke
Miami Herald—Helen Kohen
Orlando Sentinel—Charles Twardy
Palatka Daily News—Butch Prevatt
Palm Beach Daily News—Michael Gatea & Jan Sjostrom
Pensacola News-Journal—Susan Catron
Saint Augustine Record—Karen Harvey

Saint Petersburg Times—Maryanne Marger
Sarasota Herald Tribune—Joan Altabe
Tallahassee Democrat—Janie Nelson
Tampa Tribune—Pat Mitchell
West Palm Beach Post—Gary Schwan

GEORGIA

Albany Herald—Lucille Russell
(Athens) Banner-Herald & Daily News—Kim Henderson
Atlanta Journal & Constitution—Cathy Fox
Augusta Chronicle—Don Rhodes
Augusta Herald—Don Rhodes
Cartersville Daily Tribune News—Elizabeth Cochran
Columbus Enquirer—Don Coker
Columbus Times—Carol Gerdes
Macon Telegraph—Dan Maley
Savannah News—Susan Love
Waycross Journal Herald—Nicki Carter

HAWAII

Honolulu Advertiser—Ronn Ronck
(Honolulu) Star Bulletin—Mike Rovner

IDAHO

(Boise) Idaho Statesman—Camille Nichols
Coeur d'Alene Press—Barry Casebolt
(Idaho Falls) Post-Register—Paul Menser
Lewiston Morning Tribune—John McCarthy
(Pocatello) Idaho State Journal—Joy Morrison
(Twin Falls) Times-News—Darlene Huner

ILLINOIS

Alton Telegraph—Mike Leathers
Arlington Heights Daily Herald—Jean Rudolph
Bloomington Daily Pantagraph—Stephan Gleason
Centralia Sentinel—Nancy Hensley
Chicago Sun-Times—Lon Grahnke
Chicago Tribune—Alan Artner
Decatur Herald-Review—Bob Fallstrom
Ke Kalb Daily Chronicle—Bonnie Reimisch
Dixon Telegraph—Carl Maronich
(Galesburg) Register-Mail—Robert Harrison
Moline Daily Dispatch—William McElwain
Peoria Journal-Star—Gary Panetta
(Rockford) Register-Star—Gail Baruch
(Springfield) State Journal-Register—Margaret Boswell
Watseka Times Republic—Joy Claire

INDIANA

(Bedford) Times-Mail—Eleanor Himebaugh
Columbus Republic—Doug Showalter
Connersville News-Examiner—Dick Konstanzer
Crawfordsville Journal-Review—Dave Tomaro
Evansville Courier—Roger McBain
Evansville Press—Sandra Knipe
Fort Wayne News-Sentinel—Bill Carlton
Gary Post-Tribune—Curt Wagner
Huntington Herald-Press—Rob Ziegler
Indianapolis News—Zach Dunkin
Indianapolis Star—Steve Mannheimer
Muncie Star—Bruce A. Douglas
Shelbyville News—Margaret A. Huffman
South Bend Tribune—Chuck Smallcis
(Spencer) Evening World—Kevin Kleine
Washington Times-Herald—Melody Maust

IOWA

(Burlington) Hawk Eye—Bob Wilson
Cedar Rapids Gazette—Duane Crock
Centerville Iowegian—Gerald Stoddard
Des Moines Register—Eliot Nusbaum
(Iowa City) Daily Iowan—Steve Cruse
Muscatine Journal—Anita Bird

Newton Daily News—Peter Hussman
Oelwein Daily Register—Ken Schmith
Sioux City Journal—Bruce Miller
Washington Evening Journal—Brooks Taylor
Waterloo Courier—Phyllis Singer

KANSAS

Concordia Blade-Empire—Brad Lowell
Eureka Herald—Richard W. Clasen
Hutchinson News—Roger Verdon
(Independence) Daily Report—Georgia High
Lawrence Journal World—Mason King
(Liberal) Southwest Times—Karla Burt
Manhattan Mercury—Patrice Macan
Newton Kansan—Joe Sullens
Norton Daily Telegram—Mary Beth Boyd
Pratt Tribune—Conrad Easterday
Russell Daily News—Robert Estes
Salina Journal—Bob Kelly
Topeka Capital-Journal—Jane Witkoski
Wichita Eagle-Beacon—Ed Arone

KENTUCKY

(Ashland) Daily Independent—Cathie Schaffer
(Covington) Kentucky Post—Michele Day
(Elizabethtown) News-Enterprise—Mary Alice Holt
(Hopkinsville) Kentucky New Era—David Jennings
Lexington Herald-Leader—Paula Anderson
Louisville Courier-Journal—Diane Heilenman
Murray Ledger & Times—Stacey Crook
Paducah Sun—Lynn McDaniel
Winchester Sun—Amy Hogg

LOUISIANA

Alexandria Daily Town Talk—Alice Story
Bastrop Daily Enterprise—Addye Mae Mitcham
Crowley Post-Signal—Harold Gonzales
Hammond Daily Star—Joan Davis
Minden Press-Herald—Bonnie Koskie
(New Orleans) Times Picayune—Chris Waddington
Shreveport Times—Kathie Rowell
Slidell Sentry-News—John Perkins

MAINE

Bangor Daily News—Eric Zelz
(Lewiston) Sun-Journal—Heather McCarthy
Portland Press Herald—Jane Lord

MARYLAND

(Annapolis) Capital—Kathy Edwards
Baltimore Sun—John Dorsey
Columbia Flier—Geoffrey Himes & John Harding
(Hagerstown) Herald-Mail—Cindy Mills
Salisbury Daily Times—Eric Sahler

MASSACHUSETTS

(Boston) Christian Science Monitor—April Austin
Boston Globe—John Koch
Boston Hellenic Chronicle—Nancy Agris
Boston Herald—Bill Weber
Boston Phoenix—Cate McQuaid
(Brockton) Enterprise—Maureen Call
(East Boston) Post-Gazette—John Brenner & Pam Donnaruma
(Framingham) Middlesex News—Cate Prato
Haverhill Gazette—John Lockwood
Lawrence Eagle Tribune—Marjory Sherman & Brenda Smith
Lowell Sun—Ann Schecter
(Pittsfield) Berkshire Eagle—Charles Bonenti
(Quincy) Patriot Ledger—Jon Lehman
Springfield Union News—Doris Schmidt
Taunton Daily Gazette—Karen White
West Springfield Record—Marie A. Coburn
Worcester Telegram & Gazette—Dave Mawson

MICHIGAN

Alpena News—Diane Speer
Ann Arbor News—Bruce Martin
Battle Creek Enquirer—Jim Dean
Bay City Times—Jenni Laidman
(Benton Harbor-St Joseph) Herald-Palladium—Steve Pepple
Big Rapids Pioneer—Jim Bruskotter
Detroit Free Press—Marsha Miro
Detroit News—Joy Colby
Flint Journal—Michael Riha
Grand Rapids Press—Sue Wallace
Jackson Citizen Patriot—John Stewart
Kalamazoo Gazette—Doug Pullen
Lansing State Journal—Mike Hughes
Ludington Daily News—Cheryl Higginson
(Mount Clemens) Macomb Daily—Robert Russell
Muskegon Chronicle—Linda Heppe
(Pontiac) Oakland Press—Mark Rademacher
Saginaw News—Janet Martineau

MINNESOTA

Austin Daily Herald—Judy McDermott & Kimberly Masters
Duluth News Tribune & Herald—J. P. Furst
(Hibbing) Daily Tribune—Doreen Lindahl
(Minneapolis) Minnesota Daily—Nick Tangborn & Steve Dowling
Minneapolis Star & Tribune—Mary Abbe Martin
(Red Wing) Republican Eagle—James Pumarlo
(Rochester) Post-Bulletin—Janice McFarland
Saint Cloud Times—Mike Nistler
Saint Paul Pioneer Press—Diane Hellekson
(Wilmar) West Central Tribune—Forrest Peterson & Joan Wright
Worthington Daily Globe—Beth Rickers

MISSISSIPPI

(Biloxi) Sun Herald—Jean Prescott
(Greenville) Delta Democrat-Times—Sally Gresham
(Jackson) Clarion-Ledger—Orly Hood
(McComb) Enterprise-Journal—Charles M. Dunagin & Jack Ryan
Meridian Star—Dorothy Thompson
(Pascagoula) Mississippi Press—Charles Brooks
(Tupelo) Northeast Mississippi Daily Journal—Mary Farrell

MISSOURI

Brookfield News-Bulletin—Esther Willson
Farmington Press Leader—Laura Barton
Independence Examiner—Coral Beach
Jefferson City Capital News—Dwight Warren
Kansas City Star—Alice Thorson
Neosha Daily News—Rob Viehman
Saint Joseph News-Press—Preston Filbert
Saint Louis Post-Dispatch—Robert Duffy
Springfield News-Leader—Bill Tatum
West Plains Daily Quill—Vickie Taylor

MONTANA

Billings Gazette—Christine C. Meyers
(Butte) Montana Standard—Carmen Winslow
(Missoula) Missoulian—Theresa Johnson

NEBRASKA

Kearney Hub—Donna Farris
Lincoln Journal—Tom Ineck
McCook Daily Gazette—Steve Walker
Omaha World-Herald—Kyle McMillan

NEVADA

(Carson City) Nevada Appeal—Lisa Kirk
Las Vegas Review-Journal—Pat Morgan
Las Vegas Sun—Phil Hagen
Reno Gazette-Journal—Sandy Macias

NEW HAMPSHIRE

(Hanover) Dartmouth—Angela Crossman
Manchester Union Leader—Peter Swanson

NEW JERSEY

Atlantic City Press—Alice Post
Bridgeton Evening News—Diane Hill
The (Bridgewater) Courier News—Paul Grzella
(Cherry Hill) Courier-Post—Robert Baxter
(Hackensack) Record—John Zeaman
(Jersey City) Jersey Journal—Margaret Schmidt
(Morristown) Daily Record—Marion Fuller
(Neptune) Asbury Park Press—Gretchen Van Benthuysen
Newark Star Ledger—Eileen Watkins
(New Brunswick) Home News—Evelyn Apgar
(Passaic) North Jersey Herald & News—Michael Starr
(Trenton) Trentonian—Lori Reed
Woodbridge News Tribune—Nancy Cherry
(Woodbury) Gloucester County Times—John Barna & John Schoonejongen

NEW MEXICO

Albuquerque Journal—Dave Steinberg
Albuquerque Tribune—Ricardo Gandara & Kevin Hellyer
Carlsbad Current-Argus—Betty Patton
Clovis News-Journal—Maryanne Sutton
(Farmington) Daily Times—Deborah Tracy
(Grants) Cibola County Grants Beacon—Joe Looney
Hobbs Daily News-Sun—Dawn Morgan
Roswell Daily Record—Andrea Egger
(Santa Fe) New Mexican—Denise Cusel

NEW YORK

Albany Times Union—Jackie Demaline
Batavia Daily News—Elaine Thomas
(Binghamton) Press & Sun-Bulletin—Barbara Van Atta
Buffalo News—Richard Huntington
Corning Leader—Todd Franko
(Herkimer) Evening Telegram—Dan Guzewich
(Melville) Newsday—Peggy Katalinich & Sylviane Gold
Middletown Times Herald-Record—Emily Morrison
New York Daily News—Tom Ruis
New York Post—Bob Costello
New York Times—John Russell
(New York) Wall Street Journal—Raymond Sokolov
(Nyack) Rockland Journal-News—Georgette Gouveia
Pawling News-Chronicle—Mary Beth Iaquinto
Port Chester Daily Item—Georgette Gouveia
Poughkeepsie Journal—Florence Pennella
Rochester Democrat & Chronicle—Ron Netsky
Rochester Times-Union—Allison Mayer Duffey
(Saratoga Springs) Saratogian—Anne Harding
Schenectady Gazette—Margaret Wright
(Southold) Long Island Traveler/Watchman—Patricia Wood
Staten Island Advance—Michael Fressola
Staten Island Register—Diane Scalfani
Syracuse Herald-Journal—William Robinson & Kathy Schreider
Syracuse Post-Standard—Kathy Schneider
(Troy) Record—Doug DeLisle & Steve Barnes
Woodside Herald—Joe Sabba
(Yorktown Heights) North County News—Elaine Winterstein

NORTH CAROLINA

Asheville Citizen-Times—Dale Neal
Charlotte Observer—Tom Patterson
Durham Herald-Sun—Susan Broili & Jim Wise
Elizabeth City Daily Advance—Jeff Hampton
Goldsboro News-Argus—Winkie Lee
Greensboro News & Record—Abe Jones
Greenville Daily Reflector—Cherie Evans
Hendersonville Times-News—Sally Cook-Anderson
(Lumberton) Robesonian—Knight Chamberlin
(Raleigh) News & Observer—Chuck Twardy
Shelby Star—Dan Conover
Tryon Daily Bulletin—Jeffrey Byrd
Washington Daily News—Pam Nuckols

(Waynesville) Mountaineer—Ned Loemyer
Wilmington Star-News—Karen Olson
Wilson Daily Times—Harold Tarelton
Winston-Salem Journal—Tom Travin

NORTH DAKOTA

Bismarck Tribune—Vicki Voskuil
Dickinson Press—Linda Sailer
Fargo Forum—Cathleen Zaiser
Grand Forks Herald—Gail Hand
Jamestown Sun—Wayne Nelson

OHIO

Akron Beacon Journal—Dorothy Shinn
Athens Messenger—Carol James
Beavercreek News Current—Michele Grier
Canton Repository—Dan Kane
Cincinnati Enquirer—Owen Findsen & Roy Huff
Cincinnati Post—Nancy Berlier
Cleveland Plain Dealer—Helen Cullinan
Columbus Dispatch—Jacqueline Hall
Dayton Daily News & Journal Herald—Betty Dietz Krebs
Delphos Daily Herald—Esther Bielawski
Fostoria Review Times—Tim Dehnhoff
Galion Inquirer—Theresa McPeek
Portsmouth Daily Times—Jeff Henson
Sandusky Register—Kathy Lilje
Sidney Daily News—Margie Wuebker
Toledo Blade—Tom Gearhart
Troy Daily News—Kevin Aprile
Wapakoneta Daily News—Debbie Baumann
(Willoughby) News-Herald—Tricia Ambrose
(Youngstown) Vindicator—Michael A. Braun

OKLAHOMA

Blackwell Journal-Tribune—Dale McGaha
Claremore Progress—Pat Reeder
Elk City Daily News—Jo Ann Medders
Lawton Constitution—Charles Clark
Muskogee Daily Phoenix & Times-Democrat—Liz McMahan
(Oklahoma City) Daily Oklahoman—Billy Sandlin
Pryor Daily Times—Terry Aylward
Seminole Producer—Karen Anson
Tulsa Tribune—James Watts
Tulsa World—Cathy Milan

OREGON

(Coos Bay) World—Linda Meirjurgen
(Eugene) Register-Guard—Paul Denison
(Grants Pass) Daily Courier—Edith Decker
(Medford) Mail Tribune—Bill Varble
(Ontario) Argus Observer—Chris Moore & Shanna Wiggins
(Portland) Oregonian—Karen Brooks
(Salem) Statesman-Journal—Ron Cowan

PENNSYLVANIA

Allentown Morning Call—Paul Willistein
Bradford Era—J. M. Cleary
Brookville American—Randon Bartley
(Doylestown) Intelligencer—Sharon Swadis
(DuBois) Courier-Express—Denny Bonavita
Greensburg Tribune-Review—Cathy Lubenski
(Harrisburg) Patriot-News—John McGinley
(Huntingdon) Daily News—Sue McElwee
Johnstown Tribune Democrat—Bruce Wissinger
(Lancaster) Sunday News—Jim Ruth
(Levittown) Bucks County Courier Times—Larry Printz
(Lewistown) Sentinel—Brad Siddons & Scott Franco
(Lock Haven) Express—Charles R. Ryan
(New Kensington-Tarentum) Valley News-Dispatch—Pat Vido
Philadelphia Daily News—Sandra Shea
Philadelphia Guide Newspapers, Inc.—Bob Jacobs
Philadelphia Inquirer—Ed Sozanski
Philadelphia New Observer—James Spady & Frank Green
Pittsburgh Post-Gazette—Donald Miller

Pittsburgh Press—Pat Lowry
(Primos) Daily Times—Trish Cofiell
(Reading) Times—George Hatza
Scranton Times—Daniel F. Cusick
(Towanda) Daily Review—Dennis Irvine
(Wilkes-Barre) Times Leader—Paul Gallagher
York Dispatch—Pam Saylor

RHODE ISLAND

Providence Journal-Bulletin—Mick Cochran
(South Kingstown) Narragansett Times—Karen Bousquet

SOUTH CAROLINA

Anderson Independent-Mail—Kristin Norton
Beaufort Gazette—Debbie Radford
Charleston News & Courier—Gill Guerry
Columbia Black News—Bernard Legette
(Columbia) State—William Starr
Florence Morning News—Jeff Johnson
Greenville News—Debra Richardson-Moore
Orangeburg Times & Democrat—Joyce W. Milkie
(Spartanburg) Herald-Journal—Jill Jones

SOUTH DAKOTA

(Mitchell) Republic—Barb Dykstra
(Sioux Falls) Argus Leader—Ann Grauvogl

TENNESSEE

Chattanooga News-Free Press—Ann Nichols
Chattanooga Times—Randy Arnold
(Clarksville) Leaf Chronicle—Doug Ray
(Columbia) Daily Herald—Marvine Sugg
Elizabethton Starr—Rozella Hardin
Jackson Sun—Delores Ballard
Johnson City Press—Lisa Paine-Brooks
Kingsport Times-News—Becky Whitlock
Knoxville News-Sentinel—Bob Alexander
Lebanon Democrat—Marcia Poley
(Memphis) Commercial Appeal—Frederic Koeppel
(Morristown) Citizen Tribune—Page Brewer
(Murfreesboro) Daily News Journal—Suzanne Ghianni
Nashville Banner—Beth Monin
Nashville Tennessean—Richard Schweid & Clara Hieronymous
(Oak Ridge) Oak Ridger—Michael Frazier & Kay Dillon

TEXAS

Abilene Reporter-News—Bob Lapham
Amarillo Daily News—Kay Mohr
Austin American-Statesman—Ed Crowell
Beaumont Enterprise—Roy Bray
Big Spring Herald—Debbie Lincecum
(Clute) Brazosport Facts—Linda Heath
(Corpus Christi) Caller-Times—Ron George
Dallas Morning News—Janet Kutner
El Paso Herald-Post—Robbie Farley-Villalobos
El Paso Times—Josi Weber
Fort Worth Star-Telegram—Janet Tyson
Gonzales Inquirer—Bradley Avant
Houston Chronicle—Patricia Johnson
Houston Post—Mark Hanna
(Hurst) Mid-City News—Ginny Adams
(Lubbock) Avalanche Journal—Bill Kerns
Midland Reporter-Telegram—Georgia Temple
(Nacogdoches) Daily Sentinel—J. Lynn Carl & Gary Borders
Odessa American—Judy Paine
Orange Leader—Karen Snipes
Pecos Enterprise—Karen Oglesby
Plainview Daily Herald—Nicki Logan
Port Arthur News—Darragh Doiron
San Angelo Standard Times—Nejla Desctl
San Antonio Express-News—Kristina Paledes
San Antonio Light—Carolyn Warmbold
San Marcos Daily Record—Rowe Ray

(Tyler) Courier Times—Danny Mogle
Waco Tribune Herald—Carl Hoover
Waxahachie Daily Light—Sandra Minatra
Wichita Falls Times Record News—Maria Weaver

UTAH

Logan Herald Journal—Jennifer Hines
Ogden Standard-Examiner—Vanessa Zimmer
Provo Daily Herald—Renee Nelson
(Salt Lake City) Deseret News—Richard Christenson
Salt Lake Tribune—Helen Forsberg

VERMONT

Burlington Free Press—Julie Metzer
Saint Albans Messenger—Cathy Brauner & Gary Rutowski

VIRGINIA

(Arlington) USA Today—David Zimmerman
Bristol Herald Courier—Brian Reese
(Covington) Virginian Review—Horton P. Beirne
(Fredericksburg) Free Lance-Star—Gwen Woolf
Hopewell News—Virginia Dail
(Lynchburg) News & Advance—Cecil Mullan
Newport News Daily Press—Mark Erickson
(Norfolk) Ledger-Star—Diane Goldsmith
(Norfolk) Virginian-Pilot—Diane Goldsmith
Richmond Times-Dispatch—Robert Meritt
Roanoke Times & World News—Ann Mansfield
(Waynesboro) News-Virginian—Richard Prior

WASHINGTON

(Aberdeen) Daily World—Micki Colwell
Ellensburg Daily Record—Karol Ludtka
(Everett) Herald—Mike Murray
(Moses Lake) Columbia Basin Herald—Dan Black
Seattle Times—Delores Ament
Seattle Weekly—Katherine Koberg
Spokane Spokesman-Review—Kathryn DeLong
Tacoma News Tribune—Don Ruiz
(Vancouver) Columbian—Lynn Matthews
Wenatchee World—David Kraft

WEST VIRGINIA

Bluefield Daily Telegraph—Samantha Myers
Charleston Daily Mail—Julie Kemp
Charleston Gazette—Jane Claymore
Huntington Herald-Dispatch—Kelly Bragg
(Martinsburg) Journal—Greg Stepanich
(Wheeling) News-Register—Don Fise

WISCONSIN

(Appleton) Post-Crescent—Maureen Blaney
(Chippewa Falls) Chippewa Herald-Telegram—Mark Baker
(Eau Claire) Leader-Telegram—Bill Foy
Green Bay Press-Gazette—Warren Gerds
Kenosha News—Elizabeth Snyder
(Madison) Capital Times—Jake Stockinger
(Madison) Wisocnsin State Journal—Brian Howell
Milwaukee Journal—James Auer
Milwaukee Sentinel—Janis Paine

(Racine) Journal Times—Barbara Schuet
(Superior) Evening Telegram—Finley Stalvig
Wausau Daily Herald—Sara Kuhl

WYOMING

(Casper) Star-Tribune—Wyoma Groenenberg
(Cheyenne) Wyoming Eagle & State Tribune—Leah Noonan
Riverton Ranger—Dave Perry
Rock Springs Daily Rocket-Miner—Bruce Yoder

PUERTO RICO

(San Juan) El Mundo—Norma Borges & Jose Rodriguez
(San Juan) El Nuevo Dia—Samuel Cherson
(San Juan) El Vocero de Puerto Rico—Elia Gonzales-Ramos

CANADA

ALBERTA

Calgary Herald—Nancy Tousley
Calgary Sun—Lisa Shaw
Edmonton Journal—Rick Pape
Edmonton Sun—Fred Curatolo

BRITISH COLUMBIA

Vancouver Province—Peter Clough
Vancouver Sun—Iva Butler
Victoria Times-Colonist—Adrian Chamberlin & Michael D. Reid

MANITOBA

Winnipeg Free Press—Gordon Preece

NOVA SCOTIA

Halifax Chronicle Herald—Elissa B. Ernard

ONTARIO

Hamilton Spectator—Mike Baldwin
(Kitchener) Waterloo Record—Robert Reid
London Free Press—Doug Bale
Ottawa Citizen—Nancy Baele
Toronto Globe & Mail—John B. Mays
Toronto Star—Christopher Hume
Toronto Sun—Lisa Balfour Bowen
Windsor Star—Owen Jones

QUEBEC

Montreal Gazette—Ann Duncan
(Montreal) La Presse Ltee—Mario Roy
(Montreal) Le Journal de Montreal—Gilles Crevier
(Quebec) Le Journal de Quebec—Denise Martel
(Quebec) Le Soleil—Marc Samson

SASKATCHEWAN

Regina Leader-Post—Pat Davitt
(Saskatoon) Star Phoenix—Sheila Robertson

Scholarships and Fellowships

OFFERED BY	AMOUNT	OPEN TO	DURATION	WHEN OFFERED
ACA College of Design, 2528 Kemper Lane, Cincinnati, OH 45206	$5,300	First-year ACA student who has completed 11 months	One year	Annually
Academy of the Arts, 106 South St, Easton, MD 21601	$15-$120	Students 18 yrs and under to participate in Academy arts classes	Per class	Ongoing
Adrian College, 110 S Madison, Adrian, MI 49221	$750-$1500	Freshmen	Renewable up to 4 years	Annually to incoming Freshmen
	$500	Upperclass	Renewable	Annually
	$1000	Upperclass art major	One year	Annually
	$2000	Incoming freshmen HS GPA 3.3; can be combined with any of the above	Renewable for 4 years	Annually
American Academy of Art, 122 S Michigan Ave, Chicago, IL 60603	$16,000	High school seniors and currently enrolled AAA students	One or more school semesters	Bi-annually
American Antiquarian Society, 185 Salisbury St, Worcester, MA 01609	Maximum available stipend $30,000 (AAS-NEH Fellowships)	Qualified scholars in American history and culture to 1877. Degree candidates are not eligible	Six months-one year at the Society's library	Annually
	Peterson Fellowships, $850 per month	Qualified scholars in American history & culture to 1877 & open to grad students at work on dissertations	One-three months at the Society's library	Annually
	AAS-ASECS Fellowships, $850 per month	Qualified scholars in any area of American eighteenth-century studies. Degree candidates not eligible	One-three months at the Society's library	Annually
American Numismatic Society, Broadway at 155th St, New York, NY 10032	$2000 stipend in support of summer study	Students who have completed one year graduate study in classics, archaeology, history, art history and related fields	Summer	Deadline March 1
	$3500 dissertatiohn fellowship	Individuals who have completed the ANS Graduate Seminar & general examinations for the doctorate	Academic year	Deadline March 1
	$2000 Frances M Schwartz Fellowship	Individuals who have completed the B.A.	Academic year	Deadline March 1
	Louise Wallace Hackney Fellowship for the Study of Chinese Art—$7000	Post-Doctoral and Doctoral students who are U.S. citizens	One year	July 1st to June 30th
American Scandinavian Foundation, Exchange Division, 725 Park Ave, New York, NY 10021	$2500-$15,000	Applicants with an undergraduate degree (unrestricted fields) for Denmark, Finland, Iceland, Norway and Sweden	Up to one year	Annually, deadline Nov. 1
Aquinas College, 1607 Robinson Rd SE, Grand Rapids, MI 49506	$500-$4500	Incoming Freshmen	4 years	Annually
Arizona Commission on the Arts, 417 West Roosevelt St, Phoenix, AZ 85003	$5000-$7500	Residents of Arizona, over 18; students are not eligible	One year	Annually
	Performing Arts Fellowship	Same as above	One year	Annually
	Writers Fellowship	Same as above	One year	Annually
	Visual Arts Fellowships			

OFFERED BY	AMOUNT	OPEN TO	DURATION	WHEN OFFERED
Arkansas State University, Dept of Art, State University, AR 72467	$100-$800 range, full or partial tuition grants up to 4 each semester	Entering and current undergraduates	One semester-Eight semesters	Reviewed each semester
Arrowmont School of Arts and Crafts, 556 Parkway, Box 567, Gatlinburg, TN 37738	$175-$300 (12-15)	Needy students	One or two weeks	Spring and summer
	Assistantships covering room and board and class tuition in exchange for work (14)	Students with experience in particular medium	Two to six weeks	Spring and summer
Art Association of Richmond, McGuire Memorial Hall, 350 Whitewater Blvd, Richmond, IN 47374	$500	Richmond high school senior studying art	One year	Annually
	Anna Belle Henthorne Art Scholarship, $350	Richmond High School senior studying art	One year	Annually
Art Center College of Design, 1700 Lida St, PO Box 7197, Pasadena, CA 91109	Variable	All students	1 or 2 semesters at a time	Every semester
Art Institute for the Permain Basin, 4909 E University Blvd, Odessa, TX 79762-8144	Tuition	Area children & adults who need tuition help	One semester	Per semester
Art Institute of Boston, 700 Beacon St, Boston, MA 02215	$500 to $3500	Accepted or enrolled students at the Art Institute	One-four years	Annually; deadline Feb 20,
The Art Institute of Dallas, Two North Park, 8080 Park Lane, Dallas TX 75231	$76,000	High school seniors	18-27 months	Annually
Art Institute of Philadelphia, 1622 Chestnut St, Philadelphia, PA 19103	Varied	Eligible students	One year	Annually
Art Institute of Pittsburgh, 526 Penn Ave, Pittsburgh, PA 15222	$1650	Current students	One quarter	Quarterly
Art Institute of Seattle, 2323 Elliott Ave, Seattle, WA 98121	Full tuition	High school seniors	Full program	Annually
	Variable merit scholarship	New & continuing students (based on need)	Annual	Quarterly
Artpark, Box 371, Lewiston, NY 14092	Three week residence	Artists of all media	Three weeks during the summer	Deadline Oct. 30
	Sculpture project funding	Sculptors of all media	Variable	Deadline Oct. 30
Art Students League of New York, 215 W. 57th St, New York, NY 10019	Tuition $7000 Traveling Scholarships (2) and Awards for Advanced study including living and travel expenses; also other scholarships	League students	One year	Annually
Arts Council of Spartanburg County, Inc, 385 S Spring St, Spartanburg, SC 29306	Varies	Residents	Variable	Annually
	Mary Wheeler Davis Scholarship $1000	Spatanburg couty students pursuing studies toward career in the arts	One year	Annually; application deadline March 1
Artworks, 19 Everett Alley, Trenton, NJ 08611	$100-$150	Students enrolled in Artworks classes	One year	Annually
Ashland University Dept of Art, College Ave, Ashland, OH 44805	$500-$1000	Entering Freshmen	One Year, renewable	Annually
Atlanta College of Art, 1280 Peachtree St. NE, Atlanta, GA 30309	$500-$2500	Prospective students	Year	Annually
Atlantic Christian College, Art Department, Wilson, NC 27893	Determined by interest on principle	All art majors	Determined by Art Faculty	Spring for following fall
Augusta College, Dept of Fine Arts, 2500 Walton Way, Augusta, GA 30904	Variable	Freshmen, Sopomores, Juniors	One year	Annually
Augustana College, Art & Art History Dept, 3701 7th Ave, Rock Island, IL 61201	$2000	Studio art majors beginning in freshman year	One to four years	Annually
Austin College Art Dept, PO Box 1177, Sherman, TX 75090	$500	Incoming freshmen and transfer students	Four years	Annually
Austin Peay State Univ, Dept of Art, Clarksville, TN 37044	Variable	High school art seniors in central Tennessee and transfer students	One year	Annually
Baldwin Historical Society & Museum, 1980 Grand Ave, Baldwin, NY 11510	$100	Local high school students in American History	One year	Annually

OFFERED BY	AMOUNT	OPEN TO	DURATION	WHEN OFFERED
Ball State University, 2000 University Ave, Muncie, IN 47306	$5100 graduate assistantship academic year (tuition waived)	Undergraduate degree in art students	One year (assistantship)	Annually
Banff Centre for the Arts, PO Box 1020, Banff, AB T0L 0G0, Canada	Contact Sponsor	All Accepted Applicants	Length of program (residency) accepted into	On acceptance
Bassist College, 2000 SW Fifth Ave, Portland, OR 97201	$22,090 (The total represents the combined amounts for the first and second year students)	Bassist College Students	One and two years	Annually
F. Lammot Belin Arts Scholarship, Waverly Community House, Waverly, PA 18471	$9000	Exceptional ability in chosen field. Must be a U.S. citizen. Must have been or presently be a resident of the Abingtons or Pocono Northeast of PA	One year	Annually, deadline Dec. 15
Bennington College, Bennington, VT 05201	$5,450 (tuition remission), one-half of Tuition	Qualified graduate applicants who will in exchange for their assistantships, work in the studios	Two years	Annually
Berry College, Art Department, Mt. Berry, GA 30149	$300-$500	Freshman art majors	One year	Annually
Berkshire Artisans, 28 Renne Ave, Pittsfield, MA 01201	$3800	Massachusetts Artists only	One year	Semi-annually
Blanden Memorial Art Museum, 920 Third Ave S, Fort Dodge, IA 50501	$400	Local high school students when recommended by high school art teachers for participation at the University of Iowa Summer Workshop for high school students	One summer workshop	Annually
Bloomsburg University, Dept of Art, Blakeless Center for the Humanities, Old Science Hall, Bloomsburg, PA 17815	$500	Freshmen	One year	Annually
Bob Jones University, School of Fine Arts, Wade Hampton Blvd, Greenville, SC 29614	$125 to $325 per month	Undergraduate students with demonstrated financial need and satisfactory school record. Campus work assignment required.	One semester (renewable)	Semi-annually
Bradley University, Div of Art, Heuser Art Center, Peoria, IL 61625	Undergraduate art merit scholarships $650 to $2000; Additional university scholarships to total full tuition in certain situations. 5 graduate assistantships and scholarships covering almost all tuition & fees to all tuition & fees dependent upon qualifications	Any student in or entering the art program	One year, two year, four year	Annually
	George & Norma Kuttemann $2000	Sculpture students upper division including graduate students	One year	Annually
Brewton-Parker College, Art Dept, Box 202, Mt. Vernon, GA 30445	Variable	Freshmen art majors, dormitory students preferred	One year	Quarterly
Briar Cliff College, 3303 Rebecca St, Sioux City, IA 51104	One-half tuition	Freshmen	Four year (renewable each year)	Annually
Brigham Young University, Harris Fine Arts Center, C-502 HFAC, Provo, UT 84602	Full and half tuition	Qualified freshmen applicants, transfer students and continuing students	One year	Annually
Bucknell University, Dept of Art, Lewisburg, PA 17837	$6300 plus tuition	Registered graduate students	One year (renewable)	Annually
Cabots Old Indian Pueblo Museum, 67616 E Desert View Ave, Desert Hot Springs, CA 92240	$1000	Students specializing in art & history museums	One year	Annually
California College of Arts and Crafts, 5212 Broadway, Oakland, CA 94618	Variable. Scholarships, loans, grants	Grants & loans, open to all students; based on need & merit	One year, renewable	Annually
California Institute of the Arts/School of Art, 24700 McBean Pkwy, Valencia, CA 91355	Variable	Enrolled students	One year	Annually
California State University, Chico, Art Department, First & Normal, Chico, CA 95929-0820	Ahlquist, Hamilton, Ravekes, Morrow Scholarships—varies	Art Majors	One year	Annually
California State University, Fullerton, Art Dept, Fullerton, CA 92634	$500-$2000	Enrolled students	One year	Annually
California State University, Hayward, Art Dept, Hayward, CA 94542	Variable	Any art student	One year	Annually
California State University, Los Angeles, Art Dept, 5151 State Univ Drive, Los Angeles, CA 90032	Varies	Undergraduates and graduates	One year	Annually

OFFERED BY	AMOUNT	OPEN TO	DURATION	WHEN OFFERED
Cameron University, Art Dept, 2800 W Gore Blvd, Lawton, OR 73505	Tuition	All	Semester & year	Semi-annually
Campbellsville College, Fine Arts Div, 200 W College St, Campbellsville, KY 42718	Varied	All applicants who can show proficiency	Four years (renewable)	Semi-annually
Canadian Scandinavian Foundation, McGill Univ, 805 Sherbrook St. W, Montreal, PQ H3G 3G1	Brucebo scholarship, 5,000 SEK for travel, food stipend & cottage use	Talented, young Canadian artist-painter	Two months in Gotland	Annually
Canadian Society of Painters, c/o Visual Arts Ontario, 439 Wellington St. W, Toronto, ON M5V 1E7	$100	Art Students at selected Canadian colleges of art	One year	Annually
	Swedish Institute Bursary Grant	Canadian citizens wishing to pursue studies/research in Scandinavia	four-eight months	Annually
	CSF Special Travel Grants, $1000	Same as above		Annually
	Sylwia Weldon Scholarship for Norway $1000-$1500	Same as above		Annually
Canton Art Institute, 1001 Market Ave N, Canton, OH 44702	$45	Students in our art classes	12 weeks	
Cardinal Stritch College, 6801 N. Yates Rd, Milwaukee, WI 53217	$1000	Students pursuing a Bachelor of Fine Arts (4 yr) degree	4 years if requirements met	Annually
Carroll College, 100 N East Ave, Waukesha, WI 53186	$500	Freshmen (art majors)	One year	Annually
Case Western Reserve University, Dept of Art History & Art, Mather House, Cleveland, OH 44106	$17,394	MA & PhD candidates	One year	Annually
Casper College, Dept of Visual Arts, 125 College Dr, Casper, WY 82601	Tuition and some supplies	Full-time enrollees	Semester	Semi-annually
The Catholic University of America, Dept of Art, Michigan Ave, Washington, DC 20064	Variable	All applicants		Annually
Cazenovia College, Cazenovia, NY 13035	$100-$1000	Advertising Design majors	Academic year (renewable)	Annually
	$100-$1000	Art majors	Academic year (renewable)	Annually
	$100-$1000	Interior Design majors	Academic year (renewable)	Annually
	$100-$1000	Fashion Design majors	Academic year (renewable)	Annually
	$100-$1000	Commercial Illustration majors	Academic year (renewable)	Annually
Center for Creative Studies, College of Art and Design, 245 E. Kirby St, Detroit, MI 48202	one-fourth tuition to full tuition	Transfer students and graduating high school seniors, continuing CRS-CAD students	One year	Annually
Central University of Iowa, Art Dept, 812 University, Pella, IA 50219	$2500	Review of portfolio	Four years	Annually
Central Wyoming College, Art Center, 2660 Peck Ave, Riverton, WY 82501	$500-$2000+	All applicants	One year, renewable	Semi-annually
Chadron State College, Department of Art, Chadron, NE 69337	Up to full in-state tuition for first year; Up to full in-state tuition or a percentage thereof subsequent years	No restrictions		Annually
Chaffey College, 5885 Haven Ave, Alta Loma, CA 91701	Variable	Qualified students	One year	Annually
Chautauqua Institution/The Art School, Box 1098, Dept 6, Chautauqua, NY 14722	$27,000	Full term students	Eight weeks	Annually
Cintas Fellowship Program, Institute of International Education, 809 United Nations Plaza, New York, NY 10017	$10,000	Professional artists who are Cuban or of Cuban lineage. Intended for professionals who have completed their academic and technical training	One year	Annually
Claremont Graduate School, Art Dept, 251 E 10th St, Claremont CA 91711	$6000	All	One year	Annually
Clark College, Art Dept, 1800 E. McLoughlin Blvd, Vancouver, WA 98663	Tuition waver (up to $275/term)	All new or returning students who enroll for at least 6 credits	One year	Annually
Clarke College, 1550 Clarke Dr, Dubuque, IA 52001	$500-$2000	Entering freshmen of any age-based on portfolio presentation	One year, (renewable for 4 years)	Annually

OFFERED BY	AMOUNT	OPEN TO	DURATION	WHEN OFFERED
Cleveland State University, Department of Art, Euclid Ave. at E. 24th St, Cleveland, OH 44115	Tuition (part or full)	Incoming high school students, transfer students, and continuing full time studio art majors based on merit. State residents only	One year	Annually
Coe College, Art Department, 1221 First Ave. NE, Cedar Rapids, IA 52402	$2500 - full tuition	Incoming freshmen and transfer students	Four years	3 times per year
Coker College, Art Dept, College Ave, Martsville, SC 29550	$2000	Incoming freshmen	Four years	Annually
Colby Community College, Visual Arts Department, 1255 S. Range, Colby, KS 67701	$100 up to full tuition and fees	Any applicant, juried portfolio	Two years	Annually
College of Charleston, School of the Arts, Charleston, SC 29424	$5000 new scholarships	Incoming students and to students enrolled in Music, Theatre, Art and Art History	Variable	Annually
College of Mt. Saint Joseph, Art Department, 5701 Delhi Road, Cincinnati, OH 45233-1670	Full tuition Scholastic Art Scholarship	High school graduates	One year (renewable)	Annually
	$2000 Fine Arts Scholarship	High school graduates	One year (renewable)	Annually
	$2000 Selections Scholarship	High school graduates	One year (renewable)	Biannually
	$1000 Ohio Governor's Youth Art Scholarship	High school graduates	One year (renewable)	Annually
	$1000 S. Augusta Zimmer Scholarship	High school graduates	One year	As available
College of New Rochelle, School of Arts & Sciences, New Rochelle, NY 10805	Variable	Incoming freshman with portfolio	Four years renewable	Annually
College of St. Benedict, Benedicta Arts Center, St. Joseph, MN 56374	$350-$1000 per year	Incoming art majors and present art majors	One to four years	Annually
College of St. Catherine, Art Dept, 2004 Randolph, St. Paul, MN 55105	Variable	Art majors	One year	Annually
College of Saint Mary, Art Dept, 1901 S. 72nd St, Omaha, NE 68124	Variable	High school graduates	Renewable up to 4 yrs	Annually
The College of Santa Fe, Saint Michaels Dr, Santa Fe, NM 87501	$500-$6000	By portfolio review and interview on a competitive basis	One year (renewable for 4 years)	Annually
College of Southern Idaho, Art Dept, PO Box 1238, Twin Falls, ID 83301	$500-$1000	All applicants	Semester & year	Annually, April
Colorado Institute of Art, 200 E. Ninth Ave, Denver, CO 80203	$85000	High school seniors	Full program tuition	Annually
Colorado State University, Dept of Art, Fort Collins, CO 80523	Varies	All	One year	Semi-annually
Columbia University, School of the Arts, 615 Dodge, New York, NY 10027	Variable	All registered students in competition		Annually
Concordia College, Art Department, 901 So. Eighth, Moorhead, MN 56562	Variable	Entering freshmen and upper classmen	One year	Annually
Converse College, Dept of Art, PO Box 29, Spartanburg, SC 29302	Varies	Scholastic & athletic students	One year	Annually
Cornell College, Mt. Vernon, IA 52314	$6000	Selected on recommendation of Art Dept.	Four years if student remains art major in good academic standing	Annually to freshmen
Cornish College of the Arts, 710 East Roy St, Seattle, WA 98102	Kreielsheimer Scholarship: Full tuition plus books & supplies	residents of WA, OR and AK; must be recent (within two years) high school graduate or earned GED	Four years	Annually
Cottey College, Fine Arts Division, Nevada, MO 64772	$600	Students interested in art who are attending Cottey College	One year (renewable)	Annually
	$400 (Harry Chew Memorial Scholarship)	Students interested in art who are attending Cottey College	One year (renewable)	Annually
Crazy Horse Memorial Foundation, Avenue of the Chiefs, Crazy Horse, SD 57730	Over $10,000	College students from South Dakota Indian reservations	One year	Annually
Crowder College, 601 La Crede, Neosho, MO 64850	Full tuition	District resident and Missouri resident	2 year	Semi-annually

OFFERED BY	AMOUNT	OPEN TO	DURATION	WHEN OFFERED
Cumberland College, Art Dept, Box 523, Williamsburg, KY 40769	$1200	All	One year (renewable)	Annually
Dana College, Blair, NE 68008	$500-$2000	Entering students	4 year with annual review	Annually
Dean Junior College, Visual and Performing Arts Department, 99 Main St, Franklin, MA 02038	Variable	Full-time students	One year	Annually
Denison University, PO Box M, Granville, OH 43023	Vail Scholarships in the Arts-$1500	All students, competitive. Awarded on the basis of portfolio and general academic ability	One year (renewable)	Annually, deadline March 1
Detroit Artists Market, 300 River Place, Suite 1650, Detroit, MI 48207	Varies	Any qualified student who is attending the specific school whose turn it is to receive the scholarship; given on rotating basis to Center for Creative Studies, Wayne State University and Cranbrook Academy of Art	One year	Annually
Dickinson College, Fine Arts Department, Weiss Center for the Arts, Carlisle, PA 17013	Varies according to number of recipients	Fine arts majors	One year	Annually
Dickinson State University, Department of Fine Arts & Humanities, Dickinson, ND 58601	$500 TMI Systems Design Corporation Scholarship	Any art or business student	One year	Annually
	$300 Tom Niemitalo Memorial Art Scholarship	Any art major or minor	One year	Annually
	$100 DSU Alumni Foundation Scholarships	Freshmen	One year	Annually
	$300 Clinton A. Sheffield Memorial Art Scholarship	Art education students	One year	Annually
	$250 David Huether Memorial Art Scholarship	Art students	One year	Annually
Drake University, Art Dept, 25th & University Ave, Des Moines, IA 50311	Variable	Art majors	One year (renewable)	Annually
Dunedin Fine Arts & Cultural Center, 1143 Michigan Blvd, Dunedin, FL 34698	Variable	Students sixth grade and above with sincere interest and/or talent and financial need; some collegiate assistance available	5, 8 and 10 weeks depending upon length of class	Annually
East Carolina University, School of Art, Greenville, NC 27858-4353	$175-$1000	All art majors, communication art and art education majors	One semester	Annually
	$475	All out-of-state entering freshmen art majors, based on a portfolio review during NASAD portfolio days	One semester	Annually
East Central Community College, Art Dept, PO Box 27, Decatur, MS 39327	$1300 (2 years)	Art majors	Two years	Annually
East Central College, PO Box 529, Union, MO 63084	$600	High school seniors or older who display artistic ability & discipline	One semester	Semi-annually
East Tennessee State University, Carroll Reece Museum, Johnson City, TN 37614	$2000	High school seniors, college students & other persons from the region wishing to continue their art education	One year	Annually
Eastern Washington University, Dept of Art, Chene, WA 99004	Varies	Art majors only	One year	Annually
Edinboro University of Pennsylvania, Dept of Art, Edinboro, PA 16444	$3400 & tuition (16) Graduate $98,000 total 201 currently receiving	MFA students-Graduate, Undergraduate, BFA - Fine Arts, BA - Art History, Art Education. Special honors scholarships work study available based on need	One year (renewable)	Annually
Emory University, Art History Dept, Atlanta, GA 30322	Competitive	PhD candidates	4 years	Annually
Endicott College, Art Dept, 376 Hale St, Beverly, MA 01915	Varies to need	All applicants	4 years	Annually
Fairbanks Arts Association, PO Box 72786, Fairbanks, AK 99707	$400	Junior high students attending the University of Alaska summer fine arts camp	One year	Annually
Fairmont State College, Art Dept, Fairmont, WV 26554	$2000-$5000	Qualified freshmen-seniors	One year	Annually
Fashion Institute of Dallas, The Art Institute of Dallas, 2 N Park East, Dallas, TX 75231	$40,200	High school seniors	18-27 months	Annually

OFFERED BY	AMOUNT	OPEN TO	DURATION	WHEN OFFERED
Fashion Institute of Technology, 227 W. 27th St, New York, NY 10001	Variable	All students who qualify	Renewable	Annually
Flagler College, Visual Arts Dept, 74 King St, Saint Augustine, FL 32084	$500 per year	Applicants with slides of portfolio (freshmen)	One year	Annually
Florida A & M University, Dept of Visual Arts, Humanity & Theatre, Tallahassee, FL 32307	$500	Freshmem	One year; can be renewed if in good standing	Semi-annually
Florida International University, Visual Arts Dept, University Park Campus Bldg DM-382, Miami, FL 33199	$500-$750	Current visual arts majors (full time)	Semester	Annually
Fort Hays State University, Visual Arts Center, 600 Park St, Hays, KS 67601	$16,500 $400 each	Graduate Assistantships Undergraduate Scholarships	One year One year	Annually Annually
Franklin and Marshall College, Art Dept, PO Box 3003, Lancaster, PA 17604-3003	Variable	Advanced students with experience	Summer	At request of professors
	$3,000	A sophomore major	Summer travel grant to study or research abroad	Annually
Franklin College, Art Dept, 501 E Monroe, Franklin, IN 46131	$400	Art majors	One year	Annually
Friends of Photography, 250 Forth St, San Francisco, CA 94103	Variable	Photographer who has demonstrated excellence in and commitment to the field of creative photography	One year	Annually
Friends University, Art Department, 2100 University Ave, Wichita, KS 67213	$600 and up	All art majors	One to four years if grades & work standards are maintained	Annually
Fuller Lodge Art Center & Gallery, 2132 Central Ave, PO Box 790, Los Alamos, NM 87544	$500	A qualified Los Alamos high school graduating senior majoring in art in college	One year	Annually
Georgetown College, Georgetown, KY 40324	$250-$1000 plus financial aid on a need basis & academic scholarships	All graduates of accredited secondary schools. A portfolio is required for an art grant but not for admission to the program	As long as academic progress is being made and the recipient is majoring in art	Semi-annually
Georgia State University, School of Art Design, University Plaza, Atlanta, GA 30303	$600	Graduate students	One year	Quarterly
Georgian Court College, Lakewood Ave, Lakewood, NJ 08701	$1000 and $750 per yr	High school graduates who plan to major in art	Renewable for 4 years	Annually
The Glassell School of Art, The Museum of Fine Arts, Houston, 5101 Montrose Blvd, Houston TX 77006	$3200	Post-graduate artists	9 months	Annually
Goshen College, 1700 S Main, Goshen, IN 46526	Varies	Based on academic ability and/or need	One to four years	Annually
Grants for Graduate Study Abroad. Write: U.S. Student Programs, Institute of International Education, 809 United Nations Plaza, New York, NY 10017		People in the arts may apply for any of these awards (Fulbright-Hays and Foreign Governments, Lusk Memorial Fellowships, Kade Memorial Fellowships), but they must be affiliated with an educational institute abroad while pursuing their studies	One academic year	Annually
Green Mountain College, Dept of Art, Poultney, VT 05764	$3,000	Art applicants; freshmen	4 years	Annually
John Simon Guggenheim Memorial Foundation, 90 Park Ave, New York, NY 10016	Adjusted to needs of fellows	Advanced professionals, citizens or permanent residents of U.S., Canada, Latin America and the Caribbean	Six months to one year	Annually
Gustavus Adolphus College, Art Dept, Schaefer Fine Arts Center, Saint Peter, MN 56082	$300-$850	40 studio and art history students	One year	Annually
Hardin-Simmons University, Art Dept, Hickory at Ambler St, PO Box 1151 Univ Station, Abilene, TX 79698	Up to $500 per semester	Art majors, full-time students	One year	Annually
Hannibal-LaGrange College, 2800 Palmyra Road, Hannibal, MI 63401	$2000, $250 per semester	Beginning freshmen	Per semester	Annually
Harding University, Department of Art, Box 2253, Searcy, AR 72149	Variable	Art majors	One year	Annual

OFFERED BY	AMOUNT	OPEN TO	DURATION	WHEN OFFERED
Hartford Art School, University of Hartford, 200 Bloomfield Ave, West Harrford, CT 06117	Up to full-tuition	Open to qualified applicants for full time study	One year, renewable	Annually
Hill College, Fine Arts Dept, PO Box 619, Hillsboro, TX 76645	$100 per semester plus dorm room	Area high school students	Semester	Semi-annually
Hofstra University, 1000 Fulton Ave, Hempstead, NY 11550	$15,000	Undergrads	Variable	Annually
Holland College Centre of Creative Arts, 50 Burns Ave, Charlottetown, Prince Edward Island C1E 1H7, Canada	$1000	Craft program students	Two years	Annually
Hope College, Art Department, De Pree Art Center, Holland, MI 49423	Four scholarships of $2500 each	Prospective Art majors	Four years (renewable)	Annually
Houston Center for Photography, 1441 W Alabama, Houston, TX 77006	$1000 & exhibition	Houston area photographers, and artists who incorporate photographic media in their work	One year	Annually
Huguenot Historical Society, PO Box 339, New Paltz, NY 12561	$1000	Students in the museum field summer jobs	One year	Annually
The Huntington Library and Art Gallery, San Marino, CA 91108	$1800	Scholars doing research on British & American art	One to three months	Annually; applications recieved October 1 to December 15 for awards begininng the following June 1
Hutchinson Art Association, 1520 N Main, Hutchinson, KS 67501	$250	Hutchinson Community College students	One year	Annually
Illinois State University, Art Dept, CUA119, Normal, IL 61761	Varied	All students	One year	Annually
Illinois Wesleyan University, School of Art, Bloomington, IL 61702	$2000-$6800 per year	Entering freshmen	4 yr (renewable)	Annually
Imperial Valley College, Art Dept, PO Box 158, Imperial, CA 92251	Vaied	All students	One year	Annually
Indiana Purdue University, Dept of Fine Arts, 2101 Coliseum Blvd E, Fort Wayne, IN 46805-1499	Varied	Full-time degree students	One year	Annually
Indiana State University, Department of Art, Terre Haute, IN 47809	$2600	MFA, MS, MA	One year	Annually
	$1100	BFA Freshmen	Four years	Annually
		Juniors/Seniors Painting	One year	
	$350-$1500	BS, BFA	One year	Annually
Indiana University, Hope School of Fine Arts, Fine Arts 123, Bloomington, IN 47405	$6000 plus fee scholarship	Beginning graduates	One year	Annually
Indiana University of Pennsylvania, Dept of Arts & Art Education, 114 Sprawls Hall, Indiana, PA 15705	$100-4500	Graduate students	One year	Annually
Indian Hills Community College, Ottumwa Campus, Dept. of Art, Grandview at Elm, Ottumwa, IA 52501	$100-$400	Full-time students in art	One year	Annually
James Madison University, College of Fine Arts and Communication, Dept of Art, Harrisonburg, VA 22807	$1000-$4000	Undergraduate art major who plans to enter the career of architecture (pre-architecture program available)	One year (renewable)	Annually
Jersey City State College, Art Dept, 2039 Kennedy Blvd, Jersey City, NJ 07305	Varies	Applicants with appropriate SAT scores, recommendations	Varies	Annually
Johnson Atelier, Technical Institute of Sculpture, 60 Ward Ave Extension, Mercerville, NJ 08619	$4800 (tuition grant)	Accepted students	One year	Annually
Joliet Jr College, Fine Arts Dept., 1216 Houbolt Ave, Joliet, IL 60436	Variable	All art students by application & portfolio	One year	Annually
Kalamazoo College, 1200 Academy, Kalamazoo, MI, 49007	$1500	Accepted applicants	One year (renewable)	Annually
Kansas City Art Institute, 4415 Warwick Blvd, Kansas City, MO 64111	$500-$9000	All eligible students	Varies; need based for one year; competitive based on GPA year-to-year	Varies

OFFERED BY	AMOUNT	OPEN TO	DURATION	WHEN OFFERED
Kansas State University, Department of Art, Manhattan, KS 66506	Variable scholarship awards	Freshmen-senior undergraduates & graduates in MFA program	One year	Annually
Kappa Pi International Honorary Art Fraternity, 9321 Paul Adrian Dr, Crestwood, MO 63126	$200, $300 & $500-$1000	Active student members only	One year	Annually
Kellogg Community College, 450 North Ave, Battle Creek, MI 49017	$30-$200	Departmental majors	Per semester	Semi-annually
Kent State University, School of Art, Kent, OH 44242	$500 per year; graduate fellowships, graduate teaching assistants (tuition waiver)	One year	Varies	Annually
Kentucky Art & Craft Gallery, 609 W Main St, Louisville, KY 40202	$2000-$4000	Kentucky crafts people & artists		Annually & semi-annually
Maude I. Kerns, Art Center, 1910 E. 15th Ave., Eugene, OR 97401	$50	Children	Two weeks	Annually (summer program)
Keystone Junior College, Fine Arts Dept, PO Box 50, La Plume PA 18440	$1000-$2500	Students in upper 2/5 of graduating class	One year (renewable)	Annually
Knox College, Dept of Art, Galesburg, IL 61401	Based on need	Based on need; also fine arts scholarships	One year; renewable	Annually
Lane Community College, 4000 East 30th Ave, Eugene, OR 97405	$276	Graphic design students	One year	Annually
Lansing Community College, PO Box 40010, Lansing MI 48901-7210	Full tuition	Residents who demonstrate merit (talent, high GPA, etc.)	2-year	Annually
Laramie County Community College, Div of Humanities, 1400 E Colege Dr, Cheyenne, WY 82007	Two at $346	All applicants	One year	Semi-annually
Limestone College, 1115 College Dr, Geffrey, SC 29340	$1500	Majors - studio & art ed	One year (renewable)	Annually
Lindenwood Colleges, Art Department, St. Charles, MO 63301	Variable	Basis of merit & financial need	One year (renewable)	Annually & semi-annually
Linfield College, Art Dept, McMinnville, OR 97128	Up to $10,000	Students participating in competitive scholarship progrm	4 years	Annually
Lock Haven University, Lock Haven, PA 17745	Varies	Variable	One year	
Long Island University, Brooklyn Center, Art Dept, University Plaza, Brooklyn, NY 11201	One-half tuition	Art Majors with 3.0 average	One year	Annually
Long Island University, C.W. Post Campus, Art Dept, Northern Blvd, Brookville, NY 11548	$1000	Incoming undergraduates	One year	Annually
Longwood College, Dept of Art, Pine St, Varmville, VA 23901	$3500 total	Current students only	One year	Annually
Louisiana College, 1140 College Dr, Pineville, LA 71359	$500 per semester	Qualified art majors	Variable	Semi-annually
Loyola Marymount University, Art Dept, Communications & Fine Arts, Loyola Blvd & W 80th St, Los Angeles, CA90045	Varies	Returning studio arts and art history majors	One year	Annually
Lubbock Christian University, 5601 W 19th, Lubbock, TX 79407	$150-$200	Based on portfolio	One year	Annually
Luther College, Department of Art, Decorah, IA 52101	1 at $1000 5 at $400	High school seniors	One year	Annually
Lycoming College, Art Dept, Williamsport, PA 17701	$1,500	Entering students	Renewable for four years	Semi-annually
Mansfield University, Art Dept, Allen Hall, Mansfield, PA 16933	Varies	Freshmen	One year	Annually
Marian College, Art Dept, 45 S National Ave, Fond du Lac, WI 54935	$500	Art, art education, and humanities majors	One year	Annually
Marion Art Center, 80 Pleasant, Box 602, Marion, MA 02738	$500	High school seniors	One year	Annually
Maryland College of Art & Design, 10500 Georgia Ave, Silver Spring, MD 20902	Up to $1500	Degree-seeking students	One year	Annually

OFFERED BY	AMOUNT	OPEN TO	DURATION	WHEN OFFERED
Marymount College, Art Dept, Neperhan Rd, Tarrytown, NY 10591	Varies (up to $500)	Full-time students	One year	Annually
Marywood College, Art Dept, 2300 Adams Ave, Scranton, PA 18509	Varies	All students; undergraduate and graduate	Undergraduate, 4 years; graduate, one year renewable	Annually
McMurry University, Art Department, PO Box 308, McMurry Station, Abilene, TX 79697	$2200	Art students who show special ability	One year	Annually
	$3000 with $1000 added each remaining year	Art scholarship (based on portfolio judging from local area high schools)		Annually
Memphis College of Art, 1930 Poplar Ave, Overton Pk, Memphis, TN 38104	Varies-$200 to half-tuition	High school graduates and transfers, based on merit	Four years (renewable)	Annually
Mercyhurst College, Dept of Art, Glenwood Hills, Erie, PA 16546	$20,000	All freshmen art applicants, recent high school graduates	One year (renewable)	Annually
Mesa Community College, Dept of Art, 1833 W Southern Ave, Mesa, AZ 85202	$4000	Enrolled students and high school seniors	One year or semester	Annually (spring)
Metropolitan Museum of Art, Office of Academic Affairs, 1000 Fifth Ave, New York, NY 10028	Variable	Scholars researching art historical fields relating to Metropolitan Museum of Art collections & Conservators	One year	Deadline Nov. 17, 1989 for art historical fellowships and January 13, 1989 for conservation fellowships
Miami-Dade Community College, Visual Arts Dept, 11011 SW 104 St, Miami, FL 33176	$350-$500 per term	New and continuing art majors, two at $1200 per year	Varies	Annually; semi-annually
Midland College, Art Dept, 3600 N Garfield, Midland, TX 79705	Full tuition and fees	Full time student (12hrs) art major, at least 6 credits per semester	One semester continuing for one additional semester	Semi-annually
	$100 per semester	Any student in art	One semester	Semi-annually
Midwestern State University, Div of Fine Arts, 3400 Taft Blvd, Wichita Falls, TX 76308	Varies	All students	One year	Annually
Miles Community College, Art Department, 2715 Dickinson St, Miles City, MT 59301	Based on need	Art students	One year	Annually
Millikin University, Art Department, 1184 W Main, Decatur, IL 62522	$500 to one-half tuition	Qualified students	Four years	Annually
Mills College, Art Department, 5000 MacArthur Blvd, PO Box 9975, Oakland, CA 94613	Variable	Mills graduate students		Annually
	Eleanor Crum Award in Ceramics	Graduating seniors & MFA's		Annually
	Catherine Morgan Trefethen Award	Merit Award to 2nd yr. MFA's		Annually
	Aurelia Henry Reinhardt Faculty Purse	Graduating seniors for further study		Annually
Milwaukee Institute of Art & Design, 273 E Erie St, Milwaukee, WI 53202	$3000-$9800	Open to new full-time students who attend two or more semesters-based on merit and performance	One year-4 year awards	Annually; (portfolio competition held each spring)
Minneapolis College of Art & Design, 2501 Stevens Ave S, Minneapolis, MN 55404	Varies	All	One year	Annually
Minnesota Museum of Art Landmark Center, Fifth at Market, Saint Paul, MN 55104	Varies	Children from low income families	One year	Annually
Minnesota State Arts Board, 432 Summit Ave, Saint Paul, MN 55102	$6000 (Fellowships only)	Professional artists in all disciplines who are residents of the state of Minnesota	One year	Annually
Missouri Southern State College, Art Department, Newman & Duquesne Rds, Joplin, MO 64801	Henry Hornsby $1000 Thomas Hart Benton $1150 (4) Warten Fine Arts $1150 BL Parker $500	Top quality students with art skills and financial needs	One year	Annually
Missouri Western State College, Art Department, 4525 Downs Dr, St. Joseph, MO 64507	Variable	Any qualifying student majoring in art	By semester	By semester
Mitchell Community College, Visual Art Department, E. Broad St, Statesville, NC 28677	Full tuition (3)	Full time student — Fellowship; sophomore already enrolled	One year	Annually

OFFERED BY	AMOUNT	OPEN TO	DURATION	WHEN OFFERED
Mohawk Valley Community College, 1101 Sherman Dr, Utica, NY 13510	Varies	Students in curriculum		Annually
Montana State University, School of Art, Bozeman, MT 59717	(1) $4500 teaching assistantship	Graduate students	10 months	Annually-March 1
	(2) $1000 presidential scholarship	Graduate students	10 months	Annually
Montay College, Art Dept, 3750 W. Peterson Ave, Chicago, IL 60659	$500	Seniors	One year	Annually
Montclair Art Museum, Art School, 3 S. Mountain Ave, PO Box 1582, Montclair, NJ 07042	Adults $140 Children $100	Adults & children	One term	Fall & Spring
Monterey Peninsula Museum of Art, 559 Pacific St, Monterey, CA 93940	$100 monthly	All students	Monthly	Annually, deadline for application Nov. 15
Montserrat College of Art, Dunham Rd, PO Box 26, Beverly, MA 01915	Merit Awards $1000	Incoming freshmen	One year	At time of admission
	Alumni Scholarship $1000	Continuing students who are eligible for financial aid	One year	Spring for following year
	Montserrat grants varying to $3000	Students eligible for financial aid	One year	Spring for following year
Mount Allison University, Dept of Fine Arts, Sackville, NB E0A 3C0	$1000	Students entering the first year of the Bachelor of Fine Arts degree program	One year	Annually
Mount Hood Community College, Visual Arts Center, 26000 SE Stack St, Bresham, OR 97030	Varies	Varies	Quarterly; annually	Annually; semi-annually; quarterly
Mount Mary College, 2900 N Menomonee River Pkwy, Milwaukee, WI 53222	$2000	Freshmen	Continuing	Annually
Mount Royal College, Dept of Interior Design, 4825 Richard Rd SW, Calgary, AB T3E 6K6, Canada	$3,000	Second-year students and program graduates	One year	Annually
Murray State University, Dept of Art, 15th St, Murray, KY 42071	Variable (Presidential, University Scholars and Academic Scholarships)	Graduating high school seniors	One to four years	Annually, February 15 deadline
	$500 to $2000 departmental/collegiate scholarships	Incoming freshman and students majoring in art at Murray State University (portfolio required)	One year	Annually February 15 deadline
Museum of Early Southern Decorative Arts Summer Institute, PO Box 10310, Winston-Salem, NC 27108	Fellowship for partial tuition	Graduate students in history, art history, preservation, museum studies; museum personnel	June-July (four weeks)	Annually
Muskingum College, Art Dept., Johnson Hall, New Concord, OH 43762	$1800	Art majors and minors	One year	Annually
National Gallery of Art, Center of Advanced Study in the Visual Arts, Constitution Ave at Fourth St NW, Washington, DC 20565	$11,000	Ph.D. candidates	3 years	Annually
	$11,000 Paul Mellon Fellowship	Ph.D. candidates	3 year	Annually
	$11,000 Samuel H. Kress Fellowship	Ph.D. candidates	Two years	Annually
	$11,000 Mary Davis Fellowship	Ph.D. candidates	Two years	Annually
	$11,000 Wyeth Fellowship	Ph.D. candidates	Two years	Annually
	$11,000 Ittleson Fellowship	Ph.D. candidates	Two years	Annually
	$11,000 Andrew W Mellon Fellowship	Ph.D. candidates	Two years	Annually
	$11,000 Robert H and Clarice Smith Fellowship	Ph.D. candidates	One year	Annually
	$11,000 Chester Dale Fellowships (2)	Ph.D. candidates	One Year	Annually
National League of American Pen Women, 1300 17th St, NW, Washington, DC 20036	$500 & $1000 each in Letters, Music & Art	Pen Arts Grant to a deserving Pen Woman, Mature Women Scholarship		Biennial on even numbered years
Navarro College, Art Dept, 3200 N. Hwy 31, Corsicana, TX 75110	$200-$600 Each (20)	Art majors or any art field, granted based on a portfolio review & interview	One year	Annually
Nazareth College of Rochester, Art Department, 4245 East Ave, Rochester, NY 14610	1000	Qualified high school graduates	Four years	Annually

OFFERED BY	AMOUNT	OPEN TO	DURATION	WHEN OFFERED
Newark School of Fine & Industrial Art, 550 Dr. M. L. King Boulevard, Newark, NJ 07102	$300	Newark Residents — Full Tuition; Others — Partial ($300)	One year (some scholarships are renewable)	Annually
New Jersey Summer Arts Institute, at Rutgers University, PO Box 352, New Brunswick, NJ 08903	$100-$2400	Accepted talented middle and high school students with demonstrated or potential talent in the arts, writing, dance, theater, art & technology, vocal and instrumental music, visual arts and inter arts	Summer (5 weeks)	Annually
New Mexico State University, Art Department, Box 30001, Las Cruces, NM 88003	$3000-$7000 (graduate assistantships)	Graduate students	One-two years	Annually
New York Academy of Art, Graduate School of Figurative Art, 419 Lafayette St, New York, NY 10003	$500-$5000	MFA candidates	Two years	Annually
New York School of Interior Design, 155 E. 56th St, New York, NY 10022	Variable	Full time students	One year	Semi-annually
Niagara University, Castellani Art Gallery, 3100 Lewiston Rd., Niagura Falls, NY 14109	$10,000	Minorities	One year	When grant funded
Nicholls State University, Dept of Art, Thibodaux, LA 70310	$100-500	Art majors	One year	Annually
North Carolina Wesleyan, Dept of Art, 3400 N Wesleyan Blvd, Rocky Mount, NC 27804-8630	Varies	Based on need, academic qualifications, or both	Varies	Annually
North Dakota State University, Div of Fine Arts, Box 5691, State University Station, Fargo, ND 58105	$1,800	Junniors and Seniors	One year	Annually
North Iowa Area Community College, Dept of Art, 500 College Dr, Mason City, IA 50401	$500	Art majors	One year	Annually
Northeast Louisiana University, Dept of Art, 700 University Ave, Stubbs 141, Monroe, LA 71209	$200	Top 5 full-time art students with portfolio	One year	Annually
Northeast Missouri State University, Division of Fine Arts, Kirksville, MO 63501	Varing amounts	High school seniors; other awards available to junior college graduates	One year (renewable)	Annually
Northeastern Illinois University, Art Department, 5500 N St. Louis, Chicago, IL 60625	$659.80 (Lower Level) $683.80 (Upper Level)	Board of Governors Talent Scholarships available to gifted art students	One term	Annually
Northeastern Oklahoma A&M College, Art Dept. Miami, OK 74354	Tuition(3) Full-$1600(1)	Art majors Art majors	One year One year	Annually Annually
Northern Illinois University, School of Art, DeKalb, IL 60115-2883	Jack Arends Scholarship-about $1000	Art majors with 3.0 overall grade point average, one year residence at NIU, portfolio, and 3 recommendations (2 from NIU Art Department)	One year	Annually
	James P. Bates Memorial Scholarship-about $500	Rotated among majors in the various areas of the Art Department	One year	Annually
	Richard Keefer Scholarship-about $400	Art majors-rotated among four areas-Art History and Art Education; Drawing, Painting & Printmaking; Crafts & Sculpture; Design & Photography	One year	Annually
	NIU Tuition Waiver-tuition fee for Illinois residents	In-coming art majors; must maintain 2.5 overall grade point average and 3.0 art grade point average; awarded by Portfolio Competition	One year	Annually
	John X. Koznarek Memorial Scholarship-about $1000	Accepted or enrolled majors in studio art. Portfolio and three recommendations	One year	Annually
	Cora B. Miner Scholarship-about $400	Preferably to student from DeKalb County with interest in realistic art	One year	Annually
	Frances E. Gates Memorial Scholarship-about $300	Preferably a graduate student specializing in watercolor	One year	Annually
	Peg Bond scholarship-about $1000	Awarded to an undergraduate art education major; minimum 3.0 GPA overall, art portfolio and brief paper on subject of the teaching of art as a profession must be submitted.	One year	Annually

OFFERED BY	AMOUNT	OPEN TO	DURATION	WHEN OFFERED
Northern Michigan University, Dept of Art, Marquette, MI 49855	$500-$1000	Entering freshmen & upper level students	One year	Annually
Northwest College, Powell, WY 82435	Maximum $800 per person per year, plus 3, $1000 scholarships/yr	All students, portfolio required	Two years	Annually
Northwest Missouri State University, Department of Art, Maryville, MO 64468	$600-$1000	Freshmen & Seniors	One year	Annually, in March
Northwestern College, Art Department, Orange City, IA 51041	$500	Art majors competing as entering freshmen in competitive exhibition	One year (renewable)	Annually
Nova Scotia College of Art & Design, 5163 Duke St, Halifax, NS B3J 3J6, Canada	$500-$1500 (Canadian $)	Students at NSCAD	One year	Annually
Oberlin College, Department of Art, Oberlin, OH 44074	$5400 plus tuition remission (3-4 graduate assistantships)	Graduates with BA degrees who qualify	One year (renewable)	Annually
Ohio State University, Dept of History of Art, 100 Hayes Hall, Columbus, OH 43210	$6660 for first year students, to $7425 for fifth year students, plus tuition waiver for teaching associatships	Students who demonstrate accomplishment and evidence of potential excellence in teaching scholarship and/or research in History of Art	Up to 200 credit hours	Annually
	University fellowship of $900 per month plus tuition waiver	First year students	One year	Annually
Ohio State University, Graduate School, Department of Art Education, Columbus, OH 43210	(1) Graduate Associates-9 mo. start at $6,210 plus tuition waivers; (2) Fellowships-12 mo. start at $10,260 plus tuition waivers	All MA and PhD candidates (special minority fellowships are also awarded)	9-12 months (renewable for three years)	Annually, deadline Feb.
Ohio University, School of Art, College of Fine Arts, Athens, OH 45701	Tuition scholarship, graduate teaching assistantships	Undergraduate students and graduates	One year (renewable)	Annually
Ohio University-Chillicothe Campus, Fine Arts & Humanities Div, 571 W 5th St, PO Box 629, Chillicothe, OH 45601	Four at $400	Freshmen and sophomores	One year	Annually
Oklahoma City University, 2501 N. Blackwelder, Oklahoma City, OK 73106	$1000-$1250	Freshmen, junior & senior art majors	One year	Annually
	5 Regular Norick Art Scholarships $1000	Freshmen	One year	Annually
	3 Native American Norick Art Scholarships $1000	Freshmen	One year	Annually
	Petree Scholarship in Art $1000	Freshmen	Four year	Annually
	Ruth Jeanette Brooks Scholarship in Fine Arts $3000	Sophomore and above	One year (renewable)	Annually
	Iva B. Kelly Art Scholarship $2500	Juniors and seniors	One year (renewable)	Annually
	Roberta M. Miller Art Scholarship $1500	Sophomore and above	One year (renewable)	Annually
	Fritz Ford Art Award $200	Sophomore and above	One year (renewable)	Annually
	2 Norick Art Center League Scholarships $500	Sophomore and above	One semester (renewable)	Per semester
Old Dominion University, Art Dept, Norfolk, VI 23529	Charles K. Sibley Scholarship $3000	Undergraduate studio and history majors	One year	Annually
	$500	All graduate students	One year	Annually
	Ralph Margolius Memorial Scholarship $1000	Undergraduate studio majors	One year	Annually
	Barbara Gorlinsky Memorial Scholarship $1500	Undergraduate majors; based on financial need	One year	Annually
	Graduate Fellowships $5500	All graduate students	One year	Annually
Ontario College of Art, 100 McCaul St, Toronto, ON M5T 1W1, Canada	Variable	Ontario College of Art students only	One year	Annually
Oregon School of Arts and Crafts, 8245 SW Barnes Rd, Portland, OR 97225	Variable	Full-time certificate programs students	One year	End of winter quarter, for next academic year

OFFERED BY	AMOUNT	OPEN TO	DURATION	WHEN OFFERED
Otis School of Art and Design, 2401 Wilshire Blvd, Los Angeles, CA 90057	Variable	Students enrolled at Otis in the BFA or MFA degree programs	Academic year	Annually
Our Lady of the Lake University, 411 SW 24th St, San Antonio, TX 78285	Tuition scholarship based on current tuition rate	Any student with a high school GPA of 3.00 and the composite score made on the SAT test or the ACT test	Current semester/year	Annually
Pacific Lutheran University, School of the Arts, Tacoma, WA 98447	$500-$3000	All enrolled students	One year	Annually
Pacific Northwest College of Art, 1219 SW Park St, Portland, OR 97205	Variable	Enrolled students	One school year	Annually
	Variable	Incoming freshmen	One school year	Annually
Palomar College, 1140 W Mission Rd, San Marcos, CA 92069	$200 Lake San Marcos Art League Award	Returning sophomore majoring in art		June
	$100 Catherine Ann (Tim) Sawday Memorial Scholarship	Deserving student majoring in art or science		June
	$250 Fallbrook Art Association	Fallbrook resident, full time art student at a two year community college		June
	$150 Showcase of the Arts-Evelyn Surface Memorial	Two awards-one for art student returning to Palomar and one for a graduating art student going on to a 4-year institution		June
	Ivie Frances Wickam Scholarships $1500-$5000	Current women graduates of Palomar College who are evident of financial need, evidence of scholastic record; preference is given to art and/or education students		June
	$200 John Barlow	Returning or transfer students		June
	$500 Misty Hills	Four transfering art majors		June
Pasadena City College, Art Department, 1570 E. Colorado Blvd, Pasadena, CA 91106	$12,000 (14)	Art majors completing five courses at PCC with a college-wide GPA of 3.0 & art GPA of 3.5		Annually
Peabody & Essex Museum, 132 Essex St, Salem, MA 01970	Variable	Graduate students in American studies at Boston University	One year	Annually
Pembroke State University, Art Dept, PO Box 5064, Pembroke, NC 28372	Varies	Talented and/or academic gifted students	One year (renewable)	Annually
Peoria Art Guild, 1831 N. Knoxville Ave, Peoria, IL 61603	$25-$50	Local children, adults & students who would benefit from artistic instruction, but who would be otherwise unable to attend art classes	8 weeks	4 times each year
Philadelphia College of Art & Design, Broad & Pine Sts, Philadelphia, PA 19102	$4000	High school students, all incoming freshmen	One year	Annually
Plum Tree Fine Arts Program, PO Box 1-A, Pilar, NM 97531	50% of tuition	Residents of New Mexico	Workshop session	Annually
Plymouth State College, Plymouth, New Hampshire 03264	Various	Various criteria, including high scholarship and achievement	Scholarships one year, fellowships one semester	Annually
Pomona College, Art Dept, 333 College Way, Claremont, CA 91711	Based on need	Enrolled students	Academic period	Annually
The Ponca City Art Association, Box 1394, 819 E. Central, Ponca City, OK 74602	$250	Local art student	One year	Annually
Portage & District Arts Centre, 160 Saskatchewan Ave W, Portage la Prairie, MB RIN OMI, Canada	$500	Canadian citizen who has been a resident of Portage la Prairie for one year	One year	Annually
Portland State University, Dept of Art, PO Box 751, Portland, OR 97207	Varied	Art major with 20 hrs in art at time of application. Good accumulative GPA and portfolio also required	Academic year	Annually-Spring
Rensselaer County Historical Society, 59 Second St, Troy NY 12180	Volunteer summer museum intern program	Juniors & seniors with art history, history majors & some museum training	Ten weeks	Annually during the summer
Rhode Island School of Design, Two College St, Providence, RI 02903	Variable	Accepted degree candidates on undergraduate & graduate level based on financial need	One year	Annually
Rice University, Dept of Art & Art History, PO Box 1892, Houston, TX 77251	$1000-$7500 (plus tuition waiver)	Candidates of the Master of Arts degree in Art History and Classical Archaeology	One year, renewable	Annually

OFFERED BY	AMOUNT	OPEN TO	DURATION	WHEN OFFERED
Ricks College, Department of Art, Rexburg, ID 83440	$200-$400	Art majors	One year	Fall
Ringling School of Art & Design, 2700 N Tamiami Trail, Sarasota, FL 34234	$500-$2500	All full-time Ringling students	One year, some semester grants, renewable	Annually
Rocky Mountain College of Art and Design, 6875 E Evans Ave, Denver, CO 80224	$750	Full-time students	One trimester (renewable)	Each trimester
Sacred Heart University, Dept of Art, 5151 Park Ave, Fairfield, CT 06432-1000	$500-$2000	Full-time art majors	One year	Annually
Saint Andrews Presbyterian College, Art Program, Laurinburg, NC 28352	$500-$2000	Freshmen and transfer students	Renewable for four years total	Annually
Saint Xavier College, Dept of Art, 3700 W 103rd St, Chicago, IL 60655	Varies; covers cource tuition	Smith Scholarship to School of Art Institute of Chicago open to Saint Xavier art majors	Per course	Annually
Salisbury State University, Art Dept, College & Camden Ave, Salisbury, MD 21801	BFA $500 each	First-year students	One year, renewable	Annually
Salmagundi Club, 47 Fifth Ave, New York, NY 10003	Membership	Qualified applicants, artists under 30 years of age, three examples of work to be submitted for approval by committee	Four years	
	$600 (3 art scholarship)	Sophomore or above, art major with artistic aptitude and ability	One year	Annually
Salve Regina - The Newport College, Art Dept, Ochre Point Ave, Newport, RI 02840	Variable	Based on financial need	One year	Annually
San Antonio Art Institute, 6000 N. New Braunfels, PO Box 6092, San Antonio, TX 78209	Full & partial tuition	All students	One semester & full year	March 1st, April 1st, Oct. 15th
San Diego State University, College of Professional Studies & Fine Arts, Dept of Art, San Diego, CA 92182	Isabel Kraft Sculpture Scholarship, $3000	Sculpture students	Fall	Annually
	Patricia Clapp Scholarship, $500	Art majors	Fall	Annually
	Haystack Mountain School of Crafts Scholarship, summer fees paid for program in Deer Isle, ME	Crafts undergraduates & graduates	Spring	Annually
	Darryl Groover Memorial Scholarship ($500)	Painting students	Spring	Annually
	Paul Lingren Memorial Scholarship ($750)	Undergraduate studio students	Spring	Annually
	SDSU Art Council Scholarships ($500)	Undergraduate art majors	Spring	Annually
San Francisco Art Institute, 800 Chestnut St, San Francisco, CA 94133	Tuition scholarships	Undergraduate and graduate students with demonstrated financial need	Academic year	Semi-annually
Saskatchewan Association of Architects, Marr Residence, 326-11th St. E., Saskatoon, SK S7N 0E7	$2000	Permanent residents of Saskatchewan, and full time University students in Architecture		Annually
Colby Sawyer College, New London, NH 03257	$1200	All students-often split into smaller amounts for more students	One year (renewable)	Annually
Scholastic Awards, Scholastic Inc. 730 Broadway, New York, NY 10003	Varies; scholarship nominations to participating colleges and art institutions	Students graduating high school who submit outstanding portfolios of art and/or photography	Varies	Annually; entries accepted early Feb only, write for details
	Portfolio Awards; 5 at $5000 each	Students graduating high school entering the scholarship nominations program (above)	One year	Annually; entries accepted early Feb only, write for details
The School of Fashion Design, 136 Newbury St, Boston, MA 02116	$1000	All curently enrolled full time students	One year	Annually (in May for Sept enrollment)
School of Fine Arts, 38660 Mentor Ave, Willoughby, OH 44094	Tuition	Talent plus need	One year	Annually
School of the Art Institute of Chicago, Columbus Dr. at Jackson Blvd, Chicago, IL 60603	$500-$5500	Full-time degree students in need and undergraduate degree students with merit, regardless of need	One year, renewable upon updated application	Annually

OFFERED BY	AMOUNT	OPEN TO	DURATION	WHEN OFFERED
School of the Museum of Fine Arts, 230 The Fenway, Boston, MA 02115	Varies	Deserving students	One year	Annually
The School of the Ozarks, Department of Art, Point Lookout, MO 65726	Full tuition, room and board, Work/Study Grant	Preference to scholarship, financial need, geographic location	Four years	Each semester
School of Visual Arts, 209 E. 23rd St, New York, NY 10010	$1,000,000 Full and partial tuition	Undergraduate; High school seniors; Graduate	Four year BFA, two year MFA	Annually through admissions process
Schoolcraft College, Dept of Art & Design, 18600 Haggerty Rd, Livonia, MI 48152	Varies	All students	One year	Annually
Seton Hill College, Greensburg, PA 15601	$1000 toward tuition	Incoming freshmen art majors	One year	Annually
Siena Heights College, Studio Angelico-Art Dept, 1247 Siena Heights Dr Adrian, MI 49221	Varies	Undergraduates	One year	Annually
Skowhegan School of Painting and Sculpture, 329 E 68th St, New York, NY 10021-5606	Full scholarships $4300 (9)	Qualified art students 18 years of age and over, slide review	Nine weeks June to August	Annually
	Partial scholarships (45)	Qualified art students 18 years of age and over, slide review	Nine weeks June to August	Annually
Smithsonian Institute, Office of Fellowships & Grants, 955 L'Enfant Plaza, Suite 7000, Washington, DC 20560	$21,000	Post-doctoral scholars in American art history, Oriental art history and African art	Six months to one year	Deadline Jan. 15
	$13,000	Dissertation research for Doctoral candidates in American art history, Oriental art history and African art	Six months to one year	Deadline Jan. 15
Smithsonian Institution, Internship Coordinator, Freer Gallery, Washington, DC 20560	Freer Gallery Internship	Interns must have working knowledge of one or more of the pertinent Oriental languages & submit a proposal relevant to the Freer collections		
	Harold P Stern Memorial Fund at Freer Gallery	Selection of recipients is by invitation only & is based upon outstanding scholarly achievements in the field of Japanese art		
Smithsonian Institution, Internship Coordinator, Hirshhorn Museum & Sculpture Garden, Washington, DC 20560	Hirshhorn Museum & Sculpture Garden Internship	College juniors & seniors who have completed at least 12 semester hours in art history.	Ten weeks	Deadline March 1
		Graduate student internships are available for students in accredited art history graduate programs	One Semester	Deadline March 1
Smithsonian Institution, Internship Coordinator, National Museum of African Art, Washington, DC 20560	National Museum of African Art Internship	People enrolled in undergraduate & graduate programs of study & for people interested in exploring museum professions		
Smithsonian Institution, Internship Coordinator, National Museum of American Art, Washington, DC 20560	National Museum of American Art Internship	Museum training for college senior graduate students, in art history, studio art and American studies	Nine weeks, commence in June	Deadline Feb. 15
Smithsonian Institution, Internship Coordinator, National Portrait Gallery, Washington, DC 20560	National Portrait Gallery Internship		Three months	
Smithsonian Institution, Internship Coordinator, Cooper-Hewitt, New York, NY 10128	Sidney & Celia Siegel Fellowship Program at Cooper-Hewitt	Applicants with two years of college education, preference given to those without previous museum experience	Ten weeks	Deadline April 1
Society of Architectural Historians, 1232 Pine St, Philadelphia, PA 19107	One given to participate in annual tour	Outstanding students engaged in graduate work in architecture, architectural history, city planning or urban history, landscape history or landscape design & current member of the Society of Architectural Historians		Annually
	Alice Davis Hitchock Book Award			Annually
	Founders' Award	Student must be engaged in graduate study that involves some aspect of the history of architecture		Annually
South Carolina Arts Commission, 1800 Gervais St, Columbia, SC 29201	$5000 (6)	SC professional artists: visual arts (2), crafts (1), literary arts (2), music performance (1)	One year	Annually

OFFERED BY	AMOUNT	OPEN TO	DURATION	WHEN OFFERED
South Dakota Art Museum, Medary Ave. at Harvey Dunn St, Brookings, SD 57007	$250	Art students of South Dakota State Univ	One year	Annually
Southampton Campus, Long Island University Fine Arts Division, Southampton, NY 11968	$1000-$3000	Freshmen and transfer students who have applied for admission	Up to four years	Bi-annually
Southern Illinois University, Carbondale, School of Art and Design, Carbondale, IL 62901-4301	$201,575	Graduating seniors, entering freshmen, graduate students, some continuing undergraduates	One year	Annually
Southern Methodist University, Art Div, Dallas, TX 75275-0356	Varies	Undergraduates and graduates	One year	Annually
Southern Oregon State College, Dept of Art, 1250 Siskiyou Blvd, Ashland, OR 97520	$550-$750	Enrolled art students	Tuition deferment	Annually
Southern Utah State University, Department of Art, Cedar City, UT 84720	Part tuition	Residents of Utah and nonresidents	One year	Annually and quarterly
	$700 up	Freshmen, sophomores, juniors and seniors	One year	Annually
South Florida Art Institute of Hollywood, 1301 S. Ocean Dr, Hollywood, FL 33019	$8000 yearly	Elementary, senior and junior high school graduates	One, two and four years	Annually
	$3000	Senior citizens	One, two and four years	Annually
Southwest Missouri State University, Department of Art, 901 S. National, Springfield, MO 65804	$150-$800 (12)	Art majors currently enrolled	One year	Annually
	$800 (2)	Entering freshmen	One year	Annually
Southwestern College, 100 College St, Winfield, KS 67156	$150-$800	Entering students	One year	Annually
Southwestern Community College, Art Dept, 1501 W Townline rd, Creston, IA 50801	$200	Art majors	Semester	Semi-annually
Southwestern Louisiana State University, Dept of Visual Arts, PO Box 765, Hammond, LA 70402	$200	Sophomores	One year	Annually
Springfield Art Center, 107 Cliff Park Rd, Springfield, OH 45501	$25-$100	Children, some adults	Ten weeks	Each quarter
Springfield College, 263 Alden St, Springfield, MA 01109	Variable	Qualified students based on financial need	One year	Annually
Springfield College in Illinois, Dept of Art, 1500 N Fifth, Springfield, IL 62702	Varies	All students	One year	Semi-annually
State University of New York at Binghamton, Department of Art and Art History, Binghamton, NY 13901	Variable	Art history graduate students, with additional fellowships open to minorities	One year	Annually
State University of New York, College at Brockport, Dept of Art, Tower Fine Arts, Brockport, NY 14420	$300-$400	Enrolled art majors	One year	Annually
State University of New York, College at Geneseo, Dept of Art, Geneseo, NY 14454	$500	Art studio & art history majors, minors, concentrates — juniors	One year	Annually
State University of New York at Plattsburgh, Art Dept, Myers Fine Arts Bldg, Plattsburgh, NY 12901	$3,000	All art majors	One Year	Annually
Stephen F. Austin State University, Art Dept, Box 13001, Nacogdoches, TX 75962	$5200	Graduates	Six semesters for MFA candidates, four semesters for MA candidates	Annually
Margaret Woodbury Strong Museum, One Manhattan Sq, Rochester, NY 14607	H. J. Swinney Museum Studies Internship Program	Graduate students who aspire to a career in the museum profession	Three months (summer)	Annually
Sul Ross State University, Dept of Art, C-90, Alpine, TX 79832	$150 per semester	All art majors, including graduate	One Year	Annually
Sullivan County Community College, LeRoy Road, Loch Saez Drake, NY 12759	Variable	Students in commerical art or photography	Varies	Annually

OFFERED BY	AMOUNT	OPEN TO	DURATION	WHEN OFFERED
Summer Arts Institute, New Jersey School of the Arts, Carriage House, Douglass Campus of Rutgers University, New Brunswick, NJ 08903	$100-$1500	Accepted talented high school students with demonstrated or potential talent in the arts	Summer	Annually
Sunbury Shores Arts and Nature Centre, Inc, 139 Water St, PO Box 100, St. Andrews, NB EOG 2X0, Canada	Approx $400 each; all costs covered	New Brunswick residents ages 12-21 inclusive	One to three weeks varying with art course	Annually, for July and Aug. Submit application by Mar. 31
Swarthmore College, 500 College Ave, Swarthmore, PA 19081	Varies	All students	Variable	Annually
Syracuse University, School of Art, 203 Crouse College, Syracuse, NY 13244-1010	$1000 for undergraduates, partial & full tuition scholarships for graduates, $8775 fellowships for graduates, half & full assistantships for graduates		One year	Annually
Teikyo Westmar University, 1002 3rd Ave SE, Le Mars, IA 51031	$250	Art majors	One year	Annually
Tennessee Arts Commission, 320 Sixth Ave N, Suite 100, Nashville, TN 37243-0780	$2500	Fellowship for professional artists who are residents of Tennessee	One year	Annually
Texas A&M University, College of Architecture, College Station, TX 77843-3137	$40,000	Based on scholarship	One year	Annually
Texas State Technical College, Commerial Art Dept, PO Box 11197, Amarillo, TX 79111	$100-$200	(1 year) continuing students	One quarter	Semi-annually
Texas Tech University, Dept of Art, Lubbock, TX 79409	$200-$10,000	BFA, MAS, MFA, PhD applicants	One year, renewable	Annually
Tobe-Coburn School for Fashion Careers, 686 Broadway, New York, NY 10012	$1000-$1500	Students of the school		Annually
The Toledo Museum of Art, PO Box 1013, Toledo, OH 43697	W. Sinclair Walbridge Scholarship, variable: $3-$700 avg	Students enrolled as majors in art, art history or art education through the Dept. of Art of the University of Toledo at The Toledo Museum of Art	One year	Annually
	Art Interests, Inc. Scholarship for Entering Freshmen, variable: $600-$1000	Students enrolled as majors in art, art history or art education through the Dept. of Art of the University of Toledo at the Toledo Museum of Art	One year	Annually
	Douglas Mark Palmer Memorial Scholarship, variable: $3-$800	Art History majors at U of Toledo	One year	Annually
	James G. Southworth Scholarship for Ceramic Art Study $500	Open competition; portfolio review required	One year	Annually
	Curtis W. Davis, Sr. Scholarship for Glass Art Study, $600 & use of glass-blowing facility	Open competition; portfolio review required	One year	Annually
Treasure Valley Community College, Art Dept, 650 College Blvd, Ontario, OR 97914	Varies	Art majors	One year	Annually
Truro Center for the Arts at Castle Hill, PO Box 756, Truro, MA 02666	1 5-day course	Local school children, AIDS patients, etc.		Annually
Tucson Museum of Art, Attn: Julie Willson, 140 N Main, Tucson, AZ 85701	Varied	Talented needy and minority students for TMA school classes only	Each session	Quarterly
Tufts University, Fine Arts Dept, 11 Talbot Ave, Medford, MA 02155	$13,800 tuition remission	Graduate students	One year	Annually
Union University, Highway 45 Bypass, Jackson, TN 38305	Maximum $800	Incoming freshmen & transfers and returning students	One year (renewable)	Annually
Universal Technical Institute, Commercial Art Div, 4001 S 24th St, Omaha, NE 68107	Varies	High school graduates	One year	Annually
The University of Akron School of Art, Folk Hall, Akron, OH 44325	$20,000 total scholarship fund	All art students	One year renewable	Annually
University of Alabama, Dept of Art, Huntsville, AL 35899	Varied	Art major with 2.5 average on 4.0 scale	One year	Annually
University of Alaska, Anchorage, Dept of Arts & Sciences, 3211 Providence Dr, Anchorage, AK 99508	$800-$1000	Continuing students	One or two semesters	Annually

OFFERED BY	AMOUNT	OPEN TO	DURATION	WHEN OFFERED
University of Alaska, Fairbanks, Dept of Art, Fine Arts Complex, Fairbanks, AK 99775-0200	Tuition	Entering students	One year	Annually
University of Alberta, Dept of Art & Design, 3-98 Fine Arts Bldg, Edmonton, AB T6G 2C9	$9000	Incoming graduate students in MVA program	One year	Annually
University of Arizona, Faculty of Fine Arts, Department of Art, Tucson, AZ 85721	Variable	Students enrolled in art program at UA	One year	Annually
University of Arkansas, Art Dept, Fayetteville, AR 72701	Tuition	Freshmen, sophomore	One year	Annually
	Tuition & up to $5100 (GTA)	MFA Grad Students	One year	April 1st each year—Annually
University of California, Department of Art History, Santa Barbara, CA 93106	Variable	Graduate students approved by Art History Department chairman. MA and PhD candidates are also eligible for consideration for departmental Vidda Foundation and Art Affiliate Awards	Academic year	
University of Central Oklahoma, Dept of Visual Arts & Design, 100 North University Dr, Edmond, OK 73034-0180	$450	Under graduate students	One semester	Semi-annually
University of Cincinnati, School of Art, 839C DAAP, ML 16, Cincinnati, OH 45221	Undergraduate, $500; Graduate, stipend & full tuition	Fine arts freshmen; SOA freshmen; University Graduate Scholarships and Minority Fellowships	One year	Annually
University of Connecticut, Art Dept, Storrs, CT 06269-1099	$300-$1000	Freshmen	One year	Annually
University of Delaware, Dept of History, Newark, DE 19716	$9100, MA candidates; $10,080, PhD candidates	Students enrolled as MA candidates and/or PhD candidates	2 to 4 yr program	Deadline Jan 1
University of Denver, School of Art, 2121 East Asbury, Denver, CO 80208	$50,000	Graduate & undergraduate students	One year	Annually
University of Hawaii at Manoa, 2535 The Mall, Honolulu, HI 96822	Varies	All	One year, one semester	Annually, semi-annually
University of Idaho, Department of Art & Architecture, Moscow, ID 83843	Variable	All majors in art, undergraduate and graduate, based on ability alone	One year	Annually
	$400 (Commemorative Art Scholarship)	Upper division undergraduates in art, based on need and ability		Annually in the Spring for Fall semester
University of Illinois, Urbana-Champaign, College of Fine and Applied Arts, 110 Architecture Bldg, 608 E. Lorado Taft Dr, Champaign, IL, 61820	Kate Neal Kinley Memorial Fellowship-Major Amount 2 or 3 of $7000; 2 or 3 of $1000	Graduates of the College of Fine and Applied Arts of the University of Illinois, Urbana-Champaign and to graduates of similar institutions of equal educational standing. Preference is given to applicants under 25 years of age	One academic year	Annually; applications are due Feb 15
University of Indianapolis, Art Dept, 1400 E Hanna Ave, Indianapolis, IN 46227	$9820	Entering freshmen majors and returning majors	One year	Annually
University of Kansas, Department of Art and Music Education and Music Therapy, 311 Bailey Hall, Lawrence, KS 66045	Variable up to $6000	Undergraduates in Art Education and graduate students in Art Education; also graduate students in art museum education	One academic year (renewable)	Annually
University of Lethbridge, Department of Art, 4401 University Dr, Lethbridge, AB, Canada	Variable	Qualified students on entry		Annually
	Art Department Faculty $100	Full-time second/third year student-art major; outstanding accomplishment in an area of Studio Art over at least one full year at the University		Annually
	George Varzari Sculpture Award $100	Full-time student currently enrolled in a sculpture course at the University of Lethbridge - outstanding in area of sculpture. Works sculpted during current academic year		
	George and Olive Spinks $500	3rd and 4th year students majoring in the fine arts	One year	Annually
	Agnes Turcotte Memorial $1700	3rd and 4th year students majoring in the fine arts	One year	Annually

OFFERED BY	AMOUNT	OPEN TO	DURATION	WHEN OFFERED
	Fine Arts Entrance - Art $1000	New freshman or transfer students with majors in the fine arts	One year	Annually
University of Louisville, Allen R Hite Art Institute, Dept of Fine Arts, Belkamp Campus, Louisville, KY 40292	Varies	All students	One year; 4-year full scholarship for incoming freshmen	Annually
University of Maryland, Dept of Art History, College Park, MD 20742	$500	Undergraduates (Reed Scholarship), graduates, museum interns, teaching assistantships, Maryland fellowships, dean's fellows	One year	Annually, semi-annually
University of Miami, Dept of Art and Art History, PO Box 248106, Coral Gables, FL 33124-4410	Partial tuition waiver	Qualified students	One year (renewable)	Annually; application deadline March 15
University of Michigan, Ann Arbor, History of Art Dept. Ann Arbor, MI 48109-1357	Charles L. Freer Scholarship in Oriental Art, amounts vary to $5000	Graduate students in Oriental art	One year	Annually
	Charles L. Freer Fellowships in Oriental Art, amounts vary to $3000	Advanced graduate students in Oriental art, residence at Freer Gallery, Washington, DC	Half year	Annually
	Graduate Fellowships offered by Horace H. Rackham School of Graduate Studies, amounts vary to $4000	Graduate students	One year	Annually
	Rackham Predoctoral Fellowship, $5000	Predoctoral student	One year	Annually
	Regents Fellowships, First Year Fellowship, $7500 plus tuition & fees	Beginning graduate students	Three years	Annually
	Teaching Fellowships up to $6000 plus full tuition waiver	Graduate students of the second year & beyond	One year	Annually
	Luce Fellowships	Advanced graduate student	One year	Annually
	Michigan Minority Merit Fellowship offered by Horace H. Rackham School of Graduate Studies, tuition plus up to $9000	Beginning minority graduate students	Up to 5 years	Annually
University of Minnesota, Duluth, Department of Art, 317 Humanities Bldg, Duluth, MN 55812	$5000 Grad Teaching assistantships (4-6)	Graduate students	One year	Annually
	$250 scholarships (4)	Undergraduate	Summer session only	
	$1000 awards (6)	Undergrad/graduate	One year	Annually
	$600 scholarships (5)	Undergraduate and/or graduate	One year	Annually
University of Minnesota, Minneapolis, Art History, 27 Pleasant St. SE, 108 Jones Hall, Minneapolis, MN 55455	$500-$4000 or 10,500 graduate school fellowship	Graduate students	One year	Annually
University of Minnesota, Minneapolis, Department of Studio Art, Minneapolis, MN 55455	$200-$4000	Undergraduate and/or graduate	One year	Annually
University of Mississippi, Art Dept, University, MS 38677	$2250-$6500 plus tuition	Qualified students	Three years (renewable)	Annually
University of Montevallo, Montevallo, AL 35115	Full tuition and fee waiver	Freshmen and transfer students	Four years	Annually
University of Nebraska, Kearney, Dept of Art & Art History, Kearney, NE 68849	$400 tuition wavier in Art (25), variable scholarships $130-$1000	Entering freshmen	One year	Annually
University of Nebraska-Lincoln, Department of Art, Woods Hall, Lincoln, NE 68588	Thomas Coleman Memorial Scholarship in Printmaking awards of $100 each	Outstanding graduate and undergraduate student in prints	One year	Annually
	Francis Vreeland Award in Art $1600	Outstanding graduate and undergraduate students in studio art	One year	Annually
	E. Evelyn Peterson Memorial Fine Arts Scholarships $10,000	Outstanding students, sophomore and above, with high potential in art	One year	Annually
	Ruth Ann Sack Memorial Scholarship in Photography and Painting, 5 at $100	Outstanding upper division students in photography and painting	One year	Annually as income available
	Louise Esterday Munday Fine Arts Scholarship $600	Determined by financial need	One year	Annually

OFFERED BY	AMOUNT	OPEN TO	DURATION	WHEN OFFERED
	Shelly Arnold Waggoner Memorial Scholarship Fund, 4 awards of $600 each	Based on exceptional talent	One year	Annually
	Art & Art History Dept Scholarships, 3 awards of $100 each	Demonstrated talent and need	One year	Annually
	Nellis Polly Hills & John Hills Scholarship $2400	Based on scholastic achievement, Willard professional potential and financial need	One year	Annually
	Henry Grabowski Memorial Award $100	Based on creativity in any medium		Annually
University of New Mexico, Albuquerque, NM 87131	Varies	Undergraduates and graduates	Variable	ANnually
University of North Alabama, Dept of Art, PO Box 5006, Florence, AL 35632-0001	$250-$1000	Entering freshmen, sophomore, juniors, seniors & transfers	One year (renewable)	Annually
University of North Carolina-Chapel Hill, Department of Art, CB# 3405, Hanes Art Center, Chapel Hill, NC 27599-3405	Emily Pollard Fellowships, $2000-$5000	Graduate students only	One year	Annually
	UNC-CH Merit Assistantship $9000	Graduate students only	One year	First year
	Minority presence awards $9000	Graduate students only	One year, option to renew	Annually
University of North Carolina at Charlotte, Dept of Visual Arts, Charlotte, NC 28223	$300	Undergraduate students	One semester	Annually
University of North Dakota, Dept of Visual Arts, PO Box 8134, Grand Forks, ND 58202	Varies	All	Varies	Semi-annually
University of North Texas, Art Dept, PO Box 5098, UNT, Denton, TX 76203	$3000 per semester, full fellowship	Qualified graduate students on a competitive basis	One year	Annually
University of Notre Dame, Graduate School, Art, Art History & Design Dept. Notre Dame, IN 46556	Tuition $14,530, Stipend $7700	Teaching assistants chosen by faculty	Up to three years	Annually
University of the Pacific, 3601 Pacific Ave, Stockton, CA 95211	Varies	All students	Varies	Annually
University of Pittsburgh, Henry Clay Frick Dept of Art History and Architecture, Pittsburgh, PA 15260	$8830-TA, $9280-TF, $11,000-Mellon Tuition scholarships	Fine arts graduate students (art history)	One year, renewable	Annually
University of Puget Sound, 1500 N Warner St, Tacoma, WA 98416	$1000	Freshmen, transfers and upper class	Renewable	Annually
University of San Diego, Art History Area, Fine Arts Dept, Alcala Park, San Diego, CA 92123	Variable		One year	Annually, semi-annually
University of Saskatchewan, Dept of Art & History, Saskatoon, SK S7N 0W0	$100-$1000	Second, third and fourth year students		Annually
University of South Carolina, Dept of Art, Sloan College, Columbia, SC 29208	Varies	Entering freshmen	One year	Annually
University of South Dakota, Art Dept, CFA 179, Vermillion, SD 57069	Undergraduate Scholarships-$200 (5)		Academic year	Annually
	Oscar Howe Scholarship-$750	Outstanding art student	Academic year	Annually
	A B Gunderson Scholarship-$750 (1)	Senior	Academic year	Annually
	Graduate Assistantships-$4000 (5)		Academic year by contract	Annually
The University of the South, Department of Fine Arts, Sewanee, TN 37375	$30	Studio art major	One year	Annually
University of Southern California, School of Fine Arts, Watt Hall 104, University Park, Los Angeles, CA 90089-0292	Variable	Fine arts majors	One year	Annually
	$10,000-J. Paul Getty Memorial Scholarship	Graduate student, Art History	One year	Annually

OFFERED BY	AMOUNT	OPEN TO	DURATION	WHEN OFFERED
	Graduate teaching assistantships (tuition credit and stipend)-contact School of Fine Arts	Graduate students, Art History and Studio Art	One to three years	Annually
	Museum Studies Fellowships-contact School of Fine Arts	Graduate students, Museum Studies Program	One to three years	Annually
	Graduate Fellowships-contact USC Graduate School, UGR 105, USC, University Park, Los Angeles, CA 90089-4015	Graduate students	Generally one to three years	Annually
University of Tennessee, Dept of Art, 1715 Volunteer Blvd, Knoxville, TN 37996-2410	$5000	Currently enrolled art majors	One year	Annually
University of Texas at San Antonio, Division of Art & Architecture, San Antonio, TX 78285	$200	Graduate MFA applicants	One year	Fall
University of Texas-Pan American, Department of Art, Edinburg, TX 78539	$600-$650 per semester	Entering freshmen or art majors with 2.5 average (4.00 system), 30 hours completed study	One year	Fall & Spring (deadline to apply: Dec 1)
University of Utah, Art Dept AAC 161, Salt Lake City, UT 84112	Varied	Docents	One year	Annually
University of Virginia, Bayly Art Museum, Rugby Rd, Charlottesville, VA 22903	$4000	Graduate students in the Department of Art History, University of Virginia	One year (10 hrs/week)	Annually
	$12,000	Advanced graduate students in the Dept of Art History, University of Virginia	One year (20 hrs/week)	Annually
University of West Florida, Dept of Art, 11000 University Pkwy, Pensacola, FL 32514	Varies	Freshmen and junior college transfers	One-time and 4-year	Annually
University of Windsor, School of Visual Arts, Windsor, ON, N9B 3P4, Canada	Variable	Visual arts students	One year	Annually
University of Wisconsin-Eau Claire, Dept of Art, Park and Garfield Aves, Eau Claire, WI 54701	Variable	Qualified students	One year	Annually
University of Wisconsin-Green Bay, Dean of Arts Programs, Green Bay, WI 54311-7001	Variable	Majors (art, music, theatre)	One year, semester	Annual
University of Wisconsin-Milwaukee, Art History Dept, PO Box 413, Mitchell Hall 151, Milwaukee, WI 53201	$5800 and $7200; also small cash grants to specific research projects	All students	Academic year	Annually
University of Wisconsin-Superior, Superior, WI 54880	Varied	Candidates with Bachelors degree and competitive portfolio	Academic year	Annually deadline Mar. 15
	Varied	Undergrads, based upon class rank or portfolio. Must have a high school diploma or equivalent		
University of Wyoming, Art Dept, PO Box 3138, Laramie, WY 82071	$12,500	Freshmen, transfer and continuing art majors (studio)	One year	Annually
	Six assistantships $6600 stipend plus full tuition	Graduate students	One year	Annually
Valdosta State College, Dept of Art, N Paterson St, Valdosta, CA 31698	$425 per quarter	Art majors	Until graduation	As current recients graduate
	$100-$350	Art majors	Freshmen year	Annually
Vanderbilt University, Dept of Fine Arts, 23rd Ave S at West End Ave, PO Box 1801, Station B, Nashville, TN 37235	$6700 (plus tuition)	Entering graduate students in art history	One year	Annually
Vermont State Craft Center at Frog Hollow, Mill St, Middlebury, VT 05753	Open	Applicants who demonstrate a need	One class session	Quarterly
Vermont Studio Center, PO Box 613, Johnson, VT 05656	$650-$1300 per month	Painters, sculptors & writers	One month Critics' Program or 1 and 2 month residencies	Ongoing
Wabash College, Art Dept, 301 W Wabash Ave, Crawfordsville, IN 47933	40% through full scholarship	All students	4 years	Annually

OFFERED BY	AMOUNT	OPEN TO	DURATION	WHEN OFFERED
Wartburg College, Art Department, 222 9th St NW, PO Box 1003, Waverly, IA 50677	$500	Those deemed artistically and academically qualified by the art department chairperson	One year	Annually
Washington and Lee University, Dept of Fine Arts, Lexington, VA 24450	Varies according to need	Art majors, coed	One year (renewable up to four years)	Annually
Wayland Baptist University, Div of Christian Communication Arts, PO Box 249, 1900 W 7th, Plainview, TX 79072	Varies	Art students	One year	Annually
Wayne State College, Wayne, NE	$500	Undergraduate	One year renewable	Semi-annually
Wayne State University, Dept of Art & Art History, 150 Community Arts Bldg, Detroit, MI 48202	$6000	Entering undergraduate students in fine arts	Four years	Annually
	$50,000	Graduate students in fine arts and fashion design	One year; renewable	Annually
	$6,500	Fine art undergraduate and graduate students	One year	Annually
	$3000	Fashion desgn students	One year	Annually
	$1750	Art history students	One year	Annually
Weber State University, Dept of Visual Arts, Ogden, UT 84409	Tuition wavier	Art students	One year	Annually
Webster University, Hunt Travel Award, Art Dept, 470 E. Lockwood, Webster Groves, MO 63119	$1000	Junior or senior art majors	One semester	Annually
Wenatchee Valley College, Art Dept, 1300 5th St, Wenatchee, WA 98801	$371 (3 quarters) (4)	Best qualified applicants	On-going	Annually
Wesleyan College, Forsyth Rd, Macon, GA 31297	$500-$3000	Any female who has made application and submits a portfolio	Until student leaves Wesleyan	Annually, before June
West Georgia College, Carrollton, GA 30118	$14,000	Art majors	One year	Annually
Westchester Community College, Art Workshop, Westchester County Center, White Plains, NY 10607		Disabled and in need of financial assistance		
Western Illinois University Art Department, West Adams, Macomb, IL 61455	$500	Students matriculating or new students with outstanding portfolios	Each semester	Semi-annually
	Tuition	Incoming freshmen with art portfolio	Semester	Semi-annually
Western Michigan University, Dept of Art, Kalamazoo, MI 49008	Varies	Undergraduate and graduate	One year	Annually
Western Montana College, 710 S Atlantic, Dillon, MT 59725	$1000	All art education students	One year	Annually
Western New Mexico University, Expressive Arts Dept, PO Box 680, Silver City, NM 88062	$500-$5000	Undergraduate or graduate majors in art	One year	Annually
Western Wyoming Community College, PO Box 428, Rock Springs, WY 82901	Full tuition board & books	Art majors	One year (renewable)	Annually
Westminster College, New Wilmington, PA 16172	Varied	All students	One year	Annually
Whitney Museum of American Art, Independent Study Program, 384 Broadway, 4th floor, New York, NY 10013	$3995 Helena Rubenstein Fellowships (10) & tuition $900	Students of outstanding academic achievement	Two semesters	Annually
	$900 and full tuition available studio program (15)	Graduates and advanced undergraduates	Two semesters	Annually
Witchita Art Association, School of Art, 9112 Central, Witchita, KS 67206	Tuition	Based on talent and need	Varies	Annually
Wilkes University, Dept of Art, Wilkes-Barre, PA 18766	Up to full tuition	Art: scholastic art awards national winners, College-wide: all majors academically qualified	One year	Annually
Williams College, Department of Art, Williamstown, MA 01267	$6000 Hubbard Hutchinson Memorial Scholarship	Williams senior for two years of graduate work	Two years at $6000 a year	Annually

OFFERED BY	AMOUNT	OPEN TO	DURATION	WHEN OFFERED
	Florence & Horace Mayer Scholarship	Williams (financial aid) student majoring in art or music	One year (may be extended second year)	Annually
	Beatrice Stone Scholarship	Williams financial aid student majoring in art or music	One year (may be extended second year)	Annually
Wingate College, Div of Fine Arts, Wingate, NC 28174	$500 (2)	Incoming freshmen	One year	Semi-annually
Winthrop College, Rock Hill, SC 29733	$100-$500	Freshmen	One year	Annually
Woodstock School of Art, PO Box 338AD, Woodstock, NY 12498	Variable	All who qualify by reason of merit and need	One month or longer	Annually
	Free studio space	Painters, sculptors, printmakers may apply	3-5 weeks	Spring & Fall
Worcester Center for Crafts, 25 Sagamore Rd, Worcester, MA 01605	$500-$1500	Full time students in 2 year program	One year	Annually
Wright State University, Dept of Art and Art History, Dayton, OH 45435	Variable, $1000 minimum	Art majors	Variable, one year minimum	Annually
Helene Wurlitzer Foundation of New Mexico, Box 545, Taos, NM 87571	Free rent & utilities	Any artist in all media & allied fields, creative, not interpretive	April 1 to Sept. 30	Annually
Xavier University, Dept of Art, 3800 Victory Pkwy, Cincinnati OH 45207-2311	$105,000	Graduating high school seniors	Four years	Annually
Yale Center for British Art, Yale University, 1080 Chapel St, PO Box 2120 Yale Station, New Haven, CT 06520	Short-term resident visiting fellowships	Scholars in post-doctoral or equivalent research related to British art	One month	Monthly
	Andrew W Mellon Fellowship, $12,000 plus travel	Predoctoral candidate from British or other non-American University	One year	Annually
Yale University, School of Art, 1605A Yale Station, New Haven, CT 06520	Variable	Eligible MFA students	Academic year	Annually, GAPSFAS deadline Mar. 1
Yard School of Art, 99 S. Fullerton Ave, Montclair, NJ, 07042	$350	Talented physically handicapped talented children	One year	Anytime
York College, Art Dept, Ninth & Kiplinger St, Box 246, York, NE 68467	$500	Art students	One year	Annually
Young Harris College, Department of Art, Young Harris, GA 30582	$1000 (3)	Art majors	One year	Annually

ARIZONA

SCOTTSDALE ARTS FESTIVAL, Scottsdale. Annual, mid-March. Any media. Juried. Entry Slides due Nov. 14 - prospectus mailed out in Sept. For further information write Scottsdale Center for the Arts, 7383 Scottsdale Mall, Scottsdale, AZ 85251. Phone (602)994-2301.

ARKANSAS

ARKANSAS ARTS CENTER DELTA ART EXHIBITION, Little Rock. Annual, Oct-Nov. All paintings & sculpture (not over 500 pounds). Open to artists born in or residing in Ark, La, Miss, Mo, Okla, Tenn & Tex. Juried by slides, Cash Awards: (1)$1500 "Grand Award". (2) $500 (each) "Delta Awards". Fee $10 per entry, limit two. Deadline for slides usually mid-August. For further information write Collections and Exhibitions, The Arkansas Arts Center, MacArthur Park, PO Box 2137, Little Rock, AR 72203

ARKANSAS ARTS CENTER PRINTS, DRAWINGS & PHOTOGRAPHS EXHIBITIONS, Little Rock. Bi-Annual, May-June. Prints in all media; drawings in all media; photographs in color and/or monochrome. Open to artists born in or residing in Ark, La, Miss, Mo, Okla, Tenn & Tex. Juried by object, awards & $2000 purchase prizes. Fee $7.50 for each entry, limit two. Entry deadline: April 10, 1989. For further information write Collections and Exhibitions. The Arkansas Arts Center, MacArthur Park, PO Box 2137, Little Rock, AR 72203.

ARKANSAS ARTS CENTER REGIONAL CRAFT BIENNIAL, Little Rock. Biennial, Sept.-Oct. 1994. Objects made of craft media - clay, fiber, glass, metal, wood and mixed-media. Open to artists born in or residing in Arkansas, Louisiana, Oklahoma, Mississippi, Missouri, Tennessee and Texas. Juried by slides. Juror's Award and up to $2000 in additional Purchase Awards. Fee $10 per entry, limit three. Deadline for slides usually late June. For further information write Decorative Arts Museum, The Arkansas Arts Center, MacArthur Park, P.O. Box 2137, Little Rock, AR 72203.

ARKANSAS ARTS CENTER TOYS DESIGNED BY ARTISTS EXHIBITION, Little Rock. Annual, Nov-Jan. Toys in all Media. Open to all artists. Work Must have been completed within past two years. $3000 in purchase awards. Fee $10.00 per entry, limit 3. Jury. Dates for entry cards and work due to be announced. For further information write Decorative Arts Museum, The Arkansas Arts Center, MAcArthur Park, PO Box 2137, Little Rock, AR 72203.

CALIFORNIA

BURBANK ART EXHIBITION, Burbank. Annual, September. Drawing, graphics, mixed media, painting, photography, prints, sculpture and watercolor. $2000 cash and purchase awards. Fee $7 per entry non members, $5 per entry members. Slides due July 29, accepted work due August 16, 17 (*Hand deliveries only*) S.A.S.E. Required. for further information write Creative Arts Center, PO Box 6459, Burbank, CA 91510.

INK AND CLAY, Pomona. Annual, for California artists only. Prints, drawings, ceramic ware or sculpture. Juried, purchase awards. Fee $10 for one or two entries. For further information write Art Department California State Polytechnic University, 3801 W. Temple Blvd, Pomona, CA 91768.

OLIVE HYDE ART GALLERY ANNUAL TEXTILE COMPETITION, Annual. March 19-April 25, 1993. Textiles. Open to any artist working in predominately fiber media. Juried, awards. Fee $5 per item, limit 3. Work must be hand delivered. Jury by March 12-13. For further information write Olive Hyde Art Gallery, City of Fremont, Leisure Services Department, PO Box 5006, Fremont, CA 94537.

SAN BERNARDINO ART ASSOCIATION INLAND EXHIBITION. Annual, Oct. Oil, acrylic, watercolor, mixed, collage, graphics (no sculpture or photography). Open to all California artists. Cash awards & purchase awards. Fee $5 per entry, limit 3, 30% comn. For further information write San Bernardino Art Association, PO Box 3754, San Bernardino, CA 92404.

COLORADO

GILPIN COUNTY ARTS ASSOCIATION EXHIBITION, Central City. June-Sept. Painting, sculpture, crafts & photography. Open to Colo artists. Fee $6 per entry. For further information write Gilpin County Arts Assoc, Eureka St. PO Box 161, Central City, CO 80427.

CONNECTICUT

CELEBRATION OF AMERICAN CRAFTS, New Haven. Annual, Nov-Dec. Crafts. Open to US artists. Juried. Deadline for slides June 15. For prospectus send SASE to Creative Arts Workshop, 80 Audubon St, New Haven, CT 06510.

NEW HAVEN PAINT AND CLAY CLUB. Annual, March. Oil, watercolor, acrylic, graphics & sculpture. Open to artists from the New England states & NY. Prizes & purchase awards. Fee $10 for first entry, $6 for second, 20% comn. Entry forms mailed out in Jan & Feb. For further information write NHP & C Club Secretary, 51 Trumbull St., New Haven, CT 06510.

SLATER MEMORIAL MUSEUM, Norwich. Annual, Mar 7-Apr 22, 1993. Sculpture, painting, drawing and prints. Open to all resident Connecticut artists. Jury, prizes. Fee $10 first entry, $8 second entry. Members may submit one entry free of charge; sculpture limited to 200 pounds. No work to exceed 72" horizontally. For further information write The Slater Memorial Museum, 108 Crescent St, Norwich, CT 06360.

DELAWARE

DELAWARE ART MUSEUM'S REGIONAL BIENNIAL, Wilmington, July 9-Sept 5, 1993. All media (except video), must be original work executed by entrants. Open only to artists who reside in the following states and counties: New Castle, Kent and Sussex, Delaware; Chester, Delaware, and Philadelphia, Pennsylvania; Cecil County, Maryland; and Salem County, New Jersey. Juror: Roy Slade, President, Cranbrook Academy of Art.; Director, Cranbrook Academy of Art Museum. Juried by slides with cash prizes. Fee; limit of three works per person. For prospectus send SASE to: Jenine Culligan, Delaware Art Museum, 2301 Kentmere Parkway, Wilmington, DE 19806. Tel 302-571-9590.

DISTRICT OF COLUMBIA

ANNUAL EXHIBITION, MINIATURE SOCIETY OF WASHINGTON, DC. Annual, Nov. Painting, graphics, sculpture, carving, & nontraditional, 5x8 inches, including frame, sculpture limited to 8 inches. Cash awards. Fee, local nonmembers, $20 for 3 entries; out-of-town nonmembers, $25 for 3 entries. For further information write Margaret Wisdon, 5812 Massachusetts Ave., NW, Washington DC 20816.

FLORIDA

MIAMI BEACH OUTDOOR FESTIVAL OF THE ARTS. Miami Beach. Annual, Feb. All media $45,000 in awards. Fee $150. Entry slides due Nov. 1. For further information write Miami Beach Fine Arts Board, Dept. FL, PO Bin O, Miami Beach, FL 33119.

SOCIETY OF THE FOUR ARTS EXHIBITION OF CONTEMPORARY AMERICAN PAINTINGS. Palm Beach. Annual. Dec. Oils, watercolors, drawings, mixed & flat collages completed since Jan. Open to artists residing in the U.S. $16,000 cash award. Fee $10. Limit 2 entries; comn 15%. Specific dates on which entry cards & work are due are announced in prospectus available upon request in Sept. For further information write The Society of the Four Arts, Four Arts Plaza, Palm Beach, FL 33480.

ILLINOIS

AMERICAN CENTER FOR DESIGN, The 100 Show, Chicago. Annual. Books, brochures, announcements, invitations, stationery, annual reports, house organs, calendars, catalogs, posters, manuals, corporate graphics, packages, logos and trademarks. Fee $25 per entry for non members, $20 per entry for members. Entry due early June. For further information write American Center for Design, 233 E. Ontario, Suite 500, Chicago, IL 60611.

INDIANA

EVANSVILLE MUSEUM OF ARTS AND SCIENCE ANNUAL MID-STATES ART EXHIBITION. Annual; Write or call for application in May-August. Painting, drawing, watercolor, graphic arts (no photographs), collage, and sculpture. Open to residents of Indiana, Ohio, Kentucky, Illinois, Missouri, and Tennessee. Juried awards. Fee $15.00. For further information write Art Committee, Evansville Museum of Arts & Science, 411 S.E. Riverside Dr, Evansville, IN 47713; or call 812-425-2406.

EVANSVILLE MUSEUM OF ARTS AND SCIENCE ANNUAL MID-STATES CRAFT EXHIBITION. Annual; Write or call for application in October-December. Ceramic, textile, metalwork, glass, wood, enamel, and handcrafted materials. Open to residents of Indiana, Ohio, Kentucky, Illinois, Missouri, and Tennessee. Juried awards. Fee $15.00. For further information write Art Committee, Evansville Museum of Arts & Science, 411 S.E. Riverside Dr., Evansville, IN 47713; or call 812-425-2406.

EVANSVILLE MUSEUM OF ARTS AND SCIENCE ANNUAL REALISM TO-DAY EXHIBITION. Annual; write or call for application in February/March. Painting, drawing, watercolor, graphic arts (no photographs), and collage. Open to residents of Indiana, Ohio, Kentucky, Illinois, Missouri, and Tennessee. Juried awards. Fee $15.00. For further information write Art Committee, Evansville Museum of Arts & Science, 411 S.E. Riverside Dr., Evansville, IN 47713; or call 812-425-2406.

IOWA

IOWA CRAFTS ANNUAL, Mason city. Annual, Oct-Nov-Dec. Open to any and all craft media, such as clay, fiber, metals, and others. Open to all artists, craftspersons residing within the State of Iowa. Juried by submission of the work, up to $2500 in cash awards. No fee. Entry deadline three weeks prior to opening of show. For further information write Richard Leet, Director, Charles H MacNider Museum, 303 Second St. SE., Mason City, IA 50401.

LOUISIANA

NEW ORLEANS MUSEUM OF ART. Triennial. Focus on contemporary art in all media by professional artists from thirteen-state region of Southeastern US. Single guest curator purchases. No fee. Next exhibition in series: 1995. For further information write New Orleans Triennial, New Orleans Museum of Art, PO Box 19123, Lelong Ave, City Park, New Orleans, LA 70179.

MARYLAND

CUMBERLAND VALLEY ARTISTS ANNUAL EXHIBITION, Hagerstown. Annual, June. Open media. Open to residents & former residents of the Cumberland Valley region. Juried, prizes & awards. Fee $10. Entries due May 11. For further information write Washington County Museum of Fine Arts, PO Box 423, Hagerstown, MD 21741.

MICHIGAN

MID-MICHIGAN ANNUAL EXHIBITION, Midland. Annual, fall. All media & mixed media (painting, drawing, prints, sculpture, plastics, ceramics, textiles, jewelry, enameling, metalwork, woodwork, photography). Open to Mich artists 18 years and over, only original work completed within the past 2 years. Juried, prizes & awards. Fee $15 per artist, limit three entries; $10 fee for MAC members. Preliminary jurying from slides. Entries due Sept. for further information write the Midland Art Council of Midland Center for the Arts, Inc. 1801 West St Andrews, Midland, MI 48640.

MINNESOTA

WHITE BEAR ARTS COUNCIL & LAKEWOOD COMMUNITY COLLEGE NORTHERN LIGHTS, White Bear Lake. Annual, Mar-Apr. Paintings, sculpture, drawings, hand-pulled prints. Open to artists in MN, WI, IA, ND, SD. Juried, prizes, ribbons, money awards & purchase awards. Fee $6 first entry, $4 second entry, two entries per artist. Entries due Feb 12. For further information write White Bear Arts Council, Box 10715, White Bear Lake, MN 55110.

MISSOURI

PHOTOSPIVA, Joplin. Nov-Dec. All photography processes. Open to US artists. Juried, $1500 in cash awards. Fee $10, limit 4. For further information write Spiva Art Center, 3950 Newman Rd, Joplin, MO 64801.

NEW JERSEY

BOARDWALK INDIAN SUMMMER ART SHOW, Atlantic City. Annual, Sept. All media. $3000 in awards. For further information write Florence Miller, Dir, 205 N. Montpelier Ave., Atlantic City, NJ 08401.

N.J. CENTER FOR VISUAL ARTS JURIED SHOW, Summit. Jan-Feb. All media. Juried $1550 in awards. Fee $15, limit 2 slides. For further information write N.J. Center for Visual Arts, 68 Elm St., Summit, NJ 07901.

RUTGERS NATIONAL WORKS ON PAPER, Camden. Mar-Apr. Works on paper surface traditional or experimental techniques, excluding print & photography. Open to US artists. Juried, $5000 minimum in purchase awards. For further information write Stedman Art Gallery, Rutgers Univ., Camden, NJ 08102.

NEW YORK

CHAUTAUQUA ART ASSOCIATION GALLERIES, Chautauqua Institution, National Exhibition of American Art. Open to US artists. Juror: Randall Williams, Metropolitan Museum of Art. Media: Oil, Acrylic, Watercolor, Drawing, Prints, Mixed Media, Photography, 3 Dimensional, Electronically Generated 2D, Fibers. Juried by slides, over $5000 in cash and purchase awards. Fee $6 for each slide, minimum 3 slides required in each media category entered. Send self-addressed-stamped-envelope for entry forms to : Jeffrey Crist, Director CAA, Box 999, Chautauqua, New York, 14722.

COOPERSTOWN ART ASSOCIATION NATIONAL EXHIBITION. Annual, July-Aug. Painting, graphics, sculpture & crafts (no photography). Open to any adult in the US. Over $3000 in prizes. Fee $15 each entry. 25% comn. Mailed entries due in the hands of agent by June 8th. Hand delivered entries June 10th & 11th. For further information write Majorie Walters, Director, Cooperstown Art Association, 22 Main St., Cooperstown, NY 13326.

EVERSON MUSEUM OF ART EVERSON BIENNIAL, Syracuse, NY. Biennial, held during even years. Painting, prints, drawing, collage, photographs, sculpture, fiber. Open to artists over 18 years of age who reside in NY. Fee for non-members, CERAMIC NATIONAL. Syracuse, NY, a triennial exhibit held in the spring, open to artists 21 years of age or older who reside in the U.S. Purchase prices. Fee. Artwork must be predominatly of fired clay. For further information write Everson Museum of Art, Public Info Dept., 401 Harrison St. Syracuse, NY 13202.

NATIONAL SCULPTURE SOCIETY, New York. Annual. Sculpture only. Open to all American sculptors on a juried basis. Jury prizes & awards. Write for prospectus approx Jan 1. For further information write National Sculpture Society, 15 E. 26th St., New York, NY 10010.

NATONAL SOCIETY OF PAINTERS IN CASEIN & ACRYLIC, New York. Annual, Mar. Casein and acrylic. Open to all artists. Juried, $3200 cash awards & medals. Fee $15. Slides due Jan 15. For further information write Dorothy Barberis, Corr. Sec, 217 Lincoln Ave., Elmswood Park, NJ 07407.

NORTH CAROLINA

NORTH CAROLINA ARTISTS EXHBITION, Raleigh. Triennial, Oct-Dec, 1993. All media. Open to current North Carolina residents. For further information write Curatorial Dept. North Carolina Museum of Art, 2110 Blue Ridge Rd. Raleigh, NC 27607.

SHELBY ART LEAGUE, Shelby. Annual, Juried, $4000 in cash awards. For further information write before August, 1993, to Shelby Art League, PO Box 1708, Shelby, NC 28150.

SOUTHEASTERN CENTER FOR CONTEMPORARY ART, Winston-Salem. Annual NEA/SECCA Southeastern Artists Fellowship Competition. Media as specified. Open to all artists, 18 years & older, residing in the eleven southeastern states & Washington, DC. Juried. For further information write Southeastern Center for Contemporary Art, 750 Marguerite Dr., Winston-Salem, NC 27106.

NORTH DAKOTA

18TH BIENNIAL NATIONAL JURIED ART EXHIBITION. Open to all artists. Awards cash & purchases. Fee $10 for first piece; $5 for each additional piece up to 3 entries per artist. For information write 2nd Crossing Gallery, 200 N Central, Valley City, ND 58072. Tel 701-845-2690.

OHIO

SUMMERFAIR, Cincinnati. Annual, June. Juried exhibition & sale. All fine arts & crafts. Over $9,000 in cash awards. Fee $150; Processing fee $20. Entries due February 13. For further information write Summerfair Dept AAD, PO Box 8287, Cincinnati, OH 45208. Phone (513)531-0050.

OREGON

WILLAMETTE VALLEY JURIED EXHIBITION, Corvallis. Annual, Non-functional media. Open to Willamette Valley artists. Juried, $1000 cash awards. No fee, limit 2. Juried from slides. Send SASE for prospectus. For further information write Corvallis Arts Center, 700 SW Madison Ave, Corvallis, OR 97333.

PENNSYLVANIA

ANNUAL INTERNATIONAL COMPETITION, Philadelphia. Annual, fall. Even years - prints, Odd years - photographs. Juried, purchase & other awards (over $8000). Purchase prizes offered to the Permanent Collection of the Philadelphia Museum of Art. Fee $25 (covers participation and 1 yr membership in club, catalogue). For further information send SASE to The Print Club, Center for Prints and Photographs, 1614 Latimer St., Philadelphia, PA 19103.

HAZLETON ART LEAGUE REGIONAL ART EXHIBIT, Hazleton. Annual, Apr. Paintings, sculpture, drawings & graphics. Hand delivered. Open to artists within 100 miles of Hazleton. Juried, cash & purchase awards. For further information write E Ruth Howe, 416 W Broad St, Hazleton, PA 18201.

THREE RIVERS ARTS FESTIVAL, Pittsburgh, Annual, 17 days, June. Juried Painting, Sculpture, Crafts, Photography, Video, and Artists' Market. Cash and Exhibit awards. Juried Visual Arts exhibition. Open to artists in DE, DC, IL, IN, KY, MD, NJ, NY, OH, PA, VA & WV. Artists' Market open to artists in all 50 states. Fee $15. Entry Slides due early February. For information and entry forms: Three Rivers Arts Festival, 207 Sweetbriar St., Pittsburgh, PA 15211.

WASHINGTON & JEFFERSON COLLEGE NATIONAL PAINTING SHOW, Washington. Annual, Mar-Apr. All painting. Open to any US artists, 18 yrs old. Prizes & purchase awards. Fee $10 for each slide entry. Entry cards & slides due Jan, work due Mar. For further information write Paul B Edwards, Olin Art Center, Washington & Jefferson College, Washington, PA 15301.

RHODE ISLAND

PROVIDENCE ART CLUB. Three open shows every year. scheduled at different times & varied from season to season; for instance, an open small sculpture show, an open drawing or print show, or perhaps a painting or craft show. For further information write Mrs. Tore Dalenius, Providence Art Club, 11 Thomas St., Providence, RI 02903.

SOUTH DAKOTA

RED CLOUD INDIAN ART SHOW, Pine Ridge. June-Aug. Paintings, graphics, mixed media, 3-D work. Open to any tribal member of the native people of North America. Juried, $5500 in merit & purchase awards. Entries due May 22. For further information write Red Cloud Indian Art Show, Red Cloud Indian School, Pine Ridge, SD 57770.

TEXAS

EL PASO MUSEUM OF ART NATIONAL SUN CARNIVAL. Biennial, Dec. All painting. Open to any US citizen residing in the US and its territories. Juried, purchase awards. For further information write Kevin Donovan, Curator of Collections, El Paso Museum of Art, 1211 Montana, El Paso, TX 79902.

MUSEUMS OF ABILENE. Annual competition of contemporary two-dimensional art. Open to Texas artists. Exhibition, Mar-April. For information, write MOA Annual Art Competition, Museums of Abilene, 102 Cypress, Abilene, TX 79601 or call 915-673-4587. Juried. Cash prizes & solo exhibition awarded. Call for entries mailed in fall.

WORKS ON PAPER ANNUAL EXHIBITION, San Marcos. Annual. Media on or of paper. Open to all artists. Juried. Fee $18 per 2 entries. Purchase awards. For further information write Randall T. Reid, Art Dept., University Drive, Southwest Texas State University, San Marcos, TX 78666-4616. 512/245-2611.

UTAH

UTAH STATEWIDE ANNUAL COMPETITION AND EXHIBITION, Salt Lake City. This juried exhibit sponsored by the Utah Arts Council has a tradition spanning more than ninety years. Open to Utah artists only at no charge, this exhibition is selected by at least one out-of-state juror. The annual format is hosted by the Utah Museum of Fine Arts with rotating disciplines. Up to $10,000 is allocated for cash awards and purchases. For further information write Utah Arts Council, 617 East South Temple, Salt Lake City, UT 84102. Tel 801-533-4195.

WEST VIRGINIA

HUNTINGTON MUSEUM OF ART-EXHIBITION 280. Mar-June. Open to artists above high school age, living within 280 miles of Huntington. Jury, awards. Slides due Jan. For further information write Exhibition 280, Curatorial Assistant, Huntington Museum of Art 2033 McCoy Rd, Huntington, WV 25701.

WISCONSIN

LAKEFRONT FESTIVAL OF ARTS, Milwaukee. Annual. June. Multi-media. Open to professional artists and craftsmen from across the country. $10,000 in prizes. Fee $22. For further information write Milwaukee Art Museum, 750 N Lincoln Memorial Dr, Milwaukee, WI 53202.

Traveling Exhibition Booking Agencies

ALBRIGHT-KNOX ART GALLERY, 1285 Elmwood Ave, Buffalo, NY 14222. *Chief Cur* Michael G Auping; *Cur* Cheryl Brutvan; *Dir* Douglas G Schlutz. *Exhibits*—Jenny Holzer: The Venice Installation; Hamish Fulton: Selected Walks 1969-1989; Abstract Expressionism: The Critical Developments; Structure to Resemblance: Work by Eight American Sculptors; Susan Rothenberg: Paintings and Drawings; Clyfford Still: The Buffalo and San Francisco Collections; Jess: A Grand Collage, 1951-1993.

AMARILLO ART CENTER, 2200 S Van Buren, PO Box 447, Amarillo, TX 79178. *Dir* Patrick McCrachen. *Exhibits*—Russell Lee in Texas: Photographs; Last of a Breed: Western Photographs by Matrin Schreiber; American Images: FSA Photographs. Rental Fees $500 and up. Brochures available.

AMERICAS SOCIETY INC, 680 Park Avenue, New York, NY 10021. Tel 212-249-8950, FAX 212-249-5868. *Dir Visual Arts* Fatima Bercht; *Visual Arts and Education Programs Admin* Barbara Berger. *Exhibits*—Latin American, Caribbean and Canadian art from pre-Columbian to contemporary times. Details of programs available from Department of Visual Arts. Rental fees are dependent on the nature of the exhibition.

ART CENTER OF BATTLE CREEK, 265 E Emmett St, Battle Creek, MI 49017. *Dir* A W Concannon; *Cur* Timothy Norris. *Exhibits*—Women Artists of Michigan; Michigan's African American Artists; Signature Group; Rhythm & Repetition; The Print: Varieties of Technique. Rental fees $200-$400 for 4 weeks. Shipping fees are responsibility of rentor.

ART GALLERY OF YORK UNIVERSITY, 4700 Keele St, Rm N145, Ross Bldg, North York, ON M3J 1P3, Canada. *Dir & Cur* Loretta Yarlow; *Asst Cur* Catherine Crowston. *Exhibits*—Diagnosis: Marc de Guerre, Mark Lewis, Kiki Smith, Jana Sterback; Meeting Place: Robert Gober, Liz Magor, Juan Munoz; Living in the Hot House: Tony Brown; Jocelyn Alloucherie; Lynne Cohen; Tom Dean; Rene Daniels/Shirley Wiitasalo.

THE ASIA SOCIETY GALLERIES, 725 Park Ave, New York, NY 10021. *Dir* Vishakha Desai. *Exhibits*—Asian art, usually on closely focused topics. Rental fee varies. Shipping fee varies.

ASSOCIATION OF SCIENCE-TECHNOLOGY CENTERS (ASTC), 1025 Vermont Ave NW, Suite 500, Washington, DC 20005-3516. Tel 202-783-7200, FAX 202-783-7207. *Traveling Exhibitions* Beth Porter & Celia Lowe. *Exhibits*—Museum quality exhibitions on science, technology, science art, natural history, and related subjects. Exhibition formats included are photography shows, art work and artifact collections and "hands-on" exhibits emphasizing viewer participation. Examples of current offerings are: About Faces: a 1500 square-foot exhibition from the Reuben H Fleet Science Center exploring the nature of visual memory and recognition; Amazing Feets: in the process of exploring how animals move, this whimsical participatory exhibition from the NC Museum of Life and Science examines bugs' feet, horses' knees, and birds on their perches; Leonardo: an extensive collection of hands-on models based on Leonardo da Vinci's scientific and technical drawings including life-sized reproductions of a printing press, helicopter, military tank, automobile, and airplane. Rental fees are charged for exhibitions, and host museums are responsible for paying inbound shipping costs and for providing a secure display space and professional handling. For a catalog and details and information on availability, contact Beth Porter or Celia Lowe.

AUGUSTANA COLLEGE ART GALLERY, Art & Art History Dept, 3701 7th Ave, Rock Island, IL 61201. *Dir* Sherry C Maurer. *Exhibits*—Swedish American Artists. Rental fees $2000. Shipping fees $1500.

BALZEKAS MUSEUM OF LITHUANIAN CULTURE, 6500 South Pulaski Rd, Chicago, IL 60629. *Pres* Stanley Balzekas Jr. Six small portable cases which include history, maps, and some memorabilia on Lithuania dating back 300 years. Rental fee is $150 plus transportation.

BOYCE CAMPUS, COMMUNITY COLLEGE OF ALLEGHENY COUNTY, Beatty Road, Monroeville, PA 15146. *Profs* Bruno Sorento & Jeanne Moffatt Connors. *Exhibits*—Traveling Art Show: High quality student art works displayed in folding panels, sealed under glass. Free-standing and attractive. No rental fee.

BREVARD ART CENTER AND MUSEUM, PO Box 360835, 1463 Highland Ave, Melbourne, FL 32936-0835. *Exec Dir* Randall A Hayes; *Cur* Amy Vigilante. *Exhibits*—Contemporary works on paper.

BURCHFIELD ART CENTER, State University College, 1300 Elmwood Ave, Buffalo, NY 14222. *Dir* Anthony Bannon. *Exhibits*—Charles E Burchfield: The Sacred Woods; Robert Lax and Concrete Poetry. Rental fees $1,500-$10,000.

CENTRO CULTURAL DE LA RAZA, 2004 Park Blvd, San Diego, CA 92102. Tel 619-235-6135. Various exhibits reflective of Mexican, Indian and Chicano art and culture. Rental fees vary.

COLORADO SPRINGS FINE ARTS CENTER, 30 W Dale St, Colorado Springs, CO 80903. Tel 719-634-5581; FAX 719-634-0570. *Exec Dir* David J Wagner; *Dir of Collections* Cathy Wright; *Exhibition Coordr* Kathy Reynolds. *Exhibits*—Walt Kuhn: An Imaginary History of the West; John James Audubon's The Birds of America: Double Elephant Folio; Posada: Major Works from the Taylor Museum Collection; Contemporary Native American Prints. Rental fees $1,000-$7,500, not including shipping.

CORNING MUSEUM OF GLASS, One Museum Way, Corning, NY 14830-2253. Tel 607-937-5371. *Exhibits*—Liquid Refreshment: 2,000 Years of Drinks and Drinking Glasses (April 24-Oct 17, 1993); Stanislav Libensky and Jaroslava Brychtova: A 45 Year Retrospective (April 23-Oct 16, 1994).

CUSTER COUNTY ART CENTER, Water Plant Road, PO Box 1284, Miles City, MT 59301. *Dir* Susan McDaniel. *Exhibits*—Images of an Idyllic Past—The Photographs of Edward S Curtis. Rental fee $500.

ERIE ART MUSEUM, 411 State St, Erie, PA 16501. *Dir* John Vanco. *Exhibits*—The Tactile Vessel: New Basket Forms; Take a Good Look; Daumier Lithographs; Art of the Comic Book; Edward Sheriff Curtis: People of the Pueblos. Rental fees $500-$2800. Shipping fees: borrower pays one-way shipping to next site.

FRENCH CULTURAL SERVICES, Exhibitions Dept, 972 Fifth Ave, New York, NY 10021. *Exhibits*—Photography, documentary & art exhibits available. Rental fees and insurance obligations vary. One way shipping cost paid by exhibitor. Catalogs available.

GALERIE RESTIGOUCHE GALLERY, 39 rue Andrew Street, CP/PO Box 674, Campbellton, NB E3N 3H1, Canada. *Dir & Cur* Colette Bourgoin. *Exhibits*—Couleurs d'Acadie: Color photographs of brightly painted houses phenomena. 120 running feet. No rental fee. Borrower pays cost of transportation both ways. Catalog available.

THE SOLOMON R GUGGENHEIM MUSEUM, 1071 Fifth Ave, New York, NY 10128. *Deputy Dir* Diane Waldman; *Cur* Vivian Barnett. *Exhibits*—Concentrations of individual artists; Eureopean painting & sculpture; modern sculpture; European sources of American abstraction; American abstract painting and works on paper from the 1930's & 1940's; postwar American painting; postwar European painting; postwar art; Latin American art; works on paper. Borrowing institutions will remain responsible for shipping, insurance costs, packing & other charges. In addition, some loan exhibitions organized by the museum are available for travel tours.

HIBEL MUSEUM OF ART, 150 Royal Poinciana Plaza, Palm Beach, FL 33480. Tel 407-833-6870. *Exec Trustee* Andy Plotkin, PhD.
Exhibits—From as little as one piece to as many as one hundred or more in the following categories: paintings, original stone lithographs, serigraphs, sculptures, porcelain art, and drawings (rarely shown to the public) by world renowned artist Edna Hibel. Support materials available include: posters, catalogues, brochures & press materials, museum gift items, films, videotapes, and invitations for opening. Major exhibitions now available: A Golden Bridge; The Magic of Porcelain; A Celebration of Life; Hibel on Lithography; and Idyllic Days: Early Watercolors.

HUNTERDON ART CENTER, Seven Lower Center St, Clinton, NJ 08809. *Exec Dir* Sue Knapp-Steen.
Exhibits—Treasures of Prints; National Print Exhibition, art selected from an annual juried show, which numbers over 350 prints by such artists as Red Grooms, Ben Shahn, Stefan Martin, Salvador Dali, Lynd Ward and Edward Coker.

HUNT INSTITUTE FOR BOTANICAL DOCUMENTATION, Carnegie Mellon University, Pittsburgh, PA 15213. *Cur of Art* James J White.
Exhibits—International Exhibition; State Flowers: Watercolors by Anne Ophelia Dowden; Marilena Pistoia: Botanical Watercolors; Poisonous Plants; Orchids from the Hunt Institute Collection. Rental fees $300-$750. Shipping fees vary.

INDEPENDENT CURATORS INCORPORATED, 799 Broadway, #205, New York, NY 10003. *Assoc Dir* Judith Richards; *Exec Dir* Susan Sollins.
Exhibits—After Perestroika: Kitchenmaids or Stateswomen; Critiques of Pure Abstraction; Dark Decor; Departures: Photography 1923-1990; Drawn in the Nineties; Empty Dress: Clothing as Surrogate in Recent Art; The First Generation: Women and Video, 1970-75; Froom Media to Metaphor: Art About AIDS; Good Stories Well Told: Video Art for Young Audiences; Image and Memory: Latin American Photography, 1880-1992; Monumental Propaganda; Print Portfolio: The Print and the Photographic Image. Rental fees $500-$15,000, varying with exhibition.

ISLIP ART MUSEUM, 50 Irish Ave, East Islip, NY 11730-2098. *Exec Dir* Mary Lou Cohalan; *Dir of Collections & Exhibitions* Catherine Valenza.
Exhibits—20 Years Ago Today: 20th Anniversary at the Museum.

KANSAS STATE UNIVERSITY, Manhattan KS 66506. *Dept Head* Charles Stroh; *Cur* Jessica Reichman.
Exhibits—Moments Without Proper Names: Photographs by Gordon Parks; Contemporary Printmaking in India. Rental & shipping vees vary. Write for information.

KERN COUNTY MUSEUM, 3801 Chester Ave, Bakersfield, CA 93301. Tel 805-861-2132. *Asst Dir* David R McCauley.
Exhibits—Black Women: Achievements Against the Odds: photographs, quotations, and histories of inspiring African American women.

KITCHENER-WATERLOO ART GALLERY, 101 Queen St N, Kitchener, ON N2H 6P7, Canada. *Exten Cur & Educ Officer* Paul Blain.
Exhibits—Abstract Art; Animal Images—Part II; Art: A Study of Realism; Arthur Lismer; Canadian Landscape; Children in Art; Drawing: Canadian Trends; Inuit Art; Lawren Harris; Progression Proof Silkscreen

LAGUNA ART MUSEUM, 307 Cliff Drive, Laguna Beach, CA 92651. Tel 714-494-8971; FAX 714-494-1530. *Dir* Charles Desmarais.
Exhibits—Art in Los Angeles Prior to 1900; I Thought California Would Be Different: New Work in Los Angeles; Paintings from Paradise: Selections from the Laguna Art Museum Collection of California Impressionism; John McLaughlin: A Retrospective; Custom Culture: Von Dutch, Ed "Big Daddy" Roth, Robert Williams and Their Influence; The San Francisco School of Abstract Expressionism; "Self-Help" Graphics: Art in East L.A.; Genesis and the Crucifixion in the Art of Rico Lebrun. Fees range from $2,500 to $20,000.

LAS VEGAS-CLARK COUNTY LIBRARY DISTRICT, 833 Las Vegas Blvd N, Las Vegas, NV 89101. Tel 702-382-3493, ext 249. *Program Coordr* Margaret Trasatti; *Gallery Mgr* Denise Shapiro.
Exhibits—Regular monthly exhibits in eight galleries located in various library facilities throughout the greater Las Vegas area. Coordinate the annual festival of the arts and regional fine arts competition. Call for further information.

MAITLAND ART CENTER TRAVELING EXHIBITION SERVICE (MACTES), 231 W Packwood Ave, Maitland, FL 32751-5596. Tel 407-539-2181. *Cur* Dorothy T Van Arsdale.
Exhibits—Currently 12 exhibitions of lithographs, watercolors, photography, textiles, sculpture, mixed-media, both foreign and American, range from 25-50 pieces per exhibit. Rental fees $500-$1,000 for 4-week booking period. The exhibitor is responsible for outgoing shipping. Annual and periodic catalogs available.

MEMORIAL UNIVERSITY OF NEWFOUNDLAND, Art Gallery, Arts & Culture Centre, St John's NF A1C 5S7, Canada. *Cur* Patricia Grattan.

Exhibits—Contemporary art; folk art; traditional craft of Newfoundland & Labrador. Rental & shipping fees vary.

MIDMARCH ARTS, 300 Riverside Dr, New York, NY 10025. *Exec Dir* Cynthia Navaretta.
Exhibits—Six crooked photographers: Alternative processes. Rental & shipping fees $6,000.

MIDWEST MUSEUM OF AMERICAN ART, PO Box 1812, 429 S Main, Elkhart, IN 46515. *Dir* Jane Burns; *Cur* Brian D Byrn.
Exhibits—American Masters of Photography (30 works); Viktoras Petravicius: Master of the Monoprint (30 works); John Doyle: Prints of Social Satire; William Gropper Prints. Rental fees $900 each.

MONTANA HISTORICAL SOCIETY, 225 N Roberts, PO Box 201201, Helena, MT 59620-1201. *Cur Educ* Joan Haefer.
Exhibits—Children in Montana: 1864-1930; Montana Collage: Our History through Photography, 1880-1910; F Jay Haynes: Fifty Views; Photographing Montana 1894-1928: The World of Evelyn Cameron. Write for information.

MONTEREY PENINSULA MUSEUM OF ART, 559 Pacific St, Monterey, CA 93940. *Dir* Jo Farb Hernandez; *Art Dir* Marc D'Estout.
Exhibits—The Monterey Photographic Tradition; The Weston Years; Colors and Impressions: The Early Work of E C Fortune: The Eye of the Child (International Folk Art); The Expressive Sculpture of Alvin Light; Photogravures: Edward Curtis; The Chicago Federal Act Project: WPA Prints; Joe Cole: A New Life's Work (Folk artist: oil pastels on paper); Wonderful Colors: The Paintings of August Gay; Jeannette Marfield Lewis: A Centennial Salute (prints and paintings).

MUSEUM OF CONTEMPORARY ART, SAN DIEGO, 700 Prospect St, La Jolla, CA 92037. *Dir* Dr Hugh Marlais Davies.
Exhibits—Vernon Fisher; Peter Shelton: Waxworks; Emilio Ambasz; Alfredo Jarr; Richard Long; Robert Moskowitz; Maurizio Pellegrin; Celia Munoz; Allan Wexler; Anish Kapoor; Noboru Tsubaki; Julie Bozzi; Antony Gormley; Jana Sterbak.

THE MUSEUM OF EAST TEXAS, 503 N Second St, Lufkin, TX 75901. *Exec Dir* Mark Tullos.
Exhibits—Mountain Plains Regional Competition; Janet Turner: Prints and Drawings; Mexican Folk Art Collection; Doing the Dishes: Contemporary Glass; Approaching a New Century: Artists Gary Justis, Dean McNiel and Taro Suzuki; The Medieval Mind: Illuminate Manuscripts. Rental fees $1000-$3000.

MUSEUM OF FINE ARTS, University of Montana, Missoula, MT 59812. *Dir & Cur* Dennis Kern.
Exhibits—Stettner Photographs; Atget Photographs; Contemporary British Prints; Daumier Prints; Fra Dana Collection; W.P.A. Prints; Rockwell Kent Prints. Rental fees $300-$2000.

MUSEUM OF MODERN ART, 11 W 53rd St, New York, NY 10019.
Exhibition Program: *Coordr of Exhibitions* Richard L Palmer; *Assoc Coordr* Eleni Cocordas.
A number of exhibitions directed by members of the Museum's curatorial staff are offered to other qualified museums on a participating basis. These exhibitions are generally either full-scale projects or reduced versions of shows initially presented at The Museum of Modern Art. Although exhibitions are not necessarily available at all times in all media, the traveling program does cover the entire range of the Museum's New York program—painting, sculpture, drawings, prints, photography, architecture and design. Participating fees usually begin at $2000 for smaller exhibitions and range up to several thousand dollars for major exhibitions. Tour participants are also asked to cover pro-rated transport costs.

International Program: *Dir, International Prog* Waldo Rasmussen; *Assoc Dir* Elizabeth Streibert.
The primary function of the program is to encourage cultural exchange in all the visual arts on a broad international level. Exhibitions of painting, sculpture, drawings, prints, photography, architecture, design, and film are circulated by the Museum to foreign countries under the auspices of The International Council of The Museum of Modern Art. Rental fee plus pro-rated transportation fee. Programs with overseas libraries and visiting foreign specialists.

Circulating Film & Video Library: *Librarian* William Sloan.
Films and programs are drawn from the Museum's international archive of films as well as being distributed on behalf of independent producers; these are made available for rental and, in some cases, for lease. The films exemplify or illustrate the history, development, scale and technical diversity of the motion picture. Programming assistance is available upon request. Rental or lease fee plus shipping and handling costs. Catalogs and supplements list more than 1300 titles ranging from the films of the 1890's to recent independent productions.

NATIONAL WATERCOLOR SOCIETY, 18220 S Hoffman Ave, Cerritos, CA 90701. *Pres* Jim Salchak.

Exhibits—Travel Shows are juried from the Annual Exhibitions and the All-Membership Shows. Works are aquamedia on paper under plexi. The approximate number of works in each show is 30-100. NWS travel shows are available only to museums and galleries with adequate security and supervision. Commercial galleries are not eligible. National Watercolor Society requires that exhibiting galleries provide insurance during the exhibit and pay transportation and in-transit insurance one way. No other fee is charged. A limited number of Annual Exhibition catalogs are available for a nominal fee.

NICOLAYSEN ART MUSEUM, 400 E Collins Dr, Casper, WY 82601. *Interim Dir* Alex Efinoff.
Exhibits—Historic Ranches of Wyoming—80 black & white photographs with book length catalog. Rental fee $500 per month.

NORTH CENTRAL WASHINGTON MUSEUM, 127 South Mission, Wenatchee, WA 98801. *Museum Dir* Keith Williams; *Art Gallery Coordr* Terri White.
Exhibits—Japanese Woodblock Print: The Ronin Story (52 prints by the artist Ichiysuai Kuniyoshi based on one of Japan's most famous stories). Rental fees, shipping fees vary.

ORLANDO MUSEUM OF ART, 2416 North Mills Ave, Orlando, FL 32803. *Exec Dir* Marina Grant Morrisey; *Cur of Contemporary Art* Sue Scott; *Cur of 19th Century American Art* Valerie Leeds; *Cur of Exhibitions* Hansen Mulford.
Exhibits—Jennifer Bartlett: A Print Retrospective, rental fee $4000; My People: The Portraits of Robert Henri, rental fee $22,000.

OWATONNA ARTS CENTER, 435 Dunnell Dr, PO Box 134, Owatonna, MN 55060. *Dir* Silvan Durben.
Exhibits—The Marianne Young Costume Collection. This collection includes 98 garments from 25 countries and is complete with accessories such as hats, jewelry, gloves and boots. The collection includes caftans, saris, coats, kimonos, evening gowns and French originals. Examples of the gowns in the collection include: a dress from South Africa made completely of white ostrich feathers; a long gown from Pakistan covered with mirrors held in place by embroidery; a bright blue poncho cape from Bali (used in formal dances) which is painted in gold, yellow and shocking pink; a wine-red caracul skin coat from Afghanistan embroidered in gold with black caracul edging. The costumes, all in her own petite size, were collected and worn by Marianne Young during 50 years of travel. Rental fee $600 plus transportation. The center also has a sculpture garden that was designed by Brooks Cavin, and has four works by Minnesota sculptors: Reflections III by Paul T Granlund; Spirit of Peace by Charles Gangon; Winged Figure by John Rood, and Compass by Donald Hammel. Brochure available on request.

PLAINS ART MUSEUM, 521 Main Ave, PO Box 2338, Moorhead, MN 56560. *Dir* Elizabeth Hannaher; *Business Mgr* Paul Carlson; *Communications Mgr* Laurie Baker.
Exhibits—On the Border: Native American Weaving Traditions of the Great Lakes and Prairie; Kirk Lybeckin: A Hard Look-Photorealism. Rental fees available upon request.

PRAIRIE GALLERY, 10209 99th St, Grande Prairie, AB T8V 2H3, Canada. Tel 403-532-8111; FAX 403-539-1991. *Dir & Cur* Elizabeth Ginn.
Exhibits—Terry Emrick: Travelog; Susan Mills: Books; Valory Webber: Private Voices Whispering in Public; Carmen Haakstad: Beyond the Game, Behind the Ballot Box; Bloom/Stocking: Street Photographs from the Third World; Dean Tatum Reeves, Christine Koch: River Gods; Dan Campbell: Myth/Metaphor; Ben Wong: All Schools-All Art; Come Walk with Me: A Luke Lindoe Retrospective; some forty exhibitions are produced by the Prairie Gallery.

THE PRINT CONSORTIUM, 6121 NW 77th St, Kansas City, MO 64151. *Exec Dir* Dr William S Eickhorst.
Exhibits—Museum quality exhibits of works by established American & European printmakers. Rental fee $300-$750 plus shipping. Catalog available.

C M RUSSELL MUSEUM, 400 13th Street N, Great Falls, MT 59401. *Dir* Lorne E Renders; *Registrar* Jan Postler.
Exhibits—C M Russell Cowboy Artist (20 to 50 pieces); Uncle Sam (50-250 pieces); Winold Reiss (approximately 60 pieces). Rental fees $2500-$3500.

SMITHSONIAN INSTITUTION TRAVELING EXHIBITION SERVICE (SITES), Washington, DC 20560. Tel 202-357-2700. *Dir* Anna R Cohn.
Exhibits—Architecture, cultural history, decorative arts, design, environment, paintings, prints & drawing, photography, science & technology. Available to educational, scientific, cultural and, on occasion, commercial institutions. Educational materials and program activities supplement the exhibits. Catalogs, posters and brochures accompany specific exhibits. Annual catalog "Update" available to exhibitors on request. Quarterly newsletter "Siteline" available now.

SOUTH CAROLINA ARTS COMMISSION MEDIA ARTS CENTER, 1800 Gervais St, Columbia, SC 29201. *Exhibit Coordr* Susan Leonard.
Exhibits—Southern Circuit (film/video artist tour).

TEXAS FINE ARTS ASSOCIATION, 3809-B W 35th St, Austin, TX 78703. Tel 512-453-5312. *Dir* Sandra Gregor.
Exhibits—New American Talent: At the Edge; Beyond Photography. Rental fees $900-$1500. Currently touring only in Texas; may expand regionally.

TWEED MUSEUM OR ART, University of Minnesota-Duluth, 10 University Dr, Duluth, MN 55812. *Dir* Martin DeWitt.
Exhibits—The Mounty Legend: The Potlach collection of illustrations from the Tweed Museum of Art; American Prints & Drawings from the Tweed Museum; Three American Regionalists: Benton, Curry, Wood Lithos. Rental fees $1200-$15,000.

THE UKRAINIAN MUSEUM, 203 Second Ave, New York, NY 10003. *Dir* Maria Shust.
Exhibits—Masterpieces in Wood: Houses of Worship in Ukraine; Ukraine Fold Art; To Preserve a Heritage: The Story of the Ukrainian Immigration in the USA. Rental fees $450-$1000. Packets of information on particular traveling exhibitions are available.

UNIVERSITY MUSEUMS, Southern Illinois University, Edwardsville, ILL 62026-1150. *Dir* David C Huntley; *Cur* Michael E Mason.
Exhibits—Louis H Sullivan: Unison with Nature. Rental fee $50 (weekly).

UNIVERSITY MUSEUMS, The University of Mississippi, University, MS 38677. *Dir* Bonnie J Krause; *Coordr* Susan V Hannah.
Exhibits—Olynthus 348 BC: The Destruction and Resurrection of a Greek City (photographic). $100 rental, shipping one way.

UNIVERSITY OF HAWAII ART GALLERY, Dept of Art, Honolulu, HI 96822. *Dir* Tom Klobe.
Exhibits—The Fifth International Shoe Box Sculpture Exhibition; Jean Charlot: A Retrospective; Baskets: Redefining Volume and Meaning; PARTS. Rental fees vary.

UNIVERSITY OF MINNESOTA ART MUSEUM, 110 Northrop Auditorium, 84 Church St SE, Minneapolis, MN 55455. Tel 612-624-9560. *Asst Dir for Touring* Colleen Sheehy.
Statewide touring exhibitions include the exhibit, educational catalog or brochure, and a humanities program related to the themes of the exhibition. Rental fees $300-$3500. Shipping fees prorated for national tourings. Call for further information on statewide, regional and national traveling exhibitions.

UNIVERSITY OF PUGET SOUND, Art Dept, 1500 N Warner, Tacoma, WA 98416. *Chmn Art Dept* Ken Stevens; *Gallery Dir* Greg Bell.
Exhibits—Smithsonian Sites Exhibition, American Federation of Arts, Exhibit Travel Services (ETS). Rental fees $2500 per year. Shipping fees $1000 per year.

UNIVERSITY OF SOUTH DAKOTA, Vermillion, SD 57069. *Dir* John A Day.
Exhibits—Works from permanent collection: Contemporary Prints/Drawings; Oscar Howe Paintings. Rental fee is cost plus $100-$500 depending on size of show.

UNIVERSITY OF TENNESSEE, Dept of Art, 1715 Volunteer Blvd, Rm 213, Knoxville, TN 37996-2410. *Dir Ewing Gallery of Art & Architecture* Sam Yates.
Exhibits—Yugoslavian Architectural Drawings; Byron McKeeby Retrospective; Joseph Delaney Retrospective; Fact/Fiction/Fantasy: Recent Narrative Art in the Southeast. Fees vary with exhibition, often includ catalogs.

U.S. NAVAL ACADEMY MUSEUM, Annapolis, MD 21402. Tel 410-267-2108. *Dir* Kenneth J Hagan; *Assoc Dir & Senior Cur* James W Cheevers.
Exhibits—Currier & Ives Navy. Rental & shipping fees vary.

UTAH ARTS COUNCIL, 617 E South Temple, Salt Lake City, UT 84102. Tel 801-533-5757.
Exhibits—The exhibition program is designed to provide traveling exhibitions to a statewide audience. Approximately twenty exhibitions are available which vary in size and subject matter. They include works from the permanent collections of the Utah Arts Council, the Utah Museum of Fine Arts and from special collections contributed by organizations and individuals. Exhibitions are scheduled for one month at $50 per exhibit. They may be booked by museums, college and public galleries, community groups or institutions such as libraries, schools, or other non-profit organizations. The Visual Arts staff transports the exhibitions and supervises installation.

WHARTON ESHERICK MUSEUM, Horseshoe Trail, PO Box 595, Paoli, PA 19301. Tel 215-644-5822.
Exhibits—Half a Century in Wood: 1920-1970—a photographic exhibition of furniture created by Wharton Esherick including a catalog. Rental fees $250. Shipping fees $50-$100. Contact Museum Director.

WHITNEY MUSEUM OF AMERICAN ART, 945 Madison Ave, New York, NY 10021. *Admin* Nancy A McGary.
Exhibits—Vary; primarily 20th Century American Art.

THE WINNIPEG ART GALLERY, 300 Memorial Blvd, Winnipeg, MB R3C 1V1, Canada. *Exten Serv Coordr* Robert Epp. Tel 204-786-6641. FAX 204-788-4998.
Exhibits—Several exhibitions of contemporary Canadian art organized each year by the Winnipeg Art Gallery are offered to other qualified galleries and museums in Canada, the United States, and abroad, on a participating basis. Borrowing fees and loan terms vary.

LEIGH YAWKEY WOODSON ART MUSEUM, 700 N 12th St, Wausau, WI 54401-5007. Tel 715-845-7010; FAX 715-845-7103. *Assoc Dir* Marcia M Theel; *Cur of Exhib* Andrew J McGivern; *Cur of Coll* Jane Weinke.
Exhibits—Wildlife: The Artist's View: Fifty paintings and 10 sculptures by an international selection of artists. Rental fee $7000 plus pro-rated freight. 100 catalogs included in rental fee. Birds in Arts: Fifty paintings and 10 sculptures by international artists who specialize in artistic depiction of birds. Rental fee $7800 plus pro-rated freight. 100 catalogs included in rental fee. Naturally Drawn: a sampling of wildlife drawings, sketches and field studies from the Museum's evolving drawing collection; 60 works. Rental fee $2000 plus outgoing shipping.

IV INDEXES

Subject

Personnel

Organizational

Subject Index

Major subjects are listed first, followed by named collections.

AMERICAN WESTERN ART

The Albrecht-Kemper Museum of Art, Saint Joseph MO

Albuquerque Museum of Art, History & Science, Albuquerque NM

Amerind Foundation, Inc, Amerind Museum, Fulton-Hayden Memorial Art Gallery, Dragoon AZ

Anchorage Museum of History and Art, Anchorage AK

Artesia Historical Museum & Art Center, Artesia NM

Art Gallery of Hamilton, Hamilton ON

Art Institute for the Permian Basin, Odessa TX

Birmingham Museum of Art, Birmingham AL

Brigham Young University, B F Larsen Gallery, Provo UT

Buffalo Bill Memorial Association, Buffalo Bill Historical Center, Cody WY

Canajoharie Art Gallery, Canajoharie NY

Carson County Square House Museum, Panhandle TX

Amon Carter Museum, Fort Worth TX

Cedar Rapids Museum of Art, Cedar Rapids IA

Church of Jesus Christ of Latter-day Saints, Museum of Church History & Art, Salt Lake City UT

Cincinnati Institute of Fine Arts, Taft Museum, Cincinnati OH

Continental Bank Corporation, Art Collection, Chicago IL

Crook County Museum and Art Gallery, Sundance WY

Dickinson College, Trout Gallery, Carlisle PA

East Carolina University, Wellington B Gray Gallery, Greenville NC

Favell Museum of Western Art & Indian Artifacts, Klamath Falls OR

Frontier Times Museum, Bandera TX

Genesee Country Museum, John L Wehle Gallery of Sporting Art, Mumford NY

Charles B Goddard Center for the Visual and Performing Arts, Ardmore OK

Nora Eccles Harrison Museum of Art, Logan UT

Idaho Historical Museum, Boise ID

Joslyn Art Museum, Omaha NE

Leanin' Tree Museum of Western Art, Boulder CO

Los Angeles County Museum of Natural History, William S Hart Museum, Newhall CA

Marietta College, Grover M Hermann Fine Arts Center, Marietta OH

Mississippi Museum of Art, Jackson MS

Arthur Roy Mitchell Memorial Inc, Museum of Western Art, Trinidad CO

MonDak Heritage Center, Sidney MT

Monterey Peninsula Museum of Art Association, Monterey CA

Museum of Fine Arts, Saint Petersburg, Florida, Inc, Saint Petersburg FL

Museum of Western Art, Denver CO

National Cowboy Hall of Fame and Western Heritage Center, Oklahoma City OK

National Museum of Women in the Arts, Washington DC

National Park Service, Hubbell Trading Post National Historic Site, Ganado AZ

Nevada Museum Of Art, Reno NV

R W Norton Art Gallery, Shreveport LA

Oklahoma Historical Society, State Museum of History, Oklahoma City OK

Pioneer Town, Pioneer Museum of Western Art, Wimberley TX

Redding Museum of Art & History, Redding CA

Red Rock State Park, Museum, Church Rock NM

Sid W Richardson Foundation, Collection of Western Art, Fort Worth TX

The Rockwell Museum, Corning NY

Roswell Museum and Art Center, Roswell NM

C M Russell Museum, Great Falls MT

Sangre de Cristo Arts & Conference Center, Pueblo CO

Southwest Museum, Los Angeles CA

Stanford University, Art Gallery, Stanford CA

Nelda C & H J Lutcher Stark Foundation, Stark Museum of Art, Orange TX

Texas Tech University, Museum, Lubbock TX

United States Military Academy, West Point Museum, West Point NY

University of Colorado at Colorado Springs, Gallery of Contemporary Art, Colorado Springs CO

University of Rhode Island, Fine Arts Center Galleries, Kingston RI

University of Texas at Austin, Archer M Huntington Art Gallery, Austin TX

Wyoming State Museum, State Art Gallery, Cheyenne WY

ANTHROPOLOGY

Amerind Foundation, Inc, Amerind Museum, Fulton-Hayden Memorial Art Gallery, Dragoon AZ

Anchorage Museum of History and Art, Anchorage AK

Bay County Historical Society, Historical Museum of Bay County, Bay City MI

Beloit College, Wright Museum of Art, Beloit WI

Bowdoin College, Peary-MacMillan Arctic Museum, Brunswick ME

Chelan County Public Utility District, Rocky Reach Dam, Wenatchee WA

Dewitt Historical Society of Tompkins County, Ithaca NY

Douglas County Historical Society, Fairlawn Mansion & Museum, Superior WI

East Carolina University, Wellington B Gray Gallery, Greenville NC

Five Civilized Tribes Museum, Muskogee OK

Hampton University, University Museum, Hampton VA

Indiana University, William Hammond Mathers Museum, Bloomington IN

Luna County Historical Society, Inc, Deming Luna Mimbres Museum, Deming NM

McAllen International Museum, McAllen TX

Maryhill Museum of Art, Goldendale WA

Milwaukee Public Museum, Milwaukee WI

Arthur Roy Mitchell Memorial Inc, Museum of Western Art, Trinidad CO

Mohave Museum of History and Arts, Kingman AZ

Monterey Peninsula Museum of Art Association, Monterey CA

Museum of New York, Rock Hill SC

Oklahoma Historical Society, State Museum of History, Oklahoma City OK

Phelps County Historical Society, Phelps County Museum, Holdrege NE

Red Rock State Park, Museum, Church Rock NM

Roberts County Museum, Miami TX

Royal Ontario Museum, Toronto ON

Sheldon Jackson Museum, Sitka AK

State Historical Society of Wisconsin, State Historical Museum, Madison WI

State Museum of Pennsylvania, Pennsylvania Historical & Museum Commission, Harrisburg PA

University of Pennsylvania, University Museum of Archaelogy & Anthropology, Philadelphia PA

University of Pennsylvania, Library, Philadelphia PA

University of Washington, Thomas Burke Memorial Washington State Museum, Seattle WA

ANTIQUITIES - ASSYRIAN

Cincinnati Museum Association, Cincinnati Art Museum, Cincinnati OH

Florida State University Foundation - Central Florida Community College Foundation, The Appleton Museum of Art, Ocala FL

Kimbell Art Museum, Fort Worth TX

The Metropolitan Museum of Art, New York NY

Rosicrucian Egyptian Museum and Art Gallery, San Jose CA

Toledo Museum of Art, Toledo Museum of Art, Toledo OH

University of Chicago, Oriental Institute Museum, Chicago IL

University of Missouri, Museum of Art and Archaeology, Columbia MO

University of Rochester, Memorial Art Gallery, Rochester NY

Walters Art Gallery, Baltimore MD

ANTIQUITIES - BYZANTINE

Cincinnati Museum Association, Cincinnati Art Museum, Cincinnati OH

Detroit Institute of Arts, Detroit MI

Florida State University Foundation - Central Florida Community College Foundation, The Appleton Museum of Art, Ocala FL

Harvard University, Dumbarton Oaks Research Library and Collections, Washington DC

The Metropolitan Museum of Art, New York NY

Newark Museum Association, The Newark Museum, Newark NJ

Princeton University, The Art Museum, Princeton NJ

University of Delaware, University Gallery, Newark DE

University of Illinois, World Heritage Museum, Champaign IL

University of Missouri, Museum of Art and Archaeology, Columbia MO

Walters Art Gallery, Baltimore MD

ANTIQUITIES - EGYPTIAN

Albany Museum of Art, Albany GA

Lyman Allyn Art Museum, New London CT

Beloit College, Wright Museum of Art, Beloit WI

Berkshire Museum, Pittsfield MA

Brevard Art Center and Museum, Inc, Melbourne FL

Cincinnati Museum Association, Cincinnati Art Museum, Cincinnati OH

Cleveland Museum of Art, Cleveland OH

Detroit Institute of Arts, Detroit MI

Emory University, Museum of Art & Archaeology, Atlanta GA

Evansville Museum of Arts and Science, Evansville IN

Fine Arts Museums of San Francisco, M H de Young Memorial Museum and California Palace of the Legion of Honor, San Francisco CA

Florida State University Foundation - Central Florida Community College Foundation, The Appleton Museum of Art, Ocala FL

Freeport Art Museum & Cultural Center, Freeport IL

Hamilton College, Fred L Emerson Gallery, Clinton NY

Harvard University, William Hayes Fogg Art Museum, Cambridge MA

Harvard University, Semitic Museum, Cambridge MA

Johns Hopkins University, Archaeological Collection, Baltimore MD

Kimbell Art Museum, Fort Worth TX

The Metropolitan Museum of Art, New York NY

Milwaukee Art Museum, Milwaukee WI

Mount Holyoke College, Art Museum, South Hadley MA

Museum of Fine Arts, Boston MA

Newark Museum Association, The Newark Museum, Newark NJ

Princeton University, The Art Museum, Princeton NJ

Purdue University Galleries, West Lafayette IN

Putnam Museum of History & Natural Science, Davenport IA

Queens College, City University of New York, Godwin-Ternbach Museum, Flushing NY

Rosicrucian Egyptian Museum and Art Gallery, San Jose CA

Saint Gregory's Abbey and College, Mabee-Gerrer Museum of Art, Shawnee OK

The Saint Louis Art Museum, Saint Louis MO

Toledo Museum of Art, Toledo Museum of Art, Toledo OH

Tufts University, Art Gallery, Medford MA

University of Chicago, Oriental Institute Museum, Chicago IL

University of Delaware, University Gallery, Newark DE

University of Illinois, World Heritage Museum, Champaign IL

University of Michigan, Kelsey Museum of Archaeology, Ann Arbor MI

University of Missouri, Museum of Art and Archaeology, Columbia MO

Walters Art Gallery, Baltimore MD
Yale University, Art Gallery, New Haven CT

ARCHAEOLOGY

Alabama Department of Archives and History Museum, Museum Galleries, Montgomery AL
Amerind Foundation, Inc, Amerind Museum, Fulton-Hayden Memorial Art Gallery, Dragoon AZ
Anchorage Museum of History and Art, Anchorage AK
Archaeological Society of Ohio, Indian Museum of Lake County, Ohio, Painesville OH
Artesia Historical Museum & Art Center, Artesia NM
Augusta Richmond County Museum, Augusta GA
Aurora University, Schingoethe Center for Native American Cultures, Aurora IL
Bay County Historical Society, Historical Museum of Bay County, Bay City MI
Beloit College, Wright Museum of Art, Beloit WI
Canadian Museum of Civilization, Hull ON
Chelan County Public Utility District, Rocky Reach Dam, Wenatchee WA
The City of Petersburg Museums, Petersburg VA
County of Henrico, Meadow Farm Museum, Glen Allen VA
Defense Language Institute Foreign Language Center, Presidio of Monterey Historical Holding, Presidio of Monterey CA
Department of Culture & Multi-Culturalism, Provincial Museum of Alberta, Edmonton AB
Dewitt Historical Society of Tompkins County, Ithaca NY
Douglas County Historical Society, Fairlawn Mansion & Museum, Superior WI
El Paso Museum of Art, Wilderness Park Museum, El Paso TX
Emory University, Museum of Art & Archaeology, Atlanta GA
Eskimo Museum, Churchill MB
Fairfield University, Thomas J Walsh Art Gallery, Fairfield CT
Fudan Museum Foundation, Ambler PA
Greene County Historical Society, Xenia OH
Hampton University, University Museum, Hampton VA
Heard Museum, Phoenix AZ
Hebrew Union College, Skirball Museum, Los Angeles CA
Historical and Cultural Affairs, Delaware State Museums, Dover DE
Institute of the Great Plains, Museum of the Great Plains, Lawton OK
The Jewish Museum, New York NY
Johns Hopkins University, Homewood House Museum, Baltimore MD
Lakeview Museum of Arts and Sciences, Peoria IL
Louisiana State Exhibit Museum, Shreveport LA
Loveland Museum and Gallery, Loveland CO
McPherson Museum, McPherson KS
Arthur Roy Mitchell Memorial Inc, Museum of Western Art, Trinidad CO
Mohave Museum of History and Arts, Kingman AZ
Museum of New York, Rock Hill SC
Museum of Northern Arizona, Flagstaff AZ
Native American Center for the Living Arts, Niagara Falls NY
Oklahoma Historical Society, State Museum of History, Oklahoma City OK
Frank Phillips Foundation Inc, Woolaroc Museum, Bartlesville OK
Ponca City Cultural Center & Museum, Ponca City OK
Putnam Museum of History & Natural Science, Davenport IA
Redding Museum of Art & History, Redding CA
Red Rock State Park, Museum, Church Rock NM
Riverside Municipal Museum, Riverside CA
Roberts County Museum, Miami TX
Rome Historical Society Museum, Rome NY
Royal Ontario Museum, Toronto ON
Saint Augustine Historical Society, Oldest House and Museums, Saint Augustine FL
Spertus Museum, Chicago IL
State Art Museum of Florida, John & Mable Ringling Museum of Art, Sarasota FL

State Historical Society of Wisconsin, State Historical Museum, Madison WI
State Museum of Pennsylvania, Pennsylvania Historical & Museum Commission, Harrisburg PA
Tomoka State Park Museum, Fred Dana Marsh Museum, Ormond Beach FL
University of California, Los Angeles, Fowler Museum of Cultural History, Los Angeles CA
University of Illinois, World Heritage Museum, Champaign IL
University of Pennsylvania, Arthur Ross Gallery, Philadelphia PA
University of Pennsylvania, University Museum of Archaelogy & Anthropology, Philadelphia PA
University of Pennsylvania, Library, Philadelphia PA
University of Puerto Rico, Museum of Anthropology, History & Art, Rio Piedras PR
University of Tennessee, Frank H McClung Museum, Knoxville TN
Vancouver Museum Association, Vancouver Museum, Vancouver BC
Vassar College, Vassar Art Gallery, Poughkeepsie NY
Wade House & Wesley W Jung Carriage Museum, Historic House & Carriage Museum, Greenbush WI
Wayne County Historical Society, Museum, Honesdale PA
Western Kentucky University, Kentucky Museum, Bowling Green KY
Wethersfield Historical Society Inc, Wethersfield CT

ARCHITECTURE

Allentown Art Museum, Allentown PA
Artesia Historical Museum & Art Center, Artesia NM
The Art Institute of Chicago, Chicago IL
Association for the Preservation of Virginia Antiquities, John Marshall House, Richmond VA
Athenaeum of Philadelphia, Philadelphia PA
Baltimore Museum of Art, Baltimore MD
The Bartlett Museum, Amesbury MA
Beloit College, Wright Museum of Art, Beloit WI
Boston Public Library, Albert H Wiggin Gallery & Print Department, Boston MA
Cedar Rapids Museum of Art, Cedar Rapids IA
Chatillon-DeMenil House Foundation, DeMenil Mansion, Saint Louis MO
Chattahoochee Valley Art Museum, LaGrange GA
Chicago Architecture Foundation, Glessner House, Chicago IL
Church of Jesus Christ of Latter-day Saints, Museum of Church History & Art, Salt Lake City UT
CIGNA Corporation, CIGNA Museum & Art Collection, Philadelphia PA
Cincinnati Institute of Fine Arts, Taft Museum, Cincinnati OH
The City of Petersburg Museums, Petersburg VA
City of Springdale, Shiloh Museum, Springdale AR
Clemson University, Rudolph E Lee Gallery, Clemson SC
Cooper-Hewitt, National Museum of Design, New York NY
Cosanti Foundation, Scottsdale AZ
County of Henrico, Meadow Farm Museum, Glen Allen VA
Cranbrook Academy of Art Museum, Bloomfield Hills MI
Dewitt Historical Society of Tompkins County, Ithaca NY
Eccles Community Art Center, Ogden UT
Wharton Esherick Museum, Wharton Esherick Studio, Paoli PA
Federal Reserve Board, Art Gallery, Washington DC
Edsel & Eleanor Ford House, Grosse Pointe Shores MI
Fort Totten State Historic Site, Pioneer Daughters Museum, Fort Totten ND
Historical and Cultural Affairs, Delaware State Museums, Dover DE

Historical Society of Washington DC, Christian Heurich Mansion, Washington DC
Hudson River Museum, Yonkers NY
Jefferson County Open Space, Hiwan Homestead Museum, Evergreen CO
Jersey City Museum, Jersey City NJ
The Jewish Museum, New York NY
Johns Hopkins University, Homewood House Museum, Baltimore MD
Kemerer Museum of Decorative Arts, Bethlehem PA
Landmark Society of Western New York, Inc, Rochester NY
Library of Congress, Prints and Photographs Division, Washington DC
Litchfield Historical Society, Litchfield CT
Lockwood-Mathews Mansion Museum, Norwalk CT
Longfellow-Evangeline State Commemorative Area, Saint Martinville LA
Louisa May Alcott Memorial Association, Orchard House, Concord MA
Maine Historical Society, Wadsworth-Longfellow House, Portland ME
Maryland Historical Society, Museum of Maryland History, Baltimore MD
Massachusetts Institute of Technology, MIT Museum, Cambridge MA
Milwaukee Art Museum, Milwaukee WI
Mission San Luis Rey Museum, San Luis Rey CA
Arthur Roy Mitchell Memorial Inc, Museum of Western Art, Trinidad CO
Monterey Peninsula Museum of Art Association, Monterey CA
Morris-Jumel Mansion, Inc, New York NY
Munson-Williams-Proctor Institute, Museum of Art, Utica NY
Museum of Modern Art, New York NY
The National Park Service, United States Department of the Interior, The Statue of Liberty National Monument, New York NY
Nebraska State Capitol, Lincoln NE
New Haven Colony Historical Society, New Haven CT
Norfolk Historical Society Inc, Museum, Norfolk CT
North Miami Center of Contemporary Art, North Miami FL
Penobscot Marine Museum, Searsport ME
Phelps County Historical Society, Phelps County Museum, Holdrege NE
Philadelphia Museum of Art, Philadelphia PA
Purdue University Galleries, West Lafayette IN
Riley County Historical Museum, Manhattan KS
Rowland Evans Robinson Memorial Association, Rokeby Museum, Ferrisburgh VT
Royal Ontario Museum, Toronto ON
San Francisco Museum of Modern Art, San Francisco CA
Shaker Village of Pleasant Hill, Harrodsburg KY
Society for the Preservation of New England Antiquities, Archives, Boston MA
State University of New York College at Fredonia, M C Rockefeller Arts Center Gallery, Fredonia NY
Tallahassee Museum of History & Natural Science, Tallahassee FL
United States Capitol, Architect of the Capitol, Washington DC
University of California, Santa Barbara, University Art Museum, Santa Barbara CA
University of Pennsylvania, Arthur Ross Gallery, Philadelphia PA
University of Rhode Island, Fine Arts Center Galleries, Kingston RI
Vassar College, Vassar Art Gallery, Poughkeepsie NY
Wade House & Wesley W Jung Carriage Museum, Historic House & Carriage Museum, Greenbush WI
Westover, Charles City VA
Kemper & Leila Williams Foundation, New Orleans LA
Woodrow Wilson House, Washington DC
Frank Lloyd Wright Pope-Leighey House, Mount Vernon VA
York Institute Museum, Saco ME

CARPETS & RUGS

Asian Art Museum of San Francisco, Avery
  Brundage Collection, San Francisco CA
Cincinnati Institute of Fine Arts, Taft Museum,
  Cincinnati OH
Clinton County Historical Association, Clinton
  County Historical Museum, Plattsburgh NY
County of Henrico, Meadow Farm Museum, Glen
  Allen VA
Edsel & Eleanor Ford House, Grosse Pointe Shores
  MI
General Board of Discipleship, The United
  Methodist Church, The Upper Room Chapel &
  Museum, Nashville TN
Greene County Historical Society, Xenia OH
Hermitage Foundation Museum, Norfolk VA
Huntington Museum of Art, Huntington WV
Iowa State Education Association, Salisbury House,
  Des Moines IA
The Jewish Museum, New York NY
Kemerer Museum of Decorative Arts, Bethlehem
  PA
Marquette University, Haggerty Museum of Art,
  Milwaukee WI
Arthur Roy Mitchell Memorial Inc, Museum of
  Western Art, Trinidad CO
Nevada Museum Of Art, Reno NV
Pasadena Historical Society, Pasadena CA
Penobscot Marine Museum, Searsport ME
Phelps County Historical Society, Phelps County
  Museum, Holdrege NE
Portland Art Museum, Portland OR
Putnam Museum of History & Natural Science,
  Davenport IA
The Rosenbach Museum and Library, Philadelphia
  PA
George Walter Vincent Smith Art Museum,
  Springfield MA
Topeka Public Library, Gallery of Fine Arts,
  Topeka KS
US Department of State, Diplomatic Reception
  Rooms, Washington DC
University of Pennsylvania, Arthur Ross Gallery,
  Philadelphia PA
Vizcaya Museum and Gardens, Miami FL
Willard House and Clock Museum, Inc, Grafton
  MA
Woodmere Art Museum, Philadelphia PA
York Institute Museum, Saco ME

CARTOONS

Cartoon Art Museum, San Francisco CA
Hartwick College, Foreman Gallery, Oneonta NY
Herbert Hoover Presidential Library & Museum,
  West Branch IA
International Museum of Cartoon Art, Montreal PQ
The Jewish Museum, New York NY
Kansas State Historical Society, Kansas Museum of
  History, Topeka KS
National Art Museum of Sport, Indianapolis IN
State Historical Society of Missouri, Columbia MO
Syracuse University, Art Collection, Syracuse NY
United States Military Academy, West Point
  Museum, West Point NY

CERAMICS

Alabama Department of Archives and History
  Museum, Museum Galleries, Montgomery AL
Albany Institute of History and Art, Albany NY
Albion College, Bobbitt Visual Arts Center, Albion
  MI
Charles Allis Art Museum, Milwaukee WI
American Swedish Institute, Minneapolis MN
Arizona State University, University Art Museum,
  Tempe AZ
Art Institute for the Permian Basin, Odessa TX
Asian Art Museum of San Francisco, Avery
  Brundage Collection, San Francisco CA
Baldwin Historical Society Museum, Baldwin NY
Baltimore Museum of Art, Baltimore MD
Bass Museum of Art, Miami Beach FL
Berea College, Doris Ulmann Galleries, Berea KY
Boulder Historical Society Inc, Museum of History,
  Boulder CO
Brandeis University, Rose Art Museum, Waltham
  MA

Brigham City Museum-Gallery, Brigham City UT
Bradford Brinton Memorial Museum & Historic
  Ranch, Big Horn WY
Butler Institute of American Art, Art Museum,
  Youngstown OH
Calvin College, Center Art Gallery, Grand Rapids
  MI
Canadian Museum of Nature, Musee Canadien de
  la Nature, Ottawa ON
Charleston Museum, Charleston SC
Chester County Historical Society, West Chester
  PA
CIGNA Corporation, CIGNA Museum & Art
  Collection, Philadelphia PA
Cincinnati Institute of Fine Arts, Taft Museum,
  Cincinnati OH
Clay Studio, Philadelphia PA
Cleveland Museum of Art, Cleveland OH
Cleveland State University, Art Gallery, Cleveland
  OH
Clinton County Historical Association, Clinton
  County Historical Museum, Plattsburgh NY
College of Saint Benedict, Art Gallery, Saint Joseph
  MN
College of William and Mary, Joseph & Margaret
  Muscarelle Museum of Art, Williamsburg VA
Columbus Museum, Columbus GA
Columbus Museum of Art, Columbus OH
Concordia College, Marx Hausen Art Gallery,
  Seward NE
Cosanti Foundation, Scottsdale AZ
County of Henrico, Meadow Farm Museum, Glen
  Allen VA
Cranbrook Academy of Art Museum, Bloomfield
  Hills MI
Creighton University, Fine Arts Gallery, Omaha
  NE
DAR Museum, National Society Daughters of the
  American Revolution, Washington DC
East Baton Rouge Parks & Recreation Commission,
  Baton Rouge Gallery Inc, Baton Rouge LA
Erie Art Museum, Erie PA
Wharton Esherick Museum, Wharton Esherick
  Studio, Paoli PA
Everson Museum of Art, Syracuse NY
Edsel & Eleanor Ford House, Grosse Pointe Shores
  MI
Galleries of the Claremont Colleges, Claremont CA
George R Gardiner Museum of Ceramic Art,
  Toronto ON
Goucher College, Rosenberg Gallery, Towson MD
Greene County Historical Society, Xenia OH
Harrison County Historical Museum, Marshall TX
Nora Eccles Harrison Museum of Art, Logan UT
Harvard University, William Hayes Fogg Art
  Museum, Cambridge MA
Haystack Mountain School of Crafts, Gallery, Deer
  Isle ME
Historic Deerfield, Inc, Deerfield MA
Honolulu Academy of Arts, Honolulu HI
Hyde Park Art Center, Chicago IL
Idaho Historical Museum, Boise ID
Indianapolis Museum of Art, Indianapolis IN
Institute of American Indian Arts Museum, Santa
  Fe NM
Iowa State University, Brunnier Gallery Museum,
  Ames IA
Jersey City Museum, Jersey City NJ
The Jewish Museum, New York NY
Johns Hopkins University, Homewood House
  Museum, Baltimore MD
Kemerer Museum of Decorative Arts, Bethlehem
  PA
Maude I Kerns Art Center, Henry Korn Gallery,
  Eugene OR
Lemoyne Art Foundation, Inc, Tallahassee FL
Lightner Museum, Saint Augustine FL
Litchfield Historical Society, Litchfield CT
Longfellow-Evangeline State Commemorative Area,
  Saint Martinville LA
Longue Vue House and Gardens, New Orleans LA
Louisa May Alcott Memorial Association, Orchard
  House, Concord MA
Loyola Marymount University, Laband Art Gallery,
  Los Angeles CA
Charles H MacNider Museum, Mason City IA
Maine Historical Society, Wadsworth-Longfellow
  House, Portland ME

Maryland Art Place, Baltimore MD
Mercer County Community College, The Gallery,
  Trenton NJ
Arthur Roy Mitchell Memorial Inc, Museum of
  Western Art, Trinidad CO
James Monroe Museum, Fredericksburg VA
Mount Saint Vincent University, Art Gallery,
  Halifax NS
Musee d'Art de Saint-Laurent, Saint-Laurent PQ
The Museum, Greenwood SC
The Museum at Drexel University, Philadelphia PA
Museum of Art, Fort Lauderdale, Fort Lauderdale
  FL
Museum of New York, Rock Hill SC
National Museum of American History,
  Washington DC
National Museum of Women in the Arts,
  Washington DC
National Museum of Women in the Arts, Library &
  Research Center, Washington DC
Nelson-Atkins Museum of Art, Kansas City MO
Nevada Museum Of Art, Reno NV
North Central Washington Museum, Art Gallery,
  Wenatchee WA
North Miami Center of Contemporary Art, North
  Miami FL
Northwestern College, Te Paske Gallery of
  Rowenhorst, Orange City IA
Oak Ridge Art Center, Oak Ridge TN
Oglebay Institute, Mansion Museum, Wheeling WV
Old Salem Inc, Museum of Early Southern
  Decorative Arts, Winston-Salem NC
Palm Beach Community College Foundation,
  Museum of Art, Lake Worth FL
Palm Beach County Parks & Recreation
  Department, Morikami Museum & Japanese
  Gardens, Delray Beach FL
Pasadena Historical Society, Pasadena CA
Peabody & Essex Museum, Salem MA
Pennsylvania State University, Palmer Museum of
  Art, University Park PA
Penobscot Marine Museum, Searsport ME
Phelps County Historical Society, Phelps County
  Museum, Holdrege NE
Philbrook Museum of Art, Tulsa OK
Phillips County Museum, Helena AR
Portland Art Museum, Portland OR
Principia College, School of Nations Museum,
  Elsah IL
Purdue University Galleries, West Lafayette IN
Putnam Museum of History & Natural Science,
  Davenport IA
Randall Museum Junior Museum, San Francisco
  CA
Randolph-Macon Woman's College, Maier Museum
  of Art, Lynchburg VA
Redding Museum of Art & History, Redding CA
Santa Barbara Museum of Art, Santa Barbara CA
Santa Clara University, de Saisset Museum, Santa
  Clara CA
Ella Sharp Museum, Jackson MI
Shelburne Museum, Shelburne VT
Abigail Adams Smith Museum, New York NY
George Walter Vincent Smith Art Museum,
  Springfield MA
Society for the Preservation of New England
  Antiquities, Archives, Boston MA
Society of the Cincinnati, Anderson House
  Museum, Washington DC
Southern Alleghenies Museum of Art, Loretto PA
Southern Illinois University, University Museum,
  Carbondale IL
State University of New York at Geneseo, Bertha V
  B Lederer Gallery, Geneseo NY
Syracuse University, Art Collection, Syracuse NY
Toledo Museum of Art, Toledo Museum of Art,
  Toledo OH
Topeka Public Library, Gallery of Fine Arts,
  Topeka KS
Triton Museum of Art, Santa Clara CA
The Ukrainian Museum, New York NY
US Coast Guard Museum, New London CT
United States Naval Academy Museum, Annapolis
  MD
University of Akron, University Galleries, Akron
  OH
University of Colorado, Art Galleries, Boulder CO

CRAFTS

Albuquerque Museum of Art, History & Science, Albuquerque NM

American Craft Council, American Craft Museum, New York NY

Anchorage Museum of History and Art, Anchorage AK

Arizona State University, University Art Museum, Tempe AZ

Art Patrons League of Mobile, Mobile AL

Bay County Historical Society, Historical Museum of Bay County, Bay City MI

Bradford Brinton Memorial Museum & Historic Ranch, Big Horn WY

Bucks County Historical Society, Mercer Museum, Doylestown PA

Burchfield Art Center, Buffalo NY

Chinese Culture Foundation, Chinese Culture Center Gallery, San Francisco CA

CIGNA Corporation, CIGNA Museum & Art Collection, Philadelphia PA

City of Pittsfield, Berkshire Artisans, Pittsfield MA

City of Springdale, Shiloh Museum, Springdale AR

Clark County Historical Society, Pioneer - Krier Museum, Ashland KS

Cleveland State University, Art Gallery, Cleveland OH

College of Saint Benedict, Art Gallery, Saint Joseph MN

Columbus Museum, Columbus GA

Concordia Historical Institute, Saint Louis MO

Confederation Centre Art Gallery and Museum, Charlottetown PE

Contemporary Crafts Association and Gallery, Portland OR

Cosanti Foundation, Scottsdale AZ

County of Henrico, Meadow Farm Museum, Glen Allen VA

Craft and Folk Art Museum, Los Angeles CA

Dewitt Historical Society of Tompkins County, Ithaca NY

Douglas County Historical Society, Fairlawn Mansion & Museum, Superior WI

Durham Art Guild Inc, Durham NC

East Tennessee State University, Carroll Reece Museum, Johnson City TN

Enook Galleries, Waterloo ON

Wharton Esherick Museum, Wharton Esherick Studio, Paoli PA

Essex Historical Society, Essex Shipbuilding Museum, Essex MA

Evansville Museum of Arts and Science, Evansville IN

Favell Museum of Western Art & Indian Artifacts, Klamath Falls OR

Fillmore County Historical Society, Fountain MN

Georgetown College Gallery, Georgetown KY

Heritage Center of Lancaster County, Lancaster PA

Indian Arts and Crafts Board, Sioux Indian Museum, Rapid City SD

Institute of American Indian Arts Museum, Santa Fe NM

Jersey City Museum, Jersey City NJ

Maude I Kerns Art Center, Henry Korn Gallery, Eugene OR

Leelanau Historical Museum, Leland MI

Long Beach Museum of Art, Long Beach CA

Longfellow-Evangeline State Commemorative Area, Saint Martinville LA

McAllen International Museum, McAllen TX

Carrie McLain Museum, Nome AK

Maison Saint-Gabriel Museum, Montreal PQ

Mankato State University, Conkling Gallery Art Dept, Mankato MN

Marietta College, Grover M Hermann Fine Arts Center, Marietta OH

Maryland Art Place, Baltimore MD

Massillon Museum, Massillon OH

Minnesota Museum of American Art, Saint Paul MN

Arthur Roy Mitchell Memorial Inc, Museum of Western Art, Trinidad CO

Moose Jaw Art Museum and National Exhibition Centre, Art & History Museum, Moose Jaw SK

Mountain View Doukhobor Museum, Grand Forks BC

Museum of the Plains Indian & Crafts Center, Browning MT

National Museum of American Art, Renwick Gallery, Washington DC

National Museum of Women in the Arts, Washington DC

National Museum of Women in the Arts, Library & Research Center, Washington DC

New Visions Gallery, Inc, Marshfield WI

Nova Scotia Museum, Maritime Museum of the Atlantic, Halifax NS

Noyes Museum, Oceanville NJ

Oakland Museum, Art Dept, Oakland CA

Okefenokee Heritage Center, Inc, Waycross GA

Old Dartmouth Historical Society, New Bedford Whaling Museum, New Bedford MA

Palos Verdes Art Center, Rancho Palos Verdes CA

Pasadena Historical Society, Pasadena CA

Penobscot Marine Museum, Searsport ME

Phelps County Historical Society, Phelps County Museum, Holdrege NE

Principia College, School of Nations Museum, Elsah IL

Randall Museum Junior Museum, San Francisco CA

Red Rock State Park, Museum, Church Rock NM

Lauren Rogers Museum of Art, Laurel MS

San Diego State University, University Art Gallery, San Diego CA

South Carolina State Museum, Columbia SC

Southern Plains Indian Museum, Anadarko OK

Southwest Museum, Los Angeles CA

Stamford Museum and Nature Center, Stamford CT

Ukrainian Canadian Archives & Museum of Alberta, Edmonton AB

The Ukrainian Museum, New York NY

United Society of Shakers, Shaker Museum, Poland Spring ME

University of Colorado at Colorado Springs, Gallery of Contemporary Art, Colorado Springs CO

Utah Arts Council, Chase Home Museum of Utah Folk Art, Salt Lake City UT

Vermont State Craft Center at Frog Hollow, Middlebury VT

Volcano Art Center, Hawaii National Park HI

Wade House & Wesley W Jung Carriage Museum, Historic House & Carriage Museum, Greenbush WI

Worcester Center for Crafts, Worcester MA

DECORATIVE ARTS

Alabama Department of Archives and History Museum, Museum Galleries, Montgomery AL

Albuquerque Museum of Art, History & Science, Albuquerque NM

Lyman Allyn Art Museum, New London CT

Americas Society, New York NY

Ari Museum of Western Virginia, Roanoke VA

Arkansas Arts Center, Little Rock AR

Art Gallery of Greater Victoria, Victoria BC

The Art Institute of Chicago, Chicago IL

Art Patrons League of Mobile, Mobile AL

Arts and Science Center, Statesville NC

Asian Art Museum of San Francisco, Avery Brundage Collection, San Francisco CA

Association for the Preservation of Virginia Antiquities, John Marshall House, Richmond VA

Athenaeum of Philadelphia, Philadelphia PA

Atlanta Historical Society Inc, Atlanta History Center, Atlanta GA

Atlanta Museum, Atlanta GA

Augusta Richmond County Museum, Augusta GA

Baltimore Museum of Art, Baltimore MD

Bass Museum of Art, Miami Beach FL

Bay County Historical Society, Historical Museum of Bay County, Bay City MI

Bennington Museum, Bennington VT

Jesse Besser Museum, Alpena MI

Birmingham Museum of Art, Birmingham AL

Bower's Museum, Santa Ana CA

Bowne House Historical Society, Flushing NY

Bradford Brinton Memorial Museum & Historic Ranch, Big Horn WY

Brooklyn Historical Society, Brooklyn NY

Canton Art Institute, Canton OH

Carnegie Institute, Carnegie Museum of Art, Pittsburgh PA

Charleston Museum, Charleston SC

Chatillon-DeMenil House Foundation, DeMenil Mansion, Saint Louis MO

Cheekwood-Tennessee Botanical Gardens & Museum of Art, Nashville TN

Chicago Historical Society, Chicago IL

Church of Jesus Christ of Latter-day Saints, Museum of Church History & Art, Salt Lake City UT

CIGNA Corporation, CIGNA Museum & Art Collection, Philadelphia PA

Cincinnati Institute of Fine Arts, Taft Museum, Cincinnati OH

Cincinnati Museum Association, Cincinnati Art Museum, Cincinnati OH

City of Holyoke Museum-Wistariahurst, Holyoke MA

The City of Petersburg Museums, Petersburg VA

Cleveland Museum of Art, Cleveland OH

Clinton County Historical Association, Clinton County Historical Museum, Plattsburgh NY

College of William and Mary, Joseph & Margaret Muscarelle Museum of Art, Williamsburg VA

Colonial Williamsburg Foundation, DeWitt Wallace Decorative Arts Gallery, Williamsburg VA

Columbia County Historical Society, Columbia County Museum, Kinderhook NY

Columbia Museum of Art, Columbia SC

Columbus Museum, Columbus GA

Cooper-Hewitt, National Museum of Design, New York NY

County of Henrico, Meadow Farm Museum, Glen Allen VA

Cranbrook Academy of Art Museum, Bloomfield Hills MI

Crocker Art Museum, Sacramento CA

Cummer Gallery of Art, DeEtte Holden Cummer Museum Foundation, Jacksonville FL

The Currier Gallery of Art, Manchester NH

Delaware Art Museum, Wilmington DE

Detroit Institute of Arts, Detroit MI

Dewitt Historical Society of Tompkins County, Ithaca NY

The Dixon Gallery & Gardens, Memphis TN

Douglas County Historical Society, Fairlawn Mansion & Museum, Superior WI

Ellis County Museum Inc, Waxahachie TX

El Paso Museum of Art, El Paso TX

Wharton Esherick Museum, Wharton Esherick Studio, Paoli PA

Essex Historical Society, Essex Shipbuilding Museum, Essex MA

Evansville Museum of Arts and Science, Evansville IN

Fall River Historical Society, Fall River MA

Farmington Village Green and Library Association, Stanley-Whitman House, Farmington CT

William A Farnsworth Library and Art Museum, Rockland ME

Fetherston Foundation, Packwood House Museum, Lewisburg PA

Fine Arts Museums of San Francisco, M H de Young Memorial Museum and California Palace of the Legion of Honor, San Francisco CA

Flint Institute of Arts, Flint MI

Edsel & Eleanor Ford House, Grosse Pointe Shores MI

Galleries of the Claremont Colleges, Claremont CA

Getty Center for the History of Art & the Humanities Trust Museum, Santa Monica CA

Getty Center for the History of Art & the Humanities Trust Museum, The J Paul Getty Museum, Santa Monica CA

Girard College, Stephen Girard Collection, Philadelphia PA

Grand Rapids Art Museum, Grand Rapids MI

Greene County Historical Society, Xenia OH

Gunston Hall Plantation, Lorton VA

Harvard University, Dumbarton Oaks Research Library and Collections, Washington DC

Harvard University, William Hayes Fogg Art Museum, Cambridge MA

Heritage Center of Lancaster County, Lancaster PA

Hermitage Foundation Museum, Norfolk VA

Hershey Museum, Hershey PA

Hinckley Foundation Museum, Ithaca NY

Hispanic Society of America, Museum, New York NY

Westmoreland Museum of Art, Greensburg PA
Wheaton College, Watson Gallery, Norton MA
Willard House and Clock Museum, Inc, Grafton MA
Williams College, Museum of Art, Williamstown MA
Woodrow Wilson House, Washington DC
Winterthur Museum and Gardens, Winterthur DE
Leigh Yawkey Woodson Art Museum, Inc, Wausau WI
Workman & Temple Family Homestead Museum, City of Industry CA
Wyoming State Museum, State Art Gallery, Cheyenne WY
York Institute Museum, Saco ME

DIORAMAS

Anchorage Museum of History and Art, Anchorage AK
The Bartlett Museum, Amesbury MA
CIGNA Corporation, CIGNA Museum & Art Collection, Philadelphia PA
Clinton County Historical Association, Clinton County Historical Museum, Plattsburgh NY
Defense Language Institute Foreign Language Center, Presidio of Monterey Historical Holding, Presidio of Monterey CA
Essex Historical Society, Essex Shipbuilding Museum, Essex MA
Loveland Museum and Gallery, Loveland CO
Maricopa County Historical Society, Desert Caballeros Western Museum, Wickenburg AZ
Museum of New York, Rock Hill SC
Penobscot Marine Museum, Searsport ME
Roberts County Museum, Miami TX
Will Rogers Memorial and Museum, Media Center Library, Claremore OK
Safety Harbor Museum of Regional History, Safety Harbor FL
Trotting Horse Museum, Goshen NY
United States Military Academy, West Point Museum, West Point NY
West Baton Rouge Historical Association, Museum, Port Allen LA
Zigler Museum, Jennings LA

DOLLS

Lyman Allyn Art Museum, New London CT
Anchorage Museum of History and Art, Anchorage AK
Arts and Science Center, Statesville NC
Atlanta Historical Society Inc, Atlanta History Center, Atlanta GA
Bennington Museum, Bennington VT
Brooklyn Historical Society, Brooklyn OH
Cambria Historical Society, New Providence NJ
Carnegie Institute, Carnegie Museum of Art, Pittsburgh PA
City of Springdale, Shiloh Museum, Springdale AR
Clinton County Historical Association, Clinton County Historical Museum, Plattsburgh NY
Dartmouth Heritage Museum, Dartmouth NS
Fillmore County Historical Society, Fountain MN
Houston Museum of Decorative Arts, Chattanooga TN
Iowa State University, Brunnier Gallery Museum, Ames IA
Jersey City Museum, Jersey City NJ
Kemerer Museum of Decorative Arts, Bethlehem PA
Maude I Kerns Art Center, Henry Korn Gallery, Eugene OR
Livingston County Historical Society, Cobblestone Museum, Geneseo NY
Longfellow-Evangeline State Commemorative Area, Saint Martinville LA
Luna County Historical Society, Inc, Deming Luna Mimbres Museum, Deming NM
MonDak Heritage Center, Sidney MT
The Museums at Stony Brook, Stony Brook NY
Oregon State University, Horner Museum, Corvallis OR
Palm Beach County Parks & Recreation Department, Morikami Museum & Japanese Gardens, Delray Beach FL
Pasadena Historical Society, Pasadena CA

Peabody & Essex Museum, Salem MA
Penobscot Marine Museum, Searsport ME
Phelps County Historical Society, Phelps County Museum, Holdrege NE
Presidential Museum, Odessa TX
Principia College, School of Nations Museum, Elsah IL
Putnam Museum of History & Natural Science, Davenport IA
Rhode Island Historical Society, John Brown House, Providence RI
Riley County Historical Museum, Manhattan KS
Roberts County Museum, Miami TX
Santa Barbara Museum of Art, Santa Barbara CA
Shelburne Museum, Shelburne VT
University of Mississippi, University Museums, Oxford MS
Willard House and Clock Museum, Inc, Grafton MA

DRAWINGS

The Albrecht-Kemper Museum of Art, Saint Joseph MO
American University, Watkins Collectiony, Washington DC
Arkansas Arts Center, Little Rock AR
Art Gallery of Nova Scotia, Halifax NS
Art Institute for the Permian Basin, Odessa TX
The Art Institute of Chicago, Chicago IL
Art Museum of the Americas, Washington DC
Arts and Science Center, Statesville NC
Leo Baeck Institute, New York NY
Baldwin-Wallace College, Fawick Art Gallery, Berea OH
Ball State University, Museum of Art, Muncie IN
Baltimore Museum of Art, Baltimore MD
Baylor University, Martin Museum of Art, Waco TX
Beaverbrook Art Gallery, Fredericton NB
Roy Boyd Gallery, Chicago IL
Brigham Young University, B F Larsen Gallery, Provo UT
Brooklyn Historical Society, Brooklyn NY
Brown University, David Winton Bell Gallery, Providence RI
The Buffalo Fine Arts Academy, Albright-Knox Art Gallery, Buffalo NY
Butler Institute of American Art, Art Museum, Youngstown OH
California Historical Society, El Molino Viejo, San Marino CA
California State University Stanislaus, University Art Gallery, Turlock CA
Calvin College, Center Art Gallery, Grand Rapids MI
Canadian Museum of Nature, Musee Canadien de la Nature, Ottawa ON
Carnegie Institute, Carnegie Museum of Art, Pittsburgh PA
Cedar Rapids Museum of Art, Cedar Rapids IA
CIGNA Corporation, CIGNA Museum & Art Collection, Philadelphia PA
Cincinnati Museum Association, Cincinnati Art Museum, Cincinnati OH
City of Pittsfield, Berkshire Artisans, Pittsfield MA
Sterling and Francine Clark Art Institute, Williamstown MA
Cleveland State University, Art Gallery, Cleveland OH
Clinton County Historical Association, Clinton County Historical Museum, Plattsburgh NY
College of Saint Benedict, Art Gallery, Saint Joseph MN
College of William and Mary, Joseph & Margaret Muscarelle Museum of Art, Williamsburg VA
Colorado Springs Fine Arts Center, Colorado Springs CO
Columbus Museum of Art, Columbus OH
Concordia University, Leonard & Bina Ellen Art Gallery, Montreal PQ
Cooper-Hewitt, National Museum of Design, New York NY
Corcoran Gallery of Art, Washington DC
Cornell University, Herbert F Johnson Museum of Art, Ithaca NY
Creighton University, Fine Arts Gallery, Omaha NE

Del Mar College, Joseph A Cain Memorial Art Gallery, Corpus Christi TX
Wharton Esherick Museum, Wharton Esherick Studio, Paoli PA
Essex Historical Society, Essex Shipbuilding Museum, Essex MA
Fayette Art Museum, Fayette AL
Federal Reserve Board, Art Gallery, Washington DC
Fitchburg Art Museum, Fitchburg MA
Edsel & Eleanor Ford House, Grosse Pointe Shores MI
Fort Hays State University, Moss-Thorns Gallery of Arts, Hays KS
Frick Collection, New York NY
Getty Center for the History of Art & the Humanities Trust Museum, Santa Monica CA
Getty Center for the History of Art & the Humanities Trust Museum, The J Paul Getty Museum, Santa Monica CA
Goucher College, Rosenberg Gallery, Towson MD
Grand Rapids Art Museum, Grand Rapids MI
Greenville College, Richard W Bock Sculpture Collection, Greenville IL
Grinnell College, Print & Drawing Study Room/ Gallery, Grinnell IA
Solomon R Guggenheim Museum, New York NY
Hamilton College, Fred L Emerson Gallery, Clinton NY
Hampton University, University Museum, Hampton VA
Hartwick College, Foreman Gallery, Oneonta NY
Harvard University, William Hayes Fogg Art Museum, Cambridge MA
Heckscher Museum, Huntington NY
Housatonic Community College, Housatonic Museum of Art, Bridgeport CT
Hyde Park Art Center, Chicago IL
Illinois Wesleyan University, Merwin & Wakeley Galleries, Bloomington IL
Indianapolis Museum of Art, Indianapolis IN
Indiana University, Art Museum, Bloomington IN
International Museum of Cartoon Art, Montreal PQ
Jersey City Museum, Jersey City NJ
The Jewish Museum, New York NY
Kalamazoo Institute of Arts, Kalamazoo MI
Kemerer Museum of Decorative Arts, Bethlehem PA
Maude I Kerns Art Center, Henry Korn Gallery, Eugene OR
Kitchener-Waterloo Art Gallery, Kitchener ON
La Salle University, Art Museum, Philadelphia PA
Liberty Memorial Museum & Archives, Kansas City MO
Library of Congress, Prints and Photographs Division, Washington DC
Litchfield Historical Society, Litchfield CT
Long Beach Museum of Art, Long Beach CA
Los Angeles County Museum of Art, Los Angeles CA
Louisiana State University, Museum of Arts, Baton Rouge LA
The Robert McLaughlin Gallery, Oshawa ON
McMaster University, Art Gallery, Hamilton ON
Madison Art Center, Madison WI
Mankato State University, Conkling Gallery Art Dept, Mankato MN
Maryland Art Place, Baltimore MD
Massachusetts Institute of Technology, List Visual Arts Center, Cambridge MA
Meridian Museum of Art, Meridian MS
The Metropolitan Museum of Art, New York NY
MEXIC-ARTE Museum, Austin TX
James A Michener Arts Center, Doylestown PA
Middlebury College, Museum of Art, Middlebury VT
Millikin University, Perkinson Gallery, Decatur IL
Mills College, Art Gallery, Oakland CA
Minneapolis Society of Fine Arts, Minneapolis Institute of Arts, Minneapolis MN
Minnesota Museum of American Art, Saint Paul MN
Mississippi University for Women, Fine Arts Gallery, Columbus MS
Mobil Corporation, Art Collection, Fairfax VA
Montclair Art Museum, Montclair NJ
Morris Communications Corporation, Morris Museum of Art, Augusta GA

Mount Holyoke College, Art Museum, South Hadley MA
Munson-Williams-Proctor Institute, Museum of Art, Utica NY
Murray State University, Eagle Gallery, Murray KY
Museum of Arts and Sciences, Inc, Macon GA
Museum of Modern Art, New York NY
National Air and Space Museum, Washington DC
National Art Museum of Sport, Indianapolis IN
National Museum of American Art, Washington DC
National Museum of Women in the Arts, Library & Research Center, Washington DC
Nevada Museum Of Art, Reno NV
New Mexico State University, University Art Gallery, Las Cruces NM
The John A Noble Collection, Staten Island NY
North Miami Center of Contemporary Art, North Miami FL
Noyes Museum, Oceanville NJ
Oakland Museum, Art Dept, Oakland CA
Oak Ridge Art Center, Oak Ridge TN
Oklahoma City Art Museum, Oklahoma City OK
Olana State Historic Site, Hudson NY
Owensboro Museum of Fine Art, Owensboro KY
Pennsylvania Academy of the Fine Arts, Galleries, Philadelphia PA
Pennsylvania State University, Palmer Museum of Art, University Park PA
Penobscot Marine Museum, Searsport ME
Phillips Academy, Addison Gallery of American Art, Andover MA
Plains Art Museum, Moorhead MN
Portland Art Museum, Portland OR
Potsdam College of the State University of New York, Roland Gibson Gallery, Potsdam NY
Print Club of Albany, Museum, Albany NY
Putnam Museum of History & Natural Science, Davenport IA
Quincy University, The Gray Gallery, Quincy IL
Randall Museum Junior Museum, San Francisco CA
Randolph-Macon Woman's College, Maier Museum of Art, Lynchburg VA
Walter Cecil Rawls Museum, Courtland VA
Roberson Museum & Science Center, Binghamton NY
The Rosenbach Museum and Library, Philadelphia PA
The Saint Louis Art Museum, Saint Louis MO
San Jose Museum of Art, San Jose CA
Santa Barbara Museum of Art, Santa Barbara CA
SLA Arch-Couture Inc, Art Collection, Denver CO
Smith College, Museum of Art, Northampton MA
Southern Alleghenies Museum of Art, Loretto PA
Southern Illinois University, University Museum, Carbondale IL
Springfield Art Museum, Springfield MO
State Art Museum of Florida, John & Mable Ringling Museum of Art, Sarasota FL
State University of New York at Albany, University Art Gallery, Albany NY
State University of New York at Purchase, Neuberger Museum, Purchase NY
Syracuse University, Art Collection, Syracuse NY
3M, Art Collection, Saint Paul MN
Trenton State College, College Art Gallery, Trenton NJ
Tulane University, University Art Collection, New Orleans LA
The Ukrainian Museum, New York NY
Ulster County Community College, Muroff-Kotler Visual Arts Gallery, Stone Ridge NY
US Coast Guard Museum, New London CT
United States Military Academy, West Point Museum, West Point NY
United States Naval Academy Museum, Annapolis MD
University of Calgary, The Nickle Arts Museum, Calgary AB
University of Chicago, David and Alfred Smart Museum of Art, Chicago IL
University of Colorado, Art Galleries, Boulder CO
University of Colorado at Colorado Springs, Gallery of Contemporary Art, Colorado Springs CO
University of Delaware, University Gallery, Newark DE

University of Georgia, Georgia Museum of Art, Athens GA
University of Illinois, Krannert Art Museum, Champaign IL
University of Iowa, Museum of Art, Iowa City IA
University of Louisville, Allen R Hite Art Institute Gallery, Louisville KY
University of Massachusetts, Amherst, University Gallery, Amherst MA
University of Minnesota, University Art Museum, Minneapolis MN
University of Mississippi, University Museums, Oxford MS
University of Missouri, Museum of Art and Archaeology, Columbia MO
University of Nebraska, Lincoln, Sheldon Memorial Art Gallery, Lincoln NE
University of New Hampshire, The Art Gallery, Durham NH
University of New Mexico, University Art Museum, Albuquerque NM
University of North Carolina at Greensboro, Weatherspoon Art Gallery, Greensboro NC
University of Notre Dame, Snite Museum of Art, Notre Dame IN
University of Pennsylvania, Arthur Ross Gallery, Philadelphia PA
University of Pittsburgh, University Art Gallery, Pittsburgh PA
University of Rhode Island, Fine Arts Center Galleries, Kingston RI
University of Southern Colorado, College of Liberal & Fine Arts, Pueblo CO
University of South Florida, Contemporary Art Museum, Tampa FL
University of Texas at Austin, Archer M Huntington Art Gallery, Austin TX
University of Vermont, Robert Hull Fleming Museum, Burlington VT
University of Washington, Henry Art Gallery, Seattle WA
University of Wisconsin Oshkosh, Allen R Priebe Gallery, Oshkosh WI
University of Wisconsin-Stout, J Furlong Gallery, Menomonie WI
Valparaiso University, Museum of Art, Valparaiso IN
Vassar College, Vassar Art Gallery, Poughkeepsie NY
Walker Art Center, Minneapolis MN
Washington County Museum of Fine Arts, Hagerstown MD
Waterworks Visual Arts Center, Salisbury NC
Westminster College, Art Gallery, New Wilmington PA
Wheaton College, Watson Gallery, Norton MA
Whitney Museum of American Art, New York NY
Wichita Art Museum, Wichita KS
Kemper & Leila Williams Foundation, New Orleans LA

EMBROIDERY

Art Institute for the Permian Basin, Odessa TX
Asian Art Museum of San Francisco, Avery Brundage Collection, San Francisco CA
Baltimore Museum of Art, Baltimore MD
The City of Petersburg Museums, Petersburg VA
Clinton County Historical Association, Clinton County Historical Museum, Plattsburgh NY
County of Henrico, Meadow Farm Museum, Glen Allen VA
Fillmore County Historical Society, Fountain MN
Historic Deerfield, Inc, Deerfield MA
The Jewish Museum, New York NY
Kemerer Museum of Decorative Arts, Bethlehem PA
Maude I Kerns Art Center, Henry Korn Gallery, Eugene OR
Litchfield Historical Society, Litchfield CT
Longfellow-Evangeline State Commemorative Area, Saint Martinville LA
Maine Historical Society, Wadsworth-Longfellow House, Portland ME
Mountain View Doukhobor Museum, Grand Forks BC
National Museum of Women in the Arts, Library & Research Center, Washington DC

Pasadena Historical Society, Pasadena CA
Penobscot Marine Museum, Searsport ME
Phelps County Historical Society, Phelps County Museum, Holdrege NE
Putnam Museum of History & Natural Science, Davenport IA
The Ukrainian Museum, New York NY
Ukrainian National Museum and Library, Chicago IL
West Baton Rouge Historical Association, Museum, Port Allen LA

ENAMELS

Asian Art Museum of San Francisco, Avery Brundage Collection, San Francisco CA
Loyola University of Chicago, Martin D'Arcy Gallery of Art, Chicago IL
USS Constitution Museum Foundation Inc, Boston National Historical Park, Museum, Boston MA

ESKIMO ART

Alaska State Museum, Juneau AK
Anchorage Museum of History and Art, Anchorage AK
Archaeological Society of Ohio, Indian Museum of Lake County, Ohio, Painesville OH
Art Gallery of Hamilton, Hamilton ON
Aurora University, Schingoethe Center for Native American Cultures, Aurora IL
Bowdoin College, Peary-MacMillan Arctic Museum, Brunswick ME
Brevard Art Center and Museum, Inc, Melbourne FL
Chilkat Valley Historical Society, Sheldon Museum & Cultural Center, Haines AK
CIGNA Corporation, CIGNA Museum & Art Collection, Philadelphia PA
College of William and Mary, Joseph & Margaret Muscarelle Museum of Art, Williamsburg VA
Eskimo Museum, Churchill MB
Genesee Country Museum, John L Wehle Gallery of Sporting Art, Mumford NY
Heritage Center, Inc, Pine Ridge SD
Johnson-Humrickhouse Museum, Coshocton OH
Kendall Whaling Museum, Sharon MA
Louisiana Arts and Science Center, Baton Rouge LA
Luna County Historical Society, Inc, Deming Luna Mimbres Museum, Deming NM
MacDonald Stewart Art Centre Art Center, Guelph ON
Carrie McLain Museum, Nome AK
Maryhill Museum of Art, Goldendale WA
Moravian Historical Society, Whitefield House Museum, Nazareth PA
National Art Museum of Sport, Indianapolis IN
Portland Art Museum, Portland OR
Science Museums of Charlotte, Inc, Discovery Place, Charlotte NC
Sheldon Jackson Museum, Sitka AK
US Coast Guard Museum, New London CT
United States Department of the Interior Museum, Washington DC
United States Tobacco Manufacturing Company Inc, Museum of Tobacco & History, Nashville TN
University of Delaware, University Gallery, Newark DE
University of Michigan, Museum of Art, Ann Arbor MI
Vancouver Museum Association, Vancouver Museum, Vancouver BC
Winnipeg Art Gallery, Winnipeg MB
York University, Art Gallery of York University, North York ON
Yugtarvik Regional Museum & Bethel Visitors Center, Bethel AK

ETCHINGS & ENGRAVINGS

The Albrecht-Kemper Museum of Art, Saint Joseph MO
American University, Watkins Collectiony, Washington DC
Art Gallery of Hamilton, Hamilton ON
Art Institute for the Permian Basin, Odessa TX

Baldwin Historical Society Museum, Baldwin NY

Brown University, David Winton Bell Gallery, Providence RI

Cedar Rapids Museum of Art, Cedar Rapids IA

CIGNA Corporation, CIGNA Museum & Art Collection, Philadelphia PA

Cleveland State University, Art Gallery, Cleveland OH

Clinton Art Association Gallery, Clinton IA

College of William and Mary, Joseph & Margaret Muscarelle Museum of Art, Williamsburg VA

Concordia Historical Institute, Saint Louis MO

Concordia University, Leonard & Bina Ellen Art Gallery, Montreal PQ

Delaware Art Museum, Wilmington DE

Durham Art Guild Inc, Durham NC

East Baton Rouge Parks & Recreation Commission, Baton Rouge Gallery Inc, Baton Rouge LA

Federal Reserve Board, Art Gallery, Washington DC

Edsel & Eleanor Ford House, Grosse Pointe Shores MI

Galleries of the Claremont Colleges, Claremont CA

Grinnell College, Print & Drawing Study Room/ Gallery, Grinnell IA

Hamilton College, Fred L Emerson Gallery, Clinton NY

Jersey City Museum, Jersey City NJ

The Jewish Museum, New York NY

Maude I Kerns Art Center, Henry Korn Gallery, Eugene OR

Lincoln National Life Insurance Co, Lincoln Museum, Fort Wayne IN

Lockwood-Mathews Mansion Museum, Norwalk CT

Charles H MacNider Museum, Mason City IA

Marcella Sembrich Memorial Association Inc, Opera Museum, Bolton Landing NY

Maryhill Museum of Art, Goldendale WA

Mary Washington College, The Gari Melchers Estate & Memorial Gallery, Fredericksburg VA

Michelson-Reves Museum of Art, Marshall TX

Mohawk Valley Heritage Association, Inc, Walter Elwood Museum, Amsterdam NY

Murray State University, Eagle Gallery, Murray KY

National Art Museum of Sport, Indianapolis IN

National Museum of Women in the Arts, Washington DC

National Museum of Women in the Arts, Library & Research Center, Washington DC

Nevada Museum Of Art, Reno NV

New Haven Colony Historical Society, New Haven CT

New Mexico State University, University Art Gallery, Las Cruces NM

New Visions Gallery, Inc, Marshfield WI

Northern Illinois University, NIU Art Museum, De Kalb IL

North Miami Center of Contemporary Art, North Miami FL

Northwestern College, Te Paske Gallery of Rowenhorst, Orange City IA

Oklahoma City Art Museum, Oklahoma City OK

The Parrish Art Museum, Southampton NY

Philadelphia Sketch Club, Inc, Philadelphia PA

Portland Art Museum, Portland OR

Print Club of Albany, Museum, Albany NY

Provincetown Art Association and Museum, Provincetown MA

Randolph-Macon Woman's College, Maier Museum of Art, Lynchburg VA

The Rockwell Museum, Corning NY

Saint Gregory's Abbey and College, Mabee-Gerrer Museum of Art, Shawnee OK

SLA Arch-Couture Inc, Art Collection, Denver CO

State Capitol Museum, Olympia WA

Syracuse University, Art Collection, Syracuse NY

The Ukrainian Museum, New York NY

US Coast Guard Museum, New London CT

United States Military Academy, West Point Museum, West Point NY

University of Colorado at Colorado Springs, Gallery of Contemporary Art, Colorado Springs CO

University of Delaware, University Gallery, Newark DE

University of New Hampshire, The Art Gallery, Durham NH

University of Pennsylvania, Arthur Ross Gallery, Philadelphia PA

Ursinus College, Philip & Muriel Berman Museum of Art, Collegeville PA

Vassar College, Vassar Art Gallery, Poughkeepsie NY

Wichita State University, Edwin A Ulrich Museum of Art, Wichita KS

Winterthur Museum and Gardens, Winterthur DE

ETHNOLOGY

Amerind Foundation, Inc, Amerind Museum, Fulton-Hayden Memorial Art Gallery, Dragoon AZ

Aurora University, Schingoethe Center for Native American Cultures, Aurora IL

Bowdoin College, Peary-MacMillan Arctic Museum, Brunswick ME

Canadian Museum of Civilization, Hull ON

Centenary College of Louisiana, Meadows Museum of Art, Shreveport LA

Chief Plenty Coups Museum, Pryor MT

Chilkat Valley Historical Society, Sheldon Museum & Cultural Center, Haines AK

Dawson City Museum & Historical Society, Dawson City YT

Department of Culture & Multi-Culturalism, Provincial Museum of Alberta, Edmonton AB

Dewitt Historical Society of Tompkins County, Ithaca NY

Eskimo Museum, Churchill MB

Institute of the Great Plains, Museum of the Great Plains, Lawton OK

Kenosha Public Museum, Kenosha WI

Loyola Marymount University, Laband Art Gallery, Los Angeles CA

McCord Museum of Canadian History, Montreal PQ

Mohave Museum of History and Arts, Kingman AZ

Museum of New York, Rock Hill SC

The National Park Service, United States Department of the Interior, The Statue of Liberty National Monument, New York NY

Newburyport Maritime Society, Custom House Maritime Museum, Newburyport MA

New York State Museum, Albany NY

Oklahoma Historical Society, State Museum of History, Oklahoma City OK

Queen's University, Agnes Etherington Art Centre, Kingston ON

Red Rock State Park, Museum, Church Rock NM

Riverside Municipal Museum, Riverside CA

Shelburne Museum, Shelburne VT

Sheldon Jackson Museum, Sitka AK

Spertus Museum, Chicago IL

The Ukrainian Museum, New York NY

University of Alaska, Museum, Fairbanks AK

University of Pennsylvania, University Museum of Archaelogy & Anthropology, Philadelphia PA

University of Vermont, Robert Hull Fleming Museum, Burlington VT

FOLK ART

Albuquerque Museum of Art, History & Science, Albuquerque NM

Ari Museum of Western Virginia, Roanoke VA

Art Institute for the Permian Basin, Odessa TX

Arts and Science Center, Statesville NC

Aurora University, Schingoethe Center for Native American Cultures, Aurora IL

Balzekas Museum of Lithuanian Culture, Chicago IL

Brigham City Museum-Gallery, Brigham City UT

Bucks County Historical Society, Mercer Museum, Doylestown PA

Canadian Museum of Civilization, Hull ON

Cardinal Stritch College, Layton Honor Gallery, Milwaukee WI

Center for Puppetry Arts, Atlanta GA

Chattahoochee Valley Art Museum, LaGrange GA

Chicano Humanities & Arts Council, Denver CO

Church of Jesus Christ of Latter-day Saints, Museum of Church History & Art, Salt Lake City UT

City of Springdale, Shiloh Museum, Springdale AR

Cleveland State University, Art Gallery, Cleveland OH

Colonial Williamsburg Foundation, Abby Aldrich Rockefeller Folk Art Center, Williamsburg VA

Columbus Museum, Columbus GA

Continental Bank Corporation, Art Collection, Chicago IL

Cortland County Historical Society, Suggett House Museum, Cortland NY

County of Henrico, Meadow Farm Museum, Glen Allen VA

Craft and Folk Art Museum, Los Angeles CA

Douglas County Historical Society, Fairlawn Mansion & Museum, Superior WI

East Carolina University, Wellington B Gray Gallery, Greenville NC

Eastern Illinois University, Tarble Arts Center, Charleston IL

Enook Galleries, Waterloo ON

Essex Historical Society, Essex Shipbuilding Museum, Essex MA

Everhart Museum, Scranton PA

Fayette Art Museum, Fayette AL

Frostburg State University, The Stephanie Ann Roper Gallery, Frostburg MD

Galeria de la Raza, Studio 24, San Francisco CA

Genesee Country Museum, John L Wehle Gallery of Sporting Art, Mumford NY

Halifax Historical Society, Inc, Halifax Historical Museum, Daytona Beach FL

Heritage Center, Inc, Pine Ridge SD

Heritage Plantation of Sandwich, Sandwich MA

High Point Historical Society Inc, Museum, High Point NC

Hinckley Foundation Museum, Ithaca NY

Historical Society of York County, York PA

Hyde Park Art Center, Chicago IL

Illinois State Museum, Illinois Art Gallery & Lockport Gallery, Springfield IL

Illinois State Museum, State of Illinois Art Gallery, Chicago IL

Indiana University, William Hammond Mathers Museum, Bloomington IN

Jamestown-Yorktown Foundation, Yorktown VA

Jefferson County Open Space, Hiwan Homestead Museum, Evergreen CO

Jersey City Museum, Jersey City NJ

Kemerer Museum of Decorative Arts, Bethlehem PA

Key West Art and Historical Society, East Martello Museum and Gallery, Key West FL

Kiah Museum, Savannah GA

Leelanau Historical Museum, Leland MI

Louisa May Alcott Memorial Association, Orchard House, Concord MA

Loyola Marymount University, Laband Art Gallery, Los Angeles CA

Luna County Historical Society, Inc, Deming Luna Mimbres Museum, Deming NM

McAllen International Museum, McAllen TX

McCord Museum of Canadian History, Montreal PQ

Mercer County Community College, The Gallery, Trenton NJ

Mexican Fine Arts Center Museum, Chicago IL

Mexican Museum, San Francisco CA

Miami University Art Museum, Oxford OH

Milwaukee Public Museum, Milwaukee WI

Mingei International, Inc, Mingei International Museum of World Folk Art, San Diego CA

Monterey Peninsula Museum of Art Association, Monterey CA

Moravian Historical Society, Whitefield House Museum, Nazareth PA

Morris Communications Corporation, Morris Museum of Art, Augusta GA

Musee d'Art de Saint-Laurent, Saint-Laurent PQ

Museum of American Folk Art, New York NY

Museum of New Mexico, Museum of International Folk Art, Santa Fe NM

Museum of the Americas, Brookfield VT

The National Park Service, United States Department of the Interior, The Statue of Liberty National Monument, New York NY

New York State Historical Association, Fenimore House, Cooperstown NY

Northern Kentucky University Gallery, Highland Heights KY

North Miami Center of Contemporary Art, North Miami FL

Norwich Free Academy, Slater Memorial Museum & Converse Art Gallery, Norwich CT

Oatlands, Inc, Leesburg VA

Olana State Historic Site, Hudson NY

Old Colony Historical Society, Museum, Taunton MA

Old Dartmouth Historical Society, New Bedford Whaling Museum, New Bedford MA

Old Jail Art Center, Albany TX

Old Salem Inc, Museum of Early Southern Decorative Arts, Winston-Salem NC

Old York Historical Society, Gaol Museum, York ME

Oysterponds Historical Society, Museum, Orient NY

Pasadena Historical Society, Pasadena CA

Patterson Homestead, Dayton OH

Peabody & Essex Museum, Salem MA

Philadelphia Museum of Art, Philadelphia PA

Philbrook Museum of Art, Tulsa OK

Pilgrim Society, Pilgrim Hall Museum, Plymouth MA

Marjorie Merriweather Post Foundation of DC, Hillwood Museum, Washington DC

Putnam County Historical Society, Foundry School Museum, Cold Spring NY

Putnam Museum of History & Natural Science, Davenport IA

Quapaw Quarter Association, Inc, Villa Marre, Little Rock AR

Frederic Remington Art Museum, Ogdensburg NY

Rhode Island School of Design, Museum of Art, Providence RI

Riley County Historical Museum, Manhattan KS

Roberson Museum & Science Center, Binghamton NY

Roberts County Museum, Miami TX

Rowland Evans Robinson Memorial Association, Rokeby Museum, Ferrisburgh VT

Rock Ford Foundation, Inc, Rock Ford Plantation & Kauffman Museum, Lancaster PA

Saint Louis County Historical Society, Duluth MN

Salem Art Association, Bush House, Salem OR

San Diego Museum of Art, San Diego CA

Santa Clara University, de Saisset Museum, Santa Clara CA

Shaker Village of Pleasant Hill, Harrodsburg KY

Ella Sharp Museum, Jackson MI

Shirley Plantation, Charles City VA

Abigail Adams Smith Museum, New York NY

Society of the Cincinnati, Anderson House Museum, Washington DC

Springfield Library & Museums Association, Connecticut Valley Historical Museum, Springfield MA

T C Steele State Historic Site, Nashville IN

Summit County Historical Society, Akron OH

United Society of Shakers, Shaker Museum, Poland Spring ME

US Department of State, Diplomatic Reception Rooms, Washington DC

University of Montana, Paxson Gallery, Missoula MT

University of San Diego, Founders' Gallery, San Diego CA

University of Tampa, Henry B Plant Museum, Tampa FL

University of Tennessee, Frank H McClung Museum, Knoxville TN

University of Tennessee, Eleanor Dean Audigier Art Collection, Knoxville TN

University of Utah, Utah Museum of Fine Arts, Salt Lake City UT

University of Wisconsin-Madison, Elvehjem Museum of Art, Madison WI

Van Cortlandt Mansion & Museum, Bronx NY

Vermilion County Museum Society, Danville IL

Virginia Museum of Fine Arts, Richmond VA

Vizcaya Museum and Gardens, Miami FL

Wade House & Wesley W Jung Carriage Museum, Historic House & Carriage Museum, Greenbush WI

Wayne County Historical Society, Museum, Honesdale PA

Western Kentucky University, Kentucky Museum, Bowling Green KY

Wethersfield Historical Society Inc, Wethersfield CT

White House, Washington DC

Willard House and Clock Museum, Inc, Grafton MA

Woodrow Wilson House, Washington DC

Winterthur Museum and Gardens, Winterthur DE

Woodmere Art Museum, Philadelphia PA

Workman & Temple Family Homestead Museum, City of Industry CA

York Institute Museum, Saco ME

GLASS

Academy of the New Church, Glencairn Museum, Bryn Athyn PA

Albany Institute of History and Art, Albany NY

Albion College, Bobbitt Visual Arts Center, Albion MI

American Swedish Institute, Minneapolis MN

Arizona State University, University Art Museum, Tempe AZ

Arts and Science Center, Statesville NC

Baldwin Historical Society Museum, Baldwin NY

Ball State University, Museum of Art, Muncie IN

Baltimore Museum of Art, Baltimore MD

Baylor University, Martin Museum of Art, Waco TX

Bennington Museum, Bennington VT

Bergstrom Mahler Museum, Neenah WI

Boulder Historical Society Inc, Museum of History, Boulder CO

Bower's Museum, Santa Ana CA

Brigham City Museum-Gallery, Brigham City UT

Brooklyn Historical Society, Brooklyn OH

Brown University, David Winton Bell Gallery, Providence RI

Cambria Historical Society, New Providence NJ

Charleston Museum, Charleston SC

Chrysler Museum, Norfolk VA

City of Holyoke Museum-Wistariahurst, Holyoke MA

City of Pittsfield, Berkshire Artisans, Pittsfield MA

Cleveland State University, Art Gallery, Cleveland OH

Clinton Art Association Gallery, Clinton IA

Columbus Chapel & Boal Mansion Museum, Boalsburg PA

Cooper-Hewitt, National Museum of Design, New York NY

Corning Museum of Glass, Corning NY

The Currier Gallery of Art, Manchester NH

DAR Museum, National Society Daughters of the American Revolution, Washington DC

Dartmouth Heritage Museum, Dartmouth NS

Dewitt Historical Society of Tompkins County, Ithaca NY

Fillmore County Historical Society, Fountain MN

Flint Institute of Arts, Flint MI

Edsel & Eleanor Ford House, Grosse Pointe Shores MI

Fort Totten State Historic Site, Pioneer Daughters Museum, Fort Totten ND

Freer Gallery of Art, Washington DC

Fuller Museum of Art, Brockton MA

Harvard University, Semitic Museum, Cambridge MA

Hastings Museum, Hastings NE

Historical and Cultural Affairs, Delaware State Museums, Dover DE

Historical Society of Cheshire County, Colony House Museum, Keene NH

Houston Museum of Decorative Arts, Chattanooga TN

Huguenot Historical Society of New Paltz, Locust Lawn, Gardiner NY

Hunter Museum of Art, Chattanooga TN

Iowa State University, Brunnier Gallery Museum, Ames IA

Maude I Kerns Art Center, Henry Korn Gallery, Eugene OR

Kings County Historical Society and Museum, Hampton NB

Livingston County Historical Society, Cobblestone Museum, Geneseo NY

Lockwood-Mathews Mansion Museum, Norwalk CT

Longfellow-Evangeline State Commemorative Area, Saint Martinville LA

Luna County Historical Society, Inc, Deming Luna Mimbres Museum, Deming NM

McCord Museum of Canadian History, Montreal PQ

Marcella Sembrich Memorial Association Inc, Opera Museum, Bolton Landing NY

Maryland Historical Society, Museum of Maryland History, Baltimore MD

Memphis Brooks Museum of Art, Memphis TN

Mitchell Museum, Mount Vernon IL

Montreal Museum of Fine Arts, Montreal PQ

The Museum, Greenwood SC

National Museum of American History, Washington DC

National Society of Colonial Dames of America in the State of Maryland, Mount Clare Mansion, Baltimore MD

Nevada Museum Of Art, Reno NV

Newark Museum Association, The Newark Museum, Newark NJ

New Haven Colony Historical Society, New Haven CT

North Miami Center of Contemporary Art, North Miami FL

Oglebay Institute, Mansion Museum, Wheeling WV

Oklahoma City Art Museum, Oklahoma City OK

Old Salem Inc, Museum of Early Southern Decorative Arts, Winston-Salem NC

Oshkosh Public Museum, Oshkosh WI

Palm Beach Community College Foundation, Museum of Art, Lake Worth FL

Pasadena Historical Society, Pasadena CA

Philadelphia Museum of Art, Philadelphia PA

Philbrook Museum of Art, Tulsa OK

Phillips County Museum, Helena AR

Portland Museum of Art, Portland ME

Principia College, School of Nations Museum, Elsah IL

Putnam Museum of History & Natural Science, Davenport IA

Queens College, City University of New York, Godwin-Ternbach Museum, Flushing NY

Rahr-West Art Museum, Manitowoc WI

Walter Cecil Rawls Museum, Courtland VA

Frederic Remington Art Museum, Ogdensburg NY

Riley County Historical Museum, Manhattan KS

Rowland Evans Robinson Memorial Association, Rokeby Museum, Ferrisburgh VT

Nelda C & H J Lutcher Stark Foundation, Stark Museum of Art, Orange TX

State University of New York at Geneseo, Bertha V B Lederer Gallery, Geneseo NY

Summit County Historical Society, Akron OH

Syracuse University, Art Collection, Syracuse NY

Toledo Museum of Art, Toledo Museum of Art, Toledo OH

Topeka Public Library, Gallery of Fine Arts, Topeka KS

Triton Museum of Art, Santa Clara CA

United States Tobacco Manufacturing Company Inc, Museum of Tobacco & History, Nashville TN

University of Colorado at Colorado Springs, Gallery of Contemporary Art, Colorado Springs CO

University of Mississippi, University Museums, Oxford MS

Valentine Museum, Richmond VA

Village of Potsdam Public Museum, Potsdam NY

Volcano Art Center, Hawaii National Park HI

Washington County Museum of Fine Arts, Hagerstown MD

Wayne County Historical Society, Museum, Honesdale PA

Wellfleet Historical Society Museum & Rider House, Wellfleet MA

Wheaton College, Watson Gallery, Norton MA

White House, Washington DC

Willard House and Clock Museum, Inc, Grafton MA

GOLD

Beloit College, Wright Museum of Art, Beloit WI
Dawson City Museum & Historical Society, Dawson City YT
Franklin Mint Museum, Franklin Center PA
Freer Gallery of Art, Washington DC
Loyola University of Chicago, Martin D'Arcy Gallery of Art, Chicago IL
Museum of Fine Arts, Houston, Houston TX
Old Salem Inc, Museum of Early Southern Decorative Arts, Winston-Salem NC
United States Figure Skating Association, World Figure Skating Hall of Fame and Museum, Colorado Springs CO
Willard House and Clock Museum, Inc, Grafton MA

GRAPHICS

Alberta College of Art, Illingworth Kerr Gallery, Calgary AB
Art Gallery of Hamilton, Hamilton ON
Art Museum of Southeast Texas, Beaumont TX
Augusta Richmond County Museum, Augusta GA
Baltimore City Community College, Art Gallery, Baltimore MD
Baltimore Museum of Art, Baltimore MD
Balzekas Museum of Lithuanian Culture, Chicago IL
Baylor University, Martin Museum of Art, Waco TX
Beloit College, Wright Museum of Art, Beloit WI
Blanden Memorial Art Museum, Fort Dodge IA
Canton Art Institute, Canton OH
Capital University, Schumacher Gallery, Columbus OH
Cheekwood-Tennessee Botanical Gardens & Museum of Art, Nashville TN
Chelan County Public Utility District, Rocky Reach Dam, Wenatchee WA
Chicago Historical Society, Chicago IL
Clemson University, Rudolph E Lee Gallery, Clemson SC
Cleveland State University, Art Gallery, Cleveland OH
College of William and Mary, Joseph & Margaret Muscarelle Museum of Art, Williamsburg VA
Colorado Springs Fine Arts Center, Colorado Springs CO
Columbia Museum of Art, Columbia SC
Concordia University Wisconsin, Fine Art Gallery, Mequon WI
Cornell University, Herbert F Johnson Museum of Art, Ithaca NY
Creighton University, Fine Arts Gallery, Omaha NE
Cummer Gallery of Art, DeEtte Holden Cummer Museum Foundation, Jacksonville FL
C W Post Campus of Long Island University, Hillwood Art Museum, Brookville NY
Delaware Art Museum, Wilmington DE
Detroit Institute of Arts, Detroit MI
Dickinson State University, Mind's Eye Gallery, Dickinson ND
Edmundson Art Foundation, Inc, Des Moines Art Center, Des Moines IA
Erie Art Museum, Erie PA
Evansville Museum of Arts and Science, Evansville IN
Fine Arts Museums of San Francisco, M H de Young Memorial Museum and California Palace of the Legion of Honor, San Francisco CA
Galleries of the Claremont Colleges, Claremont CA
Georgetown College Gallery, Georgetown KY
Georgetown University, Art and History Museum, Washington DC
George Washington University, The Dimock Gallery, Washington DC
Grinnell College, Print & Drawing Study Room/ Gallery, Grinnell IA
Gertrude Herbert Memorial Institute of Art, Augusta GA
Howard University, Gallery of Art, Washington DC
Illinois State Museum, Illinois Art Gallery & Lockport Gallery, Springfield IL
Institute of American Indian Arts Museum, Santa Fe NM

John C Calhoun State Community College, Art Gallery, Decatur AL
Joslyn Art Museum, Omaha NE
Kalamazoo Institute of Arts, Kalamazoo MI
Maude I Kerns Art Center, Henry Korn Gallery, Eugene OR
Lehigh University Art Galleries, Bethlehem PA
Louisiana Arts and Science Center, Baton Rouge LA
Louisiana State University, Museum of Arts, Baton Rouge LA
L'Universite Laval, Ecole des Arts Visuels, Quebec PQ
Marion Koogler McNay Art Museum, San Antonio TX
Judah L Magnes Museum, Berkeley CA
Manufacturers Hanover, New York NY
Mark Twain Bancshares, Saint Louis MO
Maryland Art Place, Baltimore MD
Mitchell Museum, Mount Vernon IL
Montgomery Museum of Fine Arts, Montgomery AL
Mount Allison University, Owens Art Gallery, Sackville NB
Muscatine Art Center, Muscatine IA
Museum of Art, Fort Lauderdale, Fort Lauderdale FL
Museum of Fine Arts, Springfield MA
Museum of Modern Art, New York NY
New Orleans Museum of Art, New Orleans LA
Niagara University, Castellani Art Museum, New York NY
North Carolina State University, Visual Arts Programs, Raleigh NC
North Miami Center of Contemporary Art, North Miami FL
Oklahoma City Art Museum, Oklahoma City OK
Old Jail Art Center, Albany TX
Owensboro Museum of Fine Art, Owensboro KY
Pennsylvania State University, Palmer Museum of Art, University Park PA
Portland Art Museum, Portland OR
Print Club of Albany, Museum, Albany NY
Provincetown Art Association and Museum, Provincetown MA
Queen's University, Agnes Etherington Art Centre, Kingston ON
Rhode Island School of Design, Museum of Art, Providence RI
San Jose State University, Union Gallery, San Jose CA
Santa Clara University, de Saisset Museum, Santa Clara CA
Shell Canada Ltd, Calgary AB
Siena Heights College, Klemm Gallery, Studio Angelico, Adrian MI
Simon Fraser University, Simon Fraser Gallery, Burnaby BC
Norton Simon Museum, Pasadena CA
State University of New York at Geneseo, Bertha V B Lederer Gallery, Geneseo NY
Stephens College, Lewis James & Nellie Stratton Davis Art Gallery, Columbia MO
Syracuse University, Art Collection, Syracuse NY
Tryon Palace Historic Sites & Gardens, New Bern NC
Tufts University, Art Gallery, Medford MA
The Ukrainian Museum, New York NY
United States Military Academy, West Point Museum, West Point NY
United States Navy, Art Gallery, Washington DC
University of Connecticut, William Benton Museum of Art - Connecticut's State Art Museum, Storrs CT
University of Delaware, University Gallery, Newark DE
University of Georgia, Georgia Museum of Art, Athens GA
University of Kansas, Spencer Museum of Art, Lawrence KS
University of Kentucky, Art Museum, Lexington KY
University of Sherbrooke, Art Gallery, Sherbrooke PQ
University of Utah, Utah Museum of Fine Arts, Salt Lake City UT
University of Wisconsin, University Art Museum, Milwaukee WI

Wichita State University, Edwin A Ulrich Museum of Art, Wichita KS
Wilkes Art Gallery, North Wilkesboro NC
Woodmere Art Museum, Philadelphia PA

HISPANIC ART

Albuquerque Museum of Art, History & Science, Albuquerque NM
Art Institute for the Permian Basin, Odessa TX
Bradford Brinton Memorial Museum & Historic Ranch, Big Horn WY
Chicano Humanities & Arts Council, Denver CO
City of Pittsfield, Berkshire Artisans, Pittsfield MA
Cleveland State University, Art Gallery, Cleveland OH
Concordia Historical Institute, Saint Louis MO
East Baton Rouge Parks & Recreation Commission, Baton Rouge Gallery Inc, Baton Rouge LA
East Carolina University, Wellington B Gray Gallery, Greenville NC
Federal Reserve Board, Art Gallery, Washington DC
Intar Latin American Gallery, New York NY
Loyola Marymount University, Laband Art Gallery, Los Angeles CA
Maryland Art Place, Baltimore MD
MEXIC-ARTE Museum, Austin TX
Monterey Peninsula Museum of Art Association, Monterey CA
Museum of Fine Arts, Saint Petersburg, Florida, Inc, Saint Petersburg FL
Museum of New Mexico, Museum of International Folk Art, Santa Fe NM
National Museum of Women in the Arts, Library & Research Center, Washington DC
New Mexico State University, University Art Gallery, Las Cruces NM
North Miami Center of Contemporary Art, North Miami FL
Roswell Museum and Art Center, Roswell NM
Royal Ontario Museum, Toronto ON
South Carolina State Museum, Columbia SC
University of Pennsylvania, Arthur Ross Gallery, Philadelphia PA
University of Puerto Rico, Museum of Anthropology, History & Art, Rio Piedras PR
Wustum Museum Art Association, Racine WI

HISTORICAL MATERIAL

Adams County Historical Society, Museum & Cultural Center, Brighton CO
Alabama Department of Archives and History Museum, Museum Galleries, Montgomery AL
Alaska State Museum, Juneau AK
Albuquerque Museum of Art, History & Science, Albuquerque NM
Amerind Foundation, Inc, Amerind Museum, Fulton-Hayden Memorial Art Gallery, Dragoon AZ
Anchorage Museum of History and Art, Anchorage AK
Appaloosa Museum, Inc, Moscow ID
Arlington Historical Society Inc, Museum, Arlington VA
Artesia Historical Museum & Art Center, Artesia NM
Arts and Science Center, Statesville NC
Ashland Historical Society, Ashland MA
Ateneo Puertorriqueno, San Juan PR
Atlanta Historical Society Inc, Atlanta History Center, Atlanta GA
Baker University, Old Castle Museum, Baldwin City KS
The Bartlett Museum, Amesbury MA
Battleship North Carolina, Wilmington NC
Bay County Historical Society, Historical Museum of Bay County, Bay City MI
Beverly Historical Society, Cabot, Hale and Balch House Museums, Beverly MA
Boulder Historical Society Inc, Museum of History, Boulder CO
Bowdoin College, Peary-MacMillan Arctic Museum, Brunswick ME
Brant Historical Society, Brant County Museum, Brantford ON
Brick Store Museum, Kennebunk ME

California State University Stanislaus, University Art Gallery, Turlock CA
Canadian Museum of Civilization, Hull ON
Canajoharie Art Gallery, Canajoharie NY
Casa Amesti, Monterey CA
Center for Puppetry Arts, Atlanta GA
Chatillon-DeMenil House Foundation, DeMenil Mansion, Saint Louis MO
Chelan County Public Utility District, Rocky Reach Dam, Wenatchee WA
Chesapeake Bay Maritime Museum, Saint Michaels MD
Chief Plenty Coups Museum, Pryor MT
Chinese Culture Foundation, Chinese Culture Center Gallery, San Francisco CA
Church of Jesus Christ of Latter-day Saints, Museum of Church History & Art, Salt Lake City UT
City of Springdale, Shiloh Museum, Springdale AR
Clark County Historical Society, Springfield OH
Clark County Historical Society, Pioneer - Krier Museum, Ashland KS
Cleveland State University, Art Gallery, Cleveland OH
Clinton Historical Museum Village, Clinton NJ
Cliveden, Philadelphia PA
Cohasset Historical Society, Cohasset Maritime Museum, Cohasset MA
The Coley Homestead & Barn Museum, Weston CT
Columbus and Lowndes County Historical Society, Florence McLeod Hazard Museum, Columbus MS
Columbus Museum, Columbus GA
Connecticut Historical Commission, Sloane-Stanley Museum, Kent CT
Connecticut Historical Society, Hartford CT
Dacotah Prairie Museum, Lamont Gallery, Aberdeen SD
Dawson City Museum & Historical Society, Dawson City YT
Defense Language Institute Foreign Language Center, Presidio of Monterey Historical Holding, Presidio of Monterey CA
Department of Natural Resources of Missouri, Missouri State Museum, Jefferson City MO
Dickinson College, Trout Gallery, Carlisle PA
Eva Brook Donly Museum, Simcoe ON
Douglas County Historical Society, Fairlawn Mansion & Museum, Superior WI
Drew County Historical Society, Museum, Monticello AR
East Bay Asian Local Development Corp, Asian Resource Gallery, Oakland CA
East Tennessee State University, Carroll Reece Museum, Johnson City TN
Eberdt Museum of Communications, Heritage Sutton, Sutton PQ
Emily Carr Gallery Archives, Victoria BC
Erie Art Museum, Erie PA
Fillmore County Historical Society, Fountain MN
Five Civilized Tribes Museum, Muskogee OK
Floyd County Museum, New Albany IN
Fort Morgan Heritage Foundation, Fort Morgan CO
Fort Ticonderoga Association, Ticonderoga NY
Fort Totten State Historic Site, Pioneer Daughters Museum, Fort Totten ND
Gadsden Museum, Mesilla NM
Gananoque Historical Museum, Gananoque ON
General Board of Discipleship, The United Methodist Church, The Upper Room Chapel & Museum, Nashville TN
Thomas Gilcrease Institute of American History & Art, Tulsa OK
Glenbow Museum, Calgary AB
Goshen Historical Society, Goshen CT
Great Lakes Historical Society, Vermilion OH
Greene County Historical Society, Xenia OH
Hampton University, University Museum, Hampton VA
Harrison County Historical Museum, Marshall TX
Headquarters Fort Monroe, Dept of Army, Casemate Museum, Fort Monroe VA
Historical Society of Bloomfield, Bloomfield NJ
Historical Society of Old Newbury, Cushing House Museum, Newburyport MA
Historical Society of Washington DC, Christian Heurich Mansion, Washington DC

Idaho Historical Museum, Boise ID
Illinois State Museum, State of Illinois Art Gallery, Chicago IL
Indiana University, William Hammond Mathers Museum, Bloomington IN
Institute of the Great Plains, Museum of the Great Plains, Lawton OK
Jackson County Historical Society, 1859 Jail, Marshal s Home & Museum, Independence MO
Jamestown-Yorktown Foundation, Yorktown VA
Jefferson County Historical Museum, Pine Bluff AR
Jefferson County Open Space, Hiwan Homestead Museum, Evergreen CO
Jordan Historical Museum of The Twenty, Jordan ON
Kansas State Historical Society, Kansas Museum of History, Topeka KS
Kelowna Centennial Museum and National Exhibit Centre, Kelowna BC
Kentucky Historical Society, Old State Capitol & Annex, Frankfort KY
Kern County Museum, Bakersfield CA
Klamath County Museum, Klamath Falls OR
Lafayette Museum Association, Lafayette Museum, Lafayette LA
Landmark Society of Western New York, Inc, Rochester NY
LeSueur Museum, LeSueur MN
Lightner Museum, Saint Augustine FL
Long Branch Historical Museum, Long Branch NJ
Longfellow-Evangeline State Commemorative Area, Saint Martinville LA
Louisa May Alcott Memorial Association, Orchard House, Concord MA
Louisiana State Exhibit Museum, Shreveport LA
Loveland Museum and Gallery, Loveland CO
Luna County Historical Society, Inc, Deming Luna Mimbres Museum, Deming NM
Lyme Historical Society, Florence Griswold Museum, Old Lyme CT
McCord Museum of Canadian History, Montreal PQ
McPherson Museum, McPherson KS
Marcella Sembrich Memorial Association Inc, Opera Museum, Bolton Landing NY
The Market Gallery of the City of Toronto Archives, Toronto ON
Maryhill Museum of Art, Goldendale WA
Mission San Luis Rey Museum, San Luis Rey CA
Missouri Historical Society, Saint Louis MO
Mohave Museum of History and Arts, Kingman AZ
MonDak Heritage Center, Sidney MT
Monterey Peninsula Museum of Art Association, Monterey CA
Moravian Historical Society, Whitefield House Museum, Nazareth PA
Mountain View Doukhobor Museum, Grand Forks BC
Multicultural Heritage Centre, Stony Plain AB
Muscatine Art Center, Muscatine IA
Museum of Fine Arts, Saint Petersburg, Florida, Inc, Saint Petersburg FL
Museum of New York, Rock Hill SC
Museum of Northern British Columbia, Ruth Harvey Art Gallery, Prince Rupert BC
National Archives & Records Administration, Franklin D Roosevelt Museum, Hyde Park NY
National Archives and Records Service, John F Kennedy Library and Museum, Boston MA
National Art Museum of Sport, Indianapolis IN
National Museum of the American Indian, New York NY
The National Park Service, United States Department of the Interior, The Statue of Liberty National Monument, New York NY
Naval War College Museum, Newport RI
Nebraska State Capitol, Lincoln NE
Newfoundland Museum, Saint John's NF
New Hampshire Antiquarian Society, Hopkinton NH
New Haven Colony Historical Society, New Haven CT
The John A Noble Collection, Staten Island NY
No Man's Land Historical Society Museum, Goodwell OK
Norfolk Historical Society Inc, Museum, Norfolk CT

North Central Washington Museum, Art Gallery, Wenatchee WA
Northeastern Nevada Historical Society Museum, Elko NV
The Ohio Historical Society, Inc, Campus Martius Museum and Ohio River Museum, Marietta OH
Oklahoma Historical Society, State Museum of History, Oklahoma City OK
Old Salem Inc, Museum of Early Southern Decorative Arts, Winston-Salem NC
Old York Historical Society, Gaol Museum, York ME
Oregon Historical Society, Portland OR
Palo Alto Cultural Center, Palo Alto CA
Pennsylvania State University, Palmer Museum of Art, University Park PA
Phelps County Historical Society, Phelps County Museum, Holdrege NE
Philipse Manor Hall State Historic Site, Yonkers NY
Pope County Historical Society Museum, Glenwood MN
Portsmouth Historical Society, John Paul Jones House, Portsmouth NH
Putnam County Historical Society, Foundry School Museum, Cold Spring NY
Putnam Museum of History & Natural Science, Davenport IA
Redding Museum of Art & History, Redding CA
Red Rock State Park, Museum, Church Rock NM
Rensselaer County Historical Society, Hart-Cluett Mansion, 1827, Troy NY
Ringwood Manor House Museum, Ringwood NJ
Roberts County Museum, Miami TX
Rowland Evans Robinson Memorial Association, Rokeby Museum, Ferrisburgh VT
Rome Historical Society Museum, Rome NY
Royal Ontario Museum, Toronto ON
Safety Harbor Museum of Regional History, Safety Harbor FL
Saint Bernard Foundation and Monastery, North Miami Beach FL
Saint-Gaudens National Historic Site, Cornish NH
Saint Louis County Historical Society, Duluth MN
Seneca Falls Historical Society Museum, Seneca Falls NY
Sheldon Jackson Museum, Sitka AK
Sheldon Museum, Middlebury VT
Society for the Preservation of New England Antiquities, Archives, Boston MA
Southern Oregon Historical Society, Jacksonville Museum of Southern Oregon History, Jacksonville OR
State Historical Society of Wisconsin, State Historical Museum, Madison WI
State Museum of Pennsylvania, Pennsylvania Historical & Museum Commission, Harrisburg PA
Tallahassee Museum of History & Natural Science, Tallahassee FL
Tennessee State Museum, Nashville TN
Totem Heritage Center, Ketchikan AK
Towson State University, The Holtzman Art Gallery, Towson MD
Trail of '98 Museum, Skagway AK
Transylvania University, Morlan Gallery, Lexington KY
Ukrainian Canadian Archives & Museum of Alberta, Edmonton AB
The Ukrainian Museum, New York NY
United Methodist Historical Society, Library, Baltimore MD
United Society of Shakers, Shaker Museum, Poland Spring ME
US Coast Guard Museum, New London CT
US Navy Supply Corps School, Museum, Athens GA
United States Tobacco Manufacturing Company Inc, Museum of Tobacco & History, Nashville TN
University of Illinois, World Heritage Museum, Champaign IL
University of Pennsylvania, Arthur Ross Gallery, Philadelphia PA
USS Constitution Museum Foundation Inc, Boston National Historical Park, Museum, Boston MA
Van Cortlandt Mansion & Museum, Bronx NY

Ventura County Historical Society Museum, Ventura CA
Vermilion County Museum Society, Danville IL
Wade House & Wesley W Jung Carriage Museum, Historic House & Carriage Museum, Greenbush WI
Harold Warp Pioneer Village Foundation, Minden NE
Waterville Historical Society, Redington Museum, Waterville ME
Waterworks Visual Arts Center, Salisbury NC
Wayne County Historical Society, Museum, Honesdale PA
Wayne County Historical Society, Wooster OH
Western Kentucky University, Kentucky Museum, Bowling Green KY
Western Reserve Historical Society, Cleveland OH
Westminster College, Winston Churchill Memorial & Library in the United States, Fulton MO
Wethersfield Historical Society Inc, Wethersfield CT
Willard House and Clock Museum, Inc, Grafton MA
Williams College, Museum of Art, Williamstown MA
Woodrow Wilson Birthplace Foundation, Staunton VA
Woodrow Wilson House, Washington DC
Woodstock Artists Association, Woodstock NY

ISLAMIC ART

Dickinson College, Trout Gallery, Carlisle PA
Harvard University, Arthur M Sackler Museum, Cambridge MA
Los Angeles County Museum of Art, Los Angeles CA
Monterey Peninsula Museum of Art Association, Monterey CA
Ohio State University, Slide & Photograph Library, Columbus OH
Williams College, Museum of Art, Williamstown MA

IVORY

Anchorage Museum of History and Art, Anchorage AK
Beloit College, Wright Museum of Art, Beloit WI
Bowdoin College, Peary-MacMillan Arctic Museum, Brunswick ME
The Bruce Museum, Greenwich CT
Chilkat Valley Historical Society, Sheldon Museum & Cultural Center, Haines AK
Harvard University, Dumbarton Oaks Research Library and Collections, Washington DC
Iowa State University, Brunnier Gallery Museum, Ames IA
Loyola University of Chicago, Martin D'Arcy Gallery of Art, Chicago IL
Mitchell Museum, Mount Vernon IL
The Museum, Greenwood SC
Oklahoma Center for Science and Art, Kirkpatrick Center, Oklahoma City OK
Rahr-West Art Museum, Manitowoc WI
Robert W Ryerss Library and Museum, Philadelphia PA
Saint John's University, Chung-Cheng Art Gallery, Jamaica NY
Santa Clara University, de Saisset Museum, Santa Clara CA
Sheldon Jackson Museum, Sitka AK
Toronto Dominion Bank, Toronto ON
University of Michigan, Kelsey Museum of Archaeology, Ann Arbor MI
Yugtarvik Regional Museum & Bethel Visitors Center, Bethel AK

JADE

Beloit College, Wright Museum of Art, Beloit WI
Freer Gallery of Art, Washington DC
Harvard University, William Hayes Fogg Art Museum, Cambridge MA
Hermitage Foundation Museum, Norfolk VA
Indianapolis Museum of Art, Indianapolis IN
Mitchell Museum, Mount Vernon IL

Norton Gallery and School of Art, West Palm Beach FL
Pennsylvania State University, Palmer Museum of Art, University Park PA
Marjorie Merriweather Post Foundation of DC, Hillwood Museum, Washington DC
Saint John's University, Chung-Cheng Art Gallery, Jamaica NY
Seattle Art Museum, Seattle WA
Virginia Museum of Fine Arts, Richmond VA
Washington County Museum of Fine Arts, Hagerstown MD

JEWELRY

Art Institute for the Permian Basin, Odessa TX
Baldwin Historical Society Museum, Baldwin NY
Baltimore Museum of Art, Baltimore MD
Beloit College, Wright Museum of Art, Beloit WI
Bradford Brinton Memorial Museum & Historic Ranch, Big Horn WY
Chicano Humanities & Arts Council, Denver CO
Harvard University, Dumbarton Oaks Research Library and Collections, Washington DC
Haystack Mountain School of Crafts, Gallery, Deer Isle ME
Institute of American Indian Arts Museum, Santa Fe NM
Maude I Kerns Art Center, Henry Korn Gallery, Eugene OR
Kings County Historical Society and Museum, Hampton NB
James Monroe Museum, Fredericksburg VA
National Museum of Women in the Arts, Washington DC
National Museum of Women in the Arts, Library & Research Center, Washington DC
Nevada Museum Of Art, Reno NV
North Miami Center of Contemporary Art, North Miami FL
Ohio University, Trisolini Gallery, Athens OH
Palos Verdes Art Center, Rancho Palos Verdes CA
Randall Museum Junior Museum, San Francisco CA
Riley County Historical Museum, Manhattan KS
Rollins College, George D and Harriet W Cornell Fine Arts Museum, Winter Park FL
The Ukrainian Museum, New York NY
United States Figure Skating Association, World Figure Skating Hall of Fame and Museum, Colorado Springs CO
USS Constitution Museum Foundation Inc, Boston National Historical Park, Museum, Boston MA
Valentine Museum, Richmond VA
Virginia Museum of Fine Arts, Richmond VA

JUDAICA

American Jewish Historical Society, Waltham MA
Leo Baeck Institute, New York NY
B'nai B'rith International, B'nai B'rith Klutznick National Jewish Museum, Washington DC
Gershon & Rebecca Fenster Museum of Jewish Art, Tulsa OK
Hebrew Union College, Skirball Museum, Los Angeles CA
Hebrew Union College - Jewish Institute of Religion, Skirball Museum-Cincinnati Branch, Cincinnati OH
Lightner Museum, Saint Augustine FL
Long Beach Jewish Community Center, Center Gallery, Long Beach CA
Judah L Magnes Museum, Berkeley CA
Museum of Fine Arts, Saint Petersburg, Florida, Inc, Saint Petersburg FL
Spertus Museum, Chicago IL
The Temple, The Temple Museum of Religious Art, Cleveland OH
Temple Beth Israel, Plotkin Juddica Museum, Phoenix AZ
Vancouver Museum Association, Vancouver Museum, Vancouver BC
Yeshiva University Museum, New York NY

JUVENILE ART

Art Institute for the Permian Basin, Odessa TX
Murray State University, Eagle Gallery, Murray KY
South Carolina State Museum, Columbia SC

LACES

Baltimore Museum of Art, Baltimore MD
The City of Petersburg Museums, Petersburg VA
Cooper-Hewitt, National Museum of Design, New York NY
Litchfield Historical Society, Litchfield CT
Longfellow-Evangeline State Commemorative Area, Saint Martinville LA
Montreal Museum of Fine Arts, Montreal PQ
National Museum of Women in the Arts, Library & Research Center, Washington DC
Portland Art Museum, Portland OR
Marjorie Merriweather Post Foundation of DC, Hillwood Museum, Washington DC
Syracuse University, Art Collection, Syracuse NY
Washington County Museum of Fine Arts, Hagerstown MD

LANDSCAPES

The Albrecht-Kemper Museum of Art, Saint Joseph MO
Art Institute for the Permian Basin, Odessa TX
Arts and Science Center, Statesville NC
Bay County Historical Society, Historical Museum of Bay County, Bay City MI
Cedar Rapids Museum of Art, Cedar Rapids IA
Church of Jesus Christ of Latter-day Saints, Museum of Church History & Art, Salt Lake City UT
City of Pittsfield, Berkshire Artisans, Pittsfield MA
College of William and Mary, Joseph & Margaret Muscarelle Museum of Art, Williamsburg VA
Concordia University, Leonard & Bina Ellen Art Gallery, Montreal PQ
Connecticut Historical Commission, Sloane-Stanley Museum, Kent CT
Durham Art Guild Inc, Durham NC
East Baton Rouge Parks & Recreation Commission, Baton Rouge Gallery Inc, Baton Rouge LA
Fayette Art Museum, Fayette AL
Federal Reserve Board, Art Gallery, Washington DC
Landmark Society of Western New York, Inc, Rochester NY
Maine Historical Society, Wadsworth-Longfellow House, Portland ME
Marcella Sembrich Memorial Association Inc, Opera Museum, Bolton Landing NY
The Market Gallery of the City of Toronto Archives, Toronto ON
Maryhill Museum of Art, Goldendale WA
Maryland Art Place, Baltimore MD
Maui Historical Society, Bailey House, Wailuku HI
Moravian College, Payne Gallery, Bethlehem PA
Morris Communications Corporation, Morris Museum of Art, Augusta GA
National Museum of Women in the Arts, Washington DC
Nevada Museum Of Art, Reno NV
New Haven Colony Historical Society, New Haven CT
New Mexico State University, University Art Gallery, Las Cruces NM
North Miami Center of Contemporary Art, North Miami FL
Old Salem Inc, Museum of Early Southern Decorative Arts, Winston-Salem NC
C M Russell Museum, Great Falls MT
SLA Arch-Couture Inc, Art Collection, Denver CO
Syracuse University, Art Collection, Syracuse NY
The Ukrainian Museum, New York NY
United Society of Shakers, Shaker Museum, Poland Spring ME
University of Colorado at Colorado Springs, Gallery of Contemporary Art, Colorado Springs CO
University of Delaware, University Gallery, Newark DE
University of New Hampshire, The Art Gallery, Durham NH
University of Pennsylvania, Arthur Ross Gallery, Philadelphia PA

Waterworks Visual Arts Center, Salisbury NC

LATIN AMERICAN ART

Arizona State University, University Art Museum, Tempe AZ
Aurora University, Schingoethe Center for Native American Cultures, Aurora IL
Beloit College, Wright Museum of Art, Beloit WI
Brown University, David Winton Bell Gallery, Providence RI
California State University Stanislaus, University Art Gallery, Turlock CA
Center for Puppetry Arts, Atlanta GA
Chicano Humanities & Arts Council, Denver CO
Cleveland State University, Art Gallery, Cleveland OH
East Carolina University, Wellington B Gray Gallery, Greenville NC
Federal Reserve Board, Art Gallery, Washington DC
Institute of Puerto Rican Culture, Museo de Bellas Artes, San Juan PR
Intar Latin American Gallery, New York NY
Loyola Marymount University, Laband Art Gallery, Los Angeles CA
McAllen International Museum, McAllen TX
Mexican Fine Arts Center Museum, Chicago IL
MEXIC-ARTE Museum, Austin TX
Monterey Peninsula Museum of Art Association, Monterey CA
National Museum of Women in the Arts, Washington DC
North Miami Center of Contemporary Art, North Miami FL
Roswell Museum and Art Center, Roswell NM
University of Colorado at Colorado Springs, Gallery of Contemporary Art, Colorado Springs CO
University of Florida, University Gallery, Gainesville FL
University of Texas at Austin, Archer M Huntington Art Gallery, Austin TX
Ursinus College, Philip & Muriel Berman Museum of Art, Collegeville PA
Williams College, Museum of Art, Williamstown MA
Wustum Museum Art Association, Racine WI

LEATHER

Bowdoin College, Peary-MacMillan Arctic Museum, Brunswick ME
Fort Totten State Historic Site, Pioneer Daughters Museum, Fort Totten ND
Luna County Historical Society, Inc, Deming Luna Mimbres Museum, Deming NM
Nebraska State Capitol, Lincoln NE
Nevada Museum Of Art, Reno NV

MANUSCRIPTS

American Jewish Historical Society, Waltham MA
Amerind Foundation, Inc, Amerind Museum, Fulton-Hayden Memorial Art Gallery, Dragoon AZ
Archives of American Art, Washington DC
Atlanta Historical Society Inc, Atlanta History Center, Atlanta GA
Baldwin Historical Society Museum, Baldwin NY
The Bartlett Museum, Amesbury MA
Boulder Historical Society Inc, Museum of History, Boulder CO
Brigham Young University, B F Larsen Gallery, Provo UT
Chicago Historical Society, Chicago IL
The City of Petersburg Museums, Petersburg VA
City of Springdale, Shiloh Museum, Springdale AR
The Coley Homestead & Barn Museum, Weston CT
Concordia Historical Institute, Saint Louis MO
Dawson City Museum & Historical Society, Dawson City YT
Fillmore County Historical Society, Fountain MN
Freer Gallery of Art, Washington DC
General Board of Discipleship, The United Methodist Church, The Upper Room Chapel & Museum, Nashville TN
Getty Center for the History of Art & the Humanities Trust Museum, Santa Monica CA

Getty Center for the History of Art & the Humanities Trust Museum, The J Paul Getty Museum, Santa Monica CA
Greene County Historical Society, Xenia OH
La Casa del Libro Museum, San Juan PR
LeSueur Museum, LeSueur MN
Liberty Memorial Museum & Archives, Kansas City MO
Litchfield Historical Society, Litchfield CT
Litchfield Historical Society, Ingraham Memorial Research Library, Litchfield CT
Louisa May Alcott Memorial Association, Orchard House, Concord MA
McCord Museum of Canadian History, Montreal PQ
Judah L Magnes Museum, Berkeley CA
Maine Historical Society, Wadsworth-Longfellow House, Portland ME
Marcella Sembrich Memorial Association Inc, Opera Museum, Bolton Landing NY
Mohave Museum of History and Arts, Kingman AZ
Naval War College Museum, Newport RI
Nevada Museum Of Art, Reno NV
The John A Noble Collection, Staten Island NY
Old York Historical Society, Gaol Museum, York ME
Putnam Museum of History & Natural Science, Davenport IA
Redding Museum of Art & History, Redding CA
Rowland Evans Robinson Memorial Association, Rokeby Museum, Ferrisburgh VT
The Rosenbach Museum and Library, Philadelphia PA
Shaker Village of Pleasant Hill, Harrodsburg KY
Abigail Adams Smith Museum, New York NY
Nelda C & H J Lutcher Stark Foundation, Stark Museum of Art, Orange TX
US Coast Guard Museum, New London CT
United States Figure Skating Association, World Figure Skating Hall of Fame and Museum, Colorado Springs CO
United States Naval Academy Museum, Annapolis MD
University of Pennsylvania, Arthur Ross Gallery, Philadelphia PA
Vermilion County Museum Society, Danville IL
Washington County Museum of Fine Arts, Hagerstown MD
Wayne County Historical Society, Museum, Honesdale PA
White House, Washington DC
Winterthur Museum and Gardens, Winterthur DE

MAPS

Alabama Department of Archives and History Museum, Museum Galleries, Montgomery AL
Atlanta Historical Society Inc, Atlanta History Center, Atlanta GA
Baldwin Historical Society Museum, Baldwin NY
The Bartlett Museum, Amesbury MA
Bowdoin College, Peary-MacMillan Arctic Museum, Brunswick ME
City of Springdale, Shiloh Museum, Springdale AR
The Coley Homestead & Barn Museum, Weston CT
Dawson City Museum & Historical Society, Dawson City YT
Fillmore County Historical Society, Fountain MN
Fort Totten State Historic Site, Pioneer Daughters Museum, Fort Totten ND
Greene County Historical Society, Xenia OH
Kern County Museum, Library, Bakersfield CA
La Casa del Libro Museum, San Juan PR
LeSueur Museum, LeSueur MN
Liberty Memorial Museum & Archives, Kansas City MO
McPherson Museum, McPherson KS
The Market Gallery of the City of Toronto Archives, Toronto ON
Massachusetts Institute of Technology, MIT Museum, Cambridge MA
Massachusetts Institute of Technology, Hart Nautical Galleries and Collections, Cambridge MA
Moravian Historical Society, Whitefield House Museum, Nazareth PA
Naval War College Museum, Newport RI

Norfolk Historical Society Inc, Museum, Norfolk CT
Old Salem Inc, Museum of Early Southern Decorative Arts, Winston-Salem NC
Oysterponds Historical Society, Museum, Orient NY
Putnam Museum of History & Natural Science, Davenport IA
Redding Museum of Art & History, Redding CA
Rensselaer County Historical Society, Hart-Cluett Mansion, 1827, Troy NY
Roberts County Museum, Miami TX
David M Stewart Museum, Montreal PQ
Towson State University, The Holtzman Art Gallery, Towson MD
Vermilion County Museum Society, Danville IL
Wayne County Historical Society, Museum, Honesdale PA
Westminster College, Winston Churchill Memorial & Library in the United States, Fulton MO
Wethersfield Historical Society Inc, Wethersfield CT
York Institute Museum, Saco ME

MARINE PAINTING

The Albrecht-Kemper Museum of Art, Saint Joseph MO
The Bostonian Society, Old State House Museum, Boston MA
Butler Institute of American Art, Art Museum, Youngstown OH
Calvert Marine Museum, Solomons MD
Chattahoochee Valley Art Museum, LaGrange GA
Columbia River Maritime Museum, Astoria OR
Douglas County Historical Society, Fairlawn Mansion & Museum, Superior WI
Federal Reserve Board, Art Gallery, Washington DC
Great Lakes Historical Society, Vermilion OH
Kendall Whaling Museum, Sharon MA
Maine Maritime Museum, Bath ME
The Mariners' Museum, Newport News VA
The Market Gallery of the City of Toronto Archives, Toronto ON
Massachusetts Institute of Technology, MIT Museum, Cambridge MA
Massachusetts Institute of Technology, Hart Nautical Galleries and Collections, Cambridge MA
Monterey History and Art Association, Maritime Museum of Monterey, Monterey CA
Naval Historical Center, The Navy Museum, Washington DC
Naval War College Museum, Newport RI
Nevada Museum Of Art, Reno NV
Newburyport Maritime Society, Custom House Maritime Museum, Newburyport MA
New Haven Colony Historical Society, New Haven CT
The John A Noble Collection, Staten Island NY
Nova Scotia Museum, Maritime Museum of the Atlantic, Halifax NS
Oysterponds Historical Society, Museum, Orient NY
Provincetown Art Association and Museum, Provincetown MA
San Diego Maritime Museum, San Diego CA
San Francisco Maritime National Historical Park, National Maritime Museum, San Francisco CA
Society for the Preservation of New England Antiquities, Archives, Boston MA
South Street Seaport Museum, New York NY
Towson State University, The Holtzman Art Gallery, Towson MD
USS Constitution Museum Foundation Inc, Boston National Historical Park, Museum, Boston MA
Woodstock Artists Association, Woodstock NY
Yarmouth County Historical Society, Yarmouth County Museum, Yarmouth NS

MEDIEVAL ART

Academy of the New Church, Glencairn Museum, Bryn Athyn PA
Lyman Allyn Art Museum, New London CT
Beloit College, Wright Museum of Art, Beloit WI
General Board of Discipleship, The United Methodist Church, The Upper Room Chapel & Museum, Nashville TN
Marion Koogler McNay Art Museum, San Antonio TX
The Metropolitan Museum of Art, New York NY
Museum of Fine Arts, Houston, Houston TX
Rensselaer Newman Foundation Chapel and Cultural Center, The Gallery, Troy NY
Royal Ontario Museum, Toronto ON
Saint Mary's College of California, Hearst Art Gallery, Moraga CA
Toledo Museum of Art, Toledo Museum of Art, Toledo OH
University of Illinois, Krannert Art Museum, Champaign IL
University of Rochester, Memorial Art Gallery, Rochester NY
University of Vermont, Robert Hull Fleming Museum, Burlington VT
University of Wisconsin-Madison, Elvehjem Museum of Art, Madison WI
Vassar College, Vassar Art Gallery, Poughkeepsie NY
Williams College, Museum of Art, Williamstown MA
Worcester Art Museum, Worcester MA

METALWORK

Beloit College, Wright Museum of Art, Beloit WI
Chilkat Valley Historical Society, Sheldon Museum & Cultural Center, Haines AK
Durham Art Guild Inc, Durham NC
Freer Gallery of Art, Washington DC
Harvard University, Dumbarton Oaks Research Library and Collections, Washington DC
McCord Museum of Canadian History, Montreal PQ
Maryland Historical Society, Museum of Maryland History, Baltimore MD
Musee d'Art de Saint-Laurent, Saint-Laurent PQ
Old Salem Inc, Museum of Early Southern Decorative Arts, Winston-Salem NC
Pioneer Town, Pioneer Museum of Western Art, Wimberley TX
Principia College, School of Nations Museum, Elsah IL
Randall Museum Junior Museum, San Francisco CA
St Clair County Community College, Jack R Hennesey Art Galleries, Port Huron MI
Southern Illinois University, University Museum, Carbondale IL
The Ukrainian Museum, New York NY
United States Naval Academy Museum, Annapolis MD

MEXICAN ART

Americas Society, New York NY
Art Institute for the Permian Basin, Odessa TX
Aurora University, Schingoethe Center for Native American Cultures, Aurora IL
Brown University, David Winton Bell Gallery, Providence RI
Chicano Humanities & Arts Council, Denver CO
Cleveland State University, Art Gallery, Cleveland OH
Craft and Folk Art Museum, Los Angeles CA
Davenport Museum of Art, Davenport IA
Defense Language Institute Foreign Language Center, Presidio of Monterey Historical Holding, Presidio of Monterey CA
East Carolina University, Wellington B Gray Gallery, Greenville NC
El Paso Museum of Art, El Paso TX
Fresno Arts Center & Museum, Fresno CA
Guadalupe Historic Foundation, Santuario de Guadalupe, Santa Fe NM
Intar Latin American Gallery, New York NY
Jefferson County Open Space, Hiwan Homestead Museum, Evergreen CO

McAllen International Museum, McAllen TX
Mercer County Community College, The Gallery, Trenton NJ
Mexican Fine Arts Center Museum, Chicago IL
Mexican Museum, San Francisco CA
MEXIC-ARTE Museum, Austin TX
Monterey Peninsula Museum of Art Association, Monterey CA
Museum of New Mexico, Museum of Fine Arts, Santa Fe NM
Phoenix Art Museum, Phoenix AZ
Plaza de la Raza Cultural Center, Los Angeles CA
Roswell Museum and Art Center, Roswell NM
University of Colorado at Colorado Springs, Gallery of Contemporary Art, Colorado Springs CO
University of Houston, Sarah Campbell Blaffer Gallery, Houston TX
University of Illinois, World Heritage Museum, Champaign IL
Wichita Art Museum, Wichita KS
Wustum Museum Art Association, Racine WI

MILITARY ART

Alabama Department of Archives and History Museum, Museum Galleries, Montgomery AL
The City of Petersburg Museums, Petersburg VA
Clark County Historical Society, Pioneer - Krier Museum, Ashland KS
Defense Language Institute Foreign Language Center, Presidio of Monterey Historical Holding, Presidio of Monterey CA
Fort Totten State Historic Site, Pioneer Daughters Museum, Fort Totten ND
Headquarters Fort Monroe, Dept of Army, Casemate Museum, Fort Monroe VA
Liberty Memorial Museum & Archives, Kansas City MO
Naval War College Museum, Newport RI
Oklahoma Historical Society, State Museum of History, Oklahoma City OK
David M Stewart Museum, Montreal PQ
Stratford Historical Society, Stratford CT
US Navy Supply Corps School, Museum, Athens GA
USS Constitution Museum Foundation Inc, Boston National Historical Park, Museum, Boston MA

MINIATURES

Arts and Science Center, Statesville NC
Carolina Art Association, Gibbes Museum of Art, Charleston SC
Litchfield Historical Society, Litchfield CT
Maine Historical Society, Wadsworth-Longfellow House, Portland ME
Maryhill Museum of Art, Goldendale WA
National Museum of American Art, Washington DC
Naval War College Museum, Newport RI
New Jersey Historical Society Museum, Newark NJ
New Orleans Museum of Art, New Orleans LA
R W Norton Art Gallery, Shreveport LA
South Carolina State Museum, Columbia SC
United States Figure Skating Association, World Figure Skating Hall of Fame and Museum, Colorado Springs CO
University of Cincinnati, Tangeman Fine Arts Gallery, Cincinnati OH
USS Constitution Museum Foundation Inc, Boston National Historical Park, Museum, Boston MA
Willard House and Clock Museum, Inc, Grafton MA
York Institute Museum, Saco ME

MOSAICS

Baltimore Museum of Art, Baltimore MD
Harvard University, Dumbarton Oaks Research Library and Collections, Washington DC
Worcester Art Museum, Worcester MA

ORIENTAL ART

Allentown Art Museum, Allentown PA
Lyman Allyn Art Museum, New London CT
Amherst College, Mead Art Museum, Amherst MA
Ari Museum of Western Virginia, Roanoke VA
Art Gallery of Greater Victoria, Victoria BC
The Art Institute of Chicago, Chicago IL
Art Patrons League of Mobile, Mobile AL
Baltimore Museum of Art, Baltimore MD
Bates College, Museum of Art, Lewiston ME
Beloit College, Wright Museum of Art, Beloit WI
Berkshire Museum, Pittsfield MA
Blanden Memorial Art Museum, Fort Dodge IA
Boise Art Museum, Boise ID
California State University Stanislaus, University Art Gallery, Turlock CA
Carnegie Institute, Carnegie Museum of Art, Pittsburgh PA
Carolina Art Association, Gibbes Museum of Art, Charleston SC
China Institute in America, China House Gallery, New York NY
Chrysler Museum, Norfolk VA
Cleveland Museum of Art, Cleveland OH
Colby College, Musuem of Art, Waterville ME
The College at New Paltz State University of New York, College Art Gallery, New Paltz NY
Columbus Museum of Art, Columbus OH
Cummer Gallery of Art, DeEtte Holden Cummer Museum Foundation, Jacksonville FL
Danville Museum of Fine Arts & History, Danville VA
Davenport Museum of Art, Davenport IA
Dayton Art Institute, Dayton OH
Denver Art Museum, Denver CO
Dickinson College, Trout Gallery, Carlisle PA
Drew University, Elizabeth P Korn Gallery, Madison NJ
Evansville Museum of Arts and Science, Evansville IN
Everhart Museum, Scranton PA
Everson Museum of Art, Syracuse NY
Flint Institute of Arts, Flint MI
Florence Museum, Florence SC
Freeport Art Museum & Cultural Center, Freeport IL
Fresno Arts Center & Museum, Fresno CA
Galleries of the Claremont Colleges, Claremont CA
Isabella Stewart Gardner Museum, Boston MA
Greenville College, Richard W Bock Sculpture Collection, Greenville IL
Hammond-Harwood House Association, Inc, Annapolis MD
Harvard University, Arthur M Sackler Museum, Cambridge MA
Headley-Whitney Museum, Lexington KY
Hermitage Foundation Museum, Norfolk VA
Hofstra University, Hofstra Museum, Hempstead NY
Honolulu Academy of Arts, Honolulu HI
Indianapolis Museum of Art, Indianapolis IN
Johns Hopkins University, Evergreen House, Baltimore MD
Johnson-Humrickhouse Museum, Coshocton OH
Kenosha Public Museum, Kenosha WI
Memphis Brooks Museum of Art, Memphis TN
The Metropolitan Museum of Art, New York NY
Minneapolis Society of Fine Arts, Minneapolis Institute of Arts, Minneapolis MN
Monterey Peninsula Museum of Art Association, Monterey CA
The Museum at Drexel University, Philadelphia PA
Museum of Fine Arts, Springfield MA
Museum of Fine Arts, Boston MA
Museum of Fine Arts, Houston, Houston TX
Museum of Oriental Cultures, Corpus Christi TX
National Society of Colonial Dames of America in the State of Maryland, Mount Clare Mansion, Baltimore MD
Nelson-Atkins Museum of Art, Kansas City MO
Newark Museum Association, The Newark Museum, Newark NJ
Norman Mackenzie Art Gallery, Regina SK
North Carolina State University, Chinqua-Penn Plantation House, Garden & Greenhouses, Reidsville NC
Oakland University, Meadow Brook Art Gallery, Rochester MI

Oberlin College, Allen Memorial Art Museum, Oberlin OH
Oklahoma Center for Science and Art, Kirkpatrick Center, Oklahoma City OK
Oregon State University, Horner Museum, Corvallis OR
Pacific - Asia Museum, Pasadena CA
Pacific University, Old College Hall, Pacific University Museum, Forest Grove OR
The Parrish Art Museum, Southampton NY
Philadelphia Museum of Art, Philadelphia PA
Philbrook Museum of Art, Tulsa OK
Phoenix Art Museum, Phoenix AZ
Portland Art Museum, Portland OR
Princeton University, The Art Museum, Princeton NJ
Rhode Island Historical Society, John Brown House, Providence RI
Rhode Island School of Design, Museum of Art, Providence RI
Saginaw Art Museum, Saginaw MI
Saint John's University, Chung-Cheng Art Gallery, Jamaica NY
St Lawrence University, Richard F Brush Art Gallery, Canton NY
The Saint Louis Art Museum, Saint Louis MO
San Diego Museum of Art, San Diego CA
Santa Barbara Museum of Art, Santa Barbara CA
Scripps College, Clark Humanities Museum, Claremont CA
Seattle Art Museum, Seattle WA
George Walter Vincent Smith Art Museum, Springfield MA
Society of the Cincinnati, Anderson House Museum, Washington DC
Sonoma State University, Art Gallery, Rohnert Park CA
Stanford University, Art Gallery, Stanford CA
Stratford Historical Society, Stratford CT
Syracuse University, Art Collection, Syracuse NY
Tucson Museum of Art, Tucson AZ
University of Alabama at Birmingham, Visual Arts Gallery, Birmingham AL
University of Chicago, David and Alfred Smart Museum of Art, Chicago IL
University of Florida, University Gallery, Gainesville FL
University of Illinois, Krannert Art Museum, Champaign IL
University of Illinois, World Heritage Museum, Champaign IL
University of Kansas, Spencer Museum of Art, Lawrence KS
University of Miami, Lowe Art Museum, Coral Gables FL
University of Missouri, Museum of Art and Archaeology, Columbia MO
University of North Carolina at Greensboro, Weatherspoon Art Gallery, Greensboro NC
University of Notre Dame, Snite Museum of Art, Notre Dame IN
University of Oregon, Museum of Art, Eugene OR
University of Tampa, Henry B Plant Museum, Tampa FL
University of Vermont, Robert Hull Fleming Museum, Burlington VT
University of Wisconsin, University Art Museum, Milwaukee WI
University of Wisconsin-Madison, Elvehjem Museum of Art, Madison WI
Vancouver Museum Association, Vancouver Museum, Vancouver BC
Vanderbilt University, Fine Arts Gallery, Nashville TN
Vassar College, Vassar Art Gallery, Poughkeepsie NY
Village of Potsdam Public Museum, Potsdam NY
Washington County Museum of Fine Arts, Hagerstown MD
Wayne Center for the Arts, Wooster OH
Wesleyan University, Davison Art Center, Middletown CT
Widener University, Art Museum, Chester PA
Williams College, Museum of Art, Williamstown MA
Woodmere Art Museum, Philadelphia PA
Yale University, Art Gallery, New Haven CT

PAINTING - AMERICAN

Albany Institute of History and Art, Albany NY
Alberta College of Art, Illingworth Kerr Gallery, Calgary AB
Albertson College of Idaho, Rosenthal Art Gallery, Caldwell ID
The Albrecht-Kemper Museum of Art, Saint Joseph MO
Albright College, Freedman Gallery, Reading PA
Albuquerque Museum of Art, History & Science, Albuquerque NM
Allegheny College, Bowman, Megahan and Penelec Galleries, Meadville PA
Allentown Art Museum, Allentown PA
Charles Allis Art Museum, Milwaukee WI
American University, Watkins Collectiony, Washington DC
Amerind Foundation, Inc, Amerind Museum, Fulton-Hayden Memorial Art Gallery, Dragoon AZ
Anchorage Museum of History and Art, Anchorage AK
Anna Maria College, Saint Luke's Gallery, Paxton MA
Arizona State University, University Art Museum, Tempe AZ
Arkansas Arts Center, Little Rock AR
Art Complex Museum, Duxbury MA
Artesia Historical Museum & Art Center, Artesia NM
Art Gallery of Hamilton, Hamilton ON
Art Gallery of Nova Scotia, Halifax NS
Art Gallery of Ontario, Toronto ON
The Art Institute of Chicago, Chicago IL
Artists' Cooperative Gallery, Omaha NE
The Art Museum of Santa Cruz County, Santa Cruz CA
Art Museum of Southeast Texas, Beaumont TX
Art Patrons League of Mobile, Mobile AL
Asheville Art Museum, Asheville NC
Ashland Historical Society, Ashland MA
Atlanta Museum, Atlanta GA
Attleboro Museum, Center for the Arts, Attleboro MA
Augusta Richmond County Museum, Augusta GA
Bakersfield Art Foundation, Bakersfield Museum of Art, Bakersfield CA
Baldwin Historical Society Museum, Baldwin NY
Baldwin-Wallace College, Fawick Art Gallery, Berea OH
Ball State University, Museum of Art, Muncie IN
Baltimore City Community College, Art Gallery, Baltimore MD
Baltimore City Life Museums, Baltimore MD
Baltimore Museum of Art, Baltimore MD
Bard College, William Cooper Procter Art Center, Annandale-on-Hudson NY
John D Barrow Art Gallery, Skaneateles NY
The Bartlett Museum, Amesbury MA
Bass Museum of Art, Miami Beach FL
Bates College, Museum of Art, Lewiston ME
Baylor University, Martin Museum of Art, Waco TX
Beaumont Art League, Beaumont TX
Beloit College, Wright Museum of Art, Beloit WI
Berea College, Doris Ulmann Galleries, Berea KY
Bergstrom Mahler Museum, Neenah WI
Berkshire Museum, Pittsfield MA
Birmingham Museum of Art, Birmingham AL
Blanden Memorial Art Museum, Fort Dodge IA
Board of Parks & Recreation, The Parthenon, Nashville TN
Boise Art Museum, Boise ID
Boulder Historical Society Inc, Museum of History, Boulder CO
Bowdoin College, Peary-MacMillan Arctic Museum, Brunswick ME
Roy Boyd Gallery, Chicago IL
Brandeis University, Rose Art Museum, Waltham MA
Brandywine River Museum, Chadds Ford PA
Brigham Young University, B F Larsen Gallery, Provo UT
Bradford Brinton Memorial Museum & Historic Ranch, Big Horn WY
Brown University, David Winton Bell Gallery, Providence RI
The Bruce Museum, Greenwich CT

The Buffalo Fine Arts Academy, Albright-Knox Art Gallery, Buffalo NY
Burchfield Art Center, Buffalo NY
Butler Institute of American Art, Art Museum, Youngstown OH
California State University Stanislaus, University Art Gallery, Turlock CA
Canadian Wildlife & Wilderness Art Museum, Ottawa ON
Canajoharie Art Gallery, Canajoharie NY
Canton Art Institute, Canton OH
Capital University, Schumacher Gallery, Columbus OH
Cardinal Stritch College, Layton Honor Gallery, Milwaukee WI
Carnegie Institute, Carnegie Museum of Art, Pittsburgh PA
Carolina Art Association, Gibbes Museum of Art, Charleston SC
Amon Carter Museum, Fort Worth TX
Cedar Rapids Museum of Art, Cedar Rapids IA
Chatillon-DeMenil House Foundation, DeMenil Mansion, Saint Louis MO
Chattahoochee Valley Art Museum, LaGrange GA
Cheekwood-Tennessee Botanical Gardens & Museum of Art, Nashville TN
Chrysler Museum, Norfolk VA
Church of Jesus Christ of Latter-day Saints, Museum of Church History & Art, Salt Lake City UT
Cincinnati Museum Association, Cincinnati Art Museum, Cincinnati OH
City of Pittsfield, Berkshire Artisans, Pittsfield MA
Clark County Historical Society, Pioneer - Krier Museum, Ashland KS
Clemson University, Rudolph E Lee Gallery, Clemson SC
Cleveland Museum of Art, Cleveland OH
Cleveland State University, Art Gallery, Cleveland OH
Clinton Art Association Gallery, Clinton IA
Colby College, Musuem of Art, Waterville ME
The College at New Paltz State University of New York, College Art Gallery, New Paltz NY
College of Saint Benedict, Art Gallery, Saint Joseph MN
Colorado Springs Fine Arts Center, Colorado Springs CO
Columbia County Historical Society, Columbia County Museum, Kinderhook NY
Columbia Museum of Art, Columbia SC
Columbus Chapel & Boal Mansion Museum, Boalsburg PA
Columbus Museum, Columbus GA
Columbus Museum of Art, Columbus OH
Concordia Historical Institute, Saint Louis MO
Confederation Centre Art Gallery and Museum, Charlottetown PE
Connecticut Historical Commission, Sloane-Stanley Museum, Kent CT
Coos Art Museum, Coos Bay OR
Corcoran Gallery of Art, Washington DC
Cornell University, Herbert F Johnson Museum of Art, Ithaca NY
Crane Collection Gallery, Boston MA
Crawford County Historical Society, Baldwin-Reynolds House Museum, Meadville PA
Crazy Horse Memorial, Indian Museum of North America, Crazy Horse SD
Creighton University, Fine Arts Gallery, Omaha NE
Cripple Creek District Museum, Cripple Creek CO
Crocker Art Museum, Sacramento CA
Cummer Gallery of Art, DeEtte Holden Cummer Museum Foundation, Jacksonville FL
The Currier Gallery of Art, Manchester NH
Dallas Museum of Art, Dallas TX
DAR Museum, National Society Daughters of the American Revolution, Washington DC
Davenport Museum of Art, Davenport IA
Dayton Art Institute, Dayton OH
Delaware Art Museum, Wilmington DE
Denver Art Museum, Denver CO
Dezign House, Jefferson OH
Dickinson State University, Mind's Eye Gallery, Dickinson ND
Dixie College, Southwestern Utah Art Gallery, Saint George UT

New Mexico State University, University Art Gallery, Las Cruces NM
New Orleans Museum of Art, New Orleans LA
Newport Harbor Art Museum, Newport Beach CA
New York University, Grey Art Gallery and Study Center, New York NY
Niagara University, Castellani Art Museum, New York NY
North Carolina Central University, Art Museum, Durham NC
North Carolina Museum of Art, Raleigh NC
North Dakota State University, Memorial Union Art Gallery, Fargo ND
Northern Illinois University, NIU Art Museum, De Kalb IL
North Miami Center of Contemporary Art, North Miami FL
Norton Gallery and School of Art, West Palm Beach FL
R W Norton Art Gallery, Shreveport LA
Norwest Bank of Minneapolis, Art Collection, Minneapolis MN
Norwich Free Academy, Slater Memorial Museum & Converse Art Gallery, Norwich CT
Noyes Museum, Oceanville NJ
Oakland Museum, Art Dept, Oakland CA
Oak Ridge Art Center, Oak Ridge TN
Oberlin College, Allen Memorial Art Museum, Oberlin OH
Ogunquit Museum of American Art, Ogunquit ME
Ohio State University, Wexner Center for the Arts, Columbus OH
Ohio University, Trisolini Gallery, Athens OH
Okefenokee Heritage Center, Inc, Waycross GA
Oklahoma Center for Science and Art, Kirkpatrick Center, Oklahoma City OK
Oklahoma City Art Museum, Oklahoma City OK
Oklahoma Historical Society, State Museum of History, Oklahoma City OK
Olana State Historic Site, Hudson NY
Old Dartmouth Historical Society, New Bedford Whaling Museum, New Bedford MA
Orlando Museum of Art, Orlando FL
Owensboro Museum of Fine Art, Owensboro KY
Palm Springs Desert Museum, Inc, Palm Springs CA
Panhandle-Plains Histoical Society Museum, Canyon TX
The Parrish Art Museum, Southampton NY
Peabody & Essex Museum, Salem MA
Pennsylvania Academy of the Fine Arts, Galleries, Philadelphia PA
Pennsylvania State University, Palmer Museum of Art, University Park PA
Philadelphia Museum of Art, Philadelphia PA
Philadelphia Sketch Club, Inc, Philadelphia PA
Philbrook Museum of Art, Tulsa OK
Phillips Academy, Addison Gallery of American Art, Andover MA
The Phillips Collection, Washington DC
Phillips County Museum, Helena AR
Portland Art Museum, Portland OR
Portland Museum of Art, Portland ME
Portsmouth Athenaeum, Portsmouth NH
Portsmouth Museums, Arts Center, Portsmouth VA
Potsdam College of the State University of New York, Roland Gibson Gallery, Potsdam NY
Princeton University, The Art Museum, Princeton NJ
Provincetown Art Association and Museum, Provincetown MA
Putnam County Historical Society, Foundry School Museum, Cold Spring NY
Queebsborough Community College, Art Gallery, Bayside NY
Rahr-West Art Museum, Manitowoc WI
Rapid City Fine Arts Council, Dahl Fine Arts Center, Rapid City SD
Reading Public Museum and Art Gallery, Reading PA
Red Rock State Park, Museum, Church Rock NM
Frederic Remington Art Museum, Ogdensburg NY
Reynolda House Museum of American Art, Winston-Salem NC
Rhode Island School of Design, Museum of Art, Providence RI
Sid W Richardson Foundation, Collection of Western Art, Fort Worth TX

R J R Nabisco, Inc, New York NY
Roberson Museum & Science Center, Binghamton NY
Rowland Evans Robinson Memorial Association, Rokeby Museum, Ferrisburgh VT
The Rockwell Museum, Corning NY
Rogers House Museum Gallery, Ellsworth KS
Lauren Rogers Museum of Art, Laurel MS
Rollins College, George D and Harriet W Cornell Fine Arts Museum, Winter Park FL
Roswell Museum and Art Center, Roswell NM
Round Top Center for the Arts Inc, Arts Gallery, Damariscotta ME
C M Russell Museum, Great Falls MT
Robert W Ryerss Library and Museum, Philadelphia PA
Saginaw Art Museum, Saginaw MI
St Clair County Community College, Jack R Hennesey Art Galleries, Port Huron MI
Saint Gregory's Abbey and College, Mabee-Gerrer Museum of Art, Shawnee OK
Saint Johnsbury Athenaeum, Saint Johnsbury VT
Saint John's Museum of Art, Wilmington NC
St Lawrence University, Richard F Brush Art Gallery, Canton NY
The Saint Louis Art Museum, Saint Louis MO
San Diego Museum of Art, San Diego CA
San Diego State University, University Art Gallery, San Diego CA
San Francisco Museum of Modern Art, San Francisco CA
San Joaquin Pioneer and Historical Society, The Haggin Museum, Stockton CA
San Jose Museum of Art, San Jose CA
San Jose State University, Union Gallery, San Jose CA
Santa Barbara Museum of Art, Santa Barbara CA
Santa Clara University, de Saisset Museum, Santa Clara CA
Schenectady Museum, Planetarium & Visitors Center, Schenectady NY
Seattle Art Museum, Seattle WA
Ella Sharp Museum, Jackson MI
Shelburne Museum, Shelburne VT
Shell Canada Ltd, Calgary AB
Silverado Museum, Saint Helena CA
SLA Arch-Couture Inc, Art Collection, Denver CO
Smith College, Museum of Art, Northampton MA
George Walter Vincent Smith Art Museum, Springfield MA
Society for the Preservation of New England Antiquities, Archives, Boston MA
Society of the Cincinnati, Anderson House Museum, Washington DC
South Carolina State Museum, Columbia SC
South Dakota State University, South Dakota Art Museum, Brookings SD
Southern Alleghenies Museum of Art, Loretto PA
Southern Illinois University, University Museum, Carbondale IL
Southern Utah University, Braithwaite Fine Arts Gallery, Cedar City UT
Springfield Art Museum, Springfield MO
Springfield Library & Museums Association, Connecticut Valley Historical Museum, Springfield MA
Springville Museum of Art, Springville UT
Stamford Museum and Nature Center, Stamford CT
Nelda C & H J Lutcher Stark Foundation, Stark Museum of Art, Orange TX
State Historical Society of Missouri, Columbia MO
Staten Island Institute of Arts and Sciences, Staten Island NY
State University of New York at Albany, University Art Gallery, Albany NY
State University of New York at Geneseo, Bertha V B Lederer Gallery, Geneseo NY
State University of New York at Oswego, Tyler Art Gallery, Oswego NY
State University of New York at Purchase, Neuberger Museum, Purchase NY
T C Steele State Historic Site, Nashville IN
Stephens College, Lewis James & Nellie Stratton Davis Art Gallery, Columbia MO
Stetson University, Duncan Gallery of Art, De Land FL
Stratford Historical Society, Stratford CT

Sunrise Museum, Inc, Sunrise Art Museum, Sunrise Children's Museum & Planatarium, Charleston WV
SVACA - Sheyenne Valley Arts and Crafts Association, Bjarne Ness Gallery, Fort Ransom ND
Sheldon Swope Art Museum, Terre Haute IN
Syracuse University, Art Collection, Syracuse NY
Tacoma Art Museum, Tacoma WA
Terra Museum of American Art, Chicago IL
Timken Museum of Art, San Diego CA
Toledo Museum of Art, Toledo Museum of Art, Toledo OH
Tomoka State Park Museum, Fred Dana Marsh Museum, Ormond Beach FL
Triton Museum of Art, Santa Clara CA
Tryon Palace Historic Sites & Gardens, New Bern NC
Tucson Museum of Art, Tucson AZ
Tufts University, Art Gallery, Medford MA
Tulane University, University Art Collection, New Orleans LA
Edwin A Ulrich Museum, Hyde Park NY
Ulster County Community College, Muroff-Kotler Visual Arts Gallery, Stone Ridge NY
United Society of Shakers, Shaker Museum, Poland Spring ME
United States Capitol, Architect of the Capitol, Washington DC
US Department of State, Diplomatic Reception Rooms, Washington DC
United States Department of the Interior Museum, Washington DC
United States Figure Skating Association, World Figure Skating Hall of Fame and Museum, Colorado Springs CO
United States Naval Academy Museum, Annapolis MD
University of Alabama at Birmingham, Visual Arts Gallery, Birmingham AL
University of Chicago, David and Alfred Smart Museum of Art, Chicago IL
University of Colorado, Art Galleries, Boulder CO
University of Connecticut, William Benton Museum of Art - Connecticut's State Art Museum, Storrs CT
University of Delaware, University Gallery, Newark DE
University of Florida, University Gallery, Gainesville FL
University of Georgia, Georgia Museum of Art, Athens GA
University of Illinois, Krannert Art Museum, Champaign IL
University of Iowa, Museum of Art, Iowa City IA
University of Kansas, Spencer Museum of Art, Lawrence KS
University of Kentucky, Art Museum, Lexington KY
University of Maryland, College Park, Art Gallery, College Park MD
University of Minnesota, University Art Museum, Minneapolis MN
University of Minnesota, Duluth, Tweed Museum of Art, Duluth MN
University of Montana, Paxson Gallery, Missoula MT
University of Nebraska, Lincoln, Sheldon Memorial Art Gallery, Lincoln NE
University of New Mexico, University Art Museum, Albuquerque NM
University of North Carolina at Greensboro, Weatherspoon Art Gallery, Greensboro NC
University of Northern Iowa, Gallery of Art, Cedar Falls IA
University of Notre Dame, Snite Museum of Art, Notre Dame IN
University of Oregon, Museum of Art, Eugene OR
University of Pittsburgh, University Art Gallery, Pittsburgh PA
University of Rhode Island, Fine Arts Center Galleries, Kingston RI
University of Southern California, Fisher Gallery, Los Angeles CA
University of South Florida, Contemporary Art Museum, Tampa FL
University of Southwestern Louisiana, University Art Museum, Lafayette LA

University of Texas at Arlington, Center for Research & Contemporary Arts, Arlington TX
University of Texas at Austin, Archer M Huntington Art Gallery, Austin TX
University of Wisconsin, University Art Museum, Milwaukee WI
University of Wisconsin-Madison, Wisconsin Union Galleries, Madison WI
University of Wisconsin-Madison, Elvehjem Museum of Art, Madison WI
University of Wisconsin-Stout, J Furlong Gallery, Menomonie WI
University of Wyoming, Art Museum, Laramie WY
USS Constitution Museum Foundation Inc, Boston National Historical Park, Museum, Boston MA
Valentine Museum, Richmond VA
Valparaiso University, Museum of Art, Valparaiso IN
Vassar College, Vassar Art Gallery, Poughkeepsie NY
Virginia Commonwealth University, Anderson Gallery, Richmond VA
Walker Art Center, Minneapolis MN
Washburn University, Mulvane Art Museum, Topeka KS
Washington County Museum of Fine Arts, Hagerstown MD
Waterworks Visual Arts Center, Salisbury NC
Wayne Center for the Arts, Wooster OH
Wayne County Historical Society, Museum, Honesdale PA
Western Kentucky University, Kentucky Museum, Bowling Green KY
Western State College of Colorado, Quigley Hall Art Gallery, Gunnison CO
Westminster College, Art Gallery, New Wilmington PA
Westmoreland Museum of Art, Greensburg PA
Wethersfield Historical Society Inc, Wethersfield CT
White House, Washington DC
Whitney Museum of American Art, New York NY
Wichita Art Museum, Wichita KS
Wichita State University, Edwin A Ulrich Museum of Art, Wichita KS
Widener University, Art Museum, Chester PA
Wilkes Art Gallery, North Wilkesboro NC
Wilkes University, Sordoni Art Gallery, Wilkes-Barre PA
Woodrow Wilson House, Washington DC
Winnipeg Art Gallery, Winnipeg MB
Winterthur Museum and Gardens, Winterthur DE
Wiregrass Museum of Art, Dothan AL
Wood Art Gallery, Montpelier VT
Woodmere Art Museum, Philadelphia PA
Woodstock Artists Association, Woodstock NY
Worcester Art Museum, Worcester MA
Wustum Museum Art Association, Racine WI
Wustum Museum Art Association, Charles A Wustum Museum of Fine Arts, Racine WI
Yale University, Art Gallery, New Haven CT
York Institute Museum, Saco ME
York University, Art Gallery of York University, North York ON
Zigler Museum, Jennings LA

PAINTING - AUSTRALIAN

Federal Reserve Board, Art Gallery, Washington DC
Historical Society of the Town of Greenwich, Inc, Bush-Holley House, Cos Cob CT

PAINTING - BRITISH

Albany Institute of History and Art, Albany NY
Arnot Art Museum, Elmira NY
Art Gallery of Hamilton, Hamilton ON
Baltimore Museum of Art, Baltimore MD
Bass Museum of Art, Miami Beach FL
Bates College, Museum of Art, Lewiston ME
Beaverbrook Art Gallery, Fredericton NB
Beloit College, Wright Museum of Art, Beloit WI
Bradford Brinton Memorial Museum & Historic Ranch, Big Horn WY
Corcoran Gallery of Art, Washington DC
Davenport Museum of Art, Davenport IA
Delaware Art Museum, Wilmington DE

The Dixon Gallery & Gardens, Memphis TN
Gunston Hall Plantation, Lorton VA
Henry E Huntington Library, Art Collections & Botanical Gardens, San Marino CA
Kendall Whaling Museum, Sharon MA
Louisiana State University, Museum of Arts, Baton Rouge LA
McMaster University, Art Gallery, Hamilton ON
Maryhill Museum of Art, Goldendale WA
Mellon Bank, Pittsburgh PA
Mint Museum of Art, Charlotte NC
Montreal Museum of Fine Arts, Montreal PQ
Museum of Fine Arts, Springfield MA
Museum of the Americas, Brookfield VT
New Orleans Museum of Art, New Orleans LA
Niagara University, Castellani Art Museum, New York NY
Owensboro Museum of Fine Art, Owensboro KY
Pennsylvania State University, Palmer Museum of Art, University Park PA
Princeton University, The Art Museum, Princeton NJ
The Rosenbach Museum and Library, Philadelphia PA
San Diego Museum of Art, San Diego CA
University of Florida, University Gallery, Gainesville FL
University of Notre Dame, Snite Museum of Art, Notre Dame IN
University of Southern California, Fisher Gallery, Los Angeles CA
University of Utah, Utah Museum of Fine Arts, Salt Lake City UT
Walters Art Gallery, Baltimore MD
Worcester Art Museum, Worcester MA
Yale University, Yale Center for British Art, New Haven CT

PAINTING - CANADIAN

Bowdoin College, Peary-MacMillan Arctic Museum, Brunswick ME
Canadian Museum of Nature, Musee Canadien de la Nature, Ottawa ON
Concordia University, Leonard & Bina Ellen Art Gallery, Montreal PQ
Edmonton Art Gallery, Edmonton AB
Enook Galleries, Waterloo ON
Estevan National Exhibition Centre Inc, Estevan SK
Heritage Center, Inc, Pine Ridge SD
Kitchener-Waterloo Art Gallery, Kitchener ON
L'Universite Laval, Ecole des Arts Visuels, Quebec PQ
McCord Museum of Canadian History, Montreal PQ
McMaster University, Art Gallery, Hamilton ON
The Market Gallery of the City of Toronto Archives, Toronto ON
Montreal Museum of Fine Arts, Montreal PQ
National Gallery of Canada, Ottawa ON
Niagara University, Castellani Art Museum, New York NY
Prince George Art Gallery, Prince George BC
Provincial Archives of Manitoba, Winnipeg MB
Toronto Dominion Bank, Toronto ON
University of Calgary, The Nickle Arts Museum, Calgary AB
Vancouver Art Gallery, Vancouver BC
Peter and Catharine Whyte Foundation, Whyte Museum of the Canadian Rockies, Banff AB
Winnipeg Art Gallery, Winnipeg MB
York University, Art Gallery of York University, North York ON

PAINTING - DUTCH

Arnot Art Museum, Elmira NY
Bass Museum of Art, Miami Beach FL
Bates College, Museum of Art, Lewiston ME
Chrysler Museum, Norfolk VA
Sterling and Francine Clark Art Institute, Williamstown MA
Corcoran Gallery of Art, Washington DC
Evansville Museum of Arts and Science, Evansville IN
Isabella Stewart Gardner Museum, Boston MA
Kendall Whaling Museum, Sharon MA

McMaster University, Art Gallery, Hamilton ON
Memphis Brooks Museum of Art, Memphis TN
Montreal Museum of Fine Arts, Montreal PQ
Museum of Fine Arts, Springfield MA
Oberlin College, Allen Memorial Art Museum, Oberlin OH
San Diego Museum of Art, San Diego CA
Timken Museum of Art, San Diego CA
University of California, Santa Barbara, University Art Museum, Santa Barbara CA
University of Southern California, Fisher Gallery, Los Angeles CA
Western Kentucky University, Kentucky Museum, Bowling Green KY
Worcester Art Museum, Worcester MA

PAINTING - EUROPEAN

Allentown Art Museum, Allentown PA
American University, Watkins Collection, Washington DC
Art Complex Museum, Duxbury MA
Art Gallery of Greater Victoria, Victoria BC
Art Gallery of Hamilton, Hamilton ON
Art Gallery of Ontario, Toronto ON
Ball State University, Museum of Art, Muncie IN
Bass Museum of Art, Miami Beach FL
Bates College, Museum of Art, Lewiston ME
Berkshire Museum, Pittsfield MA
Blanden Memorial Art Museum, Fort Dodge IA
Bob Jones University, Museum & Art Gallery, Greenville SC
Boise Art Museum, Boise ID
The Buffalo Fine Arts Academy, Albright-Knox Art Gallery, Buffalo NY
Carnegie Institute, Carnegie Museum of Art, Pittsburgh PA
Cincinnati Museum Association, Cincinnati Art Museum, Cincinnati OH
Cleveland Museum of Art, Cleveland OH
Columbia Museum of Art, Columbia SC
Columbus Museum of Art, Columbus OH
Corcoran Gallery of Art, Washington DC
Cornell University, Herbert F Johnson Museum of Art, Ithaca NY
Crocker Art Museum, Sacramento CA
Cummer Gallery of Art, DeEtte Holden Cummer Museum Foundation, Jacksonville FL
The Currier Gallery of Art, Manchester NH
Dallas Museum of Art, Dallas TX
Davenport Museum of Art, Davenport IA
Dayton Art Institute, Dayton OH
Denver Art Museum, Denver CO
Detroit Institute of Arts, Detroit MI
Dezign House, Jefferson OH
Edmonton Art Gallery, Edmonton AB
Evansville Museum of Arts and Science, Evansville IN
Everhart Museum, Scranton PA
Fairbanks Museum and Planetarium, Saint Johnsbury VT
Fairfield University, Thomas J Walsh Art Gallery, Fairfield CT
William A Farnsworth Library and Art Museum, Rockland ME
Fine Arts Museums of San Francisco, M H de Young Memorial Museum and California Palace of the Legion of Honor, San Francisco CA
Flint Institute of Arts, Flint MI
Frick Collection, New York NY
Grand Rapids Art Museum, Grand Rapids MI
Solomon R Guggenheim Museum, New York NY
Harvard University, Busch-Reisinger Museum, Cambridge MA
Harvard University, William Hayes Fogg Art Museum, Cambridge MA
Headley-Whitney Museum, Lexington KY
Gertrude Herbert Memorial Institute of Art, Augusta GA
Hirshhorn Museum and Sculpture Garden, Washington DC
Hofstra University, Hofstra Museum, Hempstead NY
Honolulu Academy of Arts, Honolulu HI
Huntington Museum of Art, Huntington WV
Hyde Collection Trust, Glens Falls NY
Indianapolis Museum of Art, Indianapolis IN
Joslyn Art Museum, Omaha NE

Kendall Whaling Museum, Sharon MA
Kimbell Art Museum, Fort Worth TX
La Salle University, Art Museum, Philadelphia PA
Los Angeles County Museum of Art, Los Angeles CA
Loyola University of Chicago, Martin D'Arcy Gallery of Art, Chicago IL
McAllen International Museum, McAllen TX
McMaster University, Art Gallery, Hamilton ON
Marion Koogler McNay Art Museum, San Antonio TX
Merrick Art Gallery, New Brighton PA
The Metropolitan Museum of Art, New York NY
Milwaukee Art Museum, Milwaukee WI
Minneapolis Society of Fine Arts, Minneapolis Institute of Arts, Minneapolis MN
Mint Museum of Art, Charlotte NC
Mount Holyoke College, Art Museum, South Hadley MA
Munson-Williams-Proctor Institute, Museum of Art, Utica NY
Musee d'Art de Joliette, Joliette PQ
Museum of Arts and Sciences, Inc, Macon GA
Museum of Fine Arts, Springfield MA
Museum of Fine Arts, Houston TX
Muskegon Museum of Art, Muskegon MI
Nevada Museum Of Art, Reno NV
New Orleans Museum of Art, New Orleans LA
New York University, Grey Art Gallery and Study Center, New York NY
North Carolina Museum of Art, Raleigh NC
North Country Museum of Arts, Park Rapids MN
Northwestern College, Te Paske Gallery of Rowenhorst, Orange City IA
R W Norton Art Gallery, Shreveport LA
Oklahoma City Art Museum, Oklahoma City OK
Panhandle-Plains Histoical Society Museum, Canyon TX
Philadelphia Museum of Art, Philadelphia PA
Philbrook Museum of Art, Tulsa OK
The Phillips Collection, Washington DC
Portland Art Museum, Portland OR
Portland Museum of Art, Portland ME
Princeton University, The Art Museum, Princeton NJ
Queens College, City University of New York, Godwin-Ternbach Museum, Flushing NY
Reading Public Museum and Art Gallery, Reading PA
Frederic Remington Art Museum, Ogdensburg NY
Lauren Rogers Museum of Art, Laurel MS
Rollins College, George D and Harriet W Cornell Fine Arts Museum, Winter Park FL
Saginaw Art Museum, Saginaw MI
Saint Gregory's Abbey and College, Mabee-Gerrer Museum of Art, Shawnee OK
St Lawrence University, Richard F Brush Art Gallery, Canton NY
The Saint Louis Art Museum, Saint Louis MO
San Diego Museum of Art, San Diego CA
San Joaquin Pioneer and Historical Society, The Haggin Museum, Stockton CA
Santa Barbara Museum of Art, Santa Barbara CA
Seattle Art Museum, Seattle WA
Shelburne Museum, Shelburne VT
Smith College, Museum of Art, Northampton MA
George Walter Vincent Smith Art Museum, Springfield MA
Southern Illinois University, University Museum, Carbondale IL
State Art Museum of Florida, John & Mable Ringling Museum of Art, Sarasota FL
State University of New York at Purchase, Neuberger Museum, Purchase NY
Toledo Museum of Art, Toledo Museum of Art, Toledo OH
Tucson Museum of Art, Tucson AZ
Tulane University, University Art Collection, New Orleans LA
University of Chicago, David and Alfred Smart Museum of Art, Chicago IL
University of Cincinnati, Tangeman Fine Arts Gallery, Cincinnati OH
University of Connecticut, William Benton Museum of Art - Connecticut's State Art Museum, Storrs CT
University of Illinois, Krannert Art Museum, Champaign IL

University of Iowa, Museum of Art, Iowa City IA
University of Kansas, Spencer Museum of Art, Lawrence KS
University of Kentucky, Art Museum, Lexington KY
University of Missouri, Museum of Art and Archaeology, Columbia MO
University of North Carolina at Greensboro, Weatherspoon Art Gallery, Greensboro NC
University of Northern Iowa, Gallery of Art, Cedar Falls IA
University of Notre Dame, Snite Museum of Art, Notre Dame IN
University of Oklahoma, Fred Jones Jr Museum of Art, Norman OK
University of Wisconsin-Madison, Elvehjem Museum of Art, Madison WI
University of Wyoming, Art Museum, Laramie WY
Vanderbilt University, Fine Arts Gallery, Nashville TN
Vassar College, Vassar Art Gallery, Poughkeepsie NY
Virginia Museum of Fine Arts, Richmond VA
Walters Art Gallery, Baltimore MD
Washburn University, Mulvane Art Museum, Topeka KS
Widener University, Art Museum, Chester PA
Wilkes University, Sordoni Art Gallery, Wilkes-Barre PA
Woodmere Art Museum, Philadelphia PA
Yale University, Art Gallery, New Haven CT
Zigler Museum, Jennings LA

PAINTING - FLEMISH

Arnot Art Museum, Elmira NY
Bass Museum of Art, Miami Beach FL
Capital University, Schumacher Gallery, Columbus OH
Chrysler Museum, Norfolk VA
Sterling and Francine Clark Art Institute, Williamstown MA
Clemson University, Fort Hill, Clemson SC
Columbus Chapel & Boal Mansion Museum, Boalsburg PA
Corcoran Gallery of Art, Washington DC
Evansville Museum of Arts and Science, Evansville IN
The Frick Art Museum, Pittsburgh PA
Isabella Stewart Gardner Museum, Boston MA
Memphis Brooks Museum of Art, Memphis TN
Oberlin College, Allen Memorial Art Museum, Oberlin OH
San Diego Museum of Art, San Diego CA
University of California, Santa Barbara, University Art Museum, Santa Barbara CA
University of Southern California, Fisher Gallery, Los Angeles CA
Virginia Museum of Fine Arts, Richmond VA
Worcester Art Museum, Worcester MA

PAINTING - FRENCH

Charles Allis Art Museum, Milwaukee WI
Arnot Art Museum, Elmira NY
The Art Institute of Chicago, Chicago IL
Baltimore Museum of Art, Baltimore MD
Bates College, Museum of Art, Lewiston ME
Centenary College of Louisiana, Meadows Museum of Art, Shreveport LA
Chrysler Museum, Norfolk VA
Sterling and Francine Clark Art Institute, Williamstown MA
Corcoran Gallery of Art, Washington DC
Davenport Museum of Art, Davenport IA
The Dixon Gallery & Gardens, Memphis TN
The Frick Art Museum, Pittsburgh PA
Isabella Stewart Gardner Museum, Boston MA
Grand Rapids Art Museum, Grand Rapids MI
Hill-Stead Museum, Farmington CT
Lockwood-Mathews Mansion Museum, Norwalk CT
McMaster University, Art Gallery, Hamilton ON
Montreal Museum of Fine Arts, Montreal PQ
The Museum at Drexel University, Philadelphia PA
Museum of Fine Arts, Springfield MA
Niagara University, Castellani Art Museum, New York NY

Norton Gallery and School of Art, West Palm Beach FL
Oklahoma City Art Museum, Oklahoma City OK
The Saint Louis Art Museum, Saint Louis MO
San Joaquin Pioneer and Historical Society, The Haggin Museum, Stockton CA
Syracuse University, Art Collection, Syracuse NY
Tacoma Art Museum, Tacoma WA
Telfair Academy of Arts and Sciences Inc, Savannah GA
Timken Museum of Art, San Diego CA
Tufts University, Art Gallery, Medford MA
Tulane University, University Art Collection, New Orleans LA
University of Notre Dame, Snite Museum of Art, Notre Dame IN
University of Rochester, Memorial Art Gallery, Rochester NY
University of Southern California, Fisher Gallery, Los Angeles CA
Worcester Art Museum, Worcester MA

PAINTING - GERMAN

Arnot Art Museum, Elmira NY
Columbus Chapel & Boal Mansion Museum, Boalsburg PA
Davenport Museum of Art, Davenport IA
Grand Rapids Art Museum, Grand Rapids MI
McMaster University, Art Gallery, Hamilton ON
The Metropolitan Museum of Art, New York NY
Milwaukee Art Museum, Milwaukee WI
The Museum at Drexel University, Philadelphia PA
Niagara University, Castellani Art Museum, New York NY
The Saint Louis Art Museum, Saint Louis MO
Syracuse University, Art Collection, Syracuse NY
Telfair Academy of Arts and Sciences Inc, Savannah GA
Tufts University, Art Gallery, Medford MA
University of Kansas, Spencer Museum of Art, Lawrence KS

PAINTING - ISRAELI

Temple Beth Israel, Plotkin Juddica Museum, Phoenix AZ

PAINTING - ITALIAN

American Classical College, Classical Art Gallery, Albuquerque NM
Arnot Art Museum, Elmira NY
Ball State University, Museum of Art, Muncie IN
Bates College, Museum of Art, Lewiston ME
Canton Art Institute, Canton OH
Chrysler Museum, Norfolk VA
Sterling and Francine Clark Art Institute, Williamstown MA
Columbia Museum of Art, Columbia SC
Columbus Chapel & Boal Mansion Museum, Boalsburg PA
The Frick Art Museum, Pittsburgh PA
Frick Collection, New York NY
Galleries of the Claremont Colleges, Claremont CA
Isabella Stewart Gardner Museum, Boston MA
Grand Rapids Art Museum, Grand Rapids MI
Howard University, Gallery of Art, Washington DC
Hyde Collection Trust, Glens Falls NY
Indianapolis Museum of Art, Clowes Fund Collection, Indianapolis IN
Memphis Brooks Museum of Art, Memphis TN
Museum of Fine Arts, Springfield MA
The Parrish Art Museum, Southampton NY
Philbrook Museum of Art, Tulsa OK
Potsdam College of the State University of New York, Roland Gibson Gallery, Potsdam NY
San Diego Museum of Art, San Diego CA
Timken Museum of Art, San Diego CA
University of Arizona, Museum of Art, Tucson AZ
University of California, Santa Barbara, University Art Museum, Santa Barbara CA
University of Notre Dame, Snite Museum of Art, Notre Dame IN
University of Southern California, Fisher Gallery, Los Angeles CA
University of Tennessee, Eleanor Dean Audigier Art Collection, Knoxville TN

University of Utah, Utah Museum of Fine Arts, Salt Lake City UT
Vanderbilt University, Fine Arts Gallery, Nashville TN
Vassar College, Vassar Art Gallery, Poughkeepsie NY
Virginia Museum of Fine Arts, Richmond VA
Western Kentucky University, Kentucky Museum, Bowling Green KY

PAINTING - JAPANESE

Cleveland Museum of Art, Cleveland OH
General Board of Discipleship, The United Methodist Church, The Upper Room Chapel & Museum, Nashville TN
Hofstra University, Hofstra Museum, Hempstead NY
Honolulu Academy of Arts, Honolulu HI
Japan Society, Inc, Japan Society Gallery, New York NY
Johns Hopkins University, Evergreen House, Baltimore MD
Kendall Whaling Museum, Sharon MA
New Orleans Museum of Art, New Orleans LA
Palm Beach County Parks & Recreation Department, Morikami Museum & Japanese Gardens, Delray Beach FL
Potsdam College of the State University of New York, Roland Gibson Gallery, Potsdam NY
Saint John's University, Chung-Cheng Art Gallery, Jamaica NY
Seattle Art Museum, Seattle WA

PAINTING - POLISH

Polish Museum of America, Chicago IL
St Mary's Galeria, Orchard Lake MI

PAINTING - RUSSIAN

Concordia University Wisconsin, Fine Art Gallery, Mequon WI
Michelson-Reves Museum of Art, Marshall TX
Marjorie Merriweather Post Foundation of DC, Hillwood Museum, Washington DC
University of Wisconsin-Madison, Elvehjem Museum of Art, Madison WI

PAINTING - SCANDINAVIAN

American Swedish Historical Foundation and Museum, Philadelphia PA
American Swedish Institute, Minneapolis MN

PAINTING - SPANISH

Arnot Art Museum, Elmira NY
Canton Art Institute, Canton OH
Columbus Chapel & Boal Mansion Museum, Boalsburg PA
Mission San Luis Rey Museum, San Luis Rey CA
Montreal Museum of Fine Arts, Montreal PQ
San Diego Museum of Art, San Diego CA
Timken Museum of Art, San Diego CA

PERIOD ROOMS

Adams National Historic Site, Quincy MA
Alabama Department of Archives and History Museum, Museum Galleries, Montgomery AL
Allentown Art Museum, Allentown PA
Artesia Historical Museum & Art Center, Artesia NM
Ashland Historical Society, Ashland MA
Atlanta Historical Society Inc, Atlanta History Center, Atlanta GA
The Bartlett Museum, Amesbury MA
Bartow-Pell Mansion Museum and Garden, New York NY
Bay County Historical Society, Historical Museum of Bay County, Bay City MI
Boulder Historical Society Inc, Museum of History, Boulder CO
Brick Store Museum, Kennebunk ME
Bradford Brinton Memorial Museum & Historic Ranch, Big Horn WY
Kit Carson Historic Museum, Taos NM

Chateau Ramezay Museum, Montreal PQ
Chatillon-DeMenil House Foundation, DeMenil Mansion, Saint Louis MO
Chester County Historical Society, West Chester PA
Chicago Architecture Foundation, Glessner House, Chicago IL
Cincinnati Museum Association, Cincinnati Art Museum, Cincinnati OH
City of Holyoke Museum-Wistariahurst, Holyoke MA
The City of Petersburg Museums, Petersburg VA
City of Springdale, Shiloh Museum, Springdale AR
Clark County Historical Society, Pioneer - Krier Museum, Ashland KS
Clemson University, Fort Hill, Clemson SC
Cliveden, Philadelphia PA
Colonel Black Mansion, Ellsworth ME
Columbus Museum, Columbus GA
Concord Museum, Concord MA
Crane Collection Gallery, Boston MA
Crawford County Historical Society, Baldwin-Reynolds House Museum, Meadville PA
Creek Council House Museum, Okmulgee OK
The Dixon Gallery & Gardens, Memphis TN
Douglas County Historical Society, Fairlawn Mansion & Museum, Superior WI
East Tennessee State University, Carroll Reece Museum, Johnson City TN
Environment Canada - Canadian Parks Service, Laurier House, Ottawa ON
Farmington Village Green and Library Association, Stanley-Whitman House, Farmington CT
Fillmore County Historical Society, Fountain MN
Henry Morrison Flagler Museum, Whitehall Mansion, Palm Beach FL
The Frick Art Museum, Pittsburgh PA
Gananoque Historical Society, Gananoque ON
Gibson Society, Inc, Gibson House Museum, Boston MA
Girard College, Stephen Girard Collection, Philadelphia PA
Greene County Historical Society, Xenia OH
Hancock Shaker Village, Inc, Pittsfield MA
Historical and Cultural Affairs, Delaware State Museums, Dover DE
Historical Society of Washington DC, Christian Heurich Mansion, Washington DC
Historic Cherry Hill, Albany NY
Hopewell Museum, Hopewell NJ
House of Roses, Senator Wilson Home, Deadwood SD
Stan Hywet Hall & Gardens, Inc, Akron OH
Idaho Historical Museum, Boise ID
Imperial Calcasieu Museum, Lake Charles LA
Independence National Historical Park, Philadelphia PA
Indianapolis Museum of Art, Indianapolis IN
Jackson County Historical Society, 1859 Jail, Marshal s Home & Museum, Independence MO
Jefferson County Open Space, Hiwan Homestead Museum, Evergreen CO
Thomas Jefferson Memorial Foundation, Monticello, Charlottesville VA
Johns Hopkins University, Homewood House Museum, Baltimore MD
Jordan Historical Museum of The Twenty, Jordan ON
Kentucky Historical Society, Old State Capitol & Annex, Frankfort KY
Ladies Library and Art Association, Independence Museum, Independence KS
Lehigh County Historical Society, Allentown PA
Liberty Hall Historic Site, Liberty Hall Museum, Frankfort KY
Lockwood-Mathews Mansion Museum, Norwalk CT
Longfellow-Evangeline State Commemorative Area, Saint Martinville LA
Longfellow National Historic Site, Cambridge MA
Longfellow's Wayside Inn Museum, South Sudbury MA
Loveland Museum and Gallery, Loveland CO
McPherson Museum, McPherson KS
Maine Historical Society, Wadsworth-Longfellow House, Portland ME
Manitoba Historical Society, Dalnavert Museum, Winnipeg MB

Mattatuck Historical Society Museum, Waterbury CT
Minneapolis Society of Fine Arts, Minneapolis Institute of Arts, Minneapolis MN
MonDak Heritage Center, Sidney MT
Morris-Jumel Mansion, Inc, New York NY
Mount Vernon Ladies' Association of the Union, Mount Vernon VA
Muchnic Foundation and Atchison Art Association, Muchnic Gallery, Atchison KS
Museum of Fine Arts, Boston MA
Museum of Fine Arts, Saint Petersburg, Florida, Inc, Saint Petersburg FL
National Museum of American Art, Renwick Gallery, Washington DC
National Trust for Historic Preservation, Decatur House, Washington DC
Nelson-Atkins Museum of Art, Kansas City MO
New Haven Colony Historical Society, New Haven CT
New York State Historical Association, Farmers' Museum, Inc, Cooperstown NY
New York State Office of Parks Recreation & Historic Preservation, John Jay Homestead State Historic Site, Katonah NY
New York State Office of Parks, Recreation & Historical Preservation, Mills Mansion State Historical Site, Staatsburg NY
Oatlands, Inc, Leesburg VA
Oglebay Institute, Mansion Museum, Wheeling WV
Oklahoma Historical Society, State Museum of History, Oklahoma City OK
Old Barracks Museum, Trenton NJ
Old Fort Harrod State Park Mansion Museum, Harrodsburg KY
Old York Historical Society, Elizabeth Perkins House, York ME
Paine Art Center and Arboretum, Oshkosh WI
Peabody & Essex Museum, Salem MA
Peoria Historical Society, Peoria IL
Phelps County Historical Society, Phelps County Museum, Holdrege NE
Philadelphia Museum of Art, Philadelphia PA
Piatt Castles, West Liberty OH
Portsmouth Historical Society, John Paul Jones House, Portsmouth NH
Putnam County Historical Society, Foundry School Museum, Cold Spring NY
Rhode Island Historical Society, John Brown House, Providence RI
Riley County Historical Museum, Manhattan KS
Rowland Evans Robinson Memorial Association, Rokeby Museum, Ferrisburgh VT
Rock Ford Foundation, Inc, Rock Ford Plantation & Kauffman Museum, Lancaster PA
Roswell Museum and Art Center, Roswell NM
C M Russell Museum, Great Falls MT
Robert W Ryerss Library and Museum, Philadelphia PA
Saint Augustine Historical Society, Oldest House and Museums, Saint Augustine FL
Saint-Gaudens National Historic Site, Cornish NH
Schuyler-Hamilton House, Morristown NJ
Schuyler Mansion State Historic Site, Albany NY
Seneca Falls Historical Society Museum, Seneca Falls NY
Shelburne Museum, Shelburne VT
Sheldon Museum, Middlebury VT
Abigail Adams Smith Museum, New York NY
Society for the Preservation of New England Antiquities, Archives, Boston MA
Nelda C & H J Lutcher Stark Foundation, Stark Museum of Art, Orange TX
Stratford Historical Society, Stratford CT
Sturdivant Hall, Selma AL
Tallahassee Museum of History & Natural Science, Tallahassee FL
Telfair Academy of Arts and Sciences Inc, Savannah GA
Temple Beth Israel, Plotkin Juddica Museum, Phoenix AZ
Tippecanoe County Historical Museum, Lafayette IN
The Trustees of Reservations, The Mission House, Stockbridge MA
Mark Twain Birthplace Museum, Stoutsville MO
United Society of Shakers, Shaker Museum, Poland Spring ME

US Department of State, Diplomatic Reception Rooms, Washington DC

Utah Department of Natural Resources, Division of Parks & Recreation, Territorial Statehouse, Fillmore UT

Vermilion County Museum Society, Danville IL

Wade House & Wesley W Jung Carriage Museum, Historic House & Carriage Museum, Greenbush WI

Mamie McFaddin Ward Heritage Historic Foundation, Beaumont TX

Wellfleet Historical Society Museum & Rider House, Wellfleet MA

Western Kentucky University, Kentucky Museum, Bowling Green KY

Western Reserve Historical Society, Cleveland OH

Wethersfield Historical Society Inc, Wethersfield CT

Woodrow Wilson House, Washington DC

Winterthur Museum and Gardens, Winterthur DE

PEWTER

Albany Institute of History and Art, Albany NY

Baker University, Old Castle Museum, Baldwin City KS

Franklin Mint Museum, Franklin Center PA

Historic Deerfield, Inc, Deerfield MA

Johns Hopkins University, Homewood House Museum, Baltimore MD

Livingston County Historical Society, Cobblestone Museum, Geneseo NY

New Canaan Historical Society, New Canaan CT

Oglebay Institute, Mansion Museum, Wheeling WV

Peabody & Essex Museum, Salem MA

Wellfleet Historical Society Museum & Rider House, Wellfleet MA

Winterthur Museum and Gardens, Winterthur DE

PHOTOGRAPHY

Adirondack Historical Association, Adirondack Museum, Blue Mountain Lake NY

Alberta College of Art, Illingworth Kerr Gallery, Calgary AB

Albright College, Freedman Gallery, Reading PA

Albuquerque Museum of Art, History & Science, Albuquerque NM

Anchorage Museum of History and Art, Anchorage AK

Artesia Historical Museum & Art Center, Artesia NM

Art Gallery of Hamilton, Hamilton ON

Art Institute for the Permian Basin, Odessa TX

The Art Institute of Chicago, Chicago IL

Art Museum of Southeast Texas, Beaumont TX

Atlanta Historical Society Inc, Atlanta History Center, Atlanta GA

Baldwin Historical Society Museum, Baldwin NY

Baltimore City Life Museums, Baltimore MD

Bay County Historical Society, Historical Museum of Bay County, Bay City MI

Beloit College, Wright Museum of Art, Beloit WI

Berea College, Doris Ulmann Galleries, Berea KY

Jesse Besser Museum, Alpena MI

Boise Art Museum, Boise ID

Boston Public Library, Albert H Wiggin Gallery & Print Department, Boston MA

Boulder Historical Society Inc, Museum of History, Boulder CO

Bowdoin College, Peary-MacMillan Arctic Museum, Brunswick ME

Roy Boyd Gallery, Chicago IL

Brooklyn Historical Society, Brooklyn NY

Brown University, David Winton Bell Gallery, Providence RI

Burchfield Art Center, Buffalo NY

California State University Stanislaus, University Art Gallery, Turlock CA

Canadian Museum of Contemporary Photography, Ottawa ON

Canadian Museum of Nature, Musee Canadien de la Nature, Ottawa ON

Canajoharie Art Gallery, Canajoharie NY

Carnegie Institute, Carnegie Museum of Art, Pittsburgh PA

Amon Carter Museum, Fort Worth TX

Cedar Rapids Museum of Art, Cedar Rapids IA

Center for Puppetry Arts, Atlanta GA

Chattahoochee Valley Art Museum, LaGrange GA

Chilkat Valley Historical Society, Sheldon Museum & Cultural Center, Haines AK

Church of Jesus Christ of Latter-day Saints, Museum of Church History & Art, Salt Lake City UT

Cincinnati Museum Association, Cincinnati Art Museum, Cincinnati OH

City of Pittsfield, Berkshire Artisans, Pittsfield MA

City of Springdale, Shiloh Museum, Springdale AR

Clark County Historical Society, Pioneer - Krier Museum, Ashland KS

Clinton Art Association Gallery, Clinton IA

The Coley Homestead & Barn Museum, Weston CT

Columbia College, The Museum of Contemporary Photography, Chicago IL

Columbus Museum of Art, Columbus OH

Continental Bank Corporation, Art Collection, Chicago IL

Corcoran Gallery of Art, Washington DC

Cornell University, Herbert F Johnson Museum of Art, Ithaca NY

Creighton University, Fine Arts Gallery, Omaha NE

Crocker Art Museum, Sacramento CA

Defense Language Institute Foreign Language Center, Presidio of Monterey Historical Holding, Presidio of Monterey CA

Delaware Art Museum, Wilmington DE

Durham Art Guild Inc, Durham NC

DuSable Museum of African American History, Chicago IL

East Baton Rouge Parks & Recreation Commission, Baton Rouge Gallery Inc, Baton Rouge LA

East Bay Asian Local Development Corp, Asian Resource Gallery, Oakland CA

Eccles Community Art Center, Ogden UT

Edmonton Art Gallery, Edmonton AB

Fayette Art Museum, Fayette AL

Federal Reserve Board, Art Gallery, Washington DC

Fillmore County Historical Society, Fountain MN

Fort Totten State Historic Site, Pioneer Daughters Museum, Fort Totten ND

The Friends of Photography, Ansel Adams Center for Photography, San Francisco CA

Galleries of the Claremont Colleges, Claremont CA

George Washington University, The Dimock Gallery, Washington DC

Getty Center for the History of Art & the Humanities Trust Museum, Santa Monica CA

Getty Center for the History of Art & the Humanities Trust Museum, The J Paul Getty Museum, Santa Monica CA

Goshen Historical Society, Goshen CT

Goucher College, Rosenberg Gallery, Towson MD

Grinnell College, Print & Drawing Study Room/Gallery, Grinnell IA

Grossmont Community College, Hyde Gallery, El Cajon CA

Guild Hall of East Hampton, Inc, Guild Hall Museum, East Hampton NY

Hallmark Cards, Inc, Fine Art Programs, Kansas City MO

Harvard University, William Hayes Fogg Art Museum, Cambridge MA

Headquarters Fort Monroe, Dept of Army, Casemate Museum, Fort Monroe VA

Historic Northampton Museum, Northampton MA

Hofstra University, Hofstra Museum, Hempstead NY

Hudson River Museum, Yonkers NY

Hunter Museum of Art, Chattanooga TN

Huntsville Museum of Art, Huntsville AL

Hyde Park Art Center, Chicago IL

Illinois State Museum, Illinois Art Gallery & Lockport Gallery, Springfield IL

Illinois State Museum, State of Illinois Art Gallery, Chicago IL

Institute of American Indian Arts Museum, Santa Fe NM

Intar Latin American Gallery, New York NY

International Center of Photography, New York NY

International Museum of Photography at George Eastman House, Rochester NY

Kalamazoo Institute of Arts, Kalamazoo MI

Lafayette College, Morris R Williams Center for the Arts, Art Gallery, Easton PA

Lehigh University Art Galleries, Bethlehem PA

LeSueur Museum, LeSueur MN

Liberty Memorial Museum & Archives, Kansas City MO

Library of Congress, Prints and Photographs Division, Washington DC

Louisa May Alcott Memorial Association, Orchard House, Concord MA

Louisiana Arts and Science Center, Baton Rouge LA

Louisiana Department of Culture, Recreation and Tourism, Louisiana State Museum, New Orleans LA

Loyola Marymount University, Laband Art Gallery, Los Angeles CA

McCord Museum of Canadian History, Montreal PQ

McLean County Historical Society, Bloomington IL

Maine Coast Artists, Art Gallery, Rockport ME

Mark Twain Bancshares, Saint Louis MO

Marquette University, Haggerty Museum of Art, Milwaukee WI

Massachusetts Institute of Technology, List Visual Arts Center, Cambridge MA

Meridian Museum of Art, Meridian MS

The Metropolitan Museum of Art, New York NY

Mexican Fine Arts Center Museum, Chicago IL

Miami-Dade Community College, Kendal Campus, Art Gallery, Miami FL

Miami University Art Museum, Oxford OH

Middle Tennessee State University, Photographic Gallery, Murfreesboro TN

Midwest Museum of American Art, Elkhart IN

Mills College, Art Gallery, Oakland CA

Milwaukee Public Museum, Milwaukee WI

Minneapolis Society of Fine Arts, Minneapolis Institute of Arts, Minneapolis MN

Monterey Peninsula Museum of Art Association, Monterey CA

Mountain View Doukhobor Museum, Grand Forks BC

Murray State University, Eagle Gallery, Murray KY

The Museum, Greenwood SC

Museum of American Textile History, North Andover MA

Museum of Fine Arts, Houston, Houston TX

Museum of Holography - Chicago, Chicago IL

Museum of Modern Art, New York NY

Museum of the City of New York, New York NY

National Museum of Women in the Arts, Washington DC

The National Park Service, United States Department of the Interior, The Statue of Liberty National Monument, New York NY

Nevada Museum Of Art, Reno NV

New Orleans Museum of Art, New Orleans LA

Newport Harbor Art Museum, Newport Beach CA

Niagara University, Castellani Art Museum, New York NY

Norfolk Historical Society Inc, Museum, Norfolk CT

Norwest Bank of Minneapolis, Art Collection, Minneapolis MN

Noyes Museum, Oceanville NJ

Oakland Museum, Art Dept, Oakland CA

Ohio University, Trisolini Gallery, Athens OH

Oklahoma City Art Museum, Oklahoma City OK

Olana State Historic Site, Hudson NY

Open Space, Victoria BC

Phillips Academy, Addison Gallery of American Art, Andover MA

Photographers Gallery, Saskatoon SK

Plains Art Museum, Moorhead MN

Portland Art Museum, Portland OR

Provincetown Art Association and Museum, Provincetown MA

Provincial Archives of Manitoba, Winnipeg MB

Randall Museum Junior Museum, San Francisco CA

Redding Museum of Art & History, Redding CA

Riley County Historical Museum, Manhattan KS

Roberson Museum & Science Center, Binghamton NY

Rome Historical Society Museum, Rome NY

St Lawrence University, Richard F Brush Art Gallery, Canton NY

The Saint Louis Art Museum, Saint Louis MO
San Francisco Maritime National Historical Park, National Maritime Museum, San Francisco CA
San Francisco Museum of Modern Art, San Francisco CA
Santa Clara University, de Saisset Museum, Santa Clara CA
Shell Canada Ltd, Calgary AB
Silverado Museum, Saint Helena CA
Smith College, Museum of Art, Northampton MA
Society for the Preservation of New England Antiquities, Boston MA
South Carolina State Museum, Columbia SC
Southern Illinois University, University Museum, Carbondale IL
Stamford Museum and Nature Center, Stamford CT
Stanley Museum, Inc, Kingfield ME
State Historical Society of Wisconsin, State Historical Museum, Madison WI
State University of New York at Purchase, Neuberger Museum, Purchase NY
Stratford Historical Society, Stratford CT
The Studio Museum in Harlem, New York NY
Swedish American Museum Association of Chicago, Chicago IL
3M, Art Collection, Saint Paul MN
Tomoka State Park Museum, Fred Dana Marsh Museum, Ormond Beach FL
Tufts University, Art Gallery, Medford MA
Tulane University, University Art Collection, New Orleans LA
Ulster County Community College, Muroff-Kotler Visual Arts Gallery, Stone Ridge NY
United Methodist Historical Society, Lovely Lane Museum, Baltimore MD
United Society of Shakers, Shaker Museum, Poland Spring ME
United States Figure Skating Association, World Figure Skating Hall of Fame and Museum, Colorado Springs CO
University of Akron, University Galleries, Akron OH
University of Alabama at Birmingham, Visual Arts Gallery, Birmingham AL
University of Alaska, Museum, Fairbanks AK
University of Arizona, Center for Creative Photography, Tucson AZ
University of Calgary, The Nickle Arts Museum, Calgary AB
University of Colorado, Art Galleries, Boulder CO
University of Colorado at Colorado Springs, Gallery of Contemporary Art, Colorado Springs CO
University of Florida, University Gallery, Gainesville FL
University of Iowa, Museum of Art, Iowa City IA
University of Kentucky, Photographic Archives, Lexington KY
University of Massachusetts, Amherst, University Gallery, Amherst MA
University of Michigan, Museum of Art, Ann Arbor MI
University of Nebraska, Lincoln, Sheldon Memorial Art Gallery, Lincoln NE
University of New Hampshire, The Art Gallery, Durham NH
University of New Mexico, University Art Museum, Albuquerque NM
University of Notre Dame, Snite Museum of Art, Notre Dame IN
University of Oklahoma, Fred Jones Jr Museum of Art, Norman OK
University of Rhode Island, Fine Arts Center Galleries, Kingston RI
University of South Florida, Contemporary Art Museum, Tampa FL
University of Washington, Henry Art Gallery, Seattle WA
University of West Florida, Art Gallery, Pensacola FL
University of Wisconsin, University Art Museum, Milwaukee WI
University of Wisconsin-Madison, Wisconsin Union Galleries, Madison WI
USS Constitution Museum Foundation Inc, Boston National Historical Park, Museum, Boston MA
Utah Arts Council, Chase Home Museum of Utah Folk Art, Salt Lake City UT

Utah Department of Natural Resources, Division of Parks & Recreation, Territorial Statehouse, Fillmore UT
Valentine Museum, Richmond VA
Village of Potsdam Public Museum, Potsdam NY
Virginia Commonwealth University, Anderson Gallery, Richmond VA
Volcano Art Center, Hawaii National Park HI
Walker Art Center, Minneapolis MN
Waterworks Visual Arts Center, Salisbury NC
Wayne County Historical Society, Museum, Honesdale PA
Wesleyan University, Davison Art Center, Middletown CT
Wethersfield Historical Society Inc, Wethersfield CT
Whatcom Museum of History and Art, Bellingham WA
Kemper & Leila Williams Foundation, New Orleans LA
Woodstock Artists Association, Woodstock NY
Peter Yegen Jr Yellowstone County Museum, Billings MT
Yosemite Museum, Yosemite National Park CA

PORCELAIN

Allentown Art Museum, Allentown PA
American Swedish Institute, Minneapolis MN
Art Institute for the Permian Basin, Odessa TX
Association for the Preservation of Virginia Antiquities, John Marshall House, Richmond VA
Atlanta Historical Society Inc, Atlanta History Center, Atlanta GA
Atlanta Museum, Atlanta GA
Baltimore Museum of Art, Baltimore MD
Beaverbrook Art Gallery, Fredericton NB
Bellingrath Gardens and Home, Theodore AL
Beloit College, Wright Museum of Art, Beloit WI
The Bradford Museum of Collector's Plates, Niles IL
The Bruce Museum, Greenwich CT
Campbell Museum, Camden NJ
Chatillon-DeMenil House Foundation, DeMenil Mansion, Saint Louis MO
Cheekwood-Tennessee Botanical Gardens & Museum of Art, Nashville TN
Sterling and Francine Clark Art Institute, Williamstown MA
Cranbrook Academy of Art Museum, Bloomfield Hills MI
Cummer Gallery of Art, DeEtte Holden Cummer Museum Foundation, Jacksonville FL
Danville Museum of Fine Arts & History, Danville VA
The Dixon Gallery & Gardens, Memphis TN
Everson Museum of Art, Syracuse NY
Fort Smith Art Center, Fort Smith AR
Fort Totten State Historic Site, Pioneer Daughters Museum, Fort Totten ND
Franklin Mint Museum, Franklin Center PA
The Frick Art Museum, Pittsburgh PA
Frick Collection, New York NY
General Board of Discipleship, The United Methodist Church, The Upper Room Chapel & Museum, Nashville TN
Girard College, Stephen Girard Collection, Philadelphia PA
Hammond-Harwood House Association, Inc, Annapolis MD
Headley-Whitney Museum, Lexington KY
Hill-Stead Museum, Farmington CT
Historical and Cultural Affairs, Delaware State Museums, Dover DE
Herbert Hoover Presidential Library & Museum, West Branch IA
Indianapolis Museum of Art, Indianapolis IN
Johns Hopkins University, Homewood House Museum, Baltimore MD
Lehigh University Art Galleries, Bethlehem PA
Longfellow-Evangeline State Commemorative Area, Saint Martinville LA
Maryland Historical Society, Museum of Maryland History, Baltimore MD
Memphis Brooks Museum of Art, Memphis TN
Montreal Museum of Fine Arts, Montreal PQ
Museum of Fine Arts, Boston MA

National Society of Colonial Dames of America in the State of Maryland, Mount Clare Mansion, Baltimore MD
Pennsylvania State University, Palmer Museum of Art, University Park PA
Philadelphia Museum of Art, Philadelphia PA
Marjorie Merriweather Post Foundation of DC, Hillwood Museum, Washington DC
Frederic Remington Art Museum, Ogdensburg NY
Rhode Island School of Design, Museum of Art, Providence RI
The Rosenbach Museum and Library, Philadelphia PA
Robert W Ryerss Library and Museum, Philadelphia PA
Saint John's University, Chung-Cheng Art Gallery, Jamaica NY
The Saint Louis Art Museum, Saint Louis MO
Seattle Art Museum, Seattle WA
Ella Sharp Museum, Jackson MI
Ships of The Sea Museum, Savannah GA
Nelda C & H J Lutcher Stark Foundation, Stark Museum of Art, Orange TX
US Department of State, Diplomatic Reception Rooms, Washington DC
United States Tobacco Manufacturing Company Inc, Museum of Tobacco & History, Nashville TN
University of Notre Dame, Snite Museum of Art, Notre Dame IN
University of Tampa, Henry B Plant Museum, Tampa FL
University of Tennessee, Eleanor Dean Audigier Art Collection, Knoxville TN
Virginia Museum of Fine Arts, Richmond VA
Wayne Center for the Arts, Wooster OH
T T Wentworth Jr Museum, Florida State Museum, Pensacola FL
White House, Washington DC
Wichita Art Museum, Wichita KS
Winterthur Museum and Gardens, Winterthur DE
Woodmere Art Museum, Philadelphia PA

PORTRAITS

Art Institute for the Permian Basin, Odessa TX
Ashland Historical Society, Ashland MA
Baltimore Museum of Art, Baltimore MD
The Bartlett Museum, Amesbury MA
Beloit College, Wright Museum of Art, Beloit WI
Canton Art Institute, Canton OH
Carolina Art Association, Gibbes Museum of Art, Charleston SC
Cedar Rapids Museum of Art, Cedar Rapids IA
Chatillon-DeMenil House Foundation, DeMenil Mansion, Saint Louis MO
Chelan County Public Utility District, Rocky Reach Dam, Wenatchee WA
Church of Jesus Christ of Latter-day Saints, Museum of Church History & Art, Salt Lake City UT
Delaware Art Museum, Wilmington DE
Durham Art Guild Inc, Durham NC
Everson Museum of Art, Syracuse NY
Fort Totten State Historic Site, Pioneer Daughters Museum, Fort Totten ND
Historical and Cultural Affairs, Delaware State Museums, Dover DE
Huntington Museum of Art, Huntington WV
Idaho Historical Museum, Boise ID
Independence National Historical Park, Philadelphia PA
Indianapolis Museum of Art, Indianapolis IN
Jekyll Island Museum, Jekyll Island GA
Lincoln National Life Insurance Co, Lincoln Museum, Fort Wayne IN
Livingston County Historical Society, Cobblestone Museum, Geneseo NY
Longfellow-Evangeline State Commemorative Area, Saint Martinville LA
Louisa May Alcott Memorial Association, Orchard House, Concord MA
Marcella Sembrich Memorial Association Inc, Opera Museum, Bolton Landing NY
The Market Gallery of the City of Toronto Archives, Toronto ON
Michelson-Reves Museum of Art, Marshall TX
James Monroe Museum, Fredericksburg VA

Moravian Historical Society, Whitefield House Museum, Nazareth PA
Morris Communications Corporation, Morris Museum of Art, Augusta GA
Murray State University, Eagle Gallery, Murray KY
Musee Regional de Vaudreuil-Soulanges, Vaudreuil PQ
Nevada Museum Of Art, Reno NV
New Haven Colony Historical Society, New Haven CT
New Jersey Historical Society Museum, Newark NJ
New York State Office of Parks Recreation & Historic Preservation, John Jay Homestead State Historic Site, Katonah NY
Norfolk Historical Society Inc, Museum, Norfolk CT
R W Norton Art Gallery, Shreveport LA
Oklahoma City Art Museum, Oklahoma City OK
Oshkosh Public Museum, Oshkosh WI
The Parrish Art Museum, Southampton NY
Philipse Manor Hall State Historic Site, Yonkers NY
Presidential Museum, Odessa TX
Riley County Historical Museum, Manhattan KS
Rowland Evans Robinson Memorial Association, Rokeby Museum, Ferrisburgh VT
Rollins College, George D and Harriet W Cornell Fine Arts Museum, Winter Park FL
Royal Ontario Museum, Canadian Decorative Arts Department, Toronto ON
Shirley Plantation, Charles City VA
SLA Arch-Couture Inc, Art Collection, Denver CO
Society for the Preservation of New England Antiquities, Archives, Boston MA
Stratford Historical Society, Stratford CT
Gilbert Stuart Memorial Association, Inc, Museum, Saunderstown RI
Summit County Historical Society, Akron OH
Telfair Academy of Arts and Sciences Inc, Savannah GA
Tomoka State Park Museum, Fred Dana Marsh Museum, Ormond Beach FL
Transylvania University, Morlan Gallery, Lexington KY
University of Southern California, Fisher Gallery, Los Angeles CA
Wayne County Historical Society, Museum, Honesdale PA
White House, Washington DC
Winterthur Museum and Gardens, Winterthur DE
Woodstock Artists Association, Woodstock NY

POSTERS

American Jewish Historical Society, Waltham MA
American University, Watkins Collectiony, Washington DC
Art Institute for the Permian Basin, Odessa TX
Beloit College, Wright Museum of Art, Beloit WI
Canadian Museum of Nature, Musee Canadien de la Nature, Ottawa ON
Cedar Rapids Museum of Art, Cedar Rapids IA
Center for Puppetry Arts, Atlanta GA
Chicano Humanities & Arts Council, Denver CO
Defense Language Institute Foreign Language Center, Presidio of Monterey Historical Holding, Presidio of Monterey CA
Delaware Art Museum, Wilmington DE
Fairfield University, Thomas J Walsh Art Gallery, Fairfield CT
Greenville College, Richard W Bock Sculpture Collection, Greenville IL
Herbert Hoover Presidential Library & Museum, West Branch IA
International Museum of Cartoon Art, Montreal PQ
La Casa del Libro Museum, San Juan PR
Liberty Memorial Museum & Archives, Kansas City MO
Livingston County Historical Society, Cobblestone Museum, Geneseo NY
Museum of Modern Art, New York NY
Museum of Movie Art, Calgary AB
Museum of New York, Rock Hill SC
National Archives of Canada, Documentary Art and Photography, Ottawa ON
Nebraska State Capitol, Lincoln NE
New Jersey Historical Society Museum, Newark NJ

Temple Beth Israel, Plotkin Juddica Museum, Phoenix AZ
Tomoka State Park Museum, Fred Dana Marsh Museum, Ormond Beach FL
United States Tobacco Manufacturing Company Inc, Museum of Tobacco & History, Nashville TN

POTTERY

Alabama Department of Archives and History Museum, Museum Galleries, Montgomery AL
Allegheny College, Bowman, Megahan and Penelec Galleries, Meadville PA
Art Association of Jacksonville, David Strawn Art Gallery, Jacksonville IL
Atlanta Historical Society Inc, Atlanta History Center, Atlanta GA
Baker University, Old Castle Museum, Baldwin City KS
Brevard College, Sims Art Center, Brevard NC
Church of Jesus Christ of Latter-day Saints, Museum of Church History & Art, Salt Lake City UT
City of Pittsfield, Berkshire Artisans, Pittsfield MA
Clinton Art Association Gallery, Clinton IA
Creighton University, Fine Arts Gallery, Omaha NE
Enook Galleries, Waterloo ON
Fayette Art Museum, Fayette AL
Freeport Art Museum & Cultural Center, Freeport IL
Gadsden Museum, Mesilla NM
Grand Rapids Art Museum, Grand Rapids MI
Grossmont Community College, Hyde Gallery, El Cajon CA
Halifax Historical Society, Inc, Halifax Historical Museum, Daytona Beach FL
Harvard University, Dumbarton Oaks Research Library and Collections, Washington DC
High Point Historical Society Inc, Museum, High Point NC
Historical Society of Cheshire County, Colony House Museum, Keene NH
Johnson-Humrickhouse Museum, Coshocton OH
Kenosha Public Museum, Kenosha WI
Livingston County Historical Society, Cobblestone Museum, Geneseo NY
McCord Museum of Canadian History, Montreal PQ
Maryland Historical Society, Museum of Maryland History, Baltimore MD
Meridian Museum of Art, Meridian MS
Monterey Peninsula Museum of Art Association, Monterey CA
Mount Saint Vincent University, Art Gallery, Halifax NS
Musee Regional de Vaudreuil-Soulanges, Vaudreuil PQ
Nelson-Atkins Museum of Art, Kansas City MO
R W Norton Art Gallery, Shreveport LA
Oak Ridge Art Center, Oak Ridge TN
Peoria Historical Society, Peoria IL
Phelps County Historical Society, Phelps County Museum, Holdrege NE
Saint John's Museum of Art, Wilmington NC
Summit County Historical Society, Akron OH
Tomoka State Park Museum, Fred Dana Marsh Museum, Ormond Beach FL
Tulane University, University Art Collection, New Orleans LA
University of Delaware, University Gallery, Newark DE
University of Michigan, Kelsey Museum of Archaeology, Ann Arbor MI
University of Washington, Henry Art Gallery, Seattle WA
Village of Potsdam Public Museum, Potsdam NY
Virginia Museum of Fine Arts, Richmond VA
West Baton Rouge Historical Association, Museum, Port Allen LA

PRE-COLUMBIAN ART

Americas Society, New York NY
Art Association of Jacksonville, David Strawn Art Gallery, Jacksonville IL
Aurora University, Schingoethe Center for Native American Cultures, Aurora IL
Beloit College, Wright Museum of Art, Beloit WI
Birmingham Museum of Art, Birmingham AL
Bower's Museum, Santa Ana CA
Brandeis University, Rose Art Museum, Waltham MA
Brevard Art Center and Museum, Inc, Melbourne FL
California State University Stanislaus, University Art Gallery, Turlock CA
Center for Puppetry Arts, Atlanta GA
Chicano Humanities & Arts Council, Denver CO
Colgate University, Picker Art Gallery, Hamilton NY
The College at New Paltz State University of New York, College Art Gallery, New Paltz NY
Concordia University, Leonard & Bina Ellen Art Gallery, Montreal PQ
Continental Bank Corporation, Art Collection, Chicago IL
Dallas Museum of Art, Dallas TX
Dartmouth College, Hood Museum of Art, Hanover NH
East Tennessee State University, Carroll Reece Museum, Johnson City TN
Hampton University, University Museum, Hampton VA
Harvard University, Dumbarton Oaks Research Library and Collections, Washington DC
Hofstra University, Hofstra Museum, Hempstead NY
Jacksonville Art Museum, Jacksonville FL
Kimbell Art Museum, Fort Worth TX
MEXIC-ARTE Museum, Austin TX
Minneapolis Society of Fine Arts, Minneapolis Institute of Arts, Minneapolis MN
Mint Museum of Art, Charlotte NC
Monterey Peninsula Museum of Art Association, Monterey CA
Mount Holyoke College, Art Museum, South Hadley MA
Munson-Williams-Proctor Institute, Museum of Art, Utica NY
Musee d'Art de Joliette, Joliette PQ
Museum of Fine Arts, Houston, Houston TX
Museum of Fine Arts, Saint Petersburg, Florida, Inc, Saint Petersburg FL
Museum of the Americas, Brookfield VT
National Museum of the American Indian, New York NY
Natural History Museum of Los Angeles County, Los Angeles CA
Newark Museum Association, The Newark Museum, Newark NJ
New Mexico State University, University Art Gallery, Las Cruces NM
New Orleans Museum of Art, New Orleans LA
Niagara University, Castellani Art Museum, New York NY
North Carolina Museum of Art, Raleigh NC
Oakland University, Meadow Brook Art Gallery, Rochester MI
Oklahoma Center for Science and Art, Kirkpatrick Center, Oklahoma City OK
Orlando Museum of Art, Orlando FL
Portland Art Museum, Portland OR
Princeton University, The Art Museum, Princeton NJ
Rhode Island School of Design, Museum of Art, Providence RI
Rice University, Sewall Art Gallery, Houston TX
Roswell Museum and Art Center, Roswell NM
Royal Ontario Museum, Toronto ON
C M Russell Museum, Great Falls MT
Saint Gregory's Abbey and College, Mabee-Gerrer Museum of Art, Shawnee OK
The Saint Louis Art Museum, Saint Louis MO
Science Museums of Charlotte, Inc, Discovery Place, Charlotte NC
Southern Connecticut State University, Art Gallery, New Haven CT
Southwest Museum, Los Angeles CA
Tampa Museum of Art, Tampa FL

Tucson Museum of Art, Tucson AZ
University of Florida, University Gallery, Gainesville FL
University of Houston, Sarah Campbell Blaffer Gallery, Houston TX
University of Illinois, Krannert Art Museum, Champaign IL
University of Iowa, Museum of Art, Iowa City IA
University of Kentucky, Art Museum, Lexington KY
University of Miami, Lowe Art Museum, Coral Gables FL
University of Missouri, Museum of Art and Archaeology, Columbia MO
University of Notre Dame, Snite Museum of Art, Notre Dame IN
University of South Florida, Contemporary Art Museum, Tampa FL
Vancouver Museum Association, Vancouver Museum, Vancouver BC
Wichita Art Museum, Wichita KS
Williams College, Museum of Art, Williamstown MA
Worcester Art Museum, Worcester MA
Wustum Museum Art Association, Racine WI

PRIMITIVE ART

Lyman Allyn Art Museum, New London CT
Art Gallery of Greater Victoria, Victoria BC
The Art Institute of Chicago, Chicago IL
Beloit College, Wright Museum of Art, Beloit WI
Boise Art Museum, Boise ID
Bowdoin College, Peary-MacMillan Arctic Museum, Brunswick ME
The Buffalo Fine Arts Academy, Albright-Knox Art Gallery, Buffalo NY
Capital University, Schumacher Gallery, Columbus OH
Church of Jesus Christ of Latter-day Saints, Museum of Church History & Art, Salt Lake City UT
City of Springdale, Shiloh Museum, Springdale AR
The College at New Paltz State University of New York, College Art Gallery, New Paltz NY
Columbus Museum, Columbus GA
Enook Galleries, Waterloo ON
Fayette Art Museum, Fayette AL
Field Museum of Natural History, Chicago IL
Fine Arts Museums of San Francisco, M H de Young Memorial Museum and California Palace of the Legion of Honor, San Francisco CA
Gallery of Prehistoric Paintings, New York NY
Heritage Plantation of Sandwich, Sandwich MA
Illinois Historic Preservation Agency, Bishop Hill State Historis Site, Bishop Hill IL
Indiana University, Art Museum, Bloomington IN
Lightner Museum, Saint Augustine FL
The Metropolitan Museum of Art, New York NY
Monterey Peninsula Museum of Art Association, Monterey CA
Morris Communications Corporation, Morris Museum of Art, Augusta GA
Museum of Fine Arts, Springfield MA
Museum of Fine Arts, Houston, Houston TX
Olivet College, Armstrong Museum of Art and Archaeology, Olivet MI
Roswell Museum and Art Center, Roswell NM
Royal Ontario Museum, Toronto ON
Science Museums of Charlotte, Inc, Discovery Place, Charlotte NC
Seattle Art Museum, Seattle WA
Southwest Museum, Los Angeles CA
Staten Island Institute of Arts and Sciences, Staten Island NY
Stephens College, Lewis James & Nellie Stratton Davis Art Gallery, Columbia MO
University of Missouri, Museum of Art and Archaeology, Columbia MO
University of Rochester, Memorial Art Gallery, Rochester NY

PRINTS

Adirondack Historical Association, Adirondack Museum, Blue Mountain Lake NY
Albertson College of Idaho, Rosenthal Art Gallery, Caldwell ID
Albion College, Bobbitt Visual Arts Center, Albion MI
The Albrecht-Kemper Museum of Art, Saint Joseph MO
Albright College, Freedman Gallery, Reading PA
Aldrich Museum of Contemporary Art, Ridgefield CT
American University, Watkins Collectiony, Washington DC
Ari Museum of Western Virginia, Roanoke VA
Arizona State University, University Art Museum, Tempe AZ
Arkansas Arts Center, Little Rock AR
Art Gallery of Nova Scotia, Halifax NS
Art Institute for the Permian Basin, Odessa TX
The Art Institute of Chicago, Chicago IL
Art Museum of South Texas, Corpus Christi TX
Art Museum of the Americas, Washington DC
Art Patrons League of Mobile, Mobile AL
Attleboro Museum, Center for the Arts, Attleboro MA
Augustana College, Art Gallery, Rock Island IL
Austin College, Ida Green Gallery, Sherman TX
Leo Baeck Institute, New York NY
Baldwin-Wallace College, Fawick Art Gallery, Berea OH
Ball State University, Museum of Art, Muncie IN
Baltimore City Life Museums, Baltimore MD
Baltimore Museum of Art, Baltimore MD
Bard College, William Cooper Procter Art Center, Annandale-on-Hudson NY
Bates College, Museum of Art, Lewiston ME
Baylor University, Martin Museum of Art, Waco TX
Beaverbrook Art Gallery, Fredericton NB
Beloit College, Wright Museum of Art, Beloit WI
Berea College, Doris Ulmann Galleries, Berea KY
Jesse Besser Museum, Alpena MI
Boston Public Library, Albert H Wiggin Gallery & Print Department, Boston MA
Roy Boyd Gallery, Chicago IL
Brandeis University, Rose Art Museum, Waltham MA
Brevard College, Sims Art Center, Brevard NC
Brigham City Museum-Gallery, Brigham City UT
Brigham Young University, B F Larsen Gallery, Provo UT
Bradford Brinton Memorial Museum & Historic Ranch, Big Horn WY
Brooklyn Historical Society, Brooklyn NY
Brown University, David Winton Bell Gallery, Providence RI
The Buffalo Fine Arts Academy, Albright-Knox Art Gallery, Buffalo NY
Burnaby Art Gallery, Burnaby BC
Butler Institute of American Art, Art Museum, Youngstown OH
Calvin College, Center Art Gallery, Grand Rapids MI
Canadian Museum of Nature, Musee Canadien de la Nature, Ottawa ON
Capital University, Schumacher Gallery, Columbus OH
Carnegie Institute, Carnegie Museum of Art, Pittsburgh PA
Carolina Art Association, Gibbes Museum of Art, Charleston SC
Amon Carter Museum, Fort Worth TX
Cedar Rapids Museum of Art, Cedar Rapids IA
Central Michigan University, Art Gallery, Mount Pleasant MI
Cincinnati Museum Association, Cincinnati Art Museum, Cincinnati OH
City of Pittsfield, Berkshire Artisans, Pittsfield MA
Clinton Art Association Gallery, Clinton IA
The College at New Paltz State University of New York, College Art Gallery, New Paltz NY
College of Eastern Utah, Gallery East, Price UT
College of Saint Benedict, Art Gallery, Saint Joseph MN
Columbus Museum of Art, Columbus OH
Concordia College, Marx Hausen Art Gallery, Seward NE

Concordia University, Leonard & Bina Ellen Art Gallery, Montreal PQ
Confederation Centre Art Gallery and Museum, Charlottetown PE
Cooper-Hewitt, National Museum of Design, New York NY
Coos Art Museum, Coos Bay OR
Cranbrook Academy of Art Museum, Bloomfield Hills MI
Creighton University, Fine Arts Gallery, Omaha NE
Crocker Art Museum, Sacramento CA
Danville Museum of Fine Arts & History, Danville VA
DAR Museum, National Society Daughters of the American Revolution, Washington DC
Dartmouth College, Hood Museum of Art, Hanover NH
Delaware Art Museum, Wilmington DE
Durham Art Guild Inc, Durham NC
DuSable Museum of African American History, Chicago IL
Eastern Illinois University, Tarble Arts Center, Charleston IL
East Tennessee State University, Carroll Reece Museum, Johnson City TN
Eccles Community Art Center, Ogden UT
El Camino College Art Gallery, Torrance CA
Estevan National Exhibition Centre Inc, Estevan SK
Everhart Museum, Scranton PA
Fairfield University, Thomas J Walsh Art Gallery, Fairfield CT
Federal Reserve Board, Art Gallery, Washington DC
Findlay College, Egner Fine Arts Center, Findlay OH
Fitchburg Art Museum, Fitchburg MA
Fort Hays State University, Moss-Thorns Gallery of Arts, Hays KS
Fort Wayne Museum of Art, Inc, Fort Wayne IN
Freeport Art Museum & Cultural Center, Freeport IL
Frick Collection, New York NY
Frostburg State University, The Stephanie Ann Roper Gallery, Frostburg MD
George Washington University, The Dimock Gallery, Washington DC
Wendell Gilley Museum, Southwest Harbor ME
Gonzaga University, Ad Art Gallery, Spokane WA
Goucher College, Rosenberg Gallery, Towson MD
Grand Rapids Art Museum, Grand Rapids MI
Grinnell College, Print & Drawing Study Room/ Gallery, Grinnell IA
Grossmont Community College, Hyde Gallery, El Cajon CA
Solomon R Guggenheim Museum, New York NY
Guild Hall of East Hampton, Inc, Guild Hall Museum, East Hampton NY
Hamilton College, Fred L Emerson Gallery, Clinton NY
Hammond-Harwood House Association, Inc, Annapolis MD
Hartwick College, Foreman Gallery, Oneonta NY
Harvard University, William Hayes Fogg Art Museum, Cambridge MA
Headquarters Fort Monroe, Dept of Army, Casemate Museum, Fort Monroe VA
Heckscher Museum, Huntington NY
Hill-Stead Museum, Farmington CT
Honolulu Academy of Arts, Honolulu HI
House of Roses, Senator Wilson Home, Deadwood SD
Howard University, Gallery of Art, Washington DC
Hunterdon Art Center, Clinton NJ
Hunter Museum of Art, Chattanooga TN
Huntington Museum of Art, Huntington WV
Huntsville Museum of Art, Huntsville AL
Hyde Collection Trust, Glens Falls NY
Hyde Park Art Center, Chicago IL
Illinois Wesleyan University, Merwin & Wakeley Galleries, Bloomington IL
Indianapolis Museum of Art, Indianapolis IN
Indiana University, Art Museum, Bloomington IN
Jacksonville Art Museum, Jacksonville FL
Jamestown-Yorktown Foundation, Yorktown VA
Johnson-Humrickhouse Museum, Coshocton OH

Keene State College, Thorne-Sagendorph Art Gallery, Keene NH
Kent State University, School of Art Gallery, Kent OH
Kitchener-Waterloo Art Gallery, Kitchener ON
Lafayette College, Morris R Williams Center for the Arts, Art Gallery, Easton PA
La Salle University, Art Museum, Philadelphia PA
Library of Congress, Prints and Photographs Division, Washington DC
Lindenwood College, Harry D Hendren Gallery, Saint Charles MO
Long Beach Museum of Art, Long Beach CA
Longfellow's Wayside Inn Museum, South Sudbury MA
Long Island Graphic Eye Gallery, Port Washington NY
Los Angeles County Museum of Art, Los Angeles CA
Lycoming College Gallery, Williamsport PA
McAllen International Museum, McAllen TX
McCord Museum of Canadian History, Montreal PQ
MacDonald Stewart Art Centre Art Center, Guelph ON
The Robert McLaughlin Gallery, Oshawa ON
McMaster University, Art Gallery, Hamilton ON
Charles H MacNider Museum, Mason City IA
McPherson College Gallery, McPherson KS
Madison Art Center, Madison WI
Judah L Magnes Museum, Berkeley CA
Maine Coast Artists, Art Gallery, Rockport ME
Mankato State University, Conkling Gallery Art Dept, Mankato MN
The Market Gallery of the City of Toronto Archives, Toronto ON
Marquette University, Haggerty Museum of Art, Milwaukee WI
Maryville College, Fine Arts Center Gallery, Maryville TN
Mary Washington College, The Gari Melchers Estate & Memorial Gallery, Fredericksburg VA
Massachusetts Institute of Technology, List Visual Arts Center, Cambridge MA
Meridian Museum of Art, Meridian MS
Mexican Fine Arts Center Museum, Chicago IL
Miami-Dade Community College, Kendal Campus, Art Gallery, Miami FL
Miami University Art Museum, Oxford OH
Michelson-Reves Museum of Art, Marshall TX
Michigan State University, Kresge Art Museum, East Lansing MI
Middlebury College, Museum of Art, Middlebury VT
Millikin University, Perkinson Gallery, Decatur IL
Mills College, Art Gallery, Oakland CA
Minneapolis Society of Fine Arts, Minneapolis Institute of Arts, Minneapolis MN
Minnesota Museum of American Art, Saint Paul MN
Mississippi University for Women, Fine Arts Gallery, Columbus MS
Mobil Corporation, Art Collection, Fairfax VA
Montclair Art Museum, Montclair NJ
Moravian College, Payne Gallery, Bethlehem PA
Morehead State University, Claypool-Young Art Gallery, Morehead KY
Mount Holyoke College, Art Museum, South Hadley MA
Mount Mary College, Tower Gallery, Milwaukee WI
Munson-Williams-Proctor Institute, Museum of Art, Utica NY
Murray State University, Eagle Gallery, Murray KY
Museum of American Textile History, North Andover MA
Museum of Arts and History, Port Huron MI
Museum of Arts and Sciences, Inc, Macon GA
Museum of Fine Arts, Boston MA
Museum of Modern Art, New York NY
Museum of Movie Art, Calgary AB
Museum of the City of New York, New York NY
Museums of Abilene, Inc, Abilene TX
Nassau Community College, Firehouse Art Gallery, Garden City NY
Nassau County Museum of Fine Art, Roslyn NY
National Air and Space Museum, Washington DC

National Archives of Canada, Documentary Art and Photography, Ottawa ON
National Museum of American Art, Washington DC
National Museum of Racing and Hall of Fame, Saratoga Springs NY
Naval Historical Center, The Navy Museum, Washington DC
Nebraska Wesleyan University, Elder Gallery, Lincoln NE
Nevada Museum Of Art, Reno NV
New Mexico State University, University Art Gallery, Las Cruces NM
New Visions Gallery, Inc, Marshfield WI
New York University, Grey Art Gallery and Study Center, New York NY
Niagara University, Castellani Art Museum, New York NY
The John A Noble Collection, Staten Island NY
North Central Washington Museum, Art Gallery, Wenatchee WA
Northern Kentucky University Gallery, Highland Heights KY
Northwestern College, Te Paske Gallery of Rowenhorst, Orange City IA
Norwest Bank of Minneapolis, Art Collection, Minneapolis MN
Noyes Museum, Oceanville NJ
Oakland Museum, Art Dept, Oakland CA
Oak Ridge Art Center, Oak Ridge TN
Ohio University, Trisolini Gallery, Athens OH
Okefenokee Heritage Center, Inc, Waycross GA
Oklahoma Center for Science and Art, Kirkpatrick Center, Oklahoma City OK
Old Dartmouth Historical Society, New Bedford Whaling Museum, New Bedford MA
Olivet College, Armstrong Museum of Art and Archaeology, Olivet MI
Order Sons of Italy in America, Garibaldi & Meucci Meuseum, Staten Island NY
Pennsylvania Academy of the Fine Arts, Galleries, Philadelphia PA
Pennsylvania State University, Palmer Museum of Art, University Park PA
Philbrook Museum of Art, Tulsa OK
Phillips Academy, Addison Gallery of American Art, Andover MA
Plains Art Museum, Moorhead MN
Portland Art Museum, Portland OR
Portland Museum of Art, Portland ME
Portsmouth Museums, Arts Center, Portsmouth VA
Potsdam College of the State University of New York, Roland Gibson Gallery, Potsdam NY
Print Club of Albany, Museum, Albany NY
Provincetown Art Association and Museum, Provincetown MA
Provincial Archives of Manitoba, Winnipeg MB
Putnam Museum of History & Natural Science, Davenport IA
Queebsborough Community College, Art Gallery, Bayside NY
Queen's University, Agnes Etherington Art Centre, Kingston ON
Quincy University, The Gray Gallery, Quincy IL
Rahr-West Art Museum, Manitowoc WI
Reed College, Douglas F Cooley Memorial Art Gallery, Portland OR
Reynolda House Museum of American Art, Winston-Salem NC
Rhode Island School of Design, Museum of Art, Providence RI
Rice University, Sewall Art Gallery, Houston TX
R J R Nabisco, Inc, New York NY
Roberson Museum & Science Center, Binghamton NY
The Rockwell Museum, Corning NY
Rogers House Museum Gallery, Ellsworth KS
Rollins College, George D and Harriet W Cornell Fine Arts Museum, Winter Park FL
The Rosenbach Museum and Library, Philadelphia PA
Robert W Ryerss Library and Museum, Philadelphia PA
Saint Anselm College, Chapel Art Center, Manchester NH
St Clair County Community College, Jack R Hennesey Art Galleries, Port Huron MI

Saint Gregory's Abbey and College, Mabee-Gerrer Museum of Art, Shawnee OK
St Lawrence University, Richard F Brush Art Gallery, Canton NY
The Saint Louis Art Museum, Saint Louis MO
Saint Mary's College, Moreau Gallery, Notre Dame IN
Salisbury State University, University Gallery, Salisbury MD
San Diego Museum of Art, San Diego CA
San Diego State University, University Art Gallery, San Diego CA
San Jose Museum of Art, San Jose CA
Scottsdale Center for the Arts, Scottsdale AZ
Seattle Art Museum, Seattle WA
Ella Sharp Museum, Jackson MI
Silvermine Guild Arts Center, Silvermine Galleries, New Canaan CT
Skidmore College, Schick Art Gallery, Saratoga Springs NY
Smith College, Museum of Art, Northampton MA
Sonoma State University, Art Gallery, Rohnert Park CA
Southern Alleghenies Museum of Art, Loretto PA
Southern Arkansas University, Art Dept Gallery & Magale Art Gallery, Magnolia AR
Southern Illinois University, University Museum, Carbondale IL
Springfield Art Museum, Springfield MO
Stamford Museum and Nature Center, Stamford CT
State Art Museum of Florida, John & Mable Ringling Museum of Art, Sarasota FL
Staten Island Institute of Arts and Sciences, Staten Island NY
State University of New York at Albany, University Art Gallery, Albany NY
State University of New York at Oswego, Tyler Art Gallery, Oswego NY
State University of New York at Purchase, Neuberger Museum, Purchase NY
State University of New York College at Fredonia, M C Rockefeller Arts Center Gallery, Fredonia NY
Stetson University, Duncan Gallery of Art, De Land FL
3M, Art Collection, Saint Paul MN
Toledo Museum of Art, Toledo Museum of Art, Toledo OH
Toronto Dominion Bank, Toronto ON
Towson State University, The Holtzman Art Gallery, Towson MD
Trenton State College, College Art Gallery, Trenton NJ
Trotting Horse Museum, Goshen NY
Tufts University, Art Gallery, Medford MA
Tulane University, University Art Collection, New Orleans LA
Ulster County Community College, Muroff-Kotler Visual Arts Gallery, Stone Ridge NY
United States Figure Skating Association, World Figure Skating Hall of Fame and Museum, Colorado Springs CO
United States Naval Academy Museum, Annapolis MD
United States Tobacco Manufacturing Company Inc, Museum of Tobacco & History, Nashville TN
University of Alabama at Birmingham, Visual Arts Gallery, Birmingham AL
University of Calgary, The Nickle Arts Museum, Calgary AB
University of California, Santa Barbara, University Art Museum, Santa Barbara CA
University of Colorado, Art Galleries, Boulder CO
University of Colorado at Colorado Springs, Gallery of Contemporary Art, Colorado Springs CO
University of Delaware, University Gallery, Newark DE
University of Florida, University Gallery, Gainesville FL
University of Houston, Sarah Campbell Blaffer Gallery, Houston TX
University of Illinois, Krannert Art Museum, Champaign IL
University of Iowa, Museum of Art, Iowa City IA
University of Louisville, Allen R Hite Art Institute Gallery, Louisville KY

University of Maryland, College Park, Art Gallery, College Park MD
University of Massachusetts, Amherst, University Gallery, Amherst MA
University of Minnesota, University Art Museum, Minneapolis MN
University of Minnesota, Duluth, Tweed Museum of Art, Duluth MN
University of Missouri, Museum of Art and Archaeology, Columbia MO
University of Nebraska at Omaha, Art Gallery, Omaha NE
University of Nebraska, Lincoln, Sheldon Memorial Art Gallery, Lincoln NE
University of New Brunswick, Art Centre, Fredericton NB
University of New Hampshire, The Art Gallery, Durham NH
University of New Mexico, University Art Museum, Albuquerque NM
University of North Carolina at Greensboro, Weatherspoon Art Gallery, Greensboro NC
University of Notre Dame, Snite Museum of Art, Notre Dame IN
University of Pittsburgh, University Art Gallery, Pittsburgh PA
University of Rhode Island, Fine Arts Center Galleries, Kingston RI
University of Rochester, Memorial Art Gallery, Rochester NY
University of Southern Colorado, College of Liberal & Fine Arts, Pueblo CO
University of South Florida, Contemporary Art Museum, Tampa FL
University of Texas at Austin, Archer M Huntington Art Gallery, Austin TX
University of Vermont, Robert Hull Fleming Museum, Burlington VT
University of Washington, Henry Art Gallery, Seattle WA
University of West Florida, Art Gallery, Pensacola FL
University of Wisconsin, University Art Museum, Milwaukee WI
University of Wisconsin-Madison, Wisconsin Union Galleries, Madison WI
University of Wisconsin Oshkosh, Allen R Priebe Gallery, Oshkosh WI
University of Wisconsin-Stout, J Furlong Gallery, Menomonie WI
University of Wyoming, Art Museum, Laramie WY
USS Constitution Museum Foundation Inc, Museum, Boston National Historical Park, Museum, Boston MA
Utah Department of Natural Resources, Division of Parks & Recreation, Territorial Statehouse, Fillmore UT
Valentine Museum, Richmond VA
Valparaiso University, Museum of Art, Valparaiso IN
Vanderbilt University, Fine Arts Gallery, Nashville TN
Virginia Commonwealth University, Anderson Gallery, Richmond VA
Wake Forest University, A Lewis Aycock Art Slide Library & Print Collection, Winston Salem NC
Walker Art Center, Minneapolis MN
Washburn University, Mulvane Art Museum, Topeka KS
Washington County Museum of Fine Arts, Hagerstown MD
Washington State University, Museum of Art, Pullman WA
Waterworks Visual Arts Center, Salisbury NC
Wayne Center for the Arts, Wooster OH
Wayne State College, Nordstrand Visual Arts Gallery, Wayne NE
Wesleyan University, Davison Art Center, Middletown CT
Western Michigan University-Art Dept, Gallery II, Kalamazoo MI
Western State College of Colorado, Quigley Hall Art Gallery, Gunnison CO
Westminster College, Art Gallery, New Wilmington PA
Westmoreland Museum of Art, Greensburg PA
Wheaton College, Watson Gallery, Norton MA
White House, Washington DC
Whitney Museum of American Art, New York NY

Wichita Falls Museum and Art Center, Wichita Falls TX
Wichita State University, Edwin A Ulrich Museum of Art, Wichita KS
Kemper & Leila Williams Foundation, New Orleans LA
Witter Gallery, Storm Lake IA
Woodstock Artists Association, Woodstock NY
Worcester Art Museum, Worcester MA
Wustum Museum Art Association, Charles A Wustum Museum of Fine Arts, Racine WI
Yellowstone Art Center, Billings MT

RELIGIOUS ART

Amerind Foundation, Inc, Amerind Museum, Fulton-Hayden Memorial Art Gallery, Dragoon AZ
Archives of the Archdiocese of St Paul & Minneapolis, Saint Paul MN
Art Complex Museum, Duxbury MA
Art Gallery of Hamilton, Hamilton ON
Art Institute for the Permian Basin, Odessa TX
Leo Baeck Institute, New York NY
Biblical Arts Center, Dallas TX
Bob Jones University, Museum & Art Gallery, Greenville SC
Cathedral of Saint John the Divine, New York NY
Center for Puppetry Arts, Atlanta GA
Church of Jesus Christ of Latter-day Saints, Museum of Church History & Art, Salt Lake City UT
Church of Jesus Christ of Latter Day Saints, Mormon Visitors' Center, Independence MO
Fairfield University, Thomas J Walsh Art Gallery, Fairfield CT
General Board of Discipleship, The United Methodist Church, The Upper Room Chapel & Museum, Nashville TN
Georgetown University, Art and History Museum, Washington DC
Guadalupe Historic Foundation, Santuario de Guadalupe, Santa Fe NM
Harvard University, Dumbarton Oaks Research Library and Collections, Washington DC
Institute of Puerto Rican Culture, Dominican Convent Museum, San Juan PR
Institute of Puerto Rican Culture, Museo de Arte Religioso Porta Coeli, San Juan PR
The Interchurch Center, The Interchurch Center Galleries, New York NY
Kateri Tekakwitha Shrine, Musee Kateri Tekakwitha, Kahnawake PQ
Los Angeles County Museum of Art, Los Angeles CA
Louisiana Arts and Science Center, Baton Rouge LA
Loyola Marymount University, Laband Art Gallery, Los Angeles CA
Mission San Luis Rey Museum, San Luis Rey CA
Mission San Miguel Museum, San Miguel CA
Moravian Historical Society, Whitefield House Museum, Nazareth PA
Musee d'Art de Joliette, Joliette PQ
Museum of Fine Arts, Saint Petersburg, Florida, Inc, Saint Petersburg FL
National Council on Art in Jewish Life, New York NY
Newark Museum Association, The Newark Museum, Newark NJ
New Mexico State University, University Art Gallery, Las Cruces NM
North Park College, Carlson Tower Gallery, Chicago IL
Oklahoma City Art Museum, Oklahoma City OK
Rensselaer Newman Foundation Chapel and Cultural Center, The Gallery, Troy NY
Millicent Rogers Museum, Taos NM
Saint Bernard Foundation and Monastery, North Miami Beach FL
Saint Gregory's Abbey and College, Mabee-Gerrer Museum of Art, Shawnee OK
Saint Mary's College of California, Hearst Art Gallery, Moraga CA
San Carlos Cathedral, Monterey CA
Southern Baptist Theological Seminary, Joseph A Callaway Archaeological Museum, Louisville KY

Temple Beth Israel, Plotkin Juddica Museum, Phoenix AZ
Timken Museum of Art, San Diego CA
Tulane University, University Art Collection, New Orleans LA
United Methodist Church Commission on Archives and History, Madison NJ
United Methodist Historical Society, Lovely Lane Museum, Baltimore MD
United Society of Shakers, Shaker Museum, Poland Spring ME
University of Illinois, World Heritage Museum, Champaign IL
University of Wisconsin, University Art Museum, Milwaukee WI
University of Wisconsin-Madison, Elvehjem Museum of Art, Madison WI
Valparaiso University, Museum of Art, Valparaiso IN
Waterworks Visual Arts Center, Salisbury NC
Williams College, Museum of Art, Williamstown MA
Yeshiva University Museum, New York NY

RENAISSANCE ART

Charles Allis Art Museum, Milwaukee WI
Lyman Allyn Art Museum, New London CT
Art Institute for the Permian Basin, Odessa TX
Ball State University, Museum of Art, Muncie IN
Baltimore Museum of Art, Baltimore MD
Berea College, Doris Ulmann Galleries, Berea KY
Columbia Museum of Art, Columbia SC
Columbia Museum of Art, Columbia Art Association, Columbia SC
Dickinson College, Trout Gallery, Carlisle PA
East Los Angeles College, Vincent Price Gallery, Monterey Park CA
El Paso Museum of Art, El Paso TX
Fairfield University, Thomas J Walsh Art Gallery, Fairfield CT
Flint Institute of Arts, Flint MI
Frick Collection, New York NY
Grand Rapids Art Museum, Grand Rapids MI
Guadalupe Historic Foundation, Santuario de Guadalupe, Santa Fe NM
Hartwick College, Foreman Gallery, Oneonta NY
Harvard University, Busch-Reisinger Museum, Cambridge MA
Gertrude Herbert Memorial Institute of Art, Augusta GA
Honolulu Academy of Arts, Honolulu HI
Howard University, Gallery of Art, Washington DC
Indianapolis Museum of Art, Clowes Fund Collection, Indianapolis IN
Memphis Brooks Museum of Art, Memphis TN
Mint Museum of Art, Charlotte NC
Montclair State College, Art Gallery, Upper Montclair NJ
New Orleans Museum of Art, New Orleans LA
The Parrish Art Museum, Southampton NY
Portland Art Museum, Portland OR
Rhode Island School of Design, Museum of Art, Providence RI
San Diego Museum of Art, San Diego CA
University of Arizona, Museum of Art, Tucson AZ
University of Illinois, World Heritage Museum, Champaign IL
University of Michigan, Museum of Art, Ann Arbor MI
University of Rochester, Memorial Art Gallery, Rochester NY
University of Utah, Utah Museum of Fine Arts, Salt Lake City UT
University of Wisconsin-Madison, Elvehjem Museum of Art, Madison WI
Vanderbilt University, Fine Arts Gallery, Nashville TN
Virginia Museum of Fine Arts, Richmond VA
Williams College, Museum of Art, Williamstown MA

REPRODUCTIONS

Appaloosa Museum, Inc, Moscow ID
Chattahoochee Valley Art Museum, LaGrange GA
Clark County Historical Society, Pioneer - Krier Museum, Ashland KS
General Board of Discipleship, The United Methodist Church, The Upper Room Chapel & Museum, Nashville TN
Museum of Movie Art, Calgary AB
Western Kentucky University, Kentucky Museum, Bowling Green KY

RESTORATIONS

Center for Puppetry Arts, Atlanta GA
Huntington Museum of Art, Huntington WV
Johns Hopkins University, Homewood House Museum, Baltimore MD
Landmark Society of Western New York, Inc, Rochester NY
Lockwood-Mathews Mansion Museum, Norwalk CT
Louisa May Alcott Memorial Association, Orchard House, Concord MA
Mission San Luis Rey Museum, San Luis Rey CA
Mohave Museum of History and Arts, Kingman AZ
The National Park Service, United States Department of the Interior, The Statue of Liberty National Monument, New York NY
Nebraska State Capitol, Lincoln NE
Nelda C & H J Lutcher Stark Foundation, Stark Museum of Art, Orange TX
Vermilion County Museum Society, Danville IL

SCRIMSHAW

Anchorage Museum of History and Art, Anchorage AK
Chilkat Valley Historical Society, Sheldon Museum & Cultural Center, Haines AK
Enook Galleries, Waterloo ON
Heritage Plantation of Sandwich, Sandwich MA
Kendall Whaling Museum, Sharon MA
Old Dartmouth Historical Society, New Bedford Whaling Museum, New Bedford MA
Ships of The Sea Museum, Savannah GA

SCULPTURE

Albany Institute of History and Art, Albany NY
Albright College, Freedman Gallery, Reading PA
American Swedish Institute, Minneapolis MN
American University, Watkins Collectiony, Washington DC
Anna Maria College, Saint Luke's Gallery, Paxton MA
Arizona State University, University Art Museum, Tempe AZ
Art Gallery of Nova Scotia, Halifax NS
Art Gallery of Ontario, Toronto ON
Art Institute for the Permian Basin, Odessa TX
The Art Institute of Chicago, Chicago IL
The Art Museum of Santa Cruz County, Santa Cruz CA
Art Museum of Southeast Texas, Beaumont TX
Art Museum of the Americas, Washington DC
Art Patrons League of Mobile, Mobile AL
The Aspen Art Museum, Aspen CO
Atlanta Museum, Atlanta GA
Augusta Richmond County Museum, Augusta GA
Leo Baeck Institute, New York NY
Baldwin-Wallace College, Fawick Art Gallery, Berea OH
Baltimore Museum of Art, Baltimore MD
Bard College, William Cooper Procter Art Center, Annandale-on-Hudson NY
The Bartlett Museum, Amesbury MA
Baylor University, Martin Museum of Art, Waco TX
Beaumont Art League, Beaumont TX
Beaverbrook Art Gallery, Fredericton NB
Beloit College, Wright Museum of Art, Beloit WI
Bergstrom Mahler Museum, Neenah WI
Berkshire Museum, Pittsfield MA
Birmingham Museum of Art, Birmingham AL
Blanden Memorial Art Museum, Fort Dodge IA
Boise Art Museum, Boise ID

Bowdoin College, Peary-MacMillan Arctic Museum, Brunswick ME
Roy Boyd Gallery, Chicago IL
Brigham Young University, B F Larsen Gallery, Provo UT
Bradford Brinton Memorial Museum & Historic Ranch, Big Horn WY
Brookgreen Gardens, Murrells Inlet SC
Brooklyn Historical Society, Brooklyn NY
Brown University, David Winton Bell Gallery, Providence RI
The Buffalo Fine Arts Academy, Albright-Knox Art Gallery, Buffalo NY
Butler Institute of American Art, Art Museum, Youngstown OH
California State University Stanislaus, University Art Gallery, Turlock CA
Calvin College, Center Art Gallery, Grand Rapids MI
Canadian Wildlife & Wilderness Art Museum, Ottawa ON
Canton Art Institute, Canton OH
Capital University, Schumacher Gallery, Columbus OH
Carnegie Institute, Carnegie Museum of Art, Pittsburgh PA
Amon Carter Museum, Fort Worth TX
Cedar Rapids Museum of Art, Cedar Rapids IA
Chattahoochee Valley Art Museum, LaGrange GA
Church of Jesus Christ of Latter-day Saints, Museum of Church History & Art, Salt Lake City UT
Cincinnati Museum Association, Cincinnati Art Museum, Cincinnati OH
City of Pittsfield, Berkshire Artisans, Pittsfield MA
Sterling and Francine Clark Art Institute, Williamstown MA
Cleveland Museum of Art, Cleveland OH
Clinton Art Association Gallery, Clinton IA
College of Saint Benedict, Art Gallery, Saint Joseph MN
Colorado Springs Fine Arts Center, Colorado Springs CO
Columbia County Historical Society, Columbia County Museum, Kinderhook NY
Columbia Museum of Art, Columbia Art Association, Columbia SC
Columbus Museum of Art, Columbus OH
Concordia University, Leonard & Bina Ellen Art Gallery, Montreal PQ
Coos Art Museum, Coos Bay OR
Cornell University, Herbert F Johnson Museum of Art, Ithaca NY
Cranbrook Academy of Art Museum, Bloomfield Hills MI
Crazy Horse Memorial, Indian Museum of North America, Crazy Horse SD
Creighton University, Fine Arts Gallery, Omaha NE
Crocker Art Museum, Sacramento CA
Cummer Gallery of Art, DeEtte Holden Cummer Museum Foundation, Jacksonville FL
Delaware Art Museum, Wilmington DE
Del Mar College, Joseph A Cain Memorial Art Gallery, Corpus Christi TX
Durham Art Guild Inc, Durham NC
DuSable Museum of African American History, Chicago IL
East Baton Rouge Parks & Recreation Commission, Baton Rouge Gallery Inc, Baton Rouge LA
Edmundson Art Foundation, Inc, Des Moines Art Center, Des Moines IA
El Camino College Art Gallery, Torrance CA
Wharton Esherick Museum, Wharton Esherick Studio, Paoli PA
Everhart Museum, Scranton PA
Everson Museum of Art, Syracuse NY
Federal Reserve Board, Art Gallery, Washington DC
Fine Arts Center for the New River Valley, Pulaski VA
Flint Institute of Arts, Flint MI
Florida State University, Fine Arts Gallery & Museum, Tallahassee FL
Fort Wayne Museum of Art, Inc, Fort Wayne IN
Freeport Art Museum & Cultural Center, Freeport IL
Frick Collection, New York NY

Fruitlands Museum, Inc, Harvard MA
Gaston County Museum of Art & History, Dallas NC
General Board of Discipleship, The United Methodist Church, The Upper Room Chapel & Museum, Nashville TN
Georgetown College Gallery, Georgetown KY
Georgetown University, Art and History Museum, Washington DC
George Washington University, The Dimock Gallery, Washington DC
Getty Center for the History of Art & the Humanities Trust Museum, Santa Monica CA
Getty Center for the History of Art & the Humanities Trust Museum, The J Paul Getty Museum, Santa Monica CA
Girard College, Stephen Girard Collection, Philadelphia PA
Charles B Goddard Center for the Visual and Performing Arts, Ardmore OK
Goucher College, Rosenberg Gallery, Towson MD
Grand Rapids Art Museum, Grand Rapids MI
Greenville College, Richard W Bock Sculpture Collection, Greenville IL
Solomon R Guggenheim Museum, New York NY
Guild Hall of East Hampton, Inc, Guild Hall Museum, East Hampton NY
Hartwick College, Foreman Gallery, Oneonta NY
Harvard University, Dumbarton Oaks Research Library and Collections, Washington DC
Harvard University, William Hayes Fogg Art Museum, Cambridge MA
Heard Museum, Phoenix AZ
Heckscher Museum, Huntington NY
Gertrude Herbert Memorial Institute of Art, Augusta GA
Hirshhorn Museum and Sculpture Garden, Washington DC
Hispanic Society of America, Museum, New York NY
Historic Landmarks Foundation of Indiana, Morris-Butler House, Indianapolis IN
Honolulu Academy of Arts, Honolulu HI
Housatonic Community College, Housatonic Museum of Art, Bridgeport CT
Howard University, Gallery of Art, Washington DC
Hudson River Museum, Yonkers NY
Hunter Museum of Art, Chattanooga TN
Henry E Huntington Library, Art Collections & Botanical Gardens, San Marino CA
Huntsville Museum of Art, Huntsville AL
Hyde Collection Trust, Glens Falls NY
Hyde Park Art Center, Chicago IL
Illinois State Museum, Illinois Art Gallery & Lockport Gallery, Springfield IL
Illinois State Museum, State of Illinois Art Gallery, Chicago IL
Institute for Contemporary Art, The Clocktower Gallery, Long Island City NY
Institute of American Indian Arts Museum, Santa Fe NM
Intar Latin American Gallery, New York NY
Iowa State Education Association, Salisbury House, Des Moines IA
Iowa State University, Brunnier Gallery Museum, Ames IA
Joslyn Art Museum, Omaha NE
Kalamazoo Institute of Arts, Kalamazoo MI
Kent State University, School of Art Gallery, Kent OH
Kimbell Art Museum, Fort Worth TX
Laumeier Sculpture Park, Saint Louis MO
Leanin' Tree Museum of Western Art, Boulder CO
Lehigh University Art Galleries, Bethlehem PA
Lightner Museum, Saint Augustine FL
Long Beach Museum of Art, Long Beach CA
Los Angeles County Museum of Art, Los Angeles CA
Loyola University of Chicago, Martin D'Arcy Gallery of Art, Chicago IL
L'Universite Laval, Ecole des Arts Visuels, Quebec PQ
The Robert McLaughlin Gallery, Oshawa ON
Marion Koogler McNay Art Museum, San Antonio TX
Charles H MacNider Museum, Mason City IA
Maine Coast Artists, Art Gallery, Rockport ME

University of Pittsburgh, University Art Gallery, Pittsburgh PA
University of Rhode Island, Fine Arts Center Galleries, Kingston RI
University of San Diego, Founders' Gallery, San Diego CA
University of South Florida, Contemporary Art Museum, Tampa FL
University of Tennessee, Eleanor Dean Audigier Art Collection, Knoxville TN
University of Wisconsin, University Art Museum, Milwaukee WI
University of Wisconsin-Madison, Wisconsin Union Galleries, Madison WI
University of Wisconsin-Stout, J Furlong Gallery, Menomonie WI
University of Wyoming, Art Museum, Laramie WY
Utah Arts Council, Chase Home Museum of Utah Folk Art, Salt Lake City UT
Valentine Museum, Richmond VA
Vassar College, Vassar Art Gallery, Poughkeepsie NY
Virginia Museum of Fine Arts, Richmond VA
Volcano Art Center, Hawaii National Park HI
Walker Art Center, Minneapolis MN
Washburn University, Mulvane Art Museum, Topeka KS
Washington County Museum of Fine Arts, Hagerstown MD
Waterworks Visual Arts Center, Salisbury NC
Western Washington University, Western Gallery, Bellingham WA
Westmoreland Museum of Art, Greensburg PA
Wheaton College, Watson Gallery, Norton MA
White House, Washington DC
Whitney Museum of American Art, New York NY
Wichita Art Museum, Wichita KS
Wichita State University, Edwin A Ulrich Museum of Art, Wichita KS
Widener University, Art Museum, Chester PA
Wilkes Art Gallery, North Wilkesboro NC
Wilkes University, Sordoni Art Gallery, Wilkes-Barre PA
Winnipeg Art Gallery, Winnipeg MB
Woodmere Art Museum, Philadelphia PA
Woodstock Artists Association, Woodstock NY
Yale University, Art Gallery, New Haven CT
York University, Art Gallery of York University, North York ON
Zigler Museum, Jennings LA

SILVER

Albany Institute of History and Art, Albany NY
Allentown Art Museum, Allentown PA
Lyman Allyn Art Museum, New London CT
Art Institute for the Permian Basin, Odessa TX
Baltimore Museum of Art, Baltimore MD
The Bartlett Museum, Amesbury MA
Beloit College, Wright Museum of Art, Beloit WI
Berea College, Doris Ulmann Galleries, Berea KY
Berkshire Museum, Pittsfield MA
Birmingham Museum of Art, Birmingham AL
Sterling and Francine Clark Art Institute, Williamstown MA
The Currier Gallery of Art, Manchester NH
DAR Museum, National Society Daughters of the American Revolution, Washington DC
Detroit Institute of Arts, Detroit MI
The Frick Art Museum, Pittsburgh PA
Girard College, Stephen Girard Collection, Philadelphia PA
Hammond-Harwood House Association, Inc, Annapolis MD
Harvard University, William Hayes Fogg Art Museum, Cambridge MA
Hill-Stead Museum, Farmington CT
Historical and Cultural Affairs, Delaware State Museums, Dover DE
Historical Society of Cheshire County, Colony House Museum, Keene NH
Historic Deerfield, Inc, Deerfield MA
Huntington Museum of Art, Huntington WV
Johns Hopkins University, Homewood House Museum, Baltimore MD
Livingston County Historical Society, Cobblestone Museum, Geneseo NY

Louisiana State University, Museum of Arts, Baton Rouge LA
Loyola University of Chicago, Martin D'Arcy Gallery of Art, Chicago IL
Maryland Historical Society, Museum of Maryland History, Baltimore MD
Mitchell Museum, Mount Vernon IL
James Monroe Museum, Fredericksburg VA
Montclair Art Museum, Montclair NJ
Musee d'Art de Saint-Laurent, Saint-Laurent PQ
Museum of Arts and Sciences, Cuban Museum, Daytona Beach FL
Museum of Fine Arts, Boston MA
National Society of Colonial Dames of America in the State of Maryland, Mount Clare Mansion, Baltimore MD
Nevada Museum Of Art, Reno NV
R W Norton Art Gallery, Shreveport LA
Old Colony Historical Society, Museum, Taunton MA
Peabody & Essex Museum, Salem MA
Portland Art Museum, Portland OR
Putnam Museum of History & Natural Science, Davenport IA
Walter Cecil Rawls Museum, Courtland VA
Frederic Remington Art Museum, Ogdensburg NY
Lauren Rogers Museum of Art, Laurel MS
The Rosenbach Museum and Library, Philadelphia PA
San Diego Museum of Art, San Diego CA
Santa Clara University, de Saisset Museum, Santa Clara CA
Shirley Plantation, Charles City VA
Abigail Adams Smith Museum, New York NY
Spertus Museum, Chicago IL
Summit County Historical Society, Akron OH
Temple Beth Israel, Plotkin Juddica Museum, Phoenix AZ
US Department of State, Diplomatic Reception Rooms, Washington DC
United States Naval Academy Museum, Annapolis MD
University of Iowa, Museum of Art, Iowa City IA
University of South Carolina, McKissick Museum, Columbia SC
University of Tennessee, Eleanor Dean Audigier Art Collection, Knoxville TN
University of Utah, Utah Museum of Fine Arts, Salt Lake City UT
Valentine Museum, Richmond VA
Virginia Museum of Fine Arts, Richmond VA
Yale University, Art Gallery, New Haven CT

SOUTHWESTERN ART

Albuquerque Museum of Art, History & Science, Albuquerque NM
Amerind Foundation, Inc, Amerind Museum, Fulton-Hayden Memorial Art Gallery, Dragoon AZ
Artesia Historical Museum & Art Center, Artesia NM
Art Institute for the Permian Basin, Odessa TX
Aurora University, Schingoethe Center for Native American Cultures, Aurora IL
Beloit College, Wright Museum of Art, Beloit WI
Bradford Brinton Memorial Museum & Historic Ranch, Big Horn WY
Chicano Humanities & Arts Council, Denver CO
Church of Jesus Christ of Latter-day Saints, Museum of Church History & Art, Salt Lake City UT
Colorado Springs Fine Arts Center, Colorado Springs CO
Dickinson College, Trout Gallery, Carlisle PA
Douglas Art Association, Little Gallery, Douglas AZ
Enook Galleries, Waterloo ON
Genesee Country Museum, John L Wehle Gallery of Sporting Art, Mumford NY
Heard Museum, Phoenix AZ
Heritage Center, Inc, Pine Ridge SD
Intar Latin American Gallery, New York NY
Jefferson County Open Space, Hiwan Homestead Museum, Evergreen CO
Maricopa County Historical Society, Desert Caballeros Western Museum, Wickenburg AZ
Mission San Luis Rey Museum, San Luis Rey CA

Museum of Fine Arts, Saint Petersburg, Florida, Inc, Saint Petersburg FL
New Mexico State University, University Art Gallery, Las Cruces NM
Northern Arizona University, Art Museum & Galleries, Flagstaff AZ
Ohio University, Trisolini Gallery, Athens OH
Palm Springs Desert Museum, Inc, Palm Springs CA
Red Rock State Park, Museum, Church Rock NM
Roswell Museum and Art Center, Roswell NM
Royal Ontario Museum, Toronto ON
C M Russell Museum, Great Falls MT
Nelda C & H J Lutcher Stark Foundation, Stark Museum of Art, Orange TX
University of Colorado at Colorado Springs, Gallery of Contemporary Art, Colorado Springs CO
University of Michigan, Museum of Art, Ann Arbor MI
University of New Mexico, The Harwood Foundation, Taos NM
Wichita Art Museum, Wichita KS
Yuma Fine Arts Association, Art Center, Yuma AZ

STAINED GLASS

Academy of the New Church, Glencairn Museum, Bryn Athyn PA
The Art Institute of Chicago, Chicago IL
Church of Jesus Christ of Latter-day Saints, Museum of Church History & Art, Salt Lake City UT
Corcoran Gallery of Art, Washington DC
General Board of Discipleship, The United Methodist Church, The Upper Room Chapel & Museum, Nashville TN
Higgins Armory Museum, Worcester MA
Jekyll Island Museum, Jekyll Island GA
Workman & Temple Family Homestead Museum, City of Industry CA

TAPESTRIES

American Swedish Institute, Minneapolis MN
Baltimore Museum of Art, Baltimore MD
City of Pittsfield, Berkshire Artisans, Pittsfield MA
Corcoran Gallery of Art, Washington DC
Cummer Gallery of Art, DeEtte Holden Cummer Museum Foundation, Jacksonville FL
The Frick Art Museum, Pittsburgh PA
General Board of Discipleship, The United Methodist Church, The Upper Room Chapel & Museum, Nashville TN
Higgins Armory Museum, Worcester MA
Hyde Collection Trust, Glens Falls NY
Iowa State Education Association, Salisbury House, Des Moines IA
Nebraska State Capitol, Lincoln NE
Nemours Mansion & Gardens, Wilmington DE
Nevada Museum Of Art, Reno NV
R W Norton Art Gallery, Shreveport LA
Santa Clara University, de Saisset Museum, Santa Clara CA
Norton Simon Museum, Pasadena CA
Society of the Cincinnati, Anderson House Museum, Washington DC
Temple Beth Israel, Plotkin Juddica Museum, Phoenix AZ
University of Houston, Sarah Campbell Blaffer Gallery, Houston TX
University of San Diego, Founders' Gallery, San Diego CA
University of Utah, Utah Museum of Fine Arts, Salt Lake City UT
Virginia Museum of Fine Arts, Richmond VA
Vizcaya Museum and Gardens, Miami FL
Wayne Center for the Arts, Wooster OH

TEXTILES

Alabama Department of Archives and History Museum, Museum Galleries, Montgomery AL
Allentown Art Museum, Allentown PA
American Swedish Institute, Minneapolis MN
Aurora University, Schingoethe Center for Native American Cultures, Aurora IL
Baltimore Museum of Art, Baltimore MD

Balzekas Museum of Lithuanian Culture, Chicago IL
Bay County Historical Society, Historical Museum of Bay County, Bay City MI
Beloit College, Wright Museum of Art, Beloit WI
Berea College, Doris Ulmann Galleries, Berea KY
Boulder Historical Society Inc, Museum of History, Boulder CO
Bower's Museum, Santa Ana CA
Calvin College, Center Art Gallery, Grand Rapids MI
Cedar Rapids Museum of Art, Cedar Rapids IA
Charleston Museum, Charleston SC
Church of Jesus Christ of Latter-day Saints, Museum of Church History & Art, Salt Lake City UT
Cincinnati Museum Association, Cincinnati Art Museum, Cincinnati OH
City of Pittsfield, Berkshire Artisans, Pittsfield MA
Clark County Historical Society, Pioneer - Krier Museum, Ashland KS
Cleveland Museum of Art, Cleveland OH
Columbia Museum of Art, Columbia SC
Columbia Museum of Art, Columbia Art Association, Columbia SC
Cooper-Hewitt, National Museum of Design, New York NY
Cranbrook Academy of Art Museum, Bloomfield Hills MI
The Currier Gallery of Art, Manchester NH
Dawson County Historical Society, Museum, Lexington NE
Detroit Institute of Arts, Detroit MI
Douglas County Historical Society, Fairlawn Mansion & Museum, Superior WI
Durham Art Guild Inc, Durham NC
Flint Institute of Arts, Flint MI
Freeport Art Museum & Cultural Center, Freeport IL
Gaston County Museum of Art & History, Dallas NC
Harvard University, Dumbarton Oaks Research Library and Collections, Washington DC
High Point Historical Society Inc, Museum, High Point NC
Historic Deerfield, Inc, Deerfield MA
Historic Northampton Museum, Northampton MA
Honolulu Academy of Arts, Honolulu HI
Hyde Park Art Center, Chicago IL
Idaho Historical Museum, Boise ID
Indianapolis Museum of Art, Indianapolis IN
Institute of American Indian Arts Museum, Santa Fe NM
Johns Hopkins University, Homewood House Museum, Baltimore MD
Kelowna Centennial Museum and National Exhibit Centre, Kelowna BC
Lightner Museum, Saint Augustine FL
Livingston County Historical Society, Cobblestone Museum, Geneseo NY
Longfellow-Evangeline State Commemorative Area, Saint Martinville LA
Longue Vue House and Gardens, New Orleans LA
Los Angeles County Museum of Art, Los Angeles CA
Loyola University of Chicago, Martin D'Arcy Gallery of Art, Chicago IL
McAllen International Museum, McAllen TX
McCord Museum of Canadian History, Montreal PQ
Manufacturers Hanover, New York NY
Maryland Historical Society, Museum of Maryland History, Baltimore MD
Mellon Bank, Pittsburgh PA
Memphis Brooks Museum of Art, Memphis TN
Miami University Art Museum, Oxford OH
Minnesota Museum of American Art, Saint Paul MN
Mission San Luis Rey Museum, San Luis Rey CA
Morris Communications Corporation, Morris Museum of Art, Augusta GA
Murray State University, Eagle Gallery, Murray KY
Musee d'Art de Saint-Laurent, Saint-Laurent PQ
The Museum at Drexel University, Philadelphia PA
Museum of American Textile History, North Andover MA
Museum of New Mexico, Museum of International Folk Art, Santa Fe NM

Museum of New York, Rock Hill SC
The Museums at Stony Brook, Stony Brook NY
National Museum of American History, Washington DC
Nevada Museum Of Art, Reno NV
North Carolina State University, Visual Arts Programs, Raleigh NC
Norwich Free Academy, Slater Memorial Museum & Converse Art Gallery, Norwich CT
Ohio University, Trisolini Gallery, Athens OH
Olana State Historic Site, Hudson NY
Old Colony Historical Society, Museum, Taunton MA
Palm Beach County Parks & Recreation Department, Morikami Museum & Japanese Gardens, Delray Beach FL
Philadelphia College of Textiles and Science, Paley Design Center, Philadelphia PA
Principia College, School of Nations Museum, Elsah IL
Putnam Museum of History & Natural Science, Davenport IA
Quapaw Quarter Association, Inc, Villa Marre, Little Rock AR
Rhodes College, Jessie L Clough Art Memorial for Teaching, Memphis TN
Riley County Historical Museum, Manhattan KS
Rome Historical Society Museum, Rome NY
Saginaw Art Museum, Saginaw MI
Scalamandre Museum of Textiles, New York NY
Schenectady Museum, Planetarium & Visitors Center, Schenectady NY
Scripps College, Clark Humanities Museum, Claremont CA
Shaker Village of Pleasant Hill, Harrodsburg KY
Shelburne Museum, Shelburne VT
Abigail Adams Smith Museum, New York NY
Society for the Preservation of New England Antiquities, Archives, Boston MA
South Carolina State Museum, Columbia SC
Spertus Museum, Chicago IL
T C Steele State Historic Site, Nashville IN
Stratford Historical Society, Stratford CT
Temple Beth Israel, Plotkin Juddica Museum, Phoenix AZ
Textile Museum, Washington DC
3M, Art Collection, Saint Paul MN
United Society of Shakers, Shaker Museum, Poland Spring ME
University of California, Los Angeles, Fowler Museum of Cultural History, Los Angeles CA
University of Colorado at Colorado Springs, Gallery of Contemporary Art, Colorado Springs CO
University of Delaware, University Gallery, Newark DE
University of Miami, Lowe Art Museum, Coral Gables FL
University of Michigan, Museum of Art, Ann Arbor MI
University of Michigan, Kelsey Museum of Archaeology, Ann Arbor MI
University of Oregon, Museum of Art, Eugene OR
University of San Diego, Founders' Gallery, San Diego CA
University of Washington, Henry Art Gallery, Seattle WA
Wethersfield Historical Society Inc, Wethersfield CT
Wheaton College, Watson Gallery, Norton MA
Wichita Art Museum, Wichita KS
Winterthur Museum and Gardens, Winterthur DE

WATERCOLORS

The Albrecht-Kemper Museum of Art, Saint Joseph MO
American University, Watkins Collectiony, Washington DC
Art Institute for the Permian Basin, Odessa TX
Baylor University, Martin Museum of Art, Waco TX
Beloit College, Wright Museum of Art, Beloit WI
Roy Boyd Gallery, Chicago IL
Brevard College, Sims Art Center, Brevard NC
Brooklyn Historical Society, Brooklyn NY
Burchfield Art Center, Buffalo NY
Butler Institute of American Art, Art Museum, Youngstown OH

California Historical Society, El Molino Viejo, San Marino CA
Canadian Museum of Nature, Musee Canadien de la Nature, Ottawa ON
Chattahoochee Valley Art Museum, LaGrange GA
Church of Jesus Christ of Latter-day Saints, Museum of Church History & Art, Salt Lake City UT
City of Pittsfield, Berkshire Artisans, Pittsfield MA
Corcoran Gallery of Art, Washington DC
East Baton Rouge Parks & Recreation Commission, Baton Rouge Gallery Inc, Baton Rouge LA
Eastern Illinois University, Tarble Arts Center, Charleston IL
Eccles Community Art Center, Ogden UT
Fayette Art Museum, Fayette AL
Ford Motor Company, Dearborn MI
Girard College, Stephen Girard Collection, Philadelphia PA
Grinnell College, Print & Drawing Study Room/ Gallery, Grinnell IA
Hamilton College, Fred L Emerson Gallery, Clinton NY
Howard University, Gallery of Art, Washington DC
Huntsville Museum of Art, Huntsville AL
Indianapolis Museum of Art, Indianapolis IN
Joslyn Art Muscum, Omaha NE
Kalamazoo Institute of Arts, Kalamazoo MI
La Salle University, Art Museum, Philadelphia PA
Louisiana State University, Museum of Arts, Baton Rouge LA
Charles H MacNider Museum, Mason City IA
McPherson College Gallery, McPherson KS
Maine Coast Artists, Art Gallery, Rockport ME
The Market Gallery of the City of Toronto Archives, Toronto ON
MEXIC-ARTE Museum, Austin TX
Michelson-Reves Museum of Art, Marshall TX
Millikin University, Perkinson Gallery, Decatur IL
Mobil Corporation, Art Collection, Fairfax VA
Moravian Historical Society, Whitefield House Museum, Nazareth PA
Mount Mary College, Tower Gallery, Milwaukee WI
National Archives of Canada, Documentary Art and Photography, Ottawa ON
Naval Historical Center, The Navy Museum, Washington DC
Nevada Museum Of Art, Reno NV
New York University, Grey Art Gallery and Study Center, New York NY
Niagara University, Castellani Art Museum, New York NY
Northern Illinois University, NIU Art Museum, De Kalb IL
Oak Ridge Art Center, Oak Ridge TN
Oklahoma City Art Museum, Oklahoma City OK
Philbrook Museum of Art, Tulsa OK
Provincetown Art Association and Museum, Provincetown MA
Putnam Museum of History & Natural Science, Davenport IA
Rapid City Fine Arts Council, Dahl Fine Arts Center, Rapid City SD
Frederic Remington Art Museum, Ogdensburg NY
Sid W Richardson Foundation, Collection of Western Art, Fort Worth TX
Springfield Art Museum, Springfield MO
Stetson University, Duncan Gallery of Art, De Land FL
3M, Art Collection, Saint Paul MN
Tulane University, University Art Collection, New Orleans LA
United States Department of the Interior Museum, Washington DC
University of Calgary, The Nickle Arts Museum, Calgary AB
University of Colorado, Art Galleries, Boulder CO
University of Colorado at Colorado Springs, Gallery of Contemporary Art, Colorado Springs CO
University of Wisconsin-Madison, Wisconsin Union Galleries, Madison WI
Valentine Museum, Richmond VA
Vassar College, Vassar Art Gallery, Poughkeepsie NY
Waterworks Visual Arts Center, Salisbury NC
Wichita Art Museum, Wichita KS
Woodstock Artists Association, Woodstock NY

Wustum Museum Art Association, Charles A Wustum Museum of Fine Arts, Racine WI

WOODCARVINGS

Art Gallery of Hamilton, Hamilton ON
Art Institute for the Permian Basin, Odessa TX
Beaumont Art League, Beaumont TX
Beloit College, Wright Museum of Art, Beloit WI
Canadian Museum of Nature, Musee Canadien de la Nature, Ottawa ON
Center for Puppetry Arts, Atlanta GA
Chilkat Valley Historical Society, Sheldon Museum & Cultural Center, Haines AK
Church of Jesus Christ of Latter-day Saints, Museum of Church History & Art, Salt Lake City UT
Clark County Historical Society, Pioneer - Krier Museum, Ashland KS
Clinton Art Association Gallery, Clinton IA
Enook Galleries, Waterloo ON
Wharton Esherick Museum, Wharton Esherick Studio, Paoli PA
Fayette Art Museum, Fayette AL
General Board of Discipleship, The United Methodist Church, The Upper Room Chapel & Museum, Nashville TN
Wendell Gilley Museum, Southwest Harbor ME
Gloridale Partnership, National Museum of Woodcarving, Custer SD
Hermitage Foundation Museum, Norfolk VA
Higgins Armory Museum, Worcester MA
Historical Society of Washington DC, Christian Heurich Mansion, Washington DC
Iowa State University, Brunnier Gallery Museum, Ames IA
Kiah Museum, Savannah GA
Maine Coast Artists, Art Gallery, Rockport ME
MEXIC-ARTE Museum, Austin TX
Mitchell Museum, Mount Vernon IL
Musee d'Art de Saint-Laurent, Saint-Laurent PQ
The Museum, Greenwood SC
Museum of New York, Rock Hill SC
Nebraska State Capitol, Lincoln NE
Nevada Museum Of Art, Reno NV
Noyes Museum, Oceanville NJ
Ohio University, Trisolini Gallery, Athens OH
Phelps County Historical Society, Phelps County Museum, Holdrege NE
Putnam Museum of History & Natural Science, Davenport IA
Rhodes College, Jessie L Clough Art Memorial for Teaching, Memphis TN
C M Russell Museum, Great Falls MT
St Clair County Community College, Jack R Hennesey Art Galleries, Port Huron MI
SVACA - Sheyenne Valley Arts and Crafts Association, Bjarne Ness Gallery, Fort Ransom ND
Tomoka State Park Museum, Fred Dana Marsh Museum, Ormond Beach FL
Trotting Horse Museum, Goshen NY
Ukrainian National Museum and Library, Chicago IL
University of Cincinnati, Tangeman Fine Arts Gallery, Cincinnati OH
Warther Museum Inc, Dover OH
Waterworks Visual Arts Center, Salisbury NC
Wichita Art Museum, Wichita KS

WOODCUTS

The Albrecht-Kemper Museum of Art, Saint Joseph MO
American University, Watkins Collectiony, Washington DC
Beloit College, Wright Museum of Art, Beloit WI
Carnegie Institute, Carnegie Museum of Art, Pittsburgh PA
Carolina Art Association, Gibbes Museum of Art, Charleston SC
City of Pittsfield, Berkshire Artisans, Pittsfield MA
Clinton Art Association Gallery, Clinton IA
Colgate University, Picker Art Gallery, Hamilton NY
Coos Art Museum, Coos Bay OR
Eccles Community Art Center, Ogden UT

Wharton Esherick Museum, Wharton Esherick Studio, Paoli PA
Grinnell College, Print & Drawing Study Room/ Gallery, Grinnell IA
Charles H MacNider Museum, Mason City IA
Maine Coast Artists, Art Gallery, Rockport ME
MEXIC-ARTE Museum, Austin TX
MonDak Heritage Center, Sidney MT
Museum of Fine Arts, Springfield MA
Nevada Museum Of Art, Reno NV
New Mexico State University, University Art Gallery, Las Cruces NM
New Visions Gallery, Inc, Marshfield WI
Niagara University, Castellani Art Museum, New York NY
Northern Illinois University, NIU Art Museum, De Kalb IL
Northwestern College, Te Paske Gallery of Rowenhorst, Orange City IA
Ohio University, Trisolini Gallery, Athens OH
Oklahoma City Art Museum, Oklahoma City OK
The Parrish Art Museum, Southampton NY
Print Club of Albany, Museum, Albany NY
Provincetown Art Association and Museum, Provincetown MA
State Capitol Museum, Olympia WA
University of Alabama at Birmingham, Visual Arts Gallery, Birmingham AL
University of Colorado at Colorado Springs, Gallery of Contemporary Art, Colorado Springs CO
Woodstock Artists Association, Woodstock NY

Collections

Accounting Books
Oysterponds Historical Society, Museum, Orient NY

Adler Collection
Lehigh University Art Galleries, Bethlehem PA

Blanche Adler Graphic Arts Collection
Baltimore Museum of Art, Baltimore MD

Adolf Collection of Austrian Academic Paintings
Pennsylvania State University, Palmer Museum of Art, University Park PA

Aerobatic Airplane
Clark County Historical Society, Pioneer - Krier Museum, Ashland KS

Agricultural Equipment
Dawson County Historical Society, Museum, Lexington NE

Agricultural & Woodworking Tools
Rowland Evans Robinson Memorial Association, Rokeby Museum, Ferrisburgh VT

Agriculture
Adams County Historical Society, Museum & Cultural Center, Brighton CO

Aldrich Collection
Aldrich Museum of Contemporary Art, Ridgefield CT

Lucy Truman Aldrich Collection of Porcelains & Textiles
Rhode Island School of Design, Museum of Art, Providence RI

Washington Allston Trust Collection
University of Miami, Lowe Art Museum, Coral Gables FL

American Art
Saint Mary's College of California, Hearst Art Gallery, Moraga CA

Animation
International Museum of Cartoon Art, Montreal PQ

Antiquities - Cycladic
Kimbell Art Museum, Fort Worth TX

Karel Appel Graphics Collection
Art Gallery of Hamilton, Hamilton ON

Archdiocese Santa Fe Collection
Guadalupe Historic Foundation, Santuario de Guadalupe, Santa Fe NM

Archival Materials
Oysterponds Historical Society, Museum, Orient NY

Archives; Photos & Maps; Trade & Business Items
Arizona Historical Society-Yuma, Century House Museum & Garden, Yuma AZ

Arensberg Collection
Philadelphia Museum of Art, Philadelphia PA

J Chester Armstrong
Zigler Museum, Jennings LA

Grant Arnold Fine Print Collection
State University of New York at Oswego, Tyler Art Gallery, Oswego NY

Matthias H Arnot Collection
Arnot Art Museum, Elmira NY

Art History
Adams County Historical Society, Museum & Cultural Center, Brighton CO

Artists books
Washington Project for the Arts, Washington DC

Art Preservation

The Bartlett Museum, Amesbury MA

Asnis Collection

Sonoma State University, Art Gallery, Rohnert Park CA

Assyrian & Babylonian Seals & Cyclinders

Rosicrucian Egyptian Museum and Art Gallery, San Jose CA

Lady Nancy Astor Collection of English China

Virginia Museum of Fine Arts, Richmond VA

Eleanor Deane Audigier Art Collection

University of Tennessee, Frank H McClung Museum, Knoxville TN

Autio Ceramics Collection

University of Montana, Paxson Gallery, Missoula MT

Alice Baber Midwest Collection

Greater Lafayette Museum of Art, Lafayette IN

Manson F Backus Print Collection

Seattle Art Museum, Seattle WA

Baker Collection of Porcelain

Lehigh University Art Galleries, Bethlehem PA

Bryant Baker Sculpture Collection

Ponca City Cultural Center & Museum, Ponca City OK

Ball-Kraft Collection of Roman and Syrian Glass

Ball State University, Museum of Art, Muncie IN

Bancroft Collection

Delaware Art Museum, Wilmington DE

John Chandler Bancroft Collection of Japanese Prints

Worcester Art Museum, Worcester MA

Barbed Wire Collection

Clark County Historical Society, Pioneer - Krier Museum, Ashland KS

Barberini-Kress Foundation Collection

Philadelphia Museum of Art, Philadelphia PA

Virgil Barker Collection

University of Miami, Lowe Art Museum, Coral Gables FL

Alfred I Barton Collection

University of Miami, Lowe Art Museum, Coral Gables FL

Bernard Baruch Silver Collection

University of South Carolina, McKissick Museum, Columbia SC

Antoine Louis Barye Collection of Bronzes

Corcoran Gallery of Art, Washington DC

Bauhaus Archives

Harvard University, Busch-Reisinger Museum, Cambridge MA

Ellen H Bayard Painting Collection

Baltimore Museum of Art, Baltimore MD

Zoe Beiler Paintings Collection

Dickinson State University, Mind's Eye Gallery, Dickinson ND

Bell Collection

Luna County Historical Society, Inc, Deming Luna Mimbres Museum, Deming NM

Thomas E Benesch Memorial Drawing Collection

Baltimore Museum of Art, Baltimore MD

Bennington Pottery Collection

Bennington Museum, Bennington VT

Berman Collection

Lehigh University Art Galleries, Bethlehem PA
Ursinus College, Philip & Muriel Berman Museum of Art, Collegeville PA

Bernat Oriental Collection

Colby College, Musuem of Art, Waterville ME

Harry A Bernstein Memorial Painting Collection

Baltimore Museum of Art, Baltimore MD

Biggs Sculpture Collection

Red River Valley Museum, Vernon TX

Biographies, Memoirs, Military Mannuals from 17th & 18th centuries

Fort Ticonderoga Association, Ticonderoga NY

Birds of America

Audubon Wildlife Sanctuary, Audubon PA

Vyvyan Blackford Collection

Fort Hays State University, Moss-Thorns Gallery of Arts, Hays KS

Wendel Black Print Collection

Oregon State University, Fairbanks Gallery, Corvallis OR

Edwin M Blake Memorial Collection

Trinity College, Austin Arts Center, Hartford CT

Aubrey Bodine Collection

Calvert Marine Museum, Solomons MD

Bodmer Collection

Joslyn Art Museum, Omaha NE

Boehm Collection

Bellingrath Gardens and Home, Theodore AL

J S Bohannon Folk Art Steamboat Collection

Calvert Marine Museum, Solomons MD

Bones, Skulls & Skelton Collection

SLA Arch-Couture Inc, Art Collection, Denver CO

Frederick T Bonham Collection

University of Tennessee, Frank H McClung Museum, Knoxville TN

Bradley Collection

Milwaukee Art Museum, Milwaukee WI

Branch Collection of Renaissance Art

Virginia Museum of Fine Arts, Richmond VA

Constantin Brancusi Sculpture Collection

Solomon R Guggenheim Museum, New York NY

Saidye & Samuel Bronfman Collection of Canadian Art

Montreal Museum of Fine Arts, Montreal PQ

Ailsa Mellon Bruce Collection of Decorative Arts

Virginia Museum of Fine Arts, Richmond VA

Pierre Brunet Collection

United States Figure Skating Association, World Figure Skating Hall of Fame and Museum, Colorado Springs CO

Buchanan Collection of City of Lethbridge

Southern Alberta Art Gallery, Lethbridge AB

Buddhist Art Collection

Jacques Marchais Center of Tibetan Art, Tibetan Museum, Staten Island NY

George Burchett Collection

Tattoo Art Museum, San Francisco CA

Burnap Collection

Nelson-Atkins Museum of Art, Kansas City MO

Burnap English Pottery Collection

Village of Potsdam Public Museum, Potsdam NY

Burrison Folklife Collection

Atlanta Historical Society Inc, Atlanta History
   Center, Atlanta GA

James F Byrnes Collection

University of South Carolina, McKissick Museum,
   Columbia SC

Caballeria Collection of Oils

Southwest Museum, Los Angeles CA

B G Canton Gallery

Stanford University, Art Gallery, Stanford CA

Caplan Collection

Children's Museum, Rauh Memorial Library,
   Indianapolis IN

Carder Steuben Glass Collection

The Rockwell Museum, Corning NY

Carnegie Collection of Prints

Dickinson College, Trout Gallery, Carlisle PA

Carrington Collection of Chinese Art

Rhode Island Historical Society, John Brown
   House, Providence RI

Robert Carter Collection

Gunston Hall Plantation, Library, Lorton VA

Carter Collection of Peruvian Art

Florida State University, Fine Arts Gallery &
   Museum, Tallahassee FL

Clarence Carter Paintings

Southern Ohio Museum Corporation, Southern
   Ohio Museum & Cultural Center, Portsmouth
   OH

George Washington Carver Artifacts

Tuskegee Institute National Historic Site, George
   Washington Carver & The Oaks, Tuskegee
   Institute AL

**John H Cassell Collection of Political
Cartoons**

Hartwick College, Foreman Gallery, Oneonta NY

Cass Wedgewood Collection

Wheaton College, Watson Gallery, Norton MA

Lynn Chadwick Sculpture Collection

Ursinus College, Philip & Muriel Berman Museum
   of Art, Collegeville PA

Mark Chagall Stained Glass Collection

The Art Institute of Chicago, Chicago IL

Conrad Wise Chapman Oils Collection

Valentine Museum, Richmond VA

Christopher Columbus Collection of Arts

New Jersey State Museum, Trenton NJ

Frederic Edwin Church Collection

Olana State Historic Site, Hudson NY

Winston Churchill Oil Painting Collection

Westminster College, Winston Churchill Memorial
   & Library in the United States, Fulton MO

Cinema Arts

American Museum of the Moving Image, Astoria
   NY

Civil War Artifacts

Drew County Historical Society, Museum,
   Monticello AR

Civil War Collection

Chicago Historical Society, Chicago IL
Kiah Museum, Savannah GA
Library of Congress, Prints and Photographs
   Division, Washington DC
Museum of Arts and History, Port Huron MI
Phillips County Museum, Helena AR
Kemper & Leila Williams Foundation, New Orleans
   LA

Civil War Period Collection

Jackson County Historical Society, John Wornall
   House Museum, Independence MO

Clark European Collection

Corcoran Gallery of Art, Washington DC

Clewell Pottery Collection

Jesse Besser Museum, Alpena MI

Jack Clifton Paintings Collection

Headquarters Fort Monroe, Dept of Army,
   Casemate Museum, Fort Monroe VA

Laura A Clubb Collection of Paintings

Philbrook Museum of Art, Tulsa OK

Jean Cocteau Collection

Severin Wunderman Museum, Irvine CA

Coe Collection

Coe College, Gordon Fennell Gallery & Marvin
   Cone Gallery, Cedar Rapids IA

Colburn Collection of Indian Bastketry

United States Department of the Interior Museum,
   Washington DC

Colburn Gemstone Collection

University of South Carolina, McKissick Museum,
   Columbia SC

**Cole Collection of Oriental & Decorative
Arts**

Dickinson College, Trout Gallery, Carlisle PA

**George W Cole Smith and Wesson Gun
Collection**

Hastings Museum, Hastings NE

Comic Books

International Museum of Cartoon Art, Montreal PQ

Comic Strips

International Museum of Cartoon Art, Montreal PQ

Marvin Cone Collection

Coe College, Gordon Fennell Gallery & Marvin
   Cone Gallery, Cedar Rapids IA

Cone Collection of French Art

Baltimore Museum of Art, Baltimore MD

Container Corporation of America Collection

National Museum of American Art, Washington
   DC

Contemporary Art

Burnaby Art Gallery, Burnaby BC
Hyde Park Art Center, Chicago IL
Lane Community College, Art Dept Gallery,
   Eugene OR
Los Angeles Contemporary Exhibitions, Los
   Angeles CA
University of Colorado at Colorado Springs, Gallery
   of Contemporary Art, Colorado Springs CO
Washington Project for the Arts, Washington DC

Contemporary Art Galleries

Rosicrucian Egyptian Museum and Art Gallery, San
   Jose CA

Contemporary Art of Western Montana

Missoula Museum of the Arts, Missoula MT

Contemporary Art, prints

The Art Museum of Santa Cruz County, Santa Cruz
   CA

Contemporary Native American Arts

Jesse Besser Museum, Alpena MI

Coons Collection

Carrie McLain Museum, Nome AK

Copeland Collection

Delaware Art Museum, Wilmington DE
Gunston Hall Plantation, Library, Lorton VA

Cosla Collection

Saint Mary's Romanian Orthodox Church,
    Romanian Ethnic Museum, Cleveland OH

Cosla Collection of Renaissance Art

Montclair State College, Art Gallery, Upper
    Montclair NJ

Cotter Collection

Saint Mary's College, Moreau Gallery, Notre Dame
    IN

Cowan Collection

Board of Parks & Recreation, The Parthenon,
    Nashville TN

Craig Collection of Edna Hibel

Edna Hibel Art Foundation, Hibel Museum of Art,
    Palm Beach FL

Charles Cristadoro Sculptures

Los Angeles County Museum of Natural History,
    William S Hart Museum, Newhall CA

Crozier Collection of Chinese Art

Philadelphia Museum of Art, Philadelphia PA

Cummings Collection

Colby College, Musuem of Art, Waterville ME

Edward S Curtis Photographic Collection

Custer County Art Center, Miles City MT

Charles Cutts Collection

Nevada Museum Of Art, Reno NV

Cybis Collection

Mercer County Community College, The Gallery,
    Trenton NJ

**Elise Agnus Daingerfield 18th Century
Collection**

Baltimore Museum of Art, Baltimore MD

Chester Dale Collection

National Gallery of Art, Washington DC

Cyrus Dallin Bronze Collection

Springville Museum of Art, Springville UT

Dana Collection

University of Montana, Paxson Gallery, Missoula
    MT

**Joseph E Davies Collection of Russian Icons
& Paintings**

University of Wisconsin-Madison, Elvehjem
    Museum of Art, Madison WI

Jacqueline Davis China Collection

Henry Phipps Ross & Sarah Juliette Ross Memorial
    Museum, Saint Andrews NB

Cecil Clark Davis Collection

Marion Art Center, Marion MA

Norman Davis Collection of Classical Art

Seattle Art Museum, Seattle WA

D'Berger Collection

Santa Clara University, de Saisset Museum, Santa
    Clara CA

Deeds

Oysterponds Historical Society, Museum, Orient
    NY

**Agnes Delano Watercolor and Print
Collection**

Howard University, Gallery of Art, Washington DC

**Thomas S Dickey Civil War Ordinance
Collection**

Atlanta Historical Society Inc, Atlanta History
    Center, Atlanta GA

**John G Diefenbaker Memorabilia &
Archives**

University of Saskatchewan, John G Diefenbaker
    Centre, Saskatoon SK

**Frank & Mary Alice Diener Collection of
Ancient Snuff Bottles**

Fresno Metropolitan Museum, Fresno CA

Digget Collection of Wooden Models

Halifax Historical Society, Inc, Halifax Historical
    Museum, Daytona Beach FL

Maynard Dixon Collection

Brigham Young University, B F Larsen Gallery,
    Provo UT

**F B Doane Collection of Western American
Art**

Frontier Times Museum, Bandera TX

Domestic Arts

Hinckley Foundation Museum, Ithaca NY

Dorflinger Glass Collection

Everhart Museum, Scranton PA

Doughty Bird Collection

Reynolda House Museum of American Art,
    Winston-Salem NC

Grace G Drayton Collection

G G Drayton Club, Salem OH

Marie Dressler Collection

Kiah Museum, Savannah GA

**Anthony J Drexel Collection of 19th
Century Paintings & Sculptures**

The Museum at Drexel University, Philadelphia PA

Driebe Collection of Paintings

Lehigh University Art Galleries, Bethlehem PA

Jose Drudis-Blada Collection

Mount Saint Mary's College, Jose Drudis-Biada Art
    Gallery, Los Angeles CA

DuBose Civil War Collection

Atlanta Historical Society Inc, Atlanta History
    Center, Atlanta GA

Dunbarton Print Collection

Saint Mary's College, Moreau Gallery, Notre Dame
    IN

Duncan Collection

University of Montana, Paxson Gallery, Missoula
    MT

**Dunnigan Collection of 19th Century
Etchings**

The Parrish Art Museum, Southampton NY

Harvey Dunn Paintings Collection

South Dakota State University, South Dakota Art
    Museum, Brookings SD

Dura-Europes Archaeological Collection

Yale University, Art Gallery, New Haven CT

**Hanson Rawlings Duval Jr Memorial
Collection**

Baltimore Museum of Art, Baltimore MD

**James Earle Studio Collection of Western
Art**

National Cowboy Hall of Fame and Western
    Heritage Center, Oklahoma City OK

Early Indian Art

Appaloosa Museum, Inc, Moscow ID

Editorial Cartoons

International Museum of Cartoon Art, Montreal PQ

Egyptology

University of Pennsylvania, Library, Philadelphia
    PA

Henry Eichheim Collection

Santa Barbara Museum of Art, Santa Barbara CA

Abram Eisenberg French Painting Collection

Baltimore Museum of Art, Baltimore MD

Elkins Collection of Old Masters

Philadelphia Museum of Art, Philadelphia PA

Elliott Collection of 20th Century European Art

University of Iowa, Museum of Art, Iowa City IA

Lincoln Ellsworth Collection

Mid-America All-Indian Center, Wichita KS

Clarence Ellsworth Painting

Los Angeles County Museum of Natural History, William S Hart Museum, Newhall CA

Jacob Epstein Old Masters Collection

Baltimore Museum of Art, Baltimore MD

Esso Collection

University of Miami, Lowe Art Museum, Coral Gables FL

Ethnographic Arts

Cornell University, Herbert F Johnson Museum of Art, Ithaca NY

European and American Posters

United States Military Academy, West Point Museum, West Point NY

Eustis Collection of Furniture

Oatlands, Inc, Leesburg VA

William T Evans Collection

National Museum of American Art, Washington DC

Florence Naftzger Evans Collection of Porcelain

Wichita Art Museum, Wichita KS

Mrs Arthur Kelly Evans Collection of Pottery and Porcelain

Virginia Museum of Fine Arts, Richmond VA

Peter Carl Faberge Collection of Czarist Jewels

Virginia Museum of Fine Arts, Richmond VA

Faberge objets d'art

Marjorie Merriweather Post Foundation of DC, Hillwood Museum, Washington DC

Fairbanks Collection of Paintings

Fort Wayne Museum of Art, Inc, Fort Wayne IN

Farm Machinery

Clark County Historical Society, Pioneer - Krier Museum, Ashland KS

F B Housser Memorial Collection

London Regional Art & Historical Museums, London ON

Lyonel Feininger Archives

Harvard University, Busch-Reisinger Museum, Cambridge MA

Dexter M Ferry Collection

Vassar College, Vassar Art Gallery, Poughkeepsie NY

Louis Feuchter Collection

Calvert Marine Museum, Solomons MD

Clark Field Collection of American Indian Crafts

Philbrook Museum of Art, Tulsa OK

Film

American Museum of the Moving Image, Astoria NY

Museum of Modern Art, New York NY

Fire Fighting; Material Culture

CIGNA Corporation, CIGNA Museum & Art Collection, Philadelphia PA

Elizabeth Parke Firestone Collection of French Silver

Detroit Institute of Arts, Detroit MI

Fisher Collection

Parson Fisher House, Jonathan Fisher Memorial, Inc, Blue Hill ME
University of Southern California, Fisher Gallery, Los Angeles CA

Fisher Memorial Collection

Beloit College, Wright Museum of Art, Beloit WI

Flagg Collection

Milwaukee Art Museum, Milwaukee WI

James M Flagg Painting

Los Angeles County Museum of Natural History, William S Hart Museum, Newhall CA

Charles & Katherine Fleetwood Pre-Columbian Collection

University of Houston, Sarah Campbell Blaffer Gallery, Houston TX

Julius Fleischman Collection

University of Cincinnati, Tangeman Fine Arts Gallery, Cincinnati OH

Folding Fans

Ellis County Museum Inc, Waxahachie TX

Fowler Collection of Paintings, Sculpture & Porcelain

Gadsden Museum of Fine Arts, Inc, Gadsden AL

Charles L Franck Photograph Collection

Kemper & Leila Williams Foundation, New Orleans LA

Simon Fraser Collection

Simon Fraser University, Simon Fraser Gallery, Burnaby BC

Laura G Fraser Studio Collection of Western Art

National Cowboy Hall of Fame and Western Heritage Center, Oklahoma City OK

Elizabeth L Frelinghuysen Collection

Gunston Hall Plantation, Library, Lorton VA

Samuel Friedenberg Collection of Plaques & Medals

The Jewish Museum, New York NY

Harry G Friedman Collection of Ceremonial Objects

The Jewish Museum, New York NY

Toni Frissell Collection

Library of Congress, Prints and Photographs Division, Washington DC

Patricia & Phillip Frost Collection

National Museum of American Art, Washington DC

Laura Anne Fry American Art Pottery & Art Glass

Greater Lafayette Museum of Art, Lafayette IN

Eugene Fuller Memorial Collection of Chinese Jades

Seattle Art Museum, Seattle WA

Fulton-Meyer Collection of African Art

University of Mississippi, University Museums, Oxford MS

Armand Hammer Collection

University of Southern California, Fisher Gallery, Los Angeles CA

Thomas Handforth Etching Collection

State Capitol Museum, Olympia WA

Armin Hansen Collection

Monterey Peninsula Museum of Art Association, Monterey CA

H C Hanson Naval Architecture Collection

Whatcom Museum of History and Art, Bellingham WA

Harmon Foundation Collection of African Wood Carvings

Kiah Museum, Savannah GA

Robert Harris Collection

Confederation Centre Art Gallery and Museum, Charlottetown PE

Harstone Carving Collection

Lizzardo Museum of Lapidary Art, Elmhurst IL

Marsden Hartley Drawing Collection

Bates College, Museum of Art, Lewiston ME

Fred Harvey Collection

Heard Museum, Phoenix AZ

Olga Hasbrouck Collection of Chinese Ceramics

Vassar College, Vassar Art Gallery, Poughkeepsie NY

Hawaiian Art

Volcano Art Center, Hawaii National Park HI

William Randolph Hearst Collection of Arms & Armour

Detroit Institute of Arts, Detroit MI

Heeramaneck Collection of Asian Art

Virginia Museum of Fine Arts, Richmond VA

Heeramaneck Collection of Primitive Art

Seattle Art Museum, Seattle WA

Herbert Waide Hemphill Jr Collection

National Museum of American Art, Washington DC

Edward F Heyne Pre-Columbian Collection

University of Houston, Sarah Campbell Blaffer Gallery, Houston TX

Abby Williams Hill Collection

University of Puget Sound, Kittredge Art Gallery, Tacoma WA

Hinkhouse Contemporary Art Collection

Coe College, Gordon Fennell Gallery & Marvin Cone Gallery, Cedar Rapids IA

Hirschberg Collection of West African Arts

Topeka Public Library, Gallery of Fine Arts, Topeka KS

Hirsch Collection of Oriental Rugs

Portland Art Museum, Portland OR

Joseph H Hirshhorn Collection

Hirshhorn Museum and Sculpture Garden, Washington DC

Hispanic Collection

Hispanic Society of America, Museum, New York NY
Library of Congress, Prints and Photographs Division, Washington DC

Historical Material, Nautical Prints

Massachusetts Institute of Technology, MIT Museum, Cambridge MA

Historic Newspapers & Magazines

Rowland Evans Robinson Memorial Association, Rokeby Museum, Ferrisburgh VT

History of Holyoke 1850-1930

City of Holyoke Museum-Wistariahurst, Holyoke MA

HMS Debraak, 18th century British Warship

Historical and Cultural Affairs, Delaware State Museums, Dover DE

Morris Henry Hobbs Print Collection

Kemper & Leila Williams Foundation, New Orleans LA

Roy Hofheinz Tapestry Collection

University of Houston, Sarah Campbell Blaffer Gallery, Houston TX

Willitts J Hole Collection

University of California, Los Angeles, Wight Art Gallery, Los Angeles CA

Mary Hollen Collection

Huronia Museum, Midland ON

Holliday Collection of Neo-Impressionist Paintings

Indianapolis Museum of Art, Indianapolis IN

Oliver Wendell Holmes Stereographic Collection

Canton Art Institute, Canton OH

Winslow Homer Collection

Colby College, Musuem of Art, Waterville ME

Winslow Homer Woodcut Collection

State Capitol Museum, Olympia WA

Samuel Houghton Great Basin Collection

Nevada Museum Of Art, Reno NV

J Harry Howard Gemstone Collection

University of South Carolina, McKissick Museum, Columbia SC

Oscar Howe Collection

University of South Dakota Art Galleries, Vermillion SD

Joe and Lucy Howorth Collection

Delta State University, Fielding L Wright Art Center, Cleveland MS

Anna C Hoyt Collection of Old Masters

Vanderbilt University, Fine Arts Gallery, Nashville TN

Gardiner Greene Hubbard Endowment Collection of Prints

Library of Congress, Prints and Photographs Division, Washington DC

Winifred Kimball Hudnut Collection

University of Utah, Utah Museum of Fine Arts, Salt Lake City UT

Marie Hull Collection

Delta State University, Fielding L Wright Art Center, Cleveland MS

J Marvin Hunter Western Americana Collection

Frontier Times Museum, Bandera TX

Charles & Elsa Hutzler Memorial Collection of Contemporary Sculpture

Baltimore Museum of Art, Baltimore MD

Illinois Art, historical & contemporary

Illinois State Museum, State of Illinois Art Gallery, Chicago IL

Illuminated Manuscripts

Nelda C & H J Lutcher Stark Foundation, Stark Museum of Art, Orange TX

Illustrated Books

Museum of Modern Art, New York NY

Illustrated Maps

Tomoka State Park Museum, Fred Dana Marsh Museum, Ormond Beach FL

Illustrations

International Museum of Cartoon Art, Montreal PQ

Tools Implements of Pioneer Lifeways

Coos County Historical Society Museum, North Bend OR

Incunabula

La Casa del Libro Museum, San Juan PR

Indian Baskets

Luna County Historical Society, Inc, Deming Luna Mimbres Museum, Deming NM

Industrial Design

Craft and Folk Art Museum, Los Angeles CA

William Inge Memorabilia Collection

Ladies Library and Art Association, Independence Museum, Independence KS

Installation

Washington Project for the Arts, Washington DC

Inuit Art

Aurora University, Schingoethe Center for Native American Cultures, Aurora IL
Bowdoin College, Peary-MacMillan Arctic Museum, Brunswick ME
Capital University, Schumacher Gallery, Columbus OH
Dawson City Museum & Historical Society, Dawson City YT
Toronto Dominion Bank, Toronto ON

Isaacson Porcelain Collection

Seattle Art Museum, Seattle WA

Harry L Jackson Print Collection

Murray State University, Eagle Gallery, Murray KY

Mary Frick Jacobs European Art Collection

Baltimore Museum of Art, Baltimore MD

James McNeill Collection

Isabella Stewart Gardner Museum, Boston MA

Japanese Ceramics, Decorative Arts, Design & Architecture, Fine Arts, Graphic Arts, Sculpture, Textiles, Woodblock Prints

Japan Society, Inc, Japan Society Gallery, New York NY

Japanese Print Collection

Oregon State University, Fairbanks Gallery, Corvallis OR

Jarves Collection of Italian Paintings

Yale University, Art Gallery, New Haven CT

C Paul Jennewein Collection

Tampa Museum of Art, Tampa FL

Jens Jensen Archive of Landscape Architecture & Drawings

University of Michigan, Art & Architecture Library & Computer Lab, Ann Arbor MI

Jette Collection

Colby College, Musuem of Art, Waterville ME

Franz Johnson Collection

Huronia Museum, Midland ON
Saint Louis County Historical Society, Duluth MN

Johnson Collection of Art

Topeka Public Library, Gallery of Fine Arts, Topeka KS

John G Johnson Collection of Old Masters

Philadelphia Museum of Art, Philadelphia PA

S C Johnson & Son Collection

National Museum of American Art, Washington DC

F B Johnston Collection

Library of Congress, Prints and Photographs Division, Washington DC
National Museum of American Art, Washington DC

T Catesby Jones Collection of 20th Century European Art

Virginia Museum of Fine Arts, Richmond VA

Raymond Jonson Reserved Retrospective Collection of Paintings

University of New Mexico, Jonson Gallery, Albuquerque NM

Journals

Oysterponds Historical Society, Museum, Orient NY

A Juley & Son Collection

National Museum of American Art, Washington DC

Vasily Kandinsky Collection

Solomon R Guggenheim Museum, New York NY

William Keith Paintings Collection

Saint Mary's College of California, Hearst Art Gallery, Moraga CA

Kempsmith Collection

Lehigh University Art Galleries, Bethlehem PA

Marie Kendall Photography Collection

Norfolk Historical Society Inc, Museum, Norfolk CT

Victor Kiam Painting Collection

New Orleans Museum of Art, New Orleans LA

Darius Kinsey Photograph Collection

Whatcom Museum of History and Art, Bellingham WA

Paul Klee Collection

Solomon R Guggenheim Museum, New York NY

Kolb Graphics Collection

Santa Clara University, de Saisset Museum, Santa Clara CA

Korean Pottery Collection

Allegheny College, Bowman, Megahan and Penelec Galleries, Meadville PA

Krannert Memorial Collection

University of Indianapolis, Leah Ransburg Art Gallery, Indianapolis IN

Samuel H Kress Collection

Allentown Art Museum, Allentown PA
Columbia Museum of Art, Columbia SC
El Paso Museum of Art, El Paso TX
Howard University, Gallery of Art, Washington DC
Memphis Brooks Museum of Art, Memphis TN
National Gallery of Art, Washington DC
North Carolina Museum of Art, Raleigh NC
Philbrook Museum of Art, Tulsa OK
Portland Art Museum, Portland OR
Trinity College, Austin Arts Center, Hartford CT
University of Arizona, Museum of Art, Tucson AZ
University of Miami, Lowe Art Museum, Coral Gables FL
Vanderbilt University, Fine Arts Gallery, Nashville TN

Samuel H Kress Collection of Renaissance Art

Berea College, Doris Ulmann Galleries, Berea KY
Honolulu Academy of Arts, Honolulu HI
New Orleans Museum of Art, New Orleans LA

Samuel H Kress Study Collection

University of Georgia, Georgia Museum of Art, Athens GA
University of Notre Dame, Snite Museum of Art, Notre Dame IN

Irma Kruse Collection

Hastings Museum, Hastings NE

Kurdian Collection of Mexican Art

Wichita Art Museum, Wichita KS

Mary Andresw Ladd Collection of Japanese Prints

Portland Art Museum, Portland OR

William S Ladd Collection of Pre-Columbian Art

Portland Art Museum, Portland OR

B Lafon Drawing Collection

Kemper & Leila Williams Foundation, New Orleans LA

Norman LaLiberte Collection

Saint Mary's College, Moreau Gallery, Notre Dame IN

Robert L Lambdin Painting

Los Angeles County Museum of Natural History, William S Hart Museum, Newhall CA

John D Lankenau Collection of 19th Century Paintings & Sculptures

The Museum at Drexel University, Philadelphia PA

Larson Drawing Collection

Austin Peay State University, Margaret Fort Trahern Gallery, Clarksville TN

Mauricio Lasansky Print Collection

University of Iowa, Museum of Art, Iowa City IA

Samuel K Lathrop Collection

University of Miami, Lowe Art Museum, Coral Gables FL

Latino Chicano Art

Chicano Humanities & Arts Council, Denver CO

Plaza de la Raza Cultural Center, Los Angeles CA

Latter-Schlesinger Miniature Collection

New Orleans Museum of Art, New Orleans LA

Clarence Laughlin Photograph Collection

Kemper & Leila Williams Foundation, New Orleans LA

Roberta Campbell Lawson Collection of Indian Artifacts

Philbrook Museum of Art, Tulsa OK

Lawther Collection of Ethiopian Crosses

Portland Art Museum, Portland OR

Layton Collection

Milwaukee Art Museum, Milwaukee WI

Robert Lehman Collection

The Metropolitan Museum of Art, New York NY

Roy C Leventritt Collection

Asian Art Museum of San Francisco, Avery Brundage Collection, San Francisco CA

Dr Louis Levy Collection of American Prints

Memphis Brooks Museum of Art, Memphis TN

Robert H & Ryda Levy Collection of Contemporary Sculpture

Baltimore Museum of Art, Baltimore MD

Julius Levy Memorial Collection of Oriental Art

Baltimore Museum of Art, Baltimore MD

Lewis Collection of Classical Antiquities

Portland Art Museum, Portland OR

Lewis-Kneberg Collection

University of Tennessee, Frank H McClung Museum, Knoxville TN

Lewisohn Collection of Caribbean Art

University of Mississippi, University Museums, Oxford MS

Dan Leyrer Photograph Collection

Kemper & Leila Williams Foundation, New Orleans LA

Lida Hilton Print Collection

Montclair State College, Art Gallery, Upper Montclair NJ

Jonas Lie Collection of Panama Canal Oils

United States Military Academy, West Point Museum, West Point NY

Liedesdorf Collection of European Armor

United States Military Academy, West Point Museum, West Point NY

Jacques Lipchitz Sculpture Collection

University of Arizona, Museum of Art, Tucson AZ

Liquor Bottle Collection

Luna County Historical Society, Inc, Deming Luna Mimbres Museum, Deming NM

Lithophane Collection

Blair Museum of Lithophanes and Carved Waxes, Toledo OH

Alain Locke Collection of African Art

Howard University, Gallery of Art, Washington DC

Lockwood-deForest Collection

Mark Twain Memorial, Hartford CT

Loomis Wildlife Collection

Roberson Museum & Science Center, Binghamton NY

Ted Lord Collection

Huronia Museum, Midland ON

George A Lucas Collection

Baltimore Museum of Art, Baltimore MD

Ernst Mahler Collection of Germanic Glass

Bergstrom Mahler Museum, Neenah WI

Make-up

American Museum of the Moving Image, Astoria NY

Richard Mandell Collection

University of South Carolina, McKissick Museum, Columbia SC

Mildred Many Memorial Collection

Mid-America All-Indian Center, Wichita KS

Marghab Linens Collection

South Dakota State University, South Dakota Art Museum, Brookings SD

John Marin Collection

Colby College, Musuem of Art, Waterville ME

Maritime Archaeology

Historical and Cultural Affairs, Delaware State Museums, Dover DE

Maritime Objects Collection

Coos County Historical Society Museum, North Bend OR

Markley Collection of Ancient Peruvian Ceramics

Pennsylvania State University, Palmer Museum of Art, University Park PA

Marks Collection of Pre-Columbian Art

East Tennessee State University, Carroll Reece Museum, Johnson City TN

Jacob Marks Memorial Collection

Memphis College of Art, G Pillow Lewis Memorial Library, Memphis TN

Fred Dana Marsh Collection

Tomoka State Park Museum, Fred Dana Marsh Museum, Ormond Beach FL

Masonic Collection

Museum of Our National Heritage, Lexington MA

Mason-Mercer Rare Book Collection

Gunston Hall Plantation, Library, Lorton VA

Material Culture

American Museum of the Moving Image, Astoria NY

A W Mauach Permanent Collection

Palette & Chisel Academy of Fine Arts, Chicago IL

Mayan Studies

University of Pennsylvania, Library, Philadelphia PA

Saidie A May Collection

Baltimore Museum of Art, Baltimore MD

McClelland Collection

Rosemount Victorian House Museum, Pueblo CO

McCrellis Doll Collection

Rhode Island Historical Society, John Brown House, Providence RI

Manley McDonald Originals

Hastings County Museum, Belleville ON

McFadden Collection of Old Masters

Philadelphia Museum of Art, Philadelphia PA

Gladys McFerron Collection

United States Figure Skating Association, World Figure Skating Hall of Fame and Museum, Colorado Springs CO

McGill Collection

University of Montana, Paxson Gallery, Missoula MT

McGowen Doll House Collection

Nicolaysen Art Museum and Discovery Center, Childrens Discovery Center, Casper WY

McLain Collection

Carrie McLain Museum, Nome AK

McLanahan Memorial Collection

Baltimore Museum of Art, Baltimore MD

George F McMurray Collection

Trinity College, Austin Arts Center, Hartford CT

Paul McPharlin Collection of Theatre & Graphic Arts

Detroit Institute of Arts, Detroit MI

Algur H Meadows Collection of Spanish Paintings

Southern Methodist University, Meadows Museum, Dallas TX

Media Arts

San Francisco Museum of Modern Art, San Francisco CA

Hamilton King Meek Memorial Collection

London Regional Art & Historical Museums, London ON

Meissen Porcelain Collection

Cummer Gallery of Art, DeEtte Holden Cummer Museum Foundation, Jacksonville FL
Virginia Museum of Fine Arts, Richmond VA

Andrew W Mellon Collection

National Gallery of Art, Washington DC

Photographs Memorabilia

Ellis County Museum Inc, Waxahachie TX

Mendocino County History

Mendocino County Museum, Willits CA

Conger Metcalf Collection

Coe College, Gordon Fennell Gallery & Marvin Cone Gallery, Cedar Rapids IA

Mexican Folk Art

Chicano Humanities & Arts Council, Denver CO

Michael Silver Collection

University of Utah, Utah Museum of Fine Arts, Salt Lake City UT

Michener Collection of American Paintings

University of Texas at Austin, Archer M Huntington Art Gallery, Austin TX

Michener Collection of Prints & Paintings

Kent State University, School of Art Gallery, Kent OH

Mielke Collection

Carrie McLain Museum, Nome AK

Military Art Collection

Fort George G Meade Museum, Fort Meade MD
National Infantry Museum, Fort Benning GA

Military equipment relating to mech Cavalry & Armor

Cavalry - Armor Foundation, Patton Museum of Cavalry & Armor, Fort Knox KY

Samuel & Tobie Miller Collection

Baltimore Museum of Art, Baltimore MD

Anna L Miller Paintings

Viterbo College Art Gallery, La Crosse WI

John Miller Photography Collection

Delta State University, Fielding L Wright Art Center, Cleveland MS

Millington-Barnard Collection

University of Mississippi, University Museums, Oxford MS

Rose & Benjamin Mintz Collection of Eastern European Art

The Jewish Museum, New York NY

Albert K Mitchell Russell-Remington Collection

National Cowboy Hall of Fame and Western Heritage Center, Oklahoma City OK

Andrew Molles Collection

Riverside Art Museum, Riverside CA

James Montgomery Ward Permanent Collection

Palette & Chisel Academy of Fine Arts, Chicago IL

Monumental Outdoor Art

Tomoka State Park Museum, Fred Dana Marsh Museum, Ormond Beach FL

Marianne Moore Archive Collection

The Rosenbach Museum and Library, Philadelphia PA

Moore Collection

London Regional Art & Historical Museums, London ON
University of Illinois, Krannert Art Museum, Champaign IL
University of Tennessee, Frank H McClung Museum, Knoxville TN

Henry Moore Sculpture Collection

Art Gallery of Ontario, Toronto ON

Thomas Moran & J M W/Turner Original Prints, Watercolor & Oil Collections

The Turner Museum, Denver CO

Morgenroth Collection of Renaissance Medals

University of California, Santa Barbara, University Art Museum, Santa Barbara CA

Mormon Collection

Church of Jesus Christ of Latter-day Saints, Museum of Church History & Art, Salt Lake City UT

Howard J Morrison Jr Osteological Collection

Kiah Museum, Savannah GA

Morse Collection

Beloit College, Wright Museum of Art, Beloit WI
Wichita Art Museum, Library, Wichita KS

William Moser Collection of African Art

Fort Wayne Museum of Art, Inc, Fort Wayne IN

Mountain Sculpture-Carving

Crazy Horse Memorial, Indian Museum of North
America, Crazy Horse SD

**William Sidney Mount Collection; carriages-
horse drawn transportation, decoys;
miniature rooms**

The Museums at Stony Brook, Stony Brook NY

Arnold Mountfort Collection

Santa Clara University, de Saisset Museum, Santa
Clara CA

Mourot Collection of Meissen Porcelain

Virginia Museum of Fine Arts, Richmond VA

Movie Posters

American Museum of the Moving Image, Astoria
NY

Mowat Loyalist Collection

Henry Phipps Ross & Sarah Juliette Ross Memorial
Museum, Saint Andrews NB

**Roland P Murdock Collection of American
Art**

Wichita Art Museum, Wichita KS

Musical Instruments

The Metropolitan Museum of Art, New York NY

**Gwen Houston Naftzger Collection of
Porcelain Birds**

Wichita Art Museum, Wichita KS

**L S and Ida L Naftzger Collection of Prints
and Drawings**

Wichita Art Museum, Wichita KS

**M C Naftzger Collection of Russell
Paintings**

Wichita Art Museum, Wichita KS

**Nagel Collection of Chinese & Tibetan
Sculpture & Textiles**

Scripps College, Clark Humanities Museum,
Claremont CA

Joseph Nassy Collection

Severin Wunderman Museum, Irvine CA

Native American Art

Florence Museum, Florence SC
Newark Museum Association, The Newark
Museum, Newark NJ

Native American artifacts

Artesia Historical Museum & Art Center, Artesia
NM
Coos County Historical Society Museum, North
Bend OR

Native American Basketry

Redding Museum of Art & History, Redding CA

Native American Ethno-graphic Material

City of Holyoke Museum-Wistariahurst, Holyoke
MA

Native American Fine Art

Heard Museum, Phoenix AZ

Elizabeth S Navas Collection

Wichita Art Museum, Library, Wichita KS

Robert Lyn Nelson Graphics Collection

Nicolaysen Art Museum and Discovery Center,
Childrens Discovery Center, Casper WY

Leslie Fenton Netsuke Collection

Hartnell College Gallery, Salinas CA

Otto Neumann Collection

Tampa Museum of Art, Tampa FL

Newcomb Pottery Collection

West Baton Rouge Historical Association, Museum,
Port Allen LA

New England History

Springfield Library & Museums Association,
Connecticut Valley Historical Museum,
Springfield MA

**Chief Justice Robert N C Nix Sr Collection
of Legal Writings & Memorabilia**

Afro-American Historical & Cultural Museum,
Philadelphia PA

North American Artifacts

Crazy Horse Memorial, Indian Museum of North
America, Crazy Horse SD

Harry T Norton Collection of Glass

Montreal Museum of Fine Arts, Montreal PQ

Alice B Nunn Silver Collection

Portland Art Museum, Portland OR

Ohilia Buerger Collection of Ancient coins

Lawrence University, Wriston Art Center Galleries,
Appleton WI

Olsen Collection

University of Illinois, Krannert Art Museum,
Champaign IL

Elizabeth O'Neill Verner Collection

Tradd Street Press, Elizabeth O'Neill Verner Studio
Museum, Charleston SC

**Oppenheimer Collection of Late Medieval &
Early Renaissance Sculpture & Paintings**

Marion Koogler McNay Art Museum, San Antonio
TX

Ernst Oppler Collection

Brevard Art Center and Museum, Inc, Melbourne
FL

Oriental Furniture Collection

Nelson-Atkins Museum of Art, Kansas City MO

**Oriental Rugs Collection; African, Pre-
Columbian works; Ethnographic Collection**

Birmingham Museum of Art, Birmingham AL

Leslie Oursler Collection

Calvert Marine Museum, Solomons MD

Painting: Chinese Genealogy

Chinese Culture Foundation, Chinese Culture
Center Gallery, San Francisco CA

Paintings

Art Museum of the Americas, Washington DC
National Museum of Women in the Arts,
Washington DC
Order Sons of Italy in America, Garibaldi &
Meucci Meuseum, Staten Island NY

Paper

Order Sons of Italy in America, Garibaldi &
Meucci Meuseum, Staten Island NY

Parish Collection of Furniture

Frederic Remington Art Museum, Ogdensburg NY

Parker Lace Collection

Montreal Museum of Fine Arts, Montreal PQ

**Samuel Parrish Collection of Renaissance
Art**

The Parrish Art Museum, Southampton NY

Patterns

Essex Historical Society, Essex Shipbuilding
Museum, Essex MA

J G D'Arcy Paul Collection

Baltimore Museum of Art, Baltimore MD

The Paulson Collection of Ancient Near Eastern Coins

University of Georgia, Georgia Museum of Art, Athens GA

John Barton Payne Collection

Virginia Museum of Fine Arts, Richmond VA

Peabody Institute Collection

Baltimore Museum of Art, Baltimore MD

Adelaide Pearson Collection

Colby College, Musuem of Art, Waterville ME

Samuel Pees Contemporary Painting Collection

Allegheny College, Bowman, Megahan and Penelec Galleries, Meadville PA

Pendleton Collection

Kelly-Griggs House Museum, Red Bluff CA

Pendleton House Decorative Arts Collection

Rhode Island School of Design, Museum of Art, Providence RI

Joseph Pennell Collection

George Washington University, The Dimock Gallery, Washington DC

Pennell Endowment Collection of Prints

Library of Congress, Prints and Photographs Division, Washington DC

Pfeffer Moser Glass Collection

University of the Ozarks, Stephens Gallery, Clarksville AR

Leonard Pfeiffer Collection

University of Arizona, Museum of Art, Tucson AZ

Phelps Collection

Delaware Art Museum, Wilmington DE

Walter J Phillips Collection

Banff Centre, Walter Phillips Gallery, Banff AB

George Phippen Memorial Western Bronze Collection

Maricopa County Historical Society, Desert Caballeros Western Museum, Wickenburg AZ

Duncan Phyfe Furniture Collection

Cincinnati Institute of Fine Arts, Taft Museum, Cincinnati OH

Albert Pilavin Collection of 20th Century American Arts

Rhode Island School of Design, Museum of Art, Providence RI

Lucile Pillow Porcelain Collection

Montreal Museum of Fine Arts, Montreal PQ

Pioneer Memorabilia

Crazy Horse Memorial, Indian Museum of North America, Crazy Horse SD

Pitkin Collection of Asian Art

Beloit College, Wright Museum of Art, Beloit WI

Plans

Essex Historical Society, Essex Shipbuilding Museum, Essex MA

Pohl Collection - German Expressionism

Lawrence University, Wriston Art Center Galleries, Appleton WI

William J Pollock Collection of American Indian Art

Colby College, Musuem of Art, Waterville ME

H V Poor

Birger Sandzen Memorial Gallery, Lindsborg KS

Porter-Phelps-Huntington Family Collection

Porter-Phelps-Huntington Foundation, Inc Foundation, Inc, Historic House Museum, Hadley MA

Potamkin Collection of 19th & 20th Century Work

Dickinson College, Trout Gallery, Carlisle PA

Potlatch Collection of Royal Canadian Mounted Police Illustrations

University of Minnesota, Duluth, Tweed Museum of Art, Duluth MN

Charles Pratt Collection of Chinese Jades

Vassar College, Vassar Art Gallery, Poughkeepsie NY

Lillian Thomas Pratt Collection of Czarist Jewels

Virginia Museum of Fine Arts, Richmond VA

Pre-Columbian Art

Blanden Memorial Art Museum, Fort Dodge IA

William Henry Price Memorial Collection of Oil Paintings

Oregon State University, Memorial Union Art Gallery, Corvallis OR

Puerto Rican Art

University of Puerto Rico, Museum of Anthropology, History & Art, Rio Piedras PR

Puppetry

Center for Puppetry Arts, Atlanta GA

Putnam Collection

Timken Museum of Art, San Diego CA

Quadrupeds of North America Collection

Audubon Wildlife Sanctuary, Audubon PA

Quaker Art Collection

Swarthmore College, Friends Historical Library, Swarthmore PA

Freda & Clara Radoff Mexican Print Collection

University of Houston, Sarah Campbell Blaffer Gallery, Houston TX

Natacha Rambova Egyptian Collection

University of Utah, Utah Museum of Fine Arts, Salt Lake City UT

Rand Collection of American Indian Art

Montclair Art Museum, Montclair NJ

Rare Books

Nelda C & H J Lutcher Stark Foundation, Stark Museum of Art, Orange TX

Rasmussen Collection of Eskimo Arts

Portland Art Museum, Portland OR

W T Rawleigh Collection

Freeport Art Museum & Cultural Center, Freeport IL

Ray American Indian Collection

Red River Valley Museum, Vernon TX

Lester Raymer

Birger Sandzen Memorial Gallery, Lindsborg KS

Recreational & Working Historic Small Craft (boats), Models (full rigged ship & half hulls), Tools

Penobscot Marine Museum, Searsport ME

Regional Folk Art

Columbus Museum of Art, Columbus OH

Frederic Remington Collection

Bradford Brinton Memorial Museum & Historic Ranch, Big Horn WY
Buffalo Bill Memorial Association, Buffalo Bill Historical Center, Cody WY
R W Norton Art Gallery, Shreveport LA
St Lawrence University, Richard F Brush Art Gallery, Canton NY

Remington Drawings

Headquarters Fort Monroe, Dept of Army, Casemate Museum, Fort Monroe VA

Frederic Remington Western Art Paintings

Sid W Richardson Foundation, Collection of Western Art, Fort Worth TX

Richards Coin Collection

Hastings Museum, Hastings NE

General Lawrason Riggs Collection

Baltimore Museum of Art, Baltimore MD

Rindisbacher Watercolor Collection

United States Military Academy, West Point Museum, West Point NY

William Ritschel Collection

Monterey Peninsula Museum of Art Association, Monterey CA

Rloss Photo Collection

United States Figure Skating Association, World Figure Skating Hall of Fame and Museum, Colorado Springs CO

David Roberts Collection

Riverside County Museum, Edward-Dean Museum, Cherry Valley CA

Roberts Sculpture Collection

Portland Art Museum, Portland OR

Marion Sharp Robinson Collection

University of Utah, Utah Museum of Fine Arts, Salt Lake City UT

David Robinson Collection of Antiquities

University of Mississippi, University Museums, Oxford MS

Sara Roby Foundation Collection

National Museum of American Art, Washington DC

Abby Aldrich Rockefeller Collection of Japanese Art

Rhode Island School of Design, Museum of Art, Providence RI

Norman Rockwell Collection

Norman Rockwell Museum at Stockbridge, Stockbridge MA

Robert F Rockwell Foundation Collection

The Rockwell Museum, Corning NY

Rodeo Portrait Collection

National Cowboy Hall of Fame and Western Heritage Center, Oklahoma City OK

Rodman Collection of Popular Art

The Art Galleries of Ramapo College, Mahwah NJ

Nicholas Roerich Collection

Nicholas Roerich Museum, New York NY

John Rogers Sculpture Collection

Saginaw Art Museum, Saginaw MI

August H O Rolle/Collection

Calvert Marine Museum, Solomons MD

Edward Rose Collection of Ceramics

Brandeis University, Rose Art Museum, Waltham MA

Ross Decorative Art Collection

Henry Phipps Ross & Sarah Juliette Ross Memorial Museum, Saint Andrews NB

Guy Rowe Wax Drawings Collections

Angelo State University, Houston Harte University Center, San Angelo TX

Peter Paul Rubens Collection

State Art Museum of Florida, John & Mable Ringling Museum of Art, Sarasota FL

Rugs

Luna County Historical Society, Inc, Deming Luna Mimbres Museum, Deming NM

Charles M Russell Collection

Bradford Brinton Memorial Museum & Historic Ranch, Big Horn WY
Buffalo Bill Memorial Association, Buffalo Bill Historical Center, Cody WY
R W Norton Art Gallery, Shreveport LA
C M Russell Museum, Great Falls MT

Charles M Russell Paintings

Wichita Art Museum, Wichita KS

Charles M Russell Western Art Paintings

Sid W Richardson Foundation, Collection of Western Art, Fort Worth TX

Russian & Baltic Photography

Roy Boyd Gallery, Chicago IL

Sackler Collection

The Metropolitan Museum of Art, New York NY

Oscar & Maria Salzer Collection of Still Life & Trompe L'oeil Paintings

Fresno Metropolitan Museum, Fresno CA

Oscar & Maria Salzer Collection of 16th & 17th Century Dutch & Flemish Paintings

Fresno Metropolitan Museum, Fresno CA

Wilbur Sandison Photography Collection

Whatcom Museum of History and Art, Bellingham WA

Sandwich Glass Collection

Fuller Museum of Art, Brockton MA

Birger Sandzen

Birger Sandzen Memorial Gallery, Lindsborg KS

Sargent Collection of American Indian Art

Montclair Art Museum, Montclair NJ

Sawhill Artifact Collection

James Madison University, Sawhill Gallery, Harrisonburg VA

Jonathan Sax Print Collection

University of Minnesota, Duluth, Tweed Museum of Art, Duluth MN

Richard Schmid Permanent Collection

Palette & Chisel Academy of Fine Arts, Chicago IL

Alice F Schott Doll Collection

Santa Barbara Museum of Art, Santa Barbara CA

Schreyvogel Collection

National Cowboy Hall of Fame and Western Heritage Center, Oklahoma City OK

Charles Schreyvogel Painting

Los Angeles County Museum of Natural History, William S Hart Museum, Newhall CA

Schuette Woodland Indian Collection

Rahr-West Art Museum, Manitowoc WI

Schwartz Collection of Chinese Ivories

Rahr-West Art Museum, Manitowoc WI

Scotese Collection of Graphics

Columbia Museum of Art, Columbia SC

Philip Sears Sculpture Collection

Fruitlands Museum, Inc, Harvard MA

Seibels Collection of Renaissance Art

Columbia Museum of Art, Columbia SC

Shaker Collection

Hancock Shaker Village, Inc, Pittsfield MA
Shaker Museum, Old Chatham NY

Sharp Collection of Glass

Frederic Remington Art Museum, Ogdensburg NY

Sheet Music Covers

Liberty Memorial Museum & Archives, Kansas City
MO

Inglis Sheldon-Williams Collection

Regina Public Library, Dunlop Art Gallery, Regina
SK

**William Ludwell Sheppard Watercolor
Collection**

Valentine Museum, Richmond VA

Ship Models

Essex Historical Society, Essex Shipbuilding
Museum, Essex MA
US Coast Guard Museum, New London CT

**David M Shoup Collection of Korean
Pottery**

Allegheny College, Bowman, Megahan and Penelec
Galleries, Meadville PA

B Simon Lithography Collection

Kemper & Leila Williams Foundation, New Orleans
LA

John Singer Sargent Collection

Isabella Stewart Gardner Museum, Boston MA

Dorothy D Skewis Print Collection

Witter Gallery, Storm Lake IA

Sloan Collection

Valparaiso University, Museum of Art, Valparaiso
IN

Eric Sloane Collection

Connecticut Historical Commission, Sloane-Stanley
Museum, Kent CT

Helen S Slosberg Collection of Oceanic Art

Brandeis University, Rose Art Museum, Waltham
MA

**C R Smith Collection of Western American
Art**

University of Texas at Austin, Archer M
Huntington Art Gallery, Austin TX

Smith Painting Collection

Woodmere Art Museum, Philadelphia PA

Smith-Patterson Memorial Collection

Delta State University, Fielding L Wright Art
Center, Cleveland MS

Snelgrove Historical Collection

Gadsden Museum of Fine Arts, Inc, Gadsden AL

Soldiers' Art & Crafts

Liberty Memorial Museum & Archives, Kansas City
MO

Sonnenschein Collection

Cornell College, Armstrong Gallery, Mount Vernon
IA

Spanish Colonial Folk Art

Chicano Humanities & Arts Council, Denver CO

Leon Spilliaert Collection

The Metropolitan Museum of Art, New York NY

Sporting Art

Genesee Country Museum, John L Wehle Gallery
of Sporting Art, Mumford NY

Springfield & Connecticut Valley History

Springfield Library & Museums Association,
Connecticut Valley Historical Museum,
Springfield MA

Benton Spruance Print Collection

Beaver College Art Gallery, Glenside PA

Staff Training

The Bartlett Museum, Amesbury MA

Stamps

Order Sons of Italy in America, Garibaldi &
Meucci Meuseum, Staten Island NY

Anisoara Stan Collection

Saint Mary's Romanian Orthodox Church,
Romanian Ethnic Museum, Cleveland OH

Stanford Family Collection

Stanford University, Art Gallery, Stanford CA

Staples Collection of Indonesian Art

James Madison University, Sawhill Gallery,
Harrisonburg VA

Statuary Hall

Alabama Department of Archives and History
Museum, Museum Galleries, Montgomery AL

**John Steele Collection of Furniture, Silver &
Paintings**

Jamestown-Yorktown Foundation, Yorktown VA

John Steele Print Collection

East Tennessee State University, Carroll Reece
Museum, Johnson City TN

**Harry J Stein-Samuel Friedenberg
Collection of Coins from the Holy Land**

The Jewish Museum, New York NY

Stern Collection

Philadelphia Museum of Art, Philadelphia PA

Harold P Stern Collection of Oriental Art

Vanderbilt University, Fine Arts Gallery, Nashville
TN

Stern-Davis Collection of Peruvian Painting

New Orleans Museum of Art, New Orleans LA

Dorothy Stevens Collection

United States Figure Skating Association, World
Figure Skating Hall of Fame and Museum,
Colorado Springs CO

Robert Louis Stevenson Collection

Silverado Museum, Saint Helena CA

Stiegel Glass Collection

Philadelphia Museum of Art, Philadelphia PA

Alfred Stieglitz Collection

Fisk University Museum of Art, University
Galleries, Nashville TN

Clyfford Still Collection

San Francisco Museum of Modern Art, San
Francisco CA

**Thomas D Stimson Memorial Collection of
Far Eastern Art**

Seattle Art Museum, Seattle WA

Stoddard Collection of Greek Vases

Yale University, Art Gallery, New Haven CT

Ala Story Print Collection

University of California, Santa Barbara, University
Art Museum, Santa Barbara CA

**Warda Stevens Stout Collection of 18th
Century German Porcelain**

The Dixon Gallery & Gardens, Memphis TN

Sully Portrait Collection

United States Military Academy, West Point Museum, West Point NY

Swiss Art & Literature

Swiss Institute, New York NY

Tabor Collection of Oriental Art

Philbrook Museum of Art, Tulsa OK

Robert H Tannahill Collection of Impressionist & Post Impressionist Paintings

Detroit Institute of Arts, Detroit MI

Alfredo S G Taylor Architect;

Norfolk Historical Society Inc, Museum, Norfolk CT

Taylor Collection of Southwestern Art

Colorado Springs Fine Arts Center, Colorado Springs CO

Technological Implements

Ellis County Museum Inc, Waxahachie TX

Television

American Museum of the Moving Image, Astoria NY

Textile Collection

The Art Institute of Chicago, Chicago IL

Justin K Thannhauser Collection of Impressionist & Post-Impressionist Paintings

Solomon R Guggenheim Museum, New York NY

Thatcher Family Collection

Rosemount Victorian House Museum, Pueblo CO

Thieme Collection of Paintings

Fort Wayne Museum of Art, Inc, Fort Wayne IN

Thorne Miniature Collection

The Art Institute of Chicago, Chicago IL

Tibetan Art Collection

Jacques Marchais Center of Tibetan Art, Tibetan Museum, Staten Island NY

Louis Comfort Tiffany Collection

Charles Morse Museum of American Art, Winter Park FL

Tiffany Glass Collection

Johns Hopkins University, Evergreen House, Baltimore MD
Mark Twain Memorial, Hartford CT

Tobin Theatre Arts Collection Related to Opera, Ballet & Musical Stage

Marion Koogler McNay Art Museum, San Antonio TX

Tools

Essex Historical Society, Essex Shipbuilding Museum, Essex MA

James Townes Medal Collection

Delta State University, Fielding L Wright Art Center, Cleveland MS

Toys

Rowland Evans Robinson Memorial Association, Rokeby Museum, Ferrisburgh VT

Trees Collection

University of Illinois, Krannert Art Museum, Champaign IL

Trovwer Silver Collection

University of Utah, Utah Museum of Fine Arts, Salt Lake City UT

Tucker Porcelain Collection

Philadelphia Museum of Art, Philadelphia PA

Tufnell Watercolor Collection

Calvert Marine Museum, Solomons MD

J M W Turner Watercolor Collection

Indianapolis Museum of Art, Indianapolis IN

Lyle Tuttle Collection

Tattoo Art Museum, San Francisco CA

George P Tweed Memorial Collection of American & European Paintings

University of Minnesota, Duluth, Tweed Museum of Art, Duluth MN

Tyson Collection

Philadelphia Museum of Art, Philadelphia PA

Ukrainian Paintings; Archives

The Ukrainian Museum, New York NY

Doris Ulmann Photography Collection

Berea College, Doris Ulmann Galleries, Berea KY

The Alfred H & Eva Underhill Holbrook Collection of American Art

University of Georgia, Georgia Museum of Art, Athens GA

Nora S Unwin Collection of Wood Engravings, Drawings, Watercolors

Sharon Arts Center, Sharon NH

Edward Virginius Valentine Sculpture Collection

Valentine Museum, Richmond VA

Vanderpoel Collection

Norwich Free Academy, Slater Memorial Museum & Converse Art Gallery, Norwich CT

Van Ess Collection of Renaissance and Baroque Art

Hartwick College, Foreman Gallery, Oneonta NY

Edward Burr Van Vleck Collection of Japanese Prints

University of Wisconsin-Madison, Elvehjem Museum of Art, Madison WI

Matthew Vassar Collection

Vassar College, Vassar Art Gallery, Poughkeepsie NY

James Ven Der Zee Photography Collection

The Studio Museum in Harlem, New York NY

David T Vernon Indian Arts Collection

Grand Teton National Park Service, Colter Bay Indian Arts Museum, Moose WY

Victor Talking Machine Company Phonographs & Records

Historical and Cultural Affairs, Delaware State Museums, Dover DE

Voertman Collection

University of North Texas, University Art Gallery, Denton TX

Von Schleinitz Collection

Milwaukee Art Museum, Milwaukee WI

Wagner Collection of African Sculpture

Scripps College, Clark Humanities Museum, Claremont CA

Walker Collection of French Impressionists

Corcoran Gallery of Art, Washington DC

C G Wallace Collection

Heard Museum, Phoenix AZ

Cloud Wampler Collection of Oriental Art

Everson Museum of Art, Syracuse NY

Felix M Warburg Collection of Medieval Sculpture

Vassar College, Vassar Art Gallery, Poughkeepsie NY

Austen D Warburton Native American Art & Artifacts Collection

Triton Museum of Art, Santa Clara CA

Andy Warhol Collection

University of Maryland, College Park, Art Gallery, College Park MD

Booker T Washington Collection

Tuskegee Institute National Historic Site, George Washington Carver & The Oaks, Tuskegee Institute AL

George Washington Memorabilia

Mount Vernon Ladies' Association of the Union, Mount Vernon VA

Wassenberg Collection

Wassenberg Art Center, Van Wert OH

Watkins Collection of American and European Paintings

American University, Watkins Collectiony, Washington DC

Homer Watson Collection

Kitchener-Waterloo Art Gallery, Kitchener ON

William Watson Collection of Ceramics

Lemoyne Art Foundation, Inc, Tallahassee FL

Ernest C & Jane Werner Watson Collection of Indian Miniatures

University of Wisconsin-Madison, Elvehjem Museum of Art, Madison WI

Samuel Bell, Frederick J & Coulten Waugh Collection

Edwin A Ulrich Museum, Hyde Park NY

Ulrich Collection of Frederick J Waugh Paintings

Wichita State University, Edwin A Ulrich Museum of Art, Wichita KS

Wax Collection

Blair Museum of Lithophanes and Carved Waxes, Toledo OH

John Wayne Collection

National Cowboy Hall of Fame and Western Heritage Center, Oklahoma City OK

Weaponry

Ellis County Museum Inc, Waxahachie TX

Weatherhead Collection of Contemporary Graphics

Fort Wayne Museum of Art, Inc, Fort Wayne IN

Weaving

Palos Verdes Art Center, Rancho Palos Verdes CA

Wedgwood Collection

R W Norton Art Gallery, Shreveport LA

Teresa Jackson Weill Collection

Brandeis University, Rose Art Museum, Waltham MA

J Alden Weir Collection

Brigham Young University, B F Larsen Gallery, Provo UT

Wellington Collection of Wood Engravings

Art Patrons League of Mobile, Mobile AL

Ward Wells Anchorage Photo Collection

Anchorage Museum of History and Art, Archives, Anchorage AK

Benjamin West Collection

Bob Jones University, Museum & Art Gallery, Greenville SC

Western Art

Ohio State University, Slide & Photograph Library, Columbus OH

Western & Contemporary Western

Warren Hall Coutts III Memorial Museum of Art, El Dorado KS

Maurice Wetheim Collection

Harvard University, William Hayes Fogg Art Museum, Cambridge MA

Candace Wheeler Collection

Mark Twain Memorial, Hartford CT

James McNeill Whistler Collection

Freer Gallery of Art, Washington DC

Peter Whitebird Collection of WPA Project Paintings

Viterbo College Art Gallery, La Crosse WI

White Collection

Baltimore Museum of Art, Baltimore MD
Philadelphia Museum of Art, Philadelphia PA
Sumter Gallery of Art, Sumter SC

Whitney Silver Collection

Montclair Art Museum, Montclair NJ

Whittington Memorial Collection

Delta State University, Fielding L Wright Art Center, Cleveland MS

Wiant Collection of Chinese Art

Ohio State University, Wexner Center for the Arts, Columbus OH

Bartlett Wicks Collection

University of Utah, Utah Museum of Fine Arts, Salt Lake City UT

Widener Collection

National Gallery of Art, Washington DC

Albert H Wiggin Collection

Boston Public Library, Albert H Wiggin Gallery & Print Department, Boston MA

Wilder Collection of Art Glass & Pottery

Topeka Public Library, Gallery of Fine Arts, Topeka KS

Wildlife Art (North American & European)

Genesee Country Museum, John L Wehle Gallery of Sporting Art, Mumford NY

Willard Clocks Collection

Willard House and Clock Museum, Inc, Grafton MA

Archibald M Willard Paintings Collection

Southern Lorain County Historical Society, Spirit of '76 Museum, Wellington OH

Will Collection of Paintings & Drawings

Jersey City Museum, Jersey City NJ

William Rufus King Collection

Alabama Department of Archives and History Museum, Museum Galleries, Montgomery AL

Adolph D and Wilkins C Williams Collection

Virginia Museum of Fine Arts, Richmond VA

Lois Wilson Collection

Fayette Art Museum, Fayette AL
Huntington College, Robert E Wilson Art Gallery, Huntington IN
Lehigh University Art Galleries, Bethlehem PA

Wilstach Collection of Old Masters

Philadelphia Museum of Art, Philadelphia PA

Wingert Collection of African & Oceanic Art

Montclair State College, Art Gallery, Upper Montclair NJ

Ella Witter Collection

Witter Gallery, Storm Lake IA

Women Artists

La Centrale Powerhouse Gallery, Montreal PQ

Grant Wood Collection

Davenport Museum of Art, Davenport IA
Huronia Museum, Midland ON

William Woodward Collection

Baltimore Museum of Art, Baltimore MD

Theodore Wores Collection

Triton Museum of Art, Santa Clara CA

World War I Covers

Liberty Memorial Museum & Archives, Kansas City
   MO

Frank Lloyd Wright Collection

Allentown Art Museum, Allentown PA
George Washington University, The Dimock
   Gallery, Washington DC

Wutzburger Collection

Baltimore Museum of Art, Baltimore MD

Wyeth Family Collection

Brandywine River Museum, Chadds Ford PA

Mahonri Young Collection of Manuscripts

Brigham Young University, B F Larsen Gallery,
   Provo UT

Karl Zerbe Collection of Serigraphs

Lemoyne Art Foundation, Inc, Tallahassee FL

Zogbaum Drawings

Headquarters Fort Monroe, Dept of Army,
   Casemate Museum, Fort Monroe VA

Aaboe-Milligan, Betty Ann, *Cur,* Dartmouth Heritage Museum, Dartmouth NS

Aakhus, Michael, *Asst Prof,* University of Southern Indiana, Art Dept, Evansville IN (S)

Aaron, Herve, *VPres,* National Antique & Art Dealers Association of America, New York NY

Aarons, Phillip E, *Treas,* Artists Space, New York NY

Aaronson, Diana, *Exec Dir,* Gershon & Rebecca Fenster Museum of Jewish Art, Tulsa OK

Abatelli, Carol, *Reference-Visual Arts Specialist,* State University of New York at Purchase, Library, Purchase NY

Abbe, Pat, *Development Dir,* Owatonna Arts Center, Community Arts Center, Owatonna MN

Abbott, Fred, *Chmn Board,* Glenbow Museum, Calgary AB

Abbott, Sharon, *Cur of Education,* Anchorage Museum of History and Art, Anchorage AK

Abby, Ronald, *Prog Coordr,* Housatonic Community College, Art Dept, Bridgeport CT (S)

Abeepe, Louise Vander, *VPres,* Musee d'Art de Saint-Laurent, Saint-Laurent PQ

Abeles, Sigmund, *Prof,* University of New Hampshire, Dept of the Arts, Durham NH (S)

Abell, Mary, *Instr,* Dowling College, Dept of Visual Arts, Oakdale NY (S)

Abelman, Arthur, *Treas,* Sculpture Center Inc, New York NY

Abel-Vidor, Suzanne, *Dir,* City of Ukiah, Grace Hudson Museum & The Sun House, Ukiah CA

Aber, Robert W, *Dir,* Roberson Museum & Science Center, Binghamton NY

Abid, Ann B, *Librn,* Cleveland Museum of Art, Ingalls Library, Cleveland OH

Abide, Joe, *Instr,* Delta State University, Dept of Art, Cleveland MS (S)

Abiko, Bonnie, *Asst Prof,* Oakland University, Dept of Art and Art History, Rochester MI (S)

Able, Edward H, *Dir,* American Association of Museums, International Council of Museums Committee, Washington DC

Abler, Timothy, *Asst Prof,* Cardinal Stritch College, Art Dept, Milwaukee WI (S)

Ablow, Joseph, *Prof,* Boston University, School of Visual Arts, Boston MA (S)

Abraham, Richard, *Instr,* Central Community College - Platte Campus, Business & Arts Cluster, Columbus NE (S)

Abrahams, Joe, *Adminr Parks, Recreation & Cultural Serv,* City of Tampa, Art in Public Places, Tampa FL

Abrahamson, Roy E, *Academic Area Head,* Southern Illinois University, School of Art & Design, Carbondale IL (S)

Abrams, Jan, *VPres,* Sculpture Center Inc, New York NY

Abrams, Jean, *Coordr,* Mississippi Delta Community College, Dept of Fine Arts, Moorhead MS (S)

Abrams, Joseph R, *Chmn,* Mississippi Delta Community College, Dept of Fine Arts, Moorhead MS (S)

Abrans, Barbara, *Educ Dir,* Oregon Historical Society, Portland OR

Abt, Jeffrey, *Chmn,* Wayne State University, Dept of Art and Art History, Detroit MI (S)

Ach, Roger, *Chmn,* Contemporary Arts Center, Cincinnati OH

Acker, Brenda, *Registrar,* Oshkosh Public Museum, Oshkosh WI

Acker, Karen, *Chmn,* Goucher College, Art Dept, Towson MD (S)

Ackerman, Doris, *Dir Development & Public Relations,* New Jersey Center for Visual Arts, Summit NJ

Ackerman, Rudy, *Chmn Art Dept,* Moravian College, Payne Gallery, Bethlehem PA

Ackerman, Rudy S, *Chmn Dept,* Moravian College, Dept of Art, Bethlehem PA (S)

Ackerson, Anne W, *Dir,* Rensselaer County Historical Society, Hart-Cluett Mansion, 1827, Troy NY

Ackley, Clifford, *Cur Prints & Drawings,* Museum of Fine Arts, Boston MA

Acomb, Merlin, *Exhibition Designer & Preparator,* University of Vermont, Robert Hull Fleming Museum, Burlington VT

Acorn, Eleanor, *Head Librn,* John M Cuelenaere Library, Grace Campbell Gallery, Prince Albert SK

Acorn, John, *Head Dept,* Clemson University, College of Architecture, Clemson SC (S)

Acosta, Jeffrey, *Cur,* MacArthur Memorial, Norfolk VA

Acosta-Colon, Marie, *Exec Dir,* Mexican Museum, San Francisco CA

Acree, Robert, *Adjunct Instr,* Maryville University of Saint Louis, Art Division, Saint Louis MO (S)

Acs, Alajos, *Midwest Representative,* American Society of Artists, Inc, Chicago IL

Acton, David L, *Cur Prints & Drawings,* Worcester Art Museum, Worcester MA

Adair, John M, *Coordr,* Cumberland County College, Humanities Div, Vineland NJ (S)

Adamakos, Peter, *Pres,* International Museum of Cartoon Art, Montreal PQ

Adamchick, Kathryn, *Dir Education,* Hudson River Museum, Yonkers NY

Adames, David, *Head Historical Interpreter,* Dundurn Castle, Hamilton ON

Adames, Jean, *Adjunct Prof,* Wilkes University, Dept of Art, Wilkes-Barre PA (S)

Adams, Anne, *Registrar,* Kimbell Art Museum, Fort Worth TX

Adams, Barbara, *Office Mgr,* Art Center of Battle Creek, Michigan Art & Artist Archives, Battle Creek MI

Adams, Bebo, *Business Mgr,* Canton Art Institute, Canton OH (S)

Adams, Betty B, *Chmn Dept,* Saint Mary's College, Art Dept, Raleigh NC (S)

Adams, Bryding, *Cur Decorative Arts,* Birmingham Museum of Art, Birmingham AL

Adams, Celeste, *Assoc Dir Spec Projects,* Museum of Fine Arts, Houston, Houston TX

Adams, Daniel, *Asst Prof,* Harding University, Dept of Art, Searcy AR (S)

Adams, Eloise, *Dir,* Stephen F Austin State University, SFA Gallery, Nacogdoches TX

Adams, Henry, *Samuel Sosland Cur American Art,* Nelson-Atkins Museum of Art, Kansas City MO

Adams, Idie, *Ceramic Coordr,* Butte College, Dept of Fine Arts, Oroville CA (S)

Adams, Jack, *Pres,* Association of Hawaii Artists, Honolulu HI

Adams, Jacqueline, *Picture Specialist,* San Diego Public Library, Art & Music Section, San Diego CA

Adams, James R C, *Chmn Dept,* Manchester College, Art Dept, North Manchester IN (S)

Adams, Jean C, *Asst Dir,* Wilkes University, Sordoni Art Gallery, Wilkes-Barre PA

Adams, Jeanne, *Instr,* Main Line Center for the Arts, Haverford PA (S)

Adams, Jennifer, *Membership & Gallery Coordr,* Contemporary Arts Center, Cincinnati OH

Adams, J Michael, *Dean,* Drexel University, Nesbitt College of Design Arts, Philadelphia PA (S)

Adams, Joy, *Asst Prof,* Ithaca College, Fine Art Dept, Ithaca NY (S)

Adams, Kenneth D, *Business Mgr,* Canton Art Institute, Canton OH

Adams, Mac, *Chmn,* State University of New York College at Old Westbury, Visual Arts Department, Old Westbury NY (S)

Adams, Marie-Louise, *Coordr,* St Tammany Art Association, Covington LA

Adams, Marlin C, *Chmn Div,* Frank Phillips College, Art Dept, Borger TX (S)

Adams, Meg, *Educ,* Blanden Memorial Art Museum, Fort Dodge IA

Adams, Nancy, *Co-Dir,* Mobius Inc, Boston MA

Adams, Nicholas, *Prof,* Vassar College, Art Dept, Poughkeepsie NY (S)

Adams, Robert, *Prof,* Alabama A & M University, Art and Art Education, Normal AL (S)

Adams, Robert, *Secy,* Smithsonian Institution, Washington DC

Adams, Roger J, *Assoc Prof,* Nazareth College of Rochester, Art Dept, Rochester NY (S)

Adams, Sally, *Business Mgr,* Western Reserve Historical Society, Cleveland OH

Adams, Sharon, *Specialist Ceramic Educ,* Duke University Union, Durham NC

Adams, Stan, *Instr,* Illinois Central College, Dept of Fine Arts, East Peoria IL (S)

Adams, Virginia M, *Librn,* Old Dartmouth Historical Society, Whaling Museum Library, New Bedford MA

Adamson, Jim, *Instr,* Sierra College, Art Dept, Rocklin CA (S)

Adamson, Scott, *Adminr,* Genesee Country Museum, John L Wehle Gallery of Sporting Art, Mumford NY

Adamy, George E, *Dir,* Adamy's Concrete and Cast Paper Workshops, Larchmont NY (S)

Aday, Jerry L, *Exec Dir,* Mid-America All-Indian Center, Wichita KS

Addams, Cynthia, *Exec Dir,* Salem Art Association, Salem OR

Addams, Cynthia, *Exec Dir,* Salem Art Association, Bush Barn Art Center, Salem OR

Addington, Aldon, *Assoc Prof,* Southern Illinois University, School of Art & Design, Carbondale IL (S)

Addison, Betty, *Librn,* Morris Museum, Library, Morristown NJ

Addison, B Kent, *Prof,* Maryville University of Saint Louis, Art Division, Saint Louis MO (S)

Addison, Deborah, *Dir Development,* Ohio State University, Wexner Center for the Arts, Columbus OH

Addison, Elizabeth, *Dir External Affairs,* Art Gallery of Ontario, Toronto ON

Addison, E W, *Dir,* Brewton-Parker College, Visual Arts, Mount Vernon GA (S)

Addison, Les, *Instr,* Maryville University of Saint Louis, Art Division, Saint Louis MO (S)

Ade, Shirley, *Museum Dir,* McPherson Museum, McPherson KS

Adelman, Charles, *Assoc Prof,* University of Northern Iowa, Dept of Art, Cedar Falls IA (S)

Adelman, Everett, *Instr,* Munson-Williams-Proctor Institute, School of Art, Utica NY (S)

Adelman, Everett Mayo, *Instr,* North Carolina Wesleyan College, Dept of Visual & Performing Arts, Rocky Mount NC (S)

Adelman, Jean S, *Librn,* University of Pennsylvania, Library, Philadelphia PA

Adelmann, Arthur R, *Prof,* Weber State University, Dept of Visual Arts, Ogden UT (S)

Adkins, Margie, *Prof,* Texas Christian University, Art & Art History Dept, Fort Worth TX (S)

Adney, Carol, *Dir,* City of San Rafael, Falkirk Cultural Center, San Rafael CA

Adrian, Barbara, *Treas,* Pen and Brush, Inc, New York NY

Aframe, Debby, *Slide Librn,* Worcester Art Museum, Library, Worcester MA

Agard, James, *Assoc Prof,* Gettysburg College, Dept of Art, Gettysburg PA (S)

Agee, Nelle, *Asst Prof,* Oklahoma Baptist University, Art Dept, Shawnee OK (S)

Agee, Sheila, *Executive Dir,* Civic Fine Arts Center, Sioux Falls SD

Agee, Sheila, *Exec Dir,* Civic Fine Arts Center, Library, Sioux Falls SD

Ageloff, Scott, *Asst Prof,* Marymount College, Art Dept, Tarrytown NY (S)

Aglio, Henry, *Asst Prof,* West Virginia University at Parkersburg, Art Dept, Parkersburg WV (S)

Agnew, Ellen Schall, *Dir,* Randolph-Macon Woman's College, Maier Museum of Art, Lynchburg VA

Agnew, L Jack, *Prof,* Sullivan County Community College, Division of Commercial Art and Photography, Loch Sheldrake NY (S)

Agricoa, Jack, *Chmn,* Millsaps College, Dept of Art, Jackson MS (S)

Aguado, William, *Council Dir,* Bronx Council on the Arts, Longwood Arts Gallery, Bronx NY

Aguilo, Sister, *Instr,* University of North Carolina at Charlotte, Dept of Visual Arts, Charlotte NC (S)

Ahearn, Maureen, *Dir,* Keene State College, Thorne-Sagendorph Art Gallery, Keene NH

Ahlstrom, Romaine, *Dept Mgr,* Los Angeles Public Library, Arts & Recreation Dept, Los Angeles CA

Ahmad, Sufi, *Assoc Prof,* Saint Francis College, Art Dept, Fort Wayne IN (S)

Aho, Charles, *Adjunct Instr,* Le Moyne College, Fine Arts Dept, Syracuse NY (S)

Ahr, John, *Asst Dir,* Severin Wunderman Museum, Irvine CA

Ahrens, Kent, *Dir,* The Rockwell Museum, Corning NY

Ahrens, Kent, *Dir,* The Rockwell Museum, Library, Corning NY

Ahysen, Harry J, *Prof,* Sam Houston State University, Art Dept, Huntsville TX (S)

Aichele, K Porter, *Head,* University of North Carolina at Greensboro, Art Dept, Greensboro NC (S)

Aiello, Eugene, *Treas,* Arthur Roy Mitchell Memorial Inc, Museum of Western Art, Trinidad CO

Aiken, Edward A, *Dir,* Syracuse University, Joe and Emily Lowe Art Gallery, Syracuse NY

Aiken, Jane, *Prof,* Virginia Polytechnic Institute & State University, Dept of Art & Art History, Blacksburg VA (S)

Aiken, Suzanne, *Instr,* University of Evansville, Art Dept, Evansville IN (S)

Aikin, Roger, *Instr,* Creighton University, Fine and Performing Arts Dept, Omaha NE (S)

Aikman, John, *Instr,* Linn Benton Community College, Fine & Applied Art Dept, Albany OR (S)

Ainslie, Patricia, *Acting Chief Cur,* Glenbow Museum, Calgary AB

Ainslie, Patricia, *Cur Art,* Glenbow Museum, Calgary AB

Aistars, John, *Dir Art Prog,* Cazenovia College, Chapman Art Center Gallery, Cazenovia NY

Aistars, John, *Chmn,* Cazenovia College, Center for Art & Design Studies, Cazenovia NY (S)

Aitken, T, *Instr,* Community College of Rhode Island, Dept of Art, Warwick RI (S)

Aker, Susie, *Registrar,* Nevada Museum Of Art, Reno NV

Akgulian, Mark, *Exhibits Cur,* Spertus Museum, Chicago IL

Akin, Lew S, *Chmn,* Abraham Baldwin Agricultural College, Art & Humanities Dept, Tifton GA (S)

Akiyama, Patricia, *Pres,* Wind Luke Asian Museum Memorial Foundation, Inc, Seattle WA

Akuna-Hanson, Chris, *Gallery Dir,* Rio Hondo College Art Gallery, Whittier CA

Albacete, Manuel J, *Gallery Dir,* Canton Art Institute, Canton OH

Albacete, Manuel J, *Exec Dir,* Canton Art Institute, Art Library, Canton OH

Albacete, Manuel J, *Dir,* Canton Art Institute, Canton OH (S)

Albert, Karen, *Exhibit Designer & Preparation,* Hofstra University, Hofstra Museum, Hempstead NY

Albo, James, *Pres & Chief Exec Officer,* Security Pacific Bank Arizona, Phoenix AZ

Albrecht, Carl, *Head Natural History,* Ohio Historical Society, Columbus OH

Albrecht, Sterling, *Dir Libraries,* Brigham Young University, Harold B Lee Library, Provo UT

Albritton, Leigh, *Registrar,* Milwaukee Art Museum, Milwaukee WI

Alderette, Bob, *Assoc Prof,* University of Southern California, School of Fine Arts, Los Angeles CA (S)

Aldern, Robert, *Asst Prof,* Augustana College, Art Dept, Sioux Falls SD (S)

Alders, Patricia, *Asst,* De Anza College, Euphrat Gallery, Cupertino CA

Alderson, Ingrid, *Exec Dir,* Community Arts Council of Vancouver, Vancouver BC

Alderson, Marge, *Treas,* Art League, Alexandria VA

Aldrich, Jonathan, *Instr,* Portland School of Art, Portland ME (S)

Aldridge, Alexander Q, *VPres Development,* Philadelphia Museum of Art, Philadelphia PA

Aleci, Linda, *Asst Prof,* Franklin and Marshall College, Art Dept, Lancaster PA (S)

Alexander, Andrew, *Dir,* Mason City Public Library, Mason City IA

Alexander, Barbara, *Asst Prof,* University of Alaska, Dept of Art, Fairbanks AK (S)

Alexander, Brian, *Dir,* Shelburne Museum, Shelburne VT

Alexander, Brian, *Dir,* Shelburne Museum, Library, Shelburne VT

Alexander, Brooke, *Cur,* Fried, Frank, Harris, Shriver & Jacobson, Art Collection, New York NY

Alexander, Forsyth, *Pub Dir,* Old Salem Inc, Museum of Early Southern Decorative Arts, Winston-Salem NC

Alexander, Irene, *Dir,* Stephens College, Lewis James & Nellie Stratton Davis Art Gallery, Columbia MO

Alexander, James, *Assoc Prof,* University of Alabama in Birmingham, Dept of Art, Birmingham AL (S)

Alexander, Kathie, *Public Relations Representative,* First Tennessee National Corp, First Tennessee Heritage Collection, Memphis TN

Alexander, Lo, *Pres,* Arts on the Park, Lakeland FL

Alexander, Mary Veitch, *Owner,* Gadsden Museum, Mesilla NM

Alexander, Richard, *Admin Asst,* Public Corporation for the Arts, Visual & Performing Arts Registry, Long Beach CA

Alexander, Ronald J, *Head Dept,* Northeast Louisiana University, Dept of Art, Monroe LA (S)

Alexander, Ron J, *Head,* Northeast Louisiana University, Bry Gallery, Monroe LA

Alexander, Vikky, *Asst Prof,* University of Victoria, Dept of Visual Arts, Victoria BC (S)

Alexick, David, *Faculty,* Christopher Newport College, Arts & Communications, Newport News VA (S)

Alfano, Domenic, *Asst Prof,* New York Institute of Technology, Fine Arts Dept, Old Westbury NY (S)

Alford, Constance, *Assoc Prof,* Alcorn State University, Dept of Fine Arts, Lorman MS (S)

Alford, John, *Instr,* Mississippi University for Women, Division of Fine & Performing Arts, Columbus MS (S)

Algermissen, Elizabeth, *Asst Dir Exhib,* Los Angeles County Museum of Art, Los Angeles CA

Ali, Ronald, *Instr,* Indiana University of Pennsylvania, Dept of Art and Art Education, Indiana PA (S)

Alkema, Chester, *Prof,* Grand Valley State University, Art & Design Dept, Allendale MI (S)

Alkens, Martha, *Supt,* Independence National Historical Park, Philadelphia PA

Allaben, Craig, *Gallery Mgr,* University of Massachusetts, Amherst, University Gallery, Amherst MA

Allan, Helen W, *Dir & Cur,* Clinton County Historical Association, Clinton County Historical Museum, Plattsburgh NY

Allan, Ruth, *Instr,* Wenatchee Valley College, Art Dept, Wenatchee WA (S)

Allard, L, *Chief Librn,* Musee du Quebec, Bibliotheque des Arts, Quebec PQ

Allen, Bruce, *Chmn Dept & Assoc Prof,* Centenary College of Louisiana, Dept of Art, Shreveport LA (S)

Allen, Carol K, *Coordr Exhib,* Museum of Fine Arts, Saint Petersburg, Florida, Inc, Saint Petersburg FL

Allen, Catherine, *Instr,* Main Line Center for the Arts, Haverford PA (S)

Allen, Don, *Cur,* Favell Museum of Western Art & Indian Artifacts, Klamath Falls OR

Allen, Dottie, *Art Prog Coordr,* Hill College, Fine Arts Dept, Hillsboro TX (S)

Allen, Earlene, *Prof,* Marshall University, Dept of Art, Huntington WV (S)

Allen, Eleanor, *Prof,* Florida Community College at Jacksonville, South Campus, Art Dept, Jacksonville FL (S)

Allen, Emille, *Pres Bd of Mgrs,* University of Rochester, Memorial Art Gallery, Rochester NY

Allen, Estherly, *Lectr,* Cardinal Stritch College, Art Dept, Milwaukee WI (S)

Allen, Francie, *Bookstore Mgr,* Fort Worth Art Association, Modern Art Museum of Fort Worth, Fort Worth TX

Allen, Frederick E, *Dean Instruction,* Butte College, Dept of Fine Arts, Oroville CA (S)

Allen, F Robert, *Instructor,* Saint Louis Community College at Meramec, Art Dept, Saint Louis MO (S)

Allen, Gwen, *Dir,* Plainsman Museum, Aurora NE

Allen, Jan, *Assoc Cur,* Queen's University, Agnes Etherington Art Centre, Kingston ON

Allen, Jane E, *Cur,* Philadelphia Maritime Museum, Philadelphia PA

Allen, Jere H, *Prof,* University of Mississippi, Dept of Art, University MS (S)

Allen, Jim, *Instr,* Springfield College in Illinois, Dept of Art, Springfield IL (S)

Allen, Judith, *Dir,* Minot Art Association, Minot Art Gallery, Minot ND

Allen, Jules, *Asst Prof,* Queensborough Community College, Dept of Art and Photography, Bayside NY (S)

Allen, Kay, *Asst to Dir,* University of Southern California, Fisher Gallery, Los Angeles CA

Allen, Lynne, *Asst Prof,* Rutgers, the State University of New Jersey, Mason Gross School of the Arts, New Brunswick NJ (S)

Allen, Margaret, *Fine Arts Reference Librn,* Grace A Dow Memorial Library, Fine Arts Dept, Midland MI

Allen, Mary L, *Asst Dir,* Gunston Hall Plantation, Lorton VA

Allen, Nancy S, *Chief Librn,* Museum of Fine Arts, William Morris Hunt Memorial Library, Boston MA

Allen, Rachel, *Actg Chief Research & Scholars Center,* National Museum of American Art, Washington DC

Allen, Ray, *Dean,* Portland School of Art, Portland ME (S)

Allen, Roger, *Chmn,* West Virginia University at Parkersburg, Art Dept, Parkersburg WV (S)

Allen, Skip, *Instr,* Millsaps College, Dept of Art, Jackson MS (S)

Allen, Stan, *Chmn Div Urban Design,* Columbia University, Graduate School of Architecture, Planning & Preservation, New York NY (S)

Allen, Velma, *Dir,* Drew County Historical Society, Museum, Monticello AR

Allen, Virginia, *Chmn Critical Studies,* Massachusetts College of Art, Boston MA (S)

Allen, Walter, *Instr,* James H Faulkner Community College, Bay Minette AL (S)

Allen, William, *Prof,* Arkansas State University, Dept of Art, Jonesboro AR (S)

Alley, Jon, *Instr,* Bucks County Community College, Fine Arts Dept, Newtown PA (S)

Alley, Perry, *Treas,* Hudson Valley Art Association, Flushing NY

Allina, Babette, *Asst Cur,* Equitable Life Assurance Society, New York NY

Alling, Clarence, *Dir,* Waterloo Museum of Art, Waterloo IA

Allison, Brooke, *Instr,* Dunedin Fine Arts and Cultural Center, Dunedin FL (S)

Allison, Clement, *Div Head,* Tusculum College, Fine Arts Dept, Greeneville TN (S)

Allison, Glenn, *Dir,* The Art Gallery of Southwestern Manitoba, Brandon MB

Allman, Anne, *Assoc Prof,* College of the Ozarks, Dept of Art, Point Lookout MO (S)

Allman, Marion, *Pres,* ACA College of Design, Cincinnati OH (S)

Allo, Anthony, *Chmn Fine Arts,* Indian River Community College, Fine Arts Dept, Fort Pierce FL (S)

Allodi, M, *Cur-in-Charge,* Royal Ontario Museum, Canadian Decorative Arts Department, Toronto ON

Allred, Osral, *Chmn,* Snow College, Art Dept, Ephraim UT (S)

Allsopp, Robert, *Adjunct Prof,* University of Toronto, Programme in Landscape Architecture, Toronto ON (S)

Allumbaugh, James, *Chmn Art Ed,* East Texas State University, Dept of Art, East Texas Station, Commerce TX (S)

Almanza, Miguel, *Asst Prof,* Weber State University, Dept of Visual Arts, Ogden UT (S)

Almquist, Robert, *Discipline Coordr,* Lewis-Clark State College, Art Dept, Lewiston ID (S)

Alonso-Mendoza, Emeilo, *Development,* Center for the Fine Arts, Miami FL

Alpay, Beverly, *Pres,* Palos Verdes Art Center, Rancho Palos Verdes CA

Alperson, Phillip, *Journal Ed,* American Society for Aesthetics, Edmonton AB

Alston, Littleton, *Artist-in-Res,* Creighton University, Fine and Performing Arts Dept, Omaha NE (S)

Altemus, Anne R, *Lectr,* Johns Hopkins University, School of Medicine, Dept of Art as Applied to Medicine, Baltimore MD (S)

Alter-Muri, Simone, *Asst Prof,* Springfield College, Dept of Visual and Performing Arts, Springfield MA (S)

Altman, Patricia B, *Cur of Textiles & Folk Art,* University of California, Los Angeles, Fowler Museum of Cultural History, Los Angeles CA

Altshuler, Bruce, *Dir,* Isamu Noguchi Foundation, Garden Museum, Long Island City NY

Altshuler, Linda, *Exec Dir,* The Barnum Museum, Bridgeport CT

Aluzzo, Adrienne, *Librn,* Archives of American Art, Midwest Regional Center, Washington DC

Alvarez, Jose B, *Instr,* Inter American University of Puerto Rico, Dept of Art, San German PR (S)

Alves, C Douglass, *Dir,* Calvert Marine Museum, Solomons MD

Alviti, John V, *Exec Dir,* Historical Society of Washington DC, Christian Heurich Mansion, Washington DC

Alward, Sharon, *Chmn Drawing,* University of Manitoba, School of Art, Winnipeg MB (S)

Amack, Rex, *Dir,* Game and Parks Commission, Arbor Lodge State Historical Park, Nebraska City NE

Amato, Cheryl, *Asst Dir,* Visual Arts Center of Northwest Florida, Panama City FL

Amatore, Edward, *Registrar,* State Art Museum of Florida, John & Mable Ringling Museum of Art, Sarasota FL

Amazeen, Lauren, *Exec Dir,* The Kitchen Center, New York NY

Ambroge, Patti, *Assoc Prof,* Rochester Institute of Technology, School of Photographic Arts & Sciences, Rochester NY (S)

Ambrose, Gail, *Recording Secy,* South County Art Association, Kingston RI

Ambrose, Gordon, *Caretaker & Installation Technician,* Moose Jaw Art Museum and National Exhibition Centre, Art & History Museum, Moose Jaw SK

Ambrose, Richard, *Prog Dir,* Fresno Metropolitan Museum, Fresno CA

Ambrosino, Thomas, *Prof,* Sullivan County Community College, Division of Commercial Art and Photography, Loch Sheldrake NY (S)

Ambrosio, Katherine, *Shop Mgr,* Carmel Mission and Gift Shop, Carmel CA

Ambrson, Rodd, *Instr,* Marylhurst College, Art Dept, Marylhurst OR (S)

Amerson, L Price, *Dir,* University of California, Richard L Nelson Gallery & Fine Arts Collection, Davis CA

Ames, Edward A, *Pres,* Art Commission of the City of New York, New York NY

Ames, Jennifer D, *Pres,* The Art Institute of Chicago, Auxiliary Board, Chicago IL

Ames, Madge, *Treas,* Kennebec Valley Art Association, Harlow Gallery, Hallowell ME

Ames, M M, *Dir,* University of British Columbia, Museum of Anthropology, Vancouver BC

Ames, Robert, *Pres,* Timken Museum of Art, San Diego CA

Ames, Samuel B, *Chmn,* Rhode Island College, Art Dept, Providence RI (S)

Ames-Bell, Linda, *Prof,* University of Toledo, Dept of Art, Toledo OH (S)

Ames Petersen, Nancy, *Dir,* Timken Museum of Art, San Diego CA

Amhert, Pat, *Dir,* Oscar Howe Art Center, Mitchell SD

Ammons, Betty, *Asst Librn,* United Methodist Historical Society, Library, Baltimore MD

Amols, Abigail, *Dir,* Cooperstown Art Association, Cooperstown NY

Amory, Claudia, *Dir,* School 33 Art Center, Baltimore MD

Amory, Dita, *Cur Drawings, Prints & Paintings,* National Academy of Design, New York NY

Amos, Emma, *Prof,* Rutgers, the State University of New Jersey, Mason Gross School of the Arts, New Brunswick NJ (S)

Amos, Maria, *Admin Asst,* Oklahoma City University, Hulsey Gallery-Norick Art Center, Oklahoma City OK

Amrhein, John, *Dean Library Serv,* California State University Stanislaus, Vasche Library, Turlock CA

Amsler, Cory, *Cur Coll,* Bucks County Historical Society, Mercer Museum, Doylestown PA

Amt, Richard, *Chief Photographic Services,* National Gallery of Art, Washington DC

Amundson, Dale, *Dir,* University of Manitoba, Gallery III, Winnipeg MB

Amyx, Chet, *Instr,* Cuesta College, Art Dept, San Luis Obispo CA (S)

Amyx, Guyla Call, *Instr,* Cuesta College, Art Dept, San Luis Obispo CA (S)

Anacker, John, *Gallery Dir,* Montana State University, Haynes Fine Arts Gallery, Bozeman MT

Ananian, Elissa, *Prof,* Salem State College, Art Dept, Salem MA (S)

Anastasi, John, *Pres,* New York Society of Architects, New York NY

Anawalt, Patricia, *Consulting Cur of Costumes & Textiles,* University of California, Los Angeles, Fowler Museum of Cultural History, Los Angeles CA

Anaya, Mikki, *Pres,* Guadalupe Historic Foundation, Santuario de Guadalupe, Santa Fe NM

Anchors, Barbara, *Librn,* Ships of The Sea Museum, Library, Savannah GA

Anderl, Robert, *Head Information Access Servs,* University of Alaska, Elmer E Rasmuson Library, Fairbanks AK

Andersen, Jay, *Adminr,* Grand Marais Art Colony, Grand Marais MN (S)

Andersen, Jeffrey W, *Dir,* Lyme Historical Society, Florence Griswold Museum, Old Lyme CT

Andersen, Paul, *Registrar,* Fine Arts Museum of Long Island, Hempstead NY

Andersen, Stephen, *Gallery Dir,* Valdosta State College, Art Gallery, Valdosta GA

Anderson, Ann, *Cur Educ,* Ward Foundation, Ward Museum of Wildfowl Art, Salisbury MD

Anderson, Arthur, *Assoc Prof,* York College of the City University of New York, Fine and Performing Arts, Jamaica NY (S)

Anderson, Barbara, *Membership Secy,* Bergstrom Mahler Museum, Neenah WI

Anderson, Barbara, *Membership Secy,* Bergstrom Mahler Museum, Library, Neenah WI

Anderson, Barbara, *Instr,* Concordia College, Art Dept, Moorhead MN (S)

Anderson, Betsy, *Lectr,* Saint Joseph's University, Dept of Fine & Performing Arts, Philadelphia PA (S)

Anderson, Carolyn, *Registrar,* Sheldon Swope Art Museum, Terre Haute IN

Anderson, Chris, *Instr,* Virginia Intermont College, Fine Arts Division, Bristol VA (S)

Anderson, C Paul, *Dean Div Fine & Performing Arts,* Dixie College, Art Dept, Saint George UT (S)

Anderson, Craig, *Assoc Dir,* NAB Gallery, Chicago IL

Anderson, Daniel J, *Head Ceramic,* Southern Illinois University at Edwardsville, Dept of Art & Design, Edwardsville IL (S)

Anderson, Dorothy, *Prog Dir,* Lizzadro Museum of Lapidary Art, Elmhurst IL

Anderson, Dorthea, *Cur,* Plymouth Antiquarian Society, Plymouth MA

Anderson, Douglas, *Asst Prof,* University of Hartford, Hartford Art School, West Hartford CT (S)

Anderson, Ellen, *Assoc Prof,* Saint Mary's College, Art Dept, Raleigh NC (S)

Anderson, Eric, *Instr,* University of North Carolina at Charlotte, Dept of Visual Arts, Charlotte NC (S)

Anderson, Gail, *Registrar,* University of Oklahoma, Fred Jones Jr Museum of Art, Norman OK

Anderson, Gail, *Head Arts & Recreation,* Calgary Public Library, Arts & Recreation Dept, Calgary AB

Anderson, Hugh B, *Dir,* Polk Community College, Art, Letters & Social Sciences, Winter Haven FL (S)

Anderson, James C, *Cur,* University of Louisville, Photographic Archives, Louisville KY

Anderson, Jeffrey C, *Assoc Prof,* George Washington University, Dept of Art, Washington DC (S)

Anderson, Jim, *Chmn,* Armstrong State College, Art & Music Dept, Savannah GA (S)

Anderson, Joan, *Music Librn & Cataloger,* California Institute of the Arts Library, Santa Clarita CA

Anderson, Joe, *Achaeologist,* Institute of the Great Plains, Museum of the Great Plains, Lawton OK

Anderson, John, *Business Mgr,* Brandywine River Museum, Chadds Ford PA

Anderson, John, *Assoc Prof,* Framingham State College, Art Dept, Framingham MA (S)

Anderson, Jon, *Prof,* Utah State University, Dept of Art, Logan UT (S)

Anderson, Joseph, *Pres,* Columbia Museum of Art, Columbia Art Association, Columbia SC

Anderson, Judi, *Head Technical Servs,* Ponca City Library, Art Dept, Ponca City OK

Anderson, Julia, *Art Cur,* Safeco Insurance Company, Art Collection, Seattle WA

Anderson, Ken, *Assoc Prof,* University of Missouri-Saint Louis, Art Dept, Saint Louis MO (S)

Anderson, Ken, *Asst Prof,* Peru State College, Art Dept, Peru NE (S)

Anderson, Kristin, *Chmn,* Augsburg College, Art Dept, Minneapolis MN (S)

Anderson, Larry, *Drawing Chmn,* Atlanta College of Art, Atlanta GA (S)

Anderson, Leon, *Assoc Prof,* Saint Louis Community College at Forest Park, Art Dept, Saint Louis MO (S)

Anderson, Lynn, *Cur Educ,* Norton Gallery and School of Art, West Palm Beach FL

Anderson, Mark, *Prof,* Presbyterian College, Fine Arts Dept, Clinton SC (S)

Anderson, Maxwell L, *Adjunct Prof,* Emory University, Art History Dept, Atlanta GA (S)

Anderson, Maxwell L, *Dir,* Emory University, Museum of Art & Archaeology, Atlanta GA

Anderson, Maynard, *Prof,* Wartburg College, Dept of Art, Waverly IA (S)

Anderson, Nancy, *Cur Asst,* Manitoba Historical Society, Dalnavert Museum, Winnipeg MB

Anderson, Nancy B, *Exec Dir,* Museum of Arts and Sciences, Inc, Macon GA

Anderson, Neil, *Prof,* Bucknell University, Dept of Art, Lewisburg PA (S)

Anderson, Patricia, *Dir,* New Rochelle Public Library, Art Section, New Rochelle NY

Anderson, Peter, *VPres Prog,* Museum of Science and Industry, Chicago IL

Anderson, Richita, *Librn,* Aesthetic Realism Foundation, Eli Siegel Collection, New York NY

Anderson, Richita, *Librn,* Aesthetic Realism Foundation, Library, New York NY

Anderson, Robert, *Prof,* West Virginia University, College of Creative Arts, Morgantown WV (S)

Anderson, Stanford, *Head Dept,* Massachusetts Institute of Technology, School of Architecture and Planning, Cambridge MA (S)

Anderson, Susan, *Development Officer,* Bellevue Art Museum, Bellevue WA

Anderson, Susan, *Cur Exhib,* Laguna Art Museum, Laguna Beach CA

Anderson, Susan, *Dir,* Bloomington Art Center, Bloomington MN

Anderson, Sven, *Asst Prof,* West Texas State University, Art, Communication & Theatre Dept, Canyon TX (S)

Anderson, Terrance A, *Dir,* Savannah State College, Dept of Fine Arts, Savannah GA (S)

Anderson, Terry, *Instr,* Northeast Mississippi Junior College, Art Dept, Booneville MS (S)

Anderson, Tom, *Comptroller,* Alberta College of Art, Calgary AB (S)

Anderson, Tom, *Chmn,* Florida State University, Art Education Dept, Tallahassee FL (S)

Anderson, W, *Instr,* Humboldt State University, College of Arts & Humanities, Arcata CA (S)

Anderson, Wayne, *Assoc Prof,* Wayne State College, Art Dept, Wayne NE (S)

Anderson, Wyatt, *Interim Dean,* University of Georgia, Franklin College of Arts & Sciences, Dept of Art, Athens GA (S)

Andors, Rhoda, *Pres,* National Society of Mural Painters, Inc, New York NY

Andraka, Judith, *Chmn,* Prince George's Community College, Art Dept, Largo MD (S)

Andrea, Martha, *Assoc Prof,* Colby-Sawyer College, Dept of Fine & Performing Arts, New London NH (S)

Andress, Thomas, *Print Selection Committee Chmn,* Print Club of Albany, Museum, Albany NY

Andrews, Edwin, *Asst Prof,* Northeastern University, Dept of Art & Architecture, Boston MA (S)

Andrews, Hazel, *Chmn,* Lynnwood Arts Centre, Simcoe ON

Andrews, Luann, *Cur Educ,* University of Missouri, Museum of Art and Archaeology, Columbia MO

Andrews, Nancy, *Librn,* Mingei International, Inc, Reference Library, San Diego CA

Andrews, Richard, *Dir,* University of Washington, Henry Art Gallery, Seattle WA

Andrews, Victoria, *Asst Dir Research Progs,* Museum of New Mexico, Office of Cultural Affairs of New Mexico, The Governor's Gallery, Santa Fe NM

Andrus, Beryl, *Branch Adminr,* Las Vegas-Clark County Library District, Las Vegas NV

Andrus-Walck, Kathryn, *Asst Prof,* University of Colorado-Colorado Springs, Fine Arts Dept, Colorado Springs CO (S)

Angel, Catherine, *Asst Prof,* University of Wisconsin-Stevens Point, Dept of Art & Design, Stevens Point WI (S)

Angel, Dennis, *Asst Prof,* University of Wisconsin-Stevens Point, Dept of Art & Design, Stevens Point WI (S)

Angelillo, Kathy, *Business Adminr,* Fresno Metropolitan Museum, Fresno CA

Angeline, M, *Prof,* Madonna College, Art Dept, Livonia MI (S)

Angeloch, Robert, *Instr,* Woodstock School of Art, Inc, Woodstock NY (S)

Angert, Joe C, *Instr,* Saint Louis Community College at Forest Park, Art Dept, Saint Louis MO (S)

Anglin, B, *Prof,* Christopher Newport College, Arts & Communications, Newport News VA (S)

Anglin, Barbara, *Technical Services Librn,* Lee County Library, Tupelo MS

Angus, Judy, *Vis Asst Prof,* Adams State College, Dept of Visual Arts, Alamosa CO (S)

Annis, Norman, *Prof,* Gettysburg College, Dept of Art, Gettysburg PA (S)

Annis, Susan, *Dir, Cultural Human Resources,* Canadian Conference of the Arts, Ottawa ON

Anreus, Alehandro, *Cur Coll,* Montclair Art Museum, Montclair NJ

Anreus, Alejandro, *Asst Cur,* Montclair Art Museum, Art School, Montclair NJ (S)

Ansbacher, Theodore H, *Dir Education,* Museum of Science and Industry, Chicago IL

Ansell, Joseph, *Chmn,* Otterbein College, Dept of Visual Arts, Westerville OH (S)

Antaki, Karen, *Acting Cur,* Concordia University, Leonard & Bina Ellen Art Gallery, Montreal PQ

Antel, Barbara, *Cur & Consultant,* Westinghouse Electric Corporation, Art Collection, Pittsburgh PA

Anthony, Carolyn, *Dir,* Skokie Public Library, Skokie IL

Anthony, David, *Dean,* Golden West College, Visual Art Dept, Huntington Beach CA (S)

Anthony, Jan, *Office Mgr,* Mount Saint Vincent University, Art Gallery, Halifax NS

Anthony, Lawrence, *Prof,* Rhodes College, Dept of Art, Memphis TN (S)

Anthony, Stuart, *Asst Dir,* Exit Art, New York NY

Anthony, Vincent, *Exec Dir,* Center for Puppetry Arts, Atlanta GA

Antognini, Alfredo, *Paintings Conservator,* Balboa Art Conservation Center, San Diego CA

Antoine, Janeen, *Exec Dir Sicangu Lakato Tribe,* American Indian Contemporary Arts, San Francisco CA

Anton, D, *Instr,* Humboldt State University, College of Arts & Humanities, Arcata CA (S)

Anton, Don, *Instr,* Olympic College, Social Sciences & Humanities Division, Bremerton WA (S)

Anton, Waldo, *Treas,* Guadalupe Historic Foundation, Santuario de Guadalupe, Santa Fe NM

Antonetti, Martin, *Librn,* Grolier Club Library, New York NY

Antonovics, Lilian, *Admin Asst,* Duke University Museum of Art, Durham NC

Antonsen, Lasse, *Coordr Gallery,* University of Massachusetts Dartmouth, College of Visual and Performing Arts, North Dartmouth MA (S)

Antrim, Craig, *Vis Asst Prof,* Loyola Marymount University, Art & Art History Dept, Los Angeles CA (S)

Antrim, Elizabeth, *Slide Cur,* San Jose State University, Robert D Clark Library, San Jose CA

Apesos, Anthony, *Chmn Fine Arts Dept,* Art Institute of Boston, Boston MA (S)

Apfelstadt, Eric, *Asst Prof,* Santa Clara University, Art Dept, Santa Clara CA (S)

Apollini, Robert, *Dir,* Highland Community College, Freeport IL (S)

Appelhof, Ruth Stevens, *Exec Dir,* Ari Museum of Western Virginia, Roanoke VA

Appleman, David, *Instr,* Bob Jones University, School of Fine Arts, Greenville SC (S)

Apraxime, Pierre, *Cur,* The Gilman Paper Company, New York NY

Aquero, Clara, *Asst Prof,* Savannah State College, Dept of Fine Arts, Savannah GA (S)

Aquilino, Marie, *Asst Prof,* University of Kansas, Kress Foundation Dept of Art History, Lawrence KS (S)

Aranoff, June B, *Special Events Coordr,* Yeshiva University Museum, New York NY

Arbitman, Kahren Jones, *Dir,* Pennsylvania State University, Palmer Museum of Art, University Park PA

Arbour, Rosemarie, *Dept Head,* Universite du Quebec a Montreal, Famille des Arts, Montreal PQ (S)

Arbury, Stephen, *Instr,* Radford University, Art Dept, Radford VA (S)

Arceneaux, Pamela D, *Reference Librn,* Kemper & Leila Williams Foundation, Historic New Orleans Collection, New Orleans LA

Arceo, Rene, *Visual Arts Coord,* Mexican Fine Arts Center Museum, Chicago IL

Archabal, Nina M, *Dir,* Minnesota Historical Society, Saint Paul MN

Archer, Jim, *Instr,* Clark College, Art Dept, Vancouver WA (S)

Archer, Leslie, *Financial Dir,* Danforth Museum of Art, Framingham MA

Archer, Richard, *Asst Prof,* Southern Illinois University, School of Art & Design, Carbondale IL (S)

Archer, Sheila, *Visual Arts Coordr,* Organization of Saskatchewan Arts Councils (OSAC), Regina SK

Archibald, Dale, *Chief Cur,* Oregon Historical Society, Portland OR

Archibald, Robert, *Pres,* Missouri Historical Society, Saint Louis MO

Archuleta, Margaret, *Cur of fine Art,* Heard Museum, Phoenix AZ

Ard, Tim, *Media Instr,* Grayson County College, Art Dept, Denison TX (S)

Arellanes, Audrey Spencer, *Dir & Ed,* American Society of Bookplate Collectors & Designers, Alhambra CA

Arendse, Basil, *Exhibition Production Chief,* National Museum of African Art, Washington DC

Arentz, Donald, *Asst Prof Philosophy,* LeMoyne College, Wilson Art Gallery, Syracuse NY

Arimitsu, Joe, *Chmn Art 3-D Media,* California State University, Northridge, Dept of Art-Two Dimensional Media, Northridge CA (S)

Arksey, Laura, *Cur Spec Coll & Archives,* Eastern Washington State Historical Society, Library, Spokane WA

Armijo-Beeson, Isabel, *Prog Dir,* Chicano Humanities & Arts Council, Denver CO

Arminio, Roberta Y, *Dir,* Museum of Ossining Historical Society, Ossining NY

Armstrong, Elizabeth, *Cur,* Walker Art Center, Minneapolis MN

Armstrong, Kathy, *Registrar,* Fairbanks Museum and Planetarium, Saint Johnsbury VT

Armstrong, Lilian, *Chmn,* Wellesley College, Art Dept, Wellesley MA (S)

Armstrong, Richard, *Cur Contemporary Art,* Carnegie Institute, Carnegie Museum of Art, Pittsburgh PA

Armstrong, Rodney, *Dir & Librn,* Boston Athenaeum, Boston MA

Armstrong, Susan, *Asst Prof,* Malone College, Dept of Art, Canton OH (S)

Arnade, Valerie, *Ed of Publications,* Walters Art Gallery, Baltimore MD

Arnason, Charles, *Pres,* Minnesota Historical Society, Saint Paul MN

Arndt, Susan, *Art Instr,* Red Rocks Community College, Arts & Humanities Department, Lakewood CO (S)

Arning, Bill, *Exec Dir,* White Columns, New York NY

Arnold, Arleen, *Dir of Admin Servs,* Ferguson Library, Stamford CT

Arnold, Craig, *Librn,* San Diego Maritime Museum, San Diego CA

Arnold, Dorothea, *Cur Egyptian Art,* The Metropolitan Museum of Art, New York NY

Arnold, Mary Koniz, *Development Assoc,* Dutchess County Arts Council, Poughkeepsie NY

Arnold, Ralph, *Prof,* Loyola University of Chicago, Fine Arts Dept, Chicago IL (S)

Arnold, Willard B, *Pres Historical Society,* Waterville Historical Society, Redington Museum, Waterville ME

Arntson, Amy E, *Chmn,* University of Wisconsin-Whitewater, Dept of Art, Whitewater WI (S)

Aronson, Carol, *Prof,* University of New Hampshire, Dept of the Arts, Durham NH (S)

Arp, Kimberly, *Prof,* Louisiana State University, School of Art, Baton Rouge LA (S)

Arpadi, Allen, *Instr,* Saint Louis Community College at Forest Park, Art Dept, Saint Louis MO (S)

Arpag, Bekir E, *Assoc Prof,* Rochester Institute of Technology, School of Printing, Rochester NY (S)

Arraras, Maria Teresa, *Dir,* La Casa del Libro Museum, San Juan PR

Arrasmith, Lynnda, *Registrar,* Canton Art Institute, Canton OH (S)

Arrington, Gerald C, *Prof,* Concord College, Fine Art Division, Athens WV (S)

Arrington, Jacquline, *Board Pres,* Jamaica Arts Center, Jamaica NY

Arrington, Michael, *Dean School Arts & Science,* Ouachita Baptist University, Dept of Art, Arkadelphia AR (S)

Arrowo, Inna, *Chmn,* Eastern Connecticut State University, Fine Arts Dept, Willimantic CT (S)

Arroyo, Paul, *Office Mgr,* Sheldon Swope Art Museum, Terre Haute IN

Arsem, Marilyn, *Co-Dir,* Mobius Inc, Boston MA

Arsenault-Desfosses, Helene, *Project Leader Temporary Exhib,* Canadian Museum of Nature, Musee Canadien de la Nature, Ottawa ON

Arseneault, Celine, *Botanist & Librn,* Jardin Botanique de Montreal, Bibliotheque, Montreal PQ

Arthur, Kathleen, *Prof,* James Madison University, Dept of Art, Harrisonburg VA (S)

Artzberger, John A, *Dir,* Oglebay Institute, Mansion Museum, Wheeling WV

Arvanetes, Jan White, *Instr,* Alma College, Clack Art Center, Alma MI (S)

Asano, Hisako, *Adjunct Asst Prof,* University of Southern California, School of Fine Arts, Los Angeles CA (S)

Asch, Howard, *Dir Public Prog,* Jamaica Arts Center, Jamaica NY

Aseltine, Terry, *Public Relations Mgr,* Winnipeg Art Gallery, Winnipeg MB

Ash, Carla Caccamise, *Cur,* Joseph E Seagram & Sons, Inc, Gallery, New York NY

Ash, Dorothy, *Chmn,* West Hills Community College, Fine Arts Dept, Coalinga CA (S)

Ash, Marilyn, *Dir,* Sharon Arts Center, Sharon NH (S)

Ash, Marilyn, *Dir,* Sharon Arts Center, Sharon NH

Ash, Richard, *Art Coordr,* Midwestern State University, Div of Fine Arts, Wichita Falls TX (S)

Ashbaugh, Sue, *Educ Coordr,* Jefferson County Open Space, Hiwan Homestead Museum, Evergreen CO

Ashby, Anna Lou, *Assoc Cur Printed Books,* Pierpont Morgan Library, New York NY

Ashcroft, Ira, *Chmn Art Committee,* Wilfrid Laurier Univer2ity, Art Gallery, Waterloo ON

Asher, Catherine, *Asst Prof,* University of Minnesota, Minneapolis, Art History, Minneapolis MN (S)

Asher, Frederick, *Chmn,* University of Minnesota, Minneapolis, Art History, Minneapolis MN (S)

Asher, Karen, *Pub Relations Officer,* Lyman Allyn Art Museum, New London CT

Asher, Martha, *Registrar,* Sterling and Francine Clark Art Institute, Williamstown MA

Asherman, Adrian, *Pres,* Barn Gallery Associates, Inc, Ogunquit ME

Ashley, Francis, *Secy-Treas & Dir,* Intermuseum Conservation Association, Oberlin OH

Ashley, James, *VPres,* Gadsden Museum of Fine Arts, Inc, Gadsden AL

Ashlstrom, Ed, *Chmn,* Montgomery College, Dept of Art, Rockville MD (S)

Ashman, Stuart, *Cur,* Museum of New Mexico, Office of Cultural Affairs of New Mexico, The Governor's Gallery, Santa Fe NM

Ashton, Jean, *Dir,* New York Historical Society, Library, New York NY

Ashton, Rick J, *Librn,* Denver Public Library, Humanities Dept, Denver CO

Ashworth, Judie, *Mgr,* Franklin Mint Museum, Franklin Center PA

Asimakos, John, *Assoc Prof,* Mount Allison University, Fine Arts Dept, Sackville NB (S)

Aspell, Amy, *Supr,* City of Irvine, Irvine Fine Arts Center, Irvine CA

Aspell, Amy, *Supv,* City of Irvine, Fine Arts Center, Irvine CA (S)

Asper, Lynn, *Chmn,* Grand Rapids Junior College, Art Dept, Grand Rapids MI (S)

Aszling, Jill, *Registrar,* Massachusetts Institute of Technology, List Visual Arts Center, Cambridge MA

Aten, Duane, *Dir,* College of Marin, Art Gallery, Kentfield CA

Atha, Barbara, *Pres,* Octagon Center for the Arts, Ames IA

Athan, Jean, *Art Consultant,* Wilmington Trust Company, Wilmington DE

Atherly, Mary, *Registrar & Assoc Cur,* Iowa State University, Brunnier Gallery Museum, Ames IA

Atherton, Beth, *Cur,* Silverado Museum, Saint Helena CA

Atherton, Beth, *Cur,* Silverado Museum, Reference Library, Saint Helena CA

Atherton, Charles H, *Secy,* United States Commission of Fine Arts, Washington DC

Atkins, Bill, *Dir,* Triton Museum of Art, Santa Clara CA

Atkins, Captain A J, *Pres,* Sturdivant Hall, Selma AL

Atkins, Karen, *Prog Chmn,* Texas State Technical College, Commercial Art in Advertising, Amarillo TX (S)

Atkinson, Daniel, *Prog Dir,* Library Association of La Jolla, Athenaeum Music and Arts Library, La Jolla CA

Atkinson, D Scott, *Cur,* Terra Museum of American Art, Chicago IL

Atkinson, Leslie, *Pres & Chief Exec Officer,* SLA Arch-Couture Inc, Art Collection, Denver CO

Atkinson, Tammy, *Head Librn,* Lauren Rogers Museum of Art, Library, Laurel MS

Atkinson, Tammy D, *Head Librn,* Lauren Rogers Museum of Art, Laurel MS

Atrnandez, Daniel, *Board VPres,* Centro Cultural De La Raza, San Diego CA

Attenborough, Debra, *Cur of Education,* Rodman Hall Arts Centre, Saint Catharines ON

Attenborough, Debra, *Librn,* Rodman Hall Arts Centre, Library, Saint Catharines ON

Attie, Diana, *Prof,* University of Toledo, Dept of Art, Toledo OH (S)

Atton, William G, *Pres,* Wichita Center for the Arts, Wichita KS (S)

Atwell, Kathleen, *Develop Dir,* Tippecanoe County Historical Museum, Lafayette IN

Atwell, Michael, *Asst Dir,* Purdue University Galleries, West Lafayette IN

Atz, Anne L, *Pres,* Florida Artist Group Inc, Punta Gorda FL

Au, Jeri, *Asst Prof,* Webster University, Art Dept, Webster Groves MO (S)

Aubourg, Vickie, *Slide Librn,* University of California, Art Dept Library, Davis CA

Auchincloss, Katharine, *Chmn Board,* New Jersey Historical Society Museum, Newark NJ

Auchstetter, Rosann, *Asst Librn,* Indiana University, Fine Arts Library, Bloomington IN

Audet, M, *Asst Librn,* Musee du Quebec, Bibliotheque des Arts, Quebec PQ

Audrey, Laura, *Instr,* University of Southern Colorado, Belmont Campus, Dept of Art, Pueblo CO (S)

Audrus, Lisa, *Assoc Prof,* Portland State University, Dept of Art, Portland OR (S)

Auerbach, Seymour, *Prof,* Catholic University of America, School of Architecture & Planning, Washington DC (S)

Aufderheide, Larry, *Chmn & Dir of Humanities Div,* Lakeland Community College, Visual Arts Dept, Mentor OH (S)

Augaitis, Daina, *Chief Cur,* Banff Centre, Walter Phillips Gallery, Banff AB

Auger, Jane, *Cur & Caretaker,* South County Art Association, Kingston RI

August, James, *Assoc Dir, Development & Communications,* Winnipeg Art Gallery, Winnipeg MB

Augustine, Tracy, *Prog Advisor,* University of Tennessee, University of Tennessee Exhibits Committee, Knoxville TN

Augusztiny, Roxana, *Asst Dir,* University of Washington, Thomas Burke Memorial Washington State Museum, Seattle WA

Aumann, Karen, *Asst Prof,* Philadelphia Community College, Dept of Art, Philadelphia PA (S)

Aunspaugh, Richard, *Chmn,* Young Harris College, Dept of Art, Young Harris GA (S)

Auping, Michael G, *Chief Cur,* The Buffalo Fine Arts Academy, Albright-Knox Art Gallery, Buffalo NY

Aurbach, Michael, *Assoc Prof,* Vanderbilt University, Dept of Fine Arts, Nashville TN (S)

Aurellan, Frank J, *Asst Dir,* Woodrow Wilson House, Washington DC

Aurino-Martel, Kari, *Financial Aid,* Rocky Mountain College of Art & Design, Denver CO (S)

Ausfeld, Margaret, *Cur, Painting & Sculpture,* Montgomery Museum of Fine Arts, Montgomery AL

Austin, Carole, *Cur,* San Francisco Craft and Folk Art Museum, San Francisco CA

Austin, Helen C, *Instr,* John C Calhoun State Community College, Division of Fine Arts, Decatur AL (S)

Austin, Helen C, *Dir,* John C Calhoun State Community College, Art Gallery, Decatur AL

Austin, Howard, *Instructor,* Milwaukee Area Technical College, Graphic Arts Dept, Milwaukee WI (S)

Austin, James G, *Asst Prof,* Salem College, Art Dept, Winston-Salem NC (S)

Austin, Jerry, *Grad Studies Coordr,* University of North Texas, School of Visual Arts, Denton TX (S)

Austin, Jerry, *Ceramics Coordr,* University of North Texas, School of Visual Arts, Denton TX (S)

Austin, Jon, *Dir,* Rome Historical Society Museum, Rome NY

Austin, Lisa, *Public Relations Dir,* Portland Museum of Art, Portland ME

Austin, Robin, *Development Dir,* New Jersey Historical Society Museum, New Jersey State Museum at Morven, Newark NJ

Auth, Catherine T, *Exec Dir,* National Artists Equity Association Inc, Washington DC

Auth, Susan H, *Cur Classical Collection,* Newark Museum Association, The Newark Museum, Newark NJ

Autry, Carolyn, *Assoc Prof,* University of Toledo, Dept of Art, Toledo OH (S)

Baker, Patsy Collins, *Gallery Dir & Admin Asst,* New Orleans Academy of Fine Arts, Academy Gallery, New Orleans LA

Baker, Paul, *Acting Chair Lib Arts Studies,* Ontario College of Art, Toronto ON (S)

Baker, Robert, *Cur Natural Science Research Lab,* Texas Tech University, Museum, Lubbock TX

Baker, Roger, *Instr,* Clark College, Art Dept, Vancouver WA (S)

Baker, Sandra, *Instr,* Brazosport College, Art Dept, Lake Jackson TX (S)

Baker, Susan, *Instr,* Vincennes University Junior College, Art Dept, Vincennes IN (S)

Baker, Van, *Exec Dir,* Ward Foundation, Ward Museum of Wildfowl Art, Salisbury MD

Baker, Victoria, *Asst Cur Early Canadian Art,* National Gallery of Canada, Ottawa ON

Baker, W Lowell, *Chmn Dept,* University of Alabama, Art Dept, Tuscaloosa AL (S)

Bakke, Julie, *Registrar,* Menil Collection, Houston TX

Bakker, Dirk, *Photographer,* Detroit Institute of Arts, Detroit MI

Bakovych, A, *Asst Prof,* Northern Arizona University, School of Art & Design, Flagstaff AZ (S)

Balado, Jose, *Dir Fine Arts,* Institute of Puerto Rican Culture, Escuela de Artes Plasticas, San Juan PR (S)

Balakier, Ann, *Asst Prof,* University of South Dakota, Dept of Art, Vermillion SD (S)

Balamuth, Eva, *Librn,* The Parrish Art Museum, Aline B Saarinen Library, Southampton NY

Balas, Shawna, *Cur,* Ukrainian Cultural and Educational Centre, Winnipeg MB

Balas, Shawna, *Gallery Cur,* Ukrainian Cultural and Educational Centre, Gallery, Winnipeg MB

Balch, Inge, *Assoc Prof,* Baker University, Dept of Art, Baldwin City KS (S)

Balchen, Arthur, *Pres,* Ojai Valley Art Center, Ojai CA

Baldaia, Peter, *Cur,* Rockford Art Museum, Rockford IL

Balderacchi, Christa, *Asst to Dir,* Institute of Contemporary Art, Boston MA

Balderson, Lance, *Instr,* Ocean City Art Center, Ocean City NJ (S)

Baldridge, Mark, *HeadDept,* Longwood College, Dept of Art, Farmville VA (S)

Baldwin, Dana, *Coordr of Educ Prog,* Contemporary Arts Museum, Houston TX

Baldwin, Geraldine, *Libr Dir,* Alice Curtis Desmond & Hamilton Fish Library, Hudson River Reference Collection, Garrison NY

Baldwin, Guy, *Assoc Prof,* University of Minnesota, Minneapolis, Dept of Studio Art, Minneapolis MN (S)

Baldwin, Larry, *Asst Dir,* Birmingham Museum of Art, Birmingham AL

Baldwin, Robert, *Instr,* Connecticut College, Dept of Art History, New London CT (S)

Baldwin, Robert A, *Assoc Prof,* Vanderbilt University, Dept of Fine Arts, Nashville TN (S)

Balentine, Susan, *Theatre Dir,* Hill Country Arts Foundation, Ingram TX

Balester, John, *Chmn,* American Academy of Art, Chicago IL (S)

Baley, Susan G, *Museum Educator,* University of Oklahoma, Fred Jones Jr Museum of Art, Norman OK

Balinsky, Alvin, *Chmn Fine Arts,* Milwaukee Institute of Art and Design, Milwaukee WI (S)

Balistreri, Becky, *Chmn Design Dept,* Milwaukee Institute of Art and Design, Milwaukee WI (S)

Balkcum, Bea, *Instr,* Wayne Community College, Liberal Arts Dept, Goldsboro NC (S)

Ball, Isabel, *Dean,* Our Lady of the Lake University, Dept of Art, San Antonio TX (S)

Ball, Jeff, *Instr,* William Woods-Westminster Colleges, Art Dept, Fulton MO (S)

Ball, Kathy, *Registrar,* Lafayette Natural History Museum, Planetarium and Nature Station, Lafayette LA

Ball, Martin, *Asst Prof,* Rutgers, the State University of New Jersey, Mason Gross School of the Arts, New Brunswick NJ (S)

Ball, Rex, *Exec Dir,* The University of Texas, Institute of Texan Cultures, San Antonio TX

Ball, Rolaine D, *Admin Asst,* National Trust for Historic Preservation, Chesterwood Museum, Glendale MA

Ball, Susan L, *Exec Dir,* College Art Association, New York NY

Ballaine, Jerrold, *Prof,* University of California, Berkeley, College of Letters & Sciences-Art Dept, Berkeley CA (S)

Ballance, Stephen, *Chmn Dept,* Northwestern Michigan College, Art Dept, Traverse City MI (S)

Ballantine, Robert, *Graphic Designer,* London Regional Art & Historical Museums, London ON

Ballard, Diane, *Development Assoc,* Museum of Photographic Arts, Balboa Park CA

Ballard, Helen, *Chief Visitors Services,* Lightner Museum, Saint Augustine FL

Ballard, Lockett Ford, *Exec Dir,* Rock Ford Foundation, Inc, Rock Ford Plantation & Kauffman Museum, Lancaster PA

Ballard, Maria, *Office Administrator,* University of South Carolina, McKissick Museum, Columbia SC

Ballatore, Sandy, *Asst Cur Contemporary Art,* Museum of New Mexico, Museum of Fine Arts, Santa Fe NM

Ballentine, Don M, *Head Dept,* Atlanta Area Technical School, Dept of Commercial Art, Atlanta GA (S)

Ballinger, James K, *Dir,* Phoenix Art Museum, Phoenix AZ

Ballschmider, Mary Jo, *Mgr of Admin Svcs,* Sheboygan Arts Foundation, Inc, John Michael Kohler Arts Center, Sheboygan WI

Balmos, Don, *Chmn,* McLennan Community College, Fine Arts Dept, Waco TX (S)

Balmuth, Miriam, *Prof,* Tufts University, Dept of Art & Art History, Medford MA (S)

Balogh, Anthony, *Instr,* Madonna College, Art Dept, Livonia MI (S)

Balogh, Christa, *Instr,* Southeastern Community College, Dept of Art, Whiteville NC (S)

Balshaw, Paul, *Dean,* Marshall University, Dept of Art, Huntington WV (S)

Balthrope, David, *Prof,* Christopher Newport College, Arts & Communications, Newport News VA (S)

Baltrushunas, John, *Asst Prof,* Maryville University of Saint Louis, Art Division, Saint Louis MO (S)

Balzekas, Stanley, *Pres,* Balzekas Museum of Lithuanian Culture, Chicago IL

Balzer, G, *Assoc Prof,* Northern Arizona University, School of Art & Design, Flagstaff AZ (S)

Bambrick, Barbara, *Exec Dir,* Saint Bernard Foundation and Monastery, North Miami Beach FL

Banas, Lillian, *Treas,* Jesse Besser Museum, Alpena MI

Banasiak, John, *Assoc Prof,* University of South Dakota, Dept of Art, Vermillion SD (S)

Banchs, William, *Pres,* National Foundation for Advancement in the Arts, Miami FL

Bancou, Marielle, *Exec Dir,* Color Association of The US, New York NY

Bandes, Susan, *Dir,* Michigan State University, Kresge Art Museum, East Lansing MI

Bandy, Mary Lea, *Dir Dept Film,* Museum of Modern Art, New York NY

Bandy, Nancy, *Prof,* Victoria College, Victoria TX (S)

Bang, Peggy L, *Instr,* North Iowa Area Community College, Dept of Art, Mason City IA (S)

Banian, Nancy, *Admin Asst,* Manchester Institute of Arts and Sciences Gallery, Manchester NH

Baniassad, E, *Dean,* Technical University of Nova Scotia, Faculty of Architecture, Halifax NS (S)

Banka, Lynn, *Instr,* Creighton University, Fine and Performing Arts Dept, Omaha NE (S)

Banks, Barbara, *Membership & Program Liaison,* Madison Art Center, Madison WI

Banks, Charles, *Dir,* Butera School of Art, Boston MA (S)

Banks, John, *Pres Bd Trustees,* Stratford Art Association, The Gallery Stratford, Stratford ON

Banks, Miranda, *Clocktower Coordr,* Institute for Contemporary Art, The Clocktower Gallery, Long Island City NY

Bannard, Darby, *Chmn,* University of Miami, Dept of Art & Art History, Coral Gables FL (S)

Bannett, Lendy, *Dir of Sales,* Cleveland Center for Contemporary Art, Cleveland OH

Bannon, Anthony, *Dir,* Burchfield Art Center, Buffalo NY

Bantel, Linda, *Dir Museum,* Pennsylvania Academy of the Fine Arts, Galleries, Philadelphia PA

Bantens, Robert, *Art Historian,* University of South Alabama, Dept of Art, Mobile AL (S)

Baptie, Sue M, *Dir,* Vancouver City Archives, Vancouver BC

Baptista, Danille, *Instr,* University of Alabama in Birmingham, Dept of Art, Birmingham AL (S)

Barabe, Bryon, *Secy,* Xicanindio, Inc, Mesa AZ

Baraetucci, Mauricio, *Gallery Chmn,* Santa Monica College Art Gallery, Santa Monica CA

Baranchuk, Maria, *Asst Dir,* Louisa May Alcott Memorial Association, Orchard House, Concord MA

Baranetski, Walter, *Pres,* Ukrainian Institute of America, Inc, New York NY

Barbash, Steven, *Prof,* State University of New York, College at Cortland, Art Dept, Cortland NY (S)

Barber, Earle N, *VPres,* Woodmere Art Museum, Philadelphia PA

Barber, Ronald, *Dir,* Port of History Museum, Philadelphia PA

Barberio, Laura, *Ursuline Gallery Mgr,* Southwest Craft Center, Emily Edwards & Ursuline Sales Gallery, San Antonio TX

Barberis, Dorothy, *Corresp Secy,* National Society of Painters in Casein & Acrylic, Inc, Whitehall PA

Barbier, Sally, *Prog Coordr Ceramics,* Alberta College of Art, Calgary AB (S)

Barbieri, Frances, *Education Coordr,* Seneca Falls Historical Society Museum, Seneca Falls NY

Barboni, Gwen, *Exec Dir,* Meadville Council on the Arts, Meadville PA

Barbre, M J, *Museum Shop Mgr,* Philbrook Museum of Art, Tulsa OK

Barch, Nancy, *Instr,* Wayne Art Center, Wayne PA (S)

Bard, Perry, *Instr,* Bard College, Milton Avery Graduate School of the Arts, Annandale-on-Hudson NY (S)

Barde, Alex, *Assoc Prof,* Pittsburg State University, Art Dept, Pittsburg KS (S)

Bardel, Penelope K, *Assoc Dir,* The Metropolitan Museum of Art, New York NY

Barden, John, *Librn,* Tryon Palace Historic Sites & Gardens, Library, New Bern NC

Barden, John R, *Historian,* Tryon Palace Historic Sites & Gardens, New Bern NC

Bardenheuer, Lee, *Treas,* Kent Art Association, Inc, Gallery, Kent CT

Bardes, Leo N, *Dir Fine Arts,* College of San Mateo, Creative Arts Dept, San Mateo CA (S)

Bardon, Donna, *Friends of Lovejoy Library,* Southern Illinois University, Lovejoy Library, Edwardsville IL

Barensfeld, Mark, *Instr,* Art Academy of Cincinnati, Cincinnati OH (S)

Barham, Jane G, *Dir,* Imperial Calcasieu Museum, Lake Charles LA

Barilleaux, Rene Paul, *Gallery Dir,* College of Charleston, Halsey Gallery, Charleston SC

Barish, Esther, *Chmn,* Jersey City State College, Art Dept, Jersey City NJ (S)

Barkan, Leonard, *Prof,* University of Michigan, Ann Arbor, Dept of History of Art, Ann Arbor MI (S)

Barker, Jimmy H, *Dept Head,* Sam Houston State University, Art Dept, Huntsville TX (S)

Barker, Norman, *Instr,* Johns Hopkins University, School of Medicine, Dept of Art as Applied to Medicine, Baltimore MD (S)

Barker, Patricia, *Admin Asst,* Noah Webster Foundation & Historical Society of West Hartford, Inc, Noah Webster's House, West Hartford CT

Barker, Samuel M C, *Pres,* Newport Historical Society, Newport RI

Barkley, Alan, *Pres,* Emily Carr College of Art & Design, Vancouver BC (S)

Barletta, Barbara, *Assoc Prof,* University of Florida, Dept of Art, Gainesville FL (S)

Barley, Gerlinde, *Head of Reference,* The College at New Paltz State University of New York, Sojourner Truth Library, New Paltz NY

Barlow, Barbara, *Pres,* Blacksburg Regional Art Association, Christiansburg VA

Barlow, Deborah, *Fine Arts Subject Specialist & Reference Librn,* University of North Texas, Willis Library, Denton TX

Barlow, Deborah, *Reference Librn,* University of Southern California, Helen Topping Architecture & Fine Arts Library, Los Angeles CA

Barmann, Floyd, *Exec Dir & Cur Museum,* Clark County Historical Society, Springfield OH

Barmann, Floyd, *Dir,* Clark County Historical Society, Library, Springfield OH

Barnard, Marbo, *Pres,* Pastel Society of the West Coast, Sacramento Fine Arts Center, Carmichael CA

Barnes, Art, *Chmn Dept,* Lenoir Rhyne College, Dept of Art, Hickory NC (S)

Barnes, Bernadine, *Asst Prof,* Wake Forest University, Dept of Art, Winston-Salem NC (S)

Barnes, Carl F, *Prof,* Oakland University, Dept of Art and Art History, Rochester MI (S)

Barnes, Donna, *Dir Exhib,* Fuller Museum of Art, Brockton MA

Barnes, Gary, *Assoc Prof,* Arkansas Tech University, Dept of Art, Russellville AR (S)

Barnes, Kathy Chan, *Festivals Committee Dir,* American Society of Artists, Inc, Chicago IL

Barnes, Laurie, *Cur of Asian Art,* Detroit Institute of Arts, Detroit MI

Barnes, Lisa Tremper, *Dir,* Ursinus College, Philip & Muriel Berman Museum of Art, Collegeville PA

Barnes, Marilyn, *Office Mgr,* Oakville Galleries, Centennial Gallery and Gairloch Gallery, Oakville ON

Barnes, Raymond S, *Asst Prof,* Muhlenberg College, Dept of Art, Allentown PA (S)

Barnes, Reinaldo, *Mgr,* Longfellow-Evangeline State Commemorative Area, Saint Martinville LA

Barnes, Robert, *Prof,* Indiana University, Bloomington, Henry Radford Hope School of Fine Arts, Bloomington IN (S)

Barnes, Ron, *Secy,* Prescott Fine Arts Association, Gallery, Prescott AZ

Barnes, Sharron, *Assoc Prof,* Gulf Coast Community College, Division of Fine Arts, Panama City FL (S)

Barnes, Susan, *Sr Cur Western Art,* Dallas Museum of Art, Dallas TX

Barnes, Ted, *Asst Prof,* Louisiana College, Dept of Art, Pineville LA (S)

Barnes, William, *Assoc Prof,* College of William and Mary, Dept of Fine Arts, Williamsburg VA (S)

Barnett, Edith, *Secy,* Lincoln County Historical Association, Maine Art Gallery, Old Academy, Wiscasset ME

Barnett, James F, *Dir Historic Properties,* Mississippi Department of Archives and History, State Historical Museum, Jackson MS

Barnett, John, *Prof,* California State University, Art Dept, Turlock CA (S)

Barnett, John D, *Acting Cur,* United States Navy, Art Gallery, Washington DC

Barnett, Loretta, *Prof,* Colby-Sawyer College, Dept of Fine & Performing Arts, New London NH (S)

Barnett, Patricia J, *Systems Reference Librn,* The Metropolitan Museum of Art, Thomas J Watson Library, New York NY

Barnett, Richard, *Prof,* College of Mount Saint Vincent, Fine Arts Dept, Riverdale NY (S)

Barnett, Robert, *Secy Board of Trustees,* Royal Ontario Museum, Toronto ON

Barnett, Vivian Endicott, *Cur,* Solomon R Guggenheim Museum, New York NY

Barnette, Joan, *Dir,* Red Rock State Park, Museum, Church Rock NM

Barnhart, Audrey, *Museum Technician,* Oregon Trail Museum Association, Scotts Bluff National Monument, Gering NE

Barnhill, Georgia, *Pres,* Fitchburg Art Museum, Fitchburg MA

Barnhill, Georgia B, *Cur Graphic Arts,* American Antiquarian Society, Worcester MA

Barnitz, Downing, *Dir,* Florida Southern College, Melvin Art Gallery, Lakeland FL

Barnitz, Downing, *Chmn Dept,* Florida Southern College, Art Dept, Lakeland FL (S)

Barnitz, Gwenda, *Vol Coordr,* Salvador Dali Museum, Saint Petersburg FL

Barnum, Amy, *Librn,* New York State Historical Association, Library, Cooperstown NY

Baroff, Debby, *Cur Spec Coll,* Institute of the Great Plains, Museum of the Great Plains, Lawton OK

Baroff, Deborah, *Cur Spec Coll,* Institute of the Great Plains, Research Library, Lawton OK

Baron, Ronald, *Instr,* Dowling College, Dept of Visual Arts, Oakdale NY (S)

Baron, Stuart, *Dir,* Boston University, School of Visual Arts, Boston MA (S)

Barone, Deborah, *Cur,* Connecticut State Library, Museum of Connecticut History, Hartford CT

Barr, David, *Prof,* Macomb Community College, Art Dept, Warren MI (S)

Barr, David, *Assoc Dir Project Management,* Royal Ontario Museum, Toronto ON

Barr, Donald, *Assoc Prof,* College of the Ozarks, Dept of Art, Point Lookout MO (S)

Barr, Elaine, *Business Mgr,* Ashtabula Arts Center, Ashtabula OH

Barr, John W, *Chmn Board of Governors,* J B Speed Art Museum, Louisville KY

Barr, Keith L, *Dir,* Peoria Historical Society, Peoria IL

Barraclough, Dennis, *Dir,* Daemen College, Fanette Goldman & Carolyn Greenfield Gallery, Amherst NY

Barraclough, Dennis, *Chmn Dept,* Daemen College, Art Dept, Amherst NY (S)

Barrager, Roberta, *Assoc Prof,* Pierce College, Art Dept, Woodland Hills CA (S)

Barreda Ynonge, Frederico, *Head Dept,* University of Puerto Rico, Dept of Fine Arts, Rio Piedras PR (S)

Barreras del Rio, Petra, *Exec Dir,* El Museo del Barrio, New York NY

Barrett, Marguerite, *Asst Librn,* Rutgers, The State University of New Jersey, Art Library, New Brunswick NJ

Barrett, Nancy, *Cur Photography,* New Orleans Museum of Art, New Orleans LA

Barrett, Robert, *Dir & Chief Cur,* Fresno Arts Center & Museum, Fresno CA

Barrett, S Barre, *Art Chair,* Jacksonville University, Dept of Art, Jacksonville FL (S)

Barrett, Terry, *Assoc Prof,* Ohio State University, Dept of Art Education, Columbus OH (S)

Barrett, Wayne, *Dir Editorial Services,* Colonial Williamsburg Foundation, Williamsburg VA

Barrie, Brooke, *Acad Dir,* Johnson Atelier Technical Institute of Sculpture, Mercerville NJ (S)

Barrie, Shirley, *Adminr,* Canadian Society of Painters in Watercolour, Toronto ON

Barringer, George M, *Special Collections Librn,* Georgetown University, Lauinger Library-Special Collections Division, Washington DC

Barrington, Susan T, *Supt,* Old Fort Harrod State Park Mansion Museum, Harrodsburg KY

Barron, Stephanie, *Cur 20th Century Art,* Los Angeles County Museum of Art, Los Angeles CA

Barry, Maria, *Bulletin Educ,* Special Libraries Association, Museum, Arts and Humanities Division, Washington DC

Barsotti, Frank, *Prof,* School of the Art Institute of Chicago, Chicago IL (S)

Bart, Sharon, *Supv Branches,* Miami-Dade Public Library, Miami FL

Bartel, Marvin, *Prof,* Goshen College, Art Dept, Goshen IN (S)

Bartell, Lori, *Second VPres,* Springfield Museum of Art, Springfield OH

Bartelo, Jose, *Dir,* Institute of Puerto Rican Culture, Escuela de Artes Plasticas Galleria, San Juan PR

Bartelo, Jose, *Dir,* Institute of Puerto Rican Culture, Museo de Bellas Artes, San Juan PR

Bartelo, Jose, *Dir,* Institute of Puerto Rican Culture, Dr Jose C Barbosa Museum and Library, San Juan PR

Bartelo, Jose, *Dir,* Institute of Puerto Rican Culture, Dominican Convent Museum, San Juan PR

Bartelo, Jose, *Dir,* Institute of Puerto Rican Culture, Museo de Arte Religioso Porta Coeli, San Juan PR

Bartelo, Jose, *Dir,* Institute of Puerto Rican Culture, Museo de Historia Naval y Militar de Puerto Rico, San Juan PR

Bartelo, Jose, *Dir,* Institute of Puerto Rican Culture, Museo de la Familia Puertorriquena del Siglo XIX, San Juan PR

Bartelo, Jose, *Dir,* Institute of Puerto Rican Culture, Museo de la Farmacia Puertorriquena, San Juan PR

Bartelo, Jose, *Dir,* Institute of Puerto Rican Culture, Museo y Parque Historico de Caparra, San Juan PR

Barter, Judith, *Cur American Arts,* The Art Institute of Chicago, Chicago IL

Bartfield, Ira, *Coordr of Photography,* National Gallery of Art, Washington DC

Barth, Charles, *Prof,* Mount Mercy College, Art Dept, Cedar Rapids IA (S)

Barth, Cynthia M, *Librn,* Munson-Williams-Proctor Institute, Art Reference Library, Utica NY

Barth, Miles, *Cur of Coll,* International Center of Photography, New York NY

Barth, Uta, *Asst Prof,* University of California, Riverside, Dept of Art, Riverside CA (S)

Bartholomew, Terese Tse, *Cur Indian Art,* Asian Art Museum of San Francisco, Avery Brundage Collection, San Francisco CA

Bartkiewicz, Mibs, *Admin Asst,* Louisiana State University, Museum of Arts, Baton Rouge LA

Bartlett, Christopher, *Dir,* Towson State University, The Holtzman Art Gallery, Towson MD

Bartlett, Christopher, *Prof,* Maryland College of Art and Design, Silver Spring MD (S)

Bartlett, Jack, *Assoc Prof,* Mississippi State University, Art Dept, Mississippi State MS (S)

Bartlett, Kathie, *Second VPres,* Sierra Arts Foundation, Reno NV

Bartner, Howard C, *Asst Prof,* Johns Hopkins University, School of Medicine, Dept of Art as Applied to Medicine, Baltimore MD (S)

Barton, Brigid, *Chmn,* Santa Clara University, Art Dept, Santa Clara CA (S)

Barton, James, *Pres,* Johnson Atelier Technical Institute of Sculpture, Mercerville NJ (S)

Bartram, Robert, *Head Librn,* Johns Hopkins University, George Peabody Library, Baltimore MD

Bartsch, Martha, *Prof,* Pace University, Dyson College of Arts & Sciences, Pleasantville NY (S)

Barwick, Kent, *Pres,* Municipal Art Society of New York, New York NY

Barzman, Karen-edis, *Asst Prof,* Cornell University, Dept of the History of Art, Ithaca NY (S)

Bascom, Ruth E, *Pres,* Wharton Esherick Museum, Wharton Esherick Studio, Paoli PA

Basha, Regine, *Cur,* Saidye Bronfman Centre, Montreal PQ

Bashkoff, Tracey R, *Assoc Cur & Registrar,* Guild Hall of East Hampton, Inc, Guild Hall Museum, East Hampton NY

Basinger, Jeanine, *Prof,* Wesleyan University, Art Dept, Middletown CT (S)

Basista, Paul, *Exec Dir,* Graphic Artists Guild, New York NY

Baskin, Gere, *Dir,* Detroit Focus, Detroit MI

Basquin, Kit, *Cur of Education and Public Prog,* Marquette University, Haggerty Museum of Art, Milwaukee WI

Bass, Pat, *VPres,* Crooked Tree Arts Council, Virginia M McCune Community Arts Center, Petoskey MI

Bass, W Clayton, *Exhib Design Supv,* Emory University, Museum of Art & Archaeology, Atlanta GA

Bassett, Hilary, *Dir,* Midland Art Council, Midland MI

Bassett, Lynne, *Cur Colls,* Historic Northampton Museum, Northampton MA

Bassett, Ruth, *Librn,* Brandywine River Museum, Chadds Ford PA

Bassett, Ruth, *Librn,* Brandywine River Museum, Library, Chadds Ford PA

Bassin, Joan, *Executive Dir,* National Institute for Architectural Education, New York NY

Bassinger, Marily, *Dir,* Art Institute for the Permian Basin, Odessa TX

Bassist, Donald H, *Pres,* Bassist College Library, Portland OR

Bassist, Norma, *VPres & Secy,* Bassist College Library, Portland OR

Bassist, Norma, *Librn,* Bassist College Library, Portland OR

Baster, Victoria V, *Asst Cur,* University of Lethbridge, Art Gallery, Lethbridge AB

Bastian, Duane, *Prof,* University of Toledo, Dept of Art, Toledo OH (S)

Bastin, Kimberly, *Dir Development,* Arts United of Greater Fort Wayne, Fort Wayne IN

Bastoni, Gerald R, *Dir,* Kemerer Museum of Decorative Arts, Bethlehem PA

Batchelor, Anthony, *Chmn,* Art Academy of Cincinnati, Cincinnati OH (S)

Batchelor, Elisabeth, *Asst Dir for Coll,* Cincinnati Museum Association, Cincinnati Art Museum, Cincinnati OH

Batdorff, Jon, *Instr,* Goddard College, Visual Arts Dept, Plainfield VT (S)

Bates, Bruce B, *Chmn,* International Museum of Photography at George Eastman House, Rochester NY

Bates, Craig D, *Cur Ethnography,* Yosemite Museum, Yosemite National Park CA

Bates, Geoff, *Asst Prof,* Salem College, Art Dept, Winston-Salem NC (S)

Bates, Marjorie, *Exec Dir,* Craftsmen's Guild of Mississippi, Inc, Agriculture & Forestry Museum, Jackson MS

Bates, P Martin, *Prof,* University of Victoria, Dept of Visual Arts, Victoria BC (S)

Bates, Sara, *Dir Exhib & Prog Cherokee Tribe,* American Indian Contemporary Arts, San Francisco CA

Bates, Tom, *Prof,* La Roche College, Division of Graphics, Design & Communication, Pittsburgh PA (S)

Bathurst, Rosemary, *Instr,* Siena Heights College, Studio Angelico-Art Dept, Adrian MI (S)

Batista, Kenneth, *Chmn,* University of Pittsburgh, Dept of Studio Arts, Pittsburgh PA (S)

Batkin, Jonathan, *Dir,* Wheelwright Museum of the American Indian, Santa Fe NM

Batson, Darrell, *Branch Adminr,* Las Vegas-Clark County Library District, Las Vegas NV

Batson, Gayle, *Instr,* The Arkansas Arts Center, Museum School, Little Rock AR (S)

Batson, Joan, *Program Dir,* Bemis Foundation, New Gallery, Omaha NE

Battaglini, Charles, *Instr,* Indiana University of Pennsylvania, Dept of Art and Art Education, Indiana PA (S)

Batteen, Sue, *Cur Coll,* Dacotah Prairie Museum, Ruth Bunker Memorial Library, Aberdeen SD

Battis, Nicholas, *Registrar,* Pratt Institute Library, Rubelle & Norman Schafler Gallery, Brooklyn NY

Battle, Martha, *Treas,* North Carolina Museums Council, Raleigh NC

Batty, Ellen, *Circulation Librn,* Athenaeum of Philadelphia, Philadelphia PA

Batty, Ellen, *Circulation Librn,* Athenaeum of Philadelphia, Library, Philadelphia PA

Batzka, Stephen, *Assoc Prof,* Manchester College, Art Dept, North Manchester IN (S)

Bauche, Dean, *Cur,* Allen Sapp Gallery, North Battleford SK

Bauer, Brent A, *Asst Prof,* Johns Hopkins University, School of Medicine, Dept of Art as Applied to Medicine, Baltimore MD (S)

Bauer, Susie, *Asst to Dir,* Oklahoma City Art Museum, Oklahoma City OK

Bauknight, Alice R, *Cur of Exhib,* University of South Carolina, McKissick Museum, Columbia SC

Bauman, Patricia, *Pres,* G G Drayton Club, Salem OH

Bauman, Thomas, *VPres,* G G Drayton Club, Salem OH

Baumann, Edward, *Assoc Prof,* University of Missouri, Art History and Archaeology Dept, Columbia MO (S)

Baumann, Richard, *Instr,* Columbia College, Art Dept, Columbia MO (S)

Baumel, Dina, *Coordr Book Distribution,* Visual Studies Workshop, Rochester NY

Baver, Florence, *Pres,* Pennsylvania Dutch Folk Culture Society Inc, Pennsylvania Dutch Folklife Museum, Lenhartsville PA

Bawin, Art, *Instr,* Solano Community College, Division of Fine & Applied Art, Suisun City CA (S)

Baxter, Joan, *Exec Secy,* Greene County Historical Society, Xenia OH

Baxter, Joseph, *Treas,* Woodmere Art Museum, Philadelphia PA

Baxter, Paula A, *Cur Art & Arch Coll,* The New York Public Library, Art, Prints and Photographs Division, New York NY

Baxter, Violet, *VPres,* New York Artists Equity Association, Inc, New York NY

Bay, Sonja, *Librn,* Solomon R Guggenheim Museum, New York NY

Bay, Sonja, *Librn,* Solomon R Guggenheim Museum, Library, New York NY

Bayersdorfer, Fred, *Dir,* Old Dominion University, Gallery, Norfolk VA

Bayersdorfer, Fred, *Gallery Dir,* Old Dominion University, Art Dept, Norfolk VA (S)

Bayles, Jennifer, *Cur Education,* The Buffalo Fine Arts Academy, Albright-Knox Art Gallery, Buffalo NY

Bayless, Frederick, *Treas,* Almond Historical Society, Inc, Hagadorn House The 1800-37 Museum, Almond NY

Bayless, Stephen, *Prof,* Georgia Southern University, Dept of Art, Statesboro GA (S)

Bayrus, Kristin, *Catalog Librn,* Moore College of Art & Design, Library, Philadelphia PA

Bayuzick, Dennis, *Assoc Prof,* University of Wisconsin-Parkside, Art Dept, Kenosha WI (S)

Baza, Larry, *Board Exec Dir,* Centro Cultural De La Raza, San Diego CA

Bazin, Renee, *Dir Public Information,* Arts & Education Council of Greater Saint Louis, Saint Louis MO

Beach, Milo, *Dir,* Freer Gallery of Art, Washington DC

Beach, Milo, *Adjunct Prof,* University of Michigan, Ann Arbor, Dept of History of Art, Ann Arbor MI (S)

Beach, Milo C, *Dir,* Freer Gallery of Art & The Arthur M Sackler Gallery Gallery, Washington DC

Beachum, Sharon G, *Chmn,* Hampton University, Art Dept, Hampton VA (S)

Beafore, Shirley, *Activities Coordr,* Chrysler Museum, Norfolk VA

Beagle, Charles, *Dir Facility Servs & Security,* Memphis Brooks Museum of Art, Memphis TN

Beal, Bruce, *Commissioner,* Boston Art Commission of the City of Boston, Boston MA

Beal, Graham W J, *Dir,* Joslyn Art Museum, Omaha NE

Beal, Maggie, *Chmn,* Wisconsin Painters & Sculptors, Inc, Milwaukee WI

Beale, Arthur, *Dir Research,* Museum of Fine Arts, Boston MA

Beale, M Cohn, *Dir Conservation,* Harvard University, William Hayes Fogg Art Museum, Cambridge MA

Bealer, Jan, *VPres,* Kemerer Museum of Decorative Arts, Bethlehem PA

Beall, Burtch, *Chmn,* Utah Arts Council, Chase Home Museum of Utah Folk Art, Salt Lake City UT

Beall, Mary, *Head Programming Dept,* Englewood Library, Fine Arts Dept, Englewood NJ

Beals, Stuart, *Instr,* Johnson County Community College, Visual Arts Program, Overland Park KS (S)

Beam, Amy, *Media Relations Asst,* National Art Museum of Sport, Indianapolis IN

Beam, Michael, *Asst Registrar,* Westmoreland Museum of Art, Greensburg PA

Beam, Philip C, *Emeritus Prof,* Bowdoin College, Art Dept, Brunswick ME (S)

Beamer, Karl, *Assoc Prof,* Bloomsburg University, Dept of Art, Bloomsburg PA (S)

Bean, Carole, *Instr,* Creighton University, Fine and Performing Arts Dept, Omaha NE (S)

Beane, Frances A, *Deputy Dir,* Harvard University, Harvard University Art Museums, Cambridge MA

Beane, Frances A, *Deputy Dir,* Harvard University, William Hayes Fogg Art Museum, Cambridge MA

Beane, Frances A, *Deputy Dir,* Harvard University, Arthur M Sackler Museum, Cambridge MA

Bear, Marcelle, *VPres,* Florida Artist Group Inc, Punta Gorda FL

Beard, Kimberly, *Registrar,* Port Authority of New York & New Jersey, Art Collection, New York NY

Beard, Rick, *Exec Dir,* Atlanta Historical Society Inc, Atlanta History Center, Atlanta GA

Beardman, John, *Prof,* Oakland University, Dept of Art and Art History, Rochester MI (S)

Beardsley, Kelcy, *Instr,* Marylhurst College, Art Dept, Marylhurst OR (S)

Beardsley, Margaret, *Pres,* Parson Fisher House, Jonathan Fisher Memorial, Inc, Blue Hill ME

Beardsley, Theodore S, *Dir,* Hispanic Society of America, Museum, New York NY

Bearnson, Dorothy, *Prof,* University of Utah, Art Dept, Salt Lake City UT (S)

Bearor, Karen, *Asst Prof,* Florida State University, Art History Dept (R133B), Tallahassee FL (S)

Beasley, Elizabeth, *Dir Development,* Norton Gallery and School of Art, West Palm Beach FL

Beatty, Norman G, *VPres Media & Government Relations,* Colonial Williamsburg Foundation, Williamsburg VA

Beauchamp, Sharon, *Secy,* Lubbock Art Association, Inc, Lubbock TX

Beaudoin-Ross, Jacqueline, *Cur Costume,* McCord Museum of Canadian History, Montreal PQ

Beaule, Denise, *Secy,* Saint Anselm College, Chapel Art Center, Manchester NH

Bechet, Ron, *Asst Prof,* Southern University in New Orleans, Art Dept, New Orleans LA (S)

Bechwith, Wendy, *Instr,* La Roche College, Division of Graphics, Design & Communication, Pittsburgh PA (S)

Beck, Albert, *Prof,* Culver-Stockton College, Division of Fine Arts, Canton MO (S)

Beck, Brian, *Public Relations,* University of Arizona, Museum of Art, Tucson AZ

Beck, Martin, *Curatorial Registrar,* Montclair Art Museum, Montclair NJ

Beck, Patty, *Registrar,* San Antonio Art Institute, San Antonio TX (S)

Beck, Sachiko, *Asst Prof,* Framingham State College, Art Dept, Framingham MA (S)

Beckelman, John, *Chmn Art Dept,* Coe College, Gordon Fennell Gallery & Marvin Cone Gallery, Cedar Rapids IA

Beckelman, John, *Chmn & Assoc Prof,* Coe College, Dept of Art, Cedar Rapids IA (S)

Becker, Carol, *Grad Division Chair,* School of the Art Institute of Chicago, Chicago IL (S)

Becker, David, *Prof,* University of Wisconsin, Madison, Dept of Art, Madison WI (S)

Beckerman, Lilyan, *Treas,* Hollywood Art Museum, Hollywood FL

Beckman, Judy, *Coordr,* Kenyon College, Art Gallery, Gambier OH

Beckwith, Alice, *Assoc Prof,* Providence College, Art and Art History Dept, Providence RI (S)

Beckwith, Claudia, *Head Collections Management & Security,* Greenville County Museum of Art, Greenville SC

Beckwith, Herbert, *Technical Services,* San Francisco Maritime National Historical Park, J Porter Shaw Library, San Francisco CA

Bedard, Robert J, *Treas,* Art PAC, Washington DC

Bedeaux, Joan, *Treas,* New Mexico Art League, Gallery, Albuquerque NM

Bedell, Cindy, *Asst Cur Educ,* Tippecanoe County Historical Museum, Lafayette IN

Bedell, Rober, *Chmn,* Southern Seminary College, Buena Vista VA (S)

Bedgood, Jill, *Lectr,* Southwest Texas State University, Dept of Art, San Marcos TX (S)

Bedigian, Deena, *Registrar,* Louisiana Department of Culture, Recreation and Tourism, Louisiana State Museum, New Orleans LA

Beecher, Raymond, *Librn,* Greene County Historical Society, Bronck Museum, Coxsackie NY

Beeching, Lynne, *Development,* Hidalgo County Historical Museum, Edinburg TX

Beelick, Susan, *Humanities Reference & Slide Librn,* California State University at Sacramento, Library - Humanities Reference Dept, Sacramento CA

Beer MA, Kenneth J, *Assoc Prof,* James Madison University, Dept of Art, Harrisonburg VA (S)

Beerman, Miriam, *Instr,* Montclair Art Museum, Art School, Montclair NJ (S)

Beesch, Ruth K, *Dir,* University of North Carolina at Greensboro, Weatherspoon Art Gallery, Greensboro NC

Begland, Mary Ann, *Assoc Prof,* Rochester Institute of Technology, School of Art and Design, Rochester NY (S)

Begley, Holly, *Dir,* Old Slater Mill Association, Slater Mill Historic Site, Pawtucket RI

Begley, John P, *Exec Dir,* Louisville Visual Art Association, Louisville KY

Behler, Mark, *Cur,* North Central Washington Museum, Art Gallery, Wenatchee WA

Behlke, James, *Instr,* University of Alaska, Dept of Art, Fairbanks AK (S)

Behnk, Elisa, *Media Relations Mgr,* Carnegie Institute, Carnegie Museum of Art, Pittsburgh PA

Behrens, Fred, *Head Dept,* Columbia State Community College, Dept of Art, Columbia TN (S)

Behrnes, Roy, *Prof,* University of Northern Iowa, Dept of Art, Cedar Falls IA (S)

Beiersdorfer, Ann, *Prof,* Xavier University, Dept of Art, Cincinnati OH (S)

Beim, Elizabeth, *Development Pub Affairs Officer,* National Museum of the American Indian, New York NY

Beiman, Frances, *Supv Art & Music Div,* Newark Public Library, Art & Music Div, Newark NJ

Beitzel, Ross, *Head,* Gloucester County College, Liberal Arts Dept, Sewell NJ (S)

Beizer, S, *Chmn Jewelry Design,* Fashion Institute of Technology, Art & Design Division, New York NY (S)

Belan, Kyra, *Gallery Dir,* Broward Community College - South Campus, Art Gallery, Pembroke Pines FL

Beland, Mario, *Conservator Early Art,* Musee du Quebec, Quebec PQ

Belanger, Alain, *Coordr,* Vu Centre D'Animation Et De Diffusion De La Photographie, Quebec PQ

Belasco, Ruth, *Chmn,* Spring Hill College, Fine Arts Dept, Mobile AL (S)

Belcheff, Koste, *Chmn Art & Music,* Angelo State University, Art and Music Dept, San Angelo TX (S)

Belcher, Patty, *Reference Librn,* Bernice Pauahi Bishop Museum, Library, Honolulu HI

Belfield, Sandra, *Asst Prof,* Pittsburg State University, Art Dept, Pittsburg KS (S)

Belfort-Chalat, Jacqueline, *Chmn & Prof,* Le Moyne College, Fine Arts Dept, Syracuse NY (S)

Belknap, Beth, *Asst,* College of Mount Saint Joseph, Art Dept, Cincinnati OH (S)

Belknap, Waldron Phoenix, *Dir & Librn,* Winterthur Museum and Gardens, Library, Winterthur DE

Belko, Kathleen, *Exec Dir,* New Hampshire Antiquarian Society, Hopkinton NH

Bell, Betty, *Treas,* DuPage Art League School & Gallery, Wheaton IL

Bell, Clair C, *Exec Dir,* Staunton Fine Arts Association, Staunton Augusta Art Center, Staunton VA

Bell, Donald, *Chmn Dept,* State University of New York at Binghamton, Dept of Art & Art History, Binghamton NY (S)

Bell, Eugene, *Instr,* Cuyahoga Valley Art Center, Cuyahoga Falls OH (S)

Bell, Eunice, *Exec Dir,* Ocean City Art Center, Ocean City NJ

Bell, Eunice, *Exec Dir,* Ocean City Art Center, Art Library, Ocean City NJ

Bell, Greg, *Dir,* University of Puget Sound, Kittredge Art Gallery, Tacoma WA

Bell, Kathy, *Instr,* Bob Jones University, School of Fine Arts, Greenville SC (S)

Bell, Larry, *Second VPres,* Buffalo Society of Artists, Kenmore NY

Bell, Roberley, *Instr,* Villa Maria College of Buffalo, Art Dept, Buffalo NY (S)

Bell, Robert, *Instr,* Umpqua Community College, Fine & Performing Arts Dept, Roseburg OR (S)

Bell, Trevor, *Prof,* Florida State University, Art Dept, Tallahassee FL (S)

Bellah, Mary S, *Cur,* Carnegie Art Museum, Oxnard CA

Bellamy, Jan, *Marketing,* Ella Sharp Museum, Jackson MI

Bellas, Gerald, *Dir,* College of Mount Saint Joseph, Studio San Giuseppe, Cincinnati OH

Bellas, Gerry, *Asst Prof,* College of Mount Saint Joseph, Art Dept, Cincinnati OH (S)

Bellerby, Greg, *Cur,* Emily Carr College of Art & Design, The Charles H Scott Gallery, Vancouver BC

Belley, L, *Asst Librn,* Musee du Quebec, Bibliotheque des Arts, Quebec PQ

Bellingham, Susan, *Special Coll Librn,* University of Waterloo, Dana Porter Library, Waterloo ON

Bellion, Wendy, *Library Asst,* National Museum of Women in the Arts, Library & Research Center, Washington DC

Bello, Jane Arce, *Exec Dir,* Association of Hispanic Arts, New York NY

Belluscio, Lynne, *Dir,* Leroy Historical Society, Leroy NY

Belson, Anne, *Cultural Affairs Coordr,* Federal Reserve Bank of Boston, Boston MA

Belvo, Hazel, *Faculty,* Grand Marais Art Colony, Grand Marais MN

Belvo, Hazel, *Chmn Fine Arts,* Minneapolis College of Art and Design, Minneapolis MN (S)

Belz, Carl I, *Dir,* Brandeis University, Rose Art Museum, Waltham MA

Benckenstein, Eunice R, *VChmn,* Nelda C & H J Lutcher Stark Foundation, Stark Museum of Art, Orange TX

Bendel, D, *Prof,* Northern Arizona University, School of Art & Design, Flagstaff AZ (S)

Bender, David R, *Exec Dir,* Special Libraries Association, Museum, Arts and Humanities Division, Washington DC

Bender, Jeffrey, *Instr,* University of Evansville, Art Dept, Evansville IN (S)

Bender, Jennifer, *Asst Dir,* Art Com-La Mamelle, Inc, San Francisco CA

Bender, June, *Admin Asst,* Vernon Art Gallery, Vernon BC

Benedetti, Joan M, *Museum Librn,* Craft and Folk Art Museum, Research Library, Los Angeles CA

Benedict, Bro, *Dir,* Saint Gregory's Abbey and College, Mabee-Gerrer Museum of Art, Shawnee OK

Benedict, Mary Jane, *Librn,* J B Speed Art Museum, Art Reference Library, Louisville KY

Benefield, Richard, *Adminr,* Brown University, David Winton Bell Gallery, Providence RI

Benet, Linda, *Chmn,* Santa Barbara City College, Fine Arts Dept, Santa Barbara CA (S)

Benezra, Neal, *Chief Cur,* Hirshhorn Museum and Sculpture Garden, Washington DC

Bengston, Charlotte, *Treas,* Essex Historical Society, Essex Shipbuilding Museum, Essex MA

Bengstrom, Rod, *Gallery Dir,* University of Akron, University Galleries, Akron OH

Benio, Pauleve, *Chmn Art Dept,* Adrian College, Art Dept, Adrian MI (S)

Beniston, Susan, *Instr,* Toronto School of Art, Toronto ON (S)

Benjamin, Brent, *Asst Dir Spec Projects & Prog,* Museum of Fine Arts, Boston MA

Benjamin, Karl, *Prof,* Pomona College, Art Dept, Claremont CA (S)

Benjamin, Karl, *Prof,* Claremont Graduate School, Dept of Fine Arts, Claremont CA (S)

Benjamin, Martin, *Chmn Visual Arts,* Union College, Dept of the Arts, Schenectady NY (S)

Benn, Carl, *Cur,* Toronto Historical Board, Historic Fort York, Toronto ON

Bennedict, Burton, *Dir,* University of California, Phoebe Apperson Hearst Museum of Anthropology, Berkeley CA

Bennett, Archie, *Instr,* Surry Community College, Art Dept, Dobson NC (S)

Bennett, Barbara, *Instr,* The Arkansas Arts Center, Museum School, Little Rock AR (S)

Bennett, David, *Dept Head, Advertising Design,* Art Institute of Houston, Houston TX (S)

Bennett, Don, *Chmn,* San Joaquin Delta College, Art Dept, Stockton CA (S)

Bennett, Fernanda, *Registrar,* Nassau County Museum of Fine Art, Roslyn NY

Bennett, James, *Assoc Prof,* Norwich University, Dept of Philosophy, Religion and Fine Arts, Northfield VT (S)

Bennett, K Sharon, *Archivist,* Charleston Museum, Charleston SC

Bennett, K Sharon, *Librn,* Charleston Museum, Library, Charleston SC

Bennett, Laura, *Educ Dir,* Owensboro Museum of Fine Art, Owensboro KY

Bennett, Lloyd, *Assoc Prof,* Xavier University of Louisiana, Dept of Fine Arts, New Orleans LA (S)

Bennett, Scott, *Head Art Dept,* Houghton College, Art Dept, Houghton NY (S)

Bennett, Shelley, *Adjunct Asst Prof,* University of Southern California, School of Fine Arts, Los Angeles CA (S)

Bennett, Shelley M, *Cur British & Continental Art,* Henry E Huntington Library, Art Collections & Botanical Gardens, San Marino CA

Bennett, Swannee, *Cur,* Arkansas Territorial Restoration, Little Rock AR

Bennett, Swannee, *Cur,* Arkansas Territorial Restoration, Library, Little Rock AR

Benoy, Cecilia, *Cur of Education,* Gaston County Museum of Art & History, Dallas NC

Bensen, James Q, *Secy,* The National Art Museum of Sport, Indianapolis IN

Benson, Anita, *Instr,* Monterey Peninsula College, Art Dept, Monterey CA (S)

Benson, Barbara E, *Exec Dir,* Historical Society of Delaware, Old Town Hall Museum, Wilmington DE

Benson, Barbara E, *Exec Dir,* Historical Society of Delaware, Library, Wilmington DE

Benson, Bob, *Chmn,* College of the Redwoods, Arts, Humanities & Social Sciences Division, Eureka CA (S)

Benson, Eugenia, *Fine Arts,* Silas Bronson Library, Art, Theatre & Music Services, Waterbury CT

Benson, Jack, *Emeritus Prof,* University of Massachusetts, Amherst, Art History Program, Amherst MA (S)

Benson, Mark, *Asst Prof,* Auburn University at Montgomery, Dept of Fine Arts, Montgomery AL (S)

Benson, M D, *Instr,* Humboldt State University, College of Arts & Humanities, Arcata CA (S)

Benson, Richard, *Prof,* Yale University, School of Art, New Haven CT (S)

Benson, Timothy, *Cur,* Los Angeles County Museum of Art, Robert Gore Rifkind Center for German Expressionist Studies, Los Angeles CA

Bentcourt, Savannah, *Treas,* Coquille Valley Art Association, Coquille OR

Bentley, Eden R, *Librn,* Johnson Atelier Technical Institute of Sculpture, Johnson Atelier Library, Mercerville NJ

Bently, Martha, *Librn,* Monterey History and Art Association, Library, Monterey CA

Benton, Ann C S, *Supervising Librn,* The New York Public Library, Mid-Manhattan Library, Art Collection, New York NY

Benton, Janetta, *Prof,* Pace University, Dyson College of Arts & Sciences, Pleasantville NY (S)

Bentor, Eli, *Asst Prof,* Winthrop College, Dept of Art & Design, Rock Hill SC (S)

Bentor, Ray, *Publicity,* Iowa State University, Brunnier Gallery Museum, Ames IA

Benvenuti, Noella, *Registrar,* San Bernardino County Museum, Fine Arts Institute, Redlands CA

Ben'zvi, Paul, *Instr,* Indiana University of Pennsylvania, Dept of Art and Art Education, Indiana PA (S)

Berard, Guy, *Chmn,* St Lawrence University, Dept of Fine Arts, Canton NY (S)

Berardi, Marianne, *Dir,* The Albrecht-Kemper Museum of Art, Saint Joseph MO

Bercht, Fatima, *Dir Visual Arts Program,* Americas Society, New York NY

Berchuck, Rhonda, *Art Cur,* State Street Bank & Trust Co, Boston MA

Berg, Barbara, *Secy,* Shoreline Historical Museum, Seattle WA

Berg, Eric, *Treas,* Society of Animal Artists, Inc, Bronx NY

Berg, Kathy L, *Librn,* Worcester Art Museum, Library, Worcester MA

Berg, Mona, *Gallery Dir,* Purdue University Galleries, West Lafayette IN

Berg, Niels, *VPres,* Ages of Man Fellowship, Amenia NY

Berg, Susan, *Dir,* Colonial Williamsburg Foundation, Library, Williamsburg VA

Bergeman, Rich, *Instr,* Linn Benton Community College, Fine & Applied Art Dept, Albany OR (S)

Bergen, Philip S, *Librn,* The Bostonian Society, Library, Boston MA

Berger, Jerry A, *Dir,* Springfield Art Museum, Springfield MO

Berger, M, *Ref Librn,* McGill University, Blackader-Lauterman Library of Architecture and Art, Montreal PQ

Berger, Mark, *Dir Visual Arts,* Rutgers, the State University of New Jersey, Mason Gross School of the Arts, New Brunswick NJ

Berger, Patricia, *Cur Chinese Art,* Asian Art Museum of San Francisco, Avery Brundage Collection, San Francisco CA

Berger, Richard, *Chmn Sculpture Dept,* San Francisco Art Institute, San Francisco CA (S)

Berger, Robert, *Adjunct Assoc Prof,* Pennsylvania State University, University Park, Dept of Art History, University Park PA (S)

Bergeron, Andre, *Artistic Cur,* Saint Joseph's Oratory, Museum, Montreal PQ

Bergeron, Claudette, *Admin Secy,* La Galerie Montcalm la galerie d'art de la Villede Hull, Hull PQ

Bergeron, Jack, *Asst Prof,* Lansing Community College, Media Dept, Lansing MI (S)

Bergeron, Yves, *Cur,* Musee du Seminaire de Quebec, Quebec PQ

Bergfeld, Mary Ann, *Assoc Prof,* Saint Xavier University, Dept of Art, Chicago IL (S)

Berg-Johnson, Karen, *Asst Prof,* Bethel College, Dept of Art, Saint Paul MN (S)

Berglass, Nancy, *Exec Dir,* Arts Council of San Mateo County, Belmont CA

Berglin, Merlin, *Office Supv,* Pope County Historical Society Museum, Glenwood MN

Berglund, R P, *Dir Cultural Prog,* International Business Machines Corp, IBM Gallery of Science & Art, New York NY

Bergman, Joseph, *Assoc Prof,* Siena Heights College, Studio Angelico-Art Dept, Adrian MI (S)

Bergman, Robert P, *Dir,* Walters Art Gallery, Baltimore MD

Bergmann, Frank, *Assoc Dean Humanities,* Utica College of Syracuse University, Division of Humanities, Utica NY (S)

Bergmann, Merrie, *Chmn,* Town of Cummington Historical Commission, Kingman Tavern Historical Museum, Cummington MA

Bergquiste, Michael, *Treas,* Erie Art Museum, Erie PA

Bergrson, Mary T, *Dir Marketing, Communications, Mem & Development,* Indianapolis Museum of Art, Indianapolis IN

Bergs, Lilita, *Public Relations & Marketing Mgr,* The Rockwell Museum, Corning NY

Bergsieker, David, *Instr,* Illinois Valley Community College, Div of Humanities and Fine Arts, Oglesby IL (S)

Berhalter, Kathleen, *Art Dept Chmn,* Delaware State College, Dept of Art and Art Education, Dover DE (S)

Berke, Debra, *Museum Cur,* United States Department of the Interior Museum, Washington DC

Berkowitz, Rita, *Asst Prof,* Bradford College, Creative Arts Division, Bradford MA (S)

Berkowitz, Roger M, *Deputy Dir,* Toledo Museum of Art, Toledo Museum of Art, Toledo OH

Berks, Linda, *Technican Museums Coll & Exhib,* London Regional Art & Historical Museums, London ON

Berl, Kathe, *VPres,* Artist-Craftsmen of New York, New York NY

Berle, Lila W, *Pres,* Norman Rockwell Museum at Stockbridge, Stockbridge MA

Berlo, Janet, *Prof,* University of Missouri-Saint Louis, Art Dept, Saint Louis MO (S)

Berlyn, Judith, *Librn,* Chateau Ramezay Museum, Library, Montreal PQ

Berman, Gert, *Librn,* Palm Beach County Parks & Recreation Department, Donald B Gordon Memorial Library, Delray Beach FL

Berman, Mary Jane, *Dir,* Wake Forest University, Museum of Anthropology, Winston Salem NC

Berman, Nancy, *Dir,* Hebrew Union College, Skirball Museum, Los Angeles CA

Berman, Philip, *Chmn Board,* Philadelphia Museum of Art, Philadelphia PA

Bermann, Beate, *Instr,* San Diego Mesa College, Fine Arts Dept, San Diego CA (S)

Bermingham, Peter, *Dir & Chief Cur,* University of Arizona, Museum of Art, Tucson AZ

Bernal, Rudy, *Preparator,* University of Chicago, David and Alfred Smart Museum of Art, Chicago IL

Bernard, Richard M, *Dean,* Bethany College, Dept of Fine Arts, Bethany WV (S)

Bernardi, Rosemarie, *Assoc Prof Painting & Drawing,* University of Arizona, Dept of Art, Tucson AZ (S)

Bernatowicz, Rita, *Head Dept,* Castleton State College, Art Dept, Castleton VT (S)

Berner, Andrew, *Dir,* University Club Library, New York NY

Berns, Marla, *Dir,* University of California, Santa Barbara, University Art Museum, Santa Barbara CA

Bernstein, Ed, *Assoc Prof,* Indiana University, Bloomington, Henry Radford Hope School of Fine Arts, Bloomington IN (S)

Bernstein, Joanne, *Prof Hist,* Mills College, Art Dept, Oakland CA (S)

Bernstein, Joseph C, *Dir,* Union of American Hebrew Congregations, Synagogue Art and Architectural Library, New York NY

Bernstein, Lawrence A, *Assoc Prof,* Southern Illinois University, School of Art & Design, Carbondale IL (S)

Bernstein, Roberta, *Art Historian,* State University of New York at Albany, Art Dept Slide Library, Albany NY

Bernstein, Roberta, *Asst Prof,* State University of New York at Albany, Art Dept, Albany NY (S)

Bernsten, Ray, *Regional Mgr,* Chief Plenty Coups Museum, Pryor MT

Bernstock, Judith E, *Assoc Prof,* Cornell University, Dept of the History of Art, Ithaca NY (S)

Bernstorff, Marietta, *Gallery Coordr,* Social & Public Art Resource Center, (SPARC), Venice CA

Beroza, Barbara, *Coll Mgr,* Yosemite Museum, Yosemite National Park CA

Berre, Philip, *Dir,* Hudson River Museum, Yonkers NY

Berreth, David, *Dir,* Mary Washington College, The Gari Melchers Estate & Memorial Gallery, Fredericksburg VA

Berrin, Kathleen, *Cur African, Oceania & the Americas,* Fine Arts Museums of San Francisco, M H de Young Memorial Museum and California Palace of the Legion of Honor, San Francisco CA

Berry, Betty, *Chmn,* Ouachita Baptist University, Dept of Art, Arkadelphia AR (S)

Berry, E Raymond, *Chmn,* Randolph-Macon College, Dept of the Arts, Ashland VA (S)

Berry, Ethan, *Printmaking,* Monserrat College of Art, Beverly MA (S)

Berry, Lloyd, *Pres,* North Central Washington Museum, Art Gallery, Wenatchee WA

Berry, Paul, *Librn,* Calvert Marine Museum, Library, Solomons MD

Bersson, Robert, *Assoc Prof,* James Madison University, Dept of Art, Harrisonburg VA (S)

Berthol, Jake, *Instr,* New York Studio School of Drawing, Painting and Sculpture, New York NY (S)

Bertlesman, Robert, *Operations Mgr,* Nassau County Museum of Fine Art, Roslyn NY

Bertoia, Roberto, *Assoc Prof,* Cornell University, Dept of Art, Ithaca NY (S)

Bertorelli, Eugene, *Pres,* Museo Italo Americano, San Francisco CA

Bertorelli, Eugene, *Pres,* Museo Italo Americano, Library, San Francisco CA

Bertos, R, *Assoc Prof,* McGill University, Department of Art History, Montreal PQ (S)

Besant, Larry X, *Dir,* Morehead State University, Camden-Carroll Library, Morehead KY

Besemer, Linda, *Dir,* Foundation for Art Resources, Los Angeles CA

Beslanovits, Denise, *Asst to Dir,* Lehigh University Art Galleries, Bethlehem PA

Besom, Bob, *Dir,* City of Springdale, Shiloh Museum, Springdale AR

Best, Jonathan, *Prof,* Wesleyan University, Art Dept, Middletown CT (S)

Best, Sherry L, *Instr,* Clarion University of Pennsylvania, Dept of Art, Clarion PA (S)

Betancourt, Philip, *Chmn Art History,* Temple University, Tyler School of Art, Philadelphia PA (S)

Beth, Dana, *Art & Architecture Librn,* Washington University, Art & Architecture Library, Saint Louis MO

Bethany, Adeline, *Chmn Dept,* Cabrini College, Dept of Fine Arts, Radnor PA (S)

Bethke, Karl, *Prof,* University of Minnesota, Minneapolis, Dept of Studio Art, Minneapolis MN (S)

Betsch, William, *Asst Prof,* University of Miami, Dept of Art & Art History, Coral Gables FL (S)

Betts, Katheleen, *Dir,* Society of the Cincinnati, Anderson House Museum, Washington DC

Betts, Thomas W, *Prof,* Lakeland Community College, Visual Arts Dept, Mentor OH (S)

Beveridge, Nancy, *Librn,* Litchfield Historical Society, Ingraham Memorial Research Library, Litchfield CT

Bevis, Teresa, *Adjunct Instr Art Educ,* Southwestern College, Art Dept, Winfield KS (S)

Bey, Amir, *Gallery Coordr,* BRONX RIVER ART CENTER, Gallery, Bronx NY

Beyer, Al, *Head Dept,* University of South Carolina at Aiken, Dept of Fine Arts, Aiken SC (S)

Beyer, John, *Pres,* New Mexico Art League, Gallery, Albuquerque NM

Bhargava, Sudeep, *Business Mgr,* Norman Mackenzie Art Gallery, Regina SK

Bhattacharya, Sunand, *Asst Prof,* Southern Illinois University, School of Art & Design, Carbondale IL (S)

Bialy, Mark G, *Prof,* Passaic County Community College, Division of Humanities, Paterson NJ (S)

Bianco, Joseph P, *Exec VPres,* Detroit Institute of Arts, Founders Society, Detroit MI

Biasiny-Rivera, Charles B, *Exec Dir,* En Foco, Inc, Bronx NY

Biblarz, Dora, *Assoc Dean Coll Development,* Arizona State University, Hayden Library, Tempe AZ

Bibler, Helen Ann, *Dir,* Ravalli County Museum, Hamilton MT

Bibler, Robert, *Instr,* Chemeketa Community College, Dept of Humanities & Communications, Salem OR (S)

Bice, Megan, *Pres,* Ontario Association of Art Galleries, Toronto ON

Bicher, John Willen, *Commissioner,* Art Commission of the City of New York, Associates of the Art Commission, Inc, New York NY

Bickford, Christopher P, *Dir,* Connecticut Historical Society, Hartford CT

Bickley, Steve, *Prof,* Virginia Polytechnic Institute & State University, Dept of Art & Art History, Blacksburg VA (S)

Bickley-Green, Cynthia, *Asst Prof,* University of Northern Iowa, Dept of Art, Cedar Falls IA (S)

Biddle, Mark, *Prof,* Weber State University, Dept of Visual Arts, Ogden UT (S)

Bidstrup, Wendy, *Dir,* Marion Art Center, Marion MA

Bied, Donald, *Asst Prof,* Daemen College, Art Dept, Amherst NY (S)

Biedenham, Jack, *Asst Prof,* Indian River Community College, Fine Arts Dept, Fort Pierce FL (S)

Biegon, Glenn, *Assoc Prof,* College of Associated Arts, Saint Paul MN (S)

Biel, Joseph, *Instr,* Southwest Texas State University, Dept of Art, San Marcos TX (S)

Bielski, Mark, *Chmn Interior Design,* Woodbury University, Dept of Graphic Design, Burbank CA (S)

Bier, Carol, *Cur Eastern Hemisphere,* Textile Museum, Washington DC

Bier, Martha, *Librn,* Polk Museum of Art, Penfield Library, Lakeland FL

Bierley, Annamary, *Chmn Fine Arts,* Sinclair Community College, Div of Performing & Fine Arts, Dayton OH (S)

Biers, Jane C, *Cur Ancient Art,* University of Missouri, Museum of Art and Archaeology, Columbia MO

Biers, William R, *Prof,* University of Missouri, Art History and Archaeology Dept, Columbia MO (S)

Biferie, Dan, *Prof,* Daytona Beach Community College, Dept of Fine Arts & Visual Arts, Daytona Beach FL (S)

Bigazzi, Anna, *Library Coordr,* University of Hartford, Anne Bunce Cheney Library, West Hartford CT

Bigazzi, Anna, *Library Asst,* University of Hartford, Anne Bunce Cheney Library, West Hartford CT

Bigelow, Gerald F, *Cur,* Bowdoin College, Peary-MacMillan Arctic Museum, Brunswick ME

Bigler, Steve, *Prof,* University of Northern Iowa, Dept of Art, Cedar Falls IA (S)

Bilger, Betsy, *Instr,* University of North Carolina at Charlotte, Dept of Visual Arts, Charlotte NC (S)

Bilick, Phyllis, *Asst Cur,* The Queens Museum of Art, Flushing NY

Bilicke, M Angelene, *Head Dept,* Ancilla College, Art Dept, Donaldson IN (S)

Billings, Linda, *Gallery Cur,* University of Minnesota, Paul Whitney Larson Gallery, Saint Paul MN

Billings, Loren, *Dir,* Museum of Holography - Chicago, Chicago IL

Billings, Loren, *Exec Dir,* Museum of Holography - Chicago, David Wender Library, Chicago IL

Billings, Robert, *Secy,* Museum of Holography - Chicago, Chicago IL

Billings, Robert H, *Chmn Humanities & Fine Arts,* Los Angeles Harbor College, Art Dept, Wilmington CA (S)

Billington, James H, *Librn,* Library of Congress, Prints and Photographs Division, Washington DC

Bilsky, Thelma, *Registrar,* Temple Beth Israel, Plotkin Juddica Museum, Phoenix AZ

Bilyeu, Faith, *Registrar,* San Joaquin Pioneer and Historical Society, The Haggin Museum, Stockton CA

Binai, Paul, *Cur,* Southern Alleghenies Museum of Art, Loretto PA

Binder, Donald J, *Dir & Cur,* Yankton County Historical Society, Dakota Territorial Museum, Yankton SD

Binkley, David A, *Assoc Cur Africa, Oceania & the Americas,* Nelson-Atkins Museum of Art, Kansas City MO

Binks, Ronald, *Prof,* University of Texas at San Antonio, Division of Art & Architecture, San Antonio TX (S)

Bippes, Bill, *Division Dir Music Arts,* Spring Arbor College, Art Dept, Spring Arbor MI (S)

Birch, Emile, *Lectr,* New England College, Art & Art History, Henniker NH (S)

Birch, James A, *Cur Education,* Cleveland Museum of Art, Cleveland OH

Bird, Donal, *Dean,* Howard Payne University, Dept of Art, Brownwood TX (S)

Bird, Kevin, *Technician,* Alberta College of Art, Illingworth Kerr Gallery, Calgary AB

Bird, Mary Alice, *Development Dir,* William A Farnsworth Library and Art Museum, Rockland ME

Bird, Richard, *Instr,* Ricks College, Dept of Art, Rexburg ID (S)

Bird, Richard, *Assoc Prof,* Chadron State College, Dept of Art, Speech & Theatre, Chadron NE (S)

Birkett, Barbara, *Prof,* Rochester Institute of Technology, School of Printing, Rochester NY (S)

Birkett, William H, *Assoc Prof,* Rochester Institute of Technology, School of Printing, Rochester NY (S)

Birmingham, Doris A, *Prof,* New England College, Art & Art History, Henniker NH (S)

Birstins, Inese, *Gallery Admin,* Calgary Contemporary Arts Society, Triangle Gallery of Visual Arts, Calgary AB

Birth, Helga, *Librn,* Rochester Institute of Technology, Technical & Education Center of the Graphic Arts, Rochester NY

Bisaillon, Blaise, *Dir,* Forbes Library, Northampton MA

Bisaillon, Ed, *Dir,* Hastings Museum, Hastings NE

Bischof, Susan Kirkpatrick, *Exec Dir,* Santa Cruz Art League, Inc, Santa Cruz CA

Bischoff, William L, *Cur Coin Collection,* Newark Museum Association, The Newark Museum, Newark NJ

Bishop, Carol, *Div Chmn Fine & Applied Art,* Solano Community College, Division of Fine & Applied Art, Suisun City CA (S)

Bishop, Christine, *Dir,* Carnegie Art Center, Walla Walla WA

Bishop, Clarence M, *Regent,* Mount Vernon Ladies' Association of the Union, Mount Vernon VA

Bishop, Jerold, *Assoc Prof Graphic Illustration,* University of Arizona, Dept of Art, Tucson AZ (S)

Bishop, John, *Pres Board of Dir,* Santa Barbara Contemporary Arts Forum, Santa Barbara CA

Bishop, Linda, *Treas,* Prince George Art Gallery, Prince George BC

Bishop, Michael, *Dir,* California State University, Chico, University Art Gallery, Chico CA

Bishop, Michael, *Instr,* California State University, Chico, Art Dept, Chico CA (S)

Bishop, Richard, *Treasurer,* The Greenwich Art Society Inc, Greenwich CT

Bishop, Samuel, *Assoc Prof,* Northeastern University, Dept of Art & Architecture, Boston MA (S)

Bishop, Steve, *Assoc Prof,* Murray State University, Art Dept, Murray KY (S)

Bissaccia, Giusseppe, *Cur of Manuscripts,* Boston Public Library, Rare Book & Manuscripts Dept, Boston MA

Bissell, R Ward, *Prof,* University of Michigan, Ann Arbor, Dept of History of Art, Ann Arbor MI (S)

Bissonnette, Daniel, *Dir,* Musee Regional de Vaudreuil-Soulanges, Vaudreuil PQ

Bittain, Patsy, *Admin Asst,* Art Museum of Southeast Texas, Beaumont TX

Bitz, Gwen, *Registrar,* Walker Art Center, Minneapolis MN

Bitzan, Robert, *Public Information & Special Events,* University of Minnesota, University Art Museum, Minneapolis MN

Bizzarro, Tina Walduier, *Chmn Div,* Rosemont College, Division of the Arts, Rosemont PA (S)

Bjelajac, David, *Asst Prof,* George Washington University, Dept of Art, Washington DC (S)

Black, Bonnie, *Asst Prof,* Arkansas State University, Dept of Art, Jonesboro AR (S)

Black, Craig C, *Dir,* Natural History Museum of Los Angeles County, Los Angeles CA

Black, Debbie, *Asst to Dir,* Greater Lafayette Museum of Art, Lafayette IN

Black, Jack, *Board Chmn & Cur,* Fayette Art Museum, Fayette AL

Black, James R, *Prof,* Schoolcraft College, Dept of Art and Design, Livonia MI (S)

Black, Larry, *Dir,* Public Library of Columbus and Franklin County, Columbus Metropolitan Library, Columbus OH

Black, Steve, *Instr,* Vincennes University Junior College, Art Dept, Vincennes IN (S)

Blackaby, Anita D, *Dir,* State Museum of Pennsylvania, Harrisburg PA

Blackaby, Anita D, *Dir,* State Museum of Pennsylvania, Pennsylvania Historical & Museum Commission, Harrisburg PA

Blackbeard, Bill, *Dir,* San Francisco Academy of Comic Art, Library, San Francisco CA

Blackburn, Robert, *Dir,* Printmaking Workshop, New York NY

Blackburn, Selma, *Instr,* The Arkansas Arts Center, Museum School, Little Rock AR (S)

Blackburn Wright, Rachael, *Registrar,* Fort Worth Art Association, Modern Art Museum of Fort Worth, Fort Worth TX

Blackley, Terrence, *Chmn Division Fine Arts,* Fullerton College, Division of Fine Arts, Fullerton CA (S)

Blackman, Pat, *Librn,* Marion Koogler McNay Art Museum, Reference Library, San Antonio TX

Blackman, Patricia, *Acting Librn,* Marion Koogler McNay Art Museum, San Antonio TX

Blackmon, Mary Collins, *Cur,* Elisabet Ney Museum, Austin TX

Blackmun, Barbara, *Instr,* San Diego Mesa College, Fine Arts Dept, San Diego CA (S)

Blackstone, Mary, *Dean Faculty Fine Arts,* University of Regina, Dept of Art Education, Regina SK (S)

Blackwelder, Lynda, *Dir Public Programs,* Indiana State Museum, Indianapolis IN

Blackwell, Henry B, *Pres,* Hoosier Salon Patrons Association, Hoosier Salon Art Gallery, Indianapolis IN

Blackwell, J V, *Prof Emeritus,* University of Nebraska at Omaha, Dept of Art, Omaha NE (S)

Blackwood, C Roy, *Chmn,* Southeastern Louisiana University, Dept of Visual Arts, Hammond LA (S)

Blackwood, Nancy, *Chmn,* Northeastern Oklahoma A & M College, Art Dept, Miami OK (S)

Blade, Timothy T, *Cur Decorative Arts,* University of Minnesota, Goldstein Gallery, Saint Paul MN

Blades, Margaret Bleecker, *Museum Cur,* Chester County Historical Society, West Chester PA

Bladon, Patty, *Interim Dir,* Memphis Brooks Museum of Art, Memphis TN

Blain, Brad, *Dir,* Kitchener-Waterloo Art Gallery, Kitchener ON

Blain, Brad, *Dir,* Kitchener-Waterloo Art Gallery, Eleanor Calvert Memorial Library, Kitchener ON

Blain, Sandra J, *Dir,* Arrowmont School of Arts and Crafts, Gatlinburg TN (S)

Blair, Brent, *Instr,* Gettysburg College, Dept of Art, Gettysburg PA (S)

Blair, Carl, *Instr,* Bob Jones University, School of Fine Arts, Greenville SC (S)

Blair, Edward, *Pres,* The Art Institute of Chicago, Print and Drawing Dept, Chicago IL

Blair, Laurel G, *Cur,* Blair Museum of Lithophanes and Carved Waxes, Toledo OH

Blair, Linda, *Mem Coordr,* San Diego Museum of Art, San Diego CA

Blair, Robert, *Chmn,* St Lawrence College, Dept of Visual & Creative Arts, Cornwall ON (S)

Blair, Terri, *Instr,* Grayson County College, Art Dept, Denison TX (S)

Blaisdell, Phillip, *Instr,* Joe Kubert School of Cartoon & Graphic Art, Inc, Dover NJ (S)

Blake, Brooke, *Chmn,* The American Federation of Arts, New York NY

Blake, Daniel, *Dir,* University of Illinois, Museum of Natural History, Champaign IL

Blake, Hortense, *Dir,* Clinton Art Association Gallery, Clinton IA

Blake, Jeff, *Lectr,* Saint Joseph's University, Dept of Fine & Performing Arts, Philadelphia PA (S)

Blake, Jody, *Prof,* Bucknell University, Dept of Art, Lewisburg PA (S)

Blakely, Edward, *Chmn City & Regional Planning,* University of California, Berkeley, College of Environmental Design, Berkeley CA (S)

Blakely, George C, *Prof,* Florida State University, Art Dept, Tallahassee FL (S)

Blakely, Glen, *Prof,* Dixie College, Art Dept, Saint George UT (S)

Blanchette, Antoine, *VPres,* Musee d'Art de Joliette, Joliette PQ

Bland, Carol, *Pres,* Brown County Art Gallery Association Inc, Nashville IN

Bland, Joe, *Dir Operations,* Owensboro Museum of Fine Art, Owensboro KY

Blandford, Robert, *Assoc Dir,* Children's Museum of Manhattan, New York NY

Blanelli, Stephanie, *Acting Chmn,* Brevard College, Division of Fine Arts, Brevard NC (S)

Blank, Peter, *Librn,* The Metropolitan Museum of Art, Robert Goldwater Library, New York NY

Blankenship, Tiska, *Assoc Cur,* University of New Mexico, Jonson Library, Albuquerque NM

Blankenshop, Tiska, *Assoc Cur,* University of New Mexico, Jonson Gallery, Albuquerque NM

Blankinship, Sue, *Museum Store Mgr,* University of Tampa, Henry B Plant Museum, Tampa FL

Blanton, Jackson L, *Cur & Asst VPres,* Federal Reserve Bank of Richmond, Richmond VA

Blasdel, Gregg, *Asst Prof,* St Michael's College, Fine Arts Dept, Colchester VT (S)

Blatti, Jo, *Dir,* Stowe-Day Foundation, Harriet Beecher Stowe House, Hartford CT

Blatti, Jo, *Dir,* Stowe-Day Foundation, Library, Hartford CT

Blaugher, Kurt E, *Prof,* Mount Saint Mary's College, Visual & Performing Arts Dept, Emmitsburg MD (S)

Blaugrund, Annette, *Sr Cur,* New York Historical Society, New York NY

Blazier, Wendy M, *Dir,* Art And Culture Center Of Hollywood, Hollywood FL

Blazina, Vesna, *Chef de Bibliotheque,* Universite de Montreal, Bibliotheque d'Amenagement, Montreal PQ

Blebin, Margo, *Lectr,* Davis and Elkins College, Dept of Art, Elkins WV (S)

Bleck, Carol, *Business Mgr,* Tucson Museum of Art, Tucson AZ

Bleek-Byrne, Gabrielle, *Asst Prof,* Salve Regina College, Art Dept, Newport RI (S)

Bleha, Bernie, *Chmn & Instr,* Green River Community College, Art Dept, Auburn WA (S)

Bleicher, Steven, *Asst Dean,* Fashion Institute of Technology, Art & Design Division, New York NY (S)

Bleifeld, Stanley, *Pres,* National Sculpture Society, New York NY

Blevins, Tedd, *Instr,* Virginia Intermont College, Fine Arts Division, Bristol VA (S)

Blier, Suzanne Preston, *Dir Grad Studies,* Columbia University, Dept of Art History and Archaeology, New York NY (S)

Blinderman, Barry, *Dir,* Illinois State University, University Galleries, Normal IL

Blinn, Gene, *Sr Librn in Charge,* Oakland Public Library, Art, Music & Recreation Section, Oakland CA

Blisard, Herb, *Faculty,* Yakima Valley Community College, Art Dept, Yakima WA (S)

Bliss, Harry E, *Assoc Prof,* Palomar Community College, Art Dept, San Marcos CA (S)

Bliss, Jerry, *Adj Asst Prof,* Colby-Sawyer College, Dept of Fine & Performing Arts, New London NH (S)

Blizard, William, *Chmn Dept,* Springfield College, Dept of Visual and Performing Arts, Springfield MA (S)

Bloch, Kathleen, *Admin Librn,* Spertus Museum, Asher Library, Chicago IL

Blochowiak, Mary, *Publications,* Oklahoma Historical Society, State Museum of History, Oklahoma City OK

Block, Diana, *Gallery Dir,* University of North Texas, University Art Gallery, Denton TX

Block, Holly, *Exec Dir,* Art in General, New York NY

Block, Jane, *Librn,* University of Illinois, Ricker Library of Architecture and Art, Champaign IL

Block, Laura, *Pres,* Pastel Society of Oregon, Roseburg OR

Block, Philip, *Dir Educ,* International Center of Photography, New York NY

Blocton, Lula, *Asst Prof,* Eastern Connecticut State University, Fine Arts Dept, Willimantic CT (S)

Bloedhorn, Gene, *Cur,* University of Wisconsin-Stout, J Furlong Gallery, Menomonie WI

Bloedorn, Gene, *Prof,* University of Wisconsin-Stout, Dept of Art & Design, Menomonie WI (S)

Bloedorn, Glen, *Head Dept,* University of Wisconsin-Stout, Dept of Art & Design, Menomonie WI (S)

Blondin, Bruce, *Instr,* Solano Community College, Division of Fine & Applied Art, Suisun City CA (S)

Bloom, Arthur W, *Dean,* Kutztown University, College of Visual & Performing Arts, Kutztown PA (S)

Bloom, Billie, *Adminr,* Missoula Museum of the Arts, Missoula MT

Bloom, Ken, *Cur Exhib,* Spirit Square Center for the Arts, Charlotte NC

Bloom, Sharon, *Chmn,* West Shore Community College, Division of Humanities and Fine Arts, Scottville MI (S)

Bloom, Stephen, *Library Dir,* University of the Arts, Albert M Greenfield Library, Philadelphia PA

Bloom, Sue, *Asst Prof,* Western Maryland College, Art Dept, Westminster MD (S)

Bloomberg, Louise, *Cur of Slides & Art History,* University of Massachusetts, Amherst, Dorothy W Perkins Slide Library, Amherst MA

Bloomberg, Sally, *Shop Mgr,* Farmington Valley Arts Center, Avon CT

Bloomer, Jerry M, *Secy of the Board,* R W Norton Art Gallery, Shreveport LA

Bloomer, Jerry M, *Librn,* R W Norton Art Gallery, Library, Shreveport LA

Bloomfield, Debra, *Instr,* Solano Community College, Division of Fine & Applied Art, Suisun City CA (S)

Blore, Bill, *Vol Coordr,* Craigdarroch Castle Historical Museum Society, Victoria BC

Blosser, John, *Head Dept,* Hesston College, Hesston KS (S)

Blouin, Joy, *Cur,* University of Michigan, Slide and Photograph Collection, Ann Arbor MI

Blount, Alice, *Cur Earth Sciences,* Newark Museum Association, The Newark Museum, Newark NJ

Blount Radford, Lori, *Development Dir,* Artists Space, New York NY ·

Blovits, Larry, *Prof,* Aquinas College, Art Dept, Grand Rapids MI (S)

Blum, Zevi, *Assoc Prof,* Cornell University, Dept of Art, Ithaca NY (S)

Blume, Peter F, *Dir,* Allentown Art Museum, Allentown PA

Blumenthal, Arthur R, *Dir,* Rollins College, George D and Harriet W Cornell Fine Arts Museum, Winter Park FL

Blumenthal, Elizabeth, *Asst Prof,* Johns Hopkins University, School of Medicine, Dept of Art as Applied to Medicine, Baltimore MD (S)

Blundell, Harry, *Dir of Theatre,* Council of Ozark Artists and Craftsmen, Inc, Arts Center of the Ozarks Gallery, Springdale AR

Blundell, Kathi, *Dir,* Council of Ozark Artists and Craftsmen, Inc, Arts Center of the Ozarks Gallery, Springdale AR

Bluthardt, Valerie C, *Registrar & Prog Coordr,* San Angelo Museum of Fine Arts, San Angelo TX

Bob, Murray L, *Dir,* James Prendergast Library Association, Jamestown NY

Bober, Phyllis B, *Prof,* Bryn Mawr College, Dept of the History of Art, Bryn Mawr PA (S)

Bobick, Bruce, *Chmn,* West Georgia College, Art Dept, Carrollton GA (S)

Bobier, David, *Assoc Prof,* Mount Allison University, Fine Arts Dept, Sackville NB (S)

Bock, Catherine, *Prof,* School of the Art Institute of Chicago, Chicago IL (S)

Bockrath, Mark F, *Paintings Conservator,* Pennsylvania Academy of the Fine Arts, Galleries, Philadelphia PA

Bockwoldt, Michael, *VPres,* House of Roses, Senator Wilson Home, Deadwood SD

Bocz, George, *Assoc Prof,* Florida State University, Art Dept, Tallahassee FL (S)

Bodem, Dennis R, *Dir,* Jesse Besser Museum, Alpena MI

Bodem, Dennis R, *Dir,* Jesse Besser Museum, Philip M Park Library, Alpena MI

Bodily, Vince, *Instr,* Ricks College, Dept of Art, Rexburg ID (S)

Bodine, Paul, *Assoc Prof,* Eastern Illinois University, Art Dept, Charleston IL (S)

Bodnaruk, V, *Chmn Art,* City Colleges of Chicago, Daley College, Chicago IL (S)

Boe, Michael, *Asst Librn,* Minneapolis Society of Fine Arts, Art Reference Library, Minneapolis MN

Boehm, Louise Kirtland, *Assoc Prof,* Palomar Community College, Art Dept, San Marcos CA (S)

Boehme, Sarah, *Cur Whitney Gallery,* Buffalo Bill Memorial Association, Buffalo Bill Historical Center, Cody WY

Boelhauer, Gary, *Chmn Arts & Humanities,* Marian College, Art Dept, Fond Du Lac WI (S)

Boelts, Jackson, *Assoc Prof Graphic Design-Illustration,* University of Arizona, Dept of Art, Tucson AZ (S)

Boemer, Cathy, *Asst to Dir,* Museum of Photographic Arts, Balboa Park CA

Boen, Sandra, *Exec Dir,* Koochiching County Historical Society Museum, International Falls MN

Boetcher, Chris, *Cur Arts,* Randall Museum Junior Museum, San Francisco CA

Boettcher, Nancee, *Business Mgr,* Paine Art Center and Arboretum, Oshkosh WI

Bogart, Michele H, *Assoc Prof,* State University of New York at Stony Brook, Art Dept, Stony Brook NY (S)

Bogart, Michele H, *Asst Prof,* State University of New York at Stony Brook, Art Dept, Stony Brook NY (S)

Bogdanov, Branka, *Dir & Video Producer,* Institute of Contemporary Art, Boston MA

Bogdanovitch, George, *Prof,* Denison University, Dept of Art, Granville OH (S)

Boggess, Lynn, *Prof,* Fairmont State College, Div of Fine Arts, Fairmont WV (S)

Boggs, David, *Chmn,* Concordia College, Art Dept, Moorhead MN (S)

Bogin, M, *Chmn,* Hobart and William Smith Colleges, Art Dept, Geneva NY (S)

Bogle, Jon Raven, *Prof,* Lycoming College, Art Dept, Williamsport PA (S)

Bogue, Laura, *Instr,* Avila College, Art Division, Dept of Performing and Visual Art, Kansas City MO (S)

Bogusky, Alf, *Dir,* Art Gallery of Windsor, Windsor ON

Bogusky, Alf, *Exec Dir,* Edmonton Art Gallery, Edmonton AB

Bogusky, Alf, *Dir,* Edmonton Art Gallery, Library, Edmonton AB

Bohan, Ruth, *Asst Prof,* University of Missouri-Saint Louis, Art Dept, Saint Louis MO (S)

Bohanon, Gloria, *Prof,* Los Angeles City College, Dept of Art, Los Angeles CA (S)

Bohen, Barbara E, *Dir,* University of Illinois, World Heritage Museum, Champaign IL

Bohler, Matthew, *Asst Prof,* Shorter College, Art Dept, Rome GA (S)

Bohn, Babette, *Prof,* Texas Christian University, Art & Art History Dept, Fort Worth TX (S)

Bohnert, Thomas, *Coordr,* Charles Stewart Mott Community College, Art Area, School of Arts & Humanities, Flint MI (S)

Bohrer, Fred, *Assoc Prof,* Hood College, Dept of Art, Frederick MD (S)

Boisture, Richard, *Pres Board Trustees,* Zigler Museum, Jennings LA

Boisvert, Tom, *Instr,* Greenfield Community College, Art, Graphic Design & Media Communication Dept, Greenfield MA (S)

Boker, Hans, *Chmn,* McGill University, Department of Art History, Montreal PQ (S)

Bokovec, Emily, *Coordr,* Kent State University, Stark Campus, School of Art, Canton OH (S)

Boland, Lucy E, *Dir,* Danbury Scott-Fanton Museum and Historical Society, Inc, Danbury CT

Boland, Lucy E, *Dir & Cur,* Danbury Scott-Fanton Museum and Historical Society, Inc, Library, Danbury CT

Bolden, Joyce, *Chmn,* Alcorn State University, Dept of Fine Arts, Lorman MS (S)

Bolding, Gary, *Dir,* Stetson University, Duncan Gallery of Art, De Land FL

Boles, Pat, *Chairperson Dept Art,* Monterey Peninsula College, Art Dept, Monterey CA (S)

Bolge, George S, *Exec Dir,* New Jersey Center for Visual Arts, Summit NJ

Bolger, Doreen, *Cur of Painting & Sculpture,* Amon Carter Museum, Fort Worth TX

Bolger, Stuart B, *Dir,* Genesee Country Museum, John L Wehle Gallery of Sporting Art, Mumford NY

Bolis, Valda, *Librn,* The Art Institute of Boston, Library, Boston MA

Bolles, Martha, *Instr,* Mount Mary College, Art Dept, Milwaukee WI (S)

Bolling, Jennie, *Gallery Adminr,* University of Alabama at Huntsville, Gallery of Art, Huntsville AL

Bollinger, Michelle, *Asst Prof,* University of Evansville, Art Dept, Evansville IN (S)

Bolls, Debbie, *Deputy Dir,* Museums of Abilene, Inc, Abilene TX

Bolster, Donna, *Art Educator,* Winnipeg Art Gallery, Winnipeg MB

Bolton, Bruce D, *Dir,* David M Stewart Museum, Montreal PQ

Bolton, Larry, *Treas,* Hutchinson Art Association Gallery, Hutchinson KS

Bolton, Richard, *Chmn Dept,* University of California, Santa Barbara, Dept of Art Studio, Santa Barbara CA (S)

Bona, Elvia, *Gallery Asst,* Colgate University, Picker Art Gallery, Hamilton NY

Bonadies, Tony, *Dir,* Southern Connecticut State University, Art Gallery, New Haven CT

Bond, Art, *Cur,* John C Calhoun State Community College, Art Gallery, Decatur AL

Bond, Arthur, *Div Chair,* John C Calhoun State Community College, Division of Fine Arts, Decatur AL (S)

Bond, Gordon C, *Dean,* Auburn University, Dept of Art, Auburn AL (S)

Bond, Hallie, *Cur,* Adirondack Historical Association, Adirondack Museum, Blue Mountain Lake NY

Bond, Kener E, *Prof,* Rochester Institute of Technology, School of Art and Design, Rochester NY (S)

Bond, Randall, *Fine Arts Librn,* Syracuse University, Library, Syracuse NY

Bonifay, William, *Instructor,* Milwaukee Area Technical College, Graphic Arts Dept, Milwaukee WI (S)

Bonjorni, Mary, *Instr,* University of Nevada, Las Vegas, Dept of Art, Las Vegas NV (S)

Bonnellgal, Bill, *Pres,* Color Association of The US, New York NY

Bonnelly, Claude, *Dir General Library System,* L'Universite Laval, Library, Quebec PQ

Bonner, Angela, *Deputy Dir,* California Afro-American Museum, Los Angeles CA

Bonner, Bethany, *Instr,* Ocean City Art Center, Ocean City NJ (S)

Bonner, Evelyn K, *Dir Library Services,* Sheldon Jackson Museum, Stratton Library, Sitka AK

Bonner-Ganter, Deanna, *Librn,* Maine Photographic Workshops, Workshop Library, Rockport ME

Bonzelaar, Helen, *Prof,* Calvin College, Art Dept, Grand Rapids MI (S)

Booher, Margaret, *Interim Dir,* InterCultura, Inc, Fort Worth TX

Book, Michael, *Assoc Prof,* Louisiana State University, School of Art, Baton Rouge LA (S)

Booker, Robert J, *Chief Exec Officer,* Beck Cultural Exchange Center, Knoxville TN

Booko, Sharon, *Chmn Art Dept,* Barat College, Dept of Art, Lake Forest IL (S)

Boon, Susan, *Business Mgr,* Southeastern Center for Contemporary Art, Winston-Salem NC

Boone, Charles, *Asst Prof,* College of DuPage, Humanities Division, Glen Ellyn IL (S)

Boone, Edward J, *Archivist,* MacArthur Memorial, Library & Archives, Norfolk VA

Boone-Bradley, Jeanne, *Dir,* Virginia Commonwealth University, School of The Arts Library, Richmond VA

Boorsch, Suzanne, *Instr,* Sarah Lawrence College, Dept of Art History, Bronxville NY (S)

Booth, David W, *Instr,* Universite de Montreal, Dept of Art History, Montreal PQ (S)

Booth, Donald, *Chmn,* Hofstra University, Department of Fine Arts, Hempstead NY (S)

Booth, Michael, *Chmn,* Blue Mountain Community College, Fine Arts Dept, Pendleton OR (S)

Booth, Robert, *Chmn,* State University College, Dept of Art, Fredonia NY (S)

Boothe, Berresford, *Assoc Prof,* Lehigh University, Dept of Art and Architecture, Bethlehem PA (S)

Bopp, Emery, *Chmn Division of Art,* Bob Jones University, School of Fine Arts, Greenville SC (S)

Boppel, Todd, *Prof,* University of Wisconsin-Stout, Dept of Art & Design, Menomonie WI (S)

Borchardt, Susan, *Cur,* Gunston Hall Plantation, Library, Lorton VA

Borchert, Gary, *Head Dept,* Oklahoma State University, Graphic Arts Dept, Okmulgee OK (S)

Borchuck, F, *Dir,* East Tennessee State University, C C Sherrod Library, Johnson City TN

Borcoman, James, *Cur Photography Coll,* National Gallery of Canada, Ottawa ON

Bordeau, Bill, *Prof,* Marymount Manhattan College, Fine & Performing Arts Dept, New York NY (S)

Bordelon, Kathleen, *Exhib Designer,* Norfolk Historical Society Inc, Museum, Norfolk CT

Borden, Donald, *Archives,* Peter and Catharine Whyte Foundation, Whyte Museum of the Canadian Rockies, Banff AB

Borden, Donald, *Archives,* Peter and Catharine Whyte Foundation, Gallery Library, Banff AB

Borden, Tamika, *Dir,* Cambria Historical Society, New Providence NJ

Bordo, Robert, *Instr,* New York Studio School of Drawing, Painting and Sculpture, New York NY (S)

Borge, John, *Instr,* Concordia College, Art Dept, Moorhead MN (S)

Borge, John, *Instr,* Concordia College, Art Dept, Moorhead MN (S)

Borge, Rich, *Asst Prof,* Western Carolina University, Dept of Art, Cullowhee NC (S)

Borges, Richard, *Dir,* Old York Historical Society, York ME

Borges, Richard, *Exec Dir,* Old York Historical Society, Jefferds Tavern, York ME

Borges, Richard, *Exec Dir,* Old York Historical Society, John Hancock Warehouse, York ME

Borges, Richard, *Exec Dir,* Old York Historical Society, Gaol Museum, York ME

Borgeson, Diane, *Treas,* Fairbanks Arts Association, Fairbanks AK

Borg-Russell, Betty, *Instr,* The Arkansas Arts Center, Museum School, Little Rock AR (S)

Borgwardt, Barbara, *Instr,* Mount Mary College, Art Dept, Milwaukee WI (S)

Born, Richard, *Dir,* University of Chicago, David and Alfred Smart Museum of Art, Chicago IL

Bornarth, Philip W, *Prof,* Rochester Institute of Technology, School of Art and Design, Rochester NY (S)

Bornhuetter, Robert, *Grad Coordr,* Northern Illinois University, School of Art, De Kalb IL (S)

Bornstein, Erica, *Prog Dir,* Beyond Baroque Foundation, Beyond Baroque Literary/Arts Center, Venice CA

Borowic, Andrew, *Dir,* University of Akron, University Galleries, Akron OH

Borowiec, Andrew, *Dept Head,* University of Akron, School of Art, Akron OH (S)

Borowski, Elena, *Historical Cur,* Canajoharie Art Gallery, Canajoharie NY

Borowski, Elena, *Historical Cur,* Canajoharie Art Gallery, Library, Canajoharie NY

Borrowdule-Cox, Deborah, *Cur Educ,* Santa Barbara Museum of Art, Santa Barbara CA

Borrup, Tom, *Exec Dir,* Intermedia Arts Minnesota, Minneapolis MN

Borst, Kim, *Lectr,* University of Wisconsin-Superior, Programs in the Visual Arts, Superior WI (S)

Borstein, Elena, *Coordr Fine Arts,* York College of the City University of New York, Fine and Performing Arts, Jamaica NY (S)

Bosca, David, *Dir,* American Council for the Arts, Library, New York NY

Bosco, Bob, *Instr,* Creighton University, Fine and Performing Arts Dept, Omaha NE (S)

Bose, Arvn, *Assoc Prof,* Herbert H Lehman College, Art Dept, Bronx NY (S)

Boshart, Jeff, *Asst Prof,* Eastern Illinois University, Art Dept, Charleston IL (S)

Boshart, Jon D, *Chmn,* Saint Peter's College, Fine Arts Dept, Jersey City NJ (S)

Bosley, Edward, *Dir,* Univ of Southern California, Greene & Greene Library of the Arts & Crafts Movement, San Marino CA

Bossert, Carol, *Dir Science Dept & Cur Biology,* Newark Museum Association, The Newark Museum, Newark NJ

Bostick, Claudia, *Performing Arts Dir,* Jamaica Arts Center, Jamaica NY

Boterf, C A, *Prof,* Rice University, Dept of Art and Art History, Houston TX (S)

Botkin, John, *Prof,* Delaware County Community College, Communications and Humanities House, Media PA (S)

Bott, John, *Assoc Prof,* Colby-Sawyer College, Dept of Fine & Performing Arts, New London NH (S)

Bottoms, Bill, *Pres,* Colorado Institute of Art, Denver CO (S)

Botwinick, Michael, *Dir,* Newport Harbor Art Museum, Newport Beach CA

Bouc, Rod, *Asst Registrar,* Columbus Museum of Art, Columbus OH

Bouchard, Karen, *Assoc Cur,* Brown University, Art Slide Library, Providence RI

Boudreau, Anne, *Dir,* East Baton Rouge Parks & Recreation Commission, Baton Rouge Gallery Inc, Baton Rouge LA

Bouille, Alvine, *Dir Museum,* Musee des Augustines de l'Hotel Dieu of Quebec, Quebec PQ

Bouille, Alvine, *Dir of Museum,* Musee des Augustines de l'Hotel Dieu of Quebec, Library, Quebec PQ

Bouillon, Tony, *Instr,* Saint Francis College, Art Dept, Fort Wayne IN (S)

Bourcier, Claudette, *Gift Shop Mgr,* Cascade County Historical Society, Cascade County Historical Museum & Archives, Great Falls MT

Bourgeois, Arthur P, *Div Chmn,* Governors State University, College of Arts & Science, Art Dept, University Park IL (S)

Bourgoin, Colette, *Dir & Cur,* Galerie Restigouche Gallery, Campbellton NB

Bourke, Patrick, *Dean,* Saint Clair County Community College, Art Dept, Port Huron MI (S)

Bourque, Paul, *Technician,* Galerie d'art de l'Universite de Moncton, Moncton NB

Bous, Klaus, *Managing Dir,* SIAS International Art Society, Sherwood Park AB

Bousson, Connie, *Gallery Dir,* Huntsville Art League and Museum Association Inc, Huntsville AL

Bouyack, Kay, *Co-Dir,* Southern Ohio Museum Corporation, Southern Ohio Museum & Cultural Center, Portsmouth OH

Bova, Joe, *Dir,* Ohio University, Seigfred Gallery, Athens OH

Bovey, John A, *Dir,* British Columbia Archives & Records Service, Victoria BC

Bovey, Patricia A, *Dir,* Art Gallery of Greater Victoria, Victoria BC

Bowden, Billy, *Exec Dir,* Oklahoma Center for Science and Art, Kirkpatrick Center, Oklahoma City OK

Bowen, Amanda W, *Librn,* Smith College, Hillyer Art Library, Northampton MA

Bowen, Jean, *Music Cur,* The New York Public Library, Shelby Cullom Davis Museum, New York NY

Bowen, Nancy, *Instr,* Sarah Lawrence College, Dept of Art History, Bronxville NY (S)

Bowen, Paul, *Instr,* Truro Center for the Arts at Castle Hill, Inc, Truro MA (S)

Bowen, Virginia, *Pres,* Bowne House Historical Society, Flushing NY

Bowenkamp, Lynne, *Registrar,* University of Georgia, Georgia Museum of Art, Athens GA

Bower, Bob, *Div Chmn,* Southwestern Oregon Community College, Visual Arts Dept, Coos Bay OR (S)

Bower, Gary, *Prof,* Antioch College, Visual Arts Institute, Yellow Springs OH (S)

Bower, Gerald, *Prof,* Louisiana State University, School of Art, Baton Rouge LA (S)

Bower, Peter, *Provincial Archivist,* Provincial Archives of Manitoba, Winnipeg MB

Bower, Sharon, *Asst Prof,* Wilkes University, Dept of Art, Wilkes-Barre PA (S)

Bowers, Sally, *Chief Adminr,* The Robert McLaughlin Gallery, Oshawa ON

Bowes, Jerry, *Chair Env Design,* Ontario College of Art, Toronto ON (S)

Bowie, Lucille, *Librn,* Southern University, Art and Architecture Library, Baton Rouge LA

Bowie, Mary Ann, *Registrar,* Rollins College, George D and Harriet W Cornell Fine Arts Museum, Winter Park FL

Bowles, Bryan, *Dir,* Polynesian Cultural Center, Laie HI

Bowles, Sandra, *Advertising Dir,* Handweavers Guild of America, Bloomfield CT

Bowley, Michael, *Instr,* Marylhurst College, Art Dept, Marylhurst OR (S)

Bowlt, John, *Adjunct Prof,* University of Southern California, School of Fine Arts, Los Angeles CA (S)

Bowman, Brice, *Instr,* Solano Community College, Division of Fine & Applied Art, Suisun City CA (S)

Bowman, John, *Dept Chmn,* Prairie State College, Art Dept, Chicago Heights IL (S)

Bowman, Karmien, *Assoc Prof,* Tarrant County Junior College, Art Dept, Northeast Campus, Hurst TX (S)

Bowman, Leah, *Prof,* School of the Art Institute of Chicago, Chicago IL (S)

Bowman, Leslie, *Adjunct Asst Prof,* University of Southern California, School of Fine Arts, Los Angeles CA (S)

Bowman, Roger, *Assoc Prof,* University of Central Arkansas, Art Dept, Conway AR (S)

Bowman, Russell, *Dir,* Milwaukee Art Museum, Milwaukee WI

Bowman, S Curtis, *Exhib Designer,* Calvert Marine Museum, Solomons MD

Bowman, Stanley J, *Assoc Prof,* Cornell University, Dept of Art, Ithaca NY (S)

Bowsher, Linda, *Pres,* Louisiana State University, Museum of Arts, Baton Rouge LA

Boyagian, E, *Pres,* Rodman Hall Arts Centre, Saint Catharines ON

Boyce, Margaret, *Treas,* Shoreline Historical Museum, Seattle WA

Boyce, Robert, *Dir,* Berea College, Doris Ulmann Galleries, Berea KY

Boyce, Robert, *Assoc Prof,* Berea College, Art Dept, Berea KY (S)

Boyd, Ann, *Co-Dir,* Roy Boyd Gallery, Chicago IL

Boyd, Karen W, *Prof,* Murray State University, Art Dept, Murray KY (S)

Boyd, Patti, *Marketing Dir,* Wildlife of the American West Art Museum, Jackson WY

Boyd, Roy, *Co-Dir,* Roy Boyd Gallery, Chicago IL

Boyd, Willard L, *Pres,* Field Museum of Natural History, Chicago IL

Boyd, William L, *Assoc Prof,* Alabama A & M University, Art and Art Education, Normal AL (S)

Boyer, Barbara, *Acting Chmn,* California State University, Los Angeles, Art Dept, Los Angeles CA (S)

Boyer, Irene, *Cur Asst Decorative Art,* Illinois State Museum, Illinois Art Gallery & Lockport Gallery, Springfield IL

Boyer, John, *Executive Dir,* Mark Twain Memorial, Hartford CT

Boyer, John, *Exec Dir,* Mark Twain Memorial, Research Library, Hartford CT

Boyer, Lise, *Public Relations,* Musee du Quebec, Quebec PQ

Boyer, Marietta P, *Librn,* Pennsylvania Academy of the Fine Arts, Library, Philadelphia PA

Boyer, Penny, *Asst Dir,* National Association of Artists' Organizations (NAAO), Washington DC

Boyer, R H, *Head Dept,* Saint Norbert College, Div of Humanities & Fine Arts, De Pere WI (S)

Boyko, Lee, *Dir & Cur,* Sooke Region Museum & Art Gallery, Sooke BC

Boylan, James, *Pres,* Porter-Phelps-Huntington Foundation, Inc Foundation, Inc, Historic House Museum, Hadley MA

Boyle, Allen, *Gallery Adminr,* Latitude 53 Society of Artists, Edmonton AB

Boyle, Erin T, *Asst Chief Librn,* Medicine Hat Public Library, Medicine Hat AB

Boyle, Faye, *Admin Asst,* University of Maine, Museum of Art, Orono ME

Boyle, Kevin, *Exhib Designer,* University of California, California Museum of Photography, Riverside CA

Boyle, Michael, *Lectr,* Cardinal Stritch College, Art Dept, Milwaukee WI (S)

Boyle, Pam Seyring, *Dir,* University of Cincinnati, Tangeman Fine Arts Gallery, Cincinnati OH

Boyles, Karen, *Exec Asst,* SLA Arch-Couture Inc, Art Collection, Denver CO

Boysen, Bill H, *Crafts Area Head,* Southern Illinois University, School of Art & Design, Carbondale IL (S)

Brabham, Heather, *Admin Asst,* University of Tampa, Henry B Plant Museum, Tampa FL

Bracci-McInode, Connie, *Lectr,* Georgian Court College, Dept of Art, Lakewood NJ (S)

Bracco, Sal, *Treas,* New York Society of Architects, New York NY

Brack, Lillie, *Central Reference Coordr,* Kansas City Public Library, Kansas City MO

Brackbill, Eleanor, *Head of Musuem Education,* State University of New York at Purchase, Neuberger Museum, Purchase NY

Bracket, Donald, *Exec Adminr,* Professional Art Dealers Association of Canada, Toronto ON

Brackman Sharp, Judith, *Instr,* Vancouver Community College, Langara Campus, Dept of Fine Arts, Vancouver BC (S)

Brackney, Kathryn S, *Librn,* Georgia Institute of Technology, College of Architecture Library, Atlanta GA

Braden, Karen, *Exec Dir,* Portage and District Arts Council, Portage la Prairie MB

Bradford, Colleen H, *Chmn,* Brigham City Museum-Gallery, Brigham City UT

Bradford, David, *Chmn,* Laney College, Art Dept, Oakland CA (S)

Bradford, Wilson G, *Pres,* Lyme Historical Society, Florence Griswold Museum, Old Lyme CT

Bradley, Barbara, *Dir Illustration,* Academy of Art College, Fine Arts Dept, San Francisco CA (S)

Bradley, David, *Development Dir,* Virginia Museum of Fine Arts, Richmond VA

Bradley, Douglas, *Cur,* University of Notre Dame, Snite Museum of Art, Notre Dame IN

Bradley, Laura, *Archivist,* Yarmouth County Historical Society, Yarmouth County Museum, Yarmouth NS

Bradley, Mark, *Instr,* Campbellsville College, Fine Arts Division, Campbellsville KY (S)

Bradley, Norman, *Assoc Prof,* Indiana-Purdue University, Dept of Fine Arts, Fort Wayne IN (S)

Bradley, Ollie, *Pres,* African American Historical and Cultural Society, San Francisco CA

Bradley, Phillip, *Pres,* Summit County Historical Society, Akron OH

Bradley, Robert B, *Museum Cur,* Alabama Department of Archives and History Museum, Museum Galleries, Montgomery AL

Bradley, Ross, *VPres,* Canadian Crafts Council, Conseil Canadien de l'Artisanat, Ottawa ON

Bradley, Steve, *Assoc Prof,* College of New Rochelle School of Arts and Sciences, Art Dept, New Rochelle NY (S)

Bradley, Tim, *Photography Dept Chmn,* Art Center College of Design, Pasadena CA (S)

Bradley, Wm Steven, *Dir,* Davenport Museum of Art, Davenport IA

Bradley-Johnson, Gayle V, *Gallery Dir,* North Park College, Carlson Tower Gallery, Chicago IL

Bradley-Johnson, Gayle V, *Prof,* North Park College, Art Dept, Chicago IL (S)

Brady, Barbara, *Registrar,* University of North Carolina at Greensboro, Weatherspoon Art Gallery, Greensboro NC

Brady, Patricia, *Dir Publications & Academic Affairs,* Kemper & Leila Williams Foundation, New Orleans LA

Brady, Robert J, *Mgr Bldgs & Secy,* Frick Collection, New York NY

Brafford, C J, *Cur,* Grand Teton National Park Service, Colter Bay Indian Arts Museum, Moose WY

Brage, Carl W, *Pres,* Portsmouth Historical Society, John Paul Jones House, Portsmouth NH

Bragg, Cheryl, *Business Mgr,* Anniston Museum of Natural History, Anniston AL

Bragg, Nicholas B, *Exec Dir,* Reynolda House Museum of American Art, Winston-Salem NC

Braide, Carol, *Admin Asst,* International Museum of African Art, New York NY

Braig, Betty, *Pres,* Arizona Artist Guild, Phoenix AZ

Braig, Kathryn B, *Asst to Librn,* The Mariners' Museum, Library, Newport News VA

Braillard, Ariane, *Admin,* Swiss Institute, New York NY

Brake, Diane, *Asst to the Dir,* Panhandle-Plains Histoical Society Museum, Canyon TX

Brako, Jeanne, *Coll Mgr,* Colorado Historical Society, Museum, Denver CO

Branch, Harrison, *Prof,* Oregon State University, Dept of Art, Corvallis OR (S)

Branden, Mack, *Chmn,* California Baptist College, Art Dept, Riverside CA (S)

Branden, Shirley, *Head Reference Dept,* University of Delaware, Morris Library, Newark DE

Brandenburg, Judith, *Dean,* Columbia University, Teachers Col Program in Art & Art Education, New York NY (S)

Brander, Susan, *Admin Dir,* Museum of the Hudson Highlands, Cornwall on Hudson NY

Brandoli, Susan, *Dir,* Vernon Art Gallery, Vernon BC

Brandon, Elinore, *Chmn Illustration,* Fashion Institute of Technology, Art & Design Division, New York NY (S)

Brandon, Reiko, *Cur Textile Coll,* Honolulu Academy of Arts, Honolulu HI

Brands, Lyn, *Asst Prof,* University of Central Arkansas, Art Dept, Conway AR (S)

Brandson, Lorraine, *Cur,* Eskimo Museum, Churchill MB

Brandson, Lorraine, *Cur,* Eskimo Museum, Library, Churchill MB

Brandyberg, Tyrone, *Museum Technician,* Tuskegee Institute National Historic Site, George Washington Carver & The Oaks, Tuskegee Institute AL

Brann, Cathy, *Technician,* Bowdoin College, Peary-MacMillan Arctic Museum, Brunswick ME

Brannan, Beverly W, *Photographs,* Library of Congress, Prints and Photographs Division, Washington DC

Brannan, Ed, *Instr,* Green River Community College, Art Dept, Auburn WA (S)

Brannigan, Pat, *First VPres,* New Jersey Water-Color Society, Red Bank NJ

Bransford, Pamela, *Registrar,* Montgomery Museum of Fine Arts, Montgomery AL

Branson, Edward V, *Instr,* Yavapai College, Visual & Performing Arts Division, Prescott AZ (S)

Bransten, Rena, *Secy,* The Friends of Photography, Ansel Adams Center for Photography, San Francisco CA

Branston, Stu, *Chmn,* Oral Roberts University, Fine Arts Dept, Tulsa OK (S)

Branston, Stuart, *Asst Prof,* Oral Roberts University, Fine Arts Dept, Tulsa OK (S)

Brant, Patricia, *Acting Dir,* Widener University, Art Museum, Chester PA

Brasher, Louise, *Asst Cur,* Duke University Museum of Art, Durham NC

Bratcher, Donna, *Assoc Prof,* Claflin College, Dept of Art, Orangeburg SC (S)

Bratton, Ronald B, *Deputy Dir Admin,* Los Angeles County Museum of Art, Los Angeles CA

Brauer, Daniel R, *Publications Dir,* University of California, Los Angeles, Fowler Museum of Cultural History, Los Angeles CA

Brauer, Richard H W, *Dir & Cur,* Valparaiso University, Museum of Art, Valparaiso IN

Braufman, Sheila, *Cur,* Judah L Magnes Museum, Berkeley CA

Braun, Bettina, *Adjunct Instr,* Maryville University of Saint Louis, Art Division, Saint Louis MO (S)

Braun, Suzan, *Prof,* Eastern Illinois University, Art Dept, Charleston IL (S)

Bravender, Suzanne, *Acting Area Head Art,* Pasadena City College, Art Dept, Pasadena CA (S)

Bravo, M, *Instr,* Humboldt State University, College of Arts & Humanities, Arcata CA (S)

Brawley, Robert, *Chmn*, University of Kansas, Dept of Art, Lawrence KS (S)

Braxton, Anne, *Art Librn*, Ohio University, Fine Arts Library, Athens OH

Bray, Ann, *Vis Instr*, Claremont Graduate School, Dept of Fine Arts, Claremont CA (S)

Bray, Jim, *Dir Dept*, Missouri Southern State College, Dept of Art, Joplin MO (S)

Bray, Marsha, *VPres*, Missouri Historical Society, Saint Louis MO

Bray, Michele, *Educ Coordr*, Tulane University, Gallier House Museum, New Orleans LA

Brazil, Judy, *Instr*, Johnson County Community College, Visual Arts Program, Overland Park KS (S)

Brazile, Orella R, *Dir*, Southern University Library, Shreveport LA

Breault, Colette, *Educ Dir*, Noah Webster Foundation & Historical Society of West Hartford, Inc, Noah Webster's House, West Hartford CT

Breaux, Kathryn, *Pres*, Lafayette Museum Association, Lafayette Museum, Lafayette LA

Brechner, Michael, *Preparator*, University of Kentucky, Art Museum, Lexington KY

Bredbeck, Nancy Preston, *Coordr Library*, Newport Art Museum, Library, Newport RI

Bredendick, Joan, *Vis Lectr*, North Central College, Dept of Art, Naperville IL (S)

Breeding, Kent, *Asst Prof*, Bethany College, Mingenback Art Center, Lindsborg KS

Brehm, Georgia L, *Dir*, Black River Historical Society, Black River Academy Museum, Ludlow VT

Breimayer, Mary Phyllis, *Prof*, Georgian Court College, Dept of Art, Lakewood NJ (S)

Breitenbach, Eric, *Prof*, Daytona Beach Community College, Dept of Fine Arts & Visual Arts, Daytona Beach FL (S)

Breitenbach, William J, *Prof*, Sam Houston State University, Art Dept, Huntsville TX (S)

Breitman, Ellen, *Dir Educ*, Newport Harbor Art Museum, Newport Beach CA

Brekke, Michael, *Assoc Prof*, Atlanta College of Art, Atlanta GA (S)

Bremmer, Allen, *Chmn*, State University of New York College at Oswego, Art Dept, Oswego NY (S)

Bremser, Sarah, *Asst Cur Western Art*, Honolulu Academy of Arts, Honolulu HI

Brendel-PanDich, Susanne, *Dir*, Lyndhurst, Tarrytown NY

Breneisen, Frank, *Chmn*, Morningside College, Art Dept, Sioux City IA (S)

Brener, R, *Prof*, University of Victoria, Dept of Visual Arts, Victoria BC (S)

Brennan, Anne, *Cur of Registry & Coll*, Saint John's Museum of Art, Wilmington NC

Brennan, Beth, *Librn*, Mitchell Museum, Library, Mount Vernon IL

Brennan, Linda C, *Cur*, Plumas County Museum, Quincy CA

Brennan, Linda C, *Cur*, Plumas County Museum, Museum Archives, Quincy CA

Brennan, Margaret, *Head*, Art Gallery of Ontario, Edward P Taylor Audio-Visual Centre, Toronto ON

Brennan, Mary, *Public Information Officer*, Heard Museum, Phoenix AZ

Brennan, Nancy, *Dir*, Baltimore City Life Museums, Baltimore MD

Brennan, Ruth, *Exec Dir*, Rapid City Fine Arts Council, Dahl Fine Arts Center, Rapid City SD

Brenneman, Jan, *Dir*, Sid W Richardson Foundation, Collection of Western Art, Fort Worth TX

Brenner, M Diane, *Archivist*, Anchorage Museum of History and Art, Anchorage AK

Brenner, M Diane, *Museum Archivist*, Anchorage Museum of History and Art, Archives, Anchorage AK

Breslauer, David, *Dir*, Clinton Historical Museum Village, Clinton NJ

Breslauer, Jessica, *Dir School*, Evanston Art Center, Evanston IL

Bresnahan, Edith, *Chmn*, Dominican College of San Rafael, Art Dept, San Rafael CA (S)

Bressler, Sandra Gross, *Exec Dir*, Philadelphia Art Commission, Philadelphia PA

Brettell, Richard, *Dir*, Dallas Museum of Art, Dallas TX

Brett-Smith, Sara, *Asst Prof*, Rutgers, the State University of New Jersey, Graduate Program in Art History, New Brunswick NJ (S)

Brevda, Shirley, *Vol Librn*, Heckscher Museum, Library, Huntington NY

Brewer, Barbara, *Cur Colls*, Cascade County Historical Society, Cascade County Historical Museum & Archives, Great Falls MT

Brewer, Douglas, *Assoc Dir*, University of Illinois, Museum of Natural History, Champaign IL

Brewster, Michael, *Assoc Prof*, Claremont Graduate School, Dept of Fine Arts, Claremont CA (S)

Brewster, Riley, *Instr*, New York Studio School of Drawing, Painting and Sculpture, New York NY (S)

Brezzo, Steven L, *Dir*, San Diego Museum of Art, San Diego CA

Bride, Duffy, *Secy*, Sierra Arts Foundation, Reno NV

Bridenstine, James A, *Executive Dir*, Kalamazoo Institute of Arts, Kalamazoo MI

Bridgeford, Robert G, *Dir*, Portland Children's Museum, Portland OR

Bridges, Edwin C, *Dir*, Alabama Department of Archives and History Museum, Museum Galleries, Montgomery AL

Bridgman, Susan, *Visual Materials Librn*, Vancouver Public Library, Fine Arts & Music Div, Vancouver BC

Bridson, Gavin D R, *Bibliographer*, Carnegie Mellon University, Hunt Institute for Botanical Documentation, Pittsburgh PA

Bridwell, Nancy, *Adjunct Instr*, Maryville University of Saint Louis, Art Division, Saint Louis MO (S)

Brienza, Barney, *Chmn Dept*, Western Montana College, Art Dept, Dillon MT (S)

Brierley, David, *Cur*, San Diego Maritime Museum, San Diego CA

Briggs, Dawn, *Membership Secy*, Tucson Museum of Art, Tucson AZ

Briggs, Larry S, *Design Area Head*, Southern Illinois University, School of Art & Design, Carbondale IL (S)

Briggs, Larry S, *Assoc Prof*, Southern Illinois University, School of Art & Design, Carbondale IL (S)

Briggs, Peter, *Cur of Coll*, University of Arizona, Museum of Art, Tucson AZ

Brighamy, Gretchen, *Pres*, Saint Louis Artists' Guild, Saint Louis MO

Bright, Jane, *Cur*, Roberts County Museum, Miami TX

Briley, John B, *Mgr*, The Ohio Historical Society, Inc, Campus Martius Museum and Ohio River Museum, Marietta OH

Brill, Margaret, *Prof*, Corning Community College, Division of Humanities, Corning NY (S)

Brill, Peter S, *Cur Exhibits*, National Museum of the American Indian, New York NY

Brill, Robert H, *Research Scientist*, Corning Museum of Glass, Corning NY

Brill, Wayne, *Instr*, Interlochen Arts Academy, Dept of Visual Art, Interlochen MI (S)

Brilla, Maureen, *Asst Prof*, Nazareth College of Rochester, Art Dept, Rochester NY (S)

Brinder, Rose, *Admin Asst*, Jewish Community Centre of Toronto, The Koffler Gallery, North York ON

Brinder, Rose, *Dir*, Koffler Gallery School of Visual Art, North York ON (S)

Bringle, Edwina, *Instr*, University of North Carolina at Charlotte, Dept of Visual Arts, Charlotte NC (S)

Bringle, Mel, *Chmn Dept Humanities & Fine Arts*, Saint Andrews Presbyterian College, Art Program, Laurinburg NC (S)

Brinkerhoff, Dericksen M, *Prof*, University of California, Riverside, Dept of the History of Art, Riverside CA (S)

Brinkman, Sheryl, *Office Mgr*, Lancaster County Art Association, Lancaster PA

Brinson, Karen, *Instr*, Bob Jones University, School of Fine Arts, Greenville SC (S)

Brion, Donna, *Public Relations Officer*, Newark Museum Association, The Newark Museum, Newark NJ

Briscoe, Wayne, *Public Servs Librn*, Lethbridge Community College, Buchanan Gallery, Lethbridge AB

Brisebois, Marcel, *Dir*, Musee d'art contemporain de Montreal, Montreal PQ

Brissan, Harriet, *Prof*, Rhode Island College, Art Dept, Providence RI (S)

Bristow, William A, *Prof*, Trinity University, Dept of Art, San Antonio TX (S)

Britch, Carroll, *Prof*, Springfield College, Dept of Visual and Performing Arts, Springfield MA (S)

Britt, Sam Glenn, *Prof*, Delta State University, Dept of Art, Cleveland MS (S)

Britton, Bonnie, *Instr*, Monterey Peninsula College, Art Dept, Monterey CA (S)

Britton, R E Neil, *Prof*, Virginia Wesleyan College, Art Dept of the Humanities Division, Norfolk VA (S)

Broad, Deborah, *Assoc Prof*, Moorhead State University, Dept of Art, Moorhead MN (S)

Broberg-Quintana, Lisa, *Cur*, New Haven Colony Historical Society, New Haven CT

Broches, Alexandra, *Instr*, Dean Junior College, Visual and Performing Art Dept, Franklin MA (S)

Brock, Bess, *Museum Asst*, Campbell Museum, Camden NJ

Brock, Clifford, *Asst Dean*, Delaware County Community College, Communications and Humanities House, Media PA (S)

Brock, Lee, *Asst Dean*, Olympic College, Social Sciences & Humanities Division, Bremerton WA (S)

Brockett, C, *Prof*, Christopher Newport College, Arts & Communications, Newport News VA (S)

Brode, Carol, *Dir Gallery & Instr*, Seton Hill College, Dept of Art, Greensburg PA (S)

Broderick, Herbert, *Asst Prof*, Herbert H Lehman College, Art Dept, Bronx NY (S)

Broderick, James, *Div Dir*, University of Texas at San Antonio, Division of Art & Architecture, San Antonio TX (S)

Broderick-Lockhart, Catherine, *Instr*, Vancouver Community College, Langara Campus, Dept of Fine Arts, Vancouver BC (S)

Brodeur, Danyelle, *Coordr*, Dorval Cultural Centre, Dorval PQ

Brodie, Scott, *Asst Prof*, College of Saint Rose, Dept of Art, Albany NY (S)

Brodsky, Alan, *Instr*, Dowling College, Dept of Visual Arts, Oakdale NY (S)

Brodsky, Judith, *Prof*, Rutgers, the State University of New Jersey, Mason Gross School of the Arts, New Brunswick NJ (S)

Brodsky, Michael, *Assoc Prof*, Loyola Marymount University, Art & Art History Dept, Los Angeles CA (S)

Brody, Arthur W, *Prof*, University of Alaska, Dept of Art, Fairbanks AK (S)

Brody, Lucy, *School Dir*, Rockland Center for the Arts, West Nyack NY (S)

Brody, Myron, *Prof*, University of Arkansas, Art Dept, Fayetteville AR (S)

Brohel, Edward R, *Dir*, State University of New York, SUNY Plattsburgh Art Museum, Plattsburgh NY

Broker, Karin, *Assoc Prof*, Rice University, Dept of Art and Art History, Houston TX (S)

Bromberg, Anne R, *Assoc Cur Ancient Art*, Dallas Museum of Art, Dallas TX

Bromley, Diana, *Asst Dir*, Arts and Science Center, Statesville NC

Bromley, Kimble, *Asst Prof*, Kentucky Wesleyan College, Dept Art, Owensboro KY (S)

Broner, Megan, *VPres*, Canadian Crafts Council, Conseil Canadien de l'Artisanat, Ottawa ON

Bronzo, Andrea, *Asst Dir*, Associated Artists of Winston-Salem, Winston-Salem NC

Broodwell, Caroyln, *Prof*, Napa Valley College, Art Dept, Napa CA (S)

Brook, A B, *Assoc Dir*, Ogunquit Museum of American Art, Ogunquit ME

Brooke, Anna, *Librn*, Hirshhorn Museum and Sculpture Garden, Library, Washington DC

Brooke, David S, *Dir,* Sterling and Francine Clark Art Institute, Williamstown MA

Brookhouse, Jon, *Chairperson Dept,* Suomi College, Fine Arts Dept, Hancock MI (S)

Brooks, Carol, *Cur,* Arizona Historical Society-Yuma, Century House Museum & Garden, Yuma AZ

Brooks, Drex, *Assoc Prof,* Weber State University, Dept of Visual Arts, Ogden UT (S)

Brooks, Fran, *Dir of Classes,* The Greenwich Art Society Inc, Greenwich CT

Brooks, Gordon, *Dir,* University of Southwestern Louisiana, School of Art and Architecture, Lafayette LA (S)

Brooks, Helen M, *Dir,* Arts & Science Center for Southeast Arkansas, Pine Bluff AR

Brooks, James, *Instr,* Bob Jones University, School of Fine Arts, Greenville SC (S)

Brooks, Jamie, *VPres,* Art League, Alexandria VA

Brooks, John H, *Assoc Dir,* Sterling and Francine Clark Art Institute, Williamstown MA

Brooks, Leonard, *Dir,* United Society of Shakers, The Shaker Library, Poland Spring ME

Brooks, Leonard L, *Dir,* United Society of Shakers, Shaker Museum, Poland Spring ME

Brooks, Roger L, *Dir,* Baylor University, Armstrong Browning Library, Waco TX

Brooks, Ruth, *Assoc Educ,* Old Salem Inc, Museum of Early Southern Decorative Arts, Winston-Salem NC

Brooks, Shelley, *Sr Curatorial Asst,* Portsmouth Museums, Arts Center, Portsmouth VA

Brooks, Steven, *Photographer,* University of California, Architectural Slide Library, Berkeley CA

Brooks, Susan, *Instr,* Ocean City Art Center, Ocean City NJ (S)

Brooks, Wendell, *Asst Prof,* Trenton State College, Art Dept, Trenton NJ (S)

Brooky, Judith, *Chmn,* Muskegon Community College, Dept of Creative and Performing Arts, Muskegon MI (S)

Bross, John, *Instr,* Greenfield Community College, Art, Graphic Design & Media Communication Dept, Greenfield MA (S)

Brothers, Darrell W, *Chmn,* Thomas More College, Art Dept, Crestview Hills KY (S)

Brothers, Leslie, *Registrar,* Virginia Commonwealth University, Anderson Gallery, Richmond VA

Broude, Norma, *Prof,* American University, Dept of Art, Washington DC (S)

Broudo, J David, *Head Dept,* Endicott College, Art Dept, Beverly MA (S)

Brouillard, Pierre, *Dir,* Chateau Ramezay Museum, Montreal PQ

Brouillet, Johanne, *Dir,* University of Sherbrooke, Art Gallery, Sherbrooke PQ

Brouillette, Carol, *Coordr,* La Centrale Powerhouse Gallery, Montreal PQ

Broun, Elizabeth, *Dir,* National Museum of American Art, Washington DC

Broussard, Jeanne, *Asst Prof,* Texas Woman's University, Dept of Visual Arts, Denton TX (S)

Brouwer, Bert, *Chmn,* Albright College, Dept of Art, Reading PA (S)

Brouwer, Charles, *Asst Prof,* Radford University, Art Dept, Radford VA (S)

Brouwer, Norman, *Historian & Librn,* South Street Seaport Museum, New York NY

Brouwer, Norman, *Historian & Librn,* South Street Seaport Museum, Library, New York NY

Brown, Ann Barton, *Dir,* American Swedish Historical Foundation and Museum, Philadelphia PA

Brown, Barbara J, *Head Librn,* Washington & Lee University, University Library, Lexington VA

Brown, Beverly Louise, *Asst Dir Programs & Academic Servs & Cur Exhibitions,* Kimbell Art Museum, Fort Worth TX

Brown, Brad, *Display Artist,* City of Lethbridge, Sir Alexander Galt Museum, Lethbridge AB

Brown, Bruce R, *Assoc Prof,* Monroe Community College, Art Dept, Rochester NY (S)

Brown, Carey, *Treas,* Knoxville Museum of Art, Knoxville TN

Brown, Carolyn S, *Dir Exhib & Prog,* Roberson Museum & Science Center, Binghamton NY

Brown, Cee, *Exec Dir,* Creative Time, New York NY

Brown, Charlotte V, *Dir,* North Carolina State University, Visual Arts Programs, Raleigh NC

Brown, Chelsea, *Dir, Public Relations,* San Francisco Museum of Modern Art, San Francisco CA

Brown, Christopher, *Prof,* University of California, Berkeley, College of Letters & Sciences-Art Dept, Berkeley CA (S)

Brown, Clinton, *Prof,* Oregon State University, Dept of Art, Corvallis OR (S)

Brown, C Reynolds, *Dir,* Saint John's Museum of Art, Wilmington NC

Brown, David, *Cur Renaissance Painting,* National Gallery of Art, Washington DC

Brown, David, *Dir,* Maryland Institute, College of Art Exhibitions, Baltimore MD

Brown, David H, *Asst Prof,* Emory University, Art History Dept, Atlanta GA (S)

Brown, David R, *Pres,* Art Center College of Design, Pasadena CA (S)

Brown, Don, *Faculty,* Idaho State University, Dept of Art, Pocatello ID (S)

Brown, Dorothy D, *Chmn,* Georgia College, Art Dept, Milledgeville GA (S)

Brown, Dottie, *Instr,* Sierra College, Art Dept, Rocklin CA (S)

Brown, Edward, *Prof,* Barton College, Communication, Performaing & Visual Arts, Wilson NC (S)

Brown, Elizabeth, *Cur,* University of California, Santa Barbara, University Art Museum, Santa Barbara CA

Brown, Ellsworth H, *Pres,* Chicago Historical Society, Chicago IL

Brown, En Marquis, *Pres,* Marblehead Arts Association, Inc, Marblehead MA

Brown, Gerald F, *Exec Dir,* Paint 'N Palette Club, Grant Wood & Memorial Park Gallery, Anamosa IA

Brown, Glen, *Asst Prof,* Texas Tech University, Dept of Art, Lubbock TX (S)

Brown, Holly, *Secy,* The Museum, Greenwood SC

Brown, Irene, *Cur,* Shorncliffe Park Improvement Assoc, Prairie Panorama Museum, Czar AB

Brown, Jack Perry, *Dir of Libraries,* The Art Institute of Chicago, Ryerson and Burnham Libraries, Chicago IL

Brown, J Carter, *Chmn,* United States Commission of Fine Arts, Washington DC

Brown, Jeanne, *Admin Asst,* The Frick Art Museum, Pittsburgh PA

Brown, Jeff, *Chmn Fine Arts,* Jones County Junior College, Art Dept, Ellisville MS (S)

Brown, Jim, *Pres,* American Tapestry Alliance, Chiloquin OR

Brown, J Mike, *Pres,* Creative Arts Guild, Dalton GA

Brown, Joe, *Dean,* Texas Wesleyan University, Dept of Art, Fort Worth TX (S)

Brown, Joseph E, *Assoc Prof,* Rochester Institute of Technology, School of Printing, Rochester NY (S)

Brown, Linda, *Instr,* University of North Carolina at Charlotte, Dept of Visual Arts, Charlotte NC (S)

Brown, Lindie K, *Development Officer,* Anniston Museum of Natural History, Anniston AL

Brown, Lisa, *Admin Asst,* Burchfield Art Center, Buffalo NY

Brown, Louise Freshman, *Prof,* University of North Florida, Dept of Communications & Visual Arts, Jacksonville FL (S)

Brown, Maria, *Cur Educ,* Schenectady Museum, Planetarium & Visitors Center, Schenectady NY

Brown, Marilyn R, *Assoc Prof,* Tulane University, Sophie H Newcomb Memorial College, New Orleans LA (S)

Brown, Mark, *Asst Dir & Art Coordr,* Community Council for the Arts, Kinston NC

Brown, Mary, *Instr,* The Arkansas Arts Center, Museum School, Little Rock AR (S)

Brown, Michael, *Exec Dir,* Berkeley Art Center, Berkeley CA

Brown, Michael, *Cur Bayou Bend,* Museum of Fine Arts, Houston, Houston TX

Brown, Mildred, *Pres,* Paint 'N Palette Club, Grant Wood & Memorial Park Gallery, Anamosa IA

Brown, Milton W, *Res Prof,* City University of New York, PhD Program in Art History, New York NY (S)

Brown, Natalie, *Communications Serv,* Southern Oregon Historical Society, Jacksonville Museum of Southern Oregon History, Jacksonville OR

Brown, Osa, *Dir Publications,* Museum of Modern Art, New York NY

Brown, Pamela Wedd, *Co-Chmn,* Studio Gallery, Washington DC

Brown, Pat, *Prof,* Princeton University, Dept of Art and Archaeology, Princeton NJ (S)

Brown, Patricia L, *Instr,* Delta State University, Dept of Art, Cleveland MS (S)

Brown, Paul, *Prof,* Mississippi State University, Art Dept, Mississippi State MS (S)

Brown, Peter, *Acting Pres of School,* The Art Institute of Chicago, Chicago IL

Brown, Peter, *Acting Pres,* School of the Art Institute of Chicago, Chicago IL (S)

Brown, Richard, *Academic VPres,* Newberry Library, Chicago IL

Brown, Robert, *Dir,* Archives of American Art, New England Regional Center, Washington DC

Brown, Robert, *Dir,* Fort Missoula Historical Museum, Missoula MT

Brown, Robin, *Chmn Dept,* Southern Illinois University at Edwardsville, Dept of Art & Design, Edwardsville IL (S)

Brown, Robin, *Photography & Graphic Design,* Southern Illinois University at Edwardsville, Dept of Art & Design, Edwardsville IL (S)

Brown, Ruth, *Asst Dir,* Luna County Historical Society, Inc, Deming Luna Mimbres Museum, Deming NM

Brown, Sandra, *Assoc Prof,* Southwest Baptist University, Art Dept, Bolivar MO (S)

Brown, Shary, *Art Fair Dir,* Michigan Guild of Artists & Artisans, Michigan Guild Gallery, Ann Arbor MI

Brown, Shoko, *Cur Exhib,* Palm Beach County Parks & Recreation Department, Morikami Museum & Japanese Gardens, Delray Beach FL

Brown, Stephen, *Asst Prof,* University of Hartford, Hartford Art School, West Hartford CT (S)

Brown, Susan, *Art Prof,* Richard Bland College, Art Dept, Petersburg VA (S)

Brown, Terrence, *Dir,* Society of Illustrators, Museum of American Illustration, New York NY

Brown, Terry, *Dir,* Society of Illustrators, New York NY

Brown, Thack, *Dir Public Affairs,* Burroughs Wellcome Company, Art Collection, Research Triangle Park NC

Brown, Virginia H, *Dir,* Sheldon Museum, Middlebury VT

Brown, William, *Cur Glass,* Zanesville Art Center, Zanesville OH

Brown, William, *Asst Prof,* University of Evansville, Art Dept, Evansville IN (S)

Brown, William A, *Lectr,* Emory University, Art History Dept, Atlanta GA (S)

Brown, Yvonne S, *Head Art Information Center,* Chicago Public Library, Harold Washington Library Center, Chicago IL

Brownawell, Christopher, *Dir & Cur,* Academy of the Arts, Easton MD

Browne, Charles C, *Dir,* Fairbanks Museum and Planetarium, Saint Johnsbury VT

Browne, Joseph P, *Dir,* University of Portland, Wilson W Clark Memorial Library, Portland OR

Browne, J Prentiss, *Pres,* Star-Spangled Banner Flag House Association, Flag House & 1812 Museum, Baltimore MD

Browne, Kathleen, *Asst Prof,* Eastern Illinois University, Art Dept, Charleston IL (S)

Brownell, Charles, *Prof,* Virginia Commonwealth University, Art History Department, Richmond VA (S)

Brownfield, John, *Gallery Dir,* University of Redlands, Peppers Gallery, Redlands CA

Brownfield, John, *Chmn,* University of Redlands, Dept of Art, Redlands CA (S)

Browning, Rob, *Preparator,* University of Virginia, Bayly Art Museum, Charlottesville VA

Brown-Lee, Barbara, *Cur Educ & Actg Cur Decorative Arts,* Milwaukee Art Museum, Milwaukee WI

Brownlee, Donna, *Head Dept,* Sterling College, Art Dept, Sterling KS (S)

Brownrigg, Elizabeth, *Dir,* Omaha Childrens Museum, Inc, Omaha NE

Brozovich, Tom J, *Instr,* American River College, Dept of Art, Sacramento CA (S)

Brozynski, Dennis, *Coordr Fashion Design,* Columbia College, Art Dept, Chicago IL (S)

Brubaker, Ann, *Dir,* Nelson-Atkins Museum of Art, Creative Arts Center, Kansas City MO

Brubaker, Bob, *Head Fine Arts Dept,* Allen County Public Library, Fine Arts Dept, Fort Wayne IN

Bruce, Bonnie, *Instr,* Marylhurst College, Art Dept, Marylhurst OR (S)

Bruce, Chris, *Sr Cur,* University of Washington, Henry Art Gallery, Seattle WA

Bruce, Dan, *Asst Cur,* Kelowna Centennial Museum and National Exhibit Centre, Kelowna BC

Bruce, Donald, *Cur,* Cambria Historical Society, New Providence NJ

Bruce, Gwen, *Deputy Dir,* Indiana University, Art Museum, Bloomington IN

Bruce, Suzy, *Cur Education,* Art Museum of Southeast Texas, Beaumont TX

Bruce, Suzy, *Educ Cur,* Art Museum of Southeast Texas, Library, Beaumont TX

Bruck, Clifford, *VPres,* Star-Spangled Banner Flag House Association, Flag House & 1812 Museum, Baltimore MD

Bruckner, Rebecca, *Prof,* Seattle University, Fine Arts Dept, Division of Art, Seattle WA (S)

Brueing, Don, *Prof,* Daytona Beach Community College, Dept of Fine Arts & Visual Arts, Daytona Beach FL (S)

Bruening, Barbara, *Dept Dir Finance & Admin,* State Art Museum of Florida, John & Mable Ringling Museum of Art, Sarasota FL

Bruggen, William, *Dir Budget & Finance,* Indiana State Museum, Indianapolis IN

Bruhl, Win, *Chmn,* Concordia College, Art Dept, Saint Paul MN (S)

Bruhn, Thomas P, *Cur of Collections,* University of Connecticut, William Benton Museum of Art - Connecticut's State Art Museum, Storrs CT

Bruker, David, *Exhibits Mgr,* Indiana University, William Hammond Mathers Museum, Bloomington IN

Brumbaugh, Mary, *Exec Dir,* Lynchburg Fine Arts Center Inc, Lynchburg VA

Brumgardt, John R, *Dir,* Charleston Museum, Charleston SC

Brunelle, Edelgard, *Cur,* Pence Gallery, Davis CA

Bruner, Paul, *Dir Undergrad Prog,* Rutgers, the State University of New Jersey, Mason Gross School of the Arts, New Brunswick NJ (S)

Brunet, Margaret, *Distribution Coordr,* Art Metropole Archives, Toronto ON

Brunet, Roxanne, *Pres,* Galerie de l'Atelier, Laval PQ

Bruni, Stephen T, *Dir,* Delaware Art Museum, Wilmington DE

Brunkus, Richard, *Prof,* Albion College, Dept of Visual Arts, Albion MI (S)

Brunner, Christal, *Reference Librn,* Mexico-Audrain County Library, Mexico MO

Bruno, Ana Basso, *Prof,* Catholic University of Puerto Rico, Dept of Fine Arts, Ponce PR (S)

Brusati, Celeste, *Assoc Prof,* University of Michigan, Ann Arbor, Dept of History of Art, Ann Arbor MI (S)

Brusca, Maureen, *VPres Finance Admin,* Pennsylvania Academy of the Fine Arts, Galleries, Philadelphia PA

Brush, Gloria D, *Head Dept,* University of Minnesota, Duluth, Art Dept, Duluth MN (S)

Brush, Leif, *Prof,* University of Minnesota, Duluth, Art Dept, Duluth MN (S)

Brust, John, *Assoc Prof,* Roanoke College, Fine Arts Dept-Art, Salem VA (S)

Brutger, James H, *Assoc Prof,* University of Minnesota, Duluth, Art Dept, Duluth MN (S)

Brutvan, Cheryl A, *Cur,* The Buffalo Fine Arts Academy, Albright-Knox Art Gallery, Buffalo NY

Bruya, Marilyn, *Assoc Prof,* University of Montana, Dept of Art, Missoula MT (S)

Bruzelius, Caroline, *Chmn,* Duke University, Dept of Art and Art History, Durham NC (S)

Bryan, Betsy, *Cur Near Eastern & Egyptian Art,* Johns Hopkins University, Archaeological Collection, Baltimore MD

Bryan, Charles F, *Dir,* Virginia Historical Society, Library, Richmond VA

Bryan, Jack, *Chmn,* Cameron University, Art Dept, Lawton OK (S)

Bryan, James B, *Dean of Faculty,* Manhattanville College, Brownson Art Gallery, Purchase NY

Bryan Hood, Mary, *Dir,* Owensboro Museum of Fine Art, Owensboro KY

Bryans, John, *Head Dept,* McLean Arts Center, Art Dept, McLean VA (S)

Bryant, Anne L, *Exec Dir,* American Association of University Women, Washington DC

Bryant, Bill, *Pres,* Cuyahoga Valley Art Center, Cuyahoga Falls OH (S)

Bryant, Gene, *Chmn,* Central Piedmont Community College, Visual & Performing Arts, Charlotte NC (S)

Bryant, Jill, *Pubic Relations,* Triton Museum of Art, Library, Santa Clara CA

Bryant, Julia, *Faculty,* Florida College, Division of Art, Temple Terrace FL (S)

Bryant, Susan, *Assoc Prof,* Austin Peay State University, Dept of Art, Clarksville TN (S)

Brydon, Irene Ward, *Executive Dir,* Creative Growth Art Center, Oakland CA

Bryk, Donald, *Music & Art Librn,* Queensborough Community College Library, Bayside NY

Bryner, Dale W, *Prof,* Weber State University, Dept of Visual Arts, Ogden UT (S)

Bryner, James S, *Pres,* Allegany County Historical Society, History House, Cumberland MD

Brynolf, Anita, *Instr,* San Diego Mesa College, Fine Arts Dept, San Diego CA (S)

Brynteson, Susan, *University Libraries,* University of Delaware, Morris Library, Newark DE

Bryon, Charles, *Dir,* Virginia Historical Society, Richmond VA

Bucci, Ralph, *Asst Prof,* Salve Regina College, Art Dept, Newport RI (S)

Buchach, Carolyn, *Dept Head,* Ray College of Design, Chicago IL (S)

Buchanan, John, *Dir,* The Dixon Gallery & Gardens, Memphis TN

Buchanan, Richard, *Head,* Carnegie Mellon University, Dept of Design, Pittsburgh PA (S)

Buchanan, Sidney, *Prof,* University of Nebraska at Omaha, Dept of Art, Omaha NE (S)

Buchanan, William C, *Asst Prof,* Western Carolina University, Dept of Art, Cullowhee NC (S)

Bucher, Francois, *Prof,* Florida State University, Art History Dept (R133B), Tallahassee FL (S)

Buchman, James, *Asst Prof,* State University of New York at Albany, Art Dept, Albany NY (S)

Buchner, Ernest, *Dir,* Pilgrim Society, Pilgrim Hall Museum, Plymouth MA

Buchter, Thomas, *Head of gardens,* Winterthur Museum and Gardens, Winterthur DE

Buck, Ann, *Second VPres,* Berks Art Alliance, Reading PA

Buck, Diane, *Doll Cur,* Wenham Museum, Wenham MA

Buck, Patricia R, *Dir Public Affairs,* State Art Museum of Florida, John & Mable Ringling Museum of Art, Sarasota FL

Buck, Robert T, *Dir,* Brooklyn Museum, Brooklyn NY

Buckingham, Jim, *Exec Dir,* St Thomas Elgin Art Gallery, Saint Thomas ON

Buckland, Alex, *Instr,* Lincoln Memorial University, Division of Humanities, Harrogate TN (S)

Buckley, Daniel, *Pres,* Chatham Historical Society, Old Atwood House, Chatham MA

Buckley, Margaret, *Librn,* Edmundson Art Foundation, Inc, Library, Des Moines IA

Buckley, R F, *Assoc Prof,* Florida International University, Visual Arts Dept, Miami FL (S)

Buckson, Deborah, *Exhib & Prog Coordr,* Winterthur Museum and Gardens, Historic Houses of Odessa, Winterthur DE

Budahl, Lee P, *Assoc Prof,* Western Carolina University, Dept of Art, Cullowhee NC (S)

Budd, Beth, *Asst Dir Programs,* Duke University Union, Durham NC

Buenger, Barbara C, *Assoc Prof,* University of Wisconsin, Madison, Dept of Art History, Madison WI (S)

Buettner, Brigitte, *Asst Prof,* Smith College, Art Dept, Northampton MA (S)

Buffalo, Jo, *Assoc Prof,* Cazenovia College, Center for Art & Design Studies, Cazenovia NY (S)

Buffington, Rod, *Exec Dir,* Springfield Art Association of Edwards Place, Springfield IL

Buffington, Ron, *Gallery Coordr,* University of Tennessee at Chattanooga, George Ayres Cress Gallery of Art, Chattanooga TN

Buhler, Ken, *Registrar & Preparator,* Artists Space, New York NY

Buie, Sarah, *Dir,* Clark University, The University Gallery at Goddard Library, Worcester MA

Bujnowski, Don, *Chmn Crafts,* Rochester Institute of Technology, School of Art and Design, Rochester NY (S)

Buki, Zoltan, *Cur Fine Arts,* New Jersey State Museum, Trenton NJ

Bukowski, William, *Head of Dept,* Bethany Lutheran College, Art Dept, Mankato MN (S)

Buksbaum, Ronald, *Prof,* Greater Hartford Community College, Humanities Division & Art Dept, Hartford CT (S)

Bulick, Bill, *Dir,* Metropolitan Arts Commission, Metropolitan Center for Public Arts, Portland OR

Bull, C Jumping, *Pres,* Heritage Center, Inc, Pine Ridge SD

Bull, James, *Chmn,* Hillsborough Community College, Fine Arts Dept, Tampa FL (S)

Bullard, Diane, *Admin Asst,* Rapid City Fine Arts Council, Dahl Fine Arts Center, Rapid City SD

Bullard, E John, *Dir,* New Orleans Museum of Art, New Orleans LA

Bullens, Donald F, *Chmn,* Worcester State College, Media, Arts, and Philosophy, Worcester MA (S)

Bullock, Robert S, *Lectr,* Azusa Pacific University, College of Liberal Arts, Art Dept, Azusa CA (S)

Bullock, Susanne B, *Secy,* Guild Hall of East Hampton, Inc, Guild Hall Museum, East Hampton NY

Bullock, Virginia, *Dir of Exhib,* Calvin College, Center Art Gallery, Grand Rapids MI

Bumgardner, David Q, *Pres,* Gaston County Museum of Art & History, Dallas NC

Bumpass, Terry, *Instr,* New Mexico Junior College, Arts & Sciences, Hobbs NM (S)

Bumper, Donald, *Instr,* Eastern Community College, Dept of Art, Venice Beach CA (S)

Bunce, William, *Dir,* University of Wisconsin-Madison, Kohler Art Library, Madison WI

Bunge, Jean, *Co - Dir,* Nobles County Art Center Gallery, Worthington MN

Bunge, Martin, *Co - Dir,* Nobles County Art Center Gallery, Worthington MN

Bunker, John S, *Assoc Dir,* Jacksonville Art Museum, Jacksonville FL

Bunn, Ann, *Educ Consultant,* California State University, Long Beach, University Art Museum, Long Beach CA

Bunn, David, *Assoc Prof,* University of Southern California, School of Fine Arts, Los Angeles CA (S)

Bunnell, Max, *Head Art Dept,* Dixie College, Art Dept, Saint George UT (S)

Bunnell, Max E, *Dir,* Dixie College, Southwestern Utah Art Gallery, Saint George UT

Bunnell, Peter, *Prof,* Princeton University, Dept of Art and Archaeology, Princeton NJ (S)

Bunner, Patty, *Instr,* Southwestern Michigan College, Fine & Performing Arts Dept, Dowagiac MI (S)

Bunse, Don, *Prof,* University of Montana, Dept of Art, Missoula MT (S)

Buntman, Helene, *Museum Store Mgr,* Palm Beach County Parks & Recreation Department, Morikami Museum & Japanese Gardens, Delray Beach FL

Buonagurio, Toby, *Prof,* State University of New York at Stony Brook, Art Dept, Stony Brook NY (S)

Burant, Jim, *Documentary Art Acquisition,* National Archives of Canada, Documentary Art and Photography, Ottawa ON

Burback, William, *Dir Education,* Museum of Fine Arts, Boston MA

Burbank, Doris, *Chmn,* Alvin Community College, Art Dept, Alvin TX (S)

Burch, Emeritus J Lindsey, *Asst Prof,* Johns Hopkins University, School of Medicine, Dept of Art as Applied to Medicine, Baltimore MD (S)

Burch, Juliana Wuan, *Lectr,* University of Missouri-Saint Louis, Art Dept, Saint Louis MO (S)

Burchett, Claudette, *Chmn Humanities,* City Colleges of Chicago, Malcolm X College, Chicago IL (S)

Burchett, Jayme, *Prof,* College of the Ozarks, Dept of Art, Point Lookout MO (S)

Burchett, Kenneth, *Chair,* University of Central Arkansas, Art Dept, Conway AR (S)

Burdick, Todd, *Cur Educ Serv,* Hancock Shaker Village, Inc, Pittsfield MA

Burdick, Vanroy R, *Dir Libraries,* California College of Arts and Crafts Library, Oakland CA

Burgess, Cynthia A, *Hostess,* Baylor University, Armstrong Browning Library, Waco TX

Burgess, James L, *Chmn,* Salisbury State University, Art Dept, Salisbury MD (S)

Burgess, James L, *Art Dept Chmn,* Salisbury State University, University Gallery, Salisbury MD

Burgess, Julie, *Development Dir,* Ann Arbor Art Association, Ann Arbor MI

Burgess, Lowry, *Dean,* Carnegie Mellon University, College of Fine Arts, Pittsburgh PA (S)

Burggraf, Ray, *Assoc Prof,* Florida State University, Art Dept, Tallahassee FL (S)

Burgis, G C, *Dir,* Brampton Public Library, Art Gallery, Brampton ON

Burgland, John, *Pres,* Galesburg Civic Art Center, Galesburg IL

Burgner, Kelly, *Instr,* Ricks College, Dept of Art, Rexburg ID (S)

Burhans, Ira, *Instr,* Dunedin Fine Arts and Cultural Center, Dunedin FL (S)

Burke, Adele, *Education Coordr,* Hebrew Union College, Skirball Museum, Los Angeles CA

Burke, Daniel, *Dir,* La Salle University, Art Museum, Philadelphia PA

Burke, Ellin, *Registrar,* Yeshiva University Museum, New York NY

Burke, G, *Technician,* University of Saskatchewan, John G Diefenbaker Centre, Saskatoon SK

Burke, James, *Prof,* Louisiana State University, School of Art, Baton Rouge LA (S)

Burke, James D, *Dir,* The Saint Louis Art Museum, Saint Louis MO

Burke, Jonathan, *Chmn Fine Arts,* Art Institute of Southern California, Ruth Salyer Library, Laguna Beach CA

Burke, Mary, *Dir Educ,* The Art Center, Waco TX

Burke, Mary, *Dir Educ & Library,* The Art Center, Library, Waco TX

Burke, Mary A, *Pres,* Phillips County Museum, Helena AR

Burke, M L, *VPres,* Shoreline Historical Museum, Seattle WA

Burke, Rebecca, *Head Dept,* Mount Allison University, Fine Arts Dept, Sackville NB (S)

Burke, William J, *Assoc Prof,* Florida International University, Visual Arts Dept, Miami FL (S)

Burke-Kelly, Kathy, *Chmn Division,* Glendale Community College, Dept of Fine Arts, Glendale CA (S)

Burkett, Nancy, *Assoc Librn,* American Antiquarian Society, Library, Worcester MA

Burkhart, Vanessa, *Registrar,* Indianapolis Museum of Art, Indianapolis IN

Burko, Diane, *Prof,* Philadelphia Community College, Dept of Art, Philadelphia PA (S)

Burks, Tom, *Cur,* Texas Ranger Hall of Fame and Museum, Waco TX

Burleigh, Kimberly, *Dir MFA Prog,* University of Cincinnati, School of Art, Cincinnati OH (S)

Burley, William, *Treas,* Boothbay Region Art Foundation, Inc, Brick House Gallery, Boothbay Harbor ME

Burlingham, Cynthia, *Assoc Dir & Cur,* University of California, Los Angeles, Grunwald Center for the Graphic Arts, Los Angeles CA

Burmeister, Paul, *Asst Prof,* Winona State University, Dept of Art, Winona MN (S)

Burndorfer, Hans, *Head Librn,* University of British Columbia, Fine Arts Library, Vancouver BC

Burnell, M E, *Dir,* Portsmouth Museums, Arts Center, Portsmouth VA

Burnett, Brian, *Instr,* Toronto School of Art, Toronto ON (S)

Burnett, Eustace O, *Reference Coordr,* New York City Technical College, Namm Hall Library and Learning Resource Center, Brooklyn NY

Burnett, Virgil, *Prof,* University of Waterloo, Fine Arts Dept, Waterloo ON (S)

Burnette, Alice, *Asst Secy for Institutional Initiatives,* Smithsonian Institution, Washington DC

Burnette, Charles, *Chmn Industrial Design,* University of the Arts, Philadelphia College of Art & Design, Philadelphia PA (S)

Burnham, James, *Dir,* Sloss Furnaces National Historic Landmark, Birmingham AL

Burnley, Gary, *Instr,* Sarah Lawrence College, Dept of Art History, Bronxville NY (S)

Burns, A Lee, *Assoc Prof,* Smith College, Art Dept, Northampton MA (S)

Burns, Ann, *Treas,* LeSueur Museum, LeSueur MN

Burns, Carol, *Asst Prof,* Bloomsburg University, Dept of Art, Bloomsburg PA (S)

Burns, Cecil, *Asst,* SLA Arch-Couture Inc, Art Collection, Denver CO

Burns, Chuck, *Cur,* The Lindsay Gallery, Linsay ON

Burns, David W, *VPres,* Everson Museum of Art, Syracuse NY

Burns, Gerald, *VPres Educ Svcs,* International Correspondence Schools, School of Interior Design, Scranton PA (S)

Burns, Gerald, *VPres Educ,* International Correspondence Schools, School of Art, Scranton PA (S)

Burns, H Michael, *Chmn Bd Trustees,* McMichael Canadian Art Collection, Kleinburg ON

Burns, Jane, *Dir,* Midwest Museum of American Art, Elkhart IN

Burns, Kevin, *Chief of Grants, State of NY,* New York Office of Parks, Recreation & Historic Preservation, Natural Heritage Trust, Albany NY

Burns, Richard D, *Pres,* Midwest Museum of American Art, Elkhart IN

Burns, Robert P, *Head Architecture Dept,* North Carolina State University at Raleigh, School of Design, Raleigh NC (S)

Burns, Sarah, *Assoc Prof,* Indiana University, Bloomington, Henry Radford Hope School of Fine Arts, Bloomington IN (S)

Burns, William K, *Asst Prof,* Seton Hall University, College of Arts & Sciences, South Orange NJ (S)

Burns-Resch, Pamela, *Gift Shop Coordr,* Vernon Art Gallery, Vernon BC

Burr, Annette, *Librn,* Virginia Polytechnic Institute & State University, Art & Architecture Library, Blacksburg VA

Burr, Brooks, *Adjunct Cur Zoology,* Southern Illinois University, University Museum, Carbondale IL

Burrell, William, *Prof,* Amarillo College, Art Dept, Amarillo TX (S)

Burrough, Margaret T, *Founder,* DuSable Museum of African American History, Chicago IL

Burroughs, Ann, *Exhib Coordr,* California State University, Northridge, Art Galleries, Northridge CA

Burson, Nancy, *Admin Asst,* Scripps College, Clark Humanities Museum, Claremont CA

Burtin, Kay, *Dir,* Saint Augustine Art Association Gallery, Saint Augustine FL

Burton, Ann Betts, *Lectr,* Trinity College, Art Dept, Washington DC (S)

Burton, Douglas, *Asst Prof,* Lenoir Rhyne College, Dept of Art, Hickory NC (S)

Burton, Judith, *Dir,* Columbia University, Teachers Col Program in Art & Art Education, New York NY (S)

Burton, Margaret, *Mgr,* Forest Lawn Museum, Glendale CA

Burwell, Sandra, *Instr,* Indiana University of Pennsylvania, Dept of Art and Art Education, Indiana PA (S)

Busby, James, *Chmn,* Houston Baptist University, Dept of Art, Houston TX (S)

Busceme, Greg, *Dir,* The Art Studio Inc, Beaumont TX

Busch, Cindy, *Dir Public Relations,* Indiana State Museum, Indianapolis IN

Busch, W Larry, *Assoc Prof,* Southern Illinois University, School of Art & Design, Carbondale IL (S)

Bush, Anne, *Asst Prof,* Florida State University, Art Dept, Tallahassee FL (S)

Bush, Barbara, *Pres,* Westfield Athenaeum, Jasper Rand Art Museum, Westfield MA

Bush, Kimberly, *Registrar,* Dallas Museum of Art, Dallas TX

Bush, Robert E, *Pres,* Arts United of Greater Fort Wayne, Fort Wayne IN

Butcher, Joanne, *Academic & Community Liaison,* Miami-Dade Community College, Wolfson Campus, Frances Wolfson Art Gallery, Miami FL

Butcher, Joanne, *Academic & Community Liaison,* Miami-Dade Community College, Wolfson Campus, InterAmerican Art Gallery, Miami FL

Butcher, Joanne, *Academic & Community Liaison,* Miami-Dade Community College, Wolfson Campus, Centre Gallery, Miami FL

Butcher, Larry, *Assoc Prof,* Delta College, Art Dept, University Center MI (S)

Butchovitz, Dean, *Instr,* University of North Carolina at Charlotte, Dept of Visual Arts, Charlotte NC (S)

Butera, Joseph L, *Pres,* Butera School of Art, Boston MA (S)

Buth-Furness, Christine, *VPres-Nominations,* Coalition of Women's Art Organizations, Port Washington WI

Butler, Charles T, *Dir,* Huntington Museum of Art, Huntington WV

Butler, Cornelia, *Cur Contemporary Art,* State University of New York at Purchase, Neuberger Museum, Purchase NY

Butler, David, *Dir,* Hamilton College, Fred L Emerson Gallery, Clinton NY

Butler, Jerry E, *Chmn,* Madison Area Technical College, Art Dept, Madison WI (S)

Butler, Joseph T, *Cur,* Historic Hudson Valley, Tarrytown NY

Butler, Joyce, *Manuscripts Cur,* Brick Store Museum, Library, Kennebunk ME

Butler, Ken, *Instr,* Marylhurst College, Art Dept, Marylhurst OR (S)

Butler, Kenneth, *Treas,* Contemporary Arts Center, Cincinnati OH

Butler, Mike, *Nature Park Mgr,* Iroquois Indian Museum, Howes Cave NY

Butler, Owen, *Assoc Prof,* Rochester Institute of Technology, School of Photographic Arts & Sciences, Rochester NY (S)

Butler, Ruth, *Co-Chmn,* University of Massachusetts at Boston, Art Dept, Boston MA (S)

Butor, Melvin, *Prof,* University of Wisconsin, Madison, Dept of Art, Madison WI (S)

Butt, Harlan, *Jewelry & Metalsmithing Coordr,* University of North Texas, School of Visual Arts, Denton TX (S)

Butterfield, Michelle, *Registrar,* Portland Museum of Art, Portland ME

Butterfield, Thomas F, *Art Dir,* Virginia Polytechnic Institute & State University, Perspective Gallery, Blacksburg VA

Butterworth, James M, *Dean College Fine Arts,* Western Illinois University, Art Dept, Macomb IL (S)

Butterworth, Lynne, *Dir Communictions,* Philbrook Museum of Art, Tulsa OK

Butts, H Daniel, *Dir,* Mansfield Fine Arts Guild, Mansfield Art Center, Mansfield OH

Butts, H Daniel, *Art Dir,* Mansfield Fine Arts Guild, Library, Mansfield OH

Butts, Patricia, *Asst to the Dir,* Columbus Museum, Columbus GA

Buttwinick, Edward, *Dir,* Brentwood Art Center, Los Angeles CA (S)

Buyers, Jane, *Asst Prof,* University of Waterloo, Fine Arts Dept, Waterloo ON (S)

Byard, Paul S, *Pres,* Architectural League of New York, New York NY

Byer, Charles, *VPres Admin,* Philadelphia Art Alliance, Philadelphia PA

Byers, Larry, *Chmn Div,* Saint Louis Community College at Florissant Valley, Division of Communications & Arts, Ferguson MO (S)

Byers, Laura, *Cur Rare Books,* Norfolk Historical Society Inc, Museum, Norfolk CT

Byers, Rosemarie, *Dir,* Grace A Dow Memorial Library, Fine Arts Dept, Midland MI

Bynum, Judy B, *Dir Development,* Arts Council of Spartanburg County, Inc, Spartanburg Arts Center, Spartanburg SC

Byrd, Al, *Instructor,* Sacramento City College, Art Dept, Sacramento CA (S)

Byrd, Jeff, *Asst Prof,* University of Northern Iowa, Dept of Art, Cedar Falls IA (S)

Byrd, Joan, *Assoc Prof,* Western Carolina University, Dept of Art, Cullowhee NC (S)

Byrdsong, George, *VPres,* Fairbanks Arts Association, Fairbanks AK

Byrn, Brian D, *Cur Exhibitions & Education,* Midwest Museum of American Art, Elkhart IN

Byrne, Elizabeth, *Head,* University of California, Environmental Design Library, Berkeley CA

Byrne, Jeri, *Fine Art Librn,* Beverly Hills Public Library, Fine Arts Library, Beverly Hills CA

Byrne, Lorraine, *Head of Graphics,* Westerly Public Library, Hoxie Gallery, Westerly RI

Byrne, Nadene, *Dir,* School of the Art Institute of Chicago, John M Flaxman Library, Chicago IL

Byrnes, David J, *Dir,* Lockwood-Mathews Mansion Museum, Norwalk CT

Byrnes, Kevin, *Pres,* Baltimore City Life Museums, Baltimore MD

Byron, Merrillee, *Prof,* University of Bridgeport, Art Dept, Bridgeport CT (S)

Byrum, Donald R, *Instr,* University of North Carolina at Charlotte, Dept of Visual Arts, Charlotte NC (S)

Bytnerowicz, Dasia, *Exhib Designer,* Riverside Municipal Museum, Riverside CA

Bywaters, Diane, *Asst Prof,* University of Wisconsin-Stevens Point, Dept of Art & Design, Stevens Point WI (S)

Bzdak, Michael J, *Art Cur,* Johnson & Johnson, Art Program, New Brunswick NJ

Cabarga, Paul, *Bookstore Mgr,* University of Washington, Henry Art Gallery, Seattle WA

Cabe, Linda, *Instr,* James Madison University, Dept of Art, Harrisonburg VA (S)

Cabezas, Connie, *Dir,* Saint Edward's University, Fine Arts Exhibit Program, Austin TX

Caddell, Foster, *Head Dept,* Foster Caddell's Art School, Voluntown CT (S)

Cadigan, Edward, *Supv of Operations,* Memorial University of Newfoundland, Art Gallery, Saint John's NF

Cadogan, Jean, *Cur European Paintings, Sculpture, Drawings & Prints,* Wadsworth Atheneum, Hartford CT

Cadogan, Jean, *Assoc Prof,* Trinity College, Dept of Fine Arts, Hartford CT (S)

Caement, Louise, *Dir,* La Societe des Decorateurs-Ensembliers du Quebec, Interior Designers Society of Quebec, Montreal PQ

Cafesjian, Gerard L, *VPres,* West Publishing Company, Art & the Law, Eagan MN

Cagen, Stephen, *Asst Prof,* Rutgers, the State University of New Jersey, Mason Gross School of the Arts, New Brunswick NJ (S)

Caggiano, John, *Pres,* Rockport Art Association, Rockport MA

Cagle, Sue, *Registration Asst,* Columbus Museum, Columbus GA

Caglioti, Victor, *Assoc Prof,* University of Minnesota, Minneapolis, Dept of Studio Art, Minneapolis MN (S)

Cahn, Walter, *Pres,* International Center of Medieval Art, Inc, New York NY

Caine, Joan, *Asst Dir,* University of Washington, Henry Art Gallery, Seattle WA

Cairns, R Christopher, *Prof,* Haverford College, Fine Arts Dept, Haverford PA (S)

Cairns, Roger, *Assoc Prof,* Montgomery County Community College, Art Dept, Blue Bell PA (S)

Caison, Mary Jane, *Exec Dir,* Sumter Gallery of Art, Sumter SC

Caivano, Nicholas, *Lectr,* Georgian Court College, Dept of Art, Lakewood NJ (S)

Cajori, Charles, *Instr,* New York Studio School of Drawing, Painting and Sculpture, New York NY (S)

Caker, Richard, *Lectr,* University of Wisconsin-Stout, Dept of Art & Design, Menomonie WI (S)

Calabrese, John A, *Assoc Prof,* Texas Woman's University, Dept of Visual Arts, Denton TX (S)

Calabro, Richard, *Prof,* University of Rhode Island, Dept of Art, Kingston RI (S)

Caldarelli, Janet, *Gallery Assoc,* International Images, Ltd, Sewickley PA

Calden, Lisa, *Coll & Exhib Admin,* University of California, University Art Museum, Berkeley CA

Calderwood, Kathy, *Assoc Prof,* Nazareth College of Rochester, Art Dept, Rochester NY (S)

Caldewey, Sandra S, *Asst Dir Museum on Wheels,* Monterey Peninsula Museum of Art Association, Monterey CA

Caldwell, Blaine, *Prof,* University of the Ozarks, Dept of Art, Clarksville AR (S)

Caldwell, C, *Assoc Prof,* Northern Arizona University, School of Art & Design, Flagstaff AZ (S)

Caldwell, Cathy, *Asst Prof,* University of Central Arkansas, Art Dept, Conway AR (S)

Caldwell, Desiree, *Asst Dir Exhibit,* Museum of Fine Arts, Boston MA

Caldwell, Jody, *Reference Librn,* Drew University, Art Dept Library, Madison NJ

Caldwell, Martha B, *Prof,* James Madison University, Dept of Art, Harrisonburg VA (S)

Caldwell, Michael, *Chmn,* Seattle Pacific University, Art Dept, Seattle WA (S)

Cale, David, *Prof,* Amarillo College, Art Dept, Amarillo TX (S)

Calhoun, Larry, *Chmn Art Dept,* MacMurray College, Art Dept, Jacksonville IL (S)

Calhoun, Paul S, *Instr,* Johns Hopkins University, School of Medicine, Dept of Art as Applied to Medicine, Baltimore MD (S)

Calhoun, Ralph E, *Instr,* Guilford Technical Community College, Commercial Art Dept, Jamestown NC (S)

Calhoun, William, *Exec Dir,* Greensboro Artists' League, Greensboro NC

Calinescu, Adriana, *Cur Ancient Art,* Indiana University, Art Museum, Bloomington IN

Calisch, Douglas, *Chmn,* Wabash College, Art Dept, Crawfordsville IN (S)

Calkins, Harry, *Lectr,* University of Alaska, Dept of Art, Fairbanks AK (S)

Calkins, Robert G, *Prof,* Cornell University, Dept of the History of Art, Ithaca NY (S)

Calkins, Roger E, *Dir,* Schenectady Museum, Planetarium & Visitors Center, Schenectady NY

Callahan, Carol, *Cur,* Chicago Architecture Foundation, Glessner House, Chicago IL

Callahan, Diane, *Asst Prof,* Southwest Baptist University, Art Dept, Bolivar MO (S)

Callahan, Jerry, *Division Chmn Fine Arts,* San Jacinto Junior College, Div of Fine Arts, Pasadena TX (S)

Callahan, Nancy, *Instr,* State University of New York College at Oneonta, Dept of Art, Oneonta NY (S)

Callahan-Dolcater, Katrina, *Dir,* Dickinson State University, Mind's Eye Gallery, Dickinson ND

Callahan-Dolcater, Katrina, *Prof,* Dickinson State University, Dept of Art, Dickinson ND (S)

Callan, Josi I, *Dir,* San Jose Museum of Art, San Jose CA

Callander, Lee A, *Registrar,* National Museum of the American Indian, New York NY

Callaway, Carol, *Prof,* Christopher Newport College, Arts & Communications, Newport News VA (S)

Callaway, Martha, *Second VPres,* Brown County Art Gallery Association Inc, Nashville IN

Calleri, Daniel V, *Instr,* Villa Maria College of Buffalo, Art Dept, Buffalo NY (S)

Callery, Bernadette, *VPres,* Guild of Book Workers, New York NY

Callis, Dan, *Assoc Prof,* Biola University, Art Dept, La Mirada CA (S)

Callow, Bette Ray, *Slide Cur,* Memphis College of Art, Library, Memphis TN

Calman, Wendy, *Assoc Prof,* Indiana University, Bloomington, Henry Radford Hope School of Fine Arts, Bloomington IN (S)

Calvert, Jean W, *Dir,* Mason County Museum, Maysville KY

Calvert, Sheena, *Asst Prof,* Rutgers, the State University of New Jersey, Mason Gross School of the Arts, New Brunswick NJ (S)

Calza, Susan, *Sculpture Instr,* Johnson State College, Dept Fine Arts, Dibden Gallery, Johnson VT (S)

Camarata, Martin, *Chmn Dept,* California State University, Art Dept, Turlock CA (S)

Camarigg, Elizabeth, *Art Librn,* Mason City Public Library, Mason City IA

Camber, Diane W, *Dir,* Bass Museum of Art, Miami Beach FL

Cameron, Ben, *Instr,* Columbia College, Art Dept, Columbia MO (S)

Cameron, E, *Head,* University of Calgary, Dept of Art, Calgary AB (S)

Cameron, John B, *Prof,* Oakland University, Dept of Art and Art History, Rochester MI (S)

Camfield, William A, *Prof,* Rice University, Dept of Art and Art History, Houston TX (S)

Camp, Edward, *Prof,* Manatee Community College, Dept of Art & Humanities, Bradenton FL (S)

Camp, Kenneth, *Chmn,* Illinois Central College, Dept of Fine Arts, East Peoria IL (S)

Camp, Orton P, *VPres,* Mattatuck Historical Society Museum, Waterbury CT

Camp, R, *Instr,* Golden West College, Visual Art Dept, Huntington Beach CA (S)

Campa, Griseloa, *Gallery Coordr,* Texas A & M University, Visual Arts Committee, College Station TX

Campagna, Hal, *Instr,* Joe Kubert School of Cartoon & Graphic Art, Inc, Dover NJ (S)

Campbell, Bob, *Deputy Dir,* California Museum of Science and Industry, Los Angeles CA

Campbell, Catherine, *Recording Secy,* Bowne House Historical Society, Flushing NY

Campbell, Diana, *Admin Asst,* Fayetteville Museum of Art, Inc, Fayetteville NC

Campbell, Francis D, *Librn,* American Numismatic Society, New York NY

Campbell, Francis D, *Librn,* American Numismatic Society, Library, New York NY

Campbell, James, *Librn,* New Haven Colony Historical Society, Whitney Library, New Haven CT

Campbell, Jane, *VPres,* Monterey Peninsula Museum of Art Association, Monterey CA

Campbell, Kathleen, *Assoc Cur of Decorative Art,* Winnipeg Art Gallery, Winnipeg MB

Campbell, Krista, *Adminr Coordr,* Cincinnati Artists' Group Effort, Cincinnati OH

Campbell, Laura, *Dir Development & Marketing,* Please Touch Museum, Philadelphia PA

Campbell, Lynne, *Registrar,* Michigan State University, Kresge Art Museum, East Lansing MI

Campbell, Mary, *Asst Prof,* Jersey City State College, Art Dept, Jersey City NJ (S)

Campbell, Mary L, *Supv,* Robert W Ryerss Library and Museum, Philadelphia PA

Campbell, Mary L, *Librn,* Robert W Ryerss Library and Museum, Library, Philadelphia PA

Campbell, Mei Wan, *Cur Clothing & Textile,* Texas Tech University, Museum, Lubbock TX

Campbell, Michael, *Asst Prof,* Shippensburg University, Art Dept, Shippensburg PA (S)

Campbell, Nancy, *Chmn,* Mount Holyoke College, Art Dept, South Hadley MA (S)

Campbell, Nancy, *Cur,* MacDonald Stewart Art Centre Art Center, Guelph ON

Campbell, Phil, *Dir,* Southern Oregon State College, Stevenson Union Gallery, Ashland OR

Campbell, Priscilla, *Comptroller,* The Dixon Gallery & Gardens, Memphis TN

Campbell, Richard, *Dir,* L A Art Association, Los Angeles CA

Campbell, Richard, *Cur Prints & Drawings,* Minneapolis Society of Fine Arts, Minneapolis Institute of Arts, Minneapolis MN

Campbell, Rochelle, *Instr,* Keystone Junior College, Fine Arts Dept, Factoryville PA (S)

Campbell, Sara, *Chief Cur,* Norton Simon Museum, Pasadena CA

Campbell, Tom, *Instr,* Toronto School of Art, Toronto ON (S)

Campbell, Walter A, *Prof,* Rochester Institute of Technology, School of Printing, Rochester NY (S)

Campbell, Wayne, *Media Librn,* Greenwich Library, Greenwich CT

Campbell-Smith, Douglas, *Prof,* Central Oregon Community College, Dept of Art, Bend OR (S)

Campell, Nancy, *Exec Dir,* Wayne Art Center, Wayne PA (S)

Campion, William, *Pres,* Central Florida Community College Art Collection, Ocala FL

Campolo, Sandie, *Artists in Educ Dir,* Arizona Commission on the Arts, Phoenix AZ

Campton, Bill, *Prof,* University of Nebraska, Kearney, Dept of Art & Art History, Kearney NE (S)

Campulli, Eleanor, *Prof,* Jersey City State College, Art Dept, Jersey City NJ (S)

Campus, Peter, *Assoc Prof,* New York University, Dept of Art & Art Professions, New York NY (S)

Camrud, Madelyn, *Dir Audience Development,* North Dakota Museum of Art, Grand Forks ND

Camurati, Al, *Pres,* Hudson Valley Art Association, Flushing NY

Camurati, Al, *VPres,* National Art League Inc, Douglaston NY

Canady, Leander, *Dept Chmn,* Clinch Valley College of the University of Virginia, Visual & Performing Arts Dept, Wise VA (S)

Canaves, Marie, *Prof,* Cape Cod Community College, Art Dept, West Barnstable MA (S)

Candau, Eugenie, *Librn,* San Francisco Museum of Modern Art, Louise Sloss Ackerman Fine Arts Library, San Francisco CA

Candel, Sol, *General Mgr,* Museum of Movie Art, Calgary AB

Canedy, Norman, *Prof,* University of Minnesota, Minneapolis, Art History, Minneapolis MN (S)

Canepa, Jack, *Prof,* Webster University, Art Dept, Webster Groves MO (S)

Cannell, Susan, *Asst Prof,* Florida State University, Art Dept, Tallahassee FL (S)

Canning, Susan, *Assoc Prof,* College of New Rochelle School of Arts and Sciences, Art Dept, New Rochelle NY (S)

Cannino, Vince, *Cur Exhib & Colls,* High Point Historical Society Inc, Museum, High Point NC

Cannon, Robert, *Dir,* Public Library of Charlotte and Mecklenburg County, Charlotte NC

Cannuli, Br Richard, *Prof,* Villanova University, Dept of Art and Art History, Villanova PA (S)

Cannup, John, *Dir Facilities Management,* The Mariners' Museum, Newport News VA

Canter, Millicent, *Dir,* Longview Museum and Arts Center, Longview TX

Canter, Millicent, *Dir,* Longview Museum and Arts Center, Library, Longview TX

Canter, William, *Lectr,* Notre Dame College, Art Dept, Manchester NH (S)

Cantieni, Graham, *Section Head,* University of Quebec, Trois Rivieres, Fine Arts Section, Trois Rivieres PQ (S)

Cantor, Dorothy, *Education Dir,* Mattatuck Historical Society Museum, Waterbury CT

Cantor, Mira, *Asst Prof,* Northeastern University, Dept of Art & Architecture, Boston MA (S)

Cantrell, Carol S, *Admin Human Resources,* The Metropolitan Museum of Art, New York NY

Cantrell, Gary, *Performing Arts Librn,* Adelphi University, Fine & Performing Arts Library, Garden City NY

Cantrell, Jimmy, *Instr,* John C Calhoun State Community College, Division of Fine Arts, Decatur AL (S)

Capa, Cornell, *Dir,* International Center of Photography, New York NY

Capa, Cornell, *Dir,* International Center of Photography, Midtown, New York NY

Capawana, Sara, *Instr,* Mesa Community College, Dept of Art & Art History, Mesa AZ (S)

Capen, Gary, *Pres,* Walker Art Center, Minneapolis MN

Capener, Richard, *Dir,* Algonquin Arts Council, Bancroft Art Gallery, Bancroft ON

Capers, Valerie, *Chmn,* Bronx Community College, Music & Art Dept, Bronx NY (S)

Capet, Mitjl, *Asst Prof Art,* Imperial Valley College, Art Dept, Imperial CA (S)

Caplan, Louis, *Interim Dir,* Fort Hays State University, Forsyth Library, Hays KS

Capo, Laurence G, *Chmn Bd of Trustees,* Artworks, The Visual Art School of Princeton and Trenton, Trenton NJ

Capozzi, John, *Dir & Cur,* Saint Bonaventure University, Art Collection, Saint Bonaventure NY

Capps, Patricia, *Admin Mgr,* University of California, Los Angeles, Wight Art Gallery, Los Angeles CA

Cappuccio, Thomas, *Prof,* Northern Michigan University, Dept of Art and Design, Marquette MI (S)

Caputo, John, *Gallery Dir,* University of South Carolina at Spartanburg, Art Gallery, Art Gallery, Spartanburg SC

Carambat, John, *Asst Prof,* Louisiana State University, School of Art, Baton Rouge LA (S)

Carboni, Tamra, *Dir of Programs,* Louisiana Department of Culture, Recreation and Tourism, Louisiana State Museum, New Orleans LA

Cardiff, Gene, *Cur Natural History,* San Bernardino County Museum, Fine Arts Institute, Redlands CA

Cardiff, Janet, *Asst Prof,* University of Lethbridge, Dept of Art, Lethbridge AB (S)

Cardoni, Edmund, *Dir,* Hallwalls Contemporary Arts Center, Buffalo NY

Carey, Brian, *Collections Mgr,* National Archives of Canada, Documentary Art and Photography, Ottawa ON

Carey, Ellen, *Asst Prof,* University of Hartford, Hartford Art School, West Hartford CT (S)

Carey, John, *Acting Acad Dean,* Tunxis Community College, Graphic Design Dept, Farmington CT (S)

Carey Lester, William, *Prof,* Delta State University, Dept of Art, Cleveland MS (S)

Carfagna, Catherine, *Dir of Development,* Burchfield Art Center, Buffalo NY

Cargile, Ellen, *Chmn,* Fort Lewis College, Art Dept, Durango CO (S)

Cariolano, Jody, *Asst Prof,* Our Lady of the Lake University, Dept of Art, San Antonio TX (S)

Carlberg, Norman, *Dir,* Maryland Institute, Rinehart School of Sculpture, Baltimore MD (S)

Carlblom, Lucy, *Prog Coordr,* SVACA - Sheyenne Valley Arts and Crafts Association, Bjarne Ness Gallery, Fort Ransom ND

Carley, Michal Ann, *Assoc Cur,* University of Wisconsin, University Art Museum, Milwaukee WI

Carlin, Jane, *DAAP Librn,* University of Cincinnati, Design, Architecture, Art & Planning Library, Cincinnati OH

Carline, Gina, *Gift Shop Mgr,* Nelda C & H J Lutcher Stark Foundation, Stark Museum of Art, Orange TX

Carlisle, John, *Admin & Chmn Art Committee,* Purdue University Calumet, Bicentennial Library Gallery, Hammond IN

Carlisle, Macleah, *Dir,* Hinckley Foundation Museum, Ithaca NY

Carlisle, Roger, *Assoc Prof,* Arkansas State University, Dept of Art, Jonesboro AR (S)

Carlozzi, Annette, *Exec Dir,* Contemporary Arts Center, New Orleans LA

Carlsgaard, Lynn, *Asst Prof,* Northern State University, Art Dept, Aberdeen SD (S)

Carlson, Bertha, *Treas,* Swedish American Museum Association of Chicago, Chicago IL

Carlson, Denise, *Head Reference Serv,* Minnesota Historical Society, Library, Saint Paul MN

Carlson, Donna, *Dir of Admin,* Art Dealers Association of America, Inc, New York NY

Carlson, Eleanor, *Chmn Music Dept,* University of Massachusetts Dartmouth, College of Visual and Performing Arts, North Dartmouth MA (S)

Carlson, Eric, *Prof,* State University of New York College at Purchase, Art History Board of Study, Purchase NY (S)

Carlson, June, *Treas,* Swedish American Museum Association of Chicago, Chicago IL

Carlson, Lance, *Dean,* Rio Hondo College, Fine Arts - Humanitites Division, Whittier CA (S)

Carlson, Paul, *Business Mgr,* Plains Art Museum, Moorhead MN

Carlson, Richard, *Lectr,* Notre Dame College, Art Dept, Manchester NH (S)

Carlson, Victor, *Sr Cur Prints & Drawings,* Los Angeles County Museum of Art, Los Angeles CA

Carlson, William, *In Charge Ceramics, Glass & Metal,* University of Illinois, Urbana-Champaign, School of Art and Design, Champaign IL (S)

Carlton, Caroline, *Librn,* North Carolina State University, Harrye Lyons Design Library, Raleigh NC

Carlton, Lance, *Division Dean,* Rio Hondo College Art Gallery, Whittier CA

Carlton, Rosemary, *Interpretation Specialist,* Sheldon Jackson Museum, Sitka AK

Carman, William, *Instr,* Cardinal Stritch College, Art Dept, Milwaukee WI (S)

Carmichael, Jae, *VPres,* L A Art Association, Los Angeles CA

Carmichael, Lisa, *Asst to Dir,* Ball State University, Museum of Art, Muncie IN

Carmichael, Wade, *Dir Design & Graphics,* Indiana State Museum, Indianapolis IN

Carmin, James H, *Reference Librn,* University of Oregon, Architecture and Allied Arts Library, Eugene OR

Carnat, Sarabeth, *Prog Coordr Jewelry,* Alberta College of Art, Calgary AB (S)

Carnes, Sandra, *Chmn Fine Arts,* Malone College, Dept of Art, Canton OH (S)

Carney, Trish, *Media Asst,* San Francisco Art Institute, Anne Bremer Memorial Library, San Francisco CA

Carns, Janet, *Membership & Development Secy,* Westmoreland Museum of Art, Greensburg PA

Carol, Jane, *Instr,* Lincoln University, Dept Fine Arts, Jefferson City MO (S)

Caron, Jacqueline, *Dir,* Institut Des Arts Au Saguenay, Centre National D'Exposition A Jonquiere, Jonquiere PQ

Caron, Linda, *Chmn,* Wright State University, Dept of Art & Art History, Dayton OH (S)

Carothers, Peggy, *Adjunct Instr,* Maryville University of Saint Louis, Art Division, Saint Louis MO (S)

Carp, Richard M, *Chmn, School of Art,* Northern Illinois University, School of Art, De Kalb IL (S)

Carpenter, Cheslie, *Treas,* South County Art Association, Kingston RI

Carpenter, Janice, *Travel Publications Specialist,* Utah Travel Council, Salt Lake City UT

Carpenter, Margot, *Exec Dir,* Aesthetic Realism Foundation, New York NY (S)

Carpenter, Mary Jo, *Dir of Public Relations,* Sterling and Francine Clark Art Institute, Williamstown MA

Carpenter, Richard, *Pres,* John C Calhoun State Community College, Art Gallery, Decatur AL

Carpenter, Scott, *Museum Technician & Preparator,* Oberlin College, Allen Memorial Art Museum, Oberlin OH

Carpenter, Syd, *Asst Prof,* Swarthmore College, Dept of Art, Swarthmore PA (S)

Carpenter, Thomas, *Prof,* Virginia Polytechnic Institute & State University, Dept of Art & Art History, Blacksburg VA (S)

Carr, Angela, *Chmn,* Carleton University, Dept of Art History, Ottawa ON (S)

Carr, Jeffery, *Assoc Prof,* Saint Mary's College of Maryland, Arts and Letters Division, Saint Mary's City MD (S)

Carr, Margaret S, *Museum Registrar,* East Tennessee State University, Carroll Reece Museum, Johnson City TN

Carr, Richard, *Treas,* Beverly Historical Society, Cabot, Hale and Balch House Museums, Beverly MA

Carr, Timothy, *Librn,* Anacostia Museum, Research Library, Washington DC

Carracio, Kahleen, *Lectr,* Coe College, Dept of Art, Cedar Rapids IA (S)

Carrageorge, Adrianne, *Asst Prof,* Rochester Institute of Technology, School of Photographic Arts & Sciences, Rochester NY (S)

Carrard, Mary, *Prof,* American University, Dept of Art, Washington DC (S)

Carraro, Francine, *Asst Prof,* Southwest Texas State University, Dept of Art, San Marcos TX (S)

Carrera, Magali, *Chmn Art History,* University of Massachusetts Dartmouth, College of Visual and Performing Arts, North Dartmouth MA (S)

Carrero, Jaime, *Dir,* Inter American University of Puerto Rico, Dept of Art, San German PR (S)

Carriere, Karen, *Instr,* St Lawrence College, Dept of Visual & Creative Arts, Cornwall ON (S)

Carrigan, Jeanne, *Asst Prof Art Educ,* University of Arizona, Dept of Art, Tucson AZ (S)

Carris, Barbara, *Pres,* Rutland Area Art Association, Inc, Chaffee Art Center, Rutland VT

Carrl, Carolyn, *Deputy Dir,* National Portrait Gallery, Washington DC

Carrol, Charles, *Registrar,* Museum of Fine Arts, Houston, Houston TX

Carroll, David, *Registrar,* University of Utah, Utah Museum of Fine Arts, Salt Lake City UT

Carroll, E A, *Prof,* Vassar College, Art Dept, Poughkeepsie NY (S)

Carroll, James F L, *Dir,* New Arts Program Inc, Gallery, Kutztown PA

Carroll, Janet, *School Coordr,* Plaza de la Raza Cultural Center, Los Angeles CA

Carroll, Karen, *Dir,* Maryland Institute, Art Education Graduate Studies, Baltimore MD (S)

Carroll, Linda, *Instr,* Main Line Center for the Arts, Haverford PA (S)

Carroll, Margaret D, *Asst Prof,* Wellesley College, Art Dept, Wellesley MA (S)

Carroll, Roger, *Division Head,* Dallas Public Library, Fine Arts Division, Dallas TX

Carroll, U A, *Prof,* Vassar College, Art Dept, Poughkeepsie NY (S)

Carroll-de Sousa, Sheelagh, *Gallery Cur,* Chatham Cultural Centre, Thames Art Gallery, Chatham ON

Carroway, Rosemary, *Lectr,* Lambuth University, Dept of Human Ecology & Visual Arts, Jackson TN (S)

Carsen, Joann, *Asst Prof,* State University of New York at Albany, Art Dept, Albany NY (S)

Carson, Chris, *Cur & Educator,* Prairie Gallery, Grande Prairie AB

Carson, Gail, *Cultural Affairs Asst,* Federal Reserve Bank of Boston, Boston MA

Carson, Karen, *Vis Instr,* Claremont Graduate School, Dept of Fine Arts, Claremont CA (S)

Carson, Lew, *Prof,* California State University, Hayward, University Art Gallery, Hayward CA

Carson, Nan, *Performing Arts Coordr,* Organization of Saskatchewan Arts Councils (OSAC), Regina SK

Carson Williams, Doris, *Dir Marketing,* Carnegie Institute, Carnegie Museum of Art, Pittsburgh PA

Carstens, Jon, *Chmn,* Pacific Union College, Art Dept, Angwin CA (S)

Cart, Doran L, *Dir,* Liberty Memorial Museum & Archives, Kansas City MO

Carter, Alice T, *Librn,* Montgomery Museum of Fine Arts, Library, Montgomery AL

Carter, Charles Hill, *Owner,* Shirley Plantation, Charles City VA

Carter, Curtis L, *Dir,* Marquette University, Haggerty Museum of Art, Milwaukee WI

Carter, David, *Instr,* Dowling College, Dept of Visual Arts, Oakdale NY (S)

Carter, Floretta, *Cur,* Clark County Historical Society, Pioneer - Krier Museum, Ashland KS

Carter, Harold, *Assoc Prof,* Mansfield University, Art Dept, Mansfield PA (S)

Carter, John S, *Dir,* Philadelphia Maritime Museum, Philadelphia PA

Carter, Joseph, *Dir,* Will Rogers Memorial and Museum, Claremore OK

Carter, Joseph, *Dir,* Will Rogers Memorial and Museum, Media Center Library, Claremore OK

Carter, Kieth, *Adjunct Instr,* Lamar University, Art Dept, Beaumont TX (S)

Carter, Lee A, *Chmn Bd & Pres,* Cincinnati Institute of Fine Arts, Cincinnati OH

Carter, Lee Ault, *Chmn Cincinnati Inst of Fine Arts,* Cincinnati Institute of Fine Arts, Taft Museum, Cincinnati OH

Carter, Lynn, *Dir,* American-Scandinavian Foundation, New York NY

Carter, Mary, *Dir,* Museum of Neon Art, Los Angeles CA

Carter, May, *Asst Prof,* Lynchburg College, Art Dept, Lynchburg VA (S)

Carter, Nathan, *Dept Chmn,* Morgan State University, Dept of Art, Baltimore MD (S)

Carter, Rita, *Producer,* Center for Puppetry Arts, Atlanta GA

Carter, Robert, *Chmn Art Dept,* Saint Andrews Presbyterian College, Art Program, Laurinburg NC (S)

Carter, Robert, *Prof,* Nassau Community College, Art Dept, Garden City NY (S)

Carter, Ron, *Chmn,* Indiana University-East, Humanities Dept, Richmond IN (S)

Carter, Shirley S, *Assoc Prof,* University of North Florida, Dept of Communications & Visual Arts, Jacksonville FL (S)

Carter, Susan, *Cur & Registrar,* University of Tampa, Henry B Plant Museum, Tampa FL

Carter, Yvonne, *Prof,* University of the District of Columbia, Art Dept, Washington DC (S)

Carter-Carter, Susan, *VPres,* Society of American Graphic Artists, New York NY

Carter-Smith, Sharon, *Cur,* Persis Corporation, Art Collection, Honolulu HI

Cartland, John, *First VPres,* Arts Club of Chicago, Chicago IL

Cartmell, Robert, *Assoc Prof,* State University of New York at Albany, Art Dept, Albany NY (S)

Cartmell, Timothy, *Sr Museum Guide,* Board of Parks & Recreation, The Parthenon, Nashville TN

Cartwright, Guenther, *Assoc Prof,* Rochester Institute of Technology, School of Photographic Arts & Sciences, Rochester NY (S)

Cartwright, Rick, *Asst Prof,* Saint Francis College, Art Dept, Fort Wayne IN (S)

Cartwright, Roy, *Prof Fine Arts,* University of Cincinnati, School of Art, Cincinnati OH (S)

Caruthers, Robert, *Prof,* West Texas State University, Art, Communication & Theatre Dept, Canyon TX (S)

Carvahio, Mario, *Assoc Dean,* University of Manitoba, Faculty of Architecture, Winnipeg MB (S)

Carvalho, Joseph, *Dir,* Springfield Library & Museums Association, Connecticut Valley Historical Museum, Springfield MA

Carver, Dan, *Exec Dir,* Yeiser Art Center Inc, Paducah Art Guild Inc Gallery, Paducah KY

Carver, Melvin, *Chmn,* North Carolina Central University, Art Dept, Durham NC (S)

Carver Wees, Beth, *Cur of Decorative Arts,* Sterling and Francine Clark Art Institute, Williamstown MA

Cary, Richard, *Assoc Prof,* Mars Hill College, Art Dept, Mars Hill NC (S)

Cascieri, Arcangelo, *Dean,* Boston Architectural Center, Boston MA

Casey, Jacquelyn F, *Registrar,* Hunter Museum of Art, Chattanooga TN

Cashman, Norine D, *Cur,* Brown University, Art Slide Library, Providence RI

Caslin, Jean, *Exec Dir,* Houston Center For Photography, Houston TX

Casper, Joseph, *Pres,* Caspers, Inc, Art Collection, Tampa FL

Cassara, Tina, *Prof,* Cleveland Institute of Art, Cleveland OH (S)

Cassels-Brown, R, *Librn,* Saint Paul's School, Ohrstrom Library, Concord NH

Cassey, Robert, *VChmn,* Detroit Artists Market, Detroit MI

Cassidy, Brendan, *Dir,* Princeton University, Index of Christian Art, Princeton NJ

Cassill, Carroll, *Prof,* Cleveland Institute of Art, Cleveland OH (S)

Cassino, Michael, *Prof,* Adrian College, Art Dept, Adrian MI (S)

Cassone, John, *Assoc Prof,* Los Angeles Harbor College, Art Dept, Wilmington CA (S)

Castellani, Carla, *Museum Shop,* Niagara University, Castellani Art Museum, New York NY

Castelli, Marc, *Instr,* Main Line Center for the Arts, Haverford PA (S)

Castello, Katherine, *VPres,* Coquille Valley Art Association, Coquille OR

Castelnuovo, Sheri, *Cur Educ & Public Programming,* Madison Art Center, Madison WI

Casteras, Nancy, *Prog Coordr,* Woodbridge Township Cultural Arts Commission, Barron Arts Center, Woodbridge NJ

Castile, Rand, *Dir,* Asian Art Museum of San Francisco, Avery Brundage Collection, San Francisco CA

Castle, Charles, *Assoc Dir,* Museum of Contemporary Art, San Diego, La Jolla CA

Castle, Dalphine, *Regisgtrar & Technician,* Craigdarroch Castle Historical Museum Society, Victoria BC

Castle, Lynn, *Cur Art,* Art Museum of Southeast Texas, Beaumont TX

Castle, Wendell, *Prof,* Rochester Institute of Technology, School of Art and Design, Rochester NY (S)

Castleberry, May, *Librn,* Whitney Museum of American Art, New York NY

Castleberry, May, *Librn,* Whitney Museum of American Art, Library, New York NY

Castleman, Riva, *Deputy Dir Curatorial Affairs,* Museum of Modern Art, New York NY

Casto, Don M, *Pres,* Columbus Museum of Art, Columbus OH

Castonguay, Gerald, *Chmn,* Clark University, Dept of Visual & Performing Arts, Worcester MA (S)

Castriota, David, *Instr,* Sarah Lawrence College, Dept of Art History, Bronxville NY (S)

Castro, Louis, *Pres,* Triton Museum of Art, Santa Clara CA

Caswell, James O, *Head,* University of British Columbia, Dept of Fine Arts, Vancouver BC (S)

Caswell, Lucy Shelton, *Cur,* Ohio State University, Cartoon, Graphic & Photographic Arts Research Library, Columbus OH

Catalano, Laura, *Registrar,* The Buffalo Fine Arts Academy, Albright-Knox Art Gallery, Buffalo NY

Cate, Phillip Dennis, *Dir,* Rutgers, The State University of New Jersey, Jane Voorhees Zimmerli Art Museum, New Brunswick NJ

Cateforts, David, *Asst Prof,* University of Kansas, Kress Foundation Dept of Art History, Lawrence KS (S)

Catling, William, *Asst Prof,* Azusa Pacific University, College of Liberal Arts, Art Dept, Azusa CA (S)

Catron, Joanna D, *Cur,* Mary Washington College, The Gari Melchers Estate & Memorial Gallery, Fredericksburg VA

Catterall, John E, *Chmn,* University of Florida, Dept of Art, Gainesville FL (S)

Caulk, Douglas, *Museum Mgr,* State University of New York at Purchase, Neuberger Museum, Purchase NY

Caulkins, Deborah, *Coordr,* Lycoming College Gallery, Williamsport PA

Causey, Dorothy, *Registrar,* Edison Community College, Gallery of Fine Art, Fort Myers FL

Cauthen, Gene, *Dir Fine Arts Gallery,* Mount Wachusett Community College, Art Galleries, Gardner MA

Cavalaieri, Corliss, *Cur Exhibits,* Port of History Museum, Philadelphia PA

Cavalier, Joseph, *Prof,* School of the Art Institute of Chicago, Chicago IL (S)

Cavallaro, Marie A, *Assoc Prof,* Salisbury State University, Art Dept, Salisbury MD (S)

Cavalli, Annie, *Pres Board of Dir,* Lake County Civic Center Association, Inc, Heritage Museum and Gallery, Leadville CO

Cavan, Ralph, *Instr,* Mount Mary College, Art Dept, Milwaukee WI (S)

Cavanagh, T, *Instr,* Technical University of Nova Scotia, Faculty of Architecture, Halifax NS (S)

Cavanaugh, Marianne L, *Assoc Librn,* The Saint Louis Art Museum, Richardson Memorial Library, Saint Louis MO

Cave, Deborah, *Pres,* New Jersey Center for Visual Arts, Summit NJ

Cavener, Nancy, *Dir Educ,* Cheekwood-Tennessee Botanical Garden Museum of Art, Education Dept, Nashville TN (S)

Cavener, Nancy, *Educational Specialist,* Cheekwood-Tennessee Botanical Gardens & Museum of Art, Nashville TN

Caviness, Madeline H, *Prof,* Tufts University, Dept of Art & Art History, Medford MA (S)

Cawthron, Ruby, *Cur,* Colorado City Historical Museum, Colorado City TX

Cazort, Mimi, *Cur Prints & Drawings,* National Gallery of Canada, Ottawa ON

Cecere, James G, *Chmn Dept,* Mansfield University, Art Dept, Mansfield PA (S)

Cecil, Sarah, *Asst Dir Development,* Worcester Art Museum, Worcester MA

Cederna, Ann, *Vis Asst Prof,* Catholic University of America, School of Architecture & Planning, Washington DC (S)

Celenko, Ted, *Cur African, S Pacific, Pre-Columbian,* Indianapolis Museum of Art, Indianapolis IN

Cellini, Nicholas, *Supv Fine Arts Servs,* Beverly Hills Public Library, Fine Arts Library, Beverly Hills CA

Cembrola, Robert, *Sr Cur,* Naval War College Museum, Newport RI

Cemey, Kelly, *Lectr,* Mount Allison University, Fine Arts Dept, Sackville NB (S)

Centini, Gail, *Exec Dir,* Georgia Volunteer Lawyers for the Arts, Inc, Atlanta GA

Centofanti, Louis M, *Chmn,* Niagara University, Fine Arts Dept, Niagara Falls NY (S)

Cepek, Larry, *Dept Chmn,* Ohio Dominican College, Art Dept, Columbus OH (S)

Cernighia, Alice, *Cur Historical Educ,* Ella Sharp Museum, Jackson MI

Cernuschi, Claude, *Asst Prof,* Duke University, Dept of Art and Art History, Durham NC (S)

Cerny, Charlene, *Dir,* Museum of New Mexico, Museum of International Folk Art, Santa Fe NM

Cerretti, Richard, *Instr,* Hannibal La Grange College, Art Dept, Hannibal MO (S)

Ceruti, Mary, *Prog Mgr,* Capp Street Project, San Francisco CA

Cervantes, James, *Cur Military History,* Heritage Plantation of Sandwich, Sandwich MA

Cetlin, Cynthia, *Asst Prof,* Ohio Wesleyan University, Fine Arts Dept, Delaware OH (S)

Chabot, Aurore, *Assoc Prof Ceramics,* University of Arizona, Dept of Art, Tucson AZ (S)

Chacin de Fuchs, Mercedes, *Lectr,* Toronto Art Therapy Institute, Toronto ON (S)

Chadbourne, Janice, *Cur of Fine Arts,* Boston Public Library, Fine Arts Dept, Boston MA

Chaffee, Tom, *Assoc Prof,* Arkansas State University, Dept of Art, Jonesboro AR (S)

Chait, Andrew, *Secy,* National Antique & Art Dealers Association of America, New York NY

Chalker, Cynthia, *Cur Educ,* Please Touch Museum, Philadelphia PA

Challener, Elizbeth, *Exec Dir,* Montalvo Center for the Arts, Saratoga CA

Chalmers, E Laurence, *Pres,* San Antonio Museum Association, Inc, San Antonio TX

Chalmers, J Kim, *Chmn,* Coker College, Art Dept, Hartsville SC (S)

Chamber, Don S, *Chairperson Div Creative Arts,* Monterey Peninsula College, Art Dept, Monterey CA (S)

Chamberlain, Amelia, *Coordr Children's Prog,* Southern Oregon Historical Society, Jacksonville Museum of Southern Oregon History, Jacksonville OR

Chamberlain, Ann, *Program Dir,* Headlands Center for the Arts, Sausalito CA

Chamberlain, Anne, *Pres,* Art Information Center, Inc, New York NY

Chamberlain, Bill, *Chmn,* Southeast Missouri State University, Dept of Art, Cape Girardeau MO (S)

Chamberlain, Harold, *VPres,* Madison County Historical Society, Cottage Lawn, Oneida NY

Chamberlain, Owen, *Dept Chmn,* Portland Community College, Visual & Performing Arts Division, Portland OR (S)

Chamberlain, Peter, *Asst Prof,* Elmira College, Art Dept, Elmira NY (S)

Chamberland, Alan, *Supt,* Sterling and Francine Clark Art Institute, Williamstown MA

Chamberlin, Marsha, *Executive Dir,* Ann Arbor Art Association, Ann Arbor MI

Chamberlin, Robin, *Conservator,* University of California, Los Angeles, Fowler Museum of Cultural History, Los Angeles CA

Chamberlin, Scott, *Preparator,* University of Southern California, Fisher Gallery, Los Angeles CA

Chamberlin-Hellman, Maria, *Chmn,* Marymount College, Art Dept, Tarrytown NY (S)

Chambliss, Charles, *Pres,* Arts Council of Richmond, Inc, Richmond VA

Chambliss, George, *Exec Dir Jekyll Island,* Jekyll Island Museum, Jekyll Island GA

Champlin, Norma, *Executive Secy,* San Antonio Art League, San Antonio TX

Chan, Suzy, *Fine Art Librn,* Beverly Hills Public Library, Fine Art Library, Beverly Hills CA

Chance, JoNell, *Asst to Dir,* Art Museum of Southeast Texas, Beaumont TX

Chandlee, Truda, *Pres,* L A Art Association, Los Angeles CA

Chandler, John, *Dir,* Attleboro Museum, Center for the Arts, Attleboro MA

Chang, F Ming, *Assoc Prof,* Seton Hall University, College of Arts & Sciences, South Orange NJ (S)

Chang, John K, *Deputy Dir,* Vancouver City Archives, Vancouver BC

Chang, Joseph, *Research Asst Oriental Art,* Nelson-Atkins Museum of Art, Kansas City MO

Chang, Phyllis, *Museum Educator,* Craft and Folk Art Museum, Los Angeles CA

Chanlatte, Luis A, *Archaeologist,* University of Puerto Rico, Museum of Anthropology, History & Art, Rio Piedras PR

Channing, Laurence, *Chief Ed Museum Publications,* Cleveland Museum of Art, Cleveland OH

Channing, Susan R, *Dir,* Spaces, Cleveland OH

Chao, Paul, *Assoc Dean,* Seton Hall University, Library, South Orange NJ

Chapin, Leslie A, *Treas,* Westfield Athenaeum, Jasper Rand Art Museum, Westfield MA

Chapin, Mona L, *Head Librn,* Cincinnati Museum Association, Mary R Schiff Library, Cincinnati OH

Chaplin, George, *Prof,* Trinity College, Dept of Fine Arts, Hartford CT (S)

Chaplock, Sharon Kayne, *Dir Audio-Visual,* Milwaukee Public Museum, Milwaukee WI

Chapman, Angela, *Communications Officer,* Hickory Museum of Art, Inc, Hickory NC

Chapman, Gary, *Pres,* Cherokee National Historical Society, Inc, Tahlequah OK

Chapman, Gary, *Asst Prof,* University of Alabama in Birmingham, Dept of Art, Birmingham AL (S)

Chapman, Gretel, *Assoc Prof,* Southern Illinois University, School of Art & Design, Carbondale IL (S)

Chapman, Jefferson, *Dir,* University of Tennessee, Frank H McClung Museum, Knoxville TN

Chapman, Jefferson, *Dir,* University of Tennessee, Eleanor Dean Audigier Art Collection, Knoxville TN

Chapp, Belena S, *Dir,* University of Delaware, University Gallery, Newark DE

Chapp, Belena S, *Dir/Cur,* University of Delaware, University Gallery, Newark DE

Chappell, Berkley, *Prof,* Oregon State University, Dept of Art, Corvallis OR (S)

Chappell, Miles, *Prof,* College of William and Mary, Dept of Fine Arts, Williamsburg VA (S)

Charette, Luc, *Dir,* Galerie d'art de l'Universite de Moncton, Moncton NB

Charles, Ellen MacNeile, *Pres,* Marjorie Merriweather Post Foundation of DC, Hillwood Museum, Washington DC

Charles, Peter, *Instr,* Georgetown University, Dept of Fine Arts, Washington DC (S)

Charles, Sophie, *Museum Shop Mgr & Arts & Crafts Dir,* Yugtarvik Regional Museum & Bethel Visitors Center, Bethel AK

Charles/MA, Charles, *Assoc Prof,* University of North Florida, Dept of Communications & Visual Arts, Jacksonville FL (S)

Charlton, Deborah, *Mgr Sales & Info,* Frick Collection, New York NY

Charlton, Kathy, *Dir Development,* Cleveland Center for Contemporary Art, Cleveland OH

Charnefski, John, *Cur,* Malaspina College, Nanaimo Art Gallery & Exhibition Centre, Nanaimo BC

Charnow, Elliott, *Chmn,* Chabot College, Humanities Division, Hayward CA (S)

Chase, Ann, *Dir,* College of Mount Saint Joseph, Archbishop Alter Library, Cincinnati OH

Chase, Guy M, *Dir & Cur,* Greenville College, Richard W Bock Sculpture Collection, Greenville IL

Chase, Guy M, *Librn,* Greenville College, The Richard W Bock Sculpture Collection & Art Library, Greenville IL

Chase, Guy M, *Dept Head,* Greenville College, Division of Language, Literature & Fine Arts, Greenville IL (S)

Chase, Harriet Remington, *VPres,* Fall River Historical Society, Fall River MA

Chase, W T, *Head Conservator & Technical Laboratory,* Freer Gallery of Art, Washington DC

Chatelain, Gary, *Prof,* James Madison University, Dept of Art, Harrisonburg VA (S)

Chatfield, Margaret, *Art Librn Asst,* Old Dominion University, Elise N Hofheimer Art Library, Norfolk VA

Chatfield Taylor, Adele, *Pres,* American Academy in Rome, New York NY (S)

Chatterjee, Sankar, *Cur Vertebrate Paleontology,* Texas Tech University, Museum, Lubbock TX

Chauteau, Suzanne, *Prof,* Xavier University, Dept of Art, Cincinnati OH (S)

Chaves, Frances, *Cur,* The Reader's Digest Association Inc, Pleasantville NY

Chavez, Eduardo, *Instr,* Woodstock School of Art, Inc, Woodstock NY (S)

Chavez, Patricia, *Dir,* Fuller Lodge Art Center, Los Alamos NM

Chavez, Patricio, *Cur,* Centro Cultural De La Raza, San Diego CA

Chavez, Thomas, *Assoc Dir,* Museum of New Mexico, Palace of Governors, Santa Fe NM

Chavka, Rich, *Exhib Designer,* Southern Oregon Historical Society, Jacksonville Museum of Southern Oregon History, Jacksonville OR

Cheatham, Frank, *Prof,* Texas Tech University, Dept of Art, Lubbock TX (S)

Cheatham, Jackson, *Dir Visual Arts,* Morgan County Foundation, Inc, Madison-Morgan Cultural Center, Madison GA

Cheatham, Jane, *Assoc Prof,* Texas Tech University, Dept of Art, Lubbock TX (S)

Cheatham, Richard, *Dean,* Southwest Texas State University, Dept of Art, San Marcos TX (S)

Checefsky, Bruce, *Gallery Dir,* Cleveland Institute of Art, Reinberger Galleries, Cleveland OH

Chee, Cheng-Khee, *Assoc Prof,* University of Minnesota, Duluth, Art Dept, Duluth MN (S)

Cheek, Belinda, *Techician,* North Central College, Oesterle Library, Naperville IL

Cheevers, James W, *Senior Cur,* United States Naval Academy Museum, Annapolis MD

Chehab, Hafez, *Asst Prof,* State University of New York College at Brockport, Dept of Art & Art History, Brockport NY (S)

Chellstrop, Marjorie, *Instr,* Madonna College, Art Dept, Livonia MI (S)

Chen, Chiong-Yiao, *Asst Prof,* University of North Alabama, Dept of Art, Florence AL (S)

Chen, Lynn, *Librn,* American Numismatic Association, Library, Colorado Springs CO

Chen, Michael, *Instr,* Joe Kubert School of Cartoon & Graphic Art, Inc, Dover NJ (S)

Cheney, Iris, *Prof,* University of Massachusetts, Amherst, Art History Program, Amherst MA (S)

Cheney, J, *Fine Arts Conservator,* Mount Allison University, Owens Art Gallery, Sackville NB

Cheney, Liana, *Chairperson Dept,* University of Massachusetts at Lowell, Dept of Art, Lowell MA (S)

Cheng, Jane, *Cataloger,* Nelson-Atkins Museum of Art, Kenneth and Helen Spencer Art Reference Library, Kansas City MO

Chepp, Mark, *Dir,* Springfield Museum of Art, Springfield OH (S)

Chepp, Mark J, *Dir,* Springfield Museum of Art, Springfield OH

Chepulis, Kyle, *Technical Dir,* Brooklyn Arts Council, BACA Downtown, Brooklyn NY

Chermayeff, Ivan, *Art Consultant,* Mobil Corporation, Art Collection, Fairfax VA

Chernow, Burt, *Faculty,* Housatonic Community College, Art Dept, Bridgeport CT (S)

Cherol, John, *Pres,* Cheekwood-Tennessee Botanical Garden Museum of Art, Education Dept, Nashville TN (S)

Cherol, John A, *Dir,* Cheekwood-Tennessee Botanical Gardens & Museum of Art, Nashville TN

Cherry, Schroeder, *Dir Education,* Baltimore Museum of Art, Baltimore MD

Cherwick, Eugene, *Exec Dir,* Ukrainian Cultural and Educational Centre, Winnipeg MB

Cheshire, Craig, *Prof,* Portland State University, Dept of Art, Portland OR (S)

Cheshire, Julie, *Planned Giving Grants Coordr,* San Diego Museum of Art, San Diego CA

Chesser, Bruce, *Chmn,* Ohio Northern University, Dept of Art, Ada OH (S)

Chester, Timothy J, *Dir,* Public Museum of Grand Rapids, Grand Rapids MI

Chevian, Margaret, *Specialist,* Providence Public Library, Art & Music Services, Providence RI

Chew, Elizabeth, *Asst Cur,* The Phillips Collection, Washington DC

Chew, Paul A, *CEO & Dir,* Westmoreland Museum of Art, Greensburg PA

Chew, Paul A, *Dir,* Westmoreland Museum of Art, Art Reference Library, Greensburg PA

Chew, Ron, *Dir,* Wind Luke Asian Museum Memorial Foundation, Inc, Seattle WA

Chiburis, Nick J, *Prof Art,* Iowa Western Community College, Art Dept, Council Bluffs IA (S)

Chickanzeff, Sharon, *Dir,* New York University, Stephen Chan Library of Fine Arts, New York NY

Chickering, F William, *Dean,* Pratt Institute Library, Art & Architecture Dept, Brooklyn NY

Chieffo, Beverly, *Instr,* Albertus Magnus College, Art Dept, New Haven CT (S)

Chieffo, Clifford, *Prof,* Georgetown University, Dept of Fine Arts, Washington DC (S)

Chieffo, Clifford T, *Cur,* Georgetown University, Art and History Museum, Washington DC

Chieffo, Patricia H, *Assoc Cur,* Georgetown University, Art and History Museum, Washington DC

Chieffo, Patricia H, *Intern Origrams Officer,* National Museum of American Art, Washington DC

Chiego, William J, *Dir,* Marion Koogler McNay Art Museum, San Antonio TX

Chiesa, Wilfredo, *Assoc Prof,* University of Massachusetts at Boston, Art Dept, Boston MA (S)

Chiger, Eleanor, *Office Mgr,* Yeshiva University Museum, New York NY

Chijioke, Mary Ellen, *Cur,* Swarthmore College, Friends Historical Library, Swarthmore PA

Child, Abigail, *Instr,* Sarah Lawrence College, Dept of Art History, Bronxville NY (S)

Child, Kent, *Gallery Advisor & Humanities Division Dir,* Gavilan College, Art Gallery, Gilroy CA

Child Debs, Katherine, *Coll Mgr,* Los Angeles County Museum of Natural History, William S Hart Museum, Newhall CA

Childs, Bruce, *Assoc Prof,* Austin Peay State University, Dept of Art, Clarksville TN (S)

Childs, William A P, *Chmn Prog in Classical Archaelogy,* Princeton University, Dept of Art and Archaeology, Princeton NJ (S)

Chilla, Benigna, *Instr,* Berkshire Community College, Dept of Fine Arts, Pittsfield MA (S)

Chillman, Helen, *Slide & Photograph,* Yale University, Art and Architecture Library, New Haven CT

Chilton, Meredith, *Cur,* George R Gardiner Museum of Ceramic Art, Toronto ON

Chimy, Myron, *Dir,* Basilian Fathers, Mundare AB

Chin, Cecelia H, *Chief Librn,* National Portrait Gallery, Library, Washington DC

Chin, Cecilia, *Chief Librn,* National Museum of American Art, Library of the National Museum of American Art and the National Portrait Gallery, Washington DC

Chin, Veronica, *Dept Head,* Ray College of Design, Chicago IL (S)

Chin, Wanda W, *Coordr Exhibits & Exhibits Designer,* University of Alaska, Museum, Fairbanks AK

Chipley, Sheila M, *Asst Prof,* Concord College, Fine Art Division, Athens WV (S)

Chira, Victor, *VPres Development,* Pennsylvania Academy of the Fine Arts, Galleries, Philadelphia PA

Chism, Jim, *VPres,* Wisconsin Painters & Sculptors, Inc, Milwaukee WI

Chisolm, Donna, *Site & Museum Cur,* Longfellow-Evangeline State Commemorative Area, Saint Martinville LA

Chiss, Judy, *Assoc Executive Dir,* Chicago Children's Museum, Chicago IL

Chmel, Patrick, *Chmn,* Rider College, Dept of Fine Arts, Lawrenceville NJ (S)

Chmielewski, Wendy, *Cur Peace Collection,* Swarthmore College, Friends Historical Library, Swarthmore PA

Choate, Glenda, *Dir,* Trail of '98 Museum, Skagway AK

Choate, Jerry, *Instructor,* Northeastern Oklahoma State University, Tahlequah OK (S)

Chodkowski, Henry J, *Prof,* University of Louisville, Allen R Hite Art Institute, Louisville KY (S)

Chojecki, Randolph, *Ref Librn,* Daemen College, Marian Library, Amherst NY

Chong, Alan, *Cur Paintings,* Cleveland Museum of Art, Cleveland OH

Chouinard, Denise, *Pres,* La Societe des Decorateurs-Ensembliers du Quebec, Interior Designers Society of Quebec, Montreal PQ

Chouinard, Gaetan, *Secy-General,* Musee du Quebec, Quebec PQ

Chow, David, *Instr,* Columbia University, School of the Arts, Division of Painting & Sculpture, New York NY (S)

Chretien, Heidi, *Asst Prof,* University of North Carolina at Wilmington, Dept of Fine Arts - Division of Art, Wilmington NC (S)

Chrisman, Diane J, *Deputy Dir Public Services,* Buffalo and Erie County Public Library, Buffalo NY

Chrisman, George, *Dir,* Avila College, Thornhill Art Gallery, Kansas City MO

Chrisman, Joann, *House Adminr,* Charleston Museum, Heyward-Washington House, Charleston SC

Christensen, V A, *Dir,* Spiva Art Center, Inc, Joplin MO

Christenson, Edwin, *Asst Prof,* Elmira College, Art Dept, Elmira NY (S)

Christenson, Elroy, *Head Dept,* North Seattle Community College, Art Dept, Seattle WA (S)

Christian, Marni, *Dir Annual Giving & Membership,* Pennsylvania Academy of the Fine Arts, Galleries, Philadelphia PA

Christian, Martha, *Instr,* Rhodes College, Dept of Art, Memphis TN (S)

Christian, Roger, *Lectr,* Southwest Texas State University, Dept of Art, San Marcos TX (S)

Christiana, Michael, *Prof,* Northwestern Connecticut Community College, Fine Arts Dept, Winsted CT (S)

Christison, Muriel, *Lectr,* College of William and Mary, Dept of Fine Arts, Williamsburg VA (S)

Christ-Janer, Arland F, *Pres,* Ringling School of Art and Design, Sarasota FL (S)

Christman, David C, *Acting Dir,* Hofstra University, Hofstra Museum, Hempstead NY

Christman, George, *Instr,* Avila College, Art Division, Dept of Performing and Visual Art, Kansas City MO (S)

Christofides, Constantine, *Dir,* University of Washington, School of Art, Seattle WA (S)

Christopher, Theresa, *Registrar,* DuSable Museum of African American History, Chicago IL

Christovich, Mary Louise, *Pres of Board,* Kemper & Leila Williams Foundation, New Orleans LA

Chu, Petra, *Chmn,* Seton Hall University, College of Arts & Sciences, South Orange NJ (S)

Chu, Petrateu Doesschate, *Dir,* Seton Hall University, South Orange NJ

Chumley, Jere, *Assoc Prof,* Cleveland State Community College, Dept of Art, Cleveland TN (S)

Chung, Robert Y, *Asst Prof,* Rochester Institute of Technology, School of Printing, Rochester NY (S)

Church, John, *Instr,* Interlochen Arts Academy, Dept of Visual Art, Interlochen MI (S)

Churches, Roger, *Prof,* La Sierra University, Art Dept, Riverside CA (S)

Churchill, Angiola R, *Prof,* New York University, Dept of Art & Art Professions, New York NY (S)

Churchman, Michael, *Dir Development,* Nelson-Atkins Museum of Art, Kansas City MO

Churchwell, Beth, *Development Coordr,* San Angelo Museum of Fine Arts, San Angelo TX

Churdar, Janice, *Staff Supvr,* Bob Jones University, Museum & Art Gallery, Greenville SC

Chwast, Seymore, *VPres,* Art Directors Club, Inc, New York NY

Chytilo, Lynne, *Asst Prof,* Albion College, Dept of Visual Arts, Albion MI (S)

Ciampa, John, *Chmn American Video Institute,* Rochester Institute of Technology, School of Photographic Arts & Sciences, Rochester NY (S)

Ciampa, Rose, *Secy,* The Queens Museum of Art, Flushing NY

Cianfoni, Emilio, *Chief Conservator,* Vizcaya Museum and Gardens, Miami FL

Ciccione, Felice, *Cur Coll,* The National Park Service, United States Department of the Interior, The Statue of Liberty National Monument, New York NY

Ciccone, Amy Navratil, *Head Librn,* University of Southern California, Helen Topping Architecture & Fine Arts Library, Los Angeles CA

Cichy, Barbara, *Chmn,* Bismarck Junior College, Fine Arts Dept, Bismarck ND (S)

Cicotello, Louis, *Chmn,* University of Colorado-Colorado Springs, Fine Arts Dept, Colorado Springs CO (S)

Cieslak, Judith, *Chmn Humanities,* City Colleges of Chicago, Olive-Harvey College, Chicago IL (S)

Cikovsky, Nicholai, *Cur American Art,* National Gallery of Art, Washington DC

Cilella, Sal, *Executive Dir,* Columbia Museum School, Columbia SC (S)

Cilella, Salvatore G, *Dir,* Columbia Museum of Art, Columbia SC

Cilella, Salvatore G, *Dir,* Columbia Museum of Art, Columbia Art Association, Columbia SC

Ciminera, Marjorie, *Exec Dir,* Mystic Art Association, Inc, Mystic CT

Cinelli, Michael J, *Head Dept,* Northern Michigan University, Dept of Art and Design, Marquette MI (S)

Cipriano, M, *Chmn Dept,* Central Connecticut State University, Dept of Art, New Britain CT (S)

Cirillo, Joan, *Public Information,* Cheekwood-Tennessee Botanical Gardens & Museum of Art, Nashville TN

Cirone, Christie, *Instr,* Illinois Central College, Dept of Fine Arts, East Peoria IL (S)

Ciscle, George, *Dir,* The Contemporary, Museum for Contemporary Arts, Baltimore MD

Ciski, Maria T, *Registrar,* Wichita State University, Edwin A Ulrich Museum of Art, Wichita KS

Citrin, Susie, *Pres,* Birmingham-Bloomfield Art Association, Birmingham MI

Citron, Harvey, *Instr,* New York Academy of Art, Graduate School of Figurative Art, New York NY (S)

Citty, Betty, *Admin Sec,* North Carolina State University, Chinqua-Penn Plantation House, Garden & Greenhouses, Reidsville NC

Clahassey, Patricia, *Prof,* College of Saint Rose, Dept of Art, Albany NY (S)

Claiborne, Herbert A, *Pres,* Virginia Museum of Fine Arts, Richmond VA

Clancy, Patrick, *Chmn Photography,* Kansas City Art Institute, Kansas City MO (S)

Clapp, Anne, *Prof,* Wellesley College, Art Dept, Wellesley MA (S)

Clarien, Gary, *Workshop Supv,* Palo Alto Cultural Center, Palo Alto CA

Clark, Andrea, *Registrar,* Norton Simon Museum, Pasadena CA

Clark, A Wm, *Prof,* Fairleigh Dickinson University, Fine Arts Dept, Rutherford NJ (S)

Clark, B, *Cur American Art,* Chrysler Museum, Norfolk VA

Clark, Betty, *Communications Officer,* Queen's University, Agnes Etherington Art Centre, Kingston ON

Clark, Bob, *Head Dept,* Southwestern Community College, Commercial Art and Advertising Design Dept, Sylva NC (S)

Clark, Erica, *Dir Development,* The Museum of Contemporary Art, Los Angeles CA

Clark, Gary F, *Asst Prof,* Bloomsburg University, Dept of Art, Bloomsburg PA (S)

Clark, Ian Christie, *Pres,* Nova Scotia College of Art and Design, Halifax NS (S)

Clark, Ian Christie, *Pres,* Nova Scotia College of Art and Design, Anna Leonowens Gallery, Halifax NS

Clark, James, *Exec Dir,* Clay Studio, Philadelphia PA

Clark, James M, *Chmn,* Blackburn College, Dept of Art, Carlinville IL (S)

Clark, James M, *Exec Dir,* Public Art Fund, Inc, New York NY

Clark, Jennifer S, *Exec Dir,* Nebraska Arts Council Library, Omaha NE

Clark, Jeri, *Pres,* Licking County Art Association Gallery, Newark OH

Clark, Jessica, *Public Information Asst,* University of Chicago, David and Alfred Smart Museum of Art, Chicago IL

Clark, Joan, *Head Main Library,* Cleveland Public Library, Fine Arts & Special Collections Dept, Cleveland OH

Clark, John B, *Dir,* The Bruce Museum, Greenwich CT

Clark, Jon, *Chmn Crafts,* Temple University, Tyler School of Art, Philadelphia PA (S)

Clark, Joyce, *Cur Asst,* Regina Public Library, Dunlop Art Gallery, Regina SK

Clark, Kinball, *Cataloger,* National Portrait Gallery, Library, Washington DC

Clark, Laurie Beth, *Assoc Prof,* University of Wisconsin, Madison, Dept of Art, Madison WI (S)

Clark, L Kimball, *Cataloger,* National Museum of American Art, Library of the National Museum of American Art and the National Portrait Gallery, Washington DC

Clark, Lynda, *Dir,* Northern Illinois University, NIU Art Museum, De Kalb IL

Clark, Marcene R, *Exec Dir,* Touchstone Center for Crafts, Uniontown PA

Clark, Marcene R, *Exec Dir,* Touchstone Center for Crafts, Uniontown PA (S)

Clark, Margot, *Assoc Prof,* University of New Hampshire, Dept of the Arts, Durham NH (S)

Clark, Mark A, *Cur Decorative Arts,* Chrysler Museum, Norfolk VA

Clark, Michael, *Sr Library Asst,* Emily Carr College of Art & Design, Library, Vancouver BC

Clark, Moira, *Instr,* Toronto School of Art, Toronto ON (S)

Clark, Pam, *Gift Adminr,* University of Lethbridge, Art Gallery, Lethbridge AB

Clark, Patricia J, *Chmn,* California State University, Long Beach, Art Dept, Long Beach CA (S)

Clark, Peter P, *Registrar,* National Baseball Hall of Fame and Museum, Inc, Art Collection, Cooperstown NY

Clark, R, *Instr,* Community College of Rhode Island, Dept of Art, Warwick RI (S)

Clark, Richard, *Cur Design,* United States Military Academy, West Point Museum, West Point NY

Clark, R J, *Prof,* Princeton University, Dept of Art and Archaeology, Princeton NJ (S)

Clark, Robin, *Instr,* Indiana University of Pennsylvania, Dept of Art and Art Education, Indiana PA (S)

Clark, Ronald, *Head Independent Study Prog,* Whitney Museum of American Art, New York NY

Clark, Sara B, *Staff Asst,* Saginaw Valley State University, Dept of Art and Design, University Center MI (S)

Clark, Sonia, *Pres,* Rosemount Victorian House Museum, Pueblo CO

Clark, Sylvia, *Head Dept Interiors & Graphic Studies,* Drexel University, Nesbitt College of Design Arts, Philadelphia PA (S)

Clark, Tommy, *Asst Prof,* Campbellsville College, Fine Arts Division, Campbellsville KY (S)

Clark, Tony, *Dir,* Severin Wunderman Museum, Irvine CA

Clark, Tony, *Librn,* Severin Wunderman Museum, Research Library, Irvine CA

Clark, Trinkett, *Cur Contemporary Art,* Chrysler Museum, Norfolk VA

Clark, Vicky A, *Assoc Cur Contemporary Art,* Carnegie Institute, Carnegie Museum of Art, Pittsburgh PA

Clark, Wayne, *Exec Dir,* Museum of New York, Rock Hill SC

Clark, William, *Asst Prof,* Cedar Crest College, Art Dept, Allentown PA (S)

Clark, Willy, *Prof,* Shoreline Community College, Humanities Division, Seattle WA (S)

Clarke, Allan, *Exhib Officer,* Newfoundland Museum, Saint John's NF

Clarke, Allan, *Head Public Programming,* Newfoundland Museum, Newfoundland Museum at the Murray Premises, Saint John's NF

Clarke, Ann, *Prof,* Lakehead University, Dept of Visual Arts, Thunder Bay ON (S)

Clarke, Eugenia, *Archivist,* Planting Fields Foundation, Coe Hall at Planting Fields Arboretum, Oyster Bay NY

Clarke, James, *Pres,* National Art Education Association, Reston VA

Clarke, Jude, *Art Educ,* Vernon Art Gallery, Vernon BC

Clarke, Julie, *Pres,* Prescott Fine Arts Association, Gallery, Prescott AZ

Clarke, Robert, *Asst Prof,* Mohawk Valley Community College, Advertising Design and Production, Utica NY (S)

Clarke, Sherman, *Asst Librn,* Amon Carter Museum, Library, Fort Worth TX

Clarke, Sterling, *Dir Photography,* Art Institute of Fort Lauderdale, Fort Lauderdale FL (S)

Clarkin, William, *Librn & Archivist,* Print Club of Albany, Museum, Albany NY

Clark-Langager, Sarah, *Dir,* Western Washington University, Western Gallery, Bellingham WA

Clary, Morse, *Instr,* Columbia Basin College, Art Dept, Pasco WA (S)

Classen, Kathy, *Cur,* Barr Colony Heritage Cultural Centre, Lloydminster SK

Classen, Kathy, *Cur,* Imhoff Art Gallery, Lloydminster SK

Classen, Linda M, *Head,* Birmingham Public Library, Arts, Music & Recreation Department, Birmingham AL

Claus, Ruth S, *Dir Educ,* Hunterdon Art Center, Clinton NJ

Claussen, Louise Keith, *Dir,* Morris Communications Corporation, Morris Museum of Art, Augusta GA

Claxton-Oldfield, Patricia, *Librn,* The Robert McLaughlin Gallery, Library, Oshawa ON

Clay, Phillip L, *Urban Studies & Planning,* Massachusetts Institute of Technology, School of Architecture and Planning, Cambridge MA (S)

Clay, Vaughn, *Gallery Dir,* Indiana University of Pennsylvania, Kipp Gallery, Indiana PA

Clay, Vaughn, *Instr,* Indiana University of Pennsylvania, Dept of Art and Art Education, Indiana PA (S)

Clayson, Hollis, *Assoc Prof,* Northwestern University, Evanston, Dept of Art History, Evanston IL (S)

Clayton, Greg, *Asst Prof,* Harding University, Dept of Art, Searcy AR (S)

Clayton, Richard, *Pres,* Concord Museum, Concord MA

Clearwater, David A, *Librn,* Southern Alberta Art Gallery, Library, Lethbridge AB

Cleary, Cindy, *Mgr & Gallery Dir,* Brand Library & Art Galleries, Glendale CA

Cleary, James, *Pres,* Madison County Historical Society, Cottage Lawn, Oneida NY

Cleary, John R, *Assoc Prof,* Salisbury State University, Art Dept, Salisbury MD (S)

Cleary, Manon, *Prof,* University of the District of Columbia, Art Dept, Washington DC (S)

Cleaver, J D, *Cur of Coll,* Oregon Historical Society, Portland OR

Cleland, Camille, *Asst Dir for Technical Services,* Skokie Public Library, Skokie IL

Clemans, H, *Instr,* Golden West College, Visual Art Dept, Huntington Beach CA (S)

Clemenson, Gay, *Dir,* Jackson County Historical Society, 1859 Jail, Marshal s Home & Museum, Independence MO

Clement, Constance, *Asst Dir,* Yale University, Yale Center for British Art, New Haven CT

Clement, Louise, *Instr,* Samuel S Fleisher Art Memorial, Philadelphia PA (S)

Clement, Russell T, *Fine Arts Librn,* Brigham Young University, Harold B Lee Library, Provo UT

Clementi, Anthony, *Asst Prof,* New York Institute of Technology, Fine Arts Dept, Old Westbury NY (S)

Clementi, Bobbie, *Prof,* Daytona Beach Community College, Dept of Fine Arts & Visual Arts, Daytona Beach FL (S)

Cleminshaw, Doug, *Asst Prof,* Rochester Institute of Technology, School of Art and Design, Rochester NY (S)

Clemmer, Edwin L, *Prof,* Adams State College, Dept of Visual Arts, Alamosa CO (S)

Clemmer, Joel, *Library Dir,* MacAlester College, DeWitt Wallace Library, Saint Paul MN

Clemmons, Sara, *Chmn Fine Arts Division,* Chipola Junior College, Division of Fine Arts and Humanities, Marianna FL (S)

Clervi, Paul, *Assoc Prof,* William Woods-Westminster Colleges, Art Dept, Fulton MO (S)

Clervi, Paul, *Dir,* William Woods College, Art Gallery, Fulton MO

Cleverdon, John, *Printmaker,* University of South Alabama, Dept of Art, Mobile AL (S)

Clevett, Don, *Asst Dir Exhibits & Visitor Servs,* Department of Culture & Multi-Culturalism, Provincial Museum of Alberta, Edmonton AB

Cliff, Denis, *Instr,* Toronto School of Art, Toronto ON (S)

Cliff, Tom, *VChmn,* Detroit Artists Market, Detroit MI

Clifford, Christina, *Librn,* San Diego Public Library, Art & Music Section, San Diego CA

Clifton, James, *Chmn,* Rhodes College, Dept of Art, Memphis TN (S)

Cline, Fred A, *Librn,* Asian Art Museum of San Francisco, Avery Brundage Collection, San Francisco CA

Cline, Fred A, *Librn,* Asian Art Museum of San Francisco, Library, San Francisco CA

Cline, Mary Alice, *Dir,* Riverside Art Museum, Riverside CA

Cline-Cordonier, Susan, *Dir Historic Houses,* Clemson University, Fort Hill, Clemson SC

Clinger, Melinda, *Admin Asst,* Fulton County Historical Society Inc, Fulton County Museum & Round Barn Museum, Rochester IN

Clisby, Roger, *Dir Coll,* Columbus Museum of Art, Columbus OH

Clisby, Roger D, *Chief Cur,* Chrysler Museum, Norfolk VA

Close, Nancy, *Instr,* Grand Rapids Junior College, Art Dept, Grand Rapids MI (S)

Close, Tim, *Dir,* Arlington Arts Center, Arlington VA

Clothier, Richard I, *Chmn Fine Arts,* Graceland College, Fine Arts Dept, Lamoni IA (S)

Collier-Charlton, Janine, *Treas,* Chicago Society of Artists, Inc, Chicago IL

Collin, Margot, *Reference Librn,* Santa Barbara Public Library, Faulkner Memorial Art Wing, Santa Barbara CA

Collings, Ed, *Chmn,* Columbia College, Art Dept, Columbia MO (S)

Collins, Ann, *Librn,* Payette Associates Architects Planners, Library, Boston MA

Collins, Brad, *Chmn Art History,* University of South Carolina, Dept of Art, Columbia SC (S)

Collins, Dana, *Instr,* Illinois Valley Community College, Div of Humanities and Fine Arts, Oglesby IL (S)

Collins, D Cheryl, *Dir,* Riley County Historical Museum, Manhattan KS

Collins, Debra, *Registrar,* Fall River Historical Society, Fall River MA

Collins, Jeanne, *Dir Public Information,* Museum of Modern Art, New York NY

Collins, Joel, *Prof,* Mount Union College, Dept of Art, Alliance OH (S)

Collins, Kathleen, *Dean,* New York State College of Ceramics at Alfred University, School of Art & Design, Alfred NY (S)

Collins, Kelly, *Public Services Librn,* North Central College, Oesterle Library, Naperville IL

Collins, Lee, *Educational Affairs,* Ford Motor Company, Dearborn MI

Collins, Susan, *State Archaeologist,* Colorado Historical Society, Museum, Denver CO

Collischan, Judy, *Dir,* C W Post Campus of Long Island University, Hillwood Art Museum, Brookville NY

Colo, Papo, *Co-Founder-Official Poet,* Exit Art, New York NY

Colodny, Lou Anne, *Dir,* North Miami Center of Contemporary Art, North Miami FL

Colom, Carola, *Assoc Prof,* University of Puerto Rico, Dept of Fine Arts, Rio Piedras PR (S)

Colombik, Roger, *Asst Prof,* Southwest Texas State University, Dept of Art, San Marcos TX (S)

Colpitt, Frances, *Asst Prof,* University of Texas at San Antonio, Division of Art & Architecture, San Antonio TX (S)

Colton, Jeff, *Pres,* Ann Arbor Art Association, Ann Arbor MI

Colton, Judith J, *Dir Grad Studies,* Yale University, Dept of the History of Art, New Haven CT (S)

Colton, Stan, *Library Development,* Las Vegas-Clark County Library District, Las Vegas NV

Colvin, Richard D, *Exhibit Designer,* Rollins College, George D and Harriet W Cornell Fine Arts Museum, Winter Park FL

Comba, Steve, *Registrar,* Galleries of the Claremont Colleges, Claremont CA

Combs, Doug, *Secy,* French Art Colony, Gallipolis OH

Comella, Frank, *Mgr Marketing,* Art Gallery of Ontario, Toronto ON

Comer, Eugenia, *Asst Prof,* Augusta College, Dept of Fine Arts, Augusta GA (S)

Comer, Fred, *Exec Dir,* Iowa State Education Association, Salisbury House, Des Moines IA

Cominotto, Gary, *Instr,* Mount San Jacinto College, Art Dept, San Jacinto CA (S)

Comport, Jean, *First Asst Art & Literature Dept,* Detroit Public Library, Art & Literature Dept, Detroit MI

Compton, Douglas, *Instr,* Joe Kubert School of Cartoon & Graphic Art, Inc, Dover NJ (S)

Compton, Julie M, *Mgr,* Atlanta Public Library, Art-Humanities Dept, Atlanta GA

Compton, Lisa A, *Dir,* Old Colony Historical Society, Museum, Taunton MA

Compton, Lisa A, *Dir,* Old Colony Historical Society, Library, Taunton MA

Comstock, Jane, *Sr Instr,* University of Colorado at Denver, Dept of Fine Arts, Denver CO (S)

Comstock, Joy, *Dir Education,* Buffalo Bill Memorial Association, Buffalo Bill Historical Center, Cody WY

Conant, Pat, *Chmn,* Westfield State College, Art Dept, Westfield MA (S)

Conarroe, Joel, *Pres,* John Simon Guggenheim Memorial Foundation, New York NY

Conaway, Beverly, *VPres,* West Hills Unitarian Fellowship, Portland OR

Conaway, James, *Prof,* Hamline University, Art Dept, Saint Paul MN (S)

Conaway, James D, *Cur Permanent Colls & Exhib Dir,* Hamline University Learning Center Gallery, Saint Paul MN

Concannon, Ann, *Dir,* Art Center of Battle Creek, Michigan Art & Artist Archives, Battle Creek MI

Concannon, Ann Worth, *Dir,* Art Center of Battle Creek, Battle Creek MI

Concannon, L O, *Pres,* First State Bank, Norton KS

Concholar, Dan, *Dir,* Art Information Center, Inc, New York NY

Condax, Philip, *Dir Technology Coll,* International Museum of Photography at George Eastman House, Rochester NY

Condon, Lorna, *Cur Archives,* Society for the Preservation of New England Antiquities, Archives, Boston MA

Condra, Edward M, *Dir,* MacArthur Memorial, Norfolk VA

Cone, John, *Asst Prof of Art,* Thomas College, Humanities Division, Thomasville GA (S)

Cone, Lisa, *Resources Coordr,* City of Irvine, Irvine Fine Arts Center, Irvine CA

Cone, Lisa, *Resources Coordr,* City of Irvine, Fine Arts Center, Irvine CA (S)

Conforti, Michael, *Chief Cur & Cur Decorative Arts,* Minneapolis Society of Fine Arts, Minneapolis Institute of Arts, Minneapolis MN

Conger, Clement E, *Chmn Fine Arts Committee,* US Department of State, Diplomatic Reception Rooms, Washington DC

Conger, William, *Chmn Art Dept,* Northwestern University, Evanston, Dept of Art Theory & Practice, Evanston IL (S)

Conisbee, Philip, *Cur European Paintings & Sculpture,* Los Angeles County Museum of Art, Los Angeles CA

Conklin, Jo-Ann, *Cur Graphic Arts,* University of Iowa, Museum of Art, Iowa City IA

Conley, Alston, *Cur,* Boston College, Museum of Art, Chestnut Hill MA

Conley, B, *Chmn,* Golden West College, Visual Art Dept, Huntington Beach CA (S)

Conley, James D, *VPres,* Historic Landmarks Foundation of Indiana, Information Center Library, Indianapolis IN

Conley, Kenneth, *Lectr,* Trinity College, Art Dept, Washington DC (S)

Conlon, James, *Sculptor,* University of South Alabama, Dept of Art, Mobile AL (S)

Conn, David, *Dir,* Texas Christian University, Moudy Exhibition Hall, Fort Worth TX

Conn, Richard, *Cur Native Arts Department,* Denver Art Museum, Frederic H Douglas Library, Denver CO

Connell, E Jane, *Cur European Art,* Columbus Museum of Art, Columbus OH

Connell, Jim, *Asst Prof,* Winthrop College, Dept of Art & Design, Rock Hill SC (S)

Connell, Muriel, *Librn,* Cheekwood-Tennessee Botanical Gardens & Museum of Art, Botanic Hall Library, Nashville TN

Connell, Stephen, *Assoc Prof,* University of Montana, Dept of Art, Missoula MT (S)

Connelly, Christy, *Dir Student Services,* Antonelli Institute of Art & Photography, Cincinnati OH (S)

Connelly, Linda M, *Historic Site Mgr II,* New York State Office of Parks Recreation & Historic Preservation, John Jay Homestead State Historic Site, Katonah NY

Conner, Ann Louise, *Assoc Prof,* University of North Carolina at Wilmington, Dept of Fine Arts - Division of Art, Wilmington NC (S)

Conner, Jill, *Librn,* Brand Library & Art Galleries, Glendale CA

Conner, Mary Rebecca, *Dept Chmn,* Saint Mary College, Art Dept, Leavenworth KS (S)

Conner, Neppie, *Prof Emeritus,* University of Arkansas, Art Dept, Fayetteville AR (S)

Connett, Dee, *Prof,* Hutchinson Community Junior College, Visual Arts Dept, Hutchinson KS (S)

Connolly, Bruce E, *Dir,* New York State College of Ceramics at Alfred University, Scholes Library of Ceramics, Alfred NY

Connolly, Felicia, *Office Admin,* Wenham Museum, Wenham MA

Connor, Cynthia, *Registrar,* Columbia Museum of Art, Columbia SC

Connors, Becky, *Dir,* Freeport Art Museum & Cultural Center, Freeport IL

Connors, Becky, *Dir,* Freeport Art Museum & Cultural Center, Library, Freeport IL

Connors, Jeanne Moffatt, *Prof,* Community College of Allegheny County, Boyce Campus, Art Dept, Monroeville PA (S)

Connors, William E, *Dir,* The College at New Paltz State University of New York, Sojourner Truth Library, New Paltz NY

Connorton, Judy, *Librn,* City College of the City University of New York, Architecture Library, New York NY

Conover, Robin, *Instr,* Ocean City Art Center, Ocean City NJ (S)

Conrad, Geoffrey W, *Dir,* Indiana University, William Hammond Mathers Museum, Bloomington IN

Conrad, John, *Chmn,* San Diego Mesa College, Fine Arts Dept, San Diego CA (S)

Conrads, Margaret C, *Asst Cur American Art,* Nelson-Atkins Museum of Art, Kansas City MO

Conragra, Pier, *Instr,* Columbia University, School of the Arts, Division of Painting & Sculpture, New York NY (S)

Conrey, J, *Prof,* Camden County College, Dept of Art, Blackwood NJ (S)

Conrey, Joseph, *Coordr,* Ocean County College, Humanities Dept, Toms River NJ (S)

Conroy, Marcia, *Asst Dir Education & Community Relations,* Massachusetts Institute of Technology, MIT Museum, Cambridge MA

Conroy, Michel, *Assoc Prof,* Southwest Texas State University, Dept of Art, San Marcos TX (S)

Conroy, W Peter, *Cur National History,* Anniston Museum of Natural History, Anniston AL

Consey, Kevin, *Dir,* Museum of Contemporary Art, Chicago IL

Consolati, John, *Assoc Prof,* University of Toronto, Programme in Landscape Architecture, Toronto ON (S)

Constable, Leslie, *Exec Dir,* Acme Art Co, Columbus OH

Constans, Mary, *Prof,* Portland State University, Dept of Art, Portland OR (S)

Constantine, Gregory, *Prof,* Andrews University, Dept of Art, Art History & Design, Berrien Springs MI (S)

Constantine, John, *Instr,* North Seattle Community College, Art Dept, Seattle WA (S)

Contes, Anna, *Instr,* Woodstock School of Art, Inc, Woodstock NY (S)

Contiguglia, Georgiana, *Cur Decorative & Fine Arts,* Colorado Historical Society, Museum, Denver CO

Convertino, Karen, *Asst Dir,* College of New Rochelle, Castle Gallery, New Rochelle NY

Conway, Patricia, *Dean,* University of Pennsylvania, Graduate School of Fine Arts, Philadelphia PA (S)

Conwill, Kinshasha Holman, *Exec Dir,* The Studio Museum in Harlem, New York NY

Conyers, Wayne, *Asst Prof,* McPherson College, Art Dept, McPherson KS (S)

Cook, Alexander B, *VPres,* Great Lakes Historical Society, Vermilion OH

Cook, David, *Chmn,* Bridgewater College, Art Dept, Bridgewater VA (S)

Cook, Ian, *Chmn,* Red Deer College, Dept of Art and Design, Red Deer AB (S)

Cook, James, *Dir,* Birmingham Southern College, Doris Wainwright Kennedy Art Center, Birmingham AL

Cook, James, *Chmn Div Fine & Performing Arts,* Birmingham-Southern College, Art Dept, Birmingham AL (S)

Cook, Janet, *Cur Educ,* Montclair Art Museum, Montclair NJ

Cook, Jennifer, *Visual Art Cur,* Sangre de Cristo Arts & Conference Center, Pueblo CO

Cook, Lia, *Textiles,* California College of Arts and Crafts, Oakland CA (S)

Cook, Madelyn, *Cataloger,* University of Arizona, College of Architecture Library, Tucson AZ

Cook, Mishawn J, *Coordr,* University of Minnesota, Coffman Union Third Floor Gallery, Minneapolis MN

Cook, Nancy, *Controller,* Museum of Contemporary Art, Chicago IL

Cook, Pam, *Finance Mgr,* Shaker Museum, Old Chatham NY

Cook, Richard L, *Chmn,* College of Santa Fe, Visual Arts Dept, Santa Fe NM (S)

Cook, Ruth, *Asst,* Lincoln National Life Insurance Co, Lincoln Museum, Fort Wayne IN

Cook, William, *Acting Dir,* Ohio State University, Wexner Center for the Arts, Columbus OH

Cooke, Adrian G, *Chief Preparator,* University of Lethbridge, Art Gallery, Lethbridge AB

Cooke, Carol, *Instr,* University of North Carolina at Charlotte, Dept of Visual Arts, Charlotte NC (S)

Cooke, Constance B, *Dir,* Queens Borough Public Library, Fine Arts & Recreation Division, Jamaica NY

Cooke, Elizabeth, *Pres,* Bronx Museum of the Arts, Bronx NY

Cooke, Judith M, *Asst Dir of Development & Membership,* Nelson-Atkins Museum of Art, Friends of Art, Kansas City MO

Cooke, Robert T, *Assoc Prof,* Rutgers, the State University of New Jersey, Mason Gross School of the Arts, New Brunswick NJ (S)

Cooke, Sarah, *Archivist,* Tippecanoe County Historical Museum, Alameda McCollough Library, Lafayette IN

Cooke, S Tucker, *Chmn,* University of North Carolina at Asheville, Dept of Art, Asheville NC (S)

Coolidge, Christina, *Asst Librn,* Mount Wachusett Community College, Library, Gardner MA

Coombe, JoAnne, *Dir,* Saint Louis County Historical Society, Duluth MN

Coomer, Sue, *Librn,* Watkins Institute, Library, Nashville TN

Coon, A W, *VPres of the Board,* R W Norton Art Gallery, Shreveport LA

Coones, R C, *Instructor,* Northeastern Oklahoma State University, Tahlequah OK (S)

Cooney, Anthony, *Mgr Museum Shop,* Glenbow Museum, Calgary AB

Cooper, Charisse, *Facility Coordr,* Philbrook Museum of Art, Tulsa OK

Cooper, David, *Chmn,* Butte College, Dept of Fine Arts, Oroville CA (S)

Cooper, Diana, *Cur,* Potsdam College of the State University of New York, Roland Gibson Gallery, Potsdam NY

Cooper, Diana, *Reference Librn,* University of British Columbia, Fine Arts Library, Vancouver BC

Cooper, Ginnie, *Dir,* Multnomah County Library, Henry Failing Art and Music Dept, Portland OR

Cooper, Helen, *Cur American Painting,* Yale University, Art Gallery, New Haven CT

Cooper, Jack, *Communications Dir,* High Desert Museum, Bend OR

Cooper, Ken, *Community Services Dir,* Gavilan College, Art Gallery, Gilroy CA

Cooper, Linda G, *Asst VPres,* Wachovia Bank of North Carolina, Winston-Salem NC

Cooper, Michael, *Instr,* De Anza College, Creative Arts Div, Cupertino CA (S)

Cooper, Nan, *Instructor,* The Art Institutes International, The Art Institute of Seattle, Seattle WA (S)

Cooper, Patty, *Exec VPres,* South Carolina State Museum, Columbia SC

Cooper, Paula, *Cur,* Fried, Frank, Harris, Shriver & Jacobson, Art Collection, New York NY

Cooper, Rhonda, *Dir,* State University of New York at Stony Brook, Art Gallery, Stony Brook NY

Cooper, Wendy, *Cur Decorative Arts,* Baltimore Museum of Art, Baltimore MD

Cootner, Cathryn, *Cur Rugs,* Fine Arts Museums of San Francisco, M H de Young Memorial Museum and California Palace of the Legion of Honor, San Francisco CA

Cope, Mary, *Acting Exec Dir,* Cheltenham Center for the Arts, Cheltenham PA (S)

Copeland, Betty D, *Chmn,* Texas Woman's University, Dept of Visual Arts, Denton TX (S)

Copeland, Jan, *Instr,* The Arkansas Arts Center, Museum School, Little Rock AR (S)

Coppage, Carol B, *Exec Dir,* Northwood Institute, Alden B Dow Creativity Center, Midland MI (S)

Coppedge, Arthur, *VPres,* New York Artists Equity Association, Inc, New York NY

Coppenger, Michael, *Instructoral Dean Fine Arts & Communication,* Cerritos Community Center, Art Dept, Norwalk CA (S)

Copper, Melissa, *Asst to Dir,* National Art Museum of Sport, Indianapolis IN

Coppin, Kerry, *Assoc Prof,* Rochester Institute of Technology, School of Photographic Arts & Sciences, Rochester NY (S)

Coppola, Regina, *Cur,* University of Massachusetts, Amherst, University Gallery, Amherst MA

Coraor, John E, *Dir,* Heckscher Museum, Huntington NY

Corbett, Roy G, *Asst Dir Admin,* Walters Art Gallery, Baltimore MD

Corbin, George, *Chmn,* Herbert H Lehman College, Art Dept, Bronx NY (S)

Corcoran, Kathryn, *Art Librn,* Joslyn Art Museum, Omaha NE

Corcoran, Kathryn L, *Art Librn,* Joslyn Art Museum, Art Reference Library, Omaha NE

Corcoran, Rosemary E, *Pres Bd Trustees,* Beck Center for the Cultural Arts, Lakewood OH

Corder, Ronald, *Sr Exhibit Specialist,* United States Naval Academy Museum, Annapolis MD

Cordova, Ralph, *Pres,* Movimiento Artistico del Rio Salado, Inc (MARS), Phoenix AZ

Corey, John J, *Cur,* Kings County Historical Society and Museum, Hampton NB

Corey, Liz, *Volunteer Coordr,* Pacific - Asia Museum, Pasadena CA

Corey, Peter, *Cur Coll,* Sheldon Jackson Museum, Sitka AK

Corley, Elke G, *Supv Corporate Admin Serv,* Times Mirror Company, Los Angeles CA

Cormack, Malcolm, *Cur Paintings,* Yale University, Yale Center for British Art, New Haven CT

Cormier, Robert, *Chmn,* Boston Art Commission of the City of Boston, Boston MA

Cormier, Robert J, *Pres,* Guild of Boston Artists, Boston MA

Cornacchione, Matthew, *Business Mgr,* Indianapolis Museum of Art, Indianapolis IN

Corneau, Lucie, *Secy,* Institut Des Arts Au Saguenay, Centre National D'Exposition A Jonquiere, Jonquiere PQ

Cornelius, Phil, *Acting Area Head Ceramics,* Pasadena City College, Art Dept, Pasadena CA (S)

Cornell, Beth, *Sr Adviser,* Pennsylvania Department of Education, Arts in Education Program, Harrisburg PA

Cornell, Roger C, *Pres,* Mingei International, Inc, Mingei International Museum of World Folk Art, San Diego CA

Cornell, Thomas B, *Prof,* Bowdoin College, Art Dept, Brunswick ME (S)

Cornett, J, *Assoc Prof,* Northern Arizona University, School of Art & Design, Flagstaff AZ (S)

Cornett, James W, *Cur Natural Science,* Palm Springs Desert Museum, Inc, Palm Springs CA

Cornett, James W, *Natural Sciences,* Palm Springs Desert Museum, Inc, Library, Palm Springs CA

Cornfeld, Michael, *Chmn,* Marshall University, Dept of Art, Huntington WV (S)

Corning, Marilyn, *Librn,* Wenham Museum, Timothy Pickering Library, Wenham MA

Cornish, Glenn, *Music Instr,* Edison Community College, Dept of Fine and Performing Arts, Fort Myers FL (S)

Corr, Jim, *Cur,* Western Montana College, Art Gallery/Museum, Dillon MT

Correia, Peter, *Prof,* Ulster County Community College, Dept of Visual Arts, Stone Ridge NY (S)

Correro, Guido, *Prof,* Herkimer County Community College, Social Sciences & Humanities Division, Herkimer NY (S)

Corrie, Rebecca, *Chmn,* Bates College, Art Dept, Lewiston ME (S)

Corrigan, David J, *Cur,* Connecticut State Library, Museum of Connecticut History, Hartford CT

Corrigan, Dennis, *Instr,* Joe Kubert School of Cartoon & Graphic Art, Inc, Dover NJ (S)

Corrin, Lisa, *Asst Dir,* The Contemporary, Museum for Contemporary Arts, Baltimore MD

Corsaro, James, *Assoc Librn,* New York State Library, Manuscripts and Special Collections, Albany NY

Corser, James B, *Business Mgr,* Fort Worth Art Association, Modern Art Museum of Fort Worth, Fort Worth TX

Corson-Finnerty, Adam, *Dir Development,* Historical Society of Pennsylvania, Philadelphia PA

Corwin, Nancy, *Cur European & American Art,* University of Kansas, Spencer Museum of Art, Lawrence KS

Corwin, Nancy, *Assoc Prof,* University of Kansas, Kress Foundation Dept of Art History, Lawrence KS (S)

Costanzo, Nancy, *Chmn Dept,* Our Lady of Elms College, Dept of Fine Arts, Chicopee MA (S)

Costello, Michael J, *School Dir,* Silvermine Guild Arts Center, Silvermine Galleries, New Canaan CT

Costello, Michael J, *Dir,* Guild Art Center, New Canaan CT (S)

Costello, Thomas, *Pres,* Springfield City Library & Museums Association, Art & Music Dept, Springfield MA

Costigan, Constance C, *Prof,* George Washington University, Dept of Art, Washington DC (S)

Cote, Alan, *Instr,* Bard College, Milton Avery Graduate School of the Arts, Annandale-on-Hudson NY (S)

Cote, Claire, *Dir Cultural Serv,* Pointe Claire Cultural Centre, Stewart Hall Art Gallery, Pointe Claire PQ

Cote, Marc, *Asst Prof,* Framingham State College, Art Dept, Framingham MA (S)

Cothren, Michael, *Chairperson Dept Art,* Swarthmore College, Dept of Art, Swarthmore PA (S)

Cotter, Ann, *Ed,* Cincinnati Museum Association, Cincinnati Art Museum, Cincinnati OH

Cotter, Arlen L, *VPres,* Columbia Museum of Art, Columbia SC

Cotter, James H, *Treas,* Old Jail Art Center, Albany TX

Cotterill, Janna, *Public Relations,* Columbia Museum of Art, Columbia SC

Cottrell, J Thomas, *Pres,* Fall River Historical Society, Fall River MA

Cottrill, Thomas, *Dean Arts & Letters,* Northeastern Oklahoma State University, Tahlequah OK (S)

Cotugno, H Arthur P, *Supt Greater Amsterdam School Dist,* Mohawk Valley Heritage Association, Inc, Walter Elwood Museum, Amsterdam NY

Couch, N C Christopher, *Asst Prof,* Smith College, Art Dept, Northampton MA (S)

Couch, Urban, *Prof,* West Virginia University, College of Creative Arts, Morgantown WV (S)

Couchon, Marie-Paule, *Archivist,* Musee des Augustines de l'Hotel Dieu of Quebec, Library, Quebec PQ

Coughin, Marge, *Dir Special Events,* American Society of Artists, Inc, Chicago IL

Coughlin, Caroline M, *Dir,* Drew University, Art Dept Library, Madison NJ

Coughlin, Joan Hopkins, *Cur,* Wellfleet Historical Society Museum & Rider House, Wellfleet MA

Coulet du Gard, Dominique, *Cur Exhib,* Historical and Cultural Affairs, Delaware State Museums, Dover DE

Coull, John, *Acting Chair Technol Studies,* Ontario College of Art, Toronto ON (S)

Coulter, Gary, *Chmn,* Fort Hays State University, Moss-Thorns Gallery of Arts, Hays KS

Coulter, Gary, *Prof,* New Mexico Highlands University, School of Liberal & Fine Arts, Las Vegas NM (S)

Coulter, Gary, *Chmn,* Fort Hays State University, Dept of Art, Hays KS (S)

Coulter, Jerry L, *Prof,* James Madison University, Dept of Art, Harrisonburg VA (S)

Coumbe, Robert E, *Dir,* Free Public Library, Art and Music Dept, Trenton NJ

Counselman, Jerry, *Asst Prof,* University of Alabama in Huntsville, Dept of Art & Art History, Huntsville AL (S)

Couper, James M, *Prof,* Florida International University, Visual Arts Dept, Miami FL (S)

Coursin, Jill, *Vol Coordr & Museum Shop Mgr,* Mingei International, Inc, Mingei International Museum of World Folk Art, San Diego CA

Court, Elizabeth, *Chief Paintings Conservator,* Balboa Art Conservation Center, San Diego CA

Courtemanche, Susan, *Dir Development & Membership,* Worcester Art Museum, Worcester MA

Courtemanche, Susan, *Development,* Isabella Stewart Gardner Museum, Boston MA

Courtney, Kathleen, *Lectr,* Mount Marty College, Art Dept, Yankton SD (S)

Courvoisier, Lois, *Librn,* Crocker Art Museum, Research Library, Sacramento CA

Cousineau, Lois, *Pres,* Rogue Valley Art Association, Rogue Gallery, Medford OR

Cousins, Charles, *Gallery Display Artist,* Alberta College of Art, Illingworth Kerr Gallery, Calgary AB

Coutant, Tricia, *Dept Head,* Jacksonville Public Library, Fine Arts & Recreation Dept, Jacksonville FL

Coutellier, Francis, *Chmn,* Universite de Moncton, Department of Visual Arts, Moncton NB (S)

Couture, Marie, *Co-Chmn,* Rivier College, Art Dept, Nashua NH (S)

Couture, Theresa, *Co-Chmn,* Rivier College, Art Dept, Nashua NH (S)

Covarrubias, Charles A, *Pres,* Ventura County Historical Society Museum, Ventura CA

Covert, George, *Photo Archivist,* Seneca Falls Historical Society Museum, Seneca Falls NY

Covington, Betsy, *Dir of Development,* Columbus Museum, Columbus GA

Covington, Joseph F, *Dir Education,* North Carolina Museum of Art, Raleigh NC

Covington-Vogl, Laurel, *Assoc Prof,* Fort Lewis College, Art Dept, Durango CO (S)

Coward, Amelia B, *Trustee Adminr,* Florida Gulf Coast Art Center, Inc, Belleair FL

Cowart, Jack, *Assoc Dir,* Corcoran Gallery of Art, Washington DC

Cowden, Chris, *Dir,* Women And Their Work, Austin TX

Cowden, Dorothy, *Dir,* University of Tampa, Lee Scarfone Gallery, Tampa FL

Cowdery, Sue, *Registrar,* Mid-America All-Indian Center, Library, Wichita KS

Cowette, Thomas, *Assoc Prof,* University of Minnesota, Minneapolis, Dept of Studio Art, Minneapolis MN (S)

Cowles, Charles, *Chmn,* New York Studio School of Drawing, Painting & Sculpture, Gallery, New York NY

Cox, Abbe Rose, *Instr,* Surry Community College, Art Dept, Dobson NC (S)

Cox, Beverly, *Cur Exhib,* National Portrait Gallery, Washington DC

Cox, David N, *Prof,* Weber State University, Dept of Visual Arts, Ogden UT (S)

Cox, Dennis, *Assoc Prof,* Pacific Lutheran University, Dept of Art, Tacoma WA (S)

Cox, Harryette, *Dir Development,* Asheville Art Museum, Asheville NC

Cox, Jean, *Assoc Prof,* Oakland City College, Division of Fine Arts, Oakland City IN (S)

Cox, Jon, *Instr,* Central Wyoming College, Art Center, Riverton WY (S)

Cox, Kiersten, *Keeper, Lending Center,* Honolulu Academy of Arts, Honolulu HI

Cox, Michael, *Dean,* University of Manitoba, Faculty of Architecture, Winnipeg MB (S)

Cox, P Lynn, *Dir,* Westminster College, Art Gallery, New Wilmington PA

Cox, Richard, *Prof,* Louisiana State University, School of Art, Baton Rouge LA (S)

Cox, Sharon, *Chmn,* Jamestown College, Art Dept, Jamestown ND (S)

Cox, Valerie, *Dir,* Cartoon Art Museum, San Francisco CA

Cox, William, *Gallery Dir,* Edinboro University of Pennsylvania, Art Dept, Edinboro PA (S)

Coxe, Polly, *Archives Technician,* The Saint Louis Art Museum, Richardson Memorial Library, Saint Louis MO

Cox-Smith, Susan, *Membership Coordr,* Southern Oregon Historical Society, Jacksonville Museum of Southern Oregon History, Jacksonville OR

Coyle, Jack, *Registrar,* Independent Curators Incorporated, New York NY

Coyner, Lewis, *Chmn,* Chatham College, Art Gallery, Pittsburgh PA

Coyner, Louis, *Chmn,* Chatham College, Fine & Performing Arts, Pittsburgh PA (S)

Crabb, Patrick, *Instr,* Rancho Santiago College, Art Dept, Santa Ana CA (S)

Crabb, Ted, *Dir & Secy,* University of Wisconsin-Madison, Wisconsin Union Galleries, Madison WI

Crable, James, *Prof,* James Madison University, Dept of Art, Harrisonburg VA (S)

Craddock, Robert, *Visual Arts Dir,* Jamaica Arts Center, Jamaica NY

Craig, Andrew B, *Pres & Chmn,* The Boatmen's National Bank of St Louis, Art Collection, Saint Louis MO

Craig, B, *Corresp Secy,* San Bernardino Art Association, Inc, San Bernardino CA

Craig, Christina, *Asst Prof,* Trenton State College, Art Dept, Trenton NJ (S)

Craig, Gerry, *Art Dir,* Detroit Artists Market, Detroit MI

Craig, Lois A, *Assoc Dean,* Massachusetts Institute of Technology, School of Architecture and Planning, Cambridge MA (S)

Craig, Susan V, *Librn,* University of Kansas, Murphy Library of Art and Architecture, Lawrence KS

Craig, W Frederick, *Chmn Management Division,* Rochester Institute of Technology, School of Printing, Rochester NY (S)

Craighead, Linda, *Dir,* Palo Alto Cultural Center, Palo Alto CA

Cramer, Ann, *Pres,* Seneca Falls Historical Society Museum, Seneca Falls NY

Cramer, George, *Assoc Prof,* University of Wisconsin, Madison, Dept of Art, Madison WI (S)

Cramer, James P, *Exec VPres,* American Institute of Architects, Washington DC

Cramer, Patricia T, *Dir,* Westfield Athenaeum, Jasper Rand Art Museum, Westfield MA

Cramer, Robin, *Dir Museum Shop,* The Jewish Museum, New York NY

Cramer, Sam, *Instr,* Luzerne County Community College, Commercial Art Dept, Nanticoke PA (S)

Crammond, Elizabeth, *Pres,* Society of Canadian Artists, Toronto ON

Crampton, Nancy, *Head Weaving Dept,* Kalamazoo Institute of Arts, KIA School, Kalamazoo MI (S)

Crandall, Leo, *Dir,* Rome Art and Community Center, Rome NY

Crandall, William, *Instructor,* Milwaukee Area Technical College, Graphic Arts Dept, Milwaukee WI (S)

Crane, Barbara, *Prof,* School of the Art Institute of Chicago, Chicago IL (S)

Crane, Bonnie L, *Pres,* Crane Collection Gallery, Boston MA

Crane, David, *Prof,* Virginia Polytechnic Institute & State University, Dept of Art & Art History, Blacksburg VA (S)

Crane, Diane, *Instr,* Viterbo College, Art Dept, La Crosse WI (S)

Crane, Elizabeth, *Cur Asst,* Aurora University, Schingoethe Center for Native American Cultures, Aurora IL

Crane, James, *Prof,* Eckerd College, Art Dept, Saint Petersburg FL (S)

Crane, Lois F, *Librn,* Wichita Art Museum, Library, Wichita KS

Crane, Michael, *Dir,* University of Colorado, Art Galleries, Boulder CO

Crane, Tim, *Chmn,* Viterbo College, Art Dept, La Crosse WI (S)

Crane, Tim, *Dir,* Viterbo College Art Gallery, La Crosse WI

Crasco, Gael, *Asst to Pres,* Crane Collection Gallery, Boston MA

Crask, R M, *Coordr Fine Arts & Prof,* Jefferson Community College, Fine Arts, Louisville KY (S)

Craven, Roy, *Prof,* University of Florida, Dept of Art, Gainesville FL (S)

Crawfor, Henry, *Registrar,* Texas Tech University, Museum, Lubbock TX

Crawford, Cameron, *Instr,* Cottey College, Art Dept, Nevada MO (S)

Crawford, J, *Instr,* Humboldt State University, College of Arts & Humanities, Arcata CA (S)

Crawford, James, *Chmn,* Humboldt State University, College of Arts & Humanities, Arcata CA (S)

Crawford, James, *Cur Educ,* Rome Historical Society Museum, William E Scripture Memorial Library, Rome NY

Crawford, James D, *VPres,* Print Club Center for Prints & Photographs, Philadelphia PA

Crawford, Rebecca H, *Pres,* Florence Museum, Florence SC

Creamer, George, *Foundation Dept,* Monserrat College of Art, Beverly MA (S)

Creamer, George, *Sculpture,* Monserrat College of Art, Beverly MA (S)

Creasy, June, *Assoc Prof,* Lambuth University, Dept of Human Ecology & Visual Arts, Jackson TN (S)

Creighton, Sandra, *Visitor Services,* National Gallery of Art, Washington DC

Crespo, Michael, *Dir,* Louisiana State University, School of Art, Baton Rouge LA (S)

Cressotti, Frank, *Chmn,* Holyoke Community College, Dept of Art, Holyoke MA (S)

Crew, Roger T, *Archivist,* The Mariners' Museum, Library, Newport News VA

Crew, Spencer, *Deputy Dir,* National Museum of American History, Washington DC

Crews, Britt, *Cur,* Cape Ann Historical Association, Gallery, Gloucester MA

Crews, Britt, *Cur,* Cape Ann Historical Association, Library, Gloucester MA

Crews, Polly, *Dir,* Fort Smith Art Center, Fort Smith AR

Crews-Lynch, Cheryl, *Instr,* Ocean City Art Center, Ocean City NJ (S)

Cribb, Marigold, *Exhib Coordr,* Saskatchewan Craft Gallery, Saskatoon SK

Crider, Gail, *Deputy Dir,* Arizona Commission on the Arts, Phoenix AZ

Crilley, Sue, *Cur Cultural History,* New Jersey State Museum, Trenton NJ

Crilley, Suzanne, *Cur Cultural History,* New Jersey Historical Society Museum, New Jersey State Museum at Morven, Newark NJ

Crilly, Carol, *Cur,* Workman & Temple Family Homestead Museum, City of Industry CA

Crimson, Linda, *Adjunct Asst Prof,* Indiana University South Bend, Fine Arts Dept, South Bend IN (S)

Cripe, Dianne M, *Information Specialist,* Arizona State University, University Art Museum, Tempe AZ

Cripps, Andrew, *Coordr Art Placement,* Visual Arts Ontario, Toronto ON

Crisp, Donna, *VPres,* San Angelo Museum of Fine Arts, San Angelo TX

Crisp, Lynn, *Librn Asst,* North Carolina State University, Harrye Lyons Design Library, Raleigh NC

Crispino, Luigi, *Instr,* Franklin College, Art Dept, Franklin IN (S)

Critchfield, Ann, *Head Visual Communications & Graphic Arts,* Art Institute of Atlanta, Atlanta GA (S)

Critoph, Mark, *Pres,* Canadian Society of Painters in Watercolour, Toronto ON

Croce, Judith, *Chmn,* Caldwell College, Art Dept, Caldwell NJ (S)

Crocker, Kyle, *Prof,* Bemidji State University, Visual Arts Dept, Bemidji MN (S)

Crockett, Gillian, *Educ Coordr,* Wiregrass Museum of Art, Dothan AL

Crockett, Pamela, *Prof,* Mount Saint Mary's College, Visual & Performing Arts Dept, Emmitsburg MD (S)

Croft, Michael, *Prof Jewelry & Metalsmithing,* University of Arizona, Dept of Art, Tucson AZ (S)

Cromer, Bob, *Asst Prof,* Baylor University, Dept of Art, Waco TX (S)

Cromwell-Lacy, Sherry, *Dir Exhib,* Kansas City Art Institute, Kemper Museum of Contemporary Art & Design, Kansas City MO

Crone, Ted, *Dir,* Friends University, Whittier Fine Arts Gallery, Wichita KS

Croneberger, Robert B, *Dir,* Carnegie Institute, Library, Pittsburgh PA

Cronin, Mary, *Supv Educ,* Brandywine River Museum, Chadds Ford PA

Crooker, M J A, *Assoc Prof,* Mount Allison University, Fine Arts Dept, Sackville NB (S)

Crosbie, Tom, *Treas,* Owatonna Arts Center, Community Arts Center, Owatonna MN

Crosby, Anna, *Pres,* Coquille Valley Art Association, Coquille OR

Crosby, Ranice W, *Dir Emeritus & Assoc Prof,* Johns Hopkins University, School of Medicine, Dept of Art as Applied to Medicine, Baltimore MD (S)

Crosman, Christopher B, *Dir,* William A Farnsworth Library and Art Museum, Rockland ME

Cross, Jennifer, *Asst Prof,* Southampton Campus of Long Island University, Fine Arts Division, Southampton NY (S)

Cross, Judy, *VPres,* Arts Council of San Mateo County, Belmont CA

Cross, Ruth C, *Adminr,* University of Virginia, Bayly Art Museum, Charlottesville VA

Cross, Tony, *Instr,* Cuyahoga Valley Art Center, Cuyahoga Falls OH (S)

Crossett, Arlene, *Asst Librn,* Manchester Historic Association, Library, Manchester NH

Crossman, Rodney, *Instr,* Indiana Wesleyan University, Art Dept, Marion IN (S)

Crost, Mary, *Publicist,* Severin Wunderman Museum, Irvine CA

Croston, Robert B, *Assoc Prof,* Southern Illinois University, School of Art & Design, Carbondale IL (S)

Crotchett, Susan I, *Asst Prof,* Greenville College, Division of Language, Literature & Fine Arts, Greenville IL (S)

Croton, Lynn, *Dean Visual & Performing Arts,* C W Post Center of Long Island University, School of Visual & Performing Arts, Greenvale NY (S)

Crouch, D E, *Instr,* Western Illinois University, Art Dept, Macomb IL (S)

Crouther, Betty, *Asst Prof,* University of Mississippi, Dept of Art, University MS (S)

Crowder, Charles, *Dir of Music,* The Phillips Collection, Washington DC

Crowe, Ann G, *Prof,* Virginia Commonwealth University, Art History Department, Richmond VA (S)

Crowe, Ann G, *Asst Prof,* Virginia Commonwealth University, Art History Department, Richmond VA (S)

Crowe, Edith, *Art Reference Librn,* San Jose State University, Robert D Clark Library, San Jose CA

Crowe, John, *Prof,* Bridgewater State College, Art Dept, Bridgewater MA (S)

Crowe, M, *Lectr,* Mount Ida College, Chamberlayne School of Design & Merchandising, Boston MA (S)

Crowley, J Anthony, *Instr,* Grinnell College, Dept of Art, Grinnell IA (S)

Crowley, William, *Dir Museum,* State Historical Society of Wisconsin, State Historical Museum, Madison WI

Crown, Patricia, *Assoc Prof,* University of Missouri, Art History and Archaeology Dept, Columbia MO (S)

Crown, Roberta, *Executive Coordr,* Women in the Arts Foundation, Inc, New York NY

Crowston, Catherine, *Asst Cur,* York University, Art Gallery of York University, North York ON

Croydon, Michael, *Chmn,* Lake Forest College, Dept of Art, Lake Forest IL (S)

Crozier, Richard F, *Deputy Dir Finance & Adminr,* Winterthur Museum and Gardens, Winterthur DE

Crozier, Ron, *Librn,* Santa Barbara Museum of Art, Library, Santa Barbara CA

Crum, Katherine B, *Dir,* Mills College, Art Gallery, Oakland CA

Crumbley, Amelia, *VPres,* Mississippi Art Colony, Meridian MS

Crusan, Ronald L, *Exec Dir,* Waterworks Visual Arts Center, Salisbury NC

Cruz, Alfred, *Instr,* Our Lady of the Lake University, Dept of Art, San Antonio TX (S)

Cruz, Dennis, *Asst Dir Admin,* Millicent Rogers Museum, Taos NM

Cruz, Michele A, *Instr,* North Carolina Wesleyan College, Dept of Visual & Performing Arts, Rocky Mount NC (S)

Cruz, Patricia, *Deputy Dir Progs,* The Studio Museum in Harlem, New York NY

Cubbeck-Meche, Elizabeth, *Cur,* Alexandria Museum of Art, Alexandria LA

Cucchi, Paolo, *Dean,* Drew University, Elizabeth P Korn Gallery, Madison NJ

Cuevas, Carlos, *Chmn of Board,* Bronx Museum of the Arts, Bronx NY

Culbertson, Margaret, *Librn,* University of Houston, Architecture and Art Library, Houston TX

Culity, Brian, *Cur Art Museum,* Heritage Plantation of Sandwich, Sandwich MA

Cullen, Charles T, *Pres & Librn,* Newberry Library, Chicago IL

Culley, Lou Ann, *Assoc Prof,* Kansas State University, Art Dept, Manhattan KS (S)

Culley, Paul T, *Technical Ref & ILL Librn,* New York State College of Ceramics at Alfred University, Scholes Library of Ceramics, Alfred NY

Culver, Michael, *Cur,* Ogunquit Museum of American Art, Ogunquit ME

Cumine, R B, *Pres,* Lyceum Club and Women's Art Association of Canada, Toronto ON

Cumming, Doug, *Prof,* University of Wisconsin-Stout, Dept of Art & Design, Menomonie WI (S)

Cumming, Nan, *Head Museum Servs,* Maine Historical Society, Wadsworth-Longfellow House, Portland ME

Cumming, Nan, *Cur Museum Coll & Longfellow House,* Maine Historical Society, Library, Portland ME

Cumming, William, *Instructor,* The Art Institutes International, The Art Institute of Seattle, Seattle WA (S)

Cummings, Denise, *Inter-Library Loan Librn,* Bethany College, Library, Lindsborg KS

Cummings, Hildegard, *Cur of Education,* University of Connecticut, William Benton Museum of Art - Connecticut's State Art Museum, Storrs CT

Cummings, Mary Lou, *Cur & Registrar,* Knights of Columbus Supreme Council, Headquarters Museum, New Haven CT

Cummings, Paul, *Pres,* The Drawing Society, New York NY

Cummings, Terri, *Coordr Indian Gallery,* Oklahoma Center for Science and Art, Kirkpatrick Center, Oklahoma City OK

Cummins, Karen, *Cur Education,* New Jersey State Museum, Trenton NJ

Cunard, Gail, *Adminr & Asst Treas,* Trotting Horse Museum, Goshen NY

Cundiff, Linda, *Asst Prof,* Campbellsville College, Fine Arts Division, Campbellsville KY (S)

Cuneo, Pia, *Asst Prof Art History,* University of Arizona, Dept of Art, Tucson AZ (S)

Cuneo, Robert, *Assoc Prof,* University of Bridgeport, Art Dept, Bridgeport CT (S)

Cunning, John, *Site Admin,* Mark Twain Birthplace Museum, Stoutsville MO

Cunningham, Beth, *Registrar,* Cheekwood-Tennessee Botanical Garden Museum of Art, Education Dept, Nashville TN (S)

Cunningham, David, *Designer,* University of British Columbia, Museum of Anthropology, Vancouver BC

Cunningham, Dennis, *Instr,* Marylhurst College, Art Dept, Marylhurst OR (S)

Cunningham, Denyse M, *Asst Cur,* Aurora University, Schingoethe Center for Native American Cultures, Aurora IL

Cunningham, Elizabeth, *Registrar,* Cheekwood-Tennessee Botanical Gardens & Museum of Art, Nashville TN

Cunningham, Karlene, *Acting Area Head Apparel Arts,* Pasadena City College, Art Dept, Pasadena CA (S)

Cunningham, Linda, *Chmn Dept,* Franklin and Marshall College, Art Dept, Lancaster PA (S)

Cunningham, Michael R, *Cur Japanese Art,* Cleveland Museum of Art, Cleveland OH

Cunningham, Nancy, *VChmn,* Detroit Artists Market, Detroit MI

Cunninghan, William, *Chmn,* Cheyney University of Pennsylvania, Dept of Art, Cheyney PA (S)

Cuno, James, *Dir,* Harvard University, Harvard University Art Museums, Cambridge MA

Cuno, James, *Dir,* Harvard University, William Hayes Fogg Art Museum, Cambridge MA

Cuno, James, *Dir,* Harvard University, Arthur M Sackler Museum, Cambridge MA

Curcic, Slobodan, *Prof,* Princeton University, Dept of Art and Archaeology, Princeton NJ (S)

Curcio, Robert, *Dir,* Ward-Nasse Gallery, New York NY

Curckford-Peters, Sue, *Acting Librn,* Yale University, Art and Architecture Library, New Haven CT

Cureton, Sara, *Assoc Dir,* Old Barracks Museum, Trenton NJ

Curfman, Robert, *Asst Prof,* Indiana Wesleyan University, Art Dept, Marion IN (S)

Curhan, Ronald C, *Pres,* American Jewish Historical Society, Waltham MA

Curl, Alan, *Admin Cur,* Riverside Municipal Museum, Riverside CA

Curl, David, *Prof,* Kalamazoo College, Art Dept, Kalamazoo MI (S)

Curl, Sheila, *Librn,* University of Notre Dame, Architecture Library, Notre Dame IN

Curler, Dawna, *Staff Development Specialist,* Southern Oregon Historical Society, Jacksonville Museum of Southern Oregon History, Jacksonville OR

Curley, Arthur, *Dir,* Boston Public Library, Central Library, Boston MA

Curling, Marianne, *Cur,* Mark Twain Memorial, Hartford CT

Curling, Marianne, *Cur,* Mark Twain Memorial, Research Library, Hartford CT

Curran, Darryl J, *Chmn Dept,* California State University, Fullerton, Art Dept, Fullerton CA (S)

Curran, John, *VPres Merchandising Activities,* The Metropolitan Museum of Art, New York NY

Curren, Kathleen, *Asst Prof,* Trinity College, Dept of Fine Arts, Hartford CT (S)

Currie, Quentin, *Asst Prof,* Winthrop College, Dept of Art & Design, Rock Hill SC (S)

Curry, Anna, *Dir,* Enoch Pratt Free Library of Baltimore City, Baltimore MD

Curry, David Park, *Deputy Dir Coll,* Virginia Museum of Fine Arts, Richmond VA

Curry, G, *Assoc Prof,* University of Victoria, Dept of Visual Arts, Victoria BC (S)

Curry, Laurie, *Dir of Coll,* Shaker Village of Pleasant Hill, Harrodsburg KY

Curry, Michael P, *Dir,* City of Hampton, Hampton Arts Commission, Hampton VA

Curtin-Stevenson, Mary, *Librn,* Massachusetts College of Art, Morton R Godine Library, Boston MA

Curtis, Brian, *Asst Prof,* University of Miami, Dept of Art & Art History, Coral Gables FL (S)

Curtis, David, *Dept Head,* Virginia Western Community College, Commercial Art, Fine Art & Photography, Roanoke VA (S)

Curtis, George H, *Asst Dir,* National Archives & Records Administration, Harry S Truman Library, Independence MO

Curtis, Howard W, *Dir,* Haverhill Public Library, Art Dept, Haverhill MA

Curtis, Jean T, *Library Dir,* Detroit Public Library, Art & Literature Dept, Detroit MI

Curtis, Leslie Stewart, *Asst Prof,* College of Saint Rose, Dept of Art, Albany NY (S)

Curtis, Roger, *Treas,* North Shore Arts Association, Inc, Art Gallery, Gloucester MA

Curtis, Roger W, *Treas,* Guild of Boston Artists, Boston MA

Curtis, Steven, *Cur Historic Bldgs,* Historical and Cultural Affairs, Delaware State Museums, Dover DE

Curtis, Verna, *Photographs,* Library of Congress, Prints and Photographs Division, Washington DC

Curtis, Walter D, *Asst Prof,* University of Arkansas, Art Dept, Fayetteville AR (S)

Cushing, John D, *Pres,* Essex Historical Society, Essex Shipbuilding Museum, Essex MA

Cushman, Brad, *Chmn,* Southeastern Oklahoma State University, Art Dept, Durant OK (S)

Cushner, Samuel A, *Pres,* Danville Museum of Fine Arts & History, Danville VA

Custen, George, *Chmn,* College of Staten Island, Performing & Creative Arts Dept, Staten Island NY (S)

Cutler, Jerry, *Assoc Prof,* University of Florida, Dept of Art, Gainesville FL (S)

Cutler, Julian, *Coll Mgr,* Saint Gregory's Abbey and College, Mabee-Gerrer Museum of Art, Shawnee OK

Cutler, Phyllis L, *Librn,* Williams College, Sawyer Library, Williamstown MA

Cutler, Walter L, *Pres, Ambassador,* Meridian House International, Washington DC

Cutting, Richard W, *Treas,* The Buffalo Fine Arts Academy, Albright-Knox Art Gallery, Buffalo NY

Cyr, Lisa, *Lectr,* Notre Dame College, Art Dept, Manchester NH (S)

Cyr, Louis, *Dir,* Kateri Tekakwitha Shrine, Musee Kateri Tekakwitha, Kahnawake PQ

Cyr, Paul, *Dept Head Genealogy & Whaling Coll,* New Bedford Free Public Library, Art Dept, New Bedford MA

Czaplewski, Russ, *Cur,* Kern County Museum, Bakersfield CA

Czarnecki, James, *Assoc Prof,* University of Nebraska at Omaha, Dept of Art, Omaha NE (S)

Czarniecki, M J, *Dir,* Minnesota Museum of American Art, Saint Paul MN

Czestochowski, Joseph S, *Dir,* Cedar Rapids Museum of Art, Cedar Rapids IA

Czichos, Raymond L, *Dir,* Pioneer Town, Pioneer Museum of Western Art, Wimberley TX

Czuma, Stanislaw, *Cur SE Asian Art,* Cleveland Museum of Art, Cleveland OH

Dabakis, Melissa, *Asst Prof,* Kenyon College, Art Dept, Gambier OH (S)

Dabash, Adrian G, *Assoc Prof,* Providence College, Art and Art History Dept, Providence RI (S)

Dabertin, Thomas, *Dir Operations,* Museum of Science and Industry, Chicago IL

Da Costa Nunes, Jadviga, *Assoc Prof,* Muhlenberg College, Dept of Art, Allentown PA (S)

da Cunha, Constance Vieiva, *lectr,* Trinity College, Art Dept, Washington DC (S)

Daden, Laurence, *Deputy Chmn for Management,* National Endowment for the Arts, Washington DC

Dagenais, Mr Yves, *Deputy Dir Business,* National Gallery of Canada, Ottawa ON

D'Agostino, Fernanda, *Instr,* Marylhurst College, Art Dept, Marylhurst OR (S)

Daily, Patrick, *Exec Dir,* Tippecanoe County Historical Museum, Lafayette IN

Dajani, Virginia, *Executive Dir,* American Academy of Arts & Letters, New York NY

Dake, Dennis, *Coordr Art Educ,* Iowa State University, Dept of Art and Design, Ames IA (S)

Dake, Pat, *Librn,* Muskegon Museum of Art, Library, Muskegon MI

Dale, Cindi, *Dir Educ & Community Develop,* University of California, Los Angeles, Grunwald Center for the Graphic Arts, Los Angeles CA

Dale, Cindi, *Dir Educ & Community Develop,* University of California, Los Angeles, Wight Art Gallery, Los Angeles CA

Dale, Ron, *Assoc Prof,* University of Mississippi, Dept of Art, University MS (S)

Dalenius, Majory, *Gallery Secy,* Providence Art Club, Providence RI

D'Alessandro, Tiffany, *Asst Cur,* University of Chicago, David and Alfred Smart Museum of Art, Chicago IL

Daley, Judy, *Asst Cur,* Art Gallery of Peel, Library, Brampton ON

Daley, William, *Chmn Board,* Haystack Mountain School of Crafts, Gallery, Deer Isle ME

Daley, William, *Instr,* Chautauqua Institution, School of Art, Chautauqua NY (S)

Dalkey, F, *Instr,* Sacramento City College, Art Dept, Sacramento CA (S)

Dalton, Tessa, *Office & Sales Mgr,* Bradford Brinton Memorial Museum & Historic Ranch, Big Horn WY

Daly, Charles, *Dir,* National Archives and Records Service, John F Kennedy Library and Museum, Boston MA

Daly, Jean, *Registrar,* Clinton Historical Museum Village, Clinton NJ

Daly, Jean, *Registrar,* Clinton Historical Museum Village, Library, Clinton NJ

Damaska, Maureen, *Admin Officer,* National Museum of American Art, Washington DC

Damer, Jack, *Prof,* University of Wisconsin, Madison, Dept of Art, Madison WI (S)

Damiam, Carol, *Instr & Art Historian,* Florida International University, Visual Arts Dept, Miami FL (S)

Damkoehler, David, *Head Dept,* University of Wisconsin-Green Bay, Art-Communication & the Arts, Green Bay WI (S)

Danahy, John, *Asst Prof,* University of Toronto, Programme in Landscape Architecture, Toronto ON (S)

Danciger, Alain, *Asst Dir,* Saidye Bronfman Centre, Montreal PQ

Dandois, Leslie, *ARTLINKS Coordr,* Nevada Museum Of Art, Reno NV

Danehower, George Ann, *Gallery Dir,* Bradley University, Hartman Center Gallery, Peoria IL

Danford, Gerald, *VPres,* Fort Morgan Heritage Foundation, Fort Morgan CO

D'Angelo, Joseph, *Pres,* International Museum of Cartoon Art, Boca Raton FL

D'Angelo, Olga, *Cur Asst,* State University of New York at Purchase, Neuberger Museum, Purchase NY

Daniel, Betty, *Circulation & Reserve Supv,* Washington University, Art & Architecture Library, Saint Louis MO

Daniel, Mike, *Instr,* Long Beach City College, Dept of Art, Long Beach CA (S)

Daniel, Therese, *Pres,* Witter Gallery, Storm Lake IA

Daniels, Christopher, *Preparator,* Greenville Museum of Art, Inc, Greenville NC

Daniels, Eve, *Registar,* Roberson Museum & Science Center, Binghamton NY

Daniels, John P, *Dir,* Historic Pensacola Preservation Board, Historic Pensacola Village, Pensacola FL

Daniels, Maygene, *Gallery Archivist,* National Galiery of Art, Washington DC

Danielson, Deborah, *Asst Prof,* Siena Heights College, Studio Angelico-Art Dept, Adrian MI (S)

Danioth, David, *Instructor,* The Art Institutes International, The Art Institute of Seattle, Seattle WA (S)

Danish, Dr, *Pres,* Maryland College of Art and Design, Silver Spring MD (S)

Danly, Susan, *Cur,* Pennsylvania Academy of the Fine Arts, Galleries, Philadelphia PA

Dann, Marquis, *Asst Cur,* Red Rock State Park, Museum, Church Rock NM

Danoff, I Michael, *Dir,* Edmundson Art Foundation, Inc, Des Moines Art Center, Des Moines IA

Danz, Lidia, *Resident Cur,* Waterville Historical Society, Redington Museum, Waterville ME

Danz, Richard, *Resident Cur,* Waterville Historical Society, Redington Museum, Waterville ME

Daraska, Jessie, *Librn,* Balzekas Museum of Lithuanian Culture, Research Library, Chicago IL

d'Argencourt, Louise, *Cur European Art,* Montreal Museum of Fine Arts, Montreal PQ

Darien, Gwen, *Exec Dir,* Los Angeles Contemporary Exhibitions, Los Angeles CA

Darling, Barry, *Adjunct Asst Prof,* Le Moyne College, Fine Arts Dept, Syracuse NY (S)

Darner, Ron, *Acting Dir,* San Antonio Public Library, Dept of Fine Arts, San Antonio TX

Daro, Hazel E, *Asst to Dir,* University of Alaska, Museum, Fairbanks AK

Darr, Alan, *Cur European Sculpture & Decorative Arts,* Detroit Institute of Arts, Detroit MI

Darr, Katherine, *Librn,* Museum of Art, Fort Lauderdale, Library, Fort Lauderdale FL

Darriau, Jean-Paul, *Assoc Prof,* Indiana University, Bloomington, Henry Radford Hope School of Fine Arts, Bloomington IN (S)

Darrow, Thelma, *VPres,* Paint 'N Palette Club, Grant Wood & Memorial Park Gallery, Anamosa IA

Darst, Lise, *Museum Cur,* Rosenberg Library, Galveston TX

Dart, Donna, *Instr,* Silver Lake College, Art Dept, Manitowoc WI (S)

Dasher, Glenn T, *Chmn Art & Art History Dept,* University of Alabama in Huntsville, Dept of Art & Art History, Huntsville AL (S)

DaSilva, Marilyn, *Jewelry & Metal Arts,* California College of Arts and Crafts, Oakland CA (S)

D'Astolfo, Frank, *Chmn,* Rutgers University, Newark, Newark Col Arts & Sciences, Newark NJ (S)

Datte, Bonnie, *Office Mgr,* Midland Art Council, Midland MI

Daubert, Debra, *Cur,* Oshkosh Public Museum, Oshkosh WI

Daugherty, Michael, *Prof,* Louisiana State University, School of Art, Baton Rouge LA (S)

Daughnette, Mark, *Cur Exhib,* Alaska State Museum, Juneau AK

Daulton, Christine, *Conservator,* Westmoreland Museum of Art, Greensburg PA

D'Avanzo, Suzanne H, *Asst Prof,* Providence College, Art and Art History Dept, Providence RI (S)

Davenny, Ward, *Asst Prof,* Dickinson College, Fine Arts Dept, Carlisle PA (S)

Davenport, Ellen, *VPres,* Plastic Club, Art Club for Women, Philadelphia PA

Davenport, Martin, *Pres,* Plastic Club, Art Club for Women, Philadelphia PA

Davezac, Bertrand, *Chief Cur,* Menil Collection, Houston TX

Davezac, Shehira, *Assoc Prof,* Indiana University, Bloomington, Henry Radford Hope School of Fine Arts, Bloomington IN (S)

Davi, Susan A, *Reference Librn (Art & Art History),* University of Delaware, Morris Library, Newark DE

David, Michelle, *Admin Asst,* Fort Morgan Heritage Foundation, Fort Morgan CO

Davidhazy, Andrew, *Chmn Imaging & Photographic Technology,* Rochester Institute of Technology, School of Photographic Arts & Sciences, Rochester NY (S)

Davidson, Bernice, *Research Cur,* Frick Collection, New York NY

Davidson, David, *Assoc Dean,* New York Academy of Art, Graduate School of Figurative Art, New York NY (S)

Davidson, Mary, *Cur of Exhibits,* The National Park Service, United States Department of the Interior, The Statue of Liberty National Monument, New York NY

Davidson, Richard, *Chmn Trustees,* Longfellow's Wayside Inn Museum, South Sudbury MA

Davidson, Todd, *Mgr,* City of Scarborough, Cedar Ridge Creative Centre, Scarborough ON

Davies, Bruce W, *Exec Dir,* Craigdarroch Castle Historical Museum Society, Victoria BC

Davies, Hanlyn, *Chmn Dept,* University of Massachusetts, Amherst, College of Arts and Sciences, Amherst MA (S)

Davies, Harry, *Chmn & Prof,* Adelphi University, Dept of Art and Art History, Garden City NY (S)

Davies, Hugh M, *Dir,* Museum of Contemporary Art, San Diego, La Jolla CA

Davies, Mary Butler, *Dir,* Johns Hopkins University, Homewood House Museum, Baltimore MD

Davila, Arturo, *Prof,* University of Puerto Rico, Dept of Fine Arts, Rio Piedras PR (S)

Davis, Angelina, *Chmn,* Blue Lake Fine Arts Camp, Art Dept, Twin Lake MI (S)

Davis, Ann, *Dir,* University of Calgary, The Nickle Arts Museum, Calgary AB

Davis, Ann Marie, *Co-Dir,* Tyringham Art Galleries, Tyringham MA

DeFalla, Josie E, *Dir,* Maryhill Museum of Art, Goldendale WA

de Fato, Elizabeth, *Librn,* Seattle Art Museum, Library, Seattle WA

DeFazio, Raymond, *Assoc Prof,* Seton Hill College, Dept of Art, Greensburg PA (S)

Defenbaugh, Deni, *Asst Prof,* Rochester Institute of Technology, School of Photographic Arts & Sciences, Rochester NY (S)

Defoor, T, *Music Instr,* Edison Community College, Dept of Fine and Performing Arts, Fort Myers FL (S)

DeFurio, A G, *Chairperson,* Indiana University of Pennsylvania, Dept of Art and Art Education, Indiana PA (S)

Degraeve, Christine, *Asst Prof,* Moorhead State University, Dept of Art, Moorhead MN (S)

de Grassi, Leonard, *Prof,* Glendale Community College, Dept of Fine Arts, Glendale CA (S)

DeGrazia, Diane, *Cur Southern Baroque Painting,* National Gallery of Art, Washington DC

Dehnert, Edmund, *Chmn Humanities,* City Colleges of Chicago, Truman College, Chicago IL (S)

De Hoet, Robert, *Prog Educational-Community Servs Coordr,* Southern Illinois University, University Museum, Carbondale IL

De Hoff, William, *Lectr,* University of Wisconsin-Stout, Dept of Art & Design, Menomonie WI (S)

Dehoney, Martyvonne, *Prof,* Drew University, Art Dept, Madison NJ (S)

Deichler, Deborah, *Instr,* Main Line Center for the Arts, Haverford PA (S)

Deighton, Edwin J, *Asst Dir,* University of Oklahoma, Fred Jones Jr Museum of Art, Norman OK

Deihl, Charles L, *Pres,* Kendall College of Art & Design, Grand Rapids MI (S)

Deihl, Charles L, *Pres,* Kendall College of Art & Design, Frank & Lyn Van Steenberg Library, Grand Rapids MI

Deitrick, Pam, *Head Librn,* Public Library of Des Moines, Fine Arts Dept, Des Moines IA

DeJaager, Alfred R, *Chmn,* West Liberty State College, Art Dept, West Liberty WV (S)

Dejardin, Fiona, *Asst Prof,* Hartwick College, Art Dept, Oneonta NY (S)

DeJong, J D, *Asst Prof,* Central University of Iowa, Art Dept, Pella IA (S)

de Kat, Joan, *Asst Cur,* Brant Historical Society, Brant County Museum, Brantford ON

De Kleden, Dino, *VPres,* Guadalupe Historic Foundation, Santuario de Guadalupe, Santa Fe NM

Delacote, Goery, *Dir,* Exploratorium, San Francisco CA

Delahoyd, Mary, *Instr,* Sarah Lawrence College, Dept of Art History, Bronxville NY (S)

Delamater, Peg, *Asst Prof,* Winthrop College, Dept of Art & Design, Rock Hill SC (S)

DeLand, Michelle, *Pub Relations,* K Mart Corp, Troy MI

DeLaney, Charles, *Dean,* New York Institute of Photography, New York NY (S)

Delaney, Esmeralda, *Res Artist,* Grand Canyon University, Art Dept, Phoenix AZ (S)

Delaney, Richard, *Chmn,* California State University, Fresno, Art Dept, Fresno CA (S)

Delaney, Robert L, *Chmn,* Arts United of Greater Fort Wayne, Fort Wayne IN

Delaney, Susan, *Instr,* Miracosta College, Art Dept, Oceanside CA (S)

Delaney, Thomas, *Cur,* Sheldon Swope Art Museum, Terre Haute IN

de Lange, Stephany, *Instr,* Pepperdine University, Seaver College, Dept of Art, Malibu CA (S)

DeLap, Amy, *Instr,* Vincennes University Junior College, Art Dept, Vincennes IN (S)

De Lape, Christine, *Asst Dir,* The College at New Paltz State University of New York, College Art Gallery, New Paltz NY

Del-Ariew, Isabel Farrel, *Dir,* Pennsylvania State University, HUB Galleries, University Park PA

de la Torre, David, *Assoc Dir,* Honolulu Academy of Arts, Honolulu HI

Delbo, Jose, *Instr,* Joe Kubert School of Cartoon & Graphic Art, Inc, Dover NJ (S)

Delchanty, Suzanne, *Dir,* Contemporary Arts Museum, Houston TX

de Leon, Perla, *Exec Dir,* FOTOGRAFICA, New York NY

Delin, Nancy, *Art Librn,* Hewlett-Woodmere Public Library, Hewlett NY

Dell, Irve, *Asst Prof,* Saint Olaf College, Art Dept, Northfield MN (S)

Dell, Roger, *Educ Dir,* Museum of Contemporary Art, Chicago IL

della Cioppa, Margaret, *Mgr,* The Chase Manhattan Bank, NA, Art Collection, New York NY

Della-Piana, Elissa, *Illustration,* Monserrat College of Art, Beverly MA (S)

Dellavalle, Jacques A, *Prof,* Daytona Beach Community College, Dept of Fine Arts & Visual Arts, Daytona Beach FL (S)

Dellecese, Laurie, *Spec Events Coordr,* Museum of Fine Arts, Springfield MA

Deller, Harris, *Prof,* Southern Illinois University, School of Art & Design, Carbondale IL (S)

Dellis, Arlene, *Registrar,* Center for the Fine Arts, Miami FL

Dell'Olio, L, *Prof,* Camden County College, Dept of Art, Blackwood NJ (S)

Delluva, Patricia, *Registrar,* Allentown Art Museum, Allentown PA

DeLong, Marilyn, *Costume Cur,* University of Minnesota, Goldstein Gallery, Saint Paul MN

De Long, Paul, *Assoc Prof,* University of Wisconsin-Stout, Dept of Art & Design, Menomonie WI (S)

DeLong, Paul, *Lectr,* University of Wisconsin-Stout, Dept of Art & Design, Menomonie WI (S)

de Looper, Willem, *Consulting Cur,* The Phillips Collection, Washington DC

DeLorenzo, Joseph, *Chmn,* Herkimer County Community College, Social Sciences & Humanities Division, Herkimer NY (S)

DeLorme, Harry H, *Cur Educ,* Telfair Academy of Arts and Sciences Inc, Savannah GA

Delos, Kate, *Instr,* Solano Community College, Division of Fine & Applied Art, Suisun City CA (S)

DeLuca, E P, *Chmn Division Fine Arts, Language, Literature,* Peace College, Art Dept, Raleigh NC (S)

deLuise, Alexandra, *Cur,* Queens College, City University of New York, Queens College Art Center, Flushing NY

deLuise, Alexandra, *Art Librn,* Queens College, City University of New York, Art Library, Flushing NY

del Valle, Ed, *Assoc Prof,* Florida International University, Visual Arts Dept, Miami FL (S)

DelValle, Helen, *VPres,* American Society of Artists, Inc, Chicago IL

Delvin, Robert C, *Fine Arts Librn,* Illinois Wesleyan University, Slide Library, Bloomington IL

De Marcos, Sally, *Asst Prof,* New Community College of Baltimore, Dept of Fine Arts, Baltimore MD (S)

Demaree, Robert W, *Chmn,* Indiana University South Bend, Fine Arts Dept, South Bend IN (S)

DeMay, Susan, *Lectr,* Vanderbilt University, Dept of Fine Arts, Nashville TN (S)

DeMedeiros, Melissa, *Librn,* M Knoedler & Co, Inc, Library, New York NY

DeMeio, Albina, *Admin Exhib & Registration,* New York Historical Society, New York NY

DeMelim, John, *Prof,* Rhode Island College, Art Dept, Providence RI (S)

De Menil, Dominique, *Pres,* Menil Collection, Houston TX

Demerling, Rod, *Installations & Registrar,* Oakville Galleries, Centennial Gallery and Gairloch Gallery, Oakville ON

Demers, Carol A, *Asst Dir Adminstration,* University of Lethbridge, Art Gallery, Lethbridge AB

Demers, Francois, *Faculty Dean of Arts,* Universite Laval Cite Universitaire, School of Visual Arts, Quebec PQ (S)

Demeter, Michael, *Prof,* Lake Erie College-Garfield Senior College, Fine Arts Dept, Painesville OH (S)

Demetrion, James, *Dir,* Hirshhorn Museum and Sculpture Garden, Washington DC

D'Emilio, Sandra, *Cur Painting,* Museum of New Mexico, Museum of Fine Arts, Santa Fe NM

Deming, David L, *Dean,* University of Texas, Dept of Art & Art History, Austin TX (S)

Deming, Greg, *Asst Prof,* Eastern New Mexico University, Dept of Art, Portales NM (S)

de Montebello, Philippe, *Dir,* The Metropolitan Museum of Art, New York NY

DeMoss, Max, *Instr,* Mount San Jacinto College, Art Dept, San Jacinto CA (S)

DeMots, Lois, *Instr,* Siena Heights College, Studio Angelico-Art Dept, Adrian MI (S)

Demott, Judith, *Dir of Development,* Penobscot Marine Museum, Searsport ME

DeMoulpied, Deborah, *Prof,* University of Maine, Art Dept, Orono ME (S)

de Moura Sobral, Luis, *Dir Dept Art History,* Universite de Montreal, Dept of Art History, Montreal PQ (S)

Dempsey, Bruce H, *Dir,* Jacksonville Art Museum, Jacksonville FL

Dempsey, Charles, *Chmn,* Johns Hopkins University, Dept of the History of Art, Baltimore MD (S)

Dempsey, Don, *Asst Prof,* Mohawk Valley Community College, Advertising Design and Production, Utica NY (S)

Dempster, Dora, *Asst Dir Reference Div,* Metropolitan Toronto Library Board, Arts Dept, Toronto ON

Demulder, Kum, *Instr,* Joe Kubert School of Cartoon & Graphic Art, Inc, Dover NJ (S)

De Natale, Doug, *State Folk Arts Coordr,* University of South Carolina, McKissick Museum, Columbia SC

Denby, Greg, *Head Preparator,* University of Notre Dame, Snite Museum of Art, Notre Dame IN

Denerstein, Carolyn, *Pres,* Morris-Jumel Mansion, Inc, New York NY

Dengate, James, *Cur Numismatics,* University of Illinois, World Heritage Museum, Champaign IL

Deniarinis, Lucia, *Instr,* St Lawrence College, Dept of Visual & Creative Arts, Cornwall ON (S)

Denison, Cara D, *Cur Drawings & Prints,* Pierpont Morgan Library, New York NY

Denison, Dirk, *Asst Dean,* Illinois Institute of Technology, College of Architecture, Chicago IL (S)

Denker, Bert, *Librn in Charge Visual Resources Coll,* Winterthur Museum and Gardens, Library, Winterthur DE

Denning, Catherine, *Cur,* Brown University, Annmary Brown Memorial, Providence RI

Dennis, David, *Technical Dir,* University of Iowa, Museum of Art, Iowa City IA

Dennis, James M, *Prof,* University of Wisconsin, Madison, Dept of Art History, Madison WI (S)

Dennis, Jim, *VPres,* Keokuk Art Center, Keokuk IA

Dennis, Tom, *Asst Prof,* University of Nebraska, Kearney, Dept of Art & Art History, Kearney NE (S)

Dennison, Lisa, *Asst Cur,* Solomon R Guggenheim Museum, New York NY

Dennison, Nan, *Dir,* Historical Society of Palm Beach County, West Palm Beach FL

Dennison, Tom, *Performance & Video Coordr,* Los Angeles Contemporary Exhibitions, Los Angeles CA

Denny, Paul, *Chmn,* Phillips University, Dept of Art, Enid OK (S)

Denny, Richard A, *Chmn Board of Dir,* High Museum of Art, Atlanta GA

Denny, Walter, *Honorary Cur Rugs,* Harvard University, Arthur M Sackler Museum, Cambridge MA

Denny, Walter B, *Prof,* University of Massachusetts, Amherst, Art History Program, Amherst MA (S)

Densham, Robert, *Prof,* California Polytechnic State University at San Luis Obispo, Dept of Art and Design, San Luis Obispo CA (S)

De Nunzio, John, *Chmn,* Lackawanna Junior College, Art Dept, Scranton PA (S)

DePalma-Sadzkoski, Elaine, *Museum Educator,* Munson-Williams-Proctor Institute, Museum of Art, Utica NY

dePeyster, James A, *VPres,* The Society of the Four Arts, Palm Beach FL

Dimico, Sam, *Instructor,* The Art Institutes International, The Art Institute of Seattle, Seattle WA (S)

Dimond, Thomas, *Asst Prof Art,* Eastern Oregon State College, Arts & Humanities Dept, La Grande OR (S)

Dinan, Kathi, *Prog Coordr,* Pelham Art Center, Pelham NY

Dingler, John, *Preparator,* University of California, University Art Gallery, Riverside CA

Dingus, Rick, *Assoc Prof,* Texas Tech University, Dept of Art, Lubbock TX (S)

Dingwall, Kenneth, *Vis Prof,* Cleveland Institute of Art, Cleveland OH (S)

Dinkelspiel, Edgar N, *Pres,* Long Branch Historical Museum, Long Branch NJ

Dinsmore, John N, *Prof,* University of Nebraska, Kearney, Dept of Art & Art History, Kearney NE (S)

diPetta, Angelo, *Chair Applied Art & Design,* Ontario College of Art, Toronto ON (S)

Dippolito, Frank, *Art Dept Chmn,* Tacoma Community College, Art Dept, Tacoma WA (S)

Di Rienzi, Anthony, *Treas,* Pennsylvania Academy of the Fine Arts, Fellowship of the Pennsylvania Academy of the Fine Arts, Philadelphia PA

Dirks, John, *Dir,* Ogunquit Museum of American Art, Ogunquit ME

Dirkse, Lorrie, *Assoc Ed,* Dialogue Inc, Columbus OH

DiSalvi, Margaret, *Librn,* Newark Museum Association, Newark Museum Library, Newark NJ

Disantis, Dian, *Art Librn,* Mayfield Regional Library, Mayfield Village OH

Dismore, Grant, *Instr,* La Roche College, Division of Graphics, Design & Communication, Pittsburgh PA (S)

Dismuke, Alan, *Facility Dir,* Humboldt Arts Council, Eureka CA

Disney, Betty, *Dir,* Cypress College, Fine Arts Gallery, Cypress CA

DiStefano, Lynne, *Chief Cur Museums,* London Regional Art & Historical Museums, London ON

Distefano, Lynne, *Chief Cur of Museums,* London Regional Art & Historical Museums, London ON

DiTeresa, Neil, *Prof,* Berea College, Art Dept, Berea KY (S)

Dittman, Reidar, *Prof,* Saint Olaf College, Art Dept, Northfield MN (S)

Divelbess, Diane, *Prof,* California State Polytechnic University, Pomona, Art Dept, Pomona CA (S)

Divelbiss, Maggie, *Dir,* Sangre de Cristo Arts & Conference Center, Pueblo CO

Divola, John, *Chmn,* University of California, Riverside, Dept of Art, Riverside CA (S)

Dixon, Arthur L, *Chmn,* J Sargeant Reynolds Community College, Humanities & Social Science Division, Richmond VA (S)

Dixon, Bob, *Assoc Prof,* Sangamon State University, Visual Arts Program, Springfield IL (S)

Dixon, David, *Asst Prof,* East Tennessee State University, Fine Arts Dept, Johnson City TN (S)

Dixon, F Eugene, *Pres,* The Society of the Four Arts, Palm Beach FL

Dixon, Gerald, *VPres,* No Man's Land Historical Society Museum, Goodwell OK

Dixon, Jack, *Chair Foundation Studies,* Ontario College of Art, Toronto ON (S)

Dixon, Jeannette, *Librn,* Museum of Fine Arts, Houston, Hirsch Library, Houston TX

Dixon, Ken, *Prof,* Texas Tech University, Dept of Art, Lubbock TX (S)

Dixon, Laurinda, *Prof,* Syracuse University, Dept of Fine Arts (Art History), Syracuse NY (S)

Dixon, Yvonne, *Head Dept,* Trinity College, Art Dept, Washington DC (S)

Dixson, Henry, *Instr,* Avila College, Art Division, Dept of Performing and Visual Art, Kansas City MO (S)

Dixson, Lauren, *Adminr,* Craftsmen's Guild of Mississippi, Inc, Agriculture & Forestry Museum, Jackson MS

Dixson, Pauline, *Asst Prof,* Mary Baldwin College, Dept of Art, Staunton VA (S)

D'Lugosz, Joseph, *Instructor,* Milwaukee Area Technical College, Graphic Arts Dept, Milwaukee WI (S)

Dmytria, Charles, *Prof,* Northwestern Connecticut Community College, Fine Arts Dept, Winsted CT (S)

Doagan, Peggy Bailey, *Prof,* University of Arizona, Dept of Art, Tucson AZ (S)

Doak, Gale L, *Asst Prof,* Florida Southern College, Art Dept, Lakeland FL (S)

Dobb, Theodore C, *Librn,* Simon Fraser University, Library, Burnaby BC

Dobbins, Stella, *Dir,* Rice University, Sewall Art Gallery, Houston TX

Dobbins, Stella, *Lectr,* Rice University, Dept of Art and Art History, Houston TX (S)

Dobbs, John, *Assoc Prof,* John Jay College of Criminal Justice, Dept of Art, Music and Philosophy, New York NY (S)

Dobbs, Paul, *Archivist,* Massachusetts College of Art, Morton R Godine Library, Boston MA

Dobell, Colin, *Pres,* Vancouver Art Gallery, Vancouver BC

Dobereiner, Wendy, *Asst Prof,* University of British Columbia, Dept of Fine Arts, Vancouver BC (S)

Dobrinsky, Larry, *Dir of Finance & Admin,* The Mariners' Museum, Newport News VA

Dobson, Diane, *Admin Asst,* St Thomas Elgin Art Gallery, Saint Thomas ON

Docherty, Linda, *Prof,* Bowdoin College, Art Dept, Brunswick ME (S)

Dockery, Michael, *Chmn,* Harrisburg Area Community College, Division of Communication and the Arts, Harrisburg PA (S)

Doctorow, Erica, *Fine Arts Librn,* Adelphi University, Fine & Performing Arts Library, Garden City NY

Doctorow, Erica, *Dir,* Adelphi University, Swirbul Library Gallery, Garden City NY

Dodd, Jerry, *Chmn Sculpture,* East Texas State University, Dept of Art, East Texas Station, Commerce TX (S)

Doddoli, Adolfo, *Coordr Foundation,* Indiana University-Purdue University, Indianapolis, Herron School of Art, Indianapolis IN (S)

Dodds, Jed, *Museum Asst,* The Contemporary, Museum for Contemporary Arts, Baltimore MD

Dodds, Richard J, *Cur Maritime History,* Calvert Marine Museum, Solomons MD

Dodge, John W, *Asst,* The First National Bank of Chicago, Art Collection, Chicago IL

Dodge, Robert, *Instr,* Bucks County Community College, Fine Arts Dept, Newtown PA (S)

Dodson, Gray, *Museum Shop Mgr,* Virginia Beach Center for the Arts, Virginia Beach VA

Dodson, Howard, *Chief,* The New York Public Library, Schomburg Center for Research in Black Culture, New York NY

Dodson, Roy, *Prof,* Sul Ross State University, Dept of Fine Arts & Communications, Alpine TX (S)

Dodson, Susan, *Chmn,* McPherson College, Art Dept, McPherson KS (S)

Dodson, Susan W, *Dir,* McPherson College Gallery, McPherson KS

Dodson, Thomas A, *Dean Colls,* University of New Mexico, College of Fine Arts, Albuquerque NM (S)

Doe, Donald Bartlett, *Dir,* Washburn University, Mulvane Art Museum, Topeka KS

D'Oench, Ellen, *Adjunct Prof,* Wesleyan University, Art Dept, Middletown CT (S)

D'Oench, Ellen G, *Cur,* Wesleyan University, Davison Art Center, Middletown CT

Doeppel-Horn, Diane, *Cur Educ,* Carolina Art Association, Gibbes Museum of Art, Charleston SC

Doerner, P Parker, *Instr,* Indiana University of Pennsylvania, Dept of Art and Art Education, Indiana PA (S)

Doerner, Richard L, *Curatorial Asst,* United States Senate Commission on Art, Washington DC

Dogu, Hikemt, *Library Dir,* Parsons School of Design, Adam & Sophie Gimbel Design Library, New York NY

Doherty, Ann, *Deputy Dir for Development,* International Center of Photography, New York NY

Doherty, Brian, *Supervisory Park Ranger,* Longfellow National Historic Site, Cambridge MA

Doherty, Mary Lou, *Pres,* Lowell Art Association, Whistler House Museum of Art, Lowell MA

Doherty, Peggy, *Dir,* Northern Illinois University, Art Gallery in Chicago, Chicago IL

Dohner, Luke, *Preparations,* Illinois State Museum, State of Illinois Art Gallery, Chicago IL

Dolan, Susan, *Registrar,* Tucson Museum of Art, Tucson AZ

Dole, Bob, *VChmn,* United States Senate Commission on Art, Washington DC

Dolezal, Chris, *Admin Asst,* University of Arizona, Museum of Art, Tucson AZ

Dolin, John, *Prof,* Marshall University, Dept of Art, Huntington WV (S)

Doll, Linda, *Treas,* National Watercolor Society, Cerritos CA

Doll, Nancy, *Dir,* Santa Barbara Contemporary Arts Forum, Santa Barbara CA

Dombrowski, Mark, *Dir Instructional Servs,* Siena Heights College, Art Library, Adrian MI

Domine, Doug, *Instr,* Northwestern Michigan College, Art Dept, Traverse City MI (S)

Dominguez, Frank, *Chmn,* Bucks County Community College, Hicks Art Center, Newtown PA

Dominguez, Frank, *Chmn Dept,* Bucks County Community College, Fine Arts Dept, Newtown PA (S)

Dominick, Alfred S, *Sr VPres Advertising & Public Relations,* The Boatmen's National Bank of St Louis, Art Collection, Saint Louis MO

Dominquez, David, *Corporate Press Officer,* Public Corporation for the Arts, Visual & Performing Arts Registry, Long Beach CA

Domkoski, David, *Dir Handforth Gallery,* Tacoma Public Library, Handforth Gallery, Tacoma WA

Dommasch, Hans S, *Head,* University of Saskatchewan, Dept of Art & Art History, Saskatoon SK (S)

Donadio, Emmie, *Asst Dir,* Middlebury College, Museum of Art, Middlebury VT

Donahue, Michael, *Chmn,* Temple Junior College, Art Dept, Temple TX (S)

Donahue, Michael, *Academic Dean,* Camden County College, Dept of Art, Blackwood NJ (S)

Donaldson, P, *Instr,* Golden West College, Visual Art Dept, Huntington Beach CA (S)

Donaldson, Shirley, *Gallery Dir,* Coe College, Gordon Fennell Gallery & Marvin Cone Gallery, Cedar Rapids IA

Donaldson, Sue, *Dir,* Open Space, Victoria BC

Donaldson, Thomas E, *Prof,* Cleveland State University, Art Dept, Cleveland OH (S)

Donathan, Michael, *Assoc Prof Music,* Clinch Valley College of the University of Virginia, Visual & Performing Arts, Wise VA (S)

Donato, James, *Instr,* Antonelli Institute, Professional Photography, Commercial Art & Interior Design, Plymouth Meeting PA (S)

Donley, Robert, *Chmn Dept,* DePaul University, Dept of Art, Chicago IL (S)

Donlon, Claudette, *Asst Dir Adminr,* The Jewish Museum, New York NY

Donnan, Christopher B, *Dir,* University of California, Los Angeles, Fowler Museum of Cultural History, Los Angeles CA

Donnelley, Robert, *Dir,* Terra Museum of American Art, Chicago IL

Donnelly, John, *Instr,* Mount Vernon Nazarene College, Art Dept, Mount Vernon OH (S)

Donnelly, Maureen, *Registrar,* Kemper & Leila Williams Foundation, New Orleans LA

Donnelly, Peter, *Pres,* Corporate Council for the Arts, Seattle WA

Donoho, Ronan, *Pres,* Portsmouth Athenaeum, Portsmouth NH

Donovan, Margorie, *Vol Coordr,* Iowa City - Johnson County Arts Council, Arts Center, Iowa City IA

Donovan, Nancy, *Resource Coordr,* University of Calgary, Faculty of Environmental Design, Calgary AB

Donovan, Thom, *Dir,* Nippon Club Gallery, New York NY

Doolan, John M, *Asst Dir*, Kateri Galleries, The National Shrine of the North American Martyrs, Auriesville NY

Dooley, William, *Dir*, University of Alabama, Moody Gallery of Art, Tuscaloosa AL

Doolittle, Cindy, *Instr*, Mohawk Valley Community College, Advertising Design and Production, Utica NY (S)

Dopp, Alice, *Technical Serv*, Las Vegas-Clark County Library District, Las Vegas NV

Doran, Claudette, *Exhib Dir*, Valley Cottage Library, Gallery, Valley Cottage NY

Doran, Faye, *Prof*, Harding University, Dept of Art, Searcy AR (S)

Doran, Pat, *Dean Grad & Continuing Educ*, Massachusetts College of Art, Boston MA (S)

Dore, William, *Chmn*, Seattle University, Fine Arts Dept, Division of Art, Seattle WA (S)

Dorell, Mary, *VPres Educ*, DuPage Art League School & Gallery, Wheaton IL

Doremus, William, *Pres*, Halifax Historical Society, Inc, Halifax Historical Museum, Daytona Beach FL

Dorethy, Rex, *Head Dept*, University of Wisconsin-Stevens Point, Dept of Art & Design, Stevens Point WI (S)

Dorian, Gerard, *Pres*, Museum of Ossining Historical Society, Ossining NY

Dorman, Jenan, *Deputy Dir External Affairs*, Kentucky Derby Museum, Louisville KY

Dormer, James T, *Chmn*, Colorado State University, Dept of Art, Fort Collins CO (S)

Dorn, Gordon, *Div Coordr*, Northern Illinois University, School of Art, De Kalb IL (S)

Dorn, Sue B, *Deputy Dir, Development & Public Affairs*, Museum of Modern Art, New York NY

Dornbach, Vernon, *Pres*, Redlands Art Association, Redlands CA

Dornoff, H, *Secy Exhib*, University of Michigan, Slusser Gallery, Ann Arbor MI

Doroshenko, Peter, *Engelhard Cur*, Contemporary Arts Museum, Houston TX

Dorrien, Carlos, *Asst Prof*, Wellesley College, Art Dept, Wellesley MA (S)

Dorsey, Henry, *Chmn*, Coahoma Community College, Art Education & Fine Arts Dept, Clarksdale MS (S)

Dorsey, Lucia I, *Coordr*, University of Pennsylvania, Arthur Ross Gallery, Philadelphia PA

Dorsey, Michael, *Acting Dean*, East Carolina University, School of Art, Greenville NC (S)

Dorsi, Sybil, *VPres*, The Allied Artists of America, Inc, New York NY

Dortch, Ann, *Asst to Dir*, University of North Carolina at Greensboro, Weatherspoon Art Gallery, Greensboro NC

Dorval, Karen A, *Head Art & Music Dept*, Springfield City Library & Museums Association, Art & Music Dept, Springfield MA

Dotson, Esther G, *Prof Emeritus*, Cornell University, Dept of the History of Art, Ithaca NY (S)

Dougall, William G, *Historic Resources Dir*, Riverside Municipal Museum, Riverside CA

Dougherty, Dick, *Chmn*, Murray State University, Eagle Gallery, Murray KY

Dougherty, Marijo, *Interim Dir*, State University of New York at Albany, University Art Gallery, Albany NY

Dougherty, Peggy, *Dir Development*, Newark Museum Association, The Newark Museum, Newark NJ

Dougherty, Richard, *Chmn*, Murray State University, Art Dept, Murray KY (S)

Douglas, Camille, *Assoc Prof*, Murray State University, Art Dept, Murray KY (S)

Douglas, Dee, *Information Coordr*, Art Gallery of Windsor, Windsor ON

Douglas, Diane, *Dir & Cur*, Bellevue Art Museum, Bellevue WA

Douglas, Edwin P, *Instr*, Portland School of Art, Portland ME (S)

Douglas, F, *Assoc Prof*, University of Victoria, Dept of Visual Arts, Victoria BC (S)

Douglas, Larry, *Dir*, Brigham City Museum-Gallery, Brigham City UT

Douglas, Leah, *Dir Exhib*, University of the Arts, Philadelphia PA

Douglas, Stella, *Dir Sewall Art Gallery*, Rice University, Dept of Art and Art History, Houston TX (S)

Douglas-Edwards, Camille, *Comptroller*, Arts United of Greater Fort Wayne, Fort Wayne IN

Douglass, Nancy, *Treas*, Oysterponds Historical Society, Museum, Orient NY

Douke, Daniel, *Dir*, California State University, Los Angeles, Fine Arts Gallery, Los Angeles CA

Doumato, Lamia, *Reader Services Librn*, National Gallery of Art, Library, Washington DC

Dove, J A, *Horticulturist*, Tryon Palace Historic Sites & Gardens, New Bern NC

Dove, Ronald, *Pres*, Hussian School of Art, Inc, Commercial Art Dept, Philadelphia PA (S)

Dovman, Claudia, *Asst Librn*, Historic Hudson Valley, Library, Tarrytown NY

Dowd, Sandra, *Dir*, Navarro College, Art Dept, Corsicana TX (S)

Dowdy, William, *Chmn Dept*, Blue Mountain College, Art Dept, Blue Mountain MS (S)

Dowell, Cheryl, *Asst Site Mgr*, Illinois Historic Preservation Agency, Bishop Hill State Historis Site, Bishop Hill IL

Dowell-Dennis, Terri, *Educ Coordr*, Southeastern Center for Contemporary Art, Winston-Salem NC

Dowhie, Leonard, *Asst Prof*, University of Southern Indiana, Art Dept, Evansville IN (S)

Dowis, William S, *VPres*, Florence Museum, Florence SC

Dowley, Jennifer, *Exec Dir*, Headlands Center for the Arts, Sausalito CA

Dowlin, Kenneth E, *Dir*, San Francisco Public Library, Art and Music Dept, San Francisco CA

Dowling, Kathy, *Asst Dir*, Birmingham-Bloomfield Art Association, Birmingham MI

Dowling, Russell, *Chmn Bd*, High Plains Museum, McCook NE

Downes-LeGuin, Nancy, *Prog Coordr C-Sac*, Craft and Folk Art Museum, Research Library, Los Angeles CA

Downey, Leo, *Regional Prog Specialist*, New York Office of Parks, Recreation & Historic Preservation, Natural Heritage Trust, Albany NY

Downey, Martha J, *Site Mgr*, Illinois Historic Preservation Agency, Bishop Hill State Historis Site, Bishop Hill IL

Downey, Susan B, *Dept Chmn*, University of California, Los Angeles, Dept Art History, Los Angeles CA (S)

Downing, Barry L, *Chmn Board*, Wichita Center for the Arts, Wichita KS

Downs, Linda, *Cur Educ*, National Gallery of Art, Washington DC

Downs, Stuart, *Instr*, James Madison University, Dept of Art, Harrisonburg VA (S)

Downs, Stuart C, *Gallery Dir*, James Madison University, Sawhill Gallery, Harrisonburg VA

Doxey, Don, *Prof*, Westminster College of Salt Lake City, Dept of Arts, Salt Lake City UT (S)

Doyle, Cheri, *Registrar*, Southwest Museum, Los Angeles CA

Doyle, Leo, *Instr*, California State University, San Bernardino, Art Dept, San Bernardino CA (S)

Doyle Riesenberg, Cherie, *Cur*, MacAlester College, Galleries, Saint Paul MN

Doyon-Bernard, Suzette J, *Asst Prof*, University of West Florida, Dept of Art, Pensacola FL (S)

Dozier, Deborah, *Asst Dir*, University of California, University Art Gallery, Riverside CA

Dozier, James, *Dir*, Film in the Cities Gallery, Saint Paul MN

Drabenstott, Larry, *Pres*, Wayne County Historical Society, Wooster OH

Drach, Mary, *Asst Dir*, Boston University, Art Gallery, Boston MA

Drachler, Carole, *Instr*, Mesa Community College, Dept of Art & Art History, Mesa AZ (S)

Draghi, Robert, *Dean*, Marymount University of Virginia, School of Arts & Sciences Division, Arlington VA (S)

Dragon, Ric Pike, *Instr*, Woodstock School of Art, Inc, Woodstock NY (S)

Drahos, Dean, *Dir*, Baldwin-Wallace College, Fawick Art Gallery, Berea OH

Drahos, Dean, *Head Dept*, Baldwin-Wallace College, Dept of Art, Berea OH (S)

Drake, Bob, *Archivist*, Payette Associates Architects Planners, Library, Boston MA

Dransfield, Charles, *Second VPres*, Kent Art Association, Inc, Gallery, Kent CT

Draper, Jerry L, *Dean School Visual Arts*, Florida State University, Art History Dept (R133B), Tallahassee FL (S)

Draper, Stacy F Pomeroy, *Cur*, Rensselaer County Historical Society, Hart-Cluett Mansion, 1827, Troy NY

Draxler, Vesna, *Pres*, Burke Arts Council, Jailhouse Galleries, Morganton NC

Drayton-Hill, Mary, *Development Officer*, National Association of Artists' Organizations (NAAO), Washington DC

Dreeszen, Craig, *Dir*, Arts Extension Service, Amherst MA

Drehrer, Warren, *Co-Cur*, Walnut Creek Regional Center for the Arts, Bedford Gallery, Walnut Creek CA

Dreiling, Janet, *Registrar*, University of Kansas, Spencer Museum of Art, Lawrence KS

Dreiss, Joseph, *Prof*, Mary Washington College, Art Dept, Fredericksburg VA (S)

Dreisthoon, Doug, *Cur Contemporary*, Tampa Museum of Art, Tampa FL

Drennen, Barbara, *Assoc Prof*, Malone College, Dept of Art, Canton OH (S)

Drescher, Judith, *Dir*, Memphis-Shelby County Public Library and Information Center, Dept of Art, Music & Films, Memphis TN

Dressel, Barry, *Dir*, Berkshire Museum, Pittsfield MA

Drew, Melissa, *Chmn Exhib*, Klamath Falls Art Association, Klamath Art Gallery, Klamath Falls OR

Drewal, Henry J, *Prof*, University of Wisconsin, Madison, Dept of Art History, Madison WI (S)

Dreydoppel, Susan, *Exec Dir*, Moravian Historical Society, Whitefield House Museum, Nazareth PA

Dreyer, Sally, *Board Dir*, Artists' Cooperative Gallery, Omaha NE

Dreyer, Wallace E, *Adjunct Instr*, Old Dominion University, Art Dept, Norfolk VA (S)

Dreyfus, Jeffrey, *Pres Board of Dirs*, Second Street Gallery, Charlottesville VA

Dreyfus, Renee, *Cur Interpretation*, Fine Arts Museums of San Francisco, M H de Young Memorial Museum and California Palace of the Legion of Honor, San Francisco CA

Drieband, Laurence, *Fine Arts Dept Chmn*, Art Center College of Design, Pasadena CA (S)

Driesbach, Janice T, *Cur*, Crocker Art Museum, Sacramento CA

Drinkard, Joel F, *Cur*, Southern Baptist Theological Seminary, Joseph A Callaway Archaeological Museum, Louisville KY

Drinker, Sandy, *Librn*, Woodmere Art Museum, Library, Philadelphia PA

Drittler, John, *Librn*, Museum of Ossining Historical Society, Library, Ossining NY

Droega, Anthony, *Adjunct Asst Prof*, Indiana University South Bend, Fine Arts Dept, South Bend IN (S)

Droege, John, *Prof*, Bridgewater State College, Art Dept, Bridgewater MA (S)

Dronberger, Jane, *VPres*, Hutchinson Art Association Gallery, Hutchinson KS

Druback, Diana, *Asst*, Ohio State University, Fine Arts Library, Columbus OH

Druick, Douglas, *Cur European Painting*, The Art Institute of Chicago, Chicago IL

Druick, Douglas, *Cur Prints & Drawings*, The Art Institute of Chicago, Chicago IL

Drumheller, Grant, *Asst Prof*, University of New Hampshire, Dept of the Arts, Durham NH (S)

Drumm, Nelde, *Secy*, Fitchburg Art Museum, Fitchburg MA

Drummer, Carlee, *Public Relations Dir*, The New York Public Library, Shelby Cullom Davis Museum, New York NY

Drummey, Peter, *Librn*, Massachusetts Historical Society, Library, Boston MA

Drummond, Derek, *Prof*, McGill University, School of Architecture, Montreal PQ (S)

Drury, J, *Registrar,* Dundas Valley School of Art, Dundas ON (S)

Drury, Marjorie, *Museum Resource Specialist,* Columbus Museum, Columbus GA

Dryer-Kaplan, Ellen, *Project Americana Coordr,* Hebrew Union College, Skirball Museum, Los Angeles CA

Dryfhout, John H, *Supt & Cur,* Saint-Gaudens National Historic Site, Cornish NH

D'Spain, Pat, *Pres,* Frontier Times Museum, Bandera TX

Duarte, Jema, *Pres,* Xicanindio, Inc, Mesa AZ

Dubansky, Mindell, *Conservation Librn,* The Metropolitan Museum of Art, Thomas J Watson Library, New York NY

DuBay, Bren, *Lectr,* Rice University, Dept of Art and Art History, Houston TX (S)

Dubberly, Ronald A, *Dir,* Atlanta Public Library, Art-Humanities Dept, Atlanta GA

Dubinsky, John, *Chief Exec Officer,* Mark Twain Bancshares, Saint Louis MO

Dubler, Linda, *Cur Media Art,* High Museum of Art, Atlanta GA

DuBois, Daniel, *Dir,* New Britain Institute, New Britain Museum of American Art, New Britain CT

DuBois, Doug, *Asst Prof,* New Mexico State University, Art Dept, Las Cruces NM (S)

DuBois, Henry J, *Art Bibliographer,* California State University, Long Beach, University Library, Long Beach CA

DuBois, Jeanne, *Head Cur,* Housatonic Community College, Housatonic Museum of Art, Bridgeport CT

Du Boise, Kim R, *Instr,* Pearl River Community College, Art Dept, Division of Fine Arts, Poplarville MS (S)

DuBourdieu, Judee, *Cur,* North Canton Public Library, Little Art Gallery, North Canton OH

Dubreuil-Blondin, Nicole, *Instr,* Universite de Montreal, Dept of Art History, Montreal PQ (S)

DuBuske, Sandy, *In Charge Art Awards Prog,* M Grumbacher Inc, Cranbury NJ

Duce, Scott, *Assoc Prof,* Wesleyan College, Art Dept, Macon GA (S)

Duchesneau, Guy P E, *Mgr,* David M Stewart Museum, Montreal PQ

Duckworth, W Donald, *Dir,* Bernice Pauahi Bishop Museum, Honolulu HI

Ductiweicz, Scott, *Librn,* Wind Luke Asian Museum Memorial Foundation, Inc, Library, Seattle WA

Dudek, Steve, *Instr,* Barton County Community College, Fine Arts Dept, Great Bend KS (S)

Dudics MFA, Kitty, *Assoc Prof,* Del Mar College, Art Dept, Corpus Christi TX (S)

Dudko, Alice, *Gallery Dir,* Niagara County Community College Art Gallery, Sanborn NY

Dudley, Brooke F, *Exec Dir,* San Antonio Art Institute, San Antonio TX (S)

Dudley, Janice Stafford, *Admin Asst,* MacArthur Memorial, Norfolk VA

Dudley, Peter, *Instr,* Greenfield Community College, Art, Graphic Design & Media Communication Dept, Greenfield MA (S)

Duensing, Sally, *Professional Internship Prog,* Exploratorium, San Francisco CA

Duerksen, George L, *Chmn Dept,* University of Kansas, Dept of Art & Music Education & Music Therapy, Lawrence KS (S)

Duethman, Karen, *Cur Art Coll,* Commerce Bancshares, Inc, Art Collection, Kansas City MO

Duff, James H, *Dir,* Brandywine River Museum, Chadds Ford PA

Duffek, Robert, *Asst Prof,* Mohawk Valley Community College, Advertising Design and Production, Utica NY (S)

Duffy, Brian R, *Chmn,* Villa Maria College of Buffalo, Art Dept, Buffalo NY (S)

Duffy, John, *VPres,* Chicago Society of Artists, Inc, Chicago IL

Duffy, Michael, *Pres,* Rensselaer Newman Foundation Chapel and Cultural Center, The Gallery, Troy NY

Dufilho, Diane, *Assoc Dir Educ,* Asheville Art Museum, Asheville NC

DuFort, Robert, *Prof,* Schoolcraft College, Dept of Art and Design, Livonia MI (S)

Dufour, Gary, *Senior Cur,* Vancouver Art Gallery, Vancouver BC

Dufour, Lydia, *Reference Letters,* Frick Art Reference Library, New York NY

Du Fresne, John, *Lectr,* University of Wisconsin-Stout, Dept of Art & Design, Menomonie WI (S)

Dufresne, Laura, *Asst Prof,* Winthrop College, Dept of Art & Design, Rock Hill SC (S)

Dugan, Alan, *Instr,* Truro Center for the Arts at Castle Hill, Inc, Truro MA (S)

Dugan, Charles H, *Asst Prof,* Clarion University of Pennsylvania, Dept of Art, Clarion PA (S)

Dugan, Ellen, *Cur Photography,* High Museum of Art, Atlanta GA

Dugan, George, *Prof,* State University of New York, College at Cortland, Art Dept, Cortland NY (S)

Dugdale, James, *Instr,* Joliet Junior College, Fine Arts Dept, Joliet IL (S)

Duggan, Lynn, *Assoc Prof,* Nazareth College of Rochester, Art Dept, Rochester NY (S)

Duggan, Rosemary, *Pres,* Tobe-Coburn School, New York NY (S)

Duhigg, Thad, *Prof,* Texas Christian University, Art & Art History Dept, Fort Worth TX (S)

Duillo, John, *Pres,* Society of American Historical Artists, Jericho NY

Dumble, Jim, *Dir,* Arizona Watercolor Association, Phoenix AZ

Dunbar, Burton, *Chmn,* University of Missouri-Kansas City, Dept of Art and Art History, Kansas City MO (S)

Dunbeck, Helen, *Adminr,* Museum of Contemporary Art, Chicago IL

Duncan, Carol, *Prof Art History,* Ramapo College of New Jersey, School of Contemporary Arts, Mahwah NJ (S)

Duncan, Genny, *Prog Coordr,* Women And Their Work, Austin TX

Duncan, George, *VPres,* Lowell Art Association, Whistler House Museum of Art, Lowell MA

Duncan, Gloria, *Instr,* Oklahoma Baptist University, Art Dept, Shawnee OK (S)

Duncan, Karen, *Registrar,* University of Minnesota, University Art Museum, Minneapolis MN

Duncan, Katherine, *Interim Exec Dir,* Hot Springs Art Center, Fine Arts Center, Hot Springs AR

Duncan, Lorna, *VPres,* Revelstoke Art Group, Revelstoke BC

Duncan, Nancy, *Asst Dir,* University of Washington, Henry Art Gallery, Seattle WA

Duncan, Pat, *Admin Asst,* Eastern Shore Art Association, Inc, Art Center, Fairhope AL

Duncan, Richard, *Assoc Prof,* Florida International University, Visual Arts Dept, Miami FL (S)

Duncan, Robert, *Chmn,* Nebraska Arts Council Library, Omaha NE

Dundon, Margo, *Executive Dir,* Museum Science & History, Jacksonville FL

Dunifon, Don, *Prof,* Wittenberg University, Art Dept, Springfield OH (S)

Dunkerley, Susan, *Instr,* Dowling College, Dept of Visual Arts, Oakdale NY (S)

Dunkley, Diane, *Museum Dir & Chief Cur,* DAR Museum, National Society Daughters of the American Revolution, Washington DC

Dunkley, Tina, *Dir,* Georgia State University, Art Gallery, Atlanta GA

Dunlap, Ellen S, *Dir,* The Rosenbach Museum and Library, Philadelphia PA

Dunlap, Ellen S, *Pres,* American Antiquarian Society, Worcester MA

Dunlop, Betty, *Pres,* Rhode Island Watercolor Society, Pawtucket RI

Dunn, Jacque F, *Asst Dir,* University of Missouri, Museum of Art and Archaeology, Columbia MO

Dunn, Joy B, *Prog Dir,* Southern Oregon Historical Society, Jacksonville Museum of Southern Oregon History, Jacksonville OR

Dunn, Mary Maple, *VPres,* Historic Deerfield, Inc, Deerfield MA

Dunn, Nancy, *Dir,* Artesia Historical Museum & Art Center, Artesia NM

Dunn, Robert, *VPres,* National Society of Painters in Casein & Acrylic, Inc, Whitehall PA

Dunn, Roger, *Prof,* Bridgewater State College, Art Dept, Bridgewater MA (S)

Dunn, Sandra, *Mgr Resource Centre,* Ontario Crafts Council, Toronto ON

Dunn, Tracy, *Instr,* Creighton University, Fine and Performing Arts Dept, Omaha NE (S)

Dunn, Warren, *Dept Coordr,* Clark College, Art Dept, Vancouver WA (S)

Dunning, Clara, *VPres,* Arthur Roy Mitchell Memorial Inc, Museum of Western Art, Trinidad CO

Dunwoodie, Jane, *Librn,* Dayton Art Institute, Library, Dayton OH

Dunworth, Joseph, *Dir Institutional Development,* The Museums at Stony Brook, Stony Brook NY

duPont, Diana, *Cur 20th Century Art,* Santa Barbara Museum of Art, Santa Barbara CA

Dupont, Inge, *Head Reader Serv,* Pierpont Morgan Library, New York NY

Durand, Carol, *Exec Dir,* Lowell Art Association, Whistler House Museum of Art, Lowell MA

Durben, Silvan A, *Dir & Cur,* Owatonna Arts Center, Community Arts Center, Owatonna MN

Durbin, Mary L, *Asst Dir,* Southern Alleghenies Museum of Art, Loretto PA

Durel, John W, *Asst Dir,* Baltimore City Life Museums, Baltimore MD

Durham, David, *Chmn Dept,* Saint Louis Community College at Meramec, Art Dept, Saint Louis MO (S)

Durkan, Lisa, *Shop Mgr & Special Events,* Memphis Brooks Museum of Art, Memphis TN

Durland, Don, *Prof,* Texas Tech University, Dept of Art, Lubbock TX (S)

Durrant, G D, *Assoc Prof,* Palomar Community College, Art Dept, San Marcos CA (S)

dur Russell, Kent, *Educ Dir,* The Parrish Art Museum, Southampton NY

Dursi, Pat A, *Registrar,* United States Military Academy, West Point Museum, West Point NY

Dursum, Brian, *Dir,* University of Miami, Lowe Art Museum, Coral Gables FL

Dusenbury, Carolyn, *Art Librn,* California State University, Chico, Meriam Library, Chico CA

Dutton, Richard, *Dept Head,* Indian Hills Community College, Ottumwa Campus, Dept of Art, Ottumwa IA (S)

Dutton, Richard H, *Head Dept,* Indian Hills Community College, Dept of Art, Centerville IA (S)

Duty, Michael, *Exec Dir,* Eiteljorg Museum of American Indian & Western Art, Indianapolis IN

Duval, Cynthia, *Asst Dir & Cur Decorative Arts,* Museum of Fine Arts, Saint Petersburg, Florida, Inc, Saint Petersburg FL

Duvall, Debbie, *Office Mgr,* Cherokee National Historical Society, Inc, Tahlequah OK

Duval Reese, Becky, *Asst Dir,* University of Texas at Austin, Archer M Huntington Art Gallery, Austin TX

Duvigneaud, Diane, *Prof Emeritus,* North Central College, Dept of Art, Naperville IL (S)

Dvorak, Anna, *Librn,* North Carolina Museum of Art, Raleigh NC

Dvorak, Anna, *Librn,* North Carolina Museum of Art, Reference Library, Raleigh NC

Dwyer, Eugene J, *Assoc Prof,* Kenyon College, Art Dept, Gambier OH (S)

Dwyer, Penny, *Asst Cur,* George Washington University, The Dimock Gallery, Washington DC

Dwyer, Rob, *Dir,* Quincy Society of Fine Arts, Quincy IL

Dyck, Arthur P, *Head Dept,* Mount Saint Clare College, Art Dept, Clinton IA (S)

Dye, Carol, *Membership Coordr,* University of California, California Museum of Photography, Riverside CA

Dye, David, *Assoc Prof,* Hillsborough Community College, Fine Arts Dept, Tampa FL (S)

Dye, Donna, *Dir State Historical Museum,* Mississippi Department of Archives and History, State Historical Museum, Jackson MS

Dye, Donna, *Dir,* Mississippi Department of Archives & History, Mississippi State Historical Museum, Jackson MS

Dyer, E May, *Chmn,* Lock Haven University, Art Dept, Lock Haven PA (S)

Dyer, Joan, *First VPres,* Sierra Arts Foundation, Reno NV

Dyer, J T, *Cur Art,* Marine Corps Museum, Art Collection, Washington DC

Dyer, M Wayne, *Assoc Prof,* East Tennessee State University, Fine Arts Dept, Johnson City TN (S)

Dykes, Stephen E, *Deputy Dir Admin,* Fine Arts Museums of San Francisco, M H de Young Memorial Museum and California Palace of the Legion of Honor, San Francisco CA

Dyki, Judy, *Head Librn,* Cranbrook Academy of Art Museum, Library, Bloomfield Hills MI

Dykstra, Steve, *Cur,* American University, Watkins Collectiony, Washington DC

Dynneson, Donald, *Prof,* Concordia College, Art Dept, Seward NE (S)

Dyson, Robert H, *Dir & Near East Section Cur,* University of Pennsylvania, University Museum of Archaelogy & Anthropology, Philadelphia PA

Eads, Hannah, *Prof,* Eastern Illinois University, Art Dept, Charleston IL (S)

Eagar, Jorge, *VPres,* Xicanindio, Inc, Mesa AZ

Eagen, Kip, *Dir,* Palm Beach Community College Foundation, Museum of Art, Lake Worth FL

Eager, Gerald, *Head Dept,* Bucknell University, Dept of Art, Lewisburg PA (S)

Eagerton, Robert, *Coordr Fine Arts,* Indiana University-Purdue University, Indianapolis, Herron School of Art, Indianapolis IN (S)

Eakin, Judy, *Cur Exhibits,* Loveland Museum and Gallery, Loveland CO

Ealer, William, *Asst Prof,* Pennsylvania College of Technology, Dept of Design & Communiation Arts, Williamsport PA (S)

Eardley, Anthony, *Dean,* University of Toronto, School of Architecture & Landscape Architecture, Toronto ON (S)

Earenfight, Phillip, *Asst Cur,* Johnson & Johnson, Art Program, New Brunswick NJ

Earl, Nancy, *Prog Coordr Painting,* Alberta College of Art, Calgary AB (S)

Earle, Edward W, *Cur,* University of California, California Museum of Photography, Riverside CA

Earle, Michael, *Instr,* Toronto School of Art, Toronto ON (S)

Earley, Steven, *VPres,* Koochiching County Historical Society Museum, International Falls MN

Earls-Solari, Bonnie, *Cur,* Bank of America Galleries, San Francisco CA

Early, James, *Asst Secy for Educ & Public Progs,* Smithsonian Institution, Washington DC

Earnest, Nancy, *Slide Cur,* East Tennessee State University, Carroll Reece Museum, Johnson City TN

Easby, Rebecca, *Asst Prof,* Trinity College, Art Dept, Washington DC (S)

Eason, Robert, *Theatre Librn,* Dallas Public Library, Fine Arts Division, Dallas TX

Eastman, Gene M, *Prof,* Sam Houston State University, Art Dept, Huntsville TX (S)

Eastwood, R, *Pres,* Manitoba Association of Architects, Winnipeg MB

Eaton, Charlotte, *Cur,* Putnam County Historical Society, Foundry School Museum, Cold Spring NY

Eaton, Leonard J, *Chmn Executive Committee,* Bank of Oklahoma NA, Art Collection, Tulsa OK

Eaton, Nancy, *Dir Humanities,* Bay Path College, Dept of Art, Longmeadow MA (S)

Eaton, Tim, *Lectr,* University of Wisconsin-Stout, Dept of Art & Design, Menomonie WI (S)

Ebben, James, *Pres,* Edgewood College, DeRicci Gallery, Madison WI

Ebeling, Klaus, *Prof,* Jefferson Community College, Art Dept, Watertown NY (S)

Eberdt, Edmund, *Cur,* Eberdt Museum of Communications, Heritage Sutton, Sutton PQ

Eberhard, John, *Head,* Carnegie Mellon University, Dept of Architecture, Pittsburgh PA (S)

Eberhardt, Jeanie, *Exec Dir,* Peters Valley Craft Center, Layton NJ

Ebert, D, *Instr,* Golden West College, Visual Art Dept, Huntington Beach CA (S)

Ebie, Teresa, *Registrar,* Roswell Museum and Art Center, Roswell NM

Ebie, William D, *Dir,* Roswell Museum and Art Center, Roswell NM

Ebitz, David, *Dir,* State Art Museum of Florida, John & Mable Ringling Museum of Art, Sarasota FL

Eby, Jeff, *Asst Dir Finance & Admin,* Seattle Art Museum, Seattle WA

Echevarria, Agustin, *Dir,* Institute of Puerto Rican Culture, Instituto de Cultura Puertorriquena, San Juan PR

Echeverria, Durand, *Co-Cur,* Wellfleet Historical Society Museum & Rider School, Wellfleet MA

Echeverria, Felipe, *Prof,* University of Northern Iowa, Dept of Art, Cedar Falls IA (S)

Ecker, David W, *Prof,* New York University, Dept of Art & Art Professions, New York NY (S)

Ecker, Gary, *Restoration Specialist,* Riverside Municipal Museum, Riverside CA

Eckerle, Robin, *Interpretive Programs Asst,* Olana State Historic Site, Hudson NY

Eckert, Charles, *Head of Dept,* Middlesex Community College, Fine Arts Div, Middletown CT (S)

Eckert, W Dean, *Chmn,* Lindenwood College, Harry D Hendren Gallery, Saint Charles MO

Eckert, W Dean, *Chmn Dept,* Lindenwood College, Art Dept, Saint Charles MO (S)

Eckhardt, Susan, *Educ Dir,* Art Center of Battle Creek, Battle Creek MI

Eckley, Thomas, *Pres,* Cincinnati Art Club, Cincinnati OH

Eckmann, Inge Lise, *Deputy Dir,* San Francisco Museum of Modern Art, San Francisco CA

Eckstein, Karen, *Adminr,* Oklahoma City Art Museum, Oklahoma City OK

Eckstein, Karen, *Business Mgr,* Oklahoma City Art Museum, Library, Oklahoma City OK

Edborg, Judy A, *American Artisans Dir,* American Society of Artists, Inc, Chicago IL

Eddey, Roy R, *Deputy Dir,* Brooklyn Museum, Brooklyn NY

Eddy, Becky, *Asst Dean Admin,* Rochester Institute of Technology, College of Imaging Arts & Sciences, Rochester NY (S)

Eddy, Warren S, *Dir,* Cortland Free Library, Cortland NY

Edelman, Carol, *Board Chmn,* American Craft Council, New York NY

Edelson, Gilbert, *Admin VPres & Counsel,* Art Dealers Association of America, Inc, New York NY

Edelson, Michael, *Assoc Prof,* State University of New York at Stony Brook, Art Dept, Stony Brook NY (S)

Edelstein, Teri J, *Deputy Dir,* The Art Institute of Chicago, Chicago IL

Edens, Marjorie, *Oral Historian,* Southern Oregon Historical Society, Jacksonville Museum of Southern Oregon History, Jacksonville OR

Eder, Elizabeth, *Asst Dir,* Sculpture Center Inc, New York NY

Edgar, Walter, *Media Servs,* Sheldon Jackson Museum, Stratton Library, Sitka AK

Edgerton, Samuel Y, *Dir Grad Progam,* Williams College, Dept of Art, Williamstown MA (S)

Edgerton, Van, *Development Dir,* Grand Rapids Art Museum, Grand Rapids MI

Edgy, James, *Asst Dir Developemtn,* Cincinnati Museum Association, Cincinnati Art Museum, Cincinnati OH

Edison, Carol, *Folk Arts Coordr,* Utah Arts Council, Chase Home Museum of Utah Folk Art, Salt Lake City UT

Edmonds, Anne, *Dir,* Mount Holyoke College, Art Library, South Hadley MA

Edmonds, Nicolas, *Assoc Prof,* Boston University, School of Visual Arts, Boston MA (S)

Edmondson-Haney, Kristine, *Assoc Prof,* University of Massachusetts, Amherst, Art History Program, Amherst MA (S)

Edmunds, Allan L, *Pres & Exec Dir,* Brandywine Workshop, Philadelphia PA

Edmundson, Gerald, *Assoc Prof,* East Tennessee State University, Fine Arts Dept, Johnson City TN (S)

Edson, Gary, *Dir,* Texas Tech University, Museum, Lubbock TX

Edward, Deborah, *Dir,* Austin Children's Museum, Austin TX

Edwards, Beth, *Asst Prof,* University of Dayton, Visual Arts Dept, Dayton OH (S)

Edwards, Brian, *Prof,* Shoreline Community College, Humanities Division, Seattle WA (S)

Edwards, Glen, *Prof,* Utah State University, Dept of Art, Logan UT (S)

Edwards, Jean, *Asst Prof,* Winthrop College, Dept of Art & Design, Rock Hill SC (S)

Edwards, Jim, *Chmn Studio,* University of South Carolina, Dept of Art, Columbia SC (S)

Edwards, Kathleen, *Dir,* Print Club Center for Prints & Photographs, Philadelphia PA

Edwards, Lucy, *Instr,* Wayne Art Center, Wayne PA (S)

Edwards, Mary Jane, *Head Dept,* University of Wyoming, Dept of Art, Laramie WY (S)

Edwards, Melvin, *Prof,* Rutgers, the State University of New Jersey, Mason Gross School of the Arts, New Brunswick NJ (S)

Edwards, Page, *Dir,* Saint Augustine Historical Society, Oldest House and Museums, Saint Augustine FL

Edwards, Paul B, *Gallery Dir,* Washington & Jefferson College, Olin Art Gallery, Washington PA

Edwards, Paul B, *Chmn Art Dept,* Washington and Jefferson College, Art Dept, Washington PA (S)

Edwards, Richard, *Prof Emeritus,* University of Michigan, Ann Arbor, Dept of History of Art, Ann Arbor MI (S)

Edwards, Susan C S, *Dir,* Brick Store Museum, Kennebunk ME

Edwards, William, *Secy & Dir,* Oregon State University, Memorial Union Art Gallery, Corvallis OR

Edwards, William, *Chmn Board of Trustees,* Visual Studies Workshop, Rochester NY

Edwins, Steve, *Asst Prof,* Saint Olaf College, Art Dept, Northfield MN (S)

Efinoff, Alex, *Interim Dir,* Nicolaysen Art Museum and Discovery Center, Childrens Discovery Center, Casper WY

Efinoff, Alex, *Interim Dir,* Nicolaysen Art Museum and Discovery Center, Museum, Casper WY

Efland, Arthur, *Prof,* Ohio State University, Dept of Art Education, Columbus OH (S)

Egan, Karen, *Adjunct Instr,* Saginaw Valley State University, Dept of Art and Design, University Center MI (S)

Egan, William C, *Coordr,* Tomoka State Park Museum, Fred Dana Marsh Museum, Ormond Beach FL

Egen, Paul, *Co-Pres,* The Greenwich Art Society Inc, Greenwich CT

Eggebrecht, David, *Academic Dean,* Concordia University Wisconsin, Fine Art Gallery, Mequon WI

Eggler-Gerozissis, Marianne, *Prog Coordr,* City of Tampa, Art in Public Places, Tampa FL

Eggleston, William, *Treas,* Katonah Museum of Art, Katonah NY

Egleston, Robert, *Dir,* New Haven Colony Historical Society, New Haven CT

Eglinski, Edmund, *Chairperson,* University of Kansas, Kress Foundation Dept of Art History, Lawrence KS (S)

Egolof, Jacklyn, *Public Services Librn,* North Central College, Oesterle Library, Naperville IL

Ehrenthal, Michael, *VPres,* National Council on Art in Jewish Life, New York NY

Ehrhardt, Ursula M, *Asst Prof,* Salisbury State University, Art Dept, Salisbury MD (S)

Ehrlich, Abigail, *Public Relations & Marketing Coordr,* Bellevue Art Museum, Bellevue WA

Ehrlich, Martha, *Exhib Coordr,* Beacon Street Gallery, Uptown, Chicago IL

Ehrlich, Martha, *Exhib Coordr,* Beacon Street Gallery, Gallery at the School, Chicago IL

Ehses, Hanno, *Chmn Design Div,* Nova Scotia College of Art and Design, Halifax NS (S)

Eichhold, Teresa, *Instr,* Antonelli Institute of Art & Photography, Cincinnati OH (S)

Eichhorn, Theresa, *Chmn,* Fetherston Foundation, Packwood House Museum, Lewisburg PA

Eickhorst, William, *Chmn Dept,* Missouri Western State College, Art Dept, Saint Joseph MO (S)

Eickhorst, William, *Chmn Department of Art,* Missouri Western State College, Fine Arts Gallery, Saint Joseph MO

Eickoff, Harold, *Pres,* Trenton State College, College Art Gallery, Trenton NJ

Eide, Joel S, *Dir,* Northern Arizona University, Art Museum & Galleries, Flagstaff AZ

Eide, John, *Instr,* Portland School of Art, Portland ME (S)

Eidel, Marcia, *Asst Dir of Administration,* Marquette University, Haggerty Museum of Art, Milwaukee WI

Eidelberg, Martin, *Prof,* Rutgers, the State University of New Jersey, Graduate Program in Art History, New Brunswick NJ (S)

Eige, G Eason, *Chief Cur,* Huntington Museum of Art, Huntington WV

Eike, Claire, *Librn,* San Diego Museum of Art, Art Reference Library, San Diego CA

Eikelmann, Renate, *Cur Early Western Art,* Cleveland Museum of Art, Cleveland OH

Eiland, William, *Actg Museum Adminr,* University of Georgia, Georgia Museum of Art, Athens GA

Eilers, F Farny, *Pres,* New Haven Colony Historical Society, New Haven CT

Einarson, Bernice, *Adminr,* Dauphin & District Allied Arts Council, Dauphin MB

Einreinhofer, Nancy, *Dir,* William Paterson College of New Jersey, Ben Shahn Galleries, Wayne NJ

Einzig, Stern, *Assoc Prof,* C W Post Center of Long Island University, School of Visual & Performing Arts, Greenvale NY (S)

Eis, Andrea, *Lectr,* Oakland University, Dept of Art and Art History, Rochester MI (S)

Eis, Ruth, *Cur,* Judah L Magnes Museum, Berkeley CA

Eisenberg, Marvin, *Prof Emeritus,* University of Michigan, Ann Arbor, Dept of History of Art, Ann Arbor MI (S)

Eisenmenger, Michael, *Asst Prof,* Rutgers, the State University of New Jersey, Mason Gross School of the Arts, New Brunswick NJ (S)

Eisman, Hy, *Instr,* Joe Kubert School of Cartoon & Graphic Art, Inc, Dover NJ (S)

Eiswerth, Barbara, *Instr,* Marylhurst College, Art Dept, Marylhurst OR (S)

Eiteljorg, Harrison, *Chmn,* Eiteljorg Museum of American Indian & Western Art, Indianapolis IN

Ekdahl, Janis, *Asst Dir,* Museum of Modern Art, Library, New York NY

Ekins, Roger, *Assoc Dean,* Butte College, Dept of Performing Arts, Oroville CA (S)

Ekiss, Joan, *Librn,* Springfield Art Association of Edwards Place, Michael Victor II Art Library, Springfield IL

Ekiss, Margaret, *Dir of Public Relations,* Rosemount Victorian House Museum, Pueblo CO

Eknoian, Gerald, *Instr,* De Anza College, Creative Arts Div, Cupertino CA (S)

Ela, Patrick, *Exec Dir,* Craft and Folk Art Museum, Los Angeles CA

Elam, Leslie A, *Dir & Secy,* American Numismatic Society, New York NY

Elder, Alan, *Exec Dir,* Ontario Crafts Council, Toronto ON

Elder, Bev, *Reference,* Mason City Public Library, Mason City IA

Elder, Sarah M, *Coordr Alaska Native Heritage Film Project,* University of Alaska, Museum, Fairbanks AK

Elder, William Voss, *Consultant Cur Decorative Arts,* Baltimore Museum of Art, Baltimore MD

Elderfield, John, *Dir Dept Drawings,* Museum of Modern Art, New York NY

Eldred, Dale, *Chmn Sculpture,* Kansas City Art Institute, Kansas City MO (S)

Eldredge, Bruce B, *Dir,* Nelda C & H J Lutcher Stark Foundation, Stark Museum of Art, Orange TX

Eldredge, Charles, *Prof,* University of Kansas, Kress Foundation Dept of Art History, Lawrence KS (S)

Eldridge, Jan, *Instr,* Solano Community College, Division of Fine & Applied Art, Suisun City CA (S)

Eldridge, Karen, *Asst Dir,* Association of Collegiate Schools of Architecture, Washington DC

Elesh, Pam, *Pres,* North Shore Art League, Winnetka IL

Elesh, Pam, *Pres,* North Shore Art League, Winnetka IL (S)

Eley, Margaret, *Dir,* California Historical Society, El Molino Viejo, San Marino CA

Eley, Margaret, *Dir Southern California,* California Historical Society, El Molino Viejo, San Marino CA

Elfers, John, *Music Librn,* Dallas Public Library, Fine Arts Division, Dallas TX

Elfvin, John T, *VPres,* The Buffalo Fine Arts Academy, Albright-Knox Art Gallery, Buffalo NY

Elias, Margery M, *Assoc,* Dezign House, Jefferson OH

Elias, Ramon J, *Dir,* Dezign House, Jefferson OH

Elias, Ramon J, *Dir,* Dezign House, Library, Jefferson OH

Eliasoph, Philip, *Dir Walsh Art Gallery,* Fairfield University, Thomas J Walsh Art Gallery, Fairfield CT

Elicker, Sandra, *Instr,* Main Line Center for the Arts, Haverford PA (S)

Eliot, Paula, *Dir Public Relations,* Thomas Gilcrease Institute of American History & Art, Tulsa OK

Elkington, Richard N, *Assoc Prof,* Providence College, Art and Art History Dept, Providence RI (S)

Ellingson, JoAnn, *Dir,* Saint Xavier University, Byrne Memorial Library, Chicago IL

Ellingson, Susan Pierson, *Instr,* Concordia College, Art Dept, Moorhead MN (S)

Ellingwood, Sue A, *Supv Art & Music Dept,* Saint Paul Public Library, Art & Music Dept, Saint Paul MN

Elliot, Barbara, *Dir of Admis,* University of the Arts, Philadelphia College of Art & Design, Philadelphia PA (S)

Elliot, Gillian, *Dir,* Place des Arts, Coquitlam BC

Elliot, Gregory, *Asst Prof,* Louisiana State University, School of Art, Baton Rouge LA (S)

Elliot, Helen, *VPres,* Roswell Museum and Art Center, Roswell NM

Elliot, Mary Gene, *Cur,* Atlanta Museum, Atlanta GA

Elliot, Robert, *Technology,* New Brunswick Museum, Saint John NB

Elliott, Bob, *Instr,* William Woods-Westminster Colleges, Art Dept, Fulton MO (S)

Elliott, Elizabeth, *Shows,* Society of Canadian Artists, Toronto ON

Elliott, Gerald A, *Dept Head,* Lenoir Community College, Dept of Visual Art, Kinston NC (S)

Elliott, J H, *Dir,* Atlanta Museum, Atlanta GA

Elliott, John T, *Pres,* Oil Pastel Association, Nyack NY

Elliott, Joseph, *Asst Prof,* Muhlenberg College, Dept of Art, Allentown PA (S)

Elliott, Mary, *Instr,* Mount Mary College, Art Dept, Milwaukee WI (S)

Elliott, Sheila, *Executive Dir,* Oil Pastel Association, Nyack NY

Elliott, Susan, *River Museum Mgr,* Mississippi River Museum at Mud-Island, Memphis TN

Elliott-Parker, Joan, *Spec Coll,* Willard Library, Dept of Fine Arts, Evansville IN

Ellis, Anita, *Cur Decorative Arts,* Cincinnati Museum Association, Cincinnati Art Museum, Cincinnati OH

Ellis, David M, *Pres,* Crawford County Historical Society, Baldwin-Reynolds House Museum, Meadville PA

Ellis, Don, *Head Dept,* McMurry University, Art Dept, Abilene TX (S)

Ellis, George R, *Dir,* Honolulu Academy of Arts, Honolulu HI

Ellis, Greg, *City Archivist,* City of Lethbridge, Sir Alexander Galt Museum, Lethbridge AB

Ellis, Henry, *VPres,* American Tapestry Alliance, Chiloquin OR

Ellis, Liz, *Admin Asst to Dir,* Moose Jaw Art Museum and National Exhibition Centre, Art & History Museum, Moose Jaw SK

Ellis, Mary Ann, *Dir of Educ,* Museum of Arts and Sciences, Inc, Macon GA

Ellis, Mel, *Business Mgr,* New Britain Institute, New Britain Museum of American Art, New Britain CT

Ellis, Robert M, *Dir,* University of New Mexico, The Harwood Foundation, Taos NM

Ellis, Sandy, *Board Dirs Pres,* Sioux City Art Center, Sioux City IA

Ellis, Sharon, *Pres,* Lansing Art Gallery, Lansing MI

Ellis, Steve, *Preparator,* Columbus Museum, Columbus GA

Ellis, Susan, *Center Adminr,* Lafayette College, Morris R Williams Center for the Arts, Art Gallery, Easton PA

Ellis, Timothy, *Treas,* Barn Gallery Associates, Inc, Ogunquit ME

Ellison, Kathryn, *Public Relations,* Hidalgo County Historical Museum, Edinburg TX

Ellison, Mary K, *Dir Public Relations & Marketing,* Columbus Museum of Art, Columbus OH

Ellison, Rosemary, *Cur,* Southern Plains Indian Museum, Anadarko OK

Elloian, Peter, *Prof,* University of Toledo, Dept of Art, Toledo OH (S)

Elmendorf, Diane, *Exec Dir,* New York Society of Architects, New York NY

Elmore, Dennis, *Prof,* Los Angeles City College, Dept of Art, Los Angeles CA (S)

Elrick, Krista, *Visual Arts Dir,* Arizona Commission on the Arts, Phoenix AZ

Elson, James M, *Executive Dir,* Patrick Henry Memorial Foundation, Red Hill National Memorial, Brookneal VA

Elstein, Rochelle S, *Bibliographer,* Northwestern University, Art Library, Evanston IL

Elswick, Peery, *Cur of Education,* Parkersburg Art Center, Parkersburg WV

Elswick, Peery, *Educ Coordr,* Parkersburg Art Center, Art Center, Parkersburg WV

Ely, Ervin, *Instr,* Bismarck Junior College, Fine Arts Dept, Bismarck ND (S)

Elzea, Rowland P, *Assoc Dir & Chief Cur,* Delaware Art Museum, Wilmington DE

Emack-Cambra, Jane, *Cur,* Old Colony Historical Society, Library, Taunton MA

Emack-Cambra, Jane M, *Cur,* Old Colony Historical Society, Museum, Taunton MA

Emanuel, Martin, *Prof,* Atlanta College of Art, Atlanta GA (S)

Emboden, William, *Research Dir,* Severin Wunderman Museum, Irvine CA

Emerick, Judson, *Assoc Prof,* Pomona College, Art Dept, Claremont CA (S)

Emerson, Kathryn, *Admin,* Virginia Commonwealth University, Anderson Gallery, Richmond VA

Emerson, Nancy, *Library Asst,* San Diego Museum of Art, Art Reference Library, San Diego CA

Emerson, Robert L, *Dir,* State Museum of Pennsylvania, Railroad Museum of Pennsylvania, Harrisburg PA

Emert, Carol, *Registrar,* Washburn University, Mulvane Art Museum, Topeka KS

Emery, Margot, *Dir Development,* USS Constitution Museum Foundation Inc, Boston National Historical Park, Museum, Boston MA

Emig, Kay, *Res Artist,* Grand Canyon University, Art Dept, Phoenix AZ (S)

Eminent, Morris, *Scholar in Art,* Augusta College, Dept of Fine Arts, Augusta GA (S)

Emlen, Robert P, *Pres,* Providence Art Club, Providence RI

Emmendorfer, Marianne, *Cur,* Appaloosa Museum, Inc, Moscow ID

Emmerich, Andre, *Pres,* Art Dealers Association of America, Inc, New York NY

Emmerich, Carl, *Prof,* Eastern Illinois University, Art Dept, Charleston IL (S)

Emmons, Julia, *Chmn,* Movimiento Artistico del Rio Salado, Inc (MARS), Phoenix AZ

Emodi, T, *Instr,* Technical University of Nova Scotia, Faculty of Architecture, Halifax NS (S)

Emont-Scott, Deborah, *Lectr,* University of Kansas, Kress Foundation Dept of Art History, Lawrence KS (S)

Endacott, Pamela, *Treas,* Sculptors Guild, Inc, New York NY

Endress, Lawrence, *Instr,* Saint Francis College, Art Dept, Fort Wayne IN (S)

Eng, James, *Chmn,* Framingham State College, Art Dept, Framingham MA (S)

Engelbrecht, Lloyd, *Prof Art History,* University of Cincinnati, School of Art, Cincinnati OH (S)

Engell, Bettianne, *Office Mgr,* Lynnwood Arts Centre, Simcoe ON

Engelmann, Lothar K, *Prof,* Rochester Institute of Technology, School of Photographic Arts & Sciences, Rochester NY (S)

Engels, Elizabeth, *Asst Cur,* Norton Simon Museum, Pasadena CA

England, Ann, *Photographer Asst,* Georgia State University, School of Art & Design, Visual Resource Library & Reading Room, Atlanta GA

Englar, Gerald, *Assoc Prof,* University of Toronto, Programme in Landscape Architecture, Toronto ON (S)

Engle, Barbara D, *Secy Admin Asst,* Morgan County Foundation, Inc, Madison-Morgan Cultural Center, Madison GA

Englehart, Stanton, *Prof,* Fort Lewis College, Art Dept, Durango CO (S)

English, Lloyd C, *Chmn,* Western Oklahoma State College, Art Dept, Altus OK (S)

Engman, John, *Exec Dir,* Chicago Architecture Foundation, Chicago IL

Engman, Margaret, *VPres,* Pennsylvania Academy of the Fine Arts, Fellowship of the Pennsylvania Academy of the Fine Arts, Philadelphia PA

Enos, Chris, *Asst Prof,* University of New Hampshire, Dept of the Arts, Durham NH (S)

Enriquez, Carola R, *Dir,* Kern County Museum, Bakersfield CA

Enstice, Wayne, *Chmn Art Dept,* Indiana State University, Turman Art Gallery, Terre Haute IN

Enstice, Wayne, *Chmn,* Indiana State University, Dept of Art, Terre Haute IN (S)

Entin, Daniel, *Exec Dir,* Nicholas Roerich Museum, New York NY

Entwistle, Jeannette, *Cur Educ,* University of New Mexico, University Art Museum, Albuquerque NM

Enyeart, James L, *Dir,* International Museum of Photography at George Eastman House, Rochester NY

Enzweiler, Joan, *Asst Dir,* Thomas More College, TM Gallery, Crestview KY

Eppell, F, *Instr,* Technical University of Nova Scotia, Faculty of Architecture, Halifax NS (S)

Eppich, Linda, *Museum Cur,* Rhode Island Historical Society, Providence RI

Eppich, Linda, *Cur,* Rhode Island Historical Society, Aldrich House, Providence RI

Epstein, Beatrice, *Asst Museum Librn,* The Metropolitan Museum of Art, Photograph and Slide Library, New York NY

Epstein, Robert, *Chmn Ceramics,* Corcoran School of Art, Washington DC (S)

Epstein, Ruth, *Lectr,* Toronto Art Therapy Institute, Toronto ON (S)

Epting, Marion, *Graduate Advisor,* California State University, Chico, Art Dept, Chico CA (S)

Epting, Marion, *Instr,* California State University, Chico, Art Dept, Chico CA (S)

Erb, Melissa, *Coordr Educ,* Heckscher Museum, Huntington NY

Erbar, Otto, *Dir Visual Display,* Fuller Museum of Art, Brockton MA

Erbarcher, Ann E, *Registrar,* Nelson-Atkins Museum of Art, Kansas City MO

Erbe, Gary, *VPres,* The Allied Artists of America, Inc, New York NY

Erdmann, Mariella, *Assoc Prof,* Silver Lake College, Art Dept, Manitowoc WI (S)

Erdreich, Gina, *Research & Reference Librn,* Philadelphia Museum of Art, Library, Philadelphia PA

Erf, Greg, *Dir,* Eastern New Mexico University, Dept of Art, Portales NM

Erf, Greg, *Chmn,* Eastern New Mexico University, Dept of Art, Portales NM (S)

Erger, Patricia, *Adminr,* Adams County Historical Society, Museum & Cultural Center, Brighton CO

Erhard, Peter, *Prof,* Andrews University, Dept of Art, Art History & Design, Berrien Springs MI (S)

Erickson, Alden, *Instr,* Solano Community College, Division of Fine & Applied Art, Suisun City CA (S)

Erickson, Elizabeth, *Faculty,* Grand Marais Art Colony, Grand Marais MN (S)

Erickson, Erwin, *Chmn,* University of Wisconsin-La Crosse, Art Dept, La Crosse WI (S)

Erickson, Reif, *VPres,* Pastel Society of the West Coast, Sacramento Fine Arts Center, Carmichael CA

Erickson, Robert, *Asst Prof,* University of Wisconsin-Stevens Point, Dept of Art & Design, Stevens Point WI (S)

Erickson, Sally, *Public Servs Mgr,* University of Washington, Thomas Burke Memorial Washington State Museum, Seattle WA

Ericson, Sandra, *Acting Gallery Dir,* Muhlenberg College Center for the Arts, Frank Martin Gallery, Allentown PA

Ericsson, Dwight, *Dir,* Huntington College, Robert E Wilson Art Gallery, Huntington IN

Eriksen, Carl, *Dean,* Humber College of Applied Arts and Technology, Applied & Creative Arts Division, Etobicoke ON (S)

Erlandson, Molly, *Asst Prof,* West Virginia State College, Art Dept, Institute WV (S)

Ermenc, Christine, *Dir of Education,* Connecticut Historical Society, Hartford CT

Erntz, Wendy, *Asst Prof,* University of Alaska, Dept of Art, Fairbanks AK (S)

Erwin, John, *Third VPres,* Arizona Watercolor Association, Phoenix AZ

Erwin, Sarah, *Cur Archival Colls,* Thomas Gilcrease Institute of American History & Art, Library, Tulsa OK

Esch, Pam, *Dir Educ,* Cleveland Center for Contemporary Art, Cleveland OH

Escobar, Gloria, *Asst Prof,* Hartwick College, Art Dept, Oneonta NY (S)

Eshelman, Diane, *Pres,* Southeastern Center for Contemporary Art, Winston-Salem NC

Esherick, Helen, *Secy,* Wharton Esherick Museum, Wharton Esherick Studio, Paoli PA

Eshoo, Robert, *Supv Currier Art Center,* The Currier Gallery of Art, Manchester NH

Eshoo, Virginia H, *Mgr Museum Progs,* The Currier Gallery of Art, Manchester NH

Eskend, Robert, *Cur Coll,* Atwater Kent Museum, Philadelphia PA

Eskind, Andrew, *Mgr Information Technologies,* International Museum of Photography at George Eastman House, Rochester NY

Esler, Jennifer, *Exec Dir,* Cliveden, Philadelphia PA

Esparza, Richard, *Exec Dir,* Nevada Museum Of Art, Art Library, Reno NV

Esparza, Richard R, *Exec Dir,* Nevada Museum Of Art, Reno NV

Espey, Jule Adele, *Asst Prof,* Our Lady of the Lake University, Dept of Art, San Antonio TX (S)

Espino, Steve E, *Board Pres,* Centro Cultural De La Raza, San Diego CA

Esposito, Cecilia, *Dir,* Hyde Collection Trust, Glens Falls NY

Esposito, Cecilia, *Dir,* Hyde Collection Trust, Library, Glens Falls NY

Esquibel, George A, *Instr,* Sacramento City College, Art Dept, Sacramento CA (S)

Essar, Gary, *Assoc Cur of Historical Art,* Winnipeg Art Gallery, Winnipeg MB

Esslinger, Claudia J H, *Chmn,* Kenyon College, Art Dept, Gambier OH (S)

Estes, Jim, *Dept Head, Photography,* Art Institute of Houston, Houston TX (S)

Estes, Jim, *Prof,* Missouri Western State College, Art Dept, Saint Joseph MO (S)

Etier, Marc, *Instr,* East Central University, Art Dept, Ada OK (S)

Eubank, Douglas E, *Head Div,* Chowan College, Division of Art, Murfreesboro NC (S)

Eugene, Robert, *Adminr,* Princeton Antiques Bookservice, Art Marketing Reference Library, Atlantic City NJ

Eugenietsai, Eugenie, *Gallery Dir,* Kean College of New Jersey, Union NJ

Evan, Yael, *Asst Prof,* University of Missouri-Saint Louis, Art Dept, Saint Louis MO (S)

Evans, Anne B, *Adminr,* National Gallery of Art, Washington DC

Evans, Bruce, *Chief Librn,* Medicine Hat Public Library, Medicine Hat AB

Evans, Bruce, *Dir,* Mint Museum of Art, Charlotte NC

Evans, Charles, *Development Officer,* Huntington Museum of Art, Huntington WV

Evans, Constance, *Exec Dir Admin,* Skowhegan School of Painting and Sculpture, Skowhegan ME (S)

Evans, Dan, *Assoc Prof,* Philadelphia Community College, Dept of Art, Philadelphia PA (S)

Evans, Deborah, *Dir,* Adirondack Lakes Center for the Arts, Blue Mountain Lake NY

Evans, Donald H, *Assoc Prof,* Vanderbilt University, Dept of Fine Arts, Nashville TN (S)

Evans, Dorinda, *Chmn,* Emory University, Art History Dept, Atlanta GA (S)

Evans, Elaine A, *Cur Coll,* University of Tennessee, Frank H McClung Museum, Knoxville TN

Evans, Elaine A, *Cur,* University of Tennessee, Eleanor Dean Audigier Art Collection, Knoxville TN

Evans, Garth, *Instr,* New York Studio School of Drawing, Painting and Sculpture, New York NY (S)

Evans, Nancy, *Cur Education,* Kenosha Public Museum, Kenosha WI

Evans, Paul, *Librn,* East Carolina University, Art Library, Greenville NC

Evans, Peggy, *Treasurer,* French Art Colony, Gallipolis OH

Evans, Ray, *Chmn,* Feather River Community College, Art Dept, Quincy CA (S)

Evans, Robert J, *Dir,* Danforth Museum of Art, Framingham MA

Evans, Scott, *Faculty,* Idaho State University, Dept of Art, Pocatello ID (S)

Evans, Stuart B, *Dir Admin,* Cummer Gallery of Art, DeEtte Holden Cummer Museum Foundation, Jacksonville FL

Evarts, Wilbur, *Executive Dir,* Paint 'N Palette Club, Grant Wood & Memorial Park Gallery, Anamosa IA

Everett, C, *Assoc Prof,* Northern Arizona University, School of Art & Design, Flagstaff AZ (S)

Everett, J, *Assoc Prof,* Northern Arizona University, School of Art & Design, Flagstaff AZ (S)

Everhart, Stacy, *Marketing Coordr,* Sangre de Cristo Arts & Conference Center, Pueblo CO

Everidge, Janice, *Registrar,* University of Florida, University Gallery, Gainesville FL

Evers, Fred, *Asst Prof,* Bradford College, Creative Arts Division, Bradford MA (S)

Everson, Dona, *Gallery Mgr,* Silvermine Guild Arts Center, Silvermine Galleries, New Canaan CT

Ewers, Don, *Lectr,* Incarnate Word College, Art Dept, San Antonio TX (S)

Ewing, Lauren, *Assoc Prof,* Rutgers, the State University of New Jersey, Mason Gross School of the Arts, New Brunswick NJ (S)

Exon, Randall L, *Assoc Prof,* Swarthmore College, Dept of Art, Swarthmore PA (S)

Eyerdam, Pamela, *Supvr Art Serv,* Cleveland State University, Library & Art Services, Cleveland OH

Eyestone, June, *Asst Prof,* Florida State University, Art Education Dept, Tallahassee FL (S)

Eymard, Pat, *Cur,* Louisiana Historical Association, Confederate Museum, New Orleans LA

Eyraud, Cole H, *Pres,* Cabot's Old Indian Pueblo Museum, Pueblo Art Gallery, Desert Hot Springs CA

Fabbri, Anne R, *Dir,* Philadelphia College of Textiles and Science, Paley Design Center, Philadelphia PA

Faber, Carol, *Instr,* North Iowa Area Community College, Dept of Art, Mason City IA (S)

Faber, David, *Assoc Prof,* Wake Forest University, Dept of Art, Winston-Salem NC (S)

Faber, Mindy, *Assoc Dir,* School of Art Institute of Chicago, Video Data Bank, Chicago IL

Faberman, Hilarie, *Cur of Modern & Contemporary,* Stanford University, Art Gallery, Stanford CA

Fabiano, Daniel, *Prof,* University of Wisconsin-Stevens Point, Dept of Art & Design, Stevens Point WI (S)

Fabiano, Michele, *Instr,* University of North Alabama, Dept of Art, Florence AL (S)

Fabing, Suzannah J, *Dir & Chief Cur,* Smith College, Museum of Art, Northampton MA

Fabrycki, William, *Instr,* Joliet Junior College, Fine Arts Dept, Joliet IL (S)

Facci, Domenico, *VPres,* National Sculpture Society, New York NY

Faccinto, Victor, *Gallery Dir,* Wake Forest University, Dept of Art, Winston-Salem NC (S)

Faccinto, Victor, *Dir,* Wake Forest University, Fine Arts Gallery, Winston Salem NC

Facos, Michelle, *Asst Prof,* Case Western Reserve University, Dept of Art History & Art, Cleveland OH (S)

Faegenburg, Bernice, *Pres,* National Association of Women Artists, Inc, New York NY

Fagaly, William A, *Asst Dir for Art,* New Orleans Museum of Art, New Orleans LA

Fagan, Charlin Chang, *Librn,* Sarah Lawrence College Library, Esther Raushenbush Library, Bronxville NY

Fagan, Harry, *VPres,* Peninsula Fine Arts Center, Newport News VA

Faggioli, Renzo, *Ceramist-in-Residence,* Moravian College, Dept of Art, Bethlehem PA (S)

Fago, Nancy E, *Colls Mgr,* Ursinus College, Philip & Muriel Berman Museum of Art, Collegeville PA

Fahlen, Charles, *Chmn 3-D Fine Arts,* Moore College of Art & Design, Philadelphia PA (S)

Fahlund, Michael J, *Asst Dir,* Carnegie Institute, Carnegie Museum of Art, Pittsburgh PA

Fahy, Everett, *Chmn European Paintings,* The Metropolitan Museum of Art, New York NY

Fainhauz, David, *Head Librn,* Balzekas Museum of Lithuanian Culture, Research Library, Chicago IL

Fair, Barry, *Registrar & Cur Historical Art,* London Regional Art & Historical Museums, London ON

Fairbairn, Monica, *Executive Dir,* Museum of Afro-American History, Boston MA

Fairbanks, Jonathan, *Cur American Decorative Arts,* Museum of Fine Arts, Boston MA

Fairbanks, Judy, *Retail Marketing Mgr,* Indian Pueblo Cultural Center, Albuquerque NM

Fairbanks, Maureen, *Corresp Secy,* Arizona Artist Guild, Phoenix AZ

Fairbrother, Trevor, *Cur Contemporary Art,* Museum of Fine Arts, Boston MA

Fairchild, Thomas, *Treas,* Hoosier Salon Patrons Association, Hoosier Salon Art Gallery, Indianapolis IN

Fairchild MFA, Martha, *Prof,* La Roche College, Division of Graphics, Design & Communication, Pittsburgh PA (S)

Fairchild-Shepler, Martha, *Chairperson,* La Roche College, Division of Graphics, Design & Communication, Pittsburgh PA (S)

Faircloth, Norman D, *Head,* Guilford Technical Community College, Commercial Art Dept, Jamestown NC (S)

Falana, Kenneth, *Prof,* Florida A & M University, Dept of Visual Arts, Humanities & Theatre, Tallahassee FL (S)

Falcone, Paul, *Asst Prof,* Northwest Missouri State University, Dept of Art, Maryville MO (S)

Falk, Jane, *Registrar,* Akron Art Museum, Akron OH

Falk, Karen, *Dir,* Jewish Community Center of Greater Washington, Jane L & Robert H Weiner Judaic Museum, Rockville MD

Falk, Lorne, *Head Art Studio,* Banff Centre for the Arts, Banff AB (S)

Falke, Herman, *Treas,* Sculptor's Society of Canada, Toronto ON

Falke, Terry, *Instr at Interim,* East Texas State University, Dept of Art, East Texas Station, Commerce TX (S)

Falkner, Avery, *Instr,* Pepperdine University, Seaver College, Dept of Art, Malibu CA (S)

Falkner, Lorett, *Asst Prof,* Rochester Institute of Technology, School of Photographic Arts & Sciences, Rochester NY (S)

Fall, Clifford, *Head Dept,* Nebraska Wesleyan University, Art Dept, Lincoln NE (S)

Fallert, Carrol, *Pres,* St Genevieve Museum, Sainte Genevieve MO

Fallon, Steven, *VPres,* Attleboro Museum, Center for the Arts, Attleboro MA

Fallows, Lionel H, *Pres,* Mohawk Valley Heritage Association, Inc, Walter Elwood Museum, Amsterdam NY

Falls, David, *Installations Officer & Registrar,* University of Western Ontario, McIntosh Art Gallery, London ON

Falsetta, Vincent, *Painting and Drawing Coordr,* University of North Texas, School of Visual Arts, Denton TX (S)

Fane, Diana, *Chmn African, Oceanic & New World Art,* Brooklyn Museum, Brooklyn NY

Fanizza, Michael, *Asst Prof,* Old Dominion University, Art Dept, Norfolk VA (S)

Fannin, Bill, *Cur Exhib,* Department of Natural Resources of Missouri, Missouri State Museum, Jefferson City MO

Fanning, Alexandra, *Cur,* Wells Fargo & Co, History Museum, Los Angeles CA

Faquin, Jane, *Vol Coordr,* The Dixon Gallery & Gardens, Memphis TN

Farah, Priscilla, *Chief Librn,* The Metropolitan Museum of Art, Photograph and Slide Library, New York NY

Farber, Janet, *Assoc Cur 20th Century Art,* Joslyn Art Museum, Omaha NE

Faries, Molly, *Prof,* Indiana University, Bloomington, Henry Radford Hope School of Fine Arts, Bloomington IN (S)

Faris, Brunel, *Dir,* Oklahoma City University, Hulsey Gallery-Norick Art Center, Oklahoma City OK

Farley, T C, *Dir,* University of Wisconsin Oshkosh, Allen R Priebe Gallery, Oshkosh WI

Farlowe, Horace, *Sculpture,* University of Georgia, Franklin College of Arts & Sciences, Dept of Art, Athens GA (S)

Farmer, Ann, *Tour Coordr,* Fort Worth Art Association, Modern Art Museum of Fort Worth, Fort Worth TX

Farmer, Gregory, *VPres,* Porter-Phelps-Huntington Foundation, Inc Foundation, Inc, Historic House Museum, Hadley MA

Farmer, James, *Prof,* Virginia Commonwealth University, Art History Department, Richmond VA (S)

Farmer, Janice, *Development Dir,* Southern Oregon Historical Society, Jacksonville Museum of Southern Oregon History, Jacksonville OR

Farmer, Serene, *Pres,* Ashtabula Arts Center, Ashtabula OH

Farney, Cindy, *Admin Asst,* Museum of East Texas, Lufkin TX

Farnham, Katherine G, *Asst Dir,* Atlanta Historical Society Inc, Atlanta History Center, Atlanta GA

Farquhar, James Douglas, *Chmn,* University of Maryland, Dept of Art History, College Park MD (S)

Farr, Carol, *Asst Prof,* University of Alabama in Huntsville, Dept of Art & Art History, Huntsville AL (S)

Farr, Dorothy, *Cur,* Queen's University, Agnes Etherington Art Centre, Kingston ON

Farrell, Anne, *Development Dir,* Museum of Contemporary Art, San Diego, La Jolla CA

Farrell, Bill, *Prof,* School of the Art Institute of Chicago, Chicago IL (S)

Farrell, C F, *Chmn,* University of Minnesota, Morris, Humanities Division, Morris MN (S)

Farrell, Nancy, *Gallery Dir,* University of the Ozarks, Stephens Gallery, Clarksville AR

Farrell, Nancy, *Asst Prof,* University of the Ozarks, Dept of Art, Clarksville AR (S)

Farrer-Bornarth, Sylvia, *Exec Dir,* Seneca Falls Historical Society Museum, Seneca Falls NY

Farrington, Rusty, *Instr,* Iowa Central Community College, Dept of Art, Fort Dodge IA (S)

Farver, Suzanne, *Dir,* The Aspen Art Museum, Aspen CO

Farwell, Robert D, *Dir,* Fruitlands Museum, Inc, Harvard MA

Fasanella, Marc, *Asst Prof,* Southampton Campus of Long Island University, Fine Arts Division, Southampton NY (S)

Fasolino, William, *Dean,* Pratt Institute, School of Art and Design, Brooklyn NY (S)

Fass, Philip, *Asst Prof,* University of Northern Iowa, Dept of Art, Cedar Falls IA (S)

Fastuca, Carol, *Assoc Prof,* University of Maryland, Baltimore County, Visual Arts Dept, Baltimore MD (S)

Fattal, Laura, *Cur Educ,* Rutgers, The State University of New Jersey, Jane Voorhees Zimmerli Art Museum, New Brunswick NJ

Faud, Renee, *Pres Elect,* Art Guild of Burlington, Arts for Living Center, Burlington IA

Faude, Wilson H, *Exec Dir,* Old State House, Hartford CT

Faudie, Fred, *Prof,* University of Massachusetts at Lowell, Dept of Art, Lowell MA (S)

Faul, Karene, *Chairperson,* College of Saint Rose, Dept of Art, Albany NY (S)

Faulds, W Rod, *Assoc Dir,* Williams College, Museum of Art, Williamstown MA

Faulkes, Eve, *Prof,* West Virginia University, College of Creative Arts, Morgantown WV (S)

Faulkner, Norman, *Prog Coordr Glass,* Alberta College of Art, Calgary AB (S)

Faunce, Sarah, *Cur European Paintings & Sculpture,* Brooklyn Museum, Brooklyn NY

Faunt, Peggy, *Secy,* Monroe County Community College, Humanities Division, Monroe MI (S)

Fauntleroy, Carma C, *Assoc Dir,* Rutgers, The State University of New Jersey, Jane Voorhees Zimmerli Art Museum, New Brunswick NJ

Faust, Charles B, *Asst Cur,* Bradford Brinton Memorial Museum & Historic Ranch, Big Horn WY

Favell, Gene H, *Pres,* Favell Museum of Western Art & Indian Artifacts, Klamath Falls OR

Favell, Winifred L, *VPres & Treas,* Favell Museum of Western Art & Indian Artifacts, Klamath Falls OR

Faver, Jack, *Chmn,* Kansas Wesleyan University, Art Dept, Salina KS (S)

Favis, Roberta, *Head Dept,* Stetson University, Art Dept, De Land FL (S)

Fawcett, Linda D, *Chmn,* Hardin-Simmons University, Art Dept, Abilene TX (S)

Fawcett, W Peyton, *Librn,* Field Museum of Natural History, Library, Chicago IL

Fawkes, Tom, *Instr,* Pacific Northwest College of Art, Portland OR (S)

Faxon, Susan, *Asst Dir,* Phillips Academy, Addison Gallery of American Art, Andover MA

Faxon, Susan, *Cur Paintings, Sculpture, Prints & Drawings,* Phillips Academy, Addison Gallery of American Art, Andover MA

Fay, Peggy, *Grants Writer,* Iowa State University, Brunnier Gallery Museum, Ames IA

Fazekas, Catherine, *Prog Coordr,* Montclair Art Museum, Art School, Montclair NJ (S)

Fazzini, Richard, *Cur Egyptian & Classical Art,* Brooklyn Museum, Brooklyn NY

Fearon, Chris, *Museum Educator,* University of Vermont, Robert Hull Fleming Museum, Burlington VT

Fears, Eileen, *Prof,* California State Polytechnic University, Pomona, Art Dept, Pomona CA (S)

FeBland, Harriet, *Dir,* Harriet FeBland Art Workshop, New York NY (S)

Febock, Jane, *Asst Prof,* Mount Mary College, Art Dept, Milwaukee WI (S)

Fecho, Susan, *Prof,* Chowan College, Division of Art, Murfreesboro NC (S)

Fechter, Claudia Z, *Museum Dir,* The Temple, The Temple Museum of Religious Art, Cleveland OH

Fechter, Earl, *Assoc Prof,* Norwich University, Dept of Philosophy, Religion and Fine Arts, Northfield VT (S)

Fechter, Richard M, *Cur,* The Temple, Library, Cleveland OH

Federighi, Christine, *Prof,* University of Miami, Dept of Art & Art History, Coral Gables FL (S)

Fedorko, Beth, *Registrar,* Flint Institute of Arts, Library, Flint MI

Feeney, Larry, *Dir of Gallery, Cur of Museum & Permanent Coll,* Mississippi University for Women, Fine Arts Gallery, Columbus MS

Feeny, Lawrence, *Prof,* Mississippi University for Women, Division of Fine & Performing Arts, Columbus MS (S)

Fees, Paul, *Cur Buffalo Bill Museum*, Buffalo Bill Memorial Association, Buffalo Bill Historical Center, Cody WY

Fehlig, Teresa Anne, *Architecture Librn*, Oklahoma State University, Architecture Library, Stillwater OK

Fehr, Shirley, *Commercial Artist*, Saskpower, Gallery on the Roof, Regina SK

Fehrenbach, Julie, *Assoc Dir*, Spaces, Cleveland OH

Feid, Paula, *Library Dir*, Moore College of Art & Design, Library, Philadelphia PA

Feighan, M Clare, *Admin Dir*, Maude I Kerns Art Center, Henry Korn Gallery, Eugene OR

Feiman, Debra, *VPres*, Organization of Independent Artists, New York NY

Feinberg, David, *Assoc Prof*, University of Minnesota, Minneapolis, Dept of Studio Art, Minneapolis MN (S)

Feinberg, Jean, *Instr*, Bard College, Milton Avery Graduate School of the Arts, Annandale-on-Hudson NY (S)

Feinberg, Jean E, *Cur Contemporary Art*, Cincinnati Museum Association, Cincinnati Art Museum, Cincinnati OH

Feiss, Hugh, *Head Librn*, Mount Angel Abbey Library, Saint Benedict OR

Fekner, John, *Asst Prof*, C W Post Center of Long Island University, School of Visual & Performing Arts, Greenvale NY (S)

Felberbaum, Carol A, *Adjunct Instr*, Maryville University of Saint Louis, Art Division, Saint Louis MO (S)

Feldberg, Michael, *Exec Dir*, American Jewish Historical Society, Waltham MA

Feldhaus, Paul, *Instr*, California State University, Chico, Art Dept, Chico CA (S)

Feldman, Bob, *Pres*, Key West Art and Historical Society, East Martello Museum and Gallery, Key West FL

Feldman, Joel B, *Assoc Prof*, Southern Illinois University, School of Art & Design, Carbondale IL (S)

Feldman, Roger, *Assoc Prof*, Biola University, Art Dept, La Mirada CA (S)

Feldman, Sally, *Branch Adminr*, Las Vegas-Clark County Library District, Las Vegas NV

Feldstein, Barbara, *Dir Public Information*, Worcester Art Museum, Worcester MA

Fellechner, Rick, *AV Specialist*, Moore College of Art & Design, Library, Philadelphia PA

Felling, Wendy Thomas, *Cur Educ*, Nevada Museum Of Art, Reno NV

Felling, Wendy Thomas, *Cur Educ & Library Coordr*, Nevada Museum Of Art, Art Library, Reno NV

Fellner, Thomas, *Chmn Dept*, Franklin College, Art Dept, Franklin IN (S)

Felos, Charlene, *Chairperson*, Cypress College, Cypress CA (S)

Felter, Susan, *Assoc Prof*, Santa Clara University, Art Dept, Santa Clara CA (S)

Felton, Craig, *Assoc Prof*, Smith College, Art Dept, Northampton MA (S)

Fengler-Stephany, Christie, *Chmn*, University of Vermont, Dept of Art, Burlington VT (S)

Fenivick, Roly, *Instr*, Southampton Art School, Southampton ON (S)

Fennell, Patricia, *Assoc Prof*, University of Wisconsin, Madison, Dept of Art, Madison WI (S)

Fenno, John, *Pres of Board*, Canajoharie Art Gallery, Canajoharie NY

Fenno, John, *Pres of Board*, Canajoharie Art Gallery, Library, Canajoharie NY

Fenster, Fred, *Prof*, University of Wisconsin, Madison, Dept of Art, Madison WI (S)

Fenuku, Gertis, *Librn*, Howard University, Architecture & Planning Library, Washington DC

Ferber, Linda, *Cur American Paintings & Sculpture*, Brooklyn Museum, Brooklyn NY

Ferber, Linda S, *Chief Cur and Cur American Paintings & Sculpture*, Brooklyn Museum, Brooklyn NY

Feren, Steve, *Assoc Prof*, University of Wisconsin, Madison, Dept of Art, Madison WI (S)

Ferenbach, Carl, *Pres*, Brooklyn Historical Society, Brooklyn NY

Fergus, Victoria, *Prof*, West Virginia University, College of Creative Arts, Morgantown WV (S)

Ferguson, Carra, *Instr*, Georgetown University, Dept of Fine Arts, Washington DC (S)

Ferguson, Charles F, *Trustee*, Hill-Stead Museum, Farmington CT

Ferguson, Claire, *Pres*, United States Figure Skating Association, World Figure Skating Hall of Fame and Museum, Colorado Springs CO

Ferguson, Heather, *Fine Arts & Photograph Asst*, Skidmore College, Lucy Scribner Library, Saratoga Springs NY

Ferguson, John, *Instructor*, Saint Louis Community College at Meramec, Art Dept, Saint Louis MO (S)

Ferguson, Judy, *Cur Exhib & Prog*, Museum of East Texas, Lufkin TX

Ferguson, Judy, *Educ Coordr*, Witter Gallery, Storm Lake IA

Ferguson, Ken, *Business Mgr*, Art Gallery of Windsor, Windsor ON

Ferguson, Kenneth, *Chmn Ceramics*, Kansas City Art Institute, Kansas City MO (S)

Ferguson, Ray, *Assoc Prof*, University of Florida, Dept of Art, Gainesville FL (S)

Ferguson, Susan K, *Asst Horticulturist*, Tryon Palace Historic Sites & Gardens, New Bern NC

Ferguson, Willie J, *Installation Supv*, East Tennessee State University, Carroll Reece Museum, Johnson City TN

Fergusson, Mary E D'Aquin, *Asst Dir*, Longue Vue House and Gardens, New Orleans LA

Fergusson, Peter J, *Prof*, Wellesley College, Art Dept, Wellesley MA (S)

Fern, Alan, *Dir*, National Portrait Gallery, Washington DC

Fernandez, Leo, *Dir*, Western Kentucky University, University Gallery, Bowling Green KY

Fernandez, Leo, *Chmn*, Western Kentucky University, Art Dept, Bowling Green KY (S)

Fernandez, Rafael A, *Cur Prints & Drawings*, Sterling and Francine Clark Art Institute, Williamstown MA

Ferrar, Marie Elisa, *Chief*, Saint-Louis-Maillet, Dept of Visual Arts, Edmundston NB (S)

Ferreira, Teresa, *Bookstore Mgr*, Laguna Art Museum, Laguna Beach CA

Ferrell, John, *Co-Dir*, 1078 Gallery, Chico CA

Ferrell, Mike, *Cur Exhib & Design*, San Joaquin Pioneer and Historical Society, The Haggin Museum, Stockton CA

Ferris, Daniel B, *Dir*, Amos Eno Gallery, New York NY

Ferris, Robert, *Treas*, Cortland County Historical Society, Suggett House Museum, Cortland NY

Ferstrom, Katharine, *Assoc Cur Art Of Africa, Americas, Oceania*, Baltimore Museum of Art, Baltimore MD

Fertitta, Robert, *Secy*, Society for Folk Arts Preservation, Inc, New York NY

Feszczak, Zenon, *Design Dir*, Port of History Museum, Philadelphia PA

Fetchko, Peter, *Dir*, Peabody & Essex Museum, Salem MA

Fetterolf, Susan, *Pres*, Organization of Independent Artists, New York NY

Fetzer, Rachel, *Treas*, Wayne County Historical Society, Wooster OH

Fey, Mike, *Dir Exhibits*, South Carolina State Museum, Columbia SC

Fichner-Rathus, Lois, *Assoc Prof*, Trenton State College, Art Dept, Trenton NJ (S)

Fichter, Robert, *Prof*, Florida State University, Art Dept, Tallahassee FL (S)

Fickle, Dorothy H, *Assoc Cur Southeast Asian & Indian Art*, Nelson-Atkins Museum of Art, Kansas City MO

Fidler, Spencer, *Prof*, New Mexico State University, Art Dept, Las Cruces NM (S)

Field, Charles, *Prof*, University of Texas at San Antonio, Division of Art & Architecture, San Antonio TX (S)

Field, James, *Technical Dir*, Bank of Boston, Gallery, Boston MA

Field, Marshall, *Chmn Board of Trustees*, The Art Institute of Chicago, Chicago IL

Field, Richard Henning, *Dir*, Dartmouth Heritage Museum, Dartmouth NS

Field, Richard S, *Cur Prints, Drawings & Photographs*, Yale University, Art Gallery, New Haven CT

Field, Susan F, *Cur*, Uptown Center Hull House Assn, Beacon Street Gallery & Performance Company, Chicago IL

Fielden, M, *Library Supv*, Norman Mackenzie Art Gallery, Fine Arts Library, Regina SK

Fieldman, David, *Head Development*, Art Gallery of Ontario, Toronto ON

Fields, Catherine Keene, *Dir*, Litchfield Historical Society, Litchfield CT

Fields, Catherine Keene, *Dir*, Litchfield Historical Society, Ingraham Memorial Research Library, Litchfield CT

Fields, Cay, *Pres & Dir*, Norfolk Historical Society Inc, Museum, Norfolk CT

Fields, Laura Kemper, *Dir Art Coll*, Commerce Bancshares, Inc, Art Collection, Kansas City MO

Fields, Robert, *Prof*, Virginia Polytechnic Institute & State University, Dept of Art & Art History, Blacksburg VA (S)

Fife, Edward, *Chmn*, University of Toronto, Programme in Landscape Architecture, Toronto ON (S)

Fife, Lin, *Prof*, University of Colorado-Colorado Springs, Fine Arts Dept, Colorado Springs CO (S)

Figg, Laurann, *Textiles Cur & Conservator*, Vesterheim Norwegian-American Museum, Decorah IA

Figueroa, Paul C, *Dir*, Carolina Art Association, Gibbes Museum of Art, Charleston SC

Fikaris, Peter, *Asst Prof*, Jersey City State College, Art Dept, Jersey City NJ (S)

Fike, Charles, *Technical Coordr*, Ashtabula Arts Center, Ashtabula OH

File, M Jeanne, *Prof*, Daemen College, Art Dept, Amherst NY (S)

Filkosky, Josefa, *Prof*, Seton Hill College, Dept of Art, Greensburg PA (S)

Fillin-Yeh, Susan, *Cur*, Reed College, Douglas F Cooley Memorial Art Gallery, Portland OR

Fillos, Debra A, *Cur & Librn*, Lyme Historical Society, Florence Griswold Museum, Old Lyme CT

Fillos, Debra A, *Cur*, Lyme Historical Society, Archives, Old Lyme CT

Filo, Barbara, *Chmn*, Whitworth College, Art Dept, Spokane WA (S)

Finch, Don, *Dir Air Space Museum*, Oklahoma Center for Science and Art, Kirkpatrick Center, Oklahoma City OK

Finch, Robert, *Instr*, Main Line Center for the Arts, Haverford PA (S)

Findlay, James, *Head Librn*, Wolfsonian Foundation, Miami Beach FL

Findlen, Rose Ann, *Dean*, Anoka Ramsey Community College, Art Dept, Coon Rapids MN (S)

Fine, Jud, *Prof*, University of Southern California, School of Fine Arts, Los Angeles CA (S)

Fine, Milton, *Chmn Museum of Art Committee*, Carnegie Institute, Carnegie Museum of Art, Pittsburgh PA

Fine, Sally S, *Instr*, Truro Center for the Arts at Castle Hill, Inc, Truro MA (S)

Fine, Sandy, *International Child Art Coordr*, Cultural Affairs Department City of Los Angeles, Junior Arts Center, Los Angeles CA

Finger, H Ellis, *Center Dir*, Lafayette College, Morris R Williams Center for the Arts, Art Gallery, Easton PA

Fink, John, *Prof*, Nassau Community College, Art Dept, Garden City NY (S)

Fink, Lois M, *Cur Research*, National Museum of American Art, Washington DC

Fink, Mary, *Pres*, Crooked Tree Arts Council, Virginia M McCune Community Arts Center, Petoskey MI

Finkel, Kenneth, *Cur of Prints*, Library Company of Philadelphia, Print Dept, Philadelphia PA

Finkler, Robert, *Chmn*, Mankato State University, Art Dept, Mankato MN (S)

Finlayson, Lesley, *Instr,* Vancouver Community College, Langara Campus, Dept of Fine Arts, Vancouver BC (S)

Finman, Richard, *Prof,* Northwestern Connecticut Community College, Fine Arts Dept, Winsted CT (S)

Finnegan, D B, *Dir,* Beyond Baroque Foundation, Beyond Baroque Literary/Arts Center, Venice CA

Finneran, Mary, *Asst Prof,* Eastern New Mexico University, Dept of Art, Portales NM (S)

Finney, Barbara, *Office Mgr,* Crawford County Historical Society, Baldwin-Reynolds House Museum, Meadville PA

Fiorentino, Francis, *Instr,* Munson-Williams-Proctor Institute, School of Art, Utica NY (S)

Fiori, Dennis, *Dir,* Concord Museum, Concord MA

Firestone, Evan, *Dept Head,* University of Georgia, Dept of Art, Athens GA

Firestone, Evan R, *Head Dept,* University of Georgia, Franklin College of Arts & Sciences, Dept of Art, Athens GA (S)

Firmani, Debra, *Asst to Dir,* University of Maryland, College Park, Art Gallery, College Park MD

Firmani, Domenico, *Asst Prof,* College of Notre Dame of Maryland, Art Dept, Baltimore MD (S)

Fisch, Amalia, *Admin Asst,* Cornish College of the Arts, Cornish Galleries, Seattle WA

Fisch, Robert W, *Cur Weapons,* United States Military Academy, West Point Museum, West Point NY

Fischer, Billie, *Chmn Dept,* Kalamazoo College, Art Dept, Kalamazoo MI (S)

Fischer, Carl, *Secy,* Art Directors Club, Inc, New York NY

Fischer, Daryl, *Dir Educ,* Indianapolis Museum of Art, Indianapolis IN

Fischer, Ellen E, *Cur,* Greater Lafayette Museum of Art, Lafayette IN

Fischer, Gail, *Lectr,* Southwest Texas State University, Dept of Art, San Marcos TX (S)

Fischer, Martin, *Executive Dir,* Toronto Art Therapy Institute, Toronto ON (S)

Fischer, Susan, *Pres & Board Dir,* Copper Village Museum & Arts Center, Anaconda MT

Fischler, Carmen, *Dir,* Museo de Arte de Ponce, Ponce Art Museum, Ponce PR

Fish, Alida, *Chmn Photography & Film,* University of the Arts, Philadelphia College of Art & Design, Philadelphia PA (S)

Fish, Meg, *Instr,* Main Line Center for the Arts, Haverford PA (S)

Fish, Patricia, *Pres,* Wayne Art Center, Wayne PA (S)

Fish, Vinnie, *Pres,* Gallery North, Setauket NY

Fishberg, Ethel, *VPres for South Jersey,* Federated Art Associations of New Jersey, Inc, Westfield NJ

Fisher, B C, *Owner,* Westover, Charles City VA

Fisher, Bruce, *Coordr Sanamu African Gallery,* Oklahoma Center for Science and Art, Kirkpatrick Center, Oklahoma City OK

Fisher, Carol, *Educ Coordr,* Michigan State University, Kresge Art Museum, East Lansing MI

Fisher, Debra, *Asst Prof,* Denison University, Dept of Art, Granville OH (S)

Fisher, Elaine, *Chmn Design,* University of Massachusetts Dartmouth, College of Visual and Performing Arts, North Dartmouth MA (S)

Fisher, Fred J, *Dir,* Marjorie Merriweather Post Foundation of DC, Hillwood Museum, Washington DC

Fisher, F S, *Mgr,* Westover, Charles City VA

Fisher, James L, *Cur of Prints and Asst Dir,* Fort Worth Art Association, Modern Art Museum of Fort Worth, Fort Worth TX

Fisher, Jay M, *Pres,* Print Council of America, Baltimore MD

Fisher, Larry, *Acting Chair,* East Stroudsburg University, Art Dept, East Stroudsburg PA (S)

Fisher, Mac, *Instr,* Samuel S Fleisher Art Memorial, Philadelphia PA (S)

Fisher, Nora, *Cur Textiles,* Museum of New Mexico, Museum of International Folk Art, Santa Fe NM

Fisher, Richard, *Asst Prof,* College of Santa Fe, Visual Arts Dept, Santa Fe NM (S)

Fisher, Robert A, *Dir,* Yakima Valley Community College, Art Dept, Yakima WA (S)

Fisher, Stephen, *Asst Dir,* Albertson College of Idaho, Rosenthal Art Gallery, Caldwell ID

Fisher, Stephen, *Asst to Registrar,* Museum of Fine Arts, Reference Library, Springfield MA

Fisher, Stephen, *Asst Prof,* Rhode Island College, Art Dept, Providence RI (S)

Fishman, Beverly, *Head Painting Dept,* Cranbrook Academy of Art, Bloomfield Hills MI (S)

Fishman, Elizabeth, *Asst to Librn,* Walters Art Gallery, Library, Baltimore MD

Fishman, Paul, *Exec Dir,* Boston Center for Adult Education, Boston MA (S)

Fisk, Ann, *Exec Dir,* Rockport Art Association, Rockport MA

Fiske, Timothy, *Assoc Dir,* Minneapolis Society of Fine Arts, Minneapolis Institute of Arts, Minneapolis MN

Fitch, Diane, *Assoc Prof,* Wright State University, Dept of Art & Art History, Dayton OH (S)

Fitch, Kenith, *Pres,* Salmagundi Club, New York NY

Fitch, Kenith, *Librn,* Salmagundi Club, Library, New York NY

Fitts, Catherine, *Coll & Exhibits Coordr,* Supreme Court of the United States, Washington DC

Fitzgerald, Alice, *Secy,* Colby College, Musuem of Art, Waterville ME

Fitzgerald, Anita, *Assoc Prof,* Cazenovia College, Center for Art & Design Studies, Cazenovia NY (S)

Fitzgerald, Dori, *Cur,* City of Irvine, Irvine Fine Arts Center, Irvine CA

Fitzgerald, Dori, *Cur,* City of Irvine, Fine Arts Center, Irvine CA (S)

Fitzgerald, Kevin, *Visual Coll Cur,* Atlanta College of Art Library, Atlanta GA

Fitzgerald, Mary, *Asst Prof,* Roanoke College, Fine Arts Dept-Art, Salem VA (S)

Fitzgerald, Michael, *Asst Prof,* Trinity College, Dept of Fine Arts, Hartford CT (S)

Fitzgerald, Oscar P, *Dir,* Naval Historical Center, The Navy Museum, Washington DC

Fitzgerald, Richard P, *Cur,* The Southland Corporation, Art Collection, Dallas TX

Fitzgerald, Thomas, *Comptroller,* Museum of Fine Arts, Boston MA

Fitzpatrick, James B, *Pres Meadow Brook Gallery Assocs,* Oakland University, Meadow Brook Art Gallery, Rochester MI

Fitzpatrick, Nancy, *Treas,* Beaumont Art League, Beaumont TX

Fitzpatrick, Philip, *Assoc Prof,* Lamar University, Art Dept, Beaumont TX (S)

Fitzpatrick, Sue, *Secy,* University of Notre Dame, Snite Museum of Art, Notre Dame IN

Fitzpatrick, Wanda, *Cur & Mgr,* Frontier Times Museum, Bandera TX

Fixx, Kimberly, *Acting Registrar,* Oberlin College, Allen Memorial Art Museum, Oberlin OH

Flahaven, James, *Asst Prof,* Clarion University of Pennsylvania, Dept of Art, Clarion PA (S)

Flam, Jack, *Prof,* City University of New York, PhD Program in Art History, New York NY (S)

Flanagan, Jeanne, *Dir,* College of Saint Rose, Picotte Art Gallery, Albany NY

Flanagan, Leo, *Dir,* Silas Bronson Library, Art, Theatre & Music Services, Waterbury CT

Flanagan, Michael, *Dir,* University of Wisconsin, University Art Museum, Milwaukee WI

Flanagan, Nancy, *Asst Prof,* Assumption College, Dept of Art & Music, Worcester MA (S)

Flannery, Louis, *Chief Librn,* Oregon Historical Society, Library, Portland OR

Flannery, Merle, *Assoc Prof,* University of Florida, Dept of Art, Gainesville FL (S)

Flannery, Richard E, *Pres Board of Trustees,* Hoyt Institute of Fine Arts, New Castle PA

Flashner, Dale, *Asst Prof,* Adelphi University, Dept of Art and Art History, Garden City NY (S)

Flat Lip, Lawrence, *Int,* Chief Plenty Coups Museum, Pryor MT

Fleck, Michael, *Personnel Mgr,* Kalani Honua Institute for Cultural Studies, Pahoa HI (S)

Fleck, Rudolf, *Prof,* Loyola Marymount University, Art & Art History Dept, Los Angeles CA (S)

Flecker, Maurice, *Dean,* Suffolk County Community College, Art Dept, Selden NY (S)

Flecky, Michael, *Asst Prof,* Creighton University, Fine and Performing Arts Dept, Omaha NE (S)

Fleischer, Arthur, *Chmn,* Fried, Frank, Harris, Shriver & Jacobson, Art Collection, New York NY

Fleischer, Donna H, *Exec Dir,* Franchise Finance Corporation of America, The Fleischer Museum, Scottsdale AZ

Fleischer, Mary, *Chmn,* Marymount Manhattan College, Fine & Performing Arts Dept, New York NY (S)

Fleischer, Roland E, *Prof,* Pennsylvania State University, University Park, Dept of Art History, University Park PA (S)

Fleischer, Roland E, *Graduate Officer,* Pennsylvania State University, University Park, Dept of Art History, University Park PA (S)

Fleischman, Lawrence, *Chmn,* Kennedy Galleries, Art Gallery, New York NY

Fleischman, Stephen, *Dir,* Madison Art Center, Madison WI

Fleming, Jeff, *Asst Cur,* Southeastern Center for Contemporary Art, Winston-Salem NC

Fleming, John, *Pres,* African American Museums Association, Wilberforce OH

Fleming, Larry, *Chmn Art Direction,* Center for Creative Studies, College of Art & Design, Detroit MI (S)

Fleming, Linda, *Sculpture,* California College of Arts and Crafts, Oakland CA (S)

Fleming, Marnie, *Cur Contemporary Art,* Oakville Galleries, Centennial Gallery and Gairloch Gallery, Oakville ON

Fleming, Penelope, *Instr,* Main Line Center for the Arts, Haverford PA (S)

Fleming, Timothy, *Chmn,* San Jacinto College-North, Art Dept, Houston TX (S)

Fleminger, Susan, *Dir,* Louis Abrons Art Center, New York NY

Fletcher, Donna, *Membership & Coordr,* Museum of Fine Arts, Saint Petersburg, Florida, Inc, Saint Petersburg FL

Fletcher, Dorothy, *Lectr,* Emory University, Art History Dept, Atlanta GA (S)

Fletcher, H George, *Cur Printed Books & Bindings,* Pierpont Morgan Library, New York NY

Fletcher, Nettie, *Exec Asst,* Portage and District Arts Council, Portage la Prairie MB

Fletcher, Peter, *Assoc Prof,* Viterbo College, Art Dept, La Crosse WI (S)

Flewwelling, Morris, *Pres,* Canadian Museums Association, Association des Musees Canadiens, Ottawa ON

Flewwelling, Morris, *Dir,* Normandeau Cultural & Natural History Society, Red Deer & District Museum & Archives, Red Deer AB

Flewwelling, Morris, *Dir,* Normandeau Cultural & Natural History Society, Red Deer & District Museum Exhibition Centre, Red Deer AB

Flick, Robbert, *Prof,* University of Southern California, School of Fine Arts, Los Angeles CA (S)

Flick, Tim, *Exhibit Designer,* Columbus Museum, Columbus GA

Flickenger, Paul, *Instr,* West Shore Community College, Division of Humanities and Fine Arts, Scottville MI (S)

Flint, Suzanne, *Cur,* Pocumtuck Valley Memorial Association, Memorial Hall, Deerfield MA

Flint-Gohlke, Lucy, *Asst Dir,* Wellesley College, Museum, Wellesley MA

Flomenhaft, Eleanor, *Sir,* Fine Arts Museum of Long Island, Hempstead NY

Flood, James W, *Dept Chmn,* Towson State University, Dept of Art, Baltimore MD (S)

Floreen, Joyce, *Pres,* Berks Art Alliance, Reading PA

Flori, R A, *Pres,* American Fine Arts Society, New York NY

Florio, R A, *Exec Dir,* Art Students League of New York, New York NY (S)

Florio, Rosina A, *Exec Dir & Dir Libr,* Art Students League of New York, New York NY

Florio, Rosina A, *Dir,* Art Students League of New York, Library, New York NY

Floss, Michael M, *Exec Dir,* Pro Arts, Oakland CA

Flowers, Eileen, *Library Dir,* North Canton Public Library, Little Art Gallery, North Canton OH

Flowers, Randolph, *Assoc Prof,* Del Mar College, Art Dept, Corpus Christi TX (S)

Floyd, Margaret H, *Assoc Prof,* Tufts University, Dept of Art & Art History, Medford MA (S)

Floyd, Phylis, *Cur,* Michigan State University, Kresge Art Museum, East Lansing MI

Fluegel, Kathleen, *Development Officer,* University of Minnesota, University Art Museum, Minneapolis MN

Flumiani, C M, *Pres,* American Classical College, Classical Art Gallery, Albuquerque NM

Flumiani, C M, *Pres,* American Classical College, Trecento Art Library, Albuquerque NM

Flumiani, C M, *Dir,* American Classical College, Albuquerque NM (S)

Flynn, Angela, *Financial Adminr,* Beaverbrook Art Gallery, Fredericton NB

Flynn, Charles, *Instructor,* Virginia State University, Fine & Commercial Art, Petersburg VA (S)

Flynn, Judith, *Chmn,* Penn Valley Community College, Art Dept, Kansas City MO (S)

Flynt, Henry N, *Pres,* Historic Deerfield, Inc, Deerfield MA

Fogarty, Mary Beth, *Artist-in-Res,* Creighton University, Fine and Performing Arts Dept, Omaha NE (S)

Fogarty, Neil, *Pres,* Art Centre of New Jersey, East Orange NJ (S)

Fogerty, Lee, *Co-Dir,* Springfield City Library & Museums Association, Art & Music Dept, Springfield MA

Fogt, Rex, *Assoc Prof,* University of Toledo, Dept of Art, Toledo OH (S)

Folda, Jaroslav, *Prof,* University of North Carolina at Chapel Hill, Art Dept, Chapel Hill NC (S)

Foley, Bob, *Head Librn,* Banff Centre, Centre for the Arts Library, Banff AB

Foley, Suzanne, *Cur,* University of Virginia, Bayly Art Museum, Charlottesville VA

Foley, Virginia, *VPres,* Cleveland Museum of Art, Print Club of Cleveland, Cleveland OH

Folgarait, Leonard, *Assoc Prof,* Vanderbilt University, Dept of Fine Arts, Nashville TN (S)

Follett, Nancy, *Mgr,* Detroit Artists Market, Detroit MI

Folley, Ann, *Cur,* Wenham Museum, Wenham MA

Folsom, James, *Dir Botanical Gardens,* Henry E Huntington Library, Art Collections & Botanical Gardens, San Marino CA

Foltz, Diane, *Instr,* La Roche College, Division of Graphics, Design & Communication, Pittsburgh PA (S)

Foltz, Patrick A, *Exec Dir,* Historical Society of York County, York PA

Fomin, Elizabeth, *Asst Prof,* Rochester Institute of Technology, School of Art and Design, Rochester NY (S)

Fondaw, Ron, *Assoc Prof,* University of Miami, Dept of Art & Art History, Coral Gables FL (S)

Fong, Lawrence, *Registrar,* University of Oregon, Museum of Art, Eugene OR

Fong, Wen, *Chmn Prog Chinese and Japanese Art and Archaeology,* Princeton University, Dept of Art and Archaeology, Princeton NJ (S)

Fong, Wen, *Special Consultant for Asian Affairs,* The Metropolitan Museum of Art, New York NY

Fontaine, Jeannette, *Cur,* Chatham Historical Society, Old Atwood House, Chatham MA

Fontana, Lilia M, *Asst to Dir,* Miami-Dade Community College, Kendal Campus, Art Gallery, Miami FL

Fontenot, Bill, *Cur Natural Science,* Lafayette Natural History Museum, Planetarium and Nature Station, Lafayette LA

Foose, Robert James, *Chair,* University of Kentucky, Dept of Art, Lexington KY (S)

Foote, Susan, *Lectr,* Lambuth University, Dept of Human Ecology & Visual Arts, Jackson TN (S)

Forbes, Cindy, *Museum Secy,* Art Museum of Southeast Texas, Beaumont TX

Forbes, Donna M, *Dir,* Yellowstone Art Center, Billings MT

Forbes, James, *Dir Development,* Fine Arts Museums of San Francisco, M H de Young Memorial Museum and California Palace of the Legion of Honor, San Francisco CA

Forbes, Pamela, *Editor Triptych,* Fine Arts Museums of San Francisco, M H de Young Memorial Museum and California Palace of the Legion of Honor, San Francisco CA

Forbes, Wayne, *Instr,* Illinois Central College, Dept of Fine Arts, East Peoria IL (S)

Forbis, John, *Staff Librn,* The Carnegie Library of Pittsburgh, Pittsburgh PA

Ford, Beth M, *Asst Prof,* Florida Southern College, Art Dept, Lakeland FL (S)

Ford, Derna, *Chmn Fine Arts Dept,* Barry University, Dept of Fine Arts, Miami Shores FL (S)

Ford, Hermine, *Pres,* Artists Space, New York NY

Ford, Howard, *Dir & Cur,* Gallery Lambton, Sarnia ON

Ford, Janice, *Gallery Dir,* Pikeville College, Humanities Division, Pikeville KY (S)

Ford, Linda, *Exec Dir,* The Light Factory, Inc, Charlotte NC

Ford, Margaret, *Assoc Librn,* Museum of Fine Arts, Houston, Hirsch Library, Houston TX

Ford, Sharon, *Instr,* Rancho Santiago College, Art Dept, Santa Ana CA (S)

Fordan, Carolyn, *Chmn Dept Humanities,* Imperial Valley College, Art Dept, Imperial CA (S)

Forell, Jean, *Cur of Education,* Flint Institute of Arts, Flint MI

Foresta, Merry, *Cur Photography,* National Museum of American Art, Washington DC

Forester, Alice, *VPres,* Leigh Yawkey Woodson Art Museum, Inc, Wausau WI

Forest Wilson, Ernest, *Prof,* Catholic University of America, School of Architecture & Planning, Washington DC (S)

Forgang, David M, *Chief Cur,* Yosemite Museum, Yosemite National Park CA

Forge, Andrew, *Prof,* Yale University, School of Art, New Haven CT (S)

Forino, Alan, *Chmn,* Point Park College, Performing Arts Dept, Pittsburgh PA (S)

Formigoni, Mauri, *Asst Prof,* Sangamon State University, Visual Arts Program, Springfield IL (S)

Formo, Peter L, *VPres,* Amerind Foundation, Inc, Amerind Museum, Fulton-Hayden Memorial Art Gallery, Dragoon AZ

Formo, Peter L, *VPres,* Amerind Foundation, Inc, Fulton-Hayden Memorial Library, Dragoon AZ

Formosa, Gerald, *Instr,* Vancouver Community College, Langara Campus, Dept of Fine Arts, Vancouver BC (S)

Forney, Darrell, *Instr,* Sacramento City College, Art Dept, Sacramento CA (S)

Forney, David G, *Pres,* Doshi Center for Contemporary Art, Harrisburg PA

Forrester, Vivian, *House Mgr,* North Carolina State University, Chinqua-Penn Plantation House, Garden & Greenhouses, Reidsville NC

Forsha, Lynda, *Cur,* Museum of Contemporary Art, San Diego, La Jolla CA

Forst, George William, *Instr,* Sterling College, Art Dept, Sterling KS (S)

Forster-Hahn, Francoise, *Prof,* University of California, Riverside, Dept of the History of Art, Riverside CA (S)

Forsthoffer, Joe, *Pub Information Coordr,* Ward Foundation, Ward Museum of Wildfowl Art, Salisbury MD

Forsyth, Ilene H, *Prof,* University of Michigan, Ann Arbor, Dept of History of Art, Ann Arbor MI (S)

Fort, LiFran, *Instr,* Fisk University, Art Dept, Nashville TN (S)

Fort, Tom, *Asst Dir & Cur Exhibits,* Hidalgo County Historical Museum, Edinburg TX

Forte, Joseph C, *Instr,* Sarah Lawrence College, Dept of Art History, Bronxville NY (S)

Fortier, Rollin, *Preparator,* University of California, Santa Barbara, University Art Museum, Santa Barbara CA

Fortreide, Steven, *Assoc Dir,* Allen County Public Library, Fine Arts Dept, Fort Wayne IN

Fortson, Kay, *Pres,* Kimbell Art Museum, Fort Worth TX

Foshay, Susan, *Exhib Cur,* Art Gallery of Nova Scotia, Halifax NS

Foss, Maggie, *Cur of Education,* San Bernardino County Museum, Fine Arts Institute, Redlands CA

Foster, Anthony, *Exhib Designer,* Southern Methodist University, Meadows Museum, Dallas TX

Foster, April, *Instr,* Art Academy of Cincinnati, Cincinnati OH (S)

Foster, Barbara Ann, *Secy,* Colonel Black Mansion, Ellsworth ME

Foster, Bill, *Dir,* Portland Art Museum, Northwest Film Center, Portland OR

Foster, David, *Chmn Art Dept,* Lake Tahoe Community College, Art Dept, South Lake Tahoe CA (S)

Foster, Elaine, *Prof,* Jersey City State College, Art Dept, Jersey City NJ (S)

Foster, Hal, *Assoc Prof,* Cornell University, Dept of the History of Art, Ithaca NY (S)

Foster, John, *Instr Photo & Art,* Victor Valley College, Art Dept, Victorville CA (S)

Foster, Kathleen, *Cur 19th & 20th Century Art,* Indiana University, Art Museum, Bloomington IN

Foster, Keith, *Dir,* Redding Museum of Art & History, Redding CA

Foster, Michael, *Treas,* Kemerer Museum of Decorative Arts, Bethlehem PA

Foti, Arlene, *Instr,* Grand Canyon University, Art Dept, Phoenix AZ (S)

Foti, Mollie, *Gallery Dir,* The Gallery at Hawaii Loa College, Marinda Lee Gallery, Kaneohe HI

Foti-Soublet, Silvana, *Chmn,* Methodist College, Art Dept, Fayetteville NC (S)

Foulos, Don, *Gallery Cur,* University of Saskatchewan, Gordon Snelgrove Art Gallery, Saskatoon SK

Founds, George, *Assoc Prof,* La Roche College, Division of Graphics, Design & Communication, Pittsburgh PA (S)

Fournet, Annette, *Gallery Dir,* University of New Orleans, Fine Arts Gallery, New Orleans LA

Fournet, Annette E, *Assoc Prof,* University of New Orleans-Lake Front, Dept of Fine Arts, New Orleans LA (S)

Fowler, Harriet, *Dir,* University of Kentucky, Art Museum, Lexington KY

Fox, Anne, *House Adminr,* Charleston Museum, Joseph Manigault House, Charleston SC

Fox, Carson, *Instr,* Main Line Center for the Arts, Haverford PA (S)

Fox, Chris, *Instr,* Main Line Center for the Arts, Haverford PA (S)

Fox, Edward, *Prof,* Nassau Community College, Art Dept, Garden City NY (S)

Fox, Elizabeth P, *Cur,* Connecticut Historical Society, Hartford CT

Fox, Gail, *Instr,* Delaware County Community College, Communications and Humanities House, Media PA (S)

Fox, Howard, *Cur Contemporary Art,* Los Angeles County Museum of Art, Los Angeles CA

Fox, Hugh R, *Asst Prof,* Rochester Institute of Technology, School of Printing, Rochester NY (S)

Fox, John, *Asst Prof,* Finger Lakes Community College, Visual & Performing Arts Dept, Canandaigua NY (S)

Fox, Juidth Hoos, *Cur,* Wellesley College, Museum, Wellesley MA

Fox, Paulette, *Coordr of Museum Information,* Tennessee State Museum, Nashville TN

Fox, Randall, *Supt,* Game and Parks Commission, Arbor Lodge State Historical Park, Nebraska City NE

Fox, Robert, *Chmn,* National Institute for Architectural Education, New York NY

Fox, Ross, *Cur European Art,* Amherst College, Mead Art Museum, Amherst MA

Fox, Terri, *Admin Asst,* The Art Studio Inc, Beaumont TX

Foxley, William C, *Pres,* Museum of Western Art, Denver CO

Foxworth, Eugenia C, *Dir,* Soho 20 Gallery, New York NY

Foy, Donna, *Chmn,* Saint Mary-of-the-Woods College, Art Dept, Saint Mary-of-the-Woods IN (S)

Foy, Jessica, *Cur of Coll,* Mamie McFaddin Ward Heritage Historic Foundation, Beaumont TX

Fraas, Kathleen, *Registrar,* Niagara University, Castellani Art Museum, New York NY

Fraher, James, *Dept Head,* Ray College of Design, Chicago IL (S)

Frajzyngier, Anna, *Library Asst,* University of Colorado, Art and Architecture Library, Boulder CO

Fraley, Carolyn J, *Prof,* Mount Saint Mary's College, Visual & Performing Arts Dept, Emmitsburg MD (S)

Frampton, Doris, *Dir Annual Giving,* Philbrook Museum of Art, Tulsa OK

Francey, Mary F, *Asst Prof,* University of Utah, Art Dept, Salt Lake City UT (S)

Francis, Cortez, *Chmn,* Manatee Community College, Dept of Art & Humanities, Bradenton FL (S)

Francis, Frances, *Registrar,* High Museum of Art, Atlanta GA

Francis, Irma Talabi, *Asst Dir Spec Projects,* Fondo del Sol, Visual Art & Media Center, Washington DC

Francis, Kathleen, *Textile Conservator,* Museum of American Textile History, North Andover MA

Francis, Richard, *Chief Cur,* Museum of Contemporary Art, Chicago IL

Francis, Tom, *Painting Chmn,* Atlanta College of Art, Atlanta GA (S)

Francis, Wayne, *Gallery Dir,* Northern Michigan University, Lee Hall Gallery, Marquette MI

Franco, Ann, *Assoc Prof,* Concordia College, Bronxville NY (S)

Frandrup, Dennis, *Asst Prof,* College of Saint Benedict, Art Dept, Saint Joseph MN (S)

Franits, Wayne, *Prof,* Syracuse University, Dept of Fine Arts (Art History), Syracuse NY (S)

Frank, Barbara, *Asst Prof,* State University of New York at Stony Brook, Art Dept, Stony Brook NY (S)

Frank, Charles, *Executive Dir,* Fine Arts Association, School of Fine Arts, Willoughby OH

Frank, Charles M, *Dir,* School of Fine Arts, Visual Arts Dept, Willoughby OH (S)

Frank, David, *Prof,* Mississippi University for Women, Division of Fine & Performing Arts, Columbus MS (S)

Frank, Denise, *Dir Fine Arts,* Chattanooga State Technical Community College, Advertising Arts Dept, Chattanooga TN (S)

Frank, Henry B, *VPres,* Detroit Institute of Arts, Founders Society, Detroit MI

Frank, Irene, *Art Reference Librn,* University of South Florida, Library, Tampa FL

Frank, Richard, *Pres,* Oysterponds Historical Society, Museum, Orient NY

Frank, Stuart M, *Dir,* Kendall Whaling Museum, Sharon MA

Franke, Ken, *Exec Dir,* San Diego Maritime Museum, San Diego CA

Frankel, Dextra, *Dir,* California State University Fullerton, Art Gallery, Visual Arts Center, Fullerton CA

Frankel, Martha, *Chief Cur,* Oshkosh Public Museum, Oshkosh WI

Frankel, Robert H, *Dir,* Chrysler Museum, Norfolk VA

Franki, James, *Instr,* Moravian College, Dept of Art, Bethlehem PA (S)

Franklin, Barbara-Decker, *Dir Educational Center,* Craft Alliance Gallery & Education Center, Saint Louis MO

Franklin, Carolyn, *Catalog Librn,* San Francisco Art Institute, Anne Bremer Memorial Library, San Francisco CA

Franklin, Dwayne, *Registrar & Exhib Preparator,* Dickinson College, Trout Gallery, Carlisle PA

Franklin, Hardy R, *Dir Library,* Public Library of the District of Columbia, Art Division, Washington DC

Franklin, Jane, *Admin,* Washington University, Gallery of Art, Saint Louis MO

Franklin, Oliver, *Educ,* Hidalgo County Historical Museum, Edinburg TX

Franklin, Ruth, *Cur of African & Oceanic Art,* Stanford University, Art Gallery, Stanford CA

Franklin-Smith, Constance, *Dir,* ArtNetwork, Renaissance CA

Franks, Mary, *Asst Cur Educ,* George Walter Vincent Smith Art Museum, Springfield MA

Franks, Steffi, *Instr,* Chautauqua Institution, School of Art, Chautauqua NY (S)

Frankston, Leon, *Chmn,* Nassau Community College, Art Dept, Garden City NY (S)

Frantz, Alice, *Head Div,* Huron University, Arts & Sciences Division, Huron SD (S)

Frantz, Barry, *Chmn Fine Arts Div,* Cuesta College, Art Dept, San Luis Obispo CA (S)

Frantz, James H, *Conservator Objects,* The Metropolitan Museum of Art, New York NY

Frantz, Susanne, *Cur 20th Century Glass,* Corning Museum of Glass, Corning NY

Frappier, Gilles, *Dir,* Ottawa Public Library, Fine Arts Dept, Ottawa ON

Frasczak, Mary Beth, *Librn,* College of the Associated Arts, Library, Saint Paul MN

Fraser, A Ian, *Cur,* Indianapolis Museum of Art, Clowes Fund Collection, Indianapolis IN

Fraser, James, *Libr Dir,* Fairleigh Dickinson University, Florham Madison Campus Library - Art Dept, Madison NJ

Fraser, Jon, *Div Dir,* Southampton Campus of Long Island University, Fine Arts Division, Southampton NY (S)

Fraser, Judith, *Fine Arts Librn,* Long Beach Public Library, Long Beach CA

Fraser, Ted, *Dir,* Confederation Centre Art Gallery and Museum, Charlottetown PE

Fraser, Ted, *Dir,* Confederation Centre Art Gallery and Museum, Library, Charlottetown PE

Frauchiger, Fritz, *Dir,* Palm Springs Desert Museum, Inc, Palm Springs CA

Frauchiger, Fritz, *Dir,* Palm Springs Desert Museum, Inc, Library, Palm Springs CA

Fraunfelter, George, *Adj Cur Geology,* Southern Illinois University, University Museum, Carbondale IL

Fraze, Denny, *Chmn,* Amarillo College, Art Dept, Amarillo TX (S)

Frazer, John, *Prof,* Wesleyan University, Art Dept, Middletown CT (S)

Frazier, Bill, *Instr,* San Jacinto College-North, Art Dept, Houston TX (S)

Frazier, Clifton T, *Assoc Prof,* Rochester Institute of Technology, School of Printing, Rochester NY (S)

Frechette, Suzy Enns, *Mgr Fine Arts Dept,* Saint Louis Public Library, Saint Louis MO

Fred, Morris A, *Dir,* Spertus Museum, Chicago IL

Frederick, Helen C, *Artistic Dir,* Pyramid Atlantic, Riverdale MD

Fredericks, Maria, *Assoc Conservator for Libr Colls,* Winterthur Museum and Gardens, Library, Winterthur DE

Fredrick, Charles, *Chair,* California State Polytechnic University, Pomona, Art Dept, Pomona CA (S)

Freeburg, Charles, *Pres,* Lubbock Art Association, Inc, Lubbock TX

Freed, Denise Lisiecki, *Head of Painting & Drawing Dept,* Kalamazoo Institute of Arts, KIA School, Kalamazoo MI (S)

Freed, Michael, *Dir,* Individual Artists of Oklahoma, Oklahoma City OK

Freed, Rita, *Cur Egyptian & Ancient Near Eastern,* Museum of Fine Arts, Boston MA

Freedman, Ben, *Prof,* West Virginia University, College of Creative Arts, Morgantown WV (S)

Freedman, Susan K, *Pres,* Public Art Fund, Inc, New York NY

Freehling, Stanley M, *Pres,* Arts Club of Chicago, Chicago IL

Freeman, Carla C, *Art Librn,* New York State College of Ceramics at Alfred University, Scholes Library of Ceramics, Alfred NY

Freeman, David, *Prof,* Winthrop College, Dept of Art & Design, Rock Hill SC (S)

Freeman, Jeff, *Assoc Prof,* University of South Dakota, Dept of Art, Vermillion SD (S)

Freeman, Kirk, *Assoc Prof,* Bethel College, Dept of Art, Saint Paul MN (S)

Freeman, Lorraine, *2nd VPres,* Halifax Historical Society, Inc, Halifax Historical Museum, Daytona Beach FL

Freeman, Louis M, *Pres of Board,* New Orleans Museum of Art, New Orleans LA

Freeman, Mary Ann C, *Exec Dir,* Museum of Art, Science and Industry, Discovery Museum, Bridgeport CT

Freeman, Muriel C, *Pres,* National League of American Pen Women, Washington DC

Freeman, Nancy, *Pres,* Round Top Center for the Arts Inc, Arts Gallery, Damariscotta ME

Freeman, Rob, *VPres,* Ontario Association of Art Galleries, Toronto ON

Freeman, Robert, *Dir,* Stratford Art Association, The Gallery Stratford, Stratford ON

Freeman, Scott, *Dir Public Prog,* University of Washington, Thomas Burke Memorial Washington State Museum, Seattle WA

Freer, Elene J, *Cur,* Muskoka Arts & Crafts Inc, Chapel Gallery, Bracebridge ON

Fregin, Nancy J, *Pres,* American Society of Artists, Inc, Chicago IL

Freiberg, Jack, *Asst Prof,* Florida State University, Art History Dept (R133B), Tallahassee FL (S)

Freitag, Sally, *Registrar,* National Gallery of Art, Washington DC

French, Earl, *Education Coordr,* Stowe-Day Foundation, Harriet Beecher Stowe House, Hartford CT

French, Jeannie, *Asst Prof,* South Dakota State University, Dept of Visual Arts, Brookings SD (S)

French, Kate Pearson, *Exec Dir,* Wave Hill, Bronx NY

French, La Wanda, *Dir,* Ponca City Cultural Center & Museum, Ponca City OK

French, La Wanda, *Dir,* Ponca City Cultural Center & Museum, Library, Ponca City OK

French, Sandra, *Office Asst,* Art League of Manatee County, Bradenton FL

French, Sandra, *Office Asst,* Art League of Manatee County, Library, Bradenton FL

French, Stephanie, *VPres,* The American Federation of Arts, New York NY

French, Stephanie, *VPres Corporate Contributions & Cultural Affairs,* Philip Morris Company Inc, New York NY

Frenderheim, Tom L, *VPres,* The American Federation of Arts, New York NY

Frets, Paul W, *Prof,* Radford University, Art Dept, Radford VA (S)

Fretwell, Jacqueline, *Ed & Dir Research,* Saint Augustine Historical Society, Library, Saint Augustine FL

Freudenheim, Tom, *Asst Secy for Arts & Humanities,* Smithsonian Institution, Washington DC

Freund, David, *Assoc Prof Photography,* Ramapo College of New Jersey, School of Contemporary Arts, Mahwah NJ (S)

Frew, Rachel, *Libr Asst,* University of North Carolina at Chapel Hill, Joseph Curtis Sloane Art Library, Chapel Hill NC

Frey, Barbara, *Dir,* East Texas State University, University Gallery, Commerce TX

Frey, Barbara, *Chmn Ceramics,* East Texas State University, Dept of Art, East Texas Station, Commerce TX (S)

Frey, Mary, *Asst Prof,* University of Hartford, Hartford Art School, West Hartford CT (S)

Frey, Nancy, *Artistic Dir,* Maude I Kerns Art Center School, Eugene OR (S)

Frey, Richard, *Asst to Dir,* Print Club Center for Prints & Photographs, Philadelphia PA

Frey, Viola, *Ceramics,* California College of Arts and Crafts, Oakland CA (S)

Freye, Melissa, *Coordr Development & Public Relations,* Muskegon Museum of Art, Muskegon MI

Friary, Donald R, *Executive Dir & Secy,* Historic Deerfield, Inc, Deerfield MA

Frick, Aida, *Asst Prof,* Wartburg College, Dept of Art, Waverly IA (S)

Frick, Arthur C, *Dept Head,* Wartburg College, Dept of Art, Waverly IA (S)

Frick, Henry Clay, *Pres,* Frick Collection, New York NY

Fricker, Geoff, *Prof,* Butte College, Dept of Fine Arts, Oroville CA (S)

Friebert, Judith, *Assoc Librn,* Toledo Museum of Art, Library, Toledo OH

Friedland, R, *Chmn Advertising Design,* Fashion Institute of Technology, Art & Design Division, New York NY (S)

Friedman, Alice T, *Assoc Prof,* Wellesley College, Art Dept, Wellesley MA (S)

Friedman, Barbara, *Prof,* Pace University, Dyson College of Arts & Sciences, Pleasantville NY

Friedman, Betty, *Exec Dir,* Farmington Valley Arts Center, Avon CT

Friedman, Donna, *Coordr Visual Studies,* Iowa State University, Dept of Art and Design, Ames IA (S)

Friedman, Maxine, *Pres,* Tracey-Warner School, Philadelphia PA (S)

Friedman, Paula, *Public Relations,* Judah L Magnes Museum, Berkeley CA

Friedman, Robert, *Instr,* Stephens College, Art & Fashion Dept, Columbia MO (S)

Friedmann, Cynthia, *Public Relations,* Harvard University, Harvard University Art Museums, Cambridge MA

Friend, Miles E, *Faculty,* Idaho State University, Dept of Art, Pocatello ID (S)

Frier, Scottie, *Asst Dir,* Barn Gallery Associates, Inc, Ogunquit ME

Frinta, Mojmir, *Prof,* State University of New York at Albany, Art Dept, Albany NY (S)

Frisbee, John, *Dir,* New Hampshire Historical Society, Concord NH

Frisch, Jefferey, *Dir,* Orange County Center for Contemporary Art, Santa Ana CA

Frisch, Marianne Brunson, *Asst Cur,* The Reader's Digest Association Inc, Pleasantville NY

Fritsch, Peter, *Consultant,* Pennsylvania Dutch Folk Culture Society Inc, Pennsylvania Dutch Folklife Museum, Lenhartsville PA

Fritz, Berry, *Public Relations,* McAllen International Museum, McAllen TX

Fritz, Judith, *Exec Dir,* Taos Art Association Inc, Stables Art Center, Taos NM

Fritzsche, Mary W, *Education Dir,* Virginia Museum of Fine Arts, Richmond VA

Frizzell, Deborah, *Cur of Education,* New Britain Institute, New Britain Museum of American Art, New Britain CT

Frizzle, Donald, *Secy,* Pocumtuck Valley Memorial Association, Memorial Hall, Deerfield MA

Froehlich, Conrad G, *Dir,* Martin & Osa Johnson Safari Museum, Inc, Chanute KS

Froehlich, Conrad G, *Dir,* Martin & Osa Johnson Safari Museum, Inc, Imperato Collection of West African Artifacts, Chanute KS

Froehlich, Conrad G, *Dir,* Martin & Osa Johnson Safari Museum, Inc, Johnson Collection of Photographs, Movies & Memorabilia, Chanute KS

Froehlich, Conrad G, *Dir,* Martin & Osa Johnson Safari Museum, Inc, Selsor Gallery of Art, Chanute KS

Froehlich, Conrad G, *Dir,* Martin & Osa Johnson Safari Museum, Inc, Scott Explorers Library, Chanute KS

Fromboluti, Iona, *Dir,* Prince Street Gallery, New York NY

Fromer, Seymour, *Dir,* Judah L Magnes Museum, Berkeley CA

Fromm, Annette B, *Project Dir,* Creek Council House Museum, Library, Okmulgee OK

Fronmuller, Regina Marie, *Head Dept,* Springfield College in Illinois, Dept of Art, Springfield IL (S)

Frontz, Stephanie J, *Librn,* University of Rochester, Art Library, Rochester NY

Frost, A, *Instr,* Technical University of Nova Scotia, Faculty of Architecture, Halifax NS (S)

Frost, Christa, *Chmn Div Communications & Humanities,* Aims Community College, Design & Creative Studies Dept, Greeley CO (S)

Frost, J William, *Dir,* Swarthmore College, Friends Historical Library, Swarthmore PA

Frudakis, Anthony, *Instr,* Ocean City Art Center, Ocean City NJ (S)

Frudakis, Tony, *Asst Prof,* Hillsdale College, Art Dept, Hillsdale MI (S)

Fruhan, Catherine, *Asst Prof,* DePauw University, Art Dept, Greencastle IN (S)

Frushour, Steve, *Museum Contact,* Toledo Federation of Art Societies, Inc, Toledo OH

Fry, Eileen, *Slide Librn,* Indiana University, Fine Arts Library, Bloomington IN

Fry, George, *Dir,* New Brunswick College of Craft & Design, Fredericton NB

Fry, George F, *Dir of Craft School,* New Brunswick College of Craft & Design, Fredericton NB (S)

Fryberger, Betsy G, *Cur of Prints & Drawings,* Stanford University, Art Gallery, Stanford CA

Fryd, Vivien G, *Asst Prof,* Vanderbilt University, Dept of Fine Arts, Nashville TN (S)

Frye, Melinda Y, *Assoc Cur,* United States Senate Commission on Art, Washington DC

Frye, Steve, *Dir,* John P Barclay Memorial Gallery, Pittsburgh PA

Fryhle, Corinne, *Acting Cur Educ Prog,* Oberlin College, Allen Memorial Art Museum, Oberlin OH

Fu, Shen, *Cur Chinese Art,* Freer Gallery of Art, Washington DC

Fuchs, Angele, *Chmn,* Mount Mary College, Tower Gallery, Milwaukee WI

Fuchs, Angelee, *Chmn,* Mount Mary College, Art Dept, Milwaukee WI (S)

Fuchsen, Charlyn, *Dept Head,* Ray College of Design, Chicago IL (S)

Fudge, John, *Prof,* University of Colorado at Denver, Dept of Fine Arts, Denver CO (S)

Fuentes, Leopoldo, *Asst Prof,* State University of New York College at Brockport, Dept of Art & Art History, Brockport NY (S)

Fuentes, Tina, *Assoc Prof,* Texas Tech University, Dept of Art, Lubbock TX (S)

Fuglie, Gordon, *Dir,* Loyola Marymount University, Laband Art Gallery, Los Angeles CA

Fukuda, Ellyn, *Secy,* Queen's Medical Center Auxiliary, Queen Emma Gallery, Honolulu HI

Fuller, Richard A, *Chmn & Prof,* Wilkes University, Dept of Art, Wilkes-Barre PA (S)

Fullerton, Byron, *Dir,* Cowboy Artists of America Museum Foundation, Kerrville TX

Fullerton, Joan, *Instr,* Laramie County Community College, Division of Arts & Humanities, Cheyenne WY (S)

Fullford, Gladys, *Business Mgr,* Whatcom Museum of History and Art, Bellingham WA

Fulton, Carol, *Registrar,* Craft and Folk Art Museum, Los Angeles CA

Fulton, Duncan, *Pres,* Amerind Foundation, Inc, Fulton-Hayden Memorial Library, Dragoon AZ

Fulton, Ken, *Instr,* Northwest Community College, Dept of Art, Powell WY (S)

Fulton, Marianne, *Sr Cur,* International Museum of Photography at George Eastman House, Rochester NY

Fulton, William Duncan, *Pres,* Amerind Foundation, Inc, Amerind Museum, Fulton-Hayden Memorial Art Gallery, Dragoon AZ

Fumasi, Eddie, *Registrar & Cur,* Frederick R Weisman Art Foundation, Los Angeles CA

Fundenburke, Amy, *Exhib Cur,* Arts Council, Inc, Winston-Salem NC

Funderburk, Brent, *Assoc Prof,* Mississippi State University, Art Dept, Mississippi State MS (S)

Fundingsland, Marilyn, *Exhib Coordr,* North Dakota Museum of Art, Grand Forks ND

Funk, Charlotte, *Instr,* Texas Tech University, Dept of Art, Lubbock TX (S)

Funk, Kathryn, *Dir,* San Jose Institute of Contemporary Art, San Jose CA

Funk, Robert, *Pres,* Cornish College of the Arts, Art Dept, Seattle WA (S)

Funk, Tamara, *Cur Educ,* Historical Society of York County, York PA

Funk, Tom, *Prof,* Ocean County College, Humanities Dept, Toms River NJ (S)

Funk, Verne, *Prof,* Texas Tech University, Dept of Art, Lubbock TX (S)

Furches, Harry, *Assoc Prof,* Murray State University, Art Dept, Murray KY (S)

Furchgott, David, *Exec Dir,* International Sculpture Center, Washington DC

Furdell, William J, *Div Chmn & Prof,* College of Great Falls, Humanities Div, Great Falls MT (S)

Furgol, Edward, *Cur,* Naval Historical Center, The Navy Museum, Washington DC

Furman, David, *Prof Ceramics & Pottery,* Pitzer College, Dept of Art, Claremont CA (S)

Furman, Evelyn E, *Cur,* Tabor Opera House Museum, Leadville CO

Furman, Roy L, *Treas,* Guild Hall of East Hampton, Inc, Guild Hall Museum, East Hampton NY

Furman, Serena, *Designer,* Museum of Our National Heritage, Lexington MA

Furst, Donald, *Asst Prof,* University of North Carolina at Wilmington, Dept of Fine Arts - Division of Art, Wilmington NC (S)

Furstenberg, James H, *Cur Public Prog,* Honolulu Academy of Arts, Honolulu HI

Furtak, Rosemary, *Librn,* Walker Art Center, Staff Reference Library, Minneapolis MN

Furubotn, Eric, *Instr,* Dowling College, Dept of Visual Arts, Oakdale NY (S)

Fusco, Pet, *Cur of European Sculpture & Works of Art,* Getty Center for the History of Art & the Humanities Trust Museum, The J Paul Getty Museum, Santa Monica CA

Fusco, Peter, *Cur of European Sculpture & Works of Art,* Getty Center for the History of Art & the Humanities Trust Museum, Santa Monica CA

Fusich, Monica, *Art Selector,* University of California, Library, Riverside CA

Fustukian, Sam, *Dir,* University of South Florida, Library, Tampa FL

Futernick, Robert, *Conservator Paper,* Fine Arts Museums of San Francisco, M H de Young Memorial Museum and California Palace of the Legion of Honor, San Francisco CA

Fyfe, Jo, *Dept Chmn,* Spokane Falls Community College, Fine & Applied Arts Div, Spokane WA (S)

Fzalay, Marilyn, *Instr,* Cuyahoga Community College, Dept of Art, Cleveland OH (S)

Gabak, Peter, *Cur,* Cayuga Museum of History and Art, Auburn NY

Gabak, Peter, *Acting Librn,* Cayuga Museum of History and Art, Library, Auburn NY

Gabarra, Ed, *Adminr,* Mission San Luis Rey Museum, San Luis Rey CA

Gabarro, Marilyn, *Co-Chmn Design,* Massachusetts College of Art, Boston MA (S)

Gabel, David, *Preparator,* Syracuse University, Art Collection, Syracuse NY

Gabel, Marlene, *Exec Dir,* Contemporary Crafts Association and Gallery, Portland OR

Gaber-Hotchkiss, Magda, *Assoc Librn,* Hancock Shaker Village, Inc, Library, Pittsfield MA

Gabriel, Robert, *Dir,* Southern Highland Handicraft Guild, Folk Art Center, Asheville NC

Gaddis, Robert, *Div Head,* Campbellsville College, Fine Arts Division, Campbellsville KY (S)

Gadson, James, *Assoc Prof,* University of North Carolina at Chapel Hill, Art Dept, Chapel Hill NC (S)

Gaetz, Georgina, *Dir,* Revelstoke Art Group, Revelstoke BC

Gaffney, Gary, *Chmn,* Art Academy of Cincinnati, Cincinnati OH (S)

Gaffney, Richard W, *Chmn,* Wagner College, Performing & Visual Arts Dept, Staten Island NY (S)

Gage, Frances, *Instr,* Toronto School of Art, Toronto ON (S)

Gage, Mary M, *Dir,* Mohawk Valley Heritage Association, Inc, Walter Elwood Museum, Amsterdam NY

Gage, Robert, *Chmn,* Waubonsee Community College, Art Dept, Sugar Grove IL (S)

Gagnier, Bruce, *Instr,* New York Studio School of Drawing, Painting and Sculpture, New York NY (S)

Gagnon, Francois Marc, *Instr,* Universite de Montreal, Dept of Art History, Montreal PQ (S)

Gagnon, Paulette, *Cur,* Musee d'art contemporain de Montreal, Montreal PQ

Gagnon, Sylvie, *Dir,* Societe Des Musees Quebecois, Montreal PQ

Gaiber, Maxine, *Public Relations,* Newport Harbor Art Museum, Newport Beach CA

Gaige, Helen, *Chmn,* State University of New York College at New Paltz, Art Education Dept, New Paltz NY (S)

Gaillard, K, *Admin Services,* Heublein, Inc, Farmington CT

Gaines, C T, *Prof,* Presbyterian College, Fine Arts Dept, Clinton SC (S)

Gaines, Helen E, *Dir,* Las Vegas Art Museum, Las Vegas NV

Gaither, Edmund B, *Dir & Cur,* Museum of the National Center of Afro-American Artists, Boston MA

Gaither, James L, *Instr,* Casper College, Dept of Visual Arts, Casper WY (S)

Galassi, Peter, *Dir Dept Photography,* Museum of Modern Art, New York NY

Galavaris, G, *Prof,* McGill University, Department of Art History, Montreal PQ (S)

Galbraith, Lynn, *Asst Prof Art Educ,* University of Arizona, Dept of Art, Tucson AZ (S)

Galczenski, Marian, *Instr,* Cuesta College, Art Dept, San Luis Obispo CA (S)

Galembo, Phyllis, *Assoc Prof,* State University of New York at Albany, Art Dept, Albany NY (S)

Galer, Beth, *Dir Development,* Fuller Museum of Art, Brockton MA

Gallacci, Paul, *Midwest Representative,* American Society of Artists, Inc, Chicago IL

Gallagher, Christy, *Secy,* New Haven Paint and Clay Club, Inc, New Haven CT

Gallagher, Edward P, *Dir,* National Academy School of Fine Arts, New York NY (S)

Gallagher, Edward P, *Dir,* National Academy of Design, New York NY

Gallagher, Edward P, *Dir,* National Academy of Design, Archives, New York NY

Gallagher, Frank, *Pres,* Nevada Museum Of Art, Reno NV

Gallagher, James, *Pres,* Philadelphia College of Textiles & Science, School of Textiles, Philadelphia PA (S)

Gallagher, Jean, *Instr,* California State University, Chico, Art Dept, Chico CA (S)

Gallagher, Marsha V, *Chief Cur, Cur Material Culture,* Joslyn Art Museum, Omaha NE

Gallahen, Ulla, *Board Dir,* Artists' Cooperative Gallery, Omaha NE

Gallant, Michele, *Registrar & Preparator,* Dalhousie University, Art Gallery, Halifax NS

Gallas, Ron, *Asst Prof,* Saint Olaf College, Art Dept, Northfield MN (S)

Gallatin, Gaile, *Chmn,* Muskingum College, Art Department, New Concord OH (S)

Gallett, Kelly, *Admin Asst,* Tempe Arts Center, Tempe AZ

Galligan, David, *Admin Dir,* Walker Art Center, Minneapolis MN

Gallo, Frank, *In Charge Sculpture,* University of Illinois, Urbana-Champaign, School of Art and Design, Champaign IL (S)

Galloway, Elizabeth, *VPres & Dir,* Art Center College of Design, James Lemont Fogg Memorial Library, Pasadena CA

Galloway, Gail, *Cur,* Supreme Court of the United States, Washington DC

Galloway, Helen, *Prof,* Saint Mary's College of Minnesota, Art Dept No 18, Winona MN (S)

Galloway, Hugh, *Chmn,* McMaster University, Dept of Art and Art History, Hamilton ON (S)

Galloway, Jan, *Dir,* Crook County Museum and Art Gallery, Sundance WY

Galloway, John, *Lectr,* California Lutheran University, Art Dept, Thousand Oaks CA (S)

Galloway, Mary Lou, *Mgr IL Artisans Shop,* Illinois State Museum, Southern Illinois Arts & Crafts Marketplace, Chicago IL

Galloway, Patricia, *Dir Special Projects,* Mississippi Department of Archives and History, State Historical Museum, Jackson MS

Galloway, Robert, *Chmn Dept Art,* Mesa Community College, Dept of Art & Art History, Mesa AZ (S)

Galloway, Thomas D, *Dean,* Georgia Institute of Technology, College of Architecture, Atlanta GA (S)

Galvin, Susan A, *Trustee,* Hill-Stead Museum, Farmington CT

Gamache, Alan, *Assoc Prof,* University of Wisconsin-Stout, Dept of Art & Design, Menomonie WI (S)

Gambill, Norman, *Head Dept,* South Dakota State University, Dept of Visual Arts, Brookings SD (S)

Gamble, Steven G, *Pres,* Southern Arkansas University, Art Dept Gallery & Magale Art Gallery, Magnolia AR

Gamblin, Noriko, *Cur,* Long Beach Museum of Art, Long Beach CA

Gammon, Helen, *Treas,* Keokuk Art Center, Keokuk IA

Gammon, Lynda, *Assoc Prof,* University of Victoria, Dept of Visual Arts, Victoria BC (S)

Gamwell, Lyn, *Dir,* State University of New York at Binghamton, University Art Gallery, Vestal NY

Gandara, Nancy, *Asst Dir,* San Antonio Public Library, Dept of Fine Arts, San Antonio TX

Gandee, Cynthia, *Dir,* University of Tampa, Henry B Plant Museum, Tampa FL

Gandy, Janice, *Art Historian,* University of South Alabama, Dept of Art, Mobile AL (S)

Ganem, Cynthia, *Treas,* Arizona Artist Guild, Phoenix AZ

Gangitano, Lia, *Asst Registrar,* Institute of Contemporary Art, Boston MA

Gann, Dan, *Division Head,* Indianapolis Marion County Public Library, Arts Division, Indianapolis IN

Ganong, Overton G, *Exec Dir,* South Carolina State Museum, Columbia SC

Gans, Lucy, *Prof,* Lehigh University, Dept of Art and Architecture, Bethlehem PA (S)

Ganser, Debbie, *Dept Secy,* University of Wisconsin, Madison, Dept of Art History, Madison WI (S)

Ganstrom, Linda, *Instr,* Barton County Community College, Fine Arts Dept, Great Bend KS (S)

Gant, Ella, *Instr,* Hamilton College, Art Dept, Clinton NY (S)

Gant, Sally, *Educ Coordr,* Old Salem Inc, Museum of Early Southern Decorative Arts, Winston-Salem NC

Ganteaume, Cecile R, *Asst Cur,* National Museum of the American Indian, New York NY

Gantner, Ellen, *Dir ILL Artisans Prog,* Illinois State Museum, Illinois Artisans Shop, Chicago IL

Gantner, Ellen, *Dir ILL Artisans Prog,* Illinois State Museum, Southern Illinois Arts & Crafts Marketplace, Chicago IL

Gantner, Ellen, *Dir IL Artisans Prog,* Illinois State Museum, Lincoln Home National Historic Site, Chicago IL

Ganz, Howard, *Instr,* Miracosta College, Art Dept, Oceanside CA (S)

Gappmayer, Sam, *Dir,* Salt Lake Art Center, Salt Lake City UT

Garand, Henri, *Chmn,* Mount Royal College, Dept of Interior Design, Calgary AB (S)

Garay, Olga, *Dir Cultural Affairs,* Miami-Dade Community College, Wolfson Campus, Frances Wolfson Art Gallery, Miami FL

Garay, Olga, *Dir Cultural Affairs,* Miami-Dade Community College, Wolfson Campus, InterAmerican Art Gallery, Miami FL

Garay, Olga, *Dir Cultural Affairs,* Miami-Dade Community College, Wolfson Campus, Centre Gallery, Miami FL

Garballey, Jim, *Head Sign Painting,* Butera School of Art, Boston MA (S)

Garbee, Robert, *Asst Prof,* Lynchburg College, Art Dept, Lynchburg VA (S)

Garcia, Hector, *Assoc Prof,* Indiana-Purdue University, Dept of Fine Arts, Fort Wayne IN (S)

Garcia, Maria Teresa, *Cur of Educ,* Southern Methodist University, Meadows Museum, Dallas TX

Garcia-Gutierrez, Enrique, *Assoc Prof,* University of Puerto Rico, Dept of Fine Arts, Rio Piedras PR (S)

Gard, Bruce, *Dept Head,* North Dakota State School of Science, Dept of Graphic Arts, Wahpeton ND (S)

Gardiner, Allen R, *Instr,* Portland School of Art, Portland ME (S)

Gardiner, George, *Pres,* Gilbert Stuart Memorial Association, Inc, Museum, Saunderstown RI

Gardiner, Paul, *Temporary Exhibits,* Alaska State Museum, Juneau AK

Gardner, Doll, *Office Admin,* West Hills Unitarian Fellowship, Portland OR

Gardner, Frederick, *Dean,* California Institute of the Arts Library, Santa Clarita CA

Gardner, Frederick, *Head, Computer Serv,* California Institute of the Arts Library, Santa Clarita CA

Gardner, Jack, *Branch Adminr,* Las Vegas-Clark County Library District, Las Vegas NV

Gardner, Janet, *Dir,* Spoon River College, Art Dept, Canton IL (S)

Gardner, Sandra, *Educator,* Pasadena Historical Society, Pasadena CA

Gardner, William, *Chmn Div Communications & Humanities,* Lewis and Clark Community College, Art Dept, Godfrey IL (S)

Gardner, William F, *Chmn,* North Florida Junior College, Dept Humanities & Art, Madison FL (S)

Garfield, Alan, *Chmn,* Teikyo Marycrest University, Art and Computer Graphics Dept, Davenport IA (S)

Garhart, Martin, *Prof,* Kenyon College, Art Dept, Gambier OH (S)

Garibaldi, Linn D, *Pres,* Anson County Historical Society, Inc, Wadesboro NC

Gariepy, Luce, *Asst Librn,* Musee du Quebec, Bibliotheque des Arts, Quebec PQ

Gariff, David, *Asst Prof,* Cleveland State University, Art Dept, Cleveland OH (S)

Garland, Deb, *Registrar,* Indiana University, Art Museum, Bloomington IN

Garman, Mary S, *Chmn Board,* Crook County Museum and Art Gallery, Sundance WY

Garner, William, *In Charge Art Coll & Program,* First Commercial Bank in Little Rock, Little Rock AR

Garoza, Valdis, *Chmn,* Marietta College, Grover M Hermann Fine Arts Center, Marietta OH

Garoza, Valdis, *Assoc Prof,* Marietta College, Art Dept, Marietta OH (S)

Garreck, Dennis, *Exec Dir,* Organization of Saskatchewan Arts Councils (OSAC), Regina SK

Garrels, Gary, *Cur,* Walker Art Center, Minneapolis MN

Garren, Robert F, *Chmn,* Southern College of Seventh-Day Adventists, Art Dept, Collegedale TN (S)

Garrett, James, *Ethnic Art Studies,* California College of Arts and Crafts, Oakland CA (S)

Garrett, Sidney, *Prof,* Louisiana State University, School of Art, Baton Rouge LA (S)

Garrett, Stephen, *Dir,* Armand Hammer Museum of Art & Cultural Center, Los Angeles CA

Garrison, Ann, *Office Mgr,* Birmingham-Bloomfield Art Association, Birmingham MI

Garrison, Helene, *Chmn Liberal Arts,* Art Institute of Southern California, Ruth Salyer Library, Laguna Beach CA

Garrison, Jim, *Instr,* Mesa Community College, Dept of Art & Art History, Mesa AZ (S)

Garrison, William, *Colls Mgr,* Saratoga County Historical Society, Brookside Museum, Ballston Spa NY

Garrity, Noreen Scott, *Asst Dir Educ,* Rutgers University, Stedman Art Gallery, Camden NJ

Garrott, Martha, *Dir,* Mississippi Crafts Center, Ridgeland MS

Garrow, Pascale, *Instr,* Dowling College, Dept of Visual Arts, Oakdale NY (S)

Garten, Beverly, *Asst Dean,* Eastern Illinois University, Art Dept, Charleston IL (S)

Garten, Clifford, *Prof,* Hamline University, Art Dept, Saint Paul MN (S)

Gartenmann, Donna, *City of Boulder Arts Commission,* Boulder Public Library and Gallery, Dept of Fine Arts Gallery, Boulder CO

Garthwaite, Ernest, *Assoc Prof,* York College of the City University of New York, Fine and Performing Arts, Jamaica NY (S)

Gartner, Mary, *Cur,* LeSueur Museum, LeSueur MN

Gartrell, Roberta, *Asst,* Ponca City Cultural Center & Museum, Library, Ponca City OK

Garvens, Ellen, *Asst Prof,* Oberlin College, Dept of Art, Oberlin OH (S)

Garvey, Susan Gibson, *Cur,* Dalhousie University, Art Gallery, Halifax NS

Garvey, Timothy, *Instr,* Illinois Wesleyan University, School of Art, Bloomington IL (S)

Garvin, D B, *Cur,* New Hampshire Historical Society, Concord NH

Garwell, Robert, *Dean of Fine Arts,* Texas Christian University, Art & Art History Dept, Fort Worth TX (S)

Gary, Anne-Bridget, *Asst Prof,* University of Wisconsin-Stevens Point, Dept of Art & Design, Stevens Point WI (S)

Gascon, France, *Chief Cur,* McCord Museum of Canadian History, Montreal PQ

Gasnell, Ivan, *Cur Painting,* Harvard University, William Hayes Fogg Art Museum, Cambridge MA

Gasparro, Frank, *Instr,* Samuel S Fleisher Art Memorial, Philadelphia PA (S)

Gass, Katherine, *Registrar,* The Chase Manhattan Bank, NA, Art Collection, New York NY

Gastonguay, N, *Asst Librn,* Musee du Quebec, Bibliotheque des Arts, Quebec PQ

Gastony, Endre, *Asst Prof,* Augustana College, Art Dept, Sioux Falls SD (S)

Gates, Carole C, *Instr,* Villa Maria College of Buffalo, Art Dept, Buffalo NY (S)

Gates, Elaine, *Assoc Prof,* Hood College, Dept of Art, Frederick MD (S)

Gates, H I, *Assoc Prof,* George Washington University, Dept of Art, Washington DC (S)

Gates, Jay, *Dir,* Seattle Art Museum, Seattle WA

Gates, Leigh, *Head Slide Librn,* The Art Institute of Chicago, Ryerson and Burnham Libraries, Chicago IL

Gates, Thomas P, *Art Librn,* Southern Methodist University, Hamon Arts Library, Dallas TX

Gates, Valery, *Asst Prof,* Virginia State University, Fine & Commercial Art, Petersburg VA (S)

Gatewood, Maud F, *Prof,* Averett College, Art Dept, Danville VA (S)

Gatlin, Sally, *Gallery Mgr,* Coppini Academy of Fine Arts, San Antonio TX

Gauchier, Michelle, *Librn,* Musee d'art contemporain de Montreal, Mediatheque, Montreal PQ

Gaudieri, Millicent Hall, *Exec Dir,* Association of Art Museum Directors, New York NY

Gaudreault, Andre, *Instr,* Universite de Montreal, Dept of Art History, Montreal PQ (S)

Gaughan, Tom, *Instr,* Samuel S Fleisher Art Memorial, Philadelphia PA (S)

Gaul, Elaine, *Designer,* Indiana University, William Hammond Mathers Museum, Bloomington IN

Gaul, Mitchell, *Head of Design & Installation,* San Diego Museum of Art, San Diego CA

Gauthier, Gerard J, *In Charge,* Denison University, Art Dept Slide Library, Granville OH

Gauvreau, Robert, *Division Dean,* Modesto Junior College, Arts Humanities and Speech Division, Modesto CA (S)

Gavin, Carney E S, *Exec Dir,* Harvard University, Semitic Museum, Cambridge MA

Gavin, Robin Farwell, *Cur Spanish Colonial Coll,* Museum of New Mexico, Museum of International Folk Art, Santa Fe NM

Gavio, Denise, *Asst Librn,* Princeton University, Marquand Library, Princeton NJ

Gay, Robert, *Instr,* Waynesburg College, Dept of Fine Arts, Waynesburg PA (S)

Gay, William, *Prof,* Tuskegee University, College of Arts & Sciences, Art Dept, Tuskegee Institute AL (S)

Gayer, Don, *Vol Librn,* Vizcaya Museum and Gardens, Library, Miami FL

Gaylor, Gregory, *Dir,* Sweetwater Community Fine Arts Center, Rock Springs WY

Gaylor, Robert B, *Dir,* The Center for Contemporary Arts of Santa Fe, Santa Fe NM

Gaynor, Kathy, *Asst to Dir,* Friends University, Edmund Stanley Library Gallery, Wichita KS

Gaynor, Matthew, *Instr,* California State University, San Bernardino, Art Dept, San Bernardino CA (S)

Gazda, Elaine K, *Dir,* University of Michigan, Kelsey Museum of Archaeology, Ann Arbor MI

Gazda, Elaine K, *Dir Kelsey Museum,* University of Michigan, Ann Arbor, Dept of History of Art, Ann Arbor MI (S)

Gealt, Adelheid, *Dir,* Indiana University, Art Museum, Bloomington IN

Gealt, Barry, *Prof,* Indiana University, Bloomington, Henry Radford Hope School of Fine Arts, Bloomington IN (S)

Gearey, Dave, *Instr,* Sarah Lawrence College, Dept of Art History, Bronxville NY (S)

Geary-Furniss, Judy, *Assoc Dir,* Lakeview Museum of Arts and Sciences, Peoria IL

Gebb, Wayne, *Instr,* Midway College, Art Dept, Midway KY (S)

Gebhard, David, *Cur of Architectural Drawings,* University of California, Santa Barbara, University Art Museum, Santa Barbara CA

Geddes, Eric, *Cur,* University of Oregon, Aperture Photo Gallery - EMU Art Gallery, Eugene OR

Geddes, Mathew, *Instr,* Ricks College, Dept of Art, Rexburg ID (S)

Gedeon, Lucinda H, *Dir,* State University of New York at Purchase, Neuberger Museum, Purchase NY

Gehret, L Alan, *Asst to Cur,* Audubon Wildlife Sanctuary, Audubon PA

Gehrke, Ted, *Dir,* San Jose State University, Union Gallery, San Jose CA

Gehrm, Barbara, *Archives,* Ward Foundation, Ward Museum of Wildfowl Art, Salisbury MD

Geibert, Ron, *Prof,* Wright State University, Dept of Art & Art History, Dayton OH (S)

Geibert, Ron, *Assoc Prof,* Wright State University, Dept of Art & Art History, Dayton OH (S)

Geiger, Alison, *Cur Coll,* Historical Society of Rockland County, New City NY

Geiger, Gail L, *Assoc Prof,* University of Wisconsin, Madison, Dept of Art History, Madison WI (S)

Geil, Peter Gus, *First VPres,* Springfield Museum of Art, Springfield OH

Geimzer, Eugene, *Asst Prof,* Loyola University of Chicago, Fine Arts Dept, Chicago IL (S)

Geis, Mary Christina, *Dir,* Georgian Court College Gallery, M Christina Geis Gallery, Lakewood NJ

Geis, Mary Christina, *Head Dept,* Georgian Court College, Dept of Art, Lakewood NJ (S)

Geischer, Geraldine, *Instructor,* Milwaukee Area Technical College, Graphic Arts Dept, Milwaukee WI (S)

Geisinger, William, *Instr,* De Anza College, Creative Arts Div, Cupertino CA (S)

Geist, Ronnie, *Dir of Programming,* Women's Interart Center, Inc, Interart Gallery, New York NY

Gekht, Rita R, *Artist,* New York Tapestry Artists, Carmel NY

Gelbman, Lois, *Instr,* Lakewood Community College, Humanities Dept, White Bear Lake MN (S)

Geldin, Sherri, *Assoc Dir,* The Museum of Contemporary Art, Los Angeles CA

Geller, Beatrice, *Assoc Prof,* Pacific Lutheran University, Dept of Art, Tacoma WA (S)

Gellert, J, *Dean Faculty of Arts & Sciences,* Lakehead University, Dept of Visual Arts, Thunder Bay ON (S)

Gelles, Ann, *Comptroller,* Nassau County Museum of Fine Art, Roslyn NY

Gellman, Lola B, *Chmn,* Queensborough Community College, Dept of Art and Photography, Bayside NY (S)

Geltmaker, John, *Pres,* Floyd County Museum, New Albany IN

Geltner, Frank, *Asst Dir,* University of Oregon, Aperture Photo Gallery - EMU Art Gallery, Eugene OR

Gemme, Teresa, *Gallery Coordr,* Liberty National Bank, Liberty Gallery, Louisville KY

Gendel, Bonnie, *Fine Arts Mgr,* Alverno College Gallery, Milwaukee WI

Gendel, Bonnie, *Dir,* Alverno College, Art Dept, Milwaukee WI (S)

Geneau, Rachelle, *Cur Asst,* The Canadian Craft Museum, Vancouver BC

General, John, *Dir Electronics & Kinetics,* Museum of Holography - Chicago, Chicago IL

Genevro, Rosalie, *Executive Dir,* Architectural League of New York, New York NY

Genshaft, Carole, *Educator for Schools, Prog & Resources,* Columbus Museum of Art, Resource Center, Columbus OH

Gensler, Alma, *Mgr,* Arts Club of Washington, James Monroe House, Washington DC

Genszler, Leslie, *Gallery Shop Mgr,* Madison Art Center, Madison WI

Gentner, Norma, *Asst Facility Supv,* Robert W Ryerss Library and Museum, Philadelphia PA

Gentner, Norma, *Asst Librn,* Robert W Ryerss Library and Museum, Library, Philadelphia PA

Gentry, James, *Instr,* Eastern Arizona College, Art Dept, Thatcher AZ (S)

Gentry, Kathryn, *Pres,* Headley-Whitney Museum, Lexington KY

Gentry, Sandra, *Admin Asst,* Pensacola Museum of Art, Pensacola FL

Geoffrion, Moira, *Prof Sculpture,* University of Arizona, Dept of Art, Tucson AZ (S)

George, David N, *Prof,* Truett-McConnell College, Arts Dept, Cleveland GA (S)

George, Susan, *Public Relations Officer,* Fraunces Tavern Museum, New York NY

George, Theresa, *Asst Treas,* Rhode Island Watercolor Society, Pawtucket RI

Georgia, Olivia, *Dir Visual Arts,* Snug Harbor Cultural Center, Newhouse Center for Contemporary Art, Staten Island NY

Georgias, Andrew, *Prof,* Glendale Community College, Dept of Fine Arts, Glendale CA (S)

Georgiou, Tyrone, *Chmn,* University at Buffalo, State University of New York, Dept of Art, Buffalo NY (S)

Gerard, Tim, *Pres,* Art Guild of Burlington, Arts for Living Center, Burlington IA

Gerardine, M, *Dir,* Caldwell College, Art Gallery, Caldwell NJ

Gerber, John, *Dir,* Ohio University, Trisolini Gallery, Athens OH

Gerber, Phyllis, *Dir Vol Servs,* Douglas County Historical Society, Fairlawn Mansion & Museum, Superior WI

Gergo, Gabor, *Assoc Prof,* University of Bridgeport, Art Dept, Bridgeport CT (S)

Gerharz, Ellen, *Dir,* Lewistown Art Center, Lewistown MT

Gerhold, William H, *Assoc Prof,* Marietta College, Art Dept, Marietta OH (S)

Gerholz, Barbara F, *Business Mgr,* Flint Institute of Arts, Flint MI

Geritz, Kathy, *Assoc Film Cur,* University of California, Pacific Film Archive, Berkeley CA

Gerlach, Monte, *Assoc Prof,* Saint Xavier University, Dept of Art, Chicago IL (S)

Gersan, Denise, *Cur of Exhib,* University of Miami, Lowe Art Museum, Coral Gables FL

Gersan, Denise, *Cur,* University of Miami, Lowe Art Museum Reference Library, Coral Gables FL

Gershon, Bob, *Asst Prof,* Castleton State College, Art Dept, Castleton VT (S)

Gershon, Stacy, *Asst Cur,* The Chase Manhattan Bank, NA, Art Collection, New York NY

Gerson, Paula, *Treas,* International Center of Medieval Art, Inc, New York NY

Gerstein, Marc, *Assoc Prof,* University of Toledo, Dept of Art, Toledo OH (S)

Gerstner, Crace, *Admin Asst,* University of Colorado at Colorado Springs, Gallery of Contemporary Art, Colorado Springs CO

Gertjejansen, Doyle J, *Prof,* University of New Orleans-Lake Front, Dept of Fine Arts, New Orleans LA (S)

Gertmenian, Doris N, *Library Chmn,* Univ of Southern California, Greene & Greene Library of the Arts & Crafts Movement, San Marino CA

Gervais, Sylvie, *Consultation of Coll,* National Archives of Canada, Documentary Art and Photography, Ottawa ON

Gesualdi, Cani, *Mgr,* City of Gainesville, Thomas Center Galleries - Cultural Affairs, Gainesville FL

Gettinger, Edmond, *Chmn Art Dept,* Western Illinois University, Art Dept, Macomb IL (S)

Getty, Louanne, *Instr,* Hamilton College, Art Dept, Clinton NY (S)

Getz, Lowell, *Cur Malacology,* University of Illinois, Museum of Natural History, Champaign IL

Gevins, Jack, *Instr,* Bucks County Community College, Fine Arts Dept, Newtown PA (S)

Geyer, Eddie Joyce, *Vol Coordr,* Saint Augustine Historical Society, Oldest House and Museums, Saint Augustine FL

Geyer, George E, *Instr,* Rancho Santiago College, Art Dept, Santa Ana CA (S)

Ghannam, Edward, *Assoc Prof,* University of Miami, Dept of Art & Art History, Coral Gables FL (S)

Gheen, Donald, *Sculptor,* Madonna College, Art Dept, Livonia MI (S)

Ghez, Susanne, *Dir,* The Renaissance Society, Chicago IL

Ghirrardo, Raymond, *Prof,* Ithaca College, Fine Art Dept, Ithaca NY (S)

Ghiz, Ronald, *Assoc Prof,* University of Maine, Art Dept, Orono ME (S)

Giacoletti, Larry, *Exhib Asst,* National Art Museum of Sport, Indianapolis IN

Gianini, Paul, *Pres,* Valencia Community College, Art Gallery-East Campus, Orlando FL

Gianvito, John, *Asst Prof,* University of Massachusetts at Boston, Art Dept, Boston MA (S)

Giarrizzo, John, *Instr,* Northwest Community College, Dept of Art, Powell WY (S)

Gibbons, Arthur, *Dir Program,* Bard College, Milton Avery Graduate School of the Arts, Annandale-on-Hudson NY (S)

Gibbons, Cathleen, *Educ Coordr,* University of Chicago, David and Alfred Smart Museum of Art, Chicago IL

Gibbons, Hugh, *Prof,* Texas Tech University, Dept of Art, Lubbock TX (S)

Gibbons, Janice, *Instr,* John C Calhoun State Community College, Division of Fine Arts, Decatur AL (S)

Gibbons, Jerry, *Chmn of Humanities Div,* Williams Baptist College, Dept of Art, College City AR (S)

Gibbons, Jim, *Asst Prof,* Shorter College, Art Dept, Rome GA (S)

Gibbs, Barbara K, *Dir,* Crocker Art Museum, Sacramento CA

Gibbs, Bonnie, *Cur,* Principia College, School of Nations Museum, Elsah IL

Gibbs, Jocelyn, *Consultant,* Saving & Preserving Arts & Cultural Environments, Spaces Library and Archive, Los Angeles CA

Gibbs, Judy, *Development Coordr,* Amon Carter Museum, Fort Worth TX

Gibbs, Katherine, *Coordr Drawing & Painting,* Iowa State University, Dept of Art and Design, Ames IA (S)

Gibbs, Lora Lee, *Cur Educ,* Newport Art Museum, Newport RI

Gibbs, Maurice E, *Exec Dir,* Nantucket Historical Association, Historic Nantucket, Nantucket MA

Gibbs, Sally, *Asst to Dir,* Jackson County Historical Society, John Wornall House Museum, Independence MO

Gibbs, Tom, *Instr,* Loras College, Dept of Art, Dubuque IA (S)

Gibson, Ben, *Fine Arts Representative,* Edinboro University of Pennsylvania, Art Dept, Edinboro PA (S)

Gibson, Candis, *Admin Asst,* Bakersfield Art Foundation, Bakersfield Museum of Art, Bakersfield CA

GIbson, Cathy, *Educ Office,* Malaspina College, Nanaimo Art Gallery & Exhibition Centre, Nanaimo BC

Gibson, Edward, *Dir,* Jones Memorial Library, Jones Memorial Library, Lynchburg VA

Gibson, E M, *Dir,* Simon Fraser University, Simon Fraser Gallery, Burnaby BC

Gibson, Jay, *Asst Dir,* Sculpture Center Inc, New York NY

Gibson, Jim, *Prof,* Northern State University, Art Dept, Aberdeen SD (S)

Gibson, Jim, *Gallery Dir,* Northern State University, Art Galleries, Aberdeen SD

Gibson, Michael, *Gallery Store Supvr,* Mendel Art Gallery and Civic Conservatory, Saskatoon SK

Gibson, Robert, *Asst Prof,* Mississippi University for Women, Division of Fine & Performing Arts, Columbus MS (S)

Gibson, Sandra, *Exec Dir,* Public Corporation for the Arts, Visual & Performing Arts Registry, Long Beach CA

Gibson, Sarah S, *Librn,* Sterling and Francine Clark Art Institute, Clark Art Institute Library, Williamstown MA

Gibson, Walter, *Prof,* Case Western Reserve University, Dept of Art History & Art, Cleveland OH (S)

Gibson, Wend Enger, *Exhibit Chmn,* Middlesex County Cultural & Heritage Commission, Artists League of Central New Jersey, North Brunswick NJ

Gibson-Wood, Carol, *Asst Prof,* University of Victoria, Dept of History in Art, Victoria BC (S)

Gide, Thomas D, *Head Sculpture,* Southern Illinois University at Edwardsville, Dept of Art & Design, Edwardsville IL (S)

Giebel, Douglas, *Assoc Prof,* Roberts Wesleyan College, Art Dept, Rochester NY (S)

Gieber, Terry, *Chmn,* Gonzaga University, Dept of Art, Spokane WA (S)

Giese, David, *Dept Chmn,* University of Idaho, College of Art & Architecture, Moscow ID (S)

Giffen, Sarah, *Educator,* Old York Historical Society, Gaol Museum, York ME

Giffiths, Marion, *Gallery Dir,* Sculpture Center Inc, New York NY

Gifford, Dorenda J, *Cur Educ,* Alexandria Museum of Art, Alexandria LA

Giffuni, Flora B, *Pres,* Pastel Society of America, National Arts Club Gallery, New York NY

Gikas, Carol S, *Exec Dir,* Louisiana Arts and Science Center, Baton Rouge LA

Gikas, Carol S, *Exec Dir,* Louisiana Arts and Science Center, Library, Baton Rouge LA

Gilbart, Helen, *Acting Dir,* Saint Petersburg Junior College, Humanities Dept, Saint Petersburg FL (S)

Gilbert, Ann, *Archivist,* United Society of Shakers, Shaker Museum, Poland Spring ME

Gilbert, Anne, *Archivist,* United Society of Shakers, The Shaker Library, Poland Spring ME

Gilbert, Barbara, *Cur,* Hebrew Union College, Skirball Museum, Los Angeles CA

Gilbert, Cathy, *Cur,* Riverside County Museum, Edward-Dean Museum, Cherry Valley CA

Gilbert, Gail R, *Head Art Library,* University of Louisville, Margaret M Bridwell Art Library, Louisville KY

Gilbert, Humphrey, *Assoc Prof,* University of Wisconsin-Stout, Dept of Art & Design, Menomonie WI (S)

Gilbert, Johnnie Mae, *Pres,* Tougaloo College, Art Dept, Tougaloo MS (S)

Gilbert, Samantha, *Adminr,* The Jewish Museum, New York NY

Gilbert, S Parker, *Pres,* Pierpont Morgan Library, New York NY

Gilchrist, John, *Public Relations,* Glenbow Museum, Calgary AB

Gilden, Anita, *Librn,* Philadelphia Museum of Art, Library, Philadelphia PA

Gilens, Todd, *Exhibition Coordr,* The Community Education Center, Philadelphia PA

Giles, Christine, *Head Register,* Wolfsonian Foundation, Miami Beach FL

Giles, Linda Mary, *Financial Officer,* Art Gallery of Greater Victoria, Victoria BC

Giles, Mary, *Asst Archivist,* Charleston Museum, Library, Charleston SC

Giles, Millie, *Adjunct Asst Prof,* Texas Woman's University, Dept of Visual Arts, Denton TX (S)

Gilg, Karen, *Prof,* University of Maine at Augusta, Division of Fine & Performing Arts, Augusta ME (S)

Gilg, Keran, *Dir,* University of Maine at Augusta, Jewett Gallery, Augusta ME

Gilizee, M, *Dir Photography,* Art Institute of Fort Lauderdale, Fort Lauderdale FL (S)

Gilkey, Gordon, *Instr,* Pacific Northwest College of Art, Portland OR (S)

Gill, Cecil, *Dir,* Roberts County Museum, Miami TX

Gill, Charles, *Printmaking,* California College of Arts and Crafts, Oakland CA (S)

Gill, Madeline, *Pres,* St Tammany Art Association, Covington LA

Gillentine, Jane, *Librn,* School of American Research, Library, Santa Fe NM

Gillerman, David, *Asst Prof,* Providence College, Art and Art History Dept, Providence RI (S)

Gillespie, David M, *Dir,* Frostburg State University, Lewis J Ort Library, Frostburg MD

Gillespie, Gary, *Chmn,* Glenville State College, Dept of Fine Arts, Glenville WV (S)

Gillett, Marnie, *Dir,* San Francisco Camerawork Inc, San Francisco CA

Gilleylen, Tom, *Facilities & Security Mgr,* The Phillips Collection, Washington DC

Gillham, Margaret, *Cur,* Art Museum of South Texas, Corpus Christi TX

Gilliam, Scott, *Sculpture Chmn,* Atlanta College of Art, Atlanta GA (S)

Gilligan, Lorraine, *Cur,* Planting Fields Foundation, Coe Hall at Planting Fields Arboretum, Oyster Bay NY

Gilliland, Cynthia, *Asst Registrar,* Dartmouth College, Hood Museum of Art, Hanover NH

Gillis, Jean, *Cur Botanical Science,* Heritage Plantation of Sandwich, Sandwich MA

Gillis, Margaret J, *Chmn,* Dominican College of Blauvelt, Art Dept, Orangeburg NY (S)

Gillis, Margaret K, *VPres,* Detroit Institute of Arts, Founders Society, Detroit MI

Gillison, David, *Asst Prof,* Herbert H Lehman College, Art Dept, Bronx NY (S)

Gilmore, Jean A, *Registrar,* Brandywine River Museum, Chadds Ford PA

Gilmore, Jerry, *Art Dir,* Movimiento Artistico del Rio Salado, Inc (MARS), Phoenix AZ

Gilmore, Peter, *Dir Operations,* The Drawing Center, New York NY

Gilmore, R, *Prof,* Gonzaga University, Dept of Art, Spokane WA (S)

Gilmore, Roger, *Pres,* Portland School of Art, Portland ME (S)

Gilow, Betty, *Instr,* Rhodes College, Dept of Art, Memphis TN (S)

Gilpin, Risa, *Head Adult Servs,* Providence Athenaeum, Library, Providence RI

Gil-Roberts, H, *Treas,* Lyme Art Association, Inc, Old Lyme CT

Gimbel, Paul A, *VPres,* Mattatuck Historical Society Museum, Waterbury CT

Gimse, Malcolm, *Prof,* Saint Olaf College, Art Dept, Northfield MN (S)

Ginn, Elizabeth, *Dir,* Prairie Gallery, Grande Prairie AB

Gioello, D, *Chmn Fashion Design,* Fashion Institute of Technology, Art & Design Division, New York NY (S)

Gioffre, Dolores, *Chmn,* Woodbridge Township Cultural Arts Commission, Barron Arts Center, Woodbridge NJ

Giordana, Enrico, *Prof,* College of Mount Saint Vincent, Fine Arts Dept, Riverdale NY (S)

Gips, Terry, *Dir,* University of Maryland, College Park, Art Gallery, College Park MD

Giral, Angela, *Librn,* Columbia University, Avery Architectural and Fine Arts Library, New York NY

Girard, Jack, *Prog Dir,* Transylvania University, Studio Arts Dept, Lexington KY (S)

Girshman, Beth, *Adult Service Librn,* Jones Library, Inc, Amherst MA

Gitner, Fred J, *Library Dir,* French Institute-Alliance Francaise, Library, New York NY

Giuliano, Marie, *Business Office Supvr,* Ferguson Library, Stamford CT

Giuntini, Gilles, *Assoc Prof,* University of Hartford, Hartford Art School, West Hartford CT (S)

Givnish, Gerry, *Exec Dir,* Painted Bride Art Center, The Gallery at the Painted Bride, Philadelphia PA

Gladstone, Caroline T, *Mgr Vol Services,* Philadelphia Museum of Art, Mount Pleasant, Philadelphia PA

Glanton, Richard H, *Pres Board of Trustees,* Barnes Foundation, Merion Station PA

Glantz, Johnnie, *Chmn,* Art And Culture Center Of Hollywood, Hollywood FL

Glaser, Bruce, *Prof,* University of Bridgeport, Art Dept, Bridgeport CT (S)

Glaser, Lewis, *Prof,* Texas Christian University, Art & Art History Dept, Fort Worth TX (S)

Glaser, Walter, *Prof,* California State Polytechnic University, Pomona, Art Dept, Pomona CA (S)

Glasgow, Andrew, *Educ Dir,* Southern Highland Handicraft Guild, Folk Art Center, Asheville NC

Glasgow, Vaughn L, *Dir Spec Projects,* Louisiana Department of Culture, Recreation and Tourism, Louisiana State Museum, New Orleans LA

Glass, Charles, *VChmn,* Detroit Artists Market, Detroit MI

Glass, Christopher, *Vis Instr,* Bowdoin College, Art Dept, Brunswick ME (S)

Glass, Ritha R, *Pres,* Cumberland Art Society Inc, Cookeville Art Gallery, Cookeville TN

Glass, Simon, *Instr,* Toronto School of Art, Toronto ON (S)

Glassell, Alfred C, *Chmn Board,* Museum of Fine Arts, Houston, Houston TX

Glassford, C, *Instr,* Golden West College, Visual Art Dept, Huntington Beach CA (S)

Glassgald, Elissa, *Instr,* Main Line Center for the Arts, Haverford PA (S)

Glasson, Lloyd, *Prof,* University of Hartford, Hartford Art School, West Hartford CT (S)

Glavin, Ellen M, *Chmn Art Dept,* Emmanuel College, Art Dept, Boston MA (S)

Glazer, Helen, *Exhib Dir & Coll Coordr,* Goucher College, Rosenberg Gallery, Towson MD

Glazer, Steve, *Asst Prof,* Concord College, Fine Art Division, Athens WV (S)

Gleason, Mary Joan, *Ref Librn,* Daemen College, Marian Library, Amherst NY

Gleason, Ron, *Dir,* Tyler Museum of Art, Tyler TX

Gleason, Ron, *Dir,* Tyler Museum of Art, Reference Library, Tyler TX

Gleeman, E L, *Instr,* Normandale Community College, Bloomington MN (S)

Gleeson, Larry, *Art History Coordr,* University of North Texas, School of Visual Arts, Denton TX (S)

Glenn, Constance W, *Dir & Chief Cur,* California State University, Long Beach, University Art Museum, Long Beach CA

Glenn, Edna, *Adjunct Assoc,* College of Santa Fe, Visual Arts Dept, Santa Fe NM (S)

Glenn, Ralph F, *Chmn Art Dept,* Madonna College, Art Dept, Livonia MI (S)

Glenn, T, *Assoc Prof,* McGill University, Department of Art History, Montreal PQ (S)

Glennon, Rose M, *Cur Educ,* Marion Koogler McNay Art Museum, San Antonio TX

Gleysteen, William H, *Pres Japan Society,* Japan Society, Inc, Japan Society Gallery, New York NY

Glick, Eleanor, *Asst Cur,* Queens College, City University of New York, Godwin-Ternbach Museum, Flushing NY

Glickberg, Randy R, *Adminr,* Yeshiva University Museum, New York NY

Glidden, Germain G, *Pres,* The National Art Museum of Sport, Indianapolis IN

Glier, Nancy, *Businexx Mgr,* Contemporary Arts Center, Cincinnati OH

Globus, Dorothy Twining, *Exhib Coordr,* Cooper-Hewitt, National Museum of Design, New York NY

Gloeckler, Raymond, *Prof,* University of Wisconsin, Madison, Dept of Art, Madison WI (S)

Gloeckler, Terry, *Asst Prof,* Eastern Oregon State College, Arts & Humanities Dept, La Grande OR (S)

Gloger, Brooke, *VPres,* Washington Art Association, Washington Depot CT

Glotzbach, Tim, *Chmn,* Eastern Kentucky University, Art Dept, Richmond KY (S)

Glover, Rob, *Asst Prof,* Texas Tech University, Dept of Art, Lubbock TX (S)

Gluhman, Joseph W, *Head,* Auburn University, Dept of Art, Auburn AL (S)

Glynn, Edward, *Dean,* Maryland College of Art and Design, Silver Spring MD (S)

Goad, Albert, *Chmn,* Ashland College Arts and Humanities Gallery, Ashland OH

Goad, Albert W, *Chmn,* Ashland University, Art Dept, Ashland OH (S)

Gobble, Bonnie, *VPres,* Davidson County Art Guild Gallery, Inc, Lexington NC

Gobel, David, *Instr,* Marylhurst College, Art Dept, Marylhurst OR (S)

Goddard, Stephen, *Cur Prints,* University of Kansas, Spencer Museum of Art, Lawrence KS

Goddard, Stephen, *Assoc Prof,* University of Kansas, Kress Foundation Dept of Art History, Lawrence KS (S)

Godel, Larry, *Chmn Dept,* Northeast Community College, Dept of Liberal Arts, Norfolk NE (S)

Godfrey, Judy, *Dir,* Centenary College of Louisiana, Meadows Museum of Art, Shreveport LA

Godfrey, Martha, *Asst Cur,* University of California, Los Angeles, Visual Resource Collection, Los Angeles CA

Godfrey, Robert, *Head Dept,* Western Carolina University, Dept of Art, Cullowhee NC (S)

Godfrey, William, *Pres,* The Art Guild, Farmington CT

Godlewski, Henry, *Assoc Prof,* Mohawk Valley Community College, Advertising Design and Production, Utica NY (S)

Godlewski, Susan Glover, *Assoc Librn & Head Reference Dept,* The Art Institute of Chicago, Ryerson and Burnham Libraries, Chicago IL

Godsey, William, *Instr,* John C Calhoun State Community College, Division of Fine Arts, Decatur AL (S)

Godwin, Stan, *Asst Prof,* East Texas State University, Dept of Art, East Texas Station, Commerce TX (S)

Goehlich, John, *Dept Head,* Ray College of Design, Chicago IL (S)

Goeke, Mary Ellen, *Registrar,* Cincinnati Museum Association, Cincinnati Art Museum, Cincinnati OH

Goering, Douglas, *Chmn Dept Visual Arts,* Albion College, Dept of Visual Arts, Albion MI (S)

Goering, Douglas, *Assoc Prof,* Albion College, Dept of Visual Arts, Albion MI (S)

Goering, Karen M, *Exec VPres,* Missouri Historical Society, Saint Louis MO

Goetemann, Gordon, *Prof,* College of Saint Benedict, Art Dept, Saint Joseph MN (S)

Goetz, Linda, *Librn,* West Bend Gallery of Fine Arts, West Bend WI

Goetz, Mary Anna, *Instr,* Woodstock School of Art, Inc, Woodstock NY (S)

Goetz, Nancy, *Asst Prof,* Colby College, Art Dept, Waterville ME (S)

Goff, Lila J, *Asst to Dir for Libraries & Museum Coll,* Minnesota Historical Society, Saint Paul MN

Goffe, Gwen, *Assoc Dir Finance & Admin,* Museum of Fine Arts, Houston, Houston TX

Goffen, Rona, *Prof,* Rutgers, the State University of New Jersey, Graduate Program in Art History, New Brunswick NJ (S)

Goist, David, *Chief Conservator,* North Carolina Museum of Art, Raleigh NC

Golahny, Amy, *Chmn Dept Asst Prof,* Lycoming College, Art Dept, Williamsport PA (S)

Gold, Lawrence, *Assoc Prof,* Pacific Lutheran University, Dept of Art, Tacoma WA (S)

Goldberg, Glenn, *Instr,* New York Studio School of Drawing, Painting and Sculpture, New York NY (S)

Goldberg, Joshua, *Cur of Education,* University of Arizona, Museum of Art, Tucson AZ

Goldberg, Kenneth, *Information Specialist,* Northeast Ohio Areawide Coordinating Agency (NOACA), Information Resource Center, Cleveland OH

Goldberg, Monica, *Instr,* Ocean City Art Center, Ocean City NJ (S)

Goldberg, Shirley, *Co Chair Interior Design,* Academy of Art College, Fine Arts Dept, San Francisco CA (S)

Goldberg, Steven, *Art Specialist,* Portland Public Library, Art Dept, Portland ME

Goldblat, Aaron, *Dir Exhibits,* Please Touch Museum, Philadelphia PA

Golden, Jackie, *Vis Asst Prof,* University of Arkansas, Art Dept, Fayetteville AR (S)

Golden, Joe, *Pres,* Spirit Square Center for the Arts, Charlotte NC

Golden, Judith, *Prof Photography,* University of Arizona, Dept of Art, Tucson AZ (S)

Golden, Morton, *Deputy Dir,* Museum of Fine Arts, Boston MA

Golden, Thelma, *Branch Dir,* Whitney Museum of American Art, Whitney Museum at Philip Morris, New York NY

Golden, Vivian, *Trustee,* Foundation for Today's Art, Nexus Gallery, Philadelphia PA

Goldfarb, Barbara, *First VPres,* Monmouth Museum and Cultural Center, Lincroft NJ

Goldfarb, Hilliard T, *Cur,* Isabella Stewart Gardner Museum, Boston MA

Goldich, Louis, *Registrar,* San Diego Museum of Art, San Diego CA

Goldin, Ellen, *Instr,* Dowling College, Dept of Visual Arts, Oakdale NY (S)

Goldman, Nancy, *Library Head,* University of California, Pacific Film Archive, Berkeley CA

Goldman, Shifra, *Instr,* Rancho Santiago College, Art Dept, Santa Ana CA (S)

Goldman, Shirley, *Pres,* Pence Gallery, Davis CA

Goldman, Stewart, *Chmn,* Art Academy of Cincinnati, Cincinnati OH (S)

Goldman, Susan, *Resident Printer,* Pyramid Atlantic, Riverdale MD

Goldner, George, *Cur Paintings & Drawings,* Getty Center for the History of Art & the Humanities Trust Museum, Santa Monica CA

Goldner, George, *Cur Paintings & Drawings,* Getty Center for the History of Art & the Humanities Trust Museum, The J Paul Getty Museum, Santa Monica CA

Goldsborough, Jennifer, *Chief Cur,* Maryland Historical Society, Library, Baltimore MD

Goldsborough, Jennifer F, *Chief Cur,* Maryland Historical Society, Museum of Maryland History, Baltimore MD

Goldschmidt, Eva, *Catalog Librn,* French Institute-Alliance Francaise, Library, New York NY

Goldsleger, Cheryl, *Dept Head,* Piedmont College, Art Dept, Demorest GA (S)

Goldsmith, B D, *VChmn,* Town of Cummington Historical Commission, Kingman Tavern Historical Museum, Cummington MA

Goldsmith, Christopher, *Admin Dir,* Milwaukee Art Museum, Milwaukee WI

Goldsmith, Robert B, *Deputy Dir Admin,* Frick Collection, New York NY

Goldstein, Alan, *Instr,* Bucks County Community College, Fine Arts Dept, Newtown PA (S)

Goldstein, Andrea, *Librn,* Temple University, Tyler School of Art Library, Philadelphia PA

Goldstein, Audrey, *Chmn Fine Arts,* New England School of Art & Design, Boston MA (S)

Goldstein, Gabriel, *Asst Cur,* Yeshiva University Museum, New York NY

Goldstein, Howard, *Chmn Dept,* Trenton State College, Art Dept, Trenton NJ (S)

Goldstein, Howard, *Chmn,* Trenton State College, College Art Gallery, Trenton NJ

Goldstein, Karen, *Cur Exhib,* Pilgrim Society, Pilgrim Hall Museum, Plymouth MA

Goldstein, Linda, *Dir,* Frank Lloyd Wright Pope-Leighey House, Mount Vernon VA

Goldstein, Linda, *Dir,* Woodlawn Plantation, Mount Vernon VA

Goldstein, Marilyn, *Prof,* C W Post Center of Long Island University, School of Visual & Performing Arts, Greenvale NY (S)

Goldstein, Nathan, *Chmn Found Dept,* Art Institute of Boston, Boston MA (S)

Goldstine, Stephen, *Graduate Studies,* California College of Arts and Crafts, Oakland CA (S)

Goldstone, Lois, *Pres,* Boothbay Region Art Foundation, Inc, Brick House Gallery, Boothbay Harbor ME

Goler, Robert, *Cur Decorative Arts,* Chicago Historical Society, Chicago IL

Goley, Mary Anne, *Dir,* Federal Reserve Board, Art Gallery, Washington DC

Golik, Jay, *Prof,* Napa Valley College, Art Dept, Napa CA (S)

Golino, Michael, *Exhibit Designer,* Museum of Photographic Arts, Balboa Park CA

Gollier, J, *Chmn Photography,* Fashion Institute of Technology, Art & Design Division, New York NY (S)

Golomb, Katherine, *Dir of Public Servs,* Ferguson Library, Stamford CT

Gomas, Ralph, *Instr,* College of the Sequoias, Art Dept, Visalia CA (S)

Gomez, Elisa, *Pres,* Kean College of New Jersey, Union NJ

Gomez, Martin, *Dir Library Servs,* Oakland Public Library, Art, Music & Recreation Section, Oakland CA

Gomez, Mirta, *Assoc Prof,* Florida International University, Visual Arts Dept, Miami FL (S)

Gomez, Peter J, *Pres,* Pilgrim Society, Pilgrim Hall Museum, Plymouth MA

Gonchar, Nancy, *Exec Dir,* New Langton Arts, San Francisco CA

Goncher, Dennis D, *Dir,* School of Airbrush Arts, Villa Park IL (S)

Gong, Stephen, *Gen Mgr,* University of California, Pacific Film Archive, Berkeley CA

Gontz, Richard A, *Exec Dir,* Indiana State Museum, Indianapolis IN

Gonzales, Felice, *VPres,* Guadalupe Historic Foundation, Santuario de Guadalupe, Santa Fe NM

Gonzales, Paul, *Dir,* Institute of American Indian Arts Museum, Santa Fe NM

Gonzales, Paul, *Dir,* Institute of American Indian Arts Museum, Santa Fe NM (S)

Gonzalez, Anna, *Managing Dir,* Installation Gallery, San Diego CA

Gonzalez, Manuel, *Exec Dir & VPres,* The Chase Manhattan Bank, NA, Art Collection, New York NY

Gonzalez, Ondina, *Dir,* Berry College, Memorial Library, Mount Berry GA

Gonzalez, Ray, *Literature Prog Dir,* Guadalupe Cultural Arts Center, San Antonio TX

Gonzalez, Ruben, *Artist-in-Residence,* Western New Mexico University, Dept of Expressive Arts, Silver City NM (S)

Gooch, Peter, *Asst Prof,* University of Dayton, Visual Arts Dept, Dayton OH (S)

Good, Mary, *Dir Advertising Design & Fashion Illustration,* Art Institute of Fort Lauderdale, Fort Lauderdale FL (S)

Goodale, David, *Pres,* Kauai Museum, Lihue HI

Goode, Carm, *Assoc Prof,* Loyola Marymount University, Art & Art History Dept, Los Angeles CA (S)

Goodenough, Daniel W, *Pres,* Academy of the New Church, Glencairn Museum, Bryn Athyn PA

Goodheart, John, *Dir,* Indiana University, Bloomington, Henry Radford Hope School of Fine Arts, Bloomington IN (S)

Goodhue, Timothy, *Registrar,* Yale University, Yale Center for British Art, New Haven CT

Goodison, Michael, *Prog Coordr & Archivist,* Smith College, Museum of Art, Northampton MA

Goodkind, Joan, *Librn,* Simon's Rock College of Bard, Library, Great Barrington MA

Goodman, Bill, *Instr,* Hibbing Community College, Art Dept, Hibbing MN (S)

Goodman, Herb, *Asst Prof,* Louisiana State University, School of Art, Baton Rouge LA (S)

Goodman, Marilyn J S, *Executive Dir,* Philadelphia Art Alliance, Philadelphia PA

Goodman, Michael, *Dir Nexus Press,* Nexus Contemporary Art Center, Atlanta GA

Goodman, Sherry, *Cur Educ,* University of California, University Art Museum, Berkeley CA

Goodman, Susan T, *Chief Cur,* The Jewish Museum, New York NY

Goodrich, James R, *Coordr of Reader Serv,* The College at New Paltz State University of New York, Sojourner Truth Library, New Paltz NY

Goodrich, James W, *Exec Dir,* State Historical Society of Missouri, Columbia MO

Goodrich, James W, *Dir & Librn,* State Historical Society of Missouri, Library, Columbia MO

Goodrich, Margaret, *Librn,* Denver Art Museum, Frederic H Douglas Library, Denver CO

Goodrich, William, *Head Librn,* Willard Library, Dept of Fine Arts, Evansville IN

Goodridge, James, *Instr,* University of Evansville, Art Dept, Evansville IN (S)

Goodridge, Lawrence W, *Instr,* Art Academy of Cincinnati, Cincinnati OH (S)

Goodson, Lucy, *Asst Prof,* Coe College, Dept of Art, Cedar Rapids IA (S)

Goodspeed, Barbara, *Pres,* Kent Art Association, Inc, Gallery, Kent CT

Goodstein, Barbara, *Instr,* Chautauqua Institution, School of Art, Chautauqua NY (S)

Goodwin, David, *Assoc Prof,* Coe College, Dept of Art, Cedar Rapids IA (S)

Goodwin, John, *Dir,* Printed Matter, Inc, New York NY

Goodwin, Mary, *Instr,* California State University, San Bernardino, Art Dept, San Bernardino CA (S)

Goodwin, Mary, *Exec Dir,* Fine Arts Center for the New River Valley, Pulaski VA

Goodwin, Priscilla, *Visitor Prog Coordr,* Supreme Court of the United States, Washington DC

Goodyear, Frank H, *Pres,* Pennsylvania Academy of the Fine Arts, Galleries, Philadelphia PA

Goodyear, John, *Prof,* Rutgers, the State University of New Jersey, Mason Gross School of the Arts, New Brunswick NJ (S)

Gootee, Marita, *Asst Prof,* Mississippi State University, Art Dept, Mississippi State MS (S)

Gopalan, Sunjata, *Instr,* Southeastern Louisiana University, Dept of Visual Arts, Hammond LA (S)

Gordan, Anette, *Registrar Asst,* Tampa Museum of Art, Library, Tampa FL

Gorden, Bette, *Technical Services Asst,* The Saint Louis Art Museum, Richardson Memorial Library, Saint Louis MO

Gordening, Genice, *Asst Dir,* Dawson County Historical Society, Museum, Lexington NE

Gordon, Alden R, *Assoc Prof,* Trinity College, Dept of Fine Arts, Hartford CT (S)

Gordon, Amorita, *Registrar,* Lauren Rogers Museum of Art, Laurel MS

Gordon, Dan, *Prog Coordr Photography,* Alberta College of Art, Calgary AB (S)

Gordon, David, *Gallery Dir,* St Lawrence College, Art Gallery, Kingston ON

Gordon, Edward, *Adminr,* Gibson Society, Inc, Gibson House Museum, Boston MA

Gordon, Elliott, *Dean,* Pratt Institute, Pratt Manhattan, New York NY (S)

Gordon, Elliott, *Chmn,* Pratt Manhattan, New York NY

Gordon, Geri, *School Dir,* Art League, Alexandria VA

Gordon, Irene, *Lectr,* John Jay College of Criminal Justice, Dept of Art, Music and Philosophy, New York NY (S)

Gordon, Jane A, *Pres Board Trustees,* Edmundson Art Foundation, Inc, Des Moines Art Center, Des Moines IA

Gordon, Jayne, *Coordr of Educ,* Concord Museum, Concord MA

Gordon, Jennifer, *Asst Prof,* University of Lethbridge, Dept of Art, Lethbridge AB (S)

Gordon, John, *VPres,* Beaumont Art League, Beaumont TX

Gordon, Joy L, *Exec Dir,* Guild Hall of East Hampton, Inc, Guild Hall Museum, East Hampton NY

Gordon, Kate, *Dir,* Passaic County Historical Society, Paterson NJ

Gordon, Kathy, *Dir,* Colby Community College, Visual Arts Dept, Colby KS (S)

Gordon, Lewis, *Assoc Head Music,* Saint Joseph's University, Dept of Fine & Performing Arts, Philadelphia PA (S)

Gordon, Louis, *Dir Educ,* Fine Arts Museums of San Francisco, M H de Young Memorial Museum and California Palace of the Legion of Honor, San Francisco CA

Gordon, Lynn, *Prof,* Radford University, Art Dept, Radford VA (S)

Gordon, Martha, *Asst Prof,* Tarrant County Junior College, Art Dept, Northeast Campus, Hurst TX (S)

Gordon, Peter, *Cur,* San Jose Museum of Art, San Jose CA

Gordon, Richard, *Asst Cur,* Alberta College of Art, Illingworth Kerr Gallery, Calgary AB

Gordon, Thelma, *Head of AV Services,* Westport Public Library, Westport CT

Gordon, Wendy, *Cur Educ,* Boulder Historical Society Inc, Museum of History, Boulder CO

Gore, Eugenia, *VPres for North Jersey,* Federated Art Associations of New Jersey, Inc, Westfield NJ

Gore, Jefferson A, *Cur Fine Arts,* Reading Public Museum and Art Gallery, Reading PA

Gore, Michael, *Exec Dir,* Belle Grove Plantation, Middletown VA

Gore, Sam, *Head Dept,* Mississippi College, Art Dept, Clinton MS (S)

Goree, Joan, *Instr,* John C Calhoun State Community College, Division of Fine Arts, Decatur AL (S)

Gorewitz, Shalom, *Dir,* Ramapo College of New Jersey, School of Contemporary Arts, Mahwah NJ (S)

Goring, Rich, *Historic Site Mgr,* Palisades Interstate Park Commission, Senate House State Historic Site, Kingston NY

Goring, Rich, *Historic Site Mgr,* Palisades Interstate Park Commission, Reference Library, Kingston NY

Gorka, Paul, *Instr,* Wayne Art Center, Wayne PA (S)

Gorman, Donna, *Exec Dir,* The Art Guild, Farmington CT

Gorman, William D, *Pres,* American Watercolor Society, New York NY

Gormley, Brian, *Artistic Exec Dir,* Silvermine Guild Arts Center, Silvermine Galleries, New Canaan CT

Gormley, Nina Z, *Exec Dir,* Wendell Gilley Museum, Southwest Harbor ME

Gorny, Anthony, *Instr,* Samuel S Fleisher Art Memorial, Philadelphia PA (S)

Gorove, Margaret, *Dir,* University of Mississippi, University Gallery, Oxford MS

Gorove, Margaret, *Chmn,* University of Mississippi, Dept of Art, University MS (S)

Gorse, George, *Chmn Art Dept,* Pomona College, Art Dept, Claremont CA (S)

Gorski, Daniel, *Dir,* Glassell School of Art, Houston TX (S)

Gorton, Julie, *Dir,* Sun Valley Center for the Arts and Humanities, Dept of Fine Art, Sun Valley ID (S)

Gorton, Tonda, *Public Information Officer,* Arizona Commission on the Arts, Phoenix AZ

Gorton, Tonda, *Public Information Officer,* Arizona Commission on the Arts, Reference Library, Phoenix AZ

Gosling, Craig, *Pres,* Association of Medical Illustrators, Atlanta GA

Goss, Charles, *Asst,* Cazenovia College, Center for Art & Design Studies, Cazenovia NY (S)

Goss, Hanna, *Public Relations,* Arkansas Territorial Restoration, Library, Little Rock AR

Goss, Hanna Bartsch, *Public Relations,* Arkansas Territorial Restoration, Little Rock AR

Goss, Nancy, *Dir of Public Relations,* Ferguson Library, Stamford CT

Gossel, Deborah S, *Asst to Dir,* Flint Institute of Arts, Flint MI

Gosselin, Gaetan, *Dir,* Vu Centre D'Animation Et De Diffusion De La Photographie, Quebec PQ

Gostin, Arlene, *Lectr,* University of Pennsylvania, Graduate School of Fine Arts, Philadelphia PA (S)

Gotlieb, Marc J, *Asst Prof,* Emory University, Art History Dept, Atlanta GA (S)

Gotlob, Mark, *Deputy Dir,* The American Federation of Arts, New York NY

Gott, Wesley A, *Chmn,* Southwest Baptist University, Art Dept, Bolivar MO (S)

Gottfried, Michael D, *Cur of Paleontology,* Calvert Marine Museum, Solomons MD

Gottlieb, Dan, *Chief Designer,* North Carolina Museum of Art, Raleigh NC

Gottlieb, Peter, *Archivist,* State Historical Society of Wisconsin, Archives, Madison WI

Gottlieb, Susan, *Public Relations Dir,* Norton Gallery and School of Art, West Palm Beach FL

Gottlieb, Wendy, *Public Affairs Asst Dir,* Kimbell Art Museum, Fort Worth TX

Gottschalk, Roger, *Chmn,* University of Wisconsin-Platteville, Dept of Fine Art, Platteville WI (S)

Gottsegen, Peter, *Chmn Bd of Trustees,* Caramoor Center for Music & the Arts, Inc, Caramoor House Museum, Katonah NY

Gottselig, Len, *Librn,* Glenbow Museum, Library, Calgary AB

Gough-DiJulio, Betsy, *Dir Educ,* Virginia Beach Center for the Arts, Virginia Beach VA

Goughnour, David, *Instr,* Iowa Lakes Community College, Dept of Art, Estherville IA (S)

Gould, Diane, *Chmn,* Shoreline Community College, Humanities Division, Seattle WA (S)

Gould, Kenton, *Admin Asst,* Rogue Valley Art Association, Rogue Gallery, Medford OR

Gould, Monica, *Cur Coll,* Loveland Museum and Gallery, Loveland CO

Gould, Virginia, *VPres Exhibits,* DuPage Art League School & Gallery, Wheaton IL

Gouma-Pederson, Thalia, *Prof,* College of Wooster, Dept of Art, Wooster OH (S)

Gourley, Hugh J, *Dir,* Colby College, Musuem of Art, Waterville ME

Gowen, John R, *Prof,* Ocean County College, Humanities Dept, Toms River NJ (S)

Grabania, Nadine, *Asst Cur & Registrar,* The Frick Art Museum, Pittsburgh PA

Grabbe, Kaye, *Admin Librn,* Lake Forest Library, Fine Arts Dept, Lake Forest IL

Grabill, Vin, *Assoc Prof,* University of Maryland, Baltimore County, Visual Arts Dept, Baltimore MD (S)

Grabowski, Beth, *Asst Prof,* University of North Carolina at Chapel Hill, Art Dept, Chapel Hill NC (S)

Graboys, Caroline, *Dir,* Fuller Museum of Art, Brockton MA

Grace, Laura, *Slide Cur,* University of Arkansas, Art Slide Library, Little Rock AR

Grachos, Louis, *Cur Exhib,* Metro-Dade Center, Center for the Fine Arts, Miami FL

Grachos, Louis P, *Dir Exhib,* The Queens Museum of Art, Flushing NY

Graft, James, *Dir of Educ,* Colorado Institute of Art, Denver CO (S)

Grah, Bill, *Instr,* Montclair Art Museum, Art School, Montclair NJ (S)

Graham, Ann, *Slide Cur,* University of North Texas, Visual Resources Collection, Denton TX

Graham, Anne, *Coordr Jewelry,* University of Delaware, Dept of Art, Newark DE (S)

Graham, Carann, *Instr,* Salem College, Art Dept, Winston-Salem NC (S)

Graham, Conrad, *Cur Decorative Arts,* McCord Museum of Canadian History, Montreal PQ

Graham, Cynthia, *Vis Prof,* Atlanta College of Art, Atlanta GA (S)

Graham, Douglas, *Founder & Treas,* The Turner Museum, Denver CO

Graham, Edward W, *Museum Asst,* Audubon Wildlife Sanctuary, Audubon PA

Graham, Greg, *Dir,* Canadian Artists' Representation-Le Front Des Artistes Canadiens, Ottawa ON

Graham, John R, *Cur Exhib,* Western Illinois University, Art Gallery-Museum, Macomb IL

Graham, Julia, *Lectr,* Rhodes College, Dept of Art, Memphis TN (S)

Graham, Linda, *Dir & VPres,* The Turner Museum, Denver CO

Graham, Richard, *Instr,* Salt Lake Community College, Graphic Design Dept, Salt Lake City UT (S)

Graham, Robert, *Prof,* Virginia Polytechnic Institute & State University, Dept of Art & Art History, Blacksburg VA (S)

Gralapp, Marcelee, *Library Dir,* Boulder Public Library and Gallery, Dept of Fine Arts Gallery, Boulder CO

Grams, Sheri D, *Controller,* Marion Koogler McNay Art Museum, San Antonio TX

Granche, Pierre, *Instr,* Universite de Montreal, Dept of Art History, Montreal PQ (S)

Grand, Stanley I, *Dir,* University of Wisconsin-Stevens Point, Carlsten Art Gallery, Stevens Point WI

Graneto, Doug, *Mgr,* Southern Oregon State College, Stevenson Union Gallery, Ashland OR

Graney, Carol Homan, *Assoc Dir,* University of the Arts, Albert M Greenfield Library, Philadelphia PA

Granger, Robert, *Faculty,* Idaho State University, Dept of Art, Pocatello ID (S)

Granger, Steven T, *Archivist,* Archives of the Archdiocese of St Paul & Minneapolis, Saint Paul MN

Granne, Regina, *Instr,* Bard College, Milton Avery Graduate School of the Arts, Annandale-on-Hudson NY (S)

Granof, Corinne, *Educ & Tours,* Northwestern University, Mary & Leigh Block Gallery, Evanston IL

Grant, Jerry, *Asst Dir Coll & Research,* Shaker Museum, Old Chatham NY

Grant, Marion, *Dir Art Educ,* Berkshire Museum, Pittsfield MA

Grant, Michele, *Exec Dir,* Prints In Progress, Philadelphia PA

Grant, Susan K, *Assoc Prof,* Texas Woman's University, Dept of Visual Arts, Denton TX (S)

Grant, Wendy, *Instr,* St Lawrence College, Dept of Visual & Creative Arts, Cornwall ON (S)

Granzow, Carl, *Assoc Prof,* University of Lethbridge, Dept of Art, Lethbridge AB (S)

Grattan, Patricia, *Dir,* Memorial University of Newfoundland, Art Gallery, Saint John's NF

Grau, Janet, *Instr,* Main Line Center for the Arts, Haverford PA (S)

Graubart, Maria K, *Librn,* The Currier Gallery of Art, Library, Manchester NH

Gravel, Claire, *Conservatrice en Art Contemporain,* Le Musee Regional de Rimouski, Centre National d' Exposition, Rimouski PQ

Gravel, Louise, *Technician,* La Galerie Montcalm la galerie d'art de la Villede Hull, Hull PQ

Graveline, Michelle, *Chmn,* Assumption College, Dept of Art & Music, Worcester MA (S)

Graves, Charles E, *Chmn,* Xavier University of Louisiana, Dept of Fine Arts, New Orleans LA (S)

Graves, Helen, *Registrar,* Art Museum of Southeast Texas, Beaumont TX

Graves, Jane, *Fine & Performing Arts Librn,* Skidmore College, Lucy Scribner Library, Saratoga Springs NY

Graves, Robert, *Prof,* Wenatchee Valley College, Art Dept, Wenatchee WA (S)

Graves, Sid F, *Dir,* Carnegie Public Library, Delta Blues Museum, Clarksdale MS

Gray, Anne, *Operations Coordr,* Bellevue Art Museum, Bellevue WA

Gray, Beth, *Dir,* East Hampton Library, Pennypacker Long Island Collection, East Hampton NY

Gray, Brian, *Dir Design & Facility,* Newport Harbor Art Museum, Newport Beach CA

Gray, Donald, *Chmn,* Community College of Rhode Island, Dept of Art, Warwick RI (S)

Gray, Donald F, *Chmn,* Community College of Rhode Island, Art Department Gallery, Warwick RI

Gray, Lynn, *Assoc Prof,* University of Minnesota, Minneapolis, Dept of Studio Art, Minneapolis MN (S)

Gray, Marillyn, *Development & Public Relations Dir,* Danforth Museum of Art, Framingham MA

Gray, Noel, *Coordr,* Chadron State College, Arts Gallery, Chadron NE

Gray, Noel, *Prof,* Chadron State College, Dept of Art, Speech & Theatre, Chadron NE (S)

Gray, Richard, *VPres,* Art Dealers Association of America, Inc, New York NY

Gray, Rosa, *Secy,* San Angelo Art Club, Helen King Kendall Memorial Art Gallery, San Angelo TX

Gray, Sandra, *Librn,* University of Utah, Owen Library, Salt Lake City UT

Gray, Sharon R, *Asst Dir,* Springville Museum of Art, Springville UT

Gray, Sonia, *Dir Neighborhood Art Prog,* San Francisco City & County Arts Commission, San Francisco CA

Graybill, Maribeth, *Assoc Prof,* Swarthmore College, Dept of Art, Swarthmore PA (S)

Grayson, Lynn, *Marketing Public Relations Specialist,* Science Museums of Charlotte, Inc, Discovery Place, Charlotte NC

Greathouse, W S, *Pres & Dir,* Charles and Emma Frye Art Museum, Seattle WA

Greathouse, W S, *Pres,* Charles and Emma Frye Art Museum, Library, Seattle WA

Greco, Anthony, *Prof,* Atlanta College of Art, Atlanta GA (S)

Green, Alfred E, *Prof,* Texas Woman's University, Dept of Visual Arts, Denton TX (S)

Green, Art, *Assoc Prof,* University of Waterloo, Fine Arts Dept, Waterloo ON (S)

Green, Bill, *Instr,* West Texas State University, Art, Communication & Theatre Dept, Canyon TX (S)

Green, Brent, *Head Dept,* Abilene Christian University, Dept of Art, Abilene TX (S)

Green, Charles, *Dir,* International Museum of Cartoon Art, Boca Raton FL

Green, Christine, *Cur,* Anderson Fine Arts Center, Anderson IN

Green, Elwood, *Executive Dir,* Native American Center for the Living Arts, Niagara Falls NY

Green, James, *Cur of Printed Books,* Library Company of Philadelphia, Print Dept, Philadelphia PA

Green, Jane Whipple, *Dir,* Federated Art Associations of New Jersey, Inc, Westfield NJ

Green, John, *Asst Dir,* Plainsman Museum, Aurora NE

Green, John B, *Cur Coll,* Tryon Palace Historic Sites & Gardens, New Bern NC

Green, Jonathan W, *Dir,* University of California, California Museum of Photography, Riverside CA

Green, Marilyn, *Pres,* Las Vegas Art Museum, Las Vegas NV

Green, Marla, *Cur Educ,* Plains Art Museum, Moorhead MN

Green, Michael, *Assoc Prof,* College of Southern Idaho, Art Dept, Twin Falls ID (S)

Green, Mike, *Gallery Dir,* College of Southern Idaho, Herrett Museum & Art Gallery, Twin Falls ID

Green, Nancy E, *Cur Prints & Photographs,* Cornell University, Herbert F Johnson Museum of Art, Ithaca NY

Green, Nancy E, *Chair,* Old Jail Art Center, Albany TX

Green, Richard, *Instr,* Eastern Arizona College, Art Dept, Thatcher AZ (S)

Green, Tom, *Chmn Fine Arts,* Corcoran School of Art, Washington DC (S)

Green, Wilder, *VPres,* The Drawing Society, New York NY

Green, William, *Asst Prof,* New Mexico State University, Art Dept, Las Cruces NM (S)

Greenberg, Barbara, *Cur of Education,* Lakeview Museum of Arts and Sciences, Peoria IL

Greenberg, Barbara, *Pres,* Allied ArtsGallery of the Yakima Valley, Yakima WA

Greenberg, Gary, *Asst Prof,* Clarion University of Pennsylvania, Dept of Art, Clarion PA (S)

Greenberg, Pearl, *Coordr Art Educ,* Kean College of New Jersey, Fine Arts Dept, Union NJ (S)

Greenberg, Ted, *Registrar,* Fine Arts Museums of San Francisco, M H de Young Memorial Museum and California Palace of the Legion of Honor, San Francisco CA

Greenblatt, Arthur, *Pres,* Monserrat College of Art, Beverly MA (S)

Greene, Allison, *Assoc Cur of 20th Century Art,* Museum of Fine Arts, Houston, Houston TX

Greene, James, *VPres,* Burlington County Historical Society, Burlington NJ

Greene, Janice, *Instr,* University of Evansville, Art Dept, Evansville IN (S)

Greene, J Craig, *Chmn,* Meredith College, Art Dept, Raleigh NC (S)

Greene, Ken, *Instr,* William Woods-Westminster Colleges, Art Dept, Fulton MO (S)

Greene, Ryland W, *Prof,* Cedar Crest College, Art Dept, Allentown PA (S)

Greene, Tom, *Instr,* ACA College of Design, Cincinnati OH (S)

Greenfield, Sylvia R, *Prof,* Southern Illinois University, School of Art & Design, Carbondale IL (S)

Greenhill, Patricia, *Coordr of Public Information,* State University of New York at Purchase, Neuberger Museum, Purchase NY

Greenland, Dorothy, *Sr Libr Specialist,* University of Utah, Marriott Library, Salt Lake City UT

Greenlee, Hugh, *Prof,* Cleveland Institute of Art, Cleveland OH (S)

Greenshields, Monte, *Dir,* Photographers Gallery, Saskatoon SK

Greenshields, Monte, *Dir,* Photographers Gallery, Library, Saskatoon SK

Greenspan, Sheila, *Head Educ Servs,* Art Gallery of Ontario, Toronto ON

Greenwall, Steven R, *Dept Head,* Allen County Community College, Art Dept, Iola KS (S)

Greenwell, Jolene, *Cur & Exec Dir,* Kentucky New State Capitol, Office of Historic Properties, Frankfort KY

Greenwold, Mark, *Assoc Prof,* State University of New York at Albany, Art Dept, Albany NY (S)

Greer, Carole, *Assoc Prof,* Southwest Texas State University, Dept of Art, San Marcos TX (S)

Greer, Dwaine, *Prof Art Educ,* University of Arizona, Dept of Art, Tucson AZ (S)

Gregerman, Marjorie, *Assoc Prof,* Johns Hopkins University, School of Medicine, Dept of Art as Applied to Medicine, Baltimore MD (S)

Gregersen, Thomas, *Cur,* Palm Beach County Parks & Recreation Department, Morikami Museum & Japanese Gardens, Delray Beach FL

Gregg, Jonathan, *Dir,* Vermont Studio Center, Johnson VT (S)

Gregoire, Collene Z, *Assoc Prof,* Baker University, Dept of Art, Baldwin City KS (S)

Gregor, Sandra, *Dir,* Texas Fine Arts Association, Austin TX

Gregory, Diane, *Asst Prof,* Southwest Texas State University, Dept of Art, San Marcos TX (S)

Gregory, Fred, *Assoc Prof,* Atlanta College of Art, Atlanta GA (S)

Gregory, Peg, *VPres,* South County Art Association, Kingston RI

Gregory, Shirley, *Dir,* Barton College, Library, Wilson NC

Gregory, Tim, *Archivist,* Pasadena Historical Society, Pasadena CA

Gregson, Christopher, *Asst Historic Preservation Supv,* County of Henrico, Meadow Farm Museum, Glen Allen VA

Greig, Rick E, *Program Dir,* Angelo State University, Houston Harte University Center, San Angelo TX

Greiner, William, *Asst Prof,* Olivet Nazarene University, Dept of Art, Kankakee IL (S)

Greives, Tom, *Pres,* Greater Lafayette Museum of Art, Lafayette IN

Greives, Tom, *Pres,* Greater Lafayette Museum of Art, Library, Lafayette IN

Grenda, C, *Prof,* City Colleges of Chicago, Daley College, Chicago IL (S)

Grenville, Bruce, *Cur,* Mendel Art Gallery and Civic Conservatory, Saskatoon SK

Greone Bowman, Leslie, *Cur Decorative Arts,* Los Angeles County Museum of Art, Los Angeles CA

Gresham, Paul A, *Instructor,* Oklahoma State University, Graphic Arts Dept, Okmulgee OK (S)

Gressom, Harriette, *Asst Prof,* Atlanta College of Art, Atlanta GA (S)

Gribbon, Michael, *Coordr Colls, Prints, Drawings & Photographs,* National Gallery of Canada, Ottawa ON

Grider, George, *Cur,* Ephraim McDowell-Cambus-Kenneth Foundation, McDowell House & Apothecary Shop, Danville KY

Griesell, Mary, *Coordr,* Lewis and Clark Community College, Art Dept, Godfrey IL (S)

Griesemer, Allan, *Dir,* San Bernardino County Museum, Fine Arts Institute, Redlands CA

Griesinger, Pamela, *Prof,* Daytona Beach Community College, Dept of Fine Arts & Visual Arts, Daytona Beach FL (S)

Griffel, Lois, *Dir,* Cape Cod School of Art, Provincetown MA (S)

Griffen, Richard, *Instr,* Hannibal La Grange College, Art Dept, Hannibal MO (S)

Griffin, Anita, *Instructor,* The Art Institutes International, The Art Institute of Seattle, Seattle WA (S)

Griffin, Cathryn, *Asst Prof,* Western Carolina University, Dept of Art, Cullowhee NC (S)

Griffin, Fred, *Instructor,* The Art Institutes International, The Art Institute of Seattle, Seattle WA (S)

Griffin, Gary, *Head Metalsmithing Dept,* Cranbrook Academy of Art, Bloomfield Hills MI (S)

Griffin, Gerald, *Instr,* Ricks College, Dept of Art, Rexburg ID (S)

Griffin, Janice, *Cur,* Chicago Architecture Foundation, Henry B Clarke House Museum, Chicago IL

Griffin, Jerri, *Ceramics & Sculpture Instr,* Hutchinson Community Junior College, Visual Arts Dept, Hutchinson KS (S)

Griffin, Kathleen, *Sr Librn,* San Diego Public Library, Art & Music Section, San Diego CA

Griffin, Penny, *Asst Prof,* Salem College, Art Dept, Winston-Salem NC (S)

Griffin, Stephen L, *Assoc Prof,* Mary Washington College, Art Dept, Fredericksburg VA (S)

Griffin, Tommy, *Cur Exhib,* University of Oregon, Museum of Art, Eugene OR

Griffin-Hughes, Donna, *Educator,* San Angelo Museum of Fine Arts, San Angelo TX

Griffis, Larry, *Chief Exec Officer,* Ashford Hollow Foundation for Visual & Performing Arts, Griffis Sculpture Park, East Otto NY

Griffis, Larry L, *Dir,* Birger Sandzen Memorial Gallery, Lindsborg KS

Griffis, Mark, *Dir,* Ashford Hollow Foundation for Visual & Performing Arts, Griffis Sculpture Park, East Otto NY

Griffis, Simon, *Assoc Dir,* Ashford Hollow Foundation for Visual & Performing Arts, Griffis Sculpture Park, East Otto NY

Griffiss, M Keating, *Head of Dept,* Chattanooga-Hamilton County Bicentennial Library, Fine Arts & Audio Visuals Department, Chattanooga TN

Griffith, Alison, *Research Assoc,* Severin Wunderman Museum, Irvine CA

Griffith, Bill, *Asst Dir,* Arrowmont School of Arts and Crafts, Gatlinburg TN (S)

Griffith, Daniel, *Div Dir,* Historical and Cultural Affairs, Delaware State Museums, Dover DE

Griffith, David, *Pres,* Artrain, Inc, Ann Arbor MI

Griffith, Elizabeth, *Exec Dir,* Ogden Union Station, Union Station Museums, Ogden UT

Griffith, Fuller O, *Asst Prof,* George Washington University, Dept of Art, Washington DC (S)

Griffith, June B, *Librn,* Lehigh County Historical Society, Allentown PA

Griffith, Laura S, *Asst Dir,* Fairmount Park Art Association, Philadelphia PA

Griffith, Marion, *Gallery Dir,* Sculpture Center Gallery & School, New York NY (S)

Griffith, Robert, *Assoc Prof,* University of Massachusetts at Lowell, Dept of Art, Lowell MA (S)

Griffith, Roberta, *Prof,* Hartwick College, Art Dept, Oneonta NY (S)

Griffith, Sheryl, *Librn,* National Archives & Records Administration, Library, Hyde Park NY

Griffiths, June B, *Librn,* Lehigh County Historical Society, Scott Andrew Trexler II Library, Allentown PA

Grilli, Stephanie, *Asst Prof,* University of Colorado at Denver, Dept of Fine Arts, Denver CO (S)

Grillo, Michael, *Vis Asst Lecturer,* Trinity College, Dept of Fine Arts, Hartford CT (S)

Grillo, Michael, *Asst Prof,* University of Maine, Art Dept, Orono ME (S)

Grim, Jerrine, *Coordr,* Friends of the Arts and Sciences, Hilton Leech Studio, Leech Studio Workshops, Sarasota FL (S)

Grimaldi, Mary Ellen, *Historic Site Asst,* Schuyler Mansion State Historic Site, Albany NY

Grimes, Carroll, *Chmn,* University of Pittsburgh at Johnstown, Dept of Fine Arts, Johnstown PA (S)

Grimes, Joann, *Pres,* Middletown Fine Arts Center, Middletown OH

Grimm, Albert, *Cur,* Southern Lorain County Historical Society, Spirit of '76 Museum, Wellington OH

Grinnell, Nancy W, *Librn,* Art Complex Museum, Library, Duxbury MA

Grinstead, Richard, *Dept Chmn,* California University of Pennsylvania, Dept of Art, California PA (S)

Grinstein, Elyse, *Pres Cultural Affairs Commission,* City of Los Angeles, Cultural Affairs Dept, Los Angeles CA

Gristina, Mary Campbell, *Asst to Dir,* Cummer Gallery of Art, DeEtte Holden Cummer Museum Foundation, Jacksonville FL

Griswold, Mac, *Instr,* Sarah Lawrence College, Dept of Art History, Bronxville NY (S)

Griswold, Scott, *Instr,* Ocean City Art Center, Ocean City NJ (S)

Griswold, Scott, *Board Pres,* Ocean City Art Center, Ocean City NJ

Gritcher, Peter, *Dir,* Mountain View Doukhobor Museum, Grand Forks BC

Grittner, James, *Chmn,* University of Wisconsin-Superior, Programs in the Visual Arts, Superior WI (S)

Grizzell, Kenneth, *Prof,* University of South Dakota, Dept of Art, Vermillion SD (S)

Groce, Susan, *Prof,* University of Maine, Art Dept, Orono ME (S)

Groell, Joseph, *Instr,* New York Academy of Art, Graduate School of Figurative Art, New York NY (S)

Groeneveld, Paul, *Asst to Dir,* Civic Fine Arts Center, Sioux Falls SD

Grogan, John, *VPres,* Children's Museum, Rauh Memorial Library, Indianapolis IN

Grogan, Kevin, *Dir,* Fisk University Museum of Art, University Galleries, Nashville TN

Grohlinghorst, Martin, *Asst Prof,* Missouri Western State College, Art Dept, Saint Joseph MO (S)

Grootkerk, Paul, *Assoc Prof,* Mississippi State University, Art Dept, Mississippi State MS (S)

Groover, Charles, *Head,* Jacksonville State University, Art Dept, Jacksonville AL (S)

Grose, Donald, *Dir,* University of North Texas, Willis Library, Denton TX

Grose, Virginia M, *VPres,* South Carolina National Bank, Columbia SC

Grosowsky, Vern, *Instr,* Solano Community College, Division of Fine & Applied Art, Suisun City CA (S)

Gross, Charles M, *Prof,* University of Mississippi, Dept of Art, University MS (S)

Gross, Kelly M, *Dir,* Art Association of Jacksonville, David Strawn Art Gallery, Jacksonville IL

Gross, Kenneth R, *Dir,* Birmingham-Bloomfield Art Association, Birmingham MI

Gross, Kenneth R, *Executive Dir,* Birmingham-Bloomfield Art Association, Birmingham MI (S)

Gross, Laurence F, *Cur,* Museum of American Textile History, North Andover MA

Gross, Margarete K, *Picture Coll Librn,* Chicago Public Library, Harold Washington Library Center, Chicago IL

Grossman, Barbara, *Instr,* Chautauqua Institution, School of Art, Chautauqua NY (S)

Grossman, Cissy, *Cur,* Congregation Emanu-El, New York NY

Grossman, Ellen, *Pres,* The Society of Arts and Crafts, Boston MA

Grossman, Gilda S, *Senior Art Therapist,* Toronto Art Therapy Institute, Toronto ON (S)

Grossman, Grace Cohen, *Cur,* Hebrew Union College, Skirball Museum, Los Angeles CA

Grossman, Orin, *Chmn,* Fairfield University, Fine Arts Dept, Fairfield CT (S)

Grosvenor, Walter, *Assoc Prof,* Whitworth College, Art Dept, Spokane WA (S)

Grote, Bob, *Exec Dir,* Pittsburgh Center for the Arts, Pittsburgh PA

Grote, William M, *Chmn,* Loyola University of New Orleans, Dept of Visual Arts, New Orleans LA (S)

Grotfielt, Deborah, *Asst Dir,* Diverse Works, Houston TX

Grothus, Barbara, *Pres,* Albuquerque United Artists, Albuquerque NM

Ground, Perry, *Museum Educator,* Iroquois Indian Museum, Howes Cave NY

Grouse, Michael G, *Prof,* University of Alabama in Huntsville, Dept of Art & Art History, Huntsville AL (S)

Grow, Mary, *Pres,* Rome Historical Society Museum, Rome NY

Growborg, Erik, *Instr,* Miracosta College, Art Dept, Oceanside CA (S)

Grubb, Alice, *Office Mgr,* Boulder Art Center, Boulder CO

Grubb, Rochelle T, *Pres,* Davidson County Art Guild Gallery, Inc, Lexington NC

Grubb, Tom, *Dir,* Fayetteville Museum of Art, Inc, Fayetteville NC

Grube, Dick Dewayne, *Dir,* National Infantry Museum, Fort Benning GA

Gruber, Doris, *Periodicals,* Trinity College Library, Washington DC

Grudzinski, Bruce, *Chmn Foundations Dept,* Milwaukee Institute of Art and Design, Milwaukee WI (S)

Gruenwald, Helen, *Asst Prof,* Kirkwood Community College, Dept of Fine Arts, Cedar Rapids IA (S)

Gruenwald, Larry, *Technician,* University of Minnesota, Duluth, Tweed Museum of Art, Duluth MN

Grundberg, Andy, *Exec Dir,* The Friends of Photography, Ansel Adams Center for Photography, San Francisco CA

Grunebaum, Gabriele, *VPres,* Ukiyo-e Society of America, Inc, New York NY

Gruner, Charles J, *Dir Lecture & Demonstration Serv,* American Society of Artists, Inc, Chicago IL

Grupe, Barbara, *Asst to Dir,* The Phillips Collection, Washington DC

Grupp, Carl A, *Chmn,* Augustana College, Art Dept, Sioux Falls SD (S)

Gruss, David, *Cur Permanent Coll,* San Jose State University, Union Gallery, San Jose CA

Grzesiak, Marion, *Cur of Education,* Montclair Art Museum, Art School, Montclair NJ (S)

Gualtieri, Joseph P, *Dir,* Norwich Free Academy, Slater Memorial Museum & Converse Art Gallery, Norwich CT

Guan, Kathleen, *Exec Dir,* Chinese Culture Foundation, Chinese Culture Center Gallery, San Francisco CA

Guary, Cindy, *Admin Asst,* Prairie Gallery, Grande Prairie AB

Guava, Sig, *Chmn Div Urban Planning,* Columbia University, Graduate School of Architecture, Planning & Preservation, New York NY (S)

Gubelmann, William S, *Secy,* The Society of the Four Arts, Palm Beach FL

Gudger, Bob, *Mgr Cultural & Community Affairs,* Xerox Corporation, Art Collection, Stamford CT

Guenther, Bruce, *Chief Cur,* Newport Harbor Art Museum, Newport Beach CA

Guenthler, John R, *Assoc Prof,* Indiana University-Southeast, Fine Arts Dept, New Albany IN (S)

Guerin, Charles Allan, *Dir,* University of Wyoming, Art Museum, Laramie WY

Guernsey, David T, *Exec Dir,* Ships of The Sea Museum, Savannah GA

Guest, Peter, *Instr,* Malden Bridge School of Art, Malden Bridge NY (S)

Guetzko, Becky, *Instr,* University of Charleston, Carleton Varney Dept of Art & Design, Charleston WV (S)

Guffin, Raymond L, *Prof,* Stillman College, Stillman Art Gallery and Art Dept, Tuscaloosa AL (S)

Guichet, Melody, *Prof,* Louisiana State University, School of Art, Baton Rouge LA (S)

Guiffre, Samuel L, *School Dir,* Mount Ida College, Chamberlayne School of Design & Merchandising, Boston MA (S)

Guilbaut, Serge, *Prof,* University of British Columbia, Dept of Fine Arts, Vancouver BC (S)

Guilfoile, William J, *Assoc Dir,* National Baseball Hall of Fame and Museum, Inc, Art Collection, Cooperstown NY

Guilfoyle, Marvin, *Acquisitions Librn,* University of Evansville, University Library, Evansville IN

Guilmain, Jacques, *Prof,* State University of New York at Stony Brook, Art Dept, Stony Brook NY (S)

Guip, David, *Prof,* University of Toledo, Dept of Art, Toledo OH (S)

Guitian, Jose, *Registrar,* University of Miami, Lowe Art Museum, Coral Gables FL

Gulacsy, Elizabeth, *Reference Librn & Archivist,* New York State College of Ceramics at Alfred University, Scholes Library of Ceramics, Alfred NY

Gulbranson, Rex, *Design/Organization Development Dir,* Arizona Commission on the Arts, Phoenix AZ

Gull, Robert, *Pres,* Art Gallery of Greater Victoria, Victoria BC

Gumarman, Elizabeth, *Office Mgr,* University of California, Los Angeles, Grunwald Center for the Graphic Arts, Los Angeles CA

Gumpper, Jean, *Assoc Prof,* Concordia College, Art Dept, Moorhead MN (S)

Gund, Agnes, *Pres,* Museum of Modern Art, New York NY

Gundersheimer, Werner, *Dir,* Folger Shakespeare Library, Washington DC

Gunderson, Barry, *Assoc Prof,* Kenyon College, Art Dept, Gambier OH (S)

Gunderson, Jeff, *Librn,* San Francisco Art Institute, Anne Bremer Memorial Library, San Francisco CA

Gunn, Nancy, *Asst Dir for Public Relations & Development,* Wellesley College, Museum, Wellesley MA

Gunnion, Vernon S, *Cur Collections,* Landis Valley Museum, Lancaster PA

Guraedy, J Bruce, *Head Dept,* East Central Community College, Art Dept, Decatur MS (S)

Gursoy, Ahmet, *VPres,* Federation of Modern Painters & Sculptors, New York NY

Gurth, Barbara, *Exec Dir,* Arts Council of the Mid-Columbia Region, Kennewick WA

Gussow, Jill, *Asst Prof,* State University of New York College at Brockport, Dept of Art & Art History, Brockport NY (S)

Gustafson, Dwight, *Dean,* Bob Jones University, School of Fine Arts, Greenville SC (S)

Gustafson, Roger, *Instr,* Elgin Community College, Fine Arts Dept, Elgin IL (S)

Gutekunst, B, *Head Humanities Division,* Catholic University of America, Humanities Division, Mullen Library, Washington DC

Gutenkauf, Diane, *Cur,* Old Barracks Museum, Trenton NJ

Guthrie, Barbara, *Registrar,* Huntsville Museum of Art, Huntsville AL

Guthrie, Carole, *Instr,* Bay Path College, Dept of Art, Longmeadow MA (S)

Guthrie, Jill, *Managing Ed,* Princeton University, The Art Museum, Princeton NJ

Gutierrez, Luis, *Instr,* San Jose City College, School of Fine Arts, San Jose CA (S)

Gutierrez, Rafael, *Dir,* Indian Pueblo Cultural Center, Albuquerque NM

Gutierrez-Solana, Carlos, *Dir,* Artists Space, New York NY

Gutierrez-Solana, Carlos, *Dir,* Artists Space, Artists Space Gallery, New York NY

Gutridge, Delbert R, *Registrar,* Cleveland Museum of Art, Cleveland OH

Gutwirth, Sarah, *Asst Prof,* State University of New York College at Potsdam, Dept of Fine Arts, Potsdam NY (S)

Guy, Jody, *Dir,* Silver Eye Center for Photography, Pittsburgh PA

Guy, Linda, *Prof,* Texas Christian University, Art & Art History Dept, Fort Worth TX (S)

Guzman, Diane, *Librn,* Brooklyn Museum, Wilbour Library of Egyptology, Brooklyn NY

Haak, Kellen, *Registrar,* Dartmouth College, Hood Museum of Art, Hanover NH

Haarer, Ann, *Chmn Dept,* College of Saint Elizabeth, Art Dept, Morristown NJ (S)

Haas, Charles W, *Asst Prof,* Monroe Community College, Art Dept, Rochester NY (S)

Haber, Mark, *Assoc Dean,* Pratt Institute, School of Architecture, Brooklyn NY (S)

Haberland, Jody, *Head,* Arlington County Department of Public Libraries, Fine Arts Section, Arlington VA

Haberman, David, *Prof,* Cuyahoga Community College, Dept of Art, Cleveland OH (S)

Haberman, Patty, *Exhib Coordr,* Tempe Arts Center, Tempe AZ

Haberstroh, Matthew, *Slide Cur,* School of Visual Arts Library, New York NY

Hack, Rosalinda I, *Head Visual & Performing Arts Div,* Chicago Public Library, Harold Washington Library Center, Chicago IL

Hacker, Katherine, *Asst Prof,* University of British Columbia, Dept of Fine Arts, Vancouver BC (S)

Hacker, Robert G, *Paul & Louise Miller Prof,* Rochester Institute of Technology, School of Printing, Rochester NY (S)

Hackett, Phoebe, *Asst Dir Admin,* Massachusetts Institute of Technology, MIT Museum, Cambridge MA

Hacklin, Alan, *Chmn,* Columbia University, School of the Arts, Division of Painting & Sculpture, New York NY (S)

Hadaway, Sandra S, *Admin,* Telfair Academy of Arts and Sciences Inc, Savannah GA

Hadd, Br Arnold, *Cur,* United Society of Shakers, Shaker Museum, Poland Spring ME

Hadd, Br Arnold, *Cur,* United Society of Shakers, The Shaker Library, Poland Spring ME

Haddad, Farid A, *Prof,* New England College, Art & Art History, Henniker NH (S)

Hadden, Helen, *Librn,* Art Gallery of Hamilton, Muriel Isabel Bostwick Library, Hamilton ON

Haddock, Brent, *Chmn,* College of Eastern Utah, Gallery East, Price UT

Hadler, Mona, *Assoc Prof,* City University of New York, PhD Program in Art History, New York NY (S)

Hadley, John W B, *Chairman Board Trustees,* Heckscher Museum, Huntington NY

Hadley, Richard, *Head Div Humanities & Fine Arts,* Fayetteville State University, Fine Arts & Communications, Fayetteville NC (S)

Hadley, Stephen, *Dir Progs,* Historical Society of Rockland County, New City NY

Hadley, Trevor, *Serials Librn,* The Metropolitan Museum of Art, Thomas J Watson Library, New York NY

Haefliger, Kathleen, *Music Librn,* Pennsylvania State University, Pattee Library, University Park PA

Haefner, Scott, *Learning Librn Intern,* Schenectady County Historical Society, Library, Schenectady NY

Hafeli, Mary, *Educ Dir,* Ann Arbor Art Association, Ann Arbor MI

Hafer, Linda, *Asst Dir,* Art League, Alexandria VA

Hafertepe, Kenneth, *Dir Academic Programs,* Historic Deerfield, Inc, Deerfield MA

Hagaman, S, *Chmn Div,* Purdue University, West Lafayette, Dept of Visual & Performaing Arts, Div of Art & Design, West Lafayette IN (S)

Hagan, Kay, *Instructor,* Saint Louis Community College at Meramec, Art Dept, Saint Louis MO (S)

Hagan, Kenneth, *Dir,* United States Naval Academy Museum, Annapolis MD

Hagan, Kenneth J, *Dir,* United States Naval Academy Museum, Library, Annapolis MD

Hagedorn, Bernard, *Instr,* Vincennes University Junior College, Art Dept, Vincennes IN (S)

Hagedorn, Deborah, *Instr,* Vincennes University Junior College, Art Dept, Vincennes IN (S)

Hagel, Cynthia, *Dir,* Valley City Arts & Gallery Association, Second Crossing Gallery Staus Mall, Valley City ND

Hageman, Dennis, *Dept Head,* Iowa Lakes Community College, Dept of Art, Estherville IA (S)

Hageman, Lee, *Chmn Dept Art,* Northwest Missouri State University, DeLuce Art Gallery, Maryville MO

Hageman, Lee, *Chmn,* Northwest Missouri State University, Dept of Art, Maryville MO (S)

Hagemeyer, Jim, *Chmn,* Heidelberg College, Dept of Art, Tiffin OH (S)

Hagen, Gary, *Assoc Prof,* University of Wisconsin-Stevens Point, Dept of Art & Design, Stevens Point WI (S)

Hager, Hellmut, *Dept Head,* Pennsylvania State University, University Park, Dept of Art History, University Park PA (S)

Hagerstrand, Martin A, *Pres Board Trustees,* Oklahoma Historical Society, State Museum of History, Oklahoma City OK

Haglich, Bianca, *Prof,* Marymount College, Art Dept, Tarrytown NY (S)

Hagloch, Jennifer, *Bush House Cur,* Salem Art Association, Bush House, Salem OR

Hagloch, Jennifer, *Cur,* Salem Art Association, Archives, Salem OR

Hagman, Jean, *Dir,* Oklahoma City Art Museum, Library, Oklahoma City OK

Hagman, Jean Cassels, *Dir,* Oklahoma City Art Museum, Oklahoma City OK

Hagstrom, Robert A, *Div Chmn,* Jamestown Community College, Visual & Performing Arts Division, Jamestown NY (S)

Hague, Thomas M, *Pres,* Canton Art Institute, Canton OH

Hahn, Cynthia J, *Assoc Prof,* Florida State University, Art History Dept (R133B), Tallahassee FL (S)

Hahn, Jean, *Secy,* Mingei International, Inc, Mingei International Museum of World Folk Art, San Diego CA

Hahn, Martha, *Dir,* Allegany County Historical Society, History House, Cumberland MD

Hahne, Freddie, *Pres,* Eyes and Ears Foundation, San Francisco CA

Haight, Bonnie, *Gallery Mgr,* Creative Growth Art Center, Oakland CA

Haiman, Kurt, *Pres,* Art Directors Club, Inc, New York NY

Haines, Melissa J, *Site Coordr,* Association for the Preservation of Virginia Antiquities, John Marshall House, Richmond VA

Hair, Norman J, *Chmn,* Gulf Coast Community College, Division of Fine Arts, Panama City FL (S)

Hajduczok, Lydia, *Public Relations,* The Ukrainian Museum, New York NY

Hajic, Maria, *Cur,* Wildlife of the American West Art Museum, Jackson WY

Hakala, Sue, *Supv,* Galeria Mesa, Mesa Arts Center, Mesa AZ

Halasz, Piri, *Asst Prof Art History,* Bethany College, Dept of Fine Arts, Bethany WV (S)

Halbreich, Kathy, *Dir,* Walker Art Center, Minneapolis MN

Halcro, Kathleen, *Site Dir,* Jackson County Historical Society, Research Library and Archives, Independence MO

Hale, Angie, *Membership Dir,* Association of American Editorial Cartoonists, Raleigh NC

Hale, David, *Instr,* Goddard College, Visual Arts Dept, Plainfield VT (S)

Hale, Laura, *Instr,* Georgia Southern University, Dept of Art, Statesboro GA (S)

Hale, Nathan Cabot, *Pres,* Ages of Man Fellowship, Amenia NY

Hales, David, *Head Alaska & Polar Regions Colls,* University of Alaska, Elmer E Rasmuson Library, Fairbanks AK

Haley, Roger, *Librn,* United States Senate Commission on Art, Reference Library, Washington DC

Halkin, Theodore, *Prof,* School of the Art Institute of Chicago, Chicago IL (S)

Halkovic, Marilyn, *Art Librn,* University of Georgia, University of Georgia Libraries, Athens GA

Hall, Alla, *Dir of Fine Arts,* Armand Hammer Museum of Art & Cultural Center, Los Angeles CA

Hall, Andrew, *Instr,* Cedar Crest College, Art Dept, Allentown PA (S)

Hall, Angela, *Librn,* Birmingham Public Library, Arts, Music & Recreation Department, Birmingham AL

Hall, Annette, *Chmn,* University of Arkansas at Monticello, Fine Arts Dept, Monticello AR (S)

Hall, Audrey, *Cur Art,* Museum of the Hudson Highlands, Cornwall on Hudson NY

Hall, Bonnie, *Assoc Dir & Adminr,* Laguna Art Museum, Laguna Beach CA

Hall, Doug, *Prof,* Kirkwood Community College, Dept of Fine Arts, Cedar Rapids IA (S)

Hall, Doug, *Facilities Dept,* R J R Nabisco, Inc, New York NY

Hall, James, *Dir Finance,* Please Touch Museum, Philadelphia PA

Hall, Jane, *Coordr,* Aesthetic Realism Foundation, Terrain Gallery, New York NY

Hall, Janice, *Asst Dir Curatorial Servs,* Putnam Museum of History & Natural Science, Davenport IA

Hall, Jean C, *Asst to Dir,* Cummer Gallery of Art, DeEtte Holden Cummer Museum Foundation, Jacksonville FL

Hall, Lana, *Instr,* Salt Lake Community College, Graphic Design Dept, Salt Lake City UT (S)

Hall, Lane, *Asst Prof,* Teikyo Marycrest University, Art and Computer Graphics Dept, Davenport IA (S)

Hall, Mark, *Instr,* Marian College, Art Dept, Indianapolis IN (S)

Hall, Martha, *Visual Resources Librn,* University of the Arts, Albert M Greenfield Library, Philadelphia PA

Hall, Mary-Anne, *Docent,* Norwich Free Academy, Slater Memorial Museum & Converse Art Gallery, Norwich CT

Hall, Priscilla, *Museum Shop Mgr,* Bennington Museum, Bennington VT

Hall, Rick, *Instr,* The Arkansas Arts Center, Museum School, Little Rock AR (S)

Hall, Robert, *Chmn,* Flagler College, Visual Arts Dept, Saint Augustine FL (S)

Hall, Robert, *Education Specialist,* Anacostia Museum, Washington DC

Hall, Shawn, *Asst Dir,* Northeastern Nevada Historical Society Museum, Library, Elko NV

Hall, Thomas, *Chmn Fine Arts,* York College of Pennsylvania, Dept of English & Humanities, York PA (S)

Hall, Walter, *Assoc Prof,* University of Hartford, Hartford Art School, West Hartford CT (S)

Hall, Wendy, *Fine Arts Librn,* Columbia College, Library, Chicago IL

Hallam, John, *Chmn,* Pacific Lutheran University, Dept of Art, Tacoma WA (S)

Hallatt, Kim, *Asst Dir Admin,* University of Rochester, Memorial Art Gallery, Rochester NY

Hall-Duncan, Nancy, *Cur Art,* The Bruce Museum, Greenwich CT

Hallet, Robert, *First VPs,* National Watercolor Society, Cerritos CA

Hallet, Stanley I, *Dean,* Catholic University of America, School of Architecture & Planning, Washington DC (S)

Halliday, Richard, *Prog Coordr Drawing,* Alberta College of Art, Calgary AB (S)

Hallman, Gary, *Assoc Prof,* University of Minnesota, Minneapolis, Dept of Studio Art, Minneapolis MN (S)

Hall-Smith, Arthur, *Prof,* George Washington University, Dept of Art, Washington DC (S)

Hallum, John, *Colls Mgr,* Sitka Historical Society, Isabel Miller Museum, Sitka AK

Halpern, Linda, *Asst Prof,* James Madison University, Dept of Art, Harrisonburg VA (S)

Halpern, Nora, *Instr,* Pepperdine University, Seaver College, Dept of Art, Malibu CA (S)

Halpin, Marjorie M, *Cur Ethnology,* University of British Columbia, Museum of Anthropology, Vancouver BC

Halsband, Frances, *Dean,* Pratt Institute, School of Architecture, Brooklyn NY (S)

Halsey, Anthony P, *Treas,* Mystic Art Association, Inc, Mystic CT

Halter, Ellen F, *Asst Prof,* Concordia College, Bronxville NY (S)

Halverson, Wayne, *Asst Prof,* University of Wisconsin-Stevens Point, Dept of Art & Design, Stevens Point WI (S)

Halvorsen, Liza, *Store Mgr,* Bellevue Art Museum, Bellevue WA

Hamady, Sue, *Dean of Student Affairs,* Kendall College of Art & Design, Frank & Lyn Van Steenberg Library, Grand Rapids MI

Hamady, Susanne, *Dean of Student Affairs,* Kendall College of Art & Design, Grand Rapids MI (S)

Hamady, Walter, *Prof,* University of Wisconsin, Madison, Dept of Art, Madison WI (S)

Hamann, Carol, *Mgr,* Atlantic Gallery, New York NY

Hambourg, Maria, *Cur Photographs,* The Metropolitan Museum of Art, New York NY

Hamburger, Jeffrey, *Assoc Prof,* Oberlin College, Dept of Art, Oberlin OH (S)

Hamersky, Al, *Pres,* Lincoln Arts Council, Lincoln NE

Hames, Alma, *Secy,* Wayne County Historical Society, Museum, Honesdale PA

Hames, Charles, *Treas,* Wayne County Historical Society, Museum, Honesdale PA

Hamic, Steve, *Treas,* Arts on the Park, Lakeland FL

Hamil, Sherrie, *Dir,* Gadsden Museum of Fine Arts, Inc, Gadsden AL

Hamilton, David Verner, *Pres,* Tradd Street Press, Elizabeth O'Neill Verner Studio Museum, Charleston SC

Hamilton, Esley, *Adjunct Instr,* Maryville University of Saint Louis, Art Division, Saint Louis MO (S)

Hamilton, John, *Cur Colls,* Museum of Our National Heritage, Lexington MA

Hamilton, Mort, *Dir,* Charles B Goddard Center for the Visual and Performing Arts, Ardmore OK

Hamilton, Philip, *Prof,* University of Wisconsin, Madison, Dept of Art, Madison WI (S)

Hamilton, Robert, *Instr,* Indiana University of Pennsylvania, Dept of Art and Art Education, Indiana PA (S)

Hamilton, Shirley, *Exec Mgr,* Allied Arts Council of Lethbridge, Bowman Arts Center, Lethbridge AB

Hamister, Lynette, *Pres,* Center for Exploratory & Perceptual Art, CEPA Gallery, Buffalo NY

Hamm, Jack, *Artist-in-Residence,* Dallas Baptist University, Dept of Art, Dallas TX (S)

Hamm, Virginia, *Cur Educ,* National Art Museum of Sport, Indianapolis IN

Hamma, Kenneth, *Adjunct Asst Prof,* University of Southern California, School of Fine Arts, Los Angeles CA (S)

Hammack, Louis, *Head Technical Services,* The Art Institute of Chicago, Ryerson and Burnham Libraries, Chicago IL

Hammell, Peter, *Dir,* National Museum of Racing and Hall of Fame, Saratoga Springs NY

Hammer, Betty W, *Admin Dir of Development,* Westmoreland Museum of Art, Greensburg PA

Hammett, Beverly, *Asst Librn,* Webster Parish Library, Minden LA

Hammock, Virgil, *Prof,* Mount Allison University, Fine Arts Dept, Sackville NB (S)

Hammond, Claristie, *Assoc Archivist,* Lincoln Memorial Shrine, Redlands CA

Hammond, Harmony, *Prof Painting & Drawing,* University of Arizona, Dept of Art, Tucson AZ (S)

Hammond, Jean, *Chmn Dept of Graphic Design,* New England School of Art & Design, Boston MA (S)

Hammond, Pete, *Pres,* San Antonio Art League, San Antonio TX

Hammond, Tom, *Grad Coordr,* University of Georgia, Franklin College of Arts & Sciences, Dept of Art, Athens GA (S)

Hammond, Tom, *Printmaking,* University of Georgia, Franklin College of Arts & Sciences, Dept of Art, Athens GA (S)

Hammond, Wayne G, *Asst Librn,* Williams College, Chapin Library, Williamstown MA

Hamm Walsh, Dawna, *Asst Prof,* Dallas Baptist University, Dept of Art, Dallas TX (S)

Hampton, Suzanne, *Asst to Dir,* Cartoon Art Museum, San Francisco CA

Hamshaw, Rallou, *Acting Dir,* First Street Gallery, New York NY

Hanawalt, Margaret, *Childrens Room,* Mason City Public Library, Mason City IA

Hanchrow, Grace M, *Asst Dir for Development,* Montgomery Museum of Fine Arts, Montgomery AL

Hancock, Barbara, *Asst Dir,* Lake George Arts Project, Courthouse Gallery, Lake George NY

Hancock, Beverlye, *Ed Cur,* Wake Forest University, Museum of Anthropology, Winston Salem NC

Hancock, Constance Cann, *In Charge,* Nations Bank, Art Collection, Richmond VA

Hancock, Elliott, *Music Dir,* Ozark Folk Center, Mountain View AR

Hancock, John, *Asst Prof,* Barton College, Communication, Performaing & Visual Arts, Wilson NC (S)

Hancock, Kathleen, *Instr,* Roger Williams College, Art Dept, Bristol RI (S)

Hancock, Lisa, *Registrar,* Virginia Museum of Fine Arts, Richmond VA

Hand, Donald, *Horticulture,* National Gallery of Art, Washington DC

Hand, Ronald, *Exhib Designer,* Pennsylvania State University, Palmer Museum of Art, University Park PA

Hanft, Margie, *Film & Reference Librn,* California Institute of the Arts Library, Santa Clarita CA

Hanhardt, John G, *Cur Film & Video,* Whitney Museum of American Art, New York NY

Hankey, Robert E, *Pres,* College of the Associated Arts, Saint Paul MN

Hankey, Robert E, *Pres,* College of Associated Arts, Saint Paul MN (S)

Hankins, Antoinette, *Public Relations,* Maricopa County Historical Society, Desert Caballeros Western Museum, Wickenburg AZ

Hankins, Roger, *Dir,* University of California, Memorial Union Art Gallery, Davis CA

Hanley, Lynn, *Instr,* Gettysburg College, Dept of Art, Gettysburg PA (S)

Hanlon, Meg, *Publications,* Dallas Muscum of Art, Dallas TX

Hanna, Annette Adrian, *Dir,* Blackwell Street Center for the Arts, Dover NJ

Hanna, James, *Assoc Prof,* Texas Tech University, Dept of Art, Lubbock TX (S)

Hanna, Martha, *Asst Cur,* Canadian Museum of Contemporary Photography, Ottawa ON

Hanna, Paul, *Prof,* Texas Tech University, Dept of Art, Lubbock TX (S)

Hanna, Susan, *Registrar,* State Museum of Pennsylvania, Pennsylvania Historical & Museum Commission, Harrisburg PA

Hanna, Wayne, *Dept Head,* Ray College of Design, Chicago IL (S)

Hanna, William J, *Dir Records Management,* Mississippi Department of Archives and History, State Historical Museum, Jackson MS

Hannah, Susan, *Prog Coordr,* University of Mississippi, University Museums, Oxford MS

Hannaher, Elizabeth, *Dir,* Plains Art Museum, Moorhead MN

Hannan, William, *Assoc Prof,* Black Hawk College, Art Dept, Moline IL (S)

Hanner, Frank, *Cur,* National Infantry Museum, Fort Benning GA

Hanni, Margaret, *Dir,* Phillips Exeter Academy, Frederic R Mayer Art Center & Lamont Gallery, Exeter NH

Hannibal, Joe, *Prof,* California State Polytechnic University, Pomona, Art Dept, Pomona CA (S)

Hanniford, Sultana, *Recording Secy,* Lyme Art Association, Inc, Old Lyme CT

Hannon, Brian, *Dir,* Center for Book Arts, Inc, New York NY

Hanon, Stan, *Dir,* University of Saskatchewan, John G Diefenbaker Centre, Saskatoon SK

Hansen, Chris, *Instructor,* Milwaukee Area Technical College, Graphic Arts Dept, Milwaukee WI (S)

Hansen, Elisa, *Dir Adult Educ,* State Art Museum of Florida, John & Mable Ringling Museum of Art, Sarasota FL

Hansen, Ingrid, *Chmn,* The Washington Center For Photography, Washington DC

Hansen, Jim, *Assoc Prof Art & Cur Installations,* Bradley University, Hartman Center Gallery, Peoria IL

Hansen, John, *Instructor,* The Art Institutes International, The Art Institute of Seattle, Seattle WA (S)

Hansen, Mark R, *Pres-Elect,* National Art Education Association, Reston VA

Hansen, Pearl, *Prof,* Wayne State College, Art Dept, Wayne NE (S)

Hansen, Rena, *Ed,* Midmarch Associates, Women Artists News Archive, New York NY

Hansen, Roland, *Head Readers Services,* School of the Art Institute of Chicago, John M Flaxman Library, Chicago IL

Hansen, Shardlow, *VPres,* Galesburg Civic Art Center, Galesburg IL

Hansen, Steve, *Instr,* Andrews University, Dept of Art, Art History & Design, Berrien Springs MI (S)

Hansen, Trudy, *Cur Prints & Drawings,* Rutgers, The State University of New Jersey, Jane Voorhees Zimmerli Art Museum, New Brunswick NJ

Hanson, Carol, *Secy,* Headquarters Fort Monroe, Dept of Army, Casemate Museum, Fort Monroe VA

Hanson, David A, *Chmn,* Fairleigh Dickinson University, Fine Arts Dept, Rutherford NJ (S)

Hanson, Doug, *Chmn Dept of Art,* Cornell College, Armstrong Gallery, Mount Vernon IA

Hanson, Doug, *Head Dept,* Cornell College, Art Dept, Mount Vernon IA (S)

Hanson, Emma, *Cur Plains Indian Museum,* Buffalo Bill Memorial Association, Buffalo Bill Historical Center, Cody WY

Hanson, Lowell, *Chmn,* Everett Community College, Art Dept, Everett WA (S)

Hanson, Robert, *Instr,* Pacific Northwest College of Art, Portland OR (S)

Hanson, Steven, *Circulations Supv,* Art Center College of Design, James Lemont Fogg Memorial Library, Pasadena CA

Hanson, Susan, *Asst Prof,* College of Wooster, Dept of Art, Wooster OH (S)

Hanson, Susan, *Historic Preservation Supv,* County of Henrico, Meadow Farm Museum, Glen Allen VA

Happus, Adrien, *Asst Prof,* Augustana College, Art Dept, Sioux Falls SD (S)

Harada, Gwen, *Slide Coll,* Honolulu Academy of Arts, Honolulu HI

Harakal, Eileen E, *Exec Dir Public Affairs,* The Art Institute of Chicago, Chicago IL

Haralson, Dianne, *Dir,* Five Civilized Tribes Museum, Library, Muskogee OK

Haralson, Dianne S, *Dir,* Five Civilized Tribes Museum, Muskogee OK

Harasimowicz, Alan, *Exhibits Designer,* Southern Illinois University, University Museum, Carbondale IL

Harber, Margaret Neiman, *Pres,* Society of Scribes, Ltd, New York NY

Harbison, Carol, *Library Mgr,* Southern Oregon Historical Society, Library, Jacksonville OR

Harbison, Craig, *Prof,* University of Massachusetts, Amherst, Art History Program, Amherst MA (S)

Hard, Michael W, *Treas,* Amerind Foundation, Inc, Amerind Museum, Fulton-Hayden Memorial Art Gallery, Dragoon AZ

Hard, Michael W, *Treas,* Amerind Foundation, Inc, Fulton-Hayden Memorial Library, Dragoon AZ

Hardberger, Linda, *Cur Tobin Theatre Coll & Library,* Marion Koogler McNay Art Museum, San Antonio TX

Harders, Faith, *Librn,* University of Kentucky, Hunter M Adams Architecture Library, Lexington KY

Hardesty, David, *Chmn,* Oregon State University, Dept of Art, Corvallis OR (S)

Hardesty, Patricia, *Serials Librn,* Harvard University, Library, Washington DC

Hardey, Sharon, *Registrar,* Illinois State University, Museum Library, Normal IL

Hardginski, Jean, *Mgr Bldg Servs,* The Pillsbury Company, Art Collection, Minneapolis MN

Hardiman, George W, *In Charge Art Educ,* University of Illinois, Urbana-Champaign, School of Art and Design, Champaign IL (S)

Hardin, Kris, *African Section Asst Cur,* University of Pennsylvania, University Museum of Archaeology & Anthropology, Philadelphia PA

Hardin, Laura Vookles, *Cur,* Hudson River Museum, Yonkers NY

Harding, Ann, *Prof,* Louisiana State University, School of Art, Baton Rouge LA (S)

Harding, Carol S, *Deputy Dir External Affairs,* Winterthur Museum and Gardens, Winterthur DE

Harding, Catherine, *Asst Prof,* University of Victoria, Dept of History in Art, Victoria BC (S)

Harding, Suzanne, *Assoc Prof,* Seton Hill College, Dept of Art, Greensburg PA (S)

Harding, Thomas, *Instr,* The Arkansas Arts Center, Museum School, Little Rock AR (S)

Hardman, Barbara, *Pres,* Arts Council of San Mateo County, Belmont CA

Hardwig, Scott, *Assoc Prof,* Roanoke College, Fine Arts Dept-Art, Salem VA (S)

Hardy, Chantal, *Instr,* Universite de Montreal, Dept of Art History, Montreal PQ (S)

Hardy, David, *Gallery Supt & Preparator,* University of Utah, Utah Museum of Fine Arts, Salt Lake City UT

Hardy, Dominick, *Prog Asst,* Art Gallery of Peterborough, Peterborough ON

Hardy, Leah, *Asst Prof,* Sam Houston State University, Art Dept, Huntsville TX (S)

Hardy, Neil, *Asst Prof,* Johns Hopkins University, School of Medicine, Dept of Art as Applied to Medicine, Baltimore MD (S)

Hardy, Saralyn Reece, *Dir,* Salina Art Center, Salina KS

Hardy-Pilon, Claudette, *Pres,* Canadian Crafts Council, Conseil Canadien de l'Artisanat, Ottawa ON

Hare, John, *Chief Preparator,* Hunter Museum of Art, Chattanooga TN

Hare, William E, *Dir,* New London County Historical Society, New London CT

Haren, John Van, *Dept Head,* Eastern Michigan University, Ford Gallery, Ypsilanti MI

Harger, Dale R, *Pres,* Higgins Armory Museum, Worcester MA

Hargett, Marty, *Assoc Prof,* Lincoln College, Art Dept, Lincoln IL (S)

Hargrove, Mary, *Secy,* Hudson Valley Art Association, Flushing NY

Harington, Donald, *Assoc Prof,* University of Arkansas, Art Dept, Fayetteville AR (S)

Harkavy, Donna, *Cur Contemporary Art,* Worcester Art Museum, Worcester MA

Harkins, William E, *Pres,* Ukiyo-e Society of America, Inc, New York NY

Harless, Susan, *Cur of Exhibits,* High Desert Museum, Bend OR

Harlow, Ann, *Dir,* Saint Mary's College of California, Hearst Art Gallery, Moraga CA

Harm, Nancy, *Registrar,* Cornell University, Herbert F Johnson Museum of Art, Ithaca NY

Harman, Julia, *Dir & Cur,* Houston Museum of Decorative Arts, Chattanooga TN

Harman, Maryann, *Prof,* Virginia Polytechnic Institute & State University, Dept of Art & Art History, Blacksburg VA (S)

Harmes, Michael, *Acad Dean,* Ontario College of Art, Toronto ON (S)

Harmon, Charles, *Asst Prof,* Winthrop College, Dept of Art & Design, Rock Hill SC (S)

Harmon, Foster, *Dir,* Foster Harmon Galleries of American Art, Sarasota FL

Harmon, Foster, *Dir,* Foster Harmon Galleries of American Art, Library, Sarasota FL

Harmon, Jean, *Assoc Prof,* Missouri Western State College, Art Dept, Saint Joseph MO (S)

Harmon, Rick, *Quarterly Ed,* Oregon Historical Society, Library, Portland OR

Harmsen, Jeri, *Educ Officer,* Queen's University, Agnes Etherington Art Centre, Kingston ON

Harmsen, Phyllis, *Secy,* Augustana College, Center for Western Studies, Sioux Falls SD

Harmsen, Phyllis, *Secy,* Augustana College, Center for Western Studies, Sioux Falls SD

Harned, Hal C, *Exec Dir,* Lexington Art League, Inc, Lexington KY

Harnly, Marc, *Paper Conservator,* Balboa Art Conservation Center, San Diego CA

Harper, David, *Pres of Board,* Fort Smith Art Center, Fort Smith AR

Harper, George D, *Asst Prof,* Glenville State College, Dept of Fine Arts, Glenville WV (S)

Harper, Katherine, *Assoc Prof,* Loyola Marymount University, Art & Art History Dept, Los Angeles CA (S)

Harper, Lucy Bjorklund, *Librn,* University of Rochester, Charlotte W Allen Memorial Art Gallery Library, Rochester NY

Harper, Margaret, *Div Chair Arts & Science,* Oakland City College, Division of Fine Arts, Oakland City IN (S)

Harper, Paula, *Assoc Prof,* University of Miami, Dept of Art & Art History, Coral Gables FL (S)

Harper, Prudence O, *Chmn Ancient Near Eastern Art,* The Metropolitan Museum of Art, New York NY

Harper, Robert W, *Exec Dir,* Lightner Museum, Saint Augustine FL

Harper, Suzanne, *Dir of Fine Arts,* Museum of Arts and Sciences, Inc, Macon GA

Harrigan, Kenneth W, *Chmn Board of Trustees,* Royal Ontario Museum, Toronto ON

Harrington, Peggy, *Dir,* Cathedral of Saint John the Divine, New York NY

Harrington, Ruthanne, *Lectr,* Notre Dame College, Art Dept, Manchester NH (S)

Harrington, Susan, *Prof,* Texas Christian University, Art & Art History Dept, Fort Worth TX (S)

Harris, Al, *Dir,* University of Texas at Arlington, Center for Research & Contemporary Arts, Arlington TX

Harris, Albert, *Museum Coordr,* Portsmouth Museums, Arts Center, Portsmouth VA

Harris, Alisas, *Treas,* Artworks, The Visual Art School of Princeton and Trenton, Trenton NJ

Harris, Allyn O, *Gallery Dir,* Baltimore City Community College, Art Gallery, Baltimore MD

Harris, Allyn O, *Prof,* New Community College of Baltimore, Dept of Fine Arts, Baltimore MD (S)

Harris, A Peter, *Dir,* Rodman Hall Arts Centre, Saint Catharines ON

Harris, Caroline, *Dir Development,* The Drawing Center, New York NY

Harris, David J, *Instr,* North Seattle Community College, Art Dept, Seattle WA (S)

Harris, Donald, *Dean Col,* Ohio State University, College of the Arts, Columbus OH (S)

Harris, Ellen, *Dir,* Montclair Art Museum, Montclair NJ

Harris, Ellen, *Dir,* Montclair Art Museum, Art School, Montclair NJ (S)

Harris, Frann, *Educ Liaison,* University of Saskatchewan, John G Diefenbaker Centre, Saskatoon SK

Harris, Gene E, *Cur Coll,* Brandywine River Museum, Chadds Ford PA

Harris, Joe, *Technical Theater & Visual Arts,* Culver-Stockton College, Division of Fine Arts, Canton MO (S)

Harris, Karen, *Dir,* Marymount Manhattan College Gallery, New York NY

Harris, Lou, *Division Chmn,* University of Tampa, Dept of Art, Tampa FL (S)

Harris, Marie Joan, *Aceadmic Dean,* Avila College, Thornhill Art Gallery, Kansas City MO

Harris, Michael, *Coordr Photography Hall Fame,* Oklahoma Center for Science and Art, Kirkpatrick Center, Oklahoma City OK

Harris, Michele, *Dir Finance,* Mississippi Museum of Art, Jackson MS

Harris, Miriam B, *Dir,* Colorado State University, Curfman Gallery, Fort Collins CO

Harris, Mona, *Gallery Dir,* Lahaina Arts Society, Art Organization, Lahaina HI

Harris, Patrick, *Gallery Dir,* College of Santa Fe, Visual Arts Dept, Santa Fe NM (S)

Harris, Rhonda, *Prog Coordr,* The Light Factory, Inc, Charlotte NC

Harris, Robert A, *Dir,* Helen M Plum Memorial Library, Lombard IL

Harris, Ronna, *Asst Prof,* Tulane University, Sophie H Newcomb Memorial College, New Orleans LA (S)

Harris, Stanley, *Communications Dir,* The Albrecht-Kemper Museum of Art, Saint Joseph MO

Harrison, Alexandra, *Community Relations,* Art Gallery of Hamilton, Hamilton ON

Harrison, Cheryl, *Chmn,* High Point College, Fine Arts Dept, High Point NC (S)

Harrison, Ed, *Pres Bd of Governors,* Natural History Museum of Los Angeles County, Los Angeles CA

Harrison, Helen, *VPres,* Key West Art and Historical Society, East Martello Museum and Gallery, Key West FL

Harrison, Jeff, *Cur European Art,* Chrysler Museum, Norfolk VA

Harrison, Joan, *Assoc Prof,* C W Post Center of Long Island University, School of Visual & Performing Arts, Greenvale NY (S)

Harrison, Lucy, *Dance & Theater Librn,* California Institute of the Arts Library, Santa Clarita CA

Harrison, Pam, *Cur,* Pasadena Historical Society, Pasadena CA

Harrison, Tony, *Instr,* Columbia University, School of the Arts, Division of Painting & Sculpture, New York NY (S)

Harrist, Robert, *Asst Prof,* Oberlin College, Dept of Art, Oberlin OH (S)

Harrity, Gail, *Admin,* Solomon R Guggenheim Museum, New York NY

Hart, Ann, *Studio Arts,* Wiregrass Museum of Art, Dothan AL

Hart, Arnold, *Instr,* Okaloosa-Walton Junior College, Dept of Fine and Performing Arts, Niceville FL (S)

Hart, Barbara A, *Assoc Dir for Admin,* National Portrait Gallery, Washington DC

Hart, Diane, *Registrar,* Williams College, Museum of Art, Williamstown MA

Hart, E J, *Dir,* Peter and Catharine Whyte Foundation, Whyte Museum of the Canadian Rockies, Banff AB

Hart, Katherine, *Cur Academic Progs,* Dartmouth College, Hood Museum of Art, Hanover NH

Hart, Robert G, *Gen Mgr,* United States Department of the Interior, Indian Arts & Crafts Board, Washington DC

Hart, Vincent, *Lectr,* Georgian Court College, Dept of Art, Lakewood NJ (S)

Hartcourt, Glenn, *Asst Prof,* University of Southern California, School of Fine Arts, Los Angeles CA (S)

Hartfield, Ronne, *Exec Dir Museum Educ,* The Art Institute of Chicago, Chicago IL

Harth, Marjorie L, *Dir,* Galleries of the Claremont Colleges, Claremont CA

Harthorn, Sandy, *Cur of Exhibitions,* Boise Art Museum, Boise ID

Hartigan, Grace, *Dir,* Maryland Institute, Hoffberger School of Painting, Baltimore MD (S)

Hartke, Mary, *VPres,* Iroquois County Historical Society Museum, Old Courthouse Museum, Watseka IL

Hartman, Bruce, *Dir Art Gallery,* Johnson County Community College, Visual Arts Program, Overland Park KS (S)

Hartman, Eleanor, *Librn,* Los Angeles County Museum of Art, Los Angeles CA

Hartman, Eleanor C, *Librn,* Los Angeles County Museum of Art, Library, Los Angeles CA

Hartman, Hedy, *Pres & Chief Exec Officer,* Staten Island Institute of Arts and Sciences, Staten Island NY

Hartman, Mark, *Planetarium Dir,* Museum of the Southwest, Midland TX

Hartman, Mark, *Planetarium Dir,* Museum of the Southwest, Library, Midland TX

Hartman, Mark A, *Cur Astronomy,* Hastings Museum, Hastings NE

Hartman, Terry L, *Instr,* Modesto Junior College, Arts Humanities and Speech Division, Modesto CA (S)

Hartmere, Anne, *Architecture & Urban Planning Librn,* University of California, Los Angeles, Arts Library, Los Angeles CA

Hartshom, Janet, *Information Receptionist,* London Regional Art & Historical Museums, London ON

Hartshorn, Willis, *Deputy Dir for Prog,* International Center of Photography, New York NY

Hartswick, Kim, *Assoc Prof,* George Washington University, Dept of Art, Washington DC (S)

Hartt, Kathleen, *Archivist,* Museum of Fine Arts, Houston, Hirsch Library, Houston TX

Hartwell, Carroll T, *Cur Photography,* Minneapolis Society of Fine Arts, Minneapolis Institute of Arts, Minneapolis MN

Hartwell, Janice E, *Assoc Prof,* Florida State University, Art Dept, Tallahassee FL (S)

Harty, Lela, *Dir,* Lela Harty School of Art, San Diego CA (S)

Hartz, Jill, *Community Relations Coordr,* Cornell University, Herbert F Johnson Museum of Art, Ithaca NY

Hartzad, Susan, *Cur,* McLean County Historical Society, Bloomington IL

Hartzell, Helen F, *Mgr Museum Store,* Westmoreland Museum of Art, Greensburg PA

Harvath, John, *Mgr, Fine Arts & Recreation,* Houston Public Library, Houston TX

Harvey, Bruce, *Dir,* Housatonic Community College, Library, Bridgeport CT

Harvey, Bunny, *Assoc Prof,* Wellesley College, Art Dept, Wellesley MA (S)

Harvey, Clifford, *Prof,* West Virginia University, College of Creative Arts, Morgantown WV (S)

Harvey, D, *Prof,* University of Victoria, Dept of Visual Arts, Victoria BC (S)

Harvey, Edward, *Head,* Allan Hancock College, Fine Arts Dept, Santa Maria CA (S)

Harvey, Emily, *Chmn,* Rockland Community College, Graphic Arts & Advertising Tech Dept, Suffern NY (S)

Harvey, George, *VPres,* Pope County Historical Society Museum, Glenwood MN

Harvey, Lois, *Librn,* Art And Culture Center Of Hollywood, Art Reference Library, Hollywood FL

Harvey, Marjorie, *Mgr Exhib,* High Museum of Art, Atlanta GA

Harvey, Phillis, *Asst Dir,* Society of Illustrators, Museum of American Illustration, New York NY

Harvey, Robert, *Chmn,* Merced College, Arts Division, Merced CA (S)

Harwick, James A, *Cur Antique Auto Museum,* Heritage Plantation of Sandwich, Sandwich MA

Harwick, Joanne, *Assoc Prof,* Fort Hays State University, Dept of Art, Hays KS (S)

Harwit, Martin, *Dir,* National Air and Space Museum, Washington DC

Hasbrouck, Kenneth E, *Pres,* Huguenot Historical Society of New Paltz, Locust Lawn, Gardiner NY

Hasen, Irwin, *Instr,* Joe Kubert School of Cartoon & Graphic Art, Inc, Dover NJ (S)

Hashimoto, Alan, *Asst Prof,* Utah State University, Dept of Art, Logan UT (S)

Haskell, Barbara, *Cur,* Whitney Museum of American Art, New York NY

Haskell, Eric, *Dir,* Scripps College, Clark Humanities Museum, Claremont CA

Haskell, Heather, *Cur Coll,* Museum of Fine Arts, Springfield MA

Haskin, Daniel, *Recording Secy,* Buffalo Society of Artists, Kenmore NY

Hasrold, Carol, *Librn,* Vesterheim Norwegian-American Museum, Reference Library, Decorah IA

Hasselbalch, Kurt, *Cur,* Massachusetts Institute of Technology, Hart Nautical Galleries and Collections, Cambridge MA

Hasselfelt, Karen, *Dir,* Surrey Art Gallery, Surrey BC

Hassey, Bob, *Dir Finance & Administration,* USS Constitution Museum Foundation Inc, Boston National Historical Park, Museum, Boston MA

Hassrick, Peter H, *Dir,* Buffalo Bill Memorial Association, Buffalo Bill Historical Center, Cody WY

Hastanan, Skowmon, *Asst to Dir,* Lehman College Art Gallery, Bronx NY

Hastedt, Cathy, *Registrar Art,* Texas A & M University, University Center Galleries, College Station TX

Hastings, Patti, *Vis Instr,* Atlanta College of Art, Atlanta GA (S)

Haswell, Susan, *Site Mgr,* Schuyler Mansion State Historic Site, Albany NY

Hatch, Ann, *Pres,* Capp Street Project, San Francisco CA

Hatch, Bill, *Dept Head,* San Juan College, Art Dept, Farmington NM (S)

Hatcher, Keith, *Dept Head,* Southern Connecticut State University, Dept of Art, New Haven CT (S)

Hatfield, Barbara, *Dir,* North Dakota State University, Memorial Union Art Gallery, Fargo ND

Hatfield, Thomas A, *Exec Dir,* National Art Education Association, Reston VA

Hathaway, Carol J, *Instr,* Roger Williams College, Art Dept, Bristol RI (S)

Hathaway, Joan, *Asst Dir,* Fitchburg Art Museum, Fitchburg MA

Hauck, Judy, *Registrar,* Alaska State Museum, Juneau AK

Haug, Donald R, *Dir,* Chautauqua Art Association Galleries, Chautauqua NY

Hauge, Lila, *Dir,* Mayville State University Gallery, Mayville ND

Hauge, Lila, *Art Dept Chmn,* Valley City State College, Art Dept, Valley City ND (S)

Haught, Roy, *Prof,* Loras College, Dept of Art, Dubuque IA (S)

Hauptman, Kathy, *Div Performing Arts,* Wichita Center for the Arts, Wichita KS (S)

Hausey, Robert, *Prof,* Louisiana State University, School of Art, Baton Rouge LA (S)

Hausrath, Joan, *Prof,* Bridgewater State College, Art Dept, Bridgewater MA (S)

Haut, Sheryl, *Research Librn,* Davenport Museum of Art, Davenport IA

Haut, Sheryl, *Librn,* Davenport Museum of Art, Art Reference Library, Davenport IA

Havas, Edwin, *Instr,* Montclair Art Museum, Art School, Montclair NJ (S)

Havas, Edwin, *Asst Prof,* Seton Hall University, College of Arts & Sciences, South Orange NJ (S)

Havas, Sandy, *Dir,* Eccles Community Art Center, Ogden UT

Havel, Joseph, *Prof,* Austin College, Art Dept, Sherman TX (S)

Havelak, Sharon, *Chmn Fine Arts,* Lourdes College, Art Dept, Sylvania OH (S)

Havemeyer, Ann, *Archivist,* Norfolk Historical Society Inc, Museum, Norfolk CT

Haven, Mark, *Assoc Prof,* Rochester Institute of Technology, School of Photographic Arts & Sciences, Rochester NY (S)

Havens, Neil, *Prof,* Rice University, Dept of Art and Art History, Houston TX (S)

Havens, Sarah, *Exec Dir,* American Council for the Arts, New York NY

Haver, Ronald, *Dir Film Programs,* Los Angeles County Museum of Art, Los Angeles CA

Hawes, Louis, *Prof,* Indiana University, Bloomington, Henry Radford Hope School of Fine Arts, Bloomington IN (S)

Hawk, Steven, *Librn & Dir,* Akron-Summit County Public Library, Fine Arts Division, Akron OH

Hawkes, Carol, *Dean,* Western Connecticut State University, School of Arts & Sciences, Danbury CT (S)

Hawkins, Ashton, *Exec VPres & Counsel,* The Metropolitan Museum of Art, New York NY

Hawkins, John, *Prof,* Queensborough Community College, Dept of Art and Photography, Bayside NY (S)

Hawkins, Laura Kat, *Interim Dir,* Western Montana College, Art Gallery/Museum, Dillon MT

Hawkins, Lewis, *Asst Prof,* Maryland College of Art and Design, Silver Spring MD (S)

Hawkins, Pamela S, *Asst Dir,* Pyramid Arts Center, Rochester NY

Hawley, Anne, *Dir,* Isabella Stewart Gardner Museum, Boston MA

Hawley, Henry, *Chief Cur Later Western Art,* Cleveland Museum of Art, Cleveland OH

Haworth, Stephen K, *Asst Prof,* University of West Florida, Dept of Art, Pensacola FL (S)

Hawryliuk, Phyllis, *Exec Asst,* Ukrainian Cultural and Educational Centre, Winnipeg MB

Haxthausen, Charles, *Assoc Prof,* University of Minnesota, Minneapolis, Art History, Minneapolis MN (S)

Hayano, Carl, *VPres for Academic Affairs,* Kendall College of Art & Design, Frank & Lyn Van Steenberg Library, Grand Rapids MI

Hayashi, Masumi, *Assoc Prof,* Cleveland State University, Art Dept, Cleveland OH (S)

Haydel, Douglas, *Div Chmn,* Thomas College, Humanities Division, Thomasville GA (S)

Hayden, Cynthia L, *Museum Technician,* Fort George G Meade Museum, Fort Meade MD

Hayden, Jackie, *Instr,* Chautauqua Institution, School of Art, Chautauqua NY (S)

Hayden, Sally, *Managing Ed & Public Relations,* University of Kansas, Spencer Museum of Art, Lawrence KS

Haydu, John R, *Assoc Prof,* Central Missouri State University, Art Dept, Warrensburg MO (S)

Hayes, Ann Marie, *Museum Educator,* Davenport Museum of Art, Davenport IA

Hayes, Bonnie, *Asst Prof,* Beaver College, Dept of Fine Arts, Glenside PA (S)

Hayes, Cheryl A, *Asst Prof,* University of New Orleans-Lake Front, Dept of Fine Arts, New Orleans LA (S)

Hayes, Janet, *Recording Secy,* Key West Art and Historical Society, East Martello Museum and Gallery, Key West FL

Hayes, Joe, *Cur Anthropology,* Institute of the Great Plains, Museum of the Great Plains, Lawton OK

Hayes, Philip, *Illustration Chmn,* Art Center College of Design, Pasadena CA (S)

Hayes, Randall, *Executive Dir,* Brevard Art Center and Museum, Inc, Melbourne FL

Hayes, Stephen, *Instr,* Marylhurst College, Art Dept, Marylhurst OR (S)

Hayes, Trisha, *Dir Public Relations,* Southern Vermont Art Center, Manchester VT

Haymaker, James, *Dir,* Pfeiffer College, Art Program, Misenheimer NC (S)

Haynes, Sandra, *Acting Area Head History,* Pasadena City College, Art Dept, Pasadena CA (S)

Haynie, Ron, *Dir,* American University, Watkins Collection, Washington DC

Hays, Audrey, *Head Librn,* Norfolk Public Library, Feldman Fine Arts & Audio Visual Dept, Norfolk VA

Hays, Margo, *Asst Cur,* Sloss Furnaces National Historic Landmark, Birmingham AL

Hayton, Greg, *Chief Librn,* Cambridge Public Library and Gallery, Cambridge ON

Hayum, Andree, *Division Chmn,* Fordham University, Art Dept, New York NY (S)

Hayward, Jane, *Cur,* The Metropolitan Museum of Art, The Cloisters, New York NY

Hazelgrove, Nancy, *Cur,* University of Toronto, Blackwood Gallery, Mississauga ON

Hazelhurst, Gail, *Gallery Dir,* The Gallery at Hawaii Loa College, Marinda Lee Gallery, Kaneohe HI

Hazelroth, Susan, *Dir Student Educ,* State Art Museum of Florida, John & Mable Ringling Museum of Art, Sarasota FL

Hazelwood, Carl, *Art Dir,* Aljira Center for Contemporary Art, Newark NJ

Hazelwood, Donna, *Asst Prof,* Oakland City College, Division of Fine Arts, Oakland City IN (S)

Hazen, Ellen Z, *Registrar,* Kendall Whaling Museum, Sharon MA

Hazlehurst, F Hamilton, *Prof,* Vanderbilt University, Dept of Fine Arts, Nashville TN (S)

Hazleton, Jayne, *Registrar,* Oklahoma City Art Museum, Oklahoma City OK

Hazlett, Ann R, *VPres,* First State Bank, Norton KS

Hazlitt, Donald, *Instr,* Columbia University, School of the Arts, Division of Painting & Sculpture, New York NY (S)

Hazlitt, Donald, *Faculty,* Columbia University, School of the Arts, Division of Painting & Sculpture, New York NY (S)

Heacock, Scott, *Treas,* Toledo Federation of Art Societies, Inc, Toledo OH

Head, Robert W, *Prof,* Murray State University, Art Dept, Murray KY (S)

Heafner, Donald, *VPres,* Southern Arkansas University, Art Dept Gallery & Magale Art Gallery, Magnolia AR

Heald, David, *Photographer,* Solomon R Guggenheim Museum, New York NY

Healey, Ann, *Pres,* San Francisco City & County Arts Commission, San Francisco CA

Healy, Anne, *Chmn,* University of California, Berkeley, College of Letters & Sciences-Art Dept, Berkeley CA (S)

Healy, Timothy S, *Pres,* The New York Public Library, New York NY

Heaphy, Maryann, *Dir Library,* Englewood Library, Fine Arts Dept, Englewood NJ

Heard, J, *Instr,* Golden West College, Visual Art Dept, Huntington Beach CA (S)

Heard, Virginia, *Dir,* Sandwich Historical Society, Center Sandwich NH

Hearth, Dale, *Dir Performing Arts ,* Palm Springs Desert Museum, Inc, Palm Springs CA

Heasley, Charles, *Assoc Prof,* State University of New York, College at Cortland, Art Dept, Cortland NY (S)

Heath, Anne, *Chmn General Studies,* California State University, Northridge, Dept of Art-Two Dimensional Media, Northridge CA (S)

Heath, Samuel K, *Dir,* Southern Methodist University, Meadows Museum, Dallas TX

Heaton, Jim, *Pres Chilkat Valley Historical Society,* Chilkat Valley Historical Society, Sheldon Museum & Cultural Center, Haines AK

Hebb, Grace, *Secy & Bookkeeper,* Douglas County Historical Society, Fairlawn Mansion & Museum, Superior WI

Hebert, Al, *Prof,* Macomb Community College, Art Dept, Warren MI (S)

Hebert, Arline, *Chmn,* Toronto School of Art, Toronto ON (S)

Hecht, Suzanne, *Division Chmn,* Wells College, Dept of Art, Aurora NY (S)

Hecker, Frances E, *Head,* Tulane University, Architecture Library, New Orleans LA

Hecker, Jennifer, *Asst Prof,* State University of New York College at Brockport, Dept of Art & Art History, Brockport NY (S)

Hecksher, Morrison H, *Cur American Decorative Art,* The Metropolitan Museum of Art, New York NY

Hedblom, Bette, *Dir,* Arizona Watercolor Association, Phoenix AZ

Heder, Terence, *Dir,* Meridian Museum of Art, Meridian MS

Hedin, Thomas F, *Prof,* University of Minnesota, Duluth, Art Dept, Duluth MN (S)

Hedman, Donn, *Instr,* Indiana University of Pennsylvania, Dept of Art and Art Education, Indiana PA (S)

Hedquist, Valerie, *Prof,* Washington and Lee University, Division of Art, Lexington VA (S)

Hedyschultz, Eleen, *Pres,* Society of Illustrators, New York NY

Heeger, Gerald A, *Dean,* New School for Social Research, Adult Education Division, New York NY (S)

Heekin, Susan, *Dir,* University of Cincinnati, Tangeman Fine Arts Gallery, Cincinnati OH

Heelis, Sharon Lyn, *Art Gallery Secy,* Brigham Young University, B F Larsen Gallery, Provo UT

Heffley, Lynda, *Cur,* City of Charleston, City Hall Council Chamber Gallery, Charleston SC

Heffley, Scott, *Asst Conservator,* Nelson-Atkins Museum of Art, Kansas City MO

Heffner, Jinger, *Exhibit Coordr,* Los Angeles Contemporary Exhibitions, Los Angeles CA

Heffner, Terry, *Assoc Dir,* Meredith Gallery, Baltimore MD

Heflin, Patricia, *Fine Arts Support Specialist,* US Department of State, Diplomatic Reception Rooms, Washington DC

Hegarty, Kevin, *Dir,* Tacoma Public Library, Handforth Gallery, Tacoma WA

Hegarty, Marianna, *Cur,* Gilbert Stuart Memorial Association, Inc, Museum, Saunderstown RI

Hegarty, Melinda, *Asst Prof,* Eastern Illinois University, Art Dept, Charleston IL (S)

Hegarty, Michael, *Cur,* Gilbert Stuart Memorial Association, Inc, Museum, Saunderstown RI

Hehman, Jennifer, *Assoc Librn,* Indiana University - Purdue University at Indianapolis, Herron School of Art Library, Indianapolis IN

Heideman, Susan, *Chmn Art Dept,* Smith College, Art Dept, Northampton MA (S)

Heil, Elizabeth, *Asst Prof,* Roanoke College, Fine Arts Dept-Art, Salem VA (S)

Heil, Harry, *Gallery Dir,* Western State College of Colorado, Quigley Hall Art Gallery, Gunnison CO

Heineman, Jan, *Secy,* Maricopa County Historical Society, Desert Caballeros Western Museum, Wickenburg AZ

Heineman, Stephanie, *Dir,* Northport-East Northport Public Library, Northport NY

Heinenman, Laureen, *Pres of Board,* Oshkosh Public Museum, Oshkosh WI

Heinicke, Janet, *Chairperson Dept,* Simpson College, Art Dept, Indianola IA (S)

Heinicke, Janet, *Head Art Dept,* Simpson College, Farnham Gallery, Indianola IA

Heinrich, Milton, *Prof,* Dana College, Art Dept, Blair NE (S)

Heinrich, Roberta, *Visual Arts & Community Programs Dir,* Sun Valley Center for the Arts and Humanities, Dept of Fine Art, Sun Valley ID (S)

Heinson, Lillian, *Slide Librn,* York University, Fine Arts Phase II Slide Library, North York ON

Heintzman, John, *Cur Coll & Exhib,* Lakeview Museum of Arts and Sciences, Peoria IL

Heinzen, Mary Ann, *Pres,* National Art League Inc, Douglaston NY

Heipp, Richard, *Assoc Prof,* University of Florida, Dept of Art, Gainesville FL (S)

Heisch, Melvena, *Preservation Dir,* Oklahoma Historical Society, State Museum of History, Oklahoma City OK

Heischman, Robert, *Prof,* Rochester Institute of Technology, School of Art and Design, Rochester NY (S)

Heise, Lane, *Instr,* Harcum Junior College, Dept of Fine Arts, Bryn Mawr PA (S)

Heislar, Franklyn, *Cur,* Muttart Art Gallery, Calgary AB

Heiss, Alanna, *Exec Dir Institute,* Institute for Contemporary Art, Project Studio One (P S 1), Long Island City NY

Heit, Dorothea, *Vis Prof,* Oral Roberts University, Fine Arts Dept, Tulsa OK (S)

Heitz, Thomas R, *Historian,* National Baseball Hall of Fame and Museum, Inc, Art Collection, Cooperstown NY

Held, Nancy L, *Lectr,* Johns Hopkins University, School of Medicine, Dept of Art as Applied to Medicine, Baltimore MD (S)

Held, Peter, *Gallery Dir,* Salem Art Association, Bush Barn Art Center, Salem OR

Helfrich/ MFA, Paul, *Assoc Prof,* College of William and Mary, Dept of Fine Arts, Williamsburg VA (S)

Hellberg, Ray, *Prof,* Utah State University, Dept of Art, Logan UT (S)

Heller, Angelica, *VPres,* The National Art Museum of Sport, Indianapolis IN

Heller, Barbara, *Head Conservator,* Detroit Institute of Arts, Detroit MI

Heller, John, *Prof,* Bridgewater State College, Art Dept, Bridgewater MA (S)

Heller, Kevin, *Asst Supv,* Newark Museum Association, Junior Museum, Newark NJ

Heller, Susanna, *Instr,* Sarah Lawrence College, Dept of Art History, Bronxville NY (S)

Hellier, Bob, *Preparator,* Tampa Museum of Art, Tampa FL

Helm, Alison, *Prof,* West Virginia University, College of Creative Arts, Morgantown WV (S)

Helm, David, *Vis Asst Prof,* Wake Forest University, Dept of Art, Winston-Salem NC (S)

Helpern, Frank, *Bibliographer,* Free Library of Philadelphia, Rare Book Dept, Philadelphia PA

Helsell, Charles, *Cur, Art Coll,* 3M, Art Collection, Saint Paul MN

Helzel, Florence, *Cur,* Judah L Magnes Museum, Berkeley CA

Helzer, Richard, *Dir Art,* Montana State University, School of Art, Bozeman MT (S)

Hemdahl-Owen, Ann, *Assoc Prof,* Jefferson Community College, Fine Arts, Louisville KY (S)

Hemphill, Ingrid, *First VPres,* Berks Art Alliance, Reading PA

Hench, Robert, *Gallery Dir,* University of Southern Colorado, College of Liberal & Fine Arts, Pueblo CO

Hench, Robert, *Assoc Prof,* University of Southern Colorado, Belmont Campus, Dept of Art, Pueblo CO (S)

Hendershot, James, *Assoc Prof,* Saint John's University, Art Dept, Collegeville MN (S)

Henderson, Barry, *Librn,* Beaverbrook Art Gallery, Library, Fredericton NB

Henderson, Doug, *Branch Adminr,* Las Vegas-Clark County Library District, Las Vegas NV

Henderson, Janet, *Office Mgr,* Maryland-National Capital Park & Planning Commission, Montpelier Cultural Arts Center, Laurel MD

Henderson, John T, *Pres,* Jefferson Community College, Art Dept, Watertown NY (S)

Henderson, Jon M, *Mgr Library Services,* Hallmark Cards, Inc, Creative Library, Kansas City MO

Henderson, Lana, *Prof,* North Carolina Central University, Art Dept, Durham NC (S)

Henderson, Lyman, *Pres,* Arts and Letters Club of Toronto, Toronto ON

Henderson, Maren, *Prof,* California State Polytechnic University, Pomona, Art Dept, Pomona CA (S)

Henderson, Ruth, *Acting Chief Librn,* City College of the City University of New York, Morris Raphael Cohen Library, New York NY

Henderson, Thomas, *Assoc Prof,* Mount Allison University, Fine Arts Dept, Sackville NB (S)

Hendig, Cathy, *Instr,* Monterey Peninsula College, Art Dept, Monterey CA (S)

Hendley, B, *Dean,* University of Waterloo, Fine Arts Dept, Waterloo ON (S)

Hendley, Susan, *Pres Board Dir,* Zanesville Art Center, Zanesville OH

Hendrick, Joe, *Assoc Prof,* Monroe Community College, Art Dept, Rochester NY (S)

Hendricks, Barkley L, *Prof,* Connecticut College, Dept of Art, New London CT (S)

Hendricks, Geoffrey, *Prof,* Rutgers, the State University of New Jersey, Mason Gross School of the Arts, New Brunswick NJ (S)

Hendricks, Joan, *Registrar,* State University of New York at Purchase, Neuberger Museum, Purchase NY

Hendricks, Larry, *Dir Humanities & Fine Arts,* Sacramento City College, Art Dept, Sacramento CA (S)

Hendricks, Leta, *Librn,* Ohio State University, Human Ecology Library, Columbus OH

Hendrickson, Bill, *Pres,* Mason County Museum, Maysville KY

Hendrickson, Morry, *Prof,* Shoreline Community College, Humanities Division, Seattle WA (S)

Hendrickson, Ted, *Asst Prof,* Connecticut College, Dept of Art, New London CT (S)

Hendrikx, Gim, *Assoc Prof,* Mount Vernon Nazarene College, Art Dept, Mount Vernon OH (S)

Hendrix, Randy P, *Asst to the Dir,* Westminster College, Winston Churchill Memorial & Library in the United States, Fulton MO

Henisch, Heinz, *Prof,* Pennsylvania State University, University Park, Dept of Art History, University Park PA (S)

Henke, Dellas, *Assoc Prof,* Grand Valley State University, Art & Design Dept, Allendale MI (S)

Henke, Jerry D, *Executive Dir,* Fillmore County Historical Society, Fountain MN

Henkel, James, *Assoc Prof,* University of Minnesota, Minneapolis, Dept of Studio Art, Minneapolis MN (S)

Hennage, David E, *VPres for Admin,* Museum of Science and Industry, Chicago IL

Hennessey, Colleen, *Archivist,* Freer Gallery of Art & The Arthur M Sackler Gallery Gallery, Library, Washington DC

Hennessey, Maureen Hart, *Cur,* Norman Rockwell Museum at Stockbridge, Stockbridge MA

Hennessey, Maureen Hart, *Cur,* Norman Rockwell Museum at Stockbridge, Library, Stockbridge MA

Hennessey, William, *Dir,* University of Michigan, Museum of Art, Ann Arbor MI

Hennessy, William, *Dir Museum Art,* University of Michigan, Ann Arbor, Dept of History of Art, Ann Arbor MI (S)

Hennigar, Robert, *Computer Graphics Chmn,* Art Center College of Design, Pasadena CA (S)

Henning, Darrell D, *Dir,* Vesterheim Norwegian-American Museum, Decorah IA

Henning, Jean, *Coordr Young People's Program,* Nassau County Museum of Fine Art, Roslyn NY

Henning, Jean, *Membership,* Ward Foundation, Ward Museum of Wildfowl Art, Salisbury MD

Henning, Robert, *Asst Dir Curatorial Affairs,* Santa Barbara Museum of Art, Santa Barbara CA

Henning, Roni, *Master Printer,* New York Institute of Technology, Fine Arts Dept, Old Westbury NY (S)

Henning, William, *Cur,* University of Kentucky, Art Museum, Lexington KY

Hennum, Paulette, *Registrar,* Crocker Art Museum, Sacramento CA

Henrickson, Steve, *Cur Coll,* Alaska State Museum, Juneau AK

Henriques, Beth, *Asst Dir,* The Queens Museum of Art, Flushing NY

Henry, Ed, *Deputy Dir for Admin & Finance,* Museum of the City of New York, New York NY

Henry, Hugh, *Education Coordr,* Swift Current National Exhibition Centre, Swift Current SK

Henry, Jean, *Dir & Cur,* The Museum at Drexel University, Philadelphia PA

Henry, John, *Coordr of Galleries,* St Clair County Community College, Jack R Hennesey Art Galleries, Port Huron MI

Henry, Karen, *Dir & Cur,* Burnaby Art Gallery, Burnaby BC

Henry, Martha, *Traveling Exhib Dir,* New England Center for Contemporary Art, Brooklyn CT

Henry, Michelle, *Asst to Dir,* Jamestown Community College, The Forum Gallery, Jamestown NY

Henry, Renee, *Dir Visitors Serv,* Please Touch Museum, Philadelphia PA

Henry, Sara, *Prof,* Drew University, Art Dept, Madison NJ (S)

Henry, Sue, *Acting Dir,* Riverside County Museum, Edward-Dean Museum, Cherry Valley CA

Henry, Sue, *VPres,* Biloxi Art Association Inc & Gallery, Biloxi MS

Henry, Wayne, *Dir,* Arapahoe Community College, Colorado Gallery of the Arts, Littleton CO

Henshall, Barbara E, *Cur,* Martin & Osa Johnson Safari Museum, Inc, Chanute KS

Hensler, Ruth, *Instructor,* Saint Louis Community College at Meramec, Art Dept, Saint Louis MO (S)

Hensley, Fred Owen, *Prof,* University of North Alabama, Dept of Art, Florence AL (S)

Hensley, John, *Dir,* Department of Natural Resources of Missouri, Missouri State Museum, Jefferson City MO

Hensley, John, *Dir,* Department of Natural Resources of Missouri, Elizabeth Rozier Gallery, Jefferson City MO

Hentchel, Fred, *Instr,* Illinois Central College, Dept of Fine Arts, East Peoria IL (S)

Henton, Marty, *Dir,* Living Arts & Science Center, Inc, Lexington KY

Hentz, Christopher, *Prof,* Louisiana State University, School of Art, Baton Rouge LA (S)

Hepler, Paul H, *Chmn,* State University of New York College at Geneseo, Dept of Art, Geneseo NY (S)

Hepner, Edward D, *Operations Mgr & Preparator,* Marion Koogler McNay Art Museum, San Antonio TX

Heppell, Shirley, *Librn,* Cortland County Historical Society, Kellogg Memorial Research Library, Cortland NY

Hepper, Ann, *Adminr,* Contemporary Art Gallery society of British Columbia, Vancouver BC

Hepworth, Russell, *Assoc Prof,* College of Southern Idaho, Art Dept, Twin Falls ID (S)

Herard, Marvin T, *Prof,* Seattle University, Fine Arts Dept, Division of Art, Seattle WA (S)

Herbeck, Edward, *Vis Lectr,* North Central College, Dept of Art, Naperville IL (S)

Herberg, Mayde, *Instr,* Rancho Santiago College, Art Dept, Santa Ana CA (S)

Herbert, Frank, *Chmn,* Kilgore College, Art Dept, Kilgore TX (S)

Herbert, Linda M, *Public Information Officer,* Everson Museum of Art, Syracuse NY

Herbert, Lynn, *Asst Cur,* Contemporary Arts Museum, Houston TX

Herbert, Sharon, *Cur,* University of Michigan, Kelsey Museum of Archaeology, Ann Arbor MI

Heredia, Ruben, *Vis Prof,* Butte College, Dept of Fine Arts, Oroville CA (S)

Herfurth, Sharon, *First Asst,* Dallas Public Library, Fine Arts Division, Dallas TX

Heriard, Robert T, *Chair Reference Servs,* University of New Orleans, Earl K Long Library, New Orleans LA

Heric, John, *Assoc Prof Sculpture,* University of Arizona, Dept of Art, Tucson AZ (S)

Hering, Michael J, *Mgr Coll,* School of American Research, Santa Fe NM

Herle, Father Clifford, *Dir,* Mission San Miguel Museum, San Miguel CA

Herman, Eleanor, *Dir Development,* International Museum of Photography at George Eastman House, Rochester NY

Herman, Judy, *Exec Dir,* Main Line Center of the Arts, Haverford PA

Herman, Judy S, *Admin Exec Dir,* Main Line Center for the Arts, Haverford PA (S)

Herman, Ladell, *Technical Advisor,* Hickory Museum of Art, Inc, Hickory NC

Herman, Lloyd, *Cur,* The Canadian Craft Museum, Vancouver BC

Hermann, Frank, *Prof Fine Arts,* University of Cincinnati, School of Art, Cincinnati OH (S)

Hernandez, Alberto H, *Librn,* University of Northern Iowa, Art & Music Section Rod Library, Cedar Falls IA

Hernandez, Gary, *Pres of Board,* Art League of Houston, Houston TX

Hernandez, Jo Farb, *Dir,* Monterey Peninsula Museum of Art Association, Monterey CA

Hernandez, Sam, *Assoc Prof,* Santa Clara University, Art Dept, Santa Clara CA (S)

Hernandez-Cruz, Luis, *Prof,* University of Puerto Rico, Dept of Fine Arts, Rio Piedras PR (S)

Herod, Dave D, *Senior Cur Anthropologist,* University of California, Phoebe Apperson Hearst Museum of Anthropology, Berkeley CA

Heron, Reginald, *Assoc Prof,* Indiana University, Bloomington, Henry Radford Hope School of Fine Arts, Bloomington IN (S)

Herr, Marcianne, *Dir Educ,* Akron Art Museum, Akron OH

Herr, Marcianne, *Educ Dir,* Akron Art Museum, Martha Stecher Reed Art Library, Akron OH

Herrero, Susana, *Assoc Prof,* University of Puerto Rico, Dept of Fine Arts, Rio Piedras PR (S)

Herrick, Daniel, *Treas,* National Gallery of Art, Washington DC

Herrick, Kristine, *Asst Prof,* College of Saint Rose, Dept of Art, Albany NY (S)

Herrick, Pam, *Dir,* Van Cortlandt Mansion & Museum, Bronx NY

Herring, Howard, *Exec Dir,* Caramoor Center for Music & the Arts, Inc, Caramoor House Museum, Katonah NY

Herrington, Dennis, *Preparator,* Contemporary Arts Center, Cincinnati OH

Herrington, Thomas E, *Chief Preparator,* New Orleans Museum of Art, New Orleans LA

Herrity, Carol M, *Asst Librn,* Lehigh County Historical Society, Scott Andrew Trexler II Library, Allentown PA

Herrold, David, *Asst Prof,* DePauw University, Art Dept, Greencastle IN (S)

Herron, Cliff, *Chmn,* Okaloosa-Walton Junior College, Dept of Fine and Performing Arts, Niceville FL (S)

Herschman, Judith, *Librn,* University of California, Los Angeles, Fowler Museum of Cultural History, Los Angeles CA

Hersh, Lela, *Registrar,* Museum of Contemporary Art, Chicago IL

Hershberger, Abner, *Chmn,* Goshen College, Art Dept, Goshen IN (S)

Herskowitz, Richard, *Adjunct Cur Film & Video,* Cornell University, Herbert F Johnson Museum of Art, Ithaca NY

Herskowitz, Sylvia A, *Dir,* Yeshiva University Museum, New York NY

Hersrud, Cher, *Mem & Development,* Plains Art Museum, Moorhead MN

Hertel, C H, *Prof Art,* Pitzer College, Dept of Art, Claremont CA (S)

Hertel, Christiane, *Asst Prof,* Bryn Mawr College, Dept of the History of Art, Bryn Mawr PA (S)

Herter, Raymond, *Chmn of Board,* Monmouth Museum and Cultural Center, Lincroft NJ

Hertz, Betti-Sue, *Admin Dir,* Bronx Council on the Arts, Longwood Arts Gallery, Bronx NY

Hertz, Richard, *Liberal Arts, Sciences & Graduate Studies Chmn,* Art Center College of Design, Pasadena CA (S)

Hertzi, Joseph R, *Cur Exhibits,* Canton Art Institute, Canton OH (S)

Herz, Nicole, *Admin Asst,* Organization of Independent Artists, New York NY

Herzer, Frankie, *Dir & Cur,* Plains Indians & Pioneers Historical Foundation, Museum & Art Center, Woodward OK

Hess, Anthony P, *Librn,* Colby College, Bixler Art & Music Library, Waterville ME

Hess, Honee A, *Dir Education,* Worcester Art Museum, Worcester MA

Hess, Robert, *Dir,* Willamette University, George Putnam University Center, Salem OR

Hess, Sally, *Mgr,* Chicago Architecture Foundation, Chicago IL

Hess, Teresa, *Art History Instr,* Hutchinson Community Junior College, Visual Arts Dept, Hutchinson KS (S)

Hessburg, Aloyse, *Assoc Prof,* Mount Mary College, Art Dept, Milwaukee WI (S)

Hesselman, Dorothy K, *Ref Librn & Cataloger,* The Metropolitan Museum of Art, Irene Lewisohn Costume Reference Library, New York NY

Hessemer, Peter, *Assoc Prof,* Oakton Community College, Art & Architecture Dept, Des Plaines IL (S)

Hester, Randolf, *Chmn Landscape Archit,* University of California, Berkeley, College of Environmental Design, Berkeley CA (S)

Hethcox, Jarrell, *Chmn,* Columbus College, Dept of Art, Fine Arts Hall, Columbus GA (S)

Hethcox, Jarrell, *Dept Head,* Columbus College, The Gallery, Columbus GA

Heuer, Curt, *Concentration Chmn,* University of Wisconsin-Green Bay, Art-Communication & the Arts, Green Bay WI (S)

Heuler, Henry J, *Assoc Prof,* University of West Florida, Dept of Art, Pensacola FL (S)

Heuser, Frederick J, *Dir,* Presbyterian Historical Society, Philadelphia PA

Hewitt, Clarissa, *Prof,* California Polytechnic State University at San Luis Obispo, Dept of Art and Design, San Luis Obispo CA (S)

Hewitt, David, *Head of Publications & Sales,* San Diego Museum of Art, San Diego CA

Hewitt, Tim, *Cur Educ,* Presidential Museum, Odessa TX

Hext, Charles R, *Prof,* Sul Ross State University, Dept of Fine Arts & Communications, Alpine TX (S)

Heyduck, Bill, *Prof,* Eastern Illinois University, Art Dept, Charleston IL (S)

Heyer, Paul, *Pres,* New York School of Interior Design, New York NY (S)

Heyler, Joanne, *Asst Cur,* Broad Inc, Kaufman & Broad Home Corp Collection, Los Angeles CA

Heyman, Ellen H, *Assoc Prof,* Clinton Community College, Art Dept, Plattsburgh NY (S)

Heyman, Therese, *Sr Cur Prints & Photographs,* Oakland Museum, Art Dept, Oakland CA

Hibbard, James, *Prof,* Portland State University, Dept of Art, Portland OR (S)

Hibbs, Vivian A, *Cur Archaeology,* Hispanic Society of America, Museum, New York NY

Hickey, Carol, *Instr,* Franklin and Marshall College, Art Dept, Lancaster PA (S)

Hickey, Christopher, *Chmn Dept,* Clark-Atlanta University, School of Arts & Sciences, Atlanta GA (S)

Hickey, Margaret, *Chmn Design,* Massachusetts College of Art, Boston MA (S)

Hickman, Paul, *Asst Prof,* Arkansas State University, Dept of Art, Jonesboro AR (S)

Hickman, Susan Lopez, *Gallery Coordr,* Durham Art Guild Inc, Durham NC

Hickman, Theresa, *Mem Secy,* Norton Gallery and School of Art, West Palm Beach FL

Hickok, Robert, *Dean,* University of California, Irvine, Studio Art Dept, Irvine CA (S)

Hicks, Herbert A, *Assoc Prof,* University of Lethbridge, Dept of Art, Lethbridge AB (S)

Hicks, Hilarie M, *Cur Interpretation,* Tryon Palace Historic Sites & Gardens, New Bern NC

Hicks, Jim, *Instr,* Pacific Northwest College of Art, Portland OR (S)

Hicks, Laurie, *Asst Prof,* University of Maine, Art Dept, Orono ME (S)

Hicks, Leon, *Assoc Prof,* Webster University, Art Dept, Webster Groves MO (S)

Hicks, Leslie, *Cur of Educ,* Jekyll Island Museum, Jekyll Island GA

Hicks, Linda, *Admin,* University of Pittsburgh, University Art Gallery, Pittsburgh PA

Hicks, Ron, *Instr,* Johnson County Community College, Visual Arts Program, Overland Park KS (S)

Hicks, Steve, *Chmn,* Oklahoma Baptist University, Art Dept, Shawnee OK (S)

Hickson, Howard, *Museum Dir,* Northeastern Nevada Historical Society Museum, Elko NV

Hickson, Howard, *Dir,* Northeastern Nevada Historical Society Museum, Library, Elko NV

Hiers, C, *Dir,* Northern Arizona University, School of Art & Design, Flagstaff AZ (S)

Hiester, Jan, *Registrar,* Charleston Museum, Charleston SC

Higa, Kaz, *Prof,* Los Angeles City College, Dept of Art, Los Angeles CA (S)

Higa, Yosh, *Prof,* Southampton Campus of Long Island University, Fine Arts Division, Southampton NY (S)

Higbee, Lisa A, *Exec Dir,* Rosemount Victorian House Museum, Pueblo CO

Higgins, Isabelle, *Librn,* Brooks Institute Photography Library, Santa Barbara CA

Higgins, Larkin, *Instr,* California Lutheran University, Art Dept, Thousand Oaks CA (S)

Higgins, Steven, *Co-Chmn Painting,* University of Manitoba, School of Art, Winnipeg MB (S)

Higgins-Jacob, Coleen, *Treas,* John Simon Guggenheim Memorial Foundation, New York NY

Higginson, Genevra, *Special Events Officer,* National Gallery of Art, Washington DC

High, Steven, *Dir,* Virginia Commonwealth University, Anderson Gallery, Richmond VA

Hightower, Caroline, *Exec Dir,* American Institute of Graphic Arts, New York NY

Hightower, Luann, *Registrar,* Sharon Arts Center, Sharon NH

Hightower, Nancy, *Finance Officer,* Laguna Art Museum, Laguna Beach CA

Higley, David P, *Pres,* Art Institute of Fort Lauderdale, Fort Lauderdale FL (S)

Higtie, Jessie, *Asst Dir,* University of Texas at Austin, Archer M Huntington Art Gallery, Austin TX

Hild, Glen, *Assoc Prof,* Eastern Illinois University, Art Dept, Charleston IL (S)

Hildebrand, Danna, *Instr,* Sheridan College, Art Dept, Sheridan WY (S)

Hildreth MFA, Joseph, *Chmn,* State University of New York College at Potsdam, Dept of Fine Arts, Potsdam NY (S)

Hile, Jeanette, *Assoc Prof,* Seton Hall University, College of Arts & Sciences, South Orange NJ (S)

Hileman, Jayne, *Chmn,* Saint Xavier University, Dept of Art, Chicago IL (S)

Hiles, Bruce, *Chief Cur,* Huntsville Museum of Art, Huntsville AL

Hilgeman, Lese, *Dir & Cur Art Gallery,* Indiana University - Purdue University at Indianapolis, Indianapolis Center for Contemporary Art-Herron Gallery, Indianapolis IN

Hilger, Charles, *Dir,* The Art Museum of Santa Cruz County, Santa Cruz CA

Hill, Amy, *Instr,* The Arkansas Arts Center, Museum School, Little Rock AR (S)

Hill, Barbara, *Ed Coordr,* Florida Gulf Coast Art Center, Inc, Belleair FL (S)

Hill, Barbara, *Dir Instructional Prog,* Hand Workshop, Virginia Center for the Craft Arts, Richmond VA

Hill, Barbara Anderson, *Cur,* Florida Gulf Coast Art Center, Inc, Belleair FL

Hill, Charles, *Cur Canadian Art,* National Gallery of Canada, Ottawa ON

Hill, Chris, *Lectr,* Southwest Texas State University, Dept of Art, San Marcos TX (S)

Hill, Dennis, *Music Instr,* Edison Community College, Dept of Fine and Performing Arts, Fort Myers FL (S)

Hill, G A, *Librn,* McMaster University, Library, Hamilton ON

Hill, Heidi, *Site Asst,* Olana State Historic Site, Hudson NY

Hill, James K, *Head Dept,* Southwest Missouri State University, Dept of Art & Design, Springfield MO (S)

Hill, Jan, *Chairman Museum Bd of Trustees,* Chilkat Valley Historical Society, Sheldon Museum & Cultural Center, Haines AK

Hill, Jennifer, *Curatorial Asst Preparator,* Columbia College, The Museum of Contemporary Photography, Chicago IL

Hill, John R, *Historical Sites,* Oklahoma Historical Society, State Museum of History, Oklahoma City OK

Hill, Melinda M, *Public Relations,* Rhode Island School of Design, Providence RI (S)

Hill, Peter, *Prof,* University of Nebraska at Omaha, Dept of Art, Omaha NE (S)

Hill, Ron, *Transportation Design Chmn,* Art Center College of Design, Pasadena CA

Hill, Sara, *Development Dir,* Old Barracks Museum, Trenton NJ

Hill, Thom, *Dean of Fine & Performing Arts,* Rancho Santiago College, Art Dept, Santa Ana CA (S)

Hill, Tom, *Librn,* Vassar College, Art Library, Poughkeepsie NY

Hillbruner, Fred, *Asst Dir & Head Technical Services,* School of the Art Institute of Chicago, John M Flaxman Library, Chicago IL

Hillding, John, *Instructor,* The Art Institutes International, The Art Institute of Seattle, Seattle WA (S)

Hiller, Edward, *Chmn,* SVACA - Sheyenne Valley Arts and Crafts Association, Bjarne Ness Gallery, Fort Ransom ND

Hilliard, Elbert R, *Dir,* Mississippi Department of Archives and History, State Historical Museum, Jackson MS

Hillier, John, *Instr,* Kilgore College, Art Dept, Kilgore TX (S)

Hillman, Arthur, *Chmn Art Dept,* Simon's Rock College of Bard, Great Barrington MA

Hillman, Arthur, *Chmn Studio Arts Dept,* Simon's Rock of Bard College, Visual Arts Dept, Great Barrington MA (S)

Hillman, Arthur, *Instr,* Simon's Rock of Bard College, Visual Arts Dept, Great Barrington MA (S)

Hillman, Elizabeth, *Dir,* South Peace Art Society, Dawson Creek Art Gallery, Dawson Creek BC

Hillman, Judy, *Instr,* Hope College, Art Dept, Holland MI (S)

Hillyer, Debbie, *Instructor Arts & Crafts,* Palo Alto Junior Museum, Palo Alto CA

Hilton, Alison, *Instr,* Georgetown University, Dept of Fine Arts, Washington DC (S)

Hilty, Thomas, *Dir,* Bowling Green State University, School of Art, Bowling Green OH (S)

Hime, Gary D, *Asst Librn,* Wichita Public Library, Wichita KS

Himmel, Betty, *Pres,* Katonah Museum of Art, Katonah NY

Himmelstein, Paul, *Pres,* American Institute for Conservation of Historic & Artistic Works (AIC), Washington DC

Hinckley, Robert L, *VPres,* Wendell Gilley Museum, Southwest Harbor ME

Hindman, Sandra, *Prof,* Northwestern University, Evanston, Dept of Art History, Evanston IL (S)

Hinds, Jill, *Instr,* Northwestern Michigan College, Art Dept, Traverse City MI (S)

Hinds, Pat, *Prof,* Antelope Valley College, Art Dept, Division of Fine Arts, Lancaster CA (S)

Hindson, Bradley T, *Assoc Prof,* Rochester Institute of Technology, School of Photographic Arts & Sciences, Rochester NY (S)

Hines, Adrienne G, *Exec Dir,* Arts Council of Richmond, Inc, Richmond VA

Hines, Carol, *Chmn,* Old Dominion University, Art Dept, Norfolk VA (S)

Hines, Carol, *Assoc Prof,* Old Dominion University, Art Dept, Norfolk VA (S)

Hines, Carol S, *Art Chmn,* Old Dominion University, Gallery, Norfolk VA

Hines, Claire, *Librn,* Brownsville Art League Museum, Brownsville TX

Hines, James, *Prof,* Christopher Newport College, Arts & Communications, Newport News VA (S)

Hines, Jean, *Art & Architecture Librn,* Pratt Institute Library, Art & Architecture Dept, Brooklyn NY

Hines, Jessica, *Asst Prof,* Georgia Southern University, Dept of Art, Statesboro GA (S)

Hines, Joseph, *Cur Exhib,* Anniston Museum of Natural History, Anniston AL

Hines, Mary Anne, *Chief of Reference,* Library Company of Philadelphia, Print Dept, Philadelphia PA

Hines, Norman, *Prof,* Pomona College, Art Dept, Claremont CA (S)

Hing, Allan, *Interior Design Chmn,* Atlanta College of Art, Atlanta GA (S)

Hinken, Susan, *Technical Services Librn,* University of Portland, Wilson W Clark Memorial Library, Portland OR

Hinkhouse, Jim, *Prof,* Fort Hays State University, Dept of Art, Hays KS (S)

Hinkley, James, *Dir of Educ,* Carson County Square House Museum, Panhandle TX

Hinson, Mary Joan, *Prof,* Florida Community College at Jacksonville, South Campus, Art Dept, Jacksonville FL (S)

Hinson, Mary Joan, *Dir,* Florida Community College at Jacksonville, South Gallery, Jacksonville FL

Hinson, Tom E, *Cur Contemporary Art,* Cleveland Museum of Art, Cleveland OH

Hinton, William, *Dir & Cur,* Louisburg College, Art Gallery, Louisburg NC

Hintz, Glen, *Asst Prof,* Rochester Institute of Technology, School of Art and Design, Rochester NY (S)

Hintze, Rick, *Prof,* Kirkwood Community College, Dept of Fine Arts, Cedar Rapids IA (S)

Hios, Theo, *VPres,* Federation of Modern Painters & Sculptors, New York NY

Hippel, Bruce, *Instr,* Ocean City Art Center, Ocean City NJ (S)

Hipple, Rebecca, *Admin Secy,* Davenport Museum of Art, Davenport IA

Hipsley, Vicky, *Artist,* San Bernardino County Museum, Fine Arts Institute, Redlands CA

Hirano, M, *Assoc Prof,* American University, Dept of Art, Washington DC (S)

Hirata, Evelyn, *Electronic Arts Chmn (computer),* Atlanta College of Art, Atlanta GA (S)

Hiratsuka, Yuji, *Assoc Prof,* Oregon State University, Dept of Art, Corvallis OR (S)

Hirsch, Barron, *Prof,* Saginaw Valley State University, Dept of Art and Design, University Center MI (S)

Hirsch, Richard, *Prof,* Rochester Institute of Technology, School of Art and Design, Rochester NY (S)

Hirsch, Steve, *Asst Prof,* Trenton State College, Art Dept, Trenton NJ (S)

Hirsch, Steven, *Asst Prof,* Pennsylvania College of Technology, Dept of Design & Communiation Arts, Williamsport PA (S)

Hirschel, Anthony, *Dir,* University of Virginia, Bayly Art Museum, Charlottesville VA

Hirschfeld, Susan B, *Asst Cur,* Solomon R Guggenheim Museum, New York NY

Hirschfeld, Jim, *Asst Prof,* University of North Carolina at Chapel Hill, Art Dept, Chapel Hill NC (S)

Hirschl, Milton, *Prof,* Pierce College, Art Dept, Woodland Hills CA (S)

Hirschorn, Paul, *Head Dept Architecture,* Drexel University, Nesbitt College of Design Arts, Philadelphia PA (S)

Hirsh, Joanne, *VPres,* Print Club Center for Prints & Photographs, Philadelphia PA

Hirsh, Sharon, *Prof,* Dickinson College, Fine Arts Dept, Carlisle PA (S)

Hirshen, Sanford, *Dir,* University of British Columbia, School of Architecture, Vancouver BC (S)

Hiscox, Ingeborg, *Art Gallery Dir,* Pointe Claire Cultural Centre, Stewart Hall Art Gallery, Pointe Claire PQ

Hislop, David, *First VPres,* Rochester Historical Society, Rochester NY

Hitch, Henry C, *Pres,* No Man's Land Historical Society Museum, Goodwell OK

Hitchcock, Alix, *Instr,* Wake Forest University, Dept of Art, Winston-Salem NC (S)

Hitchcock, D Michael, *Assoc Prof,* George Washington University, Dept of Art, Washington DC (S)

Hitchcock, Dorothy, *Instr,* Casper College, Dept of Visual Arts, Casper WY (S)

Hitchings, Sinclair H, *Keeper of Prints,* Boston Public Library, Albert H Wiggin Gallery & Print Department, Boston MA

Hitner, Chuck, *Prof Painting & Drawing,* University of Arizona, Dept of Art, Tucson AZ (S)

Hitt, Terri, *Asst Prof,* University of Dayton, Visual Arts Dept, Dayton OH (S)

Hixson, Nancy S, *Registrar,* University of Houston, Sarah Campbell Blaffer Gallery, Houston TX

Hlad, Richard, *Asst Prof,* Tarrant County Junior College, Art Dept, Northeast Campus, Hurst TX (S)

Hluszok, Zenon, *Archivist,* Ukrainian Cultural and Educational Centre, Winnipeg MB

Ho, Abraham P, *Cur,* Saint John's University, Chung-Cheng Art Gallery, Jamaica NY

Ho, Rosa, *Cur Art & Public Prog,* University of British Columbia, Museum of Anthropology, Vancouver BC

Ho, Wai-Kam, *Lectr,* University of Kansas, Kress Foundation Dept of Art History, Lawrence KS (S)

Hoadley, Mary, *Admin,* Cosanti Foundation, Scottsdale AZ

Hoadley, Mary, *Administration,* Cosanti Foundation, Arcosanti, Scottsdale AZ

Hoar, Bill, *Assoc Prof,* Northern State University, Art Dept, Aberdeen SD (S)

Hoard, Curtis, *Prof,* University of Minnesota, Minneapolis, Dept of Studio Art, Minneapolis MN (S)

Hobbie, Margaret, *Dir,* Dewitt Historical Society of Tompkins County, Ithaca NY

Hobbs, Don, *Interim Dir,* Boulder Art Center, Boulder CO

Hobbs, Frank, *Prof,* Mary Baldwin College, Dept of Art, Staunton VA (S)

Hobbs, Moria, *Dir,* Thomas More College, TM Gallery, Crestview KY

Hobgood, E Wade, *Prof,* Winthrop College, Dept of Art & Design, Rock Hill SC (S)

Hobson, Kitty A, *Archivist,* Oshkosh Public Museum, Library, Oshkosh WI

Hobson, Marlena, *Sr Member,* Mary Baldwin College, Dept of Art, Staunton VA (S)

Hochstetler, Max, *Chmn,* Austin Peay State University, Dept of Art, Clarksville TN (S)

Hock, Jerome, *Instr Commercial Art,* Honolulu Community College, Honolulu HI (S)

Hock, Nancy, *Cur S E Asia,* Asian Art Museum of San Francisco, Avery Brundage Collection, San Francisco CA

Hockett, Roland L, *Assoc Prof,* Gulf Coast Community College, Division of Fine Arts, Panama City FL (S)

Hocking, Christopher, *Prof,* West Virginia University, College of Creative Arts, Morgantown WV (S)

Hocking, Sheldon, *Instr,* Sierra College, Art Dept, Rocklin CA (S)

Hodecker, Paula, *Instr,* Springfield College, Dept of Visual and Performing Arts, Springfield MA (S)

Hodge, Leta, *Exec Dir,* Audrain County Historical Society, Graceland Museum & American Saddlehorse Museum, Mexico MO

Hodgell, Lois, *Coordr,* University of Minnesota, Morris, Humanities Division, Morris MN (S)

Hodges, Rhoda, *Chmn Board,* Warren Hall Coutts III Memorial Museum of Art, El Dorado KS

Hodgson, J Trevor, *Dir,* Dundas Valley School of Art, Dundas ON (S)

Hodgson, Julie, *Curatorial Asst Prints & Drawings,* National Gallery of Canada, Ottawa ON

Hodik, Barbara, *Prof,* Rochester Institute of Technology, School of Art and Design, Rochester NY (S)

Hodne, Thomas, *Prof,* University of Manitoba, Faculty of Architecture, Winnipeg MB (S)

Hodnicki, Jill, *Chmn Holyoke Historical Commission,* City of Holyoke Museum-Wistariahurst, Holyoke MA

Hodosy, Kenneth, *Dir,* Roswell P Flower Memorial Library, Watertown NY

Hodsoll, Frank, *Chmn,* National Endowment for the Arts, Washington DC

Hodson, Carol, *Asst Prof,* Webster University, Art Dept, Webster Groves MO (S)

Hoeber, Daniel, *VPres Acad Affairs,* Mercy College of Detroit, Art Dept, Detroit MI (S)

Hoel, Randall, *Gallery Mgr,* Sharon Arts Center, Sharon NH

Hoell, Peter, *Instructor,* Saint Louis Community College at Meramec, Art Dept, Saint Louis MO (S)

Hoeltzel, Susan, *Dir,* Lehman College Art Gallery, Bronx NY

Hoerner, Julia, *Assoc Prof,* University of Colorado-Colorado Springs, Fine Arts Dept, Colorado Springs CO (S)

Hoever, Buzz, *Asst Dir Finances Admin,* Monterey Peninsula Museum of Art Association, Monterey CA

Hofacket, Katy, *Coordr,* Luna County Historical Society, Inc, Deming Luna Mimbres Museum, Deming NM

Hoff, Roger, *VPres,* Wustum Museum Art Association, Racine WI

Hoff, Terry, *Area Coordr,* Columbia College, Fine Arts, Columbia CA (S)

Hoffer, Paul, *Dir Exhibits,* Museum of Science and Industry, Chicago IL

Hoffman, Barbara, *Business Mgr & Cur,* Playboy Enterprises, Inc, Chicago IL

Hoffman, Dan, *Head Architecture Dept,* Cranbrook Academy of Art, Bloomfield Hills MI (S)

Hoffman, Eva, *Asst Prof,* Tufts University, Dept of Art & Art History, Medford MA (S)

Hoffman, John, *Chmn,* Loras College, Dept of Art, Dubuque IA (S)

Hoffman, Katherine, *Chmn,* Saint Anselm College, Dept of Fine Arts, Manchester NH (S)

Hoffman, Kim, *Assoc Prof,* Western Oregon State College, Creative Arts Division, Visual Arts, Monmouth OR (S)

Hoffman, Lawrence, *Chief Conservator,* Hirshhorn Museum and Sculpture Garden, Washington DC

Hoffman, Lee, *Painting & Design,* University of South Alabama, Dept of Art, Mobile AL (S)

Hoffman, Lorre, *Asst Prof,* University of Colorado at Denver, Dept of Fine Arts, Denver CO (S)

Hoffman, Lothar, *Chmn Graphic Design,* Center for Creative Studies, College of Art & Design, Detroit MI (S)

Hoffman, Margaret, *Treas,* East Windsor Historical Society, Inc, Scantic Academy Museum, East Windsor CT

Hoffman, Marilyn F, *Dir,* The Currier Gallery of Art, Manchester NH

Hoffman, Neil J, *Pres,* California College of Arts and Crafts, Oakland CA (S)

Hoffman, Susan, *Exec Dir,* California Confederation of the Arts, Sacramento CA

Hoffman, William M, *Chmn,* Rutgers University, Camden, Art Dept, Camden NJ (S)

Hoffmann, John, *Dir Research,* Museum of Holography - Chicago, Chicago IL

Hoffmann, Robert, *Asst Secy for the Sciences,* Smithsonian Institution, Washington DC

Hoffory, Fernando, *Project Dir,* Public Art Fund, Inc, Library, New York NY

Hoffroy, Fernando, *Project Dir,* Public Art Fund, Inc, New York NY

Hofland, M, *Asst to Dir,* Mount Allison University, Owens Art Gallery, Sackville NB

Hofman, Michael, *Gallery Mgr,* Eye Gallery, San Francisco CA

Hogan, Dan, *Instr,* Cincinnati Academy of Design, Cincinnati OH (S)

Hogan, Dorothy G, *Dir,* The Sandwich Historical Society, Inc, Sandwich Glass Museum, Sandwich MA

Hogan, Dorothy G, *Dir,* The Sandwich Historical Society, Inc, Library, Sandwich MA

Hogan, Irmfrieda, *Lectr,* Lake Forest College, Dept of Art, Lake Forest IL (S)

Hogan, James, *College Librn,* College of the Holy Cross, Dinand Library, Worcester MA

Hogarty, Ellen S, *Pres,* Rensselaer County Historical Society, Hart-Cluett Mansion, 1827, Troy NY

Hoge, Robert W, *Museum Cur,* American Numismatic Association, Museum, Colorado Springs CO

Hogu, Barbara J, *Asst Prof,* City Colleges of Chicago, Malcolm X College, Chicago IL (S)

Hohri, Cynthia, *Dir Communications,* The Museum of Contemporary Art, Los Angeles CA

Hoi, Samuel, *Dean,* Corcoran School of Art, Washington DC (S)

Hoitt, Will, *Cur,* Clemson University, Fort Hill, Clemson SC

Holahan, Elizabeth G, *Pres,* Rochester Historical Society, Rochester NY

Holahan, Mary, *Registrar,* Delaware Art Museum, Wilmington DE

Holan, Rose, *VPres Organization,* DuPage Art League School & Gallery, Wheaton IL

Holbach, Joseph, *Registrar,* The Phillips Collection, Washington DC

Holbrook, Gary, *VPres,* San Bernardino County Museum, Fine Arts Institute, Redlands CA

Holbrook, W Paul, *Exec Dir,* American Ceramic Society, Westerville OH

Holcomb, Ann, *Dir Nexus Gallery,* Nexus Contemporary Art Center, Atlanta GA

Holcomb, Grant, *Dir,* University of Rochester, Memorial Art Gallery, Rochester NY

Holcomb, Richard, *Chmn,* Palm Beach Community College, Dept of Art, Lake Worth FL (S)

Holcombe, Anna, *Assoc Prof,* State University of New York College at Brockport, Dept of Art & Art History, Brockport NY (S)

Holcombe, Anna Calluori, *Dir,* State University of New York, College at Brockport, Tower Fine Arts Gallery, Brockport NY

Holden, John, *Asst Prof,* Bemidji State University, Visual Arts Dept, Bemidji MN (S)

Holden, Lynn, *Assoc Dean,* Carnegie Mellon University, College of Fine Arts, Pittsburgh PA (S)

Holden, Wendy, *Sr Assoc Cur,* University of Michigan, Asian Art Archives, Ann Arbor MI

Holden, Wendy, *Sr Assoc Cur & Asian Art Archives,* University of Michigan, Slide and Photograph Collection, Ann Arbor MI

Holder, Thomas J, *Instr,* University of Nevada, Las Vegas, Dept of Art, Las Vegas NV (S)

Holeb, Marshall, *Secy,* Arts Club of Chicago, Chicago IL

Holgate, Edward, *Gallery Coordr,* Lawrence University, Wriston Art Center Galleries, Appleton WI

Hollad, John Boyd, *Prof,* Moorhead State University, Dept of Art, Moorhead MN (S)

Holland, Dana, *Lectr,* Southwest Texas State University, Dept of Art, San Marcos TX (S)

Holland, Jane, *Dir of Conservation,* London Regional Art & Historical Museums, London ON

Holland, Raymond E, *Pres,* Kemerer Museum of Decorative Arts, Bethlehem PA

Holleran, Owen, *Admin Officer,* Chattahoochee Valley Art Museum, LaGrange GA

Holliday, Judith, *Librn,* Cornell University, Fine Arts Library, Ithaca NY

Holliday, Peter, *Instr,* California State University, San Bernardino, Art Dept, San Bernardino CA (S)

Hollihan, Dean, *VPres,* Safety Harbor Museum of Regional History, Safety Harbor FL

Holliman, Lilly, *Treas,* Biloxi Art Association Inc & Gallery, Biloxi MS

Hollingsworth, Harry W, *VPres,* Antonelli Institute, Professional Photography, Commercial Art & Interior Design, Plymouth Meeting PA (S)

Hollingsworth, Priscilla, *Instr,* Vincennes University Junior College, Art Dept, Vincennes IN (S)

Hollingworth, Keith, *Art Historian,* Greenfield Community College, Art, Graphic Design & Media Communication Dept, Greenfield MA (S)

Hollingworth, Keith, *Art Historian,* Greenfield Community College, Art, Graphic Design & Media Communication Dept, Greenfield MA (S)

Hollinshead, Mary, *Asst Prof,* University of Rhode Island, Dept of Art, Kingston RI (S)

Hollis, Sara, *Chmn,* Southern University in New Orleans, Art Dept, New Orleans LA (S)

Hollis, Wayne, *Instr,* Iowa Lakes Community College, Dept of Art, Estherville IA (S)

Hollister, Mary, *Blair Art Extension Coordr,* Southern Alleghenies Museum of Art, Loretto PA

Hollister, Mary, *Coordr,* Southern Alleghenies Museum of Art, Blair Art Museum, Loretto PA

Hollister-Didier, Jennie, *Dir,* Liberty Village Arts Center and Gallery, Chester MT

Hollomon, James W, *Cur of Coll & Exhib,* Gaston County Museum of Art & History, Dallas NC

Holloway, Amy, *Librn,* African American Historical and Cultural Society, Library, San Francisco CA

Holloway, Bea, *Librn,* Art Museum of Southeast Texas, Library, Beaumont TX

Hollrah, Warren, *Archivist,* Westminster College, Winston Churchill Memorial & Library in the United States, Fulton MO

Holly, Michael Ann, *Chmn,* University of Rochester, Dept of Art & Art History, Rochester NY (S)

Holm, Jack, *Asst Prof,* Rochester Institute of Technology, School of Photographic Arts & Sciences, Rochester NY (S)

Holm, Susanne, *Treas,* Monterey Peninsula Museum of Art Association, Monterey CA

Holman, Julia, *Coordr of Tennessee State Museum Foundation,* Tennessee State Museum, Nashville TN

Holman, L Bruce, *Instr,* Cottey College, Art Dept, Nevada MO (S)

Holman, Nancy, *Pres,* Salt Lake Art Center, Salt Lake City UT

Holmes, Barry, *Instr,* Vancouver Community College, Langara Campus, Dept of Fine Arts, Vancouver BC (S)

Holmes, Beth, *Pres,* Victoria Society of Maine, Victoria Mansion - Morse Libby House, Portland ME

Holmes, Daphne, *Public Relations Dir,* Denver Art Museum, Denver CO

Holmes, David, *Prof,* University of Wisconsin-Parkside, Art Dept, Kenosha WI (S)

Holmes, H T, *Dir Archives & Library,* Mississippi Department of Archives and History, State Historical Museum, Jackson MS

Holmes, Ira, *Chmn,* Central Florida Community College, Humanities Dept, Ocala FL (S)

Holmes, J, *Cur Asst,* Royal Ontario Museum, Canadian Decorative Arts Department, Toronto ON

Holmes, Jennifer, *Cur,* Northwestern University, Mary & Leigh Block Gallery, Evanston IL

Holmes, Larry, *Chmn,* University of Delaware, Dept of Art, Newark DE (S)

Holmes, LeRoy F, *Chmn,* North Carolina Agricultural and Technical State University, Art Dept, Greensboro NC (S)

Holmes, Martha, *Asst Prof,* Fort Hays State University, Dept of Art, Hays KS (S)

Holmes, Wendy, *Prof,* University of Rhode Island, Dept of Art, Kingston RI (S)

Holmes, Willard, *Dir,* Vancouver Art Gallery, Vancouver BC

Holmgren, Erin, *Instr,* Mount Mary College, Art Dept, Milwaukee WI (S)

Holo, Selma, *Adjunct Assoc Prof,* University of Southern California, School of Fine Arts, Los Angeles CA (S)

Holo, Selma, *Dir,* University of Southern California, Fisher Gallery, Los Angeles CA

Holownia, Thaddeus, *Prof,* Mount Allison University, Fine Arts Dept, Sackville NB (S)

Holsing, Marilyn, *Chmn Univ Art & Art Educ,* Temple University, Tyler School of Art, Philadelphia PA (S)

Holt, Alison, *Catalog Librn,* Art Center College of Design, James Lemont Fogg Memorial Library, Pasadena CA

Holt, Bonnie, *Vook Librn,* University of California, Art Dept Library, Davis CA

Holt, Daniel, *Dir,* Dwight D Eisenhower Presidential Library, Abilene KS

Holt, David, *Asst Prof,* Marymount College, Art Dept, Tarrytown NY (S)

Holt, Laura, *Librn,* Museum of New Mexico, Laboratory of Anthropology, Santa Fe NM

Holt, Leigh, *Dir Dept Arts & Science,* Dominican College of Blauvelt, Art Dept, Orangeburg NY (S)

Holt, Leon C, *Pres Board Trustees,* Allentown Art Museum, Allentown PA

Holt, Louise, *Dir,* Haymarket Art Gallery, Lincoln NE

Holte, Bettye, *Dir,* Austin Peay State University, Margaret Fort Trahern Gallery, Clarksville TN

Holte, Bettye, *Asst Prof,* Austin Peay State University, Dept of Art, Clarksville TN (S)

Holte-Lucas, Bettye, *Gallery Cur,* Austin Peay State University, Art Dept Library, Clarksville TN

Holtgrewe, Douglas, *Chmn,* Elmira College, Art Dept, Elmira NY (S)

Holubec, Marie, *Slide Librn,* York University, Fine Arts Phase II Slide Library, North York ON

Holubizky, Ihor, *Contemporary Cur,* Art Gallery of Hamilton, Muriel Isabel Bostwick Library, Hamilton ON

Holz, Ronald W, *Div Head Music & Art,* Asbury College, Art Dept, Wilmore KY (S)

Holzer, Harold, *Dir Communiations,* The Metropolitan Museum of Art, New York NY

Hom, Meiling, *Asst Prof,* Philadelphia Community College, Dept of Art, Philadelphia PA (S)

Homan, Geoff, *Exec Dir,* Association of Artist-Run Galleries, New York NY

Homan, Ralph, *Instructor,* College of the Sequoias, Art Dept, Visalia CA (S)

Hommel, William L, *Chmn,* University of Central Oklahoma, Dept of Visual Arts & Design, Edmond OK (S)

Honaman, Dee Dee, *Prog Developer,* Museum Science & History, Jacksonville FL

Hong, Lynda, *Slide Librn Cur,* Montclair State College, Slide Library, Upper Montclair NJ

Hong, Shen, *Dir Grad Studies,* City College of New York, Art Dept, New York NY (S)

Honig, Elizabeth, *Asst Prof,* Tufts University, Dept of Art & Art History, Medford MA (S)

Honsa, Vlasta, *Branch Adminr,* Las Vegas-Clark County Library District, Las Vegas NV

Hood, Craig, *Asst Prof,* University of New Hampshire, Dept of the Arts, Durham NH (S)

Hood, Eugene, *Dir,* University of Wisconsin-Eau Claire, Foster Gallery, Eau Claire WI

Hood, Gail, *Assoc Prof,* Southeastern Louisiana University, Dept of Visual Arts, Hammond LA (S)

Hood, Gary A, *Cur Art,* Museum of the Southwest, Midland TX

Hood, Graham S, *Dir & Cur Coll,* Colonial Williamsburg Foundation, Williamsburg VA

Hood, Mary Bryan, *Dir,* Owensboro Museum of Fine Art, Owensboro KY

Hood, Susan, *Asst Prof,* Indiana University South Bend, Fine Arts Dept, South Bend IN (S)

Hood, William, *Prof,* Oberlin College, Dept of Art, Oberlin OH (S)

Hoogstoel, Jewel, *Development Assoc,* State University of New York at Purchase, Neuberger Museum, Purchase NY

Hook, Charles E, *Assoc Prof,* Florida State University, Art Dept, Tallahassee FL (S)

Hooks, Earl J, *Chmn,* Fisk University, Art Dept, Nashville TN (S)

Hoone, Jeff, *Dir,* Light Work, Syracuse NY

Hooper, Letha, *Asst Cur,* Art Institute for the Permian Basin, Odessa TX

Hoopingarner, Tim, *Dir,* Colorado Mountain College, Fine Arts Gallery, Breckenridge CO

Hoort, Rebecca, *Sr Cur,* University of Michigan, Slide and Photograph Collection, Ann Arbor MI

Hooten, Joseph, *Instr,* Long Beach City College, Dept of Art, Long Beach CA (S)

Hoover, Bobbye, *Admin Asst,* Museum of Fine Arts, Saint Petersburg, Florida, Inc, Saint Petersburg FL

Hoover, David, *Registrar,* Carson County Square House Museum, Panhandle TX

Hoover, Elizabeth, *Dir of Admissions,* School of the Art Institute of Chicago, Chicago IL (S)

Hoover, Heather, *Instr,* University of North Carolina at Charlotte, Dept of Visual Arts, Charlotte NC (S)

Hoover, Jamie Gwyn, *Cur & Registrar,* California State University Stanislaus, University Art Gallery, Turlock CA

Hope, Samuel, *Executive Dir,* National Association of Schools of Art & Design, Reston VA

Hopkins, Debra, *Asst Dir Visual Arts,* Scottsdale Center for the Arts, Scottsdale AZ

Hopkins, Henry T, *Chmn,* University of California, Los Angeles, Dept of Art, Los Angeles CA (S)

Hopkins, Henry T, *Dir,* University of California, Los Angeles, Wight Art Gallery, Los Angeles CA

Hopkins, Joe, *Prof,* Sullivan County Community College, Division of Commercial Art and Photography, Loch Sheldrake NY (S)

Hopkins, Susan, *Instr,* Ocean City Art Center, Ocean City NJ (S)

Hopkins, Terri, *Instr,* Marylhurst College, Art Dept, Marylhurst OR (S)

Hopkins, William, *Instr,* Ocean City Art Center, Ocean City NJ (S)

Hoppe, David, *Instr,* California State University, Chico, Art Dept, Chico CA (S)

Hopper, James, *Chmn,* Mount Union College, Dept of Art, Alliance OH (S)

Hopper, Janette, *Instr,* Columbia Basin College, Art Dept, Pasco WA (S)

Hopper, W Kenneth, *Instr,* Huntington College, Art Dept, Huntington IN (S)

Horak, Jan-Christopher, *Cur Film Coll,* International Museum of Photography at George Eastman House, Rochester NY

Horan, Pam, *Reference Librn,* University of Portland, Wilson W Clark Memorial Library, Portland OR

Horcajo, Tamara L, *Adminr,* Maui Historical Society, Bailey House, Wailuku HI

Horchler, Eleanor, *Dir,* River Vale Public Library, Art Dept, River Vale NJ

Horewitz, Deborah, *Instr,* College of the Canyons, Art Dept, Valencia CA (S)

Hori, Robert, *Gallery Dir,* Japanese American Cultural & Community Center, George J Doizaki Gallery, Los Angeles CA

Horigan, Evelyn, *Art & Slide Librn,* California Institute of the Arts Library, Santa Clarita CA

Horiuchi, Yozo, *Asst Librn,* Japan Society, Inc, Library, New York NY

Horlbeck, Frank R, *Prof,* University of Wisconsin, Madison, Dept of Art History, Madison WI (S)

Horn, B, *Assoc Prof,* Northern Arizona University, School of Art & Design, Flagstaff AZ (S)

Horn, Larry, *Pres,* Safety Harbor Museum of Regional History, Safety Harbor FL

Horn, Robert, *Assoc Dir,* NAB Gallery, Chicago IL

Horn, Sam, *Instr,* The Arkansas Arts Center, Museum School, Little Rock AR (S)

Horn, Susan, *Vis Prof,* Nebraska Wesleyan University, Art Dept, Lincoln NE (S)

Hornaday, Richard, *Instr,* California State University, Chico, Art Dept, Chico CA (S)

Hornbuckle, Heather, *Acting Coll Mgr,* Marion Koogler McNay Art Museum, San Antonio TX

Horne, Adele, *Membership Asst,* Houston Center For Photography, Houston TX

Horne, Catherine W, *Chief Cur,* University of South Carolina, McKissick Museum, Columbia SC

Horne, Marie Vickers, *Membership & Public Relations Assoc,* Library Association of La Jolla, Athenaeum Music and Arts Library, La Jolla CA

Horne, Meade B, *Dir,* Edgecombe County Cultural Arts Council, Inc, Blount-Bridgers House, Hobson Pittman Memorial Gallery, Tarboro NC

Horne, Ralph, *Prof,* Pennsylvania College of Technology, Dept of Design & Communiation Arts, Williamsport PA (S)

Horne, Walter G, *Chmn Photography Plates & Press Division,* Rochester Institute of Technology, School of Printing, Rochester NY (S)

Horner, Elizabeth, *Asst,* Tucson Museum of Art, Library, Tucson AZ

Hornik, Heidi, *Dir,* Baylor University, Martin Museum of Art, Waco TX

Hornik, Heidi J, *Asst Prof,* Baylor University, Dept of Art, Waco TX (S)

Horning, Jerome, *Chmn Dept,* Creighton University, Fine and Performing Arts Dept, Omaha NE (S)

Horning, Jerome K, *Chmn Fine & Performing Arts Dept,* Creighton University, Fine Arts Gallery, Omaha NE

Hornor, Elizabeth S, *Coordr Education Progs,* Emory University, Museum of Art & Archaeology, Atlanta GA

Horowicz, Kari E, *Librn,* The Buffalo Fine Arts Academy, G Robert Strauss Jr Memorial Library, Buffalo NY

Horowitz, Corinne Gilletz, *Cur of Education,* University of California, Santa Barbara, University Art Museum, Santa Barbara CA

Horowitz, Emily, *Asst to Dir,* Texas Fine Arts Association, Austin TX

Horowitz, Marvin, *Prof,* New York Institute of Technology, Fine Arts Dept, Old Westbury NY (S)

Horras, Nancy, *Pres Art Assoc,* Fairfield Public Library, Fairfield Art Association, Fairfield IA

Horrell, Jeffrey L, *Librn,* Harvard University, Fine Arts Library, Cambridge MA

Horrocks, Sandra, *Public Relations Mgr,* Philadelphia Museum of Art, Philadelphia PA

Horsey, Ann, *Cur Coll,* Historical and Cultural Affairs, Delaware State Museums, Dover DE

Horsfield, Kate, *Dir,* School of Art Institute of Chicago, Video Data Bank, Chicago IL

Horsting, Archana, *Exec Dir,* Kala Institute, Berkeley CA

Horstman, Neil W, *Resident Dir,* Mount Vernon Ladies' Association of the Union, Mount Vernon VA

Hortas, Carlos, *Dean,* Hunter College, Art Dept, New York NY (S)

Horton, Alfred F, *Assoc Prof,* Rochester Institute of Technology, School of Printing, Rochester NY (S)

Horton, Anna, *First Asst,* Public Library of Cincinnati & Hamilton County, Art & Music Department, Cincinnati OH

Horton, Christopher, *Assoc Prof,* University of Hartford, Hartford Art School, West Hartford CT (S)

Horton, Frank L, *Dir Emeritus,* Old Salem Inc, Museum of Early Southern Decorative Arts, Winston-Salem NC

Horton, Lon, *Pres,* Wisconsin Fine Arts Association, Inc, Ozaukee Art Center, Cedarburg WI

Horton, Lynne M, *Cur Hist,* The Sandwich Historical Society, Inc, Sandwich Glass Museum, Sandwich MA

Horton, Ray, *Cur,* Nassau Community College, Firehouse Art Gallery, Garden City NY

Horvat, Krisjohn O, *Prof,* Rhode Island College, Art Dept, Providence RI (S)

Horvitz, Suzanne, *Foundation Dir & Trustee,* Foundation for Today's Art, Nexus Gallery, Philadelphia PA

Hose, Henry, *Gallery Dir,* Mercer County Community College, The Gallery, Trenton NJ

Hose, Henry, *Cur,* Mercer County Community College, Arts & Communications, Trenton NJ (S)

Hoshino, Osamu, *Deputy Dir,* Utah Travel Council, Salt Lake City UT

Hoskin, Denise, *Office Mgr,* Dalhousie University, Art Gallery, Halifax NS

Hoskisson, Don, *Head Art Dept,* Western Oregon State College, Campbell Hall Gallery, Monmouth OR

Hosley, William, *Cur Decorative Arts,* Wadsworth Atheneum, Hartford CT

Hostetter, David, *Cur Planetarium,* Lafayette Natural History Museum, Planetarium and Nature Station, Lafayette LA

Hotheinz, Rudolph H, *Assoc Prof,* Virginia Western Community College, Commercial Art, Fine Art & Photography, Roanoke VA (S)

Hough, Katherine, *Cur,* Palm Springs Desert Museum, Inc, Library, Palm Springs CA

Hough, Katherine Plake, *Cur Art,* Palm Springs Desert Museum, Inc, Palm Springs CA

Hough, Melissa, *Dir,* CIGNA Corporation, CIGNA Museum & Art Collection, Philadelphia PA

Houghton, Amory, *Deputy Dir External Affairs,* Whitney Museum of American Art, New York NY

Houghton, Barbara, *Chmn,* Northern Kentucky University, Art Dept, Highland Heights KY (S)

Houlihan, Patrick T, *Dir,* Millicent Rogers Museum, Taos NM

House, Thomas, *Photographic Archivist,* University of Kentucky, Photographic Archives, Lexington KY

House, William, *Chmn Industrial Design,* Center for Creative Studies, College of Art & Design, Detroit MI (S)

Householder, Johanna, *Acting Chair New Media,* Ontario College of Art, Toronto ON (S)

Houseman, Anne, *Pres Board of Trustees,* Burnaby Art Gallery, Burnaby BC

Houser, Caroline, *Assoc Prof,* Smith College, Art Dept, Northampton MA (S)

Housman, Russell, *Prof,* Nassau Community College, Art Dept, Garden City NY (S)

Houston, David, *Dir,* Clemson University, Rudolph E Lee Gallery, Clemson SC

Houston, David, *Visual Arts Dir,* South Carolina Arts Commission, Columbia SC

Houston, Shirley, *First VPres,* Jesse Besser Museum, Alpena MI

Hovind, Mary, *Specialist,* University of Wisconsin-Stout, Dept of Art & Design, Menomonie WI (S)

Howard, Angela, *Asst Prof,* Rutgers, the State University of New Jersey, Graduate Program in Art History, New Brunswick NJ (S)

Howard, Bert, *Dir,* Art Association School, Spartanburg SC (S)

Howard, Carolyn, *Instr,* Wayne Art Center, Wayne PA (S)

Howard, Cecil, *Prof,* Western New Mexico University, Dept of Expressive Arts, Silver City NM (S)

Howard, Cordelia, *Dir Libr Servs,* Long Beach Public Library, Long Beach CA

Howard, Evan, *Local Minister,* Mission San Luis Rey Museum, San Luis Rey CA

Howard, Jan, *Assoc Cur Prints Drawings & Photographs,* Baltimore Museum of Art, Baltimore MD

Howard, Jerry, *Coordr Museum Serv,* Alaska State Museum, Juneau AK

Howard, John, *Co-Pres,* The Greenwich Art Society Inc, Greenwich CT

Howard, Jonas, *Art Dir,* Floyd County Museum, New Albany IN

Howard, Jonas A, *Prof,* Indiana University-Southeast, Fine Arts Dept, New Albany IN (S)

Howard, Nora, *Dir,* Wethersfield Historical Society Inc, Old Academy Library, Wethersfield CT

Howard, Nora, *Dir,* Wethersfield Historical Society Inc, Wethersfield CT

Howat, John K, *Chmn American Art Dept,* The Metropolitan Museum of Art, New York NY

Howe, Catherine, *Asst Dir,* White Columns, New York NY

Howe, Eunice, *Assoc Prof,* University of Southern California, School of Fine Arts, Los Angeles CA (S)

Howe, Jeffery, *Chmn,* Boston College, Fine Arts Dept, Newton MA (S)

Howe, Katherine, *Cur Decorative Arts,* Museum of Fine Arts, Houston, Houston TX

Howe, Richard, *Pres,* Haystack Mountain School of Crafts, Gallery, Deer Isle ME

Howe, Thomas, *Chmn,* Southwestern University, Art Dept, Georgetown TX (S)

Howell, Anne, *Development Officer,* Heckscher Museum, Huntington NY

Howell, Anne, *Museum Technician,* United States Department of the Interior Museum, Washington DC

Howell, Anthony, *Prof,* Western New Mexico University, Dept of Expressive Arts, Silver City NM (S)

Howell, Bob, *Prof,* Hardin-Simmons University, Art Dept, Abilene TX (S)

Howell, Bronwen, *Public Relations,* Contemporary Arts Center, Cincinnati OH

Howell, Charles, *Cur Entomology,* San Bernardino County Museum, Fine Arts Institute, Redlands CA

Howell, Janet, *Dir & Cur,* Newburyport Maritime Society, Custom House Maritime Museum, Newburyport MA

Howell, Joseph, *Secy & Registrar,* Zanesville Art Center, Zanesville OH

Howell, Joseph, *Registrar & Librn,* Zanesville Art Center, Library, Zanesville OH

Howell, Joyce B, *Asst Prof,* Virginia Wesleyan College, Art Dept of the Humanities Division, Norfolk VA (S)

Howell, Nancy, *Pres,* New England Watercolor Society, Boston MA

Howell, Robert D, *Prof,* California Polytechnic State University at San Luis Obispo, Dept of Art and Design, San Luis Obispo CA (S)

Howell, Tom, *Chmn,* Porterville College, Dept of Fine Arts, Porterville CA (S)

Howett, Catherine, *Secy,* Emory University, Museum of Art & Archaeology, Atlanta GA

Howett, Catherine T, *Asst Dir,* Emory University, Museum of Art & Archaeology, Atlanta GA

Howett, John, *Prof,* Emory University, Art History Dept, Atlanta GA (S)

Howk, Cynthia, *Res Coordr,* Landmark Society of Western New York, Inc, Wenrich Memorial Library, Rochester NY

Howkins, Mary Ball, *Assoc Prof,* Rhode Island College, Art Dept, Providence RI (S)

Howland, Dave, *Treas,* Redding Museum of Art & History, Redding CA

Howland, Margaret, *Visitor Servs,* Harvard University, Harvard University Art Museums, Cambridge MA

Howsam, Robert, *Assoc Exec Dir,* Colorado Springs Fine Arts Center, Colorado Springs CO

Howsare, Susan, *Asst Prof,* Waynesburg College, Dept of Fine Arts, Waynesburg PA (S)

Howze, Jim, *Prof,* Texas Tech University, Dept of Art, Lubbock TX (S)

Hoy, Harold, *Dir,* Lane Community College, Art Dept Gallery, Eugene OR

Hoydysh, Daria, *Cur,* Ukrainian Institute of America, Inc, New York NY

Hoyle, Glen, *Dir,* Art Instruction Schools, Education Dept, Minneapolis MN (S)

Hrehov, John, *Asst Prof,* Indiana-Purdue University, Dept of Fine Arts, Fort Wayne IN (S)

Hruska, Dorothy I, *Dir & Museologist,* LeSueur County Historical, Museum, Chapter One, Elysian MN

Hruska, Dorothy I, *Dir,* LeSueur County Historical, Collections Library, Elysian MN

Hrycelak, George, *Dir & Pres,* Ukrainian National Museum and Library, Chicago IL

Hu, Zheng, *Preparator,* State University of New York at Albany, University Art Gallery, Albany NY

Hubbard, Elizabeth, *Dir of Personnel,* The Phillips Collection, Washington DC

Hubbard, John, *Theatre Coordr,* Ashtabula Arts Center, Ashtabula OH

Hubbard, John D, *Prof,* Northern Michigan University, Dept of Art and Design, Marquette MI (S)

Hubbard, Peggy, *Dir Development,* University of Rochester, Memorial Art Gallery, Rochester NY

Hubbard, Rita, *Head Dept,* Christopher Newport College, Arts & Communications, Newport News VA (S)

Hubbard, William, *VPres,* Pocumtuck Valley Memorial Association, Memorial Hall, Deerfield MA

Hubel, Vello, *Chair Industrial Design,* Ontario College of Art, Toronto ON (S)

Huber, Caroline, *Co-Dir,* Diverse Works, Houston TX

Huber, Gerard, *Coordr Grad Programs,* East Texas State University, Dept of Art, East Texas Station, Commerce TX (S)

Huber, Mary, *Dir,* City of Cedar Falls, Iowa, James & Meryl Hearst Center for the Arts, Cedar Falls IA

Huberman, Brian, *Assoc Prof,* Rice University, Dept of Art and Art History, Houston TX (S)

Hubert, Thomas, *Dept Chmn,* Mercyhurst College, Dept of Art, Erie PA (S)

Hubschmitt, William, *Instr,* State University of New York College at Oneonta, Dept of Art, Oneonta NY (S)

Huculak, Larry, *Dir,* Basilian Fathers, Library, Mundare AB

Hudgins, Rena, *Head Librn,* Chrysler Museum, Norfolk VA

Hudgins, Rena, *Chief Librn,* Chrysler Museum, Jean Outland Chrysler Library, Norfolk VA

Hudnut, David, *Pres,* California Historical Society, El Molino Viejo, San Marino CA

Hudson, Bradley, *Registrar & Preparator,* Syracuse University, Joe and Emily Lowe Art Gallery, Syracuse NY

Hudson, Carol J, *Public Information,* Schenectady Museum, Planetarium & Visitors Center, Schenectady NY

Hudson, David C, *Pres & Exec Dir,* Arts Council, Inc, Winston-Salem NC

Hudson, Eldred, *Instr,* University of North Carolina at Charlotte, Dept of Visual Arts, Charlotte NC (S)

Hudson, Judith B, *Cur Art,* Valley National Bank of Arizona, Phoenix AZ

Hudson, Myrna, *Adult Serv Division Coordr,* Wichita Public Library, Wichita KS

Hudson, Nancy, *Asst Dir,* Las Vegas-Clark County Library District, Las Vegas NV

Hudson, Ralph M, *VPres,* Kappa Pi International Honorary Art Fraternity, Crestwood MO

Huebner, Carla, *Asst Prof,* Mount Mary College, Art Dept, Milwaukee WI (S)

Huebner, Gregory, *Prof,* Wabash College, Art Dept, Crawfordsville IN (S)

Huenink, Peter, *Chmn,* Vassar College, Art Dept, Poughkeepsie NY (S)

Huether, Mary, *Asst Instr,* Dickinson State University, Dept of Art, Dickinson ND (S)

Huff, John, *Interior Design,* University of Georgia, Franklin College of Arts & Sciences, Dept of Art, Athens GA (S)

Huff, Robert, *Chmn Dept Kendall Campus,* Miami-Dade Community College, Visual Arts Dept, Miami FL (S)

Huffman, Lorilee, *Cur Colls,* Southern Illinois University, University Museum, Carbondale IL

Huffman, Walker, *Pres Board Trustees,* Zanesville Art Center, Zanesville OH

Hufford, Gary, *Instr,* The Arkansas Arts Center, Museum School, Little Rock AR (S)

Huggins, Victor, *Prof,* Virginia Polytechnic Institute & State University, Dept of Art & Art History, Blacksburg VA (S)

Hughes, Carolyn, *Dir Coll,* The Bostonian Society, Old State House Museum, Boston MA

Hughes, Danny R, *Dir Spec Projects,* Arts Council of Spartanburg County, Inc, Spartanburg Arts Center, Spartanburg SC

Hughes, Gary, *Chief Cur,* New Brunswick Museum, Saint John NB

Hughes, Inez H, *Dir,* Harrison County Historical Museum, Marshall TX

Hughes, Jeffrey, *Asst Prof,* Webster University, Art Dept, Webster Groves MO (S)

Hughes, John, *Assoc Prof,* Missouri Western State College, Art Dept, Saint Joseph MO (S)

Hughes, Kenneth, *Assoc Dean Design,* Emily Carr College of Art & Design, Vancouver BC (S)

Hughes, Kevin, *Instr,* Vincennes University Junior College, Art Dept, Vincennes IN (S)

Hughes, Mary Jo, *Assoc Cur,* Queen's University, Agnes Etherington Art Centre, Kingston ON

Hughes, Shirley, *Division Chmn,* Burlington County College, Humanities & Fine Art Div, Pemberton NJ (S)

Hughes, Woody, *Instr,* Dowling College, Dept of Visual Arts, Oakdale NY (S)

Hughley, John, *Prof,* North Carolina Central University, Art Dept, Durham NC (S)

Hughston, Milan R, *Librn,* Amon Carter Museum, Library, Fort Worth TX

Huisman, Carl J, *Prof,* Calvin College, Art Dept, Grand Rapids MI (S)

Hujsak, Mary D, *Librn,* American Craft Council, Craft Information Center, New York NY

Hulet, Grant, *Prof,* Salt Lake Community College, Graphic Design Dept, Salt Lake City UT (S)

Hull, David, *Principal Librn,* San Francisco Maritime National Historical Park, J Porter Shaw Library, San Francisco CA

Hull, Jim, *Dept Chmn,* Mount Vernon College, Art Dept, Washington DC (S)

Hull, Joan C, *Exec Dir,* The Bostonian Society, Old State House Museum, Boston MA

Hull, John, *Asst Prof,* University of Mississippi, Dept of Art, University MS (S)

Hull, Vida, *Asst Prof,* East Tennessee State University, Fine Arts Dept, Johnson City TN (S)

Hulstrom, Richard L, *Art Consultant,* Lutheran Brotherhood Gallery, Minneapolis MN

Hulten, Kim, *Bookkeeper,* Cascade County Historical Society, Cascade County Historical Museum & Archives, Great Falls MT

Hults, Linda, *Assoc Prof,* College of Wooster, Dept of Art, Wooster OH (S)

Humble, Douglas, *Galleries Asst,* Galleries of the Claremont Colleges, Claremont CA

Humble, Jody L, *Librn,* Canadian Conference of the Arts, Ottawa ON

Hume, Robert, *Instr,* San Jacinto College-North, Art Dept, Houston TX (S)

Hummer, Philip W, *Treas,* Chicago Historical Society, Chicago IL

Humphery, Meeghan, *Admin Asst & visual Arts & Exhibit Coordr,* Ashtabula Arts Center, Ashtabula OH

Humphrey, John, *Assoc Prof,* University of Michigan, Ann Arbor, Dept of History of Art, Ann Arbor MI (S)

Humphrey, Rebecca, *Prof,* James Madison University, Dept of Art, Harrisonburg VA (S)

Humphrey, Rita S, *Admin Asst,* Baylor University, Armstrong Browning Library, Waco TX

Humphries, Dave, *Dir & Cur,* Swift Current National Exhibition Centre, Swift Current SK

Huneault, Kristina, *Curatorial Asst,* Concordia University, Leonard & Bina Ellen Art Gallery, Montreal PQ

Hungerford, Constance Cain, *Prof,* Swarthmore College, Dept of Art, Swarthmore PA (S)

Hunnibell, S, *Instr,* Community College of Rhode Island, Dept of Art, Warwick RI (S)

Hunsberger, Charles W, *Dir,* Las Vegas-Clark County Library District, Las Vegas NV

Hunt, Ashley, *Mgr,* International Museum of Cartoon Art, Boca Raton FL

Hunt, David, *Cur Western American Art,* Joslyn Art Museum, Omaha NE

Hunt, David, *Assoc Prof,* Fort Lewis College, Art Dept, Durango CO (S)

Hunt, Doris, *Pres,* Pine Castle Folk Art Center, Orlando FL

Hunt, Dot, *Librn Asst,* North Carolina State University, Harrye Lyons Design Library, Raleigh NC

Hunt, Garrett, *Visual Arts Dir,* Council of Ozark Artists and Craftsmen, Inc, Arts Center of the Ozarks Gallery, Springdale AR

Hunt, John P, *Executive Secy,* Marblehead Historical Society, Marblehead MA

Hunt, Lyn, *Chmn Board,* Morgan County Foundation, Inc, Madison-Morgan Cultural Center, Madison GA

Hunt, Susan, *Prof,* University of Wisconsin-Stout, Dept of Art & Design, Menomonie WI (S)

Hunt, Susan, *Asst Prof,* University of Wisconsin-Stout, Dept of Art & Design, Menomonie WI (S)

Hunter, Carolyn, *Art Librn,* Public Library of Charlotte and Mecklenburg County, Charlotte NC

Hunter, James, *Dir,* Huronia Museum, Midland ON

Hunter, John, *Art & Theatre Arts Chmn,* Washburn University of Topeka, Dept of Art & Theatre Arts, Topeka KS (S)

Hunter, John, *Chmn,* Cleveland State University, Art Dept, Cleveland OH (S)

Hunter, John, *Prof,* Cleveland State University, Art Dept, Cleveland OH (S)

Hunter, Judith, *Exec Dir,* Pasadena Historical Society, Pasadena CA

Hunter, Ron, *Principal,* Nutana Collegiate Institute, Memorial Library and Art Gallery, Saskatoon SK

Hunter, Rosetta, *Chmn,* Seattle Central Community College, Humanities - Social Sciences Division, Seattle WA (S)

Hunter, Terry K, *Instr,* South Carolina State University, Art Dept, Orangeburg SC (S)

Huntley, Reginald D, *Controller,* Southwest Museum, Los Angeles CA

Huntting, Nancy, *Coordr,* Aesthetic Realism Foundation, Terrain Gallery, New York NY

Huret, Laquita, *Office Mgr,* Carson County Square House Museum, Panhandle TX

Hurlbert, Susan, *Clerk,* Burbank Public Library, Warner Research Collection, Burbank CA

Hurley, K, *Asst Dean,* Technical University of Nova Scotia, Faculty of Architecture, Halifax NS (S)

Hurlstone, Robert, *Chmn 3-D Studies,* Bowling Green State University, School of Art, Bowling Green OH (S)

Hurry, Robert J, *Registrar,* Calvert Marine Museum, Solomons MD

Hurst, Andrew W, *Exhib Coordr,* University of Tennessee, Frank H McClung Museum, Knoxville TN

Hurst, Andrew W, *Exhibits Coodr,* University of Tennessee, Eleanor Dean Audigier Art Collection, Knoxville TN

Hurst, Louann, *Acting Dir,* Lee County Library, Tupelo MS

Hurt, Susanne, *Recording Secy,* American Artists Professional League, Inc, New York NY

Husband, Elizabeth F, *Secy,* Amerind Foundation, Inc, Amerind Museum, Fulton-Hayden Memorial Art Gallery, Dragoon AZ

Husband, Timothy, *Assoc Cur,* The Metropolitan Museum of Art, The Cloisters, New York NY

Huseboe, Arthur R, *Exec Dir,* Augustana College, Center for Western Studies, Sioux Falls SD

Huseboe, Arthur R, *Dir,* Augustana College, Center for Western Studies, Sioux Falls SD

Huser, Diane, *Membership Coordr,* National Art Museum of Sport, Indianapolis IN

Huskey, Susan, *Instr,* Dunedin Fine Arts and Cultural Center, Dunedin FL (S)

Huskinson, Ann G, *Exec Dir,* Red River Valley Museum, Vernon TX

Huston, Alan, *Assoc Prof,* Winthrop College, Dept of Art & Design, Rock Hill SC (S)

Huston, Kathleen, *City Librn,* Milwaukee Public Library, Art, Music & Recreation Dept, Milwaukee WI

Hutchens, Edie, *Mgr,* Wilkes Art Gallery, North Wilkesboro NC

Hutchins, Lee, *Exec Dir,* Society for Photographic Education, Dallas TX

Hutchinson, Albert, *Comptroller,* International Museum of African Art, New York NY

Hutchinson, Don, *Instr,* Vancouver Community College, Langara Campus, Dept of Fine Arts, Vancouver BC (S)

Hutchinson, Max, *Pres,* Max Hutchinson's Sculpture Fields, Kenoza Lake NY

Hutchinson, Valerie, *Asst Prof,* Arkansas State University, Dept of Art, Jonesboro AR (S)

Hutchinson, William, *Acting Chmn,* University of California, Los Angeles, Dept of Design, Los Angeles CA (S)

Hutchison, Jane C, *Art History Dept Chmn,* University of Wisconsin, Madison, Dept of Art History, Madison WI (S)

Huth, Nancy, *Cur Educ & Asst Dir,* Ball State University, Museum of Art, Muncie IN

Hutsell, Barbara, *Dir,* Atlanta College of Art Library, Atlanta GA

Hutslar, Don, *Actg Head History,* Ohio Historical Society, Columbus OH

Hutson, Bill, *Instr,* Creighton University, Fine and Performing Arts Dept, Omaha NE (S)

Hutson, Janet H, *Development Dir,* Handweavers Guild of America, Bloomfield CT

Hutterer, Karl, *Dir,* University of Washington, Thomas Burke Memorial Washington State Museum, Seattle WA

Hutton, Joan, *Pres,* Minneapolis Society of Fine Arts, Friends of the Institute, Minneapolis MN

Hutton, John, *Asst Prof,* Lansing Community College, Media Dept, Lansing MI (S)

Hutton, John, *Instr,* Salem College, Art Dept, Winston-Salem NC (S)

Hutton, Robert, *Prof,* Marshall University, Dept of Art, Huntington WV (S)

Hutton Turner, Elizabeth, *Assoc Cur,* The Phillips Collection, Washington DC

Huvwitz, Jeffrey, *Photographer in Residence,* Moravian College, Dept of Art, Bethlehem PA (S)

Huyke, Hector J, *Dir,* University of Puerto Rico, Mayaguez, Dept of Humanities, College of Arts & Sciences, Mayaguez PR (S)

Hyde, Marion R, *Head,* Utah State University, Dept of Art, Logan UT (S)

Hyde, Susan, *Graphic Designer,* University of Kansas, Spencer Museum of Art, Lawrence KS

Hyde, T Budge, *Head Art Dept,* Greenfield Community College, Art, Graphic Design & Media Communication Dept, Greenfield MA (S)

Hyke, Stewart, *Dir Office Cultural Affairs Oakland Univ,* Oakland University, Meadow Brook Art Gallery, Rochester MI

Hyland, Douglas, *Dir,* San Antonio Museum Association, Inc, San Antonio Museum of Art, San Antonio TX

Hyland, John W, *Chmn,* American Academy in Rome, New York NY (S)

Hyland, William, *VPres,* Monterey Peninsula Museum of Art Association, Monterey CA

Hyldelund, Douglas, *Instr,* Mohawk Valley Community College, Advertising Design and Production, Utica NY (S)

Hyleck, Walter, *Dept Chair,* Berea College, Art Dept Library, Berea KY

Hyleck, Walter, *Chmn,* Berea College, Art Dept, Berea KY (S)

Hyman, Lewis B, *VPres,* Wilmington Trust Company, Wilmington DE

Hynes, William, *Chmn Art Dept,* Shippensburg University, Art Dept, Shippensburg PA (S)

Hynes, William Q, *Dir,* Shippensburg University, Kauffman Gallery, Shippensburg PA

Hysell, David M, *Prof,* Rhode Island College, Art Dept, Providence RI (S)

Hysinger, Paula, *Pub Relations Officer,* Greenville County Museum of Art, Greenville SC

Hyslin, Richard, *Chmn Dept,* University of Texas Pan American, Art Dept, Edinburg TX (S)

Iacono, Domenic J, *Asst Dir,* Syracuse University, Art Collection, Syracuse NY

Ianni, Ronald W, *VPres,* Art Gallery of Windsor, Windsor ON

Ibbitson, R, *Fine Arts Technician,* Mount Allison University, Owens Art Gallery, Sackville NB

Iberg, Kim, *Lectr,* Southwest Texas State University, Dept of Art, San Marcos TX (S)

Ice, Joyce, *Asst Dir,* Museum of New Mexico, Museum of International Folk Art, Santa Fe NM

Igwe, Kod, *Chmn,* Claflin College, Dept of Art, Orangeburg SC (S)

Ikedo, Yoshiro, *Prof,* Kansas State University, Art Dept, Manhattan KS (S)

Iler, Henry, *Prof,* Georgia Southern University, Dept of Art, Statesboro GA (S)

Iles, Bill R, *Chmn,* McNeese State University, Dept of Visual Arts, Lake Charles LA (S)

Imami-Paydar, Niloo, *Asst Cur Textiles & Costumes,* Indianapolis Museum of Art, Indianapolis IN

Imm, Eumie, *Assoc Librn Reference,* Museum of Modern Art, Library, New York NY

Immaculatum, Cor, *Chairperson Dept,* Marywood College, Art Dept, Scranton PA (S)

Incardona, Lisa, *Registrar,* The Dixon Gallery & Gardens, Memphis TN

Incardona, Lisa, *Registrar,* The Dixon Gallery & Gardens, Library, Memphis TN

Indeck, Karen, *Dir,* University of Illinois At Chicago, Gallery 400, Chicago IL

Infantino, Cynthia, *Adult Servs Coordr,* Lake Forest Library, Fine Arts Dept, Lake Forest IL

Ingber, Rabbi Abie, *Exec Dir,* Hillel Foundation, Hillel Jewish Student Center Gallery, Cincinnati OH

Ingberman, Jeannette, *Dir,* Exit Art, New York NY

Ingersoll, Jonathan, *Assoc Prof,* Saint Mary's College of Maryland, Arts and Letters Division, Saint Mary's City MD (S)

Ingersoll, Jonathan, *Dir,* St Mary's College of Maryland, The Dwight Frederick Boyden Gallery, Saint Mary City MD

Ingersoll, Lynn, *Dir Photography,* Academy of Art College, Fine Arts Dept, San Francisco CA (S)

Ingle, J Addison, *Pres,* Charleston Museum, Charleston SC

Inglis, Elspeth, *Dir Educ,* Bennington Museum, Bennington VT

Ingram, Marilyn, *Cur Education,* Kimbell Art Museum, Fort Worth TX

Ingram, Sharilyn J, *Depty Chief Admin,* Art Gallery of Ontario, Toronto ON

Ingram, Tom, *VChmn,* Knoxville Museum of Art, Knoxville TN

Inks, Ed, *Instr,* University of Nevada, Las Vegas, Dept of Art, Las Vegas NV (S)

Inlow, Terry, *Prof,* Wilmington College, Art Dept, Wilmington OH (S)

Inman, Jan, *Instr,* La Sierra University, Art Dept, Riverside CA (S)

Innes, David, *Business Mgr,* Allentown Art Museum, Allentown PA

Insalaco, Thomas F, *Prof,* Finger Lakes Community College, Visual & Performing Arts Dept, Canandaigua NY (S)

Ippoldo, Diane, *Instr,* Wayne Art Center, Wayne PA (S)

Ipson, Daniel A, *Chmn Fine Arts,* Hartnell College, Art and Photography Dept, Salinas CA (S)

Irby, Frank, *Instr,* Pacific Northwest College of Art, Portland OR (S)

Ireland, Martha, *Cur,* Princeton Antiques Bookservice, Art Marketing Reference Library, Atlantic City NJ

Irvine, Betty Jo, *Head Librn,* Indiana University, Fine Arts Library, Bloomington IN

Irvine, Brenda, *Acting Cur,* Woodstock Public Library, Art Gallery, Woodstock ON

Irwin, Millard, *Chmn,* Cabrillo College, Visual Arts Division, Aptos CA (S)

Isaacson, Gene, *Instr,* Rancho Santiago College, Art Dept, Santa Ana CA (S)

Isaacson, Gene, *Advisor to Board,* Orange County Center for Contemporary Art, Santa Ana CA

Isaacson, Joel, *Prof,* University of Michigan, Ann Arbor, Dept of History of Art, Ann Arbor MI (S)

Isaacson, M, *Instr,* Humboldt State University, College of Arts & Humanities, Arcata CA (S)

Isaacson, Marcia, *Assoc Prof,* University of Florida, Dept of Art, Gainesville FL (S)

Isabelle, Margot, *Librn,* Massachusetts College of Art, Morton R Godine Library, Boston MA

Isenberg, E Duane, *Asst Prof,* Mohawk Valley Community College, Advertising Design and Production, Utica NY (S)

Ishee, Charles, *Head Art & Music Dept,* Public Library of Cincinnati & Hamilton County, Art & Music Department, Cincinnati OH

Ishikawa, Joseph, *Dir Emeritus,* Michigan State University, Kresge Art Museum, East Lansing MI

Isman, Bonnie, *Dir,* Jones Library, Inc, Amherst MA

Isoline, Charles J, *Assoc Prof,* Baylor University, Dept of Art, Waco TX (S)

Ison, Mary M, *Head Reference Section,* Library of Congress, Prints and Photographs Division, Washington DC

Ison, Susan, *Dir,* Loveland Museum and Gallery, Loveland CO

Israels, Sarah, *Dir Development,* London Regional Art & Historical Museums, London ON

Isto, Ted, *Instr,* Umpqua Community College, Fine & Performing Arts Dept, Roseburg OR (S)

Italiano, J N, *Assoc Prof,* College of the Holy Cross, Dept of Visual Arts, Worcester MA (S)

Itsell, Mary K, *Asst Cur,* US Department of State, Diplomatic Reception Rooms, Washington DC

Ittelson, Mary I, *Assoc Dir,* Museum of Contemporary Art, Chicago IL

Itter, William, *Prof,* Indiana University, Bloomington, Henry Radford Hope School of Fine Arts, Bloomington IN (S)

Ittu, George, *Pres,* Saint Mary's Romanian Orthodox Church, Romanian Ethnic Museum, Cleveland OH

Ivers, Bernadette, *Asst Dean,* Illinois Institute of Technology, College of Architecture, Chicago IL (S)

Ivers, Louise H, *Chairwoman,* California State University, Dominguez Hills, Art Dept, Carson CA (S)

Ives, Colta, *VPres,* Print Council of America, Baltimore MD

Ives, Colta, *Cur-in-Charge Prints & Illustrated Books,* The Metropolitan Museum of Art, New York NY

Ives, Colta, *Cur in Charge,* The Metropolitan Museum of Art, Dept of Prints & Illustrated Books, New York NY

Ives, Jack, *Asst Dir Archaelogy & Ethnology,* Department of Culture & Multi-Culturalism, Provincial Museum of Alberta, Edmonton AB (S)

Ivey, Paul, *Asst Prof Art History,* University of Arizona, Dept of Art, Tucson AZ (S)

Ivins, Mildred, *Chmn Fashion Illustration,* Moore College of Art & Design, Philadelphia PA (S)

Ivory, Carol, *Asst Prof,* Winthrop College, Dept of Art & Design, Rock Hill SC (S)

Ivory, Paul W, *Dir,* National Trust for Historic Preservation, Chesterwood Museum, Glendale MA

Izquierdo, Manuel, *Instr,* Pacific Northwest College of Art, Portland OR (S)

Jablow, Lisa, *Chmn,* Johnson State College, Dept Fine Arts, Dibden Gallery, Johnson VT (S)

Jack, Marlene, *Assoc Prof,* College of William and Mary, Dept of Fine Arts, Williamsburg VA (S)

Jacka, Doris, *First VPres,* San Bernardino Art Association, Inc, San Bernardino CA

Jack MFA, Meredith M, *Assoc Prof,* Lamar University, Art Dept, Beaumont TX (S)

Jackovich, Sheila, *Gallery Hostess,* Pemaquid Group of Artists, Pemaquid Point ME

Jacks, Frank, *Chmn,* Pikeville College, Humanities Division, Pikeville KY (S)

Jackson, A, *Instr,* Golden West College, Visual Art Dept, Huntington Beach CA (S)

Jackson, A, *Instr,* Technical University of Nova Scotia, Faculty of Architecture, Halifax NS (S)

Jackson, Amy, *Ed Art,* Illinois State Museum, Illinois State Art Gallery & Lockport Gallery, Springfield IL

Jackson, Anke, *Assoc Dir,* The Parrish Art Museum, Southampton NY

Jackson, Arnold, *Dir Promotional Servs,* American Society of Artists, Inc, Chicago IL

Jackson, B, *Secy-Registrar,* University of Victoria, Maltwood Art Museum and Gallery, Victoria BC

Jackson, Bev, *Adminr,* Favell Museum of Western Art & Indian Artifacts, Klamath Falls OR

Jackson, Bill, *First VPres,* Rome Historical Society Museum, Rome NY

Jackson, Craig, *Reference Librn,* Mechanics' Institute Library, San Francisco CA

Jackson, Dale, *Dir Art Dept,* Southwestern Community College, Art Dept, Creston IA (S)

Jackson, Dana, *Cur & Conservator Objects,* Vesterheim Norwegian-American Museum, Decorah IA

Jackson, David, *Asst Prof,* Murray State University, Art Dept, Murray KY (S)

Jackson, Doug, *Dir,* Chatham Cultural Centre, Thames Art Gallery, Chatham ON

Jackson, Duke, *Chmn Fine Arts,* Georgia Southwestern College, Art Gallery, Americus GA

Jackson, Duke, *Chmn,* Georgia Southwestern College, Dept of Fine Arts, Americus GA (S)

Jackson, Harry, *Cur Education,* National Portrait Gallery, Washington DC

Jackson, Herb, *Dir,* Davidson College Art Gallery, Davidson NC

Jackson, Herb, *Chmn,* Davidson College, Art Dept, Davidson NC (S)

Jackson, Ilene, *Office Coordr,* Portage and District Arts Council, Portage la Prairie MB

Jackson, Jan, *Dir & Chmn Exhib Committee,* State University of New York at Geneseo, Bertha V B Lederer Gallery, Geneseo NY

Jackson, Jed, *Asst Prof,* Southern Illinois University, School of Art & Design, Carbondale IL (S)

Jackson, Marsha, *Deputy Dir,* Museum of New Mexico, Santa Fe NM

Jackson, Mary Gaissert, *Dir,* The Athenaeum, Alexandria VA

Jackson, Milton, *Div Chmn of Music,* James H Faulkner Community College, Bay Minette AL (S)

Jackson, Patsy, *Educ Mgr,* Texas Tech University, Museum, Lubbock TX

Jackson, Robin, *Chmn,* Treasure Valley Community College, Art Dept, Ontario OR (S)

Jackson, Steve, *Cur Art & Photography,* Montana State University, Museum of the Rockies, Bozeman MT

Jackson, Susan, *Prof,* Marshall University, Dept of Art, Huntington WV (S)

Jackson, Ward, *Archivist,* Solomon R Guggenheim Museum, New York NY

Jackson, William, *Instr,* Simon's Rock of Bard College, Visual Arts Dept, Great Barrington MA (S)

Jackson, William M, *Asst Dir,* Pierpont Morgan Library, New York NY

Jackson Beck, Lauren, *Asst Museum Librn,* The Metropolitan Museum of Art, The Cloisters Library, New York NY

Jacob, John, *Cur,* Photographic Resource Center, Boston MA

Jacob, Susan, *Development Dir,* Intermedia Arts Minnesota, Minneapolis MN

Jacobi, Richard, *Instr,* Casper College, Dept of Visual Arts, Casper WY (S)

Jacobs, David L, *Chmn,* University of Houston, Dept of Art, Houston TX (S)

Jacobs, Ellen, *Prof,* Florida International University, Visual Arts Dept, Miami FL (S)

Jacobs, Fredrika H, *Asst Prof,* Virginia Commonwealth University, Art History Department, Richmond VA (S)

Jacobs, James, *Assoc Prof,* Weber State University, Dept of Visual Arts, Ogden UT (S)

Jacobs, Joseph, *Cur Painting & Sculpture,* Newark Museum Association, The Newark Museum, Newark NJ

Jacobs, Joyce, *Asst Prof,* Georgian Court College, Dept of Art, Lakewood NJ (S)

Jacobs, Lynn, *Asst Prof,* University of Arkansas, Art Dept, Fayetteville AR (S)

Jacobs, Nina S, *Dir,* Jersey City Museum, Jersey City NJ

Jacobs, P J, *Adminr,* University of Nebraska, Lincoln, Sheldon Memorial Art Gallery, Lincoln NE

Jacobs, Robert A, *Exec Dir,* Leo Baeck Institute, New York NY

Jacobs, Stan, *Chmn,* Midland College, Allison Fine Arts Dept, Midland TX (S)

Jacobsen, Jamia, *First VPres,* Hoosier Salon Patrons Association, Hoosier Salon Art Gallery, Indianapolis IN

Jacobsen, Robert, *Cur Oriental Arts,* Minneapolis Society of Fine Arts, Minneapolis Institute of Arts, Minneapolis MN

Jacobsen, Terry D, *Asst Dir,* Carnegie Mellon University, Hunt Institute for Botanical Documentation, Pittsburgh PA

Jacobson, Debra, *Publicity Dir,* American Jewish Art Club, Evanston IL

Jacobson, Frank, *Dir,* Scottsdale Center for the Arts, Scottsdale AZ

Jacobson, Jake, *Assoc Prof,* University of Nebraska, Kearney, Dept of Art & Art History, Kearney NE (S)

Jacobson, Lee, *Instr,* Chemeketa Community College, Dept of Humanities & Communications, Salem OR (S)

Jacobson, Leslie, *VPres,* Katonah Museum of Art, Katonah NY

Jacobson, Paul, *Chairperson Div Language & Arts,* Western Nebraska Community College, Division of Language and Arts, Scottsbluff NE (S)

Jacobson, Thora E, *Dir,* Philadelphia Museum of Art, Samuel S Fleisher Art Memorial, Philadelphia PA

Jacobson, Thora E, *Dir,* Samuel S Fleisher Art Memorial, Philadelphia PA (S)

Jacoby, Florence, *Instr,* Umpqua Community College, Fine & Performing Arts Dept, Roseburg OR (S)

Jacoby, Jerry, *Board Dir,* Artists' Cooperative Gallery, Omaha NE

Jacoby, Mark, *Pres,* National Antique & Art Dealers Association of America, New York NY

Jacoby, Patricia, *Dir Development,* Museum of Fine Arts, Boston MA

Jacoby, Thomas J, *Head,* University of Connecticut, Art & Design Library, Storrs CT

Jacomini, Ronald, *Chmn Design Studies,* Bowling Green State University, School of Art, Bowling Green OH (S)

Jacquard, Jerry, *Prof,* Indiana University, Bloomington, Henry Radford Hope School of Fine Arts, Bloomington IN (S)

Jaeger, Al, *Lectr,* Notre Dame College, Art Dept, Manchester NH (S)

Jaenike, Vaughn, *Dean,* Eastern Illinois University, Art Dept, Charleston IL (S)

Jaffe, Alan, *VPres,* Mingei International, Inc, Mingei International Museum of World Folk Art, San Diego CA

Jaffe, Amamda, *Prof,* New Mexico State University, Art Dept, Las Cruces NM (S)

Jaffe, John G, *Dir,* Sweet Briar College, Martin C Shallenberger Art Library, Sweet Briar VA

Jaffe, Richard P, *Pres,* Print Club Center for Prints & Photographs, Philadelphia PA

Jagooa, Peter, *Pres,* Society of North American Goldsmiths, Jacksonville FL

Jahns, Tim, *Educ Coordr,* City of Irvine, Irvine Fine Arts Center, Irvine CA

Jahns, Tim, *Educ Coordr,* City of Irvine, Fine Arts Center, Irvine CA (S)

Jahos, Catherine, *Prog Adminr,* Monmouth Museum and Cultural Center, Lincroft NJ

Jalenak, Maia, *Cur,* Louisiana Arts and Science Center, Baton Rouge LA

James, Christopher, *Chmn Photography Dept,* Art Institute of Boston, Boston MA (S)

James, David, *Assoc Prof,* University of Montana, Dept of Art, Missoula MT (S)

James, Mary, *Instr,* Woodstock School of Art, Inc, Woodstock NY (S)

James, Philip, *Head Dept,* James Madison University, Dept of Art, Harrisonburg VA (S)

James, Portia P, *Historian,* Anacostia Museum, Washington DC

James, Sally, *Asst Prof,* Bemidji State University, Visual Arts Dept, Bemidji MN (S)

James, Theodore, *Coll & Exhib Mgr,* Joslyn Art Museum, Omaha NE

Jameson, Nancy O, *Dir,* Old Island Restoration Foundation Inc, Wrecker's Museum, Key West FL

Jamieson, Geoffrey, *Pres,* Alberta Society of Artists, Calgary AB

Jamison, John, *Pres,* The Mariners' Museum, Newport News VA

Jamison, Roger A, *Chmn,* Mercer University, Art Dept, Macon GA (S)

Janecek, James, *Asst Prof,* Providence College, Art and Art History Dept, Providence RI (S)

Janes, R, *Dir,* Glenbow Museum, Calgary AB

Janick, Richard, *Instr,* Monterey Peninsula College, Art Dept, Monterey CA (S)

Jankowski, Edward, *Asst Prof,* Monmouth College, Dept of Art, West Long Branch NJ (S)

Jannotta, Edgar D, *VChmn,* Chicago Historical Society, Chicago IL

Janovy, Karen, *Education Coordr,* University of Nebraska, Lincoln, Sheldon Memorial Art Gallery, Lincoln NE

Jansen, Catherine, *Instr,* Bucks County Community College, Fine Arts Dept, Newtown PA (S)

Jansen, James, *Chmn Fine Arts Dept,* Loyola University of Chicago, Fine Arts Dept, Chicago IL (S)

Jansky, Rollin, *Assoc Prof,* University of Wisconsin-Parkside, Art Dept, Kenosha WI (S)

Janson, Tony, *Chief Cur,* North Carolina Museum of Art, Raleigh NC

Janzen, Joan, *Educ Coordr,* Hastings Museum, Hastings NE

Jappen, Janet, *Exec Dir,* Mid-Hudson Arts and Science Center, Poughkeepsie NY

Jaquith, Robin, *Treas,* Arts Council of San Mateo County, Belmont CA

Jaramillo, Gloria, *Deputy Dir,* Mexican Museum, San Francisco CA

Jareckie, Stephen B, *Cur Photography,* Worcester Art Museum, Worcester MA

Jaremba, Tom, *Prof,* School of the Art Institute of Chicago, Chicago IL (S)

Jarvis, Elizabeth, *Cur,* Historical Society of Pennsylvania, Philadelphia PA

Jarvis, R C, *Chmn,* Alberta Foundation For The Arts, Edmonton AB

Jarzombek, Nancy Allyn, *Assoc Cur Painting & Sculpture,* Cornell University, Herbert F Johnson Museum of Art, Ithaca NY

Jaskevich, Jane, *Prof,* Polk Community College, Art, Letters & Social Sciences, Winter Haven FL (S)

Jaskowiak, Jennifer, *Exhib Coordr,* University of Southern California, Fisher Gallery, Los Angeles CA

Jastrebsky, Barbara, *Registrar,* Randolph-Macon Woman's College, Maier Museum of Art, Lynchburg VA

Javan, Marjorie, *Pres,* Boston Printmakers, Boston MA

Javorski, Susanne, *Art Librn,* Wesleyan University, Art Library, Middletown CT

Jaworek, Joe, *Membership Servs Coordr,* Michigan Guild of Artists & Artisans, Michigan Guild Gallery, Ann Arbor MI

Jaxtheimer, Betsy, *Educ Outreach Coordr,* Randolph-Macon Woman's College, Maier Museum of Art, Lynchburg VA

Jay, Robert, *Chmn Dept Art,* University of Hawaii at Manoa, Art Gallery, Honolulu HI

Jay, Robert, *Chmn,* University of Hawaii at Manoa, Dept of Art, Honolulu HI (S)

Jay, Stephen, *Dean, College of Performing Arts,* University of the Arts, Philadelphia College of Art & Design, Philadelphia PA (S)

Jayo, Norman, *Editor,* National Alliance for Media Arts & Culture (NAMAC), Oakland CA

Jeanes, Mary Bradshaw, *Exec Dir,* Visual Arts Center of Northwest Florida, Panama City FL

Jedda, Barbara, *Chief Cur,* Craft Alliance Gallery & Education Center, Saint Louis MO

Jefcoat MFA, Joe, *VPres of Arts & Educ,* Spirit Square Center for the Arts, Charlotte NC

Jeffers, Ellie, *Dir Sales Shop,* Colorado Springs Fine Arts Center, Colorado Springs CO

Jeffers, Susan, *Instr Asst,* Ulster County Community College, Dept of Visual Arts, Stone Ridge NY (S)

Jeffords, James, *Acting Chmn,* Congressional Arts Caucus, Washington DC

Jeffrey, Brooks, *Slide Cur,* University of Arizona, College of Architecture Library, Tucson AZ

Jeffreys, Harold, *Chmn,* City Of Raleigh Arts Commission, Municipal Building Art Exhibitions, Raleigh NC

Jendrzejewski, Andrew, *Chmn,* Vincennes University Junior College, Art Dept, Vincennes IN (S)

Jendyk, Christine, *Cur,* Ukrainian Canadian Archives & Museum of Alberta, Edmonton AB

Jenkens, Garlan G, *Dir Visual Art & Education,* Arts & Science Center for Southeast Arkansas, Pine Bluff AR

Jenkins, Bruce, *Dir Film & Video,* Walker Art Center, Minneapolis MN

Jenkins, Donald, *Cur Asian Art,* Portland Art Museum, Portland OR

Jenkins, Dorothy, *Pres,* Polk Museum of Art, Lakeland FL

Jenkins, J, *Admin Asst,* Johns Hopkins University, George Peabody Library, Baltimore MD

Jenkins, Norma P H, *Librn,* Corning Museum of Glass, Rakow Library, Corning NY

Jenkins, Rupert, *Assoc Dir,* San Francisco Camerawork Inc, San Francisco CA

Jenkins, Suzanne, *Registrar,* National Portrait Gallery, Washington DC

Jenkinson, Pamela, *Public Information Programs,* Los Angeles County Museum of Art, Los Angeles CA

Jenkner, Ingrid, *Asst Cur,* Regina Public Library, Dunlop Art Gallery, Regina SK

Jenneman, Eugene A, *Museum Dir,* Northwestern Michigan College, Dennos Museum Center, Traverse City MI

Jennen, Tim, *Media Relations Supv,* Minnesota Museum of American Art, Saint Paul MN

Jennings, Corrine, *Dir,* Kenkeleba House, Inc, Kenkeleba Gallery, New York NY

Jennings, C W, *Prof,* California Polytechnic State University at San Luis Obispo, Dept of Art and Design, San Luis Obispo CA (S)

Jennings, DeAnn, *Instructor,* Los Angeles Harbor College, Art Dept, Wilmington CA (S)

Jennings, Emily, *Lectr,* McMurry University, Art Dept, Abilene TX (S)

Jennings, Susan, *Pres Bd Trustees,* Milwaukee Art Museum, Milwaukee WI

Jensen, Carl, *Art Dept Chmn,* University of Southern Colorado, College of Liberal & Fine Arts, Pueblo CO

Jensen, Carl, *Chmn,* University of Southern Colorado, Belmont Campus, Dept of Art, Pueblo CO (S)

Jensen, Carl, *Asst Prof,* University of Southern Colorado, Belmont Campus, Dept of Art, Pueblo CO (S)

Jensen, James, *Assoc Dir,* The Contemporary Museum, Honolulu HI

Jensen, James, *Asst Prof,* Loyola University of Chicago, Fine Arts Dept, Chicago IL (S)

Jensen, Ken, *Chief Librn,* Regina Public Library, Art Dept, Regina SK

Jensen, Robert A, *Prof,* Calvin College, Art Dept, Grand Rapids MI (S)

Jensen, Robin, *Chmn Dept,* Calvin College, Art Dept, Grand Rapids MI (S)

Jensen, Sue, *Asst Prof,* Auburn University at Montgomery, Dept of Fine Arts, Montgomery AL (S)

Jensen, Thomas, *Cur Horticulture,* Paine Art Center and Arboretum, Oshkosh WI

Jensen, William M, *Prof,* Baylor University, Dept of Art, Waco TX (S)

Jercich, George, *Assoc Prof,* California Polytechnic State University at San Luis Obispo, Dept of Art and Design, San Luis Obispo CA (S)

Jerenigan, Jeremy, *Asst Prof,* Tulane University, Sophie H Newcomb Memorial College, New Orleans LA (S)

Jergens, Robert, *Prof,* Cleveland Institute of Art, Cleveland OH (S)

Jernigan, Bonnie, *Publicity Coordr,* Art Complex Museum, Duxbury MA

Jesburg, Bob, *Treas,* L A Art Association, Los Angeles CA

Jess, Larry, *First VPres,* Huntsville Art League and Museum Association Inc, Huntsville AL

Jessiman, John, *Prof,* State University of New York, College at Cortland, Art Dept, Cortland NY (S)

Jessop, Brad, *Instr,* East Central University, Art Dept, Ada OK (S)

Jessup, Philip C, *Secy & Gen Counsel,* National Gallery of Art, Washington DC

Jessup, Robert, *Asst Prof,* University of Hartford, Hartford Art School, West Hartford CT (S)

Jessup, Robert, *Basic Drawing Coordr,* University of North Texas, School of Visual Arts, Denton TX (S)

Jetter, Charyl, *Instr,* Andrews University, Dept of Art, Art History & Design, Berrien Springs MI (S)

Jewel, Debbie, *Business Mgr,* Sunrise Museum, Inc, Sunrise Art Museum, Sunrise Children's Museum & Planatarium, Charleston WV

Jewell, Frank, *Dir,* Valentine Museum, Richmond VA

Jiang, Zhe-Zhou, *Instr,* Wayne Art Center, Wayne PA (S)

Jicha, Jon, *Assoc Prof,* Western Carolina University, Dept of Art, Cullowhee NC (S)

Jilg, Michael, *Assoc Prof,* Fort Hays State University, Dept of Art, Hays KS (S)

Johnston, Phillip M, *Dir,* Carnegie Institute, Carnegie Museum of Art, Pittsburgh PA

Johnston, Randy, *Instr,* Rochester Community College, Art Dept, Rochester MN (S)

Johnston, Richard, *Chmn Art Dept & Gallery Dir,* California State University, San Bernardino, University Art Galleries, San Bernardino CA

Johnston, Richard M, *Chmn Dept,* California State University, San Bernardino, Art Dept, San Bernardino CA (S)

Johnston, Sally, *Public Affairs,* Historic Hudson Valley, Tarrytown NY

Johnston, Sona, *Cur Painting & Sculpture Before 1900,* Baltimore Museum of Art, Baltimore MD

Johnston, William R, *Assoc Dir,* Walters Art Gallery, Baltimore MD

Johnston, W Robert, *Chief External Affairs,* National Museum of American Art, Washington DC

Jokinen, David, *Asst Prof,* Denison University, Dept of Art, Granville OH (S)

Jolliff, Joyce, *Undergrad Admissions,* Southern Illinois University, School of Art & Design, Carbondale IL (S)

Jolly, Angela, *Dir,* Rocky Mount Arts Center, Rocky Mount NC

Jonas, Allen, *Prof,* Bluefield State College, Art Dept, Bluefield WV (S)

Jonas, Joe, *Dept Chmn,* North Idaho College, Art Dept, Coeur D'Alene ID (S)

Jones, Angela R, *Reference Librn & Cataloger,* University of Southern Mississippi, McCain Library & Archives, Hattiesburg MS

Jones, Anita, *Assoc Cur Textiles,* Baltimore Museum of Art, Baltimore MD

Jones, Ann, *Serials Librn,* The Art Institute of Chicago, Ryerson and Burnham Libraries, Chicago IL

Jones, Anne C, *Asst to Dir Development,* North Carolina Museum of Art, Raleigh NC

Jones, Ben, *Prof,* Jersey City State College, Art Dept, Jersey City NJ (S)

Jones, Betty, *Office Secy,* Danville Museum of Fine Arts & History, Danville VA

Jones, Bob, *Chmn of the Board,* Bob Jones University, Museum & Art Gallery, Greenville SC

Jones, Brian H, *Coordr & Assoc Prof,* Indiana University-Southeast, Fine Arts Dept, New Albany IN (S)

Jones, Cal, *Instr,* Marian College, Art Dept, Fond Du Lac WI (S)

Jones, Charles E, *Librn,* University of Chicago, Oriental Institute Research Archives, Chicago IL

Jones, Dennis, *Prof Sculpture,* University of Arizona, Dept of Art, Tucson AZ (S)

Jones, Don R, *Chmn,* Iowa Wesleyan College, Art Dept, Mount Pleasant IA (S)

Jones, Doris, *Guild Dir,* Danville Museum of Fine Arts & History, Danville VA

Jones, Eileen, *Pres,* Lahaina Arts Society, Art Organization, Lahaina HI

Jones, Eleanor, *Assoc Cur American Art,* Dallas Museum of Art, Dallas TX

Jones, Elliott, *Asst Prof,* Old Dominion University, Art Dept, Norfolk VA (S)

Jones, F G, *Instr,* Western Illinois University, Art Dept, Macomb IL (S)

Jones, Frank, *Assoc Prof,* Palomar Community College, Art Dept, San Marcos CA (S)

Jones, Frederick N, *Instr,* Guilford Technical Community College, Commercial Art Dept, Jamestown NC (S)

Jones, George, *Assoc Prof,* Saint Thomas Aquinas College, Art Dept, Sparkhill NY (S)

Jones, Gerard, *Secy,* Louis Comfort Tiffany Foundation, New York NY

Jones, Glory, *Public Affairs Coordr,* Solomon R Guggenheim Museum, New York NY

Jones, Harvey L, *Deputy Cur Art,* Oakland Museum, Art Dept, Oakland CA

Jones, Joseph Howard, *Prof,* University of New Orleans-Lake Front, Dept of Fine Arts, New Orleans LA (S)

Jones, Judy Voss, *Assoc Prof,* Converse College, Art Dept, Spartanburg SC (S)

Jones, Julie, *Cur Arts of Africa, Oceania & the Americas,* The Metropolitan Museum of Art, New York NY

Jones, Justin, *Conservator,* Saint Gregory's Abbey and College, Mabee-Gerrer Museum of Art, Shawnee OK

Jones, Kathleen, *Registrar,* University of Illinois, Krannert Art Museum, Champaign IL

Jones, Kent, *Head Dept Visual Arts,* Memorial University of Newfoundland, School of Fine Arts, Visual Arts Dept, Corner Brook NF (S)

Jones, Kirsten, *Public Art Coordr,* City of Eugene, Hult Center, Jacobs Gallery, Eugene OR

Jones, Leonard, *Assoc Prof,* Virginia State University, Fine & Commercial Art, Petersburg VA (S)

Jones, Lial, *Dir Educ,* Delaware Art Museum, Wilmington DE

Jones, Lynn, *Asst Prof,* Brenau College, Art Dept, Gainesville GA (S)

Jones, Margaret, *Children's Librn,* Mexico-Audrain County Library, Mexico MO

Jones, Marvin H, *Prof,* Cleveland State University, Art Dept, Cleveland OH (S)

Jones, Mary Mahon, *Coordr Educ,* Norman Mackenzie Art Gallery, Regina SK

Jones, Mike, *Animal Cur,* Tallahassee Museum of History & Natural Science, Tallahassee FL

Jones, Pamela, *Asst Prof,* University of Massachusetts at Boston, Art Dept, Boston MA (S)

Jones, Peter, *Dir,* Cayuga Museum of History and Art, Auburn NY

Jones, Reba, *Registrar,* Amarillo Art Association, Amarillo Art Center, Amarillo TX

Jones, Richard, *Chmn,* Russell Sage College, Visual and Performing Arts Dept, Troy NY (S)

Jones, R L, *Chmn,* Shepherd College, Art Dept, Shepherdstown WV (S)

Jones, Robert, *Acting Dean,* Seton Hall University, Library, South Orange NJ

Jones, Sonja, *Librn,* Balboa Art Conservation Center, Richard D Buck Memorial Library, San Diego CA

Jones, Steven, *Dir,* Nashua Center for Arts, Nashua NH (S)

Jones, Susan, *Gallery Dir,* Firelands Association for the Visual Arts, Oberlin OH

Jones, Thomas W, *Dir,* Danville Museum of Fine Arts & History, Danville VA

Jones, William, *Dir,* Tongass Historical Museum, Ketchikan AK

Jones Hill, Sharon, *Assoc Prof,* Virginia Commonwealth University, Art History Department, Richmond VA (S)

Jones MLS, Dolores A, *Cur,* University of Southern Mississippi, McCain Library & Archives, Hattiesburg MS

Jonson AACR, Laurence, *Coll Conservator,* Deere & Company, Moline IL

Jordan, Carole, *Instr,* Muskingum College, Art Department, New Concord OH (S)

Jordan, Catherine, *Registrar,* Chrysler Museum, Norfolk VA

Jordan, Daniel P, *Dir,* Thomas Jefferson Memorial Foundation, Monticello, Charlottesville VA

Jordan, Douglas, *Asst Prof,* Salt Lake Community College, Graphic Design Dept, Salt Lake City UT (S)

Jordan, Eddie J, *Prof,* Southern University in New Orleans, Art Dept, New Orleans LA (S)

Jordan, Kathryn, *Cur,* Clinton Historical Museum Village, Clinton NJ

Jordan, Sandra, *Chmn,* University of Montevallo, College of Fine Arts, Montevallo AL (S)

Jordon, Martha, *Instr,* The Arkansas Arts Center, Museum School, Little Rock AR (S)

Jordon, Shelley, *Assoc Prof,* Oregon State University, Dept of Art, Corvallis OR (S)

Jorgensen, Sandra, *Prof,* Elmhurst College, Art Dept, Elmhurst IL (S)

Joselow, Beth, *Chmn Academic Studies,* Corcoran School of Art, Washington DC (S)

Joselyn, Cathie, *Prof,* Clarion University of Pennsylvania, Dept of Art, Clarion PA (S)

Joseph, Phil, *Art Coordr,* Miami University, Dept Fine Arts, Hamilton OH (S)

Josepher, Susan, *Chmn,* Metropolitan State College of Denver, Art Dept, Denver CO (S)

Josephson, Ken, *Prof,* School of the Art Institute of Chicago, Chicago IL (S)

Josey, Alley, *Dir,* Art Community Center, Art Center of Corpus Christi, Corpus Christi TX

Josias, Steven, *Trustee Pres,* Museum of Discovery & Science, Fort Lauderdale FL

Joslin, Richard, *Lecturer,* Smith College, Art Dept, Northampton MA (S)

Joyal, Me Serge, *VPres,* Musee d'Art de Joliette, Joliette PQ

Joyaux, Alain, *Dir,* Ball State University, Museum of Art, Muncie IN

Joyce, Daniel, *Cur Ex & Coll,* Kenosha Public Museum, Kenosha WI

Joyce, Thomas J, *Secy,* Rockwell International Corporation Trust, Pittsburgh PA

Joyner, Charles, *Head Design Dept,* North Carolina State University at Raleigh, School of Design, Raleigh NC (S)

Juchniewich, Daniel, *Asst Dir,* Rahr-West Art Museum, Manitowoc WI

Juckem, Irene, *Secy,* Marquette University, Haggerty Museum of Art, Milwaukee WI

Judge, R, *Instr,* Community College of Rhode Island, Dept of Art, Warwick RI (S)

Judson, William D, *Cur Film and Video,* Carnegie Institute, Carnegie Museum of Art, Pittsburgh PA

Judy, Carole, *Librn,* Eastern Michigan University, Art Dept Slide Collection, Ypsilanti MI

Judy, David J, *Head Dept,* Bethany College, Dept of Fine Arts, Bethany WV (S)

Juergensen, Virginia, *Prof,* Mohawk Valley Community College, Advertising Design and Production, Utica NY (S)

Julian, Joanne, *Head Dept,* College of the Canyons, Art Dept, Valencia CA (S)

Jumonville, Florence, *Head Librn,* Kemper & Leila Williams Foundation, New Orleans LA

Jumonville, Florence M, *Head Librn,* Kemper & Leila Williams Foundation, Historic New Orleans Collection, New Orleans LA

Juncker, Art, *Chmn,* Gavilan College, Art Dept, Gilroy CA (S)

Juneau, Andre, *Dir,* Musee du Seminaire de Quebec, Quebec PQ

Jung, Michael, *Dir,* Denison University, Art Gallery, Granville OH

Jung, Michael, *Prof,* Denison University, Dept of Art, Granville OH (S)

Junkins, Larry, *Prof,* University of Wisconsin, Madison, Dept of Art, Madison WI (S)

Junnila, Maria, *Assoc Prof,* College of Associated Arts, Saint Paul MN (S)

Jurgensmeyer, Marne, *Dir,* Fort Morgan Heritage Foundation, Fort Morgan CO

Juristo, Michelle S, *Cur,* University of South Florida, Contemporary Art Museum, Tampa FL

Juska, Phillip, *Interim Pres & Dir Educ,* Art Institute of Philadelphia, Philadelphia PA (S)

Just, William, *Exec Dir,* Association of Medical Illustrators, Atlanta GA

Kabana, Palmera, *3rd VPres,* Halifax Historical Society, Inc, Halifax Historical Museum, Daytona Beach FL

Kabil, Leila, *Exhib Coordr,* McAllen International Museum, McAllen TX

Kabriel, J Ronald, *Asst Prof,* Catholic University of America, School of Architecture & Planning, Washington DC (S)

Kach, Claire, *Division Mgr,* Queens Borough Public Library, Fine Arts & Recreation Division, Jamaica NY

Kachel, Harold S, *Museum Dir,* No Man's Land Historical Society Museum, Goodwell OK

Kachel, Joan Overton, *Cur & Secy,* No Man's Land Historical Society Museum, Goodwell OK

Kadas, Deborah, *Instr,* Oregon State University, Dept of Art, Corvallis OR (S)

Kadis, Averil, *Chief Public Relations Division,* Enoch Pratt Free Library of Baltimore City, Baltimore MD

Kadish, Skip, *Instr,* Monterey Peninsula College, Art Dept, Monterey CA (S)

Kaericher, John, *Exhib Coordr*, Northwestern College, Te Paske Gallery of Rowenhorst, Orange City IA

Kaericher, John, *Chmn*, Northwestern College, Art Dept, Orange City IA (S)

Kagan, Larry, *Chmn*, Rensselaer Polytechnic Institute, Dept of Art, Troy NY (S)

Kager, Stephen J, *Dir*, Woodbridge Township Cultural Arts Commission, Barron Arts Center, Woodbridge NJ

Kagle, Joseph A, *Dir*, The Art Center, Waco TX

Kahan, Mitchell, *Dir*, Akron Art Museum, Akron OH

Kahle, David, *Dept Head*, Mount Marty College, Art Dept, Yankton SD (S)

Kahler, Bruce, *Asst Prof*, Bethany College, Mingenback Art Center, Lindsborg KS

Kahler, Caroline, *Head Art Dept*, Bethany College, Art Dept, Lindsborg KS (S)

Kahler, Carolyn, *Chmn Dept*, Bethany College, Mingenback Art Center, Lindsborg KS

Kahler Berg, Lynn, *Dir*, Art Services International, Alexandria VA

Kahmeyer, Ray, *Prof*, Bethany College, Mingenback Art Center, Lindsborg KS

Kahn, David M, *Exec Dir*, Brooklyn Historical Society, Brooklyn NY

Kahn, Debora, *Asst Prof*, American University, Dept of Art, Washington DC (S)

Kahn, Deborah, *Prof*, Princeton University, Dept of Art and Archaeology, Princeton NJ (S)

Kahn, E J, *Instr*, Truro Center for the Arts at Castle Hill, Inc, Truro MA (S)

Kahn, Elizabeth, *Assoc Prof*, St Lawrence University, Dept of Fine Arts, Canton NY (S)

Kahn, Herbert, *Cur*, Exchange National Bank of Chicago, Chicago IL

Kahn, James S, *Pres & Dir*, Museum of Science and Industry, Chicago IL

Kahn, Jeanne, *Pres*, Scottsdale Artists' League, Scottsdale AZ

Kahn, Miriam, *Cur Asian & Pacific Ethnology*, University of Washington, Thomas Burke Memorial Washington State Museum, Seattle WA

Kahute, Robert M, *Assoc Prof*, Rochester Institute of Technology, School of Art and Design, Rochester NY (S)

Kaimal, Padma, *Asst Prof*, Colgate University, Dept of Art & Art History, Hamilton NY (S)

Kain, Evelyn, *Chmn*, Ripon College Art Gallery, Ripon WI

Kain, Evelyn, *Chmn*, Ripon College, Art Dept, Ripon WI (S)

Kain, Jay, *Prof*, James Madison University, Dept of Art, Harrisonburg VA (S)

Kainer, Michael, *Preparator*, Pacific Grove Art Center, Pacific Grove CA

Kaiser, Charles, *Prof*, Mount Mary College, Art Dept, Milwaukee WI (S)

Kaiser, Mary Anne, *Program Coordr*, Hunter Museum of Art, Chattanooga TN

Kaiser, Michael, *Instr Commercial Art*, Honolulu Community College, Honolulu HI (S)

Kaiser, Shawn, *Office Mgr*, Arts Council of San Mateo County, Belmont CA

Kaiser-Brinklow, Joyce, *Asst Librn*, Art Institute of Fort Lauderdale, Technical Library, Fort Lauderdale FL

Kajitani, Nobuko, *Conservator Textiles*, The Metropolitan Museum of Art, New York NY

Kakas, Karen, *Chmn Art Educ*, Bowling Green State University, School of Art, Bowling Green OH (S)

Kakudo, Yoshiko, *Cur Japanese Art*, Asian Art Museum of San Francisco, Avery Brundage Collection, San Francisco CA

Kalb, Marty J, *Prof*, Ohio Wesleyan University, Fine Arts Dept, Delaware OH (S)

Kale, Louise, *Registrar*, College of William and Mary, Joseph & Margaret Muscarelle Museum of Art, Williamsburg VA

Kalemkerian, Nairy, *Adminr*, Guilde Canadienne des Metiers d'Art, Quebec, Canadian Guild of Crafts, Quebec, Montreal PQ

Kalin, Louise, *Dir*, Gallery North, Setauket NY

Kalinovska, Milena, *Dir*, Institute of Contemporary Art, Boston MA

Kallaugher, Kevin, *Pres-Elect*, Association of American Editorial Cartoonists, Raleigh NC

Kallenberger, Christine, *Dir Exhib & Coll*, Philbrook Museum of Art, Tulsa OK

Kallies, Flora, *Admin Asst*, Canadian Artists' Representation-Le Front Des Artistes Canadiens, Ottawa ON

Kallos, Kay Klein, *Instr*, Atlanta College of Art, Atlanta GA (S)

Kalmbach, Ann, *Exec Dir*, Women's Studio Workshop, Inc, Rosendale NY

Kaloyamides, Michael G, *Chmn*, University of New Haven, Dept of Visual & Performing Arts & Philosophy, West Haven CT (S)

Kamansky, David, *Dir*, Pacific - Asia Museum, Pasadena CA

Kamerling, Leonard J, *Coordr Alaska Native Heritage Film Project*, University of Alaska, Museum, Fairbanks AK

Kamin, Benjamin Alon, *Sr Rabbi*, The Temple, The Temple Museum of Religious Art, Cleveland OH

Kaminsky, Lauren, *Dir & Cur*, Fraunces Tavern Museum, New York NY

Kaminsky, Vera, *Coordr Fibers*, University of Delaware, Dept of Art, Newark DE (S)

Kamm, James J, *Assoc Dir*, Wolfsonian Foundation, Miami Beach FL

Kamm, Keith A, *Bibliographer*, Athenaeum of Philadelphia, Philadelphia PA

Kammermeyer, Michael, *Chmn*, California State University, Long Beach, Design Dept, Long Beach CA (S)

Kampen, Michael, *Instr*, University of North Carolina at Charlotte, Dept of Visual Arts, Charlotte NC (S)

Kamradt, Doris, *Educ Asst*, Leigh Yawkey Woodson Art Museum, Inc, Art Library, Wausau WI

Kamyszew, Krzysztof, *Cur*, Polish Museum of America, Chicago IL

Kamyszew, Krzysztof, *Cur*, Polish Museum of America, Research Library, Chicago IL

Kan, Michael, *Cur African, Oceanic & New World Cultures Art*, Detroit Institute of Arts, Detroit MI

Kane, Katherine, *Dir Coll Servs*, Colorado Historical Society, Museum, Denver CO

Kane, Mary Ann, *Dir*, Cortland County Historical Society, Suggett House Museum, Cortland NY

Kane, Maureen, *Pres*, Riverside Art Museum, Riverside CA

Kane, Patricia, *Cur American Decorative Arts*, Yale University, Art Gallery, New Haven CT

Kane, Susan, *Chmn*, Oberlin College, Dept of Art, Oberlin OH (S)

Kane, Susan, *Assoc Prof*, Oberlin College, Dept of Art, Oberlin OH (S)

Kane, Virginia C, *Assoc Prof*, University of Michigan, Ann Arbor, Dept of History of Art, Ann Arbor MI (S)

Kaneshiro, Carolyn, *Instr*, Mount San Jacinto College, Art Dept, San Jacinto CA (S)

Kangas, Gene, *Prof*, Cleveland State University, Art Dept, Cleveland OH (S)

Kanter, Laurence, *Cur Robert Lehman Collection*, The Metropolitan Museum of Art, New York NY

Kany, Susan L, *Mgr Corporate & Foundation Relations*, Harvard University, Harvard University Art Museums, Cambridge MA

Kapelke, Steve, *Chmn Liberal Arts & Art History*, Milwaukee Institute of Art and Design, Milwaukee WI (S)

Kapitan, Lynn, *Asst Prof*, Mount Mary College, Art Dept, Milwaukee WI (S)

Kaplan, Debbie, *Instr*, Main Line Center for the Arts, Haverford PA (S)

Kaplan, Helene J, *Dir*, Octagon Center for the Arts, Ames IA

Kaplan, Ilee, *Assoc Dir*, California State University, Long Beach, University Art Museum, Long Beach CA

Kaplan, Janet, *Chmn Liberal Arts*, Moore College of Art & Design, Philadelphia PA (S)

Kaplan, Julius, *Instr*, California State University, San Bernardino, Art Dept, San Bernardino CA (S)

Kaplan, Lena Biorck, *Pres*, American-Scandinavian Foundation, New York NY

Kaplan, Lester, *Exec Dir*, Jewish Community Center of Greater Washington, Jane L & Robert H Weiner Judaic Museum, Rockville MD

Kaplan, Paul, *Coordr*, State University of New York College at Purchase, Art History Board of Study, Purchase NY (S)

Kaplan, Ruth, *Public Information Officer*, National Gallery of Art, Washington DC

Kaplan, Stanley, *Prof*, Nassau Community College, Art Dept, Garden City NY (S)

Kaplan, Sue, *Fine Art Librn*, Beverly Hills Public Library, Fine Arts Library, Beverly Hills CA

Kaplan, Susan A, *Dir*, Bowdoin College, Peary-MacMillan Arctic Museum, Brunswick ME

Kaplan, Wendy Tarlow, *Cur*, Art Complex Museum, Duxbury MA

Kaplowitz, Kenneth, *Assoc Prof*, Trenton State College, Art Dept, Trenton NJ (S)

Kappes, Ann, *Museum Mgr*, Mingei International, Inc, Mingei International Museum of World Folk Art, San Diego CA

Kapplinger, Kent, *Lectr*, North Dakota State University, Div of Fine Arts, Fargo ND (S)

Kaprelian, Charles, *Chmn Basic Arts*, Moore College of Art & Design, Philadelphia PA (S)

Kapty, Judy, *Secy*, Ukrainian Cultural and Educational Centre, Winnipeg MB

Karagheus-Murphy, Marsha, *Prof*, Xavier University, Dept of Art, Cincinnati OH (S)

Karamer, Alison, *Registrar*, Phillips Academy, Addison Gallery of American Art, Andover MA

Karasch, Barrie, *Secy*, Brookfield Craft Center, Inc, Gallery, Brookfield CT

Karber, Jennifer, *Adminr*, Jefferson County Open Space, Hiwan Homestead Museum, Evergreen CO

Karcheski, Walter J, *Cur & Librn*, Higgins Armory Museum, Library, Worcester MA

Kardon, Carol, *Instr*, Main Line Center for the Arts, Haverford PA (S)

Kardon, Janet, *Dir*, American Craft Council, American Craft Museum, New York NY

Kardon, Peter, *Dir Planning & Latin America Prog*, John Simon Guggenheim Memorial Foundation, New York NY

Kares, Jean, *VPres*, Canadian Crafts Council, Conseil Canadien de l'Artisanat, Ottawa ON

Karetzky, Patricia, *Instr*, Sarah Lawrence College, Dept of Art History, Bronxville NY (S)

Karew, John H, *Dir*, Okefenokee Heritage Center, Inc, Waycross GA

Karg, Anita L, *Archivist*, Carnegie Mellon University, Hunt Institute for Botanical Documentation, Pittsburgh PA

Karl, Brian, *Dir*, Harvestworks, Inc, New York NY

Karl, Robert, *Adjunct Asst Prof*, Virginia Wesleyan College, Art Dept of the Humanities Division, Norfolk VA (S)

Karlen, Mark, *Chmn Interior Design*, Moore College of Art & Design, Philadelphia PA (S)

Karlins, Mary Lee, *Asst Prof*, Bradford College, Creative Arts Division, Bradford MA (S)

Karlowicz, T M, *Instr*, Western Illinois University, Art Dept, Macomb IL (S)

Karlstrom, Ann, *Publications Mgr*, Fine Arts Museums of San Francisco, M H de Young Memorial Museum and California Palace of the Legion of Honor, San Francisco CA

Karlstrom, Paul J, *Regional Dir*, Archives of American Art, Huntington Library Memorial Museum, Washington DC

Karnes, Andrea, *Curatorial Asst*, Fort Worth Art Association, Modern Art Museum of Fort Worth, Fort Worth TX

Karoly, Elizabeth, *Cur*, Nassau Community College, Firehouse Art Gallery, Garden City NY

Karp, Essie, *Exec Dir*, Women's Caucus For Art, Philadelphia PA

Karp, Karen, *2nd VChmn*, Guild Hall of East Hampton, Inc, Guild Hall Museum, East Hampton NY

Karp, Marilynn, *Faculty Dir*, New York University, 80 Washington Square East Galleries, New York NY

Karp, Marilynn G P, *Prof,* New York University, Dept of Art & Art Professions, New York NY (S)

Karpen, John E, *Prof,* Rochester Institute of Technology, School of Photographic Arts & Sciences, Rochester NY (S)

Karpinski, Helen, *Librn,* Memphis Brooks Museum of Art, Memphis TN

Karpinski, Helen, *Librn,* Memphis Brooks Museum of Art, Library, Memphis TN

Karpiscak, Adeline, *Asst Dir,* University of Arizona, Museum of Art, Tucson AZ

Karpowicz, Maria, *Librn,* Polish Museum of America, Research Library, Chicago IL

Karraker, Gene, *Equipment Technician,* California State University Fullerton, Art Gallery, Visual Arts Center, Fullerton CA

Karraker, Jack, *Chmn Dept,* University of Nebraska, Kearney, Dept of Art & Art History, Kearney NE (S)

Karras, Tiana, *Designer,* Winnipeg Art Gallery, Winnipeg MB

Karsina, James, *Assoc Prof,* Aquinas College, Art Dept, Grand Rapids MI (S)

Kartzinel, Wayne, *Dir,* Westchester Community College, Westchester Art Workshop, White Plains NY (S)

Karzen, Michael, *VPres,* American Jewish Art Club, Evanston IL

Kaserman, Roberta, *Head Dept,* Adams State College, Dept of Visual Arts, Alamosa CO (S)

Kasfir, Sidney L, *Asst Prof,* Emory University, Art History Dept, Atlanta GA (S)

Kaspar, Thomas L, *Preservation,* Nebraska State Capitol, Lincoln NE

Kasper, Janice, *Museum Teacher,* Penobscot Marine Museum, Searsport ME

Kasprzak, Constance, *Dir Display & Design,* Museum of Holography - Chicago, Chicago IL

Kass, Emily, *Dir,* Fort Wayne Museum of Art, Inc, Fort Wayne IN

Kass, Emily, *Pres,* Intermuseum Conservation Association, Oberlin OH

Kass, Ray, *Prof,* Virginia Polytechnic Institute & State University, Dept of Art & Art History, Blacksburg VA (S)

Kassing, Gayle, *Dean,* Florida School of the Arts, Visual Arts, Palatka FL (S)

Kassoy, Bernard, *Instructor,* Harriet FeBland Art Workshop, New York NY (S)

Kastin, Judith B, *Treas,* Society of Scribes, Ltd, New York NY

Kaszanits, Robert, *Asst Dir Museum Servs,* National Gallery of Canada, Ottawa ON

Katauskas, Joseph, *VPres,* Balzekas Museum of Lithuanian Culture, Chicago IL

Katchen, Michael, *Dir Coll Management,* Franklin Furnace Archive, Inc, New York NY

Katcher, Roanne, *Mem & Volunteer Coordr,* Center for the Fine Arts, Miami FL

Kates, Sam W, *Dir,* Wiregrass Museum of Art, Dothan AL

Kato, Bruce, *Chief Cur,* Alaska State Museum, Juneau AK

Katsaros, Aliki, *Asst to the Dir,* Fitchburg Art Museum, Fitchburg MA

Katsiaficas, Mary Diane, *Prof,* University of Minnesota, Minneapolis, Dept of Studio Art, Minneapolis MN (S)

Katsiff, Bruce, *Dir,* James A Michener Arts Center, Doylestown PA

Katsimpalis, Tom, *Cur Education,* Loveland Museum and Gallery, Loveland CO

Katsourides, Andrew, *Asst Prof,* Central Missouri State University, Art Dept, Warrensburg MO (S)

Katz, April, *Chmn,* Clarion University of Pennsylvania, Dept of Art, Clarion PA (S)

Katz, Jonathan, *Exec Dir,* National Assembly of State Arts Agencies, Washington DC

Katz, Lillian R, *Dir of Media Serv,* Port Washington Public Library, Port Washington NY

Katz, Lynda, *Instr,* Southeastern Louisiana University, Dept of Visual Arts, Hammond LA (S)

Katz, Melvin, *Prof,* Portland State University, Dept of Art, Portland OR (S)

Katz, Milton, *Chmn Liberal Arts,* Kansas City Art Institute, Kansas City MO (S)

Katz, Paul, *Exec Dir,* Carson County Square House Museum, Panhandle TX

Katz, Robert, *Prof,* University of Maine at Augusta, Division of Fine & Performing Arts, Augusta ME (S)

Katz, Roberta Gray, *Dir Educ,* Terra Museum of American Art, Chicago IL

Katzinger, Leon, *Pres,* Bay County Historical Society, Historical Museum of Bay County, Bay City MI

Kauders, Audrey, *Deputy Dir,* Joslyn Art Museum, Omaha NE

Kaufman, Barbara, *Assoc Prof,* Seton Hall University, College of Arts & Sciences, South Orange NJ (S)

Kaufman, Glen, *Fabric Design,* University of Georgia, Franklin College of Arts & Sciences, Dept of Art, Athens GA (S)

Kaufman, Jim, *Chmn,* Ohio State University, Dept of Industrial Design, Columbus OH (S)

Kaufman, Jolene, *Business Mgr,* Oregon Trail Museum Association, Scotts Bluff National Monument, Gering NE

Kaufman, Joshua, *Exec Dir,* Lawyers Committee for the Arts, Volunteer Lawyers for the Arts, Washington DC

Kaufman, Robert, *Instr,* University of North Carolina at Charlotte, Dept of Visual Arts, Charlotte NC (S)

Kaufman, Faith, *Art & Music Librn,* Forbes Library, Northampton MA

Kaufmann, Robert C, *Head Librn,* The Metropolitan Museum of Art, Irene Lewisohn Costume Reference Library, New York NY

Kaufmann, Thomas, *Prof,* Princeton University, Dept of Art and Archaeology, Princeton NJ (S)

Kaul, Marley, *Chmn,* Bemidji State University, Visual Arts Dept, Bemidji MN (S)

Kaulbach, Peggy, *Dir Research & Archives,* Butler Institute of American Art, Hopper Resource Library, Youngstown OH

Kaulback, Peggy, *Dir of Research & Archives,* Butler Institute of American Art, Art Museum, Youngstown OH

Kaumeyer, Kenneth, *Cur of Estuarine Biology,* Calvert Marine Museum, Solomons MD

Kavanagh, Thomas, *Cur Coll,* Indiana University, William Hammond Mathers Museum, Bloomington IN

Kay, Mary, *Asst Prof,* Bethany College, Mingenback Art Center, Lindsborg KS

Kay, Mary, *Prof,* Bethany College, Art Dept, Lindsborg KS (S)

Kay, Terry, *Dir System Development,* Museum of Holography - Chicago, Chicago IL

Kaya, Kathy, *Librn,* Montana State University, Creative Arts Library, Bozeman MT

Kaye, Sheldon, *Dir,* Portland Public Library, Art Dept, Portland ME

Kays, Elena, *Instr, Interior Design,* Centenary College, Div of Fine Arts, Hackettstown NJ (S)

Kayser, Peggy, *Adminr,* Hebrew Union College, Skirball Museum, Los Angeles CA

Kayser, Robert, *Assoc Prof,* Rochester Institute of Technology, School of Photographic Arts & Sciences, Rochester NY (S)

Keane, Richard, *Prof,* School of the Art Institute of Chicago, Chicago IL (S)

Keane, Terence, *Exec Dir,* Museums of Abilene, Inc, Abilene TX

Kearney, John, *Co-Dir,* Contemporary Art Workshop, Chicago IL

Kearney, Lynn, *Co-Dir,* Contemporary Art Workshop, Chicago IL

Kearney, Lynn, *Dir,* Contemporary Art Workshop, Chicago IL (S)

Kearns, Lola, *Dir Arts in Special Education Project,* Pennsylvania Department of Education, Arts in Education Program, Harrisburg PA

Keating, John, *Librn,* Massachusetts College of Art, Morton R Godine Library, Boston MA

Keating, Linda, *Dir Educ,* Fuller Museum of Art, Brockton MA

Keating, T Gerard, *VPres,* Cohasset Historical Society, Caleb Lothrop House, Cohasset MA

Keator, Carol, *Dir,* Santa Barbara Public Library, Faulkner Memorial Art Wing, Santa Barbara CA

Keaveney, Sydney Starr, *Asst Dean,* Pratt Institute Library, Art & Architecture Dept, Brooklyn NY

Keckeisen, Robert, *Museum Dir,* Kansas State Historical Society, Kansas Museum of History, Topeka KS

Kecskes, Lily C J, *Head Librn,* Freer Gallery of Art & The Arthur M Sackler Gallery Gallery, Library, Washington DC

Kedts, Norman, *Prof,* University of Wisconsin-Stevens Point, Dept of Art & Design, Stevens Point WI (S)

Keech, John, *Assoc Prof,* Arkansas State University, Dept of Art, Jonesboro AR (S)

Keefe, Ann, *Co-Dir,* Springfield City Library & Museums Association, Art & Music Dept, Springfield MA

Keefe, Charles P, *Dir,* Brown County Art Gallery Association Inc, Nashville IN

Keefe, Jill, *Librn,* Museum of American Folk Art, Library, New York NY

Keefe, John W, *Cur Decorative Arts,* New Orleans Museum of Art, New Orleans LA

Keefe, Maureen, *Prog Dir,* San Francisco Artspace & Artspace Annex, San Francisco CA

Keegan, Dan, *Chmn,* West Virginia Wesleyan College, Dept of Fine Arts, Buckhannon WV (S)

Keegan, Daniel, *Coordr,* Avila College, Art Division, Dept of Performing and Visual Art, Kansas City MO (S)

Keegan, Kim, *Program & Educ Coordr,* Manchester Institute of Arts and Sciences Gallery, Manchester NH

Keenan, Jon, *Prof,* Colby-Sawyer College, Dept of Fine & Performing Arts, New London NH (S)

Keenan, Joseph, *Dir,* Free Public Library of Elizabeth, Fine Arts Dept, Elizabeth NJ

Keenan-McCormick, Bernadette, *Caretaker/Hostess,* Colonel Black Mansion, Ellsworth ME

Keene, Charles, *Dir,* Museum of the Hudson Highlands, Cornwall on Hudson NY

Keene, Sally, *Dir,* Thomas College Art Gallery, Waterville ME

Keene, Sally, *Dir Public Relations,* Thomas College Art Gallery, Library, Waterville ME

Keeney, Bill, *Chmn Graphic Design,* Woodbury University, Dept of Graphic Design, Burbank CA (S)

Keesee, Delores, *Textile Conservator,* Indiana State Museum, Indianapolis IN

Keggi, Julia Q, *Pres,* Mattatuck Historical Society Museum, Waterbury CT

Keiser, Sandra, *Assoc Prof,* Mount Mary College, Art Dept, Milwaukee WI (S)

Keitel, Mary Jane, *Dir of Government Affairs & Foundation Relations,* The Art Institute of Chicago, Chicago IL

Keith, Gary, *Galleries Mgr,* Galleries of the Claremont Colleges, Claremont CA

Keith, Marie C, *Assoc Librn,* Frick Art Reference Library, New York NY

Kekke, Rhonda, *Head Dept,* Kirkwood Community College. Dept of Fine Arts, Cedar Rapids IA (S)

Kelder, Diane, *Prof,* City University of New York, PhD Program in Art History, New York NY (S)

Keller, Candace, *Assoc Prof,* Wayland Baptist University, Dept of Art, Plainview TX (S)

Keller, Carol, *Dir,* Auraria Higher Education Center, Auraria Library Gallery, Denver CO

Keller, Carol, *Dir,* Auraria Higher Education Center, Emmanuel Gallery, Denver CO

Keller, Deane, *Instr,* Woodstock School of Art, Inc, Woodstock NY (S)

Keller, Diane, *Lectr,* University of Pennsylvania, Graduate School of Fine Arts, Philadelphia PA (S)

Keller, Dorothy Bosch, *Chmn Dept,* Saint Joseph College, Dept of Fine Arts, West Hartford CT (S)

Keller, Emily, *Cultural Arts Mgr,* Brea Civic & Cultural Center Gallery, Brea CA

Keller, John, *Assoc Prof,* Harding University, Dept of Art, Searcy AR (S)

Keller, Judith, *Cur of Prints and Drawings,* University of Texas at Austin, Archer M Huntington Art Gallery, Austin TX

Keller, Linn, *Dir,* North Carolina State University, Chinqua-Penn Plantation House, Garden & Greenhouses, Reidsville NC

Keller, Marjorie, *Prof,* University of Rhode Island, Dept of Art, Kingston RI (S)

Keller, Patricia J, *Dir & Cur,* Heritage Center of Lancaster County, Lancaster PA

Keller, Peter, *Exec Dir,* Bower's Museum, Santa Ana CA

Keller, Stephen, *Asst Dean,* University of Hartford, Hartford Art School, West Hartford CT (S)

Keller, Tim, *Chmn,* Knoxville Museum of Art, Knoxville TN

Keller, Ulrich, *Adjunct Cur Photography,* University of California, Santa Barbara, University Art Museum, Santa Barbara CA

Kelley, Clarence, *Cur Asian Art,* Dayton Art Institute, Dayton OH

Kelley, Donald C, *Art Gallery Dir,* Boston Athenaeum, Boston MA

Kelley, Edward, *Coordr Art History,* Indiana University-Purdue University, Indianapolis, Herron School of Art, Indianapolis IN (S)

Kelley, Fred, *Museum Shop Mgr,* Pennsylvania Academy of the Fine Arts, Galleries, Philadelphia PA

Kelley, Regina, *Instr,* Portland School of Art, Portland ME (S)

Kelley, Terry, *Pres,* Team Bank Fort Worth, Fort Worth TX

Kellner, Tana, *Artistic Dir,* Women's Studio Workshop, Inc, Rosendale NY

Kellogg, Lisa, *Prog Dir,* Women's Studio Workshop, Inc, Rosendale NY

Kellum, Barbara, *Asst Prof,* Smith College, Art Dept, Northampton MA (S)

Kelly, Cathie, *Asst Prof,* University of Nevada, Las Vegas, Dept of Art, Las Vegas NV (S)

Kelly, Christina, *Registrar,* University of Vermont, Robert Hull Fleming Museum, Burlington VT

Kelly, Daisy, *Education Dir,* Adirondack Historical Association, Adirondack Museum, Blue Mountain Lake NY

Kelly, David C, *Head Dept,* University of Connecticut, Art Dept, Storrs CT (S)

Kelly, D J, *Instr,* Western Illinois University, Art Dept, Macomb IL (S)

Kelly, Elizabeth M, *Fine Arts Librn,* Amherst College, Frost Library, Amherst MA

Kelly, Gemey, *Dir,* Mount Allison University, Owens Art Gallery, Sackville NB

Kelly, James, *Cur Spec Coll,* Virginia Historical Society, Richmond VA

Kelly, Jennifer, *Gallery Coordr,* Ohio University, Trisolini Gallery, Athens OH

Kelly, Keith, *National Dir,* Canadian Conference of the Arts, Ottawa ON

Kelly, Margaret, *Cur,* Forbes Inc, New York NY

Kelly, Margaret E, *Sr VPres,* Florida Artist Group Inc, Punta Gorda FL

Kelly, Nancy, *Dir Community Relations,* Florida Gulf Coast Art Center, Inc, Belleair FL

Kelly, Nancy, *Dir,* University of Nebraska at Omaha, Art Gallery, Omaha NE

Kelly, Robert, *Instr,* Bard College, Milton Avery Graduate School of the Arts, Annandale-on-Hudson NY (S)

Kelly, Vincent N, *Chmn,* Yavapai College, Visual & Performing Arts Division, Prescott AZ (S)

Kelly, William, *Assoc Prof,* Bemidji State University, Visual Arts Dept, Bemidji MN (S)

Kelly-Zimmers, Claire, *Assoc Prof,* Portland State University, Dept of Art, Portland OR (S)

Kelm, Bonnie G, *Dir,* Miami University Art Museum, Oxford OH

Kelman, M, *Instr,* Community College of Rhode Island, Dept of Art, Warwick RI (S)

Kelsey, Josephine, *Pres,* Center for Creative Studies, College of Art & Design, Detroit MI (S)

Kelsey, Linda D, *Deputy Dir,* The Mariners' Museum, Newport News VA

Kelsey, Mary, *Prof,* Cape Cod Community College, Art Dept, West Barnstable MA (S)

Kemp, Arnold, *Mgr,* New Langton Arts, San Francisco CA

Kemp, Paul Z, *Prof,* Baylor University, Dept of Art, Waco TX (S)

Kemp, Weston D, *Prof,* Rochester Institute of Technology, School of Photographic Arts & Sciences, Rochester NY (S)

Kemper, David W, *Chief Exec Officer & Pres,* Commerce Bancshares, Inc, Art Collection, Kansas City MO

Kemper, Mark, *Asst Supt,* Game and Parks Commission, Arbor Lodge State Historical Park, Nebraska City NE

Kemper, R Crosby, *Chmn,* United Missouri Bancshares, Inc, Kansas City MO

Kempton, Peggy, *Admin Dir,* Morgan County Foundation, Inc, Madison-Morgan Cultural Center, Madison GA

Kenan, Bruce A, *VPres,* Everson Museum of Art, Syracuse NY

Kendall, Donald M, *Executive Committee Chmn,* PepsiCo Inc, Purchase NY

Kendall, Ginny, *Instr,* Main Line Center for the Arts, Haverford PA (S)

Kendall, M M, *Librn,* Mason County Museum, Maysville KY

Kendall, Thomas, *Dir KIA School,* Kalamazoo Institute of Arts, KIA School, Kalamazoo MI (S)

Kendall, William, *Prof,* Bridgewater State College, Art Dept, Bridgewater MA (S)

Kendra, A Walter, *Dir,* Central Connecticut State University, Art Dept Museum, New Britain CT

Kendrick, Diane, *Coordr,* Averett College, Art Dept, Danville VA (S)

Kendrick, Teresa, *Dir Public Information,* Laguna Gloria Art Museum, Austin TX

Keneally, Michael, *Cur Exhib,* Dacotah Prairie Museum, Lamont Gallery, Aberdeen SD

Kenfield, John F, *Assoc Prof,* Rutgers, the State University of New Jersey, Graduate Program in Art History, New Brunswick NJ (S)

Kennedy, Arlene, *Dir,* University of Western Ontario, McIntosh Art Gallery, London ON

Kennedy, Bridget, *Vis Asst Prof,* Trinity College, Dept of Fine Arts, Hartford CT (S)

Kennedy, Carol Jean, *Educ Dir,* Arizona Commission on the Arts, Phoenix AZ

Kennedy, Chris, *Dir Retail Operations,* Terra Museum of American Art, Chicago IL

Kennedy, Elizabeth, *Dir,* Paris Gibson Square, Museum of Art, Great Falls MT

Kennedy, Greg, *Visual Arts Chmn,* Idyllwild School of Music and the Arts, Idyllwild CA (S)

Kennedy, Harriet F, *Asst Dir,* Museum of the National Center of Afro-American Artists, Boston MA

Kennedy, Helen, *Secy,* Waterloo Art Association, Waterloo IA

Kennedy, James E, *Head,* University of South Alabama, Ethnic American Slide Library, Mobile AL

Kennedy, James E, *Chmn,* University of South Alabama, Dept of Art, Mobile AL (S)

Kennedy, Janet, *Assoc Prof,* Indiana University, Bloomington, Henry Radford Hope School of Fine Arts, Bloomington IN (S)

Kennedy, John, *Exhib Officer,* Mount Saint Vincent University, Art Gallery, Halifax NS

Kennedy, Linda, *Instr,* Texas Tech University, Dept of Art, Lubbock TX (S)

Kennedy, Nella, *Prof,* Northwestern College, Art Dept, Orange City IA (S)

Kennedy, Patrick, *Chmn Dept,* Orange County Community College, Art Dept, Middletown NY (S)

Kennedy, Philip, *Exhibits Designer Art,* Illinois State Museum, Illinois Art Gallery & Lockport Gallery, Springfield IL

Kennedy, Roger G, *Dir,* National Museum of American History, Washington DC

Kennedy, Ronald, *Prof,* Southeastern Louisiana University, Dept of Visual Arts, Hammond LA (S)

Kennedy, Terrence, *Cur,* Institute for Creative Arts, Fairfield IA

Kennell, Elizabeth, *Head Exhib,* McCord Museum of Canadian History, Montreal PQ

Kenney, James, *Pres,* Clark County Historical Society, Springfield OH

Kennington, Sarah J, *Registrar,* University of California, Los Angeles, Fowler Museum of Cultural History, Los Angeles CA

Kennon, Arthur B, *Pres,* Kappa Pi International Honorary Art Fraternity, Crestwood MO

Kenseth, Joy, *Chmn,* Dartmouth College, Dept of Art History, Hanover NH (S)

Kent, Budge, *Chmn Finance Committee,* Danville Museum of Fine Arts & History, Danville VA

Kent, Diane, *Recording Secy,* Arizona Artist Guild, Phoenix AZ

Kent, Renee, *Slide Librn,* Sarah Lawrence College Library, Esther Raushenbush Library, Bronxville NY

Kenwood, Cindy, *VPres,* Southern Alberta Art Gallery, Lethbridge AB

Kenyon, Colleen, *Exec Dir,* Catskill Center for Photography, Inc, Woodstock NY

Keogh, Michael, *Instr,* Casper College, Dept of Visual Arts, Casper WY (S)

Kerber, Gwen, *Vis Asst Prof,* Trinity College, Dept of Fine Arts, Hartford CT (S)

Kerber, Gwen, *Instr,* Bucks County Community College, Fine Arts Dept, Newtown PA (S)

Kern, Arthur E, *Prof,* Tulane University, Sophie H Newcomb Memorial College, New Orleans LA (S)

Kern, Dennis D, *Dir,* University of Montana, Gallery of Visual Arts, Missoula MT

Kern, Dennis D, *Cur,* University of Montana, Paxson Gallery, Missoula MT

Kern, Steven, *Cur of Paintings,* Sterling and Francine Clark Art Institute, Williamstown MA

Kerns, Ginger, *Head Dept,* Eastern Community College, Dept of Art, Venice Beach CA (S)

Kerr, Donald, *Prof,* Grand Valley State University, Art & Design Dept, Allendale MI (S)

Kerr, Donald M, *Pres,* High Desert Museum, Bend OR

Kerr, Gloria, *Exec Asst,* London Regional Art & Historical Museums, London ON

Kerr, Joellen, *Dir,* University of Charleston, Carleton Varney Dept of Art & Design, Charleston WV (S)

Kerr, Myrtle, *Treas,* Kappa Pi International Honorary Art Fraternity, Crestwood MO

Kerr, Norwood, *Archival Librn,* Alabama Department of Archives and History Museum, Library, Montgomery AL

Kerr, Robert, *Prof,* Rochester Institute of Technology, School of Art and Design, Rochester NY (S)

Kerrigan, Thomas, *Prof,* University of Minnesota, Duluth, Art Dept, Duluth MN (S)

Kerrin, Jessica, *Dir,* Nova Scotia College of Art and Design, Anna Leonowens Gallery, Halifax NS

Kershaw, Rock, *Executive Dir,* Artspace Inc, Raleigh NC

Kerslake, Kenneth A, *Prof,* University of Florida, Dept of Art, Gainesville FL (S)

Kerstetter, Ricki Jayne-Walter, *Acting Museum Adminr,* Fetherston Foundation, Packwood House Museum, Lewisburg PA

Kersting, Irene, *Asst Dir,* Albuquerque Museum of Art, History & Science, Albuquerque NM

Kerswill, Margaret, *Deputy Dir,* C W Post Campus of Long Island University, Hillwood Art Museum, Brookville NY

Kertess, Klaus, *Adjunct Cur Drawings,* Whitney Museum of American Art, New York NY

Kessler, Kendall, *Instr,* Radford University, Art Dept, Radford VA (S)

Kestenbaum, Stuart J, *Dir,* Haystack Mountain School of Crafts, Gallery, Deer Isle ME

Kestenbaum, Stuart J, *Dir,* Haystack Mountain School of Crafts, Library, Deer Isle ME

Kestenbaum, Stuart J, *Dir,* Haystack Mountain School of Crafts, Deer Isle ME (S)

Kester, Susanne, *Media Resources Coordr,* Hebrew Union College, Skirball Museum, Los Angeles CA

Kester, William, *Asst Dean Humanities & Social Science,* San Jose City College, School of Fine Arts, San Jose CA (S)

Kesterson-Bollen, Sharon, *Prof,* College of Mount Saint Joseph, Art Dept, Cincinnati OH (S)

Ketchum, Cavaliere, *Prof,* University of Wisconsin, Madison, Dept of Art, Madison WI (S)

Ketchum, James R, *Cur,* United States Senate Commission on Art, Washington DC

Kirtland-Boehm, Louise, *Gallery Dir,* Palomar Community College, Boehm Gallery, San Marcos CA

Kiser, Kimmerly, *Assoc Prof,* Wright State University, Dept of Art & Art History, Dayton OH (S)

Kislow, Karen, *Registrar,* Winnipeg Art Gallery, Winnipeg MB

Kisluk, Anna J, *Dir,* International Foundation for Art Research, Inc, Art Loss Register, New York NY

Kismaric, Carole, *Publications Dir,* Institute for Contemporary Art, Project Studio One (P S 1), Long Island City NY

Kissane, Michael, *Asst Prof,* Randolph-Macon College, Dept of the Arts, Ashland VA (S)

Kistler, Kathleen, *Dir Division Fine Arts,* Shasta College, Art Dept, Fine Arts Division, Redding CA (S)

Kitao, T Kaori, *Prof,* Swarthmore College, Dept of Art, Swarthmore PA (S)

Kitchen, Janaan, *VPres,* Alaska Artists' Guild, Anchorage AK

Kitnick, Jill, *Secy,* Santa Barbara Contemporary Arts Forum, Santa Barbara CA

Kitt, Bill, *Asst Prof,* Saint Mary's College of Minnesota, Art Dept No 18, Winona MN (S)

Kitt Chappell, Sally, *Prof,* DePaul University, Dept of Art, Chicago IL (S)

Kittle, Barbara, *Librn,* University of Arizona, Museum of Art Library, Tucson AZ

Kittredge, Cindy, *Dir & Cur,* Cascade County Historical Society, Cascade County Historical Museum & Archives, Great Falls MT

Kitzing, Erna, *Bookkeeper,* Springfield Free Public Library, Donald B Palmer Museum, Springfield NJ

Kiuchi, Frank, *Treas,* Wind Luke Asian Museum Memorial Foundation, Inc, Seattle WA

Kivy, Peter, *Pres,* American Society for Aesthetics, Edmonton AB

Kizik, Roger, *Preparator,* Brandeis University, Rose Art Museum, Waltham MA

Klaffky, Susan E, *Dir,* Woodrow Wilson Birthplace Foundation, Staunton VA

Klassen, John, *Dir,* Massillon Museum, Massillon OH

Klausmeyer, David, *VPres,* Norman Rockwell Museum at Stockbridge, Stockbridge MA

Klaven, Marvin L, *Dir,* Millikin University, Perkinson Gallery, Decatur IL

Klaven, Marvin L, *Chmn Art Dept,* Millikin University, Art Dept, Decatur IL (S)

Klazek, Nancy, *Educ Officer,* Art Gallery of Greater Victoria, Victoria BC

Kleckler, Curtis, *Financial Officer,* Rockford Art Museum, Rockford IL

Kleeblatt, Norman, *Cur of Collections,* The Jewish Museum, New York NY

Kleeman, Richard, *Head Dept,* Allegheny College, Art Dept, Meadville PA (S)

Klein, Caroline, *Pres,* Guild of Creative Art, Shrewsbury NJ (S)

Klein, Ellen Lee, *Adminr,* National Academy School of Fine Arts, New York NY (S)

Klein, Henry, *Chmn,* Los Angeles Valley College, Art Dept, Van Nuys CA (S)

Klein, John, *Asst Prof,* University of Missouri, Art History and Archaeology Dept, Columbia MO (S)

Klein, Leanne, *Assoc Cur,* Minnesota Museum of American Art, Saint Paul MN

Klein, Leanne, *Assoc Cur Coll Management,* Minnesota Museum of American Art, Library, Saint Paul MN

Klein, Pat, *Chmn Painting Dept,* San Francisco Art Institute, San Francisco CA (S)

Klein, Roberta, *Children's Instr,* Montclair Art Museum, Art School, Montclair NJ (S)

Klein, Shirley, *Second VPres,* New York Society of Architects, New York NY

Kleinbauer, Eugene, *Prof,* Indiana University, Bloomington, Henry Radford Hope School of Fine Arts, Bloomington IN (S)

Klein Friskey, Ellen, *Pres,* Douglas Art Association, Little Gallery, Douglas AZ

Kleinman, Alan, *Development Assoc,* Artists Space, New York NY

Kleinman, Alan, *Developmental Assoc,* Artists Space, Artists Space Gallery, New York NY

Kleinschmidt, Kelly A, *Dir Public Relations,* Stan Hywet Hall & Gardens, Inc, Akron OH

Kleinschmidt, Robert W, *Prof,* University of Utah, Art Dept, Salt Lake City UT (S)

Kleinsmith, Gene, *Chmn,* Victor Valley College, Art Dept, Victorville CA (S)

Kleinsmith, Louise, *Instr,* Adrian College, Art Dept, Adrian MI (S)

Klem, Alan, *Instr,* Creighton University, Fine and Performing Arts Dept, Omaha NE (S)

Klema, Stephen A, *Graphic Design Coordr,* Tunxis Community College, Graphic Design Dept, Farmington CT (S)

Klenk, William, *Prof,* University of Rhode Island, Dept of Art, Kingston RI (S)

Klett, Imy, *Instr,* Olympic College, Social Sciences & Humanities Division, Bremerton WA (S)

Klima, Stefan, *Fine Art Librn,* Beverly Hills Public Library, Fine Arts Library, Beverly Hills CA

Kliman, Eve, *Assoc Prof,* University of Waterloo, Fine Arts Dept, Waterloo ON (S)

Klimaszewski, Cathy, *Ames Coordr for Univrsity Educ,* Cornell University, Herbert F Johnson Museum of Art, Ithaca NY

Klimiades, Mario Nick, *Librn,* Heard Museum, Phoenix AZ

Klimiades, Mario Nick, *Librn & Archivist,* Heard Museum, Library & Archives, Phoenix AZ

Kline, Benjamin F G, *Cur,* State Museum of Pennsylvania, Railroad Museum of Pennsylvania, Harrisburg PA

Kline, Katy, *Dir,* Massachusetts Institute of Technology, List Visual Arts Center, Cambridge MA

Kline, Michelle, *Public Relations & Membership Coordr,* Southern Alleghenies Museum of Art, Loretto PA

Kline, Paul, *Dept Head,* Bridgewater College, Art Dept, Bridgewater VA (S)

Klingensmith, Ann, *Asst Prof,* Iowa Wesleyan College, Art Dept, Mount Pleasant IA (S)

Klingman, Berry J, *Prof,* Baylor University, Dept of Art, Waco TX (S)

Klingman, John, *Assoc Dean,* Tulane University, School of Architecture, New Orleans LA (S)

Klinkner, Marti, *Prog Dir,* Walnut Creek Regional Center for the Arts, Bedford Gallery, Walnut Creek CA

Klinkon, Heinz, *Asst Prof,* Rochester Institute of Technology, School of Art and Design, Rochester NY (S)

Klinkowstein, Tom, *Asst Prof,* Trenton State College, Art Dept, Trenton NJ (S)

Klobe, Tom, *Dir,* University of Hawaii at Manoa, Art Gallery, Honolulu HI

Klonarides, Carole Ann, *Media Arts Cur,* Long Beach Museum of Art, Long Beach CA

Kloongian, Harold, *Pres,* North Shore Arts Association, Inc, Art Gallery, Gloucester MA

Klopfer, Dennis, *Asst Prof,* Mount Mary College, Art Dept, Milwaukee WI (S)

Kloppenburg, Henry, *Pres,* Mendel Art Gallery and Civic Conservatory, Saskatoon SK

Klos, Sheila M, *Head Librn,* University of Oregon, Architecture and Allied Arts Library, Eugene OR

Klosky, Linda, *Co-Dir,* The Center for Contemporary Arts of Santa Fe, Santa Fe NM

Klosky, Peter, *Chief Designer,* Roberson Museum & Science Center, Binghamton NY

Klotter, James, *Dir,* Kentucky Historical Society, Old State Capitol & Annex, Frankfort KY

Klotter, James, *Dir,* Kentucky Historical Society, Library, Frankfort KY

Kluba, William, *Instr,* Tunxis Community College, Graphic Design Dept, Farmington CT (S)

Klueg, James, *Asst Prof,* University of Minnesota, Duluth, Art Dept, Duluth MN (S)

Kluessandorf, Joanna, *Museum Cur,* University of Illinois, Museum of Natural History, Champaign IL

Kluge, Janice, *Asst Prof,* University of Alabama in Birmingham, Dept of Art, Birmingham AL (S)

Klyberg, Albert T, *Dir,* Rhode Island Historical Society, Providence RI

Knab, Bernie, *Dir,* Chemeketa Community College, Dept of Humanities & Communications, Salem OR (S)

Knachel, Philip A, *Assoc Dir,* Folger Shakespeare Library, Washington DC

Knapp, M Jason, *Chmn,* Anderson University, Art Dept, Anderson IN (S)

Knapp-Steen, Sue, *Exec Dir,* Hunterdon Art Center, Clinton NJ

Knasinski, Ralph, *Vis Instr,* Beloit College, Dept of Art, Beloit WI (S)

Knaub, Donald E, *Dir,* Wichita State University, Edwin A Ulrich Museum of Art, Wichita KS

Knauer, Del, *Dir,* Hutchinson Art Association Gallery, Hutchinson KS

Knauss, Carol, *Asst Dir,* University of Illinois, World Heritage Museum, Champaign IL

Knauth, Sharon, *Dir,* Butte Silver Bow Arts Chateau, Butte MT

Knebel, Mary, *Reference Librn,* Hallmark Cards, Inc, Creative Library, Kansas City MO

Knecht, John, *Asso Prof,* Colgate University, Dept of Art & Art History, Hamilton NY (S)

Knecht, Samuel, *Dir,* Hillsdale College, Art Dept, Hillsdale MI (S)

Kneeland, Donna, *Development Dir,* Monterey Peninsula Museum of Art Association, Monterey CA

Knepper, Ben, *Exhib Designer,* Ohio State University, Wexner Center for the Arts, Columbus OH

Kneubuhl, Victoria, *Educ Spec,* Judiciary History Center, Honolulu HI

Knicely, Carol, *Asst Prof,* University of British Columbia, Dept of Fine Arts, Vancouver BC (S)

Knierim, Mark, *Technical Services Librn,* Portland School of Art, Library, Portland ME

Knight, David, *Dir,* Northern Kentucky University Gallery, Highland Heights KY

Knight, Mary, *Treas,* Wayne County Historical Society, Wooster OH

Knight, Mary Ann, *Head Dept Music & Arts Serv,* Berkshire Athenaeum Library, Pittsfield MA

Knight, Robert, *Dir Visual Arts,* Scottsdale Center for the Arts, Scottsdale AZ

Knight MA, Katie, *Instr,* Suomi College, Fine Arts Dept, Hancock MI (S)

Knights, T, *Assoc Prof,* Northern Arizona University, School of Art & Design, Flagstaff AZ (S)

Knipe, James, *Chmn,* Radford University, Art Dept, Radford VA (S)

Knodel, Gerhardt, *Head Fiber Dept,* Cranbrook Academy of Art, Bloomfield Hills MI (S)

Knoll, Ann M, *Dir,* Saginaw Art Museum, Saginaw MI

Knopf, David, *Business Mgr,* J B Speed Art Museum, Louisville KY

Knott, Robert, *Prof,* Wake Forest University, Dept of Art, Winston-Salem NC (S)

Knowles, Elizabeth P, *Dir,* Lyman Allyn Art Museum, New London CT

Knowles, Karen, *Asst to Cur,* University of Louisville, Slide Collection, Louisville KY

Knowlton, Kenn, *Instr,* Art Academy of Cincinnati, Cincinnati OH (S)

Knox, Northrup R, *VPres,* The Buffalo Fine Arts Academy, Albright-Knox Art Gallery, Buffalo NY

Knox, Seymour H, *Pres,* The Buffalo Fine Arts Academy, Albright-Knox Art Gallery, Buffalo NY

Knutsen, Jim, *Dir,* Black Hills State College, Ruddell Gallery, Spearfish SD

Knutson, Glenda, *Dir,* Michelson-Reves Museum of Art, Marshall TX

Knutson, Norman, *Prof,* Adrian College, Art Dept, Adrian MI (S)

Kobrynich, Bill, *Dir Interior Design,* Art Institute of Fort Lauderdale, Fort Lauderdale FL (S)

Koch, Bruno, *Prof,* Christopher Newport College, Arts & Communications, Newport News VA (S)

Koch, Cynthia, *Dir,* Old Barracks Museum, Trenton NJ

Koch, George, *Pres,* United States Committee of the International Association of Art, Inc, Washington DC

Koch, George C, *Pres,* National Artists Equity Association Inc, Washington DC

Koch, Loretta, *Acting Humanities Librn,* Southern Illinois University, Humanities Library, Carbondale IL

Kocher, Edward G, *Pres,* West Bend Gallery of Fine Arts, West Bend WI

Kocher, Robert, *Prof,* Coe College, Dept of Art, Cedar Rapids IA (S)

Kochheiser, Thomas, *Lectr,* University of Missouri-Saint Louis, Art Dept, Saint Louis MO (S)

Kochheiser, Thomas H, *Dir,* University of Missouri, Saint Louis, Gallery 210, Saint Louis MO

Kochka, Al, *Dir,* Muskegon Museum of Art, Muskegon MI

Koczwara, Chris Trella, *VPres,* Cumberland Art Society Inc, Cookeville Art Gallery, Cookeville TN

Koehler, Catherine, *Instr,* Delta State University, Dept of Art, Cleveland MS (S)

Koehler, Ron, *Assoc Prof,* Delta State University, Dept of Art, Cleveland MS (S)

Koehn, Judd R, *Assoc Prof Art,* Eastern Oregon State College, Arts & Humanities Dept, La Grande OR (S)

Koenig, Audrey, *Curatorial Adminr & Registrar,* Newark Museum Association, The Newark Museum, Newark NJ

Koenig, Robert J, *Dir,* Noyes Museum, Oceanville NJ

Koepke, Dave, *Acting Plant & Security Supvr,* Minnesota Museum of American Art, Saint Paul MN

Koepnick, Pat, *Public Relations,* Dayton Art Institute, Dayton OH

Koerlin, Ernest, *Assoc Prof,* Wright State University, Dept of Art & Art History, Dayton OH (S)

Koerth, Harold, *Head Dept,* Coffeyville Community College, Art Dept, Coffeyville KS (S)

Koetter, Fred, *Dean,* Yale University, School of Architecture, New Haven CT (S)

Koetting, Delores, *Treas,* St Genevieve Museum, Sainte Genevieve MO

Koffman, David, *Librn,* University of Georgia, Dept of Art, Athens GA

Kohl, Allan, *Slide Librn,* Minneapolis College of Art & Design, Library & Media Center, Minneapolis MN

Kohn, Hannah, *House Chmn,* Plastic Club, Art Club for Women, Philadelphia PA

Kohnstamm, Ricka, *Acting Asst Dir Development & Membership,* Minnesota Museum of American Art, Saint Paul MN

Kokot, Sharon, *Dir of Education,* Columbus Museum of Art, Columbus OH

Kola, Marcia, *Instr,* Dean Junior College, Visual and Performing Art Dept, Franklin MA (S)

Kolb, Carolyn J, *Prof,* University of New Orleans-Lake Front, Dept of Fine Arts, New Orleans LA (S)

Kolb, Nancy D, *Exec Dir,* Please Touch Museum, Philadelphia PA

Kolberg, Persijs, *Dir,* Jefferson County Historical Society, Watertown NY

Kolberg, Persijs, *Dir,* Jefferson County Historical Society, Library, Watertown NY

Koldoff, Patsy, *Cur,* First Interstate Bank of Arizona, Phoenix AZ

Kolinski, Laura, *Cur Educ,* Canton Art Institute, Canton OH (S)

Kolisnyk, Anne, *Exec Dir,* Ontario Association of Art Galleries, Toronto ON

Kolkka, Karen, *Instr,* Main Line Center for the Arts, Haverford PA (S)

Kollasch, Sheila, *Cur,* Maricopa County Historical Society, Desert Caballeros Western Museum, Wickenburg AZ

Kolmstetter, Ursual, *Reference Librn,* Indianapolis Museum of Art, Stout Reference Library, Indianapolis IN

Kolok, William, *Chmn,* Kentucky Wesleyan College, Dept Art, Owensboro KY (S)

Kolt, Ingrid, *Public Progs Coordr,* Surrey Art Gallery, Surrey BC

Koltun, Lilly, *Dir,* National Archives of Canada, Documentary Art and Photography, Ottawa ON

Koltun, Nancy, *First VPres,* North Shore Art League, Winnetka IL

Komanecky, Michael, *Cur,* The Currier Gallery of Art, Manchester NH

Komas, James, *Lectr,* Cardinal Stritch College, Art Dept, Milwaukee WI (S)

Komechak, Michael E, *Head,* Illinois Benedictine College, Fine Arts Dept, Lisle IL (S)

Komives, Eugene, *Chief of Security,* Westmoreland Museum of Art, Greensburg PA

Konaty, Gerald, *Cur Ethnology,* Glenbow Museum, Calgary AB

Konkus, Helene, *Lending Dept Supv,* Newark Museum Association, The Newark Museum, Newark NJ

Konowitz, Ellen, *Asst Prof,* Vanderbilt University, Dept of Fine Arts, Nashville TN (S)

Koob, Richard, *Exec Dir,* Kalani Honua Institute for Cultural Studies, Pahoa HI (S)

Koons, Darrel, *Instr,* Bob Jones University, School of Fine Arts, Greenville SC (S)

Koop, Kathy, *Head Dept,* Westminster College, Art Dept, New Wilmington PA (S)

Koop, Rebecca, *Instr,* William Jewell College, Art Dept, Liberty MO (S)

Koopman, Patricia, *Asst Prof,* University of Wisconsin-Stevens Point, Dept of Art & Design, Stevens Point WI (S)

Koos, Greg, *Exec Dir,* McLean County Historical Society, Bloomington IL

Kootchick, Rebecca, *Prog Asst,* Main Line Center of the Arts, Haverford PA

Kopatz, Kim, *Slide Cur,* University of Rochester, Art Library, Rochester NY

Kopf, Vicki, *Asst Dir,* Southeastern Center for Contemporary Art, Winston-Salem NC

Koplin, Bruce M, *Acting Chmn,* Virginia Commonwealth University, Art History Department, Richmond VA (S)

Koppy, Ann, *Dir,* Coos County Historical Society Museum, North Bend OR

Kopran, Eileen, *Public Servs Dir,* Dickinson State University, Stoxen Library, Dickinson ND

Koras, George, *Prof,* State University of New York at Stony Brook, Art Dept, Stony Brook NY (S)

Kord, Victor, *Chmn Dept,* Cornell University, Dept of Art, Ithaca NY (S)

Kordich, Diane D, *Prof,* Northern Michigan University, Dept of Art and Design, Marquette MI (S)

Korenic, Lynette, *Head Arts Library,* University of California, Santa Barbara, Arts Library, Santa Barbara CA

Kornacki, Frances E, *Asst to Dir,* Norwich Free Academy, Slater Memorial Museum & Converse Art Gallery, Norwich CT

Kornblum, Susan, *Pres,* Long Beach Art League, Island Park NY

Kornetchuk, Elena, *Pres,* International Images, Ltd, Sewickley PA

Kornhauser, Stephen, *Head Conservator,* Wadsworth Atheneum, Hartford CT

Kornwolf, James D, *Prof,* College of William and Mary, Dept of Fine Arts, Williamsburg VA (S)

Korol, Atta, *Pres,* Chautauqua Art Association Galleries, Chautauqua NY

Korol, Korene, *Arts Specialist,* Patterson Library & Art Gallery, Westfield NY

Koroscik, Judith, *Assoc Prof,* Ohio State University, Dept of Art Education, Columbus OH (S)

Korpita, Terrie, *Admin Asst,* Historic Northampton Museum, Northampton MA

Korshak, Yvonne, *Prof,* Adelphi University, Dept of Art and Art History, Garden City NY (S)

Korte, Gerald, *Faculty,* Grand Marais Art Colony, Grand Marais MN (S)

Korten, Noel, *Prog Dir,* Los Angeles Municipal Art Gallery, Los Angeles CA

Kortenhaus, Lynne M, *Cur,* Ritz-Carlton Hotel Company, Art Collection, Atlanta GA

Kortenhaus, Lynne M, *Fine Arts Advisor,* Ritz-Carlton Hotel Company, Art Collection, Atlanta GA

Kortum, Karl, *Chief Cur,* San Francisco Maritime National Historical Park, National Maritime Museum, San Francisco CA

Korza, Pam, *Spec Projects Coordr,* Arts Extension Service, Amherst MA

Korzun, Jonathan, *Instr,* Southwestern Michigan College, Fine & Performing Arts Dept, Dowagiac MI (S)

Kosan, Julius T, *Assoc Prof,* Bowling Green State University, Art Dept, Huron OH (S)

Kosche, Eugene R, *Cur History,* Bennington Museum, Bennington VT

Koschmann, Edward, *VPres,* Brooklyn Historical Society, Brooklyn OH

Koshalek, Richard, *Dir,* The Museum of Contemporary Art, Los Angeles CA

Koshel, Terry, *Instr,* Sarah Lawrence College, Dept of Art History, Bronxville NY (S)

Koski, Ann L, *Dir,* Neville Public Museum, Green Bay WI

Koslosky, Robert, *Prof,* Bloomsburg University, Dept of Art, Bloomsburg PA (S)

Koslowsky, Deborah, *Library Asst,* Textile Museum, Arthur D Jenkins Library, Washington DC

Koss, Allen, *Chmn Graphic Arts & Design,* Temple University, Tyler School of Art, Philadelphia PA (S)

Koss, Gene H, *Assoc Prof,* Tulane University, Sophie H Newcomb Memorial College, New Orleans LA (S)

Kostant, Amy, *Assoc Dir,* B'nai B'rith International, B'nai B'rith Klutznick National Jewish Museum, Washington DC

Koster, Ann, *Coll Mgr & Public Relations Officer,* Santa Clara University, de Saisset Museum, Santa Clara CA

Kosuge, Michihiro, *Prof,* Portland State University, Dept of Art, Portland OR (S)

Koszarski, Richard, *Head of Colls,* American Museum of the Moving Image, Astoria NY

Kotik, Charlotta, *Cur Contemporary Art,* Brooklyn Museum, Brooklyn NY

Kotin, David B, *Mgr History Dept,* Metropolitan Toronto Library Board, History Dept, Toronto ON

Koutecky, Judy, *Admin Asst,* Mendel Art Gallery and Civic Conservatory, Saskatoon SK

Koutroulis, Aris, *Chmn Fine Arts,* Center for Creative Studies, College of Art & Design, Detroit MI (S)

Kovach, Chris, *Financial Mgr,* Mexican Museum, San Francisco CA

Kovach, Ruth Ann, *Chmn Dept,* Waldorf College, Art Dept, Forest City IA (S)

Kovach, Sally, *Chmn,* University of North Carolina at Charlotte, Dept of Visual Arts, Charlotte NC (S)

Kovacs, Rudy, *Faculty,* Idaho State University, Dept of Art, Pocatello ID (S)

Kovacs, Thomas, *In Charge Graphic Design,* University of Illinois, Urbana-Champaign, School of Art and Design, Champaign IL (S)

Kowal, Calvin, *Instr,* Art Academy of Cincinnati, Cincinnati OH (S)

Kowalczyk, Susan, *Registrar,* The Rockwell Museum, Corning NY

Kowall, Tom, *Registrar,* Ontario College of Art, Toronto ON (S)

Kowalski, Libby, *Instr,* Chautauqua Institution, School of Art, Chautauqua NY (S)

Kowalski, Libby, *Assoc Prof,* State University of New York, College at Cortland, Art Dept, Cortland NY (S)

Kowaski, Paul, *Adjunct Instr,* Saginaw Valley State University, Dept of Art and Design, University Center MI (S)

Kowski, Robert, *Assoc Prof,* Greensboro College, Dept of Art, Division of Fine Arts, Greensboro NC (S)

Kowski, Robert, *Assoc Prof,* Greensboro College, Irene Cullis Gallery, Greensboro NC

Kozik, Patricia, *Dir,* University of Wisconsin, Union Art Gallery, Milwaukee WI

Kozloff, Arielle P, *Cur Ancient Art,* Cleveland Museum of Art, Cleveland OH

Kozlowski, Barbara, *Assoc Dir for Public Services,* Skokie Public Library, Skokie IL

Kozlowski, Ronald S, *Dir,* Miami-Dade Public Library, Miami FL

Kraball, Merrill, *Chmn,* Bethel College, Dept of Art, North Newton KS (S)

Krackeler, Robert, *Chmn,* Albany Institute of History and Art, Albany NY

Kraemer, Pat, *Instr,* Rochester Community College, Art Dept, Rochester MN (S)

Kraft, Ann, *Asst to Dir,* Solomon R Guggenheim Museum, New York NY

Kraft, Ellen, *Exec Dir,* USS Constitution Museum Foundation Inc, Boston National Historical Park, Museum, Boston MA

Kraft, James, *Asst Dir Development & Membership,* Whitney Museum of American Art, New York NY

Krainak, Paul, *Prof,* West Virginia University, College of Creative Arts, Morgantown WV (S)

Kramer, Edith, *Cur Film,* University of California, University Art Museum, Berkeley CA

Kramer, Edith, *Cur Film,* University of California, Pacific Film Archive, Berkeley CA

Kramer, Gerald, *Prof,* Cuyahoga Community College, Dept of Art, Cleveland OH (S)

Kramer, Jim, *Gallery Operations Mgr,* Madison Art Center, Madison WI

Kramer, Larry, *Pres,* Avila College, Thornhill Art Gallery, Kansas City MO

Kramer, Leslie, *Dir,* Elmira College, George Waters Gallery, Elmira NY

Kramer, Leslie, *Asst Prof,* Elmira College, Art Dept, Elmira NY (S)

Kramer, Linda, *Cur Prints & Drawings,* Brooklyn Museum, Brooklyn NY

Kramer, Trudy, *Dir,* The Parrish Art Museum, Southampton NY

Krammes, Barry A, *Chmn Dept,* Biola University, Art Dept, La Mirada CA (S)

Krane, Susan, *Cur 20th Century Art,* High Museum of Art, Atlanta GA

Kraning, Al, *Assoc Prof,* University of Nebraska, Kearney, Dept of Art & Art History, Kearney NE (S)

Krashes, Barbara, *VPres,* Federation of Modern Painters & Sculptors, New York NY

Kraskin, Sandra, *Dir,* Baruch College of the City University of New York, Gallery, New York NY

Kraus, Russell C, *Prof,* Rochester Institute of Technology, School of Photographic Arts & Sciences, Rochester NY (S)

Krause, Bonnie J, *Dir,* University of Mississippi, University Museums, Oxford MS

Krause, Bonnie J, *Dir,* University of Mississippi, University Museums Library, Oxford MS

Krause, Darrell R, *Park Mgr,* Florida Department of Natural Resources, Stephen Foster State Folk Culture Center, White Springs FL

Krause, Lawrence, *Prof,* Cleveland Institute of Art, Cleveland OH (S)

Krause, Martin F, *Cur Prints & Drawings,* Indianapolis Museum of Art, Indianapolis IN

Krauss, James A, *Chmn & Prof,* Oakton Community College, Art & Architecture Dept, Des Plaines IL (S)

Krauss, Rosalind, *Distinguished Prof,* City University of New York, PhD Program in Art History, New York NY (S)

Krauss, Rosalind, *Prof,* City University of New York, PhD Program in Art History, New York NY (S)

Kraut, Adrienne, *Art Educ Coordn,* San Jose State University, School of Art & Design, San Jose CA (S)

Kravitz, Joanne, *Interior Designer,* Glendale Federal Savings, Glendale CA

Kravitz, Susan, *Prof,* Nassau Community College, Art Dept, Garden City NY (S)

Kray, Gordon, *Adjunct Prof,* Trinity College, Art Dept, Washington DC (S)

Kray, Hazele, *Cur,* The Bartlett Museum, Amesbury MA

Krebs, Jerry, *Assoc Prof,* Radford University, Art Dept, Radford VA (S)

Kreft, Barbara, *Prof,* Hamline University, Art Dept, Saint Paul MN (S)

Kreger, Philip, *Chief of Exhibits,* Tennessee State Museum, Nashville TN

Krehbiel, James, *Assoc Prof,* Ohio Wesleyan University, Fine Arts Dept, Delaware OH (S)

Krehe, Lynette, *Co-Dir,* 1078 Gallery, Chico CA

Kreischer, Patricia, *Graphic Artist,* Lake Forest Library, Fine Arts Dept, Lake Forest IL

Kreisher, Katharine, *Chmn,* Hartwick College, Art Dept, Oneonta NY (S)

Krejcarek, Philip, *Assoc Prof,* Carroll College, Art Dept, Waukesha WI (S)

Kremer, Bruce, *Facilities Mgr,* Headlands Center for the Arts, Sausalito CA

Kremer, William, *Chmn,* University of Notre Dame, Dept of Art, Art History & Design, Notre Dame IN (S)

Kremgold, David, *Assoc Prof,* University of Florida, Dept of Art, Gainesville FL (S)

Kren, Margo, *Assoc Prof,* Kansas State University, Art Dept, Manhattan KS (S)

Kren, Thom, *Cur Manuscripts,* Getty Center for the History of Art & the Humanities Trust Museum, Santa Monica CA

Kren, Thomas, *Cur Manuscripts,* Getty Center for the History of Art & the Humanities Trust Museum, The J Paul Getty Museum, Santa Monica CA

Kreneck, Lynwood, *Prof,* Texas Tech University, Dept of Art, Lubbock TX (S)

Krens, Thomas, *Dir,* Solomon R Guggenheim Museum, New York NY

Kreplin, Bill, *Lectr,* Webster University, Art Dept, Webster Groves MO (S)

Krepps, Jerald, *Assoc Prof,* University of Minnesota, Minneapolis, Dept of Studio Art, Minneapolis MN (S)

Kresse, Bridget, *Instr,* The Arkansas Arts Center, Museum School, Little Rock AR (S)

Kresse, Cynthia, *Instr,* The Arkansas Arts Center, Museum School, Little Rock AR (S)

Kresse, Kevin, *Instr,* The Arkansas Arts Center, Museum School, Little Rock AR (S)

Kret, Robert, *Dir,* Ella Sharp Museum, Jackson MI

Kret, Virginia, *VPres,* Toledo Artists' Club, Toledo OH

Kreuter, Gretchen, *Interim Pres,* Olivet College, Armstrong Museum of Art and Archaeology, Olivet MI

Kreuzer, Terry, *Cur of Art,* Wyoming State Museum, State Art Gallery, Cheyenne WY

Krevenas, Michele, *Cur,* Laumeier Sculpture Park, Saint Louis MO

Kreyling, Christine, *Cur Coll,* Cheekwood-Tennessee Botanical Garden Museum of Art, Education Dept, Nashville TN (S)

Kreyling, Christine, *Cur Coll & Exhib,* Cheekwood-Tennessee Botanical Gardens & Museum of Art, Nashville TN

Kridel, Craig, *Cur Education Museum,* University of South Carolina, McKissick Museum, Columbia SC

Kriefal, Maria, *Sales Mgr,* Vermont State Craft Center at Frog Hollow, Middlebury VT

Krieg, Peter, *Pastor,* Mission San Miguel Museum, San Miguel CA

Krieger, Brad, *Vis Prof,* Nebraska Wesleyan University, Art Dept, Lincoln NE (S)

Kriele, Shelby, *Cur,* Greene County Historical Society, Bronck Museum, Coxsackie NY

Kriley, James D, *Dean,* University of Montana, Paxson Gallery, Missoula MT

Krist, Andrea, *Managing Dir,* Beck Center for the Cultural Arts, Lakewood OH

Krist, Dennis, *Asst Prof,* Indiana-Purdue University, Dept of Fine Arts, Fort Wayne IN (S)

Kristof, Jane, *Assoc Prof,* Portland State University, Dept of Art, Portland OR (S)

Kritselis, Alexander, *Dir,* Pasadena City College, Art Gallery, Pasadena CA

Krivitz, James, *Deputy Operations Dir,* Milwaukee Public Museum, Milwaukee WI

Kroesing, Mickey, *Gift Shop Mgr,* Muskegon Museum of Art, Muskegon MI

Kroff, Linda, *Instr,* University of North Carolina at Charlotte, Dept of Visual Arts, Charlotte NC (S)

Krol, Penne, *Instr,* Greenfield Community College, Art, Graphic Design & Media Communication Dept, Greenfield MA (S)

Kroll, James, *Head Dept,* Denver Public Library, Humanities Dept, Denver CO

Kromm, Jane, *Asst Prof,* State University of New York College at Purchase, Art History Board of Study, Purchase NY (S)

Krommenhoek, Hans, *Instructor,* Milwaukee Area Technical College, Graphic Arts Dept, Milwaukee WI (S)

Krone, Ted, *Chmn,* Friends University, Art Dept, Wichita KS (S)

Kronewetter, Justin, *Chmn,* Ohio Wesleyan University, Fine Arts Dept, Delaware OH (S)

Kroning, Melissa, *Registrar,* National Museum of American Art, Washington DC

Kroop, Bernie, *Instructional Asst,* Sullivan County Community College, Division of Commercial Art and Photography, Loch Sheldrake NY (S)

Krouse, Linda, *Chief Finance Officer,* Bellevue Art Museum, Bellevue WA

Krouse, Millicent, *Treas,* American Color Print Society, Philadelphia PA

Krueger, Donald W, *Dir Studio Art Prog,* Clark University, Dept of Visual & Performing Arts, Worcester MA (S)

Krueger, Lothar, *Prof Emeritus,* University of Arkansas, Art Dept, Fayetteville AR (S)

Krueger, Pamela, *Dir,* Laurentian University, Museum & Art Centre, Sudbury ON

Krueger, Pamela, *Dir,* Laurentian University, Art Centre Library, Sudbury ON

Krug, Harry E, *Chairperson,* Pittsburg State University, Art Dept, Pittsburg KS (S)

Krug, Kersti, *Public Information Officer,* University of British Columbia, Museum of Anthropology, Vancouver BC

Krule, Bernard K, *Assoc Prof,* Oakton Community College, Art & Architecture Dept, Des Plaines IL (S)

Krull, Jeffrey R, *Dir,* Allen County Public Library, Fine Arts Dept, Fort Wayne IN

Krumenauer, Kris, *Instr,* Marian College, Art Dept, Fond Du Lac WI (S)

Kruse, Carolyn, *VPres,* United States Figure Skating Association, World Figure Skating Hall of Fame and Museum, Colorado Springs CO

Kruse, Donald, *Assoc Prof,* Indiana-Purdue University, Dept of Fine Arts, Fort Wayne IN (S)

Kruse, Gerald, *Assoc Prof,* South Dakota State University, Dept of Visual Arts, Brookings SD (S)

Krushenisky, Laurie, *Educ Coordr,* Michelson-Reves Museum of Art, Marshall TX

Kruss, W Paul, *VChmn,* Chicago Historical Society, Chicago IL

Krute, Carol, *Cur Costume & Textiles,* Wadsworth Atheneum, Hartford CT

Kruth, Leslie M, *VPres,* American Institute for Conservation of Historic & Artistic Works (AIC), Washington DC

Kryszak, Bonnie C, *Chief Art Div,* Public Library of the District of Columbia, Art Division, Washington DC

Kryszko, Karen, *Assoc Prof,* Saint Mary's College of Minnesota, Art Dept No 18, Winona MN (S)

Kuan, Baulu, *Assoc Prof,* College of Saint Benedict, Art Dept, Saint Joseph MN (S)

Kubasiewicz, Jan, *Asst Prof,* University of Hartford, Hartford Art School, West Hartford CT (S)

Kubert, Joe, *Pres,* Joe Kubert School of Cartoon & Graphic Art, Inc, Dover NJ (S)

Kubiak, Kathy, *Instr,* Mount Mary College, Art Dept, Milwaukee WI (S)

Kubo, Duane, *Acting Dean Creative Arts,* De Anza College, Creative Arts Div, Cupertino CA (S)

Kuchar, Kathleen, *Prof,* Fort Hays State University, Dept of Art, Hays KS (S)

Kucharski, Malcolm, *Asst Prof,* Pittsburg State University, Art Dept, Pittsburg KS (S)

Kuchta, Ronald A, *Dir,* Everson Museum of Art, Syracuse NY

Kuczynski, John D, *Art Dept Chmn,* Pierce College, Art Dept, Woodland Hills CA (S)

Kudder-Sullivan, P, *Asst Prof,* Southampton Campus of Long Island University, Fine Arts Division, Southampton NY (S)

Kudla, Joanne, *Registrar,* Buffalo Bill Memorial Association, Buffalo Bill Historical Center, Cody WY

Kudlawiec, Dennis P, *Chmn,* Livingston University, Division of Fine Arts, Livingston AL (S)

Kuegel, Bob, *Dir,* Tucson Museum of Art School, Tucson AZ (S)

Kuegel, Robert, *School Mgr,* Tucson Museum of Art, Tucson AZ

Kuehn, Claire, *Archivist & Librn,* Panhandle-Plains Histoical Society Museum, Library, Canyon TX

Kuehn, Gary, *Prof,* Rutgers, the State University of New Jersey, Mason Gross School of the Arts, New Brunswick NJ (S)

Kuehne, Kleda, *Asst Dir,* Valley City Arts & Gallery Association, Second Crossing Gallery Staus Mall, Valley City ND

Kueppers, Brigitte, *Arts Special Coll Librn,* University of California, Los Angeles, Arts Library, Los Angeles CA

Kugel, Richard C, *Sr Cur,* Old Dartmouth Historical Society, New Bedford Whaling Museum, New Bedford MA

Kugler, Sharon, *Asst Mgr,* Queens Borough Public Library, Fine Arts & Recreation Division, Jamaica NY

Kuhl, Nora, *Exec Dir,* Dinnerware Artist's Cooperative, Tucson AZ

Kuiper, James, *Instr,* California State University, Chico, Art Dept, Chico CA (S)

Kukla, Jon, *Dir,* Kemper & Leila Williams Foundation, New Orleans LA

Kukuchka, Andy, *Ranch Foreman,* Bradford Brinton Memorial Museum & Historic Ranch, Big Horn WY

Kulhawy, Ken, *Instr,* Lakewood Community College, Humanities Dept, White Bear Lake MN (S)

Kuluk, Tony, *Pres,* Manitoba Society of Artists, Winnipeg MB

Kumnick, Charles, *Asst Prof,* Trenton State College, Art Dept, Trenton NJ (S)

Kuncevich, Michael, *Pres,* American Color Print Society, Philadelphia PA

Kundar, Cynthia A, *Dir & Educ Dir,* Merrick Art Gallery, New Brighton PA

Kuniholm, Peter I, *Assoc Prof,* Cornell University, Dept of the History of Art, Ithaca NY (S)

Kunkel, Jerry W, *Chmn,* University of Colorado, Boulder, Dept of Fine Arts, Boulder CO (S)

Kuntz, Karen, *Coll Development,* Chicago Public Library, Harold Washington Library Center, Chicago IL

Kuo, James K Y, *Prof,* Daemen College, Art Dept, Amherst NY (S)

Kuoni, Carin, *Dir,* Swiss Institute, New York NY

Kupferberg, Kenneth, *Treas,* Bowne House Historical Society, Flushing NY

Kupper, Ketti, *Chmn,* University of Bridgeport, Art Dept, Bridgeport CT (S)

Kupper, Ketti, *Art Dept Chmn,* University of Bridgeport, Carlson Gallery, Bridgeport CT

Kupris, Valdis, *Prof,* New York Institute of Technology, Fine Arts Dept, Old Westbury NY (S)

Kuras, Jean, *Pres,* Historical Society of Bloomfield, Bloomfield NJ

Kuretsky, Susan D, *Prof,* Vassar College, Art Dept, Poughkeepsie NY (S)

Kurka, Donald F, *Head Art Dept,* University of Tennessee, Knoxville, Dept of Art, Knoxville TN (S)

Kuronen, Dennis, *Dept Chmn,* Beaver College Art Gallery, Glenside PA

Kuronen, Dennis, *Chmn,* Beaver College, Dept of Fine Arts, Glenside PA (S)

Kurriger, Patricia, *Prof,* College of DuPage, Humanities Division, Glen Ellyn IL (S)

Kurtich, John, *Prof,* School of the Art Institute of Chicago, Chicago IL (S)

Kurutz, K D, *Cur Education,* Crocker Art Museum, Sacramento CA

Kurytnik, Kevin, *Pres,* Quickdraw Animation Society, Calgary AB

Kusaba, Yoshio, *Instr,* California State University, Chico, Art Dept, Chico CA (S)

Kushner, Marilyn S, *Cur of Coll,* Montclair Art Museum, Art School, Montclair NJ (S)

Kusnerz, P A, *Librn,* University of Michigan, Art & Architecture Library & Computer Lab, Ann Arbor MI

Kuspit, Donald B, *Prof,* State University of New York at Stony Brook, Art Dept, Stony Brook NY (S)

Kustner, Anne, *Instr,* Mount Mary College, Art Dept, Milwaukee WI (S)

Kutbay, Bonnie, *Instr,* Mansfield University, Art Dept, Mansfield PA (S)

Kuwayama, George, *Cur Far Eastern Art,* Los Angeles County Museum of Art, Los Angeles CA

Kuypers, Jan, *VPres,* Royal Canadian Academy of Arts, Toronto ON

Kuzminski, Catherine, *Chmn Fine Arts Program,* Westminster College of Salt Lake City, Dept of Arts, Salt Lake City UT (S)

Kwan, Michael, *Asst Dir Admin,* Santa Barbara Museum of Art, Santa Barbara CA

Kwon, Miwon, *ISP Coordr,* Whitney Museum of American Art, Downtown at Federal Reserve Plaza, New York NY

Kwong, Mary, *Dir,* Revelstoke Art Group, Revelstoke BC

Kyle, Jane, *Chief Academic Officer,* Oregon School of Arts and Crafts, Hoffman Gallery, Portland OR

Kynkor, Ellen M, *Personnel Officer,* National City Bank, Atrium Gallery, Cleveland OH

Kyral, JoAnn, *Supt,* Oregon Trail Museum Association, Scotts Bluff National Monument, Gering NE

Kyriakakis, Stella, *Dir,* Art Metropole Archives, Toronto ON

LaBarbera, Anne, *Museum Shop,* Niagara University, Castellani Art Museum, New York NY

LaBat, Karen, *Textile Cur,* University of Minnesota, Goldstein Gallery, Saint Paul MN

Labat, Ton, *Chmn Performance & Video Dept,* San Francisco Art Institute, San Francisco CA (S)

Labbe, Armand J, *Chief Cur,* Bower's Museum, Santa Ana CA

Labe, Paul, *Prof,* Harford Community College, Fine & Applied Arts Dept, Div of Arts & Sciences, Bel Air MD (S)

LaBelle, Marguarite, *Assoc Prof,* Jersey City State College, Art Dept, Jersey City NJ (S)

Laber, Philip, *Olive DeLuce Art Gallery Coll Cur,* Northwest Missouri State University, DeLuce Art Gallery, Maryville MO

Laber, Philip, *Assoc Prof,* Northwest Missouri State University, Dept of Art, Maryville MO (S)

LaBlanc, Necol, *Secy,* Galerie d'art de l'Universite de Moncton, Moncton NB

LaBonte, Linelle, *Prof,* College of Notre Dame of Maryland, Art Dept, Baltimore MD (S)

LaBossiere, Holly, *Head Public Servs,* Ponca City Library, Art Dept, Ponca City OK

Labranche, John, *Cur,* Old York Historical Society, Gaol Museum, York ME

Labuz, Ronald, *Head Dept,* Mohawk Valley Community College, Advertising Design and Production, Utica NY (S)

Lacasse, Yves, *Cur Early Canadian Art,* Montreal Museum of Fine Arts, Montreal PQ

Lacey, Thomas, *Instr,* Indiana University of Pennsylvania, Dept of Art and Art Education, Indiana PA (S)

Lachapelle, Francois, *Dir Museum,* Le Musee Regional de Rimouski, Centre National d' Exposition, Rimouski PQ

Lachman, Diane, *Instr,* Main Line Center for the Arts, Haverford PA (S)

Lachman, Diane, *Instr,* Main Line Center for the Arts, Haverford PA (S)

Lackey, Jane, *Chmn Fiber,* Kansas City Art Institute, Kansas City MO (S)

Lackore, Dale Raddatz, *Head Dept,* Luther College, Art Dept, Decorah IA (S)

Lackowski, Daniel, *Chmn,* City Colleges of Chicago, Wright College, Chicago IL (S)

LaCour, Beth, *Instr,* Yavapai College, Visual & Performing Arts Division, Prescott AZ (S)

LaCroix, Catherine, *Education Dir,* Museum of Oriental Cultures, Corpus Christi TX

LaCroix, Julie, *Dir, Gallery,* Sierra Nevada College, Art Dept, Incline Village NV (S)

Laczko, Gina, *Education Servs Mgr,* Heard Museum, Phoenix AZ

Ladely, Dan, *Cur Mary Riepma Ross Film Theater,* University of Nebraska, Lincoln, Sheldon Memorial Art Gallery, Lincoln NE

Ladkin, Nicola, *Coll Mgr (Anthropology),* Texas Tech University, Museum, Lubbock TX

Ladnier, Paul, *Assoc Prof,* University of North Florida, Dept of Communications & Visual Arts, Jacksonville FL (S)

LaDouceur, Philip A, *Dir,* Blanden Memorial Art Museum, Fort Dodge IA

LaDouceur, Philip A, *Dir,* Blanden Memorial Art Museum, Museum Library, Fort Dodge IA

Lafargue, Philippe, *Conservator,* Tryon Palace Historic Sites & Gardens, New Bern NC

Laferriere, David, *Pres,* Attleboro Museum, Center for the Arts, Attleboro MA

Lafferty, Daniel, *Dir of Education,* The Art Institutes International, The Art Institute of Seattle, Seattle WA (S)

Lafo, Rachel, *Cur,* DeCordova Museum & Sculpture Park, Lincoln MA

LaFollette, Curtis K, *Prof,* Rhode Island College, Art Dept, Providence RI (S)

La Follette, Laetitia, *Asst Prof,* University of Massachusetts, Amherst, Art History Program, Amherst MA (S)

LaFond, Louise, *Assoc Prof,* Colorado College, Dept of Art, Colorado Springs CO (S)

LaFountain, Wes, *Educ Dir,* Portland Museum of Art, Portland ME

Laframboise, Alain, *Instr,* Universite de Montreal, Dept of Art History, Montreal PQ (S)

La France, Liselle, *Dir,* Historic Cherry Hill, Albany NY

LaFrance, Michael, *VPres,* LeSueur County Historical, Museum, Chapter One, Elysian MN

Lagatutta, Bill, *Tamarind Master Printer & Studio Mgr,* University of New Mexico, Tamarind Institute, Albuquerque NM (S)

Lagimodiere, Claudette, *Assoc Dir, Interpretive Servs,* Winnipeg Art Gallery, Winnipeg MB

Lagrisola, Terri, *Public Relations Dir,* Embarcadero Center Ltd, San Francisco CA

LaGue, Mary, *Registrar,* Ari Museum of Western Virginia, Roanoke VA

Lahaye, Francois, *Dir,* Centre Culturel de Trois Rivieres, Trois Rivieres PQ

Lai, Waihang, *Faculty,* Kauai Community College, Dept of Art, Lihue HI (S)

Laing, Aileen H, *Prof,* Sweet Briar College, Art History Dept, Sweet Briar VA (S)

Lainhoff, Thomas A, *Dir,* Gunston Hall Plantation, Lorton VA

Laiou, Angeliki, *Dir,* Harvard University, Dumbarton Oaks Research Library and Collections, Washington DC

Laird, Diane, *Instr,* Trenton State College, Art Dept, Trenton NJ (S)

Laird, Lucinda, *Dir Public Relations,* Brandywine River Museum, Chadds Ford PA

Laird, Walter J, *Chmn,* Winterthur Museum and Gardens, Winterthur DE

Lake, Ellen, *Head Dept,* Central Community College - Platte Campus, Business & Arts Cluster, Columbus NE (S)

Lake, Jerry L, *Prof,* George Washington University, Dept of Art, Washington DC (S)

Laliberte-Bourque, A, *Dir,* Musee du Quebec, Quebec PQ

L'Allier, Pierre, *Conservator Modern Art,* Musee du Quebec, Quebec PQ

Lalonde, Jerome, *Asst Prof,* Mohawk Valley Community College, Advertising Design and Production, Utica NY (S)

La Malfa, James, *Head Dept,* University of Wisconsin Center-Marinette County, Art Dept, Marinette WI (S)

Laman, Jean, *Prof,* Southwest Texas State University, Dept of Art, San Marcos TX (S)

Lamar, Kent, *Prof,* University of Science and Arts of Oklahoma, Arts Dept, Chickasha OK (S)

Lamarche, Lise, *Instr,* Universite de Montreal, Dept of Art History, Montreal PQ (S)

Lamarche, William, *Public Relations Officer,* Maryhill Museum of Art, Goldendale WA

LaMarcz, Howard, *Chmn,* C W Post Center of Long Island University, School of Visual & Performing Arts, Greenvale NY (S)

Lamarre, Blanche, *Chmn,* Notre Dame College, Art Dept, Manchester NH (S)

Lamb, Kurt H, *Dir,* Mexico-Audrain County Library, Mexico MO

Lamb, Sheila, *Coordr General Studies,* Ontario College of Art, Toronto ON (S)

Lambard, Richard, *Owner,* Art Questers, Cottonwood AZ

Lambe, Jane, *Education,* Hastings County Museum, Belleville ON

Lambert, Anne, *Cur Education,* University of Wisconsin-Madison, Elvehjem Museum of Art, Madison WI

Lambert, Anne, *Childrens Librn,* Willard Library, Dept of Fine Arts, Evansville IN

Lambert, D Keith, *Dept Chmn,* Gaston College, Art Dept, Dallas NC (S)

Lambert, Fredrick A, *Exec Dir,* Oglebay Institute, Mansion Museum, Wheeling WV

Lambert, Kirby, *Cur Coll,* Montana Historical Society, Library, Helena MT

Lambert, William E, *Dir,* Del Mar College, Joseph A Cain Memorial Art Gallery, Corpus Christi TX

Lambert, William E, *Chmn,* Del Mar College, Art Dept, Corpus Christi TX (S)

Lambeth, Karen, *Exec Dir,* Palette & Chisel Academy of Fine Arts, Chicago IL

Lambl, Christopher, *Asst Prof,* Clarion University of Pennsylvania, Dept of Art, Clarion PA (S)

Lambrechts, Lillian, *Dir & Cur,* Bank of Boston, Gallery, Boston MA

Lamia, Stephen, *Div Coordr,* Dowling College, Dept of Visual Arts, Oakdale NY (S)

Lammers, E, *Fine Arts Chmn,* Queens College, Fine Arts Dept, Charlotte NC (S)

LaMotta, Janice, *Cur,* New Britain Institute, New Britain Museum of American Art, New Britain CT

Lamoureux, Johanne, *Instr,* Universite de Montreal, Dept of Art History, Montreal PQ (S)

La Moy, William T, *Dir,* Peabody & Essex Museum, James Duncan Phillips Library, Salem MA

Lamp, Frederick, *Cur Art of Africa, Americas, Oceania,* Baltimore Museum of Art, Baltimore MD

Lampe, Susan, *Fund Development,* Honolulu Academy of Arts, Honolulu HI

Lampe, William, *Preparator,* University of Minnesota, University Art Museum, Minneapolis MN

Lampela, Laurel, *Asst Prof,* Cleveland State University, Art Dept, Cleveland OH (S)

Lampela, Laurel, *Prof,* Marshall University, Dept of Art, Huntington WV (S)

Lamy, Whitney, *Dir,* Peabody & Essex Museum, Cotting-Smith-Assembly House, Salem MA

Lance, Kathleen A, *Public Service,* Sweet Briar College, Martin C Shallenberger Art Library, Sweet Briar VA

Lancet, Marc, *Instr,* Solano Community College, Division of Fine & Applied Art, Suisun City CA (S)

Land, Chris, *Art Handler,* Columbus Museum, Columbus GA

Land, Norman, *Prof,* University of Missouri, Art History and Archaeology Dept, Columbia MO (S)

Landa, Albert W, *Dean,* New York Academy of Art, Graduate School of Figurative Art, New York NY (S)

Landa, Robin, *Coordr Visual Communications,* Kean College of New Jersey, Fine Arts Dept, Union NJ (S)

Landau, Laureen, *Instr,* Sacramento City College, Art Dept, Sacramento CA (S)

Landau, Linda, *Project Coordr,* Severin Wunderman Museum, Irvine CA

Landefeld, Anne, *Secy,* Cleveland Museum of Art, Print Club of Cleveland, Cleveland OH

Landes, Bernard, *Gallery Dir,* Long Beach Jewish Community Center, Center Gallery, Long Beach CA

Landes, Jennifer, *Gallery Coordr,* Whitney Museum of American Art, Whitney Museum of American Art at Champion, New York NY

Landis, Ellen J, *Cur of Art,* Albuquerque Museum of Art, History & Science, Albuquerque NM

Landon, Morris, *Pres,* San Diego Maritime Museum, San Diego CA

Landry, David, *Assoc Dir,* Queen's Medical Center Auxiliary, Queen Emma Gallery, Honolulu HI

Landry, Jean, *Assoc Prof,* Notre Dame College, Art Dept, Manchester NH (S)

Landry, Pierre, *Asst Cur Later Canadian Art,* National Gallery of Canada, Ottawa ON

Landus, Matt, *Prog Asst,* University of Louisville, Allen R Hite Art Institute Gallery, Louisville KY

Land-Weber, E, *Instr,* Humboldt State University, College of Arts & Humanities, Arcata CA (S)

Landwehr, William C, *Exec Dir,* Paine Art Center and Arboretum, Oshkosh WI

Lane, Barbara G, *Chmn,* Queens College, Art Dept, Flushing NY (S)

Lane, Bruce, *Asst Prof,* Rochester Institute of Technology, School of Photographic Arts & Sciences, Rochester NY (S)

Lane, Diane, *Admin Asst,* Art Gallery of Windsor, Windsor ON

Lane, Donetta, *Exec Dir,* African American Historical and Cultural Society, San Francisco CA

Lane, John R, *Dir,* San Francisco Museum of Modern Art, San Francisco CA

Lane, Kerstin B, *Exec Dir,* Swedish American Museum Association of Chicago, Chicago IL

Lane, Mark, *Dir,* San Antonio Museum Association, Inc, Witte Museum, San Antonio TX

Lane, Richard, *Treas-Secy,* The American Federation of Arts, New York NY

Lane, Rosemary, *Coordr Printmaking,* University of Delaware, Dept of Art, Newark DE (S)

Lane, Sally, *Board Dirs,* Owatonna Arts Center, Community Arts Center, Owatonna MN

Lane, Serena, *Dir,* The American Federation of Arts, New York NY

Lane, Sheila, *Performing Arts Coordr,* St Mary's University, Art Gallery, Halifax NS

Lane, Thomas, *Assoc Prof,* University of Minnesota, Minneapolis, Dept of Studio Art, Minneapolis MN (S)

Lang, James, *Prof,* La Salle University, Dept of Art, Philadelphia PA (S)

Lang, Norma, *Dir,* Moose Jaw Art Museum and National Exhibition Centre, Art & History Museum, Moose Jaw SK

Lang, Tom, *Adminr,* Webster University, Loretto-Hilton Center Gallery, Saint Louis MO

Lang, Tom, *Chmn,* Webster University, Art Dept, Webster Groves MO (S)

Lang, William, *Head Librn,* Art Dept, Free Library of Philadelphia, Art Dept, Philadelphia PA

Langdon, Ann, *Secy,* Connecticut Women Artists, Inc, Guiford CT

Langdon, George, *Pres,* American Museum of Natural History, New York NY

Langevin, Ann, *Extension Serv,* Las Vegas-Clark County Library District, Las Vegas NV

Langford, Martha, *Dir Museum,* Canadian Museum of Contemporary Photography, Ottawa ON

Langland, Harold, *Prof,* Indiana University South Bend, Fine Arts Dept, South Bend IN (S)

Langley, LeRoy, *Master Woodcarver,* Calvert Marine Museum, Solomons MD

Langmann, Karen, *Trustee,* Hill-Stead Museum, Farmington CT

Langston-Harrison, Lee, *Cur,* James Monroe Museum, Fredericksburg VA

Langston-Harrison, Lee, *Cur,* James Monroe Museum, Fredericksburg VA

Lanids, Tim, *Business Mgr,* Ward Foundation, Ward Museum of Wildfowl Art, Salisbury MD

Lanier, David, *Prof,* University of the District of Columbia, Art Dept, Washington DC (S)

Lankford, Judy, *Deputy Dir,* Valentine Museum, Richmond VA

Lankford, Louis, *Assoc Prof,* Ohio State University, Dept of Art Education, Columbus OH (S)

Lanmon, Dwight P, *Dir,* Winterthur Museum and Gardens, Winterthur DE

Lanning, Dixie M, *Librn,* Bethany College, Library, Lindsborg KS

Lanoriauct, Joanne, *Instr,* St Lawrence College, Dept of Visual & Creative Arts, Cornwall ON (S)

Lansbury, Edgar, *Pres,* Nicholas Roerich Museum, New York NY

Lansdown, Robert R, *Dir,* Frank Phillips Foundation Inc, Woolaroc Museum, Bartlesville OK

Lansdown, Robert R, *Dir,* Frank Phillips Foundation Inc, Library, Bartlesville OK

Lantz, Janie, *Dept Chmn,* Crowder College, Art & Design, Neosho MO (S)

Lantz, Sherrye, *Assoc Prof,* Virginia Western Community College, Commercial Art, Fine Art & Photography, Roanoke VA (S)

Lantzy, Donald M, *Dean,* Syracuse University, College of Visual and Performing Arts, Syracuse NY (S)

Lanzi, Elisa, *Membership & Public Relations Coordr,* Bennington Museum, Bennington VT

Lanzl, Christina, *Dir,* Bromfield Gallery, Boston MA

Lanzone, Dale M, *Dir,* General Services Administration, Washington DC

Lanzone, Modesto, *Chmn,* Museo Italo Americano, San Francisco CA

Lao, Lincoln, *Chairperson Dept of Art & Design & Prof,* Schoolcraft College, Dept of Art and Design, Livonia MI (S)

Lapalombara, David, *Chmn,* Antioch College, Visual Arts Institute, Yellow Springs OH (S)

Lapcek, Barbara, *Exec Dir Prog,* Skowhegan School of Painting and Sculpture, Skowhegan ME (S)

Lapcek, Barbara, *Dir,* Skowhegan School of Painting and Sculpture, New York NY (S)

Lapilio, Lani, *Dir,* Judiciary History Center, Honolulu HI

LaPlant, Don, *Children's Theatre Coordr,* Arts & Science Center for Southeast Arkansas, Pine Bluff AR

LaPlantz, D M, *Instr,* Humboldt State University, College of Arts & Humanities, Arcata CA (S)

LaPointe, M, *Library Technician,* Sheridan College of Applied Arts and Technology, Visual Arts & Crafts Library, Oakville ON

La Porte, Mary, *Assoc Prof,* California Polytechnic State University at San Luis Obispo, Dept of Art and Design, San Luis Obispo CA (S)

Laporte, Norbert, *Gallery Dir,* William Bonifas Fine Art Center Gallery, Alice Powers Art Gallery, Escanaba MI

Lappin, Richard, *Controller & Chief Financial Officer,* Institute of Contemporary Art, Boston MA

Laracuente, Mahir, *Prof,* Catholic University of Puerto Rico, Dept of Fine Arts, Ponce PR (S)

Larimer, Angela, *Business Mgr,* Cincinnati Institute of Fine Arts, Taft Museum, Cincinnati OH

Larimer, Cindy, *Acting Head,* University of Maryland, College Park, Architecture Library, College Park MD

Laris, Georgia, *Instr,* San Diego Mesa College, Fine Arts Dept, San Diego CA (S)

Lark, Tom, *Cur of Collections,* Albuquerque Museum of Art, History & Science, Albuquerque NM

Larken, Dan, *Lectr,* Rochester Institute of Technology, School of Photographic Arts & Sciences, Rochester NY (S)

Larkin, Alan, *Assoc Prof,* Indiana University South Bend, Fine Arts Dept, South Bend IN (S)

Larkin, Frank Y, *VChmn,* Museum of Modern Art, New York NY

Larkins, Ellen C, *Dept Chmn,* Alabama State University, Art Dept, Montgomery AL (S)

Larmer, Oscar V, *Prof,* Kansas State University, Art Dept, Manhattan KS (S)

Larned, Ron, *Chmn & Prof,* Rollins College, Dept of Art, Main Campus, Winter Park FL (S)

Larner, John, *Instr,* Mount Mary College, Art Dept, Milwaukee WI (S)

LaRoche, Christian S, *Dir,* Historical Society of Okaloosa & Walton Counties, Inc, Historical Society Museum, Valparaiso FL

Larouche, Michel, *Instr,* Universite de Montreal, Dept of Art History, Montreal PQ (S)

Larrick, Jim, *Pres,* Association of American Editorial Cartoonists, Raleigh NC

Larris, Jeffrey, *Asst Dir,* College Art Association, New York NY

Larry, Charles, *Arts Librn,* Northern Illinois University, Library, De Kalb IL

Larry, John, *Instr,* Johnson County Community College, Visual Arts Program, Overland Park KS (S)

Larsen, Dinah W, *Coordr Ethnology,* University of Alaska, Museum, Fairbanks AK

Larsen, Donna, *Dir,* Santa Rosa Junior College, Art Gallery, Santa Rosa CA

Larsen, Ken, *Assoc Dir,* California Confederation of the Arts, Sacramento CA

Larsen, Patrick, *Prof,* University of Central Arkansas, Art Dept, Conway AR (S)

Larsen, Richard, *Chmn,* Barr Colony Heritage Cultural Centre, Lloydminster SK

Larsen-Martin, Susan, *Prof,* University of Southern California, School of Fine Arts, Los Angeles CA (S)

Larson, Betty, *Secy,* Pensacola Junior College, Visual Arts Gallery, Pensacola FL

Larson, Bradley, *Dir,* Oshkosh Public Museum, Oshkosh WI

Larson, Daniel, *Chmn,* Avila College, Art Division, Dept of Performing and Visual Art, Kansas City MO (S)

Larson, Daniel, *Chmn Humanities,* Avila College, Thornhill Art Gallery, Kansas City MO

Larson, Gregg, *Registrar, Librn & Archivist,* Ella Sharp Museum, Jackson MI

Larson, Jan, *VPres Board Dir,* Plains Art Museum, Moorhead MN

Larson, John, *Archivist,* University of Chicago, Oriental Institute Museum, Chicago IL

Larson, Judy, *Cur American Art,* High Museum of Art, Atlanta GA

Larson, June, *Asst Dir,* Vermilion County Museum Society, Danville IL

Larson, Karen, *Asst Dir Educ,* Putnam Museum of History & Natural Science, Davenport IA

Larson, Mary, *Library Technician,* University of Colorado, Art and Architecture Library, Boulder CO

Larson, Mike, *Prof,* Shoreline Community College, Humanities Division, Seattle WA (S)

Larson, Preston K, *Chmn,* Brigham Young University, Hawaii Campus, Division of Fine Arts, Laie HI (S)

Larson, Sidney, *Cur,* State Historical Society of Missouri, Columbia MO

Larson, Sidney, *Instr,* Columbia College, Art Dept, Columbia MO (S)

Larson, Will, *Dir,* Maryland Institute, Graduate Photography, Baltimore MD (S)

Lasansky, Leonardo, *Prof,* Hamline University, Art Dept, Saint Paul MN (S)

Lasansky, William, *Prof,* Bucknell University, Dept of Art, Lewisburg PA (S)

Lashbrook, Dee, *Pres,* Fairbanks Arts Association, Fairbanks AK

Laske, Lyle, *Prof,* Moorhead State University, Dept of Art, Moorhead MN (S)

Laskin, Harriette C F, *Assoc Prof,* Tidewater Community College, Art Dept, Portsmouth VA (S)

Lasko, Maureen, *Inter-Library Loan Librn,* The Art Institute of Chicago, Ryerson and Burnham Libraries, Chicago IL

Lasky, Carole, *Adjunct Instr,* Maryville University of Saint Louis, Art Division, Saint Louis MO (S)

Lasseter, Sam, *Coordr Marketing & Development,* Houston Center For Photography, Houston TX

Lassiter, Christine Moss, *Cur,* Port Authority of New York & New Jersey, Art Collection, New York NY

Lassiter, Kathleen, *Dir,* State of Hawaii, Dept of Land & Natural Resources, Wailoa Visitor Center, Hilo HI

Laszkiewicz, Magdalena, *Lectr,* University of Wisconsin-Stout, Dept of Art & Design, Menomonie WI (S)

Laszlo, Elaine, *Membership Clerk,* London Regional Art & Historical Museums, London ON

Latham, Ron, *Dir,* Berkshire Athenaeum Library, Pittsfield MA

Lathrop, Randi, *Gallery Mgr,* The Society of Arts and Crafts, Boston MA

Latka, Nick, *Asst Prof,* University of Southern Colorado, Belmont Campus, Dept of Art, Pueblo CO (S)

Latour, Terry S, *Archivist,* University of Southern Mississippi, McCain Library & Archives, Hattiesburg MS

Latta, Douglas, *Asst Prof,* Oral Roberts University, Fine Arts Dept, Tulsa OK (S)

Latta, George, *Emeritus Prof,* William Woods-Westminster Colleges, Art Dept, Fulton MO (S)

Lattimore, Walter, *Asst Prof,* University of the District of Columbia, Art Dept, Washington DC (S)

Latzki, Eric, *Publicity Dir,* The Kitchen Center, New York NY

Latzko, Walter, *Registrar,* Trotting Horse Museum, Goshen NY

Lauder, Ronald S, *VPres,* Museum of Modern Art, New York NY

Lauderdale, M, *Dir,* Jacksonville University, Alexander Brest Museum & Gallery, Jacksonville FL

Lauer, Jeanett, *Dean,* United States International University, School of Performing and Visual Arts, San Diego CA (S)

Laughlin, Margarita, *Registrar,* Museum of Fine Arts, Saint Petersburg, Florida, Inc, Saint Petersburg FL

Laughlin, Page, *Asst Prof,* Wake Forest University, Dept of Art, Winston-Salem NC (S)

Lauitt, Edward, *First VPres,* Society for Folk Arts Preservation, Inc, New York NY

Launer, Lisa, *Arts Coordr,* City of San Rafael, Falkirk Cultural Center, San Rafael CA

Laurette, Sandra, *Pres,* Beaumont Art League, Beaumont TX

Laurin, Gordon, *Asst Dir & Cur,* St Mary's University, Art Gallery, Halifax NS

Lautanen-Raleigh, Marcia, *Cur,* Aurora University, Schingoethe Center for Native American Cultures, Aurora IL

Lauvao, Fa'ailoilo, *Cur,* Jean P Haydon Museum, Pago Pago, American Samoa PI

LaVallee, Adrian, *Coordr Exhib,* Saint Anselm College, Chapel Art Center, Manchester NH

Lavallee, Paul, *Dir Admin,* Montreal Museum of Fine Arts, Montreal PQ

Lavender, Candi, *Museum Educ,* Wake Forest University, Museum of Anthropology, Winston Salem NC

Laverty, Bruce, *Architectural Archivist,* Athenaeum of Philadelphia, Philadelphia PA

Lavery, Jean, *Assoc Dir Public Communication,* Royal Ontario Museum, Toronto ON

Lavey, Mary, *Adjunct Prof,* Adams State College, Dept of Visual Arts, Alamosa CO (S)

Lavin, Marguerite, *Rights & Reproductions,* Museum of the City of New York, Library, New York NY

Lavine, Steven D, *Pres,* California Institute of the Arts, School of Art, Valencia CA (S)

Law, Aaron, *Coordr Visual Communications,* Indiana University-Purdue University, Indianapolis, Herron School of Art, Indianapolis IN (S)

Law, Craig, *Assoc Prof,* Utah State University, Dept of Art, Logan UT (S)

Lawal, Dr, *Prof,* Virginia Commonwealth University, Art History Department, Richmond VA (S)

Lawhorn, James C, *Adminr,* Huntington Museum of Art, Huntington WV

Lawler, Joyce, *Dir Development,* Creative Time, New York NY

Lawler, Patric K, *Asst Prof,* Sam Houston State University, Art Dept, Huntsville TX (S)

Lawler, Sarah M, *Museum Asst,* Danforth Museum of Art, Framingham MA

Lawless, Patrick, *Music Librn,* Banff Centre, Centre for the Arts Library, Banff AB

Lawn, Robert, *Dir,* Nassau Community College, Firehouse Art Gallery, Garden City NY

Lawn, Robert, *Prof,* Nassau Community College, Art Dept, Garden City NY (S)

Lawrason, Helena, *Cur,* Shorncliffe Park Improvement Assoc, Prairie Panorama Museum, Czar AB

Lawrence, Camille, *Chmn,* Davidson County Community College, Fine Arts & Humanities Div, Lexington NC (S)

Lawrence, David, *Head Dept,* San Bernardino Valley College, Art Dept, San Bernardino CA (S)

Lawrence, Deirdre, *Librn,* Brooklyn Museum, Brooklyn NY

Lawrence, Deirdre E, *Librn,* Brooklyn Museum, Libraries/Archives, Brooklyn NY

Lawrence, Ellen, *Vis Lectr,* College of the Holy Cross, Dept of Visual Arts, Worcester MA (S)

Lawrence, Jacob, *Board Dir Member,* Art Information Center, Inc, New York NY

Lawrence, John, *Chief Cur,* Kemper & Leila Williams Foundation, New Orleans LA

Lawrence, John D, *Dept Head,* La Grange College, Lamar Dodd Art Center Museum, La Grange GA (S)

Lawrence, John D, *Dir,* La Grange College, Lamar Dodd Art Center Museum, La Grange GA

Lawrence, Katherine, *Asst Dir,* The Dixon Gallery & Gardens, Memphis TN

Lawrence, Laura, *Periodicals,* Las Vegas-Clark County Library District, Las Vegas NV

Lawrence, Molly, *Marketing Mgr,* Caspers, Inc, Art Collection, Tampa FL

Lawrence, Patricia, *Prof,* Louisiana State University, School of Art, Baton Rouge LA (S)

Lawrence, Priscilla, *Coll Mgr,* Kemper & Leila Williams Foundation, New Orleans LA

Lawrence, Sallee, *Cur,* Saint Johnsbury Athenaeum, Saint Johnsbury VT

Lawrence, Sally, *Dir,* Pacific Northwest College of Art, Portland OR (S)

Lawrence, Sidney, *Public Affairs Officer,* Hirshhorn Museum and Sculpture Garden, Washington DC

Lawrie, Irene L, *Registrar,* Lightner Museum, Saint Augustine FL

Lawson, Edward P, *Chief Education Dept,* Hirshhorn Museum and Sculpture Garden, Washington DC

Lawson, Jeannette, *Dir of Education,* Philbrook Museum of Art, Tulsa OK

Lawson, Jim, *Head Dept,* Sheridan College, Art Dept, Sheridan WY (S)

Lawson, Noel G, *Prof,* Radford University, Art Dept, Radford VA (S)

Lawson, Pam F, *Asst Prof,* Radford University, Art Dept, Radford VA (S)

Lawson, Roger, *Catalogue Librn,* National Gallery of Art, Library, Washington DC

Lawson, Scott, *Asst Cur,* Plumas County Museum, Museum Archives, Quincy CA

Lawson, Scott J, *Asst Cur,* Plumas County Museum, Quincy CA

Lawson, Thomas, *Dean,* California Institute of the Arts, School of Art, Valencia CA (S)

Lawton, Brad, *Lectr,* Southwest Texas State University, Dept of Art, San Marcos TX (S)

Lawton, Carol, *Chmn,* Lawrence University, Dept of Art, Appleton WI (S)

Lawton, Rebecca E, *Cur,* Vassar College, Vassar Art Gallery, Poughkeepsie NY

Lawyer, Shauna, *Dir Public Relations & Marketing,* Oklahoma City Art Museum, Oklahoma City OK

Lawyer, Shauna, *Dir Public Relations,* Oklahoma City Art Museum, Library, Oklahoma City OK

Lazar, Arthur, *Lectr,* Lake Forest College, Dept of Art, Lake Forest IL (S)

Lazar, Howard, *Coordr Street Artist Prog,* San Francisco City & County Arts Commission, San Francisco CA

Lazarus, Alan H, *Chmn,* William Paterson College, Art Dept, Wayne NJ (S)

Lazarus, Eleanor, *Assoc Dir Education,* DeCordova Museum & Sculpture Park, Lincoln MA

Lazarus, Fred, *Pres,* Maryland Institute, College of Art Exhibitions, Baltimore MD

Lazarus, Fred, *Pres,* Maryland Institute, College of Art, Baltimore MD (S)

Lazarus, Mell, *Pres,* National Cartoonists Society, New York NY

Lazich, Lynn, *Educ Dir,* Green Hill Center for North Carolina Art, Greensboro NC

Lazzari, Margaret, *Assoc Prof,* University of Southern California, School of Fine Arts, Los Angeles CA (S)

Lazzaro, Claudia, *Assoc Prof,* Cornell University, Dept of the History of Art, Ithaca NY (S)

Lazzaro, Richard, *Prof,* University of Wisconsin, Madison, Dept of Art, Madison WI (S)

Lea, Kathy, *Mgr Library Servs,* Lethbridge Community College, Buchanan Gallery, Lethbridge AB

Leach, David, *Assoc Prof,* Wright State University, Dept of Art & Art History, Dayton OH (S)

Leach, Sally, *Assoc Dir,* University of Texas at Austin, Harry Ransom Humanities Research Center, Austin TX

Leadingham, Jo, *Gallery Coordr,* Kentucky State University, Jackson Hall Gallery, Frankfort KY

Leaf, Bill, *Instr,* University of Nevada, Las Vegas, Dept of Art, Las Vegas NV (S)

Leahy, John Louise, *Assoc Prof,* Marygrove College, Visual & Performing Arts Div, Detroit MI (S)

Leamon, David L, *Dir,* Topeka Public Library, Gallery of Fine Arts, Topeka KS

Lean, Larry, *Chmn,* Mount Olive College, Dept of Art, Mount Olive NC (S)

Leary, Edward, *Assoc Prof,* Boston University, School of Visual Arts, Boston MA (S)

Leary, Lisa, *Registrar,* Brandeis University, Rose Art Museum, Waltham MA

Leary, Nadine, *Exec Secy,* Captain Robert Bennet Forbes House, Milton MA

Leath, Susan, *Dir,* Florence Museum, Florence SC

Leatherbarrow, David, *Chmn,* University of Pennsylvania, Dept of Architecture, Philadelphia PA (S)

Leatherman, Donna, *Cur,* Autozone, Autozone Corporation Collection, Memphis TN

Leavenn, Ileana, *Prof,* Seattle Central Community College, Humanities - Social Sciences Division, Seattle WA (S)

Leavitt, Rita Doyle, *Recording Secy,* Chicago Society of Artists, Inc, Chicago IL

Leavitt, Ruth, *Assoc Prof,* University of Maryland, Baltimore County, Visual Arts Dept, Baltimore MD (S)

Leax, Ronald A, *Assoc Dean School,* Washington University, School of Fine Arts, Saint Louis MO (S)

Lebeau, Leon, *Prof,* University of Illinois, Chicago, Health Science Center, Biomedical Visualizations, Chicago IL (S)

Lebeck, Steven, *Instr,* Elgin Community College, Fine Arts Dept, Elgin IL (S)

Leblanc, Anne, *Office Mgr,* Temiskaming Art Gallery, Haileybury ON

LeBlanc, Anne-Marie, *Assoc Prof,* Indiana-Purdue University, Dept of Fine Arts, Fort Wayne IN (S)

LeBlonde, Daniel W, *VPres,* Cincinnati Institute of Fine Arts, Cincinnati OH

Lecky, James, *VPres,* Gallery North, Setauket NY

Lecky, James, *Chmn,* New York Academy of Art, Graduate School of Figurative Art, New York NY (S)

Leclerc, Denise, *Asst Cur Later Canadian Art,* National Gallery of Canada, Ottawa ON

LeCount, Sarah W, *Cur,* Kemerer Museum of Decorative Arts, Bethlehem PA

Le Dain, Bruce, *Pres,* Royal Canadian Academy of Arts, Toronto ON

Ledbetter, Ben, *Asst Prof,* Wesleyan University, Art Dept, Middletown CT (S)

Lederer, Carrie, *Cur,* City of San Rafael, Falkirk Cultural Center, San Rafael CA

Lee, Cenetta, *Dir of Branch Servs,* Ferguson Library, Stamford CT

Lee, Charles, *Inst,* San Diego Mesa College, Fine Arts Dept, San Diego CA (S)

Lee, Christopher G, *Dir,* Columbus Chapel & Boal Mansion Museum, Boalsburg PA

Lee, Chui-chun, *Coordr of Computer Serv,* The College at New Paltz State University of New York, Sojourner Truth Library, New Paltz NY

Lee, Colin, *Instr,* Dowling College, Dept of Visual Arts, Oakdale NY (S)

Lee, Diane, *Exec Dir,* Anderson County Arts Council, Anderson SC

Lee, Ellen, *Chief Cur,* Indianapolis Museum of Art, Indianapolis IN

Lee, Hyosoo, *Technical Servs Librn,* Cleveland Institute of Art, Jessica Gund Memorial Library, Cleveland OH

Lee, J May, *Dir,* China Institute in America, China House Gallery, New York NY

Lee, John M, *Head Div Fine Arts,* Northeast Missouri State University, Art Dept, Kirksville MO (S)

Lee, Katharine C, *Dir,* Virginia Museum of Fine Arts, Richmond VA

Lee, Marge, *Dir Public Information,* Baltimore Museum of Art, Baltimore MD

Lee, Martha J, *Registrar,* Yosemite Museum, Yosemite National Park CA

Lee, Mary Esther, *Planning Coordr,* Public Museum of Grand Rapids, Grand Rapids MI

Lee, Mathilde Boal, *Pres,* Columbus Chapel & Boal Mansion Museum, Boalsburg PA

Lee, Michelle, *Museum Shop Mgr,* The Studio Museum in Harlem, New York NY

Lee, Ok Hi, *Registrar,* Pennsylvania State University, Palmer Museum of Art, University Park PA

Lee, Robert, *Dir,* Asian American Arts Centre, New York NY

Lee, Robert J, *Assoc Prof,* Marymount College, Art Dept, Tarrytown NY (S)

Lee, Roger, *Head,* University of Regina, Dept of Visual Arts, Regina SK (S)

Lee, Seung, *Instr,* Dowling College, Dept of Visual Arts, Oakdale NY (S)

Lee, Shwu Ting, *Instr,* California State University, San Bernardino, Art Dept, San Bernardino CA (S)

Lee, Tatwina, *Pres,* Chinese Culture Foundation, Chinese Culture Center Gallery, San Francisco CA

Lee, Tiffany, *Cur of Education,* Saint John's Museum of Art, Wilmington NC

Lee, Vicky, *Arts Coordr,* King County Arts Commission, Seattle WA

Lee, Wynn, *Dir & Exec Dir,* Balboa Art Conservation Center, San Diego CA

Leean, Arch, *Prof,* Saint Olaf College, Art Dept, Northfield MN (S)

Leece, Curtis, *Adjunct Instr,* Saginaw Valley State University, Dept of Art and Design, University Center MI (S)

Leek, Lisa, *Educator,* College of William and Mary, Joseph & Margaret Muscarelle Museum of Art, Williamsburg VA

Leeper, John P, *Dir Emeritus,* Marion Koogler McNay Art Museum, San Antonio TX

Lees, Gary P, *Dir Dept & Assoc Prof,* Johns Hopkins University, School of Medicine, Dept of Art as Applied to Medicine, Baltimore MD (S)

Leese, Marianne, *Publications,* Historical Society of Rockland County, New City NY

Leet, Richard E, *Dir,* Charles H MacNider Museum, Mason City IA

Leete, William, *Prof,* University of Rhode Island, Dept of Art, Kingston RI (S)

Leete, William C, *Prof,* Northern Michigan University, Dept of Art and Design, Marquette MI (S)

Leffel, Larry, *Chmn,* Bay De Noc Community College, Art Dept, Escanaba MI (S)

Leger, Danielle, *Librn,* Artexte Information Centre, Montreal PQ

Leggett, Laura, *Asst Cur & Registrar,* Mississippi Museum of Art, Jackson MS

Legree, Carson, *Instr,* Treasure Valley Community College, Art Dept, Ontario OR (S)

Lehman, Arnold L, *Dir,* Baltimore Museum of Art, Baltimore MD

Lehman, Harry, *Pres,* House of Roses, Senator Wilson Home, Deadwood SD

Lehman, Mark, *Asst Prof,* Trenton State College, Art Dept, Trenton NJ (S)

Lehr, Lydia, *Instr,* Main Line Center for the Arts, Haverford PA (S)

Lehr, Lydia, *Instr,* Main Line Center for the Arts, Haverford PA (S)

Lehrer, Leonard, *Chmn,* New York University, Dept of Art & Art Professions, New York NY (S)

Lehrer, Leonard, *Chmn,* International Center for Advanced Studies in Art, New York NY

Lehrer, Susan Frisch, *Asst Dir,* National Trust for Historic Preservation, Chesterwood Museum, Glendale MA

Lehrer, Susan Frisch, *Asst Museum Dir,* National Trust for Historic Preservation, Museum Library & Archives, Glendale MA

Leibert, Peter, *Chmn,* Connecticut College, Dept of Art, New London CT (S)

Leibold, Cheryl, *Archivist,* Pennsylvania Academy of the Fine Arts, Archives, Philadelphia PA

Leibow-Giegerich, Nicole, *Librn,* The Metropolitan Museum of Art, Robert Lehman Collection Library, New York NY

Leichty, Erle, *Akkadian Cur,* University of Pennsylvania, University Museum of Archaelogy & Anthropology, Philadelphia PA

Leider, Karen, *Dir,* Trinity College Library, Washington DC

Leidich, David, *Asst to Dir,* Moravian College, Payne Gallery, Bethlehem PA

Leidy, Denise P, *Cur Galleries,* The Asia Society Galleries, New York NY

Leifer, Elizabeth, *Instr,* Suomi College, Fine Arts Dept, Hancock MI (S)

Leinroth, Martha, *Asst Prof,* Rochester Institute of Technology, School of Photographic Arts & Sciences, Rochester NY (S)

Leipzig, Mel, *Prof,* Mercer County Community College, Arts & Communications, Trenton NJ (S)

Leiser, Jo Ann, *Treas,* New York Artists Equity Association, Inc, New York NY

Leisy, Ray, *VPres,* Wayne County Historical Society, Wooster OH

Leiter, Franziska Kruschen, *Dir,* Acadia University Art Gallery, Wolfville NS

Leites, Susan, *Lectr,* University of Pennsylvania, Graduate School of Fine Arts, Philadelphia PA (S)

Leith, Christine, *Div Chmn,* Emma Willard School, Arts Division, Troy NY (S)

Leivick, Joe, *Cur of Photography,* Stanford University, Art Gallery, Stanford CA

Leja, Ilga, *Dir,* Nova Scotia College of Art and Design, Library, Halifax NS

Leja, Michael, *Asst Prof,* Northwestern University, Evanston, Dept of Art History, Evanston IL (S)

Lemakis, Suzy, *Cur,* Citibank, NA, Long Island City NY

Lemanski, Maryjo, *Head Children's Prog,* Kalamazoo Institute of Arts, KIA School, Kalamazoo MI (S)

Lemco van Ginkel, Blanche, *Sec,* Royal Canadian Academy of Arts, Toronto ON

LeMelle, Veronique, *Exec Dir,* Jamaica Arts Center, Jamaica NY

Lemme, Rosalie, *Asst Prof,* Dallas Baptist University, Dept of Art, Dallas TX (S)

Lemmerman, Harold, *Dir,* Jersey City State College, Courtney Art Gallery, Jersey City NJ

Lemmerman, Harold, *Dir,* Jersey City State College, Art Space, Jersey City NJ

Lemmerman, Harold, *Prof,* Jersey City State College, Art Dept, Jersey City NJ (S)

Lemmon, Alfred, *Cur of Manuscripts,* Kemper & Leila Williams Foundation, New Orleans LA

Lemmon, Colette, *Dir Children's Museum,* Iroquois Indian Museum, Howes Cave NY

Lemons, Charles R, *Cur,* Cavalry - Armor Foundation, Patton Museum of Cavalry & Armor, Fort Knox KY

Lemp, Frank J, *Chmn,* Ottawa University, Dept of Art, Ottawa KS (S)

Lemstrom-Sheedy, Kaarin, *Sales Adminr,* Whitney Museum of American Art, New York NY

Lenderman, Max, *Prof,* Rochester Institute of Technology, School of Art and Design, Rochester NY (S)

Lenfestey, Harriett, *Cur Educ,* University of Tampa, Henry B Plant Museum, Tampa FL

Lengyel, Paul, *VPres,* Print Club of Albany, Museum, Albany NY

Lennig, Arthur, *Assoc Prof,* State University of New York at Albany, Art Dept, Albany NY (S)

Lentz, Tom, *Asst Dir,* Freer Gallery of Art, Washington DC

Lenz, Mary Jane, *Assoc Cur,* National Museum of the American Indian, New York NY

Leoin, Pamela, *Assoc Dir,* Temple Beth Israel, Plotkin Juddica Museum, Phoenix AZ

Leonard, Catherine, *Asst Prof,* Mount Mary College, Art Dept, Milwaukee WI (S)

Leonard, David, *Provincial Archivist,* Department of Culture & Multi-Culturalism, Provincial Archives of Alberta, Edmonton AB

Leonard, Glen, *Dir,* Church of Jesus Christ of Latter-day Saints, Museum of Church History & Art, Salt Lake City UT

Leonard, Robert, *Dir,* Wharton Esherick Museum, Wharton Esherick Studio, Paoli PA

Leonard, Susan, *Exhibitions Coordr,* South Carolina Arts Commission, Columbia SC

Leonard-Cravens, Mary, *Assoc Prof,* Eastern Illinois University, Art Dept, Charleston IL (S)

Leonardi, Joe, *Mgr Media Arts Center,* Long Beach Museum of Art, Long Beach CA

Leondar, Arnold, *Chmn,* Tarrant County Junior College, Art Dept, Northeast Campus, Hurst TX (S)

Leonhard, Aimee, *Asst Conservator,* University of Missouri, Museum of Art and Archaeology, Columbia MO

Lepine, Micheline, *Business Operations Mgr,* Burchfield Art Center, Buffalo NY

Lequire, Stephen, *Assoc Prof,* University of North Carolina at Wilmington, Dept of Fine Arts - Division of Art, Wilmington NC (S)

Lerch, Dawn, *Public Relations,* M Grumbacher Inc, Cranbury NJ

Lerner, A, *Prof,* City Colleges of Chicago, Daley College, Chicago IL (S)

Lerner, Alexandra, *Trustee,* Foundation for Today's Art, Nexus Gallery, Philadelphia PA

Lerner, Martin, *Cur Asian Art,* The Metropolitan Museum of Art, New York NY

Lerner, Norman, *Assoc Prof,* California Polytechnic State University at San Luis Obispo, Dept of Art and Design, San Luis Obispo CA (S)

Lerner-Rosenberg, Rachel, *Public Information Officer,* University of Chicago, David and Alfred Smart Museum of Art, Chicago IL

Leroy, Hugh, *Chmn,* York University, Dept of Visual Arts, North York ON (S)

LeSage, Randy, *Instr,* Dean Junior College, Visual and Performing Art Dept, Franklin MA (S)

Lesher, Pete, *Cur,* Chesapeake Bay Maritime Museum, Saint Michaels MD

Lesher, Pete, *Cur,* Chesapeake Bay Maritime Museum, Library, Saint Michaels MD

LeShock, Ed, *Asst Prof,* Radford University, Art Dept, Radford VA (S)

Lesko, Diana, *Sr Cur of Coll & Exhib,* Museum of Fine Arts, Saint Petersburg, Florida, Inc, Saint Petersburg FL

Leslie, Nancy, *Lectr,* State University of New York College at Brockport, Dept of Art & Art History, Brockport NY (S)

Lessard, Elizabeth, *Librn,* Manchester Historic Association, Library, Manchester NH

Lesser, Ann, *Pres & CEO,* Crary Art Gallery Inc, Warren PA

Lessman-Moss, Janice, *Div Coordr Crafts,* Kent State University, School of Art, Kent OH (S)

Lester, Howard, *Assoc Prof,* Rochester Institute of Technology, School of Photographic Arts & Sciences, Rochester NY (S)

Lester, Laura, *Dir of Public Affairs,* The Phillips Collection, Washington DC

LeSueur, Bill, *Design & Installation,* Fort Worth Art Association, Modern Art Museum of Fort Worth, Fort Worth TX

LeSueur, Marc, *Art History,* California College of Arts and Crafts, Oakland CA (S)

Letson, Christine, *Secy,* Oysterponds Historical Society, Museum, Orient NY

Letson, Frederick, *VPres,* Oysterponds Historical Society, Museum, Orient NY

Lettenstrom, Dean R, *Assoc Prof,* University of Minnesota, Duluth, Art Dept, Duluth MN (S)

Lettenstrom, Nancy, *Asst Prof,* University of Minnesota, Duluth, Art Dept, Duluth MN (S)

Lettieri, Robin, *Dir,* Port Chester Public Library, Fine Arts Dept, Port Chester NY

Leval, Susana Torruella, *Chief Cur,* El Museo del Barrio, New York NY

Levanovsky, Odelia, *Asst Librn,* French Institute-Alliance Francaise, Library, New York NY

Levant, Ginger, *Instr,* Dowling College, Dept of Visual Arts, Oakdale NY (S)

LeVant, Howard, *Assoc Prof,* Rochester Institute of Technology, School of Photographic Arts & Sciences, Rochester NY (S)

Levensky-Vogel, Elayne, *Instr,* Green River Community College, Art Dept, Auburn WA (S)

Leventhal, Nathan, *Pres,* Lincoln Center for the Performing Arts, Cork Gallery, New York NY

Leverette, Carlton, *Coordr,* New Community College of Baltimore, Dept of Fine Arts, Baltimore MD (S)

Levi, Toby, *Admin Officer,* Massachusetts Institute of Technology, List Visual Arts Center, Cambridge MA

Levin, David S, *Dean,* Mercer County Community College, Arts & Communications, Trenton NJ (S)

Levin, Ruth, *Registrar,* Bennington Museum, Bennington VT

Levine, Julius S, *Assoc Prof,* Catholic University of America, School of Architecture & Planning, Washington DC (S)

Levine, Kathy, *Instr,* Dowling College, Dept of Visual Arts, Oakdale NY (S)

Levine, Louis D, *Dir & Asst Commissioner,* New York State Museum, Albany NY

Levine, Mark, *Vice Chmn,* American Craft Council, New York NY

Levine, Martin, *Asst Prof,* State University of New York at Stony Brook, Art Dept, Stony Brook NY (S)

Levine, May, *Dir,* The American Foundation for the Arts, Miami FL

LeVine, Newton, *Assoc Prof Architecture,* Ramapo College of New Jersey, School of Contemporary Arts, Mahwah NJ (S)

Levine, Phyllis, *Public Information Dir,* International Center of Photography, New York NY

Levine, Sam, *Treasurer,* National Council on Art in Jewish Life, New York NY

Levine, Steven, *Prof,* Bryn Mawr College, Dept of the History of Art, Bryn Mawr PA (S)

Levinson, Diane, *Art School Dir,* San Jose Museum of Art, San Jose CA

Levinson, Jude, *Chmn Theater,* Idyllwild School of Music and the Arts, Idyllwild CA (S)

Levitan, Melissa, *Cur Textiles,* Fine Arts Museums of San Francisco, M H de Young Memorial Museum and California Palace of the Legion of Honor, San Francisco CA

Levitt, Isabell, *Prof,* North Carolina Central University, Art Dept, Durham NC (S)

Levitz, Dale R, *Asst Prof,* Johns Hopkins University, School of Medicine, Dept of Art as Applied to Medicine, Baltimore MD (S)

Levitz, Martin, *Secy,* Ukiyo-e Society of America, Inc, New York NY

Levy, David, *Pres,* Corcoran Gallery of Art, Washington DC

Levy, Jane, *Librn,* Judah L Magnes Museum, Berkeley CA

Levy, Jane, *Librn,* Judah L Magnes Museum, Blumenthal Rare Book & Manuscript Library, Berkeley CA

Levy, Marjorie, *Dir,* Pilchuck Glass School, Seattle WA (S)

Levy, Sue, *Cur,* CIGNA Corporation, CIGNA Museum & Art Collection, Philadelphia PA

Lew, Jack, *Chmn Design,* Kansas City Art Institute, Kansas City MO (S)

Lew, Norman, *Exec VPres,* Chinese Culture Foundation, Chinese Culture Center Gallery, San Francisco CA

Lew, William W, *Head Dept,* University of Northern Iowa, Dept of Art, Cedar Falls IA (S)

Lewallen, Glenn, *Pres,* San Angelo Art Club, Helen King Kendall Memorial Art Gallery, San Angelo TX

Lewandoswki, Niles, *Co-Chmn Foundation Prog,* University of the Arts, Philadelphia College of Art & Design, Philadelphia PA (S)

Lewin, Jacqueline, *Cur Hist & Librn,* Saint Joseph Museum, Saint Joseph MO

LeWinter, Stephen S, *Asst Prof,* University of Tennessee at Chattanooga, Dept of Art, Chattanooga TN (S)

Lewis, Allice, *Head Archives,* Woodstock Artists Association, Woodstock NY

Lewis, Arnold, *Chmn,* College of Wooster, Dept of Art, Wooster OH (S)

Lewis, Barbara, *Prof,* James Madison University, Dept of Art, Harrisonburg VA (S)

Lewis, Carole, *Secy,* Sculptors Guild, Inc, New York NY

Lewis, C Douglas, *Cur Sculpture,* National Gallery of Art, Washington DC

Lewis, Charles, *Prof Theatre,* Clinch Valley College of the University of Virginia, Visual & Performing Arts Dept, Wise VA (S)

Lewis, C Stanley, *Prof,* American University, Dept of Art, Washington DC (S)

Lewis, Elma, *Artistic Dir,* Museum of the National Center of Afro-American Artists, Boston MA

Lewis, Gay, *Registrar Asst,* National Art Museum of Sport, Indianapolis IN

Lewis, Jack R, *Art Coordr,* Georgia Southwestern College, Art Gallery, Americus GA

Lewis, Janet, *Chmn Fashion Design,* Moore College of Art & Design, Philadelphia PA (S)

Lewis, Jerry, *Chmn Dept,* Joliet Junior College, Fine Arts Dept, Joliet IL (S)

Lewis, Louise, *Dir,* California State University, Northridge, Art Galleries, Northridge CA

Lewis, Marcia, *Co-Dir,* Springfield City Library & Museums Association, Art & Music Dept, Springfield MA

Lewis, Marcia, *Instr,* Long Beach City College, Dept of Art, Long Beach CA (S)

Lewis, Mary, *Vis Asst Prof,* Trinity College, Dept of Fine Arts, Hartford CT (S)

Lewis, Michael H, *Chmn & Prof,* University of Maine, Art Dept, Orono ME (S)

Lewis, Monty, *Dir,* Coronado School of Fine Arts, Coronado CA (S)

Lewis, Nina, *Asst to Dir,* North Dakota Museum of Art, Grand Forks ND

Lewis, Richard, *Asst Prof,* Bradford College, Creative Arts Division, Bradford MA (S)

Lewis, Robert E, *Chmn Dept,* Memphis State University, Dept of Art, Memphis TN (S)

Lewis, Russell, *Ed,* Chicago Historical Society, Chicago IL

Lewis, Samella, *Founder,* Museum of African American Art, Los Angeles CA

Lewis, Stanley, *Instr,* Chautauqua Institution, School of Art, Chautauqua NY (S)

Lewis, Susan, *Chief Librn,* Boston Architectural Center, Memorial Library, Boston MA

Lewis, Tim, *Archivist,* Rome Historical Society Museum, William E Scripture Memorial Library, Rome NY

Lewis, Tom, *Controller,* Art Gallery of Ontario, Toronto ON

Lewitin, Margot, *Artistic Dir,* Women's Interart Center, Inc, Interart Gallery, New York NY

Lewton, Val, *Chief of Design & Production,* National Museum of American Art, Washington DC

Ley, Sean, *Dir,* Crooked Tree Arts Council, Virginia M McCune Community Arts Center, Petoskey MI

Leys, Dale, *Prof,* Murray State University, Art Dept, Murray KY (S)

Leyva, Maria, *Cur Reference Center,* Art Museum of the Americas, Washington DC

Leznicki, Bojana H, *Artist,* New York Tapestry Artists, Carmel NY

Lhote, Jean-Francois, *Instr,* Universite de Montreal, Dept of Art History, Montreal PQ (S)

Li, Chu-tsing, *Res Cur Far Eastern Art,* Nelson-Atkins Museum of Art, Kansas City MO

Li, Chu-tsing, *Prof Emeritus,* University of Kansas, Kress Foundation Dept of Art History, Lawrence KS (S)

Liakos, J Dimitri, *Div Coordr,* Northern Illinois University, School of Art, De Kalb IL (S)

Liang, Alice, *Registrar,* San Jose State University, Union Gallery, San Jose CA

Libby, Gary Russell, *Dir,* Museum of Arts and Sciences, Cuban Museum, Daytona Beach FL

Libby, Liz, *Asst Prof,* University of Maine at Augusta, Division of Fine & Performing Arts, Augusta ME (S)

Liberatore, Claudia, *Sr Lectr,* Aquinas College, Art Dept, Grand Rapids MI (S)

Libermann, Ruth, *Gallery Coordr,* Art in General, New York NY

Libin, Laurence, *Cur Musical Instruments,* The Metropolitan Museum of Art, New York NY

Lichtman, Eve, *Librn,* Brand Library & Art Galleries, Glendale CA

Lidtke, Thomas D, *Exec Dir,* West Bend Gallery of Fine Arts, West Bend WI

Lidtke, Thomas D, *Exec Dir,* West Bend Gallery of Fine Arts, Library, West Bend WI

Lie, Henry, *Dir Center for Conservation & Technical Studies,* Harvard University, Harvard University Art Museums, Cambridge MA

Lieb, Kathi, *Educational Cur,* Spertus Museum, Chicago IL

Lieber, Beth, *Exec Dir,* Ashtabula Arts Center, Ashtabula OH

Lieberman, Jack, *Instr,* Cuyahoga Valley Art Center, Cuyahoga Falls OH (S)

Lieberman, William S, *Chmn Twentieth Century Art,* The Metropolitan Museum of Art, New York NY

Liebman, Steven, *Instr,* Hamilton College, Art Dept, Clinton NY (S)

Lien, Lary, *Instr,* Interlochen Arts Academy, Dept of Visual Art, Interlochen MI (S)

Lierheimer, Violet, *Acquisitions Librn,* Mexico-Audrain County Library, Mexico MO

Lifschitz, Edward, *Cur Education,* National Museum of African Art, Washington DC

Lightfoot, Thomas, *Asst Prof,* Rochester Institute of Technology, School of Art and Design, Rochester NY (S)

Lightner, Karen, *Ref Librn,* Free Library of Philadelphia, Rare Book Dept, Philadelphia PA

Ligo, Larry L, *Prof,* Davidson College, Art Dept, Davidson NC (S)

Ligon, Claude M, *Dir,* Maryland Museum of African Art, Columbia MD

Ligon, Doris Hillian, *Exec Dir,* Maryland Museum of African Art, Columbia MD

Ligon, Margaret, *Dir Marketing,* Morgan County Foundation, Inc, Madison-Morgan Cultural Center, Madison GA

Ligon, Margy, *Dir Education,* Walker Art Center, Minneapolis MN

Liles, Robbie, *VPres,* Anson County Historical Society, Inc, Wadesboro NC

Lillehoj, Elizabeth, *Asst Prof,* DePaul University, Dept of Art, Chicago IL (S)

Lilley, Ann, *Secy,* Mattatuck Historical Society Museum, Waterbury CT

Lillich, Meredith, *Prof,* Syracuse University, Dept of Fine Arts (Art History), Syracuse NY (S)

Lillie, Lloyd, *Prof,* Boston University, School of Visual Arts, Boston MA (S)

Lilly, Paige, *Librn,* Penobscot Marine Museum, Searsport ME

Lilly, Paige, *Librn,* Penobscot Marine Museum, Stephen Phillips Memorial Library, Searsport ME

Lilyquist, Christine, *Lila Acheson Wallace Research Cur Egyptology,* The Metropolitan Museum of Art, New York NY

Lim, Susan, *Chmn Music,* Idyllwild School of Music and the Arts, Idyllwild CA (S)

Limondjian, Hilde, *Program Mgr Concerts & Lectures,* The Metropolitan Museum of Art, New York NY

LiMouze, Dorothy, *Asst Prof,* St Lawrence University, Dept of Fine Arts, Canton NY (S)

Lincer, Catherin, *Libr Dir,* Cochise College, Charles Di Peso Library, Douglas AZ

Lincoln, Louise, *Cur Ethnographic Arts,* Minneapolis Society of Fine Arts, Minneapolis Institute of Arts, Minneapolis MN

Lincoln, Louise, *Cur African Oceanic New World Cultures,* Minneapolis Society of Fine Arts, Minneapolis Institute of Arts, Minneapolis MN

Lind, Jennifer, *Registrar,* University of Massachusetts, Amherst, University Gallery, Amherst MA

Linda, Mary F, *Asst Dir,* Pennsylvania State University, Palmer Museum of Art, University Park PA

Lindblom, Michelle, *Instr,* Bismarck Junior College, Fine Arts Dept, Bismarck ND (S)

Lindbloom, Terri, *Asst Prof,* Florida State University, Art Dept, Tallahassee FL (S)

Linden, Barbara, *Facilities Mgr,* Massachusetts Institute of Technology, MIT Museum, Cambridge MA

Lindenberger, Beth, *Instr,* Cuyahoga Valley Art Center, Cuyahoga Falls OH (S)

Lindenheim, Diane, *Instr,* Bucks County Community College, Fine Arts Dept, Newtown PA (S)

Linder, Bradford, *Historic Resource Dir,* Southern Oregon Historical Society, Jacksonville Museum of Southern Oregon History, Jacksonville OR

Linder, Robert, *Dean Fine Arts,* Houston Baptist University, Dept of Art, Houston TX (S)

Lindgren, Bernice, *Treas,* Phelps County Historical Society, Phelps County Museum, Holdrege NE

Lindgren, Don, *Pres,* Phelps County Historical Society, Phelps County Museum, Holdrege NE

Lindholm, Lisa, *Asst Prof,* University of Hartford, Hartford Art School, West Hartford CT (S)

Lindland, Pauline, *Art Cur,* Petro-Canada Inc, Corporate Art Programme, Calgary AB

Lindner, Harry, *Instr,* Northeast Community College, Dept of Liberal Arts, Norfolk NE (S)

Lindquist, Evan, *Prof,* Arkansas State University, Dept of Art, Jonesboro AR (S)

Lindquist, Fred, *Chmn Board Dir,* Atwater Kent Museum, Philadelphia PA

Lindsay, Betsy, *Instr,* Pacific Northwest College of Art, Portland OR (S)

Lindsey, Anne, *Assoc Prof,* University of Tennessee at Chattanooga, Dept of Art, Chattanooga TN (S)

Lindsey, Jack, *Cur American Decorative Arts,* Philadelphia Museum of Art, Mount Pleasant, Philadelphia PA

Lindsey, Kathy, *Instr,* The Arkansas Arts Center, Museum School, Little Rock AR (S)

Lindsley, James Elliott, *Pres,* Columbia County Historical Society, Columbia County Museum, Kinderhook NY

Lindsley, James Elliott, *Pres,* Columbia County Historical Society, Library, Kinderhook NY

Lindstrom, Janet, *Exec Dir,* New Canaan Historical Society, New Canaan CT

Line, David, *Pres,* Sierra Arts Foundation, Reno NV

Lineberry, Heather, *Cur,* Arizona State University, University Art Museum, Tempe AZ

Linehan, James, *Prof,* University of Maine, Art Dept, Orono ME (S)

Lineker, Bruce, *Cur Exhib,* Montgomery Museum of Fine Arts, Montgomery AL

Lingeman, Thomas, *Assoc Prof,* University of Toledo, Dept of Art, Toledo OH (S)

Lingerfelt, Marilyn, *VPres & Exhib Chmn,* Coppini Academy of Fine Arts, San Antonio TX

Lingerfelt, Marilyn, *Pres,* Coppini Academy of Fine Arts, Library, San Antonio TX

Lingner, Fern, *Pres,* Boca Raton Museum of Art, Boca Raton FL

Linhares, Philip, *Chief Cur Art,* Oakland Museum, Art Dept, Oakland CA

Linhares, Philip, *Chief Cur Art,* Oakland Museum, Library, Oakland CA

Linhart, Lucie E, *Registrar,* University of Lethbridge, Art Gallery, Lethbridge AB

Linker, Wayne, *Exec VPres,* American Academy in Rome, New York NY (S)

Linn, Bruce, *Registrar,* University of Chicago, David and Alfred Smart Museum of Art, Chicago IL

Linowitz, June, *Dir,* Studio Gallery, Washington DC

Lintault, M Joan, *Prof,* Southern Illinois University, School of Art & Design, Carbondale IL (S)

Lintault, Roger, *Instr,* California State University, San Bernardino, Art Dept, San Bernardino CA (S)

Linton, Henri, *Dept Chmn,* University of Arkansas at Pine Bluff, Art Dept, Pine Bluff AR (S)

Linton, Laura, *Development Officer,* Barnes Foundation, Merion Station PA

Lionette, Gina, *Dir Public Affairs,* Worcester Art Museum, Worcester MA

Lipfert, Nathan, *Library Dir,* Maine Maritime Museum, Archives Library, Bath ME

Lipinski, Marlene, *Coordr Graphics,* Columbia College, Art Dept, Chicago IL (S)

Lipowicz, Edward, *Cur,* Canajoharie Art Gallery, Canajoharie NY

LiPowski, Mike, *Asst Cur,* Toronto Historical Board, Historic Fort York, Toronto ON

Lipp, Frederick, *Prof,* Rochester Institute of Technology, School of Art and Design, Rochester NY (S)

Lippincott, Bertram, *Librn,* Newport Historical Society, Library, Newport RI

Lippman, Barbara, *Interim Dir Continuing Studies,* University of the Arts, Philadelphia College of Art & Design, Philadelphia PA (S)

Lippman, Irvin, *Asst Dir,* Amon Carter Museum, Fort Worth TX

Lippman, Judith, *Dir,* Meredith Gallery, Baltimore MD

Lipschutz, Jeff, *Chmn,* University of Wisconsin-Oshkosh, Dept of Art, Oshkosh WI (S)

Lipsett, Katherine, *Art Cur,* Peter and Catharine Whyte Foundation, Whyte Museum of the Canadian Rockies, Banff AB

Lipsitt, Cyrus D, *Executive Dir,* Worcester Center for Crafts, Worcester MA

Lipsitt, Cyrus D, *Exec Dir,* Worcester Center for Crafts, Worcester MA (S)

Lipsmeyer, Elizabeth, *Asst Prof,* Old Dominion University, Art Dept, Norfolk VA (S)

Lipton, Barbara, *Dir,* Jacques Marchais Center of Tibetan Art, Tibetan Museum, Staten Island NY

Lipton, Leah, *Prof,* Framingham State College, Art Dept, Framingham MA (S)

Lis, Edward, *Instr,* Wayne Art Center, Wayne PA (S)

Lisanti, Dominic A, *Business Adminr,* Newark Museum Association, The Newark Museum, Newark NJ

Liscomb, Kathlyn, *Asst Prof,* University of Victoria, Dept of History in Art, Victoria BC (S)

Lisk, Susan J, *Dir,* Porter-Phelps-Huntington Foundation, Inc Foundation, Inc, Historic House Museum, Hadley MA

List, Kathleen, *Dir,* Beeghly Library, Delaware OH

Lister, Ardele, *Asst Prof,* Rutgers, the State University of New Jersey, Mason Gross School of the Arts, New Brunswick NJ (S)

Lister, Peter, *Lectr,* Rosemont College, Division of the Arts, Rosemont PA (S)

Littell, David, *Adjunct Instr,* Saginaw Valley State University, Dept of Art and Design, University Center MI (S)

Little, Bruce, *Asst Prof,* Georgia Southern University, Dept of Art, Statesboro GA (S)

Little, Cynthia, *VPres Interpretation,* Historical Society of Pennsylvania, Philadelphia PA

Little, Katherine, *Prof,* Harcum Junior College, Dept of Fine Arts, Bryn Mawr PA (S)

Little, Ken, *Assoc Prof,* University of Texas at San Antonio, Division of Art & Architecture, San Antonio TX (S)

Little, Kenneth D, *Registrar,* University of Arizona, Museum of Art, Tucson AZ

Little, Robert, *Cur Non-Canadian Decorative Arts,* Montreal Museum of Fine Arts, Montreal PQ

Little, Stephen, *Cur Asian Art,* Honolulu Academy of Arts, Honolulu HI

Littlefield, Doris B, *Chief Cur,* Vizcaya Museum and Gardens, Miami FL

Litwin, Sharon, *Asst Dir for Develop,* New Orleans Museum of Art, New Orleans LA

Litzer, Doris, *Instr,* Linn Benton Community College, Fine & Applied Art Dept, Albany OR (S)

Liu, Hung, *Asst Prof,* Mills College, Art Dept, Oakland CA (S)

Liu, Lily, *Asst Prof,* Lansing Community College, Media Dept, Lansing MI (S)

Lively, Carter, *Dir,* Liberty Hall Historic Site, Liberty Hall Museum, Frankfort KY

Lively, Carter, *Dir,* Liberty Hall Historic Site, Library, Frankfort KY

Lively, Carter, *Dir,* Liberty Hall Historic Site, Orlando Brown House, Frankfort KY

Livengood, Eleanor, *Executive Secy,* Marblehead Arts Association, Inc, Marblehead MA

Livermore, Marie, *Membership Chmn,* Blacksburg Regional Art Association, Christiansburg VA

Livesay, Thomas, *Dir,* Museum of New Mexico, Santa Fe NM

Livingston, Sherrill, *Asst Dir for Admin,* Pacific - Asia Museum, Pasadena CA

Lizardi, Oscar, *Pres,* Pimeria Alta Historical Society, Nogales AZ

Lizzadro, John S, *Dir,* Lizzadro Museum of Lapidary Art, Elmhurst IL

Llewellyn, Frederick, *Dir,* Forest Lawn Museum, Glendale CA

Lloyd, Anita, *General Mgr,* Chilliwack Community Arts Council, Chilliwack BC

Lloyd, David, *Assoc Pres,* Marcella Sembrich Memorial Association Inc, Opera Museum, Bolton Landing NY

Lloyd, Geri, *Secy,* Art Guild of Burlington, Arts for Living Center, Burlington IA

Lloyd, Jackie, *Art Adminr,* Leanin' Tree Museum of Western Art, Boulder CO

Lloyd, Judith, *Educ & Public Relations,* Illinois State Museum, State of Illinois Art Gallery, Chicago IL

Lloyd, June, *Librn,* Historical Society of York County, Library, York PA

Lloyd, Marie, *Marketing Coord,* Chatham Cultural Centre, Thames Art Gallery, Chatham ON

Lo, Beth, *Assoc Prof,* University of Montana, Dept of Art, Missoula MT (S)

LoaFond, Kevin, *Treas,* Portsmouth Athenaeum, Portsmouth NH

Loar, Peggy A, *Dir,* Wolfsonian Foundation, Miami Beach FL

Loar, Steve, *Asst Dean,* Rochester Institute of Technology, College of Imaging Arts & Sciences, Rochester NY (S)

Loar, Steve, *Assoc Prof,* Rochester Institute of Technology, School of Art and Design, Rochester NY (S)

Lobbig, David, *Facilities Tech,* Washington University, Gallery of Art, Saint Louis MO

Lobe, Robert, *Chief Librn,* School of Visual Arts Library, New York NY

Locatelli, Rev Paul, *Academic Pres,* Santa Clara University, de Saisset Museum, Santa Clara CA

Loccisano, Joe, *Prof,* Manatee Community College, Dept of Art & Humanities, Bradenton FL (S)

Locey, Jean, *Assoc Prof,* Cornell University, Dept of Art, Ithaca NY (S)

Lochead, Mary, *Head Librn,* University of Manitoba, Architecture & Fine Arts Library, Winnipeg MB

Lock, Barbara, *Instr,* Adrian College, Art Dept, Adrian MI (S)

Lock, Diana, *Exec Secy,* Paine Art Center and Arboretum, Oshkosh WI

Lockard, Ray Anne, *Librn,* University of Pittsburgh, Henry Clay Frick Fine Arts Library, Pittsburgh PA

Locke, Angus, *Admin,* New Hampshire Art Association, Inc, Manchester NH

Locke, Jaye, *Coordr,* Rice University, Sewall Art Gallery, Houston TX

Locke, John A, *Prof,* Ulster County Community College, Dept of Visual Arts, Stone Ridge NY (S)

Locker, David, *Adult Serv,* Willard Library, Dept of Fine Arts, Evansville IN

Lockett, Robbin, *Dir,* Arts Club of Chicago, Chicago IL

Lockett, Sandra B, *Supvr Central Servs,* Milwaukee Public Library, Art, Music & Recreation Dept, Milwaukee WI

Lockhart, Susan Melton, *Registrar,* University of California, Los Angeles, Grunwald Center for the Graphic Arts, Los Angeles CA

Lockhart, Susan Melton, *Registrar,* University of California, Los Angeles, Wight Art Gallery, Los Angeles CA

Lockman, Lisa, *Vis Prof,* Nebraska Wesleyan University, Art Dept, Lincoln NE (S)

Lockpez, Inverna, *Dir,* Intar Latin American Gallery, New York NY

Loeb, Barbara, *Assoc Prof,* Oregon State University, Dept of Art, Corvallis OR (S)

Loeb, Jean R, *Secy & Treas,* Mississippi Art Colony, Meridian MS

Loeblein, Christopher, *Cur History,* Charleston Museum, Charleston SC

Loeffler, Carl E, *Exec Dir,* Art Com-La Mamelle, Inc, San Francisco CA

Loehr, Thomas, *Asst Prof,* Spring Hill College, Fine Arts Dept, Mobile AL (S)

Loescher, Robert, *Prof,* School of the Art Institute of Chicago, Chicago IL (S)

Loeser, Tom, *Asst Prof,* University of Wisconsin, Madison, Dept of Art, Madison WI (S)

Loesl, Sue, *Instr,* Mount Mary College, Art Dept, Milwaukee WI (S)

Lofgren, Ron, *Chmn,* William Penn College, Art Dept, Oskaloosa IA (S)

Lofquist, Ann, *Prof,* Bowdoin College, Art Dept, Brunswick ME (S)

Loft, Deborah, *Chmn,* College of Marin, Dept of Art, Kentfield CA (S)

Loftis, Deborah, *Librn,* Birmingham Public Library, Arts, Music & Recreation Department, Birmingham AL

Loftus, Erin, *Acting Slide Librn,* Museum of Fine Arts, Houston, Hirsch Library, Houston TX

Logan, Anne-Marie, *Librn,* Yale University, Art Reference Library, New Haven CT

Logan, David, *Prof,* East Tennessee State University, Fine Arts Dept, Johnson City TN (S)

Logan, Fern, *Instr,* Elmhurst College, Art Dept, Elmhurst IL (S)

Logan, Kathryn, *Head,* The Carnegie Library of Pittsburgh, Pittsburgh PA

Logan, Oscar, *Assoc Prof,* Alabama A & M University, Art and Art Education, Normal AL (S)

Logan, Serge E, *Pres,* Wustum Museum Art Association, Racine WI

Logan-Peters, Kay, *Assoc Prof,* University of Nebraska, Lincoln, Architecture Library, Lincoln NE

Logback, Nadine, *Display Arrangement,* McPherson Museum, McPherson KS

Logenecker, Martha, *Exec Dir,* Mingei International, Inc, Mingei International Museum of World Folk Art, San Diego CA

Loggin, Rosalie, *Instr,* University of Texas at Tyler, Dept of Art, Tyler TX (S)

Logue, Kathy, *Instr,* Main Line Center for the Arts, Haverford PA (S)

Lohf, Kenneth A, *Pres,* Grolier Club Library, New York NY

Lohin, Ro, *Prog Dir,* New York Studio School of Drawing, Painting and Sculpture, New York NY (S)

Lohner, Harold, *Gallery Dir,* Russell Sage College, Gallery, Troy NY

Loizeaux, Dan, *Chmn Dept,* Connecticut Institute of Art, Greenwich CT (S)

Lokensgard, Lynn, *Asst Prof,* Lamar University, Art Dept, Beaumont TX (S)

Lomahaftewa, Gloria, *Asst Cur,* Heard Museum, Phoenix AZ

Lomas, Ronald, *Registrar,* Montclair Art Museum, Art School, Montclair NJ (S)

Lombard, Deborah, *Educ Coordr,* Iowa State University, Brunnier Gallery Museum, Ames IA

Lombard, Lynette, *Asst Prof,* Knox College, Dept of Art, Galesburg IL (S)

Lombardi, Nancy, *Prog Dir Art,* Lansing Community College, Media Dept, Lansing MI (S)

Lombardo, Dan, *Cur,* Jones Library, Inc, Amherst MA

Lomber, Elaine, *Chmn,* Finger Lakes Community College, Visual & Performing Arts Dept, Canandaigua NY (S)

Lonergan, Mary Ann, *Instructor,* Briar Cliff College, Art Dept, Sioux City IA (S)

Long, Barbara, *Pres,* Maui Historical Society, Bailey House, Wailuku HI

Long, Betty, *Registrar,* Maryhill Museum of Art, Goldendale WA

Long, Jennifer, *Accounting Mgr,* Memphis Brooks Museum of Art, Memphis TN

Long, John M, *Dean School of Fine Arts,* Troy State University, School of Art & Classics, Troy AL (S)

Long, Lois, *Photograph Coll Coordr,* Supreme Court of the United States, Washington DC

Long, Martha, *Business Mgr,* Great Lakes Historical Society, Vermilion OH

Long, Mary, *Prof,* Texarkana College, Art Dept, Texarkana TX (S)

Long, Mary Louise, *Instr,* Montclair Art Museum, Art School, Montclair NJ (S)

Long, Randy, *Assoc Prof,* Indiana University, Bloomington, Henry Radford Hope School of Fine Arts, Bloomington IN (S)

Long, Richard, *Prof,* University of Wisconsin, Madison, Dept of Art, Madison WI (S)

Long, Robert, *Asst Prof,* Mississippi State University, Art Dept, Mississippi State MS (S)

Longhauser, Elsa, *Gallery Dir,* Moore College of Art & Design, Golden Paley Gallery, Philadelphia PA

Longhenry, Susan, *Cur Education,* University of Georgia, Georgia Museum of Art, Athens GA

Longley, Lillian, *Instr,* Malden Bridge School of Art, Malden Bridge NY (S)

Longman, Debbie, *Education Coordr,* Fraunces Tavern Museum, New York NY

Longmire, Sam, *Cur Educ,* Evansville Museum of Arts and Science, Evansville IN

Longo, Judith A, *Asst Dean of Humanities,* Ocean County College, Humanities Dept, Toms River NJ (S)

Longstreth-Brown, Kitty, *Registrar,* University of New Mexico, University Art Museum, Albuquerque NM

Longtin, Barbara C, *Dir,* Muscatine Art Center, Muscatine IA

Lonnberg, Thomas R, *Asst Cur,* Evansville Museum of Arts and Science, Evansville IN

Lonsdorf, Alice B, *Pres,* Philadelphia Museum of Art, Women's Committee, Philadelphia PA

Lonsdors, George, *Head Admin,* The Metropolitan Museum of Art, The Cloisters, New York NY

Loomis, Ormond H, *Dir,* Florida Folklife Programs, White Springs FL

Loomis, Tom, *Assoc Prof,* Mansfield University, Art Dept, Mansfield PA (S)

Looney, Roberto, *Exec Dir,* Wayne Center for the Arts, Wooster OH

Loonsk, Susan, *Asst Prof,* University of Wisconsin-Superior, Programs in the Visual Arts, Superior WI (S)

Loord, Leon, *Pres,* American Society of Portrait Artists (ASOPA), Montgomery AL

Loord McRae, Joy, *Treas,* American Society of Portrait Artists (ASOPA), Montgomery AL

Loosle, Richard, *Asst Prof,* Catholic University of America, School of Architecture & Planning, Washington DC (S)

Lopez, Barbara, *Business Mgr,* Tulane University, Gallier House Museum, New Orleans LA

Lopez, Diana, *Cur Archaeology,* University of Puerto Rico, Museum of Anthropology, History & Art, Rio Piedras PR

Lopez, Gildardo, *Museum Asst,* Spanish Governor's Palace, San Antonio TX

Lopez, Jan, *Asst Cur,* University of Delaware, University Gallery, Newark DE

Lopez, Tom, *Asst Prof,* Rochester Institute of Technology, School of Photographic Arts & Sciences, Rochester NY (S)

Lopez-Woodward, Dina, *Exec Dir,* Xicanindio, Inc, Mesa AZ

Lopina, Celeste N, *Cur & Registrar,* Paine Art Center and Arboretum, Oshkosh WI

Lorance, Jane, *Branch Adminr,* Las Vegas-Clark County Library District, Las Vegas NV

Lorance, Loretta, *Instr,* Dowling College, Dept of Visual Arts, Oakdale NY (S)

Loranth, Alice N, *Head Fine Arts & Special Colls Dept,* Cleveland Public Library, Fine Arts & Special Collections Dept, Cleveland OH

Lorber, Elaine, *Exec Dir,* City Of Raleigh Arts Commission, Municipal Building Art Exhibitions, Raleigh NC

Lord, Catharine, *Dir,* University of California, Irvine, Fine Art Gallery, Irvine CA

Lord, Catherine, *Chmn,* University of California, Irvine, Studio Art Dept, Irvine CA (S)

Lord, Jane, *Committee Chmn,* Colonel Black Mansion, Ellsworth ME

Lordi, Michael, *Librn,* California College of Arts and Crafts Library, Oakland CA

Lorenz, Mary, *Cur Colls,* Mississippi Department of Archives & History, Mississippi State Historical Museum, Jackson MS

Loria, Joan, *Asst Dir Exhibits,* Massachusetts Institute of Technology, MIT Museum, Cambridge MA

Loriaux, Maurice, *Dir,* Southwest Art League Seminars, Santa Fe NM (S)

Lorinskas, Robert, *Museology,* Southern Illinois University, University Museum, Carbondale IL

Lorio, George, *Chmn,* Guilford College, Art Dept, Greensboro NC (S)

Losario, Sam, *Asst Prof,* University of Florida, Dept of Art, Gainesville FL (S)

Losch, Michael, *Asst Prof,* Western Maryland College, Art Dept, Westminster MD (S)

Lottes, John W, *Pres,* Art Institute of Southern California, Laguna Beach CA (S)

Lottes, John W, *Pres,* Art Institute of Southern California, Ruth Salyer Library, Laguna Beach CA

Lott-Gerlach, Linda, *Librn,* Harvard University, Studies in Landscape Architecture & Garden Library, Washington DC

Lottis, Lynnea, *Outreach Coordr,* Ella Sharp Museum, Jackson MI

Loucks, John, *Chmn Humanities,* Seward County Community College, Art Dept, Liberal KS (S)

Louer, Albert O, *Dir Media Relations,* Colonial Williamsburg Foundation, Williamsburg VA

Loundon, George W, *Exec Dir,* Allied ArtsGallery of the Yakima Valley, Yakima WA

Loutenschlager, Madeline, *Guide,* Mark Twain Birthplace Museum, Stoutsville MO

Lovano-Kerr, Jessie, *Prof,* Florida State University, Art Education Dept, Tallahassee FL (S)

Lovato, Manuelita, *Cur Coll,* Institute of American Indian Arts Museum, Santa Fe NM (S)

Love, Ed, *Prof,* Florida State University, Art Dept, Tallahassee FL (S)

Love, Josephine H, *Dir,* Your Heritage House, Detroit MI

Loveday, Amos, *Chief Educ Division,* Ohio Historical Society, Columbus OH

Lovejoy, Barbara, *Registrar,* University of Kentucky, Art Museum, Lexington KY

Lovejoy, Jake, *Instr,* Solano Community College, Division of Fine & Applied Art, Suisun City CA (S)

Lovejoy, Martha L, *Dir,* Dubuque Art Association, Dubuque Museum of Art, Dubuque IA

Lovejoy, Tom, *Asst Secy for External Affairs,* Smithsonian Institution, Washington DC

Loveless, Jim, *Prof,* Colgate University, Dept of Art & Art History, Hamilton NY (S)

Loveless, Jim, *Prof,* Colgate University, Dept of Art & Art History, Hamilton NY (S)

Lovell, Barbra, *Membership Coordr,* Spertus Museum, Chicago IL

Lovell, Carol, *Dir,* Kauai Museum, Lihue HI

Lovell, Charles Muir, *Gallery Dir,* East Carolina University, Wellington B Gray Gallery, Greenville NC

Lovell, Julianna, *Coordr,* Castleton State College, Art Dept, Castleton VT (S)

Lovell, William, *Chmn,* Iona College, Seton School of Associate Degree Studies, Art Dept, Yonkers NY (S)

Lovett, Margaret, *Cur,* Kauai Museum, Lihue HI

Loveys, Geraldine, *Registrar,* McMaster University, Art Gallery, Hamilton ON

Loving, Al, *Dir Evening Session,* City College of New York, Art Dept, New York NY (S)

Loving, Charles, *Asst Dir,* University of Utah, Utah Museum of Fine Arts, Salt Lake City UT

Loving, Richard, *Prof,* School of the Art Institute of Chicago, Chicago IL (S)

Lovins, Mona, *Dir,* Hollywood Art Center School, Hollywood CA (S)

Low, Bill, *Asst Cur,* Bates College, Museum of Art, Lewiston ME

Low, Julian, *National Dir,* National Alliance for Media Arts & Culture (NAMAC), Oakland CA

Low, Markus J, *Dir, Corporate Art Servs,* Ciba-Geigy Corporation, Art Collection, Ardsley NY

Lowe, Constance, *Asst Prof,* University of Texas at San Antonio, Division of Art & Architecture, San Antonio TX (S)

Lowe, Donna, *Librn,* National Infantry Museum, Library, Fort Benning GA

Lowe, George, *Asst Prof,* University of Florida, Dept of Art, Gainesville FL (S)

Lowe, J Michael, *Prof,* St Lawrence University, Dept of Fine Arts, Canton NY (S)

Lowe, Marvin, *Prof,* Indiana University, Bloomington, Henry Radford Hope School of Fine Arts, Bloomington IN (S)

Lowe, Mary, *Instr,* Dunedin Fine Arts and Cultural Center, Dunedin FL (S)

Lowe, Maurice C, *Assoc Prof,* University of Pennsylvania, Graduate School of Fine Arts, Philadelphia PA (S)

Lowe, Patricia, *Librn,* Will Rogers Memorial and Museum, Media Center Library, Claremore OK

Lowe, Phillip, *Music Prog Coordr,* Hill College, Fine Arts Dept, Hillsboro TX (S)

Lowe, Truman, *Assoc Prof,* University of Wisconsin, Madison, Dept of Art, Madison WI (S)

Lowe, Trumman, *Chmn,* University of Wisconsin, Madison, Dept of Art, Madison WI (S)

Lowell, Barbara, *Dir of Mem & Museum Servs,* Newark Museum Association, The Newark Museum, Newark NJ

Lowenthal, Constance, *Executive Dir,* International Foundation for Art Research, Inc, New York NY

Lowenthal, Elaine, *Asst Librn Cataloging,* Harrington Institute of Interior Design, Design Library, Chicago IL

Lowenthal, Elaine, *Circulation Specialist,* Harrington Institute of Interior Design, Design Library, Chicago IL

Lowery, Stephen, *Assoc Prof,* Aurora University, Art Dept, Aurora IL (S)

Lowman, Joyce, *Instr,* John C Calhoun State Community College, Division of Fine Arts, Decatur AL (S)

Lowman, Sandra, *Archivist Librn,* The Seagram Museum, Library, Waterloo ON

Lowney, Bruce, *Artist in Residence,* Fort Lewis College, Art Dept, Durango CO (S)

Lowrey, Annie, *Dir Educ,* Wichita Center for the Arts, Wichita KS (S)

Lowrey, Charles B, *University Librn,* Carnegie Mellon University, Hunt Library, Pittsburgh PA

Lowrie, Pamela B, *Prof,* College of DuPage, Humanities Division, Glen Ellyn IL (S)

Lowry, Glen, *Dir,* Art Gallery of Ontario, Toronto ON

Lowry, Keith, *Prof,* University of Nebraska, Kearney, Dept of Art & Art History, Kearney NE (S)

Loy, Jessica, *Instr,* College of Saint Rose, Dept of Art, Albany NY (S)

Loy, John, *Instr,* Munson-Williams-Proctor Institute, School of Art, Utica NY (S)

Lubben, Anne, *Instr,* Teikyo Westmar University, Art Dept, LeMars IA (S)

Lubbin, Ann, *Dir,* Teikyo Westmar University, Mock Library Art Dept, LeMars IA

Lubbin, Anne, *Gallery Dir,* Teikyo Westmar University, Westmar Art Gallery, LeMars IA

Luber, Harvey, *Instr,* The Arkansas Arts Center, Museum School, Little Rock AR (S)

Lubin, David, *Assoc Prof,* Colby College, Art Dept, Waterville ME (S)

Lubot, Eugene S, *Dean,* Albright College, Freedman Gallery, Reading PA

Lubowsky, Susan, *Dir,* Southeastern Center for Contemporary Art, Winston-Salem NC

Lucarelli, Carolyn, *Asst Museum Librn,* The Metropolitan Museum of Art, Photograph and Slide Library, New York NY

Lucas, Cindy, *Business Mgr,* College of William and Mary, Joseph & Margaret Muscarelle Museum of Art, Williamsburg VA

Lucas, Dan, *Library Dir,* Portland Art Museum, Rex Arragon Library, Portland OR

Lucas, Donald, *VChair,* Old Jail Art Center, Albany TX

Lucas, Judith S, *Cur,* Hebrew Union College - Jewish Institute of Religion, Skirball Museum-Cincinnati Branch, Cincinnati OH

Lucas, Margaret, *Prof,* West Virginia University, College of Creative Arts, Morgantown WV (S)

Lucas, Margaret, *Dean Col,* Rochester Institute of Technology, College of Imaging Arts & Sciences, Rochester NY (S)

Luce, Charles, *Chmn & Prof,* County College of Morris, Art Dept, Randolph NJ (S)

Luce, Ken, *Instr,* San Jacinto College-North, Art Dept, Houston TX (S)

Luce, Ray, *Head Historic Preservation,* Ohio Historical Society, Columbus OH

Lucero, Fred, *Instr,* California State University, Chico, Art Dept, Chico CA (S)

Lucero, Helen, *Cur of New Mexico Hispanic Crafts & Textiles,* Museum of New Mexico, Museum of International Folk Art, Santa Fe NM

Lucey, Susan, *Assoc Prof,* University of Minnesota, Minneapolis, Dept of Studio Art, Minneapolis MN (S)

Luchinsky, Ellen, *Dept Head,* Enoch Pratt Free Library of Baltimore City, Baltimore MD

Luckey, Laura C, *Dir,* Bennington Museum, Bennington VT

Luckman, Stewart, *Prof,* Bethel College, Dept of Art, Saint Paul MN (S)

Luckner, Kurt T, *Cur of Ancient Art,* Toledo Museum of Art, Toledo Museum of Art, Toledo OH

Luderowski, Barbara, *Exec Dir,* Mattress Factory, Pittsburgh PA

Ludwig, Coy L, *Dir,* State University of New York at Oswego, Tyler Art Gallery, Oswego NY

Ludwig, Daniel, *Asst Prof,* Salve Regina College, Art Dept, Newport RI (S)

Lue, Joanne, *Admin Asst,* State University of New York at Albany, University Art Gallery, Albany NY

Luebbers, Leslie L, *Dir,* Memphis State University, University Gallery, Memphis TN

Luecking, Stephen, *Assoc Prof,* DePaul University, Dept of Art, Chicago IL (S)

Lueders, Nano Nore, *Instr,* William Jewell College, Art Dept, Liberty MO (S)

Luehrman, Richard, *Prof,* Central Missouri State University, Art Dept, Warrensburg MO (S)

Luers, William H, *Pres,* The Metropolitan Museum of Art, New York NY

Lugo, Anthony J, *Assoc Prof,* Palomar Community College, Art Dept, San Marcos CA (S)

Lujan, Roy, *Dean,* New Mexico Highlands University, School of Liberal & Fine Arts, Las Vegas NM (S)

Lukas, Malte, *VPres,* Fitchburg Art Museum, Fitchburg MA

Lukas, Vicki A, *Dept Head Technical Service,* New Bedford Free Public Library, Art Dept, New Bedford MA

Luke, Suzanne, *Membership Coordr & Admin Asst,* Visual Arts Ontario, Toronto ON

Lukehart, Peter, *Asst Prof,* Dickinson College, Fine Arts Dept, Carlisle PA (S)

Lukehart, Peter M, *Dir,* Dickinson College, Trout Gallery, Carlisle PA

Lum, Harry, *Chmn Art Dept,* Grossmont Community College, Hyde Gallery, El Cajon CA

Lum, Harry, *Head Dept,* Grossmont College, Art Dept, El Cajon CA (S)

Luman, Mitch, *Science Planetarium Dir,* Evansville Museum of Arts and Science, Evansville IN

Lumpkin, Farnese, *Asst Prof,* Savannah State College, Dept of Fine Arts, Savannah GA (S)

Lumsden, Ian G, *Dir,* Beaverbrook Art Gallery, Fredericton NB

Lunceford, Charles R, *Dean of Arts & Sciences,* Indian River Community College, Fine Arts Dept, Fort Pierce FL (S)

Lunceford, Ray C, *Div Dir of Art & Science,* Indian River Community College, Fine Arts Dept, Fort Pierce FL (S)

Lund, David, *Instr,* Chautauqua Institution, School of Art, Chautauqua NY (S)

Lund, Judith N, *Registrar,* Old Dartmouth Historical Society, New Bedford Whaling Museum, New Bedford MA

Lund, Raymond, *Asst Prof,* Johns Hopkins University, School of Medicine, Dept of Art as Applied to Medicine, Baltimore MD (S)

Lund, Richard, *Prof,* College of DuPage, Humanities Division, Glen Ellyn IL (S)

Lundstrom, Mike, *Instr,* Treasure Valley Community College, Art Dept, Ontario OR (S)

Lunsford, W Hal, *Chmn,* Middle Georgia College, Dept of Art, Cochran GA (S)

Luongo, Daniel, *Chmn,* East Stroudsburg University, Art Dept, East Stroudsburg PA (S)

Lupia, Archy L, *Pres,* Moody County Historical Society, Flandreau SD

Lupin, E Ralph, *Chmn,* Louisiana Department of Culture, Recreation and Tourism, Louisiana State Museum, New Orleans LA

Lurie, Janice, *Asst Librn,* The Buffalo Fine Arts Academy, G Robert Strauss Jr Memorial Library, Buffalo NY

Lussier, Real, *Dir of Traveling Exhib,* Musee d'art contemporain de Montreal, Montreal PQ

Lutchmansingh, Larry D, *Prof,* Bowdoin College, Art Dept, Brunswick ME (S)

Luther, Lacinda, *Asst Cur,* Wells Fargo & Co, History Museum, Los Angeles CA

Lutjeans, Phyllis J, *Museum Scientist,* University of California, Irvine, Fine Art Gallery, Irvine CA

Lutomski, James, *Assoc Prof,* Marygrove College, Visual & Performing Arts Div, Detroit MI (S)

Luton, Barbara, *Development Dir,* Santa Barbara Museum of Art, Santa Barbara CA

Lutsch, Gail, *Assoc Prof,* Bethel College, Dept of Art, North Newton KS (S)

Lutzker, Mary-Ann, *Prof Hist,* Mills College, Art Dept, Oakland CA (S)

Lybarger, Mary, *Faculty,* Edgewood College, Art Dept, Madison WI (S)

Lydecker, Kent, *Deputy Dir Educ,* The Metropolitan Museum of Art, New York NY

Lyke, Linda, *Chmn,* Occidental College, Dept of Art History & Visual Arts, Los Angeles CA (S)

Lykins, Anne, *Staff Site Interpreter,* Patterson Homestead, Dayton OH

Lykins, Jere, *Asst Prof,* Berry College, Art Dept, Mount Berry GA (S)

Lyle, Charles, *Dir,* Maryland Historical Society, Library, Baltimore MD

Lyle, Charles T, *Dir,* Maryland Historical Society, Museum of Maryland History, Baltimore MD

Lyle, Janice, *Assoc Dir & Dir Educ,* Palm Springs Desert Museum, Inc, Palm Springs CA

Lyle, Janice, *Education,* Palm Springs Desert Museum, Inc, Library, Palm Springs CA

Lyle, Janice, *Assoc Dir & Dir Educ,* Palm Springs Desert Museum, Inc, Library, Palm Springs CA

Lyman, David H, *Founder & Dir,* Maine Photographic Workshops, Rockport ME

Lyman, David H, *Founder & Dir,* Maine Photographic Workshops, Rockport ME (S)

Lymon, Keith, *Asst Bookstore Mgr,* Fort Worth Art Association, Modern Art Museum of Fort Worth, Fort Worth TX

Lynagh, Pat, *Asst Librn,* National Portrait Gallery, Library, Washington DC

Lynagh, Patricia, *Asst Librn,* National Museum of American Art, Library of the National Museum of American Art and the National Portrait Gallery, Washington DC

Lynch, John, *Pres,* Colonel Black Mansion, Ellsworth ME

Lynch, John W, *Asst Prof,* Central Missouri State University, Art Dept, Warrensburg MO (S)

Lynch, Robert, *Pres & Chief Exec Officer,* National Assembly of Local Arts Agencies, Washington DC

Lynde, Donna, *Instr,* Cottey College, Art Dept, Nevada MO (S)

Lynde, Richard, *VPres,* Montclair State College, Art Gallery, Upper Montclair NJ

Lyndrup, Allen, *Chmn Theatre Dept,* College of Charleston, School of the Arts, Charleston SC (S)

Lynes, Lisa, *Instr,* North Idaho College, Art Dept, Coeur D'Alene ID (S)

Lyon, Jean, *Shop,* New England Maple Museum, Rutland VT

Lyon, Joyce, *Assoc Prof,* University of Minnesota, Minneapolis, Dept of Studio Art, Minneapolis MN (S)

Lyon, Robert, *Dir,* Louisiana State University, School of Art Gallery, Baton Rouge LA

Lyon, Robert, *Prof,* Louisiana State University, School of Art, Baton Rouge LA (S)

Lyon, Sally, *Chief Reference Div,* City College of the City University of New York, Morris Raphael Cohen Library, New York NY

Lyons, Anne, *Asst Librn,* Wadsworth Atheneum, Auerbach Art Library, Hartford CT

Lyons, Deborah, *Advisor Hopper Collection,* Whitney Museum of American Art, New York NY

Lyons, Mark, *Dir,* New York Office of Parks, Recreation & Historic Preservation, Natural Heritage Trust, Albany NY

Lyons, Nathan, *Dir,* Visual Studies Workshop, Rochester NY

Lysniak, Wolodymyr, *Admin Dir,* Ukrainian Institute of America, Inc, New York NY

Lyss, Michael, *Adjunct Instr,* Maryville University of Saint Louis, Art Division, Saint Louis MO (S)

Lytjen, M Lora, *Asst Dir,* University of New Hampshire, The Art Gallery, Durham NH

Lytle, Hubert, *Pres,* Iroquois County Historical Society Museum, Old Courthouse Museum, Watseka IL

Lytle, Richard, *Prof,* Yale University, School of Art, New Haven CT (S)

Lytle, Sarah A, *Dir,* Hill-Stead Museum, Farmington CT

Maag, Albert, *Dir,* Capital University, Art Library, Columbus OH

Maakestad, John, *Prof,* Saint Olaf College, Art Dept, Northfield MN (S)

Maas, Bernard, *Chmn Crafts,* Edinboro University of Pennsylvania, Art Dept, Edinboro PA (S)

Maass, Andrew, *Dir,* Tampa Museum of Art, Tampa FL

Maberry, Sue, *Dir,* Otis Art Institute of Parsons School of Design Gallery, Library, Los Angeles CA

MacAdam, Barbara, *Cur for American Art,* Dartmouth College, Hood Museum of Art, Hanover NH

Macalik, M, *Instr,* Technical University of Nova Scotia, Faculty of Architecture, Halifax NS (S)

MacArthur, Ann, *Pres of Association,* Charles Morse Museum of American Art, Winter Park FL

MaCaulay, Roder, *Development Dir,* Memphis Brooks Museum of Art, Memphis TN

Macaulay, Scott, *Prog Dir,* The Kitchen Center, New York NY

Macaulay, Thomas, *Prof,* Wright State University, Dept of Art & Art History, Dayton OH (S)

Mac Boggs, Mayo, *Dir,* Converse College, Milliken Art Gallery, Spartanburg SC

MacCollum, Lisa, *Exhibit Coordr,* Heard Museum, Phoenix AZ

MacDonald, Anne, *Dir,* San Francisco Artspace & Artspace Annex, San Francisco CA

MacDonald, Bruce K, *Dean,* School of the Museum of Fine Arts, Boston MA (S)

MacDonald, Elizabeth, *Treas,* Plastic Club, Art Club for Women, Philadelphia PA

MacDonald, George, *Dir,* Canadian Museum of Civilization, Hull ON

MacDonald, Gerald J, *Cur,* Hispanic Society of America, Library, New York NY

MacDonald, John, *Dir Corp Affairs,* Rothmans, Benson & Hedges, Art Collection, Don Mills ON

Macdonald, Paige, *Prog Coordr,* Adirondack Lakes Center for the Arts, Blue Mountain Lake NY

Macdonald, Robert R, *Dir,* Museum of the City of New York, New York NY

MacDonald, Ruby, *Owner,* Clyde Farnell Folk Art Park, Sticks & Stones House, Corner Brook NF

MacDonald, Sara, *Reference Librn,* University of the Arts, Albert M Greenfield Library, Philadelphia PA

MacDonald, Scott, *Instr,* Hamilton College, Art Dept, Clinton NY (S)

MacDonald-McInerney, Jane, *Educ Dir,* Firelands Association for the Visual Arts, Oberlin OH

MacDougall, Elisabeth, *Pres,* Society of Architectural Historians, Philadelphia PA

MacDougall, Scott, *Dean & Chmn Craft Div,* Nova Scotia College of Art and Design, Halifax NS (S)

Mace, Mary, *Librn,* Berkshire Museum, Pittsfield MA

MacEachran, David F, *Assoc Prof,* New England College, Art & Art History, Henniker NH (S)

Macechak, Jeffrey, *Chief Historical Interpreter,* Old Barracks Museum, Trenton NJ

MacGregor, Greg, *Prof,* California State University, Hayward, University Art Gallery, Hayward CA

MacGregor, Gregory, *Chmn,* California State University, Hayward, Art Dept, Hayward CA (S)

Machek, Frank, *Gallery Dir,* Albion College, Bobbitt Visual Arts Center, Albion MI

Mack, Angela D, *Cur Coll,* Carolina Art Association, Gibbes Museum of Art, Charleston SC

Mack, James, *Chmn Humanities,* City Colleges of Chicago, Harold Washington College, Chicago IL (S)

MacKay, Don, *Chmn Dept,* University of Waterloo, Fine Arts Dept, Waterloo ON (S)

MacKay, Robert, *Dir Educ,* Museum of Our National Heritage, Lexington MA

MacKay-Lyons, B, *Instr,* Technical University of Nova Scotia, Faculty of Architecture, Halifax NS (S)

Mackenzie, Lynn, *Asst Prof,* College of DuPage, Humanities Division, Glen Ellyn IL (S)

MacKenzie, Warren, *Prof Emeritus,* University of Minnesota, Minneapolis, Dept of Studio Art, Minneapolis MN (S)

Mackey, David, *Pres,* Hopewell Museum, Hopewell NJ

Mackie, Elizabeth, *Asst Prof,* Trenton State College, Art Dept, Trenton NJ (S)

MacKillop, Rod, *Instr,* University of North Carolina at Charlotte, Dept of Visual Arts, Charlotte NC (S)

Macklin, A D, *Chmn,* Jackson State University, Dept of Art, Jackson MS (S)

MacLean, Dougald, *VPres,* Bowne House Historical Society, Flushing NY

MacLean, Douglas, *Asst Prof,* Lake Forest College, Dept of Art, Lake Forest IL (S)

MacLeish, A Bruce, *Cur Coll,* New York State Historical Association, Fenimore House, Cooperstown NY

MacLennan, Toby, *Assoc Prof,* Rutgers, the State University of New Jersey, Mason Gross School of the Arts, New Brunswick NJ (S)

MacNabb, Vicki, *Admin Dir,* Women's Art Registry of Minnesota Gallery, Saint Paul MN

Macneil, Tonia, *Art Coordr,* San Francisco City & County Arts Commission, San Francisco CA

MacNeill, Daniel S, *Dir,* Union County Public Library Gallery, Monroe NC

MacNulty, Thomas, *Asst Prof,* Adelphi University, Dept of Art and Art History, Garden City NY (S)

MacTaggart, Alan, *Chmn,* Lander University, Dept of Art, Greenwood SC (S)

Madaus, Howard M, *Cur Cody Firearms Museum,* Buffalo Bill Memorial Association, Buffalo Bill Historical Center, Cody WY

Maddaus, Elsie, *Archivist Librn,* Schenectady County Historical Society, Library, Schenectady NY

Madden, J Robert, *Prof,* Lamar University, Art Dept, Beaumont TX (S)

Maddison, Jean, *Instr,* Toronto School of Art, Toronto ON (S)

Maddock, Pam, *Instr,* American River College, Dept of Art, Sacramento CA (S)

Maddox, Gene, *Instr,* College of the Sequoias, Art Dept, Visalia CA (S)

Maddux, Sue Ellen, *Pres,* Community Council for the Arts, Kinston NC

Mader, Daniel, *Chmn,* College of Mount Saint Joseph, Art Dept, Cincinnati OH (S)

Madigan, Kathleen, *Adj Prof,* Washington and Jefferson College, Art Dept, Washington PA (S)

Madill, Shirley, *Cur of Contemporary Art,* Winnipeg Art Gallery, Winnipeg MB

Madison, Willie C, *Park Supt,* Tuskegee Institute National Historic Site, George Washington Carver & The Oaks, Tuskegee Institute AL

Madkour, Christopher, *Dir,* Southern Vermont Art Center, Manchester VT

Madonia, Ann, *Cur,* College of William and Mary, Joseph & Margaret Muscarelle Museum of Art, Williamsburg VA

Madsen, Michelle, *Prof,* Hamline University, Art Dept, Saint Paul MN (S)

Madura, Nancy, *Instr,* Casper College, Dept of Visual Arts, Casper WY (S)

Madzeno, Laurence W, *Dean,* Mesa College, Art Dept, Grand Junction CO (S)

Maeckelbergh, Kenneth, *Instr,* Lakewood Community College, Humanities Dept, White Bear Lake MN (S)

Maeda, Robert, *Chmn,* Brandeis University, Dept of Fine Arts, Waltham MA (S)

Maeder, Edward, *Cur Costumes & Textiles,* Los Angeles County Museum of Art, Los Angeles CA

Maeder, Edward, *Adjunct Asst Prof,* University of Southern California, School of Fine Arts, Los Angeles CA (S)

Magavern, William J, *VPres,* The Buffalo Fine Arts Academy, Albright-Knox Art Gallery, Buffalo NY

Magden, Norman, *Div Coordr,* Northern Illinois University, School of Art, De Kalb IL (S)

Magee, Eileen, *Program Coordr,* Athenaeum of Philadelphia, Philadelphia PA

Maggiacomo, Amy, *Coll Coordr,* Art Metropole Archives, Toronto ON

Maggio, Ron, *Asst Prof,* Springfield College, Dept of Visual and Performing Arts, Springfield MA (S)

Maggio, Ronald, *Coordr,* Springfield College, Hasting Gallery, Springfield MA

Magher, Tena, *Instr,* Young Harris College, Dept of Art, Young Harris GA (S)

Maginnis, Ann, *Librn,* Corcoran Gallery of Art, Library, Washington DC

Magleby, McRay, *Prof,* University of Utah, Art Dept, Salt Lake City UT (S)

Magnan, Oscar, *Dir,* Saint Peter's College, Art Gallery, Jersey City NJ

Magness, Jodie, *Asst Prof,* Tufts University, Dept of Art & Art History, Medford MA (S)

Magnoni, Corinne, *Assoc Dir,* University of Wisconsin-Madison, Elvehjem Museum of Art, Madison WI

Magnusson, Paul, *Pres,* Oregon School of Arts and Crafts, Portland OR (S)

Magnusson, Paul, *Pres,* Oregon School of Arts and Crafts, Hoffman Gallery, Portland OR

Magowan, Robert A, *VPres,* The Society of the Four Arts, Palm Beach FL

Magri, Ken, *Instr,* American River College, Dept of Art, Sacramento CA (S)

Magruder, Lane, *Gallery Coordr,* University of the South, University Gallery, Sewanee TN

Maguire, Eunice, *Cur,* University of Illinois, Krannert Art Museum, Champaign IL

Maguire, Nancy, *Asst Dir for Progs & Admin,* Rutgers University, Stedman Art Gallery, Camden NJ

Maguire, William, *Prof,* Florida International University, Visual Arts Dept, Miami FL (S)

Mahar, William J, *Head Humanities,* Penn State Harrisburg, Humanities Division, Middletown PA (S)

Maher, James B, *Librn,* Brooks Institute Photography Library, Santa Barbara CA

Maher, Kathleen, *Asst Dir,* Lockwood-Mathews Mansion Museum, Norwalk CT

Maher, Kim L, *Exec Dir,* Museum of Discovery & Science, Fort Lauderdale FL

Mahey, John A, *Dir,* Flint Institute of Arts, Flint MI

Mahlke, Ernest, *Instr,* State University of New York College at Oneonta, Dept of Art, Oneonta NY (S)

Mahlke, Ernest D, *Chmn Art Dept,* State University of New York College at Oneonta, Art Gallery & Sculpture Court, Oneonta NY

Mahoney, Michael, *Chmn Dept Fine Arts,* Trinity College, Austin Arts Center, Hartford CT

Mahoney, Michael R T, *Chmn,* Trinity College, Dept of Fine Arts, Hartford CT (S)

Mahsun, Carol Anne, *Asst Prof,* Hope College, Art Dept, Holland MI (S)

Mahut, Jane, *Dir,* Jewish Community Centre of Toronto, The Koffler Gallery, North York ON

Mahy, Gordon, *Chmn,* Mars Hill College, Art Dept, Mars Hill NC (S)

Mai, James, *Prof,* Wenatchee Valley College, Art Dept, Wenatchee WA (S)

Mailloux, Ken, *Admin,* New Jersey Historical Society Museum, New Jersey State Museum at Morven, Newark NJ

Mainardi, Patricia, *Assoc Prof,* City University of New York, PhD Program in Art History, New York NY (S)

Maines, Clark, *Chmn,* Wesleyan University, Art Dept, Middletown CT (S)

Maines, Clark, *Prof,* Wesleyan University, Art Dept, Middletown CT (S)

Mainiero, Elizabeth, *Dir,* Greenwich Library, Greenwich CT

Maize, Shirley, *Dir of Visual Arts,* Tennessee Valley Art Association and Center, Tuscumbia AL

Majeske, Robert, *Instr,* Illinois Central College, Dept of Fine Arts, East Peoria IL (S)

Majeski, Thomas, *Chmn Dept,* University of Nebraska at Omaha, Dept of Art, Omaha NE (S)

Majewski, Shirley, *Library Aide,* Historic Deerfield, Inc, Henry N Flynt Library, Deerfield MA

Major, Sharon, *Public Relations Coordr,* University of California, Santa Barbara, University Art Museum, Santa Barbara CA

Majors, Elaine, *Instr,* Creighton University, Fine and Performing Arts Dept, Omaha NE (S)

Majusiak, Anne, *Gallery Dir,* Vermont State Craft Center at Frog Hollow, Middlebury VT

Makela, Laurie, *Graphic Designer,* Walker Art Center, Minneapolis MN

Maki, Michael, *Dir Educ,* Art Institute of Houston, Houston TX (S)

Makov, Susan, *Prof,* Weber State University, Dept of Visual Arts, Ogden UT (S)

Makow, Yoram, *Prof,* California State Polytechnic University, Pomona, Art Dept, Pomona CA (S)

Malak, Greg, *Cur,* Will Rogers Memorial and Museum, Media Center Library, Claremore OK

Malak, Gregory, *Cur,* Will Rogers Memorial and Museum, Claremore OK

Malarkey, Jean, *Dean Admissions,* Oregon School of Arts and Crafts, Portland OR (S)

Malavet, Juanita, *Museum Shop Mgr,* The Rockwell Museum, Corning NY

Malcolm-Arnold, Gloria, *VPres,* Kent Art Association, Inc, Gallery, Kent CT

Malde, Pradip, *Chmn Dept,* University of the South, Dept of Fine Arts, Sewanee TN (S)

Malesky, Barney J, *Cur Education,* San Diego Museum of Art, San Diego CA

Malgeri, Dina G, *Librn,* Malden Public Library, Art Dept & Gallery, Malden MA

Malinski, Richard M, *Chief Librn,* Ryerson Polytechnical Institute, Library, Toronto ON

Malkoff Moon, Susan, *Head Librn,* Nelson-Atkins Museum of Art, Kenneth and Helen Spencer Art Reference Library, Kansas City MO

Mallard, Michael, *Chmn,* Union University, Dept of Art, Jackson TN (S)

Malles, Evelyn, *Slide Librn,* Center for Creative Studies, College of Art & Design Library, Detroit MI

Malley, Richard C, *Registrar,* Connecticut Historical Society, Hartford CT

Mallory, Michael, *Acting Chmn,* Brooklyn College, Art Dept, Brooklyn NY (S)

Mallory, Nina, *Prof,* State University of New York at Stony Brook, Art Dept, Stony Brook NY (S)

Malloy, Susan, *Dir,* Central Iowa Art Association, Inc, Marshalltown IA

Malloy, Susan, *Dir,* Central Iowa Art Association, Inc, Art Reference Library, Marshalltown IA

Malloy, Susan, *Division Head,* Public Library of Columbus and Franklin County, Columbus Metropolitan Library, Columbus OH

Malm, Linda, *Chmn Dept,* Pasadena City College, Art Dept, Pasadena CA (S)

Malmstrom, Susan, *Member Serv Liaison,* Public Corporation for the Arts, Visual & Performing Arts Registry, Long Beach CA

Malone, Carla, *Dir,* University of the Pacific, Stockton CA

Malone, Carolyn, *Assoc Prof,* University of Southern California, School of Fine Arts, Los Angeles CA (S)

Malone, Delores, *Secy,* Fine Arts Museums of San Francisco, M H de Young Memorial Museum and California Palace of the Legion of Honor, San Francisco CA

Malone, Leslie, *Instr,* University of North Carolina at Charlotte, Dept of Visual Arts, Charlotte NC (S)

Malone, Peter, *Gallery Asst,* Kingsborough Community College, City University of New York, Art Gallery, Brooklyn NY

Malone, Robert R, *Head Printmaking,* Southern Illinois University at Edwardsville, Dept of Art & Design, Edwardsville IL (S)

Maloney, Irene, *Art Dir,* Montay College, Art Dept, Chicago IL (S)

Maloney, Kathleen, *Marketing & Public Relations Dir,* Intermedia Arts Minnesota, Minneapolis MN

Maloney, Leslie, *Curatorial Asst Preparator,* Phillips Academy, Addison Gallery of American Art, Andover MA

Maloney, Patricia, *Asst Prof,* Washington and Jefferson College, Art Dept, Washington PA (S)

Malt, Carol, *Dir,* Pensacola Museum of Art, Pensacola FL

Malt, Carol, *Dir,* Pensacola Museum of Art, Harry Thornton Library, Pensacola FL

Maltais, Marie, *Dir,* University of New Brunswick, Art Centre, Fredericton NB

Malus, Mary June, *Coordr,* Imperial Calcasieu Museum, Gibson Barham Gallery, Lake Charles LA

Malus, Mary June, *Coordr,* Imperial Calcasieu Museum, Gibson Library, Lake Charles LA

Mancoff, Debra, *Assoc Prof,* Beloit College, Dept of Art, Beloit WI (S)

Mancuso, Bill, *Dir of Permanent Coll,* Thiel College, Sampson Art Gallery, Greenville PA

Mandarino, Joseph, *Acting Assoc Dir Curatorial,* Royal Ontario Museum, Toronto ON

Mandaville, Erik, *Instr,* Houston Baptist University, Dept of Art, Houston TX (S)

Mandel, Gerry, *VPres,* Children's Art Foundation, Santa Cruz CA

Mandle, Roger, *Deputy Dir,* National Gallery of Art, Washington DC

Maneen, Thomas, *Instr,* Mohawk Valley Community College, Advertising Design and Production, Utica NY (S)

Manger, Barbara, *Lectr,* Cardinal Stritch College, Art Dept, Milwaukee WI (S)

Mangers, Marvin, *Gen Mgr,* Harold Warp Pioneer Village Foundation, Minden NE

Manhart, Marcia, *Dir,* Philbrook Museum of Art, Tulsa OK

Manhart, Thomas A, *Dir,* University of Tulsa, Alexandre Hogue Gallery, Tulsa OK

Manifold, Gregory, *Dir Marketing,* Arts United of Greater Fort Wayne, Fort Wayne IN

Manilla, Morton, *Chmn Educ Committee,* Toronto Art Therapy Institute, Toronto ON (S)

Maniscalco, Nelson R, *Chmn,* Cedar Crest College, Art Dept, Allentown PA (S)

Manley, Beverley, *Pres,* Arthur Manley Society, Tampa FL

Mann, Jack, *Assoc Prof,* Wittenberg University, Art Dept, Springfield OH (S)

Mann, John, *Dir Music & Video Business,* Art Institute of Fort Lauderdale, Fort Lauderdale FL (S)

Mann, Katinka, *Treas,* American Abstract Artists, New York NY

Mann, Lois, *Dir Development,* Dayton Art Institute, Dayton OH

Mann, Richard, *Admin Dir,* Allied Arts of Seattle, Inc, Seattle WA

Mann, Tina, *Instr,* William Woods-Westminster Colleges, Art Dept, Fulton MO (S)

Mann, Vivian B, *Cur of Judaica,* The Jewish Museum, New York NY

Mann, Vivian B, *Cur of Judaica,* The Jewish Museum, Library, New York NY

Mannheimer, Marc, *Asst Prof,* Bradford College, Creative Arts Division, Bradford MA (S)

Mannikka, Eleanor, *Instr,* University of Michigan, Ann Arbor, Dept of History of Art, Ann Arbor MI (S)

Manning, Larry, *Instructor,* Jefferson Davis Community College, Art Dept, Brewton AL (S)

Manning, Les, *Head Ceramics Studio,* Banff Centre for the Arts, Banff AB (S)

Manning, Mary, *Dir,* Minneapolis College of Art & Design, Library & Media Center, Minneapolis MN

Mano, Charlene, *Educ Coordr,* Wind Luke Asian Museum Memorial Foundation, Inc, Seattle WA

Manoogian, Richard, *Pres,* Detroit Institute of Arts, Founders Society, Detroit MI

Manos, George, *Asst to Dir of Music,* National Gallery of Art, Washington DC

Manriquez, Dion, *Asst Prof,* University of Wisconsin-Stout, Dept of Art & Design, Menomonie WI (S)

Mansell, A, *Chmn,* University of Western Ontario, Dept of Visual Arts, London ON (S)

Mansfield, Meribah, *Library Dir,* Public Library of Columbus and Franklin County, Columbus Metropolitan Library, Columbus OH

Mansfield, Pat, *Pres,* Surface Design Association, Inc, Oakland CA

Manson, Martha, *Instr,* Monterey Peninsula College, Art Dept, Monterey CA (S)

Manthorne, Katherine, *In Charge Art History,* University of Illinois, Urbana-Champaign, School of Art and Design, Champaign IL (S)

Mantin, Regina, *Cur Art,* New Brunswick Museum, Saint John NB

Manton, Jill, *Art Coordr,* San Francisco City & County Arts Commission, San Francisco CA

Mantz, Cheryl, *Instr,* Mount Mary College, Art Dept, Milwaukee WI (S)

Manuele, Lisa, *Instr,* Springfield College in Illinois, Dept of Art, Springfield IL (S)

Mapes, Maria, *Registrar,* California State University, Long Beach, University Art Museum, Long Beach CA

Mapp, Thomas, *Dir,* University of Chicago, Lorado Taft Midway Studios, Chicago IL

Mappus, Cynthia, *Public Information,* Carolina Art Association, Gibbes Museum of Art, Charleston SC

Mar, Louis, *Pres,* Coppini Academy of Fine Arts, San Antonio TX

Marak, L B, *Instr,* Humboldt State University, College of Arts & Humanities, Arcata CA (S)

Marandel, J Patrice, *Cur European Paintings,* Detroit Institute of Arts, Detroit MI

Marasco, Rose, *Chmn,* University of Southern Maine, Art Dept, Gorham ME (S)

March, Paula, *Membership Mgr,* Fine Arts Museums of San Francisco, The Museum Society, San Francisco CA

Marchand, Andre, *Dean Communication & Head Educative Serv,* Musee du Quebec, Quebec PQ

Marchant, Beverly, *Asst Prof,* La Salle University, Dept of Art, Philadelphia PA (S)

Marchese, James, *First VPres,* Art Centre of New Jersey, East Orange NJ (S)

Marchlinski, Mark, *Asst Prof,* University of Alabama in Huntsville, Dept of Art & Art History, Huntsville AL (S)

Marconi, Nello, *Chief Design & Production,* National Portrait Gallery, Washington DC

Marcou, George T, *Prof,* Catholic University of America, School of Architecture & Planning, Washington DC (S)

Marcum-Estes, Leah, *Dir,* Oak Ridge Art Center, Oak Ridge TN

Marcum-Estes, Leah, *Dir,* Oak Ridge Art Center, Library, Oak Ridge TN

Marcus, Evelyn, *Cur for Exhib,* Dartmouth College, Hood Museum of Art, Hanover NH

Marcus, James, *1st VChmn,* Guild Hall of East Hampton, Inc, Guild Hall Museum, East Hampton NY

Marcus, Susan Bass, *Artifact Center Cur,* Spertus Museum, Chicago IL

Marcus, Terry, *Librn,* Milwaukee Institute of Art Design, Library, Milwaukee WI

Marcusen, Richard B, *Instr,* Yavapai College, Visual & Performing Arts Division, Prescott AZ (S)

Marczuk, Katherine, *Dir,* Center on Contemporary Art, Seattle WA

Marden, Fred, *VPres,* Brookfield Craft Center, Inc, Gallery, Brookfield CT

Marder, Tod, *Assoc Prof,* Rutgers, the State University of New Jersey, Graduate Program in Art History, New Brunswick NJ (S)

Marecha, Lisa, *Instr,* Marylhurst College, Art Dept, Marylhurst OR (S)

Marein, Shirley, *Prof,* New York Institute of Technology, Fine Arts Dept, Old Westbury NY (S)

Margolin, Victor, *Chmn Dept Hist of Architecture & Art,* University of Illinois at Chicago, College of Architecture, Art and Urban Planning, Chicago IL (S)

Margulies, Stephen, *Cur Works on Paper,* University of Virginia, Bayly Art Museum, Charlottesville VA

Marichal, Flavia, *Cur Art,* University of Puerto Rico, Museum of Anthropology, History & Art, Rio Piedras PR

Marien, Mary, *Prof,* Syracuse University, Dept of Fine Arts (Art History), Syracuse NY (S)

Marin, Donna, *Dir,* Chatillon-DeMenil House Foundation, DeMenil Mansion, Saint Louis MO

Marin, Jim, *Dir,* Los Angeles Valley College, Art Gallery, Van Nuys CA

Marincola, Paula, *Gallery Dir,* Beaver College Art Gallery, Glenside PA

Maring, Joel, *Adj Cur Anthropology,* Southern Illinois University, University Museum, Carbondale IL

Marino, Charles, *Assoc Prof,* University of Southern Colorado, Belmont Campus, Dept of Art, Pueblo CO (S)

Marioni, Tom, *Dir,* Archives of MOCA (Museum of Conceptual Art), San Francisco CA

Marioni, Tom, *Dir,* Archives of MOCA (Museum of Conceptual Art), Library, San Francisco CA

Mariott, W B, *VPres,* Ventura County Historical Society Museum, Ventura CA

Mark, Joseph, *Instr,* Pennsylvania College of Technology, Dept of Design & Communiation Arts, Williamsport PA (S)

Mark, Peter, *Assoc Prof,* Wesleyan University, Art Dept, Middletown CT (S)

Mark, Phyllis, *VPres Publications,* Sculptors Guild, Inc, New York NY

Markey, Mary, *Supv,* Baltimore City Life Museums, Library, Baltimore MD

Marklay, Judy R, *Dir Development,* Public Art Fund, Inc, New York NY

Markman, Ronald, *Prof,* Indiana University, Bloomington, Henry Radford Hope School of Fine Arts, Bloomington IN (S)

Markoe, Glenn E, *Cur Classical, Near Eastern Art,* Cincinnati Museum Association, Cincinnati Art Museum, Cincinnati OH

Markovitz, Geraldine, *Assoc Cur Fine Arts,* Sunrise Museum, Inc, Sunrise Art Museum, Sunrise Children's Museum & Planatarium, Charleston WV

Markowski, Gene, *Adjunct Prof,* Trinity College, Art Dept, Washington DC (S)

Marks, Andrea, *Assoc Prof,* Oregon State University, Dept of Art, Corvallis OR (S)

Marks, Arthur S, *Chmn,* University of North Carolina at Chapel Hill, Art Dept, Chapel Hill NC (S)

Marks, Graham, *Head Ceramics Dept,* Cranbrook Academy of Art, Bloomfield Hills MI (S)

Marks, Judy, *Sr Dir,* American Institute of Architects, AIA Library & Archives, Washington DC

Marks, Robert C, *Dean,* Harrington Institute of Interior Design, Chicago IL (S)

Markson, Eileen, *Head Librn,* Bryn Mawr College, Art and Archaeology Library, Bryn Mawr PA

Markstein, Annabelle, *Asst to Dir,* Franchise Finance Corporation of America, The Fleischer Museum, Scottsdale AZ

Markusen, Tom, *Chmn,* State University of New York College at Brockport, Dept of Art & Art History, Brockport NY (S)

Marlais, Michael, *Assoc Prof,* Colby College, Art Dept, Waterville ME (S)

Marlier, Rita, *Adjunct Instr,* Old Dominion University, Art Dept, Norfolk VA (S)

Marlin, W, *Prof,* Camden County College, Dept of Art, Blackwood NJ (S)

Marling, Karal Ann, *Prof,* University of Minnesota, Minneapolis, Art History, Minneapolis MN (S)

Marlowe, Claudia, *Library Asst,* San Francisco Art Institute, Anne Bremer Memorial Library, San Francisco CA

Marmor, Max, *Reference Librn,* New York University, Stephen Chan Library of Fine Arts, New York NY

Marohn, Pat, *Dir,* Santa Cruz Valley Art Association, Tubac Center of the Arts, Tubac AZ

Marotta, Joseph, *Chmn,* University of Utah, Art Dept, Salt Lake City UT (S)

Marquardt, Bonnie, *Dir,* Moody County Historical Society, Flandreau SD

Marquardt-Cherry, Janet, *Chmn,* University of South Florida, Art Dept, Tampa FL (S)

Marquardt-Cherry, Janet, *Assoc Prof,* Eastern Illinois University, Art Dept, Charleston IL (S)

Marquet, Cynthia, *Librn,* Historical Society of the Cocalico Valley, Ephrata PA

Marra, Mary Ella, *Gallery Dir,* Kutztown University, Sharadin Art Gallery, Kutztown PA

Marriott, William, *Foundation,* University of Georgia, Franklin College of Arts & Sciences, Dept of Art, Athens GA (S)

Marron, Donald B, *VChmn,* Museum of Modern Art, New York NY

Marron, Donald B, *Pres,* Paine Webber Inc, New York NY

Marrow, James, *Prof,* Princeton University, Dept of Art and Archaeology, Princeton NJ (S)

Mars, Robert E, *Exec VPres Admin Affairs,* The Art Institute of Chicago, Chicago IL

Marschlek, Doug, *Assoc Prof,* University of Wisconsin, Madison, Dept of Art, Madison WI (S)

Marsden, Lorna, *Pres,* Wilfrid Laurier Univer2ity, Art Gallery, Waterloo ON

Marsden-Atlass, Lynn, *Asst Dir,* Colby College, Musuem of Art, Waterville ME

Marsh, Elizabeth D, *Librn,* Eastern Shore Art Association, Inc, Library, Fairhope AL

Marsh, Julie Brown, *Public Relations,* Huntington Museum of Art, Huntington WV

Marsh, Pricilla, *VPres,* Lubbock Art Association, Inc, Lubbock TX

Marsh, Robert, *Prof,* Averett College, Art Dept, Danville VA (S)

Marsh, Stephen, *Prog Mgr,* Daytona Beach Community College, Dept of Fine Arts & Visual Arts, Daytona Beach FL (S)

Marsh, Steve, *Deputy Dir,* Mint Museum of Art, Charlotte NC

Marshall, Ann, *Asst Dir,* Heard Museum, Phoenix AZ

Marshall, Don, *VPres & Exec Dir,* St Tammany Art Association, Covington LA

Marshall, Gordon, *Asst Librn,* Library Company of Philadelphia, Print Dept, Philadelphia PA

Marshall, Grant, *Head Dept Interior Design,* University of Manitoba, Faculty of Architecture, Winnipeg MB (S)

Marshall, Howard, *Prof,* University of Missouri, Art History and Archaeology Dept, Columbia MO (S)

Marshall, Lane L, *Dean,* Kansas State University, College of Architecture and Design, Manhattan KS (S)

Marshall, Nancy, *Lectr,* Emory University, Art History Dept, Atlanta GA (S)

Marshall, Rhoda, *Exec Dir,* Art Directors Club, Inc, New York NY

Marshall, Richard, *Cur,* Whitney Museum of American Art, New York NY

Marshall, Robert, *Chmn,* Brigham Young University, Dept of Art, Provo UT (S)

Marshall, Thomas, *Chmn,* Barton College, Communication, Performaing & Visual Arts, Wilson NC (S)

Marshall, W, *Pres of Bd,* Hermitage Foundation Museum, Norfolk VA

Marshall, William J, *Dir Special Collections & Archives,* University of Kentucky, Photographic Archives, Lexington KY

Marshman, Robert, *Assoc Prof,* University of West Florida, Dept of Art, Pensacola FL (S)

Marsolais, Gilles, *Instr,* Universite de Montreal, Dept of Art History, Montreal PQ (S)

Martel, Jean, *Admin Dir,* Ottawa Public Library, Fine Arts Dept, Ottawa ON

Martell, Charles, *Dean,* California State University at Sacramento, Library - Humanities Reference Dept, Sacramento CA

Marteney, Susan, *Educ Coordr,* Schweinfurth Art Center, Auburn NY

Marter, Joan, *Prof,* Rutgers, the State University of New Jersey, Graduate Program in Art History, New Brunswick NJ (S)

Martin, Anna, *Asst Prof,* University of Northern Iowa, Dept of Art, Cedar Falls IA (S)

Martin, Don, *Assoc Prof,* Flagler College, Visual Arts Dept, Saint Augustine FL (S)

Martin, Edeen, *Pres,* Mid-America Arts Alliance & Exhibits USA, Kansas City MO

Martin, Francis, *Acting Chmn,* University of Central Florida, Art Dept, Orlando FL (S)

Martin, Frank, *Instr,* Chautauqua Institution, School of Art, Chautauqua NY (S)

Martin, Frank, *Cur Colls & Exhib,* South Carolina State University, Art Dept, Orangeburg SC (S)

Martin, Gaylene, *Dir,* Turtle Mountain Chippewa Historical Society, Turtle Mountain Heritage Center, Belcourt ND

Martin, I A, *Chief Exec Officer,* The Pillsbury Company, Art Collection, Minneapolis MN

Martin, Jane, *VPres & Dir,* Saint Mary's Romanian Orthodox Church, Romanian Ethnic Museum, Cleveland OH

Martin, Jean, *Dir,* Farmington Village Green and Library Association, Stanley-Whitman House, Farmington CT

Martin, Jeff, *Dir & Exhib Coordr,* Parkersburg Art Center, Parkersburg WV

Martin, Jeff, *Registrar,* University of Iowa, Museum of Art, Iowa City IA

Martin, Jeffry, *Exec Dir,* Parkersburg Art Center, Art Center, Parkersburg WV

Martin, Jerry P, *Gift Shop Mgr & Tours,* Mid-America All-Indian Center, Wichita KS

Martin, Jerry P, *Dir,* Mid-America All-Indian Center, Library, Wichita KS

Martin, Julie, *Asst Librn,* Dayton Art Institute, Library, Dayton OH

Martin, Kathryn, *Dean,* University of Illinois, Urbana-Champaign, College of Fine and Applied Arts, Champaign IL (S)

Martin, Kenneth, *Instr,* Campbellsville College, Fine Arts Division, Campbellsville KY (S)

Martin, Linda, *Development Dir,* Headlands Center for the Arts, Sausalito CA

Martin, Linda, *Adminr,* Malaspina College, Nanaimo Art Gallery & Exhibition Centre, Nanaimo BC

Martin, Lori, *Instr,* Sterling College, Art Dept, Sterling KS (S)

Martin, Marie, *Gallery Coordr,* National Center on Arts & Aging-National Council on The Aging, NCOA Gallery Patina, Washington DC

Martin, Martha, *Instr,* Main Line Center for the Arts, Haverford PA (S)

Martin, Martha Kent, *Instr,* Main Line Center for the Arts, Haverford PA (S)

Martin, Mary Hyde, *Pres,* Klamath Falls Art Association, Klamath Art Gallery, Klamath Falls OR

Martin, Michel, *Conservator Contemporary Art,* Musee du Quebec, Quebec PQ

Martin, Patsy, *Admin Asst,* Columbia Museum of Art, Columbia SC

Martin, Peter, *Asst Prof,* College of Associated Arts, Saint Paul MN (S)

Martin, Phil, *Dir,* Angelo State University, Houston Harte University Center, San Angelo TX

Martin, Polly, *Instr,* Chautauqua Institution, School of Art, Chautauqua NY (S)

Martin, Rachael E, *Exec Dir,* Douglas County Historical Society, Fairlawn Mansion & Museum, Superior WI

Martin, Ray, *Prof,* School of the Art Institute of Chicago, Chicago IL (S)

Martin, Richard, *Dir,* Fashion Institute of Technology Galleries, New York NY

Martin, Richard, *Cur Costume Institute,* The Metropolitan Museum of Art, New York NY

Martin, Rita, *Sales,* Turtle Mountain Chippewa Historical Society, Turtle Mountain Heritage Center, Belcourt ND

Martin, Rosemary H, *Exec Dir,* Associated Artists of Winston-Salem, Winston-Salem NC

Martin, Roy B, *Pres of Board of Trustees,* Chrysler Museum, Norfolk VA

Martin, Terry, *Instr,* William Woods-Westminster Colleges, Art Dept, Fulton MO (S)

Martin, Terry, *Instr,* Salt Lake Community College, Graphic Design Dept, Salt Lake City UT (S)

Martin, Thomas, *Assoc Prof,* New York Institute of Technology, Fine Arts Dept, Old Westbury NY (S)

Martin, Tony, *Acting Dir,* Idaho State University, John B Davis Gallery of Fine Art, Pocatello ID

Martin, Tony, *Faculty,* Idaho State University, Dept of Art, Pocatello ID (S)

Martin, Vernon, *Dept Head,* Hartford Public Library, Art Dept, Hartford CT

Martin, William J, *Dir,* The City of Petersburg Museums, Petersburg VA

Martinez, Albert, *Dir,* Ghost Ranch Living Museum, Abiquiu NM

Martinez, Diego, *Environmental Educ,* Ghost Ranch Living Museum, Abiquiu NM

Martinez, Ed W, *Chmn Dept,* University of Nevada, Reno, Art Dept, Reno NV (S)

Martinez, Juan, *Instr & Art Historian,* Florida International University, Visual Arts Dept, Miami FL (S)

Martinez, Katharine, *Research Librn of American Painting,* Winterthur Museum and Gardens, Library, Winterthur DE

Martinez, Larry, *Pres,* Taos Art Association Inc, Stables Art Center, Taos NM

Martinez, Laura, *Librn,* Fort Worth Art Association, Modern Art Museum of Fort Worth, Fort Worth TX

Martinez, Laura, *Librn,* Fort Worth Art Association, Library, Fort Worth TX

Martinez, Manual, *Instr,* Cochise College, Art Dept, Douglas AZ (S)

Martinez, Rick, *Gallery Dir,* Southern Oregon State College, Central Art Gallery, Ashland OR

Martinez, Rosita, *Chmn,* Valencia Community College - West Campus, Art Dept, Orlando FL (S)

Martinez, Vincente, *Asst Cur Exhib,* Millicent Rogers Museum, Taos NM

Martin-Felton, Zora, *Acting Dir Educ & Research,* Anacostia Museum, Washington DC

Martins, Michael, *Cur,* Fall River Historical Society, Fall River MA

Martyka, Paul, *Assoc Prof,* Winthrop College, Dept of Art & Design, Rock Hill SC (S)

Martz, Jean-Marie, *Chmn Dance,* Idyllwild School of Music and the Arts, Idyllwild CA (S)

Martz, Jim, *Acquisition Dir,* Dickinson State University, Stoxen Library, Dickinson ND

Martz, Mary J, *Handicapped Services Coordr,* Cultural Affairs Department City of Los Angeles, Junior Arts Center, Los Angeles CA

Marvin, Anne, *Cur Fine Art,* Kansas State Historical Society, Kansas Museum of History, Topeka KS

Marvin, Miranola, *Prof,* Wellesley College, Art Dept, Wellesley MA (S)

Marwah, Armarjit S, *Pres Cultural Heritage Commission,* City of Los Angeles, Cultural Affairs Dept, Los Angeles CA

Marx, Robert, *Exec Dir,* The New York Public Library, Shelby Cullom Davis Museum, New York NY

Marxhausen, Reinhold P, *Prof,* Concordia College, Art Dept, Seward NE (S)

Marzio, Peter C, *Dir,* Museum of Fine Arts, Houston, Houston TX

Marzo, Janet, *Cur,* Nassau Community College, Firehouse Art Gallery, Garden City NY

Marzolf, Helen, *Dir & Cur,* Regina Public Library, Dunlop Art Gallery, Regina SK

Masel, Marjorie, *Prof,* Seattle University, Fine Arts Dept, Division of Art, Seattle WA (S)

Mashiko, M, *VPres Admissions,* Sculptors Guild, Inc, New York NY

Masich, Andrew E, *VPres,* Colorado Historical Society, Museum, Denver CO

Maskerman, Dawn, *Admin Asst,* Schweinfurth Art Center, Auburn NY

Mason, Bonnie C, *Cur of Educ,* Miami University Art Museum, Oxford OH

Mason, Charles E, *Honorary Cur of Prints,* Boston Athenaeum, Boston MA

Mason, Glenn, *Dir,* Eastern Washington State Historical Society, Cheney Cowles Museum, Spokane WA

Mason, Henri, *Dir,* Drew County Historical Society, Museum, Monticello AR

Mason, Jeffrey, *Chmn,* California State University, Bakersfield, Fine Arts Dept, Bakersfield CA (S)

Mason, Joel, *Chmn,* New York City Technical College of the City University of New York, Dept of Art and Advertising Design, Brooklyn NY (S)

Mason, Kathleen, *Dir Human Resources,* Indianapolis Museum of Art, Indianapolis IN

Mason, Marilyn Gell, *Dir,* Cleveland Public Library, Fine Arts & Special Collections Dept, Cleveland OH

Mason, Molly, *Asst Prof,* State University of New York at Stony Brook, Art Dept, Stony Brook NY (S)

Mason, Penelope E, *Assoc Prof,* Florida State University, Art History Dept (R133B), Tallahassee FL (S)

Massar, Phyllis, *Arts & Media Supvr,* Ferguson Library, Stamford CT

Massaroni, Dino, *Instr,* Cuyahoga Valley Art Center, Cuyahoga Falls OH (S)

Massarsky, Tara, *Asst Librn,* Solomon R Guggenheim Museum, New York NY

Massarsky, Tara, *Asst Librn,* Solomon R Guggenheim Museum, Library, New York NY

Massey, Bryan, *Asst Prof,* University of Central Arkansas, Art Dept, Conway AR (S)

Massidda, Mary, *Pres,* Springfield Art League, Springfield MA

Massie-Lane, Rebecca, *Dir,* Sweet Briar College, Art Gallery, Sweet Briar VA

Massier, John, *Asst Cur,* Jewish Community Centre of Toronto, The Koffler Gallery, North York ON

Massing, Peter, *Prof,* Marshall University, Dept of Art, Huntington WV (S)

Masson, Ann M, *Dir,* Tulane University, Gallier House Museum, New Orleans LA

Mastai, Judith, *Head Public Progs,* Vancouver Art Gallery, Vancouver BC

Masteller, Barry, *Co-Dir,* Pacific Grove Art Center, Pacific Grove CA

Master-Karnik, Paul, *Dir,* DeCordova Museum & Sculpture Park, Lincoln MA

Masterson, Judith P, *Gallery Coordr,* Trenton State College, College Art Gallery, Trenton NJ

Masterson, Nancy, *Color & Graphic Instr,* Hutchinson Community Junior College, Visual Arts Dept, Hutchinson KS (S)

Mastin, Catharine, *Cur,* Art Gallery of Windsor, Windsor ON

Mates, Judy, *Instr,* Joe Kubert School of Cartoon & Graphic Art, Inc, Dover NJ (S)

Mather, Charles E, *Pres,* Fairmount Park Art Association, Philadelphia PA

Matherly, John, *Tech,* Hudson River Museum, Yonkers NY

Matheson, Susan, *Assoc Cur Ancient Art,* Yale University, Art Gallery, New Haven CT

Mathews, Edgar H H, *Cur Museum Educ,* Florida State University Foundation - Central Florida Community College Foundation, The Appleton Museum of Art, Ocala FL

Mathews, John, *Instr,* Bucks County Community College, Fine Arts Dept, Newtown PA (S)

Mathews, Nancy Mowll, *Prendergast Cur,* Williams College, Museum of Art, Williamstown MA

Mathews, Patricia, *Assoc Prof,* Oberlin College, Dept of Art, Oberlin OH (S)

Mathis, Doyle, *VPres,* Berry College, Moon Gallery, Mount Berry GA

Matilsky, Barbara, *Cur,* The Queens Museum of Art, Flushing NY

Mato, Nancy, *Deputy Dir,* The Society of the Four Arts, Palm Beach FL

Matson, Isabel, *Asst to Dir,* Wayne Center for the Arts, Wooster OH

Matson, Mellisa, *Educ,* Edgecombe County Cultural Arts Council, Inc, Blount-Bridgers House, Hobson Pittman Memorial Gallery, Tarboro NC

Matsumoto, Moritaka, *Assoc Prof,* University of British Columbia, Dept of Fine Arts, Vancouver BC (S)

Mattecheck, Marianna, *1st VPres Board,* Coos Art Museum, Coos Bay OR

Matter, Mercedes, *Instr,* New York Studio School of Drawing, Painting and Sculpture, New York NY (S)

Matteson, Charles C, *Chmn Art Dept,* State University of New York, Agricultural and Technical College, Art Dept, Cobleskill NY (S)

Matteson, Lynn, *Dean,* University of Southern California, School of Fine Arts, Los Angeles CA (S)

Matthews, Bill, *Exhibit Specialist,* Headquarters Fort Monroe, Dept of Army, Casemate Museum, Fort Monroe VA

Matthews, Eugene, *Assoc Chmn,* University of Colorado, Boulder, Dept of Fine Arts, Boulder CO (S)

Matthews, Gail, *Cur Community Servs,* University of South Carolina, McKissick Museum, Columbia SC

Matthews, Harriett, *Prof,* Colby College, Art Dept, Waterville ME (S)

Matthews, Henry, *Asst Dir & Cur Coll & Exhib,* Muskegon Museum of Art, Muskegon MI

Matthews, Julia, *Head Librn,* Royal Ontario Museum, Library & Archives, Toronto ON

Matthews, T, *VPres,* University of Victoria, Maltwood Art Museum and Gallery, Victoria BC

Matthias, Diana, *Coordr Community Prog,* University of Notre Dame, Snite Museum of Art, Notre Dame IN

Matthias, Susan M, *Assoc Prof,* Indiana University-Southeast, Fine Arts Dept, New Albany IN (S)

Mattison, Robert S, *Dept Head,* Lafayette College, Dept of Art, Easton PA (S)

Mattson, J C, *Site Supv III,* Fort Totten State Historic Site, Pioneer Daughters Museum, Fort Totten ND

Mattson, Robert, *Staff,* Willmar Community College, Willmar MN (S)

Mattusch, Carol C, *Prof,* George Mason University, Dept of Art & Art History, Fairfax VA (S)

Mattys, Joe, *Assoc Prof,* Randolph-Macon College, Dept of the Arts, Ashland VA (S)

Matuszawski, Fred, *Pres,* Manchester Historic Association, Manchester NH

Mauck, Marchita, *Prof,* Louisiana State University, School of Art, Baton Rouge LA (S)

Maudlin-Jeronimo, John, *Exec Dir,* National Architectural Accrediting Board, Inc, Washington DC

Mauer, Ernest, *Prof Emeriti,* Old Dominion University, Art Dept, Norfolk VA (S)

Mauersberger, George, *Assoc Prof,* Cleveland State University, Art Dept, Cleveland OH (S)

Maughan, William, *Co Chair Fine Art,* Academy of Art College, Fine Arts Dept, San Francisco CA (S)

Mauldin, Barbara, *Cur American & Latin American Coll,* Museum of New Mexico, Museum of International Folk Art, Santa Fe NM

Mauldin, Estelle M, *Pres,* The Museum, Greenwood SC

Mauner, George L, *Prof,* Pennsylvania State University, University Park, Dept of Art History, University Park PA (S)

Mauren, Paul, *Assoc Prof,* College of Saint Rose, Dept of Art, Albany NY (S)

Maurer, Evan, *Dir,* Minneapolis Society of Fine Arts, Minneapolis Institute of Arts, Minneapolis MN

Maurer, Neil, *Assoc Prof,* University of Texas at San Antonio, Division of Art & Architecture, San Antonio TX (S)

Maurer, Sherry C, *Gallery Dir,* Augustana College, Art Gallery, Rock Island IL

Mauro, Robert, *Assoc Prof,* Beaver College, Dept of Fine Arts, Glenside PA (S)

Maveety, Patrick, *Cur of Oriental Art,* Stanford University, Art Gallery, Stanford CA

Mavigliano, George, *Assoc Prof,* Southern Illinois University, School of Art & Design, Carbondale IL (S)

Mavor, Carol, *Asst Prof,* University of North Carolina at Chapel Hill, Art Dept, Chapel Hill NC (S)

Mavrogenes, Sylvia, *Youth Serv Adminr,* Miami-Dade Public Library, Miami FL

Maw, Nicholas, *Instr,* Bard College, Milton Avery Graduate School of the Arts, Annandale-on-Hudson NY (S)

Mawdsley, Richard, *Prof,* Southern Illinois University, School of Art & Design, Carbondale IL (S)

Maxwell, Allan, *Prof,* Daytona Beach Community College, Dept of Fine Arts & Visual Arts, Daytona Beach FL (S)

Maxwell, Howard, *College Pres,* Girard College, Stephen Girard Collection, Philadelphia PA

Maxwell, James, *Prog Coordr,* Mendocino Art Center, Mendocino CA (S)

Maxwell, Kathleen, *Lectr,* Santa Clara University, Art Dept, Santa Clara CA (S)

Maxwell, K C, *Assoc Prof,* Shoreline Community College, Humanities Division, Seattle WA (S)

Maxwell, Margaret, *VPres,* Children's Museum, Rauh Memorial Library, Indianapolis IN

Maxwell, Melanie, *Media Relation Specialist,* Indiana State Museum, Indianapolis IN

Maxwell, Stephanie, *Asst Prof,* Rochester Institute of Technology, School of Photographic Arts & Sciences, Rochester NY (S)

Maxwell, William C, *Chmn,* College of New Rochelle School of Arts and Sciences, Art Dept, New Rochelle NY (S)

May, D L, *Instr,* Andrews University, Dept of Art, Art History & Design, Berrien Springs MI (S)

May, Hayden B, *Dean School Fine Arts,* Miami University, Art Dept, Oxford OH (S)

May, James E, *Gallery Asst,* Indiana University - Purdue University at Indianapolis, Indianapolis Center for Contemporary Art-Herron Gallery, Indianapolis IN

May, James M, *Asst Prof,* University of Nebraska, Kearney, Dept of Art & Art History, Kearney NE (S)

May, Larry, *Instr,* Art Academy of Cincinnati, Cincinnati OH (S)

May, Robert E, *Pres,* Woodmere Art Museum, Philadelphia PA

May, Wally, *Prog Coordr Sculpture,* Alberta College of Art, Calgary AB (S)

Maya, Gloria, *Prof,* Western New Mexico University, Dept of Expressive Arts, Silver City NM (S)

Maybank, Mary Rose, *Dir of Fellows & Special Programs,* Harvard University, Harvard University Art Museums, Cambridge MA

Mayberry, Alberta, *Dir Library,* Langston University, Melvin B Tolson Black Heritage Center, Langston OK

Mayer, Carol, *Cur Collections,* University of British Columbia, Museum of Anthropology, Vancouver BC

Mayer, Edward, *Prof,* State University of New York at Albany, Art Dept, Albany NY (S)

Mayer, Ernest, *Photographer,* Winnipeg Art Gallery, Winnipeg MB

Mayer, Jesse, *Treas,* Essex Art Association, Inc, Essex CT

Mayer, John, *Dir,* Manchester Historic Association, Manchester NH

Mayer, Lance, *Conservator,* Lyman Allyn Art Museum, New London CT

Mayer, Robert, *Pres,* Cleveland Institute of Art, Cleveland Art Association, Cleveland OH

Mayer, Robert A, *Pres,* Cleveland Institute of Art, Reinberger Galleries, Cleveland OH

Mayer, Robert A, *Pres,* Cleveland Institute of Art, Cleveland OH (S)

Mayer, Roger, *Chmn,* Brown University, Dept of Visual Art, Providence RI (S)

Mayer, Susan M, *Educational Coordr,* University of Texas at Austin, Archer M Huntington Art Gallery, Austin TX

Mayer, William, *Chmn,* Hope College, Art Dept, Holland MI (S)

Mayes, Bud, *Dir,* Wilkes Community College, Arts and Science Division, Wilkesboro NC (S)

Mayes, Stephen L, *Dir,* Arkansas State University-Art Department, Jonesboro, Fine Arts Center Gallery, Jonesboro AR

Mayes, Steven L, *Prof,* Arkansas State University, Dept of Art, Jonesboro AR (S)

Mayfield, Signe, *Cur,* Palo Alto Cultural Center, Palo Alto CA

Mayfield, Stephen, *Member Secy,* Art Museum of Southeast Texas, Beaumont TX

Mayhall, Dorothy, *Dir of Art,* Stamford Museum and Nature Center, Stamford CT

Maylone, R Russell, *Head Special Art Library,* Northwestern University, Art Library, Evanston IL

Maynihan, William J, *Dir,* American Museum of Natural History, New York NY

Mayo, David, *Exhib Designer,* University of California, Los Angeles, Fowler Museum of Cultural History, Los Angeles CA

Mayo, Marti, *Dir,* University of Houston, Sarah Campbell Blaffer Gallery, Houston TX

Mayor, Babette, *Asst Prof,* California State Polytechnic University, Pomona, Art Dept, Pomona CA (S)

Mayor, Robin, *Pres,* Alberta College of Art, Calgary AB (S)

Mays, Clarence C, *Chmn Div Human,* Virginia Western Community College, Commercial Art, Fine Art & Photography, Roanoke VA (S)

Mays, Shirley, *Librn,* Independence National Historical Park, Library, Philadelphia PA

Mazanowski V, Ron, *Div Coordr,* Northern Illinois University, School of Art, De Kalb IL (S)

Maze, Clarence, *Pres,* Richard Bland College, Art Dept, Petersburg VA (S)

Mazeika, George, *Registrar,* University of Connecticut, William Benton Museum of Art - Connecticut's State Art Museum, Storrs CT

Mazonowicz, Douglas, *Dir,* Gallery of Prehistoric Paintings, New York NY

Mazonowicz, Douglas, *Dir,* Gallery of Prehistoric Paintings, Library, New York NY

Mazur, Jim, *Preparator,* Marquette University, Haggerty Museum of Art, Milwaukee WI

Mazur, Robert, *Chmn 2-D Studies,* Bowling Green State University, School of Art, Bowling Green OH (S)

Mazur, Susan, *Libr Technical Asst II,* University of Maryland, College Park, Art Library, College Park MD

McAdams, Jean, *Librn,* Washington Art Association, Library, Washington Depot CT

McAdams, Margaret, *Asst Prof,* Ohio University-Chillicothe Campus, Fine Arts & Humanities Division, Chillicothe OH (S)

McAfee, Michael J, *Cur History,* United States Military Academy, West Point Museum, West Point NY

McAleer, P, *Instr,* Technical University of Nova Scotia, Faculty of Architecture, Halifax NS (S)

McAlister, Judith, *Cur,* Adams National Historic Site, Quincy MA

McAlister, Richard A, *Assoc Prof,* Providence College, Art and Art History Dept, Providence RI (S)

McAllister, Gerry, *Dir,* University of California-San Diego, Mandeville Gallery, La Jolla CA

McAllister, Lowell, *Dir,* Frederic Remington Art Museum, Ogdensburg NY

McAllister, Lowell, *Exec Dir,* Frederic Remington Art Museum, Library, Ogdensburg NY

McAllister, Michael, *Chmn Dept,* North Carolina Wesleyan College, Dept of Visual & Performing Arts, Rocky Mount NC (S)

McAllister, Sue, *First VPres,* Brown County Art Gallery Association Inc, Nashville IN

McAlpine, D, *Head Natural Sciences,* New Brunswick Museum, Saint John NB

McArt, Craig, *Prof,* Rochester Institute of Technology, School of Art and Design, Rochester NY (S)

McArthur, Seonaid, *Educ Cur,* Museum of Contemporary Art, San Diego, La Jolla CA

McAusland, Randyy, *Deputy Chmn for Programs,* National Endowment for the Arts, Washington DC

McAvity, John G, *Exec Dir,* Canadian Museums Association, Association des Musees Canadiens, Ottawa ON

McBeth, James, *Cur,* Lightner Museum, Saint Augustine FL

McBeth, James R, *Chmn,* Weber State University, Dept of Visual Arts, Ogden UT (S)

McBoggs, Mayo, *Assoc Prof,* Converse College, Art Dept, Spartanburg SC (S)

McBratney-Stapleton, Deborah, *Exec Dir,*
Anderson Fine Arts Center, Anderson IN

McBride, Carolyn N, *Secy,* National Hall of Fame
for Famous American Indians, Anadarko OK

McBride, Joe, *Dir & Exec VPres,* National Hall of
Fame for Famous American Indians, Anadarko
OK

McBride, Peggy, *Reference Librn,* University of
British Columbia, Fine Arts Library, Vancouver
BC

McCabe, Mary Kennedy, *Exec Dir,* Mid-America
Arts Alliance & Exhibits USA, Kansas City MO

McCabe, Maureen, *Prof,* Connecticut College, Dept
of Art, New London CT (S)

McCabe, Michael, *Librn,* Brevard College, James A
Jones Library, Brevard NC

McCabe, Monica, *Exhib Coordr,* Middlebury
College, Museum of Art, Middlebury VT

McCabe, Nancy, *Development Officer,* John Simon
Guggenheim Memorial Foundation, New York
NY

McCabe, Sharon, *Business Mgr,* Montana Historical
Society, Helena MT

McCafferty, Jay, *Instructor,* Los Angeles Harbor
College, Art Dept, Wilmington CA (S)

McCaffrey, Kristi, *Secy,* National Art Museum of
Sport, Indianapolis IN

McCaffrey, Morra, *Cur Ethnology,* McCord
Museum of Canadian History, Montreal PQ

McCain, Diana, *Public Information Officer,*
Connecticut Historical Society, Hartford CT

McCalister, Lonnie, *Chmn,* Lee College, Dept of
Music & Fine Arts, Cleveland TN (S)

McCallig, Patrick, *VPres,* Museum of Holography -
Chicago, Chicago IL

McCallister, Sandra, *Asst Prof,* Southwest Texas
State University, Dept of Art, San Marcos TX
(S)

McCallum, Charles, *Pres,* University of Alabama at
Birmingham, Visual Arts Gallery, Birmingham
AL

McCallum, David, *VPres,* Artists' Cooperative
Gallery, Omaha NE

McCallum, Tracy, *Librn,* University of New
Mexico, Library, Taos NM

McCampbell, Jerry, *Chmn Math & Science,*
Idyllwild School of Music and the Arts, Idyllwild
CA (S)

McCann, Michael, *Exec Dir,* Center for Safety in
the Arts, Art Hazards Information Center, New
York NY

McCann, Ted, *Co-Dir,* Carnegie Mellon University,
Forbes Gallery, Pittsburgh PA

McCardell/PhD, Nora, *Dir Student Services,*
Ontario College of Art, Toronto ON

McCargish, Lori, *Dir,* Acme Art Co, Columbus OH

McCarren, Paul, *Instr,* Georgetown University,
Dept of Fine Arts, Washington DC (S)

McCarroll, B J, *Chmn,* University of Lethbridge,
Dept of Art, Lethbridge AB (S)

McCarter, Mickey, *Undergrad Coordr,* University
of North Texas, School of Visual Arts, Denton
TX (S)

McCarter, Robert, *Chmn Div Architecture,*
Columbia University, Graduate School of
Architecture, Planning & Preservation, New
York NY (S)

McCarthy, Frank, *Corp Council,* North Central Life
Insurance Company, Art Collection, Saint Paul
MN

McCarthy, John R, *Treas,* Artists' Fellowship, Inc,
New York NY

McCarthy, Kevin, *Dir of Personnel,* Ferguson
Library, Stamford CT

McCarthy, Meg, *Educ,* American Association of
Museums, International Council of Museums
Committee, Washington DC

McCarthy, Paul H, *Dir,* University of Alaska,
Elmer E Rasmuson Library, Fairbanks AK

McCarthy, Rita, *Cur,* Loyola University of Chicago,
Martin D'Arcy Gallery of Art, Chicago IL

McCarthy, Rita, *Cur,* Loyola University of Chicago,
Library, Chicago IL

McCartney, Henry, *Dir,* Landmark Society of
Western New York, Inc, Rochester NY

McCarty, Gayle, *Dir,* Hinds Junior College District,
Marie Hull Gallery, Raymond MS

McCarty, Ruth, *Pres,* Marin Society of Artists Inc,
Ross CA

McCaslin, Jack, *Prof,* James Madison University,
Dept of Art, Harrisonburg VA (S)

McCaulay, Janet, *Mgr Arts Center,* Arts United of
Greater Fort Wayne, Fort Wayne IN

McCauley, Ann, *Asst Prof,* University of
Massachusetts at Boston, Art Dept, Boston MA
(S)

McCauley, David, *Asst Dir,* Kern County Museum,
Bakersfield CA

McCauley, Joan E, *Group Leader Humanities of
Fine Arts,* California State University, Long
Beach, University Library, Long Beach CA

McCauley, Robert N, *Chmn Dept Fine Arts,*
Rockford College, Dept of Fine Arts, Rockford
IL (S)

McClain, Bruce, *Chmn,* Gustavus Adolphus
College, Art & Art History Dept, Saint Peter
MN (S)

McClain, Sam, *Treas,* Alaska Artists' Guild,
Anchorage AK

McClanahan, John D, *Chmn & Prof,* Baylor
University, Dept of Art, Waco TX (S)

McClary, Kathleen, *Cur Flat Textiles,* Indiana State
Museum, Indianapolis IN

McClary, Larry, *Drawing,* California College of
Arts and Crafts, Oakland CA (S)

McCleary, M Cecile, *Museum Supv,* City of
Lethbridge, Sir Alexander Galt Museum,
Lethbridge AB

McCleery, Steve, *Dean,* New Mexico Junior
College, Arts & Sciences, Hobbs NM (S)

McClellan, Douglas, *Chmn,* University of
California, Santa Cruz, Board of Studies in Art,
Santa Cruz CA (S)

McClellan, Lynette, *Cur,* Gananoque Historical
Museum, Gananoque ON

McClellan, Nancy, *Exec Dir,* Firehouse Art Center,
Norman OK

McClemey-Brooker, Cheryl, *VPres External Affairs,*
Philadelphia Museum of Art, Philadelphia PA

McCloat, Elizabeth, *Dir,* Bryant Library, Roslyn
NY

McClure, Dorothy, *Public Relations Dir,* Memphis
Brooks Museum of Art, Memphis TN

McClure, Michael, *Dir CE,* Art Institute of
Houston, Houston TX (S)

McCluskey, Holly, *Cur of Educ,* Oglebay Institute,
Mansion Museum, Wheeling WV

McComb, Ronald G, *Librn,* Cornish College of the
Arts, Cornish Library, Seattle WA

McCombs, Bruce, *Assoc Prof,* Hope College, Art
Dept, Holland MI (S)

McCommons, Richard, *Exec Dir,* Association of
Collegiate Schools of Architecture, Washington
DC

McConathy, Deirdre, *Asst Prof,* University of
Illinois, Chicago, Health Science Center,
Biomedical Visualizations, Chicago IL (S)

McConnaughy, James, *Treas,* National Antique &
Art Dealers Association of America, New York
NY

McConnell, Mary Apple, *Chmn Dept,* Texas
Wesleyan University, Dept of Art, Fort Worth
TX (S)

McConnell, Michael, *Prof,* University of New
Hampshire, Dept of the Arts, Durham NH (S)

McCool, Gary, *Coordr Public Servs,* Plymouth
State College, Herbert H Lamson Library,
Plymouth NH

McCormic, Mickie, *Dir,* Oysterponds Historical
Society, Museum, Orient NY

McCormick, Cathy, *Second VPres Exhib,* Arizona
Artist Guild, Phoenix AZ

McCormick, Charles James, *Chmn,* Georgetown
College, Art Dept, Georgetown KY (S)

McCormick, Daniel Y, *Operations & Finance,*
International Museum of Photography at George
Eastman House, Rochester NY

McCormick, Donald, *Recordings Cur,* The New
York Public Library, Shelby Cullom Davis
Museum, New York NY

McCormick, James, *Chmn,* Georgetown College
Gallery, Georgetown KY

McCormick, James, *Art Dept Chmn,* University of
Nevada, Sheppard Fine Art Gallery, Reno NV

McCormick, John, *Assoc Prof,* Delta College, Art
Dept, University Center MI (S)

McCormick, Maureen, *Registrar,* Princeton
University, The Art Museum, Princeton NJ

McCormick, Pauline, *Cataloger,* Worcester Art
Museum, Library, Worcester MA

McCormick, Peggy H, *Exec Dir,* Cottonlandia
Museum, Greenwood MS

McCosker, Jane, *Second VPres,* Monmouth
Museum and Cultural Center, Lincroft NJ

McCoy, Bruce G, *Pres,* Arlington Historical Society
Inc, Museum, Arlington VA

McCoy, Katherine, *Co-Head Design Dept,*
Cranbrook Academy of Art, Bloomfield Hills MI
(S)

McCoy, Katie, *Exhib Designer,* City of Springdale,
Shiloh Museum, Springdale AR

McCoy, L Frank, *Dean,* University of Montevallo,
College of Fine Arts, Montevallo AL (S)

McCoy, Melinda, *Secy,* Knoxville Museum of Art,
Knoxville TN

McCoy, Michael, *Co-Head Design Dept,* Cranbrook
Academy of Art, Bloomfield Hills MI (S)

McCoy, Olga, *Educ Dir,* Fayetteville Museum of
Art, Inc, Fayetteville NC

McCoy, Paul A, *Asst Prof,* Baylor University, Dept
of Art, Waco TX (S)

McCoy, Robert S, *Pres,* Columbia Museum of Art,
Columbia SC

McCracken, Patrick, *Dir & Cur,* Amarillo Art
Association, Amarillo Art Center, Amarillo TX

McCracken, Ursula E, *Dir,* Textile Museum,
Washington DC

McCrea, Ann, *Dir Publications,* Worcester Art
Museum, Worcester MA

McCrea, Kay, *Pres,* Kansas Watercolor Society,
Wichita Art Museum, Wichita KS

McCready, Eric, *Dir,* University of Texas at Austin,
Archer M Huntington Art Gallery, Austin TX

McCready, William, *Academic Dean,* Queen's
University, Dept of Art, Kingston ON (S)

McCredie, James R, *Dir,* New York University,
Institute of Fine Arts, New York NY (S)

McCreight, Tim, *Instr,* Portland School of Art,
Portland ME (S)

McCroskey, Nancy, *Asst Prof,* Indiana-Purdue
University, Dept of Fine Arts, Fort Wayne IN
(S)

McCrosky, Jean, *Dir Educ,* Fitchburg Art Museum,
Fitchburg MA

McCue, Donald, *Cur,* Lincoln Memorial Shrine,
Redlands CA

McCue, Harry, *Chmn,* Ithaca College, Fine Art
Dept, Ithaca NY (S)

McCughey, Patrick, *Dir,* Wadsworth Atheneum,
Hartford CT

McCulla, George Ann, *Pres,* Mississippi Art
Colony, Meridian MS

McCullagh, Janice, *Asst Prof,* Baylor University,
Dept of Art, Waco TX (S)

McCullagh, Suzanne, *Cur Prints & Drawings,* The
Art Institute of Chicago, Chicago IL

McCullen, Mark, *Instr,* Main Line Center for the
Arts, Haverford PA (S)

McCulley, Clyde E, *Dir,* Munson-Williams-Proctor
Institute, School of Art, Utica NY (S)

McCulloch, Judith, *Admin,* Cape Ann Historical
Association, Gallery, Gloucester MA

McCulloch, Judith, *Admin,* Cape Ann Historical
Association, Museum, Gloucester MA

McCune, John, *Pres,* Monterey History and Art
Association, Monterey CA

McDade, George C, *Prof,* Monroe Community
College, Art Dept, Rochester NY (S)

McDaniel, Craig, *Dir,* Indiana State University,
Turman Art Gallery, Terre Haute IN

McDaniel, Dennis K, *Adminr,* State Museum of
Pennsylvania, Brandywine Battlefield Park,
Harrisburg PA

McDaniel, Mike, *Dir,* Arizona Watercolor
Association, Phoenix AZ

McDaniel, Nancy, *Community Development
Coordr,* Boise Art Museum, Boise ID

McDaniel, Richard, *Instr,* Woodstock School of
Art, Inc, Woodstock NY (S)

McDaniel, Susan, *Admin Asst,* Memphis Brooks
Museum of Art, Memphis TN

McKenna, John, *Correspondence Secy,* Salmagundi Club, New York NY

McKenzie, Carissa, *Programs,* University of Kansas, Spencer Museum of Art, Lawrence KS

McKenzie, Elaine, *Office Mgr,* North Dakota Museum of Art, Grand Forks ND

McKenzie, Karen, *Chief Librn,* Art Gallery of Ontario, Edward P Taylor Research Library & Archives, Toronto ON

McKenzie, Stephen, *Arts Workshop Supv,* Newark Museum Association, The Newark Museum, Newark NJ

McKibbin, Robert, *Chmn Dept,* Grinnell College, Dept of Art, Grinnell IA (S)

McKiernan, Susan, *Asst Dir,* University of Akron, University Galleries, Akron OH

McKim, Hazel, *Librn,* Redding Museum of Art & History, Museum Research Library, Redding CA

McKim-Smith, Gridley, *Prof,* Bryn Mawr College, Dept of the History of Art, Bryn Mawr PA (S)

McKinney, Hal, *Assoc Dir Admin,* North Carolina Museum of Art, Raleigh NC

McKinney, Nancy, *Assoc Ed Publications,* California Afro-American Museum, Los Angeles CA

McKinney, Thomas R, *Dir,* Ataloa Lodge Museum, Muskogee OK

McKinstry, Richard, *Librn in Charge Joseph Downs Coll of Manuscripts & Printed Ephemera,* Winterthur Museum and Gardens, Library, Winterthur DE

McKinzie, Mack P, *Dir Institutional Advancement,* Indianapolis Museum of Art, Indianapolis IN

McKirahan, John, *Asst Prof,* University of Nebraska, Kearney, Dept of Art & Art History, Kearney NE (S)

McKnight, Marni, *Admin Asst,* Estevan National Exhibition Centre Inc, Estevan SK

McKnight, William, *Cur Biology,* Indiana State Museum, Indianapolis IN

McLachlan, Elizabeth, *Assoc Prof,* Rutgers, the State University of New Jersey, Graduate Program in Art History, New Brunswick NJ (S)

McLain, Guy A, *Head of Library & Archive Coll,* Springfield Library & Museums Association, Connecticut Valley Historical Museum, Springfield MA

McLain, Nancy, *Financial Mgr,* Dartmouth College, Hood Museum of Art, Hanover NH

McLallen, Helen, *Cur,* Columbia County Historical Society, Columbia County Museum, Kinderhook NY

McLane, Michael, *Dir,* State University of New York at Oswego, Penfield Library, Oswego NY

McLaughlin, Kevin, *Instr,* Albert Lea - Mankato Technical College, Commercial and Technical Art Dept, North Mankato MN (S)

McLaughlin, Bettye, *Clerical Hostess,* Red River Valley Museum, Vernon TX

McLaughlin, Claudia, *Education Dir,* Saratoga County Historical Society, Brookside Museum, Ballston Spa NY

McLaughlin, Jan, *Cur,* University of Oregon, Aperture Photo Gallery - EMU Art Gallery, Eugene OR

McLaughlin, Jane, *Admins Asst,* Ursinus College, Philip & Muriel Berman Museum of Art, Collegeville PA

McLaughlin, Louise, *Dir,* Mankato State University, Conkling Gallery Art Dept, Mankato MN

McLaughlin, Rosemary, *Asst Cur,* New Mexico State University, University Art Gallery, Las Cruces NM

McLaughlin, Ursula, *Spec Prog Admin,* College of William and Mary, Joseph & Margaret Muscarelle Museum of Art, Williamsburg VA

McLean, Genetta, *Dir,* Bates College, Museum of Art, Lewiston ME

McLean, Peter, *Assoc Prof,* University of Hartford, Hartford Art School, West Hartford CT (S)

McLemore, Mary, *Dir Division Liberal Arts,* Motlow State Community College, Art Dept, Tullahoma TN (S)

McLendon, Kirk, *Chmn Dept,* Henry Ford Community College, Art Dept, Dearborn MI (S)

McLendon, Marty, *Chmn,* Northeast Mississippi Junior College, Art Dept, Booneville MS (S)

McLennan, Bill, *Graphic Designer, Photographer,* University of British Columbia, Museum of Anthropology, Vancouver BC

McLoone, Patricia, *Instr,* Ellsworth Community College, Dept of Fine Arts, Iowa Falls IA (S)

McMahan, Evadine, *Admin Asst,* Tennessee State Museum, Nashville TN

McMahan, Robert, *Prof,* Antelope Valley College, Art Dept, Division of Fine Arts, Lancaster CA (S)

McMahon, James, *Prof,* Manatee Community College, Dept of Art & Humanities, Bradenton FL (S)

McMahon, Maggie, *Assoc Prof,* University of Tennessee at Chattanooga, Dept of Art, Chattanooga TN (S)

McMahon, Sharon, *Chairperson,* Saint Mary's University of San Antonio, Dept of Fine Arts, San Antonio TX (S)

McManus, James, *Instr,* California State University, Chico, Art Dept, Chico CA (S)

McMillan, Alan C, *Dir Student Services,* Emily Carr College of Art & Design, Vancouver BC (S)

McMillan, Barbara, *Librn,* Mount Vernon Ladies' Association of the Union, Mount Vernon VA

McMillan, David, *Chmn Photography,* University of Manitoba, School of Art, Winnipeg MB (S)

McMillan, Ken, *VPres,* Saint Augustine Art Association Gallery, Saint Augustine FL

McMillan, Patsy, *Dir,* Klamath County Museum, Klamath Falls OR

McMillan, Patsy, *Dir,* Klamath County Museum, Research Library, Klamath Falls OR

McMillan, Patsy, *Dir,* Klamath County Museum, Baldwin Hotel Museum Annex, Klamath Falls OR

McMillan, R Bruce J, *Dir,* Illinois State Museum, Illinois Art Gallery & Lockport Gallery, Springfield IL

McMillan, Richard, *Instr,* La Sierra University, Art Dept, Riverside CA (S)

McMillian, Kenneth L, *Chmn,* University of North Florida, Dept of Communications & Visual Arts, Jacksonville FL (S)

McMinn, William, *Dean College,* Cornell University, Dept of Art, Ithaca NY (S)

McMorris, Penny, *Cur,* Owens-Corning Fiberglass Corporation, Art Collection, Toledo OH

McNair, Amy, *Asst Prof,* University of Kansas, Kress Foundation Dept of Art History, Lawrence KS (S)

McNair, Lee, *Chmn,* Des Moines Area Community College, Art Dept, Boone IA (S)

McNally, Colleen, *Lectr,* Lake Forest College, Dept of Art, Lake Forest IL (S)

McNally, Dennis, *Chmn,* Saint Joseph's University, Dept of Fine & Performing Arts, Philadelphia PA (S)

McNamara, Carole A, *Registrar,* University of Michigan, Museum of Art, Ann Arbor MI

McNamara, Walter, *Gallery Cur,* University of Nevada, Sheppard Fine Art Gallery, Reno NV

McNamee, Donald W, *Chief Librn,* Natural History Museum of Los Angeles County, Research Library, Los Angeles CA

McNaughton, James W, *Prof,* University of Southern Indiana, Art Dept, Evansville IN (S)

McNaughton, Mary, *Cur of Exhibitions,* Galleries of the Claremont Colleges, Claremont CA

McNaughton, Patrick, *Assoc Prof,* Indiana University, Bloomington, Henry Radford Hope School of Fine Arts, Bloomington IN (S)

McNaul, Nancy, *Dir Educ Prog,* The University of Texas, Institute of Texan Cultures, San Antonio TX

McNayr, Linda, *Cur,* Emily Carr Gallery Archives, Victoria BC

McNeal, Brenda, *Registrar,* Florida State University Foundation - Central Florida Community College Foundation, The Appleton Museum of Art, Ocala FL

McNeal, Meridith, *Dir of Educ,* The Fund for the Borough of Brooklyn, The Rotunda Gallery, Brooklyn NY

McNealy, Terry A, *Librn,* Bucks County Historical Society, Spruance Library, Doylestown PA

McNear, Sarah A, *Cur,* Allentown Art Museum, Allentown PA

McNeely, Stephen, *Pres,* Audubon Artists, Inc, New York NY

McNeil, Donald B, *Art Cur,* General Mills, Inc, Art Collection, Minneapolis MN

McNeil, Donna, *Dir,* Barn Gallery Associates, Inc, Ogunquit ME

McNeil, W K, *Folklorist,* Ozark Folk Center, Mountain View AR

McNeill, Janice, *Librn,* Chicago Historical Society, Chicago IL

McNeill, John, *Dir,* Royal Ontario Museum, Toronto ON

McNeill, Lloyd, *Assoc Prof,* Rutgers, the State University of New Jersey, Mason Gross School of the Arts, New Brunswick NJ (S)

McNeill, Regan, *Asst to Artistic Dir,* Social & Public Art Resource Center, (SPARC), Venice CA

McNicholas, Mary Ann, *Adminr,* San Francisco Craft and Folk Art Museum, San Francisco CA

McNutt, James, *Adj Prof,* Washington and Jefferson College, Art Dept, Washington PA (S)

McNutt, Jim, *Dir Coll,* The University of Texas, Institute of Texan Cultures, San Antonio TX

McPhail, Edna, *Treas,* South Peace Art Society, Dawson Creek Art Gallery, Dawson Creek BC

McPhearson, Ginia, *Pres,* Arts Council of Tuscaloosa County, Inc, Tuscaloosa AL

McPherson, Heather, *Asst Prof,* University of Alabama in Birmingham, Dept of Art, Birmingham AL (S)

McQuade, Millie, *Curatorial Asst,* Artesia Historical Museum & Art Center, Artesia NM

McQueen, Barbara, *Pres,* Sunbury Shores Arts and Nature Centre, Inc, Gallery, Saint Andrews NB

McQuillin, Max, *Corresp Secy,* Key West Art and Historical Society, East Martello Museum and Gallery, Key West FL

McQuire, Edward, *Dean,* College of Charleston, School of the Arts, Charleston SC (S)

McQuiston, William, *Dir,* Rensselaer Newman Foundation Chapel and Cultural Center, The Gallery, Troy NY

McRae, Jane, *Librn,* Birmingham Museum of Art, Library, Birmingham AL

McRaven, Donald B, *Prof,* Moorhead State University, Dept of Art, Moorhead MN (S)

McRoberts, Jerry, *Assoc Prof,* Eastern Illinois University, Art Dept, Charleston IL (S)

McSherry, Dorothy, *Asst Prof,* New Mexico Highlands University, School of Liberal & Fine Arts, Las Vegas NM (S)

McTavish, David, *Dir,* Queen's University, Agnes Etherington Art Centre, Kingston ON

McThail, Donald, *Treas,* Print Club Center for Prints & Photographs, Philadelphia PA

McVaugh, Robert, *Chmn,* Colgate University, Dept of Art & Art History, Hamilton NY (S)

McVay, Kathleen, *Bookshop,* University of Kansas, Spencer Museum of Art, Lawrence KS

McVicar, Ann Lamont, *Librn,* Millicent Rogers Museum, Library, Taos NM

McVicker, Charles, *Asst Prof,* Trenton State College, Art Dept, Trenton NJ (S)

McVity, Patsy B, *Cur,* Concord Art Association, Concord MA

McWayne, Barry J, *Coordr Fine Arts,* University of Alaska, Museum, Fairbanks AK

McWeeney, Jim, *Instr,* Joe Kubert School of Cartoon & Graphic Art, Inc, Dover NJ (S)

McWhorter, Mark, *Instructor,* Indian Hills Community College, Dept of Art, Centerville IA (S)

McWhorter, Mark, *Instr,* Indian Hills Community College, Ottumwa Campus, Dept of Art, Ottumwa IA (S)

McWilliams, Mary, *Acting Dir,* Evanston Historical Society, Charles Gates Dawes House, Evanston IL

Mead, Christopher, *Chmn,* University of New Mexico, Dept of Art & Art History, Albuquerque NM (S)

Mead, Gerald, *Educ Cur,* Burchfield Art Center, Buffalo NY

Mead-Donaldson, Susan, *Technical Serv Adminr,* Miami-Dade Public Library, Miami FL

Meade, Celia, *Gallery Asst,* Calgary Contemporary Arts Society, Triangle Gallery of Visual Arts, Calgary AB

Meade, Joanne, *Cur,* Alcan Aluminium Ltd, Montreal PQ

Meader, Abbott, *Assoc Prof,* Colby College, Art Dept, Waterville ME (S)

Meader, Robert F W, *Librn,* Hancock Shaker Village, Inc, Library, Pittsfield MA

Meador-Woodruff, Robin, *Coordr of Coll,* University of Michigan, Kelsey Museum of Archaeology, Ann Arbor MI

Meadows, Christine, *Cur,* Mount Vernon Ladies' Association of the Union, Mount Vernon VA

Meadows, Warren, *Secy,* Springfield Art Museum, Springfield MO

Meadows-Rogers, Robert, *Asst Prof,* Concordia College, Art Dept, Moorhead MN (S)

Meany, Phillip, *Assoc Prof,* University of Minnesota, Duluth, Art Dept, Duluth MN (S)

Mear, Margaret, *Assoc Prof,* Saint Mary's College of Minnesota, Art Dept No 18, Winona MN (S)

Mears, Peter, *Interim Dir & Cur,* Laguna Gloria Art Museum, Austin TX

Meatyard, Jerry, *Assoc Prof,* Hillsborough Community College, Fine Arts Dept, Tampa FL (S)

Mecklenburg, Virginia, *Chief Cur,* National Museum of American Art, Washington DC

Medeiros, Rosemary, *Dir,* New Bedford Free Public Library, Art Dept, New Bedford MA

Medeiros, Sylvia, *Dir,* Hayward Area Forum of the Arts, Sun Gallery, Hayward CA

Medina, Dennis, *Museum Cur,* Dwight D Eisenhower Presidential Library, Abilene KS

Medlock, Rudy, *Head Art Dept,* Asbury College, Student Center Gallery, Wilmore KY

Medlock, Rudy, *Art Dept Head,* Asbury College, Art Dept, Wilmore KY (S)

Meech, Nancy, *Treas,* Kings County Historical Society and Museum, Hampton NB

Meehan, Tracy, *Registrar,* Adirondack Historical Association, Adirondack Museum, Blue Mountain Lake NY

Meek, A J, *Prof,* Louisiana State University, School of Art, Baton Rouge LA (S)

Meek, Ken, *Cur Coll,* Frank Phillips Foundation Inc, Woolaroc Museum, Bartlesville OK

Meeks, Donna, *Cur of Educ,* Eastern Illinois University, Tarble Arts Center, Charleston IL

Meeks, Jackie, *Membership & Museum Store,* Oklahoma City Art Museum, Oklahoma City OK

Meeks, Jim, *Preparator,* Oklahoma City Art Museum, Oklahoma City OK

Meeks, Sally, *Registrar,* El Paso Museum of Art, El Paso TX

Megorden, Winston, *Instr,* California State University, Chico, Art Dept, Chico CA (S)

Mehl, Richard, *Instr,* Portland School of Art, Portland ME (S)

Mehring, Gretchen, *Asst Dir Marketing,* Cincinnati Museum Association, Cincinnati Art Museum, Cincinnati OH

Meier, Tom, *Dir,* Boulder Historical Society Inc, Museum of History, Boulder CO

Meiers, Susanna, *Dir,* El Camino College Art Gallery, Torrance CA

Meillon, Eileen, *Librn,* David M Stewart Museum, Library, Montreal PQ

Meisner, Ann, *Cur Capricorn Asunder Gallery,* San Francisco City & County Arts Commission, San Francisco CA

Meissner, Marilyn, *Communications Asst,* Marquette University, Haggerty Museum of Art, Milwaukee WI

Meister, Mark J, *Pres,* Archaeological Institute of America, Boston MA

Meixner, Laura L, *Assoc Prof,* Cornell University, Dept of the History of Art, Ithaca NY (S)

Mejer, Robert Lee, *Gallery Dir,* Quincy University, The Gray Gallery, Quincy IL

Mejer, Robert Lee, *Prof Art,* Quincy University, Dept of Art, Quincy IL (S)

Mekas, Adolfas, *Instr,* Bard College, Milton Avery Graduate School of the Arts, Annandale-on-Hudson NY (S)

Melchert, James, *Prof,* University of California, Berkeley, College of Letters & Sciences-Art Dept, Berkeley CA (S)

Meley, Tricia, *Cur Education,* Heritage Center of Lancaster County, Lancaster PA

Melick, Susan, *Librn,* The Metropolitan Museum of Art, Photograph and Slide Library, New York NY

Melion, Walter S, *Assoc Prof,* Emory University, Art History Dept, Atlanta GA (S)

Melis, Alan, *Assoc Prof,* University of Toledo, Dept of Art, Toledo OH (S)

Mella, Joseph S, *Dir,* Vanderbilt University, Fine Arts Gallery, Nashville TN

Mellick/MFA, James, *Assoc Prof,* Calvin College, Art Dept, Grand Rapids MI (S)

Mellon, Andrew W, *Librn,* Frick Art Reference Library, New York NY

Mellon, Marc Richard, *Pres,* Artists' Fellowship, Inc, New York NY

Mello-nee, Mary, *Coordr Educ,* Charles H MacNider Museum, Mason City IA

Mellott, Richard, *Cur Educ,* Asian Art Museum of San Francisco, Avery Brundage Collection, San Francisco CA

Melson, Claudia F, *Cur Registration,* Historical and Cultural Affairs, Delaware State Museums, Dover DE

Melton, Rachel, *Educ Specialist,* Washburn University, Mulvane Art Museum, Topeka KS

Melton, Sonja, *Library Asst,* Kansas State University, Paul Weigel Library of Architecture & Design, Manhattan KS

Meltzer, Meryl, *VPres,* Artists Space, New York NY

Meltzer, Robert M, *Pres,* The American Federation of Arts, New York NY

Melvin, David Skene, *Librn,* Arts and Letters Club of Toronto, Library, Toronto ON

Melvin, Douglas, *Chmn,* North Central Michigan College, Art Dept, Petoskey MI (S)

Melvin, Ellen, *Educ Officer Natural Science,* New Brunswick Museum, Saint John NB

Menard, Lloyd, *Prof,* University of South Dakota, Dept of Art, Vermillion SD (S)

Menard, Michael J, *Exec Dir,* Koshare Indian Museum, Inc, La Junta CO

Menard, Regent, *Instr,* St Lawrence College, Dept of Visual & Creative Arts, Cornwall ON (S)

Mendell, Cyndi, *Instr,* ACA College of Design, Cincinnati OH (S)

Mendelson, Haim, *Pres,* Federation of Modern Painters & Sculptors, New York NY

Mendelson, Haim, *Gallery Dir,* Hudson Guild Neighborhood House, Art Gallery, New York NY

Mendelson, Shari, *Instr,* Chautauqua Institution, School of Art, Chautauqua NY (S)

Mendenhall, John, *Prof,* California Polytechnic State University at San Luis Obispo, Dept of Art and Design, San Luis Obispo CA (S)

Mendoza, Mary, *VPres,* Long Beach Art League, Island Park NY

Mendro, Donna, *Recordings Librn,* Dallas Public Library, Fine Arts Division, Dallas TX

Meneray, Bill, *Chmn Memorial Hall Committee,* Louisiana Historical Association, Confederate Museum, New Orleans LA

Meng, Charles, *Dir Works on Paper Exhib,* Southwest Texas State University, Dept of Art, San Marcos TX (S)

Mengel, Claudia, *Cur,* Manufacturers Hanover, New York NY

Menger, Linda, *Chmn Dept,* Delta College, Art Dept, University Center MI (S)

Menges, Gary, *Librn,* University of Washington, Suzzallo Library, Seattle WA

Menken, Ingrid, *Treas,* Haystack Mountain School of Crafts, Gallery, Deer Isle ME

Menn, Richard J, *Cur,* Carmel Mission and Gift Shop, Carmel CA

Menna, Sari, *Recording Coordr,* Women in the Arts Foundation, Inc, New York NY

Menning, Daleene, *Assoc Prof,* Grand Valley State University, Art & Design Dept, Allendale MI (S)

Menocal, Narciso G, *Prof,* University of Wisconsin, Madison, Dept of Art History, Madison WI (S)

Mensch, Judy, *Dir,* The Children's Aid Society, Visual Arts Program of the Greenwich Village Center, New York NY (S)

Mensing, Iris, *Auditorium Mgr & Book Store Mgr,* University of Notre Dame, Snite Museum of Art, Notre Dame IN

Menzies, Janet, *Registrar,* Simon Fraser University, Simon Fraser Gallery, Burnaby BC

Menzonares, Rick F, *Exec Mgr,* Chicano Humanities & Arts Council, Denver CO

Meranus, Philip, *Dir Public Affairs,* The Jewish Museum, New York NY

Mercado, Marianne, *Tour Coordr,* The Bradford Museum of Collector's Plates, Niles IL

Mercede, Nevin, *Instr,* Indiana University of Pennsylvania, Dept of Art and Art Education, Indiana PA (S)

Mercer, David, *Instructor,* The Art Institutes International, The Art Institute of Seattle, Seattle WA (S)

Mercer, Dorothy, *Asst Prof,* Radford University, Art Dept, Radford VA (S)

Mercer, John, *Chmn,* Phoenix College, Dept of Art & Photography, Phoenix AZ (S)

Merchant, Ailine, *Asst Mgr,* Brand Library & Art Galleries, Glendale CA

Merchant, John, *Instr,* Lakeland Community College, Visual Arts Dept, Mentor OH (S)

Merdzinski, Marilyn, *Colls Mgr,* Public Museum of Grand Rapids, Grand Rapids MI

Meredith, Andrew, *Cur of Exhib & Designs,* Nelson-Atkins Museum of Art, Kansas City MO

Meredith, George, *Asst Shop Mgr,* Memphis Brooks Museum of Art, Memphis TN

Meredith, Janet, *Head Marketing Development,* Vancouver Art Gallery, Vancouver BC

Merendino, Janice, *Lectr,* Rosemont College, Division of the Arts, Rosemont PA (S)

Meretta, Anne, *Museum Shop Mgr,* Rhode Island School of Design, Museum of Art, Providence RI

Merkel, Bernadette, *Chmn Graphic Design,* Rochester Institute of Technology, School of Art and Design, Rochester NY (S)

Merriam, Mary-Linda, *Pres,* Moore College of Art & Design, Philadelphia PA (S)

Merrick, Robert S, *Trustee,* Merrick Art Gallery, New Brighton PA

Merrihew, Levan, *Treas,* Gallery North, Setauket NY

Merrill, Anne, *Dir of Development,* Palm Beach County Parks & Recreation Department, Morikami Museum & Japanese Gardens, Delray Beach FL

Merrill, Don, *Chmn,* Salt Lake Community College, Graphic Design Dept, Salt Lake City UT (S)

Merrill, Joyce, *Exec Asst,* Indian Pueblo Cultural Center, Albuquerque NM

Merrill, Ross, *Chief Conservation,* National Gallery of Art, Washington DC

Merriman, Janette, *Cur Coll,* Southern Oregon Historical Society, Jacksonville Museum of Southern Oregon History, Jacksonville OR

Merriman, Janette, *Cur Coll,* Southern Oregon Historical Society, Library, Jacksonville OR

Merriman, Larry, *Dir,* Cecelia Coker Bell Gallery, Hartsville SC

Merritt, Jake, *Pres,* Colorado City Historical Museum, Colorado City TX

Merson, Jeanne, *Adjunct Instr,* Maryville University of Saint Louis, Art Division, Saint Louis MO (S)

Mertens, Joan R, *Cur Greek & Roman Art,* The Metropolitan Museum of Art, New York NY

Merwin, Nancy S, *Pres,* McLean County Art Association, Arts Center, Bloomington IL

Meschutt, David, *Cur Art,* United States Military Academy, West Point Museum, West Point NY

Messer, David, *Dir,* Bergen Museum of Art & Science, Paramus NJ

Messersmith, Harry, *Exec Dir,* DeLand Museum of Art, DeLand FL

Messersmith, Linda, *Library Assoc,* University of Notre Dame, Architecture Library, Notre Dame IN

Messersmith, Mark, *Assoc Prof,* Florida State University, Art Dept, Tallahassee FL (S)

Messick, Kathy, *Store Mgr,* Virginia Commonwealth University, Anderson Gallery, Richmond VA

Messimer, Susan, *Assoc Cur,* Heritage Center of Lancaster County, Lancaster PA

Messina, Mitchell, *Asst Prof,* Nazareth College of Rochester, Art Dept, Rochester NY (S)

Mester, Clark, *Gallery Dir,* Bowie State University, Fine Arts Dept, Bowie MD (S)

Mesun, Brian, *Asst Prof,* Carroll College, Art Dept, Waukesha WI (S)

Meszaros, Cheryl, *Educ Coordr,* Mendel Art Gallery and Civic Conservatory, Saskatoon SK

Metcalf, Preston, *Asst to Dir,* Triton Museum of Art, Santa Clara CA

Metcalf, William E, *Chief Cur,* American Numismatic Society, New York NY

Metcalfe, Elizabeth, *Adjunct Instr,* Maryville University of Saint Louis, Art Division, Saint Louis MO (S)

Metcoff, Donald, *Chicago Representative,* American Society of Artists, Inc, Chicago IL

Metcoff, Donald, *Librn,* American Society of Artists, Inc, Library Organization, Chicago IL

Metraux, M, *Cur,* York University, Fine Arts Phase II Slide Library, North York ON

Mettala, Teri, *Mgr,* Ojai Valley Art Center, Ojai CA

Metts, Thomas S, *Finance Officer,* Museum of Fine Arts, Saint Petersburg, Florida, Inc, Saint Petersburg FL

Metz, Carolyn J, *Dir Educational Resources,* Indianapolis Museum of Art, Indianapolis IN

Metz, Carolyn J, *Dir Educational Resources,* Indianapolis Museum of Art, Stout Reference Library, Indianapolis IN

Metz, Christie, *Board Trustees,* Sioux City Art Center, Sioux City IA

Metz, Janice, *Instr,* College of the Canyons, Art Dept, Valencia CA (S)

Metz, Martha A, *Community Outreach,* Dickinson College, Trout Gallery, Carlisle PA

Metz, Rinda, *Assoc Prof,* Ohio Wesleyan University, Fine Arts Dept, Delaware OH (S)

Metzger, Michael, *Coordr Studio Prog,* Kean College of New Jersey, Fine Arts Dept, Union NJ (S)

Metzker, Dale, *Assoc Prof,* Pennsylvania College of Technology, Dept of Design & Communiation Arts, Williamsport PA (S)

Meunier, Brian A, *Assoc Prof,* Swarthmore College, Dept of Art, Swarthmore PA (S)

Meunier, John, *Dean,* Arizona State University, College of Architecture & Environmental Design, Tempe AZ (S)

Mew, T J, *Chmn,* Berry College, Art Dept, Mount Berry GA (S)

Mew, T J, *Prof of Art,* Berry College, Memorial Library, Mount Berry GA

Mey, Andree, *Cur Coll,* Lehigh County Historical Society, Allentown PA

Meyer, Elisabeth, *Assoc Prof,* Cornell University, Dept of Art, Ithaca NY (S)

Meyer, Ellen, *Pres,* Atlanta College of Art, Atlanta GA (S)

Meyer, Fred, *Head Dept,* West Virginia Institute of Technology, Creative Arts Dept, Montgomery WV (S)

Meyer, Helen, *Pres,* LeSueur Museum, LeSueur MN

Meyer, Hugo, *Prof,* Princeton University, Dept of Art and Archaeology, Princeton NJ (S)

Meyer, Jerry D, *Asst Chmn,* Northern Illinois University, School of Art, De Kalb IL (S)

Meyer, Joan L, *Head Technical Servs,* Springfield Free Public Library, Donald B Palmer Museum, Springfield NJ

Meyer, Jon, *Dept Head,* University of Arizona, Dept of Art, Tucson AZ (S)

Meyer, R, *Faculty Lectr,* McGill University, Department of Art History, Montreal PQ (S)

Meyer, Robert, *Dean Humanities,* Sierra College, Art Dept, Rocklin CA (S)

Meyer, Ruth K, *Dir Taft Museum,* Cincinnati Institute of Fine Arts, Taft Museum, Cincinnati OH

Meyer, Ursula, *Prof Emeritus,* Herbert H Lehman College, Art Dept, Bronx NY (S)

Meyer, Wayne, *Librn,* Ball State University, Architecture Library, Muncie IN

Meyers, Amy, *Cur American Art,* Henry E Huntington Library, Art Collections & Botanical Gardens, San Marino CA

Meyers, Dale, *Active Honorary Pres,* American Watercolor Society, New York NY

Meyers, Frances, *Assoc Prof,* University of Wisconsin, Madison, Dept of Art, Madison WI (S)

Meyers, Kathryn, *Instr,* Main Line Center for the Arts, Haverford PA (S)

Meyers, Mary, *Librn,* Cowboy Artists of America Museum Foundation, Library, Kerrville TX

Meyers, Pieter, *Head Conservation,* Los Angeles County Museum of Art, Los Angeles CA

Mezei, Gabor P, *Instr,* Southampton Art School, Southampton ON (S)

Mezzatesta, Joanna, *VPres,* Society of Scribes, Ltd, New York NY

Mezzatesta, Michael P, *Dir,* Duke University Museum of Art, Durham NC

Mhire, Herman, *Dir,* University of Southwestern Louisiana, University Art Museum, Lafayette LA

Mhiripiri, Julie, *Co-Owner,* Mhiripiri Gallery, Minneapolis MN

Mhiripiri, Rex, *Co-Owner,* Mhiripiri Gallery, Minneapolis MN

Miao, Jean, *Press Officer,* Craft and Folk Art Museum, Los Angeles CA

Miazga, John, *Production Asst,* Institute of Contemporary Art, Boston MA

Micchelli, Tom, *Slide & Picture,* Cooper Union for the Advancement of Science & Art, Library, New York NY

Micco, T, *Assoc Prof,* Northern Arizona University, School of Art & Design, Flagstaff AZ (S)

Michael, Shirley, *Head Art & Music Dept,* Free Public Library, Art and Music Dept, Trenton NJ

Michael, Simon, *Head Dept,* Simon Michael School of Fine Arts, Rockport TX (S)

Michaelides, C, *Dean School,* Washington University, School of Architecture, Saint Louis MO (S)

Michaels, Bonni-Dara, *Asst Cur,* Yeshiva University Museum, New York NY

Michaels, Marion, *Dean School Liberal Arts,* Auburn University at Montgomery, Dept of Fine Arts, Montgomery AL (S)

Michaels, Rachel, *Instr,* International Correspondence Schools, School of Interior Design, Scranton PA (S)

Michaels, Rachel, *Chief Instr,* International Correspondence Schools, School of Art, Scranton PA (S)

Michaels, Rebecca, *Asst Prof,* Beaver College, Dept of Fine Arts, Glenside PA (S)

Michaels-Paque, John, *Lectr,* Cardinal Stritch College, Art Dept, Milwaukee WI (S)

Michala, Mollie, *Lectr,* Emory University, Art History Dept, Atlanta GA (S)

Michaud, Monique, *Animatrice,* Le Musee Regional de Rimouski, Centre National d' Exposition, Rimouski PQ

Michaux, Henry G, *Assoc Prof,* South Carolina State University, Art Dept, Orangeburg SC (S)

Michel, Delbert, *Prof,* Hope College, Art Dept, Holland MI (S)

Michel, Peter, *Dir Library & Archives,* Missouri Historical Society, Library & Collections Center, Saint Louis MO

Micheli, Julio, *Prof,* Catholic University of Puerto Rico, Dept of Fine Arts, Ponce PR (S)

Michie, Thomas, *Cur Decorative Arts,* Rhode Island School of Design, Museum of Art, Providence RI

Mick, Chery, *Financial Adminr,* D-Art, A Visual Arts Center for Dallas, Dallas TX

Mickelson, Duane, *Asst Prof,* Concordia College, Art Dept, Moorhead MN (S)

Mickenberg, David, *Dir,* Northwestern University, Mary & Leigh Block Gallery, Evanston IL

Micklewright, Nancy, *Asst Prof,* University of Victoria, Dept of History in Art, Victoria BC (S)

Midas, Liz, *Rights & Reproductions,* Norton Simon Museum, Pasadena CA

Miele, John, *Dir Fashion Illustration,* Art Institute of Fort Lauderdale, Fort Lauderdale FL (S)

Miesel, Victor H, *Prof,* University of Michigan, Ann Arbor, Dept of History of Art, Ann Arbor MI (S)

Migliori, Larry, *Asst Prof,* Mohawk Valley Community College, Advertising Design and Production, Utica NY (S)

Migliovino, Laura, *Instr,* Anoka Ramsey Community College, Art Dept, Coon Rapids MN (S)

Mihailovic, Olivera, *Cur,* University of Chicago, Art Slide Collection, Chicago IL

Mihal, Milan, *Assoc Prof,* Vanderbilt University, Dept of Fine Arts, Nashville TN (S)

Miho, James, *Communication Design Chmn,* Art Center College of Design, Pasadena CA (S)

Mikkelson, Rick, *Chmn,* State University of New York at Plattsburgh, Art Dept, Plattsburgh NY (S)

Mikos, Mike, *Chmn Illustration,* Center for Creative Studies, College of Art & Design, Detroit MI (S)

Mikus, Eleanore, *Assoc Prof,* Cornell University, Dept of Art, Ithaca NY (S)

Milakovich, Jeannie, *Chmn,* Gogebic Community College, Fine Arts Dept, Ironwood MI (S)

Milbrandt, L, *Head Dept,* Valdosta State College, Dept of Art, Valdosta GA (S)

Milbrandt, Lanny, *Head Art Dept,* Valdosta State College, Art Gallery, Valdosta GA

Mileaf, Janine, *Registrar,* Wesleyan University, Davison Art Center, Middletown CT

Miles, Carolyn, *Dir,* Atrium Gallery, Saint Louis MO

Miles, Christine M, *Dir,* Albany Institute of History and Art, Albany NY

Miles, David, *Prof,* Ohio University-Belmont County Campus, Dept Comparative Arts, Saint Clairsville OH (S)

Miles, Sheila, *Cur,* Yellowstone Art Center, Billings MT

Miley, Bonnie, *Chmn,* Iowa Western Community College, Art Dept, Council Bluffs IA (S)

Miley, E J, *Assoc Prof,* Lincoln College, Art Dept, Lincoln IL (S)

Miley, Les, *Chmn Art Dept,* University of Evansville, Krannert Gallery, Evansville IN

Miley, Les, *Dept Head,* University of Evansville, Art Dept, Evansville IN (S)

Miley, Les, *Prof,* University of Evansville, Art Dept, Evansville IN (S)

Miley, Mimi C, *Chief Cur,* Allentown Art Museum, Allentown PA

Milford, Frances, *Chmn of Trustees,* John D Barrow Art Gallery, Skaneateles NY

Milkovich, Michael, *Dir,* Museum of Fine Arts, Saint Petersburg, Florida, Inc, Saint Petersburg FL

Millan, Nelson, *Instr,* University of Puerto Rico, Dept of Fine Arts, Rio Piedras PR (S)

Millard, Charles, *Dir,* University of North Carolina at Chapel Hill, Ackland Art Museum, Chapel Hill NC

Millard, Elizabeth Wright, *Exec Dir,* Forum for Contemporary Arts, Saint Louis MO

Mille, John, *Vis Instr,* Claremont Graduate School, Dept of Fine Arts, Claremont CA (S)

Millen, Bruce, *Assoc Cur,* Queen's University, Agnes Etherington Art Centre, Kingston ON

Miller, Amelia, *Pres,* Pocumtuck Valley Memorial Association, Memorial Hall, Deerfield MA

Miller, Arthur, *Chmn Humanities Division,* New College of the University of South Florida, Fine Arts Dept, Humanities Division, Sarasota FL (S)

Miller, Barbara, *Chmn,* Maui Community College, Art Dept, Kahului HI (S)

Miller, Barbara S, *Chmn,* Eastern Washington University, Dept of Art, Cheney WA (S)

Miller, Cheryl, *Cur,* Historical Society of Washington DC, Christian Heurich Mansion, Washington DC

Miller, Christina, *Book & Gift Shop Mgr,* San Jose Museum of Art, San Jose CA

Miller, Darby, *Museum Relations,* University of Tampa, Henry B Plant Museum, Tampa FL

Miller, David, *Secy,* Lyman Allyn Art Museum, New London CT

Miller, David, *Dir,* Skidmore College, Schick Art Gallery, Saratoga Springs NY

Miller, Donald R, *Pres,* The Queens Museum of Art, Flushing NY

Miller, Doretta M, *Chmn,* Skidmore College, Dept of Art & Art History, Saratoga Springs NY (S)

Miller, Dusty, *Dir,* University of Oregon, Aperture Photo Gallery - EMU Art Gallery, Eugene OR

Miller, Edward C, *Assoc Prof,* Rochester Institute of Technology, School of Art and Design, Rochester NY (S)

Miller, Elaine, *Asst Librn Photos,* Washington State Historical Society, Hewitt Memorial Library, Tacoma WA

Miller, Elizabeth J, *Dir,* Maine Historical Society, Portland ME

Miller, George, *Dir,* California State University, Hayward, C E Smith Museum of Anthropology, Hayward CA

Miller, Glen, *Asst Prof,* Rochester Institute of Technology, School of Photographic Arts & Sciences, Rochester NY (S)

Miller, Greg, *Instr,* Mount Mary College, Art Dept, Milwaukee WI (S)

Miller, Harriet S, *Dir,* Cultural Affairs Department City of Los Angeles, Junior Arts Center, Los Angeles CA

Miller, Jack, *Librn,* High Museum of Art, Library, Atlanta GA

Miller, Jane, *Instr,* Monterey Peninsula College, Art Dept, Monterey CA (S)

Miller, Jerry, *Chair Dept,* Central Missouri State University, Art Dept, Warrensburg MO (S)

Miller, Jim, *Education Coordr,* McAllen International Museum, McAllen TX

Miller, John B, *Prof,* Texas Woman's University, Dept of Visual Arts, Denton TX (S)

Miller, John Franklin, *Exec Dir,* Stan Hywet Hall & Gardens, Inc, Akron OH

Miller, John J, *Asst Prof,* South Dakota State University, Dept of Visual Arts, Brookings SD (S)

Miller, John P, *Preparator,* Vassar College, Vassar Art Gallery, Poughkeepsie NY

Miller, John V, *VPres,* Summit County Historical Society, Akron OH

Miller, Joseph, *Dir Grad Studies,* Catholic University of America, School of Architecture & Planning, Washington DC (S)

Miller, J Robert, *Lectr,* McMurry University, Art Dept, Abilene TX (S)

Miller, Karen, *Secy,* Lafayette Natural History Museum, Planetarium and Nature Station, Lafayette LA

Miller, Kate, *Admin Asst,* Emily Carr College of Art & Design, The Charles H Scott Gallery, Vancouver BC

Miller, Lee, *Dir,* French Art Colony, Gallipolis OH

Miller, Lee Anne, *Dean,* Cooper Union School of Art, New York NY (S)

Miller, Lenore D, *Dir,* George Washington University, The Dimock Gallery, Washington DC

Miller, Leslie, *Cur Special Events,* Oberlin College, Allen Memorial Art Museum, Oberlin OH

Miller, Lillian B, *Ed Charles Wilson Peale Papers,* National Portrait Gallery, Washington DC

Miller, Lynette, *Cur,* Wheelwright Museum of the American Indian, Santa Fe NM

Miller, Lynette, *Cur,* Wheelwright Museum of the American Indian, Mary Cabot Wheelwright Research Library, Santa Fe NM

Miller, Lynn, *Dir,* Houston Baptist University, Museum of American Architecture and Decorative Arts, Houston TX

Miller, Marc H, *Cur,* The Queens Museum of Art, Flushing NY

Miller, Margaret A, *Dir & Chief Cur,* University of South Florida, Contemporary Art Museum, Tampa FL

Miller, Marie Celeste, *Prof,* Aquinas College, Art Dept, Grand Rapids MI (S)

Miller, Marjorie, *First VPres,* Arizona Watercolor Association, Phoenix AZ

Miller, Marjorie, *Ref & Special Collections,* Fashion Institute of Technology Galleries, Library, New York NY

Miller, Marlene, *Instr,* Bucks County Community College, Fine Arts Dept, Newtown PA (S)

Miller, Marlene, *Instr,* Illinois Central College, Dept of Fine Arts, East Peoria IL (S)

Miller, Mary, *Chmn,* Yale University, Dept of the History of Art, New Haven CT (S)

Miller, Mary M, *Librn,* Springfield Museum of Art, Library, Springfield OH

Miller, Michael, *Prof,* School of the Art Institute of Chicago, Chicago IL (S)

Miller, Michael, *Chmn Painting,* East Texas State University, Dept of Art, East Texas Station, Commerce TX (S)

Miller, Pamela, *Archivist,* McCord Museum of Canadian History, Montreal PQ

Miller, Robin, *Slide Librn,* Philadelphia Museum of Art, Slide Library, Philadelphia PA

Miller, Roger, *Asst Dir,* Battleship North Carolina, Wilmington NC

Miller, Roger, *Pres,* Brattleboro Museum & Art Center, Brattleboro VT

Miller, Ron, *Dir,* World Archaeological Society, Information Center & Library, Hollister MO

Miller, Ruane, *Assoc Prof,* Trenton State College, Art Dept, Trenton NJ (S)

Miller, Ruth, *Instr,* New York Studio School of Drawing, Painting and Sculpture, New York NY (S)

Miller, Samuel C, *Dir,* Newark Museum Association, The Newark Museum, Newark NJ

Miller, Steve, *Assoc Prof,* Palomar Community College, Art Dept, San Marcos CA (S)

Miller, Steve, *Asst Dir,* World Archaeological Society, Information Center & Library, Hollister MO

Miller, Steven, *Dir Museum,* Western Reserve Historical Society, Cleveland OH

Miller, Susan V, *Exec Dir,* Hoyt Institute of Fine Arts, New Castle PA

Miller, William B, *Librn,* Waterville Historical Society, Redington Museum, Waterville ME

Miller Clark, Denise, *Dir ,* Columbia College, The Museum of Contemporary Photography, Chicago IL

Miller-Keller, Andrea, *Cur of Contemporary Art,* Wadsworth Atheneum, Hartford CT

Milley, John C, *Chief Museum Operations,* Independence National Historical Park, Philadelphia PA

Millie, Elena G, *Posters,* Library of Congress, Prints and Photographs Division, Washington DC

Milligan, Barbara J, *Dir & Cur,* Plymouth Antiquarian Society, Plymouth MA

Milligan, Frank, *Dir,* New Brunswick Museum, Saint John NB

Milligan, Shirley Miller, *Admin Asst to Chmn,* Blount Inc, Montgomery AL

Millin, Laura J, *Dir,* Missoula Museum of the Arts, Missoula MT

Milloff, Mark, *Chmn Dept,* Berkshire Community College, Dept of Fine Arts, Pittsfield MA (S)

Millon, Henry A, *Dean, Center for Advanced Study in Visual Arts,* National Gallery of Art, Washington DC

Mills, Anne, *Executive Secy,* University of Notre Dame, Snite Museum of Art, Notre Dame IN

Mills, Daniel T, *Cur,* The First National Bank of Chicago, Art Collection, Chicago IL

Mills, David, *Dir,* Newfoundland Museum, Saint John's NF

Mills, Don, *Chief Librn,* Mississauga Library System, Mississauga ON

Mills, James, *Pres,* Montclair Art Museum, Montclair NJ

Mills, James, *Prof,* East Tennessee State University, Fine Arts Dept, Johnson City TN (S)

Mills, Lawrence, *Assoc Prof,* Central University of Iowa, Art Dept, Pella IA (S)

Mills, Lea, *Dir,* College of the Redwoods, Arts, Humanities & Social Sciences Division, Eureka CA (S)

Mills, Richard, *Prof,* Auburn University at Montgomery, Dept of Fine Arts, Montgomery AL (S)

Mills, Richard, *Asst Prof,* C W Post Center of Long Island University, School of Visual & Performing Arts, Greenvale NY (S)

Mills, Ron, *Chmn Dept,* Linfield College, Art Dept, McMinnville OR (S)

Millsaps, Lucy, *Assoc Prof,* Millsaps College, Dept of Art, Jackson MS (S)

Mills-Varnell, Ruth B, *Dir,* Art Association of Richmond, Richmond Art Museum, Richmond IN

Mills-Varnell, Ruth B, *Dir,* Art Association of Richmond, Library, Richmond IN

Milne, Norman F, *Clerk,* The Currier Gallery of Art, Manchester NH

Milne, Robert, *Treas,* Cleveland Museum of Art, Print Club of Cleveland, Cleveland OH

Milner, Angela, *Secy,* Long Island Graphic Eye Gallery, Port Washington NY

Milner, Sue, *Head Dept,* Eastern Wyoming College, Art Dept, Torrington WY (S)

Milnes, Robert, *Dir,* San Jose State University, School of Art & Design, San Jose CA (S)

Milosevich, Joe, *Instr,* Joliet Junior College, Fine Arts Dept, Joliet IL (S)

Milosevich, Joe B, *Gallery Dir,* Joliet Junior College, Laura A Sprague Art Gallery, Joliet IL

Milot, Barbara, *Asst Prof,* Framingham State College, Art Dept, Framingham MA (S)

Milovich, Rose M, *Assoc Cur,* Nora Eccles Harrison Museum of Art, Logan UT

Milrod, Linda, *Dir,* Contemporary Art Gallery society of British Columbia, Vancouver BC

Milrod, Linda, *Dir,* Contemporary Art Gallery society of British Columbia, Art Library Service, Vancouver BC

Milroy, Elizabeth, *Asst Prof,* Wesleyan University, Art Dept, Middletown CT (S)

Milroy, John, *Pres,* Jesse Besser Museum, Alpena MI

Mimeault, Mme Sonia, *Registrar,* Musee du Seminaire de Quebec, Quebec PQ

Mimms, Julia M, *Admin Asst,* Maitland Art Center, Library, Maitland FL

Mimms, Julie, *Prog Coordr,* Maitland Art Center, Maitland FL

Mims, Michael, *Acting Area Head Photography,* Pasadena City College, Art Dept, Pasadena CA (S)

Minar, Virginia, *Instr,* Mount Mary College, Art Dept, Milwaukee WI (S)

Mindencupp, Cecila, *Dir Development,* University of Virginia, Bayly Art Museum, Charlottesville VA

Minet, Cynthia, *Asst Prof,* Antelope Valley College, Art Dept, Division of Fine Arts, Lancaster CA (S)

Mink, Abby, *Dir,* Jackson County Historical Society, John Wornall House Museum, Independence MO

Minkkinen, Arno, *Assoc Prof,* University of Massachusetts at Lowell, Dept of Art, Lowell MA (S)

Minkler, Christine, *Dept Public Programming,* Columbia Museum of Art, Columbia SC

Minkoff, Dolores, *Corresponding Secy,* Chicago Society of Artists, Inc, Chicago IL

Minnelli, Peter, *Area Mgr,* Environment Canada - Canadian Parks Service, Laurier House, Ottawa ON

Mino, Yutaka, *Cur Asian Art,* The Art Institute of Chicago, Department of Asian Art, Chicago IL

Minogue, Eileen, *Asst Dir,* Northport-East Northport Public Library, Northport NY

Mintich, Mary, *Prof,* Winthrop College, Dept of Art & Design, Rock Hill SC (S)

Mintz, Ward, *Asst Dir Programs,* The Jewish Museum, New York NY

Minvielle, Shereen H, *Dir,* Shadows-on-the-Teche, New Iberia LA

Miraglia, Anthony J, *Chmn Fine Art,* University of Massachusetts Dartmouth, College of Visual and Performing Arts, North Dartmouth MA (S)

Mirakian, Sherry, *Instr,* Ocean City Art Center, Ocean City NJ (S)

Mirzoeff, Nicholas D, *Asst Prof,* University of Wisconsin, Madison, Dept of Art History, Madison WI (S)

Misfeldt, Willard, *Chmn Art History,* Bowling Green State University, School of Art, Bowling Green OH (S)

Mishkin, Janet, *Dir,* Monroe County Historical Association, Elizabeth D Walters Library, Stroudsburg PA

Mishler, John, *Asst Prof,* Goshen College, Art Dept, Goshen IN (S)

Misik, Sharon, *Cur Education,* Old Barracks Museum, Trenton NJ

Misner, Mary, *Coordr Cultural Servs,* Cambridge Public Library and Gallery, Cambridge ON

Missal, Paul, *Instr,* Pacific Northwest College of Art, Portland OR (S)

Mita, DiAnne, *Gallery Asst,* St Mary's College of Maryland, The Dwight Frederick Boyden Gallery, Saint Mary City MD

Mitch, Dale, *Dir,* United States Figure Skating Association, World Figure Skating Hall of Fame and Museum, Colorado Springs CO

Mitchell, Alex F, *Prof,* Lake Forest College, Dept of Art, Lake Forest IL (S)

Mitchell, Charles, *VPres,* Headley-Whitney Museum, Lexington KY

Mitchell, David, *Exec Dir,* Saratoga County Historical Society, Brookside Museum, Ballston Spa NY

Mitchell, Deborah, *Cur,* Missoula Museum of the Arts, Missoula MT

Mitchell, Dolores, *Instr,* California State University, Chico, Art Dept, Chico CA (S)

Mitchell, Donald, *Assoc Dir Human Resources,* Royal Ontario Museum, Toronto ON

Mitchell, F Jeannette, *Librn,* Portsmouth Athenaeum, Library, Portsmouth NH

Mitchell, George, *Chmn,* United States Senate Commission on Art, Washington DC

Mitchell, Jeannette, *Librn,* Portsmouth Athenaeum, Portsmouth NH

Mitchell, Jean S, *Office Mgr,* Cliveden, Philadelphia PA

Mitchell, Katherine, *Lectr,* Emory University, Art History Dept, Atlanta GA (S)

Mitchell, Maggie, *Dir,* Tom Thomson Memorial Art Gallery, Owen Sound ON

Mitchell, Maggie, *Dir,* Tom Thomson Memorial Art Gallery, Library, Owen Sound ON

Mitchell, Marian, *Chmn Board Trustees,* Atwater Kent Museum, Philadelphia PA

Mitchell, Martha, *Asst Prof,* Muskingum College, Art Department, New Concord OH (S)

Mitchell, Marty, *Asst Prof Art,* Adams State College, Dept of Visual Arts, Alamosa CO (S)

Mitchell, Ned, *Dir Development,* Craft Alliance Gallery & Education Center, Saint Louis MO

Mitchell, Pauline, *Registrar,* Shelburne Museum, Shelburne VT

Mitchell, Ramona, *Lectr,* Lake Forest College, Dept of Art, Lake Forest IL (S)

Mitchell, Robert, *Bus Mgr,* Society of North American Goldsmiths, Jacksonville FL

Mitchell, Robert O H, *VPres,* Peninsula Fine Arts Center, Newport News VA

Mitchell, Sandy, *Librn,* Jesse Besser Museum, Philip M Park Library, Alpena MI

Mitchell, Stanley A, *Prof,* Chowan College, Division of Art, Murfreesboro NC (S)

Mitchell, Starr, *Educ Coordr,* Arkansas Territorial Restoration, Little Rock AR

Mitchell, Starr, *Education Coordr,* Arkansas Territorial Restoration, Library, Little Rock AR

Mitchell, Taylor, *Asst Prof,* Incarnate Word College, Art Dept, San Antonio TX (S)

Mitchell, Timothy, *Prof,* University of Kansas, Kress Foundation Dept of Art History, Lawrence KS (S)

Mitchell, William J, *Dean,* Massachusetts Institute of Technology, School of Architecture and Planning, Cambridge MA (S)

Mitchellrgrast, Ellen, *Secy,* Fine Arts Center for the New River Valley, Pulaski VA

Mithen, Jeanne C, *Archivist,* Riley County Historical Museum, Manhattan KS

Mithen, Jeanne C, *Archivist,* Riley County Historical Museum, Seaton Library, Manhattan KS

Mitsanas, D, *Instr,* Humboldt State University, College of Arts & Humanities, Arcata CA (S)

Mittelgluek, E L, *Dir,* Mount Vernon Public Library, Fine Art Dept, Mount Vernon NY

Mittler, Gene, *Prof,* Texas Tech University, Dept of Art, Lubbock TX (S)

Miura, Carol, *Instr,* Rancho Santiago College, Art Dept, Santa Ana CA (S)

Mixon, Jamie, *Asst Prof,* Mississippi State University, Art Dept, Mississippi State MS (S)

Miyasaki, George, *Prof,* University of California, Berkeley, College of Letters & Sciences-Art Dept, Berkeley CA (S)

Miyata, Masako, *Prof,* James Madison University, Dept of Art, Harrisonburg VA (S)

Miyata, Wayne A, *Faculty,* Kauai Community College, Dept of Art, Lihue HI (S)

Miyazaki, Hiroshi, *Instr,* San Diego Mesa College, Fine Arts Dept, San Diego CA (S)

Mizuno, Alex, *Creative Dir,* Japantown Art & Media Workshop, San Francisco CA

Mnick, Krysia, *Public Relations Dir,* Pyramid Arts Center, Rochester NY

Mnuchin, Adrian, *Chmn,* International Museum of African Art, New York NY

Mo, Charles, *Dir Curatorial Serv,* Mint Museum of Art, Charlotte NC

Moak, Mark, *Chmn Dept,* Rocky Mountain College, Art Dept, Billings MT (S)

Moats, Tamara, *Cur of Education,* University of Washington, Henry Art Gallery, Seattle WA

Mobley, Karen R, *Gallery Dir,* New Mexico State University, University Art Gallery, Las Cruces NM

Mobley, Russell, *Instr,* Campbellsville College, Fine Arts Division, Campbellsville KY (S)

Mochon, Anne, *Assoc Prof,* University of Massachusetts, Amherst, Art History Program, Amherst MA (S)

Modder, Susan, *Acting Admin Dir,* Charles Allis Art Museum, Milwaukee WI

Mode, Robert L, *Chmn,* Vanderbilt University, Dept of Fine Arts, Nashville TN (S)

Mode, Robert L, *Assoc Prof,* Vanderbilt University, Dept of Fine Arts, Nashville TN (S)

Modica, Andrea, *Instr,* State University of New York College at Oneonta, Dept of Art, Oneonta NY (S)

Moe, Richard, *Pres,* National Trust for Historic Preservation, Washington DC

Moeller, Gary E, *Dir,* Rogers State College, Art Dept, Claremore OK (S)

Moeller, Madelyn, *Adminr,* Old Salem Inc, Museum of Early Southern Decorative Arts, Winston-Salem NC

Moesch, Susan, *Pres,* DuPage Art League School & Gallery, Wheaton IL

Moffatt, Constance, *Assoc Prof,* Pierce College, Art Dept, Woodland Hills CA (S)

Moffatt, David, *Asst Dir Operations,* Museum of Fine Arts, Boston MA

Moffatt, Laurie Norton, *Dir,* Norman Rockwell Museum at Stockbridge, Stockbridge MA

Moffett, Charles S, *Dir,* The Phillips Collection, Washington DC

Moffett, Kenworth W, *Exec Dir,* Museum of Art, Fort Lauderdale FL

Moffett, William, *Instr,* Wilkes Community College, Arts and Science Division, Wilkesboro NC (S)

Moffett, William A, *Dir Library,* Henry E Huntington Library, Art Collections & Botanical Gardens, San Marino CA

Moffett, W L, *Instr,* Western Illinois University, Art Dept, Macomb IL (S)

Moffitt, Ann, *Publicist,* Penobscot Marine Museum, Searsport ME

Moffitt, John, *Prof,* New Mexico State University, Art Dept, Las Cruces NM (S)

Mohanty, Gail Fowler, *Cur,* Old Slater Mill Association, Slater Mill Historic Site, Pawtucket RI

Mohn, Wallace D, *Deputy Dir Support Services,* Buffalo and Erie County Public Library, Buffalo NY

Mohr, John, *Cur Exhibits,* New Jersey State Museum, Trenton NJ

Mohr, Ken, *Adjunct Instr,* Maryville University of Saint Louis, Art Division, Saint Louis MO (S)

Moir, Alfred, *Adjunct Cur Drawings,* University of California, Santa Barbara, University Art Museum, Santa Barbara CA

Moisan, Micheline, *Cur Prints & Drawings,* Montreal Museum of Fine Arts, Montreal PQ

Moky, Wayne, *Pres,* Swedish American Museum Association of Chicago, Chicago IL

Moldenhauer, Richard, *Acting Dir & Business Mgr,* Mendel Art Gallery and Civic Conservatory, Saskatoon SK

Moldenhauer, Susan, *Cur Museum & Progs,* University of Wyoming, Art Museum, Laramie WY

Moldroski, Dick, *Prof,* Eastern Illinois University, Art Dept, Charleston IL (S)

Molen, Jan, *Dir,* Napa Valley College, Art Dept, Napa CA (S)

Molina, Samuel B, *Assoc Prof,* George Washington University, Dept of Art, Washington DC (S)

Molinaro, Monica, *Lectr,* Oakland University, Dept of Art and Art History, Rochester MI (S)

Mollett, David, *Instr,* University of Alaska, Dept of Art, Fairbanks AK (S)

Molnar, Lynette, *Dir,* Eye Gallery, San Francisco CA

Molnar, Mike, *Instr,* Luzerne County Community College, Commercial Art Dept, Nanticoke PA (S)

Molner, Frank, *Instr,* Rancho Santiago College, Art Dept, Santa Ana CA (S)

Mominee, John, *Dir,* University of Wisconsin - Platteville, Harry Nohr Art Gallery, Platteville WI

Monaco, Theresa, *Prof,* Emmanuel College, Art Dept, Boston MA (S)

Monaghan, Kathleen, *Branch Dir,* Whitney Museum of American Art, Whitney at Equitable Center, New York NY

Monaghan, Susan, *Dir of Operations,* Ann Arbor Art Association, Ann Arbor MI

Monahan, Michael, *Instr,* California State University, Chico, Art Dept, Chico CA (S)

Moncries, Bill, *Pres,* South Arkansas Arts Center, El Dorado AR

Mondrus, Martin, *Prof,* Glendale Community College, Dept of Fine Arts, Glendale CA (S)

Mongeon, Sandra, *Corp Program Dir,* DeCordova Museum & Sculpture Park, Lincoln MA

Monisey, Marna Grant, *VPres,* The American Federation of Arts, New York NY

Monje, Andrew, *Asst Prof,* Marymount University of Virginia, School of Arts & Sciences Division, Arlington VA (S)

Monkelien, Sheryl, *Instr,* Bismarck Junior College, Fine Arts Dept, Bismarck ND (S)

Monkhouse, Christopher, *Cur Architecture,* Carnegie Institute, Carnegie Museum of Art, Pittsburgh PA

Monkman, Betty C, *Assoc Cur,* White House, Washington DC

Monks, Dierdre, *Asst Prof,* Lycoming College, Art Dept, Williamsport PA (S)

Monroe, Arthur, *Registrar,* Oakland Museum, Art Dept, Oakland CA

Monroe, Dan L, *Pres & Chief Exec Officer,* Portland Art Museum, Portland OR

Monroe, Gary, *Prof,* Daytona Beach Community College, Dept of Fine Arts & Visual Arts, Daytona Beach FL (S)

Monroe, Michael, *Cur-in-charge,* National Museum of American Art, Renwick Gallery, Washington DC

Monroe, Michael, *Registrar,* Nicolaysen Art Museum and Discovery Center, Childrens Discovery Center, Casper WY

Monroe, Michael, *Registrar,* Nicolaysen Art Museum and Discovery Center, Museum, Casper WY

Monroe, P Jensen, *Supv Public Programs,* The Rockwell Museum, Corning NY

Monson, Richard D, *Prof,* Central Missouri State University, Art Dept, Warrensburg MO (S)

Montana, Daniela, *Dir Technical Assistance,* Association of Hispanic Arts, New York NY

Montgomery, Carlton, *Community Events Mgr,* Knight Publishing Company, Charlotte NC

Montgomery, Edward, *Prof,* Miami University, Dept Fine Arts, Hamilton OH (S)

Montgomery, Jane, *Registrar,* Harvard University, Harvard University Art Museums, Cambridge MA

Montgomery, Jane M, *Secy,* Cottonlandia Museum, Greenwood MS

Montgomery, Katherine, *Instr,* Davidson County Community College, Fine Arts & Humanities Div, Lexington NC (S)

Montgomery, Pat, *Admin Asst,* Alaska State Museum, Juneau AK

Montgomery, Renee, *Registrar,* Los Angeles County Museum of Art, Los Angeles CA

Montgomery, Roger, *Dean Environmental Design,* University of California, Berkeley, College of Environmental Design, Berkeley CA (S)

Monti, Laura, *In Charge Keeper,* Boston Public Library, Rare Book & Manuscripts Dept, Boston MA

Montileaux, Paulette, *Cur,* Indian Arts and Crafts Board, Sioux Indian Museum, Rapid City SD

Moody, Barbara, *Dean,* Monserrat College of Art, Beverly MA (S)

Moody, Larrie, *Asst Prof,* Pittsburg State University, Art Dept, Pittsburg KS (S)

Moon, Marvin, *Assoc Prof,* Texas Tech University, Dept of Art, Lubbock TX (S)

Moon, Steve, *Asst Architecture Librn,* Clemson University, Emery A Gunnin Architectural Library, Clemson SC

Mooney, Allen, *Asst Prof,* State University of New York, College at Cortland, Art Dept, Cortland NY (S)

Mooney, Sandra, *Librn,* Louisiana State University, Design Resource Center, Baton Rouge LA

Mooney, Tom, *Librn,* Cherokee National Historical Society, Inc, Library, Tahlequah OK

Mooney, Wanda, *Admin Staff Specialist,* Memorial University of Newfoundland, Art Gallery, Saint John's NF

Moore, Ann, *Asst Cur Educ,* New Orleans Museum of Art, New Orleans LA

Moore, Anne, *VPres,* Intermuseum Conservation Association, Oberlin OH

Moore, Anne F, *Dir,* Oberlin College, Allen Memorial Art Museum, Oberlin OH

Moore, Bill, *Instr,* Pacific Northwest College of Art, Portland OR (S)

Moore, Christine, *Admin Asst,* Southern Methodist University, Meadows Museum, Dallas TX

Moore, Craig, *Dir,* Taylor University, Chronicle-Tribune Art Gallery, Upland IN

Moore, Craig, *Chmn,* Taylor University, Art Dept, Upland IN (S)

Moore, C Witaker, *VPres,* Columbia Museum of Art, Columbia SC

Moore, Dan, *Pres,* American Association of Museums, International Council of Museums Committee, Washington DC

Moore, Dawn, *Gallery Assoc,* International Images, Ltd, Sewickley PA

Moore, Donald Everett, *Acting Chmn,* Mitchell Community College, Visual Art Dept, Statesville NC (S)

Moore, Elaine, *Dir & Cur,* Museum of Northern British Columbia, Ruth Harvey Art Gallery, Prince Rupert BC

Moore, Elaine, *Dir,* Museum of Northern British Columbia, Library, Prince Rupert BC

Moore, George S, *Pres,* Hispanic Society of America, Museum, New York NY

Moore, Jack, *Art Teacher,* Motlow State Community College, Art Dept, Tullahoma TN (S)

Moore, James C, *Dir,* Albuquerque Museum of Art, History & Science, Albuquerque NM

Moore, Jennifer W, *Exec Dir & Cur,* Green Hill Center for North Carolina Art, Greensboro NC

Moore, Jerry, *Dir of Operations,* High Desert Museum, Bend OR

Moore, Jerry C, *Assoc Dean,* University of Kansas, School of Fine Arts, Lawrence KS (S)

Moore, Jim, *Instr,* Campbellsville College, Fine Arts Division, Campbellsville KY (S)

Moore, John, *Prof,* Boston University, School of Visual Arts, Boston MA (S)

Moore, John, *Asst Prof,* Smith College, Art Dept, Northampton MA (S)

Moore, Julia Muney, *Exhib Cur,* Indianapolis Art League, Churchman-Fehsenfeld Gallery, Indianapolis IN

Moore, Julia Muney, *Resource Coordr,* Indianapolis Art League, Library, Indianapolis IN

Moore, Kathleen, *Asst to Art Librn,* University of Louisville, Margaret M Bridwell Art Library, Louisville KY

Moore, Kemille, *Asst Prof,* University of North Carolina at Wilmington, Dept of Fine Arts - Division of Art, Wilmington NC (S)

Moore, Lester, *Pres & Gen Mgr,* Polynesian Cultural Center, Laie HI

Moore, Marilyn, *Asst to Dir,* California State University Fullerton, Art Gallery, Visual Arts Center, Fullerton CA

Moore, Marshall, *Chmn,* Ward Foundation, Ward Museum of Wildfowl Art, Salisbury MD

Moore, Melodye, *Historic Site Mgr,* New York State Office of Parks, Recreation & Historical Preservation, Mills Mansion State Historical Site, Staatsburg NY

Moore, Nevalyn, *Instr,* Campbellsville College, Fine Arts Division, Campbellsville KY (S)

Moore, Owen, *Collections Mgr,* University of California, Los Angeles, Fowler Museum of Cultural History, Los Angeles CA

Moore, Patti, *Public Prog Officer,* St Thomas Elgin Art Gallery, Saint Thomas ON

Moore, Susan, *Chmn Painting, Drawing, & Sculpture,* Temple University, Tyler School of Art, Philadelphia PA (S)

Moorill, Rowena, *Instr,* Joe Kubert School of Cartoon & Graphic Art, Inc, Dover NJ (S)

Mooz, R Peter, *Dir,* Dallas Historical Society, Hall of State, Dallas TX

Moppett, George, *Asst Cur,* Mendel Art Gallery and Civic Conservatory, Saskatoon SK

Moppett, Ron, *Dir & Cur,* Alberta College of Art, Illingworth Kerr Gallery, Calgary AB

Morais, Lee, *Asst Dir Educ,* New Orleans Museum of Art, New Orleans LA

Morales, Raymond, *Assoc Prof,* University of Utah, Art Dept, Salt Lake City UT (S)

Morales-Coll, Eduardo, *Pres,* Ateneo Puertorriqueno, San Juan PR

Morales-Coll, Eduardo, *Pres,* Ateneo Puertorriqueno, Library, San Juan PR

Moran, Diane D, *Chmn,* Sweet Briar College, Art History Dept, Sweet Briar VA (S)

Moran, George F, *Treas,* National Hall of Fame for Famous American Indians, Anadarko OK

Moran, Joe, *Instr,* California State University, San Bernardino, Art Dept, San Bernardino CA (S)

Moran, Judy, *Exec Dir,* Public Art Works, San Rafael CA

Moran, Lois, *Editor-in-Chief American Craft Magazine,* American Craft Council, New York NY

Moran, Mark W, *Asst Prof,* Baylor University, Dept of Art, Waco TX (S)

Moran, Sara, *Executive Dir,* The Community Education Center, Philadelphia PA

Moran, Susan, *Admin Asst,* John P Barclay Memorial Gallery, Pittsburgh PA

Moran, Susan, *Admin Asst,* John P Barclay Memorial Gallery, Resource Center, Pittsburgh PA

Morandi, Thomas, *Prof,* Oregon State University, Dept of Art, Corvallis OR (S)

Morandi, Thomas, *Asst Prof,* Oregon State University, Dept of Art, Corvallis OR (S)

Mordecai, Jo, *Coordr Exhib,* Schenectady County Historical Society, Schenectady NY

More, Mary Thomas, *Librn,* Lourdes College, Duns Scotus Library, Sylvania OH

Morec, Marti, *Librn,* Berkeley Public Library, Berkeley CA

Morehouse, Dorothy V, *Pres,* Monmouth Museum and Cultural Center, Lincroft NJ

Morel, Sylvie, *Dir Exhib,* Canadian Museum of Civilization, Hull ON

Morell, Abelardo, *Chmn Media,* Massachusetts College of Art, Boston MA (S)

Morelli, Dina, *Instr,* Loras College, Dept of Art, Dubuque IA (S)

Morello, Samuel E, *Instr,* Charles Stewart Mott Community College, Art Area, School of Arts & Humanities, Flint MI (S)

Moreno, Barry, *Libr Technician,* The National Park Service, United States Department of the Interior, The Statue of Liberty National Monument, New York NY

Moreno, Ignacio, *Visual Resources Coordr,* The Phillips Collection, Washington DC

Moreno, Laura, *Deputy Dir,* Caribbean Cultural Center, New York NY

Moreno, Maria L, *Asst Prof,* University of Puerto Rico, Dept of Fine Arts, Rio Piedras PR (S)

Moreno Vega, Marta, *Exec Dir,* Caribbean Cultural Center, New York NY

Moretta, Eleanor, *Dir Exhib,* Pratt Institute Library, Rubelle & Norman Schafler Gallery, Brooklyn NY

Morey, Mark, *Cur Education,* Amarillo Art Association, Amarillo Art Center, Amarillo TX

Morgam, Donna, *Lectr,* Davis and Elkins College, Dept of Art, Elkins WV (S)

Morgan, Bonnie, *Coordr Public Progs,* London Regional Art & Historical Museums, London ON

Morgan, Carol, *Actig Dir Educ,* Museum of Modern Art, New York NY

Morgan, Chris, *Lectr,* Texas Woman's University, Dept of Visual Arts, Denton TX (S)

Morgan, Clarence, *Assoc Prof,* University of Minnesota, Minneapolis, Dept of Studio Art, Minneapolis MN (S)

Morgan, Dahlia, *Gallery Dir & Lecturer,* Florida International University, Visual Arts Dept, Miami FL (S)

Morgan, Dahlia, *Dir,* Florida International University, The Art Museum at FIU, Miami FL

Morgan, Elizabeth, *Development Dir,* Reynolda House Museum of American Art, Winston-Salem NC

Morgan, George, *Dir,* Massachusetts College of Art, Morton R Godine Library, Boston MA

Morgan, Helen, *Prof,* South Dakota State University, Dept of Visual Arts, Brookings SD (S)

Morgan, Keith, *Second VPres,* Society of Architectural Historians, Philadelphia PA

Morgan, Kenneth, *Asst Prof Studio Art,* Bethany College, Dept of Fine Arts, Bethany WV (S)

Morgan, Laura, *Serials,* Chicago Public Library, Harold Washington Library Center, Chicago IL

Morgan, Linda D, *Instructional Media Specialist,* University of South Carolina, Art Library, Columbia SC

Morgan, M, *Instr,* Humboldt State University, College of Arts & Humanities, Arcata CA (S)

Morgan, Richard, *Cur Artistic Prog,* Charles Allis Art Museum, Milwaukee WI

Morgan, Risa, *Exec Dir,* City Art Works, Pratt Fine Arts Center, Seattle WA (S)

Morgan, Robert C, *Prof,* Rochester Institute of Technology, School of Art and Design, Rochester NY (S)

Morgan, Theodora, *Librn,* National Sculpture Society, Library, New York NY

Morgan, William, *Prof,* University of Wisconsin-Superior, Programs in the Visual Arts, Superior WI (S)

Morgan, Windle, *Preparator,* Cheekwood-Tennessee Botanical Gardens & Museum of Art, Nashville TN

Morgenstern, Joan, *Pres,* Houston Center For Photography, Houston TX

Mori, John, *Asst Prof,* Arkansas Tech University, Dept of Art, Russellville AR (S)

Moriarty, Marcia, *Instr,* Mount Mary College, Art Dept, Milwaukee WI (S)

Moriarty, Peter, *Photography Dept Head,* Johnson State College, Dept Fine Arts, Dibden Gallery, Johnson VT (S)

Morin, Jeffrey, *Asst Prof,* University of Tennessee at Chattanooga, Dept of Art, Chattanooga TN (S)

Moriority, Kaleen, *Asst Prof,* Rochester Institute of Technology, School of Photographic Arts & Sciences, Rochester NY (S)

Morison, John H, *VPres,* The Currier Gallery of Art, Manchester NH

Morita, Linda, *Librn & Archivist,* McMichael Canadian Art Collection, Library, Kleinburg ON

Moritz, Terry, *Pres,* The Art Institute of Chicago, Society for Contemporary Arts, Chicago IL

Morlan, Jenny, *Prof,* DePaul University, Dept of Art, Chicago IL (S)

Morley, Geraldine, *Asst,* Fine Arts Museum of Long Island, Hempstead NY

Morley, Stephen H, *Dir,* Academy of the New Church, Glencairn Museum, Bryn Athyn PA

Mornes, Joon, *Library Head,* University of Minnesota, Architecture Library, Minneapolis MN

Morningstar, William, *Assoc Prof,* Berea College, Art Dept, Berea KY (S)

Morr, Lynell, *Librn,* State Art Museum of Florida, John & Mable Ringling Museum of Art, Sarasota FL

Morr, Lynell A, *Librn,* State Art Museum of Florida, Art Research Library, Sarasota FL

Morrell, John, *Instr,* Georgetown University, Dept of Fine Arts, Washington DC (S)

Morrill, Allen, *Library Dir,* Kansas City Art Institute, Library, Kansas City MO

Morrill, Julie, *Dir Public Relations,* Colorado Springs Fine Arts Center, Colorado Springs CO

Morrin, Peter, *Dir,* J B Speed Art Museum, Louisville KY

Morris, Angie, *Facility Mgr,* Artspace Inc, Raleigh NC

Morris, Anne, *Exhib Dir,* Palos Verdes Art Center, Rancho Palos Verdes CA

Morris, Anne O, *Librn,* Toledo Museum of Art, Library, Toledo OH

Morris, Daniel, *Chmn,* Waynesburg College, Dept of Fine Arts, Waynesburg PA (S)

Morris, Daphne, *Archivist,* Town of Cummington Historical Commission, Kingman Tavern Historical Museum, Cummington MA

Morris, Earl W, *Head Dept,* University of Minnesota, Dept of Design, Housing & Apparel, Saint Paul MN (S)

Morris, Jeffory, *Cur,* Galeria Mesa, Mesa Arts Center, Mesa AZ

Morris, Joyce, *Secy,* Berry College, Moon Gallery, Mount Berry GA

Morris, Kathleen, *Mgr,* Ontario Crafts Council, Craft Resource Centre, Toronto ON

Morris, Kim, *Head Reference Librn,* James Prendergast Library Association, Jamestown NY

Morris, Leslie A, *Cur Books & Manuscripts,* The Rosenbach Museum and Library, Philadelphia PA

Morris, Paula, *Dir,* Wilkes Art Gallery, North Wilkesboro NC

Morris, Phillip S, *Dean,* Memphis College of Art, G Pillow Lewis Memorial Library, Memphis TN

Morris, Phillip S, *Exec VPres,* Memphis College of Art, Memphis TN (S)

Morris, Robert L, *Head Art Dept,* Penn Valley Community College, Art Dept, Kansas City MO (S)

Morris, Stephen, *Treas,* Maricopa County Historical Society, Desert Caballeros Western Museum, Wickenburg AZ

Morris, Wayne, *Chmn 2-D Fine Arts,* Moore College of Art & Design, Philadelphia PA (S)

Morris, W S, *Chmn & CEO,* Morris Communications Corporation, Augusta GA

Morris, W S, *Chmn Board,* Morris Communications Corporation, Morris Museum of Art, Augusta GA

Morrisey, Bob, *Prof,* Polk Community College, Art, Letters & Social Sciences, Winter Haven FL (S)

Morrisey, Marena Grant, *Dir,* Orlando Museum of Art, Orlando FL

Morrisey, Marena Grant, *Executive Dir,* Orlando Museum of Art, Art Library, Orlando FL

Morrison, Alan E, *Librn,* University of Pennsylvania, Fisher Fine Arts Library - Art Dept, Philadelphia PA

Morrison, Anise, *Asst Cur,* Chattahoochee Valley Art Museum, LaGrange GA

Morrison, Ann, *Progs Coordr,* Mississippi Department of Archives & History, Mississippi State Historical Museum, Jackson MS

Morrison, George, *Instr,* Grand Marais Art Colony, Grand Marais MN (S)

Morrison, Keith, *Chmn,* University of Maryland, Department of Art, College Park MD (S)

Morrison, Ken, *Thesis Dir,* Toronto Art Therapy Institute, Toronto ON (S)

Morrison, M Christine, *Librn,* National Endowment for the Arts, Library, Washington DC

Morrison, Phil, *Installer,* Severin Wunderman Museum, Irvine CA

Morrison, Philip, *Instr,* College of the Canyons, Art Dept, Valencia CA (S)

Morrison, Philip R, *Dir,* Hermitage Foundation Museum, Norfolk VA

Morrison, Philip R, *Dir,* Hermitage Foundation Museum, Library, Norfolk VA

Morrison, Sue, *Chmn Design Dept,* Art Institute of Boston, Boston MA (S)

Morrison, Theo, *Bookkeeper,* Lahaina Arts Society, Art Organization, Lahaina HI

Morrissey, T, *Instr,* Community College of Rhode Island, Dept of Art, Warwick RI (S)

Morrissey, Tom, *Dir & Librn,* Community College of Rhode Island, Flanagan Valley Campus Art Gallery, Warwick RI

Morrow, Delores, *Photograph Cur,* Montana Historical Society, Library, Helena MT

Morrow, Lisa, *Dir Grants & Development,* University of California, California Museum of Photography, Riverside CA

Morrow, Terry, *Prof,* Texas Tech University, Dept of Art, Lubbock TX (S)

Morsches, Richard, *VPres Operations,* The Metropolitan Museum of Art, New York NY

Morse, A Reynolds, *Pres,* Salvador Dali Museum, Saint Petersburg FL

Morse, Bart, *Assoc Prof,* University of Arizona, Dept of Art, Tucson AZ (S)

Mortenson, K Hauser, *Instr,* Golden West College, Visual Art Dept, Huntington Beach CA (S)

Mortimer, Ann, *Pres,* Ontario Crafts Council, Toronto ON

Mortimer, Kristin A, *Dir,* Mount Holyoke College, Art Museum, South Hadley MA

Mortimer, Ruth, *Lectr,* Smith College, Art Dept, Northampton MA (S)

Morton, Gregory, *Cur Educ,* Chattahoochee Valley Art Museum, LaGrange GA

Morton, Pat, *Art Coordr,* NOVA Corporation of Alberta, NOVA Garden Court Gallery, Calgary AB

Morton, Robert, *Head Dept,* Plymouth State College, Art Dept, Plymouth NH (S)

Mortonson, Sheila, *Librn,* Tucson Museum of Art, Tucson AZ

Mortonson, Sheila, *Librn,* Tucson Museum of Art, Library, Tucson AZ

Mosby, Dewey F, *Dir,* Colgate University, Picker Art Gallery, Hamilton NY

Mosby, Norma, *Librn,* University of Arkansas, Fine Arts Library, Fayetteville AR

Moseley, Bruce M, *Cur,* Fort Ticonderoga Association, Ticonderoga NY

Moseley, Bruce M, *Cur,* Fort Ticonderoga Association, Thompson-Pell Research Center, Ticonderoga NY

Moseley, Debra, *Instr,* The Arkansas Arts Center, Museum School, Little Rock AR (S)

Moser, Christopher L, *Cur Anthropology,* Riverside Municipal Museum, Riverside CA

Moser, Erika, *Second VPres,* Society for Folk Arts Preservation, Inc, New York NY

Moser, Jan, *Head,* Merced College, Arts Division, Merced CA (S)

Moser, Joann G, *Cur Graphic Arts,* National Museum of American Art, Washington DC

Moser, Ken, *Chief Conservator,* Brooklyn Museum, Brooklyn NY

Moses, Eva W, *Asst Librn,* R W Norton Art Gallery, Library, Shreveport LA

Moses, H Vincent, *Cur History,* Riverside Municipal Museum, Riverside CA

Moses, Jennifer, *Asst Prof,* University of New Hampshire, Dept of the Arts, Durham NH (S)

Moses, Marshall, *Pres,* Yarmouth County Historical Society, Yarmouth County Museum, Yarmouth NS

Moses, Norma, *Secy,* State University of New York at Binghamton, University Art Gallery, Vestal NY

Moskowitz, Anita, *Assoc Prof,* State University of New York at Stony Brook, Art Dept, Stony Brook NY (S)

Moskowitz, Bob, *Adjunct Instr,* Maryville University of Saint Louis, Art Division, Saint Louis MO (S)

Mosman, Tim, *Asst Dir,* Mills College, Art Gallery, Oakland CA

Moss, Dena, *Pres,* Redding Museum of Art & History, Redding CA

Moss, Frances, *Instr,* John C Calhoun State Community College, Division of Fine Arts, Decatur AL (S)

Moss, Joe, *Coordr Sculpture,* University of Delaware, Dept of Art, Newark DE (S)

Moss, Michael E, *Dir Museum,* United States Military Academy, West Point Museum, West Point NY

Moss, Myrna, *Admin,* Cherokee National Historical Society, Inc, Tahlequah OK

Moss, Rick, *Cur History,* California Afro-American Museum, Los Angeles CA

Moss, Roger W, *Dir,* Athenaeum of Philadelphia, Philadelphia PA

Most, Gregory P J, *Chief Slide Librn,* National Gallery of Art, Slide Library, Washington DC

Motes, J Barry, *Asst Prof,* Jefferson Community College, Fine Arts, Louisville KY (S)

Motherwell, M K, *Educ Coordr,* City of Springdale, Shiloh Museum, Springdale AR

Motley, A J, *Cur Manuscripts Collections,* Chicago Historical Society, Chicago IL

Motsinger, Connie, *Instr,* Antonelli Institute of Art & Photography, Cincinnati OH (S)

Mottram, Ron, *Chmn,* Illinois State University, Art Dept, Normal IL (S)

Moty, Eleanor, *Prof,* University of Wisconsin, Madison, Dept of Art, Madison WI (S)

Motz, Leslie P, *Chmn,* Indiana-Purdue University, Dept of Fine Arts, Fort Wayne IN (S)

Moulton, Alice, *Secy,* Concord Art Association, Concord MA

Mount, Sigrid Docken, *Librn,* Vanderbilt University, Arts Library, Nashville TN

Mousseau, P J, *Prof,* Moorhead State University, Dept of Art, Moorhead MN (S)

Mowbray, Caire, *Lectr,* Notre Dame College, Art Dept, Manchester NH (S)

Mower, D Roger, *Adminr,* Audubon Wildlife Sanctuary, Audubon PA

Mowery, Frank, *Pres,* Guild of Book Workers, New York NY

Mowery, Veronica, *Secy,* Shippensburg University, Kauffman Gallery, Shippensburg PA

Mowry, Elizabeth, *Instr,* Woodstock School of Art, Inc, Woodstock NY (S)

Mowry, Robert, *Cur Chinese Art,* Harvard University, Harvard University Art Museums, Cambridge MA

Mowry, Robert, *Cur Chinese Art,* Harvard University, Arthur M Sackler Museum, Cambridge MA

Moxey, Keith, *Chmn,* Columbia University, Barnard College, New York NY (S)

Moxley, Richard, *Dir,* Agecroft Association, Richmond VA

Moy, Henry, *Dir,* Beloit College, Wright Museum of Art, Beloit WI

Moy, Henry, *Dir Art Museum,* Beloit College, Dept of Art, Beloit WI (S)

Moynahan, Alberta, *Asst Dir,* Ephraim McDowell-Cambus-Kenneth Foundation, McDowell House & Apothecary Shop, Danville KY

Moynihan, Jeanne, *Lectr,* Cardinal Stritch College, Art Dept, Milwaukee WI (S)

Mrja, Karen L, *Dir Fine Arts,* College of Saint Benedict, Art Gallery, Saint Joseph MN

Mroczek, Russell, *Chmn Design,* Minneapolis College of Art and Design, Minneapolis MN (S)

Mroczkowski, Dennis, *Dir,* Headquarters Fort Monroe, Dept of Army, Casemate Museum, Fort Monroe VA

Mross, Jean, *Instr,* The Arkansas Arts Center, Museum School, Little Rock AR (S)

Muccifori, Sarah M, *Development Dir,* Printmaking Council of New Jersey, North Branch NJ

Muehlig, Linda, *Assoc Cur Paintings,* Smith College, Museum of Art, Northampton MA

Mueller, Garry, *Chmn,* Pacific University in Oregon, Arts Division, Forest Grove OR (S)

Mueller, John C, *Prof,* University of Detroit Mercy, School of Architecture, Detroit MI (S)

Mueller, Marlene, *Assoc Prof,* Wayne State College, Art Dept, Wayne NE (S)

Mueller, Martha A, *Cataloging & Serials Librn,* New York State College of Ceramics at Alfred University, Scholes Library of Ceramics, Alfred NY

Mueller, Robert, *Asst Prof,* University of Florida, Dept of Art, Gainesville FL (S)

Mugar, Martin, *Dir Gallery,* The Art Institute of Boston, Gallery East, Boston MA

Muhlert, Jan Keene, *Dir,* Amon Carter Museum, Fort Worth TX

Muhn, B G, *Instr,* Georgetown University, Dept of Fine Arts, Washington DC (S)

Muick, Paul C, *Prof,* Mary Washington College, Art Dept, Fredericksburg VA (S)

Muir, James, *VPres,* Society of American Historical Artists, Jericho NY

Muir, Tom, *Cur,* T T Wentworth Jr Museum, Florida State Museum, Pensacola FL

Muir, Tom, *Museum Admnr,* Historic Pensacola Preservation Board, Historic Pensacola Village, Pensacola FL

Muir, Tom, *Museum Admnr,* Historic Pensacola Preservation Board, Library, Pensacola FL

Muirhead, Robert, *Instr,* Hamilton College, Art Dept, Clinton NY (S)

Muka, Cheryl L H, *Chief Adminr,* Cornell University, Herbert F Johnson Museum of Art, Ithaca NY

Muldavin-Smirle, Phyllis, *Chmn,* Los Angeles City College, Dept of Art, Los Angeles CA (S)

Muldoon, William, *VPres for Mgt,* Meridian House International, Washington DC

Mules, Helen, *Assoc Cur Drawings,* The Metropolitan Museum of Art, New York NY

Mulford, Linda M, *Librn,* Fairfield Historical Society, Library, Fairfield CT

Mulgrew, John, *Chmn,* Pace University, Dyson College of Arts & Sciences, Pleasantville NY (S)

Muliero, Diane, *Education Coordr,* Art Complex Museum, Duxbury MA

Mullan, Patricia, *Head Reference,* Berkeley Public Library, Berkeley CA

Mullen, Denise, *Assoc Prof,* Jersey City State College, Art Dept, Jersey City NJ (S)

Mullen, James, *Chmn,* State University of New York College at Oneonta, Dept of Art, Oneonta NY (S)

Mullen, Nancy Jo, *Dir,* Rogue Valley Art Association, Rogue Gallery, Medford OR

Mullen, Philip, *Prof,* University of South Carolina, Dept of Art, Columbia SC (S)

Mullen, Ruth, *Librn,* Reynolda House Museum of American Art, Library, Winston-Salem NC

Muller, Arlene, *Gift Shop Mgr,* Eccles Community Art Center, Ogden UT

Muller, Max P, *Gallery Dir,* Sarasota Visual Art Center, Sarasota FL

Muller, Nicholas, *Dir,* State Historical Society of Wisconsin, State Historical Museum, Madison WI

Muller, Priscilla E, *Cur Mus Paintings & Metalwork,* Hispanic Society of America, Museum, New York NY

Muller, Richard, *Prof,* Portland State University, Dept of Art, Portland OR (S)

Muller, Sheila, *Assoc Prof,* University of Utah, Art Dept, Salt Lake City UT (S)

Mulligan, Catherine, *Lectr,* North Dakota State University, Div of Fine Arts, Fargo ND (S)

Mullin, A G, *Instr,* Western Illinois University, Art Dept, Macomb IL (S)

Mullin, John R, *Dept Head,* University of Massachusetts, Amherst, Dept of Landscape Architecture & Regional Planning, Amherst MA (S)

Mullin, Timothy J, *Site Dir,* Historical Society of Delaware, George Read II House, Wilmington DE

Mullineaux, Connie, *Art Education,* Edinboro University of Pennsylvania, Art Dept, Edinboro PA (S)

Mulvany, John, *Chairperson Art & Photography Depts,* Columbia College, Art Dept, Chicago IL (S)

Mulvany, John, *Museum Coordr & Chmn Dept Art & Photography,* Columbia College, The Museum of Contemporary Photography, Chicago IL

Muncaster, Ian, *Treas,* Professional Art Dealers Association of Canada, Toronto ON

Munce, James C, *Assoc Prof,* Kansas State University, Art Dept, Manhattan KS (S)

Munchaca, Belinda, *Dance Prog Dir,* Guadalupe Cultural Arts Center, San Antonio TX

Munden, Carol, *Cur,* Mississippi Valley Conservation Authority, Mill of Kintail Museum, Almonte ON

Mundy, James, *Dir,* Vassar College, Vassar Art Gallery, Poughkeepsie NY

Munford, M B, *Asst Cur Decorative of Arts,* Baltimore Museum of Art, Baltimore MD

Munhall, Edgar, *Cur,* Frick Collection, New York NY

Muniz, Maria L, *Communications Specialist,* Tryon Palace Historic Sites & Gardens, New Bern NC

Munk, Rosalyn, *Dir,* Arizona State University, Memorial Union Gallery, Tempe AZ

Munns, Lynn R, *Div Head,* Casper College, Dept of Visual Arts, Casper WY (S)

Muno, Ed, *Art Dir,* National Cowboy Hall of Fame and Western Heritage Center, Oklahoma City OK

Munoz, Teresa, *Chmn,* Loyola Marymount University, Art & Art History Dept, Los Angeles CA (S)

Munro, Alan, *Prof,* Oregon State University, Dept of Art, Corvallis OR (S)

Munroe, Valerie, *Treas,* Revelstoke Art Group, Revelstoke BC

Munson, Richard, *Chmn,* University of Northern Colorado, Dept of Visual Arts, Greeley CO (S)

Munzenrider, Claire, *Conservator,* Museum of New Mexico, Museum of International Folk Art, Santa Fe NM

Munzner, Aribert, *Acting Visual Studies,* Minneapolis College of Art and Design, Minneapolis MN (S)

Murakami, Jean, *Asst Prof,* East Tennessee State University, Fine Arts Dept, Johnson City TN (S)

Murakishi, Steve, *Head Printmaking Dept,* Cranbrook Academy of Art, Bloomfield Hills MI (S)

Murch, Anna Valentina, *Asst Prof,* Mills College, Art Dept, Oakland CA (S)

Murdoch, Elena, *Financial Officer,* Portland Museum of Art, Portland ME

Murdock, Kathy, *Executive Secy,* The Stained Glass Association of America, Kansas City MO

Murgia, Pierre, *Publications,* Musee du Quebec, Quebec PQ

Muri, Wendy, *Admin Asst,* Swift Current National Exhibition Centre, Swift Current SK

Murillo, Stephen, *Asst Cur,* Wichita State University, Edwin A Ulrich Museum of Art, Wichita KS

Murphy, Brian, *Registrar,* Memorial University of Newfoundland, Art Gallery, Saint John's NF

Murphy, Charlotte, *Exec Dir,* National Association of Artists' Organizations (NAAO), Washington DC

Murphy, Debra E, *Asst Prof,* University of North Florida, Dept of Communications & Visual Arts, Jacksonville FL (S)

Murphy, Donn, *Prof,* Georgetown University, Dept of Fine Arts, Washington DC (S)

Murphy, Edith, *Registrar,* William A Farnsworth Library and Art Museum, Rockland ME

Murphy, Franklin D, *Chmn Bd of Trustees,* National Gallery of Art, Washington DC

Murphy, Greg, *Co-Chair Drawing & Painting,* Ontario College of Art, Toronto ON (S)

Murphy, Helen, *Asst Dir Communications & Marketing,* National Gallery of Canada, Ottawa ON

Murphy, Janet, *Pres,* Missouri Western State College, Fine Arts Gallery, Saint Joseph MO

Murphy, John Satre, *Assoc Prof,* University of Wisconsin-Parkside, Art Dept, Kenosha WI (S)

Murphy, Kenneth, *Instr,* Mohawk Valley Community College, Advertising Design and Production, Utica NY (S)

Murphy, Margaret H, *Chmn,* Alabama Southern Community College, Art Dept, Monroeville AL (S)

Murphy, Marilyn, *Librn,* Mount Mercy College, Library, Cedar Rapids IA

Murphy, Marilyn, *Assoc Prof,* Vanderbilt University, Dept of Fine Arts, Nashville TN (S)

Murphy, Marjorie, *Pres,* Wayne County Historical Society, Museum, Honesdale PA

Murphy, Melinda, *Store Mgr,* Morris Communications Corporation, Morris Museum of Art, Augusta GA

Murphy, Michaela A, *Cur Photography,* Norfolk Historical Society Inc, Museum, Norfolk CT

Murphy, Patricia, *Dir & Cur,* Beacon Street Gallery, Uptown, Chicago IL

Murphy, Patrick, *Assoc Prof,* Pennsylvania College of Technology, Dept of Design & Communiation Arts, Williamsport PA (S)

Murphy, Patrick T, *Dir,* Institute of Contemporary Art, Philadelphia PA

Murphy, Rivers, *Head Dept,* Northwestern State University of Louisiana, Dept of Art, Natchitoches LA (S)

Murphy, Ronald J, *Pres,* Louisville Visual Art Association, Louisville KY

Murras, Amerigo, *Spec Dir Ecotec,* Storefront for Art & Architecture, New York NY

Murray, Ann, *Dir,* Wheaton College, Watson Gallery, Norton MA

Murray, Diana T, *VPres Finance & Treas,* The Metropolitan Museum of Art, New York NY

Murray, Eileen M, *Exec Dir,* Hyde Park Art Center, Chicago IL

Murray, G, *Chmn Display Design,* Fashion Institute of Technology, Art & Design Division, New York NY (S)

Murray, Gale, *Assoc Prof,* Colorado College, Dept of Art, Colorado Springs CO (S)

Murray, Holly, *Instr,* Springfield College, Dept of Visual and Performing Arts, Springfield MA (S)

Murray, I, *Librn,* McGill University, Blackader-Lauterman Library of Architecture and Art, Montreal PQ

Murray, Joan, *Dir,* The Robert McLaughlin Gallery, Oshawa ON

Murray, John, *Chmn,* New York Institute of Technology, Gallery, Old Westbury NY

Murray, John, *Chmn,* New York Institute of Technology, Fine Arts Dept, Old Westbury NY (S)

Murray, John W, *Pres,* Beverly Historical Society, Cabot, Hale and Balch House Museums, Beverly MA

Murray, Julia K, *Asst Prof,* University of Wisconsin, Madison, Dept of Art History, Madison WI (S)

Murray, Kenneth, *Chmn Div,* Wingate College, Division of Fine Arts, Wingate NC (S)

Murray, Merrill, *Library-LRC Dir,* Art Institute of Fort Lauderdale, Technical Library, Fort Lauderdale FL

Murray, Neale, *Chmn Dept,* North Park College, Art Dept, Chicago IL (S)

Murray, Reuben, *Exec Dir,* South Arkansas Arts Center, Library, El Dorado AR

Murray, Richard, *Cur Painting & Sculpture,* National Museum of American Art, Washington DC

Murray, Rueben, *Exec Dir,* South Arkansas Arts Center, El Dorado AR

Murray, Ruth Anne, *Publicity & Promotion Coordr,* London Regional Art & Historical Museums, London ON

Murray, Sarah, *Paintings Conservator,* Balboa Art Conservation Center, San Diego CA

Murray, Susan, *Dir Development,* Cleveland Center for Contemporary Art, Cleveland OH

Murray, Tim, *Dir,* Brevard College, Sims Art Center, Brevard NC

Murray, Timothy G, *Prof,* Brevard College, Division of Fine Arts, Brevard NC (S)

Murro, Sue F, *Dir Summer School,* Virginia Commonwealth University, School of the Arts, Richmond VA (S)

Murrow, Nila West, *Head Dept,* Southern Nazarene University, Art Dept, Bethany OK (S)

Murtagh, Gina, *Asst Dir,* Light Work, Syracuse NY

Muscat, Ann, *Deputy Dir,* California Museum of Science and Industry, Los Angeles CA

Musgnug, Kristin, *Asst Prof,* University of Arkansas, Art Dept, Fayetteville AR (S)

Musi, Susan, *Gallery Dir,* Western Washington University, Viking Union Gallery, Bellingham WA

Muskovitz, Rosalyn, *Assoc Prof,* Grand Valley State University, Art & Design Dept, Allendale MI (S)

Must, Raymond, *Assoc Prof,* Wright State University, Dept of Art & Art History, Dayton OH (S)

Muth, Tom J, *Asst Dir,* Topeka Public Library, Gallery of Fine Arts, Topeka KS

Mycue, David, *Cur Archaeology & Coll,* Hidalgo County Historical Museum, Edinburg TX

Myers, Adele, *Instr,* Saint Thomas Aquinas College, Art Dept, Sparkhill NY (S)

Myers, Chris, *Chmn Graphic Design,* University of the Arts, Philadelphia College of Art & Design, Philadelphia PA (S)

Myers, Derek, *Head Art Dept,* Virginia Polytechnic Institute & State University, Armory Art Gallery, Blacksburg VA

Myers, Derek, *Head Dept,* Virginia Polytechnic Institute & State University, Dept of Art & Art History, Blacksburg VA (S)

Myers, Fred A, *Dir,* Thomas Gilcrease Institute of American History & Art, Tulsa OK

Myers, Gay, *Conservator,* Lyman Allyn Art Museum, New London CT

Myers, Joanne, *Asst to Dir,* Fruitlands Museum, Inc, Harvard MA

Myers, John, *Chmn,* University of North Carolina at Wilmington, Dept of Fine Arts - Division of Art, Wilmington NC (S)

Myers, John, *Assoc Prof,* University of North Carolina at Wilmington, Dept of Fine Arts - Division of Art, Wilmington NC (S)

Myers, Lynn R, *Dir,* University of South Carolina, McKissick Museum, Columbia SC

Myers, Malcolm, *Prof Emeritus,* University of Minnesota, Minneapolis, Dept of Studio Art, Minneapolis MN (S)

Myers, Mary L, *Cur,* The Metropolitan Museum of Art, Dept of Prints & Illustrated Books, New York NY

Myers, Paulette, *Head Fiber & Fabric,* Southern Illinois University at Edwardsville, Dept of Art & Design, Edwardsville IL (S)

Myers, Roy, *Acting Chief Exec Officer,* Pennsylvania State University at New Kensington, Depts of Art & Architecture, New Kensington PA (S)

Myers, Suzita, *Cur,* Sandwich Historical Society, Center Sandwich NH

Myers, William G, *Head Collections,* Ohio Historical Society, Archives-Library Division, Columbus OH

Myerson, Susan, *Chief Cataloguer,* Harvard University, Fine Arts Library, Cambridge MA

Myford, James, *Chmn Dept,* Slippery Rock University of Pennsylvania, Dept of Art, Slippery Rock PA (S)

Mylorie, Rosyln D, *Cataloger,* School of Visual Arts Library, New York NY

Mynatt, Ron, *Instr,* The Arkansas Arts Center, Museum School, Little Rock AR (S)

Naar, Harry I, *Assoc Prof of Art & Dir,* Rider College, Art Gallery, Lawrenceville NJ

Nacke, Bruce, *Interior Design Coordr,* University of North Texas, School of Visual Arts, Denton TX (S)

Nadel, Joshua, *Prof,* University of Maine at Augusta, Division of Fine & Performing Arts, Augusta ME (S)

Nadolny, Kathi, *Asst Dir,* Arts United of Greater Fort Wayne, Fort Wayne IN

Naef, Weston, *Cur Photographs,* Getty Center for the History of Art & the Humanities Trust Museum, Santa Monica CA

Naef, Weston, *Cur Photographs,* Getty Center for the History of Art & the Humanities Trust Museum, The J Paul Getty Museum, Santa Monica CA

Nagai, Mona, *Film Coll Mgr,* University of California, University Art Museum, Berkeley CA

Nagano, Karen, *Instr,* Monterey Peninsula College, Art Dept, Monterey CA (S)

Nagar, Devvrat, *Instr,* La Roche College, Division of Graphics, Design & Communication, Pittsburgh PA (S)

Nagel, John, *Instructor,* Saint Louis Community College at Meramec, Art Dept, Saint Louis MO (S)

Nagel, Stewart, *Dir,* Bloomsburg University of Pennsylvania, Haas Gallery of Art, Bloomsburg PA

Nagel, Stewart, *Prof,* Bloomsburg University, Dept of Art, Bloomsburg PA (S)

Nager, Arthur, *Assoc Prof,* University of Bridgeport, Art Dept, Bridgeport CT (S)

Nagle, Ron, *Prof,* Mills College, Art Dept, Oakland CA (S)

Nahas, Christopher, *Slide File Coordr,* Artists Space, New York NY

Nakamura, Caroline, *Chmn,* University of Hawaii, Kapiolani Community College, Honolulu HI (S)

Nakashima, Thomas, *Assoc Prof,* Catholic University of America, Dept of Art, Washington DC (S)

Nakazato, Hitoshi, *Asst Prof,* University of Pennsylvania, Graduate School of Fine Arts, Philadelphia PA (S)

Nance, William W, *Assoc Prof,* Alabama A & M University, Art and Art Education, Normal AL (S)

Nanna, Susan, *Shop Mgr,* Craft Alliance Gallery & Education Center, Saint Louis MO

Naos, Theodore, *Assoc Prof,* Catholic University of America, School of Architecture & Planning, Washington DC (S)

Napolitano, Kaye, *Mgr,* Oatlands, Inc, Leesburg VA

Napran, Laura, *Cur,* Enook Galleries, Waterloo ON

Narad, Regina L, *Executive Asst to Dir,* Westmoreland Museum of Art, Greensburg PA

Naragon, Dwain, *Dept Head,* University of Alaska, Dept of Art, Fairbanks AK (S)

Narrow, Kathryn, *Gen Mgr,* Clay Studio, Philadelphia PA

Narwicz, Christina, *Development Asst,* Bemis Foundation, New Gallery, Omaha NE

Nasby, Judith, *Dir,* MacDonald Stewart Art Centre Art Center, Guelph ON

Nasgaard, Roald, *Chief Cur,* Art Gallery of Ontario, Toronto ON

Nash, Anedith, *Liberal Arts,* Minneapolis College of Art and Design, Minneapolis MN (S)

Nash, James, *Prog Mgr,* Piatt Castles, West Liberty OH

Nash, Steven, *Assoc Dir & Chief Cur,* Fine Arts Museums of San Francisco, M H de Young Memorial Museum and California Palace of the Legion of Honor, San Francisco CA

Nash-Wright, Holly, *Dean,* Elgin Community College, Fine Arts Dept, Elgin IL (S)

Nasisse, Andy, *Ceramics,* University of Georgia, Franklin College of Arts & Sciences, Dept of Art, Athens GA (S)

Naso, Albert, *Chmn,* Bakersfield College, Art Dept, Bakersfield CA (S)

Nasse, Harry, *Chmn of the Board,* Ward-Nasse Gallery, New York NY

Natella, Dora, *Head Sculpture Dept,* Kalamazoo Institute of Arts, KIA School, Kalamazoo MI (S)

Natella, Dora, *Asst Prof,* Indiana University, Bloomington, Henry Radford Hope School of Fine Arts, Bloomington IN (S)

Nathan, Jacqueline, *Gallery Dir,* Bowling Green State University, School of Art, Bowling Green OH (S)

Nathan, Jacqueline S, *Exhib Prog Adminr,* Bowling Green State University, School of Art, Bowling Green OH

Nathanson, Carol, *Assoc Prof,* Wright State University, Dept of Art & Art History, Dayton OH (S)

Nathanson, Jeff, *Exec Dir,* Richmond Art Center, Civic Center Plaza, Richmond CA

Nation, Morna, *Chmn,* Wharton County Junior College, Art Dept, Wharton TX (S)

Naubert-Riser, Constance, *Instr,* Universite de Montreal, Dept of Art History, Montreal PQ (S)

Naujoks, Robert, *Chmn Dept,* Mount Mercy College, Art Dept, Cedar Rapids IA (S)

Nauman, Lynn, *Educ Coordr,* Redding Museum of Art & History, Redding CA

Nauts, Alan, *Instr,* Saint Francis College, Art Dept, Fort Wayne IN (S)

Navaretta, Cynthia, *Exec Dir,* Midmarch Associates, Women Artists News Archive, New York NY

Navel, Joseph, *Assoc Dir,* Glassell School of Art, Houston TX (S)

Navidi, Sheherzad, *Librn,* Saint Augustine Historical Society, Library, Saint Augustine FL

Navin, Patrick, *Instr,* Green River Community College, Art Dept, Auburn WA (S)

Navrat, Dennis, *Chmn,* University of South Dakota, Dept of Art, Vermillion SD (S)

Nawrocki, Thomas, *Prof,* Mississippi University for Women, Division of Fine & Performing Arts, Columbus MS (S)

Naylor, David, *Dir Visual Arts,* Universite Laval Cite Universitaire, School of Visual Arts, Quebec PQ (S)

Nazar, D, *VPres,* Rodman Hall Arts Centre, Saint Catharines ON

Nazionale, Nina, *Reference,* School of Visual Arts Library, New York NY

Neaderland, Louise, *Dir,* International Society of Copier Artists (ISCA), New York NY

Neal, Berna, *Architecture Librn,* Arizona State University, Hayden Library, Tempe AZ

Neal, Berna E, *Dept Head,* Arizona State University, Architecture and Environmental Design Library, Tempe AZ

Neal, Christine Crafts, *Assoc Cur European & American Art,* University of Missouri, Museum of Art and Archaeology, Columbia MO

Neal, Gilbert L, *Chmn Dept,* Hastings College, Art Dept, Hastings NE (S)

Neal, Stephanie B, *Dir Development,* The Currier Gallery of Art, Manchester NH

Neal, Tracy, *Asst to Dir,* Temple University, Tyler School of Art-Galleries, Tyler Gallery, Philadelphia PA

Neary, Patrica, *Cur Exhibits,* Heard Museum, Phoenix AZ

Neault, Carolyn, *Cur,* Columbus and Lowndes County Historical Society, Florence McLeod Hazard Museum, Columbus MS

Nedelka, Helen, *Treas,* Brooklyn Historical Society, Brooklyn OH

Needham, Richard H, *Chmn,* Chicago Historical Society, Chicago IL

Neely, John, *Assoc Prof,* Utah State University, Dept of Art, Logan UT (S)

Neeper, Rita, *Pres,* Balboa Art Conservation Center, San Diego CA

Neff, George, *Chmn Dept,* Rowan College of New Jersey, Dept of Art, Glassboro NJ (S)

Neff, John Hallmark, *Dir Art Prog,* The First National Bank of Chicago, Art Collection, Chicago IL

Neff, Mary, *Coordr,* Marian College, Art Dept, Fond Du Lac WI (S)

Negrych, Love, *Reference Librn,* University of Manitoba, Architecture & Fine Arts Library, Winnipeg MB

Neill, Mary G, *Dir,* Yale University, Art Gallery, New Haven CT

Neill, Peter, *Pres,* South Street Seaport Museum, New York NY

Neils, Jenifer, *Chmn,* Case Western Reserve University, Dept of Art History & Art, Cleveland OH (S)

Neimanas, Joyce, *Prof,* School of the Art Institute of Chicago, Chicago IL (S)

Nellermoe, John, *Chmn,* Texas Lutheran College, Dept of Visual Arts, Seguin TX (S)

Nell-Smith, Bruce, *Head Dept,* Newberry College, Dept of Art, Newberry SC (S)

Nelsen, Betty, *Instr,* American River College, Dept of Art, Sacramento CA (S)

Nelsen, Kenneth, *Assoc Prof,* Northwest Missouri State University, Dept of Art, Maryville MO (S)

Nelson, Atephen, *Chief Librn,* Woodstock Public Library, Art Gallery, Woodstock ON

Nelson, Burton R, *Cur Exhib,* Hastings Museum, Hastings NE

Nelson, Carolyn, *Lectr,* Centenary College of Louisiana, Dept of Art, Shreveport LA (S)

Nelson, Christina H, *Cur Decorative Arts & Assoc Cur European Decorative Arts,* Nelson-Atkins Museum of Art, Kansas City MO

Nelson, Craig, *Co Chair Fine Art,* Academy of Art College, Fine Arts Dept, San Francisco CA (S)

Nelson, David, *Pres,* Strasburg Museum, Strasburg VA

Nelson, Dean, *Museum Adminr,* Connecticut State Library, Museum of Connecticut History, Hartford CT

Nelson, Fred, *Coordr Illustration,* Columbia College, Art Dept, Chicago IL (S)

Nelson, Halfrid, *Exec Dir,* Humboldt Arts Council, Eureka CA

Nelson, Harold, *Dir,* Long Beach Museum of Art, Long Beach CA

Nelson, Irving, *Librn,* Navajo Nation Library, Window Rock AZ

Nelson, Jean, *Secy,* Blacksburg Regional Art Association, Christiansburg VA

Nelson, Julie D, *Dir,* University of Northern Iowa, Gallery of Art, Cedar Falls IA

Nelson, Kirk J, *Cur Glass,* The Sandwich Historical Society, Inc, Sandwich Glass Museum, Sandwich MA

Nelson, Lucie, *Cur,* State University of New York at Binghamton, University Art Gallery, Vestal NY

Nelson, Magee, *Dir,* Hockaday Center for the Arts, Kalispell MT

Nelson, Marion, *Prof,* University of Minnesota, Minneapolis, Art History, Minneapolis MN (S)

Nelson, Mary Carroll, *Founder,* Society of Layerists in Multi Media, Albuquerque NM

Nelson, Norman, *Garden Cur,* Palm Beach County Parks & Recreation Department, Morikami Museum & Japanese Gardens, Delray Beach FL

Nelson, Paula, *Dir,* Woodstock School of Art, Inc, Woodstock NY (S)

Nelson, Rebecca, *Dir Sheldon Museum,* Chilkat Valley Historical Society, Sheldon Museum & Cultural Center, Haines AK

Nelson, Robert, *Chmn,* University of Chicago, Dept of Art History and Committee on Art and Design, Chicago IL (S)

Nelson, Sarah, *Educ Cur,* Lehigh County Historical Society, Allentown PA

Nelson, Shannon, *Dept Head Interior Design,* Art Institute of Houston, Houston TX (S)

Nelson, Susan, *Instr,* Saint Mary College, Art Dept, Leavenworth KS (S)

Nelson, Susan, *Assoc Prof,* Indiana University, Bloomington, Henry Radford Hope School of Fine Arts, Bloomington IN (S)

Nelson, Vance, *Site Supv I,* Fort Totten State Historic Site, Pioneer Daughters Museum, Fort Totten ND

Nelson, Warren C, *VPres & Treas,* Naples Art Gallery, Naples FL

Nelson Hoyle, Karen, *Cur,* University of Minnesota, Children's Literature Research Collections, Minneapolis MN

Nelson-Kise, James, *Pres,* Philadelphia Museum of Art, Samuel S Fleisher Art Memorial, Philadelphia PA

Nelson-Mayson, Lin, *Cur Colls,* Columbia Museum of Art, Columbia SC

Nemiroff, Diane, *Assoc Cur Contemporary Art,* National Gallery of Canada, Ottawa ON

Nemsik, Jim, *Instr,* Rancho Santiago College, Art Dept, Santa Ana CA (S)

Neperud, Ronald, *Prof,* University of Wisconsin, Madison, Dept of Art, Madison WI (S)

Neri, Jean, *Exec Dir,* Museum of Oriental Cultures, Corpus Christi TX

Nervig, Denis J, *Photographer,* University of California, Los Angeles, Fowler Museum of Cultural History, Los Angeles CA

Nesbitt, Bill, *Cur,* Dundurn Castle, Hamilton ON

Neshat, Shirin, *Dir,* Storefront for Art & Architecture, New York NY

Nesin, Jeffrey D, *Pres,* Memphis College of Art, G Pillow Lewis Memorial Library, Memphis TN

Ness, Gary C, *Dir,* Ohio Historical Society, Columbus OH

Ness, Kim G, *Dir,* McMaster University, Art Gallery, Hamilton ON

Nestor, James, *Instr,* Indiana University of Pennsylvania, Dept of Art and Art Education, Indiana PA (S)

Neth, Ted, *Chmn Performing Arts Div,* Columbia Basin College, Art Dept, Pasco WA (S)

Netsky, Ron, *Head Dept,* Nazareth College of Rochester, Art Dept, Rochester NY (S)

Nettles, Bea, *In Charge Photography,* University of Illinois, Urbana-Champaign, School of Art and Design, Champaign IL (S)

Netzer, Nancy, *Dir,* Boston College, Museum of Art, Chestnut Hill MA

Neubert, George W, *Dir,* University of Nebraska, Lincoln, Sheldon Memorial Art Gallery, Lincoln NE

Neumaiere, Diane, *Asst Prof,* Rutgers, the State University of New Jersey, Mason Gross School of the Arts, New Brunswick NJ (S)

Neuman, Robert M, *Assoc Prof,* Florida State University, Art History Dept (R133B), Tallahassee FL (S)

Neuman de Vegvar, Carol, *Assoc Prof,* Ohio Wesleyan University, Fine Arts Dept, Delaware OH (S)

Neumann, J E, *Instr,* Western Illinois University, Art Dept, Macomb IL (S)

Neumann, Timothy C, *Dir,* Pocumtuck Valley Memorial Association, Memorial Hall, Deerfield MA

Neupert, James, *Instr,* Whitworth College, Art Dept, Spokane WA (S)

Neuroth, Karl O, *Chmn Fine Arts,* Keystone Junior College, Fine Arts Dept, Factoryville PA (S)

Nevadomi, Kenneth, *Prof,* Cleveland State University, Art Dept, Cleveland OH (S)

Nevins, Christopher B, *Cur,* Fairfield Historical Society, Fairfield CT

Nevins, Jerome, *Prof,* Albertus Magnus College, Art Dept, New Haven CT (S)

Nevins, Jerry, *Chmn,* Albertus Magnus College, Art Dept, New Haven CT (S)

Nevitt, Steve, *Chmn,* Columbia College, Dept of Art, Columbia SC (S)

Newberry, James, *Prof,* East Texas State University, Dept of Art, East Texas Station, Commerce TX (S)

Newberry, Susan, *Dir Education,* Newark Museum Association, The Newark Museum, Newark NJ

Newbold, Theodore T, *Treas,* Fairmount Park Art Association, Philadelphia PA

Newbold, Theodore T, *Pres,* Philadelphia Art Commission, Philadelphia PA

Newkirk, Dale, *Prof,* New Mexico State University, Art Dept, Las Cruces NM (S)

Newkirk, Sally, *Coordr,* Floyd County Museum, New Albany IN

Newlun, Jeanie, *Secy,* Colgate University, Picker Art Gallery, Hamilton NY

Newman, Alan B, *Exec Dir Photographic Serv,* The Art Institute of Chicago, Chicago IL

Newman, Constance Berry, *Under Secy,* Smithsonian Institution, Washington DC

Newman, Geoffrey, *Dean,* Montclair State College, Fine Arts Dept, Upper Montclair NJ (S)

Newman, Geoffrey, *Dean,* Montclair State College, Art Gallery, Upper Montclair NJ (S)

Newman, Heather, *Head Librn,* Sarasota Visual Art Center, Library, Sarasota FL

Newman, Jerry, *Prof,* Lamar University, Art Dept, Beaumont TX (S)

Newman, John, *Asst Prof,* University of Arkansas, Art Dept, Fayetteville AR (S)

Newman, Richard, *Chmn,* Bradford College, Creative Arts Division, Bradford MA (S)

Newman, Ruth D, *Dir,* New York University, 80 Washington Square East Galleries, New York NY

Newman, Susi, *Pres,* Art Association of Jacksonville, David Strawn Art Gallery, Jacksonville IL

Newmeyer, Sarah, *Admin Officer,* Freer Gallery of Art, Washington DC

Newsome, Steven, *Dir,* Anacostia Museum, Washington DC

Newton, Earle W, *Dir,* Museum of the Americas, Brookfield VT

Newton, Earle W, *Dir,* Museum of the Americas, Library, Brookfield VT

Newton, Earle W, *Exec Dir,* Historic Saint Augustine Preservation Board, Saint Augustine FL

Newton, Harold, *Instr,* Pennsylvania College of Technology, Dept of Design & Communiation Arts, Williamsport PA (S)

Newton, Verne W, *Dir,* National Archives & Records Administration, Franklin D Roosevelt Museum, Hyde Park NY

Ney, Cheri S, *Office Mgr,* State Museum of Pennsylvania, Railroad Museum of Pennsylvania, Harrisburg PA

Ney, Susan, *Chmn Dept,* Azusa Pacific University, College of Liberal Arts, Art Dept, Azusa CA (S)

Ng, Anthony, *Pub Relations & Develpment Dir,* Afro-American Historical & Cultural Museum, Philadelphia PA

Ng, W Tin, *Exec Dir,* Alberta Foundation For The Arts, Edmonton AB

Ngote, Lisa, *Lectr,* Oakland University, Dept of Art and Art History, Rochester MI (S)

Nian, Zhang Hong, *Instr,* Woodstock School of Art, Inc, Woodstock NY (S)

Nicandri, David, *Dir,* Washington State Historical Society, Tacoma WA

Nicard, Gary, *Progm Coordr,* Artists Space, New York NY

Niceley, H T, *Chmn Dept,* Carson-Newman College, Art Dept, Jefferson City TN (S)

Nichelson, Jack C, *Prof,* University of Florida, Dept of Art, Gainesville FL (S)

Nicholas, Frederick M, *Chmn,* The Museum of Contemporary Art, Los Angeles CA

Nicholas, Grace, *Admin Asst,* The 1890 House-Museum & Center for Victorian Arts, Cortland NY

Nicholls, Dave, *Cur of Exhibits,* Anchorage Museum of History and Art, Anchorage AK

Nichols, Adele, *Gallery Dir,* Kennebec Valley Art Association, Harlow Gallery, Hallowell ME

Nichols, Charlotte, *Asst Prof,* Seton Hall University, College of Arts & Sciences, South Orange NJ (S)

Nichols, Cheryl G, *Exec Dir,* Quapaw Quarter Association, Inc, Villa Marre, Little Rock AR

Nichols, Frank, *Prof,* Fort Hays State University, Dept of Art, Hays KS (S)

Nichols, Joan, *Tour Guide,* Historical Society of Cheshire County, Colony House Museum, Keene NH

Nichols, Judy, *Youth Serv Division Coordr,* Wichita Public Library, Wichita KS

Nichols, Kay, *Cur Education,* Museum of Fine Arts, Springfield MA

Nichols, Kay, *Cur Education,* George Walter Vincent Smith Art Museum, Springfield MA

Nichols, Kay, *Cur,* George Walter Vincent Smith Art Museum, Springfield MA

Nichols, Lawrence, *Cur European Painting & Sculpture Before 1900,* Toledo Museum of Art, Toledo Museum of Art, Toledo OH

Nichols, Lawrence W, *Assoc Cur,* Philadelphia Museum of Art, John G Johnson Collection, Philadelphia PA

Nichols, Madeleine, *Dance Cur,* The New York Public Library, Shelby Cullom Davis Museum, New York NY

Nichols, Sarah, *Cur Section Antiquities, Oriental & Decorative Arts,* Carnegie Institute, Carnegie Museum of Art, Pittsburgh PA

Nichols, Walter, *Prof,* Mount Saint Mary's College, Visual & Performing Arts Dept, Emmitsburg MD (S)

Nicholson, Freda, *Chief Exec Officer,* Science Museums of Charlotte, Inc, Discovery Place, Charlotte NC

Nicholson, Gail, *Exec Dir,* Center for Exploratory & Perceptual Art, CEPA Gallery, Buffalo NY

Nicholson, Jane, *Cur Educ,* Paine Art Center and Arboretum, Oshkosh WI

Nicholson, Lisa, *Visitor Servs,* Sheldon Jackson Museum, Sitka AK

Nicholson, Roy, *Assoc Prof,* Southampton Campus of Long Island University, Fine Arts Division, Southampton NY (S)

Nicholson, Sally, *General Mgr,* Association of American Editorial Cartoonists, Raleigh NC

Nicholson, Scott, *Educ Coordr,* Estevan National Exhibition Centre Inc, Estevan SK

Nickel, Lorene, *Assoc Prof,* Mary Washington College, Art Dept, Fredericksburg VA (S)

Nickol, Michael, *VPres,* Midwest Museum of American Art, Elkhart IN

Nickson, Graham, *Dean,* New York Studio School of Drawing, Painting and Sculpture, New York NY (S)

Nickson, Graham, *Dean,* New York Studio School of Drawing, Painting & Sculpture, Gallery, New York NY

Nickson, Guy, *Asst Dir,* Randolph Street Gallery, Chicago IL

Nicoll, Jessica, *Cur Coll,* Portland Museum of Art, Portland ME

Nicolosi, Anthony S, *Dir,* Naval War College Museum, Newport RI

Niederlander, Carol, *Chmn,* Saint Louis Community College at Forest Park, Art Dept, Saint Louis MO (S)

Nielsen, Ann T, *Pres,* Monterey Peninsula Museum of Art Association, Monterey CA

Nielsen, Erik, *Prof,* Southwest Texas State University, Dept of Art, San Marcos TX (S)

Nielsen, Thomas L, *Instr Pottery,* Red Rocks Community College, Arts & Humanities Department, Lakewood CO (S)

Nielson, Nancy, *Head of Circulation,* The College at New Paltz State University of New York, Sojourner Truth Library, New Paltz NY

Niemiec, Ted, *Dir Educ,* Museum of Holography - Chicago, Chicago IL

Nienhuis, Pamela, *Cur,* Arts Council of Spartanburg County, Inc, The Gallery, Spartanburg SC

Nierrengarten-Smith, Beej, *Dir,* Laumeier Sculpture Park, Saint Louis MO

Nies, Laura, *Dir Permanent Coll,* Earlham College, Leeds Gallery, Richmond IN

Nihart, F B, *Deputy Dir,* Marine Corps Museum, Art Collection, Washington DC

Niki, Kenji, *Librn,* Saint John's University, Asian Collection, Jamaica NY

Niles, Fred, *Assoc Prof,* University of Dayton, Visual Arts Dept, Dayton OH (S)

Niles, Katherine F, *Dir Art Prog,* PepsiCo Inc, Purchase NY

Nill, Annegreth, *Assoc Cur Contemporary Art,* Dallas Museum of Art, Dallas TX

Nilsen, Norman, *Museum School Dir,* Philbrook Museum of Art, Tulsa OK

Nilsen, Norman, *Asst Prof,* University of Montana, Dept of Art, Missoula MT (S)

Nilsson, Joan H, *Dir Visual Servs,* University of Washington, Art Slide Collection, Seattle WA

Niman, Marti, *Gallery Mgr,* Gilpin County Arts Association, Central City CO

Nimmer, Dean, *Chmn Fine Arts, 2D,* Massachusetts College of Art, Boston MA (S)

Nipp, Francis M, *Chmn,* Liberty Life Insurance Company, Greenville SC

Nippard, Mary Helen, *Admnr,* Star-Spangled Banner Flag House Association, Library, Baltimore MD

Nisbet, Peter, *Cur,* Harvard University, Busch-Reisinger Museum, Cambridge MA

Nisenholt, Mark, *Prof,* Lakehead University, Dept of Visual Arts, Thunder Bay ON (S)

Nishioka, Reiko, *Educ Dir,* Palm Beach County Parks & Recreation Department, Morikami Museum & Japanese Gardens, Delray Beach FL

Nivens, Charles, *Assoc Prof,* Eastern Illinois University, Art Dept, Charleston IL (S)

Nix, W Robert, *Art Education,* University of Georgia, Franklin College of Arts & Sciences, Dept of Art, Athens GA (S)

Nixon, Emily, *Art Consultant,* Continental Bank Corporation, Art Collection, Chicago IL

Noble, Cynthia, *Asst Prof,* Springfield College, Dept of Visual and Performing Arts, Springfield MA (S)

Noble, Dorothy, *VPres,* Wayne County Historical Society, Museum, Honesdale PA

Noblett, Duane, *Assoc Prof,* Kansas State University, Art Dept, Manhattan KS (S)

Noce, Gary, *Coll Documentation Systems Mgr,* Roberson Museum & Science Center, Binghamton NY

Nochberg, Edwin, *VPres,* Sculpture Center Inc, New York NY

Nochin, Gail J, *Library Dir,* Paier College of Art, Inc, Library, Hamden CT

Nock, Walter J, *Museum Specialist,* United States Military Academy, West Point Museum, West Point NY

Nodal, Adolfo V, *General Mgr,* City of Los Angeles, Cultural Affairs Dept, Los Angeles CA

Noe, Cindy, *Asst Dir,* Women And Their Work, Austin TX

Noe, Jerry, *Asst Chmn Studio Art,* University of North Carolina at Chapel Hill, Art Dept, Chapel Hill NC (S)

Noe, Jerry, *Prof,* University of North Carolina at Chapel Hill, Art Dept, Chapel Hill NC (S)

Noe, Lendon H, *Asst Prof,* Lambuth University, Dept of Human Ecology & Visual Arts, Jackson TN (S)

Noeding, Faye S, *Owner,* Bent Museum & Gallery, Taos NM

Noeding, Otto T, *Owner,* Bent Museum & Gallery, Taos NM

Noffke, Gary, *Jewelry & Metalwork,* University of Georgia, Franklin College of Arts & Sciences, Dept of Art, Athens GA (S)

Nofziger, Lori, *Circulation Supvr,* Cleveland Institute of Art, Jessica Gund Memorial Library, Cleveland OH

Noga, Joseph L, *Coordr Grad Program,* Rochester Institute of Technology, School of Printing, Rochester NY (S)

Nokes, Jack, *Dir Admin,* Laguna Gloria Art Museum, Austin TX

Nolan, Dennis, *Asst Prof,* University of Hartford, Hartford Art School, West Hartford CT (S)

Nolan, Ed, *Librn,* Washington State Historical Society, Hewitt Memorial Library, Tacoma WA

Nolan, Liesel, *Head Art & Architecture Library,* University of Colorado, Art and Architecture Library, Boulder CO

Nolan, Patricia E, *Special Arts Servs Dir,* American Society of Artists, Inc, Chicago IL

Nolan, William, *Visual Studies Chmn,* Atlanta College of Art, Atlanta GA (S)

Nolen, Eliott C, *Commissioner,* Art Commission of the City of New York, Associates of the Art Commission, Inc, New York NY

Nolf, Richard A, *Dir,* Saint Joseph Museum, Saint Joseph MO

Nolin, Anne-Marie, *Dir Communications,* Montclair Art Museum, Montclair NJ

Noll, Anna C, *Cur,* Heckscher Museum, Huntington NY

Nonn, Thomas I, *Chmn,* Kingsborough Community College, Dept of Art, Brooklyn NY (S)

Noon, Patrick, *Cur Prints Drawings & Rare Books,* Yale University, Yale Center for British Art, New Haven CT

Nooter, Polly, *Asst Cur,* International Museum of African Art, New York NY

Norberg, Deborah, *Deputy Dir,* San Jose Museum of Art, San Jose CA

Norbut, Tess, *Photo Research Cur,* Art Center College of Design, James Lemont Fogg Memorial Library, Pasadena CA

Nordberg, Paul C, *Instr,* Pierce College, Art Dept, Woodland Hills CA (S)

Nordimann, Marie, *Registrar,* Washington University, Gallery of Art, Saint Louis MO

Nordman, Russ, *Exhib Coordr,* College of Saint Benedict, Art Gallery, Saint Joseph MN

Nordstrom, Alison, *Dir,* Daytona Beach Community College, Southeast Museum of Photography, Daytona Beach FL

Norick, Frank A, *Principal Anthropologist,* University of California, Phoebe Apperson Hearst Museum of Anthropology, Berkeley CA

Norman, Grace, *Asst Prof of Art,* Adams State College, Dept of Visual Arts, Alamosa CO (S)

Norman, Guy, *Asst Prof of Art,* Trenton State College, Art Dept, Trenton NJ (S)

Norman, Janis, *Chmn Educ,* University of the Arts, Philadelphia College of Art & Design, Philadelphia PA (S)

Norman, John, *Chmn,* College of the Desert, Art Dept, Palm Desert CA (S)

Norman, Julyen, *Dir,* 1708 East Main Gallery, Richmond VA

Norman, Wayne, *Pres,* Dubuque Art Association, Dubuque Museum of Art, Dubuque IA

Norris, Andrea, *Dir,* University of Kansas, Spencer Museum of Art, Lawrence KS

Norris, E George, *Asst Dir,* University of West Florida, Art Gallery, Pensacola FL

Norris, Emile, *Curatorial Assoc,* Harvard University, Busch-Reisinger Museum, Cambridge MA

North, Kenda, *Chmn,* University of Texas at Arlington, Dept of Art & Art History, Arlington TX (S)

Northern, Tamara, *Sr Cur & Cur for Ethnographic Art,* Dartmouth College, Hood Museum of Art, Hanover NH

Northerner, Sara, *Asst Prof,* Utah State University, Dept of Art, Logan UT (S)

Northey, Doris, *Prog Coordr,* Normandeau Cultural & Natural History Society, Red Deer & District Museum & Archives, Red Deer AB

Northrop, Eileen, *Dir Admissions,* Art Institute of Fort Lauderdale, Fort Lauderdale FL (S)

Northrup, Jim, *Instr,* Grand Marais Art Colony, Grand Marais MN (S)

Northup, Marjorie, *Cur of Educ,* Reynolda House Museum of American Art, Winston-Salem NC

Norton, Ann, *Vis Asst Prof,* Trinity College, Dept of Fine Arts, Hartford CT (S)

Norton, Bernice, *Secy,* Willard House and Clock Museum, Inc, Grafton MA

Norton, Paul, *Prof,* University of Massachusetts, Amherst, Art History Program, Amherst MA (S)

Norton, Richard W, *Pres of the Board,* R W Norton Art Gallery, Shreveport LA

Norton, William, *Instr,* Columbia University, School of the Arts, Division of Painting & Sculpture, New York NY (S)

Norwicki, Erv, *Treas,* Wisconsin Painters & Sculptors, Inc, Milwaukee WI

Nosanow, Barbara Shissler, *Dir,* Portland Museum of Art, Portland ME

Notari, Carrie, *Prof,* North Park College, Art Dept, Chicago IL (S)

Novacek, Vera, *Secy,* Art Gallery of Peterborough, Peterborough ON

Novak, Allen, *AV Librn,* Ringling School of Art & Design Library, Sarasota FL

Novak, Janos, *Frames Technician,* Balboa Art Conservation Center, San Diego CA

Novak, Philip, *Asst Dir,* Stamford Museum and Nature Center, Stamford CT

Novelli, Martin, *Chmn Dept,* Ocean County College, Humanities Dept, Toms River NJ (S)

Noyes, Alex, *Studio Mgr,* Harvestworks, Inc, New York NY

Noyes, Julie, *Instr,* Northeast Community College, Dept of Liberal Arts, Norfolk NE (S)

Noyes, Nicholas, *Dir Library Servs,* Maine Historical Society, Library, Portland ME

Nozynski, John H, *Dir,* The 1890 House-Museum & Center for Victorian Arts, Cortland NY

Nuchims, Paul, *Chmn,* West Virginia State College, Art Dept, Institute WV (S)

Nuetzel, Ron, *Adjunct Instr,* Maryville University of Saint Louis, Art Division, Saint Louis MO (S)

Nuetzmann, Amy, *Asst to Dir,* Jackson County Historical Society, John Wornall House Museum, Independence MO

Nugent, Kristina, *Dir,* Miracosta College, Art Dept, Oceanside CA (S)

Nugent, Patricia, *Assoc Prof,* Rosemont College, Division of the Arts, Rosemont PA (S)

Nunnelley, Robert, *Prof,* Fairleigh Dickinson University, Fine Arts Dept, Rutherford NJ (S)

Nurse, Margaret, *Treas,* Society of Canadian Artists, Toronto ON

Nusbaum, Daniel C, *Chmn,* Mount Saint Mary's College, Visual & Performing Arts Dept, Emmitsburg MD (S)

Nussle, William H, *Instr,* Nossi School of Art, Goodlettsville TN (S)

Nuvayestewa, Grace, *Library Asst,* Institute of American Indian Arts Museum, Alaska Native Culture and Arts Development, Santa Fe NM

Nuzum, Thomas, *Instr,* Charles Stewart Mott Community College, Art Area, School of Arts & Humanities, Flint MI (S)

Nyerges, Alex, *Dir,* Dayton Art Institute, Dayton OH

Nygren, Edward J, *Cur Art Div,* Henry E Huntington Library, Art Collections & Botanical Gardens, San Marino CA

Nylander, Jane, *Dir,* Society for the Preservation of New England Antiquities, Boston MA

Nyman, William, *Asst Prof,* Trenton State College, Art Dept, Trenton NJ (S)

Oaks, Dallin H, *Chmn Bd,* Polynesian Cultural Center, Laie HI

Oaks, Gary, *Asst Prof,* Southern University in New Orleans, Art Dept, New Orleans LA (S)

Oates, Robert, *Mgr Personnel,* Toledo Museum of Art, Toledo Museum of Art, Toledo OH

Oatway, Martha, *Chmn & Dir,* Lincoln County Historical Association, Maine Art Gallery, Old Academy, Wiscasset ME

Oberschmidt, Ervin, *Exec Dir,* Cincinnati Institute of Fine Arts, Cincinnati OH

Oberweiser, Don, *Staff Artist,* Oshkosh Public Museum, Oshkosh WI

Obetz, Tim, *Production Asst,* Institute of Contemporary Art, Boston MA

O'Brian, Ellen M, *Pres,* Biloxi Art Association Inc & Gallery, Biloxi MS

O/Brian, John, *Assoc Prof,* University of British Columbia, Dept of Fine Arts, Vancouver BC (S)

O'Brien, Carole, *Dir Educ,* Butler Institute of American Art, Art Museum, Youngstown OH

O'Brien, Cookie, *Info Officer,* Historic Saint Augustine Preservation Board, Saint Augustine FL

O'Brien, Kevin, *Dir,* Everhart Museum, Scranton PA

O'Brien, Mern, *Dir,* Dalhousie University, Art Gallery, Halifax NS

O'Brien, Patrick M, *Dir,* Alexandria Library, Alexandria VA

O'Brien, Walt, *Instr,* Umpqua Community College, Fine & Performing Arts Dept, Roseburg OR (S)

O'Brien, William, *Sales Mgr,* Walters Art Gallery, Baltimore MD

Occhiuto, Joseph, *Rector,* San Carlos Cathedral, Monterey CA

Ocepek, Louis, *Dept Head & Prof,* New Mexico State University, Art Dept, Las Cruces NM (S)

Ochershausen, Cindylou, *Conservator,* National Portrait Gallery, Washington DC

Ochoa, Jody, *Registrar,* Idaho Historical Museum, Boise ID

Ochs, Steven, *Asst Prof,* Southern Arkansas University, Dept of Art, Magnolia AR (S)

Ockman, Carol, *Chmn Art History,* Williams College, Dept of Art, Williamstown MA (S)

O'Connell, Bonnie, *Asst Prof,* University of Nebraska at Omaha, Dept of Art, Omaha NE (S)

O'Connell, Clare, *Assoc Dir Development,* Worcester Art Museum, Worcester MA

O'Connell, Daniel M, *Commissioner of Cultural Affairs & Artistic Dir,* City of Pittsfield, Berkshire Artisans, Pittsfield MA

O'Connell, Donald, *Instructor,* Milwaukee Area Technical College, Graphic Arts Dept, Milwaukee WI (S)

O'Connell, Kenneth R, *Prof,* University of Oregon, Dept of Fine & Applied Arts, Eugene OR (S)

O'Conner, B A, *Gallery Dir,* Monserrat College of Art, Beverly MA (S)

O'Conner, David, *VPres,* Thornton W Burgess Society, Inc, Museum, Sandwich MA

O'Conner, Jim, *Finance Mgr,* Omaha Childrens Museum, Inc, Omaha NE

O'Connor, Brenda A, *Dir,* Lewis County Historical Museum, Chehalis WA

O'Connor, Brenda A, *Dir,* Lewis County Historical Museum, Library, Chehalis WA

O'Connor, David, *Egyptian Section Cur,* University of Pennsylvania, University Museum of Archaeology & Anthropology, Philadelphia PA

O'Connor, John A, *Prof,* University of Florida, Dept of Art, Gainesville FL (S)

O'Connor, Mallory, *Gallery Coordr,* City of Gainesville, Thomas Center Galleries - Cultural Affairs, Gainesville FL

O'Connor, Robert, *Chmn Board,* Staten Island Institute of Arts and Sciences, Staten Island NY

O'Connor, Stanley J, *Prof,* Cornell University, Dept of the History of Art, Ithaca NY (S)

O'Connor, Thom, *Chair Dept,* State University of New York at Albany, Art Dept, Albany NY (S)

O'Connor, Thom, *Prof,* State University of New York at Albany, Art Dept, Albany NY (S)

O'Day, Kathy, *Pres,* Art League, Alexandria VA

Odell, Franklin, *Head Outside Art Prog,* Foundation for Art Resources, Los Angeles CA

Odell, John B, *Registrar,* United States Senate Commission on Art, Washington DC

Odevseff, Barbara, *Registrar,* Wichita Art Museum, Wichita KS

Odom, Anne, *Cur,* Marjorie Merriweather Post Foundation of DC, Hillwood Museum, Washington DC

Odom, Patt, *Instr,* Mississippi Gulf Coast Community College-Jackson County Campus, Art Dept, Gautier MS (S)

Odoms, Carol, *Mgr,* Intermountain Cultural Center & Museum, Weiser ID

O'Donnell, Hugh, *Instr,* New York Studio School of Drawing, Painting and Sculpture, New York NY (S)

O'Donnell, Kendra, *Principal,* Phillips Exeter Academy, Frederic R Mayer Art Center & Lamont Gallery, Exeter NH

O'Donnell, Patricia, *Secy,* Art Complex Museum, Duxbury MA

O'Donnell, Shauna, *Prog Dir,* New Langton Arts, San Francisco CA

Oedel, William, *Asst Prof,* University of Massachusetts, Amherst, Art History Program, Amherst MA (S)

Oehlschlaeger, Frank, *Asst Prof,* Notre Dame College, Art Dept, Manchester NH (S)

Oertel, Dawn, *Instr,* Mount Mary College, Art Dept, Milwaukee WI (S)

Oettel, Russell L, *Prof,* Indiana-Purdue University, Dept of Fine Arts, Fort Wayne IN (S)

Oettinger, Marion, *Cur Folk Art,* San Antonio Museum Association, Inc, San Antonio Museum of Art, San Antonio TX

Offner, Elliot, *Prof,* Smith College, Art Dept, Northampton MA (S)

Ogden, Dale, *Cur History,* Indiana State Museum, Indianapolis IN

Ogle, Jimmy, *General Mgr,* Mississippi River Museum at Mud-Island, Memphis TN

Ogle, Philip, *Assoc Prof,* College of Associated Arts, Saint Paul MN (S)

Oglesby, Linwood, *Exec Dir,* American Council for the Arts, New York NY

O'Gorman, James F, *Prof,* Wellesley College, Art Dept, Wellesley MA (S)

O'Hara, Betsy, *Forum Ed,* Kansas City Artists Coalition, Kansas City MO

O'Hara, Bruce, *Assoc Prof,* Tougaloo College, Art Dept, Tougaloo MS (S)

O'Hara, Cate, *Publications,* Cincinnati Institute of Fine Arts, Taft Museum, Cincinnati OH

O'Hara, Donal J, *Prof,* University of Bridgeport, Art Dept, Bridgeport CT (S)

O'Hara, Edward, *Librn,* Manhattanville College, Library, Purchase NY

O'Hara, J, *Assoc Prof,* Northern Arizona University, School of Art & Design, Flagstaff AZ (S)

O'Hara, Virginia, *Assoc Cur,* Brandywine River Museum, Chadds Ford PA

O'Hare, Marita, *Development & Membership Dir,* The American Federation of Arts, New York NY

O'Hayes, Patrick, *Secy,* Newport Historical Society, Newport RI

O'Hear, James, *Assoc Dean,* Catholic University of America, School of Architecture & Planning, Washington DC (S)

O'Hern, Dianne, *Asst Prof,* Southern Arkansas University, Dept of Art, Magnolia AR (S)

O'Hern, Dianne, *Asst Prof,* Southern Arkansas University, Art Dept Gallery & Magale Art Gallery, Magnolia AR

O'Hern, John D, *Dir,* Arnot Art Museum, Elmira NY

Ojala, Meg, *Asst Prof,* Saint Olaf College, Art Dept, Northfield MN (S)

Okada, Connie, *Librn,* University of Washington, Art Library, Seattle WA

Okaya, Michiko, *Gallery Dir,* Lafayette College, Morris R Williams Center for the Arts, Art Gallery, Easton PA

Okazaki, Arthur, *Prof,* Tulane University, Sophie H Newcomb Memorial College, New Orleans LA (S)

O'Keefe, Michael J, *Chmn,* Oklahoma Christian University of Science & Arts, Department of Art & Design, Oklahoma City OK (S)

O'Keefe, Paul, *Div Coordr Painting,* Kent State University, School of Art, Kent OH (S)

Okner, Annette, *VPres,* Chicago Society of Artists, Inc, Chicago IL

Oko, Andrew, *Dir,* Norman Mackenzie Art Gallery, Regina SK

Okoye, Ikem, *Lectr,* Northwestern University, Evanston, Dept of Art History, Evanston IL (S)

Olason, LuAnn, *Prom Dir,* Battleship North Carolina, Wilmington NC

O'Laughlin, Thomas C, *Cur,* El Paso Museum of Art, Wilderness Park Museum, El Paso TX

Olbrantz, John, *Deputy Dir,* Whatcom Museum of History and Art, Bellingham WA

Olcott, Susan, *Exhib Coordr,* Public Library of Columbus and Franklin County, Columbus Metropolitan Library, Columbus OH

Oldach, Linda R, *Dir,* Mount Wachusett Community College, Library, Gardner MA

Oldaker, William, *Instr,* West Virginia Wesleyan College, Dept of Fine Arts, Buckhannon WV (S)

Oldenburg, Richard E, *Dir Museum,* Museum of Modern Art, New York NY

Olds, Clifton C, *Prof,* Bowdoin College, Art Dept, Brunswick ME (S)

Olds, Joyce, *Instr,* The Arkansas Arts Center, Museum School, Little Rock AR (S)

Oleary, Daniel, *Asst Cur,* Minneapolis Society of Fine Arts, Minneapolis Institute of Arts, Minneapolis MN

O'Leary, Dennis, *Dir,* Boise Art Museum, Boise ID

O'Leary, Jay, *Division Chmn of Fine Arts,* Wayne State College, Nordstrand Visual Arts Gallery, Wayne NE

O'Leary, Jay, *Div Chmn,* Wayne State College, Art Dept, Wayne NE (S)

Olesen, Darcy, *Dir Development,* Laguna Gloria Art Museum, Austin TX

Olijnyk, Michael, *Cur,* Mattress Factory, Pittsburgh PA

Oliner, Stan, *Cur Books & Manuscripts,* Colorado Historical Society, Museum, Denver CO

Olivant, David, *Instr,* Southwest Texas State University, Dept of Art, San Marcos TX (S)

Oliver, Cornelia, *Prof,* Mary Washington College, Art Dept, Fredericksburg VA (S)

Oliver, Donna, *Dir Tours,* Edsel & Eleanor Ford House, Grosse Pointe Shores MI

Oliver, Judith, *Assoc Prof,* Colgate University, Dept of Art & Art History, Hamilton NY (S)

Oliver, Patricia, *Environmental Design Chmn,* Art Center College of Design, Pasadena CA (S)

Olivero, Ray, *Graduate Coordr,* Wichita State University, Division of Art, Wichita KS (S)

Olivo, Sandra, *Asst Dir,* Sheldon Museum, Middlebury VT

Ollman, Arthur, *Exec Dir,* Museum of Photographic Arts, Balboa Park CA

O'Looney, James, *Assoc Prof,* Mohawk Valley Community College, Advertising Design and Production, Utica NY (S)

Olpin, Robert S, *Dir,* University of Utah, Owen Library, Salt Lake City UT

Olpin, Robert S, *Dean,* University of Utah, Art Dept, Salt Lake City UT (S)

Olsen, Caren, *Cur,* Honeywell Inc, Art Collection, Minneapolis MN

Olsen, Charles, *Chmn,* St Francis College, Fine Arts Dept, Loretto PA (S)

Olsen, Dean, *Dir,* Stephen Brew Gallery, Madison WI

Olsen, Dennis, *Assoc Prof,* University of Texas at San Antonio, Division of Art & Architecture, San Antonio TX (S)

Olsen, Jim, *Dept Head,* Dana College, Art Dept, Blair NE (S)

Olsen, Karen, *Instr,* Mount Mary College, Art Dept, Milwaukee WI (S)

Olsen, Mel, *Prof,* University of Wisconsin-Superior, Programs in the Visual Arts, Superior WI (S)

Olsen, Sandra H, *Dir,* Niagara University, Castellani Art Museum, New York NY

Olsen, Steven, *Operation Mgr,* Church of Jesus Christ of Latter-day Saints, Museum of Church History & Art, Salt Lake City UT

Olsen, Susan, *Exec Dir,* Key West Art and Historical Society, East Martello Museum and Gallery, Key West FL

Olshan, Bernarl, *Pres,* American Society of Contemporary Artists, Bronx NY

Olson, Dennis, *Instr,* Amarillo College, Art Dept, Amarillo TX (S)

Olson, Diane, *Development Dir,* Huntsville Museum of Art, Huntsville AL

Olson, Dona, *Cur & Mgr,* New England Maple Museum, Rutland VT

Olson, Elizabeth, *Development Dir,* Fresno Metropolitan Museum, Fresno CA

Olson, Gary, *Prog Coordr Printmaking,* Alberta College of Art, Calgary AB (S)

Olson, George, *Prof,* College of Wooster, Dept of Art, Wooster OH (S)

Olson, Janis, *Cur of Collections,* Whatcom Museum of History and Art, Bellingham WA

Olson, Jim, *Chief of Exhib,* Natural History Museum of Los Angeles County, Los Angeles CA

Olson, Joann, *Librn,* Miami University Art Museum, Wertz Art & Architecture Library, Oxford OH

Olson, Joanne, *Curatorial Asst,* Art Complex Museum, Duxbury MA

Olson, Joseph, *Prof,* Georgia Southern University, Dept of Art, Statesboro GA (S)

Olson, Kristina, *Cur,* West Virginia University, Art Galleries, Morgantown WV

Olson, Kristina, *Cur,* West Virginia University, Creative Arts Center and Gallery, Morgantown WV

Olson, Linda, *Dir,* Minot State University, University Galleries, Minot ND

Olson, Maude, *Treas,* Pemaquid Group of Artists, Pemaquid Point ME

Olson, Rebecca, *Dir Membership,* Walker Art Center, Minneapolis MN

Olson, Richard W P, *Prof,* Beloit College, Dept of Art, Beloit WI (S)

Olson, Roberta J M, *Chmn Dept,* Wheaton College, Art Dept, Norton MA (S)

Olson, Thomas H, *Pres,* New England Maple Museum, Rutland VT

Olson-Janjic, Kathleen, *Asst Prof,* Washington and Lee University, Division of Art, Lexington VA (S)

Olszewski, Edward J, *Prof,* Case Western Reserve University, Dept of Art History & Art, Cleveland OH (S)

Olszewski, Michael, *Chmn Textile Design,* Moore College of Art & Design, Philadelphia PA (S)

Olton, Charles S, *Dean,* Parsons School of Design, New York NY (S)

Oltvedt, Carl, *Prof,* Moorhead State University, Dept of Art, Moorhead MN (S)

Olvera, John, *Prof,* Winthrop College, Dept of Art & Design, Rock Hill SC (S)

O'Malley, Dennis M, *Dir,* Rhode Island College, Edward M Bannister Gallery, Providence RI

O'Malley, Karen, *Instr,* Marylhurst College, Art Dept, Marylhurst OR (S)

O'Malley, Kathleen, *Assoc Registrar,* Dartmouth College, Hood Museum of Art, Hanover NH

O'Malley, William, *Instr,* Charles Stewart Mott Community College, Art Area, School of Arts & Humanities, Flint MI (S)

Omar, Margit, *Assoc Prof,* University of Southern California, School of Fine Arts, Los Angeles CA (S)

O'Meara, Nancy C, *Projects Coordr,* Philadelphia Museum of Art, Women's Committee, Philadelphia PA

Omelia, John F, *Asst Prof,* Manhattan College, School of Arts and Sciences, Bronx NY (S)

O'Neal, Mary, *Prof,* University of California, Berkeley, College of Letters & Sciences-Art Dept, Berkeley CA (S)

O'Neil, Dennis, *Chmn Printmaking,* Corcoran School of Art, Washington DC (S)

O'Neil, Elaine, *Dir,* Rochester Institute of Technology, School of Photographic Arts & Sciences, Rochester NY (S)

O'Neil, Elaine, *Dir,* Rochester Institute of Technology, College of Graphic Arts & Photography, Rochester NY (S)

O'Neil, John, *Chmn,* University of South Carolina, Dept of Art, Columbia SC (S)

O'Neil, Karen, *Instr,* Woodstock School of Art, Inc, Woodstock NY (S)

O'Neil, William, *Pres,* Massachusetts College of Art, Boston MA (S)

O'Neill, Robert G, *Head Dept,* Lamar University, Art Dept, Beaumont TX (S)

O'Neill, Yvette, *Instr,* Lower Columbia College, Longview WA (S)

Oney, Charles, *Pres,* Southern Lorain County Historical Society, Spirit of '76 Museum, Wellington OH

Ong, John D, *VPres,* Historic Deerfield, Inc, Deerfield MA

Onken, Michael O, *Grad Studies,* Southern Illinois University, School of Art & Design, Carbondale IL (S)

Onorato, Ronald J, *Chmn,* University of Rhode Island, Dept of Art, Kingston RI (S)

Ony, Donna, *Dir,* Revelstoke Art Group, Revelstoke BC

Opar, Barbara A, *Architecture Librn & Dept Head,* Syracuse University, Library, Syracuse NY

Opar, Tamara L, *Chief Librn,* Winnipeg Art Gallery, Clara Lander Library, Winnipeg MB

Opar, Tamara L, *Librn,* Ukrainian Cultural and Educational Centre, Library and Archives, Winnipeg MB

Opodocer, Paul, *Cur Native American Art,* Bower's Museum, Santa Ana CA

Oppenheim, Ellen G, *Dir,* Old Jail Art Center, Albany TX

Oppenheim, Phyllis, *Cur Colls,* College of Southern Idaho, Herrett Museum & Art Gallery, Twin Falls ID

Opper, Edward, *Acad Dean Educ,* Greenville Technical College, Art History Dept, Greenville SC (S)

Oppler, Ellen, *Prof,* Syracuse University, Dept of Fine Arts (Art History), Syracuse NY (S)

Oravez, Dave, *Chmn,* Boise State University, Art Dept, Boise ID (S)

Ore, Joyce, *Dir Pub Relations,* Hastings College, Art Dept, Hastings NE (S)

Orgera, Laura, *Marketing & Prog Coordr,* National Art Museum of Sport, Indianapolis IN

Orlebeke, Charles, *Dir School Urban Planning,* University of Illinois at Chicago, College of Architecture, Art and Urban Planning, Chicago IL (S)

Orloff, Chet, *Exec Dir,* Oregon Historical Society, Portland OR

Orman, Paul, *Deputy Dir,* Minnesota Museum of American Art, Saint Paul MN

Ormond, Mark, *Dir,* Center for the Fine Arts, Miami FL

Ormond, Mark, *Dir,* Metro-Dade Center, Center for the Fine Arts, Miami FL

Ornelas, La Verne, *Chmn,* Northeastern Illinois University, Art Dept, Chicago IL (S)

Ornstein, Jeannette, *Educ Dir,* Yeshiva University Museum, New York NY

O'Rourke, Marilyn, *Librn,* New Canaan Historical Society, New Canaan CT

Orozco, Sylvia, *Co-Dir,* MEXIC-ARTE Museum, Austin TX

Orr, Amy, *Asst Prof,* Rosemont College, Division of the Arts, Rosemont PA (S)

Orr, Darlene, *Dir,* Carrie McLain Museum, Nome AK

Orr, Estelle, *Instr,* Rancho Santiago College, Art Dept, Santa Ana CA (S)

Orr-Cahall, Christina, *Dir,* Norton Gallery and School of Art, West Palm Beach FL

Orr-Cahall, Christina, *Dir,* Norton Gallery and School of Art, West Palm Beach FL

Orth, Fredrick, *Chmn,* San Diego State University, University Art Gallery, San Diego CA

Orth, Fredrick, *Chmn,* San Diego State University, Dept of Art, San Diego CA (S)

Ortiz, Emilio I, *Dir,* Guadalupe Historic Foundation, Santuario de Guadalupe, Santa Fe NM

Ortiz, Rafael, *Prof,* Rutgers, the State University of New Jersey, Mason Gross School of the Arts, New Brunswick NJ (S)

Ortner, Frederick, *Chmn,* Knox College, Dept of Art, Galesburg IL (S)

Orwig, Rosemarie, *Arts Outreach Coordr,* Redding Museum of Art & History, Redding CA

Ory, Norma R, *Dean Jr School & Community Outreach Prog,* Glassell School of Art, Houston TX (S)

Osaki, Amy, *Cur Educ,* Portland Art Museum, Portland OR

Osborne, Carol, *Assoc Dir & Cur Coll,* Stanford University, Art Gallery, Stanford CA

Osborne, Frederick S, *Dir,* Pennsylvania Academy of the Fine Arts, Philadelphia PA (S)

Osborne, #John L, *Prof,* University of Victoria, Dept of History in Art, Victoria BC (S)

Osbrone, Jack, *Pres Board Trustees,* Hastings Museum, Hastings NE

Osbun, Jack, *Chmn,* Wittenberg University, Art Dept, Springfield OH (S)

Oser, Marilyn, *Public Relations Dir,* Wave Hill, Bronx NY

Osgood, William B, *Commissioner,* Boston Art Commission of the City of Boston, Boston MA

O'Shello, Wanda, *Editor Arts Quarterly,* New Orleans Museum of Art, New Orleans LA

Ostby, Lloyd, *Head Art, Music & Films,* Memphis-Shelby County Public Library and Information Center, Dept of Art, Music & Films, Memphis TN

Osterman, Greg, *Instr,* Grand Canyon University, Art Dept, Phoenix AZ (S)

Osterman, William, *Asst Prof,* Rochester Institute of Technology, School of Photographic Arts & Sciences, Rochester NY (S)

Ostermiller, Jerry, *Exec Dir,* Columbia River Maritime Museum, Astoria OR

Ostheimer, Andy, *Dir,* San Jose State University, Art Gallery, San Jose CA

Ostrow, Mindy, *Asst Dir,* State University of New York at Oswego, Tyler Art Gallery, Oswego NY

Ostrow, Stephen E, *Chief,* Library of Congress, Prints and Photographs Division, Washington DC

O'Sullivan, Constance, *Exec Dir,* Peninsula Fine Arts Center, Newport News VA

O'Sullivan, Thomas, *Cur Art,* Minnesota Historical Society, Library, Saint Paul MN

Oswald, Marianne, *Secy,* Santa Clara University, de Saisset Museum, Santa Clara CA

Oswald, Rose B, *Secy,* Stanley Museum, Inc, Kingfield ME

Oszuscik, Philipe, *Art Historian,* University of South Alabama, Dept of Art, Mobile AL (S)

Otis, Helen K, *Conservator-in-Charge Paper,* The Metropolitan Museum of Art, New York NY

Otis, James, *Facilities Chmn,* Print Club of Albany, Museum, Albany NY

O'Toole, Judith, *Adjunct Prof,* Wilkes University, Dept of Art, Wilkes-Barre PA (S)

O'Toole, Judith H, *Dir,* Wilkes University, Sordoni Art Gallery, Wilkes-Barre PA

O'Toole, Kevin, *Adjunct Prof,* Wilkes University, Dept of Art, Wilkes-Barre PA (S)

Ott, Frank, *Assoc Prof,* C W Post Center of Long Island University, School of Visual & Performing Arts, Greenvale NY (S)

Ott, Greg, *Headmaster,* Delphian School, Sheridan OR (S)

Ott, Lili, *Dir,* Johns Hopkins University, Evergreen House, Baltimore MD

Ott, Wendell, *Dir,* Museum of the Southwest, Midland TX

Ottaviano, Scotty, *Assoc Prof,* Cazenovia College, Center for Art & Design Studies, Cazenovia NY (S)

Ottmann, Klaus, *Cur Exhibitions,* Wesleyan University, Ezra and Cecile Zilkha Gallery, Middletown CT

Otto, Gretchen, *Gallery Dir,* Eastern Michigan University, Ford Gallery, Ypsilanti MI

Otto, Guttorn, *Instr,* Southampton Art School, Southampton ON (S)

Otto, Martha, *Head Archaeology,* Ohio Historical Society, Columbus OH

Otton, William, *Pres,* Wichita Center for the Arts, Wichita KS

Otton, William, *Pres,* Wichita Center for the Arts, Maude Schollenberger Memorial Library, Wichita KS

Ottulich, John, *VPres,* The Queens Museum of Art, Flushing NY

Oubre, Jean, *Coordr,* Crowley Art Association, The Gallery, Crowley LA

Ouchie, Eugene, *Prog Coordr Visual Communications,* Alberta College of Art, Calgary AB (S)

Ouellette, David, *Dir Galleries,* Florida School of the Arts, Visual Arts, Palatka FL (S)

Ourecky, Irma, *Pres,* Wilber Czech Museum, Wilber NE

Ovellet, Jacque, *Managing Dir,* Canadian Museum of Civilization, Hull ON

Overby, Osmund, *Prof,* University of Missouri, Art History and Archaeology Dept, Columbia MO (S)

Overson, Kristin, *Asst to Dir,* The One Club for Art & Copy, New York NY

Overstreet, Joe, *Art Dir,* Kenkeleba House, Inc, Kenkeleba Gallery, New York NY

Overton, Harold, *Chmn,* Charleston Southern University, Dept of Language & Visual Art, Charleston SC (S)

Overvoorde, Chris Stoffel, *Prof,* Calvin College, Art Dept, Grand Rapids MI (S)

Owczarek, Robert, *Div Chmn,* Pine Manor College, Visual Arts Dept, Chestnut Hill MA (S)

Owczarski, Marian, *Dir,* St Mary's Galeria, Orchard Lake MI

Owen, Andra Jean, *Admin Secy,* University of Louisville, Allen R Hite Art Institute Gallery, Louisville KY

Owen, Lin, *Dir,* Wichita Falls Museum and Art Center, Wichita Falls TX

Owen, Paula, *Dir,* Hand Workshop, Virginia Center for the Craft Arts, Richmond VA

Owen, Thomas G, *Dean,* Jacksonville University, Dept of Art, Jacksonville FL (S)

Owens, Arthur, *Asst Dir Operations,* Los Angeles County Museum of Art, Los Angeles CA

Owens, Carlotta, *Asst Cur,* National Gallery of Art, Index of American Design, Washington DC

Owens, David, *Instr,* Okaloosa-Walton Junior College, Dept of Fine and Performing Arts, Niceville FL (S)

Owens, Helen McKenzie, *Pres,* Kelly-Griggs House Museum, Red Bluff CA

Owens, Marian, *Cur Education,* Huntington Museum of Art, Huntington WV

Owens, Robert, *Dept Head,* Fayetteville State University, Fine Arts & Communications, Fayetteville NC (S)

Owens, Robert L, *Chmn,* North Georgia College, Fine Arts Dept, Dahlonega GA (S)

Ownbey, Ronald B, *Chmn,* Mount San Antonio College, Art Dept, Walnut CA (S)

Oxman, M, *Assoc Prof,* American University, Dept of Art, Washington DC (S)

Ozdogan, Turker, *Prof,* George Washington University, Dept of Art, Washington DC (S)

Ozlu, Nina, *Deputy Dir,* International Sculpture Center, Washington DC

Ozols, Auseklis, *Dir,* New Orleans Academy of Fine Arts, Academy Gallery, New Orleans LA

Pabst, K T, *Dir,* Mechanics' Institute Library, San Francisco CA

Pace, Gary, *Asst Dir,* Board of Parks & Recreation, The Parthenon, Nashville TN

Pace, James, *Assoc Prof,* University of Texas at Tyler, Dept of Art, Tyler TX (S)

Pace, Lorenzo, *Dir,* Montclair State College, Art Gallery, Upper Montclair NJ

Packard, Daniel, *Prof,* University of South Dakota, Dept of Art, Vermillion SD (S)

Packard, Leo, *Dir SIACM,* Illinois State Museum, Southern Illinois Arts & Crafts Marketplace, Chicago IL

Packer, Mark, *Cur of Art Educ,* Ella Sharp Museum, Jackson MI

Paddock, Eric, *Cur Photography,* Colorado Historical Society, Museum, Denver CO

Padfield, Clive, *Dir Arts Branch,* Department of Culture & Multi-Culturalism, Arts Branch Resource Center, Edmonton AB

Padgett, James, *Advisor,* Wilberforce University, Art Dept, Wilberforce OH (S)

Padgett, Michael, *Assoc Cur,* Princeton University, The Art Museum, Princeton NJ

Padgett, Michael, *Gallery Dir,* University of Wisconsin, Gallery 101, River Falls WI

Padgett, Michael, *Chmn,* University of Wisconsin-River Falls, Art Dept, River Falls WI (S)

Padgett, R Paul, *Assoc Prof,* West Liberty State College, Art Dept, West Liberty WV (S)

Pafco, Rob, *Humanities Chmn,* Idyllwild School of Music and the Arts, Idyllwild CA (S)

Page, Abbie, *Treas,* Concord Art Association, Concord MA

Page, Colin, *Dir of Admissions,* Pacific Northwest College of Art, Portland OR (S)

Page, Greg, *Assoc Prof,* Cornell University, Dept of Art, Ithaca NY (S)

Page, Kathryn, *Archivist & Cur Maps & Manuscripts,* Louisiana Department of Culture, Recreation and Tourism, Louisiana Historical Center Library, New Orleans LA

Page, Marcia, *Project Dir,* Craft and Folk Art Museum, Los Angeles CA

Page, Richard C, *Dir Botanical Gardens,* Cheekwood-Tennessee Botanical Garden Museum of Art, Education Dept, Nashville TN (S)

Pagel, Angelika, *Assoc Prof,* Weber State University, Dept of Visual Arts, Ogden UT (S)

Paggie, Michael, *Business Mgr,* Madison Art Center, Madison WI

Pagh, Barbara, *Asst Prof,* University of Rhode Island, Dept of Art, Kingston RI (S)

Pahl, James R, *Asst Dir,* Mingei International, Inc, Mingei International Museum of World Folk Art, San Diego CA

Paier, Edward T, *Pres,* Paier College of Art, Inc, Hamden CT (S)

Paier, Edward T, *Pres,* Paier College of Art, Inc, Library, Hamden CT

Paier, Jonathan E, *VPres,* Paier College of Art, Inc, Library, Hamden CT

Paige, Claire, *Asst Prof,* Xavier University of Louisiana, Dept of Fine Arts, New Orleans LA (S)

Paige, J M, *Librn,* Art Gallery of Greater Victoria, Library, Victoria BC

Paige, Robert, *Prof,* Philadelphia Community College, Dept of Art, Philadelphia PA (S)

Paine, Wesley M, *Dir,* Board of Parks & Recreation, The Parthenon, Nashville TN

Painter, Hal, *Treas,* American Tapestry Alliance, Chiloquin OR

Painter, Jerry E, *Instr,* Guilford Technical Community College, Commercial Art Dept, Jamestown NC (S)

Paizy, Guy, *Instr,* University of Puerto Rico, Dept of Fine Arts, Rio Piedras PR (S)

Pajak, Fraz, *Assoc Prof,* Converse College, Art Dept, Spartanburg SC (S)

Pal, Pratapaditya, *Cur Indian & Southeast Asian Art,* Los Angeles County Museum of Art, Los Angeles CA

Palazzolo, T, *Prof,* City Colleges of Chicago, Daley College, Chicago IL (S)

Palca, Doris, *Head Publications,* Whitney Museum of American Art, New York NY

Palchick, Bernard, *Prof,* Kalamazoo College, Art Dept, Kalamazoo MI (S)

Palermo, F, *Instr,* Technical University of Nova Scotia, Faculty of Architecture, Halifax NS (S)

Palermo, James, *Dir Admissions,* Art Institute of Philadelphia, Philadelphia PA (S)

Paley, William S, *Chmn Emeritus,* Museum of Modern Art, New York NY

Palijczuk, Wasyl, *Gallery Dir,* Western Maryland College, Gallery One, Westminster MD

Palijczuk, Wasyl, *Prof,* Western Maryland College, Art Dept, Westminster MD (S)

Palisin, B, *Instr,* Sacramento City College, Art Dept, Sacramento CA (S)

Palladino-Craig, Allys, *Dir,* Florida State University, Fine Arts Gallery & Museum, Tallahassee FL

Pallas, James, *Prof,* Macomb Community College, Art Dept, Warren MI (S)

Palmer, Anne, *Adminr,* Akron Art Museum, Akron OH

Palmer, Charles, *Dir,* Rehoboth Art League, Inc, Rehoboth Beach DE (S)

Palmer, Charles, *Dir,* Rehoboth Art League, Inc, Rehoboth Beach DE

Palmer, David, *Dir of Exhibitions,* Newark Museum Association, The Newark Museum, Newark NJ

Palmer, Richard, *Coordr Exhib,* Museum of Modern Art, New York NY

Palmer, Robert, *Prof,* University of Richmond, Dept of Art & Art History, Richmond VA (S)

Palmer, Robert, *Assoc Prof,* Cleveland Institute of Art, Cleveland OH (S)

Palmer, Sharon S, *Exec Dir,* Columbia County Historical Society, Columbia County Museum, Kinderhook NY

Palusky, Robert, *Instr,* Hamilton College, Art Dept, Clinton NY (S)

Pamer, Lawrence, *Cur Exhib,* Museum of Art, Fort Lauderdale, Fort Lauderdale FL

Panagakos, Despina, *Admin,* The Museum, Greenwood SC

Panciera, David J, *Dir,* Westerly Public Library, Hoxie Gallery, Westerly RI

Pancoast, Helene M, *Dir,* Bakehouse Art Complex, Inc, Miami FL

Pancoast, Virgilia H, *Dir,* International Foundation for Art Research, Inc, Authentication Service, New York NY

Panczenko, Russell, *Dir,* University of Wisconsin-Madison, Elvehjem Museum of Art, Madison WI

Pang, Philip, *Communications Coordr,* Pacific - Asia Museum, Pasadena CA

Pankow, David P, *Asst Prof,* Rochester Institute of Technology, School of Printing, Rochester NY (S)

Pantazzi, Michael, *Assoc Cur European Art,* National Gallery of Canada, Ottawa ON

Pantell, Richard, *Instr,* Woodstock School of Art, Inc, Woodstock NY (S)

Pantezzi, Gail, *Chmn of Board of Trustees,* Hammond Museum & Japanese Stroll Garden, Cross-Cultural Center, North Salem NY

Panyard, Gerry, *Instr,* Madonna College, Art Dept, Livonia MI (S)

Panzer, Mary, *Cur Photographs,* National Portrait Gallery, Washington DC

Panzer, Robert, *Exec Dir,* Visual Artists & Galleries Association (VAGA), New York NY

Paoletta, Donald, *Chmn,* University of Texas at Tyler, Dept of Art, Tyler TX (S)

Paoletti, John T, *Prof,* Wesleyan University, Art Dept, Middletown CT (S)

Paolini, Carl, *Instr,* Joe Kubert School of Cartoon & Graphic Art, Inc, Dover NJ (S)

Paolini, Shirley, *Dean,* Barry University, Dept of Fine Arts, Miami Shores FL (S)

Papadopoulos, Joan, *First VPres,* Swedish American Museum Association of Chicago, Chicago IL

Papageorge, Tod, *Prof,* Yale University, School of Art, New Haven CT (S)

Pape, Eva, *Cur,* New England Center for Contemporary Art, Brooklyn CT

Papier, Maurice A, *Head Dept,* Saint Francis College, Art Dept, Fort Wayne IN (S)

Papineau, Karen, *Registrar,* Museum of Fine Arts, Springfield MA

Papineau, Karen, *Registrar,* George Walter Vincent Smith Art Museum, Springfield MA

Pappas, Marilyn, *Chmn Fine Arts, 3-D,* Massachusetts College of Art, Boston MA (S)

Papt, Roy, *Pres,* Phoenix Art Museum, Phoenix AZ

Paquette, Susanne, *Coordr,* La Centrale Powerhouse Gallery, Montreal PQ

Paragas, Betsye, *Public Relations Dir,* Omaha Childrens Museum, Inc, Omaha NE

Paratley, Rob, *Asst Dir Business Operations,* Cornell University, Herbert F Johnson Museum of Art, Ithaca NY

Paratore, Philip, *Prof,* University of Maine at Augusta, Division of Fine & Performing Arts, Augusta ME (S)

Parcell, S, *Instr,* Technical University of Nova Scotia, Faculty of Architecture, Halifax NS (S)

Parch, Elizabeth, *Admin Asst,* Richmond Art Center, Civic Center Plaza, Richmond CA

Pardington, Ralph, *Instr,* College of Santa Fe, Visual Arts Dept, Santa Fe NM (S)

Pardo, Jorge, *Circulation Supv,* Art Center College of Design, James Lemont Fogg Memorial Library, Pasadena CA

Pardo, Jorge, *Public Arts Mgr,* Public Corporation for the Arts, Visual & Performing Arts Registry, Long Beach CA

Pardo, Mary, *Asst Chmn Art Hist,* University of North Carolina at Chapel Hill, Art Dept, Chapel Hill NC (S)

Pardon, Jackie, *Slide & Photograph Asst,* Skidmore College, Schick Art Gallery, Saratoga Springs NY

Pardue, Diana, *Cur of Coll,* Heard Museum, Phoenix AZ

Pardue, Diana, *Chief Cur,* The National Park Service, United States Department of the Interior, The Statue of Liberty National Monument, New York NY

Pare, Jean-Pierre, *Asst to Cur,* Musee du Seminaire de Quebec, Quebec PQ

Parente, R A, *Chmn Art Dept,* Anna Maria College, Saint Luke's Gallery, Paxton MA

Parente, Ralph, *Chmn Dept,* Anna Maria College, Dept of Art, Paxton MA (S)

Paret, John J, *Dir,* Kateri Galleries, The National Shrine of the North American Martyrs, Auriesville NY

Parfenoff, Michael S, *Dir,* Blackhawk Mountain School of Art Gallery, Blackhawk CO

Parg, Shelagh, *Dir Finance & Personnel,* London Regional Art & Historical Museums, London ON

Parish, W Ray, *Head Dept,* University of Texas at El Paso, Dept of Art, El Paso TX (S)

Parisi, Beulah, *Acting Librn,* Contemporary Crafts Association and Gallery, Library, Portland OR

Park, Christy, *Chmn Art,* Massachusetts College of Art, Boston MA (S)

Park, Hye Ok, *Dir of Computer Serv,* Ferguson Library, Stamford CT

Park, Kyong, *Founder,* Storefront for Art & Architecture, New York NY

Park, Leland, *Librn,* Davidson College Art Gallery, Library, Davidson NC

Park, Marlene, *Prof,* John Jay College of Criminal Justice, Dept of Art, Music and Philosophy, New York NY (S)

Park, Marlene, *Prof,* City University of New York, PhD Program in Art History, New York NY (S)

Park, Seho, *Asst Prof,* Winona State University, Dept of Art, Winona MN (S)

Parke, David L, *Dir,* Hershey Museum, Hershey PA

Parker, Barry, *Exec VPres,* Sculptors Guild, Inc, New York NY

Parker, Barry, *Chmn Fine Arts Dept,* University of the Arts, Philadelphia College of Art & Design, Philadelphia PA (S)

Parker, Bart, *Prof,* University of Rhode Island, Dept of Art, Kingston RI (S)

Parker, Cheryl Ann, *Asst Dir,* West Bend Gallery of Fine Arts, West Bend WI

Parker, C J, *Head Dept,* Peace College, Art Dept, Raleigh NC (S)

Parker, Collier B, *Chmn Dept,* Delta State University, Fielding L Wright Art Center, Cleveland MS

Parker, Collier B, *Chmn,* Delta State University, Dept of Art, Cleveland MS (S)

Parker, Cynthia, *Office Mgr,* Ella Sharp Museum, Jackson MI

Parker, Donna, *Cur of Exhib,* Western Kentucky University, Kentucky Museum, Bowling Green KY

Parker, Harry S, *Dir,* Fine Arts Museums of San Francisco, M H de Young Memorial Museum and California Palace of the Legion of Honor, San Francisco CA

Parker, Jennifer, *Archivist,* Jackson County Historical Society, Research Library and Archives, Independence MO

Parker, Joe, *Chmn,* Limestone College, Art Dept, Gaffney SC (S)

Parker, Phil, *Coordr Graphic Design,* Florida School of the Arts, Visual Arts, Palatka FL (S)

Parker, Robert J, *Dean Faculty Fine Arts,* Concordia University, Faculty of Fine Arts, Montreal PQ (S)

Parker, S M, *Instr,* Western Illinois University, Art Dept, Macomb IL (S)

Parker, Stephanie, *Pres,* South County Art Association, Kingston RI

Parker, Thomas, *Chmn Dept,* Drury College, Art and Art History Dept, Springfield MO (S)

Parker, Tim Ann, *Asst Head,* University of Connecticut, Art & Design Library, Storrs CT

Parker-Smith, Betty, *VPres Academic Affairs,* Tougaloo College, Art Collection, Tougaloo MS

Parkerson, Jane, *Cur Educ,* Polk Museum of Art, Lakeland FL

Parkinson, Carol, *Dir,* Harvestworks, Inc, New York NY

Parkinson, George, *Division Chief & State Archivist,* Ohio Historical Society, Archives-Library Division, Columbus OH

Parkinson, John, *VPres & Treas,* Museum of Modern Art, New York NY

Parks, Ann B, *Asst Dir,* Landmark Society of Western New York, Inc, Wenrich Memorial Library, Rochester NY

Parks, Robert, *Cur Autograph Manuscripts,* Pierpont Morgan Library, New York NY

Parks-Kirby, Carie, *Assoc Prof,* Alma College, Clack Art Center, Alma MI

Parmet, Joe, *Exec Dir,* Long Beach Jewish Community Center, Center Gallery, Long Beach CA

Parrino, George, *Dean,* State University of New York College at Purchase, Division of Visual Arts, Purchase NY (S)

Parris, David, *Cur Science,* New Jersey State Museum, Trenton NJ

Parrish, Maurice, *Deputy Dir,* Detroit Institute of Arts, Detroit MI

Parry, Lee, *Prof Art History,* University of Arizona, Dept of Art, Tucson AZ (S)

Parry, Pamela, *Registrar,* Norton Gallery and School of Art, West Palm Beach FL

Parry, Pamela J, *Exec Dir,* Art Libraries Society of North America, Tucson AZ

Parshall, Robert, *Assoc Prof,* University of Illinois, Chicago, Health Science Center, Biomedical Visualizations, Chicago IL (S)

Parsley, Jacque, *Dir,* Liberty National Bank, Liberty Gallery, Louisville KY

Parson, David, *Lectr,* College of William and Mary, Dept of Fine Arts, Williamsburg VA (S)

Parson, Del, *Asst Prof,* Dixie College, Art Dept, Saint George UT (S)

Parson, Leon, *Instr,* Ricks College, Dept of Art, Rexburg ID (S)

Parsons, Bernard, *Pres,* Arthur Roy Mitchell Memorial Inc, Museum of Western Art, Trinidad CO

Parsons, Jean, *Chmn Dept,* Interlochen Arts Academy, Dept of Visual Art, Interlochen MI (S)

Parsons, Jean, *Instr,* Interlochen Arts Academy, Dept of Visual Art, Interlochen MI (S)

Parsons, Marcia M, *Fine Arts Librn,* University of Texas at Austin, Fine Arts Library, Austin TX

Parsons, Mary, *Asst Dir,* City of Springdale, Shiloh Museum, Springdale AR

Parsons, Merribell, *Dir,* Columbus Museum of Art, Columbus OH

Parsons, Michael J, *Chmn Dept,* Ohio State University, Dept of Art Education, Columbus OH (S)

Parsons, Richard, *Prof,* Lakeland Community College, Visual Arts Dept, Mentor OH (S)

Parsons, Sheila, *Instr,* The Arkansas Arts Center, Museum School, Little Rock AR (S)

Partin, Bruce, *Chmn,* Roanoke College, Fine Arts Dept-Art, Salem VA (S)

Partridge, Kathleen, *Instr,* Mohawk Valley Community College, Advertising Design and Production, Utica NY (S)

Parvis, Paul B, *Asst Dir,* Connecticut Historical Society, Hartford CT

Paschen, Stephen H, *Dir,* Summit County Historical Society, Akron OH

Pascoe, Clara, *Dir Educ,* Westmoreland Museum of Art, Greensburg PA

Pasinski, Irene, *Pres,* Associated Artists of Pittsburgh, Pittsburgh PA

Paskus, Wendy, *Dir Community Relations,* Artrain, Inc, Ann Arbor MI

Pass, Dwayne, *Instr,* Tulsa Junior College, Art Dept, Tulsa OK (S)

Passanise, Gary, *Artist-in-Residence,* Webster University, Art Dept, Webster Groves MO (S)

Pastan, Elizabeth, *Asst Prof,* Indiana University, Bloomington, Henry Radford Hope School of Fine Arts, Bloomington IN (S)

Pasternack, Derick, *Chief Exec Officer,* Lovelace Medical Foundation, Art Collection, Albuquerque NM

Pasternak, Anne, *Gallery Cur,* Real Art Ways (RAW), Hartford CT

Pastore, Shiela, *Volunteer Coordr,* Palo Alto Cultural Center, Palo Alto CA

Patanella, Paul, *Librn,* Art Institute of Philadelphia Library, Philadelphia PA

Patano, Tony, *Coordr Interior Design,* Columbia College, Art Dept, Chicago IL (S)

Patch, Charles, *Syst Dir,* Kemper & Leila Williams Foundation, New Orleans LA

Patel, Vipule, *Educ Asst,* University of Chicago, David and Alfred Smart Museum of Art, Chicago IL

Paterakis, Angela, *Prof,* School of the Art Institute of Chicago, Chicago IL (S)

Paterniti, John, *Accounting Mgr,* San Diego Museum of Art, San Diego CA

Paterson, Pamela, *Admin Asst,* The Saint Louis Art Museum, Richardson Memorial Library, Saint Louis MO

Patierno, Mary, *Instr,* Sarah Lawrence College, Dept of Art History, Bronxville NY (S)

Patitucci, Joe, *Chmn,* American River College, Dept of Art, Sacramento CA (S)

Patnaude, Francis, *VPres,* Washington Art Association, Washington Depot CT

Patnode, J Scott, *Prof,* Gonzaga University, Dept of Art, Spokane WA (S)

Patnode, J Scott, *Dir,* Gonzaga University, Ad Art Gallery, Spokane WA

Patrick, Brian, *Assoc Prof,* University of Utah, Art Dept, Salt Lake City UT (S)

Patrick, Darry, *Assoc Prof,* Sam Houston State University, Art Dept, Huntsville TX (S)

Patrick, Jill, *Dir,* Ontario College of Art, Dorothy H Hoover Library, Toronto ON

Patrick, Rick, *Chmn Dept,* Holy Names College, Art Dept, Oakland CA (S)

Patrick, Stephen E, *Exec Dir,* Hammond-Harwood House Association, Inc, Annapolis MD

Patrick, Vernon, *Chmn,* California State University, Chico, Art Dept, Chico CA (S)

Patrick, Vernon, *Instr,* California State University, Chico, Art Dept, Chico CA (S)

Patrick, Victoria, *Dir,* Johnson State College, Dept Fine Arts, Dibden Gallery, Johnson VT (S)

Patridge, Margaret, *Public Information,* Walker Art Center, Minneapolis MN

Patrizio, Maurice, *Dir Visitor Servs,* State Museum of Pennsylvania, Brandywine Battlefield Park, Harrisburg PA

Patt, Susan, *Prof,* La Sierra University, Art Dept, Riverside CA (S)

Patten, Barbara, *Asst Prof,* Spring Hill College, Fine Arts Dept, Mobile AL (S)

Patten, James, *Cur Contemporary Art,* London Regional Art & Historical Museums, London ON

Pattern, Lloyd, *Ceramisist,* University of South Alabama, Dept of Art, Mobile AL (S)

Patterson, Aubrey B, *Pres,* Bank of Mississippi, Art Collection, Tupelo MS

Patterson, Belinda A, *Lectr,* Lambuth University, Dept of Human Ecology & Visual Arts, Jackson TN (S)

Patterson, Curtis, *Assoc Prof,* Atlanta College of Art, Atlanta GA (S)

Patterson, Michelle, *Prof,* North Carolina Central University, Art Dept, Durham NC (S)

Patterson, Myron, *Fine Arts Librn,* University of Utah, Marriott Library, Salt Lake City UT

Patterson, Richard, *Instr,* Marian College, Art Dept, Indianapolis IN (S)

Patterson, Vivian, *Assoc Cur Coll,* Williams College, Museum of Art, Williamstown MA

Patterson, Willis R, *Head Dept,* Central Wyoming College, Art Center, Riverton WY (S)

Patton, Larry, *Chmn,* Butler County Community College, Art Dept, El Dorado KS (S)

Patton, Sharon, *Cur,* The Studio Museum in Harlem, New York NY

Patton, Sharon, *Assoc Prof,* University of Michigan, Ann Arbor, Dept of History of Art, Ann Arbor MI (S)

Patton, Thomas, *Chmn,* University of Missouri-Saint Louis, Art Dept, Saint Louis MO (S)

Pattou, Suzanne, *Secy,* The Art Institute of Chicago, Antiquarian Society, Chicago IL

Paukert, Karel, *Chief Cur Musical Arts,* Cleveland Museum of Art, Cleveland OH

Paul, Alison, *Exec Dir,* Pelham Art Center, Pelham NY

Paul, Didier, *Cur Old Masters,* Montreal Museum of Fine Arts, Montreal PQ

Paul, John, *VPres,* Heritage Center, Inc, Pine Ridge SD

Paul, Kathy, *Dir Development & Community Relations,* Madison Art Center, Madison WI

Paul, Shannon L, *Librn,* University of Arizona, College of Architecture Library, Tucson AZ

Pauldine, David, *Pres,* The Art Institutes International, The Art Institute of Seattle, Seattle WA (S)

Paulette, Paula M, *Dir,* Maine Coast Artists, Art Gallery, Rockport ME

Paulmier, Emily, *Instr,* Main Line Center for the Arts, Haverford PA (S)

Paulsen, Richard, *Chmn,* Elmhurst College, Art Dept, Elmhurst IL (S)

Paulson, Alan, *Prof,* Gettysburg College, Dept of Art, Gettysburg PA (S)

Paulson, Robert, *Two-Dimensional Area Head,* Southern Illinois University, School of Art & Design, Carbondale IL (S)

Paulson, Robert, *Prof,* Southern Illinois University, School of Art & Design, Carbondale IL (S)

Pavlik, John, *Dir,* Fisher Scientific Company, Fisher Collection of Alchemical and Historical Pictures, Pittsburgh PA

Pavovic, Miutin, *Preparator,* Telfair Academy of Arts and Sciences Inc, Savannah GA

Pawel, Nancy, *Lectr,* Incarnate Word College, Art Dept, San Antonio TX (S)

Pawlowicz, Peter, *Asst Prof,* East Tennessee State University, Fine Arts Dept, Johnson City TN (S)

Pawlowski, Andrew, *Pres,* Sculptor's Society of Canada, Toronto ON

Payne, Christopher, *Asst Prof,* Huntingdon College, Dept of Art, Montgomery AL (S)

Payne, Couric, *General Mgr Museum Stores,* Fine Arts Museums of San Francisco, M H de Young Memorial Museum and California Palace of the Legion of Honor, San Francisco CA

Payton, Neal, *Vis Asst Prof,* Catholic University of America, School of Architecture & Planning, Washington DC (S)

Payton, Tamara, *Secy,* US Department of State, Diplomatic Reception Rooms, Washington DC

Peace, Bernie K, *Prof,* West Liberty State College, Art Dept, West Liberty WV (S)

Peacock, Barbara, *Library Technical Asst,* University of Michigan, Fine Arts Library, Ann Arbor MI

Peacock, Jan, *Coordr MFA Prog,* Nova Scotia College of Art and Design, Halifax NS (S)

Peak, Marianne, *Supt,* Adams National Historic Site, Quincy MA

Peake, John Gay, *Chmn Bd,* Art Patrons League of Mobile, Mobile AL

Pear, William H, *Cur,* Nichols House Museum, Inc, Boston MA

Pearce, John N, *Dir of Planning & Prog,* James Monroe Museum, Fredericksburg VA

Peard Lawson, Karol Anne, *Chief Cur,* Columbus Museum, Columbus GA

Pearlstein, Connie, *Office Mgr,* Pacific Grove Art Center, Pacific Grove CA

Pearlstein, Elinor, *Assoc Cur Chinese Art,* The Art Institute of Chicago, Department of Asian Art, Chicago IL

Pearlstine, Norman, *Chmn,* New York Historical Society, New York NY

Pearson, Clifton, *Head Dept,* Alabama A & M University, Art and Art Education, Normal AL (S)

Pearson, Duane, *Superintendent,* Roosevelt-Vanderbilt National Historic Sites, Hyde Park NY

Pearson, Jim, *Instr,* Vincennes University Junior College, Art Dept, Vincennes IN (S)

Pearson, John, *Prof,* Oberlin College, Dept of Art, Oberlin OH (S)

Pearson, J Robert, *Exec Dir,* Bellingrath Gardens and Home, Theodore AL

Pearson, Mary, *Gallery Mgr,* Green Hill Center for North Carolina Art, Greensboro NC

Pease, David, *Dean,* Yale University, School of Art, New Haven CT (S)

Pease, Edwin, *Prof,* College of William and Mary, Dept of Fine Arts, Williamsburg VA (S)

Peatross, C Ford, *Cur Architecture,* Library of Congress, Prints and Photographs Division, Washington DC

Peavy, Nancy, *VPres,* National Center on Arts & Aging-National Council on The Aging, NCOA Gallery Patina, Washington DC

Pebworth, Charles A, *Prof,* Sam Houston State University, Art Dept, Huntsville TX (S)

Pecchenino, J Ronald, *Chmn,* University of the Pacific, College of the Pacific, Dept of Art, Stockton CA (S)

Pechanec, Mary, *Asst Dir for Development,* Pacific - Asia Museum, Pasadena CA

Peck, Judith, *Prof,* Ramapo College of New Jersey, School of Contemporary Arts, Mahwah NJ (S)

Peck, Marshall, *Pres,* Southern Vermont Art Center, Manchester VT

Peck, William H, *Cur Ancient Art,* Detroit Institute of Arts, Detroit MI

Peckam, Cynthia A, *Cur,* Sandy Bay Historical Society, Sewall Scripture House-Old Castle, Rockport MA

Pecoraro, Sal, *Instr,* De Anza College, Creative Arts Div, Cupertino CA (S)

Pecoravo, Patricia, *Asst Registrar & Cur Traveling Exhib,* New Orleans Museum of Art, New Orleans LA

Pedigo, Ruth, *Historical Preservation Dir,* Safety Harbor Museum of Regional History, Safety Harbor FL

Pedley, John G, *Prof,* University of Michigan, Ann Arbor, Dept of History of Art, Ann Arbor MI (S)

Peebles, Phoebe, *Archivist,* Harvard University, Harvard University Art Museums, Cambridge MA

Peebles, Phoebe, *Archivist,* Harvard University, William Hayes Fogg Art Museum, Cambridge MA

Peele, Jim, *Assoc Dir,* University of Illinois, Krannert Art Museum, Champaign IL

Peer, Charles, *Head Dept,* John Brown University, Art Dept, Siloam Springs AR (S)

Pefferman, Curt, *Instr,* Eastern Iowa Community College, Art Dept, Clinton IA (S)

Peglau, Michael, *Adjunct Asst Prof,* Drew University, Art Dept, Madison NJ (S)

Peirce, John, *Funding,* Alaska Artists' Guild, Anchorage AK

Peircy, Leslie, *Registrar,* Dawson City Museum & Historical Society, Dawson City YT

Peiser, Judy, *Exec Dir,* Center for Southern Folklore, Memphis TN

Pelfrey, Robert, *Instr,* Cuesta College, Art Dept, San Luis Obispo CA (S)

Pelkey, Brenda, *Admin Coordr,* Photographers Gallery, Saskatoon SK

Pell, John B, *Pres,* Fort Ticonderoga Association, Ticonderoga NY

Pellegrini, Francis N, *Dept Chmn,* State University of New York at Farmingdale, Advertising Art Design Dept, Farmingdale NY (S)

Pellerito, Marlene, *Adjunct Instr,* Saginaw Valley State University, Dept of Art and Design, University Center MI (S)

Pelly, Charles, *Pres,* Industrial Designers Society of America, Great Falls VA

Pelrine, Diane, *Cur African & Oceanic Pre Columbian Art,* Indiana University, Art Museum, Bloomington IN

Pels, Marsha, *Instr,* Sarah Lawrence College, Dept of Art History, Bronxville NY (S)

Peltier, Cynthia, *Asst to Dir,* Bucknell University, Center Gallery, Lewisburg PA

Pelto, Nicole, *Registrar,* Lyman Allyn Art Museum, New London CT

Pelton, Dolores, *Pres,* Munson Gallery, New Haven CT

Pelton, Robert, *Cur,* The Barnum Museum, Bridgeport CT

Peluso, Marta, *Dir,* Cuesta College, Cuesta College Art Gallery, San Luis Obispo CA

Pelzel, Thomas O, *Assoc Prof,* University of California, Riverside, Dept of the History of Art, Riverside CA (S)

Pence, Marc, *Registrar,* Portland Art Museum, Portland OR

Pendell, David, *Assoc Prof,* University of Utah, Art Dept, Salt Lake City UT (S)

Pendercast, Len, *Projects Officer,* Visual Arts Ontario, Toronto ON

Pendergast, Carol, *Asst Prof,* University of Massachusetts at Lowell, Dept of Art, Lowell MA (S)

Pendergraft, Norman, *Prof,* North Carolina Central University, Art Dept, Durham NC (S)

Pendergraft, Norman E, *Dir,* North Carolina Central University, Art Museum, Durham NC

Pendlebury, Theresa, *Slide Cur,* Art Center College of Design, James Lemont Fogg Memorial Library, Pasadena CA

Pendleton, Debbie, *Asst Dir Public Services,* Alabama Department of Archives and History Museum, Museum Galleries, Montgomery AL

Peniston, Ann, *Dir,* Lake County Civic Center Association, Inc, Heritage Museum and Gallery, Leadville CO

Peniston, Robert C, *Dir,* Washington & Lee University, Lee Chapel and Museum, Lexington VA

Peniston, Robert C, *Dir,* Washington & Lee University, Lee Chapel and Museum, Lexington VA

Penn, Barbara, *Assoc Prof Painting & Drawing,* University of Arizona, Dept of Art, Tucson AZ (S)

Penn, Beverly, *Asst Prof,* Southwest Texas State University, Dept of Art, San Marcos TX (S)

Pennella, Lisa, *Dir,* Schweinfurth Art Center, Auburn NY

Pennell Doiron, Jeannette, *Chmn,* Beaumont Arts Council, Beaumont TX

Pennington, Beth, *Treas,* Lubbock Art Association, Inc, Lubbock TX

Pennington, Claudia L, *Assoc Dir,* Naval Historical Center, The Navy Museum, Washington DC

Pennington, Estill Curtis, *Cur,* Morris Communications Corporation, Morris Museum of Art, Augusta GA

Pennington, Mary Anne, *Dir,* Lauren Rogers Museum of Art, Laurel MS

Penny, A, *Instr,* Technical University of Nova Scotia, Faculty of Architecture, Halifax NS (S)

Penny, Carl, *Librn,* New Orleans Museum of Art, New Orleans LA

Penny, Carl O, *Librn,* New Orleans Museum of Art, Felix J Dreyfous Library, New Orleans LA

Penny, Simon, *Asst Prof,* University of Florida, Dept of Art, Gainesville FL (S)

Penuel, Jaime, *Lectr,* North Dakota State University, Div of Fine Arts, Fargo ND (S)

Penwell, Donna, *Dir,* Monterey History and Art Association, Maritime Museum of Monterey, Monterey CA

Peoples, Wade, *Chmn,* Judson College, Division of Fine Arts, Marion AL (S)

Pepail, Rosalinci, *Cur Canadian Decorative Arts,* Montreal Museum of Fine Arts, Montreal PQ

Pepich, Bruce W, *Dir,* Wustum Museum Art Association, Racine WI

Pepich, Bruce W, *Dir,* Wustum Museum Art Association, Charles A Wustum Museum of Fine Arts, Racine WI

Pepich, Bruce W, *Dir,* Wustum Museum Art Association, Wustum Art Library, Racine WI

Pepin, Suzanne, *Visual Arts Coordr,* City of Eugene, Hult Center, Jacobs Gallery, Eugene OR

Pepion, Loretta F, *Cur,* Museum of the Plains Indian & Crafts Center, Browning MT

Pepper, Jerold L, *Librn,* Adirondack Historical Association, Library, Blue Mountain Lake NY

Peranteau, Michael, *Co-Dir,* Diverse Works, Houston TX

Percy, Ann, *Cur Drawings,* Philadelphia Museum of Art, Philadelphia PA

Peres, Michael, *Chmn Biomedical Photography Communications,* Rochester Institute of Technology, School of Photographic Arts & Sciences, Rochester NY (S)

Perez, Angel, *Institute of Puerto Rican Culture,* Centro Ceremonial de Caguana, San Juan PR

Perinet, Francine, *Dir,* Oakville Galleries, Centennial Gallery and Gairloch Gallery, Oakville ON

Perkins, Dean, *Assoc Prof,* Norwich University, Dept of Philosophy, Religion and Fine Arts, Northfield VT (S)

Perkins, Margaret, *Assoc Cur of Education,* University of Arizona, Museum of Art, Tucson AZ

Perkins, Pamela G, *Head Branch Museums,* Whitney Museum of American Art, New York NY

Perkins, Tristine, *Coll Mgr,* Indiana University, William Hammond Mathers Museum, Bloomington IN

Perlin, Ruth, *Head Educ Resources Progs,* National Gallery of Art, Washington DC

Perlman, Bill, *VPres,* Women's Interart Center, Inc, Interart Gallery, New York NY

Perlman, Lawrence, *Chmn Board,* Walker Art Center, Minneapolis MN

Perlus, Barry, *Assoc Prof,* Cornell University, Dept of Art, Ithaca NY (S)

Pernish, Paul, *Dept Head,* Contra Costa Community College, Dept of Art, San Pablo CA (S)

Pernot, M M, *Dir,* Burlington County Historical Society, Burlington NJ

Perper, Harold, *VPres,* Boca Raton Museum of Art, Boca Raton FL

Perreault, Martine, *Gallery Dir,* Ann Arbor Art Association, Ann Arbor MI

Perri, John, *Prof,* University of Wisconsin-Stout, Dept of Art & Design, Menomonie WI (S)

Perron, Michell, *Dir,* Musee d'Art de Joliette, Joliette PQ

Perrot, Paul N, *Dir,* Santa Barbara Museum of Art, Santa Barbara CA

Perry, Birthe, *Pres,* Allied Arts Council of Lethbridge, Bowman Arts Center, Lethbridge AB

Perry, Candice, *Museum Cur,* The Filson Club, Louisville KY

Perry, Donald, *Chmn,* Emporia State University, Division of Art, Emporia KS (S)

Perry, Donald, *Dir,* Emporia State University, Norman R Eppink Art Gallery, Emporia KS

Perry, Elizabeth, *Corporate Relations Officer,* National Gallery of Art, Washington DC

Perry, Jeanne, *Registrar,* Severin Wunderman Museum, Irvine CA

Perry, Kenneth, *Dir,* Museum of Western Colorado, Grand Junction CO

Perry, Nancy S, *Dir,* Jamestown-Yorktown Foundation, Yorktown VA

Perry, Patricia, *Business Mgr,* Maryhill Museum of Art, Goldendale WA

Perry, Richard, *Dir of Development,* Museum of Photographic Arts, Balboa Park CA

Person, Ann I, *Educ Coordr,* Danforth Museum of Art, Framingham MA

Persons, Cecil, *Instr,* The Arkansas Arts Center, Museum School, Little Rock AR (S)

Pertl, Susan, *Cur,* McDonald's Corporation, Art Collection, Oakbrook IL

Pesold, Nicole, *Prog Dir,* Pointe Claire Cultural Centre, Stewart Hall Art Gallery, Pointe Claire PQ

Pessin, I Marc, *Sr Instr,* University of British Columbia, Dept of Fine Arts, Vancouver BC (S)

Pestel, Michael, *Prof,* Chatham College, Art Gallery, Pittsburgh PA

Pestel, Michael, *Asst Prof,* Chatham College, Fine & Performing Arts, Pittsburgh PA (S)

Petch, H, *Pres,* University of Victoria, Maltwood Art Museum and Gallery, Victoria BC

Petcoff, Jessie, *Registrar,* Duke University Museum of Art, Durham NC

Peters, Jennifer, *Membership Coordr,* Historical Society of Pennsylvania, Philadelphia PA

Peters, Larry D, *Gallery Dir,* Topeka Public Library, Gallery of Fine Arts, Topeka KS

Peters, P J, *Vis Prof,* Nebraska Wesleyan University, Art Dept, Lincoln NE (S)

Peters, Rick L, *Dept Head,* Southwestern College, Art Dept, Winfield KS (S)

Peters, Robert, *Chmn Graphic Design,* University of Manitoba, School of Art, Winnipeg MB (S)

Peters, Susan Dodge, *Asst Dir Educ,* University of Rochester, Memorial Art Gallery, Rochester NY

Peters, Thomas, *Prof,* Lehigh University, Dept of Art and Architecture, Bethlehem PA (S)

Peters, Wallace, *Assoc Prof,* Philadelphia Community College, Dept of Art, Philadelphia PA (S)

Peters, Wendy, *Instr,* Ohio Wesleyan University, Fine Arts Dept, Delaware OH (S)

Petersen, Daniel W, *Instr,* Modesto Junior College, Arts Humanities and Speech Division, Modesto CA (S)

Petersen, Karen, *Dir,* Rowland Evans Robinson Memorial Association, Rokeby Museum, Ferrisburgh VT

Petersen, Leonard, *Prof,* University of Wisconsin-Superior, Programs in the Visual Arts, Superior WI (S)

Peterson, Allan, *Head Dept,* Pensacola Junior College, Dept of Visual Arts, Pensacola FL (S)

Peterson, Allan, *Dir,* Pensacola Junior College, Visual Arts Gallery, Pensacola FL

Peterson, C, *Assoc Prof,* Northern Arizona University, School of Art & Design, Flagstaff AZ (S)

Peterson, Carole, *Registrar for Art,* Illinois State Museum, Illinois Art Gallery & Lockport Gallery, Springfield IL

Peterson, Christine, *Librn,* Oregon School of Arts and Crafts, Library, Portland OR

Peterson, Chuck, *VPres,* Caspers, Inc, Art Collection, Tampa FL

Peterson, Dean A, *Asst Prof,* Salisbury State University, Art Dept, Salisbury MD (S)

Peterson, D R, *Instr,* Normandale Community College, Bloomington MN (S)

Peterson, Fred, *Pres,* Arts and Crafts Association of Meriden Inc, Gallery 53, Meriden CT

Peterson, Frederick, *Coordr,* University of Minnesota, Morris, Humanities Division, Morris MN (S)

Peterson, Gaylen, *Head Dept,* Lutheran Brethren Schools, Art Dept, Fergus Falls MN (S)

Peterson, Glen L, *Instr,* Yavapai College, Visual & Performing Arts Division, Prescott AZ (S)

Peterson, Harold, *Librn,* Minneapolis Society of Fine Arts, Art Reference Library, Minneapolis MN

Peterson, Heidi, *Instr,* Wartburg College, Dept of Art, Waverly IA (S)

Peterson, James, *Head Dept Fine & Performing Arts,* Edison Community College, Dept of Fine and Performing Arts, Fort Myers FL (S)

Peterson, James, *Asst Prof,* Franklin and Marshall College, Art Dept, Lancaster PA (S)

Peterson, John D, *Exec Dir,* Morris Museum, Morristown NJ

Peterson, John E, *Cur Archives,* Lutheran Theological Seminary, Krauth Memorial Library, Philadelphia PA

Peterson, Judith, *Dir,* Muckenthaler Cultural Center, Fullerton CA

Peterson, Kendall, *Admin Asst,* Art Community Center, Art Center of Corpus Christi, Corpus Christi TX

Peterson, Kip, *Registrar,* Memphis Brooks Museum of Art, Memphis TN

Peterson, Larry D, *Prof,* University of Nebraska, Kearney, Dept of Art & Art History, Kearney NE (S)

Peterson, Margaret, *Dir,* Sunbury Shores Arts and Nature Centre, Inc, Gallery, Saint Andrews NB

Peterson, Margaret, *Assoc Prof,* Central Missouri State University, Art Dept, Warrensburg MO (S)

Peterson, Margaret Ray, *Dir,* Sunbury Shores Arts and Nature Centre, Inc, Library, Saint Andrews NB

Peterson, Martin E, *Cur American Art,* San Diego Museum of Art, San Diego CA

Peterson, Nick, *Display Technician,* College of Southern Idaho, Herrett Museum & Art Gallery, Twin Falls ID

Peterson, Pauline M, *Reference Librn,* Jones Library, Inc, Amherst MA

Peterson, Penny, *First VPres,* Arizona Artist Guild, Phoenix AZ

Peterson, Robert, *Film Dept Chmn,* Art Center College of Design, Pasadena CA (S)

Peterson, Robyn G, *Cur,* The Rockwell Museum, Corning NY

Peterson, Russell O, *Dean of Curriculum & Adult Educ,* College of Lake County, Art Dept, Grayslake IL (S)

Peterson, Willard, *Prof,* Roberts Wesleyan College, Art Dept, Rochester NY (S)

Petheo, Bela, *Chmn,* College of Saint Benedict, Art Dept, Saint Joseph MN (S)

Petheo, Bela, *Prof,* Saint John's University, Art Dept, Collegeville MN (S)

Petheo, Bela, *Chmn of Art Dept,* College of Saint Benedict, Art Gallery, Saint Joseph MN

Petrick, Mary Anna, *Instructor,* Milwaukee Area Technical College, Graphic Arts Dept, Milwaukee WI (S)

Petrie, Claire, *Reference Librn,* Parsons School of Design, Adam & Sophie Gimbel Design Library, New York NY

Petrik, Virgil, *Lectr,* Mount Marty College, Art Dept, Yankton SD (S)

Petrochuz, Ron, *Assoc Prof,* University of Maryland, Baltimore County, Visual Arts Dept, Baltimore MD (S)

Petroff, Angela, *Interim Dir,* Creative Art Center, Pontiac MI (S)

Petroff, Angela, *Interim Dir,* Creative Arts Center, Pontiac MI

Petrosky, Ed, *Prof,* West Virginia University, College of Creative Arts, Morgantown WV (S)

Petrovich-Mwaniki, Lois, *Asst Prof,* Western Carolina University, Dept of Art, Cullowhee NC (S)

Petruchyk, Jon, *Prof,* Christopher Newport College, Arts & Communications, Newport News VA (S)

Petrulis, Elizabeth, *Preparator,* Sheldon Swope Art Museum, Terre Haute IN

Petry, Mary Ann, *Assoc Prof,* West Texas State University, Art, Communication & Theatre Dept, Canyon TX (S)

Petterplace, Jennifer, *Preparator,* McMaster University, Art Gallery, Hamilton ON

Pettibone, John W, *Executive Dir & Cur,* Hammond Castle Museum, Gloucester MA

Peven, Michael, *Dept Chairperson,* University of Arkansas, Art Dept, Fayetteville AR (S)

Pevny, Chrystyna, *Archivist,* The Ukrainian Museum, New York NY

Peyrat, Jean, *Librn,* Center for Creative Studies, College of Art & Design Library, Detroit MI

Pezzerd, L Candace, *Cur Education,* Rhode Island Historical Society, Providence RI

Pfaff, Larry, *Deputy Librn,* Art Gallery of Ontario, Edward P Taylor Research Library & Archives, Toronto ON

Pfanschmidt, Martha, *Instr,* Marylhurst College, Art Dept, Marylhurst OR (S)

Pfeifer, Natalie, *Gallery Dir,* Volcano Art Center, Hawaii National Park HI

Pfeiff, Janette, *VPres,* Seneca Falls Historical Society Museum, Seneca Falls NY

Pfingstaff, Benjamin, *Asst Prof,* Norwich University, Dept of Philosophy, Religion and Fine Arts, Northfield VT (S)

Pfleger, Claire, *Lectr,* Cardinal Stritch College, Art Dept, Milwaukee WI (S)

Pfliger, Terry, *Dept Coordr,* St Lawrence College, Art Gallery, Kingston ON

Pfotenhauer, Louise, *In Charge,* Neville Public Museum, Library, Green Bay WI

Pfrehm, Paul, *Asst Prof,* Southeastern Oklahoma State University, Art Dept, Durant OK (S)

Pfzff, Judy, *Instr*, Columbia University, School of the Arts, Division of Painting & Sculpture, New York NY (S)

Phegley, John, *Exhibition Designer*, University of Notre Dame, Snite Museum of Art, Notre Dame IN

Phelam, Dr, *Dir*, University of Oklahoma, School of Art, Norman OK (S)

Phelan, Thomas, *Treas*, Rensselaer Newman Foundation Chapel and Cultural Center, The Gallery, Troy NY

Phelps, Bill, *Chmn*, Ellsworth Community College, Dept of Fine Arts, Iowa Falls IA (S)

Phelps, Brent, *Photography Coordr*, University of North Texas, School of Visual Arts, Denton TX (S)

Phelps, Jon J, *Union Dir*, Duke University Union, Durham NC

Phelps, Mason, *Pres Board of Trustees*, Museum of Contemporary Art, San Diego, La Jolla CA

Phelps, Timothy H, *Assoc Prof*, Johns Hopkins University, School of Medicine, Dept of Art as Applied to Medicine, Baltimore MD (S)

Phetts, Meg, *Cur*, Ventura County Historical Society Museum, Ventura CA

Philbin, Ann, *Dir*, The Drawing Center, New York NY

Philbin, Kathleen A, *Exec Dir*, Doshi Center for Contemporary Art, Harrisburg PA

Philbrick, Harry, *Cur Educ*, Aldrich Museum of Contemporary Art, Ridgefield CT

Philbrick, Ruth, *Cur Photo Archives*, National Gallery of Art, Washington DC

Philbrick, Ruth, *Cur*, National Gallery of Art, Photographic Archives, Washington DC

Philipps, Alice, *Financial Coordr*, Women in the Arts Foundation, Inc, New York NY

Phillips, Anthony, *Prof*, School of the Art Institute of Chicago, Chicago IL (S)

Phillips, Barbara L, *Dir Planning & Development*, Allentown Art Museum, Allentown PA

Phillips, Carol, *VPres Educ*, Banff Centre for the Arts, Banff AB (S)

Phillips, Cindy, *Pres Board Dir*, Plains Art Museum, Moorhead MN

Phillips, Duane L, *Asst Prof*, University of North Alabama, Dept of Art, Florence AL (S)

Phillips, Francis, *Dir*, Intersection for the Arts, San Francisco CA

Phillips, Gifford, *VChmn*, Museum of Modern Art, New York NY

Phillips, Helen, *Prof*, University of Central Arkansas, Art Dept, Conway AR (S)

Phillips, Kathryn D, *Librn*, Freer Gallery of Art & The Arthur M Sackler Gallery Gallery, Library, Washington DC

Phillips, Kris, *Instr*, Sarah Lawrence College, Dept of Art History, Bronxville NY (S)

Phillips, Laura, *Instr*, The Arkansas Arts Center, Museum School, Little Rock AR (S)

Phillips, Lisa, *Cur*, Whitney Museum of American Art, New York NY

Phillips, Mary, *Cur Dir*, Phillips University, Grace Phillips Johnson Art Gallery, Enid OK

Phillips, Mary, *Assoc Prof*, Phillips University, Dept of Art, Enid OK (S)

Phillips, Patricia C, *Chmn Art Studio & Art Educ*, State University of New York College at New Paltz, Art Studio Dept, New Paltz NY (S)

Phillips, Quitman E, *Asst Prof*, University of Wisconsin, Madison, Dept of Art History, Madison WI (S)

Phillips, Robert F, *Cur of Contemporary Art*, Toledo Museum of Art, Toledo Museum of Art, Toledo OH

Phillips, Susan, *Dir Fashion Design*, Art Institute of Fort Lauderdale, Fort Lauderdale FL (S)

Phillips-Abbott, Rebecca, *Admin Dir*, National Museum of Women in the Arts, Washington DC

Phillpot, Clive, *Dir*, Museum of Modern Art, Library, New York NY

Phinney, Gail, *Coordr Museum Guides*, Muskegon Museum of Art, Muskegon MI

Phipps, Richard, *Chmn*, Capital University, Fine Arts Dept, Columbus OH (S)

Piasecki, Jane, *Assoc Dir*, Newport Harbor Art Museum, Newport Beach CA

Piatt, Margaret, *Dir*, Piatt Castles, West Liberty OH

Piazza, Paul J, *Controller*, International Museum of Photography at George Eastman House, Rochester NY

Picco, Ronald, *Prof*, College of Santa Fe, Visual Arts Dept, Santa Fe NM (S)

Piche, Thomas, *Cur*, Everson Museum of Art, Syracuse NY

Pickens, Susan, *Asst Prof*, Ithaca College, Fine Art Dept, Ithaca NY (S)

Pickett, Anna, *Dir & Cur*, Prince George Art Gallery, Prince George BC

Pickett, Victor, *Prof*, Old Dominion University, Art Dept, Norfolk VA (S)

Picon, Carlos A, *Cur-in-Charge Greek & Roman Art*, The Metropolitan Museum of Art, New York NY

Pidot, Ronald K, *Museum Scientist Zoology*, Riverside Municipal Museum, Riverside CA

Piehl, Walter, *Instr*, Minot State University, Dept of Art, Division of Humanities, Minot ND (S)

Piejko, Alex, *Instr*, Mohawk Valley Community College, Advertising Design and Production, Utica NY (S)

Piene, Otto, *Dir*, Massachusetts Institute of Technology, Center for Advanced Visual Studies, Cambridge MA (S)

Pier, Gwen M, *Exec Dir*, National Sculpture Society, New York NY

Pierce, Ann, *Instr*, California State University, Chico, Art Dept, Chico CA (S)

Pierce, Beverly, *Adminr*, Hirshhorn Museum and Sculpture Garden, Washington DC

Pierce, Carol, *Prof*, Christopher Newport College, Arts & Communications, Newport News VA (S)

Pierce, Charles E, *Dir*, Pierpont Morgan Library, New York NY

Pierce, Christopher, *Asst Prof*, Berea College, Art Dept, Berea KY (S)

Pierce, Donald, *Cur Decorative Art*, High Museum of Art, Atlanta GA

Pierce, Rita, *Dir*, Springfield Art & Historical Society, Springfield VT

Pierce, Sally, *Print Dept Cur*, Boston Athenaeum, Boston MA

Pierro, Lenny, *Chmn*, Kean College of New Jersey, Fine Arts Dept, Union NJ (S)

Piersol, Daniel, *Chief Cur Exhib*, New Orleans Museum of Art, New Orleans LA

Pierson, Gary, *Instr*, Ricks College, Dept of Art, Rexburg ID (S)

Pierson, Richard, *Dean Admissions*, Clark University, Dept of Visual & Performing Arts, Worcester MA (S)

Pierson, Ridgely, *Pres*, Quincy Art Center, Quincy IL

Pierson, Ridgely, *Pres*, Quincy Art Center, Library, Quincy IL

Pierson, Sallie, *Dir*, Estevan National Exhibition Centre Inc, Estevan SK

Piesentin, Joe, *Instr*, Pepperdine University, Seaver College, Dept of Art, Malibu CA (S)

Pietrzak, Ted, *Dir*, Art Gallery of Hamilton, Hamilton ON

Pigott, Vincent, *Assoc Dir*, University of Pennsylvania, University Museum of Archaelogy & Anthropology, Philadelphia PA

Pike, Jo, *Dir Visitor Servs*, Museum of Modern Art, New York NY

Pike, Kermit J, *Librn*, Western Reserve Historical Society, Cleveland OH

Pike, Kermit J, *Librn Dir*, Western Reserve Historical Society, Library, Cleveland OH

Pikkoja, Vilma, *Vol Librn*, French Art Colony, Library, Gallipolis OH

Pilat, Peter, *Instr*, Monterey Peninsula College, Art Dept, Monterey CA (S)

Pilgram, Suzanne, *Asst Prof*, Georgian Court College, Dept of Art, Lakewood NJ (S)

Pilgrim, Dianne, *Dir*, Cooper-Hewitt, National Museum of Design, New York NY

Pili, Leala, *Exec Dir*, Jean P Haydon Museum, Pago Pago, American Samoa PI

Pilia, Jorge, *Theater Arts Prog Dir*, Guadalupe Cultural Arts Center, San Antonio TX

Pillsbury, Edmund P, *Dir*, Kimbell Art Museum, Fort Worth TX

Pinardi, Brenda, *Prof*, University of Massachusetts at Lowell, Dept of Art, Lowell MA (S)

Pincoe, William, *Treas*, Canton Art Institute, Canton OH

Pincus, Debra, *Assoc Prof*, University of British Columbia, Dept of Fine Arts, Vancouver BC (S)

Pincus-Witten, Robert, *Prof*, City University of New York, PhD Program in Art History, New York NY (S)

Pindak, Zoe, *Deputy Dir Admin*, Baltimore Museum of Art, Baltimore MD

Pindell, Howardena, *Prof*, State University of New York at Stony Brook, Art Dept, Stony Brook NY (S)

Pinder, Joseph, *Vis Lectr*, North Central College, Dept of Art, Naperville IL (S)

Pinedo, Maria, *Dir*, Galeria de la Raza, Studio 24, San Francisco CA

Pines, Doralynn, *Acquisitions Librn & Bibliographer*, The Metropolitan Museum of Art, Thomas J Watson Library, New York NY

Pines, Philip A, *Dir*, Trotting Horse Museum, Goshen NY

Ping, Donn Britt, *Asst Prof*, Converse College, Art Dept, Spartanburg SC (S)

Pink, Jim, *Instr*, University of Nevada, Las Vegas, Dept of Art, Las Vegas NV (S)

Pinkel, Sheila, *Assoc Prof*, Pomona College, Art Dept, Claremont CA (S)

Pinkham, Katherine, *Cur*, Beverly Historical Society, Cabot, Hale and Balch House Museums, Beverly MA

Pinkney, Valerie, *Art Librn*, Dallas Public Library, Fine Arts Division, Dallas TX

Pinson, Penelope, *VPres*, Arts on the Park, Lakeland FL

Pintea, June C, *Dir*, Erie Historical Museum & Planetarium, Erie PA

Pinto, John, *Prof*, Princeton University, Dept of Art and Archaeology, Princeton NJ (S)

Piotrowski, C, *Assoc Prof*, Northern Arizona University, School of Art & Design, Flagstaff AZ (S)

Piotrowski, Ronald, *Prof*, Northern Arizona University, School of Art & Design, Flagstaff AZ (S)

Piper, Bill, *Instr*, Walla Walla Community College, Art Dept, Walla Walla WA (S)

Pippin, Ruth Ann, *Asst Dir Business Management*, Brevard Art Center and Museum, Inc, Melbourne FL

Pisciotta, Henry, *Fine Arts Librn*, Carnegie Mellon University, Hunt Library, Pittsburgh PA

Piskoti, James, *Prof*, California State University, Art Dept, Turlock CA (S)

Pitelka, Vince, *Dept Coordr*, North Dakota State University, Div of Fine Arts, Fargo ND (S)

Pitman, Bonnie, *Deputy Dir*, University of California, University Art Museum, Berkeley CA

Pitman, Dianne, *Asst Prof*, Northeastern University, Dept of Art & Architecture, Boston MA (S)

Pitman, Ursula, *Dir of Docents*, Fitchburg Art Museum, Fitchburg MA

Pitsch, Barbara A, *Dir Educ*, The Currier Gallery of Art, Manchester NH

Pitt, Paul, *Prof*, Harding University, Dept of Art, Searcy AR (S)

Pitt, Sheila, *Asst Prof Gallery Management*, University of Arizona, Dept of Art, Tucson AZ (S)

Pittenger, Charles, *Registrar*, J B Speed Art Museum, Louisville KY

Pitts, Bill, *State Museum Dir*, Oklahoma Historical Society, State Museum of History, Oklahoma City OK

Pitts, Dannell, *Communications Dir*, Columbus Museum, Columbus GA

Pitts, Lyna, *Instr*, Southeastern Louisiana University, Dept of Visual Arts, Hammond LA (S)

Pitts, Terence, *Dir*, University of Arizona, Center for Creative Photography, Tucson AZ

Pittsley, Rich, *Dir*, Chief Plenty Coups Museum, Pryor MT

Pivorun, Phyllis, *Media Resources Cur*, Clemson University, Emery A Gunnin Architectural Library, Clemson SC

Pivovar, Ronald, *Dir,* Thiel College, Sampson Art Gallery, Greenville PA

Pivovar, Ronald A, *Chmn Dept,* Thiel College, Dept of Art, Greenville PA (S)

Pizzollo, Sissy, *Dir,* Muse Art Gallery, Philadelphia PA

Plantz, John, *Treas,* Luna County Historical Society, Inc, Deming Luna Mimbres Museum, Deming NM

Plater, Daryl, *Instr,* Vancouver Community College, Langara Campus, Dept of Fine Arts, Vancouver BC (S)

Platou, Dode, *Dir Emerita,* Kemper & Leila Williams Foundation, New Orleans LA

Platt, Nicholas, *Pres,* The Asia Society Galleries, New York NY

Plaut, Anthony, *Dir Gallery,* Cornell College, Armstrong Gallery, Mount Vernon IA

Plax, Julie, *Asst Prof Art History,* University of Arizona, Dept of Art, Tucson AZ (S)

Plear, Scott, *Chmn Dept,* Vancouver Community College, Langara Campus, Dept of Fine Arts, Vancouver BC (S)

Plehaty, Phyllis, *Cur Costumes,* Boulder Historical Society Inc, Museum of History, Boulder CO

Plosky, Charles, *Assoc Prof,* Jersey City State College, Art Dept, Jersey City NJ (S)

Plotkin, Andy, *Exec Trustee,* Edna Hibel Art Foundation, Hibel Museum of Art, Palm Beach FL

Plotkin, Andy, *Exec Trustee,* Edna Hibel Art Foundation, Library, Palm Beach FL

Plotkin, Theodore, *Pres,* Edna Hibel Art Foundation, Hibel Museum of Art, Palm Beach FL

Plummer, Ann, *Asst Prof,* Winona State University, Dept of Art, Winona MN (S)

Plummer, John H, *Cur Medieval & Renaissance Manuscripts,* Pierpont Morgan Library, New York NY

Podl, Tom, *Pres,* Polish Museum of America, Chicago IL

Poeschl, Paul, *Prog Coordr,* Oshkosh Public Museum, Oshkosh WI

Poese, Neil, *Executive Dir,* Kit Carson Historic Museum, Taos NM

Poggemeyer, Karen, *Asst Dir,* Eccles Community Art Center, Ogden UT

Pogue, Dwight, *Assoc Prof,* Smith College, Art Dept, Northampton MA (S)

Pogue, Larry, *Chmn,* East Central College, Art Dept, Union MO (S)

Pohl, Frances, *Assoc Prof,* Pomona College, Art Dept, Claremont CA (S)

Pohlkamp, Mark, *Lectr,* University of Wisconsin-Stevens Point, Dept of Art & Design, Stevens Point WI (S)

Pohlman, Lynette, *Dir,* Iowa State University, Brunnier Gallery Museum, Ames IA

Pohlmann, Ken, *Preparator,* Middlebury College, Museum of Art, Middlebury VT

Poindexter, Edith C, *Admin Asst,* Patrick Henry Memorial Foundation, Red Hill National Memorial, Brookneal VA

Poirier, Ivanhoe, *Pastor & Dir,* Musee de la Basilique Notre-Dame, Montreal PQ

Pokinski, Deborah, *Instr,* Hamilton College, Art Dept, Clinton NY (S)

Polan, Louise, *Cur Exhib,* Huntington Museum of Art, Huntington WV

Poland, Barbara, *Research Librn,* Warner Bros Research Library, North Hollywood CA

Polcari, Stephen, *Dir,* Archives of American Art, New York Regional Center, Washington DC

Polenberg, Marcia, *Dir,* Central Michigan University, Art Gallery, Mount Pleasant MI

Polera, Josephine, *Financial Aid Officer,* Ontario College of Art, Toronto ON (S)

Poleskie, Steve, *Prof,* Cornell University, Dept of Art, Ithaca NY (S)

Poley, Albert, *Prof,* Rochester Institute of Technology, School of Art and Design, Rochester NY (S)

Poling, Clark V, *Prof,* Emory University, Art History Dept, Atlanta GA (S)

Poliszczuk, Orest S, *Prof,* Montgomery College, Dept of Art, Rockville MD (S)

Polito, Ronald, *Co-Chmn,* University of Massachusetts at Boston, Art Dept, Boston MA (S)

Polk, Andrew, *Assoc Prof Printmaking,* University of Arizona, Dept of Art, Tucson AZ (S)

Polk, Tom, *Art History,* University of Georgia, Franklin College of Arts & Sciences, Dept of Art, Athens GA (S)

Pollack, Rhoda-Gale, *Dean,* University of Kentucky, Dept of Art, Lexington KY (S)

Pollan, Andrea, *Cur,* Arlington Arts Center, Arlington VA

Pollini, John, *Prof,* University of Southern California, School of Fine Arts, Los Angeles CA (S)

Polskin, Philippa, *Pres,* Ruder Finn & Rotman Inc, New York NY

Polster, Nancy, *Chmn Dept & Coordr Interior Design,* Iowa State University, Dept of Art and Design, Ames IA (S)

Poltz, John, *Cur Photography,* University of Kansas, Spencer Museum of Art, Lawrence KS

Polus, Judith Ann, *Bemis Art School Dir,* Colorado Springs Fine Arts Center, Colorado Springs CO

Pomeroy, Dan, *Chief Cur of Collections,* Tennessee State Museum, Nashville TN

Pomeroy, Dan, *Chief Cur,* Tennessee State Museum, Library, Nashville TN

Pomeroy, Lily, *Asst Prof,* Dickinson State University, Dept of Art, Dickinson ND (S)

Pomeroy Draper, Stacy, *Cur,* Rensselaer County Historical Society, Library, Troy NY

Pondone, Marc, *Instr,* Solano Community College, Division of Fine & Applied Art, Suisun City CA (S)

Ponzo, Gary, *Asst Art Placement,* Visual Arts Ontario, Toronto ON

Poole, Nancy, *Exec Dir,* London Regional Art & Historical Museums, London ON

Pooley, David, *Registrar,* Eastern Illinois University, Tarble Arts Center, Charleston IL

Poor, Robert, *Prof,* University of Minnesota, Minneapolis, Art History, Minneapolis MN (S)

Pope, Edward, *Assoc Prof,* University of Wisconsin, Madison, Dept of Art, Madison WI (S)

Pope, John C, *Trustee,* Hill-Stead Museum, Farmington CT

Pope, Linda, *Dir,* University of California - Santa Cruz, Eloisa Pickard Smith Gallery, Santa Cruz CA

Pope, Patricia, *VPres,* Barn Gallery Associates, Inc, Ogunquit ME

Pope, Thomas, *VPres,* Key West Art and Historical Society, East Martello Museum and Gallery, Key West FL

Popovic, Tanya, *Chmn & Librn,* LeMoyne College, Wilson Art Gallery, Syracuse NY

Popovich, Ljubica D, *Assoc Prof,* Vanderbilt University, Dept of Fine Arts, Nashville TN (S)

Popowcer, Stuart, *Controller,* Terra Museum of American Art, Chicago IL

Popp, Jan, *Asst Dir,* Capital University, Schumacher Gallery, Columbus OH

Porada, Edith, *Honorary Cur Seals & Tablets,* Pierpont Morgan Library, New York NY

Poras, Linda, *Cur,* Fitchburg Art Museum, Fitchburg MA

Porcari, George, *Acquisitions Librn,* Art Center College of Design, James Lemont Fogg Memorial Library, Pasadena CA

Porps, Ernest O, *Prof,* University of Colorado at Denver, Dept of Fine Arts, Denver CO (S)

Porta, Siena, *Chmn Board of Dir,* Cultural Council Foundation, Fourteen Sculptors Gallery, New York NY

Porteous, Timothy, *Pres,* Ontario College of Art, Toronto ON (S)

Porter, Ann, *Dir,* University of Vermont, Robert Hull Fleming Museum, Burlington VT

Porter, Dave, *Media Dir,* Utah Travel Council, Salt Lake City UT

Porter, David S, *Assoc Prof,* University of North Florida, Dept of Communications & Visual Arts, Jacksonville FL (S)

Porter, Dean A, *Dir,* University of Notre Dame, Snite Museum of Art, Notre Dame IN

Porter, Deborah, *Instr,* Stephens College, Art & Fashion Dept, Columbia MO (S)

Porter, Dolores, *Shop Mgr,* B'nai B'rith International, B'nai B'rith Klutznick National Jewish Museum, Washington DC

Porter, Edward, *Pres College,* International Fine Arts College, Miami FL (S)

Porter, Elwin, *Dir,* South Florida Art Institute of Hollywood, Dania FL (S)

Porter, Jane M, *Keeper,* Portsmouth Athenaeum, Portsmouth NH

Porter, Jeanne Chenault, *Assoc Prof,* Pennsylvania State University, University Park, Dept of Art History, University Park PA (S)

Porter, John, *Prof,* Gavilan College, Art Dept, Gilroy CA (S)

Porter, John R, *Chief Conservator,* Montreal Museum of Fine Arts, Montreal PQ

Porter, Robert, *Dir Publishing, Policy & Planning,* American Council for the Arts, New York NY

Portera, Michael, *Instr,* Miracosta College, Art Dept, Oceanside CA (S)

Portwood, Fiona, *Curatorial Asst,* Prairie Gallery, Grande Prairie AB

Posner, Helaine, *Cur,* Massachusetts Institute of Technology, List Visual Arts Center, Cambridge MA

Post, J B, *Head,* Free Library of Philadelphia, Print and Picture Dept, Philadelphia PA

Post, John, *Cur Education,* Hickory Museum of Art, Inc, Hickory NC

Post, William, *Dir Libr Colls,* California State University, Chico, Meriam Library, Chico CA

Post, William, *Cur Ornithology,* Charleston Museum, Charleston SC

Poster, Amy, *Cur Asian Art,* Brooklyn Museum, Brooklyn NY

Postler, Janet W, *Registrar,* C M Russell Museum, Great Falls MT

Postler, Janet W, *Librn,* C M Russell Museum, Frederic G Renner Memorial Library, Great Falls MT

Potoff, Reeva, *Instr,* Columbia University, School of the Arts, Division of Painting & Sculpture, New York NY (S)

Potratz, Wayne, *Chmn Dept,* University of Minnesota, Minneapolis, Dept of Studio Art, Minneapolis MN (S)

Potter, Ann, *Secy,* Paint 'N Palette Club, Grant Wood & Memorial Park Gallery, Anamosa IA

Potter, G W, *Instr,* Western Illinois University, Art Dept, Macomb IL (S)

Potter, Jan, *Public Communication Coordr,* K Mart Corp, Troy MI

Potter, Joann, *Registrar,* Vassar College, Vassar Art Gallery, Poughkeepsie NY

Potters, Stephen, *VChmn,* National Institute for Architectural Education, New York NY

Potts, Daria, *Prog Coordr,* Midland Art Council, Midland MI

Poulet, Anne, *Cur European Decorative Arts & Sculpture,* Museum of Fine Arts, Boston MA

Poulos, Basilios N, *Chmn,* Rice University, Dept of Art and Art History, Houston TX (S)

Poulos, Helen, *Pres,* Federated Art Associations of New Jersey, Inc, Westfield NJ

Poulton, M, *Instr,* Technical University of Nova Scotia, Faculty of Architecture, Halifax NS (S)

Poundstone, Sally H, *Dir,* Westport Public Library, Westport CT

Pover, Bonnie Bird, *Asst Dir,* Noyes Museum, Oceanville NJ

Pover, Bonnie Bird, *Asst to Dir,* Noyes Museum, Library, Oceanville NJ

Powell, Deanna, *Secy,* Algonquin Arts Council, Bancroft Art Gallery, Bancroft ON

Powell, Earl A, *Dir,* National Gallery of Art, Washington DC

Powell, Janice J, *Librn,* Princeton University, Marquand Library, Princeton NJ

Powell, JoAnne, *Secy,* North Carolina Museums Council, Raleigh NC

Powell, Linda, *Cur of Educ,* Fort Worth Art Association, Modern Art Museum of Fort Worth, Fort Worth TX

Powell, Lyne, *Pres,* South Peace Art Society, Dawson Creek Art Gallery, Dawson Creek BC

Powell, Michael, *Chmn,* Metropolitan Arts Commission, Metropolitan Center for Public Arts, Portland OR

Powell, Nancy, *Registrar,* CIGNA Corporation, CIGNA Museum & Art Collection, Philadelphia PA

Powell, Patricia, *Ed,* University of Wisconsin-Madison, Elvehjem Museum of Art, Madison WI

Powell, Phillip, *Chmn,* Carthage College, Art Dept, Kenosha WI (S)

Powell, Richard, *Asst Prof,* Duke University, Dept of Art and Art History, Durham NC (S)

Powell, Richard, *Chmn,* Tulane University, University Art Collection, New Orleans LA

Powell, Robert, *Chmn,* Ricks College, Dept of Art, Rexburg ID (S)

Powelson, Rosemary, *Art Instr,* Lower Columbia College, Longview WA (S)

Power, Christine T, *Cur,* Federal Reserve Bank of Minneapolis, Minneapolis MN

Powers, Dave, *Cur,* National Archives and Records Service, John F Kennedy Library and Museum, Boston MA

Powers, Diane, *VPres,* Mingei International, Inc, Mingei International Museum of World Folk Art, San Diego CA

Powers, James, *Dir Educ,* Missouri Historical Society, Saint Louis MO

Powers, JoAnn, *Assoc Prof,* C W Post Center of Long Island University, School of Visual & Performing Arts, Greenvale NY (S)

Powers, Martin, *Assoc Prof,* University of Michigan, Ann Arbor, Dept of History of Art, Ann Arbor MI (S)

Powers, Mary, *Pres,* Kings County Historical Society and Museum, Hampton NB

Powers, Mary Ann, *Instr,* Assumption College, Dept of Art & Music, Worcester MA (S)

Powers, Mary Ann, *Asst Prof,* Assumption College, Dept of Art & Music, Worcester MA (S)

Powers, Ramon, *Exec Dir,* Kansas State Historical Society, Kansas Museum of History, Topeka KS

Powers, Sandra L, *Dir,* Society of the Cincinnati, Anderson House Library, Washington DC

Poynor, Robin, *Assoc Prof,* University of Florida, Dept of Art, Gainesville FL (S)

Pozzatti, Rudy, *Prof,* Indiana University, Bloomington, Henry Radford Hope School of Fine Arts, Bloomington IN (S)

P'Pool, Kenneth M, *Dir Historic Preservation,* Mississippi Department of Archives and History, State Historical Museum, Jackson MS

Pramuk, Ed, *Prof,* Louisiana State University, School of Art, Baton Rouge LA (S)

Prater, Teresa, *Chmn Dept,* Converse College, Art Dept, Spartanburg SC (S)

Pratt, Bartram J, *Pres,* Cohasset Historical Society, Caleb Lothrop House, Cohasset MA

Pratt, Donald, *Chmn Board of Governors,* Kansas City Art Institute, Kemper Museum of Contemporary Art & Design, Kansas City MO

Pratt, George, *Instr,* Joe Kubert School of Cartoon & Graphic Art, Inc, Dover NJ (S)

Pratt, Vernon, *Assoc Prof,* Duke University, Dept of Art and Art History, Durham NC (S)

Pratt, William C, *Dir,* Twin City Art Foundation, Masur Museum of Art, Monroe LA

Pratzon, Jill, *Painting Restorer,* Illustration House Inc, Gallery, New York NY

Pratzon, Jim, *Gallery Mgr,* Illustration House Inc, Gallery, New York NY

Pray, John Noell, *Dir & Cur,* Hamline University Learning Center Gallery, Library, Saint Paul MN

Prchal, Polly, *City Mgr,* Carrie McLain Museum, Nome AK

Prekop, Martin, *Undergrad Division Chmn,* School of the Art Institute of Chicago, Chicago IL (S)

Prelinger, Elizabeth, *Instr,* Georgetown University, Dept of Fine Arts, Washington DC (S)

Prendeville, Jet M, *Art Librn,* Rice University, Alice Pratt Brown Library of Art, Architecture & Music, Houston TX

Press, Elizabeth, *Dir,* Historical Society of Martin County, Elliott Museum, Stuart FL

Prestiano, Robert, *Coordr,* Angelo State University, Art and Music Dept, San Angelo TX (S)

Preston, Carola, *Education Office Asst,* Memphis Brooks Museum of Art, Memphis TN

Preston, Jim, *Dir Human Resources,* M Grumbacher Inc, Cranbury NJ

Prete, Cosmo, *Instr,* Dowling College, Dept of Visual Arts, Oakdale NY (S)

Pretti, Brad, *Pres Board Trustees,* Roswell Museum and Art Center, Roswell NM

Prevost, Beth, *Cur Field Exhib,* Department of Natural Resources of Missouri, Missouri State Museum, Jefferson City MO

Price, B Byron, *Exec Dir,* National Cowboy Hall of Fame and Western Heritage Center, Oklahoma City OK

Price, B Byron, *Executive Dir,* National Cowboy Hall of Fame and Western Heritage Center, Museum, Oklahoma City OK

Price, Bonnie, *Dir Communications,* National Watercolor Society, Cerritos CA

Price, Boyce, *Pres,* Essex Art Association, Inc, Essex CT

Price, Joan, *Supervisor Art Education,* City College of New York, Art Dept, New York NY (S)

Price, L, *Instr,* Humboldt State University, College of Arts & Humanities, Arcata CA (S)

Price, Marla, *Dir,* Fort Worth Art Association, Modern Art Museum of Fort Worth, Fort Worth TX

Price, Mary Jo, *Exhib Librn,* Frostburg State University, Lewis J Ort Library, Frostburg MD

Price, Mary Sue Sweeney, *Deputy Dir,* Newark Museum Association, The Newark Museum, Newark NJ

Price, Michael, *Chmn,* Hamline University Learning Center Gallery, Library, Saint Paul MN

Price, Michael, *Exec Dir,* Providence Athenaeum, Providence RI

Price, Michael, *Head Dept,* Hamline University, Art Dept, Saint Paul MN (S)

Price, Pam, *Library Dir,* Mercer County Community College, Library, Trenton NJ

Price, Pam, *Chmn,* University of Texas of Permian Basin, Dept of Art, Odessa TX (S)

Price, Priscilla B, *Registrar,* Corning Museum of Glass, Corning NY

Price, Ramon, *Chief Cur,* DuSable Museum of African American History, Chicago IL

Price, Richard W, *Managing Editor,* Corning Museum of Glass, Corning NY

Price, Rob, *Assoc Prof,* University of Wisconsin-Stout, Dept of Art & Design, Menomonie WI (S)

Price, Rob, *Asst Prof,* University of Wisconsin-Stout, Dept of Art & Design, Menomonie WI (S)

Price, Sally Irwin, *Dir,* Baycrafters, Inc, Bay Village OH

Priede, Zigmunds, *Instr,* Johnson County Community College, Visual Arts Program, Overland Park KS (S)

Priest, Terri, *Assoc Prof,* College of the Holy Cross, Dept of Visual Arts, Worcester MA (S)

Priester, Anne, *Adjunct Prof,* Lehigh University, Dept of Art and Architecture, Bethlehem PA (S)

Prieve, E Arthur, *Dir,* University of Wisconsin, Madison, Graduate School of Business, Center for Arts Administration, Madison WI (S)

Prince, David, *Cur,* Syracuse University, Art Collection, Syracuse NY

Prince, Paul, *Designer of Exhib,* University of California, Santa Barbara, University Art Museum, Santa Barbara CA

Prince, Richard, *Assoc Prof,* University of British Columbia, Dept of Fine Arts, Vancouver BC (S)

Pritchard, C William, *Assoc Exec Dir,* Iowa State Education Association, Salisbury House, Des Moines IA

Pritchett, Frances, *Paper Conservator,* Balboa Art Conservation Center, San Diego CA

Privatsky, Benni, *Assoc Dir,* Dickinson State University, Mind's Eye Gallery, Dickinson ND

Privett, Rev Stephen A, *Academic VPres,* Santa Clara University, de Saisset Museum, Santa Clara CA

Privitt, Bob, *Instr,* Pepperdine University, Seaver College, Dept of Art, Malibu CA (S)

Probe, Suzanne, *Asst Cur,* Regina Public Library, Dunlop Art Gallery, Regina SK

Probes, Anna Greidanus, *Asst Prof,* Calvin College, Art Dept, Grand Rapids MI (S)

Procos, D, *Instr,* Technical University of Nova Scotia, Faculty of Architecture, Halifax NS (S)

Prokof, Carol, *Asst Cur,* Surrey Art Gallery, Surrey BC

Prokop, Clifton A, *Assoc Prof,* Keystone Junior College, Fine Arts Dept, Factoryville PA (S)

Prokopoff, Stephen S, *Dir,* University of Iowa, Museum of Art, Iowa City IA

Prol, Elbertus, *Cur,* Ringwood Manor House Museum, Ringwood NJ

Prom, James, *Instr,* Rochester Community College, Art Dept, Rochester MN (S)

Proper, David R, *Librn,* Historic Deerfield, Inc, Henry N Flynt Library, Deerfield MA

Propersi, August, *Dir,* Connecticut Institute of Art, Greenwich CT (S)

Propersi, August, *Pres & Dir,* Connecticut Institute of Art Galleries, Greenwich CT

Propersi, Joann, *VPres,* Connecticut Institute of Art, Greenwich CT (S)

Propersi, Joann, *VPres,* Connecticut Institute of Art Galleries, Greenwich CT

Propersi, Linda, *Asst Dir,* Connecticut Institute of Art, Greenwich CT (S)

Propersi, Linda, *Asst,* Connecticut Institute of Art Galleries, Greenwich CT

Propersi, Michael, *Adminr,* Connecticut Institute of Art, Greenwich CT (S)

Propersi, Michael, *Adminr,* Connecticut Institute of Art Galleries, Greenwich CT

Proske, Beatrice G, *Cur Emeritus Sculpture,* Hispanic Society of America, Museum, New York NY

Prosperetti, Leopoldine, *Registrar,* Walters Art Gallery, Baltimore MD

Prosser, Judy, *Archivist,* Museum of Western Colorado, Grand Junction CO

Protzen, Jean-Pierre, *Chmn Architecture,* University of California, Berkeley, College of Environmental Design, Berkeley CA (S)

Prouty, Sharman, *Asst Librn,* Historic Deerfield, Inc, Henry N Flynt Library, Deerfield MA

Provan, Archibald D, *Assoc Prof,* Rochester Institute of Technology, School of Printing, Rochester NY (S)

Provencher, Alfred, *Assoc Prof,* Monmouth College, Dept of Art, West Long Branch NJ (S)

Provine, William, *Instr,* John C Calhoun State Community College, Division of Fine Arts, Decatur AL (S)

Provis, Dorothy, *Pres,* Coalition of Women's Art Organizations, Port Washington WI

Provo, Daniel, *Dir,* Wildlife of the American West Art Museum, Jackson WY

Pruett, James W, *Chief of Music,* The John F Kennedy Center for the Performing Arts, Performing Arts Library, Washington DC

Pruett, Pam, *Educ Assoc,* Columbus Museum, Columbus GA

Pruitt, Helen, *Pres Board,* Carolina Art Association, Gibbes Museum of Art, Charleston SC

Pruner, Gary L, *Instr,* American River College, Dept of Art, Sacramento CA (S)

Prusak, Patricia, *Dep Dir,* Georgia Volunteer Lawyers for the Arts, Inc, Atlanta GA

Pruss, Mary, *Treasurer,* Safety Harbor Museum of Regional History, Safety Harbor FL

Pryor, Gerald, *Artist-in-Residence,* New York University, Dept of Art & Art Professions, New York NY (S)

Pryor, Jerome, *Prof,* Xavier University, Dept of Art, Cincinnati OH (S)

Przybilla, Carrie, *Assoc Cur 20th Century Art,* High Museum of Art, Atlanta GA

Przybylek, Leslie, *Instr,* Gettysburg College, Dept of Art, Gettysburg PA (S)

Przybylek, Stephanie E, *Cur,* Crawford County Historical Society, Baldwin-Reynolds House Museum, Meadville PA

Puccinelli, Lydia, *Cur,* National Museum of African Art, Washington DC

Puckett, Richard L, *Dir,* Lemoyne Art Foundation, Inc, Tallahassee FL

Pudles, Lynne, *Asst Prof,* Lake Forest College, Dept of Art, Lake Forest IL (S)

Pufahl, John K, *Dir,* University of Windsor, School of Visual Arts, Windsor ON (S)

Puffer, John, *Instr,* Vincennes University Junior College, Art Dept, Vincennes IN (S)

Pugh, Judith Novak, *Dir,* Westminster College, Winston Churchill Memorial & Library in the United States, Fulton MO

Puglisi, Catherine, *Assoc Prof,* Rutgers, the State University of New Jersey, Graduate Program in Art History, New Brunswick NJ (S)

Pujol, Elliott, *Prof,* Kansas State University, Art Dept, Manhattan KS (S)

Pulido, Pio, *Co-Dir,* MEXIC-ARTE Museum, Austin TX

Pulin, Carol, *Fine Prints,* Library of Congress, Prints and Photographs Division, Washington DC

Pulinka, Steven M, *Site Adminr,* Winterthur Museum and Gardens, Historic Houses of Odessa, Winterthur DE

Pulitzer, Emily Rauh, *Pres,* Forum for Contemporary Arts, Saint Louis MO

Pullman, Patricia, *Asst to Dir,* New York Experimental Glass Workshop, Brooklyn NY

Pulsifer, Dorothy, *Chmn,* Bridgewater State College, Art Dept, Bridgewater MA (S)

Pultorak, Marceil, *Chairperson,* Carroll College, Art Dept, Waukesha WI (S)

Pumphrey, Richard G, *Chmn,* Lynchburg College, Art Dept, Lynchburg VA (S)

Puniello, Francoise S, *Cur,* Douglass College-Rutgers the State University, Mary H Dana Women Artists Series, New Brunswick NJ

Punnett, Robert, *Pres,* Museum of Northern British Columbia, Ruth Harvey Art Gallery, Prince Rupert BC

Punt, Gerry, *Instr,* Augustana College, Art Dept, Sioux Falls SD (S)

Pura, William, *Chmn Printmaking,* University of Manitoba, School of Art, Winnipeg MB (S)

Purdy, Henry, *Dir,* Holland College, Centre of Creative Arts Library & Gallery, Charlottetown PE

Purdy, Henry, *Dir,* Holland College, Centre of Creative Arts, Charlottetown PE (S)

Purdy, John M, *Dir,* Cavalry - Armor Foundation, Patton Museum of Cavalry & Armor, Fort Knox KY

Purdy, Tine, *Pres,* Huntsville Art League and Museum Association Inc, Huntsville AL

Purrington, Robert H, *Innkeeper,* Longfellow's Wayside Inn Museum, South Sudbury MA

Pursell, Clay, *Adjunct Instr,* Maryville University of Saint Louis, Art Division, Saint Louis MO (S)

Purves-Smith, Phyllis, *Chmn Illustration,* University of the Arts, Philadelphia College of Art & Design, Philadelphia PA (S)

Purvis, Alston, *Assoc Prof,* Boston University, School of Visual Arts, Boston MA (S)

Purvis, Mike, *Dir Exhib,* Maryland Hall for the Creative Arts, Cardinal Gallery, Annapolis MD

Pushkin, Grace, *Admin Asst,* Columbia University, School of the Arts, Division of Painting & Sculpture, New York NY (S)

Pusti, Judy, *Admin Asst,* Institute Of Alaska Native Arts, Inc, Fairbanks AK

Puterbaugh, David, *Pres,* Peoria Historical Society, Peoria IL

Putka, Robert, *Instr,* Cuyahoga Valley Art Center, Cuyahoga Falls OH (S)

Putman, Sumi, *Printmaker,* University of South Alabama, Dept of Art, Mobile AL (S)

Putnam, Karen H, *Vice Dir Development,* Brooklyn Museum, Brooklyn NY

Putterman, Florence, *VPres,* Society of American Graphic Artists, New York NY

Pyhrberg, Marilyn, *Development Dir,* Portland Museum of Art, Portland ME

Pyhrr, Stuart, *Cur Arms & Armor,* The Metropolitan Museum of Art, New York NY

Pylant, Carol, *Assoc Prof,* University of Wisconsin, Madison, Dept of Art, Madison WI (S)

Pylyshenko, Wolodymyr, *Assoc Prof,* State University of New York College at Brockport, Dept of Art & Art History, Brockport NY (S)

Quackenbush, Laura, *Cur & Adminr,* Leelanau Historical Museum, Leland MI

Quadhamer, Roger, *Dean Div,* El Camino College, Division of Fine Arts, Torrance CA (S)

Quarcoopome, Nii, *Asst Prof,* University of Michigan, Ann Arbor, Dept of History of Art, Ann Arbor MI (S)

Quealey, Natalie, *Educ,* Huronia Museum, Midland ON

Quets, Anne Marie, *Librn Asst,* Indianapolis Museum of Art, Stout Reference Library, Indianapolis IN

Quick, Betsy, *Educ Dir,* University of California, Los Angeles, Fowler Museum of Cultural History, Los Angeles CA

Quick, Edward, *Dir,* Sheldon Swope Art Museum, Research Library, Terre Haute IN

Quick, Edward R, *Dir,* Sheldon Swope Art Museum, Terre Haute IN

Quick, Joh, *Instr,* Ohio Wesleyan University, Fine Arts Dept, Delaware OH (S)

Quick, Michael, *Cur American Art,* Los Angeles County Museum of Art, Los Angeles CA

Quick, Richard, *Dir,* Rahr-West Art Museum, Manitowoc WI

Quick, Richard, *Dir,* Rahr-West Art Museum, Library, Manitowoc WI

Quigley, Lidia, *Conservator,* Museo de Arte de Ponce, Ponce Art Museum, Ponce PR

Quigley, Suzanne, *Registrar,* Detroit Institute of Arts, Detroit MI

Quimby, Frank, *Prof,* Salem State College, Art Dept, Salem MA (S)

Quinby, Carol, *Dir,* Order Sons of Italy in America, Garibaldi & Meucci Meuseum, Staten Island NY

Quinlan, Barbara, *Dir Public Serv,* Mississauga Library System, Central Library, Art Department, Mississauga ON

Quinlan, Catherine, *Dir,* University of Western Ontario, D B Weldon Library, London ON

Quinlan, Suzanne, *Treas,* The Washington Center For Photography, Washington DC

Quinn, Kristin, *Assoc Prof,* Saint Ambrose University, Art Dept, Davenport IA (S)

Quinn, Mairin, *Secy,* Rensselaer Newman Foundation Chapel and Cultural Center, The Gallery, Troy NY

Quinn, William, *Dir,* Kent State University, School of Art, Kent OH (S)

Quinonez, Gary, *Instr,* Monterey Peninsula College, Art Dept, Monterey CA (S)

Quint, California, *Vol,* Redding Museum of Art & History, Museum Research Library, Redding CA

Quintanilla, Faustino, *Dir,* Queebsborough Community College, Art Gallery, Bayside NY

Quirarte, Jacinto, *Prof,* University of Texas at San Antonio, Division of Art & Architecture, San Antonio TX (S)

Quirk, James, *Prof,* Northern Michigan University, Dept of Art and Design, Marquette MI (S)

Quirk, John, *Asst Prof,* Wartburg College, Dept of Art, Waverly IA (S)

Quiros, Alfred, *Asst Prof Painting & Drawing,* University of Arizona, Dept of Art, Tucson AZ (S)

Raab, Judith M, *Asst to Dir,* Williams College, Museum of Art, Williamstown MA

Raack, Robert, *Visual Arts Coordr,* School of Fine Arts, Visual Arts Dept, Willoughby OH (S)

Rab, Harry, *Asst Prof,* Rochester Institute of Technology, School of Printing, Rochester NY (S)

Rabe, Michael, *Assoc Prof,* Saint Xavier University, Dept of Art, Chicago IL (S)

Rabinovitch, Cecil, *Exec Dir,* Saidye Bronfman Centre, Montreal PQ

Racalbuto, Dave, *VPres,* Hollywood Art Museum, Hollywood FL

Racker, Barbara, *Cur,* Paris Gibson Square, Museum of Art, Great Falls MT

Rackow, Marcia, *Coordr,* Aesthetic Realism Foundation, Terrain Gallery, New York NY

Raczka, Robert, *Gallery Dir,* Allegheny College, Bowman, Megahan and Penelec Galleries, Meadville PA

Radan, George, *Prof,* Villanova University, Dept of Art and Art History, Villanova PA (S)

Radecki, Martin J, *Chief Conservator,* Indianapolis Museum of Art, Indianapolis IN

Radell, Lloyd, *Chmn,* Mercy College of Detroit, Art Dept, Detroit MI (S)

Rademacher, Richard J, *Head Librn,* Wichita Public Library, Wichita KS

Rades, Bill, *Dept Head,* Fort Steilacoom Community College, Fine Arts Dept, Tacoma WA (S)

Radford, Jim, *Asst Chmn Advertising Design,* Art Institute of Fort Lauderdale, Fort Lauderdale FL (S)

Radford, Mathew, *Instr,* New York Studio School of Drawing, Painting and Sculpture, New York NY (S)

Radke, Don, *Adjunct Asst Prof,* Texas Woman's University, Dept of Visual Arts, Denton TX (S)

Radke, Gary, *Prof,* Syracuse University, Dept of Fine Arts (Art History), Syracuse NY (S)

Radosh, Sondra M, *Asst Dir,* Jones Library, Inc, Amherst MA

Rafael, Ruth, *Archivist,* Judah L Magnes Museum, Berkeley CA

Rafat, Pasha, *Instr,* University of Nevada, Las Vegas, Dept of Art, Las Vegas NV (S)

Rafferty, Emily, *VPres Development & Membership,* The Metropolitan Museum of Art, New York NY

Ragan, J Thomas, *Dean,* North Carolina State University at Raleigh, School of Design, Raleigh NC (S)

Ragan, Sherry, *Exec Dir,* Institute for Design & Experimental Art (IDEA), Sacramento CA

Raggio, Olga, *Chmn European Sculture & Decorative Arts,* The Metropolitan Museum of Art, New York NY

Rago, Juliet, *Prof,* Loyola University of Chicago, Fine Arts Dept, Chicago IL (S)

Raguin, Virginia C, *Prof,* College of the Holy Cross, Dept of Visual Arts, Worcester MA (S)

Rahm, Bob, *Acting Area Head Design,* Pasadena City College, Art Dept, Pasadena CA (S)

Raia, Frank, *Dir Educ,* Art Institute of Fort Lauderdale, Fort Lauderdale FL (S)

Raines, D O, *Chmn,* Presbyterian College, Fine Arts Dept, Clinton SC (S)

Raines, Kevin, *Chairperson,* College of Notre Dame of Maryland, Art Dept, Baltimore MD (S)

Raines, Kevin, *Prof,* College of Notre Dame of Maryland, Art Dept, Baltimore MD (S)

Rainwater, Robert, *Asst Dir for Art, Prints & Photographs & Cur Spencer Coll,* The New York Public Library, Spencer Collection, New York NY

Rainwater, Robert, *Asst Dir,* The New York Public Library, Art, Prints and Photographs Division, New York NY

Rait, Elearnor, *Cur Coll,* Hofstra University, Hofstra Museum, Hempstead NY

Raithel, Jan, *Dept Chmn,* Chaffey Community College, Art Dept, Rancho Cucamonga CA (S)

Raizman, David, *Head Dept Fashion & Visual Studies,* Drexel University, Nesbitt College of Design Arts, Philadelphia PA (S)

Rajam, Margaret, *Prof,* West Virginia University, College of Creative Arts, Morgantown WV (S)

Rakonczay, Arlene, *Exec Dir,* Chicago Artists' Coalition, Chicago IL

Ralph, Liala, *Museum Shop Mgr,* Joslyn Art Museum, Omaha NE

Ramage, Andrew, *Prof,* Cornell University, Dept of the History of Art, Ithaca NY (S)

Raman, Anne, *Gallery Dir,* Foundation for Today's Art, Nexus Gallery, Philadelphia PA

Ramberg, W Dodd, *Prof,* Catholic University of America, School of Architecture & Planning, Washington DC (S)

Ramers, Del, *Asst Cur,* Temple University, Slide Library, Philadelphia PA

Ramirez, Adrian N, *Prof,* Catholic University of Puerto Rico, Dept of Fine Arts, Ponce PR (S)

Ramirez, Alejandro H, *Art Asst,* Newark Museum Association, Junior Museum, Newark NJ

Ramirez, Jeffrey, *Deputy Dir,* Bronx Museum of the Arts, Bronx NY

Ramirez, Luis, *Prof,* North Park College, Art Dept, Chicago IL (S)

Ramirez, Luis, *Chmn & Prof,* La Sierra University, Art Dept, Riverside CA (S)

Ramonis, Val, *Exec Dir,* Balzekas Museum of Lithuanian Culture, Chicago IL

Ramos, Jim, *Instr,* Gettysburg College, Dept of Art, Gettysburg PA (S)

Ramos , Julianne, *Exec Dir,* Rockland Center for the Arts, West Nyack NY

Ramos, Julianne, *Exec Dir,* Rockland Center for the Arts, West Nyack NY (S)

Ramsaran, Helen, *Assoc Prof,* John Jay College of Criminal Justice, Dept of Art, Music and Philosophy, New York NY (S)

Ramsay, George, *Prof,* Wittenberg University, Art Dept, Springfield OH (S)

Ramsey, Peter, *Dir,* Evergreen State College, Evergreen Galleries, Olympia WA

Rand, Anne Gimes, *Cur,* USS Constitution Museum Foundation Inc, Boston National Historical Park, Museum, Boston MA

Rand, Archie, *Instr,* Bard College, Milton Avery Graduate School of the Arts, Annandale-on-Hudson NY (S)

Rand, Archie, *Instr,* Columbia University, School of the Arts, Division of Painting & Sculpture, New York NY (S)

Rand, Duncan, *Librn,* Lethbridge Public Library, Art Gallery, Lethbridge AB

Rand, Harry, *Cur Painting & Sculpture,* National Museum of American Art, Washington DC

Rand, Olan A, *Asst Prof,* Northwestern University, Evanston, Dept of Art History, Evanston IL (S)

Rand, Richard, *Cur for European Art,* Dartmouth College, Hood Museum of Art, Hanover NH

Randall, Lawrence E, *Dir,* State University of New York at Purchase, Library, Purchase NY

Randall, Lilian M C, *Research Cur of Manuscripts and Rare Books,* Walters Art Gallery, Baltimore MD

Randall, Ross, *Development Officer,* Maryhill Museum of Art, Goldendale WA

Randazzo, Angelo, *Dir,* Manchester Institute of Arts and Sciences Gallery, Manchester NH

Randazzo, Angelo, *Exec Dir,* Manchester Institute of Arts and Sciences, Manchester NH (S)

Randolph, Karen, *Chmn,* Lubbock Christian University, Art Dept, Lubbock TX (S)

Rands, Robert L, *Adj Cur Archaeology,* Southern Illinois University, University Museum, Carbondale IL

Rankin, Shan, *Executive Dir,* Hidalgo County Historical Museum, Edinburg TX

Rankin, Tom, *Assoc Prof,* University of Mississippi, Dept of Art, University MS (S)

Ranspach, Ernest, *Instr,* College of Boca Raton, Art & Design Dept, Boca Raton FL (S)

Rantoul, T Neal, *Assoc Prof,* Northeastern University, Dept of Art & Architecture, Boston MA (S)

Rappaport, Jane W, *Prog Coordr,* Newark Museum Association, The Newark Museum, Newark NJ

Rarick, Ronald D, *Chmn Dept,* University of Indianapolis, Art Dept, Indianapolis IN (S)

Rasbury, Patricia, *Cur of Education,* Tennessee State Museum, Nashville TN

Rash, Brennan, *Public Affairs Officer,* National Portrait Gallery, Washington DC

Rash, Nancy, *Chmn,* Connecticut College, Dept of Art History, New London CT (S)

Rasmussen, Gerald E, *Dir,* Stamford Museum and Nature Center, Stamford CT

Rasmussen, Jack, *Exec Dir,* Maryland Art Place, Baltimore MD

Rasmussen, Keith, *Exec Dir,* Chattahoochee Valley Art Museum, LaGrange GA

Rasmussen, Marie, *Chmn Fine & Performing Arts,* Umpqua Community College, Fine & Performing Arts Dept, Roseburg OR (S)

Rasmussen, Waldo, *Dir International Prog,* Museum of Modern Art, New York NY

Rasmussen, Warren, *Dean,* San Francisco State University, Art Dept, San Francisco CA (S)

Rassweiler, Janet, *Dir Educ,* South Street Seaport Museum, New York NY

Ratajczak, Peter, *Dir,* Peace Museum, Chicago IL

Rathbone, Eliza, *Chief Cur,* The Phillips Collection, Washington DC

Rathbun, James W, *Pres,* Museum of the Hudson Highlands, Cornwall on Hudson NY

Rathgeb, Donald A, *Chmn,* St Michael's College, Fine Arts Dept, Colchester VT (S)

Rathke, Jan, *Shop Mgr,* Iowa State University, Brunnier Gallery Museum, Ames IA

Rathwell, George, *VPrincipal,* Nutana Collegiate Institute, Memorial Library and Art Gallery, Saskatoon SK

Ratner, Peter, *Asst Prof,* James Madison University, Dept of Art, Harrisonburg VA (S)

Ratner, Rhoda, *Librn,* National Museum of American History, Branch Library, Washington DC

Rattner, Carl, *Prof,* Saint Thomas Aquinas College, Art Dept, Sparkhill NY (S)

Rattray, Alexander, *Head Landscape Archit,* University of Manitoba, Faculty of Architecture, Winnipeg MB (S)

Rau, David D J, *Asst Cur,* Cranbrook Academy of Art Museum, Bloomfield Hills MI

Rauch, Judy, *VPres,* Peninsula Fine Arts Center, Newport News VA

Raudzens, Ingrida, *Prof,* Salem State College, Art Dept, Salem MA (S)

Rauf, Barbara, *Assoc Prof,* Thomas More College, Art Dept, Crestview Hills KY (S)

Raulston, Linda, *Cur,* Oklahoma Center for Science and Art, Kirkpatrick Center, Oklahoma City OK

Rausch, Elisa, *Instr,* Northwest Community College, Dept of Art, Powell WY (S)

Rauschenberg, Brad, *Dir of Research,* Old Salem Inc, Museum of Early Southern Decorative Arts, Winston-Salem NC

Rauschenberg, Bradford L, *Dir of Research,* Old Salem Inc, Library, Winston-Salem NC

Rauschenberg, Chris, *Dir,* Blue Sky, Oregon Center for the Photographic Arts, Portland OR

Rauschenberg, Christopher, *Instr,* Marylhurst College, Art Dept, Marylhurst OR (S)

Rautman, Marcus, *Assoc Prof,* University of Missouri, Art History and Archaeology Dept, Columbia MO (S)

Ravenal, C, *Assoc Prof,* American University, Dept of Art, Washington DC (S)

Ravenel, Gaillard, *Chief of Design & Installation,* National Gallery of Art, Washington DC

Ravenhill, Philip, *Chief Cur,* National Museum of African Art, Washington DC

Raveson, Art, *Instr,* Joe Kubert School of Cartoon & Graphic Art, Inc, Dover NJ (S)

Rawlings, Greg, *Planetarium Dir,* Sunrise Museum, Inc, Sunrise Art Museum, Sunrise Children's Museum & Planatarium, Charleston WV

Rawlinson, Kate, *Gallery Dir,* Miami-Dade Community College, Wolfson Campus, Frances Wolfson Art Gallery, Miami FL

Rawlinson, Kate, *Gallery Dir,* Miami-Dade Community College, Wolfson Campus, InterAmerican Art Gallery, Miami FL

Rawlinson, Kate, *Gallery Dir,* Miami-Dade Community College, Wolfson Campus, Centre Gallery, Miami FL

Rawls, James A, *Chmn,* Pearl River Community College, Art Dept, Division of Fine Arts, Poplarville MS (S)

Rawson, Gale, *Museum Registrar,* Pennsylvania Academy of the Fine Arts, Galleries, Philadelphia PA

Rawstern, Sherri, *Cur Educ,* Dacotah Prairie Museum, Lamont Gallery, Aberdeen SD

Ray, David, *Dept Head,* Ray College of Design, Chicago IL (S)

Ray, Jeffrey, *Cur Coll,* Atwater Kent Museum, Philadelphia PA

Ray, Lawrence A, *Chmn,* Lambuth University, Dept of Human Ecology & Visual Arts, Jackson TN (S)

Ray, Lisa, *Cur Exhib,* Columbia Museum of Art, Columbia SC

Ray, R Kenneth, *Prof,* University of Wisconsin, Madison, Dept of Art, Madison WI (S)

Ray, Timothy, *Chmn,* Moorhead State University, Dept of Art, Moorhead MN (S)

Ray, Wade, *Pres,* Ray College of Design, Chicago IL (S)

Rayen, James W, *Prof,* Wellesley College, Art Dept, Wellesley MA (S)

Raymond, Jo, *Chmn,* Guild Hall of East Hampton, Inc, Guild Hall Museum, East Hampton NY

Raz, Robert, *Dir Library,* Grand Rapids Public Library, Music & Art Dept, Grand Rapids MI

Rea, Douglas F, *Assoc Prof,* Rochester Institute of Technology, School of Photographic Arts & Sciences, Rochester NY (S)

Rea, Jacqueline, *Art Cur,* Leo Baeck Institute, New York NY

Read, Bob, *Art Dir,* New Mexico Highlands University, Arrott Art Gallery, Las Vegas NM

Read, Pamela, *Admnr,* Alice Curtis Desmond & Hamilton Fish Library, Hudson River Reference Collection, Garrison NY

Read, Rick, *Contact,* Pacific University, Old College Hall, Pacific University Museum, Forest Grove OR

Real, William A, *Conservator,* Carnegie Institute, Carnegie Museum of Art, Pittsburgh PA

Reardon, Michael J, *Regional Dir,* Blackhawk Mountain School of Art Gallery, Blackhawk CO

Reaves, Wendy W, *Cur Prints,* National Portrait Gallery, Washington DC

Reber, Demi, *Project Dir,* Antioch College, Noyes & Read Galleries, Yellow Springs OH

Reber, Mick, *Prof,* Fort Lewis College, Art Dept, Durango CO (S)

Reber, Wally, *Asst Dir,* Buffalo Bill Memorial Association, Buffalo Bill Historical Center, Cody WY

Reboli, John, *Dept Chmn Visual Arts,* College of the Holy Cross, Dinand Library, Worcester MA

Reboli, John P, *Chair,* College of the Holy Cross, Dept of Visual Arts, Worcester MA (S)

Rebsamen, Werner, *Assoc Prof,* Rochester Institute of Technology, School of Printing, Rochester NY (S)

Reck, Pat, *Museum Coordr,* Indian Pueblo Cultural Center, Albuquerque NM

Red, Virginia, *Provost,* University of the Arts, Philadelphia PA

Red, Virginia, *Provost,* University of the Arts, Philadelphia College of Art & Design, Philadelphia PA (S)

Redd, Richard, *Assoc Prof,* Lehigh University, Dept of Art and Architecture, Bethlehem PA (S)

Reddington, Dorothy, *Asst Dir Public Affairs,* Cornell University, Herbert F Johnson Museum of Art, Ithaca NY

Reddy, David, *Folklife Admnr,* Florida Folklife Programs, White Springs FL

Reddy, N Krishna, *Artist-in-Residence,* New York University, Dept of Art & Art Professions, New York NY (S)

Reddyhoff, Gillian, *Cur,* The Market Gallery of the City of Toronto Archives, Toronto ON

Redemer, Gloria, *Mgr IL Artisans Shop,* Illinois State Museum, Lincoln Home National Historic Site, Chicago IL

Redford, Marcia, *Dir,* Fort Saskatchewan Municipal Library, Exhibit Room, Fort Saskatchewan AB

Redpath, Lisa, *Music & Visual Arts Librn,* College of the Holy Cross, Dinand Library, Worcester MA

Reece, Ann, *Public Relations,* Art Museum of Southeast Texas, Beaumont TX

Reece, Janice, *Librn,* Texas Ranger Hall of Fame and Museum, Library, Waco TX

Reece, Raymond, *Art Librn,* University of California, Los Angeles, Arts Library, Los Angeles CA

Reed, Alan, *Assoc Prof,* Saint John's University, Art Dept, Collegeville MN (S)

Reed, Barbara E, *Librn,* Dartmouth College, Sherman Art Library, Hanover NH

Reed, Barry C, *Assoc Prof,* Palomar Community College, Art Dept, San Marcos CA (S)

Reed, Carl, *Assoc Prof,* Colorado College, Dept of Art, Colorado Springs CO (S)

Reed, Charles, *Prof,* Ocean County College, Humanities Dept, Toms River NJ (S)

Reed, Dorothy B, *Registrar,* Plymouth Antiquarian Society, Plymouth MA

Reed, James, *Exec Dir,* Craft Alliance Gallery & Education Center, Saint Louis MO

Reed, Jane, *Asst Dir,* University Club Library, New York NY

Reed, Jesse F, *Chmn,* Davis and Elkins College, Dept of Art, Elkins WV (S)

Reed, Joan, *VPres,* Chautauqua Art Association Galleries, Chautauqua NY

Reed, John, *Asst Dir,* Pilchuck Glass School, Seattle WA (S)

Reed, Kurt, *VPres,* Wayne County Historical Society, Museum, Honesdale PA

Reed, Madeline, *Dir,* Watkins Institute, School of Art, Nashville TN (S)

Reed, Madeline, *Art Dir,* Watkins Institute, Nashville TN

Reed, Mary Ellen, *Instr,* Marian College, Art Dept, Indianapolis IN (S)

Reed, Nancy, *Assoc Prof,* Texas Tech University, Dept of Art, Lubbock TX (S)

Reed, Robert, *Prof,* Yale University, School of Art, New Haven CT (S)

Reed, Roger, *VPres,* Illustration House Inc, Gallery, New York NY

Reed, Rosalie, *Registrar,* Yale University, Art Gallery, New Haven CT

Reed, Sandy, *Student Dir,* Thiel College, Sampson Art Gallery, Greenville PA

Reed, Scott, *Instr,* Colby College, Art Dept, Waterville ME (S)

Reed, Shirley M, *Dir,* Community Gallery of Lancaster County, Lancaster PA

Reed, Steve, *Dir,* Watkins Institute, Nashville TN

Reed, Todd, *Instr,* West Shore Community College, Division of Humanities and Fine Arts, Scottville MI (S)

Reed, Walt, *Pres,* Illustration House Inc, Gallery, New York NY

Reeder, Ellen, *Cur of Ancient Art,* Walters Art Gallery, Baltimore MD

Reedy, Robert, *Dir Div of Art,* Bradley University, Hartman Center Gallery, Peoria IL

Reedy, Robert, *Dir,* Bradley University, Division of Art, Peoria IL (S)

Reeg, Rachelle, *Educ Dir,* Chatillon-DeMenil House Foundation, DeMenil Mansion, Saint Louis MO

Reents-Budet, Dorie, *Cur Pre-Colombian Art,* Duke University Museum of Art, Durham NC

Reents-Budet, Dorie, *Adjunct Asst Prof,* Duke University, Dept of Art and Art History, Durham NC (S)

Rees, James C, *Asst Dir,* Mount Vernon Ladies' Association of the Union, Mount Vernon VA

Rees, Michael, *Asst Prof,* Oberlin College, Dept of Art, Oberlin OH (S)

Rees, Norma, *Pres,* California State University, Hayward, University Art Gallery, Hayward CA

Rees, Philip, *Art Librn,* University of North Carolina at Chapel Hill, Joseph Curtis Sloane Art Library, Chapel Hill NC

Rees, Tony, *Archivist,* Glenbow Museum, Library, Calgary AB

Reese, Becky Duval, *Dir,* El Paso Museum of Art, El Paso TX

Reese, Becky Duval, *Dir,* El Paso Museum of Art, Library, El Paso TX

Reese, Judy, *Pres,* Toledo Artists' Club, Toledo OH

Reese, Lillian, *Recording Secy,* Art Centre of New Jersey, East Orange NJ (S)

Reese, Richard, *Prof,* University of Wisconsin, Madison, Dept of Art, Madison WI (S)

Reese, Robe, *Exec Dir,* Presidential Museum, Odessa TX

Reese, Thomas W, *Assoc Dir,* Getty Center for the History of Art & the Humanities Trust Museum, Santa Monica CA

Reeve, Gordon, *Chmn Sculpture,* University of Manitoba, School of Art, Winnipeg MB (S)

Reeves, Don, *Coll Cur,* National Cowboy Hall of Fame and Western Heritage Center, Oklahoma City OK

Reeves, James, *Dir,* Surry Community College, Art Dept, Dobson NC (S)

Reeves, Jonathan, *Chmn Art History,* University of Cincinnati, School of Art, Cincinnati OH (S)

Reeves V, I S K, *Pres,* Architects Design Group Inc, Winter Park FL

Reff, Richard, *Pres,* Jewish Community Center of Greater Washington, Jane L & Robert H Weiner Judaic Museum, Rockville MD

Regan, Kathie, *Instr,* Main Line Center for the Arts, Haverford PA (S)

Reger, Lawrence L, *Pres,* National Institute for the Conservation of Cultural Property, Washington DC

Rehm-Mott, Denise, *Assoc Prof,* Eastern Illinois University, Art Dept, Charleston IL (S)

Reibach, Lois, *Head Technical Servs,* Lutheran Theological Seminary, Krauth Memorial Library, Philadelphia PA

Reich, Christopher J, *Dir,* Anniston Museum of Natural History, Anniston AL

Reichardt, George, *Pres Board,* Board of Parks & Recreation, The Parthenon, Nashville TN

Reichardt, Paul, *Actg Dir,* University of Alaska, Museum, Fairbanks AK

Reichel, Kealii, *Dir,* Maui Historical Society, Bailey House, Wailuku HI

Reichert, Marilyn F, *Dir,* Hebrew Union College - Jewish Institute of Religion, Skirball Museum-Cincinnati Branch, Cincinnati OH

Reid, Donna, *Instr,* Chemeketa Community College, Dept of Humanities & Communications, Salem OR (S)

Reid, Eve, *Head Paper Making,* Kalamazoo Institute of Arts, KIA School, Kalamazoo MI (S)

Reid, Harry F, *Treas,* Star-Spangled Banner Flag House Association, Flag House & 1812 Museum, Baltimore MD

Reid, Helen K, *Educ Coordr,* University of New Hampshire, The Art Gallery, Durham NH

Reid, Irvin, *Pres,* Montclair State College, Art Gallery, Upper Montclair NJ

Reid, Jane Caffrey, *Junior Museum Supv,* Newark Museum Association, Junior Museum, Newark NJ

Reid, Joan-Elisabeth, *Registrar,* Worcester Art Museum, Worcester MA

Reid, Margaret, *Instr,* Guilford Technical Community College, Commercial Art Dept, Jamestown NC (S)

Reid, Megan, *Division Dir,* Arizona Historical Society-Yuma, Century House Museum & Garden, Yuma AZ

Reid, Randall, *Asst Prof,* Southwest Texas State University, Dept of Art, San Marcos TX (S)

Reid, Richard, *Div Chmn,* Lane Community College, Art and Applied Design Dept, Eugene OR (S)

Reid, Susan, *Secy,* Eva Brook Donly Museum, Simcoe ON

Reidhaar, James, *Assoc Prof,* Indiana University, Bloomington, Henry Radford Hope School of Fine Arts, Bloomington IN (S)

Reidy, Robin, *Dir,* 911 Arts Media Center, Seattle WA

Reilly, Bernard F, *Popular & Applied Graphic Arts,* Library of Congress, Prints and Photographs Division, Washington DC

Reilly, Dorothy, *Asst Dir,* Jacques Marchais Center of Tibetan Art, Tibetan Museum, Staten Island NY

Reilly, Gerald I, *Cur of Collections,* Oglebay Institute, Mansion Museum, Wheeling WV

Reilly, James, *Assoc Prof,* Rochester Institute of Technology, School of Photographic Arts & Sciences, Rochester NY (S)

Reilly, Jerry M, *Instr,* Modesto Junior College, Arts Humanities and Speech Division, Modesto CA (S)

Reilly, Jovanne D, *Adminr,* Museo Italo Americano, San Francisco CA

Reilly, Thomas J, *Pres,* Philadelphia Art Alliance, Philadelphia PA

Reily, William A, *Prof,* Incarnate Word College, Art Dept, San Antonio TX (S)

Reina, Charles, *Adjunct Prof,* Nassau Community College, Art Dept, Garden City NY (S)

Reinckens, Sharon, *Deputy Dir,* Anacostia Museum, Washington DC

Reinelt, Jack, *VPres,* Ann Arbor Art Association, Ann Arbor MI

Reinertson, Lisa, *Instr,* California State University, Chico, Art Dept, Chico CA (S)

Reinhardt, Debbie, *Cur,* Laumeier Sculpture Park, Saint Louis MO

Reinhart, Susan, *Assoc Prof,* University of Bridgeport, Art Dept, Bridgeport CT (S)

Reinhold, Allen, *Prof,* Salt Lake Community College, Graphic Design Dept, Salt Lake City UT (S)

Reinke, Bernnett, *Librn Dir,* Dickinson State University, Stoxen Library, Dickinson ND

Reis, Victoria, *Admin Asst,* National Association of Artists' Organizations (NAAO), Washington DC

Reisenfeld, Robin, *Instr,* Dickinson College, Fine Arts Dept, Carlisle PA (S)

Reising, Christine, *Dir,* Siena Heights College, Klemm Gallery, Studio Angelico, Adrian MI

Reising, Christine, *Assoc Prof,* Siena Heights College, Studio Angelico-Art Dept, Adrian MI (S)

Reiss, Anna, *Dir,* Kentucky Guild of Artists and Craftsmen Inc, Berea KY

Reiss, Ellen, *Class Chmn Aesthetic Realism,* Aesthetic Realism Foundation, New York NY (S)

Reiss, Roland, *Chmn,* Claremont Graduate School, Dept of Fine Arts, Claremont CA (S)

Reissman, Elyse, *Dir Development,* Montclair Art Museum, Montclair NJ

Reith, Mary, *Secy,* Plastic Club, Art Club for Women, Philadelphia PA

Reitmeyer, Jennifer, *Assoc Prof,* Barton College, Communication, Performaing & Visual Arts, Wilson NC (S)

Rejcevich, Linda, *Dir Marketing & Public Relations,* Joslyn Art Museum, Omaha NE

Rekedael, Jane, *Prof,* Gavilan College, Art Dept, Gilroy CA (S)

Reker, Les, *Asst Prof,* Moravian College, Dept of Art, Bethlehem PA (S)

Reker, Les, *Dir,* Moravian College, Payne Gallery, Bethlehem PA

Remer, Robert R, *Acting Commissioner,* Chicago Public Library, Harold Washington Library Center, Chicago IL

Remington, Lillian, *Executive Secy,* Marblehead Arts Association, Inc, Marblehead MA

Remington, Lynne, *Public Relations & Development,* Northwestern University, Mary & Leigh Block Gallery, Evanston IL

Remington, R Roger, *Prof,* Rochester Institute of Technology, School of Art and Design, Rochester NY (S)

Remirez, Paul, *Gallery Coordr,* Brooklyn Arts Council, BACA Downtown, Brooklyn NY

Remsing, J Gary, *Instr,* Modesto Junior College, Arts Humanities and Speech Division, Modesto CA (S)

Renald, Steven, *Animateur Technician,* Institut Des Arts Au Saguenay, Centre National D'Exposition A Jonquiere, Jonquiere PQ

Renau, Lynn, *Cur,* Kentucky Derby Museum, Louisville KY

Renault, George, *Chmn,* Benedictine College, Art Dept, Atchison KS (S)

Render, Lorne E, *Dir,* C M Russell Museum, Great Falls MT

Rendon, Joanne, *Librn,* The Society of the Four Arts, Library, Palm Beach FL

Renehart, Margaret, *Artist in Res,* Avila College, Art Division, Dept of Performing and Visual Art, Kansas City MO (S)

Renick, Pat, *Prof Fine Arts,* University of Cincinnati, School of Art, Cincinnati OH (S)

Reninger, Lisa, *Development Assoc,* Fraunces Tavern Museum, New York NY

Renkl, W, *Asst Prof,* Austin Peay State University, Dept of Art, Clarksville TN (S)

Rennie, Heather, *Exec Dir,* Algonquin Arts Council, Bancroft Art Gallery, Bancroft ON

Rennie, Mark, *Exec Dir,* Eyes and Ears Foundation, San Francisco CA

Rensberger, John, *Cur Vertebrate Paleontology,* University of Washington, Thomas Burke Memorial Washington State Museum, Seattle WA

Rentof, Beryl, *Ref Head,* Fashion Institute of Technology Galleries, Library, New York NY

Reoutt, Steve, *Graphic Design,* California College of Arts and Crafts, Oakland CA (S)

Replogle, Ray, *Prof,* Wayne State College, Art Dept, Wayne NE (S)

Replogle, Rex, *Assoc Prof,* Kansas State University, Art Dept, Manhattan KS (S)

Resch, Francis X, *Assoc Cur,* Alternative Museum, New York NY

Resnick, Robert M, *Dir,* Antonelli Institute of Art & Photography, Cincinnati OH (S)

Ressel, Richard, *Pres,* Lancaster County Art Association, Lancaster PA

Restivo, John P, *Dir Sales & Marketing,* Canadiana Sport Art Collection, Canadian Sport and Fitness Centre, Gloucester ON

Retallack, John, *Assoc Prof,* Rochester Institute of Technology, School of Photographic Arts & Sciences, Rochester NY (S)

Retfalvi, A, *Librn,* University of Toronto, Fine Art Library, Toronto ON

Reusch, Johann, *Graduate Mentor,* Trinity College, Dept of Fine Arts, Hartford CT (S)

Reusch, Johann J K, *Cur,* Marquette University, Haggerty Museum of Art, Milwaukee WI

Reuter, Laurel J, *Dir & Head Cur,* North Dakota Museum of Art, Grand Forks ND

ReVille, Jac F, *Pres,* Portraits South, Raleigh NC

Revor, Remy, *Prof,* Mount Mary College, Art Dept, Milwaukee WI (S)

Rewald, John, *Distinguished Prof Emeritus,* City University of New York, PhD Program in Art History, New York NY (S)

Reynolds, Harold M, *Asst Prof,* Central Missouri State University, Art Dept, Warrensburg MO (S)

Reynolds, Jock, *Dir,* Phillips Academy, Addison Gallery of American Art, Andover MA

Reynolds, John R, *Chief Preparator & Exhibition Designer,* Worcester Art Museum, Worcester MA

Reynolds, Jonathan, *Asst Prof,* University of Michigan, Ann Arbor, Dept of History of Art, Ann Arbor MI (S)

Reynolds, Liz, *Registrar,* Brooklyn Museum, Brooklyn NY

Reynolds, Robert, *Prof,* California Polytechnic State University at San Luis Obispo, Dept of Art and Design, San Luis Obispo CA (S)

Reynolds, Robert, *Cur Earth Sciences,* San Bernardino County Museum, Fine Arts Institute, Redlands CA

Reynolds, Ron, *Head Dept,* Arkansas Tech University, Dept of Art, Russellville AR (S)

Reynolds, Stephen, *Prof,* University of Texas at San Antonio, Division of Art & Architecture, San Antonio TX (S)

Reynolds, Tom, *Pres,* Southern Ohio Museum Corporation, Southern Ohio Museum & Cultural Center, Portsmouth OH

Reynolds, Valrae, *Cur Oriental Coll,* Newark Museum Association, The Newark Museum, Newark NJ

Reynolds, Vic, *Assoc Prof,* Wayne State College, Art Dept, Wayne NE (S)

Reynolds, Virginia, *Lectr,* New England College, Art & Art History, Henniker NH (S)

Reynolds, Wiley R, *VPres,* The Society of the Four Arts, Palm Beach FL

Rhea, Richard, *Instr,* Tacoma Community College, Art Dept, Tacoma WA (S)

Rhei, Marylin, *Prof,* Smith College, Art Dept, Northampton MA (S)

Rhie, Marylin, *Asst Prof,* Smith College, Art Dept, Northampton MA (S)

Rhoades, Mark, *Asst Prof,* University of Richmond, Dept of Art & Art History, Richmond VA (S)

Rhodes, A Talley, *Cur Educ,* Hunter Museum of Art, Chattanooga TN

Rhodes, David, *Pres,* School of Visual Arts, New York NY (S)

Rhodes, Ed, *Instr,* Ouachita Baptist University, Dept of Art, Arkadelphia AR (S)

Rhodes, Jim, *Adult Serv Dept,* Topeka Public Library, Gallery of Fine Arts, Topeka KS

Rhodes, Lisa, *Admin Dir,* Center for Puppetry Arts, Atlanta GA

Rhodes, Marcus A, *Pres,* Old Colony Historical Society, Museum, Taunton MA

Rhodes, Milton, *Pres & CEO,* American Council for the Arts, New York NY

Rhodes, Reilly, *Exec Dir,* National Art Museum of Sport, Indianapolis IN

Rhodes, Rita, *Exec Dir,* Arts and Science Center, Statesville NC

Rhodes, Silas H, *Chmn,* School of Visual Arts, New York NY (S)

Ribkoff, Natalie, *Art Admin,* Toronto Dominion Bank, Toronto ON

Ricciardelli, Catherine, *Registrar,* Minneapolis Society of Fine Arts, Minneapolis Institute of Arts, Minneapolis MN

Ricciardi, Dana D, *Dir,* Captain Robert Bennet Forbes House, Milton MA

Ricciotti, Dominic, *Chmn,* Winona State University, Dept of Art, Winona MN (S)

Rice, Arthur, *Head Landscape Architecture Dept,* North Carolina State University at Raleigh, School of Design, Raleigh NC (S)

Rice, Danielle, *Cur Educ,* Philadelphia Museum of Art, Philadelphia PA

Rice, James, *Chmn Photographic Processing & Finishing Management,* Rochester Institute of Technology, School of Photographic Arts & Sciences, Rochester NY (S)

Rice, Jane G, *Dep Dir,* San Diego Museum of Art, San Diego CA

Rice, Joyce, *Corresp Secy,* Toledo Federation of Art Societies, Inc, Toledo OH

Rice, Kevin, *Registrar,* Confederation Centre Art Gallery and Museum, Charlottetown PE

Rice, Kevin, *Registrar,* Confederation Centre Art Gallery and Museum, Library, Charlottetown PE

Rice, Nancy, *Prof,* Maryville University of Saint Louis, Art Division, Saint Louis MO (S)

Rice, Nancy N, *Gallery Dir,* Maryville University Saint Louis, Morton J May Foundation Gallery, Saint Louis MO

Rich, Danny C, *Secy,* Inter-Society Color Council, Lawrenceville NJ

Rich, Libby, *Librn,* Columbia Museum of Art, Library, Columbia SC

Rich, Merle, *Registrar,* Artesia Historical Museum & Art Center, Artesia NM

Rich, Patricia, *Pres,* Arts & Education Council of Greater Saint Louis, Saint Louis MO

Richard, Harold James, *Prof,* University of New Orleans-Lake Front, Dept of Fine Arts, New Orleans LA (S)

Richard, Jack, *Dir,* Richard Gallery and Almond Tea Gallery, Divisions of Studios of Jack Richard, Cuyahoga Falls OH

Richard, Jack, *Dir,* Studios of Jack Richard Creative School of Design, Cuyahoga Falls OH (S)

Richard, Nancy, *Dir Foundation,* University of Southwestern Louisiana, University Art Museum, Lafayette LA

Richard, Paul, *VPres,* Children's Museum, Rauh Memorial Library, Indianapolis IN

Richards, Anita, *Admin Dir,* Marcella Sembrich Memorial Association Inc, Opera Museum, Bolton Landing NY

Richards, Evann, *Asst Prof,* Saint Louis Community College at Forest Park, Art Dept, Saint Louis MO (S)

Richards, Evann, *Adjunct Instr,* Maryville University of Saint Louis, Art Division, Saint Louis MO (S)

Richards, Heidi, *Chmn Dept of Interior Design,* New England School of Art & Design, Boston MA (S)

Richards, Judith Olch, *Assoc Dir,* Independent Curators Incorporated, New York NY

Richards, Katherine M, *Pres,* Special Libraries Association, Museum, Arts and Humanities Division, Washington DC

Richards, Lenore, *Co-Chair Env Design,* Ontario College of Art, Toronto ON (S)

Richards, L Jane, *Cur,* Fort Missoula Historical Museum, Missoula MT

Richards, Margaret, *Secy,* San Bernardino Art Association, Inc, San Bernardino CA

Richards, Peter, *Artist Coordr,* Exploratorium, San Francisco CA

Richards, Ronald, *Cur in Charge,* Indiana State Museum, Indianapolis IN

Richards, Rosalyn, *Prof,* Bucknell University, Dept of Art, Lewisburg PA (S)

Richardson, Brenda, *Deputy Dir & Cur Modern Paintings & Sculpture,* Baltimore Museum of Art, Baltimore MD

Richardson, Douglas, *Pres of Board,* Yellowstone Art Center, Billings MT

Richardson, Frederick, *Treas,* Springfield Art & Historical Society, Springfield VT

Richardson, Hubbard, *Pres,* Springfield Art & Historical Society, Springfield VT

Richardson, Jim, *Instructor,* The Art Institutes International, The Art Institute of Seattle, Seattle WA (S)

Richardson, John A, *Head Art History,* Southern Illinois University at Edwardsville, Dept of Art & Design, Edwardsville IL (S)

Richardson, Linda, *Dir,* Jefferson County Historical Museum, Pine Bluff AR

Richardson, Martha, *Chmn Fine Arts Dept,* Mississippi Gulf Coast Community College-Jackson County Campus, Art Dept, Gautier MS (S)

Richardson, Paul, *Research Specialist,* Southern Oregon Historical Society, Jacksonville Museum of Southern Oregon History, Jacksonville OR

Richardson, Terry, *Instr,* Rochester Community College, Art Dept, Rochester MN (S)

Richardson, Trevor, *Cur of Exhib,* University of North Carolina at Greensboro, Weatherspoon Art Gallery, Greensboro NC

Richardson, Wallace, *Chmn,* Mid-America Arts Alliance & Exhibits USA, Kansas City MO

Richbourg, Lance, *Asst Prof,* St Michael's College, Fine Arts Dept, Colchester VT (S)

Richert, Clark, *Exhib Coordr,* Boulder Public Library and Gallery, Dept of Fine Arts Gallery, Boulder CO

Richert, Phyllis, *Cur,* Chalet of the Golden Fleece, New Glarus WI

Richiuso, John-Paul, *Archivist,* Staten Island Institute of Arts and Sciences, Staten Island NY

Richman, Gary, *Prof,* University of Rhode Island, Dept of Art, Kingston RI (S)

Richman, Irwin, *Prof,* Penn State Harrisburg, Humanities Division, Middletown PA (S)

Richmond, Cindy, *Cur Exhib,* Norman Mackenzie Art Gallery, Regina SK

Richmond, R, *Asst Prof,* University of Maine at Augusta, Division of Fine & Performing Arts, Augusta ME (S)

Richmond, William, *Asst Prof,* University of Evansville, Art Dept, Evansville IN (S)

Richter, Susan, *Prog Dir,* Vermilion County Museum Society, Danville IL

Richter, Susan E, *Prog Dir,* Vermilion County Museum Society, Library, Danville IL

Rickards, Gail, *Mgr & Video Art Coordr,* Spaces, Cleveland OH

Rickels, Robert E, *Prof,* Concordia College, Art Dept, Saint Paul MN (S)

Ricketts, Missy, *Asst Dir,* Tennessee Valley Art Association and Center, Tuscumbia AL

Ricketts, Nancy, *VPres,* Sitka Historical Society, Isabel Miller Museum, Sitka AK

Rideout, Janice, *Historian,* Marblehead Historical Society, Library, Marblehead MA

Ridge, Michele M, *Dir,* Erie County Library System, Plavcan Gallery, Erie PA

Ridgeway, Teresa M, *Registrar,* Bower's Museum, Santa Ana CA

Rieben, John, *Asst Prof,* University of Wisconsin, Madison, Dept of Art, Madison WI (S)

Rieder-Hudd, Jacquie, *Treas,* Orange County Center for Contemporary Art, Santa Ana CA

Riedinger, Robert J, *Correspondence Secy,* Artists' Fellowship, Inc, New York NY

Riegel, James, *Head Photography Dept,* Kalamazoo Institute of Arts, KIA School, Kalamazoo MI (S)

Rieger, Sonja, *Chmn Dept,* University of Alabama in Birmingham, Dept of Art, Birmingham AL (S)

Riemer, Milton, *Chmn,* Concordia Lutheran College, Dept of Fine Arts, Austin TX (S)

Rienhoff, William, *Mgr,* Municipal Art Society of Baltimore City, Baltimore MD

Riese, Beatrice, *Pres,* American Abstract Artists, New York NY

Rietman, Susan, *Dean,* Fashion Institute of Technology, Art & Design Division, New York NY (S)

Riffee, Steven, *Preparator,* College of William and Mary, Joseph & Margaret Muscarelle Museum of Art, Williamsburg VA

Riffle, Brenda, *Librn,* Hampshire County Public Library, Romney WV

Rifkin, Ned, *Dir,* High Museum of Art, Atlanta GA

Rigall, Barbara A, *Exec Dir,* Florida Center for Contemporary Art-Artist Alliance Inc, Tampa FL

Rigby, Bruce, *Prof,* Trenton State College, Art Dept, Trenton NJ (S)

Rigby, Eda K, *Art History Grad Coordr,* San Diego State University, Dept of Art, San Diego CA (S)

Rigdon, Lois, *Dir,* Art Guild of Burlington, Arts for Living Center, Burlington IA

Rigg, Margaret, *Assoc Prof,* Eckerd College, Art Dept, Saint Petersburg FL (S)

Riggins, Lois, *Dir,* Tennessee State Museum, Nashville TN

Riggs, Gerry, *Dir & Cur,* University of Colorado at Colorado Springs, Gallery of Contemporary Art, Colorado Springs CO

Riggs Liroff, Sylvia, *Dir Art Center,* National Center on Arts & Aging-National Council on The Aging, NCOA Gallery Patina, Washington DC

Rights, Edith A, *Librn,* Montclair Art Museum, LeBrun Library, Montclair NJ

Riker, Janet, *Dir,* The Fund for the Borough of Brooklyn, The Rotunda Gallery, Brooklyn NY

Riley, Audrey, *Instr,* Saint Francis College, Art Dept, Fort Wayne IN (S)

Riley, Dixie, *Head Librn,* Chappell Memorial Library and Art Gallery, Chappell NE

Riley, G Patrick, *Chmn,* Southwestern Oklahoma State University, Art Dept, Weatherford OK (S)

Riley, Jan, *Cur,* Contemporary Arts Center, Cincinnati OH

Riley, Michael, *Cur of Educ,* Boise Art Museum, Boise ID

Riley, Sara, *Librn,* Kendall Whaling Museum, Library, Sharon MA

Riley, Terence, *Dir Dept Architecture & Design,* Museum of Modern Art, New York NY

Riley-Land, Sara, *Instr,* Stephens College, Art & Fashion Dept, Columbia MO (S)

Riley-Land, Sarah, *Actg Dir,* Stephens College, Lewis James & Nellie Stratton Davis Art Gallery, Columbia MO

Rinder, Lawrence, *Cur,* University of California, University Art Museum, Berkeley CA

Rindfleisch, Jan, *Dir,* De Anza College, Euphrat Gallery, Cupertino CA

Rindlisbacher, David, *Assoc Prof,* West Texas State University, Art, Communication & Theatre Dept, Canyon TX (S)

Riner, Camille, *Instr,* Southwestern Michigan College, Fine & Performing Arts Dept, Dowagiac MI (S)

Ring, Dan, *Extension Coordr,* Mendel Art Gallery and Civic Conservatory, Saskatoon SK

Ringering, Dennis L, *Head Drawing,* Southern Illinois University at Edwardsville, Dept of Art & Design, Edwardsville IL (S)

Ringle, Stephen, *Exhibits Preparator,* University of Maine, Museum of Art, Orono ME

Rinne, Cindy, *Pres,* San Bernardino County Museum, Fine Arts Institute, Redlands CA

Riof-Metcalf, Silva, *Prof,* Gavilan College, Art Dept, Gilroy CA (S)

Riopelle, Christopher, *Assoc Cur,* Philadelphia Museum of Art, Rodin Museum of Philadelphia, Philadelphia PA

Riordan, John, *Prof,* State University of New York College at Potsdam, Dept of Fine Arts, Potsdam NY (S)

Riordan, Bernard, *Dir,* Art Gallery of Nova Scotia, Halifax NS

Rios, Sylvia, *Gallery Dir,* Gavilan College, Art Gallery, Gilroy CA

Ripley, Robert C, *Mgr Capitol Restoration & Promotion,* Nebraska State Capitol, Lincoln NE

Rippee, Marilyn, *Dir Omniplex,* Oklahoma Center for Science and Art, Kirkpatrick Center, Oklahoma City OK

Rippon, Thomas, *Interim Chmn,* University of Montana, Dept of Art, Missoula MT (S)

Risatti, Howard, *Assoc Prof,* Virginia Commonwealth University, Art History Department, Richmond VA (S)

Risberg, Debra, *Cur,* Illinois State University, University Galleries, Normal IL

Riseman, Henry, *Dir,* New England Center for Contemporary Art, Brooklyn CT

Rishel, Joseph, *Cur of Pre-1900 European Painting & Sculpture,* Philadelphia Museum of Art, Rodin Museum of Philadelphia, Philadelphia PA

Rishel, Joseph, *Cur,* Philadelphia Museum of Art, John G Johnson Collection, Philadelphia PA

Risley, Mary, *Adjunct Assoc Prof,* Wesleyan University, Art Dept, Middletown CT (S)

Rison, Carolyn, *Admin Asst,* Cincinnati Institute of Fine Arts, Taft Museum, Cincinnati OH

Risse, Robert, *Assoc Prof,* University of Massachusetts at Boston, Art Dept, Boston MA (S)

Ritch, Irene R, *Cur,* Henry Phipps Ross & Sarah Juliette Ross Memorial Museum, Saint Andrews NB

Ritchie, Charles, *Asst Cur,* National Gallery of Art, Index of American Design, Washington DC

Ritchie, Sherri, *Coordr,* Edmonton Public Library, Foyer Gallery, Edmonton AB

Ritson, Kate, *Prof,* Trinity University, Dept of Art, San Antonio TX (S)

Rittenhouse, Cheri, *Prof,* Rock Valley College, Dept of Art, Rockford IL (S)

Ritter, Josef, *Assoc Prof,* Cazenovia College, Center for Art & Design Studies, Cazenovia NY (S)

Ritts, Edwin, *Exec Dir,* Asheville Art Museum, Asheville NC

Ritzler, Claire, *Educ Dir,* Center for Puppetry Arts, Atlanta GA

Rivard, Paul, *Dir,* Museum of American Textile History, North Andover MA

Rivard-Shaw, Nancy, *Cur American Art,* Detroit Institute of Arts, Detroit MI

Rivera, Concha, *Community Development Officer,* University of California, California Museum of Photography, Riverside CA

Rivera, Frank, *Prof,* Mercer County Community College, Arts & Communications, Trenton NJ (S)

Rivera, George, *Cur,* Triton Museum of Art, Santa Clara CA

Rivera de Figueroa, Carmen A, *Assoc Prof,* University of Puerto Rico, Dept of Fine Arts, Rio Piedras PR (S)

Rivera-Garcia, Rafael, *Prof,* University of Puerto Rico, Dept of Fine Arts, Rio Piedras PR (S)

Rivers, Kathy, *Art Dept Chair,* Grand Canyon University, Art Dept, Phoenix AZ (S)

Rives, Elizabeth, *Pres,* Washington Art Association, Washington Depot CT

Rivo, Lisa, *Mgr Public Information,* Institute of Contemporary Art, Boston MA

Rizk, Ron, *Prof,* University of Southern California, School of Fine Arts, Los Angeles CA (S)

Riznik, Helen, *Mgr Museum Shop,* Kauai Museum, Lihue HI

Roach, Donald, *Chmn Museum Committee,* Rhode Island School of Design, Museum of Art, Providence RI

Roach, T, *Assoc Prof,* St Francis Xavier University, Fine Arts Dept, Antigonish NS (S)

Roane, Teresa, *Librn,* Valentine Museum, Library, Richmond VA

Roark, John, *Asst Prof,* Lynchburg College, Art Dept, Lynchburg VA (S)

Roatz Myers, Dorothy, *Secy,* New York Artists Equity Association, Inc, New York NY

Robb, Carole, *Instr,* New York Studio School of Drawing, Painting and Sculpture, New York NY (S)

Robb, David M, *Dir,* Huntsville Museum of Art, Huntsville AL

Robb, Phyllis L, *Secy,* The Art Institute of Chicago, Chicago IL

Robbin, C Roxanne, *Prof,* California State University, Art Dept, Turlock CA (S)

Robbins, Carol, *Cur Textiles,* Dallas Museum of Art, Dallas TX

Robbins, Judy, *Editor,* Handweavers Guild of America, Bloomfield CT

Robbins, Warren M, *Senior Scholar & Founding Dir Emeritus,* National Museum of African Art, Washington DC

Roberds, Gene, *Coordr Fine Art,* Florida School of the Arts, Visual Arts, Palatka FL (S)

Roberson, Karen, *Asst Prof,* University of Texas at Tyler, Dept of Art, Tyler TX (S)

Robert, Henry Flood, *Dir,* Knoxville Museum of Art, Knoxville TN

Robert-Deutsch, Maria, *Dept Head,* Honolulu Community College, Honolulu HI (S)

Roberts, Ann, *Lectr,* Centenary College of Louisiana, Dept of Art, Shreveport LA (S)

Roberts, Ann, *Prof,* University of Waterloo, Fine Arts Dept, Waterloo ON (S)

Roberts, Brady, *Cur of Coll,* Davenport Museum of Art, Davenport IA

Roberts, Carla A, *Exec Dir,* Atlatl, Phoenix AZ

Roberts, Carol, *Board Chmn,* Detroit Artists Market, Detroit MI

Roberts, Eileen, *Assoc Prof,* Northern Michigan University, Dept of Art and Design, Marquette MI (S)

Roberts, Gail, *Studio Grad Coordr,* San Diego State University, Dept of Art, San Diego CA (S)

Roberts, Helene, *Cur of Visual Coll,* Harvard University, Fine Arts Library, Cambridge MA

Roberts, Jane, *Dir & Cur,* Wood Art Gallery, Montpelier VT

Roberts, Jeff, *Dir Development,* Ari Museum of Western Virginia, Roanoke VA

Roberts, J P L, *Dean of Faculty Fine Arts,* University of Calgary, Dept of Art, Calgary AB (S)

Roberts, Karen, *Admin Secy,* Arizona Historical Society-Yuma, Century House Museum & Garden, Yuma AZ

Roberts, Marie, *Asst Prof,* Fairleigh Dickinson University, Fine Arts Dept, Rutherford NJ (S)

Roberts, Patti, *Library Technician,* Ringling School of Art & Design Library, Sarasota FL

Roberts, Perri Lee, *Asst Prof,* University of Miami, Dept of Art & Art History, Coral Gables FL (S)

Roberts, Prudence, *Cur American & European Art,* Portland Art Museum, Portland OR

Roberts, Wesley, *Instr,* Campbellsville College, Fine Arts Division, Campbellsville KY (S)

Robertshaw, Mary Jane, *Assoc Prof,* College of New Rochelle School of Arts and Sciences, Art Dept, New Rochelle NY (S)

Roberts-Manganelli, Susan, *Registrar & Asst Cur,* Stanford University, Art Gallery, Stanford CA

Roberts-Manganelli, Susan, *Registrar & Asst Cur,* Stanford University, Art Gallery, Stanford CA

Robertson, Anne, *Assoc Dir,* College of New Rochelle, Castle Gallery, New Rochelle NY

Robertson, Barbara, *Educ Coordr,* Williams College, Museum of Art, Williamstown MA

Robertson, Charles, *Deputy Dir,* National Museum of American Art, Washington DC

Robertson, David, *Dir,* Loyola University of Chicago, Martin D'Arcy Gallery of Art, Chicago IL

Robertson, David, *Dir,* Loyola University of Chicago, Library, Chicago IL

Robertson, David J, *Prof,* Rochester Institute of Technology, School of Photographic Arts & Sciences, Rochester NY (S)

Robertson, Donna, *Dean,* Tulane University, School of Architecture, New Orleans LA (S)

Robertson, F, *Instr,* Community College of Rhode Island, Dept of Art, Warwick RI (S)

Robertson, Jack, *Librn,* University of Virginia, Fiske Kimball Fine Arts Library, Charlottesville VA

Robertson, Joan E, *Art Cur,* Kemper National Insurance Companies, Long Grove IL

Robertson, Karen, *Dir,* Morgan State University, Library, Baltimore MD

Robertson, Linda C, *Dir of Development,* Kemerer Museum of Decorative Arts, Bethlehem PA

Robertson, Roderick, *Head Dept,* Saint Mary's College of Minnesota, Art Dept No 18, Winona MN (S)

Robertson, Scott, *Chmn,* University of Wisconsin-Eau Claire, Dept of Art, Eau Claire WI (S)

Robin, Madeleine, *Dir Art,* L'Universite Laval, Library, Quebec PQ

Robings, Edward, *Exec Dir,* Ventura County Historical Society Museum, Ventura CA

Robinow, Pat, *Slide Cur,* Wright State University, Dept of Art and Art History Resource Center & Slide Library, Dayton OH

Robins, Henriann, *Ref Dept,* Springfield Free Public Library, Donald B Palmer Museum, Springfield NJ

Robins, Rosemary Gay, *Asst Prof,* Emory University, Art History Dept, Atlanta GA (S)

Robinson, Art, *Business Mgr,* New Brunswick Museum, Saint John NB

Robinson, Barbara, *Chmn,* National Assembly of State Arts Agencies, Washington DC

Robinson, Bonnie, *Dir Gallery,* The Art Institute of Boston, Gallery East, Boston MA

Robinson, C David, *Pres,* The Friends of Photography, Ansel Adams Center for Photography, San Francisco CA

Robinson, David, *Exec Dir,* Eastern Shore Art Association, Inc, Art Center, Fairhope AL

Robinson, Don D, *Chmn Dept,* Harding University, Dept of Art, Searcy AR (S)

Robinson, Douglas, *Registrar,* Hirshhorn Museum and Sculpture Garden, Washington DC

Robinson, Duncan, *Dir,* Yale University, Yale Center for British Art, New Haven CT

Robinson, Fern, *Young Adult,* Mason City Public Library, Mason City IA

Robinson, Franklin W, *Co-Dir,* Cornell University, Herbert F Johnson Museum of Art, Ithaca NY

Robinson, Franklin W, *Dir,* Cornell University, Museum Library, Ithaca NY

Robinson, George, *Prof,* Bethel College, Dept of Art, Saint Paul MN (S)

Robinson, James, *Cur Oriental Art,* Indianapolis Museum of Art, Indianapolis IN

Robinson, Kristine, *Cur,* Historic Cherry Hill, Albany NY

Robinson, Lilien, *Chmn,* George Washington University, Dept of Art, Washington DC (S)

Robinson, Orvetta, *Librn,* Illinois State Museum, Library, Springfield IL

Robinson, Patricia, *Dir Development,* Painted Bride Art Center, The Gallery at the Painted Bride, Philadelphia PA

Robinson, Pearl, *Educ Dir,* Afro-American Historical & Cultural Museum, Philadelphia PA

Robinson, Peter, *VPres Sales,* Blount Inc, Library, Montgomery AL

Robinson, Roger W, *Pres,* Willard House and Clock Museum, Inc, Grafton MA

Robinson, Roger W, *Dir,* Willard House and Clock Museum, Inc, Grafton MA

Robinson, Sally, *Exhib Coordr,* Dawson City Museum & Historical Society, Dawson City YT

Robinson, Sandra, *Instr,* Mount San Jacinto College, Art Dept, San Jacinto CA (S)

Robinson, Steve, *Prog Coordr,* MacDonald Stewart Art Centre Art Center, Guelph ON

Robinson, Sue Ann, *Educator,* Long Beach Museum of Art, Long Beach CA

Robinson, Susan, *Prof,* Loyola Marymount University, Art & Art History Dept, Los Angeles CA (S)

Robinson, William, *Acting Head,* Purdue University Calumet, Dept of Communication & Creative Arts, Hammond IN (S)

Robinson, William W, *Cur Drawings,* Harvard University, William Hayes Fogg Art Museum, Cambridge MA

Robinson-Hubbuch, Jocelyn, *Exec Dir,* African American Museums Association, Wilberforce OH

Robison, Andrew, *Sr Cur Print, Drawing & Sculpture,* National Gallery of Art, Washington DC

Robison, Jan, *Registrar of Coll,* Florida State University, Fine Arts Gallery & Museum, Tallahassee FL

Robison, Tim, *Dir Admissions,* San Francisco Art Institute, San Francisco CA (S)

Roby, Thomas, *Chmn,* City Colleges of Chicago, Kennedy-King College, Chicago IL (S)

Roche, James, *Prof,* Florida State University, Art Dept, Tallahassee FL (S)

Roche, Joanne, *Librn III & Head Dept,* Yonkers Public Library, Fine Arts Dept, Yonkers NY

Roche, Valerie, *Instr,* Creighton University, Fine and Performing Arts Dept, Omaha NE (S)

Rochette, Edward C, *Pres,* American Numismatic Association, Museum, Colorado Springs CO

Rochfort, Desmond, *Chmn,* University of Alberta, Dept of Art and Design, Edmonton AB (S)

Rockefeller, David, *Chmn of Board,* Museum of Modern Art, New York NY

Rockefeller, John D, *Pres Emeritus,* Museum of Modern Art, New York NY

Rockefeller, Steven C, *Pres,* Wendell Gilley Museum, Southwest Harbor ME

Rockett, Will, *Dean,* University of Wisconsin-Milwaukee, Dept of Art, Milwaukee WI (S)

Rockhill, King, *Pres,* Appaloosa Museum, Inc, Moscow ID

Rockwood, Lynda, *Asst Prof,* Webster University, Art Dept, Webster Groves MO (S)

Rodda, Jenni, *Cur,* New York University, Institute of Fine Arts Visual Resources Collection, New York NY

Roddam, Dot, *Museum Coordr,* Ogden Union Station, Union Station Museums, Ogden UT

Roddy, Hilda, *Instr,* The Arkansas Arts Center, Museum School, Little Rock AR (S)

Rode, Meredith, *Prof,* University of the District of Columbia, Art Dept, Washington DC (S)

Roderick, Marty, *Gallery Mgr,* Mendocino Art Center, Gallery, Mendocino CA

Rodes, David S, *Dir,* University of California, Los Angeles, Grunwald Center for the Graphic Arts, Los Angeles CA

Rodger, Judith, *Chief Cur Gallery,* London Regional Art & Historical Museums, London ON

Rodgers, Bill, *Prog Coordr Foundation,* Alberta College of Art, Calgary AB (S)

Rodgers, Dan, *Instr,* ACA College of Design, Cincinnati OH (S)

Rodgers, Dick, *Chmn Dept,* Earlham College, Art Dept, Richmond IN (S)

Rodgers, Richard, *Art Dept,* Earlham College, Leeds Gallery, Richmond IN

Rodgers, Timothy R, *Cur,* Lawrence University, Wriston Art Center Galleries, Appleton WI

Rodriguez, Anita, *Instr,* Mount San Jacinto College, Art Dept, San Jacinto CA (S)

Rodriguez, Belgica, *Dir,* Art Museum of the Americas, Washington DC

Rodriguez, Geno, *Dir,* Alternative Museum, New York NY

Rodriguez, Pedro A, *Exec Dir,* Guadalupe Cultural Arts Center, San Antonio TX

Rodriguez, Ruth, *Admin Asst,* University of Puerto Rico, Museum of Anthropology, History & Art, Rio Piedras PR

Rodriguiz, Sandria, *Assoc Dean,* College of Lake County, Art Dept, Grayslake IL (S)

Roe, Ruth, *Librn,* Newport Harbor Art Museum, Library, Newport Beach CA

Roe, Tom, *Chmn,* Ventura College, Fine Arts Dept, Ventura CA (S)

Roemer, Carol, *Instr,* Long Beach City College, Dept of Art, Long Beach CA (S)

Roese, Ronnie L, *Dir,* Biblical Arts Center, Dallas TX

Roever, James, *VPres,* Missouri Western State College, Fine Arts Gallery, Saint Joseph MO

Roeyer, Mark, *Exhib Designer,* University of Kansas, Spencer Museum of Art, Lawrence KS

Rogal, Samuel J, *Chmn,* Illinois Valley Community College, Div of Humanities and Fine Arts, Oglesby IL (S)

Roger, Leon, *Mgr,* Virginia Commonwealth University, Anderson Gallery, Richmond VA

Rogers, Barbara, *Prof Painting & Drawing,* University of Arizona, Dept of Art, Tucson AZ (S)

Rogers, Byran, *Head,* Carnegie Mellon University, Dept of Art, Pittsburgh PA (S)

Rogers, Cynthia J, *Archivist,* Liberty Memorial Museum & Archives, Kansas City MO

Rogers, Dan, *Instr,* Bismarck Junior College, Fine Arts Dept, Bismarck ND (S)

Rogers, James W, *Prof,* Glenville State College, Dept of Fine Arts, Glenville WV (S)

Rogers, Judith, *Instr,* Linn Benton Community College, Fine & Applied Art Dept, Albany OR (S)

Rogers, Millard F, *Dir,* Cincinnati Museum Association, Cincinnati Art Museum, Cincinnati OH

Rogers, Nancy M, *Exec Dir,* Wooster Community Art Center, Danbury CT

Rogers, Patricia J, *Assoc Librn Book Coll,* Harvard University, Fine Arts Library, Cambridge MA

Rogers, Paul, *Austin Fellow,* Trinity College, Dept of Fine Arts, Hartford CT (S)

Rogers, Robert, *Assoc Prof,* Queensborough Community College, Dept of Art and Photography, Bayside NY (S)

Rogers, Ruth E, *Dir,* Rogers House Museum Gallery, Ellsworth KS

Rogers, Sarah, *Vis Asst Prof,* University of Arkansas, Art Dept, Fayetteville AR (S)

Rogers, Wendy, *Admin Asst,* The Canadian Craft Museum, Vancouver BC

Rogers-Lafferty, Sarah, *Chief Cur & Dir Exhib,* Ohio State University, Wexner Center for the Arts, Columbus OH

Rohlfing, John, *Asst Prof,* University of Hartford, Hartford Art School, West Hartford CT (S)

Rohm, Robert H, *Prof,* University of Rhode Island, Dept of Art, Kingston RI (S)

Rohn, Megan, *Chmn & Instr,* Marian College, Art Dept, Indianapolis IN (S)

Rohrer, Judith, *Asst Prof,* Emory University, Art History Dept, Atlanta GA (S)

Rohrer, Thelma, *Asst Prof,* Albion College, Dept of Visual Arts, Albion MI (S)

Rohwer, Sievert, *Cur Birds,* University of Washington, Thomas Burke Memorial Washington State Museum, Seattle WA

Roison, Morrie, *Prof,* Gavilan College, Art Dept, Gilroy CA (S)

Rojas, Christina, *Registrar,* Mingei International, Inc, Mingei International Museum of World Folk Art, San Diego CA

Rokfalusi, J Mark, *Asst Prof,* Atlanta College of Art, Atlanta GA (S)

Rokfalusi, Mark, *Acting Communication Design Chmn,* Atlanta College of Art, Atlanta GA (S)

Roland, Craig, *Asst Prof,* University of Florida, Dept of Art, Gainesville FL (S)

Roll, Donn, *Asst Dir,* Foster Harmon Galleries of American Art, Sarasota FL

Roll, Donn, *Asst Dir,* Foster Harmon Galleries of American Art, Library, Sarasota FL

Roll, Jon, *Gallery Mgr,* Massachusetts Institute of Technology, List Visual Arts Center, Cambridge MA

Roll, Jonah, *Cur Educ,* Port of History Museum, Philadelphia PA

Roller, Marion, *First VPres,* Pen and Brush, Inc, New York NY

Roller, Marion, *Pres,* The Allied Artists of America, Inc, New York NY

Roller, Marion, *Treas,* Audubon Artists, Inc, New York NY

Roller, Marion, *Secy,* National Sculpture Society, New York NY

Roller, Scott, *Cur of Historical Coll,* Putnam Museum of History & Natural Science, Davenport IA

Roller, Terry M, *Assoc Prof,* Baylor University, Dept of Art, Waco TX (S)

Rollins, Caroline, *Membership, Sales & Publications,* Yale University, Art Gallery, New Haven CT

Rollins, Jane, *Events Coordr,* Ward Foundation, Ward Museum of Wildfowl Art, Salisbury MD

Rollins, Ken, *Executive Dir,* Polk Museum of Art, Lakeland FL

Rollins, Rich, *Instr,* Marylhurst College, Art Dept, Marylhurst OR (S)

Rolnick, Neil, *Dir of Graduate Programs,* Rensselaer Polytechnic Institute, Dept of Art, Troy NY (S)

Rom, Cristine, *Library Dir,* Cleveland Institute of Art, Jessica Gund Memorial Library, Cleveland OH

Rom, Cynthia, *Registrar,* Corcoran Gallery of Art, Washington DC

Romano, Enola R, *Art Asst,* Newark Museum Association, Junior Museum, Newark NJ

Romano, Filomena, *Instr,* Dowling College, Dept of Visual Arts, Oakdale NY (S)

Romano, Jaime, *Asst Prof,* University of Puerto Rico, Dept of Fine Arts, Rio Piedras PR (S)

Romano, Salvatore, *Asst Prof,* Herbert H Lehman College, Art Dept, Bronx NY (S)

Rome, Jay, *Treas,* Fitchburg Art Museum, Fitchburg MA

Romejko, Paul, *Photography & Graphics,* University of South Alabama, Dept of Art, Mobile AL (S)

Romero, Orlando, *Librn,* Museum of New Mexico, Palace of Governors Library, Santa Fe NM

Romine, June, *Public Relations Dir,* Palos Verdes Art Center, Rancho Palos Verdes CA

Ronalds, William, *Chmn,* Saint John's University, Dept of Fine Arts, Jamaica NY (S)

Ronzone, Jamey, *Children's Prog,* Palo Alto Cultural Center, Palo Alto CA

Rood, Margaret, *Dir,* Thousand Islands Craft School & Textile Museum, Clayton NY (S)

Roode, William, *Assoc Prof,* University of Minnesota, Minneapolis, Dept of Studio Art, Minneapolis MN (S)

Rooney, Steve, *Deputy Dir for Adminr,* International Center of Photography, New York NY

Rooney, Thomas, *Assoc Prof,* Catholic University of America, Dept of Art, Washington DC (S)

Roop, Ophelia, *Head Librn,* Indiana University - Purdue University at Indianapolis, Herron School of Art Library, Indianapolis IN

Roos, Sandra, *General Studies,* California College of Arts and Crafts, Oakland CA (S)

Roosa, Wayne L, *Assoc Prof,* Bethel College, Dept of Art, Saint Paul MN (S)

Roosevelt, Janice, *Dir Public Relations,* Winterthur Museum and Gardens, Winterthur DE

Root, Margaret, *Prof,* University of Michigan, Ann Arbor, Dept of History of Art, Ann Arbor MI (S)

Root, Margaret C, *Assoc Cur,* University of Michigan, Kelsey Museum of Archaeology, Ann Arbor MI

Root, Nina J, *Dir Library Servs,* American Museum of Natural History, Library, New York NY

Ropp, Ann, *Dir Exhib,* East Tennessee State University, Elizabeth Slocumb Galleries, Johnson City TN

Rosand, David, *Chmn,* Columbia University, Dept of Art History and Archaeology, New York NY (S)

Rosasco, Betsy, *Assoc Cur,* Princeton University, The Art Museum, Princeton NJ

Rose, George, *Instr,* Chautauqua Institution, School of Art, Chautauqua NY (S)

Rose, George, *Assoc Prof,* Northwest Missouri State University, Dept of Art, Maryville MO (S)

Rose, Isabel, *Mgr of Arts Dept,* Metropolitan Toronto Library Board, Arts Dept, Toronto ON

Rose, Joshua, *Prof,* New Mexico State University, Art Dept, Las Cruces NM (S)

Rose, Patricia, *Chmn,* Florida State University, Art History Dept (R133B), Tallahassee FL (S)

Rose, Robert, *Asst Dir,* University of Northern Iowa, Art & Music Section Rod Library, Cedar Falls IA

Rose, Robert, *Supt,* Davenport Museum of Art, Davenport IA

Rose, Sharon, *Development Coordr,* Bellevue Art Museum, Bellevue WA

Rose, Susan, *VPres,* Santa Barbara Contemporary Arts Forum, Santa Barbara CA

Rose, Thomas, *Prof,* University of Minnesota, Minneapolis, Dept of Studio Art, Minneapolis MN (S)

Roseberry, Helen, *Museum Dir,* East Tennessee State University, Carroll Reece Museum, Johnson City TN

Rosell, Karen, *Chmn Dept,* Juniata College, Dept of Art, Huntingdon PA (S)

Roseman, Barry, *Asst Prof,* University of Tennessee at Chattanooga, Dept of Art, Chattanooga TN (S)

Rosen, Ann, *Dept Head,* Ray College of Design, Chicago IL (S)

Rosen, Barry H, *Dir,* Milwaukee Public Museum, Milwaukee WI

Rosen, James, *Asst Prof,* Augusta College, Dept of Fine Arts, Augusta GA (S)

Rosen, Leila, *Librn,* Aesthetic Realism Foundation, Eli Siegel Collection, New York NY

Rosen, M, *Prof,* City Colleges of Chicago, Daley College, Chicago IL (S)

Rosen, Seymour, *Dir,* Saving & Preserving Arts & Cultural Environments, Los Angeles CA

Rosen, Shelly, *Instr,* Main Line Center for the Arts, Haverford PA (S)

Rosen, Steven W, *Dir & Chief Cur,* Nora Eccles Harrison Museum of Art, Logan UT

Rosen, Sue, *Dir Marketing,* Kentucky Art & Craft Gallery, Louisville KY

Rosenbaum, Allen, *Dir,* Princeton University, The Art Museum, Princeton NJ

Rosenbaum, Arthur, *Drawing & Painting,* University of Georgia, Franklin College of Arts & Sciences, Dept of Art, Athens GA (S)

Rosenbaum, Joan H, *Dir,* The Jewish Museum, New York NY

Rosenberg, Ahuva, *Cataloger,* Spertus Museum, Asher Library, Chicago IL

Rosenberg, Barry A, *Dir,* Aldrich Museum of Contemporary Art, Ridgefield CT

Rosenberg, Eric, *Asst Prof,* Tufts University, Dept of Art & Art History, Medford MA (S)

Rosenberg, Herbert, *Assoc Prof,* Jersey City State College, Art Dept, Jersey City NJ (S)

Rosenberg, Lisa, *Advisor,* Western Washington University, Viking Union Gallery, Bellingham WA

Rosenberg, Marcia, *Dir,* Danforth Museum of Art School, Framingham MA (S)

Rosenberg, Martin, *Assoc Prof,* University of Nebraska at Omaha, Dept of Art, Omaha NE (S)

Rosenberg, Sarah Z, *Exec Dir,* American Institute for Conservation of Historic & Artistic Works (AIC), Washington DC

Rosenberg, Steve, *Chmn Music Dept,* College of Charleston, School of the Arts, Charleston SC (S)

Rosenberger, Pat, *Executive Dir,* Valley Art Center Inc, Clarkston WA

Rosenberger, Stephen, *Ref & Ill,* Fashion Institute of Technology Galleries, Library, New York NY

Rosenberger, Suann, *Dir Educ,* Octagon Center for the Arts, Ames IA

Rosenblatt, Lisa, *Museum Resources Assoc,* B'nai B'rith International, B'nai B'rith Klutznick National Jewish Museum, Washington DC

Rosenblum, Peter, *Assoc Prof,* Seton Hall University, College of Arts & Sciences, South Orange NJ (S)

Rosenfeld, Susan, *Asst Cur,* University of California, Los Angeles, Visual Resource Collection, Los Angeles CA

Rosenstein, Lynne, *Asst Dir,* Long Beach Jewish Community Center, Center Gallery, Long Beach CA

Rosensweig, Larry, *Dir,* Palm Beach County Parks & Recreation Department, Morikami Museum & Japanese Gardens, Delray Beach FL

Rosenthal, Donald, *Dir,* Saint Anselm College, Chapel Art Center, Manchester NH

Rosenthal, Ellen, *Pres,* Hunterdon Art Center, Clinton NJ

Rosenthal, Jean Trapido, *Library Dir,* Saint Augustine Historical Society, Library, Saint Augustine FL

Rosenthal, Richard, *Pres,* Contemporary Arts Center, Cincinnati OH

Rosenzweig, Warren, *Dir,* Brooklyn Arts Council, BACA Downtown, Brooklyn NY

Rosevear, Carol, *Head,* New Brunswick Museum, Library, Saint John NB

Rosholt, Don, *Pres,* Pope County Historical Society Museum, Glenwood MN

Rosier, Ken, *Asst Prof,* Del Mar College, Art Dept, Corpus Christi TX (S)

Rosine, Gary, *Chmn,* Cardinal Stritch College, Layton Honor Gallery, Milwaukee WI

Rosine, Gary, *Prof,* Cardinal Stritch College, Art Dept, Milwaukee WI (S)

Rosing, Katherine, *Chmn,* Arc Gallery, Chicago IL

Roskam, Sherry, *Business Mgr,* Freeport Art Museum & Cultural Center, Freeport IL

Roskill, Mark, *Prof,* University of Massachusetts, Amherst, Art History Program, Amherst MA (S)

Roskos, Nancy, *Pres,* Community Gallery of Lancaster County, Lancaster PA

Roslak, Robyn, *Asst Prof,* University of Minnesota, Duluth, Art Dept, Duluth MN (S)

Rosler, Martha, *Dir Graduate Prog,* Rutgers, the State University of New Jersey, Mason Gross School of the Arts, New Brunswick NJ (S)

Rosnow, Nancy, *Coordr,* Frostburg State University, The Stephanie Ann Roper Gallery, Frostburg MD

Rosnow, Nancy P, *Head Dept,* Frostburg State University, Dept of Visual Arts, Frostburg MD (S)

Rosovsky, Nitza, *Cur Exhibits,* Harvard University, Semitic Museum, Cambridge MA

Ross, Alex, *Librn,* Stanford University, Art Library, Stanford CA

Ross, Barbara, *Assoc Cur,* Princeton University, The Art Museum, Princeton NJ

Ross, Carole, *Assoc Dean Grad Studies,* University of Kansas, School of Fine Arts, Lawrence KS (S)

Ross, Colleen, *Accounts Receivable & Donations Clerk,* London Regional Art & Historical Museums, London ON

Ross, Cynthia, *Instr,* Goddard College, Visual Arts Dept, Plainfield VT (S)

Ross, David A, *Dir,* Whitney Museum of American Art, New York NY

Ross, David A, *Exec Dir,* McAllen International Museum, McAllen TX

Ross, Doran H, *Asst Dir & Cur Africa, Oceania & Indonesia,* University of California, Los Angeles, Fowler Museum of Cultural History, Los Angeles CA

Ross, Gail, *Exec Dir,* Burke Arts Council, Jailhouse Galleries, Morganton NC

Ross, Gayle, *Temporary Asst Prof,* Arkansas State University, Dept of Art, Jonesboro AR (S)

Ross, Harold, *Dean,* Cottey College, Art Dept, Nevada MO (S)

Ross, Johnnie, *Instr,* Portland School of Art, Portland ME (S)

Ross, Malcolm C, *Chmn Fine Arts Div,* Florida Keys Community College, Art Dept, Key West FL (S)

Ross, Marilyn, *Museum Shop Mgr,* Danforth Museum of Art, Framingham MA

Ross, Mary Anne, *Assoc Prof,* Delta State University, Dept of Art, Cleveland MS (S)

Ross, Novelene, *Chief Cur,* Wichita Art Museum, Wichita KS

Ross, Robert, *Assoc Prof,* University of Arkansas, Art Dept, Fayetteville AR (S)

Ross, Robert, *Asst Prof,* Catholic University of America, Dept of Art, Washington DC (S)

Ross, S, *Instr,* Humboldt State University, College of Arts & Humanities, Arcata CA (S)

Ross, W Ogden, *VPres,* Newport Historical Society, Newport RI

Rossen, Arlene, *Dir Development,* Akron Art Museum, Akron OH

Rossen, Susan F, *Exec Dir Publications,* The Art Institute of Chicago, Chicago IL

Rosser, Warren, *Chmn Painting & Printmaking,* Kansas City Art Institute, Kansas City MO (S)

Rosset, Carole, *Coll Mgr & Registrar,* University of California, Richard L Nelson Gallery & Fine Arts Collection, Davis CA

Rossi, Dianna, *Memberships,* Pastel Society of the West Coast, Sacramento Fine Arts Center, Carmichael CA

Rossley, Bruce R, *Commissioner,* Boston Art Commission of the City of Boston, Boston MA

Rossman, Michelle, *Slide Librn,* Cleveland Institute of Art, Jessica Gund Memorial Library, Cleveland OH

Rossol, Monona, *Pres,* Artist-Craftsmen of New York, New York NY

Roszel, James, *Admin Asst,* Boston Visual Artists Union, Boston MA

Rote, Carey, *Dir,* Corpus Christi State University, Weil Art Gallery, Corpus Christi TX

Roters, Carlene, *Asst Prof,* Northern State University, Art Dept, Aberdeen SD (S)

Roth, Arnold, *Liaison,* National Cartoonists Society, New York NY

Roth, Dan, *Cur,* US Navy Supply Corps School, Museum, Athens GA

Roth, Darlene, *Dir Prog,* Atlanta Historical Society Inc, Atlanta History Center, Atlanta GA

Roth, Kathy, *Instr,* St Lawrence College, Dept of Visual & Creative Arts, Cornwall ON (S)

Roth, Moira, *Prof Art Hist,* Mills College, Art Dept, Oakland CA (S)

Roth, Rachel, *Supvr,* New Jersey Institute of Technology, Architectural Information Center, Newark NJ

Roth, Rob, *Arts Coordr,* King County Arts Commission, Seattle WA

Roth, Tom, *Instr,* Springfield College in Illinois, Dept of Art, Springfield IL (S)

Rothchild, Richard, *Pres Bd Trustees,* Silvermine Guild Arts Center, Silvermine Galleries, New Canaan CT

Rothenberg, Jerome, *Dept Chmn,* University of California, San Diego, Visual Arts Dept, La Jolla CA (S)

Rothermel, Barbara, *Cur Art,* Everhart Museum, Scranton PA

Rothermel, Joan Ashley, *Treas,* American Watercolor Society, New York NY

Rothman, Barbara, *Secy,* DuPage Art League School & Gallery, Wheaton IL

Rothman, Deborah, *Public Relations Mgr,* University of Rochester, Memorial Art Gallery, Rochester NY

Rothman, Louise, *Asst Prof,* University of Florida, Dept of Art, Gainesville FL (S)

Rothove, Billi, *Gallery Dir,* Central Missouri State University, Art Center Gallery, Warrensburg MO

Rothrock, Kathy, *History Specialist,* Headquarters Fort Monroe, Dept of Army, Casemate Museum, Fort Monroe VA

Rothschild, Deborah Menaker, *Assoc Cur Exhib,* Williams College, Museum of Art, Williamstown MA

Rothweile, Rae, *In Charge,* Crestar Bank, Art Collection, Richmond VA

Rotondi, Michael, *Dir,* Southern California Institute of Architecture, Los Angeles CA (S)

Rouillard, Cynthia, *Admin Asst,* Yuma Fine Arts Association, Art Center, Yuma AZ

Rouleau, Bishop Reynald, *Dir,* Eskimo Museum, Churchill MB

Rourke, Orland, *Assoc Prof,* Concordia College, Art Dept, Moorhead MN (S)

Rouse, Terrie S, *Dir,* California Afro-American Museum, Los Angeles CA

Roush, Elizabeth, *Dir of Finance,* Columbus Museum of Art, Columbus OH

Rousseau, T Marshall, *Acting Dir,* Salvador Dali Museum, Saint Petersburg FL

Routen, David, *Chmn Graduate Committee,* University of Nebraska-Lincoln, Dept of Art & Art History, Lincoln NE (S)

Routledge, Marie, *Asst Cur Inuit Art,* National Gallery of Canada, Ottawa ON

Roux, F, *Curatorial Asst,* McGill University, Blackader-Lauterman Library of Architecture and Art, Montreal PQ

Rovetti, Paul F, *Dir,* University of Connecticut, William Benton Museum of Art - Connecticut's State Art Museum, Storrs CT

Row, Brian G, *Chmn,* Southwest Texas State University, Dept of Art, San Marcos TX (S)

Rowan, George, *Assoc Prof,* University of New Orleans-Lake Front, Dept of Fine Arts, New Orleans LA (S)

Rowan, George H, *Assoc Prof,* University of New Orleans-Lake Front, Dept of Fine Arts, New Orleans LA (S)

Rowan, Gerald, *Prog Coordr,* Northampton Community College, Art Dept, Bethlehem PA (S)

Rowan, Herman, *Prof,* University of Minnesota, Minneapolis, Dept of Studio Art, Minneapolis MN (S)

Rowan, Peter J, *Prog Dir,* Lesley College, Arts Institute, Cambridge MA (S)

Rowars, Lorelei, *Gift Shop Supv,* Newark Museum Association, The Newark Museum, Newark NJ

Rowe, Ann P, *Cur New World,* Textile Museum, Washington DC

Rowe, Charles, *Coordr Illustration,* University of Delaware, Dept of Art, Newark DE (S)

Rowe, Donald, *Dir,* Olivet College, Armstrong Museum of Art and Archaeology, Olivet MI

Rowe, Donald, *Prof,* Olivet College, Art Dept, Olivet MI (S)

Rowe, Duane, *Dir of Marketing,* First Interstate Bank of Fort Collins, Fort Collins CO

Rowe, Kenneth, *Dir,* United Methodist Church Commission on Archives and History, Library, Madison NJ

Rowe, Martha, *Research Assoc,* Old Salem Inc, Museum of Early Southern Decorative Arts, Winston-Salem NC

Rowe, Martha, *Research Assoc,* Old Salem Inc, Library, Winston-Salem NC

Rowe, Robert, *Prof,* Marshall University, Dept of Art, Huntington WV (S)

Rowe, Sandra, *Asst Prof,* California State Polytechnic University, Pomona, Art Dept, Pomona CA (S)

Rowe, Susan, *Instructor,* Olivet College, Art Dept, Olivet MI (S)

Rowe, William, *Assoc Prof,* Arkansas State University, Dept of Art, Jonesboro AR (S)

Rowitch, Jerry, *Owner,* Venice Place Sculpture Gardens, Venice CA (S)

Rowland, Lisa, *Communications Mgr,* Arts & Science Center for Southeast Arkansas, Pine Bluff AR

Rowland, William, *Deputy Dir,* Virginia Museum of Fine Arts, Richmond VA

Rowlands, Eliot, *Asst Cur European Art,* Nelson-Atkins Museum of Art, Kansas City MO

Roworth, Wendy, *Prof,* University of Rhode Island, Dept of Art, Kingston RI (S)

Roy, Constance, *Assoc Prof,* Cazenovia College, Center for Art & Design Studies, Cazenovia NY (S)

Roy, Denise, *Instr,* Marylhurst College, Art Dept, Marylhurst OR (S)

Roy, James, *Chmn,* Saint Cloud State University, Dept of Art, Saint Cloud MN (S)

Roy, Randy, *Exec Dir,* Kentucky Derby Museum, Louisville KY

Roy, Roxanne, *Admin Asst,* Historical Society of Cheshire County, Colony House Museum, Keene NH

Royal, Don, *Chmn Dept,* Olivet Nazarene University, Dept of Art, Kankakee IL (S)

Royce, Diana, *Head Librn,* Stowe-Day Foundation, Library, Hartford CT

Royer, Jean, *Pres,* Musee d'Art de Saint-Laurent, Saint-Laurent PQ

Rozene, Janette, *Cat Head,* Fashion Institute of Technology Galleries, Library, New York NY

Rozier, Robert, *Chmn,* Alma College, Clack Art Center, Alma MI (S)

Rozman, Joseph, *Prof,* Mount Mary College, Art Dept, Milwaukee WI (S)

Roznoy, Cynthia, *Mgr,* Whitney Museum of American Art, Whitney Museum of American Art at Champion, New York NY

Rozsa, Allen, *Dir,* Church of Jesus Christ of Latter Day Saints, Mormon Visitors' Center, Independence MO

Rub, Timothy, *Dir,* Dartmouth College, Hood Museum of Art, Hanover NH

Rubel, William, *Pres,* Children's Art Foundation, Santa Cruz CA

Rubenstein, Elliott, *Assoc Prof,* Rochester Institute of Technology, School of Photographic Arts & Sciences, Rochester NY (S)

Rubenstein, T Ephraim, *Asst Prof,* University of Richmond, Dept of Art & Art History, Richmond VA (S)

Rubey, Debra, *Head Art, Music & Drama Dept,* Flint Public Library, Fine Arts Dept, Flint MI

Rubin, David, *Chief Cur,* Cleveland Center for Contemporary Art, Cleveland OH

Rubin, Esta, *Treas,* Long Island Graphic Eye Gallery, Port Washington NY

Rubin, James, *Chmn,* State University of New York at Stony Brook, Art Dept, Stony Brook NY (S)

Rubin, Michael, *Dir,* Education Alliance, Art School, New York NY (S)

Rubin, Robert S, *Chmn Board of Trustees,* Brooklyn Museum, Brooklyn NY

Rubin, Virginia C, *Dir Development,* San Francisco Museum of Modern Art, San Francisco CA

Rubinger, M, *Instr,* Technical University of Nova Scotia, Faculty of Architecture, Halifax NS (S)

Rubini, Gail, *Chairperson Studio Art,* Florida State University, Art Dept, Tallahassee FL (S)

Rubio, Pablo, *Asst Prof,* University of Puerto Rico, Dept of Fine Arts, Rio Piedras PR (S)

Rubis, James, *Librn,* Fairfield Public Library, Fairfield Art Association, Fairfield IA

Ruby, Julianne, *Archives,* Cascade County Historical Society, Cascade County Historical Museum & Archives, Great Falls MT

Ruby, William G, *Dir Educ,* New Jersey Center for Visual Arts, Summit NJ

Rudey, Liz, *Chmn,* Long Island University, Brooklyn Center, Art Dept, Brooklyn NY (S)

Rudolph, Conrad, *Chmn,* University of California, Riverside, Dept of the History of Art, Riverside CA (S)

Rudolph, Jeffrey N, *Executive Dir,* California Museum of Science and Industry, Los Angeles CA

Rudolph, Wanda, *Librn,* Springfield Art Museum, Springfield MO

Rudolph, Wanda, *Librn,* Springfield Art Museum, Library, Springfield MO

Rudolph, Wolf, *Assoc Prof,* Indiana University, Bloomington, Henry Radford Hope School of Fine Arts, Bloomington IN (S)

Rudquist, Jerry, *Head Dept,* MacAlester College, Dept of Art, Saint Paul MN (S)

Rudy, Jenny, *Development Officer,* Nevada Museum Of Art, Reno NV

Rudy, John, *Coordr Research Center,* Visual Studies Workshop, Research Center, Rochester NY

Ruedy, Don, *Assoc Prof,* University of Wisconsin, Center-Barron County, Dept of Art, Rice Lake WI (S)

Ruege, Ruth, *Coordr Fine Arts,* Milwaukee Public Library, Art, Music & Recreation Dept, Milwaukee WI

Rueppel, Merrill, *Dir,* The Contemporary Museum, Honolulu HI

Ruess, Diane, *Acting Head Instructional Media Serv,* University of Alaska, Elmer E Rasmuson Library, Fairbanks AK

Rufe, Laurie J, *Asst Dir,* Roswell Museum and Art Center, Roswell NM

Ruff, Eric, *Cur,* Yarmouth County Historical Society, Yarmouth County Museum, Yarmouth NS

Ruffer, David G, *Pres,* Albright College, Freedman Gallery, Reading PA

Ruffo, Joseph M, *Chmn & Dir,* University of Nebraska, Lincoln, The Gallery of the Department of Art & Art History, Lincoln NE

Ruffo, Joseph M, *Chmn Dept,* University of Nebraska-Lincoln, Dept of Art & Art History, Lincoln NE (S)

Ruffolo, Robert E, *Pres,* Princeton Antiques Bookservice, Art Marketing Reference Library, Atlantic City NJ

Rufo, Christy R, *Pres,* New England School of Art & Design, Boston MA (S)

Rugg, Ruth Ann, *Public Affairs,* Amon Carter Museum, Fort Worth TX

Ruggeri, JoAnne, *Acting Dir,* Greenwich House Pottery, New York NY (S)

Ruggie Saunders, Cathie, *Assoc Prof,* Saint Xavier University, Dept of Art, Chicago IL (S)

Ruggles, Janet E, *Chief Paper Conservator,* Balboa Art Conservation Center, San Diego CA

Ruggles, Joanne, *Prof,* California Polytechnic State University at San Luis Obispo, Dept of Art and Design, San Luis Obispo CA (S)

Rugila, Elaine, *Pres,* Monroe City Community College, Fine Arts Council, Monroe MI

Ruhl, Elizabeth, *Pres,* Cody Country Art League, Cody WY

Ruhstaller, Tod, *Dir & Cur of History,* San Joaquin Pioneer and Historical Society, The Haggin Museum, Stockton CA

Ruhstaller, Tod, *Acting Librn,* San Joaquin Pioneer and Historical Society, Petzinger Memorial Library, Stockton CA

Ruiz, Ben, *Instr,* Joe Kubert School of Cartoon & Graphic Art, Inc, Dover NJ (S)

Ruiz, Mike, *Chairperson,* City College of San Francisco, Art Dept, San Francisco CA (S)

Ruiz de Fischler, Carmen T, *Asst Prof,* University of Puerto Rico, Dept of Fine Arts, Rio Piedras PR (S)

Rule, Amy, *Archivist,* University of Arizona, Center for Creative Photography, Tucson AZ

Rumford, Beatrix T, *VPres Museums,* Colonial Williamsburg Foundation, Williamsburg VA

Rumrill, Alan, *Dir,* Historical Society of Cheshire County, Colony House Museum, Keene NH

Rumrill, Alan, *Dir,* Historical Society of Cheshire County, Archive Center of the Society, Keene NH

Rundquist, Leisa, *Cur,* South Bend Regional Museum of Art, South Bend IN

Runge, Tedd, *Design & Creative Studies Dept Coordr,* Aims Community College, Design & Creative Studies Dept, Greeley CO (S)

Runtsch, Alice, *Pres,* Oak Ridge Art Center, Oak Ridge TN

Runyan, Timothy J, *Pres,* Great Lakes Historical Society, Vermilion OH

Runyon, Dianne, *Registrar,* Art Institute of Philadelphia, Philadelphia PA (S)

Runyon, John M, *Prof,* Corning Community College, Division of Humanities, Corning NY (S)

Rupinski, Jill, *Instr,* Wayne Art Center, Wayne PA (S)

Rupp, Cora, *Exec Dir,* Art League, Alexandria VA

Ruprecht, Carl, *Supt of Grounds,* Stan Hywet Hall & Gardens, Inc, Akron OH

Rusak, Halina, *Art Librn,* Rutgers, The State University of New Jersey, Art Library, New Brunswick NJ

Rush, Dorothy, *Librn,* The Filson Club, Reference and Research Library, Louisville KY

Rush, Kent, *Assoc Prof,* University of Texas at San Antonio, Division of Art & Architecture, San Antonio TX (S)

Rush, Sallee, *Instr,* Main Line Center for the Arts, Haverford PA (S)

Rushing, Kim, *Instr,* Delta State University, Dept of Art, Cleveland MS (S)

Rushing, Sandra, *Registrar,* University of California, Santa Barbara, University Art Museum, Santa Barbara CA

Ruskey, John, *Acting Cur,* Carnegie Public Library, Delta Blues Museum, Clarksdale MS

Rusnell, Wesley A, *Cur Coll,* Roswell Museum and Art Center, Roswell NM

Russell, Donald, *Exec Dir,* Washington Project for the Arts, Washington DC

Russell, Douglas, *Gallery Dir,* Oregon State University, Fairbanks Gallery, Corvallis OR

Russell, Douglas, *Gallery Dir,* Oregon State University, Giustina Gallery, Corvallis OR

Russell, Douglas, *Sr Resident Asst,* Oregon State University, Dept of Art, Corvallis OR (S)

Russell, Jennifer, *Deputy Dir Internal Affairs,* Whitney Museum of American Art, New York NY

Russell, John I, *Lectr,* John Jay College of Criminal Justice, Dept of Art, Music and Philosophy, New York NY (S)

Russell, John I, *Exec Dir,* Brookfield Craft Center, Inc, Gallery, Brookfield CT

Russell, Kay, *Corresponding Secy,* Gilpin County Arts Association, Central City CO

Russell, Marilyn M, *Cur Educ,* Carnegie Institute, Carnegie Museum of Art, Pittsburgh PA

Russell, Pamela, *Cur Antiquity,* Tampa Museum of Art, Tampa FL

Russell, Robert, *Prof,* Pittsburg State University, Art Dept, Pittsburg KS (S)

Russell, Robert, *Chmn Art Educ,* University of Cincinnati, School of Art, Cincinnati OH (S)

Russell, Thomas, *Instr,* Roger Williams College, Art Dept, Bristol RI (S)

Russo, Donna, *Dir,* Bowne House Historical Society, Flushing NY

Russo, Kathleen, *Chmn,* Florida Atlantic University, Art Dept, Boca Raton FL (S)

Rust, Brian, *Instr,* Augusta College, Dept of Fine Arts, Augusta GA (S)

Rustige, Rona, *Cur,* Hastings County Museum, Belleville ON

Rustman, Mark, *Fine Arts Dept Head,* Topeka Public Library, Gallery of Fine Arts, Topeka KS

Rutenberg, Brigitte, *Pres,* Pennsylvania Academy of the Fine Arts, Fellowship of the Pennsylvania Academy of the Fine Arts, Philadelphia PA

Rutkovsky , Paul, *Asst Prof,* Florida State University, Art Dept, Tallahassee FL (S)

Rutkowski, Walter, *Prof,* Louisiana State University, School of Art, Baton Rouge LA (S)

Rutledge, Natalie, *Head Ref Librn,* West Virginia University, Evansdale Library, Morgantown WV

Rutstein, Roz, *Coordr,* Hagerstown Junior College, Art Dept, Hagerstown MD (S)

Ruttinger, Jacquelyn, *Exhib Dir,* Western Michigan University-Art Dept, Gallery II, Kalamazoo MI

Ryan, Ann, *Museum Shop Mgr,* University of Connecticut, William Benton Museum of Art - Connecticut's State Art Museum, Storrs CT

Ryan, David, *Cur Coll,* Norwest Bank of Minneapolis, Art Collection, Minneapolis MN

Ryan, George, *Dir,* Rochester Institute of Technology, School of Printing, Rochester NY (S)

Ryan, James, *Historic Site Mgr,* Olana State Historic Site, Hudson NY

Ryan, James, *Historic Site Mgr,* Olana State Historic Site, Archives, Hudson NY

Ryan, Linda Lee, *Instr,* Casper College, Dept of Visual Arts, Casper WY (S)

Ryan, Martin, *Assoc Prof,* Monmouth College, Dept of Art, West Long Branch NJ (S)

Ryan, Maureen, *Asst Prof,* University of British Columbia, Dept of Fine Arts, Vancouver BC (S)

Ryan, Patricia, *Asst Cur,* Honeywell Inc, Art Collection, Minneapolis MN

Ryan, Paul, *Instr,* Southeastern Louisiana University, Dept of Visual Arts, Hammond LA (S)

Ryan, Rebecca, *Registrar,* National Art Museum of Sport, Indianapolis IN

Rychlewski, Karen, *Prof,* West Liberty State College, Art Dept, West Liberty WV (S)

Rydell, Christine, *Instr,* Solano Community College, Division of Fine & Applied Art, Suisun City CA (S)

Ryer, Laurie, *Asst Dir,* Mattatuck Historical Society Museum, Waterbury CT

Rykwert, Joseph, *Chmn Grad Group,* University of Pennsylvania, Dept of Architecture, Philadelphia PA (S)

Ryman, Robert, *Commissioner,* Art Commission of the City of New York, Associates of the Art Commission, Inc, New York NY

Ryuto, Setsuko, *Admin Asst,* San Joaquin Pioneer and Historical Society, The Haggin Museum, Stockton CA

Saab, Nina, *Librn,* California College of Arts and Crafts Library, Oakland CA

Sabatella, Joseph, *Prof,* University of Florida, Dept of Art, Gainesville FL (S)

Sabin, Peter, *Lectr,* New England College, Art & Art History, Henniker NH (S)

Sacher, Pamela, *Instr,* Greenfield Community College, Art, Graphic Design & Media Communication Dept, Greenfield MA (S)

Sachs, Samuel, *Dir,* Detroit Institute of Arts, Detroit MI

Sack, Carol, *Assoc Dean Col,* Rochester Institute of Technology, College of Imaging Arts & Sciences, Rochester NY (S)

Sack, Wendy, *Asst Dean,* Tulane University, School of Architecture, New Orleans LA (S)

Sackman, Elmer, *Librn,* Fort Worth Public Library, Fine Arts Section, Fort Worth TX

Saczawa, Janet, *Gallery Asst,* Huntsville Museum of Art, Reference Library, Huntsville AL

Sadinsky, Rachael, *Cur Collection,* Arnot Art Museum, Elmira NY

Sadler, Louis, *Head,* University of Illinois, Chicago, Health Science Center, Biomedical Visualizations, Chicago IL (S)

Sadlerner, Rob, *Treas,* Saint Louis Artists' Guild, Saint Louis MO

Safford, Herbert D, *Dir,* University of Northern Iowa, Art & Music Section Rod Library, Cedar Falls IA

Safrin, Robert W, *Dir,* The Society of the Four Arts, Palm Beach FL

Sagan Alvim, Maureen, *Registrar,* Ohio State University, Wexner Center for the Arts, Columbus OH

Saganic, Livio, *Chmn Art Dept,* Drew University, Elizabeth P Korn Gallery, Madison NJ

Saganic, Livio, *Chmn Dept,* Drew University, Art Dept, Madison NJ (S)

Sagawa, Susan, *Assoc Cur,* Bellevue Art Museum, Bellevue WA

Sager, Rochelle, *Dir,* Fashion Institute of Technology Galleries, Library, New York NY

Sahlstrand, James, *Dir Art Gallery,* Central Washington University, Sarah Spurgeon Gallery, Ellensburg WA

Sahnabel, Harry H, *Cur,* US Department of State, Diplomatic Reception Rooms, Washington DC

Saidel, Alice, *Ref Librn,* Dayton Art Institute, Library, Dayton OH

Sainte-Marie, G, *Dir,* National Museum of Science & Technology, Ottawa ON

Sajadian, Morteza, *Dir,* University of Missouri, Museum of Art and Archaeology, Columbia MO

Sakal, John A, *Preparator & Registrar,* Westmoreland Museum of Art, Greensburg PA

Sakamoto, Kerri, *Writer,* Art in General, New York NY

Sakowski, Robert C, *Dir,* University of Manitoba, School of Art, Winnipeg MB (S)

Sal, Jack, *Chmn Photography,* Moore College of Art & Design, Philadelphia PA (S)

Salam, Halide, *Prof,* Radford University, Art Dept, Radford VA (S)

Salay, David, *Dir & Cur Ranching Heritage Center,* Texas Tech University, Museum, Lubbock TX

Salberg, Lester, *Pres,* Rock Valley College, Dept of Art, Rockford IL (S)

Saler, Karen, *Co-Chmn Foundation Program,* University of the Arts, Philadelphia College of Art & Design, Philadelphia PA (S)

Sallee, Tiffany C, *Admnr,* Historic Landmarks Foundation of Indiana, Morris-Butler House, Indianapolis IN

Sally, Dana, *Head Librn,* West Virginia University, Evansdale Library, Morgantown WV

Salmon, Mark, *Academic Dean,* Atlanta College of Art, Atlanta GA (S)

Salmon, Ray, *Instr,* Solano Community College, Division of Fine & Applied Art, Suisun City CA (S)

Salmon, Robin, *VPres Academic Affairs & Cur,* Brookgreen Gardens, Murrells Inlet SC

Salmon, Robin, *VPres & Cur,* Brookgreen Gardens, Library, Murrells Inlet SC

Salmond, Wendy, *Chmn,* Chapman University, Art Dept, Orange CA (S)

Salo, Bob, *Pres,* Hartland Art Council, Hartland MI

Salomon, Carol, *Engineering & Science,* Cooper Union for the Advancement of Science & Art, Library, New York NY

Salomon, Judith, *Assoc Prof,* Cleveland Institute of Art, Cleveland OH (S)

Salstrom, Joanne, *Gallery Asst,* Sonoma State University, Art Gallery, Rohnert Park CA

Saltalamacchia, Karen, *Adjunct Instr,* Emmanuel College, Art Dept, Boston MA (S)

Salter, Anne, *Dir Library & Archives,* Atlanta Historical Society Inc, Atlanta History Center, Atlanta GA

Saltzman, Marvin, *Prof,* University of North Carolina at Chapel Hill, Art Dept, Chapel Hill NC (S)

Saluato, Michael, *Asst Prof,* Philadelphia Community College, Dept of Art, Philadelphia PA (S)

Salvage, Barbara, *Art Librn,* Jacksonville Art Museum, Jacksonville FL

Salvage, Barbara, *Art Librn,* Jacksonville Art Museum, Library, Jacksonville FL

Salveson, Douglas, *Dir,* Findlay College, Egner Fine Arts Center, Findlay OH

Salvest, John J, *Asst Prof,* Arkansas State University, Dept of Art, Jonesboro AR (S)

Salzillo, Marjorie, *Instr,* Munson-Williams-Proctor Institute, School of Art, Utica NY (S)

Salzillo, William, *Instr,* Hamilton College, Art Dept, Clinton NY (S)

Samaras, Isabel, *Prog Dir,* Franklin Furnace Archive, Inc, New York NY

Samaras, Valessia, *Dir Membership,* Institute of Contemporary Art, Boston MA

Samko, Patrice, *Librn,* Burbank Public Library, Warner Research Collection, Burbank CA

Sammon, Christine E, *Library Dir,* Alberta College of Art, Luke Lindoe Library, Calgary AB

Sammons, Richard, *Instr,* Bismarck Junior College, Fine Arts Dept, Bismarck ND (S)

Samms, Mary, *Librn,* Textile Museum, Arthur D Jenkins Library, Washington DC

Samogis, Nancy, *Instr,* Creighton University, Fine and Performing Arts Dept, Omaha NE (S)

Sample, George, *Asst Prof,* Central Missouri State University, Art Dept, Warrensburg MO (S)

Sampson, Cheryl E, *Staff Asst,* Nora Eccles Harrison Museum of Art, Logan UT

Sampson, Gary, *Asst Prof,* Grand Valley State University, Art & Design Dept, Allendale MI (S)

Samson, Bruce, *Pres,* University of Tampa, Lee Scarfone Gallery, Tampa FL

Samuels, Clifford, *Dir,* Trova Foundation, Philip Samuels Fine Art, St Louis MO

Samuels, Philip, *Pres,* Trova Foundation, Philip Samuels Fine Art, St Louis MO

Samuelson, Jerry, *Dean School of Arts,* California State University, Fullerton, Art Dept, Fullerton CA (S)

Sanchez, Beatrice Rivas, *Pres,* Kansas City Art Institute, Kansas City MO (S)

Sand, Viki, *Dir,* Shaker Museum, Old Chatham NY

Sand, Viki, *Dir,* Shaker Museum, Emma B King Library, Old Chatham NY

Sande, Theodore A, *Exec Dir,* Western Reserve Historical Society, Cleveland OH

Sandeen, Janice, *Woodwork & Furniture Design,* California College of Arts and Crafts, Oakland CA (S)

Sanden, Michael H, *Dir,* Lakeview Museum of Arts and Sciences, Peoria IL

Sanderbeck, Kelly, *Development Dir,* City Art Works, Pratt Fine Arts Center, Seattle WA (S)

Sanders, Albert E, *Cur Natural History,* Charleston Museum, Charleston SC

Sanders, Gary, *Dir,* Kimball Art Center, Park City UT

Sanders, James, *Dir Building Servs,* Worcester Art Museum, Worcester MA

Sanders, James H, *Executive Dir,* Sawtooth Center for Visual Art, Winston-Salem NC (S)

Sanders, Jenny, *Instr,* Saint Francis College, Art Dept, Fort Wayne IN (S)

Sanders, Ralph, *Instr,* Chattanooga State Technical Community College, Advertising Arts Dept, Chattanooga TN (S)

Sanders, Robert, *Cur Herpetology,* San Bernardino County Museum, Fine Arts Institute, Redlands CA

Sanders, Scott, *Dir,* South Carolina Arts Commission, Columbia SC

Sanders, Scott, *Dir,* South Carolina Arts Commission, Media Center, Columbia SC

Sanders, Val, *Chmn,* Palomar Community College, Art Dept, San Marcos CA (S)

Sanders, William, *Instr,* Surry Community College, Art Dept, Dobson NC (S)

Sanderson, Chica, *Dir of Development,* Philbrook Museum of Art, Tulsa OK

Sanderson, Dennis C, *Chmn,* Francis Marion University, Fine Arts Dept, Florence SC (S)

Sanderson, Robert, *Pres,* Mid-Hudson Arts and Science Center, Poughkeepsie NY

Sanderson, Ruth E, *Exec Dir,* Kansas Watercolor Society, Wichita Art Museum, Wichita KS

Sandin, Karl, *Asst Prof,* Denison University, Dept of Art, Granville OH (S)

Sandler, Irving, *Prof,* State University of New York College at Purchase, Art History Board of Study, Purchase NY (S)

Sandman, Keith, *Instr,* Munson-Williams-Proctor Institute, School of Art, Utica NY (S)

Sandmeier, Carol, *Dir Admin,* Los Angeles County Museum of Natural History, William S Hart Museum, Newhall CA

Sandone, Corrine, *Asst Prof,* Johns Hopkins University, School of Medicine, Dept of Art as Applied to Medicine, Baltimore MD (S)

Sandoval, Gema, *Exec Dir,* Plaza de la Raza Cultural Center, Los Angeles CA

Sandweiss, Martha, *Dir,* Amherst College, Mead Art Museum, Amherst MA

Sanematsu, Helen, *Publicity,* University of California, California Museum of Photography, Riverside CA

Sanford, Beverly, *Dir Educ & Prog,* Science Museums of Charlotte, Inc, Discovery Place, Charlotte NC

Sangcola, Hugh, *Dir Mem,* Color Association of The US, New York NY

Sanger, Helen, *Librn,* Frick Art Reference Library, New York NY

Sangster, Gary, *Cur,* Jersey City Museum, Jersey City NJ

Sanguinetti, E F, *Dir,* University of Utah, Utah Museum of Fine Arts, Salt Lake City UT

San Juan, Rose Marie, *Assoc Prof,* University of British Columbia, Dept of Fine Arts, Vancouver BC (S)

Sankey, Eric, *Chmn,* Mount Hood Community College, Visual Arts Center, Gresham OR (S)

Sano, Emily J, *Sr Cur Non-Western Art,* Dallas Museum of Art, Dallas TX

Santelli, Thomas, *Lectr,* College of Saint Rose, Dept of Art, Albany NY (S)

Santiago, Alfonso, *Head Dept,* Catholic University of Puerto Rico, Dept of Fine Arts, Ponce PR (S)

Santiago, Fernando, *Auxiliary Prof,* Inter American University of Puerto Rico, Dept of Art, San German PR (S)

Santiago, Raymond, *Asst Dir,* Miami-Dade Public Library, Miami FL

Santiago de Curet, Annie, *Dir,* University of Puerto Rico, Museum of Anthropology, History & Art, Rio Piedras PR

Santis, Jorge, *Cur Coll,* Museum of Art, Fort Lauderdale, Fort Lauderdale FL

Santomasso, Eugene A, *Assoc Prof,* City University of New York, PhD Program in Art History, New York NY (S)

Santoro, Geraldine, *Registrar,* The National Park Service, United States Department of the Interior, The Statue of Liberty National Monument, New York NY

Sapp, Willy, *Vis Prof,* Nebraska Wesleyan University, Art Dept, Lincoln NE (S)

Sara, Heidi, *Tour Coordr & Secy,* London Regional Art & Historical Museums, London ON

Sarachman, Diane, *Slide Cur,* Temple University, Slide Library, Philadelphia PA

Sarchet, Diane, *Dir,* Pine Castle Folk Art Center, Orlando FL

Sargent, John T, *Commissioner,* Art Commission of the City of New York, Associates of the Art Commission, Inc, New York NY

Sargent, Mary T, *Pres,* Hill-Stead Museum, Farmington CT

Sargent, Warren, *VPres,* Octagon Center for the Arts, Ames IA

Sarkowski, Faye, *Pres Board,* Seattle Art Museum, Seattle WA

Sarner, Amy, *Instr,* Main Line Center for the Arts, Haverford PA (S)

Sarner, Amy, *Instr,* Main Line Center for the Arts, Haverford PA (S)

Sarro, Maureen, *Museum Asst,* Fraunces Tavern Museum, New York NY

Sarton, Jay, *Dir Science,* Roberson Museum & Science Center, Binghamton NY

Sartorius, Tara, *Cur Educ,* Montgomery Museum of Fine Arts, Montgomery AL

Sarvay, James, *Pres,* Cortland County Historical Society, Suggett House Museum, Cortland NY

Sassa, Reiko, *Dir,* Japan Society, Inc, Library, New York NY

Sasso, Paul, *Assoc Prof,* Murray State University, Art Dept, Murray KY (S)

Satchell, Ernest R, *Coordr Art Education,* University of Maryland Eastern Shore, Art & Technology Dept, Princess Anne MD (S)

Sather, Jane, *Technician,* Regina Public Library, Dunlop Art Gallery, Regina SK

Satlof, Ellen, *Public Relations,* Laguna Art Museum, Laguna Beach CA

Satoda, Ikuko, *Controller,* San Francisco Museum of Modern Art, San Francisco CA

Satre, Paul, *Chmn,* Judson College, Division of Fine Arts, Elgin IL (S)

Satterfield, Debra, *Asst Prof,* Arkansas State University, Dept of Art, Jonesboro AR (S)

Sauberli, Ronald, *Library Asst,* Illinois State Museum, Library, Springfield IL

Saucedo, Christopher, *Asst Prof,* University of New Orleans-Lake Front, Dept of Fine Arts, New Orleans LA (S)

Sauer, Jean S, *Coordr of Technical Serv,* The College at New Paltz State University of New York, Sojourner Truth Library, New Paltz NY

Sauer, Timothy, *Business Mgr,* Creative Growth Art Center, Oakland CA

Saulnier, Nancy, *Gallery Dir,* Art League, Alexandria VA

Saunders, Ann O, *Assoc Prof,* Southern Illinois University, School of Art & Design, Carbondale IL (S)

Saunders, Cheryl A, *Registrar,* Carnegie Institute, Carnegie Museum of Art, Pittsburgh PA

Saunders, Joseph, *Chief Exec Officer,* Art Services International, Alexandria VA

Saunders, Joyan, *Asst Prof New Genre,* University of Arizona, Dept of Art, Tucson AZ (S)

Saunders, Juliet, *Asst Dir,* Providence Athenaeum, Providence RI

Saunders, Juliet, *Asst Librn,* Providence Athenaeum, Library, Providence RI

Saunders, Kathy, *Comptroller,* Huntington Museum of Art, Huntington WV

Saunders, Richard H, *Dir,* Middlebury College, Museum of Art, Middlebury VT

Saunders, Susanna T, *Instr,* Main Line Center for the Arts, Haverford PA (S)

Sausser, Nancy, *Asst Dir,* Maryland-National Capital Park & Planning Commission, Montpelier Cultural Arts Center, Laurel MD

Sautter, Dianne L, *Executive Dir,* Chicago Children's Museum, Chicago IL

Sauvage, Danielle, *Dir Communications,* Montreal Museum of Fine Arts, Montreal PQ

Savage, Cort, *Asst Prof,* Davidson College, Art Dept, Davidson NC (S)

Savage, Dorothy, *Cur,* Bradford Brinton Memorial Museum & Historic Ranch, Big Horn WY

Savage, Jerome, *In Charge Painting,* University of Illinois, Urbana-Champaign, School of Art and Design, Champaign IL (S)

Savage, Melody, *VPres Finance,* Newberry Library, Chicago IL

Savage-Hutchinson, Joan, *Instr,* College of Boca Raton, Art & Design Dept, Boca Raton FL (S)

Savalas, Penelope, *Dir,* Morris-Jumel Mansion, Inc, New York NY

Savary, Lee, *Cur Exhibits,* University of New Mexico, University Art Museum, Albuquerque NM

Savery, Suzanne, *Cur,* The City of Petersburg Museums, Petersburg VA

Saville, Jeniffer, *Cur Western Art,* Honolulu Academy of Arts, Honolulu HI

Savini, Richard, *Vis Prof,* California State University, Art Dept, Turlock CA (S)

Saw, James T, *Assoc Prof,* Palomar Community College, Art Dept, San Marcos CA (S)

Sawchuk, Michele, *Reference & Coll Development Librn - Fine Arts & Architecture,* University of Waterloo, Dana Porter Library, Waterloo ON

Sawycky, Roman, *Asst Dir & Head Art Dept,* Free Public Library of Elizabeth, Fine Arts Dept, Elizabeth NJ

Sawyer, Bert, *Exec Dir,* MonDak Heritage Center, Sidney MT

Sawyer, Bert, *Exec Dir,* MonDak Heritage Center, Willo Ralston Library for Historical Research, Sidney MT

Sawyer, Donna, *Public Information Officer,* Chrysler Museum, Norfolk VA

Sawyer, Ellen, *Development Dir,* Marion Koogler McNay Art Museum, San Antonio TX

Sawyer, Henry W, *VPres,* Fairmount Park Art Association, Philadelphia PA

Sawyer, Marie, *Exec Dir,* MonDak Heritage Center, Sidney MT

Sawyer, Marie, *Exec Dir,* MonDak Heritage Center, Willo Ralston Library for Historical Research, Sidney MT

Sayre, Henry, *Assoc Prof,* Oregon State University, Dept of Art, Corvallis OR (S)

Sbarra, Carol, *Treas,* Wichita Center for the Arts, Wichita KS

Scafetta, Stefano, *Sr Conservator,* National Museum of American Art, Washington DC

Scala, Mark, *Dir Education,* Art Museum of Western Virginia, Roanoke VA

Scalera, Michelle, *Conservator,* State Art Museum of Florida, John & Mable Ringling Museum of Art, Sarasota FL

Scarborough, J Banks, *Treas,* Florence Museum, Florence SC

Scarbrough, Cleve K, *Dir,* Hunter Museum of Art, Chattanooga TN

Scarola, Vito Leonard, *Chmn Visual Communications,* Art Institute of Southern California, Ruth Salyer Library, Laguna Beach CA

Scarpitta, Salvatore, *Faculty,* Maryland Institute, Mount Royal School of Art, Baltimore MD (S)

Scepanski, Jordan, *Dir,* California State University, Long Beach, University Library, Long Beach CA

Schaad, Dee, *Prof,* University of Indianapolis, Art Dept, Indianapolis IN (S)

Schaber, Ken, *Instr,* Lake Michigan College, Dept of Art, Benton Harbor MI (S)

Schaefer, Fred, *Asst Prof,* Pennsylvania College of Technology, Dept of Design & Communiation Arts, Williamsport PA (S)

Schaeffer, Barbara, *Cur Colls,* Rome Historical Society Museum, William E Scripture Memorial Library, Rome NY

Schafer, Michael L, *Pres,* Mohawk Valley Community College, Advertising Design and Production, Utica NY (S)

Schafer, Sheldon, *Science Planetarium Dir,* Lakeview Museum of Arts and Sciences, Peoria IL

Schaffer, Anne Louise, *Asst Cur Africa, Oceania & the Americas,* Museum of Fine Arts, Houston, Houston TX

Schaffer, Bonnie, *Coordr Communications,* Norman Mackenzie Art Gallery, Regina SK

Schaffer, Dale E, *Co-owner,* Gloridale Partnership, National Museum of Woodcarving, Custer SD

Schaffer, Gloria, *Co-owner,* Gloridale Partnership, National Museum of Woodcarving, Custer SD

Schaffer, Jo, *Cur,* State University of New York College at Cortland, Art Slide Library, Cortland NY

Schaffer, Joelien, *Dir,* Clarion University, Hazel Sandford Gallery, Clarion PA

Schaffer, Joeliene, *Instr,* Clarion University of Pennsylvania, Dept of Art, Clarion PA (S)

Schaffer, John, *Head Dept,* Augusta College, Dept of Fine Arts, Augusta GA (S)

Schaffer, Richard, *Asst Registrar,* University of Arizona, Museum of Art, Tucson AZ

Schafroth, Colleen, *Cur Education,* Maryhill Museum of Art, Goldendale WA

Schall, Jan, *Asst Prof,* University of Florida, Dept of Art, Gainesville FL (S)

Schaller, Gertrude, *Admin Asst,* Forest Hills Adult Center, Forest Hills NY (S)

Schaller, Heidi, *Dir,* Saint John's College, Elizabeth Myers Mitchell Art Gallery, Annapolis MD

Schalnat, Teresa, *Curatorial Consultant,* Wright State University, Dayton Art Institute, Dayton OH

Schantz, Michael W, *Dir,* Woodmere Art Museum, Philadelphia PA

Schapiro, Taylor, *Educ Dir,* Huntsville Museum of Art, Huntsville AL

Schapp, Rebecca M, *Dir,* Santa Clara University, de Saisset Museum, Santa Clara CA

Schar, Stuart, *Dean,* University of Hartford, Hartford Art School, West Hartford CT (S)

Scharf, Lee, *Cur Art,* Museum of Art, Science and Industry, Discovery Museum, Bridgeport CT

Scharfenberg, D F, *Instr,* Western Illinois University, Art Dept, Macomb IL (S)

Schatz, Charlotte, *Instr,* Bucks County Community College, Fine Arts Dept, Newtown PA (S)

Schatz, Julius, *Pres,* National Council on Art in Jewish Life, New York NY

Schatz, Julius, *Pres,* National Council on Art in Jewish Life, Library, New York NY

Schau, Madeline, *Corresp Secy,* Bowne House Historical Society, Flushing NY

Schauer, Rudolph, *Prof,* University of Minnesota, Duluth, Art Dept, Duluth MN (S)

Schechke, R, *Chmn Fine Arts,* Fashion Institute of Technology, Art & Design Division, New York NY (S)

Schechter, Emanuel, *Librn,* Boca Raton Museum of Art, Library, Boca Raton FL

Schedl, Naomi, *Pres,* Iowa City - Johnson County Arts Council, Arts Center, Iowa City IA

Scheer, Elaine, *Asst Prof,* University of Wisconsin, Madison, Dept of Art, Madison WI (S)

Scheer, Lisa, *Asst Prof,* Saint Mary's College of Maryland, Arts and Letters Division, Saint Mary's City MD (S)

Scheer, Malcolm E, *Librn,* New York School of Interior Design Library, New York NY

Scheer, Stephen, *Instr,* Bard College, Milton Avery Graduate School of the Arts, Annandale-on-Hudson NY (S)

Scheer, Stephen, *Photographic Design,* University of Georgia, Franklin College of Arts & Sciences, Dept of Art, Athens GA (S)

Scheer, Steven S, *Chmn,* Saint Meinrad College, Humanities Dept, Saint Meinrad IN (S)

Schefcik, Jerry, *Dir,* University of Nevada, Las Vegas, Art Gallery, Las Vegas NV

Scheiblberg, Leslie, *Cur,* Ormond Memorial Art Museum and Gardens, Ormond Beach FL

Scheifler, Linda, *Conservator,* Asian Art Museum of San Francisco, Avery Brundage Collection, San Francisco CA

Scheiser, Edward, *Chief Exhib,* Hirshhorn Museum and Sculpture Garden, Washington DC

Schelhof, Rudolph B, *VPres,* The American Federation of Arts, New York NY

Schell, Edwin, *Executive Secy,* United Methodist Historical Society, Lovely Lane Museum, Baltimore MD

Schell, Edwin, *Librn,* United Methodist Historical Society, Library, Baltimore MD

Schell, William H, *Dir,* Martin Memorial Library, York PA

Scheller, Bonnie, *Instr,* Villa Maria College of Buffalo, Art Dept, Buffalo NY (S)

Schellhorn, Mary, *Dir,* Columbia College, Library, Chicago IL

Schelling, George, *Instr,* Luzerne County Community College, Commercial Art Dept, Nanticoke PA (S)

Schelshorn, Christine, *Dir Visual & Sound Archives,* State Historical Society of Wisconsin, State Historical Museum, Madison WI

Schenck, Marvin, *Cur,* Saint Mary's College of California, Hearst Art Gallery, Moraga CA

Schenk, Joseph B, *Dir,* Art Patrons League of Mobile, Mobile AL

Scher, Anne J, *Dir Public Relations,* The Jewish Museum, New York NY

Scher, Reda, *Instr,* Main Line Center for the Arts, Haverford PA (S)

Scherer, Herbert G, *Librn,* University of Minnesota, Art Book Collection, Minneapolis MN

Scherpereel, Richard, *Dir,* Texas A & I University, Art Gallery, Kingsville TX

Scherpereel, Richard, *Chmn,* Texas A & I University, Art Dept, Kingsville TX (S)

Schetzsle, Letha, *Registrar & Cur,* Denison University, Art Gallery, Granville OH

Scheu, David R, *Dir,* Battleship North Carolina, Wilmington NC

Scheuner, Mary, *Dir Educ,* Memphis Brooks Museum of Art, Memphis TN

Schick, Gillian, *Public Relations Asst,* The Canadian Craft Museum, Vancouver BC

Schick, Marjorie, *Prof,* Pittsburg State University, Art Dept, Pittsburg KS (S)

Schienbaum, David, *Asst Prof,* College of Santa Fe, Visual Arts Dept, Santa Fe NM (S)

Schier, Peter, *Assoc Prof,* University of Bridgeport, Art Dept, Bridgeport CT (S)

Schieve, Barbara, *VPres,* Brooklyn Historical Society, Brooklyn OH

Schiff, Jeffrey, *Asst Prof,* Wesleyan University, Art Dept, Middletown CT (S)

Schiffer, Tim, *VPres,* Santa Barbara Contemporary Arts Forum, Santa Barbara CA

Schifferli, Mary, *Acting Librn,* Albany Institute of History and Art, Albany NY

Schifferli, Mary, *Acting Librn,* Albany Institute of History and Art, McKinley Library, Albany NY

Schiffers, Richard, *Assoc Dir,* California State University at Sacramento, University Union Exhibit Lounge, Sacramento CA

Schiffman, Janice, *Acting Dir,* Albright College, Freedman Gallery, Reading PA

Schiffman, Sedra, *VPres,* Woodmere Art Museum, Philadelphia PA

Schimelfenig, Rachel Kay, *Educ Mgr,* Aurora University, Schingoethe Center for Native American Cultures, Aurora IL

Schimenti, Margie, *Pres,* Artists' Cooperative Gallery, Omaha NE

Schimmelman, Janice C, *Assoc Prof,* Oakland University, Dept of Art and Art History, Rochester MI (S)

Schindle, A, *Instr,* Western Illinois University, Art Dept, Macomb IL (S)

Schira, Peter, *Deputy Chmn,* Bronx Community College, Music & Art Dept, Bronx NY (S)

Schiwek, Joseph, *Librn,* Bassist College Library, Portland OR

Schlanger, Gregg, *Asst Prof,* Austin Peay State University, Dept of Art, Clarksville TN (S)

Schlankey, Margaret, *Rare Books Librn,* Rosenberg Library, Galveston TX

Schlawin, Judy, *Prof,* Winona State University, Dept of Art, Winona MN (S)

Schleier, Joan, *Pres,* Keokuk Art Center, Keokuk IA

Schlitt, Melinda, *Asst Prof,* Dickinson College, Fine Arts Dept, Carlisle PA (S)

Schloder, John, *Dir,* Birmingham Museum of Art, Birmingham AL

Schlossberg, Leon, *Assoc Prof,* Johns Hopkins University, School of Medicine, Dept of Art as Applied to Medicine, Baltimore MD (S)

Schlosser, Anne G, *Head Librn,* University of Southern California, Cinema-Television Library & Archives of Performing Arts, Los Angeles CA

Schlosser, Anne G, *Dir,* Warner Bros Research Library, North Hollywood CA

Schlosser, Ira, *Dir Admin & Finance,* Peabody & Essex Museum, Salem MA

Schlosser, Tom, *Chmn Dept,* College of Saint Mary, Art Dept, Omaha NE (S)

Schlossman, Jenni, *Registrar & Asst Cur,* Colgate University, Picker Art Gallery, Hamilton NY

Schlough, Steven, *Public Relations Officer,* Whitney Museum of American Art, New York NY

Schmaeling, Susan, *Public Information Officer,* Contemporary Arts Museum, Houston TX

Schmaljohn, Russell, *Asst Prof,* Northwest Missouri State University, Dept of Art, Maryville MO (S)

Schmalz, Lydia H, *Cur,* Longue Vue House and Gardens, New Orleans LA

Schmats, Kathleen, *VPres,* Summit County Historical Society, Akron OH

Schmidlapp, Don, *Assoc Prof,* Winona State University, Dept of Art, Winona MN (S)

Schmidt, Bernard L, *Dir,* Xavier University, Xavier Art Gallery, Cincinnati OH

Schmidt, Bernard L, *Chmn,* Xavier University, Dept of Art, Cincinnati OH (S)

Schmidt, Corine, *Coordr,* Wenatchee Valley College, Gallery 76, Wenatchee WA

Schmidt, Edward, *Instr,* New York Academy of Art, Graduate School of Figurative Art, New York NY (S)

Schmidt, Eleanore, *Assoc Dir Adult Servs,* Long Beach Public Library, Long Beach CA

Schmidt, Elizabeth, *Cur,* Agecroft Association, Richmond VA

Schmidt, Fern, *Pres,* San Bernardino Art Association, Inc, San Bernardino CA

Schmidt, Fred, *Instr,* The Arkansas Arts Center, Museum School, Little Rock AR (S)

Schmidt, Katherine, *Dir,* Colorado Mountain College, Visual & Performing Arts, Vale CO (S)

Schmidt, Kathleen, *Instructor,* Northeastern Oklahoma State University, Tahlequah OK (S)

Schmidt, Kirsten, *Dir Public Relations & Publications,* California State University, Long Beach, University Art Museum, Long Beach CA

Schmidt, Lawrence, *Military Historian,* Old Barracks Museum, Trenton NJ

Schmidt, Phyllis, *Reference Librn,* Fort Hays State University, Forsyth Library, Hays KS

Schmidt, Sherri, *Dean University Libraries,* Arizona State University, Hayden Library, Tempe AZ

Schmidt, Susan S, *Assoc Prof,* College of the Holy Cross, Dept of Visual Arts, Worcester MA (S)

Schmiegel, Karol A, *Registrar,* Winterthur Museum and Gardens, Winterthur DE

Schmits, John W, *Chmn,* Saint Ambrose University, Art Dept, Davenport IA (S)

Schmitt, Helmut, *Dir,* Merritt College, Art Dept, Oakland CA (S)

Schmitz, Robert, *Prof,* Rochester Institute of Technology, School of Art and Design, Rochester NY (S)

Schmutzhart, Berthold, *Chmn Sculpture,* Corcoran School of Art, Washington DC (S)

Schnabel, JoAnn, *Asst Prof,* University of Northern Iowa, Dept of Art, Cedar Falls IA (S)

Schnee, Alix Sandra, *Project Dir,* Philipse Manor Hall State Historic Site, Yonkers NY

Schneider, Beth, *Eduction Dir,* Museum of Fine Arts, Houston, Houston TX

Schneider, Cynthia, *Instr,* Georgetown University, Dept of Fine Arts, Washington DC (S)

Schneider, Elsa, *Education Cur,* Kemper & Leila Williams Foundation, New Orleans LA

Schneider, Emery E, *Chmn Design Composition Division,* Rochester Institute of Technology, School of Printing, Rochester NY (S)

Schneider, Karen, *Librn,* The Phillips Collection, Washington DC

Schneider, Karen, *Librn,* The Phillips Collection, Library, Washington DC

Schneider, Laurie, *Prof,* John Jay College of Criminal Justice, Dept of Art, Music and Philosophy, New York NY (S)

Schneider, Russell, *Chmn,* Hinds Junior College District, Marie Hull Gallery, Raymond MS

Schneider, Russell, *Chmn,* Hinds Community College, Dept of Art, Raymond MS (S)

Schneider, U, *Instr,* Sarah Lawrence College, Dept of Art History, Bronxville NY (S)

Schneiderman, Nancy, *Cur,* Rochester Historical Society, Rochester NY

Schneiderman, Richard S, *Dir,* North Carolina Museum of Art, Raleigh NC

Schneider-Wilson, Nancy, *Instr,* Johnson County Community College, Visual Arts Program, Overland Park KS (S)

Schnell, Ann, *Photographer,* Tougaloo College, Art Collection, Tougaloo MS

Schnell, Frank T, *Cur of Archaeology,* Columbus Museum, Columbus GA

Schnell, Marianne B, *VPres,* New York Artists Equity Association, Inc, New York NY

Schnell, Ron, *Dir,* Tougaloo College, Art Collection, Tougaloo MS

Schnell, Ronald, *Chmn Dept,* Tougaloo College, Art Dept, Tougaloo MS (S)

Schnellman, Lew, *Instr,* Lakewood Community College, Humanities Dept, White Bear Lake MN (S)

Schnepf, Scott, *Asst Prof,* University of New Hampshire, Dept of the Arts, Durham NH (S)

Schnepper, Mary, *Cur of Coll,* Evansville Museum of Arts and Science, Evansville IN

Schnepper, Mary, *Cur,* Evansville Museum of Arts and Science, Henry R Walker Jr Memorial Art Library, Evansville IN

Schnitz, Gary, *Chmn,* Association of Medical Illustrators, Atlanta GA

Schnorr, Emil, *Adjunct Prof,* Springfield College, Dept of Visual and Performing Arts, Springfield MA (S)

Schnorr, Emil G, *Conservator,* George Walter Vincent Smith Art Museum, Springfield MA

Schnur, Barbara, *Mgr Cataloging Servs,* Presbyterian Historical Society, Philadelphia PA

Schoenborn, Amy, *Acting Dir Development,* Mexican Museum, San Francisco CA

Schoenfeld, William, *Prof,* Ocean County College, Humanities Dept, Toms River NJ (S)

Schoenherr, Douglas, *Assoc Cur European & American Prints & Drawings,* National Gallery of Canada, Ottawa ON

Schofield, Peg, *Lectr,* Saint Joseph's University, Dept of Fine & Performing Arts, Philadelphia PA (S)

Schonlau, Ree, *Dir,* Bemis Foundation, New Gallery, Omaha NE

Schoommaker, Donna, *Instr,* Cuyahoga Valley Art Center, Cuyahoga Falls OH (S)

Schor, Mira, *Instr,* Sarah Lawrence College, Dept of Art History, Bronxville NY (S)

Schorr, David, *Prof,* Wesleyan University, Art Dept, Middletown CT (S)

Schorsch, Ismar, *Pres,* Leo Baeck Institute, New York NY

Schory, Karen, *Instr,* Johnson County Community College, Visual Arts Program, Overland Park KS (S)

Schott, Gene A, *Dir,* Heritage Plantation of Sandwich, Sandwich MA

Schousen, Steve, *Chmn Dept,* Aquinas College, Art Dept, Grand Rapids MI (S)

Schouten, Marion, *Asst Prof,* College of the Holy Cross, Dept of Visual Arts, Worcester MA (S)

Schrader, John E, *Chmn Dept,* East Tennessee State University, Fine Arts Dept, Johnson City TN (S)

Schreider, Carol, *Dir Educ,* Colorado Historical Society, Museum, Denver CO

Schreier, Barbara, *Cur Costumes,* Chicago Historical Society, Chicago IL

Schrock, Eileen, *VPres,* Phelps County Historical Society, Phelps County Museum, Holdrege NE

Schrock, Peggy, *Asst Prof,* Murray State University, Art Dept, Murray KY (S)

Schroeder, George, *Chmn,* Hiram College, Art Dept, Hiram OH (S)

Schroth, Sarah, *Cur,* University of North Carolina at Chapel Hill, Ackland Art Museum, Chapel Hill NC

Schuchard, Oliver A, *Chmn,* University of Missouri, Art Dept, Columbia MO (S)

Schueckler, Valerie, *Asst Comptroller,* Sterling and Francine Clark Art Institute, Williamstown MA

Schueler, Dean A, *Dev Dir,* Augustana College, Center for Western Studies, Sioux Falls SD

Schueler, Dean A, *Dev Dir,* Augustana College, Center for Western Studies, Sioux Falls SD

Schueler, Donna, *Asst Dir,* Saint John's College, Elizabeth Myers Mitchell Art Gallery, Annapolis MD

Schuette, Lynn, *Dir,* Sushi-Performance & Visual Art Gallery, San Diego CA

Schuler, Hans C, *Dir,* Schuler School of Fine Arts, Baltimore MD (S)

Schuler, Jane, *Prof,* York College of the City University of New York, Fine and Performing Arts, Jamaica NY (S)

Schulman, William, *Assoc Prof,* University of Wisconsin-Stout, Dept of Art & Design, Menomonie WI (S)

Schulte, Greg, *Asst Prof,* Utah State University, Dept of Art, Logan UT (S)

Schultz, Bernard, *Chmn,* West Virginia University, College of Creative Arts, Morgantown WV (S)

Schultz, Douglas G, *Dir,* The Buffalo Fine Arts Academy, Albright-Knox Art Gallery, Buffalo NY

Schultz, Gary, *Div Dean,* Riverside Community College, Dept of Art & Mass Media, Riverside CA (S)

Schultz, Jeffrey, *Dir,* Wade House & Wesley W Jung Carriage Museum, Historic House & Carriage Museum, Greenbush WI

Schultz, Mike, *Head Librn,* Western Montana College, Lucy Carson Memorial Library, Dillon MT

Schultz, Tom, *Pres,* Arizona Watercolor Association, Phoenix AZ

Schultze, Raymond W, *Prof,* University of Nebraska, Kearney, Dept of Art & Art History, Kearney NE (S)

Schulze, Franz, *Prof Emeritus,* Lake Forest College, Dept of Art, Lake Forest IL (S)

Schumacher, Ann, *Asst Prof,* Berea College, Art Dept, Berea KY (S)

Schumaker, Rita, *Instr,* University of North Carolina at Charlotte, Dept of Visual Arts, Charlotte NC (S)

Schuman, Vincent B, *Pres,* Baldwin Historical Society Museum, Baldwin NY

Schumann, Elka, *Mgr,* Bread & Puppet Theater, Museum, Glover VT

Schumann, Peter, *Artist,* Bread & Puppet Theater, Museum, Glover VT

Schupackitz, Vera, *VPres Annual Exhib,* Sculptors Guild, Inc, New York NY

Schuster, Adeline, *Library Dir,* Harrington Institute of Interior Design, Design Library, Chicago IL

Schuster, David, *Chmn Illustration Dept,* Art Institute of Boston, Boston MA (S)

Schuster, Kenneth L, *Dir,* Bradford Brinton Memorial Museum & Historic Ranch, Big Horn WY

Schuster, Sarah, *Asst Prof,* Oberlin College, Dept of Art, Oberlin OH (S)

Schutte, Richard, *Treas,* Valley Art Center Inc, Clarkston WA

Schutte, Thomas F, *Pres,* Rhode Island School of Design, Providence RI (S)

Schutz, Suzanne, *Pres,* Historical Society of the Town of Greenwich, Inc, Bush-Holley House, Cos Cob CT

Schuweiler-Daab, Suzanne, *Asst Prof,* Converse College, Art Dept, Spartanburg SC (S)

Schuyler, Michael, *Music Librn,* Munson-Williams-Proctor Institute, Art Reference Library, Utica NY

Schuyler, Robert L, *Am Hist Arch Assoc Cur,* University of Pennsylvania, University Museum of Archaeology & Anthropology, Philadelphia PA

Schvetze, Frederick, *Asst Prof,* Bradford College, Creative Arts Division, Bradford MA (S)

Schwab, Alice Ann, *VPres,* Doshi Center for Contemporary Art, Harrisburg PA

Schwab, Lis, *Development & Membership,* Judah L Magnes Museum, Berkeley CA

Schwab, Norman, *Chmn & Prof,* Mount Saint Mary's College, Art Dept, Los Angeles CA (S)

Schwabach, James Bruce, *Instr,* Herkimer County Community College, Social Sciences & Humanities Division, Herkimer NY (S)

Schwager, Michael, *Dir,* Sonoma State University, Art Gallery, Rohnert Park CA

Schwager, Sue, *Assoc Secy,* John Simon Guggenheim Memorial Foundation, New York NY

Schwalenberg, Pat, *Gift Shop Mgr,* Paine Art Center and Arboretum, Oshkosh WI

Schwalm, Terry, *Dir,* Saskatchewan Craft Gallery, Saskatoon SK

Schwanke, Harriet, *Supv Branches,* Miami-Dade Public Library, Miami FL

Schwartwood, Larry, *Art Exhib Dir,* Eastern New Mexico University, Golden Library, Portales NM

Schwartz, Abby S, *Cur of Education,* Cincinnati Institute of Fine Arts, Taft Museum, Cincinnati OH

Schwartz, Constance, *Dir Admin & Chief Cur,* Nassau County Museum of Fine Art, Roslyn NY

Schwartz, Dan, *Dir Educ,* USS Constitution Museum Foundation Inc, Boston National Historical Park, Museum, Boston MA

Schwartz, David, *Head of Film & Video,* American Museum of the Moving Image, Astoria NY

Schwartz, Douglas W, *Dir,* School of American Research, Santa Fe NM

Schwartz, Joan M, *Photography Acquisition,* National Archives of Canada, Documentary Art and Photography, Ottawa ON

Schwartz, Judith, *Dir,* University of Toronto, Justina M Barnicke Gallery, Toronto ON

Schwartz, Judith S, *Dir Undergraduate Studies,* New York University, Dept of Art & Art Professions, New York NY (S)

Schwartz, L C, *Instr,* Western Illinois University, Art Dept, Macomb IL (S)

Schwartz, Marianne S, *Secy,* Detroit Institute of Arts, Founders Society, Detroit MI

Schwartz, Melanie, *Instr,* Southwestern Oregon Community College, Visual Arts Dept, Coos Bay OR (S)

Schwartz, Michael, *Asst Prof,* Augusta College, Dept of Fine Arts, Augusta GA (S)

Schwartz, Richard J, *Co-Dir,* Cornell University, Herbert F Johnson Museum of Art, Ithaca NY

Schwartz, Robert T, *Exec Dir,* Industrial Designers Society of America, Great Falls VA

Schwartzbaum, Paul, *Conservator,* Solomon R Guggenheim Museum, New York NY

Schwarz, Joseph, *Head Dept,* Auburn University at Montgomery, Dept of Fine Arts, Montgomery AL (S)

Schwarzbek, Ellen, *Registrar,* Hickory Museum of Art, Inc, Hickory NC

Schwarzer, Joseph Karl, *Dir,* Higgins Armory Museum, Worcester MA

Schwarzer, Lynn, *Asst Prof,* Colgate University, Dept of Art & Art History, Hamilton NY (S)

Schwebel, Renata Manasse, *VPres Spec Exhib,* Sculptors Guild, Inc, New York NY

Schwein, Florence, *Dir,* University of Texas at El Paso, El Paso TX

Schweitzer, Josh, *Pres,* Los Angeles Center For Photographic Studies, Los Angeles CA

Schweizer, Paul D, *Dir,* Munson-Williams-Proctor Institute, Museum of Art, Utica NY

Schwenger, Frances, *Libr Bd Dir,* Metropolitan Toronto Library Board, Arts Dept, Toronto ON

Schwenger, Kathryn, *Museum Cur,* Chatham Cultural Centre, Thames Art Gallery, Chatham ON

Schwerdtfeger, Toshiko, *Asst Dir,* Saint Cloud State University, Atwood Center Gallery Lounge, Saint Cloud MN

Schwoeffermann, Catherine, *Cur Folklife,* Roberson Museum & Science Center, Binghamton NY

Scillia, Charles, *Chmn,* John Carroll University, Dept of Art History & Humanities, Cleveland OH (S)

Scoates, Chris, *Cur,* Washington University, Gallery of Art, Saint Louis MO

Scoggins, Lillian, *Asst Librn,* Lutheran Theological Seminary, Krauth Memorial Library, Philadelphia PA

Scopinich, June, *Dean Humanities,* Southwestern College, Art Gallery, Chula Vista CA

Scotello, Frank, *Asst Prof,* Marian College, Art Dept, Fond Du Lac WI (S)

Scott, A M, *Instr,* Humboldt State University, College of Arts & Humanities, Arcata CA (S)

Scott, Bill, *Instr,* Main Line Center for the Arts, Haverford PA (S)

Scott, Charles, *Chmn Ceramics,* University of Manitoba, School of Art, Winnipeg MB (S)

Scott, Charles C, *Prof,* Glenville State College, Dept of Fine Arts, Glenville WV (S)

Scott, Charles F, *Cur Furniture & Decorative Arts,* University of Connecticut, William Benton Museum of Art - Connecticut's State Art Museum, Storrs CT

Scott, Deborah R Emont, *Sanders Sosland Cur 20th Century Art,* Nelson-Atkins Museum of Art, Kansas City MO

Scott, Eric, *Comptroller,* National Art Museum of Sport, Indianapolis IN

Scott, Gerry, *Cur Western Antiquities,* San Antonio Museum Association, Inc, San Antonio Museum of Art, San Antonio TX

Scott, James, *Instructor,* The Art Institutes International, The Art Institute of Seattle, Seattle WA (S)

Scott, Jim, *Exhib Designer,* Ohio State University, Wexner Center for the Arts, Columbus OH

Scott, John, *Assoc Prof,* University of Florida, Dept of Art, Gainesville FL (S)

Scott, John T, *Prof,* Xavier University of Louisiana, Dept of Fine Arts, New Orleans LA (S)

Scott, Kevin, *Dir Design & Production,* Colorado Historical Society, Museum, Denver CO

Scott, Larry, *Dir,* Western Kentucky University, Kentucky Museum, Bowling Green KY

Scott, Laurel, *Assoc Prof,* University of Wisconsin-Superior, Programs in the Visual Arts, Superior WI (S)

Scott, Mark, *VPres,* International Museum of Cartoon Art, Montreal PQ

Scott, Robert Montgomery, *Pres,* Philadelphia Museum of Art, Philadelphia PA

Scott, Sandra, *Head,* Mississippi Valley State University, Fine Arts Dept, Itta Bena MS (S)

Scott, Sharon, *Cataloger,* Toledo Museum of Art, Library, Toledo OH

Scott-Stewart, Diane, *Exec Dir,* Nova Scotia Association of Architects, Halifax NS

Scouten, Rex W, *Cur,* White House, Washington DC

Scrimager, Brenda, *Instr,* The Arkansas Arts Center, Museum School, Little Rock AR (S)

Scroggins, Barbara, *Slide Librn,* University of New Hampshire, Dept of the Arts Slide Library, Durham NH

Scucchi, Robie, *Assoc Prof,* Mississippi State University, Art Dept, Mississippi State MS (S)

Scully, S, *Chmn of Board,* University of Victoria, Maltwood Art Museum and Gallery, Victoria BC

Seabold, Tom, *Dir,* Keokuk Art Center, Keokuk IA

Seabury, Linda, *Public Relations & Membership Coordr,* Manchester Institute of Arts and Sciences Gallery, Manchester NH

Seal, Dale, *Instr,* The Arkansas Arts Center, Museum School, Little Rock AR (S)

Seals, Joan, *Spec Events Coordr,* Port of History Museum, Philadelphia PA

Seaman, Anne T, *Librn,* Honolulu Academy of Arts, Robert Allerton Library, Honolulu HI

Seamans, Warren A, *Dir,* Massachusetts Institute of Technology, MIT Museum, Cambridge MA

Seames, Stephen T, *Research & Reference Asst,* Maine Historical Society, Library, Portland ME

Seamonds, Maureen, *Assoc Prof,* Iowa Central Community College, Dept of Art, Fort Dodge IA (S)

Searing, Helen, *Prof,* Smith College, Art Dept, Northampton MA (S)

Searles, Rose, *Head Circulation Dept,* Springfield Free Public Library, Donald B Palmer Museum, Springfield NJ

Searls-McConnel, Maryse, *Assoc Prof,* University of New Hampshire, Dept of the Arts, Durham NH (S)

Sears, Elizabeth, *Asst Prof,* University of Michigan, Ann Arbor, Dept of History of Art, Ann Arbor MI (S)

Sears, L Dennis, *Chmn,* Huntingdon College, Dept of Art, Montgomery AL (S)

Seaton, Elizabeth, *Children's Instr,* Montclair Art Museum, Art School, Montclair NJ (S)

Sebastian, Magdalyn, *Dir Museum Colls,* Missouri Historical Society, Library & Collections Center, Saint Louis MO

Seckelson, Linda, *Reader Servs Librn,* The Metropolitan Museum of Art, Thomas J Watson Library, New York NY

Seckinger, Linda, *Assoc Prof,* Mississippi State University, Art Dept, Mississippi State MS (S)

Secrest, Donna, *Office Mgr,* Ponca City Art Association, Ponca City OK

Sedberry, Connie, *Dir,* Penland School of Crafts, Penland NC (S)

Sedler, Barbara, *Instr,* Loras College, Dept of Art, Dubuque IA (S)

Sedlock, Timothy, *Preparator,* Williams College, Museum of Art, Williamstown MA

Seeber, Frances M, *Chief Archivist,* National Archives & Records Administration, Library, Hyde Park NY

Seed, John, *Instr,* Mount San Jacinto College, Art Dept, San Jacinto CA (S)

Seeley, J, *Prof,* Wesleyan University, Art Dept, Middletown CT (S)

Seely, Ella, *Head Art & Music Dept,* Multnomah County Library, Henry Failing Art and Music Dept, Portland OR

Seem, Olga, *Gallery Dir,* Mount Saint Mary's College, Jose Drudis-Biada Art Gallery, Los Angeles CA

Seeman, Helene Zucker, *Dir Art Program,* Prudential Insurance Collection, Newark NJ

Seeman, Rebecca, *Instr,* Art Academy of Cincinnati, Cincinnati OH (S)

Seeney, Lynn, *Exec Dir,* BRONX RIVER ART CENTER, Gallery, Bronx NY

Sefcik, James F, *Dir,* Louisiana Department of Culture, Recreation and Tourism, Louisiana Historical Center Library, New Orleans LA

Segal, Beatrice, *Treas,* Second Street Gallery, Charlottesville VA

Segall, Andrea, *Librn,* Berkeley Public Library, Berkeley CA

Segalman, Richard, *Instr,* Woodstock School of Art, Inc, Woodstock NY (S)

Segger, Martin, *Dir & Cur,* University of Victoria, Maltwood Art Museum and Gallery, Victoria BC

Seid, Steve, *Asst Cur Video,* University of California, University Art Museum, Berkeley CA

Seidelman, James E, *Interim Dir,* Headley-Whitney Museum, Lexington KY

Seidelman, James E, *Dir,* Headley-Whitney Museum, Library, Lexington KY

Seiden, Don, *Prof,* School of the Art Institute of Chicago, Chicago IL (S)

Seif, Denise, *Gallery Dir,* Parkland College, Art Gallery, Champaign IL

Seifert, Jan E, *Fine Arts Librn,* University of Oklahoma, Fine Arts Library, Norman OK

Seiger, William, *Instr,* DePaul University, Dept of Art, Chicago IL (S)

Seiler, Jessica, *Asst Librn,* Atlanta College of Art Library, Atlanta GA

Seiler, Mike, *Instr,* Muskingum College, Art Department, New Concord OH (S)

Seivert, Lisa A, *Research Librn,* Buffalo Museum of Science, Research Library, Buffalo NY

Seiz, Janet, *Faculty,* Saint Ambrose University, Art Dept, Davenport IA (S)

Seiz, John, *Instr,* Springfield College in Illinois, Dept of Art, Springfield IL (S)

Selby, Pat, *Instr,* Cuyahoga Valley Art Center, Cuyahoga Falls OH (S)

Selby, Roger, *Exec Dir,* Boca Raton Museum of Art, Boca Raton FL

Selchak, John, *Pres,* National Watercolor Society, Cerritos CA

Seley, Beverly, *Assoc Prof,* Grand Valley State University, Art & Design Dept, Allendale MI (S)

Self, Stephen, *Chmn,* Mount Vernon Nazarene College, Art Dept, Mount Vernon OH (S)

Seligman, Thomas K, *Dir,* Stanford University, Art Gallery, Stanford CA

Seligsohn, Valerie, *Assoc Prof,* Philadelphia Community College, Dept of Art, Philadelphia PA (S)

Seline, Janice, *Acting Asst Cur Contemporary Art,* National Gallery of Canada, Ottawa ON

Selip, Bonnie, *Prof,* Lake Erie College-Garfield Senior College, Fine Arts Dept, Painesville OH (S)

Sellars, Beth, *Cur Art,* Eastern Washington State Historical Society, Cheney Cowles Museum, Spokane WA

Sellars, Bette J, *Instr,* Graceland College, Fine Arts Dept, Lamoni IA (S)

Sellars, Judith, *Librn,* Museum of New Mexico, Museum of International Folk Art, Santa Fe NM

Sellars, Judith, *Librn,* Museum of New Mexico, Library, Santa Fe NM

Selle, Kay, *Fashion Design Coordr,* University of North Texas, School of Visual Arts, Denton TX (S)

Selle, Thomas, *Asst Prof,* Carroll College, Art Dept, Waukesha WI (S)

Sellers, Kate, *Dir of Development,* Walters Art Gallery, Baltimore MD

Sellett, Barbara, *Dir,* Rockford Art Museum, Rockford IL

Selter, Dan S, *Prof,* Transylvania University, Studio Arts Dept, Lexington KY (S)

Selvar, Jane Cumming, *Dir,* Bronxville Public Library, Bronxville NY

Selz, Paul, *Chmn Museum Committee,* Fairfield Public Library, Fairfield Art Association, Fairfield IA

Semergieff, Chris, *Instr,* Chautauqua Institution, School of Art, Chautauqua NY (S)

Semiven, Douglas, *Instr,* Madonna College, Art Dept, Livonia MI (S)

Semmel, Bwetty, *Admin Asst,* Plains Indians & Pioneers Historical Foundation, Museum & Art Center, Woodward OK

Semmel, Joan, *Prof,* Rutgers, the State University of New Jersey, Mason Gross School of the Arts, New Brunswick NJ (S)

Semmens, Beverly, *Treas,* Surface Design Association, Inc, Oakland CA

Semowich, Charles, *Pres,* Print Club of Albany, Museum, Albany NY

Senie, Harriette, *Deputy Chair,* City College of New York, Art Dept, New York NY (S)

Senior, Diana, *Pres,* The Art Institute of Chicago, Textile Society, Chicago IL

Senior, William J, *Dir,* Yard School of Art, Montclair NJ (S)

Senn, Barbara, *Admin Asst,* Galleries of the Claremont Colleges, Claremont CA

Senn, Carol Johnson, *Dir,* Ephraim McDowell-Cambus-Kenneth Foundation, McDowell House & Apothecary Shop, Danville KY

Senn, Greg, *Asst Prof,* Eastern New Mexico University, Dept of Art, Portales NM (S)

Sennett, Arthur, *Prof,* State University of New York College at Potsdam, Dept of Fine Arts, Potsdam NY (S)

Senton, Luis, *Pres,* Casa Amesti, Monterey CA

Serafin, Pricilla, *Graphic Design,* Monserrat College of Art, Beverly MA (S)

Serebrennikov, Nina, *Asst Prof,* Davidson College, Art Dept, Davidson NC (S)

Seremet, Peter M, *Corporate VPres,* Heublein, Inc, Farmington CT

Serenco, Henry, *Assoc Prof,* University of Nebraska at Omaha, Dept of Art, Omaha NE (S)

Serenyi, Peter, *Chmn,* Northeastern University, Dept of Art & Architecture, Boston MA (S)

Serepca, Mark, *Dir Communications,* Special Libraries Association, Museum, Arts and Humanities Division, Washington DC

Serfaty, Gail F, *Assoc Cur,* US Department of State, Diplomatic Reception Rooms, Washington DC

Sergio, Jeaniene, *Treas,* Arizona Watercolor Association, Phoenix AZ

Sergovic, John, *VPres Finance,* Philadelphia Museum of Art, Philadelphia PA

Serlin-Cobb, Fran, *Dir Marketing & Communications,* Milwaukee Art Museum, Milwaukee WI

Serroes, Richard, *Instr,* Modesto Junior College, Arts Humanities and Speech Division, Modesto CA (S)

Service, Donna, *Lectr,* Centenary College of Louisiana, Dept of Art, Shreveport LA (S)

Sestac, Barbara, *Assoc Prof,* Portland State University, Dept of Art, Portland OR (S)

Sesteak, Barbara, *Dept Head,* Portland State University, Dept of Art, Portland OR (S)

Setford, David, *Cur,* Norton Gallery and School of Art, West Palm Beach FL

Setford, David F, *Cur,* Norton Gallery and School of Art, Library, West Palm Beach FL

Settle, Suzanne, *Instr,* Delta College, Art Dept, University Center MI (S)

Settle-Cooney, Mary, *Exec Dir,* Tennessee Valley Art Association and Center, Tuscumbia AL

Setzer, Barbara, *Asst Dir,* Waterworks Visual Arts Center, Salisbury NC

Sevelius, Helen, *Academic Dean Fine Arts,* Alberta College of Art, Calgary AB (S)

Sever, Ziya, *Instr,* Western Nebraska Community College, Division of Language and Arts, Scottsbluff NE (S)

Severance, Betsy, *Registrar,* Newport Harbor Art Museum, Newport Beach CA

Severtson, Johan, *Chmn Graphic Design,* Corcoran School of Art, Washington DC (S)

Sewell, Darrel, *McNeil Cur American Art,* Philadelphia Museum of Art, Philadelphia PA

Sexton, Ginny, *Mgr Public Relations,* The Bradford Museum of Collector's Plates, Niles IL

Seyller, Anna, *Business Mgr,* University of Vermont, Robert Hull Fleming Museum, Burlington VT

Seymour, Gayle, *Assoc Prof,* University of Central Arkansas, Art Dept, Conway AR (S)

Sfirri, Mark, *Instr,* Bucks County Community College, Fine Arts Dept, Newtown PA (S)

Sfollite, Shelia, *Chmn,* George Mason University, Dept of Art & Art History, Fairfax VA (S)

Sha, Marjorie, *Head of Reference,* New Rochelle Public Library, Art Section, New Rochelle NY

Shackelford, George, *Cur of European Art,* Museum of Fine Arts, Houston, Houston TX

Shackelford, Margie, *Dir of Development,* Newport Harbor Art Museum, Newport Beach CA

Shacklette, Nancy, *Head Childrens Dept,* Springfield Free Public Library, Donald B Palmer Museum, Springfield NJ

Shadle, Selina, *Admin Asst,* African American Historical and Cultural Society, San Francisco CA

Shady, Ronald, *Asst Prof,* University of North Alabama, Dept of Art, Florence AL (S)

Shaeffer, Dana, *Dept Head,* Grand View College, Art Dept, Des Moines IA (S)

Shafer, Laura, *Admin Asst,* Children's Art Foundation, Santa Cruz CA

Shaffer, Barbara Dadd, *Adminr,* Sitka Historical Society, Isabel Miller Museum, Sitka AK

Shaffer, Fern, *Pres Emeritus,* Artemisia Gallery, Chicago IL

Shaffer, Harrison, *Pres,* Gilpin County Arts Association, Central City CO

Shaffer, Marcy, *Educ Dir,* Rensselaer County Historical Society, Hart-Cluett Mansion, 1827, Troy NY

Shaffer, Mary, *Art Head,* Northwest Nazarene College, Art Dept, Nampa ID (S)

Shaffer, Sarah Saville, *Asst Dir,* National Trust for Historic Preservation, Decatur House, Washington DC

Shaffstall, James W, *Chmn Dept,* Hanover College, Dept of Art, Hanover IN (S)

Shahriar, Shahnaz, *Prof,* Marshall University, Dept of Art, Huntington WV (S)

Shain, Charles, *Dir,* Arts Council of Greater Kingsport, Kingsport TN

Shakespeare, Valerie, *Pres,* Actual Art Foundation, New York NY

Shakir, Adib, *Pres,* Tougaloo College, Art Collection, Tougaloo MS

Shalit, Willa, *Artist-in-Res,* College of Santa Fe, Visual Arts Dept, Santa Fe NM (S)

Shamblin, Barbara, *Chmn,* Salve Regina College, Art Dept, Newport RI (S)

Shamon, Kate, *Special Events Coordr,* Institute of Contemporary Art, Boston MA

Shamy, Pat, *Treas,* New Jersey Water-Color Society, Red Bank NJ

Shaner, Carol, *Exhibits Librn,* Sarah Lawrence College Library, Esther Raushenbush Library, Bronxville NY

Shanley, Kevin, *Pres & Chmn Bd of Trustees,* Newark Museum Association, The Newark Museum, Newark NJ

Shannahan, John W, *Dir,* Connecticut Historical Commission, Sloane-Stanley Museum, Kent CT

Shannon, Dolly, *Archives,* Luna County Historical Society, Inc, Deming Luna Mimbres Museum, Deming NM

Shannon, George Ward, *Dir,* Louisiana State Exhibit Museum, Shreveport LA

Shannon, Joseph, *Prof,* Trenton State College, Art Dept, Trenton NJ (S)

Shannon, Mary O, *Exec Secy,* Boston Art Commission of the City of Boston, Boston MA

Shapero, Janet, *Asst Prof,* Utah State University, Dept of Art, Logan UT (S)

Shapiro, Babe, *Faculty,* Maryland Institute, Mount Royal School of Art, Baltimore MD (S)

Shapiro, Denise, *Dir,* Las Vegas-Clark County Library District, Flamingo Gallery, Las Vegas NV

Shapiro, Michael A, *Dir,* Los Angeles County Museum of Art, Los Angeles CA

Shapiro, Samuel, *Pres,* Sarasota Visual Art Center, Sarasota FL

Sharer, Robert, *Am Section Cur,* University of Pennsylvania, University Museum of Archaeology & Anthropology, Philadelphia PA

Sharma, Sue, *Division Chief,* Brooklyn Public Library, Art and Music Division, Brooklyn NY

Sharon, Dan, *Reference Librn,* Spertus Museum, Asher Library, Chicago IL

Sharp, Elbert L, *Chief Preparator,* Memphis Brooks Museum of Art, Memphis TN

Sharp, Ellen, *Graphic Arts,* Detroit Institute of Arts, Detroit MI

Sharp, Lewis, *Dir,* Denver Art Museum, Denver CO

Sharp, Pamela, *Art Educ Coordr,* San Jose State University, School of Art & Design, San Jose CA (S)

Sharp, Paula, *Dir Development,* Newport Art Museum, Newport RI

Sharpe, Yolanda, *Instr,* State University of New York College at Oneonta, Dept of Art, Oneonta NY (S)

Sharshal, Stan, *Lectr,* Emory University, Art History Dept, Atlanta GA (S)

Shartin, Anastasia, *Gallery Mgr,* Capp Street Project, San Francisco CA

Shaskan, I, *Instr,* Sacramento City College, Art Dept, Sacramento CA (S)

Shatto, Gloria, *Pres,* Berry College, Moon Gallery, Mount Berry GA

Shatzman, Merrill, *Artist in Residence,* Duke University, Dept of Art and Art History, Durham NC (S)

Shaughnessy, Robert, *Prof,* Southampton Campus of Long Island University, Fine Arts Division, Southampton NY (S)

Shaw, Catherine Elliot, *Cur,* University of Western Ontario, McIntosh Art Gallery, London ON

Shaw, Courtney, *Head Art Library,* University of Maryland, College Park, Art Library, College Park MD

Shaw, Gean, *Pres,* Muttart Art Gallery, Calgary AB

Shaw, H Allen, *Instructor,* Oklahoma State University, Graphic Arts Dept, Okmulgee OK (S)

Shaw, J W, *Chmn,* University of Toronto, Dept of Fine Art, Toronto ON (S)

Shaw, Karen, *Cur,* Islip Art Museum, East Islip NY

Shaw, Louise, *Exec Dir,* Nexus Contemporary Art Center, Atlanta GA

Shaw, Mary Beth, *Cur,* Mendocino County Museum, Willits CA

Shaw, Meg, *Librn,* University of Kentucky, Edward Warder Rannells Art Library, Lexington KY

Shaw, Richard, *Prof,* University of California, Berkeley, College of Letters & Sciences-Art Dept, Berkeley CA (S)

Shaw, Rodney, *Dir,* Rochester Institute of Technology, College of Imaging Arts & Sciences, Rochester NY (S)

Shaw, Wayne, *Dept Head,* Belleville Area College, Art Dept, Belleville IL (S)

Shay, Jim, *Cur,* Longfellow National Historic Site, Cambridge MA

Shea, Robert, *Actg Chmn,* Ohio State University, Dept of Art, Columbus OH (S)

Sheaks, Barclay, *Dir,* Virginia Wesleyan College, Art Dept of the Humanities Division, Norfolk VA (S)

Shealy, Ernest, *House Adminr,* Charleston Museum, Aiken-Rhett House, Charleston SC

Shear, T Leslie, *Prof,* Princeton University, Dept of Art and Archaeology, Princeton NJ (S)

Sheardy, Robert, *Chmn Art History & Liberal Arts,* Kendall College of Art & Design, Grand Rapids MI (S)

Sheardy, Robert, *Chmn Art History & Liberal Arts,* Kendall College of Art & Design, Frank & Lyn Van Steenberg Library, Grand Rapids MI

Shearer, Linda, *Dir,* Williams College, Museum of Art, Williamstown MA

Shearman, John, *Chmn Dept,* Harvard University, Dept of Fine Arts, Sackler Museum, Cambridge MA (S)

Shechter, Jack, *Dir,* University of Judaism, Dept of Continuing Education, Los Angeles CA (S)

Sheckler, Allyson, *Asst Prof,* Florida Southern College, Art Dept, Lakeland FL (S)

Shedd, Peggy, *Museum Shop Mgr,* Flint Institute of Arts, Flint MI

Sheedy, Madelon, *Johnstown Art Extension Coordr,* Southern Alleghenies Museum of Art, Loretto PA

Sheedy, Madelon, *Cur,* Southern Alleghenies Museum of Art, Johnstown Art Museum, Loretto PA

Sheehan, Linda, *Secy,* University of Louisville, Allen R Hite Art Institute Gallery, Louisville KY

Sheehan, Lori, *Rentals Coordr,* Sangre de Cristo Arts & Conference Center, Pueblo CO

Sheehan, Michael T, *Dir,* Woodrow Wilson House, Washington DC

Sheehy, Carolyn A, *Dir,* North Central College, Oesterle Library, Naperville IL

Sheehy, Colleen, *Asst Dir for Touring,* University of Minnesota, University Art Museum, Minneapolis MN

Sheets, Allen, *Assoc Prof,* Moorhead State University, Dept of Art, Moorhead MN (S)

Sheff, Donald, *Dir,* New York Institute of Photography, New York NY (S)

Shekore, Mark, *Chmn,* Northern State University, Art Dept, Aberdeen SD (S)

Sheldon, James L, *Cur Photography,* Phillips Academy, Addison Gallery of American Art, Andover MA

Sheldon, Janine, *Development Dir,* University of California, University Art Museum, Berkeley CA

Sheley, David, *Dir & Cur,* Turner House Museum, Hattiesburg MS

Shelkrot, Elliot, *Library Pres & Dir,* Free Library of Philadelphia, Art Dept, Philadelphia PA

Shelnutt, Gregory, *Asst Prof,* University of Mississippi, Dept of Art, University MS (S)

Shelton, Carol, *Gallery Asst,* Saint Paul's School, Art Center in Hargate, Concord NH

Shelton, Kay, *Head Librn,* Alaska State Library, Historical Library Section, Juneau AK

Shelton, L T, *Cur Coll,* Department of Natural Resources of Missouri, Missouri State Museum, Jefferson City MO

Shepard, Charles, *Asst Prof,* University of Maine, Art Dept, Orono ME (S)

Shepard, Charles A, *Dir,* University of Maine, Museum of Art, Orono ME

Shepard, Fred, *Preparator,* Santa Clara University, de Saisset Museum, Santa Clara CA

Shepard, Fred, *Prof,* Murray State University, Art Dept, Murray KY (S)

Shepard, Piper, *Instr,* Chautauqua Institution, School of Art, Chautauqua NY (S)

Shepard, Sandy, *Cur Educ,* Tyler Museum of Art, Tyler TX

Shepard, Sandy, *Cur Educ,* Tyler Museum of Art, Reference Library, Tyler TX

Shepherd, Elizabeth, *Cur Exhibit,* University of California, Los Angeles, Wight Art Gallery, Los Angeles CA

Shepherd, Gyde, *Asst Dir Public Prog,* National Gallery of Canada, Ottawa ON

Shepherd, Lori, *Art Consultant,* Mobil Corporation, Art Collection, Fairfax VA

Shepherd, Murray, *University Librn,* University of Waterloo, Dana Porter Library, Waterloo ON

Shepp, James G, *Exec Dir,* Maitland Art Center, Maitland FL

Shepp, James G, *Dir,* Maitland Art Center, Library, Maitland FL

Sheppard, Luvon, *Assoc Prof,* Rochester Institute of Technology, School of Art and Design, Rochester NY (S)

Sheridan, Clare, *Librn,* Museum of American Textile History, Library, North Andover MA

Sheridan, Matt, *Contact,* Utah Department of Natural Resources, Division of Parks & Recreation, Territorial Statehouse, Fillmore UT

Sheridan, Patricia, *Treas,* Rhode Island Watercolor Society, Pawtucket RI

Sheriff, Mary, *Assoc Prof,* University of North Carolina at Chapel Hill, Art Dept, Chapel Hill NC (S)

Sherin, Pamela, *Dir Cultural Relations,* Bristol-Myers Squibb Co, Princeton NJ

Sherk, Jeffrey L, *Librn,* Maritz, Inc, Library, Fenton MO

Sherk, Scott, *Assoc Prof,* Muhlenberg College, Dept of Art, Allentown PA (S)

Sherman, Barbara, *Secy,* American Fine Arts Society, New York NY

Sherman, Curt, *Asst Chmn & Prof,* Winthrop College, Dept of Art & Design, Rock Hill SC (S)

Sherman, Joseph, *Ed,* Confederation Centre Art Gallery and Museum, Charlottetown PE

Sherman, Michael, *Dir,* Vermont Historical Society, Museum, Montpelier VT

Sherman, Michael, *Dir,* Vermont Historical Society, Library, Montpelier VT

Sherman, Nancy, *Real Estate Adminr,* Pittsburgh National Bank, Art Collection, Pittsburgh PA

Sherman, Paul T, *Admin Services Librn,* New York City Technical College, Namm Hall Library and Learning Resource Center, Brooklyn NY

Sherman, Todd, *Asst Prof,* University of Alaska, Dept of Art, Fairbanks AK (S)

Sherman, Tom, *Dir,* Syracuse University, College of Visual and Performing Arts, Syracuse NY (S)

Sherrill, Martine, *Cur Slides & Prints,* Wake Forest University, A Lewis Aycock Art Slide Library & Print Collection, Winston Salem NC

Sherwin, Michael, *Pres,* Cleveland Museum of Art, Cleveland OH

Sherwood, Bruce T, *Dir,* Victoria Society of Maine, Victoria Mansion - Morse Libby House, Portland ME

Sherwood, Corinne, *Co-Chmn,* Polk Museum of Art, Penfield Library, Lakeland FL

Sherwood, Katherine, *Prof,* University of California, Berkeley, College of Letters & Sciences-Art Dept, Berkeley CA (S)

Sherwood, Leland, *Prof,* Peru State College, Art Dept, Peru NE (S)

Shestack, Alan, *Dir,* Museum of Fine Arts, Boston MA

Shetabi, Mark, *Asst Gallery Dir,* Western Washington University, Viking Union Gallery, Bellingham WA

Shevburn, Earl, *Community Arts Dir,* City of Los Angeles, Cultural Affairs Dept, Los Angeles CA

Shiba, Hiromi, *Registrar,* Museo de Arte de Ponce, Ponce Art Museum, Ponce PR

Shick, Andrew, *Cur,* Passaic County Historical Society, Paterson NJ

Shickman, Allan, *Assoc Prof,* University of Northern Iowa, Dept of Art, Cedar Falls IA (S)

Shieh, Suewhei T, *Cur,* Towson State University, Asian Arts Center, Towson MD

Shield, Jan, *Assoc Prof,* Pacific University in Oregon, Arts Division, Forest Grove OR (S)

Shields, David, *Asst Prof,* Southwest Texas State University, Dept of Art, San Marcos TX (S)

Shields, D H, *Asst Librn,* University of Michigan, Art & Architecture Library & Computer Lab, Ann Arbor MI

Shields, Paul M, *Asst Prof,* York College, Art Dept, York NE (S)

Shields, Tom, *Asst Prof,* Augustana College, Art Dept, Sioux Falls SD (S)

Shields, William, *Chief Admin Officer,* Royal Architectural Institute of Canada, Ottawa ON

Shiffman, Jacqueline, *Dir of Development,* Franklin Furnace Archive, Inc, New York NY

Shifman, Barry, *Cur Decorative Arts,* Indianapolis Museum of Art, Indianapolis IN

Shifrin, Susan, *Cur,* Philadelphia College of Textiles and Science, Paley Design Center, Philadelphia PA

Shigaki, Betty Jean, *Dir,* Rochester Art Center, Rochester MN

Shih, Chia-Chun, *Librn,* Kimbell Art Museum, Fort Worth TX

Shih, Chia-Chun, *Librn,* Kimbell Art Museum, Library, Fort Worth TX

Shikowitz, Joyce, *Assoc Prof,* Rochester Institute of Technology, School of Art and Design, Rochester NY (S)

Shimizu, Yoshiaki, *Prof,* Princeton University, Dept of Art and Archaeology, Princeton NJ (S)

Shine, Mary Beth, *Asst to Dir & Librn,* New York University, Grey Art Gallery and Study Center, New York NY

Shiner, Roger A, *Secy-Treas,* American Society for Aesthetics, Edmonton AB

Shipley, Anne, *Chmn,* Sierra Nevada College, Art Dept, Incline Village NV (S)

Shipley, Carole, *Reference Librn,* Library Association of La Jolla, Athenaeum Music and Arts Library, La Jolla CA

Shipley, Roger, *Co-Dir,* Lycoming College Gallery, Williamsport PA

Shipley, Roger Douglas, *Prof,* Lycoming College, Art Dept, Williamsport PA (S)

Shipley, Walter B, *Instr,* Okaloosa-Walton Junior College, Dept of Fine and Performing Arts, Niceville FL (S)

Shippee Lambert, Lisa, *Head Special Coll,* Rosenberg Library, Galveston TX

Shippen, Gerald, *Instr,* Central Wyoming College, Art Center, Riverton WY (S)

Shireman, Candace, *Cur,* Historical Society of Washington DC, Christian Heurich Mansion, Washington DC

Shirley, Karen, *Prof,* Antioch College, Visual Arts Institute, Yellow Springs OH (S)

Shirley, Margaret, *Instr,* Marylhurst College, Art Dept, Marylhurst OR (S)

Shiroki, Kathy, *Coordr,* Nicolaysen Art Museum and Discovery Center, Childrens Discovery Center, Casper WY

Shiroki, Kathy, *Discovery Center Coordr,* Nicolaysen Art Museum and Discovery Center, Museum, Casper WY

Shives, Christine, *Admin Asst,* Washington County Museum of Fine Arts, Hagerstown MD

Shives, Rebecca, *Adult Servs,* Martin Memorial Library, York PA

Shmiliar, M, *Pres,* Ukrainian Canadian Archives & Museum of Alberta, Edmonton AB

Shockley, Richard, *Museum Technician,* City of Lethbridge, Sir Alexander Galt Museum, Lethbridge AB

Shoemake, Gayla, *Asst Dean,* North Hennepin Community College, Art Dept, Minneapolis MN (S)

Shoemaker, Ed, *Library Resources,* Oklahoma Historical Society, State Museum of History, Oklahoma City OK

Shoemaker, Edward C, *Dir Library Resources Div,* Oklahoma Historical Society, Library Resources Division, Oklahoma City OK

Shoemaker, George, *Chmn Art Dept,* Edinboro University of Pennsylvania, Art Dept, Edinboro PA (S)

Shoemaker, Innis, *Sr Cur Prints, Drawings & Photographs,* Philadelphia Museum of Art, Philadelphia PA

Shoger, Jan, *Chmn,* Saint Olaf College, Art Dept, Northfield MN (S)

Shoger, Jan, *Assoc Prof,* Saint Olaf College, Art Dept, Northfield MN (S)

Shogren, Samuel W, *Cur,* Penobscot Marine Museum, Searsport ME

Shook, Larry, *Head Dept,* Victoria College, Victoria TX (S)

Shook, Melissa, *Assoc Prof,* University of Massachusetts at Boston, Art Dept, Boston MA (S)

Shoptaw, Alisa, *Museum Shop Mgr,* The Dixon Gallery & Gardens, Memphis TN

Shore, Francine, *Instr,* Main Line Center for the Arts, Haverford PA (S)

Shore, Susan, *Tour Coordr,* Spertus Museum, Chicago IL

Shoreman, Mike, *Assoc Dir Adminr & Finance,* Royal Ontario Museum, Toronto ON

Shores, Ken, *Prof,* Lewis & Clark College, Dept of Art, Portland OR (S)

Shorr, Ken, *Assoc Prof Photography,* University of Arizona, Dept of Art, Tucson AZ (S)

Short, Bradley H, *Creative Arts Librn,* Brandeis University, Leonard L Farber Library, Waltham MA

Short, Frank, *Chmn,* Montgomery County Community College, Art Dept, Blue Bell PA (S)

Short, Rebekah, *Asst Prof,* Goshen College, Art Dept, Goshen IN (S)

Short, Robert, *Instr,* Green River Community College, Art Dept, Auburn WA (S)

Short, William M, *Cur,* Rhodes College, Jessie L Clough Art Memorial for Teaching, Memphis TN

Shortt, A J (Fred), *Cur,* National Museum of Science & Technology Corporation, National Aviation Museum, Ottawa ON

Shoulders, Patrick, *Pres Board Dir,* Evansville Museum of Arts and Science, Evansville IN

Shoulet, Susan, *Exec Dir,* College of New Rochelle, Castle Gallery, New Rochelle NY

Showman, Richard K, *Ed, Nathanael Green Papers,* Rhode Island Historical Society, Providence RI

Shriver, Karen, *Instr,* West Virginia State College, Art Dept, Institute WV (S)

Shrum, L Vance, *Asst to Dir,* Cummer Gallery of Art, DeEtte Holden Cummer Museum Foundation, Jacksonville FL

Shtern, Adele, *Assoc Prof,* University of Bridgeport, Art Dept, Bridgeport CT (S)

Shubert, Joseph, *State Librn-Assoc Commissioner for Libraries,* New York State Library, Manuscripts and Special Collections, Albany NY

Shuck, Patrick, *Instructor,* Saint Louis Community College at Meramec, Art Dept, Saint Louis MO (S)

Shuckerow, Tim, *Asst Prof,* Case Western Reserve University, Dept of Art History & Art, Cleveland OH (S)

Shuebrook, Ronald L, *Chmn,* University of Guelph, Fine Art Dept, Guelph ON (S)

Shugart, Katie, *Vol Coordr,* Wake Forest University, Museum of Anthropology, Winston Salem NC

Shultes, Stephanie, *Cur,* Iroquois Indian Museum, Howes Cave NY

Shultz, Jay, *Assoc Prof,* Palomar Community College, Art Dept, San Marcos CA (S)

Shuman, Geraldine S, *Museum Coordr,* Hastings Museum, Hastings NE

Shunk, Hal, *Asst Prof,* Wilmington College, Art Dept, Wilmington OH (S)

Shurkus, Marie, *Communications Coordr,* Randolph Street Gallery, Chicago IL

Shurtleff, Carol B, *Staff Coordr,* Maitland Art Center, Maitland FL

Shurtleff, Carol B, *Educ Coordr,* Maitland Art Center, Library, Maitland FL

Shust, Maria, *Dir,* The Ukrainian Museum, New York NY

Shust, Maria, *Dir,* The Ukrainian Museum, Library, New York NY

Shutt, Susan, *Instr,* Pepperdine University, Seaver College, Dept of Art, Malibu CA (S)

Shuttleworth, Roseanne, *VPres,* Allegany County Historical Society, History House, Cumberland MD

Sias, James H, *Prof,* Rochester Institute of Technology, School of Art and Design, Rochester NY (S)

Sibley, William A, *VPres,* University of Alabama at Birmingham, Visual Arts Gallery, Birmingham AL

Sichel, Kim, *Dir,* Boston University, Art Gallery, Boston MA

Sicola, Kimberly, *Coll Mgr,* County of Henrico, Meadow Farm Museum, Glen Allen VA

Siddons, Vera Jo, *Prof,* University of Northern Iowa, Dept of Art, Cedar Falls IA (S)

Sider, Sandra, *Cur Manuscripts & Rare Bks,* Hispanic Society of America, Library, New York NY

Sider, Sandra, *Instr,* Sarah Lawrence College, Dept of Art History, Bronxville NY (S)

Sides, Wayne, *Asst Prof,* University of North Alabama, Dept of Art, Florence AL (S)

Sido, Lee T, *Assoc Prof,* University of Nevada, Las Vegas, Dept of Art, Las Vegas NV (S)

Sieber, Roy, *Assoc Dir,* National Museum of African Art, Washington DC

Sieber, Roy, *Prof,* Indiana University, Bloomington, Henry Radford Hope School of Fine Arts, Bloomington IN (S)

Sieg, Robert, *Chmn,* East Central University, Art Dept, Ada OK (S)

Siegal, Matthew, *Exhib Mgr & Registrar,* Institute of Contemporary Art, Boston MA

Siegel, Cheryl A, *Librn,* Vancouver Art Gallery, Library, Vancouver BC

Siegel, Dianne, *VPres & Mgr,* First Interstate Bank, Los Angeles CA

Siegel, Judith, *Dir Educ,* The Jewish Museum, New York NY

Siegel, Peter, *Finance Dir,* Artists Space, New York NY

Siegesmund, Richard, *Chief Cur,* San Francisco Museum of Modern Art, San Francisco CA

Siegfried, Jay, *Chmn,* Middlesex County College, Visual Arts Dept, Edison NJ (S)

Siegman, William, *Cur African, Oceanic & New World Cultures,* Brooklyn Museum, Brooklyn NY

Siegner, Mark, *Pres,* Latitude 53 Society of Artists, Edmonton AB

Siekert, John, *VPres,* Art Guild of Burlington, Arts for Living Center, Burlington IA

Siers, Pamela, *Exec Dir,* Vermont State Craft Center at Frog Hollow, Middlebury VT

Siersma, Betsy, *Dir,* University of Massachusetts, Amherst, University Gallery, Amherst MA

Sievers, Ann H, *Assoc Cur Prints,* Smith College, Museum of Art, Northampton MA

Sievert, Mary-Ann, *Artist,* New York Tapestry Artists, Carmel NY

Siewart, Debra, *Cur Costumes,* Indiana State Museum, Indianapolis IN

Sigala, Stephanie C, *Librn,* The Saint Louis Art Museum, Richardson Memorial Library, Saint Louis MO

Sigel, Milt, *Instr,* Bucks County Community College, Fine Arts Dept, Newtown PA (S)

Sigerson, Marge, *Librn,* Museum of Arts and Sciences, Library, Daytona Beach FL

Sigler, Doug, *Prof,* Rochester Institute of Technology, School of Art and Design, Rochester NY (S)

Sigmund, Dina, *Corp Art Dir,* Illinois Bell, Chicago IL

Silas, Anna, *Dir,* Hopi Cultural Center Museum, Second Mesa AZ

Silberman, Robert, *Assoc Prof,* University of Minnesota, Minneapolis, Art History, Minneapolis MN (S)

Silcox, Ginsley, *Dir,* Southern Methodist University, Hamon Arts Library, Dallas TX

Silhan, William A, *Prof,* University of West Florida, Dept of Art, Pensacola FL (S)

Silliman, Thomas, *Dir,* East Los Angeles College, Vincent Price Gallery, Monterey Park CA

Sillings, M, *Wildlife Biologist,* Museum of the Hudson Highlands, Cornwall on Hudson NY

Sillius, I, *Library Technician,* Sheridan College of Applied Arts and Technology, Visual Arts & Crafts Library, Oakville ON

Sillman, Sewell, *Lectr,* University of Pennsylvania, Graduate School of Fine Arts, Philadelphia PA (S)

Silosky, Daniel, *Registrar,* Huntington Museum of Art, Huntington WV

Silver, Adele Z, *Mgr Public Information,* Cleveland Museum of Art, Cleveland OH

Silver, Beverly, *Educ Coordr,* Bellevue Art Museum, Bellevue WA

Silver, Julius L, *Prof,* Rochester Institute of Technology, School of Printing, Rochester NY (S)

Silver, Larry, *VPres,* College Art Association, New York NY

Silver, Larry, *Prof,* Northwestern University, Evanston, Dept of Art History, Evanston IL (S)

Silverberg, David, *Prof,* Mount Allison University, Fine Arts Dept, Sackville NB (S)

Silverman, Gilbert B, *Treas,* Detroit Institute of Arts, Founders Society, Detroit MI

Silverman, Monroe, *Pres,* Stamford Museum and Nature Center, Stamford CT

Silversides, Brock, *Chief A-V Archivist,* Department of Culture & Multi-Culturalism, Provincial Archives of Alberta, Edmonton AB

Silverstein, Susan, *Public Prog,* Naval Historical Center, The Navy Museum, Washington DC

Silverstein, Teil, *Dir Development,* Institute of Contemporary Art, Boston MA

SilverThorne, Jeanette, *Admin Asst,* York University, Art Gallery of York University, North York ON

Silverthorne, Jeffrey, *Asst Prof,* C W Post Center of Long Island University, School of Visual & Performing Arts, Greenvale NY (S)

Silvestro, Clement M, *Dir,* Museum of Our National Heritage, Lexington MA

Sim, Richard, *Prof,* Antelope Valley College, Art Dept, Division of Fine Arts, Lancaster CA (S)

Simak, Ellen, *Cur Coll,* Hunter Museum of Art, Chattanooga TN

Simerly, Dolores, *In Charge of Art Coll,* First Tennesse Bank, Maryville TN

Simile, Robert, *Assoc Prof,* West Virginia Institute of Technology, Creative Arts Dept, Montgomery WV (S)

Simkin, Phillips, *Assoc Prof,* York College of the City University of New York, Fine and Performing Arts, Jamaica NY (S)

Simmerly, Scott, *Preparator,* Cleveland State University, Art Gallery, Cleveland OH

Simmermacher, Rebecca, *Designer,* University of Kentucky, Art Museum, Lexington KY

Simmons, Catherine T, *Community Relations Coordr,* Maitland Art Center, Library, Maitland FL

Simmons, Charles B, *Dir,* Henry Morrison Flagler Museum, Whitehall Mansion, Palm Beach FL

Simmons, E H, *Dir,* Marine Corps Museum, Art Collection, Washington DC

Simmons, Henry L, *Librn,* University of Southern Mississippi, McCain Library & Archives, Hattiesburg MS

Simmons, Mary Jean, *Acting Dir,* Gordon College, Dept of Fine Arts, Barnesville GA (S)

Simmons, Michael, *Instr,* California State University, Chico, Art Dept, Chico CA (S)

Simmons, Terry K, *Exhib Chmn,* Delta State University, Fielding L Wright Art Center, Cleveland MS

Simmons, Terry K, *Assoc Prof,* Delta State University, Dept of Art, Cleveland MS (S)

Simon, Alf, *Dir Exhib,* University of Manitoba, Faculty of Architecture Exhibition Centre, Winnipeg MB

Simon, Ann, *Instr,* Main Line Center for the Arts, Haverford PA (S)

Simon, Carol, *Registrar,* Beloit College, Wright Museum of Art, Beloit WI

Simon, C M, *Dir,* Heritage Center, Inc, Pine Ridge SD

Simon, David, *Prof,* Colby College, Art Dept, Waterville ME (S)

Simon, Dorothy, *Asst Cur,* New York University, Institute of Fine Arts Visual Resources Collection, New York NY

Simon, Meryl, *Librn,* Aesthetic Realism Foundation, Eli Siegel Collection, New York NY

Simon, Michael, *Chmn,* Beloit College, Dept of Art, Beloit WI (S)

Simon, Norton, *Pres,* Norton Simon Museum, Pasadena CA

Simon, Sherri, *Cur Educ & Progs,* High Point Historical Society Inc, Museum, High Point NC

Simon, Sonia, *Assoc Prof,* Colby College, Art Dept, Waterville ME (S)

Simon, Sonia, *Asst Prof,* Colby College, Art Dept, Waterville ME (S)

Simon, Suzanne, *Cur,* Historical Society of Old Newbury, Cushing House Museum, Newburyport MA

Simons, Anneke Prins, *Prof,* Jersey City State College, Art Dept, Jersey City NJ (S)

Simons, Chris, *Prof,* Shoreline Community College, Humanities Division, Seattle WA (S)

Simons, Patricia, *Assoc Prof,* University of Michigan, Ann Arbor, Dept of History of Art, Ann Arbor MI (S)

Simons, Sheri, *Instr,* California State University, Chico, Art Dept, Chico CA (S)

Simonsson, Maria, *Asst Executive Dir,* Art League, Alexandria VA

Simor, Marilyn L, *Dir & Cur,* Queens College, City University of New York, Godwin-Ternbach Museum, Flushing NY

Simor, Suzanna, *Dir,* Queens College, City University of New York, Queens College Art Center, Flushing NY

Simor, Suzanna, *Head,* Queens College, City University of New York, Art Library, Flushing NY

Simpson, Barbara, *Librn,* Kean College of New Jersey, Nancy Thompson Library, Union NJ

Simpson, Ellen, *Library Dir,* Valley Cottage Library, Gallery, Valley Cottage NY

Simpson, Gayle, *VPres,* Conejo Valley Art Museum, Thousand Oaks CA

Simpson, Glen C, *Prof,* University of Alaska, Dept of Art, Fairbanks AK (S)

Simpson, Janet F, *Executive Dir,* Kansas City Artists Coalition, Kansas City MO

Simpson, Leslie T, *Dir,* Winfred L & Elizabeth C Post Foundation, Post Memorial Art Reference Library, Joplin MO

Simpson, Marc, *Cur American Painting,* Fine Arts Museums of San Francisco, M H de Young Memorial Museum and California Palace of the Legion of Honor, San Francisco CA

Simpson, Marianna, *Cur Near Eastern Art,* Freer Gallery of Art, Washington DC

Simpson, Pamela H, *Head of Art Div,* Washington and Lee University, Division of Art, Lexington VA (S)

Simpson, Paula, *Dir,* Monterey Public Library, Art & Architecture Dept, Monterey CA

Simpson, Ruth D, *Cur Archaeology,* San Bernardino County Museum, Fine Arts Institute, Redlands CA

Simpson, Shannon, *Cur,* Ellis County Museum Inc, Waxahachie TX

Sims, Carol, *Guild Dir,* Silvermine Guild Arts Center, Silvermine Galleries, New Canaan CT

Sims, Judith, *Dir Prog,* Laguna Gloria Art Museum, Austin TX

Sims, William R, *Chmn Dept,* Cornell University, New York State College of Human Ecology, Ithaca NY (S)

Sinclair, Jane, *Prof,* Chapman University, Art Dept, Orange CA (S)

Sinclair, Sarah Lentz, *Pres,* Harrison County Historical Museum, Marshall TX

Sinclair, Susan, *Librn & Archivist,* Isabella Stewart Gardner Museum, Rare Book Collection & Archives, Boston MA

Sincox, Kim Robinson, *Cur,* Battleship North Carolina, Wilmington NC

Sindelar, Norma, *Archivist,* The Saint Louis Art Museum, Richardson Memorial Library, Saint Louis MO

Sindelir, Robert J, *Dir & Cur,* Miami-Dade Community College, Kendal Campus, Art Gallery, Miami FL

Sing, Susan, *Instr,* Glendale Community College, Dept of Fine Arts, Glendale CA (S)

Singer, Clyde, *Assoc Dir,* Butler Institute of American Art, Art Museum, Youngstown OH

Singer, Liz, *Secy,* Lahaina Arts Society, Art Organization, Lahaina HI

Singleton, David, *Deputy Dir,* Philbrook Museum of Art, Tulsa OK

Singleton, Katherine, *Pres,* Arts Council of Greater Kingsport, Kingsport TN

Sinicrope, Donna, *Educ Coordr,* Florida Gulf Coast Art Center, Inc, Belleair FL

Sinicrope, Donna, *Educ Coordr,* Florida Gulf Coast Art Center, Inc, Art Reference Library, Belleair FL

Sinsheimer, Karen, *Cur Photography,* Santa Barbara Museum of Art, Santa Barbara CA

Sipiorski, Dennis, *Art Dept Head,* Nicholls State University, Dept of Art, Thibodaux LA (S)

Sippel, Jeffrey, *Educ Dir,* University of New Mexico, Tamarind Institute, Albuquerque NM (S)

Sirkus, Susan, *Development Dir,* Craft and Folk Art Museum, Los Angeles CA

Sirna, Jessie, *Instr,* Charles Stewart Mott Community College, Art Area, School of Arts & Humanities, Flint MI (S)

Siry, Joseph, *Assoc Prof,* Wesleyan University, Art Dept, Middletown CT (S)

Sischka, Kathy, *VPres,* Prescott Fine Arts Association, Gallery, Prescott AZ

Siska, Patricia D, *Cataloguer,* Frick Art Reference Library, New York NY

Siskind, Erica, *Library Asst,* University of California, Architectural Slide Library, Berkeley CA

Sislen, Dayne, *Adjunct Instr,* Maryville University of Saint Louis, Art Division, Saint Louis MO (S)

Sisto, Elena, *Instr,* New York Studio School of Drawing, Painting and Sculpture, New York NY (S)

Sistrunk, Allen, *Dir Gardens,* Atlanta Historical Society Inc, Atlanta History Center, Atlanta GA

Sit, Elaine, *Communications Dir,* Headlands Center for the Arts, Sausalito CA

Sitterly, Glenn F, *Cur,* Baldwin Historical Society Museum, Baldwin NY

Sivers, Cora, *Cur of Marghab Collection,* South Dakota State University, South Dakota Art Museum, Brookings SD

Sivertson, Howard, *Faculty,* Grand Marais Art Colony, Grand Marais MN (S)

Sjoberg, Ake W, *Babylonian Section Tablet Coll Cur,* University of Pennsylvania, University Museum of Archaelogy & Anthropology, Philadelphia PA

Sjogren, Margaret, *Chmn Dept Art,* Southern Oregon State College, Dept of Art, Ashland OR (S)

Sjogren, Margaret L, *Chmn Dept Art,* Southern Oregon State College, Central Art Gallery, Ashland OR

Skaggs, Robert, *Prof,* School of the Art Institute of Chicago, Chicago IL (S)

Skeel, Sharin, *Public Information Officer,* Pennsylvania Academy of the Fine Arts, Galleries, Philadelphia PA

Skelley, Robert C, *Prof,* University of Florida, Dept of Art, Gainesville FL (S)

Skelton, Carl, *Instr,* Toronto School of Art, Toronto ON (S)

Skelton, Scott, *Asst Mgr,* Houston Public Library, Houston TX

Skidmore, Gail, *Exec Dir,* Arts Council of Tuscaloosa County, Inc, Tuscaloosa AL

Skidmore, Margaret, *Assoc Dir Development,* Museum of Fine Arts, Houston, Houston TX

Skidmore, Mercedes C, *Asst Dir Admin,* The Rockwell Museum, Corning NY

Skidmore, Steve, *Dir,* Ponca City Library, Art Dept, Ponca City OK

Skiles, Jackie, *Newsletter Editor,* Women in the Arts Foundation, Inc, New York NY

Skinezelewski, Kelly, *Gallery Coordr,* Banc One Wisconsin Corp, Milwaukee WI

Skinner, Arthur, *Asst Prof,* Eckerd College, Art Dept, Saint Petersburg FL (S)

Skinner, Bill, *Chmn Div of Communications & Arts,* North Arkansas Community College, Art Dept, Harrison AR (S)

Skinner, Dan, *VPres,* Lahaina Arts Society, Art Organization, Lahaina HI

Skinner, Greg, *Dir,* Cornish College of the Arts, Cornish Galleries, Seattle WA

Skinner, Robert, *Prof,* Southampton Campus of Long Island University, Fine Arts Division, Southampton NY (S)

Skjelstad, Lucy, *Dir,* Oregon State University, Horner Museum, Corvallis OR

Sklar, Hinda F, *Librn,* Harvard University, Frances Loeb Library, Cambridge MA

Sklarski, Bonnie, *Prof,* Indiana University, Bloomington, Henry Radford Hope School of Fine Arts, Bloomington IN (S)

Skoog, William, *Chmn,* Southwestern Michigan College, Fine & Performing Arts Dept, Dowagiac MI (S)

Skory, Gary, *Dir,* Midland County Historical Society, Midland MI

Skotheim, Robert Allen, *Pres,* Henry E Huntington Library, Art Collections & Botanical Gardens, San Marino CA

Skousen, Nola, *Librn,* Museum of Our National Heritage, Lexington MA

Skredergard, Helen, *Exec Dir,* Indian Arts & Crafts Association, Albuquerque NM

Skurkis, Barry, *Chmn,* North Central College, Dept of Art, Naperville IL (S)

Skurkis, Barry, *Pres,* Chicago Society of Artists, Inc, Chicago IL

Sky, Carol, *VPres,* National Artists Equity Association Inc, Washington DC

Slack, Barbara, *Librn,* Webster Parish Library, Minden LA

Slade, Rona, *Assoc Dean of Faculty,* Corcoran School of Art, Washington DC (S)

Slade, Roy, *Dir Museum,* Cranbrook Academy of Art Museum, Bloomfield Hills MI

Slade, Roy, *Pres,* Cranbrook Academy of Art, Bloomfield Hills MI (S)

Slade, Terry, *Asst Prof,* Hartwick College, Art Dept, Oneonta NY (S)

Slagle, Nancy, *Asst Prof,* Texas Tech University, Dept of Art, Lubbock TX (S)

Slammon, Robert, *Researcher,* Burchfield Art Center, Archives, Buffalo NY

Slaney, Debra, *Registrar,* Heard Museum, Phoenix AZ

Slanger, George, *Chmn Div Humanities,* Minot State University, Dept of Art, Division of Humanities, Minot ND (S)

Slattery, Michael, *Instr,* Bob Jones University, School of Fine Arts, Greenville SC (S)

Slatton, Ralph, *Asst Prof,* East Tennessee State University, Fine Arts Dept, Johnson City TN (S)

Slaughter, Ann Marie, *Exec Ed,* Dialogue Inc, Columbus OH

Slavish, Peter J, *Prof,* Blackburn College, Dept of Art, Carlinville IL (S)

Slawson, Brian, *Asst Prof,* University of Florida, Dept of Art, Gainesville FL (S)

Sledd, Michael, *Instr,* Columbia College, Art Dept, Columbia MO (S)

Slenker, Elizabeth, *Instr,* Saint Thomas Aquinas College, Art Dept, Sparkhill NY (S)

Slenker, Jean, *Instr,* Indiana University of Pennsylvania, Dept of Art and Art Education, Indiana PA (S)

Slenker, Robert, *Instr,* Indiana University of Pennsylvania, Dept of Art and Art Education, Indiana PA (S)

Slick, John, *Dir,* Wayne State University, Community Arts Gallery, Detroit MI

Slimon, Gary, *Dir,* Canadian Wildlife & Wilderness Art Museum, Ottawa ON

Slimon, Gary, *Dir,* Canadian Wildlife & Wilderness Art Museum, Library, Ottawa ON

Sloan, Charles, *Preparator,* Museum of New Mexico, Museum of Fine Arts, Santa Fe NM

Sloan, John, *Chmn,* Whittier College, Dept of Art, Whittier CA (S)

Sloan, Marcus, *Dir Exhib,* InterCultura, Inc, Fort Worth TX

Sloan, Mark, *Dir,* Potsdam College of the State University of New York, Roland Gibson Gallery, Potsdam NY

Slocumb, Franklyn, *Supt,* Norton Gallery and School of Art, West Palm Beach FL

Slorp, John S, *Pres,* Minneapolis College of Art and Design, Minneapolis MN (S)

Sloshberg, Leah P, *Dir,* New Jersey State Museum, Trenton NJ

Slouffman, Jim, *Dir Educ,* Antonelli Institute of Art & Photography, Cincinnati OH (S)

Slovin, Rochelle, *Dir,* American Museum of the Moving Image, Astoria NY

Slowinski, Mary, *Prog Dir,* City Art Works, Pratt Fine Arts Center, Seattle WA (S)

Slusarenko, Kay, *Chairperson,* Marylhurst College, Art Dept, Marylhurst OR (S)

Sluterbeck, Kay R, *Office Mgr,* Wassenberg Art Center, Van Wert OH

Slutsky, Madeleine, *Dept Head,* Ray College of Design, Chicago IL (S)

Slyfield, Donna, *Readers' Services,* Helen M Plum Memorial Library, Lombard IL

Small, Carol, *Instr,* Gettysburg College, Dept of Art, Gettysburg PA (S)

Small, James, *Asst Prof,* Rutgers, the State University of New Jersey, Graduate Program in Art History, New Brunswick NJ (S)

Small, Janus, *Exec Dir,* New Organization for the Visual Arts, (NOVA), Cleveland OH

Small, Jocelyn, *Prof,* Rutgers, the State University of New Jersey, Graduate Program in Art History, New Brunswick NJ (S)

Small, Marcella, *Instr,* Delta State University, Dept of Art, Cleveland MS (S)

Small, Martha, *Registrar,* Wadsworth Atheneum, Hartford CT

Smallenberg, Harry, *Chmn General Studies,* Center for Creative Studies, College of Art & Design, Detroit MI (S)

Smalley, David, *Prof,* Connecticut College, Dept of Art, New London CT (S)

Smalley, Jennifer, *Admin Asst,* Nevada Museum Of Art, Reno NV

Smalley, Stephen, *Prof,* Bridgewater State College, Art Dept, Bridgewater MA (S)

Smar, Joyce, *Mgr Performing Arts,* Toledo Museum of Art, Toledo Museum of Art, Toledo OH

Smart, Sonny, *CEO & General Mgr,* Chelan County Public Utility District, Rocky Reach Dam, Wenatchee WA

Smart, Tom, *Cur,* Beaverbrook Art Gallery, Fredericton NB

Smedstad, Ivar, *Editing Post Production Facility,* Electronic Arts Intermix, Inc, New York NY

Smemo, Suzanne, *Instr,* Concordia College, Art Dept, Moorhead MN (S)

Smigocki, Stephen, *Prof,* Fairmont State College, Div of Fine Arts, Fairmont WV (S)

Smigrod, Claudia, *Chmn Photography,* Corcoran School of Art, Washington DC (S)

Smirl, Sharon, *Asst Dir Admin,* Tyler Museum of Art, Tyler TX

Smirl, Sharon, *Asst Dir Admin,* Tyler Museum of Art, Reference Library, Tyler TX

Smith, Aj, *Instr,* The Arkansas Arts Center, Museum School, Little Rock AR (S)

Smith, Alice, *Cur Education,* Springfield Library & Museums Association, Connecticut Valley Historical Museum, Springfield MA

Smith, Allessandra, *Admin Asst,* Captain Robert Bennet Forbes House, Milton MA

Smith, Andrea, *Cur,* T C Steele State Historic Site, Nashville IN

Smith, Ann, *Dir,* Mattatuck Historical Society Museum, Waterbury CT

Smith, Barbara A, *Gallery Mgr,* Guild of Boston Artists, Boston MA

Smith, B G, *Supt,* Texas Ranger Hall of Fame and Museum, Waco TX

Smith, Bill, *Photographer & Cur,* Huronia Museum, Midland ON

Smith, B J, *Dir,* Oklahoma State University, Gardiner Art Gallery, Stillwater OK

Smith, Bonnie Oehlert, *Adminr,* Door County, Miller Art Center, Sturgeon Bay WI

Smith, Brad, *Media Center Dir,* Minneapolis College of Art & Design, Library & Media Center, Minneapolis MN

Smith, Brian, *Photo Lab Technician,* Institute of the Great Plains, Museum of the Great Plains, Lawton OK

Smith, Brydon, *Asst Dir Coll & Research,* National Gallery of Canada, Ottawa ON

Smith, C, *Instr,* Community College of Rhode Island, Dept of Art, Warwick RI (S)

Smith, Catherine, *Instr,* Charles Stewart Mott Community College, Art Area, School of Arts & Humanities, Flint MI (S)

Smith, Claude, *Chmn,* Western New Mexico University, Dept of Expressive Arts, Silver City NM (S)

Smith, Claudia, *Prof,* University of Wisconsin-Stout, Dept of Art & Design, Menomonie WI (S)

Smith, Claudia, *Assoc Prof,* University of Wisconsin-Stout, Dept of Art & Design, Menomonie WI (S)

Smith, C Martin, *Product Design Chmn,* Art Center College of Design, Pasadena CA (S)

Smith, Dan, *Instr,* Claflin College, Dept of Art, Orangeburg SC (S)

Smith, Darold, *Prof,* West Texas State University, Art, Communication & Theatre Dept, Canyon TX (S)

Smith, David, *Faculty,* Edgewood College, Art Dept, Madison WI (S)

Smith, David, *Assoc Prof,* University of New Hampshire, Dept of the Arts, Durham NH (S)

Smith, David, *Art Lecturer,* Edgewood College, DeRicci Gallery, Madison WI

Smith, David L, *Assoc Prof,* University of Wisconsin-Stevens Point, Dept of Art & Design, Stevens Point WI (S)

Smith, Donald C, *Prof,* Rhode Island College, Art Dept, Providence RI (S)

Smith, Donna, *Asst Librn,* Lauren Rogers Museum of Art, Library, Laurel MS

Smith, Dorothy V, *Publicity,* Leatherstocking Brush & Palette Club Inc, Cooperstown NY

Smith, Doug, *Instr,* Modesto Junior College, Arts Humanities and Speech Division, Modesto CA (S)

Smith, Ed, *Instr,* Chautauqua Institution, School of Art, Chautauqua NY (S)

Smith, Elizabeth B, *Assoc Prof,* Pennsylvania State University, University Park, Dept of Art History, University Park PA (S)

Smith, Elsie, *Asst Prof,* Millsaps College, Dept of Art, Jackson MS (S)

Smith, Evelyn, *Children's Prog Specialist,* Hampshire County Public Library, Romney WV

Smith, Frank Anthony, *Prof,* University of Utah, Art Dept, Salt Lake City UT (S)

Smith, Fred T, *Dir,* Kent State University, School of Art Gallery, Kent OH

Smith, Fred T, *Div Coordr Art History,* Kent State University, School of Art, Kent OH (S)

Smith, Gary N, *Dir,* Mamie McFaddin Ward Heritage Historic Foundation, Beaumont TX

Smith, Gary T, *Dir,* Hartnell College Gallery, Salinas CA

Smith, George, *Assoc Prof,* Rice University, Dept of Art and Art History, Houston TX (S)

Smith, George, *Asst Prof,* University of the District of Columbia, Art Dept, Washington DC (S)

Smith, Gerald, *Librn,* Fine Arts Museums of San Francisco, Library, San Francisco CA

Smith, Gerald D, *Dean,* Huntington College, Art Dept, Huntington IN (S)

Smith, Graham, *Prof,* University of Michigan, Ann Arbor, Dept of History of Art, Ann Arbor MI (S)

Smith, Gregory Allgire, *Dir,* Telfair Academy of Arts and Sciences Inc, Savannah GA

Smith, Gregory H, *VPres,* Ventura County Historical Society Museum, Ventura CA

Smith, Greta, *Asst Librn,* Old Colony Historical Society, Library, Taunton MA

Smith, Heather, *Dir,* Dawson City Museum & Historical Society, Dawson City YT

Smith, Helen, *Instr,* Duke University, Dept of Art and Art History, Durham NC (S)

Smith, Hoppy, *Gallery Dir,* The Gallery at Hawaii Loa College, Marinda Lee Gallery, Kaneohe HI

Smith, Howard, *Slide Cur,* University of Southern California, Helen Topping Architecture & Fine Arts Library, Los Angeles CA

Smith, J, *Instr,* Western Illinois University, Art Dept, Macomb IL (S)

Smith, James L, *Pres,* Waterloo Art Association, Waterloo IA

Smith, Jan, *Cur,* Bergstrom Mahler Museum, Neenah WI

Smith, Janet, *Store Mgr,* Museum of Contemporary Art, Chicago IL

Smith, Jean, *Librn,* Woodrow Wilson Birthplace Foundation, Library, Staunton VA

Smith, Jean, *Studio Admin,* Gibbes Museum School, Gibbes Museum Studio, Charleston SC (S)

Smith, Jenny, *Dir,* International Fine Arts College, Miami FL (S)

Smith, Jerry, *Publicity,* The Washington Center For Photography, Washington DC

Smith, Jil, *Instr,* The Arkansas Arts Center, Museum School, Little Rock AR (S)

Smith, Jo, *Office Mgr,* Marin Society of Artists Inc, Ross CA

Smith, John, *Archivist,* The Art Institute of Chicago, Ryerson and Burnham Libraries, Chicago IL

Smith, Joseph E, *Assoc Prof,* Oakland City College, Division of Fine Arts, Oakland City IN (S)

Smith, Judith Chiba, *Cur European & American Coll,* Museum of New Mexico, Museum of International Folk Art, Santa Fe NM

Smith, June L, *Dept Chmn,* East Los Angeles College, Art Dept, Monterey Park CA (S)

Smith, J Weldon, *Dir,* San Francisco Craft and Folk Art Museum, San Francisco CA

Smith, K, *Departmental Asst,* Royal Ontario Museum, Canadian Decorative Arts Department, Toronto ON

Smith, Karen Burgess, *Dir Art Center,* Saint Paul's School, Art Center in Hargate, Concord NH

Smith, Katherine, *Receptionist,* Fort Worth Art Association, Modern Art Museum of Fort Worth, Fort Worth TX

Smith, Kathryn S, *Pres,* Historical Society of Washington DC, Christian Heurich Mansion, Washington DC

Smith, Kent, *Asst Prof,* University of Nebraska, Kearney, Dept of Art & Art History, Kearney NE (S)

Smith, Kent J, *Dir of Art,* Illinois State Museum, Illinois Art Gallery & Lockport Gallery, Springfield IL

Smith, Kimberly, *VPres,* African American Historical and Cultural Society, San Francisco CA

Smith, Lawry, *Dir & Cur,* Lamama La Galleria, New York NY

Smith, Luther, *Prof,* Texas Christian University, Art & Art History Dept, Fort Worth TX (S)

Smith, Lynn, *Asst Prof,* Winthrop College, Dept of Art & Design, Rock Hill SC (S)

Smith, Maggie, *Recording Secy,* Kent Art Association, Inc, Gallery, Kent CT

Smith, Margaret, *Asst Prof,* University of Richmond, Dept of Art & Art History, Richmond VA (S)

Smith, Margaret Supplee, *Prof,* Wake Forest University, Dept of Art, Winston-Salem NC (S)

Smith, Marilyn, *Adminr,* Art Museum of South Texas, Corpus Christi TX

Smith, Mark, *Chmn,* Austin College, Art Dept, Sherman TX (S)

Smith, Mark Stephen, *Dir,* Austin College, Ida Green Gallery, Sherman TX

Smith, Mary E, *Prof,* Tulane University, Sophie H Newcomb Memorial College, New Orleans LA (S)

Smith, Mary Elizabeth, *Cur,* Liberty Hall Historic Site, Liberty Hall Museum, Frankfort KY

Smith, Mary Kay, *Co-Chmn,* Polk Museum of Art, Penfield Library, Lakeland FL

Smith, Maureen, *Finance Dir,* Southern Oregon Historical Society, Jacksonville Museum of Southern Oregon History, Jacksonville OR

Smith, Melinda, *Exec Dir,* Davidson County Art Guild Gallery, Inc, Lexington NC

Smith, Melinda K, *Registrarial Asst,* United States Senate Commission on Art, Washington DC

Smith, Merrill W, *Assoc Librn & Col Mgr,* Massachusetts Institute of Technology, Rotch Library of Architecture & Planning, Cambridge MA

Smith, Michael, *Assoc Prof,* East Tennessee State University, Fine Arts Dept, Johnson City TN (S)

Smith, Michael J, *Dir,* Putnam Museum of History & Natural Science, Davenport IA

Smith, Michael J, *Head Painting,* Southern Illinois University at Edwardsville, Dept of Art & Design, Edwardsville IL (S)

Smith, Michele L, *Dir,* Wassenberg Art Center, Van Wert OH

Smith, Michelle, *Registrar,* Plains Art Museum, Moorhead MN

Smith, Moishe, *Prof,* Utah State University, Dept of Art, Logan UT (S)

Smith, Monica, *Conservator,* Vancouver Art Gallery, Vancouver BC

Smith, Nan, *Assoc Prof,* University of Florida, Dept of Art, Gainesville FL (S)

Smith, Nancy M, *Exec Dir,* Rosenberg Library, Galveston TX

Smith, Owen, *Asst Prof,* University of Maine, Art Dept, Orono ME (S)

Smith, Patricia, *Exec Dir,* Sierra Arts Foundation, Reno NV

Smith, Patricia, *Chmn Printmaking,* University of the Arts, Philadelphia College of Art & Design, Philadelphia PA (S)

Smith, Patricia, *Head Technical Serv,* Columbia College, Library, Chicago IL

Smith, Paul, *VPres,* Louis Comfort Tiffany Foundation, New York NY

Smith, Priscilla, *Asst Prof,* Colgate University, Dept of Art & Art History, Hamilton NY (S)

Smith, Quinn, *Secy,* Crary Art Gallery Inc, Warren PA

Smith, Randy, *Asst Library Dir,* Boulder Public Library and Gallery, Dept of Fine Arts Gallery, Boulder CO

Smith, Richard Norton, *Library Dir,* Herbert Hoover Presidential Library & Museum, West Branch IA

Smith, Robynn, *Instr,* Monterey Peninsula College, Art Dept, Monterey CA (S)

Smith, Ronald C, *Supvr,* Spokane Falls Community College, Fine & Applied Arts Div, Spokane WA (S)

Smith, Sam, *Instr,* Marian College, Art Dept, Indianapolis IN (S)

Smith, Scott, *Treas,* Attleboro Museum, Center for the Arts, Attleboro MA

Smith, Scott, *Theater Coordr,* Brooklyn Arts Council, BACA Downtown, Brooklyn NY

Smith, Sharon, *Instr,* California State University, Chico, Art Dept, Chico CA (S)

Smith, Shaw, *Assoc Prof,* Davidson College, Art Dept, Davidson NC (S)

Smith, Stacy, *Curatorial Asst & Registrar,* Noyes Museum, Oceanville NJ

Smith, Thomas G, *Aquirium Dir,* Berkshire Museum, Pittsfield MA

Smith, Thomas O, *Chmn,* Grambling State University, Art Dept, Grambling LA (S)

Smith, Walter, *Prof,* Pierce College, Art Dept, Woodland Hills CA (S)

Smith, Willard, *Prof,* College of DuPage, Humanities Division, Glen Ellyn IL (S)

Smith EdD, John W, *Assoc Prof,* University of Arkansas, Art Dept, Fayetteville AR (S)

Smith-Fisher, Laura, *Development Officer,* National Gallery of Art, Washington DC

Smith-Hunter, Susan, *Chairperson,* Green Mountain College, Dept of Art, Poultney VT (S)

Smith-Hurd, Diane, *Instr,* Art Academy of Cincinnati, Cincinnati OH (S)

Smith-Rubenzahl, Ian, *Reprography Coordr,* Visual Arts Ontario, Toronto ON

Smith Shafts, Karen, *Asst Keeper of Prints,* Boston Public Library, Albert H Wiggin Gallery & Print Department, Boston MA

Smith-Willow, Neal, *Asst Prof,* Brenau College, Art Dept, Gainesville GA (S)

Smits, Kathy, *Secy,* Bergstrom Mahler Museum, Neenah WI

Smogor, Robert, *Registrar,* University of Notre Dame, Snite Museum of Art, Notre Dame IN

Smoke, Joe, *Dir,* Los Angeles Center For Photographic Studies, Los Angeles CA

Smotherman, Ann, *Art Teacher,* Motlow State Community College, Art Dept, Tullahoma TN (S)

Smyrnios, Arleigh, *Instr,* Kalamazoo Valley Community College, Humanities Development Center, Kalamazoo MI (S)

Smyser, Michael, *Assoc Prof,* Montgomery County Community College, Art Dept, Blue Bell PA (S)

Smyth, Frances, *Editor,* National Gallery of Art, Washington DC

Smyth, Linda, *Instr,* St Lawrence College, Dept of Visual & Creative Arts, Cornwall ON (S)

Smythe, James E, *Prof,* Western Carolina University, Dept of Art, Cullowhee NC (S)

Snapp, Ronald, *Assoc Prof,* Old Dominion University, Art Dept, Norfolk VA (S)

Snavely, Loanne, *Arts & Architecture Librn,* Pennsylvania State University, Pattee Library, University Park PA

Sneddeker, Duane, *Cur Photographs,* Missouri Historical Society, Saint Louis MO

Snellenberger, Earl, *Prof,* University of Indianapolis, Art Dept, Indianapolis IN (S)

Snellenberger, Earl G, *Dir,* University of Indianapolis, Leah Ransburg Art Gallery, Indianapolis IN

Snibbe, Robert M, *Pres,* Napoleonic Society of America, Library, Clearwater FL

Snider, Laurence, *Exec Dir,* Artworks, Library, Trenton NJ

Snider, Lawrence, *Exec Dir,* Artworks, The Visual Art School of Princeton and Trenton, Trenton NJ

Snoddy, Donald, *Museum Dir,* Union Pacific Railroad, Historical Museum, Omaha NE

Snodgrass, John, *Treas,* Charles B Goddard Center for the Visual and Performing Arts, Ardmore OK

Snooks, A Nancy, *Asst Prof,* Pierce College, Art Dept, Woodland Hills CA (S)

Snovak, Katherine, *Staff Librn,* The Carnegie Library of Pittsburgh, Pittsburgh PA

Snow, Helen, *Pres,* Virginia Beach Center for the Arts, Virginia Beach VA

Snow, Marina, *Humanities Reference Librn,* California State University at Sacramento, Library - Humanities Reference Dept, Sacramento CA

Snow, Maryly, *Librn,* University of California, Architectural Slide Library, Berkeley CA

Snowden, Gilda, *Gallery Dir,* Detroit Repertory Theatre Gallery, Detroit MI

Snowden, Mary, *Painting,* California College of Arts and Crafts, Oakland CA (S)

Snowden, Pennell, *Cur,* Muchnic Foundation and Atchison Art Association, Muchnic Gallery, Atchison KS

Snowman, Tracy, *Instr,* Spoon River College, Art Dept, Canton IL (S)

Snydacker, Daniel, *Exec Dir,* Newport Historical Society, Newport RI

Snydacker, William, *Pres,* Muscatine Art Center, Muscatine IA

Snyder, Barry, *Prof,* Fairmont State College, Div of Fine Arts, Fairmont WV (S)

Snyder, Craig, *Dir,* Gallery West Ltd, Alexandria VA

Snyder, George E, *Asst Dir for Operations,* Cincinnati Museum Association, Cincinnati Art Museum, Cincinnati OH

Snyder, Iris, *Head Librn,* Delaware Art Museum, Helen Farr Sloan Library, Wilmington DE

Snyder, James, *Deputy Dir, Planning & Prog Support,* Museum of Modern Art, New York NY

Snyder, Mary, *Dir of Non-Print Coll,* Nova Scotia College of Art and Design, Library, Halifax NS

Snyder, R B, *Pres,* Norton Gallery and School of Art, West Palm Beach FL

Snyder, Robert, *Prof,* School of the Art Institute of Chicago, Chicago IL (S)

Snyder, Suzanne, *Chmn,* Fairmont State College, Div of Fine Arts, Fairmont WV (S)

Soave, Sergio, *Prof,* West Virginia University, College of Creative Arts, Morgantown WV (S)

Sobel, Margaret, *Admin,* National Society of Colonial Dames of America in the State of Maryland, Mount Clare Mansion, Baltimore MD

Sobieszek, Robert A, *Cur Photography,* Los Angeles County Museum of Art, Los Angeles CA

Sobol, Judith, *Dir,* Grand Rapids Art Museum, Grand Rapids MI

Sobol, Leah, *Dir Stables Gallery,* Taos Art Association Inc, Stables Art Center, Taos NM

Sobre, Judith, *Prof,* University of Texas at San Antonio, Division of Art & Architecture, San Antonio TX (S)

Socha, Dan, *In Charge Printmaking,* University of Illinois, Urbana-Champaign, School of Art and Design, Champaign IL (S)

Socha, H Norman, *Dir,* Enook Galleries, Waterloo ON

Sockol, Michael, *Public Relations Dir,* DeCordova Museum & Sculpture Park, Lincoln MA

Soderberg, Robert, *Pres,* Skaneateles Library Association, Skaneateles NY

Soderberg, Vicki, *Adminr,* William Bonifas Fine Art Center Gallery, Alice Powers Art Gallery, Escanaba MI

Sodervick, Bruce, *Assoc Prof,* Rochester Institute of Technology, School of Art and Design, Rochester NY (S)

Soellner, Walt, *Treas,* Society of North American Goldsmiths, Jacksonville FL

Sohi, Marilyn, *Registrar,* Madison Art Center, Madison WI

Soklin, Susan, *Pres,* Boulder Art Center, Boulder CO

Sokolec, Stephanie, *Membership Coordr,* Terra Museum of American Art, Chicago IL

Sokolowski, Thomas W, *Dir,* New York University, Grey Art Gallery and Study Center, New York NY

Soldate, Joseph, *Assoc Chmn,* California State University, Los Angeles, Art Dept, Los Angeles CA (S)

Solem, John, *Chmn,* California Lutheran University, Art Dept, Thousand Oaks CA (S)

Soleri, Paolo, *Pres,* Cosanti Foundation, Scottsdale AZ

Soleri, Paolo, *Pres,* Cosanti Foundation, Arcosanti, Scottsdale AZ

Soles, Kathleen A, *Asst Prof,* Emmanuel College, Art Dept, Boston MA (S)

Solheim, David, *Chmn,* Dickinson State University, Dept of Art, Dickinson ND (S)

Sollins, Susan, *Exec Dir,* Independent Curators Incorporated, New York NY

Solmon, Dan, *Co-Chair Drawing & Painting,* Ontario College of Art, Toronto ON (S)

Solmssen, Peter, *Pres,* University of the Arts, Philadelphia PA

Solmssen, Peter, *Pres,* University of the Arts, Philadelphia College of Art & Design, Philadelphia PA (S)

Solomon, Bernard, *Assoc Prof,* Georgia Southern University, Dept of Art, Statesboro GA (S)

Solomon, Elke, *Instr,* Columbia University, School of the Arts, Division of Painting & Sculpture, New York NY (S)

Solomon, Martin, *Treas,* Art Directors Club, Inc, New York NY

Solomon, Richard E, *VPres,* Museum of Modern Art, New York NY

Solomon-Kiefer, C, *Asst Prof,* McGill University, Department of Art History, Montreal PQ (S)

Solot, E V, *Instr,* Western Illinois University, Art Dept, Macomb IL (S)

Soloway, Lynn, *Dir,* Concordia College, Marx Hausen Art Gallery, Seward NE

Soloway, Lynn, *Prof,* Concordia College, Art Dept, Seward NE (S)

Solt, Mary, *Exec Dir of Museum Registration,* The Art Institute of Chicago, Chicago IL

Soltes, Ori Z, *Dir,* B'nai B'rith International, B'nai B'rith Klutznick National Jewish Museum, Washington DC

Solvick, Shirley, *Chief Art & Literature Dept,* Detroit Public Library, Art & Literature Dept, Detroit MI

Sombille, Marilyn, *Dean,* Rutgers, the State University of New Jersey, Mason Gross School of the Arts, New Brunswick NJ (S)

Somers, David, *Cur,* Art Gallery of Peel, Peel Heritage Complex, Brampton ON

Somers, David, *Cur,* Art Gallery of Peel, Library, Brampton ON

Somers, Eric, *Dir,* Dutchess Community College, Dept of Visual Arts, Poughkeepsie NY (S)

Somerville, Mary, *Asst Dir,* Miami-Dade Public Library, Miami FL

Sommer, Susan, *Chief Librn Circulations Coll Mgr,* The New York Public Library, Shelby Cullom Davis Museum, New York NY

Sommers, Joyce, *Exec Dir,* Indianapolis Art League, Churchman-Fehsenfeld Gallery, Indianapolis IN

Somogyi, George, *Prof,* Lakeland Community College, Visual Arts Dept, Mentor OH (S)

Sonday, Milton, *Cur Textiles,* Cooper-Hewitt, National Museum of Design, New York NY

Sonderegger, John, *Preparator,* University of Minnesota, University Art Museum, Minneapolis MN

Sonkevitch, Anatole, *Assoc Prof,* University of Michigan, Ann Arbor, Dept of History of Art, Ann Arbor MI (S)

Sonneborn, Sydney R, *Head Dept,* Miles Community College, Dept of Fine Arts and Humanities, Miles City MT (S)

Sonnema, Roy, *Asst Prof,* Georgia Southern University, Dept of Art, Statesboro GA (S)

Sons, Ruth, *Controller,* Tucson Museum of Art, Tucson AZ

Sontag, Roz, *Admin Asst,* Rollins College, George D and Harriet W Cornell Fine Arts Museum, Winter Park FL

Sopher, Sonja, *Conservator,* Portland Art Museum, Portland OR

Sopher, Vicki, *Dir,* National Trust for Historic Preservation, Decatur House, Washington DC

Sopka, Elaine C, *Dir,* Newark School of Fine and Industrial Art, Newark NJ (S)

Soreff, Stephen, *Prof,* C W Post Center of Long Island University, School of Visual & Performing Arts, Greenvale NY (S)

Sorensen, Lee, *Librn & Art Bibliographer,* Duke University Museum of Art, East Campus Library, Durham NC

Sorensen, R O, *Chmn,* Furman University, Dept of Art, Greenville SC (S)

Sorento, Bruno, *Prof,* Community College of Allegheny County, Boyce Campus, Art Dept, Monroeville PA (S)

Sorge, Walter, *Prof,* Eastern Illinois University, Art Dept, Charleston IL (S)

Sorgenti, Harold A, *Chmn Bd,* Pennsylvania Academy of the Fine Arts, Galleries, Philadelphia PA

Sorkow, Janice, *Dir,* Museum of Fine Arts, Dept of Photographic Services, Boston MA

Sormson, Lillian, *Cataloging Dir,* Dickinson State University, Stoxen Library, Dickinson ND

Sorokan, Lisa, *Admin Asst,* Community Arts Council of Vancouver, Vancouver BC

Sorrell, Robert, *Asst Prof,* College of Santa Fe, Visual Arts Dept, Santa Fe NM (S)

Sorrell, Sonya, *Instr,* Pepperdine University, Seaver College, Dept of Art, Malibu CA (S)

Sossa, Oscar, *Gallery Asst,* Queebsborough Community College, Art Gallery, Bayside NY

Soto, Anita, *Commissioner,* Art Commission of the City of New York, Associates of the Art Commission, Inc, New York NY

Soto, Raymond, *Film & Television Librn,* University of California, Los Angeles, Arts Library, Los Angeles CA

Soucy, Don, *Head Art Educ,* University of New Brunswick, Art Education Section, Fredericton NB (S)

Soule, Robert, *Supt,* Yale University, Art Gallery, New Haven CT

Sourakli, Judy, *Cur of Coll,* University of Washington, Henry Art Gallery, Seattle WA

Sousa, Jean, *Assoc Dir of Museum Educ,* The Art Institute of Chicago, Kraft General Food Education Center Museum, Chicago IL

South, Carissa, *Asst Cur Colls & Exhibit,* Art Museum of Western Virginia, Roanoke VA

Southall, Tom, *Cur Photographic Coll,* Amon Carter Museum, Fort Worth TX

Southam, Thomas, *Cur of Exhibitions,* University of Utah, Utah Museum of Fine Arts, Salt Lake City UT

Southard, Edna, *Cur of Coll,* Miami University Art Museum, Oxford OH

Southerland, Louise, *Dolls & Toys,* Luna County Historical Society, Inc, Deming Luna Mimbres Museum, Deming NM

Southerland, Ted, *Dir,* Luna County Historical Society, Inc, Deming Luna Mimbres Museum, Deming NM

Southern, Kathy, *Pres,* Sculpture Center Inc, New York NY

Southworth, Miles F, *Prof,* Rochester Institute of Technology, School of Printing, Rochester NY (S)

Sowards, Liz, *Acting Chmn,* Wichita State University, Division of Art, Wichita KS (S)

Sowiski, Peter, *Chmn,* State University College at Buffalo, Fine Arts Dept, Buffalo NY (S)

Spack, Carol, *Business Dir,* Boston Visual Artists Union, Boston MA

Spadaccinni, Carol, *Public Relations,* Rhode Island Historical Society, Providence RI

Spaid, Gregory P, *Assoc Prof,* Kenyon College, Art Dept, Gambier OH (S)

Spain, Susan M, *Asst to Dir,* Edgecombe County Cultural Arts Council, Inc, Blount-Bridgers House, Hobson Pittman Memorial Gallery, Tarboro NC

Spakes, Larry, *Artist in Residence,* Phillips County Community College, Dept of English and Fine Arts, Helena AR (S)

Spalatin, Ivana, *Chmn Art History,* East Texas State University, Dept of Art, East Texas Station, Commerce TX (S)

Spalding, Ann E, *Educ Coordr,* Maitland Art Center, Maitland FL

Spalding, David A E, *Exec Dir,* British Columbia Museums Association, Victoria BC

Spalding, Jeffrey, *Assoc Prof,* University of Lethbridge, Dept of Art, Lethbridge AB (S)

Spalding, Jeffrey, *Gallery Dir & Cur,* University of Lethbridge, Art Gallery, Lethbridge AB

Spangenberg, Kristin L, *Cur Prints & Drawings,* Cincinnati Museum Association, Cincinnati Art Museum, Cincinnati OH

Spangler, Cindy, *Registrar,* University of Tennessee, Ewing Gallery of Art and Architecture, Knoxville TN

Sparagana, John, *Asst Prof,* Rice University, Dept of Art and Art History, Houston TX (S)

Sparks, Henry, *Prof,* Christopher Newport College, Arts & Communications, Newport News VA (S)

Sparks, Jonathan, *Dir,* Friends University, Edmund Stanley Library Gallery, Wichita KS

Sparks, Tammy, *Asst Prof,* University of Dayton, Visual Arts Dept, Dayton OH (S)

Sparling, Mary, *Dir Art Gallery,* Mount Saint Vincent University, Art Gallery, Halifax NS

Sparrow, Diane, *Dir,* Boston Architectural Center, Boston MA

Spartz, India, *Photographs Librn,* Alaska State Library, Historical Library Section, Juneau AK

Spater, Susan Clarke, *Dir,* Pimeria Alta Historical Society, Nogales AZ

Spaull, Malcom, *Chmn Film/Video,* Rochester Institute of Technology, School of Photographic Arts & Sciences, Rochester NY (S)

Spave, Pari, *Cur,* Equitable Life Assurance Society, New York NY

Spear, Cheryl, *Secy,* Owatonna Arts Center, Community Arts Center, Owatonna MN

Spear, Richard, *Prof,* Oberlin College, Dept of Art, Oberlin OH (S)

Spears, Kimberly, *Prog Dir,* Anderson County Arts Council, Anderson SC

Speck, Lawrence, *Acting Dean,* University of Texas, School of Architecture, Austin TX (S)

Spector, Jack J, *Prof,* Rutgers, the State University of New Jersey, Graduate Program in Art History, New Brunswick NJ (S)

Speed, John S, *Pres Board Governor,* J B Speed Art Museum, Louisville KY

Speed, Karen, *Admin Asst,* University of California, University Art Gallery, Riverside CA

Speight, Jerry, *Assoc Prof,* Murray State University, Art Dept, Murray KY (S)

Speller, Randall, *Reference Librn,* Art Gallery of Ontario, Edward P Taylor Research Library & Archives, Toronto ON

Speller, Virginia, *Librn,* Old York Historical Society, George Marshall Store Library, York ME

Spellman, Bryan D, *Admin Officer,* University of Montana, Gallery of Visual Arts, Missoula MT

Spellman, Bryan D, *Admin Officer,* University of Montana, Paxson Gallery, Missoula MT

Spencer, Anne M, *Cur Ethnological Coll,* Newark Museum Association, The Newark Museum, Newark NJ

Spencer, Bruce, *Pres,* Lighthouse Gallery, Tequesta FL

Spencer, David M, *Branch Librn,* National Air and Space Museum, Library MRC 314, Washington DC

Spencer, Deirdre, *Head Fine Arts Library,* University of Michigan, Fine Arts Library, Ann Arbor MI

Spencer, Howard DaLee, *Cur,* Nevada Museum Of Art, Reno NV

Spencer, John, *Prof,* Duke University, Dept of Art and Art History, Durham NC (S)

Spencer, Marilyn, *Coordr of Vol & Membership,* Southern Methodist University, Meadows Museum, Dallas TX

Spencer, Paul, *Assoc Cur,* Minnesota Museum of American Art, Saint Paul MN

Spencer, Ruth, *Reference Librn,* Art Center College of Design, James Lemont Fogg Memorial Library, Pasadena CA

Spencer, Sue, *Pres Heritage Foundation,* Fort Morgan Heritage Foundation, Fort Morgan CO

Spencer, T W, *Admin VPres,* Transco Energy Company Inc, Transco Gallery, Houston TX

Spencer, William T, *Cur Exhibits,* National Baseball Hall of Fame and Museum, Inc, Art Collection, Cooperstown NY

Speranza, Kathy, *Painting,* Monserrat College of Art, Beverly MA (S)

Sperath, Albert, *Gallery Dir,* Murray State University, Eagle Gallery, Murray KY

Sperath, Albert, *Gallery Dir,* Murray State University, Art Dept, Murray KY (S)

Sperber, Barbara, *Dir Admin,* The Queens Museum of Art, Flushing NY

Sperling, Christine, *Asst Prof,* Bloomsburg University, Dept of Art, Bloomsburg PA (S)

Sperling, L Joy, *Chmn Dept,* Denison University, Dept of Art, Granville OH (S)

Sperow, Donna Wilt, *Adminr,* Bakehouse Art Complex, Inc, Miami FL

Speth, Constance W, *Chmn,* Central Washington University, Dept of Art, Ellensburg WA (S)

Spevers, Franklin, *Assoc Prof,* Calvin College, Art Dept, Grand Rapids MI (S)

Sphar, Carol, *Dir, Summer Art Prog,* Sierra Nevada College, Art Dept, Incline Village NV (S)

Spielmann, Diane, *Archivist,* Leo Baeck Institute, Library, New York NY

Spigel, Bernice, *Dir,* Creative Arts Guild, Dalton GA

Spikes, Tracy, *Cur,* Historic Saint Augustine Preservation Board, Saint Augustine FL

Spiller, Harley, *Adminr,* Franklin Furnace Archive, Inc, New York NY

Spillman, Jane, *cur American Glass,* Corning Museum of Glass, Corning NY

Spinar, Melvin, *Assoc Prof,* South Dakota State University, Dept of Visual Arts, Brookings SD (S)

Spindler, Virginia, *Mgr School & Teacher Prog,* Terra Museum of American Art, Chicago IL

Spink, Walter M, *Prof,* University of Michigan, Ann Arbor, Dept of History of Art, Ann Arbor MI (S)

Spink, William B, *Pres,* Naples Art Gallery, Naples FL

Spinski, Victor, *Coordr Ceramics,* University of Delaware, Dept of Art, Newark DE (S)

Spirn, Anne Whiston, *Chairperson,* University of Pennsylvania, Dept of Landscape Architecture & Regional Planning, Philadelphia PA (S)

Spiro, Edmund, *Treas,* Middlesex County Cultural & Heritage Commission, Artists League of Central New Jersey, North Brunswick NJ

Spiro, Stephen B, *Cur,* University of Notre Dame, Snite Museum of Art, Notre Dame IN

Spitler, Carol, *Assoc Prof,* Oakland City College, Division of Fine Arts, Oakland City IN (S)

Spitzer, Laura, *Prof,* Bucknell University, Dept of Art, Lewisburg PA (S)

Spitzmueller, Pamela, *Librn,* Guild of Book Workers, Library, New York NY

Splendore, Patricia, *Prog Dir,* American-Scandinavian Foundation, New York NY

Spoerner, Thomas, *Chmn,* Ball State University, Dept of Art, Muncie IN (S)

Spohn, Jennifer, *Chief Conservator,* Worcester Art Museum, Worcester MA

Sponenberg, Susan, *Coordr,* Luzerne County Community College, Commercial Art Dept, Nanticoke PA (S)

Spoo, Corinne H, *Librn,* Paine Art Center and Arboretum, George P Nevitt Library, Oshkosh WI

Spoon, Jennifer, *Asst Prof,* Radford University, Art Dept, Radford VA (S)

Sporny, Stan, *Prof,* Marshall University, Dept of Art, Huntington WV (S)

Spradling, Kim, *Asst Prof,* Northwest Missouri State University, Dept of Art, Maryville MO (S)

Sprague, Jack, *Advertising Design Coordr,* University of North Texas, School of Visual Arts, Denton TX (S)

Sprague, Mary, *Instructor,* Saint Louis Community College at Meramec, Art Dept, Saint Louis MO (S)

Sprigg, June, *Cur Coll,* Hancock Shaker Village, Inc, Pittsfield MA

Spring, Kathy, *Dir of Public Relations,* Ella Sharp Museum, Jackson MI

Springer, Clinton, *Chmn,* Warner House Association, MacPheadris-Warner House, Portsmouth NH

Sprout, Sally, *Art Cur,* Transco Energy Company Inc, Transco Gallery, Houston TX

Spurgin, John E, *VPres Academic Affairs,* Milwaukee Institute of Art and Design, Milwaukee WI (S)

Spurling, Noreer, *Treas,* Buffalo Society of Artists, Kenmore NY

Squier, Jack L, *Prof,* Cornell University, Dept of Art, Ithaca NY (S)

Squires, William, *Art Appreciation,* University of Georgia, Franklin College of Arts & Sciences, Dept of Art, Athens GA (S)

Srsen, Judy, *Asst to Dir,* Owatonna Arts Center, Community Arts Center, Owatonna MN

Stacey, Robert, *Supvr,* New York University, Stephen Chan Library of Fine Arts, New York NY

Stachura, Irene, *Reference,* San Francisco Maritime National Historical Park, J Porter Shaw Library, San Francisco CA

Stack, Danial M, *Dean,* International Fine Arts College, Miami FL (S)

Stack, Lotus, *Cur Textiles,* Minneapolis Society of Fine Arts, Minneapolis Institute of Arts, Minneapolis MN

Stack, Trudy Wilner, *Cur,* University of Arizona, Center for Creative Photography, Tucson AZ

Stackhouse, Mary, *Dir,* Truro Center for the Arts at Castle Hill, Inc, Truro MA (S)

Stackman, Robert, *Pres,* Greene County Historical Society, Bronck Museum, Coxsackie NY

Stackpole, Renny A, *Dir,* Penobscot Marine Museum, Searsport ME

Stacy, Betty, *Librn,* Virginia Museum of Fine Arts, Library, Richmond VA

Staebell, Sandra, *Cur of Coll & Registrar,* Western Kentucky University, Kentucky Museum, Bowling Green KY

Staebler, Tom, *VPres & Art Dir,* Playboy Enterprises, Inc, Chicago IL

Staffne, Dennis, *Prof,* Northern Michigan University, Dept of Art and Design, Marquette MI (S)

Stafford, F Eugene, *Instr,* Guilford Technical Community College, Commercial Art Dept, Jamestown NC (S)

Stafford, Jennifer, *Registrar,* Nelda C & H J Lutcher Stark Foundation, Stark Museum of Art, Orange TX

Stager, Lawrence, *Dir & Prof,* Harvard University, Semitic Museum, Cambridge MA

Staggs, Joe, *Library Technician,* University of Kentucky, Hunter M Adams Architecture Library, Lexington KY

Stahl, David G, *Pres,* New Hampshire Historical Society, Concord NH

Stahl, David G, *Pres,* New Hampshire Historical Society, Library, Concord NH

Stahl, Judith R, *Art Dir,* Louisiana State University, Union Art Gallery, Baton Rouge LA

Stahl, Stef, *Chmn Museum Educ,* Toledo Museum of Art, Toledo Museum of Art, Toledo OH

Stahler, Hank, *Building Dir,* Institute for Contemporary Art, Project Studio One (P S 1), Long Island City NY

Staiger, Paul, *Graduate Program Coordr,* San Jose State University, School of Art & Design, San Jose CA (S)

Staley, Thomas F, *Dir,* University of Texas at Austin, Harry Ransom Humanities Research Center, Austin TX

Stalnaker, Budd, *Prof,* Indiana University, Bloomington, Henry Radford Hope School of Fine Arts, Bloomington IN (S)

Stalsworth, Lee, *Chief Photography,* Hirshhorn Museum and Sculpture Garden, Washington DC

Stalvey, Dorrance, *Dir Music Programs,* Los Angeles County Museum of Art, Los Angeles CA

Stam, Deirdre C, *Pres,* Art Libraries Society of North America, Tucson AZ

Stamm, Geoffrey E, *Asst General Mgr,* United States Department of the Interior, Indian Arts & Crafts Board, Washington DC

Stammler, Ursula, *Dir,* University of Kansas, Architectural Resource Center, Lawrence KS

Stamper, Malcolm, *Chmn,* Seattle Art Museum, Seattle WA

Stampfle, Felice, *Emeritus Cur Drawings & Prints,* Pierpont Morgan Library, New York NY

Stancliffe, Thomas, *Asst Prof,* University of Northern Iowa, Dept of Art, Cedar Falls IA (S)

Stanczak, Julian, *Prof,* Cleveland Institute of Art, Cleveland OH (S)

Standridge, Christine, *Admin Asst,* Nassau County Museum of Fine Art, Roslyn NY

Stanfield, Alyson B, *Asst Cur,* Oklahoma City Art Museum, Oklahoma City OK

Stanfield, Alyson B, *Cur,* Oklahoma City Art Museum, Library, Oklahoma City OK

Stanford, Linda O, *Chmn,* Michigan State University, Dept of Art, East Lansing MI (S)

Stanford, Michael, *Adjunct Prof,* Wilkes University, Dept of Art, Wilkes-Barre PA (S)

Stangland-Cameron, Lyn, *Asst Prof,* Dean Junior College, Visual and Performing Art Dept, Franklin MA (S)

Stanislaus, Grace, *Dir,* Bronx Museum of the Arts, Bronx NY

Stanitz, Mark, *Prof,* Rochester Institute of Technology, School of Art and Design, Rochester NY (S)

Stanley, David, *Assoc Prof,* University of Florida, Dept of Art, Gainesville FL (S)

Stanley, Janet L, *Librn,* National Museum of African Art, The Warren M Robbins Library, Washington DC

Stanley, John S, *Asst to Dir,* Toledo Museum of Art, Toledo Museum of Art, Toledo OH

Stanley, Linda, *VPres Coll,* Historical Society of Pennsylvania, Philadelphia PA

Stanley, Robert A, *Prof,* Oakton Community College, Art & Architecture Dept, Des Plaines IL (S)

Stanley, T, *Instr,* Humboldt State University, College of Arts & Humanities, Arcata CA (S)

Stanley, Tom, *Dir,* Winthrop University Galleries, Rock Hill SC

Stanola, Sally, *Dir,* Tulane University, Dept Art Newcomb Col Art Galleries, New Orleans LA

Stansbury, George, *Chmn,* University of Mary Hardin-Baylor, Dept of Fine Arts, Belton TX (S)

Stanton, Barbara, *Membership Secy,* Ella Sharp Museum, Jackson MI

Staples, Wayne, *Chmn & Prof,* Acadia University, Art Dept, Wolfville NS (S)

Stapp, William F, *Sr Cur,* International Museum of Photography at George Eastman House, Rochester NY

Star, Doug, *Business Mgr,* Columbus Museum, Columbus GA

Starensier, Adele, *Adjunct Asst Prof,* Drew University, Art Dept, Madison NJ (S)

Stark, David, *Cur Education,* Rhode Island School of Design, Museum of Art, Providence RI

Stark, Nelda C, *Chmn,* Nelda C & H J Lutcher Stark Foundation, Stark Museum of Art, Orange TX

St-Arnaud, Jacques, *Guide,* Musee des Augustines de l'Hotel Dieu of Quebec, Quebec PQ

Starr, Daniel, *Assoc Librn Cataloguing,* Museum of Modern Art, Library, New York NY

Starr, Lori, *Head Public Information,* Getty Center for the History of Art & the Humanities Trust Museum, Santa Monica CA

Starr, Lori, *Head Public Information,* Getty Center for the History of Art & the Humanities Trust Museum, The J Paul Getty Museum, Santa Monica CA

Stasko, Joseph, *Exec Dir,* Organization of Independent Artists, New York NY

Statlander, Raymond, *Assoc Prof,* Jersey City State College, Art Dept, Jersey City NJ (S)

Staubo, Karl, *Dir,* Viridian Gallery, New York NY

Staudt, Christina, *Instr,* Dowling College, Dept of Visual Arts, Oakdale NY (S)

Staudt, Dennis, *Pres,* Art Gallery of Windsor, Windsor ON

Staum, Sonja, *Librn,* Museum of Contemporary Art, Library, Chicago IL

Staum, Sonja, *Librn,* Museum of Contemporary Art, Library, Chicago IL

Stautberg, Robert E, *Chmn Museum Committee,* Cincinnati Institute of Fine Arts, Taft Museum, Cincinnati OH

Stayner, Mary Ann, *Personnel Mgr,* Winnipeg Art Gallery, Winnipeg MB

Stayton, Kevin, *Cur Decorative Arts,* Brooklyn Museum, Brooklyn NY

St Claire, Archer, *Dir Prog,* Rutgers, the State University of New Jersey, Graduate Program in Art History, New Brunswick NJ (S)

Steadman, Clinton, *Treas,* Rochester Historical Society, Rochester NY

Steadman, David, *Dir,* Toledo Federation of Art Societies, Inc, Toledo OH

Steadman, David W, *Dir,* Toledo Museum of Art, Toledo Museum of Art, Toledo OH

Steadman, David W, *VPres,* The American Federation of Arts, New York NY

Steadman, Thomas, *Asst Prof,* Georgia Southern University, Dept of Art, Statesboro GA (S)

Steans, Joan, *Asst Prof,* Jersey City State College, Art Dept, Jersey City NJ (S)

Stebbins, Joan, *Dir & Cur,* Southern Alberta Art Gallery, Lethbridge AB

Stebbins, Theodore E, *Cur American Painting,* Museum of Fine Arts, Boston MA

Stebinger, Patricia, *Instr,* Marylhurst College, Art Dept, Marylhurst OR (S)

Stecchine, Brendan, *Dir,* Zone Art Center, Springfield MA

Stecchini, Brendan, *Instr,* Springfield College, Dept of Visual and Performing Arts, Springfield MA (S)

Stecher, Barbara, *Librn,* DeCordova Museum & Sculpture Park, DeCordova Museum Library, Lincoln MA

Steel, LaVar, *Chmn,* College of Southern Idaho, Art Dept, Twin Falls ID (S)

Steel, Rebecca D, *Head Librn,* Kalamazoo Institute of Arts, Library, Kalamazoo MI

Steel, Virginia Oberlin, *Dir,* Rutgers University, Stedman Art Gallery, Camden NJ

Steele, Brian, *Asst Prof,* Texas Tech University, Dept of Art, Lubbock TX (S)

Steele, Chris, *Photography,* Massachusetts Historical Society, Library, Boston MA

Steele, Curtis, *Chmn,* Arkansas State University, Dept of Art, Jonesboro AR (S)

Steele, John, *Assoc Prof,* East Tennessee State University, Fine Arts Dept, Johnson City TN (S)

Steele, Karen, *Adminr,* National Society of the Colonial Dames, Wilton House Museum, Richmond VA

Steele, Lisa, *Academic Dean,* Rocky Mountain College of Art & Design, Denver CO (S)

Steele, Steven M, *Dir,* Rocky Mountain College of Art & Design, Denver CO (S)

Steele, Tim, *Assoc Prof,* South Dakota State University, Dept of Visual Arts, Brookings SD (S)

Steele-Marsh, Ann, *Pres,* Associated Artists of New Jersey, Dover NJ

Steen, Karen, *Instr,* Cazenovia College, Center for Art & Design Studies, Cazenovia NY (S)

Steenberg, Gerald W, *Dir Library,* Saint Paul Public Library, Art & Music Dept, Saint Paul MN

Stefanko, Micheal, *Chmn Arts Dept,* Community College of Allegheny County, Fine Arts Dept, West Mifflin PA (S)

Steffen, Pamela, *Asst Prof,* Mount Mary College, Art Dept, Milwaukee WI (S)

Stegeman, Charles, *Chmn & Prof,* Haverford College, Fine Arts Dept, Haverford PA (S)

Steight, Carlton, *Cur,* Sturdivant Hall, Selma AL

Stein, Ed, *Chmn,* Brookdale Community College, Art Dept, Lincroft NJ (S)

Stein, Gael B, *Librn, Dir,* Saint Johnsbury Athenaeum, Saint Johnsbury VT

Stein, Jan, *Asst to Dir,* DeLand Museum of Art, DeLand FL

Stein, Judith E, *Cur,* Pennsylvania Academy of the Fine Arts, Galleries, Philadelphia PA

Stein, Julie, *Cur Archaeology,* University of Washington, Thomas Burke Memorial Washington State Museum, Seattle WA

Stein, Leslie, *Mgr,* Scalamandre Museum of Textiles, New York NY

Stein, Michael, *Faculty,* Housatonic Community College, Art Dept, Bridgeport CT (S)

Steinberg, David, *Asst Prof,* Case Western Reserve University, Dept of Art History & Art, Cleveland OH (S)

Steinberg, Rita, *Exec Dir,* Kentucky Art & Craft Gallery, Louisville KY

Steinberg, Ronald M, *Prof,* Rhode Island College, Art Dept, Providence RI (S)

Steinberg, Ronald M, *Prof,* Rhode Island College, Art Dept, Providence RI (S)

Steinbright, Janet, *Prog Servs Asst,* Institute Of Alaska Native Arts, Inc, Fairbanks AK

Steiner, Chris, *Cur of Education,* Albuquerque Museum of Art, History & Science, Albuquerque NM

Steiner, Frederick, *Chmn Planning,* Arizona State University, College of Architecture & Environmental Design, Tempe AZ (S)

Steiner, Suzanne, *Assoc Chmn,* Carlow College, Art Dept, Pittsburgh PA (S)

Steinhoff Morrison, Judith, *Dir Sewall Art Gallery,* Rice University, Dept of Art and Art History, Houston TX (S)

Steinke, Earl, *VPres Building & Grounds,* DuPage Art League School & Gallery, Wheaton IL

Steinman, Louise, *Spec Events Coordr,* Cultural Affairs Department City of Los Angeles, Junior Arts Center, Los Angeles CA

Steinsiek, Tommy A, *Dir,* Creek Council House Museum, Okmulgee OK

Steinway, Kate, *Cur Prints & Photographs,* Connecticut Historical Society, Hartford CT

Steir, Paul, *Treas,* Ukiyo-e Society of America, Inc, New York NY

Steirnagle, Michael, *Assoc Prof,* Palomar Community College, Art Dept, San Marcos CA (S)

Steiro, Carol, *Prog Mgr,* Museum of New Mexico, Museum of International Folk Art, Santa Fe NM

Stellwagen, Anne, *Acting Cur Educ,* Wadsworth Atheneum, Hartford CT

Stelzer, Stuart, *Library Dir,* University of the Ozarks, Dobson Memorial Library, Clarksville AR

Stene, Larry M, *Asst Prof,* Washington and Lee University, Division of Art, Lexington VA (S)

Stephanian, C, *Media Dir,* San Francisco Art Institute, Anne Bremer Memorial Library, San Francisco CA

Stephanic, Jeffrey L, *Assoc Prof,* George Washington University, Dept of Art, Washington DC (S)

Stephany, Jerry, *Assoc Prof,* University of Maryland, Baltimore County, Visual Arts Dept, Baltimore MD (S)

Stephen, Virginia, *Educ Cur,* Art Gallery of Nova Scotia, Halifax NS

Stephens, Bonnie, *Exec Dir,* Utah Arts Council, Chase Home Museum of Utah Folk Art, Salt Lake City UT

Stephens, Claude, *Education Dir,* Tallahassee Museum of History & Natural Science, Tallahassee FL

Stephens, Dennis, *Collection Development Officer,* University of Alaska, Elmer E Rasmuson Library, Fairbanks AK

Stephens, Elisa, *Pres,* Academy of Art College, Fine Arts Dept, San Francisco CA (S)

Stephens, Robert, *Instr,* John C Calhoun State Community College, Division of Fine Arts, Decatur AL (S)

Stephens, Roger, *Instr,* Southwestern Community College, Commercial Art and Advertising Design Dept, Sylva NC (S)

Stephens, Scott, *Acting Gallery Dir,* University of Montevallo, The Gallery, Montevallo AL

Stephens, Tom, *Dir,* University of Northern Colorado, John Mariani Art Gallery, Greeley CO

Stephens, William B, *Prof,* University of Texas at Tyler, Dept of Art, Tyler TX (S)

Stephenson, Christie, *Asst Librn Acquisitions,* University of Virginia, Fiske Kimball Fine Arts Library, Charlottesville VA

Stephenson, James, *Dir School of Visual Arts,* Pennsylvania State University, University Park, School of Visual Arts, University Park PA (S)

Stephenson, John H, *Interim Dean,* University of Michigan, Slusser Gallery, Ann Arbor MI

Stephenson, John H, *Interim Dean,* University of Michigan, Ann Arbor, School of Art, Ann Arbor MI (S)

Stephenson, Michael, *Dir,* Mitchell Museum, Mount Vernon IL

Stepheson, Richard, *Head Div,* Regis College, Fine Arts Dept, Denver CO (S)

Stepic, Barbara, *Pres,* Brooklyn Historical Society, Brooklyn OH

Stepney, Philip H R, *Dir,* Department of Culture & Multi-Culturalism, Provincial Museum of Alberta, Edmonton AB

Sterba, Lynn, *Asst,* University of Houston, Architecture and Art Library, Houston TX

Sterling, Cathy Card, *Dir of Corporate & Foundation Relations,* The Phillips Collection, Washington DC

Sterling, Peter, *Pres,* Children's Museum, Rauh Memorial Library, Indianapolis IN

Sterling, William, *Assoc Prof,* Wilkes University, Dept of Art, Wilkes-Barre PA (S)

Sterm, Stacey, *Development Asst,* Bellevue Art Museum, Bellevue WA

Stern, Evelyn, *Exec Dir,* Society for Folk Arts Preservation, Inc, New York NY

Stern, Lanning, *Assoc Chair, Design,* San Jose State University, School of Art & Design, San Jose CA (S)

Stern, Zelda, *PR-Development Dir,* Williams College, Museum of Art, Williamstown MA

Sternal, Thomas, *Dir,* Morehead State University, Claypool-Young Art Gallery, Morehead KY

Sternal, Tom, *Chmn,* Morehead State University, Art Dept, Morehead KY (S)

Sternfeld, Joel, *Instr,* Sarah Lawrence College, Dept of Art History, Bronxville NY (S)

Sterrenburg, Joan, *Prof,* Indiana University, Bloomington, Henry Radford Hope School of Fine Arts, Bloomington IN (S)

Sterritt, Coleen, *Vis Instr,* Claremont Graduate School, Dept of Fine Arts, Claremont CA (S)

Stetson, Daniel E, *Dir,* Laguna Gloria Art Museum, Austin TX

Stetson, Linda, *Treas,* Lincoln County Historical Association, Maine Art Gallery, Old Academy, Wiscasset ME

Stetson, Martha, *Dir,* Lincoln County Historical Association, Pownalborough Court House, Wiscasset ME

Stetson, Martha, *Dir,* Lincoln County Historical Association, Library, Wiscasset ME

Stetson, Martha, *Dir,* Lincoln County Historical Association, Lincoln County Museum & Pre-Revolutionary Court House, Wiscasset ME

Stevanov, Zoran, *Assoc Prof,* Fort Hays State University, Dept of Art, Hays KS (S)

Stevens, Arthur, *Chmn Dept,* Scripps College, Art Dept, Claremont CA (S)

Stevens, Edward, *Lectr,* University of Wisconsin-Stout, Dept of Art & Design, Menomonie WI (S)

Stevens, Edward B, *Pres,* Museum of American Textile History, North Andover MA

Stevens, Jane, *Admin Asst & Registration,* Illinois State Museum, State of Illinois Art Gallery, Chicago IL

Stevens, John, *Prof,* Manchester Community College, Fine Arts Dept, Manchester CT (S)

Stevens, Ken, *Chmn,* University of Puget Sound, Art Dept, Tacoma WA (S)

Stevens, Lynnette, *Periodical Librn,* LeMoyne College, Wilson Art Gallery, Syracuse NY

Stevens, Mark B, *Preparator,* Burnaby Art Gallery, Burnaby BC

Stevens, Michael, *State Historian,* State Historical Society of Wisconsin, State Historical Museum, Madison WI

Stevens, Nancy, *Ed,* Amon Carter Museum, Fort Worth TX

Stevens, N Lee, *Sr Cur Art Coll,* State Museum of Pennsylvania, Harrisburg PA

Stevens, N Lee, *Sr Cur Art,* State Museum of Pennsylvania, Pennsylvania Historical & Museum Commission, Harrisburg PA

Stevens, Susan, *Treas,* Florida Artist Group Inc, Punta Gorda FL

Stevens, Teresa Cummings, *Head Librn,* Maryland College of Art & Design Library, Silver Spring MD

Stevenson, Alma Gallanos, *Head Dept,* Stevenson Academy of Traditional Painting, Sea Cliff NY (S)

Stevenson, Cynthia, *Assoc Cur,* University of Louisville, Photographic Archives, Louisville KY

Stevenson, Frances, *Publications Officer,* National Portrait Gallery, Washington DC

Stevenson, John R, *Pres,* National Gallery of Art, Washington DC

Stevenson, Robert, *VPres Government & Pub Relations,* K Mart Corp, Troy MI

Stevenson, Ruth Carter, *Pres,* Amon Carter Museum, Fort Worth TX

Steward, Cynthia, *Gift Shop Mgr,* Tulane University, Gallier House Museum, New Orleans LA

Steward, James, *Cur,* University of California, University Art Museum, Berkeley CA

Steward, Karla, *Head of Fine Arts Div,* Akron-Summit County Public Library, Fine Arts Division, Akron OH

Steward, Martha J, *Dir of IRC,* California Polytechnic State University, College of Architecture & Environmental Design-Art Collection, San Luis Obispo CA

Stewart, Ann, *Assoc Cur of Education,* University of Utah, Utah Museum of Fine Arts, Salt Lake City UT

Stewart, Arch W L, *Head Library & Archives,* Canadian Museum of Nature, Musee Canadien de la Nature, Ottawa ON

Stewart, David, *Asst Prof,* University of Alabama in Huntsville, Dept of Art & Art History, Huntsville AL (S)

Stewart, Dennis, *Cur of Educ,* Southern Ohio Museum Corporation, Southern Ohio Museum & Cultural Center, Portsmouth OH

Stewart, Dorothy, *Corresp Secy,* Kent Art Association, Inc, Gallery, Kent CT

Stewart, Dorothy C, *Recording Secy,* Florida Artist Group Inc, Punta Gorda FL

Stewart, Duncan E, *Dir,* University of West Florida, Art Gallery, Pensacola FL

Stewart, Duncan E, *Assoc Prof,* University of West Florida, Dept of Art, Pensacola FL (S)

Stewart, Ian R, *Deputy Dir,* Minnesota Historical Society, Saint Paul MN

Stewart, James, *Assoc Dean,* Ohio University, School of Art, Athens OH (S)

Stewart, James A, *Adminr,* Historical and Cultural Affairs, Delaware State Museums, Dover DE

Stewart, John, *Asst State Archivist,* Ohio Historical Society, Archives-Library Division, Columbus OH

Stewart, John, *Business Adminr,* Ontario College of Art, Toronto ON (S)

Stewart, John, *Chmn,* Eastfield College, Humanities Division, Art Dept, Mesquite TX (S)

Stewart, John, *Prof Fine Arts,* University of Cincinnati, School of Art, Cincinnati OH (S)

Stewart, Larry, *Second VPres Exhib,* Arizona Artist Guild, Phoenix AZ

Stewart, Lizbeth, *Chmn Crafts,* University of the Arts, Philadelphia College of Art & Design, Philadelphia PA (S)

Stewart, Mark, *Communications Officer,* J B Speed Art Museum, Louisville KY

Stewart, Milo V, *Assoc Dir,* New York State Historical Association, Fenimore House, Cooperstown NY

Stewart, Paula, *Archivist,* Amon Carter Museum, Library, Fort Worth TX

Stewart, Priscilla, *Prof,* Manatee Community College, Dept of Art & Humanities, Bradenton FL (S)

Stewart, Regina, *Pres,* New York Artists Equity Association, Inc, New York NY

Stewart, Rick, *Cur Western Paintings,* Amon Carter Museum, Fort Worth TX

Stewart, Robert, *Assoc Prof,* Atlanta College of Art, Atlanta GA (S)

Stewart, Robert G, *Cur Paintings & Sculpture,* National Portrait Gallery, Washington DC

Stewart, Rowena, *Exec Dir,* Afro-American Historical & Cultural Museum, Philadelphia PA

Stewart, Shelia, *Exec Dir,* Art Museum of Southeast Texas, Beaumont TX

Stewart, Wes, *Photographer Technician,* Old Salem Inc, Museum of Early Southern Decorative Arts, Winston-Salem NC

Stewart, William G, *General Mgr,* Willet Stained Glass Studios, Philadelphia PA

Steyaert, John, *Assoc Prof,* University of Minnesota, Minneapolis, Art History, Minneapolis MN (S)

St Gelais, R, *Asst Librn,* Musee du Quebec, Bibliotheque des Arts, Quebec PQ

St Germain, Cheryl, *Membership & Vol Coordr,* Old York Historical Society, York ME

St Hours, Harry, *Assoc Prof,* Hood College, Dept of Art, Frederick MD (S)

Stick, Gordon M F, *VPres,* Star-Spangled Banner Flag House Association, Flag House & 1812 Museum, Baltimore MD

Stickney, Laura, *Teacher Outreach Coordr,* Cultural Affairs Department City of Los Angeles, Junior Arts Center, Los Angeles CA

Stidsen, Donald, *Asst Cur Exhibits,* Massachusetts Institute of Technology, MIT Museum, Cambridge MA

Stiebeling, D, *Asst Prof,* McGill University, Department of Art History, Montreal PQ (S)

Stieber, Nancy, *Asst Prof,* University of Massachusetts at Boston, Art Dept, Boston MA (S)

Stier, Maggie, *Cur,* Fruitlands Museum, Inc, Harvard MA

Stier, Margaret, *Cur,* Fruitlands Museum, Inc, Library, Harvard MA

Stiff, Juanita, *Treas,* Roswell Museum and Art Center, Roswell NM

Stiger, Lucille, *Registrar,* University of Wisconsin-Madison, Elvehjem Museum of Art, Madison WI

Stiles, Claire, *Chmn,* Eckerd College, Art Dept, Saint Petersburg FL (S)

Stiles, Kristine, *Asst Prof,* Duke University, Dept of Art and Art History, Durham NC (S)

Still, Chris, *Instr,* Dunedin Fine Arts and Cultural Center, Dunedin FL (S)

Stillman, Diane Brandt, *Dir of Education,* Walters Art Gallery, Baltimore MD

Stillman, Wadell, *Dir Admin & Finance,* Historic Hudson Valley, Tarrytown NY

Stinchcomb, Donna, *Dir Educ,* Sangre de Cristo Arts & Conference Center, Pueblo CO

Stinespring, John, *Asst Prof,* Texas Tech University, Dept of Art, Lubbock TX (S)

Stipe Maas, Jim, *Actg Preparator,* University of Georgia, Georgia Museum of Art, Athens GA

Stirn-Ainslie, Suzanne, *Dir,* Abigail Adams Smith Museum, New York NY

Stitt, Susan, *Pres,* Historical Society of Pennsylvania, Philadelphia PA

Stiver, Greg, *Instr,* Oral Roberts University, Fine Arts Dept, Tulsa OK (S)

Stivers, David, *Archivist,* Nabisco Brands, Inc, East Hanover NJ

St James, Gerald, *Dean,* Leeward Community College, Arts and Humanities Division, Pearl City HI (S)

St John, Terry, *Head Dept,* College of Notre Dame, Dept of Art, Belmont CA (S)

St Lawrence, Frances, *Business Mgr,* Birmingham-Bloomfield Art Association, Birmingham MI

Stock, Karen, *Dir,* Lansing Art Gallery, Lansing MI

Stocker, Eric, *Librn,* Redwood Library and Athenaeum, Newport RI

Stockton, Diana H, *Admin,* Essex Historical Society, Essex Shipbuilding Museum, Essex MA

Stockwell, Ross, *Instr,* San Diego Mesa College, Fine Arts Dept, San Diego CA (S)

Stoddard, Brooks, *Assoc Prof,* University of Maine at Augusta, Division of Fine & Performing Arts, Augusta ME (S)

Stoessell, Pamela, *Prof,* Marymount University of Virginia, School of Arts & Sciences Division, Arlington VA (S)

Stoker, E, *Prof,* Incarnate Word College, Art Dept, San Antonio TX (S)

Stoker, Jim, *Chmn,* Trinity University, Dept of Art, San Antonio TX (S)

Stokes, Charlotte, *Chmn Dept,* Oakland University, Dept of Art and Art History, Rochester MI (S)

Stokes, David, *Asst Prof,* Winthrop College, Dept of Art & Design, Rock Hill SC (S)

Stokes, Leonard, *Chmn,* University of Pennsylvania, Graduate School of Fine Arts, Philadelphia PA (S)

Stokes, Sally Sims, *Cur NTL,* University of Maryland, College Park, Architecture Library, College Park MD

Stokes, Sally Sims, *Librn,* University of Maryland, College Park, Historic Preservation Library, College Park MD

Stokstad, Marilyn, *Research Cur,* University of Kansas, Spencer Museum of Art, Lawrence KS

Stokstad, Marilyn, *Consult Cur Medieval Art,* Nelson-Atkins Museum of Art, Kansas City MO

Stokstad, Marilyn, *Pres,* International Center of Medieval Art, Inc, New York NY

Stokstad, Marilyn, *Prof,* University of Kansas, Kress Foundation Dept of Art History, Lawrence KS (S)

Stolar, Katrusia, *Educ Exten Coordr,* Ukrainian Cultural and Educational Centre, Winnipeg MB

Stolper, Carolyn, *Dir Development,* Museum of Contemporary Art, Chicago IL

Stone, Caroline, *Educ & Exhib Cur,* Memorial University of Newfoundland, Art Gallery, Saint John's NF

Stone, Carolyn, *Chmn Art Education,* Delta State University, Fielding L Wright Art Center, Cleveland MS

Stone, Carolyn Rea, *Prof,* Delta State University, Dept of Art, Cleveland MS (S)

Stone, Denise, *Asst Prof,* University of Kansas, Dept of Art & Music Education & Music Therapy, Lawrence KS (S)

Stone, Elizabeth, *Pres,* Wenham Museum, Wenham MA

Stone, Gaylund, *Gallery Dir,* Concordia University Wisconsin, Fine Art Gallery, Mequon WI

Stone, Gerald, *Information Services Section,* National Archives of Canada, Documentary Art and Photography, Ottawa ON

Stone, Harold, *Instr,* Lakewood Community College, Humanities Dept, White Bear Lake MN (S)

Stone, James, *Chmn,* Hannibal La Grange College, Art Dept, Hannibal MO (S)

Stone, Lawre, *Dir of Education,* Isamu Noguchi Foundation, Garden Museum, Long Island City NY

Stone, Robert L, *Folk Arts Coordr,* Florida Folklife Programs, White Springs FL

Stone, Thelma, *Arts Unit Mgr,* Fort Worth Public Library, Fine Arts Section, Fort Worth TX

Stone-Ferrier, Linda, *Grad Advisory & Assoc Prof,* University of Kansas, Kress Foundation Dept of Art History, Lawrence KS (S)

Stoneham, John, *Librn,* Maryland Institute, Library, Baltimore MD

Stonelaws, Linda, *Cur Art,* Frank Phillips Foundation Inc, Woolaroc Museum, Bartlesville OK

Stone-Miller, Rebecca, *Asst Prof,* Emory University, Art History Dept, Atlanta GA (S)

Stonestreet, Robert, *Dir & Treas,* Public Library of Cincinnati & Hamilton County, Art & Music Department, Cincinnati OH

Stooker, Hendrik, *Dir,* Occidental College, Weingart & Coons Galleries, Los Angeles CA

Stoops, Susan, *Cur,* Brandeis University, Rose Art Museum, Waltham MA

Stopka, Christina, *Librn,* Buffalo Bill Memorial Association, Buffalo Bill Historical Center, Cody WY

Stopka, Tina, *Librn & Archivist,* Buffalo Bill Memorial Association, Harold McCracken Research Library, Cody WY

Stoppert, Mary, *Coordr & Prof,* Northeastern Illinois University, Gallery, Chicago IL

Storr/, robert, *Vis Instr,* Claremont Graduate School, Dept of Fine Arts, Claremont CA (S)

Storwick, Michael, *Spec Serv Librn,* University of Portland, Wilson W Clark Memorial Library, Portland OR

Story, Charlotte, *Asst Prof,* American University, Dept of Art, Washington DC (S)

Story, Dana A, *Historian,* Essex Historical Society, Essex Shipbuilding Museum, Essex MA

Story, Jean, *Registrar,* Contemporary Arts Museum, Houston TX

Stoughton, Kathleen, *Instr,* San Diego Mesa College, Fine Arts Dept, San Diego CA (S)

Stoughton, Michael, *Assoc Prof,* University of Minnesota, Minneapolis, Art History, Minneapolis MN (S)

Stout, Charles, *Museum Cur,* University of Illinois, Museum of Natural History, Champaign IL

Stout, Ken, *Assoc Prof,* University of Arkansas, Art Dept, Fayetteville AR (S)

Stout, Sara, *Lectr,* Trinity College, Art Dept, Washington DC (S)

Stout, William G, *Registrar,* Frick Collection, New York NY

Stovel, Bud, *Pres & Dir,* Revelstoke Art Group, Revelstoke BC

Stover, Cathy, *Supervisory & Archivist,* Archives of American Art, New York Regional Center, Washington DC

Stover, Donald L, *Cur American Decorative Arts,* Fine Arts Museums of San Francisco, M H de Young Memorial Museum and California Palace of the Legion of Honor, San Francisco CA

Stover, Kathy, *Museum Shop,* Museum of Fine Arts, Saint Petersburg, Florida, Inc, Saint Petersburg FL

Stowell, Don, *Dir,* North Dakota State University, Div of Fine Arts, Fargo ND (S)

Stowell, Michael W, *Dir,* Saint Cloud State University, Kiehle Gallery, Saint Cloud MN

Stowens, Doris, *Registrar,* American Craft Council, American Craft Museum, New York NY

Stowers, John Walter, *Pres,* Montgomery Museum of Fine Arts, Montgomery AL

Stowers, Robert, *Assoc Prof,* University of Wisconsin-Stevens Point, Dept of Art & Design, Stevens Point WI (S)

Strachota, John, *Instructor,* Milwaukee Area Technical College, Graphic Arts Dept, Milwaukee WI (S)

Straight, Robert, *Coordr Foundations,* University of Delaware, Dept of Art, Newark DE (S)

Stranahan, Duane, *Pres,* Toledo Museum of Art, Toledo Museum of Art, Toledo OH

Strandberg, Kevin, *Instr,* Illinois Wesleyan University, School of Art, Bloomington IL (S)

Strange, Georgia, *Assoc Prof,* Indiana University, Bloomington, Henry Radford Hope School of Fine Arts, Bloomington IN (S)

Strange, Tom, *Dir,* Daniel Boone Regional Library, Columbia MO

Strassfield, Christina Mossaides, *Cur,* Guild Hall of East Hampton, Inc, Guild Hall Museum, East Hampton NY

Strathman-Becker, Randy, *Art Prog Dir,* Teikyo Westmar University, Art Dept, LeMars IA (S)

Stratton, John, *Asst Librn,* Bethany College, Library, Lindsborg KS

Stratton, Priscilla, *Operations Mgr,* University of Chicago, David and Alfred Smart Museum of Art, Chicago IL

Stratyner, Barbara, *Cur Exhibits,* The New York Public Library, Shelby Cullom Davis Museum, New York NY

Straub, Dale, *Prof,* Pennsylvania College of Technology, Dept of Design & Communiation Arts, Williamsport PA (S)

Strauber, Susan, *Instr,* Grinnell College, Dept of Art, Grinnell IA (S)

Strauss, Linda, *Cur Visual Resources Coll,* Columbia University, Dept of Art History & Archeology, New York NY

Strawn, Martha, *Instr,* University of North Carolina at Charlotte, Dept of Visual Arts, Charlotte NC (S)

Strecker, Eleanor, *Childrens Dept Head,* Topeka Public Library, Gallery of Fine Arts, Topeka KS

Streed, Crit, *Assoc Prof,* University of Northern Iowa, Dept of Art, Cedar Falls IA (S)

Street, Betty, *Assoc Prof,* Texas Tech University, Dept of Art, Lubbock TX (S)

Streetman, Evon, *Prof,* University of Florida, Dept of Art, Gainesville FL (S)

Streetman, John W, *Dir,* Evansville Museum of Arts and Science, Evansville IN

Strehlke, Carl B, *Adjunct Cur,* Philadelphia Museum of Art, John G Johnson Collection, Philadelphia PA

Streitz, Ronald, *Artistic Dir,* Pewabic Society Inc, Detroit MI

Stremsterfer, Marianne, *Instr,* Springfield College in Illinois, Dept of Art, Springfield IL (S)

Streng, Barbara, *Adminr,* Boise Art Museum, Boise ID

Stretch, Cynthia, *Acting Adminr,* Rosicrucian Egyptian Museum and Art Gallery, San Jose CA

Stricevic, George, *Prof Art History,* University of Cincinnati, School of Art, Cincinnati OH (S)

Strickland, Alice, *Exec Dir,* Goldsboro Art Center, Goldsboro NC (S)

Strickland, Barbour, *Exec Dir,* Greenville Museum of Art, Inc, Greenville NC

Strickland, Barbour, *Exec Dir,* Greenville Museum of Art, Inc, Reference Library, Greenville NC

Strickland, Eycke, *Lectr,* Emory University, Art History Dept, Atlanta GA (S)

Strickland, Melissa, *Registrar,* Saint Gregory's Abbey and College, Mabee-Gerrer Museum of Art, Shawnee OK

Strickler, Susan E, *Dir Curatorial Affairs,* Worcester Art Museum, Worcester MA

Stricklin, Linda, *Dept Chmn & Gallery Dir,* McMurry University, Ryan Fine Arts Center, Abilene TX

Stringer, Candace, *Instr,* Wayne Art Center, Wayne PA (S)

Stringer, Mary Evelyn, *Prof,* Mississippi University for Women, Division of Fine & Performing Arts, Columbus MS (S)

Stringfield, Susan, *Chief Librn,* Miami Dade Public Library, Miami Beach Branch, Miami Beach FL

Strohm, Robert, *Assoc Dir,* Virginia Historical Society, Richmond VA

Strohman, Barbara J, *Assoc Prof,* Bloomsburg University, Dept of Art, Bloomsburg PA (S)

Strombotne, James S, *Prof,* University of California, Riverside, Dept of Art, Riverside CA (S)

Strong, Deidre, *Dir Public Relations,* Austin Children's Museum, Austin TX

Strong, Donald, *Chmn Art History,* California State University, Northridge, Dept of Art-Two Dimensional Media, Northridge CA (S)

Strong, Donald S, *Chmn,* California State University, Northridge, Art History Dept, Northridge CA (S)

Strong, John, *Dir,* Lake George Arts Project, Courthouse Gallery, Lake George NY

Strong, Karin, *Pres,* Catharine Lorillard Wolfe Art Club, Inc, New York NY

Strong, Scott M, *Museum Specialist,* United States Senate Commission on Art, Washington DC

Stroot, Scott, *Asst Prof,* Bradford College, Creative Arts Division, Bradford MA (S)

Strope, Mary, *Exec Dir,* Michigan Guild of Artists & Artisans, Michigan Guild Gallery, Ann Arbor MI

Strother, Joseph W, *Dir,* Louisiana Tech University, School of Art and Architecture, Ruston LA (S)

Strother, Robert A, *Coordr,* Greenville County Museum of Art, Museum School of Art, Greenville SC (S)

Stroud, Betty, *Dept Head,* Union College, Art Dept, Barbourville KY (S)

Stroud, Jane, *Partner,* Stroud Waller Inc, Highland Park IL

Stroup, Joanne, *Dir & Cur,* Wabaunsee County Historical Museum, Alma KS

Stroup, Rodger, *Dir Coll & Interpretation,* South Carolina State Museum, Columbia SC

Stroup, Timothy, *Chmn,* John Jay College of Criminal Justice, Dept of Art, Music and Philosophy, New York NY (S)

Strouse, Norman H, *Dir,* Silverado Museum, Saint Helena CA

Strueber, Michael M, *Dir,* Southern Alleghenies Museum of Art, Loretto PA

Struthers, Sharon, *Instr,* The Arkansas Arts Center, Museum School, Little Rock AR (S)

Stuart, Joseph, *Dir,* South Dakota State University, South Dakota Art Museum, Brookings SD

Stuart, Joseph, *Prof,* South Dakota State University, Dept of Visual Arts, Brookings SD (S)

Stuart, Nancy, *Chmn Applied Photography,* Rochester Institute of Technology, School of Photographic Arts & Sciences, Rochester NY (S)

Stuart, Nancy, *Assoc Prof,* Rochester Institute of Technology, School of Photographic Arts & Sciences, Rochester NY (S)

Stuart, Signey, *Prof,* South Dakota State University, Dept of Visual Arts, Brookings SD (S)

Stubbs, Sharon, *Treas,* Iowa City - Johnson County Arts Council, Arts Center, Iowa City IA

Stuckenbruck, Corky, *Dir,* Texas Woman's University Art Gallery, Denton TX

Stuckenbruck, Linda, *Assoc Prof,* Texas Woman's University, Dept of Visual Arts, Denton TX (S)

Stuckey, Charles, *Cur 20th Century Painting & Sculpture,* The Art Institute of Chicago, Chicago IL

Stuhlman, Rachel, *Librn,* International Museum of Photography at George Eastman House, Library, Rochester NY

Stuhr, Pat, *Asst Prof,* Ohio State University, Dept of Art Education, Columbus OH (S)

Stule, Will, *Prof,* Butte College, Dept of Fine Arts, Oroville CA (S)

Stull, Donald L, *Commissioner,* Boston Art Commission of the City of Boston, Boston MA

Stull, Staci, *Slide Cur,* Massachusetts College of Art, Morton R Godine Library, Boston MA

Stupay, Diane, *VPres,* Cleveland Museum of Art, Print Club of Cleveland, Cleveland OH

Stupler, Harvey, *Instr,* Long Beach City College, Dept of Art, Long Beach CA (S)

Sturgeon, Mary, *Prof,* University of North Carolina at Chapel Hill, Art Dept, Chapel Hill NC (S)

Sturgeon, Thelma M, *Exec Coordr,* Bicentennial Art Center & Museum, Paris IL

Sturges, Hollister, *Dir,* Museum of Fine Arts, Springfield MA

Sturges, Hollister, *Dir,* George Walter Vincent Smith Art Museum, Springfield MA

Sturgess, Louise, *Exec Dir,* Pittsburgh History & Landmarks Foundation, James D Van Trump Library, Pittsburgh PA

Sturr, Ed, *Prof,* Kansas State University, Art Dept, Manhattan KS

Sturr, Ed, *Assoc Prof,* Kansas State University, Art Dept, Manhattan KS (S)

Stutts, Lora, *Gallery Dir,* Barton College, Case Art Gallery & Rackley Room Gallery, Wilson NC

Stutts, Lora, *Instr,* Barton College, Communication, Performaing & Visual Arts, Wilson NC (S)

Styka, Wanda Magdeleine, *Archivist,* National Trust for Historic Preservation, Museum Library & Archives, Glendale MA

Styron, Thomas W, *Exec Dir,* Greenville County Museum of Art, Greenville SC

Subler, Craig, *Dir,* University of Missouri-Kansas City, Gallery of Art, Kansas City MO

Sudano, G R, *Head Dept,* Purdue University, West Lafayette, Dept of Visual & Performaing Arts, Div of Art & Design, West Lafayette IN (S)

Suddith, John T, *Chmn,* Louisiana College, Dept of Art, Pineville LA (S)

Sudeburg, Erika, *Assoc Prof,* University of California, Riverside, Dept of Art, Riverside CA (S)

Sudman, Sharon, *Instr,* Saint Olaf College, Art Dept, Northfield MN (S)

Suelflow, August R, *Dir,* Concordia Historical Institute, Saint Louis MO

Sugarman, Matthew, *Assoc Prof,* University of Northern Iowa, Dept of Art, Cedar Falls IA (S)

Sugg, Joel D, *Pres,* San Angelo Museum of Fine Arts, San Angelo TX

Suggs, Marianne Stevens, *Chmn,* Appalachian State University, Dept of Art, Boone NC (S)

Sulkin, Robert, *Chmn,* Hollins College, Art Dept, Roanoke VA (S)

Sullivan, Anne, *Registrar,* University of Arizona, Center for Creative Photography, Tucson AZ

Sullivan, Brenda, *Dir,* Photographic Resource Center, Boston MA

Sullivan, Catherine, *Asst Dir,* California State University, Chico, University Art Gallery, Chico CA

Sullivan, Donna, *Dept Head Fashion Marketing,* Art Institute of Houston, Houston TX (S)

Sullivan, Eugene, *Prof,* Framingham State College, Art Dept, Framingham MA (S)

Sullivan, Gerald P, *Sr Lect,* Santa Clara University, Art Dept, Santa Clara CA (S)

Sullivan, Jacqueline, *Asst Dir for Admin,* New Orleans Museum of Art, New Orleans LA

Sullivan, James E, *Assoc Prof,* Southern Illinois University, School of Art & Design, Carbondale IL (S)

Sullivan, John, *Assoc Prof,* Arkansas Tech University, Dept of Art, Russellville AR (S)

Sullivan, Kyra, *VPres-Programs,* Coalition of Women's Art Organizations, Port Washington WI

Sullivan, Linda S, *Exec Dir,* Mississippi Museum of Art, Jackson MS

Sullivan, Mark, *Asst Prof,* Villanova University, Dept of Art and Art History, Villanova PA (S)

Sullivan, Martin, *Dir,* Heard Museum, Phoenix AZ

Sullivan, Patricia, *Asst Librn,* Cornell University, Fine Arts Library, Ithaca NY

Sullivan, Ronald Dee, *Prof,* Del Mar College, Art Dept, Corpus Christi TX (S)

Sullivan, Scott, *Acting Dean,* University of North Texas, School of Visual Arts, Denton TX (S)

Sullivan, Scott A, *Pres,* Midwest Art History Society, Denton TX

Sultan, Larry, *Photography,* California College of Arts and Crafts, Oakland CA (S)

Sultan, Terrie, *Cur,* Corcoran Gallery of Art, Washington DC

Sulzberger, Arthur Ochs, *Chmn Board Trustees,* The Metropolitan Museum of Art, New York NY

Sulzner, Nathalie, *Slide Librn,* University of Massachusetts, Amherst, Dorothy W Perkins Slide Library, Amherst MA

Summa, Terry, *Dean,* Foothill College, Fine Arts and Communications Div, Los Altos Hills CA (S)

Summers, Betty, *Secy,* Manitoba Historical Society, Dalnavert Museum, Winnipeg MB

Summers, Cherie, *Registrar,* Santa Barbara Museum of Art, Santa Barbara CA

Summers, David, *Chmn,* University of Virginia, McIntire Dept of Art, Charlottesville VA (S)

Summers, Gene, *Chmn Architecture,* Illinois Institute of Technology, College of Architecture, Chicago IL (S)

Summers, Nancy, *Instr,* Woodstock School of Art, Inc, Woodstock NY (S)

Sumner, Stephen, *Acting Chmn,* University of Tulsa, Dept of Art, Tulsa OK (S)

Sumner, William M, *Dir,* University of Chicago, Oriental Institute Museum, Chicago IL

Sumrall, Robert F, *Cur of Ship Models,* United States Naval Academy Museum, Annapolis MD

Sund, Judy, *Asst Prof,* Duke University, Dept of Art and Art History, Durham NC (S)

Sundby, Mel, *Instr,* Lakewood Community College, Humanities Dept, White Bear Lake MN (S)

Sundet, E S, *Instr,* Humboldt State University, College of Arts & Humanities, Arcata CA (S)

Sundin, Einar, *Pres,* Koochiching County Historical Society Museum, International Falls MN

Sundt, Christine L, *Slide Cur,* University of Oregon, Architecture and Allied Arts Library, Eugene OR

Sungur, Barbara Z, *Assoc Prof,* University of British Columbia, Dept of Fine Arts, Vancouver BC (S)

Sunkel, Robert, *Percival DeLuce Art Gallery Coll Cur,* Northwest Missouri State University, DeLuce Art Gallery, Maryville MO

Sunkel, Robert, *Assoc Prof,* Northwest Missouri State University, Dept of Art, Maryville MO (S)

Supancic, David, *Asst Dir,* Sangre de Cristo Arts & Conference Center, Pueblo CO

Surratt, Monte, *Instr,* Cochise College, Art Dept, Douglas AZ (S)

Surtees, Ursula, *Dir & Cur,* Kelowna Centennial Museum and National Exhibit Centre, Kelowna BC

Susi, Frank, *Grad Coordr,* Kent State University, School of Art, Kent OH (S)

Susi, Frank, *Div Coordr Art Educ,* Kent State University, School of Art, Kent OH (S)

Sussman, Robert, *Pres,* 55 Mercer, New York NY (S)

Sussman, Wendy, *Prof,* University of California, Berkeley, College of Letters & Sciences-Art Dept, Berkeley CA (S)

Sussmann, Elisabeth, *Cur,* Whitney Museum of American Art, New York NY

Susstrink, Sabrine, *Asst Prof,* Rochester Institute of Technology, School of Photographic Arts & Sciences, Rochester NY (S)

Suter, David, *Dean,* St Martins College, Humanities Dept, Lacey WA (S)

Suter, Sherwood, *Prof,* McMurry University, Art Dept, Abilene TX (S)

Sutherin, Judy, *Dir Communications,* Arts Council, Inc, Winston-Salem NC

Sutherland, Cara, *Cur of Exhibits,* Museum of Our National Heritage, Lexington MA

Suthren, V J H, *Dir,* Canadian War Museum, Ottawa ON

Sutinen, Paul, *Asst Chairperson,* Marylhurst College, Art Dept, Marylhurst OR (S)

Sutter, Gwen, *Assoc Admin,* University of Minnesota, University Art Museum, Minneapolis MN

Sutter, James, *Prof,* State University of New York College at Potsdam, Dept of Fine Arts, Potsdam NY (S)

Sutton, Judith, *Assoc Dir,* Public Library of Charlotte and Mecklenburg County, Charlotte NC

Sutton, Patricia, *Asst Prof,* University of Hartford, Hartford Art School, West Hartford CT (S)

Sutton, Peter, *Cur European Paintings,* Museum of Fine Arts, Boston MA

Svedlow, Andrew, *Assoc Dir Public Prog,* Museum of the City of New York, New York NY

Svendsen, Louise Averill, *Cur Emer,* Solomon R Guggenheim Museum, New York NY

Swain, Darlene, *Instr,* Mesa Community College, Dept of Art & Art History, Mesa AZ (S)

Swain, Tim, *Gallery Asst,* Anderson Fine Arts Center, Anderson IN

Swallow, Nancy, *Registrar,* Menil Collection, Houston TX

Swaminadhan, Anamd, *Pres,* Musee d'Art de Joliette, Joliette PQ

Swan, Susan, *Treas,* National Institute for Architectural Education, New York NY

Swanson, Erik, *Dir,* Cripple Creek District Museum, Cripple Creek CO

Swanson, Jean, *Admin Coordr,* Farmington Valley Arts Center, Avon CT

Swanson, Joann E, *Asst Prof,* University of Dayton, Visual Arts Dept, Dayton OH (S)

Swanson, Kenneth J, *Museum Adminr,* Idaho Historical Museum, Boise ID

Swanson, Laurie, *Dir Public Relations & Marketing,* Tucson Museum of Art, Tucson AZ

Swanson, Mary T, *Chmn,* University of Saint Thomas, Dept of Art History, Saint Paul MN (S)

Swanson, Roy, *Prof,* Hutchinson Community Junior College, Visual Arts Dept, Hutchinson KS (S)

Swanson, Vern G, *Dir,* Springville Museum of Art, Springville UT

Swarez, Bibiana, *Asst Prof,* DePaul University, Dept of Art, Chicago IL (S)

Swartz, Helen, *Adminr,* Boston College, Museum of Art, Chestnut Hill MA

Sweatt, Lilla, *Slide Cur,* San Diego State University, Art Department Slide Library, San Diego CA

Sweeney, Megan, *Instr,* Cuyahoga Community College, Dept of Art, Cleveland OH (S)

Sweeney, Patrick, *Curatorial Registrar,* Davenport Museum of Art, Davenport IA

Sweeney, Robert, *Chmn,* Amherst College, Dept of Fine Arts, Amherst MA (S)

Sweeney, Vincent, *Cur Archives & Library,* Staten Island Institute of Arts and Sciences, Archives Library, Staten Island NY

Sweet, Marsia, *Head Reader Serv,* National Gallery of Canada, Library, Ottawa ON

Sweet, Marvin, *Asst Prof,* Bradford College, Creative Arts Division, Bradford MA (S)

Sweetman, Rosemany, *Chmn,* Niagara County Community College, Fine Arts Div, Sanborn NY (S)

Swenson, Betty, *Chmn Div,* Jacksonville University, Dept of Art, Jacksonville FL (S)

Swenson, Christine, *Cur Graphic Arts,* Toledo Museum of Art, Toledo Museum of Art, Toledo OH

Swenson, Ida, *Admin Asst,* Wooster Community Art Center, Danbury CT

Swenson, Sonja, *Chmn,* Taft College, Division of Performing Arts, Taft CA (S)

Swensson, Lise, *Chief Cur Art,* South Carolina State Museum, Columbia SC

Swid, Steve, *Chmn,* Municipal Art Society of New York, New York NY

Swider, Bougdon, *Chmn,* Colorado College, Dept of Art, Colorado Springs CO (S)

Swider, Tony, *Instr,* University of North Carolina at Charlotte, Dept of Visual Arts, Charlotte NC (S)

Swiderski, Christine, *Cur,* Ontario College of Art, Gallery 76, Toronto ON

Swift, Lucia, *Membership Coordr,* Columbus Museum, Columbus GA

Swingle, Jane, *Art Coll Mgr,* First Bank Minneapolis, Art Collection, Minneapolis MN

Swinton, Elizabeth de Sabato, *Cur Asian Art,* Worcester Art Museum, Worcester MA

Swyrydenko, Walter, *Prof,* Lakeland Community College, Visual Arts Dept, Mentor OH (S)

Sykes, Lawrence F, *Prof,* Rhode Island College, Art Dept, Providence RI (S)

Syloid, Plotkin, *Dir,* Temple Beth Israel, Plotkin Juddica Museum, Phoenix AZ

Sylva, Ron, *Prof Art Educ,* University of Cincinnati, School of Art, Cincinnati OH (S)

Sylvester, Judith, *Conservator,* Indiana University, William Hammond Mathers Museum, Bloomington IN

Sylvester, Steve, *Art Dept Chmn,* Montana University System-Northern Montana College, Humanities & Social Sciences, Havre MT (S)

Symmes, Edwin C, *Pres,* Photographic Investments Gallery, Atlanta GA

Symmes, Marilyn, *Cur Drawings & Prints,* Cooper-Hewitt, National Museum of Design, New York NY

Sypoelt, Terrie, *Reference Librn,* Arkansas State University-Art Department, Jonesboro, Library, Jonesboro AR

Syvertson, Alma, *Asst Dir,* Fillmore County Historical Society, Fountain MN

Szabla, Joanne, *Prof,* Rochester Institute of Technology, School of Art and Design, Rochester NY (S)

Szeitz, P R, *Prof,* Moorhead State University, Dept of Art, Moorhead MN (S)

Szekely, Linda, *Curatorial Asst,* Norman Rockwell Museum at Stockbridge, Library, Stockbridge MA

Szmagaj, Kenneth, *Assoc Prof,* James Madison University, Dept of Art, Harrisonburg VA (S)

Szoke, Andrew, *Asst Prof,* Northampton Community College, Art Dept, Bethlehem PA (S)

Szott, Brian, *Dir Continuing Studies,* Minneapolis College of Art and Design, Minneapolis MN (S)

Szuszitzky, Blanche, *Treas,* North Country Museum of Arts, Park Rapids MN

Szynaka, Edward, *Library Dir,* Pasadena Public Library, Fine Arts Dept, Pasadena CA

Tabakoff, Sheila K, *Cur Coll,* The Dixon Gallery & Gardens, Memphis TN

Tabakoff, Sheila K, *Cur Coll,* The Dixon Gallery & Gardens, Library, Memphis TN

Tabbaa, Yasser, *Asst Prof,* University of Michigan, Ann Arbor, Dept of History of Art, Ann Arbor MI (S)

Taber, Marlene, *Chmn,* College of the Sequoias, Art Dept, Visalia CA (S)

Tabor, Leslie, *Librn,* Salvador Dali Museum, Library, Saint Petersburg FL

Tabor, Martha, *Co-Chmn,* Studio Gallery, Washington DC

Tacang, Lee, *Instr,* De Anza College, Creative Arts Div, Cupertino CA (S)

Tacha, Athena, *Prof,* Oberlin College, Dept of Art, Oberlin OH (S)

Tack, Catherine, *Staff Librn,* The Carnegie Library of Pittsburgh, Pittsburgh PA

Taddie, Dan, *Chmn,* Maryville College, Dept of Fine Arts, Maryville TN (S)

Taddie, Daniel, *Chmn,* Maryville College, Fine Arts Center Gallery, Maryville TN

Tadlock, Marvin, *Chmn,* Virginia Intermont College, Fine Arts Division, Bristol VA (S)

Taff, Cavett, *Cur Exhib,* Mississippi Department of Archives & History, Mississippi State Historical Museum, Jackson MS

Tafler, David, *Lectr,* Rosemont College, Division of the Arts, Rosemont PA (S)

Tafoya, Guadalupe, *Chief Cur,* Millicent Rogers Museum, Taos NM

Tafoya, Joan, *Asst Cur Coll,* Museum of New Mexico, Museum of Fine Arts, Santa Fe NM

Taft, Francis, *Prof,* Cleveland Institute of Art, Cleveland OH (S)

Taft, W Stanley, *Asst Prof,* Cornell University, Dept of Art, Ithaca NY (S)

Tai, Susan Shin-Tsu, *Cur Asian Art,* Santa Barbara Museum of Art, Santa Barbara CA

Taillefert, Marcel, *Dir,* Saint Joseph's Oratory, Museum, Montreal PQ

Tain-Alfonso, Jose, *Adminr,* The Phillips Collection, Washington DC

Taira, Masa Morioka, *Dir,* Queen's Medical Center Auxiliary, Queen Emma Gallery, Honolulu HI

Tait, Jen, *Distribution,* Art Com-La Mamelle, Inc, San Francisco CA

Takacs, John, *Instr,* Dean Junior College, Visual and Performing Art Dept, Franklin MA (S)

Takacs, Sharon, *System Librn,* North Central College, Oesterle Library, Naperville IL

Takenaga, Barbara, *Chmn Studio Art,* Williams College, Dept of Art, Williamstown MA (S)

Talalay, Kathryn, *Asst Librn,* American Academy of Arts & Letters, Library, New York NY

Talalay, Lauren E, *Asst Dir & Asst Cur Educ,* University of Michigan, Kelsey Museum of Archaeology, Ann Arbor MI

Talalay, Marjorie, *Dir,* Cleveland Center for Contemporary Art, Cleveland OH

Talalay, Marjorie, *Dir,* Cleveland Center for Contemporary Art, Library, Cleveland OH

Talarico, Sandra, *Dir,* Florida State University Foundation - Central Florida Community College Foundation, The Appleton Museum of Art, Ocala FL

Talbert, Mark, *Chmn,* Southern Utah State University, Dept of Art, Cedar City UT (S)

Talbot, Howard C, *Dir,* National Baseball Hall of Fame and Museum, Inc, Art Collection, Cooperstown NY

Talbot, William S, *Asst Dir Admin,* Cleveland Museum of Art, Cleveland OH

Talbott, Linda, *Dir,* Copper Village Museum & Arts Center, Anaconda MT

Talbott, Linda, *Dir,* Copper Village Museum & Arts Center, Library, Anaconda MT

Talbott, Ronald, *Instr,* Harrisburg Area Community College, Division of Communication and the Arts, Harrisburg PA (S)

Taliaferro, Jil Evans, *Asst Prof,* Saint Olaf College, Art Dept, Northfield MN (S)

Talley, Charles, *Ed Surface Design Journal,* Surface Design Association, Inc, Oakland CA

Talley, Dan R, *Dir,* Jamestown Community College, The Forum Gallery, Jamestown NY

Tallman, Carol W, *Librn,* State Museum of Pennsylvania, Library, Harrisburg PA

Tallon, Roy V, *Registrar,* Museum of the City of Mobile, Mobile AL

Tamisiea, Jeanne, *Asst Prof,* Black Hawk College, Art Dept, Moline IL (S)

Tamplin, Illi-Maria, *Dir,* Art Gallery of Peterborough, Peterborough ON

Tamraz, Bill, *Pres,* New Rochelle Public Library, New Rochelle Art Association, New Rochelle NY

Tamura, Ruth, *Cur,* Judiciary History Center, Honolulu HI

Tamura, Tomiaki, *Dir of Design,* Cosanti Foundation, Scottsdale AZ

Tamura, Tomiaki, *Planning,* Cosanti Foundation, Arcosanti, Scottsdale AZ

Tancin, Charlotte, *Librn,* Carnegie Mellon University, Hunt Institute for Botanical Documentation, Pittsburgh PA

Tandy, Jean C, *Chmn Dept Art,* Mount Wachusett Community College, Art Galleries, Gardner MA

Tanier, George, *Treas,* Art Information Center, Inc, New York NY

Tanier, Inger, *Board Dir Member,* Art Information Center, Inc, New York NY

Taniguchi, Dennis, *Exec Dir,* Japantown Art & Media Workshop, San Francisco CA

Tanis, Janet, *Asst Dir & Dir Educ,* Edna Hibel Art Foundation, Library, Palm Beach FL

Tanis, Janet E, *Asst Dir,* Edna Hibel Art Foundation, Hibel Museum of Art, Palm Beach FL

Tanis, Steven, *Coordr Drawing & Painting,* University of Delaware, Dept of Art, Newark DE (S)

Tannebaum, Marilyn, *Instr,* Solano Community College, Division of Fine & Applied Art, Suisun City CA (S)

Tannen, Jason, *Vis Arts Coord,* Sushi-Performance & Visual Art Gallery, San Diego CA

Tannenbaum, Barbara, *Cur Art,* Akron Art Museum, Akron OH

Tannenbaum, Judith, *Asst Dir,* Institute of Contemporary Art, Philadelphia PA

Tanner, Larry, *Dir Coll,* Louisiana Department of Culture, Recreation and Tourism, Louisiana State Museum, New Orleans LA

Tanner, Richard, *Prof,* Rochester Institute of Technology, School of Art and Design, Rochester NY (S)

Tanselle, G Thomas, *VPres & Secy,* John Simon Guggenheim Memorial Foundation, New York NY

Taormina, John J, *Cur,* Ohio State University, Slide & Photograph Library, Columbus OH

Taraba, Fred, *Asst Dir,* Illustration House Inc, Gallery, New York NY

Taragin, Davira, *Cur of 19th & 20th Century Glass,* Toledo Museum of Art, Toledo Museum of Art, Toledo OH

Tarantal, Stephen, *Dean, College of Art & Design,* University of the Arts, Philadelphia College of Art & Design, Philadelphia PA (S)

Tarbox, Gurdon, *Pres,* Brookgreen Gardens, Murrells Inlet SC

Tarbox, Gurdon, *Pres,* Brookgreen Gardens, Library, Murrells Inlet SC

Tarchi, Claudio, *Secy,* Museo Italo Americano, San Francisco CA

Tardif, Jacqueline, *Dir,* La Galerie Montcalm la galerie d'art de la Villede Hull, Hull PQ

Tardo, Barbara, *Assoc Prof,* Southeastern Louisiana University, Dept of Visual Arts, Hammond LA (S)

Tarnowski, Thomas, *Instr,* Johnson County Community College, Visual Arts Program, Overland Park KS (S)

Tarpey, Sean, *Registrar & Preparator,* Mount Holyoke College, Art Museum, South Hadley MA

Tarr, Blair, *Cur of Decorative Art,* Kansas State Historical Society, Kansas Museum of History, Topeka KS

Tarrell, Robert, *Chmn,* Edgewood College, Art Dept, Madison WI (S)

Tarrell, Robert, *Art Department Chmn,* Edgewood College, DeRicci Gallery, Madison WI

Tartakov, Gary, *Coordr Art History,* Iowa State University, Dept of Art and Design, Ames IA (S)

Tarver, Daisy D, *Cur,* Tulane University, Gallier House Museum, New Orleans LA

Tarver, Paul, *Registrar,* New Orleans Museum of Art, New Orleans LA

Tasaka, Sharon, *Assoc Dir,* University of Hawaii at Manoa, Art Gallery, Honolulu HI

Tate, Barbara, *Dir,* Henry Street Settlement Arts for Living Center, New York NY (S)

Tate, George, *Cur,* Sturdivant Hall, Selma AL

Tate, Greg, *Chmn,* Skagit Valley College, Dept of Art, Mount Vernon WA (S)

Tate, Jamie, *Dir,* Mississippi Art Colony, Meridian MS

Tate, Will, *Vis Prof,* Oral Roberts University, Fine Arts Dept, Tulsa OK (S)

Tatham, David, *Prof,* Syracuse University, Dept of Fine Arts (Art History), Syracuse NY (S)

Tatum, James, *Chmn,* Lincoln University, Dept Fine Arts, Jefferson City MO (S)

Taub, Peter, *Exec Dir,* Randolph Street Gallery, Chicago IL

Taulbee, Ann, *Instr,* Illinois Wesleyan University, School of Art, Bloomington IL (S)

Taulbee, Ann E, *Dir,* Illinois Wesleyan University, Merwin & Wakeley Galleries, Bloomington IL

Taupier, Anne, *Gallery & Bookstore Mgr,* Institute of Contemporary Art, Boston MA

Tauriello, Frank, *VPres,* American Society of Portrait Artists (ASOPA), Montgomery AL

Taurins, Irene, *Registrar,* Philadelphia Museum of Art, Philadelphia PA

Taylor, Alex, *Instr,* St Lawrence College, Dept of Visual & Creative Arts, Cornwall ON (S)

Taylor, Barry, *Pres,* Wheaton Cultural Alliance Inc, Millville NJ

Taylor, Bruce, *Asst Prof,* University of Waterloo, Fine Arts Dept, Waterloo ON (S)

Taylor, Carole, *Library Dir,* Fort Valley State College, H A Hunt Memorial Library, Fort Valley GA

Taylor, Charles, *Preparator,* Philbrook Museum of Art, Tulsa OK

Taylor, Cheryl, *Dir,* Maricopa County Historical Society, Desert Caballeros Western Museum, Wickenburg AZ

Taylor, Daniel, *Dir,* Mendocino County Museum, Willits CA

Taylor, David, *Dir,* L'Universite Laval, Ecole des Arts Visuels, Quebec PQ

Taylor, Doug, *Pres Manitoba Historical Society,* Manitoba Historical Society, Dalnavert Museum, Winnipeg MB

Taylor, Frazine, *Readi Reference Librn,* Alabama Department of Archives and History Museum, Library, Montgomery AL

Taylor, Herman W, *Prof,* Washington and Lee University, Division of Art, Lexington VA (S)

Taylor, Howard J, *Dir,* San Angelo Museum of Fine Arts, San Angelo TX

Taylor, Hugh H, *Prof,* Washington and Jefferson College, Art Dept, Washington PA (S)

Taylor, Ira M, *Prof,* Hardin-Simmons University, Art Dept, Abilene TX (S)

Taylor, Joan, *Assoc Prof,* Fairleigh Dickinson University, Fine Arts Dept, Rutherford NJ (S)

Taylor, Judson, *Public Relations,* Marion Koogler McNay Art Museum, San Antonio TX

Taylor, Julie, *Treas,* Art Guild of Burlington, Arts for Living Center, Burlington IA

Taylor, Marcia, *Assoc Prof,* Trenton State College, Art Dept, Trenton NJ (S)

Taylor, Marilyn S, *Cur Ethnology,* Saint Joseph Museum, Saint Joseph MO

Taylor, Mary Diane, *Chmn Dept Art,* Brescia College, Anna Eaton Stout Memorial Art Gallery, Owensboro KY

Taylor, Mary Diane, *Chmn,* Brescia College, Dept of Art, Owensboro KY (S)

Taylor, Mary Jane, *Dir,* Brenau College, Art Dept, Gainesville GA (S)

Taylor, Michael, *Chmn Dept,* Lewis & Clark College, Dept of Art, Portland OR (S)

Taylor, Michael, *Prof,* Rochester Institute of Technology, School of Art and Design, Rochester NY (S)

Taylor, Michael D, *Dean Col,* University of Massachusetts Dartmouth, College of Visual and Performing Arts, North Dartmouth MA (S)

Taylor, N Wayne, *Prof,* University of Wisconsin, Madison, Dept of Art, Madison WI (S)

Taylor, Odelle, *Bookkeeper,* Community Council for the Arts, Kinston NC

Taylor, Pat, *Lectr,* Southwest Texas State University, Dept of Art, San Marcos TX (S)

Taylor, Rene, *Emeritus Dir,* Museo de Arte de Ponce, Ponce Art Museum, Ponce PR

Taylor, Robert, *Theatre Cur,* The New York Public Library, Shelby Cullom Davis Museum, New York NY

Taylor, Rod A, *Head Dept,* Norfolk State University, Fine Arts Dept, Norfolk VA (S)

Taylor, Romalis, *Asst Dir Facilities,* Los Angeles County Museum of Art, Los Angeles CA

Taylor, Ron, *Instr,* University of North Carolina at Charlotte, Dept of Visual Arts, Charlotte NC (S)

Taylor, Susan, *Dir,* Wellesley College, Museum, Wellesley MA

Taylor, Tom, *Coordr Fine Arts,* Columbia College, Art Dept, Chicago IL (S)

Taylor, Walter, *VPres Operations,* Philadelphia Museum of Art, Philadelphia PA

Taylor, Warren, *Instr,* Midland College, Allison Fine Arts Dept, Midland TX (S)

Taylor, William C, *Operations Mgr,* Arts Council of Spartanburg County, Inc, Spartanburg Arts Center, Spartanburg SC

Tazian, Kegham, *Chmn,* Oakland Community College, Art Dept, Farmington Hills MI (S)

Teague, Edward H, *Architecture Fine Arts Bibliographer & Head Librn,* University of Florida, Architecture and Fine Arts Library, Gainesville FL

Teahan, John W, *Librn,* Wadsworth Atheneum, Auerbach Art Library, Hartford CT

Teats, Gloria, *Co-Chmn & Secy,* Valley Art Center Inc, Clarkston WA

Tebbens, Marianne, *Instr,* Wayne Art Center, Wayne PA (S)

Teczar, Steven, *Art Division Chmn,* Maryville University of Saint Louis, Art Division, Saint Louis MO (S)

Tedford, Catherine, *Dir,* St Lawrence University, Richard F Brush Art Gallery, Canton NY

Teeter, Emily, *Asst Cur,* University of Chicago, Oriental Institute Museum, Chicago IL

Tefft, Tom, *Art Dept Chmn,* Citrus College, Art Dept, Glendora CA (S)

Teichman, Judith, *Deputy Dir,* Asian Art Museum of San Francisco, Avery Brundage Collection, San Francisco CA

Teieda, Juan, *Xicano Music Prog Dir,* Guadalupe Cultural Arts Center, San Antonio TX

Teitelbaum, Matthew, *Cur,* Institute of Contemporary Art, Boston MA

Teixeira, Alice, *Secy,* Providence Art Club, Providence RI

Telfair, Tula, *Asst Prof,* Wesleyan University, Art Dept, Middletown CT (S)

Teller, Douglas H, *Prof,* George Washington University, Dept of Art, Washington DC (S)

Tellier, Cassandra Lee, *Dir,* Capital University, Schumacher Gallery, Columbus OH

Telseyan, Madeleine, *Dir,* Rhode Island Historical Society, Library, Providence RI

Temple, Laura, *Museum on Wheels Dir,* Monterey Peninsula Museum of Art Association, Monterey CA

Temple, Paula, *Assoc Prof,* University of Mississippi, Dept of Art, University MS (S)

Templeton, Dee, *Dir,* Gertrude Herbert Memorial Institute of Art, Augusta GA

Templeton, Rijn, *Interim Librn,* University of Iowa, Art Library, Iowa City IA

Tenabe, Gabriel S, *Dir & Cur,* Morgan State University, James E Lewis Museum of Art, Baltimore MD

Tenckhoff, Diana, *Asst Cur Asian Art,* University of Oregon, Museum of Art, Eugene OR

Tennent, Elaine, *Dir,* Tennent Art Foundation Gallery, Honolulu HI

Tennessen, Margaret, *Art Coordr,* University of Wisconsin-Madison, Wisconsin Union Galleries, Madison WI

Tenuth, Jeffrey, *Registrar,* Indiana State Museum, Indianapolis IN

Teodorowych, Oksana, *Cur,* Ukrainian National Museum and Library, Chicago IL

Teoli, Alfred, *Assoc Prof,* University of Illinois, Chicago, Health Science Center, Biomedical Visualizations, Chicago IL (S)

Teramoto, John, *Asst Prof,* University of Kansas, Kress Foundation Dept of Art History, Lawrence KS (S)

ter Elst, Hendrika, *Slide File Coordr,* Artists Space, Unaffiliated Artists File, New York NY

Terentieff, Robert, *Prof,* Mount Saint Mary's College, Visual & Performing Arts Dept, Emmitsburg MD (S)

Terenzio, Marion, *Dir Creative Arts,* Russell Sage College, Visual and Performing Arts Dept, Troy NY (S)

Terhune, Webster, *Cur,* Westerly Public Library, Hoxie Gallery, Westerly RI

Ter Molen, Larry, *Exec VPres Development & Public Affairs,* The Art Institute of Chicago, Chicago IL

Ternay, Bill, *Chmn Illustration,* Moore College of Art & Design, Philadelphia PA (S)

Terra, Daniel J, *Pres,* Terra Museum of American Art, Chicago IL

Terrell, Richard, *Head Dept,* Doane College, Dept of Art, Crete NE (S)

Terrien, George, *Pres,* Boston Architectural Center, Boston MA

Terry, Ann, *Assoc Prof,* Wittenberg University, Art Dept, Springfield OH (S)

Terry, C, *Dir,* National Museum of Science & Technology Corporation, National Aviation Museum, Ottawa ON

Terry, Carol, *Dir,* Rhode Island School of Design, Library, Providence RI

Terry, Christopher, *Asst Prof,* Utah State University, Dept of Art, Logan UT (S)

Terry, Michael, *Dir,* Spertus Museum, Asher Library, Chicago IL

Terry, Ronald, *Chmn,* First Tennessee National Corp, First Tennessee Heritage Collection, Memphis TN

Tersteeg, William, *Prof,* Keystone Junior College, Fine Arts Dept, Factoryville PA (S)

Terzian, Aram, *Dir Div Liberal Arts,* Philadelphia Community College, Dept of Art, Philadelphia PA (S)

Tesso, Jane B, *Art Admin Consultant,* B P America, Cleveland OH

Tettleton, Robert L, *Prof,* University of Mississippi, Dept of Art, University MS (S)

Threatt, Thomas K, *Asst,* Fort Worth Public Library, Fine Arts Section, Fort Worth TX

Thrift, Linda, *Keeper Catalog of American Portraits,* National Portrait Gallery, Washington DC

Throm, Qurenzia, *Chmn,* Valencia Community College, Art Gallery-East Campus, Orlando FL

Thruston, Kathleen, *Asst Dir Marketing,* Massachusetts Institute of Technology, MIT Museum, Cambridge MA

Thumsujarit, Chaiwat, *Asst Prof,* Fort Hays State University, Dept of Art, Hays KS (S)

Thurber, Davis P, *Treas,* The Currier Gallery of Art, Manchester NH

Thurman, Christa C Mayer, *Cur Textiles,* The Art Institute of Chicago, Chicago IL

Thurman, Dori, *Treas,* Queen's Medical Center Auxiliary, Queen Emma Gallery, Honolulu HI

Thurman, Henry L, *Dean,* Southern University A & M College, School of Architecture, Baton Rouge LA (S)

Thurman, Mark, *Instr,* Toronto School of Art, Toronto ON (S)

Thurner, Robert, *Dir,* Cleveland State University, Art Gallery, Cleveland OH

Thurston, Anne, *Sales Coordr,* Crooked Tree Arts Council, Virginia M McCune Community Arts Center, Petoskey MI

Thurston, Nancy, *Librn,* Bassist College Library, Portland OR

Thursz, Daniel, *Pres,* National Center on Arts & Aging-National Council on The Aging, NCOA Gallery Patina, Washington DC

Thye, David, *Chmn,* Sioux Falls College, Dept of Art, Sioux Falls SD (S)

Tibbitts, Cori, *Cur of Exhib,* Lakeview Museum of Arts and Sciences, Peoria IL

Tibboel, Carla, *Art Librn,* Public Library of Des Moines, Fine Arts Dept, Des Moines IA

Tibbs, Debbie, *Controller,* Polk Museum of Art, Lakeland FL

Tichenol, Irene, *Dir & Librn,* Brooklyn Historical Society, Library, Brooklyn NY

Tichich, Richard, *Head Dept,* Georgia Southern University, Dept of Art, Statesboro GA (S)

Ticho, Harold K, *Treas,* Mingei International, Inc, Mingei International Museum of World Folk Art, San Diego CA

Tiemann, Robert E, *Prof,* Trinity University, Dept of Art, San Antonio TX (S)

Tiernan, Terrance, *Chairperson,* Junior College of Albany, Fine Arts Division, Albany NY (S)

Tierney, Lennox, *Prof,* University of Utah, Art Dept, Salt Lake City UT (S)

Tierney, Richard, *Pres,* Laughner Brothers, Inc, Indianapolis IN

Tiessen, G, *Assoc Prof,* University of Victoria, Dept of Visual Arts, Victoria BC (S)

Tigerman, Stanly, *Dir School Architecture,* University of Illinois at Chicago, College of Architecture, Art and Urban Planning, Chicago IL (S)

Tilghman, Douglas, *Asst Dir,* University of Kansas, Spencer Museum of Art, Lawrence KS

Till, Barry, *Cur Asian Art,* Art Gallery of Greater Victoria, Victoria BC

Tilney, Cathy, *Business Mgr,* Concord Museum, Concord MA

Tilotson, Virginia, *Prof,* Brevard College, Division of Fine Arts, Brevard NC (S)

Tilton, Barbara, *Asst Prof,* University of Montana, Dept of Art, Missoula MT (S)

Timlin, Peggy, *Cur Manuscripts & Books,* Pilgrim Society, Pilgrim Hall Museum, Plymouth MA

Timlin, Peggy M, *Cur Manuscripts & Books,* Pilgrim Society, Library, Plymouth MA

Timmerman, Erik, *Assoc Prof,* Rochester Institute of Technology, School of Photographic Arts & Sciences, Rochester NY (S)

Timmerman, Mary Jane, *Asst Prof,* Murray State University, Art Dept, Murray KY (S)

Timmons, Heather, *Interim Gallery Dir,* Salisbury State University, University Gallery, Salisbury MD

Timmons, Judi B, *Dir,* The Dalles Art Association, Oregon Trail Art Gallery, The Dalles OR

Timms, Peter, *Dir,* Fitchburg Art Museum, Fitchburg MA

Timoshuk, Walter, *Executive VPres,* Norton Simon Museum, Pasadena CA

Timpano, Anne, *Dir,* Columbus Museum, Columbus GA

Tindall, Hiram, *Cur,* Stratford Historical Society, Stratford CT

Tindel, Raymond, *Registrar,* University of Chicago, Oriental Institute Museum, Chicago IL

TinNyo, Elaine, *Gallery Mgr,* White Columns, New York NY

Tintle, Debbie, *Second VPres,* New Jersey Water-Color Society, Red Bank NJ

Tio, Adrian, *Assoc Dir,* Bowling Green State University, School of Art, Bowling Green OH (S)

Tipton, Gail, *Public Program Dir,* Children's Museum of Manhattan, New York NY

Tipton, Greg, *Cur,* Museums of Abilene, Inc, Abilene TX

Tischler, Maynard, *Dir,* University of Denver, School of Art, Denver CO (S)

Tisher, Harold, *VPres,* Yankton County Historical Society, Dakota Territorial Museum, Yankton SD

Tissue, Heather, *Development Dir,* New Langton Arts, San Francisco CA

Tite, Winston, *Instr,* University of North Carolina at Charlotte, Dept of Visual Arts, Charlotte NC (S)

Titmus, Wilma, *Office Mgr,* College of Southern Idaho, Herrett Museum & Art Gallery, Twin Falls ID

Titus, Harry B, *Chmn,* Wake Forest University, Dept of Art, Winston-Salem NC (S)

Titus, H Edwin, *VPres,* Passaic County Community College, Division of Humanities, Paterson NJ (S)

Titus, William, *Registrar,* Heckscher Museum, Huntington NY

Tiura, Oliver, *Prof,* Lakehead University, Dept of Visual Arts, Thunder Bay ON (S)

Tjader, Harlan, *Instr,* Vermilion Community College, Art Dept, Ely MN (S)

Tlosker, Susan, *Cur,* Norman Mackenzie Art Gallery, Slide Library, Regina SK

Todd, James, *Prof,* University of Montana, Dept of Art, Missoula MT (S)

Todd, Mark, *Prof,* Southwest Texas State University, Dept of Art, San Marcos TX (S)

Todtz, William, *Librn & Archivist,* McLean County Historical Society, Bloomington IL

Toedetemeir, Terry, *Instr,* Pacific Northwest College of Art, Portland OR (S)

Toedtemeier, Terry, *Cur Photography,* Portland Art Museum, Portland OR

Toensing, Robert E, *Instr,* Anoka Ramsey Community College, Art Dept, Coon Rapids MN (S)

Tofte, Jon, *Teaching Specialist,* University of Minnesota, Duluth, Art Dept, Duluth MN (S)

Tokarski, Carol, *Dir,* Community Council for the Arts, Kinston NC

Toker, Franklin, *First VPres,* Society of Architectural Historians, Philadelphia PA

Tolbert, James A, *Chmn Dept,* Linn Benton Community College, Fine & Applied Art Dept, Albany OR (S)

Toliver, Harold, *Cur & Cunsultant,* Golden State Mutual Life Insurance Company, Afro-American Art Collection, Los Angeles CA

Tollefson, Wayne, *Assoc Prof,* North Dakota State University, Div of Fine Arts, Fargo ND (S)

Tolmatch, Elaine, *Registrar,* Montreal Museum of Fine Arts, Montreal PQ

Tolnick, Judith, *Galleries Dir,* University of Rhode Island, Fine Arts Center Galleries, Kingston RI

Tolstedt, Lowell, *Dean,* Columbus College of Art and Design, Fine Arts Dept, Columbus OH (S)

Toluse, Joe, *Cur,* Idaho Historical Museum, Boise ID

Tom, Robert, *Asst Prof,* Moorhead State University, Dept of Art, Moorhead MN (S)

Toma, Pamela, *Exec Dir,* Historic Northampton Museum, Northampton MA

Tomasini, Wallace J, *Dir,* University of Iowa, School of Art and Art History, Iowa City IA (S)

Tomidy, Paul, *Cur Spec Projects,* Oakland Museum, Art Dept, Oakland CA

Tomlin, Terry, *Chmn Fine Arts,* Texas Southmost College, Fine Arts Dept, Brownsville TX (S)

Tomlinson, Bill, *Cur,* Algonquin Arts Council, Bancroft Art Gallery, Bancroft ON

Tompkins, Robert S, *Asst Prof,* Rochester Institute of Technology, School of Printing, Rochester NY (S)

Tomsen, Mary, *Dir Public Relations,* North Central Washington Museum, Art Gallery, Wenatchee WA

Tomsic, Walt, *Assoc Prof,* Pacific Lutheran University, Dept of Art, Tacoma WA (S)

Toner, Rochelle, *Dean,* Temple University, Tyler School of Art-Galleries, Tyler Gallery, Philadelphia PA

Toner, Rochelle, *Dean,* Temple University, Tyler School of Art, Philadelphia PA (S)

Tong, Darlene, *Art Librn,* San Francisco State University, J Paul Leonard Library, San Francisco CA

Toone, Thomas, *Asst Prof,* Utah State University, Dept of Art, Logan UT (S)

Tootle, Ann, *Registrar,* The Albrecht-Kemper Museum of Art, Saint Joseph MO

Toperzer, Thomas R, *Dir,* University of Oklahoma, Fred Jones Jr Museum of Art, Norman OK

Topkin, William, *Pres,* Mystic Art Association, Inc, Mystic CT

Toplovich, Ann, *Exec Dir,* Tennessee Historical Society, Nashville TN

Toppan, Muriel L, *Librn,* Walters Art Gallery, Library, Baltimore MD

Torcoletti, Enzo, *Prof,* Flagler College, Visual Arts Dept, Saint Augustine FL (S)

Tornheim, N, *Instr,* Golden West College, Visual Art Dept, Huntington Beach CA (S)

Torno, Janet E, *Assoc Admin,* University of Michigan, Museum of Art, Ann Arbor MI

Torntore, Susan, *Cur Exhib,* State Capitol Museum, Olympia WA

Torrence, Suzanne, *Asst Dir,* Quapaw Quarter Association, Inc, Villa Marre, Little Rock AR

Torrenti, Thomas, *VPres,* Lyme Art Association, Inc, Old Lyme CT

Torres, Alberto, *Admin Asst,* Chicano Humanities & Arts Council, Denver CO

Torres, Harold, *Tourism Mgr,* Pueblo of San Ildefonso, Maria Martinez Museum, Santa Fe NM

Torres, Manuel, *Assoc Prof,* Florida International University, Visual Arts Dept, Miami FL (S)

Torres-Delgado, Rene, *Asst Prof,* University of Puerto Rico, Dept of Fine Arts, Rio Piedras PR (S)

Torri, Erika, *Exec Dir & Librn,* Library Association of La Jolla, Athenaeum Music and Arts Library, La Jolla CA

Torri, Erika, *Librn,* Museum of Contemporary Art, San Diego, Helen Palmer Geisel Library, La Jolla CA

Torrini, Rudolph E, *Chmn Dept,* Fontbonne College, Art Dept, Saint Louis MO (S)

Tortolero, Carlos, *Executive Dir,* Mexican Fine Arts Center Museum, Chicago IL

Toth, Carl, *Head Photography Dept,* Cranbrook Academy of Art, Bloomfield Hills MI (S)

Toth, George, *Commercial Art,* Madonna College, Art Dept, Livonia MI (S)

Toth, Richard E, *Head,* Utah State University, Dept of Landscape Architecture Environmental Planning, Logan UT (S)

Toubes, Xavier, *Assoc Prof,* University of North Carolina at Chapel Hill, Art Dept, Chapel Hill NC (S)

Touchett, Lori-Ann, *Cur,* Johns Hopkins University, Archaeological Collection, Baltimore MD

Touhey, Paula, *Dir,* Kenosha Public Museum, Kenosha WI

Tourtillotte, Bill, *Gallery Dir,* Saint Mary's College, Moreau Gallery, Notre Dame IN

Tousignant, Serge, *Instr,* Universite de Montreal, Dept of Art History, Montreal PQ (S)

Tovell, Rosemarie, *Assoc Cur Canadian Prints & Drawings,* National Gallery of Canada, Ottawa ON

Tow, Kelly, *Instr,* Antonelli Institute of Art & Photography, Cincinnati OH (S)

Towgood, Jean, *Pres,* Women's Caucus For Art, Philadelphia PA

Towner, Mark, *Asst Dir,* Davenport Museum of Art, Davenport IA

Townsend, Allen, *Librn,* Dallas Museum of Art, Library, Dallas TX

Townsend, Carol, *First VPres,* Buffalo Society of Artists, Kenmore NY

Townsend, Gavin, *Asst Prof,* University of Tennessee at Chattanooga, Dept of Art, Chattanooga TN (S)

Townsend, Richard, *Hardman Cur,* Philbrook Museum of Art, Tulsa OK

Townsend, Richard F, *Cur Africa, Oceania & the Americas,* The Art Institute of Chicago, Chicago IL

Townsend, Susan M, *Pres of Board,* Rehoboth Art League, Inc, Rehoboth Beach DE

Townsley, Beth, *Librn,* Middletown Fine Arts Center, Library, Middletown OH

Track, Soge, *Cur Native Americans,* Millicent Rogers Museum, Taos NM

Tracy, Paul, *Asst Preparator,* Memphis Brooks Museum of Art, Memphis TN

Tracy, Robert, *Chmn Dept,* University of Nevada, Las Vegas, Dept of Art, Las Vegas NV (S)

Tracz, Tim, *Assoc Prof,* Austin College, Art Dept, Sherman TX (S)

Trafford, Hal, *Head Commercial Art,* Butera School of Art, Boston MA (S)

Trager, Neil C, *Dir,* The College at New Paltz State University of New York, College Art Gallery, New Paltz NY

Trahan, Eric, *Dir,* Canajoharie Art Gallery, Canajoharie NY

Trahan, Eric, *Dir Library,* Canajoharie Art Gallery, Library, Canajoharie NY

Trakis, Louis, *Head Dept,* Manhattanville College, Art Dept, Purchase NY (S)

Tramposch, William, *Pres,* New York State Historical Association, Fenimore House, Cooperstown NY

Tramposch, William, *Pres,* New York State Historical Association, Farmers' Museum, Inc, Cooperstown NY

Tranter, Adele, *VPres,* Crary Art Gallery Inc, Warren PA

Trapani, Denise, *Assoc Dir Development,* DeCordova Museum & Sculpture Park, Lincoln MA

Trapp, Kenneth R, *Asst Cur,* Oakland Museum, Art Dept, Oakland CA

Trasatti, Margaret, *Programming,* Las Vegas-Clark County Library District, Las Vegas NV

Trask, Benjamin, *Librn,* The Mariners' Museum, Library, Newport News VA

Trauger, Susan, *Librn,* Los Angeles County Museum of Art, Robert Gore Rifkind Center for German Expressionist Studies, Los Angeles CA

Traugott, Joseph, *Cur,* University of New Mexico, Jonson Gallery, Albuquerque NM

Traverso, Daniel, *Head Dept,* Austin Community College, Dept of Commercial Art, North Ridge Campus, Austin TX (S)

Travis, Betsy, *Dir,* Village of Potsdam Public Museum, Potsdam NY

Travis, David, *Cur Photography,* The Art Institute of Chicago, Chicago IL

Travis, Jessica, *Reference Librn,* Kemper & Leila Williams Foundation, Historic New Orleans Collection, New Orleans LA

Treacy, Thomas D, *Dir,* Antonelli Institute, Professional Photography, Commercial Art & Interior Design, Plymouth Meeting PA (S)

Treadway, Beth A, *Gallery Dir,* Pace University Gallery, Pleasantville NY

Treadway, Florence Coyle, *Dir,* Longue Vue House and Gardens, New Orleans LA

Treanor, Dennis, *Art Instr,* Randall Museum Junior Museum, San Francisco CA

Trecker, Stan, *Pres,* The Art Institute of Boston, Gallery East, Boston MA

Trecker, Stan, *Pres,* Art Institute of Boston, Boston MA (S)

Trelstad, Barbara, *Registrar,* Rutgers, The State University of New Jersey, Jane Voorhees Zimmerli Art Museum, New Brunswick NJ

Tremblay, Jean-Noel, *Dir Admin,* Musee du Quebec, Quebec PQ

Tremble, Steve, *Exec Dir,* Lincoln Arts Council, Lincoln NE

Trenkle, Mary P, *Head Dept,* Wiley College, Dept of Fine Arts, Marshall TX (S)

Trent, Andrienne, *Reprography Coordr,* Visual Arts Ontario, Toronto ON

Trepp, George, *Dir,* Long Beach Public Library, Long Beach NY

Trevelyan, Amelia, *Chmn,* Gettysburg College, Dept of Art, Gettysburg PA (S)

Trevorrow, Todd F, *Head,* Olivet College, Library, Olivet MI

Triano, Anthony, *Asst Prof,* Seton Hall University, College of Arts & Sciences, South Orange NJ (S)

Tribert Williams, Renee, *Cur,* Stowe-Day Foundation, Harriet Beecher Stowe House, Hartford CT

Trick, Gordan, *Instr,* Vancouver Community College, Langara Campus, Dept of Fine Arts, Vancouver BC (S)

Trickey, Karen, *Asst Prof,* Nazareth College of Rochester, Art Dept, Rochester NY (S)

Trien, Susan, *Public Relations,* Strong Museum, Rochester NY

Trigg, Eloise, *Chmn Dept Art,* Howard Payne University, Dept of Art, Brownwood TX (S)

Triggs, Stanley, *Cur Photography,* McCord Museum of Canadian History, Montreal PQ

Tripoulas, Cindy, *Librn,* Baltimore Museum of Art, E Kirkbride Miller Art Research Library, Baltimore MD

Trippett, Lorraine, *Controller,* Craft and Folk Art Museum, Los Angeles CA

Trissel, James, *Prof,* Colorado College, Dept of Art, Colorado Springs CO (S)

Tritsehler, Susan, *Dir,* Historical Society of the Town of Greenwich, Inc, Bush-Holley House, Cos Cob CT

Tritthardt, Sylvia, *Registrar,* Mendel Art Gallery and Civic Conservatory, Saskatoon SK

Troeger, Betty J, *Assoc Prof,* Florida State University, Art Education Dept, Tallahassee FL (S)

Troemner, Deborah W, *Admin Asst,* Philadelphia Museum of Art, Mount Pleasant, Philadelphia PA

Trop, Sandra, *Assoc Dir,* Everson Museum of Art, Syracuse NY

Trosty, Francia, *Asst Prof,* Lansing Community College, Media Dept, Lansing MI (S)

Trotter, Ruth, *Chmn,* University of La Verne, Dept of Art, La Verne CA (S)

Troup, Marie, *Acting Cur,* Jordan Historical Museum of The Twenty, Jordan ON

Troxell, Robert, *Asst Prof,* Eastern Illinois University, Art Dept, Charleston IL (S)

Troxell, Robert, *Art Coordr,* Harrisburg Area Community College, Division of Communication and the Arts, Harrisburg PA (S)

Troy, John, *Instr,* Joe Kubert School of Cartoon & Graphic Art, Inc, Dover NJ (S)

Troy, Nancy J, *Prof,* Northwestern University, Evanston, Dept of Art History, Evanston IL (S)

Troy, Tim, *Librn,* University of Arizona, Center for Creative Photography, Tucson AZ

Troy, Tim, *Librn,* University of Arizona, Library, Tucson AZ

Troyen, Aimee, *Treas,* Print Council of America, Baltimore MD

Trudel, Jean, *Instr,* Universite de Montreal, Dept of Art History, Montreal PQ (S)

True, Marion, *Cur Antiquities,* Getty Center for the History of Art & the Humanities Trust Museum, Santa Monica CA

True, Marion, *Cur Antiquities,* Getty Center for the History of Art & the Humanities Trust Museum, The J Paul Getty Museum, Santa Monica CA

True, Marion, *Adjunct Asst Prof,* University of Southern California, School of Fine Arts, Los Angeles CA (S)

Trueblood, Emily, *Treas,* Society of American Graphic Artists, New York NY

Truettner, William H, *Cur Painting & Sculpture,* National Museum of American Art, Washington DC

Trumpy, Sigrid, *Cur of Robinson Coll,* United States Naval Academy Museum, Annapolis MD

Tryba, Mildred, *Assoc Prof,* Cardinal Stritch College, Art Dept, Milwaukee WI (S)

Tryon, Musa, *Librn,* Vancouver Public Library, Fine Arts & Music Div, Vancouver BC

Tsai, Eugenie, *Dir,* State University of New York College at Old Westbury, Amelie A Wallace Gallery, Old Westbury NY

Tsakirgis, Barbara, *Asst Prof,* Vanderbilt University, Dept of Fine Arts, Nashville TN (S)

Tsatsos, Irene, *Executive Dir,* NAME, Chicago IL

Tsatsos, Irene, *Dir,* NAME, NAME Documents, Chicago IL

Tschinkel, Paul, *Prof,* Queensborough Community College, Dept of Art and Photography, Bayside NY (S)

Tschudi, Alan, *Assoc Prof,* James Madison University, Dept of Art, Harrisonburg VA (S)

Tschumi, Bernard, *Dean Architectural Planning,* Columbia University, Graduate School of Architecture, Planning & Preservation, New York NY (S)

Tse, Stephen, *Chmn,* Big Bend Community College, Art Dept, Moses Lake WA (S)

Tsukashima, Rodney, *Instr,* Long Beach City College, Dept of Art, Long Beach CA (S)

Tsutakawa, Mayumi, *Exec Dir,* King County Arts Commission, Seattle WA

Tucci, J Michael, *Instr,* Mount Mary College, Art Dept, Milwaukee WI (S)

Tucci, Josephine, *Admin Asst,* Textile Museum, Washington DC

Tucci, Judy, *Instr,* Northeast Mississippi Junior College, Art Dept, Booneville MS (S)

Tuchman, Maurice, *Sr Cur 20th Century Art,* Los Angeles County Museum of Art, Los Angeles CA

Tuck, David, *VPres,* Professional Art Dealers Association of Canada, Toronto ON

Tucker, Anne, *Cur of Photography,* Museum of Fine Arts, Houston, Houston TX

Tucker, Judy, *Secy,* Memorial University of Newfoundland, Art Gallery, Saint John's NF

Tucker, Louis L, *Dir,* Massachusetts Historical Society, Boston MA

Tucker, Marcia, *Dir,* The New Museum of Contemporary Art, New York NY

Tucker, Marcia, *Dir,* The New Museum of Contemporary Art, The Soho Center Library, New York NY

Tucker, Martha, *Special Events Coordr,* Pennsylvania Academy of the Fine Arts, Galleries, Philadelphia PA

Tucker, Martin, *Prof Fine Arts,* University of Cincinnati, School of Art, Cincinnati OH (S)

Tucker, Paul, *Instr,* University of Massachusetts at Boston, Art Dept, Boston MA (S)

Tucker, Sandra, *Business Mgr,* Carolina Art Association, Gibbes Museum of Art, Charleston SC

Tucker, Yvonne, *Assoc Prof,* Florida A & M University, Dept of Visual Arts, Humanities & Theatre, Tallahassee FL (S)

Tuele, Nicholas, *Asst Dir & Chief Cur,* Art Gallery of Greater Victoria, Victoria BC

Tuggle, Catherine, *Dir of Museum Serv,* DAR Museum, National Society Daughters of the American Revolution, Washington DC

Tuhey, Ned, *Instr,* Mesa Community College, Dept of Art & Art History, Mesa AZ (S)

Tulk, Gert, *Secy,* Hollywood Art Museum, Hollywood FL

Tulk, Herbert, *Dir,* Hollywood Art Museum, Hollywood FL

Tullos, Mark, *Dir,* Alexandria Museum of Art, Alexandria LA

Tumasonis, Elizabeth, *Chmn,* University of Victoria, Dept of History in Art, Victoria BC (S)

Tumasonis, Elizabeth, *Asst Prof,* University of Victoria, Dept of History in Art, Victoria BC (S)

Tung, Wu, *Cur Asiatic Art,* Museum of Fine Arts, Boston MA

Tunison, Ron, *Treasurer,* Society of American Historical Artists, Jericho NY

Tupper, Jon, *Assoc Dir, Curatorial Servs,* Winnipeg Art Gallery, Winnipeg MB

Turak, T, *Full Prof,* American University, Dept of Art, Washington DC (S)

Turk, Elizabeth, *Photography Chmn,* Atlanta College of Art, Atlanta GA (S)

Turmel, Jean, *Admin Asst,* Hermitage Foundation Museum, Norfolk VA

Turnbull, JoAnne, *Librn,* McCord Museum of Canadian History, Montreal PQ

Turner, David, *Dir,* Museum of New Mexico, Museum of Fine Arts, Santa Fe NM

Turner, Evan H, *Dir,* Cleveland Museum of Art, Cleveland OH

Turner, Helen Mary, *Head Dept,* Maple Woods Community College, Dept of Art and Art History, Kansas City MO (S)

Turner, John D, *Asst Prof,* University of North Alabama, Dept of Art, Florence AL (S)

Turner, J Rigbie, *Cur Music Manuscripts,* Pierpont Morgan Library, New York NY

Turner, Judy, *Museum Librn,* Milwaukee Public Museum, Milwaukee WI

Turner, Opal, *Office Mgr,* Marshall University, Dept of Art, Huntington WV (S)

Turner, Paige, *Exec Dir,* Second Street Gallery, Charlottesville VA

Turner, Paul V, *Chmn Dept Art,* Stanford University, Dept of Art, Stanford CA (S)

Turner, Richard, *Prof,* Chapman University, Art Dept, Orange CA (S)

Turner, Sarah H, *Archivist,* United States Capitol, Art Reference Library, Washington DC

Turner, S Scott, *Dean,* Sheridan College, Faculty of Visual Arts, Oakville ON (S)

Turner, Tom, *Head Jewelry Dept,* Kalamazoo Institute of Arts, KIA School, Kalamazoo MI (S)

Turnure, James, *Prof,* Bucknell University, Dept of Art, Lewisburg PA (S)

Turpie, Linda, *Adminr,* Tulane University, Dept Art Newcomb Col Art Galleries, New Orleans LA

Turpin, Thomas D, *Prof,* University of Arkansas, Art Dept, Fayetteville AR (S)

Turrentine, Regina, *Chmn,* Charles B Goddard Center for the Visual and Performing Arts, Ardmore OK

Turtell, Neal, *Chief Librn,* National Gallery of Art, Washington DC

Turtell, Neal, *Exec Librn,* National Gallery of Art, Library, Washington DC

Turtletaub, Myrna, *Pres,* Long Island Graphic Eye Gallery, Port Washington NY

Turyn, Ann, *Instr,* Bard College, Milton Avery Graduate School of the Arts, Annandale-on-Hudson NY (S)

Tussing, Nan, *Pres,* New Haven Paint and Clay Club, Inc, New Haven CT

Tuthill, Reginald, *VPres,* Oysterponds Historical Society, Museum, Orient NY

Tutnam, Roger, *Chmn Trustee Committee,* George Walter Vincent Smith Art Museum, Springfield MA

Tutor, Charles, *Chmn,* Western State College of Colorado, Quigley Hall Art Gallery, Gunnison CO

Tutor, Charles, *Chmn,* Western State College of Colorado, Dept of Art & Industrial Technology, Gunnison CO (S)

Tutt, George E, *Chmn Div Fine Arts & Head Art Dept,* William Woods-Westminster Colleges, Art Dept, Fulton MO (S)

Tuttle, Jan, *Pres,* West Hills Unitarian Fellowship, Portland OR

Tuttle, Judith, *Consultant,* Tattoo Art Museum, San Francisco CA

Tuttle, Lyle, *Dir,* Tattoo Art Museum, San Francisco CA

Tuttle, Richard, *Chmn,* Tulane University, Sophie H Newcomb Memorial College, New Orleans LA (S)

Tuttle, Richard, *Chmn,* Tulane University, Dept Art Newcomb Col Art Galleries, New Orleans LA

Tuusuli, Moaali'itele, *Chmn Board of Trustees,* Jean P Haydon Museum, Pago Pago, American Samoa PI

Tweedy, Joan, *Instr,* University of North Carolina at Charlotte, Dept of Visual Arts, Charlotte NC (S)

Twiggs, Leo F, *Chmn,* South Carolina State University, Art Dept, Orangeburg SC (S)

Twist, Susan, *Dir,* Brant Historical Society, Brant County Museum, Brantford ON

Tye, Hetly, *Registrar,* Museum of Photographic Arts, Balboa Park CA

Tyler, Barbara, *Dir & CEO,* McMichael Canadian Art Collection, Kleinburg ON

Tyler, Cathie, *Chmn,* Paris Junior College, Art Dept, Paris TX (S)

Tyler, Douglas E, *Chmn,* Saint Mary's College, Dept of Art, Notre Dame IN (S)

Tymchak, Michael, *Dean of Art,* University of Regina, Dept of Art Education, Regina SK (S)

Tynemouth, Brian, *Librn,* New England School of Art & Design, Library, Boston MA

Tyrer, Nancy, *Asst Dir,* Heritage Plantation of Sandwich, Sandwich MA

Tysinger, Joan W, *Cur,* Georgia State University, School of Art & Design, Visual Resource Library & Reading Room, Atlanta GA

Tyssen, T G, *Exec Dir,* The Seagram Museum, Waterloo ON

Tyzack, Michael, *Chmn Studio Art,* College of Charleston, School of the Arts, Charleston SC (S)

Udvarhelyi, Elspeth, *Deputy Dir Museum Development,* Baltimore Museum of Art, Baltimore MD

Uebelhor, Curtis R, *Asst Dir,* The New Harmony Gallery of Contemporary Art, New Harmony IN

Ugent, Donald, *Adjunct Cur Botany,* Southern Illinois University, University Museum, Carbondale IL

Uglow, Sadie, *Librn,* Tacoma Art Museum, Reference Library, Tacoma WA

Uhde, Jan, *Assoc Prof,* University of Waterloo, Fine Arts Dept, Waterloo ON (S)

Uhrich, Kitty, *Coordr,* Indianapolis Museum of Art, Indianapolis Museum of Art at Columbus, Indianapolis IN

Ulak, James T, *Assoc Cur Japanese Art,* The Art Institute of Chicago, Department of Asian Art, Chicago IL

Ulloa, Derby, *Prof,* Florida Community College at Jacksonville, South Campus, Art Dept, Jacksonville FL (S)

Ullrich, John W, *Pres,* Leigh Yawkey Woodson Art Museum, Inc, Wausau WI

Ulrich, Edwin A, *Dir,* Edwin A Ulrich Museum, Hyde Park NY

Ulrich, Edwin A, *Dir,* Edwin A Ulrich Museum, Library, Hyde Park NY

Umamoto, Joyce, *Cur,* Archives of MOCA (Museum of Conceptual Art), San Francisco CA

Umen, Harry, *Asst Prof,* Notre Dame College, Art Dept, Manchester NH (S)

Umlauf, Karl, *Prof,* Baylor University, Dept of Art, Waco TX (S)

Unangst, George, *Secy,* Pennsylvania Dutch Folk Culture Society Inc, Pennsylvania Dutch Folklife Museum, Lenhartsville PA

Underhill, Michael, *Dir Archit,* Arizona State University, College of Architecture & Environmental Design, Tempe AZ

Underwood, Barbara, *Admin Asst,* University of California, Los Angeles, Fowler Museum of Cultural History, Los Angeles CA

Underwood, Carol, *Shop Mgr,* Sharon Arts Center, Sharon NH

Underwood, Consuelo, *Exec Dir,* Washington Lawyers for the Arts, Seattle WA

Underwood, David, *Asst Prof,* Rutgers, the State University of New Jersey, Graduate Program in Art History, New Brunswick NJ (S)

Underwood, Lori, *Cur,* San Fernando Valley Historical Society, Mission Hills CA

Underwood, Mary Lou, *Instr,* Grayson County College, Art Dept, Denison TX (S)

Underwood, Sandra L, *Assoc Prof,* Saint Mary's College of Maryland, Arts and Letters Division, Saint Mary's City MD (S)

Underwood, Tut, *Dir Public Information & Marketing,* South Carolina State Museum, Columbia SC

Unger, Howard, *Prof,* Ocean County College, Humanities Dept, Toms River NJ (S)

Ungerman, Temmi, *Instr,* Toronto Art Therapy Institute, Toronto ON (S)

Ungkavatanapong, Nopchai, *Preparator,* Miami University Art Museum, Oxford OH

Unser, Carlene, *Assoc Prof,* Viterbo College, Art Dept, La Crosse WI (S)

Unterschultz, Judy, *Exec Dir,* Multicultural Heritage Centre, Stony Plain AB

Upchurch, Diane, *Coordr,* Arizona State University, Architectural Image Library, Tempe AZ

Uphoff, Dudley, *Exec Dir,* Arts on the Park, Lakeland FL

Upton, Stephanie, *Dir,* Louisa May Alcott Memorial Association, Orchard House, Concord MA

Uraneck, Joan, *Instr,* Portland School of Art, Portland ME (S)

Urban, Erin, *Dir,* The John A Noble Collection, Staten Island NY

Urban, Ruth Harris, *Board Dir,* Artists' Cooperative Gallery, Omaha NE

Urban, Thomas, *Craft Center Coordr,* University of Oregon, Aperture Photo Gallery - EMU Art Gallery, Eugene OR

Urbizu, William, *Asst Dir & Media Relations,* Miami-Dade Public Library, Miami FL

Urista, Arturo, *Dir,* Self Help Graphics, Los Angeles CA

Urquhart, A M, *Prof,* University of Waterloo, Fine Arts Dept, Waterloo ON (S)

Urso, Josette, *Instr,* Chautauqua Institution, School of Art, Chautauqua NY (S)

Urso, Len, *Prof,* Rochester Institute of Technology, School of Art and Design, Rochester NY (S)

Ushenko, Audrey, *Assoc Prof,* Indiana-Purdue University, Dept of Fine Arts, Fort Wayne IN (S)

Ushioka, Ellen, *Asst Dir,* Columbia College, The Museum of Contemporary Photography, Chicago IL

Usui, Kiichi, *Dir,* Oakland University, Meadow Brook Art Gallery, Rochester MI

Uter, Bonnie, *Dir Public Affairs & Publications,* University of Georgia, Georgia Museum of Art, Athens GA

Utterbach, Rosalie, *Chmn Fashion Design,* Woodbury University, Dept of Graphic Design, Burbank CA (S)

Uyemura, Ken, *Prof,* University of Miami, Dept of Art & Art History, Coral Gables FL (S)

Uzureau, Linda, *Assoc Dean,* South Suburban College, Art Dept, South Holland IL (S)

Vaal, Lisa, *Lectr,* Notre Dame College, Art Dept, Manchester NH (S)

Vadeboncoeur, Guy, *Cur,* David M Stewart Museum, Montreal PQ

Vaggalis, K L, *Dir & Secy,* The Turner Museum, Denver CO

Vail, Neil, *Treas,* Wustum Museum Art Association, Racine WI

Vajda, Elizabeth, *Head Librn,* Cooper Union for the Advancement of Science & Art, Library, New York NY

Valdes, Karen, *Assoc Prof,* University of Florida, Dept of Art, Gainesville FL (S)

Val Des, Karen W, *Acting Dir,* University of Florida, University Gallery, Gainesville FL

Valdez, Helen, *Pres,* Mexican Fine Arts Center Museum, Chicago IL

Valencia, Romolo, *Instr Graphic Arts,* Honolulu Community College, Honolulu HI (S)

Valentine, Marilyn, *Libr Asst,* University of Maryland, College Park, Art Library, College Park MD

Valenza, Catherine, *Dir of Coll & Exhib,* Islip Art Museum, East Islip NY

Valenza, Dan, *Chmn,* University of New Hampshire, Dept of the Arts, Durham NH (S)

Valle, Martha, *Registrar,* Rosemount Victorian House Museum, Pueblo CO

Valley, Derek R, *Dir,* State Capitol Museum, Olympia WA

Valliant, John R, *Dir,* Chesapeake Bay Maritime Museum, Saint Michaels MD

Vallieres, Nicole, *Registrar,* McCord Museum of Canadian History, Montreal PQ

Vallila, Marja, *Asst Prof,* State University of New York at Albany, Art Dept, Albany NY (S)

Van Allen, David, *Dir,* Mount Mercy College, McAuley Gallery, Cedar Rapids IA

Van Arsdale, Dorothy T, *Traveling Exhib Cur,* Maitland Art Center, Maitland FL

Van Arsdale, Dorothy T, *Cur Traveling Exhib,* Maitland Art Center, Library, Maitland FL van Balgooy, Max A, *Dir of Education & Public Affairs,* Workman & Temple Family Homestead Museum, City of Industry CA

Van Bramer, Judie, *Membership Mgr,* University of Rochester, Memorial Art Gallery, Rochester NY

Vance, Alex, *Executive Dir,* Bergstrom Mahler Museum, Neenah WI

Vance, Joseph, *Pres,* Society of Animal Artists, Inc, Bronx NY

Vance, Lori, *Asst Prof,* Mount Mary College, Art Dept, Milwaukee WI (S)

Vanco, John, *Dir,* Erie Art Museum, Erie PA

Vandegrift, David, *Chmn Div,* Marygrove College, Visual & Performing Arts Div, Detroit MI (S)

Vandegrift, David, *Assoc Prof,* Marygrove College, Visual & Performing Arts Div, Detroit MI (S)

Van de Guchte, Maarten, *Cur,* University of Illinois, Krannert Art Museum, Champaign IL

Van De Putte, Andre S, *Dir,* Lasell College, Art & Interior Design Program, Auburndale MA (S)

Vanderbilt, Claire F, *Chmn,* Historical Society of the Town of Greenwich, Inc, Bush-Holley House, Cos Cob CT

Vanderhill, Rein, *Asst Prof,* Northwestern College, Art Dept, Orange City IA (S)

VanderMark, Bert, *Asst Prof,* Webster University, Art Dept, Webster Groves MO (S)

van der Mark, J, *Cur Twentieth Century,* Detroit Institute of Arts, Detroit MI

Vandermeuen, Jan, *Prof,* Cleveland State University, Art Dept, Cleveland OH (S)

VanDerpool, Karen, *Instr,* California State University, Chico, Art Dept, Chico CA (S)

Vandersluys, Norman, *Instr,* West Shore Community College, Division of Humanities and Fine Arts, Scottville MI (S)

Vanderway, Richard, *Education Coordr,* Whatcom Museum of History and Art, Bellingham WA

Vander Weg, Phil, *Chmn,* Western Michigan University-Art Dept, Gallery II, Kalamazoo MI

VanderWeg, Phillip, *Chairperson Dept,* Western Michigan University, Dept of Art, Kalamazoo MI (S)

Vandest, Bill, *Instr,* Creighton University, Fine and Performing Arts Dept, Omaha NE (S)

Van Dueben, Patrick, *Prof,* Daytona Beach Community College, Dept of Fine Arts & Visual Arts, Daytona Beach FL (S)

Van Dyk, Stephen, *Librn,* Cooper-Hewitt, National Museum of Design, New York NY

Van Dyk, Stephen, *Librn,* Cooper-Hewitt, National Museum of Design, Cooper-Hewitt Museum Branch Library, New York NY

Van Dyke, Fred, *Asst Prof,* Salt Lake Community College, Graphic Design Dept, Salt Lake City UT (S)

Van Dyke, Gene, *Dir, Governor's School for the Arts,* Pennsylvania Department of Education, Arts in Education Program, Harrisburg PA

Van Dyke, Mary, *Librn,* Amarillo Art Association, Library, Amarillo TX

Van Dyke, Sandra, *Pres,* Art Institute of Pittsburgh, Pittsburgh PA (S)

Vanek, Mark, *Educ Coordr,* Anderson Fine Arts Center, Anderson IN

van Everdingen, Arie, *Assoc Prof,* Monmouth College, Dept of Art, West Long Branch NJ (S)

Vango, Eugene, *Asst Prof,* Virginia State University, Fine & Commercial Art, Petersburg VA (S)

Vango, Eugene R, *Prof,* Virginia State University, Fine & Commercial Art, Petersburg VA (S)

Vangsness, Joe, *Pres,* Palette & Chisel Academy of Fine Arts, Chicago IL

Van Haaften, Julia, *Cur of Photographs,* The New York Public Library, Print Room, New York NY

Van Haren, John E, *Head Dept,* Eastern Michigan University, Dept of Art, Ypsilanti MI (S)

Van Hook, L Bailey, *Prof,* Virginia Polytechnic Institute & State University, Dept of Art & Art History, Blacksburg VA (S)

Van Hooten, Joan, *Development Officer,* Long Beach Museum of Art, Long Beach CA

Van Horn, David, *Assoc Prof,* Siena Heights College, Studio Angelico-Art Dept, Adrian MI (S)

Van Horn, Don, *Chmn,* University of Arkansas at Little Rock, Dept of Art, Little Rock AR (S)

Van Horn, Don, *Chmn,* University of Arkansas, Art Slide Library, Little Rock AR

Van Horn, Walter, *Cur of Coll,* Anchorage Museum of History and Art, Anchorage AK

Van Horne, John C, *Librn,* Library Company of Philadelphia, Print Dept, Philadelphia PA

Van Kampen, Jan, *Chair Commun & Design,* Ontario College of Art, Toronto ON (S)

VanLandingham, Mrs, *Pres,* Association for the Preservation of Virginia Antiquities, Richmond VA

Van Miegroet, Hans, *Asst Prof,* Duke University, Dept of Art and Art History, Durham NC (S)

Vann, Lowell C, *Chmn,* Samford University, Art Dept, Birmingham AL (S)

Van Over, Nancy, *Instr,* Adrian College, Art Dept, Adrian MI (S)

Van Parys, Michelle, *Prof,* State University of New York College at Potsdam, Dept of Fine Arts, Potsdam NY (S)

Van Riper, Ryn, *Admin,* Huntsville Museum of Art, Huntsville AL

Van Schaick, John, *Pres,* Schenectady County Historical Society, Schenectady NY

Van Suchtelen, Adrian, *Prof,* Utah State University, Dept of Art, Logan UT (S)

Van Tassell, Katherine, *Chief Cur,* Minnesota Museum of American Art, Saint Paul MN

Van Vleet, Barbara, *Public Information,* Toledo Museum of Art, Toledo Museum of Art, Toledo OH

VanWagoner, Richard J, *Prof,* Weber State University, Dept of Visual Arts, Ogden UT (S)

van Weringh, Reinolde, *Librn,* Queen's University, Art Library, Kingston ON

Van Westering, Karen, *Publications Dir,* The New York Public Library, Shelby Cullom Davis Museum, New York NY

Van Winkle, Mary, *Librn,* Massachusetts College of Art, Morton R Godine Library, Boston MA

VanZandt, Paul, *Chmn Dept,* Pembroke State University, Art Dept, Pembroke NC (S)

Van Zanten, David, *Chmn Dept,* Northwestern University, Evanston, Dept of Art History, Evanston IL (S)

Varady, Adrienne, *Cur,* University of Cincinnati, DAAP Slide Library, Cincinnati OH

Varga, Vincent J, *Cur,* Art Gallery of Windsor, Windsor ON

Vargas, Kathy, *Visual Arts Dir,* Guadalupe Cultural Arts Center, San Antonio TX

Varnedoe, Kirk, *Dir Dept Painting & Sculpture,* Museum of Modern Art, New York NY

Varner, Victoria Star, *Asst Prof,* Southwestern University, Art Dept, Georgetown TX (S)

Varnum, Maevernon, *Instr,* Wayne Art Center, Wayne PA (S)

Vartabedian, Bob, *Head Dept,* West Texas State University, Art, Communication & Theatre Dept, Canyon TX (S)

Vasconcellos, Anthony, *Managing Dir,* Institute for Contemporary Art, Project Studio One (P S 1), Long Island City NY

Vaslef, Irene, *Librn,* Harvard University, Library, Washington DC

Vassallo, Carol, *Library Asst,* Bryn Mawr College, Art and Archaeology Library, Bryn Mawr PA

Vasseur, Dominique, *Cur of European & Graphic Arts & Registrar,* Dayton Art Institute, Dayton OH

Vatandoost, Nossi, *Exec Dir,* Nossi School of Art, Goodlettsville TN (S)

Vatsky, Sharon, *Exec Dir,* The Queens Museum of Art, Flushing NY

Vaughan, James, *Chmn Interior Design,* Fashion Institute of Technology, Art & Design Division, New York NY (S)

Vaughan, Tom, *Cur Archival Coll,* Bisbee Mining & Historical Museum, Lemuel Shattuck Memorial Library, Bisbee AZ

Vaughn, Babs, *Registrar,* Muskegon Museum of Art, Muskegon MI

Vaux, Richard, *Prof,* Adelphi University, Dept of Art and Art History, Garden City NY (S)

Vazquez, Paul, *Prof,* University of Bridgeport, Art Dept, Bridgeport CT (S)

Veasey, Ruth, *Instr,* Ocean City Art Center, Ocean City NJ (S)

Veatch, James, *Assoc Prof,* University of Massachusetts at Lowell, Dept of Art, Lowell MA (S)

Vecchitto, Dan, *Dir Development,* Museum of Modern Art, New York NY

Veckman, Thomas, *Registrar,* Historical Society of Delaware, Old Town Hall Museum, Wilmington DE

Veerkamp, Patrick, *Assoc Prof,* Southwestern University, Art Dept, Georgetown TX (S)

Vega, Margaret, *Chmn Foundation Fine Arts,* Kendall College of Art & Design, Grand Rapids MI (S)

Vega, Margaret, *Chmn Foundation & Fine Arts,* Kendall College of Art & Design, Frank & Lyn Van Steenberg Library, Grand Rapids MI

Vegavega, Gloria A, *Librn,* Institute of Puerto Rican Culture, Library, San Juan PR

Veinus, P, *Assoc Prof,* Northern Arizona University, School of Art & Design, Flagstaff AZ (S)

Veith, Gene Edward, *Div Dir,* Concordia University, Division of Arts & Sciences, Mequon WI (S)

Veith, Ulike, *Program Coordr,* Photographers Gallery, Saskatoon SK

Vejvoda, Barbara, *Development Assoc,* Institute of Contemporary Art, Boston MA

Velasque, Geraldine, *Prof,* Georgian Court College, Dept of Art, Lakewood NJ (S)

Vena, Dante, *Chmn Art Educ,* University of Massachusetts Dartmouth, College of Visual and Performing Arts, North Dartmouth MA (S)

Vena, David, *VPres,* The Friends of Photography, Ansel Adams Center for Photography, San Francisco CA

Venable, Charles, *Cur Decorative Arts,* Dallas Museum of Art, Dallas TX

Venancio, Doria, *Assoc Dir,* SIAS International Art Society, Sherwood Park AB

Venancio, Horacio, *Assoc Dir,* SIAS International Art Society, Sherwood Park AB

Vendetti, Debra, *Education Coordr,* William A Farnsworth Library and Art Museum, Rockland ME

Venner, Thomas, *Chairperson Dept,* Siena Heights College, Studio Angelico-Art Dept, Adrian MI (S)

Ventimiglia, John T, *Instr,* Portland School of Art, Portland ME (S)

Ventura, Nina, *Secy,* Wind Luke Asian Museum Memorial Foundation, Inc, Seattle WA

Vera, Betty, *Artist,* New York Tapestry Artists, Carmel NY

Vera, Maria Garcia, *Auxiliary Prof,* Inter American University of Puerto Rico, Dept of Art, San German PR (S)

Verbrugghen, Johanna M, *Cur,* North Country Museum of Arts, Park Rapids MN

Verderber, Rob, *Coordr,* Ameritrust Company National Association, Art Collection, Cleveland OH

Verdini, G, *Chief AV Div,* Brooklyn Public Library, Art and Music Division, Brooklyn NY

Verdon, Ron, *Prof,* University of Wisconsin-Stout, Dept of Art & Design, Menomonie WI (S)

Ver Hague, James, *Prof,* Rochester Institute of Technology, School of Art and Design, Rochester NY (S)

Verkaik, May, *Dir,* Brownsville Art League Museum, Brownsville TX

Vermeule, Cornelius C, *Cur Classical Art,* Museum of Fine Arts, Boston MA

Vermillion, Emily J G, *Cur Educ,* University of Iowa, Museum of Art, Iowa City IA

Vernon, Ann D, *Dir Education,* Chrysler Museum, Norfolk VA

Vernon, Betty, *Art Dir,* Hill Country Arts Foundation, Ingram TX

Vernon, Carol, *Instr,* Southwestern Oregon Community College, Visual Arts Dept, Coos Bay OR (S)

Vernon, Marlene, *Prog Dir,* University of Minnesota, Paul Whitney Larson Gallery, Saint Paul MN

Vernon, Mary, *Chair,* Southern Methodist University, Art Div, Dallas TX (S)

Verstegen, Mark, *Technical Services Supvr,* Madison Art Center, Madison WI

Vervoort, Patricia, *Chmn,* Lakehead University, Dept of Visual Arts, Thunder Bay ON (S)

Verzar, Christine, *Chmn Dept,* Ohio State University, Dept of the History of Art, Columbus OH (S)

Vesely, Carolyn, *Dir,* Glenhyrst Art Gallery of Brant, Brantford ON

Vetroco, Marcia E, *Assoc Prof,* University of New Orleans-Lake Front, Dept of Fine Arts, New Orleans LA (S)

Vevers, Tony, *Instr,* Truro Center for the Arts at Castle Hill, Inc, Truro MA (S)

Vial, Pascale, *Office Mgr,* Albuquerque United Artists, Albuquerque NM

Viator, Della, *Asst to Dir,* University of Southwestern Louisiana, University Art Museum, Lafayette LA

Vick, Elizabeth, *Prof,* Chowan College, Division of Art, Murfreesboro NC (S)

Victor, Charlene, *Exec Dir,* Brooklyn Arts Council, BACA Downtown, Brooklyn NY

Victor, James, *Lectr,* Rosemont College, Division of the Arts, Rosemont PA (S)

Victor, Michael, *Pres,* Erie Art Museum, Erie PA

Vidal, Mary, *Prof,* Princeton University, Dept of Art and Archaeology, Princeton NJ (S)

Vidnovic, Nick, *Lectr,* University of Pennsylvania, Graduate School of Fine Arts, Philadelphia PA (S)

Viera, Ricardo, *Dir Exhib & Coll,* Lehigh University Art Galleries, Bethlehem PA

Viera, Ricardo, *Prof,* Lehigh University, Dept of Art and Architecture, Bethlehem PA (S)

Vieth, M Bruce, *Pres,* Philadelphia Sketch Club, Inc, Philadelphia PA

Vigiletti, Christine, *Asst Registrar,* Los Angeles County Museum of Art, Robert Gore Rifkind Center for German Expressionist Studies, Los Angeles CA

Vigiletti, Robert, *Chmn Photography,* Center for Creative Studies, College of Art & Design, Detroit MI (S)

Viguers, Aurelia, *Instr,* Main Line Center for the Arts, Haverford PA (S)

Viirlaid, Helle, *Registrar,* Vancouver Art Gallery, Vancouver BC

Vikan, Gary, *Asst Dir Curatorial Affairs & Cur of Medieval Art,* Walters Art Gallery, Baltimore MD

Vike, Gene, *Chmn,* Western Washington University, Art Dept, Bellingham WA (S)

Vilcins, M, *Reference Librn,* National Gallery of Canada, Library, Ottawa ON

Villa, Elizabeth, *Curatorial Asst,* Galleries of the Claremont Colleges, Claremont CA

Villaneuve, Patricia, *Asst Prof,* University of Kansas, Dept of Art & Music Education & Music Therapy, Lawrence KS (S)

Villeneuve, Rene, *Asst Cur Early Canadian Art,* National Gallery of Canada, Ottawa ON

Villenue, Pat, *Cur Education,* University of Kansas, Spencer Museum of Art, Lawrence KS

Vinc, Marty, *Education Chmn,* Huntsville Art League and Museum Association Inc, Huntsville AL

Vincent, Marcus, *Gallery Dir,* Brigham Young University, B F Larsen Gallery, Provo UT

Vincent, Ruth, *Registrar & Colls Mgr,* Wind Luke Asian Museum Memorial Foundation, Inc, Seattle WA

Vincent-Jones, Craig, *Development,* Portland Art Museum, Portland OR

Vinyard, Eugene, *Asst Prof,* Springfield College, Dept of Visual and Performing Arts, Springfield MA (S)

Violante, Pamela, *Registrar,* United States Capitol, Art Reference Library, Washington DC

Virkau, Vytas, *Assoc Prof,* North Central College, Dept of Art, Naperville IL (S)

Virtue, George, *Pres,* Southern Alberta Art Gallery, Lethbridge AB

Viscarra, Joseph, *Chief Cataloguer,* New York City Technical College, Namm Hall Library and Learning Resource Center, Brooklyn NY

VisGirda, Rimas, *Instr,* Illinois Wesleyan University, School of Art, Bloomington IL (S)

Vissat, Maureen, *Chairperson,* Seton Hill College, Dept of Art, Greensburg PA (S)

Visser, Mary, *Assoc Prof,* Southwestern University, Art Dept, Georgetown TX (S)

Visser, Susan R, *Exec Dir,* South Bend Regional Museum of Art, South Bend IN

Vitale, Lee, *Technical Servs Librn,* Daemen College, Marian Library, Amherst NY

Vitale, Thomas Jewell, *Assoc Prof,* Loras College, Dept of Art, Dubuque IA (S)

Vivoni, Paul, *Assoc Prof,* Inter American University of Puerto Rico, Dept of Art, San German PR (S)

Vlack, Donald, *Museum Head,* The New York Public Library, Shelby Cullom Davis Museum, New York NY

Voces, Yolanda, *Second VPres,* San Bernardino Art Association, Inc, San Bernardino CA

Voci, Peter, *Assoc Prof,* New York Institute of Technology, Fine Arts Dept, Old Westbury NY (S)

Voelkle, William M, *Cur Medieval & Renaissance Manuscripts,* Pierpont Morgan Library, New York NY

Vogel, Alan, *Assoc Prof,* Rochester Institute of Technology, School of Photographic Arts & Sciences, Rochester NY (S)

Vogel, Scott, *Electronic Arts Chmn (Video),* Atlanta College of Art, Atlanta GA (S)

Vogel, Susan, *Exec Dir,* International Museum of African Art, New York NY

Vogt, Allie, *Instr,* North Idaho College, Art Dept, Coeur D'Alene ID (S)

Vogt, John, *Assoc Prof,* Kansas State University, Art Dept, Manhattan KS (S)

Vogt, Margaret, *Registrar,* Massillon Museum, Massillon OH

Voigt, Gaines, *Pres,* Marion Koogler McNay Art Museum, San Antonio TX

Voit, Irene, *Business Serv,* Las Vegas-Clark County Library District, Las Vegas NV

Volk, Ulla, *Art & Architecture,* Cooper Union for the Advancement of Science & Art, Library, New York NY

Vollmer, Stephen, *Chief Cur,* El Paso Museum of Art, El Paso TX

Voltachio, John, *Prof,* Salem State College, Art Dept, Salem MA (S)

vom Baur, Daphne, *Secy,* Tradd Street Press, Elizabeth O'Neill Verner Studio Museum, Charleston SC

Von Barghahn, Barbara, *Assoc Prof,* George Washington University, Dept of Art, Washington DC (S)

Vonkeman, Anine, *Public Prog Cur,* Southern Alberta Art Gallery, Lethbridge AB

von Sonnenberg, Hubert, *Conservator Paintings,* The Metropolitan Museum of Art, New York NY

Von Stockum, R R, *Dir,* The Filson Club, Louisville KY

Von Wilken Zook, Peter, *Ceramics Coordr,* Mendocino Art Center, Mendocino CA (S)

Voos, William J, *Dean,* Indiana University-Purdue University, Indianapolis, Herron School of Art, Indianapolis IN (S)

Vos, Margaret, *Prog Dir,* Saint Cloud State University, Atwood Center Gallery Lounge, Saint Cloud MN

Voss, Cathy, *In Charge Art Coll,* Banc One Wisconsin Corp, Milwaukee WI

Voss, Jerrold, *Dir,* Ohio State University, School of Architecture, Columbus OH (S)

Voth, Andrew, *Dir,* Carnegie Art Museum, Oxnard CA

Vouk, Kathy, *Instr,* Creighton University, Fine and Performing Arts Dept, Omaha NE (S)

Vouri, Michael, *Public Relations,* Whatcom Museum of History and Art, Bellingham WA

Vruwink, J, *Chmn,* Central University of Iowa, Art Dept, Pella IA (S)

Vyse, Richard, *Head Art Dept,* The School of Fashion Design, Boston MA (S)

Waale, Kim, *Instr,* Cazenovia College, Center for Art & Design Studies, Cazenovia NY (S)

Wabnitz, Robert, *Prof,* Rochester Institute of Technology, School of Art and Design, Rochester NY (S)

Wachna, Pamela, *Cur,* The Market Gallery of the City of Toronto Archives, Toronto ON

Wachsberger, Fredrica, *VPres,* Oysterponds Historical Society, Museum, Orient NY

Wacksmith, Karen, *Asst Prof,* Randolph-Macon College, Dept of the Arts, Ashland VA (S)

Waddell, Roberta, *Cur of Prints,* The New York Public Library, Print Room, New York NY

Waddington, Murray, *Chief Librn,* National Gallery of Canada, Library, Ottawa ON

Waddington, Susan R, *Coordr,* Providence Public Library, Art & Music Services, Providence RI

Waddle, Carl, *Dean,* Fresno City College, Art Dept, Fresno CA (S)

Wade, Edward M, *Chmn,* Potomac State College, Dept of Art, Keyser WV (S)

Wade, J Blake, *Exec Dir,* Oklahoma Historical Society, State Museum of History, Oklahoma City OK

Wade, Karen Graham, *Dir,* Workman & Temple Family Homestead Museum, City of Industry CA

Wade, Warner W, *Prof Painting,* Ramapo College of New Jersey, School of Contemporary Arts, Mahwah NJ (S)

Wadhams, Hazel, *Cur,* Goshen Historical Society, Goshen CT

Wadley, William, *Head,* East Texas State University, Dept of Art, East Texas Station, Commerce TX (S)

Wadsworth, David, *Sr Cur,* Cohasset Historical Society, Caleb Lothrop House, Cohasset MA

Wadsworth, Dorothy, *Instr,* Johnson County Community College, Visual Arts Program, Overland Park KS (S)

Waelder, Kristine, *Development Officer,* Everson Museum of Art, Syracuse NY

Wageman, Susan, *Exhib Cur,* Rosicrucian Egyptian Museum and Art Gallery, San Jose CA

Wageman, Virginia, *Publications Dir,* College Art Association, New York NY

Waggoner, Allison, *VPres,* Owatonna Arts Center, Community Arts Center, Owatonna MN

Wagman, N E, *Prof,* Salem State College, Art Dept, Salem MA (S)

Wagner, Betty L, *Librn,* University of Washington, Architecture & Urban Planning Library, Seattle WA

Wagner, Catherine F, *Prof Studio Art & Chmn,* Mills College, Art Dept, Oakland CA (S)

Wagner, David, *Dir,* Colorado Springs Fine Arts Center, Colorado Springs CO

Wagner, Dee, *Registrar,* Brookfield Craft Center, Inc, Video Library, Brookfield CT

Wagner, Fred, *Asst Dir,* Pyramid Arts Center, Rochester NY

Wagner, Katherine, *Exec Dir,* D-Art, A Visual Arts Center for Dallas, Dallas TX

Wagner, Lois, *Cur,* Sterling Portfolio Inc, New York NY

Wagner, Norman, *Printmaking Chmn,* Atlanta College of Art, Atlanta GA (S)

Wagner, Patty, *Museum Educ,* McLean County Historical Society, Bloomington IL

Wagner, Robin, *Registrar & Cur Asst,* Charles H MacNider Museum, Mason City IA

Wagner, Ronald, *Instr,* Joe Kubert School of Cartoon & Graphic Art, Inc, Dover NJ (S)

Wagner, Vernon M, *Pres,* The Art Institute of Chicago, Woman's Board, Chicago IL

Wagner, Wesley, *Asst Prof,* Bethany College, Dept of Fine Arts, Bethany WV (S)

Wagner, William, *Assoc Prof,* Old Dominion University, Art Dept, Norfolk VA (S)

Wagoner, Holly, *Staff Asst,* Terra Museum of American Art, Chicago IL

Wagoner, Phillip, *Adjunct Asst Prof,* Wesleyan University, Art Dept, Middletown CT (S)

Wagoner, Ralph, *Pres,* Western Illinois University, Art Gallery-Museum, Macomb IL

Wahnee, B J, *Instr,* Haskell Indian Junior College, Art Dept, Lawrence KS (S)

Wailes, Bernard, *European Section Assoc Cur,* University of Pennsylvania, University Museum of Archaelogy & Anthropology, Philadelphia PA

Wainstein Bond, Anne, *Cur Material Culture,* Colorado Historical Society, Museum, Denver CO

Wainwright, Paige, *Asst Dir,* Sloss Furnaces National Historic Landmark, Birmingham AL

Waisbrot, Ann, *Dir,* New Visions Gallery, Inc, Marshfield WI

Waits, Nancy, *Coordr,* A I R Gallery, New York NY

Waits, Roy, *Instr,* ACA College of Design, Cincinnati OH (S)

Wakeford, Mary, *Registrar,* Hofstra University, Hofstra Museum, Hempstead NY

Walbank, Mary, *Cur Numismatics,* University of Calgary, The Nickle Arts Museum, Calgary AB

Walbridge, Barbara, *VPres,* Balboa Art Conservation Center, San Diego CA

Walch, Margaret, *Assoc Dir,* Color Association of The US, New York NY

Walch, Peter, *Dir,* University of New Mexico, University Art Museum, Albuquerque NM

Walch, Timothy, *Asst Dir,* Herbert Hoover Presidential Library & Museum, West Branch IA

Walczak, Dawne, *Exec Dir,* Tempe Arts Center, Tempe AZ

Walden, Jerry, *Chmn,* University of Southern Mississippi, Dept of Art, Hattiesburg MS (S)

Waldman, Arthur, *Prof,* Ocean County College, Humanities Dept, Toms River NJ (S)

Waldman, Diane, *Deputy Dir,* Solomon R Guggenheim Museum, New York NY

Waldner, Wolfgang, *Dir,* Austrian Cultural Institute, Gallery, New York NY

Waldon, Tricia, *Admin Asst,* City of Hampton, Hampton Arts Commission, Hampton VA

Waldorf, Gwendolyn, *Assoc Dir,* Tallahassee Museum of History & Natural Science, Tallahassee FL

Waldron, Peter, *Asst Prof,* Bradford College, Creative Arts Division, Bradford MA (S)

Wales, Kitty, *Instr,* Dean Junior College, Visual and Performing Art Dept, Franklin MA (S)

Walford, E John, *Chmn,* Wheaton College, Dept of Art, Wheaton IL (S)

Walick, Christine, *Asst Dir,* Archaeological Society of Ohio, Indian Museum of Lake County, Ohio, Painesville OH

Walk, Deborah, *Archivist,* State Art Museum of Florida, Art Research Library, Sarasota FL

Walker, Barry, *Cur Prints & Drawings,* Museum of Fine Arts, Houston, Houston TX

Walker, Brian, *Dir,* International Museum of Cartoon Art, Boca Raton FL

Walker, Caroline, *Education & Communications Officer,* Beaverbrook Art Gallery, Fredericton NB

Walker, Charles, *Instr,* De Anza College, Creative Arts Div, Cupertino CA (S)

Walker, Daniel, *Cur Islamic Art,* The Metropolitan Museum of Art, New York NY

Walker, Debra, *Exec Dir,* Historical Society of Rockland County, New City NY

Walker, Earl, *Chmn,* George Brown College of Applied Arts and Technology, Dept of Visual Arts, Toronto ON (S)

Walker, J Charles, *Div Coordr Design,* Kent State University, School of Art, Kent OH (S)

Walker, Jeffry, *Dir,* Trinity College, Austin Arts Center, Hartford CT

Walker, Kathrine, *Educ Coordr,* Lyman Allyn Art Museum, New London CT

Walker, Larry, *Dir School,* Georgia State University, School of Art & Design, Atlanta GA (S)

Walker, Larry, *Chmn Human & Fine Arts,* Garden City Community College, Art Dept, Garden City KS (S)

Walker, Mort, *Chmn,* International Museum of Cartoon Art, Boca Raton FL

Walker, Pat, *Asst Prof,* Georgia Southern University, Dept of Art, Statesboro GA (S)

Walker, Priscilla, *Dir,* Portsmouth Historical Society, John Paul Jones House, Portsmouth NH

Walker, Robert, *Instr,* College of the Canyons, Art Dept, Valencia CA (S)

Walker, Roslyn, *Cur,* National Museum of African Art, Washington DC

Walker, Sharon, *Corporate Art Admin,* Ashland Oil, Inc, Ashland KY

Walker, Wendell, *Gallery Mgr,* New York University, Grey Art Gallery and Study Center, New York NY

Walker, William B, *Chief Librn,* The Metropolitan Museum of Art, New York NY

Walker, William B, *Chief Librn,* The Metropolitan Museum of Art, Thomas J Watson Library, New York NY

Walking Stick, Kay, *Asst Prof,* State University of New York at Stony Brook, Art Dept, Stony Brook NY (S)

Walking Stick, Kay, *Asst Prof,* Cornell University, Dept of Art, Ithaca NY (S)

Wall, Brent, *Assoc Prof,* Saint Xavier University, Dept of Art, Chicago IL (S)

Wall, Brian, *Prof,* University of California, Berkeley, College of Letters & Sciences-Art Dept, Berkeley CA (S)

Wall, Constance, *Librn,* Detroit Institute of Arts, Research Library, Detroit MI

Wall, Jeff, *Prof,* University of British Columbia, Dept of Fine Arts, Vancouver BC (S)

Wallace, Alan, *Instr,* Chattanooga State Technical Community College, Advertising Arts Dept, Chattanooga TN (S)

Wallace, Betty, *Dir,* Nebraska Wesleyan University, Elder Gallery, Lincoln NE

Wallace, Bob, *Dir,* Dawson County Historical Society, Museum, Lexington NE

Wallace, Bruce, *Assoc Prof,* University of Tennessee at Chattanooga, Dept of Art, Chattanooga TN (S)

Wallace, Ian, *Assoc Dean Media,* Emily Carr College of Art & Design, Vancouver BC (S)

Wallace, Jana M, *Admin Asst,* Public Museum of Grand Rapids, Grand Rapids MI

Wallace, J E, *Dept Chmn,* Western Connecticut State University, School of Arts & Sciences, Danbury CT (S)

Wallace, Jill Snyder, *Gallery Coordr,* League of New Hampshire Craftsmen, League Gallery, Concord NH

Wallace, Keith, *Cur,* Contemporary Art Gallery society of British Columbia, Vancouver BC

Wallace, Paula, *Dept Head Reference,* New Bedford Free Public Library, Art Dept, New Bedford MA

Wallace, Richard W, *Prof,* Wellesley College, Art Dept, Wellesley MA (S)

Wallace, Scott, *Lectr,* University of Wisconsin-Stout, Dept of Art & Design, Menomonie WI (S)

Wallach, Alan, *Prof,* College of William and Mary, Dept of Fine Arts, Williamsburg VA (S)

Wallach, Eric, *Secy & Treas,* Art Dealers Association of America, Inc, New York NY

Waller, Bret, *Dir,* Indianapolis Museum of Art, Indianapolis IN

Waller, Marlene, *Partner,* Stroud Waller Inc, Highland Park IL

Waller, Susan, *Dir,* Portland School of Art, Baxter Gallery, Portland ME

Walling, Cathleen, *Asst Dir, Admin,* University of California, California Museum of Photography, Riverside CA

Walling, Cynthia, *VPres,* Middlesex County Cultural & Heritage Commission, Artists League of Central New Jersey, North Brunswick NJ

Wallis, Charline, *Prog Dir,* Tyler Junior College, Art Program, Tyler TX (S)

Wallis, Mel R, *Instr,* Olympic College, Social Sciences & Humanities Division, Bremerton WA (S)

Wall MLS, Kay L, *Dir,* University of Southern Mississippi, McCain Library & Archives, Hattiesburg MS

Wallot, Jean-Pierre, *National Archivist,* National Archives of Canada, Documentary Art and Photography, Ottawa ON

Walpole, Donald, *Assoc Prof,* Saint Meinrad College, Humanities Dept, Saint Meinrad IN (S)

Walpuck, Kenneth, *Prof,* Queensborough Community College, Dept of Art and Photography, Bayside NY (S)

Walsh, James J, *Chmn Trustees,* Everhart Museum, Scranton PA

Walsh, John, *Dir,* Getty Center for the History of Art & the Humanities Trust Museum, The J Paul Getty Museum, Santa Monica CA

Walsh, Karen, *Prog Asst,* Woodrow Wilson House, Washington DC

Walsh, Karen, *Public Programming Asst,* Newfoundland Museum, Library, Saint John's NF

Walsh, Linda, *Assoc Chair, Studio,* San Jose State University, School of Art & Design, San Jose CA (S)

Walsh, Marguerite, *Assoc Prof,* New England College, Art & Art History, Henniker NH (S)

Walsh, Michael, *Head Dept,* Milwaukee Area Technical College, Graphic Arts Dept, Milwaukee WI (S)

Walsh, Susan, *Dir,* University Of Wisconsin-Whitewater, Crossman Gallery, Whitewater WI

Walsh, Thomas, *Sculpture Area Head,* Southern Illinois University, School of Art & Design, Carbondale IL (S)

Walsh, Timothy F, *Head Dept,* Otero Junior College, Dept of Arts, La Junta CO (S)

Walter, Charles Thomas, *Asst Prof,* Bloomsburg University, Dept of Art, Bloomsburg PA (S)

Walter, Elizabeth M, *Prof,* University of North Alabama, Dept of Art, Florence AL (S)

Walter, Loyola, *Asst Prof,* College of Mount Saint Joseph, Art Dept, Cincinnati OH (S)

Walters, Bruce, *Assoc Prof,* Teikyo Marycrest University, Art and Computer Graphics Dept, Davenport IA (S)

Walters, Daniel, *Dir,* Spokane Public Library Gallery, Spokane WA

Walters, Elizabeth J, *Assoc Prof,* Pennsylvania State University, University Park, Dept of Art History, University Park PA (S)

Walters, Janet, *Sccy & Treas,* Western Canada Art Association Inc, Lethbridge AB

Walters, Janet, *Cur,* Lethbridge Public Library, Art Gallery, Lethbridge AB

Walters, Kim, *Librn & Dir,* Southwest Museum, Braun Research Library, Los Angeles CA

Walters, Louisella, *Dir,* Regis College, L J Walters Jr Gallery, Weston MA

Walters, Suzanne G, *Public Relations & Membership Coordr,* Flint Institute of Arts, Flint MI

Walters, Sylvia, *Chmn,* San Francisco State University, Art Dept, San Francisco CA (S)

Waltershausen, George L, *Chmn Dept,* Monmouth College, Dept of Art, Monmouth IL (S)

Walton, Ann T, *Cur Coll,* Burlington Northern, Saint Paul MN

Walton, John, *Dir,* Palo Alto Junior Museum, Palo Alto CA

Walton, Mary Anne, *Mgr,* Maritz, Inc, Library, Fenton MO

Walton, Thomas, *Assoc Prof,* Catholic University of America, School of Architecture & Planning, Washington DC (S)

Walusis, Michael, *Chmn,* Youngstown State University, Art Dept, Youngstown OH (S)

Wandling, Beverly, *Treas,* Octagon Center for the Arts, Ames IA

Wands, Robert, *Asst Prof,* University of Southern Colorado, Belmont Campus, Dept of Art, Pueblo CO (S)

Wang, David, *Asst Prof,* Berea College, Art Dept, Berea KY (S)

Wang, David, *Asst Prof,* Centenary College, Div of Fine Arts, Hackettstown NJ (S)

Wanggaard, Amy, *Exec Assoc,* Artists Space, New York NY

Wanserski, Martin, *Assoc Prof,* University of South Dakota, Dept of Art, Vermillion SD (S)

Wantz, John A, *Prof,* College of DuPage, Humanities Division, Glen Ellyn IL (S)

Wantz, Justine, *Assoc Prof,* Loyola University of Chicago, Fine Arts Dept, Chicago IL (S)

Wanzel, G, *Instr,* Technical University of Nova Scotia, Faculty of Architecture, Halifax NS (S)

Ward, Alfred, *Chmn & Prof,* Winthrop College, Dept of Art & Design, Rock Hill SC (S)

Ward, Bill, *Prof,* University of Miami, Dept of Art & Art History, Coral Gables FL (S)

Ward, Jan R, *Prof,* Del Mar College, Art Dept, Corpus Christi TX (S)

Ward, John L, *Prof,* University of Florida, Dept of Art, Gainesville FL (S)

Ward, Lois, *Technical Servs,* Beeghly Library, Delaware OH

Ward, Marna, *Asst Dir,* Lauren Rogers Museum of Art, Laurel MS

Ward, Nora, *Cur,* Spanish Governor's Palace, San Antonio TX

Ward, Peter, *Cur Invertebrate Paleontology,* University of Washington, Thomas Burke Memorial Washington State Museum, Seattle WA

Ward, R D, *Prof,* Randolph-Macon College, Dept of the Arts, Ashland VA (S)

Ward, Robert, *Prof,* Bridgewater State College, Art Dept, Bridgewater MA (S)

Ward, Robert, *Coordr,* Bowie State University, Fine Arts Dept, Bowie MD (S)

Ward, Roger, *Lectr,* University of Kansas, Kress Foundation Dept of Art History, Lawrence KS (S)

Ward, Roger B, *Cur European Painting & Sculpture,* Nelson-Atkins Museum of Art, Kansas City MO

Ward, Sandra, *Asst Dir,* Peters Valley Craft Center, Layton NJ

Ward, Scott, *Dir,* Downey Museum of Art, Downey CA

Ward, William, *Educator,* Philadelphia Maritime Museum, Philadelphia PA

Ward, William E, *Asst in East Indian Art & Museum Designer,* Cleveland Museum of Art, Cleveland OH

Warda, Rebecca, *Asst to Dir,* Widener University, Art Museum, Chester PA

Wardle, Alfred, *Instr,* Munson-Williams-Proctor Institute, School of Art, Utica NY (S)

Wardropper, Ian, *Cur European Decorative Arts, Sculpture & Classical Art,* The Art Institute of Chicago, Chicago IL

Wardwell, Anne E, *Cur Textiles,* Cleveland Museum of Art, Cleveland OH

Ware, Mike, *Instr,* Alice Lloyd College, Art Dept, Pippa Passes KY (S)

Warehall, Bill, *Instr,* California State University, San Bernardino, Art Dept, San Bernardino CA (S)

Warfield, Vivian Millicent, *Acting Dir,* Art Commission of the City of New York, Associates of the Art Commission, Inc, New York NY

Warger, Julia M, *Interpretive Programs Asst,* New York State Office of Parks Recreation & Historic Preservation, John Jay Homestead State Historic Site, Katonah NY

Wargo, Richard, *Cur,* Marcella Sembrich Memorial Association Inc, Opera Museum, Bolton Landing NY

Waricher, George, *Asst Prof,* Shippensburg University, Art Dept, Shippensburg PA (S)

Waring, David, *Art & Music Librn,* Greenwich Library, Greenwich CT

Warlick, Mary, *Dir,* The One Club for Art & Copy, New York NY

Warlick, Pam, *VPres,* Gaston County Museum of Art & History, Dallas NC

Warma, Susanne, *Asst Prof,* Utah State University, Dept of Art, Logan UT (S)

Warner, Craig L, *Instr,* Graceland College, Fine Arts Dept, Lamoni IA (S)

Warner, Deborah, *Dean,* Moore College of Art & Design, Philadelphia PA (S)

Warner, Dona, *Dir of Production,* Johnson Atelier Technical Institute of Sculpture, Mercerville NJ (S)

Warner, Malcolm, *Cur European Art,* San Diego Museum of Art, San Diego CA

Warner, Sarah E, *Development Officer,* Flint Institute of Arts, Flint MI

Warner, W S, *Pres,* Five Civilized Tribes Museum, Muskogee OK

Warner Slane, Kathleen, *Chmn,* University of Missouri, Art History and Archaeology Dept, Columbia MO (S)

Warp, Harold, *Pres,* Harold Warp Pioneer Village Foundation, Minden NE

Warren, Betty, *Dir,* Malden Bridge School of Art, Malden Bridge NY (S)

Warren, David, *Assoc Dir & Sr Cur,* Museum of Fine Arts, Houston, Houston TX

Warren, Katherine, *Dir,* University of California, University Art Gallery, Riverside CA

Warren, Lynne, *Assoc Cur,* Museum of Contemporary Art, Chicago IL

Warren, Peter W, *Head,* Eastern Montana College, Art Dept, Billings MT (S)

Warren, Russell, *Prof,* Davidson College, Art Dept, Davidson NC (S)

Warren, Sandra, *Business Mgr,* Indiana University, William Hammond Mathers Museum, Bloomington IN

Warren, Yolanda, *Art Librn,* Washington & Lee University, University Library, Lexington VA

Warrens, Robert, *Prof,* Louisiana State University, School of Art, Baton Rouge LA (S)

Warrick, Renee, *Finance Officer,* Chattahoochee Valley Art Museum, LaGrange GA

Warther, David, *Pres,* Warther Museum Inc, Dover OH

Warther, Mark, *General Mgr,* Warther Museum Inc, Dover OH

Wartluft, David J, *Dir Library,* Lutheran Theological Seminary, Krauth Memorial Library, Philadelphia PA

Washburn, Beverly, *Pres of Board,* Village of Potsdam Public Museum, Potsdam NY

Washburn, Joan T, *VPres,* Art Dealers Association of America, Inc, New York NY

Washington, Gary, *Asst Prof,* Southampton Campus of Long Island University, Fine Arts Division, Southampton NY (S)

Washington, John, *Inst,* Lansing Community College, Media Dept, Lansing MI (S)

Washmon, Gary, *Asst Prof,* Texas Woman's University, Dept of Visual Arts, Denton TX (S)

Washton Long, Rose-Carol, *Chmn Exec Committee,* City University of New York, PhD Program in Art History, New York NY (S)

Wass, Janice, *Cur Decorative Arts,* Illinois State Museum, Illinois Art Gallery & Lockport Gallery, Springfield IL

Wasserman, Krystyn A, *Head Librn,* National Museum of Women in the Arts, Library & Research Center, Washington DC

Watanabe, Joan, *Prof,* Glendale Community College, Dept of Fine Arts, Glendale CA (S)

Waters, Kathryn M, *Chmn,* University of Southern Indiana, Art Dept, Evansville IN (S)

Waters, Sara, *Prof,* Texas Tech University, Dept of Art, Lubbock TX (S)

Watkins, Anne E, *Registrar & Librn,* Colonial Williamsburg Foundation, Abby Aldrich Rockefeller Folk Art Center Library, Williamsburg VA

Watkins, Bonnie K, *Registrar & Cur Collection,* Saint Joseph Museum, Saint Joseph MO

Watkins, Dianne, *Cur Educ,* Western Kentucky University, Kentucky Museum, Bowling Green KY

Watkins, Karin, *Asst Comptroller,* Sterling and Francine Clark Art Institute, Williamstown MA

Watkins, Ruth, *Asst Prof,* College of Notre Dame of Maryland, Art Dept, Baltimore MD (S)

Watkinson, Barbara, *Chmn,* College of William and Mary, Dept of Fine Arts, Williamsburg VA (S)

Watkinson, James, *Preparator,* Dartmouth College, Hood Museum of Art, Hanover NH

Watkinson, Patricia, *Dir,* Washington State University, Museum of Art, Pullman WA

Watral, James, *Lectr,* Texas Woman's University, Dept of Visual Arts, Denton TX (S)

Watrous, John, *Chmn,* Santa Rosa Junior College, Art Dept, Santa Rosa CA (S)

Watrous, Rebecca, *Educ Dir,* Historic Cherry Hill, Albany NY

Watson, Barbara C, *Librn,* William A Farnsworth Library and Art Museum, Library, Rockland ME

Watson, Denise, *Center Adminr,* Muckenthaler Cultural Center, Fullerton CA

Watson, Donald, *Dean,* Rensselaer Polytechnic Institute, School of Architecture, Troy NY (S)

Watson, Joseph A, *Assoc Prof,* Rochester Institute of Technology, School of Art and Design, Rochester NY (S)

Watson, Katharine J, *Dir,* Bowdoin College, Museum of Art, Brunswick ME

Watson, Larry, *Executive Dir,* Coos Art Museum, Coos Bay OR

Watson, Larry, *Dir,* Coos Art Museum, Coos Bay OR (S)

Watson, Lorraine, *Instr,* Ocean City Art Center, Ocean City NJ (S)

Watson, Mark S, *Marketing Dir,* City of Hampton, Hampton Arts Commission, Hampton VA

Watson, Richard, *Exhib Dir,* Afro-American Historical & Cultural Museum, Philadelphia PA

Watson, Robert, *Secy,* United States Figure Skating Association, World Figure Skating Hall of Fame and Museum, Colorado Springs CO

Watson, Robert, *Dir,* Florida Atlantic University, Ritter Art Gallery, Boca Raton FL

Watson, Robyn S, *Dir,* Provincetown Art Association and Museum, Provincetown MA

Watson, Scott, *Cur,* University of British Columbia, Fine Arts Gallery, Vancouver BC

Watson, Thomas, *Instr,* Columbia College, Art Dept, Columbia MO (S)

Watson, Wendy, *Cur,* Mount Holyoke College, Art Museum, South Hadley MA

Watt, James C Y, *Sr Cur Asian Art,* The Metropolitan Museum of Art, New York NY

Wattenmaker, Richard J, *Dir,* Archives of American Art, Washington DC

Watts, Barbara, *Asst Prof,* Florida International University, Visual Arts Dept, Miami FL (S)

Watts, Christopher, *Chmn,* Washington State University, Fine Arts Dept, Pullman WA (S)

Watts, Michael, *Dir,* Eastern Illinois University, Tarble Arts Center, Charleston IL

Watts, Roland S, *Chmn,* Winston-Salem State University, Art Dept, Winston-Salem NC (S)

Watts, Steve, *Coordr,* University of Charleston, Carleton Varney Dept of Art & Design, Charleston WV (S)

Watts, Tracy, *Asst Prof,* State University of New York College at Potsdam, Dept of Fine Arts, Potsdam NY (S)

Waufle, Alan D, *Dir,* Gaston County Museum of Art & History, Dallas NC

Waufle, Alan D, *Dir,* Gaston County Museum of Art & History, Library, Dallas NC

Wauhkonen, Robert, *Chmn Liberal Arts,* Art Institute of Boston, Boston MA (S)

Way, Nancy, *Secy,* Muckenthaler Cultural Center, Fullerton CA

Wayne, Cynthia, *Exec Dir,* Pyramid Atlantic, Riverdale MD

Wayne, Kathryn, *Architectural Librn,* University of California, Environmental Design Library, Berkeley CA

Wayne, Sam, *Instructor,* Saint Louis Community College at Meramec, Art Dept, Saint Louis MO (S)

Weare, Shane, *Art Chmn,* Sonoma State University, Art Dept, Rohnert Park CA (S)

Weatherley, Glynn, *Lectr,* Lambuth University, Dept of Human Ecology & Visual Arts, Jackson TN (S)

Weaver, A M, *Dir,* Painted Bride Art Center, The Gallery at the Painted Bride, Philadelphia PA

Weaver, Betsy, *Docents,* University of Kansas, Spencer Museum of Art, Lawrence KS

Weaver, Bobby, *Asst Dir,* National Cowboy Hall of Fame and Western Heritage Center, Oklahoma City OK

Weaver, Herb, *Gallery Dir,* Brescia College, Anna Eaton Stout Memorial Art Gallery, Owensboro KY

Weaver, Judy, *Asst Dir,* Montana State University, Museum of the Rockies, Bozeman MT

Weaver, Larry E, *Assoc Prof,* University of Lethbridge, Dept of Art, Lethbridge AB (S)

Weaver, Marie, *Asst Prof,* University of Alabama in Birmingham, Dept of Art, Birmingham AL (S)

Weaver, Tonya, *Registrar,* Main Line Center of the Arts, Haverford PA

Weaver, Virginia, *Public Relations Officer,* New Orleans Museum of Art, New Orleans LA

Webb, Charles, *Equipment Coordr,* South Carolina Arts Commission, Columbia SC

Webb, Dixie, *Slide Librn,* Austin Peay State University, Art Dept Library, Clarksville TN

Webb, Dixie, *Asst Prof,* Austin Peay State University, Dept of Art, Clarksville TN (S)

Webb, Greg, *Instr,* Joe Kubert School of Cartoon & Graphic Art, Inc, Dover NJ (S)

Webb, Hugh, *Dir,* Portland Community College, North View Gallery, Portland OR

Webb, Keith, *Publication Sales Mgr,* National Gallery of Art, Washington DC

Webb, Nick, *Chmn Art Educ Div,* Nova Scotia College of Art and Design, Halifax NS (S)

Webb, Robert, *Cur,* Maine Maritime Museum, Bath ME

Webber, Bill, *Prof,* New Community College of Baltimore, Dept of Fine Arts, Baltimore MD (S)

Webber, Larry Jan, *Head,* Mississippi State University, Art Dept, Mississippi State MS (S)

Webber, Mark, *Instr,* Keystone Junior College, Fine Arts Dept, Factoryville PA (S)

Webber, Nancy E, *Asst Prof,* Los Angeles Harbor College, Art Dept, Wilmington CA (S)

Webby, Ernest J, *Dir,* Brockton Public Library System, Joseph A Driscoll Art Gallery, Brockton MA

Weber, Edward, *VPres & Treas,* Rhode Island Watercolor Society, Pawtucket RI

Weber, Jean M, *Exec Dir,* Maine Maritime Museum, Bath ME

Weber, John, *Cur Contemporary Art,* Portland Art Museum, Portland OR

Weber, John, *Prof,* Elmhurst College, Art Dept, Elmhurst IL (S)

Weber, Joseph A, *Art Education,* Southern Illinois University at Edwardsville, Dept of Art & Design, Edwardsville IL (S)

Weber, Louis, *Assoc Prof,* University of Dayton, Visual Arts Dept, Dayton OH (S)

Weber, Mark, *Adjunct Instr,* Maryville University of Saint Louis, Art Division, Saint Louis MO (S)

Weber, Michael, *Asst Prof,* Beloit College, Dept of Art, Beloit WI (S)

Weber, Robin, *Asst Dir,* Museum of Northern British Columbia, Library, Prince Rupert BC

Weberg, Lorraine, *Ref & Vertical Files,* Fashion Institute of Technology Galleries, Library, New York NY

Webster, Barry, *Mgr,* Toronto Dominion Bank, Toronto ON

Webster, Byron, *Dir,* Bell Museum of Natural History, Minneapolis MN

Webster, Donald B, *Cur,* Royal Ontario Museum, Canadian Decorative Arts Department, Toronto ON

Webster, Jenneth, *Community Relations,* Lincoln Center for the Performing Arts, Cork Gallery, New York NY

Webster, Lynn, *Dir,* Albertson College of Idaho, Rosenthal Art Gallery, Caldwell ID

Webster, Melissa, *Instr,* Walla Walla Community College, Art Dept, Walla Walla WA (S)

Webster, Paul, *Lectr,* Oakland University, Dept of Art and Art History, Rochester MI (S)

Webster, Robert J, *Assoc Prof,* Rochester Institute of Technology, School of Printing, Rochester NY (S)

Wechsler, Fredrica W, *Dir,* National Academy of Sciences, Arts in the Academy, Washington DC

Wechsler, Jeffrey, *Asst Dir, Curatorial Affairs,* Rutgers, The State University of New Jersey, Jane Voorhees Zimmerli Art Museum, New Brunswick NJ

Wechsler, Judith, *Chmn Art & Art History,* Tufts University, Dept of Art & Art History, Medford MA (S)

Weckbacher, Vernon, *Cur Colls,* McAllen International Museum, McAllen TX

Weckbacher, Vernon, *Cur Colls,* McAllen International Museum, Library, McAllen TX

Wedig, Dale, *Assoc Prof,* Northern Michigan University, Dept of Art and Design, Marquette MI (S)

Weeden, Morris S, *Pres,* The Art Institute of Chicago, Antiquarian Society, Chicago IL

Weedman, Kenneth R, *Chmn,* Cumberland College, Dept of Art, Williamsburg KY (S)

Weege, William, *Prof,* University of Wisconsin, Madison, Dept of Art, Madison WI (S)

Weekley, Carolyn, *Cur,* Colonial Williamsburg Foundation, Abby Aldrich Rockefeller Folk Art Center, Williamsburg VA

Weekly, Michelle, *Archivist & Registrar,* Burchfield Art Center, Buffalo NY

Weekly, Nancy, *Charles Cary Rumsey Cur,* Burchfield Art Center, Buffalo NY

Weeks, Dennis, *Assoc Prof,* Saint Joseph's University, Dept of Fine & Performing Arts, Philadelphia PA (S)

Wees, J Dustin, *Photograph & Slide Librn,* Sterling and Francine Clark Art Institute, Clark Art Institute Library, Williamstown MA

Wegner, Samuel J, *Exec Dir,* Southern Oregon Historical Society, Jacksonville Museum of Southern Oregon History, Jacksonville OR

Wegner, Shelley, *Asst Dir,* Midland County Historical Society, Midland MI

Wehle, Amy, *Bus Mgr,* Mount Holyoke College, Art Museum, South Hadley MA

Wei, Lilly, *Dir,* Kingsborough Community College, City University of New York, Art Gallery, Brooklyn NY

Wei, Philip, *Dir Library Services,* Plymouth State College, Herbert H Lamson Library, Plymouth NH

Weichinger, Rebecca, *Asst Prof,* University of Wisconsin-Stevens Point, Dept of Art & Design, Stevens Point WI (S)

Weidl, Beverly, *Cur,* Hopewell Museum, Hopewell NJ

Weidman, James F, *Development Dir,* Columbus Museum of Art, Columbus OH

Weidman, Jeffrey, *Art Librn,* Oberlin College, Clarence Ward Art Library, Oberlin OH

Weidner, Marsha, *Assoc Prof,* University of Kansas, Kress Foundation Dept of Art History, Lawrence KS (S)

Weidner, Timothy, *Cur History,* Roberson Museum & Science Center, Binghamton NY

Weiffenbach, Jeanie, *Gallery Dir,* San Francisco Art Institute, Galleries, San Francisco CA

Weigand, Charles J, *Assoc Prof,* Rochester Institute of Technology, School of Printing, Rochester NY (S)

Weigand, Herb, *Asst Prof,* East Stroudsburg University, Art Dept, East Stroudsburg PA (S)

Weigo, Norman, *Chmn,* Triton College, School of Arts & Sciences, River Grove IL (S)

Weil, Stephen, *Deputy Dir,* Hirshhorn Museum and Sculpture Garden, Washington DC

Weiland, Chris, *Instr,* Indiana University of Pennsylvania, Dept of Art and Art Education, Indiana PA (S)

Weiland, Julie L, *Development,* Greater Lafayette Museum of Art, Lafayette IN

Weiler, Melody, *Chmn,* Texas Tech University, Dept of Art, Lubbock TX (S)

Weill, Rose R, *Public Relations,* Art Dealers Association of America, Inc, New York NY

Weinberg, H Barbara, *Cur American Paintings & Sculpture,* The Metropolitan Museum of Art, New York NY

Weinberg, H Barbara, *Assoc Prof,* City University of New York, PhD Program in Art History, New York NY (S)

Weiner, Judith Kaufman, *Exec Dir,* East End Arts & Humanities Council, Riverhead NY

Weiner, Sarah Elliston, *Dir,* Columbia University, Gallery, New York NY

Weingarden, Lauren, *Assoc Prof,* Florida State University, Art History Dept (R133B), Tallahassee FL (S)

Weinke, Jane, *Assoc Cur,* Leigh Yawkey Woodson Art Museum, Inc, Wausau WI

Weinmann, Nury Vicens, *Instr,* Main Line Center for the Arts, Haverford PA (S)

Weinrich, Peter H, *Exec Dir,* Canadian Crafts Council, Conseil Canadien de l'Artisanat, Ottawa ON

Weinshenker, Anne Betty, *Chmn,* Montclair State College, Fine Arts Dept, Upper Montclair NJ (S)

Weinshenker, Anne Betty, *Chmn Fine Arts Dept,* Montclair State College, Art Gallery, Upper Montclair NJ

Weinstein, Margret, *Distribution Dir,* Intermedia Arts Minnesota, Minneapolis MN

Weinstein, Penny, *Pres,* Connecticut Women Artists, Inc, Guiford CT

Weinstein, Todd, *Dir,* Union Square Gallery, New York NY

Weinzapfel, Connie, *Dir,* The New Harmony Gallery of Contemporary Art, New Harmony IN

Weir, Cliff, *Pres,* Gananoque Historical Museum, Gananoque ON

Weir, Rob, *Dir,* Colonial Williamsburg Foundation, Visitor Center, Williamsburg VA

Weirich, Nancy, *Librn,* Tippecanoe County Historical Museum, Alameda McCollough Library, Lafayette IN

Weis, Anne, *Chmn,* University of Pittsburgh, Henry Clay Frick Fine Arts Dept, Pittsburgh PA (S)

Weis, Hanne, *Asst Academic Dean,* Alberta College of Art, Calgary AB (S)

Weis, Helen H, *Librn,* Willet Stained Glass Studios, Philadelphia PA

Weis, Richard, *Asst Prof,* Grand Valley State University, Art & Design Dept, Allendale MI (S)

Weisberg, Ruth, *Pres,* College Art Association, New York NY

Weisberg, Ruth, *Prof,* University of Southern California, School of Fine Arts, Los Angeles CA (S)

Weiseman, Jack, *Assoc Dean Fine Arts,* College of DuPage, Humanities Division, Glen Ellyn IL (S)

Weisenburger, Patricia, *Librn,* Kansas State University, Paul Weigel Library of Architecture & Design, Manhattan KS

Weisenburger, Ray, *Assoc Dean,* Kansas State University, College of Architecture and Design, Manhattan KS (S)

Weiser, Ronald, *Chmn,* Artrain, Inc, Ann Arbor MI

Weisgall, Hugo, *Pres,* American Academy of Arts & Letters, New York NY

Weisman, Suzy, *Librn,* Milwaukee Art Museum, Library, Milwaukee WI

Weiss, Art, *Dept Chmn,* California State University, Northridge, Dept of Art-Two Dimensional Media, Northridge CA (S)

Weiss, Glenn, *Public Arts Coordr,* King County Arts Commission, Seattle WA

Weiss, Jeff, *Assoc Prof,* Rochester Institute of Technology, School of Photographic Arts & Sciences, Rochester NY (S)

Weiss, John, *Coordr Photography,* University of Delaware, Dept of Art, Newark DE (S)

Weiss, Olga, *Registrar & Cur of Permanent Collection,* Spertus Museum, Chicago IL

Weiss, Peg, *Prof,* Syracuse University, Dept of Fine Arts (Art History), Syracuse NY (S)

Weiss, Peggy, *Arts Coordr,* King County Arts Commission, Seattle WA

Weisse, Leah, *Archivist,* Kohler Company, Art Collection, Kohler WI

Weisser, Terry Drayman, *Dir of Conservation & Technical Research,* Walters Art Gallery, Baltimore MD

Weissman, Judith Reiter, *Assoc Prof,* New York University, Dept of Art & Art Professions, New York NY (S)

Weisz, Helen, *Instr,* Bucks County Community College, Fine Arts Dept, Newtown PA (S)

Weizman, Sandra Morton, *Cur Cultural History,* Glenbow Museum, Calgary AB

Welch, Bill, *Instructor,* Oklahoma State University, Graphic Arts Dept, Okmulgee OK (S)

Welch, Brenda, *Coordr Spec Events,* Worcester Art Museum, Worcester MA

Welch, Marni, *Registrar,* Judah L Magnes Museum, Berkeley CA

Welch, S Anthony, *Dean,* University of Victoria, Dept of History in Art, Victoria BC (S)

Welch, Stuart Cary, *Cur Islamic & Later Indian Art,* Harvard University, Arthur M Sackler Museum, Cambridge MA

Welch, Vicky, *Dir of Conferences & Events,* Marian College, Allison Mansion, Indianapolis IN

Welch, William, *Pres,* Artists Association of Nantucket, Nantucket MA

Welge, William, *Indian Archives & Manuscripts,* Oklahoma Historical Society, State Museum of History, Oklahoma City OK

Weliver, Evelyn R, *Head Librn,* Interlochen, Interlochen MI

Weller, Eric, *Prof,* Southwest Texas State University, Dept of Art, San Marcos TX (S)

Weller, Laurie, *Adjunct Asst Prof,* Texas Woman's University, Dept of Visual Arts, Denton TX (S)

Welles, David, *Reference,* Las Vegas-Clark County Library District, Las Vegas NV

Welliver, Jackie, *Instr,* Pennsylvania College of Technology, Dept of Design & Communiation Arts, Williamsport PA (S)

Wellman, Leslie, *Cur Arts Educ Servs,* Dartmouth College, Hood Museum of Art, Hanover NH

Wells, Carol B, *Assoc Prof,* Villa Maria College of Buffalo, Art Dept, Buffalo NY (S)

Wells, Gerald, *Prof,* Fort Lewis College, Art Dept, Durango CO (S)

Wells, Jennifer, *Cur,* Paine Webber Inc, New York NY

Wells, Rufus, *Asst Prof,* University of the District of Columbia, Art Dept, Washington DC (S)

Wells, Suzanne, *Special Exhibitions Coordr,* Philadelphia Museum of Art, Philadelphia PA

Wells, Valerie Creighton, *Exec Dir,* Saskatchewan Arts Board, Regina SK

Welsh, Caroline, *Cur,* Adirondack Historical Association, Adirondack Museum, Blue Mountain Lake NY

Welsh, Peter, *Chief Cur,* Heard Museum, Phoenix AZ

Welter, Cole H, *Chmn,* University of Alaska Anchorage, Dept of Art, Anchorage AK (S)

Weltman, Ethel, *Admin Asst,* University of Oregon, Museum of Art, Eugene OR

Weltner, Betsey, *Exec Dir,* Georgia Council For The Arts, Atlanta GA

Welu, James A, *Dir,* Worcester Art Museum, Worcester MA

Welu, William J, *Chairperson,* Briar Cliff College, Art Dept, Sioux City IA (S)

Welych, Anita, *Instr,* Cazenovia College, Center for Art & Design Studies, Cazenovia NY (S)

Wemmlinger, Raymond, *Cur & Librn,* Players, Hampden-Booth Theatre Library, New York NY

Wendler, Walter V, *Dean,* Texas A & M University, College of Architecture, College Station TX (S)

Wenegrat, Saul, *Adminr,* Port Authority of New York & New Jersey, Art Collection, New York NY

Weng, Siegfried, *Dir Emeritus,* Evansville Museum of Arts and Science, Evansville IN

Wenig-Horswell, Judy, *Assoc Prof,* Goshen College, Art Dept, Goshen IN (S)

Weninger, Judy, *VPres,* Prince George Art Gallery, Prince George BC

Wentworth, Michael, *Cur of Collections,* Boston Athenaeum, Boston MA

Wentworth, T W, *Deputy Dir & Secy,* T T Wentworth Jr Museum, Florida State Museum, Pensacola FL

Wentz, Richard, *Dir Public Relations,* Buffalo Bill Memorial Association, Buffalo Bill Historical Center, Cody WY

Wenz, Alison, *Asst Prof,* Seton Hall University, College of Arts & Sciences, South Orange NJ (S)

Wenzel, Carol, *Business Mgr,* Historic Deerfield, Inc, Deerfield MA

Wepler, William, *Cur Popular Culture,* Indiana State Museum, Indianapolis IN

Werckmeister, Otto-Karl, *Mary Jane Crowe Distinguished Prof,* Northwestern University, Evanston, Dept of Art History, Evanston IL (S)

Werenko, John, *Asst Dean,* Indiana University-Purdue University, Indianapolis, Herron School of Art, Indianapolis IN (S)

Werfel, Gina S, *Chmn,* Randolph-Macon Woman's College, Dept of Art, Lynchburg VA (S)

Werger, Art, *Acting Chmn,* Wesleyan College, Art Dept, Macon GA (S)

Werk, Horst, *Assoc Prof,* Corning Community College, Division of Humanities, Corning NY (S)

Werle, Thomas, *Prof,* Greater Hartford Community College, Humanities Division & Art Dept, Hartford CT (S)

Werlink, Joy, *Asst Librn Manuscripts,* Washington State Historical Society, Hewitt Memorial Library, Tacoma WA

Werner, Charlotte, *Chmn Foundations,* University of Manitoba, School of Art, Winnipeg MB (S)

Werner, Don, *Designer,* National Museum of the American Indian, New York NY

Werness, Hope, *Prof,* California State University, Art Dept, Turlock CA (S)

Werness, Hope B, *Dir,* California State University Stanislaus, University Art Gallery, Turlock CA

Wertheim, Earl, *Assoc Prof,* Sullivan County Community College, Division of Commercial Art and Photography, Loch Sheldrake NY (S)

Wertheimer, Gary, *Chmn,* Olivet College, Art Dept, Olivet MI (S)

Wertkin, Gerard C, *Dir,* Museum of American Folk Art, New York NY

Werts, Adrien, *Development Asst,* Oklahoma City Art Museum, Oklahoma City OK

Wertschek, John, *Assoc Dean Foundation,* Emily Carr College of Art & Design, Vancouver BC (S)

Wesaw, Sallie, *Prof,* Central Wyoming College, Art Center, Riverton WY (S)

Wescoat, Bonna D, *Assoc Prof,* Emory University, Art History Dept, Atlanta GA (S)

Wescott, Richard, *Dir,* Augusta Richmond County Museum, Augusta GA

Weselmann, Ramona, *Personnel Supv,* Minnesota Museum of American Art, Saint Paul MN

Wesley, John, *Dept Chmn,* Bellevue Community College, Art Dept, Bellevue WA (S)

Wesley, Sherre, *Executive Dir,* Dutchess County Arts Council, Poughkeepsie NY

Wessell, Frederick, *Prof,* University of Hartford, Hartford Art School, West Hartford CT (S)

Wessell, Henry, *Chmn Photography Dept,* San Francisco Art Institute, San Francisco CA (S)

Wessell, Marion, *Chmn,* Wayne Community College, Liberal Arts Dept, Goldsboro NC (S)

Wessels, Henry, *Prof,* California Polytechnic State University at San Luis Obispo, Dept of Art and Design, San Luis Obispo CA (S)

West, Bill, *Display Artist,* College of Southern Idaho, Herrett Museum & Art Gallery, Twin Falls ID

West, Bruce, *Lectr,* Lewis & Clark College, Dept of Art, Portland OR (S)

West, Claire, *Performing Art Dir,* Arizona Commission on the Arts, Phoenix AZ

West, Coleen, *Development Dir,* Maryland Art Place, Baltimore MD

West, E F, *Exec Dir,* Fitchburg Historical Society, Fitchburg MA

West, Janet, *Cur of Spec Coll,* Port Washington Public Library, Port Washington NY

West, Matt, *Instr,* Laramie County Community College, Division of Arts & Humanities, Cheyenne WY (S)

West, Richard, *Dir,* Smithsonian Institution, National Museum of the American Indian, Washington DC

West, Richard V, *Dir,* Newport Art Museum School, Newport RI (S)

West, Richard Y, *Dir,* Newport Art Museum, Newport RI

West, Ruth, *Instr,* Springfield College, Dept of Visual and Performing Arts, Springfield MA (S)

West, Sharon, *Head of Reference & Bibliographic Instruction,* University of Alaska, Elmer E Rasmuson Library, Fairbanks AK

West, Virginia, *Chmn Art Committee,* North Canton Public Library, Little Art Gallery, North Canton OH

West, William, *Adjunct Instr,* Le Moyne College, Fine Arts Dept, Syracuse NY (S)

Westbrook, Nicholas, *Exec Dir,* Fort Ticonderoga Association, Ticonderoga NY

Westbrook, Nicholas, *Exec Dir,* Fort Ticonderoga Association, Thompson-Pell Research Center, Ticonderoga NY

Wester, Janie, *Asst Prof,* Oklahoma Baptist University, Art Dept, Shawnee OK (S)

Westerfield, Barbara, *Cur of Education,* University of Wyoming, Art Museum, Laramie WY

Westlake, Richard, *Theatre Arts Instr,* Edison Community College, Dept of Fine and Performing Arts, Fort Myers FL (S)

Westly, Kathy, *Chmn,* West Valley College, Art Dept, Saratoga CA (S)

Westpfahl, Richard, *Chmn,* Western Wisconsin Technical College, Graphics Division, La Crosse WI (S)

Westwater, Angela K, *Pres,* Louis Comfort Tiffany Foundation, New York NY

Westwood, Jefferson, *Center Dir,* State University of New York College at Fredonia, M C Rockefeller Arts Center Gallery, Fredonia NY

Westwood, Pam, *Travel Development Specialist,* Utah Travel Council, Salt Lake City UT

Wetenhall, John, *Cur Painting & Sculpture,* Birmingham Museum of Art, Birmingham AL

Wetherell, Ron, *Prof,* Florida Community College at Jacksonville, South Campus, Art Dept, Jacksonville FL (S)

Wethli, Mark C, *Chmn,* Bowdoin College, Art Dept, Brunswick ME (S)

Wetterau, Ted C, *Chmn,* Arts & Education Council of Greater Saint Louis, Saint Louis MO

Wetzel, David, *Dir Publications,* Colorado Historical Society, Museum, Denver CO

Weurding, Peggy, *Dir,* Arthur Roy Mitchell Memorial Inc, Museum of Western Art, Trinidad CO

Weyerhaeuser, Charles A, *Museum Dir,* Art Complex Museum, Duxbury MA

Whalen, Mary Grace, *Asst Museum Librn,* The Metropolitan Museum of Art, Uris Library, New York NY

Wharton, Annabel, *Assoc Prof,* Duke University, Dept of Art and Art History, Durham NC (S)

Wharton, Brenda, *Office Mgr,* Art Institute for the Permian Basin, Odessa TX

Wheat, Evie, *VPres,* Birmingham-Bloomfield Art Association, Birmingham MI

Wheat, Evie, *VChmn,* Detroit Artists Market, Detroit MI

Wheeler, Anne B, *Registrar,* Pimeria Alta Historical Society, Library, Nogales AZ

Wheeler, Geof, *Adjunct Instr,* Maryville University of Saint Louis, Art Division, Saint Louis MO (S)

Wheeler, Jane, *Coordr,* Richmond Arts Centre, Richmond BC

Wheeler, Jean, *Librn,* San Jose Museum of Art, Library, San Jose CA

Wheelock, Arthur, *Cur Northern Baroque Painting,* National Gallery of Art, Washington DC

Whelan, James, *Dir,* Lafayette Natural History Museum, Planetarium and Nature Station, Lafayette LA

Whelan, Mary, *Cur,* Mission San Luis Rey Museum, San Luis Rey CA

Whelehan, David, *Chmn,* Old State House, Hartford CT

Whisman, Rex, *Adminr,* Rocky Mountain College of Art & Design, Denver CO (S)

Whitacre, Steve, *Chmn Found,* Kansas City Art Institute, Kansas City MO (S)

Whitaker, Kathleen, *Chief Cur,* Southwest Museum, Los Angeles CA

Whitcomb, Therese T, *Dir,* University of San Diego, Founders' Gallery, San Diego CA

White, Alex, *Asst Prof,* University of Hartford, Hartford Art School, West Hartford CT (S)

White, Amos, *Chmn,* Bowie State University, Fine Arts Dept, Bowie MD (S)

White, Anna S, *Chmn Board of Trustees,* Indianapolis Museum of Art, Indianapolis IN

White, Barbara, *Assoc Dir Admin,* Kimbell Art Museum, Fort Worth TX

White, Barbara E, *Adjunct Prof,* Tufts University, Dept of Art & Art History, Medford MA (S)

White, Beverly M, *Fine Arts Librn,* Manchester City Library, Manchester NH

White, Bill, *Mgr Exhib,* Fine Arts Museums of San Francisco, M H de Young Memorial Museum and California Palace of the Legion of Honor, San Francisco CA

White, Blair, *Cur,* East Tennessee State University, Carroll Reece Museum, Johnson City TN

White, Cliff, *Pres,* Peter and Catharine Whyte Foundation, Whyte Museum of the Canadian Rockies, Banff AB

White, David O, *Museum Dir,* Connecticut Historical Commission, Sloane-Stanley Museum, Kent CT

White, Deborah, *Catalog Asst,* San Francisco Art Institute, Anne Bremer Memorial Library, San Francisco CA

White, Dennis, *Dean Fine Arts Div,* Antelope Valley College, Art Dept, Division of Fine Arts, Lancaster CA (S)

White, Donald, *Chmn Art Committee,* Angelo State University, Houston Harte University Center, San Angelo TX

White, Donald, *Mediterranean Section Cur,* University of Pennsylvania, University Museum of Archaelogy & Anthropology, Philadelphia PA

White, Douglas, *Vis Asst Prof,* Converse College, Art Dept, Spartanburg SC (S)

White, E Alan, *Head,* University of Tennessee at Chattanooga, Dept of Art, Chattanooga TN (S)

White, Ed, *Chmn Humanities Div,* Quincy Junior College, Fine Arts Dept, Quincy MA (S)

White, Eric, *Chief,* Public Library of the District of Columbia, Audiovisual Division, Washington DC

White, Fran, *Asst Dean,* Laney College, Art Dept, Oakland CA (S)

White, Gail S, *Asst Prof,* Colgate University, Dept of Art & Art History, Hamilton NY (S)

White, Gail Scott, *Asst Prof,* Cornell University, Dept of Art, Ithaca NY (S)

White, George M, *Architect of the Capitol,* United States Capitol, Architect of the Capitol, Washington DC

White, George M, *Architect,* United States Capitol, Art Reference Library, Washington DC

White, James J, *Cur of Art,* Carnegie Mellon University, Hunt Institute for Botanical Documentation, Pittsburgh PA

White, John, *Chmn Management Committee,* Manitoba Historical Society, Dalnavert Museum, Winnipeg MB

White, Joseph S, *Archivist,* Virginia Dept Historic Resources, Research Library, Richmond VA

White, Kathy, *Bookstore Mgr,* Salvador Dali Museum, Saint Petersburg FL

White, Ken, *Chmn Fine Arts Photography,* Rochester Institute of Technology, School of Photographic Arts & Sciences, Rochester NY (S)

White, Ken, *Assoc Prof,* Rochester Institute of Technology, School of Photographic Arts & Sciences, Rochester NY (S)

White, Larry, *Head Dept Art,* Long Beach City College, Dept of Art, Long Beach CA (S)

White, Larry, *Instr,* Long Beach City College, Dept of Art, Long Beach CA (S)

White, Lynda, *Asst Librn & Public Services,* University of Virginia, Fiske Kimball Fine Arts Library, Charlottesville VA

White, Mary, *Dir,* League of New Hampshire Craftsmen, Library, Concord NH

White, Mary G, *Dir,* League of New Hampshire Craftsmen, League Gallery, Concord NH

White, Matthew, *Admnr,* Mamie McFaddin Ward Heritage Historic Foundation, Beaumont TX

White, Paul Lowell, *VPres,* Mystic Art Association, Inc, Mystic CT

White, Richard L, *Dir & Cur,* Muttart Art Gallery, Calgary AB

White, Roland, *Chief Photographer,* National Portrait Gallery, Washington DC

White, Terri, *Art Gallery Coordr,* North Central Washington Museum, Art Gallery, Wenatchee WA

White, Tim, *Preparator,* University of Minnesota, University Art Museum, Minneapolis MN

Whitehead, John C, *Chmn Society Board of Trustees,* The Asia Society Galleries, New York NY

Whitehead, Lynn, *Asst Prof,* East Tennessee State University, Fine Arts Dept, Johnson City TN (S)

Whitehead, Marcia, *Head Publications,* Carnegie Institute, Carnegie Museum of Art, Pittsburgh PA

Whitehouse, David, *Dir,* Corning Museum of Glass, Corning NY

Whitehouse, Diane, *Co-Chmn Paintings,* University of Manitoba, School of Art, Winnipeg MB (S)

Whitesel, Lita, *Chmn,* California State University, Sacramento, Dept of Art, Sacramento CA (S)

Whitesell, John, *Chmn,* University of Louisville, Allen R Hite Art Institute Gallery, Louisville KY

Whiteside, Kathy, *Instr,* Texas Tech University, Dept of Art, Lubbock TX (S)

Whitesides, Patricia, *Registrar,* Toledo Museum of Art, Toledo Museum of Art, Toledo OH

Whiteside Thompson, Holly, *Office Mgr,* Firelands Association for the Visual Arts, Oberlin OH

Whitfield, Kim, *Sales Dir,* Battleship North Carolina, Wilmington NC

Whitfield, Rebeca, *Instr,* The Arkansas Arts Center, Museum School, Little Rock AR (S)

Whiting, B J, *Tour Supv,* Nemours Mansion & Gardens, Wilmington DE

Whitlock, John J, *Dir,* Southern Illinois University, University Museum, Carbondale IL

Whitman, Marina D, *Educ Cur,* Art And Culture Center Of Hollywood, Hollywood FL

Whitman, Nathan T, *Prof Emeritus,* University of Michigan, Ann Arbor, Dept of History of Art, Ann Arbor MI (S)

Whitmore, Anthony, *Div Chmn,* Potomac State College, Dept of Art, Keyser WV (S)

Whitney, Allota, *Registrar,* Heritage Plantation of Sandwich, Sandwich MA

Whitney, Debra, *Gallery Monitor,* New York University, Grey Art Gallery and Study Center, New York NY

Whitney, Patrick, *Dir,* Illinois Institute of Technology, Institute of Design, Chicago IL (S)

Whitney, Patrick, *Pres,* American Center for Design Gallery, Chicago IL

Whitney, Steve, *Asst Prof,* Coe College, Dept of Art, Cedar Rapids IA (S)

Whitney, Susan, *Pres,* Professional Art Dealers Association of Canada, Toronto ON

Whitsell, John, University of Louisville, Allen R Hite Art Institute, Louisville KY (S)

Whittaker, Shelley, *Admin Asst,* Kamloops Art Gallery, Kamloops BC

Whittemore, Gioia, *Gallery Asst,* Whitney Museum of American Art, Downtown at Federal Reserve Plaza, New York NY

Whitten, Lee, *Prof,* Los Angeles City College, Dept of Art, Los Angeles CA (S)

Whittington, E Michael, *Cur,* Albany Museum of Art, Albany GA

Whittington, Harrell, *Instr,* Bob Jones University, School of Fine Arts, Greenville SC (S)

Whittington, Jon, *Chmn,* Belhaven College, Art Dept, Jackson MS (S)

Whitworth, Kay S, *Pres,* Belle Grove Plantation, Middletown VA

Whitworth, Thomas C, *Assoc Prof,* University of New Orleans-Lake Front, Dept of Fine Arts, New Orleans LA (S)

Wholley, Jay, *Prof,* Ramapo College of New Jersey, School of Contemporary Arts, Mahwah NJ (S)

Whyte, Robert, *Cur,* Museo Italo Americano, San Francisco CA

Wible, Karen, *Dir External Relations,* The Mariners' Museum, Newport News VA

Wickkiser, Carol B, *Exec Dir,* Lehigh County Historical Society, Allentown PA

Wicklein, Helen, *Pres,* United Methodist Historical Society, Lovely Lane Museum, Baltimore MD

Wicks, Kay O, *Gallery Sales Mgr,* Kentucky Art & Craft Gallery, Louisville KY

Wickstrom, Andriette, *Dir,* Witter Gallery, Storm Lake IA

Widdifield, Stacie, *Asst Prof Art History,* University of Arizona, Dept of Art, Tucson AZ (S)

Widdows, Sue, *Dir,* Peoria Art Guild, Peoria IL

Widman, Harry, *Instr,* Pacific Northwest College of Art, Portland OR (S)

Widmer, Jason, *Instr,* Linn Benton Community College, Fine & Applied Art Dept, Albany OR (S)

Widner, Kristine E, *Membership & Vol Coordr,* University of Utah, Utah Museum of Fine Arts, Salt Lake City UT

Widrick, Melissa, *Cur Educ,* Jefferson County Historical Society, Watertown NY

Widrig, W M, *Prof,* Rice University, Dept of Art and Art History, Houston TX (S)

Wiebe, Charles M, *Dir of Exhib,* International Images, Ltd, Sewickley PA

Wiede, Lisa, *Asst General Mgr,* Ozark Folk Center, Mountain View AR

Wiedemann, D, *Prof,* City Colleges of Chicago, Daley College, Chicago IL (S)

Wiegmann, Richard, *Prof,* Concordia College, Art Dept, Seward NE (S)

Wiess, Sheila, *Education Coordr,* Pacific - Asia Museum, Pasadena CA

Wiest, Scottie, *Lectr,* Davis and Elkins College, Dept of Art, Elkins WV (S)

Wiggins, Bruce, *Dir Educ Consulting,* Delphian School, Sheridan OR (S)

Wight, Darlene, *Assoc Cur of Inuit Art,* Winnipeg Art Gallery, Winnipeg MB

Wightman, Lisa, *Instr,* Munson-Williams-Proctor Institute, School of Art, Utica NY (S)

Wigton, Robert H, *Pres,* Fine Arts Association, School of Fine Arts, Willoughby OH

Wilbers, Tim, *Asst Prof,* University of Dayton, Visual Arts Dept, Dayton OH (S)

Wilborn, Tracy, *Coordr Special Projects,* North Dakota Museum of Art, Grand Forks ND

Wilburne, Robert, *Pres,* Colonial Williamsburg Foundation, Williamsburg VA

Wilcher, Richard, *Fine Arts Dept Chmn,* Brazosport College, Art Dept, Lake Jackson TX (S)

Wilcox, David, *Assoc Cur of Anthropology,* Museum of Northern Arizona, Flagstaff AZ

Wilcox, E Ann, *Librn,* Philadelphia Maritime Museum, Philadelphia PA

Wilcox, E Ann, *Librn,* Philadelphia Maritime Museum, Library, Philadelphia PA

Wilcox, Jeffrey, *Registrar,* University of Missouri, Museum of Art and Archaeology, Columbia MO

Wilcox, Lawrence, *Instr,* New Mexico Junior College, Arts & Sciences, Hobbs NM (S)

Wilcoxson, Shirlie Bowers, *Chmn,* Saint Gregory's College, Dept of Art, Shawnee OK (S)

Wilczek, Ronald, *Coordr,* Roger Williams College, Art Dept, Bristol RI (S)

Wilde, Betty, *Assoc Dir,* En Foco, Inc, Bronx NY

Wilder, Michael, *Prof,* Southwestern College, Art Dept, Winfield KS (S)

Wilen, Carl, *Prof,* Eastern Illinois University, Art Dept, Charleston IL (S)

Wiley, Aubrey, *Asst Prof,* Lynchburg College, Art Dept, Lynchburg VA (S)

Wiley, Dyan, *Educ Coordr,* Arts Extension Service, Amherst MA

Wilfong, Terry, *Asst Archivist,* University of Chicago, Oriental Institute Research Archives, Chicago IL

Wilhelm, Stephanie, *VPres,* Museo Italo Americano, San Francisco CA

Wilkerson, Maggie, *Office Mgr,* Beaumont Art League, Beaumont TX

Wilkerson, Paula, *Exec Dir,* Urban Institute for Contemporary Arts, Race Street Gallery, Grand Rapids MI

Wilkes, Leslie, *Operations Mgr,* Women And Their Work, Austin TX

Wilkie, Everett C, *Editor,* Connecticut Historical Society, Hartford CT

Wilkie, Everett C, *Head Librn,* Connecticut Historical Society, Library, Hartford CT

Wilkie, Jo-Anne, *Exec Dir,* The Art Center, Mount Clemens MI

Wilkins, David G, *Dir,* University of Pittsburgh, University Art Gallery, Pittsburgh PA

Wilkins, Janet, *Assoc Prof,* Mary Baldwin College, Dept of Art, Staunton VA (S)

Wilkins, Will K, *Dir,* Real Art Ways (RAW), Hartford CT

Wilkinson, Betty, *Registrar,* Art Gallery of Windsor, Windsor ON

Wilkinson, Betty F, *Librn,* Art Gallery of Windsor, Reference Library, Windsor ON

Wilkinson, Carlton, *Lectr,* Vanderbilt University, Dept of Fine Arts, Nashville TN (S)

Wilkinson, J, *Coordr,* Dundas Valley School of Art, Dundas ON (S)

Wilkinson, Nancy B, *Dept Head,* Oklahoma State University, Art Dept, Stillwater OK (S)

Wilkinson, Sean, *Acting Chmn,* University of Dayton, Visual Arts Dept, Dayton OH (S)

Wilkinson, William D, *Dir,* The Mariners' Museum, Newport News VA

Will, Duncan, *Membership Public Relations,* Phillips Academy, Addison Gallery of American Art, Andover MA

Will, Vernon, *Head Conservation,* Ohio Historical Society, Archives-Library Division, Columbus OH

Willard, Shirley, *Pres,* Fulton County Historical Society Inc, Fulton County Museum & Round Barn Museum, Rochester IN

Willard, Tom, *Executive Dir,* Deaf Artists of America Inc, Rochester NY

Willard, Tracey, *Prog Dir,* Deaf Artists of America Inc, Rochester NY

Willens, Kay, *Asst Prof,* Kenyon College, Art Dept, Gambier OH (S)

Willers, Karl E, *Dir,* Whitney Museum of American Art, Downtown at Federal Reserve Plaza, New York NY

Willet, E Crosby, *Pres,* Willet Stained Glass Studios, Philadelphia PA

Willey, Chris, *Asst Prof,* Central Missouri State University, Art Dept, Warrensburg MO (S)

Williams, Ardelia, *Head Dept,* Indiana Wesleyan University, Art Dept, Marion IN (S)

Williams, Becky, *Spec Events,* Columbus Museum, Columbus GA

Williams, Deborah, *Dir,* Patterson Library & Art Gallery, Westfield NY

Williams, Diana, *Public Support Serv,* Wichita Public Library, Wichita KS

Williams, Dick, *Instr,* Iowa Lakes Community College, Dept of Art, Estherville IA (S)

Williams, Elaine, *VPres,* Haymarket Art Gallery, Lincoln NE

Williams, Emily, *Asst Prof,* Clarion University of Pennsylvania, Dept of Art, Clarion PA (S)

Williams, Gloria, *Cur,* Norton Simon Museum, Pasadena CA

Williams, Henry H, *Asst Dir for Finance & Admin,* Norman Rockwell Museum at Stockbridge, Stockbridge MA

Williams, Holly, *Educ Coordr,* Whitney Museum of American Art, Whitney Museum of American Art at Champion, New York NY

Williams, Idaherma, *VPres,* American Color Print Society, Philadelphia PA

Williams, Jane, *Agent,* Richard Gallery and Almond Tea Gallery, Divisions of Studios of Jack Richard, Cuyahoga Falls OH

Williams, Jane, *Asst Prof Art History,* University of Arizona, Dept of Art, Tucson AZ (S)

Williams, Janice, *Asst Prof,* Augusta College, Dept of Fine Arts, Augusta GA (S)

Williams, Jay, *Cur,* Edison Community College, Gallery of Fine Art, Fort Myers FL

Williams, Jennifer Frazer, *Dir,* American Society of Portrait Artists (ASOPA), Montgomery AL

Williams, Judith, *Asst Prof,* University of British Columbia, Dept of Fine Arts, Vancouver BC (S)

Williams, Judith I., *Dir,* Jacksonville Public Library, Fine Arts & Recreation Dept, Jacksonville FL

Williams, Juliana F, *Assoc Prof,* Monroe Community College, Art Dept, Rochester NY (S)

Williams, Kay P, *Dir,* Tryon Palace Historic Sites & Gardens, New Bern NC

Williams, Keith, *Dir,* North Central Washington Museum, Art Gallery, Wenatchee WA

Williams, Keith J, *Asst Prof,* Muskingum College, Art Department, New Concord OH (S)

Williams, Kenneth, *Graphic Design,* University of Georgia, Franklin College of Arts & Sciences, Dept of Art, Athens GA (S)

Williams, Lawrence, *Prof,* Rochester Institute of Technology, School of Art and Design, Rochester NY (S)

Williams, Lorraine, *Cur Archaeology-Ethnology,* New Jersey State Museum, Trenton NJ

Williams, Lyle, *Asst Cur Prints & Drawings,* Marion Koogler McNay Art Museum, San Antonio TX

Williams, Mara, *Dir,* Brattleboro Museum & Art Center, Brattleboro VT

Williams, Martin, *Instr,* Antonelli Institute of Art & Photography, Cincinnati OH (S)

Williams, Mary, *Prog Asst,* University of British Columbia, Fine Arts Gallery, Vancouver BC

Williams, Mary Jane, *Registrar,* Arizona State University, University Art Museum, Tempe AZ

Williams, Megan, *Instr,* Toronto School of Art, Toronto ON (S)

Williams, Mollie Lee, *Dir,* Patterson Homestead, Dayton OH

Williams, Nancy, *Operating Committee Chmn,* Jackson County Historical Society, 1859 Jail, Marshal s Home & Museum, Independence MO

Williams, Norman, *Chmn Foundation Studies,* Rochester Institute of Technology, School of Art and Design, Rochester NY (S)

Williams, Patricia, *Deputy Exec for Progs,* American Association of Museums, International Council of Museums Committee, Washington DC

Williams, Randolph, *Chmn,* Manhattanville College, Brownson Art Gallery, Purchase NY

Williams, Robert, *Instr,* Albert Lea - Mankato Technical College, Commercial and Technical Art Dept, North Mankato MN (S)

Williams, Roberta, *Instr,* Marian College, Art Dept, Indianapolis IN (S)

Williams, Roger, *Dir,* Art Academy of Cincinnati, Cincinnati OH (S)

Williams, Sally, *Asst Dir Public Information,* Brooklyn Museum, Brooklyn NY

Williams, Sally, *Dir,* Noah Webster Foundation & Historical Society of West Hartford, Inc, Noah Webster's House, West Hartford CT

Williams, Stephen R, *Dir,* Museum of Arts and History, Port Huron MI

Williams, Steve, *Coll Mgr (Sciences),* Texas Tech University, Museum, Lubbock TX

Williams, Sylvia H, *Dir,* National Museum of African Art, Washington DC

Williams, Thomas L, *VPres,* Contemporary Arts Center, Cincinnati OH

Williams, Tom, *Assoc Prof,* Southwest Texas State University, Dept of Art, San Marcos TX (S)

Williams, W, *Assoc Prof,* Northern Arizona University, School of Art & Design, Flagstaff AZ (S)

Williams, Wayne, *Prof,* Finger Lakes Community College, Visual & Performing Arts Dept, Canandaigua NY (S)

Williams, William E, *Prof,* Haverford College, Fine Arts Dept, Haverford PA (S)

Williamson, Brenda, *Asst Dir,* Center for the Fine Arts, Miami FL

Williamson, James S, *Instr,* Rhodes College, Dept of Art, Memphis TN (S)

Williamson, J Reid, *Pres,* Historic Landmarks Foundation of Indiana, Information Center Library, Indianapolis IN

Williford, Paul, *Librn,* Memphis College of Art, Library, Memphis TN

Williford, Paul S, *Librn,* Memphis College of Art, G Pillow Lewis Memorial Library, Memphis TN

Willis, Elizabeth, *VPres,* Wind Luke Asian Museum Memorial Foundation, Inc, Seattle WA

Willis, Jay, *Prof,* University of Southern California, School of Fine Arts, Los Angeles CA (S)

Willis, Nancy C, *Pres,* Council of Delaware Artists, Middletown DE

Willis, Tim, *Asst Dir Operations,* Department of Culture & Multi-Culturalism, Provincial Museum of Alberta, Edmonton AB

Willis, Wendy, *Instr,* Southwestern Michigan College, Fine & Performing Arts Dept, Dowagiac MI (S)

Willman, Merle, *Asst Dept Head,* University of Massachusetts, Amherst, Dept of Landscape Architecture & Regional Planning, Amherst MA (S)

Willner, Judith, *Acting Chmn,* Coppin State College, Dept Fine & Communication Arts, Baltimore MD (S)

Willock, Tom, *Dir,* Medicine Hat Museum & Art Gallery, Medicine Hat AB

Willome, Thomas, *Chmn,* San Antonio College, Visual Arts & Technology, San Antonio TX (S)

Willoughby, Karin L, *Cur Natural Science,* University of South Carolina, McKissick Museum, Columbia SC

Wills, Norman, *Dean,* Daytona Beach Community College, Dept of Fine Arts & Visual Arts, Daytona Beach FL (S)

Willse, Michael, *Assoc Prof,* Rosemont College, Division of the Arts, Rosemont PA (S)

Willumson, Glenn, *Cur,* Pennsylvania State University, Palmer Museum of Art, University Park PA

Wilmerding, John, *Chmn Dept,* Princeton University, Dept of Art and Archaeology, Princeton NJ (S)

Wilmerding, John, *Prof,* Princeton University, Dept of Art and Archaeology, Princeton NJ (S)

Wilmot, James, *VPres,* Boothbay Region Art Foundation, Inc, Brick House Gallery, Boothbay Harbor ME

Wilson, A, *Secy General,* Canadian Society for Education Through Art, Oakville ON

Wilson, Bob, *Instr,* Antonelli Institute of Art & Photography, Cincinnati OH (S)

Wilson, Bruce, *Head,* Saint Mary's College of Maryland, Arts and Letters Division, Saint Mary's City MD (S)

Wilson, Carrie, *Coordr,* Aesthetic Realism Foundation, Terrain Gallery, New York NY

Wilson, Catherine, *Librn,* Terra Museum of American Art, Chicago IL

Wilson, Catherine, *Librn,* Terra Museum of American Art, Library, Chicago IL

Wilson, Chris, *Prof,* Barton College, Communication, Performaing & Visual Arts, Wilson NC (S)

Wilson, Christine, *Dir Public Information,* Mississippi Department of Archives and History, State Historical Museum, Jackson MS

Wilson, Christopher, *Chmn,* Middlebury College, Dept of Art, Middlebury VT (S)

Wilson, Don, *Vis Prof,* Oral Roberts University, Fine Arts Dept, Tulsa OK (S)

Wilson, Dora, *Dean,* Ohio University, School of Art, Athens OH (S)

Wilson, Elizabeth, *Public Affairs,* Pierpont Morgan Library, New York NY

Wilson, Frederic W, *Cur Gilbert & Sullivan Coll,* Pierpont Morgan Library, New York NY

Wilson, Gillian, *Cur Decorative Arts,* Getty Center for the History of Art & the Humanities Trust Museum, Santa Monica CA

Wilson, Gillian, *Cur Decorative Arts,* Getty Center for the History of Art & the Humanities Trust Museum, The J Paul Getty Museum, Santa Monica CA

Wilson, Gordon, *Assoc Prof,* Whitworth College, Art Dept, Spokane WA (S)

Wilson, Jane, *Asst Dir,* Owensboro Museum of Fine Art, Owensboro KY

Wilson, Jay M, *Pres Board of Trustees,* Walters Art Gallery, Baltimore MD

Wilson, Jim, *Business Mgr,* Long Beach Museum of Art, Long Beach CA

Wilson, Jo, *Coordr Library Servs,* Delta State University, Library, Cleveland MS

Wilson, John, *Cur Painting,* Cincinnati Museum Association, Cincinnati Art Museum, Cincinnati OH

Wilson, John M, *Prof,* Hope College, Art Dept, Holland MI (S)

Wilson, John Montgomery, *Dir,* Hope College, De Pree Art Center & Gallery, Holland MI

Wilson, John R, *Prof,* Butte College, Dept of Fine Arts, Oroville CA (S)

Wilson, Joyce, *Chmn,* Bellevue College, Art Dept, Bellevue NE (S)

Wilson, Karen L, *Cur,* University of Chicago, Oriental Institute Museum, Chicago IL

Wilson, Karla, *Secy,* Loveland Museum and Gallery, Loveland CO

Wilson, Kay, *Dir,* Grinnell College, Print & Drawing Study Room/Gallery, Grinnell IA

Wilson, Keith, *Interior Architecture Design,* California College of Arts and Crafts, Oakland CA (S)

Wilson, Kenneth, *Chmn Dept of Art,* Bloomsburg University of Pennsylvania, Haas Gallery of Art, Bloomsburg PA

Wilson, Kenneth, *Chmn,* Bloomsburg University, Dept of Art, Bloomsburg PA (S)

Wilson, Keyser, *Asst Prof,* Stillman College, Stillman Art Gallery and Art Dept, Tuscaloosa AL (S)

Wilson, Laurie, *Prof,* New York University, Dept of Art & Art Professions, New York NY (S)

Wilson, Laurie, *Exec Dir,* Lakeside Studio, Lakeside MI

Wilson, M, *Chmn,* College of Saint Catherine, Visual Arts Dept, Saint Paul MN (S)

Wilson, Marc, *Dir,* Nelson-Atkins Museum of Art, Friends of Art, Kansas City MO

Wilson, Marc F, *Dir & Cur Oriental Art,* Nelson-Atkins Museum of Art, Kansas City MO

Wilson, Margaret, *Secy,* Essex Art Association, Inc, Essex CT

Wilson, Martha, *Executive Dir,* Franklin Furnace Archive, Inc, New York NY

Wilson, Moira, *Librn,* Crafts Guild of Manitoba, Inc, Library, Winnipeg MB

Wilson, Nancy, *Instr,* The Arkansas Arts Center, Museum School, Little Rock AR (S)

Wilson, Neal, *Prof,* Southwest Texas State University, Dept of Art, San Marcos TX (S)

Wilson, Palma, *Chief Ranger,* Oregon Trail Museum Association, Scotts Bluff National Monument, Gering NE

Wilson, Patsy, *Dir Library Services,* Cooke County College Library, Art Dept, Gainesville TX

Wilson, Randon, *Pres,* Utah Lawyers for the Arts, Salt Lake City UT

Wilson, Richard, *Art Dept Chmn,* Shasta College, Art Dept, Fine Arts Division, Redding CA (S)

Wilson, Richard, *Asst Prof,* Rice University, Dept of Art and Art History, Houston TX (S)

Wilson, Rob, *Arts Cur,* Redding Museum of Art & History, Redding CA

Wilson, Robb, *Assoc Prof,* University of Wisconsin-Stout, Dept of Art & Design, Menomonie WI (S)

Wilson, Roger D (Sam), *Asst Prof,* University of Utah, Art Dept, Salt Lake City UT (S)

Wilson, Stanley, *Prof,* California State Polytechnic University, Pomona, Art Dept, Pomona CA (S)

Wilson, Stephen, *Instr,* California State University, Chico, Art Dept, Chico CA (S)

Wilson, Steve, *Dir,* Institute of the Great Plains, Museum of the Great Plains, Lawton OK

Wilson, Thomas, *Exec Dir,* Southwest Museum, Los Angeles CA

Wilson, Thomas H, *Deputy Dir,* International Museum of African Art, New York NY

Wilson, Tracy, *Dir of Development,* Berkshire Museum, Pittsfield MA

Wilson, Wallace, *Prof,* University of Florida, Dept of Art, Gainesville FL (S)

Wilson, Wayne, *Asst Cur,* Kelowna Centennial Museum and National Exhibit Centre, Kelowna BC

Wilton, John, *Prof,* Daytona Beach Community College, Dept of Fine Arts & Visual Arts, Daytona Beach FL (S)

Wiltraut, Douglas, *VPres,* Audubon Artists, Inc, New York NY

Wiltrout, Douglas, *Pres,* National Society of Painters in Casein & Acrylic, Inc, Whitehall PA

Wilwerding, Justin, *Lectr,* University of Wisconsin-Stout, Dept of Art & Design, Menomonie WI (S)

Wimberly, Dick, *VPres,* New Mexico Art League, Gallery, Albuquerque NM

Wimmer, Gayle, *Prof,* University of Arizona, Dept of Art, Tucson AZ (S)

Winant, Donna, *Asst,* Worcester Art Museum, Library, Worcester MA

Wince, Charles, *Exec Dir,* Acme Art Co, Columbus OH

Wind, Geraldine, *Asst Prof,* Mount Mary College, Art Dept, Milwaukee WI (S)

Windrum, Robert, *Cur,* Ontario College of Art, Gallery 76, Toronto ON

Windsor-Liscombe, Rhodri, *Prof,* University of British Columbia, Dept of Fine Arts, Vancouver BC (S)

Wine, Jerry, *Treasurer,* G G Drayton Club, Salem OH

Winegrad, Dilys, *Dir,* University of Pennsylvania, Arthur Ross Gallery, Philadelphia PA

Wineland, Gene, *Chmn,* Pratt Community College, Art Dept, Pratt KS (S)

Wineland, John, *Cur,* Hartwick College, Foreman Gallery, Oneonta NY

Winet, Jon, *Dir,* Southern Exposure Gallery, San Francisco CA

Winiker, Barry M, *Asst Cur,* Joseph E Seagram & Sons, Inc, Gallery, New York NY

Wink, Jon D, *Chmn,* Stephen F Austin State University, Art Dept, Nacogdoches TX (S)

Winkler, Audrey, *Chmn,* Jersey City Museum, Jersey City NJ

Winkler, Paul, *Acting Dir,* Menil Collection, Houston TX

Winkler, Suzanne, *Instr,* Columbia University, School of the Arts, Division of Painting & Sculpture, New York NY (S)

Winkler, Valerie, *Educ Dir,* Children's Museum of Manhattan, New York NY

Winningham, Geoffrey, *Prof,* Rice University, Dept of Art and Art History, Houston TX (S)

Winshaip, Joan, *Dir Cultural Affairs,* San Francisco City & County Arts Commission, San Francisco CA

Winship, John, *Instr,* Gettysburg College, Dept of Art, Gettysburg PA (S)

Winslow, B B, *Studio School Coordr & Public Relations Coordr,* Midland Art Council, Midland MI

Winslow, Bruce, *Interim Dir Midland Art Council,* Midland Center for the Arts, Midland MI (S)

Winslow, Bruce, *Adjunct Instr,* Saginaw Valley State University, Dept of Art and Design, University Center MI (S)

Winslow, John, *Chmn Dept,* Catholic University of America, Dept of Art, Washington DC (S)

Winter, Gerald G, *Prof,* University of Miami, Dept of Art & Art History, Coral Gables FL (S)

Winter, John, *Conservation Scientist,* Freer Gallery of Art, Washington DC

Winter, Robert, *Asst Prof,* Lenoir Rhyne College, Dept of Art, Hickory NC (S)

Winter, William, *Pres,* Mississippi Department of Archives & History, Mississippi State Historical Museum, Jackson MS

Winter, William F, *Pres Board Trustees,* Mississippi Department of Archives and History, State Historical Museum, Jackson MS

Winters, John L, *Assoc Prof,* University of Mississippi, Dept of Art, University MS (S)

Winters, Nathan, *Prof,* University of Utah, Art Dept, Salt Lake City UT (S)

Winters, Sandra, *Assoc Prof,* Florida International University, Visual Arts Dept, Miami FL (S)

Winzenz, Karon, *Cur Art,* University of Wisconsin, Green Bay, Lawton Gallery, Green Bay WI

Wipfler, Heinz, *Asst Prof,* Queensborough Community College, Dept of Art and Photography, Bayside NY (S)

Wiprud, Theodore, *Prof,* Oregon State University, Dept of Art, Corvallis OR (S)

Wirstrom, Margaret, *Chmn Fine Arts,* Delgado College, Dept of Fine Arts, New Orleans LA (S)

Wise, Edward, *Secy,* Pemaquid Group of Artists, Pemaquid Point ME

Wise, Edward B, *Pres,* Pemaquid Group of Artists, Pemaquid Point ME

Wise, R Gordon, *Chmn,* Millersville University, Art Dept, Millersville PA (S)

Wishon, Emory, *Pres & Board of Trustees,* Fresno Metropolitan Museum, Fresno CA

Wislinski, Bob, *Dir External Affairs,* Columbia Museum of Art, Columbia SC

Wismer, Edward, *Instr,* Ocean City Art Center, Ocean City NJ (S)

Wisniewfki, Judith, *Instr,* Delaware County Community College, Communications and Humanities House, Media PA (S)

Wisniewski, Dale, *Vis Lectr,* North Central College, Dept of Art, Naperville IL (S)

Wissler-Thomas, Carrie, *Pres,* Art Association of Harrisburg, School and Galleries, Harrisburg PA

Wistar, Caroline, *Cur,* La Salle University, Art Museum, Philadelphia PA

Witcombe, Christopher, *Asst Prof,* Sweet Briar College, Art History Dept, Sweet Briar VA (S)

Witczak, Dan, *Chief Preparator & Registrar,* Cleveland Center for Contemporary Art, Cleveland OH

Witham, James, *Cur,* Essex Historical Society, Essex Shipbuilding Museum, Essex MA

Witherell, James, *Area Dir,* College of the Siskiyous, Art Dept, Weed CA (S)

Witherow, Dale, *Assoc Prof,* Mansfield University, Art Dept, Mansfield PA (S)

Withers, Benjamin, *Cur,* University of Chicago, Max Epstein Archive, Chicago IL

Witt, David, *Cur,* University of New Mexico, The Harwood Foundation, Taos NM

Witter, Robert, *Asst Prof,* City Colleges of Chicago, Malcolm X College, Chicago IL (S)

Wittersheim, John, *Assoc Prof,* Siena Heights College, Studio Angelico-Art Dept, Adrian MI (S)

Witthoft, Brucia, *Prof,* Framingham State College, Art Dept, Framingham MA (S)

Wittig-Harby, Mickey, *Public Relations Officer,* Honolulu Academy of Arts, Honolulu HI

Wittkopp, Greg, *Cur Coll,* Cranbrook Academy of Art Museum, Bloomfield Hills MI

Witty, Anne, *Cur,* Columbia River Maritime Museum, Library, Astoria OR

Witzling, Mara, *Assoc Prof,* University of New Hampshire, Dept of the Arts, Durham NH (S)

Witzmann, Hugh, *Asst Prof,* Saint John's University, Art Dept, Collegeville MN (S)

Wixom, William D, *Chmn,* The Metropolitan Museum of Art, The Cloisters, New York NY

Wixoma, William D, *Chmn Medieval Art & the Cloisters,* The Metropolitan Museum of Art, New York NY

Wodiczko, Krystov, *Adjunct Asst Prof,* New York Institute of Technology, Fine Arts Dept, Old Westbury NY (S)

Wodzicki, Halinka, *Cur Educ,* Tacoma Art Museum, Tacoma WA

Woertendyke, Ruis, *Prof,* Pace University, Dyson College of Arts & Sciences, Pleasantville NY (S)

Wohlford, Kenneth M, *Dir of Performing Arts,* Colorado Springs Fine Arts Center, Colorado Springs CO

Woike, Glenn V, *Head Librn,* Daemen College, Marian Library, Amherst NY

Wojciechowski, Barbara P, *Instr,* Villa Maria College of Buffalo, Art Dept, Buffalo NY (S)

Wojtkiewicz, Dennis, *Dir Grad Studies,* Bowling Green State University, School of Art, Bowling Green OH (S)

Wolanin, Barbara A, *Chief Cur,* United States Capitol, Architect of the Capitol, Washington DC

Wolanin, Barbara A, *Cur,* United States Capitol, Art Reference Library, Washington DC

Wolber, Paul, *Dir,* Spring Arbor College, Art Dept, Spring Arbor MI (S)

Wold, Lynn Murdock, *Librn,* Berkeley Public Library, Berkeley CA

Wold, William, *Assoc Prof,* University of South Dakota, Dept of Art, Vermillion SD (S)

Wolf, Arthur H, *Dir,* Montana State University, Museum of the Rockies, Bozeman MT

Wolf, Constance, *Cur Educ,* Whitney Museum of American Art, New York NY

Wolf, Pat, *Dir,* Northland Pioneer College, Art Dept, Holbrook AZ (S)

Wolf, Patricia B, *Dir,* Anchorage Museum of History and Art, Anchorage AK

Wolf, Richard A, *Dir,* Saint Joseph Museum, Library, Saint Joseph MO

Wolf, Robert L, *Dir Design,* Arizona State University, College of Architecture & Environmental Design, Tempe AZ (S)

Wolf, Sara, *Librn,* Mint Museum of Art, Library, Charlotte NC

Wolf, Tom, *Dir,* Bard College, William Cooper Procter Art Center, Annandale-on-Hudson NY

Wolf, Vicki, *Managing Dir,* Sushi-Performance & Visual Art Gallery, San Diego CA

Wolfe, Laurie, *Cataloger,* Free Library of Philadelphia, Rare Book Dept, Philadelphia PA

Wolfe, Leslie, *Assoc Dir,* Roy Boyd Gallery, Chicago IL

Wolfe, Lisa, *Mgr Community Relations,* Spokane Public Library Gallery, Spokane WA

Wolfe, Michael, *Chief Financial Officer,* Whitney Museum of American Art, New York NY

Wolfe, Nancy, *Dept of Education,* Indiana State Museum, Indianapolis IN

Wolfe, Townsend, *Chief Cur,* The Arkansas Arts Center, Museum School, Little Rock AR (S)

Wolfe, Townsend D, *Dir & Chief Cur,* Arkansas Arts Center, Little Rock AR

Wolfensohn, James D, *Chmn of the Board of Trustees,* The John F Kennedy Center for the Performing Arts, Washington DC

Wolff, Beverly, *Secy,* Artists Space, New York NY

Wolff, Hennie, *Exec Dir,* Visual Arts Ontario, Library, Toronto ON

Wolff, Hennie L, *Exec Dir,* Visual Arts Ontario, Toronto ON

Wolff, Martha, *Cur European Painting Before 1750,* The Art Institute of Chicago, Chicago IL

Wolfram, William R, *Head Dept,* Concordia College, Art Dept, Seward NE (S)

Wolhart, Holly, *Coll Outreach Programs Supv,* Minnesota Museum of American Art, Saint Paul MN

Wolin, Jeffrey, *Assoc Prof,* Indiana University, Bloomington, Henry Radford Hope School of Fine Arts, Bloomington IN (S)

Wolins, Inez, *Dir,* Wichita Art Museum, Wichita KS

Woliung, Laurie, *Instr,* College of Mount Saint Joseph, Art Dept, Cincinnati OH (S)

Wolk, Robert G, *Pres,* North Carolina Museums Council, Raleigh NC

Wollowitz, Charles, *Adjunct Asst Prof,* Le Moyne College, Fine Arts Dept, Syracuse NY (S)

Woloshyn, Sonyia, *Comptroller,* Montclair Art Museum, Montclair NJ

Wolschke-Bulmahn, Joachim, *Dir Studies,* Harvard University, Studies in Landscape Architecture & Garden Library, Washington DC

Wolsk, Nancy, *Dir,* Transylvania University, Morlan Gallery, Lexington KY

Wolsk, Nancy, *Instr,* Transylvania University, Studio Arts Dept, Lexington KY (S)

Woltman, Robert, *Cur of Exhibits,* Albuquerque Museum of Art, History & Science, Albuquerque NM

Wolverton, Margaret, *Admin Dir,* California Crafts Museum, San Francisco CA

Wolynetz, Lubow, *Educational Dir,* The Ukrainian Museum, New York NY

Wong, Eddie, *Prof,* University of Wisconsin-Stout, Dept of Art & Design, Menomonie WI (S)

Wong, Michele, *Registrar,* New York University, Grey Art Gallery and Study Center, New York NY

Wong, Yat-May, *Financial Asst,* Institute of Contemporary Art, Boston MA

Wong-Lida, Ed, *Chmn Design Studies,* Kendall College of Art & Design, Frank & Lyn Van Steenberg Library, Grand Rapids MI

Wong-Ligda, Ed, *Chmn Design Studies,* Kendall College of Art & Design, Grand Rapids MI (S)

Wonson, Theresa, *VPres,* North Shore Arts Association, Inc, Art Gallery, Gloucester MA

Woo, Suzanne, *Membership & Special Events,* Fort Worth Art Association, Modern Art Museum of Fort Worth, Fort Worth TX

Wood, Carol, *Cur Art,* Roberson Museum & Science Center, Binghamton NY

Wood, Cliff, *Dean Arts & Science,* Grayson County College, Art Dept, Denison TX (S)

Wood, Clifford P, *Dept Head,* California State University at Sacramento, Library - Humanities Reference Dept, Sacramento CA

Wood, Darrow, *Chief Librn,* New York City Technical College, Namm Hall Library and Learning Resource Center, Brooklyn NY

Wood, David, *Cur,* Concord Museum, Concord MA

Wood, David, *Cur,* Concord Museum, Library, Concord MA

Wood, Don, *Cur Oriental Art,* Birmingham Museum of Art, Birmingham AL

Wood, James N, *Pres & Dir,* The Art Institute of Chicago, Chicago IL

Wood, Judy, *Acq Head,* Fashion Institute of Technology Galleries, Library, New York NY

Wood, Marcia J, *Prof,* Kalamazoo College, Art Dept, Kalamazoo MI (S)

Wood, Margaret K, *Pres,* Goshen Historical Society, Goshen CT

Wood, Marilyn, *Instr,* Normandale Community College, Bloomington MN (S)

Wood, Mary Louise, *Dir,* American Association of Museums, International Council of Museums Committee, Washington DC

Wood, Richard D, *Pres Board of Trustees,* Indianapolis Museum of Art, Indianapolis IN

Wood, Robert B, *Pres Emeritus,* Halifax Historical Society, Inc, Halifax Historical Museum, Daytona Beach FL

Wood, Sally, *Cur Interpretation,* Wade House & Wesley W Jung Carriage Museum, Historic House & Carriage Museum, Greenbush WI

Wood, Sharon, *Assoc Prof,* Lansing Community College, Media Dept, Lansing MI (S)

Wood, Susan, *Assoc Prof,* Oakland University, Dept of Art and Art History, Rochester MI (S)

Wood, Theodore T, *Chmn,* Saint Louis University, Fine & Performing Arts Dept, Saint Louis MO (S)

Wood, Thomas R, *Dir Architecture,* Montana State University, School of Architecture, Bozeman MT (S)

Wood, William, *1st VPres,* Halifax Historical Society, Inc, Halifax Historical Museum, Daytona Beach FL

Wood, William P, *VPres,* Fairmount Park Art Association, Philadelphia PA

Woodard, Garr, *Head Dept,* Kansas State University, Art Dept, Manhattan KS (S)

Woodard, Marie, *Slide Librn,* Providence College, Art and Art History Dept, Providence RI (S)

Woodburn, Steven, *Adjunct Asst Prof,* New York Institute of Technology, Fine Arts Dept, Old Westbury NY (S)

Woodcock, Michael, *Prof Drawing & Painting,* Pitzer College, Dept of Art, Claremont CA (S)

Woodford, Don, *Instr,* California State University, San Bernardino, Art Dept, San Bernardino CA (S)

Woodham, Derrick, *Dir,* University of Cincinnati, School of Art, Cincinnati OH (S)

Woodham, Jean, *Pres,* Sculptors Guild, Inc, New York NY

Woodie, Rebekah, *Dir Community Relations,* Ari Museum of Western Virginia, Roanoke VA

Woodruff, Lynne, *Asst Librn,* University of Maryland, College Park, Art Library, College Park MD

Woods, Arlene, *Assoc Prof,* Salve Regina College, Art Dept, Newport RI (S)

Woods, Bill, *Asst Prof,* Philadelphia Community College, Dept of Art, Philadelphia PA (S)

Woods, James, *Dir,* College of Southern Idaho, Herrett Museum & Art Gallery, Twin Falls ID

Woods, Jean, *Dir,* Washington County Museum of Fine Arts, Hagerstown MD

Woods, Jennifer L, *Chief Conservation,* Library Company of Philadelphia, Print Dept, Philadelphia PA

Woods, Jenny, *Cur Oppertshauser House,* Multicultural Heritage Centre, Stony Plain AB

Woods, Paula, *Cur of Educ,* Tippecanoe County Historical Museum, Lafayette IN

Woods, Richard, *Pres College,* Earlham College, Leeds Gallery, Richmond IN

Woods, Shirley, *Asst Dir for Operations,* Montgomery Museum of Fine Arts, Montgomery AL

Woods, Yvette, *Instructor,* Saint Louis Community College at Meramec, Art Dept, Saint Louis MO (S)

Woodson, Doris, *Asst Prof,* Virginia State University, Fine & Commercial Art, Petersburg VA (S)

Woodson, Jim, *Prof,* Texas Christian University, Art & Art History Dept, Fort Worth TX (S)

Woodward, Anne S, *Dir Museum Division,* Historical Society of Delaware, Old Town Hall Museum, Wilmington DE

Woodward, Gary, *Assoc Prof,* Kansas State University, Art Dept, Manhattan KS (S)

Woodward, Kessler, *Asst Prof,* University of Alaska, Dept of Art, Fairbanks AK (S)

Woodward, Richard, *Assoc Dir Exhib/Prog Div,* Virginia Museum of Fine Arts, Richmond VA

Woodward, Roland H, *Exec Dir,* Chester County Historical Society, West Chester PA

Woodward, W T, *Assoc Prof,* George Washington University, Dept of Art, Washington DC (S)

Woodworth, John, *Cur,* Florida State University, Fine Arts Gallery & Museum, Tallahassee FL

Woody, Elsbeth, *Chmn,* Bernard M Baruch College of the City University of New York, Art Dept, New York NY (S)

Woody, Howard, *Prof,* University of South Carolina, Dept of Art, Columbia SC (S)

Woodyatt, Lois H, *Archival Asst,* National Academy of Design, Archives, New York NY

Woolever, Mary, *Architecture Librn,* The Art Institute of Chicago, Ryerson and Burnham Libraries, Chicago IL

Woolfolk, Charles, *Assoc Dean,* Rutgers, the State University of New Jersey, Mason Gross School of the Arts, New Brunswick NJ (S)

Woolley, Jay C, *Dir,* Utah Travel Council, Salt Lake City UT

Woollman, Lisa, *Instr,* Delaware County Community College, Communications and Humanities House, Media PA (S)

Woolson, Evelyn, *Pres,* Arts Club of Washington, James Monroe House, Washington DC

Woon, Wendy, *Education & Extension Officer,* Art Gallery of Hamilton, Hamilton ON

Woosley, Anne I, *Foundation Dir,* Amerind Foundation, Inc, Amerind Museum, Fulton-Hayden Memorial Art Gallery, Dragoon AZ

Woosley, Anne I, *Foundation Dir,* Amerind Foundation, Inc, Fulton-Hayden Memorial Library, Dragoon AZ

Wooters, David A, *Archivist,* International Museum of Photography at George Eastman House, Library, Rochester NY

Work, Lisa, *Gen Mgr,* Louisville Visual Art Association, Louisville KY

Workman, Robert, *Dir Exhib,* The American Federation of Arts, New York NY

Workman, Roger, *Pres,* Otis School of Art & Design, Fine Arts, Los Angeles CA (S)

Worley, Ken, *Adjunct Instr,* Maryville University of Saint Louis, Art Division, Saint Louis MO (S)

Worlie, Ronda, *Asst Dir,* Custer County Art Center, Miles City MT

Worsham, Beverly, *Asst Dir,* Walter Cecil Rawls Museum, Courtland VA

Worth, Robert R, *Pres,* Adirondack Historical Association, Adirondack Museum, Blue Mountain Lake NY

Worth, Timothy, *Cur,* Manitoba Historical Society, Dalnavert Museum, Winnipeg MB

Wortham, Marshall, *Prof,* Southwest Texas State University, Dept of Art, San Marcos TX (S)

Worthen, Mark, *Secy,* Louisiana State University, Museum of Arts, Baton Rouge LA

Worthen, William B, *Dir,* Arkansas Territorial Restoration, Little Rock AR

Worthington, Margart, *Lectr,* University of North Carolina at Wilmington, Dept of Fine Arts - Division of Art, Wilmington NC (S)

Worthley, Ginger, *Exhibit Dir,* Conejo Valley Art Museum, Thousand Oaks CA

Worthy-Dumbleton, Mary, *Docent,* Florida Community College at Jacksonville, South Gallery, Jacksonville FL

Wotojwicz, Robert, *Asst Prof,* Old Dominion University, Art Dept, Norfolk VA (S)

Wray, George T, *Prof,* University of Idaho, College of Art & Architecture, Moscow ID (S)

Wray, Ronald E, *Exec Dir,* National Institute of Art & Disabilities (NIAD), Richmond CA

Wright, Anetta, *Coll Mgr,* Cortland County Historical Society, Kellogg Memorial Research Library, Cortland NY

Wright, Astri, *Asst Prof,* University of Victoria, Dept of History in Art, Victoria BC (S)

Wright, Carolyn, *Asst Dir,* Rehoboth Art League, Inc, Rehoboth Beach DE

Wright, Caryl, *Pres,* Brevard Art Center and Museum, Inc, Melbourne FL

Wright, Catherine A, *Coordr Public Relations,* The Currier Gallery of Art, Manchester NH

Wright, Cathy, *Dir of Exhib,* Colorado Springs Fine Arts Center, Colorado Springs CO

Wright, Charles B, *Exec Dir,* Dia Center for the Arts, New York NY

Wright, Claire, *Exec Dir,* Licking County Art Association Gallery, Newark OH

Wright, David, *Museum Cur,* United States Tobacco Manufacturing Company Inc, Museum of Tobacco & History, Nashville TN

Wright, David W, *Registrar,* Pierpont Morgan Library, New York NY

Wright, E L, *VPres,* Danville Museum of Fine Arts & History, Danville VA

Wright, Erin, *Asst Prof,* Louisiana State University, School of Art, Baton Rouge LA (S)

Wright, James, *Dir,* University of New Mexico, Fine Arts Library, Albuquerque NM

Wright, J Franklin, *Prof,* George Washington University, Dept of Art, Washington DC (S)

Wright, Jinx, *Pres,* Hutchinson Art Association Gallery, Hutchinson KS

Wright, Kate, *Performing Arts,* Sun Valley Center for the Arts and Humanities, Dept of Fine Art, Sun Valley ID (S)

Wright, Lynda W, *Cataloger,* Chrysler Museum, Jean Outland Chrysler Library, Norfolk VA

Wright, Mary A, *Dept Head,* San Antonio Public Library, Dept of Fine Arts, San Antonio TX

Wright, Mildred, *Supervising Librn,* The New York Public Library, Mid-Manhattan Library, Picture Collection, New York NY

Wright, Nancy, *Asst Dir,* Samuel S Fleisher Art Memorial, Philadelphia PA (S)

Wright, Ona, *Chairperson,* Cooke County College, Div of Communications & Fine Arts, Gainesville TX (S)

Wright, Patricia, *Asst Dir,* Sweet Briar College, Martin C Shallenberger Art Library, Sweet Briar VA

Wright, Pope, *Lectr,* University of Wisconsin-Superior, Programs in the Visual Arts, Superior WI (S)

Wright, Ralph, *VPres,* Southern Lorain County Historical Society, Spirit of '76 Museum, Wellington OH

Wright, Rebecca, *Membership,* Harvard University, Harvard University Art Museums, Cambridge MA

Wright, Rob, *Assoc Prof,* University of Toronto, Programme in Landscape Architecture, Toronto ON (S)

Wright, Robin, *Cur Native American Art,* University of Washington, Thomas Burke Memorial Washington State Museum, Seattle WA

Wright, Sara, *Business Mgr,* Arts & Science Center for Southeast Arkansas, Pine Bluff AR

Wright, Sarah E, *Pres,* Pen and Brush, Inc, New York NY

Wright, Sarah E, *Pres,* Pen and Brush, Inc, Library, New York NY

Wright, Sharyl, *Instr,* Avila College, Art Division, Dept of Performing and Visual Art, Kansas City MO (S)

Wright, Stanley Marc, *Dir,* Wright School of Art, Stowe VT (S)

Wright, Susanne, *Public Relations & Promotions,* Kentucky Derby Museum, Louisville KY

Wright, Tony, *Head Design & Installation,* Fort Worth Art Association, Modern Art Museum of Fort Worth, Fort Worth TX

Wright, Vicki C, *Dir,* University of New Hampshire, The Art Gallery, Durham NH

Wright, Virginia L, *Assoc Librn,* Corning Museum of Glass, Rakow Library, Corning NY

Wroble, Stephen, *Prof,* Schoolcraft College, Dept of Art and Design, Livonia MI (S)

Wroblewski, Andrzej, *In Charge Industrial Design,* University of Illinois, Urbana-Champaign, School of Art and Design, Champaign IL (S)

Wu, Marshall, *Cur of Asian Art,* University of Michigan, Museum of Art, Ann Arbor MI

Wu, Marshall, *Cur,* University of Michigan, Ann Arbor, Dept of History of Art, Ann Arbor MI (S)

Wunder, Elizabeth V, *Admin Asst,* Washburn University, Mulvane Art Museum, Topeka KS

Wurmfeld, Sanford, *Chmn Art Dept,* Hunter College, Art Dept, New York NY (S)

Wurtz, John, *Pres,* Jefferson County Historical Society Museum, Madison IN

Wyancko, Ronald, *Prof,* James Madison University, Dept of Art, Harrisonburg VA (S)

Wyatt, Charles D, *Supt,* National Park Service, Hubbell Trading Post National Historic Site, Ganado AZ

Wyatt, J Leslie, *Prof,* University of Mississippi, Dept of Art, University MS (S)

Wyatt, Joseph, *Cur,* University of Waterloo, Art Gallery, Waterloo ON

Wyatt, Victoria, *Assoc Prof,* University of Victoria, Dept of History in Art, Victoria BC (S)

Wylder, Viki D, *Registrar of Exhib,* Florida State University, Fine Arts Gallery & Museum, Tallahassee FL

Wylie, Anne, *Pres,* Prince George Art Gallery, Prince George BC

Wylie, Elizabeth, *Dir,* Tufts University, Art Gallery, Medford MA

Wylie, Rolfe, *Chmn,* Texarkana College, Art Dept, Texarkana TX (S)

Wylie, William, *Instr,* University of North Carolina at Charlotte, Dept of Visual Arts, Charlotte NC (S)

Wyly, Mary, *Librn,* Newberry Library, Chicago IL

Wyman, Doris, *VPres,* New York Artists Equity Association, Inc, New York NY

Wyman, James, *Coordr Exhib,* Visual Studies Workshop, Rochester NY

Wyngaard, Susan E, *Head Librn,* Ohio State University, Fine Arts Library, Columbus OH

Wyrick, Carol, *Cur Educ,* Joslyn Art Museum, Omaha NE

Xu, Gan, *Instr,* Portland School of Art, Portland ME (S)

Yack, John L, *Coordr,* Southern Illinois University, College of Technical Careers, Carbondale IL (S)

Yager, David, *Chmn,* University of Maryland, Baltimore County, Visual Arts Dept, Baltimore MD (S)

Yaggie, Frank R, *Pres,* Yankton County Historical Society, Dakota Territorial Museum, Yankton SD

Yakstis, Gary, *Operations Dir,* University of Connecticut, Jorgensen Gallery, Storrs CT

Yalle, Tina, *Dir,* New York Experimental Glass Workshop, Brooklyn NY

Yanes, Bob, *Asst Dir,* San Jose State University, Union Gallery, San Jose CA

Yanez, Rene, *Cur Cultural Prog,* Mexican Museum, San Francisco CA

Yang, Geoffrey, *Treas,* The Friends of Photography, Ansel Adams Center for Photography, San Francisco CA

Yanik, John V, *Assoc Prof,* Catholic University of America, School of Architecture & Planning, Washington DC (S)

Yankovich, Kasha, *Mgr ILL Artisans Shop,* Illinois State Museum, Illinois Artisans Shop, Chicago IL

Yao, Winberta, *Art Specialist,* Arizona State University, Hayden Library, Tempe AZ

Yapelli, Tina, *Cur Exhibitions,* Madison Art Center, Madison WI

Yarbedra, Ronald F, *Prof,* Florida A & M University, Dept of Visual Arts, Humanities & Theatre, Tallahassee FL (S)

Yarbrough, Sonji, *Instr,* Mount Mary College, Art Dept, Milwaukee WI (S)

Yard, Sally, *Chmn,* University of San Diego, Art Dept, San Diego CA (S)

Yarden, Elie, *Instr,* Bard College, Milton Avery Graduate School of the Arts, Annandale-on-Hudson NY (S)

Yarlow, Loretta, *Dir & Cur,* York University, Art Gallery of York University, North York ON

Yarwood, Kim, *Gallery Mgr,* Niagara University, Castellani Art Museum, New York NY

Yassin, Robert A, *Dir,* Tucson Museum of Art, Tucson AZ

Yasuda, Robert, *Prof,* C W Post Center of Long Island University, School of Visual & Performing Arts, Greenvale NY (S)

Yates, Hollye, *Cur,* Museums of Abilene, Inc, Abilene TX

Yates, Miriam, *Pres,* Shoreline Historical Museum, Seattle WA

Yates, Sam, *Dir,* University of Tennessee, Ewing Gallery of Art and Architecture, Knoxville TN

Yates, Steve, *Cur Photography,* Museum of New Mexico, Museum of Fine Arts, Santa Fe NM

Yatrakis, Kathryn, *Dean,* Columbia University, Columbia College, New York NY (S)

Yavarkovsky, Jerome, *Dir,* New York State Library, Manuscripts and Special Collections, Albany NY

Yeager, Lisa, *Vol Coordr,* Bellevue Art Museum, Bellevue WA

Yeager, William, *Cur,* Eva Brook Donly Museum, Simcoe ON

Yeager, William, *Cur,* Eva Brook Donly Museum, Library, Simcoe ON

Yeates, Michael, *Asst Dir Coll,* Massachusetts Institute of Technology, MIT Museum, Cambridge MA

Yee, Ann G, *Admin Coordr,* East Bay Asian Local Development Corp, Asian Resource Gallery, Oakland CA

Yee, Kay, *Acting Area Head Jewelry,* Pasadena City College, Art Dept, Pasadena CA (S)

Yeh, Chen Hwon, *Bookkeeper,* London Regional Art & Historical Museums, London ON

Yelen, Alice Rae, *Asst to Dir,* New Orleans Museum of Art, New Orleans LA

Yeni, Lindi, *Dir,* Midtown Art Center, Houston TX

Yerdon, Lawrence J, *Dir,* Hancock Shaker Village, Inc, Pittsfield MA

Yerkovich, Sally, *Deputy Dir Membership & Development,* Museum of the City of New York, New York NY

Yes, Phyllis A, *Assoc Prof,* Lewis & Clark College, Dept of Art, Portland OR (S)

Yiengpruksawan, Mimi, *Dir Undergrad Studies,* Yale University, Dept of the History of Art, New Haven CT (S)

Ylitalo, Katherine, *Cur Art,* University of Calgary, The Nickle Arts Museum, Calgary AB

Yochim, Louise Dunn, *Pres,* American Jewish Art Club, Evanston IL

Yoder, Jonathan, *Chmn,* Northern Virginia Community College, Art Dept, Annandale VA (S)

Yohe, Perry, *Pres,* Grand Prairie Arts Council, Inc, Arts Center of the Grand Prairie, Stuttgart AR

Yolleck, Frima, *Bookkeeper,* Visual Arts Ontario, Toronto ON

Yonemura, Ann, *Assoc Cur Japanese Art,* Freer Gallery of Art, Washington DC

Yoon, Sang, *Asst Prof,* James Madison University, Dept of Art, Harrisonburg VA (S)

Yorba, Jonathan, *Interim Cur,* Mexican Museum, San Francisco CA

York, George, *Educ Coordr,* Institute for Contemporary Art, Project Studio One (P S 1), Long Island City NY

York, Hildreth, *Assoc Prof,* Rutgers, the State University of New Jersey, Graduate Program in Art History, New Brunswick NJ (S)

York, Jeffrey, *Cur Education,* Birmingham Museum of Art, Birmingham AL

York, Robert, *Instr of Art,* Edison Community College, Dept of Fine and Performing Arts, Fort Myers FL (S)

Yorty, Faith, *Cur Education,* Springfield Art Museum, Springfield MO

Yoshida, Ray, *Prof,* School of the Art Institute of Chicago, Chicago IL (S)

Yoshimine-Webster, Carol, *Chmn Div,* Centenary College, Div of Fine Arts, Hackettstown NJ (S)

Yoshimura, Reiko, *Librn,* Freer Gallery of Art & The Arthur M Sackler Gallery Gallery, Library, Washington DC

Yost, Robert, *Dir,* Mohave Museum of History and Arts, Kingman AZ

Yothers, John, *Adj Prof,* Washington and Jefferson College, Art Dept, Washington PA (S)

Youds, Robert, *Asst Prof,* University of Victoria, Dept of Visual Arts, Victoria BC (S)

Youmans, Brian, *instructional Aide,* Victor Valley College, Art Dept, Victorville CA (S)

Young, Alice, *Coordr Educ,* Agecroft Association, Richmond VA

Young, Amy L, *Asst Cur,* Wichita State University, Edwin A Ulrich Museum of Art, Wichita KS

Young, Becky, *Lectr,* University of Pennsylvania, Graduate School of Fine Arts, Philadelphia PA (S)

Young, Betsy, *Instr,* Ocean City Art Center, Ocean City NJ (S)

Young, Bill, *General Mgr,* Ozark Folk Center, Mountain View AR

Young, Brent, *Assoc Prof,* Cleveland Institute of Art, Cleveland OH (S)

Young, Carolyn, *Visitor Servs,* Sheldon Jackson Museum, Sitka AK

Young, Charles, *Assoc Prof,* Calvin College, Art Dept, Grand Rapids MI (S)

Young, Charles, *Prof,* Austin Peay State University, Dept of Art, Clarksville TN (S)

Young, Charles A, *Chairperson,* University of the District of Columbia, Art Dept, Washington DC (S)

Young, Charles A, *Prof,* University of the District of Columbia, Art Dept, Washington DC (S)

Young, Christopher R, *Cur,* Flint Institute of Arts, Flint MI

Young, C Philip, *Prof,* Hartwick College, Art Dept, Oneonta NY (S)

Young, Dana, *Museum Consultant,* San Antonio Art League, San Antonio TX

Young, Daniel, *Instr,* State University of New York College at Oneonta, Dept of Art, Oneonta NY (S)

Young, G E, *Dean Art,* Eastern Oregon State College, Arts & Humanities Dept, La Grande OR (S)

Young, Guy, *Pub Information Dir,* Sunrise Museum, Inc, Sunrise Art Museum, Sunrise Children's Museum & Planatarium, Charleston WV

Young, James L, *Dir,* College of Eastern Utah, Gallery East, Price UT

Young, Jane Anne, *Dir of Education,* University of Virginia, Bayly Art Museum, Charlottesville VA

Young, Joseph L, *Dir,* Art in Architecture, Los Angeles CA (S)

Young, Joseph L, *Dir,* Art in Architecture, Joseph Young Library, Los Angeles CA

Young, Martie, *Asst Dir Colls & Progs & Cur Asian Art,* Cornell University, Herbert F Johnson Museum of Art, Ithaca NY

Young, Martie W, *Prof,* Cornell University, Dept of the History of Art, Ithaca NY (S)

Young, Mary, *Librn,* Institute of American Indian Arts Museum, Alaska Native Culture and Arts Development, Santa Fe NM

Young, Pamela, *Assoc Registrar,* Walker Art Center, Minneapolis MN

Young, Patience, *Cur Education,* Detroit Institute of Arts, Detroit MI

Young, Patrick, *Photographer,* University of Michigan, Slide and Photograph Collection, Ann Arbor MI

Young, Retha, *Treas,* Chilkat Valley Historical Society, Sheldon Museum & Cultural Center, Haines AK

Young, Richard, *Prof,* Gavilan College, Art Dept, Gilroy CA (S)

Young, Robert, *Asst Prof,* University of British Columbia, Dept of Fine Arts, Vancouver BC (S)

Young, Thomas E, *Librn,* Philbrook Museum of Art, Chapman Library, Tulsa OK

Young, Timothy, *Assoc Prof,* Malone College, Dept of Art, Canton OH (S)

Young, Tom, *Instr,* Greenfield Community College, Art, Graphic Design & Media Communication Dept, Greenfield MA (S)

Youngberg, Kathryn B, *Museum Shop Mgr,* Longue Vue House and Gardens, New Orleans LA

Youngberg, Marcia, *Secy,* Swedish American Museum Association of Chicago, Chicago IL

Youngblood, Judy, *Printmaking Coordr,* University of North Texas, School of Visual Arts, Denton TX (S)

Youngblood, Michael S, *Assoc Prof,* Southern Illinois University, School of Art & Design, Carbondale IL (S)

Younger, Dan, *Dir Publications,* Photographic Resource Center, Boston MA

Youngers, Peter L, *Instructional Dir,* General Studies, Northeastern Junior College, Dept of Art, Sterling CO (S)

Youngman, James E, *Head Dept,* Artist Studio Centers, Inc, New York NY (S)

Youngman, Robert, *Cur Graphic Arts,* Muskegon Museum of Art, Muskegon MI

Yrigoyen, Charles, *Secy,* United Methodist Church Commission on Archives and History, Madison NJ

Yu, Chilin, *Librn,* Columbus College of Art & Design, Packard Library, Columbus OH

Yu, Sung, *Cur Asian Art,* San Diego Museum of Art, San Diego CA

Yuen, Kee-Ho, *Asst Prof,* University of Northern Iowa, Dept of Art, Cedar Falls IA (S)

Yurkanin, Sharon, *Sales Gallery,* Allentown Art Museum, Allentown PA

Zabarsky, Melvin, *Prof,* University of New Hampshire, Dept of the Arts, Durham NH (S)

Zabel, Barbara, *Instr,* Connecticut College, Dept of Art History, New London CT (S)

Zabel, Craig, *Assoc Prof,* Pennsylvania State University, University Park, Dept of Art History, University Park PA (S)

Zaborowski, Dennis, *Prof,* University of North Carolina at Chapel Hill, Art Dept, Chapel Hill NC (S)

Zachariah, Gale, *Young People's Library,* Las Vegas-Clark County Library District, Las Vegas NV

Zacharias, David, *Asst Prof,* Converse College, Art Dept, Spartanburg SC (S)

Zachman, Gina, *Educ Coordr,* University of Notre Dame, Snite Museum of Art, Notre Dame IN

Zachos, Kimon S, *Pres,* The Currier Gallery of Art, Manchester NH

Zack, Suzanne, *Asst Librn,* Stowe-Day Foundation, Library, Hartford CT

Zacnic, Ivan, *Chmn,* Lehigh University, Dept of Art and Architecture, Bethlehem PA (S)

Zahner, Mary, *Asst Prof,* University of Dayton, Visual Arts Dept, Dayton OH (S)

Zakoian, Paul, *Sculpture,* Contemporary Art Workshop, Chicago IL (S)

Zamagias, James D, *Chmn,* Allegany Community College, Art Dept, Cumberland MD (S)

Zamjahn, Bruce, *Instr,* Mount Mary College, Art Dept, Milwaukee WI (S)

Zamost, Rita, *Pres,* Long Beach Jewish Community Center, Center Gallery, Long Beach CA

Zander, Jane, *Cataloger,* Nelson-Atkins Museum of Art, Kenneth and Helen Spencer Art Reference Library, Kansas City MO

Zandler, Richard, *Dir,* Maryland-National Capital Park & Planning Commission, Montpelier Cultural Arts Center, Laurel MD

Zane, Anthony M, *Dir,* Old Dartmouth Historical Society, New Bedford Whaling Museum, New Bedford MA

Zapton, Steve, *Prof,* James Madison University, Dept of Art, Harrisonburg VA (S)

Zarov, Jonathan, *Publicist,* Madison Art Center, Madison WI

Zarse, Elaine, *Assoc Prof,* Mount Mary College, Art Dept, Milwaukee WI (S)

Zarsky, Mimi, *Program Coordr,* National Alliance for Media Arts & Culture (NAMAC), Oakland CA

Zaruba, Gary E, *Prof,* University of Nebraska, Kearney, Dept of Art & Art History, Kearney NE (S)

Zaugg, Elwood, *Dean,* Salt Lake Community College, Graphic Design Dept, Salt Lake City UT (S)

Zea, Philip, *Cur,* Historic Deerfield, Inc, Deerfield MA

Zeff, Jacqlyn, *Dean Arts & Science,* Mercy College of Detroit, Art Dept, Detroit MI (S)

Zeger, Cynthia B, *Dir,* Horizons Unlimited Supplementary Educational Center, Art Gallery, Salisbury NC

Zehnder, Marvin, *Prof,* Northern Michigan University, Dept of Art and Design, Marquette MI (S)

Zehner, Theodora, *VPres,* Surface Design Association, Inc, Oakland CA

Zehr, Connie, *Assoc Prof,* Claremont Graduate School, Dept of Fine Arts, Claremont CA (S)

Zeidan, Kimberly, *Exec Dir,* Art League of Houston, Houston TX

Zeidler, Jeanne, *Dir,* Hampton University, University Museum, Hampton VA

Zeitlin, Marilyn A, *Dir,* Arizona State University, University Art Museum, Tempe AZ

Zell, Beverly, *Photo Archivist,* Stowe-Day Foundation, Library, Hartford CT

Zeller, Frank, *Instr,* Lakewood Community College, Humanities Dept, White Bear Lake MN (S)

Zeller, Helen, *First VPres,* Toledo Federation of Art Societies, Inc, Toledo OH

Zeller, Joe, *Chmn,* University of Kansas, Dept of Design, Lawrence KS (S)

Zeller, Paulette, *Asst Prof,* Shorter College, Art Dept, Rome GA (S)

Zendejas, R E, *Dir Museum Servs,* Colorado Springs Fine Arts Center, Colorado Springs CO

Zepp, Eugene, *Librn,* Boston Public Library, Rare Book & Manuscripts Dept, Boston MA

Zernich, Ted, *Acting Dir,* University of Illinois, Krannert Art Museum, Champaign IL

Zernich, Theodore, *DirSchool,* University of Illinois, Urbana-Champaign, School of Art and Design, Champaign IL (S)

Zhou, Xiuqin, *Registrar,* Marquette University, Haggerty Museum of Art, Milwaukee WI

Zic, Virginia F, *Coordr,* Sacred Heart University, Dept of Art, Fairfield CT (S)

Zidek, Al, *Instr,* Solano Community College, Division of Fine & Applied Art, Suisun City CA (S)

Ziditz-Ward, Vera, *Asst Prof,* Bloomsburg University, Dept of Art, Bloomsburg PA (S)

Ziegler, Arthur P, *Pres,* Pittsburgh History & Landmarks Foundation, James D Van Trump Library, Pittsburgh PA

Ziegler, David, *Dir,* University of California, Los Angeles, Visual Resource Collection, Los Angeles CA

Ziegler, J E, *Assoc Prof,* College of the Holy Cross, Dept of Visual Arts, Worcester MA (S)

Ziemann, Richard, *Prof,* Herbert H Lehman College, Art Dept, Bronx NY (S)

Zierden, Martha, *Cur Historic Archaeology,* Charleston Museum, Charleston SC

Ziller, Janis, *Curatorial Asst,* Nelda C & H J Lutcher Stark Foundation, Stark Museum of Art, Orange TX

Zimmer, Jim, *Dir,* Sioux City Art Center, Sioux City IA

Zimmer, Jim, *Dir,* Sioux City Art Center, Library, Sioux City IA

Zimmer, Jim L, *Dir,* Sioux City Art Center, Sioux City IA (S)

Zimmer, Sandra, *Instr,* Linn Benton Community College, Fine & Applied Art Dept, Albany OR (S)

Zimmer, Stephen, *Dir,* Philmont Scout Ranch, Philmont Museum, Cimarron NM

Zimmer, Stephen, *Dir,* Philmont Scout Ranch, Seaton Memorial Library, Cimarron NM

Zimmerer-McKelvie, Kathy, *Gallery Dir,* University Art Gallery of California State University at Dominguez Hills, Dominguez Hills CA

Zimmerman, Edwin M, *Pres,* Textile Museum, Washington DC

Zimmerman, Fred, *Chmn,* State University of New York, College at Cortland, Art Dept, Cortland NY (S)

Zimmerman, Gerald, *Head Special Projects,* Chicago Public Library, Harold Washington Library Center, Chicago IL

Zimmerman, Jerome, *Prof,* C W Post Center of Long Island University, School of Visual & Performing Arts, Greenvale NY (S)

Zimmerman, Salli, *Prof,* Nassau Community College, Art Dept, Garden City NY (S)

Zimmermann, Corinne, *Coordr Patrons & Friends,* Brandeis University, Rose Art Museum, Waltham MA

Zindler, Debra, *Marketing Coordr,* Milwaukee Public Museum, Milwaukee WI

Zingg, Robert, *Exhibition Adminr,* Muckenthaler Cultural Center, Fullerton CA

Zink, James, *Dir,* Southeast Missouri State University, Kent Library, Cape Girardeau MO

Zins, Daniel, *Assoc Prof,* Atlanta College of Art, Atlanta GA (S)

Zinser, Jerry, *Coordr of Arts,* University of New Haven, Dept of Visual & Performing Arts & Philosophy, West Haven CT (S)

Zinser, Robert E, *Treas,* Springfield Museum of Art, Springfield OH

Ziolkowski, Anne, *Museum Dir,* Crazy Horse Memorial, Indian Museum of North America, Crazy Horse SD

Ziolkowski, Ruth, *Chief Executive Officer & Chmn Board,* Crazy Horse Memorial, Indian Museum of North America, Crazy Horse SD

Zippay, Lori, *Dir,* Electronic Arts Intermix, Inc, New York NY

Zirkle, Merle W, *Instr,* Grinnell College, Dept of Art, Grinnell IA (S)

Zivich, Matthew, *Chmn Dept,* Saginaw Valley State University, Dept of Art and Design, University Center MI (S)

Zlotsky, Deborah, *Asst Prof,* University of Northern Iowa, Dept of Art, Cedar Falls IA (S)

Organization Index

Schools are indicated by "S".

Abilene Christian University, Dept of Art, Abilene TX (S)
Abraham Baldwin Agricultural College, Art & Humanities Dept, Tifton GA (S)
Louis Abrons Art Center, New York NY (M)
ACA College of Design, Cincinnati OH (S)
Academy of Art College, Fine Arts Dept, San Francisco CA (S)
Academy of the Arts, Easton MD (M)
Academy of the New Church, Glencairn Museum, Bryn Athyn PA (M)
Acadia University, Art Dept, Wolfville NS (S)
Acadia University Art Gallery, Wolfville NS (M)
Louise Sloss Ackerman Fine Arts Library, see San Francisco Museum of Modern Art, San Francisco CA
Ackland Art Museum, see University of North Carolina at Chapel Hill, Chapel Hill NC
Acme Art Co, Columbus OH (A)
Actual Art Foundation, New York NY (A)
Ansel Adams Center for Photography, see The Friends of Photography, San Francisco CA
Adams County Historical Society, Museum & Cultural Center, Brighton CO (M,L)
Hunter M Adams Architecture Library, see University of Kentucky, Lexington KY
Adams National Historic Site, Quincy MA (M)
Adams State College, Dept of Visual Arts, Alamosa CO (S)
Adamy's Concrete and Cast Paper Workshops, Larchmont NY (S)
Addison Gallery of American Art, see Phillips Academy, Andover MA
Adelphi University, Fine & Performing Arts Library, Garden City NY (L,M)
Adelphi University, Dept of Art and Art History, Garden City NY (S)
Adirondack Historical Association, Adirondack Museum, Blue Mountain Lake NY (M,L)
Adirondack Lakes Center for the Arts, Blue Mountain Lake NY (A)
Adrian College, Art Dept, Adrian MI (S)
Aesthetic Realism Foundation, Eli Siegel Collection, New York NY (A,M,L)
Aesthetic Realism Foundation, New York NY (S)
African American Association, Wilberforce OH (O)
African American Historical and Cultural Society, San Francisco CA (A,L)
Afro-American Historical & Cultural Museum, Philadelphia PA (M)
Agecroft Association, Richmond VA (A,L)
Ages of Man Fellowship, Amenia NY (A)
Agnes Scott College, Dept of Art, Decatur GA (S)
Agriculture & Forestry Museum, see Craftsmen's Guild of Mississippi, Inc, Jackson MS
Aiken County Historical Museum, Aiken SC (M)
Aiken-Rhett House, see Charleston Museum, Charleston SC
Aims Community College, Design & Creative Studies Dept, Greeley CO (S)
A I R Gallery, New York NY (M)
Akron Art Museum, Akron OH (M,L)
Akron-Summit County Public Library, Fine Arts Division, Akron OH (L)

Alabama A & M University, Art and Art Education, Normal AL (S)
Alabama Department of Archives and History Museum, Museum Galleries, Montgomery AL (M,L)
Alabama Southern Community College, Art Dept, Monroeville AL (S)
Alabama State University, Art Dept, Montgomery AL (S)
Alaska Artists' Guild, Anchorage AK (A)
Alaska State Library, Historical Library Section, Juneau AK (L)
Alaska State Museum, Juneau AK (M)
Albany Institute of History and Art, Albany NY (M,L)
Albany Museum of Art, Albany GA (M)
Alberta College of Art, Illingworth Kerr Gallery, Calgary AB (M,L)
Alberta College of Art, Calgary AB (S)
Alberta Foundation For The Arts, Edmonton AB (A)
Alberta Society of Artists, Calgary AB (A)
Albert Lea - Mankato Technical College, Commercial and Technical Art Dept, North Mankato MN (S)
Albertson College of Idaho, Rosenthal Art Gallery, Caldwell ID (M)
Albertus Magnus College, Art Dept, New Haven CT (S)
Albion College, Bobbitt Visual Arts Center, Albion MI (M)
Albion College, Dept of Visual Arts, Albion MI (S)
The Albrecht-Kemper Museum of Art, Saint Joseph MO (M)
Albright College, Dept of Art, Reading PA (S)
Albright College, Freedman Gallery, Reading PA (M)
Albright-Knox Art Gallery, see The Buffalo Fine Arts Academy, Buffalo NY
Albuquerque Museum of Art, History & Science, Albuquerque NM (M)
Albuquerque United Artists, Albuquerque NM (M)
Alcan Aluminium Ltd, Montreal PQ (C)
Alcorn State University, Dept of Fine Arts, Lorman MS (S)
Aldrich Museum of Contemporary Art, Ridgefield CT (M)
Alexandria Library, Alexandria VA (L)
Alexandria Museum of Art, Alexandria LA (M)
Algonquin Arts Council, Bancroft Art Gallery, Bancroft ON (M)
Alice Lloyd College, Art Dept, Pippa Passes KY (S)
Aljira Center for Contemporary Art, Newark NJ (A)
Allan Hancock College, Fine Arts Dept, Santa Maria CA (S)
Allegany Community College, Art Dept, Cumberland MD (S)
Allegany County Historical Society, History House, Cumberland MD (M)
Allegheny College, Bowman, Megahan and Penelec Galleries, Meadville PA (M)
Allegheny College, Art Dept, Meadville PA (S)

Charlotte W Allen Memorial Art Gallery Library, see University of Rochester, Rochester NY
Allen County Community College, Art Dept, Iola KS (S)
Allen County Public Library, Fine Arts Dept, Fort Wayne IN (L)
Allen Memorial Art Museum, see Oberlin College, Oberlin OH
Allentown Art Museum, Allentown PA (M)
Robert Allerton Library, see Honolulu Academy of Arts, Honolulu HI
The Allied Artists of America, Inc, New York NY (O)
Allied Arts Council of Lethbridge, Bowman Arts Center, Lethbridge AB (A)
Allied ArtsGallery of the Yakima Valley, Yakima WA (A,L)
Allied Arts of Seattle, Inc, Seattle WA (A)
Charles Allis Art Museum, Milwaukee WI (M)
Allison Mansion, see Marian College, Indianapolis IN
Lyman Allyn Art Museum, New London CT (M,L)
Alma College, Clack Art Center, Alma MI (S)
Almond Historical Society, Inc, Hagadorn House The 1800-37 Museum, Almond NY (M)
Alternative Museum, New York NY (M)
Alverno College, Art Dept, Milwaukee WI (S)
Alverno College Gallery, Milwaukee WI (M)
Alvin Community College, Art Dept, Alvin TX (S)
Amarillo Art Association, Amarillo TX (A,L)
Amarillo Art Center, see Amarillo Art Association, Amarillo TX
Amarillo College, Art Dept, Amarillo TX (S)
American Abstract Artists, New York NY (O)
American Academy in Rome, New York NY (S)
American Academy of Art, Chicago IL (S)
American Academy of Arts & Letters, New York NY (O)
American Antiquarian Society, Worcester MA (O)
American Architectural Foundation, Washington DC (M,L)
American Artists Professional League, Inc, New York NY (O)
American Association of Museums, Washington DC (O)
American Association of University Women, Washington DC (O)
American Center for Design Gallery, Chicago IL (O)
American Ceramic Society, Westerville OH (O)
American Classical College, Classical Art Gallery, Albuquerque NM (M,L)
American Classical College, Albuquerque NM (S)
American Color Print Society, Philadelphia PA (O)
American Council for the Arts, New York NY (O)
American Craft Council, American Craft Museum, New York NY (M)
American Craft Council, New York NY (O)
The American Federation of Arts, New York NY (O)
American Fine Arts Society, New York NY (O)
The American Foundation for the Arts, Miami FL (O)

Barn Gallery Associates, Inc, Ogunquit ME (A)
Justina M Barnicke Gallery, see University of Toronto, Toronto ON
The Barnum Museum, Bridgeport CT (M)
Barr Colony Heritage Cultural Centre, Lloydminster SK (A)
Barron Arts Center, see Woodbridge Township Cultural Arts Commission, Woodbridge NJ
John D Barrow Art Gallery, Skaneateles NY (M)
Barry University, Dept of Fine Arts, Miami Shores FL (S)
The Bartlett Museum, Amesbury MA (M)
Barton College, Case Art Gallery & Rackley Room Gallery, Wilson NC (M,L)
Barton College, Communication, Performaing & Visual Arts, Wilson NC (S)
Barton County Community College, Fine Arts Dept, Great Bend KS (S)
Bartow-Pell Mansion Museum and Garden, New York NY (M)
Baruch College of the City University of New York, Gallery, New York NY (M)
Basilian Fathers, Mundare AB (A,L)
Bassist College Library, Portland OR (L)
Bass Museum of Art, Miami Beach FL (M)
Bates College, Museum of Art, Lewiston ME (M)
Bates College, Art Dept, Lewiston ME (S)
Baton Rouge Gallery Inc, see East Baton Rouge Parks & Recreation Commission, Baton Rouge LA
Battleship North Carolina, Wilmington NC (M)
Baver Genealogical Library, see Pennsylvania Dutch Folk Culture Society Inc, Lenhartsville PA
Baxter Gallery, see Portland School of Art, Portland ME
Bay County Historical Society, Historical Museum of Bay County, Bay City MI (M)
Baycrafters, Inc, Bay Village OH (A)
Bay De Noc Community College, Art Dept, Escanaba MI (S)
Baylor University, Dept of Art, Waco TX (S)
Baylor University, Waco TX (M,L)
Bayly Art Museum, see University of Virginia, Charlottesville VA
Bayonne Free Public Library, Art Dept, Bayonne NJ (L)
Bay Path College, Dept of Art, Longmeadow MA (S)
Beacon Street Gallery, Uptown, Chicago IL (M)
Beacon Street Gallery & Performance Company, see Uptown Center Hull House Assn, Chicago IL
Beaumont Art League, Beaumont TX (M)
Beaumont Arts Council, Beaumont TX (A)
Beaverbrook Art Gallery, Fredericton NB (M,L)
Beaver College, Dept of Fine Arts, Glenside PA (S)
Beaver College Art Gallery, Glenside PA (M)
Beck Center for the Cultural Arts, Lakewood OH (A)
Beck Cultural Exchange Center, Knoxville TN (M)
Bedford Gallery, see Walnut Creek Regional Center for the Arts, Walnut Creek CA
Beeghly Library, Delaware OH (L)
Belhaven College, Art Dept, Jackson MS (S)
Cecelia Coker Bell Gallery, Hartsville SC (M)
David Winton Bell Gallery, see Brown University, Providence RI
Belle Grove Plantation, Middletown VA (M)
Belleville Area College, Art Dept, Belleville IL (S)
Bellevue Art Museum, Bellevue WA (M)
Bellevue College, Art Dept, Bellevue NE (S)
Bellevue Community College, Art Dept, Bellevue WA (S)
Bellevue Gallery, Bloomington IN (M)
Bellingrath Gardens and Home, Theodore AL (M)
Bell Museum of Natural History, Minneapolis MN (M)
Beloit College, Wright Museum of Art, Beloit WI (M,A)
Beloit College, Dept of Art, Beloit WI (S)
Elmer Belt Library of Vinciana, see University of California, Los Angeles, Los Angeles CA
Bemidji State University, Visual Arts Dept, Bemidji MN (S)
Bemis Foundation, New Gallery, Omaha NE (M)
Benedict College, Art Department, Columbia SC (S)
Benedictine College, Art Dept, Atchison KS (S)

Bennington College, Visual Arts Division, Bennington VT (S)
Bennington Museum, Bennington VT (M,L)
Bent Museum & Gallery, Taos NM (M)
William Benton Museum of Art - Connecticut's State Art Museum, see University of Connecticut, Storrs CT
Berea College, Doris Ulmann Galleries, Berea KY (M,L)
Berea College, Art Dept, Berea KY (S)
Bergen Community College, Visual Art Dept, Paramus NJ (S)
Bergen County Historical Society, Steuben House Museum, River Edge NJ (M)
Bergen Museum of Art & Science, Paramus NJ (M)
Bergstrom Mahler Museum, Neenah WI (M,L)
Berkeley Art Center, Berkeley CA (A)
Berkeley Public Library, Berkeley CA (L)
Berks Art Alliance, Reading PA (A)
Berkshire Artisans, see City of Pittsfield, Pittsfield MA
Berkshire Athenaeum Library, Pittsfield MA (L)
Berkshire Community College, Dept of Fine Arts, Pittsfield MA (S)
Berkshire Museum, Pittsfield MA (M)
Philip & Muriel Berman Museum of Art, see Ursinus College, Collegeville PA
Bernard M Baruch College of the City University of New York, Art Dept, New York NY (S)
Berry College, Art Dept, Mount Berry GA (S)
Berry College, Moon Gallery, Mount Berry GA (M,L)
Jesse Besser Museum, Alpena MI (M,L)
Bethany College, Dept of Fine Arts, Bethany WV (S)
Bethany College, Lindsborg KS (L,M)
Bethany College, Art Dept, Lindsborg KS (S)
Bethany Lutheran College, Art Dept, Mankato MN (S)
Bethel College, Dept of Art, North Newton KS (S)
Bethel College, Mennonite Library & Archives, North Newton KS (L)
Bethel College, Dept of Art, Saint Paul MN (S)
Beverly Hills Public Library, Fine Arts Library, Beverly Hills CA (L)
Beverly Historical Society, Cabot, Hale and Balch House Museums, Beverly MA (M,L)
Beyond Baroque Foundation, Beyond Baroque Literary/Arts Center, Venice CA (A)
Biblical Arts Center, Dallas TX (M)
Bicentennial Art Center & Museum, Paris IL (M)
Big Bend Community College, Art Dept, Moses Lake WA (S)
Biloxi Art Association Inc & Gallery, Biloxi MS (A)
Biola University, Art Dept, La Mirada CA (S)
Birmingham-Bloomfield Art Association, Birmingham MI (A)
Birmingham-Bloomfield Art Association, Birmingham MI (S)
Birmingham Museum of Art, Birmingham AL (M,L)
Birmingham Public Library, Arts, Music & Recreation Department, Birmingham AL (L)
Birmingham Southern College, Doris Wainwright Kennedy Art Center, Birmingham AL (M)
Birmingham-Southern College, Art Dept, Birmingham AL (S)
Bisbee Mining & Historical Museum, Lemuel Shattuck Memorial Library, Bisbee AZ (L)
Bernice Pauahi Bishop Museum, Honolulu HI (M,L)
Bishop Hill State Historis Site, see Illinois Historic Preservation Agency, Bishop Hill IL
Bismarck Junior College, Fine Arts Dept, Bismarck ND (S)
Bixler Art & Music Library, see Colby College, Waterville ME
Blackader-Lauterman Library of Architecture and Art, see McGill University, Montreal PQ
Blackburn College, Dept of Art, Carlinville IL (S)
Black Hawk College, Art Dept, Moline IL (S)
Blackhawk Mountain School of Art Gallery, Blackhawk CO (M)
Black Hills State College, Ruddell Gallery, Spearfish SD (M,L)
Black Hills State University, Art Dept, Spearfish SD (S)

Black River Historical Society, Black River Academy Museum, Ludlow VT (M)
Blacksburg Regional Art Association, Christiansburg VA (A)
Blackwell Library, see Salisbury State University, Salisbury MD
Blackwell Street Center for the Arts, Dover NJ (A)
Blackwood Gallery, see University of Toronto, Mississauga ON
Sarah Campbell Blaffer Gallery, see University of Houston, Houston TX
Blair Art Museum, see Southern Alleghenies Museum of Art, Loretto PA
Blair Museum of Lithophanes and Carved Waxes, Toledo OH (M,L)
Blanden Memorial Art Museum, Fort Dodge IA (M,L)
Mary & Leigh Block Gallery, see Northwestern University, Evanston IL
Bloomington Art Center, Bloomington MN (M)
Bloomsburg University, Dept of Art, Bloomsburg PA (S)
Bloomsburg University of Pennsylvania, Haas Gallery of Art, Bloomsburg PA (M)
Blount-Bridgers House, Hobson Pittman Memorial Gallery, see Edgecombe County Cultural Arts Council, Inc, Tarboro NC
Blount Inc, Montgomery AL (C,L)
Bluefield State College, Art Dept, Bluefield WV (S)
Blue Lake Fine Arts Camp, Art Dept, Twin Lake MI (S)
Blue Mountain College, Art Dept, Blue Mountain MS (S)
Blue Mountain Community College, Fine Arts Dept, Pendleton OR (S)
Blue Mountain Gallery, New York NY (M)
Blue Sky, Oregon Center for the Photographic Arts, Portland OR (M)
Ernest Blumenschein Home, see Kit Carson Historic Museum, Taos NM
Blumenthal Rare Book & Manuscript Library, see Judah L Magnes Museum, Berkeley CA
B'nai B'rith International, B'nai B'rith Klutznick National Jewish Museum, Washington DC (M)
B'nai B'rith Klutznick National Jewish Museum, see B'nai B'rith International, Washington DC
Board of Parks & Recreation, The Parthenon, Nashville TN (M)
The Boatmen's National Bank of St Louis, Art Collection, Saint Louis MO (C)
Bobbitt Visual Arts Center, see Albion College, Albion MI
Bob Jones University, Museum & Art Gallery, Greenville SC (M)
Bob Jones University, School of Fine Arts, Greenville SC (S)
Boca Raton Museum of Art, Boca Raton FL (A,L)
Richard W Bock Sculpture Collection, see Greenville College, Greenville IL
The Richard W Bock Sculpture Collection & Art Library, see Greenville College, Greenville IL
Boehm Gallery, see Palomar Community College, San Marcos CA
Boise Art Museum, Boise ID (M)
Boise State University, Art Dept, Boise ID (S)
William Bonifas Fine Art Center Gallery, Alice Powers Art Gallery, Escanaba MI (M)
Daniel Boone Regional Library, Columbia MO (L)
Boothbay Region Art Foundation, Inc, Brick House Gallery, Boothbay Harbor ME (A)
Boston Architectural Center, Boston MA (A,L)
Boston Art Commission of the City of Boston, Boston MA (A)
Boston Athenaeum, Boston MA (L)
Boston Center for Adult Education, Boston MA (S)
Boston College, Museum of Art, Chestnut Hill MA (M)
Boston College, Fine Arts Dept, Newton MA (S)
The Bostonian Society, Old State House Museum, Boston MA (M,L)
Boston National Historical Park, see USS Constitution Museum Foundation Inc, Boston MA
Boston Printmakers, Boston MA (A)
Boston Public Library, Boston MA (L,M)
Boston University, School of Visual Arts, Boston MA (S)
Boston University, Art Gallery, Boston MA (M)

Boston Visual Artists Union, Boston MA (A)
Muriel Isabel Bostwick Library, see Art Gallery of Hamilton, Hamilton ON
Botanic Hall Library, see Cheekwood-Tennessee Botanical Gardens & Museum of Art, Nashville TN
Boulder Art Center, Boulder CO (A)
Boulder Historical Society Inc, Museum of History, Boulder CO (A)
Boulder Public Library and Gallery, Dept of Fine Arts Gallery, Boulder CO (L)
Bowdoin College, Peary-MacMillan Arctic Museum, Brunswick ME (M)
Bowdoin College, Art Dept, Brunswick ME (S)
Bower's Museum, Santa Ana CA (M)
Bowie State University, Fine Arts Dept, Bowie MD (S)
Bowling Green State University, School of Art, Bowling Green OH (M)
Bowling Green State University, School of Art, Bowling Green OH (S)
Bowling Green State University, Art Dept, Huron OH (S)
Bowman Arts Center, see Allied Arts Council of Lethbridge, Lethbridge AB
Bowman, Megahan and Penelec Galleries, see Allegheny College, Meadville PA
Bowne House Historical Society, Flushing NY (A)
The Dwight Frederick Boyden Gallery, see St Mary's College of Maryland, Saint Mary City MD
Roy Boyd Gallery, Chicago IL (M)
B P America, Cleveland OH (C)
Bradford College, Creative Arts Division, Bradford MA (S)
The Bradford Museum of Collector's Plates, Niles IL (M)
Bradley University, Hartman Center Gallery, Peoria IL (M)
Bradley University, Division of Art, Peoria IL (S)
Braithwaite Fine Arts Gallery, see Southern Utah University, Cedar City UT
Brampton Public Library, Art Gallery, Brampton ON (L)
Branch Banking & Trust Company, Art Collection, Charlotte NC (C)
Brandeis University, Dept of Fine Arts, Waltham MA (S)
Brandeis University, Rose Art Museum, Waltham MA (M,L)
Brand Library & Art Galleries, Glendale CA (L)
Brandywine Battlefield Park, see State Museum of Pennsylvania, Harrisburg PA
Brandywine River Museum, Chadds Ford PA (M,L)
Brandywine Workshop, Philadelphia PA (A)
Brant Historical Society, Brant County Museum, Brantford ON (M,L)
Brattleboro Museum & Art Center, Brattleboro VT (M)
Braun Research Library, see Southwest Museum, Los Angeles CA
Brazosport College, Art Dept, Lake Jackson TX (S)
Brea Civic & Cultural Center Gallery, Brea CA (M)
Bread & Puppet Theater, Museum, Glover VT (M)
Anne Bremer Memorial Library, see San Francisco Art Institute, San Francisco CA
Brenau College, Art Dept, Gainesville GA (S)
Brenner Library, see Quincy University, Quincy IL
Brentwood Art Center, Los Angeles CA (S)
Brescia College, Anna Eaton Stout Memorial Art Gallery, Owensboro KY (M)
Brescia College, Dept of Art, Owensboro KY (S)
Alexander Brest Museum & Gallery, see Jacksonville University, Jacksonville FL
Brevard Art Center and Museum, Inc, Melbourne FL (M)
Brevard College, Division of Fine Arts, Brevard NC (S)
Brevard College, Sims Art Center, Brevard NC (M,L)
Stephen Brew Gallery, Madison WI (M)
Brewton-Parker College, Visual Arts, Mount Vernon GA (S)
Briar Cliff College, Art Dept, Sioux City IA (S)
Brick House Gallery, see Boothbay Region Art Foundation, Inc, Boothbay Harbor ME
Brick Store Museum, Kennebunk ME (M,L)
Bridgewater College, Art Dept, Bridgewater VA (S)

Bridgewater State College, Art Dept, Bridgewater MA (S)
Margaret M Bridwell Art Library, see University of Louisville, Louisville KY
Brigham City Museum-Gallery, Brigham City UT (M)
Brigham Young University, Provo UT (M,L)
Brigham Young University, Dept of Art, Provo UT (S)
Brigham Young University, Hawaii Campus, Division of Fine Arts, Laie HI (S)
Bradford Brinton Memorial Museum & Historic Ranch, Big Horn WY (M)
Bristol-Myers Squibb Co, Princeton NJ (C)
British Columbia Archives & Records Service, Victoria BC (L)
British Columbia Museums Association, Victoria BC (A)
Broad Inc, Kaufman & Broad Home Corp Collection, Los Angeles CA (C)
Brockton Public Library System, Joseph A Driscoll Art Gallery, Brockton MA (L)
Bromfield Gallery, Boston MA (M)
Bronck Museum, see Greene County Historical Society, Coxsackie NY
Saidye Bronfman Centre, Montreal PQ (A)
Silas Bronson Library, Art, Theatre & Music Services, Waterbury CT (L)
Bronx Community College, Music & Art Dept, Bronx NY (S)
Bronx Council on the Arts, Longwood Arts Gallery, Bronx NY (M)
Bronx Museum of the Arts, Bronx NY (M)
BRONX RIVER ART CENTER, Gallery, Bronx NY (M)
Bronxville Public Library, Bronxville NY (L)
Brookdale Community College, Art Dept, Lincroft NJ (S)
Brookfield Craft Center, Inc, Gallery, Brookfield CT (M,L)
Brookgreen Gardens, Murrells Inlet SC (M,L)
Brooklyn Arts Council, BACA Downtown, Brooklyn NY (A)
Brooklyn College, Art Dept, Brooklyn NY (S)
Brooklyn Historical Society, Brooklyn NY (A,L)
Brooklyn Historical Society, Brooklyn OH (M)
Brooklyn Museum, Brooklyn NY (M,L)
Brooklyn Public Library, Art and Music Division, Brooklyn NY (L)
Brookside Museum, see Saratoga County Historical Society, Ballston Spa NY
Brooks Institute Photography Library, Santa Barbara CA (L)
Broward Community College - South Campus, Art Gallery, Pembroke Pines FL (M)
Alice Pratt Brown Library of Art, Architecture & Music, see Rice University, Houston TX
Annmary Brown Memorial, see Brown University, Providence RI
Brown County Art Gallery Association Inc, Nashville IN (A)
Armstrong Browning Library, see Baylor University, Waco TX
John Brown House, see Rhode Island Historical Society, Providence RI
Orlando Brown House, see Liberty Hall Historic Site, Frankfort KY
Brownson Art Gallery, see Manhattanville College, Purchase NY
Brownsville Art League Museum, Brownsville TX (M)
Brown University, Providence RI (M,L)
Brown University, Providence RI (S)
The Bruce Museum, Greenwich CT (M)
Avery Brundage Collection, see Asian Art Museum of San Francisco, San Francisco CA
Brunnier Gallery Museum, see Iowa State University, Ames IA
Richard F Brush Art Gallery, see St Lawrence University, Canton NY
Bryant Library, Roslyn NY (L)
Bry Gallery, see Northeast Louisiana University, Monroe LA
Bryn Mawr College, Art and Archaeology Library, Bryn Mawr PA (L)
Bryn Mawr College, Dept of the History of Art, Bryn Mawr PA (S)

Buchanan Gallery, see Lethbridge Community College, Lethbridge AB
Bucknell University, Center Gallery, Lewisburg PA (M)
Bucknell University, Dept of Art, Lewisburg PA (S)
Richard D Buck Memorial Library, see Balboa Art Conservation Center, San Diego CA
Bucks County Community College, Hicks Art Center, Newtown PA (M)
Bucks County Community College, Fine Arts Dept, Newtown PA (S)
Bucks County Historical Society, Mercer Museum, Doylestown PA (M,L)
Buffalo and Erie County Public Library, Buffalo NY (L)
Buffalo Bill Historical Center, see Buffalo Bill Memorial Association, Cody WY
Buffalo Bill Memorial Association, Buffalo Bill Historical Center, Cody WY (A,M,L)
The Buffalo Fine Arts Academy, Albright-Knox Art Gallery, Buffalo NY (M,L)
Buffalo Museum of Science, Research Library, Buffalo NY (L)
Buffalo Society of Artists, Kenmore NY (A)
Ruth Bunker Memorial Library, see Dacotah Prairie Museum, Aberdeen SD
Burbank Public Library, Warner Research Collection, Burbank CA (A)
Burchfield Art Center, Buffalo NY (M,L)
Thornton W Burgess Society, Inc, Museum, Sandwich MA (M)
Burke Arts Council, Jailhouse Galleries, Morganton NC (M)
Thomas Burke Memorial Washington State Museum, see University of Washington, Seattle WA
Burlington County College, Humanities & Fine Art Div, Pemberton NJ (S)
Burlington County Historical Society, Burlington NJ (A)
Burlington Northern, Saint Paul MN (C)
Burnaby Art Gallery, Burnaby BC (M)
Burroughs Wellcome Company, Art Collection, Research Triangle Park NC (C)
Busch-Reisinger Museum, see Harvard University, Cambridge MA
Bush Barn Art Center, see Salem Art Association, Salem OR
Bush-Holley House, see Historical Society of the Town of Greenwich, Inc, Cos Cob CT
Bush House, see Salem Art Association, Salem OR
Butera School of Art, Boston MA (S)
Butler County Community College, Art Dept, El Dorado KS (S)
Butler Institute of American Art, Art Museum, Youngstown OH (M,L)
Butte College, Oroville CA (S)
Butte Silver Bow Arts Chateau, Butte MT (M)
Byrne Memorial Library, see Saint Xavier University, Chicago IL
Cabot, Hale and Balch House Museums, see Beverly Historical Society, Beverly MA
Cabot's Old Indian Pueblo Museum, Pueblo Art Gallery, Desert Hot Springs CA (M)
Cabrillo College, Visual Arts Division, Aptos CA (S)
Cabrini College, Dept of Fine Arts, Radnor PA (S)
Foster Caddell's Art School, Voluntown CT (S)
Joseph A Cain Memorial Art Gallery, see Del Mar College, Corpus Christi TX
Caldwell College, Art Gallery, Caldwell NJ (M)
Caldwell College, Art Dept, Caldwell NJ (S)
Calgary Contemporary Arts Society, Triangle Gallery of Visual Arts, Calgary AB (M)
Calgary Public Library, Arts & Recreation Dept, Calgary AB (L)
John C Calhoun State Community College, Division of Fine Arts, Decatur AL (S)
California Afro-American Museum, Los Angeles CA (M)
California Baptist College, Art Dept, Riverside CA (S)
California College of Arts and Crafts, Oakland CA (S)
California College of Arts and Crafts Library, Oakland CA (L)
California Confederation of the Arts, Sacramento CA (A)

California Crafts Museum, San Francisco CA (M)

California Historical Society, El Molino Viejo, San Marino CA (M,L)

California Institute of the Arts, School of Art, Valencia CA (S)

California Institute of the Arts Library, Santa Clarita CA (L)

California Lutheran University, Art Dept, Thousand Oaks CA (S)

California Museum of Science and Industry, Los Angeles CA (M)

California Polytechnic State University, College of Architecture & Environmental Design-Art Collection, San Luis Obispo CA (L)

California Polytechnic State University at San Luis Obispo, Dept of Art and Design, San Luis Obispo CA (S)

California State Polytechnic University, Pomona, Art Dept, Pomona CA (S)

California State University, Art Dept, Turlock CA (S)

California State University at Sacramento, Sacramento CA (L,M)

California State University, Bakersfield, Fine Arts Dept, Bakersfield CA (S)

California State University, Chico, University Art Gallery, Chico CA (M,L)

California State University, Chico, Art Dept, Chico CA (S)

California State University, Dominguez Hills, Art Dept, Carson CA (S)

California State University, Fresno, Art Dept, Fresno CA (S)

California State University Fullerton, Art Gallery, Visual Arts Center, Fullerton CA (M)

California State University, Fullerton, Art Dept, Fullerton CA (S)

California State University, Hayward, University Art Gallery, Hayward CA (M)

California State University, Hayward, Art Dept, Hayward CA (S)

California State University, Long Beach, Long Beach CA (S)

California State University, Long Beach, University Art Museum, Long Beach CA (M,L)

California State University, Los Angeles, Fine Arts Gallery, Los Angeles CA (M)

California State University, Los Angeles, Art Dept, Los Angeles CA (S)

California State University, Northridge, Art Galleries, Northridge CA (M)

California State University, Northridge, Dept of Art-Two Dimensional Media, Northridge CA (S)

California State University, Sacramento, Dept of Art, Sacramento CA (S)

California State University, San Bernardino, Art Dept, San Bernardino CA (S)

California State University, San Bernardino, University Art Galleries, San Bernardino CA (M)

California State University Stanislaus, Turlock CA (M,L)

California University of Pennsylvania, Dept of Art, California PA (S)

Joseph A Callaway Archaeological Museum, see Southern Baptist Theological Seminary, Louisville KY

Eleanor Calvert Memorial Library, see Kitchener-Waterloo Art Gallery, Kitchener ON

Calvert Marine Museum, Solomons MD (M,L)

Calvin College, Center Art Gallery, Grand Rapids MI (M)

Calvin College, Art Dept, Grand Rapids MI (S)

Cambria Historical Society, New Providence NJ (M)

Cambridge Art Association, Cambridge MA (A)

Cambridge Public Library and Gallery, Cambridge ON (L)

Camden-Carroll Library, see Morehead State University, Morehead KY

Camden County College, Dept of Art, Blackwood NJ (S)

Cameron University, Art Dept, Lawton OK (S)

Grace Campbell Gallery, see John M Cuelenaere Library, Prince Albert SK

Campbell Hall Gallery, see Western Oregon State College, Monmouth OR

Campbell Museum, Camden NJ (C)

Campbellsville College, Fine Arts Division, Campbellsville KY (S)

Campus Martius Museum and Ohio River Museum, see The Ohio Historical Society, Inc, Marietta OH

Canadian Artists' Representation-Le Front Des Artistes Canadiens, Ottawa ON (A)

Canadiana Sport Art Collection, Canadian Sport and Fitness Centre, Gloucester ON (M)

Canadian Conference of the Arts, Ottawa ON (O)

The Canadian Craft Museum, Vancouver BC (M)

Canadian Crafts Council, Canadien de l'Artisanat, Ottawa ON (O)

Canadian Guild of Crafts, Quebec, see Guilde Canadienne des Metiers d'Art, Quebec, Montreal PQ

Canadian Museum of Civilization, Hull ON (M)

Canadian Museum of Contemporary Photography, Ottawa ON (M)

Canadian Museum of Nature, Musee Canadien de la Nature, Ottawa ON (M)

Canadian Museums Association, Association des Musees Canadiens, Ottawa ON (O)

Canadian Society for Education Through Art, Oakville ON (O)

Canadian Society of Painters in Watercolour, Toronto ON (O)

Canadian Sport and Fitness Centre, see Canadiana Sport Art Collection, Gloucester ON

Canadian War Museum, Ottawa ON (M)

Canadian Wildlife & Wilderness Art Museum, Ottawa ON (M,L)

Canadien de l'Artisanat, see Canadian Crafts Council, Ottawa ON

Canajoharie Art Gallery, Canajoharie NY (M,L)

Canton Art Institute, Canton OH (M,L)

Canton Art Institute, Canton OH (S)

Cape Ann Historical Association, Gallery, Gloucester MA (A,M,L)

Cape Cod Community College, Art Dept, West Barnstable MA (S)

Cape Cod School of Art, Provincetown MA (S)

Capital University, Schumacher Gallery, Columbus OH (M,L)

Capital University, Fine Arts Dept, Columbus OH (S)

Capp Street Project, San Francisco CA (M)

Caramoor Center for Music & the Arts, Inc, Caramoor House Museum, Katonah NY (M)

Cardinal Gallery, see Maryland Hall for the Creative Arts, Annapolis MD

Cardinal Stritch College, Layton Honor Gallery, Milwaukee WI (M)

Cardinal Stritch College, Art Dept, Milwaukee WI (S)

Caribbean Cultural Center, New York NY (M)

Carlen House, see Museum of the City of Mobile, Mobile AL

Carleton College, Dept of Art & Art History, Northfield MN (S)

Carleton University, Dept of Art History, Ottawa ON (S)

Carlow College, Art Dept, Pittsburgh PA (S)

Carlson Gallery, see University of Bridgeport, Bridgeport CT

Carlson Tower Gallery, see North Park College, Chicago IL

Carlsten Art Gallery, see University of Wisconsin-Stevens Point, Stevens Point WI

Carmel Mission and Gift Shop, Carmel CA (M,L)

Carnegie Art Center, Walla Walla WA (A)

Carnegie Art Museum, Oxnard CA (M)

Carnegie Institute, Carnegie Museum of Art, Pittsburgh PA (M,L)

The Carnegie Library of Pittsburgh, Pittsburgh PA (L)

Carnegie Mellon University, Pittsburgh PA (M,L)

Carnegie Mellon University, College of Fine Arts, Pittsburgh PA (S)

Carnegie Museum of Art, see Carnegie Institute, Pittsburgh PA

Carnegie Public Library, Delta Blues Museum, Clarksdale MS (M)

Carolina Art Association, Gibbes Museum of Art, Charleston SC (M,L)

Carrizo Art and Craft Workshops, Ruidoso NM (S)

Carroll College, Art Dept, Waukesha WI (S)

Carson County Square House Museum, Panhandle TX (M)

Kit Carson Historic Museum, Taos NM (A,L,M)

Lucy Carson Memorial Library, see Western Montana College, Dillon MT

Carson-Newman College, Art Dept, Jefferson City TN (S)

Amon Carter Museum, Fort Worth TX (M,L)

Carthage College, Art Dept, Kenosha WI (S)

Cartoon Art Museum, San Francisco CA (M)

George Washington Carver & The Oaks, see Tuskegee Institute National Historic Site, Tuskegee Institute AL

Casa Amesti, Monterey CA (M)

Casa Blanca Museum, see Institute of Puerto Rican Culture, San Juan PR

Cascade County Historical Society, Cascade County Historical Museum & Archives, Great Falls MT (M)

Case Art Gallery & Rackley Room Gallery, see Barton College, Wilson NC

Casemate Museum, see Headquarters Fort Monroe, Dept of Army, Fort Monroe VA

Case Western Reserve University, Dept of Art History & Art, Cleveland OH (S)

Casper College, Dept of Visual Arts, Casper WY (S)

Caspers, Inc, Art Collection, Tampa FL (C)

Castellani Art Museum, see Niagara University, New York NY

Castle Gallery, see College of New Rochelle, New Rochelle NY

Castleton State College, Art Dept, Castleton VT (S)

Cathedral of Saint John the Divine, New York NY (M)

Catholic University of America, Humanities Division, Mullen Library, Washington DC (L)

Catholic University of America, Washington DC (S)

Catholic University of Puerto Rico, Dept of Fine Arts, Ponce PR (S)

Catonsville Community College, Art Dept, Catonsville MD (S)

Catskill Center for Photography, Inc, Woodstock NY (A)

Cavalry - Armor Foundation, Patton Museum of Cavalry & Armor, Fort Knox KY (M)

Cayuga Museum of History and Art, Auburn NY (M,L)

Cazenovia College, Chapman Art Center Gallery, Cazenovia NY (M)

Cazenovia College, Center for Art & Design Studies, Cazenovia NY (S)

Cedar Crest College, Art Dept, Allentown PA (S)

Cedar Grove, see Philadelphia Museum of Art, Philadelphia PA

Cedar Rapids Museum of Art, Cedar Rapids IA (M,L)

Cedar Ridge Creative Centre, see City of Scarborough, Scarborough ON

Centenary College, Div of Fine Arts, Hackettstown NJ (S)

Centenary College of Louisiana, Dept of Art, Shreveport LA (S)

Centenary College of Louisiana, Meadows Museum of Art, Shreveport LA (M)

Centennial Gallery and Gairloch Gallery, see Oakville Galleries, Oakville ON

Centennial Library - Arts Complex, see The Art Gallery of Southwestern Manitoba, Brandon MB

Center-Barron County, Dept of Art, see University of Wisconsin, Rice Lake WI (S)

Center for Book Arts, Inc, New York NY (M)

The Center for Contemporary Arts of Santa Fe, Santa Fe NM (A)

Center for Creative Photography, see University of Arizona, Tucson AZ

Center for Creative Studies, College of Art & Design, Detroit MI (S)

Center for Creative Studies, College of Art & Design Library, Detroit MI (L)

Center for Critical Architecture, 2AES (Art & Architecture Exhibition Space), San Francisco CA (A)

Center for Exploratory & Perceptual Art, CEPA Gallery, Buffalo NY (M,L)

Center for Safety in the Arts, Art Hazards Information Center, New York NY (L)

Center for Southern Folklore, Memphis TN (A)

Center for the Fine Arts, Miami FL (M)

Center on Contemporary Art, Seattle WA (A)

Central Community College - Platte Campus, Business & Arts Cluster, Columbus NE (S)

Central Connecticut State University, Art Dept Museum, New Britain CT (M)

Central Connecticut State University, Dept of Art, New Britain CT (S)

Central Florida Community College, Humanities Dept, Ocala FL (S)

Central Florida Community College Art Collection, Ocala FL (M)

Central Iowa Art Association, Inc, Marshalltown IA (A,L)

Central Michigan University, Dept of Art, Mount Pleasant MI (S)

Central Michigan University, Art Gallery, Mount Pleasant MI (M)

Central Missouri State University, Art Center Gallery, Warrensburg MO (M)

Central Missouri State University, Art Dept, Warrensburg MO (S)

Central Oregon Community College, Dept of Art, Bend OR (S)

Central Piedmont Community College, Visual & Performing Arts, Charlotte NC (S)

Central State University, Dept of Art, Wilberforce OH (S)

Central University of Iowa, Art Dept, Pella IA (S)

Central Washington University, Sarah Spurgeon Gallery, Ellensburg WA (M)

Central Washington University, Dept of Art, Ellensburg WA (S)

Central Wyoming College, Art Center, Riverton WY (S)

Centre Culturel de Trois Rivieres, Trois Rivieres PQ (A)

Centre Gallery, see Miami-Dade Community College, Wolfson Campus, Miami FL

Centre National d' Exposition, see Le Musee Regional de Rimouski, Rimouski PQ

Centro Ceremonial de Caguana, see Institute of Puerto Rican Culture, San Juan PR

Centro Cultural De La Raza, San Diego CA (M)

Century House Museum & Garden, see Arizona Historical Society-Yuma, Yuma AZ

CEPA Gallery, see Center for Exploratory & Perceptual Art, Buffalo NY

Cerritos Community Center, Art Dept, Norwalk CA (S)

Chabot College, Humanities Division, Hayward CA (S)

Chadron State College, Arts Gallery, Chadron NE (M)

Chadron State College, Dept of Art, Speech & Theatre, Chadron NE (S)

Chaffee Art Center, see Rutland Area Art Association, Inc, Rutland VT

Chaffey Community College, Art Dept, Rancho Cucamonga CA (S)

Chalet of the Golden Fleece, New Glarus WI (M)

Chamberlayne School of Design & Merchandising, see Mount Ida College, Boston MA (S)

Stephen Chan Library of Fine Arts, see New York University, New York NY

Chapel Art Center, see Saint Anselm College, Manchester NH

Chapel Gallery, see Muskoka Arts & Crafts Inc, Bracebridge ON

Chapin Library, see Williams College, Williamstown MA

Chapman Art Center Gallery, see Cazenovia College, Cazenovia NY

Chapman Library, see Philbrook Museum of Art, Tulsa OK

Chapman University, Art Dept, Orange CA (S)

Chappell Memorial Library and Art Gallery, Chappell NE (L)

Charles River School, Creative Arts Program, Dover MA (S)

Charles Stewart Mott Community College, Art Area, School of Arts & Humanities, Flint MI (S)

Charleston Museum, Charleston SC (M,L)

Charleston Southern University, Dept of Language & Visual Art, Charleston SC (S)

Chase Home Museum of Utah Folk Art, see Utah Arts Council, Salt Lake City UT

The Chase Manhattan Bank, NA, Art Collection, New York NY (C)

Chateau Ramezay Museum, Montreal PQ (M,L)

Chatham College, Art Gallery, Pittsburgh PA (M)

Chatham College, Fine & Performing Arts, Pittsburgh PA (S)

Chatham Cultural Centre, Thames Art Gallery, Chatham ON (A)

Chatham Historical Society, Old Atwood House, Chatham MA (M)

Chatillon-DeMenil House Foundation, DeMenil Mansion, Saint Louis MO (M)

Chattahoochee Valley Art Museum, LaGrange GA (M)

Chattanooga-Hamilton County Bicentennial Library, Fine Arts & Audio Visuals Department, Chattanooga TN (L)

Chattanooga State Technical Community College, Advertising Arts Dept, Chattanooga TN (S)

Chautauqua Art Association Galleries, Chautauqua NY (M)

Chautauqua Institution, School of Art, Chautauqua NY (S)

Cheekwood-Tennessee Botanical Garden Museum of Art, Education Dept, Nashville TN (S)

Cheekwood-Tennessee Botanical Gardens & Museum of Art, Nashville TN (M,L)

Chelan County Public Utility District, Rocky Reach Dam, Wenatchee WA (M)

Cheltenham Center for the Arts, Cheltenham PA (S)

Chemeketa Community College, Dept of Humanities & Communications, Salem OR (S)

Anne Bunce Cheney Library, see University of Hartford, West Hartford CT

Cherokee National Historical Society, Inc, Tahlequah OK (A,L)

Chesapeake Bay Maritime Museum, Saint Michaels MD (M,L)

Chester County Historical Society, West Chester PA (A)

Chesterwood Museum, see National Trust for Historic Preservation, Glendale MA

Cheyney University of Pennsylvania, Dept of Art, Cheyney PA (S)

Chicago Architecture Foundation, Chicago IL (M)

Chicago Artists' Coalition, Chicago IL (A)

Chicago Children's Museum, Chicago IL (M)

Chicago Historical Society, Chicago IL (A)

Chicago Public Library, Harold Washington Library Center, Chicago IL (L)

Chicago Society of Artists, Inc, Chicago IL (A)

Chicano Humanities & Arts Council, Denver CO (A)

Chicano-Latino Arts Resource Library, see Galeria de la Raza, San Francisco CA

Chief Plenty Coups Museum, Pryor MT (M)

The Children's Aid Society, Visual Arts Program of the Greenwich Village Center, New York NY (S)

Children's Art Foundation, Santa Cruz CA (A)

Children's Museum, Rauh Memorial Library, Indianapolis IN (M)

Children's Museum of Manhattan, New York NY (M)

Chilkat Valley Historical Society, Sheldon Museum & Cultural Center, Haines AK (M,L)

Chilliwack Community Arts Council, Chilliwack BC (A)

China House Gallery, see China Institute in America, New York NY

China Institute in America, China House Gallery, New York NY (M)

Chinese Culture Foundation, Chinese Culture Center Gallery, San Francisco CA (A)

Chinqua-Penn Plantation House, Garden & Greenhouses, see North Carolina State University, Reidsville NC

Chipola Junior College, Division of Fine Arts and Humanities, Marianna FL (S)

Chowan College, Division of Art, Murfreesboro NC (S)

Christian Heurich Mansion, see Historical Society of Washington DC, Washington DC

Christopher Newport College, Arts & Communications, Newport News VA (S)

Chronicle-Tribune Art Gallery, see Taylor University, Upland IN

Jean Outland Chrysler Library, see Chrysler Museum, Norfolk VA

Chrysler Museum, Norfolk VA (M,L)

Chung-Cheng Art Gallery, see Saint John's University, Jamaica NY

Winston Churchill Memorial & Library in the United States, see Westminster College, Fulton MO

Church of Jesus Christ of Latter Day Saints, Mormon Visitors' Center, Independence MO (M)

Church of Jesus Christ of Latter-day Saints, Museum of Church History & Art, Salt Lake City UT (M,L)

Ciba-Geigy Corporation, Art Collection, Ardsley NY (C)

CIGNA Corporation, CIGNA Museum & Art Collection, Philadelphia PA (C)

Cincinnati Academy of Design, Cincinnati OH (S)

Cincinnati Art Club, Cincinnati OH (A)

Cincinnati Artists' Group Effort, Cincinnati OH (A)

Cincinnati Art Museum, see Cincinnati Museum Association, Cincinnati OH

Cincinnati Institute of Fine Arts, Taft Museum, Cincinnati OH (M)

Cincinnati Institute of Fine Arts, Cincinnati OH (A)

Cincinnati Museum Association, Cincinnati Art Museum, Cincinnati OH (M,L)

Citibank, NA, Long Island City NY (C)

Citrus College, Art Dept, Glendora CA (S)

City Art Works, Pratt Fine Arts Center, Seattle WA (S)

City College of New York, Art Dept, New York NY (S)

City College of San Francisco, Art Dept, San Francisco CA (S)

City College of the City University of New York, Morris Raphael Cohen Library, New York NY (L)

City Colleges of Chicago, Chicago IL (S)

City Gallery of Contemporary Art, Raleigh NC (M)

City of Cedar Falls, Iowa, James & Meryl Hearst Center for the Arts, Cedar Falls IA (M)

City of Charleston, City Hall Council Chamber Gallery, Charleston SC (M)

City of Eugene, Hult Center, Jacobs Gallery, Eugene OR (M)

City of Gainesville, Thomas Center Galleries - Cultural Affairs, Gainesville FL (M)

City of Hampton, Hampton Arts Commission, Hampton VA (M)

City of Holyoke Museum-Wistariahurst, Holyoke MA (M)

City of Irvine, Irvine Fine Arts Center, Irvine CA (M)

City of Irvine, Fine Arts Center, Irvine CA (S)

City of Lethbridge, Sir Alexander Galt Museum, Lethbridge AB (M)

City of Los Angeles, Cultural Affairs Dept, Los Angeles CA (M)

The City of Petersburg Museums, Petersburg VA (M)

City of Pittsfield, Berkshire Artisans, Pittsfield MA (M)

City Of Raleigh Arts Commission, Municipal Building Art Exhibitions, Raleigh NC (A)

City of San Rafael, Falkirk Cultural Center, San Rafael CA (M)

City of Scarborough, Cedar Ridge Creative Centre, Scarborough ON (M)

City of Springdale, Shiloh Museum, Springdale AR (M)

City of Tampa, Art in Public Places, Tampa FL (A)

City of Ukiah, Grace Hudson Museum & The Sun House, Ukiah CA (M)

City University of New York, PhD Program in Art History, New York NY (S)

Civic Center Plaza, see Richmond Art Center, Richmond CA

Civic Fine Arts Center, Sioux Falls SD (M,L)

Clackamas Community College, Art Dept, Oregon City OR (S)

Clack Art Center, see Alma College, Alma MI (S)

Claflin College, Dept of Art, Orangeburg SC (S)

Claremont Graduate School, Dept of Fine Arts, Claremont CA (S)

Clarion University, Hazel Sandford Gallery, Clarion PA (M)

Clarion University of Pennsylvania, Dept of Art, Clarion PA (S)

Clark-Atlanta University, School of Arts & Sciences, Atlanta GA (S)

Clark College, Art Dept, Vancouver WA (S)

Clark County Historical Society, Pioneer - Krier Museum, Ashland KS (M)

Clark County Historical Society, Springfield OH (M,L)

Clarke College, Dept of Art, Dubuque IA (S)

Henry B Clarke House Museum, see Chicago Architecture Foundation, Chicago IL

Clark Humanities Museum, see Scripps College, Claremont CA

Robert D Clark Library, see San Jose State University, San Jose CA

Sterling and Francine Clark Art Institute, Williamstown MA (M,L)

Clark University, The University Gallery at Goddard Library, Worcester MA (M)

Clark University, Dept of Visual & Performing Arts, Worcester MA (S)

Wilson W Clark Memorial Library, see University of Portland, Portland OR

Claypool-Young Art Gallery, see Morehead State University, Morehead KY

Clay Studio, Philadelphia PA (M)

Clemson University, Clemson SC (M,L)

Clemson University, College of Architecture, Clemson SC (S)

Cleveland Art Association, see Cleveland Institute of Art, Cleveland OH

Cleveland Center for Contemporary Art, Cleveland OH (M,L)

Cleveland Institute of Art, Reinberger Galleries, Cleveland OH (M,L,A)

Cleveland Institute of Art, Cleveland OH (S)

Cleveland Museum of Art, Cleveland OH (M,L,A)

Cleveland Public Library, Fine Arts & Special Collections Dept, Cleveland OH (L)

Cleveland State Community College, Dept of Art, Cleveland TN (S)

Cleveland State University, Art Dept, Cleveland OH (S)

Cleveland State University, Library & Art Services, Cleveland OH (L,M)

Clinch Valley College of the University of Virginia, Visual & Performing Arts Dept, Wise VA (S)

Clinton Art Association Gallery, Clinton IA (A)

Clinton Community College, Art Dept, Plattsburgh NY (S)

Clinton County Historical Association, Clinton County Historical Museum, Plattsburgh NY (M)

Clinton Historical Museum Village, Clinton NJ (M,L)

Cliveden, Philadelphia PA (M)

The Clocktower Gallery, see Institute for Contemporary Art, Long Island City NY

The Cloisters, see The Metropolitan Museum of Art, New York NY

Jessie L Clough Art Memorial for Teaching, see Rhodes College, Memphis TN

Clowes Fund Collection, see Indianapolis Museum of Art, Indianapolis IN

Clyde Connelly Center for Contemporary Arts, Shreveport LA (M)

Coahoma Community College, Art Education & Fine Arts Dept, Clarksdale MS (S)

Coalition of Women's Art Organizations, Port Washington WI (O)

Cobblestone Museum, see Livingston County Historical Society, Geneseo NY

Cochise College, Art Dept, Douglas AZ (S)

Cochise College, Charles Di Peso Library, Douglas AZ (L)

Cody Country Art League, Cody WY (A)

Coe College, Gordon Fennell Gallery & Marvin Cone Gallery, Cedar Rapids IA (M)

Coe College, Dept of Art, Cedar Rapids IA (S)

Coffeyville Community College, Art Dept, Coffeyville KS (S)

Coffman Union Third Floor Gallery, see University of Minnesota, Minneapolis MN

Cohasset Historical Society, Caleb Lothrop House, Cohasset MA (M)

Cohasset Maritime Museum, see Cohasset Historical Society, Cohasset MA

Morris Raphael Cohen Library, see City College of the City University of New York, New York NY

Coker College, Art Dept, Hartsville SC (S)

Francis Colburn Gallery, see University of Vermont, Burlington VT

Colby College, Musuem of Art, Waterville ME (M,L)

Colby College, Art Dept, Waterville ME (S)

Colby Community College, Visual Arts Dept, Colby KS (S)

Colby-Sawyer College, Dept of Fine & Performing Arts, New London NH (S)

Coleman Library, see Tougaloo College, Tougaloo MS

The Coley Homestead & Barn Museum, Weston CT (A)

Colgate University, Dept of Art & Art History, Hamilton NY (S)

Colgate University, Picker Art Gallery, Hamilton NY (M)

College Art Association, New York NY (O)

The College at New Paltz State University of New York, College Art Gallery, New Paltz NY (M,L)

College of Associated Arts, Saint Paul MN (S)

College of Boca Raton, Art & Design Dept, Boca Raton FL (S)

College of Charleston, School of the Arts, Charleston SC (S)

College of Charleston, Halsey Gallery, Charleston SC (M)

College of DuPage, Humanities Division, Glen Ellyn IL (S)

College of Eastern Utah, Gallery East, Price UT (M)

College of Great Falls, Humanities Div, Great Falls MT (S)

College of Lake County, Art Dept, Grayslake IL (S)

College of Marin, Art Gallery, Kentfield CA (M)

College of Marin, Dept of Art, Kentfield CA (S)

College of Mount Saint Joseph, Art Dept, Cincinnati OH (S)

College of Mount Saint Joseph, Studio San Giuseppe, Cincinnati OH (M,L)

College of Mount Saint Vincent, Fine Arts Dept, Riverdale NY (S)

College of New Rochelle, Castle Gallery, New Rochelle NY (M)

College of New Rochelle School of Arts and Sciences, Art Dept, New Rochelle NY (S)

College of Notre Dame, Dept of Art, Belmont CA (S)

College of Notre Dame of Maryland, Art Dept, Baltimore MD (S)

College of Saint Benedict, Art Dept, Saint Joseph MN (S)

College of Saint Benedict, Art Gallery, Saint Joseph MN (M)

College of Saint Catherine, Visual Arts Dept, Saint Paul MN (S)

College of Saint Elizabeth, Mahoney Library, Morristown NJ (L)

College of Saint Elizabeth, Art Dept, Morristown NJ (S)

College of Saint Francis, Fine Arts Dept, Joliet IL (S)

College of Saint Mary, Art Dept, Omaha NE (S)

College of Saint Rose, Picotte Art Gallery, Albany NY (M)

College of Saint Rose, Dept of Art, Albany NY (S)

College of San Mateo, Creative Arts Dept, San Mateo CA (S)

College of Santa Fe, Visual Arts Dept, Santa Fe NM (S)

College of Southern Idaho, Art Dept, Twin Falls ID (S)

College of Southern Idaho, Herrett Museum & Art Gallery, Twin Falls ID (M)

College of Staten Island, Performing & Creative Arts Dept, Staten Island NY (S)

College of the Associated Arts, Saint Paul MN (M,L)

College of the Canyons, Art Dept, Valencia CA (S)

College of the Desert, Art Dept, Palm Desert CA (S)

College of the Holy Cross, Dept of Visual Arts, Worcester MA (S)

College of the Holy Cross, Dinand Library, Worcester MA (L)

College of the Ozarks, Dept of Art, Point Lookout MO (S)

College of the Redwoods, Arts, Humanities & Social Sciences Division, Eureka CA (S)

College of the Sequoias, Art Dept, Visalia CA (S)

College of the Siskiyous, Art Dept, Weed CA (S)

College of Visual & Performing Arts, see Kutztown University, Kutztown PA (S)

College of William and Mary, Joseph & Margaret Muscarelle Museum of Art, Williamsburg VA (M)

College of William and Mary, Dept of Fine Arts, Williamsburg VA (S)

College of Wooster, Dept of Art, Wooster OH (S)

Colonel Black Mansion, Ellsworth ME (M)

Colonial Architecture Museum, see Institute of Puerto Rican Culture, San Juan PR

Colonial Williamsburg Foundation, Williamsburg VA (M,A,L)

Colony House Museum, see Historical Society of Cheshire County, Keene NH

Colorado City Historical Museum, Colorado City TX (M)

Colorado College, Dept of Art, Colorado Springs CO (S)

Colorado Gallery of the Arts, see Arapahoe Community College, Littleton CO

Colorado Historical Society, Museum, Denver CO (M,L)

Colorado Institute of Art, Denver CO (S)

Colorado Mountain College, Fine Arts Gallery, Breckenridge CO (M)

Colorado Mountain College, Visual & Performing Arts, Vale CO (S)

Colorado Springs Fine Arts Center, Colorado Springs CO (M,L)

Colorado State University, Dept of Art, Fort Collins CO (S)

Colorado State University, Curfman Gallery, Fort Collins CO (M)

Color Association of the US, New York NY (O)

Colter Bay Indian Arts Museum, see Grand Teton National Park Service, Moose WY

Columbia Art Association, see Columbia Museum of Art, Columbia SC

Columbia Basin College, Art Dept, Pasco WA (S)

Columbia College, Art Dept, Chicago IL (S)

Columbia College, Chicago IL (L,M)

Columbia College, Fine Arts, Columbia CA (S)

Columbia College, Art Dept, Columbia MO (S)

Columbia College, Dept of Art, Columbia SC (S)

Columbia College, see Columbia University, New York NY (S)

Columbia County Historical Society, Columbia County Museum, Kinderhook NY (M,L)

Columbia Museum of Art, Columbia SC (M,L,A)

Columbia Museum School, Columbia SC (S)

Columbia River Maritime Museum, Astoria OR (M,L)

Columbia State Community College, Dept of Art, Columbia TN (S)

Columbia University, Avery Architectural and Fine Arts Library, New York NY (L,M)

Columbia University, New York NY (S)

Columbus and Lowndes County Historical Society, Florence McLeod Hazard Museum, Columbus MS (M)

Columbus Chapel & Boal Mansion Museum, Boalsburg PA (M)

Columbus College, Dept of Art, Fine Arts Hall, Columbus GA (S)

Columbus College, The Gallery, Columbus GA (M)

Columbus College of Art and Design, Fine Arts Dept, Columbus OH (S)

Columbus College of Art & Design, Packard Library, Columbus OH (L)

Columbus Cultural Arts Center, Columbus OH (M)

Columbus Metropolitan Library, see Public Library of Columbus and Franklin County, Columbus OH

Columbus Museum, Columbus GA (M)

Columbus Museum of Art, Columbus OH (M,L)

Commerce Bancshares, Inc, Art Collection, Kansas City MO (C)

Commercial Art Division, see Universal Technical Institute, Omaha NE (S)

Community Arts Council of Vancouver, Vancouver BC (A)

Community College of Allegheny County, Fine Arts Dept, West Mifflin PA (S)

Community College of Allegheny County, Boyce Campus, Art Dept, Monroeville PA (S)

Community College of Rhode Island, Art Department Gallery, Warwick RI (M)

Community College of Rhode Island, Dept of Art, Warwick RI (S)

Community Council for the Arts, Kinston NC (A)

The Community Education Center, Philadelphia PA (A)

Community Gallery of Lancaster County, Lancaster PA (M)

Compton Community College, Compton CA (S)

Concord Art Association, Concord MA (A)

Concord College, Fine Art Division, Athens WV (S)

Concordia College, Bronxville NY (S)

Concordia College, Art Dept, Moorhead MN (S)

Concordia College, Art Dept, Saint Paul MN (S)

Concordia College, Marx Hausen Art Gallery, Seward NE (M)

Concordia College, Art Dept, Seward NE (S)

Concordia Historical Institute, Saint Louis MO (M)

Concordia Lutheran College, Dept of Fine Arts, Austin TX (S)

Concordia University, Division of Arts & Sciences, Mequon WI (S)

Concordia University, Leonard & Bina Ellen Art Gallery, Montreal PQ (M)

Concordia University, Faculty of Fine Arts, Montreal PQ (S)

Concordia University Wisconsin, Fine Art Gallery, Mequon WI (M)

Concord Museum, Concord MA (M,L)

Conejo Valley Art Museum, Thousand Oaks CA (M)

Confederate Museum, see Louisiana Historical Association, New Orleans LA

Confederation Centre Art Gallery and Museum, Charlottetown PE (M,L)

Congregation Emanu-El, New York NY (M)

Congressional Arts Caucus, Washington DC (O)

Conkling Gallery Art Dept, see Mankato State University, Mankato MN

Connecticut College, New London CT (S)

Connecticut Historical Commission, Sloane-Stanley Museum, Kent CT (M)

Connecticut Historical Society, Hartford CT (A,L)

Connecticut Institute of Art, Greenwich CT (S)

Connecticut Institute of Art Galleries, Greenwich CT (M)

Connecticut State Library, Museum of Connecticut History, Hartford CT (L)

Connecticut Valley Historical Museum, see Springfield Library & Museums Association, Springfield MA

Connecticut Women Artists, Inc, Guiford CT (A)

The Contemporary, Museum for Contemporary Arts, Baltimore MD (M)

Contemporary Art Gallery society of British Columbia, Vancouver BC (M,L)

Contemporary Arts Center, Cincinnati OH (M,L)

Contemporary Arts Center, New Orleans LA (A)

Contemporary Arts Museum, Houston TX (M)

Contemporary Art Workshop, Chicago IL (A)

Contemporary Art Workshop, Chicago IL (S)

Contemporary Crafts Association and Gallery, Portland OR (M,L)

The Contemporary Museum, Honolulu HI (M)

Continental Bank Corporation, Art Collection, Chicago IL (C)

Contra Costa Community College, Dept of Art, San Pablo CA (S)

Converse College, Art Dept, Spartanburg SC (S)

Converse College, Milliken Art Gallery, Spartanburg SC (M)

Cooke County College, Div of Communications & Fine Arts, Gainesville TX (S)

Cooke County College Library, Art Dept, Gainesville TX (L)

Cookeville Art Gallery, see Cumberland Art Society Inc, Cookeville TN

Douglas F Cooley Memorial Art Gallery, see Reed College, Portland OR

Cooper-Hewitt, National Museum of Design, New York NY (M,L)

Cooperstown Art Association, Cooperstown NY (A)

Cooper Union for the Advancement of Science & Art, Library, New York NY (L)

Cooper Union School of Art, New York NY (S)

Coos Art Museum, Coos Bay OR (M)

Coos Art Museum, Coos Bay OR (S)

Coos County Historical Society Museum, North Bend OR (M)

Copper Village Museum & Arts Center, Anaconda MT (A,L)

Coppini Academy of Fine Arts, San Antonio TX (A,L)

Coppin State College, Dept Fine & Communication Arts, Baltimore MD (S)

Coquille Valley Art Association, Coquille OR (A,L)

Corcoran Gallery of Art, Washington DC (M,L)

Corcoran School of Art, Washington DC (S)

Cork Gallery, see Lincoln Center for the Performing Arts, New York NY

Cornell College, Armstrong Gallery, Mount Vernon IA (M)

Cornell College, Art Dept, Mount Vernon IA (S)

George D and Harriet W Cornell Fine Arts Museum, see Rollins College, Winter Park FL

Cornell University, Herbert F Johnson Museum of Art, Ithaca NY (M,L)

Cornell University, Ithaca NY (S)

Corning Community College, Division of Humanities, Corning NY (S)

Corning Museum of Glass, Corning NY (M,L)

Cornish College of the Arts, Art Dept, Seattle WA (S)

Cornish College of the Arts, Cornish Galleries, Seattle WA (M,L)

Cornish Galleries, see Cornish College of the Arts, Seattle WA

Coronado School of Fine Arts, Coronado CA (S)

Corporate Council for the Arts, Seattle WA (A)

Corpus Christi State University, Weil Art Gallery, Corpus Christi TX (M)

Cortland County Historical Society, Suggett House Museum, Cortland NY (M,L)

Cortland Free Library, Cortland NY (L)

Cosanti Foundation, Scottsdale AZ (A)

Cottey College, Art Dept, Nevada MO (S)

Cotting-Smith-Assembly House, see Peabody & Essex Museum, Salem MA

Cottonlandia Museum, Greenwood MS (M)

Council of Delaware Artists, Middletown DE (A)

Council of Ozark Artists and Craftsmen, Inc, Arts Center of the Ozarks Gallery, Springdale AR (M)

County College of Morris, Art Dept, Randolph NJ (S)

County of Henrico, Meadow Farm Museum, Glen Allen VA (M)

Courtney Art Gallery, see Jersey City State College, Jersey City NJ

Couse Memorial Library, see Saginaw Art Museum, Saginaw MI

Warren Hall Coutts III Memorial Museum of Art, El Dorado KS (M)

Cowboy Artists of America Museum Foundation, Kerrville TX (M,L)

Cheney Cowles Museum, see Eastern Washington State Historical Society, Spokane WA

Craft Alliance Gallery & Education Center, Saint Louis MO (M)

Craft and Folk Art Museum, Los Angeles CA (M,L)

Crafts Guild of Manitoba, Inc, Library, Winnipeg MB (L)

Craftsmen's Guild of Mississippi, Inc, Agriculture & Forestry Museum, Jackson MS (M)

Craigdarroch Castle Historical Museum Society, Victoria BC (A)

Cranbrook Academy of Art, Bloomfield Hills MI (S)

Cranbrook Academy of Art Museum, Bloomfield Hills MI (M,L)

Crane Collection Gallery, Boston MA (M)

Crary Art Gallery Inc, Warren PA (M)

Crawford County Historical Society, Baldwin-Reynolds House Museum, Meadville PA (M)

Crazy Horse Memorial, Indian Museum of North America, Crazy Horse SD (M)

Creative Art Center, Pontiac MI (S)

Creative Arts Center, Pontiac MI (A)

Creative Arts Guild, Dalton GA (A)

Creative Growth Art Center, Oakland CA (M)

Creative Time, New York NY (A)

Creek Council House Museum, Okmulgee OK (M,L)

Creighton University, Fine Arts Gallery, Omaha NE (M)

Creighton University, Fine and Performing Arts Dept, Omaha NE (S)

George Ayres Cress Gallery of Art, see University of Tennessee at Chattanooga, Chattanooga TN

Crestar Bank, Art Collection, Richmond VA (C)

Cripple Creek District Museum, Cripple Creek CO (M)

Crocker Art Museum, Sacramento CA (M,L)

Crook County Museum and Art Gallery, Sundance WY (M)

Crooked Tree Arts Council, Virginia M McCune Community Arts Center, Petoskey MI (M)

Crossman Gallery, see University Of Wisconsin-Whitewater, Whitewater WI

Crowder College, Art & Design, Neosho MO (S)

Crowley Art Association, The Gallery, Crowley LA (A)

Crowninshield-Bentley House, see Peabody & Essex Museum, Salem MA

Crow Wing County Historical Society, Brainerd MN (M)

Cuban Museum, see Museum of Arts and Sciences, Daytona Beach FL

John M Cuelenaere Library, Grace Campbell Gallery, Prince Albert SK (M)

Cuesta College, Art Dept, San Luis Obispo CA (S)

Cuesta College, Cuesta College Art Gallery, San Luis Obispo CA (L)

Irene Cullis Gallery, see Greensboro College, Greensboro NC

Cultural Affairs Department City of Los Angeles, Junior Arts Center, Los Angeles CA (A,L)

Cultural Council Foundation, Fourteen Sculptors Gallery, New York NY (M)

Culver-Stockton College, Division of Fine Arts, Canton MO (S)

Cumberland Art Society Inc, Cookeville Art Gallery, Cookeville TN (A)

Cumberland College, Dept of Art, Williamsburg KY (S)

Cumberland County College, Humanities Div, Vineland NJ (S)

DeEtte Holden Cummer Museum Foundation, see Cummer Gallery of Art, Jacksonville FL

Cummer Gallery of Art, DeEtte Holden Cummer Museum Foundation, Jacksonville FL (M,L)

Curfman Gallery, see Colorado State University, Fort Collins CO

The Currier Gallery of Art, Manchester NH (M,L)

Cushing House Museum, see Historical Society of Old Newbury, Newburyport MA

Custer County Art Center, Miles City MT (A)

Custom House Maritime Museum, see Newburyport Maritime Society, Newburyport MA

Cuyahoga Community College, Dept of Art, Cleveland OH (S)

Cuyahoga Valley Art Center, Cuyahoga Falls OH (S)

C W Post Campus of Long Island University, Hillwood Art Museum, Brookville NY (M)

C W Post Center of Long Island University, School of Visual & Performing Arts, Greenvale NY (S)

Cypress College, Fine Arts Gallery, Cypress CA (M)

Cypress College, Cypress CA (S)

Dacotah Prairie Museum, Lamont Gallery, Aberdeen SD (M,L)

Daemen College, Fanette Goldman & Carolyn Greenfield Gallery, Amherst NY (M,L)

Daemen College, Art Dept, Amherst NY (S)

Dahl Fine Arts Center, see Rapid City Fine Arts Council, Rapid City SD

Dakota State University, College of Liberal Arts, Madison SD (S)

Dakota Territorial Museum, see Yankton County Historical Society, Yankton SD

Dutchess Community College, Dept of Visual Arts, Poughkeepsie NY (S)
Dutchess County Arts Council, Poughkeepsie NY (M)
Dyson College of Arts & Sciences, see Pace University, Pleasantville NY (S)
Eagle Gallery, see Murray State University, Murray KY
Earlham College, Leeds Gallery, Richmond IN (M)
Earlham College, Art Dept, Richmond IN (S)
East Baton Rouge Parks & Recreation Commission, Baton Rouge Gallery Inc, Baton Rouge LA (M)
East Bay Asian Local Development Corp, Asian Resource Gallery, Oakland CA (M)
East Carolina University, Wellington B Gray Gallery, Greenville NC (M,L)
East Carolina University, School of Art, Greenville NC (S)
East Central College, Art Dept, Union MO (S)
East Central Community College, Art Dept, Decatur MS (S)
East Central University, Art Dept, Ada OK (S)
East End Arts & Humanities Council, Riverhead NY (A)
Eastern Arizona College, Art Dept, Thatcher AZ (S)
Eastern Community College, Dept of Art, Venice Beach CA (S)
Eastern Connecticut State University, Fine Arts Dept, Willimantic CT (S)
Eastern Illinois University, Tarble Arts Center, Charleston IL (M)
Eastern Illinois University, Art Dept, Charleston IL (S)
Eastern Iowa Community College, Art Dept, Clinton IA (S)
Eastern Kentucky University, Art Dept, Richmond KY (S)
Eastern Michigan University, Ford Gallery, Ypsilanti MI (M,L)
Eastern Michigan University, Dept of Art, Ypsilanti MI (S)
Eastern Montana College, Art Dept, Billings MT (S)
Eastern New Mexico University, Dept of Art, Portales NM (M,L)
Eastern New Mexico University, Dept of Art, Portales NM (S)
Eastern Oregon State College, Arts & Humanities Dept, La Grande OR (S)
Eastern Shore Art Association, Inc, Art Center, Fairhope AL (A,L)
Eastern Washington State Historical Society, Cheney Cowles Museum, Spokane WA (M,L)
Eastern Washington University, Dept of Art, Cheney WA (S)
Eastern Wyoming College, Art Dept, Torrington WY (S)
Eastfield College, Humanities Division, Art Dept, Mesquite TX (S)
East Hampton Library, Pennypacker Long Island Collection, East Hampton NY (L)
East Los Angeles College, Art Dept, Monterey Park CA (S)
East Los Angeles College, Vincent Price Gallery, Monterey Park CA (M)
East Martello Museum and Gallery, see Key West Art and Historical Society, Key West FL
East Stroudsburg University, Art Dept, East Stroudsburg PA (S)
East Tennessee State University, Johnson City TN (M,L)
East Tennessee State University, Fine Arts Dept, Johnson City TN (S)
East Texas State University, University Gallery, Commerce TX (M)
East Texas State University, Dept of Art, East Texas Station, Commerce TX (S)
East Windsor Historical Society, Inc, Scantic Academy Museum, East Windsor CT (M)
Eberdt Museum of Communications, Heritage Sutton, Sutton PQ (M)
Eccles Community Art Center, Ogden UT (A)
Eckerd College, Art Dept, Saint Petersburg FL (S)
Ecole des Arts Visuels, see L'Universite Laval, Quebec PQ

Edgecombe County Cultural Arts Council, Inc, Blount-Bridgers House, Hobson Pittman Memorial Gallery, Tarboro NC (M)
Edgewood College, Art Dept, Madison WI (S)
Edgewood College, DeRicci Gallery, Madison WI (M)
Edinboro University of Pennsylvania, Art Dept, Edinboro PA (S)
Edison Community College, Gallery of Fine Art, Fort Myers FL (M)
Edison Community College, Dept of Fine and Performing Arts, Fort Myers FL (S)
Edmonton Art Gallery, Edmonton AB (M,L)
Edmonton Public Library, Foyer Gallery, Edmonton AB (L)
Edmundson Art Foundation, Inc, Des Moines Art Center, Des Moines IA (M,L)
Education Alliance, Art School, New York NY (S)
Edward-Dean Museum, see Riverside County Museum, Cherry Valley CA
Emily Edwards & Ursuline Sales Gallery, see Southwest Craft Center, San Antonio TX
Egner Fine Arts Center, see Findlay College, Findlay OH
Dwight D Eisenhower Presidential Library, Abilene KS (L)
Eiteljorg Museum of American Indian & Western Art, Indianapolis IN (M)
El Camino College, Division of Fine Arts, Torrance CA (S)
El Camino College Art Gallery, Torrance CA (M)
Elder Gallery, see Nebraska Wesleyan University, Lincoln NE
Electronic Arts Intermix, Inc, New York NY (A)
Elgin Community College, Fine Arts Dept, Elgin IL (S)
Elizabeth City State University, Dept of Art, Elizabeth City NC (S)
Leonard & Bina Ellen Art Gallery, see Concordia University, Montreal PQ
Elliott Museum, see Historical Society of Martin County, Stuart FL
Ellis County Museum Inc, Waxahachie TX (M)
Ellsworth Community College, Dept of Fine Arts, Iowa Falls IA (S)
Elmhurst College, Art Dept, Elmhurst IL (S)
Elmira College, George Waters Gallery, Elmira NY (M)
Elmira College, Art Dept, Elmira NY (S)
El Molino Viejo, see California Historical Society, San Marino CA
El Museo del Barrio, New York NY (M)
El Paso Museum of Art, El Paso TX (M,L)
Elvehjem Museum of Art, see University of Wisconsin-Madison, Madison WI
Walter Elwood Museum, see Mohawk Valley Heritage Association, Inc, Amsterdam NY
Embarcadero Center Ltd, San Francisco CA (C)
Emerald Empire Art Gallery, Springfield OR (A)
Fred L Emerson Gallery, see Hamilton College, Clinton NY
Emily Carr College of Art & Design, Vancouver BC (S)
Emily Carr College of Art & Design, The Charles H Scott Gallery, Vancouver BC (M,L)
Emily Carr Gallery Archives, Victoria BC (M)
Emmanuel College, Art Dept, Boston MA (S)
Emmanuel Gallery, see Auraria Higher Education Center, Denver CO
Emma Willard School, Arts Division, Troy NY (S)
Emory University, Art History Dept, Atlanta GA (S)
Emory University, Museum of Art & Archaeology, Atlanta GA (M)
Emporia State University, Division of Art, Emporia KS (S)
Emporia State University, Norman R Eppink Art Gallery, Emporia KS (M)
Endicott College, Art Dept, Beverly MA (S)
En Foco, Inc, Bronx NY (M)
Englewood Library, Fine Arts Dept, Englewood NJ (L)
Amos Eno Gallery, New York NY (M)
Enook Galleries, Waterloo ON (M)
Environment Canada - Canadian Parks Service, Laurier House, Ottawa ON (A)

Ephraim McDowell-Cambus-Kenneth Foundation, McDowell House & Apothecary Shop, Danville KY (M)
Norman R Eppink Art Gallery, see Emporia State University, Emporia KS
Max Epstein Archive, see University of Chicago, Chicago IL
Equitable Life Assurance Society, New York NY (C)
Erie Art Museum, Erie PA (M)
Erie County Library System, Plavcan Gallery, Erie PA (L)
Erie Historical Museum & Planetarium, Erie PA (M)
Escuela de Artes Plasticas, see Institute of Puerto Rican Culture, San Juan PR (S)
Escuela de Artes Plasticas Galleria, see Institute of Puerto Rican Culture, San Juan PR
Wharton Esherick Museum, Wharton Esherick Studio, Paoli PA (M)
Eskimo Museum, Churchill MB (M,L)
Essex Art Association, Inc, Essex CT (A)
Essex Historical Society, Essex Shipbuilding Museum, Essex MA (M)
Essex Shipbuilding Museum, see Essex Historical Society, Essex MA
Estevan National Exhibition Centre Inc, Estevan SK (M)
Agnes Etherington Art Centre, see Queen's University, Kingston ON
Ethnic American Slide Library, see University of South Alabama, Mobile AL
Euphrat Gallery, see De Anza College, Cupertino CA
Evansdale Library, see West Virginia University, Morgantown WV
Evanston Art Center, Evanston IL (A)
Evanston Historical Society, Charles Gates Dawes House, Evanston IL (M)
Evansville Museum of Arts and Science, Evansville IN (M,L)
Everett Community College, Art Dept, Everett WA (S)
Evergreen House, see Johns Hopkins University, Baltimore MD
Evergreen State College, Evergreen Galleries, Olympia WA (M)
Everhart Museum, Scranton PA (M)
Everson Museum of Art, Syracuse NY (M)
Ewing Gallery of Art and Architecture, see University of Tennessee, Knoxville TN
Exchange National Bank of Chicago, Chicago IL (C)
Exit Art, New York NY (M)
Exploratorium, San Francisco CA (A)
Eye Gallery, San Francisco CA (M)
Eyes and Ears Foundation, San Francisco CA (A)
Henry Failing Art and Music Dept, see Multnomah County Library, Portland OR
Fairbanks Arts Association, Fairbanks AK (A)
Fairbanks Gallery, see Oregon State University, Corvallis OR
Fairbanks Museum and Planetarium, Saint Johnsbury VT (M)
Fairfield Art Association, see Fairfield Public Library, Fairfield IA
Fairfield Historical Society, Fairfield CT (A,L)
Fairfield Public Library, Fairfield Art Association, Fairfield IA (L)
Fairfield University, Fine Arts Dept, Fairfield CT (S)
Fairfield University, Thomas J Walsh Art Gallery, Fairfield CT (M)
Fairlawn Mansion & Museum, see Douglas County Historical Society, Superior WI
Fairleigh Dickinson University, Florham Madison Campus Library - Art Dept, Madison NJ (L)
Fairleigh Dickinson University, Fine Arts Dept, Rutherford NJ (S)
Fairmont State College, Div of Fine Arts, Fairmont WV (S)
Fairmount Park Art Association, Philadelphia PA (A)
Falkirk Cultural Center, see City of San Rafael, San Rafael CA
Fall River Historical Society, Fall River MA (M)
Fanette Goldman & Carolyn Greenfield Gallery, see Daemen College, Amherst NY

Foundry School Museum, see Putnam County Historical Society, Cold Spring NY

Fourteen Sculptors Gallery, see Cultural Council Foundation, New York NY

Fowler Museum of Cultural History, see University of California, Los Angeles, Los Angeles CA

Foyer Gallery, see Edmonton Public Library, Edmonton AB

Framingham State College, Art Dept, Framingham MA (S)

Franchise Finance Corporation of America, The Fleischer Museum, Scottsdale AZ (A,L)

Francis Marion University, Fine Arts Dept, Florence SC (S)

Franklin and Marshall College, Art Dept, Lancaster PA (S)

Franklin College, Art Dept, Franklin IN (S)

Franklin Furnace Archive, Inc, New York NY (L)

Franklin Mint Museum, Franklin Center PA (M)

Franklin Pierce College, Dept of Fine Arts & Graphic Communications, Rindge NH (S)

Frank Phillips College, Art Dept, Borger TX (S)

Fraunces Tavern Museum, New York NY (M)

Fredericton National Exhibition Centre, Fredericton NB (M)

Freedman Gallery, see Albright College, Reading PA

Free Library of Philadelphia, Philadelphia PA (L)

Freeport Art Museum & Cultural Center, Freeport IL (M,L)

Free Public Library, Art and Music Dept, Trenton NJ (L)

Free Public Library of Elizabeth, Fine Arts Dept, Elizabeth NJ (L)

Freer Gallery of Art, Washington DC (M)

Freer Gallery of Art & The Arthur M Sackler Gallery Gallery, Washington DC (M,L)

French Art Colony, Gallipolis OH (A,L)

French Institute-Alliance Francaise, Library, New York NY (L)

Fresno Arts Center & Museum, Fresno CA (M)

Fresno City College, Art Dept, Fresno CA (S)

Fresno Metropolitan Museum, Fresno CA (M)

The Frick Art Museum, Pittsburgh PA (M)

Frick Art Reference Library, New York NY (L)

Frick Collection, New York NY (M)

Henry Clay Frick Fine Arts Dept, see University of Pittsburgh, Pittsburgh PA (S)

Henry Clay Frick Fine Arts Library, see University of Pittsburgh, Pittsburgh PA

Fried, Frank, Harris, Shriver & Jacobson, Art Collection, New York NY (C)

Lee M Friedman Memorial Library, see American Jewish Historical Society, Waltham MA

Friends Historical Library, see Swarthmore College, Swarthmore PA

The Friends of Photography, Ansel Adams Center for Photography, San Francisco CA (A)

Friends of the Arts and Sciences, Hilton Leech Studio, Leech Studio Workshops, Sarasota FL (S)

Friends of the Beloit College Museums, see Beloit College, Beloit WI

Friends University, Art Dept, Wichita KS (S)

Friends University, Wichita KS (S)

Frontier Times Museum, Bandera TX (M)

Frostburg State University, The Stephanie Ann Roper Gallery, Frostburg MD (M,L)

Frostburg State University, Dept of Visual Arts, Frostburg MD (S)

Frost Library, see Amherst College, Amherst MA

Fruitlands Museum, Inc, Harvard MA (M,L)

Charles and Emma Frye Art Museum, Seattle WA (M,L)

Fudan Museum Foundation, Ambler PA (A)

Fuller Lodge Art Center, Los Alamos NM (M)

Fuller Museum of Art, Brockton MA (A,L)

Fullerton College, Division of Fine Arts, Fullerton CA (S)

Fulton County Historical Society Inc, Fulton County Museum & Round Barn Museum, Rochester IN (M,L)

Fulton County Museum Reference Room, see Fulton County Historical Society Inc, Rochester IN

Fulton County Museum & Round Barn Museum, see Fulton County Historical Society Inc, Rochester IN

Fulton-Hayden Memorial Library, see Amerind Foundation, Inc, Dragoon AZ

The Fund for the Borough of Brooklyn, The Rotunda Gallery, Brooklyn NY (M)

J Furlong Gallery, see University of Wisconsin-Stout, Menomonie WI

Furman University, Dept of Art, Greenville SC (S)

Gadsden Museum, Mesilla NM (M)

Gadsden Museum of Fine Arts, Inc, Gadsden AL (M)

Galeria de la Raza, Studio 24, San Francisco CA (M,L)

Galeria Mesa, Mesa Arts Center, Mesa AZ (M)

Galerie d'art de l'Universite de Moncton, Moncton NB (M)

Galerie de l'Atelier, Laval PQ (M)

Galerie Restigouche Gallery, Campbellton NB (M)

Galesburg Civic Art Center, Galesburg IL (A)

Galleries of the Claremont Colleges, Claremont CA (M)

The Gallery at Hawaii Loa College, Marinda Lee Gallery, Kaneohe HI (M)

Gallery at the School, see Beacon Street Gallery, Chicago IL

Gallery East, see College of Eastern Utah, Price UT

Gallery 57, Fullerton CA (M)

Gallery Lambton, Sarnia ON (L)

Gallery North, Setauket NY (M)

Gallery of DuPont Hall, see Washington & Lee University, Lexington VA

Gallery of Prehistoric Paintings, New York NY (M,L)

Gallery on the Roof, see Saskpower, Regina SK

The Gallery Stratford, see Stratford Art Association, Stratford ON

Gallery West Ltd, Alexandria VA (M)

Gallery 76, see Wenatchee Valley College, Wenatchee WA

Gallier House Museum, see Tulane University, New Orleans LA

Sir Alexander Galt Museum, see City of Lethbridge, Lethbridge AB

Game and Parks Commission, Arbor Lodge State Historical Park, Nebraska City NE (M)

Gananoque Historical Museum, Gananoque ON (M)

Gaol Museum, see Old York Historical Society, York ME

Garden City Community College, Art Dept, Garden City KS (S)

Gardiner Art Gallery, see Oklahoma State University, Stillwater OK

George R Gardiner Museum of Ceramic Art, Toronto ON (M)

Isabella Stewart Gardner Museum, Boston MA (M,L)

Gardner-Pingree House, see Peabody & Essex Museum, Salem MA

Garibaldi & Meucci Meuseum, see Order Sons of Italy in America, Staten Island NY

Linda Garrett Reference Library, see Oklahoma City University, Oklahoma City OK

Gaston College, Art Dept, Dallas NC (S)

Gaston County Museum of Art & History, Dallas NC (M,L)

Gavilan College, Art Gallery, Gilroy CA (M)

Gavilan College, Art Dept, Gilroy CA (S)

Helen Palmer Geisel Library, see Museum of Contemporary Art, San Diego, La Jolla CA

M Christina Geis Gallery, see Georgian Court College Gallery, Lakewood NJ

General Board of Discipleship, The United Methodist Church, The Upper Room Chapel & Museum, Nashville TN (M)

General Mills, Inc, Art Collection, Minneapolis MN (C)

General Services Administration, Washington DC (O)

Genesee Country Museum, John L Wehle Gallery of Sporting Art, Mumford NY (M)

George Brown College of Applied Arts and Technology, Dept of Visual Arts, Toronto ON (S)

George Mason University, Dept of Art & Art History, Fairfax VA (S)

Georgetown College, Art Dept, Georgetown KY (S)

Georgetown College Gallery, Georgetown KY (M)

Georgetown University, Art and History Museum, Washington DC (M,L)

Georgetown University, Dept of Fine Arts, Washington DC (S)

George Washington University, The Dimock Gallery, Washington DC (M)

George Washington University, Dept of Art, Washington DC (S)

Georgia College, Art Dept, Milledgeville GA (S)

Georgia Council For The Arts, Atlanta GA (A)

Georgia Institute of Technology, College of Architecture Library, Atlanta GA (L)

Georgia Institute of Technology, College of Architecture, Atlanta GA (S)

Georgia Museum of Art, see University of Georgia, Athens GA

Georgian Court College, Dept of Art, Lakewood NJ (S)

Georgian Court College Gallery, M Christina Geis Gallery, Lakewood NJ (M)

Georgia Southern University, Dept of Art, Statesboro GA (S)

Georgia Southwestern College, Art Gallery, Americus GA (M)

Georgia Southwestern College, Dept of Fine Arts, Americus GA (S)

Georgia State University, School of Art & Design, Atlanta GA (S)

Georgia State University, School of Art & Design, Visual Resource Library & Reading Room, Atlanta GA (L,M)

Georgia Volunteer Lawyers for the Arts, Inc, Atlanta GA (A)

Getty Center for the History of Art & the Humanities Trust Museum, Santa Monica CA (L)

Gettysburg College, Dept of Art, Gettysburg PA (S)

The J Paul Getty Museum, see Getty Center for the History of Art & the Humanities Trust Museum, Santa Monica CA

Ghost Ranch Living Museum, Abiquiu NM (M)

Gibbes Museum of Art, see Carolina Art Association, Charleston SC

Gibbes Museum School, Gibbes Museum Studio, Charleston SC (S)

Gibson Barham Gallery, see Imperial Calcasieu Museum, Lake Charles LA

Gibson House Museum, see Gibson Society, Inc, Boston MA

Roland Gibson Gallery, see Potsdam College of the State University of New York, Potsdam NY

Gibson Society, Inc, Gibson House Museum, Boston MA (M)

Thomas Gilcrease Institute of American History & Art, Tulsa OK (M,L)

Wendell Gilley Museum, Southwest Harbor ME (M)

The Gilman Paper Company, New York NY (C)

Gilpin County Arts Association, Central City CO (A)

Adam & Sophie Gimbel Design Library, see Parsons School of Design, New York NY

Girard College, Stephen Girard Collection, Philadelphia PA (M)

Stephen Girard Collection, see Girard College, Philadelphia PA

Giustina Gallery, see Oregon State University, Corvallis OR

Glassell School of Art, Houston TX (S)

Glenbow Museum, Calgary AB (M,L)

Glencairn Museum, see Academy of the New Church, Bryn Athyn PA

Glendale Community College, Dept of Fine Arts, Glendale CA (S)

Glendale Federal Savings, Glendale CA (C)

Glenhyrst Art Gallery of Brant, Brantford ON (M,L)

Glenville State College, Dept of Fine Arts, Glenville WV (S)

Glessner House, see Chicago Architecture Foundation, Chicago IL

Gloridale Partnership, National Museum of Woodcarving, Custer SD (M)

Gloucester County College, Liberal Arts Dept, Sewell NJ (S)

Charles B Goddard Center for the Visual and Performing Arts, Ardmore OK (A)

Goddard College, Visual Arts Dept, Plainfield VT (S)

Morton R Godine Library, see Massachusetts College of Art, Boston MA
Godwin-Ternbach Museum, see Queens College, City University of New York, Flushing NY
Gogebic Community College, Fine Arts Dept, Ironwood MI (S)
Golden Paley Gallery, see Moore College of Art & Design, Philadelphia PA
Golden State Mutual Life Insurance Company, Afro-American Art Collection, Los Angeles CA (C)
Golden West College, Visual Art Dept, Huntington Beach CA (S)
Goldsboro Art Center, Goldsboro NC (S)
Goldstein Gallery, see University of Minnesota, Saint Paul MN
Robert Goldwater Library, see The Metropolitan Museum of Art, New York NY
Gonzaga University, Dept of Art, Spokane WA (S)
Gonzaga University, Ad Art Gallery, Spokane WA (M)
Gordon College, Dept of Fine Arts, Barnesville GA (S)
Donald B Gordon Memorial Library, see Palm Beach County Parks & Recreation Department, Delray Beach FL
Goshen College, Art Dept, Goshen IN (S)
Goshen Historical Society, Goshen CT (M)
Goucher College, Art Dept, Towson MD (S)
Goucher College, Rosenberg Gallery, Towson MD (M)
Governors State University, College of Arts & Science, Art Dept, University Park IL (S)
Grace College, Dept of Art, Winona Lake IN (S)
Graceland College, Fine Arts Dept, Lamoni IA (S)
Graceland Museum & American Saddlehorse Museum, see Audrain County Historical Society, Mexico MO
Grambling State University, Art Dept, Grambling LA (S)
Grand Canyon University, Art Dept, Phoenix AZ (S)
Grand Marais Art Colony, Grand Marais MN (S)
Grand Prairie Arts Council, Inc, Arts Center of the Grand Prairie, Stuttgart AR (A)
Grand Rapids Art Museum, Grand Rapids MI (M,L)
Grand Rapids Junior College, Art Dept, Grand Rapids MI (S)
Grand Rapids Public Library, Music & Art Dept, Grand Rapids MI (L)
Grand Teton National Park Service, Colter Bay Indian Arts Museum, Moose WY (A)
Grand Valley State University, Art & Design Dept, Allendale MI (S)
Grand View College, Art Dept, Des Moines IA (S)
Grant Wood & Memorial Park Gallery, see Paint 'N Palette Club, Anamosa IA
Graphic Artists Guild, New York NY (A)
The Gray Gallery, see Quincy University, Quincy IL
Grayson County College, Art Dept, Denison TX (S)
Wellington B Gray Gallery, see East Carolina University, Greenville NC
Greater Hartford Community College, Humanities Division & Art Dept, Hartford CT (S)
Greater Lafayette Museum of Art, Lafayette IN (M,L)
Great Lakes Historical Society, Vermilion OH (M)
Greene County Historical Society, Bronck Museum, Coxsackie NY (M)
Greene County Historical Society, Xenia OH (A)
Greene & Greene Library of the Arts & Crafts Movement, see Univ of Southern California, San Marino CA
Albert M Greenfield Library, see University of the Arts, Philadelphia PA
Greenfield Community College, Art, Graphic Design & Media Communication Dept, Greenfield MA (S)
Green Hill Center for North Carolina Art, Greensboro NC (M)
Ida Green Gallery, see Austin College, Sherman TX
Green Mountain College, Dept of Art, Poultney VT (S)
Green Research Library, see Old Jail Art Center, Albany TX

Green River Community College, Art Dept, Auburn WA (S)
Greensboro Artists' League, Greensboro NC (A)
Greensboro College, Dept of Art, Division of Fine Arts, Greensboro NC (S)
Greensboro College, Irene Cullis Gallery, Greensboro NC (M)
Greenville College, Richard W Bock Sculpture Collection, Greenville IL (M,L)
Greenville College, Division of Language, Literature & Fine Arts, Greenville IL (S)
Greenville County Museum of Art, Greenville SC (M)
Greenville County Museum of Art, Museum School of Art, Greenville SC (S)
Greenville Museum of Art, Inc, Greenville NC (A,L)
Greenville Technical College, Art History Dept, Greenville SC (S)
The Greenwich Art Society Inc, Greenwich CT (A)
Greenwich House Pottery, New York NY (S)
Greenwich Library, Greenwich CT (L)
Grey Art Gallery and Study Center, see New York University, New York NY
Griffis Sculpture Park, see Ashford Hollow Foundation for Visual & Performing Arts, East Otto NY
Grinnell College, Dept of Art, Grinnell IA (S)
Grinnell College, Print & Drawing Study Room/ Gallery, Grinnell IA (M)
Florence Griswold Museum, see Lyme Historical Society, Old Lyme CT
Grolier Club Library, New York NY (L)
Grossmont College, Art Dept, El Cajon CA (S)
Grossmont Community College, Hyde Gallery, El Cajon CA (M)
M Grumbacher Inc, Cranbury NJ (C)
Grunwald Center for the Graphic Arts, see University of California, Los Angeles, Los Angeles CA
Guadalupe Cultural Arts Center, San Antonio TX (A)
Guadalupe Historic Foundation, Santuario de Guadalupe, Santa Fe NM (M)
John Simon Guggenheim Memorial Foundation, New York NY (A)
Solomon R Guggenheim Museum, New York NY (M,L)
Guild Art Center, New Canaan CT (S)
Guilde Canadienne des Metiers d'Art, Quebec, Canadian Guild of Crafts, Quebec, Montreal PQ (A)
Guild Hall of East Hampton, Inc, Guild Hall Museum, East Hampton NY (M)
Guild of Book Workers, New York NY (O)
Guild of Boston Artists, Boston MA (A)
Guild of Creative Art, Shrewsbury NJ (S)
Guilford College, Art Dept, Greensboro NC (S)
Guilford Technical Community College, Commercial Art Dept, Jamestown NC (S)
Gulf Coast Community College, Division of Fine Arts, Panama City FL (S)
Jessica Gund Memorial Library, see Cleveland Institute of Art, Cleveland OH
Emery A Gunnin Architectural Library, see Clemson University, Clemson SC
Gunston Hall Plantation, Lorton VA (M,L)
Gustavus Adolphus College, Art & Art History Dept, Saint Peter MN (S)
Haas Gallery of Art, see Bloomsburg University of Pennsylvania, Bloomsburg PA
Hagadorn House The 1800-37 Museum, see Almond Historical Society, Inc, Almond NY
Hagerstown Junior College, Art Dept, Hagerstown MD (S)
Haggerty Museum of Art, see Marquette University, Milwaukee WI
The Haggin Museum, see San Joaquin Pioneer and Historical Society, Stockton CA
Halifax Historical Society, Inc, Halifax Historical Museum, Daytona Beach FL (M)
Hallmark Cards, Inc, Kansas City MO (C,L)
Hall of State, see Dallas Historical Society, Dallas TX
Hallwalls Contemporary Arts Center, Buffalo NY (M)
Halsey Gallery, see College of Charleston, Charleston SC

Hamilton College, Fred L Emerson Gallery, Clinton NY (M)
Hamilton College, Art Dept, Clinton NY (S)
Hamline University, Art Dept, Saint Paul MN (S)
Hamline University Learning Center Gallery, Saint Paul MN (M,L)
Hammond Castle Museum, Gloucester MA (M)
Hammond-Harwood House Association, Inc, Annapolis MD (M)
Hammond Museum & Japanese Stroll Garden, Cross-Cultural Center, North Salem NY (M)
Hamon Arts Library, see Southern Methodist University, Dallas TX
Hampden-Booth Theatre Library, see Players, New York NY
Hampshire County Public Library, Romney WV (L)
Hampton Arts Commission, see City of Hampton, Hampton VA
Hampton University, University Museum, Hampton VA (M)
Hampton University, Art Dept, Hampton VA (S)
John Hancock Warehouse, see Old York Historical Society, York ME
Hancock Shaker Village, Inc, Pittsfield MA (M,L)
Handforth Gallery, see Tacoma Public Library, Tacoma WA
Handweavers Guild of America, Bloomfield CT (A)
Hand Workshop, Virginia Center for the Craft Arts, Richmond VA (A)
Hannibal La Grange College, Art Dept, Hannibal MO (S)
Hanover College, Dept of Art, Hanover IN (S)
Dane G Hansen Memorial Museum, Logan KS (M)
Harcum Junior College, Dept of Fine Arts, Bryn Mawr PA (S)
Harding University, Dept of Art, Searcy AR (S)
Hardin-Simmons University, Art Dept, Abilene TX (S)
Harford Community College, Fine & Applied Arts Dept, Div of Arts & Sciences, Bel Air MD (S)
Harlow Gallery, see Kennebec Valley Art Association, Hallowell ME
Foster Harmon Galleries of American Art, Sarasota FL (M,L)
Harold Washington College, see City Colleges of Chicago, Chicago IL (S)
Harrington Institute of Interior Design, Chicago IL (S)
Harrington Institute of Interior Design, Design Library, Chicago IL (L)
Harrisburg Area Community College, Division of Communication and the Arts, Harrisburg PA (S)
Harrison County Historical Museum, Marshall TX (M)
Nora Eccles Harrison Museum of Art, Logan UT (M)
Houston Harte University Center, see Angelo State University, San Angelo TX
Hartford Art School, see University of Hartford, West Hartford CT
Hartford Public Library, Art Dept, Hartford CT (L)
Hartland Art Council, Hartland MI (A)
Hartman Center Gallery, see Bradley University, Peoria IL
Hart Nautical Galleries and Collections, see Massachusetts Institute of Technology, Cambridge MA
Hartnell College, Art and Photography Dept, Salinas CA (S)
Hartnell College Gallery, Salinas CA (M)
Stephen H Hart Library, see Colorado Historical Society, Denver CO
Hartwick College, Foreman Gallery, Oneonta NY (M)
Hartwick College, Art Dept, Oneonta NY (S)
William S Hart Museum, see Los Angeles County Museum of Natural History, Newhall CA
Harvard University, Cambridge MA (M,L)
Harvard University, Dept of Fine Arts, Sackler Museum, Cambridge MA (S)
Harvard University, Dumbarton Oaks Research Library and Collections, Washington DC (M,L)
Harvestworks, Inc, New York NY (A)
Ruth Harvey Art Gallery, see Museum of Northern British Columbia, Prince Rupert BC
The Harwood Foundation, see University of New Mexico, Taos NM

Haskell Indian Junior College, Art Dept, Lawrence KS (S)

Hasting Gallery, see Springfield College, Springfield MA

Hastings College, Art Dept, Hastings NE (S)

Hastings County Museum, Belleville ON (M)

Hastings Museum, Hastings NE (M)

Marx Hausen Art Gallery, see Concordia College, Seward NE

Haverford College, Fine Arts Dept, Haverford PA (S)

Haverhill Public Library, Art Dept, Haverhill MA (L)

Hayden Library, see Arizona State University, Tempe AZ

Jean P Haydon Museum, Pago Pago, American Samoa PI (M)

Haymarket Art Gallery, Lincoln NE (M)

Haynes Fine Arts Gallery, see Montana State University, Bozeman MT

Haystack Mountain School of Crafts, Gallery, Deer Isle ME (M,L)

Haystack Mountain School of Crafts, Deer Isle ME (S)

Hayward Area Forum of the Arts, Sun Gallery, Hayward CA (M)

Florence McLeod Hazard Museum, see Columbus and Lowndes County Historical Society, Columbus MS

Headlands Center for the Arts, Sausalito CA (A)

Headley-Whitney Museum, Lexington KY (M,L)

Headquarters Fort Monroe, Dept of Army, Casemate Museum, Fort Monroe VA (M)

Heard Museum, Phoenix AZ (M,L)

Hearst Art Gallery, see Saint Mary's College of California, Moraga CA

James & Meryl Hearst Center for the Arts, see City of Cedar Falls, Iowa, Cedar Falls IA

Phoebe Apperson Hearst Museum of Anthropology, see University of California, Berkeley CA

Hebrew Union College, Skirball Museum, Los Angeles CA (M)

Hebrew Union College - Jewish Institute of Religion, Skirball Museum-Cincinnati Branch, Cincinnati OH (M)

Heckscher Museum, Huntington NY (M,L)

Heidelberg College, Dept of Art, Tiffin OH (S)

Harry D Hendren Gallery, see Lindenwood College, Saint Charles MO

Jack R Hennesey Art Galleries, see St Clair County Community College, Port Huron MI

Henry Art Gallery, see University of Washington, Seattle WA

Henry Ford Community College, Art Dept, Dearborn MI (S)

Patrick Henry Memorial Foundation, Red Hill National Memorial, Brookneal VA (M)

Henry Street Settlement Arts for Living Center, New York NY (S)

Gertrude Herbert Memorial Institute of Art, Augusta GA (M)

Heritage Center Archives, see Turtle Mountain Chippewa Historical Society, Belcourt ND

Heritage Center, Inc, Pine Ridge SD (M)

Heritage Center of Lancaster County, Lancaster PA (M)

Heritage Plantation of Sandwich, Sandwich MA (M)

Heritage Sutton, see Eberdt Museum of Communications, Sutton PQ

Herkimer County Community College, Social Sciences & Humanities Division, Herkimer NY (S)

Grover M Hermann Fine Arts Center, see Marietta College, Marietta OH

Hermitage Foundation Museum, Norfolk VA (M,L)

Herrett Museum & Art Gallery, see College of Southern Idaho, Twin Falls ID

Herron School of Art, see Indiana University-Purdue University, Indianapolis, Indianapolis IN (S)

Herron School of Art Library, see Indiana University - Purdue University at Indianapolis, Indianapolis IN

Hershey Museum, Hershey PA (M)

Hesston College, Hesston KS (S)

Heublein, Inc, Farmington CT (C)

Hewitt Memorial Library, see Washington State Historical Society, Tacoma WA

Hewlett-Woodmere Public Library, Hewlett NY (L)

Heyward-Washington House, see Charleston Museum, Charleston SC

Hibbing Community College, Art Dept, Hibbing MN (S)

Edna Hibel Art Foundation, Hibel Museum of Art, Palm Beach FL (M,L)

Hickory Museum of Art, Inc, Hickory NC (M,L)

Hicks Art Center, see Bucks County Community College, Newtown PA

Hidalgo County Historical Museum, Edinburg TX (M)

Higgins Armory Museum, Worcester MA (M,L)

High Desert Museum, Bend OR (M)

Highland Community College, Freeport IL (S)

High Museum of Art, Atlanta GA (M,L)

High Plains Museum, McCook NE (M)

High Point College, Fine Arts Dept, High Point NC (S)

High Point Historical Society Inc, Museum, High Point NC (A)

Hill College, Fine Arts Dept, Hillsboro TX (S)

Hill Country Arts Foundation, Ingram TX (A)

Hillel Foundation, Hillel Jewish Student Center Gallery, Cincinnati OH (M)

Hillel Jewish Student Center Gallery, see Hillel Foundation, Cincinnati OH

Hillsborough Community College, Fine Arts Dept, Tampa FL (S)

Hillsdale College, Art Dept, Hillsdale MI (S)

Hill-Stead Museum, Farmington CT (M)

Hillwood Art Museum, see C W Post Campus of Long Island University, Brookville NY

Hillwood Museum, see Marjorie Merriweather Post Foundation of DC, Washington DC

Hillyer Art Library, see Smith College, Northampton MA

Hinckley Foundation Museum, Ithaca NY (M)

Hinds Community College, Dept of Art, Raymond MS (S)

Hinds Junior College District, Marie Hull Gallery, Raymond MS (M)

Hiram College, Art Dept, Hiram OH (S)

Hirsch Library, see Museum of Fine Arts, Houston, Houston TX

Hirshhorn Museum and Sculpture Garden, Washington DC (M,L)

Hispanic Society of America, Museum, New York NY (M,L)

Historical and Cultural Affairs, Delaware State Museums, Dover DE (M)

Historical Museum of Bay County, see Bay County Historical Society, Bay City MI

Historical Society of Bloomfield, Bloomfield NJ (M)

Historical Society of Cheshire County, Colony House Museum, Keene NH (M,L)

Historical Society of Delaware, Wilmington DE (M,L)

Historical Society of Kent County, Chestertown MD (A)

Historical Society of Martin County, Elliott Museum, Stuart FL (M)

Historical Society of Okaloosa & Walton Counties, Inc, Historical Society Museum, Valparaiso FL (M)

Historical Society of Old Newbury, Cushing House Museum, Newburyport MA (M)

Historical Society of Palm Beach County, West Palm Beach FL (A)

Historical Society of Pennsylvania, Philadelphia PA (A)

Historical Society of Rockland County, New City NY (M)

Historical Society of the Cocalico Valley, Ephrata PA (A)

Historical Society of the Town of Greenwich, Inc, Bush-Holley House, Cos Cob CT (M)

Historical Society of Washington DC, Christian Heurich Mansion, Washington DC (M,L)

Historical Society of York County, York PA (A,L)

Historic Cherry Hill, Albany NY (M)

Historic Deerfield, Inc, Deerfield MA (M,L)

Historic Houses of Odessa, see Winterthur Museum and Gardens, Winterthur DE

Historic Hudson Valley, Tarrytown NY (M,L)

Historic Landmarks Foundation of Indiana, Morris-Butler House, Indianapolis IN (M,L)

Historic Northampton Museum, Northampton MA (M)

Historic Pensacola Preservation Board, Historic Pensacola Village, Pensacola FL (A,L)

Historic Saint Augustine Preservation Board, Saint Augustine FL (A)

Allen R Hite Art Institute, see University of Louisville, Louisville KY (S)

Allen R Hite Art Institute Gallery, see University of Louisville, Louisville KY

Hiwan Homestead Museum, see Jefferson County Open Space, Evergreen CO

Hobart and William Smith Colleges, Art Dept, Geneva NY (S)

Hockaday Center for the Arts, Kalispell MT (A)

Hoffberger School of Painting, see Maryland Institute, Baltimore MD (S)

Hoffman Gallery, see Oregon School of Arts and Crafts, Portland OR

Elise N Hofheimer Art Library, see Old Dominion University, Norfolk VA

Hofstra University, Hofstra Museum, Hempstead NY (M)

Hofstra University, Hempstead NY (S)

Alexandre Hogue Gallery, see University of Tulsa, Tulsa OK

Holland College, Centre of Creative Arts Library & Gallery, Charlottetown PE (L)

Holland College, Centre of Creative Arts, Charlottetown PE (S)

Hollins College, Art Dept, Roanoke VA (S)

Hollywood Art Center School, Hollywood CA (S)

Hollywood Art Museum, Hollywood FL (M)

The Holtzman Art Gallery, see Towson State University, Towson MD

Holy Names College, Art Dept, Oakland CA (S)

Holyoke Community College, Dept of Art, Holyoke MA (S)

Homewood House Museum, see Johns Hopkins University, Baltimore MD

Honeywell Inc, Art Collection, Minneapolis MN (C)

Honolulu Academy of Arts, Honolulu HI (M,L)

Honolulu Academy of Arts, The Art Center at Linekona, Honolulu HI (S)

Honolulu Community College, Honolulu HI (S)

Hood College, Dept of Art, Frederick MD (S)

Hood Museum of Art, see Dartmouth College, Hanover NH

Hoosier Salon Patrons Association, Hoosier Salon Art Gallery, Indianapolis IN (A)

Dorothy H Hoover Library, see Ontario College of Art, Toronto ON

Herbert Hoover Presidential Library & Museum, West Branch IA (L)

Hope College, Art Dept, Holland MI (S)

Hope College, De Pree Art Center & Gallery, Holland MI (M)

Henry Radford Hope School of Fine Arts, see Indiana University, Bloomington, Bloomington IN (S)

Hopewell Museum, Hopewell NJ (M)

Hopi Cultural Center Museum, Second Mesa AZ (M)

Hopper Resource Library, see Butler Institute of American Art, Youngstown OH

Horizons Unlimited Supplementary Educational Center, Art Gallery, Salisbury NC (M)

Horner Museum, see Oregon State University, Corvallis OR

Hot Springs Art Center, Fine Arts Center, Hot Springs AR (M)

Houghton College, Art Dept, Houghton NY (S)

Housatonic Community College, Housatonic Museum of Art, Bridgeport CT (M,L)

Housatonic Community College, Art Dept, Bridgeport CT (S)

House of Happy Walls, see Jack London State Historic Park, Glen Ellen CA

House of Roses, Senator Wilson Home, Deadwood SD (M)

Houston Baptist University, Dept of Art, Houston TX (S)

Houston Baptist University, Museum of American Architecture and Decorative Arts, Houston TX (M)

International Sculpture Center, Washington DC (M)

International Society of Copier Artists (ISCA), New York NY (O)

Intersection for the Arts, San Francisco CA (A)

Inter-Society Color Council, Lawrenceville NJ (O)

Iona College, Seton School of Associate Degree Studies, Art Dept, Yonkers NY (S)

Iowa Central Community College, Dept of Art, Fort Dodge IA (S)

Iowa City - Johnson County Arts Council, Arts Center, Iowa City IA (A)

Iowa Lakes Community College, Dept of Art, Estherville IA (S)

Iowa State Education Association, Salisbury House, Des Moines IA (M)

Iowa State University, Dept of Art and Design, Ames IA (S)

Iowa State University, Brunnier Gallery Museum, Ames IA (M)

Iowa Wesleyan College, Art Dept, Mount Pleasant IA (S)

Iowa Western Community College, Art Dept, Council Bluffs IA (S)

Iroquois County Historical Society Museum, Old Courthouse Museum, Watseka IL (M)

Iroquois Indian Museum, Howes Cave NY (M)

Irvine Fine Arts Center, see City of Irvine, Irvine CA

Islip Art Museum, East Islip NY (M)

Ithaca College, Fine Art Dept, Ithaca NY (S)

Jackson County Historical Society, 1859 Jail, Marshal s Home & Museum, Independence MO (M,L)

Jackson Hall Gallery, see Kentucky State University, Frankfort KY

Jackson Square Artists Association, New Orleans LA (A)

Jackson State University, Dept of Art, Jackson MS (S)

Jacksonville Art Museum, Jacksonville FL (M,L)

Jacksonville Public Library, Fine Arts & Recreation Dept, Jacksonville FL (L)

Jacksonville State University, Art Dept, Jacksonville AL (S)

Jacksonville University, Dept of Art, Jacksonville FL (S)

Jacksonville University, Alexander Brest Museum & Gallery, Jacksonville FL (M)

Jacobs Gallery, see City of Eugene, Hult Center, Eugene OR

Jailhouse Galleries, see Burke Arts Council, Morganton NC

Jamaica Arts Center, Jamaica NY (M)

James Madison University, Sawhill Gallery, Harrisonburg VA (M)

James Madison University, Dept of Art, Harrisonburg VA (S)

Jamestown College, Art Dept, Jamestown ND (S)

Jamestown Community College, Visual & Performing Arts Division, Jamestown NY (S)

Jamestown Community College, The Forum Gallery, Jamestown NY (M)

Jamestown-Yorktown Foundation, Yorktown VA (M)

Japanese American Cultural & Community Center, George J Doizaki Gallery, Los Angeles CA (M)

Japan Society, Inc, New York NY (M,L)

Japantown Art & Media Workshop, San Francisco CA (A)

Jardin Botanique de Montreal, Bibliotheque, Montreal PQ (L)

John Jay Homestead State Historic Site, see New York State Office of Parks Recreation & Historic Preservation, Katonah NY

Jefferds Tavern, see Old York Historical Society, York ME

Jefferson Community College, Fine Arts, Louisville KY (S)

Jefferson Community College, Art Dept, Watertown NY (S)

Jefferson County Historical Museum, Pine Bluff AR (M)

Jefferson County Historical Society, Watertown NY (M,L)

Jefferson County Historical Society Museum, Madison IN (M)

Jefferson County Open Space, Hiwan Homestead Museum, Evergreen CO (M)

Jefferson Davis Community College, Art Dept, Brewton AL (S)

Thomas Jefferson Memorial Foundation, Monticello, Charlottesville VA (M)

Jekyll Island Museum, Jekyll Island GA (M)

Arthur D Jenkins Library, see Textile Museum, Washington DC

Jericho Historical Society, Jericho VT (A)

Jersey City Museum, Jersey City NJ (M)

Jersey City State College, Courtney Art Gallery, Jersey City NJ (M)

Jersey City State College, Art Dept, Jersey City NJ (S)

Jewett Gallery, see University of Maine at Augusta, Augusta ME

Jewish Community Center of Greater Washington, Jane L & Robert H Weiner Judaic Museum, Rockville MD (M)

Jewish Community Centre of Toronto, The Koffler Gallery, North York ON (M)

The Jewish Museum, New York NY (M,L)

John Brown University, Art Dept, Siloam Springs AR (S)

John Carroll University, Dept of Art History & Humanities, Cleveland OH (S)

John C Calhoun State Community College, Art Gallery, Decatur AL (M)

John Jay College of Criminal Justice, Dept of Art, Music and Philosophy, New York NY (S)

Johns Hopkins University, Baltimore MD (M,L)

Johns Hopkins University, Baltimore MD (S)

Johnson Atelier Technical Institute of Sculpture, Mercerville NJ (S)

Johnson Atelier Technical Institute of Sculpture, Johnson Atelier Library, Mercerville NJ (L)

Johnson Collection of Photographs, Movies & Memorabilia, see Martin & Osa Johnson Safari Museum, Inc, Chanute KS

Johnson County Community College, Visual Arts Program, Overland Park KS (S)

Grace Phillips Johnson Art Gallery, see Phillips University, Enid OK

Herbert F Johnson Museum of Art, see Cornell University, Ithaca NY

Johnson-Humrickhouse Museum, Coshocton OH (M,L)

John G Johnson Collection, see Philadelphia Museum of Art, Philadelphia PA

Johnson & Johnson, Art Program, New Brunswick NJ (C)

Martin & Osa Johnson Safari Museum, Inc, Chanute KS (M)

Johnson State College, Dept Fine Arts, Dibden Gallery, Johnson VT (S)

Johnstown Art Museum, see Southern Alleghenies Museum of Art, Loretto PA

Joliet Junior College, Fine Arts Dept, Joliet IL (S)

Joliet Junior College, Laura A Sprague Art Gallery, Joliet IL (M)

Jones County Junior College, Art Dept, Ellisville MS (S)

Fred Jones Jr Museum of Art, see University of Oklahoma, Norman OK

James A Jones Library, see Brevard College, Brevard NC

John Paul Jones House, see Portsmouth Historical Society, Portsmouth NH

Jones Library, Inc, Amherst MA (L)

Jones Memorial Library, Jones Memorial Library, Lynchburg VA (L)

Jones Memorial Library, see Jones Memorial Library, Lynchburg VA

Jonson Gallery, see University of New Mexico, Albuquerque NM

Jordan Historical Museum of The Twenty, Jordan ON (M)

Jorgensen Gallery, see University of Connecticut, Storrs CT

Joseloff Gallery, see University of Hartford, West Hartford CT

Joslyn Art Museum, Omaha NE (M,L)

J Sargeant Reynolds Community College, Humanities & Social Science Division, Richmond VA (S)

Judiciary History Center, Honolulu HI (M)

Judson College, Division of Fine Arts, Elgin IL (S)

Judson College, Division of Fine Arts, Marion AL (S)

Juniata College, Dept of Art, Huntingdon PA (S)

Junior Arts Center, see Cultural Affairs Department City of Los Angeles, Los Angeles CA

Junior College of Albany, Fine Arts Division, Albany NY (S)

Kala Institute, Berkeley CA (A)

Kalamazoo College, Art Dept, Kalamazoo MI (S)

Kalamazoo Institute of Arts, Kalamazoo MI (M,L)

Kalamazoo Institute of Arts, KIA School, Kalamazoo MI (S)

Kalamazoo Valley Community College, Humanities Development Center, Kalamazoo MI (S)

Kalani Honua Institute for Cultural Studies, Pahoa HI (S)

Kamloops Art Gallery, Kamloops BC (M)

Kamserloni Art Gallery, Kamloops BC (M)

Kansas City Art Institute, Kansas City MO (S)

Kansas City Art Institute, Kemper Museum of Contemporary Art & Design, Kansas City MO (M,L)

Kansas City Artists Coalition, Kansas City MO (M)

Kansas City Public Library, Kansas City MO (L)

Kansas Museum of History, see Kansas State Historical Society, Topeka KS

Kansas State Historical Society, Kansas Museum of History, Topeka KS (M)

Kansas State University, Paul Weigel Library of Architecture & Design, Manhattan KS (L)

Kansas State University, Manhattan KS (S)

Kansas Watercolor Society, Wichita Art Museum, Wichita KS (A)

Kansas Wesleyan University, Art Dept, Salina KS (S)

Kapiolani Community College, see University of Hawaii, Honolulu HI (S)

Kappa Pi International Honorary Art Fraternity, Crestwood MO (O)

Kateri Galleries, The National Shrine of the North American Martyrs, Auriesville NY (M)

Kateri Tekakwitha Shrine, Musee Kateri Tekakwitha, Kahnawake PQ (M)

Katonah Museum of Art, Katonah NY (M)

Kauai Community College, Dept of Art, Lihue HI (S)

Kauai Museum, Lihue HI (M)

Kauai Regional Library, Lihue HI (L)

Kauffman Gallery, see Shippensburg University, Shippensburg PA

Kaufman & Broad Home Corp Collection, see Broad Inc, Los Angeles CA

Kean College of New Jersey, Union NJ (M,L)

Kean College of New Jersey, Fine Arts Dept, Union NJ (S)

Keene State College, Thorne-Sagendorph Art Gallery, Keene NH (M)

Kellogg Community College, Visual & Performing Arts Dept, Battle Creek MI (S)

Kellogg Library & Reading Room, see The 1890 House-Museum & Center for Victorian Arts, Cortland NY

Kellogg Memorial Research Library, see Cortland County Historical Society, Cortland NY

Kelly-Griggs House Museum, Red Bluff CA (M)

Kelowna Centennial Museum and National Exhibit Centre, Kelowna BC (M,L)

Kelsey Museum of Archaeology, see University of Michigan, Ann Arbor MI

Kemerer Museum of Decorative Arts, Bethlehem PA (M)

Kemper Museum of Contemporary Art & Design, see Kansas City Art Institute, Kansas City MO

Kemper National Insurance Companies, Long Grove IL (C)

Kendall College of Art & Design, Grand Rapids MI (S)

Kendall College of Art & Design, Frank & Lyn Van Steenberg Library, Grand Rapids MI (L)

Helen King Kendall Memorial Art Gallery, see San Angelo Art Club, San Angelo TX

Kendall Whaling Museum, Sharon MA (M,L)

Kenkeleba House, Inc, Kenkeleba Gallery, New York NY (M)

Kennebec Valley Art Association, Harlow Gallery, Hallowell ME (A)

Doris Wainwright Kennedy Art Center, see Birmingham Southern College, Birmingham AL

Kennedy Galleries, Art Gallery, New York NY (M)

Rudolph E Lee Gallery, see Clemson University, Clemson SC

Leeward Community College, Arts and Humanities Division, Pearl City HI (S)

Lehigh County Historical Society, Allentown PA (M,L)

Lehigh University, Dept of Art and Architecture, Bethlehem PA (S)

Lehigh University Art Galleries, Bethlehem PA (M)

Lehman College Art Gallery, Bronx NY (M)

Herbert H Lehman College, Art Dept, Bronx NY (S)

Robert Lehman Collection Library, see The Metropolitan Museum of Art, New York NY

Lela Harty School of Art, San Diego CA (S)

Lemoyne Art Foundation, Inc, Tallahassee FL (M)

Le Moyne College, Fine Arts Dept, Syracuse NY (S)

LeMoyne College, Wilson Art Gallery, Syracuse NY (M)

Le Musee Regional de Rimouski, Centre National d' Exposition, Rimouski PQ (M,L)

Lenoir Community College, Dept of Visual Art, Kinston NC (S)

Lenoir Rhyne College, Dept of Art, Hickory NC (S)

J Paul Leonard Library, see San Francisco State University, San Francisco CA

Anna Leonowens Gallery, see Nova Scotia College of Art and Design, Halifax NS

Leroy Historical Society, Leroy NY (A)

Lesley College, Arts Institute, Cambridge MA (S)

LeSueur County Historical, Museum, Chapter One, Elysian MN (M,L)

LeSueur Museum, LeSueur MN (M)

Lethbridge Community College, Buchanan Gallery, Lethbridge AB (M)

Lethbridge Public Library, Art Gallery, Lethbridge AB (L)

Lewis and Clark Community College, Art Dept, Godfrey IL (S)

Lewis & Clark College, Dept of Art, Portland OR (S)

Lewis-Clark State College, Art Dept, Lewiston ID (S)

Lewis County Historical Museum, Chehalis WA (M,L)

G Pillow Lewis Memorial Library, see Memphis College of Art, Memphis TN

James E Lewis Museum of Art, see Morgan State University, Baltimore MD

Irene Lewisohn Costume Reference Library, see The Metropolitan Museum of Art, New York NY

Lewistown Art Center, Lewistown MT (A)

Lexington Art League, Inc, Lexington KY (A)

Liberty Hall Historic Site, Liberty Hall Museum, Frankfort KY (M,L)

Liberty Hall Museum, see Liberty Hall Historic Site, Frankfort KY

Liberty Life Insurance Company, Greenville SC (C)

Liberty Memorial Museum & Archives, Kansas City MO (M)

Liberty National Bank, Liberty Gallery, Louisville KY (C)

Liberty Village Arts Center and Gallery, Chester MT (M)

Library, see Universite Du Quebec, Montreal PQ

Library Association of La Jolla, Athenaeum Music and Arts Library, La Jolla CA (L)

Library Company of Philadelphia, Print Dept, Philadelphia PA (L)

Library of Congress, Prints and Photographs Division, Washington DC (L)

Licking County Art Association Gallery, Newark OH (M)

The Light Factory, Inc, Charlotte NC (M)

Lighthouse Gallery, Tequesta FL (M,L)

Lightner Museum, Saint Augustine FL (M,L)

Light Work, Syracuse NY (A)

Limestone College, Art Dept, Gaffney SC (S)

Lincoln Arts Council, Lincoln NE (A)

Lincoln Center for the Performing Arts, Cork Gallery, New York NY (M)

Lincoln College, Art Dept, Lincoln IL (S)

Lincoln County Historical Association, Pownalborough Court House, Wiscasset ME (A, L,M)

Lincoln County Museum & Pre-Revolutionary Court House, see Lincoln County Historical Association, Wiscasset ME

Lincoln Home National Historic Site, see Illinois State Museum, Chicago IL

Lincoln Memorial Shrine, Redlands CA (L)

Lincoln Memorial University, Division of Humanities, Harrogate TN (S)

Lincoln Museum, see Lincoln National Life Insurance Co, Fort Wayne IN

Lincoln National Life Insurance Co, Lincoln Museum, Fort Wayne IN (C)

Lincoln University, Dept Fine Arts, Jefferson City MO (S)

Lindenwood College, Harry D Hendren Gallery, Saint Charles MO (M)

Lindenwood College, Art Dept, Saint Charles MO (S)

Luke Lindoe Library, see Alberta College of Art, Calgary AB

The Lindsay Gallery, Linsay ON (M)

Linfield College, Art Dept, McMinnville OR (S)

Linn Benton Community College, Fine & Applied Art Dept, Albany OR (S)

Litchfield Historical Society, Litchfield CT (A,L)

Littman Gallery, see Portland State University, Portland OR

Living Arts & Science Center, Inc, Lexington KY (M)

Livingston County Historical Society, Cobblestone Museum, Geneseo NY (M)

Livingston University, Division of Fine Arts, Livingston AL (S)

Lizzadro Museum of Lapidary Art, Elmhurst IL (M)

Lock Haven University, Art Dept, Lock Haven PA (S)

Lockwood-Mathews Mansion Museum, Norwalk CT (M)

Frances Loeb Library, see Harvard University, Cambridge MA

Jack London State Historic Park, House of Happy Walls, Glen Ellen CA (M)

London Regional Art & Historical Museums, London ON (M)

Long Beach Art League, Island Park NY (A)

Long Beach City College, Dept of Art, Long Beach CA (S)

Long Beach Jewish Community Center, Center Gallery, Long Beach CA (M)

Long Beach Museum of Art, Long Beach CA (M,L)

Long Beach Public Library, Long Beach CA (L)

Long Beach Public Library, Long Beach NY (L)

Long Branch Historical Museum, Long Branch NJ (M)

Earl K Long Library, see University of New Orleans, New Orleans LA

Longfellow-Evangeline State Commemorative Area, Saint Martinville LA (M)

Longfellow National Historic Site, Cambridge MA (M)

Longfellow's Wayside Inn Museum, South Sudbury MA (M)

Long Island Graphic Eye Gallery, Port Washington NY (M)

Long Island University, Brooklyn Center, Art Dept, Brooklyn NY (S)

Longue Vue House and Gardens, New Orleans LA (M)

Longview Museum and Arts Center, Longview TX (M,L)

Longwood Arts Gallery, see Bronx Council on the Arts, Bronx NY

Longwood College, Dept of Art, Farmville VA (S)

Lorain County Community College, Art Dept, Elyria OH (S)

Loras College, Dept of Art, Dubuque IA (S)

Loretto-Hilton Center Gallery, see Webster University, Saint Louis MO

L A Art Association, Los Angeles CA (A)

Los Angeles Center For Photographic Studies, Los Angeles CA (A)

Los Angeles City College, Dept of Art, Los Angeles CA (S)

Los Angeles Contemporary Exhibitions, Los Angeles CA (M)

Los Angeles County Museum of Art, Los Angeles CA (M,L)

Los Angeles County Museum of Natural History, William S Hart Museum, Newhall CA (M)

Los Angeles Harbor College, Art Dept, Wilmington CA (S)

Los Angeles Municipal Art Gallery, Los Angeles CA (M)

Los Angeles Public Library, Arts & Recreation Dept, Los Angeles CA (L)

Los Angeles Valley College, Art Gallery, Van Nuys CA (M)

Los Angeles Valley College, Art Dept, Van Nuys CA (S)

Caleb Lothrop House, see Cohasset Historical Society, Cohasset MA

Louisa May Alcott Memorial Association, Orchard House, Concord MA (A)

Louisburg College, Art Gallery, Louisburg NC (M)

Louisiana Arts and Science Center, Baton Rouge LA (M,L)

Louisiana College, Dept of Art, Pineville LA (S)

Louisiana Department of Culture, Recreation and Tourism, Louisiana State Museum, New Orleans LA (M,L)

Louisiana Historical Association, Confederate Museum, New Orleans LA (A)

Louisiana Historical Center Library, see Louisiana Department of Culture, Recreation and Tourism, New Orleans LA

Louisiana State Exhibit Museum, Shreveport LA (M)

Louisiana State Museum, see Louisiana Department of Culture, Recreation and Tourism, New Orleans LA

Louisiana State University, Baton Rouge LA (M,L)

Louisiana State University, School of Art, Baton Rouge LA (S)

Louisiana Tech University, School of Art and Architecture, Ruston LA (S)

Louisville Visual Art Association, Louisville KY (A)

Lourdes College, Art Dept, Sylvania OH (S)

Lourdes College, Duns Scotus Library, Sylvania OH (L)

Lovejoy Library, see Southern Illinois University, Edwardsville IL

Lovelace Medical Foundation, Art Collection, Albuquerque NM (C)

Loveland Museum and Gallery, Loveland CO (M)

Lovely Lane Museum, see United Methodist Historical Society, Baltimore MD

Lowe Art Museum, see University of Miami, Coral Gables FL

Joe and Emily Lowe Art Gallery, see Syracuse University, Syracuse NY

Lowell Art Association, Whistler House Museum of Art, Lowell MA (A)

Lower Columbia College, Longview WA (S)

Loyola Marymount University, Laband Art Gallery, Los Angeles CA (M)

Loyola Marymount University, Art & Art History Dept, Los Angeles CA (S)

Loyola University of Chicago, Martin D'Arcy Gallery of Art, Chicago IL (M,L)

Loyola University of Chicago, Fine Arts Dept, Chicago IL (S)

Loyola University of New Orleans, Dept of Visual Arts, New Orleans LA (S)

Lubbock Art Association, Inc, Lubbock TX (A)

Lubbock Christian University, Art Dept, Lubbock TX (S)

Luna County Historical Society, Inc, Deming Luna Mimbres Museum, Deming NM (M)

L'Universite Laval, Ecole des Arts Visuels, Quebec PQ (M,L)

Jeannette Lusk Library Collection, see South Dakota State University, Brookings SD

Lutheran Brethren Schools, Art Dept, Fergus Falls MN (S)

Lutheran Brotherhood Gallery, Minneapolis MN (M)

Lutheran Theological Seminary, Krauth Memorial Library, Philadelphia PA (L)

Luther College, Art Dept, Decorah IA (S)

Luzerne County Community College, Commercial Art Dept, Nanticoke PA (S)

Lyceum Club and Women's Art Association of Canada, Toronto ON (A,L)

Lycoming College, Art Dept, Williamsport PA (S)

Lycoming College Gallery, Williamsport PA (M)

Mary Washington College, Art Dept, Fredericksburg VA (S)

Mary Washington College, The Gari Melchers Estate & Memorial Gallery, Fredericksburg VA (M)

Marywood College, Art Dept, Scranton PA (S)

Mason City Public Library, Mason City IA (L)

Mason County Museum, Maysville KY (M)

Mason Gross School of the Arts, see Rutgers, the State University of New Jersey, New Brunswick NJ (S)

Massachusetts College of Art, Boston MA (S)

Massachusetts College of Art, Boston MA (L)

Massachusetts Historical Society, Boston MA (A,L)

Massachusetts Institute of Technology, Cambridge MA (S)

Massachusetts Institute of Technology, Cambridge MA (M,L)

Massillon Museum, Massillon OH (M)

Masur Museum of Art, see Twin City Art Foundation, Monroe LA

William Hammond Mathers Museum, see Indiana University, Bloomington IN

Mattatuck Historical Society Museum, Waterbury CT (M,L)

Mattress Factory, Pittsburgh PA (M)

Maui Community College, Art Dept, Kahului HI (S)

Maui Historical Society, Bailey House, Wailuku HI (A)

Max Hutchinson's Sculpture Fields, Kenoza Lake NY (M)

Frederic R Mayer Art Center & Lamont Gallery, see Phillips Exeter Academy, Exeter NH

Mayfield Regional Library, Mayfield Village OH (L)

Morton J May Foundation Gallery, see Maryville University Saint Louis, Saint Louis MO

Mayville State University Gallery, Mayville ND (M)

Mead Art Museum, see Amherst College, Amherst MA

Meadow Brook Art Gallery, see Oakland University, Rochester MI

Meadow Farm Museum, see County of Henrico, Glen Allen VA

Meadows Museum, see Southern Methodist University, Dallas TX

Meadows Museum of Art, see Centenary College of Louisiana, Shreveport LA

Meadville Council on the Arts, Meadville PA (A)

Mechanics' Institute Library, San Francisco CA (L)

Medicine Hat Museum & Art Gallery, Medicine Hat AB (M)

Medicine Hat Public Library, Medicine Hat AB (L)

The Gari Melchers Estate & Memorial Gallery, see Mary Washington College, Fredericksburg VA

Mellon Bank, Pittsburgh PA (C)

Melvin Art Gallery, see Florida Southern College, Lakeland FL

Memorial Library, see Berry College, Mount Berry GA

Memorial Union Art Gallery, see Oregon State University, Corvallis OR

Memorial Union Gallery, see Arizona State University, Tempe AZ

Memorial University of Newfoundland, School of Fine Arts, Visual Arts Dept, Corner Brook NF (S)

Memorial University of Newfoundland, Art Gallery, Saint John's NF (M)

Memphis Brooks Museum of Art, Memphis TN (M,L)

Memphis College of Art, Memphis TN (L)

Memphis College of Art, Memphis TN (S)

Memphis-Shelby County Public Library and Information Center, Dept of Art, Music & Films, Memphis TN (L)

Memphis State University, Dept of Art, Memphis TN (S)

Memphis State University, Memphis TN (M,L)

Mendel Art Gallery and Civic Conservatory, Saskatoon SK (M,L)

Mendocino Art Center, Gallery, Mendocino CA (A,L)

Mendocino Art Center, Mendocino CA (S)

Mendocino County Museum, Willits CA (M)

Menil Collection, Houston TX (M)

Mennonite Library & Archives, see Bethel College, North Newton KS

Merced College, Arts Division, Merced CA (S)

Mercer County Community College, The Gallery, Trenton NJ (M,L)

Mercer County Community College, Arts & Communications, Trenton NJ (S)

Mercer Museum, see Bucks County Historical Society, Doylestown PA

Mercer University, Art Dept, Macon GA (S)

Mercy College of Detroit, Art Dept, Detroit MI (S)

Mercyhurst College, Dept of Art, Erie PA (S)

Meredith College, Art Dept, Raleigh NC (S)

Meredith Gallery, Baltimore MD (M)

Meriam Library, see California State University, Chico, Chico CA

Meridian House International, Washington DC (M)

Meridian Museum of Art, Meridian MS (M)

Merrick Art Gallery, New Brighton PA (M)

Merritt College, Art Dept, Oakland CA (S)

Merwin & Wakeley Galleries, see Illinois Wesleyan University, Bloomington IL

Mesa Arts Center, see Galeria Mesa, Mesa AZ

Mesa College, Art Dept, Grand Junction CO (S)

Mesa Community College, Dept of Art & Art History, Mesa AZ (S)

Methodist College, Art Dept, Fayetteville NC (S)

Metro-Dade Center, Center for the Fine Arts, Miami FL (M)

Metropolitan Arts Commission, Metropolitan Center for Public Arts, Portland OR (A)

Metropolitan Center for Public Arts, see Metropolitan Arts Commission, Portland OR

The Metropolitan Museum of Art, New York NY (M,L)

Metropolitan State College of Denver, Art Dept, Denver CO (S)

Metropolitan Toronto Library Board, Toronto ON (L)

Mexican Fine Arts Center Museum, Chicago IL (M)

Mexican Museum, San Francisco CA (M)

MEXIC-ARTE Museum, Austin TX (A)

Mexico-Audrain County Library, Mexico MO (L)

Mhiripiri Gallery, Minneapolis MN (M)

Miami-Dade Community College, Visual Arts Dept, Miami FL (S)

Miami-Dade Community College, Kendal Campus, Art Gallery, Miami FL (M)

Miami-Dade Community College, Wolfson Campus, Frances Wolfson Art Gallery, Miami FL (M)

Miami-Dade Public Library, Miami FL (L)

Miami Dade Public Library, Miami Beach Branch, Miami Beach FL (L)

Miami University, Dept Fine Arts, Hamilton OH (S)

Miami University, Art Dept, Oxford OH (S)

Miami University Art Museum, Oxford OH (M,L)

Simon Michael School of Fine Arts, Rockport TX (S)

Michelson-Reves Museum of Art, Marshall TX (M)

James A Michener Arts Center, Doylestown PA (M)

Michigan Art & Artist Archives, see Art Center of Battle Creek, Battle Creek MI

Michigan Guild Gallery, see Michigan Guild of Artists & Artisans, Ann Arbor MI

Michigan Guild of Artists & Artisans, Michigan Guild Gallery, Ann Arbor MI (A)

Michigan State University, Kresge Art Museum, East Lansing MI (M,L)

Michigan State University, Dept of Art, East Lansing MI (S)

Mid-America All-Indian Center, Wichita KS (M,L)

Mid-America Arts Alliance & Exhibits USA, Kansas City MO (O)

Middlebury College, Museum of Art, Middlebury VT (M)

Middlebury College, Dept of Art, Middlebury VT (S)

Middle Georgia College, Dept of Art, Cochran GA (S)

Middlesex Community College, Fine Arts Div, Middletown CT (S)

Middlesex County College, Visual Arts Dept, Edison NJ (S)

Middlesex County Cultural & Heritage Commission, Artists League of Central New Jersey, North Brunswick NJ (A)

Middle Tennessee State University, Photographic Gallery, Murfreesboro TN (M)

Middle Tennessee State University, Art Dept, Murfreesboro TN (S)

Middletown Fine Arts Center, Middletown OH (A,L)

Mid-Hudson Arts and Science Center, Poughkeepsie NY (M)

Midland Art Council, Midland MI (A)

Midland Center for the Arts, Midland MI (S)

Midland College, Allison Fine Arts Dept, Midland TX (S)

Midland County Historical Society, Midland MI (M)

Midmarch Associates, Women Artists News Archive, New York NY (L)

Midtown, see International Center of Photography, New York NY

Midtown Art Center, Houston TX (M)

Midway College, Art Dept, Midway KY (S)

Midwest Art History Society, Denton TX (O)

Midwestern State University, Div of Fine Arts, Wichita Falls TX (S)

Midwest Museum of American Art, Elkhart IN (M)

Miles Community College, Dept of Fine Arts and Humanities, Miles City MT (S)

Miller Art Center, see Door County, Sturgeon Bay WI

E Kirkbride Miller Art Research Library, see Baltimore Museum of Art, Baltimore MD

Isabel Miller Museum, see Sitka Historical Society, Sitka AK

Millersville University, Art Dept, Millersville PA (S)

Milliken Art Gallery, see Converse College, Spartanburg SC

Millikin University, Perkinson Gallery, Decatur IL (M)

Millikin University, Art Dept, Decatur IL (S)

Mill of Kintail Museum, see Mississippi Valley Conservation Authority, Almonte ON

Millsaps College, Dept of Art, Jackson MS (S)

Mills College, Art Gallery, Oakland CA (M)

Mills College, Art Dept, Oakland CA (S)

Mills Mansion State Historical Site, see New York State Office of Parks, Recreation & Historical Preservation, Staatsburg NY

Milwaukee Area Technical College, Graphic Arts Dept, Milwaukee WI (S)

Milwaukee Art Museum, Milwaukee WI (M,L)

Milwaukee Institute of Art and Design, Milwaukee WI (S)

Milwaukee Institute of Art Design, Library, Milwaukee WI (L)

Milwaukee Public Library, Art, Music & Recreation Dept, Milwaukee WI (L)

Milwaukee Public Museum, Milwaukee WI (M)

Mind's Eye Gallery, see Dickinson State University, Dickinson ND

Mingei International, Inc, Mingei International Museum of World Folk Art, San Diego CA (M,L)

Mingenback Art Center, see Bethany College, Lindsborg KS

Minneapolis College of Art and Design, Minneapolis MN (S)

Minneapolis College of Art & Design, Library & Media Center, Minneapolis MN (L)

Minneapolis Institute of Arts, see Minneapolis Society of Fine Arts, Minneapolis MN

Minneapolis Society of Fine Arts, Minneapolis Institute of Arts, Minneapolis MN (M,L,A)

Minnesota Historical Society, Saint Paul MN (A,L)

Minnesota Museum of American Art, Saint Paul MN (M,L)

Minot Art Association, Minot Art Gallery, Minot ND (M)

Minot State University, Dept of Art, Division of Humanities, Minot ND (S)

Minot State University, University Galleries, Minot ND (M)

Mint Museum of Art, Charlotte NC (M,L)

Miracosta College, Art Dept, Oceanside CA (S)

The Mission House, see The Trustees of Reservations, Stockbridge MA

Mission San Luis Rey Museum, San Luis Rey CA (M)

Mission San Miguel Museum, San Miguel CA (M)

Mississauga Library System, Mississauga ON (L)

Mississippi Art Colony, Meridian MS (A)

Mississippi College, Art Dept, Clinton MS (S)

Mississippi Crafts Center, Ridgeland MS (M)

Mississippi Delta Community College, Dept of Fine Arts, Moorhead MS (S)

Mississippi Department of Archives and History, State Historical Museum, Jackson MS (L)

Mississippi Department of Archives & History, Mississippi State Historical Museum, Jackson MS (M)

Mississippi Gulf Coast Community College-Jackson County Campus, Art Dept, Gautier MS (S)

Mississippi Museum of Art, Jackson MS (M,L)

Mississippi River Museum at Mud-Island, Memphis TN (M)

Mississippi State Historical Museum, see Mississippi Department of Archives & History, Jackson MS

Mississippi State University, Art Dept, Mississippi State MS (S)

Mississippi University for Women, Fine Arts Gallery, Columbus MS (M)

Mississippi University for Women, Division of Fine & Performing Arts, Columbus MS (S)

Mississippi Valley Conservation Authority, Mill of Kintail Museum, Almonte ON (M)

Mississippi Valley State University, Fine Arts Dept, Itta Bena MS (S)

Missoula Museum of the Arts, Missoula MT (M)

Missouri Historical Society, Saint Louis MO (M,L)

Missouri Southern State College, Dept of Art, Joplin MO (S)

Missouri State Museum, see Department of Natural Resources of Missouri, Jefferson City MO

Missouri Western State College, Art Dept, Saint Joseph MO (S)

Missouri Western State College, Fine Arts Gallery, Saint Joseph MO (M)

Arthur Roy Mitchell Memorial Inc, Museum of Western Art, Trinidad CO (M)

Mitchell Community College, Visual Art Dept, Statesville NC (S)

Elizabeth Myers Mitchell Art Gallery, see Saint John's College, Annapolis MD

Mitchell Museum, Mount Vernon IL (M,L)

MIT Museum, see Massachusetts Institute of Technology, Cambridge MA

Mobil Corporation, Art Collection, Fairfax VA (C)

Mobius Inc, Boston MA (A)

Mock Library Art Dept, see Teikyo Westmar University, LeMars IA

Modern Art Museum of Fort Worth, see Fort Worth Art Association, Fort Worth TX

Modesto Junior College, Arts Humanities and Speech Division, Modesto CA (S)

Moffatt-Ladd House, see National Society of the Colonial Dames of America, Portsmouth NH

Mohave Museum of History and Arts, Kingman AZ (M)

Mohawk Valley Community College, Advertising Design and Production, Utica NY (S)

Mohawk Valley Heritage Association, Inc, Walter Elwood Museum, Amsterdam NY (M)

MonDak Heritage Center, Sidney MT (M,L)

Monmouth College, Dept of Art, Monmouth IL (S)

Monmouth College, Dept of Art, West Long Branch NJ (S)

Monmouth Museum and Cultural Center, Lincroft NJ (M)

Monroe City Community College, Fine Arts Council, Monroe MI (A)

Monroe Community College, Art Dept, Rochester NY (S)

Monroe County Community College, Humanities Division, Monroe MI (S)

Monroe County Historical Association, Elizabeth D Walters Library, Stroudsburg PA (M)

James Monroe Museum, Fredericksburg VA (M,L)

James Monroe House, see Arts Club of Washington, Washington DC

Monserrat College of Art, Beverly MA (S)

Montalvo Center for the Arts, Saratoga CA (A)

Montana Historical Society, Helena MT (A,L)

Montana State University, Bozeman MT (M,L)

Montana State University, Bozeman MT (S)

Montana University System-Northern Montana College, Humanities & Social Sciences, Havre MT (S)

Montay College, Art Dept, Chicago IL (S)

Montclair Art Museum, Montclair NJ (M,L)

Montclair Art Museum, Art School, Montclair NJ (S)

Montclair State College, Fine Arts Dept, Upper Montclair NJ (S)

Montclair State College, Art Gallery, Upper Montclair NJ (M,L)

Monterey History and Art Association, Monterey CA (A,M,L)

Monterey Peninsula College, Art Dept, Monterey CA (S)

Monterey Peninsula Museum of Art Association, Monterey CA (A)

Monterey Public Library, Art & Architecture Dept, Monterey CA (L)

Montgomery College, Dept of Art, Rockville MD (S)

Montgomery County Community College, Art Dept, Blue Bell PA (S)

Montgomery Museum of Fine Arts, Montgomery AL (M,L)

Monticello, see Thomas Jefferson Memorial Foundation, Charlottesville VA

Montpelier Cultural Arts Center, see Maryland-National Capital Park & Planning Commission, Laurel MD

Montreal Museum of Fine Arts, Montreal PQ (M,L)

Moody County Historical Society, Flandreau SD (A)

Moody Gallery of Art, see University of Alabama, Tuscaloosa AL

Moon Gallery, see Berry College, Mount Berry GA

Moore College of Art & Design, Golden Paley Gallery, Philadelphia PA (M,L)

Moore College of Art & Design, Philadelphia PA (S)

Moorhead State University, Dept of Art, Moorhead MN (S)

Moose Jaw Art Museum and National Exhibition Centre, Art & History Museum, Moose Jaw SK (M)

Moravian College, Dept of Art, Bethlehem PA (S)

Moravian College, Payne Gallery, Bethlehem PA (M)

Moravian Historical Society, Whitefield House Museum, Nazareth PA (M)

Moreau Gallery, see Saint Mary's College, Notre Dame IN

Morehead State University, Art Dept, Morehead KY (S)

Morehead State University, Morehead KY (M,L)

Morgan County Foundation, Inc, Madison-Morgan Cultural Center, Madison GA (M)

Pierpont Morgan Library, New York NY (L)

Morgan State University, Dept of Art, Baltimore MD (S)

Morgan State University, Baltimore MD (M,L)

Morikami Museum & Japanese Gardens, see Palm Beach County Parks & Recreation Department, Delray Beach FL

Morlan Gallery, see Transylvania University, Lexington KY

Morningside College, Art Dept, Sioux City IA (S)

Morris-Butler House, see Historic Landmarks Foundation of Indiana, Indianapolis IN

Morris Communications Corporation, Augusta GA (C,M)

Morris-Jumel Mansion, Inc, New York NY (M)

Morris Library, see University of Delaware, Newark DE

Morris Museum, Morristown NJ (M,L)

Morris Museum of Art, see Morris Communications Corporation, Augusta GA

Charles Morse Museum of American Art, Winter Park FL (M)

Moss-Thorns Gallery of Arts, see Fort Hays State University, Hays KS

Motlow State Community College, Art Dept, Tullahoma TN (S)

Moudy Exhibition Hall, see Texas Christian University, Fort Worth TX

Mountain View Doukhobor Museum, Grand Forks BC (M)

Mount Allison University, Owens Art Gallery, Sackville NB (M)

Mount Allison University, Fine Arts Dept, Sackville NB (S)

Mount Angel Abbey Library, Saint Benedict OR (L)

Mount Clare Mansion, see National Society of Colonial Dames of America in the State of Maryland, Baltimore MD

Mount Holyoke College, Art Museum, South Hadley MA (M,L)

Mount Holyoke College, Art Dept, South Hadley MA (S)

Mount Hood Community College, Visual Arts Center, Gresham OR (S)

Mount Ida College, Boston MA (S)

Mount Marty College, Art Dept, Yankton SD (S)

Mount Mary College, Tower Gallery, Milwaukee WI (M)

Mount Mary College, Art Dept, Milwaukee WI (S)

Mount Mercy College, McAuley Gallery, Cedar Rapids IA (M,L)

Mount Mercy College, Art Dept, Cedar Rapids IA (S)

Mount Olive College, Dept of Art, Mount Olive NC (S)

Mount Pleasant, see Philadelphia Museum of Art, Philadelphia PA

Mount Royal College, Dept of Interior Design, Calgary AB (S)

Mount Royal School of Art, see Maryland Institute, Baltimore MD (S)

Mount Saint Clare College, Art Dept, Clinton IA (S)

Mount Saint Mary's College, Visual & Performing Arts Dept, Emmitsburg MD (S)

Mount Saint Mary's College, Art Dept, Los Angeles CA (S)

Mount Saint Mary's College, Jose Drudis-Biada Art Gallery, Los Angeles CA (M)

Mount Saint Vincent University, Art Gallery, Halifax NS (M)

Mount San Antonio College, Art Dept, Walnut CA (S)

Mount San Jacinto College, Art Dept, San Jacinto CA (S)

Mount Union College, Dept of Art, Alliance OH (S)

Mount Vernon College, Art Dept, Washington DC (S)

Mount Vernon Ladies' Association of the Union, Mount Vernon VA (M)

Mount Vernon Nazarene College, Art Dept, Mount Vernon OH (S)

Mount Vernon Public Library, Fine Art Dept, Mount Vernon NY (L)

Mount Wachusett Community College, Art Galleries, Gardner MA (M,L)

Movimiento Artistico del Rio Salado, Inc (MARS), Phoenix AZ (A)

Muchnic Foundation and Atchison Art Association, Muchnic Gallery, Atchison KS (M)

Muckenthaler Cultural Center, Fullerton CA (A)

Muhlenberg College, Dept of Art, Allentown PA (S)

Muhlenberg College Center for the Arts, Frank Martin Gallery, Allentown PA (M)

Multicultural Heritage Centre, Stony Plain AB (M)

Multnomah County Library, Henry Failing Art and Music Dept, Portland OR (L)

Mulvane Art Museum, see Washburn University, Topeka KS

Municipal Art Society of Baltimore City, Baltimore MD (A)

Municipal Art Society of New York, New York NY (A,L)

Munson Gallery, New Haven CT (M)

Munson-Williams-Proctor Institute, Museum of Art, Utica NY (M,L)

Munson-Williams-Proctor Institute, School of Art, Utica NY (S)

Muroff-Kotler Visual Arts Gallery, see Ulster County Community College, Stone Ridge NY

Murphy Library of Art and Architecture, see University of Kansas, Lawrence KS

Murray State University, Eagle Gallery, Murray KY (M)

Murray State University, Art Dept, Murray KY (S)

Joseph & Margaret Muscarelle Museum of Art, see College of William and Mary, Williamsburg VA

Muscatine Art Center, Muscatine IA (M,L)

Muse Art Gallery, Philadelphia PA (M)

Musee Canadien de la Nature, see Canadian Museum of Nature, Ottawa ON

Musee d'art contemporain de Montreal, Montreal PQ (M,L)

Musee d'Art de Joliette, Joliette PQ (M,L)

Musee d'Art de Saint-Laurent, Saint-Laurent PQ (M)

Musee de la Basilique Notre-Dame, Montreal PQ (M)

Musee des Augustines de l'Hotel Dieu of Quebec, Quebec PQ (M,L)

Musee du Quebec, Quebec PQ (M,L)

Musee du Seminaire de Quebec, Quebec PQ (M)

Musee Kateri Tekakwitha, see Kateri Tekakwitha Shrine, Kahnawake PQ

Musee Regional de Vaudreuil-Soulanges, Vaudreuil PQ (M,L)

Museo de Arte de Ponce, Ponce Art Museum, Ponce PR (M,L)

Museo de Arte Religioso Porta Coeli, see Institute of Puerto Rican Culture, San Juan PR

Museo de Historia Naval y Militar de Puerto Rico, see Institute of Puerto Rican Culture, San Juan PR

Museo de la Familia Puertorriquena del Siglo XIX, see Institute of Puerto Rican Culture, San Juan PR

Museo de la Farmacia Puertorriquena, see Institute of Puerto Rican Culture, San Juan PR

Museo del Grabado Latinoamericano, see Institute of Puerto Rican Culture, San Juan PR

Museo Italo Americano, San Francisco CA (M,L)

Museo y Parque Historico de Caparra, see Institute of Puerto Rican Culture, San Juan PR

The Museum, Greenwood SC (M)

The Museum at Drexel University, Philadelphia PA (M)

Museum of African American Art, Los Angeles CA (M)

Museum of Afro-American History, Boston MA (M)

Museum of American Folk Art, New York NY (M,L)

Museum of American Illustration, see Society of Illustrators, New York NY

Museum of American Textile History, North Andover MA (M,L)

Museum of Art, Fort Lauderdale, Fort Lauderdale FL (M,L)

Museum of Arts and History, Port Huron MI (M)

Museum of Arts and Sciences, Cuban Museum, Daytona Beach FL (M,L)

Museum of Arts and Sciences, Inc, Macon GA (M)

Museum of Art, Science and Industry, Discovery Museum, Bridgeport CT (M)

Museum of Connecticut History, see Connecticut State Library, Hartford CT

Museum of Contemporary Art, Chicago IL (M,L)

The Museum of Contemporary Art, Los Angeles CA (M)

Museum of Contemporary Art, San Diego, La Jolla CA (M,L)

The Museum of Contemporary Photography, see Columbia College, Chicago IL

Museum of Discovery & Science, Fort Lauderdale FL (M)

Museum of Early Southern Decorative Arts, see Old Salem Inc, Winston-Salem NC

Museum of East Texas, Lufkin TX (A)

Museum of Fine Arts, Boston MA (M,L)

Museum of Fine Arts, Springfield MA (M,L)

Museum of Fine Arts, Houston, Houston TX (M,L)

Museum of Fine Arts, Saint Petersburg, Florida, Inc, Saint Petersburg FL (M,L)

Museum of Holography - Chicago, Chicago IL (A,L)

Museum of Maryland History, see Maryland Historical Society, Baltimore MD

Museum of Modern Art, New York NY (M,L)

Museum of Movie Art, Calgary AB (M)

Museum of Neon Art, Los Angeles CA (M)

Museum of New Mexico, Santa Fe NM (M,L)

Museum of New Mexico, Office of Cultural Affairs of New Mexico, The Governor's Gallery, Santa Fe NM (M)

Museum of New York, Rock Hill SC (M,L)

Museum of Northern Arizona, Flagstaff AZ (M)

Museum of Northern British Columbia, Ruth Harvey Art Gallery, Prince Rupert BC (M,L)

Museum of Oriental Cultures, Corpus Christi TX (M)

Museum of Ossining Historical Society, Ossining NY (M,L)

Museum of Our National Heritage, Lexington MA (M)

Museum of Photographic Arts, Balboa Park CA (M)

Museum of Science and Industry, Chicago IL (M)

Museum of the Americas, Brookfield VT (M,L)

Museum of the City of Mobile, Mobile AL (M,L)

Museum of the City of New York, New York NY (M,L)

Museum of the Great Plains, see Institute of the Great Plains, Lawton OK

Museum of the Hudson Highlands, Cornwall on Hudson NY (M)

Museum of the National Center of Afro-American Artists, Boston MA (M)

Museum of the Plains Indian & Crafts Center, Browning MT (M)

Museum of the Southwest, Midland TX (M,L)

Museum of Western Art, Denver CO (M)

Museum of Western Colorado, Grand Junction CO (L)

The Museums at Stony Brook, Stony Brook NY (M,L)

Museum Science & History, Jacksonville FL (M)

Museums of Abilene, Inc, Abilene TX (M)

Muskegon Community College, Dept of Creative and Performing Arts, Muskegon MI (S)

Muskegon Museum of Art, Muskegon MI (M,L)

Muskingum College, Art Department, New Concord OH (S)

Muskoka Arts & Crafts Inc, Chapel Gallery, Bracebridge ON (M)

Muttart Art Gallery, Calgary AB (M)

Mystic Art Association, Inc, Mystic CT (A)

NAB Gallery, Chicago IL (M)

Nabisco Brands, Inc, East Hanover NJ (C)

NAME, Chicago IL (M,L)

Namm Hall Library and Learning Resource Center, see New York City Technical College, Brooklyn NY

Nanaimo Art Gallery & Exhibition Centre, see Malaspina College, Nanaimo BC

Nantucket Historical Association, Historic Nantucket, Nantucket MA (M)

Napa Valley College, Art Dept, Napa CA (S)

Naples Art Gallery, Naples FL (M)

Napoleonic Society of America, Library, Clearwater FL (L)

Nashua Center for Arts, Nashua NH (S)

Nassau Community College, Firehouse Art Gallery, Garden City NY (M)

Nassau Community College, Art Dept, Garden City NY (S)

Nassau County Museum of Fine Art, Roslyn NY (M)

National Academy of Design, New York NY (O)

National Academy of Sciences, Arts in the Academy, Washington DC (M)

National Academy School of Fine Arts, New York NY (S)

National Air and Space Museum, Washington DC (M,L)

National Alliance for Media Arts & Culture (NAMAC), Oakland CA (O)

National Antique & Art Dealers Association of America, New York NY (O)

National Architectural Accrediting Board, Inc, Washington DC (O)

National Archives and Records Service, John F Kennedy Library and Museum, Boston MA (M)

National Archives of Canada, Ottawa ON (L)

National Archives & Records Administration, Franklin D Roosevelt Museum, Hyde Park NY (M,L)

National Archives & Records Administration, Harry S Truman Library, Independence MO (L)

National Art Education Association, Reston VA (O)

National Artists Equity Association Inc, Washington DC (O)

National Art League Inc, Douglaston NY (A)

The National Art Museum of Sport, Indianapolis IN (M)

National Art Museum of Sport, Indianapolis IN (M)

National Assembly of Local Arts Agencies, Washington DC (O)

National Assembly of State Arts Agencies, Washington DC (O)

National Association of Artists' Organizations (NAAO), Washington DC (O)

National Association of Schools of Art & Design, Reston VA (O)

National Association of Women Artists, Inc, New York NY (O)

National Baseball Hall of Fame and Museum, Inc, Art Collection, Cooperstown NY (M)

National Cartoonists Society, New York NY (O)

National Center on Arts & Aging-National Council on The Aging, NCOA Gallery Patina, Washington DC (O)

National City Bank, Atrium Gallery, Cleveland OH (C)

National Council on Art in Jewish Life, New York NY (A,L)

National Council on Education for the Ceramic Arts (NCECA), Bandon OR (O)

National Cowboy Hall of Fame and Western Heritage Center, Oklahoma City OK (M)

National Endowment for the Arts, Washington DC (O)

National Foundation for Advancement in the Arts, Miami FL (O)

National Gallery of Art, Washington DC (M,L)

National Gallery of Canada, Ottawa ON (M,L)

National Hall of Fame for Famous American Indians, Anadarko OK (M)

National Infantry Museum, Fort Benning GA (M,L)

National Institute for Architectural Education, New York NY (O)

National Institute for the Conservation of Cultural Property, Washington DC (O)

National Institute of Art & Disabilities (NIAD), Richmond CA (A)

National League of American Pen Women, Washington DC (O)

National Maritime Museum, see San Francisco Maritime National Historical Park, San Francisco CA

National Museum of African Art, Washington DC (M,L)

National Museum of American Art, Washington DC (M,L)

National Museum of American History, Washington DC (M,A,L)

National Museum of Racing and Hall of Fame, Saratoga Springs NY (M,L)

National Museum of Science & Technology, Ottawa ON (M)

National Museum of Science & Technology Corporation, National Aviation Museum, Ottawa ON (M)

National Museum of the American Indian, New York NY (M)

National Museum of Women in the Arts, Washington DC (M,L)

National Museum of Woodcarving, see Gloridale Partnership, Custer SD

National Park Service, Hubbell Trading Post National Historic Site, Ganado AZ (M)

The National Park Service, United States Department of the Interior, The Statue of Liberty National Monument, New York NY (M)

National Portrait Gallery, Washington DC (M,L)

National Sculpture Society, New York NY (O)

The National Shrine of the North American Martyrs, see Kateri Galleries, Auriesville NY

National Society Daughters of the American Revolution, see DAR Museum, Washington DC

National Society of Colonial Dames of America in the State of Maryland, Mount Clare Mansion, Baltimore MD (M,L)

National Society of Mural Painters, Inc, New York NY (O)

National Society of Painters in Casein & Acrylic, Inc, Whitehall PA (O)

National Society of the Colonial Dames, Wilton House Museum, Richmond VA (M)

National Society of the Colonial Dames of America, Moffatt-Ladd House, Portsmouth NH (A)

National Trust for Historic Preservation, Chesterwood Museum, Glendale MA (M,L)

National Trust for Historic Preservation, Washington DC (M)

National Watercolor Society, Cerritos CA (O)

Nations Bank, Art Collection, Richmond VA (C)

Native American Center for the Living Arts, Niagara Falls NY (M)

Natural Heritage Trust, see New York Office of Parks, Recreation & Historic Preservation, Albany NY

Natural History Museum of Los Angeles County, Los Angeles CA (M,L)

Navajo Nation Library, Window Rock AZ (L)

Navajo Tribal Museum, Window Rock AZ (M)

Naval Historical Center, The Navy Museum, Washington DC (M)

Naval War College Museum, Newport RI (M)

Navarro College, Art Dept, Corsicana TX (S)

The Navy Museum, see Naval Historical Center, Washington DC

Nazareth College of Rochester, Art Dept, Rochester NY (S)

Nebraska Arts Council Library, Omaha NE (L)

Nebraska State Capitol, Lincoln NE (M)

Nebraska Wesleyan University, Elder Gallery, Lincoln NE (M)

Nebraska Wesleyan University, Art Dept, Lincoln NE (S)

Nelson-Atkins Museum of Art, Kansas City MO (M,L,A)

Richard L Nelson Gallery & Fine Arts Collection, see University of California, Davis CA

Nemours Mansion & Gardens, Wilmington DE (M)

Nesbitt College of Design Arts, see Drexel University, Philadelphia PA (S)

Bjarne Ness Gallery, see SVACA - Sheyenne Valley Arts and Crafts Association, Fort Ransom ND

Neuberger Museum, see State University of New York at Purchase, Purchase NY

Nevada Museum Of Art, Reno NV (M,L)

Neville Public Museum, Green Bay WI (M,L)

George P Nevitt Library, see Paine Art Center and Arboretum, Oshkosh WI

Newark Museum Association, The Newark Museum, Newark NJ (M,L)

Newark Public Library, Art & Music Div, Newark NJ (L)

Newark School of Fine and Industrial Art, Newark NJ (S)

New Arts Program Inc, Gallery, Kutztown PA (A)

New Bedford Free Public Library, Art Dept, New Bedford MA (L)

New Bedford Whaling Museum, see Old Dartmouth Historical Society, New Bedford MA

Newberry College, Dept of Art, Newberry SC (S)

Newberry Library, Chicago IL (L)

New Britain Institute, New Britain Museum of American Art, New Britain CT (M)

New Britain Museum of American Art, see New Britain Institute, New Britain CT

New Brunswick College of Craft & Design, Fredericton NB (A,L)

New Brunswick College of Craft & Design, Fredericton NB (S)

New Brunswick Museum, Saint John NB (M,L)

Newburyport Maritime Society, Custom House Maritime Museum, Newburyport MA (M)

New Canaan Historical Society, New Canaan CT (M)

New College of the University of South Florida, Fine Arts Dept, Humanities Division, Sarasota FL (S)

New Community College of Baltimore, Dept of Fine Arts, Baltimore MD (S)

New England Center for Contemporary Art, Brooklyn CT (M)

New England College, Art & Art History, Henniker NH (S)

New England Maple Museum, Rutland VT (M)

New England School of Art & Design, Boston MA (S)

New England School of Art & Design, Library, Boston MA (L)

New England Watercolor Society, Boston MA (O)

Newfoundland Museum, Saint John's NF (M,L)

New Hampshire Antiquarian Society, Hopkinton NH (M)

New Hampshire Art Association, Inc, Manchester NH (A)

New Hampshire Historical Society, Concord NH (A,L)

The New Harmony Gallery of Contemporary Art, New Harmony IN (M)

New Haven Colony Historical Society, New Haven CT (A,L)

New Haven Paint and Clay Club, Inc, New Haven CT (A)

Newhouse Center for Contemporary Art, see Snug Harbor Cultural Center, Staten Island NY

New Jersey Center for Visual Arts, Summit NJ (A)

New Jersey Historical Society Museum, Newark NJ (M)

New Jersey Institute of Technology, Architectural Information Center, Newark NJ (L)

New Jersey State Museum, Trenton NJ (M)

New Jersey State Museum at Morven, see New Jersey Historical Society Museum, Newark NJ

New Jersey Water-Color Society, Red Bank NJ (A)

New Langton Arts, San Francisco CA (M)

New London County Historical Society, New London CT (A)

New Mexico Art League, Gallery, Albuquerque NM (A)

New Mexico Highlands University, Arrott Art Gallery, Las Vegas NM (M)

New Mexico Highlands University, School of Liberal & Fine Arts, Las Vegas NM (S)

New Mexico Junior College, Arts & Sciences, Hobbs NM (S)

New Mexico State University, University Art Gallery, Las Cruces NM (M)

New Mexico State University, Art Dept, Las Cruces NM (S)

The New Museum of Contemporary Art, New York NY (M,L)

New Organization for the Visual Arts, (NOVA), Cleveland OH (M)

New Orleans Academy of Fine Arts, Academy Gallery, New Orleans LA (M)

New Orleans Museum of Art, New Orleans LA (M,L)

Newport Art Museum, Newport RI (M,L)

Newport Art Museum School, Newport RI (S)

Newport Harbor Art Museum, Newport Beach CA (M,L)

Newport Historical Society, Newport RI (A,L)

New Rochelle Art Association, see New Rochelle Public Library, New Rochelle NY

New Rochelle Public Library, Art Section, New Rochelle NY (L,A)

New School for Social Research, Adult Education Division, New York NY (S)

New Visions Gallery, Inc, Marshfield WI (M)

New York Academy of Art, Graduate School of Figurative Art, New York NY (S)

New York Artists Equity Association, Inc, New York NY (A)

New York City Technical College, Namm Hall Library and Learning Resource Center, Brooklyn NY (L)

New York City Technical College of the City University of New York, Dept of Art and Advertising Design, Brooklyn NY (S)

New York Experimental Glass Workshop, Brooklyn NY (A)

New York Historical Society, New York NY (A,L)

New York Institute of Photography, New York NY (S)

New York Institute of Technology, Gallery, Old Westbury NY (M,L)

New York Institute of Technology, Fine Arts Dept, Old Westbury NY (S)

New York Office of Parks, Recreation & Historic Preservation, Natural Heritage Trust, Albany NY (A)

The New York Public Library, New York NY (L,M)

New York School of Interior Design, New York NY (S)

New York School of Interior Design Library, New York NY (L)

New York Society of Architects, New York NY (A)

New York State College of Ceramics at Alfred University, Scholes Library of Ceramics, Alfred NY (L)

New York State College of Ceramics at Alfred University, School of Art & Design, Alfred NY (S)

New York State College of Human Ecology, see Cornell University, Ithaca NY (S)

New York State Historical Association, Cooperstown NY (M,L)

New York State Library, Manuscripts and Special Collections, Albany NY (L)

New York State Museum, Albany NY (M)

New York State Office of Parks, Recreation & Historic Preservation, Mills Mansion State Historical Site, Staatsburg NY (M)

New York State Office of Parks Recreation & Historic Preservation, John Jay Homestead State Historic Site, Katonah NY (A)

New York Studio School of Drawing, Painting and Sculpture, New York NY (S)

New York Studio School of Drawing, Painting & Sculpture, Gallery, New York NY (M,L)

New York Tapestry Artists, Carmel NY (A)

New York University, New York NY (M,L)

New York University, Institute of Fine Arts, New York NY (S)

Nexus Contemporary Art Center, Atlanta GA (M)

Nexus Gallery, see Foundation for Today's Art, Philadelphia PA

Elisabet Ney Museum, Austin TX (M,L)

Niagara County Community College, Fine Arts Div, Sanborn NY (S)

Niagara County Community College Art Gallery, Sanborn NY (M)

Niagara University, Castellani Art Museum, New York NY (M)

Niagara University, Fine Arts Dept, Niagara Falls NY (S)

Nicholls State University, Dept of Art, Thibodaux LA (S)

Nichols House Museum, Inc, Boston MA (M)

The Nickle Arts Museum, see University of Calgary, Calgary AB

Nicolaysen Art Museum and Discovery Center, Childrens Discovery Center, Casper WY (M,L)

911 Arts Media Center, Seattle WA (A)

Nippon Club Gallery, New York NY (M)

Noah Webster Foundation & Historical Society of West Hartford, Inc, Noah Webster's House, West Hartford CT (M)

Nobles County Art Center Gallery, Worthington MN (A)

The John A Noble Collection, Staten Island NY (M)

Isamu Noguchi Foundation, Garden Museum, Long Island City NY (M)

Harry Nohr Art Gallery, see University of Wisconsin - Platteville, Platteville WI

No Man's Land Historical Society Museum, Goodwell OK (M)

Nordstrand Visual Arts Gallery, see Wayne State College, Wayne NE

Norfolk Historical Society Inc, Museum, Norfolk CT (M)

Norfolk Public Library, Feldman Fine Arts & Audio Visual Dept, Norfolk VA (L)

Norfolk State University, Fine Arts Dept, Norfolk VA (S)

Norick Art Center, see Oklahoma City University, Oklahoma City OK (S)

Normandale Community College, Bloomington MN (S)

Normandeau Cultural & Natural History Society, Red Deer & District Museum & Archives, Red Deer AB (M)

Norman Mackenzie Art Gallery, Regina SK (M,L)

Northampton Community College, Art Dept, Bethlehem PA (S)

North Arkansas Community College, Art Dept, Harrison AR (S)

North Canton Public Library, Little Art Gallery, North Canton OH (L)

North Carolina Agricultural and Technical State University, Art Dept, Greensboro NC (S)

North Carolina Central University, Art Museum, Durham NC (M)

North Carolina Central University, Art Dept, Durham NC (S)

North Carolina Museum of Art, Raleigh NC (M,L)

North Carolina Museums Council, Raleigh NC (A)

North Carolina State University, Harrye Lyons Design Library, Raleigh NC (L,M)

North Carolina State University, Chinqua-Penn Plantation House, Garden & Greenhouses, Reidsville NC (M)

North Carolina State University at Raleigh, School of Design, Raleigh NC (S)

North Carolina Wesleyan College, Dept of Visual & Performing Arts, Rocky Mount NC (S)

North Central College, Dept of Art, Naperville IL (S)

North Central College, Oesterle Library, Naperville IL (L)

North Central Life Insurance Company, Art Collection, Saint Paul MN (C)

North Central Michigan College, Art Dept, Petoskey MI (S)

North Central Washington Museum, Art Gallery, Wenatchee WA (M)

North Country Museum of Arts, Park Rapids MN (M)

North Dakota Museum of Art, Grand Forks ND (M)

North Dakota State School of Science, Dept of Graphic Arts, Wahpeton ND (S)

North Dakota State University, Memorial Union Art Gallery, Fargo ND (M)

North Dakota State University, Div of Fine Arts, Fargo ND (S)

Northeast Community College, Dept of Liberal Arts, Norfolk NE (S)

Northeastern Illinois University, Gallery, Chicago IL (M)

Northeastern Illinois University, Art Dept, Chicago IL (S)

Northeastern Junior College, Dept of Art, Sterling CO (S)

Northeastern Nevada Historical Society Museum, Elko NV (M,L)

Northeastern Oklahoma A & M College, Art Dept, Miami OK (S)

Northeastern Oklahoma State University, Tahlequah OK (S)

Northeastern University, Dept of Art & Architecture, Boston MA (S)

Northeast Louisiana University, Dept of Art, Monroe LA (S)

Northeast Louisiana University, Bry Gallery, Monroe LA (M)

Northeast Mississippi Junior College, Art Dept, Booneville MS (S)

Northeast Missouri State University, Art Dept, Kirksville MO (S)

Northeast Ohio Areawide Coordinating Agency (NOACA), Information Resource Center, Cleveland OH (L)

Northern Arizona University, Art Museum & Galleries, Flagstaff AZ (M)

Northern Arizona University, School of Art & Design, Flagstaff AZ (S)

Northern Illinois University, Art Gallery in Chicago, Chicago IL (M)

Northern Illinois University, NIU Art Museum, De Kalb IL (M,L)

Northern Illinois University, School of Art, De Kalb IL (S)

Northern Kentucky University, Art Dept, Highland Heights KY (S)

Northern Kentucky University Gallery, Highland Heights KY (M)

Northern Michigan University, Lee Hall Gallery, Marquette MI (M)

Northern Michigan University, Dept of Art and Design, Marquette MI (S)

Northern State University, Art Dept, Aberdeen SD (S)

Northern State University, Art Galleries, Aberdeen SD (M)

Northern Virginia Community College, Art Dept, Annandale VA (S)

North Florida Junior College, Dept Humanities & Art, Madison FL (S)

North Georgia College, Fine Arts Dept, Dahlonega GA (S)

North Hennepin Community College, Art Gallery, Brooklyn Park MN (M)

North Hennepin Community College, Art Dept, Minneapolis MN (S)

North Idaho College, Art Dept, Coeur D'Alene ID (S)

North Iowa Area Community College, Dept of Art, Mason City IA (S)

Northland Pioneer College, Art Dept, Holbrook AZ (S)

North Miami Center of Contemporary Art, North Miami FL (M)

North Park College, Carlson Tower Gallery, Chicago IL (M)

North Park College, Art Dept, Chicago IL (S)

Northport-East Northport Public Library, Northport NY (L)

North Seattle Community College, Art Dept, Seattle WA (S)

North Shore Art League, Winnetka IL (A)

North Shore Art League, Winnetka IL (S)

North Shore Arts Association, Inc, Art Gallery, Gloucester MA (A)

North View Gallery, see Portland Community College, Portland OR

Northwest Community College, Dept of Art, Powell WY (S)

Northwestern College, Te Paske Gallery of Rowenhorst, Orange City IA (M)

Northwestern College, Art Dept, Orange City IA (S)

Northwestern Connecticut Community College, Fine Arts Dept, Winsted CT (S)

Northwestern Michigan College, Dennos Museum Center, Traverse City MI (M)

Northwestern Michigan College, Art Dept, Traverse City MI (S)

Northwestern State University of Louisiana, Dept of Art, Natchitoches LA (S)

Northwestern University, Evanston IL (M,L)

Northwestern University, Evanston, Evanston IL (S)

Northwest Missouri State University, DeLuce Art Gallery, Maryville MO (M)

Northwest Missouri State University, Dept of Art, Maryville MO (S)

Northwest Nazarene College, Art Dept, Nampa ID (S)

Northwood Institute, Alden B Dow Creativity Center, Midland MI (S)

Norton Gallery and School of Art, West Palm Beach FL (M,L)

R W Norton Art Gallery, Shreveport LA (M,L)

Norwest Bank of Minneapolis, Art Collection, Minneapolis MN (C)

Norwich Free Academy, Slater Memorial Museum & Converse Art Gallery, Norwich CT (M)

Norwich University, Dept of Philosophy, Religion and Fine Arts, Northfield VT (S)

Nossi School of Art, Goodlettsville TN (S)

Notre Dame College, Art Dept, Manchester NH (S)

(NOVA), see New Organization for the Visual Arts, Cleveland OH

NOVA Corporation of Alberta, NOVA Garden Court Gallery, Calgary AB (C)

Nova Scotia Association of Architects, Halifax NS (A)

Nova Scotia College of Art and Design, Halifax NS (S)

Nova Scotia College of Art and Design, Anna Leonowens Gallery, Halifax NS (M,L)

Nova Scotia Museum, Maritime Museum of the Atlantic, Halifax NS (M)

Noyes Museum, Oceanville NJ (M,L)

Noyes & Read Galleries, see Antioch College, Yellow Springs OH

Nutana Collegiate Institute, Memorial Library and Art Gallery, Saskatoon SK (L)

Oakland City College, Division of Fine Arts, Oakland City IN (S)

Oakland Community College, Art Dept, Farmington Hills MI (S)

Oakland Museum, Art Dept, Oakland CA (M,L)

Oakland Public Library, Art, Music & Recreation Section, Oakland CA (L)

Oakland University, Meadow Brook Art Gallery, Rochester MI (M)

Oakland University, Dept of Art and Art History, Rochester MI (S)

Oak Ridge Art Center, Oak Ridge TN (A,L)

Oakton Community College, Art & Architecture Dept, Des Plaines IL (S)

Oakville Galleries, Oakville ON (M)

Oatlands, Inc, Leesburg VA (M)

Oberlin College, Allen Memorial Art Museum, Oberlin OH (M,L)

Oberlin College, Dept of Art, Oberlin OH (S)

Occidental College, Weingart & Coons Galleries, Los Angeles CA (M)

Occidental College, Dept of Art History & Visual Arts, Los Angeles CA (S)

Ocean City Art Center, Ocean City NJ (S)

Ocean City Art Center, Ocean City NJ (A,L)

Ocean County College, Humanities Dept, Toms River NJ (S)

Octagon Center for the Arts, Ames IA (A)

Oesterle Library, see North Central College, Naperville IL

Office of Cultural Affairs of New Mexico, The Governor's Gallery, see Museum of New Mexico, Santa Fe NM

Office of Historic Properties, see Kentucky New State Capitol, Frankfort KY

Ogden Union Station, Ogden UT (M)

Oglebay Institute, Mansion Museum, Wheeling WV (M,L)

Ogunquit Museum of American Art, Ogunquit ME (M,L)

Ohio Dominican College, Art Dept, Columbus OH (S)

Ohio Historical Society, Columbus OH (A,L)

The Ohio Historical Society, Inc, Campus Martius Museum and Ohio River Museum, Marietta OH (M)

Ohio Northern University, Dept of Art, Ada OH (S)

Ohio State University, Columbus OH (M,L)

Ohio State University, Columbus OH (S)

Ohio University, Trisolini Gallery, Athens OH (M,L)

Ohio University, School of Art, Athens OH (S)

Ohio University-Belmont County Campus, Dept Comparative Arts, Saint Clairsville OH (S)

Ohio University-Chillicothe Campus, Fine Arts & Humanities Division, Chillicothe OH (S)

Ohio Wesleyan University, Fine Arts Dept, Delaware OH (S)

Ohrstrom Library, see Saint Paul's School, Concord NH

Oil Pastel Association, Nyack NY (A)

Ojai Valley Art Center, Ojai CA (A)

Okaloosa-Walton Junior College, Dept of Fine and Performing Arts, Niceville FL (S)

Okefenokee Heritage Center, Inc, Waycross GA (M)

Oklahoma Baptist University, Art Dept, Shawnee OK (S)

Oklahoma Center for Science and Art, Kirkpatrick Center, Oklahoma City OK (M)

Oklahoma Christian University of Science & Arts, Department of Art & Design, Oklahoma City OK (S)

Oklahoma City Art Museum, Oklahoma City OK (M,L)

Oklahoma City University, Norick Art Center, Oklahoma City OK (S)

Oklahoma City University, Hulsey Gallery-Norick Art Center, Oklahoma City OK (M,L)

Oklahoma Historical Society, State Museum of History, Oklahoma City OK (M,L)

Oklahoma State University, Graphic Arts Dept, Okmulgee OK (S)

Oklahoma State University, Gardiner Art Gallery, Stillwater OK (M,L)

Oklahoma State University, Art Dept, Stillwater OK (S)

Ringling School of Art & Design Library, Sarasota FL (L)

Ringwood Manor House Museum, Ringwood NJ (M)

Rio Hondo College, Fine Arts - Humanitites Division, Whittier CA (S)

Rio Hondo College Art Gallery, Whittier CA (M)

Ripon College, Art Dept, Ripon WI (S)

Ripon College Art Gallery, Ripon WI (M)

Ritter Art Gallery, see Florida Atlantic University, Boca Raton FL

Ritz-Carlton Hotel Company, Art Collection, Atlanta GA (C)

Riverside Art Museum, Riverside CA (M,L)

Riverside Community College, Dept of Art & Mass Media, Riverside CA (S)

Riverside County Museum, Edward-Dean Museum, Cherry Valley CA (M,L)

Riverside Municipal Museum, Riverside CA (M)

River Vale Public Library, Art Dept, River Vale NJ (L)

Rivier College, Art Dept, Nashua NH (S)

R J R Nabisco, Inc, New York NY (C)

Roanoke College, Fine Arts Dept-Art, Salem VA (S)

The Warren M Robbins Library, see National Museum of African Art, Washington DC

Roberson Museum & Science Center, Binghamton NY (M)

Roberts County Museum, Miami TX (M)

Roberts Wesleyan College, Art Dept, Rochester NY (S)

Rowland Evans Robinson Memorial Association, Rokeby Museum, Ferrisburgh VT (A)

Rochester Art Center, Rochester MN (A)

Rochester Community College, Art Dept, Rochester MN (S)

Rochester Historical Society, Rochester NY (A)

Rochester Institute of Technology, Technical & Education Center of the Graphic Arts, Rochester NY (L)

Rochester Institute of Technology, Rochester NY (S)

Abby Aldrich Rockefeller Folk Art Center, see Colonial Williamsburg Foundation, Williamsburg VA

Abby Aldrich Rockefeller Folk Art Center Library, see Colonial Williamsburg Foundation, Williamsburg VA

M C Rockefeller Arts Center Gallery, see State University of New York College at Fredonia, Fredonia NY

Rockford Art Museum, Rockford IL (A,L)

Rockford College, Dept of Fine Arts, Rockford IL (S)

Rock Ford Foundation, Inc, Rock Ford Plantation & Kauffman Museum, Lancaster PA (M)

Rock Ford Plantation & Kauffman Museum, see Rock Ford Foundation, Inc, Lancaster PA

Rockland Center for the Arts, West Nyack NY (M)

Rockland Center for the Arts, West Nyack NY (S)

Rockland Community College, Graphic Arts & Advertising Tech Dept, Suffern NY (S)

Rockport Art Association, Rockport MA (A)

Rock Valley College, Dept of Art, Rockford IL (S)

Rockwell International Corporation Trust, Pittsburgh PA (C)

The Rockwell Museum, Corning NY (M,L)

Norman Rockwell Museum at Stockbridge, Stockbridge MA (M,L)

Rocky Mountain College, Art Dept, Billings MT (S)

Rocky Mountain College of Art & Design, Denver CO (S)

Rocky Mount Arts Center, Rocky Mount NC (A)

Rocky Reach Dam, see Chelan County Public Utility District, Wenatchee WA

Rodin Museum of Philadelphia, see Philadelphia Museum of Art, Philadelphia PA

Rodman Hall Arts Centre, Saint Catharines ON (A,L)

Nicholas Roerich Museum, New York NY (M)

Rogers House Museum Gallery, Ellsworth KS (M)

Lauren Rogers Museum of Art, Laurel MS (M,L)

Millicent Rogers Museum, Taos NM (M,L)

Rogers State College, Art Dept, Claremore OK (S)

Will Rogers Memorial and Museum, Claremore OK (M,L)

Roger Williams College, Art Dept, Bristol RI (S)

Rogue Valley Art Association, Rogue Gallery, Medford OR (A)

Rohrbach Library, see Kutztown University, Kutztown PA

Rokeby Museum, see Rowland Evans Robinson Memorial Association, Ferrisburgh VT

Rollins College, George D and Harriet W Cornell Fine Arts Museum, Winter Park FL (M)

Rollins College, Dept of Art, Main Campus, Winter Park FL (S)

Rome Art and Community Center, Rome NY (A)

Rome Historical Society Museum, Rome NY (M,L)

Franklin D Roosevelt Museum, see National Archives & Records Administration, Hyde Park NY

Roosevelt-Vanderbilt National Historic Sites, Hyde Park NY (M)

The Stephanie Ann Roper Gallery, see Frostburg State University, Frostburg MD

Rose Art Museum, see Brandeis University, Waltham MA

Rosemont College, Division of the Arts, Rosemont PA (S)

Rosemount Victorian House Museum, Pueblo CO (M)

The Rosenbach Museum and Library, Philadelphia PA (M)

Rosenberg Gallery, see Goucher College, Towson MD

Rosenberg Library, Galveston TX (L)

Rosenthal Art Gallery, see Albertson College of Idaho, Caldwell ID

Rosicrucian Egyptian Museum and Art Gallery, San Jose CA (M)

Henry Phipps Ross & Sarah Juliette Ross Memorial Museum, Saint Andrews NB (M)

Roswell Museum and Art Center, Roswell NM (M,L)

Rotch Library of Architecture & Planning, see Massachusetts Institute of Technology, Cambridge MA

Rothmans, Benson & Hedges, Art Collection, Don Mills ON (C)

The Rotunda Gallery, see The Fund for the Borough of Brooklyn, Brooklyn NY

Round Top Center for the Arts Inc, Arts Gallery, Damariscotta ME (M,L)

Round Top Library, see Round Top Center for the Arts Inc, Damariscotta ME

Rowan College of New Jersey, Dept of Art, Glassboro NJ (S)

Royal Architectural Institute of Canada, Ottawa ON (O)

Royal Canadian Academy of Arts, Toronto ON (O)

Royal Ontario Museum, Toronto ON (M,L)

Elizabeth Rozier Gallery, see Department of Natural Resources of Missouri, Jefferson City MO

Rubelle & Norman Schafler Gallery, see Pratt Institute Library, Brooklyn NY

Ruddell Gallery, see Black Hills State College, Spearfish SD

Ruder Finn & Rotman Inc, New York NY (C)

C M Russell Museum, Great Falls MT (M,L)

Russell Sage College, Gallery, Troy NY (M)

Russell Sage College, Visual and Performing Arts Dept, Troy NY (S)

Rutgers, The State University of New Jersey, New Brunswick NJ (M,L)

Rutgers, the State University of New Jersey, New Brunswick NJ (S)

Rutgers University, Stedman Art Gallery, Camden NJ (M)

Rutgers University, Camden, Art Dept, Camden NJ (S)

Rutgers University, Newark, Newark Col Arts & Sciences, Newark NJ (S)

Rutland Area Art Association, Inc, Chaffee Art Center, Rutland VT (A)

Ryan Fine Arts Center, see McMurry University, Abilene TX

Ryerson and Burnham Libraries, see The Art Institute of Chicago, Chicago IL

Ryerson Polytechnical Institute, Library, Toronto ON (L)

Robert W Ryerss Library and Museum, Philadelphia PA (M,L)

Aline B Saarinen Library, see The Parrish Art Museum, Southampton NY

Arthur M Sackler Gallery, see Smithsonian Institution, Washington DC

Arthur M Sackler Museum, see Harvard University, Cambridge MA

Sacramento City College, Art Dept, Sacramento CA (S)

Sacramento Fine Arts Center, see Pastel Society of the West Coast, Carmichael CA

Sacred Heart University, Dept of Art, Fairfield CT (S)

Safeco Insurance Company, Art Collection, Seattle WA (C)

Safety Harbor Museum of Regional History, Safety Harbor FL (M)

Saginaw Art Museum, Saginaw MI (M,L)

Saginaw Valley State University, Dept of Art and Design, University Center MI (S)

Saint Ambrose University, Art Dept, Davenport IA (S)

Saint Andrews Presbyterian College, Art Program, Laurinburg NC (S)

Saint Anselm College, Chapel Art Center, Manchester NH (M)

Saint Anselm College, Dept of Fine Arts, Manchester NH (S)

Saint Augustine Art Association Gallery, Saint Augustine FL (A)

Saint Augustine Historical Society, Saint Augustine FL (M,L)

Saint Bernard Foundation and Monastery, North Miami Beach FL (M)

Saint Bonaventure University, Art Collection, Saint Bonaventure NY (M)

Saint Clair County Community College, Art Dept, Port Huron MI (S)

St Clair County Community College, Jack R Hennesey Art Galleries, Port Huron MI (M)

Saint Cloud State University, Saint Cloud MN (M)

Saint Cloud State University, Dept of Art, Saint Cloud MN (S)

Saint Edward's University, Fine Arts Exhibit Program, Austin TX (M)

Saint Francis College, Art Dept, Fort Wayne IN (S)

Saint Francis College, John Weatherhead Gallery, Fort Wayne IN (M)

St Francis College, Fine Arts Dept, Loretto PA (S)

St Francis Xavier University, Fine Arts Dept, Antigonish NS (S)

Saint-Gaudens National Historic Site, Cornish NH (M,L)

St Genevieve Museum, Sainte Genevieve MO (M)

Saint Gregory's Abbey and College, Mabee-Gerrer Museum of Art, Shawnee OK (M)

Saint Gregory's College, Dept of Art, Shawnee OK (S)

Saint Johnsbury Athenaeum, Saint Johnsbury VT (M)

Saint John's College, Elizabeth Myers Mitchell Art Gallery, Annapolis MD (M)

Saint John's Museum of Art, Wilmington NC (M,L)

Saint John's University, Art Dept, Collegeville MN (S)

Saint John's University, Chung-Cheng Art Gallery, Jamaica NY (M,L)

Saint John's University, Dept of Fine Arts, Jamaica NY (S)

Saint Joseph College, Dept of Fine Arts, West Hartford CT (S)

Saint Joseph Museum, Saint Joseph MO (M,L)

Saint Joseph's Oratory, Museum, Montreal PQ (M,L)

Saint Joseph's University, Dept of Fine & Performing Arts, Philadelphia PA (S)

St Lawrence College, Dept of Visual & Creative Arts, Cornwall ON (S)

St Lawrence College, Art Gallery, Kingston ON (M)

St Lawrence University, Richard F Brush Art Gallery, Canton NY (M)

St Lawrence University, Dept of Fine Arts, Canton NY (S)

Saint Louis Artists' Guild, Saint Louis MO (A)

The Saint Louis Art Museum, Saint Louis MO (M,L)

Saint Louis Community College at Florissant Valley, Division of Communications & Arts, Ferguson MO (S)

Saint Louis Community College at Forest Park, Art Dept, Saint Louis MO (S)

Saint Louis Community College at Meramec, Art Dept, Saint Louis MO (S)

Saint Louis County Historical Society, Duluth MN (M)

Saint-Louis-Maillet, Dept of Visual Arts, Edmundston NB (S)

Saint Louis Public Library, Saint Louis MO (L)

Saint Louis University, Fine & Performing Arts Dept, Saint Louis MO (S)

Saint Luke's Gallery, see Anna Maria College, Paxton MA

St Martins College, Humanities Dept, Lacey WA (S)

Saint Mary College, Art Dept, Leavenworth KS (S)

Saint Mary-of-the-Woods College, Art Dept, Saint Mary-of-the-Woods IN (S)

Saint Mary's College, Dept of Art, Notre Dame IN (S)

Saint Mary's College, Moreau Gallery, Notre Dame IN (M)

Saint Mary's College, Art Dept, Raleigh NC (S)

Saint Mary's College of California, Hearst Art Gallery, Moraga CA (M)

St Mary's College of Maryland, The Dwight Frederick Boyden Gallery, Saint Mary City MD (M)

Saint Mary's College of Maryland, Arts and Letters Division, Saint Mary's City MD (S)

Saint Mary's College of Minnesota, Art Dept No 18, Winona MN (S)

St Mary's Galeria, Orchard Lake MI (M)

Saint Mary's Romanian Orthodox Church, Romanian Ethnic Museum, Cleveland OH (M)

St Mary's University, Art Gallery, Halifax NS (M)

Saint Mary's University of San Antonio, Dept of Fine Arts, San Antonio TX (S)

Saint Meinrad College, Humanities Dept, Saint Meinrad IN (S)

St Michael's College, Fine Arts Dept, Colchester VT (S)

Saint Norbert College, Div of Humanities & Fine Arts, De Pere WI (S)

Saint Olaf College, Art Dept, Northfield MN (S)

Saint Paul Public Library, Art & Music Dept, Saint Paul MN (L)

Saint Paul's School, Art Center in Hargate, Concord NH (M,L)

Saint Petersburg Junior College, Humanities Dept, Saint Petersburg FL (S)

Saint Peter's College, Fine Arts Dept, Jersey City NJ (S)

Saint Peter's College, Art Gallery, Jersey City NJ (M)

St Tammany Art Association, Covington LA (A)

Saint Thomas Aquinas College, Art Dept, Sparkhill NY (S)

St Thomas Elgin Art Gallery, Saint Thomas ON (M)

Saint Xavier University, Dept of Art, Chicago IL (S)

Saint Xavier University, Byrne Memorial Library, Chicago IL (L)

Salem Art Association, Salem OR (A,M,L)

Salem College, Art Dept, Winston-Salem NC (S)

Salem State College, Art Dept, Salem MA (S)

Salina Art Center, Salina KS (M)

Salisbury House, see Iowa State Education Association, Des Moines IA

Salisbury State University, Art Dept, Salisbury MD (S)

Salisbury State University, Salisbury MD (M,L)

Salmagundi Club, New York NY (O)

Salt Lake Art Center, Salt Lake City UT (A)

Salt Lake City Public Library, Fine Arts/ Audiovisual Dept and Atrium Gallery, Salt Lake City UT (L)

Salt Lake Community College, Graphic Design Dept, Salt Lake City UT (S)

Salvador Dali Museum, Saint Petersburg FL (M,L)

Salve Regina College, Art Dept, Newport RI (S)

Ruth Salyer Library, see Art Institute of Southern California, Laguna Beach CA

Samford University, Art Dept, Birmingham AL (S)

Sam Houston State University, Art Dept, Huntsville TX (S)

Sampson Art Gallery, see Thiel College, Greenville PA

Philip Samuels Fine Art, see Trova Foundation, St Louis MO

San Angelo Art Club, Helen King Kendall Memorial Art Gallery, San Angelo TX (M)

San Angelo Museum of Fine Arts, San Angelo TX (M)

San Antonio Art Institute, San Antonio TX (S)

San Antonio Art League, San Antonio TX (A,L)

San Antonio College, Visual Arts & Technology, San Antonio TX (S)

San Antonio Museum Association, Inc, San Antonio TX (A,M)

San Antonio Public Library, Dept of Fine Arts, San Antonio TX (L)

San Bernardino Art Association, Inc, San Bernardino CA (A)

San Bernardino County Museum, Fine Arts Institute, Redlands CA (M)

San Bernardino Valley College, Art Dept, San Bernardino CA (S)

San Carlos Cathedral, Monterey CA (M)

Hazel Sandford Gallery, see Clarion University, Clarion PA

San Diego Maritime Museum, San Diego CA (M)

San Diego Mesa College, Fine Arts Dept, San Diego CA (S)

San Diego Museum of Art, San Diego CA (M,L)

San Diego Public Library, Art & Music Section, San Diego CA (L)

San Diego State University, University Art Gallery, San Diego CA (M,L)

San Diego State University, Dept of Art, San Diego CA (S)

Sandwich Historical Society, Center Sandwich NH (M)

The Sandwich Historical Society, Inc, Sandwich Glass Museum, Sandwich MA (M,L)

Sandy Bay Historical Society, Sewall Scripture House-Old Castle, Rockport MA (A)

Birger Sandzen Memorial Gallery, Lindsborg KS (M)

San Fernando Valley Historical Society, Mission Hills CA (A,L)

San Francisco Academy of Comic Art, Library, San Francisco CA (L)

San Francisco Art Institute, Galleries, San Francisco CA (M,L)

San Francisco Art Institute, San Francisco CA (S)

San Francisco Artspace & Artspace Annex, San Francisco CA (A)

San Francisco Camerawork Inc, San Francisco CA (A)

San Francisco City & County Arts Commission, San Francisco CA (A)

San Francisco Craft and Folk Art Museum, San Francisco CA (M)

San Francisco Maritime National Historical Park, National Maritime Museum, San Francisco CA (M,L)

San Francisco Museum of Modern Art, San Francisco CA (M,L)

San Francisco Public Library, Art and Music Dept, San Francisco CA (L)

San Francisco State University, Art Dept, San Francisco CA (S)

San Francisco State University, J Paul Leonard Library, San Francisco CA (L)

Sangamon State University, Visual Arts Program, Springfield IL (S)

Sangre de Cristo Arts & Conference Center, Pueblo CO (A)

San Jacinto College-North, Art Dept, Houston TX (S)

San Jacinto Junior College, Div of Fine Arts, Pasadena TX (S)

San Joaquin Delta College, Art Dept, Stockton CA (S)

San Joaquin Pioneer and Historical Society, The Haggin Museum, Stockton CA (M,L)

San Jose City College, School of Fine Arts, San Jose CA (S)

San Jose Institute of Contemporary Art, San Jose CA (M)

San Jose Museum of Art, San Jose CA (M,L)

San Jose State University, San Jose CA (M,L)

San Jose State University, School of Art & Design, San Jose CA (S)

San Juan College, Art Dept, Farmington NM (S)

Santa Barbara City College, Fine Arts Dept, Santa Barbara CA (S)

Santa Barbara Contemporary Arts Forum, Santa Barbara CA (A)

Santa Barbara Museum of Art, Santa Barbara CA (M,L)

Santa Barbara Public Library, Faulkner Memorial Art Wing, Santa Barbara CA (L)

Santa Clara University, de Saisset Museum, Santa Clara CA (M)

Santa Clara University, Art Dept, Santa Clara CA (S)

Santa Cruz Art League, Inc, Santa Cruz CA (A)

Santa Cruz Valley Art Association, Tubac Center of the Arts, Tubac AZ (A,L)

Santa Fe Institute of Fine Arts, Santa Fe NM (S)

Santa Monica College Art Gallery, Santa Monica CA (M)

Santa Rosa Junior College, Art Dept, Santa Rosa CA (S)

Santa Rosa Junior College, Santa Rosa CA (M)

Santuario de Guadalupe, see Guadalupe Historic Foundation, Santa Fe NM

Allen Sapp Gallery, North Battleford SK (M)

Sarah Lawrence College, Dept of Art History, Bronxville NY (S)

Sarah Lawrence College Library, Esther Raushenbush Library, Bronxville NY (L)

Sarasota Visual Art Center, Sarasota FL (A,L)

Saratoga County Historical Society, Brookside Museum, Ballston Spa NY (A)

Saskatchewan Arts Board, Regina SK (O)

Saskatchewan Association of Architects, Saskatoon SK (A)

Saskatchewan Craft Gallery, Saskatoon SK (M)

Saskpower, Gallery on the Roof, Regina SK (C)

Savannah State College, Dept of Fine Arts, Savannah GA (S)

Saving & Preserving Arts & Cultural Environments, Los Angeles CA (A,L)

Sawhill Gallery, see James Madison University, Harrisonburg VA

Sawtooth Center for Visual Art, Winston-Salem NC (S)

Sawyer Library, see Williams College, Williamstown MA

Scalamandre Museum of Textiles, New York NY (M)

Scantic Academy Museum, see East Windsor Historical Society, Inc, East Windsor CT

Lee Scarfone Gallery, see University of Tampa, Tampa FL

Schenectady County Historical Society, Schenectady NY (A,L)

Schenectady Museum, Planetarium & Visitors Center, Schenectady NY (M,L)

Mary R Schiff Library, see Cincinnati Museum Association, Cincinnati OH

Schingoethe Center for Native American Cultures, see Aurora University, Aurora IL

Scholes Library of Ceramics, see New York State College of Ceramics at Alfred University, Alfred NY

Maude Schollenberger Memorial Library, see Wichita Center for the Arts, Wichita KS

Schomburg Center for Research in Black Culture, see The New York Public Library, New York NY

Schoolcraft College, Dept of Art and Design, Livonia MI (S)

School of Airbrush Arts, Villa Park IL (S)

School of American Research, Santa Fe NM (M,L)

School of Art Institute of Chicago, Video Data Bank, Chicago IL (L)

The School of Fashion Design, Boston MA (S)

School of Fine Arts, Visual Arts Dept, Willoughby OH (S)

School of Nations Museum, see Principia College, Elsah IL

School of the Art Institute of Chicago, Chicago IL (S)

School of the Art Institute of Chicago, John M Flaxman Library, Chicago IL (L)

School of the Museum of Fine Arts, Boston MA (S)

School of Visual Arts, New York NY (S)
School of Visual Arts Library, New York NY (L)
School 33 Art Center, Baltimore MD (A)
Schuler School of Fine Arts, Baltimore MD (S)
Schumacher Gallery, see Capital University, Columbus OH
Schuyler-Hamilton House, Morristown NJ (M)
Schuyler Mansion State Historic Site, Albany NY (M)
Schweinfurth Art Center, Auburn NY (M)
Science Museums of Charlotte, Inc, Discovery Place, Charlotte NC (M)
Agnes Scott College, Dalton Gallery, Decatur GA (M)
Scott Explorers Library, see Martin & Osa Johnson Safari Museum, Inc, Chanute KS
Scotts Bluff National Monument, see Oregon Trail Museum Association, Gering NE
Scottsdale Artists' League, Scottsdale AZ (A)
Scottsdale Center for the Arts, Scottsdale AZ (M)
The Charles H Scott Gallery, see Emily Carr College of Art & Design, Vancouver BC
Lucy Scribner Library, see Skidmore College, Saratoga Springs NY
Scripps College, Art Dept, Claremont CA (S)
Scripps College, Clark Humanities Museum, Claremont CA (M)
William E Scripture Memorial Library, see Rome Historical Society Museum, Rome NY
Sculptors Guild, New York NY (O)
Sculptor's Society of Canada, Toronto ON (O)
Sculpture Center Gallery & School, New York NY (S)
Sculpture Center Inc, New York NY (M,L)
Sculpture Space, Inc, Utica NY (M)
Joseph E Seagram & Sons, Inc, Gallery, New York NY (C)
The Seagram Museum, Waterloo ON (M,L)
Seaton Library, see Riley County Historical Museum, Manhattan KS
Seaton Memorial Library, see Philmont Scout Ranch, Cimarron NM
Seattle Art Museum, Seattle WA (M,L)
Seattle Central Community College, Humanities - Social Sciences Division, Seattle WA (S)
Seattle Pacific University, Art Dept, Seattle WA (S)
Seattle University, Fine Arts Dept, Division of Art, Seattle WA (S)
Second Crossing Gallery Staus Mall, see Valley City Arts & Gallery Association, Valley City ND
Second Street Gallery, Charlottesville VA (M)
Security Pacific Bank Arizona, Phoenix AZ (C)
Seigfred Gallery, see Ohio University, Athens OH
Self Help Graphics, Los Angeles CA (A)
Selsor Gallery of Art, see Martin & Osa Johnson Safari Museum, Inc, Chanute KS
Semitic Museum, see Harvard University, Cambridge MA
Senate House State Historic Site, see Palisades Interstate Park Commission, Kingston NY
Seneca Falls Historical Society Museum, Seneca Falls NY (M)
Seton Hall University, South Orange NJ (M,L)
Seton Hall University, College of Arts & Sciences, South Orange NJ (S)
Seton Hill College, Dept of Art, Greensburg PA (S)
Seton Hill College, Reeves Memorial Library, Greensburg PA (L)
Seton School of Associate Degree Studies, Art Dept, see Iona College, Yonkers NY (S)
1708 East Main Gallery, Richmond VA (M)
Severin Wunderman Museum, Irvine CA (M,L)
Sewall Art Gallery, see Rice University, Houston TX
Sewall Scripture House-Old Castle, see Sandy Bay Historical Society, Rockport MA
Seward County Community College, Art Dept, Liberal KS (S)
SFA Gallery, see Stephen F Austin State University, Nacogdoches TX
Shadows-on-the-Teche, New Iberia LA (M)
Ben Shahn Galleries, see William Paterson College of New Jersey, Wayne NJ
The Shaker Library, see United Society of Shakers, Poland Spring ME
Shaker Museum, Old Chatham NY (M,L)
Shaker Museum, see United Society of Shakers, Poland Spring ME

Shaker Village of Pleasant Hill, Harrodsburg KY (M)
Martin C Shallenberger Art Library, see Sweet Briar College, Sweet Briar VA
Sharadin Art Gallery, see Kutztown University, Kutztown PA
Sharon Arts Center, Sharon NH (S)
Sharon Arts Center, Sharon NH (M)
Ella Sharp Museum, Jackson MI (M)
Shasta College, Art Dept, Fine Arts Division, Redding CA (S)
Lemuel Shattuck Memorial Library, see Bisbee Mining & Historical Museum, Bisbee AZ
Shawinigan Art Center, Shawinigan PQ (A)
J Porter Shaw Library, see San Francisco Maritime National Historical Park, San Francisco CA
Sheboygan Arts Foundation, Inc, John Michael Kohler Arts Center, Sheboygan WI (A)
Shelburne Museum, Shelburne VT (M,L)
Sheldon Jackson Museum, Sitka AK (M,L)
Sheldon Memorial Art Gallery, see University of Nebraska, Lincoln, Lincoln NE
Sheldon Museum, Middlebury VT (M)
Sheldon Museum & Cultural Center, see Chilkat Valley Historical Society, Haines AK
Shell Canada Ltd, Calgary AB (C)
Shepherd College, Art Dept, Shepherdstown WV (S)
Sheppard Fine Art Gallery, see University of Nevada, Reno NV
Sheridan College, Faculty of Visual Arts, Oakville ON (S)
Sheridan College, Art Dept, Sheridan WY (S)
Sheridan College of Applied Arts and Technology, Visual Arts & Crafts Library, Oakville ON (L)
Sherman Art Library, see Dartmouth College, Hanover NH
C C Sherrod Library, see East Tennessee State University, Johnson City TN
Shiloh Museum, see City of Springdale, Springdale AR
Shippensburg University, Art Dept, Shippensburg PA (S)
Shippensburg University, Kauffman Gallery, Shippensburg PA (M)
Ships of The Sea Museum, Savannah GA (M,L)
Shirley Plantation, Charles City VA (M)
1859 Jail, Marshal s Home & Museum, see Jackson County Historical Society, Independence MO
Shoreline Community College, Humanities Division, Seattle WA (S)
Shoreline Historical Museum, Seattle WA (M)
Shorncliffe Park Improvement Assoc, Prairie Panorama Museum, Czar AB (M)
Shorter College, Art Dept, Rome GA (S)
SIAS International Art Society, Sherwood Park AB (O)
Eli Siegel Collection, see Aesthetic Realism Foundation, New York NY
Siena College, Fine Arts Dept, Loudonville NY (S)
Siena Heights College, Klemm Gallery, Studio Angelico, Adrian MI (M,L)
Siena Heights College, Studio Angelico-Art Dept, Adrian MI (S)
Sierra Arts Foundation, Reno NV (A)
Sierra College, Art Dept, Rocklin CA (S)
Sierra Nevada College, Art Dept, Incline Village NV (S)
Silverado Museum, Saint Helena CA (M,L)
Silver Eye Center for Photography, Pittsburgh PA (A)
Silver Lake College, Art Dept, Manitowoc WI (S)
Silvermine Guild Arts Center, Silvermine Galleries, New Canaan CT (A,L)
Simon Fraser University, Simon Fraser Gallery, Burnaby BC (M,L)
Norton Simon Museum, Pasadena CA (M)
Simon's Rock College of Bard, Great Barrington MA (M,L)
Simon's Rock of Bard College, Visual Arts Dept, Great Barrington MA (S)
Simpson College, Art Dept, Indianola IA (S)
Simpson College, Farnham Gallery, Indianola IA (M)
Sims Art Center, see Brevard College, Brevard NC
Sinclair Community College, Div of Performing & Fine Arts, Dayton OH (S)
Sioux City Art Center, Sioux City IA (A,L)

Sioux City Art Center, Sioux City IA (S)
Sioux Falls College, Dept of Art, Sioux Falls SD (S)
Sioux Indian Museum, see Indian Arts and Crafts Board, Rapid City SD
Sitka Historical Society, Isabel Miller Museum, Sitka AK (M)
Skagit Valley College, Dept of Art, Mount Vernon WA (S)
Skaneateles Library Association, Skaneateles NY (A)
Skidmore College, Schick Art Gallery, Saratoga Springs NY (M,L)
Skidmore College, Dept of Art & Art History, Saratoga Springs NY (S)
Skirball Museum, see Hebrew Union College, Los Angeles CA
Skirball Museum-Cincinnati Branch, see Hebrew Union College - Jewish Institute of Religion, Cincinnati OH
Skokie Public Library, Skokie IL (L)
Skowhegan School of Painting and Sculpture, New York NY (S)
Skowhegan School of Painting and Sculpture, Skowhegan ME (S)
SLA Arch-Couture Inc, Art Collection, Denver CO (C)
Slater Memorial Museum & Converse Art Gallery, see Norwich Free Academy, Norwich CT
Slater Mill Historic Site, see Old Slater Mill Association, Pawtucket RI
Slippery Rock University of Pennsylvania, Dept of Art, Slippery Rock PA (S)
Joseph Curtis Sloane Art Library, see University of North Carolina at Chapel Hill, Chapel Hill NC
Sloane-Stanley Museum, see Connecticut Historical Commission, Kent CT
Helen Farr Sloan Library, see Delaware Art Museum, Wilmington DE
Elizabeth Slocumb Galleries, see East Tennessee State University, Johnson City TN
Sloss Furnaces National Historic Landmark, Birmingham AL (M)
Slusser Gallery, see University of Michigan, Ann Arbor MI
David and Alfred Smart Museum of Art, see University of Chicago, Chicago IL
Abigail Adams Smith Museum, New York NY (M)
C E Smith Museum of Anthropology, see California State University, Hayward, Hayward CA
Smith College, Museum of Art, Northampton MA (M,L)
Smith College, Art Dept, Northampton MA (S)
Eloisa Pickard Smith Gallery, see University of California - Santa Cruz, Santa Cruz CA
George Walter Vincent Smith Art Museum, Springfield MA (M)
Smithsonian Institution, Washington DC (M)
Gordon Snelgrove Art Gallery, see University of Saskatchewan, Saskatoon SK
Snite Museum of Art, see University of Notre Dame, Notre Dame IN
Snow College, Art Dept, Ephraim UT (S)
Snug Harbor Cultural Center, Newhouse Center for Contemporary Art, Staten Island NY (M)
Social & Public Art Resource Center, (SPARC), Venice CA (A)
Societe Des Musees Quebecois, Montreal PQ (A,L)
Society For Commercial Archeology, see National Museum of American History, Washington DC
Society for Folk Arts Preservation, Inc, New York NY (O)
Society for Photographic Education, Dallas TX (A)
Society for the Preservation of New England Antiquities, Boston MA (A,L)
Society of American Graphic Artists, New York NY (O)
Society of American Historical Artists, Jericho NY (O)
Society of Animal Artists, Inc, Bronx NY (O)
Society of Architectural Historians, Philadelphia PA (O)
The Society of Arts and Crafts, Boston MA (A)
Society of Canadian Artists, Toronto ON (O)
Society of Illustrators, New York NY (O)
Society of Illustrators, Museum of American Illustration, New York NY (M)
Society of Layerists in Multi Media, Albuquerque NM (A)

United Missouri Bancshares, Inc, Kansas City MO (C)
United Society of Shakers, Shaker Museum, Poland Spring ME (M,L)
United States Capitol, Architect of the Capitol, Washington DC (M,L)
US Coast Guard Museum, New London CT (M)
United States Commission of Fine Arts, Washington DC (A)
United States Committee of the International Association of Art, Inc, Washington DC (O)
US Department of State, Diplomatic Reception Rooms, Washington DC (M)
United States Department of the Interior, Indian Arts & Crafts Board, Washington DC (O)
United States Department of the Interior Museum, Washington DC (M)
United States Figure Skating Association, World Figure Skating Hall of Fame and Museum, Colorado Springs CO (M,L)
United States International University, School of Performing and Visual Arts, San Diego CA (S)
United States Military Academy, West Point Museum, West Point NY (M)
United States Naval Academy Museum, Annapolis MD (M,L)
United States Navy, Art Gallery, Washington DC (M)
US Navy Supply Corps School, Museum, Athens GA (M)
United States Senate Commission on Art, Washington DC (A,L)
United States Tobacco Manufacturing Company Inc, Museum of Tobacco & History, Nashville TN (C)
US West, Seattle WA (C)
United Westurne Inc, Art Collection, Montreal PQ (C)
Universal Technical Institute, Commercial Art Division, Omaha NE (S)
Universite de Moncton, Department of Visual Arts, Moncton NB (S)
Universite de Montreal, Bibliotheque d'Amenagement, Montreal PQ (L)
Universite de Montreal, Dept of Art History, Montreal PQ (S)
Universite Du Quebec, Library, Bibliotheque des Arts, Montreal PQ (L)
Universite du Quebec a Montreal, Famille des Arts, Montreal PQ (S)
Universite Laval Cite Universitaire, School of Visual Arts, Quebec PQ (S)
University Art Gallery of California State University at Dominguez Hills, Dominguez Hills CA (M)
University at Buffalo, State University of New York, Dept of Art, Buffalo NY (S)
University Club Library, New York NY (L)
University of Akron, Akron OH (M)
University of Akron, School of Art, Akron OH (S)
University of Alabama, Moody Gallery of Art, Tuscaloosa AL (M)
University of Alabama, Art Dept, Tuscaloosa AL (S)
University of Alabama at Birmingham, Visual Arts Gallery, Birmingham AL (M)
University of Alabama at Huntsville, Gallery of Art, Huntsville AL (M)
University of Alabama in Birmingham, Dept of Art, Birmingham AL (S)
University of Alabama in Huntsville, Dept of Art & Art History, Huntsville AL (S)
University of Alaska, Fairbanks AK (M,L)
University of Alaska, Dept of Art, Fairbanks AK (S)
University of Alaska Anchorage, Dept of Art, Anchorage AK (S)
University of Alberta, Dept of Art and Design, Edmonton AB (S)
University of Arizona, Tucson AZ (M,L)
University of Arizona, Dept of Art, Tucson AZ (S)
University of Arkansas, Fayetteville AR (L)
University of Arkansas, Art Dept, Fayetteville AR (S)
University of Arkansas, Art Slide Library, Little Rock AR (L)
University of Arkansas at Little Rock, Dept of Art, Little Rock AR (S)

University of Arkansas at Monticello, Fine Arts Dept, Monticello AR (S)
University of Arkansas at Pine Bluff, Art Dept, Pine Bluff AR (S)
University of Bridgeport, Art Dept, Bridgeport CT (S)
University of Bridgeport, Carlson Gallery, Bridgeport CT (M)
University of British Columbia, Vancouver BC (M,L)
University of British Columbia, Vancouver BC (S)
University of Calgary, The Nickle Arts Museum, Calgary AB (M,L)
University of Calgary, Dept of Art, Calgary AB (S)
University of California, Berkeley CA (M,L)
University of California, Davis CA (M,L)
University of California, Riverside CA (M,L)
University of California, Berkeley, Berkeley CA (S)
University of California, Davis, Art Dept, Davis CA (S)
University of California, Irvine, Fine Art Gallery, Irvine CA (M)
University of California, Irvine, Studio Art Dept, Irvine CA (S)
University of California, Los Angeles, Los Angeles CA (S)
University of California, Los Angeles, Los Angeles CA (M,L)
University of California, Riverside, Riverside CA (S)
University of California-San Diego, Mandeville Gallery, La Jolla CA (M)
University of California, San Diego, Visual Arts Dept, La Jolla CA (S)
University of California, Santa Barbara, Dept of Art Studio, Santa Barbara CA (S)
University of California, Santa Barbara, Santa Barbara CA (M,L)
University of California, Santa Cruz, Board of Studies in Art, Santa Cruz CA (S)
University of California - Santa Cruz, Eloisa Pickard Smith Gallery, Santa Cruz CA (M)
University of Central Arkansas, Art Dept, Conway AR (S)
University of Central Florida, Art Dept, Orlando FL (S)
University of Central Oklahoma, Dept of Visual Arts & Design, Edmond OK (S)
University of Charleston, Carleton Varney Dept of Art & Design, Charleston WV (S)
University of Chicago, Chicago IL (M,L)
University of Chicago, Dept of Art History and Committee on Art and Design, Chicago IL (S)
University of Cincinnati, Cincinnati OH (M,L)
University of Cincinnati, School of Art, Cincinnati OH (S)
University of Colorado, Art Galleries, Boulder CO (M,L)
University of Colorado at Colorado Springs, Gallery of Contemporary Art, Colorado Springs CO (M)
University of Colorado at Denver, Dept of Fine Arts, Denver CO (S)
University of Colorado, Boulder, Dept of Fine Arts, Boulder CO (S)
University of Colorado-Colorado Springs, Fine Arts Dept, Colorado Springs CO (S)
University of Connecticut, Storrs CT (M,L)
University of Connecticut, Art Dept, Storrs CT (S)
University of Dayton, Visual Arts Dept, Dayton OH (S)
University of Delaware, Dept of Art, Newark DE (S)
University of Delaware, Newark DE (M,L)
University of Denver, School of Art, Denver CO (S)
University of Detroit Mercy, School of Architecture, Detroit MI (S)
University of Evansville, Evansville IN (M,L)
University of Evansville, Art Dept, Evansville IN (S)
University of Findlay, Art Dept, Findlay OH (S)
University of Florida, Gainesville FL (M,L)
University of Florida, Dept of Art, Gainesville FL (S)
University of Georgia, Athens GA (M,L)
University of Georgia, Franklin College of Arts & Sciences, Dept of Art, Athens GA (S)

University of Guelph, Fine Art Dept, Guelph ON (S)
University of Hartford, Hartford Art School, West Hartford CT (S)
University of Hartford, Joseloff Gallery, West Hartford CT (M,L)
University of Hawaii, Kapiolani Community College, Honolulu HI (S)
University of Hawaii at Manoa, Art Gallery, Honolulu HI (M)
University of Hawaii at Manoa, Dept of Art, Honolulu HI (S)
University of Houston, Sarah Campbell Blaffer Gallery, Houston TX (M,L)
University of Houston, Dept of Art, Houston TX (S)
University of Idaho, College of Art & Architecture, Moscow ID (S)
University of Illinois, Champaign IL (M,L)
University of Illinois at Chicago, College of Architecture, Art and Urban Planning, Chicago IL (S)
University of Illinois At Chicago, Gallery 400, Chicago IL (M)
University of Illinois, Chicago, Health Science Center, Biomedical Visualizations, Chicago IL (S)
University of Illinois, Urbana-Champaign, College of Fine and Applied Arts, Champaign IL (S)
University of Indianapolis, Leah Ransburg Art Gallery, Indianapolis IN (M)
University of Indianapolis, Art Dept, Indianapolis IN (S)
University of Iowa, School of Art and Art History, Iowa City IA (S)
University of Iowa, Iowa City IA (M,L)
University of Judaism, Dept of Continuing Education, Los Angeles CA (S)
University of Kansas, Spencer Museum of Art, Lawrence KS (M,L)
University of Kansas, School of Fine Arts, Lawrence KS (S)
University of Kentucky, Lexington KY (M,L)
University of Kentucky, Dept of Art, Lexington KY (S)
University of Kentucky, Hunter M Adams Architecture Library, Lexington KY (L)
University of La Verne, Dept of Art, La Verne CA (S)
University of Lethbridge, Dept of Art, Lethbridge AB (S)
University of Lethbridge, Art Gallery, Lethbridge AB (M)
University of Louisville, Louisville KY (M,L)
University of Louisville, Allen R Hite Art Institute, Louisville KY (S)
University of Maine, Museum of Art, Orono ME (M)
University of Maine, Art Dept, Orono ME (S)
University of Maine at Augusta, Jewett Gallery, Augusta ME (M)
University of Maine at Augusta, Division of Fine & Performing Arts, Augusta ME (S)
University of Manitoba, Gallery III, Winnipeg MB (M,L)
University of Manitoba, Winnipeg MB (S)
University of Mary Hardin-Baylor, Dept of Fine Arts, Belton TX (S)
University of Maryland, College Park MD (S)
University of Maryland, Baltimore County, Visual Arts Dept, Baltimore MD (S)
University of Maryland, College Park, Art Gallery, College Park MD (M,L)
University of Maryland Eastern Shore, Art & Technology Dept, Princess Anne MD (S)
University of Massachusetts, Amherst, Amherst MA (M,L)
University of Massachusetts, Amherst, Amherst MA (S)
University of Massachusetts at Boston, Art Dept, Boston MA (S)
University of Massachusetts at Lowell, Dept of Art, Lowell MA (S)
University of Massachusetts Dartmouth, College of Visual and Performing Arts, North Dartmouth MA (S)
University of Miami, Lowe Art Museum, Coral Gables FL (M,L)

University of Toronto, Blackwood Gallery, Mississauga ON (M)
University of Toronto, Toronto ON (M,L)
University of Toronto, Toronto ON (S)
University of Tulsa, Dept of Art, Tulsa OK (S)
University of Tulsa, Alexandre Hogue Gallery, Tulsa OK (M)
University of Utah, Utah Museum of Fine Arts, Salt Lake City UT (M,L)
University of Utah, Art Dept, Salt Lake City UT (S)
University of Vermont, Robert Hull Fleming Museum, Burlington VT (M,L)
University of Vermont, Dept of Art, Burlington VT (S)
University of Victoria, Maltwood Art Museum and Gallery, Victoria BC (M)
University of Victoria, Victoria BC (S)
University of Virginia, Charlottesville VA (M,L)
University of Virginia, McIntire Dept of Art, Charlottesville VA (S)
University of Washington, School of Art, Seattle WA (S)
University of Washington, Seattle WA (M,L,O)
University of Waterloo, Waterloo ON (M,L)
University of Waterloo, Fine Arts Dept, Waterloo ON (S)
University of Western Ontario, McIntosh Art Gallery, London ON (M,L)
University of Western Ontario, Dept of Visual Arts, London ON (S)
University of West Florida, Art Gallery, Pensacola FL (M,L)
University of West Florida, Dept of Art, Pensacola FL (S)
University of Windsor, School of Visual Arts, Windsor ON (S)
University of Wisconsin, Milwaukee WI (M)
University of Wisconsin, Center-Barron County, Dept of Art, Rice Lake WI (S)
University of Wisconsin, Gallery 101, River Falls WI (M)
University of Wisconsin Center-Marinette County, Art Dept, Marinette WI (S)
University of Wisconsin-Eau Claire, Dept of Art, Eau Claire WI (S)
University of Wisconsin-Eau Claire, Foster Gallery, Eau Claire WI (M)
University of Wisconsin, Green Bay, Lawton Gallery, Green Bay WI (M)
University of Wisconsin-Green Bay, Art-Communication & the Arts, Green Bay WI (S)
University of Wisconsin-La Crosse, Art Dept, La Crosse WI (S)
University of Wisconsin-Madison, Madison WI (M,L)
University of Wisconsin, Madison, Madison WI (S)
University of Wisconsin-Milwaukee, Dept of Art, Milwaukee WI (S)
University of Wisconsin Oshkosh, Allen R Priebe Gallery, Oshkosh WI (M)
University of Wisconsin-Oshkosh, Dept of Art, Oshkosh WI (S)
University of Wisconsin-Parkside, Art Dept, Kenosha WI (S)
University of Wisconsin-Platteville, Dept of Fine Art, Platteville WI (S)
University of Wisconsin - Platteville, Harry Nohr Art Gallery, Platteville WI (M)
University of Wisconsin-River Falls, Art Dept, River Falls WI (S)
University of Wisconsin-Stevens Point, Dept of Art & Design, Stevens Point WI (S)
University of Wisconsin-Stevens Point, Carlsten Art Gallery, Stevens Point WI (M)
University of Wisconsin-Stout, J Furlong Gallery, Menomonie WI (M)
University of Wisconsin-Stout, Dept of Art & Design, Menomonie WI (S)
University of Wisconsin-Superior, Programs in the Visual Arts, Superior WI (S)
University of Wisconsin-Whitewater, Dept of Art, Whitewater WI (S)
University Of Wisconsin-Whitewater, Crossman Gallery, Whitewater WI (M)
University of Wyoming, Art Museum, Laramie WY (M)

University of Wyoming, Dept of Art, Laramie WY (S)
Univ of Southern California, Greene & Greene Library of the Arts & Crafts Movement, San Marino CA (L)
The Upper Room Chapel & Museum, see General Board of Discipleship, The United Methodist Church, Nashville TN
Uptown, see Beacon Street Gallery, Chicago IL
Uptown Center Hull House Assn, Beacon Street Gallery & Performance Company, Chicago IL (M)
Urban Institute for Contemporary Arts, Race Street Gallery, Grand Rapids MI (M)
Uris Library, see The Metropolitan Museum of Art, New York NY
Ursinus College, Philip & Muriel Berman Museum of Art, Collegeville PA (M)
USS Constitution Museum Foundation Inc, Boston National Historical Park, Museum, Boston MA (M)
Utah Arts Council, Chase Home Museum of Utah Folk Art, Salt Lake City UT (M)
Utah Department of Natural Resources, Division of Parks & Recreation, Territorial Statehouse, Fillmore UT (M)
Utah Lawyers for the Arts, Salt Lake City UT (A)
Utah Museum of Fine Arts, see University of Utah, Salt Lake City UT
Utah State University, Logan UT (S)
Utah Travel Council, Salt Lake City UT (A)
Utica College of Syracuse University, Division of Humanities, Utica NY (S)
Valdosta State College, Art Gallery, Valdosta GA (M)
Valdosta State College, Dept of Art, Valdosta GA (S)
Valencia Community College, Art Gallery-East Campus, Orlando FL (M)
Valencia Community College - West Campus, Art Dept, Orlando FL (S)
Valentine Museum, Richmond VA (M,L)
Valley Art Center Inc, Clarkston WA (A)
Valley City Arts & Gallery Association, Second Crossing Gallery Staus Mall, Valley City ND (M)
Valley City State College, Art Dept, Valley City ND (S)
Valley Cottage Library, Gallery, Valley Cottage NY (L)
Valley National Bank of Arizona, Phoenix AZ (C)
Valparaiso University, Museum of Art, Valparaiso IN (M)
Van Cortlandt Mansion & Museum, Bronx NY (M)
Vancouver Art Gallery, Vancouver BC (M,L)
Vancouver City Archives, Vancouver BC (L)
Vancouver Community College, Langara Campus, Dept of Fine Arts, Vancouver BC (S)
Vancouver Museum, see Vancouver Museum Association, Vancouver BC
Vancouver Museum Association, Vancouver Museum, Vancouver BC (M,L)
Vancouver Museum Library, see Vancouver Museum Association, Vancouver BC
Vancouver Public Library, Fine Arts & Music Div, Vancouver BC (M)
Vanderbilt University, Fine Arts Gallery, Nashville TN (M,L)
Vanderbilt University, Dept of Fine Arts, Nashville TN (S)
Frank & Lyn Van Steenberg Library, see Kendall College of Art & Design, Grand Rapids MI
James D Van Trump Library, see Pittsburgh History & Landmarks Foundation, Pittsburgh PA
Carleton Varney Dept of Art & Design, see University of Charleston, Charleston WV (S)
Vasche Library, see California State University Stanislaus, Turlock CA
Vassar Art Gallery, see Vassar College, Poughkeepsie NY
Vassar College, Vassar Art Gallery, Poughkeepsie NY (M,L)
Vassar College, Art Dept, Poughkeepsie NY (S)
Venice Place Sculpture Gardens, Venice CA (S)
Ventura College, Fine Arts Dept, Ventura CA (S)
Ventura County Historical Society Museum, Ventura CA (M)

Vermilion Community College, Art Dept, Ely MN (S)
Vermilion County Museum Society, Danville IL (M,L)
Vermont Historical Society, Museum, Montpelier VT (M,L)
Vermont State Craft Center at Frog Hollow, Middlebury VT (M)
Vermont Studio Center, Johnson VT (S)
Elizabeth O'Neill Verner Studio Museum, see Tradd Street Press, Charleston SC
Vernon Art Gallery, Vernon BC (M)
Vesterheim Norwegian-American Museum, Decorah IA (M,L)
Victoria College, Victoria TX (S)
Victoria Mansion - Morse Libby House, see Victoria Society of Maine, Portland ME
Victoria Society of Maine, Victoria Mansion - Morse Libby House, Portland ME (M)
Michael Victor II Art Library, see Springfield Art Association of Edwards College, Springfield IL
Victor Valley College, Art Dept, Victorville CA (S)
Viking Union Gallery, see Western Washington University, Bellingham WA
Village of Potsdam Public Museum, Potsdam NY (M)
Villa Maria College of Buffalo, Art Dept, Buffalo NY (S)
Villa Marre, see Quapaw Quarter Association, Inc, Little Rock AR
Villanova University, Dept of Art and Art History, Villanova PA (S)
Vincennes University Junior College, Art Dept, Vincennes IN (S)
Virginia Beach Center for the Arts, Virginia Beach VA (A)
Virginia Center for the Craft Arts, see Hand Workshop, Richmond VA
Virginia Commonwealth University, Richmond VA (M,L)
Virginia Commonwealth University, Richmond VA (S)
Virginia Dept Historic Resources, Research Library, Richmond VA (L)
Virginia Historical Society, Richmond VA (A,L)
Virginia Intermont College, Fine Arts Division, Bristol VA (S)
Virginia Museum of Fine Arts, Richmond VA (M,L)
Virginia Polytechnic Institute & State University, Blacksburg VA (M,L)
Virginia Polytechnic Institute & State University, Dept of Art & Art History, Blacksburg VA (S)
Virginia State University, Fine & Commercial Art, Petersburg VA (S)
Virginia Wesleyan College, Art Dept of the Humanities Division, Norfolk VA (S)
Virginia Western Community College, Commercial Art, Fine Art & Photography, Roanoke VA (S)
Viridian Gallery, New York NY (M)
Visual Artists & Galleries (VAGA), New York NY (O)
Visual Arts Center of Alaska, Anchorage AK (M)
Visual Arts Center of Northwest Florida, Panama City FL (M,L)
The Visual Art School of Princeton and Trenton, see Artworks, Trenton NJ
Visual Arts Ontario, Toronto ON (A,L)
Visual Studies Workshop, Rochester NY (M,L)
Viterbo College, Art Dept, La Crosse WI (S)
Viterbo College Art Gallery, La Crosse WI (M)
Vizcaya Museum and Gardens, Miami FL (M,L)
Volcano Art Center, Hawaii National Park HI (M)
Volunteer Lawyers for the Arts, see Lawyers Committee for the Arts, Washington DC
Volunteer Lawyers for the Arts of Massachusetts Inc, Boston MA (A)
Vu Centre D'Animation Et De Diffusion De La Photographie, Quebec PQ (M)
Wabash College, Art Dept, Crawfordsville IN (S)
Wabaunsee County Historical Museum, Alma KS (M)
Wachovia Bank of North Carolina, Winston-Salem NC (C)
Wade House & Wesley W Jung Carriage Museum, Historic House & Carriage Museum, Greenbush WI (M)
Wadsworth Atheneum, Hartford CT (M,L)

Westport Public Library, Westport CT (L)

West Publishing Company, Art & the Law, Eagan MN (C)

West Shore Community College, Division of Humanities and Fine Arts, Scottville MI (S)

West Texas State University, Art, Communication & Theatre Dept, Canyon TX (S)

West Valley College, Art Dept, Saratoga CA (S)

West Virginia Institute of Technology, Creative Arts Dept, Montgomery WV (S)

West Virginia State College, Art Dept, Institute WV (S)

West Virginia University, Morgantown WV (M,L)

West Virginia University, College of Creative Arts, Morgantown WV (S)

West Virginia University at Parkersburg, Art Dept, Parkersburg WV (S)

West Virginia Wesleyan College, Dept of Fine Arts, Buckhannon WV (S)

Wethersfield Historical Society Inc, Old Academy Library, Wethersfield CT (A)

Wethersfield Historical Society Inc, Wethersfield CT (A)

Wexner Center for the Arts, see Ohio State University, Columbus OH

Wharton County Junior College, Art Dept, Wharton TX (S)

Wharton Esherick Studio, see Wharton Esherick Museum, Paoli PA

Whatcom Museum of History and Art, Bellingham WA (M,L)

Wheaton College, Norton MA (M,L)

Wheaton College, Art Dept, Norton MA (S)

Wheaton College, Dept of Art, Wheaton IL (S)

Wheaton Cultural Alliance Inc, Millville NJ (M)

Mary Cabot Wheelwright Research Library, see Wheelwright Museum of the American Indian, Santa Fe NM

Wheelwright Museum of the American Indian, Santa Fe NM (M,L)

Whistler House Museum of Art, see Lowell Art Association, Lowell MA

White Columns, New York NY (M)

Whitefield House Museum, see Moravian Historical Society, Nazareth PA

White Gallery, see Portland State University, Portland OR

Whitehall Mansion, see Henry Morrison Flagler Museum, Palm Beach FL

White House, Washington DC (M)

Whitman College, Art Dept, Walla Walla WA (S)

Whitney at Equitable Center, see Whitney Museum of American Art, New York NY

Whitney Library, see New Haven Colony Historical Society, New Haven CT

Whitney Museum of American Art, New York NY (M,L)

Whittier College, Dept of Art, Whittier CA (S)

Whittier Fine Arts Gallery, see Friends University, Wichita KS

Whitworth College, Art Dept, Spokane WA (S)

Peter and Catharine Whyte Foundation, Whyte Museum of the Canadian Rockies, Banff AB (M,L)

Wichita Art Museum, Wichita KS (M,L)

Wichita Art Museum, see Kansas Watercolor Society, Wichita KS

Wichita Center for the Arts, Wichita KS (A,L)

Wichita Center for the Arts, Wichita KS (S)

Wichita Falls Museum and Art Center, Wichita Falls TX (M)

Wichita Public Library, Wichita KS (L)

Wichita State University, Edwin A Ulrich Museum of Art, Wichita KS (M)

Wichita State University, Division of Art, Wichita KS (S)

Widener University, Art Museum, Chester PA (M)

Albert H Wiggin Gallery & Print Department, see Boston Public Library, Boston MA

Wight Art Gallery, see University of California, Los Angeles, Los Angeles CA

Wilber Czech Museum, Wilber NE (M)

Wilberforce University, Art Dept, Wilberforce OH (S)

Wilbour Library of Egyptology, see Brooklyn Museum, Brooklyn NY

Wilbur Room Library, see University of Vermont, Burlington VT

Wilderness Park Museum, see El Paso Museum of Art, El Paso TX

Wildlife of the American West Art Museum, Jackson WY (L)

Wiley College, Dept of Fine Arts, Marshall TX (S)

Wilfrid Laurier Univer2ity, Art Gallery, Waterloo ON (M)

Wilkes Art Gallery, North Wilkesboro NC (M)

Wilkes Community College, Arts and Science Division, Wilkesboro NC (S)

Wilkes University, Sordoni Art Gallery, Wilkes-Barre PA (M)

Wilkes University, Dept of Art, Wilkes-Barre PA (S)

Willamette University, George Putnam University Center, Salem OR (M)

Willard House and Clock Museum, Inc, Grafton MA (M)

Willard Library, Dept of Fine Arts, Evansville IN (L)

Willet Stained Glass Studios, Philadelphia PA (L)

William Jewell College, Art Dept, Liberty MO (S)

William Paterson College, Art Dept, Wayne NJ (S)

William Penn College, Art Dept, Oskaloosa IA (S)

Williams Baptist College, Dept of Art, College City AR (S)

Williams College, Museum of Art, Williamstown MA (M,L)

Williams College, Dept of Art, Williamstown MA (S)

Kemper & Leila Williams Foundation, New Orleans LA (M,L)

Morris R Williams Center for the Arts, Art Gallery, see Lafayette College, Easton PA

William Woods College, Art Gallery, Fulton MO (M)

William Woods-Westminster Colleges, Art Dept, Fulton MO (S)

Willis Library, see University of North Texas, Denton TX

Willmar Community College, Willmar MN (S)

Wilmington College, Art Dept, Wilmington OH (S)

Wilmington Trust Company, Wilmington DE (C)

Wilson Art Gallery, see LeMoyne College, Syracuse NY

Captain John Wilson Historical House, see Cohasset Historical Society, Cohasset MA

Robert E Wilson Art Gallery, see Huntington College, Huntington IN

Woodrow Wilson Birthplace Foundation, Staunton VA (M,L)

Woodrow Wilson House, Washington DC (M)

Wilton House Museum, see National Society of the Colonial Dames, Richmond VA

Wind Luke Asian Museum Memorial Foundation, Inc, Seattle WA (M,L)

Wingate College, Division of Fine Arts, Wingate NC (S)

Winnipeg Art Gallery, Winnipeg MB (M,L)

Winona State University, Dept of Art, Winona MN (S)

Winston-Salem State University, Art Dept, Winston-Salem NC (S)

Winterthur Museum and Gardens, Winterthur DE (M,L)

Winthrop College, Dept of Art & Design, Rock Hill SC (S)

Winthrop University Galleries, Rock Hill SC (M)

Wiregrass Museum of Art, Dothan AL (M)

Wisconsin Fine Arts Association, Inc, Ozaukee Art Center, Cedarburg WI (A)

Wisconsin Painters & Sculptors, Inc, Milwaukee WI (A)

Wisconsin Union Galleries, see University of Wisconsin-Madison, Madison WI

Witte Museum, see San Antonio Museum Association, Inc, San Antonio TX

Wittenberg University, Art Dept, Springfield OH (S)

Witter Gallery, Storm Lake IA (M)

Wofford College, Sandor Teszler Library Gallery, Spartanburg SC (M)

Catharine Lorillard Wolfe Art Club, Inc, New York NY (A)

Frances Wolfson Art Gallery, see Miami-Dade Community College, Wolfson Campus, Miami FL

Wolfsonian Foundation, Miami Beach FL (A)

Women And Their Work, Austin TX (A)

Women Artists News Archive, see Midmarch Associates, New York NY

Women in the Arts Foundation, Inc, New York NY (A)

Women's Art Registry of Minnesota Gallery, Saint Paul MN (A)

Women's Caucus For Art, Philadelphia PA (O)

Women's Interart Center, Inc, Interart Gallery, New York NY (M)

Women's Studio Workshop, Inc, Rosendale NY (A)

Wood Art Gallery, Montpelier VT (M)

Woodbridge Township Cultural Arts Commission, Barron Arts Center, Woodbridge NJ (M)

Woodbury University, Dept of Graphic Design, Burbank CA (S)

Woodlawn Plantation, Mount Vernon VA (M)

Woodmere Art Museum, Philadelphia PA (M,L)

Leigh Yawkey Woodson Art Museum, Inc, Wausau WI (M,L)

Woodstock Artists Association, Woodstock NY (A,L)

Woodstock Public Library, Art Gallery, Woodstock ON (M)

Woodstock School of Art, Inc, Woodstock NY (S)

Woolaroc Museum, see Frank Phillips Foundation Inc, Bartlesville OK

Wooster Community Art Center, Danbury CT (A,L)

Worcester Art Museum, Worcester MA (M,L)

Worcester Center for Crafts, Worcester MA (M)

Worcester Center for Crafts, Worcester MA (S)

Worcester State College, Media, Arts, and Philosophy, Worcester MA (S)

Workman & Temple Family Homestead Museum, City of Industry CA (M)

World Archaeological Society, Information Center & Library, Hollister MO (L)

World Figure Skating Hall of Fame and Museum, see United States Figure Skating Association, Colorado Springs CO

World Heritage Museum, see University of Illinois, Champaign IL

John Wornall House Museum, see Jackson County Historical Society, Independence MO

Wrecker's Museum, see Old Island Restoration Foundation Inc, Key West FL

Wright College, see City Colleges of Chicago, Chicago IL (S)

Fielding L Wright Art Center, see Delta State University, Cleveland MS

Frank Lloyd Wright Pope-Leighey House, Mount Vernon VA (M)

Wright Museum of Art, see Beloit College, Beloit WI

Wright School of Art, Stowe VT (S)

Wright State University, Dayton OH (M,L)

Wright State University, Dept of Art & Art History, Dayton OH (S)

Wriston Art Center Galleries, see Lawrence University, Appleton WI

Wustum Art Library, see Wustum Museum Art Association, Racine WI

Charles A Wustum Museum of Fine Arts, see Wustum Museum Art Association, Racine WI

Wustum Museum Art Association, Racine WI (A, M,L)

Wyoming State Museum, State Art Gallery, Cheyenne WY (M)

Xavier Art Gallery, see Xavier University, Cincinnati OH

Xavier University, Xavier Art Gallery, Cincinnati OH (M)

Xavier University, Dept of Art, Cincinnati OH (S)

Xavier University of Louisiana, Dept of Fine Arts, New Orleans LA (S)

Xerox Corporation, Art Collection, Stamford CT (C)

Xicanindio, Inc, Mesa AZ (A)

Yager Museum, see Hartwick College, Oneonta NY

Yakima Valley Community College, Art Dept, Yakima WA (S)

Yale Center for British Art, see Yale University, New Haven CT

Yale University, New Haven CT (M,L)

Yale University, New Haven CT (S)

Yankton County Historical Society, Dakota Territorial Museum, Yankton SD (M)

Yard School of Art, Montclair NJ (S)